WHITAKER'S ALMANACK

2009

A & C BLACK

LONDON

A & C Black Publishers Ltd
36 Soho Square, London W1D 3QY

Whitaker's Almanack published annually since 1868

STANDARD EDITION
Cloth covers
978–1–4081–0422–4

CONCISE EDITION
Paperback
978–1–4081–0421–7

NORTH AMERICAN EDITION
Hardback
978–1–4144–5572–3/1–4144–5572–0
Gale, Cengage Learning

JACKET PHOTOGRAPHS
1. Adelie penguins on an iceberg in east Antarctica. © Colin Monteath/Hedgehog House/Getty Images
2. A scene from the closing ceremony of the Beijing Olympic Games in August 2008. © Julian Finney/Getty Images Sport
3. The US presidential candidate Barack Obama giving a speech in West Virginia in March 2008. © Alex Brandon/AP/PA Photos
4. Spanish football fans celebrate a goal against Russia at the European Championships in June 2008. © Daniel Ochoa de Olza/AP/PA Photos
5. Boris Johnson takes office as mayor of London in May 2008. © William Wintercross/Stringer/Getty Images News
6. The skies darken over a branch of Northern Rock bank in Newcastle, November 2007. © Getty Images

Typeset in the UK by RefineCatch Ltd, Bungay, Suffolk NR35 1EF

Printed in the UK by CPI William Clowes Beccles NR34 7TL

Whitaker's Almanack was compiled with the assistance of: Amnesty International; Christian Research; UK Hydrographic Office; Oxford Cartographers; WM/Reuters; Keesing's Worldwide; Transparency International: the global coalition against corruption; United Nations Population Division; World Gazetteer/Stefan Helders (**W** www.world-gazetteer.com) and the World Health Organisation.

Material was reproduced from (in addition to that indicated): *CIA World Factbook 2008*; *The London Diplomatic List January 2008* © Crown Copyright; *International Financial Statistics Year Book* © International Monetary Fund; *Military Balance 2008* published by Taylor & Francis; *People in Power* © Cambridge International Reference on Current Affairs (CIRCA) and 2008 *World Development Indicators* published by the World Bank. Crown copyright material is reproduced with the permission of the Controller of Her Majesty's Stationery Office.

A CIP catalogue record for this book is available from the British Library.

EDITORIAL STAFF
Editor-in-Chief: Inna Ward
UK Project Editors: Ruth Northey, Clare Slaven
International Project Editor: Mike Jakeman
Editorial Assistant: Ruth Craven
Editorial Intern: Anna Krzyzanowska

CONTRIBUTORS (where not listed)
Gordon Taylor (Astronomy); Hemant Kanitkar (Hindu calendar); John Noi (IT); Elizabeth Holmes (Education); Karen Harries-Rees (Environment); Clive Longhurst (Insurance); Duncan Murray, Chris Priestley (Legal Notes); Jill Papworth (Taxation); Edward Gibbes, Stan Greenberg (Sport); Philip Eden (Weather); Russell Ash (World in Figures) and Hilary Marsden (Countries of the World)

CONTENTS

PREFACE 7

THE YEAR 2009

2009 Calendar 10
2010 Calendar 11
Forthcoming Events 12
Centenaries 14

UNITED KINGDOM

UK in Figures 17
The National Flag 23

ROYAL FAMILY 24
Private Secretaries 26
Finance 29
Military Titles 31
Kings and Queens 34
The House of Windsor 39
Descendants of Queen Victoria 40

PRECEDENCE 42

PEERAGE 44
Hereditary Peers 46
Life Peers 66
Lords Spiritual 75
Courtesy Titles 76
Peers' Surnames 77
Orders of Chivalry 82
Baronetage and Knightage 85
Dames 114
Decorations and Medals 117
Chiefs of Clans in Scotland 120
Privy Council 122

PARLIAMENT 125
Houses of Parliament 126
Political Parties 134
Members of Parliament 137
General Election Results 145
By-elections 181

THE GOVERNMENT AND PUBLIC BODIES 182
Government Departments 184
 Executive Agencies 196
 Non-ministerial Government Departments 201
Public Bodies Directory 206

REGIONAL GOVERNMENT 234
London 234
Wales 239
Scotland 245
Northern Ireland 256

LOCAL GOVERNMENT 262
Local Government Introduction 262
Political Composition of Councils 269
England 274
 Principal Cities 276
 English County Councils 283
 District Councils 284
 Metropolitan Borough Councils 288
 Unitary Councils 289
London 291
 The City Guilds 293
 London Borough Councils 296
Wales 297
Scotland 300
Northern Ireland 305
Isle of Man 307
Channel Islands 308

EUROPEAN PARLIAMENT 310

LAW AND ORDER 313
Law Courts and Offices 313
 Scottish Judicature 321
 Northern Ireland Judicature 324
Tribunals 325
Ombudsman Services 331
Police 334
Prisons 339

DEFENCE 344
Salaries 354
Pensions 356

EDUCATION 357
The Education System 357
Education Directory 376
 Universities 376
 Professional Education 387
Independent Schools 396
National Academies 406
Research Councils 408

HEALTH 413
National Health Service 413

SOCIAL WELFARE 420
Social Services 420
National Insurance 422
Pensions 424
War Pensions 426
Tax Credits 428
Benefits 429

UTILITIES AND TRANSPORT 437
Water 437
Energy 440
Transport 445

RELIGION 455
Religion in the UK 455
Churches 462

COMMUNICATIONS **485**
Telecommunications 485
Postal Services 486
IDD Codes 488

INFORMATION TECHNOLOGY **491**
Glossary 494
Country Web Domain Names 496

THE ENVIRONMENT **498**
Conservation and Heritage 502
World Heritage Sites 508
Wildlife and Habitat 509

HERITAGE **513**
The Year in Review 513
Historic Buildings and Monuments 515
Museums and Galleries 523
Sights of London 531
Hallmarks 539

BANKING AND FINANCE **542**
British Currency 542
Banking and Personal Finance 544
Financial Services Regulation 547
National Savings 549
London Stock Exchange 551
Insurance 552
Economic Statistics 557
Cost of Living and Inflation 562

TAXATION **564**
Stamp Duty 579

LEGAL NOTES **581**
Intellectual Property 605

THE MEDIA **607**
Broadcasting 607
  Television 607
  Radio 609
The Press 619
  Newspapers 619
  Periodicals 623
Book Publishers 630

ORGANISATIONS **635**
Employers' and Trade Associations 635
Trade Unions 637
Sports Bodies 641
Clubs 646
Societies and Institutions 649

THE WORLD

The World in Figures 677
The North and South Poles 685
Air Distances From London 688
Time Zones 690
Currencies and Exchange Rates 693
Travel Overseas 697
European Union 700
International Organisations 711
Countries of the World A-Z 735
UK Overseas Territories 1069

THE YEAR 2007–8

Events 1079
  UK Affairs 1079
  Arts and Media 1082
  Business and Economic Affairs 1085
  Crimes and Legal Affairs 1087
  Environment and Science 1091
  Sport 1094
  International Events 1097
Obituaries 1111
Archaeology 1115
Architecture 1120
Art 1127
Broadcasting 1131
Business and Finance 1136
Conservation 1140
Dance 1144
Film 1148
Literature 1152
Music 1157
  Classical 1157
  Pop 1162
Opera 1165
Parliament 1170
Acts of Parliament 1176
White Papers 1178
Science and Discovery 1179
Theatre 1185
Weather 1189
Sports Results 1195
Olympic Games 2008 1217
Sports Records 1222

TIME AND SPACE

Astronomy 1227
Time Measurement and Calendars 1287
Tidal Predictions 1303

GENERAL REFERENCE

Weights and Measures 1313
  Conversion Tables 1318
The Periodic Table 1319
Nobel Prize Winners 1320

Abbreviations 1321

Index 1329
Stop Press 1369

PREFACE

Welcome to the 141st edition of *Whitaker's Almanack*. The developed world appears to be facing if not a recession, then a severe slowdown. Much of this downturn has been led by the collapse of the US economy, to which so many countries are tied. In addition to the inevitable effect of close global trade and currency links, few realised the extent of foreign banks' involvement in the American mortgage market. The knock-on effect has been tumultuous.

In the UK, the decade of consumer binge, financed by cheap debt and rising house prices, has abruptly ended and for many this is the first time the British economy is not thriving. A whole generation has not experienced life under a non-Labour government and is now tempted to vote for an alternative. This time last year, I wrote about the prolonged honeymoon enjoyed by the new prime minister. Then, there was speculation about an early general election; now, the press is riddled with feverish rumours of a leadership challenge. The tumbling public confidence in Gordon Brown is reflecting in his party's ratings. Among his government's recent errors was the package of measures to save the housing market, which had the opposite effect when the chancellor announced that he was considering lowering stamp duty. Such ill-conceived policies imply that the cabinet does not have a recovery plan. Unless something outstanding happens at the party's conference – and I suspect it won't – Labour, paralysed by its own indecision with regard to its leader, is surely in serious danger of losing the next election. This may no longer even depend on the performance of other parties.

Another election campaign proved to be somewhat more entertaining. Heads were turned when the US Republican candidate, John McCain, named his running mate as the unlikely Sarah Palin. Palin's 'improbable journey' from Alaskan beauty queen to potential vice-president raised the stakes, challenging the Democrats' hopes for the first African-American president in Barack Obama. Both McCain and Obama were eager to show off their diplomatic skills when the crisis in Georgia unfolded in early August. It remains to be seen what tit-for-tat measures will be exchanged between Russia and the West, but it is difficult not to draw parallels between responses to South Ossetia and other independence-seeking regions, such as Kosovo.

In an otherwise gloomy summer, it was easy to be swept up in the temporary euphoria induced by the performance of the British team at the Beijing Olympics. British medals aside, it was fascinating to catch a rare glimpse of China. My personal highlight was the moment a Georgian and a Russian athlete embraced in a remarkable show of unity that only the Olympics can provide. Readers can find details of all the new world records, results and the final medals table at the end of our Sports Results section.

Other new features for this edition include a section on Ombudsman Services and a fresh selection of colour maps. We have replaced lists of countries' neighbours with small diagramatic maps in Countries of the World and standardised that section further. The results of the London mayoral election can be found in the Regional Government section. As ever, every detail in the book has been scrupulously checked and updated using the most authoritative sources. We are most grateful for the assistance of thousands of organisations and individuals who respond so readily to our requests for information.

On a personal note, after eight devoted years, I am leaving Whitaker's to pursue another career. At the time of writing, the British media is full of stories about concrete ceilings, pitbulls with lipstick and the MOD's hat plans. The *Almanack* is a book I will always come back to for a measured, distilled and objective report of current affairs. I hope our readers will support this long-standing tradition and may it continue for another 140 years.

Inna Ward
Editor-in-Chief
September 2008

THE YEAR 2009

CHRONOLOGICAL CYCLES AND ERAS

Dominical Letter	D
Epact	3
Golden Number (Lunar Cycle)	XV
Julian Period	6722
Roman Indiction	2
Solar Cycle	2

	Beginning
Muslim year AH 1430*	29 Dec 2008
Japanese year Heisei 21	1 Jan
Roman year 2762 AUC	14 Jan
Chinese year of the Ox	26 Jan
Regnal year 58	6 Feb
Sikh new year	14 Mar
Indian (Saka) year 1931	27 Mar
Hindu new year (Chaitra)	27 Mar
Jewish year AM 5770*	19 Sep

* Year begins at sunset on the previous day

RELIGIOUS CALENDARS

CHRISTIAN

Epiphany	6 Jan
Presentation of Christ in the Temple	25 Feb
Ash Wednesday	25 Feb
The Annunciation	25 Mar
Maundy Thursday	9 Apr
Good Friday	10 Apr
Easter Day (western churches)	12 Apr
Easter Day (Eastern Orthodox)	19 Apr
Rogation Sunday	17 May
Ascension Day	21 May
Pentecost (Whit Sunday)	31 May
Trinity Sunday	7 June
Corpus Christi	11 June
All Saints' Day	1 Nov
Advent Sunday	29 Nov
Christmas Day	25 Dec

HINDU

Makara Sankranti	14 Jan
Vasant Panchami (Sarasvati Puja)	31 Jan
Mahashivaratri	23 Feb
Holi	10 Mar
Chaitra (Spring new year)	27 Mar
Ramanavami	3 Apr
Raksha Bandhan	5 Aug
Janmashtami	13 Aug
Ganesh Chaturthi, first day	23 Aug
Navaratri festival (Durga Puja), first day	19 Sep
Dasara	28 Sep
Diwali (New Year festival of lights), first day	15 Oct

JEWISH

Purim	10 Mar
Pesach (Passover), first day	9 Apr
Shavuoth (Feast of Weeks), first day	29 May
Rosh Hashanah (Jewish new year)	19 Sep
Yom Kippur (Day of Atonement)	28 Sept
Succoth (Feast of Tabernacles), first day	3 Oct
Hanukkah, first day	12 Dec

MUSLIM

Al-Hijra (Muslim new year)	29 Dec 2008
Ashura	7 Jan
Ramadan, first day	22 Aug
Eid-ul-Fitr	21 Sept
Hajj	26 Nov
Eid-ul-Adha	28 Nov

SIKH

Birthday of Guru Gobind Singh Ji	5 Jan
1Chet (Sikh new year)	14 Mar
Baisakhi Mela	14 Apr
Birthday of Guru Nanak Dev Ji	14 Apr†
Martyrdom of Guru Arjan Dev Ji	16 Jun
Martyrdom of Guru Tegh Bahadur Ji	24 Nov

† This festival is also currently celebrated according to the Lunar calendar

CIVIL CALENDAR

Countess of Wessex's birthday	20 Jan
Accession of the Queen	6 Feb
Duke of York's birthday	19 Feb
St David's Day	1 Mar
Earl of Wessex's birthday	10 Mar
Commonwealth Day	9 Mar
St Patrick's Day	17 Mar
Birthday of the Queen	21 Apr
St George's Day	23 Apr
Europe Day	9 May
Coronation Day	2 Jun
Duke of Edinburgh's birthday	10 Jun
The Queen's Official Birthday	13 Jun
Duchess of Cornwall's birthday	17 Jul
Princess Royal's birthday	15 Aug
Remembrance Sunday	8 Nov
Lord Mayor's Day	14 Nov
Prince of Wales' birthday	14 Nov
Wedding Day of the Queen	20 Nov
St Andrew's Day	30 Nov

LEGAL CALENDAR

LAW TERMS

Hilary Term	12 Jan to 8 Apr
Easter Term	21 Apr to 22 May
Trinity Term	2 Jun to 31 Jul
Michaelmas Term	1 Oct to 21 Dec

QUARTER DAYS *England, Wales and Northern Ireland*	TERM DAYS *Scotland*
Lady – 25 Mar	Candlemas – 28 Feb
Midsummer – 24 Jun	Whitsunday – 28 May
Michaelmas – 29 Sep	Lammas – 28 Aug
Christmas – 25 Dec	Martinmas – 28 Nov

2009

JANUARY

Sunday		4	11	18	25
Monday		5	12	19	26
Tuesday		6	13	20	27
Wednesday		7	14	21	28
Thursday	1	8	15	22	29
Friday	2	9	16	23	30
Saturday	3	10	17	24	31

FEBRUARY

Sunday	1	8	15	22
Monday	2	9	16	23
Tuesday	3	10	17	24
Wednesday	4	11	18	25
Thursday	5	12	19	26
Friday	6	13	20	27
Saturday	7	14	21	28

MARCH

Sunday	1	8	15	22	29
Monday	2	9	16	23	30
Tuesday	3	10	17	24	31
Wednesday	4	11	18	25	
Thursday	5	12	19	26	
Friday	6	13	20	27	
Saturday	7	14	21	28	

APRIL

Sunday		5	12	19	26
Monday		6	13	20	27
Tuesday		7	14	21	28
Wednesday	1	8	15	22	29
Thursday	2	9	16	23	30
Friday	3	10	17	24	
Saturday	4	11	18	25	

MAY

Sunday		3	10	17	24	31
Monday		4	11	18	25	
Tuesday		5	12	19	26	
Wednesday		6	13	20	27	
Thursday		7	14	21	28	
Friday	1	8	15	22	29	
Saturday	2	9	16	23	30	

JUNE

Sunday		7	14	21	28
Monday	1	8	15	22	29
Tuesday	2	9	16	23	30
Wednesday	3	10	17	24	
Thursday	4	11	18	25	
Friday	5	12	19	26	
Saturday	6	13	20	27	

JULY

Sunday		5	12	19	26
Monday		6	13	20	27
Tuesday		7	14	21	28
Wednesday	1	8	15	22	29
Thursday	2	9	16	23	30
Friday	3	10	17	24	31
Saturday	4	11	18	25	

AUGUST

Sunday		2	9	16	23	30
Monday		3	10	17	24	31
Tuesday		4	11	18	25	
Wednesday		5	12	19	26	
Thursday		6	13	20	27	
Friday		7	14	21	28	
Saturday	1	8	15	22	29	

SEPTEMBER

Sunday		6	13	20	27
Monday		7	14	21	28
Tuesday	1	8	15	22	29
Wednesday	2	9	16	23	30
Thursday	3	10	17	24	
Friday	4	11	18	25	
Saturday	5	12	19	26	

OCTOBER

Sunday		4	11	18	25
Monday		5	12	19	26
Tuesday		6	13	20	27
Wednesday		7	14	21	28
Thursday	1	8	15	22	29
Friday	2	9	16	23	30
Saturday	3	10	17	24	31

NOVEMBER

Sunday	1	8	15	22	29
Monday	2	9	16	23	30
Tuesday	3	10	17	24	
Wednesday	4	11	18	25	
Thursday	5	12	19	26	
Friday	6	13	20	27	
Saturday	7	14	21	28	

DECEMBER

Sunday		6	13	20	27
Monday		7	14	21	28
Tuesday	1	8	15	22	29
Wednesday	2	9	16	23	30
Thursday	3	10	17	24	31
Friday	4	11	18	25	
Saturday	5	12	19	26	

PUBLIC HOLIDAYS	*England and Wales*	*Scotland*	*Northern Ireland*
New Year	1 January†	1, 2† January	1 January†
St Patrick's Day	—	—	17 March
*Good Friday	10 April	10 April	10 April
Easter Monday	13 April	—	13 April
Early May	4 May†	4 May	4 May†
Spring	25 May	25 May†	25 May
Battle of the Boyne	—	—	13 July‡
Summer	31 August	3 August	31 August
St Andrew's Day	—	30 Nov§	—
*Christmas	25, 28 December	25, 28† December	25, 28 December

* In England, Wales and Northern Ireland, Christmas Day and Good Friday are common law holidays

† Subject to royal proclamation

‡ Subject to proclamation by the Secretary of State for Northern Ireland

§ The St Andrew's Day Holiday (Scotland) Bill was approved by parliament on 29 November 2006; it does not oblige employers to change their existing pattern of holidays but provides the legal framework in which the St Andrew's Day bank holiday could be substituted for an existing local holiday from another date in the year

Note: In the Channel Islands, Liberation Day is a bank and public holiday

2010

JANUARY

Sunday		3	10	17	24	31
Monday		4	11	18	25	
Tuesday		5	12	19	26	
Wednesday		6	13	20	27	
Thursday		7	14	21	28	
Friday	1	8	15	22	29	
Saturday	2	9	16	23	30	

FEBRUARY

Sunday		7	14	21	28
Monday	1	8	15	22	
Tuesday	2	9	16	23	
Wednesday	3	10	17	24	
Thursday	4	11	18	25	
Friday	5	12	19	26	
Saturday	6	13	20	27	

MARCH

Sunday		7	14	21	28
Monday	1	8	15	22	29
Tuesday	2	9	16	23	30
Wednesday	3	10	17	24	31
Thursday	4	11	18	25	
Friday	5	12	19	26	
Saturday	6	13	20	27	

APRIL

Sunday		4	11	18	25
Monday		5	12	19	26
Tuesday		6	13	20	27
Wednesday		7	14	21	28
Thursday	1	8	15	22	29
Friday	2	9	16	23	30
Saturday	3	10	17	24	

MAY

Sunday		2	9	16	23	30
Monday		3	10	17	24	31
Tuesday		4	11	18	25	
Wednesday		5	12	19	26	
Thursday		6	13	20	27	
Friday		7	14	21	28	
Saturday	1	8	15	22	29	

JUNE

Sunday		6	13	20	27
Monday		7	14	21	28
Tuesday	1	8	15	22	29
Wednesday	2	9	16	23	30
Thursday	3	10	17	24	
Friday	4	11	18	25	
Saturday	5	12	19	26	

JULY

Sunday		4	11	18	25
Monday		5	12	19	26
Tuesday		6	13	20	27
Wednesday		7	14	21	28
Thursday	1	8	15	22	29
Friday	2	9	16	23	30
Saturday	3	10	17	24	31

AUGUST

Sunday	1	8	15	22	29
Monday	2	9	16	23	30
Tuesday	3	10	17	24	31
Wednesday	4	11	18	25	
Thursday	5	12	19	26	
Friday	6	13	20	27	
Saturday	7	14	21	28	

SEPTEMBER

Sunday		5	12	19	26
Monday		6	13	20	27
Tuesday		7	14	21	28
Wednesday	1	8	15	22	29
Thursday	2	9	16	23	30
Friday	3	10	17	24	
Saturday	4	11	18	25	

OCTOBER

Sunday		3	10	17	24	31
Monday		4	11	18	25	
Tuesday		5	12	19	26	
Wednesday		6	13	20	27	
Thursday		7	14	21	28	
Friday	1	8	15	22	29	
Saturday	2	9	16	23	30	

NOVEMBER

Sunday		7	14	21	28
Monday	1	8	15	22	29
Tuesday	2	9	16	23	30
Wednesday	3	10	17	24	
Thursday	4	11	18	25	
Friday	5	12	19	26	
Saturday	6	13	20	27	

DECEMBER

Sunday		5	12	19	26
Monday		6	13	20	27
Tuesday		7	14	21	28
Wednesday	1	8	15	22	29
Thursday	2	9	16	23	30
Friday	3	10	17	24	31
Saturday	4	11	18	25	

PUBLIC HOLIDAYS	*England and Wales*	*Scotland*	*Northern Ireland*
New Year	1 January†	1, 4† January	1 January†
St Patrick's Day	—	—	17 March
*Good Friday	2 April	2 April	2 April
Easter Monday	5 April	—	5 April
Early May	3 May†	3 May	3 May†
Spring	31 May	31 May†	31 May
Battle of the Boyne	—	—	12 July‡
Summer	30 August	2 August	30 August
St Andrew's Day	—	30 Nov	—
*Christmas	27, 28 December	27, 28 December†	27, 28 December

* In England, Wales and Northern Ireland, Christmas Day and Good Friday are common law holidays

† Subject to royal proclamation

‡ Subject to proclamation by the Secretary of State for Northern Ireland

§ The St Andrew's Day Holiday (Scotland) Bill was approved by parliament on 29 November 2006; it does not oblige employers to change their existing pattern of holidays but provides the legal framework in which the St Andrew's Day bank holiday could be substituted for an existing local holiday from another date in the year

Note: In the Channel Islands, Liberation Day is a bank and public holiday

FORTHCOMING EVENTS

* Provisional dates
† Venue not confirmed

JANUARY

9–18	London Boat Show, Excel, London Docklands
10–25	London International Mime Festival
*11	Russian Winter Festival, Trafalgar Square, London
14–18	London Art Fair, Business Design Centre
14–1 February	Celtic Connections Music Festival, Glasgow
20–22	UK Open Dance Championships, Bournemouth International Centre
29–1 February	London Motorcycle Show, Excel, London Docklands

FEBRUARY

6–15	Leicester Comedy Festival
8	British Academy Film Awards, Royal Opera House, London
18–22	Jorvik Viking Festival, Jorvik Viking Centre, York
27–1 March	Ceramic Art London, Royal College of Art
28–8 March	Bath Literature Festival

MARCH

5	World Book Day
5–8	Crufts Dog Show, NEC, Birmingham
6–15	National Science and Engineering Week
8	International Women's Day
20–13 April	Ideal Home Show, Earls Court, London
25–31	BADA Antiques and Fine Art Fair, Duke of York's Square, London
29–5 April	Oxford Literary Festival

APRIL

20–22	London Book Fair, Earls Court, London

MAY

15–17	Battersea Contemporary Art Fair
19–23	RHS Chelsea Flower Show, Royal Hospital, Chelsea
21–31	Hay Festival, Hay-on-Wye, Hereford
*21–31 August	Glyndebourne Festival Opera season
29–31	Clothes Show London, Excel, London Docklands

JUNE

*8–16 August	Royal Academy of Arts Summer Exhibition, Burlington House, London
12–28	Aldeburgh Festival of Music and the Arts, Snape, Suffolk
13	Trooping the Colour, Horseguards Parade, London
*26–28	Glastonbury Festival of Contemporary Performing Arts, Somerset

JULY

3–18	Cheltenham Music Festival
7–12	RHS Hampton Court Palace Flower Show, Surrey
9–12	The Royal Show, Stoneleigh Park, Warwickshire
9–19	New Designers Exhibition, Business Design Centre, London
10–18	York Early Music Festival
10–28	Buxton Festival, Derbyshire
*16–25	The Welsh Proms, St David's Hall, Cardiff
*17–12 September	BBC Promenade Concerts, Royal Albert Hall, London
22–26	RHS Flower Show, Tatton Park, Cheshire
*24–26	WOMAD Festival, Charlton Park, Wiltshire
*24–2 August	Edinburgh Jazz and Blues Festival
*30–2 August	Cambridge Folk Festival

AUGUST

1–8	National Eisteddfod of Wales, Bala
7–29	Edinburgh Military Tattoo, Edinburgh Castle
8–15	Three Choirs Festival, Hereford
14–6 September	Edinburgh International Festival
18–20	RHS Wisley Flower Show, RHS Garden, Wisley
*28–1 November	Blackpool Illuminations, Blackpool Promenade
30–31	Notting Hill Carnival, Notting Hill, London

SEPTEMBER

5	Braemar Royal Highland Gathering, Aberdeenshire
8	International Literacy Day
*9	Mercury Music Prize
10–13	Heritage Open Days, England (nationwide)
14–17	TUC Annual Congress, BT Convention Centre, Liverpool
19–23	Liberal Democrat Party Autumn Conference, Bournemouth
26–30	Labour Party Conference, Brighton

OCTOBER

4–7 October	Conservative Party Conference, Manchester
9	National Poetry Day

*15–18	Frieze Art Fair, Regent's Park, London
Mid-October	Booker Prize
Mid-October	Classic Motor Show, NEC, Birmingham
Mid-October	London Film Festival
Mid-October–January	Turner Prize Exhibition, Tate Britain, London

NOVEMBER

*1	London to Brighton Veteran Car Run
14	Lord Mayor's Procession and Show, City of London
Mid-November	CBI Annual Conference, Business Design Centre, London

SPORTS EVENTS

JANUARY

*11–18	Snooker: Masters, Wembley Arena, London
29–1 February	Motor racing: World Rally Championship, Irish leg, Belfast
30–1 February	Badminton: English National Championships, Manchester

FEBRUARY

7–21 March	Rugby Union: Six Nations Championship
8–15	Squash: British National Championships, Manchester

MARCH

1	Football: League Cup Final, Wembley Stadium, London
5–7	Rugby: World Cup Sevens, Dubai
6–8	Athletics: European Indoor Championships, Turin
7–22	Cricket: Women's World Cup, Australia
29	Rowing: Oxford and Cambridge Boat Race, Putney to Mortlake, London

APRIL

2–4 April	Horse racing: Grand National, Aintree, Liverpool
18–4 May	Snooker: World Championship, Crucible Theatre, Sheffield
26	Athletics: London Marathon, London

MAY

2–3	Horse racing: Guineas Festival, Newmarket
†4	Football: FA Women's Cup Final
7–10	Equestrian: Badminton Horse Trials, Badminton
7–19	Cricket: England Test series vs Sri Lanka
14–17	Royal Windsor Horse Show, Home Park, Windsor
23	Rugby Union: Heineken Cup Final, Murrayfield Stadium, Edinburgh
27	Football: UEFA Champions League Final, Stadio Olimpico, Rome
*30	Football: Scottish FA Cup Final, Hampden Park, Glasgow
30	Football: FA Cup Final, Wembley Stadium, London
30–4 July	Rugby: British & Irish Lions Tour, South Africa

JUNE

5–21	Cricket: Twenty20 World Cup, England
6–13 June	Motorcycling: TT Races, Isle of Man
6	Horse racing: The Derby, Epsom Downs
15–20	Golf: British Amateur Golf Championship, Formby, West Lancashire
16–20	Horse racing: Royal Ascot
21	Motor racing: British Formula 1 Grand Prix, Silverstone, Northants
22–5 July	Tennis: Wimbledon Championship, All England Lawn Tennis Club, London

JULY

1–5	Rowing: Henley Royal Regatta, Henley-on-Thames
8–24 August	Cricket: England Test series vs Australia
11–25	Shooting: NRA Imperial Meeting, Bisley Camp, Surrey
16–19	Golf: Open Championship, Turnberry, Ayrshire
*25	Horse racing: King George VI and Queen Elizabeth Diamond Stakes, Ascot
30–2 August	Golf: Women's British Open, Royal Lytham & St Annes, Lancashire

AUGUST

1–8	Sailing: Cowes Week, Isle of Wight
15–23	Athletics: World Championships, Berlin
*29	Rugby League: Challenge Cup Final, Wembley Stadium, London

SEPTEMBER

3–6	Equestrian: Burghley Horse Trials, Stamford, Lincolnshire
9–12	Horse racing: St Leger, Doncaster

OCTOBER

Early-Mid October	Athletics: Great North Run, Newcastle
1–3	Horse racing: Cambridgeshire Meeting, Newmarket
*7–11	Equestrian: Horse of the Year Show, NEC, Birmingham
12–18	Gymnastics: World Championships, O2 Arena, London
16–17	Horse racing: Champions Meeting, Newmarket
Mid-October	Rugby League: Super League Final, Old Trafford, Manchester

DECEMBER

5–12	Curling: European Championships, Aberdeen

CENTENARIES

2009

1509
21 Apr Henry VII, king of England 1485–1509, died
10 Jul John Calvin, French reformationist, born

1709
18 Sep Dr Samuel Johnson, lexicographer, critic and poet, born

1809
4 Jan Louis Braille, French inventor of reading system for the blind, born
19 Jan Edgar Allen Poe, American author, poet, critic and editor, born
3 Feb Felix Mendelssohn-Bartholdy, German composer, born
12 Feb Charles Darwin, naturalist and scientist, born
12 Feb Abraham Lincoln, president of the USA 1860–5, born
27 Mar Baron G.-E. Haussmann, French civic planner, financier and architect, born
31 Mar Nikolai Gogol, Russian writer, born
31 Mar Edward Fitzgerald, poet and scholar, born
31 May Franz Joseph Haydn, Austrian composer, died
8 Jun Thomas Paine, writer, deist and radical, died
6 Aug Lord Alfred Tennyson, poet, born
27 Nov Fanny Kemble, actress and author, born
29 Dec William Gladstone, four-time prime minister, born

1909
17 Feb Geronimo, Apache Indian chief, died
10 Apr Algernon Swinburne, poet and critic, died
13 Apr Eudora Welty, American author, born
15 May James Mason, actor, born
18 May Fred Perry, tennis player, born
26 May Sir Matt Busby, football player and manager, born
6 Jun Sir Isaiah Berlin, Latvian-born writer and historian, born
20 Jun Errol Flynn, Australian actor, born
17 Jul Sir Hardy Amies, costume designer and the Queen's official dressmaker, born
25 Jul Louis Bleriot completed the first flight across the English Channel
14 Sep Sir Peter Scott, conservationist, born
28 Oct Francis Bacon, Anglo-Irish painter, born
26 Nov Eugene Ionesco, French-Romanian playwright and dramatist, born
9 Dec Douglas Fairbanks Jr, American actor, born

2010

1510
17 May Sandro Botticelli, Italian painter, died

1710
4 Jan Giovanni Pergolesi, Italian composer, born
12 Mar Thomas Arne, composer, born
28 Apr Thomas Betterton, actor and dramatist, died

1810
24 Feb Henry Cavendish, physicist and chemist, died
1 Mar Frédéric Chopin, Polish composer and pianist, born
2 Mar Pope Leo XIII, born
8 Jun Robert Schumann, German composer, born
5 Jul Phineas T. Barnum, American impresario, born
10 Aug Camillo Cavour, Italian statesman, born
29 Sep Elizabeth Gaskell, novelist, born

1910
8 Jan Galina Ulanova, Russian ballerina, born
23 Jan Django Reinhardt, Belgian-French guitarist, born
1 Mar David Niven, actor, born
21 Apr Mark Twain, American novelist and satirist, died
6 May Edward VII, king of United Kingdom 1901–10, died
12 May Prof. Dorothy Hodgkin, chemist and Nobel prize winner (1964), born
4 Jun Sir Christopher Cockerell, engineer and inventor of the hovercraft, born
11 Jun Jacques-Yves Cousteau, underwater explorer and filmmaker, born
13 Jun Mary Whitehouse, campaigner, born
23 Jun Jean Anouilh, French playwright, born
12 Jul Charles Stewart Rolls, automobile manufacturer, died
13 Aug Florence Nightingale, founder of trained nursing as a profession, died
26 Aug Mother Teresa, humanitarian and Nobel peace prize winner (1979), born
2 Sep Henri Rousseau, French painter, died
30 Oct Henri Dunant, Swiss founder of the Red Cross and Nobel peace prize winner (1901), died
20 Nov Leo Tolstoy, Russian novelist, died
26 Nov Cyril Cusack, Irish actor, born
19 Dec Jean Genet, French novelist and dramatist, born

THE UNITED KINGDOM

THE UK IN FIGURES

THE NATIONAL FLAG

THE ROYAL FAMILY

PRECEDENCE

THE PEERAGE

THE PRIVY COUNCIL

PARLIAMENT

THE GOVERNMENT

GOVERNMENT DEPARTMENTS AND PUBLIC OFFICES

REGIONAL GOVERNMENT

LOCAL GOVERNMENT

EUROPEAN PARLIAMENT

LAW COURTS AND OFFICES

TRIBUNALS

OMBUDSMAN SERVICES

POLICE

PRISONS

DEFENCE

EDUCATION

NATIONAL ACADEMIES

RESEARCH COUNCILS

HEALTH

SOCIAL WELFARE

WATER

ENERGY

TRANSPORT

RELIGION

COMMUNICATIONS

INFORMATION TECHNOLOGY

ENVIRONMENT

CONSERVATION AND HERITAGE

FINANCE

LEGAL NOTES

THE MEDIA

TRADE AND EMPLOYERS' ASSOCIATIONS

TRADE UNIONS

SPORTS BODIES

CLUBS

SOCIETIES AND INSTITUTIONS

THE UK IN FIGURES

The United Kingdom comprises Great Britain (England, Wales and Scotland) and Northern Ireland. The Isle of Man and the Channel Islands are Crown dependencies with their own legislative systems and are not part of the UK.

ABBREVIATIONS

AAS	*Annual Abstract of Statistics*
ST	*Social Trends*

All data is for the UK unless otherwise stated.

AREA OF THE UNITED KINGDOM

	sq. km	*sq. miles*
United Kingdom	242,495	93,627
England	130,279	50,301
Wales	20,733	8,005
Scotland	77,925	30,086
Northern Ireland	13,576	5,242

Source: ONS – *AAS 2008* (Crown copyright)

POPULATION

The first official census of population in England, Wales and Scotland was taken in 1801 and a census has been taken every ten years since, except in 1941 when there was no census because of war. The last official census in the UK was taken on 29 April 2001 and the next is due in April 2011.

The first official census of population in Ireland was taken in 1841. However, all figures given below refer only to the area which is now Northern Ireland. Figures for Northern Ireland in 1921 and 1931 are estimates based on the censuses taken in 1926 and 1937 respectively.

Estimates of the population of England before 1801, calculated from the number of baptisms, burials and marriages, are:

1570	4,160,221	1670	5,773,646
1600	4,811,718	1700	6,045,008
1630	5,600,517	1750	6,517,035

Further details are available on the Office for National Statistics (ONS) website (W www.statistics.gov.uk)

CENSUS RESULTS *Thousands*

	United Kingdom			England and Wales			Scotland			Northern Ireland		
	Total	*Male*	*Female*	*Total*	*Male*	*Female*	*Total*	*Male*	*Female*	*Total*	*Male*	*Female*
1801	—	—	—	8,893	4,255	4,638	1,608	739	869	—	—	—
1811	13,368	6,368	7,000	10,165	4,874	5,291	1,806	826	980	—	—	—
1821	15,472	7,498	7,974	12,000	5,850	6,150	2,092	983	1,109	—	—	—
1831	17,835	8,647	9,188	13,897	6,771	7,126	2,364	1,114	1,250	—	—	—
1841	20,183	9,819	10,364	15,914	7,778	8,137	2,620	1,242	1,378	1,649	800	849
1851	22,259	10,855	11,404	17,928	8,781	9,146	2,889	1,376	1,513	1,443	698	745
1861	24,525	11,894	12,631	20,066	9,776	10,290	3,062	1,450	1,612	1,396	668	728
1871	27,431	13,309	14,122	22,712	11,059	11,653	3,360	1,603	1,757	1,359	647	712
1881	31,015	15,060	15,955	25,974	12,640	13,335	3,736	1,799	1,936	1,305	621	684
1891	34,264	16,593	17,671	29,003	14,060	14,942	4,026	1,943	2,083	1,236	590	646
1901	38,237	18,492	19,745	32,528	15,729	16,799	4,472	2,174	2,298	1,237	590	647
1911	42,082	20,357	21,725	36,070	17,446	18,625	4,761	2,309	2,452	1,251	603	648
1921	44,027	21,033	22,994	37,887	18,075	19,811	4,882	2,348	2,535	1,258	610	648
1931	46,038	22,060	23,978	39,952	19,133	20,819	4,843	2,326	2,517	1,243	601	642
1951	50,225	24,118	26,107	43,758	21,016	22,742	5,096	2,434	2,662	1,371	668	703
1961	52,709	25,481	27,228	46,105	22,304	23,801	5,179	2,483	2,697	1,425	694	731
1971	55,515	26,952	28,562	48,750	23,683	25,067	5,229	2,515	2,714	1,536	755	781
1981	55,848	27,104	28,742	49,155	23,873	25,281	5,131	2,466	2,664	1,533*	750	783
1991	56,467	27,344	29,123	49,890	24,182	25,707	4,999	2,392	2,607	1,578	769	809
2001	58,789	28,581	30,208	52,042	25,327	26,715	5,062	2,432	2,630	1,685	821	864

* Figure includes 44,500 non-enumerated persons

ISLANDS

	Isle of Man			Jersey			Guernsey†		
	Total	*Male*	*Female*	*Total*	*Male*	*Female*	*Total*	*Male*	*Female*
1901	54,752	25,496	29,256	52,576	23,940	28,636	40,446	19,652	20,794
1921	60,284	27,329	32,955	49,701	22,438	27,263	38,315	18,246	20,069
1951	55,123	25,749	29,464	57,296	27,282	30,014	43,652	21,221	22,431
1971	56,289	26,461	29,828	72,532	35,423	37,109	51,458	24,792	26,666
1991	69,788	33,693	36,095	84,082	40,862	43,220	58,867	28,297	30,570
2001	76,315	37,372	38,943	87,186	42,485	44,701	59,807	29,138	30,669
2006	80,058	39,523	40,535						

† Includes Herm, Jethou and Lithou

Source: ONS – Census Reports (Crown copyright)

RESIDENT POPULATION

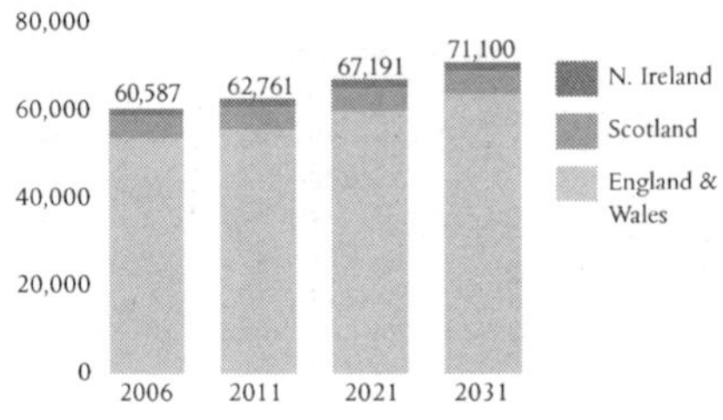

Source: ONS – AAS 2008 (Crown copyright)

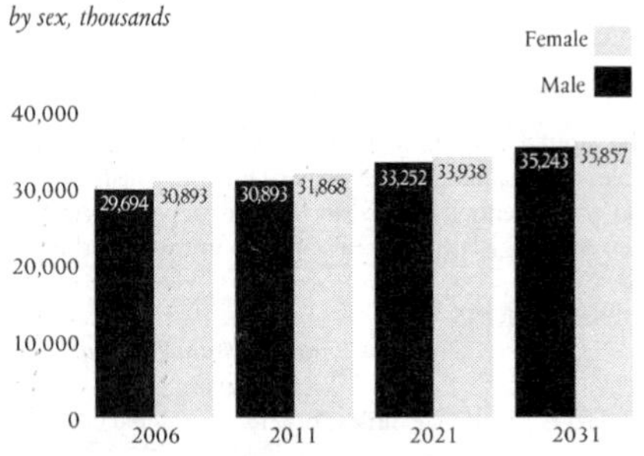

Source: ONS – AAS 2008 (Crown copyright)

BY AGE AND SEX

	Thousands Male	Female
Under 1	374	357
1–4	1,416	1,349
5–9	1,785	1,705
10–14	1,924	1,827
15–19	2,060	1,936
20–29	3,978	3,902
30–44	6,597	6,706
45–59	5,804	5,940
60–64	1,584	1,656
65–74	2,379	2,650
75–84	1,413	2,002
85+	379	864

Source: ONS – *AAS 2008* (Crown copyright)

BY ETHNIC GROUP

	Thousands
White	
British	48,424
Other	2,940
Mixed	
White and Black Caribbean	230
White and Black African	76
White and Asian	158
Other Mixed	141
Asian	
Indian	1,136
Pakistani	857
Bangladeshi	345
Other Asian	394
Black	
Black Caribbean	615
Black African	714
Black Other	55
Chinese	211
Other	836
ALL*	58,855

* Includes those who did not state their ethnic origin
Source: ONS – *AAS 2008* (Crown copyright)

IMMIGRATION

ACCEPTANCES FOR SETTLEMENT IN THE UK

*Region**	*Number of persons* 2004	2006
Europe: total†	26,585	15,800
Albania	1,105	1,185
Bulgaria	625	4,250
Romania	560	1,620
Russia	1,620	1,380
Serbia and Montenegro	9,590	2,185
Turkey	6,060	3,095
Ukraine	1,050	860
Americas: total	14,130	12,130
Canada	1,225	1,125
Colombia	1,745	880
Jamaica	2,930	2,900
USA	4,120	3,845
Africa: total	39,430	32,230
Angola	1,090	980
Dem. Rep. Congo	2,410	1,190
Ghana	2,305	2,910
Kenya	2,255	1,685
Nigeria	4,620	4,510
Sierra Leone	1,805	1,160
Somalia	3,825	2,125
South Africa	7,560	5,675
Uganda	960	685
Zimbabwe	3,765	3,420
Asia: total	53,095	69,795
Indian sub-continent: total	24,235	25,080
Bangladesh	3,115	2,860
India	11,100	11,220
Pakistan	10,020	11,000
Middle East: total	6,045	9,405
Iran	1,725	1,050
Iraq	1,725	6,875
Remainder of Asia: total	22,815	35,305
Afghanistan	1,405	7,410
China	2,515	3,365
Hong Kong	540	1,065
Japan	1,360	1,260
Malaysia	955	1,785
Nepal	515	6,940
Philippines	8,200	6,325
Sri Lanka	4,870	3,135
Thailand	985	2,425

Oceania: total	5,690	4,215
Australia	3,240	2,645
New Zealand	2,370	1,405
British Overseas Citizens	75	65
Nationality unknown	205	190
ALL NATIONALITIES	139,210	134,430

* Country specified only when the figure for 2003 or 2005 is over 1,000

† Excluding European Economic Area and Swiss nationals

Source: ONS – *AAS 2008* (Crown copyright)

BIRTHS

	Live births	*Male*	*Female*	*Birth rate**
United Kingdom	749,000	383,000	366,000	12.4
England and Wales	670,000	342,000	327,000	12.5
Scotland	56,000	28,000	27,000	10.9
Northern Ireland	23,000	12,000	11,000	13.4

* Live births per 1,000 population

Source: ONS – *AAS 2008* (Crown copyright)

FERTILITY RATES

	Live births per 1,000 women		
Age of mother at childbirth	*1971*	*1991*	*2006*
Under 20	50.1	32.9	26.4
20–24	153.9	88.9	72.0
25–29	155.6	119.9	100.1
30–34	79.4	86.5	104.6
35–39	33.9	32.0	53.4
40+	9.1	5.3	11.1
Total fertility rate*	–	1.82	1.84
Total births (thousands)	901.6	792.3	748.6

* Number of children that would be born to a woman if current patterns of fertility persisted throughout her child-bearing life

Source: ONS – *ST 2008* (Crown copyright)

TOP TEN BABY NAMES

	1954		2007	
	Girls	*Boys*	*Girls*	*Boys*
1	Susan	David	Grace	Jack
2	Linda	John	Ruby	Thomas
3	Christine	Stephen	Olivia	Oliver
4	Margaret	Michael	Emily	Joshua
5	Janet	Peter	Jessica	Harry
6	Patricia	Robert	Sophie	Charlie
7	Carol	Paul	Chloe	Daniel
8	Elizabeth	Alan	Lily	William
9	Mary	Christopher	Ella	James
10	Anne	Richard	Amelia	Alfie

Source: ONS (Crown copyright)

LEGAL ABORTIONS

	2000	*2006*
England and Wales	175,542	193,737
Scotland	11,979	13,028*

* Provisional

Source: ONS – *AAS 2008* (Crown copyright)

DEATHS

Men	*Deaths*	*Death rate**
United Kingdom	274,201	9.2
England and Wales	240,888	
Scotland	26,251	
Northern Ireland	7,062	
Women		
United Kingdom	298,023	9.6
England and Wales	261,711	
Scotland	28,842	
Northern Ireland	7,470	

* Per 1,000 population

Source: ONS – *AAS 2008* (Crown copyright)

INFANT MORTALITY RATE*

United Kingdom	5.0
England and Wales	5.0
Scotland	4.5
Northern Ireland	5.2

* Deaths of infants under one year of age per 1,000 live births

Source: ONS – *AAS 2008* (Crown copyright)

MARRIAGE AND DIVORCE

	Marriages	*Divorces*
United Kingdom*	275,140	148,141
England and Wales*	236,980	132,562
Scotland	29,898	13,014
Northern Ireland	8,259	2,565

* Provisional data

Source: ONS – *AAS 2008* (Crown copyright)

HOUSEHOLDS

BY TYPE (GREAT BRITAIN)

Percentages

	1971	*1991*	*2007*
One Person			
Under state pension age	6	11	14
Over state pension age	12	16	15
One family households			
Couple			
No children	27	28	28
1–2 dependent children	26	20	18
3 or more dependent children	9	5	3
Non-dependent children only	8	8	7
Lone parent			
Dependent children	3	6	7
Non-dependent children only	4	4	3
Two or more unrelated adults	4	3	3
Multi-family households	1	1	1
All households (=100%) *(millions)*	18.6	22.4	24.4

Source: ONS – *ST 2008* (Crown copyright)

BY SIZE (GREAT BRITAIN)

Percentages

	1971	*1991*	*2007*
One person	18	27	29
Two people	32	34	35
Three people	19	16	16
Four people	17	16	13
Five people	8	5	5
Six or more people	6	2	2
All households (=100%) *(millions)*	18.6	22.4	24.4
Average household size *(people)*	2.9	2.5	2.4

Source: ONS – *ST 2008* (Crown copyright)

DEPENDENT CHILDREN LIVING IN DIFFERENT FAMILY TYPES (GREAT BRITAIN)
Percentages

	1972	*1997*	*2007*
Couple families			
1 child	16	17	18
2 children	35	37	36
3 or more children	41	25	22
Lone mother families			
1 child	2	6	7
2 children	2	7	8
3 or more children	2	6	6
Lone father families			
1 child	–	1	1
2 or more children	1	1	1

Source: ONS – *ST 2008* (Crown copyright)

ADULTS LIVING WITH THEIR PARENTS (ENGLAND)
Percentages

	1991	*2002*	*2006*
Men			
20–24	50	56	58
25–29	19	19	22
30–34	9	8	9
Women			
20–24	32	37	39
25–29	9	10	11
30–34	5	2	3

Source: ONS – *ST 2007* (Crown copyright)

MORTGAGES

	1997	*2002*	*2007*
Mortgages* *(thousands)*	10,738	11,364	11,822
Type of mortgage for house purchase† *(percentages)*			
Standard repayment	39.6	82.8	61.1
Endowment	36.0	5.4	8.5
Other‡	24.4	11.4	30.3
Loans in arrears at end-period* *(thousands)*			
By 6–12 months	74	34	41
By 12+ months	45	17	16
Properties repossessed in period	33	12	27

* Estimates cover only members of the Council of Mortgage Lenders, which account for 98 per cent of all outstanding mortgages
† Includes new mortgages advanced by building societies and other major lenders and includes sitting tenants
‡ Includes interest only, PEP/ISA and pension
Source: ONS – *AAS 2008* (Crown copyright)

TYPE OF ACCOMMODATION (GREAT BRITAIN)
Percentages by tenure 2006

	House or bungalow			*Flat or maisonette*	
	Detached	*Semi-detached*	*Terraced*	*Purpose-built*	*Other*
Owner-occupied	31	34	27	7	2
Owned outright	36	34	21	7	2
Owned with mortgage	27	34	31	7	2
Rented from social sector	1	22	30	43	3
Council	1	24	28	45	1
Housing association	1	19	34	41	5
Rented privately	12	21	32	20	15
Furnished	8	13	29	30	20
Unfurnished	14	24	34	16	13
All tenures	23	30	28	15	3

Source: ONS – *AAS 2008* (Crown copyright)

HEALTH

DEATHS BY CAUSE

	England and Wales	*Scotland*	*N. Ireland*
Total Deaths	502,599	55,093	14,532
Deaths from natural causes	482,745	52,856	13,679
Certain infectious and parasitic diseases	7,632	791	188
Intestinal infectious diseases	3,630	128	39
Respiratory and other tuberculosis	432	43	7
Meningococcal infection	52	6	1
Viral hepatitis	205	20	4
AIDS (HIV – disease)	235	19	–
Neoplasms	138,777	15,360	3,959
Malignant neoplasm of trachea, bronchus and lung	29,332	4,062	850
Malignant neoplasm of skin	1,649	158	48
Malignant neoplasm of breast	11,011	1,112	300
Malignant neoplasm of cervix uteri	831	92	29
Malignant neoplasm of prostate	9,057	779	212
Leukaemia	3,859	362	91
Diseases of the blood and blood-forming organs and certain disorders involving the immune mechanism	1,013	113	31
Endocrine, nutritional and metabolic diseases	7,153	1,018	281
Diabetes mellitus	5,490	751	197
Mental and behavioural disorders	14,863	2,817	418
Vascular and unspecified dementia	13,289	2,101	335
Alcohol abuse	545	378	79
Drug dependence and non-dependent abuse of drugs	739	293	1
Diseases of the nervous system and sense organs	15,218	1,333	557
Meningitis (excluding meningococcal)	164	15	1
Alzheimer's disease	4,901	452	265
Diseases of the circulatory system	174,637	18,771	4,879
Ischaemic heart diseases	82,619	9,532	2,556
Cerebrovascular diseases	48,389	5,466	1,326
Diseases of the respiratory system	68,599	7,183	1,982
Influenza	17	2	1
Pneumonia	28,674	2,513	895
Bronchitis, emphysema and other chronic obstructive pulmonary diseases	23,319	2,848	616
Asthma	1,082	82	35
Diseases of the digestive system	25,786	3,208	646
Gastric and duodenal ulcer	3,145	262	57
Chronic liver disease	6,250	1,162	171
Diseases of the skin and subcutaneous tissue	1,812	130	21
Diseases of the musculo-skeletal system and connective tissue	4,238	354	79
Osteoporosis	1,390	40	11
Diseases of the genito-urinary system	10,722	1,112	359
Complications of pregnancy, childbirth and the puerperium	41	7	3
Certain conditions originating in the perinatal period*	160	139	54
Congenital malformations, deformations and chromosomal abnormalities*	1,214	151	84
Symptoms, signs and abnormal findings not classified elsewhere	10,880	369	138
Senility without mention of psychosis (old age)	9,169	206	98
Sudden infant death syndrome	143	27	1
Deaths from external causes	17,509	2,237	853
All accidents	11,824	1,264	525
Suicide and intentional self-harm	3,331	542	249
Homicide and assault	342†	115	30

* Excludes neonatal deaths (those at age under 28 days): for England and Wales neonatal deaths are included in the total number of deaths but excluded from the cause figures

† This will not be a true figure as registration of homicide and assault deaths in England and Wales is often delayed by adjourned inquests

Source: ONS – *AAS 2008* (Crown copyright)

ALCOHOL CONSUMPTION* BY AGE (GREAT BRITAIN)

Percentages

	16–24	*25–44*	*45–64*	*65+*	*All 16+*
Men					
No units	40	27	24	33	29
Up to 4 units	18	25	33	46	31
4–8 units	12	17	21	14	17
8+ units	30	31	21	7	23
Women					
No units	47	40	40	56	44
Up to 3 units	14	20	25	30	23
3–6 units	14	19	23	12	18
6+ units	25	21	12	2	15

* On at least one day in the previous week. Department of Health guidelines recommend that men should not regularly drink more than three to four units of alcohol per day and women should not regularly drink more than two to three units per day. A unit of alcohol is 8 grams by weight or 10ml by volume of pure alcohol, ie the amount contained in half a pint of ordinary strength beer or lager, a single pub measure of spirits or a small glass of ordinary strength wine

Source: ONS – *ST 2008* (Crown copyright)

NOTIFICATIONS OF INFECTIOUS DISEASES

	2000	*2006*
Measles	2,865	4,016
Mumps	3,367	15,867
Rubella	2,064	1,402
Whooping cough	866	639
Scarlet fever	2,544	2,648
Dysentery	1,613	1,238
Food poisoning	98,076	79,059
Typhoid and paratyphoid fevers	205	390
Hepatitis	4,530	5,034
Tuberculosis	7,100	8,020
Malaria	1,166	637

Source: ONS – *AAS 2008* (Crown copyright)

CONSUMPTION OF FRUIT AND VEGETABLES BY AGE (ENGLAND)

	*Average daily portions**
Men	
16–24	3.0
25–34	3.7
35–44	3.5
45–54	3.7
55–64	3.9
65–74	4.0
75+	3.8
Women	
16–24	3.3
25–34	3.9
35–44	4.0
45–54	4.2
55–64	4.5
65–74	4.1
75+	3.6

* The Department of Health recommends that a healthy diet should include at least five portions a day of a variety of fruit and vegetables (excluding potatoes)

Source: ONS – *ST 2008* (Crown copyright)

THE NATIONAL FLAG

The national flag of the United Kingdom is the Union Flag, generally known as the Union Jack.

The Union Flag is a combination of the cross of St George, patron saint of England, the cross of St Andrew, patron saint of Scotland and the cross of St Patrick, patron saint of Ireland.

Cross of St George: cross Gules in a field Argent (red cross on a white ground)

Cross of St Andrew: saltire Argent in a field Azure (white diagonal cross on a blue ground)

Cross of St Patrick: saltire Gules in a field Argent (red diagonal cross on a white ground)

The Union Flag was first introduced in 1606 after the union of the kingdoms of England and Scotland under one sovereign. The cross of St Patrick was added in 1801 after the union of Great Britain and Ireland.

See also Flags of the World colour plates.

FLYING THE UNION FLAG

The correct orientation of the Union Flag when flying is with the broader diagonal band of white uppermost in the hoist (ie near the pole) and the narrower diagonal band of white uppermost in the fly (ie furthest from the pole).

It is the practice to fly the Union Flag daily on some customs houses. In all other cases, the flying of the Union Flag on government buildings is decided by the DCMS at the Queen's command. There is no formal definition of a government building but it is generally accepted to mean a building owned or used by the Crown and predominately occupied or used by civil servants or the Armed Forces. It is now customary for the Union Flag to be flown at Buckingham Palace, Windsor Castle and Sandringham when the Queen is not in residence. Individuals, local authorities and other organisations may fly the Union Flag whenever they wish, subject to compliance with local planning requirements.

FLAGS AT HALF-MAST

Flags are flown at half-mast (ie two-thirds up between the top and bottom of the flagstaff) on the following occasions:

- from the announcement of the death up to the funeral of the sovereign, except on Proclamation Day, when flags are hoisted right up from 11am to sunset
- the funerals of members of the royal family*
- the funerals of foreign rulers*
- the funerals of prime ministers and ex-prime ministers of the UK*
- other occasions by special command of the Queen

On occasions when days for flying flags coincide with days for flying flags at half-mast, the following rules are observed. Flags are flown at full mast:

- although a member of the royal family, or a near relative of the royal family, may be lying dead, unless special commands are received from the Queen to the contrary
- although it may be the day of the funeral of a foreign ruler

If the body of a very distinguished subject is lying at a government office, the flag may fly at half-mast on that office until the body has left (provided it is a day on which the flag would fly) and then the flag is to be hoisted right up. On all other government buildings the flag will fly as usual.

DAYS FOR FLYING FLAGS

On 25 March 2008 the DCMS announced that UK government buildings in England, Scotland and Wales have the freedom to fly the Union Flag at all times, if they wish to do so, and not just on the established days listed below. In addition, on the patron saints' days of Scotland and Wales, the appropriate national flag may be flown alongside the Union Flag on Whitehall government buildings. Flags are hoisted from 8am to sunset.

Countess of Wessex's birthday	20 Jan
Accession of the Queen	6 Feb
Duke of York's birthday	19 Feb
St David's Day (in Wales only)†	1 Mar
Commonwealth Day (2009)	9 Mar
Earl of Wessex's birthday	10 Mar
St Patrick's Day (in Northern Ireland only)‡	17 Mar
Birthday of the Queen	21 Apr
St George's Day (in England only)†	23 Apr
Europe Day†	9 May
Coronation Day	2 Jun
Duke of Edinburgh's birthday	10 Jun
The Queen's Official Birthday (2009)	13 Jun
Duchess of Cornwall's birthday	17 Jul
Princess Royal's birthday	15 Aug
Remembrance Day (2009)	8 Nov
Prince of Wales' birthday	14 Nov
Wedding Day of the Queen	20 Nov
St Andrew's Day (in Scotland only)†	30 Nov
Opening of Parliament by the Queen§	
Prorogation of Parliament by the Queen§	

THE ROYAL STANDARD

The Royal Standard comprises four quarterings – two for England (three lions passant), one for Scotland¶ (a lion rampant) and one for Ireland (a harp).

The Royal Standard is flown when the Queen is in residence at a royal palace, on transport being used by the Queen for official journeys and from Victoria Tower when the Queen attends parliament. It may also be flown on any building (excluding ecclesiastical buildings) during a visit by the Queen. If the Queen is to be present in a building advice on flag flying can be obtained from the DCMS.

The Royal Standard is never flown at half-mast, even after the death of the Sovereign, as the new monarch immediately succeeds to the throne.

* Subject to special commands from the Queen in each case

† The appropriate national flag, or the European flag, may be flown in addition to the Union Flag, but not in a superior position

‡ Only the Union Flag should be flown

§ Only in the Greater London area, whether or not the Queen performs the ceremony in person

¶ In Scotland a version with two Scottish quaterings is used

THE ROYAL FAMILY

THE SOVEREIGN

ELIZABETH II, by the Grace of God, of the United Kingdom of Great Britain and Northern Ireland and of her other Realms and Territories Queen, Head of the Commonwealth, Defender of the Faith
Her Majesty Elizabeth Alexandra Mary of Windsor, elder daughter of King George VI and of HM Queen Elizabeth the Queen Mother
Born 21 April 1926, at 17 Bruton Street, London W1
Ascended the throne 6 February 1952
Crowned 2 June 1953, at Westminster Abbey
Married 20 November 1947, in Westminster Abbey, HRH the Prince Philip, Duke of Edinburgh
Official residences Buckingham Palace, London SW1A 1AA; Windsor Castle, Berks; Palace of Holyroodhouse, Edinburgh
Private residences Sandringham, Norfolk; Balmoral Castle, Aberdeenshire

HUSBAND OF THE QUEEN

HRH THE PRINCE PHILIP, DUKE OF EDINBURGH, KG, KT, OM, GBE, Royal Victorian Chain, AC, QSO, PC, Ranger of Windsor Park
Born 10 June 1921, son of Prince and Princess Andrew of Greece and Denmark, naturalised a British subject 1947, created Duke of Edinburgh, Earl of Merioneth and Baron Greenwich 1947

CHILDREN OF THE QUEEN

HRH THE PRINCE OF WALES (Prince Charles Philip Arthur George), KG, KT, GCB, OM and Great Master of the Order of the Bath, AK, QSO, PC, ADC(P)
Born 14 November 1948, created Prince of Wales and Earl of Chester 1958, succeeded as Duke of Cornwall, Duke of Rothesay, Earl of Carrick and Baron Renfrew, Lord of the Isles and Great Steward of Scotland 1952
Married (1) 29 July 1981 Lady Diana Frances Spencer (Diana, Princess of Wales (1961–97), youngest daughter of the 8th Earl Spencer and the Hon. Mrs Shand Kydd), marriage dissolved 1996; (2) 9 April 2005 Mrs Camilla Rosemary Parker Bowles, now HRH the Duchess of Cornwall (*born* 17 July 1947, daughter of Major Bruce Shand and the Hon. Mrs Rosalind Shand)
Residences Clarence House, London SW1A 1BA; Highgrove, Doughton, Tetbury, Glos GL8 8TN; Birkhall, Ballater, Aberdeenshire
Issue
1. HRH Prince William of Wales (Prince William Arthur Philip Louis), KG, *born* 21 June 1982
2. HRH Prince Henry of Wales (Prince Henry Charles Albert David), *born* 15 September 1984

HRH THE PRINCESS ROYAL (Princess Anne Elizabeth Alice Louise), KG, KT, GCVO
Born 15 August 1950, declared the Princess Royal 1987
Married (1) 14 November 1973 Captain Mark Anthony Peter Phillips, CVO (*born* 22 September 1948); marriage dissolved 1992; (2) 12 December 1992 Captain Timothy James Hamilton Laurence, MVO, RN (*born* 1 March 1955)
Residence Gatcombe Park, Minchinhampton, Glos GL6 9AT
Issue
1. Peter Mark Andrew Phillips, *born* 15 November 1977, married 17 May 2008 Autumn Patricia Kelly
2. Zara Anne Elizabeth Phillips, MBE, *born* 15 May 1981

HRH THE DUKE OF YORK (Prince Andrew Albert Christian Edward), KG, KCVO, ADC(P)
Born 19 February 1960, created Duke of York, Earl of Inverness and Baron Killyleagh 1986
Married 23 July 1986 Sarah Margaret Ferguson, now Sarah, Duchess of York (*born* 15 October 1959, younger daughter of Major Ronald Ferguson and Mrs Hector Barrantes), marriage dissolved 1996
Residence Royal Lodge, Windsor Great Park, Berks
Issue
1. HRH Princess Beatrice of York (Princess Beatrice Elizabeth Mary), *born* 8 August 1988
2. HRH Princess Eugenie of York (Princess Eugenie Victoria Helena), *born* 23 March 1990

HRH THE EARL OF WESSEX (Prince Edward Antony Richard Louis), KG, KCVO
Born 10 March 1964, created Earl of Wessex, Viscount Severn 1999
Married 19 June 1999 Sophie Helen Rhys-Jones, now HRH the Countess of Wessex (*born* 20 January 1965, daughter of Mr and Mrs Christopher Rhys-Jones)
Residence Bagshot Park, Bagshot, Surrey GU19 5HS
Issue
1. Lady Louise Windsor (Louise Alice Elizabeth Mary Mountbatten-Windsor), *born* 8 November 2003
2. Viscount Severn (James Alexander Philip Theo Mountbatten-Windsor), *born* 17 December 2007

NEPHEW AND NIECE OF THE QUEEN

Children of HRH the Princess Margaret, Countess of Snowdon and the Earl of Snowdon (*see* House of Windsor):

DAVID ALBERT CHARLES ARMSTRONG-JONES, VISCOUNT LINLEY, *born* 3 November 1961, *married* 8 October 1993 the Hon. Serena Stanhope, and has issue, Hon. Charles Patrick Inigo Armstrong-Jones, *born* 1 July 1999; Hon. Margarita Elizabeth Alleyne Armstrong-Jones, *born* 14 May 2002

LADY SARAH CHATTO (Sarah Frances Elizabeth), *born* 1 May 1964, *married* 14 July 1994 Daniel Chatto, and has issue, Samuel David Benedict Chatto, *born* 28 July 1996; Arthur Robert Nathaniel Chatto, *born* 5 February 1999

COUSINS OF THE QUEEN

Child of HRH the Duke of Gloucester and HRH Princess Alice, Duchess of Gloucester (*see* House of Windsor):

HRH THE DUKE OF GLOUCESTER (Prince Richard Alexander Walter George), KG, GCVO, Grand Prior of the Order of St John of Jerusalem

Born 26 August 1944
Married 8 July 1972 Birgitte Eva van Deurs, now HRH the Duchess of Gloucester, GCVO (*born* 20 June 1946, daughter of Asger Henriksen and Vivian van Deurs)
Residence Kensington Palace, London W8 4PU
Issue
1. Earl of Ulster (Alexander Patrick Gregers Richard), *born* 24 October 1974, *married* 22 June 2002 Dr Claire Booth, and has issue, Lord Culloden (Xan Richard Anders), *born* 12 March 2007
2. Lady Davina Lewis (Davina Elizabeth Alice Benedikte), *born* 19 November 1977, *married* 31 July 2004 Gary Lewis
3. Lady Rose Windsor (Rose Victoria Birgitte Louise), *born* 1 March 1980

Children of HRH the Duke of Kent and Princess Marina, Duchess of Kent (*see* House of Windsor):

HRH THE DUKE OF KENT (Prince Edward George Nicholas Paul Patrick), KG, GCMG, GCVO, ADC(P)
Born 9 October 1935
Married 8 June 1961 Katharine Lucy Mary Worsley, now HRH the Duchess of Kent, GCVO (*born* 22 February 1933, daughter of Sir William Worsley, Bt.)
Residence Wren House, Palace Green, London W8 4PY
Issue
1. Earl of St Andrews (George Philip Nicholas), *born* 26 June 1962, *married* 9 January 1988 Sylvana Tomaselli, and has issue, Baron Downpatrick (Edward Edmund Maximilian George), *born* 2 December 1988; Lady Marina-Charlotte Windsor (Marina-Charlotte Alexandra Katharine Helen), *born* 30 September 1992; Lady Amelia Windsor (Amelia Sophia Theodora Mary Margaret), *born* 24 August 1995
2. Lady Helen Taylor (Helen Marina Lucy), *born* 28 April 1964, *married* 18 July 1992 Timothy Taylor, and has issue, Columbus George Donald Taylor, *born* 6 August 1994; Cassius Edward Taylor, *born* 26 December 1996; Eloise Olivia Katharine Taylor, *born* 3 March 2003; Estella Olga Elizabeth Taylor, *born* 21 December 2004
3. Lord Nicholas Windsor (Nicholas Charles Edward Jonathan), *born* 25 July 1970, *married* 4 November 2006 Paola Doimi de Frankopan, and has issue, Albert Louis Philip Edward Windsor, *born* 22 September 2007

HRH PRINCESS ALEXANDRA, THE HON. LADY OGILVY (Princess Alexandra Helen Elizabeth Olga Christabel), KG, GCVO
Born 25 December 1936
Married 24 April 1963 the Rt. Hon. Sir Angus Ogilvy, KCVO (1928–2004), second son of 12th Earl of Airlie
Residence Thatched House Lodge, Richmond Park, Surrey TW10 5HP
Issue
1. James Robert Bruce Ogilvy, *born* 29 February 1964, *married* 30 July 1988 Julia Rawlinson, and has issue, Flora Alexandra Ogilvy, *born* 15 December 1994; Alexander Charles Ogilvy, *born* 12 November 1996
2. Marina Victoria Alexandra Ogilvy, *born* 31 July 1966, *married* 2 February 1990 Paul Mowatt (marriage dissolved 1997), and has issue, Zenouska May Mowatt, *born* 26 May 1990; Christian Alexander Mowatt, *born* 4 June 1993

HRH PRINCE MICHAEL OF KENT (Prince Michael George Charles Franklin), GCVO
Born 4 July 1942
Married 30 June 1978 Baroness Marie-Christine Agnes Hedwig Ida von Reibnitz, now HRH Princess Michael of Kent (*born* 15 January 1945, daughter of Baron Gunther von Reibnitz)
Residence Kensington Palace, London W8 4PU
Issue
1. Lord Frederick Windsor (Frederick Michael George David Louis), *born* 6 April 1979
2. Lady Gabriella Windsor (Gabriella Marina Alexandra Ophelia), *born* 23 April 1981

ORDER OF SUCCESSION

1	HRH the Prince of Wales
2	HRH Prince William of Wales
3	HRH Prince Henry of Wales
4	HRH the Duke of York
5	HRH Princess Beatrice of York
6	HRH Princess Eugenie of York
7	HRH the Earl of Wessex
8	Viscount Severn
9	Lady Louise Windsor
10	HRH the Princess Royal
11	Peter Phillips
12	Zara Phillips
13	Viscount Linley
14	Hon. Charles Armstrong-Jones
15	Hon. Margarita Armstrong-Jones
16	Lady Sarah Chatto
17	Samuel Chatto
18	Arthur Chatto
19	HRH the Duke of Gloucester
20	Earl of Ulster
21	Lord Culloden
22	Lady Davina Lewis
23	Lady Rose Windsor
24	HRH the Duke of Kent
25	Lady Marina-Charlotte Windsor
26	Lady Amelia Windsor
27	Lady Helen Taylor
28	Columbus Taylor
29	Cassius Taylor
30	Eloise Taylor
31	Estella Taylor
32	Lord Frederick Windsor
33	Lady Gabriella Windsor
34	HRH Princess Alexandra, the Hon. Lady Ogilvy
35	James Ogilvy
36	Alexander Ogilvy
37	Flora Ogilvy
38	Marina Ogilvy
39	Christian Mowatt

HRH Prince Michael of Kent, and the Earl of St Andrews both lost the right of succession to the throne through marriage to a Roman Catholic. Lord Nicholas Windsor and Baron Downpatrick renounced their rights to the throne on converting to Roman Catholicism in 2001 and 2003 respectively. Their children remain in succession provided that they are in communion with the Church of England.

PRIVATE SECRETARIES TO THE ROYAL FAMILY

THE QUEEN
Office: Buckingham Palace, London SW1A 1AA
T 020-7930 4832 W www.royal.gov.uk
Private Secretary to the Queen, Christopher Geidt, CVO, OBE

PRINCE PHILIP, THE DUKE OF EDINBURGH
Office: Buckingham Palace, London SW1A 1AA
T 020-7930 4832
Private Secretary, Brig. Sir Miles Hunt-Davis, KCVO, CBE

THE PRINCE OF WALES AND THE DUCHESS OF CORNWALL
Office: Clarence House, London SW1A 1BA T 020-7930 4832
Principal Private Secretary, Sir Michael Peat, KCVO

PRINCES WILLIAM AND HENRY OF WALES
Office: Clarence House, London SW1A 1BA T 020-7930 4832
Private Secretary, James Lowther-Pinkerton, MVO, MBE

THE DUKE OF YORK
Office: Buckingham Palace, London SW1A 1AA
T 020-7930 4832
Private Secretary, Alastair Watson

THE EARL AND COUNTESS OF WESSEX
Office: Bagshot Park, Surrey GU19 5PL T 01276-707040
Private Secretary, Brig. J. Smedley

THE PRINCESS ROYAL
Office: Buckingham Palace, London SW1A 1AA
T 020-7024 4199
Private Secretary, Capt. N. P. Wright, LVO, RN

THE DUKE AND DUCHESS OF GLOUCESTER
Office: Kensington Palace, London W8 4PU T 020-7368 1000
Private Secretary, Alistair Wood, MBE

THE DUKE OF KENT
Office: St James's Palace, London SW1A 1BQ T 020-7930 4872
Private Secretary, N. Adamson, LVO, OBE

THE DUCHESS OF KENT
Office: Wren House, Palace Green, London W8 4PY
T 020-7937 2730
Personal Secretary, Virginia Utley

PRINCE AND PRINCESS MICHAEL OF KENT
Office: Kensington Palace, London W8 4PU T 020-7938 3519
W www.princemichael.org.uk
Private Secretary, N. Chance

PRINCESS ALEXANDRA, THE HON. LADY OGILVY
Office: Buckingham Palace, London SW1A 1AA
T 020-7024 4270
Private Secretary, Diane Duke

ROYAL SALUTES

ENGLAND

The basic royal salute is 21 rounds with an extra 20 rounds fired at Hyde Park because it is a royal park. At the Tower of London 62 rounds are fired on royal anniversaries (21 plus a further 20 because the Tower is a royal palace and a further 21 'for the City of London') and 41 on other occasions. When the Queen's official birthday coincides with the Duke of Edinburgh's birthday, 124 rounds are fired from the Tower (62 rounds for each birthday). Gun salutes occur on the following royal anniversaries:

- Accession Day
- The Queen's birthday
- Coronation Day
- Duke of Edinburgh's birthday
- The Queen's official birthday
- state opening of parliament

Gun salutes also occur when parliament is prorogued by the sovereign, on royal births and when a visiting head of state meets the sovereign in London, Windsor or Edinburgh.

In London, salutes are fired at Hyde Park and the Tower of London although on some occasions (state visits, state opening of parliament and the Queen's birthday parade) Green Park is used instead.

Constable of the Royal Palace and Fortress of London, Gen. Sir Roger Wheeler, GCB, CBE
Lieutenant of the Tower of London, Lt.-Gen. Sir Cedric Delves, KBE, DSO
Resident Governor and Keeper of the Jewel House, Maj.-Gen. Keith Cima, CB
Master Gunner of St James's Park, Gen. Sir Alex Harley, KBE, CB
Master Gunner within the Tower, Col. Simon Garrett

SCOTLAND

Royal salutes are authorised at Edinburgh Castle and Stirling Castle. A salute of 21 guns is fired on the following occasions:

- the anniversaries of the birth, accession and coronation of the sovereign
- the anniversary of the birth of the Duke of Edinburgh

A salute of 21 guns is fired in Edinburgh on the occasion of the opening of the general assembly of the Church of Scotland. A salute of 21 guns may also be fired in Edinburgh on the arrival of HM The Queen or a member of the royal family who is a Royal Highness on an official visit. Other military saluting stations in England are at Colchester, Dover, Plymouth, Woolwich and York. Military saluting stations are also situated at Cardiff Castle in Wales, Hillsborough Castle in Northern Ireland and in Gibraltar.

ROYAL HOUSEHOLD

The PRIVATE SECRETARY is responsible for:

- informing and advising the Queen on constitutional, governmental and political matters in the UK, her other Realms and the wider Commonwealth, including communications with the prime minister and government departments
- organising the Queen's domestic and overseas official programme
- the Queen's speeches, messages, patronage, photographs, portraits and official presents
- communications in connection with the role of the royal family
- dealing with correspondence to the Queen from members of the public
- organising and coordinating royal travel
- coordinating and initiating research to support engagements by members of the royal family

The COMMUNICATIONS AND PRESS SECRETARY is in charge of Buckingham Palace's press office and reports to the private secretary. The press secretary is responsible for:

- developing communications strategies to enhance the public understanding of the role of the monarchy
- briefing the British and international media on the role and duties of the Queen and issues relating to the royal family
- responding to media enquiries
- arranging media facilities in the UK and overseas to support royal functions and engagements
- the management of the royal website

The private secretary is keeper of the royal archives and is responsible for the care of the records of the sovereign and the royal household from previous reigns, preserved in the royal archives at Windsor. As keeper, it is the private secretary's responsibility to ensure the proper management of the records of the present reign with a view to their transfer to the archives as and when appropriate. The private secretary is an *ex officio* trustee of the Royal Collection Trust.

The KEEPER OF THE PRIVY PURSE AND TREASURER to the Queen is responsible for:

- the Queen's Civil List, which is the money paid from the government's Consolidated Fund to meet official expenditure relating to the Queen's duties as head of state and head of the Commonwealth
- through the director of personnel, the planning and management of personnel policy across the royal household, the administration of all its pension schemes and private estates employees, and the allocation of employee and pensioner housing
- information technology systems
- internal audit services
- health and safety; insurance matters
- the privy purse, which is mainly financed by the net income of the Duchy of Lancaster, and meets both official and private expenditure incurred by the Queen
- liaison with other members of the royal family and their households on financial matters
- the Queen's private estates at Sandringham and Balmoral, the Queen's Racing Establishment and the Royal Studs and liaison with the Ascot Authority
- the Home Park at Windsor and liaison with the Crown Estate Commissioners concerning the Home Park and the Great Park at Windsor
- the Royal Philatelic Collection
- administrative aspects of the Military Knights of Windsor
- administration of the Royal Victorian Order, of which the keeper of the privy purse is secretary, Long and Faithful Service Medals, and the Queen's cups, medals and prizes, and policy on commemorative medals

The keeper of the privy purse is one of three royal trustees (in respect of his responsibilities for the Civil List) and is receiver-general of the Duchy of Lancaster and a member of the Duchy's Council.

The keeper of the privy purse is also responsible for property services at occupied royal palaces in England, comprising Buckingham Palace, St James's Palace, Clarence House, Marlborough House Mews, the residential and office areas of Kensington Palace, Windsor Castle and buildings in the Home and Great Parks of Windsor and Hampton Court Mews and Paddocks. The costs of property services for occupied royal palaces are met from a grant-in-aid from the Department for Culture, Media and Sport.

The DIRECTOR OF THE PROPERTY SECTION has day-to-day responsibility for the royal household's property section:

- fire safety issues
- repairs and refurbishment of buildings and new buildings work
- utilities and telecommunications
- putting up stages, tents and other work in connection with ceremonial occasions, garden parties and other official functions

The property section is also responsible, on a sub-contract basis from the DCMS, for the maintenance of Marlborough House (which is occupied by the Commonwealth Secretariat).

The keeper of the privy purse also oversees royal communications and information expenditure, which is met from the property services grant-in-aid, and the financial aspects of royal travel, met from a grant-in-aid provided by the Department for Transport.

The keeper of the privy purse is an *ex officio* trustee of the Historic Royal Palaces Trust and the Royal Collection Trust.

The Queen's Civil List and the grants-in-aid for property services and royal travel are provided by the government in return for the net surplus from the Crown Estate and other hereditary revenues.

The MASTER OF THE HOUSEHOLD is responsible for the staff and domestic arrangements at Buckingham Palace, Windsor Castle, the Palace of Holyroodhouse, Balmoral Castle and Sandringham House when the Queen is in residence. These arrangements include:

- the provision of meals for the Queen and other

members of the royal family, their guests and royal household employees
- service by liveried staff at meals, receptions and other events
- travel arrangements for employees and the movement of baggage between the royal residences
- cleaning and laundry
- furnishings and the internal decorative appearance of occupied royal palaces in collaboration with the director of the Royal Collection
- liaison with the royalty and diplomatic protection department of the Metropolitan Police concerning security procedures at occupied royal palaces
- the Queen's official entertaining, both at home and overseas, and overseeing aspects of the Queen's private entertaining

The COMPTROLLER, LORD CHAMBERLAIN'S OFFICE is responsible for:

- the organisation of all ceremonial engagements, including state visits to the Queen in the UK, royal weddings and funerals, the state opening of parliament, Guards of Honour at Buckingham Palace, investitures, and the Garter and Thistle ceremonies
- garden parties at Buckingham Palace and the Palace of Holyroodhouse (except for catering and tents)
- the Crown Jewels, which are part of the Royal Collection, when they are in use on state occasions
- coordination of the arrangements for the Queen to be represented at funerals and memorial services and at the arrival and departure of visiting heads of state
- advising on matters of precedence, style and titles, dress, flying of flags, gun salutes, mourning and other ceremonial issues
- supervising the applications from tradesmen for Royal Warrants of Appointment
- advising on the commercial use of royal emblems and contemporary royal photographs
- the ecclesiastical household, the medical household, the body guards and certain ceremonial appointments such as Gentlemen Ushers and Pages of Honour
- the lords in waiting, who represent the Queen on various occasions and escort visiting heads of state during incoming state visits
- the Queen's bargemaster and watermen and the Queen's swans
- the Royal Almonry

The comptroller is also responsible for the Royal Mews, assisted by the CROWN EQUERRY, who has day-to-day responsibility for:

- the provision of carriage processions for the state opening of parliament, state visits, Trooping of the Colour, Royal Ascot, the Garter Ceremony, the Thistle Service, the presentation of credentials to the Queen by incoming foreign ambassadors and high commissioners, and other state and ceremonial occasions
- the provision of chauffeur-driven cars
- coordinating travel arrangements by road in respect of the Queen's official engagements
- supervision and administration of the Royal Mews at Buckingham Palace, Windsor Castle, Hampton Court and the Palace of Holyroodhouse

The comptroller also has overall responsibility for the MARSHAL OF THE DIPLOMATIC CORPS, who is responsible for the relationship between the royal household and the Diplomatic Heads of Mission in London; and the SECRETARY OF THE CENTRAL CHANCERY OF THE ORDERS OF KNIGHTHOOD, who administers the Orders of Chivalry, makes arrangements for investitures and the distribution of insignia, and ensures the proper public notification of awards through the *London Gazette*.

The DIRECTOR OF THE ROYAL COLLECTION is responsible for:

- the administration and custodial control of the Royal Collection in all royal residences
- the care, display, conservation and restoration of items in the collection
- initiating and assisting research into the collection and publishing catalogues and books on the collection
- making the collection accessible to the public and educating and informing the public about the collection

The Royal Collection, which contains a large number of works of art, is held by the Queen as sovereign in trust for her successors and the nation and is not owned by her as an individual. The administration, conservation and presentation of the Royal Collection are funded by the Royal Collection Trust solely from income from visitors to Windsor Castle, Buckingham Palace and the Palace of Holyroodhouse. The Royal Collection Trust is chaired by the Prince of Wales. The Lord Chamberlain, the private secretary and the keeper of the privy purse are *ex officio* trustees and there are three external trustees appointed by the Queen.

The director of the Royal Collection is also at present the SURVEYOR OF THE QUEEN'S WORKS OF ART and is responsible for pictures and miniatures, the ROYAL LIBRARIAN is responsible for all books, manuscripts, coins and medals, insignia and works of art on paper including the watercolours, prints and drawings in the Print Room at Windsor Castle, and the SURVEYOR OF THE QUEEN'S WORKS OF ART is responsible for furniture, ceramics and the other decorative arts in the collection.

The director of the Royal Collection has overall responsibility for trading activities that fund the Royal Collection Department. These are administered by Royal Collection Enterprises Limited, the trading subsidiary of the Royal Collection Trust. The company, whose chair is the Keeper of the Privy Purse, is responsible for:

- managing access by the public to Windsor Castle (including Frogmore House), Buckingham Palace (including the Royal Mews and the Queen's Gallery) and the Palace of Holyroodhouse
- running shops at each location
- managing the images and intellectual property rights of the Royal Collection

The director of the Royal Collection is also an *ex officio* trustee of the Historic Royal Palaces Trust.

SENIOR MANAGEMENT OF THE ROYAL HOUSEHOLD

Lord Chamberlain, Earl Peel, GCVO, PC

HEADS OF DEPARTMENT
Private Secretary to The Queen, Rt. Hon. Christopher Geidt, CVO, OBE
Keeper of the Privy Purse, Sir Alan Reid, KCVO
Master of the Household, Air Vice-Marshal David Walker, OBE, MVO
Comptroller, Lord Chamberlain's Office, Lt.-Col. Andrew Ford
Director of the Royal Collection, Sir Hugh Roberts, KCVO

NON-EXECUTIVE MEMBERS
Private Secretary to the Duke of Edinburgh, Brig. Sir Miles Hunt-Davis, KCVO, CBE
Private Secretary to the Prince of Wales, Sir Michael Peat, KCVO

THE POET LAUREATE

The post of Poet Laureate was officially established when John Dryden was appointed by royal warrant as Poet Laureate and Historiographer Royal in 1668. The post is attached to the royal household and was originally conferred on the holder for life; in 1999 the length of appointment was changed to a ten-year term. It is customary for the Poet Laureate to write verse to mark events of national importance. The postholder currently receives an honorarium of £5,000 a year.
The Poet Laureate, Prof. Andrew Motion, *apptd* 1999

ROYAL FINANCES

FUNDING

CIVIL LIST

The Civil List dates back to the late 17th century. It was originally used by the sovereign to supplement hereditary revenues for paying the salaries of judges, ambassadors and other government officers as well as the expenses of the royal household. In 1760, on the accession of George III, it was decided that the Civil List would be provided by parliament to cover all relevant expenditure in return for the king surrendering the hereditary revenues of the Crown (principally the net surplus of the Crown Estate). At that time parliament undertook to pay the salaries of judges, ambassadors, etc. In 1831 parliament agreed also to meet the costs of the royal palaces in return for a reduction in the Civil List. Each sovereign has agreed to continue this arrangement. The Civil List now meets the central staff costs and running expenses of the Queen's official household.

Until 1972, the amount of money allocated annually under the Civil List was set for the duration of a reign. The system was then altered to a fixed annual payment for ten years but from 1975 high inflation made an annual review necessary. The system of payments reverted to the practice of a fixed annual payment of £7.9m for a ten year period to 31 December 2000, during this period annual Civil List expenditure reached £6.5m, and a reserve of £35m was established. In order to draw down the reserve, the annual Civil List payment was left at £7.9m for a further ten years to 31 December 2010.

The legislative requirement is for Civil List accounts to be submitted to parliament, in the form of Royal Trustees Reports, at 10-yearly intervals, but from June 2002 accounts have been published annually. The sixth annual accounts for the year ending 31 December 2007 were published in June 2008:

	2006	*2007*
Civil List payment	£7,900,000	£7,900,000
Draw-down from the Civil List reserve	£4,100,000	£4,900,000
Net Receipts	£12,000,000	£12,800,000
Net Civil List Expenditure	(£12,200,000)	(£12,700,000)

PARLIAMENTARY ANNUITIES

The Civil List Acts provide for other members of the royal family to receive parliamentary annuities from government funds to meet the expenses of carrying out their official duties. Since 1993 the Queen has reimbursed all the annuities except those paid to the late Queen Elizabeth the Queen Mother and the Duke of Edinburgh.

The Prince of Wales does not receive a parliamentary annuity. He derives his income from the revenues of the Duchy of Cornwall and these monies meet the official and private expenses of the Prince of Wales and his family (*see* Prince of Wales' Funding).

In 2000 the annual amounts payable to members of the royal family, excluding the Earl of Wessex, were reset at their 1990 levels for the next ten years. The Earl of Wessex had his annuity increased by £45,000 to £141,000 on the occasion of his marriage in 1999.

The annual payments remain as follows until December 2010:

The Duke of Edinburgh	£359,000
The Duke of York	£249,000
The Earl of Wessex	£141,000
The Princess Royal	£228,000
The Duke and Duchess of Gloucester	£175,000
The Duke and Duchess of Kent	£236,000
Princess Alexandra	£225,000
Subtotal	£1,613,000
Refunded to the Treasury by the Queen	(£1,254,000)
TOTAL	£359,000

GRANTS-IN-AID

Grants-in-aid are provided to the royal household annually by the Department for Culture, Media and Sport for property services and communications and information, and by the Department for Transport for royal travel. Property services meets the cost of property maintenance, and of utilities, telephones and related services at the occupied royal palaces in England (*see* Royal Household section for a list of occupied palaces). Communications and Information meets the cost of communication and information services in connection with official royal functions and engagements in England and Scotland. Royal travel meets the cost of official royal travel by air and rail.

GRANTS-IN-AID 2007–8:

	Grant-in-aid voted by parliament	*Total net expenditure*
Property Services	£15,000,000	£15,300,000
Marlborough House Maintenance	£600,000	£500,000
Communications and Information	£500,000	£500,000
Royal Travel	£6,400,000	£6,200,000

THE PRIVY PURSE AND THE DUCHY OF LANCASTER

The funds received by the privy purse pay for official expenses incurred by the Queen as head of state and for some of the Queen's private expenditure. The revenues of the Duchy of Lancaster are the principal source of income for the privy purse. The revenues of the Duchy were retained by George III in 1760 when the hereditary revenues were surrendered in exchange for the Civil List. The Duchy's affairs are the responsibility of the Duchy Council which reports to the Chancellor of the Duchy of Lancaster, who in turn is accountable directly to the sovereign rather than to parliament. However the chancellor does answer parliamentary questions on matters relating to the Duchy of Lancaster's responsibilities.

THE DUCHY OF LANCASTER, Lancaster Place, London WC2E 7ED **E** info@duchyoflancaster.co.uk
W www.duchyoflancaster.co.uk
Chancellor of the Duchy of Lancaster, Rt. Hon. Ed Miliband, MP, *apptd* 2007
Chair of the Council, Lord Shuttleworth
Clerk and Chief Executive, Paul Clarke, FRICS
Receiver-General, Sir Alan Reid, KCVO
Attorney-General, Robert Hildyard, QC

PERSONAL INCOME

The Queen's personal income derives mostly from investments, and is used to meet private expenditure.

EXPENDITURE MET BY GOVERNMENT DEPARTMENTS AND THE CROWN ESTATE 2007–8:

Administration of honours	£700,000
Equerries, orderlies and other personnel	£1,400,000
Maintenance of Holyroodhouse	£1,100,000
State visits to and by the Queen and liaison with the Diplomatic Corps	£700,000
Ceremonial occasions	£200,000
Maintenance of Home Park, Windsor Castle	£600,000
Other	£200,000
Total	£4,900,000

PRINCE OF WALES' FUNDING

The Duchy Estate was created in 1337 by Edward III for his son and heir Prince Edward (the Black Prince) who became the Duke of Cornwall. The Duchy's primary function is to provide an income from its assets for the Prince of Wales. Under a 1337 charter, confirmed by subsequent legislation, the Prince of Wales is not entitled to the proceeds or profit on the sale of Duchy assets but only to the annual income which is generated from these assets. The Duchy is responsible for the sustainable and commercial management of its properties, investment portfolio and approximately 54,648 hectares of land, based mostly in the southwest of England. The Prince of Wales has chosen to use a proportion of his income to meet the cost of his public and charitable work in addition to providing a private source of income. The Duchy also funds the public, charitable and private activities of the Duchess of Cornwall and princes William and Harry. Proceeds from the Duchy are voluntarily subject to income tax.

THE DUCHY OF CORNWALL, 10 Buckingham Gate, London SW1E 6L
T 0207-834 7346 **E** London@duchyofcornwall.gov.uk
W www.duchyofcornwall.org
Lord Warden of the Stannaries, Sir Nicholas Bacon, Bt.
Receiver-General, James Leigh-Pemberton
Attorney-General, Jonathan Crow, QC
Secretary and Keeper of the Records, Bertie Ross

TAXATION

The sovereign is not legally liable to pay income tax or capital gains tax. After income tax was reintroduced in 1842, some income tax was paid voluntarily by the sovereign but over a long period these payments were phased out. In 1992 the Queen offered to pay income and capital gains tax on a voluntary basis from 6 April 1993, and the Prince of Wales offered to pay tax on a voluntary basis on his income from the Duchy of Cornwall (he was already taxed in all other respects).

The main provisions for the Queen and the Prince of Wales to pay tax, set out in a Memorandum of Understanding on Royal Taxation presented to parliament on 11 February 1993, are that the Queen will pay income tax and capital gains tax in respect of her private income and assets, and on the proportion of the income and capital gains of the Privy Purse used for private purposes. Inheritance tax will be paid on the Queen's assets, except for those which pass to the next sovereign, whether automatically or by gift or bequest. The Prince of Wales will pay income tax on income from the Duchy of Cornwall used for private purposes.

The Prince of Wales has confirmed that he intends to pay tax on the same basis following his accession to the throne. Other members of the royal family are subject to tax as for any taxpayer.

MILITARY RANKS AND TITLES

THE QUEEN

ROYAL NAVY
Lord High Admiral of the United Kingdom

ARMY
Colonel-in-Chief
The Life Guards; The Blues and Royals (Royal Horse Guards and 1st Dragoons); The Royal Scots Dragoon Guards (Carabiniers and Greys); The Queen's Royal Lancers; Royal Tank Regiment; Corps of Royal Engineers; Grenadier Guards; Coldstream Guards; Scots Guards; Irish Guards; Welsh Guards; The Royal Regiment of Scotland; The Duke of Lancaster's Regiment (King's, Lancashire and Borders); The Royal Welsh; Adjutant General's Corps; The Royal Mercian and Lancastrian Yeomanry; The Governor General's Horse Guards (of Canada); The King's Own Calgary Regiment (Royal Canadian Armoured Corps); Canadian Military Engineers Branch; Royal 22e Regiment (of Canada); Governor General's Foot Guards (of Canada); The Canadian Grenadier Guards; Le Régiment de la Chaudière (of Canada); 2nd Battalion Royal New Brunswick Regiment (North Shore); 48th Highlanders of Canada; The Argyll and Sutherland Highlanders of Canada (Princess Louise's); The Calgary Highlanders; Royal Australian Engineers; Royal Australian Infantry Corps; Royal Australian Army Ordnance Corps; Royal Australian Army Nursing Corps; The Corps of Royal New Zealand Engineers; Royal New Zealand Infantry Regiment; The Malawi Rifles; The Royal Malta Artillery

Affiliated Colonel-in-Chief
The Queen's Gurkha Engineers

Captain-General
Royal Regiment of Artillery; The Honourable Artillery Company; Combined Cadet Force; Royal Regiment of Canadian Artillery; Royal Regiment of Australian Artillery; Royal Regiment of New Zealand Artillery; Royal New Zealand Armoured Corps

Royal Colonel
The Argyll and Sutherland Highlanders, 5th Battalion The Royal Regiment of Scotland

Patron
Royal Army Chaplains' Department

ROYAL AIR FORCE
Air Commodore-in-Chief
Royal Auxiliary Air Force; Royal Air Force Regiment; Air Reserve of Canada; Royal Australian Air Force Reserve; Territorial Air Force (of New Zealand)

Commandant-in-Chief
RAF College, Cranwell

Royal Honorary Air Commodore
RAF Marham; 603 (City of Edinburgh) Squadron Royal Auxiliary Air Force

PRINCE PHILIP, DUKE OF EDINBURGH

ROYAL NAVY
Admiral of the Fleet
Admiral of the Fleet, Royal Australian Navy
Admiral of the Fleet, Royal New Zealand Navy
Admiral of the Royal Canadian Sea Cadets

ROYAL MARINES
Captain-General

ARMY
Field Marshal
Field Marshal, Australian Military Forces
Field Marshal, New Zealand Army

Colonel-in-Chief
The Queen's Royal Hussars (Queen's Own and Royal Irish); The Rifles; Corps of Royal Electrical and Mechanical Engineers; Intelligence Corps; Army Cadet Force Association; The Royal Canadian Regiment; The Royal Hamilton Light Infantry (Wentworth Regiment of Canada); The Cameron Highlanders of Ottawa; The Queen's Own Cameron Highlanders of Canada; The Seaforth Highlanders of Canada; The Royal Canadian Army Cadets; The Royal Australian Corps of Electrical and Mechanical Engineers; The Australian Army Cadet Corps

Colonel
Grenadier Guards

Royal Colonel
The Highlanders, 4th Battalion The Royal Regiment of Scotland

Hon. Colonel
City of Edinburgh University Officers' Training Corps; The Trinidad and Tobago Regiment

Member
Honourable Artillery Company

ROYAL AIR FORCE
Marshal of the Royal Air Force
Marshal of the Royal Australian Air Force
Marshal of the Royal New Zealand Air Force

Air Commodore-in-Chief
Air Training Corps; Royal Canadian Air Cadets

Hon. Air Commodore
RAF Kinloss

THE PRINCE OF WALES

ROYAL NAVY
Admiral
Commodore-in-Chief
Royal Naval Command Plymouth

ARMY
General

Colonel-in-Chief
The Royal Dragoon Guards; The 22nd Cheshire Regiment; The Parachute Regiment; The Royal Gurkha Rifles; Army Air Corps; The Royal Canadian Dragoons; Lord Strathcona's Horse (Royal Canadians); The Royal Regiment of Canada; Royal Winnipeg Rifles; Royal Australian Armoured Corps; The Royal Pacific Islands Regiment; 1st The Queen's Dragoon Guards; The Black Watch (Royal Highland Regiment) of Canada; The Toronto Scottish Regiment (Queen Elizabeth The Queen Mother's Own); The Mercian Regiment

Royal Colonel
The Black Watch, 3rd Battalion The Royal Regiment of Scotland; 51st Highland, 7th Battalion The Royal Regiment of Scotland (Territorial Army); The Welsh Guards

Royal Honorary Colonel
The Queen's Own Yeomanry

ROYAL AIR FORCE
Air Chief Marshal

Hon. Air Commodore
RAF Valley

Air Commodore-in-Chief
Royal New Zealand Air Force

Colonel-in-Chief
Air Reserve Canada

THE DUCHESS OF CORNWALL

ROYAL NAVY
Commodore-in-Chief
Naval Medical Services

ARMY
Royal Colonel
4th Battalion The Rifles

PRINCE WILLIAM OF WALES

ROYAL NAVY
Commodore-in-Chief
Scotland Command; Submarines Command

ARMY
Lieutenant
The Blues and Royals (Royal Horse Guards and 1st Dragoons)

PRINCE HENRY OF WALES

ROYAL NAVY
Commodore-in-Chief
Small Ships and Diving Command

ARMY
Second Lieutenant
The Blues and Royals (Royal Horse Guards and 1st Dragoons)

THE DUKE OF YORK

ROYAL NAVY
Commander
Admiral of the Marine Society and Sea Cadets
Honorary Captain

ARMY
Colonel-in-Chief
The Royal Irish Regiment (27th (Inniskilling), 83rd, 87th and The Ulster Defence Regiment); 9th/12th Royal Lancers (The Prince of Wales's); The Royal Highland Fusiliers, 2nd Battalion The Royal Regiment of Scotland; The Yorkshire Regiment; Small Arms School Corps; The Queen's York Rangers (First Americans); Royal New Zealand Army Logistics Regiment; The Royal Highland Fusiliers of Canada; The Princess Louise Fusiliers (Canada)

ROYAL AIR FORCE
Hon. Air Commodore
RAF Lossiemouth

THE EARL OF WESSEX

ROYAL NAVY
Commodore-in-Chief
Royal Fleet Auxiliary

Patron
Royal Fleet Auxiliary Association

ARMY
Colonel-in-Chief
Hastings and Prince Edward Regiment; Saskatchewan Dragoons

Royal Hon. Colonel
Royal Wessex Yeomanry

THE COUNTESS OF WESSEX

ARMY
Colonel-in-Chief
Queen Alexandra's Royal Army Nursing Corps; The Lincoln and Welland Regiment; South Alberta Light Horse Regiment

Royal Colonel
5th Battalion, The Rifles

THE PRINCESS ROYAL

ROYAL NAVY
Rear-Admiral (Chief Commandant for Women in the Royal Navy)

ARMY
Colonel-in-Chief
The King's Royal Hussars; Royal Corps of Signals; Royal Logistic Corps; The Royal Army Veterinary Corps; 8th Canadian Hussars (Princess Louise's); Royal Newfoundland Regiment; Canadian Forces Communications and Electronics Branch; The Grey and Simcoe Foresters (Royal Canadian Armoured Corps); The Royal Regina Rifle Regiment; Canadian Forces Medical Branch; Royal Australian Corps of Signals; Royal New Zealand Corps of Signals; Royal New Zealand Nursing Corps

Affiliated Colonel-in-Chief
The Queen's Gurkha Signals; The Queen's Own Gurkha Transport Regiment

Royal Colonel
1st Battalion The Royal Regiment of Scotland; 52nd Lowland, 6th Battalion The Royal Regiment of Scotland

Colonel
The Blues and Royals (Royal Horse Guards and 1st Dragoons)

Hon. Colonel
University of London Officers' Training Corps

Commandant-in-Chief
First Aid Nursing Yeomanry (Princess Royal's Volunteer Corps)

ROYAL AIR FORCE
Hon. Air Commodore
RAF Lyneham; University of London Air Squadron

THE DUKE OF GLOUCESTER

ARMY
Colonel-in-Chief
The Royal Anglian Regiment; Royal Army Medical Corps

Deputy Colonel-in-Chief
The Royal Logistic Corps

Royal Colonel
6th Battalion, The Rifles

Hon. Colonel
Royal Monmouthshire Royal Engineers (Militia)

ROYAL AIR FORCE
Hon. Air Marshal

Hon. Air Commodore
RAF Odiham; No. 501 (County of Gloucester) Squadron Royal Auxiliary Air Force

THE DUCHESS OF GLOUCESTER

ARMY
Colonel-in-Chief
Royal Army Dental Corps; Royal Australian Army Educational Corps; Royal New Zealand Army Educational Corps; Canadian Forces Dental Services

Deputy Colonel-in-Chief
Adjutant-General's Corps

Royal Colonel
7th Battalion, The Rifles

Vice-Patron
Adjutant-General's Corps Regimental Association

Patron
Royal Army Educational Corps Association; Army Families Federation

THE DUKE OF KENT

ARMY
Field Marshal
Colonel-in-Chief
The Royal Regiment of Fusiliers; Lorne Scots (Peel, Dufferin and Hamilton Regiment)

Deputy Colonel-in-Chief
The Royal Scots Dragoon Guards (Carabiniers and Greys)

Royal Colonel
1st Battalion The Rifles

Colonel
Scots Guards

ROYAL AIR FORCE
Hon. Air Chief Marshal

Hon. Air Commodore
RAF Leuchars

THE DUCHESS OF KENT

ARMY
Deputy Colonel-in-Chief
The Royal Dragoon Guards; Adjutant-General's Corps; The Royal Logistic Corps

PRINCE MICHAEL OF KENT

ROYAL NAVY
Honorary Rear Admiral Royal Naval Reserve

ARMY
Colonel-in-Chief
Essex and Kent Scottish Regiment (Ontario)

ROYAL AIR FORCE
Hon. Air Commodore
RAF Benson

PRINCESS ALEXANDRA, THE HON. LADY OGILVY

ROYAL NAVY
Patron
Queen Alexandra's Royal Naval Nursing Service

ARMY
Colonel-in-Chief
The Queen's Own Rifles of Canada; The Canadian Scottish Regiment (Princess Mary's)

Deputy Colonel-in-Chief
The Queen's Royal Lancers

Royal Colonel
3rd Battalion The Rifles

Royal Honorary Colonel
The Royal Yeomanry

ROYAL AIR FORCE
Patron and Air Chief Commandant
Princess Mary's RAF Nursing Service

Royal Honorary Air Commodore
RAF Cottesmore

KINGS AND QUEENS

ENGLISH KINGS AND QUEENS 927 TO 1603

HOUSES OF CERDIC AND DENMARK

Reign

927–939 ÆTHELSTAN
Son of Edward the Elder, by Ecgwynn, and grandson of Alfred
Acceded to Wessex and Mercia *c.*924, established direct rule over Northumbria 927, effectively creating the Kingdom of England
Reigned 15 years

939–946 EDMUND I
Born 921, son of Edward the Elder, by Eadgifu
Married (1) Ælfgifu (2) Æthelflæd
Killed aged 25, *reigned* 6 years

946–955 EADRED
Son of Edward the Elder, by Eadgifu
Reigned 9 years

955–959 EADWIG
Born before 943, son of Edmund and Ælfgifu
Married Ælfgifu
Reigned 3 years

959–975 EDGAR I
Born 943, son of Edmund and Ælfgifu
Married (1) Æthelflæd (2) Wulfthryth (3) Ælfthryth
Died aged 32, *reigned* 15 years

975–978 EDWARD I (the Martyr)
*Born c.*962, son of Edgar and Æthelflæd
Assassinated aged *c.*16, *reigned* 2 years

978–1016 ÆTHELRED (the Unready)
*Born c.*968/969, son of Edgar and Ælfthryth
Married (1) Ælfgifu (2) Emma, daughter of Richard I, Count of Normandy
1013–14 dispossessed of kingdom by Swegn Forkbeard (King of Denmark 987–1014)
Died aged *c.*47, *reigned* 38 years

1016 EDMUND II (Ironside)
Born before 993, son of Æthelred and Ælfgifu
Married Ealdgyth
Died aged over 23, *reigned* 7 months (Apr–Nov)

1016–1035 CNUT (Canute)
*Born c.*995, son of Swegn Forkbeard, King of Denmark, and Gunhild
Married (1) Ælfgifu (2) Emma, widow of Æthelred the Unready
Gained submission of West Saxons 1015, Northumbrians 1016, Mercia 1016, King of all England after Edmund's death, King of Denmark 1019–35, King of Norway 1028–35
Died aged *c.*40, *reigned* 19 years

1035–1040 HAROLD I (Harefoot)
*Born c.*1016/17, son of Cnut and Ælfgifu
Married Ælfgifu
1035 recognised as regent for himself and his brother Harthacnut; 1037 recognised as king
Died aged *c.*23, *reigned* 4 years

1040–1042 HARTHACNUT (Harthacanute)
*Born c.*1018, son of Cnut and Emma
Titular king of Denmark from 1028
Acknowledged King of England 1035–7 with Harold I as regent; effective king after Harold's death
died aged *c.*24, *reigned* 2 years

1042–1066 EDWARD II (the Confessor)
Born between 1002 and 1005, son of Æthelred the Unready and Emma
Married Eadgyth, daughter of Godwine, Earl of Wessex
Died aged over 60, *reigned* 23 years

1066 HAROLD II (Godwinesson)
*Born c.*1020, son of Godwine, Earl of Wessex, and Gytha
Married (1) Eadgyth (2) Ealdgyth
Killed in battle aged *c.*46, *reigned* 10 months (Jan–Oct)

THE HOUSE OF NORMANDY

1066–1087 WILLIAM I (the Conqueror)
Born 1027/8, son of Robert I, Duke of Normandy; obtained the Crown by conquest
Married Matilda, daughter of Baldwin, Count of Flanders
Died aged *c.*60, *reigned* 20 years

1087–1100 WILLIAM II (Rufus)
Born between 1056 and 1060, third son of William I; succeeded his father in England only
Killed aged *c.*40, *reigned* 12 years

1100–1135 HENRY I (Beauclerk)
Born 1068, fourth son of William I
Married (1) Edith or Matilda, daughter of Malcolm III of Scotland (2) Adela, daughter of Godfrey, Count of Louvain
Died aged 67, *reigned* 35 years

1135–1154 STEPHEN
Born not later than 1100, third son of Adela, daughter of William I, and Stephen, Count of Blois
Married Matilda, daughter of Eustace, Count of Boulogne
1141 (Feb–Nov) held captive by adherents of Matilda, daughter of Henry I, who contested the crown until 1153
Died aged over 53, *reigned* 18 years

THE HOUSE OF ANJOU (PLANTAGENETS)

1154–1189 HENRY II (Curtmantle)
Born 1133, son of Matilda, daughter of Henry I, and Geoffrey, Count of Anjou
Married Eleanor, daughter of William, Duke of Aquitaine, and divorced queen of Louis VII of France
Died aged 56, *reigned* 34 years

1189–1199 RICHARD I (Coeur de Lion)
Born 1157, third son of Henry II
Married Berengaria, daughter of Sancho VI, King of Navarre
Died aged 42, *reigned* 9 years

1199–1216 JOHN (Lackland)
Born 1167, fifth son of Henry II

Married (1) Isabella or Avisa, daughter of William, Earl of Gloucester (divorced) (2) Isabella, daughter of Aymer, Count of Angoulême
Died aged 48, *reigned* 17 years

1216–1272 HENRY III
Born 1207, son of John and Isabella of Angoulême
Married Eleanor, daughter of Raymond, Count of Provence
Died aged 65, *reigned* 56 years

1272–1307 EDWARD I (Longshanks)
Born 1239, eldest son of Henry III
Married (1) Eleanor, daughter of Ferdinand III, King of Castile (2) Margaret, daughter of Philip III of France
Died aged 68, *reigned* 34 years

1307–1327 EDWARD II
Born 1284, eldest surviving son of Edward I and Eleanor
Married Isabella, daughter of Philip IV of France
Deposed Jan 1327, *killed* Sep 1327 aged 43, *reigned* 19 years

1327–1377 EDWARD III
Born 1312, eldest son of Edward II
Married Philippa, daughter of William, Count of Hainault
Died aged 64, *reigned* 50 years

1377–1399 RICHARD II
Born 1367, son of Edward (the Black Prince), eldest son of Edward III
Married (1) Anne, daughter of Emperor Charles IV (2) Isabelle, daughter of Charles VI of France
Deposed Sep 1399, *killed* Feb 1400 aged 33, *reigned* 22 years

THE HOUSE OF LANCASTER

1399–1413 HENRY IV
Born 1366, son of John of Gaunt, fourth son of Edward III, and Blanche, daughter of Henry, Duke of Lancaster
Married (1) Mary, daughter of Humphrey, Earl of Hereford (2) Joan, daughter of Charles, King of Navarre, and widow of John, Duke of Brittany
Died aged *c.*47, *reigned* 13 years

1413–1422 HENRY V
Born 1387, eldest surviving son of Henry IV and Mary
Married Catherine, daughter of Charles VI of France
Died aged 34, *reigned* 9 years

1422–1471 HENRY VI
Born 1421, son of Henry V
Married Margaret, daughter of René, Duke of Anjou and Count of Provence
Deposed Mar 1461, *restored* Oct 1470
Deposed Apr 1471, *killed* May 1471 aged 49, *reigned* 39 years

THE HOUSE OF YORK

1461–1483 EDWARD IV
Born 1442, eldest son of Richard of York (grandson of Edmund, fifth son of Edward III, and son of Anne, great-granddaughter of Lionel, third son of Edward III)
Married Elizabeth Woodville, daughter of Richard, Lord Rivers, and widow of Sir John Grey
Acceded Mar 1461, *deposed* Oct 1470, *restored* Apr 1471
Died aged 40, *reigned* 21 years

1483 EDWARD V
Born 1470, eldest son of Edward IV
Deposed Jun 1483, *died* probably Jul–Sep 1483, aged 12, *reigned* 2 months (Apr–Jun)

1483–1485 RICHARD III
Born 1452, fourth son of Richard of York
Married Anne Neville, daughter of Richard, Earl of Warwick, and widow of Edward, Prince of Wales, son of Henry VI
Killed in battle aged 32, *reigned* 2 years

THE HOUSE OF TUDOR

1485–1509 HENRY VII
Born 1457, son of Margaret Beaufort (great-granddaughter of John of Gaunt, fourth son of Edward III) and Edmund Tudor, Earl of Richmond
Married Elizabeth, daughter of Edward IV
Died aged 52, *reigned* 23 years

1509–1547 HENRY VIII
Born 1491, second son of Henry VII
Married (1) Catherine, daughter of Ferdinand II, King of Aragon, and widow of his elder brother Arthur (divorced) (2) Anne, daughter of Sir Thomas Boleyn (executed) (3) Jane, daughter of Sir John Seymour (died in childbirth) (4) Anne, daughter of John, Duke of Cleves (divorced) (5) Catherine Howard, niece of the Duke of Norfolk (executed) (6) Catherine, daughter of Sir Thomas Parr and widow of Lord Latimer
Died aged 55, *reigned* 37 years

1547–1553 EDWARD VI
Born 1537, son of Henry VIII and Jane Seymour
Died aged 15, *reigned* 6 years

1553 JANE
Born 1537, daughter of Frances (daughter of Mary Tudor, the younger daughter of Henry VII) and Henry Grey, Duke of Suffolk
Married Lord Guildford Dudley, son of the Duke of Northumberland
Deposed Jul 1553, *executed* Feb 1554 aged 16, *reigned* 9 days

1553–1558 MARY I
Born 1516, daughter of Henry VIII and Catherine of Aragon
Married Philip II of Spain
Died aged 42, *reigned* 5 years

1558–1603 ELIZABETH I
Born 1533, daughter of Henry VIII and Anne Boleyn
Died aged 69, *reigned* 44 years

BRITISH KINGS AND QUEENS SINCE 1603

THE HOUSE OF STUART

Reign

1603–1625 JAMES I (VI OF SCOTLAND)
Born 1566, son of Mary, Queen of Scots (granddaughter of Margaret Tudor, elder daughter of Henry VII), and Henry Stewart, Lord Darnley

Married Anne, daughter of Frederick II of Denmark
Died aged 58, *reigned* 22 years

1625–1649 CHARLES I
Born 1600, second son of James I
Married Henrietta Maria, daughter of Henry IV of France
Executed 1649 aged 48, *reigned* 23 years

INTERREGNUM 1649–60

1649–53 Government by a council of state
1653–8 Oliver Cromwell, Lord Protector
1658–9 Richard Cromwell, Lord Protector

Reign

1660–1685 CHARLES II
Born 1630, eldest son of Charles I
Married Catherine, daughter of John IV of Portugal
Died aged 54, *reigned* 24 years

1685–1688 JAMES II (VII OF SCOTLAND)
Born 1633, second son of Charles I
Married (1) Lady Anne Hyde, daughter of Edward, Earl of Clarendon (2) Mary, daughter of Alphonso, Duke of Modena
Reign ended with flight from kingdom Dec 1688
Died 1701 aged 67, *reigned* 3 years

INTERREGNUM
11 Dec 1688 to 12 Feb 1689

Reign

1689–1702 WILLIAM III
Born 1650, son of William II, Prince of Orange, and Mary Stuart, daughter of Charles I
Married Mary, elder daughter of James II
Died aged 51, *reigned* 13 years

and

1689–1694 MARY II
Born 1662, elder daughter of James II and Anne
Died aged 32, *reigned* 5 years

1702–1714 ANNE
Born 1665, younger daughter of James II and Anne
Married Prince George of Denmark, son of Frederick III of Denmark
Died aged 49, *reigned* 12 years

THE HOUSE OF HANOVER

1714–1727 GEORGE I (Elector of Hanover)
Born 1660, son of Sophia (daughter of Frederick, Elector Palatine, and Elizabeth Stuart, daughter of James I) and Ernest Augustus, Elector of Hanover
Married Sophia Dorothea, daughter of George William, Duke of Lüneburg-Celle
Died aged 67, *reigned* 12 years

1727–1760 GEORGE II
Born 1683, son of George I
Married Caroline, daughter of John Frederick, Margrave of Brandenburg-Anspach
Died aged 76, *reigned* 33 years

1760–1820 GEORGE III
Born 1738, son of Frederick, eldest son of George II
Married Charlotte, daughter of Charles Louis, Duke of Mecklenburg-Strelitz
Died aged 81, *reigned* 59 years

REGENCY 1811–20
Prince of Wales regent owing to the insanity of George III

Reign

1820–1830 GEORGE IV
Born 1762, eldest son of George III
Married Caroline, daughter of Charles, Duke of Brunswick-Wolfenbüttel
Died aged 67, *reigned* 10 years

1830–1837 WILLIAM IV
Born 1765, third son of George III
Married Adelaide, daughter of George, Duke of Saxe-Meiningen
Died aged 71, *reigned* 7 years

1837–1901 VICTORIA
Born 1819, daughter of Edward, fourth son of George III
Married Prince Albert of Saxe-Coburg and Gotha
Died aged 81, *reigned* 63 years

THE HOUSE OF SAXE-COBURG AND GOTHA

1901–1910 EDWARD VII
Born 1841, eldest son of Victoria and Albert
Married Alexandra, daughter of Christian IX of Denmark
Died aged 68, *reigned* 9 years

THE HOUSE OF WINDSOR

1910–1936 GEORGE V
Born 1865, second son of Edward VII
Married Victoria Mary, daughter of Francis, Duke of Teck
Died aged 70, *reigned* 25 years

1936 EDWARD VIII
Born 1894, eldest son of George V
Married (1937) Mrs Wallis Simpson
Abdicated 1936, *died* 1972 aged 77, *reigned* 10 months (20 Jan to 11 Dec)

1936–1952 GEORGE VI
Born 1895, second son of George V
Married Lady Elizabeth Bowes-Lyon, daughter of 14th Earl of Strathmore and Kinghorne
Died aged 56, *reigned* 15 years

1952– ELIZABETH II
Born 1926, elder daughter of George VI
Married Philip, son of Prince Andrew of Greece

KINGS AND QUEENS OF SCOTS 1016 TO 1603

Reign

1016–1034 MALCOLM II
Born *c.*954, son of Kenneth II
Acceded to Alba 1005, secured Lothian *c.*1016, obtained Strathclyde for his grandson Duncan *c.*1016, thus reigning over an area approximately the same as that governed by later rulers of Scotland
Died aged *c.*80, *reigned* 18 years

THE HOUSE OF ATHOL

1034–1040 DUNCAN I
Son of Bethoc, daughter of Malcolm II, and Crinan, Mormaer of Atholl
Married a cousin of Siward, Earl of Northumbria
Reigned 5 years

1040–1057 MACBETH
*Born c.*1005, son of a daughter of Malcolm II and Finlaec, Mormaer of Moray
Married Gruoch, granddaughter of Kenneth III
Killed aged *c.*52, *reigned* 17 years

1057–1058 LULACH
*Born c.*1032, son of Gillacomgan, Mormaer of Moray, and Gruoch (and stepson of Macbeth)
Died aged *c.*26, *reigned* 7 months (Aug–Mar)

1058–1093 MALCOLM III (Canmore)
*Born c.*1031, elder son of Duncan I
Married (1) Ingibiorg (2) Margaret (St Margaret), granddaughter of Edmund II of England
Killed in battle aged *c.*62, *reigned* 35 years

1093–1097 DONALD III BÁN
*Born c.*1033, second son of Duncan I
Deposed May 1094, *restored* Nov 1094, *deposed* Oct 1097, *reigned* 3 years

1094 DUNCAN II
*Born c.*1060, elder son of Malcolm III and Ingibiorg
Married Octreda of Dunbar
Killed aged *c.*34, *reigned* 6 months (May–Nov)

1097–1107 EDGAR
*Born c.*1074, second son of Malcolm III and Margaret
Died aged *c.*32, *reigned* 9 years

1107–1124 ALEXANDER I (the Fierce)
*Born c.*1077, fifth son of Malcolm III and Margaret
Married Sybilla, illegitimate daughter of Henry I of England
Died aged *c.*47, *reigned* 17 years

1124–1153 DAVID I (the Saint)
*Born c.*1085, sixth son of Malcolm III and Margaret
Married Matilda, daughter of Waltheof, Earl of Huntingdon
Died aged *c.*68, *reigned* 29 years

1153–1165 MALCOLM IV (the Maiden)
*Born c.*1141, son of Henry, Earl of Huntingdon, second son of David I
Died aged *c.*24, *reigned* 12 years

1165–1214 WILLIAM I (the Lion)
*Born c.*1142, brother of Malcolm IV
Married Ermengarde, daughter of Richard, Viscount of Beaumont
Died aged *c.*72, *reigned* 49 years

1214–1249 ALEXANDER II
Born 1198, son of William I
Married (1) Joan, daughter of John, King of England (2) Marie, daughter of Ingelram de Coucy
Died aged 50, *reigned* 34 years

1249–1286 ALEXANDER III
Born 1241, son of Alexander II and Marie
Married (1) Margaret, daughter of Henry III of England (2) Yolande, daughter of the Count of Dreux
Killed accidentally aged 44, *reigned* 36 years

1286–1290 MARGARET (the Maid of Norway)
Born 1283, daughter of Margaret (daughter of Alexander III) and Eric II of Norway
Died aged 7, *reigned* 4 years

FIRST INTERREGNUM 1290–2
Throne disputed by 13 competitors. Crown awarded to John Balliol by adjudication of Edward I of England

THE HOUSE OF BALLIOL
Reign

1292–1296 JOHN (Balliol)
*Born c.*1250, son of Dervorguilla, great-great-granddaughter of David I, and John de Balliol
Married Isabella, daughter of John, Earl of Surrey
Abdicated 1296, *died* 1313 aged *c.*63, *reigned* 3 years

SECOND INTERREGNUM 1296–1306
Edward I of England declared John Balliol to have forfeited the throne for contumacy in 1296 and took the government of Scotland into his own hands

THE HOUSE OF BRUCE
Reign

1306–1329 ROBERT I (Bruce)
Born 1274, son of Robert Bruce and Marjorie, countess of Carrick, and great-grandson of the second daughter of David, Earl of Huntingdon, brother of William I
Married (1) Isabella, daughter of Donald, Earl of Mar (2) Elizabeth, daughter of Richard, Earl of Ulster
Died aged 54, *reigned* 23 years

1329–1371 DAVID II
Born 1324, son of Robert I and Elizabeth
Married (1) Joanna, daughter of Edward II of England (2) Margaret Drummond, widow of Sir John Logie (divorced)
Died aged 46, *reigned* 41 years
1332 Edward Balliol, son of John Balliol, crowned King of Scots Sep, expelled Dec
1333–6 Edward Balliol restored as King of Scots

THE HOUSE OF STEWART

1371–1390 ROBERT II (Stewart)
Born 1316, son of Marjorie (daughter of Robert I) and Walter, High Steward of Scotland
Married (1) Elizabeth, daughter of Sir Robert Mure of Rowallan (2) Euphemia, daughter of Hugh, Earl of Ross
Died aged 74, *reigned* 19 years

1390–1406 ROBERT III
*Born c.*1337, son of Robert II and Elizabeth
Married Annabella, daughter of Sir John Drummond of Stobhall
Died aged *c.*69, *reigned* 16 years

1406–1437 JAMES I
Born 1394, son of Robert III
Married Joan Beaufort, daughter of John, Earl of Somerset
Assassinated aged 42, *reigned* 30 years

1437–1460 JAMES II
Born 1430, son of James I
Married Mary, daughter of Arnold, Duke of Gueldres
Killed accidentally aged 29, *reigned* 23 years

1460–1488 JAMES III
Born 1452, son of James II

	Married Margaret, daughter of Christian I of Denmark
	Assassinated aged 36, *reigned* 27 years
1488–1513	JAMES IV
	Born 1473, son of James III
	Married Margaret Tudor, daughter of Henry VII of England
	Killed in battle aged 40, *reigned* 25 years
1513–1542	JAMES V
	Born 1512, son of James IV
	Married (1) Madeleine, daughter of Francis I of France (2) Mary of Lorraine, daughter of the Duc de Guise
	Died aged 30, *reigned* 29 years
1542–1567	MARY
	Born 1542, daughter of James V and Mary
	Married (1) the Dauphin, afterwards Francis II of France (2) Henry Stewart, Lord Darnley (3) James Hepburn, Earl of Bothwell
	Abdicated 1567, prisoner in England from 1568, *executed* 1587, *reigned* 24 years
1567–1625	JAMES VI (and I of England)
	Born 1566, son of Mary, Queen of Scots, and Henry, Lord Darnley
	Acceded 1567 to the Scottish throne, *reigned* 58 years
	Succeeded 1603 to the English throne, so joining the English and Scottish crowns in one person. The two kingdoms remained distinct until 1707 when the parliaments of the kingdoms became conjoined

WELSH SOVEREIGNS AND PRINCES

Wales was ruled by sovereign princes from the earliest times until the death of Llywelyn in 1282. The first English Prince of Wales was the son of Edward I, who was born in Caernarvon town on 25 April 1284. According to a discredited legend, he was presented to the Welsh chieftains as their prince, in fulfilment of a promise that they should have a prince who 'could not speak a word of English' and should be native born. This son, who afterwards became Edward II, was created 'Prince of Wales and Earl of Chester' at the Lincoln Parliament on 7 February 1301.

The title Prince of Wales is borne after individual conferment and is not inherited at birth, though some Princes have been declared and styled Prince of Wales but never formally so created (*s.*). The title was conferred on Prince Charles by the Queen on 26 July 1958. He was invested at Caernarvon on 1 July 1969.

INDEPENDENT PRINCES AD 844 TO 1282

844–878	Rhodri the Great
878–916	Anarawd, son of Rhodri
916–950	Hywel Dda, the Good
950–979	Iago ab Idwal (or Ieuaf)
979–985	Hywel ab Ieuaf, the Bad
985–986	Cadwallon, his brother
986–999	Maredudd ab Owain ap Hywel Dda
999–1008	Cynan ap Hywel ab Ieuaf
1018–1023	Llywelyn ap Seisyll
1023–1039	Iago ab Idwal ap Meurig
1039–1063	Gruffydd ap Llywelyn ap Seisyll
1063–1075	Bleddyn ap Cynfyn
1075–1081	Trahaern ap Caradog
1081–1137	Gruffydd ap Cynan ab Iago
1137–1170	Owain Gwynedd
1170–1194	Dafydd ab Owain Gwynedd
1194–1240	Llywelyn Fawr, the Great
1240–1246	Dafydd ap Llywelyn
1246–1282	Llywelyn ap Gruffydd ap Llywelyn

ENGLISH PRINCES SINCE 1301

1301	Edward (Edward II)
1343	Edward the Black Prince, son of Edward III
1376	Richard (Richard II), son of the Black Prince
1399	Henry of Monmouth (Henry V)
1454	Edward of Westminster, son of Henry VI
1471	Edward of Westminster (Edward V)
1483	Edward, son of Richard III (*d.* 1484)
1489	Arthur Tudor, son of Henry VII
1504	Henry Tudor (Henry VIII)
1610	Henry Stuart, son of James I (*d.* 1612)
1616	Charles Stuart (Charles I)
*c.*1638 (*s.*)	Charles Stuart (Charles II)
1688 (*s.*)	James Francis Edward Stuart (The Old Pretender), son of James II (*d.* 1766)
1714	George Augustus (George II)
1729	Frederick Lewis, son of George II (*d.* 1751)
1751	George William Frederick (George III)
1762	George Augustus Frederick (George IV)
1841	Albert Edward (Edward VII)
1901	George (George V)
1910	Edward (Edward VIII)
1958	Charles, son of Elizabeth II

PRINCESSES ROYAL

The style Princess Royal is conferred at the sovereign's discretion on his or her eldest daughter. It is an honorary title, held for life, and cannot be inherited or passed on. It was first conferred on Princess Mary, daughter of Charles I, in approximately 1642.

*c.*1642	Princess Mary (1631–60), daughter of Charles I
1727	Princess Anne (1709–59), daughter of George II
1766	Princess Charlotte (1766–1828), daughter of George III
1840	Princess Victoria (1840–1901), daughter of Victoria
1905	Princess Louise (1867–1931), daughter of Edward VII
1932	Princess Mary (1897–1965), daughter of George V
1987	Princess Anne (*b.* 1950), daughter of Elizabeth II

THE HOUSE OF WINDSOR

King George V assumed by royal proclamation (17 July 1917) for his House and family, as well as for all descendants in the male line of Queen Victoria who are subjects of these realms, the name of Windsor.

KING GEORGE V
(George Frederick Ernest Albert), second son of King Edward VII *born* 3 June 1865 *married* 6 July 1893 HSH Princess Victoria Mary Augusta Louise Olga Pauline Claudine Agnes of Teck (Queen Mary *born* 26 May 1867 *died* 24 March 1953) *succeeded* to the throne 6 May 1910 *died* 20 January 1936. *Issue*

1. HRH PRINCE EDWARD Albert Christian George Andrew Patrick David *born* 23 June 1894 *succeeded* to the throne as King Edward VIII, 20 January 1936 *abdicated* 11 December 1936 *created* Duke of Windsor 1937 *married* 3 June 1937 Mrs Wallis Simpson (Her Grace The Duchess of Windsor *born* 19 June 1896 *died* 24 April 1986) *died* 28 May 1972

2. HRH PRINCE ALBERT Frederick Arthur George *born* 14 December 1895 *created* Duke of York 1920 *married* 26 April 1923 Lady Elizabeth Bowes-Lyon, youngest daughter of the 14th Earl of Strathmore and Kinghorne (HM Queen Elizabeth the Queen Mother *born* 4 August 1900 *died* 30 March 2002) *succeeded* to the throne as King George VI, 11 December 1936 *died* 6 February 1952. *Issue*
(1) HRH Princess Elizabeth Alexandra Mary *succeeded* to the throne as Queen Elizabeth II, 6 February 1952 (*see* Royal Family)
(2) HRH Princess Margaret Rose (later HRH The Princess Margaret, Countess of Snowdon) *born* 21 August 1930 *married* 6 May 1960 Anthony Charles Robert Armstrong-Jones, GCVO *created* Earl of Snowdon 1961 (marriage dissolved 1978) *died* 9 February 2002, having had issue (*see* Royal Family)

3. HRH PRINCESS (Victoria Alexandra Alice) MARY *born* 25 April 1897 *created* Princess Royal 1932 *married* 28 February 1922 Viscount Lascelles, later the 6th Earl of Harewood (1882–1947) *died* 28 March 1965. *Issue*
(1) George Henry Hubert Lascelles, 7th Earl of Harewood, KBE *born* 7 February 1923 *married* (1) 1949 Maria (Marion) Stein (marriage dissolved 1967) *issue (a)* David Henry George, Viscount Lascelles *born* 1950 *(b)* James Edward *born* 1953 *(c)* (Robert) Jeremy Hugh *born* 1955 (2) 1967 Mrs Patricia Tuckwell *issue (d)* Mark Hubert *born* 1964
(2) Gerald David Lascelles (1924–98) *married* (1) 1952 Miss Angela Dowding (marriage dissolved 1978) *issue (a)* Henry Ulick *born* 1953 (2) 1978 Mrs Elizabeth Colvin *issue (b)* Martin David *born* 1962

4. HRH PRINCE HENRY William Frederick Albert *born* 31 March 1900 *created* Duke of Gloucester, Earl of Ulster and Baron Culloden 1928 *married* 6 November 1935 Lady Alice Christabel Montagu-Douglas-Scott, daughter of the 7th Duke of Buccleuch and Queensberry (HRH Princess Alice, Duchess of Gloucester *born* 25 December 1901 *died* 29 October 2004) *died* 10 June 1974. *Issue*
(1) HRH Prince William Henry Andrew Frederick *born* 18 December 1941 *accidentally killed* 28 August 1972
(2) HRH Prince Richard Alexander Walter George (HRH The Duke of Gloucester)

5. HRH PRINCE GEORGE Edward Alexander Edmund *born* 20 December 1902 *created* Duke of Kent, Earl of St Andrews and Baron Downpatrick 1934 *married* 29 November 1934 HRH Princess Marina of Greece and Denmark (*born* 30 November 1906 *died* 27 August 1968) *killed on active service* 25 August 1942. *Issue*
(1) HRH Prince Edward George Nicholas Paul Patrick (HRH The Duke of Kent)
(2) HRH Princess Alexandra Helen Elizabeth Olga Christabel (HRH Princess Alexandra, the Hon. Lady Ogilvy)
(3) HRH Prince Michael George Charles Franklin (HRH Prince Michael of Kent)

6. HRH PRINCE JOHN Charles Francis *born* 12 July 1905 *died* 18 January 1919

DESCENDANTS OF QUEEN VICTORIA

I. HRH Princess Victoria Adelaide Mary Louisa, Princess Royal (1840–1901) *m* Friedrich III (1831–88), German Emperor Mar–Jun 1888

1. HIM Wilhelm II (1859–1941), German Emperor *m* (1) Princess Augusta Victoria of Schleswig-Holstein-Sonderburg-Augustenburg (1858–1921) (2) Princess Hermine of Reuss (1887–1947). *Issue* Wilhelm (1882–1951); Eitel-Friedrich (1883–1942); Adalbert (1884–1948); August Wilhelm (1887–1949); Oskar (1888–1958); Joachim (1890–1920); Viktoria Luise (1892–1980)

2. Charlotte (1860–1919) *m* Bernhard, Duke of Saxe-Meiningen (1851–1928). *Issue* Feodora (1879–1945)

3. Heinrich (1862–1929) *m* Princess Irene of Hesse (*see* III.3). *Issue* Waldemar (1889–1945); Sigismund (1896–1978); Heinrich (1900–4)

4. Sigismund (1864–6)

5. Victoria (1866–1929) *m* (1) Prince Adolf of Schaumburg-Lippe (1859–1916) (2) Alexander Zubkov (1900–36)

6. Waldemar (1868–79)

7. Sophie (1870–1932) *m* Constantine I (1868–1923), King of the Hellenes. *Issue* George II (1890–1947); Alexander I (1893–1920); Helena (1896–1982); Paul I (1901–64); Irene (1904–74); Katherine (Lady Katherine Brandram) (1913–2007)

8. Margarethe (1872–1954) *m* Prince Friedrich Karl of Hesse (1868–1940). *Issue* Friedrich Wilhelm (1893–1916); Maximilian (1894–1914); Philipp (1896–1980); Wolfgang (1896–1989); Richard (1901–69); Christoph (1901–43)

II. HRH Prince Albert Edward (HM KING EDWARD VII) (1841–1901) *succeeded* 22 Jan 1901 *m* HRH Princess Alexandra of Denmark (1844–1925)

1. Albert Victor, Duke of Clarence and Avondale (1864–92)

2. George (HM KING GEORGE V) (1865–1936) (*see* House of Windsor)

3. Louise (1867–1931), Princess Royal *m* 1st Duke of Fife (1849–1912). *Issue* Alexandra (1891–1959); Maud (1893–1945)

4. Victoria (1868–1935)

5. Maud (1869–1938) *m* Prince Carl of Denmark (1872–1957), later King Haakon VII of Norway. *Issue* Olav V (1903–91)

6. Alexander (6–7 Apr 1871)

III. HRH Princess Alice Maud Mary (1843–78) *m* Prince Ludwig (1837–92), Grand Duke of Hesse 1877–92

1. Victoria (1863–1950) *m* Prince Louis of Battenberg (1854–1921), later 1st Marquess of Milford Haven. *Issue* Alice (1885–1969); Louise (1889–1965); George (1892–1938); Louis (1900–79)

2. Elizabeth (1864–1918) *m* Grand Duke Sergius of Russia (1857–1905)

3. Irene (1866–1953) *m* Prince Heinrich of Prussia (*see* I.3)

4. Ernst Ludwig (1868–1937), Grand Duke of Hesse, *m* (1) Princess Victoria Melita of Saxe-Coburg (see IV.3) (2) Princess Eleonore of Solms-Hohensolmslich (1871–1937). *Issue* Elizabeth (1895–1903); George, Grand Duke of Hesse (1906–37); Ludwig, Prince of Hesse (1908–68)

5. Frederick William (1870–3)

6. Alix (Tsaritsa of Russia) (1872–1918) *m* Nicholas II, Tsar of All the Russias (1868–1918). *Issue* Grand Duchess Olga (1895–1918); Grand Duchess Tatiana (1897– 1918); Grand Duchess Marie (1899–1918); Grand Duchess Anastasia (1901–18); Alexis, Tsarevich of Russia (1904–18)

7. Marie (1874–8)

IV. HRH Prince Alfred Ernest Albert, Duke of Edinburgh (1844–1900) *succeeded* as Duke of Saxe-Coburg and Gotha 1893 *m* Grand Duchess Marie Alexandrovna of Russia (1853–1920)

QUEEN VICTORIA (Alexandrina Victoria) *b* 1819 *succeeded* 20 Jun 1837 *d* 1901 *m* (Francis) Albert Augustus Charles Emmanuel, Duke of Saxony, Prince of Saxe-Coburg and Gotha (HRH Albert, Prince Consort) (1819–61)

VI. HRH Princess Louise Caroline Alberta (1848–1939) *m* Marquess of Lorne (1845–1914), later 9th Duke of Argyll

VII. HRH Prince Arthur William Patrick Albert, Duke of Connaught (1850–1942) *m* Princess Louisa of Prussia (1860–1917)

1. Margaret (1882–1920) *m* Crown Prince Gustaf Adolf (1882–1973), later King of Sweden. *Issue* Gustaf Adolf, Duke of Västerbotten (1906–47); Count Sigvard Bernadotte (1907–2002); Ingrid (1910–2000); Bertil, Duke of Halland (1912–97); Count Carl Bernadotte (*b* 1916)

2. Arthur (1883–1938) *m* HH Duchess of Fife. *Issue* Alastair Arthur, 2nd Duke of Connaught (1914–43)

3. (Victoria) Patricia (1886–1974) *m* Adm. Hon. Sir Alexander Ramsay. *Issue* Alexander Ramsay of Mar (1919–2000)

VIII. HRH Prince Leopold George Duncan Albert, Duke of Albany (1853–84) *m* Princess Helena of Waldeck (1861–1922)

1. Alice (1883–1981) *m* Prince Alexander of Teck (1874–1957). *Issue* Lady May (1906–94); Rupert, Viscount Trematon (1907–28); Maurice (Mar–Sep 1910)

2. Charles Edward (1884–1954), Duke of Albany until title suspended 1917, Duke of Saxe-Coburg-Gotha, *m* Princess Victoria Adelheid of Schleswig-Holstein-Sonderburg-Glücksburg. *Issue* Johann Leopold (1906–72); Sibylla (1908–72); Dietmar Hubertus (1909–43); Caroline (1912–83); Friedrich Josias (1918–98)

IX. HRH Princess Beatrice Mary Victoria Feodore (1857–1944) *m* Prince Henry of Battenberg (1858–96)

1. Alexander, 1st Marquess of Carisbrooke (1886-1960) *m* Lady Irene Denison. *Issue* Lady Iris Mountbatten (1920–82)

2. Victoria Eugénie (1887–1969) *m* Alfonso XIII, King of Spain (1886–1941). *Issue* Alfonso (1907–38); Jaime (1908–75); Beatriz (1909–2002); Maria (1911–96); Juan (1913–93); Gonzalo (1914–34)

3. Maj. Lord Leopold Mountbatten (1889–1922)

4. Maurice (1891–1914)

1. Alfred, Prince of Saxe-Coburg (1874–99)

2. Marie (1875–1938) *m* Ferdinand (1865–1927), King of Roumania. *Issue* Carol II (1893–1953); Elisabeth (1894–1956); Marie (1900–61); Nicolas (1903–78); Ileana (1909–91); Mircea (1913–16)

3. Victoria Melita (1876–1936) *m* (1) Grand Duke Ernst Ludwig of Hesse (*see* III.4) (2) Grand Duke Kirill of Russia (1876–1938). *Issue* Marie Kirillovna (1907–51); Kira Kirillovna (1909–67); Vladimir Kirillovich (1917–92)

4. Alexandra (1878–1942) *m* Ernst, Prince of Hohenlohe Langenburg. *Issue* Gottfried (1897–1960); Maria (1899–1967); Alexandra (1901–63); Irma (1902–86)

5. Beatrice (1884–1966) *m* Alfonso of Orleans, Infante of Spain (1886–1975). *Issue* Alvaro (1910–97); Alonso (1912–36); Ataulfo (1913–74)

V. HRH Princess Helena Augusta Victoria (1846–1923) *m* Prince Christian of Schleswig-Holstein-Sonderburg-Augustenburg (1831–1917)

1. Christian Victor (1867–1900)

2. Albert (1869–1931), Duke of Schleswig-Holstein

3. Helena (1870–1948)

4. Marie Louise (1872–1956), *m* Prince Aribert of Anhalt (marriage dissolved 1900)

5. Harold (12–20 May 1876)

PRECEDENCE

ENGLAND AND WALES

The Sovereign
The Prince Philip, Duke of Edinburgh
The Prince of Wales
The Sovereign's younger sons
The Sovereign's grandsons
The Sovereign's cousins
Archbishop of Canterbury
Lord High Chancellor
Archbishop of York
The Prime Minister
Lord President of the Council
Speaker of the House of Commons
Lord Speaker
Lord Privy Seal
Ambassadors and High Commissioners
Lord Great Chamberlain
Earl Marshal
Lord Chamberlain of the Household
Lord Steward of the Household
Master of the Horse
Dukes, according to their patent of creation:
1. of England
2. of Scotland
3. of Great Britain
4. of Ireland
5. those created since the Union
Eldest sons of Dukes of the Blood Royal
Marquesses, according to their patent of creation:
1. of England
2. of Scotland
3. of Great Britain
4. of Ireland
5. those created since the Union
Dukes' eldest sons
Earls, according to their patent of creation:
1. of England
2. of Scotland
3. of Great Britain
4. of Ireland
5. those created since the Union
Younger sons of Dukes of Blood Royal
Marquesses' eldest sons
Dukes' younger sons
Viscounts, according to their patent of creation:
1. of England
2. of Scotland
3. of Great Britain
4. of Ireland
5. those created since the Union
Earls' eldest sons
Marquesses' younger sons
Bishop of London
Bishop of Durham
Bishop of Winchester
Other English Diocesan Bishops according to seniority of consecration
Suffragan Bishops, according to seniority of consecration
Secretaries of State, if of the degree of a Baron
Barons, according to their patent of creation:
1. of England
2. of Scotland
3. of Great Britain
4. of Ireland
5. those created since the Union, including Life Barons
Treasurer of the Household
Comptroller of the Household
Vice-Chamberlain of the Household
Secretaries of State under the degree of Baron
Viscounts' eldest sons
Earls' younger sons
Barons' eldest sons
Knights of the Garter
Privy Counsellors
Chancellor of the Exchequer
Chancellor of the Duchy of Lancaster
Lord Chief Justice of England and Wales
Master of the Rolls
President of the Queen's Bench Division
President of the Family Division
Chancellor of the High Court
Lords Justices of Appeal, according to seniority of appointment
Judges of the High Court, according to seniority of appointment
Viscounts' younger sons
Barons' younger sons
Sons of Life Peers and Lords of Appeal in Ordinary
Baronets, according to date of patent
Knights of the Thistle
Knights Grand Cross of the Bath
Knights Grand Commanders of the Star of India
Knights Grand Cross of St Michael and St George
Knights Grand Commanders of the Indian Empire
Knights Grand Cross of the Royal Victorian Order
Knights Grand Cross of the British Empire
Knights Commanders of the Bath
Knights Commanders of the Star of India
Knights Commanders of St Michael and St George
Knights Commanders of the Indian Empire
Knights Commanders of the Royal Victorian Order
Knights Commanders of the British Empire
Knights Bachelor
Circuit Judges, according to priority and order of their respective appointments
Companions of the Bath
Companions of the Star of India
Companions of St Michael and St George
Companions of the Indian Empire
Commanders of the Royal Victorian Order
Commanders of the British Empire
Companions of the Distinguished Service Order
Lieutenants of the Royal Victorian Order
Officers of the British Empire
Companions of the Imperial Service Order
Eldest sons of younger sons of peers
Baronets' eldest sons
Eldest sons of knights, in the same order as their fathers
Members of the Royal Victorian Order
Members of the British Empire
Younger sons of baronets
Younger sons of knights, in the same order as their fathers
Esquires
Gentlemen

WOMEN

Women take the same rank as their husbands or as their brothers; but the daughter of a peer marrying a commoner retains her title as Lady or Honourable. Daughters of peers rank next immediately after the wives of their elder brothers, and before their younger brothers' wives. Daughters of peers marrying peers of a lower degree take the same order of precedence as that of their husbands; thus the daughter of a Duke marrying a Baron becomes of the rank of Baroness only, while her sisters married to commoners retain their rank and take precedence over the Baroness. Merely official rank on the husband's part does not give any similar precedence to the wife.

Peeresses in their own right take the same precedence as peers of the same rank, ie from their date of creation.

SCOTLAND

The Sovereign
The Prince Philip, Duke of Edinburgh
The Lord High Commissioner to the General Assembly of the Church of Scotland (while that assembly is sitting)
The Duke of Rothesay (eldest son of the Sovereign)
The Sovereign's younger sons
Grandsons of the Sovereign
The Sovereign's cousins
Lord-Lieutenants
Lord Provosts of cities being *ex-officio* Lord-Lieutenants of those cities during their term of office*
Sheriffs Principal, successively, within their own localities and during holding of office
Lord Chancellor of Great Britain
Moderator of the General Assembly of the Church of Scotland
Keeper of the Great Seal of Scotland (the First Minister)
The Presiding Officer
The Secretary of State for Scotland
Hereditary High Constable of Scotland
Hereditary Master of the Household in Scotland
Dukes, in the same order as in England
Eldest sons of Dukes of the Blood Royal
Marquesses, as in England
Eldest sons of Dukes
Earls, as in England
Younger sons of Dukes of Blood Royal
Eldest sons of Marquesses
Dukes' younger sons
Lord Justice General
Lord Clerk Register
Lord Advocate
The Advocate-General
Lord Justice Clerk
Viscounts, as in England
Eldest sons of Earls
Marquesses' younger sons
Lord-Barons, as in England
Eldest sons of Viscounts
Earls' younger sons
Lord-Barons' eldest sons
Knights of the Garter
Knights of the Thistle
Privy Counsellors
Senators of College of Justice (Lords of Session)
Viscounts' younger sons
Lord-Barons' younger sons
Baronets
Knights Grand Cross and Knights Grand Commanders of orders, as in England
Knights Commanders of orders, as in England
Solicitor-General for Scotland
Lord Lyon King of Arms
Sheriffs Principal, when not within own county
Knights Bachelor
Sheriffs
Companions of Orders, as in England
Commanders of the Royal Victorian Order
Commanders of the British Empire
Companions of the Distinguished Service Order
Lieutenants of the Royal Victorian Order
Officers of the British Empire
Companions of the Imperial Service Order
Eldest sons of younger sons of peers
Eldest sons of baronets
Eldest sons of knights, as in England
Members of the Royal Victorian Order
Members of the British Empire
Baronets' younger sons
Knights' younger sons
Esquires
Gentlemen

* The Lord Provosts of the city districts of Aberdeen, Dundee, Edinburgh and Glasgow are Lord-Lieutenants for those districts *ex officio* and take precedence as such.

THE PEERAGE

ABBREVIATIONS AND SYMBOLS

S.	Scottish title
I.	Irish title
**	hereditary peer remaining in the House of Lords
°	there is no 'of' in the title
b.	born
s.	succeeded
m.	married
w.	widower or widow
M.	minor
†	heir not ascertained at time of going to press
F_	represents forename
S_	represents surname
cr.	created

The rules which govern the creation and succession of peerages are extremely complicated. There are, technically, five separate peerages, the Peerage of England, of Scotland, of Ireland, of Great Britain, and of the United Kingdom. The Peerage of Great Britain dates from 1707 when an Act of Union combined the two kingdoms of England and Scotland and separate peerages were discontinued. The Peerage of the United Kingdom dates from 1801 when Great Britain and Ireland were combined under an Act of Union. Some Scottish peers have received additional peerages of Great Britain or of the United Kingdom since 1707, and some Irish peers additional peerages of the United Kingdom since 1801.

The Peerage of Ireland was not entirely discontinued from 1801 but holders of Irish peerages, whether predating or created subsequent to the Union of 1801, were not entitled to sit in the House of Lords if they had no additional English, Scottish, Great Britain or United Kingdom peerage. However, they are eligible for election to the House of Commons and to vote in parliamentary elections. An Irish peer holding a peerage of a lower grade which enabled him to sit in the House of Lords was introduced there by the title which enabled him to sit, though for all other purposes he was known by his higher title.

In the Peerage of Scotland there is no rank of Baron; the equivalent rank is Lord of Parliament, abbreviated to 'Lord' (the female equivalent is 'Lady').

All peers of England, Scotland, Great Britain or the United Kingdom who are 21 years or over, and of British, Irish or Commonwealth nationality were entitled to sit in the House of Lords until the House of Lords Act 1999, when hereditary peers lost the right to sit. However, section two of the act provided an exception for 90 hereditary peers plus the holders of the office of Earl Marshal and Lord Great Chamberlain to remain as members of the House of Lords for their lifetime or pending further reform. Of the 90 hereditary peers, 75 were elected by the hereditary peers in their political party, or Crossbench grouping, and the remaining 15 by the whole house. Until 7 November 2002 any vacancy arising due to the death of one of the 90 excepted hereditary peers was filled by the runner-up to the original election. From 7 November 2002 any vacancy due to a death has been filled by holding a by-election. By-elections are conducted in accordance with arrangements made by the Clerk of the Parliaments and have to take place within three months of a vacancy occurring. If the vacancy is among the 75, only the excepted hereditary peers in the relevant party or Crossbench grouping are entitled to vote. If the vacancy is among the other 15, the whole house is entitled to vote.

In the list below, peers currently holding one of the 92 hereditary places in the House of Lords are indicated by ** .

In July 2008 proposed further reforms to the House of Lords were presented to parliament in a white paper *An Elected Second Chamber: Further Reform of the House of Lords* (see White Papers).

HEREDITARY WOMEN PEERS

Most hereditary peerages pass on death to the nearest male heir, but there are exceptions, and several are held by women.

A woman peer in her own right retains her title after marriage, and if her husband's rank is the superior she is designated by the two titles jointly, the inferior one second. Her hereditary claim still holds good in spite of any marriage whether higher or lower. No rank held by a woman can confer any title or even precedence upon her husband but the rank of a hereditary woman peer in her own right is inherited by her eldest son (or in some cases daughter).

After the Peerage Act 1963, hereditary women peers in their own right were entitled to sit in the House of Lords, subject to the same qualifications as men, until the House of Lords Act 1999.

LIFE PEERS

Since 1876 non-hereditary or life peerages have been conferred on certain eminent judges to enable the judicial functions of the House of Lords to be carried out. These lords are known as Lords of Appeal in Ordinary or law lords. In 2004 Baroness Hale of Richmond became the first female law lord.

Since 1958 life peerages have been conferred upon distinguished men and women from all walks of life, giving them seats in the House of Lords in the degree of Baron or Baroness. They are addressed in the same way as hereditary lords and barons, and their children have similar courtesy titles.

PEERAGES EXTINCT SINCE THE LAST EDITION

BARONIES: Chatfield (cr. 1937); Citrine (cr. 1946)

LIFE PEERAGES: Allen of Abbeydale (cr. 1976); Beaumont of Whitley (cr. 1967); Lord Blease (cr. 1978); Bridge of Harwich (cr. 1980); Bruce-Lockhart (cr. 2006); Burlison (cr. 1997); Cooke of Islandreagh (cr. 1992); Gilmour of Craigmillar (cr. 1992); Holme of Cheltenham (cr. 1990); Hunt of Tanworth (cr. 1980); Michie of Gallanach (cr. 2001); Oliver of Aylmerton (cr. 1986); Pym (cr. 1987); Russell-Johnston (cr. 1997); Stallard (cr. 1983); Stokes (cr. 1969); Thomas of Gwydir (cr. 1987); Varley (cr. 1990)

DISCLAIMER OF PEERAGES

The Peerage Act 1963 enables peers to disclaim their peerages for life. Peers alive in 1963 could disclaim within twelve months after the passing of the act (31 July 1963); a person subsequently succeeding to a peerage may disclaim within 12 months (one month if an MP) after the date of succession, or of reaching 21, if later. The disclaimer is irrevocable but does not affect the descent of the peerage after the disclaimant's death, and children of a disclaimed peer may, if they wish, retain their precedence and any courtesy titles and styles borne as children of a peer. The disclaimer permitted the disclaimant to sit in the House of Commons if elected as an MP. As the House of Lords Act 1999 removed hereditary peers from the House of Lords, they are now entitled to sit in the House of Commons without having to disclaim their titles.

The following peerages are currently disclaimed:

EARLDOM: Selkirk (1994)
VISCOUNTCY: Stansgate (1963)
BARONIES: Merthyr (1977); Reith (1972); Sanderson of Ayot (1971)
PEERS WHO ARE MINORS (ie under 21 years of age)
EARL: Craven (*b.* 1989)
VISCOUNT: Selby (*b.* 1993)
BARON: Crofton (*b.* 1988)

FORMS OF ADDRESS

Forms of address are given under the style for each individual rank of the peerage. Both formal and social forms of address are given where usage differs; nowadays, the social form is generally preferred to the formal, which increasingly is used only for official documents and on very formal occasions.

ROLL OF THE PEERAGE

Crown Office, House of Lords, London SW1A 0PW

The Roll of the Peerage is kept at the Crown Office and maintained by the Registrar of the Peerage in accordance with the terms of a 2004 royal warrant. The roll records the names of all living life peers and hereditary peers who have proved their succession to the satisfaction of the Lord Chancellor. The Roll of the Peerage is maintained in addition to the Clerk of the Parliaments' register of hereditary peers eligible to stand for election in House of Lords' by-elections.

A person whose name is not entered on the Roll of Peerage can not be addressed or mentioned by the title of a peer in any official document.

Registrar, Ian Denyer, MVO
Assistant Registrar, Grant Bavister

HEREDITARY PEERS

as at 31 August 2008

PEERS OF THE BLOOD ROYAL

Style, His Royal Highness the Duke of _/His Royal Highness the Earl of_
Style of address (*formal*) May it please your Royal Highness; *(informal)* Sir

Created	Title, order of succession, name, etc	Heir
	Dukes	
1947	*Edinburgh (1st),* HRH the Prince Philip, Duke of Edinburgh	The Prince of Wales *
1337	*Cornwall,* HRH the Prince of Wales, *s.* 1952	‡
1398 S.	*Rothesay,* HRH the Prince of Wales, *s.* 1952	‡
1986	*York (1st),* Prince Andrew, HRH the Duke of York	None
1928	*Gloucester (2nd),* Prince Richard, HRH the Duke of Gloucester, *s.* 1974	Earl of Ulster
1934	*Kent (2nd),*Prince Edward, HRH the Duke of Kent, *s.* 1942	Earl of St Andrews
	Earl	
1999	*Wessex (1st),* Prince Edward, HRH the Earl of Wessex	Viscount Severn

* In June 1999 Buckingham Palace announced that the current Earl of Wessex will be granted the Dukedom of Edinburgh when the title reverts to the Crown. The title will only revert to the Crown on both the death of the current Duke of Edinburgh and the Prince of Wales' succession as king

‡ The title is held by the sovereign's eldest son from the moment of his birth or the sovereign's accession

DUKES

Coronet, Eight strawberry leaves

Style, His Grace the Duke of _
Envelope (formal), His Grace the Duke of _; *(social),* The Duke of _. *Letter (formal),* My Lord Duke; *(social),* Dear Duke. *Spoken (formal),* Your Grace; *(social),* Duke
Wife's style, Her Grace the Duchess of _
Envelope (formal), Her Grace the Duchess of _; *(social),* The Duchess of _. *Letter (formal),* Dear Madam; *(social),* Dear Duchess. *Spoken,* Duchess
Eldest son's style, Takes his father's second title as a courtesy title (*see* Courtesy Titles)
Younger sons' style, 'Lord' before forename (F_) and surname (S_)
Envelope, Lord F_ S_. *Letter (formal),* My Lord; *(social),* Dear Lord F_. *Spoken (formal),* My Lord; *(social),* Lord F_
Daughters' style, 'Lady' before forename (F_) and surname (S_)
Envelope, Lady F_ S_. *Letter (formal),* Dear Madam; *(social),* Dear Lady F_. *Spoken,* Lady F_

Created	Title, order of succession, name, etc	Heir
1868 I.	*Abercorn (5th),* James Hamilton, KG, *b.* 1934, *s.* 1979, *m., Lord Steward*	Marquess of Hamilton, *b.* 1969
1701 S.	*Argyll (13th),* Torquhil Ian Campbell, *b.* 1968, *s.* 2001	Marquess of Lorne, *b.* 2004
1703 S.	*Atholl (11th),* John Murray, *b.* 1929, *s.* 1996, *m.*	Marquis of Tullibardine, *b.* 1960
1682	*Beaufort (11th),* David Robert Somerset, *b.* 1928, *s.* 1984, *m.*	Marquess of Worcester, *b.* 1952
1694	*Bedford (15th),* Andrew Ian Henry Russell, *b.* 1962, *s.* 2003, *m.*	Marquess of Tavistock, *b.* 2005
1663 S.	*Buccleuch (10th) and Queensberry (12th) (S. 1684),* Richard Walter John Montagu Douglas Scott, KBE, *b.* 1954, *s.* 2007, *m.*	Earl of Dalkeith, *b.* 1984
1694	*Devonshire (12th),* Peregrine Andrew Morny Cavendish, *b.* 1944, *s.* 2004, *m.*	Marquess of Hartington, *b.* 1969
1900	*Fife (3rd),* James George Alexander Bannerman Carnegie, *b.* 1929, *s.* 1959	Earl of Southesk, *b.* 1961
1675	*Grafton (11th),* Hugh Denis Charles FitzRoy, KG, *b.* 1919, *s.* 1970, *m.*	Earl of Euston, *b.* 1947
1643 S.	*Hamilton (15th) and Brandon (12th) (1711),* Angus Alan Douglas Douglas-Hamilton, *b.* 1938, *s.* 1973 *Premier Peer of Scotland*	Marquis of Douglas and Clydesdale, *b.* 1978
1766 I.	*Leinster (9th),* Maurice FitzGerald, *b.* 1948, *s.* 2004, *m. Premier Duke, Marquess and Earl of Ireland*	Lord John F., *b.* 1952

1719	*Manchester (13th),* Alexander Charles David Drogo Montagu, *b.* 1962, *s.* 2002, *m.*	Viscount Mandeville, *b.* 1993
1702	*Marlborough (11th),* John George Vanderbilt Henry Spencer-Churchill, *b.* 1926, *s.* 1972, *m.*	Marquess of Blandford, *b.* 1955
1707 S.	** *Montrose (8th),* James Graham, *b.* 1935, *s.* 1992, *m.*	Marquis of Graham, *b.* 1973
1483	** *Norfolk (18th),* Edward Wiliam Fitzalan-Howard, *b.* 1956, *s.* 2002, *m. Premier Duke and Earl Marshal*	Earl of Arundel and Surrey, *b.* 1987
1766	*Northumberland (12th),* Ralph George Algernon Percy, *b.* 1956, *s.* 1995, *m.*	Earl Percy, *b.* 1984
1675	*Richmond (10th) and Gordon (5th) (1876),* Charles Henry Gordon Lennox, *b.* 1929, *s.* 1989, *m.*	Earl of March and Kinrara, *b.* 1955
1707 S.	*Roxburghe (10th),* Guy David Innes-Ker, *b.* 1954, *s.* 1974, *m. Premier Baronet of Scotland*	Marquis of Bowmont and Cessford, *b.* 1981
1703	*Rutland (11th),* David Charles Robert Manners, *b.* 1959, *s.* 1999, *m.*	Marquess of Granby, *b.*1999
1684	*St Albans (14th),* Murray de Vere Beauclerk, *b.* 1939, *s.* 1988, *m.*	Earl of Burford, *b.* 1965
1547	*Somerset (19th),* John Michael Edward Seymour, *b.* 1952, *s.* 1984, *m.*	Lord Seymour, *b.* 1982
1833	*Sutherland (7th),* Francis Ronald Egerton, *b.* 1940, *s.* 2000, *m.*	Marquess of Stafford, *b.* 1975
1814	*Wellington (8th),* Arthur Valerian Wellesley, KG, LVO, OBE, MC, *b.* 1915, *s.* 1972, *m.*	Marquess of Douro, *b.* 1945
1874	*Westminster (6th),* Gerald Cavendish Grosvenor, KG, CB, OBE, *b.* 1951, *s.* 1979, *m.*	Earl Grosvenor, *b.* 1991

MARQUESSES

Coronet, Four strawberry leaves alternating with four silver balls

Style, The Most Hon. the Marquess (of) _ . In Scotland the spelling 'Marquis' is preferred for pre-Union creations
Envelope (formal), The Most Hon. the Marquess of _; *(social),* The Marquess of _. *Letter (formal),* My Lord; *(social),* Dear Lord _. *Spoken (formal),* My Lord; *(social),* Lord _
Wife's style, The Most Hon. the Marchioness (of) _
Envelope (formal), The Most Hon. the Marchioness of _; *(social),* The Marchioness of _. *Letter (formal),* Madam; *(social),* Dear Lady _. *Spoken,* Lady _
Eldest son's style, Takes his father's second title as a courtesy title (*see* Courtesy Titles)
Younger sons' style, 'Lord' before forename and surname, as for Duke's younger sons
Daughters' style, 'Lady' before forename and surname, as for Duke's daughter

Created	*Title, order of succession, name, etc*	*Heir*
1916	*Aberdeen and Temair (7th),* Alexander George Gordon, *b.* 1955, *s.* 2002, *m.*	Earl of Haddo, *b.* 1983
1876	*Abergavenny (6th) and 10th Earl, Abergavenny, 1784,* Christopher George Charles Nevill, *b.* 1955, *s.* 2000, *m.*	To Earldom only, David M. R. N., *b.* 1941
1821	*Ailesbury (8th),* Michael Sidney Cedric Brudenell-Bruce, *b.* 1926, *s.* 1974	Earl of Cardigan, *b.* 1952
1831	*Ailsa (8th),* Archibald Angus Charles Kennedy, *b.* 1956, *s.* 1994	Lord D. T. K., *b.* 1958
1815	*Anglesey (7th),* George Charles Henry Victor Paget, *b.* 1922, *s.* 1947, *m.*	Earl of Uxbridge, *b.* 1950
1789	*Bath (7th),* Alexander George Thynn, *b.* 1932, *s.* 1992, *m.*	Viscount Weymouth, *b.* 1974
1826	*Bristol (8th),* Frederick William Augustus Hervey, *b.* 1979, *s.* 1999	Timothy H. H., *b.* 1960
1796	*Bute (7th),* John Colum Crichton-Stuart, *b.* 1958, *s.* 1993, *m.*	Lord Mount Stuart, *b.* 1989
1812	° *Camden (6th),* David George Edward Henry Pratt, *b.* 1930, *s.* 1983	Earl of Brecknock, *b.* 1965
1815	** *Cholmondeley (7th),* David George Philip Cholmondeley, KCVO, *b.* 1960, *s.* 1990, *Lord Great Chamberlain*	Charles G. C., *b.* 1959
1816	° *Conyngham (7th),* Frederick William Henry Francis Conyngham, *b.* 1924, *s.* 1974, *m.*	Earl of Mount Charles, *b.* 1951
1791 I.	*Donegall (8th),* Arthur Patrick Chichester, *b.* 1952, *s.* 2007, *m.*	Earl of Belfast, *b.* 1990
1789 I.	*Downshire (9th),* (Arthur Francis) Nicholas Wills Hill, *b.* 1959, *s.* 2003, *m.*	Earl of Hillsborough, *b.* 1996
1801 I.	*Ely (9th),* Charles John Tottenham, *b.* 1943, *s.* 2006, *m.*	Lord Timothy C. T., *b.* 1948
1801	*Exeter (8th),* (William) Michael Anthony Cecil, *b.* 1935, *s.* 1988, *m.*	Lord Burghley, *b.* 1970

1800 I.	*Headfort (7th),* Thomas Michael Ronald Christopher Taylour, *b.* 1959, *s.* 2005, *m.*	Earl of Bective, *b.* 1989
1793	*Hertford (9th),* Henry Jocelyn Seymour, *b.* 1958, *s.* 1997, *m.*	Earl of Yarmouth, *b.* 1993
1599 S.	*Huntly (13th),* Granville Charles Gomer Gordon, *b.* 1944, *s.* 1987, *m.* *Premier Marquess of Scotland*	Earl of Aboyne, *b.* 1973
1784	*Lansdowne (9th),* Charles Maurice Mercer Nairne Petty-Fitzmaurice, LVO *b.* 1941, *s.* 1999, *m.*	Earl of Kerry, *b.* 1970
1902	*Linlithgow (4th),* Adrian John Charles Hope, *b.* 1946, *s.* 1987, *m.*	Earl of Hopetoun, *b.* 1969
1816 I.	*Londonderry (9th),* Alexander Charles Robert Vane-Tempest-Stewart, *b.* 1937, *s.* 1955, *m.*	Viscount Castlereagh, *b.* 1972
1701 S.	*Lothian (13th),* Michael Andrew Foster Jude Kerr (Michael Ancram), PC, *b.* 1945, *s.* 2004, *m.*	Lord Ralph W. F. J. K., *b.* 1957
1917	*Milford Haven (4th),* George Ivar Louis Mountbatten, *b.* 1961, *s.* 1970, *m.*	Earl of Medina, *b.* 1991
1838	*Normanby (5th),* Constantine Edmund Walter Phipps, *b.* 1954, *s.* 1994, *m.*	Earl of Mulgrave, *b.* 1994
1812	*Northampton (7th),* Spencer Douglas David Compton, *b.* 1946, *s.* 1978, *m.*	Earl Compton, *b.* 1973
1682 S.	*Queensberry (12th),* David Harrington Angus Douglas, *b.* 1929, *s.* 1954	Viscount Drumlanrig, *b.* 1967
1926	*Reading (4th),* Simon Charles Henry Rufus Isaacs, *b.* 1942, *s.* 1980, *m.*	Viscount Erleigh, *b.* 1986
1789	*Salisbury (7th) and Baron Gascoyne-Cecil (life peerage, 1999),* Robert Michael James Gascoyne-Cecil, PC, *b.* 1946, *s.* 2003, *m.*	Viscount Cranborne, *b.* 1970
1800 I.	*Sligo (11th),* Jeremy Ulick Browne, *b.* 1939, *s.* 1991, *m.*	Sebastian U. B., *b.* 1964
1787	° *Townshend (7th),* George John Patrick Dominic Townshend, *b.* 1916, *s.* 1921, *w.*	Viscount Raynham, *b.* 1945
1694 S.	*Tweeddale (14th),* Charles David Montagu Hay, *b.* 1947, *s.* 2005	(Lord) Alistair J. M. H., *b.* 1955
1789 I.	*Waterford (8th),* John Hubert de la Poer Beresford, *b.* 1933, *s.* 1934, *m.*	Earl of Tyrone, *b.* 1958
1551	*Winchester (18th),* Nigel George Paulet, *b.* 1941, *s.* 1968, *m.* *Premier Marquess of England*	Earl of Wiltshire, *b.* 1969
1892	*Zetland (4th),* Lawrence Mark Dundas, *b.* 1937, *s.* 1989, *m.*	Earl of Ronaldshay, *b.* 1965

EARLS

Coronet, Eight silver balls on stalks alternating with eight gold strawberry leaves

Style, The Rt. Hon. the Earl (of) _
Envelope (formal), The Rt. Hon. the Earl (of) _; *(social),* The Earl (of) _. *Letter (formal),* My Lord; *(social),* Dear Lord _. *Spoken (formal),* My Lord; *(social),* Lord _.
Wife's style, The Rt. Hon. the Countess (of) _
Envelope (formal), The Rt. Hon. the Countess (of) _; *(social),* The Countess (of) _. *Letter (formal),* Madam; *(social),* Lady _. *Spoken (formal),* Madam; *(social),* Lady _.
Eldest son's style, Takes his father's second title as a courtesy title (*see* Courtesy Titles)
Younger sons' style, 'The Hon.' before forename and surname, as for Baron's children
Daughters' style, 'Lady' before forename and surname, as for Duke's daughter

Created	*Title, order of succession, name, etc*	*Heir*
1639 S.	*Airlie (13th),* David George Coke Patrick Ogilvy, KT, GCVO, PC, Royal Victorian Chain, *b.* 1926, *s.* 1968, *m.*	Lord Ogilvy, *b.* 1958
1696	*Albemarle (10th),* Rufus Arnold Alexis Keppel, *b.* 1965, *s.* 1979, *m.*	Viscount Bury, *b.* 2003
1952	° *Alexander of Tunis (2nd),* Shane William Desmond Alexander, *b.* 1935, *s.* 1969, *m.*	Hon. Brian J. A., *b.* 1939
1662	*Annandale and Hartfell (11th),* Patrick Andrew Wentworth Hope Johnstone, *b.* 1941, *s.* 1983, *m.* claim established 1985	Lord Johnstone, *b.* 1971
1789 I.	° *Annesley (11th),* Philip Harrison Annesley, *b.* 1927, *s.* 2001, *m.*	Hon. Michael R. A., *b.* 1933
1785 I.	*Antrim (9th),* Alexander Randal Mark McDonnell, *b.* 1935, *s.* 1977, *m.*	Viscount Dunluce, *b.* 1967
1762 I.	** *Arran (9th),* Arthur Desmond Colquhoun Gore, *b.* 1938, *s.* 1983, *m.*	Paul A. G., CMG, CVO, *b.* 1921
1955	° ** *Attlee (3rd),* John Richard Attlee, *b.* 1956, *s.* 1991, *m.*	None
1714	*Aylesford (12th),* Charles Heneage Finch-Knightley, *b.* 1947, *s.* 2008, *m.*	Lord Guernsey, *b.* 1985

1937	** *Baldwin of Bewdley (4th),* Edward Alfred Alexander Baldwin, *b.* 1938, *s.* 1976, *w.*	Viscount Corvedale, *b.* 1973
1922	*Balfour (5th),* Roderick Francis Arthur Balfour, *b.* 1948, *s.* 2003, *m.*	Charles G. Y. B., *b.* 1951
1772	° *Bathurst (8th),* Henry Allen John Bathurst, *b.* 1927, *s.* 1943, *m.*	Lord Apsley, *b.* 1961
1919	° *Beatty (3rd),* David Beatty, *b.* 1946, *s.* 1972, *m.*	Viscount Borodale, *b.* 1973
1797 I.	° *Belmore (8th),* John Armar Lowry-Corry, *b.* 1951, *s.* 1960, *m.*	Viscount Corry, *b.* 1985
1739 I.	*Bessborough (12th),* Myles Fitzhugh Longfield Ponsonby, *b.* 1941, *s.* 2002, *m.*	Viscount Duncannon, *b.* 1974
1815	*Bradford (7th),* Richard Thomas Orlando Bridgeman, *b.* 1947, *s.* 1981, *m.*	Viscount Newport, *b.* 1980
1469	*Buchan (17th),* Malcolm Harry Erskine, *b.* 1930, *s.* 1984, *m.*	Lord Cardross, *b.* 1960
1746	*Buckinghamshire (10th),* (George) Miles Hobart-Hampden, *b.* 1944, *s.* 1983, *m.*	Sir John Hobart, Bt., *b.* 1945
1800	° *Cadogan (8th),* Charles Gerald John Cadogan, *b.* 1937, *s.* 1997, *m.*	Viscount Chelsea, *b.* 1966
1878	° *Cairns (6th),* Simon Dallas Cairns, CVO, CBE, *b.* 1939, *s.* 1989, *m.*	Viscount Garmoyle, *b.* 1965
1455	** *Caithness (20th),* Malcolm Ian Sinclair, PC, *b.* 1948, *s.* 1965, *w.*	Lord Berriedale, *b.* 1981
1800 I.	*Caledon (7th),* Nicholas James Alexander, *b.* 1955, *s.* 1980, *m.*	Viscount Alexander, *b.* 1990
1661	*Carlisle (13th),* George William Beaumont Howard, *b.* 1949, *s.* 1994	Hon. Philip C. W. H., *b.* 1963
1793	*Carnarvon (8th),* George Reginald Oliver Molyneux Herbert, *b.* 1956, *s.* 2001, *m.*	Lord Porchester, *b.* 1992
1748 I.	*Carrick (10th),* David James Theobald Somerset Butler, *b.* 1953, *s.* 1992, *m.*	Viscount Ikerrin, *b.* 1975
1800 I.	° *Castle Stewart (8th),* Arthur Patrick Avondale Stuart, *b.* 1928, *s.* 1961, *w.*	Viscount Stuart, *b.* 1953
1814	°** *Cathcart (7th),* Charles Alan Andrew Cathcart, *b.* 1952, *s.* 1999, *m.*	Lord Greenock, *b.* 1986
1647 I.	*Cavan,* The 12th Earl died in 1988.	†Roger C. Lambart, *b.* 1944
1827	° *Cawdor (7th),* Colin Robert Vaughan Campbell, *b.* 1962, *s.* 1993, *m.*	Viscount Emlyn, *b.* 1998
1801	*Chichester (9th),* John Nicholas Pelham, *b.* 1944, *s.* 1944, *m.*	Richard A. H. P., *b.* 1952
1803 I.	*Clancarty (9th),* Nicholas Power Richard Le Poer Trench, *b.* 1952, *s.* 1995	None
1776 I.	*Clanwilliam (7th),* John Herbert Meade, *b.* 1919, *s.* 1989, *w.*	Lord Gillford, *b.* 1960
1776	*Clarendon (7th),* George Frederick Laurence Hyde Villiers, *b.* 1933, *s.* 1955, *m.*	Lord Hyde, *b.* 1976
1620 I.	*Cork and Orrery (15th),* John Richard Boyle, *b.* 1945, *s.* 2003, *m.*	Viscount Dungarvan, *b.* 1978
1850	*Cottenham (9th),* Mark John Henry Pepys, *b.* 1983, *s.* 2000	Hon. Sam R. P., *b.* 1986
1762 I.	** *Courtown (9th),* James Patrick Montagu Burgoyne Winthrop Stopford, *b.* 1954, *s.* 1975, *m.*	Viscount Stopford, *b.* 1988
1697	*Coventry (13th),* George William Coventry, *b.* 1939, *s.* 2004, *m.*	David D. S. C., *b.* 1973
1857	° *Cowley (7th),* Garret Graham Wellesley, *b.* 1934, *s.* 1975, *m.*	Viscount Dangan, *b.* 1965
1892	*Cranbrook (5th),* Gathorne Gathorne-Hardy, *b.* 1933, *s.* 1978, *m.*	Lord Medway, *b.* 1968
1801 M.	*Craven (9th),* Benjamin Robert Joseph Craven, *b.* 1989, *s.* 1990	Rupert J. E. C., *b.* 1926
1398 S.	*Crawford (29th) and Balcarres (12th) (S. 1651) and Baron Balniel (life peerage, 1974),* Robert Alexander Lindsay, KT, GCVO, PC, *b.* 1927, *s.* 1975, *m. Premier Earl on Union Roll*	Lord Balniel, *b.* 1958
1861	*Cromartie (5th),* John Ruaridh Blunt Grant Mackenzie, *b.* 1948, *s.* 1989, *m.*	Viscount Tarbat, *b.* 1987
1901	*Cromer (4th),* Evelyn Rowland Esmond Baring, *b.* 1946, *s.* 1991, *m.*	Viscount Errington, *b.* 1994
1633 S.	*Dalhousie (17th),* James Hubert Ramsay, *b.* 1948, *s.* 1999, *m.*	Lord Ramsay, *b.* 1981
1725 I.	*Darnley (11th),* Adam Ivo Stuart Bligh, *b.* 1941, *s.* 1980, *m.*	Lord Clifton, *b.* 1968
1711	*Dartmouth (10th),* William Legge, *b.* 1949, *s.* 1997	Hon. Rupert L., *b.* 1951
1761	° *De La Warr (11th),* William Herbrand Sackville, *b.* 1948, *s.* 1988, *m.*	Lord Buckhurst, *b.* 1979
1622	*Denbigh (12th) and Desmond (11th) (I. 1622),* Alexander Stephen Rudolph Feilding, *b.* 1970, *s.* 1995, *m.*	Viscount Feilding, *b.* 2005
1485	*Derby (19th),* Edward Richard William Stanley, *b.* 1962, *s.* 1994, *m.*	Lord Stanley, *b.* 1998
1553	*Devon (18th),* Hugh Rupert Courtenay, *b.* 1942, *s.* 1998, *m.*	Lord Courtenay, *b.* 1975
1800 I.	*Donoughmore (8th),* Richard Michael John Hely-Hutchinson, *b.* 1927, *s.* 1981, *w.*	Viscount Suirdale, *b.* 1952
1661 I.	*Drogheda (12th),* Henry Dermot Ponsonby Moore, *b.* 1937, *s.* 1989, *m.*	Viscount Moore, *b.* 1983
1837	*Ducie (7th),* David Leslie Moreton, *b.* 1951, *s.* 1991, *m.*	Lord Moreton, *b.* 1981
1860	*Dudley (4th),* William Humble David Ward, *b.* 1920, *s.* 1969, *m.*	Viscount Ednam, *b.* 1947
1660 S.	** *Dundee (12th),* Alexander Henry Scrymgeour, *b.* 1949, *s.* 1983, *m.*	Lord Scrymgeour, *b.* 1982
1669 S.	*Dundonald (15th),* Iain Alexander Douglas Blair Cochrane, *b.* 1961, *s.* 1986, *m.*	Lord Cochrane, *b.* 1991
1686 S.	*Dunmore (12th),* Malcolm Kenneth Murray, *b.* 1946, *s.* 1995, *m.*	Hon. Geoffrey C. M., *b.*1949
1822 I.	*Dunraven and Mount-Earl (7th),* Thady Windham Thomas Wyndham-Quin, *b.* 1939, *s.* 1965, *m.*	None

1833	*Durham (7th),* Edward Richard Lambton, *b.* 1961, *s.* 2006, *m.*	Viscount Lambton, *b.* 1985
1837	*Effingham (7th),* David Mowbray Algernon Howard, *b.* 1939, *s.* 1996, *m.*	Lord Howard of Effingham, *b.* 1971
1507 S.	*Eglinton (18th) and Winton (9th) (S. 1600),* Archibald George Montgomerie, *b.* 1939, *s.* 1966, *m.*	Lord Montgomerie, *b.* 1966
1733 I.	*Egmont (12th),* Thomas Frederick Gerald Perceval, *b.* 1934, *s.* 2001, *m.*	Hon. Donald W. P., *b.* 1954
1821	*Eldon (5th),* John Joseph Nicholas Scott, *b.* 1937, *s.* 1976, *m.*	Viscount Encombe, *b.* 1962
1633 S.	*Elgin (11th) and Kincardine (15th) (S. 1647),* Andrew Douglas Alexander Thomas Bruce, KT, *b.* 1924, *s.* 1968, *m.*	Lord Bruce, *b.* 1961
1789 I.	*Enniskillen (7th),* Andrew John Galbraith Cole, *b.* 1942, *s.* 1989, *m.*	Arthur G. C., *b.* 1920
1789 I.	*Erne (6th),* Henry George Victor John Crichton, *b.* 1937, *s.* 1940, *m.*	Viscount Crichton, *b.* 1971
1452 S.	** *Erroll (24th),* Merlin Sereld Victor Gilbert Hay, *b.* 1948, *s.* 1978, *m.* *Hereditary Lord High Constable and Knight Marischal of Scotland*	Lord Hay, *b.* 1984
1661	*Essex (11th),* Frederick Paul de Vere Capell, *b.* 1944, *s.* 2005	William J. C., *b.* 1952
1711	° ** *Ferrers (13th),* Robert Washington Shirley, PC, *b.* 1929, *s.* 1954, *m.*	Viscount Tamworth, *b.* 1952
1789	° *Fortescue (8th),* Charles Hugh Richard Fortescue, *b.* 1951, *s.* 1993, *m.*	John A. F. F., *b.* 1955
1841	*Gainsborough (5th),* Anthony Gerard Edward Noel, *b.* 1923, *s.* 1927, *m.*	Viscount Campden, *b.* 1950
1623 S.	*Galloway (13th),* Randolph Keith Reginald Stewart, *b.* 1928, *s.* 1978, *w.*	Andrew C. S., *b.* 1949
1703 S.	** *Glasgow (10th),* Patrick Robin Archibald Boyle, *b.* 1939, *s.* 1984, *m.*	Viscount of Kelburn, *b.* 1978
1806 I.	*Gosford (7th),* Charles David Nicholas Alexander John Sparrow Acheson, *b.* 1942, *s.* 1966, *m.*	Hon. Patrick B. V. M. A., *b.* 1915
1945	*Gowrie (2nd),* Alexander Patrick Greysteil Hore-Ruthven, PC, *b.* 1939, *s.* 1955, *m.*	Viscount Ruthven of Canberra, *b.* 1964
1684 I.	*Granard (10th),* Peter Arthur Edward Hastings Forbes, *b.* 1957, *s.* 1992, *m.*	Viscount Forbes, *b.* 1981
1833	° *Granville (6th),* Granville George Fergus Leveson-Gower, *b.* 1959, *s.* 1996, *m.*	Lord Leveson, *b.* 1999
1806	° *Grey (6th),* Richard Fleming George Charles Grey, *b.* 1939, *s.* 1963, *m.*	Philip K. G., *b.* 1940
1752	*Guilford (10th),* Piers Edward Brownlow North, *b.* 1971, *s.* 1999, *m.*	Lord North, *b.* 2002
1619	*Haddington (13th),* John George Baillie-Hamilton, *b.* 1941, *s.* 1986, *m.*	Lord Binning, *b.* 1985
1919	° *Haig (2nd),* George Alexander Eugene Douglas Haig, OBE, *b.* 1918, *s.* 1928, *m.*	Viscount Dawick, *b.* 1961
1944	*Halifax (3rd),* Charles Edward Peter Neil Wood, *b.* 1944, *s.* 1980, *m.*	Lord Irwin, *b.* 1977
1898	*Halsbury (4th),* Adam Edward Giffard, *b.* 1934, *s.* 2000, *m.*	None
1754	*Hardwicke (10th),* Joseph Philip Sebastian Yorke, *b.* 1971, *s.* 1974	Charles E. Y., *b.* 1951
1812	*Harewood (7th),* George Henry Hubert Lascelles, KBE, *b.* 1923, *s.* 1947, *m.*	Viscount Lascelles, *b.* 1950
1742	*Harrington (11th),* William Henry Leicester Stanhope, *b.* 1922, *s.* 1929, *m.*	Viscount Petersham, *b.* 1945
1809	*Harrowby (8th),* Dudley Adrian Conroy Ryder, *b.* 1951, *s.* 2007, *m.*	Viscount Sandon, *b.* 1981
1605	** *Home (15th),* David Alexander Cospatrick Douglas-Home, CVO, CBE, *b.* 1943, *s.* 1995, *m.*	Lord Dunglass, *b.* 1987
1821	° ** *Howe (7th),* Frederick Richard Penn Curzon, *b.* 1951, *s.* 1984, *m.*	Viscount Curzon, *b.* 1994
1529	*Huntingdon (16th),* William Edward Robin Hood Hastings Bass, LVO, *b.* 1948, *s.* 1990, *m.*	Hon. Simon A. R. H. H. B., *b.* 1950
1885	*Iddesleigh (5th),* John Stafford Northcote, *b.* 1957, *s.* 2004, *m.*	Viscount St Cyres, *b.* 1985
1756	*Ilchester (10th),* Robin Maurice Fox-Strangways, *b.* 1942, *s.* 2006, *m.*	Lord Stavordale, *b.* 1972
1929	*Inchcape (4th),* (Kenneth) Peter (Lyle) Mackay, *b.* 1943, *s.* 1994, *m.*	Viscount Glenapp, *b.* 1979
1919	*Iveagh (4th),* Arthur Edward Rory Guinness, *b.* 1969, *s.* 1992	Viscount Elveden, *b.* 2003
1925	° *Jellicoe (3rd),* Patrick John Bernard Jellicoe, *b.* 1950, *s.* 2007	Viscount Brocas, *b.* 1970
1697	*Jersey (10th),* George Francis William Child Villiers, *b.* 1976, *s.* 1998 *m.*	Hon. Jamie C. C. V., *b.* 1994
1822 I.	*Kilmorey (6th),* Sir Richard Francis Needham, PC, *b.* 1942, *s.* 1977, *m.*, (does not use title)	Viscount Newry and Mourne, *b.* 1966
1866	*Kimberley (5th),* John Armine Wodehouse, *b.* 1951, *s.* 2002, *m.*	Lord Wodehouse, *b.*1978
1768 I.	*Kingston (12th),* Robert Charles Henry King-Tenison, *b.* 1969, *s.* 2002, *m.*	Viscount Kingsborough, *b.* 2000
1633 S.	*Kinnoull (15th),* Arthur William George Patrick Hay, *b.* 1935, *s.* 1938, *m.*	Viscount Dupplin, *b.* 1962
1677 S.	*Kintore (14th),* James William Falconer Keith, *b.* 1976, *s.* 2004	Lady Iona D. M. G. K., *b.* 1978
1914	° *Kitchener of Khartoum (3rd),* Henry Herbert Kitchener, TD, *b.* 1919, *s.* 1937	None
1624	*Lauderdale (17th),* Patrick Francis Maitland, *b.* 1911, *s.* 1968, *w.*	Viscount Maitland, *b.* 1937
1837	*Leicester (7th),* Edward Douglas Coke, *b.* 1936, *s.* 1994, *m.*	Viscount Coke, *b.* 1965
1641 S.	*Leven (14th) and Melville (13th) (S. 1690),* Alexander Robert Leslie Melville, *b.* 1924, *s.* 1947, *m.*	Hon. Alexander I. L. M., *b.* 1984

1831	*Lichfield (6th),* Thomas William Robert Hugh Anson, *b.* 1978, *s.* 2005	George R. A., *b.* 1960
1803 I.	*Limerick (7th),* Edmund Christopher Pery, *b.* 1963, *s.* 2003, *m.*	Viscount Glentworth, *b.* 1991
1572	*Lincoln (19th),* Robert Edward Fiennes-Clinton, *b.* 1972, *s.* 2001	Hon. William R. F.-C., *b.* 1980
1633 S.	** *Lindsay (16th),* James Randolph Lindesay-Bethune, *b.* 1955, *s.* 1989, *m.*	Viscount Garnock, *b.* 1990
1626	*Lindsey (14th) and Abingdon (9th) (1682),* Richard Henry Rupert Bertie, *b.* 1931, *s.* 1963, *m.*	Lord Norreys, *b.* 1958
1776 I.	*Lisburne (8th),* John David Malet Vaughan, *b.* 1918, *s.* 1965, *m.*	Viscount Vaughan, *b.* 1945
1822 I.	** *Listowel (6th),* Francis Michael Hare, *b.* 1964, *s.* 1997, *m.*	Hon. Timothy P. H., *b.* 1966
1905	** *Liverpool (5th),* Edward Peter Bertram Savile Foljambe, *b.* 1944, *s.* 1969, *m.*	Viscount Hawkesbury, *b.* 1972
1945	° *Lloyd George of Dwyfor (3rd),* Owen Lloyd George, *b.* 1924, *s.* 1968, *m.*	Viscount Gwynedd, *b.* 1951
1785 I.	*Longford (8th),* Thomas Frank Dermot Pakenham, *b.* 1933, *s.* 2001, *m.*, (does not use title)	Hon. Edward M. P., *b.* 1970
1807	*Lonsdale (8th),* Hugh Clayton Lowther, *b.* 1949, *s.* 2006, *m.*	Hon. William J. L., *b.* 1957
1633 S.	*Loudoun (14th),* Michael Edward Abney-Hastings, *b.* 1942, *s.* 2002, *m.*	Lord Mauchline, *b.* 1974
1838	*Lovelace (5th),* Peter Axel William Locke King, *b.* 1951, *s.* 1964, *m.*	None
1795 I.	*Lucan (7th),* Richard John Bingham, *b.* 1934, *s.* 1964, *m.* (missing since 8 November 1974)	Lord Bingham, *b.* 1967
1880	*Lytton (5th),* John Peter Michael Scawen Lytton, *b.* 1950, *s.* 1985, *m.*	Viscount Knebworth, *b.* 1989
1721	*Macclesfield (9th),* Richard Timothy George Mansfield Parker, *b.* 1943, *s.* 1992, *m.*	Hon. J. David G. P., *b.* 1945
1800	*Malmesbury (7th),* James Carleton Harris, *b.* 1946, *s.* 2000, *m.*	Viscount FitzHarris, *b.* 1970
1776	*Mansfield and Mansfield (8th) (1792),* William David Mungo James Murray, *b.* 1930, *s.* 1971, *m.*	Viscount Stormont, *b.* 1956
1565 S.	*Mar (14th) and Kellie (16th) (S. 1616) and Baron Erskine of Alloa Tower (life peerage, 2000),* James Thorne Erskine, *b.* 1949, *s.* 1994, *m.*	Hon. Alexander D. E., *b.* 1952
1785 I.	*Mayo (11th),* Charles Diarmuidh John Bourke, *b.* 1953, *s.* 2006, *m.*	Lord Naas, *b.* 1985
1627 I.	*Meath (15th),* John Anthony Brabazon, *b.* 1941, *s.* 1998, *m.*	Lord Ardee, *b.* 1977
1766 I.	*Mexborough (8th),* John Christopher George Savile, *b.* 1931, *s.* 1980, *m.*	Viscount Pollington, *b.* 1959
1813	*Minto (7th),* Gilbert Timothy George Lariston Elliot-Murray-Kynynmound, *b.* 1953, *s.* 2005, *m.*	Viscount Melgund, *b.* 1984
1562 S.	*Moray (20th),* Douglas John Moray Stuart, *b.* 1928, *s.* 1974, *m.*	Lord Doune, *b.* 1966
1815	*Morley (6th),* John St Aubyn Parker, KCVO, *b.* 1923, *s.* 1962, *m.*	Viscount Boringdon, *b.* 1956
1458	*Morton (22nd),* John Charles Sholto Douglas, *b.* 1927, *s.* 1976, *m.*	Lord Aberdour, *b.* 1952
1789	*Mount Edgcumbe (8th),* Robert Charles Edgcumbe, *b.* 1939, *s.* 1982	Piers V. E., *b.* 1946
1805	° *Nelson (9th),* Peter John Horatio Nelson, *b.* 1941, *s.* 1981, *m.*	Viscount Merton, *b.* 1971
1660 S.	*Newburgh (12th),* Don Filippo Giambattista Camillo Francesco Aldo Maria Rospigliosi, *b.* 1942, *s.* 1986, *m.*	Princess Donna Benedetta F. M. R., *b.* 1974
1827 I.	*Norbury (7th),* Richard James Graham-Toler, *b.* 1967, *s.* 2000	None
1806 I.	*Normanton (6th),* Shaun James Christian Welbore Ellis Agar, *b.* 1945, *s.* 1967, *m.*	Viscount Somerton, *b.* 1982
1647 S.	** *Northesk (14th),* David John MacRae Carnegie, *b.* 1954, *s.* 1994, *m.*	Patrick C. C., *b.* 1940
1801	** *Onslow (7th),* Michael William Coplestone Dillon Onslow, *b.* 1938, *s.* 1971, *m.*	Viscount Cranley, *b.* 1967
1696 S.	*Orkney (9th),* (Oliver) Peter St John, *b.* 1938, *s.* 1998, *m.*	Viscount Kirkwall, *b.* 1969
1328 I.	*Ormonde and Ossory (I. 1527),* The 25th/18th Earl (7th Marquess) died in 1988	†Viscount Mountgarret *b.* 1961 (*see* that title)
1925	*Oxford and Asquith (2nd),* Julian Edward George Asquith, KCMG, *b.* 1916, *s.* 1928, *w.*	Viscount Asquith, OBE, *b.* 1952
1929	° ** *Peel (3rd),* William James Robert Peel, GCVO, PC, *b.* 1947, *s.* 1969, *m.* *Lord Chamberlain*	Viscount Clanfield, *b.* 1976
1551	*Pembroke (18th) and Montgomery (15th) (1605),* William Alexander Sidney Herbert, *b.* 1978, *s.* 2003	Earl of Carnarvon *b.* 1956 (*see* that title)
1605	*Perth (18th),* John Eric Drummond, *b.* 1935, *s.* 2002, *m.*	Viscount Strathallan, *b.* 1965
1905	*Plymouth (3rd),* Other Robert Ivor Windsor-Clive, *b.* 1923, *s.* 1943, *m.*	Viscount Windsor, *b.* 1951
1785	*Portarlington (7th),* George Lionel Yuill Seymour Dawson-Damer, *b.* 1938, *s.* 1959, *m.*	Viscount Carlow, *b.* 1965
1689	*Portland (12th),* Count Timothy Charles Robert Noel Bentinck, *b.* 1953, *s.* 1997, *m.*	Viscount Woodstock, *b.* 1984
1743	*Portsmouth (10th),* Quentin Gerard Carew Wallop, *b.* 1954, *s.* 1984, *m.*	Viscount Lymington, *b.* 1981
1804	*Powis (8th),* John George Herbert, *b.* 1952, *s.* 1993, *m.*	Viscount Clive, *b.* 1979
1765	*Radnor (9th),* William Pleydell-Bouverie, *b.* 1955, *s.* 2008, *m.*	Viscount Folkestone, *b.* 1999
1831 I.	*Ranfurly (7th),* Gerald Françoys Needham Knox, *b.* 1929, *s.* 1988, *m.*	Viscount Northland, *b.* 1957
1771 I.	*Roden (10th),* Robert John Jocelyn, *b.* 1938, *s.* 1993, *m.*	Viscount Jocelyn, *b.* 1989
1801	*Romney (8th),* Julian Charles Marsham, *b.* 1948, *s.* 2004, *m.*	Viscount Marsham, *b.* 1977

1703 S.	*Rosebery (7th),* Neil Archibald Primrose, *b.* 1929, *s.* 1974, *m.*	Lord Dalmeny, *b.* 1967
1806 I.	*Rosse (7th),* William Brendan Parsons, *b.* 1936, *s.* 1979, *m.*	Lord Oxmantown, *b.* 1969.
1801	** *Rosslyn (7th),* Peter St Clair-Erskine, *b.* 1958, *s.* 1977, *m.*	Lord Loughborough, *b.* 1986
1457 S.	*Rothes (22nd),* James Malcolm David Leslie, *b.* 1958, *s.* 2005, *m.*	Hon. Alexander J. L., *b.* 1962
1861	° *Russell (6th),* Nicholas Lyulph Russell, *b.* 1968, *s.* 2004	Hon. John F. R., *b.* 1971
1915	° *St Aldwyn (3rd),* Michael Henry Hicks Beach, *b.* 1950, *s.* 1992, *m.*	Hon. David S. H. B., *b.* 1955
1815	*St Germans (10th),* Peregrine Nicholas Eliot, *b.* 1941, *s.* 1988	Lord Eliot, *b.* 2004
1660	** *Sandwich (11th),* John Edward Hollister Montagu, *b.* 1943, *s.* 1995, *m.*	Viscount Hinchingbrooke, *b.* 1969
1690	*Scarbrough (13th),* Richard Osbert Lumley, *b.* 1973, *s.* 2004	Hon. Thomas H. L., *b.* 1980
1701 S.	*Seafield (13th),* Ian Derek Francis Ogilvie-Grant, *b.* 1939, *s.* 1969, *m.*	Viscount Reidhaven, *b.* 1963
1882	** *Selborne (4th),* John Roundell Palmer, KBE, *b.* 1940, *s.* 1971, *m.*	Viscount Wolmer, *b.* 1971
1646 S.	*Selkirk,* Disclaimed for life 1994. *(see* Lord Selkirk of Douglas, Life Peers)	Master of Selkirk, *b.* 1978
1672	*Shaftesbury (12th),* Nicholas Edmund Anthony Ashley-Cooper, *b.* 1979, *s.* 2005	None
1756 I.	*Shannon (9th),* Richard Bentinck Boyle, *b.* 1924, *s.* 1963	Viscount Boyle, *b.* 1960
1442	** *Shrewsbury and Waterford (22nd) (I. 1446),* Charles Henry John Benedict Crofton Chetwynd Chetwynd-Talbot, *b.* 1952, *s.* 1980, *m. Premier Earl of England and Ireland*	Viscount Ingestre, *b.* 1978
1961	*Snowdon (1st) and Baron Armstrong-Jones (life peerage, 1999),* Antony Charles Robert Armstrong-Jones, GCVO, *b.* 1930, *m.*	Viscount Linley, *b.* 1961
1765	° *Spencer (9th),* Charles Edward Maurice Spencer, *b.* 1964, *s.* 1992, *m.*	Viscount Althorp, *b.* 1994
1703 S.	** *Stair (14th),* John David James Dalrymple, *b.* 1961, *s.* 1996, *m.*	Hon. David H. D., *b.* 1963
1984	*Stockton (2nd),* Alexander Daniel Alan Macmillan, MEP, *b.* 1943, *s.* 1986, *m.*	Viscount Macmillan of Ovenden, *b.* 1974
1821	*Stradbroke (6th),* Robert Keith Rous, *b.* 1937, *s.* 1983, *m.*	Viscount Dunwich, *b.* 1961
1847	*Strafford (8th),* Thomas Edmund Byng, *b.* 1936, *s.* 1984, *m.*	Viscount Enfield, *b.* 1964
1606 S.	*Strathmore and Kinghorne (18th) (S. 1677),* Michael Fergus Bowes Lyon, *b.* 1957, *s.* 1987, *m.*	Lord Glamis, *b.* 1986
1603	*Suffolk (21st) and Berkshire (14th) (1626),* Michael John James George Robert Howard, *b.* 1935, *s.* 1941, *m.*	Viscount Andover, *b.* 1974
1955	*Swinton (3rd),* Nicholas John Cunliffe-Lister, *b.* 1939, *s.* 2006, *m.*	Lord Masham *b.* 1970
1714	*Tankerville (10th),* Peter Grey Bennet, *b.* 1956, *s.* 1980	Adrian G. B., *b.* 1958
1822	° *Temple of Stowe (8th),* (Walter) Grenville Algernon Temple-Gore-Langton, *b.* 1924, *s.* 1988, *m.*	Lord Langton, *b.* 1955
1815	*Verulam (7th),* John Duncan Grimston, *b.* 1951, *s.* 1973, *m.*	Viscount Grimston, *b.* 1978
1729	° *Waldegrave (13th),* James Sherbrooke Waldegrave, *b.* 1940, *s.* 1995, *m.*	Viscount Chewton, *b.* 1986
1759	*Warwick (9th) and Brooke (9th) (1746),* Guy David Greville, *b.* 1957, *s.* 1996, *m.*	Lord Brooke, *b.* 1982
1633 S.	*Wemyss (12th) and March (8th),* Francis David Charteris, KT, *b.* 1912, *s.* 1937, *m.*	Lord Neidpath, *b.* 1948
1621 I.	*Westmeath (13th),* William Anthony Nugent, *b.* 1928, *s.* 1971, *m.*	Hon. Sean C. W. N., *b.* 1965
1624	*Westmorland (16th),* Anthony David Francis Henry Fane, *b.* 1951, *s.* 1993, *m.*	Hon. Harry St C. F., *b.* 1953
1876	*Wharncliffe (5th),* Richard Alan Montagu Stuart Wortley, *b.* 1953, *s.* 1987, *m.*	Viscount Carlton, *b.* 1980
1801	*Wilton (8th),* Francis Egerton Grosvenor, *b.* 1934, *s.* 1999, *m.*	Viscount Grey de Wilton, *b.*1959
1628	*Winchilsea (17th) and Nottingham (12th) (1681),* Daniel James Hatfield Finch Hatton, *b.* 1967, *s.* 1999, *m.*	Viscount Maidstone, *b.* 1998
1766	° *Winterton (8th),* (Donald) David Turnour, *b.* 1943, *s.* 1991, *m.*	Robert C. T., *b.* 1950
1956	*Woolton (3rd),* Simon Frederick Marquis, *b.* 1958, *s.* 1969, *m.*	None
1837	*Yarborough (8th),* Charles John Pelham, *b.* 1963, *s.* 1991, *m.*	Lord Worsley, *b.* 1990

COUNTESSES IN THEIR OWN RIGHT

Style, The Rt. Hon. the Countess (of) _
Envelope (formal), The Rt. Hon. the Countess (of) _; *(social),* The Countess (of) _. *Letter (formal),* Madam; *(social),* Lady _. *Spoken (formal),* Madam; *(social),* Lady _.
Husband, Untitled
Children's style, As for children of an Earl

Created	*Title, order of succession, name, etc*	*Heir*
1643 S.	*Dysart (12th in line),* Katherine Grant of Rothiemurchus, *b.* 1918, *s.* 2003 *w.*	Lord Huntingtower, *b.* 1946
c.1115 S.	** *Mar (31st in line),* Margaret of Mar, *b.* 1940, *s.* 1975, *m.* Premier Earldom of Scotland	Mistress of Mar, *b.* 1963
1947	° *Mountbatten of Burma (2nd in line),* Patricia Edwina Victoria Knatchbull, CBE, *b.* 1924, *s.* 1979, *w.*	Lord Romsey, (*also* Lord Brabourne (8th) *see* that title)
c.1235 S.	*Sutherland (24th in line),* Elizabeth Millicent Sutherland, *b.* 1921, *s.* 1963, *w.*	Lord Strathnaver, *b.* 1947

VISCOUNTS

Coronet, Sixteen silver balls

Style, The Rt. Hon. the Viscount _
Envelope (formal), The Rt. Hon. the Viscount _; *(social),* The Viscount _. *Letter (formal),* My Lord; *(social),* Dear Lord _. *Spoken,* Lord _.
Wife's style, The Rt. Hon. the Viscountess _
Envelope (formal), The Rt. Hon. the Viscountess _; *(social),* The Viscountess _. *Letter (formal),* Madam; *(social),* Dear Lady _. *Spoken,* Lady _.
Children's style, 'The Hon.' before forename and surname, as for Baron's children
In Scotland, the heir apparent to a Viscount may be styled 'The Master of _ (title of peer)'

Created	*Title, order of succession, name, etc*	*Heir*
1945	*Addison (4th),* William Matthew Wand Addison, *b.* 1945, *s.* 1992, *m.*	Hon. Paul W. A., *b.* 1973
1946	*Alanbrooke (3rd),* Alan Victor Harold Brooke, *b.* 1932, *s.* 1972	None
1919	** *Allenby (3rd),* Lt.-Col. Michael Jaffray Hynman Allenby, *b.* 1931, *s.* 1984, *m.*	Hon. Henry J. H. A., *b.* 1968
1911	*Allendale (4th),* Wentworth Peter Ismay Beaumont, *b.* 1948, *s.* 2002, *m.*	Hon. Wentworth A. I. B., *b.* 1979
1642 S.	*Arbuthnott (16th),* John Campbell Arbuthnott, KT, CBE, DSC, *b.* 1924, *s.* 1966, *m.*	Master of Arbuthnott, *b.* 1950
1751 I.	*Ashbrook (11th),* Michael Llowarch Warburton Flower, *b.* 1935, *s.* 1995, *m.*	Hon. Rowland F. W. F., *b.* 1975
1917	** *Astor (4th),* William Waldorf Astor, *b.* 1951, *s.* 1966, *m.*	Hon. William W. A., *b.* 1979
1781 I.	*Bangor (8th),* William Maxwell David Ward, *b.* 1948, *s.* 1993, *m.*	Hon. E. Nicholas W., *b.* 1953
1925	*Bearsted (5th),* Nicholas Alan Samuel, *b.* 1950, *s.* 1996, *m.*	Hon. Harry R. S., *b.* 1988
1963	*Blakenham (2nd),* Michael John Hare, *b.* 1938, *s.* 1982, *m.*	Hon. Caspar J. H., *b.* 1972
1935	** *Bledisloe (3rd),* Christopher Hiley Ludlow Bathurst, QC, *b.* 1934, *s.* 1979	Hon. Rupert E. L. B., *b.* 1964
1712	*Bolingbroke (7th) and St John (8th) (1716),* Kenneth Oliver Musgrave St John, *b.* 1927, *s.* 1974	Hon. Henry F. St J., *b.* 1957
1960	*Boyd of Merton (2nd),* Simon Donald Rupert Neville Lennox-Boyd, *b.* 1939, *s.* 1983, *m.*	Hon. Benjamin A. L.-B., *b.* 1964
1717 I.	*Boyne (11th),* Gustavus Michael Stucley Hamilton-Russell, *b.* 1965, *s.* 1995, *m.*	Hon. Gustavus A. E. H.-R., *b.* 1999
1929	*Brentford (4th),* Crispin William Joynson-Hicks, *b.* 1933, *s.* 1983, *m.*	Hon. Paul W. J.-H., *b.* 1971
1929	** *Bridgeman (3rd),* Robin John Orlando Bridgeman, *b.* 1930, *s.* 1982, *m.*	Hon. Luke R. O. B., *b.* 1971

1868	*Bridport (4th) and 7th Duke, Bronte in Sicily, 1799,* Alexander Nelson Hood, *b.* 1948, *s.* 1969, *m.*	Hon. Peregrine A. N. H., *b.* 1974
1952	** *Brookeborough (3rd),* Alan Henry Brooke, *b.* 1952, *s.* 1987, *m.*	Hon. Christopher A. B., *b.* 1954
1933	*Buckmaster (4th),* Adrian Charles Buckmaster, *b.* 1949, *s.* 2007, *m.*	Hon. Andrew N. B., *b.* 1980
1939	*Caldecote (3rd),* Piers James Hampden Inskip, *b.* 1947, *s.* 1999, *m.*	Hon. Thomas J. H. I., *b.* 1985
1941	*Camrose (4th),* Adrian Michael Berry, *b.* 1937, *s.* 2001, *m.*	Hon. Jonathan W. B., *b.* 1970
1954	*Chandos (3rd) and Baron Lyttelton of Aldershot (life peerage, 2000),* Thomas Orlando Lyttelton, *b.* 1953, *s.* 1980, *m.*	Hon. Oliver A. L., *b.* 1986
1665 I.	*Charlemont (15th),* John Dodd Caulfeild, *b.* 1966, *s.* 2001, *m.*	Hon. Shane A. C., *b.* 1996
1921	*Chelmsford (4th)* Frederic Corin Piers Thesiger, *b.* 1962, *s.* 1999, *m.*	Hon. Frederic T. *b.* 2006
1717 I.	*Chetwynd (10th),* Adam Richard John Casson Chetwynd, *b.* 1935, *s.* 1965, *m.*	Hon. Adam D. C., *b.* 1969
1911	*Chilston (4th),* Alastair George Akers-Douglas, *b.* 1946, *s.* 1982, *m.*	Hon. Oliver I. A.-D., *b.* 1973
1902	*Churchill (3rd) and 5th UK Baron Churchill (1815),* Victor George Spencer, *b.* 1934, *s.* 1973	To Barony only, Richard H. R. S., *b.* 1926
1718	*Cobham (12th),* Christopher Charles Lyttelton, *b.* 1947, *s.* 2006, *m.*	Hon. Oliver C. L., *b.* 1976
1902	** *Colville of Culross (4th),* John Mark Alexander Colville, QC, *b.* 1933, *s.* 1945, *m.*	Master of Colville, *b.* 1959
1826	*Combermere (6th),* Thomas Robert Wellington Stapleton-Cotton, *b.* 1969, *s.* 2000	Hon. David P. D. S.-C., *b.* 1932
1917	*Cowdray (4th),* Michael Orlando Weetman Pearson, *b.* 1944, *s.* 1995, *m.*	Hon. Peregrine J. D. P., *b.* 1994
1927	** *Craigavon (3rd),* Janric Fraser Craig, *b.* 1944, *s.* 1974	None
1943	*Daventry (4th),* James Edward FitzRoy Newdegate, *b.* 1960, *s.* 2000, *m.*	Hon. Humphrey J. F. N., *b.* 1995
1937	*Davidson (2nd),* John Andrew Davidson, *b.* 1928, *s.* 1970, *m.*	Hon. Malcolm W. M. D., *b.* 1934
1956	*De L'Isle (2nd),* Philip John Algernon Sidney, MBE, *b.* 1945, *s.* 1991, *m.*	Hon. Philip W. E. S., *b.* 1985
1776 I.	*De Vesci (7th),* Thomas Eustace Vesey, *b.* 1955, *s.* 1983, *m.*	Hon. Oliver I. V., *b.* 1991
1917	*Devonport (3rd),* Terence Kearley, *b.* 1944, *s.* 1973	Chester D. H. K., *b.* 1932
1964	*Dilhorne (2nd),* John Mervyn Manningham-Buller, *b.* 1932, *s.* 1980, *m.*	Hon. James E. M.-B., *b.* 1956
1622 I.	*Dillon (22nd),* Henry Benedict Charles Dillon, *b.* 1973, *s.* 1982	Hon. Richard A. L. D., *b.* 1948
1785 I.	*Doneraile (10th),* Richard Allen St Leger, *b.* 1946, *s.* 1983, *m.*	Hon. Nathaniel W. R. St J. St L., *b.* 1971
1680 I.	*Downe (12th),* Richard Henry Dawnay, *b.* 1967, *s.* 2002	Thomas P. D., *b.* 1978
1959	*Dunrossil (3rd),* Andrew William Reginald Morrison, *b.* 1953, *s.* 2000, *m.*	Hon. Callum A. B. M., *b.* 1994
1964	** *Eccles (2nd),* John Dawson Eccles, CBE, *b.* 1931, *s.* 1999, *m.*	Hon. William D. E., *b.* 1960
1897	*Esher (5th),* Christopher Lionel Baliol Brett, *b.* 1936, *s.* 2004, *m.*	Hon. Matthew C. A. B., *b.* 1963
1816	*Exmouth (10th),* Paul Edward Pellew, *b.* 1940, *s.* 1970, *m.*	Hon. Edward F. P., *b.* 1978
1620 S.	** *Falkland (15th),* Lucius Edward William Plantagenet Cary, *b.* 1935, *s.* 1984, *m. Premier Scottish Viscount on the Roll*	Master of Falkland, *b.* 1963
1720	*Falmouth (9th),* George Hugh Boscawen, *b.* 1919, *s.* 1962, *w.*	Hon. Evelyn A. H. B., *b.* 1955
1720 I.	*Gage (8th),* (Henry) Nicolas Gage, *b.* 1934, *s.* 1993, *m.*	Hon. Henry W. G., *b.* 1975
1727 I.	*Galway (12th),* George Rupert Monckton-Arundell, *b.* 1922, *s.* 1980, *m.*	Hon. J. Philip M., *b.* 1952
1478 I.	*Gormanston (17th),* Jenico Nicholas Dudley Preston, *b.* 1939, *s.* 1940, *m. Premier Viscount of Ireland*	Hon. Jenico F. T. P., *b.* 1974
1816 I.	*Gort (9th),* Foley Robert Standish Prendergast Vereker, *b.* 1951, *s.* 1995, *m.*	Hon. Robert F. P. V., *b.* 1993
1900	** *Goschen (4th),* Giles John Harry Goschen, *b.* 1965, *s.* 1977, *m.*	Hon. Alexander J. E. G., *b.* 2001
1849	*Gough (5th),* Shane Hugh Maryon Gough, *b.* 1941, *s.* 1951	None
1929	*Hailsham (3rd),* Douglas Martin Hogg, PC, QC, MP, *b.* 1945, *s.* 2001, *m.*	Hon. Quintin J. N. M. H., *b.* 1973
1891	*Hambleden (4th),* William Herbert Smith, *b.* 1930, *s.* 1948, *m.*	Hon. William H. B. S., *b.* 1955
1884	*Hampden (7th),* Francis Anthony Brand, *b.* 1970, *s.* 2008, *m.*	Hon. Lucian A. B., *b.* 2005
1936	*Hanworth (3rd),* David Stephen Geoffrey Pollock, *b.* 1946, *s.* 1996, *m.*	Harold W. C. P., *b.* 1988
1791 I.	*Harberton (11th),* Henry Robert Pomeroy, *b.* 1958, *s.* 2004, *m.*	Hon. Patrick C. P., b. 1995
1846	*Hardinge (7th),* Andrew Hartland Hardinge, *b.* 1960, *s.* 2004, *m.*	Hon. Thomas H. de M. H., *b.* 1993
1791 I.	*Hawarden (9th),* (Robert) Connan Wyndham Leslie Maude, *b.* 1961, *s.* 1991, *m.*	Hon. Varian J. C. E. M., *b.* 1997
1960	*Head (2nd),* Richard Antony Head, *b.* 1937, *s.* 1983, *m.*	Hon. Henry J. H., *b.* 1980
1550	*Hereford (19th),* Charles Robin De Bohun Devereux, *b.* 1975, *s.* 2004, *Premier Viscount of England*	Hon. Edward M. de B. D., *b.* 1977
1842	*Hill (9th),* Peter David Raymond Charles Clegg-Hill, *b.* 1945, *s.* 2003	*Hon.* Paul A. R. C.-H., *b.* 1979

1796	*Hood (8th),* Henry Lyttleton Alexander Hood, *b.* 1958, *s.* 1999, *m.*	Hon. Archibald L. S. H., *b.* 1993
1956	*Ingleby (2nd),* Martin Raymond Peake, *b.* 1926, *s.* 1966, *w.*	None
1945	*Kemsley (3rd),* Richard Gomer Berry, *b.* 1951, *s.* 1999, *m.*	Hon. Luke G. B., *b.* 1998
1911	*Knollys (3rd),* David Francis Dudley Knollys, *b.* 1931, *s.* 1966, *m.*	Hon. Patrick N. M. K., *b.* 1962
1895	*Knutsford (6th),* Michael Holland-Hibbert, *b.* 1926, *s.* 1986, *m.*	Hon. Henry T. H.-H., *b.* 1959
1954	*Leathers (3rd),* Christopher Graeme Leathers, *b.* 1941, *s.* 1996, *m.*	Hon. James F. L., *b.* 1969
1781 I.	*Lifford (9th),* (Edward) James Wingfield Hewitt, *b.* 1949, *s.* 1987, *m.*	Hon. James T. W. H., *b.* 1979
1921	*Long (4th),* Richard Gerard Long, CBE, *b.* 1929, *s.* 1967, *m.*	Hon. James R. L., *b.* 1960
1957	*Mackintosh of Halifax (3rd),* (John) Clive Mackintosh, *b.* 1958, *s.* 1980, *m.*	Hon. Thomas H. G. M., *b.* 1985
1955	*Malvern (3rd),* Ashley Kevin Godfrey Huggins, *b.* 1949, *s.* 1978	Hon. M. James H., *b.* 1928
1945	*Marchwood (3rd),* David George Staveley Penny, *b.* 1936, *s.* 1979, *w.*	Hon. Peter G. W. P., *b.* 1965
1942	*Margesson (2nd),* Francis Vere Hampden Margesson, *b.* 1922, *s.* 1965, *m.*	Capt. Hon. Richard F. D. M., *b.* 1960
1660 I.	*Massereene (14th) and Ferrard (7th) (I. 1797),* John David Clotworthy Whyte-Melville Foster Skeffington, *b.* 1940, *s.* 1992, *m.*	Hon. Charles J. C. W.-M. F. S., *b.* 1973
1802	*Melville (9th),* Robert David Ross Dundas, *b.* 1937, *s.* 1971, *m.*	Hon. Robert H. K. D., *b.* 1984
1916	*Mersey (5th),* Edward John Hallam Bigham, *b.* 1966, *s.* 2006, *m.*	Hon. David E. H. B., *b.* 1938
1717 I.	*Midleton (12th),* Alan Henry Brodrick, *b.* 1949, *s.* 1988, *m.*	Hon. Ashley R. B., *b.* 1980
1962	*Mills (3rd),* Christopher Philip Roger Mills, *b.* 1956, *s.* 1988, *m.*	None
1716 I.	*Molesworth (12th),* Robert Bysse Kelham Molesworth, *b.* 1959, *s.* 1997	Hon. William J. C. M., *b.* 1960
1801 I.	*Monck (7th),* Charles Stanley Monck, *b.* 1953, *s.* 1982 (Does not use title)	Hon. George S. M., *b.* 1957
1957	*Monckton of Brenchley (3rd),* Christopher Walter Monckton, *b.* 1952, *s.* 2006, *m.*	Hon. Timothy D. R. M., *b.* 1955
1946	** *Montgomery of Alamein (2nd),* David Bernard Montgomery, CBE, *b.* 1928, *s.* 1976, *m.*	Hon. Henry D. M., *b.* 1954
1550 I.	*Mountgarret (18th),* Piers James Richard Butler, *b.* 1961, *s.* 2004	Hon. Edmund H. R. B., *b.* 1962
1952	*Norwich (2nd),* John Julius Cooper, CVO, *b.* 1929, *s.* 1954, *m.*	Hon. Jason C. D. B. C., *b.* 1959
1651 S.	*Oxfuird (14th),* Ian Arthur Alexander Makgill, *b.* 1969, *s.* 2003	Hon. Robert E. G. M., *b.* 1969
1873	*Portman (10th),* Christopher Edward Berkeley Portman, *b.* 1958, *s.* 1999, *m.*	Hon. Luke O. B. P., *b.* 1984
1743 I.	*Powerscourt (10th),* Mervyn Niall Wingfield, *b.* 1935, *s.* 1973, *m.*	Hon. Mervyn A. W., *b.* 1963
1900	*Ridley (4th),* Matthew White Ridley, KG, GCVO, TD, *b.* 1925, *s.* 1964, *w.*	Hon. Matthew W. R., *b.* 1958
1960	*Rochdale (2nd),* St John Durival Kemp, *b.* 1938, *s.* 1993, *m.*	Hon. Jonathan H. D. K., *b.* 1961
1919	*Rothermere (4th),* (Harold) Jonathan Esmond Vere Harmsworth, *b.* 1967, *s.* 1998, *m.*	Hon. Vere R. J. H. H., *b.* 1994
1937	*Runciman of Doxford (3rd),* Walter Garrison Runciman (Garry), CBE, *b.* 1934, *s.* 1989, *m.*	Hon. David W. R., *b.* 1967
1918	*St Davids (3rd),* Colwyn Jestyn John Philipps, *b.* 1939, *s.* 1991, *m.*	Hon. Rhodri C. P., *b.* 1966
1801	*St Vincent (8th),* Edward Robert James Jervis, *b.* 1951, *s.* 2006, *m.*	Hon. James R. A. J., *b.* 1982
1937	*Samuel (3rd),* David Herbert Samuel, OBE, PHD, *b.* 1922, *s.* 1978, *m.*	Hon. Dan J. S., *b.* 1925
1911	*Scarsdale (4th),* Peter Ghislain Nathaniel Curzon, *b.* 1949, *s.* 2000, *m.*	Hon. David J. N. C., *b.* 1958
1905 M.	*Selby (6th),* Christopher Rolf Thomas Gully, *b.* 1993, *s.* 2001	Hon. (James) Edward H. G. G., *b.* 1945
1805	*Sidmouth (8th),* Jeremy Francis Addington, *b.* 1947, *s.* 2005, *m.*	Hon. Steffan A., *b.* 1966
1940	** *Simon (3rd),* Jan David Simon, *b.* 1940, *s.* 1993, *m.*	None
1960	** *Slim (2nd),* John Douglas Slim, OBE, *b.* 1927, *s.* 1970, *m.*	Hon. Mark W. R. S., *b.* 1960
1954	*Soulbury (2nd),* James Herwald Ramsbotham, *b.* 1915, *s.* 1971, *w.*	Hon. Sir Peter E. R., GCMG, GCVO, *b.* 1919
1776 I.	*Southwell (7th),* Pyers Anthony Joseph Southwell, *b.* 1930, *s.* 1960, *m.*	Hon. Richard A. P. S., *b.* 1956
1942	*Stansgate,* Anthony Neil Wedgwood Benn, *b.* 1925, *s.* 1960, *w.* Disclaimed for life 1963.	Stephen M. W. B., *b.* 1951
1959	*Stuart of Findhorn (3rd),* James Dominic Stuart, *b.* 1948, *s.* 1999, *m.*	Hon. Andrew M. S., *b.* 1957
1957	** *Tenby (3rd),* William Lloyd George, *b.* 1927, *s.* 1983, *m.*	Hon. Timothy H. G. L. G., *b.* 1962
1952	*Thurso (3rd),* John Archibald Sinclair, *b.* 1953, *s.* 1995, *m.*	Hon. James A. R. S., *b.* 1984
1721	*Torrington (11th),* Timothy Howard St George Byng, *b.* 1943, *s.* 1961, *m.*	Colin H. C.-B., *b.* 1960
1936	** *Trenchard (3rd),* Hugh Trenchard, *b.* 1951, *s.* 1987, *m.*	Hon. Alexander T. T., *b.* 1978
1921	** *Ullswater (2nd),* Nicholas James Christopher Lowther, PC, LVO, *b.* 1942, *s.* 1949, *m.*	Hon. Benjamin J. L., *b.* 1975
1622 I.	*Valentia (16th),* Frances William Dighton Annesley, *b.* 1959, *s.* 2005, *m.*	Hon. Peter J. A., *b.* 1967
1952	** *Waverley (3rd),* John Desmond Forbes Anderson, *b.* 1949, *s.* 1990	Hon. Forbes A. R. A., *b.* 1996

1938	*Weir (3rd),* William Kenneth James Weir, *b.* 1933, *s.* 1975, *m.*	Hon. James W. H. W., *b.* 1965
1918	*Wimborne (4th),* Ivor Mervyn Vigors Guest, *b.* 1968, *s.* 1993	Hon. Julien J. G., *b.* 1945
1923	*Younger of Leckie (5th),* James Edward George Younger, *b.* 1955, *s.* 2003, *m.*	Hon. Alexander W. G. Y., *b.* 1993

BARONS/LORDS

Coronet, Six silver balls

Style, The Rt. Hon. the Lord _
Envelope (formal), The Rt. Hon. Lord _; *(social),* The Lord _. *Letter (formal),* My Lord; *(social),* Dear Lord _. *Spoken,* Lord _.
In the Peerage of Scotland there is no rank of Baron; the equivalent rank is Lord of Parliament and Scottish peers should always be styled 'Lord', never 'Baron'.
Wife's style, The Rt. Hon. the Lady _
Envelope (formal), The Rt. Hon. Lady _; *(social),* The Lady _. *Letter (formal),* My Lady; *(social),* Dear Lady _. *Spoken,* Lady _
Children's style, 'The Hon.' before forename (F_) and surname (S_)
Envelope, The Hon. F_ S_. *Letter,* Dear Mr/Miss/Mrs S_. *Spoken,* Mr/Miss/Mrs S_
In Scotland, the heir apparent to a Lord may be styled 'The Master of _ (title of peer)'

Created	*Title, order of succession, name, etc*	*Heir*
1911	*Aberconway (4th),* (Henry) Charles McLaren, *b.* 1948, *s.* 2003, *m.*	Hon. Charles S. M., *b.* 1984
1873	*Aberdare (5th),* Alastair John Lyndhurst Bruce, *b.* 1947, *s.* 2005, *m.*	Hon. Hector M. N. B., *b.* 1974
1835	*Abinger (9th),* James Harry Scarlett, *b.* 1959, *s.* 2002, *m.*	Hon. Peter R. S., *b.* 1961
1869	*Acton (4th) and Acton of Bridgnorth (life peerage, 2000),* Richard Gerald Lyon-Dalberg-Acton, *b.* 1941, *s.* 1989, *m.*	Hon. John C. F. H. L.-D.-A., *b.* 1966
1887	** *Addington (6th),* Dominic Bryce Hubbard, *b.* 1963, *s.* 1982	Hon. Michael W. L. H., *b.* 1965
1896	*Aldenham (6th) and Hunsdon of Hunsdon (4th) (1923),* Vicary Tyser Gibbs, *b.* 1948, *s.* 1986, *m.*	Hon. Humphrey W. F. G., *b.* 1989
1962	*Aldington (2nd),* Charles Harold Stuart Low, *b.* 1948, *s.* 2000, *m.*	Hon. Philip T. A. L., *b.* 1990
1945	*Altrincham (3rd),* Anthony Ulick David Dundas Grigg, *b.* 1934, *s.* 2001, *m.*	Hon. (Edward) Sebastian G., *b.* 1965
1929	*Alvingham (2nd),* Maj.-Gen. Robert Guy Eardley Yerburgh, CBE, *b.* 1926, *s.* 1955, *m.*	Capt. Hon. Robert R. G. Y., *b.* 1956
1892	*Amherst of Hackney (4th),* William Hugh Amherst Cecil, *b.* 1940, *s.* 1980, *m.*	Hon. H. William A. C., *b.* 1968
1881	** *Ampthill (4th),* Geoffrey Denis Erskine Russell, CBE, PC *b.* 1921, *s.* 1973	Hon. David W. E. R., *b.* 1947
1947	*Amwell (3rd),* Keith Norman Montague, *b.* 1943, *s.* 1990, *m.*	Hon. Ian K. M., *b.* 1973
1863	*Annaly (6th),* Luke Richard White, *b.* 1954, *s.* 1990, *m.*	Hon. Luke H. W., *b.* 1990
1885	*Ashbourne (4th),* Edward Barry Greynville Gibson, *b.* 1933, *s.* 1983, *m.*	Hon. Edward C. d'O. G., *b.* 1967
1835	*Ashburton (7th),* John Francis Harcourt Baring, KG, KCVO, *b.* 1928, *s.* 1991, *m.*	Hon. Mark F. R. B., *b.* 1958
1892	*Ashcombe (4th),* Henry Edward Cubitt, *b.* 1924, *s.* 1962, *m.*	Mark E. C., *b.* 1964
1911	*Ashton of Hyde (4th),* Thomas Henry Ashton, *b.* 1958, *s.* 2008, *m.*	Hon. John E. A., *b.* 1966
1800 I.	*Ashtown (7th),* Nigel Clive Crosby Trench, KCMG, *b.* 1916, *s.* 1990, *m.*	Hon. Roderick N. G. T., *b.* 1944
1956	** *Astor of Hever (3rd),* John Jacob Astor, *b.* 1946, *s.* 1984, *m.*	Hon. Charles G. J. A., *b.* 1990
1789 I.	*Auckland (10th) and Auckland (10th) (1793),* Robert Ian Burnard Eden, *b.* 1962, *s.* 1997, *m.*	Henry V. E., *b.* 1958
1313	*Audley,* Barony in abeyance between three co-heiresses since 1997	
1900	** *Avebury (4th),* Eric Reginald Lubbock, *b.* 1928, *s.* 1971, *m.*	Hon. Lyulph A. J. L., *b.* 1954
1718 I.	*Aylmer (14th),* (Anthony) Julian Aylmer, *b.* 1951, *s.* 2006, *m.*	Hon. Michael H. A., *b.* 1991
1929	*Baden-Powell (3rd),* Robert Crause Baden-Powell, *b.* 1936, *s.* 1962, *m.*	Hon. David M. B.-P., *b.* 1940
1780	*Bagot (10th),* (Charles Hugh) Shaun Bagot, *b.* 1944, *s.* 2001, *m.*	Richard C. V. B., *b.* 1941
1953	*Baillieu (3rd),* James William Latham Baillieu, *b.* 1950, *s.* 1973, *m.*	Hon. Robert L. B., *b.* 1979
1607 S.	*Balfour of Burleigh (8th),* Robert Bruce, *b.* 1927, *s.* 1967, *m.*	Hon. Victoria B., *b.* 1973
1945	*Balfour of Inchrye (2nd),* Ian Balfour, *b.* 1924, *s.* 1988, *w.*	None
1924	*Banbury of Southam (3rd),* Charles William Banbury, *b.* 1953, *s.* 1981, *m.*	None
1698	*Barnard (11th),* Harry John Neville Vane, TD, *b.* 1923, *s.* 1964	Hon. Henry F. C. V., *b.* 1959

1887	*Basing (6th),* Stuart Anthony Whitfield Sclater-Booth, *b.* 1969, *s.* 2007, *m.*	Hon. Luke W. S.-B., *b.* 2000
1917	*Beaverbrook (3rd),* Maxwell William Humphrey Aitken, *b.* 1951, *s.* 1985, *m.*	Hon. Maxwell F. A., *b.* 1977
1647 S.	*Belhaven and Stenton (13th),* Robert Anthony Carmichael Hamilton, *b.* 1927, *s.* 1961, *m.*	Master of Belhaven, *b.* 1953
1848 I.	*Bellew (7th),* James Bryan Bellew, *b.* 1920, *s.* 1981, *w.*	Hon. Bryan E. B., *b.* 1943
1856	*Belper (5th),* Richard Henry Strutt, *b.* 1941, *s.* 1999, *m.*	Hon. Michael H. S., *b.* 1969
1421	*Berkeley (18th) and Gueterbock (life peerage, 2000),* Anthony Fitzhardinge Gueterbock, OBE, *b.* 1939, *s.* 1992, *m.*	Hon. Thomas F. G., *b.* 1969
1922	*Bethell (5th),* James Nicholas Bethell, *b.* 1967, *s.* 2007, *m.*	Hon. Jacob N. D. B., *b.* 200–
1938	*Bicester (3rd),* Angus Edward Vivian Smith, *b.* 1932, *s.* 1968	Hugh C. V. S., *b.* 1934
1903	*Biddulph (5th),* (Anthony) Nicholas Colin Maitland Biddulph, *b.* 1959, *s.* 1988, *m.*	Hon. Robert J. M. B., *b.* 1994
1938	*Birdwood (3rd),* Mark William Ogilvie Birdwood, *b.* 1938, *s.* 1962, *m.*	None
1958	*Birkett (2nd),* Michael Birkett, *b.* 1929, *s.* 1962, *w.*	Hon. Thomas B., *b.* 1982
1907	*Blyth (4th),* Anthony Audley Rupert Blyth, *b.* 1931, *s.* 1977, *m.*	Hon. James A. I. B., *b.* 1970
1797	*Bolton (8th),* Harry Algar Nigel Orde-Powlett, *b.* 1954, *s.* 2001, *m.*	Hon. Thomas O.-P., *b.* 1979
1452 S.	*Borthwick (24th),* John Hugh Borthwick, *b.* 1940, *s.* 1996, *m.*	Hon. James H. A. B. of Glengelt, *b.* 1940
1922	*Borwick (5th),* (Geoffrey Robert) James Borwick, *b.* 1955, *s.* 2007, *m.*	Hon. Edwin D. W. B., *b.* 1984
1761	*Boston (11th),* George William Eustace Boteler Irby, *b.* 1971, *s.* 2007, *m.*	Hon. Thomas W. G. B. I., *b.* 1999
1942	** *Brabazon of Tara (3rd),* Ivon Anthony Moore-Brabazon, *b.* 1946, *s.* 1974, *m.*	Hon. Benjamin R. M.-B., *b.* 1983
1880	*Brabourne (8th),* Norton Louis Philip Knatchbull, *b.* 1947, *s.* 2005, *m.* (*also* Lord Romsey heir to Countess Mountbatten of Burma, *see* that title)	Hon. Nicholas L. C. N. K., *b.* 1981
1925	*Bradbury (3rd),* John Bradbury, *b.* 1940, *s.* 1994, *m.*	Hon. John B., *b.* 1973
1962	*Brain (2nd),* Christopher Langdon Brain, *b.* 1926, *s.* 1966, *m.*	Hon. Michael C. B., *b.* 1928
1938	*Brassey of Apethorpe (3rd),* David Henry Brassey, OBE, *b.* 1932, *s.* 1967, *m.*	Hon. Edward B., *b.* 1964
1788	*Braybrooke (10th),* Robin Henry Charles Neville, *b.* 1932, *s.* 1990, *m.*	George N., *b.* 1943
1957	** *Bridges (2nd),* Thomas Edward Bridges, GCMG, *b.* 1927, *s.* 1969, *m.*	Hon. Mark T. B., *b.* 1954
1945	*Broadbridge (4th),* Martin Hugh Broadbridge, *b.* 1929, *s.* 2000, *w.*	Hon. Richard J. M. B., *b.* 1959
1933	*Brocket (3rd),* Charles Ronald George Nall-Cain, *b.* 1952, *s.* 1967, *w.*	Hon. Alexander C. C. N.-C., *b.* 1984
1860	** *Brougham and Vaux (5th),* Michael John Brougham, CBE, *b.* 1938, *s.* 1967	Hon. Charles W. B., *b.* 1971
1776	*Brownlow (7th),* Edward John Peregrine Cust, *b.* 1936, *s.* 1978, *m.*	Hon. Peregrine E. Q. C., *b.* 1974
1942	*Bruntisfield (3rd),* Michael John Victor Warrender, *b.* 1949, *s.* 2007, *m.*	Hon. John M. P. C. W., *b.* 1996
1950	*Burden (4th),* Fraser William Elsworth Burden, *b.* 1964, *s.* 2000, *m.*	Hon. Ian S. B., *b.* 1967
1529	*Burgh (8th),* (Alexander) Gregory Disney Leith, *b.* 1958, *s.* 2001, *m.*	Hon. Alexander J. S. L., *b.* 1986
1903	*Burnham (7th),* Harry Frederick Alan Lawson, *b.* 1968, *s.* 2005	None
1897	*Burton (3rd),* Michael Evan Victor Baillie, *b.* 1924, *s.* 1962, *m.*	Hon. Evan M. R. B., *b.* 1949
1643	*Byron (13th),* Robert James Byron, *b.* 1950, *s.* 1989, *m.*	Hon. Charles R. G. B., *b.* 1990
1937	*Cadman (3rd),* John Anthony Cadman, *b.* 1938, *s.* 1966, *m.*	Hon. Nicholas A. J. C., *b.* 1977
1945	*Calverley (3rd),* Charles Rodney Muff, *b.* 1946, *s.* 1971, *m.*	Hon. Jonathan E. M., *b.* 1975
1383	*Camoys (7th),* (Ralph) Thomas Campion George Sherman Stonor, GCVO, PC, *b.* 1940, *s.* 1976, *m.*	Hon. R. William R. T. S., *b.* 1974
1715 I.	*Carbery (11th),* Peter Ralfe Harrington Evans-Freke, *b.* 1920, *s.* 1970, *w.*	Hon. Michael P. E.-F., *b.* 1942
1834 I.	*Carew (7th) and Carew (7th) (1838),* Patrick Thomas Conolly-Carew, *b.* 1938, *s.* 1994, *m.*	Hon. William P. C.-C., *b.* 1973
1916	*Carnock (4th),* David Henry Arthur Nicolson, *b.* 1920, *s.* 1982	Adam N., *b.* 1957
1796 I.	*Carrington (6th) and Carrington (6th) (1797) and Carington of Upton (life peerage, 1999),* Peter Alexander Rupert Carington, KG, GCMG, CH, MC, PC, *b.* 1919, *s.* 1938, *m.*	Hon. Rupert F. J. C., *b.* 1948
1812 I.	*Castlemaine (8th),* Roland Thomas John Handcock, MBE, *b.* 1943, *s.* 1973, *m.*	Hon. Ronan M. E. H., *b.* 1989
1936	*Catto (3rd),* Innes Gordon Catto, *b.* 1950, *s.* 2001, *m.*	Hon. Alexander G. C., *b.* 1952
1918	*Cawley (4th),* John Francis Cawley, *b.* 1946, *s.* 2001, *m.*	Hon. William R. H. C., *b.* 1981
1858	*Chesham (6th),* Nicholas Charles Cavendish, *b.* 1941, *s.* 1989, *m.*	Hon. Charles G. C. C., *b.* 1974
1945	*Chetwode (2nd),* Philip Chetwode, *b.* 1937, *s.* 1950, *m.*	Hon. Roger C., *b.* 1968
1945	** *Chorley (2nd),* Roger Richard Edward Chorley, *b.* 1930, *s.* 1978, *m.*	Hon. Nicholas R. D. C., *b.* 1966
1858	*Churston (5th),* John Francis Yarde-Buller, *b.* 1934, *s.* 1991, *m.*	Hon. Benjamin F. A. Y.-B., *b.* 1974

1800 I.		*Clanmorris (8th),* Simon John Ward Bingham, *b.* 1937, *s.* 1988, *m.*	Robert D. de B. B., *b.* 1942
1672		*Clifford of Chudleigh (14th),* Thomas Hugh Clifford, *b.* 1948, *s.* 1988, *m.*	Hon. Alexander T. H. C., *b.* 1985
1299		*Clinton (22nd),* Gerard Nevile Mark Fane Trefusis, *b.* 1934, *s.* 1965, *m.*	Hon. Charles P. R. F. T., *b.* 1962
1955		*Clitheroe (2nd),* Ralph John Assheton, *b.* 1929, *s.* 1984, *m.*	Hon. Ralph C. A., *b.* 1962
1919		*Clwyd (4th),* (John) Murray Roberts, *b.* 1971, *s.* 2006	Hon. Jeremy T. R., *b.* 1973
1948		*Clydesmuir (3rd),* David Ronald Colville, *b.* 1949, *s.* 1996, *m.*	Hon. Richard C., *b.* 1980
1960	**	*Cobbold (2nd),* David Antony Fromanteel Lytton Cobbold, *b.* 1937, *s.* 1987, *m.*	Hon. Henry F. L. C., *b.* 1962
1919		*Cochrane of Cults (4th),* (Ralph Henry) Vere Cochrane, *b.* 1926, *s.* 1990, *m.*	Hon. Thomas H. V. C., *b.* 1957
1954		*Coleraine (2nd),* (James) Martin (Bonar) Law, *b.* 1931, *s.* 1980, *m.*	Hon. James P. B. L., *b.* 1975
1873		*Coleridge (5th),* William Duke Coleridge, *b.* 1937, *s.* 1984, *m.*	Hon. James D. C., *b.* 1967
1946		*Colgrain (4th),* Alastair Colin Leckie Campbell, *b.* 1951, *s.* 2008, *m.*	Hon. Thomas C. D. C., *b.* 1984
1917	**	*Colwyn (3rd),* (Ian) Anthony Hamilton-Smith, CBE, *b.* 1942, *s.* 1966, *m.*	Hon. Craig P. H.-S., *b.* 1968
1956		*Colyton (2nd),* Alisdair John Munro Hopkinson, *b.* 1958, *s.* 1996, *m.*	Hon. James P. M. H., *b.* 1983
1841		*Congleton (8th),* Christopher Patrick Parnell, *b.* 1930, *s.* 1967, *m.*	Hon. John P. C. P., *b.* 1959
1927		*Cornwallis (3rd),* Fiennes Neil Wykeham Cornwallis, OBE, *b.* 1921, *s.* 1982, *m.*	Hon. F. W. Jeremy C., *b.* 1946
1874		*Cottesloe (5th),*John Tapling Fremantle, *b.* 1927, *s.* 1994, *m.*	Hon. Thomas F. H. F., *b.* 1966
1929		*Craigmyle (4th),* Thomas Columba Shaw, *b.* 1960, *s.* 1998, *m.*	Hon. Alexander F. S., *b.* 1988
1899		*Cranworth (3rd),* Philip Bertram Gurdon, *b.* 1940, *s.* 1964, *m.*	Hon. Sacha W. R. G., *b.* 1970
1959	**	*Crathorne (2nd),* Charles James Dugdale, *b.* 1939, *s.* 1977, *m.*	Hon. Thomas A. J. D., *b.* 1977
1892		*Crawshaw (5th),* David Gerald Brooks, *b.* 1934, *s.* 1997, *m.*	Hon. John P. B., *b.* 1938
1940		*Croft (3rd),* Bernard William Henry Page Croft, *b.* 1949, *s.* 1997, *m.*	None
1797 I. M.		*Crofton (8th),* Edward Harry Piers Crofton, *b.* 1988, *s.* 2007	Francis G. C., *b.* 1915
1375		*Cromwell (7th),* Godfrey John Bewicke-Copley, *b.* 1960, *s.* 1982, *m.*	Hon. David G. B.-C., *b.* 1997
1947		*Crook (3rd),* Robert Douglas Edwin Crook, *b.* 1955, *s.* 2001, *m.*	Hon. Matthew R. C., *b.* 1990
1920		*Cullen of Ashbourne (3rd),* Edmund Willoughby Marsham Cokayne, *b.* 1916, *s.* 2000, *w.*	(Hon.) John O'B. M. C., *b.*1920
1914		*Cunliffe (3rd),* Roger Cunliffe, *b.* 1932, *s.* 1963, *m.*	Hon. Henry C., *b.* 1962
1332		*Darcy de Knayth (19th),* Caspar David Ingrams, *b.* 1962, *s.* 2008, *m.*	Hon. Thomas R. I., *b.* 1999
1927		*Daresbury (4th),* Peter Gilbert Greenall, *b.* 1953, *s.* 1996, *m.*	Hon. Thomas E. G., *b.* 1984
1924		*Darling (3rd),* (Robert) Julian Henry Darling, *b.* 1944, *s.* 2003, *m.*	Hon. Robert J. C. D., *b.* 1972
1946		*Darwen (3rd),* Roger Michael Davies, *b.* 1938, *s.* 1988, *m.*	Hon. Paul D., *b.* 1962
1932		*Davies (3rd),* David Davies, *b.* 1940, *s.* 1944, *m.*	Hon. David D. D., *b.* 1975
1812 I.		*Decies (7th),* Marcus Hugh Tristram de la Poer Beresford, *b.* 1948, *s.* 1992, *m.*	Hon. Robert M. D. de la P. B., *b.* 1988
1299		*de Clifford (27th),* John Edward Southwell Russell, *b.* 1928, *s.* 1982, *m.*	Hon. William S. R., *b.* 1930
1851		*De Freyne (7th),* Francis Arthur John French, *b.* 1927, *s.* 1935, *m.*	Hon. Fulke C. A. J. F., *b.* 1957
1821		*Delamere (5th),* Hugh George Cholmondeley, *b.* 1934, *s.* 1979, *m.*	Hon. Thomas P. G. C., *b.* 1968
1838	**	*de Mauley (7th),* Rupert Charles Ponsonby, *b.* 1957, *s.* 2002, *m.*	Ashley G. P., *b.* 1959
1937	**	*Denham (2nd),* Bertram Stanley Mitford Bowyer, KBE, PC, *b.* 1927, *s.* 1948, *m.*	Hon. Richard G. G. B., *b.* 1959
1834		*Denman (5th),* Charles Spencer Denman, CBE, MC, TD, *b.* 1916, *s.* 1971, *w.*	Hon. Richard T. S. D., *b.* 1946
1887		*De Ramsey (4th),* John Ailwyn Fellowes, *b.* 1942, *s.* 1993, *m.*	Hon. Freddie J. F., *b.* 1978
1264		*de Ros (28th),* Peter Trevor Maxwell, *b.* 1958, *s.* 1983, *m. Premier Baron of England*	Hon. Finbar J. M., *b.* 1988
1881		*Derwent (5th),* Robin Evelyn Leo Vanden-Bempde-Johnstone, LVO, *b.* 1930, *s.* 1986, *m.*	Hon. Francis P. H. V.-B.-J., *b.* 1965
1831		*de Saumarez (7th),* Eric Douglas Saumarez, *b.* 1956, *s.* 1991, *m.*	Hon. Victor T. S., *b.* 1956
1910		*de Villiers (4th),* Alexander Charles de Villiers, *b.* 1940, *s.* 2001, *m.*	None
1930		*Dickinson (2nd),* Richard Clavering Hyett Dickinson, *b.* 1926, *s.* 1943, *m.*	Hon. Martin H. D., *b.* 1961
1620 I.		*Digby (12th) and Digby (5th) (1765),* Edward Henry Kenelm Digby, KCVO, *b.* 1924, *s.* 1964, *m.*	Hon. Henry N. K. D., *b.* 1954
1615		*Dormer (17th),* Geoffrey Henry Dormer, *b.* 1920, *s.* 1995, *m.*	Hon. William R. D., *b.* 1960
1943		*Dowding (3rd),* Piers Hugh Tremenheere Dowding, *b.* 1948, *s.* 1992	Hon. Mark D. J. D., *b.* 1949
1439		*Dudley (15th),* Jim Anthony Hill Wallace, *b.* 1930, *s.* 2002, *m.*	Hon. Jeremy W. G. W., *b.* 1964
1800 I.		*Dufferin and Clandeboye (11th),* John Francis Blackwood, *b.* 1944, *s.* 1991 (claim to the peerage not yet established), *m.*	*Hon.* Francis S. B., *b.* 1979
1929		*Dulverton (3rd),* (Gilbert) Michael Hamilton Wills, *b.* 1944, *s.* 1992, *m.*	Hon. Robert A. H. W., *b.* 1983
1800 I.		*Dunalley (7th),* Henry Francis Cornelius Prittie, *b.* 1948, *s.* 1992, *m.*	Hon. Joel H. P., *b.* 1981
1324 I.		*Dunboyne (29th),* John Fitzwalter Butler, *b.* 1951, *s.* 2004, *m.*	Hon. Richard P. T. B., *b.* 1983
1892		*Dunleath (6th),* Brian Henry Mulholland, *b.* 1950, *s.* 1997, *m.*	Hon. Andrew H. M., *b.* 1981
1439 I.		*Dunsany (20th),* Edward John Carlos Plunkett, *b.* 1939, *s.* 1999, *m.*	Hon. Randal P., *b.* 1983

1780	*Dynevor (9th),* Richard Charles Uryan Rhys, *b.* 1935, *s.* 1962	Hon. Hugo G. U. R., *b.* 1966
1963	*Egremont (2nd) and Leconfield (7th) (1859),* John Max Henry Scawen Wyndham, *b.* 1948, *s.* 1972, *m.*	Hon. George R. V. W., *b.* 1983
1643	*Elibank (14th),* Alan D'Ardis Erskine-Murray, *b.* 1923, *s.* 1973, *w.*	Master of Elibank, *b.* 1964
1802	*Ellenborough (8th),* Richard Edward Cecil Law, *b.* 1926, *s.* 1945, *m.*	Maj. Hon. Rupert E. H. L., *b.* 1955
1509 S.	*Elphinstone (19th) and Elphinstone (5th) (1885),* Alexander Mountstuart Elphinstone, *b.* 1980, *s.* 1994, *m.*	Hon. Angus J. E., *b.* 1982
1934	** *Elton (2nd),* Rodney Elton, TD, *b.* 1930, *s.* 1973, *m.*	Hon. Edward P. E., *b.* 1966
1627 S.	*Fairfax of Cameron (14th),* Nicholas John Albert Fairfax, *b.* 1956, *s.* 1964, *m.*	Hon. Edward N. T. F., *b.* 1984
1961	*Fairhaven (3rd),* Ailwyn Henry George Broughton, *b.* 1936, *s.* 1973, *m.*	Maj. Hon. James H. A. B., *b.* 1963
1916	*Faringdon (3rd),* Charles Michael Henderson, KCVO, *b.* 1937, *s.* 1977, *m.*	Hon. James H. H., *b.* 1961
1756 I.	*Farnham (13th),* Simon Kenlis Maxwell, *b.* 1933, *s.* 2001, *m.*	Hon. Robin S. M., *b.* 1965
1856 I.	*Fermoy (6th),* Patrick Maurice Burke Roche, *b.* 1967, *s.* 1984, *m.*	Hon. E. Hugh B. R., *b.* 1972
1826	*Feversham (6th),* Charles Antony Peter Duncombe, *b.* 1945, *s.* 1963, *m.*	Hon. Jasper O. S. D., *b.* 1968
1798 I.	*ffrench (8th),* Robuck John Peter Charles Mario ffrench, *b.* 1956, *s.* 1986, *m.*	Hon. John C. M. J. F. ff., *b.* 1928
1909	*Fisher (3rd),* John Vavasseur Fisher, DSC, *b.* 1921, *s.* 1955, *m.*	Hon. Patrick V. F., *b.* 1953
1295	*Fitzwalter (22nd),* Julian Brook Plumptre, *b.* 1952, *s. 2004, m.*	Hon. Edward B. P., *b.* 1989
1776	*Foley (8th),* Adrian Gerald Foley, *b.* 1923, *s.* 1927, *m.*	Hon. Thomas H. F., *b.* 1961
1445	*Forbes (22nd),* Nigel Ivan Forbes, KBE, *b.* 1918, *s.* 1953, *m. Premier Lord of Scotland*	Master of Forbes, *b.* 1946
1821	*Forester (9th),* Charles Richard George Weld-Forester, *b.* 1975, *s.* 2004,	Wolstan W. W.-F., *b.* 1941
1922	*Forres (4th),* Alastair Stephen Grant Williamson, *b.* 1946, *s.* 1978, *m.*	Hon. George A. M. W., *b.* 1972
1917	*Forteviot (4th),* John James Evelyn Dewar, *b.* 1938, *s.* 1993, *w.*	Hon. Alexander J. E. D., *b.* 1971
1951	** *Freyberg (3rd),* Valerian Bernard Freyberg, *b.* 1970, *s.* 1993	Hon. Joseph J. F., *b.* 2007
1917	*Gainford (3rd),* Joseph Edward Pease, *b.* 1921, *s.* 1971, *m.*	Hon. George P., *b.* 1926
1818 I.	*Garvagh (5th),* (Alexander Leopold Ivor) George Canning, *b.* 1920, *s.* 1956, *m.*	Hon. Spencer G. S. de R. C., *b.* 1953
1942	** *Geddes (3rd),* Euan Michael Ross Geddes, *b.* 1937, *s.* 1975, *m.*	Hon. James G. N. G., *b.* 1969
1876	*Gerard (5th),* Anthony Robert Hugo Gerard, *b.* 1949, *s.* 1992, *m.*	Hon. Rupert B. C. G., *b.* 1981
1824	*Gifford (6th),* Anthony Maurice Gifford, *b.* 1940, *s.* 1961, *m.*	Hon. Thomas A. G., *b.* 1967
1917	*Gisborough (3rd),* Thomas Richard John Long Chaloner, *b.* 1927, *s.* 1951, *m.*	Hon. T. Peregrine L. C., *b.* 1961
1960	*Gladwyn (2nd),* Miles Alvery Gladwyn Jebb, *b.* 1930, *s.* 1996	None
1899	*Glanusk (5th),* Christopher Russell Bailey, *b.* 1942, *s.* 1997, *m.*	Hon. Charles H. B., *b.* 1976
1918	** *Glenarthur (4th),* Simon Mark Arthur, *b.* 1944, *s.* 1976, *m.*	Hon. Edward A. A., *b.* 1973
1911	*Glenconner (3rd),* Colin Christopher Paget Tennant, *b.* 1926, *s.* 1983, *m.*	Cody C. E. T., *b.* 1994
1964	*Glendevon (2nd),* Julian John Somerset Hope, *b.* 1950, *s.* 1996	Hon. Jonathan C. H., *b.* 1952
1922	*Glendyne (4th),* John, *b.* 1960, *s.* 2008	None
1939	** *Glentoran (3rd),* (Thomas) Robin (Valerian) Dixon, CBE, *b.* 1935, *s.* 1995, *m.*	Hon. Daniel G. D., *b.* 1959
1909	*Gorell (5th),* John Picton Gorell Barnes, *b.* 1959, *s.* 2007, *m.*	Hon. Oliver G. B., *b.* 1993
1953	** *Grantchester (3rd),* Christopher John Suenson-Taylor, *b.* 1951, *s.* 1995, *m.*	Hon. Jesse D. S.-T., *b.* 1977
1782	*Grantley (8th),* Richard William Brinsley Norton, *b.* 1956, *s.* 1995	Hon. Francis J. H. N., *b.* 1960
1794 I.	*Graves (10th),* Timothy Evelyn Graves, *b.* 1960, *s.* 2002	None
1445 S.	*Gray (23rd),* Andrew Godfrey Diarmid Stuart Campbell-Gray, *b.* 1964, *s.* 2003, *m.*	Master of Gray, *b.* 1996
1950	*Greenhill (3rd),* Malcolm Greenhill, *b.* 1924, *s.* 1989	None
1927	** *Greenway (4th),* Ambrose Charles Drexel Greenway, *b.* 1941, *s.* 1975, *m.*	Hon. Nigel. P. G., *b.* 1944
1902	*Grenfell (3rd) and Grenfell of Kilvey (life peerage, 2000),* Julian Pascoe Francis St Leger Grenfell, *b.* 1935, *s.* 1976, *m.*	Francis P. J. G., *b.* 1938
1944	*Gretton (4th),* John Lysander Gretton, *b.* 1975, *s.* 1989	Hon. John F. B. G., *b.* 2008
1397	*Grey of Codnor (6th),* Richard Henry Cornwall-Legh, *b.* 1936, *s.* 1996, *m.*	Hon. Richard S. C. C.-L., *b.* 1976
1955	*Gridley (3rd),* Richard David Arnold Gridley, *b.* 1956, *s.* 1996, *m.*	Peter A. C. G., *b.* 1940
1964	*Grimston of Westbury (3rd),* Robert John Sylvester Grimston, *b.* 1951, *s.* 2003, *m.*	Hon. Gerald C. W. G., *b.* 1953
1886	*Grimthorpe (5th),* Edward John Beckett, *b.* 1954, *s.* 2003, *m.*	Hon. Harry M. B., *b.* 1993
1945	*Hacking (3rd),* Douglas David Hacking, *b.* 1938, *s.* 1971, *m.*	Hon. Douglas F. H., *b.* 1968
1950	*Haden-Guest (5th),* Christopher Haden-Guest, *b.* 1948, *s.* 1996, *m.*	Hon. Nicholas H.-G., *b.* 1951

1886		*Hamilton of Dalzell (5th),* Gavin Goulburn Hamilton, *b.* 1968, *s.* 2006, *m.*	Hon. Robert P. H., *b.* 1971
1874		*Hampton (7th),* John Humphrey Arnott Pakington, *b.* 1964, *s.* 2003, *m.*	Hon. Charles R. C. P., *b.* 2005
1939		*Hankey (3rd),* Donald Robin Alers Hankey, *b.* 1938, *s.* 1996, *m.*	Hon. Alexander M. A. H., *b.* 1947
1958		*Harding of Petherton (2nd),* John Charles Harding, *b.* 1928, *s.* 1989, *m.*	Hon. William A. J. H., *b.* 1969
1910		*Hardinge of Penshurst (4th),* Julian Alexander Hardinge, *b.* 1945, *s.* 1997	Hon. Hugh F. H., *b.* 1948
1876		*Harlech (6th),* Francis David Ormsby-Gore, *b.* 1954, *s.* 1985, *m.*	Hon. Jasset D. C. O.-G., *b.* 1986
1939		*Harmsworth (3rd),* Thomas Harold Raymond Harmsworth, *b.* 1939, *s.* 1990, *m.*	Hon. Dominic M. E. H., *b.* 1973
1815		*Harris (8th),* Anthony Harris, *b.* 1942, *s.* 1996, *m.*	Rear-Adm. Michael G. T. H., *b.* 1941
1954		*Harvey of Tasburgh (2nd),* Peter Charles Oliver Harvey, *b.* 1921, *s.* 1968, *w.*	Charles J. G. H., *b.* 1951
1295		*Hastings (23rd),* Delaval Thomas Harold Astley, *b.* 1960, *s.* 2007, *m.*	Hon. Jacob A. A., *b.* 1991
1835		*Hatherton (8th),* Edward Charles Littleton, *b.* 1950, *s.* 1985, *m.*	Hon. Thomas E. L., *b.* 1977
1776		*Hawke (11th),* Edward George Hawke, TD, *b.* 1950, *s.* 1992, *m.*	Hon. William M. T. H., *b.* 1995
1927		*Hayter (4th),* George William Michael Chubb, *b.* 1943, *s.* 2003, *m.*	Hon. Thomas F. F. C., *b.*1986
1945		*Hazlerigg (3rd),* Arthur Grey Hazlerigg, *b.* 1951, *s.* 2002, *m.*	Hon. Arthur W. G. H. *b.* 1987
1943		*Hemingford (3rd),* (Dennis) Nicholas Herbert, *b.* 1934, *s.* 1982, *m.*	Hon. Christopher D. C. H., *b.* 1973
1906		*Hemphill (5th),* Peter Patrick Fitzroy Martyn Martyn-Hemphill, *b.* 1928, *s.* 1957, *m.*	Hon. Charles A. M. M.-H., *b.* 1954
1799 I.	**	*Henley (8th) and Northington (6th) (1885),* Oliver Michael Robert Eden, *b.* 1953, *s.* 1977, *m.*	Hon. John W. O. E., *b.* 1988
1800 I.		*Henniker (9th) and Hartismere (6th) (1866),* Mark Ian Philip Chandos Henniker-Major, *b.* 1947, *s.* 2004, *m.*	Hon. Edward G. M. H.-M., *b.* 1985
1461		*Herbert (19th),* David John Seyfried Herbert, *b.* 1952, *s.* 2002, *m.*	Hon. Oliver R. S. H., *b.* 1976
1886		*Herschell (3rd),* Rognvald Richard Farrer Herschell, *b.* 1923, *s.* 1929, *m.*	None
1935		*Hesketh (3rd),* Thomas Alexander Fermor-Hesketh, KBE, PC, *b.* 1950, *s.* 1955, *m.*	Hon. Frederick H. F.-H., *b.* 1988
1828		*Heytesbury (7th),* James William Holmes à Court, *b.* 1967, *s.* 2004, *m.*	Peter M. H.. H. à. C., *b.* 1968
1886		*Hindlip (6th),* Charles Henry Allsopp, *b.* 1940, *s.* 1993, *m.*	Hon. Henry W. A., *b.* 1973
1950		*Hives (3rd),* Matthew Peter Hives, *b.* 1971, *s.* 1997	Hon. Michael B. H., *b.* 1926
1912		*Hollenden (4th),* Ian Hampden Hope-Morley, *b.* 1946, *s.* 1999, *m.*	Hon. Edward H.-M., *b.* 1981
1897		*Holm Patrick (4th),* Hans James David Hamilton, *b.* 1955, *s.* 1991, *m.*	Hon. Ion H. J. H., *b.* 1956
1797 I.		*Hotham (8th),* Henry Durand Hotham, *b.* 1940, *s.* 1967, *m.*	Hon. William B. H., *b.* 1972
1881		*Hothfield (6th),* Anthony Charles Sackville Tufton, *b.* 1939, *s.* 1991, *m.*	Hon. William S. T., *b.* 1977
1930		*Howard of Penrith (3rd),* Philip Esme Howard, *b.* 1945, *s.* 1999, *m.*	Hon. Thomas Philip H., *b.* 1974
1960		*Howick of Glendale (2nd),* Charles Evelyn Baring, *b.* 1937, *s.* 1973, *m.*	Hon. David E. C. B., *b.* 1975
1796 I.		*Huntingfield (7th),* Joshua Charles Vanneck, *b.* 1954, *s.* 1994, *m.*	Hon. Gerard C. A. V., *b.* 1985
1866	**	*Hylton (5th),* Raymond Hervey Jolliffe, *b.* 1932, *s.* 1967, *m.*	Hon. William H. M. J., *b.* 1967
1933		*Iliffe (3rd),* Robert Peter Richard Iliffe, *b.* 1944, *s.* 1996, *m.*	Hon. Edward R. I., *b.* 1968
1543 I.		*Inchiquin (18th),* Conor Myles John O'Brien, *b.* 1943, *s.* 1982, *m.*	Conor J. A. O'B., *b.* 1952
1962		*Inchyra (2nd),* Robert Charles Reneke Hoyer Millar, *b.* 1935, *s.* 1989, *m.*	Hon. C. James C. H. M., *b.* 1962
1964	**	*Inglewood (2nd),* (William) Richard Fletcher-Vane, *b.* 1951, *s.* 1989, *m.*	Hon. Henry W. F. F.-V., *b.* 1990
1919		*Inverforth (4th),* Andrew Peter Weir, *b.* 1966, *s.* 1982	Hon. Benjamin A. W., *b.* 1997
1941		*Ironside (2nd),* Edmund Oslac Ironside, *b.* 1924, *s.* 1959, *m.*	Hon. Charles E. G. I., *b.* 1956
1952		*Jeffreys (3rd),* Christopher Henry Mark Jeffreys, *b.* 1957, *s.* 1986, *m.*	Hon. Arthur M. H. J., *b.* 1989
1906		*Joicey (5th),* James Michael Joicey, *b.* 1953, *s.* 1993, *m.*	Hon. William J. J., *b.* 1990
1937		*Kenilworth (4th),* (John) Randle Siddeley, *b.* 1954, *s.* 1981, *m.*	Hon. William R. J. S., *b.* 1992
1935		*Kennet (2nd),* Wayland Hilton Young, *b.* 1923, *s.* 1960, *m.*	Hon. W. A. Thoby Y., *b.* 1957
1776 I.		*Kensington (8th) and Kensington (5th) (1886),* Hugh Ivor Edwardes, *b.* 1933, *s.* 1981, *m.*	Hon. W. Owen A. E., *b.* 1964
1951		*Kenswood (2nd),* John Michael Howard Whitfield, *b.* 1930, *s.* 1963, *m.*	Hon. Michael C. W., *b.* 1955
1788		*Kenyon (6th),* Lloyd Tyrell-Kenyon, *b.* 1947, *s.* 1993, *m.*	Hon. Lloyd N. T.-K., *b.* 1972
1947		*Kershaw (4th),* Edward John Kershaw, *b.* 1936, *s.* 1962, *m.*	Hon. John C. E. K., *b.* 1971
1943		*Keyes (3rd),* Charles William Packe Keyes, *b.* 1951, *s.* 2005, *m.*	Hon. (Leopold R.) J. K., *b.* 1956
1909		*Kilbracken (4th),* Christopher John Godley, *b.* 1945, *s.* 2006, *m.*	Hon. James J. G., *b.* 1972
1900		*Killanin (4th),* (George) Redmond Fitzpatrick Morris, *b.* 1947, *s.* 1999, *m.*	Hon. Luke M. G. M., *b.* 1975
1943		*Killearn (3rd),* Victor Miles George Aldous Lampson, *b.* 1941, *s.* 1996, *m.*	Hon. Miles H. M. L., *b.* 1977
1789 I.		*Kilmaine (7th),* John David Henry Browne, *b.* 1948, *s.* 1978, *m.*	Hon. John F. S. B., *b.* 1983

1831	*Kilmarnock (7th),* Alastair Ivor Gilbert Boyd, *b.* 1927, *s.* 1975, *m.*	Hon. Robin J. B., *b.* 1941
1941	*Kindersley (3rd),* Robert Hugh Molesworth Kindersley, *b.* 1929, *s.* 1976, *m.*	Hon. Rupert J. M. K., *b.* 1955
1223 I.	*Kingsale (36th),* Nevinson Mark de Courcy, *b.* 1958, *s.* 2005, *m., Premier Baron of Ireland*	Joseph K. C. de C., *b.* 1955
1902	*Kinross (5th),* Christopher Patrick Balfour, *b.* 1949, *s.* 1985, *m.*	Hon. Alan I. B., *b.* 1978
1951	*Kirkwood (3rd),* David Harvie Kirkwood, PHD, *b.* 1931, *s.* 1970, *m.*	Hon. James S. K., *b.* 1937
1800 I.	*Langford (9th),* Col. Geoffrey Alexander Rowley-Conwy, OBE, *b.* 1912, *s.* 1953, *m.*	Hon. Owain G. R.-C., *b.* 1958
1942	*Latham (2nd),* Dominic Charles Latham, *b.* 1954, *s.* 1970	Anthony M. L., *b.* 1954
1431	*Latymer (9th),* Crispin James Alan Nevill Money-Coutts, *b.* 1955, *s.* 2003, *m.*	Hon. Drummond W. T. M.-C., *b.* 1986
1869	*Lawrence (5th),* David John Downer Lawrence, *b.* 1937, *s.* 1968	None
1947	*Layton (3rd),* Geoffrey Michael Layton, *b.* 1947, *s.* 1989, *m.*	Hon. David L., *b.* 1914
1839	*Leigh (6th),* Christopher Dudley Piers Leigh, *b.* 1960, *s.* 2003, *m.*	Hon. Rupert D. L., *b.* 1994
1962	*Leighton of St Mellons (3rd),* Robert William Henry Leighton Seager, *b.* 1955, *s.* 1998	Hon. Simon J. L. S., *b.* 1957
1797	*Lilford (8th),* Mark Vernon Powys, *b.* 1975, *s.* 2005	Robert C. L. P., *b.* 1930
1945	*Lindsay of Birker (3rd),* James Francis Lindsay, *b.* 1945, *s.* 1994, *m.*	Alexander S. L., *b.* 1940
1758 I.	*Lisle (9th),* (John) Nicholas Geoffrey Lysaght, *b.* 1960, *s.* 2003	Hon. David J. L., *b.* 1963
1850	*Londesborough (9th),* Richard John Denison, *b.* 1959, *s.* 1968, *m.*	Hon. James F. D., *b.* 1990
1541 I.	*Louth (16th),* Otway Michael James Oliver Plunkett, *b.* 1929, *s.* 1950, *m.*	Hon. Jonathan O. P., *b.* 1952
1458 S.	*Lovat (16th) and Lovat (5th) (1837),* Simon Fraser, *b.* 1977, *s.* 1995	Hon. Jack F., *b.* 1984
1946	*Lucas of Chilworth (3rd),* Simon William Lucas, *b.* 1957, *s.* 2001, *m.*	Hon. John R. M. L., *b.* 1995
1663	** *Lucas (11th) and Dingwall (14th) (S. 1609),* Ralph Matthew Palmer, *b.* 1951, *s.* 1991	Hon. Lewis E. P., *b.* 1987
1929	** *Luke (3rd),* Arthur Charles St John Lawson-Johnston, *b.* 1933, *s.* 1996, *m.*	Hon. Ian J. St J. L.-J., *b.* 1963
1914	** *Lyell (3rd),* Charles Lyell, *b.* 1939, *s.* 1943	None
1859	*Lyveden (7th),* Jack Leslie Vernon, *b.* 1938, *s.* 1999, *m.*	Hon. Colin R. V., *b.* 1967
1959	*MacAndrew (3rd),* Christopher Anthony Colin MacAndrew, *b.* 1945, *s.* 1989, *m.*	Hon. Oliver C. J. M., *b.* 1983
1776 I.	*Macdonald (8th),* Godfrey James Macdonald of Macdonald, *b.* 1947, *s.* 1970, *m.*	Hon. Godfrey E. H. T. M., *b.* 1982
1937	*McGowan (4th),* Harry John Charles McGowan, *b.* 1971, *s.* 2003, *m.*	Hon. Dominic J. W. McG., *b.* 1951
1922	*Maclay (3rd),* Joseph Paton Maclay, *b.* 1942, *s.* 1969, *m.*	Hon. Joseph P. M., *b.* 1977
1955	*McNair (3rd),* Duncan James McNair, *b.* 1947, *s.* 1989, *m.*	Hon. William S. A. M., *b.* 1958
1951	*Macpherson of Drumochter (2nd),* (James) Gordon Macpherson, *b.* 1924, *s.* 1965, *m.*	Hon. James A. M., *b.* 1979
1937	** *Mancroft (3rd),* Benjamin Lloyd Stormont Mancroft, *b.* 1957, *s.* 1987, *m.*	Hon. Arthur L. S. M., *b.* 1995
1807	*Manners (6th),* John Hugh Robert Manners, *b.* 1956, *s.* 2008	Hon. Richard N. M., *b.* 1924
1922	*Manton (4th),* Miles Ronald Marcus Watson, *b.* 1958, *s.* 2003, *m.*	Hon. Thomas N. C. D. W., *b.* 1985
1908	*Marchamley (4th),* William Francis Whiteley, *b.* 1968, *s.* 1994	None
1964	*Margadale (3rd),* Alastair John Morrison, *b.* 1958, *s.* 2003, *m.*	Hon. Declan J. M., *b.* 1993
1961	*Marks of Broughton (3rd),* Simon Richard Marks, *b.* 1950, *s.* 1998, *m.*	Hon. Michael M., *b.* 1989
1964	*Martonmere (2nd),* John Stephen Robinson, *b.* 1963, *s.* 1989	Hon. James I. R., *b.* 2003
1776 I.	*Massy (10th),* David Hamon Somerset Massy, *b.* 1947, *s.* 1995	Hon. John H. M., *b.* 1950
1935	*May (4th),* Jasper Bertram St John May, *b.* 1965, *s.* 2006	None
1928	*Melchett (4th),* Peter Robert Henry Mond, *b.* 1948, *s.* 1973	None
1925	*Merrivale (4th),* Derek John Philip Duke, *b.* 1948, *s.* 2007, *m.*	Hon. Thomas D., *b.* 1980
1911	*Merthyr,* Trevor Oswin Lewis, CBE, *b.* 1935, *s.* 1977, *m.* Disclaimed for life 1977	David T. L., *b.* 1977
1919	*Meston (3rd),* James Meston, *b.* 1950, *s.* 1984, *m.*	Hon. Thomas J. D. M., *b.* 1977
1838	** *Methuen (7th),* Robert Alexander Holt Methuen, *b.* 1931, *s.* 1994, *m.*	James P. A. M.-C., *b.* 1952
1711	*Middleton (12th),* (Digby) Michael Godfrey John Willoughby, MC, *b.* 1921, *s.* 1970	Hon. Michael C. J. W., *b.* 1948
1939	*Milford (4th),* Guy Wogan Philipps, *b.* 1961, *s.* 1999, *m.*	Hon. Archie S. P., *b.* 1997
1933	*Milne (3rd),* George Alexander Milne, *b.* 1941, *s.* 2005	Hon. Iain C. L. M., *b.* 1949
1951	*Milner of Leeds (3rd),* Richard James Milner, *b.* 1959, *s.* 2003, *m.*	None
1947	*Milverton (2nd), Revd* Fraser Arthur Richard Richards, *b.* 1930, *s.* 1978, *m.*	Hon. Michael H. R., *b.* 1936
1873	*Moncreiff (6th),* Rhoderick Harry Wellwood Moncreiff, *b.* 1954, *s.* 2002, *m.*	Hon. Harry J. W. M., *b.* 1986

1884	*Monk Bretton (3rd),* John Charles Dodson, *b.* 1924, *s.* 1933, *m.*	Hon. Christopher M. D., *b.* 1958
1885	*Monkswell (5th),* Gerard Collier, *b.* 1947, *s.* 1984, *m.*	Hon. James A. C., *b.* 1977
1728	** *Monson (11th),* John Monson, *b.* 1932, *s.* 1958, *m.*	Hon. Nicholas J. M., *b.* 1955
1885	** *Montagu of Beaulieu (3rd),* Edward John Barrington Douglas-Scott-Montagu, *b.* 1926, *s.* 1929, *m.*	Hon. Ralph D.-S.-M., *b.* 1961
1839	*Monteagle of Brandon (6th),* Gerald Spring Rice, *b.* 1926, *s.* 1946, *m.*	Hon. Charles J. S. R., *b.* 1953
1943	** *Moran (2nd),* (Richard) John (McMoran) Wilson, KCMG, *b.* 1924, *s.* 1977, *m.*	Hon. James M. W., *b.* 1952
1918	*Morris (3rd),* Michael David Morris, *b.* 1937, *s.* 1975, *m.*	Hon. Thomas A. S. M., *b.* 1982
1950	*Morris of Kenwood (3rd),* Jonathan David Morris, *b.* 1968, *s.* 2004, *m.*	Hon. Benjamin J. M., *b.* 1998
1831	*Mostyn (6th),* Llewellyn Roger Lloyd-Mostyn, *b.* 1948, *s.* 2000, *m.*	Hon. Gregory P. R. L.-M., *b.* 1984
1933	*Mottistone (4th),* David Peter Seely, CBE, *b.* 1920, *s.* 1966, *m.*	Hon. Peter J. P. S., *b.* 1949
1945	*Mountevans (3rd),* Edward Patrick Broke Evans, *b.* 1943, *s.* 1974, *m.*	Hon. Jeffrey de C. R. E., *b.* 1948
1283	*Mowbray (27th), Segrave (28th) (1295) and Stourton (24th) (1448),* Edward William Stephen Stourton, *b.* 1953, *s.* 2006, *m.*	Hon. James C. P. S., *b.* 1991
1932	*Moyne (3rd),* Jonathan Bryan Guinness, *b.* 1930, *s.* 1992, *m.*	Hon. Jasper J. R. G., *b.* 1954
1929	** *Moynihan (4th),* Colin Berkeley Moynihan, *b.* 1955, *s.* 1997, *m.*	Hon. Nicholas E. B. M., *b.* 1994
1781 I.	*Muskerry (9th),* Robert Fitzmaurice Deane, *b.* 1948, *s.* 1988, *m.*	Hon. Jonathan F. D., *b.* 1986
1627 S.	*Napier (14th) and Ettrick (5th) (1872),* Francis Nigel Napier, KCVO, *b.* 1930, *s.* 1954, *m.*	Master of Napier, *b.* 1962
1868	*Napier of Magdala (6th),* Robert Alan Napier, *b.* 1940, *s.* 1987, *m.*	Hon. James R. N., *b.* 1966
1940	*Nathan (3rd),* Rupert Harry Bernard Nathan, *b.* 1957, *s.* 2007, *m.*	None
1960	*Nelson of Stafford (4th),* Alistair William Henry Nelson, *b.* 1973, *s.* 2006	Hon. James J. N., *b.* 1947
1959	*Netherthorpe (3rd),* James Frederick Turner, *b.* 1964, *s.* 1982, *m.*	Hon. Andrew J. E. T., *b.* 1993
1946	*Newall (2nd),* Francis Storer Eaton Newall, *b.* 1930, *s.* 1963, *m.*	Hon. Richard H. E. N., *b.* 1961
1776 I.	*Newborough (8th),* Robert Vaughan Wynn, *b.* 1949, *s.* 1998, *m.*	Hon. Charles H. R. W., *b.* 1923
1892	*Newton (5th),* Richard Thomas Legh, *b.* 1950, *s.* 1992, *m.*	Hon. Piers R. L., *b.* 1979
1930	*Noel-Buxton (3rd),* Martin Connal Noel-Buxton, *b.* 1940, *s.* 1980, *m.*	Hon. Charles C. N.-B., *b.* 1975
1957	*Norrie (2nd),* (George) Willoughby Moke Norrie, *b.* 1936, *s.* 1977, *m.*	Hon. Mark W. J. N., *b.* 1972
1884	** *Northbourne (5th),* Christopher George Walter James, *b.* 1926, *s.* 1982, *m.*	Hon. Charles W. H. J., *b.* 1960
1866	** *Northbrook (6th),* Francis Thomas Baring, *b.* 1954, *s.* 1990, *m.*	To the Baronetcy, Peter B. *b.* 1939
1878	*Norton (8th),* James Nigel Arden Adderley, *b.* 1947, *s.* 1993, *m.*	Hon. Edward J. A. A., *b.* 1982
1906	*Nunburnholme (6th),* Stephen Charles Wilson, *b.* 1973, *s.* 2000	Hon. David M. W., *b.* 1954
1950	*Ogmore (3rd),* Morgan Rees-Williams, *b.* 1937, *s.* 2004, *m.*	Hon. Tudor D. R.-W., *b.* 1991
1870	*O'Hagan (4th),* Charles Towneley Strachey, *b.* 1945, *s.* 1961	Hon. Richard T. S., *b.* 1950
1868	*O'Neill (4th),* Raymond Arthur Clanaboy O'Neill, TD, *b.* 1933, *s.* 1944, *m.*	Hon. Shane S. C. O'N., *b.* 1965
1836 I.	*Oranmore and Browne (5th) and Mereworth (3rd) (1926),* Dominick Geoffrey Thomas Browne, *b.* 1929, *s.* 2002	Hon. Martin M. D. B., *b.* 1931
1933	** *Palmer (4th),* Adrian Bailie Nottage Palmer, *b.* 1951, *s.* 1990, *m.*	Hon. Hugo B. R. P., *b.* 1980
1914	*Parmoor (5th),* Michael Leonard Seddon Cripps, *b.* 1942, *s.* 2008, *m.*	Henry W. A. C., *b.* 1976
1937	*Pender (3rd),* John Willoughby Denison-Pender, *b.* 1933, *s.* 1965, *m.*	Hon. Henry J. R. D.-P., *b.* 1968
1866	*Penrhyn (7th),* Simon Douglas-Pennant, *b.* 1938, *s.* 2003, *m.*	Hon. Edward S. D.-P., *b.* 1966
1603	*Petre (18th),* John Patrick Lionel Petre, *b.* 1942, *s.* 1989, *m.*	Hon. Dominic W. P., *b.* 1966
1918	*Phillimore (5th),* Francis Stephen Phillimore, *b.* 1944, *s.* 1994, *m.*	Hon. Tristan A. S. P., *b.* 1977
1945	*Piercy (3rd),* James William Piercy, *b.* 1946, *s.* 1981	Hon. Mark E. P. P., *b.* 1953
1827	*Plunket (8th),* Robin Rathmore Plunket, *b.* 1925, *s.* 1975, *m.*	Hon. Shaun A. F. S. P., *b.* 1931
1831	*Poltimore (7th),* Mark Coplestone Bampfylde, *b.* 1957, *s.* 1978, *m.*	Hon. Henry A. W. B., *b.* 1985
1690 S.	*Polwarth (11th),* Andrew Walter Hepburne-Scott, *b.* 1947, *s.* 2005, *m.*	Master of Polwarth, *b.* 1973
1930	*Ponsonby of Shulbrede (4th) and Ponsonby of Roehampton (life peerage, 2000),* Frederick Matthew Thomas Ponsonby, *b.* 1958, *s.* 1990	None
1958	*Poole (2nd),* David Charles Poole, *b.* 1945, *s.* 1993, *m.*	Hon. Oliver J. P., *b.* 1972
1852	*Raglan (5th),* FitzRoy John Somerset, *b.* 1927, *s.* 1964	Hon. Geoffrey S., *b.* 1932
1932	*Rankeillour (5th),* Michael Richard Hope, *b.* 1940, *s.* 2005, *m.*	James F. H., *b.* 1968
1953	*Rathcavan (3rd),* Hugh Detmar Torrens O'Neill, *b.* 1939, *s.* 1994, *m.*	Hon. François H. N. O'N., *b.* 1984
1916	*Rathcreedan (3rd),* Christopher John Norton, *b.* 1949, *s.* 1990, *m.*	Hon. Adam G. N., *b.* 1952
1868 I.	*Rathdonnell (5th),* Thomas Benjamin McClintock-Bunbury, *b.* 1938, *s.* 1959, *m.*	Hon. William L. M.-B., *b.* 1966
1911	*Ravensdale (3rd),* Nicholas Mosley, MC, *b.* 1923, *s.* 1966, *m.*	Hon. Shaun N. M., *b.* 1949

1821	*Ravensworth (9th),* Thomas Arthur Hamish Liddell, *b.* 1954, *s.* 2004, *m.*	Hon. Henry A. T. L., *b.* 1987
1821	*Rayleigh (6th),* John Gerald Strutt, *b.* 1960, *s.* 1988, *m.*	Hon. John F. S., *b.* 1993
1937	** *Rea (3rd),* John Nicolas Rea, MD, *b.* 1928, *s.* 1981, *m.*	Hon. Matthew J. R., *b.* 1956
1628 S.	** *Reay (14th),* Hugh William Mackay, *b.* 1937, *s.* 1963, *m.*	Master of Reay, *b.* 1965
1902	*Redesdale (6th) and Mitford (life peerage 2000),* Rupert Bertram Mitford, *b.* 1967, *s.* 1991, *m.*	Hon. Bertram D. M., *b.* 2000
1940	*Reith,* Christopher John Reith, *b.* 1928, *s.* 1971, *m.* Disclaimed for life 1972.	Hon. James H. J. R., *b.* 1971
1928	*Remnant (3rd),* James Wogan Remnant, CVO, *b.* 1930, *s.* 1967, *m.*	Hon. Philip J. R., *b.* 1954
1806 I.	*Rendlesham (9th),* Charles William Brooke Thellusson, *b.* 1954, *s.* 1999, *m.*	Hon. Peter R. T., *b.* 1920
1933	*Rennell (4th),* James Roderick David Tremayne Rodd, *b.* 1978, *s.* 2006	None
1964	*Renwick (2nd),* Harry Andrew Renwick, *b.* 1935, *s.* 1973, *m.*	Hon. Robert J. R., *b.* 1966
1885	*Revelstoke (6th),* James Cecil Baring, *b.* 1938, *s.* 2003, *m.*	Hon. Alexander R. B., *b.* 1970
1905	*Ritchie of Dundee (6th),* Charles Rupert Rendall Ritchie, *b.* 1958, *s.* 2008, *m.*	Hon. Sebastian R., *b.* 2004
1935	*Riverdale (3rd),* Anthony Robert Balfour, *b.* 1960, *s.* 1998	Hon. David R. B., *b.* 1938
1961	*Robertson of Oakridge (2nd),* William Ronald Robertson, *b.* 1930, *s.* 1974, *m.*	Hon. William B. E. R., *b.* 1975
1938	*Roborough (3rd),* Henry Massey Lopes, *b.* 1940, *s.* 1992, *m.*	Hon. Massey J. H. L., *b.* 1969
1931	*Rochester (2nd),* Foster Charles Lowry Lamb, *b.* 1916, *s.* 1955, *w.*	Hon. David C. L., *b.* 1944
1934	*Rockley (3rd),* James Hugh Cecil, *b.* 1934, *s.* 1976, *m.*	Hon. Anthony R. C., *b.* 1961
1782	*Rodney (10th),* George Brydges Rodney, *b.* 1953, *s.* 1992, *m.*	Hon. John G. B. R., *b.* 1999
1651 S.	*Rollo (14th) and Dunning (5th) (1869),* David Eric Howard Rollo, *b.* 1943, *s.* 1997, *m.*	Master of Rollo, *b.* 1972
1959	*Rootes (3rd),* Nicholas Geoffrey Rootes, *b.* 1951, *s.* 1992, *m.*	William B. R., *b.* 1944
1796 I.	*Rossmore (7th) and Rossmore (6th) (1838),* William Warner Westenra, *b.* 1931, *s.* 1958, *m.*	Hon. Benedict W. W., *b.* 1983
1939	** *Rotherwick (3rd),* (Herbert) Robin Cayzer, *b.* 1954, *s.* 1996, *m.*	Hon. H. Robin C., *b.* 1989
1885	*Rothschild (4th),* (Nathaniel Charles) Jacob Rothschild, OM, GBE, *b.* 1936, *s.* 1990, *m.*	Hon. Nathaniel P. V. J. R., *b.* 1971
1911	*Rowallan (4th),* John Polson Cameron Corbett, *b.* 1947, *s.* 1993	Hon. Jason W. P. C. C., *b.* 1972
1947	*Rugby (3rd),* Robert Charles Maffey, *b.* 1951, *s.* 1990, *m.*	Hon. Timothy J. H. M., *b.* 1975
1919	*Russell of Liverpool (3rd),* Simon Gordon Jared Russell, *b.* 1952, *s.* 1981, *m.*	Hon. Edward C. S. R., *b.* 1985
1876	*Sackville (7th),* Robert Bertrand Sackville-West, *b.* 1958, *s.* 2004, *m.*	Hon. Arthur S-W., *b.* 2000
1964	*St Helens (2nd),* Richard Francis Hughes-Young, *b.* 1945, *s.* 1980, *m.*	Hon. Henry T. H.-Y., *b.* 1986
1559	** *St John of Bletso (21st),* Anthony Tudor St John, *b.* 1957, *s.* 1978, *m.*	Hon. Oliver B. St J., *b.* 1995
1887	*St Levan (4th),* John Francis Arthur St Aubyn, DSC, *b.* 1919, *s.* 1978, *w.*	James P. S. St. A., *b.* 1950
1885	*St Oswald (6th),* Charles Rowland Andrew Winn, *b.* 1959, *s.* 1999, *m.*	Hon. Rowland C. S. H. W., *b.* 1986
1960	*Sanderson of Ayot (2nd),* Alan Lindsay Sanderson, *b.* 1931, *s.* 1971, *m.* Disclaimed for life 1971.	Hon. Michael S., *b.* 1959
1945	*Sandford (2nd),* Revd John Cyril Edmondson, DSC, *b.* 1920, *s.* 1959, *m.*	Hon. James J. M. E., *b.* 1949
1871	*Sandhurst (6th),* Guy Rees John Mansfield, *b.* 1949, *s.* 2002, *m.*	Hon. Edward J. M., *b.* 1982
1802	*Sandys (7th),* Richard Michael Oliver Hill, *b.* 1931, *s.* 1961, *m.*	The Marquess of Downshire
1888	*Savile (4th),* John Anthony Thornhill Lumley-Savile, *b.* 1947, *s.* 2008, *m.*	James G. A. L-S., *b.* 1975
1447	*Saye and Sele (21st),* Nathaniel Thomas Allen Fiennes, *b.* 1920, *s.* 1968, *m.*	Hon. Martin G. F., *b.* 1961
1826	*Seaford (6th),* Colin Humphrey Felton Ellis, *b.* 1946, *s.* 1999, *m.*	Hon. Benjamin F. T. E., *b.* 1976
1932	** *Selsdon (3rd),* Malcolm McEacharn Mitchell-Thomson, *b.* 1937, *s.* 1963, *m.*	Hon. Callum M. M. M.-T., *b.* 1969
1489 S.	*Sempill (21st),* James William Stuart Whitemore Sempill, *b.* 1949, *s.* 1995, *m.*	Master of Sempill, *b.* 1979
1916	*Shaughnessy (4th),* Michael James Shaughnessy, *b.* 1946, *s.* 2003	Charles, G. P. S., *b.* 1955
1946	*Shepherd (3rd),* Graham George Shepherd, *b.* 1949, *s.* 2001, *m.*	Hon. Patrick M. S., *b.* 19–
1964	*Sherfield (3rd),* Dwight William Makins, *b.* 1951, *s.* 2006, *m.*	None
1902	*Shuttleworth (5th),* Charles Geoffrey Nicholas Kay-Shuttleworth, *b.* 1948, *s.* 1975, *m.*	Hon. Thomas E. K.-S., *b.* 1976
1950	*Silkin (3rd),* Christopher Lewis Silkin, *b.* 1947, *s.* 2001. Disclaimed for life 2001	Rory L. S., *b.* 1954
1963	*Silsoe (3rd),* Simon Rupert Trustram Eve *b.* 1966, *s.* 2005	Hon. Peter N. T. E., *b.* 1930
1947	*Simon of Wythenshawe (3rd),* Matthew Simon, *b.* 1955, *s.* 2002	Martin S., *b.* 1944
1449 S.	*Sinclair (18th),* Matthew Murray Kennedy St Clair *b.* 1968, *s.* 2004, *m.*	Hugh A. C. St C., *b.* 1957

1957		*Sinclair of Cleeve (3rd),* John Lawrence Robert Sinclair, *b.* 1953, *s.* 1985	None
1919		*Sinha (6th),* Arup Kumar Sinha, *b.* 1966, *s.* 1999	Hon. Dilip K. S., *b.* 1967
1828	**	*Skelmersdale (7th),* Roger Bootle-Wilbraham, *b.* 1945, *s.* 1973, *m.*	Hon. Andrew B.-W., *b.* 1977
1916		*Somerleyton (3rd),* Savile William Francis Crossley, GCVO, *b.* 1928, *s.* 1959, *m.*	Hon. Hugh F. S. C., *b.* 1971
1784		*Somers (9th),* Philip Sebastian Somers Cocks, *b.* 1948, *s.* 1995	Alan B. C., *b.* 1930
1780		*Southampton (6th),* Charles James FitzRoy, *b.* 1928, *s.* 1989, *m.*	Hon. Edward C. F., *b.* 1955
1959		*Spens (4th),* Patrick Nathaniel George Spens, *b.* 1968, *s.* 2001, *m.*	Hon. Peter L. S., *b.* 2000
1640		*Stafford (15th),* Francis Melfort William Fitzherbert, *b.* 1954, *s.* 1986, *m.*	Hon. Benjamin J. B. F., *b.* 1983
1938		*Stamp (4th),* Trevor Charles Bosworth Stamp, MD, *b.* 1935, *s.* 1987, *m.*	Hon. Nicholas C. T. S., *b.* 1978
1839		*Stanley of Alderley (8th), Sheffield (8th) (I. 1738) and Eddisbury (7th) (1848),* Thomas Henry Oliver Stanley, *b.* 1927, *s.* 1971, *m.*	Hon. Richard O. S., *b.* 1956
1318	**	*Strabolgi (11th),* David Montague de Burgh Kenworthy, *b.* 1914, *s.* 1953, *m.*	Andrew D. W. K., *b.* 1967
1954		*Strang (2nd),* Colin Strang, *b.* 1922, *s.* 1978, *m.*	None
1628		*Strange (17th),* Adam Humphrey Drummond of Megginch, *b.* 1953, *s.* 2005 *m.*	Hon. John A. H. D. of M. *b.* 1992
1955		*Strathalmond (3rd),* William Roberton Fraser, *b.* 1947, *s.* 1976, *m.*	Hon. William G. F., *b.* 1976
1936		*Strathcarron (3rd),* Ian David Patrick Macpherson, *b.* 1949, *s.* 2006, *m.*	Hon. Rory D. A. M., *b.* 1982
1955	**	*Strathclyde (2nd),* Thomas Galloway Dunlop du Roy de Blicquy Galbraith, PC, *b.* 1960, *s.* 1985, *m.*	Hon. Charles W. du R. de B. G., *b.* 1962
1900		*Strathcona and Mount Royal (4th),* Donald Euan Palmer Howard, *b.* 1923, *s.* 1959, *m.*	Hon. D. Alexander S. H., *b.* 1961
1836		*Stratheden (6th) and Campbell (6th) (1841),* Donald Campbell, *b.* 1934, *s.* 1987, *m.*	Hon. David A. C., *b.* 1963
1884		*Strathspey (6th),* James Patrick Trevor Grant of Grant, *b.* 1943, *s.* 1992, *m.*	Hon. Michael P. F. G., *b.* 1953
1838		*Sudeley (7th),* Merlin Charles Sainthill Hanbury-Tracy, *b.* 1939, *s.* 1941	D. Andrew J. H.-T., *b.* 1928
1786		*Suffield (11th),* Anthony Philip Harbord-Hamond, MC, *b.* 1922, *s.* 1951, *w.*	Hon. Charles A. A. H.-H., *b.* 1953
1893		*Swansea (5th),* Richard Anthony Hussey Vivian, *b.* 1957, *s.* 2005, *m.*	Hon. James H. H. V., *b.* 1999
1907		*Swaythling (5th),* Charles Edgar Samuel Montagu, *b.* 1954, *s.* 1998, *m.*	Hon. Anthony T. S. M., *b.* 1931
1919	**	*Swinfen (3rd),* Roger Mynors Swinfen Eady, *b.* 1938, *s.* 1977, *m.*	Hon. Charles R. P. S. E., *b.* 1971
1935		*Sysonby (3rd),* John Frederick Ponsonby, *b.* 1945, *s.* 1956	None
1831 I.		*Talbot of Malahide (10th),* Reginald John Richard Arundell, *b.* 1931, *s.* 1987, *m.*	Hon. Richard J. T. A., *b.* 1957
1946		*Tedder (3rd),* Robin John Tedder, *b.* 1955, *s.* 1994, *m.*	Hon. Benjamin J. T., *b.* 1985
1884		*Tennyson (6th),* David Harold Alexander Tennyson, *b.* 1960, *s.* 2006	Alan J. D. T., *b.* 1965
1918		*Terrington (6th),* Christopher Richard James Woodhouse, MB, *b.* 1946, *s.* 2001, *m.*	Hon. Jack H. L. W., *b.* 1978
1940		*Teviot (2nd),* Charles John Kerr, *b.* 1934, *s.* 1968, *m.*	Hon. Charles R. K., *b.* 1971
1616		*Teynham (20th),* John Christopher Ingham Roper-Curzon, *b.* 1928, *s.* 1972, *m.*	Hon. David J. H. I. R.-C., *b.* 1965
1964		*Thomson of Fleet (3rd),* David Kenneth Roy Thomson, *b.* 1957, *s.* 2006, *m.*	Hon. Benjamin T., *b.* 2006
1792		*Thurlow (8th),* Francis Edward Hovell-Thurlow-Cumming-Bruce, KCMG, *b.* 1912, *s.* 1971, *w.*	Hon. Roualeyn R. H.-T.-C.-B., *b.* 1952
1876		*Tollemache (5th),* Timothy John Edward Tollemache, *b.* 1939, *s.* 1975, *m.*	Hon. Edward J. H. T., *b.* 1976
1564 S.		*Torphichen (15th),* James Andrew Douglas Sandilands, *b.* 1946, *s.* 1975, *m.*	Robert P. S., *b.* 1950
1947	**	*Trefgarne (2nd),* David Garro Trefgarne, PC, *b.* 1941, *s.* 1960, *m.*	Hon. George G. T., *b.* 1970
1921		*Trevethin (4th) and Oaksey (2nd) (1947),* John Geoffrey Tristram Lawrence, OBE, *b.* 1929, *s.* 1971, *m.*	Hon. Patrick J. T. L., *b.* 1960
1880		*Trevor (5th),* Marke Charles Hill-Trevor, *b.* 1970, *s.* 1997, *m.*	Hon. Iain R. H.-T., *b.* 1971
1461 I.		*Trimlestown (21st),* Raymond Charles Barnewall, *b.* 1930, *s.* 1997	None
1940		*Tryon (3rd),* Anthony George Merrik Tryon, *b.* 1940, *s.* 1976	Hon. Charles G. B. T., *b.* 1976
1935		*Tweedsmuir (4th),* John William de l'Aigle (Toby) Buchan, *b.* 1950, *s.* 2008, *m.*	Hon. John A. G. B., *b.* 1986
1523		*Vaux of Harrowden (11th),* Anthony William Gilbey, *b.* 1940, *s.* 2002, *m.*	Hon. Richard H. G. G., *b.*1965
1800 I.		*Ventry (8th),* Andrew Wesley Daubeny de Moleyns, *b.* 1943, *s.* 1987, *m.*	Hon. Francis W. D. de M., *b.* 1965
1762		*Vernon (11th),* Anthony William Vernon-Harcourt, *b.* 1939, *s.* 2000, *m.*	Hon. Simon A. V-H., *b.* 1969
1922		*Vestey (3rd),* Samuel George Armstrong Vestey, *b.* 1941, *s.* 1954, *m.*	Hon. William G. V., *b.* 1983
1841		*Vivian (7th),* Charles Crespigny Hussey Vivian, *b.* 1966, *s.* 2004	Hon. Victor A. R. B. V., *b.* 1940

1934	*Wakehurst (3rd),* (John) Christopher Loder, *b.* 1925, *s.* 1970, *m.*	Hon. Timothy W. L., *b.* 1958
1723	** *Walpole (10th) and Walpole of Wolterton (8th) (1756),* Robert Horatio Walpole, *b.* 1938, *s.* 1989, *m.*	Hon. Jonathan R. H. W., *b.* 1967
1780	*Walsingham (9th),* John de Grey, MC, *b.* 1925, *s.* 1965, *m.*	Hon. Robert de. G., *b.* 1969
1936	*Wardington (3rd),* William Simon Pease, *b.* 1925, *s.* 2005, *m.*	None
1792 I.	*Waterpark (7th),* Frederick Caryll Philip Cavendish, *b.* 1926, *s.* 1948, *m.*	Hon. Roderick A. C., *b.* 1959
1942	*Wedgwood (4th),* Piers Anthony Weymouth Wedgwood, *b.* 1954, *s.* 1970, *m.*	Antony J. W., *b.* 1944
1861	*Westbury (6th),* Richard Nicholas Bethell, MBE, *b.* 1950, *s.* 2001, *m.*	Hon. Alexander B., *b.* 1986
1944	*Westwood (3rd),* (William) Gavin Westwood, *b.* 1944, *s.* 1991, *m.*	Hon. W. Fergus W., *b.* 1972
1544/5	*Wharton (12th),* Myles Christopher David Robertson, *b.* 1964, *s.* 2000, *m.*	Hon. Christopher J. R., *b.* 1969
1935	*Wigram (2nd),* (George) Neville (Clive) Wigram, MC, *b.* 1915, *s.* 1960, *w.*	Maj. Hon. Andrew F. C. W., *b.* 1949
1491	** *Willoughby de Broke (21st),* Leopold David Verney, *b.* 1938, *s.* 1986, *m.*	Hon. Rupert G. V., *b.* 1966
1946	*Wilson (2nd),* Patrick Maitland Wilson, *b.* 1915, *s.* 1964, *w.*	None
1937	*Windlesham (3rd) and Hennessy (life peerage, 1999),* David James George Hennessy, CVO, PC, *b.* 1932, *s.* 1962, *w.*	Hon. James R. H., *b.* 1968
1951	*Wise (2nd),* John Clayton Wise, *b.* 1923, *s.* 1968, *m.*	Hon. Christopher J. C. W., *b.* 1949
1869	*Wolverton (7th),* Christopher Richard Glyn, *b.* 1938, *s.* 1988	Miles J. G., *b.* 1966
1928	*Wraxall (3rd),* Eustace Hubert Beilby Gibbs, KCVO, CMG, *b.* 1929, *s.* 2001, *m.*	Hon. Anthony H. G., *b.* 1958
1915	*Wrenbury (3rd),* Revd John Burton Buckley, *b.* 1927, *s.* 1940, *m.*	Hon. William E. B., *b.* 1966
1838	*Wrottesley (6th),* Clifton Hugh Lancelot de Verdon Wrottesley, *b.* 1968, *s.* 1977, *m.*	Hon. Victor E. F. de V. W., *b.* 2004
1829	*Wynford (9th),* John Philip Robert Best, *b.* 1950, *s.* 2002, *m.*	Hon. Harry R. F. B., *b.* 1987
1308	*Zouche (18th),* James Assheton Frankland, *b.* 1943, *s.* 1965, *m.*	Hon. William T. A. F., *b.* 1984

BARONESSES/LADIES IN THEIR OWN RIGHT

Style, The Rt. Hon. the Lady _ , *or* The Rt. Hon. the Baroness _ , according to her preference. Either style may be used, except in the case of Scottish titles (indicated by S.), which are not baronies (*see* page 44) and whose holders are always addressed as Lady.

Envelope, may be addressed in same way as a Baron's wife or, if she prefers *(formal),* The Rt. Hon. the Baroness _; *(social),* The Baroness _. Otherwise as for a Baron's wife

Husband, Untitled

Children's style, As for children of a Baron

Created	*Title, order of succession, name, etc*	*Heir*
1664	*Arlington,* Jennifer Jane Forwood, *b.* 1939, *s.* 1999, *w.* Title called out of abeyance 1999	Hon. Patrick J. D. F., *b.* 1967
1455	*Berners (16th),* Pamela Vivien Kirkham, *b.* 1929, *s.* 1995, *m.*	Hon. Rupert W. T. K., *b.* 1953
1529	*Braye (8th),* Mary Penelope Aubrey-Fletcher, *b.* 1941, *s.* 1985, *m.*	Two co-heirs
1321	*Dacre (27th),* Rachel Leila Douglas-Home, *b.* 1929, *s.* 1970, *w.*	Hon. James T. A. D.-H., *b.* 1952
1490 S.	*Herries of Terregles (14th),* Anne Elizabeth Fitzalan-Howard, *b.* 1938, *s.* 1975, *w.*	Lady Mary Mumford, *b.* 1940
1597	*Howard de Walden (10th),* Mary Hazel Caridwen Czernin, *b.* 1935, *s.* 2004, *m.* Title called out of abeyance 2004	Hon. Peter J. J. C. *b.* 1966
1602 S.	*Kinloss (12th),* Beatrice Mary Grenville Freeman-Grenville, *b.* 1922, *s.* 1944, *w.*	Master of Kinloss, *b.* 1953
1445 S.	** *Saltoun (20th),* Flora Marjory Fraser, *b.* 1930, *s.* 1979, *w.*	Hon. Katharine I. M. I. F., *b.* 1957
1313	*Willoughby de Eresby (27th),* (Nancy) Jane Marie Heathcote-Drummond-Willoughby, *b.* 1934, *s.* 1983	Two co-heirs

LIFE PEERS

Style, The Rt. Hon. the Lord _ /The Rt. Hon. the Lady _, *or* The Rt. Hon. the Baroness _ , according to her preference
Envelope (formal), The Rt. Hon. Lord _/Lady_/ Baroness_; *(social)*, The Lord _/Lady_/Baroness_ *Letter (formal)*, My Lord/Lady; *(social)*, Dear Lord/ Lady _. *Spoken*, Lord/Lady _
Wife's style, The Rt. Hon. the Lady _
Husband, Untitled
Children's style, 'The Hon.' before forename (F_) and surname (S_)
Envelope, The Hon. F_ S_. *Letter*, Dear Mr/Miss/Mrs S_. *Spoken*, Mr/Miss/Mrs S_

NEW LIFE PEERAGES

1 September 2007 to 31 August 2008:
Prof. Haleh Afshar, OBE; Michael Walton Bates; Lady Susan Elizabeth Garden; Hon. Dame Elizabeth Manningham-Buller; Sir John (Frederick) Mogg, KCMG; Sir Robert (Haldane) Smith; Sir Nicholas Herbert Stern; Rt. Hon. James Robert Wallace, QC

SYMBOLS
* Hereditary peer who has been granted a life peerage. For further details, please refer to the Hereditary Peers section. For example, life peer *Balniel* can be found under his hereditary title *Earl of Crawford and Balcarres*
‡ Title not confirmed at time of going to press

CREATED UNDER THE APPELLATE JURISDICTION ACT 1876 (AS AMENDED)

BARONS
Created
2004 *Brown of Eaton-under-Heywood*, Simon Denis Brown, PC, *b.* 1937, *m., Lord of Appeal in Ordinary*
1991 *Browne-Wilkinson*, Nicolas Christopher Henry Browne-Wilkinson, PC, *b.* 1930, *m.*
2004 *Carswell*, Robert Douglas Carswell, PC, *b.* 1934, *m., Lord of Appeal in Ordinary*
1996 *Clyde*, James John Clyde, PC, *b.* 1932, *m.*
1986 *Goff of Chieveley*, Robert Lionel Archibald Goff, PC, *b.* 1926, *m.*
1985 *Griffiths*, (William) Hugh Griffiths, MC, PC, *b.* 1923, *m.*
1995 *Hoffmann*, Leonard Hubert Hoffmann, PC, *b.* 1934, *m. Second Senior Lord of Appeal in Ordinary*
1997 *Hutton*, (James) Brian (Edward) Hutton, PC, *b.* 1931, *m.*
1993 *Lloyd of Berwick*, Anthony John Leslie Lloyd, PC, *b.* 1929, *m.*
2005 *Mance*, Jonathan Hugh Mance, PC, *b.* 1943, *m., Lord of Appeal in Ordinary*
1998 *Millett*, Peter Julian Millett, PC, *b.* 1932, *m.*
1992 *Mustill*, Michael John Mustill, PC, *b.* 1931, *m.*
2007 *Neuberger of Abbotsbury*, David Edmond Neuberger, PC, *b.* 1948, *m., Lord of Appeal in Ordinary*
1994 *Nicholls of Birkenhead*, Donald James Nicholls, PC, *b.* 1933, *m.*
1999 *Phillips of Worth Matravers*, Nicholas Addison Phillips, b. 1938, *m. Senior Lord of Appeal in Ordinary*
1997 *Saville of Newdigate*, Mark Oliver Saville, PC, *b.* 1936, *m. Lord of Appeal in Ordinary*
2000 *Scott of Foscote*, Richard Rashleigh Folliott Scott, PC, *b.* 1934, *m. Lord of Appeal in Ordinary*
1992 *Slynn of Hadley*, Gordon Slynn, PC, *b.* 1930, *m.*
1995 *Steyn*, Johan van Zyl Steyn, PC, *b.* 1932, *m.*
1982 *Templeman*, Sydney William Templeman, MBE, PC, *b.* 1920, *w.*
2003 *Walker of Gestingthorpe*, Robert Walker, PC, *b.* 1938, *m. Lord of Appeal in Ordinary*
1992 *Woolf*, Harry Kenneth Woolf, PC, *b.* 1933, *m.*

BARONESSES
2004 *Hale of Richmond*, Brenda Marjorie Hale, DBE, PC, *b.* 1945, *m., Lord of Appeal in Ordinary*

CREATED UNDER THE LIFE PEERAGES ACT 1958

BARONS
Created
2000 **Acton of Bridgnorth*, Lord Acton, *b.* 1941, *m.* (*see* Hereditary Peers)
2001 *Adebowale*, Victor Olufemi Adebowale, CBE, *b.* 1962
2005 *Adonis*, Andrew Adonis, *b.* 1963, *m.*
1998 *Ahmed*, Nazir Ahmed, *b.* 1957, *m.*
1996 *Alderdice*, John Thomas Alderdice, *b.* 1955, *m.*
1998 *Alli*, Waheed Alli, *b.* 1964
2004 *Alliance*, David Alliance, CBE, *b.* 1932
1997 *Alton of Liverpool*, David Patrick Paul Alton, *b.* 1951, *m.*
2005 *Anderson of Swansea*, Donald Anderson, PC, *b.* 1939, *m.*
1992 *Archer of Sandwell*, Peter Kingsley Archer, PC, QC, *b.* 1926, *m.*
1992 *Archer of Weston-super-Mare*, Jeffrey Howard Archer, *b.* 1940, *m.*
1988 *Armstrong of Ilminster*, Robert Temple Armstrong, GCB, CVO, *b.* 1927, *m.*
1999 **Armstrong-Jones*, Earl of Snowdon, GCVO, *b.* 1930, *m.* (*see* Hereditary Peers)
2000 *Ashcroft*, Michael Anthony Ashcroft, KCMG,
2001 *Ashdown of Norton-sub-Hamdon*, Jeremy John Durham (Paddy) Ashdown, GCMG, KBE, PC, *b.* 1941, *m.*
1992 *Ashley of Stoke*, Jack Ashley, CH, PC, *b.* 1922, *w.*
1993 *Attenborough*, Richard Samuel Attenborough, CBE, *b.* 1923, *m.*
1998 *Bach*, William Stephen Goulden Bach, *b.* 1946, *m.*
1997 *Bagri*, Raj Kumar Bagri, CBE, *b.* 1930, *m.*
1997 *Baker of Dorking*, Kenneth Wilfred Baker, CH, PC, *b.* 1934, *m.*

2004 *Ballyedmond,* Dr Edward Haughey, OBE, *b.* 1944, *m.*
1974 **Balniel,* The Earl of Crawford and Balcarres, *b.* 1927, *m.* *(see* Hereditary Peers)
1992 *Barber of Tewkesbury,* Derek Coates Barber, *b.* 1918, *m.*
1983 *Barnett,* Joel Barnett, PC, *b.* 1923, *m.*
1997 *Bassam of Brighton,* (John) Steven Bassam, *b.* 1953
2008 *Bates,* Michael Walton Bates, *b.* 1961
1998 *Bell,* Timothy John Leigh Bell, *b.* 1941, *m.*
2000 *Bernstein of Craigweil,* Alexander Bernstein, *b.* 1936, *m.*
2001 *Best,* Richard Stuart Best, OBE, *b.* 1945, *m.*
2007 *Bew,* Prof. Paul Anthony Elliott Bew, *b.* 1950, *m.*
2001 *Bhatia,* Amirali Alibhai Bhatia, OBE, *b.* 1932, *m.*
2004 *Bhattacharyya,* Prof. (Sushantha) Kumar Bhattacharyya, CBE *b.* 1932, *m.*
2006 *Bilimoria,* Karan Faridoon Bilimoria, CBE, *b.* 1961, *m.*
2005 *Bilston,* Dennis Turner, *b.* 1942, *m.*
1996 *Bingham of Cornhill,* Thomas Henry Bingham, KG, PC, *b.* 1933, *m.*
2000 *Birt,* John Francis Hodgess Birt, *b.* 1944, *m.*
2001 *Black of Crossharbour,* Conrad Moffat Black, OC, PC, *b.* 1944, *m.*
1997 *Blackwell,* Norman Roy Blackwell, *b.* 1952, *m.*
1994 *Blaker,* Peter Allan Renshaw Blaker, KCMG, PC, *b.* 1922, *m.*
1995 *Blyth of Rowington,* James Blyth, *b.* 1940, *m.*
1996 *Borrie,* Gordon Johnson Borrie, QC, *b.* 1931, *m.*
1976 *Boston of Faversham,* Terence George Boston, QC, *b.* 1930, *m.*
1996 *Bowness,* Peter Spencer Bowness, CBE, *b.* 1943, *m.*
2003 *Boyce,* Michael Boyce, GCB, OBE, *b.* 1943
2006 *Boyd of Duncansby,* Colin David Boyd, PC, *b.* 1953, *m.*
2006 *Bradley,* Keith John Charles Bradley, PC, *b.* 1950, *m.*
1999 *Bradshaw,* William Peter Bradshaw, *b.* 1936, *m.*
1998 *Bragg,* Melvyn Bragg, *b.* 1939, *m.*
1987 *Bramall,* Edwin Noel Westby Bramall, KG, GCB, OBE, MC, *b.* 1923, *m.*
2000 *Brennan,* Daniel Joseph Brennan, QC, *b.* 1942, *m.*
1999 *Brett,* William Henry Brett, *b.* 1942, *m.*
1976 *Briggs,* Asa Briggs, FBA, *b.* 1921, *m.*
2000 *Brittan of Spennithorne,* Leon Brittan, PC, QC, *b.* 1939, *m.*
2004 *Broers,* Prof. Alec (Nigel) Broers, *b.* 1938, *m.*
1997 *Brooke of Alverthorpe,* Clive Brooke, *b.* 1942, *m.*
2001 *Brooke of Sutton Mandeville,* Peter Leonard Brooke, CH, PC, *b.* 1934, *m.*
1998 *Brookman,* David Keith Brookman, *b.* 1937, *m.*
1979 *Brooks of Tremorfa,* John Edward Brooks, *b.* 1927, *m.*
2006 *Browne of Belmont,* Wallace Hamilton Browne, *b.* 1947
2001 *Browne of Madingley,* Edmund John Phillip Browne, *b.* 1948
2006 *Burnett,* John Patrick Aubone Burnett, *b.* 1945, *m.*
1998 *Burns,* Terence Burns, GCB, *b.* 1944, *m.*
1998 *Butler of Brockwell,* (Frederick Edward) Robin Butler, KG, GCB, CVO, PC, *b.* 1938, *m.*
1978 *Buxton of Alsa,* Aubrey Leland Oakes Buxton, KCVO, MC, *b.* 1918, *m.*
2004 *Cameron of Dillington,* Ewen (James Hanning) Cameron, *b.* 1949, *m.*
1984 *Cameron of Lochbroom,* Kenneth John Cameron, PC, *b.* 1931, *m.*
1981 *Campbell of Alloway,* Alan Robertson Campbell, QC, *b.* 1917, *m.*
2001 *Campbell-Savours,* Dale Norman Campbell-Savours, *b.* 1943, *m.*
2002 *Carey of Clifton,* Rt. Revd George Leonard Carey, PC, *b.* 1935, *m.*
1999 **Carington of Upton,* Lord Carrington, GCMG, *b.* 1919, *m.* *(see* Hereditary Peers)
1999 *Carlile of Berriew,* Alexander Charles Carlile, QC, *b.* 1948, *m.*
1975 *Carr of Hadley,* (Leonard) Robert Carr, PC, *b.* 1916, *m.*
2004 *Carter of Coles,* Patrick Robert Carter, *b.* 1946, *m.*
1990 *Cavendish of Furness,* (Richard) Hugh Cavendish, *b.* 1941, *m.*
1996 *Chadlington,* Peter Selwyn Gummer, *b.* 1942, *m.*
1964 *Chalfont,* (Alun) Arthur Gwynne Jones, OBE, MC, PC, *b.* 1919, *w.*
2005 *Chidgey,* David William George Chidgey, *b.* 1942, *m.*
1987 *Chilver,* (Amos) Henry Chilver, FRS, FRENG, *b.* 1926, *m.*
1977 *Chitnis,* Pratap Chidamber Chitnis, *b.* 1936, *m.*
1998 *Christopher,* Anthony Martin Grosvenor Christopher, CBE, *b.* 1925, *m.*
2001 *Clark of Windermere,* David George Clark, PC, PHD, *b.* 1939, *m.*
1998 *Clarke of Hampstead,* Anthony James Clarke, CBE, *b.* 1932, *m.*
1998 *Clement-Jones,* Timothy Francis Clement-Jones, CBE, *b.* 1949, *m.*
1990 *Clinton-Davis,* Stanley Clinton Clinton-Davis, PC, *b.* 1928, *m.*
2000 *Coe,* Sebastian Newbold Coe, KBE, *b.* 1956, *m.*
2001 *Condon,* Paul Leslie Condon, QPM, *m.*
1997 *Cope of Berkeley,* John Ambrose Cope, PC, *b.* 1937, *m.*
2001 *Corbett of Castle Vale,* Robin Corbett, *b.* 1933, *m.*
2006 *Cotter,* Brian Joseph Michael Cotter, *b.* 1938, *m.*
1991 *Craig of Radley,* David Brownrigg Craig, GCB, OBE, *b.* 1929, *m.*
1987 *Crickhowell,* (Roger) Nicholas Edwards, PC, *b.* 1934, *m.*
2006 *Crisp,* (Edmund) Nigel (Ramsay) Crisp, KCB, *b.* 1952, *m.*
1978 *Croham,* Douglas Albert Vivian Allen, GCB, *b.* 1917, *w.*
1995 *Cuckney,* John Graham Cuckney, *b.* 1925, *m.*
2003 *Cullen of Whitekirk,* William Douglas Cullen, KT, PC, *b.* 1935, *m.*
2005 *Cunningham of Felling,* John Anderson Cunningham, PC, *b.* 1939, *m.*
1996 *Currie of Marylebone,* David Anthony Currie, *b.* 1946, *m.*
1993 *Dahrendorf,* Ralf Dahrendorf, KBE, PHD, DPHIL, FBA, *b.* 1929, *m.*
2007 *Darzi of Denham,* Ara Warkes Darzi, KBE, *b.* 1960, *m.*
2006 *Davidson of Glen Clova,* Neil Forbes Davidson, QC, *b.* 1950, *m.*
1997 *Davies of Coity,* (David) Garfield Davies, CBE, *b.* 1935, *m.*

1997 *Davies of Oldham,* Bryan Davies, PC, *b.* 1939, *m.*
1993 *Dean of Harptree,* (Arthur) Paul Dean, PC, *b.* 1924, *m.*
2006 *Dear,* Geoffrey (James) Dear, QPM, *b.* 1937, *m.*
1998 *Dearing,* Ronald Ernest Dearing, *b.* 1930, *m.*
1991 *Desai,* Prof. Meghnad Jagdishchandra Desai, PHD, *b.* 1940, *m.*
1997 *Dholakia,* Navnit Dholakia, OBE, *b.* 1937, *m.*
1997 *Dixon,* Donald Dixon, PC, *b.* 1929, *m.*
1993 *Dixon-Smith,* Robert William Dixon-Smith, *b.* 1934, *m.*
1985 *Donoughue,* Bernard Donoughue, DPHIL, *b.* 1934
2004 *Drayson,* Paul Rudd Drayson, *b.* 1960, *m.*
1994 *Dubs,* Alfred Dubs, *b.* 1932, *m.*
2004 *Dykes,* Hugh John Maxwell Dykes, *b.* 1939, *m.*
1995 *Eames,* Robert Henry Alexander Eames, OM, PHD, *b.* 1937, *m.*
1992 *Eatwell,* John Leonard Eatwell, PHD, *b.* 1945
1983 *Eden of Winton,* John Benedict Eden, PC, *b.* 1925, *m.*
1999 *Elder,* Thomas Murray Elder, *b.* 1950
1992 *Elis-Thomas,* Dafydd Elis Elis-Thomas, PC, *b.* 1946, *m.*
1985 *Elliott of Morpeth,* Robert William Elliott, *b.* 1920, *m.*
1981 *Elystan-Morgan,* Dafydd Elystan Elystan-Morgan, *b.* 1932, *w.*
2000 **Erskine of Alloa Tower,* Earl of Mar and Kellie, *b.* 1949, *m.* (*see* Hereditary Peers)
1997 *Evans of Parkside,* John Evans, *b.* 1930, *m.*
2000 *Evans of Temple Guiting,* Matthew Evans, CBE, *b.* 1941, *m.*
1998 *Evans of Watford,* David Charles Evans, *b.* 1942, *m.*
1983 *Ezra,* Derek Ezra, MBE, *b.* 1919, *m.*
1997 *Falconer of Thoroton,* Charles Leslie Falconer, QC, *b.* 1951, *m.*
1999 *Faulkner of Worcester,* Richard Oliver Faulkner, *b.* 1946, *m.*
2001 *Fearn, Ronald Cyril Fearn,* OBE, *b.* 1931, *m.*
1996 *Feldman,* Basil Feldman, *b.* 1926, *m.*
1999 *Fellowes,* Robert Fellowes, GCB, GCVO, PC, *b.* 1941, *m.*
1999 *Filkin,* David Geoffrey Nigel Filkin, CBE, *b.* 1944
1979 *Flowers,* Brian Hilton Flowers, FRS, *b.* 1924, *m.*
1999 *Forsyth of Drumlean,* Michael Bruce Forsyth, *b.* 1954, *m.*
2005 *Foster of Bishop Auckland,* Derek Foster, PC, *b.* 1937, *m.*
1999 *Foster of Thames Bank,* Norman Robert Foster, OM, *b.* 1935, *m.*
2005 *Foulkes of Cumnock,* George Foulkes, PC, *b.* 1942, *m.*
2001 *Fowler,* (Peter) Norman Fowler, PC, *b.* 1938, *m.*
1989 *Fraser of Carmyllie,* Peter Lovat Fraser, PC, QC, *b.* 1945, *m.*
1997 *Freeman,* Roger Norman Freeman, PC, *b.* 1942, *m.*
2000 *Fyfe of Fairfield,* George Lennox Fyfe, *b.* 1941, *m.*
1997 *Garel-Jones,* (William Armand) Thomas Tristan Garel-Jones, PC, *b.* 1941, *m.*
1999* *Gascoyne-Cecil,* The Marquess of Salisbury, PC , *b.* 1946, *m.* (*see* Hereditary Peers)
1999 *Gavron,* Robert Gavron, CBE, *b.* 1930, *m.*
2004 *George,* Edward (Alan John) George, GBE, PC, *b.* 1938, *m.*
2004 *Giddens,* Prof. Anthony Giddens, *b.* 1938, *m.*
1997 *Gilbert,* John William Gilbert, PC, PHD, *b.* 1927, *m.*
1977 *Glenamara,* Edward Watson Short, CH, PC, *b.* 1912, *m.*
1999 *Goldsmith,* Peter Henry Goldsmith, QC, *b.* 1950, *m.*
1997 *Goodhart,* William Howard Goodhart, QC, *b.* 1933, *m.*
2005 *Goodlad,* Alastair Robertson Goodlad, KCMG, *b.* 1943, *m.*
1997 *Gordon of Strathblane,* James Stuart Gordon, CBE, *b.* 1936, *m.*
2004 *Gould of Brookwood,* Philip Gould *b.* 1950 *m.*
1999 *Grabiner,* Anthony Stephen Grabiner, QC, *b.* 1945, *m.*
1983 *Graham of Edmonton,* (Thomas) Edward Graham, *b.* 1925, *m.*
2000 *Greaves,* Anthony Robert Greaves, *b.* 1942, *m.*
1975 *Gregson,* John Gregson, *b.* 1924
2000 **Grenfell of Kilvey,* Lord Grenfell, *b.* 1935, *m.* (*see* Hereditary Peers)
2004 *Griffiths of Burry Port,* Revd Dr Leslie John Griffiths, *b.* 1942, *m.*
1991 *Griffiths of Fforestfach,* Brian Griffiths, *b.* 1941, *m.*
2001 *Grocott,* Bruce Joseph Grocott, PC, *b.* 1940, *m.*
2000 **Gueterbock,* Lord Berkley, OBE, *b.* 1939, *m.* (*see* Hereditary Peers)
2000 *Guthrie of Craigiebank,* Charles Ronald Llewelyn Guthrie, GCB, LVO, OBE *b.* 1938, *m.*
1995 *Habgood,* Rt. Revd John Stapylton Habgood, PC, PHD, *b.* 1927, *m.*
2007 *Hameed,* Dr Khalid Hameed, *b.* 1941, *m.*
2005 *Hamilton of Epsom,* Archibald Gavin Hamilton, PC, *b.* 1941, *m.*
2001 *Hannay of Chiswick,* David Hugh Alexander Hannay, GCMG, CH, *b.* 1935, *m.*
1998 *Hanningfield,* Paul Edward Winston White, *b.* 1940
1997 *Hardie,* Andrew Rutherford Hardie, QC, PC, *b.* 1946, *m.*
2006 *Harries of Pentregarth,* Rt. Revd Richard Douglas Harries, *b.* 1936, *m.*
1998 *Harris of Haringey,* (Jonathan) Toby Harris, *b.* 1953, *m.*
1996 *Harris of Peckham,* Philip Charles Harris, *b.* 1942, *m.*
1999 *Harrison,* Lyndon Henry Arthur Harrison, *b.* 1947, *m.*
2004 *Hart of Chilton,* Garry Richard Rushby Hart, *b.* 1940, *m.*
1993 *Haskel,* Simon Haskel, *b.* 1934, *m.*
1998 *Haskins,* Christopher Robin Haskins, *b.* 1937, *m.*
2005 *Hastings of Scarisbrick,* Michael John Hastings, CBE, *b.* 1958, *m.*
1997 *Hattersley,* Roy Sidney George Hattersley, PC, *b.* 1932, *m.*
2004 *Haworth,* Alan Robert Haworth, *b.* 1948, *m.*
1992 *Hayhoe,* Bernard John (Barney) Hayhoe, PC, *b.* 1925, *m.*
1992 *Healey,* Denis Winston Healey, CH, MBE, PC, *b.* 1917, *m.*
1999 **Hennessey,* Lord Windlesham, CVO, *b.* 1932, *m.* (*see* Hereditary Peers)

2001 *Heseltine,* Michael Ray Dibdin Heseltine, CH, PC, *b.* 1933, *m.*
1997 *Higgins,* Terence Langley Higgins, KBE, PC, *b.* 1928, *m.*
2000 *Hodgson of Astley Abbotts,* Robin Granville Hodgson, CBE, *b.* 1942, *m.*
1997 *Hogg of Cumbernauld,* Norman Hogg, *b.* 1938, *m.*
1991 *Hollick,* Clive Richard Hollick, *b.* 1945, *m.*
1979 *Hooson,* (Hugh) Emlyn Hooson, QC, *b.* 1925, *m.*
2005 *Hope of Thornes,* Rt. Revd David Michael Hope, KCVO, PC, *b.* 1940
1995 *Hope of Craighead,* (James Arthur) David Hope, PC, *b.* 1938, *m. Lord of Appeal in Ordinary*
2004 *Howard of Rising,* Greville Patrick Charles Howard, *b.* 1941, *m.*
2005 *Howarth of Newport,* Alan Thomas Howarth, CBE, PC, *b.* 1944
1992 *Howe of Aberavon,* (Richard Edward) Geoffrey Howe, CH, PC, QC, *b.* 1926, *m.*
1997 *Howell of Guildford,* David Arthur Russell Howell, PC, *b.* 1936, *m.*
1978 *Howie of Troon,* William Howie, *b.* 1924, *w.*
1997 *Hoyle,* (Eric) Douglas Harvey Hoyle, *b.* 1930, *w.*
1997 *Hughes of Woodside,* Robert Hughes, *b.* 1932, *m.*
2000 *Hunt of Chesterton,* Julian Charles Roland Hunt, CBE, *b.* 1941, *m.*
1997 *Hunt of Kings Heath,* Philip Alexander Hunt, OBE, *b.* 1949, *m.*
1997 *Hunt of Wirral,* David James Fletcher Hunt, MBE, PC, *b.* 1942, *m.*
1997 *Hurd of Westwell,* Douglas Richard Hurd, CH, CBE, PC, *b.* 1930, *m.*
1978 *Hutchinson of Lullington,* Jeremy Nicolas Hutchinson, QC, *b.* 1915, *w.*
1999 *Imbert,* Peter Michael Imbert, CVO, QPM, *b.* 1933, *m.*
1997 *Inge,* Peter Anthony Inge, KG, GCB, PC, *b.* 1935, *m.*
1987 *Irvine of Lairg,* Alexander Andrew Mackay Irvine, PC, QC, *b.* 1940, *m.*
1997 *Jacobs,* (David) Anthony Jacobs, *b.* 1931, *m.*
2006 *James of Blackheath,* David Noel James, CBE, *b.* 1937, *m.*
1997 *Janner of Braunstone,* Greville Ewan Janner, QC, *b.* 1928, *w.*
2007 *Janvrin,* Robin Berry Janvrin, GCB, GCVO, PC, *b.* 1946, *m.*
2006 *Jay of Ewelme,* Michael (Hastings) Jay, GCMG, *b.* 1946, *m.*
1987 *Jenkin of Roding,* (Charles) Patrick (Fleeming) Jenkin, PC, *b.* 1926, *m.*
2000 *Joffe,* Joel Goodman Joffe, CBE, *b.* 1932, *m.*
2001 *Jones,* (Stephen) Barry Jones, *b.* 1937, *m.*
2007 *Jones of Birmingham,* Digby Marritt Jones, *b.* 1955, *m.*
2005, *Jones of Cheltenham,* Nigel David Jones, *b.* 1948, *m.*
1997 *Jopling,* (Thomas) Michael Jopling, PC, *b.* 1930, *m.*
2000 *Jordan,* William Brian Jordan, CBE, *b.* 1936, *m.*
1991 *Judd,* Frank Ashcroft Judd, *b.* 1935, *m.*
2004 *Kalms,* Harold Stanley Kalms, *b.* 1931 *m.*
2004 *Kerr of Kinlochard,* John (Olav) Kerr, GCMG, *b.* 1942, *m.*
2001 *Kilclooney,* John David Taylor, PC (NI), *b.* 1937, *m.*
1996 *Kilpatrick of Kincraig,* Robert Kilpatrick, CBE, *b.* 1926, *m.*
1985 *Kimball,* Marcus Richard Kimball, *b.* 1928, *m.*
2001 *King of Bridgwater,* Thomas Jeremy King, CH, PC, *b.* 1933, *m.*
1999 *King of West Bromwich,* Tarsem King, *b.* 1937
1993 *Kingsdown,* Robert (Robin) Leigh-Pemberton, KG, PC, *b.* 1927, *m.*
1994 *Kingsland,* Christopher James Prout, TD, PC, QC, *b.* 1942
2005 *Kinnock,* Neil Gordon Kinnock, PC, *b.* 1942, *m.*
1999 *Kirkham,* Graham Kirkham, *b.* 1944, *m.*
1975 *Kirkhill,* John Farquharson Smith, *b.* 1930, *m.*
2005 *Kirkwood of Kirkhope,* Archibald Johnstone Kirkwood, *b.* 1946, *m.*
2007 *Krebs,* Prof. John (Richard) Krebs, FRS, *b.* 1945, *m.*
1987 *Knights,* Philip Douglas Knights, CBE, QPM, *b.* 1920, *m.*
2004 *Laidlaw,* Irvine Alan Stewart Laidlaw, *b.* 1942, *m.*
1991 *Laing of Dunphail,* Hector Laing, *b.* 1923, *m.*
1999 *Laird,* John Dunn Laird, *b.* 1944, *m.*
1998 *Laming,* (William) Herbert Laming, CBE, *b.* 1936, *m.*
1998 *Lamont of Lerwick,* Norman Stewart Hughson Lamont, PC, *b.* 1942, *m.*
1990 *Lane of Horsell,* Peter Stewart Lane, *b.* 1925, *w.*
1997 *Lang of Monkton,* Ian Bruce Lang, PC, *b.* 1940, *m.*
1992 *Lawson of Blaby,* Nigel Lawson, PC, *b.* 1932, *m.*
2000 *Layard,* Peter Richard Grenville Layard, *b.* 1934, *m.*
1999 *Lea of Crondall,* David Edward Lea, OBE, *b.* 1937
2006 *Leach of Fairford,* Charles Guy Rodney Leach, *b.* 1934, *m.*
2006 *Lee of Trafford,* John Robert Louis Lee, *b.* 1942, *m.*
2004 *Leitch,* Alexander Park Leitch, *b.* 1947, *m.*
1993 *Lester of Herne Hill,* Anthony Paul Lester, QC, *b.* 1936, *m.*
1997 *Levene of Portsoken,* Peter Keith Levene, KBE, *b.* 1941, *m.*
1997 *Levy,* Michael Abraham Levy, *b.* 1944, *m.*
1989 *Lewis of Newnham,* Jack Lewis, FRS, *b.* 1928, *m.*
1999 *Lipsey,* David Lawrence Lipsey, *b.* 1948, *m.*
2001 *Livsey of Talgarth,* Richard Arthur Lloyd Livsey, CBE, *b.* 1935, *m.*
1997 *Lloyd-Webber,* Andrew Lloyd Webber, *b.* 1948, *m.*
1997 *Lofthouse of Pontefract,* Geoffrey Lofthouse, *b.* 1925, *w.*
2006 *Low of Dalston,* Prof. Colin Mackenzie Low, CBE, *b.* 1942, *m.*
2000 *Luce,* Richard Napier Luce, KG, GCVO, PC, *b.* 1936, *m.*
2005 *Lyell of Markyate,* Nicholas Walter Lyell, PC, QC, *b.* 1938, *m.*
2000 **Lyttleton of Aldershot,* The Viscount Chandos, *b.* 1953, *m. (see* Hereditary Peers)
1984 *McAlpine of West Green,* (Robert) Alistair McAlpine, *b.* 1942, *m.*
1988 *Macaulay of Bragar,* Donald Macaulay, QC, *b.* 1933, *m.*
1975 *McCarthy,* William Edward John McCarthy, DPHIL, *b.* 1925, *m.*
1976 *McCluskey,* John Herbert McCluskey, *b.* 1929, *m.*

1989 *McColl of Dulwich,* Ian McColl, CBE, FRCS, FRCSE, *b.* 1933, *m.*
1998 *Macdonald of Tradeston,* Angus John Macdonald, CBE, *b.* 1940, *m.*
1991 *Macfarlane of Bearsden,* Norman Somerville Macfarlane, KT, FRSE, *b.* 1926, *m.*
2001 *MacGregor of Pulham Market,* John Roddick Russell MacGregor, CBE, PC, *b.* 1937, *m.*
1982 *McIntosh of Haringey,* Andrew Robert McIntosh, *b.* 1933, *w.*
1979 *Mackay of Clashfern,* James Peter Hymers Mackay, KT, PC, FRSE, *b.* 1927, *m.*
1995 *Mackay of Drumadoon,* Donald Sage Mackay, PC, *b.* 1946, *m.*
2004 *McKenzie of Luton,* William David McKenzie, *b.* 1946, *m.*
1999 *Mackenzie of Culkein,* Hector Uisdean MacKenzie, *b.* 1940
1998 *Mackenzie of Framwellgate,* Brian Mackenzie, OBE, *b.* 1943, *m.*
1974 *Mackie of Benshie,* George Yull Mackie, CBE, DSO, DFC, *b.* 1919, *m.*
1996 *MacLaurin of Knebworth,* Ian Charter MacLaurin, *b.* 1937, *m.*
2001 *Maclennon of Rogart,* Robert Adam Ross Maclennan, PC, *b.* 1936, *m.*
1995 *McNally,* Tom McNally, PC, *b.* 1943, *m.*
2001 *Maginnis of Drumglass,* Kenneth Wiggins Maginnis, *b.* 1938, *m.*
2007 *Malloch-Brown,* George Mark Malloch Brown, KCMG, PC, *b.* 1953, *m.*
2006 *Marland,* Jonathan Peter Marland, *b.* 1956, *m.*
1991 *Marlesford,* Mark Shuldham Schreiber, *b.* 1931, *m.*
1981 *Marsh,* Richard William Marsh, PC, *b.* 1928, *m.*
1998 *Marshall of Knightsbridge,* Colin Marsh Marshall, *b.* 1933, *m.*
1987 *Mason of Barnsley,* Roy Mason, PC, *b.* 1924, *m.*
2005 *Mawhinney,* Brian Stanley Mawhinney, PC, *b.* 1940, *m.*
2007 *Mawson,* Revd Andrew Mawson, OBE, *b.* 1954, *m.*
2004 *Maxton,* John Alston Maxton, *b.* 1936, *m.*
2001 *May of Oxford,* Robert McCredie May, OM, *b.* 1936, *m.*
1997 *Mayhew of Twysden,* Patrick Barnabas Burke Mayhew, QC, PC, *b.* 1929, *m.*
2000 *Mitchell,* Parry Andrew Mitchell, *b.* 1943, *m.*
2000 **Mitford,* Lord Redesdale, *b.* 1967, *m. (see* Hereditary Peers)
2008 *Mogg,* John (Frederick) Mogg, KCMG, *b.* 1943 *m.*
1997 *Molyneaux of Killead,* James Henry Molyneaux, KBE, PC, *b.* 1920
2005 *Moonie,* Dr. Lewis George Moonie, *b.* 1947, *m.*
1992 *Moore of Lower Marsh,* John Edward Michael Moore, PC, *b.* 1937, *w.*
1986 *Moore of Wolvercote,* Philip Brian Cecil Moore, GCB, GCVO, CMG, PC, *b.* 1921, *m.*
2000 *Morgan,* Kenneth Owen Morgan, *b.* 1934, *m.*
2001 *Morris of Aberavon,* John Morris, KG, QC, *b.* 1931, *m.*
2006 *Morris of Handsworth,* William Manuel Morris, *b.* 1938, *m.*
1997 *Morris of Manchester,* Alfred Morris, PC, *b.* 1928, *m.*
2006 *Morrow,* Maurice George Morrow, *m.*
2001 *Moser,* Claus Adolf Moser, KCB, CBE, *b.* 1922, *m.*
1979 *Murton of Lindisfarne,* (Henry) Oscar Murton, OBE, TD, PC, *b.* 1914, *m.*
1997 *Naseby,* Michael Wolfgang Laurence Morris, PC, *b.* 1936, *m.*
1997 *Neill of Bladen,* (Francis) Patrick Neill, QC, *b.* 1926, *m.*
1997 *Newby,* Richard Mark Newby, OBE, *b.* 1953, *m.*
1997 *Newton of Braintree,* Antony Harold Newton, OBE, PC, *b.* 1937, *m.*
1994 *Nickson,* David Wigley Nickson, KBE, FRSE, *b.* 1929, *m.*
1975 *Northfield,* (William) Donald Chapman, *b.* 1923
1998 *Norton of Louth,* Philip Norton, *b.* 1951
2000 *Oakeshott of Seagrove Bay,* Matthew Alan Oakeshott, *b.* 1947, *m.*
2005 *O'Neill of Clackmannan,* Martin John O'Neill, *b.* 1945, *m.*
2001 *Ouseley,* Herman George Ouseley, *b.* 1945, *m.*
1992 *Owen,* David Anthony Llewellyn Owen, CH, PC, *b.* 1938, *m.*
1999 *Oxburgh,* Ernest Ronald Oxburgh, KBE, FRS, PHD, *b.* 1934, *m.*
1991 *Palumbo,* Peter Garth Palumbo, *b.* 1935, *m.*
2000 *Parekh,* Bhikhu Chhotalal Parekh, *b.* 1935, *m.*
1992 *Parkinson,* Cecil Edward Parkinson, PC, *b.* 1931, *m.*
1999 *Patel,* Narendra Babubhai Patel, *b.* 1938
2000 *Patel of Blackburn,* Adam Hafejee Patel, *b.* 1940
2006 *Patel of Bradford,* Prof. Kamlesh Kumar Patel, OBE, *b.* 1960 *m.*
2005 *Patten of Barnes,* Christopher Francis Patten, CH, PC, *b.* 1944, *m.*
1997 *Patten,* John Haggitt Charles Patten, PC, *b.* 1945, *m.*
1996 *Paul,* Swraj Paul, *b.* 1931, *m.*
1990 *Pearson of Rannoch,* Malcolm Everard MacLaren Pearson, *b.* 1942, *m.*
2001 *Pendry,* Thomas Pendry, *b.* 1934, *m.*
1987 *Peston,* Maurice Harry Peston, *b.* 1931, *m.*
1998 *Phillips of Sudbury,* Andrew Wyndham Phillips, OBE, *b.* 1939, *m.*
1996 *Pilkington of Oxenford,* Revd Canon Peter Pilkington, *b.* 1933, *w.*
1992 *Plant of Highfield,* Prof. Raymond Plant, PHD, *b.* 1945, *m.*
1987 *Plumb,* (Charles) Henry Plumb, *b.* 1925, *m.*
1981 *Plummer of St Marylebone,* (Arthur) Desmond (Herne) Plummer, TD, *b.* 1914, *m.*
2000 **Ponsonby of Roehampton,* Lord Ponsonby of Shulbrede, *b.* 1958 (*see* Hereditary Peers)
2000 *Powell of Bayswater,* Charles David Powell, KCMG, *b.* 1941
1987 *Prior,* James Michael Leathes Prior, PC, *b.* 1927, *m.*
1982 *Prys-Davies,* Gwilym Prys Prys-Davies, *b.* 1923, *m.*
1997 *Puttnam,* David Terence Puttnam, CBE, *b.* 1941, *m.*
1982 *Quinton,* Anthony Meredith Quinton, FBA, *b.* 1925, *m.*
1994 *Quirk,* Prof. (Charles) Randolph Quirk, CBE, FBA, *b.* 1920, *m.*
2001 *Radice,* Giles Heneage Radice, PC, *b.* 1936
2005 *Ramsbotham,* Gen. David John Ramsbotham, GCB, CBE, *b.* 1934, *m.*
2004 *Rana,* Dr Diljit Singh Rana, MBE, *b.* 1938, *m.*

1997 *Randall of St Budeaux,* Stuart Jeffrey Randall, *b.* 1938, *m.*
1997 *Razzall,* (Edward) Timothy Razzall, CBE, *b.* 1943, *m.*
1987 *Rees,* Peter Wynford Innes Rees, PC, QC, *b.* 1926, *m.*
2005 *Rees of Ludlow,* Prof. Martin John Rees, OM, *b.* 1942, *m.*
1988 *Rees-Mogg,* William Rees-Mogg, *b.* 1928, *m.*
1991 *Renfrew of Kaimsthorn,* (Andrew) Colin Renfrew, FBA, *b.* 1937, *m.*
1999 *Rennard,* Christopher John Rennard, MBE, *b.* 1960
1997 *Renton of Mount Harry,* (Ronald) Timothy Renton, PC, *b.* 1932, *m.*
1997 *Renwick of Clifton,* Robin William Renwick, KCMG, *b.* 1937, *m.*
1990 *Richard,* Ivor Seward Richard, PC, QC, *b.* 1932, *m.*
1983 *Richardson of Duntisbourne,* Gordon William Humphreys Richardson, KG, MBE, TD, PC, *b.* 1915, *w.*
1992 *Rix,* Brian Norman Roger Rix, CBE, *b.* 1924, *m.*
2004 *Roberts of Llandudno,* Revd John Roger Roberts, *b.* 1935, *m.*
1997 *Roberts of Conwy,* (Ieuan) Wyn (Pritchard) Roberts, PC, *b.* 1930, *m.*
1999 *Robertson of Port Ellen,* George Islay MacNeill Robertson, KT, GCMG, PC, *b.* 1946, *m.*
1992 *Rodger of Earlsferry,* Alan Ferguson Rodger, PC, QC, FBA, *b.* 1944, *Lord of Appeal in Ordinary*
1992 *Rodgers of Quarry Bank,* William Thomas Rodgers, PC, *b.* 1928, *w.*
1999 *Rogan,* Dennis Robert David Rogan, *b.* 1942, *m.*
1996 *Rogers of Riverside,* Richard George Rogers, CH, RA, RIBA, *b.* 1933, *m.*
2001 *Rooker,* Jeffrey William Rooker, PC, *b.* 1941, *m.*
2000 *Roper,* John Francis Hodgess Roper, PC, *b.* 1935, *m.*
2004 *Rosser,* Richard Andrew Rosser, *b.* 1944, *m.*
2006 *Rowe-Beddoe,* David (Sydney) Rowe-Beddoe, *b.* 1937, *m.*
2004 *Rowlands,* Edward Rowlands, CBE, *b.* 1940, *m.*
1997 *Ryder of Wensum,* Richard Andrew Ryder, OBE, PC, *b.* 1949, *m.*
1996 *Saatchi,* Maurice Saatchi, *b.* 1946, *m.*
1989 *Sainsbury of Preston Candover,* John Davan Sainsbury, KG, *b.* 1927, *m.*
1997 *Sainsbury of Turville,* David John Sainsbury, *b.* 1940, *m.*
1987 *St John of Fawsley,* Norman Antony Francis St John-Stevas, PC, *b.* 1929
1997 *Sandberg,* Michael Graham Ruddock Sandberg, CBE, *b.* 1927, *m.*
1985 *Sanderson of Bowden,* Charles Russell Sanderson, *b.* 1933, *m.*
1998 *Sawyer,* Lawrence (Tom) Sawyer, *b.* 1943
1997 *Selkirk of Douglas,* James Alexander Douglas-Hamilton, MSP, PC, QC, *b.* 1942, *m.*
1996 *Sewel,* John Buttifant Sewel, CBE, *b.* 1946
1999 *Sharman,* Colin Morven Sharman, OBE, *b.* 1943, *m.*
1994 *Shaw of Northstead,* Michael Norman Shaw, *b.* 1920, *m.*
2006 *Sheikh,* Mohamed Iltaf Sheikh, *b.* 1941, *m.*
2001 *Sheldon,* Robert Edward Sheldon, PC, *b.* 1923, *m.*
1994 *Sheppard of Didgemere,* Allan John George Sheppard, KCVO, *b.* 1932, *m.*
2000 *Shutt of Greetland,* David Trevor Shutt, OBE, *b.* 1942
1997 *Simon of Highbury,* David Alec Gwyn Simon, CBE, *b.* 1939, *m.*
1997 *Simpson of Dunkeld,* George Simpson, *b.* 1942, *m.*
1991 *Skidelsky,* Robert Jacob Alexander Skidelsky, DPHIL, *b.* 1939, *m.*
1997 *Smith of Clifton,* Trevor Arthur Smith, *b.* 1937, *m.*
2005 *Smith of Finsbury,* Christopher Robert Smith, PC, *b.* 1951
2008 *Smith of Kelvin,* Robert (Haldane) Smith, *b.* 1944, *m.*
1999 *Smith of Leigh,* Peter Richard Charles Smith, *b.* 1945, *m.*
2004 *Snape,* Peter Charles Snape, *b.* 1942
2005 *Soley,* Clive Stafford Soley, *b.* 1939
1990 *Soulsby of Swaffham Prior,* Ernest Jackson Lawson Soulsby, PHD, *b.* 1926, *m.*
1997 *Steel of Aikwood,* David Martin Scott Steel, KT, KBE, PC, *b.* 1938, *m.*
2004 *Steinberg,* Leonard Steinberg, *b.* 1936
1991 *Sterling of Plaistow,* Jeffrey Maurice Sterling, GCVO, CBE, *b.* 1934, *m.*
2007 *Stern of Brentford,* Nicholas Herbert Stern, *b.* 1946, *m.*
2005 *Stevens of Kirkwhelpington,* John Arthur Stevens, *b.* 1942, *m.*
1987 *Stevens of Ludgate,* David Robert Stevens, *b.* 1936, *m.*
1999 *Stevenson of Coddenham,* Henry Dennistoun Stevenson, CBE, *b.* 1945, *m.*
1992 *Stewartby,* (Bernard Harold) Ian (Halley) Stewart, RD, PC, FBA, FRSE, *b.* 1935, *m.*
1983 *Stoddart of Swindon,* David Leonard Stoddart, *b.* 1926, *m.*
1997 *Stone of Blackheath,* Andrew Zelig Stone, *b.* 1942, *m.*
2001 *Sutherland of Houndwood,* Stewart Ross Sutherland, KT, *b.* 1941, *m.*
1971 *Tanlaw,* Simon Brooke Mackay, *b.* 1934, *m.*
1996 *Taverne,* Dick Taverne, QC, *b.* 1928, *m.*
1978 *Taylor of Blackburn,* Thomas Taylor, CBE, *b.* 1929, *m.*
2006 *Taylor of Holbeach,* John Derek Taylor, CBE, *b.* 1943, *m.*
1996 *Taylor of Warwick,* John David Beckett Taylor, *b.* 1952, *m.*
1992 *Tebbit,* Norman Beresford Tebbit, CH, PC, *b.* 1931, *m.*
2001 *Temple-Morris,* Peter Temple-Morris, *b.* 1938, *m.*
2006 *Teverson,* Robin Teverson, *b.* 1952, *m.*
1996 *Thomas of Gresford,* Donald Martin Thomas, OBE, QC, *b.* 1937, *m.*
1997 *Thomas of Macclesfield,* Terence James Thomas, CBE, *b.* 1937, *m.*
1981 *Thomas of Swynnerton,* Hugh Swynnerton Thomas, *b.* 1931, *m.*
1977 *Thomson of Monifieth,* George Morgan Thomson, KT, PC, *b.* 1921, *m.*
1990 *Tombs,* Francis Leonard Tombs, FENG, *b.* 1924, *w.*
1998 *Tomlinson,* John Edward Tomlinson, *b.* 1939

1994 *Tope,* Graham Norman Tope, CBE, *b.* 1943, *m.*
1981 *Tordoff,* Geoffrey Johnson Tordoff, *b.* 1928, *m.*
2004 *Triesman,* David Maxim Triesman, *b.* 1943
2006 *Trimble,* William David Trimble, PC, *b.* 1944, *m.*
2004 *Truscott,* Dr Peter Derek Truscott, *b.* 1959 *m.*
1993 *Tugendhat,* Christopher Samuel Tugendhat, *b.* 1937, *m.*
2004 *Tunnicliffe,* Denis Tunnicliffe, CBE, *b.* 1943, *m.*
2000 *Turnberg,* Leslie Arnold Turnberg, MD, *b.* 1934, *m.*
2005 *Turnbull,* Andrew Turnbull, KCB, CVO, *b.* 1945, *m.*
2005 *Turner of Ecchinswell,* Jonathan Adair Turner, *b.* 1955, *m.*
2005 *Tyler,* Paul Archer Tyler, CBE, *b.* 1941, *m.*
2004 *Vallance of Tummel,* Iain (David Thomas) Vallance, *b.* 1943, *m.*
1996 *Vincent of Coleshill,* Richard Frederick Vincent, GBE, KCB, DSO, *b.* 1931, *m.*
1985 *Vinson,* Nigel Vinson, LVO, *b.* 1931, *m.*
1990 *Waddington,* David Charles Waddington, GCVO, PC, QC, *b.* 1929, *m.*
1990 *Wade of Chorlton,* (William) Oulton Wade, *b.* 1932, *m.*
1992 *Wakeham,* John Wakeham, PC, *b.* 1932, *m.*
1999 *Waldegrave of North Hill,* William Arthur Waldegrave, PC, *b.* 1946, *m.*
2007 *Walker of Aldringham,* Michael John Dawson Walker, GCB, CMG, CBE, *b.* 1944, *m.*
1992 *Walker of Worcester,* Peter Edward Walker, MBE, PC, *b.* 1932, *m.*
1995 *Wallace of Saltaire,* William John Lawrence Wallace, PHD, *b.* 1941, *m.*
2007 *Wallace of Tankerness,* James Robert Wallace, PC, QC, *b.* 1954, *m.*
1989 *Walton of Detchant,* John Nicholas Walton, TD, FRCP, *b.* 1922, *w.*
1998 *Warner,* Norman Reginald Warner, PC, *b.* 1940, *m.*
1997 *Watson of Invergowrie,* Michael Goodall Watson, *b.* 1949, *m.*
1999 *Watson of Richmond,* Alan John Watson, CBE, *b.* 1941, *m.*
1977 *Wedderburn of Charlton,* (Kenneth) William Wedderburn, FBA, QC, *b.* 1927, *m.*
1976 *Weidenfeld,* (Arthur) George Weidenfeld, *b.* 1919, *m.*
2007 *West of Spithead,* Adm. Alan William John West, GCB, DSC, *b.* 1948, *m.*
1996 *Whitty,* John Lawrence (Larry) Whitty, *b.* 1943, *m.*
1985 *Williams of Elvel,* Charles Cuthbert Powell Williams, CBE, *b.* 1933, *m.*
1999 *Williamson of Horton,* David (Francis) Williamson, GCMG, CB, PC, *b.* 1934, *m.*
2002 *Wilson of Dinton,* Richard Thomas James Wilson, GCB, *b.* 1942, *m.*
1992 *Wilson of Tillyorn,* David Clive Wilson, KT, GCMG, PHD, *b.* 1935, *m.*
1995 *Winston,* Robert Maurice Lipson Winston, FRCOG, *b.* 1940, *m.*
1985 *Wolfson,* Leonard Gordon Wolfson, *b.* 1927, *m.*
1991 *Wolfson of Sunningdale,* David Wolfson, *b.* 1935, *m.*
1999 *Woolmer of Leeds,* Kenneth John Woolmer, *b.* 1940, *m.*
1994 *Wright of Richmond,* Patrick Richard Henry Wright, GCMG, *b.* 1931, *m.*
2004 *Young of Norwood Green,* Anthony (Ian) Young, *b.* 1942, *m.*
1984 *Young of Graffham,* David Ivor Young, PC, *b.* 1932, *m.*

BARONESSES

Created

2005 *Adams of Craigielea,* Katherine Patricia Irene Adams, *b.* 1947, *w.*
1997 *Amos,* Valerie Ann Amos, *b.* 1954
2007 *Afshar,* Prof. Haleh Afshar, OBE, , *b.* 1944 *m.*
2000 *Andrews,* Elizabeth Kay Andrews, OBE, *b.* 1943, *m.*
1996 *Anelay of St Johns,* Joyce Anne Anelay, DBE, *b.* 1947, *m.*
1999 *Ashton of Upholland,* Catherine Margaret Ashton, PC, *b.* 1956, *m.*
1999 *Barker,* Elizabeth Jean Barker, *b.* 1961
2000 *Billingham,* Angela Theodora Billingham, DPHIL, *b.* 1939, *w.*
1987 *Blackstone,* Tessa Ann Vosper Blackstone, PHD, *b.* 1942
1999 *Blood,* May Blood, MBE, *b.* 1938
2000 *Boothroyd,* Betty Boothroyd, OM, PC, *b.* 1929
2004 *Bonham-Carter of Yarnbury,* Jane Bonham Carter, *b.* 1957, *w.*
2005 *Bottomley of Nettlestone,* Virginia Hilda Brunette Maxwell Bottomley, PC, *b.* 1948, *m.*
1998 *Buscombe,* Peta Jane Buscombe, *b.* 1954, *m.*
2006 *Butler-Sloss,* (Ann) Elizabeth (Oldfield) Butler-Sloss, GBE, PC *b.* 1933, *m.*
1996 *Byford,* Hazel Byford, DBE, *b.* 1941, *m.*
2007 *Campbell of Surbiton,* Jane Susan Campbell, DBE, *b.* 1959, *m.*
1982 *Carnegy of Lour,* Elizabeth Patricia Carnegy of Lour, *b.* 1925
1992 *Chalker of Wallasey,* Lynda Chalker, PC, *b.* 1942, *m.*
2004 *Chapman,* Nicola Jane Chapman, *b.* 1961
2005 *Clark of Calton,* Dr Lynda Margaret Clark, QC, *b.* 1949
2000 *Cohen of Pimlico,* Janet Cohen, *b.* 1940, *m.*
2005 *Corston,* Jean Ann Corston, PC, *b.* 1942, *m.*
2007 *Coussins,* Jean Coussins, *b.* 1950
1982 *Cox,* Caroline Anne Cox, *b.* 1937, *m.*
1998 *Crawley,* Christine Mary Crawley, *b.* 1950, *m.*
1990 *Cumberlege,* Julia Frances Cumberlege, CBE, *b.* 1943, *m.*
1978 *David,* Nora Ratcliff David, *b.* 1913, *w.*
1993 *Dean of Thornton-le-Fylde,* Brenda Dean, PC, *b.* 1943, *m.*
2005 *Deech,* Ruth Lynn Deech, DBE, *b.* 1943, *m.*
1974 *Delacourt-Smith of Alteryn,* Margaret Rosalind Delacourt-Smith, *b.* 1916, *m.*
2004 *D'Souza,* Dr Frances Gertrude Claire D'Souza, CMG, *b.* 1944 *m.*
1990 *Dunn,* Lydia Selina Dunn, DBE, *b.* 1940, *m.*
1990 *Eccles of Moulton,* Diana Catherine Eccles, *b.* 1933, *m.*
1972 *Elles,* Diana Louie Elles, *b.* 1921, *m.*
1997 *Emerton,* Audrey Caroline Emerton, DBE, *b.* 1935
1974 *Falkender,* Marcia Matilda Falkender, CBE, *b.* 1932
2004 *Falkner of Margravine,* Kishwer Falkner, *b.* 1955, *m.*

1994 *Farrington of Ribbleton,* Josephine Farrington, *b.* 1940, *m.*
2001 *Finlay of Llandaff,* Ilora Gillian Finlay, *b.* 1949, *m.*
1990 *Flather,* Shreela Flather, *m.*
1997 *Fookes,* Janet Evelyn Fookes, DBE, *b.* 1936
2006 *Ford,* Margaret Anne Ford, *b.* 1957, *m.*
2005 *Fritchie,* Irene Tordoff Fritchie, DBE, *b.* 1942, *m.*
1999 *Gale,* Anita Gale, *b.* 1940
2007 *Garden of Frognal,* Susan Elizabeth Garden, *b.* 1944 *m.*
1981 *Gardner of Parkes,* (Rachel) Trixie (Anne) Gardner, *b.* 1927, *w.*
2000 *Gibson of Market Rasen,* Anne Gibson, OBE, *b.* 1940, *m.*
2001 *Golding,* Llinos Golding, *b.* 1933, *m.*
1998 *Goudie,* Mary Teresa Goudie, *b.* 1946, *m.*
1993 *Gould of Potternewton,* Joyce Brenda Gould, *b.* 1932, *m.*
2001 *Greenfield,* Susan Adele Greenfield, CBE, *b.* 1950, *m.*
2000 *Greengross,* Sally Ralea Greengross, OBE, *b.* 1935, *m.*
1991 *Hamwee,* Sally Rachel Hamwee, *b.* 1947
1999 *Hanham,* Joan Brownlow Hanham, CBE, *b.* 1939, *m.*
1999 *Harris of Richmond,* Angela Felicity Harris, *b.* 1944
1996 *Hayman,* Helene Valerie Hayman, PC, *b.* 1949, *m.*
2004 *Henig,* Ruth Beatrice Henig, CBE, *b.* 1943, *m.*
1991 *Hilton of Eggardon,* Jennifer Hilton, QPM, *b.* 1936
1995 *Hogg,* Sarah Elizabeth Mary Hogg, *b.* 1946, *m.*
1990 *Hollis of Heigham,* Patricia Lesley Hollis, DPHIL, *b.* 1941, *m.*
1985 *Hooper,* Gloria Dorothy Hooper, CMG, *b.* 1939
2001 *Howarth of Breckland,* Valerie Georgina Howarth, OBE, *b.* 1940
2001 *Howe of Idlicote,* Elspeth Rosamond Morton Howe, CBE, *b.* 1932, *m.*
1999 *Howells of St Davids,* Rosalind Patricia-Anne Howells, *b.* 1931, *m.*
1991 *James of Holland Park,* Phyllis Dorothy White (P. D. James), OBE, *b.* 1920, *w.*
1992 *Jay of Paddington,* Margaret Ann Jay, PC, *b.* 1939, *m.*
2006 *Jones of Whitchurch,* Margaret Beryl Jones, *b.* 1955
1997 *Kennedy of the Shaws,* Helena Ann Kennedy, QC, *b.* 1950, *m.*
2006 *Kingsmill,* Denise Patricia Byrne Kingsmill, CBE, *b.* 1947, *m.*
1997 *Knight of Collingtree,* (Joan Christabel) Jill Knight, DBE, *b.* 1927, *w.*
1997 *Linklater of Butterstone,* Veronica Linklater, *b.* 1943, *m.*
1978 *Lockwood,* Betty Lockwood, *b.* 1924, *w.*
1997 *Ludford,* Sarah Ann Ludford, *b.* 1951
2004 *McDonagh,* Margaret Josephine McDonagh
1979 *McFarlane of Llandaff,* Jean Kennedy McFarlane, *b.* 1926
1999 *McIntosh of Hudnall,* Genista Mary McIntosh, *b.* 1946
1997 *Maddock,* Diana Margaret Maddock, *b.* 1945, *m.*
2008 *Manningham-Buller,* Elizabeth (Lydia) Manningham-Buller, DCB, *b.* 1948, *m.*
1991 *Mallalieu,* Ann Mallalieu, QC, *b.* 1945, *m.*
1970 *Masham of Ilton,* Susan Lilian Primrose Cunliffe-Lister, *b.* 1935, *w.*
1999 *Massey of Darwen,* Doreen Elizabeth Massey, *b.* 1938, *m.*
2006 *Meacher,* Molly Christine Meacher, *b.* 1940, *m.*
1998 *Miller of Chilthorne Domer,* Susan Elizabeth Miller, *b.* 1954
1993 *Miller of Hendon,* Doreen Miller, MBE, *b.* 1933, *m.*
2004 *Morgan of Drefelin,* Delyth Jane Morgan, *b.* 1961, *m.*
2001 *Morgan of Huyton,* Sally Morgan, *b.* 1959, *m.*
2004 *Morris of Bolton,* Patricia Morris, OBE, *b.* 1953
2005 *Morris of Yardley,* Estelle Morris, PC, *b.* 1952
2004 *Murphy,* Elaine Murphy, *b.* 1947, *m.*
2004 *Neuberger,* Rabbi Julia (Babette Sarah) Neuberger, DBE, *b.* 1950, *m.*
2007 *Neville-Jones,* (Lilian) Pauline Neville-Jones, DCMG, *b.* 1939
1997 *Nicholson of Winterbourne,* Emma Harriet Nicholson, MEP, *b.* 1941, *m.*
1982 *Nicol,* Olive Mary Wendy Nicol, *b.* 1923, *m.*
2000 *Noakes,* Shiela Valerie Masters, DBE, *b.* 1949, *m.*
2000 *Northover,* Lindsay Patricia Granshaw, *b.* 1954
1991 *O'Cathain,* Detta O'Cathain, OBE, *b.* 1938, *m.*
1999 *O'Neill of Bengarve,* Onora Sylvia O'Neill, CBE, PHD, *b.* 1941
1989 *Oppenheim-Barnes,* Sally Oppenheim-Barnes, PC, *b.* 1930, *m.*
2006 *Paisley of St George's,* Eileen Emily Paisley, *m.*
1990 *Park of Monmouth,* Daphne Margaret Sybil Désirée Park, CMG, OBE, *b.* 1921
1991 *Perry of Southwark,* Pauline Perry, *b.* 1931, *m.*
1997 *Pitkeathley,* Jill Elizabeth Pitkeathley, OBE, *b.* 1940
1981 *Platt of Writtle,* Beryl Catherine Platt, CBE, FENG, *b.* 1923, *m.*
1999 *Prashar,* Usha Kumari Prashar, CBE, *b.* 1948, *m.*
2004 *Prosser,* Margaret Theresa Prosser, OBE, *b.* 1937
2006 *Quin,* Joyce Gwendoline Quin, PC *b.* 1944
1996 *Ramsay of Cartvale,* Margaret Mildred (Meta) Ramsay, *b.* 1936
1994 *Rawlings,* Patricia Elizabeth Rawlings, *b.* 1939
1997 *Rendell of Babergh,* Ruth Barbara Rendell, CBE, *b.* 1930, *m.*
1998 *Richardson of Calow,* Kathleen Margaret Richardson, OBE, *b.* 1938, *m.*
2004 *Royall of Blaisdon,* Janet Anne Royall, *b.* 1955, *m.*
1997 *Scotland of Asthal,* Patricia Janet Scotland, QC, *b.* 1955, *m.*
2000 *Scott of Needham Market,* Rosalind Carol Scott, *b.* 1957
1991 *Seccombe,* Joan Anna Dalziel Seccombe, DBE, *b.* 1930, *m.*
1998 *Sharp of Guildford,* Margaret Lucy Sharp, *b.* 1938, *m.*
1973 *Sharples,* Pamela Sharples, *b.* 1923, *m.*
2005 *Shephard of Northwold,* Gillian Patricia Shephard, PC, *b.* 1940, *m.*
1995 *Smith of Gilmorehill,* Elizabeth Margaret Smith, *b.* 1940, *w.*
1999 *Stern,* Vivien Helen Stern, CBE, *b.* 1941
1996 *Symons of Vernham Dean,* Elizabeth Conway Symons, *b.* 1951
2005 *Taylor of Bolton,* Winifred Ann Taylor, PC *b.* 1947, *m.*

1992 *Thatcher,* Margaret Hilda Thatcher, KG, OM, PC, FRS, *b.* 1925, *w.*
1994 *Thomas of Walliswood,* Susan Petronella Thomas, OBE, *b.* 1935, *m.*
2006 *Thomas of Winchester,* Celia Marjorie Thomas, MBE, *b.* 1945
1998 *Thornton,* (Dorothea) Glenys Thornton, *b.* 1952, *m.*
2005 *Tonge,* Dr. Jennifer Louise Tonge, *b.* 1941, *m.*
1980 *Trumpington,* Jean Alys Barker, DCVO, PC, *b.* 1922, *w.*
1985 *Turner of Camden,* Muriel Winifred Turner, *b.* 1927, *m.*
1998 *Uddin,* Manzila Pola Uddin, *b.* 1959, *m.*
2007 *Vadera,* Shriti Vadera
2005 *Valentine,* Josephine Clare Valentine
2006 *Verma,* Sandip Verma, *b.* 1959, *m.*
2004 *Wall of New Barnet,* Margaret Mary Wall, *b.* 1941, *m.*
2000 *Walmsley,* Joan Margaret Walmsley, *b.* 1943
1985 *Warnock,* Helen Mary Warnock, DBE, *b.* 1924, *w.*
2007 *Warsi,* Sayeeda Hussain Warsi, *b.* 1971
1999 *Warwick of Undercliffe,* Diana Mary Warwick, *b.* 1945, *m.*
1999 *Whitaker,* Janet Alison Whitaker, *b.* 1936
1996 *Wilcox,* Judith Ann Wilcox, *b.* 1940, *w.*
1999 *Wilkins,* Rosalie Catherine Wilkins, *b.* 1946
1993 *Williams of Crosby,* Shirley Vivien Teresa Brittain Williams, PC, *b.* 1930, *w.*
2004 *Young of Hornsey,* Prof. Margaret Omolola Young, OBE, *b.* 1951, *m.*
1997 *Young of Old Scone,* Barbara Scott Young, *b.* 1948

LORDS SPIRITUAL

The Lords Spiritual are the Archbishops of Canterbury and York and 24 diocesan bishops of the Church of England. The Bishops of London, Durham and Winchester always have seats in the House of Lords; the other 21 seats are filled by the remaining diocesan bishops in order of seniority. The Bishop of Sodor and Man and the Bishop of Gibraltar are not eligible to sit in the House of Lords.

ARCHBISHOPS

Style, The Most Revd and Rt. Hon. the Lord Archbishop of_
Addressed as Archbishop *or* Your Grace

INTRODUCED TO HOUSE OF LORDS

2003 *Canterbury* (104th), Rowan Douglas Williams, PC, DPHIL, *b.* 1950, *m., cons.* 1992, *elected* 2002
2005 *York* (97th), John Mugabi Tucker Sentamu, PC, PHD, *b.* 1949, *m., cons.* 1996, *elected* 2005, *trans.* 2005

BISHOPS

Style, The Rt. Revd the Lord Bishop of _
Addressed as My Lord
elected date of confirmation as diocesan bishop

INTRODUCED TO HOUSE OF LORDS
(as at 31 August 2008)

1996 *London* (132nd), Richard John Carew Chartres, *b.* 1947, *m., cons.* 1992, *elected* 1995
2003 *Durham* (71st), Nicholas Thomas Wright, DPHIL, *b.* 1948, *m., cons.* 2003, *elected* 2003
1996 *Winchester* (96th), Michael Charles Scott-Joynt, *b.* 1943, *m., cons.* 1987, *elected* 1995
1997 *Southwark* (9th), Thomas Frederick Butler, *b.* 1940, *m., cons.* 1985, *elected* 1991, *trans.* 1998
1997 *Manchester* (11th), Nigel Simeon McCulloch, *b.* 1942, *m., cons.* 1986, *elected* 1992, *trans.* 2002
1998 *Salisbury* (77th), David Staffurth Stancliffe, *b.* 1942, *m., cons.* 1993, *elected* 1993
1999 *Rochester* (106th), Michael James Nazir-Ali, PHD, *b.* 1949, *m., cons.* 1984, *elected* 1994
1999 *Chelmsford* (9th), John Warren Gladwin, *b.* 1942, *m., cons.* 1994, *elected* 1994, *trans.* 2003
1999 *Portsmouth* (8th), Kenneth William Stevenson, *b.* 1949, *m., cons.* 1995, *elected* 1995
1999 *St Albans* (9th), Christopher William Herbert, *b.* 1944, *m., cons.* 1995, *elected* 1995
2001 *Peterborough* (37th), Ian Patrick Martyn Cundy, *b.* 1945, *m., cons.* 1992, *elected* 1996
2001 *Chester* (40th), Peter Robert Forster, PHD, *m., b.* 1950, *cons.* 1996, *elected* 1996
2003 *Newcastle* (11th), (John) Martin Wharton, *b.* 1944, *m., cons.* 1992, *elected* 1997
2003 *Liverpool* (7th), James Stuart Jones, *b.* 1948, *m., cons.* 1994, *elected* 1998
2003 *Leicester* (6th), Timothy John Stevens, *b.* 1946, *m., cons.* 1995, *elected* 1999
2004 *Southwell and Nottingham* (10th), George Henry Cassidy, *b.* 1942, *m., cons.* 1999, *elected* 1999
2004 *Norwich* (71st), Graham Richard James, *b.* 1951, *m., cons.* 1993, *elected* 1999
2005 *Exeter* (70th), Michael Lawrence Langrish, *b.* 1946, *m., cons.* 1993, *elected* 2000
2006 *Ripon and Leeds* (12th), John Richard Packer, *b.* 1946, *m., cons.* 1996, *elected* 2000
2007 *Ely* (68th), Dr Anthony John Russell, *b.* 1943, *m., cons.* 1988, *elected* 2000
2007 *Carlisle* (65th), (Geoffrey) Graham Dow, *b.* 1942, *m., cons.* 1985, *elected* 2000
2008 *Chichester* (102nd), John William Hind, *b.* 1945, *m., cons.* 1991, *elected* 2001
2008 *Lincoln* (71st), Dr John Charles Saxbee, *b.* 1946, *m., cons.* 1994, *elected* 2001
2008 *Bath and Wells* (77th), Peter Bryan Price, *b.* 1944, *m., cons.* 1997, *elected* 2002

BISHOPS AWAITING SEATS, in order of seniority
(as at 31 August 2008)

Bradford (9th), David Charles James, *b.* 1945, *m., cons.* 1998, *elected* 2002
Wakefield (12th), Stephen George Platten, *b.* 1947, *m., cons.* 2003, *elected* 2003
Bristol (55th), Michael Arthur Hill, *b.* 1947, *m., cons.* 1998, *elected* 2003
Lichfield (98th), Jonathan Michael Gledhill, *b.* 1949, *m., cons.* 1996, *elected* 2003
Blackburn (8th), Nicholas Stewart Reade, *b.* 1946, *m., cons.* 2004, *elected* 2004
Hereford (104th), Anthony Martin Priddis, *b.* 1948, *m., cons.* 1996, *elected* 2004
Gloucester (40th), Michael Francis Perham, *b.* 1947, *m., cons.* 2004, *elected* 2004
Guildford (9th), Christopher John Hill, *b.* 1945, *m., cons.* 1996, *elected* 2004
Derby (7th), Alastair Llewellyn John Redfern, *b.* 1948, *m., cons.* 1997, *elected* 2005
Birmingham (9th), David Andrew Urquhart, *b.* 1952, *cons.* 2000, *elected* 2006
Oxford (42nd), John Lawrence Pritchard, *b.* 1948, *m., cons.* 2002 *elected* 2007
St Edmundsbury and Ipswich (10th), (William) Nigel Stock, *b.* 1950, *m., cons.* 2000, *elected* 2007
Worcester (113th), John Geoffrey Inge, PHD, *b.* 1955, *m., cons.* 2003, *elected* 2007
Coventry (9th), Christopher John Cocksworth, PHD, *b.* 1959, *m., cons.* 2008, *elected* 2008
Truro (15th), Timothy Martin Thornton, *b.* 1957, *m., cons.* 2001, *elected* 2008
Sheffield (7th), vacant

COURTESY TITLES AND PEERS' SURNAMES

COURTESY TITLES

The heir apparent to a Duke, Marquess or Earl uses the highest of his father's other titles as a courtesy title. For example, the Marquess of Blandford is heir to the Dukedom of Marlborough, and Viscount Amberley to the Earldom of Russell. Titles of second heirs (when in use) are also given, and the courtesy title of the father of a second heir is indicated by * eg Earl of Mornington, eldest son of *Marquess of Douro.

The holder of a courtesy title is not styled 'the Most Hon.' or 'the Rt. Hon.', and in correspondence 'the' is omitted before the title. The heir apparent to a Scottish title may use the title 'Master'.

MARQUESSES

*Blandford – *Marlborough, D.*
Bowmont and Cessford – *Roxburghe, D.*
Douglas and Clydesdale – *Hamilton, D.*
*Douro – *Wellington, D.*
Graham – *Montrose, D.*
*Hamilton – *Abercorn, D.*
Hartington – *Devonshire, D.*
Lorne – *Argyll, D.*
Stafford – *Sutherland, D.*
Tavistock – *Bedford, D.*
Tullibardine – *Atholl, D.*
*Worcester – *Beaufort, D.*

EARLS

Aboyne – *Huntly, M.*
Arundel and Surrey – *Norfolk, D.*
Bective – *Headfort, M.*
Belfast – *Donegall, M.*
Brecknock – *Camden, M.*
Burford – *St Albans, D.*
*Cardigan – *Ailesbury, M.*
Compton – *Northampton, M.*
*Dalkeith – *Buccleuch, D.*
*Euston – *Grafton, D.*
Glamorgan – **Worcester, M.*
Grosvenor – *Westminster, D.*
Haddo – *Aberdeen and Temair, M.*
Hillsborough – *Downshire, M.*
Hopetoun – *Linlithgow, M.*
Kerry – *Lansdowne, M.*
March and Kinrara – *Richmond, D.*
Medina – *Milford Haven, M.*
*Mount Charles – *Conyngham, M.*
Mornington – **Douro, M.*
Mulgrave – *Normanby, M.*
Percy – *Northumberland, D.*
Ronaldshay – *Zetland, M.*
*St Andrews – *Kent, D.*
*Southesk – *Fife, D.*
Sunderland – **Blandford, M.*
*Tyrone – *Waterford, M.*
Ulster – *Gloucester, D.*
*Uxbridge – *Anglesey, M.*
Wiltshire – *Winchester, M.*
Yarmouth – *Hertford, M.*

VISCOUNTS

Alexander – *Caledon, E.*
Althorp – *Spencer, E.*
Andover – *Suffolk and Berkshire, E.*
Asquith – *Oxford and Asquith, E.*
Boringdon – *Morley, E.*
Borodale – *Beatty, E.*
Boyle – *Shannon, E.*
Brocas – *Jellicoe, E.*
Bury – *Albermarle, E.*
Campden – *Gainsborough, E.*
Carlow – *Portarlington, E.*
Carlton – *Wharncliffe, E.*
Castlereagh – *Londonderry, M.*
Chelsea – *Cadogan, E.*
Chewton – *Waldegrave, E.*
Clanfield – *Peel, E.*
Clive – *Powis, E.*
Coke – *Leicester, E.*
Corry – *Belmore, E.*
Corvedale – *Baldwin of Bewdley, E.*
Cranborne – *Salisbury, M.*
Cranley – *Onslow, E.*
Crichton – *Erne, E.*
Curzon – *Howe, E.*
Dangan – *Cowley, E.*
Dawick – *Haig, E.*
Drumlanrig – *Queensberry, M.*
Duncannon – *Bessborough, E.*
Dungarvan – *Cork and Orrery, E.*
Dunluce – *Antrim, E.*
Dunwich – *Stradbroke, E.*
Dupplin – *Kinnoull, E.*
Ednam – *Dudley, E.*
Elveden – *Iveagh, E.*
Emlyn – *Cawdor, E*
Encombe – *Eldon, E.*
Enfield – *Strafford, E.*
Erleigh – *Reading, M.*
Errington – *Cromer, E.*
Feilding – *Denbigh and Desmond, E.*
FitzHarris – *Malmesbury, E.*
Folkestone – *Radnor, E.*
Forbes – *Granard, E.*
Garmoyle – *Cairns, E.*
Garnock – *Lindsay, E.*
Glenapp – *Inchcape, E.*
Glentworth – *Limerick, E.*
Grey de Wilton – *Wilton, E.*
Grimstone – *Verulam, E.*
Gwynedd – *Lloyd George of Dwyfor, E.*
Hawkesbury – *Liverpool, E.*
Hinchingbrooke – *Sandwich, E.*
Ikerrin – *Carrick, E.*
Ingestre – *Shrewsbury, E.*
Ipswich – **Euston, E.*
Jocelyn – *Roden, E.*
Kelburn – *Glasgow, E.*
Kingsborough – *Kingston, E.*
Kirkwall – *Orkney, E.*
Knebworth – *Lytton, E.*
Lambton – *Durham, E.*
Lascelles – *Harewood, E.*
Linley – *Snowdon, E.*
Lymington – *Portsmouth, E.*
Macmillan of Ovenden – *Stockton, E.*
Maidstone – *Winchilsea, E*
Maitland – *Lauderdale, E.*
Mandeville – *Manchester, D.*
Marsham – *Romney, E.*
Melgund – *Minto, E.*
Merton – *Nelson, E.*
Moore – *Drogheda, E.*
Newport – *Bradford, E.*
Northland – *Ranfurly, E*
Newry and Mourne – *Kilmorey, E.*
Petersham – *Harrington, E.*
Pollington – *Mexborough, E*
Raynham – *Townshend, M.*
Reidhaven – *Seafield, E.*
Ruthven of Canberra – *Gowrie, E.*
St Cyres – *Iddesleigh, E.*
Sandon – *Harrowby, E.*
Savernake – **Cardigan, E.*
Severn – *Wessex, E.*
Slane – **Mount Charles, E.*
Somerton – *Normanton, E.*
Stopford – *Courtown, E.*
Stormont – *Mansfield, E.*
Strabane – **Hamilton, M.*
Strathallan – *Perth, E.*
Stuart – *Castle Stewart, E.*
Suirdale – *Donoughmore, E.*
Tamworth – *Ferrers, E.*
Tarbat – *Cromartie, E.*
Vaughan – *Lisburne, E.*
Weymouth – *Bath, M.*
Windsor – *Plymouth, E.*
Wolmer – *Selborne, E.*
Woodstock – *Portland, E.*

BARONS (LORDS)

Aberdour – *Morton, E.*
Apsley – *Bathurst, E.*
Ardee – *Meath, E.*
Balniel – *Crawford and Balcarres, E.*
Berriedale – *Caithness, E.*
Bingham – *Lucan, E.*
Binning – *Haddington, E.*
Brooke – *Warwick, E.*
Bruce – *Elgin, E.*
Burghley – *Exeter, M.*
Cardross – *Buchan, E.*
Carnegie – **Southesk, E.*
Clifton – *Darnley, E.*
Cochrane – *Dundonald, E.*
Courtenay – *Devon, E.*
Dalmeny – *Rosebery, E.*
Doune – *Moray, E.*
Downpatrick – **St Andrews, E.*
Dunglass – *Home, E.*
Eliot – *St Germans, E.*
Formartine – **Haddo, E.*
Gillford – *Clanwilliam, E.*
Glamis – *Strathmore, E.*
Greenock – *Cathcart, E.*
Guernsey – *Aylesford, E.*
Hay – *Erroll, E.*
Howard of Effingham – *Effingham, E.*
Huntingtower – *Dysart, C.*
Hyde – *Clarendon, E.*
Irwin – *Halifax, E.*

Johnstone – *Annandale and Hartfell, E.*
Langton – *Temple of Stowe, E.*
La Poer – **Tyrone, E.*
Leveson – *Granville, E*
Loughborough – *Rosslyn, E.*
Masham – *Swinton, E.*
Mauchline – *Loudoun, C.*
Medway – *Cranbrook, E.*
Montgomerie – *Eglinton and Winton, E.*
Moreton – *Ducie, E.*
Mount Stuart – *Bute, M*
Naas – *Mayo, E.*
Neidpath – *Wemyss and March, E.*
Norreys – *Lindsey and Abingdon, E.*
North – *Guilford, E.*
Ogilvy – *Airlie, E.*
Oxmantown – *Rosse, E.*
Paget de Beaudesert – **Uxbridge, E.*
Porchester – *Carnarvon, E.*
Ramsay – *Dalhousie, E.*
Romsey – *Mountbatten of Burma, C.*
Scrymgeour – *Dundee, E.*
Seymour – *Somerset, D.*
Stanley – *Derby, E.*
Stavordale – *Ilchester, E.*
Strathnaver – *Sutherland, C.*
Wodehouse – *Kimberley, E.*
Worsley – *Yarborough, E.*

PEERS' SURNAMES

The following symbols indicate the rank of the peer holding each title:

C.	Countess
D.	Duke
E.	Earl
M.	Marquess
V.	Viscount
*	Life Peer

Where no designation is given, the title is that of a hereditary Baron or Baroness.

Abney-Hastings – *Loudoun, C.*
Acheson – *Gosford, E.*
Adams – *A. of Craigielea**
Adderley – *Norton*
Addington – *Sidmouth, V.*
Adebowale – *A. of Thornes**
Agar – *Normanton, E.*
Aitken – *Beaverbrook*
Akers-Douglas – *Chilston, V.*
Alexander – *A. of Tunis, E.*
Alexander – *Caledon, E.*
Allen – *Croham**
Allsopp – *Hindlip*
Alton – *A. of Liverpool**
Anderson – *A. of Swansea**
Anderson – *Waverley, V.*
Anelay – *A. of St Johns**
Annesley – *Valentia, V.*
Anson – *Lichfield, E.*
Archer – *A. of Sandwell**
Archer – *A. of Weston-super-Mare**
Armstrong – *A. of Ilminster**
Armstrong-Jones – *Snowdon, E.*
Arthur – *Glenarthur*
Arundell – *Talbot of Malahide*
Ashdown – *A. of Norton-sub-Hamdon**
Ashley – *A. of Stoke**
Ashley-Cooper – *Shaftesbury, E.*
Ashton – *A. of Hyde*
Ashton – *A. of Upholland**
Asquith – *Oxford and Asquith, E.*
Assheton – *Clitheroe*
Astley – *Hastings*
Astor – *A. of Hever*
Aubrey-Fletcher – *Braye*
Bailey – *Glanusk*
Baillie – *Burton*
Baillie Hamilton – *Haddington, E.*
Baker – *B. of Dorking**
Baldwin – *B. of Bewdley, E.*
Balfour – *B. of Inchrye*
Balfour – *Kinross*
Balfour – *Riverdale*
Bampfylde – *Poltimore*
Banbury – *B. of Southam*
Barber – *B. of Tewkesbury**
Baring – *Ashburton*
Baring – *Cromer, E.*
Baring – *Howick of Glendale*
Baring – *Northbrook*
Baring – *Revelstoke*
Barker – *Trumpington**
Barnes – *Gorell*
Barnewall – *Trimlestown*
Bassam – *B. of Brighton**
Bathurst – *Bledisloe, V.*
Beauclerk – *St Albans, D.*
Beaumont – *Allendale, V.*
Beckett – *Grimthorpe*
Benn – *Stansgate, V.*
Bennet – *Tankerville, E.*
Bentinck – *Portland, E.*
Beresford – *Decies*
Beresford – *Waterford, M.*
Bernstein – *B. of Craigweil**
Berry – *Camrose, V.*
Berry – *Kemsley, V.*
Bertie – *Lindsey, E.*
Best – *Wynford*
Bethell – *Westbury*
Bewicke-Copley – *Cromwell*
Bigham – *Mersey, V.*
Bingham – *B. of Cornhill**
Bingham – *Clanmorris*
Bingham – *Lucan, E.*
Black – *B. of Crossharbour**
Bligh – *Darnley, E.*
Blyth – *B. of Rowington**
Bonham Carter – *B.-C. of Yarnbury**
Bootle-Wilbraham – *Skelmersdale*
Boscawen – *Falmouth, V.*
Boston – *B. of Faversham**
Bottomley – *B. of Nettlestone**
Bourke – *Mayo, E.*
Bowes Lyon – *Strathmore, E.*
Bowyer – *Denham*
Boyd – *Kilmarnock*
Boyd – *B. of Duncansby**
Boyle – *Cork and Orrery, E.*
Boyle – *Glasgow, E.*
Boyle – *Shannon, E.*
Brabazon – *Meath, E.*
Brand – *Hampden, V.*
Brassey – *B. of Apethorpe*
Brett – *Esher, V.*
Bridgeman – *Bradford, E.*
Brittan – *B. of Spennithorne**
Brodrick – *Midleton, V.*
Brooke – *Alanbrooke, V.*
Brooke – *B. of Alverthorpe**
Brooke – *Brookeborough, V.*
Brooke – *B. of Sutton Mandeville**
Brooks – *B. of Tremorfa**
Brooks – *Crawshaw*
Brougham – *Brougham and Vaux*
Broughton – *Fairhaven*
Brown – *B. of Eaton-under-Heywood**
Browne – *B. of Belmont**
Browne – *B. of Madingley**
Browne – *Kilmaine*
Browne – *Oranmore and Browne*
Browne – *Sligo, M.*
Bruce – *Aberdare*
Bruce – *Balfour of Burleigh*
Bruce – *Elgin and Kincardine, E.*
Brudenell-Bruce – *Ailesbury, M.*
Buchan – *Tweedsmuir*
Buckley – *Wrenbury*
Butler – *B. of Brockwell**
Butler – *Carrick, E.*
Butler – *Dunboyne*
Butler – *Mountgarret, V.*
Buxton – *B. of Alsa**
Byng – *Strafford, E.*
Byng – *Torrington, V.*
Cambell-Savours – *C.-S. of Allerdale**
Cameron – *C. of Dillington**
Cameron – *C. of Lochbroom**
Campbell – *Argyll, D.*
Campbell – *C. of Alloway**
Campbell – *C. of Surbiton**
Campbell – *Cawdor, E.*
Campbell – *Colgrain*
Campbell – *Stratheden and Campbell*
Campbell-Gray – *Gray*
Canning – *Garvagh*
Capell – *Essex, E.*
Carey – *C. of Clifton**
Carington – *Carrington*
Carlisle – *C. of Berriew**
Carnegie – *Fife, D.*
Carnegie – *Northesk, E.*
Carr – *C. of Hadley**
Carter – *C. of Coles**
Cary – *Falkland, V.*
Caulfeild – *Charlemont, V.*
Cavendish – *C. of Furness**
Cavendish – *Chesham*
Cavendish – *Devonshire, D.*
Cavendish – *Waterpark*
Cayzer – *Rotherwick*
Cecil – *Amherst of Hackney*
Cecil – *Exeter, M.*
Cecil – *Rockley*
Chalker – *C. of Wallasey**
Chaloner – *Gisborough*
Chapman – *C. of Leeds**
Chapman – *Northfield**
Charteris – *Wemyss and March, E.*
Chetwynd-Talbot – *Shrewsbury, E.*
Chichester – *Donegall, M.*

Child Villiers – *Jersey, E.*
Cholmondeley – *Delamere*
Chubb – *Hayter*
Clark – *C. of Calton**
Clarke – *C. of Hampstead**
Clegg-Hill – *Hill, V.*
Clifford – *C. of Chudleigh*
Cochrane – *C. of Cults*
Cochrane – *Dundonald, E.*
Cocks – *Somers*
Cohen – *C. of Pimlico**
Cokayne – *Cullen of Ashbourne*
Coke – *Leicester, E.*
Cole – *Enniskillen, E.*
Collier – *Monkswell*
Colville – *Clydesmuir*
Colville – *C. of Culross, V.*
Compton – *Northampton, M.*
Conolly-Carew – *Carew*
Cooper – *Norwich, V*
Cope – *C. of Berkeley**
Corbett – *C. of Castle Vale**.
Corbett – *Rowallan*
Cornwall-Leigh – *Grey of Condor*
Courtenay – *Devon, E.*
Craig – *C. of Radley**
Craig – *Craigavon, V.*
Crichton – *Erne, E.*
Crichton-Stuart – *Bute, M.*
Cripps – *Parmoor*
Crossley – *Somerleyton*
Cubitt – *Ashcombe*
Cunliffe-Lister – *Masham of Ilton**
Cunliffe-Lister – *Swinton, E.*
Cunningham – *C. of Felling**
Currie – *C. of Marylebone**
Curzon – *Howe, E.*
Curzon – *Scarsdale, V.*
Cust – *Brownlow*
Czernin – *Howard de Walden*
Dalrymple – *Stair, E.*
Darzi – *D. of Denham**
Daubeny de Moleyns – *Ventry*
Davidson – *D. of Glen Clova**
Davies – *D. of Coity**
Davies – *Darwen*
Davies – *D. of Oldham**
Dawnay – *Downe, V.*
Dawson-Damer – *Portarlington, E.*
Dean – *D. of Harptree**
Dean – *D. of Thornton-le-Fylde**
Deane – *Muskerry*
de Courcy – *Kingsale*
de Grey – *Walsingham*
Delacourt-Smith – *Delacourt Smith of Alteryn**
Denison – *Londesborough*
Denison-Pender – *Pender*
Devereux – *Hereford, V.*
Dewar – *Forteviot*
Dixon – *Glentoran*
Dodson – *Monk Bretton*
Douglas – *Morton, E.*
Douglas – *Queensberry, M.*
Douglas-Hamilton – *Hamilton, D.*
Douglas-Hamilton – *Selkirk, E.*
Douglas-Hamilton – *Selkirk of Douglas**
Douglas-Home – *Dacre*
Douglas-Home – *Home, E.*
Douglas-Pennant – *Penrhyn*
Douglas-Scott-Montagu – *Montagu of Beaulieu*
Drummond – *Perth, E.*
Drummond of Megginch – *Strange*
Dugdale – *Crathorne*
Duke – *Merrivale*
Duncombe – *Feversham*
Dundas – *Melville, V.*
Dundas – *Zetland, M.*
Eady – *Swinfen*
Eccles – *E. of Moulton**
Eden – *Auckland*
Eden – *E. of Winton**
Eden – *Henley*
Edgcumbe – *Mount Edgcumbe, E.*
Edmondson – *Sandford*
Edwardes – *Kensington*
Edwards – *Crickhowell**
Egerton – *Sutherland, D.*
Eliot – *St Germans, E.*
Elliott – *E. of Morpeth**
Elliot-Murray-Kynynmound – *Minto, E.*
Ellis – *Seaford*
Erskine – *Buchan, E.*
Erskine – *Mar and Kellie, E.*
Erskine-Murray – *Elibank*
Evans – *E. of Parkside**
Evans – *E. of Temple Guiting**
Evans – *E. of Watford**
Evans – *Mountevans*
Evans-Freke – *Carbery*
Eve – *Silsoe*
Fairfax – *F. of Cameron*
Falconer – *F. of Thoroton**
Falkner – *F. of Margravine**
Fane – *Westmorland, E.*
Farrington – *F. of Ribbleton**
Faulkner – *F. of Worcester**
Fearn – *F. of Southport**
Feilding – *Denbigh and Desmond, E.*
Felton – *Seaford*
Fellowes – *De Ramsey*
Fermor-Hesketh – *Hesketh*
Fiennes – *Saye and Sele*
Fiennes-Clinton – *Lincoln, E.*
Finch Hatton – *Winchilsea, E.*
Finch-Knightley – *Aylesford, E.*
Finlay – *F. of Llandaff**
Fitzalan-Howard – *Herries of Terregles*
Fitzalan-Howard – *Norfolk, D.*
FitzGerald – *Leinster, D.*
Fitzherbert – *Stafford*
FitzRoy – *Grafton, D.*
FitzRoy – *Southampton*
FitzRoy Newdegate – *Daventry, V.*
Fletcher-Vane – *Inglewood*
Flower – *Ashbrook, V.*
Foljambe – *Liverpool, E.*
Forbes – *Granard, E*
Forsyth – *F. of Drumlean**
Forwood – *Arlington*
Foster – *F. of Thames Bank**
Foulkes – *F. of Cumnock**
Fowler – *F. of Sutton Caulfield**
Fox-Strangways – *Ilchester, E.*
Frankland – *Zouche*
Fraser – *F. of Carmyllie**
Fraser – *F. of Kilmorack**
Fraser – *Lovat*
Fraser – *Saltoun*
Fraser – *Strathalmond*
Freeman-Grenville – *Kinloss*
Fremantle – *Cottesloe*
French – *De Freyne*
Fyfe – *F. of Fairfield**
Galbraith – *Strathclyde*
Garden – *G. of Frognal**
Gardner – *G. of Parkes**
Gascoyne-Cecil – *M. of Salisbury**
Gathorne-Hardy – *Cranbrook, E.*
Gibbs – *Aldenham*
Gibbs – *Wraxall*
Gibson – *Ashbourne*
Gibson – *G. of Market Rasen**
Giffard – *Halsbury, E.*
Gilbey – *Vaux of Harrowden*
Glyn – *Wolverton*
Godley – *Kilbracken*
Goff – *G. of Chieveley**
Golding – *G. of Newcastle-under-Lyme**
Gordon – *Aberdeen, M.*
Gordon – *G. of Strathblane**
Gordon – *Huntly, M.*
Gordon Lennox – *Richmond, D.*
Gore – *Arran, E.*
Gould – *G. of Brookwood**
Gould – *G. of Potternewton**
Graham – *G. of Edmonton**
Graham – *Montrose, D.*
Graham-Toler – *Norbury, E.*
Granshaw – *Northover**
Grant of Grant – *Strathspey*
Grant of Rothiemurchus – *Dysart, C.*
Granville – *G. of Eye**
Greenall – *Daresbury*
Greville – *Warwick, E.*
Griffiths – *G. of Burry Port**
Griffiths – *G. of Fforestfach**
Grigg – *Altrincham*
Grimston – *G. of Westbury*
Grimston – *Verulam, E.*
Grosvenor – *Westminster, D.*
Grosvenor – *Wilton and Ebury, E*
Guest – *Wimborne, V*
Gueterbock – *Berkeley*
Guinness – *Iveagh, E.*
Guinness – *Moyne*
Gully – *Selby, V.*
Gummer – *Chadlington**
Gurdon – *Cranworth*
Guthrie – *G. of Craigiebank**
Gwynne Jones – *Chalfont**
Hale – *H. of Richmond**
Hamilton – *Abercorn, D.*
Hamilton – *Belhaven and Stenton*
Hamilton – *H. of Dalzell*
Hamilton – *H. of Epsom**
Hamilton – *Holm Patrick*
Hamilton-Russell – *Boyne, V.*
Hamilton-Smith – *Colwyn*
Hanbury-Tracy – *Sudeley*
Handcock – *Castlemaine*
Hannay – *H. of Chiswick**
Harbord-Hamond – *Suffield*
Harding – *H. of Petherton*
Hardinge – *H. of Penshurst*
Hare – *Blakenham, V.*
Hare – *Listowel, E.*
Harmsworth – *Rothermere, V.*
Harries – *H. of Pentregarth**
Harris – *H. of Haringey**
Harris – *H. of Peckham**
Harris – *H. of Richmond**

Harris – *Malmesbury, E.*
Hart – *H. of Chilton**
Harvey – *H. of Tasburgh*
Hastings – *H. of Scarisbrick**
Hastings Bass – *Huntingdon, E.*
Haughey – *Ballyedmond**
Hay – *Erroll, E.*
Hay – *Kinnoull, E.*
Hay – *Tweeddale, M.*
Heathcote-Drummond-Willoughby – *Willoughby de Eresby*
Hely-Hutchinson – *Donoughmore, E.*
Henderson – *Faringdon*
Hennessy – *Windlesham*
Henniker-Major – *Henniker*
Hepburne-Scott – *Polwarth*
Herbert – *Carnarvon, E.*
Herbert – *Hemingford*
Herbert – *Pembroke, E.*
Herbert – *Powis, E.*
Hervey – *Bristol, M.*
Heseltine – *H. of Thenford**
Hewitt – *Lifford, V.*
Hicks Beach – *St Aldwyn, E.*
Hill – *Downshire, M.*
Hill – *Sandys*
Hill-Trevor – *Trevor*
Hilton – *H. of Eggardon**
Hobart-Hampden – *Buckinghamshire, E.*
Hodgson – *H. of Astley Abbotts**
Hogg – *Hailsham, V.*
Hogg – *H. of Cumbernauld**
Holland-Hibbert – *Knutsford, V.*
Hollis – *H. of Heigham**
Holmes à Court – *Heytesbury*
Hood – *Bridport, V.*
Hope – *Glendevon*
Hope – *H. of Craighead**
Hope – *H. of Thornes**
Hope – *Linlithgow, M.*
Hope – *Rankeillour*
Hope Johnstone – *Annandale and Hartfell, E.*
Hope-Morley – *Hollenden*
Hopkinson – *Colyton*
Hore Ruthven – *Gowrie, E.*
Hovell-Thurlow-Cumming-Bruce – *Thurlow*
Howard – *Carlisle, E.*
Howard – *Effingham, E.*
Howard – *H. of Penrith*
Howard – *H. of Rising**
Howard – *Strathcona*
Howard – *Suffolk and Berkshire, E.*
Howarth – *H. of Breckland**
Howarth – *H. of Newport**
Howe – *H. of Aberavon**
Howe – *H. of Idlicote**
Howell – *H. of Guildford**
Howells – *H. of St. Davids**
Howie – *H. of Troon**
Hubbard – *Addington*
Huggins – *Malvern, V.*
Hughes – *H. of Woodside**
Hughes-Young – *St Helens*
Hunt – *H. of Chesterton**
Hunt – *H. of Kings Heath**
Hunt – *H. of Wirral**
Hurd – *H. of Westwell**
Hutchinson – *H. of Lullington**
Ingrams – *Darcy de Knayth*
Innes-Ker – *Roxburghe, D.*
Inskip – *Caldecote, V.*
Irby – *Boston*
Irvine – *I. of Lairg**
Isaacs – *Reading, M.*
James – *J. of Blackheath**
James – *J. of Holland Park**
James – *Northbourne*
Janner – *J. of Braunstone**
Jay – *J. of Ewelme**
Jay – *J. of Paddington**
Jebb – *Gladwyn*
Jenkin – *J. of Roding**
Jervis – *St Vincent, V.*
Jocelyn – *Roden, E.*
Jolliffe – *Hylton*
Jones – *J. of Birmingham**
Jones – *J. of Cheltenham**
Jones – *J. of Deeside**
Jones – *J. of Whitchurch**
Joynson-Hicks – *Brentford, V.*
Kay-Shuttleworth – *Shuttleworth*
Kearley – *Devonport, V.*
Keith – *Kintore, E.*
Kemp – *Rochdale, V.*
Kennedy – *Ailsa, M*
Kennedy – *K. of the Shaws**
Kenworthy – *Strabolgi*
Keppel – *Albemarle, E.*
Kerr – *K. of Kinlochard**
Kerr – *Lothian, M.*
Kerr – *Teviot*
Kilpatrick – *K. of Kincraig**
King – *Lovelace, E.*
King – *K. of West Bromwich**
King-Tenison – *Kingston, E.*
Kirkham – *Berners*
Kirkwood – *K. of Kirkhope**
Kitchener – *K. of Khartoum, E.*
Knatchbull – *Brabourne*
Knatchbull – *Mountbatten of Burma, C.*
Knight – *K. of Collingtree**
Knox – *Ranfurly, E.*
Laing – *L. of Dunphail**
Lamb – *Rochester*
Lambton – *Durham, E.*
Lamont – *L. of Lerwick**
Lampson – *Killearn*
Lane – *L. of Horsell**
Lang – *L. of Monkton**
Lascelles – *Harewood, E.*
Law – *Coleraine*
Law – *Ellenborough*
Lawrence – *Trevethin and Oaksey*
Lawson – *Burnham*
Lawson – *L. of Blaby**
Lawson-Johnston – *Luke*
Lea – *L. of Crondall**
Leach – *L. of Fairford**
Lee – *L. of Trafford**
Legge – *Dartmouth, E.*
Legh – *Grey of Codnor*
Legh – *Newton*
Leigh-Pemberton – *Kingsdown**
Leith – *Burgh*
Lennox-Boyd – *Boyd of Merton, V.*
Le Poer Trench – *Clancarty, E.*
Leslie – *Rothes, E.*
Leslie Melville – *Leven and Melville, E.*
Lester – *L. of Herne Hill**
Levene – *L. of Portsoken**
Leveson-Gower – *Granville, E.*
Lewis – *L. of Newnham**
Lewis – *Merthyr*
Liddell – *Ravensworth*
Lindesay-Bethune – *Lindsay, E.*
Lindsay – *Crawford, E.*
Lindsay – *L. of Birker*
Linklater – *L. of Butterstone**
Littleton – *Hatherton*
Lloyd – *L. of Berwick**
Lloyd George – *Lloyd George of Dwyfor, E.*
Lloyd George – *Tenby, V.*
Lloyd-Mostyn – *Mostyn*
Loder – *Wakehurst*
Lofthouse – *L. of Pontefract**
Lopes – *Roborough*
Lour – *Carneggy of Lour**
Low – *Aldington*
Low – *L. of Dalston**
Lowry-Corry – *Belmore, E.*
Lowther – *Lonsdale, E.*
Lowther – *Ullswater, V.*
Lubbock – *Avebury*
Lucas – *L. of Chilworth*
Lumley – *Scarbrough, E.*
Lumley-Savile – *Savile*
Lyell – *L. of Markyate**
Lyon-Dalberg-Acton – *Acton*
Lysaght – *Lisle*
Lyttelton – *Chandos, V.*
Lyttelton – *Cobham, V.*
Lytton Cobbold – *Cobbold*
McAlpine – *M. of West Green**
Macaulay – *M. of Bragar**
McClintock-Bunbury – *Rathdonnell*
McColl – *M. of Dulwich**
Macdonald – *M. of Tradeston**
McDonnell – *Antrim, E.*
Macfarlane – *M. of Bearsden**
McFarlane – *M. of Llandaff**
MacGregor – *M. of Pulham Market**
McIntosh – *M. of Haringey**
McIntosh – *M. of Hudnall**
McKenzie – *M. of Luton**
Mackay – *Inchcape, E.*
Mackay – *M. of Clashfern**
Mackay – *M. of Drumadoon**
Mackay – *Reay*
Mackay – *Tanlaw**
MacKenzie – *M. of Culkein**
MacKenzie – *M. of Framwellgate**
Mackenzie – *Cromartie, E.*
Mackie – *M. of Benshie**
Mackintosh – *M. of Halifax, V.*
McLaren – *Aberconway*
*MacLaurin – M. of Knebworth**
MacLennan – *M. of Rogart**
Macmillan – *Stockton, E.*
Macpherson – *M. of Drumochter*
Macpherson – *Strathcarron*
Maffey – *Rugby*
Maginnis – *M. of Drumglass**
Maitland – *Lauderdale, E.*
Makgill – *Oxfuird, V.*
Makins – *Sherfield*
Manners – *Rutland, D.*
Manningham-Buller – *Dilhorne, V.*
Mansfield – *Sandhurst*
Marks – *M. of Broughton*
Marquis – *Woolton, E.*
Marshall – *M. of Knightsbridge**

Marsham – *Romney, E.*
Martyn-Hemphill – *Hemphill*
Mason – *M. of Barnsley**
Massey – *M. of Darwen**
Masters – *Noakes**
Maude – *Hawarden, V.*
Maxwell – *de Ros*
Maxwell – *Farnham*
May – *M. of Oxford**
Mayhew – *M. of Twysden**
Meade – *Clanwilliam, E.*
Mercer Nairne Petty-Fitzmaurice – *Lansdowne, M.*
Millar – *Inchyra*
Miller – *M. of Chiltorne Domer**
Miller – *M. of Hendon**
Milner – *M. of Leeds*
Mitchell-Thomson – *Selsdon*
Mitford – *Redesdale*
Molyneaux – *M. of Killead**
Monckton – *M. of Brenchley, V.*
Monckton-Arundell – *Galway, V.*
Mond – *Melchett*
Money-Coutts – *Latymer*
Montagu – *Manchester, D.*
Montagu – *Sandwich, E.*
Montagu – *Swaythling*
Montagu Douglas Scott – *Buccleuch, D.*
Montagu Stuart Wortley – *Wharncliffe, E.*
Montague – *Amwell*
Montgomerie – *Eglinton, E.*
Montgomery – *M. of Alamein, V.*
Moore – *Drogheda, E.*
Moore – *M. of Lower Marsh**
Moore – *M. of Wolvercote**
Moore-Brabazon – *Brabazon of Tara*
Moreton – *Ducie, E*
Morgan – *M. of Drefelin**
Morgan – *M. of Huyton**
Morris – *Killanin*
Morris – *M. of Aberavon**
Morris – *M. of Bolton**
Morris – *M. of Handsworth**
Morris – *M. of Manchester**
Morris – *M. of Kenwood*
Morris – *M. of Yardley**
Morris – *Naseby**
Morrison – *Dunrossil, V.*
Morrison – *Margadale*
Moser – *M. of Regents Park**
Mosley – *Ravensdale*
Mountbatten – *Milford Haven, M.*
Muff – *Calverley*
Mulholland – *Dunleath*
Murray – *Atholl, D.*
Murray – *Dunmore, E.*
Murray – *Mansfield and Mansfield, E.*
Murton – *M. of Lindisfarne**
Nall-Cain – *Brocket*
Napier – *Napier and Ettrick*
Napier – *N. of Magdala*
Needham – *Kilmorey, E.*
Neill – *N. of Bladen**
Nelson – *N. of Stafford*
Neuberger – *N. of Abbotsbury**
Nevill – *Abergavenny, M.*
Neville – *Braybrooke*
Newton – *N. of Braintree**
Nicholls – *N. of Birkenhead**
Nicolson – *Carnock*
Nicholson – *N. of Winterboune**
Nivison – *Glendyne*
Noel – *Gainsborough, E.*
North – *Guilford, E.*
Northcote – *Iddesleigh, E.*
Norton – *Grantley*
Norton – *N. of Louth**
Norton – *Rathcreedan*
Nugent – *Westmeath, E.*
Oakeshott – *O. of Seagrove Bay**
O'Brien – *Inchiquin*
Ogilvie-Grant – *Seafield, E.*
Ogilvy – *Airlie, E.*
O'Neill – *O'N. of Bengarve**
O'Neill – *O'N. of Clackmannan**
O'Neill – *Rathcavan*
Orde-Powlett – *Bolton*
Ormsby-Gore – *Harlech*
Ouseley – *O. of Peckham Rye**
Paget – *Anglesey, M.*
Paisley – *P. of St George's**
Pakenham – *Longford, E.*
Pakington – *Hampton*
Palmer – *Lucas and Dingwall*
Palmer – *Selborne, E.*
Park – *P. of Monmouth**
Parker – *Macclesfield, E.*
Parker – *Morley, E.*
Parnell – *Congleton*
Parsons – *Rosse, E.*
Patel – *P. of Blackburn**
Patel – *P. of Bradford**
Patten – *P. of Barnes**
Paulet – *Winchester, M.*
Peake – *Ingleby, V.*
Pearson – *Cowdray, V.*
Pearson – *P. of Rannoch**
Pease – *Gainford*
Pease – *Wardington*
Pelham – *Chichester, E.*
Pelham – *Yarborough, E.*
Pellew – *Exmouth, V*
Pendry – *P. of Stalybridge**.
Penny – *Marchwood, V.*
Pepys – *Cottenham, E.*
Perceval – *Egmont, E.*
Percy – *Northumberland, D.*
Perry – *P. of Southwark**
Pery – *Limerick, E.*
Philipps – *Milford*
Philipps – *St Davids, V.*
Phillips – *P. of Sudbury**
Phillips – *P. of Worth Matravers**
Phipps – *Normanby, M.*
Pilkington – *P. of Oxenford**
Plant – *P. of Highfield**
Platt – *P. of Writtle**
Pleydell-Bouverie – *Radnor, E.*
Plummer – *P. of St Marylebone**
Plumptre – *Fitzwalter*
Plunkett – *Dunsany*
Plunkett – *Louth*
Pollock – *Hanworth, V.*
Pomeroy – *Harberton, V.*
Ponsonby – *Bessborough, E.*
Ponsonby – *de Mauley*
Ponsonby – *P. of Shulbrede*
Ponsonby – *Sysonby*
Powell – *P. of Bayswater**
Powys – *Lilford*
Pratt – *Camden, M.*
Preston – *Gormanston, V.*
Primrose – *Rosebery, E.*
Prittie – *Dunalley*
Prout – *Kingsland**
Ramsay – *Dalhousie, E.*
Ramsay – *R. of Cartvale**
Ramsbotham – *Soulbury, V.*
Randall – *R. of St. Budeaux**
Rees – *R. of Ludlow**
Rees-Williams – *Ogmore*
Rendell – *R. of Babergh**
Renfrew – *R. of Kaimsthorn**
Renton – *R. of Mount Harry**
Renwick – *R. of Clifton**
Rhys – *Dynevor*
Richards – *Milverton*
Richardson – *R. of Calow**
Richardson – *R. of Duntisbourne**
Ritchie – *R. of Dundee*
Roberts – *Clwyd*
Roberts – *R. of Conway**
Roberts – *R. of Llandudno**
Robertson – *R. of Oakridge*
Robertson – *R. of Port Ellen**
Robertson – *Wharton*
Robinson – *Martonmere*
Roche – *Fermoy*
Rodd – *Rennell*
Rodger – *R. of Earlsferry**
Rodgers – *R. of Quarry Bank**
Rogers – *R. of Riverside**
Roper-Curzon – *Teynham*
Rospigliosi – *Newburgh, E.*
Rous – *Stradbroke, E.*
Rowley-Conwy – *Langford*
Royall – *R. of Blaisdon**
Runciman – *R. of Doxford, V.*
Russell – *Ampthill*
Russell – *Bedford, D.*
Russell – *de Clifford*
Russell – *R. of Liverpool*
Ryder – *Harrowby, E.*
Ryder – *R. of Wensum**
Sackville – *De La Warr, E.*
Sackville-West – *Sackville*
Sainsbury – *S. of Preston Candover**
Sainsbury – *S. of Turville**
St Aubyn – *St Levan*
St Clair – *Sinclair*
St Clair-Erskine – *Rosslyn, E.*
St John – *Bolingbroke and St John, V.*
St John – *St John of Blesto*
St John-Stevas – *St John of Fawsley**
St Leger – *Doneraile, V.*
Samuel – *Bearsted, V.*
Sanderson – *S. of Ayot*
Sanderson – *S. of Bowden**
Sandilands – *Torphichen*
Saumarez – *De Saumarez*
Savile – *Mexborough, E.*
Saville – *S. of Newdigate**
Scarlett – *Abinger*
Schreiber – *Marlesford**
Sclater-Booth – *Basing*
Scotland – *S. of Asthal**
Scott – *Eldon, E*
Scott – *S. of Foscotte**
Scott – *S. of Needham Market**.
Scrymgeour – *Dundee, E.*
Seager – *Leighton of St Mellons*
Seely – *Mottistone*
Seymour – *Hertford, M.*
Seymour – *Somerset, D.*
Sharp – *S. of Guildford**
Shaw – *Craigmyle*
Shaw – *S. of Northstead**

Shephard – *S. of Northwood**
Sheppard – *S. of Didgemere**
Shirley – *Ferrers, E.*
Short – *Glenamara**
Shutt – *S. of Greetland**
Siddeley – *Kenilworth*
Sidney – *De L'Isle, V.*
Simon – *S. of Highbury**
Simon – *S. of Wythenshawe*
Simpson – *S. of Dunkeld**
Sinclair – *Caithness, E.*
Sinclair – *S. of Cleeve*
Sinclair – *Thurso, V.*
Skeffington – *Massereene, V.*
Slynn – *S. of Hadley**
Smith – *Bicester*
Smith – *Hambleden, V.*
Smith – *Kirkhill**
Smith – *S. of Clifton**
Smith – *Smith of Finsbury**
Smith – *S. of Gilmorehill**
Smith – *S. of Kelvin**
Smith – *S. of Leigh**
Somerset – *Beaufort, D.*
Somerset – *Raglan*
Soulsby – *S. of Swaffham Prior**
Spencer – *Churchill, V.*
Spencer-Churchill – *Marlborough, D.*
Spring Rice – *Monteagle of Brandon*
Stanhope – *Harrington, E.*
Stanley – *Derby, E.*
Stanley – *of Alderley and Sheffield*
Stapleton-Cotton – *Combermere, V.*
Steel – *S. of Aikwood**
Sterling – *S. of Plaistow**
Stern – *S. of Brentford**
Stevens – *S. of Kirkwhelpington**
Stevens – *S. of Ludgate**
Stevenson – *S. of Coddenham**
Stewart – *Galloway, E.*
Stewart – *Stewartby**
Stoddart – *S. of Swindon**
Stone – *S. of Blackheath**
Stonor – *Camoys*
Stopford – *Courtown, E.*
Stourton – *Mowbray*
Strachey – *O'Hagan*
Strutt – *Belper*
Strutt – *Rayleigh*
Stuart – *Castle Stewart, E.*
Stuart – *Moray, E.*
Stuart – *S. of Findhorn, V.*
Suenson-Taylor – *Grantchester*
Sutherland – *S. of Houndwood**
Symons – *S. of Vernham Dean**
Taylor – *Kilclooney**
Taylor – *T. of Blackburn**
Taylor – *T. of Bolton**
Taylor – *T. of Holbeach**
Taylor – *T. of Warwick**
Taylour – *Headfort, M.*
Temple-Gore-Langton – *Temple of Stowe, E*
Temple-Morris – *Temple-Morris of Llandaff**
Tennant – *Glenconner*
Thellusson – *Rendlesham*
Thesiger – *Chelmsford, V.*
Thomas – *T. of Gresford**
Thomas – *T. of Macclesfield**
Thomas – *T. of Swynnerton**
Thomas – *T. of Walliswood**
Thomas – *T. of Winchester**
Thomson – *T. of Fleet*
Thomson – *T. of Monifieth**
Thynn – *Bath, M.*
Tottenham – *Ely, M.*
Trefusis – *Clinton*
Trench – *Ashtown*
Tufton – *Hothfield*
Turner – *Bilston**
Turner – *Netherthorpe*
Turner – *T. of Camden**
Turner – *T. of Ecchinswell**
Turnour – *Winterton, E.*
Tyrell-Kenyon – *Kenyon*
Vanden-Bempde-Johnstone – *Derwent*
Vane – *Barnard*
Vane-Tempest-Stewart – *Londonderry, M.*
Vanneck – *Huntingfield*
Vaughan – *Lisburne, E.*
Vereker – *Gort, V.*
Verney – *Willoughby de Broke*
Vernon – *Lyveden*
Vesey – *De Vesci, V.*
Villiers – *Clarendon, E.*
Vincent – *V. of Coleshill**
Vivian – *Swansea*
Wade – *W. of Chorlton**
Waldegrave – *W. of North Hill**
Walker – *W. of Aldringham**
Walker – *W. of Gestingthorpe**
Walker – *W. of Worcester**
Wall – *W. of New Barnett**
Wallace – *Dudley*
Wallace – *W. of Saltaire**
Wallace – *W. of Tankerness**
Wallace – *W. of Tummel**
Wallop – *Portsmouth, E.*
Walton – *W. of Detchant**
Ward – *Bangor, V.*
Ward – *Dudley, E.*
Warrender – *Bruntisfield*
Warwick – *W. of Undercliffe**
Watson – *W. of Invergowrie**
Watson – *Manton*
Watson – *W. of Richmond**
Webber – *Lloyd-Webber**
Wedderburn – *W. of Charlton**
Weir – *Inverforth*
Weld-Forester – *Forester*
Wellesley – *Cowley, E.*
Wellesley – *Wellington, D.*
West – *W. of Spithead**
Westenra – *Rossmore*
White – *Annaly*
White – *Hanningfield**
Whiteley – *Marchamley*
Whitfield – *Kenswood*
Williams – *W. of Crosby**
Williams – *W. of Elvel**
Williamson – *Forres*
Williamson – *W. of Horton**
Willoughby – *Middleton*
Wills – *Dulverton*
Wilson – *Moran*
Wilson – *Nunburnholme*
Wilson – *W. of Dinton**
Wilson – *W. of Tillyorn**
Windsor – *Gloucester, D.*
Windsor – *Kent, D.*
Windsor-Clive – *Plymouth, E.*
Wingfield – *Powerscourt, V.*
Winn – *St Oswald*
Wodehouse – *Kimberley, E.*
Wolfson – *W. of Sunningdale**
Wood – *Halifax, E.*
Woodhouse – *Terrington*
Woolmer – *W. of Leeds**
Wright – *W. of Richmond**
Wyndham – *Egremont and Leconfield*
Wyndham-Quin – *Dunraven, E.*
Wynn – *Newborough*
Yarde-Buller – *Churston*
Yerburgh – *Alvingham*
Yorke – *Hardwicke, E.*
Young – *Kennet*
Young – *Y. of Graffham**
Young – *Y. of Hornsey**
Young – *Y. of Norwood Green**
Young – *Y. of Old Scone**
Younger – *Y. of Leckie, V.*

ORDERS OF CHIVALRY

THE MOST NOBLE ORDER OF THE GARTER (1348)

KG
Ribbon, Blue
Motto, Honi soit qui mal y pense
(Shame on him who thinks evil of it)

The number of Knights and Lady Companions is limited to 24

SOVEREIGN OF THE ORDER
The Queen

LADIES OF THE ORDER
HRH The Princess Royal, 1994
HRH Princess Alexandra, The Hon. Lady Ogilvy, 2003

ROYAL KNIGHTS
HRH The Prince Philip, Duke of Edinburgh, 1947
HRH The Prince of Wales, 1958
HRH The Duke of Kent, 1985
HRH The Duke of Gloucester, 1997
HRH The Duke of York, 2006
HRH The Earl of Wessex, 2006
HRH Prince William of Wales, 2008

EXTRA KNIGHT COMPANIONS AND LADIES
Grand Duke Jean of Luxembourg, 1972
HM The Queen of Denmark, 1979
HM The King of Sweden, 1983
HM The King of Spain, 1988
HM The Queen of the Netherlands, 1989
HIM The Emperor of Japan, 1998
HM The King of Norway, 2001

KNIGHTS AND LADY COMPANIONS
Duke of Grafton, 1976
Lord Richardson of Duntisbourne, 1983
Lord Carrington, 1985
Duke of Wellington, 1990
Lord Bramall, 1990
Viscount Ridley, 1992
Lord Sainsbury of Preston Candover, 1992
Lord Ashburton, 1994
Lord Kingsdown, 1994
Sir Ninian Stephen, 1994
Baroness Thatcher, 1995
Sir Timothy Colman, 1996
Duke of Abercorn, 1999
Sir William Gladstone, 1999
Lord Inge, 2001
Sir Anthony Acland, 2001
Duke of Westminster, 2003
Lord Butler of Brockwell, 2003
Lord Morris of Aberavon, 2003
Lady Soames, 2005
Lord Bingham of Cornhill, 2005
Sir John Major, 2005
Lord Luce, 2008
Sir Thomas Dunne, 2008

Prelate, Bishop of Winchester
Chancellor, Lord Carrington, KG, GCMG, CH, MC
Register, Dean of Windsor
Garter King of Arms, Peter Gwynn-Jones, CVO
Gentleman Usher of the Black Rod, Lt.-Gen. Sir Michael Willcocks, KCB
Secretary, Patric Dickinson, LVO

THE MOST ANCIENT AND MOST NOBLE ORDER OF THE THISTLE (REVIVED 1687)

KT
Ribbon, Green
Motto, Nemo me impune lacessit
(No one provokes me with impunity)

The number of Knights and Ladies of the Thistle is limited to 16

SOVEREIGN OF THE ORDER
The Queen

ROYAL LADY OF THE ORDER
HRH The Princess Royal, 2000

ROYAL KNIGHTS
HRH The Prince Philip, Duke of Edinburgh, 1952
HRH The Prince of Wales, Duke of Rothesay, 1977

KNIGHTS AND LADIES
Earl of Wemyss and March, 1966
Earl of Elgin and Kincardine, 1981
Lord Thomson of Monifieth, 1981
Earl of Airlie, 1985
Viscount of Arbuthnott, 1996
Earl of Crawford and Balcarres, 1996
Lady Marion Fraser, 1996
Lord Macfarlane of Bearsden, 1996
Lord Mackay of Clashfern, 1997
Lord Wilson of Tillyorn, 2000
Lord Sutherland of Houndwood, 2002
Sir Eric Anderson, 2002
Lord Steel of Aikwood, 2004
Lord Robertson of Port Ellen, 2004
Lord Cullen of Whitekirk, 2007
Sir Garth Morrison, 2007

Chancellor, Earl of Airlie, KT, GCVO, PC
Dean, Very Revd Gilleasbuig Macmillan, CVO
Secretary and Lord Lyon King of Arms, David Sellar
Gentleman Usher of the Green Rod, Rear-Adm. Christopher Layman, CB, DSO, LVO

THE MOST HONOURABLE ORDER OF THE BATH (1725)

GCB *Military* GCB *Civil*

GCB	Knight (or Dame) Grand Cross
KCB	Knight Commander
DCB	Dame Commander
CB	Companion

Ribbon, Crimson
Motto, Tria juncta in uno
(Three joined in one)

Remodelled 1815, and enlarged many times since. The order is divided into civil and military divisions. Women became eligible for the order from 1 January 1971.

THE SOVEREIGN

GREAT MASTER AND FIRST OR PRINCIPAL KNIGHT GRAND CROSS
HRH The Prince of Wales, KG, KT, GCB, OM

Dean of the Order, Dean of Westminster
Bath King of Arms, Gen. Sir Brian Kenny, GCB, CBE
Registrar and Secretary, Rear-Adm. Iain Henderson, CB, CBE
Genealogist, Peter Gwynn-Jones, CVO
Gentleman Usher of the Scarlet Rod, Maj.-Gen. Charles Vyvyan, CB, CBE
Deputy Secretary, Secretary of the Central Chancery of the Orders of Knighthood

Chancery, Central Chancery of the Orders of Knighthood, St James's Palace, London SW1A 1BH

THE ORDER OF MERIT (1902)

OM *Military* OM *Civil*

OM
Ribbon, Blue and crimson

This order is designed as a special distinction for eminent men and women without conferring a knighthood upon them. The order is limited in numbers to 24, with the addition of foreign honorary members.

THE SOVEREIGN

HRH The Prince Philip, Duke of Edinburgh, 1968
Revd Prof. Owen Chadwick, KBE, 1983
Sir Andrew Huxley, 1983
Dr Frederick Sanger, 1986
Baroness Thatcher, 1990
Dame Joan Sutherland, 1991
Sir Michael Atiyah, 1992
Lucian Freud, 1993
Sir Aaron Klug, 1995
Lord Foster of Thames Bank, 1997
Sir Denis Rooke, 1997
Sir James Black, 2000
Sir Anthony Caro, 2000
Prof. Sir Roger Penrose, 2000
Sir Tom Stoppard, 2000
HRH The Prince of Wales, 2002
Lord May of Oxford, 2002
Lord Rothschild, 2002
Sir David Attenborough, 2005
Baroness Boothroyd, 2005
Sir Michael Howard, 2005
Sir Timothy Berners-Lee, KBE, 2007
Lord Eames, 2007
Lord Rees of Ludlow, 2007

Honorary Member, Nelson Mandela, 1995

Secretary and Registrar, Lord Fellowes, GCB, GCVO, PC, QSO
Chancery, Central Chancery of the Orders of Knighthood, St James's Palace, London SW1A 1BH

THE MOST DISTINGUISHED ORDER OF ST MICHAEL AND ST GEORGE (1818)

GCMG KCMG

GCMG	Knight (or Dame) Grand Cross
KCMG	Knight Commander
DCMG	Dame Commander
CMG	Companion

Ribbon, Saxon blue, with scarlet centre
Motto, Auspicium melioris aevi *(Token of a better age)*

THE SOVEREIGN

GRAND MASTER
HRH The Duke of Kent, KG, GCMG, GCVO, ADC

Prelate, Rt. Revd David Urquhart
Chancellor, Sir Christopher Mallaby, GCMG, GCVO
Secretary, Permanent Under-Secretary of State at the Foreign and Commonwealth Office and Head of the Diplomatic Service
Registrar, Lord Wilson of Tillyorn, KT, GCMG
King of Arms, Sir Jeremy Greenstock, GCMG
Gentleman Usher of the Blue Rod, Sir Anthony Figgis, KCVO, CMG
Dean, Dean of St Paul's
Deputy Secretary, Secretary of the Central Chancery of the Orders of Knighthood
Chancery, Central Chancery of the Orders of Knighthood, St James's Palace, London SW1A 1BH

THE MOST EMINENT ORDER OF THE INDIAN EMPIRE (1878)

GCIE	Knight Grand Commander
KCIE	Knight Commander
CIE	Companion

Ribbon, Imperial purple
Motto, Imperatricis auspiciis *(Under the auspices of the Empress)*

THE SOVEREIGN

Registrar, Secretary of the Central Chancery of the Orders of Knighthood
No conferments have been made since 1947

HH Maharaja Shriraj Sahib of Halvad Dhrangadhara, 1947

THE IMPERIAL ORDER OF THE CROWN OF INDIA (1877) FOR LADIES

CI

Badge, the royal cipher of Queen Victoria in jewels within an oval, surmounted by an heraldic crown and attached to a bow of light blue watered ribbon, edged white

The honour does not confer any rank or title upon the recipient

No conferments have been made since 1947

HM The Queen, 1947

THE ROYAL VICTORIAN ORDER (1896)

GCVO KCVO

GCVO	Knight or Dame Grand Cross
KCVO	Knight Commander
DCVO	Dame Commander
CVO	Commander
LVO	Lieutenant
MVO	Member

Ribbon, Blue, with red and white edges
Motto, Victoria

THE SOVEREIGN
GRAND MASTER
HRH The Princess Royal

Chancellor, Lord Chamberlain
Secretary, Keeper of the Privy Purse
Registrar, Secretary of the Central Chancery of the Orders of Knighthood
Chaplain, Chaplain of the Queen's Chapel of the Savoy
Hon. Genealogist, D. H. B. Chesshyre, CVO

THE MOST EXCELLENT ORDER OF THE BRITISH EMPIRE (1917)

GBE

KBE

The order was divided into military and civil divisions in December 1918

GBE	Knight or Dame Grand Cross
KBE	Knight Commander
DBE	Dame Commander
CBE	Commander
OBE	Officer
MBE	Member

Ribbon, Rose pink edged with pearl grey with vertical pearl stripe in centre (military division); without vertical pearl stripe (civil division)
Motto, For God and the Empire

THE SOVEREIGN

GRAND MASTER
HRH The Prince Philip, Duke of Edinburgh, KG, KT, OM, GBE, PC

Prelate, Bishop of London
King of Arms, Air Chief Marshal Sir Patrick Hine, GCB, GBE
Registrar, Secretary of the Central Chancery of the Orders of Knighthood
Secretary, Secretary of the Cabinet and Head of the Home Civil Service
Dean, Dean of St Paul's
Gentleman Usher of the Purple Rod, Sir Alexander Michael Graham, GBE, DCL
Chancery, Central Chancery of the Orders of Knighthood, St James's Palace, London SW1A 1BH

ORDER OF THE COMPANIONS OF HONOUR (1917)

CH

Ribbon, Carmine, with gold edges
This order consists of one class only and carries with it no title. The number of awards is limited to 65 (excluding honorary members).

Anthony, Rt. Hon. John, 1981
Ashley of Stoke, Lord, 1975
Attenborough, Sir David, 1995
Baker, Dame Janet, 1993
Baker of Dorking, Lord, 1992
Birtwistle, Sir Harrison, 2000
Brenner, Sydney, 1986
Brook, Peter, 1998
Brooke of Sutton Mandeville, Lord, 1992
Carrington, Lord, 1983
Christie, Sir George, 2001
Davis, Sir Colin, 2001
De Chastelain, Gen. John, 1999
Dench, Dame Judi, 2005
Fraser, Rt. Hon. Malcolm, 1977
Freud, Lucian, 1983
Glenamara, Lord, 1976
Hamilton, Richard, 1999
Hannay of Chiswick, Lord, 2003
Hawking, Prof. Stephen, 1989
Healey, Lord, 1979
Heseltine, Lord, 1997
Hobsbawm, Prof. Eric, 1998
Hockney, David, 1997
Hodgkin, Sir Howard, 2002
Howard, Sir Michael, 2002
Howe of Aberavon, Lord, 1996
Hurd of Westwell, Lord, 1995
Jones, James, 1977
King of Bridgewater, Lord, 1992
Lessing, Doris, 1999
Lovelock, Prof. James, 2002
McKellen, Sir Ian Murray, 2008
McKenzie, Prof. Dan Peter, 2003
MacKerras, Sir Charles, 2003
Mahon, Sir Denis, 2002
Major, Rt. Hon. Sir John, 1998
Owen, Lord, 1994
Patten, Rt. Hon. Lord, 1997
Pawson, Prof. Anthony James, 2006
Pinter, Harold, 2002
Riley, Bridget, 1998
Rogers of Riverside, Lord, 2008
Sanger, Dr. Frederick, 1981
Somare, Rt. Hon. Sir Michael, 1978
Talboys, Rt. Hon. Sir Brian, 1981
Tebbit, Lord, 1987

Honorary Members, Lee Kuan Yew, 1970; Prof. Amartya Sen, 2000; Bernard Haitink, 2002
Secretary and Registrar, Secretary of the Central Chancery of the Orders of Knighthood

THE DISTINGUISHED SERVICE ORDER (1886)

DSO

Ribbon, Red, with blue edges

Bestowed in recognition of especial services in action of commissioned officers in the Navy, Army and Royal Air Force and (since 1942) Mercantile Marine. The members are Companions only. A bar may be awarded for any additional act of service.

THE IMPERIAL SERVICE ORDER (1902)

ISO

Ribbon, Crimson, with blue centre

Appointment as companion of this order is open to members of the civil services whose eligibility is determined by the grade they hold. The order consists of the sovereign and companions to a number not exceeding 1,900, of whom 1,300 may belong to the home civil services and 600 to overseas civil services. The then prime minister announced in March 1993 that he would make no further recommendations for appointments to the order.

Secretary, Secretary of the Cabinet and Head of the Home Civil Service
Registrar, Secretary of the Central Chancery of the Orders of Knighthood

THE ROYAL VICTORIAN CHAIN (1902)

It confers no precedence on its holders

HM THE QUEEN

HM The King of Thailand, 1960
HM The Queen of Denmark, 1974
HM The King of Sweden, 1975
HM The Queen of the Netherlands, 1982
Gen. Antonio Eanes, 1985
HM The King of Spain, 1986
Dr Richard von Weizsäcker, 1992
HM The King of Norway, 1994
Earl of Airlie, 1997
Rt. Revd and Rt. Hon. Lord Carey of Clifton, 2002
HRH Prince Philip, Duke of Edinburgh, 2007
HM The King of Saudi Arabia, 2007

BARONETAGE AND KNIGHTAGE

BARONETS

Style, 'Sir' before forename and surname, followed by 'Bt'.
Envelope, Sir F_ S_, Bt. *Letter (formal)*, Dear Sir; *(social)*, Dear Sir F_. *Spoken*, Sir F_
Wife's style, 'Lady' followed by surname
Envelope, Lady S_. *Letter (formal)*, Dear Madam; *(social)*, Dear Lady S_. *Spoken*, Lady S_
Style of Baronetess, 'Dame' before forename and surname, followed by 'Btss.' (*see also* Dames)

There are five different creations of baronetcies: Baronets of England (creations dating from 1611); Baronets of Ireland (creations dating from 1619); Baronets of Scotland or Nova Scotia (creations dating from 1625); Baronets of Great Britain (creations after the Act of Union 1707 which combined the kingdoms of England and Scotland); and Baronets of the United Kingdom (creations after the union of Great Britain and Ireland in 1801).

Badge of Baronets of the United Kingdom

Badge of Baronets of Nova Scotia

Badge of Ulster

The patent of creation limits the destination of a baronetcy, usually to male descendants of the first baronet, although special remainders allow the baronetcy to pass, if the male issue of sons fail, to the male issue of daughters of the first baronet. In the case of baronetcies of Scotland or Nova Scotia, a special remainder of 'heirs male and of tailzie' allows the baronetcy to descend to heirs general, including women. There are four existing Scottish baronets with such a remainder.

The Official Roll of the Baronetage is kept at the Crown Office and maintained by the Registrar and Assistant Registrar of the Baronetage. Anyone who considers that he or she is entitled to be entered on the roll may apply through the Crown Office to prove their succession. Every person succeeding to a baronetcy must exhibit proofs of succession to the Lord Chancellor. A person whose name is not entered on the official roll will not be addressed or mentioned by the title of baronet or baronetess in any official document, nor will he or she be accorded precedence as a baronet of baronetess.

BARONETCIES EXTINCT SINCE THE LAST EDITION

Grierson (cr. 1685); Payne-Gallwey (cr.1812)

OFFICIAL ROLL OF THE BARONETAGE, Crown Office, House of Lords, London SW1A 0PW **T** 020-7219 2632
Registrar, Ian Denyer, MVO
Assistant Registrar, Grant Bavister

KNIGHTS

Style, 'Sir' before forename and surname, followed by appropriate post-nominal initials if a Knight Grand Cross, Knight Grand Commander or Knight Commander
Envelope, Sir F_ S_. *Letter (formal)*, Dear Sir; *(social)*, Dear Sir F_. *Spoken*, Sir F_
Wife's style, 'Lady' followed by surname
'*Envelope*, Lady S_. *Letter (formal)*, Dear Madam; *(social)*, Dear Lady S_. *Spoken*, Lady S_

The prefix 'Sir' is not used by knights who are clerics of the Church of England, who do not receive the accolade. Their wives are entitled to precedence as the wife of a knight but not to the style of 'Lady'.

ORDERS OF KNIGHTHOOD

Knight Grand Cross, Knight Grand Commander, and Knight Commander are the higher classes of the Orders of Chivalry (*see* Orders of Chivalry). Honorary knighthoods of these orders may be conferred on men who are citizens of countries of which the Queen is not head of state. As a rule, the prefix 'Sir' is not used by honorary knights.

KNIGHTS BACHELOR

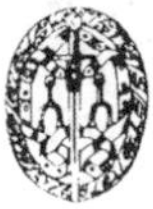

The Knights Bachelor do not constitute a royal order, but comprise the surviving representation of the ancient state orders of knighthood. The Register of Knights Bachelor, instituted by James I in the 17th century, lapsed, and in 1908 a voluntary association under the title of the Society of Knights (now the Imperial Society of Knights Bachelor) was formed with the primary objectives of continuing the various registers dating from 1257 and obtaining the uniform registration of every created Knight Bachelor. In 1926 a design for a badge to be worn by Knights Bachelor was approved and adopted; in 1974 a neck badge and miniature were added.

THE IMPERIAL SOCIETY OF KNIGHTS BACHELOR, 1 Throgmorton Avenue, London EC2N 2BY
Knight Principal, Sir Robert Balchin
Prelate, Rt. Revd and Rt. Hon. Bishop of London
Registrar, Sir Paul Judge
Hon. Treasurer, Sir Colin Berry
Clerk to the Council, Richard Jenkins, LVO, TD

LIST OF BARONETS AND KNIGHTS *as at 31 August 2008*

†	Not registered on the Official Roll of the Baronetage at the time of going to press
( )	The date of creation of the baronetcy is given in parentheses
I	Baronet of Ireland
NS	Baronet of Nova Scotia
S	Baronet of Scotland

A full entry in italic type indicates that the recipient of a knighthood died during the year in which the honour was conferred. The name is included for purposes of record. Peers are not included in this list.

Aaronson, Sir Michael John, Kt., CBE
Abbott, *Adm.* Sir Peter Charles, GBE, KCB
Abdy, Sir Valentine Robert Duff, Bt. (1850)
Acheson, *Prof.* Sir (Ernest) Donald, KBE
Ackers-Jones, Sir David, KBE, CMG
Ackroyd, Sir Timothy Robert Whyte, Bt. (1956)
Acland, Sir Antony Arthur, KG, GCMG, GCVO
Acland, *Lt.-Col.* Sir (Christopher) Guy (Dyke), Bt. (1890), MVO
Acland, Sir John Dyke, Bt. (1644)
Adam, Sir Christopher Eric Forbes, Bt. (1917)
Adam, Sir Kenneth Hugo, Kt., OBE
Adams, Sir Geoffrey Doyne, KCMG
Adams, Sir William James, KCMG
Adsetts, Sir William Norman, Kt., OBE
Adye, Sir John Anthony, KCMG
Aga Khan IV, HH Prince Karim, KBE
Agnew, Sir Crispin Hamlyn, Bt. (S. 1629)
Agnew, Sir John Keith, Bt. (1895)
Agnew, Sir Rudolph Ion Joseph, Kt.
Agnew-Somerville, Sir Quentin Charles Somerville, Bt. (1957)
Ah Koy, Sir James Michael, KBE
Aikens, *Hon.* Sir Richard John Pearson, Kt.
†Ainsworth, Sir Anthony Thomas Hugh, Bt. (1916)
Aird, *Capt.* Sir Alastair Sturgis, GCVO
Aird, Sir (George) John, Bt. (1901)
Airy, *Maj.-Gen.* Sir Christopher John, KCVO, CBE
Aitchison, Sir Charles Walter de Lancey, Bt. (1938)
Ajegbo, Sir Keith Onyema, Kt., OBE
Akenhead, *Hon.* Sir Robert, Kt.
Alberti, *Prof.* Sir Kurt George Matthew Mayer, Kt.
Albu, Sir George, Bt. (1912)
Alcock, *Air Chief Marshal* Sir (Robert James) Michael, GCB, KBE
Aldous, *Rt. Hon.* Sir William, Kt.
Alexander, Sir Charles Gundry, Bt. (1945)
Alexander, Sir Douglas, Bt. (1921)
Allen, *Prof.* Sir Geoffrey, Kt., PHD, FRS
Allen, Sir John Derek, Kt., CBE
Allen, Sir Mark John Spurgeon, Kt., CMG
Allen, *Hon.* Sir Peter Austin Philip Jermyn, Kt.
Allen, Sir Thomas Boaz, Kt., CBE
Allen, *Hon.* Sir William Clifford, KCMG
Allen, Sir William Guilford, Kt.
Alleyne, Sir George Allanmoore Ogarren, Kt.
Alleyne, *Revd* John Olpherts Campbell, Bt. (1769)
Allinson, Sir (Walter) Leonard, KCVO, CMG
Alliott, *Hon.* Sir John Downes, Kt.
Allison, *Air Chief Marshal* Sir John Shakespeare, KCB, CBE
Ambo, *Rt. Revd* George, KBE
Amet, *Hon.* Sir Arnold Karibone, Kt.
Amory, Sir Ian Heathcoat, Bt. (1874)
Anderson, *Dr* Sir James Ian Walker, Kt., CBE
Anderson, Sir John Anthony, KBE
Anderson, Sir Leith Reinsford Steven, Kt., CBE
Anderson, *Vice-Adm.* Sir Neil Dudley, KBE, CB
Anderson, *Prof.* Sir Roy Malcolm, Kt.
Anderson, Sir (William) Eric Kinloch, KT.
Anderson, *Prof.* Sir (William) Ferguson, Kt., OBE
Anderton, Sir (Cyril) James, Kt., CBE, QPM
Andrew, Sir Robert John, KCB
Andrews, Sir Derek Henry, KCB, CBE
Andrews, Sir Ian Charles Franklin, Kt., CBE, TD
Angus, Sir Michael Richardson, Kt.
Annesley, Sir Hugh Norman, Kt., QPM
Anson, *Vice-Adm.* Sir Edward Rosebery, KCB
Anson, Sir John, KCB
Anson, *Rear-Adm.* Sir Peter, Bt. CB (1831)
†Anstruther, Sir Sebastian Paten Campbell, Bt. (S. 1694)
†Anstruther, Sir Tobias Alexander Campbell, Bt. (1798)
Anstruther-Gough-Calthorpe, Sir Euan Hamilton, Bt. (1929)
Antrobus, Sir Edward Philip, Bt. (1815)
Appleyard, Sir Leonard Vincent, KCMG
Appleyard, Sir Raymond Kenelm, KBE
Arbib, Sir Martyn, Kt.
Arbuthnot, Sir Keith Robert Charles, Bt. (1823)
Arbuthnot, Sir William Reierson, Bt. (1964)
Arbuthnott, *Prof.* Sir John Peebles, Kt., PHD, FRSE
Archdale, *Capt.* Sir Edward Folmer, Bt. (1928), DSC, RN
Arculus, Sir Ronald, KCMG, KCVO
Arculus, Sir Thomas David Guy, Kt.
Armitage, *Air Chief Marshal* Sir Michael John, KCB, CBE
Armour, *Prof.* Sir James, Kt., CBE
Armstrong, Sir Christopher John Edmund Stuart, Bt. (1841), MBE
Armstrong, Sir Patrick John, Kt., CBE
Armstrong, Sir Richard, Kt., CBE
Armytage, Sir John Martin, Bt. (1738)
Arnold, Sir Thomas Richard, Kt.
Arnott, Sir Alexander John Maxwell, Bt. (1896)
Arrindell, Sir Clement Athelston, GCMG, GCVO, QC
Arthur, Sir Gavyn Farr, Kt.
Arthur, *Lt.-Gen.* Sir (John) Norman Stewart, KCB, CVO
Arthur, Sir Michael Anthony, KCMG
Arthur, Sir Stephen John, Bt. (1841)
Asbridge, Sir Jonathan Elliott, Kt.
Ash, *Prof.* Sir Eric Albert, Kt., CBE, FRS, FRENG
Ashburnham, Sir James Fleetwood, Bt. (1661)
Ashley, Sir Bernard Albert, Kt.
Ashmore, *Admiral of the Fleet* Sir Edward Beckwith, GCB, DSC
Ashworth, *Dr* Sir John Michael, Kt.
Aske, Sir Robert John Bingham, Bt. (1922)
Askew, Sir Bryan, Kt.
Asscher, Prof. Sir (Adolf) William, Kt., MD, FRCP
Astill, *Hon.* Sir Michael John, Kt.
Astley-Cooper, Sir Alexander Paston, Bt. (1821)
Aston, Sir Harold George, Kt., CBE
Astwood, *Hon.* Sir James Rufus, KBE
Atcherley, Sir Harold Winter, Kt.
Atiyah, Sir Michael Francis, Kt., OM, PHD, FRS
Atkins, *Rt. Hon.* Sir Robert James, Kt.
Atkinson, *Prof.* Sir Anthony Barnes, Kt.
Atkinson, *Air Marshal* Sir David William, KBE
Atkinson, Sir Frederick John, KCB
Atkinson, Sir John Alexander, KCB, DFC
Atkinson, Sir Robert, Kt., DSC, FRENG
Atkinson, Sir William Samuel, Kt.
Atopare, Sir Sailas, GCMG

Attenborough, Sir David Frederick, Kt., OM, CH, CVO, CBE, FRS
Aubrey-Fletcher, Sir Henry Egerton, Bt. (1782)
Audland, Sir Christopher John, KCMG
Augier, *Prof.* Sir Fitz-Roy Richard, Kt.
Auld, *Rt. Hon.* Sir Robin Ernest, Kt.
Austin, Sir Anthony Leonard, Bt. (1894)
Austin, *Air Marshal* Sir Roger Mark, KCB, AFC
Austen-Smith, *Air Marshal* Sir Roy David, KBE, CB, CVO, DFC
Avei, Sir Moi, KBE
Axford, Sir William Ian, Kt.
Ayckbourn, Sir Alan, Kt., CBE
Aykroyd, Sir James Alexander Frederic, Bt. (1929)
†Aykroyd, Sir Michael David, Bt. (1920)
Aylmer, Sir Richard John, Bt. (I. 1622)
Aynsley-Green, *Prof.* Sir Albert, Kt.
Bacha, Sir Bhinod, Kt., CMG
†Backhouse, Sir Alfred James Stott, Bt. (1901)
Bacon, Sir Nicholas Hickman Ponsonby, Bt. (1611 and 1627), *Premier Baronet of England*
Bacon, Sir Sidney Charles, Kt., CB, FRENG.
Baddeley, Sir John Wolsey Beresford, Bt. (1922)
Baddiley, *Prof.* Sir James, Kt., PHD, FRS, FRSE
Badge, Sir Peter Gilmour Noto, Kt.
Baer, Sir Jack Mervyn Frank, Kt.
Bagge, Sir (John) Jeremy Picton, Bt. (1867)
Bagnall, *Air Chief Marshal* Sir Anthony, GBE, KCB
Bailey, Sir Alan Marshall, KCB
Bailey, Sir Brian Harry, Kt., OBE
Bailey, Sir Derrick Thomas Louis, Bt. (1919), DFC
Bailey, Sir John Bilsland, KCB
Bailey, *Rt. Revd* Jonathan Sansbury, KCVO
Bailey, Sir Richard John, Kt., CBE
Bailhache, Sir Philip Martin, Kt.
Baillie, Sir Adrian Louis, Bt. (1823)
Bain, *Prof.* Sir George Sayers, Kt.
Baird, Sir Charles William Stuart, Bt. (1809)
†Baird, Sir James Andrew Gardiner, Bt. (S. 1695)
Baird, *Air Marshal* Sir John Alexander, KBE
Baird, *Vice-Adm.* Sir Thomas Henry Eustace, KCB
Bairsto, *Air Marshal* Sir Peter Edward, KBE, CB
Baker, Sir Bryan William, Kt.
Baker, *Prof.* Sir John Hamilton, Kt., QC
Baker, Sir John William, Kt., CBE
Baker, *Rt. Hon.* Sir (Thomas) Scott (Gillespie), Kt.
Balchin, Sir Robert George Alexander, Kt.
Balderstone, Sir James Schofield, Kt.
Baldwin, *Prof.* Sir Jack Edward, Kt., FRS
Baldwin, Sir Peter Robert, KCB
Ball, *Air Marshal* Sir Alfred Henry Wynne, KCB, DSO, DFC
Ball, Sir Christopher John Elinger, Kt.
Ball, *Prof.* Sir John Macleod, Kt.
Ball, Sir Richard Bentley, Bt. (1911)
Ball, *Prof.* Sir Robert James, Kt., PHD
Ballantyne, *Dr* Sir Frederick Nathaniel, GCMG
Bamford, Sir Anthony Paul, Kt.
Band, *Adm.* Sir Jonathon, GCB
Banham, Sir John Michael Middlecott, Kt.
Bannerman, Sir David Gordon, Bt., OBE (S. 1682)
Bannister, Sir Roger Gilbert, Kt., CBE, DM, FRCP
Barber, Sir Michael Bayldon, Kt.
Barber, Sir (Thomas) David, Bt. (1960)
Barbour, *Very Revd* Robert Alexander Stewart, KCVO, MC
Barclay, Sir Colville Herbert Sanford, Bt. (S. 1668)
Barclay, Sir David Rowat, Kt.
Barclay, Sir Frederick Hugh, Kt.
Barclay, Sir Peter Maurice, Kt., CBE
Barder, Sir Brian Leon, KCMG
Baring, Sir John Francis, Bt. (1911)
Barker, Sir Colin, Kt.
Barker, *Hon.* Sir (Richard) Ian, Kt.
Barling, *Hon.* Sir Gerald Edward, Kt.
Barlow, Sir Christopher Hilaro, Bt. (1803)
Barlow, Sir Frank, Kt., CBE
Barlow, Sir (George) William, Kt., FRENG
Barlow, Sir James Alan, Bt. (1902)
Barlow, Sir John Kemp, Bt. (1907)
Barnard, Sir Joseph Brian, Kt.
Barnes, *The Most Revd.* Brian James, KBE
Barnes, Sir (James) David (Francis), Kt., CBE
Barnes, Sir Kenneth, KCB
Barnewall, Sir Reginald Robert, Bt. (I. 1623)
Baron, Sir Thomas, Kt., CBE
Barran, Sir John Napoleon Ruthven, Bt. (1895)
Barratt, Sir Lawrence Arthur, Kt.
Barratt, Sir Richard Stanley, Kt., CBE, QPM
Barrett, Sir Stephen Jeremy, KCMG
†Barrett-Lennard,Sir Richard Fynes, Bt. (1801)
Barrington, Sir Benjamin, Bt. (1831)
Barrington, Sir Nicholas John, KCMG, CVO
Barrington-Ward, *Rt. Revd* Simon, KCMG
Barron, Sir Donald James, Kt.
Barrow, *Capt.* Sir Richard John Uniacke, Bt. (1835)
Barry, Sir (Lawrence) Edward (Anthony Tress), Bt. (1899)
Barter, Sir Peter Leslie Charles, Kt., OBE
†Bartlett, Sir Andrew Alan, Bt. (1913)
Barttelot, *Col.* Sir Brian Walter de Stopham, Bt. (1875), OBE
Bate, Sir David Lindsay, KBE
†Bates, Sir James Geoffrey, Bt. (1880)
Bates, Sir Malcolm Rowland, Kt.
Bates, Sir Richard Dawson Hoult, Bt. (1937)
Bateson, *Prof.* Sir Patrick, Kt.
Batho, Sir Peter Ghislain, Bt. (1928)
Bathurst, *Admiral of the Fleet* Sir (David) Benjamin, GCB
Batten, Sir John Charles, KCVO
Battersby, *Prof.* Sir Alan Rushton, Kt., FRS
Battishill, Sir Anthony Michael William, GCB
Baxendell, Sir Peter Brian, Kt., CBE, FRENG
Bayly, *Prof.* Sir Christopher Alan, Kt.
Bayne, Sir Nicholas Peter, KCMG
Baynes, Sir Christopher Rory, Bt. (1801)
Bazley, Sir Thomas John Sebastian, Bt. (1869)
Beach, *Gen.* Sir (William Gerald) Hugh, GBE, KCB, MC
Beache, *Hon.* Sir Vincent Ian, KCMG
Beale, *Lt.-Gen.* Sir Peter John, KBE, FRCP
Beamish, Sir Adrian John, KCMG
Bean, *Hon.* Sir David Michael, Kt
Beaumont, *Capt.* the Hon. Sir (Edward) Nicholas (Canning), KCVO
Beaumont, Sir George (Howland Francis), Bt. (1661)
Beaumont, Sir Richard Ashton, KCMG, OBE
Beatson, *Hon.* Sir Jack, Kt.
Beavis, *Air Chief Marshal* Sir Michael Gordon, KCB, CBE, AFC
Beck, Sir Edgar Philip, Kt.
Beckett, Sir Richard Gervase, Bt. (1921), QC
Beckett, Sir Terence Norman, KBE, FRENG
Beckwith, Sir John Lionel, Kt., CBE
Bedser, Sir Alec Victor, Kt., CBE
Beecham, Sir Jeremy Hugh, Kt.
Beecham, Sir John Stratford Roland, Bt. (1914)
Beetham, *Marshal of the Royal Air Force* Sir Michael James, GCB, CBE, DFC, AFC
Beevor, Sir Thomas Agnew, Bt. (1784)
Beith, *Rt. Hon.* Sir Alan James, Kt.
Beldam, *Rt. Hon.* Sir (Alexander) Roy (Asplan), Kt.
Belich, Sir James, Kt.
Bell, Sir Brian Ernest, KBE
Bell, Sir David Charles Maurice, Kt.
Bell, *Prof.* Sir John Irving, Kt.
Bell, Sir John Lowthian, Bt. (1885)
Bell, *Prof.* Sir Peter Robert Frank, Kt.
Bell, *Hon.* Sir Rodger, Kt.

Bell, Sir Stuart, Kt.
Bellamy, *Hon.* Sir Christopher William, Kt.
Bellingham, Sir Anthony Edward Norman, Bt. (1796)
Bender, Sir Brian Geoffrey, KCB
Benn, Sir (James) Jonathan, Bt. (1914)
Bennett, *Air Vice-Marshal* Sir Erik Peter, KBE, CB
Bennett, *Hon.* Sir Hugh Peter Derwyn, Kt.
Bennett, *Gen.* Sir Phillip Harvey, KBE, DSO
Bennett, Sir Richard Rodney, Kt., CBE
Bennett, Sir Ronald Wilfrid Murdoch, Bt. (1929)
Benson, Sir Christopher John, Kt.
Benyon, Sir William Richard, Kt.
Beresford, Sir (Alexander) Paul, Kt.
Beresford-Peirse, Sir Henry Grant de la Poer, Bt. (1814)
Berghuser, *Hon.* Sir Eric, Kt., MBE
Beringer, *Prof.* Sir John Evelyn, Kt., CBE
Berman, Sir Franklin Delow, KCMG
Berners-Lee, Sir Timothy John, OM, KBE, FRS
Bernard, Sir Dallas Edmund, Bt. (1954)
Bernstein, Sir Howard, Kt.
Berney, Sir Julian Reedham Stuart, Bt. (1620)
Berridge, *Prof.* Sir Michael John, Kt., FRS
Berrill, Sir Kenneth Ernest, GBE, KCB
Berriman, Sir David, Kt.
Berry, *Prof.* Sir Colin Leonard, Kt., FRCPATH
Berry, *Prof.* Sir Michael Victor, Kt., FRS
Berthoud, Sir Martin Seymour, KCVO, CMG
Best, Sir Richard Radford, KCVO, CBE
Best-Shaw, Sir John Michael Robert, Bt. (1665)
Bethel, Sir Baltron Benjamin, KCMG
Bett, Sir Michael, Kt., CBE
Bettison, Sir Norman George, Kt., QPM
Bevan, Sir Martyn Evan Evans, Bt. (1958)
Bevan, Sir Nicolas, Kt., CB
Bevan, Sir Timothy Hugh, Kt.
Beverley, *Lt.-Gen.* Sir Henry York La Roche, KCB, OBE, RM
Bibby, Sir Michael James, Bt. (1959)
Bichard, Sir Michael George, KCB
Bickersteth, *Rt. Revd* John Monier, KCVO
Biddulph, Sir Ian D'Olier, Bt. (1664)
Bidwell, Sir Hugh Charles Philip, GBE
Biggam, Sir Robin Adair, Kt.
Biggs, Sir Norman Paris, Kt.
Bilas, Sir Angmai Simon, Kt., OBE
Billière, *Gen.* Sir Peter Edgar de la Cour de la, KCB, KBE, DSO, MC
Bindman, Sir Geoffrey Lionel, Kt.
Bingham, *Hon.* Sir Eardley Max, Kt.
Birch, Sir John Allan, KCVO, CMG
Birch, Sir Roger, Kt., CBE, QPM
Bird, Sir Richard Geoffrey Chapman, Bt. (1922)
Birkin, Sir John Christian William, Bt. (1905)
Birkin, Sir (John) Derek, Kt., TD
Birkmyre, Sir James, Bt. (1921)
Birrell, Sir James Drake, Kt.
Birtwistle, Sir Harrison, Kt., CH
Bischoff, Sir Winfried Franz Wilhelm, Kt.
Bishop, Sir Michael David, Kt., CBE
Bisson, *Rt. Hon.* Sir Gordon Ellis, Kt.
Black, Sir James Whyte, Kt., OM, FRCP, FRS
Black, *Adm.* Sir (John) Jeremy, GBE, KCB, DSO
Black, Sir Robert David, Bt. (1922)
Blackburn, *Vice-Adm.* Sir David Anthony James, KCVO, CB, LVO
Blackburne, *Hon.* Sir William Anthony, Kt.
Blackett, Sir Hugh Francis, Bt. (1673)
Blackham, *Vice-Adm.* Sir Jeremy Joe, KCB
Blackman, Sir Frank Milton, KCVO, OBE
Blair, *Lt.-Gen.* Sir Chandos, KCVO, OBE, MC
†Blair, Sir Patrick David Hunter, Bt. (1786)
Blair, *Hon.* Sir William James Lynton, Kt.
Blair, Sir Ian Warwick, Kt., QPM
Blake, Sir Alfred Lapthorn, KCVO, MC
Blake, Sir Francis Michael, Bt. (1907)
Blake, *Hon.* Sir Nicholas John Gorrod, Kt.
Blake, Sir Peter Thomas, Kt., CBE
Blake, Sir Anthony Teilo Bruce, Bt. (I. 1622)
Blaker, Sir John, Bt. (1919)
Blakiston, Sir Ferguson Arthur James, Bt. (1763)
Blanch, Sir Malcolm, KCVO
Bland, Sir (Francis) Christopher (Buchan), Kt.
Bland, *Lt.-Col.* Sir Simon Claud Michael, KCVO
Blank, Sir Maurice Victor, Kt.
Blatherwick, Sir David Elliott Spiby, KCMG, OBE
Blelloch, Sir John Nial Henderson, KCB
Blennerhassett, Sir (Marmaduke) Adrian Francis William, Bt. (1809)
Blewitt, *Maj.* Sir Shane Gabriel Basil, GCVO
Blofeld, *Hon.* Sir John Christopher Calthorpe, Kt.
Blois, Sir Charles Nicholas Gervase, Bt. (1686)
Blom-Cooper, Sir Louis Jacques, Kt., QC
Blomefield, Sir Thomas Charles Peregrine, Bt. (1807)
Bloomfield, Sir Kenneth Percy, KCB
Blundell, Sir Thomas Leon, Kt., FRS
Blunden, Sir George, Kt.
Blunden, Sir Philip Overington, Bt. (I. 1766)
Blunt, Sir David Richard Reginald Harvey, Bt. (1720)
Blyth, Sir Charles (Chay), Kt., CBE, BEM
Boardman, *Prof.* Sir John, Kt., FSA, FBA
Bodey, *Hon.* Sir David Roderick Lessiter, Kt.
Bodmer, Sir Walter Fred, Kt., PHD, FRS
Body, Sir Richard Bernard Frank Stewart, Kt.
Bogan, Sir Nagora, KBE
Boileau, Sir Guy (Francis), Bt. (1838)
Boles, Sir Jeremy John Fortescue, Bt. (1922)
Boles, Sir John Dennis, Kt., MBE
Bolland, Sir Edwin, KCMG
Bolt, *Air Marshal* Sir Richard Bruce, KBE, CB, DFC, AFC
Bona, Sir Kina, KBE
Bonallack, Sir Michael Francis, Kt., OBE
Bond, Sir John Reginald Hartnell, Kt.
Bond, *Prof.* Sir Michael Richard, Kt., FRCPSYCH, FRCPGLAS, FRCSE
Bone, *Prof.* Sir James Drummond, Kt., FRSE
Bone, Sir Roger Bridgland, KCMG
Bonfield, Sir Peter Leahy, Kt., CBE, FRENG
Bonham, *Maj.* Sir Antony Lionel Thomas, Bt. (1852)
Bonington, Sir Christian John Storey, Kt., CBE
Bonsall, Sir Arthur Wilfred, KCMG, CBE
Bonsor, Sir Nicholas Cosmo, Bt. (1925)
Boord, Sir Nicolas John Charles, Bt. (1896)
Boorman, *Lt.-Gen.* Sir Derek, KCB
Booth, Sir Christopher Charles, Kt., MD, FRCP
Booth, Sir Clive, Kt.
Booth, Sir Douglas Allen, Bt. (1916)
Booth, Sir Gordon, KCMG, CVO
Boothby, Sir Brooke Charles, Bt. (1660)
Bore, Sir Albert, Kt.
Boreel, Sir Stephan Gerard, Bt. (1645)
Borthwick, Sir Anthony Thomas, Bt. (1908)
Borysiewicz, *Prof.* Sir Leszek Krzysztof, Kt.
Bossom, *Hon.* Sir Clive, Bt. (1953)
Boswell, *Lt.-Gen.* Sir Alexander Crawford Simpson, KCB, CBE
Bosworth, Sir Neville Bruce Alfred, Kt., CBE
Botham, Sir Ian Terence, Kt., OBE
Bottoms, *Prof.* Sir Anthony Edward, Kt.
Bottomley, Sir James Reginald Alfred, KCMG

Boughey, Sir John George Fletcher, Bt. (1798)
Boulton, Sir Clifford John, GCB
Boulton, Sir William Whytehead, Bt. (1944), CBE, TD
Bouraga, Sir Phillip, KBE
Bourn, Sir John Bryant, KCB
Bowater, Sir Euan David Vansittart, Bt. (1939)
†Bowater, Sir Michael Patrick, Bt. (1914)
Bowden, Sir Andrew, Kt., MBE
Bowden, Sir Nicholas Richard, Bt. (1915)
Bowen, Sir Barry Manfield, KCMG
Bowen, Sir Geoffrey Fraser, Kt.
Bowen, Sir Mark Edward Mortimer, Bt. (1921)
Bowes Lyon, Sir Simon Alexander, KCVO
Bowett, *Prof.* Sir Derek William, Kt., CBE, QC, FBA
†Bowlby, Sir Richard Peregrine Longstaff, Bt. (1923)
Bowman, Sir Edwin Geoffrey, KCB
Bowman, Sir Jeffery Haverstock, Kt.
Bowman-Shaw, Sir (George) Neville, Kt.
Bowness, Sir Alan, Kt., CBE
Bowyer-Smyth, Sir Thomas Weyland, Bt. (1661)
Boyce, Sir Graham Hugh, KCMG
Boyce, Sir Robert Charles Leslie, Bt. (1952)
Boyd, Sir Alexander Walter, Bt. (1916)
Boyd, Sir John Dixon Iklé, KCMG
Boyd, *Prof.* Sir Robert David Hugh, Kt.
Boyd-Carpenter, Sir (Marsom) Henry, KCVO
Boyd-Carpenter, *Lt.-Gen. Hon.* Sir Thomas Patrick John, KBE
Boyle, Sir Stephen Gurney, Bt. (1904)
Boyson, *Rt. Hon.* Sir Rhodes, Kt.
Brabham, Sir John Arthur, Kt., OBE
Bracewell-Smith, Sir Charles, Bt. (1947)
Bradbeer, Sir John Derek Richardson, Kt., OBE, TD
Bradfield, *Dr* Sir John Richard Grenfell, Kt., CBE
Bradford, Sir Edward Alexander Slade, Bt. (1902)
Brady, *Prof.* Sir John Michael, Kt., FRS
Braithwaite, *Rt. Hon.* Sir Nicholas Alexander, Kt., OBE
Braithwaite, Sir Rodric Quentin, GCMG
Bramley, *Prof.* Sir Paul Anthony, Kt.
Branson, Sir Richard Charles Nicholas, Kt.
Bratza, *Hon.* Sir Nicolas Dušan, Kt.
Breckenridge, *Prof.* Sir Alasdair Muir, Kt., CBE
Brennan, *Hon.* Sir (Francis) Gerard, KBE
Brenton, Sir Anthony Russell, KCMG
Brewer, Sir David William, Kt., CMG
Brierley, Sir Ronald Alfred, Kt.
Briggs, *Hon.* Sir Michael Townley Featherstone, Kt.
Bright, Sir Graham Frank James, Kt.
Bright, Sir Keith, Kt.
Brigstocke, *Adm.* Sir John Richard, KCB
Brinckman, Sir Theodore George Roderick, Bt. (1831)
†Brisco, Sir Campbell Howard, Bt. (1782)
Briscoe, Sir Brian Anthony, Kt.
Briscoe, Sir John Geoffrey James, Bt. (1910)
Brittan, Sir Samuel, Kt.
†Broadbent, Sir Andrew George, Bt. (1893)
Broadbent, Sir Richard John, KCB
Brocklebank, Sir Aubrey Thomas, Bt. (1885)
Brodie, Sir Benjamin David Ross, Bt. (1834)
Brodie-Hall, Sir Laurence Charles, Kt., AO, CMG
Brooke, Sir Rodney George, Kt., CBE
Brooking, Sir Trevor, Kt., CBE
Bromhead, Sir John Desmond Gonville, Bt. (1806)
Bromley, Sir Michael Roger, KBE
Bromley, Sir Rupert Charles, Bt. (1757)
Brook, *Prof.* Sir Richard John, Kt. OBE
†Brooke, Sir Alistair Weston, Bt. (1919)
Brooke, Sir Francis George Windham, Bt. (1903)
Brooke, *Rt. Hon.* Sir Henry, Kt.
Brooke, Sir (Richard) David Christopher, Bt. (1662)
Brooking, Sir Trevor David, Kt., CBE
Brooks, Sir Timothy Gerald Martin, KCVO
Brooksbank, Sir (Edward) Nicholas, Bt. (1919)
Broomfield, Sir Nigel Hugh Robert Allen, KCMG
†Broughton, Sir David Delves, Bt. (1661)
Broun, Sir Wayne Hercules, Bt. (S. 1686)
Brown, Sir (Austen) Patrick, KCB
Brown, *Adm.* Sir Brian Thomas, KCB, CBE
Brown, Sir (Cyril) Maxwell Palmer, KCB, CMG
Brown, Sir David, Kt.
Brown, *Hon.* Sir Douglas Dunlop, Kt.
Brown, Sir George Francis Richmond, Bt. (1863)
Brown, Sir George Noel, Kt.
Brown, Sir Mervyn, KCMG, OBE
Brown, Sir Peter Randolph, Kt.
Brown, *Rt. Hon.* Sir Stephen, GBE
Brown, Sir Stephen David Reid, KCVO
Browne, Sir Nicholas Walker, KBE, CMG
Brownrigg, Sir Nicholas (Gawen), Bt. (1816)
Browse, *Prof.* Sir Norman Leslie, Kt., MD, FRCS
Bruce, Sir (Francis) Michael Ian, Bt. (S. 1628)
Bruce-Clifton, Sir Hervey James Hugh, Bt. (1804)
Bruce-Gardner, Sir Robert Henry, Bt. (1945)
Brunner, Sir Hugo Laurence Joseph, KCVO
Brunner, Sir John Henry Kilian, Bt. (1895)
Brunton, Sir (Edward Francis) Lauder, Bt. (1908)
Brunton, Sir Gordon Charles, Kt.
Bryan, Sir Arthur, Kt.
Buchan-Hepburn, Sir John Alastair Trant Kidd, Bt. (1815)
Buchanan, Sir Andrew George, Bt. (1878)
Buchanan, *Vice-Adm.* Sir Peter William, KBE
Buchanan, Sir Robert Wilson (Robin), Kt.
Buchanan-Jardine, *Maj.* Sir (Andrew) Rupert (John), Bt. (1885), MC
Buckland, Sir Ross, Kt.
Buckley, Sir Michael Sidney, Kt.
Buckley, *Lt.-Cdr.* Sir (Peter) Richard, KCVO
Buckley, *Hon.* Sir Roger John, Kt.
Buckworth-Herne-Soame, Sir Charles John, Bt. (1697)
Budd, Sir Alan Peter, Kt.
Budd, Sir Colin Richard, KCMG
Bull, Sir George Jeffrey, Kt.
Bull, Sir Simeon George, Bt. (1922)
Bullock, Sir Stephen Michael, Kt.
Bultin, Sir Bato, Kt., MBE
Bunbury, Sir Michael William, Bt. (1681), KCVO
Bunyard, Sir Robert Sidney, Kt., CBE, QPM
Burbidge, Sir Peter Dudley, Bt. (1916)
Burden, Sir Anthony Thomas, Kt., QPM
Burdett, Sir Savile Aylmer, Bt. (1665)
Burgen, Sir Arnold Stanley Vincent, Kt., FRS
Burgess, *Gen.* Sir Edward Arthur, KCB, OBE
Burgess, Sir (Joseph) Stuart, Kt., CBE, PHD, FRSC
Burgh, Sir John Charles, KCMG, CB
Burke, Sir James Stanley Gilbert, Bt. (I. 1797)
Burke, Sir (Thomas) Kerry, Kt.
Burnell-Nugent, *Vice-Adm.* Sir James Michael, KCB, CBE, ADC
Burnet, Sir James William Alexander (Sir Alastair Burnet), Kt.
Burnett, *Air Chief Marshal* Sir Brian Kenyon, GCB, DFC, AFC
Burnett, Sir Charles David, Bt., (1913)
Burnett, Sir Walter John, Kt.
Burney, Sir Nigel Dennistoun, Bt. (1921)
Burns, Sir (Robert) Andrew, KCMG
Burnton, *Hon.* Sir Stanley Jeffrey, Kt.
Burrell, Sir Charles Raymond, Bt. (1774)

Burridge, *Air Chief Marshal* Sir Brian Kevin, KCB, CBE, ADC
Burston, Sir Samuel Gerald Wood, Kt., OBE
Burt, Sir Peter Alexander, Kt.
Burton, Sir Carlisle Archibald, Kt., OBE
Burton, Sir George Vernon Kennedy, Kt., CBE
Burton, *Lt.-Gen.* Sir Edmund Fortescue Gerard, KBE
Burton, Sir Graham Stuart, KCMG
Burton, *Hon.* Sir Michael John, Kt.
Burton, Sir Michael St Edmund, KCVO, CMG
Bush, *Adm.* Sir John Fitzroy Duyland, GCB, DSC
Butler, *Hon.* Sir Arlington Griffith, KCMG
Butler, Sir Michael Dacres, GCMG
Butler, Sir (Reginald) Michael (Thomas), Bt. (1922)
Butler, Sir Percy James, Kt., CBE
Butler, *Hon.* Sir Richard Clive, Kt.
Butler, Sir Richard Pierce, Bt. (1628)
Butter, *Maj.* Sir David Henry, KCVO, MC
Butterfield, *Hon.* Sir Alexander Neil Logie, Kt.
Butterfill, Sir John Valentine, Kt.
Buxton, Sir Jocelyn Charles Roden, Bt. (1840)
Buxton, *Rt. Hon.* Sir Richard Joseph, Kt.
Buzzard, Sir Anthony Farquhar, Bt. (1929)
Byatt, Sir Hugh Campbell, KCVO, CMG
Byatt, Sir Ian Charles Rayner, Kt.
Byford, Sir Lawrence, Kt., CBE, QPM
Byron, *Rt. Hon.* Sir Charles Michael Dennis, Kt.
†Cable-Alexander, Sir Patrick Desmond William, Bt. (1809)
Cadbury, Sir (George) Adrian (Hayhurst), Kt.
Cadbury, Sir (Nicholas) Dominic, Kt.
Cadogan, *Prof.* Sir John Ivan George, Kt., CBE, FRS, FRSE
Cahn, Sir Albert Jonas, Bt. (1934)
Cain, Sir Henry Edney Conrad, Kt.
Caine, Sir Michael (Maurice Micklewhite), Kt., CBE
Caines, Sir John, KCB
Caldwell, Sir Edward George, KCB
Callaghan, Sir William Henry, Kt.
Callan, Sir Ivan Roy, KCVO, CMG
Calman, *Prof.* Sir Kenneth Charles, KCB, MD, FRCP, FRCS, FRSE
Calne, *Prof.* Sir Roy Yorke, Kt., FRS
Calvert-Smith, Sir David, Kt., QC
Cameron, Sir Hugh Roy Graham, Kt., QPM
Campbell, *Prof.* Sir Colin Murray, Kt.
Campbell, Sir Ian Tofts, Kt., CBE, VRD
Campbell, Sir Ilay Mark, Bt. (1808)
Campbell, Sir James Alexander Moffat Bain, Bt. (S. 1668)
Campbell, Sir Lachlan Philip Kemeys, Bt. (1815)
Campbell, Sir Roderick Duncan Hamilton, Bt. (1831)
Campbell, Sir Robin Auchinbreck, Bt. (S. 1628)
Campbell, *Rt. Hon.* Sir Walter Menzies, Kt., CBE, QC
Campbell, *Rt. Hon.* Sir William Anthony, Kt.
Campbell-Orde, Sir John Alexander, Bt. (1790)
†Carden, Sir Christopher Robert, Bt. (1887)
†Carden, Sir John Craven, Bt. (I. 1787)
Carew, Sir Rivers Verain, Bt. (1661)
Carey, Sir de Vic Graham, Kt.
Carey, Sir Peter Willoughby, GCB
Carleton-Smith, *Maj.-Gen.* Sir Michael Edward, Kt., CBE
Carlisle, Sir James Beethoven, GCMG
Carlisle, Sir John Michael, Kt.
Carlisle, Sir Kenneth Melville, Kt.
Carnegie, *Lt.-Gen.* Sir Robin Macdonald, KCB, OBE
Carnegie, Sir Roderick Howard, Kt.
Carnwath, *Rt. Hon.* Sir Robert John Anderson, Kt., CVO
Caro, Sir Anthony Alfred, Kt., OM, CBE
Carr, Sir (Albert) Raymond (Maillard), Kt.
Carr, Sir Peter Derek, Kt., CBE
Carr, *Very Revd Dr* Arthur Wesley, KCVO
Carr-Ellison, *Col.* Sir Ralph Harry, KCVO, TD
Carrick, *Hon.* Sir John Leslie, KCMG
Carrick, Sir Roger John, KCMG, LVO
Carruthers, Sir Ian James, Kt., OBE
Carsberg, *Prof.* Sir Bryan Victor, Kt.
Carter, *Prof.* Sir David Craig, Kt., FRCSE, FRCSGLAS, FRCPE
Carter, Sir John Alexander, Kt.
Carter, Sir John Gordon Thomas, Kt.
Carter, Sir Philip David, Kt., CBE
Carter, Sir Richard Henry Alwyn, Kt.
Cartledge, Sir Bryan George, KCMG
Cary, Sir Roger Hugh, Bt. (1955)
Casey, *Rt. Hon.* Sir Maurice Eugene, Kt.
Cass, Sir Geoffrey Arthur, Kt.
Cassel, Sir Timothy Felix Harold, Bt. (1920)
Cassels, Sir John Seton, Kt., CB
Cassels, *Adm.* Sir Simon Alastair Cassillis, KCB, CBE
Cassidi, *Adm.* Sir (Arthur) Desmond, GCB
Castell, Sir William Martin, Kt.
Castledine, *Prof.* Sir George, Kt.
Catherwood, Sir (Henry) Frederick (Ross), Kt.
Catto, *Prof.* Sir Graeme Robertson Dawson, Kt.
Cave, Sir John Charles, Bt. (1896)
Cave-Browne-Cave, Sir Robert, Bt. (1641)
Cayley, Sir Digby William David, Bt. (1661)
Cayzer, Sir James Arthur, Bt. (1904)
Cazalet, *Hon.* Sir Edward Stephen, Kt.
Cazalet, Sir Peter Grenville, Kt.
Cecil, *Rear-Adm.* Sir (Oswald) Nigel Amherst, KBE, CB
Chadwick, *Rt. Hon.* Sir John Murray, Kt.
Chadwick, Sir Joshua Kenneth Burton, Bt. (1935)
Chadwick, *Revd Prof.* (William) Owen, OM, KBE, FBA
Chadwyck-Healey, Sir Charles Edward, Bt. (1919)
Chakrabarti, Sir Sumantra, KCB
Chalmers, Sir Iain Geoffrey, Kt.
Chalmers, Sir Neil Robert, Kt.
Chalstrey, Sir (Leonard) John, Kt., MD, FRCS
Chan, *Rt. Hon.* Sir Julius, GCMG, KBE
Chan, Sir Thomas Kok, Kt., OBE
Chance, Sir (George) Jeremy ffolliott, Bt. (1900)
Chandler, Sir Colin Michael, Kt.
Chandler, Sir Geoffrey, Kt., CBE
Chantler, *Prof.* Sir Cyril, Kt., MD, FRCP
Chaplin, Sir Malcolm Hilbery, Kt., CBE
Chapman, Sir David Robert Macgowan, Bt. (1958)
Chapman, Sir George Alan, Kt.
Chapman, Sir Sidney Brookes, Kt., MP
Chapple, *Field Marshal* Sir John Lyon, GCB, CBE
Charles, *Hon.* Sir Arthur William Hessin, Kt.
Charlton, Sir Robert (Bobby), Kt., CBE
Charnley, Sir (William) John, Kt., CB, FRENG
Chataway, *Rt. Hon.* Sir Christopher, Kt.
Chatfield, Sir John Freeman, Kt., CBE
†Chaytor, Sir Bruce Gordon, Bt. (1831)
Checketts, *Sqn. Ldr.* Sir David John, KCVO
Checkland, Sir Michael, Kt.
Cheshire, *Air Chief Marshal* Sir John Anthony, KBE, CB
Chessells, Sir Arthur David (Tim), Kt.
†Chetwynd, Sir Robin John Talbot, Bt. (1795)
Cheyne, Sir Patrick John Lister, Bt. (1908)
†Chichester, Sir James Henry Edward, Bt. (1641)
Chichester-Clark, Sir Robin, Kt.
Chilcot, *Rt. Hon.* Sir John Anthony, GCB
Child, Sir (Coles John) Jeremy, Bt. (1919)
Chilton, *Brig.* Sir Frederick Oliver, Kt., CBE, DSO
Chilwell, *Hon.* Sir Muir Fitzherbert, Kt.
Chinn, Sir Trevor Edwin, Kt., CVO

Chipperfield, Sir Geoffrey Howes, KCB
Chisholm, Sir John Alexander Raymond, Kt., FRENG
Chitty, Sir Thomas Willes, Bt. (1924)
Cholmeley, Sir Hugh John Frederick Sebastian, Bt. (1806)
Chow, Sir Chung Kong, Kt.
Chow, Sir Henry Francis, Kt., OBE
Christie, Sir George William Langham, Kt., CH
Christie, Sir William, Kt., MBE
Christopher, Sir Duncan Robin Carmichael, KBE, CMG
Chung, Sir Sze-yuen, GBE, FRENG
Clark, Sir Francis Drake, Bt. (1886)
Clark, Sir John Arnold, Kt.
Clark, Sir Jonathan George, Bt. (1917)
Clark, Sir Robert Anthony, Kt., DSC
Clark, Sir Terence Joseph, KBE, CMG, CVO
Clarke, *Rt. Hon.* Sir Anthony Peter, Kt.
Clarke, Sir (Charles Mansfield) Tobias, Bt. (1831)
Clarke, *Hon.* Sir Christopher Simon Courtenay Stephenson, Kt.
Clarke, Sir Christopher James, Kt., OBE
Clarke, *Hon.* Sir David Clive, Kt.
Clarke, Sir Ellis Emmanuel Innocent, GCMG
Clarke, Sir Jonathan Dennis, Kt.
Clarke, Sir Robert Cyril, Kt.
†Clarke, Sir Rupert Grant Alexander, Bt. (1882)
Clay, Sir Edward, KCMG
Clay, Sir Richard Henry, Bt. (1841)
Clayton, Sir David Robert, Bt. (1732)
Cleaver, Sir Anthony Brian, Kt.
Clementi, Sir David Cecil, Kt.
Cleminson, Sir James Arnold Stacey, KBE, MC
Clerk, Sir Robert Maxwell, Bt. (1679), OBE
Clerke, Sir John Edward Longueville, Bt. (1660)
Clifford, Sir Roger Joseph, Bt. (1887)
Clifford, Sir Timothy Peter Plint, Kt.
Clothier, Sir Cecil Montacute, KCB, QC
Clucas, Sir Kenneth Henry, KCB
Clutterbuck, *Vice-Adm.* Sir David Granville, KBE, CB
Coates, Sir Anthony Robert Milnes, Bt. (1911)
Coates, Sir David Frederick Charlton, Bt. (1921)
Coats, Sir Alastair Francis Stuart, Bt. (1905)
Coats, Sir William David, Kt.
Cochrane, Sir (Henry) Marc (Sursock), Bt. (1903)
Cockburn, Sir John Elliot, Bt. (S. 1671)
Cockburn-Campbell, Sir Alexander Thomas, Bt. (1821)
Cockshaw, Sir Alan, Kt., FRENG
†Codrington, Sir Christopher George Wayne, Bt. (1876)
Codrington, Sir William Alexander, Bt. (1721)
Coghill, Sir Patrick Kendal Farley, Bt. (1778)
Coghlin, *Hon.* Sir Patrick, Kt.
Cohen, Sir Edward, Kt.
Cohen, Sir Ivor Harold, Kt., CBE, TD
Cohen, *Prof.* Sir Philip, Kt., PHD, FRS
Cohen, Sir Ronald, Kt.
Cole, Sir (Robert) William, Kt.
Coleman, Sir Robert John, KCMG
Coleridge, *Hon.* Sir Paul James Duke, Kt.
Coles, Sir (Arthur) John, GCMG
Colfox, Sir (William) John, Bt. (1939)
Collett, Sir Christopher, GBE
Collett, Sir Ian Seymour, Bt. (1934)
Collins, Sir Alan Stanley, KCVO, CMG
Collins, *Hon.* Sir Andrew David, Kt.
Collins, Sir Bryan Thomas Alfred, Kt., OBE, QFSM
Collins, Sir John Alexander, Kt
Collins, Sir Kenneth Darlingston, Kt.
Collins, *Hon.* Sir Lawrence Antony, Kt.
Collyear, Sir John Gowen, Kt.
Colman, *Hon.* Sir Anthony David, Kt.
Colman, Sir Michael Jeremiah, Bt. (1907)
Colman, Sir Timothy, KG
†Colquhoun of Luss, Sir Malcolm Rory, Bt. (1786)
Colt, Sir Edward William Dutton, Bt. (1694)
Colthurst, Sir Charles St John, Bt. (1744)
Conant, Sir John Ernest Michael, Bt. (1954)
Connell, *Hon.* Sir Michael Bryan, Kt.
Connery, Sir Sean, Kt.
Connor, Sir William Joseph, Kt.
Conran, Sir Terence Orby, Kt.
Cons, *Hon.* Sir Derek, Kt.
Constantinou, Sir Georkios, Kt., OBE
Conway, *Prof.* Sir Gordon Richard, KCMG, FRS
Cook, Sir Christopher Wymondham Rayner Herbert, Bt. (1886)
Cook, *Prof.* Sir Peter Frederic Chester, Kt.
Cooke, *Col.* Sir David William Perceval, Bt. (1661)
Cooke, Sir Howard Felix Hanlan, GCMG, GCVO
Cooke, *Hon.* Sir Jeremy Lionel, Kt.
Cooke, *Prof.* Sir Ronald Urwick, Kt.
Cooksey, Sir David James Scott, GBE
Cooper, *Gen.* Sir George Leslie Conroy, GCB, MC
Cooper, Sir Henry, Kt.
Cooper, Sir Richard Adrian, Bt. (1905)
Cooper, *Maj.-Gen.* Sir Simon Christie, GCVO
Cooper, Sir William Daniel Charles, Bt. (1863)
Coote, Sir Christopher John, Bt. (I. 1621), *Premier Baronet of Ireland*
Copas, *Most Revd* Virgil, KBE
Copisarow, Sir Alcon Charles, Kt.
Corbett, *Maj.-Gen.* Sir Robert John Swan, KCVO, CB
Corby, Sir (Frederick) Brian, Kt.
Cordy-Simpson, *Lt.-Gen.* Sir Roderick Alexander, KBE, CB
Corfield, Sir Kenneth George, Kt., FRENG
Cormack, Sir Patrick Thomas, Kt.
Corness, Sir Colin Ross, Kt.
Cornforth, Sir John Warcup, Kt., CBE, DPHIL, FRS
Corry, Sir James Michael, Bt. (1885)
Cortazzi, Sir (Henry Arthur) Hugh, GCMG
Cory, Sir (Clinton Charles) Donald, Bt. (1919)
Cory-Wright, Sir Richard Michael, Bt. (1903)
Cossons, Sir Neil, Kt., OBE
Cotter, Sir Patrick Laurence Delaval, Bt. (I. 1763)
Cotterell, Sir John Henry Geers, Bt. (1805)
Cotton, *Hon.* Sir Robert Carrington, KCMG
Cottrell, Sir Alan Howard, Kt., PHD, FRS, FRENG
†Cotts, Sir Richard Crichton Mitchell, Bt. (1921)
Coulson, *Hon.* Sir Peter David William, Kt.
Couper, Sir James George, Bt. (1841)
Court, *Hon.* Sir Charles Walter Michael, KCMG, OBE
Courtenay, Sir Thomas Daniel, Kt.
Cousins, *Air Chief Marshal* Sir David, KCB, AFC
Coville, *Air Marshal* Sir Christopher Charles Cotton, KCB
Cowan, *Gen.* Sir Samuel, KCB, CBE
Coward, *Vice-Adm.* Sir John Francis, KCB, DSO
Cowen, *Rt. Hon. Prof.* Sir Zelman, GCMG, GCVO
Cowie, Sir Thomas (Tom), Kt., OBE
Cowper-Coles, Sir Sherard Louis, KCMG, LVO
Cox, Sir Alan George, Kt., CBE
Cox, *Prof.* Sir David Roxbee, Kt.
Cox, Sir George Edwin, Kt.
Cradock, *Rt. Hon.* Sir Percy, GCMG
Craft, *Prof.* Sir Alan William, Kt.
Craig, Sir (Albert) James (Macqueen), GCMG
Craig-Cooper, Sir (Frederick Howard) Michael, Kt., CBE, TD
Crane, *Hon.* Sir Peter Francis, Kt.
Crane, *Prof.* Sir Peter Robert, Kt.
Cranston, *Hon.* Sir Ross Frederick, Kt.
Craufurd, Sir Robert James, Bt. (1781)
Craven, Sir John Anthony, Kt.
Craven, Sir Philip Lee, Kt., MBE
Crawford, *Prof.* Sir Frederick William, Kt., FRENG
Crawford, Sir Robert William Kenneth, Kt. CBE

Crawley-Boevey, Sir Thomas Michael Blake, Bt. (1784)
Crew, Sir (Michael) Edward, Kt., QPM
Crewe, *Prof.* Sir Ivor Martin, Kt.
Cresswell, *Hon.* Sir Peter John, Kt.
Crichton-Brown, Sir Robert, KCMG, CBE, TD
Crick, *Prof.* Sir Bernard, Kt.
Crisp, Sir John Charles, Bt. (1913)
Critchett, Sir Charles George Montague, Bt. (1908)
Crockett, Sir Andrew Duncan, Kt.
Croft, Sir Owen Glendower, Bt. (1671)
Croft, Sir Thomas Stephen Hutton, Bt. (1818)
†Crofton, Sir Hugh Denis, Bt. (1801)
Crofton, *Prof.* Sir John Wenman, Kt.
†Crofton, Sir Julian Malby, Bt. (1838)
Crompton, Sir Dan, Kt., CBE, QPM
Crosby, Sir James Robert, Kt.
Crossland, *Prof.* Sir Bernard, Kt., CBE, FRENG
Crossley, Sir Sloan Nicholas, Bt. (1909)
Crowe, Sir Brian Lee, KCMG
Cruickshank, Sir Donald Gordon, Kt.
Cruthers, Sir James Winter, Kt.
Cubbon, Sir Brian Crossland, GCB
Cubitt, Sir Hugh Guy, Kt., CBE
Cullen, Sir (Edward) John, Kt., FRENG
Culme-Seymour, Sir Michael Patrick, Bt. (1809)
Culpin, Sir Robert Paul, Kt.
Cummins, Sir Michael John Austin, Kt.
Cunliffe, *Prof.* Sir Barrington, Kt., CBE
Cunliffe, Sir David Ellis, Bt. (1759)
Cunliffe-Owen, Sir Hugo Dudley, Bt. (1920)
Cunningham, *Lt.-Gen.* Sir Hugh Patrick, KBE
Cunningham, Sir Roger Keith, Kt., CBE
Cunynghame, Sir Andrew David Francis, Bt. (S. 1702)
†Currie, Sir Donald Scott, Bt. (1847)
Curry, Sir Donald Thomas Younger, Kt., CBE
Curtain, Sir Michael, KBE
Curtis, Sir Barry John, Kt.
Curtis, *Hon.* Sir Richard Herbert, Kt.
Curtis, Sir William Peter, Bt. (1802)
Curtiss, *Air Marshal* Sir John Bagot, KCB, KBE
Curwen, Sir Christopher Keith, KCMG
Cuschieri, *Prof.* Sir Alfred, Kt.
Dain, Sir David John Michael, KCVO
Dales, Sir Richard Nigel, KCVO
Dalrymple-Hay, Sir John Hugh, Bt. (1798)
†Dalrymple-White, Sir Jan Hew, Bt. (1926)
Dalton, *Vice-Adm.* Sir Geoffrey Thomas James Oliver, KCB
Dalton, Sir Richard John, KCMG
Dalyell, Sir Tam (Thomas), Bt. (NS 1685)
Daniel, Sir John Sagar, Kt., DSC
Dankworth, Sir John, Kt., CBE
Dannatt, *Lt.-Gen.* Sir Francis Richard, KCB, CBE
Darell, Sir Jeffrey Lionel, Bt. (1795), MC
Darling, Sir Clifford, GCVO
Darrington, Sir Michael John, Kt.
Darroch, Sir Nigel Kim, KCMG
Dasgupta, *Prof.* Sir Partha Sarathi, Kt.
†Dashwood, Sir Edward John Francis, Bt. (1707), *Premier Baronet of Great Britain*
Dashwood, Sir Richard James, Bt. (1684)
Daunt, Sir Timothy Lewis Achilles, KCMG
Davenport-Handley, Sir David John, Kt., OBE
David, Sir Jean Marc, Kt., CBE, QC
David, *His Hon.* Sir Robin (Robert) Daniel George, Kt.
Davies, Sir Alan Seymour, Kt.
Davies, Sir (Charles) Noel, Kt.
Davies, *Prof.* Sir David Evan Naughton, Kt., CBE, FRS, FRENG
Davies, *Hon.* Sir (David Herbert) Mervyn, Kt., MC, TD
Davies, Sir David John, Kt.
Davies, Sir Frank John, Kt., CBE
Davies, *Prof.* Sir Graeme John, Kt., FRENG
Davies, Sir John Howard, Kt.
Davies, Sir John Michael, KCB
Davies, *Vice-Adm.* Sir Lancelot Richard Bell, KBE
Davies, Sir Peter Maxwell, Kt., CBE
Davies, Sir Rhys Everson, Kt., QC
Davis, Sir Andrew Frank, Kt., CBE
Davis, Sir Colin Rex, Kt., CH, CBE
Davis, Sir Crispin Henry Lamert, Kt.
Davis, Sir John Gilbert, Bt. (1946)
Davis, *Hon.* Sir Nigel Anthony Lambert, Kt.
Davis, Sir Peter John, Kt.
Davis, *Hon.* Sir Thomas Robert Alexander Harries, KBE
Davis-Goff, Sir Robert (William), Bt. (1905)
Davison, *Rt. Hon.* Sir Ronald Keith, GBE, CMG
†Davson, Sir George Trenchard Simon, Bt. (1927)
Dawanincura, Sir John Norbert, Kt., OBE
Dawbarn, Sir Simon Yelverton, KCVO, CMG
Dawson, *Hon.* Sir Daryl Michael, KBE, CB
Dawson, Sir Hugh Michael Trevor, Bt. (1920)
Dawtry, Sir Alan (Graham), Kt., CBE, TD
Day, Sir Derek Malcolm, KCMG
Day, *Air Chief Marshal* Sir John Romney, KCB, OBE, ADC
Day, Sir (Judson) Graham, Kt.
Day, Sir Michael John, Kt., OBE
Day, Sir Simon James, Kt.
Deane, *Hon.* Sir William Patrick, KBE
Dearlove, Sir Richard Billing, KCMG, OBE
de Bellaigue, Sir Geoffrey, GCVO
†Debenham, Sir Thomas Adam, Bt. (1931)
de Deney, Sir Geoffrey Ivor, KCVO
Deeny, *Hon.* Sir Donnell Justin Patrick, Kt.
de Hoghton, Sir (Richard) Bernard (Cuthbert), Bt. (1611)
De la Bère, Sir Cameron, Bt. (1953)
de la Rue, Sir Andrew George Ilay, Bt. (1898)
De Silva, Sir George Desmond Lorenz, Kt., QC
Dellow, Sir John Albert, Kt., CBE
Delves, *Lt.-Gen.* Sir Cedric Norman George, KBE
Denholm, Sir John Ferguson (Ian), Kt., CBE
Denison-Smith, *Lt.-Gen.* Sir Anthony Arthur, KBE
Denny, Sir Anthony Coningham de Waltham, Bt. (I. 1782)
Denny, Sir Charles Alistair Maurice, Bt. (1913)
Derbyshire, Sir Andrew George, Kt.
Derham, Sir Peter John, Kt.
de Trafford, Sir Dermot Humphrey, Bt. (1841)
Deverell, *Gen.* Sir John Freegard, KCB, OBE
Devesi, Sir Baddeley, GCMG, GCVO
De Ville, Sir Harold Godfrey Oscar, Kt., CBE
Devitt, Sir James Hugh Thomas, Bt. (1916)
de Waal, Sir (Constant Henrik) Henry, KCB, QC
Dewey, Sir Anthony Hugh, Bt. (1917)
De Witt, Sir Ronald Wayne, Kt.
Dhenin, *Air Marshal* Sir Geoffrey Howard, KBE, AFC, GM, MD
Dhrangadhara, HH Maharaja Shriraj Sahib of Halvad, KCIE
Dick-Lauder, Sir Piers Robert, Bt. (S. 1690)
Dickinson, Sir Harold Herbert, Kt.
Dilke, Sir Charles John Wentworth, Bt. (1862)
Dillwyn-Venables-Llewelyn, Sir John Michael, Bt. (1890)
Dixon, Sir Jeremy, Kt.
Dixon, Sir Jonathan Mark, Bt. (1919)
Djanogly, Sir Harry Ari Simon, Kt., CBE
Dobson, *Vice-Adm.* Sir David Stuart, KBE
Dodds, Sir Ralph Jordan, Bt. (1964)
Dollery, Sir Colin Terence, Kt.
Don-Wauchope, Sir Roger (Hamilton), Bt. (S. 1667)
Donald, Sir Alan Ewen, KCMG
Donald, *Air Marshal* Sir John George, KBE
Donaldson, *Prof.* Sir Liam Joseph, Kt.
Donne, *Hon.* Sir Gaven John, KBE

Donne, Sir John Christopher, Kt.
Donnelly, Sir Joseph Brian, KBE, CMG
Dorey, Sir Graham Martyn, Kt.
Dorman, Sir Philip Henry Keppel, Bt. (1923)
Doughty, Sir Graham Martin, Kt.
Doughty, Sir William Roland, Kt.
Douglas, *Hon.* Sir Roger Owen, Kt.
Dover, *Prof.* Sir Kenneth James, Kt., DLITT, FBA, FRSE
Dowell, Sir Anthony James, Kt., CBE
Dowling, Sir Robert, Kt.
Downes, Sir Edward Thomas, Kt., CBE
Downey, Sir Gordon Stanley, KCB
Downs, Sir Diarmuid, Kt., CBE, FRENG
Downward, *Maj.-Gen.* Sir Peter Aldcroft, KCVO, CB, DSO, DFC
Dowson, Sir Philip Manning, Kt., CBE, PRA
Doyle, Sir Reginald Derek Henry, Kt., CBE
D'Oyly, Sir Hadley Gregory Bt. (1663)
Drake, *Hon.* Sir (Frederick) Maurice, Kt., DFC
Drewry, *Lt.-Gen.* Sir Christopher Francis, KCB, CBE
Drinkwater, Sir John Muir, Kt., QC
Driver, Sir Eric William, Kt.
Drury, Sir (Victor William) Michael, Kt., OBE
Dryden, Sir John Stephen Gyles, Bt. (1733 and 1795)
du Cann, *Rt. Hon.* Sir Edward Dillon Lott, KBE
†Duckworth, Sir James Edward Dyce, Bt. (1909)
du Cros, Sir Claude Philip Arthur Mallet, Bt. (1916)
Dudley-Williams, Sir Alastair Edgcumbe James, Bt. (1964)
Duff, *Prof.* Sir Gordon William, Kt.
Duff-Gordon, Sir Andrew Cosmo Lewis, Bt. (1813)
Duffell, *Lt.-Gen.* Sir Peter Royson, KCB, CBE, MC
Duffy, Sir (Albert) (Edward) Patrick, Kt., PHD
Dugdale, Sir William Stratford, Bt. (1936), MC
Duggin, Sir Thomas Joseph, Kt.
Dummett, *Prof.* Sir Michael Anthony Eardley, Kt., FBA
Dunbar, Sir Archibald Ranulph, Bt. (S. 1700)
Dunbar, Sir Robert Drummond Cospatrick, Bt. (S. 1698)
Dunbar, Sir James Michael, Bt. (S. 1694)
Dunbar of Hempriggs, Sir Richard Francis, Bt. (S. 1706)
Dunbar-Nasmith, *Prof.* Sir James Duncan, Kt., CBE
Duncan, Sir James Blair, Kt.
Dunlop, Sir Thomas, Bt. (1916)
Dunn, *Rt. Hon.* Sir Robin Horace Walford, Kt., MC
Dunne, Sir Thomas Raymond, KG, KCVO
Dunning, Sir Simon William Patrick, Bt. (1930)
Dunnington-Jefferson, Sir Mervyn Stewart, Bt. (1958)
Dunstan, *Lt.-Gen.* Sir Donald Beaumont, KBE, CB
Dunt, *Vice-Adm.* Sir John Hugh, KCB
Duntze, Sir Daniel Evans Bt. (1774)
Dupre, Sir Tumun, Kt., MBE
Dupree, Sir (Thomas William James) David, Bt. (1921)
Durand, Sir Edward Alan Christopher David Percy, Bt. (1892)
Durant, Sir (Robert) Anthony (Bevis), Kt.
Durie, Sir David Robert Campbell, KCMG
Durrant, Sir William Alexander Estridge, Bt. (1784)
Duthie, *Prof.* Sir Herbert Livingston, Kt.
Duthie, Sir Robert Grieve (Robin), Kt., CBE
Dwyer, Sir Joseph Anthony, Kt.
Dyke, Sir David William Hart, Bt. (1677)
Dymock, *Vice-Adm.* Sir Anthony Knox, KBE, CB
Dyson, Sir James, Kt., CBE
Dyson, *Rt. Hon.* Sir John Anthony, Kt.
Eady, *Hon.* Sir David, Kt.
Eardley-Wilmot, Sir Michael John Assheton, Bt. (1821)
Earle, Sir (Hardman) George (Algernon), Bt. (1869)
Easton, Sir Robert William Simpson, Kt., CBE
Eaton, *Adm.* Sir Kenneth John, GBE, KCB
Eberle, *Adm.* Sir James Henry Fuller, GCB
Ebrahim, Sir (Mahomed) Currimbhoy, Bt. (1910)
Eckersley, Sir Donald Payze, Kt., OBE
Eddington, Sir Roderick Ian, Kt.
Edge, *Capt.* Sir (Philip) Malcolm, KCVO
†Edge, Sir William, Bt. (1937)
Edmonstone, Sir Archibald Bruce Charles, Bt. (1774)
Edward, *Rt. Hon.* Sir David Alexander Ogilvy, KCMG
Edwardes, Sir Michael Owen, Kt.
Edwards, Sir Christopher John Churchill, Bt. (1866)
Edwards, *Prof.* Sir Christopher Richard Watkin, Kt.
Edwards, Sir Llewellyn Roy, Kt.
Edwards, *Prof.* Sir Samuel Frederick, Kt., FRS
†Edwards-Moss, Sir David John, Bt. (1868)
Egan, Sir John Leopold, Kt.
Ehrman, Sir William Geoffrey, KCMG
Eichelbaum, *Rt. Hon.* Sir Thomas, GBE
Elder, Sir Mark Philip, Kt., CBE
Elias, *Hon.* Sir Patrick, Kt.
Eliott of Stobs, Sir Charles Joseph Alexander, Bt. (S. 1666)
Elliot, Sir Gerald Henry, Kt.
Elliott, Sir Clive Christopher Hugh, Bt. (1917)
Elliott, Sir David Murray, KCMG, CB
Elliott, *Prof.* Sir John Huxtable, Kt., FBA
Elliott, Sir Randal Forbes, KBE
Elliott, *Prof.* Sir Roger James, Kt., FRS
Elphinstone, Sir John, Bt. (S. 1701)
Elphinstone, Sir John Howard Main, Bt. (1816)
Elsmore, Sir Lloyd, Kt., OBE
Elton, Sir Arnold, Kt., CBE
Elton, Sir Charles Abraham Grierson, Bt. (1717)
Elton, Sir Leslie, Kt.
Elvidge, Sir John, KCB
Elwes, Sir Jeremy Vernon, Kt., CBE
Elwood, Sir Brian George Conway, Kt., CBE
Elworthy, *Air Cdre. Hon.* Sir Timothy Charles, KCVO, CBE
Empey, Sir Reginald Norman Morgan, Kt., OBE
Enderby, *Prof.* Sir John Edwin, Kt. CBE, FRS
Engle, Sir George Lawrence Jose, KCB, QC
English, Sir Terence Alexander Hawthorne, KBE, FRCS
Epstein, *Prof.* Sir (Michael) Anthony, Kt., CBE, FRS
Errington, *Col.* Sir Geoffrey Frederick, Bt. (1963), OBE
Errington, Sir Lancelot, KCB
Erskine, Sir (Thomas) Peter Neil, Bt. (1821)
Erskine-Hill, Sir Alexander Rodger, Bt. (1945)
Esmonde, Sir Thomas Francis Grattan, Bt. (I. 1629)
Esplen, Sir John Graham, Bt. (1921)
Essenhigh, *Adm.* Sir Nigel Richard, GCB
Etherton, *Hon.* Sir Terence Michael Elkan Barnet, Kt.
Evans, Sir Anthony Adney, Bt. (1920)
Evans, *Rt. Hon.* Sir Anthony Howell Meurig, Kt., RD
Evans, *Prof.* Sir Christopher Thomas, Kt., OBE
Evans, *Air Chief Marshal* Sir David George, GCB, CBE
Evans, *Hon.* Sir David Roderick, Kt.
Evans, Sir Harold Matthew, Kt.
Evans, *Hon.* Sir Haydn Tudor, Kt.
Evans, *Prof.* Sir John Grimley, Kt., FRCP
Evans, Sir John Stanley, Kt., QPM
Evans, *Prof.* Sir Martin John, Kt., FRS
Evans, Sir Richard Harry, Kt., CBE
Evans, Sir Richard Mark, KCMG, KCVO
Evans, Sir Robert, Kt., CBE, FRENG
Evans-Lombe, *Hon.* Sir Edward Christopher, Kt.
†Evans-Tipping, Sir David Gwynne, Bt. (1913)

Eveleigh, *Rt. Hon.* Sir Edward Walter, Kt., ERD
Everard, Sir Robin Charles, Bt. (1911)
Every, Sir Henry John Michael, Bt. (1641)
Ewans, Sir Martin Kenneth, KCMG
†Ewart, Sir William Michael, Bt. (1887)
Ewbank, *Hon.* Sir Anthony Bruce, Kt.
Eyre, Sir Reginald Edwin, Kt.
Eyre, Sir Richard Charles Hastings, Kt., CBE
Fagge, Sir John Christopher Frederick, Bt. (1660)
Fairbairn, Sir (James) Brooke, Bt. (1869)
Fairlie-Cuninghame, Sir Robert Henry, Bt. (S. 1630)
Fairweather, Sir Patrick Stanislaus, KCMG
†Falkiner, Sir Benjamin Simon Patrick, Bt. (I. 1778)
Fall, Sir Brian James Proetel, GCVO, KCMG
Falle, Sir Samuel, KCMG, KCVO, DSC
Fang, *Prof.* Sir Harry, Kt., CBE
Fareed, Sir Djamil Sheik, Kt.
Farmer, Sir Thomas, Kt., CBE
Farquhar, Sir Michael Fitzroy Henry, Bt. (1796)
Farquharson, *Rt. Hon.* Sir Donald Henry, Kt.
Farrell, Sir Terence, Kt., CBE
Farrer, Sir (Charles) Matthew, GCVO
Farrington, Sir Henry William, Bt. (1818)
Fat, Sir (Maxime) Edouard (Lim Man) Lim, Kt.
Faulkner, Sir (James) Dennis (Compton), Kt., CBE, VRD
Fay, Sir (Humphrey) Michael Gerard, Kt.
Fayrer, Sir John Lang Macpherson, Bt. (1896)
Feachem, *Prof.* Sir Richard George Andrew, KBE
Fean, Sir Thomas Vincent, KCVO
Feilden, Sir Bernard Melchior, Kt., CBE
Feilden, Sir Henry Wemyss, Bt., (1846)
Fell, Sir David, KCB
Fender, Sir Brian Edward Frederick, Kt., CMG, PHD
Fenn, Sir Nicholas Maxted, GCMG
Fennell, *Hon.* Sir (John) Desmond Augustine, Kt., OBE
Fennessy, Sir Edward, Kt., CBE
Fenwick, Sir Leonard Raymond, Kt., CBE
Fergus, Sir Howard Archibald, KBE
Ferguson, Sir Alexander Chapman, Kt., CBE
Ferguson-Davie, Sir Michael, Bt. (1847)
Fergusson of Kilkerran, Sir Charles, Bt. (S. 1703)
Fergusson, Sir Ewan Alastair John, GCMG, GCVO
Fermor, Sir Patrick Michael Leigh, Kt., DSO, OBE
Feroze, Sir Rustam Moolan, Kt., FRCS
Fersht, *Prof.* Sir Alan Roy, Kt., FRS
Ferris, *Hon.* Sir Francis Mursell, Kt., TD
ffolkes, Sir Robert Francis Alexander, Bt. (1774), OBE
Field, Sir Malcolm David, Kt.
Field, *Hon.* Sir Richard Alan, Kt.
Fielding, Sir Colin Cunningham, Kt., CB
Fielding, Sir Leslie, KCMG
Fields, Sir Allan Clifford, KCMG
Fieldsend, *Hon.* Sir John Charles Rowell, KBE
Fiennes, Sir Ranulph Twisleton-Wykeham, Bt. (1916), OBE
Figg, Sir Leonard Clifford William, KCMG
Figgis, Sir Anthony St John Howard, KCVO, CMG
Finch, Sir Robert Gerard, Kt.
Finlay, Sir David Ronald James Bell, Bt. (1964)
Finlayson, Sir Garet Orlando, KCMG, OBE
Finney, Sir Thomas, Kt., OBE
Fison, Sir (Richard) Guy, Bt. (1905), DSC
†Fitzgerald, *Revd* Daniel Patrick, Bt. (1903)
FitzGerald, Sir Adrian James Andrew, Bt. (1880)
FitzHerbert, Sir Richard Ranulph, Bt. (1784)
Fitzpatrick, *Air Marshal* Sir John Bernard, KBE, CB
Flanagan, Sir Ronald, GBE
Flaux, *Hon.* Sir Julian Martin, Kt.
Floissac, *Hon.* Sir Vincent Frederick, Kt., CMG, OBE
Floud, *Prof.* Sir Roderick Castle, Kt.
Floyd, *Hon.* Sir Christopher David, Kt.
Floyd, Sir Giles Henry Charles, Bt. (1816)
Foley, *Lt.-Gen.* Sir John Paul, KCB, OBE, MC
Follett, *Prof.* Sir Brian Keith, Kt., FRS
Foot, Sir Geoffrey James, Kt.
Foots, Sir James William, Kt.
†Forbes, Sir James Thomas Stewart, Bt. (1823)
Forbes, *Adm.* Sir Ian Andrew, KCB, CBE
Forbes of Craigievar, Sir Andrew Iain Ochoncar, Bt. (S. 1630)
Forbes, *Vice-Adm.* Sir John Morrison, KCB
Forbes, *Hon.* Sir Thayne John, Kt.
Forbes-Leith, Sir George Ian David, Bt. (1923)
Ford, Sir Andrew Russell, Bt. (1929)
Ford, Sir David Robert, KBE, LVO
Ford, *Prof.* Sir Hugh, Kt., FRS, FRENG
Ford, Sir John Archibald, KCMG, MC
Ford, *Gen.* Sir Robert Cyril, GCB, CBE
Foreman, Sir Philip Frank, Kt., CBE, FRENG
Forestier-Walker, Sir Michael Leolin, Bt. (1835)
Forman, Sir John Denis, Kt., OBE
Forrest, *Prof.* Sir (Andrew) Patrick (McEwen), Kt.
Forte, Hon. Sir Rocco John Vincent, Kt.
Forwood, Sir Peter Noel, Bt. (1895)
Foskett, *Hon.* Sir David Robert, Kt.
Foster, Sir Andrew William, Kt.
Foster, *Prof.* Sir Christopher David, Kt.
Foster, Sir John Gregory, Bt. (1930)
Foulkes, Sir Arthur Alexander, KCMG
Foulkes, Sir Nigel Gordon, Kt.
Fountain, *Hon.* Sir Cyril Stanley Smith, Kt.
Fowden, Sir Leslie, Kt., FRS
Fowke, Sir David Frederick Gustavus, Bt. (1814)
Fowler, Sir (Edward) Michael Coulson, Kt.
Fox, Sir Christopher, Kt., QPM
Fox, Sir Paul Leonard, Kt., CBE
France, Sir Christopher Walter, GCB
Francis, Sir Horace William Alexander, Kt., CBE, FRENG
Frank, Sir Robert Andrew, Bt. (1920)
Franklin, Sir Michael David Milroy, KCB, CMG
Franks, Sir Arthur Temple, KCMG
Fraser, Sir Alasdair MacLeod, Kt.
Fraser, Sir Charles Annand, KCVO
Fraser, *Gen.* Sir David William, GCB, OBE
Fraser, Sir Iain Michael Duncan, Bt. (1943)
Fraser, Sir James Murdo, KBE
Fraser, Sir William Kerr, GCB
Frayling, *Prof.* Sir Christopher John, Kt.
Frederick, Sir Christopher St John, Bt. (1723)
Freedman, *Prof.* Sir Lawrence David, KCMG, CBE
Freeland, Sir John Redvers, KCMG
Freeman, Sir James Robin, Bt. (1945)
Freer, *Air Chief Marshal* Sir Robert William George, GBE, KCB
French, *Air Marshal* Sir Joseph Charles, KCB, CBE
Frere, *Vice-Adm.* Sir Richard Tobias, KCB
Fretwell, Sir (Major) John (Emsley), GCMG
Freud, Sir Clement Raphael, Kt.
Friend *Prof.* Sir Richard Henry, Kt.
Froggatt, Sir Leslie Trevor, Kt.
Froggatt, Sir Peter, Kt.
Frossard, Sir Charles Keith, KBE
Frost, Sir David Paradine, Kt., OBE
Fry, Sir Graham Holbrook, KCMG
Fry, Sir Peter Derek, Kt.
Fry, *Lt.-Gen.* Sir Robert Allan, KCB, CBE
Fulford, *Hon.* Sir Adrian Bruce, Kt.

Fuller, Sir James Henry Fleetwood, Bt. (1910)
Fuller, *Hon.* Sir John Bryan Munro, Kt.
Fulton, *Lt.-Gen.* Sir Robert Henry Gervase, KBE
Furness, Sir Stephen Roberts, Bt. (1913)
Gage, *Rt. Hon.* Sir William Marcus, Kt.
Gains, Sir John Christopher, Kt.
Gainsford, Sir Ian Derek, Kt.
Gaius, *Rt. Revd* Saimon, KBE
Galsworthy, Sir Anthony Charles, KCMG
Galway, Sir James, Kt., OBE
Gamble, Sir David Hugh Norman, Bt. (1897)
Gambon, Sir Michael John, Kt., CBE
Gammell, Sir William Benjamin Bowring, Kt.
Gardiner, Sir John Eliot, Kt., CBE
Gardner, *Prof.* Sir Richard Lavenham, Kt.
Gardner, Sir Roy Alan, Kt.
Garland, *Hon.* Sir Patrick Neville, Kt.
Garland, *Hon.* Sir Ransley Victor, KBE
Garner, Sir Anthony Stuart, Kt.
Garnett, *Adm.* Sir Ian David Graham, KCB
Garnier, *Rear-Adm.* Sir John, KCVO, CBE
Garrard, Sir David Eardley, Kt.
Garrett, Sir Anthony Peter, Kt., CBE
Garrick, Sir Ronald, Kt., CBE, FRENG
Garrioch, Sir (William) Henry, Kt.
Garrod, *Lt.-Gen.* Sir (John) Martin Carruthers, KCB, OBE
Garthwaite, Sir (William) Mark (Charles), Bt. (1919)
Gaskell, Sir Richard Kennedy Harvey, Kt.
Geno, Sir Makena Viora, KBE
Gent, Sir Christopher Charles, Kt.
George, Sir Arthur Thomas, Kt.
George, *Prof.* Sir Charles Frederick, MD, FRCP
George, Sir Richard William, Kt., CVO
Gerken, *Vice-Adm.* Sir Robert William Frank, KCB, CBE
Gershon, Sir Peter Oliver, Kt., CBE
Gethin, Sir Richard Joseph St Lawrence, Bt. (I. 1665)
Ghurburrun, Sir Rabindrah, Kt.
Gibb, Sir Francis Ross (Frank), Kt., CBE, FRENG
Gibbings, Sir Peter Walter, Kt.
Gibbons, Sir (John) David, KBE
Gibbons, Sir William Edward Doran, Bt. (1752)
Gibbs, *Hon.* Sir Richard John Hedley, Kt.
Gibbs, Sir Roger Geoffrey, Kt.
†Gibson, *Revd* Christopher Herbert, Bt. (1931)
Gibson, Sir Ian, Kt., CBE
Gibson, *Rt. Hon.* Sir Peter Leslie, Kt.
Gibson-Craig-Carmichael, Sir David Peter William, Bt. (S. 1702 and 1831)
Giddings, *Air Marshal* Sir (Kenneth Charles) Michael, KCB, OBE, DFC, AFC
Gieve, Sir Edward John Watson, KCB
Giffard, Sir (Charles) Sydney (Rycroft), KCMG
Gilbart-Denham, *Lt.-Col.* Sir Seymour Vivian, KCVO
Gilbert, *Air Chief Marshal* Sir Joseph Alfred, KCB, CBE
Gilbert, Sir Martin John, Kt., CBE
†Gilbey, Sir Walter Gavin, Bt. (1893)
Gill, Sir Anthony Keith, Kt.
Gill, Sir Arthur Benjamin Norman, Kt., CBE
Gillam, Sir Patrick John, Kt.
Gillen, *Hon.* Sir John de Winter, Kt.
Gillett, Sir Robin Danvers Penrose, Bt. (1959), GBE, RD
Gillinson, Sir Clive Daniel, Kt., CBE
†Gilmour, Sir John, Bt. (1897)
Gina, Sir Lloyd Maepeza, KBE
Gingell, *Air Chief Marshal* Sir John, GBE, KCB, KCVO
Giordano, Sir Richard Vincent, KBE
Girolami, Sir Paul, Kt.
Girvan, *Rt. Hon.* Sir (Frederick) Paul, Kt.
Gladstone, Sir (Erskine) William, Bt. (1846), KG
Glenn, Sir (Joseph Robert) Archibald, Kt., OBE
Glidewell, *Rt. Hon.* Sir Iain Derek Laing, Kt.
Glover, Sir Victor Joseph Patrick, Kt.
Glyn, Sir Richard Lindsay, Bt. (1759 and 1800)
Gobbo, Sir James Augustine, Kt., AC
Godber, Sir George Edward, GCB, DM
Goldberg, *Prof.* Sir David Paul Brandes, Kt.
Goldring, *Hon.* Sir John Bernard, Kt.
Gomersall, Sir Stephen John, KCMG
Gonsalves-Sabola, *Hon.* Sir Joaquim Claudino, Kt
†Gooch, Sir Miles Peter, Bt. (1866)
†Gooch, Sir Arthur Brian Sherlock Heywood, Bt. (1746)
Good, Sir John James Griffen, Kt. CBE
Goodall, Sir (Arthur) David Saunders, GCMG
Goodall, *Air Marshal* Sir Roderick Harvey, KBE, CB, AFC
Goode, Prof. Sir Royston Miles, Kt., CBE, QC
Goodenough, Sir Anthony Michael, KCMG
Goodenough, Sir William McLernon, Bt. (1943)
Goodhart, Sir Philip Carter, Kt.
Goodhart, Sir Robert Anthony Gordon, Bt. (1911)
Goodison, Sir Nicholas Proctor, Kt.
Goodman, Sir Patrick Ledger, Kt., CBE
Goodson, Sir Mark Weston Lassam, Bt. (1922)
Goodwin, Sir Frederick, KBE
Goodwin, Sir Frederick Anderson, Kt.
Goodwin, Sir Matthew Dean, Kt., CBE
Goody, *Prof.* Sir John Rankine, Kt.
†Goold, Sir George William, Bt. (1801)
Gordon, Sir Charles Addison Somerville Snowden, KCB
Gordon, Sir Donald, Kt.
Gordon, Sir Gerald Henry, Kt., CBE, QC
Gordon, Sir Robert James, Bt. (S. 1706)
Gordon-Cumming, Sir Alexander Penrose, Bt. (1804)
†Gore, Sir Nigel Hugh St George, Bt. (I. 1622)
Gore-Booth, Sir Josslyn Henry Robert, Bt. (I. 1760)
Goring, Sir William Burton Nigel, Bt. (1627)
Gorman, Sir John Reginald, Kt., CVO, CBE, MC
Gorst, Sir John Michael, Kt.
Goschen, Sir (Edward) Alexander, Bt. (1916)
Gosling, Sir (Frederick) Donald, KCVO
Goswell, Sir Brian Lawrence, Kt.
Gough, Sir Charles Brandon, Kt.
Goulden, Sir (Peter) John, GCMG
Goulding, Sir Marrack Irvine, KCMG
Goulding, Sir (William) Lingard Walter, Bt. (1904)
Gourlay, *Gen.* Sir (Basil) Ian (Spencer), KCB, OBE, MC, RM
Gourlay, Sir Simon Alexander, Kt.
Govan, Sir Lawrence Herbert, Kt.
Gow, *Gen.* Sir (James) Michael, GCB
Gowans, Sir James Learmonth, Kt., CBE, FRCP, FRS
Gozney, Sir Richard Hugh Turton, KCMG
†Graaff, Sir David de Villiers, Bt. (1911)
Grabham, Sir Anthony Henry, Kt.
Graham, *Dr* Sir Albert Cecil, Kt.
Graham, Sir Alexander Michael, GBE
Graham, Sir James Bellingham, Bt. (1662)
Graham, Sir James Fergus Surtees, Bt. (1783)
Graham, Sir James Thompson, Kt., CMG
Graham, Sir John Alexander Noble, Bt. (1906), GCMG
Graham, Sir John Alistair, Kt.
Graham, Sir John Moodie, Bt. (1964)
Graham, Sir Norman William, Kt., CB
Graham, Sir Peter, KCB, QC
Graham, Sir Peter Alfred, Kt., OBE
Graham, *Lt.-Gen.* Sir Peter Walter, KCB, CBE
†Graham, Sir Ralph Stuart, Bt. (1629)

Graham-Moon, Sir Peter Wilfred Giles, Bt. (1855)
Graham-Smith, *Prof.* Sir Francis, Kt.
Granger, *Prof.* Sir Clive William John, Kt.
Grant, Sir Archibald, Bt. (S. 1705)
Grant, Sir Clifford, Kt.
Grant, Sir (John) Anthony, Kt.
Grant, Sir John Douglas Kelso, KCMG
Grant, Sir Patrick Alexander Benedict, Bt. (S. 1688)
Grant, *Lt.-Gen.* Sir Scott Carnegie, KCB
Grant-Suttie, Sir James Edward, Bt. (S. 1702)
Granville-Chapman, *Lt.-Gen.* Sir Timothy John, GBE, KCB, ADC
Gratton-Bellew, Sir Henry Charles, Bt. (1838)
Gray, *Hon.* Sir Charles Anthony St John, Kt.
Gray, Sir Charles Ireland, Kt., CBE
Gray, *Prof.* Sir Denis John Pereira, Kt., OBE, FRCGP
Gray, Sir John Archibald Browne, Kt., SCD, FRS
Gray, *Dr.* Sir John Armstrong Muir, Kt., CBE
Gray, *Lt.-Gen.* Sir Michael Stuart, KCB, OBE
Gray, Sir Robert McDowall (Robin), Kt.
Gray, Sir William Hume, Bt. (1917)
Graydon, *Air Chief Marshal* Sir Michael James, GCB, CBE
Grayson, Sir Jeremy Brian Vincent Harrington, Bt. (1922)
Green, Sir Allan David, KCB, QC
Green, Sir Andrew Fleming, KCMG
Green, Sir Edward Patrick Lycett, Bt. (1886)
Green, Sir Gregory David, KCMG
Green, *Hon.* Sir Guy Stephen Montague, KBE
Green, Sir Kenneth, Kt.
Green, *Prof.* Sir Malcolm, Kt.
Green, Sir Owen Whitley, Kt.
Green, Sir Philip Green, Kt.
Green-Price, Sir Robert John, Bt. (1874)
Greenaway, Sir John Michael Burdick, Bt. (1933)
Greenbury, Sir Richard, Kt.
Greener, Sir Anthony Armitage, Kt.
Greengross, Sir Alan David, Kt.
Greening, *Rear-Adm.* Sir Paul Woollven, GCVO
Greenstock, Sir Jeremy Quentin, GCMG
Greenwell, Sir Edward Bernard, Bt. (1906)
Gregson, Sir Peter Lewis, GCB
Greig, Sir (Henry Louis) Carron, KCVO, CBE
Grey, Sir Anthony Dysart, Bt. (1814)
Grey-Egerton, Sir (Philip) John (Caledon), Bt. (1617)
Grierson, Sir Ronald Hugh, Kt.
Griffin, *Maj.* Sir (Arthur) John (Stewart), KCVO
Griffiths, Sir Eldon Wylie, Kt.
Grigson, *Hon.* Sir Geoffrey Douglas, Kt.
Grimshaw, Sir Nicholas Thomas, Kt., CBE
Grimwade, Sir Andrew Sheppard, Kt., CBE
Grindrod, *Most Revd* John Basil Rowland, KBE
Grinstead, Sir Stanley Gordon, Kt.
Grose, *Vice-Adm.* Sir Alan, KBE
Gross, *Hon.* Sir Peter Henry, Kt.
Grossart, Sir Angus McFarlane McLeod, Kt., CBE
Grotrian, Sir Philip Christian Brent, Bt. (1934)
Grove, Sir Charles Gerald, Bt. (1874)
Grove, Sir Edmund Frank, KCVO
Grugeon, Sir John Drury, Kt.
Grundy, Sir Mark, Kt.
Guinness, Sir Howard Christian Sheldon, Kt., VRD
Guinness, Sir John Ralph Sidney, Kt., CB
Guinness, Sir Kenelm Ernest Lee, Bt. (1867)
†Guise, Sir Christopher James, Bt. (1783)
Gull, Sir Rupert William Cameron, Bt. (1872)
Gumbs, Sir Emile Rudolph, Kt.
Gunn, Sir Robert Norman, Kt.
†Gunning, Sir Charles Theodore, Bt. (1778)
Gunston, Sir John Wellesley, Bt. (1938)
Gurdon, *Prof.* Sir John Bertrand, Kt., DPHIL, FRS
Guthrie, Sir Malcolm Connop, Bt. (1936)
Haddacks, *Vice-Adm.* Sir Paul Kenneth, KCB
Hadfield, Sir Ronald, Kt., QPM
Hadlee, Sir Richard John, Kt., MBE
Hagart-Alexander, Sir Claud, Bt. (1886)
Hague, *Prof.* Sir Douglas Chalmers, Kt., CBE
Haines, *Prof.* Sir Andrew Paul, Kt.
Haji-Ioannou, Sir Stelios, Kt.
Halberg, Sir Murray Gordon, Kt., MBE
Hall, Sir Basil Brodribb, KCB, MC, TD
Hall, *Prof.* Sir David Michael Baldock, Kt.
Hall, Sir Ernest, Kt., OBE
Hall, Sir Graham Joseph, Kt.
Hall, Sir Iain Robert, Kt.
Hall, Sir (Frederick) John (Frank), Bt. (1923)
Hall, Sir John, Kt.
Hall, Sir John Bernard, Bt. (1919)
Hall, Sir John Douglas Hoste, Bt. (S. 1687)
Hall, HE *Prof.* Sir Kenneth Octavius, GCMG
Hall, Sir Peter Edward, KBE, CMG
Hall, *Prof.* Sir Peter Geoffrey, Kt., FBA
Hall, Sir Peter Reginald Frederick, Kt., CBE
Halpern, Sir Ralph Mark, Kt.
Halsey, *Revd* John Walter Brooke, Bt. (1920)
Halstead, Sir Ronald, Kt., CBE
Hambling, Sir (Herbert) Hugh, Bt. (1924)
Hamilton, Sir Andrew Caradoc, Bt. (S. 1646)
Hamilton, Sir Edward Sydney, Bt. (1776 and 1819)
Hamilton, Sir James Arnot, KCB, MBE, FRENG
Hamilton, Sir Nigel, KCB
Hamilton-Dalrymple, *Maj.* Sir Hew Fleetwood, Bt. (S. 1697), GCVO
Hamilton-Spencer-Smith, Sir John, Bt. (1804)
Hammick, Sir Stephen George, Bt. (1834)
Hammond, Sir Anthony Hilgrove, KCB, QC
Hampel, Sir Ronald Claus, Kt.
Hampson, Sir Stuart, Kt.
Hampton, Sir (Leslie) Geoffrey, Kt.
Hampton, Sir Philip Roy, Kt.
Hanbury-Tenison, Sir Richard, KCVO
Hancock, Sir David John Stowell, KCB
Hanham, Sir Michael William, Bt. (1667), DFC
Hankes-Drielsma, Sir Claude Dunbar, KCVO
Hanley, *Rt. Hon.* Sir Jeremy James, KCMG
Hanmer, Sir John Wyndham Edward, Bt. (1774)
Hannam, Sir John Gordon, Kt.
Hanson, Sir (Charles) Rupert (Patrick), Bt. (1918)
Hanson, Sir John Gilbert, KCMG, CBE
Harcourt-Smith, *Air Chief Marshal* Sir David, GBE, KCB, DFC
Hardie Boys, *Rt. Hon.* Sir Michael, GCMG
Harding, Sir George William, KCMG, CVO
Harding, *Marshal of the Royal Air Force* Sir Peter Robin, GCB
Harding, Sir Roy Pollard, Kt., CBE
Hardy, Sir David William, Kt.
Hardy, Sir James Gilbert, Kt., OBE
Hardy, Sir Richard Charles Chandos, Bt. (1876)
Hare, Sir David, Kt., FRSL
Hare, Sir Nicholas Patrick, Bt. (1818)
Haren, *Dr* Sir Patrick Hugh, Kt.
Harford, Sir (John) Timothy, Bt. (1934)
Harington, Sir Nicholas John, Bt. (1611)
Harkness, *Very Revd* James, KCVO, CB, OBE
Harland, *Air Marshal* Sir Reginald Edward Wynyard, KBE, CB
Harley, *Gen.* Sir Alexander George Hamilton, KBE, CB
Harman, *Gen.* Sir Jack Wentworth, GCB, OBE, MC

Harman, *Hon.* Sir Jeremiah LeRoy, Kt.
Harman, Sir John Andrew, Kt.
Harmsworth, Sir Hildebrand Harold, Bt. (1922)
Harper, Sir Ewan William, Kt. CBE
Harper, *Prof.* Sir Peter Stanley, Kt., CBE
Harris, *Prof.* Sir Henry, Kt., FRCP, FRCPATH, FRS
Harris, Sir Jack Wolfred Ashford, Bt. (1932)
Harris, *Air Marshal* Sir John Hulme, KCB, CBE
Harris, *Prof.* Sir Martin Best, Kt., CBE
Harris, Sir Michael Frank, Kt.
Harris, Sir Thomas George, KBE, CMG,
Harrison, *Prof.* Sir Brian Howard, Kt.
Harrison, Sir David, Kt., CBE, FRENG
Harrison, Sir Ernest Thomas, Kt., OBE
Harrison, *Surgeon Vice-Adm.* Sir John Albert Bews, KBE
Harrison, *Hon.* Sir Michael Guy Vicat, Kt.
Harrison, Sir Michael James Harwood, Bt. (1961)
Harrison, Sir (Robert) Colin, Bt. (1922)
Harrison, Sir Terence, Kt., FRENG
Harrop, Sir Peter John, KCB
Hart, *Hon.* Sir Anthony Ronald, Kt.
Hart, Sir David Michael, Kt., OBE
Hart, Sir Graham Allan, KCB
Hartwell, Sir (Francis) Anthony Charles Peter, Bt. (1805)
Harvey, Sir Charles Richard Musgrave, Bt. (1933)
Harvie, Sir John Smith, Kt., CBE
Harvie-Watt, Sir James, Bt. (1945)
Haselhurst, *Rt. Hon.* Sir Alan Gordon Barraclough, Kt.
Haskard, Sir Cosmo Dugal Patrick Thomas, KCMG, MBE
Haslam, *Rear-Adm.* Sir David William, KBE, CB
Hastie, *Cdre* Sir Robert Cameron, KCVO, CBE, RD
Hastings, Sir Max Macdonald, Kt.
Hatter, Sir Maurice, Kt.
Havelock-Allan, Sir (Anthony) Mark David, Bt. (1858)
Hawkins, Sir Richard Caesar, Bt. (1778)
†Hawley, Sir Henry Nicholas, Bt. (1795)
Haworth, Sir Philip, Bt. (1911)
Hawthorne, *Prof.* Sir William Rede, Kt., CBE, SCD, FRS, FRENG
Hay, Sir David Osborne, Kt., CBE, DSO
Hay, Sir David Russell, Kt., CBE, FRCP, MD
Hay, Sir Hamish Grenfell, Kt.
Hay, Sir John Erroll Audley, Bt. (S. 1663)
†Hay, Sir Ronald Frederick Hamilton, Bt. (S. 1703)
Hayes, Sir Brian, Kt., CBE, QPM
Hayes, Sir Brian David, GCB
Hayman-Joyce, *Lt.-Gen.* Sir Robert John, KCB, CBE
Hayter, Sir Paul David Grenville, KCB, LVO
Hayward, Sir Anthony William Byrd, Kt.
Hayward, Sir Jack Arnold, Kt., OBE
Haywood, Sir Harold, KCVO, OBE
Head, Sir Richard Douglas Somerville, Bt. (1838)
Heap, Sir Peter William, KCMG
Heap, *Prof.* Sir Robert Brian, Kt., CBE, FRS
Hearne, Sir Graham James, Kt., CBE
Heathcote, *Brig.* Sir Gilbert Simon, Bt. (1733), CBE
†Heathcote, Sir Timothy Gilbert, Bt. (1733)
Heatley, Sir Peter, Kt., CBE
Hedley, *Hon.* Sir Mark, Kt.
Hegarty, Sir John Kevin, Kt.
Heiser, Sir Terence Michael, GCB
Henao, *Revd* Ravu, Kt., OBE
Henderson, Sir Denys Hartley, Kt.
Henderson, Sir (John) Nicholas, GCMG, KCVO
Henderson, *Hon.* Sir Launcelot Dinadan James, Kt.
Henderson, *Maj.* Sir Richard Yates, KCVO
Hennessy, Sir James Patrick Ivan, KBE, CMG
†Henniker, Sir Adrian Chandos, Bt. (1813)
Henniker-Heaton, Sir Yvo Robert, Bt. (1912)
Henriques, *Hon.* Sir Richard Henry Quixano, Kt.
Henry, *Rt. Hon.* Sir Denis Robert Maurice, Kt.
Henry, *Hon.* Sir Geoffrey Arama, KBE
†Henry, Sir Patrick Denis, Bt. (1923)
Henshaw, Sir David George, Kt.
Hepple, *Prof.* Sir Bob Alexander, Kt.
Herbecq, Sir John Edward, KCB
Herbert, *Adm.* Sir Peter Geoffrey Marshall, KCB, OBE
Hermon, Sir John Charles, Kt., OBE, QPM
Heron, Sir Conrad Frederick, KCB, OBE
Heron, Sir Michael Gilbert, Kt.
Heron-Maxwell, Sir Nigel Mellor, Bt. (S. 1683)
Hervey, Sir Roger Blaise Ramsay, KCVO, CMG
Hervey-Bathurst, Sir Frederick John Charles Gordon, Bt. (1818)
Heseltine, *Rt. Hon.* Sir William Frederick Payne, GCB, GCVO
Hewetson, Sir Christopher Raynor, Kt., TD
Hewett, Sir Richard Mark John, Bt. (1813)
Hewitt, Sir (Cyrus) Lenox (Simson), Kt., OBE
Hewitt, Sir Nicholas Charles Joseph, Bt. (1921)
Heygate, Sir Richard John Gage, Bt. (1831)
Heywood, Sir Peter, Bt. (1838)
Hibbert, Sir Jack, KCB
Hickey, Sir Justin, Kt.
Hickman, Sir (Richard) Glenn, Bt. (1903)
Hicks, Sir Robert, Kt.
Hidden, *Hon.* Sir Anthony Brian, Kt.
Hielscher, Sir Leo Arthur, Kt.
Higgins, *Rt. Hon.* Sir Malachy Joseph, Kt.
Higginson, Sir Gordon Robert, Kt., PHD, FRENG
Hill, Sir Arthur Alfred, Kt., CBE
Hill, Sir Brian John, Kt.
Hill, Sir James Frederick, Bt. (1917)
Hill, Sir John Alfred Rowley, Bt. (I. 1779)
Hill, *Vice-Adm.* Sir Robert Charles Finch, KBE, FRENG
Hill-Norton, *Vice-Adm. Hon.* Sir Nicholas John, KCB
Hill-Wood, Sir Samuel Thomas, Bt. (1921)
Hillhouse, Sir (Robert) Russell, KCB
Hills, Sir Graham John, Kt.
Hine, *Air Chief Marshal* Sir Patrick Bardon, GCB, GBE
Hirsch, *Prof.* Sir Peter Bernhard, Kt., PHD., FRS
Hirst, *Rt. Hon.* Sir David Cozens-Hardy, Kt.
Hirst, Sir Michael William, Kt.
Hoare, *Prof.* Sir Charles Anthony Richard, Kt., FRS
Hoare, Sir David John, Bt. (1786)
†Hoare, Sir Charles James, Bt. (I. 1784)
Hobart, Sir John Vere, Bt. (1914)
Hobbs, *Maj.-Gen.* Sir Michael Frederick, KCVO, CBE
Hobday, Sir Gordon Ivan, Kt.
Hobhouse, Sir Charles John Spinney, Bt. (1812)
Hobson, Sir Ronald, KCVO
†Hodge, Sir Andrew Rowland, Bt. (1921)
Hodge, *Hon.* Sir Henry Egar Garfield, Kt.
Hodge, Sir James William, KCVO, CMG
Hodgkin, Sir (Gordon) Howard (Eliot), Kt., CH, CBE
Hodgkinson, Sir Michael Stewart, Kt.
Hodgkinson, *Air Chief Marshal* Sir (William) Derek, KCB, CBE, DFC, AFC
Hodgson, Sir Maurice Arthur Eric, Kt., FRENG
Hodson, Sir Michael Robin Adderley, Bt. (I. 1789)
Hogg, Sir Christopher Anthony, Kt.
†Hogg, Sir Piers Michael James, Bt. (1846)
Holcroft, Sir Peter George Culcheth, Bt. (1921)
Holderness, Sir Martin William, Bt. (1920)
Holden, Sir Paul, Bt. (1893)
Holden, Sir John David, Bt. (1919)
Holden-Brown, Sir Derrick, Kt.
Holder, Sir John Henry, Bt. (1898)

Holdgate, Sir Martin Wyatt, Kt., CB, PHD
Holdsworth, Sir (George) Trevor, Kt., CVO
Holland, *Hon.* Sir Alan Douglas, Kt.
Holland, *Hon.* Sir Christopher John, Kt.
Holland, Sir Clifton Vaughan, Kt.
Holland, Sir Geoffrey, KCB
Holland, Sir John Anthony, Kt.
Holland, Sir Philip Welsby, Kt.
Holliday, *Prof.* Sir Frederick George Thomas, Kt., CBE, FRSE
Hollings, *Hon.* Sir (Alfred) Kenneth, Kt., MC
Hollom, Sir Jasper Quintus, KBE
Holloway, *Hon.* Sir Barry Blyth, KBE
Holm, Sir Ian (Holm Cuthbert), Kt., CBE
Holman, *Hon.* Sir (Edward) James, Kt.
Holmes, *Prof.* Sir Frank Wakefield, Kt.
Holmes, Sir John Eaton, GCVO, KBE, CMG
Holmes-Sellors, Sir Patrick John, KCVO
Holroyd, *Air Marshal* Sir Frank Martyn, KBE, CB
Holroyd, Sir Michael De Courcy Fraser, Kt., CBE
Holt, *Prof.* Sir James Clarke, Kt.
Holt, Sir Michael, Kt., CBE
Home, Sir William Dundas, Bt. (S. 1671)
Honywood, Sir Filmer Courtenay William, Bt. (1660)
†Hood, Sir John Joseph Harold, Bt. (1922)
Hookway, Sir Harry Thurston, Kt.
Hooper, *Rt. Hon.* Sir Anthony, Kt.
Hope, Sir Colin Frederick Newton, Kt.
Hope, Sir Alexander Archibald Douglas, Bt. (S. 1628)
Hope-Dunbar, Sir David, Bt. (S. 1664)
Hopkin, Sir Royston Oliver, KCMG
Hopkin, Sir (William Aylsham) Bryan, Kt., CBE
Hopkins, Sir Anthony Philip, Kt., CBE
Hopkins, Sir Michael John, Kt., CBE, RA, RIBA
Hopwood, *Prof.* Sir David Alan, Kt., FRS
Hordern, *Rt. Hon.* Sir Peter Maudslay, Kt.
Horlick, *Vice-Adm.* Sir Edwin John, KBE, FRENG
Horlick, Sir James Cunliffe William, Bt. (1914)
Horlock, *Prof.* Sir John Harold, Kt., FRS, FRENG
Horn, *Prof.* Sir Gabriel, Kt., FRS
Horn-Smith, Sir Julian Michael, Kt.
Hornby, Sir Derek Peter, Kt.
Hornby, Sir Simon Michael, Kt.
Horne, Sir Alan Gray Antony, Bt. (1929)
Horne, *Dr* Sir Alistair Allan, Kt. CBE
Horsbrugh-Porter, Sir John Simon, Bt. (1902)
Horsfall, Sir Edward John Wright, Bt. (1909)
†Hort, Sir Andrew Edwin Fenton, Bt. (1767)
Horton, Sir Robert Baynes, Kt.
Hosker, Sir Gerald Albery, KCB, QC
Hoskins, *Prof.* Sir Brian John, Kt. CBE, FRS
Hoskyns, Sir Benedict Leigh, Bt. (1676)
Hoskyns, Sir John Austin Hungerford Leigh, Kt.
Hotung, Sir Joseph Edward, Kt.
Houghton, *Lt.-Gen.* Sir John Nicholas Reynolds, KCB, CBE
Houghton, Sir John Theodore, Kt., CBE, FRS
Houldsworth, Sir Richard Thomas Reginald, Bt. (1887)
Hourston, Sir Gordon Minto, Kt.
House, *Lt.-Gen.* Sir David George, GCB, KCVO, CBE, MC
Houssemayne du Boulay, Sir Roger William, KCVO, CMG
Houstoun-Boswall, Sir (Thomas) Alford, Bt. (1836)
Howard, Sir David Howarth Seymour, Bt. (1955)
Howard, *Prof.* Sir Michael Eliot, Kt., OM, CH, CBE, MC
Howard-Dobson, *Gen.* Sir Patrick John, GCB
Howard-Lawson, Sir John Philip, Bt. (1841)
Howells, Sir Eric Waldo Benjamin, Kt., CBE
Howes, Sir Christopher Kingston, KCVO, CB
Howlett, *Gen.* Sir Geoffrey Hugh Whitby, KBE, MC
Huggins, *Hon.* Sir Alan Armstrong, Kt.
Hugh-Jones, Sir Wynn Normington, Kt., LVO
Hugh-Smith, Sir Andrew Colin, Kt.
Hughes, *Rt. Hon.* Sir Anthony Philip Gilson, Kt.
Hughes, Sir Thomas Collingwood, Bt. (1773)
Hughes, Sir Trevor Poulton, KCB
†Hughes-Morgan, Sir (Ian) Parry David, Bt. (1925)
Hull, *Prof.* Sir David, Kt.
Hulse, Sir Edward Jeremy Westrow, Bt. (1739)
Hum, Sir Christopher Owen, KCMG
Hunt, Sir John Leonard, Kt.
Hunt, *Adm.* Sir Nicholas John Streynsham, GCB, LVO
Hunt, Sir Rex Masterman, Kt., CMG
Hunt, *Dr* Sir Richard Timothy, Kt.
Hunt-Davis, *Brig.* Sir Miles Garth, KCVO, CBE
Hunter, Sir Alistair John, KCMG
Hunter, *Prof.* Sir Laurence Colvin, Kt., CBE, FRSE
Hunter, *Dr* Sir Philip John, Kt., CBE
Hunter, Sir Thomas Blane, Kt.
Huntington-Whiteley, Sir Hugo Baldwin, Bt. (1918)
Hurn, Sir (Francis) Roger, Kt.
Hurrell, Sir Anthony Gerald, KCVO, CMG
Hurst, Sir Geoffrey Charles, Kt., MBE
Husbands, Sir Clifford Straugh, GCMG
Hutchison, Sir James Colville, Bt. (1956)
Hutchison, *Rt. Hon.* Sir Michael, Kt.
Hutchison, Sir Robert, Bt. (1939)
Hutt, Sir Dexter Walter, Kt.
Huxley, *Prof.* Sir Andrew Fielding, Kt., OM, FRS
Huxtable, *Gen.* Sir Charles Richard, KCB, CBE
Ibbs, Sir (John) Robin, KBE
Imbert-Terry, Sir Michael Edward Stanley, Bt. (1917)
Imray, Sir Colin Henry, KBE, CMG
Ingham, Sir Bernard, Kt.
Ingilby, Sir Thomas Colvin William, Bt. (1866)
Inglis, Sir Brian Scott, Kt.
Inglis of Glencorse, Sir Roderick John, Bt. (S. 1703)
Ingram, Sir James Herbert Charles, Bt. (1893)
Ingram, Sir John Henderson, Kt., CBE
Inkin, Sir Geoffrey David, Kt., OBE
†Innes, Sir David Charles Kenneth Gordon, Bt. (NS 1686)
Innes of Edingight, Sir Malcolm Rognvald, KCVO
Innes, Sir Peter Alexander Berowald, Bt. (S. 1628)
Irvine, Sir Donald Hamilton, Kt., CBE, MD, FRCGP
Irving, *Prof.* Sir Miles Horsfall, Kt., MD, FRCS, FRCSE
Irwin, *Lt.-Gen.* Sir Alistair Stuart Hastings, KCB, CBE
Irwin, *Hon.* Sir Stephen John, Kt.
Isaacs, Sir Jeremy Israel, Kt.
Isham, Sir Ian Vere Gyles, Bt. (1627)
Ivory, Sir Brian Gammell, Kt., CBE
Jack, *Hon.* Sir Alieu Sulayman, Kt.
Jack, Sir David, Kt., CBE, FRS, FRSE
Jack, *Hon.* Sir Raymond Evan, Kt.
Jackling, Sir Roger Tustin, KCB, CBE
Jackson, Sir Barry Trevor, Kt.
Jackson, Sir Kenneth Joseph, Kt.
Jackson, *Gen.* Sir Michael David, GCB, CBE
Jackson, Sir Michael Roland, Bt. (1902)
Jackson, Sir Nicholas Fane St George, Bt. (1913)
Jackson, Sir Keith Arnold, Bt. (1815)
Jackson, *Hon.* Sir Rupert Matthew, Kt.
Jackson, Sir (William) Roland Cedric, Bt. (1869)
Jacob, *Rt. Hon.* Sir Robert Raphael Hayim (Robin), Kt.
Jacobi, Sir Derek George, Kt., CBE
Jacobi, *Dr* Sir James Edward, Kt., OBE
Jacobs, Sir Cecil Albert, Kt., CBE

Jacobs, *Rt. Hon.* Sir Francis Geoffrey, KCMG, QC
Jacobs, *Hon.* Sir Kenneth Sydney, KBE
Jacomb, Sir Martin Wakefield, Kt.
Jaffray, Sir William Otho, Bt. (1892)
Jagger, Sir Michael Philip, Kt.
James, Sir Cynlais Morgan, KCMG
James, Sir Jeffrey Russell, KBE
James, Sir John Nigel Courtenay, KCVO, CBE
James, Sir Stanislaus Anthony, GCMG, OBE
Jamieson, *Air Marshal* Sir David Ewan, KBE, CB
Jansen, Sir Ross Malcolm, KBE
†Jardine of Applegirth, Sir William Murray, Bt. (S. 1672)
Jardine, Sir Andrew Colin Douglas, Bt. (1916)
Jarman, *Prof.* Sir Brian, Kt., OBE
Jarratt, Sir Alexander Anthony, Kt., CB
Jarvis, Sir Gordon Ronald, Kt.
Jawara, *Hon.* Sir Dawda Kairaba, Kt.
Jay, Sir Antony Rupert, Kt., CVO
Jeewoolall, Sir Ramesh, Kt.
Jefferson, Sir George Rowland, Kt., CBE, FRENG
Jeffrey, Sir William Alexander, KCB
Jeffreys, *Prof.* Sir Alec John, Kt., FRS
Jeffries, *Hon.* Sir John Francis, Kt.
Jehangir, Sir Cowasji, Bt. (1908)
†Jejeebhoy, Sir Jehangir, Bt. (1857)
Jenkins, Sir Brian Garton, GBE
Jenkins, Sir Elgar Spencer, Kt., OBE
Jenkins, Sir James Christopher, KCB, QC
Jenkins, Sir Michael Nicholas Howard, Kt., OBE
Jenkins, Sir Michael Romilly Heald, KCMG
Jenkins, Sir Simon, Kt.
Jenkinson, Sir John Banks, Bt. (1661)
Jenks, Sir (Richard) Peter, Bt. (1932)
Jenner, *Air Marshal* Sir Timothy Ivo, KCB
Jennings, Sir John Southwood, Kt., CBE, FRSE
Jennings, Sir Peter Neville Wake, Kt., CVO
Jephcott, Sir Neil Welbourn, Bt. (1962)
Jessel, Sir Charles John, Bt. (1883)
Jewkes, Sir Gordon Wesley, KCMG
Job, Sir Peter James Denton, Kt.
John, Sir David Glyndwr, KCMG
John, Sir Elton Hercules (Reginald Kenneth Dwight), Kt., CBE
Johns, *Vice-Adm.* Sir Adrian James, KCB, CBE, ADC
Johns, *Air Chief Marshal* Sir Richard Edward, GCB, KCVO, CBE
Johnson, Sir Colpoys Guy, Bt. (1755)
Johnson, *Gen.* Sir Garry Dene, KCB, OBE, MC
Johnson, Sir John Rodney, KCMG
†Johnson, Sir Patrick Eliot, Bt. (1818)
Johnson, *Hon.* Sir Robert Lionel, Kt.
Johnson, Sir Vassel Godfrey, Kt., CBE
Johnson-Ferguson, Sir Ian Edward, Bt. (1906)
Johnston, *Lt.-Gen.* Sir Maurice Robert, KCB, CVO, OBE
Johnston, Sir Thomas Alexander, Bt. (S. 1626)
Johnstone, Sir Geoffrey Adams Dinwiddie, KCMG
Johnstone, Sir (George) Richard Douglas, Bt. (S. 1700)
Johnstone, Sir (John) Raymond, Kt., CBE
Jolliffe, Sir Anthony Stuart, GBE
Jolly, Sir Arthur Richard, KCMG
Jonas, Sir John Peter, Kt., CBE
Jones, Sir Alan Jeffrey, Kt.
Jones, Sir Harry George, Kt., CBE
Jones, Sir John Francis, Kt.
Jones, Sir Keith Stephen, Kt.
Jones, Sir Lyndon, Kt.
Jones, Sir (Owen) Trevor, Kt.
Jones, Sir Richard Anthony Lloyd, KCB
Jones, Sir Robert Edward, Kt.
Jones, Sir Roger Spencer, Kt., OBE
Jones, Sir Simon Warley Frederick Benton, Bt. (1919)
†Joseph, *Hon.* Sir James Samuel, Bt. (1943)
Jowell, *Prof.* Sir Roger Mark, Kt. CBE
Jowitt, *Hon.* Sir Edwin Frank, Kt.
Judge, *Rt. Hon.* Sir Igor, Kt.
Judge, Sir Paul Rupert, Kt.
Jugnauth, *Rt. Hon.* Sir Anerood, KCMG
Jungius, *Vice-Adm.* Sir James George, KBE
Kaberry, *Hon.* Sir Christopher Donald, Bt. (1960)
Kadoorie, *Hon.* Sir Michael David, Kt.
Kakaraya, Sir Pato, KBE
Kan Yuet-Keung, Sir, GBE
Kapi, *Hon.* Sir Mari, KCMG, CBE
Kaputin, Sir John Rumet, KBE, CMG
Kaufman, *Rt. Hon.* Sir Gerald Bernard, Kt.
Kausimae, Sir David Nanau, KBE
Kavali, Sir Thomas, Kt., OBE
Kay, *Prof.* Sir Andrew Watt, Kt.
Kay, *Rt. Hon.* Sir Maurice Ralph, Kt.
Kaye, Sir Paul Henry Gordon, Bt. (1923)
Keane, Sir Richard Michael, Bt. (1801)
Kearney, *Hon.* Sir William John Francis, Kt., CBE
Keeble, Sir (Herbert Ben) Curtis, GCMG
Keegan, Sir John Desmond Patrick, Kt., OBE
Keene, *Rt. Hon.* Sir David Wolfe, Kt.
Keith, *Hon.* Sir Brian Richard, Kt.
Keith, *Prof.* Sir James, KBE
†Kellett, Sir Stanley Charles, Bt. (1801)
Kelly, Sir Christopher William, KCB
Kelly, Sir David Robert Corbett, Kt., CBE
Kelly, *Rt. Hon.* Sir (John William) Basil, Kt.
Kemakeza, Sir Allan, Kt.
Kemball, *Air Marshal* Sir (Richard) John, KCB, CBE
Kemp-Welch, Sir John, Kt.
Kenilorea, *Rt. Hon.* Sir Peter, KBE
Kennaway, Sir John Lawrence, Bt. (1791)
Kennedy, Sir Francis, KCMG, CBE
Kennedy, *Hon.* Sir Ian Alexander, Kt.
Kennedy, *Prof.* Sir Ian McColl, Kt.
Kennedy, Sir Ludovic Henry Coverley, Kt.
†Kennedy, Sir Michael Edward, Bt., (1836)
Kennedy, *Rt. Hon.* Sir Paul Joseph Morrow, Kt.
Kennedy, *Air Chief Marshal* Sir Thomas Lawrie, GCB, AFC
Kennedy-Good, Sir John, KBE
Kenny, Sir Anthony John Patrick, Kt., DPHIL, DLITT, FBA
Kenny, *Gen.* Sir Brian Leslie Graham, GCB, CBE
Kentridge, Sir Sydney Woolf, KCMG, QC
Kenyon, Sir Nicholas Roger, Kt., CBE
Keogh, *Prof.* Sir Bruce Edward, KBE
Kermode, Sir (John) Frank, Kt., FBA
Kerr, *Rt. Hon.* Sir Brian Francis, Kt.
Kerr, *Adm.* Sir John Beverley, GCB
Kerry, Sir Michael James, KCB, QC
Kershaw, *Prof.* Sir Ian, Kt.
Kerslake, Sir Robert Walker, Kt.
Keswick, Sir John Chippendale Lindley, Kt.
Kevau, *Prof.* Sir Isi Henao, Kt., CBE
Kikau, *Ratu* Sir Jone Latianara, KBE
†Kimber, Sir Timothy Roy Henry, Bt. (1904)
King, *Prof.* Sir David Anthony, Kt., FRS
King, Sir John Christopher, Bt. (1888)
King, *Vice-Adm.* Sir Norman Ross Dutton, KBE
King, *Hon.* Sir Timothy Roger Alan, Kt.
King, Sir Wayne Alexander, Bt. (1815)
Kingman, *Prof.* Sir John Frank Charles, Kt., FRS
Kingsland, Sir Richard, Kt., CBE, DFC
Kingsley, Sir Ben, Kt.
Kinloch, Sir David, Bt. (S. 1686)
Kinloch, Sir David Oliphant, Bt. (1873)
Kipalan, Sir Albert, Kt.
Kirkpatrick, Sir Ivone Elliott, Bt. (S. 1685)
Kirkwood, *Hon.* Sir Andrew Tristram Hammett, Kt.
Kiszely, *Lt.-Gen.* Sir John Panton, KCB, MC
Kitchin, *Hon.* Sir David James Tyson, Kt.
Kitson, *Gen.* Sir Frank Edward, GBE, KCB, MC

Kitson, Sir Timothy Peter Geoffrey, Kt.
Kleinwort, Sir Richard Drake, Bt. (1909)
Klug, Sir Aaron, Kt., OM
Knight, Sir Harold Murray, KBE, DSC
Knight, Sir Kenneth John, Kt., CBE, QFSM
Knight, *Air Chief Marshal* Sir Michael William Patrick, KCB, AFC
Knight, *Prof.* Sir Peter, Kt.
†Knill, Sir Thomas John Pugin Bartholomew, Bt. (1893)
Knowles, Sir Charles Francis, Bt. (1765)
Knowles, Sir Durward Randolph, Kt., OBE
Knox, Sir David Laidlaw, Kt.
Knox, *Hon.* Sir John Leonard, Kt.
Knox-Johnston, Sir William Robert Patrick (Sir Robin), Kt., CBE, RD
Koraea, Sir Thomas, Kt.
Kornberg, *Prof.* Sir Hans Leo, Kt., DSC, SCD, PHD, FRS
Korowi, Sir Wiwa, GCMG
Kroto, *Prof.* Sir Harold Walter, Kt., FRS
Kulukundis, Sir Elias George (Eddie), Kt., OBE
Kurongku, *Most Revd* Peter, KBE
Kwok-Po Li, *Dr* Sir David, Kt., OBE
Lachmann, *Prof.* Sir Peter Julius, Kt.
Lacon, Sir Edmund Vere, Bt. (1818)
Lacy, Sir Patrick Brian Finucane, Bt. (1921)
Lacy, Sir John Trend, Kt., CBE
Laddie, *Hon.* Sir Hugh Ian Lang, Kt.
Laidlaw, Sir Christopher Charles Fraser, Kt.
Laing, Sir (John) Martin (Kirby), Kt., CBE
Laing, Sir (William) Kirby, Kt., FRENG
Laird, Sir Gavin Harry, Kt., CBE
Lake, Sir (Atwell) Graham, Bt. (1711)
Lakin, Sir Michael, Bt. (1909)
Laking, Sir George Robert, KCMG
Lamb, Sir Albert Thomas, KBE, CMG, DFC
Lambert, Sir John Henry, KCVO, CMG
†Lambert, Sir Peter John Biddulph, Bt. (1711)
Lampl, Sir Frank William, Kt.
Lampl, Sir Peter, Kt., OBE
Lamport, Sir Stephen Mark Jeffrey, KCVO
Landale, Sir David William Neil, KCVO
Landau, Sir Dennis Marcus, Kt.
Lander, Sir Stephen James, KCB
Lane, Prof. Sir David Philip, Kt.
Langham, Sir John Stephen, Bt. (1660)
Langlands, Sir Robert Alan, Kt.
Langley, *Hon.* Sir Gordon Julian Hugh, Kt.
Langrishe, Sir James Hercules, Bt. (I. 1777)
Langstaff, *Hon.* Sir Brian Frederick James, Kt.
Lankester, Sir Timothy Patrick, KCB
Lapli, Sir John Ini, GCMG
Large, Sir Andrew McLeod Brooks, Kt.
Latasi, *Rt. Hon.* Sir Kamuta, KCMG, OBE
Latham, *Rt. Hon.* Sir David Nicholas Ramsey, Kt.
Latham, Sir Michael Anthony, Kt.
Latham, Sir Richard Thomas Paul, Bt. (1919)
Latimer, Sir (Courtenay) Robert, Kt., CBE
Latimer, Sir Graham Stanley, KBE
Latour-Adrien, *Hon.* Sir Maurice, Kt.
Laughton, Sir Anthony Seymour, Kt.
Laurie, Sir Robert Bayley Emilius, Bt. (1834)
Lauterpacht, Sir Elihu, Kt., CBE, QC
Lauti, *Rt. Hon.* Sir Toaripi, GCMG
Lawes, Sir (John) Michael Bennet, Bt. (1882)
Lawler, Sir Peter James, Kt., OBE
Lawrence, Sir Clive Wyndham, Bt. (1906)
Lawrence, Sir Henry Peter, Bt. (1858)
Lawrence, Sir Ivan John, Kt., QC
Lawrence, Sir John Patrick Grosvenor, Kt., CBE
Lawrence, Sir William Fettiplace, Bt. (1867)
Lawrence-Jones, Sir Christopher, Bt. (1831)
Laws, *Rt. Hon.* Sir John Grant McKenzie, Kt.
Lawson, Sir Charles John Patrick, Bt. (1900)
Lawson, *Gen.* Sir Richard George, KCB, DSO, OBE
Lawson-Tancred, Sir Henry, Bt. (1662)
Lawton, *Prof.* Sir John Hartley, Kt., CBE, FRS
Layard, *Adm.* Sir Michael Henry Gordon, KCB, CBE
Lea, *Vice-Adm.* Sir John Stuart Crosbie, KBE
Lea, Sir Thomas William, Bt. (1892)
Leach, *Admiral of the Fleet* Sir Henry Conyers, GCB
Leahy, Sir Daniel Joseph, Kt.
Leahy, Sir John Henry Gladstone, KCMG
Leahy, Sir Terence Patrick, Kt.
Learmont, *Gen.* Sir John Hartley, KCB, CBE
Leaver, Sir Christopher, GBE
Le Bailly, *Vice-Adm.* Sir Louis Edward Stewart Holland, KBE, CB
Le Cheminant, *Air Chief Marshal* Sir Peter de Lacey, GBE, KCB, DFC
Lechmere, Sir Reginald Anthony Hungerford, Bt. (1818)
Ledger, Sir Philip Stevens, Kt., CBE, FRSE
Lee, *Brig.* Sir Leonard Henry, Kt., CBE
Lee, Sir Quo-wei, Kt., CBE
Leeds, Sir Christopher Anthony, Bt. (1812)
Lees, Sir David Bryan, Kt.
Lees, Sir Thomas Edward, Bt. (1897)
Lees, Sir Thomas Harcourt Ivor, Bt. (1804)
Lees, Sir (William) Antony Clare, Bt. (1937)
Leese, Sir Richard Charles, Kt., CBE
le Fleming, Sir David Kelland, Bt. (1705)
Legard, Sir Charles Thomas, Bt. (1660)
Legg, Sir Thomas Stuart, KCB, QC
Leggatt, *Rt. Hon.* Sir Andrew Peter, Kt.
Leggatt, Sir Hugh Frank John, Kt.
Leggett, *Prof.* Sir Anthony James, KBE
Leigh, Sir Geoffrey Norman, Kt.
Leigh, Sir Richard Henry, Bt. (1918)
Leighton, Sir Michael John Bryan, Bt. (1693)
Leitch, Sir George, KCB, OBE
Leith-Buchanan, Sir Gordon Kelly McNicol, Bt. (1775)
Le Marchant, Sir Francis Arthur, Bt. (1841)
Leng, *Gen.* Sir Peter John Hall, KCB, MBE, MC
Lennox-Boyd, The Hon. Sir Mark Alexander, Kt.
Leon, Sir John Ronald, Bt. (1911)
Leonard, *Rt. Revd Monsignor* and *Rt. Hon.* Graham Douglas, KCVO
Lepping, Sir George Geria Dennis, GCMG, MBE
Le Quesne, Sir (John) Godfray, Kt., QC
Lee-Steere, Sir Ernest Henry, KBE
Leslie, Sir Colin Alan Bettridge, Kt.
Leslie, Sir John Norman Ide, Bt. (1876)
Lester, Sir James Theodore, Kt.
Lethbridge, Sir Thomas Periam Hector Noel, Bt. (1804)
Lever, Sir Jeremy Frederick, KCMG, QC
Lever, Sir Paul, KCMG
Lever, Sir (Tresham) Christopher Arthur Lindsay, Bt. (1911)
Leveson, *Rt. Hon.* Sir Brian Henry, Kt.
Levey, Sir Michael Vincent, Kt., LVO
Levine, Sir Montague Bernard, Kt.
Levinge, Sir Richard George Robin, Bt. (I. 1704)
Lewinton, Sir Christopher, Kt.
Lewis, Sir David Courtenay Mansel, KCVO
Lewis, Sir John Anthony, Kt., OBE
Lewis, Sir Leigh Warren, KCB
Lewis, Sir Terence Murray, Kt., OBE, GM, QPM
Lewison, *Hon.* Sir Kim Martin Jordan, Kt.
Ley, Sir Ian Francis, Bt. (1905)
Li, Sir Ka-Shing, KBE
Lickiss, Sir Michael Gillam, Kt.
Liddington, Sir Bruce, Kt.

Liggins, *Prof.* Sir Graham Collingwood, Kt., CBE, FRS
Lightman, *Hon.* Sir Gavin Anthony, Kt.
Lighton, Sir Thomas Hamilton, Bt. (I. 1791)
Likierman, *Prof.* Sir John Andrew, Kt.
Lilleyman, *Prof.* Sir John Stuart, Kt.
Limon, Sir Donald William, KCB
Linacre, Sir (John) Gordon (Seymour), Kt., CBE, AFC, DFM
Lindop, Sir Norman, Kt.
Lindsay, *Hon.* Sir John Edmund Frederic, Kt.
†Lindsay, Sir James Martin Evelyn, Bt. (1962)
†Lindsay-Hogg, Sir Michael Edward, Bt. (1905)
Lipton, Sir Stuart Anthony, Kt.
Lipworth, Sir (Maurice) Sydney, Kt.
Lister-Kaye, Sir John Phillip Lister, Bt. (1812)
Lithgow, Sir William James, Bt. (1925)
Little, *Most Revd* Thomas Francis, KBE
Littler, Sir (James) Geoffrey, KCB
Llewellyn, Sir David St Vincent, Bt. (1922)
Llewellyn-Smith, *Prof.* Sir Christopher Hubert, Kt.
Lloyd, *Prof.* Sir Geoffrey Ernest Richard, Kt., FBA
Lloyd, Sir Nicholas Markley, Kt.
Lloyd, *Rt. Hon.* Sir Peter Robert Cable, Kt.
Lloyd, Sir Richard Ernest Butler, Bt. (1960)
Lloyd, *Hon.* Sir Timothy Andrew Wigram, Kt.
Lloyd-Edwards, *Capt.* Sir Norman, KCVO, RD
Lloyd-Hughes, Sir Trevor Denby, Kt.
Lloyd Jones, Sir David, Kt.
Lloyd-Jones, Sir (Peter) Hugh (Jefferd), Kt.
Loader, Air Marshal Sir Clive Robert, KCB, OBE
Loane, *Most Revd* Marcus Lawrence, KBE
Lobo, Sir Rogerio Hyndman, Kt., CBE
Lockhead, Sir Moir, Kt., OBE
†Loder, Sir Edmund Jeune, Bt. (1887)
Logan, Sir David Brian Carleton, KCMG
Logan, Sir Donald Arthur, KCMG
Lokoloko, Sir Tore, GCMG, GCVO, OBE
Longmore, *Rt. Hon.* Sir Andrew Centlivres, Kt.
Loram, *Vice-Adm.* Sir David Anning, KCB, CVO
Lord, Sir Michael Nicholson, Kt.
Lorimer, Sir (Thomas) Desmond, Kt.
Los, *Hon.* Sir Kubulan, Kt., CBE
Loughran, Sir Gerald Finbar, KCB
Louisy, *Rt. Hon.* Sir Allan Fitzgerald Laurent, KCMG
Lovell, Sir (Alfred Charles) Bernard, Kt., OBE, FRS
Lovelock, Sir Douglas Arthur, KCB
Lovill, Sir John Roger, Kt., CBE
Lowe, *Air Chief Marshal* Sir Douglas Charles, GCB, DFC, AFC
Lowe, Sir Frank Budge, Kt.
Lowe, Sir Thomas William Gordon, Bt. (1918)
Lowson, Sir Ian Patrick, Bt. (1951)
Lowther, *Col.* Sir Charles Douglas, Bt. (1824)
Lowther, Sir John Luke, KCVO, CBE
Loyd, Sir Julian St John, KCVO
Lu, Sir Tseng Chi, Kt.
Lucas, *Prof.* Sir Colin Renshaw, Kt.
Lucas, Sir Thomas Edward, Bt. (1887)
Lucas-Tooth, Sir (Hugh) John, Bt. (1920)
Luddington, Sir Donald Collin Cumyn, KBE, CMG, CVO
Lumsden, Sir David James, Kt.
Lushington, Sir John Richard Castleman, Bt. (1791)
Lyall Grant, Sir Mark Justin, KCMG
Lygo, *Adm.* Sir Raymond Derek, KCB
Lyle, Sir Gavin Archibald, Bt. (1929)
Lynch-Blosse, *Capt.* Sir Richard Hely, Bt. (1622)
Lynch-Robinson, Sir Dominick Christopher, Bt. (1920)
Lyne, Sir Roderic Michael John, KBE, CMG
Lyons, Sir John, Kt.
Lyons, Sir Michael Thomas, Kt.
McAllister, Sir Ian Gerald, Kt., CBE
McAlpine, Sir William Hepburn, Bt. (1918)
Macara, Sir Alexander Wiseman, Kt., FRCP, FRCGP
†Macara, Sir Hugh Kenneth, Bt. (1911)
McCaffrey, Sir Thomas Daniel, Kt.
McCallum, Sir Donald Murdo, Kt., CBE, FRENG
McCamley, Sir Graham Edward, KBE
McCarthy, Sir Callum, Kt.
McCartney, Sir (James) Paul, Kt., MBE
Macartney, Sir John Ralph, Bt. (I. 1799)
McClay, *Dr* Sir Allen James, Kt., CBE
McClement, *Vice-Admiral* Sir Timothy Pentreath, KCB, OBE
McClintock, Sir Eric Paul, Kt.
McColl, Sir Colin Hugh Verel, KCMG
McColl, *Gen.* Sir John Chalmers, KCB, CBE, DSO
McCollum, *Rt. Hon.* Sir William, Kt.
McCombe, *Hon.* Sir Richard George Bramwell, Kt.
McConnell, Sir Robert Shean, Bt. (1900)
MacCormac, Sir Richard Cornelius, Kt., CBE
MacCormick, *Prof.* Sir Donald Neil, Kt., MEP, QC
†McCowan, Sir David William, Bt. (1934)
McCullough, *Hon.* Sir (Iain) Charles (Robert), Kt.
MacDermott, *Rt. Hon.* Sir John Clarke, Kt.
Macdonald, Sir Alasdair Uist, Kt., CBE
Macdonald, Sir Kenneth Carmichael, KCB
Macdonald, Sir Kenneth Donald John, Kt., QC
Mcdonald, Sir Trevor, Kt., OBE
Macdonald of Sleat, Sir Ian Godfrey Bosville, Bt. (S. 1625)
McDowell, Sir Eric Wallace, Kt., CBE
Mace, *Lt.-Gen.* Sir John Airth, KBE, CB
McEwen, Sir John Roderick Hugh, Bt. (1953)
McFarland, Sir John Talbot, Bt. (1914)
MacFarlane, *Prof.* Sir Alistair George James, Kt., CBE, FRS
McFarlane, Sir Andrew Ewart, Kt.
Macfarlane, Sir (David) Neil, Kt.
McFarlane, Sir Ian, Kt.
McGrath, Sir Brian Henry, GCVO
Macgregor, Sir Ian Grant, Bt. (1828)
McGregor, Sir James David, Kt., OBE
MacGregor of MacGregor, Sir Malcolm Gregor Charles, Bt. (1795)
†McGrigor, Sir James Angus Rhoderick Neil, Bt. (1831)
McIntosh, Sir Neil William David, Kt., CBE
McIntosh, Sir Ronald Robert Duncan, KCB
McIntyre, Sir Donald Conroy, Kt., CBE
McIntyre, Sir Meredith Alister, Kt.
Mackay, *Hon.* Sir Colin Crichton, Kt.
MacKay, *Prof.* Sir Donald Iain, Kt.
MacKay, Sir Francis Henry, Kt.
McKay, Sir William Robert, KCB
Mackay-Dick, *Maj.-Gen.* Sir Iain Charles, KCVO, MBE
Mackechnie, Sir Alistair John, Kt.
McKellen, Sir Ian Murray, Kt., CH, CBE
Mackenzie, Sir (James William) Guy, Bt. (1890)
Mackenzie, *Gen.* Sir Jeremy John George, GCB, OBE
†Mackenzie, Sir Peter Douglas, Bt. (S. 1673)
†Mackenzie, Sir Roderick McQuhae, Bt. (S. 1703)
Mackerras, Sir (Alan) Charles (MacLaurin), Kt., CH, CBE
Mackeson, Sir Rupert Henry, Bt. (1954)
McKillop, Sir Thomas Fulton Wilson, Kt.
McKinnon, Sir James, Kt.
McKinnon, *Hon.* Sir Stuart Neil, Kt.
Mackintosh, Sir Cameron Anthony, Kt.
Mackworth, Sir Digby (John), Bt. (1776)
McLaren, Sir Robin John Taylor, KCMG

McLaughlin, Sir Richard, Kt.
Maclean of Dunconnell, Sir Charles Edward, Bt. (1957)
Maclean, Sir Donald Og Grant, Kt.
Maclean, Sir Lachlan Hector Charles, Bt. (NS 1631)
Maclean, Sir Murdo, Kt.
McLeod, Sir Charles Henry, Bt. (1925)
MacLeod, Sir (John) Maxwell Norman, Bt. (1924)
Macleod, Sir (Nathaniel William) Hamish, KBE
McLintock, Sir Michael William, Bt. (1934)
Maclure, Sir John Robert Spencer, Bt. (1898)
McMahon, Sir Brian Patrick, Bt. (1817)
McMahon, Sir Christopher William, Kt.
McMaster, Sir Brian John, Kt., CBE
McMichael, *Prof.* Sir Andrew James, Kt., FRS
Macmillan, Sir (Alexander McGregor) Graham, Kt.
MacMillan, *Lt.-Gen.* Sir John Richard Alexander, KCB, CBE
McMullin, *Rt. Hon.* Sir Duncan Wallace, Kt.
McMurtry, Sir David, Kt., CBE
†Macnaghten, Sir Malcolm Francis, Bt. (1836)
McNair-Wilson, Sir Patrick Michael Ernest David, Kt.
McNamara, *Air Chief Marshal* Sir Neville Patrick, KBE
Macnaughton, *Prof.* Sir Malcolm Campbell, Kt.
McNee, Sir David Blackstock, Kt., QPM
McNulty, Sir (Robert William) Roy, Kt., CBE
MacPhail, Sir Bruce Dugald, Kt.
Macpherson, Sir Ronald Thomas Steward (Tommy), CBE, MC, TD
Macpherson of Cluny, *Hon.* Sir William Alan, Kt., TD
McQuarrie, Sir Albert, Kt.
MacRae, Sir (Alastair) Christopher (Donald Summerhayes), KCMG
Macready, Sir Nevil John Wilfrid, Bt. (1923)
MacSween, *Prof.* Sir Roderick Norman McIver, Kt.
Mactaggart, Sir John Auld, Bt. (1938)
McWilliam, Sir Michael Douglas, KCMG
McWilliams, Sir Francis, GBE
Madden, Sir David Christopher Andrew, KCMG
†Madden, Sir Charles Jonathan, Bt. (1919)
Maddison, *Hon.* Sir David George, Kt.
Maddox, Sir John Royden, Kt.
Madel, Sir (William) David, Kt.
Magee, Sir Ian Bernard Vaughan, Kt., CB
Magnus, Sir Laurence Henry Philip, Bt. (1917)
Mahon, Sir (John) Denis, Kt., CH, CBE
Mahon, Sir William Walter, Bt. (1819)
Maiden, Sir Colin James, Kt., DPHIL
Maini, *Prof.* Sir Ravinder Nath, Kt.
Maino, Sir Charles, KBE
†Maitland, Sir Charles Alexander, Bt. (1818)
Maitland, Sir Donald James Dundas, GCMG, OBE
Major, *Rt. Hon.* Sir John, KG, CH
Malbon, *Vice-Adm.* Sir Fabian Michael, KBE
Malcolm, Sir James William Thomas Alexander, Bt. (S. 1665)
Malet, Sir Harry Douglas St Lo, Bt. (1791)
Mallaby, Sir Christopher Leslie George, GCMG, GCVO
Mallet, Sir William George, GCMG, CBE
Mallick, *Prof.* Sir Netar Prakash, Kt.
Mallinson, Sir William James, Bt. (1935)
Malpas, Sir Robert, Kt., CBE
Mancham, Sir James Richard Marie, KBE
†Mander, Sir (Charles) Nicholas, Bt. (1911)
Manduell, Sir John, Kt., CBE
Mann, *Hon.* Sir George Anthony, Kt.
Mann, *Rt. Revd* Michael Ashley, KCVO
Mann, Sir Rupert Edward, Bt. (1905)
Manning, Sir David Geoffrey, GCMG, CVO
Mano, Sir Koitaga, Kt., MBE
Mansel, Sir Philip, Bt. (1622)
Mansfield, *Prof.* Sir Peter, Kt.
Mantell, *Rt. Hon.* Sir Charles Barrie Knight, Kt.
Manuella, Sir Tulaga, GCMG, MBE
Manzie, Sir (Andrew) Gordon, KCB
Margetson, Sir John William Denys, KCMG
Margetts, Sir Robert John, Kt., CBE
Mark, Sir Robert, GBE
Markesinis, *Prof.* Sir Basil Spyridonos, Kt. QC
Markham, *Prof.* Sir Alexander Fred, Kt.
Markham, Sir (Arthur) David, Bt. (1911)
Marling, Sir Charles William Somerset, Bt. (1882)
Marmot, Prof. Sir Michael Gideon, Kt.
Marr, Sir Leslie Lynn, Bt. (1919)
Marriner, Sir Neville, Kt., CBE
†Marsden, Sir Simon Neville Llewelyn, Bt. (1924)
Marsh, *Prof.* Sir John Stanley, Kt., CBE
Marshall, Sir Denis Alfred, Kt.
Marshall, *Prof.* Sir (Oshley) Roy, Kt., CBE
Marshall, Sir Peter Harold Reginald, KCMG
Martin, Sir Clive Haydon, Kt., OBE
Martin, Sir George Henry, Kt., CBE
Martin, *Vice-Adm.* Sir John Edward Ludgate, KCB, DSC
Martin, *Prof.* Sir Laurence Woodward, Kt.
Martin, Sir (Robert) Bruce, Kt., QC
Marychurch, Sir Peter Harvey, KCMG
Masefield, Sir Charles Beech Gordon, Kt.
Mason, *Hon.* Sir Anthony Frank, KBE
Mason, Sir (Basil) John, Kt., CB, DSC, FRS
Mason, *Prof.* Sir David Kean, Kt., CBE
Mason, Sir Gordon Charles, Kt., OBE
Mason, Sir John Peter, Kt., CBE
Mason, Sir Peter James, KBE
Mason, *Prof.* Sir Ronald, KCB, FRS
Massie, Sir Herbert William, Kt., CBE
Matane, HE Sir Paulias Nguna, GCMG, OBE
Mathers, Sir Robert William, Kt.
Matheson of Matheson, Sir Fergus John, Bt. (1882)
Mathewson, Sir George Ross, Kt., CBE, PHD, FRSE
Matthews, Sir Terence Hedley, Kt., OBE
Maud, *Hon.* Sir Humphrey John Hamilton, KCMG
Maughan, Sir Deryck, Kt.
Mawer, Sir Philip John Courtney, Kt.
Maxwell, Sir Michael Eustace George, Bt. (S. 1681)
Maxwell-Hyslop, Sir Robert John (Robin), Kt.
Maxwell-Scott, Sir Dominic James, Bt. (1642)
May, *Rt. Hon.* Sir Anthony Tristram Kenneth, Kt.
Mayhew-Sanders, Sir John Reynolds, Kt.
Maynard, *Hon.* Sir Clement Travelyan, Kt.
Meadow, *Prof.* Sir (Samuel) Roy, Kt., FRCP, FRCPE
Medlycott, Sir Mervyn Tregonwell, Bt. (1808)
Meldrum, Sir Graham, Kt., CBE, QFSM
Melhuish, Sir Michael Ramsay, KBE, CMG
Mellon, Sir James, KCMG
Melmoth, Sir Graham John, Kt.
Melville, *Prof.* Sir David, Kt., CBE
Merifield, Sir Anthony James, KCVO, CB
†Meyer, Sir (Anthony) Ashley Frank, Bt. (1910)
Meyer, Sir Christopher John Rome, KCMG
Meyjes, Sir Richard Anthony, Kt.
†Meyrick, Sir Timothy Thomas Charlton, Bt. (1880)
Miakwe, *Hon.* Sir Akepa, KBE
Michael, Sir Duncan, Kt.
Michael, *Dr* Sir Jonathan, Kt.
Michael, Sir Peter Colin, Kt., CBE

Michels, Sir David Michael Charles, Kt.
Middleton, Sir John Maxwell, Kt.
Middleton, Sir Peter Edward, GCB
Miers, Sir (Henry) David Alastair Capel, KBE, CMG
Milbank, Sir Anthony Frederick, Bt. (1882)
Milborne-Swinnerton-Pilkington, Sir Thomas Henry, Bt. (S. 1635)
Milburn, Sir Anthony Rupert, Bt. (1905)
Miles, Sir Peter Tremayne, KCVO
Miles, Sir William Napier Maurice, Bt. (1859)
Millais, Sir Geoffrey Richard Everett, Bt. (1885)
Millard, Sir Guy Elwin, KCMG, CVO
Miller, Sir Albert Joel, KCMG, MVO, MBE, QPM, CPM
Miller, Sir Donald John, Kt., FRSE, FRENG
Miller, *Air Marshal* Sir Graham Anthony, KBE
Miller, Sir Harry Holmes, Bt. (1705)
Miller, Sir Hilary Duppa (Hal), Kt.
Miller, Sir Jonathan Wolfe, Kt., CBE
Miller, Sir Peter North, Kt.
Miller, Sir Robin Robert William, Kt.
Miller, Sir Ronald Andrew Baird, Kt., CBE
Miller of Glenlee, Sir Stephen William Macdonald, Bt. (1788)
Mills, Sir Ian, Kt.
Mills, Sir Keith, Kt.
Mills, Sir Peter Frederick Leighton, Bt. (1921)
Milman, Sir David Patrick, Bt. (1800)
Milne, Sir John Drummond, Kt.
Milne-Watson, Sir Andrew Michael, Bt. (1937)
Milner, Sir Timothy William Lycett, Bt. (1717)
Milton, Sir Simon, Kt.
Milton-Thompson, *Surgeon Vice-Adm.* Sir Godfrey James, KBE
Mirrlees, *Prof.* Sir James Alexander, Kt., FBA
Mitchell, Sir David Bower, Kt.
Mitchell, Sir Derek Jack, KCB, CVO
Mitchell, *Rt. Hon.* Sir James FitzAllen, KCMG
Mitchell, *Very Revd* Patrick Reynolds, KCVO
Mitchell, *Hon.* Sir Stephen George, Kt.
Mitting, *Hon.* Sir John Edward, Kt.
Moate, Sir Roger Denis, Kt.
Moberly, Sir Patrick Hamilton, KCMG
Moffat, Sir Brian Scott, Kt., OBE
Moffat, *Lt.-Gen.* Sir (William) Cameron, KBE
Moir, Sir Christopher Ernest, Bt. (1916)
†Molesworth-St Aubyn, Sir William, Bt. (1689)
†Molony, Sir Thomas Desmond, Bt. (1925)
Monck, Sir Nicholas Jeremy, KCB
Money-Coutts, Sir David Burdett, KCVO
Montagu, Sir Nicholas Lionel John, KCB
Montagu-Pollock, Sir Giles Hampden, Bt. (1872)
Montague, Sir Adrian Alastair, Kt., CBE
Montague-Browne, Sir Anthony Arthur Duncan, KCMG, CBE, DFC
Montgomery, Sir (Basil Henry) David, Bt. (1801), CVO
Montgomery, Sir (William) Fergus, Kt.
Montgomery-Cuninghame, Sir John Christopher Foggo, Bt. (NS 1672)
Moody-Stuart, Sir Mark, KCMG
Moollan, Sir Abdool Hamid Adam, Kt.
Moollan, *Hon.* Sir Cassam (Ismael), Kt.
†Moon, Sir Roger, Bt. (1887)
Moorcroft, Sir William, Kt.
Moore, *Most Revd* Desmond Charles, KBE
Moore, Sir Francis Thomas, Kt.
Moore, Sir John Michael, KCVO, CB, DSC
Moore, *Vice Adm.* Sir Michael Antony Claës, KBE, LVO
Moore, *Prof.* Sir Norman Winfrid, Bt. (1919)
Moore, Sir Patrick Alfred Caldwell, Kt., CBE
Moore, Sir Patrick William Eisdell, Kt., OBE
Moore, Sir Roger George, KBE
Moore, Sir William Roger Clotworthy, Bt. (1932), TD
Moore-Bick, *Rt. Hon.* Sir Martin James, Kt.
Moores, Sir Peter, Kt., CBE
Morauta, Sir Mekere, Kt.
Mordaunt, Sir Richard Nigel Charles, Bt. (1611)
Moreton, Sir John Oscar, KCMG, KCVO, MC
Morgan, *Vice-Adm.* Sir Charles Christopher, KBE
Morgan, *Hon.* Sir Charles Declan, Kt.
Morgan, Sir Graham, Kt.
Morgan, Sir John Albert Leigh, KCMG
Morgan, *Hon.* Sir Paul Hyacinth, Kt.
Morgan-Giles, *Rear-Adm.* Sir Morgan Charles, Kt., DSO, OBE, GM
Morison, *Hon.* Sir Thomas Richard Atkin, Kt.
Morland, *Hon.* Sir Michael, Kt.
Morland, Sir Robert Kenelm, Kt.
Morpeth, Sir Douglas Spottiswoode, Kt., TD
†Morris, Sir Allan Lindsay, Bt. (1806)
Morris, *Air Marshal* Sir Arnold Alec, KBE, CB
Morris, Sir Derek James, Kt.
Morris, Sir Keith Elliot Hedley, KBE, CMG
Morris, *Prof.* Sir Peter John, Kt.
Morris, Sir Trefor Alfred, Kt., CBE, QPM
Morris, *Very Revd* William James, KCVO
Morrison, Sir (Alexander) Fraser, Kt., CBE
Morrison, Sir Howard Leslie, Kt., OBE
Morrison, Sir Kenneth Duncan, Kt., CBE
Morrison, Sir (William) Garth, KT, CBE
Morrison-Bell, Sir William Hollin Dayrell, Bt. (1905)
Morrison-Low, Sir James Richard, Bt. (1908)
Morritt, *Rt. Hon.* Sir (Robert) Andrew, Kt., CVO
Morse, Sir Christopher Jeremy, KCMG
Mortimer, Sir John Clifford, Kt., CBE, QC
Moseley, Sir George Walker, KCB
Moses, *Rt. Hon.* Sir Alan George, Kt.
Moses, *Very Revd* Dr John Henry, KCVO
Moss, Sir David Joseph, KCVO, CMG
Moss, Sir Stephen Alan, Kt.
Moss, Sir Stirling Craufurd, Kt., OBE
Mostyn, Sir William Basil John, Bt. (1670)
Mott, Sir John Harmer, Bt. (1930)
Mottram, Sir Richard Clive, GCB
†Mount, Sir (William Robert) Ferdinand, Bt. (1921)
†Mountain, Sir Edward Brian Stanford, Bt. (1922)
Mountfield, Sir Robin, KCB
Mowbray, Sir John Robert, Bt. (1880)
Moylan, *Hon.* Sir Andrew John Gregory, Kt.
Muir, Sir Laurence Macdonald, Kt.
†Muir, Sir Richard James Kay, Bt. (1892)
Muir-Mackenzie, Sir Alexander Alwyne Henry Charles Brinton, Bt. (1805)
Mulcahy, Sir Geoffrey John, Kt.
Mullens, *Lt.-Gen.* Sir Anthony Richard Guy, KCB, OBE
Mummery, *Rt. Hon.* Sir John Frank, Kt.
Munby, *Hon.* Sir James Lawrence, Kt.
Munn, Sir James, Kt., OBE
Munro, Sir Alan Gordon, KCMG
†Munro, Sir Ian Kenneth, Bt. (S. 1634)
Munro, Sir Alasdair Thomas Ian, Bt. (1825)
Muria, *Hon.* Sir Gilbert John Baptist, Kt.
Murray, Sir David Edward, Kt.
Murray, *Rt. Hon.* Sir Donald Bruce, Kt.
Murray, Sir James, KCMG
Murray, *Prof.* Sir Kenneth, Kt.
Murray, Sir Nigel Andrew Digby, Bt. (S. 1628)
Murray, Sir Patrick Ian Keith, Bt. (S. 1673)
†Murray, Sir Rowland William, Bt. (S. 1630)
Mursell, Sir Peter, Kt., MBE

Musgrave, Sir Christopher John Shane, Bt. (1782)
Musgrave, Sir Christopher Patrick Charles, Bt. (1611)
Myers, Sir Philip Alan, Kt., OBE, QPM
Myers, *Prof.* Sir Rupert Horace, KBE
Mynors, Sir Richard Baskerville, Bt. (1964)
Naipaul, Sir Vidiadhar Surajprasad, Kt.
Nairn, Sir Michael, Bt. (1904)
Nairne, *Rt. Hon.* Sir Patrick Dalmahoy, GCB, MC
Naish, Sir (Charles) David, Kt.
Nalau, Sir Jerry Kasip, KBE
Nall, Sir Edward William Joseph Bt. (1954)
Namaliu, *Rt. Hon.* Sir Rabbie Langanai, KCMG
†Napier, Sir Charles Joseph, Bt. (1867)
Napier, Sir John Archibald Lennox, Bt. (S. 1627)
Napier, Sir Oliver John, Kt.
Naylor, Sir Robert, Kt.
Naylor-Leyland, Sir Philip Vyvyan, Bt. (1895)
Neal, Sir Eric James, Kt., CVO
Neale, Sir Gerrard Anthony, Kt.
Neave, Sir Paul Arundell, Bt. (1795)
Neill, *Rt. Hon.* Sir Brian Thomas, Kt.
Neill, Sir (James) Hugh, KCVO, CBE, TD
†Nelson, Sir Jamie Charles Vernon Hope, Bt. (1912)
Nelson, *Hon.* Sir Robert Franklyn, Kt.
Neubert, Sir Michael John, Kt.
New, *Maj.-Gen.* Sir Laurence Anthony Wallis, Kt., CB, CBE
Newall, Sir Paul Henry, Kt., TD
Newby, *Prof.* Sir Howard Joseph, Kt., CBE
Newington, Sir Michael John, KCMG
Newman, Sir Francis Hugh Cecil, Bt. (1912)
Newman, Sir Geoffrey Robert, Bt. (1836)
Newman, *Hon.* Sir George Michael, Kt.
Newman, Sir Kenneth Leslie, GBE, QPM
Newman, *Vice-Adm.* Sir Roy Thomas, KCB
Newman Taylor, *Prof.* Sir Anthony John, Kt., CBE
Newsam, Sir Peter Anthony, Kt.
†Newson-Smith, Sir Peter Frank Graham, Bt. (1944)
Newton, Sir (Charles) Wilfred, Kt., CBE
†Newton, *Revd* George Peter Howgill, Bt. (1900)
†Newton, Sir John Garnar, Bt. (1924)
Ngata, Sir Henare Kohere, KBE
Nice, Sir Geoffrey, Kt., QC
Nichol, Sir Duncan Kirkbride, Kt., CBE
Nicholas, Sir David, Kt., CBE
Nicholas, Sir John William, KCVO, CMG
Nicholls, Sir Nigel Hamilton, KCVO, CBE
Nichols, Sir Richard Everard, Kt.
Nicholson, Sir Bryan Hubert, GBE, Kt.
†Nicholson, Sir Charles Christian, Bt. (1912)
Nicholson, *Rt. Hon.* Sir Michael, Kt.
Nicholson, Sir Paul Douglas, Kt.
Nicholson, Sir Robin Buchanan, Kt., PHD, FRS, FRENG
Nicoll, Sir William, KCMG
Nightingale, Sir Charles Manners Gamaliel, Bt. (1628)
Nixon, Sir Simon Michael Christopher, Bt. (1906)
Noble, Sir David Brunel, Bt. (1902)
Noble, Sir Iain Andrew, Bt., OBE (1923)
Nombri, Sir Joseph Karl, Kt., ISO, BEM
Noon, Sir Gulam Kaderbhoy, Kt., MBE
Norman, Sir Arthur Gordon, KBE, DFC
Norman, Sir Mark Annesley, Bt. (1915)
Norman, Sir Robert Henry, Kt., OBE
Norman, Sir Ronald, Kt., OBE
Norman, Sir Torquil Patrick Alexander, Kt., CBE
Normington, Sir David John, KCB
Norrington, Sir Roger Arthur Carver, Kt., CBE
Norris, *Hon.* Sir Alastair Hubert, Kt.
Norriss, Air Marshal Sir Peter Coulson, KBE, CB, AFC
North, Sir Peter Machin, Kt., CBE, QC, DCL, FBA
North, Sir Thomas Lindsay, Kt.
North, Sir (William) Jonathan (Frederick), Bt. (1920)
Norton-Griffiths, Sir John, Bt. (1922)
Nossal, Sir Gustav Joseph Victor, Kt., CBE
Nott, *Rt. Hon.* Sir John William Frederic, KCB
Nourse, *Rt. Hon.* Sir Martin Charles, Kt.
Nugent, Sir John Edwin Lavallin, Bt. (I. 1795)
†Nugent, Sir Christopher George Ridley, Bt. (1806)
†Nugent, Sir (Walter) Richard Middleton, Bt. (1831)
Nunn, Sir Trevor Robert, Kt., CBE
Nunneley, Sir Charles Kenneth Roylance, Kt.
Nursaw, Sir James, KCB, QC
Nurse, Sir Paul Maxime, Kt.
†Nuttall, Sir Harry, Bt. (1922)
Nutting, Sir John Grenfell, Bt. (1903), QC
Oakeley, Sir John Digby Atholl, Bt. (1790)
Oakes, Sir Christopher, Bt. (1939)
†Oakshott, Hon. Sir Michael Arthur John, Bt. (1959)
Oates, Sir Thomas, Kt., CMG, OBE
O'Brien, Sir Frederick William Fitzgerald, Kt.
O'Brien, Sir Richard, Kt., DSO, MC
O'Brien, Sir Timothy John, Bt. (1849)
O'Brien, *Adm.* Sir William Donough, KCB, DSC
O'Connell, Sir Bernard, Kt.
O'Connell, Sir Maurice James Donagh MacCarthy, Bt. (1869)
O'Dea, Sir Patrick Jerad, KCVO
Odell, Sir Stanley John, Kt.
Odgers, Sir Graeme David William, Kt.
O'Donnell, Sir Augustine Thomas, KCB
O'Donnell, Sir Christopher John, Kt.
O'Donoghue, *Lt.-Gen.* Sir Kevin, KCB, CBE
O'Dowd, Sir David Joseph, Kt., CBE, QPM
Ogden, *Dr* Sir Peter James, Kt.
Ogden, Sir Robert, Kt., CBE
Ogilvy, Sir Francis Gilbert Arthur, Bt. (S. 1626)
Ogilvy-Wedderburn, Sir Andrew John Alexander, Bt. (1803)
Ognall, *Hon.* Sir Harry Henry, Kt.
Ohlson, Sir Brian Eric Christopher, Bt. (1920)
Oldham, *Dr* Sir John, Kt., OBE
Oliver, Sir James Michael Yorrick, Kt.
Oliver, Sir Stephen John Lindsay, Kt., QC
O'Loghlen, Sir Colman Michael, Bt. (1838)
Olver, Sir Stephen John Linley, KBE, CMG
Omand, Sir David Bruce, GCB
O'Nions, Prof. Sir Robert Keith, Kt., FRS, PHD
Ondaatje, Sir Christopher, Kt., CBE
Onslow, Sir John Roger Wilmot, Bt. (1797)
Oppenheimer, Sir Michael Bernard Grenville, Bt. (1921)
Oppenshaw, Sir Charles Peter Lawford, Kt., QC
Orde, Sir Hugh Stephen Roden, Kt., OBE
O'Regan, *Dr* Sir Stephen Gerard (Tipene), Kt.
O'Reilly, Sir Anthony John Francis, Kt.
O'Reilly, *Prof.* Sir John James, Kt.
Orr, Sir John, Kt., OBE
Orr-Ewing, Sir (Alistair) Simon, Bt. (1963)
Orr-Ewing, Sir Archibald Donald, Bt. (1886)
Osborn, Sir John Holbrook, Kt.
Osborn, Sir Richard Henry Danvers, Bt. (1662)
Osborne, Sir Peter George, Bt. (I. 1629)
O'Shea, *Prof.* Sir Timothy Michael Martin, Kt.
Osmotherly, Sir Edward Benjamin Crofton, Kt., CB
O'Sullevan, Sir Peter John, Kt., CBE
Oswald, *Admiral of the Fleet* Sir (John) Julian Robertson, GCB

Oswald, Sir (William Richard) Michael, KCVO
Otton, Sir Geoffrey John, KCB
Otton, *Rt. Hon.* Sir Philip Howard, Kt.
Oulton, Sir Antony Derek Maxwell, GCB, QC
Ouseley, *Hon.* Sir Brian Walter, Kt.
Outram, Sir Alan James, Bt. (1858)
Owen, Sir Geoffrey, Kt.
Owen, *Hon.* Sir John Arthur Dalziel, Kt.
Owen, *Hon.* Sir Robert Michael, Kt.
Owen-Jones, Sir Lindsay Harwood, KBE
Packer, Sir Richard John, KCB
Page, Sir (Arthur) John, Kt.
Paget, Sir Julian Tolver, Bt. (1871), CVO
Paget, Sir Richard Herbert, Bt. (1886)
Paine, Sir Christopher Hammon, Kt., FRCP, FRCR
Pakenham, *Hon.* Sir Michael Aiden, KBE, CMG
Palin, *Air Chief Marshal* Sir Roger Hewlett, KCB, OBE
Palliser, *Rt. Hon.* Sir (Arthur) Michael, GCMG
Palmer, Sir Albert Rocky, Kt.
Palmer, Sir (Charles) Mark, Bt. (1886)
Palmer, Sir Geoffrey Christopher John, Bt. (1660)
Palmer, *Rt. Hon.* Sir Geoffrey Winston Russell, KCMG
Palmer, Sir John Edward Somerset, Bt. (1791)
Palmer, *Maj.-Gen.* Sir (Joseph) Michael, KCVO
Palmer, Sir Reginald Oswald, GCMG, MBE
Pantlin, Sir Dick Hurst, Kt., CBE
Parbo, Sir Arvi Hillar, Kt.
Park, *Hon.* Sir Andrew Edward Wilson, Kt.
Parker, Sir Alan William, Kt., CBE
Parker, Sir Eric Wilson, Kt.
Parker, *Rt. Hon.* Sir Jonathan Frederic, Kt.
Parker, *Maj.* Sir Michael John, KCVO, CBE
Parker, Sir Richard (William) Hyde, Bt. (1681)
Parker, *Rt. Hon.* Sir Roger Jocelyn, Kt.
Parker, Sir (Thomas) John, Kt.
Parker, Sir William Peter Brian, Bt. (1844)
Parkes, Sir Edward Walter, Kt., FRENG
Parkinson, Sir Michael, Kt., CBE
Parry, Sir Emyr Jones, GCMG
Parry-Evans, *Air Chief Marshal* Sir David, GCB, CBE
Parsons, Sir John Christopher, KCVO
Parsons, Sir (John) Michael, Kt.
Parsons, Sir Richard Edmund (Clement Fownes), KCMG
Partridge, Sir Michael John Anthony, KCB
Pascoe, *Gen.* Sir Robert Alan, KCB, MBE
Pasley, Sir Robert Killigrew Sabine, Bt. (1794)
Paston-Bedingfeld, *Capt.* Sir Edmund George Felix, Bt. (1661)
Paterson, Sir Dennis Craig, Kt.
Patnick, Sir (Cyril) Irvine, Kt., OBE
Patten, *Hon.* Mr Justice, Sir Nicholas John, Kt.
Pattie, *Rt. Hon.* Sir Geoffrey Edwin, Kt.
Pattison, *Prof.* Sir John Ridley, Kt., DM, FRCPATH
Pattullo, Sir (David) Bruce, Kt., CBE
Pauncefort-Duncombe, Sir Philip Digby, Bt. (1859)
Payne, Sir Norman John, Kt., CBE, FRENG
Peach, Sir Leonard Harry, Kt.
Peacock, *Prof.* Sir Alan Turner, Kt., DSC
Pearce, Sir (Daniel Norton) Idris, Kt., CBE, TD
Pearse, Sir Brian Gerald, Kt.
Pearson, Sir Francis Nicholas Fraser, Bt. (1964)
Pearson, *Gen.* Sir Thomas Cecil Hook, KCB, CBE, DSO
Peart, *Prof.* Sir William Stanley, Kt., MD, FRS
Pease, Sir (Alfred) Vincent, Bt. (1882)
Pease, Sir Richard Thorn, Bt. (1920)
Peat, Sir Gerrard Charles, KCVO
Peat, Sir Michael Charles Gerrard, KCVO
Peck, Sir Edward Heywood, GCMG
Peckham, *Prof.* Sir Michael John, Kt.,
Pedelty, Sir Mervyn Kay, Kt.
Peek, *Vice-Adm.* Sir Richard Innes, KBE, CB, DSC
Peek, Sir Richard Grenville, Bt. (1874)
Peirse, *Air Vice-Marshal* Sir Richard Charles Fairfax, KCVO, CB
Pelgen, Sir Harry Friedrich, Kt., MBE
Peliza, Sir Robert John, KBE, ED
Pelly, Sir Richard John, Bt. (1840)
Pemberton, Sir Francis Wingate William, Kt., CBE
Pendry, *Prof.* Sir John Brian, Kt., FRS
Penrose, *Prof.* Sir Roger, Kt., OM, FRS
Penry-Davey, *Hon.* Sir David Herbert, Kt.
Pepper, *Dr.* Sir David Edwin, KCMG
Pepper, *Prof.* Sir Michael, Kt.
Perowne, *Vice-Adm.* Sir James Francis, KBE
Perring, Sir John Raymond, Bt. (1963)
Perris, Sir David (Arthur), Kt., MBE
Perry, Sir David Howard, KCB
Perry, Sir Michael Sydney, GBE
Pervez, Sir Mohammed Anwar, Kt., OBE
Peters, *Prof.* Sir David Keith, Kt., FRCP
Peterson, Sir Christopher Matthew, Kt., CBE, TD
†Petit, Sir Jehangir, Bt. (1890)
Peto, Sir Henry George Morton, Bt. (1855)
†Peto, Sir Henry Christopher Morton Bampfylde, Bt. (1927)
Peto, *Prof.* Sir Richard, Kt., FRS
Petrie, Sir Peter Charles, Bt. (1918), CMG
Pettigrew, Sir Russell Hilton, Kt.
Pettit, Sir Daniel Eric Arthur, Kt.
Pettitt, Sir Dennis, Kt.
†Philipson-Stow, Sir (Robert) Matthew, Bt. (1907)
Phillips, Sir Fred Albert, Kt., CVO
Phillips, Sir (Gerald) Hayden, GCB
Phillips, Sir John David, Kt., QPM
Phillips, Sir Peter John, Kt., OBE
Phillips, Sir Robin Francis, Bt. (1912)
Phillis, Sir Robert Weston, Kt.
Pickard, Sir (John) Michael, Kt.
Pickthorn, Sir James Francis Mann, Bt. (1959)
Pidgeon, Sir John Allan Stewart, Kt.
†Piers, Sir James Desmond, Bt. (I. 1661)
Piggott-Brown, Sir William Brian, Bt. (1903)
Pigot, Sir George Hugh, Bt. (1764)
Pigott, *Lt.-Gen.* Sir Anthony David, KCB, CBE
Pigott, Sir Berkeley Henry Sebastian, Bt. (1808)
Pike, *Lt.-Gen.* Sir Hew William Royston, KCB, DSO, MBE
Pike, Sir Michael Edmund, KCVO, CMG
Pike, Sir Philip Ernest Housden, Kt., QC
Pilditch, Sir Richard Edward, Bt. (1929)
Pile, Sir Frederick Devereux, Bt. (1900), MC
Pill, *Rt. Hon.* Sir Malcolm Thomas, Kt.
Pilling, Sir Joseph Grant, KCB
Pinsent, Sir Christopher Roy, Bt. (1938)
Pinsent, Sir Matthew Clive, Kt., CBE
Pippard, *Prof.* Sir (Alfred) Brian, Kt., FRS
Pitakaka, Sir Moses Puibangara, GCMG
Pitcher, Sir Desmond Henry, Kt.
Pitchers, *Hon.* Sir Christopher (John), Kt.
Pitchford, *Hon.* Sir Christopher John, Kt.
Pitman, Sir Brian Ivor, Kt.
Pitoi, Sir Sere, Kt., CBE
Pitt, Sir Michael Edward, Kt.
Pitts, Sir Cyril Alfred, Kt.
Plastow, Sir David Arnold Stuart, Kt.
Platt, Sir Harold Grant, Kt.
Platt, Sir Martin Philip, Bt. (1959)
Pledger, *Air Chief Marshal* Sir Malcolm David, KCB, OBE, AFC
Plender, *Hon.* Sir Richard Owen, Kt.
Plumbly, Sir Derek John, KCMG
Pogo, *Most Revd.* Ellison Leslie, KBE
Pohai, Sir Timothy, Kt., MBE
Pole, Sir (John) Richard (Walter Reginald) Carew, Bt. (1628)
Pole, Sir Peter Van Notten, Bt. (1791)

Polkinghorne, *Revd Canon* John Charlton, KBE, FRS
Pollard, Sir Charles, Kt.
†Pollen, Sir Richard John Hungerford, Bt. (1795)
Pollock, Sir George Frederick, Bt. (1866)
Ponder, *Prof.* Sir Bruce Anthony John, Kt.
Ponsonby, Sir Ashley Charles Gibbs, Bt., KCVO, MC (1956)
Poore, Sir Roger Ricardo, Bt. (1795)
Pope, Sir Joseph Albert, Kt., DSC, PHD
Popplewell, *Hon.* Sir Oliver Bury, Kt.
†Porritt, Sir Jonathon Espie, Bt. (1963)
Portal, Sir Jonathan Francis, Bt. (1901)
Porter, *Rt. Hon.* Sir Robert Wilson, Kt., PC (NI)
Posnett, Sir Richard Neil, KBE, CMG
Potter, *Rt. Hon.* Sir Mark Howard, Kt.
Potts, *Hon.* Sir Francis Humphrey, Kt.
Pound, Sir John David, Bt. (1905)
Povey, Sir Keith, Kt., QPM
Powell, Sir Nicholas Folliott Douglas, Bt. (1897)
Power, Sir Alastair John Cecil, Bt. (1924)
Power, *Hon.* Sir Noel Plunkett, Kt.
Prance, *Prof.* Sir Ghillean Tolmie, Kt., FRS
Prendergast, Sir (Walter) Kieran, KCVO, CMG
Prescott, Sir Mark, Bt. (1938)
†Preston, Sir Philip Charles Henry Hulton, Bt. (1815)
Prevost, Sir Christopher Gerald, Bt. (1805)
Price, Sir David Ernest Campbell, Kt.
Price, Sir Francis Caradoc Rose, Bt. (1815)
Price, Sir Frank Leslie, Kt.
Prickett, *Air Chief Marshal* Sir Thomas Other, KCB, DSO, DFC
Prideaux, Sir Humphrey Povah Treverbian, Kt., OBE
Priestly, Sir Julian Gordon, KCMG
†Primrose, Sir John Ure, Bt. (1903)
Pringle, *Air Marshal* Sir Charles Norman Seton, KBE, FRENG
Pringle, *Hon.* Sir John Kenneth, Kt.
Pringle, *Lt.-Gen.* Sir Steuart (Robert), Bt. (S. 1683), KCB
Pritchard, Sir Neil, KCMG
†Prichard-Jones, Sir David John Walter, Bt. (1910)
Proby, Sir William Henry, Bt. (1952)
Proctor-Beauchamp, Sir Christopher Radstock, Bt. (1745)
Prosser, Sir David John, Kt.
Prosser, Sir Ian Maurice Gray, Kt.
Pryke, Sir Christopher Dudley, Bt. (1926)
Puapua, *Rt. Hon.* Sir Tomasi, GCMG, KBE
Pugh, Sir Idwal Vaughan, KCB
Pumphrey, Sir (John) Laurence, KCMG
Purves, Sir William, Kt., CBE, DSO
Purvis, *Vice-Adm.* Sir Neville, KCB
Quan, Sir Henry (Francis), KBE
Quicke, Sir John Godolphin, Kt., CBE
Quigley, Sir (William) George (Henry), Kt., CB, PHD
Quilter, Sir Anthony Raymond Leopold Cuthbert, Bt. (1897)
Quinlan, Sir Michael Edward, GCB
Quinton, Sir James Grand, Kt.
Radcliffe, Sir Sebastian Everard, Bt. (1813)
Radda, *Prof.* Sir George Karoly, Kt., CBE, FRS
Rae, Sir William, Kt., QPM
Raeburn, Sir Michael Edward Norman, Bt. (1923)
Raikes, *Vice-Adm.* Sir Iwan Geoffrey, KCB, CBE, DSC
Raison, *Rt. Hon.* Sir Timothy Hugh Francis, Kt.
Rake, Sir Michael Derek Vaughan, Kt.
Ralli, Sir Godfrey Victor, Bt., TD (1912)
Ramdanee, Sir Mookteswar Baboolall Kailash, Kt.
Ramphal, Sir Shridath Surendranath, GCMG
Ramphul, Sir Baalkhristna, Kt.
Ramphul, Sir Indurduth, Kt.
Ramsay, Sir Alexander William Burnett, Bt. (1806)
Ramsay, Sir Allan John (Hepple), KBE, CMG
Ramsay-Fairfax-Lucy, Sir Edmund John William Hugh, Bt. (1836)
Ramsbotham, *Hon.* Sir Peter Edward, GCMG, GCVO
Ramsden, Sir John Charles Josslyn, Bt. (1689)
Ramsey, *Dr* Sir Frank Cuthbert, KCMG
Ramsey, *Hon.* Sir Vivian Arthur, Kt.
Rankin, Sir Ian Niall, Bt. (1898)
Rasch, Sir Simon Anthony Carne, Bt. (1903)
Rashleigh, Sir Richard Harry, Bt. (1831)
Ratford, Sir David John Edward, KCMG, CVO
Rattee, *Hon.* Sir Donald Keith, Kt.
Rattle, Sir Simon Dennis, Kt., CBE
Rawlins, *Surgeon Vice-Adm.* Sir John Stuart Pepys, KBE
Rawlins, *Prof.* Sir Michael David, Kt., FRCP, FRCPED
Rawlinson, Sir Anthony Henry John, Bt. (1891)
Rea, *Prof.* Sir Desmond, Kt., OBE
Read, *Air Marshal* Sir Charles Frederick, KBE, CB, DFC, AFC
Read, *Prof.* Sir David John, Kt.
Read, Sir John Emms, Kt.
†Reade, Sir Kenneth Ray, Bt. (1661)
Reardon-Smith, Sir (William) Antony (John), Bt. (1920)
Reay, *Lt.-Gen.* Sir (Hubert) Alan John, KBE
Redgrave, *Maj.-Gen.* Sir Roy Michael Frederick, KBE, MC
Redgrave, Sir Steven Geoffrey, Kt., CBE
Redmayne, Sir Nicholas, Bt. (1964)
Redwood, Sir Peter Boverton, Bt. (1911)
Reece, Sir Charles Hugh, Kt.
Reedie, Sir Craig Collins, Kt., CBE
Rees, Sir David Allan, Kt., PHD, DSC, FRS
Rees, Sir Richard Ellis Meuric, Kt., CBE
Reeve, Sir Anthony, KCMG, KCVO
Reeves, *Most Revd* Paul Alfred, GCMG, GCVO
Reffell, *Adm.* Sir Derek Roy, KCB
Refshauge, *Maj.-Gen.* Sir William Dudley, Kt., CBE
Reid, Sir Alexander James, Bt. (1897)
Reid, Sir Hugh, Bt. (1922)
Reid, Sir (Philip) Alan, KCVO
Reid, Sir Robert Paul, Kt.
Reid, Sir William Kennedy, KCB
Reiher, Sir Frederick Bernard Carl, KBE, CMG
Reilly, *Lt.-Gen.* Sir Jeremy Calcott, KCB, DSO
Renals, Sir Stanley, Bt. (1895)
Renouf, Sir Clement William Bailey, Kt.
Renshaw, Sir John David Bine, Bt. (1903)
Renwick, Sir Richard Eustace, Bt. (1921)
Reporter, Sir Shapoor Ardeshirji, KBE
Reynolds, Sir David James, Bt. (1923)
Reynolds, Sir Peter William John, Kt., CBE
Rhodes, Sir John Christopher Douglas, Bt. (1919)
Rice, *Maj.-Gen.* Sir Desmond Hind Garrett, KCVO, CBE
Rice, Sir Timothy Miles Bindon, Kt.
Richard, Sir Cliff, Kt., OBE
Richards, Sir Brian Mansel, Kt., CBE, PHD
Richards, *Hon.* Sir David Anthony Stewart, Kt.
Richards, Sir David Gerald, Kt.
Richards, *Lt.-Gen.* Sir David, Julian, KCB, CBE, DSO
Richards, Sir Francis Neville, KCMG, CVO
Richards, Sir Rex Edward, Kt., DSC, FRS
Richards, *Rt. Hon.* Sir Stephen Price, Kt.
Richardson, Sir Anthony Lewis, Bt. (1924)
Richardson, *Rt. Hon.* Sir Ivor Lloyd Morgan, Kt.
Richardson, *Lt.-Gen.* Sir Robert Francis, KCB, CVO, CBE
Richardson, Sir Thomas Legh, KCMG
Richardson-Bunbury, Sir (Richard David) Michael, Bt. (I. 1787)
Richmond, Sir David Frank, KBE, CMG
Richmond, *Prof.* Sir Mark Henry, Kt., FRS

†Ricketts, Sir Stephen Tristram, Bt. (1828)
Riddell, Sir John Charles Buchanan, Bt. (S. 1628), CVO
Ridley, Sir Adam (Nicholas), Kt.
Ridley, Sir Michael Kershaw, KCVO
Rifkind, *Rt. Hon.* Sir Malcolm Leslie, KCMG
Rigby, Sir Anthony John, Bt. (1929)
Rigby, Sir Peter, Kt.
Rimer, *Hon.* Sir Colin Percy Farquharson, Kt.
Ripley, Sir William Hugh, Bt. (1880)
Risk, Sir Thomas Neilson, Kt.
Ritako, Sir Thomas Baha, Kt., MBE
Ritblat, Sir John Henry, Kt.
Rivett-Carnac, Sir Miles James, Bt. (1836)
Rix, *Rt. Hon.* Sir Bernard Anthony, Kt.
Robati, Sir Pupuke, KBE
Robb, Sir John Weddell, Kt.
Roberts, *Hon.* Sir Denys Tudor Emil, KBE,
Roberts, Sir Derek Harry, Kt., CBE, FRS, FRENG
Roberts, *Prof.* Sir Edward Adam, KCMG
Roberts, Sir Gilbert Howland Rookehurst, Bt. (1809)
Roberts, Sir Hugh Ashley, KCVO
Roberts, Sir Ivor Anthony, KCMG
Roberts, *Dr* Sir Richard John, Kt.
Roberts, *Maj.-Gen.* Sir Sebastian John Lechmere, KCVO, OBE
Roberts, Sir Samuel, Bt. (1919)
Roberts, Sir William James Denby, Bt. (1909)
Robertson, Sir Lewis, Kt., CBE, FRSE
Robins, Sir Ralph Harry, Kt., FRENG
Robinson, Sir Albert Edward Phineas, Kt.
†Robinson, Sir Christopher Philipse, Bt. (1854)
Robinson, Sir Gerrard Jude, Kt.
Robinson, Sir Ian, Kt.
Robinson, Sir John James Michael Laud, Bt. (1660)
Robinson, *Dr* Sir Kenneth, Kt.
Robinson, Sir Wilfred Henry Frederick, Bt. (1908)
Robson, Sir John Adam, KCMG
Robson, Sir Stephen Arthur, Kt., CB
Robson, Sir Robert William, Kt., CBE
Roch, *Rt. Hon.* Sir John Ormond, Kt.
Roche, Sir David O'Grady, Bt. (1838)
Roche, Sir Henry John, Kt.
Rodgers, Sir (Andrew) Piers (Wingate Aikin-Sneath), Bt. (1964)
Rodley, *Prof.* Sir Nigel, KBE
Rodrigues, Sir Alberto Maria, Kt., CBE, ED
Rogers, *Air Chief Marshal* Sir John Robson, KCB, CBE
Rooke, Sir Denis Eric, Kt., OM, CBE, FRS, FRENG
Ropner, Sir John Bruce Woollacott, Bt. (1952)
Ropner, Sir Robert Clinton, Bt. (1904)
Rose, Sir Arthur James, Kt., CBE
Rose, *Rt. Hon.* Sir Christopher Dudley Roger, Kt.
Rose, Sir Clive Martin, GCMG
Rose, Sir David Lancaster, Bt. (1874)
Rose, *Gen.* Sir (Hugh) Michael, KCB, CBE, DSO, QGM
Rose, Sir John Edward Victor, Kt.
Rose, Sir Julian Day, Bt. (1872 and 1909)
Rose, Sir Stuart Alan Ransom, Kt.
Rosenthal, Sir Norman Leon, Kt.
Ross, *Maj.* Sir Andrew Charles Paterson, Bt. (1960)
Ross, *Lt.-Gen.* Sir Robert Jeremy, KCB, OBE
Ross, *Lt.-Col.* Sir Walter Hugh Malcolm, GCVO, OBE
Rossi, Sir Hugh Alexis Louis, Kt.
Rothschild, Sir Evelyn Robert Adrian de, Kt.
Rove, *Revd* Ikan, KBE
Rowe, *Rear-Adm.* Sir Patrick Barton, KCVO, CBE
Rowe-Ham, Sir David Kenneth, GBE
Rowland, Sir (John) David, Kt.
Rowlands, Sir David, KCB
†Rowley, Sir Richard Charles, Bt. (1836)
Rowling, Sir John Reginald, Kt.
Rowlinson, *Prof.* Sir John Shipley, Kt., FRS
Royce, *Hon.* Sir Roger John, Kt.
Royden, Sir Christopher John, Bt. (1905)
Rudd, Sir (Anthony) Nigel (Russell), Kt.
Rudge, Sir Alan Walter, Kt., CBE, FRS
Rugge-Price, Sir James Keith Peter, Bt. (1804)
Ruggles-Brise, Sir Timothy Edward, Bt. (1935)
Rumbold, Sir Henry John Sebastian, Bt. (1779)
Runchorelal, Sir (Udayan) Chinubhai Madhowlal, Bt. (1913)
Rusby, *Vice-Adm.* Sir Cameron, KCB, LVO
Rushdie, Sir (Ahmed) Salman, Kt.
†Russell, Sir (Arthur) Mervyn, Bt. (1812)
Russell, Sir Charles Dominic, Bt. (1916)
Russell, Sir George, Kt., CBE
Russell, Sir Muir, KCB
Rutter, *Prof.* Sir Michael Llewellyn, Kt., CBE, MD, FRS
Ryan, Sir Derek Gerald, Bt. (1919)
Rycroft, Sir Richard John, Bt. (1784)
Ryder, *Hon.* Sir Ernest Nigel Ryder, Kt., TD
Ryrie, Sir William Sinclair, KCB
Sacks, *Chief Rabbi Dr* Jonathan, Kt.
Sacranie, Sir Iqbal Abdul Karim Mussa, Kt., OBE
Sainsbury, *Rt. Hon.* Sir Timothy Alan Davan, Kt.
St Clair-Ford, Sir James Anson, Bt. (1793)
St George, Sir John Avenel Bligh, Bt. (I. 1766)
St John-Mildmay, Sir Walter John Hugh, Bt. (1772)
Sainty, Sir John Christopher, KCB
Salisbury, Sir Robert William, Kt.
Salt, Sir Patrick MacDonnell, Bt. (1869)
Salt, Sir (Thomas) Michael John, Bt. (1899)
Salusbury-Trelawny, Sir John Barry, Bt. (1628)
Sampson, Sir Colin, Kt., CBE, QPM
Samuel, Sir John Michael Glen, Bt. (1898)
Samuelson, Sir (Bernard) Michael (Francis), Bt. (1884)
Samuelson, Sir Sydney Wylie, Kt., CBE
Sanders, Sir Robert Tait, KBE, CMG
Sanders, Sir Ronald Michael, KCMG
Sanderson, Sir Frank Linton, Bt. (1920)
Sands, Sir Roger Blakemore, KCB
Sarei, Sir Alexis Holyweek, Kt., CBE
Sargent, Sir William Desmond, Kt., CBE
Sassoon, Sir James Meyer, Kt.
Satchwell, Sir Kevin Joseph, Kt.
Saunders, *Hon.* Sir John Henry Boulton, Kt.
Savile, Sir James Wilson Vincent, Kt., OBE
Savill, *Prof.* Sir John Stewart, Kt.
Savory, Sir Michael Berry, Kt.
Sawers, Sir Robert John, KCMG
Saxby, *Prof.* Sir Robin Keith, Kt.
Scarlett, Sir John McLeod, KCMG, OBE
Scheele, Sir Nicholas Vernon, KCMG
Schiemann, *Rt. Hon.* Sir Konrad Hermann Theodor, Kt.
Scholar, Sir Michael Charles, KCB
Scholey, Sir David Gerald, Kt., CBE
Scholey, Sir Robert, Kt., CBE, FRENG
Scholtens, Sir James Henry, KCVO
Schreier, Sir Bernard, Kt.
Schubert, Sir Sydney, Kt.
Scipio, Sir Hudson Rupert, Kt.
Scoon, Sir Paul, GCMG, GCVO, OBE
Scott, Sir Anthony Percy, Bt. (1913)
Scott, Sir David Aubrey, GCMG
Scott, *Prof.* Sir George Peter, Kt.
Scott, Sir James Jervoise, Bt. (1962)
Scott, Sir Kenneth Bertram Adam, KCVO, CMG
Scott, Sir Oliver Christopher Anderson, Bt. (1909)
Scott, *Prof.* Sir Philip John, KBE
Scott, Sir Ridley, Kt.
Scott, Sir Robert David Hillyer, Kt.
Scott, Sir Walter John, Bt. (1907)
Scott-Lee, Sir Paul Joseph, Kt., QPM
Seale, Sir Clarence David, Kt.
Seale, Sir John Henry, Bt. (1838)
Seaman, Sir Keith Douglas, KCVO, OBE
Sebastian, Sir Cuthbert Montraville, GCMG, OBE

†Sebright, Sir Rufus Hugo Giles, Bt. (1626)
Seccombe, Sir (William) Vernon Stephen, Kt.
Seconde, Sir Reginald Louis, KCMG, CVO
Sedley, *Rt. Hon.* Sir Stephen John, Kt.
Seely, Sir Nigel Edward, Bt. (1896)
Seeto, Sir Ling James, Kt., MBE
Seeyave, Sir Rene Sow Choung, Kt., CBE
Seligman, Sir Peter Wendel, Kt., CBE
Semple, Sir John Laughlin, KCB
Sergeant, Sir Patrick, Kt.
Serota, Sir Nicholas Andrew, Kt.
†Seton, Sir Charles Wallace, Bt. (S. 1683)
Seton, Sir Iain Bruce, Bt. (S. 1663)
Severne, *Air Vice-Marshal* Sir John de Milt, KCVO, OBE, AFC
Shaffer, Sir Peter Levin, Kt., CBE
Shakerley, Sir Geoffrey Adam, Bt. (1838)
Shakespeare, Sir Thomas William, Bt. (1942)
Sharp, Sir Adrian, Bt. (1922)
Sharp, Sir Kenneth Johnston, Kt., TD
Sharp, Sir Leslie, Kt., QPM
Sharp, Sir Sheridan Christopher Robin, Bt. (1920)
Sharples, Sir James, Kt., QPM
Shattock, Sir Gordon, Kt.
Shaw, Sir Brian Piers, Kt.
Shaw, Sir (Charles) Barry, Kt., CB, QC
Shaw, Sir Charles De Vere, Bt. (1821)
Shaw, *Prof.* Sir John Calman, Kt., CBE
Shaw, Sir Neil McGowan, Kt.
Shaw, Sir Roy, Kt.
Shaw, Sir Run Run, Kt., CBE
Shaw-Stewart, Sir Ludovic Houston, Bt. (S. 1667)
Shearing, Sir George Albert, Kt. OBE
Shebbeare, Sir Thomas Andrew, KCVO
Sheehy, Sir Patrick, Kt.
Sheffield, Sir Reginald Adrian Berkeley, Bt. (1755)
Shehadie, Sir Nicholas Michael, Kt., OBE
Sheil, *Rt. Hon.* Sir John, Kt.
Sheinwald, Sir Nigel Elton, KCMG
Shelley, Sir John Richard, Bt. (1611)
Shepherd, Sir Colin Ryley, Kt.
Shepherd, Sir John Alan, KCVO, CMG
Sher, Sir Antony, KBE
Sherbourne, Sir Stephen Ashley, Kt., CBE
Sherston-Baker, Sir Robert George Humphrey, Bt. (1796)
Shields, *Prof.* Sir Robert, Kt., MD
Shiffner, Sir Henry David, Bt. (1818)
Silber, *Hon.* Sir Stephen Robert, Kt.
Shinwell, Sir (Maurice) Adrian, Kt.
Shock, Sir Maurice, Kt.
Short, Sir Apenera Pera, KBE
Shortridge, Sir Jon Deacon, KCB
Shuckburgh, Sir Rupert Charles Gerald, Bt. (1660)
Sieff, *Hon.* Sir David, Kt.
Silber, *Rt. Hon.* Sir Stephen Robert, Kt.
Simeon, Sir Richard Edmund Barrington, Bt. (1815)
Simmonds, *Rt. Hon. Dr* Sir Kennedy Alphonse, KCMG
Simmons, *Air Marshal* Sir Michael George, KCB, AFC
Simmons, Sir Stanley Clifford, Kt.
Simms, Sir Neville Ian, Kt., FRENG
Simon, *Hon.* Sir Peregrine Charles Hugh, Kt.
Simonet, Sir Louis Marcel Pierre, Kt., CBE
Simpson, *Dr* Sir Peter Jeffery, Kt.
Sims, Sir Roger Edward, Kt.
Sinclair, Sir Clive Marles, Kt.
Sinclair, Sir Ian McTaggart, KCMG, QC
Sinclair, Sir Patrick Robert Richard, Bt. (S. 1704)
Sinclair, Sir Robert John, Kt.
Sinclair-Lockhart, Sir Simon John Edward Francis, Bt. (S. 1636)
Sinden, Sir Donald Alfred, Kt., CBE
Singer, *Hon.* Sir Jan Peter, Kt.
Singh, Sir Pritpal, Kt.
Singleton, Sir Roger, Kt., CBE
Sione, Sir Tomu Malaefone, GCMG, OBE
Sitwell, Sir (Sacheverell) Reresby, Bt. (1808)
Skeggs, Sir Clifford George, Kt.
Skehel, Sir John James, Kt., FRS
Skingsley, *Air Chief Marshal* Sir Anthony Gerald, GBE, KCB
Skinner, Sir (Thomas) Keith (Hewitt), Bt. (1912)
Skipwith, Sir Patrick Alexander d'Estoteville, Bt. (1622)
Slack, Sir William Willatt, KCVO, FRCS
Slade, Sir Benjamin Julian Alfred, Bt. (1831)
Slade, *Rt. Hon.* Sir Christopher John, Kt.
Slaney, *Prof.* Sir Geoffrey, KBE
Slater, *Adm.* Sir John (Jock) Cunningham Kirkwood, GCB, LVO
Sleight, Sir Richard, Bt. (1920)
Sloan, Sir Andrew Kirkpatrick, Kt., QPM
Sloman, Sir Albert Edward, Kt., CBE
Smart, Sir Jack, Kt., CBE
Smiley, *Lt.-Col.* Sir John Philip, Bt. (1903)
Smith, Sir Alan, Kt., CBE, DFC
Smith, *Hon.* Sir Andrew Charles, Kt.
Smith, Sir Andrew Thomas, Bt. (1897)
†Smith, Sir Robert Christopher Sydney Winwood, Bt. (1809)
Smith, *Prof.* Sir Colin Stansfield, Kt., CBE
Smith, Sir Cyril, Kt., MBE
Smith, *Prof.* Sir David Cecil, Kt., FRS
Smith, Sir David Iser, KCVO
Smith, Sir Dudley (Gordon), Kt.
Smith, *Prof.* Sir Eric Brian, Kt., PHD
Smith, Sir Geoffrey Johnson, Kt.
Smith, Sir John Alfred, Kt., QPM
Smith, Sir Joseph William Grenville, Kt.
Smith, Sir Kevin, Kt., CBE
Smith, Sir Michael John Llewellyn, KCVO, CMG
Smith, Sir (Norman) Brian, Kt., CBE, PHD
Smith, Sir Paul Brierley, Kt., CBE
Smith, *Hon.* Sir Peter (Winston), Kt.
Smith, Sir Robert Courtney, Kt., CBE
Smith, Sir Robert Hill, Bt. (1945)
Smith, *Gen.* Sir Rupert Anthony, KCB, DSO, OBE, QGM
Smith-Dodsworth, Sir John Christopher, Bt. (1784)
Smith-Gordon, Sir (Lionel) Eldred (Peter), Bt. (1838)
Smith-Marriott, Sir Hugh Cavendish, Bt. (1774)
Smurfit, *Dr.* Sir Michael William Joseph, KBE
Smyth, Sir Timothy John, Bt. (1955)
Snyder, Sir Michael John, Kt.
Sobers, Sir Garfield St Auburn, Kt.
Solomon, Sir Harry, Kt.
Somare, *Rt. Hon.* Sir Michael Thomas, GCMG, CH
Somerville, *Brig.* Sir John Nicholas, Kt., CBE
Sorrell, Sir John William, Kt., CBE
Sorrell, Sir Martin Stuart, Kt.
Soulsby, Sir Peter Alfred, Kt.
Soutar, *Air Marshal* Sir Charles John Williamson, KBE
Southby, Sir John Richard Bilbe, Bt. (1937)
Southern, *Prof.* Sir Edwin Mellor, Kt.
Southgate, Sir Colin Grieve, Kt.
Southgate, Sir William David, Kt.
Southward, *Dr* Sir Nigel Ralph, KCVO
Sowrey, *Air Marshal* Sir Frederick Beresford, KCB, CBE, AFC
Sparrow, Sir John, Kt.
Spearman, Sir Alexander Young Richard Mainwaring, Bt. (1840)
Spedding, *Prof.* Sir Colin Raymond William, Kt., CBE
Speed, Sir (Herbert) Keith, Kt., RD
Speelman, Sir Cornelis Jacob, Bt. (1686)
Speight, *Hon.* Sir Graham Davies, Kt.
Spencer, Sir Derek Harold, Kt., QC
Spencer, *Vice-Adm.* Sir Peter, KCB
Spencer-Nairn, Sir Robert Arnold, Bt. (1933)
Spicer, Sir James Wilton, Kt.
Spicer, Sir Nicholas Adrian Albert, Bt. (1906)
Spicer, Sir (William) Michael Hardy, Kt.
Spiers, Sir Donald Maurice, Kt., CB, TD
Spooner, Sir James Douglas, Kt.
Spratt, *Col.* Sir Greville Douglas, GBE, TD
Spring, Sir Dryden Thomas, Kt.
Squire, *Air Chief Marshal* Sir Peter Ted, GCB, DFC, AFC, ADC

Stadlen, *Hon.* Sir Nicholas Felix, Kt.
Stagg, Sir Charles Richard Vernon, KCMG
Stainton, Sir (John) Ross, Kt., CBE
Staite, Sir Richard John, Kt., OBE
Stamer, Sir (Lovelace) Anthony, Bt. (1809)
Stanhope, *Adm.* Sir Mark, KCB, OBE
Stanier, Sir Beville Douglas, Bt. (1917)
Stanley, *Rt. Hon.* Sir John Paul, Kt., MP
Staples, Sir Richard Molesworth, Bt. (I. 1628)
Starkey, Sir John Philip, Bt. (1935)
Staughton, *Rt. Hon.* Sir Christopher Stephen Thomas Jonathan Thayer, Kt.
Stear, *Air Chief Marshal* Sir Michael James Douglas, KCB, CBE
Steel, *Hon.* Sir David William, Kt.
Steer, Sir Alan William, Kt.
Stephen, *Rt. Hon.* Sir Ninian Martin, KG, GCMG, GCVO, KBE
Stephens, Sir (Edwin) Barrie, Kt.
Stephens, Sir William Benjamin Synge, Kt.
Stephenson, Sir Henry Upton, Bt. (1936)
Stephenson, Sir Paul Robert, Kt., QPM
Sternberg, Sir Sigmund, Kt.
Stevens, Sir Jocelyn Edward Greville, Kt., CVO
Stevenson, Sir Simpson, Kt.
Stewart, Sir Alan d'Arcy, Bt. (I. 1623)
Stewart, Sir Brian John, Kt., CBE
Stewart, Sir David James Henderson, Bt. (1957)
Stewart, Sir David John Christopher, Bt. (1803)
Stewart, Sir James Douglas, Kt.
Stewart, Sir James Moray, KCB
Stewart, Sir (John) Simon (Watson), Bt. (1920)
Stewart, Sir John Young, Kt., OBE
Stewart, *Lt.-Col.* Sir Robert Christie, KCVO, CBE, TD
Stewart, Sir Robertson Huntly, Kt., CBE
Stewart, Sir Robin Alastair, Bt. (1960)
Stewart, *Prof.* Sir William Duncan Paterson, Kt., FRS, FRSE
Stewart-Clark, Sir John, Bt. (1918)
Stewart-Richardson, Sir Simon Alaisdair, Bt. (S. 1630)
Stewart-Wilson, *Lt.-Col.* Sir Blair Aubyn, KCVO
Stibbon, *Gen.* Sir John James, KCB, OBE
Stirling, Sir Alexander John Dickson, KBE, CMG
Stirling, Sir Angus Duncan Aeneas, Kt.
Stirling-Hamilton, Sir Malcolm William Bruce, Bt. (S. 1673)
Stirling of Garden, *Col.* Sir James, KCVO, CBE, TD
Stirrup, *Air Chief Marshal* Sir Graham Eric (Jock), GCB, AFC, ADC
Stockdale, Sir Thomas Minshull, Bt. (1960)
Stoddart, *Prof.* Sir James Fraser, Kt.
Stoddart, *Wg Cdr.* Sir Kenneth Maxwell, KCVO, AE
Stoker, *Prof.* Sir Michael George Parke, Kt., CBE, FRCP, FRS, FRSE
Stones, Sir William Frederick, Kt., OBE
Stonhouse, *Revd* Michael Philip, Bt. (1628 and 1670)
Stonor, *Air Marshal* Sir Thomas Henry, KCB
Stoppard, Sir Thomas, Kt., OM, CBE
Storey, *Hon.* Sir Richard, Bt., CBE (1960)
Stothard, Sir Peter Michael, Kt.
Stott, Sir Adrian George Ellingham, Bt. (1920)
Stoute, Sir Michael Ronald, Kt.
Stowe, Sir Kenneth Ronald, GCB, CVO
Stracey, Sir John Simon, Bt. (1818)
Strachan, Sir Curtis Victor, Kt., CVO
Strachey, Sir Charles, Bt. (1801)
Straker, Sir Louis Hilton, KCMG
Strang Steel, Sir (Fiennes) Michael, Bt. (1938)
Street, *Hon.* Sir Laurence Whistler, KCMG
Streeton, Sir Terence George, KBE, CMG
Strickland-Constable, Sir Frederic, Bt. (1641)
Stringer, Sir Donald Edgar, Kt., CBE
Stringer, Sir Howard, Kt.
Strong, Sir Roy Colin, Kt., PHD, FSA
Stronge, Sir James Anselan Maxwell, Bt. (1803)
Stuart, Sir James Keith, Kt.
Stuart, Sir Kenneth Lamonte, Kt.
†Stuart, Sir Phillip Luttrell, Bt. (1660)
†Stuart-Forbes, Sir William Daniel, Bt. (S. 1626)
Stuart-Menteth, Sir James Wallace, Bt. (1838)
Stuart-Paul, *Air Marshal* Sir Ronald Ian, KBE
Stuart-Smith, *Rt. Hon.* Sir Murray, Kt.
Stubbs, Sir William Hamilton, Kt., PHD
Stucley, *Lt.* Sir Hugh George Coplestone Bampfylde, Bt. (1859)
Studd, Sir Edward Fairfax, Bt. (1929)
Studholme, Sir Henry William, Bt. (1956)
Sturridge, Sir Nicholas Anthony, KCVO
Stuttard, Sir John Boothman, Kt.
†Style, Sir William Frederick, Bt. (1627)
Sugar, Sir Alan Michael, Kt.
Sullivan, *Hon.* Sir Jeremy Mirth, Kt.
Sullivan, Sir Richard Arthur, Bt. (1804)
Sulston, Sir John Edward, Kt.
Sumner, *Hon.* Sir Christopher John, Kt.
Sunderland, Sir John Michael, Kt.
Sutherland, Sir John Brewer, Bt. (1921)
Sutherland, Sir William George MacKenzie, Kt.
Sutton, Sir Frederick Walter, Kt., OBE
Sutton, *Air Marshal* Sir John Matthias Dobson, KCB
Sutton, Sir Richard Lexington, Bt. (1772)
Swaffield, Sir James Chesebrough, Kt., CBE, RD
Swaine, Sir John Joseph, Kt., CBE
Swan, Sir Conrad Marshall John Fisher, KCVO, PHD
Swan, Sir John William David, KBE
Swann, Sir Michael Christopher, Bt. (1906), TD
Swartz, *Hon.* Sir Reginald William Colin, KBE, ED
Sweeney, Sir George, Kt.
Sweeting, *Prof.* Sir Martin Nicholas, Kt., OBE, FRS
Sweetnam, Sir (David) Rodney, KCVO, CBE, FRCS
Swinburn, *Lt.-Gen.* Sir Richard Hull, KCB
Swinnerton-Dyer, *Prof.* Sir (Henry) Peter (Francis), Bt. (1678), KBE, FRS
Swinton, *Maj.-Gen.* Sir John, KCVO, OBE
Swire, Sir Adrian Christopher, Kt.
Swire, Sir John Anthony, Kt., CBE
Sykes, Sir David Michael, Bt. (1921)
Sykes, Sir Francis John Badcock, Bt. (1781)
Sykes, Sir Hugh Ridley, Kt.
Sykes, *Prof.* Sir (Malcolm) Keith, Kt.
Sykes, Sir Richard, Kt.
Sykes, Sir Tatton Christopher Mark, Bt. (1783)
Symington, *Prof.* Sir Thomas, Kt., MD, FRSE
Symons, *Vice-Adm.* Sir Patrick Jeremy, KBE
Synge, Sir Robert Carson, Bt. (1801)
Synnott, Sir Hilary Nicholas Hugh, KCMG
Talboys, *Rt. Hon.* Sir Brian Edward, CH, KCB
Tang, Sir David Wing-cheung, KBE
Tangaroa, *Hon.* Sir Tangoroa, Kt., MBE
Tapps-Gervis-Meyrick, Sir George Christopher Cadafael, Bt. (1791)
Tapsell, Sir Peter Hannay Bailey, Kt., MP
Tate, Sir (Henry) Saxon, Bt. (1898)
Taureka, *Dr* Sir Reubeh, KBE
Tauvasa, Sir Joseph James, KBE
Tavare, Sir John, Kt., CBE
Tavener, *Prof.* Sir John Kenneth, Kt.
Taylor, Sir (Arthur) Godfrey, Kt.
Taylor, Sir Cyril Julian Hebden, GBE
Taylor, Sir Edward Macmillan (Teddy), Kt.
Taylor, *Rt. Revd* John Bernard, KCVO
Taylor, *Dr.* Sir John Michael, Kt., OBE

Taylor, Sir Nicholas Richard Stuart, Bt. (1917)
Taylor, *Prof.* Sir William, Kt., CBE
Taylor, Sir William George, Kt.
Teagle, *Vice-Adm.* Sir Somerford Francis, KBE
Teare, *Hon.* Sir Nigel John Martin, Kt.
Teasdale, *Prof.* Sir Graham Michael, Kt.
Tebbit, Sir Donald Claude, GCMG
Tebbit, Sir Kevin Reginald, KCB, CMG
Telito, *HE Revd* Filoimea, GCMG, MBE
Temple, *Prof.* Sir John Graham, Kt.
†Temple, Sir Richard, Bt. (1876)
Tennant, Sir Anthony John, Kt.
Tennyson-D'Eyncourt, Sir Mark Gervais, Bt. (1930)
Terry, *Air Marshal* Sir Colin George, KBE, CB
Terry, *Air Chief Marshal* Sir Peter David George, GCB, AFC
Thatcher, Sir Mark, Bt. (1990)
Thomas, Sir David John Godfrey, Bt. (1694)
Thomas, Sir Derek Morison David, KCMG
Thomas, Sir Gilbert Stanley, Kt., OBE
Thomas, Sir Jeremy Cashel, KCMG
Thomas, Sir (John) Alan, Kt.
Thomas, *Prof.* Sir John Meurig, Kt., FRS
Thomas, Sir Keith Vivian, Kt.
Thomas, *Dr* Sir Leton Felix, KCMG, CBE
Thomas, Sir Philip Lloyd, KCVO, CMG
Thomas, Sir Quentin Jeremy, Kt., CB
Thomas, *Rt. Hon.* Sir Roger John Laugharne, Kt.
Thomas, *Hon.* Sir Swinton Barclay, Kt.
Thomas, Sir William Michael, Bt. (1919)
Thomas, Sir (William) Michael (Marsh), Bt. (1918)
Thompson, Sir Christopher Peile, Bt. (1890)
Thompson, Sir Clive Malcolm, Kt.
Thompson, Sir David Albert, KCMG
Thompson, Sir Gilbert Williamson, Kt., OBE
Thompson, *Prof.* Sir Michael Warwick, Kt., DSC
Thompson, Sir Nicholas Annesley, Bt. (1963)
Thompson, Sir Nigel Cooper, KCMG, CBE
Thompson, Sir Paul Anthony, Bt. (1963)
Thompson, Sir Peter Anthony, Kt.
Thompson, *Dr* Sir Richard Paul Hepworth, KCVO
Thompson, Sir Thomas d'Eyncourt John, Bt. (1806)
Thomson, Sir (Frederick Douglas) David, Bt. (1929)
Thomson, Sir John Adam, GCMG
Thomson, Sir Mark Wilfrid Home, Bt. (1925)
Thomson, Sir Thomas James, Kt., CBE, FRCP
Thorn, Sir John Samuel, Kt., OBE
Thorne, Sir Neil Gordon, Kt., OBE, TD
Thornton, *Air Marshal* Sir Barry Michael, KCB
Thornton, Sir (George) Malcolm, Kt.
Thornton, Sir Peter Eustace, KCB
Thornton, Sir Richard Eustace, KCVO, OBE
†Thorold, Sir (Anthony) Oliver, Bt. (1642)
Thorpe, *Rt. Hon.* Sir Mathew Alexander, Kt.
Thurecht, Sir Ramon Richard, Kt., OBE
Thwaites, Sir Bryan, Kt., PHD
Tickell, Sir Crispin Charles Cervantes, GCMG, KCVO
Tidmarsh, Sir James Napier, KCVO, MBE
Tikaram, Sir Moti, KBE
Tilt, Sir Robin Richard, Kt.
Tiltman, Sir John Hessell, KCVO
Timmins, *Col.* Sir John Bradford, KCVO, OBE, TD
Tims, Sir Michael David, KCVO
Tindle, Sir Ray Stanley, Kt., CBE
Tirvengadum, Sir Harry Krishnan, Kt.
Tjoeng, Sir James Neng, KBE
Tod, *Vice-Adm.* Sir Jonathan James Richard, KCB, CBE
Todd, *Prof.* Sir David, Kt., CBE
Todd, Sir Ian Pelham, KBE, FRCS
Tollemache, Sir Lyonel Humphry John, Bt. (1793)
Tomkys, Sir (William) Roger, KCMG
Tomlinson, *Prof.* Sir Bernard Evans, Kt., CBE
Tomlinson, Sir John Rowland, Kt., CBE
Tomlinson, Sir Michael John, Kt., CBE
Tomlinson, *Hon.* Sir Stephen Miles, Kt.
Tooke, *Prof.* Sir John Edward, Kt.
Tooley, Sir John, Kt.
ToRobert, Sir Henry Thomas, KBE
Torpy, *Air Marshal* Sir Glenn Lester, GCB, CBE, DSO
Torry, Sir Peter James, GCVO, KCMG
Tory, Sir Geofroy William, KCMG
Touche, Sir Anthony George, Bt. (1920)
Touche, Sir Rodney Gordon, Bt. (1962)
Toulson, *Rt. Hon.* Sir Roger Grenfell, Kt.
Tovadek, Sir Martin, Kt. CMG
Tovey, Sir Brian John Maynard, KCMG
ToVue, Sir Ronald, Kt., OBE
Towneley, Sir Simon Peter Edmund Cosmo William, KCVO
Townsend, Sir Cyril David, Kt.
Traill, Sir Alan Towers, GBE
Treacher, *Adm.* Sir John Devereux, KCB
Treacy, *Hon.* Sir Colman Maurice, Kt.
Treacy, *Hon.* Sir (James Mary) Seamus, Kt.
Treitel, *Prof.* Sir Guenter Heinz, Kt., FBA, QC
Trescowthick, Sir Donald Henry, KBE
Trevelyan, Sir Geoffrey Washington, Bt. (1662 and 1874)
Trezise, Sir Kenneth Bruce, Kt., OBE
Trippier, Sir David Austin, Kt., RD
Tritton, Sir Anthony John Ernest, Bt. (1905)
Trollope, Sir Anthony Simon, Bt. (1642)
Trotman-Dickenson, Sir Aubrey Fiennes, Kt.
Trotter, Sir Neville Guthrie, Kt.
Trotter, Sir Ronald Ramsay, Kt.
Troubridge, Sir Thomas Richard, Bt. (1799)
Trousdell, *Lt.-Gen.* Sir Philip Charles Cornwallis, KBE, CB
Truscott, Sir Ralph Eric Nicholson, Bt. (1909)
Tsang, Sir Donald Yam-keun, KBE
Tuamure-Maoate, *Dr* Sir Terepai, KBE
Tuck, Sir Bruce Adolph Reginald, Bt. (1910)
Tucker, *Hon.* Sir Richard Howard, Kt.
Tuckey, *Rt. Hon.* Sir Simon Lane, Kt.
Tugendhat, *Hon.* Sir Michael George, Kt.
Tuita, Sir Mariano Kelesimalefo, KBE
Tuite, Sir Christopher Hugh, Bt. (1622), PHD
Tuivaga, Sir Timoci Uluiburotu, Kt.
Tully, Sir William Mark, KBE
Tupper, Sir Charles Hibbert, Bt. (1888)
Turbott, Sir Ian Graham, Kt., CMG, CVO
Turing, Sir John Dermot, Bt. (S. 1638)
Turner, Sir Colin William Carstairs, Kt., CBE, DFC
Turner, *Hon.* Sir Michael John, Kt.
Turnquest, Sir Orville Alton, GCMG, QC
Tusa, Sir John, Kt.
Tuti, *Revd* Dudley, KBE
Tweedie, *Prof.* Sir David Philip, Kt.
Tyree, Sir (Alfred) William, Kt., OBE
Tyrwhitt, Sir Reginald Thomas Newman, Bt. (1919)
Underhill, *Hon.* Sir Nicholas Edward, Kt.
Underwood, *Prof.* Sir James Cressee Elphinstone, Kt.
Unwin, Sir (James) Brian, KCB
Ure, Sir John Burns, KCMG, LVO
Urquhart, Sir Brian Edward, KCMG, MBE
Urwick, Sir Alan Bedford, KCVO, CMG
Usher, Sir Andrew John, Bt. (1899)
Utting, Sir William Benjamin, Kt., CB
Vardy, Sir Peter, Kt.

Varney, Sir David Robert, Kt.
Vasquez, Sir Alfred Joseph, Kt., CBE, QC
Vassar-Smith, Sir John Rathbone, Bt. (1917)
Vavasour, Sir Eric Michael Joseph Marmaduke, Bt. (1828)
Veness, Sir David, Kt., CBE, QPM
Venner, Sir Kenneth Dwight Vincent, KBE
Vereker, Sir John Michael Medlicott, KCB
†Verney, Sir John Sebastian, Bt. (1946)
Verney, *Hon.* Sir Lawrence John, Kt., TD
†Verney, Sir Edmund Ralph, Bt. (1818)
†Vernon, Sir James William, Bt. (1914)
Vernon, Sir (William) Michael, Kt.
Vestey, Sir Paul Edmund, Bt. (1921)
Vickers, *Prof.* Sir Brian William, Kt.
Vickers, Sir John Stuart, Kt.
Vickers, *Lt.-Gen.* Sir Richard Maurice Hilton, KCB, CVO, OBE
Viggers, *Lt-Gen.* Sir Frederick Richard, KCB, CMG, MBE
Viggers, Sir Peter John, Kt.
Vincent, Sir William Percy Maxwell, Bt. (1936)
Vineall, Sir Anthony John Patrick, Kt.
Vines, Sir William Joshua, Kt., CMG
von Schramek, Sir Eric Emil, Kt.
†Vyvyan, Sir Ralph Ferrers Alexander, Bt. (1645)
Wade-Gery, Sir Robert Lucian, KCMG, KCVO
Waena, Sir Nathaniel Rahumaea, GCMG
Waine, *Rt. Revd* John, KCVO
Waite, *Rt. Hon.* Sir John Douglas, Kt.
Waka, Sir Lucas Joseph, Kt., OBE
Wake, Sir Hereward, Bt. (1621), MC
Wakefield, Sir (Edward) Humphry (Tyrell), Bt. (1962)
Wakefield, Sir Norman Edward, Kt.
Wakefield, Sir Peter George Arthur, KBE, CMG
Wakeford, Sir Geoffrey Michael Montgomery, Kt., OBE
Wakeley, Sir John Cecil Nicholson, Bt. (1952), FRCS
†Wakeman, Sir Edward Offley Bertram, Bt. (1828)
Wald, *Prof.* Sir Nicholas John, Kt.
Wales, Sir Robert Andrew, Kt.
Waley-Cohen, Sir Stephen Harry, Bt. (1961)
Walford, Sir Christopher Rupert, Kt.
Walker, *Gen.* Sir Antony Kenneth Frederick, KCB
†Walker, Sir Christopher Robert Baldwin, Bt. (1856)
Walker, Sir David Alan, Kt.
Walker, Sir Harold Berners, KCMG
†Walker, Sir Roy Edward, Bt. (1906)
Walker, Sir James Graham, Kt., MBE
Walker, Sir John Ernest, Kt., DPHIL, FRS
Walker, *Air Marshal* Sir John Robert, KCB, CBE, AFC
Walker, Sir Miles Rawstron, Kt., CBE
Walker, Sir Patrick Jeremy, KCB
Walker, *Hon.* Sir Paul James, Kt.
Walker, Sir Rodney Myerscough, Kt.
Walker, *Hon.* Sir Timothy Edward, Kt.
Walker, Sir Victor Stewart Heron, Bt. (1868)
Walker-Okeover, Sir Andrew Peter Monro, Bt. (1886)
Walker-Smith, Sir John Jonah, Bt. (1960)
Wall, Sir John Anthony, Kt., CBE
Wall, Sir (John) Stephen, GCMG, LVO
Wall, *Rt. Hon.* Sir Nicholas Peter Rathbone, Kt.
Wall, Sir Robert William, Kt., OBE
Wallace, *Lt.-Gen.* Sir Christopher Brooke Quentin, KBE
Wallace, *Prof.* David James, Kt., CBE, FRS
Wallace, Sir Ian James, Kt., CBE
Waller, *Rt. Hon.* Sir (George) Mark, Kt.
Waller, Sir John Michael, Bt. (I. 1780)
Wallis, Sir Peter Gordon, KCVO
Wallis, Sir Timothy William, Kt.
Walmsley, *Vice-Adm.* Sir Robert, KCB
†Walsham, Sir Timothy John, Bt. (1831)
Walters, *Prof.* Sir Alan Arthur, Kt.
Walters, Sir Dennis Murray, Kt., MBE
Walters, Sir Frederick Donald, Kt.
Walters, Sir Peter Ingram, Kt.
Walters, Sir Roger Talbot, KBE, FRIBA
Wamiri, Sir Akapite, KBE
Wan, Sir Wamp, Kt., MBE
Wanless, Sir Derek, Kt.
Ward, *Rt. Hon.* Sir Alan Hylton, Kt.
Ward, Sir Austin, Kt., QC
Ward, Sir John Devereux, Kt., CBE
Ward, *Prof.* Sir John MacQueen, Kt., CBE
Ward, Sir Joseph James Laffey, Bt. (1911)
Ward, Sir Timothy James, Kt.
Wardale, Sir Geoffrey Charles, KCB
Wardlaw, Sir Henry (John), Bt. (NS. 1631)
Waring, Sir (Alfred) Holburt, Bt. (1935)
Warmington, Sir Rupert Marshall, Bt. (1908)
Warner, Sir (Edward Courtenay) Henry, Bt. (1910)
Warner, *Prof.* Sir Frederick Edward, Kt., FRS, FRENG
Warner, Sir Gerald Chierici, KCMG
Warren, Sir (Frederick) Miles, KBE
Warren, Sir Kenneth Robin, Kt.
Warren, Sir Nicholas Roger, Kt.
Wass, Sir Douglas William Gretton, GCB
Waterhouse, *Hon.* Sir Ronald Gough, GBE
Waterlow, Sir Christopher Rupert, Bt. (1873)
Waterlow, Sir (James) Gerard, Bt. (1930)
Waters, *Gen.* Sir (Charles) John, GCB, CBE
Waters, Sir (Thomas) Neil (Morris), Kt.
Waterworth, Sir Alan William, KCVO
Wates, Sir Christopher Stephen, Kt.
Watson, Sir Bruce Dunstan, Kt.
Watson, *Prof.* Sir David John, Kt., PHD
Watson, Sir (James) Andrew, Bt. (1866)
Watson, *Vice-Adm.* Sir Philip Alexander, KBE, LVO
Watson, Sir Ronald Matthew, Kt., CBE
Watson, Sir Simon Conran Hamilton, Bt. (1895)
Watt, *Gen.* Sir Charles Redmond, KCB, KCVO, CBE, ADC
Watt, *Surgeon Vice-Adm.* Sir James, KBE, FRCS
Watts, Sir John Augustus Fitzroy, KCMG, CBE
Watts, Sir Philip Beverley, KCMG
Weatherall, *Prof.* Sir David John, Kt., FRS
Weatherall, *Vice-Adm.* Sir James Lamb, KCVO, KBE
Weatherup, *Hon.* Sir Ronald Eccles, Kt.
Webb, *Prof.* Sir Adrian Leonard, Kt.
Webb-Carter, *Gen.* Sir Evelyn John, KCVO, OBE
Webster, *Vice-Adm.* Sir John Morrison, KCB
Webster, *Hon.* Sir Peter Edlin, Kt.
Wedgwood, Sir (Hugo) Martin, Bt. (1942)
Weekes, Sir Everton DeCourcey, KCMG, OBE
Weinberg, Sir Mark Aubrey, Kt.
Weir, *Hon.* Sir Reginald George, Kt.
Weir, Sir Roderick Bignell, Kt.
Welby, Sir (Richard) Bruno Gregory, Bt. (1801)
Welch, Sir John Reader, Bt. (1957)
Weldon, Sir Anthony William, Bt. (I. 1723)
Weller, Sir Arthur Burton, Kt., CBE
Wellings, Sir Jack Alfred, Kt., CBE
†Wells, Sir Christopher Charles, Bt. (1944)
Wells, Sir John Julius, Kt.
Wells, Sir William Henry Weston, Kt., FRICS
Wesker, Sir Arnold, Kt.
Westbrook, Sir Neil Gowanloch, Kt., CBE
Westmacott, Sir Peter John, KCMG
Weston, Sir Michael Charles Swift, KCMG, CVO
Weston, Sir (Philip) John, KCMG
Whalen, Sir Geoffrey Henry, Kt., CBE
Wheeler, Sir Harry Anthony, Kt., OBE
Wheeler, *Air Chief Marshal* Sir (Henry) Neil (George), GCB, CBE, DSO, DFC, AFC

Wheeler, *Rt. Hon.* Sir John Daniel, Kt.
Wheeler, Sir John Frederick, Bt. (1920)
Wheeler, *Gen.* Sir Roger Neil, GCB, CBE
Wheeler-Booth, Sir Michael Addison John, KCB
†Wheler, Sir Trevor Woodford, Bt. (1660)
Whitaker, Sir John James Ingham (Jack), Bt. (1936)
Whitchurch, Sir Graeme Ian, Kt., OBE
White, *Prof.* Sir Christopher John, Kt., CVO
White, Sir Christopher Robert Meadows, Bt. (1937)
White, Sir David (David Jason), Kt., OBE
White, Sir David Harry, Kt.
White, *Hon.* Sir Frank John, Kt.
White, Sir George Stanley James, Bt. (1904)
White, *Adm.* Sir Hugo Moresby, GCB, CBE
White, *Hon.* Sir John Charles, Kt., MBE
White, Sir John Woolmer, Bt. (1922)
White, Sir Nicholas Peter Archibald, Bt. (1802)
White, *Adm.* Sir Peter, GBE
White, Sir Willard Wentworth, Kt., CBE
Whitehead, Sir John Stainton, GCMG, CVO
†Whitehead, Sir Philip Henry Rathbone, Bt. (1889)
Whiteley, *Gen.* Sir Peter John Frederick, GCB, OBE, RM
Whitfield, Sir William, Kt., CBE
Whitmore, Sir Clive Anthony, GCB, CVO
Whitmore, Sir John Henry Douglas, Bt. (1954)
Whitney, Sir Raymond William, Kt., OBE
Whitson, Sir Keith Roderick, Kt.
Wickerson, Sir John Michael, Kt.
Wicks, Sir Nigel Leonard, GCB, CVO, CBE
†Wigan, Sir Michael Iain, Bt. (1898)
Wiggin, Sir Alfred William (Jerry), Kt., TD
†Wiggin, Sir Charles Rupert John, Bt. (1892)
†Wigram, Sir John Woolmore, Bt. (1805)
Wilbraham, Sir Richard Baker, Bt. (1776)
Wiles, *Prof.* Sir Andrew John, KBE
Wilkes, *Prof.* Sir Maurice Vincent, Kt.
Wilkes, *Gen.* Sir Michael John, KCB, CBE
Wilkie, *Hon.* Sir Alan Fraser, Kt.
Wilkinson, Sir (David) Graham (Brook) Bt. (1941)
Wilkinson, *Prof.* Sir Denys Haigh, Kt., FRS
Willcocks, Sir David Valentine, Kt., CBE, MC
Willcocks, *Lt.-Gen.* Sir Michael Alan, KCB
Williams, Sir Arthur Dennis Pitt, Kt.
Williams, Sir (Arthur) Gareth Ludovic Emrys Rhys, Bt. (1918)
Williams, *Prof.* Sir Bruce Rodda, KBE
Williams, Sir Charles Othniel, Kt.
Williams, Sir Daniel Charles, GCMG, QC
Williams, *Adm.* Sir David, GCB
Williams, *Prof.* Sir David Glyndwr Tudor, Kt.
Williams, Sir David Innes, Kt.
Williams, Sir David Reeve, Kt., CBE
Williams, *Hon.* Sir Denys Ambrose, KCMG
Williams, Sir Donald Mark, Bt. (1866)
Williams, *Prof.* Sir (Edward) Dillwyn, Kt., FRCP
Williams, Sir Francis Owen Garbett, Kt., CBE
Williams, *Hon.* Sir (John) Griffith, Kt.
Williams, Sir (Lawrence) Hugh, Bt. (1798)
Williams, Sir Osmond, Bt. (1909), MC
Williams, Sir Peter Michael, Kt.
Williams, Sir (Robert) Philip Nathaniel, Bt. (1915)
Williams, Sir Robin Philip, Bt. (1953)
Williams, *Prof.* Sir Roger, Kt.
Williams, Sir (William) Maxwell (Harries), Kt.
Williams, *Hon.* Sir Wyn Lewis
Williams-Bulkeley, Sir Richard Thomas, Bt. (1661)
Williams-Wynn, Sir David Watkin, Bt. (1688)
Williamson, Sir George Malcolm, Kt.
Williamson, *Marshal of the Royal Air Force* Sir Keith Alec, GCB, AFC
Williamson, Sir Robert Brian, Kt., CBE
Willink, Sir Charles William, Bt. (1957)
Willison, *Lt.-Gen.* Sir David John, KCB, OBE, MC
Wills, Sir David James Vernon, Bt. (1923)
Wills, Sir David Seton, Bt. (1904)
Wilmot, Sir David, Kt., QPM
Wilmot, Sir Henry Robert, Bt. (1759)
Wilmut, *Prof.* Sir Ian, Kt., OBE
Wilsey, *Gen.* Sir John Finlay Willasey, GCB, CBE
Wilshaw, Sir Michael, Kt.
Wilson, *Prof.* Sir Alan Geoffrey, Kt.
Wilson, Sir Anthony, Kt.
Wilson, *Vice-Adm.* Sir Barry Nigel, KCB
Wilson, Sir David, Bt. (1920)
Wilson, Sir David Mackenzie, Kt.
Wilson, Sir James William Douglas, Bt. (1906)
Wilson, *Brig.* Sir Mathew John Anthony, Bt. (1874), OBE, MC
Wilson, *Rt. Hon.* Sir Nicholas Allan Roy, Kt.
Wilson, Sir Robert Peter, KCMG
Wilson, *Air Chief Marshal* Sir (Ronald) Andrew (Fellowes), KCB, AFC
Wilton, Sir (Arthur) John, KCMG, KCVO, MC
Wingate, *Capt.* Sir Miles Buckley, KCVO
Winkley, Sir David Ross, Kt.
Winnington, Sir Anthony Edward, Bt. (1755)
Winship, Sir Peter James Joseph, Kt., CBE
Winter, *Dr* Sir Gregory Winter, Kt., CBE
Winterton, Sir Nicholas Raymond, Kt.
Winton, Sir Nicholas George, Kt., MBE
Wisdom, Sir Norman, Kt., OBE
Wiseman, Sir John William, Bt. (1628)
Wolfendale, *Prof.* Sir Arnold Whittaker, Kt., FRS
Wolseley, Sir Charles Garnet Richard Mark, Bt. (1628)
†Wolseley, Sir James Douglas, Bt. (I. 1745)
†Wombell, Sir George Philip Frederick, Bt. (1778)
Womersley, Sir Peter John Walter, Bt. (1945)
Woo, Sir Leo Joseph, Kt.
Woo, Sir Po-Shing, Kt.
Wood, Sir Alan Marshall Muir, Kt., FRS, FRENG
Wood, Sir Andrew Marley, GCMG
Wood, Sir Anthony John Page, Bt. (1837)
Wood, Sir Ian Clark, Kt., CBE
Wood, *Hon.* Sir John Kember, Kt., MC
Wood, Sir Martin Francis, Kt., OBE
Wood, Sir Michael Charles, KCMG
Wood, *Hon.* Sir Roderic Lionel James, Kt.
Wood, Sir Russell Dillon, KCVO, VRD
Wood, Sir William Alan, KCVO, CB
Woodard, *Rear Adm.* Sir Robert Nathaniel, KCVO
Woodcock, Sir John, Kt., CBE, QPM
Woodhead, *Vice-Adm.* Sir (Anthony) Peter, KCB
Woodhouse, *Rt. Hon.* Sir (Arthur) Owen, KBE, DSC
Woodroffe, *Most Revd* George Cuthbert Manning, KBE
Woods, Sir Robert Kynnersley, Kt., CBE
Woodward, *Hon.* Sir (Albert) Edward, Kt., OBE
Woodward, Sir Clive Ronald, Kt., OBE
Woodward, *Adm.* Sir John Forster, GBE, KCB
Woodward, Sir Thomas Jones (Tom Jones), Kt., OBE
Worsley, *Gen.* Sir Richard Edward, GCB, OBE
Worsley, Sir (William) Marcus (John), Bt. (1838)
Worsthorne, Sir Peregrine Gerard, Kt.

Wratten, *Air Chief Marshal* Sir William John, GBE, CB, AFC
Wraxall, Sir Charles Frederick Lascelles, Bt. (1813)
Wrey, Sir George Richard Bourchier, Bt. (1628)
Wrigglesworth, Sir Ian William, Kt.
Wright, Sir Allan Frederick, KBE
Wright, Sir David John, GCMG, LVO
Wright, *Hon.* Sir (John) Michael, Kt.
Wright, Sir (John) Oliver, GCMG, GCVO, DSC
Wright, *Prof.* Sir Nicholas Alcwyn, Kt.
Wright, Sir Peter Robert, Kt., CBE
Wright, *Air Marshal* Sir Robert Alfred, KBE, AFC
Wright, Sir Stephen John Leadbetter, KCMG
Wrightson, Sir Charles Mark Garmondsway, Bt. (1900)
Wrigley, *Prof.* Sir Edward Anthony (Sir Tony), Kt., PHD, PBA
Wrixon-Becher, Sir John William Michael, Bt. (1831)
Wroughton, Sir Philip Lavallin, KCVO
Wu, Sir Gordon Ying Sheung, KCMG
Yacoub, *Prof.* Sir Magdi Habib, Kt., FRCS
Yaki, Sir Roy, KBE
Yang, *Hon.* Sir Ti Liang, Kt.
Yapp, Sir Stanley Graham, Kt.
Yardley, Sir David Charles Miller, Kt., LLD
Yarrow, Sir Eric Grant, Bt. (1916), MBE
Yocklunn, Sir John (Soong Chung), KCVO
Yoo Foo, Sir (François) Henri, Kt.
Young, Sir Brian Walter Mark, Kt.
Young, Sir Colville Norbert, GCMG, MBE
Young, Sir Dennis Charles, KCMG
Young, *Rt. Hon.* Sir George Samuel Knatchbull, Bt. (1813)
Young, Sir Jimmy Leslie Ronald, Kt., CBE
Young, Sir John Kenyon Roe, Bt. (1821)
Young, *Hon.* Sir John McIntosh, KCMG
Young, Sir John Robertson, GCMG
Young, Sir Leslie Clarence, Kt., CBE
Young, Sir Nicholas Charles, Kt.
Young, Sir Robin Urquhart, KCB
Young, Sir Roger William, Kt.
Young, Sir Stephen Stewart Templeton, Bt. (1945)
Young, Sir William Neil, Bt. (1769)
Younger, Sir Julian William Richard, Bt. (1911)
Yuwi, Sir Matiabe, KBE
Zeeman, *Prof.* Sir (Erik) Christopher, Kt., FRS
Zissman, Sir Bernard Philip, Kt.
Zochonis, Sir John Basil, Kt.
Zunz, Sir Gerhard Jacob (Jack), Kt., FRENG
Zurenuoc, Sir Zibang, KBE

BARONETESS

Maxwell Macdonald (formerly Stirling-Maxwell), Dame Ann, Btss. (NS 1682)

DAMES

DAMES GRAND CROSS AND DAMES COMMANDERS

Style, 'Dame' before forename and surname, followed by appropriate post-nominal initials. Where such an award is made to a lady already in possession of a higher title, the appropriate initials follow her name
Envelope, Dame F_ S_, followed by appropriate post-nominal letters. *Letter (formal),* Dear Madam; *(social),* Dear Dame F_. *Spoken,* Dame F_
Husband, Untitled

Dame Grand Cross and Dame Commander are the higher classes for women of the Order of the Bath, the Order of St Michael and St George, the Royal Victorian Order, and the Order of the British Empire. Dames Grand Cross rank after the wives of Baronets and before the wives of Knights Grand Cross. Dames Commanders rank after the wives of Knights Grand Cross and before the wives of Knights Commanders.

Honorary Dames Commanders may be conferred on women who are citizens of countries of which the Queen is not head of state.

LIST OF DAMES
As at 31 August 2008

Women peers in their own right and life peers are not included in this list. Female members of the royal family are not included in this list; details of the orders they hold can be found within the Royal Family section.

If a dame has a double barrelled or hyphenated surname, she is listed under the first element of the name. *A full entry in italic type* indicates that the recipient of an honour died during the year in which the honour was conferred. The name is included for the purposes of record.

Abaijah, Dame Josephine, DBE
Airlie, The Countess of, DCVO
Albemarle, The Countess of, DBE
Allen, *Prof.* Dame Ingrid Victoria, DBE
Andrews, Dame Julie, DBE
Anglesey, The Marchioness of, DBE
Anson, Lady (Elizabeth Audrey), DBE
Anstee, Dame Margaret Joan, DCMG
Arden, *Rt. Hon.* Dame Mary Howarth (Mrs Mance), DBE
Atkins, Dame Eileen, DBE
Bainbridge, Dame Beryl, DBE
Baker, Dame Janet Abbott (Mrs Shelley), CH, DBE
Bakewell, Dame Joan Dawson, DBE
Barbour, Dame Margaret (Mrs Ash), DBE
Baron, *Hon.* Dame Florence Jacqueline, DBE
Barrow, Dame Jocelyn Anita (Mrs Downer), DBE
Barstow, Dame Josephine Clare (Mrs Anderson), DBE
Bassey, Dame Shirley, DBE
Beasley, *Prof.* Dame Christine Joan, DBE
Beaurepaire, Dame Beryl Edith, DBE
Beer, *Prof.* Dame Gillian Patricia Kempster, DBE, FBA
Bergquist, *Prof.* Dame Patricia Rose, DBE
Bevan, Dame Yasmin, DBE
Bewley, Dame Beulah Rosemary, DBE
Bibby, Dame Enid, DBE
Black, *Prof.* Dame Carol Mary, DBE
Black, *Hon.* Dame Jill Margaret, DBE
Blackadder, Dame Elizabeth Violet, DBE
Blaize, Dame Venetia Ursula, DBE
Blaxland, Dame Helen Frances, DBE
Blume, Dame Hilary Sharon Braverman, DBE
Booth, *Hon.* Dame Margaret Myfanwy Wood, DBE
Bowtell, Dame Ann Elizabeth, DCB
Boyd, Dame Vivienne Myra, DBE
Brain, Dame Margaret Anne (Mrs Wheeler), DBE
Brennan, Dame Maureen, DBE
Bridges, Dame Mary Patricia, DBE
Brindley, Dame Lynne Janie, DBE
Brittan, Dame Diana (Lady Brittan of Spennithorne), DBE
Browne, Lady Moyra Blanche Madeleine, DBE
Buckland, Dame Yvonne Helen Elaine, DBE
Burnell, *Prof.* Dame Susan Jocelyn Bell, DBE
Burslem, Dame Alexandra Vivien, DBE
Byatt, Dame Antonia Susan, DBE, FRSL
Bynoe, Dame Hilda Louisa, DBE
Caldicott, Dame Fiona, DBE, FRCP, FRCPSYCH
Cameron, *Prof.* Dame Averil Millicent, DBE
Campbell-Preston, Dame Frances Olivia, DCVO
Cartwright, Dame Silvia Rose, DBE
Clark, *Prof.* Dame Jill MacLeod, DBE
Clark, *Prof.* Dame (Margaret) June, DBE, PHD
Clayton, Dame Barbara Evelyn (Mrs Klyne), DBE
Cleverdon, Dame Julia Charity, DCVO, CBE
Collarbone, Dame Patricia, DBE
Contreras, *Prof.* Dame Marcela, DBE
Corsar, *Hon.* Dame Mary Drummond, DBE
Coward, Dame Pamela Sarah, DBE
Cox, *Hon.* Dame Laura Mary, DBE
Davies, *Prof.* Dame Kay Elizabeth, DBE
Davies, Dame Wendy Patricia, DBE
Davis, Dame Karlene Cecile, DBE
Daws, Dame Joyce Margaretta, DBE
Dawson, *Prof.* Dame Sandra Jane Noble, DBE
Dell, Dame Miriam Patricia, DBE
Dench, Dame Judith Olivia (Mrs Williams), CH, DBE
Descartes, Dame Marie Selipha Sesenne, DBE, BEM
Devonshire, The Duchess of, DCVO
Digby, Lady, DBE
Dobbs, *Hon.* Dame Linda Penelope, DBE
Docherty, Dame Jacqueline, DBE
Dowling, *Prof.* Dame Ann Patricia, DBE
Duffield, Dame Vivien Louise, DBE
Dumont, Dame Ivy Leona, DCMG
Dyche, Dame Rachael Mary, DBE
Elcoat, Dame Catherine Elizabeth, DBE
Ellison, Dame Jill, DBE
Else, Dame Jean, DBE
Engel, Dame Pauline Frances (Sister Pauline Engel), DBE
Esteve-Coll, Dame Elizabeth Anne Loosemore, DBE
Evans, Dame Anne Elizabeth Jane, DBE
Evans, Dame Madeline Glynne Dervel, DBE, CMG
Evison, Dame Helen June Patricia, DBE
Fenner, Dame Peggy Edith, DBE

Fielding, Dame Pauline, DBE
Finch, *Prof.* Dame Janet Valerie, DBE
Forgan, Dame Elizabeth Anne Lucy, DBE
Fort, Dame Maeve Geraldine, DCMG, DCVO
Furse, Dame Clara Hedwig Frances, DBE
Fraser, Dame Dorothy Rita, DBE
Friend, Dame Phyllis Muriel, DBE
Fry, Dame Margaret Louise, DBE
Gallagher, Dame Monica Josephine, DBE
Gardiner, Dame Helen Louisa, DBE, MVO
Ghosh, Dame Helen Frances, DCB
Glen-Haig, Dame Mary Alison, DBE
Glenn, *Prof.* Dame Hazel Gillian, DBE
Glennie, *Dr* Dame Evelyn Elizabeth Ann, DBE
Gloster, *Hon.* Dame Elisabeth (Lady Popplewell), DBE
Glover, Dame Audrey Frances, DBE, CMG
Goodall, *Dr* Dame (Valerie) Jane, DBE
Goodman, Dame Barbara, DBE
Gordon, Dame Minita Elmira, GCMG, GCVO
Gordon, *Hon.* Dame Pamela Felicity, DBE
Gow, Dame Jane Elizabeth (Mrs Whiteley), DBE
Grafton, The Duchess of, GCVO
Grant, Dame Mavis, DBE
Green, Dame Pauline, DBE
Grey, Dame Beryl Elizabeth (Mrs Svenson), DBE
Grey-Thompson, Dame Tanni Carys Davina, DBE
Griffiths, Dame Anne, DCVO
Grimthorpe, The Lady, DCVO
Guilfoyle, Dame Margaret Georgina Constance, DBE
Guthardt, *Revd Dr* Dame Phyllis Myra, DBE
Hallett, *Rt. Hon.* Dame Heather Carol, DBE
Harbison, Dame Joan Irene, DBE
Harper, Dame Elizabeth Margaret Way, DBE
Harris, Lady Pauline, DBE
Hassan, Dame Anna Patricia Lucy, DBE
Hay, Dame Barbara Logan, DCMG, MBE
Hedley-Miller, Dame Mary Elizabeth, DCVO, CB
Henderson, Dame Fiona Douglas, DCVO
Herbison, Dame Jean Marjory, DBE, CMG
Hercus, *Hon.* Dame (Margaret) Ann, DCMG
Higgins, *Prof.* Dame Joan Margaret, DBE
Higgins, *Prof.* Dame Julia Stretton, DBE, FRS
Higgins, *Prof.* Dame Rosalyn, DBE, QC
Hill, *Air Cdre* Dame Felicity Barbara, DBE
Hine, Dame Deirdre Joan, DBE, FRCP
Hodgson, Dame Patricia Anne, DBE
Hogg, *Hon.* Dame Mary Claire (Mrs Koops), DBE
Hollows, Dame Sharon, DBE
Holmes, Dame Kelly, DBE
Holroyd, Lady Margaret, DBE
Hoodless, Dame Elisabeth Anne, DBE
Hufton, *Prof.* Dame Olwen, DBE
Husband, *Prof.* Dame Janet Elizabeth Siarey, DBE
Hussey, Dame Susan Katharine (Lady Hussey of North Bradley), DCVO
Hutton, Dame Deirdre Mary, DBE
Imison, Dame Tamsyn, DBE
Isaacs, Dame Albertha Madeline, DBE
James, Dame Naomi Christine (Mrs Haythorne), DBE
Jenkins, Dame (Mary) Jennifer (Lady Jenkins of Hillhead), DBE
Johnson, *Prof.* Dame Louise Napier, DBE, FRS
Jonas, Dame Judith Mayhew
Jones, Dame Gwyneth (Mrs Haberfeld-Jones), DBE
Jordan, *Prof.* Dame Carole, DBE
Keegan, Dame Elizabeth Mary, DBE
Keegan, Dame Geraldine Mary Marcella, DBE
Kekedo, Dame Rosalina Violet, DBE
Kelleher, Dame Joan, DBE
Kellett-Bowman, Dame (Mary) Elaine, DBE
Kelly, Dame Barbara Mary, DBE
Kelly, Dame Lorna May Boreland, DBE
Kershaw, Dame Janet Elizabeth Murray (Dame Betty), DBE
Kettlewell, *Comdt.* Dame Marion Mildred, DBE
Kidu, Lady, DBE
King, *Hon.* Dame Eleanor Warwick, DBE
Kinnair, Dame Donna, DBE
Kirby, Dame Carolyn Emma, DBE
Kirby, Dame Georgina Kamiria, DBE
Kramer, *Prof.* Dame Leonie Judith, DBE
Laine, Dame Cleo (Clementine) Dinah (Lady Dankworth), DBE
Lake-Tack, *HE* Dame Louise Agnetha, GCVO
Lamb, Dame Dawn Ruth, DBE
Leather, Dame Susan Catherine, DBE
Leslie, Dame Ann Elizabeth Mary, DBE
Lewis, Dame Edna Leofrida (Lady Lewis), DBE
Lott, Dame Felicity Ann Emwhyla (Mrs Woolf), DBE
Louisy, Dame (Calliopa) Pearlette, GCMG
Lynn, Dame Vera (Mrs Lewis), DBE
MacArthur, Dame Ellen Patricia, DBE
Macdonald, Dame Mary Beaton, DBE
McDonald, Dame Mavis, DCB
Mackinnon, Dame (Una) Patricia, DBE
Macmillan of Ovenden, Katharine, Viscountess, DBE
Macur, *Hon.* Dame Julia Wendy, DBE
Mayhew, Dame Judith, DBE
Major, Dame Malvina Lorraine (Mrs Fleming), DBE
Major, Dame Norma Christina Elizabeth, DBE
Marsh, Dame Mary Elizabeth, DBE
Mason, Dame Monica Margaret, DBE
Mellor, Dame Julie Thérèse Mellor, DBE
Metge, *Dr* Dame (Alice) Joan, DBE
Middleton, Dame Elaine Madoline, DCMG, MBE
Mills, Dame Barbara Jean Lyon, DBE, QC
Mirren, Dame Helen, DBE
Moores, Dame Yvonne, DBE
Morgan, *Dr* Dame Gillian Margaret, DBE
Morrison, *Hon.* Dame Mary Anne, DCVO
Muirhead, Dame Lorna Elizabeth Fox, DBE
Muldoon, Lady Thea Dale, DBE, QSO
Mullally, *Revd* Dame Sarah Elisabeth, DBE
Mumford, Lady Mary Katharine, DCVO
Munro, Dame Alison, DBE
Murdoch, Dame Elisabeth Joy, DBE
Nelson, *Prof.* Dame Janet Laughland, DBE
Neville, Dame Elizabeth, DBE, QPM
Ogilvie, Dame Bridget Margaret, DBE, PHD, DSC
Oliver, Dame Gillian Frances, DBE
Ollerenshaw, Dame Kathleen Mary, DBE, DPHIL
O'Loan, Dame Nuala Patricia, DBE
Oxenbury, Dame Shirley Anne, DBE
Park, Dame Merle Florence (Mrs Bloch), DBE
Pauffley, *Hon.* Dame Anna Evelyn Hamilton, DBE
Penhaligon, Dame Annette (Mrs Egerton), DBE
Perkins, Dame Mary Lesley, DBE
Peters, Dame Mary Elizabeth, DBE
Pindling, Lady (Marguerite M.), DCMG
Platt, Dame Denise, DBE
Plowright, Dame Joan Ann, DBE
Polak, *Prof.* Dame Julia Margaret, DBE
Poole, Dame Avril Anne Barker, DBE
Porter, Dame Shirley (Lady Porter), DBE
Powell, Dame Sally Ann Vickers, DBE
Prendergast, Dame Simone Ruth, DBE

Price, Dame Margaret Berenice, DBE
Pugh, *Dr* Dame Gillian Mary, DBE
Purves, Dame Daphne Helen, DBE
Quinn, Dame Sheila Margaret Imelda, DBE
Rafferty, *Hon.* Dame Anne Judith, DBE
Rawson, *Prof.* Dame Jessica Mary, DBE
Rees, *Prof.* Dame Lesley Howard, DBE
Reeves, Dame Helen May, DBE
Reynolds, Dame Fiona Claire, DBE
Richardson, Dame Mary, DBE
Ridsdale, Dame Victoire Evelyn Patricia (Lady Ridsdale), DBE
Rigg, Dame Diana, DBE
Rimington, Dame Stella, DCB
Ritterman, Dame Janet, DBE
Roberts, Dame Jane Elisabeth, DBE
Robins, Dame Ruth Laura, DBE
Robottom, Dame Marlene, DBE
Roe, Dame Marion Audrey, DBE
Roe, Dame Raigh Edith, DBE
Ronson, Dame Gail, DBE
Rothwell, *Prof.* Dame Nancy Jane, DBE
Rumbold, *Rt. Hon.* Dame Angela Claire Rosemary, DBE
Runciman of Doxford, The Viscountess, DBE
Salas, Dame Margaret Laurence, DBE
Salmond, *Prof.* Dame Mary Anne, DBE
Sawyer, *Hon.* Dame Joan Augusta, DBE
Scardino, Dame Marjorie, DBE
Scott, Dame Catherine Margaret (Mrs Denton), DBE
Seward, Dame Margaret Helen Elizabeth, DBE
Shedrick, *Dr* Dame Daphne Marjorie, DBE
Shirley, Dame Stephanie, DBE
Shovelton, Dame Helena, DBE
Sibley, Dame Antoinette (Mrs Corbett), DBE
Silver, *Dr* Dame Ruth Muldoon, DBE
Smith, Dame Dela, DBE
Smith, *Rt. Hon.* Dame Janet Hilary (Mrs Mathieson), DBE
Smith, *Hon.* Dame Jennifer Meredith, DBE
Smith, Dame Margaret Natalie (Maggie) (Mrs Cross), DBE
Soames, Lady Mary, KG, DBE
Southgate, *Prof.* Dame Lesley Jill, DBE
Spencer, Dame Rosemary Jane, DCMG
Steel, *Hon.* Dame (Anne) Heather (Mrs Beattie), DBE
Stocking, Dame Barbara Mary, DBE
Strachan, Dame Valerie Patricia Marie, DCB
Strathern, *Prof.* Dame Anne Marilyn, DBE
Street, Dame Susan Ruth, DCB
Sutherland, Dame Joan (Mrs Bonynge), OM, DBE
Sutherland, Dame Veronica Evelyn, DBE, CMG
Swift, *Hon.* Dame Caroline Jane (Mrs Openshaw), DBE, QC
Symmonds, Dame Olga Patricia, DBE
Tanner, *Dr* Dame Mary Elizabeth, DBE
Taylor, Dame Elizabeth, DBE
Taylor, Dame Meg, DBE
Te Kanawa, Dame Kiri Janette, DBE
Thomas, *Prof.* Dame Jean Olwen, DBE
Thomas, Dame Maureen Elizabeth (Lady Thomas), DBE
Tinson, Dame Sue, DBE
Tizard, Dame Catherine Anne, GCMG, GCVO, DBE
Tokiel, Dame Rosa, DBE
Trotter, Dame Janet Olive, DBE
Turner-Warwick, Dame Margaret Elizabeth Harvey, DBE, FRCP, FRCPED
Uprichard, Dame Mary Elizabeth, DBE
Varley, Dame Joan Fleetwood, DBE
Wagner, Dame Gillian Mary Millicent (Lady Wagner), DBE
Wall, Dame (Alice) Anne, (Mrs Michael Wall), DCVO
Wallis, Dame Sheila Ann, DBE
Warburton, Dame Anne Marion, DCVO, CMG
Waterhouse, Dame Rachel Elizabeth, DBE, PHD
Waterman, *Dr* Dame Fanny, DBE
Webb, *Prof.* Dame Patricia, DBE
Weir, Dame Gillian Constance (Mrs Phelps), DBE
Weller, Dame Rita, DBE
Weston, Dame Margaret Kate, DBE
Westwood, Dame Vivienne Isabel, DBE
Wheldon, Dame Juliet Louise, DCB, QC
Williams, Dame Josephine, DBE
Wilson, Dame Jacqueline, DBE
Wilson-Barnett, *Prof.* Dame Jenifer, DBE
Winstone, Dame Dorothy Gertrude, DBE, CMG
Wong Yick-ming, Dame Rosanna, DBE

DECORATIONS AND MEDALS

PRINCIPAL DECORATIONS AND MEDALS
IN ORDER OF WEAR

VICTORIA CROSS (VC), 1856 (*see* below)
GEORGE CROSS (GC), 1940 (*see* below)

BRITISH ORDERS OF KNIGHTHOOD (*see also* Orders of Chivalry)
Order of the Garter
Order of the Thistle
Order of St Patrick
Order of the Bath
Order of Merit
Order of the Star of India
Order of St Michael and George
Order of the Indian Empire
Order of the Crown of India
Royal Victorian Order (Classes I, II and III)
Order of the British Empire (Classes I, II and III)
Order of the Companions of Honour
Distinguished Service Order
Royal Victorian Order (Class IV)
Order of the British Empire (Class IV)
Imperial Service Order
Royal Victorian Order (Class V)
Order of the British Empire (Class V)

BARONET'S BADGE

KNIGHT BACHELOR'S BADGE

INDIAN ORDER OF MERIT (MILITARY)

DECORATIONS
Conspicuous Gallantry Cross (CGC), 1995
Royal Red Cross Class I (RRC), 1883
Distinguished Service Cross (DSC), 1914
Military Cross (MC), December 1914
Distinguished Flying Cross (DFC), 1918
Air Force Cross (AFC), 1918
Royal Red Cross Class II (ARRC)
Order of British India
Kaisar-i-Hind Medal
Order of St John

MEDALS FOR GALLANTRY AND DISTINGUISHED CONDUCT
Union of South Africa Queen's Medal for Bravery, in Gold
Distinguished Conduct Medal (DCM), 1854
Conspicuous Gallantry Medal (CGM), 1874
Conspicuous Gallantry Medal (Flying)
George Medal (GM), 1940
Queen's Police Medal for Gallantry
Queen's Fire Service Medal for Gallantry
Royal West African Frontier Force Distinguished Conduct Medal
King's African Rifles Distinguished Conduct Medal
Indian Distinguished Service Medal
Union of South Africa Queen's Medal for Bravery, in Silver
Distinguished Service Medal (DSM), 1914
Military Medal (MM), 1916
Distinguished Flying Medal (DFM), 1918
Air Force Medal (AFM)
Constabulary Medal (Ireland)
Medal for Saving Life at Sea (Sea Gallantry Medal)
Indian Order of Merit (Civil)
Indian Police Medal for Gallantry
Ceylon Police Medal for Gallantry
Sierra Leone Police Medal for Gallantry
Sierra Leone Fire Brigades Medal for Gallantry
Colonial Police Medal for Gallantry (CPM)
Queen's Gallantry Medal (QGM), 1974
Royal Victorian Medal (RVM), Gold, Silver and Bronze
British Empire Medal (BEM)
Canada Medal
Queen's Police Medal for Distinguished Service (QPM)
Queen's Fire Service Medal for Distinguished Service (QFSM)
Queen's Volunteer Reserves Medal
Queen's Medal for Chiefs

CAMPAIGN MEDALS AND STARS
Including authorised United Nations, European Community/Union and North Atlantic Treaty Organisation medals (in order of date of campaign for which awarded)

POLAR MEDALS (in order of date)

IMPERIAL SERVICE MEDAL

POLICE MEDALS FOR VALUABLE SERVICE
Indian Police Medal for Meritorious Service
Ceylon Police Medal for Merit
Sierra Leone Police Medal for Meritorious Service
Sierra Leone Fire Brigades Medal for Meritorious Service
Colonial Police Medal for Meritorious Service

BADGE OF HONOUR

JUBILEE, CORONATION AND DURBAR MEDALS
Queen Victoria, King Edward VII, King George V, King George VI, Queen Elizabeth II, Visit Commemoration and Long and Faithful Service Medals

EFFICIENCY AND LONG SERVICE DECORATIONS AND MEDALS
Medal for Meritorious Service
Accumulated Campaign Service Medal
Medal for Long Service and Good Conduct (Military)
Naval Long Service and Good Conduct Medal
Medal for Meritorious Service (Royal Navy 1918–28)
Indian Long Service and Good Conduct Medal
Indian Meritorious Service Medal
Royal Marines Meritorious Service Medal (1849–1947)
Royal Air Force Meritorious Service Medal (1918–1928)
Royal Air Force Long Service and Good Conduct Medal
Medal for Long Service and Good Conduct (Ulster Defence Regiment)
Indian Long Service and Good Conduct Medal
Royal West African Frontier Force Long Service and Good Conduct Medal

Royal Sierra Leone Military Forces Long Service and Good Conduct Medal
King's African Rifles and Long Service and Good Conduct Medal
Indian Meritorious Service Medal
Police Long Service and Good Conduct Medal
Fire Brigade Long Service and Good Conduct Medal
African Police Medal for Meritorious Service
Royal Canadian Mounted Police Long Service Medal
Ceylon Police Long Service Medal
Ceylon Fire Services Long Service Medal
Sierra Leone Police Long Service Medal
Colonial Police Long Service Medal
Sierra Leone Fire Brigades Long Service Medal
Mauritius Police Long Service and Good Conduct Medal
Mauritius Fire Services Long Service and Good Conduct Medal
Mauritius Prisons Service Long Service and Good Conduct Medal
Colonial Fire Brigades Long Service Medal
Colonial Prison Service Medal
Hong Kong Disciplined Services Medal
Army Emergency Reserve Decoration (ERD)
Volunteer Officers' Decoration (VD)
Volunteer Long Service Medal
Volunteer Officers' Decoration (for India and the Colonies)
Volunteer Long Service Medal (for India and the Colonies)
Colonial Auxiliary Forces Officers' Decoration
Colonial Auxiliary Forces Long Service Medal
Medal for Good Shooting (Naval)
Militia Long Service Medal
Imperial Yeomanry Long Service Medal
Territorial Decoration (TD), 1908
Ceylon Armed Services Long Service Medal
Efficiency Decoration (ED)
Territorial Efficiency Medal
Efficiency Medal
Special Reserve Long Service and Good Conduct Medal
Decoration for Officers of the Royal Navy Reserve (RD), 1910
Decoration for Officers of the Royal Naval Volunteer Reserve (VRD)
Royal Naval Reserve Long Service and Good Conduct Medal
Royal Naval Volunteer Reserve Long Service and Good Conduct Medal
Royal Naval Auxiliary Sick Berth Reserve Long Service and Good Conduct Medal
Royal Fleet Reserve Long Service and Good Conduct Medal
Royal Naval Wireless Auxiliary Reserve Long Service and Good Conduct Medal
Royal Naval Auxiliary Service Medal
Air Efficiency Award (AE), 1942
Volunteer Reserves Service Medal
Ulster Defence Regiment Medal
Northern Ireland Home Service Medal
Queen's Medal (for Champion Shots of the RN and RM)
Queen's Medal (for Champion Shots of the New Zealand Naval Forces)
Queen's Medal (for Champion Shots in the Military Forces)
Queen's Medal (for Champion Shots of the Air Forces)
Cadet Forces Medal, 1950
Coastguard Auxiliary Service Long Service Medal
Special Constabulary Long Service Medal
Canadian Forces Decoration
Royal Observer Corps Medal
Civil Defence Long Service Medal
Ambulance Service (Emergency Duties) Long Service and Good Conduct Medal
Royal Fleet Auxiliary Service Medal Rhodesia Medal
Royal Ulster Constabulary Service Medal
Northern Ireland Prison Service Medal
Union of South Africa Commemoration Medal
Indian Independence Medal
Pakistan Medal
Ceylon Armed Services Inauguration Medal
Ceylon Police Independence Medal (1948)
Sierra Leone Independence Medal
Jamaica Independence Medal
Uganda Independence Medal
Malawi Independence Medal
Fiji Independence Medal
Papua New Guinea Independence Medal
Solomon Islands Independence Medal
Service Medal of the Order of St John
Badge of the Order of the League of Mercy
Voluntary Medical Service Medal (1932)
Women's Royal Voluntary Service Medal
South African Medal for War Services
Colonial Special Constabulary Medal

HONORARY MEMBERSHIP OF COMMONWEALTH ORDERS

OTHER COMMONWEALTH MEMBERS' ORDERS, DECORATIONS AND MEDALS

FOREIGN ORDERS

FOREIGN DECORATIONS

FOREIGN MEDALS

THE VICTORIA CROSS (1856)

FOR CONSPICUOUS BRAVERY

VC

Ribbon, Crimson, for all Services (until 1918 it was blue for the Royal Navy)

Instituted on 29 January 1856, the Victoria Cross was awarded retrospectively to 1854, the first being held by Lt. C. D. Lucas, RN, for bravery in the Baltic Sea on 21 June 1854 (gazetted 24 February 1857). The first 62 crosses were presented by Queen Victoria in Hyde Park, London, on 26 June 1857.

The Victoria Cross is worn before all other decorations, on the left breast, and consists of a cross-pattée of bronze, 3.8cm in diameter, with the royal crown surmounted by a lion in the centre, and beneath there is the inscription *For Valour*. Holders of the VC currently receive a tax-free annuity of £1,500, irrespective of need or other conditions. In 1911, the right to receive the cross was extended to Indian soldiers, and in 1920 to matrons, sisters and nurses, the staff of the nursing services and other services pertaining to hospitals and nursing, and to civilians of either sex regularly or temporarily under the orders, direction or supervision of the naval, military, or air forces of the crown.

SURVIVING RECIPIENTS OF THE VICTORIA CROSS
as at 31 August 2008

Apiata, *Cpl.* B. H. (New Zealand Special Air Service)
2004 *Afghanistan*
Beharry, *Pte.* J. G. (Princess of Wales's Royal Regiment)
2005 *Iraq*
Cruickshank, *Flt. Lt.* J. A. (RAFVR)
1944 *World War*
Fraser, *Lt.-Cdr.* I. E., DSC, RD and bar (RNR)
1945 *World War*
Kenna, *Pte.* E. (Australian Military Forces, 2/4th (NSW))
1945 *World War*
Lachhiman Gurung, *Havildar* (8th Gurkha Rifles)
1945 *World War*
Payne, *WO* K., DSC (USA) (Australian Army Training Team)
1969 *Vietnam*
Rambahadur Limbu, *Capt.,* MVO (10th Princess Mary's Gurkha Rifles)
1965 *Sarawak*
Speakman-Pitts, *Sgt.* W. (Black Watch, attached KOSB)
1951 *Korea*
Tulbahadur Pun, *Lt.* (6th Gurkha Rifles)
1944 *World War*
Wilson, *Lt.-Col.* E. C. T. (East Surrey Regiment)
1940 *World War*

THE GEORGE CROSS (1940)
FOR GALLANTRY

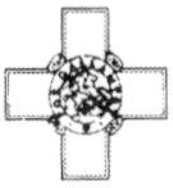

GC

Ribbon, Dark blue, threaded through a bar adorned with laurel leaves
Instituted 24 September 1940 (with amendments, 3 November 1942)

The George Cross is worn before all other decorations (except the VC) on the left breast (when worn by a woman it may be worn on the left shoulder from a ribbon of the same width and colour fashioned into a bow). It consists of a plain silver cross with four equal limbs, the cross having in the centre a circular medallion bearing a design showing St George and the Dragon. The inscription *For Gallantry* appears round the medallion and in the angle of each limb of the cross is the royal cypher 'G VI' forming a circle concentric with the medallion. The reverse is plain and bears the name of the recipient and the date of the award. The cross is suspended by a ring from a bar adorned with laurel leaves on dark blue ribbon 3.8cm wide.

The cross is intended primarily for civilians; awards to the fighting services are confined to actions for which purely military honours are not normally granted. It is awarded only for acts of the greatest heroism or of the most conspicuous courage in circumstances of extreme danger. From 1 April 1965, holders of the cross have received a tax-free annuity, which is currently £1,500. The cross has twice been awarded collectively rather than to an individual: to Malta (1942) and the Royal Ulster Constabulary (1999).

In October 1971 all surviving holders of the Albert Medal and the Edward Medal exchanged those decorations for the George Cross.

SURVIVING RECIPIENTS OF THE GEORGE CROSS
as at 31 August 2008

If the recipient originally received the Albert Medal (AM) or the Edward Medal (EM), this is indicated by the initials in parentheses.

Archer, *Col.* B. S. T., GC, OBE, ERD, 1941
Bamford, J., GC, 1952
Beaton, J., GC, CVO, 1974
Butson, *Lt.-Col.* A. R. C., GC, CD, MD (AM), 1948
Croucher, *Lance Cpl.* M., GC, 2008
Finney, *Trooper* C., GC, 2003
Flintoff, H. H., GC (EM), 1944
Gledhill, A. J., GC, 1967
Gregson, J. S., GC (AM), 1943
Johnson, *WO1 (SSM)* B., GC, 1990
Kinne, D. G., GC, 1954
Lowe, A. R., GC (AM), 1949
Norton, *Capt.* P. A., GC, 2006
Pratt, M. K., GC, 1978
Purves, Mrs M., GC (AM), 1949
Raweng, Awang anak, GC, 1951
Stevens, H. W., GC, 1958
Walker, C., GC, 1972
Walker, C. H., GC (AM), 1942
Walton, E. W. K., GC (AM), DSO, 1948
Wooding, E. A., GC (AM), 1945

CHIEFS OF CLANS IN SCOTLAND

Only chiefs of whole Names or Clans are included, except certain special instances (marked *) who, though not chiefs of a whole Name, were or are for some reason (eg the Macdonald forfeiture) independent. Under decision (*Campbell-Gray,* 1950) that a bearer of a 'double or triple-barrelled' surname cannot be held chief of a part of such, several others cannot be included in the list at present.

THE ROYAL HOUSE: HM The Queen
AGNEW: Sir Crispin Agnew of Lochnaw, Bt., QC
ANSTRUTHER: Tobias Anstruther of Anstruther and Balcaskie
ARBUTHNOTT: Viscount of Arbuthnott, KT, CBE, DSC
BANNERMAN: Sir David Bannerman of Elsick, Bt.
BARCLAY: Peter C. Barclay of Towie Barclay and of that Ilk
BORTHWICK: Lord Borthwick
BOYD: Lord Kilmarnock, MBE
BOYLE: Earl of Glasgow
BRODIE: Alexander Brodie of Brodie
BROUN OF COLSTOUN: Sir Wayne Broun of Colstoun, Bt.
BRUCE: Earl of Elgin and Kincardine, KT
BUCHAN: David Buchan of Auchmacoy
BURNETT: J. C. A. Burnett of Leys
CAMERON: Donald Cameron of Lochiel
CAMPBELL: Duke of Argyll
CARMICHAEL: Richard Carmichael of Carmichael
CARNEGIE: Duke of Fife
CATHCART: Earl Cathcart
CHARTERIS: Earl of Wemyss and March, KT
CLAN CHATTAN: K. Mackintosh of Clan Chattan
CHISHOLM: Hamish Chisholm of Chisholm *(The Chisholm)*
COCHRANE: Earl of Dundonald
COLQUHOUN: Sir Malcolm Rory Colquhoun of Luss, Bt.
CRANSTOUN: David Cranstoun of that Ilk
CUMMING: Sir Alastair Cumming of Altyre, Bt.
DARROCH: Capt. Duncan Darroch of Gourock
DAVIDSON: Alister Davidson of Davidston
DEWAR: Michael Dewar of that Ilk and Vogrie
DRUMMOND: Earl of Perth
DUNBAR: Sir James Dunbar of Mochrum, Bt.
DUNDAS: David Dundas of Dundas
DURIE: Andrew Durie of Durie, CBE
ELIOTT: Mrs Margaret Eliott of Redheugh
ERSKINE: Earl of Mar and Kellie
FARQUHARSON: Capt. A. Farquharson of Invercauld, MC
FERGUSSON: Sir Charles Fergusson of Kilkerran, Bt.
FORBES: Lord Forbes, KBE
FORSYTH: Alistair Forsyth of that Ilk
FRASER: Lady Saltoun
*FRASER (OF LOVAT): Lord Lovat
GAYRE: R. Gayre of Gayre and Nigg
GORDON: Marquess of Huntly
GRAHAM: Duke of Montrose
GRANT: Lord Strathspey
GRIERSON: Sir Michael Grierson of Lag, Bt.
GUTHRIE: Alexander Guthrie of Guthrie
HAIG: Earl Haig, OBE
HALDANE: Martin Haldane of Gleneagles
HANNAY: David Hannay of Kirkdale and of that Ilk
HAY: Earl of Erroll
HENDERSON: Alistair Henderson of Fordell
HUNTER: Pauline Hunter of Hunterston
IRVINE OF DRUM: David Irvine of Drum
JARDINE: Sir William Jardine of Applegirth, Bt.
JOHNSTONE: Earl of Annandale and Hartfell
KEITH: Earl of Kintore
KENNEDY: Marquess of Ailsa
KERR: Marquess of Lothian, PC
KINCAID: Madam Arabella Kincaid of Kincaid
LAMONT: Revd Peter Lamont of that Ilk
LEASK: Jonathan Leask of that Ilk
LENNOX: Edward Lennox of that Ilk
LESLIE: Earl of Rothes
LINDSAY: Earl of Crawford and Balcarres, KT, GCVO, PC
LIVINGSTONE (or MACLEA): Niall Livingstone of the Bachuil
LOCKHART: Angus Lockhart of the Lee
LUMSDEN: Gillem Lumsden of that Ilk and Blanerne
MACALESTER: William St J. McAlester of Loup and Kennox
MACARTHUR; John MacArthur of that Ilk
MCBAIN: J. H. McBain of McBain
MACDONALD: Lord Macdonald *(The Macdonald of Macdonald)*
*MACDONALD OF CLANRANALD: Ranald Macdonald of Clanranald
MACDONALD OF KEPPOCH: Ranald MacDonald of Keppoch
*MACDONALD OF SLEAT (CLAN HUSTEAIN): Sir Ian Macdonald of Sleat, Bt.
*MACDONELL OF GLENGARRY: Ranald MacDonell of Glengarry
MACDOUGALL: Morag MacDougall of MacDougall
MACDOWALL: Fergus Macdowall of Garthland
MACGREGOR: Sir Malcolm MacGregor of MacGregor, Bt.
MACINTYRE: Donald MacIntyre of Glenoe
MACKAY: Lord Reay
MACKENZIE: Earl of Cromartie
MACKINNON: Anne Mackinnon of Mackinnon
MACKINTOSH: John Mackintosh of Mackintosh *(The Mackintosh of Mackintosh)*
MACLACHLAN: Euan MacLachlan of MacLachlan
MACLAREN: Donald MacLaren of MacLaren and Achleskine
MACLEAN: Hon. Sir Lachlan Maclean of Duart, Bt., CVO
MACLENNAN: Ruaraidh MacLennan of MacLennan
MACLEOD: Hugh MacLeod of MacLeod
MACMILLAN: George MacMillan of MacMillan
MACNAB: J. C. Macnab of Macnab *(The Macnab)*
MACNAGHTEN: Sir Malcolm Macnaghten of Macnaghten and Dundarave, Bt.
MACNEACAIL: John Macneacail of Macneacail and Scorrybreac

MACNEIL OF BARRA: Ian Macneil of Barra *(The Macneil of Barra)*
MACPHERSON: Hon. Sir William Macpherson of Cluny, TD
MACTHOMAS: Andrew MacThomas of Finegand
MAITLAND: Earl of Lauderdale
MAKGILL: Viscount of Oxfuird
MALCOLM (MACCALLUM): Robin N. L. Malcolm of Poltalloch
MAR: Countess of Mar
MARJORIBANKS: Andrew Marjoribanks of that Ilk
MATHESON: Maj. Sir Fergus Matheson of Matheson, Bt.
MENZIES: David Menzies of Menzies
MOFFAT: Madam Moffat of that Ilk
MONCREIFFE: Hon. Peregrine Moncreiffe of that Ilk
MONTGOMERIE: Earl of Eglinton and Winton
MORRISON: Dr Iain Morrison of Ruchdi
MUNRO: Hector Munro of Foulis
MURRAY: Duke of Atholl
NESBITT (or NISBET): Mark Nesbitt of that Ilk
NICOLSON: Lord Carnock
OGILVY: Earl of Airlie, KT, GCVO, PC
OLIPHANT: Richard Oliphant of that Ilk
RAMSAY: Earl of Dalhousie
RIDDELL: Sir John Riddell of Riddell, Bt., CVO
ROBERTSON: Alexander Robertson of Struan *(Struan-Robertson)*
ROLLO: Lord Rollo
ROSE: Miss Elizabeth Rose of Kilravock
ROSS: David Ross of that Ilk and Balnagowan
RUTHVEN: Earl of Gowrie, PC
SCOTT: Duke of Buccleuch and Queensberry, KBE
SCRYMGEOUR: Earl of Dundee
SEMPILL: Lord Sempill
SHAW: John Shaw of Tordarroch
SINCLAIR: Earl of Caithness
SKENE: Danus Skene of Skene
STIRLING: Fraser Stirling of Cader
STRANGE: Maj. Timothy Strange of Balcaskie
SUTHERLAND: Countess of Sutherland
SWINTON: John Swinton of that Ilk
TROTTER: Alexander Trotter of Mortonhall
URQUHART: Kenneth Urquhart of Urquhart
WALLACE: Ian Wallace of that Ilk
WEDDERBURN: Master of Dundee
WEMYSS: Michael Wemyss of that Ilk

THE PRIVY COUNCIL

The sovereign in council, or Privy Council, was the chief source of executive power until the system of cabinet government developed in the 18th century. Now the Privy Council's main functions are to advise the sovereign and to exercise its own statutory responsibilities independent of the sovereign in council.

Membership of the Privy Council is automatic upon appointment to certain government and judicial positions in the United Kingdom, eg cabinet ministers must be Privy Counsellors and are sworn in on first assuming office. Membership is also accorded by the Queen to eminent people in the UK and independent countries of the Commonwealth of which she is Queen, on the recommendation of the British prime minister. Membership of the council is retained for life, except for very occasional removals.

The administrative functions of the Privy Council are carried out by the Privy Council Office under the direction of the president of the council, who is always a member of the cabinet. (*See also* Parliament)

President of the Council, Rt. Hon. Baroness Ashton of Upholland
Clerk of the Council, Judith Simpson

Style The Right (or Rt.) Hon._
*Envelope, The Right (or Rt.) Hon. F_ S_*
*Letter, Dear Mr/Miss/Mrs S_*
*Spoken, Mr/Miss/Mrs S_*

It is incorrect to use the letters PC after the name in conjunction with the prefix The Rt. Hon., unless the Privy Counsellor is a peer below the rank of Marquess and so is styled The Rt. Hon. because of his/her rank. In this case only, the post-nominal letters may be used in conjunction with the prefix The Rt. Hon.

MEMBERS *as at August 2008*

HRH The Duke of Edinburgh, 1951
HRH The Prince of Wales, 1977

Abernethy, *Hon.* Lord (Alastair Cameron), 2005
Ainsworth, Robert, 2005
Airlie, Earl of, 1984
Aldous, Sir William, 1995
Alebua, Ezekiel, 1988
Alexander, Douglas, 2005
Amos, Baroness, 2003
Ampthill, Lord, 1995
Ancram, Michael, 1996
Anderson of Swansea, Lord, 2000
Angiolini, Elish, 2006
Anthony, Douglas, 1971
Arbuthnot, James, 1998
Archer of Sandwell, Lord, 1977
Arden, Dame Mary, 2000
Armstrong, Hilary, 1999
Arthur, *Hon.* Owen, 1995
Ashdown of Norton-sub-Hamdon, Lord, 1989
Ashley of Stoke, Lord, 1979
Ashton of Upholland, Baroness, 2006
Atkins, Sir Robert, 1995
Auld, Sir Robin, 1995
Baker, Sir Thomas, 2002
Baker of Dorking, Lord, 1984
Balls, Ed, 2007
Barnett, Lord, 1975
Barron, Kevin, 2001
Battle, John, 2002
Beckett, Margaret, 1993
Beith, Sir Alan, 1992
Beldam, Sir Roy, 1989
Benn, Anthony, 1964
Benn, Hilary, 2003
Bingham of Cornhill, Lord, 1986
Birch, William, 1992
Bisson, Sir Gordon, 1987
Blackstone, Baroness, 2001
Blair, Anthony, 1994
Blaker, Lord, 1983
Blanchard, Peter, 1998
Blears, Hazel, 2005
Blunkett, David, 1997
Boateng, Paul, 1999
Bolger, James, 1991
Booth, Albert, 1976
Boothroyd, Baroness, 1992
Boscawen, *Hon.* Robert, 1992
Bottomley of Nettlestone, Baroness, 1992
Boyd of Duncansby, Lord, 2000
Boyson, Sir Rhodes, 1987
Bradley, Lord, 2001
Brathwaite, Sir Nicholas, 1991
Brittan of Spennithorne, Lord, 1981
Brooke, Sir Henry, 1996
Brooke of Sutton Mandeville, Lord, 1988
Brown, Gordon, 1996
Brown, Nicholas, 1997
Brown, Sir Stephen, 1983
Brown of Eaton-under-Heywood, Lord, 1992
Browne, Desmond, 2005
Browne-Wilkinson, Lord, 1983
Bruce, Malcolm, 2006
Burnham, Andy, 2007
Butler of Brockwell, Lord, 2004
Butler-Sloss, Baroness, 1988
Buxton, Sir Richard, 1997
Byers, Stephen, 1998
Byron, Sir Dennis, 2004
Caborn, Richard, 1999
Caithness, Earl of, 1990
Cameron, David, 2005
Cameron of Lochbroom, Lord, 1984
Camoys, Lord, 1997
Campbell, Sir Walter Menzies, 1999
Campbell, Sir William, 1999
Canterbury, Archbishop of, 2002
Carey of Clifton, Lord, 1991
Carnwath, Sir Robert, 2002
Carr of Hadley, Lord, 1963
Carrington, Lord, 1959
Carswell, Lord, 1993
Casey, Sir Maurice, 1986
Chadwick, Sir John, 1997
Chalfont, Lord, 1964
Chalker of Wallasey, Baroness, 1987
Chan, Sir Julius, 1981
Chataway, Sir Christopher, 1970
Chilcot, Sir John, 2004
Christie, Perry, 2004
Clark of Windermere, Lord, 1997
Clark, Helen, 1990
Clarke, Sir Anthony, 1998
Clarke, Charles, 2001
Clarke, Kenneth, 1984
Clarke, Thomas, 1997
Clegg, Nicholas, 2008
Clinton-Davis, Lord, 1998
Clwyd, Ann, 2004
Clyde, Lord, 1996
Cooper, Yvette, 2007
Cope of Berkeley, Lord, 1988
Corston, Baroness, 2003
Cosgrove, *Hon.* Lady (Hazel Cosgrove), 2003
Coulsfield, *Hon.* Lord (John Coulsfield), 2000
Cowen, Sir Zelman, 1981
Cradock, Sir Percy, 1993
Crawford and Balcarres, Earl of, 1972
Creech, *Hon.* Wyatt, 1999
Crickhowell, Lord, 1979
Cullen of Whitekirk, Lord, 1997
Cunningham of Felling, Lord, 1993
Curry, David, 1996
Darling, Alistair, 1997
Davies, Denzil, 1978
Davies, Ronald, 1997
Davies of Oldham, Lord, 2006
Davis, David, 1997
Davis, Terence, 1999
Davison, Sir Ronald, 1978
de la Bastide, Michael, 2004
Dean of Harptree, Lord, 1991
Dean of Thornton-le-Fylde, Baroness, 1998
Denham, John, 2000
Denham, Lord, 1981
Dixon, Lord, 1996
Dobson, Frank, 1997
Donaldson, Jeffrey, 2007
Dorrell, Stephen, 1994
du Cann, Sir Edward, 1964
Duncan Smith, Iain, 2001
Dunn, Sir Robin, 1980
Dyson, Sir John, 2001
Eassie, *Hon.* Lord (Ronald Mackay), 2006

East, Paul, 1998
Eden of Winton, Lord, 1972
Edward, Sir David, 2005
Eggar, Timothy, 1995
Eichelbaum, Sir Thomas, 1989
Elias, *Hon.* Dame, Sian, 1999
Elis-Thomas, Lord, 2004
Esquivel, Manuel, 1986
Evans, Sir Anthony, 1992
Eveleigh, Sir Edward, 1977
Falconer of Thoroton, Lord, 2003
Farquharson, Sir Donald, 1989
Fellowes, Lord, 1990
Ferrers, Earl, 1982
Field, Frank, 1997
Flint, Caroline, 2008
Floissac, Sir Vincent, 1992
Foot, Michael, 1974
Forsyth of Drumlean, Lord, 1995
Foster of Bishop Auckland, Lord, 1993
Foulkes of Cumnock, Lord, 2002
Fowler, Lord, 1979
Fraser, Malcolm, 1976
Fraser of Carmyllie, Lord, 1989
Freeman, John, 1966
Freeman, Lord, 1993
Gage, Sir William, 2004
Garel-Jones, Lord, 1992
Gault, Thomas, 1992
Geidt, Christopher, 2007
George, Bruce, 2000
George, Lord, 1999
Gibson, Sir Peter, 1993
Gilbert, Lord, 1978
Gill, *Hon.* Lord (Brian Gill), 2002
Girvan, Sir (Frederick) Paul, 2007
Glenamara, Lord, 1964
Glidewell, Sir Iain, 1985
Goff of Chieveley, Lord, 1982
Goldsmith, Lord, 2002
Goodlad, Lord, 1992
Gowrie, Earl of, 1984
Graham, Sir Douglas, 1998
Graham of Edmonton, Lord, 1998
Griffiths, Lord, 1980
Grocott, Lord, 2002
Gummer, John, 1985
Habgood, Rt. Revd Lord, 1983
Hague, William, 1995
Hain, Peter, 2001
Hale of Richmond, Baroness, 1999
Hallett, Dame Heather, 2005
Hamilton, *Hon.* Lord (Arthur Hamilton), 2002
Hamilton of Epsom, Lord, 1991
Hanley, Sir Jeremy, 1994
Hanson, David, 2007
Hardie, Lord, 1997
Hardie Boys, Sir Michael, 1989
Harman, Harriet, 1997
Harrison, Walter, 1977
Haselhurst, Sir Alan, 1999
Hattersley, Lord, 1975
Hayhoe, Lord, 1985
Hayman, Baroness, 2000
Healey, Lord, 1964
Heathcoat-Amory, David, 1996
Henry, Sir Denis, 1993
Henry, John, 1996
Heseltine, Lord, 1979
Heseltine, Sir William, 1986
Hesketh, Lord, 1991
Hewitt, Patricia, 2001
Higgins, Lord, 1979
Higgins, Sir Malachy, 2007
Hill, Keith, 2003
Hirst, Sir David, 1992
Hodge, Margaret, 2003
Hoffmann, Lord, 1992
Hogg, *Hon.* Douglas, 1992
Hollis of Heigham, Baroness, 1999
Hoon, Geoffrey, 1999
Hooper, Sir Anthony, 2004
Hope of Craighead, Lord, 1989
Hope of Thornes, Lord, 1991
Hordern, Sir Peter, 1993
Howard, Michael, 1990
Howarth, George, 2005
Howarth of Newport, Lord, 2000
Howe of Aberavon, Lord, 1972
Howell of Guildford, Lord, 1979
Hughes, Sir Anthony, 2006
Hughes, Beverley, 2004
Hunt, Jonathon, 1989
Hunt of Wirral, Lord, 1990
Hurd of Westwell, Lord, 1982
Hutchison, Sir Michael, 1995
Hutton, Lord, 1988
Hutton, John, 2001
Inge, Lord, 2004
Ingraham, Hubert, 1993
Ingram, Adam, 1999
Irvine of Lairg, Lord, 1997
Jack, Michael, 1997
Jacob, Sir Robert, 2004
Jacobs, Francis, 2005
Janvrin, Lord, 1998
Jay of Paddington, Baroness, 1998
Jenkin of Roding, Lord, 1973
Johnson, Alan, 2003
Johnson Smith, Sir Geoffrey, 1996
Jones, Lord, 1999
Jopling, Lord, 1979
Jowell, Tessa, 1998
Judge, Sir Igor, 1996
Jugnauth, Sir Anerood, 1987
Kaufman, Sir Gerald, 1978
Kay, Sir Maurice, 2004
Keene, Sir David, 2000
Keith, Sir Kenneth, 1998
Kelly, Sir Basil, 1984
Kelly, Ruth, 2004
Kenilorea, Sir Peter, 1979
Kennedy, Charles, 1999
Kennedy, Jane, 2003
Kennedy, Sir Paul, 1992
Kerr, Sir Brian, 2004
King of Bridgwater, Lord, 1979
Kingarth, *Hon.* Lord (Derek Emslie), 2006
Kingsdown, Lord, 1987
Kingsland, Lord, 1994
Kinnock, Lord, 1983
Kirkwood, *Hon.* Lord (Ian Kirkwood), 2000
Knight, Gregory, 1995
Lamont of Lerwick, Lord, 1986
Lang of Monkton, Lord, 1990
Latasi, Sir Kamuta, 1996
Latham, Sir David, 2000
Lauti, Sir Toaripi, 1979
Laws, Sir John, 1999
Lawson of Blaby, Lord, 1981
Leggatt, Sir Andrew, 1990
Leonard, Rt. Revd Graham, 1981
Letwin, Oliver, 2002
Leveson, Sir Brian, 2006
Liddell, Helen, 1998
Lilley, Peter, 1990
Lloyd of Berwick, Lord, 1984
Lloyd, Sir Peter, 1994
Lloyd, Sir Timothy, 2005
London, Bishop of, 1995
Longmore, Sir Andrew, 2001
Louisy, Sir Allan, 1981
Luce, Lord, 1986
Lyell of Markyate, Lord, 1990
McAvoy, Thomas, 2003
McCartney, Ian, 1999
McCollum, Sir Liam, 1997
McConnell, Jack, 2001
MacDermott, Sir John, 1987
Macdonald of Tradeston, Lord, 1999
McFall, John, 2004
MacGregor of Pulham Market, Lord, 1985
McIntosh of Haringey, Lord, 2002
Mackay, Andrew, 1998
McKay, Sir Ian, 1992
Mackay of Clashfern, Lord, 1979
Mackay of Drumadoon, Lord, 1996
McKinnon, Donald, 1992
Maclean, David, 1995
Maclean, *Hon.* Lord (Ranald MacLean), 2001
McLeish, Henry, 2000
Maclennan of Rogart, Lord, 1997
McLoughlin, Patrick, 2005
McMullin, Sir Duncan, 1980
McNally, Lord, 2005
McNulty, Anthony, 2007
MacShane, Denis, 2005
Major, Sir John, 1987
Malloch-Brown, Lord, 2007
Mance, Lord, 1999
Mandelson, Peter, 1998
Mantell, Sir Charles, 1997
Marnoch, *Hon.* Lord (Michael Marnoch), 2001
Marsh, Lord, 1966
Martin, Michael, 2000
Mason of Barnsley, Lord, 1968
Mates, Michael, 2004
Maude, *Hon.* Francis, 1992
Mawhinney, Lord, 1994
May, Sir Anthony, 1998
May, Theresa, 2003
Mayhew of Twysden, Lord, 1986
Meacher, Michael, 1997
Mellor, David, 1990
Michael, Alun, 1998
Milburn, Alan, 1998
Miliband, David, 2005
Miliband, Ed, 2007
Millan, Bruce, 1975
Millett, Lord, 1994
Mitchell, Sir James, 1985
Mitchell, Dr Keith, 2004
Molyneaux of Killead, Lord, 1983
Moore, Michael, 1990
Moore of Lower Marsh, Lord, 1986
Moore of Wolvercote, Lord, 1977
Moore-Bick, Sir Martin, 2005
Morgan, Rhodri, 2000
Morley, Elliot, 2007
Morris, Charles, 1978
Morris of Aberavon, Lord, 1970
Morris of Manchester, Lord, 1979
Morris of Yardley, Baroness, 1999
Morritt, Sir Robert, 1994
Moses, Sir Alan, 2005
Moyle, Roland, 1978
Mummery, Sir John, 1996
Murphy, Paul, 1999
Murray, *Hon.* Lord (Ronald Murray), 1974
Murray, Sir Donald, 1989
Murton of Lindisfarne, Lord, 1976
Musa, Wilbert, 2005
Mustill, Lord, 1985

Nairne, Sir Patrick, 1982
Namaliu, Sir Rabbie, 1989
Naseby, Lord, 1994
Needham, Sir Richard, 1994
Neill, Sir Brian, 1985
Neuberger of Abbotsbury, Lord, 2004
Newton of Braintree, Lord, 1988
Nicholls of Birkenhead, Lord, 1995
Nicholson, Sir Michael, 1995
Nimmo Smith, *Hon.* Lord (William Nimmo Smith), 2005
Nott, Sir John, 1979
Nourse, Sir Martin, 1985
O'Donnell, Turlough, 1979
Oppenheim-Barnes, Baroness, 1979
Osborne, *Hon.* Lord (Kenneth Osborne), 2001
Otton, Sir Philip, 1995
Owen, Lord, 1976
Paeniu, Bikenibeu, 1991
Paisley, Dr Ian, 2005
Palliser, Sir Michael, 1983
Palmer, Sir Geoffrey, 1986
Parker, Sir Jonathan, 2000
Parker, Sir Roger, 1983
Parkinson, Lord, 1981
Paton, *Hon.* Lady (Ann Paton), 2007
Patten, Lord, 1990
Patten of Barnes, Lord, 1989
Patterson, Percival, 1993
Pattie, Sir Geoffrey, 1987
Peel, Earl, 2006
Pendry, Lord, 2000
Penrose, *Hon.* Lord (George Penrose), 2000
Peters, Winston, 1998
Philip, *Hon.* Lord (Alexander Philip), 2005
Phillips of Worth Matravers, Lord, 1995
Pill, Sir Malcolm, 1995
Portillo, Michael, 1992
Potter, Sir Mark, 1996
Prescott, John, 1994
Price, George, 1982
Primarolo, Dawn, 2002
Prior, Lord, 1970
Prosser, *Hon.* Lord (William Prosser), 2000
Puapua, Sir Tomasi, 1982
Purnell, James, 2007
Quin, Baroness, 1998
Radice, Lord, 1999
Raison, Sir Timothy, 1982
Ramsden, James, 1963
Raynsford, Nick, 2001
Redwood, John, 1993
Reed, Lord, 2008
Rees, Lord, 1983
Reid, George, 2004
Reid, John, 1998
Renton of Mount Harry, Lord, 1989
Richard, Lord, 1993
Richards, Sir Stephen, 2005
Richardson, Sir Ivor, 1978
Richardson of Duntisbourne, Lord, 1976
Rifkind, Sir Malcolm, 1986
Rimer, Sir Colin, 2007
Rix, Sir Bernard, 2000
Roberts of Conwy, Lord, 1991
Robertson of Port Ellen, Lord, 1997
Robinson, Peter, 2007
Roch, Sir John, 1993
Rodger of Earlsferry, Lord, 1992
Rodgers of Quarry Bank, Lord, 1975
Rooker, Lord, 1999
Roper, Lord, 2005
Rose, Sir Christopher, 1992
Ross, *Hon.* Lord (Donald MacArthur), 1985
Royall, Baroness, 2008
Rumbold, Dame Angela, 1991
Ryan, Joan, 2007
Ryder of Wensum, Lord, 1990
Sainsbury, Sir Timothy, 1992
St John of Fawsley, Lord, 1979
Salisbury, Marquess of, 1994
Salmond, Alex, 2007
Sandiford, Erskine, 1989
Saville of Newdigate, Lord, 1994
Sawyer, Dame Joan, 2004
Schiemann, Sir Konrad, 1995
Scotland of Asthal, Baroness, 2001
Scott of Foscote, Lord, 1991
Seaga, Edward, 1981
Sedley, Sir Stephen, 1999
Selkirk of Douglas, Lord, 1996
Sheldon, Lord, 1977
Shephard of Northwold, Baroness, 1992
Sheil, Sir John, 2005
Shipley, Jennifer, 1998
Short, Clare, 1997
Simmonds, Kennedy Sir, 1984
Sinclair, Ian, 1977
Slade, Sir Christopher, 1982
Slynn of Hadley, Lord, 1992
Smith, Andrew, 1997
Smith, Dame Janet, 2002
Smith, Jacqueline, 2003
Smith of Finsbury, Lord, 1997
Somare, Sir Michael, 1977
Spellar, John, 2001
Stanley, Sir John, 1984
Staughton, Sir Christopher, 1988
Steel of Aikwood, Lord, 1977
Stephen, Sir Ninian, 1979
Stewartby, Lord, 1989
Steyn, Lord, 1992
Strang, Gavin, 1997
Strathclyde, Lord, 1995
Straw, Jack, 1997
Stuart-Smith, Sir Murray, 1988
Sutherland, *Hon.* Lord (Ranald Sutherland), 2000
Symons of Vernham Dean, Baroness, 2001
Talboys, Sir Brian, 1977
Taylor of Bolton, Baroness, 1997
Tebbit, Lord, 1981
Templeman, Lord, 1978
Thatcher, Baroness, 1970
Thomas, Edmund, 1996
Thomas, Sir Roger, 2003
Thomas, Sir Swinton, 1994
Thomson of Monifieth, Lord, 1966
Thorpe, Jeremy, 1967
Thorpe, Sir Matthew, 1995
Timms, Stephen, 2006
Tipping, Andrew, 1998
Tizard, Robert, 1986
Touhig, Don, 2006
Toulson, Sir Roger, 2007
Trefgarne, Lord, 1989
Trimble, Lord, 1997
Trumpington, Baroness, 1992
Tuckey, Sir Simon, 1998
Ullswater, Viscount, 1994
Upton, Simon, 1999
Vaz, Keith, 2006
Waddington, Lord, 1987
Waite, Sir John, 1993
Wakeham, Lord, 1983
Waldegrave of North Hill, Lord, 1990
Walker of Gestingthorpe, Lord, 1997
Walker of Worcester, Lord, 1970
Wall, Sir Nicholas, 2004
Wallace of Tankerness, Lord, 2000
Waller, Sir Mark, 1996
Ward, Sir Alan, 1995
Warner, Lord, 2006
Wheatley, *Hon.* Lord (John Wheatley), 2007
Wheeler, Sir John, 1993
Whitty, Lord, 2005
Widdecombe, Ann, 1997
Wigley, Dafydd, 1997
Williams, Alan, 1977
Williams of Crosby, Baroness, 1974
Williamson of Horton, Lord, 2007
Wilson, Brian, 2003
Wilson, Sir Nicholas, 2005
Windlesham, Lord, 1973
Winterton, Rosie, 2006
Wingti, Paias, 1987
Withers, Reginald, 1977
Woodhouse, Sir Owen, 1974
Woodward, Shaun, 2007
Woolf, Lord, 1986
York, Archbishop of, 2005
Young, Sir George, 1993
Young of Graffham, Lord, 1984
Zacca, Edward, 1992

PRIVY COUNCIL OF NORTHERN IRELAND

The Privy Council of Northern Ireland had responsibilities in Northern Ireland similar to those of the Privy Council in Great Britain until the Northern Ireland Act 1974.

Membership of the Privy Council of Northern Ireland is retained for life. Since the Northern Ireland Constitution Act 1973 no further appointments have been made. The postnominal initials PC (NI) are used to differentiate its members from those of the Privy Council.

MEMBERS *as at August 2008*
Bailie, Robin, 1971
Bleakley, David, 1971
Craig, William, 1963
Dobson, John, 1969
Kelly, Sir Basil, 1969
Kilclooney, Lord, 1970
Kirk, Herbert, 1962
Long, William, 1966
Porter, Sir Robert, 1969

PARLIAMENT

The United Kingdom constitution is not contained in any single document but has evolved over time, formed partly by statute, partly by common law and partly by convention. A constitutional monarchy, the United Kingdom is governed by ministers of the crown in the name of the sovereign, who is head both of the state and of the government.

The organs of government are the legislature (parliament), the executive and the judiciary. The executive consists of HM government (the cabinet and other ministers), government departments and local authorities (*see* Local Government, Government Departments and Public Bodies sections). The judiciary (*see* Law Courts and Offices section) pronounces on the law, both written and unwritten, interprets statutes and is responsible for the enforcement of the law; the judiciary is independent of both the legislature and the executive.

THE MONARCHY

The sovereign personifies the state and is, in law, an integral part of the legislature, head of the executive, head of the judiciary, commander-in-chief of all armed forces of the crown and supreme governor of the Church of England. The seat of the monarchy is in the United Kingdom. In the Channel Islands and the Isle of Man, which are crown dependencies, the sovereign is represented by a lieutenant-governor. In the member states of the Commonwealth of which the sovereign is head of state, her representative is a governor-general; in UK dependencies the sovereign is usually represented by a governor, who is responsible to the British government.

Although in practice the powers of the monarchy are now very limited, and restricted mainly to the advisory and ceremonial, there are important acts of government which require the participation of the sovereign. These include summoning, proroguing and dissolving parliament, giving royal assent to bills passed by parliament, appointing important office-holders, eg government ministers, judges, bishops and governors, conferring peerages, knighthoods and other honours, and granting pardon to a person wrongly convicted of a crime. The sovereign appoints the prime minister; by convention this office is held by the leader of the political party which enjoys, or can secure, a majority of votes in the House of Commons. In international affairs the sovereign as head of state has the power to declare war and make peace, to recognise foreign states and governments, to conclude treaties and to annex or cede territory. However, as the sovereign entrusts executive power to ministers of the crown and acts on the advice of her ministers, which she cannot ignore, royal prerogative powers are in practice exercised by ministers, who are responsible to parliament.

Ministerial responsibility does not diminish the sovereign's importance to the smooth working of government. She holds meetings of the Privy Council (*see* below), gives audiences to her ministers and other officials at home and overseas, receives accounts of cabinet decisions, reads dispatches and signs state papers; she must be informed and consulted on every aspect of national life; and she must show complete impartiality.

COUNSELLORS OF STATE

In the event of the sovereign's absence abroad, it is necessary to appoint counsellors of state under letters patent to carry out the chief functions of the monarch, including the holding of Privy Councils and giving royal assent to acts passed by parliament. The normal procedure is to appoint as counsellors three or four members of the royal family among those remaining in the UK.

In the event of the sovereign on accession being under the age of 18 years, or at any time unavailable or incapacitated by infirmity of mind or body for the performance of the royal functions, provision is made for a regency.

THE PRIVY COUNCIL

The sovereign in council, or Privy Council, was the chief source of executive power until the system of cabinet government developed. Its main function today is to advise the sovereign on the approval of various statutory functions and acts of the royal prerogative. These powers are exercised through orders in council and royal proclamations, approved by the Queen at meetings of the Privy Council. The council is also able to exercise a number of statutory duties without approval from the sovereign, including powers of supervision over the registering bodies for the medical and allied professions. These duties are exercised through orders in council.

Although appointment as a privy counsellor is for life, only those who are currently government ministers are involved in the day-to-day business of the council. A full council is summoned only on the death of the sovereign or when the sovereign announces his or her intention to marry. (For a full list of privy counsellors, *see* the Privy Council section.)

There are a number of advisory Privy Council committees whose meetings the sovereign does not attend. Some are prerogative committees, such as those dealing with legislative matters submitted by the legislatures of the Channel Islands and the Isle of Man or with applications for charters of incorporation; and some are provided for by statute, eg those for the universities of Oxford and Cambridge and the Scottish universities.

The Judicial Committee of the Privy Council is the court of final appeal from courts of the UK dependencies, courts of independent Commonwealth countries which have retained the right of appeal and courts of the Channel Islands and the Isle of Man.

It also has certain jurisdiction within the United Kingdom, the most important of which is that it is the court of final appeal for 'devolution issues', ie issues as to the legal competences and functions of the legislative and executive authorities established in Scotland, Wales and Northern Ireland by the devolution legislation of 1998.

The committee is composed of privy counsellors who hold, or have held, high judicial office, although usually only three or five hear each case.

Administrative work is carried out by the Privy Council Office under the direction of the Lord President of the Council, a cabinet minister.

PARLIAMENT

Parliament is the supreme law-making authority and can legislate for the UK as a whole or for any parts of it separately (the Channel Islands and the Isle of Man are crown dependencies and not part of the UK). The main functions of parliament are to pass laws, to provide (by voting taxation) the means of carrying on the work of government and to scrutinise government policy and administration, particularly proposals for expenditure. International treaties and agreements are by custom presented to parliament before ratification.

Parliament emerged during the late 13th and early 14th centuries. The officers of the king's household and the king's judges were the nucleus of early parliaments, joined by such ecclesiastical and lay magnates as the king might summon to form a prototype 'House of Lords', and occasionally by the knights of the shires, burgesses and proctors of the lower clergy. By the end of Edward III's reign a 'House of Commons' was beginning to appear; the first known Speaker was elected in 1377.

Parliamentary procedure is based on custom and precedent, partly formulated in the standing orders of both houses of parliament, and each house has the right to control its own internal proceedings and to commit for contempt. The system of debate in the two houses is similar; when a motion has been moved, the Speaker proposes the question as the subject of a debate. Members speak from wherever they have been sitting. Questions are decided by a vote on a simple majority. Draft legislation is introduced, in either house, as a bill. Bills can be introduced by a government minister or a private member, but in practice the majority of bills which become law are introduced by the government. To become law, a bill must be passed by each house (for parliamentary stages, *see* Parliamentary Information) and then sent to the sovereign for the royal assent, after which it becomes an act of parliament.

Proceedings of both houses are public, except on extremely rare occasions. The minutes (called *Votes and Proceedings in the Commons,* and *Minutes of Proceedings in the Lords*) and the speeches (*The Official Report of Parliamentary Debates,* Hansard) are published daily. Proceedings are also recorded for transmission on radio and television and stored in the Parliamentary Recording Unit before transfer to the National Sound Archive. Television cameras have been allowed into the House of Lords since 1985 and into the House of Commons since 1989; committee meetings may also be televised.

By the Parliament Act of 1911, the maximum duration of a parliament is five years (if not previously dissolved), the term being reckoned from the date given on the writs for the new parliament. The maximum life has been prolonged by legislation in such rare circumstances as the two World Wars (31 January 1911 to 25 November 1918; 26 November 1935 to 15 June 1945). Dissolution and writs for a general election are ordered by the sovereign on the advice of the prime minister. The life of a parliament is divided into sessions, usually of one year in length, beginning and ending most often in October or November.

DEVOLUTION

The Scottish parliament and the National Assembly for Wales have legislative power over all devolved matters, ie matters not reserved to Westminster or otherwise outside its powers. The Northern Ireland Assembly has legislative authority in the fields previously administered by the Northern Ireland departments. The assembly was suspended in October 2002 and dissolved in April 2003, before being reinstated on 8 May 2007. For further information, *see* the Regional Government section.

THE HOUSE OF LORDS

London SW1A 0PW
T 020-7219 3000 Information Office 020-7219 3107
E hlinfo@parliament.uk W www.parliament.uk

The House of Lords is the second chamber, or 'Upper House', of the UK's bicameral parliament. Until the beginning of the twentieth century, the House of Lords had considerable power, being able to veto any bill submitted to it by the House of Commons. Today the main functions of the House of Lords are to revise legislation, to act as a check on the government, to provide a forum of independent expertise and to act as a final court of appeal.

The House of Lords has a number of select committees. Some relate to the internal affairs of the house – such as its management and administration – while others carry out important investigative work on matters of public interest. The main areas of work are: Europe, science, the economy, the constitution and communications. House of Lords investigative committees look at broader issues and do not mirror government departments as the select committees in the House of Commons do.

The House of Lords has judicial powers as the ultimate court of appeal for courts in Great Britain and Northern Ireland, except for criminal cases in Scotland. These powers are exercised by the Lords of Appeal in Ordinary (the law lords) – (*see* Law Courts and Offices section). On 12 June 2003 the government announced reforms affecting the role of the Lord Chancellor as a judge and Speaker of the House of Lords, and establishing a separate supreme court (*see* Government Departments section). The supreme court is expected to be established in late 2009, when the judicial function of the House of Lords will cease. In 2006 the position of Lord Chancellor was significantly altered by the Constitutional Reform Act 2005. The office holder is no longer speaker of the House of Lords nor head of the judiciary in England and Wales, but remains a cabinet minister (the Lord Chancellor and Secretary of State for Justice). The function of speaker of the House of Lords was devolved to the newly created post of Lord Speaker. The Rt. Hon. Baroness Hayman was elected as the first Lord Speaker by the house on 4 July 2006.

Members of the House of Lords comprise life peers created under the Life Peerages Act 1958, 92 hereditary peers under the House of Lords Act 1999 and Lords of Appeal in Ordinary, ie law lords, under the Appellate Jurisdiction Act 1876. The Archbishops of Canterbury and York, the Bishops of London, Durham and Winchester, and the 21 senior diocesan bishops of the Church of England are also members.

The House of Lords Act provides for 90 elected hereditary peers to remain in the House of Lords until longer-term reform of the House has been carried out; 42 Conservative, 28 crossbench, three Liberal Democrat and two Labour. Elections for each of the party groups and the crossbenches were held in October and November 1999. Fifteen office holders were elected by the whole house. Two hereditary peers with royal duties, the Earl Marshal and the Lord Great Chamberlain, are also members.

Peers are disqualified from sitting in the house if they are:

- aliens, ie any peer who is not a British citizen, a Commonwealth citizen (under the British Nationality Act 1981) or a citizen of the Republic of Ireland
- under the age of 21
- undischarged bankrupts or, in Scotland, those whose estate is sequestered
- convicted of treason

Bishops retire at the age of 70 and cease to be members of the house at that time.

Members who do not wish to attend sittings of the House of Lords may apply for leave of absence for the duration of a parliament.

Members of the House of Lords are unpaid but are entitled to allowances for attendance at sittings of the house. The daily maxima, between 1 August 2007 and 31 July 2008, were £165.50 for overnight subsistence, £82.50 for day subsistence and incidental travel, and £71.50 for office costs.

COMPOSITION *as at 1 July 2008*

Archbishops and bishops	26
Life peers under the Appellate Jurisdiction Act 1876	23
Life peers under the Life Peerages Act 1958	605
Peers under the House of Lords Act 1999	92
Total	746

STATE OF THE PARTIES *as at 1 July 2008**

Conservative	202
Labour	215
Liberal Democrat	76
Crossbench	203
Archbishops and bishops	26
Other	13
Total	735

* Excluding 11 peers on leave of absence from the house

HOUSE OF LORDS PAY BANDS

Staff are placed in the following pay bands according to their level of responsibility and taking account of other factors such as experience and marketability.

Judicial group 4	£165,900
Senior band 3	£97,852–£139,974
Senior band 2	£79,433–£129,729
Senior band 1A	£66,771–£108,806
Senior band 1	£57,561–£96,477
Band A1	£56,049–£71,210
Band A2	£46,604–£58,916

OFFICERS AND OFFICIALS

The house is presided over by the Lord Speaker, whose powers differ from those of the Speaker of the House of Commons. The Lord Speaker has no power to maintain order because the House of Lords is self-regulating.

A panel of deputy speakers is appointed by Royal Commission. The first deputy speaker is the chair of committees, appointed at the beginning of each session, who is a salaried officer of the house. He or she takes the chair when the whole house is in committee and in some select committees. He or she is assisted by a panel of deputy chairs, headed by the salaried principal deputy chair of committees, who is also chair of the European Communities Committee of the house.

The Clerk of the Parliaments is the accounting officer and the chief permanent official responsible for the administration of the house. The Gentleman Usher of the Black Rod is responsible for security and other services and also has royal duties as secretary to the Lord Great Chamberlain.

Lord Speaker (£104,386), Rt. Hon. Baroness Hayman
Chair of Committees (£81,504), Lord Brabazon of Tara
Principal Deputy Chair of Committees (£76,250), Lord Grenfell
Clerk of the Parliaments (Judicial Group 4), M. G. Pownall
Clerk Assistant (Senior Band 3), D. R. Beamish, LLM
Reading Clerk and Clerk of the Overseas Office (Senior Band 2), Dr R. H. Walters, DPHIL
Clerk of the Committees (Senior Band 2), E. C. Ollard
Finance Director (Senior Band 1A), Dr F. P. Tudor
Head of Human Resources (Senior Band 1A), S. P. Bunton
Clerk of the Judicial Office and Registrar of Lords Interests (Senior Band 1A), B. P. Keith
Director of Information Services and Librarian (Senior Band 2), Dr E. Hallam Smith
Clerk of Public and Private Bill Office and Examiner of Petitions for Private Bills in the House of Lords (Senior Band 1A), T. V. Mohan
Editor of the Official Report (Senior Band 1), A. S. Nicholls
Clerk of the Records (Senior Band 1), S. K. Ellison
Deputy Finance Director and Head of Finance (Senior Band 1), J. P. Smith
Director of Public Information (Band A1), Miss M. L. Morgan
Counsel to the Chairman of Committees (Senior Band 2), M. Thomas
Second Counsel to the Chairman of Committees (Senior Band 2), Dr C. S. Kerse, CB
Legal Adviser to the Human Rights Committee (Senior Band 2), M. Hunt
Change Manager (Senior Band 1), Mrs M. E. Ollard
Clerk of the Journals (Senior Band 1), C. Johnson
Clerk of the European Union Committee (Senior Band 1A), A. Makower
Clerk of Pre-Legislative Scrutiny (Senior Band 1), Mrs K. S. Lawrence
Gentleman Usher of the Black Rod and Serjeant-at-Arms (Senior Band 2), Lt.-Gen. Sir Michael Willcocks, KCB
Yeoman Usher of the Black Rod and Deputy Serjeant-at-Arms (Band A2), Brig. H. D. C. Duncan, MBE

LORD GREAT CHAMBERLAIN'S OFFICE

Lord Great Chamberlain, Marquess of Cholmondeley
Secretary to the Lord Great Chamberlain, Lt.-Gen. Sir Michael Willcocks, KCB

SELECT COMMITTEES

The main House of Lords select committees, *as at June 2007,* are as follows:

European Union – Chair, Lord Grenfell; *Clerk,* A. Makower
European Union – Sub-committees:
A (Economic and Financial Affairs and International Trade) – Chair, Baroness Cohen of Pimlico; *Clerk,* Simon Blackburn
B (Internal Market) – Chair, Lord Freeman; *Clerk,* James Whittle

C (Foreign Affairs, Defence and Development Policy) – Chair, Lord Roper; *Clerk,* Kathryn Colvin
D (Agriculture and the Environment) – Chair, Lord Sewel; *Clerk,* Julia Labeta
E (Law and Institutions) – Chair, Lord Mance; *Clerk,* Susanna Street
F (Home Affairs) – Chair, Lord Joplin; *Clerk,* Michael Collon
G (Social and Consumer Affairs) – Chair, Baroness Howarth of Breckland; *Clerk,* Barry Werner
Constitution Committee – Chair, Lord Goodlad; *Clerk,* Tom Wilson
Delegated Powers and Regulatory Reform – Chair, Lord Goodhart; *Clerk,* A. Mackersie
Economic Affairs – Chair, Lord Wallace of Tummel; *Clerk,* Robert Graham-Harrison
Science and Technology – Chair, Lord Sutherland of Houndwood; *Clerk,* Christine Salmon Percival
I – Chair, Lord O'Neill of Clackmannan; *Clerk,* Sarah Jones
II – Chair, Lord Patel; *Clerk,* Elisa Rubio
Human Rights Joint Committee – Chair, Andrew Dismore, MP; *Lords Clerk,* Bill Sinton
Merits of Statutory Instruments Committee – Chair, Lord Filkin; *Clerk,* A. Mackersie

THE HOUSE OF COMMONS

London SW1A 0AA
T 020-7219 3000
Information office 020-7219 4272
Forthcoming business 020-7219 5532
E hcinfo@parliament.uk **W** www.parliament.uk

The members of the House of Commons are elected by universal adult suffrage. For electoral purposes, the United Kingdom is divided into constituencies, each of which returns one member to the House of Commons, the member being the candidate who obtains the largest number of votes cast in the constituency. To ensure equitable representation, the four Boundary Commissions keep constituency boundaries under review and recommend any redistribution of seats which may seem necessary because of population movements, etc. The number of seats was raised to 640 in 1945, reduced to 625 in 1948, and subsequently rose to 630 in 1955, 635 in 1970, 650 in 1983, 651 in 1992 and 659 in 1997, before falling to 646 in 2005. Of the present 646 seats, there are 529 for England, 40 for Wales, 59 for Scotland and 18 for Northern Ireland.

ELECTIONS

Elections are by secret ballot, each elector casting one vote; voting is not compulsory. For entitlement to vote in parliamentary elections, *see* Legal Notes section. When a seat becomes vacant between general elections, a by-election is held.

British subjects and citizens of the Irish Republic can stand for election as MPs provided they are 21 or over and not subject to disqualification. Those disqualified from sitting in the house include:

- undischarged bankrupts
- people sentenced to more than one year's imprisonment
- members of the House of Lords (but hereditary peers not sitting in the Lords are eligible)
- holders of certain offices listed in the House of Commons Disqualification Act 1975, eg members of the judiciary, civil service, regular armed forces, police forces, some local government officers and some members of public corporations and government commissions

A candidate does not require any party backing but his or her nomination for election must be supported by the signatures of ten people registered in the constituency. A candidate must also deposit £500 with the returning officer, which is forfeit if the candidate does not receive more than 5 per cent of the votes cast. All election expenses at a general election, except the candidate's personal expenses, are subject to a statutory limit of £7,150, plus five pence for each elector in a borough constituency or seven pence for each elector in a county constituency.

See pages 137–181 for an alphabetical list of MPs, results of the last general election in 2005 and results of by-elections since the general election.

STATE OF THE PARTIES *as at 1 September 2008**

Party	*Seats*
Labour	349
Conservative	193
Liberal Democrats	63
Democratic Unionist Party	9
Scottish National Party	7
Sinn Fein (have not taken their seats)	5
Plaid Cymru	3
Social Democratic Labour Party	3
Independent	4
Independent Conservative	1
Independent Labour	1
Respect	1
Ulster Unionist	1
UK Independence	1
The Speaker and three Deputy Speakers	4
Vacant	1
Total	646

*Working majority of 62; 349 Labour MPs less 287 of all other parties (excluding the speaker, deputy speakers and Sinn Fein)

BUSINESS

The week's business of the house is outlined each Thursday by the leader of the house, after consultation between the chief government whip and the chief opposition whip. A quarter to a third of the time will be taken up by the government's legislative programme and the rest by other business. As a rule, bills likely to raise political controversy are introduced in the Commons before going on to the Lords, and the Commons claims exclusive control in respect of national taxation and expenditure. Bills such as the finance bill, which imposes taxation, and the consolidated fund bills, which authorise expenditure, must begin in the Commons. A bill of which the financial provisions are subsidiary may begin in the Lords; and the Commons may waive its rights in regard to Lords' amendments affecting finance.

The Commons has a public register of MPs' financial and certain other interests; this is published annually as a House of Commons paper. Members must also disclose any relevant financial interest or benefit in a matter before the house when taking part in a debate, in certain other proceedings of the house, or in consultations with other MPs, with ministers or with civil servants.

MEMBERS' PAY AND ALLOWANCES

Since 1911 members of the House of Commons have received salary payments; facilities for free travel were introduced in 1924. Salary rates since 1911 are as follows:

1978 Jun	£6,897	1994 Jan	£31,687
1979 Jun	9,450	1995 Jan	33,189
1980 Jun	11,750	1996 Jan	34,085
1981 Jun	13,950	1996 Jul	43,000
1982 Jun	14,910	1997 Apr	43,860
1983 Jun	15,308	1998 Apr	45,066
1984 Jan	16,106	1999 Apr	47,008
1985 Jan	16,904	2000 Apr	48,371
1986 Jan	17,702	2001 Apr	49,822
1987 Jan	18,500	2002 Apr	55,118
1988 Jan	22,548	2003 Apr	56,358
1989 Jan	24,107	2004 Apr	57,485
1990 Jan	26,701	2005 Apr	59,095
1991 Jan	28,970	2006 Apr	59,686
1992 Jan	30,854	2007 Apr	61,181
1993 Jan	30,854	2008 Apr	61,820

In 1969 MPs were granted an annual allowance for secretarial and research expenses, revised in July 2001. Members receive an incidental expenses provision (£22,193), a staffing allowance (up to £100,205) and a communications allowance (£10,400).

Since 1972 MPs have been able to claim reimbursement for the additional cost of staying overnight away from their main residence while on parliamentary business; this is known as the additional costs allowance and from April 2008 is £24,006 per year.

Members of staff who are paid out of the allowances can benefit from a sum not exceeding 10 per cent of their gross salary which is paid into the Portcullis Pension Plan. This sum comes from a central budget.

MEMBERS' PENSIONS

Pension arrangements for MPs were first introduced in 1964. Under the Parliamentary Contributory Pension Fund (PCPF), MPs receive a pension on retirement based upon their salary in their final year, and upon their number of years' service as an MP. Members may pay a contribution rate of 10 per cent or 6 per cent and build up a pension of 2.5 per cent or 2 per cent of salary for each year of service. Pensions are normally payable at age 65; upon retirement at 65, the pension payable is subject to a maximum of 66.6 per cent of salary, inclusive of pensions from employment or self-employment prior to becoming an MP. There are provisions in place for: early retirement for those MPs who cease to serve between the ages of 50 (55 from 6 April 2010) and 65; MPs of any age who retire due to ill health; and pensions for widows/widowers of MPs. All pensions are index-linked. There is an Exchequer contribution to ensure that shortfalls are made up; currently 8.7 per cent of an MP's salary for 15 years from 2006/7.

The House of Commons Members' Fund provides for annual or lump sum grants to ex-MPs, their widows or widowers, and children of those who either ceased to serve as an MP prior to the PCPF being established or who are experiencing hardship. Members contribute £24 a year and the Exchequer £215,000 a year to the fund.

HOUSE OF COMMONS PAY BANDS

Staff are placed in the following Senior Civil Service pay bands. These pay bands apply to the most senior staff in departments and agencies.

Pay Band 1	£57,300–£116,000
Pay Band 1A	£66,600–£127,000
Pay Band 2	£81,600–£160,000
Pay Band 3	£99,960–£205,000

OFFICERS AND OFFICIALS

The House of Commons is presided over by the Speaker, who has considerable powers to maintain order. A deputy speaker, called the chairman of ways and means, and two deputy chairs may preside over sittings of the House of Commons; they are elected by the house, and, like the Speaker, neither speak nor vote other than in their official capacity.

The staff of the house are employed by a commission chaired by the Speaker. The heads of the six House of Commons departments are permanent officers of the house, not MPs. The Clerk of the House is the principal adviser to the Speaker on the privileges and procedures of the house, the conduct of the business of the house, and committees. The Serjeant-at-Arms is responsible for security and ceremonial functions of the house.

Speaker (£137,579), Rt. Hon. Michael J. Martin, MP (Glasgow Springburn)
Chairman of Ways and Means (£102,466), Sir Alan Haselhurst, MP (Saffron Walden)
First Deputy Chairman of Ways and Means (£97,543), Sylvia Heal, MP (Halesowen and Rowley Regis)
Second Deputy Chairman of Ways and Means (£97,543), Sir Michael Lord, MP (Suffolk Central and Ipswich North)
Parliamentary Commissioner for Standards in Public Life, John Lyon, CB

OFFICES OF THE SPEAKER AND CHAIRMAN OF WAYS AND MEANS

Speaker's Secretary, A. Sinclair
Chaplain to the Speaker, Revd Canon R. Wright
Secretary to the Chairman of Ways and Means, J. Whatley

DEPARTMENT OF CHAMBER AND COMMITTEE SERVICES

Clerk of the House of Commons, Dr M. R. Jack

OFFICE OF THE CHIEF EXECUTIVE

Head of Office, Ms P. Helme
Director of Internal Audit, P. Dillon-Robinson

CLERK ASSISTANT'S DIRECTORATE

Clerk Assistant, D. G. Millar
Principal Clerks
Table Office, Ms J. Sharpe
Journals, A. R. Kennon
Overseas Office, M. Hutton

VOTE OFFICE

Deliverer of the Vote, J. F. Collins
Deputy Deliverers of the Vote, O. B. T. Sweeney *(Parliamentary)*; R. Brook *(Development)*; Ms J. Pitt *(Production)*

COMMITTEE DIRECTORATE

Clerk of Committees, D. Natzler
Principal Clerk and Deputy Head of Committee Office, R. W. G. Wilson
Clerk of Domestic Committees/Secretary to the Commission, D. J. Gerhold
Select Committees, P. A. Evans; C. J. Poyser
Head of Scrutiny Unit, M. Hamlyn
Director of Broadcasting, T. Jeffes

LEGISLATION DIRECTORATE

Clerk of Legislation, R. J. Rogers

Principal Clerks
Delegated Legislation, S. J. Patrick
Bills, L. L. Smyth
National Parliament Office (Brussels), Ms L. Davidson
Ways and Means Office, M. Clark

OFFICIAL REPORT DIRECTORATE
Editor, Miss L. Sutherland
Deputy Editors, Ms V. Widgery; A. Newton

SERJEANT-AT-ARMS DIRECTORATE
Serjeant-at-Arms, Mrs J. Pay
Deputy Serjeant-at-Arms, R. M. Morton
Assistant Serjeants-at-Arms, J. M. Robertson; L. Ward

LEGAL SERVICES OFFICE
Speaker's Counsel and Head of Legal Services Office, M. Carpenter
Counsel for European Legislation, vacant
Counsel for Legislation, Peter Davis
Deputy Counsel, P. Brooksbank; Ms C. Cogger
Assistant Counsel, G. Beck; Ms V. Daly; Ms H. Emes

DEPARTMENT OF INFORMATION SERVICES
Director-General and Librarian, J. Pullinger
Directors, R. Clements *(Research Services)*; Prof. D. Cope *(Parliamentary Office of Science and Technology)*; Ms B. McInnes *(Departmental Services)*; R. Twigger *(Information Services)*; Ms A. Walker *(Public Information)*; S. Wise *(Internet Programme)*; E. Wood *(Information Management)*; Ms H. Wood *(SPIRE Programme)*
Heads of Sections, C. Barclay; Mrs D. Clark; R. Cracknell; T. Edmonds; Ms O. Gay; Mrs C. Gillie; M. Hay; V. Launert; S. McGinness; Mrs K. Marke; Ms C. Meredith; Ms V. Miller; B. Morgan; T. O'Leary; Dr C. Pond; Ms P. J. Strickland
Media and Communications Adviser, Ms E. Parratt
Parliamentary Outreach Officer, Ms C. Cowan
Visitor and Information Manager, C. Weeds

DEPARTMENT OF RESOURCES
Director-General of Resources, A. J. Walker
Director of Business Management and Development, Ms J. Rissen
Director of Operations, T. M. Bird
Director of Human Resource Management, Mrs H. Bryson
Director of Finance Policy, C. Ridley
Director, Commercial, vacant
Head of Occupational Health, Safety and Welfare Service, Dr M. McDougall

DEPARTMENT OF FACILITIES
Director-General, J. Borley
Business Management Director, vacant
Parliamentary Director of Estates, M. Barlex
Director of Accommodation Services, J. Robertson
Director of Facilities Finance, P. Collins
Executive Officer, M. Trott
Head of Human Resources and Development, J. van den Broek

CATERING AND RETAIL SERVICES DIRECTORATE
Director of Catering Services, Mrs S. Harrison
Catering Operations Manager (Outbuildings), Ms D. Herd
Food and Beverage Operations Manager, Palace of Westminster, R. Gibbs
Executive Chef, M. Hill
Retail Manager, Mrs M. DeSouza

PARLIAMENTARY INFORMATION AND COMMUNICATION TECHNOLOGY (ICT)
Director of Parliamentary ICT, Ms J. Miller
Director of Business Information Systems Directorate, I. Montgomery
Director of Operations, M. Taylor
Director of Resources, Ms E. Honer
Director of Programmes and Project Development, R. Ware

NATIONAL AUDIT OFFICE
157–197 Buckingham Palace Road, London SW1W 9SP
T 020-7798 7000 F 020-7798 7070
E enquiries@nao.gsi.gov.uk W www.nao.org.uk

The National Audit Office came into existence under the National Audit Act 1983 to replace and continue the work of the former Exchequer and Audit Department. The act reinforced the office's total financial and operational independence from the government and brought its head, the Comptroller and Auditor-General, into a closer relationship with parliament as an officer of the House of Commons.

The National Audit Office provides independent information, advice and assurance to parliament and the public about all aspects of the financial operations of government departments and many other bodies receiving public funds. It does this by examining and certifying the accounts of these organisations. It also regularly publishes reports to parliament on the results of its value for money investigations of the economy (the efficiency and effectiveness with which public resources have been used). The National Audit Office is also the auditor by agreement of the accounts of certain international and other organisations. In addition, the office authorises the issue of public funds to government departments.

Comptroller and Auditor-General, Tim Burr
Private Secretary, Janey Sacoto
Assistant Auditors-General, Gabrielle Cohen; Ed Humpherson; Wendy Kenway-Smith; Caroline Mawhood; Jim Rickleton; Martin Sinclair; Michael Whitehouse

SELECT COMMITTEES
The more significant committees, as at August 2008, are:

DEPARTMENTAL COMMITTEES
Business and Enterprise – Chair, Peter Luff, MP; *Clerk,* Eve Samson
Children, Schools and Families – Chair, Barry Sheerman, MP; *Clerk,* Kenneth Fox
Communities and Local Government – Chair, Dr Phyllis Starkey, MP; *Clerk,* Huw Yardley
Culture, Media and Sport – Chair, John Whittingdale, MP; *Clerk,* Tracey Garratty
Defence – Chair, Rt. Hon. James Arbuthnot, MP; *Clerk,* Mike Hennessy
Environment, Food and Rural Affairs – Chair, Rt. Hon. Michael Jack, MP; *Clerk,* Richard Cooke
Foreign Affairs – Chair, Mike Gapes, MP; *Clerk,* Dr Robin James
Health – Chair, Rt. Hon. Kevin Barron, MP; *Clerk,* Dr David Harrison
Home Affairs – Chair, Rt. Hon. Keith Vaz, MP; *Clerk,* Elizabeth Flood
Innovation, Universities, Science and Skills – Chair, Phil Willis, MP; *Clerk,* Sarah Davies

International Development – *Chair,* Malcolm Bruce, MP; *Clerk,* Carol Oxborough
Justice – *Chair,* Rt. Hon. Sir Alan Beith, MP; *Clerk,* Fergus Reid
Northern Ireland Affairs – *Chair,* Sir Patrick Cormack, MP; *Clerk,* David Weir
Scottish Affairs – *Chair,* Mohammad Sarwar, MP; *Clerk,* Charlotte Littleboy
Standards and Privileges – *Chair,* Rt. Hon. Sir George Young, Bt., MP; *Clerk,* Steve Priestley
Transport – *Chair,* Louise Ellman, MP; *Clerk,* Annette Toft
Treasury – *Chair,* Rt. Hon. John McFall, MP; *Clerk,* Dr John Benger
Welsh Affairs – *Chair,* Dr Hywel Francis, MP; *Clerk,* Dr Sue Griffiths
Work and Pensions – *Chair,* Terry Rooney, MP; *Clerk,* James Rhys

NON-DEPARTMENTAL COMMITTEES
Arms Export Controls – *Chair,* Roger Berry, MP; *Clerk,* Charlotte Littleboy
Environmental Audit – *Chair,* Tim Yeo, MP; *Clerk,* Gordon Clarke
European Scrutiny – *Chair,* Michael Connarty, MP; *Clerk,* Alistair Doherty
Finance and Services – *Chair,* Sir Stuart Bell, MP; *Clerk,* Dorian Gerhold
Human Rights (Joint Committee) – *Chair,* Andrew Dismore, MP; *Clerks,* Dr Mark Egan; Rebecca Neal
Modernisation of the House of Commons – *Chair,* Rt. Hon. Harriet Harman, QC, MP; *Clerk,* David Natzler
Procedure – *Chair,* Rt. Hon. Greg Knight, MP; *Clerk,* Dr Lynn Gardner
Public Accounts – *Chair,* Edward Leigh, MP; *Clerk,* Mark Etherton
Public Administration – *Chair,* Dr Tony Wright, MP; *Clerk,* Steven Mark
Regulatory Reform – *Chair,* Andrew Miller, MP; *Clerk,* John Whatley
Statutory Instruments (Joint Committee) – *Chair,* Rt. Hon. David Maclean, MP; *Clerk,* John Whatley

DOMESTIC COMMITTEE
Administration – *Chair,* Frank Doran, MP; *Clerk,* Kate Emms

OTHER COMMITTEES (CABINET OFFICE)
Intelligence and Security (Cabinet Office) – *Chair,* Rt. Hon. Margaret Beckett, MP; *Clerk,* Emma-Louise Avery

PARLIAMENTARY INFORMATION

The following is a short glossary of aspects of the work of parliament. Unless otherwise stated, references are to House of Commons procedures.

BILL – Proposed legislation is termed a bill. The stages of a public bill (for private bills, *see* below) in the House of Commons are as follows:

First reading: This stage merely constitutes an order to have the bill printed.
Second reading: The debate on the principles of the bill.
Committee stage: The detailed examination of a bill, clause by clause. In most cases this takes place in a public bill committee, or the whole house may act as a committee. Public bill committees may take evidence before embarking on detailed scrutiny of the bill. Very rarely, a bill may be examined by a select committee.
Report stage: Detailed review of a bill as amended in committee, on the floor of the house.
Third reading: Final debate on a bill.

Public bills go through the same stages in the House of Lords, but with important differences: the committee stage is taken in committee of the whole house or in a grand committee, in which any peer may participate. There are no time limits, and no selection of amendments can be made at third reading.

A bill may start in either house, and has to pass through both houses to become law. Both houses have to agree the final text of a bill, so that amendments made by the second house are then considered in the originating house, and if not agreed, sent back or themselves amended, until agreement is reached.

CHILTERN HUNDREDS – A nominal office of profit under the crown, the acceptance of which requires an MP to vacate his/her seat. The Manor of Northstead is similar. These are the only means by which an MP may resign.

CONSOLIDATED FUND BILL – A bill to authorise issue of money to maintain government services. The bill is dealt with without debate.

EARLY DAY MOTION – A motion put on the notice paper by an MP without, in general, the real prospect of its being debated. Such motions are expressions of back-bench opinion.

FATHER OF THE HOUSE – The MP whose continuous service in the House of Commons is the longest. The present Father of the House is the Rt. Hon. Alan Williams, MP.

GRAND COMMITTEES – There are three grand committees in the House of Commons, one each for Northern Ireland, Scotland and Wales; they consider matters relating specifically to that country. In the House of Lords, bills may be sent to a grand committee instead of a committee of the whole house (*see also* Bill).

HOURS OF MEETING – The House of Commons normally meets on Mondays and Tuesdays at 2.30pm, Wednesdays at 11.30am, Thursdays at 10.30am and some Fridays at 9.30am. (*See also* Westminster Hall Sittings, below.) The House of Lords normally meets at 2.30pm Mondays and Tuesdays, 3pm on Wednesdays and at 11am on Thursdays. The House of Lords often sits on Fridays at 11am.

LEADER OF THE OPPOSITION – In 1937 the office of leader of the opposition was recognised and a salary was assigned to the post. Since November 2007 this has been £132,317 (including a parliamentary salary of £61,820). The present leader of the opposition is the Rt. Hon. David Cameron, MP.

THE LORD CHANCELLOR – The office of Lord High Chancellor of Great Britain was significantly altered by the Constitutional Reform Act 2005. Previously, the Lord Chancellor was *(ex officio)* the Speaker of the House of Lords, and took part in debates and voted in divisions in the House of Lords. The Department for Constitutional Affairs was created in 2003, which became the Ministry of Justice in 2007, incorporating most of the responsibilities of the Lord Chancellor's department. The role of Speaker has been transferred to the newly created post of Lord Speaker. The Constitutional Reform Act 2005 also brought to an end the Lord Chancellor's role as head of the judiciary. A new Judicial Appointments Commission was created in April 2006, and a new supreme court (separate from the House of Lords) is being established (scheduled to open in 2009).

THE LORD SPEAKER – The first Lord Speaker of the House of Lords, the Rt. Hon. Baroness Hayman, took up office on 4 July 2006. Unlike in the case of the Lord Chancellor, the Lord Speaker is independent of the government and elected by members of the House of Lords rather than appointed by the prime minister. Although the Lord Speaker's primary role is to preside over proceedings in the House of Lords, she does not have the same powers as the speaker of the House of Commons. For example, the Lord Speaker is not responsible for maintaining order during debates, as this is the responsibility of the house as a whole. The Lord Speaker sits in the Lords on one of the woolsacks, which are couches covered in red cloth and stuffed with wool.

THE LORD GREAT CHAMBERLAIN – The Lord Great Chamberlain is a Great Officer of State, the office being hereditary since the grant of Henry I to the family of De Vere, Earls of Oxford. It is now a joint hereditary office rotating on the death of the sovereign between the Cholmondeley, Carington and Ancaster families.

The Lord Great Chamberlain, currently the Marquess of Cholmondeley, is responsible for the royal apartments in the Palace of Westminster, the Royal Gallery, the administration of the Chapel of St Mary Undercroft and, in conjunction with the Lord Speaker and the Speaker of the House of Commons, Westminster Hall. The Lord Great Chamberlain has the right to perform specific services at a coronation, he carries out ceremonial duties in the Palace of Westminster when the sovereign visits the palace and has particular responsibility for the internal administrative arrangements within the House of Lords for state openings of parliament.

OPPOSITION DAY – A day on which the topic for debate is chosen by the opposition. There are 20 such days in a normal session. On 17 days, subjects are chosen by the leader of the opposition; on the remaining three days by the leader of the next largest opposition party.

PARLIAMENT ACTS 1911 AND 1949 – Under these acts, bills may become law without the consent of the Lords, though the House of Lords has the power to delay a public bill for a parliamentary session.

PRIME MINISTER'S QUESTIONS – The prime minister answers questions from 12.00 to 12.30pm on Wednesdays.

PRIVATE BILL – A bill promoted by a body or an individual to give powers additional to, or in conflict with, the general law, and to which a special procedure applies to enable people affected to object.

PRIVATE MEMBER'S BILL – A public bill promoted by an MP or peer who is not a member of the government.

PRIVATE NOTICE QUESTION – A question adjudged of urgent importance on submission to the Speaker (in the Lords, the Lord Speaker), answered at the end of oral questions.

PRIVILEGE – The House of Commons has rights and immunities to protect it from obstruction in carrying out its duties. These are known as parliamentary privilege and enable Members of Parliament to debate freely. The most important privilege is that of freedom of speech. MPs cannot be prosecuted for sedition or sued for libel or slander over anything said during proceedings in the house. This enables them to raise in the house questions affecting the public good which might be difficult to raise outside owing to the possibility of being sued. The House of Lords has similar privileges.

QUESTION TIME – Oral questions are answered by ministers in the Commons from 2.30 to 3.30pm on Mondays and Tuesdays, 11.30am to 12.30pm on Wednesdays, and 10.30 to 11.30am on Thursdays. Questions are also taken at the start of the Lords sittings, with a daily limit of four oral questions.

ROYAL ASSENT – The royal assent is signified by letters patent to such bills and measures as have passed both Houses of Parliament (or bills which have been passed under the Parliament Acts 1911 and 1949). The sovereign has not given royal assent in person since 1854. On occasion, for instance in the prorogation of parliament, royal assent may be pronounced to the two houses by Lords Commissioners. More usually royal assent is notified to each house sitting separately in accordance with the Royal Assent Act 1967. The old French formulae for royal assent are then endorsed on the acts by the Clerk of the Parliaments.

The power to withhold assent resides with the sovereign but has not been exercised in the UK since 1707.

SELECT COMMITTEES – Consisting usually of 10 to 15 members of all parties, select committees are a means used by both houses in order to investigate certain matters.

Most select committees in the House of Commons are tied to departments: each committee investigates subjects within a government department's remit. There are other select committees dealing with matters such as public accounts (ie the spending by the government of money voted by parliament) and European legislation, and also committees advising on procedures and domestic administration of the house. Major select committees usually take evidence in public; their evidence and reports are published on the parliament website and in hard copy by TSO (The Stationery Office). House of Commons select committees are reconstituted after a general election.

In the House of Lords, select committees do not mirror government departments but cover broader issues. There is a select committee on the European Union (EU), which has seven sub-committees dealing with specific areas of EU policy, a select committee on science and technology, which appoints sub-committees to deal with specific subjects, a select committee on economic affairs and also one on the constitution. There is also a select committee on delegated powers and regulatory reform and one on the merits of statutory instruments. In addition, *ad hoc* select committees have been set up from time to time to investigate specific subjects. There are also joint committees of the two houses, eg the committees on statutory instruments and on human rights.

THE SPEAKER – The Speaker of the House of Commons is the spokesperson and chair of the Chamber. He or she is elected by the house at the beginning of each parliament or when the previous Speaker retires or dies. The Speaker neither speaks in debates nor votes in divisions except when the voting is equal.

VACANT SEATS – When a vacancy occurs in the House of Commons during a session of parliament, the writ for the by-election is moved by a whip of the party to which the member whose seat has been vacated belonged. If the house is in recess, the Speaker can issue a warrant for a writ, should two members certify to him that a seat is vacant.

WESTMINSTER HALL SITTINGS – Following a report by the Modernisation of the House of Commons Select Committee, the Commons decided in May 1999 to set up a second debating forum. It is known as 'Westminster Hall' and sittings are in the Grand Committee Room on Tuesdays from 9.30am to 2pm, Wednesdays from 9.30 to 11.30am and from 2.30 to 5pm, and Thursdays from 2.30 to 5.30pm. Sittings will be open to the public at the times indicated.

WHIPS – In order to secure the attendance of members of a particular party in parliament, particularly on the occasion of an important vote, whips (originally known as 'whippers-in') are appointed. The written appeal or circular letter issued by them is also known as a 'whip', its urgency being denoted by the number of times it is underlined. Failure to respond to a three-line whip is tantamount in the Commons to secession (at any rate temporarily) from the party. Whips are provided with office accommodation in both houses, and government and some opposition whips receive salaries from public funds.

HOUSE OF COMMONS INFORMATION OFFICE
Norman Shaw Building (North), London SW1A 2TT
T 020-7219 4272 F 020-7219 5839
E hcinfo@parliament.uk W www.parliament.uk

PARLIAMENTARY ARCHIVES
Houses of Parliament, London SW1A 0PW
T 020-7219 3074 F 020-7219 2570
E archives@parliament.uk W www.parliament.uk/archives

Since 1497, the records of parliament have been kept within the Palace of Westminster. They are in the custody of the Clerk of the Parliaments. In 1946 the House of Lords Record Office, which became the Parliamentary Archives in 2006, was established to supervise their preservation and their availability to the public. Some three million documents are preserved, including acts of parliament from 1497, journals of the House of Lords from 1510, minutes and committee proceedings from 1610, and papers laid before parliament from 1531. Amongst the records are the Petition of Right, the death warrant of Charles I, the Declaration of Breda, and the Bill of Rights. Records are available through a public search room.
Clerk of the Parliamentary Archives, S. K. Ellison

GOVERNMENT OFFICE

The government is the body of ministers responsible for the administration of national affairs, determining policy and introducing into parliament any legislation necessary to give effect to government policy. The majority of ministers are members of the House of Commons but members of the House of Lords, or of neither house, may also hold ministerial responsibility. The Lord Chancellor is always a member of the House of Lords. The prime minister is, by current convention, always a member of the House of Commons.

THE PRIME MINISTER

The office of prime minister, which had been in existence for nearly 200 years, was officially recognised in 1905 and its holder was granted a place in the table of precedence. The prime minister, by tradition also First Lord of the Treasury and Minister for the Civil Service, is appointed by the sovereign and is usually the leader of the party which enjoys, or can secure, a majority in the House of Commons. Other ministers are appointed by the sovereign on the recommendation of the prime minister, who also allocates functions amongst ministers and has the power to obtain their resignation or dismissal individually.

The prime minister informs the sovereign of state on political matters, advises on the dissolution of parliament, and makes recommendations for important crown appointments, ie the award of honours, etc.

As the chair of cabinet meetings and leader of a political party, the prime minister is responsible for translating party policy into government activity. As leader of the government, the prime minister is responsible to parliament and to the electorate for the policies and their implementation.

The prime minister also represents the nation in international affairs, eg summit conferences.

THE CABINET

The cabinet developed during the 18th century as an inner committee of the Privy Council, which was the chief source of executive power until that time. The cabinet is composed of about 20 ministers chosen by the prime minister, usually the heads of government departments (generally known as secretaries of state unless they have a special title, eg Chancellor of the Exchequer), the leaders of the two houses of parliament, and the holders of various traditional offices.

The cabinet's functions are the final determination of policy, control of government and coordination of government departments. The exercise of its functions is dependent upon enjoying majority support in the House of Commons. Cabinet meetings are held in private, taking place once or twice a week during parliamentary sittings and less often during a recess. Proceedings are confidential, the members being bound by their oath as privy counsellors not to disclose information about the proceedings.

The convention of collective responsibility means that the cabinet acts unanimously even when cabinet ministers do not all agree on a subject. The policies of departmental ministers must be consistent with the policies of the government as a whole, and once the government's policy has been decided, each minister is expected to support it or resign.

The convention of ministerial responsibility holds a minister, as the political head of his or her department, accountable to parliament for the department's work. Departmental ministers usually decide all matters within their responsibility, although on matters of political importance they normally consult their colleagues collectively. A decision by a departmental minister is binding on the government as a whole.

POLITICAL PARTIES

Before the reign of William and Mary the principal officers of state were chosen by and were responsible to the sovereign alone, and not to parliament or the nation at large. Such officers acted sometimes in concert with one another but more often independently, and the fall of one did not, of necessity, involve that of others, although all were liable to be dismissed at any moment.

In 1693 the Earl of Sunderland recommended to William III the advisability of selecting a ministry from the political party which enjoyed a majority in the House of Commons, and the first united ministry was drawn in 1696 from the Whigs, to which party the king owed his throne. This group became known as the 'Junto' and was regarded with suspicion as a novelty in the political life of the nation, being a small section meeting in secret apart from the main body of ministers. It may be regarded as the forerunner of the cabinet and in the course of time it led to the establishment of the principle of joint responsibility of ministers, so that internal disagreement caused a change of personnel or resignation of the whole body of ministers.

The accession of George I, who was unfamiliar with the English language, led to a disinclination on the part of the sovereign to preside at meetings of his ministers and caused the emergence of a prime minister, a position first acquired by Robert Walpole in 1721 and retained by him without interruption for 20 years and 326 days.

DEVELOPMENT OF PARTIES

In 1828 the Whigs became known as Liberals, a name originally given by opponents to imply laxity of principles, but gradually accepted by the party to indicate its claim to be pioneers and champions of political reform and progressive legislation. In 1861 a Liberal Registration Association was founded and Liberal Associations became widespread. In 1877 a National Liberal Federation was formed, with its headquarters in London. The Liberal Party was in power for long periods during the second half of the 19th century and for several years during the first quarter of the 20th century, but after a split in the party in 1931, the numbers elected remained small. In 1988, a majority of the Liberals agreed on a merger with the Social Democratic Party under the title Social and Liberal Democrats; since 1989 they have been known as the Liberal Democrats. A minority continue separately as the Liberal Party.

Soon after the change from Whig to Liberal, the Tory Party became known as Conservative, a name believed to have been invented by John Wilson Croker in 1830 and to have been generally adopted around the time of the passing of the Reform Act of 1832 – to indicate that the preservation of national institutions was the leading principle of the party. After the Home Rule crisis of 1886 the dissentient Liberals entered into a compact with the Conservatives, under which the latter undertook not to contest their seats, but a separate Liberal Unionist organisation was maintained until 1912, when it was united with the Conservatives.

Labour candidates for parliament made their first appearance at the general election of 1892, when there were 27 standing as Labour or Liberal-Labour. In 1900 the Labour Representation Committee (LRC) was set up in order to establish a distinct Labour group in parliament, with its own whips, its own policy, and a readiness to cooperate with any party which might be engaged in promoting legislation in the direct interests of labour. In 1906 the LRC became known as the Labour Party.

The Council for Social Democracy was announced by four former Labour cabinet ministers in January 1981 and in March 1981 the Social Democratic Party (SDP) was launched. Later that year the SDP and the Liberal Party formed an electoral alliance. In 1988 a majority of the SDP agreed on a merger with the Liberal Party but a minority continued as a separate party under the SDP title. In 1990 it was decided to wind up the party organisation and its three sitting MPs were known as independent social democrats. None were returned at the 1992 general election.

Plaid Cymru was founded in 1926 to provide an independent political voice for Wales and to campaign for self-government in Wales.

The Scottish National Party was founded in 1934 to campaign for independence for Scotland.

The Social Democratic and Labour Party was founded in 1970, emerging from the civil rights movement of the 1960s, with the aim of promoting reform, reconciliation and partnership across the sectarian divide in Northern Ireland, and of opposing violence from any quarter.

The Democratic Unionist Party was founded in 1971 to resist moves by the Ulster Unionist Party which were considered a threat to the Union. Its aim is to maintain Northern Ireland as an integral part of the UK.

The Ulster Unionist Council first met formally in 1905. Its objectives are to maintain Northern Ireland as an integral part of the UK and to promote the aims of the Ulster Unionist Party.

Sinn Fein first emerged in the 1900s as a federation of nationalist clubs. It is a left-wing republican and labour party that seeks to end British governance in Ireland and achieve a 32-county republic.

GOVERNMENT AND OPPOSITION

The government of the day is formed by the party which wins the largest number of seats in the House of Commons at a general election, or which has the support of a majority of members in the House of Commons. By tradition, the leader of the majority party is asked by the sovereign to form a government, while the largest minority party becomes the official opposition with its own leader and a shadow cabinet. Leaders of the government and opposition sit on the front benches of the Commons with their supporters (the back-benchers) sitting behind them.

FINANCIAL SUPPORT

Financial support for opposition parties in the House of Commons was introduced in 1975 and is commonly known as Short Money, after Edward Short, the leader of the house at that time, who introduced the scheme. Short Money allocation for 2008–9 is:

Conservative	£4,068,341
Liberal Democrats	£1,733,771
Plaid Cymru	£67,568
SNP	£144,035
SDLP	£60,572
Democratic Unionists	£162,524

A specific allocation for the leader of the opposition's office was introduced in April 1999 and has been set at £647,112 for the years 2008–9.

Financial support for opposition parties in the House of Lords was introduced in 1996 and is commonly known as Cranborne Money.

The parties included here are those with MPs sitting in the House of Commons in the present parliament.

CONSERVATIVE PARTY

Conservative Campaign Headquarters, 30 Millbank, London SW1P 4DP
T 020-7222 9000 F 020-7222 1135
E ccoffice@conservatives.com
W www.conservatives.com

SHADOW CABINET *as at June 2008*

Leader of the Opposition, Rt. Hon. David Cameron, MP
Senior Member and Secretary of State for Foreign Affairs, Rt. Hon. William Hague, MP
Chancellor of the Exchequer and General Election Campaign Coordinator, George Osborne, MP
Secretary of State for Home Affairs, Dominic Grieve
Party Chair, Caroline Spelman, MP
Chair of Policy Review and of Conservative Research Department, Rt. Hon. Oliver Letwin, MP
Minister for the Cabinet Office and Chancellor of the Duchy of Lancaster, Rt. Hon. Francis Maude, MP

Chair of Conservative International Office and Foreign Office Minister, David Lidington, MP
Secretary of State for Business, Enterprise and Regulatory Reform, Alan Duncan, MP
Secretary of State for Children, School and Families, Michael Gove, MP
Secretary of State for Communities and Local Government, Eric Pickles, MP
Minister for Community Cohesion and Social Action, Baroness Warsi, MP
Secretary of State for Culture, Media and Sport, Jeremy Hunt, MP
Secretary of State for Defence, Dr Liam Fox, MP
Secretary of State for Environment, Food and Rural Affairs, Peter Ainsworth, MP
Secretary of State for Health, Andrew Lansley, CBE, MP
Minister for Housing, Grant Shapps, MP
Secretary of State for Innovation, Universities and Skills, David Willetts, MP
Secretary of State for International Development, Andrew Mitchell, MP
Secretary of State for Justice, Nick Herbert, MP
Leader in the House of Commons and Minister for Women, Rt. Hon. Theresa May, MP
Leader in the House of Lords, Rt. Hon. Lord Strathclyde
Secretary of State for Northern Ireland, Owen Paterson, MP
Secretary of State for Scotland, David Mundell, MP
Minister for Security and National Security Adviser to the Leader of the Opposition, Baroness Neville-Jones, DCMG
Secretary of State for Transport, Theresa Villiers, MP
Chief Secretary to the Treasury, Philip Hammond, MP
Secretary of State for Wales, Cheryl Gillan, MP
Secretary of State for Work and Pensions, Chris Grayling, MP

CONSERVATIVE WHIPS
House of Lords, Baroness Anelay of St Johns, DBE
House of Commons, Rt. Hon. Patrick McLoughlin, MP

LABOUR PARTY

Eldon House, Regent Centre, Newcastle upon Tyne NE3 3PW
T 0870-590 0200 W www.labour.org.uk
Parliamentary Party Leader, Rt. Hon. Gordon Brown, MP
Deputy Party Leader, Leader in the Commons and Party Chair, Rt. Hon. Harriet Harman, QC, MP
Leader in the Lords, Rt. Hon. Baroness Ashton of Upholland
General Secretary, David Pitt-Watson
General Secretary, Scottish Labour Party, Colin Smyth

LIBERAL DEMOCRATS

4 Cowley Street, London SW1P 3NB
T 020-7222 7999 F 020-7799 2170
E info@libdems.org.uk W www.libdems.org.uk
President and Leader in the Commons, Simon Hughes, MP
Hon. Treasurer, Lord Razzall
Chief Executive, Lord Rennard
Parliamentary Party Leader, Rt. Hon. Nick Clegg, MP
Leader in the Lords, Rt. Hon. Lord McNally

LIBERAL DEMOCRAT SPOKESMEN *as at May 2008*
Deputy Leader and Shadow Chancellor of the Exchequer, Dr Vincent Cable, MP
Attorney-General, Lord Thomas of Gresford
Business, Enterprise and Regulatory Reform, Sarah Teather, MP
Cabinet Office, Susan Kramer, MP
Children, Schools and Families, David Laws, MP
Communities and Local Government, Julia Goldsworthy, MP
Culture, Media and Sport, Don Foster, MP
Defence, Nick Harvey, MP
Environment, Food and Rural Affairs, Prof. Steve Webb, MP
Foreign and Commonwealth Affairs, Ed Davey, MP
Health, Norman Lamb, MP
Home Affairs, Tom Brake, MP
Housing, Lembit Opik, MP
Innovation, Universities and Skills, Stephen Williams, MP
International Development, Mike Moore, MP
Justice, Jenny Willott, MP
Scotland and Northern Ireland, Mike Moore, MP
Solicitor-General, David Howarth, MP
Transport, Norman Baker, MP
Treasury, Dr Vincent Cable, MP
Wales, Roger Williams, MP
Work and Pensions, Chair of the Manifesto Group and Chief of Staff, Danny Alexander, MP
Chair of the Parliamentary Party, Lorely Burt, MP
Chair of Campaigns and Communications, Ed Davey, MP
Parliamentary Private Secretary to the Leader, Mark Hunter, MP

LIBERAL DEMOCRAT WHIPS
House of Lords, Lord Shutt of Greetland
House of Commons, Paul Burstow, MP

NORTHERN IRELAND DEMOCRATIC UNIONIST PARTY

91 Dundela Avenue, Belfast BT4 3BU
T 028-9052 1323 F 028-9052 1289
E info@dup.org.uk W www.dup.org.uk
Parliamentary Party Leader, Peter Robinson, MP, MLA
Deputy Leader, Nigel Dodds, MP, MLA
Chair, Lord Morrow, MLA
Hon. Treasurer, Gregory Campbell, MP, MLA
Party Secretary, Nigel Dodds, MP, MLA

PLAID CYMRU – THE PARTY OF WALES

Ty Gwynfor, 18 Park Grove, Cardiff CF10 3BN
T 029-2064 6000
E post@plaidcymru.org W www.plaidcymru.org
Party Leader, Ieuan Wyn Jones, AM
Party President, Dafydd Iwan
Party Vice-President, Jill Evans, MEP
Parliamentary Group Leader, Elfyn Llwyd
Chief Executive, Dr Gwenllian Lansdown

RESPECT – THE UNITY COALITION

PO Box 1109, London N4 2UU
T 0871-234 1696
E office@respectrenewal.org W www.respectrenewal.org
Chair, Linda Smith
Vice-Chair, Salma Yaqoob
National Secretary, Nick Wrack
Treasurer, Will McMahon

SCOTTISH NATIONAL PARTY

107 McDonald Road, Edinburgh EH7 4NW
T 0131-525 8900 F 0131-525 8901
E snp.hq@snp.org W www.snp.org
Westminster Parliamentary Party Leader, Alex Salmond, MP
Westminster Parliamentary Party Chief Whip, Stewart Hosie, MP
Scottish Parliamentary Party Leader, Alex Salmond, MSP

Scottish Parliamentary Party Chief Whip, Bruce Crawford, MSP
National Treasurer, Colin Beattie
National Secretary, Dr Duncan Ross
Chief Executive, Peter Murrell

SINN FEIN

53 Falls Road, Belfast BT12 4PD
T 028-9022 3000 F 028-9022 3001
E sfadmin@eircom.net W www.sinnfein.ie
Party President, Gerry Adams, MP, MLA
Vice-President, Pat Doherty, MP, MLA
Chair, Mary Lou McDonald, MEP
General Secretary, Rita O'Hare

SOCIAL DEMOCRATIC AND LABOUR PARTY

121 Ormeau Road, Belfast BT7 1SH
T 028-9024 7700 F 028-9023 6699
E info@sdlp.ie W www.sdlp.ie
Parliamentary Party Leader, Mark Durkan, MP, MLA
Deputy Leader, Dr Alasdair McDonnell, MP, MLA
Chief Whip, Patsy McGlone, MLA
Chair, Eddie McGrady, MP
Treasurer, Peter McEvoy
General Secretary, Gerry Cosgrove

ULSTER UNIONIST PARTY

Cunningham House, 429 Holywood Road, Belfast BT4 2LN
T 028-9076 5500 F 028-9076 9419
E uup@uup.org W www.uup.org
Party Leader, Sir Reg Empey, OBE, MLA
Chief Whip, David McNarry, MLA

ULSTER UNIONIST COUNCIL
Leader, Sir Reg Empey, OBE, MLA
Deputy Leader, Cllr Danny Kennedy, MLA
Party Chairman, David Campbell, CBE
Hon. Treasurer, Cllr Mark Cosgrove
Vice-Chair, Terry Wright
Party Officers, Paula Bradshaw; Kenny Donaldson; Richard Holmes; Cllr Danny Kinahan; Sandra Overend; Cllr Dr Eddie Rea; Philip Smith
Officers from Elected Representatives, David McNarry, MLA; Jim Nicholson, MEP; Cllr Trevor Wilson

The following parties have sitting MEPs, *see* European Parliament section, but no MPs.

GREEN PARTY

1A Waterlow Road, London N19 5NJ
T 020-7272 4474 F 020-7272 6653
E office@greenparty.org.uk W www.greenparty.org.uk
Party Leader, Dr Caroline Lucas, MEP
Deputy Leader, Adrian Ramsay
Chair, Richard Mallender
Finance Coordinator, Khalid Hussenbux

UK INDEPENDENCE PARTY

PO Box 408, Newton Abbot, Devon TQ12 9BG
T 01626-831290 F 01626-831348
E mail@ukip.org W www.ukip.org
Party Leader, Nigel Farage, MEP
Chair, Dr John Whittaker, MEP
Party Secretary, Michael Zuckerman
Treasurer, Marta Andreasen

MEMBERS OF PARLIAMENT as at 1 September 2008

* New MP
† Previously MP in another seat
‡ Previously MP for another party

Abbott, Diane (*b.* 1953) *Lab., Hackney North & Stoke Newington,* Maj. 7,427
Adams, Gerry (*b.* 1948) *SF, Belfast West,* Maj. 19,315
***Afriyie**, Adam (*b.* 1965) *C., Windsor,* Maj. 10,292
Ainger, Nick (*b.* 1949) *Lab., Carmarthen West & Pembrokeshire South,* Maj. 1,910
Ainsworth, Peter (*b.* 1956) *C., Surrey East,* Maj. 15,921
Ainsworth, Rt. Hon. Robert (*b.* 1952) *Lab., Coventry North East,* Maj. 14,222
***Alexander**, Danny (*b.* 1972) *LD, Inverness, Nairn, Badenoch & Strathspey,* Maj. 4,148
Alexander, Rt. Hon. Douglas (*b.* 1967) *Lab., Paisley & Renfrewshire South,* Maj. 13,232
Allen, Graham (*b.* 1953) *Lab., Nottingham North,* Maj. 12,171
Amess, David (*b.* 1952) *C., Southend West,* Maj. 8,959
Ancram, Rt. Hon. Michael (*b.* 1945) *C., Devizes,* Maj. 13,194
***Anderson**, David (*b.* 1953) *Lab., Blaydon,* Maj. 5,335
Anderson, Janet (*b.* 1949) *Lab., Rossendale & Darwen,* Maj. 3,676
Arbuthnot, Rt. Hon. James (*b.* 1952) *C., Hampshire North East,* Maj. 12,549
Armstrong, Rt. Hon. Hilary (*b.* 1945) *Lab., Durham North West,* Maj. 13,443
Atkins, Charlotte (*b.* 1950) *Lab., Staffordshire Moorlands,* Maj. 2,438
Atkinson, Peter (*b.* 1943) *C., Hexham,* Maj. 5,020
***Austin**, Ian (*b.* 1965) *Lab., Dudley North,* Maj. 5,432
Austin, John (*b.* 1944) *Lab., Erith & Thamesmead,* Maj. 11,500
Bacon, Richard (*b.* 1962) *C., Norfolk South,* Maj. 8,782
Bailey, Adrian (*b.* 1945) *Lab. (Co-op), West Bromwich West,* Maj. 10,894
Baird, Vera (*b.* 1950) *Lab., Redcar,* Maj. 12,116
Baker, Norman (*b.* 1957) *LD, Lewes,* Maj. 8,474
Baldry, Tony (*b.* 1950) *C., Banbury,* Maj. 10,797
***Balls**, Rt. Hon. Ed (*b.* 1967) *Lab. (Co-op), Normanton,* Maj. 10,002
***Banks**, Gordon (*b.* 1955) *Lab., Ochil & Perthshire South,* Maj. 688
Barker, Gregory (*b.* 1966) *C., Bexhill & Battle,* Maj. 13,449
***Barlow**, Celia (*b.* 1955) *Lab., Hove,* Maj. 420
Baron, John (*b.* 1959) *C., Billericay,* Maj. 11,206
Barrett, John (*b.* 1954) *LD, Edinburgh West,* Maj. 13,600
Barron, Rt. Hon. Kevin (*b.* 1946) *Lab., Rother Valley,* Maj. 14,224
Battle, Rt. Hon. John (*b.* 1951) *Lab., Leeds West,* Maj. 12,810
Bayley, Hugh (*b.* 1952) *Lab., York, City of,* Maj. 10,472
Beckett, Rt. Hon. Margaret (*b.* 1943) *Lab., Derby South,* Maj. 5,657
Begg, Anne (*b.* 1955) *Lab., Aberdeen South,* Maj. 1,348
Beith, Rt. Hon. Alan (*b.* 1943) *LD, Berwick-upon-Tweed,* Maj. 8,632
Bell, Sir Stuart (*b.* 1938) *Lab., Middlesbrough,* Maj. 12,567
Bellingham, Henry (*b.* 1955) *C., Norfolk North West,* Maj. 9,180
Benn, Rt. Hon. Hilary (*b.* 1953) *Lab., Leeds Central,* Maj. 11,866
Benton, Joe (*b.* 1933) *Lab., Bootle,* Maj. 16,357
***Benyon**, Richard (*b.* 1960) *C., Newbury,* Maj. 3,460
Bercow, John (*b.* 1963) *C., Buckingham,* Maj. 18,129
Beresford, Sir Paul (*b.* 1946) *C., Mole Valley,* Maj. 11,997
Berry, Dr Roger (*b.* 1948) *Lab., Kingswood,* Maj. 7,873
Betts, Clive (*b.* 1950) *Lab., Sheffield Attercliffe,* Maj. 15,967
***Binley**, Brian (*b.* 1942) *C., Northampton South,* Maj. 4,419
Blackman, Liz (*b.* 1949) *Lab., Erewash,* Maj. 7,084
***Blackman-Woods**, Dr Roberta (*b.* 1957) *Lab., Durham, City of,* Maj. 3,274
Blears, Rt. Hon. Hazel (*b.* 1956) *Lab., Salford,* Maj. 7,945
Blizzard, Bob (*b.* 1950) *Lab., Waveney,* Maj. 5,915
Blunkett, Rt. Hon. David (*b.* 1947) *Lab., Sheffield Brightside,* Maj. 13,644
Blunt, Crispin (*b.* 1960) *C., Reigate,* Maj. 10,988
***Bone**, Peter (*b.* 1952) *C., Wellingborough,* Maj. 687
Borrow, David (*b.* 1952) *Lab., Ribble South,* Maj. 2,184
Boswell, Tim (*b.* 1942) *C., Daventry,* Maj. 14,686
Bottomley, Peter (*b.* 1944) *C., Worthing West,* Maj. 9,379
Bradshaw, Ben (*b.* 1960) *Lab., Exeter,* Maj. 7,665
Brady, Graham (*b.* 1967) *C., Altrincham & Sale West,* Maj. 7,159
Brake, Tom (*b.* 1962) *LD, Carshalton & Wallington,* Maj. 1,068
Brazier, Julian (*b.* 1953) *C., Canterbury,* Maj. 7,471
Breed, Colin (*b.* 1947) *LD, Cornwall South East,* Maj. 6,507
Brennan, Kevin (*b.* 1959) *Lab., Cardiff West,* Maj. 8,167
***Brokenshire**, James (*b.* 1968) *C., Hornchurch,* Maj. 480
Brooke, Annette (*b.* 1947) *LD, Dorset Mid & Poole North,* Maj. 5,482
Brown, Rt. Hon. Gordon (*b.* 1951) *Lab., Kirkcaldy & Cowdenbeath,* Maj. 18,216
***Brown**, Lyn (*b.* 1960) *Lab., West Ham,* Maj. 9,801
Brown, Rt. Hon. Nick (*b.* 1950) *Lab., Newcastle upon Tyne East & Wallsend,* Maj. 7,565
Brown, Russell (*b.* 1951) *Lab., Dumfries & Galloway,* Maj. 2,922
Browne, Rt. Hon. Desmond (*b.* 1952) *Lab., Kilmarnock & Loudoun,* Maj. 8,703
***Browne**, Jeremy (*b.* 1970) *LD, Taunton,* Maj. 573
Browning, Angela (*b.* 1946) *C., Tiverton & Honiton,* Maj. 11,051
Bruce, Malcolm (*b.* 1944) *LD, Gordon,* Maj. 11,026
Bryant, Chris (*b.* 1962) *Lab., Rhondda,* Maj. 16,242
Buck, Karen (*b.* 1958) *Lab., Regent's Park & Kensington North,* Maj. 6,131
Burden, Richard (*b.* 1954) *Lab., Birmingham Northfield,* Maj. 6,454
Burgon, Colin (*b.* 1948) *Lab., Elmet,* Maj. 4,528
Burnham, Andy (*b.* 1970) *Lab., Leigh,* Maj. 17,272
Burns, Simon (*b.* 1952) *C., Chelmsford West,* Maj. 9,620
***Burrowes**, David (*b.* 1969) *C., Enfield Southgate,* Maj. 1,747
Burstow, Paul (*b.* 1962) *LD, Sutton & Cheam,* Maj. 2,846
Burt, Alistair (*b.* 1955) *C., Bedfordshire North East,* Maj. 12,251
***Burt**, Lorely (*b.* 1957) *LD, Solihull,* Maj. 279
***Butler**, Dawn (*b.* 1969) *Lab., Brent South,* Maj. 11,326
Butterfill, Sir John (*b.* 1941) *C., Bournemouth West,* Maj. 4,031

Byers, Rt. Hon. Stephen (*b.* 1953) *Lab., Tyneside North,* Maj. 15,037
Byrne, Liam (*b.* 1970) *Lab., Birmingham Hodge Hill,* Maj. 5,449
Cable, Dr Vincent (*b.* 1943) *LD, Twickenham,* Maj. 9,965
Caborn, Rt. Hon. Richard (*b.* 1943) *Lab., Sheffield Central,* Maj. 7,055
Cairns, David (*b.* 1966) *Lab., Inverclyde,* Maj. 11,259
Cameron, Rt. Hon. David (*b.* 1966) *C., Witney,* Maj. 14,156
Campbell, Alan (*b.* 1957) *Lab., Tynemouth,* Maj. 4,143
Campbell, Gregory (*b.* 1953) *DUP, Londonderry East,* Maj. 7,727
Campbell, Rt. Hon. Sir Menzies (*b.* 1941) *LD, Fife North East,* Maj. 12,571
Campbell, Ronnie (*b.* 1943) *Lab., Blyth Valley,* Maj. 8,527
Carmichael, Alistair (*b.* 1965) *LD, Orkney & Shetland,* Maj. 6,627
***Carswell**, Douglas (*b.* 1971) *C., Harwich,* Maj. 920
Cash, Bill (*b.* 1940) *C., Stone,* Maj. 9,089
Caton, Martin (*b.* 1951) *Lab., Gower,* Maj. 6,703
Cawsey, Ian (*b.* 1960) *Lab., Brigg & Goole,* Maj. 2,894
Challen, Colin (*b.* 1953) *Lab., Morley & Rothwell,* Maj. 12,343
Chapman, Ben (*b.* 1940) *Lab., Wirral South,* Maj. 3,724
Chaytor, David (*b.* 1949) *Lab., Bury North,* Maj. 2,926
Chope, Christopher (*b.* 1947) *C., Christchurch,* Maj. 15,559
Clapham, Michael (*b.* 1943) *Lab., Barnsley West & Penistone,* Maj. 11,314
Clappison, James (*b.* 1956) *C., Hertsmere,* Maj. 11,093
***Clark**, Greg (*b.* 1967) *C., Tunbridge Wells,* Maj. 9,988
***Clark**, Katy (*b.* 1967) *Lab., Ayrshire North & Arran,* Maj. 11,296
Clark, Paul (*b.* 1957) *Lab., Gillingham,* Maj. 254
Clarke, Rt. Hon. Charles (*b.* 1950) *Lab., Norwich South,* Maj. 3,653
Clarke, Rt. Hon. Kenneth (*b.* 1940) *C., Rushcliffe,* Maj. 12,974
Clarke, Rt. Hon. Thomas (*b.* 1941) *Lab., Coatbridge, Chryston & Bellshill,* Maj. 19,519
***Clegg**, Nick (*b.* 1967) *LD, Sheffield Hallam,* Maj. 8,682
Clelland, David (*b.* 1943) *Lab., Tyne Bridge,* Maj. 10,400
Clifton-Brown, Geoffrey (*b.* 1953) *C., Cotswold,* Maj. 9,688
Clwyd, Rt. Hon. Ann (*b.* 1937) *Lab., Cynon Valley,* Maj. 13,259
Coaker, Vernon (*b.* 1953) *Lab., Gedling,* Maj. 3,811
Coffey, Ann (*b.* 1946) *Lab., Stockport,* Maj. 9,163
Cohen, Harry (*b.* 1949) *Lab., Leyton & Wanstead,* Maj. 6,857
Connarty, Michael (*b.* 1947) *Lab., Linlithgow & Falkirk East,* Maj. 11,202
Conway, Derek (*b.* 1953) *C., Old Bexley & Sidcup,* Maj. 9,920
Cook, Frank (*b.* 1935) *Lab., Stockton North,* Maj. 12,437
***Cooper**, Rosie (*b.* 1950) *Lab., Lancashire West,* Maj. 6,084
Cooper, Yvette (*b.* 1969) *Lab., Pontefract & Castleford,* Maj. 15,246
Corbyn, Jeremy (*b.* 1949) *Lab., Islington North,* Maj. 6,716
Cormack, Sir Patrick (*b.* 1939) *C., Staffordshire South,* Maj. 8,847
Cousins, Jim (*b.* 1944) *Lab., Newcastle upon Tyne Central,* Maj. 3,982
***Cox**, Geoffrey (*b.* 1960) *C., Devon West & Torridge,* Maj. 3,236
***Crabb**, Stephen (*b.* 1973) *C., Preseli Pembrokeshire,* Maj. 607
Crausby, David (*b.* 1946) *Lab., Bolton North East,* Maj. 4,103
***Creagh**, Mary (*b.* 1967) *Lab., Wakefield,* Maj. 5,154
Cruddas, Jonathan (*b.* 1965) *Lab., Dagenham,* Maj. 7,605
Cryer, Ann (*b.* 1939) *Lab., Keighley,* Maj. 4,852
Cummings, John (*b.* 1943) *Lab., Easington,* Maj. 18,636
Cunningham, Jim (*b.* 1941) *Lab., Coventry South,* Maj. 6,255
Cunningham, Tony (*b.* 1952) *Lab., Workington,* Maj. 6,895
Curry, Rt. Hon. David (*b.* 1944) *C., Skipton & Ripon,* Maj. 11,620
Curtis-Thomas, Claire (*b.* 1958) *Lab., Crosby,* Maj. 5,840
Darling, Rt. Hon. Alistair (*b.* 1953) *Lab., Edinburgh South West,* Maj. 7,242
Davey, Edward (*b.* 1965) *LD, Kingston & Surbiton,* Maj. 8,966
David, Wayne (*b.* 1957) *Lab., Caerphilly,* Maj. 15,359
Davidson, Ian (*b.* 1950) *Lab. (Co-op), Glasgow South West,* Maj. 13,896
***Davies**, Dai (*b.* 1959) *Ind., Blaenau Gwent,* Maj. 2,484
***Davies**, David (*b.* 1970) *C., Monmouth,* Maj. 4,527
***Davies**, Philip (*b.* 1972) *C., Shipley,* Maj. 422
‡**Davies**, Quentin (*b.* 1944) *Lab., Grantham & Stamford,* Maj. 7,445
Davis, Rt. Hon. David (*b.* 1948) *C., Haltemprice & Howden,* Maj. 15,355
Dean, Janet (*b.* 1949) *Lab., Burton,* Maj. 1,421
Denham, Rt. Hon. John (*b.* 1953) *Lab., Southampton Itchen,* Maj. 9,302
***Devine**, Jim (*b.* 1953) *Lab., Livingston,* Maj. 2,680
Dhanda, Parmjit (*b.* 1971) *Lab., Gloucester,* Maj. 4,271
Dismore, Andrew (*b.* 1954) *Lab., Hendon,* Maj. 2,699
Djanogly, Jonathan (*b.* 1965) *C., Huntingdon,* Maj. 12,847
Dobbin, Jim (*b.* 1941) *Lab. (Co-op), Heywood & Middleton,* Maj. 11,083
Dobson, Rt. Hon. Frank (*b.* 1940) *Lab., Holborn & St Pancras,* Maj. 4,787
Dodds, Nigel (*b.* 1958) *DUP, Belfast North,* Maj. 5,188
Doherty, Pat (*b.* 1945) *SF, Tyrone West,* Maj. 5,005
‡**Donaldson**, Jeffrey (*b.* 1962) *DUP, Lagan Valley,* Maj. 14,117
Donohoe, Brian (*b.* 1948) *Lab., Ayrshire Central,* Maj. 10,423
Doran, Frank (*b.* 1949) *Lab., Aberdeen North,* Maj. 6,795
Dorrell, Rt. Hon. Stephen (*b.* 1952) *C., Charnwood,* Maj. 8,809
***Dorries**, Nadine (*b.* 1958) *C., Bedfordshire Mid,* Maj. 11,355
Dowd, Jim (*b.* 1951) *Lab., Lewisham West,* Maj. 9,932
Drew, David (*b.* 1952) *Lab. (Co-op), Stroud,* Maj. 350
***Duddridge**, James (*b.* 1971) *C., Rochford & Southend East,* Maj. 5,494
Duncan Smith, Rt. Hon. Iain (*b.* 1954) *C., Chingford & Woodford Green,* Maj. 10,641
Duncan, Alan (*b.* 1957) *C., Rutland & Melton,* Maj. 12,930
***Dunne**, Philip (*b.* 1958) *C., Ludlow,* Maj. 2,027
***Durkan**, Mark (*b.* 1960) *SDLP, Foyle,* Maj. 5,957
Eagle, Angela (*b.* 1961) *Lab., Wallasey,* Maj. 9,109
Eagle, Maria (*b.* 1961) *Lab., Liverpool Garston,* Maj. 7,193

Efford, Clive (*b.* 1958) *Lab., Eltham,* Maj. 3,276
Ellman, Louise (*b.* 1945) *Lab. (Co-op), Liverpool Riverside,* Maj. 10,214
***Ellwood**, Tobias (*b.* 1966) *C., Bournemouth East,* Maj. 5,244
***Engel**, Natascha (*b.* 1967) *Lab., Derbyshire North East,* Maj. 10,065
Ennis, Jeff (*b.* 1952) *Lab., Barnsley East & Mexborough,* Maj. 14,125
Etherington, Bill (*b.* 1941) *Lab., Sunderland North,* Maj. 9,995
Evans, Nigel (*b.* 1957) *C., Ribble Valley,* Maj. 14,171
†**Evennett**, David (*b.* 1949) *C., Bexleyheath & Crayford,* Maj. 4,551
Fabricant, Michael (*b.* 1950) *C., Lichfield,* Maj. 7,080
Fallon, Michael (*b.* 1952) *C., Sevenoaks,* Maj. 12,970
Farrelly, Paul (*b.* 1962) *Lab., Newcastle-under-Lyme,* Maj. 8,108
***Farron**, Tim (*b.* 1970) *LD, Westmorland & Lonsdale,* Maj. 267
***Featherstone**, Lynne (*b.* 1951) *LD, Hornsey & Wood Green,* Maj. 2,395
Field, Rt. Hon. Frank (*b.* 1942) *Lab., Birkenhead,* Maj. 12,934
Field, Mark (*b.* 1934) *C., Cities of London & Westminster,* Maj. 8,095
Fisher, Mark (*b.* 1944) *Lab., Stoke-on-Trent Central,* Maj. 9,774
Fitzpatrick, Jim (*b.* 1952) *Lab., Poplar & Canning Town,* Maj. 7,129
***Flello**, Robert (*b.* 1966) *Lab., Stoke-on-Trent South,* Maj. 8,681
Flint, Caroline (*b.* 1961) *Lab., Don Valley,* Maj. 8,598
Flynn, Paul (*b.* 1935) *Lab., Newport West,* Maj. 5,458
Follett, Barbara (*b.* 1942) *Lab., Stevenage,* Maj. 3,139
Foster, Don (*b.* 1947) *LD, Bath,* Maj. 4,638
Foster, Michael (*b.* 1946) *Lab., Hastings & Rye,* Maj. 2,026
Foster, Michael (*b.* 1963) *Lab., Worcester,* Maj. 3,144
Fox, Dr Liam (*b.* 1961) *C., Woodspring,* Maj. 6,016
Francis, Dr Hywel (*b.* 1946) *Lab., Aberavon,* Maj. 13,937
Francois, Mark (*b.* 1965) *C., Rayleigh,* Maj. 14,726
†**Fraser**, Christopher (*b.* 1962) *C., Norfolk South West,* Maj. 10,086
Gale, Roger (*b.* 1943) *C., Thanet North,* Maj. 7,634
†‡**Galloway**, George (*b.* 1954) *Respect, Bethnal Green & Bow,* Maj. 823
Gapes, Mike (*b.* 1952) *Lab. (Co-op), Ilford South,* Maj. 9,228
Gardiner, Barry (*b.* 1957) *Lab., Brent North,* Maj. 5,641
Garnier, Edward (*b.* 1952) *C., Harborough,* Maj. 3,892
***Gauke**, David (*b.* 1971) *C., Hertfordshire South West,* Maj. 8,473
George, Andrew (*b.* 1958) *LD, St Ives,* Maj. 11,609
George, Rt. Hon. Bruce (*b.* 1942) *Lab., Walsall South,* Maj. 7,946
Gerrard, Neil (*b.* 1942) *Lab., Walthamstow,* Maj. 7,993
Gibb, Nick (*b.* 1960) *C., Bognor Regis & Littlehampton,* Maj. 7,822
Gibson, Dr Ian (*b.* 1938) *Lab., Norwich North,* Maj. 5,459
Gidley, Sandra (*b.* 1957) *LD, Romsey,* Maj. 125
Gildernew, Michelle (*b.* 1970) *SF, Fermanagh & South Tyrone,* Maj. 4,582
Gillan, Cheryl (*b.* 1952) *C., Chesham & Amersham,* Maj. 13,798
Gilroy, Linda (*b.* 1949) *Lab. (Co-op), Plymouth Sutton,* Maj. 4,109
Godsiff, Roger (*b.* 1946) *Lab., Birmingham Sparkbrook & Small Heath,* Maj. 3,289
Goggins, Paul (*b.* 1953) *Lab., Wythenshawe & Sale East,* Maj. 10,827
***Goldsworthy**, Julia (*b.* 1978) *LD, Falmouth & Camborne,* Maj. 1,886
***Goodman**, Helen (*b.* 1958) *Lab., Bishop Auckland,* Maj. 10,047
Goodman, Paul (*b.* 1960) *C., Wycombe,* Maj. 7,051
***Goodwill**, Robert (*b.* 1956) *C., Scarborough & Whitby,* Maj. 1,245
***Gove**, Michael (*b.* 1967) *C., Surrey Heath,* Maj. 10,845
Gray, James (*b.* 1954) *C., Wiltshire North,* Maj. 5,303
Grayling, Chris (*b.* 1962) *C., Epsom & Ewell,* Maj. 16,447
Green, Damian (*b.* 1956) *C., Ashford,* Maj. 13,298
***Greening**, Justine (*b.* 1969) *C., Putney,* Maj. 1,766
Greenway, John (*b.* 1946) *C., Ryedale,* Maj. 10,469
Grieve, Dominic (*b.* 1956) *C., Beaconsfield,* Maj. 15,253
***Griffith**, Nia (*b.* 1956) *Lab., Llanelli,* Maj. 7,234
Griffiths, Nigel (*b.* 1955) *Lab., Edinburgh South,* Maj. 405
Grogan, John (*b.* 1961) *Lab., Selby,* Maj. 467
Gummer, Rt. Hon. John (*b.* 1939) *C., Suffolk Coastal,* Maj. 9,685
***Gwynne**, Andrew (*b.* 1974) *Lab., Denton & Reddish,* Maj. 13,498
Hague, Rt. Hon. William (*b.* 1961) *C., Richmond (Yorks),* Maj. 17,807
Hain, Rt. Hon. Peter (*b.* 1950) *Lab., Neath,* Maj. 12,710
Hall, Mike (*b.* 1952) *Lab., Weaver Vale,* Maj. 6,855
Hall, Patrick (*b.* 1951) *Lab., Bedford,* Maj. 3,383
Hamilton, David (*b.* 1950) *Lab., Midlothian,* Maj. 7,265
Hamilton, Fabian (*b.* 1955) *Lab., Leeds North East,* Maj. 5,262
Hammond, Philip (*b.* 1955) *C., Runnymede & Weybridge,* Maj. 12,349
***Hammond**, Stephen (*b.* 1962) *C., Wimbledon,* Maj. 2,301
Hancock, Mike (*b.* 1946) *LD, Portsmouth South,* Maj. 3,362
***Hands**, Greg (*b.* 1965) *C., Hammersmith & Fulham,* Maj. 5,029
Hanson, David (*b.* 1957) *Lab., Delyn,* Maj. 6,644
Harman, Rt. Hon. Harriet (*b.* 1950) *Lab., Camberwell & Peckham,* Maj. 13,483
***Harper**, Mark (*b.* 1970) *C., Forest of Dean,* Maj. 2,049
Harris, Dr Evan (*b.* 1965) *LD, Oxford West & Abingdon,* Maj. 7,683
Harris, Tom (*b.* 1964) *Lab., Glasgow South,* Maj. 10,832
Harvey, Nick (*b.* 1961) *LD, Devon North,* Maj. 4,972
Haselhurst, Rt. Hon. Sir Alan (*b.* 1937) *C., Saffron Walden,* Maj. 13,008
Havard, Dai (*b.* 1949) *Lab., Merthyr Tydfil & Rhymney,* Maj. 13,934
Hayes, John (*b.* 1958) *C., South Holland & The Deepings,* Maj. 15,780
Heal, Sylvia (*b.* 1942) *Lab., Halesowen & Rowley Regis,* Maj. 4,337
Heald, Oliver (*b.* 1954) *C., Hertfordshire North East,* Maj. 9,138
Healey, John (*b.* 1960) *Lab., Wentworth,* Maj. 15,056
Heath, David (*b.* 1954) *LD, Somerton & Frome,* Maj. 812
Heathcoat-Amory, Rt. Hon. David (*b.* 1949) *C., Wells,* Maj. 3,040
***Hemming**, John (*b.* 1960) *LD, Birmingham Yardley,* Maj. 2,672
Henderson, Doug (*b.* 1949) *Lab., Newcastle upon Tyne North,* Maj. 7,023

Hendrick, Mark (*b.* 1958) *Lab. (Co-op), Preston,* Maj. 9,407
Hendry, Charles (*b.* 1959) *C., Wealden,* Maj. 15,921
Hepburn, Stephen (*b.* 1959) *Lab., Jarrow,* Maj. 13,904
Heppell, John (*b.* 1948) *Lab., Nottingham East,* Maj. 6,939
***Herbert**, Nick (*b.* 1963) *C., Arundel & South Downs,* Maj. 11,309
Hermon, Lady Sylvia (*b.* 1956) *UUP, Down North,* Maj. 4,944
Hesford, Stephen (*b.* 1957) *Lab., Wirral West,* Maj. 1,097
Hewitt, Rt. Hon. Patricia (*b.* 1948) *Lab., Leicester West,* Maj. 9,070
Heyes, David (*b.* 1946) *Lab., Ashton-under-Lyne,* Maj. 13,952
Hill, Rt. Hon. Keith (*b.* 1943) *Lab., Streatham,* Maj. 7,466
***Hillier**, Meg (*b.* 1969) *Lab. (Co-op), Hackney South & Shoreditch,* Maj. 10,204
Hoban, Mark (*b.* 1964) *C., Fareham,* Maj. 11,702
Hodge, Rt. Hon. Margaret (*b.* 1944) *Lab., Barking,* Maj. 8,883
***Hodgson**, Sharon (*b.* 1966) *Lab., Gateshead East & Washington West,* Maj. 13,407
Hoey, Kate (*b.* 1946) *Lab., Vauxhall,* Maj. 9,977
Hogg, Rt. Hon. Douglas (*b.* 1945) *C., Sleaford & North Hykeham,* Maj. 12,705
***Hollobone**, Philip (*b.* 1964) *C., Kettering,* Maj. 3,301
***Holloway**, Adam (*b.* 1965) *C., Gravesham,* Maj. 654
Holmes, Paul (*b.* 1957) *LD, Chesterfield,* Maj. 3,045
Hood, Jimmy (*b.* 1948) *Lab., Lanark & Hamilton East,* Maj. 11,947
Hoon, Rt. Hon. Geoff (*b.* 1953) *Lab., Ashfield,* Maj. 10,213
Hope, Phil (*b.* 1955) *Lab. (Co-op), Corby,* Maj. 1,517
Hopkins, Kelvin (*b.* 1941) *Lab., Luton North,* Maj. 6,487
Horam, John (*b.* 1939) *C., Orpington,* Maj. 4,947
***Horwood**, Martin (*b.* 1962) *LD, Cheltenham,* Maj. 2,303
***Hosie**, Stewart (*b.* 1963) *SNP, Dundee East,* Maj. 383
Howard, Rt. Hon. Michael (*b.* 1941) *C., Folkestone & Hythe,* Maj. 11,680
***Howarth**, David (*b.* 1958) *LD, Cambridge,* Maj. 4,339
Howarth, Rt. Hon. George (*b.* 1949) *Lab., Knowsley North & Sefton East,* Maj. 16,269
Howarth, Gerald (*b.* 1947) *C., Aldershot,* Maj. 5,334
***Howell**, John (*b.* 1955) *C., Henley,* Maj. 10,116
Howells, Dr Kim (*b.* 1946) *Lab., Pontypridd,* Maj. 13,191
Hoyle, Lindsay (*b.* 1957) *Lab., Chorley,* Maj. 7,625
Hughes, Rt. Hon. Beverley (*b.* 1950) *Lab., Stretford & Urmston,* Maj. 7,851
Hughes, Simon (*b.* 1951) *LD, Southwark North & Bermondsey,* Maj. 5,406
***Huhne**, Chris (*b.* 1954) *LD, Eastleigh,* Maj. 568
Humble, Joan (*b.* 1951) *Lab., Blackpool North & Fleetwood,* Maj. 5,062
***Hunt**, Jeremy (*b.* 1966) *C., Surrey South West,* Maj. 5,711
***Hunter**, Mark (*b.* 1957) *LD, Cheadle,* Maj. 3,657
***Hurd**, Nick (*b.* 1962) *C., Ruislip-Northwood,* Maj. 8,910
Hutton, Rt. Hon. John (*b.* 1955) *Lab., Barrow & Furness,* Maj. 6,037
Iddon, Dr Brian (*b.* 1940) *Lab., Bolton South East,* Maj. 11,638
Illsley, Eric (*b.* 1955) *Lab., Barnsley Central,* Maj. 12,732
Ingram, Rt. Hon. Adam (*b.* 1947) *Lab., East Kilbride, Strathaven & Lesmahagow,* Maj. 14,723
Irranca-Davies, Huw (*b.* 1963) *Lab., Ogmore,* Maj. 13,703
Jack, Rt. Hon. Michael (*b.* 1946) *C., Fylde,* Maj. 12,459
Jackson, Glenda (*b.* 1936) *Lab., Hampstead & Highgate,* Maj. 3,729
***Jackson**, Stewart (*b.* 1965) *C., Peterborough,* Maj. 2,740
***James**, Sian (*b.* 1959) *Lab., Swansea East,* Maj. 11,249
Jenkin, Bernard (*b.* 1959) *C., Essex North,* Maj. 10,903
Jenkins, Brian (*b.* 1942) *Lab., Tamworth,* Maj. 2,569
Johnson, Rt. Hon. Alan (*b.* 1950) *Lab., Hull West & Hessle,* Maj. 9,450
***Johnson**, Diana (*b.* 1966) *Lab., Hull North,* Maj. 7,351
***Jones**, David (*b.* 1952) *C., Clwyd West,* Maj. 133
Jones, Helen (*b.* 1954) *Lab., Warrington North,* Maj. 12,204
Jones, Kevan (*b.* 1964) *Lab., Durham North,* Maj. 16,781
Jones, Dr Lynne (*b.* 1951) *Lab., Birmingham Selly Oak,* Maj. 8,851
Jones, Martyn (*b.* 1947) *Lab., Clwyd South,* Maj. 6,348
Jowell, Rt. Hon. Tessa (*b.* 1947) *Lab., Dulwich & West Norwood,* Maj. 8,807
Joyce, Eric (*b.* 1960) *Lab., Falkirk,* Maj. 13,475
Kaufman, Rt. Hon. Sir Gerald (*b.* 1930) *Lab., Manchester Gorton,* Maj. 5,808
***Kawczynski**, Daniel (*b.* 1972) *C., Shrewsbury & Atcham,* Maj. 1,808
Keeble, Sally (*b.* 1951) *Lab., Northampton North,* Maj. 3,960
***Keeley**, Barbara (*b.* 1952) *Lab., Worsley,* Maj. 9,368
Keen, Alan (*b.* 1937) *Lab. (Co-op), Feltham & Heston,* Maj. 6,820
Keen, Ann (*b.* 1948) *Lab., Brentford & Isleworth,* Maj. 4,411
Keetch, Paul (*b.* 1961) *LD, Hereford,* Maj. 962
Kelly, Rt. Hon. Ruth (*b.* 1968) *Lab., Bolton West,* Maj. 2,064
Kemp, Fraser (*b.* 1958) *Lab., Houghton & Washington East,* Maj. 16,065
Kennedy, Rt. Hon. Charles (*b.* 1959) *LD, Ross, Skye & Lochaber,* Maj. 14,249
Kennedy, Rt. Hon. Jane (*b.* 1958) *Lab., Liverpool Wavertree,* Maj. 5,173
Key, Robert (*b.* 1945) *C., Salisbury,* Maj. 11,142
***Khan**, Sadiq (*b.* 1970) *Lab., Tooting,* Maj. 5,381
Kidney, David (*b.* 1955) *Lab., Stafford,* Maj. 2,121
Kilfoyle, Peter (*b.* 1946) *Lab., Liverpool Walton,* Maj. 15,957
Kirkbride, Julie (*b.* 1960) *C., Bromsgrove,* Maj. 10,080
Knight, Rt. Hon. Greg (*b.* 1949) *C., Yorkshire East,* Maj. 6,283
Knight, Jim (*b.* 1965) *Lab., Dorset South,* Maj. 1,812
***Kramer**, Susan (*b.* 1950) *LD, Richmond Park,* Maj. 3,731
Kumar, Dr Ashok (*b.* 1956) *Lab., Middlesbrough South & Cleveland East,* Maj. 8,000
Ladyman, Dr Stephen (*b.* 1952) *Lab., Thanet South,* Maj. 664
Laing, Eleanor (*b.* 1958) *C., Epping Forest,* Maj. 14,358
Lait, Jacqui (*b.* 1947) *C., Beckenham,* Maj. 8,401
Lamb, Norman (*b.* 1957) *LD, Norfolk North,* Maj. 10,606
Lammy, David (*b.* 1972) *Lab., Tottenham,* Maj. 13,034
***Lancaster**, Mark (*b.* 1970) *C., Milton Keynes North East,* Maj. 1,665
Lansley, Andrew (*b.* 1956) *C., Cambridgeshire South,* Maj. 8,001
Laws, David (*b.* 1965) *LD, Yeovil,* Maj. 8,562
Laxton, Bob (*b.* 1944) *Lab., Derby North,* Maj. 3,757
Lazarowicz, Mark (*b.* 1953) *Lab. (Co-op), Edinburgh North & Leith,* Maj. 2,153
***Leech**, John (*b.* 1971) *LD, Manchester Withington,* Maj. 667

Leigh, Edward (*b.* 1950) *C., Gainsborough,* Maj. 8,003
Lepper, David (*b.* 1945) *Lab. (Co-op), Brighton Pavilion,* Maj. 5,030
Letwin, Rt. Hon. Oliver (*b.* 1956) *C., Dorset West,* Maj. 2,461
Levitt, Tom (*b.* 1954) *Lab., High Peak,* Maj. 735
Lewis, Ivan (*b.* 1967) *Lab., Bury South,* Maj. 8,912
Lewis, Dr Julian (*b.* 1951) *C., New Forest East,* Maj. 6,551
Liddell-Grainger, Ian (*b.* 1959) *C., Bridgwater,* Maj. 8,469
Lidington, David (*b.* 1956) *C., Aylesbury,* Maj. 11,065
Lilley, Rt. Hon. Peter (*b.* 1943) *C., Hitchin & Harpenden,* Maj. 11,393
Linton, Martin (*b.* 1944) *Lab., Battersea,* Maj. 163
Lloyd, Tony (*b.* 1950) *Lab., Manchester Central,* Maj. 9,776
Llwyd, Elfyn (*b.* 1951) *PC, Meirionnydd Nant Conwy,* Maj. 6,614
Lord, Sir Michael (*b.* 1938) *C., Suffolk Central & Ipswich North,* Maj. 7,856
Loughton, Tim (*b.* 1962) *C., Worthing East & Shoreham,* Maj. 8,183
Love, Andy (*b.* 1949) *Lab. (Co-op), Edmonton,* Maj. 8,075
Lucas, Ian (*b.* 1960) *Lab., Wrexham,* Maj. 6,819
Luff, Peter (*b.* 1955) *C., Worcestershire Mid,* Maj. 13,327
McAvoy, Rt. Hon. Thomas (*b.* 1943) *Lab. (Co-op), Rutherglen & Hamilton West,* Maj. 16,112
McCabe, Stephen (*b.* 1955) *Lab., Birmingham Hall Green,* Maj. 5,714
McCafferty, Christine (*b.* 1945) *Lab., Calder Valley,* Maj. 1,367
***McCarthy**, Kerry (*b.* 1965) *Lab., Bristol East,* Maj. 8,621
***McCarthy-Fry**, Sarah (*b.* 1955) *Lab. (Co-op), Portsmouth North,* Maj. 1,139
McCartney, Rt. Hon. Ian (*b.* 1951) *Lab., Makerfield,* Maj. 18,149
†McCrea, Dr William (*b.* 1948) *DUP, Antrim South,* Maj. 3,448
McDonagh, Siobhain (*b.* 1960) *Lab., Mitcham & Morden,* Maj. 12,560
***McDonnell**, Dr Alasdair (*b.* 1949) *SDLP, Belfast South,* Maj. 1,235
McDonnell, John (*b.* 1951) *Lab., Hayes & Harlington,* Maj. 10,847
***McFadden**, Pat (*b.* 1965) *Lab., Wolverhampton South East,* Maj. 10,495
McFall, Rt. Hon. John (*b.* 1944) *Lab. (Co-op), Dunbartonshire West,* Maj. 12,553
***McGovern**, James (*b.* 1956) *Lab., Dundee West,* Maj. 5,379
McGrady, Edward (*b.* 1935) *SDLP, Down South,* Maj. 9,140
McGuinness, Martin (*b.* 1950) *SF, Ulster Mid,* Maj. 10,976
McGuire, Anne (*b.* 1949) *Lab., Stirling,* Maj. 4,767
McIntosh, Anne (*b.* 1954) *C., Vale of York,* Maj. 13,712
McIsaac, Shona (*b.* 1960) *Lab., Cleethorpes,* Maj. 2,642
Mackay, Rt. Hon. Andrew (*b.* 1949) *C., Bracknell,* Maj. 12,036
McKechin, Ann (*b.* 1961) *Lab., Glasgow North,* Maj. 3,338
McKenna, Rosemary (*b.* 1941) *Lab., Cumbernauld, Kilsyth & Kirkintilloch East,* Maj. 11,562
Mackinlay, Andrew (*b.* 1949) *Lab., Thurrock,* Maj. 6,375
Maclean, Rt. Hon. David (*b.* 1953) *C., Penrith & The Border,* Maj. 11,904
McLoughlin, Rt. Hon. Patrick (*b.* 1957) *C., Derbyshire West,* Maj. 10,753
***MacNeil**, Angus (*b.* 1970) *SNP, Na h-Eileanan an Iar,* Maj. 1,441
McNulty, Tony (*b.* 1958) *Lab., Harrow East,* Maj. 4,730
MacShane, Rt. Hon. Denis (*b.* 1948) *Lab., Rotherham,* Maj. 10,681
Mactaggart, Fiona (*b.* 1953) *Lab., Slough,* Maj. 7,851
Mahmood, Khalid (*b.* 1961) *Lab., Birmingham Perry Barr,* Maj. 7,948
***Main**, Anne (*b.* 1957) *C., St Albans,* Maj. 1,361
***Malik**, Shahid (*b.* 1967) *Lab., Dewsbury,* Maj. 4,615
Malins, Humfrey (*b.* 1945) *C., Woking,* Maj. 6,612
Mallaber, Judith (*b.* 1951) *Lab., Amber Valley,* Maj. 5,275
Mann, John (*b.* 1960) *Lab., Bassetlaw,* Maj. 10,837
Maples, John (*b.* 1943) *C., Stratford-upon-Avon,* Maj. 12,184
Marris, Rob (*b.* 1955) *Lab., Wolverhampton South West,* Maj. 2,879
Marsden, Gordon (*b.* 1953) *Lab., Blackpool South,* Maj. 7,922
Marshall-Andrews, Bob (*b.* 1944) *Lab., Medway,* Maj. 213
Martin, Rt. Hon. Michael (*b.* 1945) *The Speaker, Glasgow North East,* Maj. 10,134
Martlew, Eric (*b.* 1949) *Lab., Carlisle,* Maj. 5,695
***Mason**, John (*b.* 1957) *SNP, Glasgow East,* Maj. 365
Mates, Rt. Hon. Michael (*b.* 1934) *C., Hampshire East,* Maj. 5,509
Maude, Rt. Hon. Francis (*b.* 1953) *C., Horsham,* Maj. 12,627
May, Rt. Hon. Theresa (*b.* 1956) *C., Maidenhead,* Maj. 6,231
Meacher, Rt. Hon. Michael (*b.* 1939) *Lab., Oldham West & Royton,* Maj. 10,454
Meale, Alan (*b.* 1949) *Lab., Mansfield,* Maj. 11,365
Mercer, Patrick (*b.* 1956) *C., Newark,* Maj. 6,464
Merron, Gillian (*b.* 1959) *Lab., Lincoln,* Maj. 4,614
Michael, Rt. Hon. Alun (*b.* 1943) *Lab. (Co-op), Cardiff South & Penarth,* Maj. 9,237
Milburn, Rt. Hon. Alan (*b.* 1958) *Lab., Darlington,* Maj. 10,404
Miliband, Rt. Hon. David (*b.* 1966) *Lab., South Shields,* Maj. 12,312
***Miliband**, Edward (*b.* 1969) *Lab., Doncaster North,* Maj. 12,656
Miller, Andrew (*b.* 1949) *Lab., Ellesmere Port & Neston,* Maj. 6,486
***Miller**, Maria (*b.* 1964) *C., Basingstoke,* Maj. 4,680
***Milton**, Anne (*b.* 1955) *C., Guildford,* Maj. 347
Mitchell, Andrew (*b.* 1956) *C., Sutton Coldfield,* Maj. 12,283
Mitchell, Austin (*b.* 1934) *Lab., Great Grimsby,* Maj. 7,654
Moffat, Anne (*b.* 1958) *Lab., East Lothian,* Maj. 7,620
Moffatt, Laura (*b.* 1954) *Lab., Crawley,* Maj. 37
Mole, Chris (*b.* 1958) *Lab., Ipswich,* Maj. 5,332
***Moon**, Madeleine (*b.* 1950) *Lab., Bridgend,* Maj. 6,523
Moore, Michael (*b.* 1965) *LD, Berwickshire, Roxburgh & Selkirk,* Maj. 5,901
Moran, Margaret (*b.* 1955) *Lab., Luton South,* Maj. 5,650
***Morden**, Jessica (*b.* 1968) *Lab., Newport East,* Maj. 6,838
Morgan, Julie (*b.* 1944) *Lab., Cardiff North,* Maj. 1,146
Morley, Elliot (*b.* 1952) *Lab., Scunthorpe,* Maj. 8,963
Moss, Malcolm (*b.* 1943) *C., Cambridgeshire North East,* Maj. 8,901
Mountford, Kali (*b.* 1954) *Lab., Colne Valley,* Maj. 1,501

Mudie, George (*b.* 1945) *Lab., Leeds East,* Maj. 11,578
***Mulholland**, Greg (*b.* 1970) *LD, Leeds North West,* Maj. 1,877
Mullin, Chris (*b.* 1947) *Lab., Sunderland South,* Maj. 11,059
***Mundell**, David (*b.* 1962) *C., Dumfriesshire, Clydesdale & Tweeddale,* Maj. 1,738
Munn, Meg (*b.* 1959) *Lab. (Co-op), Sheffield Heeley,* Maj. 11,370
***Murphy**, Conor (*b.* 1963) *SF, Newry & Armagh,* Maj. 8,195
Murphy, Denis (*b.* 1948) *Lab., Wansbeck,* Maj. 10,581
Murphy, Jim (*b.* 1967) *Lab., Renfrewshire East,* Maj. 6,657
Murphy, Rt. Hon. Paul (*b.* 1948) *Lab., Torfaen,* Maj. 14,791
Murrison, Dr Andrew (*b.* 1961) *C., Westbury,* Maj. 5,349
Naysmith, Dr Doug (*b.* 1941) *Lab. (Co-op), Bristol North West,* Maj. 8,962
***Neill**, Bob (*b.* 1952) *C., Bromley & Chislehurst,* Maj. 633
***Newmark**, Brooks (*b.* 1958) *C., Braintree,* Maj. 3,893
Norris, Dan (*b.* 1960) *Lab., Wansdyke,* Maj. 1,839
Oaten, Mark (*b.* 1964) *LD, Winchester,* Maj. 7,476
O'Brien, Mike (*b.* 1954) *Lab., Warwickshire North,* Maj. 7,553
O'Brien, Stephen (*b.* 1957) *C., Eddisbury,* Maj. 6,195
O'Hara, Eddie (*b.* 1937) *Lab., Knowsley South,* Maj. 17,688
Olner, Bill (*b.* 1942) *Lab., Nuneaton,* Maj. 2,280
Opik, Lembit (*b.* 1965) *LD, Montgomeryshire,* Maj. 7,173
Osborne, George (*b.* 1971) *C., Tatton,* Maj. 11,731
Osborne, Sandra (*b.* 1956) *Lab., Ayr, Carrick & Cumnock,* Maj. 9,997
Ottaway, Richard (*b.* 1945) *C., Croydon South,* Maj. 13,528
Owen, Albert (*b.* 1960) *Lab., Ynys Mon,* Maj. 1,242
Paice, James (*b.* 1949) *C., Cambridgeshire South East,* Maj. 8,624
Paisley, Revd Rt. Hon. Ian (*b.* 1926) *DUP, Antrim North,* Maj. 17,965
Palmer, Dr Nick (*b.* 1950) *Lab., Broxtowe,* Maj. 2,296
Paterson, Owen (*b.* 1956) *C., Shropshire North,* Maj. 11,020
Pearson, Ian (*b.* 1959) *Lab., Dudley South,* Maj. 4,244
***Pelling**, Andrew (*b.* 1959) *C., Croydon Central,* Maj. 75
***Penning**, Michael (*b.* 1957) *C., Hemel Hempstead,* Maj. 499
***Penrose**, John (*b.* 1964) *C., Weston-Super-Mare,* Maj. 2,079
Pickles, Eric (*b.* 1952) *C., Brentwood & Ongar,* Maj. 11,612
Plaskitt, James (*b.* 1954) *Lab., Warwick & Leamington,* Maj. 266
Pope, Greg (*b.* 1960) *Lab., Hyndburn,* Maj. 5,587
Pound, Stephen (*b.* 1948) *Lab., Ealing North,* Maj. 7,059
Prentice, Bridget (*b.* 1952) *Lab., Lewisham East,* Maj. 6,751
Prentice, Gordon (*b.* 1951) *Lab., Pendle,* Maj. 2,180
Prescott, Rt. Hon. John (*b.* 1938) *Lab., Hull East,* Maj. 11,747
Price, Adam (*b.* 1968) *PC, Carmarthen East & Dinefwr,* Maj. 6,718
Primarolo, Rt. Hon. Dawn (*b.* 1954) *Lab., Bristol South,* Maj. 11,142
Prisk, Mark (*b.* 1962) *C., Hertford & Stortford,* Maj. 13,097
***Pritchard**, Mark (*b.* 1966) *C., The Wrekin,* Maj. 942
Prosser, Gwyn (*b.* 1943) *Lab., Dover,* Maj. 4,941
Pugh, Dr John (*b.* 1948) *LD, Southport,* Maj. 3,838
Purchase, Ken (*b.* 1939) *Lab. (Co-op), Wolverhampton North East,* Maj. 8,156
Purnell, James (*b.* 1970) *Lab., Stalybridge & Hyde,* Maj. 8,348
Rammell, Bill (*b.* 1959) *Lab., Harlow,* Maj. 97
Randall, John (*b.* 1955) *C., Uxbridge,* Maj. 6,171
Raynsford, Rt. Hon. Nick (*b.* 1945) *Lab., Greenwich & Woolwich,* Maj. 10,146
Redwood, Rt. Hon. John (*b.* 1951) *C., Wokingham,* Maj. 7,240
Reed, Andy (*b.* 1964) *Lab. (Co-op), Loughborough,* Maj. 1,996
***Reed**, Jamie (*b.* 1973) *Lab., Copeland,* Maj. 6,320
Reid, Alan (*b.* 1954) *LD, Argyll & Bute,* Maj. 5,636
Reid, Rt. Hon. Dr John (*b.* 1947) *Lab., Airdrie & Shotts,* Maj. 14,084
***Rennie**, Willie (*b.* 1967) *LD, Dunfermline & Fife West,* Maj. 1,800
†**Rifkind**, Rt. Hon. Sir Malcolm (*b.* 1946) *C., Kensington & Chelsea,* Maj. 12,418
***Riordan**, Linda (*b.* 1953) *Lab. (Co-op), Halifax,* Maj. 3,417
Robathan, Andrew (*b.* 1951) *C., Blaby,* Maj. 7,873
Robertson, Angus (*b.* 1969) *SNP, Moray,* Maj. 5,676
Robertson, Hugh (*b.* 1962) *C., Faversham & Kent Mid,* Maj. 8,720
Robertson, John (*b.* 1952) *Lab., Glasgow North West,* Maj. 10,093
Robertson, Laurence (*b.* 1958) *C., Tewkesbury,* Maj. 9,892
Robinson, Geoffrey (*b.* 1938) *Lab., Coventry North West,* Maj. 9,315
Robinson, Iris (*b.* 1949) *DUP, Strangford,* Maj. 13,049
Robinson, Peter (*b.* 1948) *DUP, Belfast East,* Maj. 5,877
***Rogerson**, Dan (*b.* 1975) *LD, Cornwall North,* Maj. 3,076
Rooney, Terry (*b.* 1950) *Lab., Bradford North,* Maj. 3,511
Rosindell, Andrew (*b.* 1966) *C., Romford,* Maj. 11,589
***Rowen**, Paul (*b.* 1955) *LD, Rochdale,* Maj. 442
Roy, Frank (*b.* 1958) *Lab., Motherwell & Wishaw,* Maj. 15,222
Ruane, Christopher (*b.* 1958) *Lab., Vale of Clwyd,* Maj. 4,669
Ruddock, Joan (*b.* 1943) *Lab., Lewisham Deptford,* Maj. 11,811
Ruffley, David (*b.* 1962) *C., Bury St Edmunds,* Maj. 9,930
Russell, Bob (*b.* 1946) *LD, Colchester,* Maj. 6,277
Russell, Christine (*b.* 1945) *Lab., Chester, City of,* Maj. 915
Ryan, Joan (*b.* 1955) *Lab., Enfield North,* Maj. 1,920
Salmond, Alex (*b.* 1954) *SNP, Banff & Buchan,* Maj. 11,837
Salter, Martin (*b.* 1954) *Lab., Reading West,* Maj. 4,682
Sanders, Adrian (*b.* 1959) *LD, Torbay,* Maj. 2,029
Sarwar, Mohammad (*b.* 1952) *Lab., Glasgow Central,* Maj. 8,531
***Scott**, Lee (*b.* 1956) *C., Ilford North,* Maj. 1,653
***Seabeck**, Alison (*b.* 1954) *Lab., Plymouth Devonport,* Maj. 8,103
Selous, Andrew (*b.* 1962) *C., Bedfordshire South West,* Maj. 8,277
***Shapps**, Grant (*b.* 1968) *C., Welwyn Hatfield,* Maj. 5,946
Sharma, Virendra (*b.* 1947) *Lab., Ealing Southall,* Maj. 5,070
Shaw, Jonathan (*b.* 1966) *Lab., Chatham & Aylesford,* Maj. 2,332
Sheerman, Barry (*b.* 1940) *Lab. (Co-op), Huddersfield,* Maj. 8,351

Shepherd, Richard (*b.* 1942) *C., Aldridge-Brownhills,* Maj. 5,507
Sheridan, James (*b.* 1952) *Lab., Paisley & Renfrewshire North,* Maj. 11,001
‡**Short**, Rt. Hon. Clare (*b.* 1946) *Ind., Birmingham Ladywood,* Maj. 6,801
Simmonds, Mark (*b.* 1964) *C., Boston & Skegness,* Maj. 5,907
Simon, Sion (*b.* 1969) *Lab., Birmingham Erdington,* Maj. 9,575
Simpson, Alan (*b.* 1948) *Lab., Nottingham South,* Maj. 7,486
*__Simpson__, David (*b.* 1959) *DUP, Upper Bann,* Maj. 5,298
Simpson, Keith (*b.* 1949) *C., Norfolk Mid,* Maj. 7,560
Singh, Marsha (*b.* 1954) *Lab., Bradford West,* Maj. 3,026
Skinner, Dennis (*b.* 1932) *Lab., Bolsover,* Maj. 18,437
*__Slaughter__, Andrew (*b.* 1960) *Lab., Ealing, Acton & Shepherd's Bush,* Maj. 5,520
Smith, Rt. Hon. Andrew (*b.* 1951) *Lab., Oxford East,* Maj. 963
*__Smith__, Angela C. (*b.* 1961) *Lab., Sheffield Hillsborough,* Maj. 11,243
Smith, Angela E. (*b.* 1959) *Lab. (Co-op), Basildon,* Maj. 3,142
Smith, Geraldine (*b.* 1961) *Lab., Morecambe & Lunesdale,* Maj. 4,768
Smith, Rt. Hon. Jacqui (*b.* 1962) *Lab., Redditch,* Maj. 2,716
Smith, John (*b.* 1951) *Lab., Vale of Glamorgan,* Maj. 1,808
Smith, Sir Robert (*b.* 1958) *LD, Aberdeenshire West & Kincardine,* Maj. 7,471
*__Snelgrove__, Anne (*b.* 1957) *Lab., Swindon South* , Maj. 1,353
Soames, Hon. Nicholas (*b.* 1948) *C., Sussex Mid,* Maj. 5,890
*__Soulsby__, Sir Peter (*b.* 1948) *Lab., Leicester South,* Maj. 3,717
Southworth, Helen (*b.* 1956) *Lab., Warrington South,* Maj. 3,515
Spellar, Rt. Hon. John (*b.* 1947) *Lab., Warley,* Maj. 10,147
Spelman, Caroline (*b.* 1958) *C., Meriden,* Maj. 7,009
Spicer, Sir Michael (*b.* 1943) *C., Worcestershire West,* Maj. 2,475
Spink, Dr Robert (*b.* 1948) *C., Castle Point,* Maj. 8,201
Spring, Richard (*b.* 1946) *C., Suffolk West,* Maj. 8,909
Stanley, Rt. Hon. Sir John (*b.* 1942) *C., Tonbridge & Malling,* Maj. 13,352
Starkey, Dr Phyllis (*b.* 1947) *Lab., Milton Keynes South West,* Maj. 4,010
Steen, Anthony (*b.* 1939) *C., Totnes,* Maj. 1,947
Stewart, Ian (*b.* 1950) *Lab., Eccles,* Maj. 12,886
Stoate, Dr Howard (*b.* 1954) *Lab., Dartford,* Maj. 706
Strang, Rt. Hon. Gavin (*b.* 1943) *Lab., Edinburgh East,* Maj. 6,202
Straw, Rt. Hon. Jack (*b.* 1946) *Lab., Blackburn,* Maj. 8,009
Streeter, Gary (*b.* 1955) *C., Devon South West,* Maj. 10,141
Stringer, Graham (*b.* 1950) *Lab., Manchester Blackley,* Maj. 12,027
Stuart, Gisela (*b.* 1955) *Lab., Birmingham Edgbaston,* Maj. 2,349
*__Stuart__, Graham (*b.* 1962) *C., Beverley & Holderness,* Maj. 2,580
Stunell, Andrew (*b.* 1942) *LD, Hazel Grove,* Maj. 7,748
Sutcliffe, Gerry (*b.* 1953) *Lab., Bradford South,* Maj. 9,167
Swayne, Desmond (*b.* 1956) *C., New Forest West,* Maj. 17,285
*__Swinson__, Jo (*b.* 1980) *LD, Dunbartonshire East,* Maj. 4,061
Swire, Hugo (*b.* 1959) *C., Devon East,* Maj. 7,936
Syms, Robert (*b.* 1956) *C., Poole,* Maj. 5,988
Tami, Mark (*b.* 1963) *Lab., Alyn & Deeside,* Maj. 8,378
Tapsell, Sir Peter (*b.* 1930) *C., Louth & Horncastle,* Maj. 9,896
Taylor, Dari (*b.* 1944) *Lab., Stockton South,* Maj. 6,139
Taylor, David (*b.* 1946) *Lab. (Co-op), Leicestershire North West,* Maj. 4,477
Taylor, Ian (*b.* 1945) *C., Esher & Walton,* Maj. 7,727
Taylor, Matthew (*b.* 1963) *LD, Truro & St Austell,* Maj. 7,403
Taylor, Dr Richard (*b.* 1935) *KHHC, Wyre Forest,* Maj. 5,250
Teather, Sarah (*b.* 1974) *LD, Brent East,* Maj. 2,712
Thomas, Gareth (*b.* 1967) *Lab. (Co-op), Harrow West,* Maj. 2,028
*__Thornberry__, Emily (*b.* 1960) *Lab., Islington South & Finsbury,* Maj. 484
Thurso, John (*b.* 1953) *LD, Caithness, Sutherland & Easter Ross,* Maj. 8,168
Timms, Stephen (*b.* 1955) *Lab., East Ham,* Maj. 13,155
*__Timpson__, Edward (*b.* 1973) *C., Crewe & Nantwich,* Maj. 7,860
Tipping, Paddy (*b.* 1949) *Lab., Sherwood,* Maj. 6,652
Todd, Mark (*b.* 1954) *Lab., Derbyshire South,* Maj. 4,495
Touhig, Don (*b.* 1947) *Lab. (Co-op), Islwyn,* Maj. 15,740
Tredinnick, David (*b.* 1950) *C., Bosworth,* Maj. 5,319
Trickett, Jon (*b.* 1950) *Lab., Hemsworth,* Maj. 13,481
Truswell, Paul (*b.* 1955) *Lab., Pudsey,* Maj. 5,870
Turner, Andrew (*b.* 1953) *C., Isle of Wight,* Maj. 12,978
Turner, Dr Desmond (*b.* 1939) *Lab., Brighton Kemptown,* Maj. 2,737
Turner, Neil (*b.* 1945) *Lab., Wigan,* Maj. 11,767
Twigg, Derek (*b.* 1959) *Lab., Halton,* Maj. 14,606
Tyrie, Andrew (*b.* 1957) *C., Chichester,* Maj. 10,860
*__Ussher__, Kitty (*b.* 1971) *Lab., Burnley,* Maj. 5,778
*__Vaizey__, Ed (*b.* 1969) *C., Wantage,* Maj. 8,017
*__Vara__, Shailesh (*b.* 1960) *C., Cambridgeshire North West,* Maj. 9,833
Vaz, Keith (*b.* 1956) *Lab., Leicester East,* Maj. 15,876
Viggers, Peter (*b.* 1938) *C., Gosport,* Maj. 5,730
*__Villiers__, Theresa (*b.* 1968) *C., Chipping Barnet,* Maj. 5,960
Vis, Dr Rudi (*b.* 1941) *Lab., Finchley & Golders Green,* Maj. 741
*__Walker__, Charles (*b.* 1967) *C., Broxbourne,* Maj. 11,509
*__Wallace__, Ben (*b.* 1970) *C., Lancaster & Wyre,* Maj. 4,171
Walley, Joan (*b.* 1949) *Lab., Stoke-on-Trent North,* Maj. 10,036
Walter, Robert (*b.* 1948) *C., Dorset North,* Maj. 2,244
*__Waltho__, Lynda (*b.* 1960) *Lab., Stourbridge,* Maj. 407
Ward, Claire (*b.* 1972) *Lab., Watford,* Maj. 1,148
Wareing, Robert (*b.* 1930) *Lab., Liverpool West Derby,* Maj. 15,225
Waterson, Nigel (*b.* 1950) *C., Eastbourne,* Maj. 1,124
Watkinson, Angela (*b.* 1941) *C., Upminster,* Maj. 6,042
Watson, Tom (*b.* 1967) *Lab., West Bromwich East,* Maj. 11,652
Watts, Dave (*b.* 1951) *Lab., St Helens North,* Maj. 13,962
Webb, Prof. Steve (*b.* 1965) *LD, Northavon,* Maj. 11,033
Weir, Michael (*b.* 1957) *SNP, Angus,* Maj. 1,601

Whitehead, Dr Alan (*b.* 1950) *Lab., Southampton Test,* Maj. 7,018
Whittingdale, John (*b.* 1959) *C., Maldon & Chelmsford East,* Maj. 12,573
Wicks, Malcolm (*b.* 1947) *Lab., Croydon North,* Maj. 13,888
Widdecombe, Rt. Hon. Ann (*b.* 1947) *C., Maidstone & The Weald,* Maj. 14,856
Wiggin, Bill (*b.* 1966) *C., Leominster,* Maj. 13,187
Willetts, David (*b.* 1956) *C., Havant,* Maj. 6,508
Williams, Rt. Hon. Alan (*b.* 1930) *Lab., Swansea West,* Maj. 4,269
Williams, Betty (*b.* 1944) *Lab., Conwy,* Maj. 3,081
Williams, Hywel (*b.* 1953) *PC, Caernarfon,* Maj. 5,209
***Williams**, Mark (*b.* 1966) *LD, Ceredigion,* Maj. 219
Williams, Roger (*b.* 1948) *LD, Brecon & Radnorshire,* Maj. 3,905
***Williams**, Stephen (*b.* 1966) *LD, Bristol West,* Maj. 5,128
Willis, Phil (*b.* 1941) *LD, Harrogate & Knaresborough,* Maj. 10,429
***Willott**, Jenny (*b.* 1974) *LD, Cardiff Central,* Maj. 5,593
Wills, Michael (*b.* 1952) *Lab., Swindon North,* Maj. 2,571
Wilshire, David (*b.* 1943) *C., Spelthorne,* Maj. 9,936
***Wilson**, Phil (*b.* 1959) *Lab., Sedgefield,* Maj. 6,956
***Wilson**, Rob (*b.* 1965) *C., Reading East,* Maj. 475
***Wilson**, Sammy (*b.* 1953) *DUP, Antrim East,* Maj. 7,304
Winnick, David (*b.* 1933) *Lab., Walsall North,* Maj. 6,640
Winterton, Lady Ann (*b.* 1941) *C., Congleton,* Maj. 8,246
Winterton, Sir Nicholas (*b.* 1938) *C., Macclesfield,* Maj. 9,401
Winterton, Rosie (*b.* 1958) *Lab., Doncaster Central,* Maj. 9,802
Wishart, Peter (*b.* 1962) *SNP, Perth & Perthshire North,* Maj. 1,521
Wood, Mike (*b.* 1946) *Lab., Batley & Spen,* Maj. 5,788
Woodward, Shaun (*b.* 1958) *Lab., St Helens South,* Maj. 9,309
Woolas, Phil (*b.* 1959) *Lab., Oldham East & Saddleworth,* Maj. 3,590
Wright, Anthony (*b.* 1954) *Lab., Great Yarmouth,* Maj. 3,055
Wright, David (*b.* 1967) *Lab., Telford,* Maj. 5,406
Wright, Iain (*b.* 1972) *Lab., Hartlepool,* Maj. 7,478
***Wright**, Jeremy (*b.* 1972) *C., Rugby & Kenilworth,* Maj. 1,556
Wright, Dr Tony (*b.* 1948) *Lab., Cannock Chase,* Maj. 9,227
Wyatt, Derek (*b.* 1949) *Lab., Sittingbourne & Sheppey,* Maj. 79
Yeo, Tim (*b.* 1945) *C., Suffolk South,* Maj. 6,606
Young, Rt. Hon. Sir George (*b.* 1941) *C., Hampshire North West,* Maj. 13,264
Younger-Ross, Richard (*b.* 1953) *LD, Teignbridge,* Maj. 6,215

GENERAL ELECTION RESULTS

The results of voting in each parliamentary division at the general election of 5 May 2005 are given below. *See also* By-elections (p. 181).

SCOTTISH BOUNDARY CHANGES

The number of Scottish constituencies was reduced from 72 to 59 for the 2005 general election, bringing the average electorate of each constituency in line with that of England.

For the majority of constituencies where a boundary change has taken place, it is not appropriate to make a straight comparison between the results of 2001 and 2005. The seat of Dundee East, for example, comprises 80 per cent of the old Dundee East constituency and 30 per cent of the old Angus constituency; it cannot therefore be described as a simple gain for the Scottish National Party from Labour. The term 'notional' used here refers to a theoretical set of results, published by Professors Rallings and Thrasher of Plymouth University, that estimates the way each new constituency might have voted in the 2001 general election.

KEY

* New MP
† Previously MP in another seat
‡ Previously MP for another party
§ Notional result; *see* explanation of Scottish boundary changes
E. Electorate T. Turnout

Abbreviations

AFC	Alliance for Change
Alliance	Alliance
AP	Alternative Party
Baths	Save the Bristol North Baths Party
Bean	New Millennium Bean
BMG	Blair Must Go Party
BNP	British National Party
BPP	British Public Party
Bridges	Build Duddon and Morecambe Bridges
Burnley	Burnley First Independent
C.	Conservative
CAP	Community Action Party
CG	Community Group
CL	Communist League
Clause 28	Clause 28 Children's Protection Christian Democrats
Comm.	Communist Party
Comm. Brit.	Communist Party of Britain
Community	Community
CP	Civilisation Party
CPA	Christian Peoples Alliance
Croydon	Croydon Pensions Alliance
Currency	Virtue Currency Cognitive Appraisal Party
Cut Tax	Cut Tax on Diesel and Petrol
DDTP	Death, Dungeons & Taxes Party
Dem. Lab.	Democratic Labour Party
Dem. Soc. All.	Democratic Socialist Alliance – People Before Profit
DUP	Democratic Unionist Party
EDP	English Democratic Party
EPP	English Parliamentary Party
Elvis	Church of the Militant Elvis Party
Eng. Dem.	English Democrats Party
Eng. Ind.	English Independence Party
FF	familiesfirst.uk.net
Fit	Fit Party For Integrity And Trust
Forum	Open-Forum
FP	Freedom Party
Free Scot.	Free Scotland Party
FWP	Forward Wales Party
GBB	Get Britain Back Party
Good	Common Good
Green	Green
Green Soc.	Alliance for Green Socialism
Honesty	Demanding Honesty in Politics and Whitehall
Ind. Green	Independent Green Voice
Ind.	Independent
Ind. Pr. Lab.	Independent Progressive Labour
IP	Imperial Party
Iraq	Iraq War, Not in My Name
IWCA	Independent Working Class Association
IZB	Islam Zinda Baad Platform
JP	Justice Party
KHHC	Kidderminster Hospital and Health Concern
Lab.	Labour
Lab. (Co-op)	Labour (Cooperative)
LCA	Legalise Cannabis Alliance
LD	Liberal Democrat
Lib.	Liberal
Local	Local Community Party
Loony	Monster Raving Loony Party
Masts	Removal of Tetra Masts in Cornwall
MC	The Millenium Council
Meb. Ker.	Mebyon Kernow
MNP	Motorcycle News Party
NACVP	Newcastle Academy with Christian Values Party
NEP	New England Party
NF	National Front
Northern	Northern Progress for You
OCV	Operation Christian Vote
OFD	Organisation of Free Democrats
Online	Seeks a Worldwide Online Participatory Directory
Paisley	Pride in Paisley Party
PC	Plaid Cymru
PDP	Progressive Democratic Party
PHF	People of Horsham First
Power	Max Power Party
PPN-V	Peace Party, Non-Violence, Justice, Environment
PPS	Pensioners Party Scotland
Progress	Peace and Progress Party
Protest	Protest Vote Party
PRTYP	Personality and Rational Thinking? Yes! Party
Publican	Publican Party – Free to Smoke (Pubs)
RA	Residents Association
R & R Loony	Rock & Roll Loony Party
Respect	Respect – the Unity Coalition
RP	The Resolutionist Party
St Albans	St Albans Party
Scot. Green	Scottish Green Party
Scot. Ind.	Scottish Independence Party
Scot. Senior	Scottish Senior Citizens Party
Scot. U.	Scottish Unionist
SDLP	Social Democratic and Labour Party
Senior	Senior Citizens Party
SF	Sinn Fein
Silent	Silent Majority Party
SNH	Safeguard the National Health Service
SNP	Scottish National Party
Soc. All.	Socialist Alliance
Soc. Alt.	Socialist Alternative Party
Socialist	Socialist
Soc. Lab.	Socialist Labour Party
Soc. Unity	Socialist Unity Network
SOS	SOS! Voters Against Overdevelopment of Northampton
Speaker	The Speaker
SSCUP	Scottish Senior Citizens Unity Party
SSP	Scottish Socialist Party
Tele.	telepathicpartnership.com
TEPK	Tigers Eye the Party for Kids
Third	Third Way
TP	Their Party
UKC	UK Community Issues Party
UKIP	UK Independence Party
UK Path	UK Pathfinders
UKPP	UK Pensioners Party
UUP	Ulster Unionist Party
Veritas	Veritas
Vote Dream	Vote for Yourself Rainbow Dream Ticket
Wessex Reg.	Wessex Regionalist
Work	The People's Choice Making Politicians Work
WP	Workers' Party
WRP	Workers' Revolutionary Party
XPP	Xtraordinary People Party
YPB	Your Party (Banbury)

PARLIAMENTARY CONSTITUENCIES AS AT 5 MAY 2005 GENERAL ELECTION

ENGLAND

ALDERSHOT
E. 78,553 T. 48,141 (61.28%) C. hold
Gerald Howarth, C. 20,572
Adrian Collett, LD 15,238
Howard Linsley, Lab. 9,895
Derek Rumsey, UKIP 1,182
Gary Cowd, Eng. Dem. 701
Howling Lord Hope, Loony 553
C. maj. 5,334 (11.08%)
1.74% swing C. to LD
(2001: C. maj. 6,564 (14.49%))

ALDRIDGE-BROWNHILLS
E. 61,761 T. 39,556 (64.05%) C. hold
Richard Shepherd, C. 18,744
Jon Phillips, Lab. 13,237
Roy Sheward, LD 4,862
William Vaughan, BNP 1,620
Graham Eardley, UKIP 1,093
C. maj. 5,507 (13.92%)
1.98% swing Lab. to C.
(2001: C. maj. 3,768 (9.97%))

ALTRINCHAM & SALE WEST
E. 67,247 T. 44,310 (65.89%) C. hold
Graham Brady, C. 20,569
John Stockton, Lab. 13,410
Ian Chappell, LD 9,595
Gary Peart, UKIP 736
C. maj. 7,159 (16.16%)
4.70% swing Lab. to C.
(2001: C. maj. 2,941 (6.75%))

AMBER VALLEY
E. 75,376 T. 47,391 (62.87%) Lab. hold
Judy Mallaber, Lab. 21,593
Gillian Shaw, C. 16,318
Kate Smith, LD 6,225
Paul Snell, BNP 1,243
Alexander Stevenson, Veritas 1,224
Hugh Price, UKIP 788
Lab. maj. 5,275 (11.13%)
2.55% swing Lab. to C.
(2001: Lab. maj. 7,227 (16.24%))

ARUNDEL & SOUTH DOWNS
E. 72,535 T. 49,690 (68.50%) C. hold
*Nick Herbert, C. 24,752
Derek Deedman, LD 13,443
Sharon Whitlam, Lab. 8,482
Andrew Moffat, UKIP 2,700
Mark Stack, Protest 313
C. maj. 11,309 (22.76%)
3.55% swing C. to LD
(2001: C. maj. 13,704 (29.86%))

ASHFIELD
E. 73,403 T. 42,051 (57.29%) Lab. hold
Rt. Hon. Geoff Hoon, Lab. 20,433
Giles Inglis-Jones, C. 10,220
Wendy Johnson, LD 5,829
Roy Adkins, Ind. 2,292
Kathryn Allsop, Ind. 1,900
Sarah Hemstock, Veritas 1,108
Eddie Grenfell, Ind. 269
Lab. maj. 10,213 (24.29%)
4.72% swing Lab. to C.
(2001: Lab. maj. 13,268 (33.72%))

ASHFORD
E. 79,493 T. 51,685 (65.02%) C. hold
Damian Green, C. 26,651
Valerie Whitaker, Lab. 13,353
Chris Took, LD 8,308
Richard Boden, Green 1,753
Bernard Stroud, UKIP 1,620
C. maj. 13,298 (25.73%)
5.19% swing Lab. to C.
(2001: C. maj. 7,359 (15.35%))

ASHTON UNDER LYNE
E. 72,000 T. 36,967 (51.34%) Lab. hold
David Heyes, Lab. 21,211
Graeme Brown, C. 7,259
Les Jones, LD 5,108
Anthony Jones, BNP 2,051
Dr John Whittaker, UKIP 768
Jack Crossfield, Local 570
Lab. maj. 13,952 (37.74%)
2.82% swing Lab. to C.
(2001: Lab. maj. 15,518 (43.39%))

AYLESBURY
E. 82,428 T. 51,458 (62.43%) C. hold
David Lidington, C. 25,252
Peter Jones, LD 14,187
Mohammed Khaliel, Lab. 9,540
Christopher Adams, UKIP 2,479
C. maj. 11,065 (21.50%)
0.56% swing LD to C.
(2001: C. maj. 10,009 (20.39%))

BANBURY
E. 87,168 T. 56,209 (64.48%) C. hold
Tony Baldry, C. 26,382
Les Sibley, Lab. 15,585
Zoe Patrick, LD 10,076
Alyson Duckmanton, Green 1,590
Dianna Heimann, UKIP 1,241
James Starkey, NF 918
Christopher Rowe, YPB 417
C. maj. 10,797 (19.21%)
4.54% swing Lab. to C.
(2001: C. maj. 5,219 (10.13%))

BARKING
E. 57,658 T. 28,906 (50.13%) Lab. hold
Rt. Hon. Margaret Hodge, Lab. 13,826
Keith Prince, C. 4,943
Richard Barnbrook, BNP 4,916
Toby Wickenden, LD 3,211
Terry Jones, UKIP 803
Laurie Cleeland, Green 618
Demetrious Panton, Ind. 530
Michael Saxby, WRP 59
Lab. maj. 8,883 (30.73%)
3.61% swing Lab. to C.
(2001: Lab. maj. 9,534 (37.94%))

BARNSLEY CENTRAL
E. 60,592 T. 28,615 (47.23%) Lab. hold
Eric Illsley, Lab. 17,478
Miles Crompton, LD 4,746
Peter Morel, C. 3,813
Geoff Broadley, BNP 1,403
Donald Wood, Ind. 1,175
Lab. maj. 12,732 (44.49%)
5.22% swing Lab. to LD
(2001: Lab. maj. 15,130 (54.93%))

BARNSLEY EAST & MEXBOROUGH
E. 66,941 T. 33,026 (49.34%) Lab. hold
Jeff Ennis, Lab. 20,779
Sharron Brook, LD 6,654
Carolyn Abbott, C. 4,853
Terence Robinson, Soc. Lab. 740
Lab. maj. 14,125 (42.77%)
4.44% swing Lab. to LD
(2001: Lab. maj. 16,789 (51.64%))

BARNSLEY WEST & PENISTONE
E. 66,985 T. 36,852 (55.02%) Lab. hold
Michael Clapham, Lab. 20,372
Clive Watkinson, C. 9,058
Alison Brelsford, LD 7,422
Lab. maj. 11,314 (30.70%)
2.52% swing Lab. to C.
(2001: Lab. maj. 12,352 (35.74%))

BARROW & FURNESS
E. 61,883 T. 36,493 (58.97%) Lab. hold
Rt. Hon. John Hutton, Lab. 17,360
Bill Dorman, C. 11,323
Barry Rabone, LD 6,130
Alan Beach, UKIP 758
Timothy Bell, Bridges 409
Brian Greaves, Veritas 306
Helene Young, Ind. 207
Lab. maj. 6,037 (16.54%)
4.40% swing Lab. to C.
(2001: Lab. maj. 9,889 (25.34%))

BASILDON
E. 73,912 T. 43,141 (58.37%)
Lab. (Co-op) hold
Angela Smith, Lab. (Co-op) 18,720
Aaron Powell, C. 15,578
Martin Thompson, LD 4,473
Emma Colgate, BNP 2,055
Alix Blythe, UKIP 1,143
Vikki Copping, Green 662
Kim Gandy, Eng. Dem. 510
Lab. (Co-op) maj. 3,142 (7.28%)
5.82% swing Lab. (Co-op) to C.
(2001: Lab. (Co-op) maj. 7,738 (18.93%))

BASINGSTOKE
E. 76,404 T. 48,123 (62.98%) C. gain
*Maria Miller, C. 19,955
Paul Harvey, Lab. 15,275
Jen Smith, LD 9,952
Peter Effer, UKIP 1,044
Darren Shirley, Green 928
Roger Robertson, BNP 821
Roger Macnair, MC 148
C. maj. 4,680 (9.73%)
3.95% swing Lab. to C.
(C. gain because previous MP defected to DUP in 2004)
(2001: C. maj. 880 (1.83%))

BASSETLAW
E. 69,389 T. 40,342 (58.14%) Lab. hold
John Mann, Lab. 22,847
Jonathan Sheppard, C. 12,010
David Dobbie, LD 5,485
Lab. maj. 10,837 (26.86%)
0.90% swing C. to Lab.
(2001: Lab. maj. 9,748 (25.06%))

BATH
E. 66,824 T. 45,836 (68.59%) LD hold
Don Foster, LD 20,101
Sian Dawson, C. 15,463
Harriet Ajderian, Lab. 6,773
Eric Lucas, Green 2,494
Richard Crowder, UKIP 770
Patrick Cobbe, Ind. 177
Graham Walker, Ind. 58
LD maj. 4,638 (10.12%)
5.63% swing LD to C.
(2001: LD maj. 9,894 (21.37%))

BATLEY & SPEN
E. 62,948 T. 39,208 (62.29%) Lab. hold
Mike Wood, Lab. 17,974
Robert Light, C. 12,186
Neil Bentley, LD 5,731
Colin Auty, BNP 2,668
Clive Lord, Green 649
Lab. maj. 5,788 (14.76%)
0.81% swing C. to Lab.
(2001: Lab. maj. 5,064 (13.14%))

BATTERSEA
E. 69,548 T. 41,049 (59.02%) Lab. hold
Martin Linton, Lab. 16,569
Dominic Schofield, C. 16,406
Norsheen Bhatti, LD 6,006
Hugo Charlton, Green 1,735
Terence Jones, UKIP 333
Lab. maj. 163 (0.40%)
6.67% swing Lab. to C.
(2001: Lab. maj. 5,053 (13.73%))

BEACONSFIELD
E. 68,083 T. 43,523 (63.93%) C. hold
Dominic Grieve, C. 24,126
Peter Chapman, LD 8,873
Alex Sobel, Lab. 8,422
John Fagan, UKIP 2,102
C. maj. 15,253 (35.05%)
1.96% swing LD to C.
(2001: C. maj. 13,065 (31.07%))

BECKENHAM
E. 74,738 T. 48,964 (65.51%) C. hold
Jacqui Lait, C. 22,183
Liam Curran, Lab. 13,782
Jef Foulger, LD 10,862
James Cartwright, UKIP 1,301
Roderick Reed, Ind. 836
C. maj. 8,401 (17.16%)
3.14% swing Lab. to C.
(2001: C. maj. 4,959 (10.88%))

BEDFORD
E. 70,629 T. 42,072 (59.57%) Lab. hold
Patrick Hall, Lab. 17,557
Richard Fuller, C. 14,174
Michael Headley, LD 9,063
Peter Conquest, UKIP 995
John McCready, Ind. 283
Lab. maj. 3,383 (8.04%)
3.57% swing Lab. to C.
(2001: Lab. maj. 6,157 (15.17%))

BEDFORDSHIRE MID
E. 73,768 T. 50,420 (68.35%) C. hold
*Nadine Dorries, C. 23,345
Mark Chapman, LD 11,990
Martin Lindsay, Lab. 11,351
Richard Joselyn, UKIP 1,372
Ben Foley, Green 1,292
Howard Martin, Veritas 769
Saqhib Ali, Ind. 301
C. maj. 11,355 (22.52%)
2.55% swing C. to LD
(2001: C. maj. 8,066 (17.29%))

BEDFORDSHIRE NORTH EAST
E. 72,757 T. 49,505 (68.04%) C. hold
Alistair Burt, C. 24,725
Keith White, Lab. 12,474
Stephen Rutherford, LD 10,320
James May, UKIP 1,986
C. maj. 12,251 (24.75%)
2.9% swing Lab. to C.
(2001: C. maj. 8,577 (18.96%))

BEDFORDSHIRE SOUTH WEST
E. 74,096 T. 45,814 (61.83%) C. hold
Andrew Selous, C. 22,114
Joyce Still, Lab. 13,837
Andy Strange, LD 7,723
Tom Wise, UKIP 1,923
Kenson Gurney, Forum 217
C. maj. 8,277 (18.07%)
8.15% swing Lab. to C.
(2001: C. maj. 776 (1.77%))

BERWICK-UPON-TWEED
E. 56,944 T. 36,090 (63.38%) LD hold
Rt. Hon. Alan Beith, LD 19,052
Mike Elliott, C. 10,420
Glen Reynolds, Lab. 6,618
LD maj. 8,632 (23.92%)
0.31% swing C. to LD
(2001: LD maj. 8,458 (23.30%))

BETHNAL GREEN & BOW
E. 85,950 T. 44,007 (51.20%) Respect gain
†‡George Galloway, Respect 15,801
Oona King, Lab. 14,978
Shahagir Bakth Faruk, C. 6,244
Syed Nurul Islam Dulu, LD 4,928
John Foster, Green 1,950
Ejiro Etefia, AFC 68
Celia Pugh, CL 38
Respect maj. 823 (1.87%)
26.20% swing Lab. to Respect
(2001: Lab. maj. 10,057 (26.14%))

BEVERLEY & HOLDERNESS
E. 77,460 T. 50,202 (64.81%) C. hold
*Graham Stuart, C. 20,434
George McManus, Lab. 17,854
Brian Willie, LD 9,578
Oliver Marriott, UKIP 2,336
C. maj. 2,580 (5.14%)
1.73% swing Lab. to C.
(2001: C. maj. 781 (1.68%))

BEXHILL & BATTLE
E. 69,676 T. 46,834 (67.22%) C. hold
Greg Barker, C. 24,629
Mary Varrall, LD 11,180
Michael Jones, Lab. 8,457
Anthony Smith, UKIP 2,568
C. maj. 13,449 (28.72%)
2.63% swing LD to C.
(2001: C. maj. 10,503 (23.45%))

BEXLEYHEATH & CRAYFORD
E. 65,025 T. 42,580 (65.48%) C. gain
†David Evennett, C. 19,722
Nigel Beard, Lab. 15,171
David Raval, LD 5,144
John Dunford, UKIP 1,302
Jay Lee, BNP 1,241
C. maj. 4,551 (10.69%)
7.17% swing Lab. to C.
(2001: Lab. maj. 1,472 (3.65%))

BILLERICAY
E. 79,537 T. 48,858 (61.43%) C. hold
John Baron, C. 25,487
Anneliese Dodds, Lab. 14,281
Mike Hibbs, LD 6,471
Bryn Robinson, BNP 1,435
Seantino Callaghan, UKIP 1,184
C. maj. 11,206 (22.94%)
5.97% swing Lab. to C.
(2001: C. maj. 5,013 (10.99%))

BIRKENHEAD
E. 57,097 T. 27,786 (48.66%) Lab. hold
Rt. Hon. Frank Field, Lab. 18,059
Stuart Kelly, LD 5,125
Howard Morton, C. 4,602
Lab. maj. 12,934 (46.55%)
5.54% swing Lab. to LD
(2001: Lab. maj. 15,591 (53.82%))

BIRMINGHAM EDGBASTON
E. 64,893 T. 37,631 (57.99%) Lab. hold
Gisela Stuart, Lab. 16,465
Deirdre Alden, C. 14,116
Mike Dixon, LD 5,185
Peter Beck, Green 1,116
Stephen White, UKIP 749
Lab. maj. 2,349 (6.24%)
3.10% swing Lab. to C.
(2001: Lab. maj. 4,698 (12.45%))

BIRMINGHAM ERDINGTON
E. 64,951 T. 31,746 (48.88%) Lab. hold
Sion Simon, Lab. 16,810
Victoria Elvidge, C. 7,235
Jerry Evans, LD 5,027
Sharon Ebanks, BNP 1,512
Rannal Hepburn, UKIP 746
Terry Williams, NF 416
Lab. maj. 9,575 (30.16%)
1.20% swing Lab. to C.
(2001: Lab. maj. 9,962 (32.55%))

BIRMINGHAM HALL GREEN
E. 57,222 T. 34,536 (60.35%) Lab. hold
Stephen McCabe, Lab. 16,304
Eddie Hughes, C. 10,590
Roger Harmer, LD 6,682
David Melhuish, UKIP 960
Lab. maj. 5,714 (16.55%)
1.77% swing Lab. to C.
(2001: Lab. maj. 6,648 (20.09%))

BIRMINGHAM HODGE HILL
E. 53,903 T. 28,417 (52.72%) Lab. hold
Liam Byrne, Lab. 13,822
Nicola Davies, LD 8,373
Deborah Thomas, C. 3,768
Denis Adams, BNP 1,445
Adrian Duffen, UKIP 680
Azmat Begg, Progress 329
Lab. maj. 5,449 (19.18%)
18.29% swing Lab. to LD
(2004 July by-election: Lab. maj. 460 (2.25%))
(2001: Lab. maj. 11,618 (43.90%))

BIRMINGHAM LADYWOOD
E. 70,977 T. 33,246 (46.84%) Lab. hold
Rt. Hon. Clare Short, Lab. 17,262
Ayoub Khan, LD 10,461
Philippa Stroud, C. 3,515
Lynette Nazemi-Afshar, UKIP 2,008
Lab. maj. 6,801 (20.46%)
20.11% swing Lab. to LD
(2001: Lab. maj. 18,143 (57.61%))

BIRMINGHAM NORTHFIELD
E. 54,868 T. 31,056 (56.60%) Lab. hold
Richard Burden, Lab. 15,419
Vicky Ford, C. 8,965
Trevor Sword, LD 4,171
Mark Cattell, BNP 1,278
Gillian Chant, UKIP 641
Richard Rodgers, Good 428
Louise Houldey, Soc. Alt. 120
Francis Sweeney, WRP 34
Lab. maj. 6,454 (20.78%)
2.81% swing Lab. to C.
(2001: Lab. maj. 7,798 (26.40%))

BIRMINGHAM PERRY BARR
E. 70,126 T. 38,911 (55.49%) Lab. hold
Khalid Mahmood, Lab. 18,269
Jon Hunt, LD 10,321
Naweed Khan, C. 6,513
Dr Mohammad Naseem, Respect 2,173
Rajinder Clair, Soc. Lab. 890
Bimla Balu, UKIP 745
Lab. maj. 7,948 (20.43%)
1.61% swing Lab. to LD
(2001: Lab. maj. 8,753 (23.39%))

BIRMINGHAM SELLY OAK
E. 70,162 T. 41,740 (59.49%) Lab. hold
Dr Lynne Jones, Lab. 19,226
Joe Tildesley, C. 10,375
Richard Brighton, LD 9,591
Barney Smith, Green 1,581
Ronan Burnett, UKIP 967
Lab. maj. 8,851 (21.21%)
2.29% swing Lab. to C.
(2001: Lab. maj. 10,339 (25.78%))

BIRMINGHAM SPARKBROOK & SMALL HEATH
E. 73,721 T. 38,192 (51.81%) Lab. hold
Roger Godsiff, Lab. 13,787
Salma Yaqoob, Respect 10,498
Talib Hussain, LD 7,727
Sameer Mirza, C. 3,480
Jennifer Brookes, UKIP 1,342
Ian Jamieson, Green 855
Abdul Chaudhary, Ind. 503
Lab. maj. 3,289 (8.61%)
24.4% swing Lab. to Respect
(2001: Lab. maj. 16,246 (44.33%))

BIRMINGHAM YARDLEY
E. 50,975 T. 29,431 (57.74%) LD gain
*John Hemming, LD 13,648
Jayne Innes, Lab. 10,976
Paul Uppal, C. 2,970
Robert Purcell, BNP 1,523
Mohammed Yaqub, UKIP 314
LD maj. 2,672 (9.08%)
8.83% swing Lab. to LD
(2001: Lab. maj. 2,578 (8.59%))

BISHOP AUCKLAND
E. 67,534 T. 38,128 (56.46%) Lab. hold
*Helen Goodman, Lab. 19,065
Chris Foote-Wood, LD 9,018
Richard Bell, C. 8,736
Margaret Hopson, UKIP 1,309
Lab. maj. 10,047 (26.35%)
8.36% swing Lab. to LD
(2001: Lab. maj. 13,926 (36.12%))

BLABY
E. 75,444 T. 49,388 (65.46%) C. hold
Andrew Robathan, C. 22,487
David Morgan, Lab. 14,614
Jeff Stephenson, LD 9,382
Michael Robinson, BNP 1,704
Delroy Young, UKIP 1,201
C. maj. 7,873 (15.94%)
1.45% swing Lab. to C.
(2001: C. maj. 6,209 (13.03%))

BLACKBURN
E. 73,494 T. 41,805 (56.88%) Lab. hold
Rt. Hon. Jack Straw, Lab. 17,562
Imtiaz Ameen, C. 9,553
Tony Melia, LD 8,608
Nicholas Holt, BNP 2,263
Craig Murray, Ind. 2,082
Dorothy Baxter, UKIP 954
Graham Carter, Green 783
Lab. maj. 8,009 (19.16%)
1.90% swing Lab. to C.
(2001: Lab. maj. 9,249 (22.85%))

BLACKPOOL NORTH & FLEETWOOD
E. 74,975 T. 43,290 (57.74%) Lab. hold
Joan Humble, Lab. 20,620
Gavin Williamson, C. 15,558
Steven Bate, LD 5,533
Roy Hopwood, UKIP 1,579
Lab. maj. 5,062 (11.69%)
0.87% swing Lab. to C.
(2001: Lab. maj. 5,721 (13.44%))

BLACKPOOL SOUTH
E. 73,529 T. 38,342 (52.15%) Lab. hold
Gordon Marsden, Lab. 19,375
Michael Winstanley, C. 11,453
Doreen Holt, LD 5,552
Roy Goodwin, BNP 1,113
John Porter, UKIP 849
Lab. maj. 7,922 (20.66%)
0.32% swing Lab. to C.
(2001: Lab. maj. 8,262 (21.30%))

BLAYDON
E. 62,413 T. 39,053 (62.57%) Lab. hold
*David Anderson, Lab. 20,120
Peter Maughan, LD 14,785
Dorothy Luckhurst, C. 3,129
Norman Endacott, UKIP 1,019
Lab. maj. 5,335 (13.66%)
3.70% swing Lab. to LD
(2001: Lab. maj. 7,809 (21.06%))

BLYTH VALLEY
E. 63,640 T. 35,773 (56.21%) Lab. hold
Ronnie Campbell, Lab. 19,659
Jeffrey Reid, LD 11,132
Michael Windridge, C. 4,982
Lab. maj. 8,527 (23.84%)
5.72% swing Lab. to LD
(2001: Lab. maj. 12,188 (35.28%))

BOGNOR REGIS & LITTLEHAMPTON
E. 65,591 T. 40,747 (62.12%) C. hold
Nick Gibb, C. 18,183
George O'Neill, Lab. 10,361
Simon McDougall, LD 8,927
Adrian Lithgow, UKIP 3,276
C. maj. 7,822 (19.20%)
2.36% swing Lab. to C.
(2001: C. maj. 5,643 (14.48%))

BOLSOVER
E. 67,568 T. 38,699 (57.27%) Lab. hold
Dennis Skinner, Lab. 25,217
Denise Hawksworth, LD 6,780
Hasan Imam, C. 6,702
Lab. maj. 18,437 (47.64%)
4.53% swing Lab. to LD
(2001: Lab. maj. 18,777 (49.06%))

BOLTON NORTH EAST
E. 67,394 T. 36,911 (54.77%) Lab. hold
David Crausby, Lab. 16,874
Paul Brierley, C. 12,771
Adam Killeya, LD 6,044
Kevin Epsom, UKIP 640
Alan Ainscow, Veritas 375
Lynne Lowe, Soc. Lab. 207
Lab. maj. 4,103 (11.12%)
5.25% swing Lab. to C.
(2001: Lab. maj. 8,422 (21.62%))

BOLTON SOUTH EAST
E. 63,697 T. 31,850 (50.00%) Lab. hold
Dr Brian Iddon, Lab. 18,129
Deborah Dunleavy, C. 6,491
Frank Harasiwka, LD 6,047
Florence Bates, UKIP 840
David Jones, Veritas 343
Lab. maj. 11,638 (36.54%)
0.57% swing Lab. to C.
(2001: Lab. maj. 12,871 (37.69%))

BOLTON WEST
E. 63,836 T. 40,543 (63.51%) Lab. hold
Rt. Hon. Ruth Kelly, Lab. 17,239
Philip Allott, C. 15,175
Tim Perkins, LD 7,241
Marjorie Ford, UKIP 524
Michael Ford, Veritas 290
Kate Griggs, XPP 74
Lab. maj. 2,064 (5.09%)
4.15% swing Lab. to C.
(2001: Lab. maj. 5,518 (13.39%))

BOOTLE
E. 53,700 T. 25,622 (47.71%) Lab. hold
Joe Benton, Lab. 19,345
Chris Newby, LD 2,988
Wafik Moustafa, C. 1,580
Paul Nuttall, UKIP 1,054
Peter Glover, Soc. Alt. 655
Lab. maj. 16,357 (63.84%)
2.59% swing Lab. to LD
(2001: Lab. maj. 19,043 (69.01%))

BOSTON & SKEGNESS
E. 71,212 T. 41,869 (58.79%) C. hold
Mark Simmonds, C. 19,329
Paul Kenny, Lab. 13,422
Dr Richard Horsnell, UKIP 4,024
Alan Riley, LD 3,649
Wendy Russell, BNP 1,025
Marcus Petz, Green 420
C. maj. 5,907 (14.11%)
6.42% swing Lab. to C.
(2001: C. maj. 515 (1.28%))

BOSWORTH
E. 71,596 T. 47,499 (66.34%) C. hold
David Tredinnick, C. 20,212
Rupert Herd, Lab. 14,893
James Moore, LD 10,528
Denis Walker, UKIP 1,866
C. maj. 5,319 (11.20%)
3.07% swing Lab. to C.
(2001: C. maj. 2,280 (5.05%))

BOURNEMOUTH EAST
E. 63,426 T. 37,599 (59.28%) C. hold
*Tobias Ellwood, C. 16,925
Andrew Garratt, LD 11,681
David Stokes, Lab. 7,191
Thomas Collier, UKIP 1,802
C. maj. 5,244 (13.95%)
2.18% swing LD to C.
(2001: C. maj. 3,434 (9.59%))

BOURNEMOUTH WEST
E. 63,658 T. 33,924 (53.29%) C. hold
Sir John Butterfill, C. 14,057
Richard Renaut, LD 10,026
Dafydd Williams, Lab. 7,824
Michael Maclaire-Hillier, UKIP 2,017
C. maj. 4,031 (11.88%)
2.90% swing C. to LD
(2001: C. maj. 4,718 (14.02%))

BRACKNELL
E. 80,657 T. 51,141 (63.41%) C. hold
Rt. Hon. Andrew Mackay, C. 25,412
Janet Keene, Lab. 13,376
Lee Glendon, LD 10,128
Vincent Pearson, UKIP 1,818
Dominica Roberts, Ind. 407
C. maj. 12,036 (23.53%)
4.95% swing Lab. to C.
(2001: C. maj. 6,713 (13.64%))

BRADFORD NORTH
E. 64,515 T. 34,397 (53.32%) Lab. hold
Terry Rooney, Lab. 14,622
David Ward, LD 11,111
Teck Khong, C. 5,569
Lynda Cromie, BNP 2,061
Steve Schofield, Green 560
Umit Yildiz, Respect 474
Lab. maj. 3,511 (10.21%)
9.88% swing Lab. to LD
(2001: Lab. maj. 8,969 (25.61%))

BRADFORD SOUTH
E. 67,576 T. 36,605 (54.17%) Lab. hold
Gerry Sutcliffe, Lab. 17,954
Geraldine Carter, C. 8,787
Mike Doyle, LD 5,334
Dr James Lewthwaite, BNP 2,862
Derek Curtis, Green 695
Jason Smith, UKIP 552
Therese Muchewicz, Veritas 421
Lab. maj. 9,167 (25.04%)
1.23% swing Lab. to C.
(2001: Lab. maj. 9,662 (27.50%))

BRADFORD WEST
E. 67,356 T. 36,369 (54.00%) Lab. hold
Marsha Singh, Lab. 14,570
Haroon Rashid, C. 11,544
Mukhtar Ali, LD 6,620
Paul Cromie, BNP 2,525
Parvez Darr, Green 1,110
Lab. maj. 3,026 (8.32%)
1.27% swing Lab. to C.
(2001: Lab. maj. 4,165 (10.85%))

BRAINTREE
E. 80,458 T. 53,055 (65.94%) C. gain
*Brooks Newmark, C. 23,597
Alan Hurst, Lab. 19,704
Peter Turner, LD 7,037
James Abbott, Green 1,308
Roger Lord, UKIP 1,181
Buster Michael Nolan, Ind. 228
C. maj. 3,893 (7.34%)
4.02% swing Lab. to C.
(2001: Lab. maj. 358 (0.71%))

BRENT EAST
E. 56,227 T. 31,068 (55.25%) LD hold
Sarah Teather, LD 14,764
Yasmin Qureshi, Lab. 12,052
Kwasi Kwarteng, C. 3,193
Shahrar Ali, Green 905
Michelle Weininger, Ind. 115
Rainbow George Weiss, Vote Dream 39
LD maj. 2,712 (8.73%)
30.68% swing Lab. to LD
(2003 Sept. by-election: LD maj. 1,118 (5.36%))
(2001: Lab. maj. 13,047 (45.00%))

BRENT NORTH
E. 60,148 T. 35,682 (59.32%) Lab. hold
Barry Gardiner, Lab. 17,420
Bob Blackman, C. 11,779
Havard Hughes, LD 5,672
Babar Ahmad, Progress 685
Rainbow George Weiss, Vote Dream 126
Lab. maj. 5,641 (15.81%)
7.13% swing Lab. to C.
(2001: Lab. maj. 10,205 (30.07%))

BRENT SOUTH
E. 56,508 T. 29,764 (52.67%) Lab. hold
*Dawn Butler, Lab. 17,501
James Allie, LD 6,175
Rishi Saha, C. 4,485
Rowan Langley, Green 957
Shaun Wallace, Ind. 297
Rocky Fernandez, Ind. 288
Rainbow George Weiss, Vote Dream 61
Lab. maj. 11,326 (38.05%)
12.20% swing Lab. to LD
(2001: Lab. maj. 17,380 (60.69%))

BRENTFORD & ISLEWORTH
E. 84,366 T. 46,017 (54.54%) Lab. hold
Ann Keen, Lab. 18,329
Alexander Northcote, C. 13,918
Andrew Dakers, LD 10,477
John Hunt, Green 1,652
Phillip Andrews, Community 1,118
Michael Stoneman, NF 523
Lab. maj. 4,411 (9.59%)
6.80% swing Lab. to C.
(2001: Lab. maj. 10,318 (23.18%))

BRENTWOOD & ONGAR
E. 64,496 T. 44,145 (68.45%) C. hold
Eric Pickles, C. 23,609
Gavin Stollar, LD 11,997
John Adams, Lab. 6,579
Stuart Gulleford, UKIP 1,805
Anthony Appleton, Ind. 155
C. maj. 11,612 (26.30%)
1.91% swing LD to C.
(2001: C. maj. 2,821 (6.48%))

BRIDGWATER
E. 75,790 T. 48,109 (63.48%) C. hold
Ian Liddell-Grainger, C. 21,240
Matthew Burchell, Lab. 12,771
James Main, LD 10,940
Ray Weinstein, UKIP 1,767
Charlie Graham, Green 1,391
C. maj. 8,469 (17.60%)
1.96% swing Lab. to C.
(2001: C. maj. 4,987 (10.42%))

BRIGG & GOOLE
E. 67,364 T. 42,578 (63.21%) Lab. hold
Ian Cawsey, Lab. 19,257
Matthew Bean, C. 16,363
Gary Johnson, LD 5,690
Stephen Martin, UKIP 1,268
Lab. maj. 2,894 (6.80%)
1.43% swing Lab. to C.
(2001: Lab. maj. 3,961 (9.65%))

BRIGHTON KEMPTOWN
E. 65,985 T. 39,719 (60.19%) Lab. hold
Dr Desmond Turner, Lab. 15,858
Judith Symes, C. 13,121
Marina Pepper, LD 6,560
Simon Williams, Green 2,800
Dr James Chamberlain-Webber, UKIP 758
Caroline O'Reilly, PPN-V 172
John McLeod, Soc. Lab. 163
Elaine Cook, Ind. 127
Phil Clarke, Soc. Alt. 113
Gene Dobbs, Ind. 47
Lab. maj. 2,737 (6.89%)
2.83% swing Lab. to C.
(2001: Lab. maj. 4,922 (12.56%))

BRIGHTON PAVILION
E. 68,087 T. 43,578 (64.00%) Lab. (Co-op) hold
David Lepper, Lab. (Co-op) 15,427
Mike Weatherley, C. 10,397
Keith Taylor, Green 9,571
Hazel Thorpe, LD 7,171
Kimberley Crisp-Comotto, UKIP 508
Tony Greenstein, Green Soc. 188
Ian Fyvie, Soc. Lab. 152
Christopher Rooke, Ind. 122
Keith Jago, Ind. 42
Lab. (Co-op) maj. 5,030 (11.55%)
6.06% swing Lab. (Co-op) to C.
(2001: Lab. (Co-op) maj. 9,643 (23.68%))

BRISTOL EAST
E. 68,096 T. 41,720 (61.27%) Lab. hold
*Kerry McCarthy, Lab. 19,152
Philip James, LD 10,531
Julia Manning, C. 8,787
Arjuna Krishna-Das, Green 1,586
Jean Smith, UKIP 1,132
Paulette North, Respect 532
Lab. maj. 8,621 (20.66%)
8.59% swing Lab. to LD
(2001: Lab. maj. 13,392 (33.20%))

BRISTOL NORTH WEST
E. 77,703 T. 47,492 (61.12%) Lab. (Co-op) hold
Dr Doug Naysmith, Lab. (Co-op) 22,192
Alastair Watson, C. 13,230
Bob Hoyle, LD 9,545
Christopher Lees, UKIP 1,132
Michael Blundell, EDP 828
Graeme Jones, Soc. Alt. 565
Lab. (Co-op) maj. 8,962 (18.87%)
2.28% swing Lab. (Co-op) to C.
(2001: Lab. (Co-op) maj. 11,087 (23.74%))

BRISTOL SOUTH
E. 70,835 T. 42,328 (59.76%) Lab. hold
Rt. Hon. Dawn Primarolo, Lab. 20,778
Kay Barnard, LD 9,636
Graham Hill, C. 8,466
Charlie Bolton, Green 2,127
Mark Dent, UKIP 1,321
Lab. maj. 11,142 (26.32%)
7.86% swing Lab. to LD
(2001: Lab. maj. 14,181 (34.61%))

BRISTOL WEST
E. 81,382 T. 57,396 (70.53%) LD gain
*Stephen Williams, LD 21,987
Valerie Davey, Lab. 16,859
David Martin, C. 15,429
Justin Quinnell, Green 2,163
Simon Muir, UKIP 439
Bernard Kennedy, Soc. Lab. 329
Doug Reid, Baths 190
LD maj. 5,128 (8.93%)
8.44% swing Lab. to LD
(2001: Lab. maj. 4,426 (7.95%))

BROMLEY & CHISLEHURST
E. 71,173 T. 46,137 (64.82%) C. hold
Rt. Hon. Eric Forth, C. 23,583
Rachel Reeves, Lab. 10,241
Peter Brooks, LD 9,368
David Hooper, UKIP 1,475
Ann Garrett, Green 1,470
C. maj. 13,342 (28.92%)
4.01% swing Lab. to C.
(2001: C. maj. 9,037 (20.90%))

BROMSGROVE
E. 70,762 T. 47,810 (67.56%) C. hold
Julie Kirkbride, C. 24,387
David Jones, Lab. 14,307
Sue Haswell, LD 7,197
Paul Buckingham, UKIP 1,919
C. maj. 10,080 (21.08%)
1.63% swing Lab. to C.
(2001: C. maj. 8,138 (17.81%))

BROXBOURNE
E. 68,106 T. 40,628 (59.65%) C. hold
*Charles Walker, C. 21,878
Jamie Bolden, Lab. 10,369
Andrew Porrer, LD 4,973
Dr Andrew Emerson, BNP 1,929
Martin Harvey, UKIP 1,479
C. maj. 11,509 (28.33%)
2.28% swing Lab. to C.
(2001: C. maj. 8,993 (23.76%))

BROXTOWE
E. 71,121 T. 48,806 (68.62%) Lab. hold
Dr Nick Palmer, Lab. 20,457
Bob Seely, C. 18,161
David Watts, LD 7,837
Paul Anderson, Green 896
Patricia Wolfe, UKIP 695
Damian Hockney, Veritas 590
Mark Gregory, Ind. 170
Lab. maj. 2,296 (4.70%)
3.64% swing Lab. to C.
(2001: Lab. maj. 5,873 (11.98%))

BUCKINGHAM
E. 70,265 T. 48,307 (68.75%) C. hold
John Bercow, C. 27,748
David Greene, Lab. 9,619
Luke Croydon, LD 9,508
David Williams, UKIP 1,432
C. maj. 18,129 (37.53%)
4.05% swing Lab. to C.
(2001: C. maj. 13,325 (29.43%))

BURNLEY
E. 65,869 T. 38,983 (59.18%) Lab. hold
*Kitty Ussher, Lab. 14,999
Gordon Birtwistle, LD 9,221
Harry Brooks, Burnley 5,786
Yousuf Miah, C. 4,206
Len Starr, BNP 4,003
Dr Jeff Slater, Ind. 392
Robert McDowell, UKIP 376
Lab. maj. 5,778 (14.82%)
9.15% swing Lab. to LD
(2001: Lab. maj. 10,498 (28.46%))

BURTON
E. 78,556 T. 47,882 (60.95%) Lab. hold
Janet Dean, Lab. 19,701
Adrian Pepper, C. 18,280
Sandra Johnson, LD 6,236
Julie Russell, BNP 1,840
Philip Lancaster, UKIP 913
Brian Buxton, Veritas 912
Lab. maj. 1,421 (2.97%)
3.73% swing Lab. to C.
(2001: Lab. maj. 4,849 (10.44%))

BURY NORTH
E. 72,268 T. 44,439 (61.49%) Lab. hold
David Chaytor, Lab. 19,130
David Nuttall, C. 16,204
Wilf Davison, LD 6,514
Stewart Clough, BNP 1,790
Philip Silver, UKIP 476
Ryan O'Neill, Soc. Lab. 172
Ian Upton, Veritas 153
Lab. maj. 2,926 (6.58%)
4.00% swing Lab. to C.
(2001: Lab. maj. 6,532 (14.58%))

BURY SOUTH
E. 66,898 T. 39,154 (58.53%) Lab. hold
Ivan Lewis, Lab. 19,741
Alex Williams, C. 10,829
Victor D'Albert, LD 6,968
Jim Greenhalgh, UKIP 1,059
Yvonne Hossack, Ind. 557
Lab. maj. 8,912 (22.76%)
4.77% swing Lab. to C.
(2001: Lab. maj. 12,772 (32.30%))

BURY ST EDMUNDS
E. 79,658 T. 52,619 (66.06%) C. hold
David Ruffley, C. 24,332
David Monaghan, Lab. 14,402
David Chappell, LD 10,423
Dr John Howlett, UKIP 1,859
Graham Manning, Green 1,603
C. maj. 9,930 (18.87%)
6.95% swing Lab. to C.
(2001: C. maj. 2,503 (4.98%))

CALDER VALLEY
E. 71,325 T. 47,770 (66.98%) Lab. hold
Christine McCafferty, Lab. 18,426
Liz Truss, C. 17,059
Liz Ingleton, LD 9,027
John Gregory, BNP 1,887
Paul Palmer, Green 1,371
Lab. maj. 1,367 (2.86%)
1.83% swing Lab. to C.
(2001: Lab. maj. 3,094 (6.52%))

CAMBERWELL & PECKHAM
E. 55,739 T. 28,991 (52.01%) Lab. hold
Rt. Hon. Harriet Harman, Lab. 18,933
Richard Porter, LD 5,450
Jessica Lee, C. 2,841
Paul Ingram, Green 1,172
Derek Penhallow, UKIP 350
Margaret Sharkey, Soc. Lab. 132
Sanjay Kulkarni, WRP 113
Lab. maj. 13,483 (46.51%)
4.88% swing Lab. to LD
(2001: Lab. maj. 14,123 (56.26%))

CAMBRIDGE
E. 70,154 T. 43,569 (62.10%) LD gain
*David Howarth, LD 19,152
Anne Campbell, Lab. 14,813
Ian Lyon, C. 7,193
Martin Lucas-Smith, Green 1,245
Helene Davies, UKIP 569
Tom Woodcock, Respect 477
Suzon Forscey-Moore, Ind. 60
Graham Wilkinson, Ind. 60
LD maj. 4,339 (9.96%)
14.99% swing Lab. to LD
(2001: Lab. maj. 8,579 (20.03%))

CAMBRIDGESHIRE NORTH EAST
E. 85,079 T. 50,877 (59.80%) C. hold
Malcolm Moss, C. 24,181
Ffinlo Costain, Lab. 15,280
Alan Dean, LD 8,693
Leonard Baynes, UKIP 2,723
C. maj. 8,901 (17.50%)
2.12% swing Lab. to C.
(2001: C. maj. 6,373 (13.26%))

CAMBRIDGESHIRE NORTH WEST
E. 79,694 T. 49,092 (61.60%) C. hold
*Shailesh Vara, C. 22,504
Ayfer Orhan, Lab. 12,671
John Souter, LD 11,232
Robert Brown, UKIP 2,685
C. maj. 9,833 (20.03%)
0.80% swing Lab. to C.
(2001: C. maj. 8,101 (18.43%))

CAMBRIDGESHIRE SOUTH
E. 77,022 T. 52,648 (68.35%) C. hold
Andrew Lansley, C. 23,676
Andrew Dickson, LD 15,675
Sandra Wilson, Lab. 10,189
Robin Page, UKIP 1,556
Simon Saggers, Green 1,552
C. maj. 8,001 (15.20%)
1.09% swing C. to LD
(2001: C. maj. 8,403 (17.38%))

CAMBRIDGESHIRE SOUTH EAST
E. 85,901 T. 56,060 (65.26%) C. hold
James Paice, C. 26,374
Jonathan Chatfield, LD 17,750
Fiona Ross, Lab. 11,936
C. maj. 8,624 (15.38%)
0.97% swing C. to LD
(2001: C. maj. 8,990 (17.33%))

CANNOCK CHASE
E. 75,194 T. 43,155 (57.39%) Lab. hold
Dr Tony Wright, Lab. 22,139
Ian Collard, C. 12,912
Jenny Pinkett, LD 5,934
Roy Jenkins, UKIP 2,170
Lab. maj. 9,227 (21.38%)
2.34% swing Lab. to C.
(2001: Lab. maj. 10,704 (26.07%))

CANTERBURY
E. 72,046 T. 47,587 (66.05%) C. hold
Julian Brazier, C. 21,113
Alex Hilton, Lab. 13,642
Jenny Barnard-Langston, LD 10,059
Geoff Meaden, Green 1,521
John Moore, UKIP 926
Rocky van de Benderskum, LCA 326
C. maj. 7,471 (15.70%)
5.56% swing Lab. to C.
(2001: C. maj. 2,069 (4.58%))

CARLISLE
E. 59,508 T. 35,394 (59.48%) Lab. hold
Eric Martlew, Lab. 17,019
Mike Mitchelson, C. 11,324
Steven Tweedie, LD 5,916
Steven Cochrane, UKIP 792
Lezley Gibson, LCA 343
Lab. maj. 5,695 (16.09%)
0.12% swing Lab. to C.
(2001: Lab. maj. 5,702 (16.33%))

CARSHALTON & WALLINGTON
E. 67,844 T. 43,061 (63.47%) LD hold
Tom Brake, LD 17,357
Ken Andrew, C. 16,289
Andrew Theobald, Lab. 7,396
Francis Day, UKIP 1,111
Bob Steel, Green 908
LD maj. 1,068 (2.48%)
4.36% swing LD to C.
(2001: LD maj. 4,547 (11.20%))

CASTLE POINT
E. 69,480 T. 45,802 (65.92%) C. hold
Dr Robert Spink, C. 22,118
Luke Akehurst, Lab. 13,917
James Sandbach, LD 4,719
Neil Hamper, UKIP 3,431
Irene Willis, Green 1,617
C. maj. 8,201 (17.91%)
7.71% swing Lab. to C.
(2001: C. maj. 985 (2.48%))

CHARNWOOD
E. 76,274 T. 50,616 (66.36%) C. hold
Rt. Hon. Stephen Dorrell, C. 23,571
Richard Robinson, Lab. 14,762
Sue King, LD 9,057
Andrew Holders, BNP 1,737
Jamie Bye, UKIP 1,489
C. maj. 8,809 (17.40%)
0.68% swing Lab. to C.
(2001: C. maj. 7,739 (16.03%))

CHATHAM & AYLESFORD
E. 70,515 T. 42,080 (59.68%) Lab. hold
Jonathan Shaw, Lab. 18,387
Anne Jobson, C. 16,055
Debra Enever, LD 5,744
Jeffrey King, UKIP 1,226
Michael Russell, Eng. Dem. 668
Lab. maj. 2,332 (5.54%)
2.69% swing Lab. to C.
(2001: Lab. maj. 4,340 (10.92%))

CHEADLE
E. 68,123 T. 47,437 (69.63%) LD hold
Patsy Calton, LD 23,189
Stephen Day, C. 19,169
Martin Miller, Lab. 4,169
Vincent Cavanagh, UKIP 489
Richard Chadfield, BNP 421
LD maj. 4,020 (8.47%)
4.20% swing C. to LD
(2001: LD maj. 33 (0.08%))

CHELMSFORD WEST
E. 82,489 T. 51,052 (61.89%) C. hold
Simon Burns, C. 22,946
Stephen Robinson, LD 13,326
Russell Kennedy, Lab. 13,236
Kenneth Wedon, UKIP 1,544
C. maj. 9,620 (18.84%)
0.18% swing C. to LD
(2001: C. maj. 6,261 (13.01%))

CHELTENHAM
E. 71,541 T. 43,621 (60.97%) LD hold
*Martin Horwood, LD 18,122
Dr Vanessa Gearson, C. 15,819
Christopher Evans, Lab. 4,988
Dr Robert Hodges, Ind. 2,651
Keith Bessant, Green 908
Niall Warry, UKIP 608
Dancing Ken Hanks, Loony 525
LD maj. 2,303 (5.28%)
3.64% swing LD to C.
(2001: LD maj. 5,255 (12.56%))

CHESHAM & AMERSHAM
E. 69,217 T. 47,097 (68.04%) C. hold
Cheryl Gillan, C. 25,619
John Ford, LD 11,821
Rupa Huq, Lab. 6,610
Nick Wilkins, Green 1,656
David Samuel-Camps, UKIP 1,391
C. maj. 13,798 (29.30%)
1.53% swing LD to C.
(2001: C. maj. 11,882 (26.24%))

CHESTER, CITY OF
E. 69,785 T. 44,903 (64.34%) Lab. hold
Christine Russell, Lab. 17,458
Paul Offer, C. 16,543
Mia Jones, LD 9,818
Allan Weddell, UKIP 776
Ed Abrams, Eng. Dem. 308
Lab. maj. 915 (2.04%)
6.66% swing Lab. to C.
(2001: Lab. maj. 6,894 (15.36%))

CHESTERFIELD
E. 74,007 T. 44,121 (59.62%) LD hold
Paul Holmes, LD 20,875
Simon Rich, Lab. 17,830
Mark Kreling, C. 3,605
Christopher Brady, UKIP 997
Ian Jerram, Eng. Dem. 814
LD maj. 3,045 (6.90%)
0.54% swing Lab. to LD
(2001: LD maj. 2,586 (5.82%))

CHICHESTER
E. 78,645 T. 52,401 (66.63%) C. hold
Andrew Tyrie, C. 25,302
Alan Hilliar, LD 14,442
Jonathan Austin, Lab. 9,632
Douglas Denny, UKIP 3,025
C. maj. 10,860 (20.72%)
1.09% swing C. to LD
(2001: C. maj. 11,355 (22.93%))

CHINGFORD & WOODFORD GREEN
E. 61,386 T. 38,648 (62.96%) C. hold
Rt. Hon. Iain Duncan Smith, C. 20,555
Simon Wright, Lab. 9,914
John Beanse, LD 6,832
Michael McGough, UKIP 1,078
Barry White, Ind. 269
C. maj. 10,641 (27.53%)
6.35% swing Lab. to C.
(2001: C. maj. 5,487 (14.84%))

CHIPPING BARNET
E. 66,143 T. 42,381 (64.07%) C. hold
*Theresa Villiers, C. 19,744
Pauline Coakley-Webb, Lab. 13,784
Sean Hooker, LD 6,671
Audrey Poppy, Green 1,199
Victor Kaye, UKIP 924
Rainbow George Weiss, Vote Dream 59
C. maj. 5,960 (14.06%)
3.85% swing Lab. to C.
(2001: C. maj. 2,701 (6.36%))

CHORLEY
E. 78,838 T. 49,569 (62.87%) Lab. hold
Lindsay Hoyle, Lab. 25,131
Simon Mallett, C. 17,506
Alexander Wilson-Fletcher, LD 6,932
Lab. maj. 7,625 (15.38%)
1.11% swing Lab. to C.
(2001: Lab. maj. 8,444 (17.61%))

CHRISTCHURCH
E. 74,109 T. 51,565 (69.58%) C. hold
Christopher Chope, C. 28,208
Leslie Coman, LD 12,649
Jim King, Lab. 8,051
David Hughes, UKIP 2,657
C. maj. 15,559 (30.17%)
1.42% swing LD to C.
(2001: C. maj. 13,544 (27.32%))

CITIES OF LONDON & WESTMINSTER
E. 72,577 T. 36,487 (50.27%) C. hold
Mark Field, C. 17,260
Hywel Lloyd, Lab. 9,165
Marie-Louise Rossi, LD 7,306
Tristan Smith, Green 1,544
Colin Merton, UKIP 399
Brian Haw, Ind. 298
Jill McLachlan, CPA 246
David Harris, Veritas 218
Cass Jean-Claude Cass-Horne, Ind. 51
C. maj. 8,095 (22.19%)
4.47% swing Lab. to C.
(2001: C. maj. 4,499 (13.24%))

CLEETHORPES
E. 70,746 T. 43,589 (61.61%) Lab. hold
Shona McIsaac, Lab. 18,889
Martin Vickers, C. 16,247
Geoff Lowis, LD 6,437
Bill Hardie, UKIP 2,016
Lab. maj. 2,642 (6.06%)
3.59% swing Lab. to C.
(2001: Lab. maj. 5,620 (13.25%))

COLCHESTER
E. 79,010 T. 44,899 (56.83%) LD hold
Bob Russell, LD 21,145
Kevin Bentley, C. 14,868
Laura Bruni, Lab. 8,886
LD maj. 6,277 (13.98%)
0.64% swing C. to LD
(2001: LD maj. 5,553 (12.70%))

COLNE VALLEY
E. 74,121 T. 48,920 (66.00%) Lab. hold
Kali Mountford, Lab. 17,536
Maggie Throup, C. 16,035
Elisabeth Wilson, LD 11,822
Barry Fowler, BNP 1,430
Lesley Hedges, Green 1,295
Helen Martinek, Veritas 543
Ian Mumford, Loony 259
Lab. maj. 1,501 (3.07%)
3.40% swing Lab. to C.
(2001: Lab. maj. 4,639 (9.87%))

CONGLETON
E. 72,770 T. 46,682 (64.15%) C. hold
Lady Ann Winterton, C. 21,189
Nicholas Milton, Lab. 12,943
Eleanor Key, LD 12,550
C. maj. 8,246 (17.66%)
0.92% swing Lab. to C.
(2001: C. maj. 7,134 (15.82%))

COPELAND
E. 54,206 T. 33,757 (62.28%) Lab. hold
*Jamie Reed, Lab. 17,033
Chris Whiteside, C. 10,713
Frank Hollowell, LD 3,880
Edward Caley-Knowles, UKIP 735
Brian Earley, Ind. 734
Alan Mossop, Eng. Dem. 662
Lab. maj. 6,320 (18.72%)
2.22% swing C. to Lab.
(2001: Lab. maj. 4,964 (14.28%))

CORBY
E. 73,000 T. 48,527 (66.48%) Lab. (Co-op) hold
Phil Hope, Lab. (Co-op) 20,913
Andrew Griffith, C. 19,396
David Radcliffe, LD 6,184
Ian Gillman, UKIP 1,278
Steve Carey, Soc. Lab. 499
John Morris, Ind. 257
Lab. (Co-op) maj. 1,517 (3.13%)
4.47% swing Lab. (Co-op) to C.
(2001: Lab. (Co-op) maj. 5,700 (12.07%))

CORNWALL NORTH
E. 86,841 T. 55,982 (64.46%) LD hold
*Dan Rogerson, LD 23,842
Mark Formosa, C. 20,766
David Acton, Lab. 6,636
David Campbell-Bannerman, UKIP 3,063
Dick Cole, Meb. Ker. 1,351
Alan Eastwood, Veritas 324
LD maj. 3,076 (5.49%)
6.36% swing LD to C.
(2001: LD maj. 9,832 (18.21%))

CORNWALL SOUTH EAST
E. 80,704 T. 53,455 (66.24%) LD hold
Colin Breed, LD 24,986
Ashley Gray, C. 18,479
Colin Binley, Lab. 6,069
David Lucas, UKIP 2,693
Graham Sandercock, Meb. Ker. 769
Anne Assheton-Salton, Veritas 459
LD maj. 6,507 (12.17%)
0.89% swing C. to LD
(2001: LD maj. 5,375 (10.39%))

COTSWOLD
E. 71,039 T. 47,351 (66.65%) C. hold
Geoffrey Clifton-Brown, C. 23,326
Philip Beckerlegge, LD 13,638
Mark Dempsey, Lab. 8,457
Richard Buckley, UKIP 1,538
James Derieg, Ind. 392
C. maj. 9,688 (20.46%)
2.80% swing C. to LD
(2001: C. maj. 11,983 (26.06%))

COVENTRY NORTH EAST
E. 70,225 T. 37,195 (52.97%) Lab. hold
Rt. Hon. Robert Ainsworth, Lab. 21,178
Jaswant Singh Birdi, C. 6,956
Russell Field, LD 6,123
Dave Nellist, Soc. Alt. 1,874
Paul Sootheran, UKIP 1,064
Lab. maj. 14,222 (38.24%)
2.02% swing Lab. to C.
(2001: Lab. maj. 15,751 (42.27%))

COVENTRY NORTH WEST
E. 73,180 T. 43,438 (59.36%) Lab. hold
Geoffrey Robinson, Lab. 20,942
Brian Connell, C. 11,627
Iona Anderson, LD 7,932
David Clarke, BNP 1,556
Sandra List, UKIP 766
Nicola Downes, Soc. Alt. 615
Lab. maj. 9,315 (21.44%)
2.06% swing Lab. to C.
(2001: Lab. maj. 10,874 (25.56%))

COVENTRY SOUTH
E. 68,884 T. 40,685 (59.06%) Lab. hold
Jim Cunningham, Lab. 18,649
Heather Wheeler, C. 12,394
Vincent McKee, LD 7,228
Rob Windsor, Soc. Alt. 1,097
William Brown, UKIP 829
Irene Rogers, Ind. 344
James Rooney, FF 144
Lab. maj. 6,255 (15.37%)
2.64% swing Lab. to C.
(2001: Lab. maj. 8,279 (20.65%))

CRAWLEY
E. 71,911 T. 41,973 (58.37%) Lab. hold
Laura Moffatt, Lab. 16,411
Henry Smith, C. 16,374
Rupert Sheard, LD 6,503
Richard Trower, BNP 1,277
Ronald Walters, UKIP 935
Robin Burnham, Dem. Soc. All. 263
Arshad Khan, JP 210
Lab. maj. 37 (0.09%)
8.52% swing Lab. to C.
(2001: Lab. maj. 6,770 (17.13%))

CREWE & NANTWICH
E. 72,472 T. 43,485 (60.00%) Lab. hold
Gwyneth Dunwoody, Lab. 21,240
Eveleigh Moore-Dutton, C. 14,162
Paul Roberts, LD 8,083
Lab. maj. 7,078 (16.28%)
3.78% swing Lab. to C.
(2001: Lab. maj. 9,906 (23.84%))

CROSBY
E. 54,255 T. 36,194 (66.71%) Lab. hold
Claire Curtis-Thomas, Lab. 17,463
Debi Jones, C. 11,623
Jim Murray, LD 6,298
Dr John Whittaker, UKIP 454
Geoffrey Bottoms, Comm. Brit. 199
David Braid, Clause 28 157
Lab. maj. 5,840 (16.14%)
3.26% swing Lab. to C.
(2001: Lab. maj. 8,353 (22.66%))

CROYDON CENTRAL
E. 80,825 T. 48,957 (60.57%) C. gain
*Andrew Pelling, C. 19,974
Geraint Davies, Lab. 19,899
Jeremy Hargreaves, LD 6,384
Ian Edwards, UKIP 1,066
Bernice Golberg, Green 1,036
Marianne Bowness, Veritas 304
John Cartwright, Loony 193
Janet Stears, Work 101
C. maj. 75 (0.15%)
4.42% swing Lab. to C.
(2001: Lab. maj. 3,984 (8.69%))

CROYDON NORTH
E. 83,796 T. 43,847 (52.33%) Lab. hold
Malcolm Wicks, Lab. 23,555
Tariq Ahmad, C. 9,667
Adrian Gee-Turner, LD 7,560
Shasha Khan, Green 1,248
Henry Pearce, UKIP 770
Peter Gibson, Croydon 394
Winston McKenzie, Veritas 324
Farhan Rasheed, Ind. 197
Michelle Chambers, Work 132
Lab. maj. 13,888 (31.67%)
4.29% swing Lab. to C.
(2001: Lab. maj. 16,858 (40.25%))

CROYDON SOUTH
E. 76,872 T. 48,897 (63.61%) C. hold
Richard Ottaway, C. 25,320
Paul Smith, Lab. 11,792
Sandra Lawman, LD 10,049
James Feisenberger, UKIP 1,054
Graham Dare, Veritas 497
Mark Samuel, Work 185
C. maj. 13,528 (27.67%)
4.18% swing Lab. to C.
(2001: C. maj. 8,697 (19.30%))

DAGENHAM
E. 60,141 T. 30,841 (51.28%) Lab. hold
Jonathan Cruddas, Lab. 15,446
Michael White, C. 7,841
James Kempton, LD 3,106
Lawrence Rustem, BNP 2,870
Gerard Batten, UKIP 1,578
Lab. maj. 7,605 (24.66%)
3.43% swing Lab. to C.
(2001: Lab. maj. 8,693 (31.52%))

DARLINGTON
E. 65,281 T. 39,388 (60.34%) Lab. hold
Rt. Hon. Alan Milburn, Lab. 20,643
Anthony Frieze, C. 10,239
Robert Adamson, LD 7,269
John Hoodless, UKIP 730
Dai Davies, Veritas 507
Lab. maj. 10,404 (26.41%)
0.19% swing C. to Lab.
(2001: Lab. maj. 9,529 (23.38%))

DARTFORD
E. 74,028 T. 46,779 (63.19%) Lab. hold
Dr Howard Stoate, Lab. 19,909
Gareth Johnson, C. 19,203
Peter Bucklitsch, LD 5,036
Mark Croucher, UKIP 1,407
Michael Tibby, NEP 1,224
Lab. maj. 706 (1.51%)
2.94% swing Lab. to C.
(2001: Lab. maj. 3,306 (7.39%))

DAVENTRY
E. 88,758 T. 60,439 (68.09%) C. hold
Tim Boswell, C. 31,206
Andrew Hammond, Lab. 16,520
Hannah Saul, LD 9,964
Barry Mahoney, UKIP 1,927
Barrie Wilkins, Veritas 822
C. maj. 14,686 (24.30%)
3.64% swing Lab. to C.
(2001: C. maj. 9,649 (17.02%))

DENTON & REDDISH
E. 68,267 T. 35,442 (51.92%) Lab. hold
*Andrew Gwynne, Lab. 20,340
Alex Story, C. 6,842
Allison Seabourne, LD 5,814
John Edgar, BNP 1,326
Gerald Price, UKIP 1,120
Lab. maj. 13,498 (38.08%)
3.77% swing Lab. to C.
(2001: Lab. maj. 15,330 (45.63%))

DERBY NORTH
E. 68,173 T. 43,818 (64.27%) Lab. hold
Bob Laxton, Lab. 19,272
Richard Aitken-Davies, C. 15,515
Jeremy Beckett, LD 7,209
Martin Bardoe, Veritas 958
Michelle Medgyesy, UKIP 864
Lab. maj. 3,757 (8.57%)
3.64% swing Lab. to C.
(2001: Lab. maj. 6,982 (15.85%))

DERBY SOUTH
E. 70,397 T. 43,373 (61.61%) Lab. hold
Rt. Hon. Margaret Beckett, Lab. 19,683
Lucy Care, LD 14,026
David Brackenbury, C. 8,211
David Black, UKIP 845
Frank Leeming, Veritas 608
Lab. maj. 5,657 (13.04%)
12.05% swing Lab. to LD
(2001: Lab. maj. 13,855 (32.16%))

DERBYSHIRE NORTH EAST
E. 70,981 T. 43,434 (61.19%) Lab. hold
*Natascha Engel, Lab. 21,416
Dominic Johnson, C. 11,351
Tom Snowdon, LD 8,812
Kenneth Perkins, UKIP 1,855
Lab. maj. 10,065 (23.17%)
2.96% swing Lab. to C.
(2001: Lab. maj. 12,258 (29.10%))

DERBYSHIRE SOUTH
E. 85,049 T. 55,820 (65.63%) Lab. hold
Mark Todd, Lab. 24,823
Simon Spencer, C. 20,328
Deborah Newton-Cook, LD 7,600
David Joines, BNP 1,797
Edward Spalton, Veritas 1,272
Lab. maj. 4,495 (8.05%)
3.53% swing Lab. to C.
(2001: Lab. maj. 7,851 (15.11%))

DERBYSHIRE WEST
E. 73,865 T. 51,143 (69.24%) C. hold
Patrick McLoughlin, C. 24,378
David Menon, Lab. 13,625
Ray Dring, LD 11,408
Michael Cruddas, UKIP 1,322
Nick Delves, Loony 405
Martin Kyslun, Ind. 5
C. maj. 10,753 (21.03%)
3.23% swing Lab. to C.
(2001: C. maj. 7,370 (14.57%))

DEVIZES
E. 86,168 T. 56,146 (65.16%) C. hold
Rt. Hon. Michael Ancram, C. 27,253
Fiona Hornby, LD 14,059
Sharon Charity, Lab. 12,519
Alan Wood, UKIP 2,315
C. maj. 13,194 (23.50%)
0.84% swing C. to LD
(2001: C. maj. 11,896 (22.34%))

DEVON EAST
E. 71,000 T. 49,247 (69.36%) C. hold
Hugo Swire, C. 23,075
Tim Dumper, LD 15,139
James Court, Lab. 7,598
Colin McNamee, UKIP 3,035
Christopher Way, Ind. 400
C. maj. 7,936 (16.11%)
0.51% swing C. to LD
(2001: C. maj. 8,195 (17.13%))

DEVON NORTH
E. 76,203 T. 51,930 (68.15%) LD hold
Nick Harvey, LD 23,840
Orlando Fraser, C. 18,868
Mark Cann, Lab. 4,656
John Browne, UKIP 2,740
Richard Knight, Green 1,826
LD maj. 4,972 (9.57%)
1.76% swing C. to LD
(2001: LD maj. 2,984 (6.06%))

DEVON SOUTH WEST
E. 71,307 T. 48,885 (68.56%) C. hold
Gary Streeter, C. 21,906
Judy Evans, LD 11,765
Christopher Mavin, Lab. 11,545
Hugh Williams, UKIP 3,669
C. maj. 10,141 (20.74%)
3.86% swing C. to LD
(2001: C. maj. 7,144 (15.23%))

DEVON WEST & TORRIDGE
E. 83,489 T. 58,584 (70.17%) C. gain
*Geoffrey Cox, C. 25,013
David Walter, LD 21,777
Rebecca Richards, Lab. 6,001
Matthew Jackson, UKIP 3,790
Peter Christie, Green 2,003
C. maj. 3,236 (5.52%)
3.83% swing LD to C.
(2001: LD maj. 1,194 (2.14%))

DEWSBURY
E. 62,243 T. 38,595 (62.01%) Lab. hold
*Shahid Malik, Lab. 15,807
Sayeeda Warsi, C. 11,192
Kingsley Hill, LD 5,624
David Exley, BNP 5,066
Brenda Smithson, Green 593
Alan Girvan, Ind. 313
Lab. maj. 4,615 (11.96%)
4.18% swing Lab. to C.
(2001: Lab. maj. 7,449 (20.32%))

DON VALLEY
E. 66,993 T. 36,864 (55.03%) Lab. hold
Caroline Flint, Lab. 19,418
Adam Duguid, C. 10,820
Stewart Arnold, LD 6,626
Lab. maj. 8,598 (23.32%)
1.33% swing Lab. to C.
(2001: Lab. maj. 9,520 (25.99%))

DONCASTER CENTRAL
E. 65,731 T. 34,351 (52.26%) Lab. hold
Rosie Winterton, Lab. 17,617
Patrick Wilson, LD 7,815
Stefan Kerner, C. 6,489
John Wilkinson, BNP 1,239
Alan Simmons, UKIP 1,191
Lab. maj. 9,802 (28.53%)
8.80% swing Lab. to LD
(2001: Lab. maj. 11,999 (35.39%))

DONCASTER NORTH
E. 61,741 T. 31,578 (51.15%) Lab. hold
*Ed Miliband, Lab. 17,531
Martin Drake, C. 4,875
Doug Pickett, LD 3,800
Martin Williams, CG 2,365
Lee Hagan, BNP 1,506
Robert Nixon, UKIP 940
Michael Cassidy, Eng. Dem. 561
Lab. maj. 12,656 (40.08%)
4.17% swing Lab. to C.
(2001: Lab. maj. 15,187 (48.42%))

DORSET MID & POOLE NORTH
E. 65,924 T. 45,159 (68.50%) LD hold
Annette Brooke, LD 22,000
Simon Hayes, C. 16,518
Philip Murray, Lab. 5,221
Avril King, UKIP 1,420
LD maj. 5,482 (12.14%)
5.63% swing C. to LD
(2001: LD maj. 384 (0.88%))

DORSET NORTH
E. 74,286 T. 52,815 (71.10%) C. hold
Robert Walter, C. 23,714
Emily Gasson, LD 21,470
John Yarwood, Lab. 4,596
Richard Frampton Hobbs, UKIP 1,918
Ralph Arliss, Green 1,117
C. maj. 2,244 (4.25%)
1.85% swing C. to LD
(2001: C. maj. 3,797 (7.94%))

DORSET SOUTH
E. 70,668 T. 48,584 (68.75%) Lab. hold
Jim Knight, Lab. 20,231
Ed Matts, C. 18,419
Graham Oakes, LD 7,647
Hugh Chalker, UKIP 1,571
Vic Hamilton, LCA 282
Bernard Parkes, Respect 219
Andrew Kirkwood, PRTYP 107
Colin Bex, Wessex Reg. 83
David Marchesi, Soc. Lab. 25
Lab. maj. 1,812 (3.73%)
1.70% swing C. to Lab.
(2001: Lab. maj. 153 (0.34%))

DORSET WEST
E. 69,764 T. 53,225 (76.29%) C. hold
Rt. Hon. Oliver Letwin, C. 24,763
Justine McGuinness, LD 22,302
Dave Roberts, Lab. 4,124
Linda Guest, UKIP 1,084
Susan Greene, Green 952
C. maj. 2,461 (4.62%)
0.89% swing LD to C.
(2001: C. maj. 1,414 (2.85%))

DOVER
E. 70,884 T. 47,884 (67.55%) Lab. hold
Gwyn Prosser, Lab. 21,680
Paul Watkins, C. 16,739
Antony Hook, LD 7,607
Mike Wiltshire, UKIP 1,252
Vic Matcham, Ind. 606
Lab. maj. 4,941 (10.32%)
0.62% swing Lab. to C.
(2001: Lab. maj. 5,199 (11.56%))

DUDLEY NORTH
E. 68,766 T. 41,408 (60.22%) Lab. hold
*Ian Austin, Lab. 18,306
Ian Hillas, C. 12,874
Gerry Lewis, LD 4,257
Simon Darby, BNP 4,022
Malcolm Davis, UKIP 1,949
Lab. maj. 5,432 (13.12%)
2.26% swing Lab. to C.
(2001: Lab. maj. 6,800 (17.63%))

DUDLEY SOUTH
E. 65,228 T. 39,276 (60.21%) Lab. hold
Ian Pearson, Lab. 17,800
Marco Longhi, C. 13,556
Jonathan Bramall, LD 4,808
John Salvage, BNP 1,841
Andrew Benion, UKIP 1,271
Lab. maj. 4,244 (10.81%)
3.98% swing Lab. to C.
(2001: Lab. maj. 6,817 (18.76%))

DULWICH & WEST NORWOOD
E. 72,232 T. 41,989 (58.13%) Lab. hold
Rt. Hon. Tessa Jowell, Lab. 19,059
Jonathan Mitchell, LD 10,252
Kim Humphreys, C. 9,200
Jenny Jones, Green 2,741
Ralph Atkinson, UKIP 290
David Heather, Veritas 241
Amanda Rose, Soc. Lab. 149
Judy Weleminsky, Fit 57
Lab. maj. 8,807 (20.97%)
9.37% swing Lab. to LD
(2001: Lab. maj. 12,310 (32.19%))

DURHAM NORTH
E. 67,506 T. 37,341 (55.32%) Lab. hold
Kevan Jones, Lab. 23,932
Philip Latham, LD 7,151
Mark Watson, C. 6,258
Lab. maj. 16,781 (44.94%)
4.12% swing Lab. to LD
(2001: Lab. maj. 18,683 (48.44%))

DURHAM NORTH WEST
E. 68,130 T. 39,509 (57.99%) Lab. hold
Rt. Hon. Hilary Armstrong, Lab. 21,312
Alan Ord, LD 7,869
Jamie Devlin, C. 6,463
Watts Stelling, Ind. 3,865
Lab. maj. 13,443 (34.03%)
6.80% swing Lab. to LD
(2001: Lab. maj. 16,333 (41.64%))

DURHAM, CITY OF
E. 71,441 T. 44,364 (62.10%) Lab. hold
*Dr Roberta Blackman-Woods, Lab. 20,928
Carol Woods, LD 17,654
Ben Rogers, C. 4,179
Anthony Martin, Veritas 1,603
Lab. maj. 3,274 (7.38%)
12.51% swing Lab. to LD
(2001: Lab. maj. 13,441 (32.40%))

EALING ACTON & SHEPHERD'S BUSH
E. 70,454 T. 39,623 (56.24%) Lab. hold
*Andrew Slaughter, Lab. 16,579
Jonathan Gough, C. 11,059
Gary Malcolm, LD 9,986
Geoff Burgess, Green 1,999
Lab. maj. 5,520 (13.93%)
7.54% swing Lab. to C.
(2001: Lab. maj. 10,789 (29.00%))

EALING NORTH
E. 78,298 T. 46,507 (59.40%) Lab. hold
Stephen Pound, Lab. 20,956
Roger Curtis, C. 13,897
Francesco Fruzza, LD 9,148
Alan Outten, Green 1,319
Robin Lambert, UKIP 692
David Malindine, Veritas 495
Lab. maj. 7,059 (15.18%)
5.58% swing Lab. to C.
(2001: Lab. maj. 11,837 (26.33%))

EALING SOUTHALL
E. 83,738 T. 47,045 (56.18%) Lab. hold
Piara Khabra, Lab. 22,937
Nigel Bakhai, LD 11,497
Mark Nicholson, C. 10,147
Sarah Edwards, Green 2,175
Malkiat Bilku, WRP 289
Lab. maj. 11,440 (24.32%)
6.59% swing Lab. to LD
(2001: Lab. maj. 13,683 (29.22%))

EASINGTON
E. 61,084 T. 31,855 (52.15%) Lab. hold
John Cummings, Lab. 22,733
Christopher Ord, LD 4,097
Lucille Nicholson, C. 3,400
Ian McDonald, BNP 1,042
Dave Robinson, Soc. Lab. 583
Lab. maj. 18,636 (58.50%)
4.00% swing Lab. to LD
(2001: Lab. maj. 21,949 (66.49%))

EAST HAM
E. 78,104 T. 39,569 (50.66%) Lab. hold
Stephen Timms, Lab. 21,326
Abdul Khaliq Mian, Respect 8,171
Sarah Macken, C. 5,196
Ann Haigh, LD 4,296
David Bamber, CPA 580
Lab. maj. 13,155 (33.25%)
19.95% swing Lab. to Respect
(2001: Lab. maj. 21,032 (56.42%))

EASTBOURNE
E. 74,628 T. 48,392 (64.84%) C. hold
Nigel Waterson, C. 21,033
Stephen Lloyd, LD 19,909
Andrew Jones, Lab. 5,268
Andrew Meggs, UKIP 1,233
Clive Gross, Green 949
C. maj. 1,124 (2.32%)
1.24% swing C. to LD
(2001: C. maj. 2,154 (4.81%))

EASTLEIGH
E. 76,844 T. 49,771 (64.77%) LD hold
*Christopher Huhne, LD 19,216
Conor Burns, C. 18,648
Chris Watt, Lab. 10,238
Christopher Murphy, UKIP 1,669
LD maj. 568 (1.14%)
2.64% swing LD to C.
(2001: LD maj. 3,058 (6.43%))

ECCLES
E. 69,006 T. 34,632 (50.19%) Lab. hold
Ian Stewart, Lab. 19,702
Thelma Matuk, C. 6,816
Jane Brophy, LD 6,429
Peter Reeve, UKIP 1,685
Lab. maj. 12,886 (37.21%)
3.29% swing Lab. to C.
(2001: Lab. maj. 14,528 (43.78%))

EDDISBURY
E. 72,249 T. 45,674 (63.22%) C. hold
Stephen O'Brien, C. 21,181
Mark Green, Lab. 14,986
Joanne Crotty, LD 8,182
Steve Roxborough, UKIP 1,325
C. maj. 6,195 (13.56%)
1.64% swing Lab. to C.
(2001: C. maj. 4,568 (10.29%))

EDMONTON
E. 58,764 T. 34,703 (59.05%) Lab. (Co-op) hold
Andy Love, Lab. (Co-op) 18,456
Lionel Zetter, C. 10,381
Dr Iarla Kilbane-Dawe, LD 4,162
Nina Armstrong, Green 889
Gwyneth Rolph, UKIP 815
Lab. (Co-op) maj. 8,075 (23.27%)
2.42% swing Lab. (Co-op) to C.
(2001: Lab. (Co-op) maj. 9,772 (28.10%))

ELLESMERE PORT & NESTON
E. 68,249 T. 42,069 (61.64%) Lab. hold
Andrew Miller, Lab. 20,371
Myles Hogg, C. 13,885
Steve Cooke, LD 6,607
Henry Crocker, UKIP 1,206
Lab. maj. 6,486 (15.42%)
5.37% swing Lab. to C.
(2001: Lab. maj. 10,861 (26.15%))

ELMET
E. 68,514 T. 47,146 (68.81%) Lab. hold
Colin Burgon, Lab. 22,260
Andrew Millard, C. 17,732
Madeleine Kirk, LD 5,923
Tracy Andrews, BNP 1,231
Lab. maj. 4,528 (9.60%)
0.26% swing C. to Lab.
(2001: Lab. maj. 4,171 (9.08%))

ELTHAM
E. 57,236 T. 35,305 (61.68%) Lab. hold
Clive Efford, Lab. 15,381
Spencer Drury, C. 12,105
Ian Gerrard, LD 5,669
Jeremy Elms, UKIP 1,024
Barry Roberts, BNP 979
Andrew Graham, Ind. 147
Lab. maj. 3,276 (9.28%)
5.71% swing Lab. to C.
(2001: Lab. maj. 6,996 (20.70%))

ENFIELD NORTH
E. 66,460 T. 40,749 (61.31%) Lab. hold
Joan Ryan, Lab. 18,055
Nick de Bois, C. 16,135
Simon Radford, LD 4,642
Terence Farr, BNP 1,004
Gary Robbens, UKIP 750
Patrick Burns, Ind. 163
Lab. maj. 1,920 (4.71%)
0.63% swing Lab. to C.
(2001: Lab. maj. 2,291 (6.01%))

ENFIELD SOUTHGATE
E. 63,613 T. 42,210 (66.35%) C. gain
*David Burrowes, C. 18,830
Stephen Twigg, Lab. 17,083
Ziz Kakoulakis, LD 4,724
Trevor Doughty, Green 1,083
Brian Hall, UKIP 490
C. maj. 1,747 (4.14%)
8.69% swing Lab. to C.
(2001: Lab. maj. 5,546 (13.23%))

EPPING FOREST
E. 72,776 T. 44,860 (61.64%) C. hold
Eleanor Laing, C. 23,783
Bambos Charalambous, Lab. 9,425
Michael Heavens, LD 8,279
Julian Leppert, BNP 1,728
Andrew Smith, UKIP 1,014
Robin Tilbrook, Eng. Dem. 631
C. maj. 14,358 (32.01%)
6.07% swing Lab. to C.
(2001: C. maj. 8,426 (19.87%))

EPSOM & EWELL
E. 75,515 T. 49,879 (66.05%) C. hold
Chris Grayling, C. 27,146
Jonathan Lees, LD 10,699
Charles Mansell, Lab. 10,265
Peter Kefford, UKIP 1,769
C. maj. 16,447 (32.97%)
3.50% swing LD to C.
(2001: C. maj. 10,080 (21.61%))

EREWASH
E. 78,376 T. 50,553 (64.50%) Lab. hold
Liz Blackman, Lab. 22,472
David Simmonds, C. 15,388
Martin Garnett, LD 7,073
Robert Kilroy-Silk, Veritas 2,957
Sadie Graham, BNP 1,319
Geoffrey Kingscott, UKIP 941
R. U. Seerius, Loony 287
David Bishop, Elvis 116
Lab. maj. 7,084 (14.01%)
0.13% swing Lab. to C.
(2001: Lab. maj. 6,932 (14.26%))

ERITH & THAMESMEAD
E. 72,058 T. 37,651 (52.25%) Lab. hold
John Austin, Lab. 20,483
Chris Bromby, C. 8,983
Steven Toole, LD 5,088
Brian Ravenscroft, BNP 1,620
Barrie Thomas, UKIP 1,477
Lab. maj. 11,500 (30.54%)
1.47% swing Lab. to C.
(2001: Lab. maj. 11,167 (33.48%))

ESHER & WALTON
E. 76,926 T. 47,878 (62.24%) C. hold
Ian Taylor, C. 21,882
Mark Marsh, LD 14,155
Richard Taylor, Lab. 9,309
Bernard Collignon, UKIP 1,582
Chinners Chinnery, Loony 608
Richard Cutler, Soc. Lab. 342
C. maj. 7,727 (16.14%)
5.17% swing C. to LD
(2001: C. maj. 11,538 (25.34%))

ESSEX NORTH
E. 73,037 T. 47,959 (65.66%) C. hold
Bernard Jenkin, C. 22,811
Elizabeth Hughes, Lab. 11,908
James Raven, LD 9,831
Christopher Fox, Green 1,718
George Curtis, UKIP 1,691
C. maj. 10,903 (22.73%)
3.37% swing Lab. to C.
(2001: C. maj. 7,186 (15.99%))

EXETER
E. 84,964 T. 55,068 (64.81%) Lab. hold
Ben Bradshaw, Lab. 22,619
Peter Cox, C. 14,954
Jon Underwood, LD 11,340
Margaret Danks, Lib. 2,214
Tim Brenan, Green 1,896
Mark Fitzgeorge-Parker, UKIP 1,854
John Stuart, Ind. 191
Lab. maj. 7,665 (13.92%)
4.21% swing Lab. to C.
(2001: Lab. maj. 11,759 (22.35%))

FALMOUTH & CAMBORNE
E. 71,509 T. 48,015 (67.15%) LD gain
*Julia Goldsworthy, LD 16,747
Candy Atherton, Lab. 14,861
Ashley Crossley, C. 12,644
Michael Mahon, UKIP 1,820
David Mudd, Ind. 961
Paul Holmes, Lib. 423
Hilda Wasley, Meb. Ker. 370
Peter Gifford, Veritas 128
Richard Smith, Masts 61
LD maj. 1,886 (3.93%)
9.52% swing Lab. to LD
(2001: Lab. maj. 4,527 (9.67%))

FAREHAM
E. 72,599 T. 48,576 (66.91%) C. hold
Mark Hoban, C. 24,151
James Carr, Lab. 12,449
Richard De Ste-Croix, LD 10,551
Peter Mason-Apps, UKIP 1,425
C. maj. 11,702 (24.09%)
4.33% swing Lab. to C.
(2001: C. maj. 7,009 (15.42%))

FAVERSHAM & KENT MID
E. 66,411 T. 43,626 (65.69%) C. hold
Hugh Robertson, C. 21,690
Andrew Bradstock, Lab. 12,970
David Naghi, LD 7,204
Robert Thompson, UKIP 1,152
Norman Davidson, Loony 610
C. maj. 8,720 (19.99%)
4.90% swing Lab. to C.
(2001: C. maj. 4,183 (10.19%))

FELTHAM & HESTON
E. 75,391 T. 37,282 (49.45%)
Lab. (Co-op) hold
Alan Keen, Lab. (Co-op) 17,741
Mark Bowen, C. 10,921
Satnam Kaur Khalsa, LD 6,177
Graham Kemp, NF 975
Elizabeth Anstis, Green 815
Leon Mullett, UKIP 612
Warwick Prachar, Ind. 41
Lab. (Co-op) maj. 6,820 (18.29%)
8.35% swing Lab. (Co-op) to C.
(2001: Lab. (Co-op) maj. 12,657 (34.99%))

FINCHLEY & GOLDERS GREEN
E. 69,808 T. 43,214 (61.90%) Lab. hold
Dr Rudi Vis, Lab. 17,487
Andrew Mennear, C. 16,746
Sue Garden, LD 7,282
Noel Lynch, Green 1,136
Jeremy Jacobs, UKIP 453
Rainbow George Weiss, Vote Dream 110
Lab. maj. 741 (1.71%)
3.40% swing Lab. to C.
(2001: Lab. maj. 3,716 (8.51%))

FOLKESTONE & HYTHE
E. 70,914 T. 48,503 (68.40%) C. hold
Rt. Hon. Michael Howard, C. 26,161
Peter Carroll, LD 14,481
Maureen Tomison, Lab. 6,053
Dr Hazel Dawe, Green 688
Petrina Holdsworth, UKIP 619
Lord Toby Jug, Loony 175
Rodney Hylton-Potts, GBB 153
Grahame Leon-Smith, Senior 151
Sylvia Dunn, Progress 22
C. maj. 11,680 (24.08%)
5.60% swing LD to C.
(2001: C. maj. 5,907 (12.88%))

FOREST OF DEAN
E. 67,225 T. 47,640 (70.87%) C. gain
*Mark Harper, C. 19,474
Isabel Owen, Lab. 17,425
Christopher Coleman, LD 8,185
Patricia Hill, UKIP 1,140
Stephen Tweedie, Green 991
Anthony Reeve, Ind. 300
Gerald Morgan, EPP 125
C. maj. 2,049 (4.30%)
4.45% swing Lab. to C.
(2001: Lab. maj. 2,049 (4.59%))

FYLDE
E. 75,703 T. 45,510 (60.12%) C. hold
Rt. Hon. Michael Jack, C. 24,287
William Parbury, Lab. 11,828
Bill Winlow, LD 7,748
Tim Akeroyd, Lib. 1,647
C. maj. 12,459 (27.38%)
2.95% swing Lab. to C.
(2001: C. maj. 9,610 (21.48%))

GAINSBOROUGH
E. 70,733 T. 45,681 (64.58%) C. hold
Edward Leigh, C. 20,040
Adrian Heath, LD 12,037
John Knight, Lab. 11,744
Steven Pearson, UKIP 1,860
C. maj. 8,003 (17.52%)
1.02% swing C. to LD
(2001: C. maj. 8,071 (19.07%))

GATESHEAD EAST & WASHINGTON WEST
E. 61,421 T. 34,668 (56.44%) Lab. hold
*Sharon Hodgson, Lab. 20,997
Frank Hindle, LD 7,590
Lee Martin, C. 4,812
Jim Batty, UKIP 1,269
Lab. maj. 13,407 (38.67%)
7.29% swing Lab. to LD
(2001: Lab. maj. 17,904 (53.26%))

GEDLING
E. 68,917 T. 44,069 (63.95%) Lab. hold
Vernon Coaker, Lab. 20,329
Anna Soubry, C. 16,518
Raymond Poynter, LD 6,070
Alan Margerison, UKIP 741
Deborah Johnson, Veritas 411
Lab. maj. 3,811 (8.65%)
2.06% swing Lab. to C.
(2001: Lab. maj. 5,598 (12.78%))

GILLINGHAM
E. 72,223 T. 45,167 (62.54%) Lab. hold
Paul Clark, Lab. 18,621
Tim Butcher, C. 18,367
Andrew Stamp, LD 6,734
Craig MacKinlay, UKIP 1,191
Gordon Bryan, Ind. 254
Lab. maj. 254 (0.56%)
2.41% swing Lab. to C.
(2001: Lab. maj. 2,272 (5.38%))

GLOUCESTER
E. 82,500 T. 51,803 (62.79%) Lab. hold
Parmjit Dhanda, Lab. 23,138
Paul James, C. 18,867
Jeremy Hilton, LD 7,825
Gary Phipps, UKIP 1,116
Bryan Meloy, Green 857
Lab. maj. 4,271 (8.24%)
0.10% swing C. to Lab.
(2001: Lab. maj. 3,880 (8.05%))

GOSPORT
E. 71,119 T. 43,034 (60.51%) C. hold
Peter Viggers, C. 19,268
Richard Williams, Lab. 13,538
Roger Roberts, LD 7,145
John Bowles, UKIP 1,825
Andrea Smith, Green 1,258
C. maj. 5,730 (13.32%)
3.36% swing Lab. to C.
(2001: C. maj. 2,621 (6.59%))

GRANTHAM & STAMFORD
E. 74,074 T. 47,147 (63.65%) C. hold
Quentin Davies, C. 22,109
Ian Selby, Lab. 14,664
Patrick O'Connor, LD 7,838
Stuart Rising, UKIP 1,498
Benedict Brown, Eng. Dem. 774
John Andrews, OFD 264
C. maj. 7,445 (15.79%)
3.02% swing Lab. to C.
(2001: C. maj. 4,518 (9.76%))

GRAVESHAM
E. 68,705 T. 45,179 (65.76%) C. gain
*Adam Holloway, C. 19,739
Chris Pond, Lab. 19,085
Bruce Parmenter, LD 4,851
Geoff Coates, UKIP 850
Christopher Nickerson, Eng. Ind. 654
C. maj. 654 (1.45%)
6.29% swing Lab. to C.
(2001: Lab. maj. 4,862 (11.14%))

GREAT GRIMSBY
E. 63,711 T. 32,964 (51.74%) Lab. hold
Austin Mitchell, Lab. 15,512
Giles Taylor, C. 7,858
Andrew de Freitas, LD 6,356
Stephen Fyfe, BNP 1,338
Martin Grant, UKIP 1,239
David Brooks, Green 661
Lab. maj. 7,654 (23.22%)
5.78% swing Lab. to C.
(2001: Lab. maj. 11,484 (34.78%))

GREAT YARMOUTH
E. 68,887 T. 41,378 (60.07%) Lab. hold
Anthony Wright, Lab. 18,850
Mark Fox, C. 15,795
Stephen Newton, LD 4,585
Bertie Poole, UKIP 1,759
Michael Skipper, LCA 389
Lab. maj. 3,055 (7.38%)
1.96% swing Lab. to C.
(2001: Lab. maj. 4,564 (11.31%))

GREENWICH & WOOLWICH
E. 64,033 T. 35,615 (55.62%) Lab. hold
Rt. Hon. Nick Raynsford, Lab. 17,527
Christopher Le Breton, LD 7,381
Alistair Craig, C. 7,142
David Sharman, Green 1,579
Garry Bushell, Eng. Dem. 1,216
Stanley Gain, UKIP 709
Puvarani Nagalingam, Ind. 61
Lab. maj. 10,146 (28.49%)
8.21% swing Lab. to LD
(2001: Lab. maj. 13,433 (41.29%))

GUILDFORD
E. 75,566 T. 51,631 (68.33%) C. gain
*Anne Milton, C. 22,595
Sue Doughty, LD 22,248
Karen Landles, Lab. 5,054
John Pletts, Green 811
Martin Haslam, UKIP 645
John Morris, PPN-V 166
Victoria Lavin, Ind. 112
C. maj. 347 (0.67%)
0.90% swing LD to C.
(2001: LD maj. 538 (1.12%))

HACKNEY NORTH & STOKE NEWINGTON
E. 59,260 T. 29,380 (49.58%) Lab. hold
Diane Abbott, Lab. 14,268
James Blanchard, LD 6,841
Ertan Hurer, C. 4,218
Mischa Borris, Green 2,907
David Vail, Ind. 602
Nusrat Sen, Soc. Lab. 296
Nigel Barrow, Loony 248
Lab. maj. 7,427 (25.28%)
10.84% swing Lab. to LD
(2001: Lab. maj. 13,651 (46.09%))

HACKNEY SOUTH & SHOREDITCH
E. 64,818 T. 32,237 (49.73%) Lab. (Co-op) hold
*Meg Hillier, Lab. (Co-op) 17,048
Gavin Baylis, LD 6,844
John Moss, C. 4,524
Ipemndoh dan Iyan, Green 1,779
Dean Ryan, Respect 1,437
Benjamin Rae, Lib. 313
Monty Goldman, Comm. 200
Jonty Leff, WRP 92
Lab. (Co-op) maj. 10,204 (31.65%)
8.97% swing Lab. (Co-op) to LD
(2001: Lab. (Co-op) maj. 15,049 (49.59%))

HALESOWEN & ROWLEY REGIS
E. 65,748 T. 41,327 (62.86%) Lab. hold
Sylvia Heal, Lab. 19,243
Les Jones, C. 14,906
Martin Turner, LD 5,204
Nikki Sinclaire, UKIP 1,974
Lab. maj. 4,337 (10.49%)
4.12% swing Lab. to C.
(2001: Lab. maj. 7,359 (18.74%))

HALIFAX
E. 64,861 T. 39,659 (61.14%) Lab. (Co-op) hold
*Linda Riordan, Lab. (Co-op) 16,579
Kris Hopkins, C. 13,162
Michael Taylor, LD 7,100
Geoff Wallace, BNP 2,627
Thomas Holmes, NF 191
Lab. (Co-op) maj. 3,417 (8.62%)
3.28% swing Lab. (Co-op) to C.
(2001: Lab. (Co-op) maj. 6,129 (15.17%))

HALTEMPRICE & HOWDEN
E. 68,471 T. 48,029 (70.15%) C. hold
Rt. Hon. David Davis, C. 22,792
Jon Neal, LD 17,676
Edward Hart, Lab. 6,104
Jonathan Mainprize, BNP 798
Philip Lane, UKIP 659
C. maj. 5,116 (10.65%)
3.16% swing LD to C.
(2001: C. maj. 1,903 (4.33%))

HALTON
E. 64,379 T. 34,183 (53.10%) Lab. hold
Derek Twigg, Lab. 21,460
Colin Bloom, C. 6,854
Roger Barlow, LD 5,869
Lab. maj. 14,606 (42.73%)
3.92% swing Lab. to C.
(2001: Lab. maj. 17,428 (50.56%))

HAMMERSMITH & FULHAM
E. 79,082 T. 49,327 (62.37%) C. gain
*Greg Hands, C. 22,407
Melanie Smallman, Lab. 17,378
Alan Bullion, LD 7,116
Fiona Harrold, Green 1,933
Giles Fisher, UKIP 493
C. maj. 5,029 (10.20%)
7.35% swing Lab. to C.
(2001: Lab. maj. 2,015 (4.51%))

HAMPSHIRE EAST
E. 79,801 T. 53,139 (66.59%) C. hold
Rt. Hon. Michael Mates, C. 24,273
Ruth Bright, LD 18,764
Marjory Broughton, Lab. 8,519
David Samuel, UKIP 1,583
C. maj. 5,509 (10.37%)
3.66% swing C. to LD
(2001: C. maj. 8,890 (17.68%))

HAMPSHIRE NORTH EAST
E. 72,939 T. 47,287 (64.83%) C. hold
Rt. Hon. James Arbuthnot, C. 25,407
Adam Carew, LD 12,858
Kevin McGrath, Lab. 7,630
Paul Birch, UKIP 1,392
C. maj. 12,549 (26.54%)
1.81% swing C. to LD
(2001: C. maj. 13,257 (30.17%))

HAMPSHIRE NORTH WEST
E. 79,763 T. 51,265 (64.27%) C. hold
Rt. Hon. Sir George Young, C. 26,005
Martin Tod, LD 12,741
Michael Mumford, Lab. 10,594
Peter Sumner, UKIP 1,925
C. maj. 13,264 (25.87%)
1.50% swing C. to LD
(2001: C. maj. 12,009 (24.69%))

HAMPSTEAD & HIGHGATE
E. 68,737 T. 38,173 (55.53%) Lab. hold
Glenda Jackson, Lab. 14,615
Piers Wauchope, C. 10,886
Ed Fordham, LD 10,293
Sian Berry, Green 2,013
Magnus Nielsen, UKIP 275
Rainbow George Weiss, Vote Dream 91
Lab. maj. 3,729 (9.77%)
6.24% swing Lab. to C.
(2001: Lab. maj. 7,876 (22.24%))

HARBOROUGH
E. 74,583 T. 47,922 (64.25%) C. hold
Edward Garnier, C. 20,536
Jill Hope, LD 16,644
Peter Evans, Lab. 9,222
Marietta King, UKIP 1,520
C. maj. 3,892 (8.12%)
1.60% swing C. to LD
(2001: C. maj. 5,252 (11.31%))

HARLOW
E. 63,500 T. 39,733 (62.57%) Lab. hold
Bill Rammell, Lab. 16,453
Robert Halfon, C. 16,356
Lorna Spenceley, LD 5,002
John Felgate, UKIP 981
Anthony Bennett, Veritas 941
Lab. maj. 97 (0.24%)
6.39% swing Lab. to C.
(2001: Lab. maj. 5,228 (13.03%))

HARROGATE & KNARESBOROUGH
E. 65,622 T. 42,858 (65.31%) LD hold
Phil Willis, LD 24,113
Maggie Punyer, C. 13,684
Lorraine Ferris, Lab. 3,627
Chris Royston, UKIP 845
Colin Banner, BNP 466
John Allman, AFC 123
LD maj. 10,429 (24.33%)
1.68% swing C. to LD
(2001: LD maj. 8,845 (20.97%))

HARROW EAST
E. 84,033 T. 50,823 (60.48%) Lab. hold
Tony McNulty, Lab. 23,445
David Ashton, C. 18,715
Pash Nandhra, LD 7,747
Paul Cronin, UKIP 916
Lab. maj. 4,730 (9.31%)
6.92% swing Lab. to C.
(2001: Lab. maj. 11,124 (23.14%))

HARROW WEST
E. 74,228 T. 47,759 (64.34%)
Lab. (Co-op) hold
Gareth Thomas, Lab. (Co-op) 20,298
Mike Freer, C. 18,270
Christopher Noyce, LD 8,188
Janice Cronin, UKIP 576
Berjis Daver, Ind. 427
Lab. (Co-op) maj. 2,028 (4.25%)
4.48% swing Lab. (Co-op) to C.
(2001: Lab. (Co-op) maj. 6,156 (13.20%))

HARTLEPOOL
E. 68,776 T. 35,436 (51.52%) Lab. hold
Iain Wright, Lab. 18,251
Jody Dunn, LD 10,773
Amanda Vigar, C. 4,058
George Springer, UKIP 1,256
Frank Harrison, Soc. Lab. 373
Iris Ryder, Green 288
John Hobbs, Ind. 275
Sausage Supremo Headbanger, Loony 162
Lab. maj. 7,478 (21.10%)
11.51% swing Lab. to LD
(2004 Sept. by-election: Lab. maj. 2,033 (6.48%))
(2001: Lab. maj. 14,571 (38.29%))

HARWICH
E. 80,474 T. 50,408 (62.64%) C. gain
*Douglas Carswell, C. 21,235
Ivan Henderson, Lab. 20,315
Keith Tully, LD 5,913
Jeffrey Titford, UKIP 2,314
John Tipple, Respect 477
Christopher Humphrey, Ind. 154
C. maj. 920 (1.83%)
3.61% swing Lab. to C.
(2001: Lab. maj. 2,596 (5.40%))

HASTINGS & RYE
E. 72,765 T. 43,004 (59.10%) Lab. hold
Michael Foster, Lab. 18,107
Mark Coote, C. 16,081
Richard Stevens, LD 6,479
Terry Grant, UKIP 1,098
Sally Phillips, Green 1,032
John Ord-Clarke, Loony 207
Lab. maj. 2,026 (4.71%)
2.87% swing Lab. to C.
(2001: Lab. maj. 4,308 (10.45%))

HAVANT
E. 68,545 T. 41,351 (60.33%) C. hold
David Willetts, C. 18,370
Sarah Bogle, Lab. 11,862
Alex Bentley, LD 8,358
Timothy Dawes, Green 1,006
Steve Harris, UKIP 998
Ian Johnson, BNP 562
Russell Thomas, Veritas 195
C. maj. 6,508 (15.74%)
2.67% swing Lab. to C.
(2001: C. maj. 4,207 (10.40%))

HAYES & HARLINGTON
E. 57,493 T. 32,389 (56.34%) Lab. hold
John McDonnell, Lab. 19,009
Richard Worrall, C. 8,162
Jon Ball, LD 3,174
Tony Hazel, BNP 830
Martin Haley, UKIP 552
Brian Outten, Green 442
Paul Goddard, Ind. 220
Lab. maj. 10,847 (33.49%)
4.03% swing Lab. to C.
(2001: Lab. maj. 13,466 (41.56%))

HAZEL GROVE
E. 64,376 T. 39,117 (60.76%) LD hold
Andrew Stunell, LD 19,355
Alan White, C. 11,607
Andrew Graystone, Lab. 6,834
Keith Ryan, UKIP 1,321
LD maj. 7,748 (19.81%)
1.06% swing LD to C.
(2001: LD maj. 8,435 (21.92%))

HEMEL HEMPSTEAD
E. 73,095 T. 47,108 (64.45%) C. gain
*Michael Penning, C. 19,000
Tony McWalter, Lab. (Co-op) 18,501
Dr Richard Grayson, LD 8,089
Barry Newton, UKIP 1,518
C. maj. 499 (1.06%)
4.61% swing Lab. (Co-op) to C.
(2001: Lab. (Co-op) maj. 3,742 (8.16%))

HEMSWORTH
E. 67,339 T. 36,792 (54.64%) Lab. hold
Jon Trickett, Lab. 21,630
Jonathan Mortimer, C. 8,149
David Hall-Matthews, LD 5,766
John Burdon, Veritas 1,247
Lab. maj. 13,481 (36.64%)
3.87% swing Lab. to C.
(2001: Lab. maj. 15,636 (44.39%))

HENDON
E. 71,764 T. 41,839 (58.30%) Lab. hold
Andrew Dismore, Lab. 18,596
Dr Richard Evans, C. 15,897
Nahid Boethe, LD 5,831
David Williams, Green 754
Melvyn Smallman, UKIP 637
Rainbow George Weiss, Vote Dream 68
Michael Stewart, PDP 56
Lab. maj. 2,699 (6.45%)
5.85% swing Lab. to C.
(2001: Lab. maj. 7,417 (18.16%))

HENLEY
E. 68,538 T. 46,537 (67.90%) C. hold
Boris Johnson, C. 24,894
David Turner, LD 12,101
Kaleem Saeed, Lab. 6,862
Mark Stevenson, Green 1,518
Delphine Gray-Fisk, UKIP 1,162
C. maj. 12,793 (27.49%)
4.22% swing LD to C.
(2001: C. maj. 8,458 (19.05%))

HEREFORD
E. 71,813 T. 46,894 (65.30%) LD hold
Paul Keetch, LD 20,285
Virginia Taylor, C. 19,323
Tom Calver, Lab. 4,800
Brian Lunt, Green 1,052
Christopher Kingsley, UKIP 1,030
Peter Morton, Ind. 404
LD maj. 962 (2.05%)
0.06% swing LD to C.
(2001: LD maj. 968 (2.17%))

HERTFORD & STORTFORD
E. 73,394 T. 49,692 (67.71%) C. hold
Mark Prisk, C. 25,074
Richard Henry, Lab. 11,977
James Lucas, LD 9,129
Peter Hart, Green 1,914
David Sodey, UKIP 1,026
Debbie Le May, Veritas 572
C. maj. 13,097 (26.36%)
7.24% swing Lab. to C.
(2001: C. maj. 5,603 (11.88%))

HERTFORDSHIRE NORTH EAST
E. 72,190 T. 47,374 (65.62%) C. hold
Oliver Heald, C. 22,402
Andrew Harrop, Lab. 13,264
Iain Coleman, LD 10,147
David Hitchman, UKIP 1,561
C. maj. 9,138 (19.29%)
5.79% swing Lab. to C.
(2001: C. maj. 3,444 (7.71%))

HERTFORDSHIRE SOUTH WEST
E. 73,170 T. 50,088 (68.45%) C. hold
*David Gauke, C. 23,494
Ed Featherstone, LD 15,021
Kerron Cross, Lab. 10,466
Colin Rodden, UKIP 1,107
C. maj. 8,473 (16.92%)
0.54% swing C. to LD
(2001: C. maj. 8,181 (17.31%))

HERTSMERE
E. 67,572 T. 42,572 (63.00%) C. hold
James Clappison, C. 22,665
Kelly Tebb, Lab. 11,572
Jonathan Davies, LD 7,817
James Dry, Soc. Lab. 518
C. maj. 11,093 (26.06%)
7.12% swing Lab. to C.
(2001: C. maj. 4,902 (11.81%))

HEXHAM
E. 60,374 T. 41,513 (68.76%) C. hold
Peter Atkinson, C. 17,605
Kevin Graham, Lab. 12,585
Andrew Duffield, LD 10,673
Ian Riddell, Eng. Dem. 521
Thomas Davison, IP 129
C. maj. 5,020 (12.09%)
3.06% swing Lab. to C.
(2001: C. maj. 2,529 (5.96%))

HEYWOOD & MIDDLETON
E. 71,510 T. 39,053 (54.61%)
Lab. (Co-op) hold
Jim Dobbin, Lab. (Co-op) 19,438
Stephen Pathmarajah, C. 8,355
Crea Lavin, LD 7,261
Gary Aronsson, BNP 1,855
Phil Burke, Lib. 1,377
Dr John Whittaker, UKIP 767
Lab. (Co-op) maj. 11,083 (28.38%)
0.86% swing Lab. (Co-op) to C.
(2001: Lab. (Co-op) maj. 11,670 (30.09%))

HIGH PEAK
E. 75,275 T. 49,989 (66.41%) Lab. hold
Tom Levitt, Lab. 19,809
Andrew Bingham, C. 19,074
Marc Godwin, LD 10,000
Michael Schwartz, UKIP 1,106
Lab. maj. 735 (1.47%)
3.93% swing Lab. to C.
(2001: Lab. maj. 4,489 (9.33%))

HITCHIN & HARPENDEN
E. 67,207 T. 47,387 (70.51%) C. hold
Rt. Hon. Peter Lilley, C. 23,627
Hannah Hedges, LD 12,234
Paul Orrett, Lab. 10,499
John Saunders, UKIP 828
Peter Rigby, Ind. 199
C. maj. 11,393 (24.04%)
2.66% swing C. to LD
(2001: C. maj. 6,663 (14.83%))

HOLBORN & ST PANCRAS
E. 68,237 T. 34,359 (50.35%) Lab. hold
Rt. Hon. Frank Dobson, Lab. 14,857
Jill Fraser, LD 10,070
Margot James, C. 6,482
Adrian Oliver, Green 2,798
Rainbow George Weiss, Vote Dream 152
Lab. maj. 4,787 (13.93%)
10.98% swing Lab. to LD
(2001: Lab. maj. 11,175 (35.90%))

HORNCHURCH
E. 59,773 T. 38,169 (63.86%) C. gain
*James Brokenshire, C. 16,355
John Cryer, Lab. 15,875
Nat Green, LD 2,894
Ian Moore, BNP 1,313
Lawrence Webb, UKIP 1,033
Malvin Brown, RA 395
Graham Williamson, Third 304
C. maj. 480 (1.26%)
2.71% swing Lab. to C.
(2001: Lab. maj. 1,482 (4.17%))

HORNSEY & WOOD GREEN
E. 76,621 T. 47,330 (61.77%) LD gain
*Lynne Featherstone, LD 20,512
Barbara Roche, Lab. 18,117
Peter Forrest, C. 6,014
Jayne Forbes, Green 2,377
Roy Freshwater, UKIP 310
LD maj. 2,395 (5.06%)
14.57% swing Lab. to LD
(2001: Lab. maj. 10,614 (24.09%))

HORSHAM
E. 80,974 T. 54,495 (67.30%) C. hold
Rt. Hon. Francis Maude, C. 27,240
Rosie Sharpley, LD 14,613
Rehman Chishti, Lab. 9,320
Hugo Miller, UKIP 2,552
Jim Duggan, Ind. 416
Martin Jeremiah, PHF 354
C. maj. 12,627 (23.17%)
1.87% swing C. to LD
(2001: C. maj. 13,666 (26.92%))

HOUGHTON & WASHINGTON EAST
E. 67,089 T. 34,694 (51.71%) Lab. hold
Fraser Kemp, Lab. 22,310
Mark Greenfield, LD 6,245
Anthony Devenish, C. 4,772
John Richardson, BNP 1,367
Lab. maj. 16,065 (46.30%)
7.20% swing Lab. to LD
(2001: Lab. maj. 19,818 (58.91%))

HOVE
E. 69,939 T. 44,796 (64.05%) Lab. hold
*Celia Barlow, Lab. 16,786
Nicholas Boles, C. 16,366
Paul Elgood, LD 8,002
Anthea Ballam, Green 2,575
Stuart Bower, UKIP 575
Paddy O'Keeffe, Respect 268
Bob Dobbs, Ind. 95
Richard Franklin, Silent 78
Brian Ralfe, Ind. 51
Lab. maj. 420 (0.94%)
3.31% swing Lab. to C.
(2001: Lab. maj. 3,171 (7.55%))

HUDDERSFIELD
E. 61,723 T. 34,940 (56.61%)
Lab. (Co-op) hold
Barry Sheerman, Lab. (Co-op) 16,341
Emma Bone, LD 7,990
David Meacock, C. 7,597
Julie Stewart-Turner, Green 1,651
Karl Hanson, BNP 1,036
Theresa Quarmby, Ind. 325
Lab. (Co-op) maj. 8,351 (23.90%)
7.18% swing Lab. (Co-op) to LD
(2001: Lab. (Co-op) maj. 10,046 (28.39%))

HULL EAST
E. 65,407 T. 31,022 (47.43%) Lab. hold
Rt. Hon. John Prescott, Lab. 17,609
Andy Sloan, LD 5,862
Katy Lindsay, C. 4,038
Alan Siddle, BNP 1,022
Janet Toker, Lib. 1,018
Graham Morris, Veritas 750
Ronald Noon, Ind. 334
Linda Muir, Soc. Lab. 207
Carl Wagner, LCA 182
Lab. maj. 11,747 (37.87%)
5.88% swing Lab. to LD
(2001: Lab. maj. 15,325 (49.64%))

HULL NORTH
E. 62,590 T. 29,584 (47.27%) Lab. hold

*Diana Johnson, Lab.	15,364
Denis Healy, LD	8,013
Lydia Rivlin, C.	3,822
Martin Deane, Green	858
Brian Wainwright, BNP	766
Tineke Robinson, Veritas	389
Christopher Veasey, Northern	193
Carl Wagner, LCA	179

Lab. maj. 7,351 (24.85%)
6.30% swing Lab. to LD
(2001: Lab. maj. 10,721 (37.44%))

HULL WEST & HESSLE
E. 61,494 T. 27,818 (45.24%) Lab. hold

Rt. Hon. Alan Johnson, Lab.	15,305
David Nolan, LD	5,855
Karen Woods, C.	5,769
Stephen Wallis, Veritas	889

Lab. maj. 9,450 (33.97%)
4.66% swing Lab. to LD
(2001: Lab. maj. 10,951 (37.87%))

HUNTINGDON
E. 83,843 T. 52,418 (62.52%) C. hold

Jonathan Djanogly, C.	26,646
Julian Huppert, LD	13,799
Stephen Sartain, Lab.	9,821
Derek Norman, UKIP	2,152

C. maj. 12,847 (24.51%)
0.78% swing C. to LD
(2001: C. maj. 12,792 (26.06%))

HYNDBURN
E. 67,086 T. 39,449 (58.80%) Lab. hold

Greg Pope, Lab.	18,136
James Mawdsley, C.	12,549
Bill Greene, LD	5,577
Christian Jackson, BNP	2,444
Dr John Whittaker, UKIP	743

Lab. maj. 5,587 (14.16%)
3.66% swing Lab. to C.
(2001: Lab. maj. 8,219 (21.49%))

ILFORD NORTH
E. 70,718 T. 43,000 (60.80%) C. gain

*Lee Scott, C.	18,781
Linda Perham, Lab.	17,128
Mark Gayler, LD	5,896
Andrew Cross, UKIP	902
Martin Levin, Ind.	293

C. maj. 1,653 (3.84%)
4.55% swing Lab. to C.
(2001: Lab. maj. 2,115 (5.26%))

ILFORD SOUTH
E. 79,639 T. 42,693 (53.61%)
Lab. (Co-op) hold

Mike Gapes, Lab. (Co-op)	20,856
Stephen Metcalfe, C.	11,628
Matthew Lake, LD	8,761
Kashif Rana, BPP	763
Colin Taylor, UKIP	685

Lab. (Co-op) maj. 9,228 (21.61%)
6.14% swing Lab. (Co-op) to C.
(2001: Lab. (Co-op) maj. 13,997 (33.90%))

IPSWICH
E. 68,825 T. 41,878 (60.85%) Lab. hold

Chris Mole, Lab.	18,336
Paul West, C.	13,004
Richard Atkins, LD	8,464
Alison West, UKIP	1,134
Jervis Kay, Eng. Dem.	641
Sally Wainman, Ind.	299

Lab. maj. 5,332 (12.73%)
4.03% swing Lab. to C.
(2001 Nov. by-election: Lab. maj. 4,087 (14.91%))
(2001: Lab. maj. 8,081 (20.79%))

ISLE OF WIGHT
E. 109,046 T. 66,843 (61.30%) C. hold

Andrew Turner, C.	32,717
Anthony Rowlands, LD	19,739
Mark Chiverton, Lab.	11,484
Michael Tarrant, UKIP	2,352
Edward Corby, Ind.	551

C. maj. 12,978 (19.42%)
7.48% swing LD to C.
(2001: C. maj. 2,826 (4.45%))

ISLINGTON NORTH
E. 58,427 T. 31,494 (53.90%) Lab. hold

Jeremy Corbyn, Lab.	16,118
Laura Willoughby, LD	9,402
Nicola Talbot, C.	3,740
Jon Nott, Green	2,234

Lab. maj. 6,716 (21.32%)
10.78% swing Lab. to LD
(2001: Lab. maj. 12,958 (42.88%))

ISLINGTON SOUTH & FINSBURY
E. 57,748 T. 30,961 (53.61%) Lab. hold

*Emily Thornberry, Lab.	12,345
Bridget Fox, LD	11,861
Melanie McLean, C.	4,594
James Humphries, Green	1,471
Patricia Theophanides, UKIP	470
Andy the Hat Gardner, Loony	189
Chris Gidden, Ind.	31

Lab. maj. 484 (1.56%)
12.12% swing Lab. to LD
(2001: Lab. maj. 7,280 (25.81%))

JARROW
E. 61,814 T. 33,978 (54.97%) Lab. hold

Stephen Hepburn, Lab.	20,554
Bill Schardt, LD	6,650
Linkson Jack, C.	4,807
Alan Badger, UKIP	1,567
Roger Nettleship, SNH	400

Lab. maj. 13,904 (40.92%)
5.06% swing Lab. to LD
(2001: Lab. maj. 17,595 (51.03%))

KEIGHLEY
E. 68,229 T. 46,312 (67.88%) Lab. hold

Ann Cryer, Lab.	20,720
Karl Poulsen, C.	15,868
Nader Fekri, LD	5,484
Nick Griffin, BNP	4,240

Lab. maj. 4,852 (10.48%)
0.62% swing C. to Lab.
(2001: Lab. maj. 4,005 (9.24%))

KENSINGTON & CHELSEA
E. 62,662 T. 31,336 (50.01%) C. hold

†Rt. Hon. Sir Malcolm Rifkind, C.	18,144
Jennifer Kingsley, LD	5,726
Catherine Atkinson, Lab.	5,521
Julia Stephenson, Green	1,342
Mildred Eilorat, UKIP	395
Alfred Bovill, Ind.	107
Eddie Adams, Green Soc.	101

C. maj. 12,418 (39.63%)
0.46% swing LD to C.
(2001: C. maj. 8,771 (31.28%))

KETTERING
E. 81,887 T. 55,646 (67.95%) C. gain

*Philip Hollobone, C.	25,401
Phil Sawford, Lab.	22,100
Roger Aron, LD	6,882
Rosemarie Clark, UKIP	1,263

C. maj. 3,301 (5.93%)
3.58% swing Lab. to C.
(2001: Lab. maj. 665 (1.24%))

KINGSTON & SURBITON
E. 72,671 T. 49,750 (68.46%) LD hold

Edward Davey, LD	25,397
Kevin Davis, C.	16,431
Nick Parrott, Lab.	6,553
Barry Thornton, UKIP	657
John Hayball, Soc. Lab.	366
David Henson, Veritas	200
Rainbow George Weiss, Vote Dream	146

LD maj. 8,966 (18.02%)
6.95% swing LD to C.
(2001: LD maj. 15,676 (31.93%))

KINGSWOOD
E. 84,400 T. 56,311 (66.72%) Lab. hold

Dr Roger Berry, Lab.	26,491
Owen Inskip, C.	18,618
Geoff Brewer, LD	9,089
John Knight, UKIP	1,444
David Burnside, Ind.	669

Lab. maj. 7,873 (13.98%)
6.26% swing Lab. to C.
(2001: Lab. maj. 13,962 (26.51%))

KNOWSLEY NORTH & SEFTON EAST
E. 70,403 T. 37,053 (52.63%) Lab. hold

George Howarth, Lab.	23,461
Flo Clucas, LD	7,192
Naman Purewal, C.	5,064
Michael McDermott, BNP	872
Stephen Whatham, Soc. Lab.	464

Lab. maj. 16,269 (43.91%)
4.52% swing Lab. to LD
(2001: Lab. maj. 18,927 (50.45%))

KNOWSLEY SOUTH
E. 70,726 T. 36,444 (51.53%) Lab. hold

Eddie O'Hara, Lab.	24,820
David Smithson, LD	7,132
Andrea Leadsom, C.	4,492

Lab. maj. 17,688 (48.53%)
4.86% swing Lab. to LD
(2001: Lab. maj. 21,316 (58.26%))

LANCASHIRE WEST
E. 74,777 T. 43,155 (57.71%) Lab. hold
*Rosie Cooper, Lab. 20,746
Alf Doran, C. 14,662
Richard Kemp, LD 6,059
Alan Freeman, UKIP 871
Stephen Garrett, Eng. Dem. 525
David Braid, Clause 28 292
Lab. maj. 6,084 (14.10%)
4.17% swing Lab. to C.
(2001: Lab. maj. 9,643 (22.44%))

LANCASTER & WYRE
E. 80,739 T. 52,061 (64.48%) C. gain
*Ben Wallace, C. 22,266
Anne Sacks, Lab. 18,095
Stuart Langhorn, LD 8,453
Jon Barry, Green 2,278
John Mander, UKIP 969
C. maj. 4,171 (8.01%)
4.47% swing Lab. to C.
(2001: Lab. maj. 481 (0.92%))

LEEDS CENTRAL
E. 62,939 T. 29,186 (46.37%) Lab. hold
Rt. Hon. Hilary Benn, Lab. 17,526
Ruth Coleman, LD 5,660
Brian Cattell, C. 3,865
Mark Collett, BNP 1,201
Peter Sewards, UKIP 494
Mick Dear, Ind. 189
Oluwole Taiwo, Ind. 126
Julian Fitzgerald, AFC 125
Lab. maj. 11,866 (40.66%)
6.53% swing Lab. to LD
(2001: Lab. maj. 14,381 (52.67%))

LEEDS EAST
E. 54,691 T. 30,077 (54.99%) Lab. hold
George Mudie, Lab. 17,799
Andrew Tear, LD 6,221
Dominic Ponniah, C. 5,557
Peter Socrates, Ind. 500
Lab. maj. 11,578 (38.49%)
5.48% swing Lab. to LD
(2001: Lab. maj. 12,643 (43.51%))

LEEDS NORTH EAST
E. 63,304 T. 41,467 (65.50%) Lab. hold
Fabian Hamilton, Lab. 18,632
Matthew Lobley, C. 13,370
Jonathan Brown, LD 8,427
Celia Foote, Green Soc. 1,038
Lab. maj. 5,262 (12.69%)
2.57% swing Lab. to C.
(2001: Lab. maj. 7,089 (17.82%))

LEEDS NORTH WEST
E. 71,644 T. 44,711 (62.41%) LD gain
*Greg Mulholland, LD 16,612
Judith Blake, Lab. 14,735
George Lee, C. 11,510
Martin Hemingway, Green 1,128
Adrian Knowles, Eng. Dem. 545
Jeannie Sutton, Green Soc. 181
LD maj. 1,877 (4.20%)
9.59% swing Lab. to LD
(2001: Lab. maj. 5,236 (12.33%))

LEEDS WEST
E. 62,882 T. 33,718 (53.62%) Lab. hold
Rt. Hon. John Battle, Lab. 18,704
Darren Finlay, LD 5,894
Tim Metcalfe, C. 4,807
David Blackburn, Green 2,519
Julie Day, BNP 1,166
David Sewards, UKIP 628
Lab. maj. 12,810 (37.99%)
6.85% swing Lab. to LD
(2001: Lab. maj. 14,935 (46.54%))

LEICESTER EAST
E. 66,383 T. 41,306 (62.22%) Lab. hold
Keith Vaz, Lab. 24,015
Suella Fernandes, C. 8,139
Susan Cooper, LD 7,052
Colin Brown, Veritas 1,666
Valerie Smalley, Soc. Lab. 434
Lab. maj. 15,876 (38.44%)
2.69% swing C. to Lab.
(2001: Lab. maj. 13,442 (33.06%))

LEICESTER SOUTH
E. 72,310 T. 42,411 (58.65%) Lab. gain
*Sir Peter Soulsby, Lab. 16,688
Parmjit Singh Gill, LD 12,971
Martin McElwee, C. 7,549
Yvonne Ridley, Respect 2,720
Matthew Follett, Green 1,379
Ken Roseblade, Veritas 573
Dave Roberts, Soc. Lab. 315
Paul Lord, Ind. 216
Lab. maj. 3,717 (8.76%)
14.26% swing Lab. to LD
(2004 July by-election: LD maj.1,654 (5.62%))
(2001: Lab. maj. 13,243 (31.43%))

LEICESTER WEST
E. 62,389 T. 33,224 (53.25%) Lab. hold
Rt. Hon. Patricia Hewitt, Lab. 17,184
Sarah Richardson, C. 8,114
Zuffar Haq, LD 5,803
Geoff Forse, Green 1,571
Steve Score, Soc. Alt. 552
Lab. maj. 9,070 (27.30%)
0.86% swing Lab. to C.
(2001: Lab. maj. 9,639 (29.02%))

LEICESTERSHIRE NORTH WEST
E. 70,519 T. 47,140 (66.85%)
Lab. (Co-op) hold
David Taylor, Lab. (Co-op) 21,449
Nicola Le Page, C. 16,972
Rod Keyes, LD 5,682
John Blunt, UKIP 1,563
Clive Potter, BNP 1,474
Lab. (Co-op) maj. 4,477 (9.50%)
4.31% swing Lab. (Co-op) to C.
(2001: Lab. (Co-op) maj. 8,157 (18.12%))

LEIGH
E. 72,473 T. 36,488 (50.35%) Lab. hold
Andy Burnham, Lab. 23,097
Laurance Wedderburn, C. 5,825
Dave Crowther, LD 4,962
Ian Franzen, CAP 2,189
Thomas Hampson, LCA 415
Lab. maj. 17,272 (47.34%)
0.49% swing C. to Lab.
(2001: Lab. maj. 16,362 (46.35%))

LEOMINSTER
E. 70,587 T. 48,793 (69.12%) C. hold
Bill Wiggin, C. 25,407
Caroline Williams, LD 12,220
Paul Bell, Lab. 7,424
Felicity Norman, Green 2,191
Peter Venables, UKIP 1,551
C. maj. 13,187 (27.03%)
2.42% swing LD to C.
(2001: C. maj. 10,367 (22.19%))

LEWES
E. 67,073 T. 46,552 (69.40%) LD hold
Norman Baker, LD 24,376
Rory Love, C. 15,902
Richard Black, Lab. 4,169
Susan Murray, Green 1,071
John Petley, UKIP 1,034
LD maj. 8,474 (18.20%)
1.58% swing LD to C.
(2001: LD maj. 9,710 (21.37%))

LEWISHAM DEPTFORD
E. 59,018 T. 30,393 (51.50%) Lab. hold
Joan Ruddock, Lab. 16,902
Columba Blango, LD 5,091
James Cartlidge, C. 3,773
Darren Johnson, Green 3,367
Ian Page, Soc. Alt. 742
Dr David Holland, UKIP 518
Lab. maj. 11,811 (38.86%)
7.21% swing Lab. to LD
(2001: Lab. maj. 15,293 (52.54%))

LEWISHAM EAST
E. 59,135 T. 31,127 (52.64%) Lab. hold
Bridget Prentice, Lab. 14,263
James Cleverly, C. 7,512
Richard Thomas, LD 6,787
Anna Baker, Green 1,243
Arnold Tarling, UKIP 697
Bernard Franklin, NF 625
Lab. maj. 6,751 (21.69%)
4.12% swing Lab. to C.
(2001: Lab. maj. 8,959 (29.82%))

LEWISHAM WEST
E. 58,349 T. 31,923 (54.71%) Lab. hold
Jim Dowd, Lab. 16,611
Alex Feakes, LD 6,679
Evett McAnuff, C. 6,396
Nick Long, Green 1,464
Jens Winton, UKIP 773
Lab. maj. 9,932 (31.11%)
8.25% swing Lab. to LD
(2001: Lab. maj. 11,920 (38.68%))

LEYTON & WANSTEAD
E. 60,444 T. 33,272 (55.05%) Lab. hold
Harry Cohen, Lab. 15,234
Meher Khan, LD 8,377
Julien Foster, C. 7,393
Ashley Gunstock, Green 1,522
Nick Jones, UKIP 591
Marc Robertson, Ind. 155
Lab. maj. 6,857 (20.61%)
10.71% swing Lab. to LD
(2001: Lab. maj. 12,904 (38.27%))

LICHFIELD
E. 65,565 T. 43,744 (66.72%) C. hold
Michael Fabricant, C. 21,274
Nigel Gardner, Lab. 14,194
Ian Jackson, LD 6,804
Malcolm McKenzie, UKIP 1,472
C. maj. 7,080 (16.19%)
2.78% swing Lab. to C.
(2001: C. maj. 4,426 (10.62%))

LINCOLN
E. 65,203 T. 36,857 (56.53%) Lab. hold
Gillian Merron, Lab. 16,724
Karl McCartney, C. 12,110
Lisa Gabriel, LD 6,715
Nicholas Smith, UKIP 1,308
Lab. maj. 4,614 (12.52%)
5.08% swing Lab. to C.
(2001: Lab. maj. 8,420 (22.68%))

LIVERPOOL GARSTON
E. 63,669 T. 34,974 (54.93%) Lab. hold
Maria Eagle, Lab. 18,900
Paula Keaveney, LD 11,707
Amber Rudd, C. 3,424
Kevin Kearney, UKIP 780
David Oatley, WRP 163
Lab. maj. 7,193 (20.57%)
8.85% swing Lab. to LD
(2001: Lab. maj. 12,494 (38.27%))

LIVERPOOL RIVERSIDE
E. 75,171 T. 31,191 (41.49%) Lab. (Co-op) hold
Louise Ellman, Lab. (Co-op) 17,951
Richard Marbrow, LD 7,737
Gabrielle Howatson, C. 2,843
Peter Cranie, Green 1,707
Beth Marshall, Soc. Lab. 498
Ann Irving, UKIP 455
Lab. (Co-op) maj. 10,214 (32.75%)
10.98% swing Lab. (Co-op) to LD
(2001: Lab. (Co-op) maj. 13,950 (54.70%))

LIVERPOOL WALTON
E. 62,044 T. 27,930 (45.02%) Lab. hold
Peter Kilfoyle, Lab. 20,322
Kiron Reid, LD 4,365
Sharon Buckle, C. 1,655
Joseph Moran, UKIP 1,108
Daniel Wood, Lib. 480
Lab. maj. 15,957 (57.13%)
3.05% swing Lab. to LD
(2001: Lab. maj. 17,996 (63.24%))

LIVERPOOL WAVERTREE
E. 69,189 T. 35,171 (50.83%) Lab. hold
Rt. Hon. Jane Kennedy, Lab. 18,441
Colin Eldridge, LD 13,268
Jason Steen, C. 2,331
Mark Bill, UKIP 660
Gary Theys, Soc. Lab. 244
Paul Filby, Dem. Soc. All. 227
Lab. maj. 5,173 (14.71%)
11.81% swing Lab. to LD
(2001: Lab. maj. 12,319 (38.33%))

LIVERPOOL WEST DERBY
E. 64,591 T. 30,464 (47.16%) Lab. hold
Robert Wareing, Lab. 19,140
Patrick Maloney, LD 3,915
Steve Radford, Lib. 3,606
Peter Garrett, C. 2,567
Kai Andersen, Soc. Lab. 698
Peter Baden, UKIP 538
Lab. maj. 15,225 (49.98%)
2.66% swing Lab. to LD
(2001: Lab. maj. 15,853 (51.29%))

LOUGHBOROUGH
E. 72,351 T. 46,140 (63.77%) Lab. (Co-op) hold
Andy Reed, Lab. (Co-op) 19,098
Nicky Morgan, C. 17,102
Graeme Smith, LD 8,258
Bernard Sherratt, UKIP 1,094
John McVay, Veritas 588
Lab. (Co-op) maj. 1,996 (4.33%)
5.04% swing Lab. (Co-op) to C.
(2001: Lab. (Co-op) maj. 6,378 (14.41%))

LOUTH & HORNCASTLE
E. 75,313 T. 46,683 (61.99%) C. hold
Sir Peter Tapsell, C. 21,744
Frank Hodgkiss, Lab. 11,848
Fiona Martin, LD 9,480
Christopher Pain, UKIP 3,611
C. maj. 9,896 (21.20%)
2.10% swing Lab. to C.
(2001: C. maj. 7,554 (16.99%))

LUDLOW
E. 64,572 T. 46,540 (72.07%) C. gain
*Philip Dunne, C. 20,979
Matthew Green, LD 18,952
Nigel Knowles, Lab. 4,974
Jim Gaffney, Green 852
Michael Zuckerman, UKIP 783
C. maj. 2,027 (4.36%)
4.07% swing LD to C.
(2001: LD maj. 1,630 (3.78%))

LUTON NORTH
E. 68,175 T. 39,122 (57.38%) Lab. hold
Kelvin Hopkins, Lab. 19,062
Hannah Hall, C. 12,575
Linda Jack, LD 6,081
Colin Brown, UKIP 1,255
Kayson Gurney, Forum 149
Lab. maj. 6,487 (16.58%)
4.46% swing Lab. to C.
(2001: Lab. maj. 9,977 (25.50%))

LUTON SOUTH
E. 71,949 T. 38,918 (54.09%) Lab. hold
Margaret Moran, Lab. 16,610
Richard Stay, C. 10,960
Qurban Hussain, LD 8,778
Charles Lawman, UKIP 957
Marc Scheimann, Green 790
Mohammed Ilyas, Respect 725
Arthur Lynn, WRP 98
Lab. maj. 5,650 (14.52%)
5.62% swing Lab. to C.
(2001: Lab. maj. 10,133 (25.75%))

MACCLESFIELD
E. 72,267 T. 45,621 (63.13%) C. hold
Sir Nicholas Winterton, C. 22,628
Stephen Carter, Lab. 13,227
Catherine O'Brien, LD 8,918
John Scott, Veritas 848
C. maj. 9,401 (20.61%)
2.41% swing Lab. to C.
(2001: C. maj. 7,200 (15.79%))

MAIDENHEAD
E. 63,978 T. 45,850 (71.67%) C. hold
Rt. Hon. Theresa May, C. 23,312
Kathryn Newbound, LD 17,081
Janet Pritchard, Lab. 4,144
Tim Rait, BNP 704
Douglas Lewis, UKIP 609
C. maj. 6,231 (13.59%)
3.00% swing LD to C.
(2001: C. maj. 3,284 (7.58%))

MAIDSTONE & THE WEALD
E. 74,054 T. 48,755 (65.84%) C. hold
Rt. Hon. Ann Widdecombe, C. 25,670
Beth Breeze, Lab. 10,814
Mark Corney, LD 10,808
Anthony Robertson, UKIP 1,463
C. maj. 14,856 (30.47%)
3.92% swing Lab. to C.
(2001: C. maj. 10,318 (22.64%))

MAKERFIELD
E. 69,039 T. 35,580 (51.54%) Lab. hold
Rt. Hon. Ian McCartney, Lab. 22,494
Kulveer Ranger, C. 4,345
Trevor Beswick, LD 3,789
Peter Franzen, CAP 2,769
Dennis Shambley, BNP 1,221
Gregory Atherton, UKIP 962
Lab. maj. 18,149 (51.01%)
0.04% swing C. to Lab.
(2001: Lab. maj. 17,750 (50.92%))

MALDON & CHELMSFORD EAST
E. 69,502 T. 46,091 (66.32%) C. hold
John Whittingdale, C. 23,732
Sue Tibballs, Lab. 11,159
Matthew Lambert, LD 9,270
Jesse Pryke, UKIP 1,930
C. maj. 12,573 (27.28%)
4.05% swing Lab. to C.
(2001: C. maj. 8,462 (19.19%))

MANCHESTER BLACKLEY
E. 60,229 T. 27,591 (45.81%) Lab. hold
Graham Stringer, Lab. 17,187
Iain Donaldson, LD 5,160
Amar Ahmed, C. 3,690
Roger Bullock, UKIP 1,554
Lab. maj. 12,027 (43.59%)
6.99% swing Lab. to LD
(2001: Lab. maj. 14,464 (54.53%))

MANCHESTER CENTRAL
E. 69,656 T. 29,264 (42.01%) Lab. hold
Tony Lloyd, Lab. 16,993
Marc Ramsbottom, LD 7,217
Tom Jackson, C. 2,504
Steven Durrant, Green 1,292
Richard Kemp, NF 421
Damien O'Connor, Ind. Pr. Lab. 382
Dr John Whittaker, UKIP 272
Ronald Sinclair, Soc. Lab. 183
Lab. maj. 9,776 (33.41%)
9.80% swing Lab. to LD
(2001: Lab. maj. 13,742 (53.00%))

MANCHESTER GORTON
E. 64,696 T. 29,123 (45.02%) Lab. hold
Rt. Hon. Sir Gerald Kaufman, Lab. 15,480
Qassim Afzal, LD 9,672
Amanda Byrne, C. 2,848
Gregory Beaman, UKIP 783
Dan Waller, WRP 181
Matthew Kay, RP 159
Lab. maj. 5,808 (19.94%)
10.79% swing Lab. to LD
(2001: Lab. maj. 11,304 (41.51%))

MANCHESTER WITHINGTON
E. 67,781 T. 37,458 (55.26%) LD gain
*John Leech, LD 15,872
Rt. Hon. Keith Bradley, Lab. 15,205
Karen Bradley, C. 3,919
Brian Candeland, Green 1,595
Dr Robert Gutfreund-Walmsley, UKIP 424
Ivan Benett, Ind. 243
Yasmin Zalzala, Ind. 153
Richard Reed, TP 47
LD maj. 667 (1.78%)
17.33% swing Lab. to LD
(2001: Lab. maj. 11,524 (32.88%))

MANSFIELD
E. 69,131 T. 38,276 (55.37%) Lab. hold
Alan Meale, Lab. 18,400
Anne Wright, C. 7,035
Stewart Rickersey, Ind. 6,491
Roger Shelley, LD 5,316
Michael Harvey, Veritas 1,034
Lab. maj. 11,365 (29.69%)
0.13% swing Lab. to C.
(2001: Lab. maj. 11,038 (29.95%))

MEDWAY
E. 67,251 T. 41,093 (61.10%) Lab. hold
Bob Marshall-Andrews, Lab. 17,333
Mark Reckless, C. 17,120
Geoffrey Juby, LD 5,152
Robert Oakley, UKIP 1,488
Lab. maj. 213 (0.52%)
4.64% swing Lab. to C.
(2001: Lab. maj. 3,780 (9.79%))

MERIDEN
E. 77,342 T. 46,503 (60.13%) C. hold
Caroline Spelman, C. 22,416
Jim Brown, Lab. 15,407
William Laitinen, LD 7,113
Denis Brookes, UKIP 1,567
C. maj. 7,009 (15.07%)
3.29% swing Lab. to C.
(2001: C. maj. 3,784 (8.49%))

MIDDLESBROUGH
E. 65,924 T. 32,140 (48.75%) Lab. hold
Sir Stuart Bell, Lab. 18,562
Joe Michna, LD 5,995
Caroline Flynn-Macleod, C. 5,263
Ron Armes, BNP 819
Michael Landers, UKIP 768
Jackie Elder, Ind. 503
Derrick Arnott, Ind. 230
Lab. maj. 12,567 (39.10%)
9.03% swing Lab. to LD
(2001: Lab. maj. 16,330 (48.43%))

MIDDLESBROUGH SOUTH & CLEVELAND EAST
E. 71,883 T. 43,696 (60.79%) Lab. hold
Dr Ashok Kumar, Lab. 21,945
Mark Brooks, C. 13,945
Carl Minns, LD 6,049
Geoffrey Groves, BNP 1,099
Charlotte Bull, UKIP 658
Lab. maj. 8,000 (18.31%)
1.47% swing Lab. to C.
(2001: Lab. maj. 9,351 (21.26%))

MILTON KEYNES NORTH EAST
E. 78,758 T. 50,104 (63.62%) C. gain
*Mark Lancaster, C. 19,674
Brian White, Lab. 18,009
Jane Carr, LD 9,789
Michael Phillips, UKIP 1,400
Peter Richardson, Green 1,090
Anant Vyas, Ind. 142
C. maj. 1,665 (3.32%)
3.60% swing Lab. to C.
(2001: Lab. maj. 1,829 (3.88%))

MILTON KEYNES SOUTH WEST
E. 82,228 T. 48,709 (59.24%) Lab. hold
Dr Phyllis Starkey, Lab. 20,862
Iain Stewart, C. 16,852
Neil Stuart, LD 7,909
George Harlock, UKIP 1,750
Alan Francis, Green 1,336
Lab. maj. 4,010 (8.23%)
3.57% swing Lab. to C.
(2001: Lab. maj. 6,978 (15.38%))

MITCHAM & MORDEN
E. 65,172 T. 39,868 (61.17%) Lab. hold
Siobhain McDonagh, Lab. 22,489
Andrew Shellhorn, C. 9,929
Jo Christie-Smith, LD 5,583
Tom Walsh, Green 1,395
Adrian Roberts, Veritas 286
Rathy Alagaratnam, Ind. 186
Lab. maj. 12,560 (31.50%)
2.40% swing Lab. to C.
(2001: Lab. maj. 13,785 (36.31%))

MOLE VALLEY
E. 68,181 T. 49,415 (72.48%) C. hold
Sir Paul Beresford, C. 27,060
Nasser Butt, LD 15,063
Farmida Bi, Lab. 5,310
David Payne, UKIP 1,475
Roger Meekins, Veritas 507
C. maj. 11,997 (24.28%)
1.35% swing LD to C.
(2001: C. maj. 10,153 (21.57%))

MORECAMBE & LUNESDALE
E. 67,775 T. 41,635 (61.43%) Lab. hold
Geraldine Smith, Lab. 20,331
James Airey, C. 15,563
Alex Stone, LD 5,741
Lab. maj. 4,768 (11.45%)
0.39% swing Lab. to C.
(2001: Lab. maj. 5,092 (12.22%))

MORLEY & ROTHWELL
E. 72,248 T. 42,495 (58.82%) Lab. hold
Colin Challen, Lab. 20,570
Nick Vineall, C. 8,227
Stewart Golton, LD 6,819
Robert Finnigan, Ind. 4,608
Chris Beverley, BNP 2,271
Lab. maj. 12,343 (29.05%)
1.20% swing Lab. to C.
(2001: Lab. maj. 12,090 (31.45%))

NEW FOREST EAST
E. 68,633 T. 45,235 (65.91%) C. hold
Dr Julian Lewis, C. 21,975
Brian Dash, LD 15,424
Stephen Roberts, Lab. 5,492
Katy Davies, UKIP 2,344
C. maj. 6,551 (14.48%)
2.70% swing LD to C.
(2001: C. maj. 3,829 (9.08%))

NEW FOREST WEST
E. 69,232 T. 46,067 (66.54%) C. hold
Desmond Swayne, C. 26,004
Murari Kaushik, LD 8,719
Janice Hurne, Lab. 7,590
Brian Lawrence, UKIP 1,917
Janet Richards, Green 1,837
C. maj. 17,285 (37.52%)
3.80% swing LD to C.
(2001: C. maj. 13,191 (29.92%))

NEWARK
E. 72,249 T. 45,696 (63.25%) C. hold
Patrick Mercer, C. 21,946
Jason Reece, Lab. 15,482
Stuart Thompstone, LD 7,276
Charlotte Creasy, UKIP 992
C. maj. 6,464 (14.15%)
2.56% swing Lab. to C.
(2001: C. maj. 4,073 (9.02%))

NEWBURY
E. 75,903 T. 54,673 (72.03%) C. gain
*Richard Benyon, C. 26,771
David Rendel, LD 23,311
Oscar Van Nooijen, Lab. 3,239
David McMahon, UKIP 857
Nicholas Cornish, Ind. 409
Barrie Singleton, Ind. 86
C. maj. 3,460 (6.33%)
5.54% swing LD to C.
(2001: LD maj. 2,415 (4.75%))

NEWCASTLE-UNDER-LYME
E. 68,414 T. 39,788 (58.16%) Lab. hold
Paul Farrelly, Lab. 18,053
Jeremy Lefroy, C. 9,945
Trevor Johnson, LD 7,528
David Nixon, UKIP 1,436
John Dawson, BNP 1,390
Prof. Andrew Dobson, Green 918
Marian Harvey-Lover, Veritas 518
Lab. maj. 8,108 (20.38%)
2.72% swing Lab. to C.
(2001: Lab. maj. 9,986 (25.82%))

NEWCASTLE UPON TYNE CENTRAL
E. 62,734 T. 35,920 (57.26%) Lab. hold
Jim Cousins, Lab. 16,211
Greg Stone, LD 12,229
Wendy Morton, C. 5,749
Joe Hulm, Green 1,254
Clive Harding, NACVP 477
Lab. maj. 3,982 (11.09%)
11.10% swing Lab. to LD
(2001: Lab. maj. 11,605 (33.28%))

NEWCASTLE UPON TYNE EAST & WALLSEND
E. 56,900 T. 31,678 (55.67%) Lab. hold
Rt. Hon. Nick Brown, Lab. 17,462
David Ord, LD 9,897
Norma Dias, C. 3,532
William Hopwood, Soc. Alt. 582
Martin Levy, Comm. Brit. 205
Lab. maj. 7,565 (23.88%)
9.81% swing Lab. to LD
(2001: Lab. maj. 14,223 (43.50%))

NEWCASTLE UPON TYNE NORTH
E. 64,599 T. 38,444 (59.51%) Lab. hold
Doug Henderson, Lab. 19,224
Ron Beadle, LD 12,201
Neil Hudson, C. 6,022
Roland Wood, NF 997
Lab. maj. 7,023 (18.27%)
11.22% swing Lab. to LD
(2001: Lab. maj. 14,450 (39.73%))

NORFOLK MID
E. 81,738 T. 54,734 (66.96%) C. hold
Keith Simpson, C. 23,564
Daniel Zeichner, Lab. 16,004
Vivienne Clifford-Jackson, LD 12,988
Simon Fletcher, UKIP 2,178
C. maj. 7,560 (13.81%)
2.57% swing Lab. to C.
(2001: C. maj. 4,562 (8.68%))

NORFOLK NORTH
E. 80,784 T. 58,965 (72.99%) LD hold
Norman Lamb, LD 31,515
Iain Dale, C. 20,909
Philip Harris, Lab. 5,447
Stuart Agnew, UKIP 978
Justin Appleyard, Ind. 116
LD maj. 10,606 (17.99%)
8.56% swing C. to LD
(2001: LD maj. 483 (0.86%))

NORFOLK NORTH WEST
E. 82,171 T. 50,649 (61.64%) C. hold
Henry Bellingham, C. 25,471
Damien Welfare, Lab. 16,291
Simon Higginson, LD 7,026
Michael Stone, UKIP 1,861
C. maj. 9,180 (18.12%)
5.66% swing Lab. to C.
(2001: C. maj. 3,485 (6.81%))

NORFOLK SOUTH
E. 85,896 T. 58,974 (68.66%) C. hold
Richard Bacon, C. 26,399
Dr Ian Mack, LD 17,617
John Morgan, Lab. 13,262
Philip Tye, UKIP 1,696
C. maj. 8,782 (14.89%)
1.28% swing LD to C.
(2001: C. maj. 6,893 (12.32%))

NORFOLK SOUTH WEST
E. 88,260 T. 55,127 (62.46%) C. hold
†Christopher Fraser, C. 25,881
Charmaine Morgan, Lab. 15,795
April Pond, LD 10,207
Delia Hall, UKIP 2,738
Kim Hayes, Ind. 506
C. maj. 10,086 (18.30%)
0.30% swing Lab. to C.
(2001: C. maj. 9,366 (17.69%))

NORMANTON
E. 65,129 T. 37,424 (57.46%)
Lab. (Co-op) hold
*Ed Balls, Lab. (Co-op) 19,161
Andrew Percy, C. 9,159
Simone Butterworth, LD 6,357
John Aveyard, BNP 1,967
Mark Harrop, Ind. 780
Lab. (Co-op) maj. 10,002 (26.73%)
1.18% swing Lab. (Co-op) to C.
(2001: Lab. (Co-op) maj. 9,937 (29.09%))

NORTHAMPTON NORTH
E. 73,926 T. 42,048 (56.88%) Lab. hold
Sally Keeble, Lab. 16,905
Damian Collins, C. 12,945
Andrew Simpson, LD 10,317
John Howsam, UKIP 1,050
Paul Withrington, SOS 495
Andrew Otchie, CPA 336
Lab. maj. 3,960 (9.42%)
4.80% swing Lab. to C.
(2001: Lab. maj. 7,893 (19.02%))

NORTHAMPTON SOUTH
E. 89,722 T. 54,481 (60.72%) C. gain
*Brian Binley, C. 23,818
Tony Clarke, Lab. 19,399
Kevin Barron, LD 8,327
Derek Clark, UKIP 1,032
Anthony Green, Veritas 508
John Harrisson, SOS 437
John Percival, Loony 354
Fitzy Fitzpatrick, Ind. 346
Tim Webb, CPA 260
C. maj. 4,419 (8.11%)
4.92% swing Lab. to C.
(2001: Lab. maj. 885 (1.73%))

NORTHAVON
E. 81,800 T. 59,056 (72.20%) LD hold
Prof. Steve Webb, LD 30,872
Chris Butt, C. 19,839
Patricia Gardener, Lab. 6,277
Adrian Blake, UKIP 1,032
Alan Pinder, Green 922
Thomas Beacham, Ind. 114
LD maj. 11,033 (18.68%)
0.48% swing C. to LD
(2001: LD maj. 9,877 (17.71%))

NORWICH NORTH
E. 76,992 T. 47,033 (61.09%) Lab. hold
Dr Ian Gibson, Lab. 21,097
James Tumbridge, C. 15,638
Robin Whitmore, LD 7,616
Adrian Holmes, Green 1,252
John Youles, UKIP 1,122
Bill Holden, Ind. 308
Lab. maj. 5,459 (11.61%)
0.62% swing Lab. to C.
(2001: Lab. maj. 5,863 (12.85%))

NORWICH SOUTH
E. 70,409 T. 42,190 (59.92%) Lab. hold
Rt. Hon. Charles Clarke, Lab. 15,904
Andrew Aalders-Dunthorne, LD 12,251
Antony Little, C. 9,567
Adrian Ramsay, Green 3,101
Vandra Ahlstrom, UKIP 597
Christine Constable, Eng. Dem. 466
Don Barnard, LCA 219
Roger Blackwell, WRP 85
Lab. maj. 3,653 (8.66%)
7.09% swing Lab. to LD
(2001: Lab. maj. 8,816 (20.70%))

NOTTINGHAM EAST
E. 60,634 T. 30,091 (49.63%) Lab. hold
John Heppell, Lab. 13,787
Issan Ghazni, LD 6,848
Jim Thornton, C. 6,826
Ashley Baxter, Green 1,517
Anthony Ellwood, UKIP 740
Pete Ratcliff, Soc. Unity 373
Lab. maj. 6,939 (23.06%)
11.44% swing Lab. to LD
(2001: Lab. maj. 10,320 (34.71%))

NOTTINGHAM NORTH
E. 61,894 T. 30,383 (49.09%) Lab. hold
Graham Allen, Lab. 17,842
Priti Patel, C. 5,671
Tim Ball, LD 5,190
Irena Marriott, UKIP 1,680
Lab. maj. 12,171 (40.06%)
0.34% swing Lab. to C.
(2001: Lab. maj. 12,240 (40.74%))

NOTTINGHAM SOUTH
E. 68,921 T. 34,840 (50.55%) Lab. hold
Alan Simpson, Lab. 16,506
Sudesh Mattu, C. 9,020
Tony Sutton, LD 7,961
Ken Browne, UKIP 1,353
Lab. maj. 7,486 (21.49%)
2.90% swing Lab. to C.
(2001: Lab. maj. 9,989 (27.29%))

NUNEATON
E. 73,440 T. 45,280 (61.66%) Lab. hold
Bill Olner, Lab. 19,945
Mark Pawsey, C. 17,665
Ali Asghar, LD 5,884
Keith Tyson, UKIP 1,786
Lab. maj. 2,280 (5.04%)
6.18% swing Lab. to C.
(2001: Lab. maj. 7,535 (17.40%))

OLD BEXLEY & SIDCUP
E. 68,227 T. 44,572 (65.33%) C. hold
Derek Conway, C. 22,191
Gavin Moore, Lab. 12,271
Nickolas O'Hare, LD 6,564
Michael Barnbrook, UKIP 2,015
Claire Sayers, BNP 1,227
Gregory Peters, Ind. 304
C. maj. 9,920 (22.26%)
7.16% swing Lab. to C.
(2001: C. maj. 3,345 (7.94%))

OLDHAM EAST & SADDLEWORTH
E. 75,680 T. 43,367 (57.30%) Lab. hold
Phil Woolas, Lab. 17,968
Tony Dawson, LD 14,378
Keith Chapman, C. 7,901
Michael Treacy, BNP 2,109
Valerie Nield, UKIP 873
Philip O'Grady, Ind. 138
Lab. maj. 3,590 (8.28%)
1.14% swing LD to Lab.
(2001: Lab. maj. 2,726 (6.00%))

OLDHAM WEST & ROYTON
E. 70,496 T. 37,562 (53.28%) Lab. hold
Rt. Hon. Michael Meacher, Lab. 18,452
Sean Moore, C. 7,998
Stuart Bodsworth, LD 7,519
Anita Corbett, BNP 2,606
David Short, UKIP 987
Lab. maj. 10,454 (27.83%)
2.81% swing Lab. to C.
(2001: Lab. maj. 13,365 (33.44%))

ORPINGTON
E. 78,276 T. 54,734 (69.92%) C. hold
John Horam, C. 26,718
Chris Maines, LD 21,771
Emily Bird, Lab. 4,914
Mick Greenhough, UKIP 1,331
C. maj. 4,947 (9.04%)
4.25% swing LD to C.
(2001: C. maj. 269 (0.53%))

OXFORD EAST
E. 72,234 T. 41,790 (57.85%) Lab. hold
Rt. Hon. Andrew Smith, Lab. 15,405
Steve Goddard, LD 14,442
Virginia Morris, C. 6,992
Jacob Sanders, Green 1,813
Honest Blair, Ind. 1,485
Maurice Leen, IWCA 892
Peter Gardner, UKIP 715
Pat Mylvaganam, Ind. 46
Lab. maj. 963 (2.30%)
11.83% swing Lab. to LD
(2001: Lab. maj. 10,344 (25.96%))

OXFORD WEST & ABINGDON
E. 80,195 T. 52,600 (65.59%) LD hold
Dr Evan Harris, LD 24,336
Amanda McLean, C. 16,653
Antonia Bance, Lab. 8,725
Tom Lines, Green 2,091
Marcus Watney, UKIP 795
LD maj. 7,683 (14.61%)
1.60% swing LD to C.
(2001: LD maj. 9,185 (17.81%))

PENDLE
E. 64,917 T. 41,132 (63.36%) Lab. hold
Gordon Prentice, Lab. 15,250
Jane Ellison, C. 13,070
Shazad Anwar, LD 9,528
Thomas Boocock, BNP 2,547
Graham Cannon, UKIP 737
Lab. maj. 2,180 (5.30%)
2.73% swing Lab. to C.
(2001: Lab. maj. 4,275 (10.76%))

PENRITH & THE BORDER
E. 70,922 T. 46,882 (66.10%) C. hold
Rt. Hon. David Maclean, C. 24,046
Geyve Walker, LD 12,142
Michael Boaden, Lab. 8,958
William Robinson, UKIP 1,187
Mark Gibson, LCA 549
C. maj. 11,904 (25.39%)
3.89% swing C. to LD
(2001: C. maj. 14,677 (33.17%))

PETERBOROUGH
E. 67,499 T. 41,204 (61.04%) C. gain
*Stewart Jackson, C. 17,364
Rt. Hon. Helen Clark, Lab. 14,624
Nick Sandford, LD 6,876
Mary Herdman, UKIP 1,242
Terry Blackham, NF 931
Marc Potter, MNP 167
C. maj. 2,740 (6.65%)
6.91% swing Lab. to C.
(2001: Lab. maj. 2,854 (7.17%))

PLYMOUTH DEVONPORT
E. 72,848 T. 42,013 (57.67%) Lab. hold
*Alison Seabeck, Lab. 18,612
Richard Cuming, C. 10,509
Judith Jolly, LD 8,000
Bill Wakeham, UKIP 3,324
Keith Greene, Ind. 747
Robert Hawkins, Soc. Lab. 445
Tony Staunton, Respect 376
Lab. maj. 8,103 (19.29%)
5.98% swing Lab. to C.
(2001: Lab. maj. 13,033 (31.24%))

PLYMOUTH SUTTON
E. 67,202 T. 38,192 (56.83%)
Lab. (Co-op) hold
Linda Gilroy, Lab. (Co-op) 15,497
Oliver Colvile, C. 11,388
Karen Gillard, LD 8,685
Robert Cumming, UKIP 2,392
Rob Hawkins, Soc. Lab. 230
Lab. (Co-op) maj. 4,109 (10.76%)
4.24% swing Lab. (Co-op) to C.
(2001: Lab. (Co-op) maj. 7,517 (19.24%))

PONTEFRACT & CASTLEFORD
E. 61,871 T. 32,947 (53.25%) Lab. hold
Yvette Cooper, Lab. 20,973
Simon Jones, C. 5,727
Wesley Paxton, LD 3,942
Suzy Cass, BNP 1,835
Bob Hague, Green Soc. 470
Lab. maj. 15,246 (46.27%)
2.95% swing Lab. to C.
(2001: Lab. maj. 16,378 (52.17%))

POOLE
E. 64,178 T. 40,513 (63.13%) C. hold
Robert Syms, C. 17,571
Mike Plummer, LD 11,583
Darren Brown, Lab. 9,376
John Barnes, UKIP 1,436
Peter Pirnie, BNP 547
C. maj. 5,988 (14.78%)
2.42% swing C. to LD
(2001: C. maj. 7,166 (18.27%))

POPLAR & CANNING TOWN
E. 81,544 T. 39,010 (47.84%) Lab. hold
Jim Fitzpatrick, Lab. 15,628
Tim Archer, C. 8,499
Oliur Rahman, Respect 6,573
Janet Ludlow, LD 5,420
Terry McGrenera, Green 955
Aminul Hoque, Ind. 815
Tony Smith, Veritas 650
Simeon Ademolake, CPA 470
Lab. maj. 7,129 (18.27%)
11.55% swing Lab. to C.
(2001: Lab. maj. 14,104 (41.35%))

PORTSMOUTH NORTH
E. 62,884 T. 37,717 (59.98%)
Lab. (Co-op) hold
*Sarah McCarthy-Fry, Lab. (Co-op) 15,412
Penny Mordaunt, C. 14,273
Gary Lawson, LD 6,684
Mike Smith, UKIP 1,348
Lab. (Co-op) maj. 1,139 (3.02%)
5.45% swing Lab. (Co-op) to C.
(2001: Lab. (Co-op) maj. 5,134 (13.93%))

PORTSMOUTH SOUTH
E. 70,969 T. 40,374 (56.89%) LD hold
Mike Hancock, LD 17,047
Caroline Dinenage, C. 13,685
Mark Button, Lab. 8,714
Dennis Pierson, UKIP 928
LD maj. 3,362 (8.33%)
3.60% swing LD to C.
(2001: LD maj. 6,094 (15.54%))

PRESTON
E. 63,351 T. 34,081 (53.80%)
Lab. (Co-op) hold
Mark Hendrick, Lab. (Co-op) 17,210
Fiona Bryce, C. 7,803
William Parkinson, LD 5,701
Michael Lavalette, Respect 2,318
Ellen Boardman, UKIP 1,049
Lab. (Co-op) maj. 9,407 (27.60%)
3.22% swing Lab. (Co-op) to C.
(2001: Lab. (Co-op) maj. 12,268 (34.04%))

PUDSEY
E. 70,411 T. 46,444 (65.96%) Lab. hold
Paul Truswell, Lab. 21,261
Pamela Singleton, C. 15,391
James Keeley, LD 8,551
David Daniel, UKIP 1,241
Lab. maj. 5,870 (12.64%)
0.09% swing C. to Lab.
(2001: Lab. maj. 5,626 (12.45%))

PUTNEY
E. 61,498 T. 36,574 (59.47%) C. gain
*Justine Greening, C. 15,497
Tony Colman, Lab. 13,731
Jeremy Ambache, LD 5,965
Keith Magnum, Green 993
Anthony Gahan, UKIP 388
C. maj. 1,766 (4.83%)
6.46% swing Lab. to C.
(2001: Lab. maj. 2,771 (8.09%))

RAYLEIGH
E. 71,996 T. 46,193 (64.16%) C. hold
Mark Francois, C. 25,609
Julian Ware-Lane, Lab. 10,883
Sid Cumberland, LD 7,406
Janet Davies, UKIP 2,295
C. maj. 14,726 (31.88%)
6.25% swing Lab. to C.
(2001: C. maj. 8,290 (19.38%))

READING EAST
E. 72,806 T. 43,912 (60.31%) C. gain
*Rob Wilson, C. 15,557
Tony Page, Lab. 15,082
Prof. John Howson, LD 10,619
Rob White, Green 1,548
David Lamb, UKIP 849
Jan Lloyd, Ind. 135
Rex Hora, Ind. 122
C. maj. 475 (1.08%)
6.95% swing Lab. to C.
(2001: Lab. maj. 5,588 (12.81%))

READING WEST
E. 69,011 T. 42,103 (61.01%) Lab. hold
Martin Salter, Lab. 18,940
Ewan Cameron, C. 14,258
Denise Gaines, LD 6,663
Peter Williams, UKIP 1,180
Adrian Windisch, Green 921
Dave Boyle, Veritas 141
Lab. maj. 4,682 (11.12%)
4.98% swing Lab. to C.
(2001: Lab. maj. 8,849 (21.08%))

REDCAR
E. 66,947 T. 38,861 (58.05%) Lab. hold

Vera Baird, Lab.	19,968
Ian Swales, LD	7,852
Jonathan Lehrle, C.	6,954
Christopher McGlade, Ind.	2,379
Andrew Harris, BNP	985
Edward Walker, UKIP	564
John Taylor, Soc. Lab.	159

Lab. maj. 12,116 (31.18%)
8.25% swing Lab. to LD
(2001: Lab. maj. 13,443 (35.19%))

REDDITCH
E. 64,121 T. 40,291 (62.84%) Lab. hold

Rt. Hon. Jacqui Smith, Lab.	18,012
Karen Lumley, C.	15,296
Nigel Hicks, LD	5,602
John Ison, UKIP	1,381

Lab. maj. 2,716 (6.74%)
0.02% swing C. to Lab.
(2001: Lab. maj. 2,484 (6.71%))

REGENT'S PARK & KENSINGTON NORTH
E. 78,975 T. 40,680 (51.51%) Lab. hold

Karen Buck, Lab.	18,196
Jeremy Bradshaw, C.	12,065
Rabi Martins, LD	7,569
Dr Paul Miller, Green	1,985
Pamela Perrin, UKIP	456
Rezouk Boufas, CP	227
Abby Dharamsey, Ind.	182

Lab. maj. 6,131 (15.07%)
6.32% swing Lab. to C.
(2001: Lab. maj. 10,266 (27.71%))

REIGATE
E. 65,719 T. 42,605 (64.83%) C. hold

Crispin Blunt, C.	20,884
Jane Kulka, LD	9,896
Sam Townend, Lab.	8,896
Jeremy Wraith, UKIP	1,921
Harold Green, EDP	600
Michael Selby, Ind.	408

C. maj. 10,988 (25.79%)
0.46% swing C. to LD
(2001: C. maj. 8,025 (20.33%))

RIBBLE SOUTH
E. 75,357 T. 47,511 (63.05%) Lab. hold

David Borrow, Lab.	20,428
Lorraine Fullbrook, C.	18,244
Mark Alcock, LD	7,634
Kenneth Jones, UKIP	1,205

Lab. maj. 2,184 (4.60%)
1.82% swing Lab. to C.
(2001: Lab. maj. 3,792 (8.22%))

RIBBLE VALLEY
E. 75,692 T. 49,766 (65.75%) C. hold

Nigel Evans, C.	25,834
Julie Young, LD	11,663
Jack Davenport, Lab.	10,924
Kevin Henry, UKIP	1,345

C. maj. 14,171 (28.48%)
2.81% swing LD to C.
(2001: C. maj. 11,238 (22.85%))

RICHMOND (YORKS)
E. 69,521 T. 45,200 (65.02%) C. hold

Rt. Hon. William Hague, C.	26,722
Neil Foster, Lab.	8,915
Jacquie Bell, LD	7,982
Leslie Rowe, Green	1,581

C. maj. 17,807 (39.40%)
1.17% swing Lab. to C.
(2001: C. maj. 16,319 (37.06%))

RICHMOND PARK
E. 70,555 T. 51,374 (72.81%) LD hold

*Susan Kramer, LD	24,011
Marco Forgione, C.	20,280
James Butler, Lab.	4,768
James Page, Green	1,379
Peter Dul, UKIP	458
Peter Flower, CPA	288
Margaret Harrison, Ind.	83
Rainbow George Weiss, Vote Dream	63
Richard Meacock, Ind.	44

LD maj. 3,731 (7.26%)
1.42% swing LD to C.
(2001: LD maj. 4,964 (10.10%))

ROCHDALE
E. 69,894 T. 40,836 (58.43%) LD gain

*Paul Rowen, LD	16,787
Lorna Fitzsimons, Lab.	16,345
Khalid Hussain, C.	4,270
Derek Adams, BNP	1,773
Dr John Whittaker, UKIP	499
Samir Chatterjee, Green	448
Mohammed Salim, IZB	361
Carl Faulkner, Veritas	353

LD maj. 442 (1.08%)
7.72% swing Lab. to LD
(2001: Lab. maj. 5,655 (14.35%))

ROCHFORD & SOUTHEND EAST
E. 71,186 T. 39,462 (55.44%) C. hold

*James Duddridge, C.	17,874
Fred Grindrod, Lab.	12,380
Graham Longley, LD	5,967
John Croft, UKIP	1,913
Andrew Vaughan, Green	1,328

C. maj. 5,494 (13.92%)
2.43% swing C. to Lab.
(2001: C. maj. 7,034 (18.78%))

ROMFORD
E. 58,571 T. 36,482 (62.29%) C. hold

Andrew Rosindell, C.	21,560
Margaret Mullane, Lab.	9,971
Geoffrey Seeff, LD	3,066
John McCaffrey, BNP	1,088
Terry Murray, UKIP	797

C. maj. 11,589 (31.77%)
7.51% swing Lab. to C.
(2001: C. maj. 5,977 (16.74%))

ROMSEY
E. 72,177 T. 50,311 (69.71%) LD hold

Sandra Gidley, LD	22,465
Caroline Nokes, C.	22,340
Matthew Stevens, Lab.	4,430
Michael Wigley, UKIP	1,076

LD maj. 125 (0.25%)
2.32% swing LD to C.
(2001: LD maj. 2,370 (4.89%))

ROSSENDALE & DARWEN
E. 72,207 T. 44,437 (61.54%) Lab. hold

Janet Anderson, Lab.	19,073
Nigel Adams, C.	15,397
Mike Carr, LD	6,670
Anthony Wentworth, BNP	1,736
Graeme McIver, Green	821
David Duthie, UKIP	740

Lab. maj. 3,676 (8.27%)
1.85% swing Lab. to C.
(2001: Lab. maj. 5,223 (12.63%))

ROTHER VALLEY
E. 67,973 T. 39,495 (58.10%) Lab. hold

Rt. Hon. Kevin Barron, Lab.	21,871
Colin Phillips, C.	7,647
Phillip Bristow, LD	6,272
Nicholas Cass, BNP	2,020
Gordon Brown, UKIP	1,685

Lab. maj. 14,224 (36.01%)
2.21% swing Lab. to C.
(2001: Lab. maj. 14,882 (40.44%))

ROTHERHAM
E. 54,410 T. 29,978 (55.10%) Lab. hold

Rt. Hon. Denis MacShane, Lab.	15,840
Timothy Gordon, LD	5,159
Lee Rotherham, C.	4,966
Marlene Guest, BNP	1,986
David Cutts, UKIP	1,122
Richard Penycate, Green	905

Lab. maj. 10,681 (35.63%)
8.83% swing Lab. to LD
(2001: Lab. maj. 13,077 (44.55%))

RUGBY & KENILWORTH
E. 83,303 T. 56,949 (68.36%) C. gain

*Jeremy Wright, C.	23,447
Andy King, Lab.	21,891
Richard Allanach, LD	10,143
John Thurley, UKIP	911
Brian Hadland, Ind.	299
Lillian Pallikaropoulos, Ind.	258

C. maj. 1,556 (2.73%)
4.04% swing Lab. to C.
(2001: Lab. maj. 2,877 (5.35%))

RUISLIP-NORTHWOOD
E. 60,774 T. 39,670 (65.27%) C. hold

*Nick Hurd, C.	18,939
Mike Cox, LD	10,029
Ashley Riley, Lab.	8,323
Graham Lee, Green	892
Ian Edward, NF	841
Roland Courtenay, UKIP	646

C. maj. 8,910 (22.46%)
3.49% swing C. to LD
(2001: C. maj. 7,537 (20.29%))

RUNNYMEDE & WEYBRIDGE
E. 74,172 T. 43,524 (58.68%) C. hold

Philip Hammond, C.	22,366
Paul Greenwood, Lab.	10,017
Henry Bolton, LD	7,771
Anthony Micklethwait, UKIP	1,719
Charles Gilman, Green	1,180
Mad Crab Collett, Loony	358
Katrina Osman, UKC	113

C. maj. 12,349 (28.37%)
4.33% swing Lab. to C.
(2001: C. maj. 8,360 (19.70%))

RUSHCLIFFE
E. 79,913 T. 56,311 (70.47%) C. hold

Rt. Hon. Kenneth Clarke, C.	27,899
Edward Gamble, Lab.	14,925
Karrar Khan, LD	9,813
Simon Anthony, Green	1,692
Matthew Faithfull, UKIP	1,358
Daniel Moss, Veritas	624

C. maj. 12,974 (23.04%)
4.76% swing Lab. to C.
(2001: C. maj. 7,357 (13.51%))

RUTLAND & MELTON
E. 75,823 T. 49,284 (65.00%) C. hold
Alan Duncan, C. 25,237
Linda Arnold, Lab. 12,307
Grahame Hudson, LD 9,153
Peter Baker, UKIP 1,554
Duncan Shelley, Veritas 696
Helen Pender, Ind. 337
C. maj. 12,930 (26.24%)
3.97% swing Lab. to C.
(2001: C. maj. 8,612 (18.30%))

RYEDALE
E. 67,770 T. 44,120 (65.10%) C. hold
John Greenway, C. 21,251
Gordon Beever, LD 10,782
Paul Blanchard, Lab. 9,148
Stephen Feaster, UKIP 1,522
John Clarke, Lib. 1,417
C. maj. 10,469 (23.73%)
6.31% swing LD to C.
(2001: C. maj. 4,875 (11.11%))

SAFFRON WALDEN
E. 77,600 T. 53,020 (68.32%) C. hold
Rt. Hon. Sir Alan Haselhurst, C. 27,263
Elfreda Tealby-Watson, LD 14,255
Swatantra Nandanwar, Lab. 8,755
Raymond Tyler, UKIP 1,412
Raymond Brown, Eng. Dem. 860
Trevor Hackett, Veritas 475
C. maj. 13,008 (24.53%)
0.27% swing LD to C.
(2001: C. maj. 12,004 (23.99%))

ST ALBANS
E. 64,595 T. 45,462 (70.38%) C. gain
*Anne Main, C. 16,953
Kerry Pollard, Lab. 15,592
Michael Green, LD 11,561
Richard Evans, UKIP 707
Janet Girsman, St Albans 430
Mark Reynolds, Ind. 219
C. maj. 1,361 (2.99%)
6.60% swing Lab. to C.
(2001: Lab. maj. 4,466 (10.21%))

ST HELENS NORTH
E. 69,834 T. 39,271 (56.23%) Lab. hold
Dave Watts, Lab. 22,329
John Beirne, LD 8,367
Paul Oakley, C. 7,410
Sylvia Hall, UKIP 1,165
Lab. maj. 13,962 (35.55%)
3.99% swing Lab. to LD
(2001: Lab. maj. 15,901 (42.29%))

ST HELENS SOUTH
E. 65,441 T. 35,473 (54.21%) Lab. hold
Shaun Woodward, Lab. 19,345
Brian Spencer, LD 10,036
Una Riley, C. 4,602
Malcolm Nightingale, UKIP 847
Michael Perry, Soc. Lab. 643
Lab. maj. 9,309 (26.24%)
0.17% swing Lab. to LD
(2001: Lab. maj. 8,985 (26.58%))

ST IVES
E. 74,716 T. 50,417 (67.48%) LD hold
Andrew George, LD 25,577
Christian Mitchell, C. 13,968
Michael Dooley, Lab. 6,583
Michael Faulkner, UKIP 2,551
Katrina Slack, Green 1,738
LD maj. 11,609 (23.03%)
1.31% swing C. to LD
(2001: LD maj. 10,053 (20.41%))

SALFORD
E. 53,294 T. 22,600 (42.41%) Lab. hold
Rt. Hon. Hazel Blears, Lab. 13,007
Norman Owen, LD 5,062
Laetitia Cash, C. 3,440
Lisa Duffy, UKIP 1,091
Lab. maj. 7,945 (35.15%)
6.88% swing Lab. to LD
(2001: Lab. maj. 11,012 (48.91%))

SALISBURY
E. 80,385 T. 54,322 (67.58%) C. hold
Robert Key, C. 25,961
Richard Denton-White, LD 14,819
Clare Moody, Lab. 9,457
Frances Howard, UKIP 2,290
Hamish Soutar, Green 1,555
John Holme, Ind. 240
C. maj. 11,142 (20.51%)
1.98% swing LD to C.
(2001: C. maj. 8,703 (16.54%))

SCARBOROUGH & WHITBY
E. 73,806 T. 46,912 (63.56%) C. gain
*Robert Goodwill, C. 19,248
Lawrence Quinn, Lab. 18,003
Tania Exley-Moore, LD 7,495
Jonathan Dixon, Green 1,214
Paul Abbott, UKIP 952
C. maj. 1,245 (2.65%)
5.10% swing Lab. to C.
(2001: Lab. maj. 3,585 (7.54%))

SCUNTHORPE
E. 62,669 T. 32,664 (52.12%) Lab. hold
Elliot Morley, Lab. 17,355
Julian Sturdy, C. 8,392
Neil Poole, LD 5,556
David Baxendale, UKIP 1,361
Lab. maj. 8,963 (27.44%)
1.70% swing Lab. to C.
(2001: Lab. maj. 10,372 (30.85%))

SEDGEFIELD
E. 66,666 T. 41,483 (62.23%) Lab. hold
Rt. Hon. Tony Blair, Lab. 24,429
Grp Capt Al Lockwood, C. 5,972
Robert Browne, LD 4,935
Reg Keys, Ind. 4,252
William Brown, UKIP 646
Mark Farrell, NF 253
Fiona Luckhurst-Matthews, Veritas 218
Berony Abraham, Ind. 209
Boney Maroney, Loony 157
Jonathan Cockburn, BMG 103
Terry Pattinson, Senior 97
Cherri Gilham, UKPP 82
Helen John, Ind. 68
John Barker, Ind. 45
Julian Brennan, Ind. 17
Lab. maj. 18,457 (44.49%)
0.25% swing C. to Lab.
(2001: Lab. maj. 17,713 (44.00%))

SELBY
E. 78,111 T. 52,549 (67.27%) Lab. hold
John Grogan, Lab. 22,623
Mark Menzies, C. 22,156
Ian Cuthbertson, LD 7,770
Lab. maj. 467 (0.89%)
1.68% swing Lab. to C.
(2001: Lab. maj. 2,138 (4.25%))

SEVENOAKS
E. 65,109 T. 43,298 (66.50%) C. hold
Michael Fallon, C. 22,437
Ben Abbotts, LD 9,467
Tim Stanley, Lab. 9,101
Robert Dobson, UKIP 1,309
John Marshall, Eng. Dem. 751
Mark Ellis, UK Path 233
C. maj. 12,970 (29.96%)
1.09% swing LD to C.
(2001: C. maj. 10,154 (23.83%))

SHEFFIELD ATTERCLIFFE
E. 67,815 T. 37,019 (54.59%) Lab. hold
Clive Betts, Lab. 22,250
Kevin Moore, LD 6,283
Tracy Critchlow, C. 5,329
Jonathan Arnott, UKIP 1,680
Beverley Jones, BNP 1,477
Lab. maj. 15,967 (43.13%)
5.22% swing Lab. to LD
(2001: Lab. maj. 18,844 (52.60%))

SHEFFIELD BRIGHTSIDE
E. 51,379 T. 24,629 (47.94%) Lab. hold
Rt. Hon. David Blunkett, Lab. 16,876
Jonathan Harston, LD 3,232
Tim Clark, C. 2,205
Christopher Hartigan, BNP 1,537
Judith Clarke, UKIP 779
Lab. maj. 13,644 (55.40%)
6.37% swing Lab. to LD
(2001: Lab. maj. 17,049 (66.72%))

SHEFFIELD CENTRAL
E. 59,862 T. 29,985 (50.09%) Lab. hold
Rt. Hon. Richard Caborn, Lab. 14,950
Ali Qadar, LD 7,895
Samantha George, C. 3,094
Bernard Little, Green 1,808
Maxine Bowler, Respect 1,284
Mark Payne, BNP 539
Charlotte Arnott, UKIP 415
Lab. maj. 7,055 (23.53%)
9.09% swing Lab. to LD
(2001: Lab. maj. 12,544 (41.72%))

SHEFFIELD HALLAM
E. 59,606 T. 40,427 (67.82%) LD hold
*Nick Clegg, LD 20,710
Spencer Pitfield, C. 12,028
Mahroof Hussain, Lab. 5,110
Rob Cole, Green 1,331
Sid Cordle, CPA 441
Nigel James, UKIP 438
Ian Senior, BNP 369
LD maj. 8,682 (21.48%)
1.48% swing LD to C.
(2001: LD maj. 9,347 (24.44%))

SHEFFIELD HEELEY
E. 59,748 T. 34,093 (57.06%)
Lab. (Co-op) hold
Meg Munn, Lab. (Co-op) 18,405
Colin Ross, LD 7,035
Aster Crawshaw, C. 4,987
John Beatson, BNP 1,314
Rob Unwin, Green 1,312
Mark Suter, UKIP 775
Mark Dunnell, Soc. Alt. 265
Lab. (Co-op) maj. 11,370 (33.35%)
0.47% swing Lab. (Co-op) to LD
(2001: Lab. (Co-op) maj. 11,704 (34.28%))

SHEFFIELD HILLSBOROUGH
E. 75,706 T. 45,884 (60.61%) Lab. hold
*Angela Smith, Lab. 23,477
John Commons, LD 12,234
Jackie Doyle-Price, C. 6,890
David Wright, BNP 2,010
Maurice Patterson, UKIP 1,273
Lab. maj. 11,243 (24.50%)
4.87% swing Lab. to LD
(2001: Lab. maj. 14,569 (34.25%))

SHERWOOD
E. 75,913 T. 47,117 (62.07%) Lab. hold
Paddy Tipping, Lab. 22,824
Bruce Laughton, C. 16,172
Peter Harris, LD 6,384
Moritz Dawkins, UKIP 1,737
Lab. maj. 6,652 (14.12%)
3.15% swing Lab. to C.
(2001: Lab. maj. 9,373 (20.42%))

SHIPLEY
E. 69,575 T. 47,666 (68.51%) C. gain
*Philip Davies, C. 18,608
Christopher Leslie, Lab. 18,186
John Briggs, LD 7,018
Tom Linden, BNP 2,000
Quentin Deakin, Green 1,665
David Crabtree, Iraq 189
C. maj. 422 (0.89%)
1.99% swing Lab. to C.
(2001: Lab. maj. 1,428 (3.10%))

SHREWSBURY & ATCHAM
E. 73,193 T. 50,296 (68.72%) C. gain
*Daniel Kawczynski, C. 18,960
Michael Ion, Lab. 17,152
Richard Burt, LD 11,487
Peter Lewis, UKIP 1,349
Emma Bullard, Green 1,138
James Gollins, Ind. 126
Nigel Harris, Online 84
C. maj. 1,808 (3.59%)
5.38% swing Lab. to C.
(2001: Lab. maj. 3,579 (7.17%))

SHROPSHIRE NORTH
E. 73,477 T. 46,510 (63.30%) C. hold
Owen Paterson, C. 23,061
Sandra Samuels, Lab. 12,041
Steven Bourne, LD 9,175
Ian Smith, UKIP 2,233
C. maj. 11,020 (23.69%)
5.14% swing Lab. to C.
(2001: C. maj. 6,241 (13.42%))

SITTINGBOURNE & SHEPPEY
E. 62,950 T. 40,803 (64.82%) Lab. hold
Derek Wyatt, Lab. 17,051
Gordon Henderson, C. 16,972
Jane Nelson, LD 5,183
Stephen Dean, UKIP 926
Mad MikeYoung, R & R Loony 479
David Cassidy, Veritas 192
Lab. maj. 79 (0.19%)
4.54% swing Lab. to C.
(2001: Lab. maj. 3,509 (9.27%))

SKIPTON & RIPON
E. 76,485 T. 50,521 (66.05%) C. hold
Rt. Hon. David Curry, C. 25,100
Paul English, LD 13,480
Paul Baptie, Lab. 9,393
Ian Bannister, UKIP 2,274
Robert Leakey, Currency 274
C. maj. 11,620 (23.00%)
1.66% swing C. to LD
(2001: C. maj. 12,930 (26.32%))

SLEAFORD & NORTH HYKEHAM
E. 79,612 T. 53,397 (67.07%) C. hold
Rt. Hon. Douglas Hogg, C. 26,855
Katrina Bull, Lab. 14,150
David Harding-Price, LD 9,710
Guy Croft, UKIP 2,682
C. maj. 12,705 (23.79%)
3.05% swing Lab. to C.
(2001: C. maj. 8,622 (17.70%))

SLOUGH
E. 71,595 T. 37,095 (51.81%) Lab. hold
Fiona Mactaggart, Lab. 17,517
Sheila Gunn, C. 9,666
Thomas McCann, LD 5,739
Ajaz Khan, Respect 1,632
Geoff Howard, UKIP 1,415
David Wood, Green 759
Paul Janik, Ind. 367
Lab. maj. 7,851 (21.16%)
5.45% swing Lab. to C.
(2001: Lab. maj. 12,508 (32.07%))

SOLIHULL
E. 77,910 T. 52,313 (67.15%) LD gain
*Lorely Burt, LD 20,896
John Taylor, C. 20,617
Rory Vaughan, Lab. 8,058
Diane Carr, BNP 1,752
Andrew Moore, UKIP 990
LD maj. 279 (0.53%)
10.01% swing C. to LD
(2001: C. maj. 9,407 (19.49%))

SOMERTON & FROME
E. 77,806 T. 54,102 (69.53%) LD hold
David Heath, LD 23,759
Clive Allen, C. 22,947
Joseph Pestell, Lab. 5,865
William Lukins, UKIP 1,047
Carleton Beaman, Veritas 484
LD maj. 812 (1.50%)
0.12% swing C. to LD
(2001: LD maj. 668 (1.27%))

SOUTH HOLLAND & THE DEEPINGS
E. 77,453 T. 48,249 (62.29%) C. hold
John Hayes, C. 27,544
Linda Woodings, Lab. 11,764
Steve Jarvis, LD 6,244
Jamie Corney, UKIP 1,950
Paul Poll, Ind. 747
C. maj. 15,780 (32.71%)
4.34% swing Lab. to C.
(2001: C. maj. 11,099 (24.02%))

SOUTH SHIELDS
E. 59,403 T. 30,206 (50.85%) Lab. hold
Rt. Hon. David Miliband, Lab. 18,269
Stephen Psallidas, LD 5,957
Richard Lewis, C. 5,207
Nader Afshari-Naderi, Ind. 773
Lab. maj. 12,312 (40.76%)
2.78% swing Lab. to LD
(2001: Lab. maj. 14,090 (46.28%))

SOUTHAMPTON ITCHEN
E. 78,818 T. 43,225 (54.84%) Lab. hold
Rt. Hon. John Denham, Lab. 20,871
Flick Drummond, C. 11,569
David Goodall, LD 9,162
Kim Rose, UKIP 1,623
Lab. maj. 9,302 (21.52%)
2.80% swing Lab. to C.
(2001: Lab. maj. 11,223 (27.13%))

SOUTHAMPTON TEST
E. 72,833 T. 41,783 (57.37%) Lab. hold
Dr Alan Whitehead, Lab. 17,845
Stephen MacLoughlin, C. 10,827
Steve Sollitt, LD 10,368
John Spottiswoode, Green 1,482
Peter Day, UKIP 1,261
Lab. maj. 7,018 (16.80%)
5.08% swing Lab. to C.
(2001: Lab. maj. 11,207 (26.96%))

SOUTHEND WEST
E. 64,915 T. 39,830 (61.36%) C. hold
David Amess, C. 18,408
Peter Wexham, LD 9,449
Jan Etienne, Lab. 9,072
Carole Sampson, UKIP 1,349
Dr Marimuthu Velmurugan, Ind. 745
Jeremy Moss, Eng. Dem. 701
Dan Anslow, Power 106
C. maj. 8,959 (22.49%)
0.55% swing LD to C.
(2001: C. maj. 7,941 (21.25%))

SOUTHPORT
E. 67,977 T. 41,201 (60.61%) LD hold
Dr John Pugh, LD 19,093
Mark Bigley, C. 15,255
Paul Brant, Lab. 5,277
Terry Durrance, UKIP 749
Bill Givens, YPB 589
Harry Forster, Veritas 238
LD maj. 3,838 (9.32%)
1.00% swing C. to LD
(2001: LD maj. 3,007 (7.31%))

SOUTHWARK NORTH & BERMONDSEY
E. 77,084 T. 37,959 (49.24%) LD hold
Simon Hughes, LD 17,874
Kirsty McNeill, Lab. 12,468
David Branch, C. 4,752
Storm Poorun, Green 1,137
Linda Robson, UKIP 791
Paul Winnett, NF 704
Simi Lawanson, CPA 233
LD maj. 5,406 (14.24%)
5.94% swing LD to Lab.
(2001: LD maj. 9,632 (26.13%))

SPELTHORNE
E. 69,650 T. 42,829 (61.49%) C. hold
David Wilshire, C. 21,620
Keith Dibble, Lab. 11,684
Simon James, LD 7,318
Christopher Browne, UKIP 1,968
Caroline Schwark, UKC 239
C. maj. 9,936 (23.20%)
7.70% swing Lab. to C.
(2001: C. maj. 3,262 (7.80%))

STAFFORD
E. 70,359 T. 45,554 (64.75%) Lab. hold
David Kidney, Lab. 19,889
David Chambers, C. 17,768
Barry Stamp, LD 6,390
Frederick Goode, UKIP 1,507
Lab. maj. 2,121 (4.66%)
3.34% swing Lab. to C.
(2001: Lab. maj. 5,032 (11.34%))

STAFFORDSHIRE MOORLANDS
E. 69,136 T. 44,253 (64.01%) Lab. hold

Charlotte Atkins, Lab.	18,126
Marcus Hayes, C.	15,688
John Fisher, LD	6,927
Steve Povey, UKIP	3,512

Lab. maj. 2,438 (5.51%)
4.09% swing Lab. to C.
(2001: Lab. maj. 5,838 (13.69%))

STAFFORDSHIRE SOUTH
Deferred until 23 June 2005 due to the death of the Liberal Democrat candidate during the general election campaign (*see* by-elections)

STALYBRIDGE & HYDE
E. 66,013 T. 35,314 (53.50%) Lab. hold

James Purnell, Lab.	17,535
Lisa Boardman, C.	9,187
Viv Bingham, LD	5,532
Nigel Byrne, BNP	1,399
Mike Smee, Green	1,088
Dr John Whittaker, UKIP	573

Lab. maj. 8,348 (23.64%)
2.00% swing Lab. to C.
(2001: Lab. maj. 8,859 (27.64%))

STEVENAGE
E. 66,889 T. 41,934 (62.69%) Lab. hold

Barbara Follett, Lab.	18,003
George Freeman, C.	14,864
Julia Davies, LD	7,610
Victoria Peebles, UKIP	1,305
Antal Losonczi, Ind.	152

Lab. maj. 3,139 (7.49%)
6.35% swing Lab. to C.
(2001: Lab. maj. 8,566 (20.18%))

STOCKPORT
E. 65,593 T. 35,771 (54.53%) Lab. hold

Ann Coffey, Lab.	18,069
Elizabeth Berridge, C.	8,906
Lyn-Su Floodgate, LD	7,832
Richard Simpson, UKIP	964

Lab. maj. 9,163 (25.62%)
3.54% swing Lab. to C.
(2001: Lab. maj. 11,569 (32.70%))

STOCKTON NORTH
E. 63,271 T. 36,428 (57.57%) Lab. hold

Frank Cook, Lab.	20,012
Harriett Baldwin, C.	7,575
Neil Hughes, LD	6,869
Kevin Hughes, BNP	986
Gordon Parkin, UKIP	986

Lab. maj. 12,437 (34.14%)
3.60% swing Lab. to C.
(2001: Lab. maj. 14,647 (41.34%))

STOCKTON SOUTH
E. 71,286 T. 44,923 (63.02%) Lab. hold

Dari Taylor, Lab.	21,480
James Gaddas, C.	15,341
Mike Barker, LD	7,171
Sandra Allison, UKIP	931

Lab. maj. 6,139 (13.67%)
3.44% swing Lab. to C.
(2001: Lab. maj. 9,086 (20.55%))

STOKE-ON-TRENT CENTRAL
E. 57,643 T. 27,907 (48.41%) Lab. hold

Mark Fisher, Lab.	14,760
John Redfern, LD	4,986
Esther Baroudy, C.	4,823
Michael Coleman, BNP	2,178
Joseph Bonfiglio, UKIP	914
Jim Cessford, Soc. Alt.	246

Lab. maj. 9,774 (35.02%)
5.50% swing Lab. to LD
(2001: Lab. maj. 11,845 (41.86%))

STOKE-ON-TRENT NORTH
E. 58,422 T. 30,760 (52.65%) Lab. hold

Joan Walley, Lab.	16,191
Benjamin Browning, C.	6,155
Henry Jebb, LD	4,561
Spencer Cartlidge, BNP	2,132
Eileen Braithwaite, UKIP	696
Ian Taylor, Veritas	689
Harry Chesters, Ind.	336

Lab. maj. 10,036 (32.63%)
3.25% swing Lab. to C.
(2001: Lab. maj. 11,784 (39.13%))

STOKE-ON-TRENT SOUTH
E. 70,612 T. 37,820 (53.56%) Lab. hold

*Robert Flello, Lab.	17,727
Mark Deaville, C.	9,046
Andrew Martin, LD	5,894
Mark Leat, BNP	3,305
Neville Benson, UKIP	1,043
Grant Allen, Veritas	805

Lab. maj. 8,681 (22.95%)
3.08% swing Lab. to C.
(2001: Lab. maj. 10,489 (29.11%))

STONE
E. 70,359 T. 47,036 (66.85%) C. hold

Bill Cash, C.	22,733
Mark Davis, Lab.	13,644
Peter Stevens, LD	9,111
Michael Nattrass, UKIP	1,548

C. maj. 9,089 (19.32%)
3.05% swing Lab. to C.
(2001: C. maj. 6,036 (13.22%))

STOURBRIDGE
E. 64,479 T. 41,708 (64.68%) Lab. hold

*Lynda Waltho, Lab.	17,089
Diana Coad, C.	16,682
Chris Bramall, LD	6,850
Daniel Pui Chai Mau, UKIP	1,087

Lab. maj. 407 (0.98%)
4.29% swing Lab. to C.
(2001: Lab. maj. 3,812 (9.55%))

STRATFORD-UPON-AVON
E. 84,591 T. 58,240 (68.85%) C. hold

John Maples, C.	28,652
Dr Susan Juned, LD	16,468
Rachel Blackmore, Lab. (Co-op)	10,145
Harry Cottam, UKIP	1,621
Mick Davies, Green	1,354

C. maj. 12,184 (20.92%)
0.29% swing C. to LD
(2001: C. maj. 11,802 (21.49%))

STREATHAM
E. 79,193 T. 40,615 (51.29%) Lab. hold

Rt. Hon. Keith Hill, Lab.	18,950
Darren Sanders, LD	11,484
James Sproule, C.	7,238
Shane Collins, Green	2,245
Trevor Gittings, UKIP	396
William Colvill, WRP	127
Philippa Stone, Ind.	100
Robert West, Ind.	40
Sarah Acheng, Ind.	35

Lab. maj. 7,466 (18.38%)
10.09% swing Lab. to LD
(2001: Lab. maj. 14,270 (38.57%))

STRETFORD & URMSTON
E. 61,979 T. 38,101 (61.47%) Lab. hold

Rt. Hon. Beverley Hughes, Lab.	19,417
Damian Hinds, C.	11,566
Faraz Bhatti, LD	5,323
Mark Krantz, Respect	950
Michael McManus, UKIP	845

Lab. maj. 7,851 (20.61%)
6.71% swing Lab. to C.
(2001: Lab. maj. 13,239 (33.97%))

STROUD
E. 79,748 T. 56,875 (71.32%)
Lab. (Co-op) hold

David Drew, Lab. (Co-op)	22,527
Neil Carmichael, C.	22,177
Peter Hirst, LD	8,026
Martin Whiteside, Green	3,056
Edward Noble, UKIP	1,089

Lab. (Co-op) maj. 350 (0.62%)
4.26% swing Lab. (Co-op) to C.
(2001: Lab. (Co-op) maj. 5,039 (9.13%))

SUFFOLK CENTRAL & IPSWICH NORTH
E. 76,271 T. 50,866 (66.69%) C. hold

Sir Michael Lord, C.	22,333
Neil MacDonald, Lab.	14,477
Andrew Houseley, LD	10,709
John West, UKIP	1,754
Martin Wolfe, Green	1,593

C. maj. 7,856 (15.44%)
4.04% swing Lab. to C.
(2001: C. maj. 3,469 (7.36%))

SUFFOLK COASTAL
E. 77,423 T. 52,557 (67.88%) C. hold

Rt. Hon. John Gummer, C.	23,415
David Rowe, Lab.	13,730
David Young, LD	11,637
Richard Curtis, UKIP	2,020
Paul Whitlow, Green	1,755

C. maj. 9,685 (18.43%)
4.92% swing Lab. to C.
(2001: C. maj. 4,326 (8.58%))

SUFFOLK SOUTH
E. 70,237 T. 48,707 (69.35%) C. hold

Tim Yeo, C.	20,471
Kathy Pollard, LD	13,865
Kevin Craig, Lab.	11,917
James Carver, UKIP	2,454

C. maj. 6,606 (13.56%)
1.45% swing C. to LD
(2001: C. maj. 5,081 (11.22%))

SUFFOLK WEST
E. 72,856 T. 44,205 (60.67%) C. hold
Richard Spring, C. 21,682
Michael Jefferys, Lab. 12,773
Adrian Graves, LD 7,573
Ian Smith, UKIP 2,177
C. maj. 8,909 (20.15%)
5.02% swing Lab. to C.
(2001: C. maj. 4,295 (10.12%))

SUNDERLAND NORTH
E. 58,146 T. 28,913 (49.72%) Lab. hold
Bill Etherington, Lab. 15,719
Stephen Daughton, C. 5,724
James Hollern, LD 4,277
Neil Herron, Ind. 2,057
Debra Hiles, BNP 1,136
Lab. maj. 9,995 (34.57%)
5.11% swing Lab. to C.
(2001: Lab. maj. 13,354 (44.78%))

SUNDERLAND SOUTH
E. 62,256 T. 30,712 (49.33%) Lab. hold
Chris Mullin, Lab. 17,982
Robert Oliver, C. 6,923
Gareth Kane, LD 4,492
David Guynan, BNP 1,166
Rosalyn Warner, Loony 149
Lab. maj. 11,059 (36.01%)
3.91% swing Lab. to C.
(2001: Lab. maj. 13,667 (43.82%))

SURREY EAST
E. 73,948 T. 49,253 (66.60%) C. hold
Peter Ainsworth, C. 27,659
Jeremy Pursehouse, LD 11,738
James Bridge, Lab. 7,288
Tony Stone, UKIP 2,158
Winston Matthews, LCA 410
C. maj. 15,921 (32.32%)
2.13% swing LD to C.
(2001: C. maj. 13,203 (28.06%))

SURREY HEATH
E. 76,090 T. 47,858 (62.90%) C. hold
*Michael Gove, C. 24,642
Rosalyn Harper, LD 13,797
Chris Lowe, Lab. 7,989
Steve Smith, UKIP 1,430
C. maj. 10,845 (22.66%)
0.66% swing C. to LD
(2001: C. maj. 10,819 (23.99%))

SURREY SOUTH WEST
E. 72,977 T. 52,409 (71.82%) C. hold
*Jeremy Hunt, C. 26,420
Simon Cordon, LD 20,709
Thomas Sleigh, Lab. 4,150
Timothy Clark, UKIP 958
Glenn Platt, Veritas 172
C. maj. 5,711 (10.90%)
4.58% swing LD to C.
(2001: C. maj. 861 (1.74%))

SUSSEX MID
E. 72,114 T. 49,494 (68.63%) C. hold
Hon. Nicholas Soames, C. 23,765
Serena Tierney, LD 17,875
Robert Fromant, Lab. 6,280
Harold Piggott, UKIP 1,574
C. maj. 5,890 (11.90%)
1.58% swing C. to LD
(2001: C. maj. 6,898 (15.05%))

SUTTON & CHEAM
E. 63,319 T. 41,932 (66.22%) LD hold
Paul Burstow, LD 19,768
Richard Willis, C. 16,922
Anand Shukla, Lab. 4,954
Rainbow George Weiss, Vote Dream 288
LD maj. 2,846 (6.79%)
2.02% swing LD to C.
(2001: LD maj. 4,304 (10.84%))

SUTTON COLDFIELD
E. 72,995 T. 46,318 (63.45%) C. hold
Andrew Mitchell, C. 24,308
Robert Pocock, Lab. 12,025
Craig Drury, LD 7,710
Stephen Shorrock, UKIP 2,275
C. maj. 12,283 (26.52%)
1.63% swing Lab. to C.
(2001: C. maj. 10,104 (23.25%))

SWINDON NORTH
E. 73,636 T. 44,885 (60.96%) Lab. hold
Michael Wills, Lab. 19,612
Justin Tomlinson, C. 17,041
Mike Evemy, LD 6,831
Robert Tingey, UKIP 998
Andy Newman, Soc. Unity 208
Ernest Reynolds, Ind. 195
Lab. maj. 2,571 (5.73%)
6.71% swing Lab. to C.
(2001: Lab. maj. 8,105 (19.15%))

SWINDON SOUTH
E. 72,267 T. 43,472 (60.15%) Lab. hold
*Anne Snelgrove, Lab. 17,534
Robert Buckland, C. 16,181
Sue Stebbing, LD 7,322
Bill Hughes, Green 1,234
Stephen Halden, UKIP 955
Alan Hayward, Ind. 193
John Williams, Ind. 53
Lab. maj. 1,353 (3.11%)
6.90% swing Lab. to C.
(2001: Lab. maj. 7,341 (16.92%))

TAMWORTH
E. 71,675 T. 43,740 (61.03%) Lab. hold
Brian Jenkins, Lab. 18,801
Christopher Pincher, C. 16,232
Phillip Bennion, LD 6,175
Patrick Eston, Veritas 1,320
Tom Simpson, UKIP 1,212
Lab. maj. 2,569 (5.87%)
2.78% swing Lab. to C.
(2001: Lab. maj. 4,598 (11.42%))

TATTON
E. 64,140 T. 41,414 (64.57%) C. hold
George Osborne, C. 21,447
Justin Madders, Lab. 9,716
Ainsley Arnold, LD 9,016
Diane Bowler, UKIP 996
Michael Gibson, Ind. 239
C. maj. 11,731 (28.33%)
3.73% swing Lab. to C.
(2001: C. maj. 8,611 (20.86%))

TAUNTON
E. 85,466 T. 59,528 (69.65%) LD gain
*Jeremy Browne, LD 25,764
Adrian Flook, C. 25,191
Andrew Govier, Lab. 7,132
Helen Miles, UKIP 1,441
LD maj. 573 (0.96%)
0.69% swing C. to LD
(2001: C. maj. 235 (0.43%))

TEIGNBRIDGE
E. 88,674 T. 60,898 (68.68%) LD hold
Richard Younger-Ross, LD 27,808
Stanley Johnson, C. 21,593
Chris Sherwood, Lab. 6,931
Trevor Colman, UKIP 3,881
Reginald Wills, Lib. 685
LD maj. 6,215 (10.21%)
2.56% swing C. to LD
(2001: LD maj. 3,011 (5.08%))

TELFORD
E. 59,277 T. 34,206 (57.71%) Lab. hold
David Wright, Lab. 16,506
Stella Kyriazis, C. 11,100
Ian Jenkins, LD 4,941
Tom McCartney, UKIP 1,659
Lab. maj. 5,406 (15.80%)
5.67% swing Lab. to C.
(2001: Lab. maj. 8,383 (27.15%))

TEWKESBURY
E. 72,145 T. 45,453 (63.00%) C. hold
Laurence Robertson, C. 22,339
Alistair Cameron, LD 12,447
Charles Mannan, Lab. 9,179
Robert Rendell, Green 1,488
C. maj. 9,892 (21.76%)
0.96% swing LD to C.
(2001: C. maj. 8,663 (19.17%))

THANET NORTH
E. 72,734 T. 43,732 (60.13%) C. hold
Roger Gale, C. 21,699
Iris Johnston, Lab. 14,065
Mark Barnard, LD 6,279
Timothy Stocks, UKIP 1,689
C. maj. 7,634 (17.46%)
0.79% swing Lab. to C.
(2001: C. maj. 6,650 (15.88%))

THANET SOUTH
E. 63,436 T. 41,242 (65.01%) Lab. hold
Dr Stephen Ladyman, Lab. 16,660
Mark MacGregor, C. 15,996
Guy Voizey, LD 5,431
Nigel Farage, UKIP 2,079
Howard Green, Green 888
Maude Kinsella, Ind. 188
Lab. maj. 664 (1.61%)
1.47% swing Lab. to C.
(2001: Lab. maj. 1,792 (4.54%))

THURROCK
E. 79,545 T. 43,692 (54.93%) Lab. hold
Andrew Mackinlay, Lab. 20,636
Garry Hague, C. 14,261
Earnshaw Palmer, LD 4,770
Nick Geri, BNP 2,526
Carol Jackson, UKIP 1,499
Lab. maj. 6,375 (14.59%)
6.08% swing Lab. to C.
(2001: Lab. maj. 9,997 (26.76%))

TIVERTON & HONITON
E. 83,375 T. 58,168 (69.77%) C. hold
Angela Browning, C. 27,838
David Nation, LD 16,787
Fiona Bentley, Lab. 7,944
Robert Edwards, UKIP 2,499
Roy Collins, Lib. 1,701
Colin Matthews, Green 1,399
C. maj. 11,051 (19.00%)
3.87% swing LD to C.
(2001: C. maj. 6,284 (11.26%))

TONBRIDGE & MALLING
E. 68,444 T. 46,063 (67.30%) C. hold
Rt. Hon. Sir John Stanley, C. 24,357
Victoria Hayman, Lab. 11,005
John Barstow, LD 8,980
David Waller, UKIP 1,721
C. maj. 13,352 (28.99%)
4.77% swing Lab. to C.
(2001: C. maj. 8,250 (19.44%))

TOOTING
E. 70,504 T. 41,568 (58.96%) Lab. hold
*Sadiq Khan, Lab. 17,914
James Bethell, C. 12,533
Stephanie Dearden, LD 8,110
Siobhan Vitelli, Green 1,695
Ali Zaidi, Respect 700
Strachan McDonald, UKIP 424
Ian Perkin, Ind. 192
Lab. maj. 5,381 (12.95%)
7.36% swing Lab. to C.
(2001: Lab. maj. 10,400 (27.67%))

TORBAY
E. 76,474 T. 47,303 (61.86%) LD hold
Adrian Sanders, LD 19,317
Marcus Wood, C. 17,288
David Pedrick-Friend, Lab. 6,972
Graham Booth, UKIP 3,726
LD maj. 2,029 (4.29%)
4.91% swing LD to C.
(2001: LD maj. 6,708 (14.10%))

TOTNES
E. 74,744 T. 50,575 (67.66%) C. hold
Anthony Steen, C. 21,112
Michael Treleaven, LD 19,165
Valerie Burns, Lab. 6,185
Roger Knapman, UKIP 3,914
Michael Thompson, Ind. 199
C. maj. 1,947 (3.85%)
1.73% swing C. to LD
(2001: C. maj. 3,597 (7.30%))

TOTTENHAM
E. 66,231 T. 31,664 (47.81%) Lab. hold
David Lammy, Lab. 18,343
Wayne Hoban, LD 5,309
William MacDougall, C. 4,278
Janet Alder, Respect 2,014
Pete McAskie, Green 1,457
Jaamit Durrani, Soc. Lab. 263
Lab. maj. 13,034 (41.16%)
8.39% swing Lab. to LD
(2001: Lab. maj. 16,916 (53.53%))

TRURO & ST AUSTELL
E. 80,256 T. 51,564 (64.25%) LD hold
Matthew Taylor, LD 24,089
Dr Fiona Kemp, C. 16,686
Dr Charlotte Mackenzie, Lab. 6,991
David Noakes, UKIP 2,736
Conan Jenkin, Meb. Ker. 1,062
LD maj. 7,403 (14.36%)
0.84% swing LD to C.
(2001: LD maj. 8,065 (16.04%))

TUNBRIDGE WELLS
E. 64,630 T. 42,482 (65.73%) C. hold
*Greg Clark, C. 21,083
Laura Murphy, LD 11,095
Jacqui Jedrzejewski, Lab. 8,736
Victor Webb, UKIP 1,568
C. maj. 9,988 (23.51%)
0.35% swing C. to LD
(2001: C. maj. 9,730 (24.20%))

TWICKENHAM
E. 72,015 T. 51,687 (71.77%) LD hold
Dr Vincent Cable, LD 26,696
Paul Maynard, C. 16,731
Brian Whitington, Lab. 5,868
Henry Gower, Green 1,445
Douglas Orchard, UKIP 766
Brian Gilbert, Ind. 117
Rainbow George Weiss, Vote Dream 64
LD maj. 9,965 (19.28%)
1.98% swing C. to LD
(2001: LD maj. 7,655 (15.33%))

TYNE BRIDGE
E. 53,565 T. 26,383 (49.25%) Lab. hold
David Clelland, Lab. 16,151
Chris Boyle, LD 5,751
Tom Fairhead, C. 2,962
Kevin Scott, BNP 1,072
Jill Russell, Respect 447
Lab. maj. 10,400 (39.42%)
9.35% swing Lab. to LD
(2001: Lab. maj. 14,889 (57.19%))

TYNEMOUTH
E. 64,023 T. 42,859 (66.94%) Lab. hold
Alan Campbell, Lab. 20,143
Michael McIntyre, C. 16,000
Colin Finlay, LD 6,716
Lab. maj. 4,143 (9.67%)
5.05% swing Lab. to C.
(2001: Lab. maj. 8,678 (19.77%))

TYNESIDE NORTH
E. 64,634 T. 36,939 (57.15%) Lab. hold
Rt. Hon. Stephen Byers, Lab. 22,882
Duncan McLellan, C. 7,845
Gillian Ferguson, LD 6,212
Lab. maj. 15,037 (40.71%)
7.09% swing Lab. to C.
(2001: Lab. maj. 20,668 (55.01%))

UPMINSTER
E. 55,075 T. 34,676 (62.96%) C. hold
Angela Watkinson, C. 16,820
Keith Darvill, Lab. 10,778
Peter Truesdale, LD 3,128
Ronald Ower, RA 1,455
Chris Roberts, BNP 1,173
Alan Hindle, UKIP 701
Melanie Collins, Green 543
David Durant, Third 78
C. maj. 6,042 (17.42%)
6.88% swing Lab. to C.
(2001: C. maj. 1,241 (3.67%))

UXBRIDGE
E. 57,878 T. 34,378 (59.40%) C. hold
John Randall, C. 16,840
Rod Marshall, Lab. 10,669
Dr Tariq Mahmood, LD 4,544
Cliff Le May, BNP 763
Stephen Young, Green 725
Robert Kerby, UKIP 553
Peter Shaw, NF 284
C. maj. 6,171 (17.95%)
5.84% swing Lab. to C.
(2001: C. maj. 2,098 (6.28%))

VALE OF YORK
E. 76,000 T. 50,378 (66.29%) C. hold
Anne McIntosh, C. 26,025
David Scott, Lab. 12,313
Jeremy Wilcock, LD 12,040
C. maj. 13,712 (27.22%)
0.70% swing Lab. to C.
(2001: C. maj. 12,517 (25.81%))

VAUXHALL
E. 79,637 T. 37,353 (46.90%) Lab. hold
Kate Hoey, Lab. 19,744
Charles Anglin, LD 9,767
Edward Heckels, C. 5,405
Tim Summers, Green 1,705
Robert McWhirter, UKIP 271
Daniel Lambert, Socialist 240
Janus Polenceus, Eng. Dem. 221
Lab. maj. 9,977 (26.71%)
6.14% swing Lab. to LD
(2001: Lab. maj. 13,018 (38.99%))

WAKEFIELD
E. 73,118 T. 43,381 (59.33%) Lab. hold
*Mary Creagh, Lab. 18,802
Alec Shelbrooke, C. 13,648
David Ridgway, LD 7,063
Grant Rowe, BNP 1,328
Derek Hardcastle, Green 1,297
John Upex, UKIP 467
Paul McEnhill, Eng. Dem. 356
Mick Griffiths, Soc. Alt. 319
Linda Sheridan, Soc. Lab. 101
Lab. maj. 5,154 (11.88%)
3.70% swing Lab. to C.
(2001: Lab. maj. 7,954 (19.28%))

WALLASEY
E. 63,764 T. 36,671 (57.51%) Lab. hold
Angela Eagle, Lab. 20,085
Leah Fraser, C. 10,976
Joanna Pemberton, LD 4,770
Philip Griffiths, UKIP 840
Lab. maj. 9,109 (24.84%)
4.02% swing Lab. to C.
(2001: Lab. maj. 12,276 (32.87%))

WALSALL NORTH
E. 63,268 T. 33,428 (52.84%) Lab. hold
David Winnick, Lab. 15,990
Ian Lucas, C. 9,350
Douglas Taylor, LD 4,144
William Locke, BNP 1,992
Anthony Lenton, UKIP 1,182
Peter Smith, Dem. Lab. 770
Lab. maj. 6,640 (19.86%)
4.60% swing Lab. to C.
(2001: Lab. maj. 9,391 (29.06%))

WALSALL SOUTH
E. 60,370 T. 35,315 (58.50%) Lab. hold
Rt. Hon. Bruce George, Lab. 17,633
Kabir Sabar, C. 9,687
Mohamed Hanif Asmal, LD 3,240
Derek Bennett, UKIP 1,833
Kevin Smith, BNP 1,776
Nadia Fazal, Respect 1,146
Lab. maj. 7,946 (22.50%)
2.98% swing Lab. to C.
(2001: Lab. maj. 9,931 (28.46%))

WALTHAMSTOW
E. 63,079 T. 34,444 (54.60%) Lab. hold
Neil Gerrard, Lab. 17,323
Farid Ahmed, LD 9,330
Jane Wright, C. 6,254
Robert Brock, UKIP 810
Nancy Taaffe, Soc. Alt. 727
Lab. maj. 7,993 (23.21%)
12.18% swing Lab. to LD
(2001: Lab. maj. 15,181 (44.09%))

WANSBECK
E. 63,096 T. 36,809 (58.34%) Lab. hold
Denis Murphy, Lab. 20,315
Simon Reed, LD 9,734
Ginny Scrope, C. 5,515
Dr Nic Best, Green 1,245
Lab. maj. 10,581 (28.75%)
3.13% swing Lab. to LD
(2001: Lab. maj. 13,101 (35.01%))

WANSDYKE
E. 70,359 T. 50,933 (72.39%) Lab. hold
Dan Norris, Lab. 20,686
Chris Watt, C. 18,847
Gail Coleshill, LD 10,050
Peter Sandell, UKIP 1,129
Geoffrey Parkes, Ind. 221
Lab. maj. 1,839 (3.61%)
3.86% swing Lab. to C.
(2001: Lab. maj. 5,113 (10.42%))

WANTAGE
E. 76,156 T. 51,931 (68.19%) C. hold
*Ed Vaizey, C. 22,354
Andrew Crawford, LD 14,337
Mark McDonald, Lab. 12,464
Adam Twine, Green 1,332
Nikolai Tolstoy-Miloslavsky, UKIP 798
Gerald Lambourne, Eng. Dem. 646
C. maj. 8,017 (15.44%)
1.92% swing LD to C.
(2001: C. maj. 5,600 (11.40%))

WARLEY
E. 56,171 T. 32,087 (57.12%) Lab. hold
Rt. Hon. John Spellar, Lab. 17,462
Karen Bissell, C. 7,315
Tony Ferguson, LD 4,277
Simon Smith, BNP 1,761
Malcolm Connigale, Soc. Lab. 637
David Matthews, UKIP 635
Lab. maj. 10,147 (31.62%)
3.05% swing Lab. to C.
(2001: Lab. maj. 11,850 (37.72%))

WARRINGTON NORTH
E. 73,352 T. 40,418 (55.10%) Lab. hold
Helen Jones, Lab. 21,632
Andrew Ferryman, C. 9,428
Peter Walker, LD 7,699
John Kirkham, UKIP 1,086
Mike Hughes, CAP 573
Lab. maj. 12,204 (30.19%)
4.38% swing Lab. to C.
(2001: Lab. maj. 15,156 (38.95%))

WARRINGTON SOUTH
E. 75,724 T. 46,797 (61.80%) Lab. hold
Helen Southworth, Lab. 18,972
Fiona Bruce, C. 15,457
Ian Marks, LD 11,111
Gerald Kelley, UKIP 804
Paul Kennedy, Ind. 453
Lab. maj. 3,515 (7.51%)
4.37% swing Lab. to C.
(2001: Lab. maj. 7,387 (16.24%))

WARWICK & LEAMINGTON
E. 81,205 T. 54,784 (67.46%) Lab. hold
James Plaskitt, Lab. 22,238
Chris White, C. 21,972
Linda Forbes, LD 8,119
Ian Davison, Green 1,534
Greville Warwick, UKIP 921
Lab. maj. 266 (0.49%)
5.32% swing Lab. to C.
(2001: Lab. maj. 5,953 (11.12%))

WARWICKSHIRE NORTH
E. 75,435 T. 46,939 (62.22%) Lab. hold
Mike O'Brien, Lab. 22,561
Ian Gibb, C. 15,008
Jerry Roodhouse, LD 6,212
Michaela Mackenzie, BNP 1,910
Iain Campbell, UKIP 1,248
Lab. maj. 7,553 (16.09%)
2.81% swing Lab. to C.
(2001: Lab. maj. 9,639 (21.71%))

WATFORD
E. 76,280 T. 49,394 (64.75%) Lab. hold
Claire Ward, Lab. 16,575
Sal Brinton, LD 15,427
Ali Miraj, C. 14,634
Steve Rackett, Green 1,466
Kenneth Wight, UKIP 1,292
Lab. maj. 1,148 (2.32%)
12.75% swing Lab. to LD
(2001: Lab. maj. 5,555 (11.98%))

WAVENEY
E. 77,138 T. 49,653 (64.37%) Lab. hold
Bob Blizzard, Lab. 22,505
Peter Aldous, C. 16,590
Nick Bromley, LD 7,497
Brian Aylett, UKIP 1,861
Graham Elliott, Green 1,200
Lab. maj. 5,915 (11.91%)
3.11% swing Lab. to C.
(2001: Lab. maj. 8,553 (18.13%))

WEALDEN
E. 82,261 T. 55,653 (67.65%) C. hold
Charles Hendry, C. 28,975
Christopher Wigley, LD 13,054
Dudley Rose, Lab. 9,360
Julian Salmon, Green 2,150
Keith Riddle, UKIP 2,114
C. maj. 15,921 (28.61%)
1.25% swing LD to C.
(2001: C. maj. 13,772 (26.11%))

WEAVER VALE
E. 69,072 T. 39,420 (57.07%) Lab. hold
Mike Hall, Lab. 18,759
Jonathan Mackie, C. 11,904
Nigel Griffiths, LD 7,723
Brenda Swinscoe, UKIP 1,034
Lab. maj. 6,855 (17.39%)
3.58% swing Lab. to C.
(2001: Lab. maj. 9,637 (24.54%))

WELLINGBOROUGH
E. 79,679 T. 53,005 (66.52%) C. gain
*Peter Bone, C. 22,674
Paul Stinchcombe, Lab. 21,987
Richard Church, LD 6,147
James Wrench, UKIP 1,214
Nicholas Alex, Veritas 749
Andy Dickson, Soc. Lab. 234
C. maj. 687 (1.30%)
2.96% swing Lab. to C.
(2001: Lab. maj. 2,355 (4.62%))

WELLS
E. 77,842 T. 52,965 (68.04%) C. hold
Rt. Hon. David Heathcoat-Amory, C. 23,071
Tessa Munt, LD 20,031
Dan Whittle, Lab. 8,288
Steven Reed, UKIP 1,575
C. maj. 3,040 (5.74%)
0.15% swing LD to C.
(2001: C. maj. 2,796 (5.45%))

WELWYN HATFIELD
E. 65,617 T. 44,716 (68.15%) C. gain
*Grant Shapps, C. 22,172
Melanie Johnson, Lab. 16,226
Sara Bedford, LD 6,318
C. maj. 5,946 (13.30%)
8.05% swing Lab. to C.
(2001: Lab. maj. 1,196 (2.79%))

WENTWORTH
E. 63,561 T. 35,596 (56.00%) Lab. hold
John Healey, Lab. 21,225
Mark Hughes, C. 6,169
Keith Orrell, LD 4,800
Jonathan Pygott, BNP 1,798
John Wilkinson, UKIP 1,604
Lab. maj. 15,056 (42.30%)
3.20% swing Lab. to C.
(2001: Lab. maj. 16,449 (48.70%))

WEST BROMWICH EAST
E. 60,565 T. 35,512 (58.63%) Lab. hold
Tom Watson, Lab. 19,741
Rosemary Bromwich, C. 8,089
Ian Garrett, LD 4,386
Carl Butler, BNP 2,329
Steven Grey, UKIP 607
Judith Sambrook, Soc. Lab. 200
Margaret Macklin, Ind. 160
Lab. maj. 11,652 (32.81%)
1.46% swing C. to Lab.
(2001: Lab. maj. 9,763 (29.89%))

WEST BROMWICH WEST
E. 66,752 T. 34,917 (52.31%) Lab. (Co-op) hold
Adrian Bailey, Lab. (Co-op) 18,951
Mimi Harker, C. 8,057
Martyn Smith, LD 3,583
James Lloyd, BNP 3,456
Kevin Walker, UKIP 870
Lab. (Co-op) maj. 10,894 (31.20%)
2.23% swing Lab. (Co-op) to C.
(2001: Lab. (Co-op) maj. 11,355 (35.66%))

WEST HAM
E. 62,184 T. 30,966 (49.80%) Lab. hold
*Lyn Brown, Lab. 15,840
Lindsey German, Respect 6,039
Chris Whitbread, C. 3,618
Alexandra Sugden, LD 3,364
Jane Lithgow, Green 894
Stephen Hammond, CPA 437
Henry Mayhew, UKIP 409
Generoso Alcantara, Veritas 365
Lab. maj. 9,801 (31.65%)
19.12% swing Lab. to Respect
(2001: Lab. maj. 15,645 (53.45%))

WESTBURY
E. 83,039 T. 55,604 (66.96%) C. hold
Dr Andrew Murrison, C. 24,749
Duncan Hames, LD 19,400
Phil Gibby, Lab. 9,640
Lincoln Williams, UKIP 1,815
C. maj. 5,349 (9.62%)
0.42% swing C. to LD
(2001: C. maj. 5,294 (10.46%))

WESTMORLAND & LONSDALE
E. 69,363 T. 49,636 (71.56%) LD gain
*Tim Farron, LD 22,569
Tim Collins, C. 22,302
John Reardon, Lab. 3,796
Robert Gibson, UKIP 660
Anthony Kemp, Ind. 309
LD maj. 267 (0.54%)
3.55% swing C. to LD
(2001: C. maj. 3,147 (6.57%))

WESTON-SUPER-MARE
E. 74,900 T. 49,095 (65.55%) C. gain
*John Penrose, C. 19,804
Brian Cotter, LD 17,725
Damien Egan, Lab. 9,169
Paul Spencer, UKIP 1,207
Clive Courtney, BNP 778
William Human, Ind. 225
Paul Hemingway-Arnold, Honesty 187
C. maj. 2,079 (4.23%)
2.48% swing LD to C.
(2001: LD maj. 338 (0.72%))

WIGAN
E. 64,267 T. 34,278 (53.34%) Lab. hold
Neil Turner, Lab. 18,901
John Coombes, C. 7,134
Denise Capstick, LD 6,051
Dr John Whittaker, UKIP 1,166
Kevin Williams, CAP 1,026
Lab. maj. 11,767 (34.33%)
3.29% swing Lab. to C.
(2001: Lab. maj. 13,743 (40.91%))

WILTSHIRE NORTH
E. 80,896 T. 56,061 (69.30%) C. hold
James Gray, C. 26,282
Paul Fox, LD 20,979
David Nash, Lab. 6,794
Neil Dowdney, UKIP 1,428
Philip Allnatt, Ind. 578
C. maj. 5,303 (9.46%)
1.07% swing LD to C.
(2001: C. maj. 3,878 (7.32%))

WIMBLEDON
E. 63,714 T. 43,404 (68.12%) C. gain
*Stephen Hammond, C. 17,886
Roger Casale, Lab. 15,585
Stephen Gee, LD 7,868
Giles Barrow, Green 1,374
Andrew Mills, UKIP 408
Christopher Coverdale, Ind. 211
Alastair Wilson, TEPK 50
Rainbow George Weiss, Vote Dream 22
C. maj. 2,301 (5.30%)
7.20% swing Lab. to C.
(2001: Lab. maj. 3,744 (9.11%))

WINCHESTER
E. 85,810 T. 61,658 (71.85%) LD hold
Mark Oaten, LD 31,225
George Hollingbery, C. 23,749
Patrick Davies, Lab. 4,782
Dr David Abbott, UKIP 1,321
Arthur Uther Pendragon, Ind. 581
LD maj. 7,476 (12.12%)
2.08% swing LD to C.
(2001: LD maj. 9,634 (16.29%))

WINDSOR
E. 68,290 T. 43,693 (63.98%) C. hold
*Adam Afriyie, C. 21,646
Antony Wood, LD 11,354
Mark Muller, Lab. 8,339
David Black, UKIP 1,098
Derek Wall, Green 1,074
Peter Hooper, Ind. 182
C. maj. 10,292 (23.56%)
1.22% swing LD to C.
(2001: C. maj. 8,889 (21.11%))

WIRRAL SOUTH
E. 58,834 T. 39,704 (67.48%) Lab. hold
Ben Chapman, Lab. 16,892
Carl Cross, C. 13,168
Simon Holbrook, LD 8,568
David Scott, UKIP 616
Laurence Jones, Ind. 460
Lab. maj. 3,724 (9.38%)
1.65% swing Lab. to C.
(2001: Lab. maj. 5,049 (12.68%))

WIRRAL WEST
E. 61,050 T. 41,233 (67.54%) Lab. hold
Stephen Hesford, Lab. 17,543
Esther McVey, C. 16,446
Jeff Clarke, LD 6,652
John Moore, UKIP 429
Roger Taylor, AP 163
Lab. maj. 1,097 (2.66%)
3.65% swing Lab. to C.
(2001: Lab. maj. 4,035 (9.97%))

WITNEY
E. 78,053 T. 53,869 (69.02%) C. hold
David Cameron, C. 26,571
Liz Leffman, LD 12,415
Tony Gray, Lab. 11,845
Richard Dossett-Davies, Green 1,682
Paul Wesson, UKIP 1,356
C. maj. 14,156 (26.28%)
0.79% swing LD to C.
(2001: C. maj. 7,973 (16.20%))

WOKING
E. 72,676 T. 46,045 (63.36%) C. hold
Humfrey Malins, C. 21,838
Anne Lee, LD 15,226
Ellie Blagbrough, Lab. 7,507
Matthew Davies, UKIP 1,324
Michael Osman, UKC 150
C. maj. 6,612 (14.36%)
0.70% swing C. to LD
(2001: C. maj. 6,759 (15.75%))

WOKINGHAM
E. 68,614 T. 46,072 (67.15%) C. hold
Rt. Hon. John Redwood, C. 22,174
Prue Bray, LD 14,934
David Black, Lab. 6,991
Frank Carstairs, UKIP 994
Top Cat Owen, Loony 569
Richard Colborne, BNP 376
Michael Hall, Tele. 34
C. maj. 7,240 (15.71%)
1.02% swing LD to C.
(2001: C. maj. 5,994 (13.67%))

WOLVERHAMPTON NORTH EAST
E. 60,595 T. 32,956 (54.39%)
Lab. (Co-op) hold
Ken Purchase, Lab. (Co-op) 17,948
Alexandra Robson, C. 9,792
David Jack, LD 3,845
Lydia Simpson, UKIP 1,371
Lab. (Co-op) maj. 8,156 (24.75%)
3.45% swing Lab. (Co-op) to C.
(2001: Lab. (Co-op) maj. 9,965
(31.64%))

WOLVERHAMPTON SOUTH EAST
E. 54,047 T. 28,251 (52.27%) Lab. hold
*Pat McFadden, Lab. 16,790
James Fairbairn, C. 6,295
David Murray, LD 3,682
Kevin Simmons, UKIP 1,484
Lab. maj. 10,495 (37.15%)
4.26% swing Lab. to C.
(2001: Lab. (Co-op) maj. 12,464
(45.66%))

WOLVERHAMPTON SOUTH WEST
E. 67,096 T. 41,679 (62.12%) Lab. hold
Rob Marris, Lab. 18,489
Sandy Verma, C. 15,610
Colin Ross, LD 5,568
Douglas Hope, UKIP 1,029
Edward Mullins, BNP 983
Lab. maj. 2,879 (6.91%)
0.81% swing Lab. to C.
(2001: Lab. maj. 3,487 (8.53%))

WOODSPRING
E. 71,662 T. 51,618 (72.03%) C. hold
Dr Liam Fox, C. 21,587
Mike Bell, LD 15,571
Chanel Stevens, Lab. 11,249
Rebecca Lewis, Green 1,309
Anthony Butcher, UKIP 1,269
Michael Howson, BNP 633
C. maj. 6,016 (11.65%)
3.90% swing C. to LD
(2001: C. maj. 8,798 (18.04%))

WORCESTER
E. 72,384 T. 46,388 (64.09%) Lab. hold
Michael Foster, Lab. 19,421
Margaret Harper, C. 16,277
Mary Dhonau, LD 7,557
Richard Chamings, UKIP 1,113
Martin Roberts, BNP 980
Chris Lennard, Green 921
Prudence Dowson, Ind. 119
Lab. maj. 3,144 (6.78%)
3.13% swing Lab. to C.
(2001: Lab. maj. 5,766 (13.04%))

WORCESTERSHIRE MID
E. 71,546 T. 48,127 (67.27%) C. hold
Peter Luff, C. 24,783
Matt Gregson, Lab. 11,456
Margaret Rowley, LD 9,796
Tony Eaves, UKIP 2,092
C. maj. 13,327 (27.69%)
2.01% swing Lab. to C.
(2001: C. maj. 10,627 (23.67%))

WORCESTERSHIRE WEST
E. 66,999 T. 47,077 (70.27%) C. hold
Sir Michael Spicer, C. 20,959
Tom Wells, LD 18,484
Qamar Bhatti, Lab. 4,945
Caroline Bovey, UKIP 1,590
Malcolm Victory, Green 1,099
C. maj. 2,475 (5.26%)
3.37% swing C. to LD
(2001: C. maj. 5,374 (11.99%))

WORKINGTON
E. 61,441 T. 39,737 (64.68%) Lab. hold
Tony Cunningham, Lab. 19,554
Judith Pattinson, C. 12,659
Kate Clarkson, LD 5,815
Mark Richardson, UKIP 1,328
John Peacock, LCA 381
Lab. maj. 6,895 (17.35%)
4.30% swing Lab. to C.
(2001: Lab. maj. 10,850 (25.94%))

WORSLEY
E. 69,534 T. 36,946 (53.13%) Lab. hold
*Barbara Keeley, Lab. 18,859
Graham Evans, C. 9,491
Richard Clayton, LD 6,902
Bernard Gill, UKIP 1,694
Lab. maj. 9,368 (25.36%)
3.99% swing Lab. to C.
(2001: Lab. maj. 11,787 (33.33%))

WORTHING EAST & SHOREHAM
E. 72,302 T. 44,543 (61.61%) C. hold
Tim Loughton, C. 19,548
Daniel Yates, Lab. 11,365
James Doyle, LD 10,844
Richard Jelf, UKIP 2,109
Chris Baldwin, LCA 677
C. maj. 8,183 (18.37%)
2.06% swing Lab. to C.
(2001: C. maj. 6,139 (14.25%))

WORTHING WEST
E. 71,780 T. 44,941 (62.61%) C. hold
Peter Bottomley, C. 21,383
Claire Potter, LD 12,004
Antony Bignell, Lab. 8,630
Timothy Cross, UKIP 2,374
Chris Baldwin, LCA 550
C. maj. 9,379 (20.87%)
0.02% swing C. to LD
(2001: C. maj. 9,037 (20.91%))

WREKIN, THE
E. 67,291 T. 45,054 (66.95%) C. gain
*Mark Pritchard, C. 18,899
Peter Bradley, Lab. 17,957
Bill Tomlinson, LD 6,608
Bruce Lawson, UKIP 1,590
C. maj. 942 (2.09%)
5.37% swing Lab. to C.
(2001: Lab. maj. 3,587 (8.65%))

WYCOMBE
E. 71,464 T. 44,427 (62.17%) C. hold
Paul Goodman, C. 20,331
Julia Wassell, Lab. 13,280
James Oates, LD 8,780
Robert Davis, UKIP 1,735
David Fitton, Ind. 301
C. maj. 7,051 (15.87%)
4.41% swing Lab. to C.
(2001: C. maj. 3,168 (7.04%))

WYRE FOREST
E. 73,192 T. 46,987 (64.20%) KHHC hold
Dr Richard Taylor, KHHC 18,739
Mark Garnier, C. 13,489
Marc Bayliss, Lab. 10,716
Fran Oborski, Lib. 2,666
Rustie Lee, UKIP 1,074
Bert Priest, Loony 303
KHHC maj. 5,250 (11.17%)
13.92% swing KHHC to C.
(2001: KHHC maj. 17,630 (35.93%))

WYTHENSHAWE & SALE EAST
E. 71,766 T. 36,184 (50.42%) Lab. hold
Paul Goggins, Lab. 18,878
Jane Meehan, C. 8,051
Alison Firth, LD 7,766
William Ford, UKIP 1,120
Lynn Worthington, Soc. Alt. 369
Lab. maj. 10,827 (29.92%)
3.02% swing Lab. to C.
(2001: Lab. maj. 12,608 (35.97%))

YEOVIL
E. 77,668 T. 49,913 (64.26%) LD hold
David Laws, LD 25,658
Ian Jenkins, C. 17,096
Colin Rolfe, Lab. 5,256
Graham Livings, UKIP 1,903
LD maj. 8,562 (17.15%)
4.50% swing C. to LD
(2001: LD maj. 3,928 (8.16%))

YORK, CITY OF
E. 75,555 T. 46,597 (61.67%) Lab. hold
Hugh Bayley, Lab. 21,836
Clive Booth, C. 11,364
Andrew Waller, LD 10,166
Andy D'Agorne, Green 2,113
Richard Jackson, UKIP 832
Ken Curran, Ind. 121
Damien Fleck, DDTP 93
Andrew Hinkles, Ind. 72
Lab. maj. 10,472 (22.47%)
3.12% swing Lab. to C.
(2001: Lab. maj. 13,779 (28.72%))

YORKSHIRE EAST
E. 76,648 T. 46,925 (61.22%) C. hold
Rt. Hon. Greg Knight, C. 21,215
Emma Hoddinott, Lab. 14,932
Jim Wastling, LD 9,075
Christopher Tresidder, UKIP 1,703
C. maj. 6,283 (13.39%)
1.29% swing Lab. to C.
(2001: C. maj. 4,682 (10.81%))

WALES

ABERAVON
E. 51,080 T. 30,104 (58.94%) Lab. hold
Dr Hywel Francis, Lab. 18,077
Claire Waller, LD 4,140
Philip Evans, PC 3,545
Annunziata Rees-Mogg, C. 3,064
Walter Wright, Veritas 768
Miranda La Vey, Green 510
Lab. maj. 13,937 (46.30%)
3.57% swing Lab. to LD
(2001: Lab. maj. 16,108 (53.36%))

ALYN & DEESIDE
E. 58,939 T. 35,496 (60.22%) Lab. hold
Mark Tami, Lab. 17,331
Lynne Hale, C. 8,953
Paul Brighton, LD 6,174
Richard Coombs, PC 1,320
William Crawford, UKIP 918
Klaus Armstrong-Braun, FWP 378
Judith Kilshaw, Ind. 215
Glyn Davies, Comm Brit 207
Lab. maj. 8,378 (23.60%)
1.22% swing Lab. to C.
(2001: Lab. maj. 9,222 (26.04%))

BLAENAU GWENT
E. 53,301 T. 35,251 (66.14%) Ind. gain
*Peter Law, Ind. 20,505
Maggie Jones, Lab. 11,384
Brian Thomas, LD 1,511
John Price, PC 843
Dr Phillip Lee, C. 816
Peter Osborne, UKIP 192
Ind. maj. 9,121 (25.87%)
43.38% swing Lab. to Ind.
(2001: Lab. maj. 19,313 (60.88%))

BRECON & RADNORSHIRE
E. 55,171 T. 38,341 (69.49%) LD hold
Roger Williams, LD 17,182
Andrew Davies, C. 13,277
Leighton Veale, Lab. 5,755
Mabon ap Gwynfor, PC 1,404
Elizabeth Phillips, UKIP 723
LD maj. 3,905 (10.18%)
4.09% swing C. to LD
(2001: LD maj. 751 (2.00%))

BRIDGEND
E. 63,936 T. 37,859 (59.21%) Lab. hold
*Madeleine Moon, Lab. 16,410
Helen Baker, C. 9,887
Paul Warren, LD 7,949
Gareth Clubb, PC 2,527
Jonathan Spink, Green 595
Kunnathur Rajan, UKIP 491
Lab. maj. 6,523 (17.23%)
4.96% swing Lab. to C.
(2001: Lab. maj. 10,045 (27.15%))

CAERNARFON
E. 46,393 T. 27,999 (60.35%) PC hold
Hywel Williams, PC 12,747
Martin Eaglestone, Lab. 7,538
Melfyn ab Owain, LD 3,508
Guy Opperman, C. 3,483
Elwyn Williams, UKIP 723
PC maj. 5,209 (18.60%)
3.26% swing Lab. to PC
(2001: PC maj. 3,511 (12.08%))

CAERPHILLY
E. 66,939 T. 39,229 (58.60%) Lab. hold
Wayne David, Lab. 22,190
Lindsay Whittle, PC 6,831
Stephen Watson, C. 5,711
Ashgar Ali, LD 3,861
Graeme Beard, FWP 636
Lab. maj. 15,359 (39.15%)
1.00% swing PC to Lab.
(2001: Lab. maj. 14,425 (37.15%))

CARDIFF CENTRAL
E. 61,001 T. 36,132 (59.23%) LD gain
*Jenny Willott, LD 17,991
Jon Owen Jones, Lab. (Co-op) 12,398
Gotz Mohindra, C. 3,339
Richard Grigg, PC 1,271
Raja Gul Raiz, Respect 386
Frank Hughes, UKIP 383
Anne Savoury, Ind. 168
Captain Beany, Bean 159
Catherine Taylor-Dawson, Vote Dream 37
LD maj. 5,593 (15.48%)
8.69% swing Lab. (Co-op) to LD
(2001: Lab. (Co-op) maj. 659 (1.89%))

CARDIFF NORTH
E. 64,341 T. 45,360 (70.50%) Lab. hold
Julie Morgan, Lab. 17,707
Jonathan Morgan, C. 16,561
John Dixon, LD 8,483
John Rowlands, PC 1,936
Don Hulston, UKIP 534
Alison Hobbs, FWP 138
Catherine Taylor-Dawson, Vote Dream 1
Lab. maj. 1,146 (2.53%)
5.87% swing Lab. to C.
(2001: Lab. maj. 6,165 (14.26%))

CARDIFF SOUTH & PENARTH
E. 65,710 T. 36,912 (56.17%) Lab. (Co-op) hold
Rt. Hon. Alun Michael, Lab. (Co-op) 17,447
Victoria Green, C. 8,210
Gavin Cox, LD 7,529
Jason Toby, PC 2,023
John Matthews, Green 729
Jennifer Tuttle, UKIP 522
Dave Bartlett, Soc. Alt. 269
Andrew Taylor, Ind. 104
Catherine Taylor-Dawson, Vote Dream 79
Lab. (Co-op) maj. 9,237 (25.02%)
4.67% swing Lab. (Co-op) to C.
(2001: Lab. (Co-op) maj. 12,287 (34.37%))

CARDIFF WEST
E. 59,847 T. 34,561 (57.75%) Lab. hold
Kevin Brennan, Lab. 15,729
Simon Baker, C. 7,562
Alison Goldsworthy, LD 6,060
Neil McEvoy, PC 4,316
Joe Callan, UKIP 727
Catherine Taylor-Dawson, Vote Dream 167
Lab. maj. 8,167 (23.63%)
4.79% swing Lab. to C.
(2001: Lab. maj. 11,321 (33.22%))

CARMARTHEN EAST & DINEFWR
E. 53,484 T. 38,291 (71.59%) PC hold
Adam Price, PC 17,561
Ross Hendry, Lab. 10,843
Suzy Davies, C. 5,235
Juliana Hughes, LD 3,719
Mike Squires, UKIP 661
Sid Whitworth, LCA 272
PC maj. 6,718 (17.54%)
5.37% swing Lab. to PC
(2001: PC maj. 2,590 (6.81%))

CARMARTHEN WEST & PEMBROKESHIRE SOUTH
E. 56,245 T. 37,863 (67.32%) Lab. hold
Nick Ainger, Lab. 13,953
David Morris, C. 12,043
John Dixon, PC 5,582
John Allen, LD 5,399
Josie MacDonald, UKIP 545
Alex Daszak, LCA 237
Nick Turner, Ind. 104
Lab. maj. 1,910 (5.04%)
3.62% swing Lab. to C.
(2001: Lab. maj. 4,538 (12.29%))

CEREDIGION
E. 53,493 T. 35,947 (67.20%) LD gain
*Mark Williams, LD 13,130
Simon Thomas, PC 12,911
John Harrison, C. 4,455
Alun Davies, Lab. 4,337
Dave Bradney, Green 846
Iain Sheldon, Veritas 268
LD maj. 219 (0.61%)
6.00% swing PC to LD
(2001: PC maj. 3,944 (11.40%))

CLWYD SOUTH
E. 52,353 T. 32,931 (62.90%) Lab. hold
Martyn Jones, Lab. 14,808
Tom Biggins, C. 8,460
Deric Burnham, LD 5,105
Mark Strong, PC 3,111
Alwyn Humphreys, FWP 803
Nick Powell, UKIP 644
Lab. maj. 6,348 (19.28%)
3.64% swing Lab. to C.
(2001: Lab. maj. 8,898 (26.56%))

CLWYD WEST
E. 55,642 T. 35,614 (64.01%) C. gain
*David Jones, C. 12,909
Gareth Thomas, Lab. 12,776
Frank Taylor, LD 4,723
Eilian Williams, PC 3,874
Warwick Nicholson, UKIP 512
Jimmy James, Ind. 507
Patrick Keenan, Soc. Lab. 313
C. maj. 133 (0.37%)
1.80% swing Lab. to C.
(2001: Lab. maj. 1,115 (3.22%))

CONWY
E. 53,987 T. 33,657 (62.34%) Lab. hold
Betty Williams, Lab. 12,479
Guto Bebb, C. 9,398
Gareth Roberts, LD 6,723
Paul Rowlinson, PC 3,730
Jim Killock, Green 512
David Lloyd Jones, Soc. Lab. 324
Kenneth Khambatta, UKIP 298
Tim Evans, LCA 193
Lab. maj. 3,081 (9.15%)
4.47% swing Lab. to C.
(2001: Lab. maj. 6,219 (18.10%))

CYNON VALLEY
E. 45,369 T. 26,647 (58.73%) Lab. hold
Rt. Hon. Ann Clwyd, Lab. 17,074
Geraint Benney, PC 3,815
Margaret Phelps, LD 2,991
Antonia Dunn, C. 2,062
Susan Davies, UKIP 705
Lab. maj. 13,259 (49.76%)
0.77% swing PC to Lab.
(2001: Lab. maj. 12,998 (48.22%))

DELYN
E. 52,766 T. 34,004 (64.44%) Lab. hold
David Hanson, Lab. 15,540
John Bell, C. 8,896
Tudor Jones, LD 6,089
Phil Thomas, PC 2,524
May Crawford, UKIP 533
Nigel Williams, Ind. 422
Lab. maj. 6,644 (19.54%)
2.65% swing Lab. to C.
(2001: Lab. maj. 8,605 (24.84%))

GOWER
E. 60,925 T. 39,542 (64.90%) Lab. hold
Martin Caton, Lab. 16,786
Mike Murray, C. 10,083
Nick Tregoning, LD 7,291
Sian Caiach, PC 3,089
Richard Lewis, UKIP 1,264
Rhodri Griffiths, Green 1,029
Lab. maj. 6,703 (16.95%)
1.42% swing Lab. to C.
(2001: Lab. maj. 7,395 (19.80%))

ISLWYN
E. 50,595 T. 30,865 (61.00%) Lab. (Co-op) hold
Don Touhig, Lab. (Co-op) 19,687
Jim Criddle, PC 3,947
Lee Dillon, LD 3,873
Phillip Howells, C. 3,358
Lab. (Co-op) maj. 15,740 (51.00%)
0.67% swing PC to Lab. (Co-op)
(2001: Lab. (Co-op) maj. 15,309 (48.31%))

LLANELLI
E. 55,678 T. 35,344 (63.48%) Lab. hold
*Nia Griffith, Lab. 16,592
Neil Baker, PC 9,358
Adrian Phillips, C. 4,844
Ken Rees, LD 4,550
Lab. maj. 7,234 (20.47%)
1.39% swing PC to Lab.
(2001: Lab. maj. 6,403 (17.69%))

MEIRIONNYDD NANT CONWY
E. 33,443 T. 20,640 (61.72%) PC hold
Elfyn Llwyd, PC 10,597
Rhodri Jones, Lab. 3,983
Dan Munford, C. 3,402
Adrian Fawcett, LD 2,192
Francis Wykes, UKIP 466
PC maj. 6,614 (32.04%)
2.53% swing Lab. to PC
(2001: PC maj. 5,684 (26.98%))

MERTHYR TYDFIL & RHYMNEY
E. 54,579 T. 29,976 (54.92%) Lab. hold

Dai Havard, Lab.	18,129
Ceirion Rees, LD	4,195
Noel Turner, PC	2,972
Roger Berry, C.	2,680
Neil Greer, FWP	1,030
Gwyn Parry, UKIP	699
Ina Marsden, Soc. Lab.	271

Lab. maj. 13,934 (46.48%)
3.88% swing Lab. to LD
(2001: Lab. maj. 14,923 (47.10%))

MONMOUTH
E. 63,093 T. 45,653 (72.36%) C. gain

*David Davies, C.	21,396
Huw Edwards, Lab.	16,869
Phil Hobson, LD	5,852
Jonathan Clark, PC	993
John Bufton, UKIP	543

C. maj. 4,527 (9.92%)
5.39% swing Lab. to C.
(2001: Lab. maj. 384 (0.86%))

MONTGOMERYSHIRE
E. 46,766 T. 30,097 (64.36%) LD hold

Lembit Opik, LD	15,419
Simon Baynes, C.	8,246
David Tinline, Lab.	3,454
Ellen ap Gwynn, PC	2,078
Clive Easton, UKIP	900

LD maj. 7,173 (23.83%)
1.16% swing C. to LD
(2001: LD maj. 6,234 (21.51%))

NEATH
E. 57,607 T. 35,817 (62.17%) Lab. hold

Rt. Hon. Peter Hain, Lab.	18,835
Geraint Owen, PC	6,125
Sheila Waye, LD	5,112
Harri Lloyd Davies, C.	4,136
Susan Jay, Green	658
Gerry Brienza, Ind.	360
Pat Tabram, LCA	334
Heather Falconer, Respect	257

Lab. maj. 12,710 (35.49%)
3.41% swing Lab. to PC
(2001: Lab. maj. 14,816 (42.31%))

NEWPORT EAST
E. 54,956 T. 31,825 (57.91%) Lab. hold

*Jessica Morden, Lab.	14,389
Ed Townsend, LD	7,551
Matthew Collings, C.	7,459
Mohammad Asghar, PC	1,221
Roger Thomas, UKIP	945
Liz Screen, Soc. Lab.	260

Lab. maj. 6,838 (21.49%)
9.60% swing Lab. to LD
(2001: Lab. maj. 9,874 (31.56%))

NEWPORT WEST
E. 60,287 T. 35,732 (59.27%) Lab. hold

Paul Flynn, Lab.	16,021
Dr William Morgan, C.	10,563
Nigel Flanagan, LD	6,398
Tony Salkeld, PC	1,278
Hugh Moelwyn Hughes, UKIP	848
Peter Varley, Green	540
Saeid Arjomand, Ind.	84

Lab. maj. 5,458 (15.27%)
5.63% swing Lab. to C.
(2001: Lab. maj. 9,304 (26.54%))

OGMORE
E. 52,349 T. 30,278 (57.84%) Lab. hold

Huw Irranca-Davies, Lab.	18,295
Jackie Radford, LD	4,592
Dr Norma Lloyd-Nesling, C.	4,243
John Williams, PC	3,148

Lab. maj. 13,703 (45.26%)
2.01% swing Lab. to LD
(2002 Feb. by-election: Lab maj. 5,721 (31.13%))
(2001: Lab. maj. 14,574 (48.02%))

PONTYPRIDD
E. 65,074 T. 39,634 (60.91%) Lab. hold

Dr Kim Howells, Lab.	20,919
Mike Powell, LD	7,728
Quentin Gwynne Edwards, C.	5,321
Julie Richards, PC	4,420
David Bevan, UKIP	1,013
Robert Griffiths, Comm.	233

Lab. maj. 13,191 (33.28%)
7.91% swing Lab. to LD
(2001: Lab. maj. 17,684 (46.16%))

PRESELI PEMBROKESHIRE
E. 55,502 T. 38,587 (69.52%) C. gain

*Stephen Crabb, C.	14,106
Sue Hayman, Lab.	13,499
Dewi Smith, LD	4,963
Matt Mathias, PC	4,752
James Carver, UKIP	498
Molly Scott-Cato, Green	494
Trish Bowen, Soc. Lab.	275

C. maj. 607 (1.57%)
4.79% swing Lab. to C.
(2001: Lab. maj. 2,946 (8.01%))

RHONDDA
E. 51,041 T. 31,148 (61.03%) Lab. hold

Chris Bryant, Lab.	21,198
Layton Percy Jones, PC	4,956
Karen Roberts, LD	3,264
Paul Stuart-Smith, C.	1,730

Lab. maj. 16,242 (52.14%)
2.48% swing PC to Lab.
(2001: Lab. maj. 16,047 (47.19%))

SWANSEA EAST
E. 58,813 T. 30,834 (52.43%) Lab. hold

*Sian James, Lab.	17,457
Robert Speht, LD	6,208
Ellenor Bland, C.	3,103
Carolyn Shan Couch, PC	2,129
Kevin Holloway, BNP	770
Timothy Jenkins, UKIP	674
Tony Young, Green	493

Lab. maj. 11,249 (36.48%)
9.27% swing Lab. to LD
(2001: Lab. maj. 16,148 (53.70%))

SWANSEA WEST
E. 57,946 T. 33,086 (57.10%) Lab. hold

Rt. Hon. Alan Williams, Lab.	13,833
Rene Kinzett, LD	9,564
Mohammed Abdel-Haq, C.	5,285
Harri Roberts, PC	2,150
Martyn Shrewsbury, Green	738
Martyn Ford, UKIP	609
Yvonne Holley, Veritas	401
Robert Williams, Soc. Alt.	288
Steve Pank, LCA	218

Lab. maj. 4,269 (12.90%)
9.64% swing Lab. to LD
(2001: Lab. maj. 9,550 (29.75%))

TORFAEN
E. 60,669 T. 35,979 (59.30%) Lab. hold

Rt. Hon. Paul Murphy, Lab.	20,472
Nick Ramsay, C.	5,681
Veronica Watkins, LD	5,678
Aneurin Preece, PC	2,242
David Rowlands, UKIP	1,145
Richard Turner-Thomas, Ind.	761

Lab. maj. 14,791 (41.11%)
2.54% swing Lab. to C.
(2001: Lab. maj. 16,280 (46.19%))

VALE OF CLWYD
E. 51,982 T. 32,313 (62.16%) Lab. hold

Christopher Ruane, Lab.	14,875
Felicity Elphick, C.	10,206
Elizabeth Jewkes, LD	3,820
Mark Jones, PC	2,309
Mark Young, Ind.	442
Edna Khambatta, UKIP	375
Jeff Ditchfield, LCA	286

Lab. maj. 4,669 (14.45%)
1.68% swing Lab. to C.
(2001: Lab. maj. 5,761 (17.81%))

VALE OF GLAMORGAN
E. 68,657 T. 47,324 (68.93%) Lab. hold

John Smith, Lab.	19,481
Alun Cairns, C.	17,673
Mark Hooper, LD	6,140
Barry Shaw, PC	2,423
Richard Suchorzewski, UKIP	840
Karl-James Langford, Lib.	605
Paul Mules, Soc. Lab.	162

Lab. maj. 1,808 (3.82%)
3.29% swing Lab. to C.
(2001: Lab. maj. 4,700 (10.40%))

WREXHAM
E. 48,016 T. 30,385 (63.28%) Lab. hold

Ian Lucas, Lab.	13,993
Tom Rippeth, LD	7,174
Dr Therese Coffey, C.	6,079
Sion Owen, PC	1,744
John Walker, BNP	919
Janet Williams, FWP	476

Lab. maj. 6,819 (22.44%)
6.72% swing Lab. to LD
(2001: Lab. maj. 9,188 (30.58%))

YNYS MON
E. 52,512 T. 35,462 (67.53%) Lab. hold

Albert Owen, Lab.	12,278
Eurig Wyn, PC	11,036
Peter Rogers, Ind.	5,216
James Roach, C.	3,915
Sarah Green, LD	2,418
Elaine Gill, UKIP	367
Tim Evans, LCA	232

Lab. maj. 1,242 (3.50%)
0.58% swing PC to Lab.
(2001: Lab. maj. 800 (2.35%))

SCOTLAND

ABERDEEN NORTH
E. 65,714 T. 36,634 (55.75%) Lab. win
Frank Doran, Lab. 15,557
Steve Delaney, LD 8,762
Kevin Stewart, SNP 8,168
David Anderson, C. 3,456
John Connon, SSP 691
Lab. maj. 6,795 (18.55%)
§ 9.25% swing Lab. to LD
(§ 2001 Lab. maj. 9,294 (23.66%))

ABERDEEN SOUTH
E. 67,012 T. 41,621 (62.11%) Lab. win
Anne Begg, Lab. 15,272
Vicki Harris, LD 13,924
Stewart Whyte, C. 7,134
Maureen Watt, SNP 4,120
Rhonda Reekie, Scot. Green 768
Donald Munro, SSP 403
Lab. maj. 1,348 (3.24%)
§ 3.13% swing Lab. to LD
(§ 2001 Lab. maj. 3,931 (9.49%))

ABERDEENSHIRE WEST & KINCARDINE
E. 65,548 T. 41,648 (63.54%) LD win
Sir Robert Smith, LD 19,285
Alex Johnstone, C. 11,814
James Barrowman, Lab. 5,470
Caroline Little, SNP 4,700
Lorna Grant, SSP 379
LD maj. 7,471 (17.94%)
§ 2.25% swing C. to LD
(§ 2001 LD maj. 5,146 (13.44%))

AIRDRIE & SHOTTS
E. 61,955 T. 33,158 (53.52%) Lab. win
Rt. Hon. Dr John Reid, Lab. 19,568
Malcolm Balfour, SNP 5,484
Helen Watt, LD 3,792
Stuart Cottis, C. 3,271
Fraser Coats, SSP 706
Joseph Rowan, Scot. Ind. 337
Lab. maj. 14,084 (42.48%)
§ 1.51% swing SNP to Lab.
(§ 2001 Lab. maj. 13,545 (39.46%))

ANGUS
E. 63,093 T. 38,186 (60.52%) SNP win
Mike Weir, SNP 12,840
Sandy Bushby, C. 11,280
Douglas Bradley, Lab. 6,850
Scott Rennie, LD 6,660
Alan Manley, SSP 556
SNP maj. 1,601 (4.20%)
§ 1.34% swing C. to SNP
(§ 2001 SNP maj. 532 (1.52%))

ARGYLL & BUTE
E. 67,325 T. 43,229 (64.21%) LD win
Alan Reid, LD 15,786
James McGrigor, C. 10,150
Carolyn Manson, Lab. 9,696
Isobel Strong, SNP 6,716
Deirdre Henderson, SSP 881
LD maj. 5,636 (13.04%)
§ 1.94% swing C. to LD
(§ 2001 LD maj. 3,832 (9.16%))

AYR, CARRICK & CUMNOCK
E. 73,448 T. 45,048 (61.33%) Lab. win
Sandra Osborne, Lab. 20,433
Mark Jones, C. 10,436
Colin Waugh, LD 6,341
Charles Brodie, SNP 5,932
Donald Sharp, SSCUP 592
Murray Steele, SSP 554
James McDaid, Soc. Lab. 395
Bryan McCormack, UKIP 365
Lab. maj. 9,997 (22.19%)
§ 2.18% swing Lab. to C.
(§ 2001 Lab. maj. 12,387 (26.56%))

AYRSHIRE CENTRAL
E. 68,643 T. 42,871 (62.46%) Lab. win
Brian Donohoe, Lab. 19,905
Garry Clark, C. 9,482
Iain Kennedy, LD 6,881
Jahangir Hanif, SNP 4,969
Denise Morton, SSP 820
Robert Cochrane, Soc. Lab. 468
Jim Groves, UKIP 346
Lab. maj. 10,423 (24.31%)
§ 0.68% swing C. to Lab.
(§ 2001 Lab. maj. 9,772 (22.96%))

AYRSHIRE NORTH & ARRAN
E. 72,986 T. 44,205 (60.57%) Lab. win
*Katy Clark, Lab. 19,417
Stewart Connell, C. 8,121
Tony Gurney, SNP 7,938
George White, LD 7,264
Colin Turbett, SSP 780
John Pursley, UKIP 382
Louise McDaid, Soc. Lab. 303
Lab. maj. 11,296 (25.55%)
§ 2.68% swing Lab. to C.
(§ 2001 Lab. maj. 12,140 (27.33%))

BANFF & BUCHAN
E. 65,570 T. 37,216 (56.76%) SNP win
Alex Salmond, SNP 19,044
Sandy Wallace, C. 7,207
Eleanor Anderson, LD 4,952
Rami Okasha, Lab. 4,476
Victor Ross, OCV 683
Kathleen Kemp, UKIP 442
Steve Will, SSP 412
SNP maj. 11,837 (31.81%)
§ 2.22% swing C. to SNP
(§ 2001 SNP maj. 9,744 (27.37%))

BERWICKSHIRE, ROXBURGH & SELKIRK
E. 71,702 T. 45,388 (63.30%) LD win
Michael Moore, LD 18,993
John Lamont, C. 13,092
Sam Held, Lab. 7,206
Aileen Orr, SNP 3,885
John Hein, Lib. 916
Graeme McIver, SSP 695
Peter Neilson, UKIP 601
LD maj. 5,901 (13.00%)
§ 5.90% swing LD to C.
(§ 2001 LD maj. 10,770 (24.80%))

CAITHNESS, SUTHERLAND & EASTER ROSS
E. 46,837 T. 27,663 (59.06%) LD win
John Thurso, LD 13,957
Alan Jamieson, Lab. 5,789
Karen Shirron, SNP 3,686
Angus Ross, C. 2,835
Gordon Campbell, Ind. 848
Luke Ivory, SSP 548
LD maj. 8,168 (29.53%)
§ 7.60% swing Lab. to LD
(§ 2001 LD maj. 4,078 (14.33%))

COATBRIDGE, CHRYSTON & BELLSHILL
E. 67,385 T. 38,344 (56.90%) Lab. win
Rt. Hon. Thomas Clarke, Lab. 24,725
Duncan Ross, SNP 5,206
Rodney Ackland, LD 4,605
Lindsay Paterson, C. 2,775
Joan Kinloch, SSP 1,033
Lab. maj. 19,519 (50.90%)
§ 1.82% swing Lab. to SNP
(§ 2001 Lab. maj. 22,092 (54.55%))

CUMBERNAULD, KILSYTH & KIRKINTILLOCH EAST
E. 64,748 T. 39,088 (60.37%) Lab. win
Rosemary McKenna, Lab. 20,251
James Hepburn, SNP 8,689
Hugh O'Donnell, LD 5,817
James Boswell, C. 2,718
Willie O'Neill, SSP 1,141
Patrick Elliott, OCV 472
Lab. maj. 11,562 (29.58%)
§ 1.11% swing Lab. to SNP
(§ 2001 Lab. maj. 12,667 (31.79%))

DUMFRIES & GALLOWAY
E. 74,273 T. 50,891 (68.52%) Lab. win
Russell Brown, Lab. 20,924
Peter Duncan, C. 18,002
Douglas Henderson, SNP 6,182
Keith Legg, LD 4,259
John Schofield, Scot. Green 745
John Dennis, SSP 497
Mark Smith, OCV 282
Lab. maj. 2,922 (5.74%)
§ 2.73% swing C. to Lab.
(§ 2001 Lab. maj. 141 (0.28%))

DUMFRIESSHIRE, CLYDESDALE & TWEEDDALE
E. 66,045 T. 44,616 (67.55%) C. win
*David Mundell, C. 16,141
Sean Marshall, Lab. 14,403
Patsy Kenton, LD 9,046
Andrew Wood, SNP 4,075
Sarah MacTavish, SSP 521
Tony Lee, UKIP 430
C. maj. 1,738 (3.90%)
§ 7.98% swing Lab. to C.
(§ 2001 Lab. maj. 5,254 (12.06%))

DUNBARTONSHIRE EAST
E. 64,763 T. 46,724 (72.15%) LD win
*Jo Swinson, LD 19,533
John Lyons, Lab. 15,472
David Jack, C. 7,708
Chris Sagan, SNP 2,716
Stuart Callison, Scot. Green 876
Pamela Page, SSP 419
LD maj. 4,061 (8.69%)
§ 7.49% swing Lab. to LD
(§ 2001 Lab. maj. 2,601 (6.29%))

DUNBARTONSHIRE WEST
E. 67,805 T. 41,589 (61.34%) Lab. (Co-op) win
Rt. Hon. John McFall, Lab. (Co-op) 21,600
Tom Chalmers, SNP 9,047
Niall Walker, LD 5,999
Campbell Murdoch, C. 2,679
Les Robertson, SSP 1,708
Bryan Maher, UKIP 354
Marlon Dawson, OCV 202
Lab. (Co-op) maj. 12,553 (30.18%)
§ 4.65% swing Lab. (Co-op) to SNP
(§ 2001 Lab. (Co-op) maj. 18,169 (39.49%))

DUNDEE EAST
E. 63,335 T. 39,540 (62.43%) SNP win
*Stewart Hosie, SNP 14,708
Iain Luke, Lab. 14,325
Christopher Bustin, C. 5,061
Clive Sneddon, LD 4,498
Harvey Duke, SSP 537
Donald Low, UKIP 292
David Allison, Ind. 119
SNP maj. 383 (0.97%)
§ 1.13% swing Lab. to SNP
(§ 2001 Lab. maj. 496 (1.29%))

DUNDEE WEST
E. 65,857 T. 36,936 (56.09%) Lab. win
*James McGovern, Lab. 16,468
Joe Fitzpatrick, SNP 11,089
Nykoma Garry, LD 5,323
Christopher McKinlay, C. 3,062
Jim McFarlane, SSP 994
Lab. maj. 5,379 (14.56%)
§ 3.99% swing Lab. to SNP
(§ 2001 Lab. maj. 8,410 (22.54%))

DUNFERMLINE & FIFE WEST
E. 70,775 T. 42,394 (59.90%) Lab. win
Rachel Squire, Lab. 20,111
David Herbert, LD 8,549
Douglas Chapman, SNP 8,026
Roger Smillie, C. 4,376
Susan Archibald, SSP 689
Ian Borland, UKIP 643
Lab. maj. 11,562 (27.27%)
§ 6.47% swing Lab. to LD
(§ 2001 Lab. maj. 14,845 (36.64%))

EAST KILBRIDE, STRATHAVEN & LESMAHAGOW
E. 75,132 T. 47,733 (63.53%) Lab. win
Rt. Hon. Adam Ingram, Lab. 23,264
Douglas Edwards, SNP 8,541
John Oswald, LD 7,904
Tony Lewis, C. 4,776
Kirsten Robb, Scot. Green 1,575
Rose Gentle, Ind. 1,513
John Houston, Ind. 160
Lab. maj. 14,723 (30.84%)
§ 0.78% swing SNP to Lab.
(§ 2001 Lab. maj. 13,999 (29.29%))

EAST LOTHIAN
E. 70,989 T. 45,776 (64.48%) Lab. win
Anne Picking, Lab. 18,983
Chris Butler, LD 11,363
William Stevenson, C. 7,315
Paul McLennan, SNP 5,995
Michael Collie, Scot. Green 1,132
Gary Galbraith, SSP 504
Eric Robb, UKIP 306
William Thompson, OCV 178
Lab. maj. 7,620 (16.65%)
§ 7.54% swing Lab. to LD
(§ 2001 Lab. maj. 14,011 (31.73%))

EDINBURGH EAST
E. 64,826 T. 39,709 (61.25%) Lab. win
Rt. Hon. Gavin Strang, Lab. 15,899
Gordon Mackenzie, LD 9,697
Stefan Tymkewycz, SNP 6,760
Mev Brown, C. 4,093
Cara Gillespie, Scot. Green 2,266
Catriona Grant, SSP 868
Brett Harris, DDTP 89
Peter Clifford, Ind. 37
Lab. maj. 6,202 (15.62%)
§ 8.47% swing Lab. to LD
(§ 2001 Lab. maj. 12,808 (32.56%))

EDINBURGH NORTH & LEITH
E. 68,038 T. 42,640 (62.67%) Lab. (Co-op) win
Mark Lazarowicz, Lab. (Co-op) 14,597
Mike Crockart, LD 12,444
Iain Whyte, C. 7,969
Davie Hutchison, SNP 4,344
Mark Sydenham, Scot. Green 2,482
Bill Scott, SSP 804
Lab. (Co-op) maj. 2,153 (5.05%)
§ 8.26% swing Lab. (Co-op) to LD
(§ 2001 Lab. (Co-op) maj. 8,688 (21.56%))

EDINBURGH SOUTH
E. 60,993 T. 42,698 (70.00%) Lab. win
Nigel Griffiths, Lab. 14,188
Marilyne MacLaren, LD 13,783
Gavin Brown, C. 10,291
Graham Sutherland, SNP 2,635
Dr Steve Burgess, Scot. Green 1,387
Morag Robertson, SSP 414
Lab. maj. 405 (0.95%)
§ 6.50% swing Lab. to LD
(§ 2001 Lab. maj. 5,785 (13.95%))

EDINBURGH SOUTH WEST
E. 67,135 T. 43,926 (65.43%) Lab. win
Rt. Hon. Alistair Darling, Lab. 17,476
Gordon Buchan, C. 10,234
Simon Clark, LD 9,252
Nick Elliott-Cannon, SNP 4,654
John Blair-Fish, Scot. Green 1,520
Pat Smith, SSP 585
William Boys, UKIP 205
Lab. maj. 7,242 (16.49%)
§ 0.71% swing Lab. to C.
(§ 2001 Lab. maj. 7,951 (17.91%))

EDINBURGH WEST
E. 65,741 T. 45,265 (68.85%) LD win
John Barrett, LD 22,417
David Brogan, C. 8,817
Navraj Singh Ghaleigh, Lab. 8,433
Sheena Cleland, SNP 4,124
Ailsa Spindler, Scot. Green 964
Gary Clark, SSP 510
LD maj. 13,600 (30.05%)
§ 6.71% swing C. to LD
(§ 2001 LD maj. 5,320 (11.86%))

FALKIRK
E. 76,784 T. 45,750 (59.58%) Lab. win
Eric Joyce, Lab. 23,264
Laura Love, SNP 9,789
Callum Chomczuk, LD 7,321
David Potts, C. 4,538
Danny Quinlan, SSP 838
Lab. maj. 13,475 (29.45%)
§ 0.36% swing Lab. to SNP
(§ 2001 Lab. maj. 13,555 (30.17%))

FIFE NORTH EAST
E. 62,057 T. 38,556 (62.13%) LD win
Rt. Hon. Sir Menzies Campbell, LD 20,088
Mike Scott-Hayward, C. 7,517
Anthony King, Lab. 4,920
Rod Campbell, SNP 4,011
Jim Park, Scot. Green 1,071
Dr Duncan Pickard, UKIP 533
Jack Ferguson, SSP 416
LD maj. 12,571 (32.60%)
§ 3.20% swing C. to LD
(§ 2001 LD maj. 9,686 (26.20%))

GLASGOW CENTRAL
E. 64,053 T. 28,037 (43.77%) Lab. win
Mohammad Sarwar, Lab. 13,518
Isabel Nelson, LD 4,987
Bill Kidd, SNP 4,148
Richard Sullivan, C. 1,757
Gordon Masterton, Scot. Green 1,372
Marie Gordon, SSP 1,110
Walter Hamilton, BNP 671
Ian Johnson, Soc. Lab. 255
Thomas Greig, OCV 139
Elinor McKenzie, Comm. Brit. 80
Lab. maj. 8,531 (30.43%)
§ 7.36% swing Lab. to LD
(§ 2001 Lab. maj. 9,382 (33.82%))

GLASGOW EAST
E. 64,130 T. 30,939 (48.24%) Lab. win
David Marshall, Lab. 18,775
Lachlan McNeill, SNP 5,268
David Jackson, LD 3,665
Carl Thomson, C. 2,135
George Savage, SSP 1,096
Lab. maj. 13,507 (43.66%)
§ 1.48% swing Lab. to SNP
(§ 2001 Lab. maj. 15,238 (46.62%))

GLASGOW NORTH
E. 55,419 T. 27,921 (50.38%) Lab. win
Ann McKechin, Lab. 11,001
Amy Rodger, LD 7,663
Kenneth McLean, SNP 3,614
Brian Pope, C. 2,441
Martin Bartos, Scot. Green 2,135
Nick Tarlton, SSP 1,067
Lab. maj. 3,338 (11.96%)
§ 8.70% swing Lab. to LD
(§ 2001 Lab. maj. 8,023 (29.36%))

GLASGOW NORTH EAST
E. 62,042 T. 28,418 (45.80%) Speaker win
Rt. Hon. Michael Martin, Speaker 15,153
John McLaughlin, SNP 5,019
Doris Kelly, Soc. Lab. 4,036
Graham Campbell, SSP 1,402
Daniel Houston, Scot. U. 1,266
Scott McLean, BNP 920
Joe Chambers, Ind. 622
Speaker maj. 10,134 (35.66%)
§ 6.62% swing Speaker to SNP
(§ 2001 Speaker maj. 15,203 (48.90%))

GLASGOW NORTH WEST
E. 61,880 T. 34,061 (55.04%) Lab. win
John Robertson, Lab. 16,748
Paul Graham, LD 6,655
Graeme Hendry, SNP 4,676
Murray Roxburgh, C. 3,262
Martha Wardrop, Scot. Green 1,333
Anthea Irwin, SSP 1,108
Colin Muir, Soc. Lab. 279
Lab. maj. 10,093 (29.63%)
§ 6.80% swing Lab. to LD
(§ 2001 Lab. maj. 13,231 (38.83%))

GLASGOW SOUTH
E. 68,837 T. 38,431 (55.83%) Lab. win
Tom Harris, Lab. 18,153
Arthur Sanderson, LD 7,321
Finlay MacLean, SNP 4,860
Dr Janette McAlpine, C. 4,836
Kay Allan, Scot. Green 1,692
Ronnie Stevenson, SSP 1,303
Dorothy Entwistle, Soc. Lab. 266
Lab. maj. 10,832 (28.19%)
§ 4.93% swing Lab. to LD
(§ 2001 Lab. maj. 13,042 (33.15%))

GLASGOW SOUTH WEST
E. 62,005 T. 30,977 (49.96%)
Lab. (Co-op) win
Ian Davidson, Lab. (Co-op) 18,653
James Dornan, SNP 4,757
Katy Gordon, LD 3,593
Scott Brady, C. 1,786
Keith Baldassara, SSP 1,666
Alistair McConnachie, Ind. Green 379
Violet Shaw, Soc. Lab. 143
Lab. (Co-op) maj. 13,896 (44.86%)
§ 0.22% swing SNP to Lab. (Co-op)
(§ 2001 Lab. (Co-op) maj. 14,687 (44.42%))

GLENROTHES
E. 66,563 T. 37,366 (56.14%) Lab. win
John MacDougall, Lab. 19,395
John Beare, SNP 8,731
Elizabeth Riches, LD 4,728
Belinda Don, C. 2,651
George Rodger, PPS 716
Morag Balfour, SSP 705
Paul Smith, UKIP 440
Lab. maj. 10,664 (28.54%)
§ 2.71% swing Lab. to SNP
(§ 2001 Lab. maj. 12,988 (33.95%))

GORDON
E. 71,925 T. 44,438 (61.78%) LD win
Malcolm Bruce, LD 20,008
Iain Brotchie, Lab. 8,982
Philip Atkinson, C. 7,842
Joanna Strathdee, SNP 7,098
Tommy Paterson, SSP 508
LD maj. 11,026 (24.81%)
§ 3.73% swing Lab. to LD
(§ 2001 LD maj. 6,845 (17.36%))

INVERCLYDE
E. 59,291 T. 36,098 (60.88%) Lab. win
David Cairns, Lab. 18,318
Stuart McMillan, SNP 7,059
Douglas Herbison, LD 6,123
Gordon Fraser, C. 3,692
David Landels, SSP 906
Lab. maj. 11,259 (31.19%)
§ 2.51% swing Lab. to SNP
(§ 2001 Lab. maj. 11,314 (29.06%))

INVERNESS, NAIRN, BADENOCH & STRATHSPEY
E. 69,636 T. 44,255 (63.55%) LD win
*Danny Alexander, LD 17,830
David Stewart, Lab. 13,682
David Thompson, SNP 5,992
Robert Rowantree, C. 4,579
Donnie MacLeod, Scot. Green 1,065
Donald Lawson, Publican 678
George MacDonald, SSP 429
LD maj. 4,148 (9.37%)
§ 6.01% swing Lab. to LD
(§ 2001 Lab. maj. 1,134 (2.65%))

KILMARNOCK & LOUDOUN
E. 72,851 T. 44,383 (60.92%) Lab. win
Rt. Hon. Desmond Browne, Lab. 20,976
Daniel Coffey, SNP 12,273
Gary Smith, C. 5,026
Kevin Lang, LD 4,945
Hugh Kerr, SSP 833
Ronnie Robertson, UKIP 330
Lab. maj. 8,703 (19.61%)
§ 5.45% swing Lab. to SNP
(§ 2001 Lab. maj. 13,621 (30.51%))

KIRKCALDY & COWDENBEATH
E. 71,606 T. 41,796 (58.37%) Lab. win
Rt. Hon. Gordon Brown, Lab. 24,278
Alan Bath, SNP 6,062
Alex Cole-Hamilton, LD 5,450
Stuart Randall, C. 4,308
Steve West, SSP 666
Peter Adams, UKIP 516
James Parker, Scot. Senior 425
Elizabeth Kwantes, Ind. 47
Pat Sargent, Ind. 44
Lab. maj. 18,216 (43.58%)
§ 1.84% swing SNP to Lab.
(§ 2001 Lab. maj. 16,238 (39.91%))

LANARK & HAMILTON EAST
E. 73,736 T. 43,589 (59.11%) Lab. win
Jimmy Hood, Lab. 20,072
Fraser Grieve, LD 8,125
John Wilson, SNP 7,746
Robert Pettigrew, C. 5,576
Dennis Reilly, SSP 802
Donald Mackay, UKIP 437
Duncan McFarlane, Ind. 416
Robin Mawhinney, OCV 415
Lab. maj. 11,947 (27.41%)
§ 5.89% swing Lab. to LD
(§ 2001 Lab. maj. 12,861 (28.59%))

LINLITHGOW & FALKIRK EAST
E. 76,739 T. 46,389 (60.45%) Lab. win
Michael Connarty, Lab. 22,121
Gordon Guthrie, SNP 10,919
Stephen Glenn, LD 7,100
Michael Veitch, C. 5,486
Ally Hendry, SSP 763
Lab. maj. 11,202 (24.15%)
§ 1.16% swing Lab. to SNP
(§ 2001 Lab. maj. 11,796 (26.46%))

LIVINGSTON
E. 76,353 T. 44,337 (58.07%) Lab. win
Rt. Hon. Robin Cook, Lab. 22,657
Angela Constance, SNP 9,560
Charles Dundas, LD 6,832
Alison Ross, C. 4,499
Steven Nimmo, SSP 789
Lab. maj. 13,097 (29.54%)
§ 1.17% swing Lab. to SNP
(§ 2001 Lab. maj. 13,638 (31.88%))

MIDLOTHIAN
E. 60,644 T. 37,704 (62.17%) Lab. win
David Hamilton, Lab. 17,153
Fred Mackintosh, LD 9,888
Colin Beattie, SNP 6,400
Iain McGill, C. 3,537
Norman Gilfillan, SSP 726
Lab. maj. 7,265 (19.27%)
§ 6.98% swing Lab. to LD
(§ 2001 Lab. maj. 12,017 (31.29%))

MORAY
E. 66,463 T. 38,793 (58.37%) SNP win
Angus Robertson, SNP 14,196
Jamie Halcro-Johnston, C. 8,520
Kevin Hutchens, Lab. 7,919
Linda Gorn, LD 7,460
Norma Anderson, SSP 698
SNP maj. 5,676 (14.63%)
§ 4.07% swing C. to SNP
(§ 2001 SNP maj. 1,852 (5.06%))

MOTHERWELL & WISHAW
E. 66,987 T. 37,109 (55.40%) Lab. win
Frank Roy, Lab. 21,327
Ian MacQuarrie, SNP 6,105
Conor Snowden, LD 4,464
Peter Finnie, C. 3,440
Gregor MacEwan, SSP 1,019
Dallas Carter, Free Scot. 384
Coral Thompson, OCV 370
Lab. maj. 15,222 (41.02%)
§ 2.35% swing SNP to Lab.
(§ 2001 Lab. maj. 13,778 (36.33%))

NA H-EILEANAN AN IAR
E. 21,576 T. 13,836 (64.13%) SNP gain
*Angus MacNeil, SNP 6,213
Calum MacDonald, Lab. 4,772
Dr Jean Davis, LD 1,096
James Hargreaves, OCV 1,048
Andy Maciver, C. 610
Joanne Telfer, SSP 97
SNP maj. 1,441 (10.41%)
9.29% swing Lab. to SNP
(2001: Lab. maj. 1,074 (8.16%))

OCHIL & PERTHSHIRE SOUTH
E. 70,731 T. 46,697 (66.02%) Lab. win
*Gordon Banks, Lab. 14,645
Annabelle Ewing, SNP 13,957
Elizabeth Smith, C. 10,021
Catherine Whittingham, LD 6,218
George Baxter, Scot. Green 978
Iain Campbell, SSP 420
David Bushby, UKIP 275
Maitland Kelly, Free Scot. 183
Lab. maj. 688 (1.47%)
§ 0.18% swing Lab. to SNP
(§ 2001 Lab. maj. 821 (1.83%))

ORKNEY & SHETLAND
E. 33,048 T. 17,742 (53.69%) LD hold
Alistair Carmichael, LD 9,138
Richard Meade, Lab. 2,511
Frank Nairn, C. 2,357
John Mowat, SNP 1,833
John Aberdein, SSP 992
Scott Dyble, UKIP 424
Paul Cruickshank, LCA 311
Brian Nugent, Free Scot. 176
LD maj. 6,627 (37.35%)
8.29% swing Lab. to LD
(2001: LD maj. 3,475 (20.77%))

PAISLEY & RENFREWSHIRE NORTH
E. 63,076 T. 40,885 (64.82%) Lab. win
James Sheridan, Lab. 18,697
Bill Wilson, SNP 7,696
Lewis Hutton, LD 7,464
Philip Lardner, C. 5,566
Angela McGregor, SSP 646
Katharine McGavigan, Soc. Lab. 444
John Pearson, UKIP 372
Lab. maj. 11,001 (26.91%)
§ 1.34% swing Lab. to SNP
(§ 2001 Lab. maj. 12,417 (29.58%))

PAISLEY & RENFREWSHIRE SOUTH
E. 60,181 T. 37,860 (62.91%) Lab. win
Douglas Alexander, Lab. 19,904
Eileen McCartin, LD 6,672
Andrew Doig, SNP 6,653
Thomas Begg, C. 3,188
Iain Hogg, SSP 789
Gordon Matthew, Paisley 381
Robert Rodgers, Ind. 166
Howard Broadbent, Soc. Lab. 107
Lab. maj. 13,232 (34.95%)
§ 6.24% swing Lab. to LD
(§ 2001 Lab. maj. 13,968 (36.10%))

PERTH & PERTHSHIRE NORTH
E. 70,895 T. 45,930 (64.79%) SNP win
Peter Wishart, SNP 15,469
Douglas Taylor, C. 13,948
Doug Maughan, Lab. 8,601
Gordon Campbell, LD 7,403
Philip Stott, SSP 509
SNP maj. 1,521 (3.31%)
§ 3.85% swing SNP to C.
(§ 2001 SNP maj. 5,020 (11.01%))

RENFREWSHIRE EAST
E. 65,714 T. 47,405 (72.14%) Lab. hold
Jim Murphy, Lab. 20,815
Richard Cook, C. 14,158
Dr Gordon Macdonald, LD 8,659
Osama Bhutta, SNP 3,245
Ian Henderson, SSP 528
Lab. maj. 6,657 (14.04%)
2.43% swing Lab. to C.
(2001: Lab. maj. 9,141 (18.90%))

ROSS, SKYE & LOCHABER
E. 50,507 T. 32,538 (64.42%) LD win
Rt. Hon. Charles Kennedy, LD 19,100
Christine Conniff, Lab. 4,851
John Hodgson, C. 3,275
Mhairi Will, SNP 3,119
David Jardine, Scot. Green 1,097
Phillip Anderson, UKIP 500
Anne Macleod, SSP 412
Morris Grant, Ind. 184
LD maj. 14,249 (43.79%)
§ 11.27% swing Lab. to LD
(§ 2001 LD maj. 6,567 (21.26%))

RUTHERGLEN & HAMILTON WEST
E. 73,998 T. 43,261 (58.46%)
Lab. (Co-op) win
Rt. Hon. Thomas McAvoy,
Lab. (Co-op) 24,054
Ian Robertson, LD 7,942
Margaret Park, SNP 6,023
Peter Crerar, C. 3,621
Bill Bonnar, SSP 1,164
Janice Murdoch, UKIP 457
Lab. (Co-op) maj. 16,112 (37.24%)
§ 5.37% swing Lab. (Co-op) to LD
(§ 2001 Lab. (Co-op) maj. 18,504
(44.42%))

STIRLING
E. 64,554 T. 43,691 (67.68%) Lab. win
Anne McGuire, Lab. 15,729
Stephen Kerr, C. 10,962
Kelvin Holdsworth, LD 9,052
Frances McGlinchey, SNP 5,503
Duncan Illingworth, Scot. Green 1,302
Rowland Sheret, SSP 458
James McDonald, Ind. 261
Michael Willis, OCV 215
Matthew Desmond, UKIP 209
Lab. maj. 4,767 (10.91%)
§ 4.18% swing Lab. to C.
(§ 2001 Lab. maj. 8,303 (19.28%))

NORTHERN IRELAND

ANTRIM EAST
E. 58,335 T. 31,767 (54.46%)
DUP gain
*Sammy Wilson, DUP 15,766
Roy Beggs, UUP 8,462
Sean Neeson, Alliance 4,869
Danny O'Connor, SDLP 1,695
James McKeown, SF 828
David Kerr, Vote Dream 147
DUP maj. 7,304 (22.99%)
11.67% swing UUP to DUP
(2001: UUP maj. 128 (0.36%))

ANTRIM NORTH
E. 74,450 T. 45,926 (61.69%)
DUP hold
Revd Ian Paisley, DUP 25,156
Philip McGuigan, SF 7,191
Rodney McCune, UUP 6,637
Sean Farren, SDLP 5,585
Jayne Dunlop, Alliance 1,357
DUP maj. 17,965 (39.12%)
0.47% swing DUP to SF
(2001: DUP maj. 14,224 (28.90%))

ANTRIM SOUTH
E. 66,931 T. 37,957 (56.71%)
DUP gain
†Revd William McCrea, DUP 14,507
David Burnside, UUP 11,059
Noreen McClelland, SDLP 4,706
Henry Cushinan, SF 4,407
David Ford, Alliance 3,278
DUP maj. 3,448 (9.08%)
5.69% swing UUP to DUP
(2001: UUP maj. 1,011 (2.29%))

BELFAST EAST
E. 53,176 T. 30,831 (57.98%)
DUP hold
Peter Robinson, DUP 15,152
Sir Reg Empey, UUP 9,275
Naomi Long, Alliance 3,746
Deborah Devenny, SF 1,029
Mary Muldoon, SDLP 844
Alan Greer, C. 434
Joe Bell, WP 179
Lynda Gilby, Vote Dream 172
DUP maj. 5,877 (19.06%)
0.13% swing DUP to UUP
(2001: DUP maj. 7,117 (19.32%))

BELFAST NORTH
E. 52,853 T. 30,540 (57.78%)
DUP hold
Nigel Dodds, DUP 13,935
Gerry Kelly, SF 8,747
Alban Maginness, SDLP 4,950
Fred Cobain, UUP 2,154
Marjorie Hawkins, Alliance 438
Marcella Delaney, WP 165
Lynda Gilby, Vote Dream 151
DUP maj. 5,188 (16.99%)
0.69% swing SF to DUP
(2001: DUP maj. 6,387 (15.60%))

BELFAST SOUTH
E. 52,668 T. 32,028 (60.81%)
SDLP gain
*Dr Alasdair McDonnell, SDLP 10,339
James Spratt, DUP 9,104
Michael McGimpsey, UUP 7,263
Alex Maskey, SF 2,882
Geraldine Rice, Alliance 2,012
Lynda Gilby, Vote Dream 235
Paddy Lynn, WP 193
SDLP maj. 1,235 (3.86%)
11.91% swing UUP to SDLP
(2001: UUP maj. 5,399 (14.23%))

BELFAST WEST
E. 53,831 T. 34,545 (64.17%) SF hold
Gerry Adams, SF 24,348
Alex Attwood, SDLP 5,033
Diane Dodds, DUP 3,652
Chris McGimpsey, UUP 779
John Lowry, WP 432
Lynda Gilby, Vote Dream 154
Liam Kennedy, Ind. 147
SF maj. 19,315 (55.91%)
4.36% swing SDLP to SF
(2001: SF maj. 19,342 (47.20%))

DOWN NORTH
E. 59,748 T. 32,290 (54.04%)
UUP hold

Lady Sylvia Hermon, UUP	16,268
Peter Weir, DUP	11,324
David Alderdice, Alliance	2,451
Liam Logan, SDLP	1,009
Julian Robertson, C.	822
Christopher Carter, Ind.	211
Janet McCrory, SF	205

UUP maj. 4,944 (15.31%)
20.35% swing UUP to DUP
(2001: UUP maj. 7,324 (19.69%))

DOWN SOUTH
E. 73,668 T. 48,177 (65.40%)
SDLP hold

Edward McGrady, SDLP	21,557
Caitriona Ruane, SF	12,417
Jim Wells, DUP	8,815
Dermot Nesbitt, UUP	4,775
Julian Crozier, Alliance	613

SDLP maj. 9,140 (18.97%)
3.82% swing SDLP to SF
(2001: SDLP maj. 13,858 (26.61%))

FERMANAGH & SOUTH TYRONE
E. 67,174 T. 48,793 (72.64%) SF hold

Michelle Gildernew, SF	18,638
Arlene Foster, DUP	14,056
Tom Elliott, UUP	8,869
Tommy Gallagher, SDLP	7,230

SF maj. 4,582 (9.39%)
12.35% swing SF to DUP
(2001: SF maj. 53 (0.10%))

FOYLE
E. 69,207 T. 45,609 (65.90%)
SDLP hold

*Mark Durkan, SDLP	21,119
Mitchel McLaughlin, SF	15,162
William Hay, DUP	6,557
Eammon McCann, Soc EA	1,649
Earl Storey, UUP	1,091
Ben Reel, Vote Dream	31

SDLP maj. 5,957 (13.06%)
5.28% swing SDLP to SF
(2001: SDLP maj. 11,550 (23.63%))

LAGAN VALLEY
E. 70,742 T. 42,572 (60.18%)
DUP gain

‡Jeffrey Donaldson, DUP	23,289
Basil McCrea, UUP	9,172
Seamus Close, Alliance	4,316
Paul Butler, SF	3,197
Patricia Lewsley, SDLP	2,598

DUP maj. 14,117 (33.16%)
38.13% swing UUP to DUP
(2001: UUP maj. 18,342 (39.93%))

LONDONDERRY EAST
E. 58,861 T. 35,504 (60.32%)
DUP hold

Gregory Campbell, DUP	15,225
David McClarty, UUP	7,498
John Dallat, SDLP	6,077
Billy Leonard, SF	5,709
Yvonne Boyle, Alliance	924
Malcolm Samuel, Ind.	71

DUP maj. 7,727 (21.76%)
8.50% swing UUP to DUP
(2001: DUP maj. 1,901 (4.77%))

NEWRY & ARMAGH
E. 72,448 T. 50,696 (69.98%) SF gain

*Conor Murphy, SF	20,965
Dominic Bradley, SDLP	12,770
Paul Berry, DUP	9,311
Danny Kennedy, UUP	7,025
Gerry Markey, Ind.	625

SF maj. 8,195 (16.16%)
11.30% swing SDLP to SF
(2001: SDLP maj. 3,575 (6.43%))

STRANGFORD
E. 69,040 T. 37,032 (53.64%)
DUP hold

Iris Robinson, DUP	20,921
Gareth McGimpsey, UUP	7,872
Kieran McCarthy, Alliance	3,332
Joe Boyle, SDLP	2,496
Terry Dick, C.	1,462
Dermot Kennedy, SF	949

DUP maj. 13,049 (35.24%)
16.34% swing UUP to DUP
(2001: DUP maj. 1,110 (2.57%))

TYRONE WEST
E. 60,286 T. 43,487 (72.13%) SF hold

Pat Doherty, SF	16,910
Dr Kieran Deeny, Ind.	11,905
Thomas Buchanan, DUP	7,742
Eugene McMenamin, SDLP	3,949
Derek Hussey, UUP	2,981

SF maj. 5,005 (11.51%)
14.65% swing SF to Ind.
(2001: SF maj. 5,040 (10.39%))

ULSTER MID
E. 62,666 T. 45,426 (72.49%) SF hold

Martin McGuinness, SF	21,641
Ian McCrea, DUP	10,665
Patsy McGlone, SDLP	7,922
Billy Armstrong, UUP	4,853
Francis Donnelly, WP	345

SF maj. 10,976 (24.16%)
2.12% swing DUP to SF
(2001: SF maj. 9,953 (19.93%))

UPPER BANN
E. 72,402 T. 44,422 (61.35%)
DUP gain

*David Simpson, DUP	16,679
David Trimble, UUP	11,381
John O'Dowd, SF	9,305
Dolores Kelly, SDLP	5,747
Alan Castle, Alliance	955
Tom French, WP	355

DUP maj. 5,298 (11.93%)
7.98% swing UUP to DUP
(2001: UUP maj. 2,058 (4.03%))

BY-ELECTIONS 2005–8

Abbreviations of parties standing in the 2005–8 by-elections (see also General Election Results):

Com.	The Common Good
FPP	The Fur Play Party
MGB	Independent (Miss Great Britain) Party
Money	Money Reform Party
SCP	Scottish Christian Party (formerly Operation Christian Vote)
SPGB	Socialist Party of Great Britain
Tolls	Abolish Forth Bridge Tolls Party

BLAENAU GWENT
E. 52,508 T. 27,165 (51.73%) Ind hold
*Dai Davis, Ind. 12,543
Owen Smith, Lab. 10,059
Steffan Lewis, PC 1,755
Amy Kitcher, LD 1,477
Margrit Williams, C. 1,013
Alan Hope, Loony 318
Ind maj. 2,484 (9.14%)
8.37% swing Ind. to Lab.
(2005: Ind. maj. 9,121 (25.81%))

BROMLEY & CHISLEHURST
E. 71,818 T. 29,052 (40.45%) C. hold
*Bob Neill, C. 11,621
Ben Abbotts, LD 10,988
Nigel Farage, UKIP 2,347
Rachel Reeves, Lab 1,925
Anne Garrett, Green 811
Paul Winnett, NF 476
John Hemming-Clarke, Ind. 442
Stevens Uncles, Eng. Dem. 212
John Cartwright, Loony 132
Nick Hadziannis, Ind. 65
Anne Belsey, Money 33
C. maj. 633 (2.18%)
14.32% swing C. to LD
(2005: C. maj. 13,342 (28.92%))

CHEADLE
E. 68,051 T. 37,567 (55.20%) LD hold
*Mark Hunter, LD 19,593
Stephen Day, C. 15,936
Martin Miller, Lab. 1,739
Leslie Leggett, Veritas 218
John Allman, AFC 81
LD maj. 3,657 (9.73%)
0.63% swing C. to LD
(2005: LD maj. 4,020 (8.47%))

CREWE & NANTWICH
E. 71,963 T. 41,856 (58.16%) C. gain
Edward Timpson, C. 20,539
Tamsin Dunwoody, Lab. 12,679
Elizabeth Shenton, LD 6,040
Mike Nattrass, UKIP 922
Robert Smith, Green 359
David Roberts, Eng. Dem. 275
The Flying Brick, Loony 236
Mark Walklate, Ind. 217
Paul Thorogood, Cut Tax 118
Gemma Garrett, MGB 113
C. maj. 7,860 (18.9%)
17.6% swing Lab. to C.
(2005: Lab maj. 7,078 (16.28%))

DUNFERMLINE & FIFE WEST
E. 71,017 T. 34,578 (48.69%) LD gain
*Willie Rennie, LD 12,391
Catherine Stihler, Lab. 10,591
Douglas Chapman, SNP 7,261
Carrie Ruxton, C. 2,702
John McAllion, SSP 537
James Hargreaves, SCP 411
Thomas Minogue, Tolls 374
Ian Borland, UKIP 208
Dick Rodgers, Good 103
LD maj. 1,800 (5.21%)
16.24% swing Lab. to LD
(2005: Lab maj. 11,562 (27.27%))

EALING SOUTHALL
E. 85,423 T. 36,618 (42.87%) Lab. hold
*Virendra Sharma, Lab. 15,188
Nigel Bakhai, LD 10,118
Tony Lit, C. 8,230
Sarah Edwards, Green 1,135
Salvinder Dhillon, Respect 588
Dr Kunnathur Rajan, UKIP 285
Yaqub Masih, Christian Party 280
Jasdev Rai, Ind. 275
John Cartwright, Loony 188
Sati Chaggar, Eng. Dem. 152
Gulbash Singh, Ind. 92
Kuldeep Grewal, Ind. 87
Lab. maj. 5,070 (13.85%)
5.24% swing Lab. to LD
(2005: Lab. maj. 11,440 (24.32%))

GLASGOW EAST
E. 62,051 T. 26,174 (42.18%) SNP gain
John Mason, SNP 11,277
Margaret Curran, Lab. 10,912
Davena Rankin, C. 1,639
Ian Robertson, LD 915
Frances Curran, SSP 555
Tricia McLeish, Solidarity 512
Eileen Duke, Green 232
Chris Creighton, Ind. 67
Hamish Howett, Choice 65
SNP maj. 365 (1.39%)
22.53% swing Lab. to SNP
(2005: Lab. maj. 13,507 (43.66%))

HALTEMPRICE AND HOWDEN*
E. 70,266 T. 23,911 (34.03%) C. hold
David Davis, C. 17,113
Shan Oakes, Green 1,758
Joanne Robinson, Eng. Dem. 1,714
Tess Culnane, NF 544
Gemma Garrett, MGB 521
Jill Saward, Ind. 492
Mad Cow-Girl, Loony 412
Walter Sweeney, Ind. 238
David Craig, Ind. 135
David Pinder, New Party 135
David Icke, ND 110
C. maj. 15,355 (64.22%)
(2005 election, C. maj. 5,116 (10.65%))
* candidates that received less than 100 votes have not been included

HENLEY
E. 69,086 T. 34,761 (50.32%) C. hold
John Howell, C. 19,796
Stephen Kearney, LD 9,690
Mark Stevenson, Green 1,321
Timothy Rait, BNP 1,243
Richard McKenzie, Lab. 1,066
Chris Adams, UKIP 843
Bananaman Owen, Loony 242
Derek Allpass, Eng. Dem. 157
Amanda Harrington, MGB 128
Dick Rodgers, Com. 121
Louise Cole, MGB 91
Harry Bear, FPP 73
C. maj. 10,116 (56.95%)
0.81% swing LD to C.
(2005: C. maj. 12,793 (27.49%))

LIVINGSTON
E. 76,376 T. 29,477 (38.59%) Lab. hold
*Jim Devine, Lab. 12,319
Angela Constance, SNP 9,639
Charles Dundas, LD 4,362
Gordon Lindhurst, C. 1,993
David Robertson, Green 529
Steven Nimmo, SSP 407
Peter Adams, UKIP 108
Melville Brown, Ind. 55
John Allman, AFC 33
Brian Gardner, SPGB 32
Lab. maj. 2,680 (9.09%)
10.22% swing Lab. to SNP
(2005: Lab. maj. 13,097 (29.54%))

SEDGEFIELD
E. 67,339 T. 27,980 (41.55%) Lab. hold
*Phil Wilson, Lab. 12,528
Greg Stone, LD 5,572
Graham Robb, C. 4,082
Andrew Spence, BNP 2,494
Paul Gittins, Ind. 1,885
Toby Horton, UKIP 536
Chris Haine, Green 348
Stephen Gash, Eng. Dem. 177
Tim Grainger, Christian Party 177
Alan Hope, Loony 129
Norman Scarth, Anti-Crime Party 34
Lab. maj. 6,956 (24.86%)
11.06% swing Lab. to LD
(2005: Lab. maj. 18,457 (44.49%))

STAFFORDSHIRE SOUTH
E. 68,763 T. 25,635 (37.28%) C. hold
Sir Patrick Cormack, C. 13,343
Paul Kalinauckas, Lab. 4,496
Jo Crotty, LD 3,540
Malcolm Hurst, UKIP 2,675
Garry Bushell, Eng. Dem. 643
Kate Spohrer, Green 437
Adrian Davies, FP 434
The Revd David Braid, Clause 28 67
C. maj. 8,847 (34.51%)
9.10% swing Lab. to C.
(2001: C. maj. 6,881 (16.31%))

THE GOVERNMENT

as at 1 September 2008

THE CABINET

Prime Minister, First Lord of the Treasury and Minister for the Civil Service
Rt. Hon. Gordon Brown, MP (since June 2007)
Chancellor of the Exchequer
Rt. Hon. Alistair Darling, MP (since June 2007)
Chancellor of the Duchy of Lancaster and Minister for the Cabinet Office
Rt. Hon. Ed Miliband, MP (since June 2007)
Chief Secretary to the Treasury
Rt. Hon. Yvette Cooper, MP (since January 2008)
Leader of the House of Commons and Lord Privy Seal, Deputy Leader and Chair of Labour Party, and Minister for Women and Equalities
Rt. Hon. Harriet Harman, QC, MP (since June 2007)
Leader of the House of Lords and Lord President of the Council
Rt. Hon. Baroness Ashton of Upholland (since June 2007)
Parliamentary Secretary to the Treasury and Chief Whip
Rt. Hon. Geoff Hoon, MP (since June 2007)
Secretary of State for Business, Enterprise and Regulatory Reform
Rt. Hon. John Hutton, MP (since June 2007)
Secretary of State for Children, Schools and Families
Rt. Hon. Ed Balls, MP (since June 2007)
Secretary of State for Communities and Local Government
Rt. Hon. Hazel Blears, MP (since June 2007)
Secretary of State for Culture, Media and Sport
Rt. Hon. Andy Burnham, MP (since January 2008)
Secretary of State for Defence (since May 2006) *and Secretary of State for Scotland* (since June 2007)
Rt. Hon. Des Browne, MP
Secretary of State for Environment, Food and Rural Affairs
Rt. Hon. Hilary Benn, MP (since June 2007)
Secretary of State for Foreign and Commonwealth Affairs
Rt. Hon. David Miliband, MP (since June 2007)
Secretary of State for Health
Rt. Hon. Alan Johnson, MP (since June 2007)
Secretary of State for the Home Department
Rt. Hon. Jacqui Smith, MP (since June 2007)
Secretary of State for Innovation, Universities and Skills
Rt. Hon. John Denham, MP (since June 2007)
Secretary of State for International Development
Rt. Hon. Douglas Alexander, MP (since June 2007)
Secretary of State for Justice and Lord Chancellor
Rt. Hon. Jack Straw, MP (since June 2007)
Secretary of State for Northern Ireland
Rt. Hon. Shaun Woodward, MP (since June 2007)
Secretary of State for Transport
Rt. Hon. Ruth Kelly, MP (since June 2007)
Secretary of State for Wales
Rt. Hon. Paul Murphy, MP (since January 2008)
Secretary of State for Work and Pensions
Rt. Hon. James Purnell, MP (since January 2008)

The Attorney-General (Rt. Hon. Baroness Scotland of Asthal, QC), the Minister of State for the Olympics and London (Rt. Hon. Tessa Jowell, MP), the Minister of State for Housing (Rt. Hon. Caroline Flint, MP), the Minister of State for Africa, Asia and the UN (Lord Malloch Brown, KCMG), the Minister for the North-West and Minister for Children (Rt. Hon Beverley Hughes, MP), the Parliamentary Private Secretary to the Prime Minister (Ian Austin, MP) and the Chief Whip in the House of Lords and Captain of the Gentlemen-at-Arms (Rt. Hon. Baroness Royall of Blaisdon) attend cabinet meetings although they are not members of the cabinet.

LAW OFFICERS

Attorney-General
Rt. Hon. Baroness Scotland of Asthal, QC (since June 2007)
Solicitor-General
Vera Baird, QC, MP (since June 2007)
Advocate-General for Scotland
Lord Davidson of Glen Clova, QC (since May 2006)

MINISTERS OF STATE

Business, Enterprise and Regulatory Reform
Lord Jones of Birmingham, Kt.*
Pat McFadden, MP
Malcolm Wicks, MP
Cabinet Office
Rt. Hon. Ed Miliband, MP *(Chancellor of the Duchy of Lancaster)*
Rt. Hon. Tessa Jowell, MP
Children, Schools and Families
Rt. Hon. Beverley Hughes, MP
Jim Knight, MP
Communities and Local Government
Rt. Hon. Caroline Flint, MP
John Healey, MP
Culture, Media and Sport
Rt. Hon. Margaret Hodge, MBE, MP
Defence
Rt. Hon. Bob Ainsworth, MP
Environment, Food and Rural Affairs
Rt. Hon. Lord Rooker
Phil Woolas, MP
Equalities Office
Rt. Hon. Harriet Harman, QC, MP
Foreign and Commonwealth Office
Dr Kim Howells, MP
Lord Malloch Brown, KCMG
Rt. Hon. Jim Murphy, MP
Health
Ben Bradshaw, MP
Rt. Hon. Dawn Primarolo, MP
Home Office
Liam Byrne, MP
Tony McNulty, MP
Innovation, Universities and Skills
Ian Pearson, MP
Bill Rammell, MP

Justice
Rt. Hon. David Hanson, MP
Michael Wills, MP
Northern Ireland Office
Paul Goggins, MP
Scotland Office
David Cairns, MP
Transport
Rt. Hon. Rosie Winterton, MP
Work and Pensions
Mike O'Brien, MP
Rt. Hon. Stephen Timms, MP

* Also works in the Foreign and Commonwealth Office

UNDER-SECRETARIES OF STATE

Business, Enterprise and Regulatory Reform
Gareth Thomas, MP†
Baroness Vadera
Children, Schools and Families
Lord Adonis
Kevin Brennan, MP
Communities and Local Government
Baroness Andrews, OBE
Parmjit Dhanda, MP
Iain Wright, MP
Culture, Media and Sport
Gerry Sutcliffe, MP
Defence
Rt. Hon. Baroness Taylor of Bolton
Derek Twigg, MP
Environment, Food and Rural Affairs
Joan Ruddock, MP
Jonathan Shaw, MP
Foreign and Commonwealth Office
Meg Munn, MP
Government Equalities Office
Barbara Follett, MP
Health
Lord Darzi of Denham, KBE
Ann Keen, MP
Ivan Lewis, MP
Home Office
Vernon Coaker, MP
Meg Hillier, MP
Lord West of Spithead
Innovation, Universities and Skills
David Lammy, MP
Baroness Morgan of Drefelin
International Development
Shahid Malik, MP
Gillian Merron, MP
Justice
Maria Eagle, MP
Lord Hunt of King's Heath, OBE
Bridget Prentice, MP
Transport
Jim Fitzpatrick, MP
Tom Harris, MP
Wales Office
Huw Irranca-Davies, MP
Work and Pensions
Anne McGuire, MP
Lord McKenzie of Luton
James Plaskitt, MP

† Also in the Department for International Development

OTHER MINISTERS

Parliamentary Private Secretary to the Prime Minister
Ian Austin, MP
Cabinet Office
Rt. Hon. Tessa Jowell, MP *(Paymaster-General)*
Phil Hope, MP *(Parliamentary Secretary)*
Tom Watson, MP *(Parliamentary Secretary)*
Leader of the Commons
Harriet Harman, QC, MP *(Lord Privy Seal, Labour Party Chair and Minister for Women and Equalities)*
Helen Goodman, MP *(Parliamentary Secretary and Deputy Leader of the Commons)*
Treasury
Rt. Hon. Jane Kennedy, MP *(Financial Secretary)*
Kitty Ussher, MP *(Economic Secretary)*
Angela Eagle, MP *(Exchequer Secretary)*

GOVERNMENT WHIPS

HOUSE OF LORDS

Captain of the Honourable Corps of the Gentlemen-at-Arms (Chief Whip)
Rt. Hon. Baroness Royall of Blaisdon
Captain of the Queen's Bodyguard of the Yeomen of the Guard (Deputy Chief Whip)
Rt. Hon. Lord Davies of Oldham
Lords-in-Waiting
Lord Bach
Lord Bassam of Brighton
Baronesses-in-Waiting
Baroness Crawley
Baroness Farrington of Ribbleton
Baroness Morgan of Drefelin
Baroness Thornton

HOUSE OF COMMONS

Parliamentary Secretary to the Treasury (Chief Whip)
Rt. Hon. Geoff Hoon, MP
Treasurer of HM Household (Deputy Chief Whip)
Rt. Hon. Nicholas Brown, MP
Comptroller of HM Household
Rt. Hon. Thomas McAvoy, MP
Vice-Chamberlain of HM Household
Liz Blackman, MP
Lords Commissioners of HM Treasury
Alan Campbell, MP; Stephen McCabe, MP; Frank Roy, MP; Claire Ward, MP; Dave Watts, MP
Assistant Whips
Bob Blizzard, MP; Tony Cunningham, MP; Wayne David, MP; Michael Foster, MP; Diana R. Johnson, MP; Sadiq Khan, MP; Siobhain McDonagh, MP; Alison Seabeck, MP; Mark Tami, MP

GOVERNMENT DEPARTMENTS

THE CIVIL SERVICE

Under the Next Steps programme, launched in 1988, many semi-autonomous executive agencies were established to carry out much of the work of the civil service. Executive agencies operate within a framework set by the responsible minister which specifies policies, objectives and available resources. All executive agencies are set annual performance targets by their minister. Each agency has a chief executive, who is responsible for the day-to-day operations of the agency and who is accountable to the minister for the use of resources and for meeting the agency's targets. The minister accounts to parliament for the work of the agency. Nearly 75 per cent of civil servants now work in executive agencies. In April 2008 there were 523,260 permanent civil servants, down from about 537,000 in June 2005.

The Senior Civil Service was created in 1996 and on 1 April 2008 comprised 4,001 staff from permanent secretary to the former grade 5 level, including all agency chief executives. All government departments and executive agencies are now responsible for their own pay and grading systems for civil servants outside the Senior Civil Service.

SALARIES 2007–8

MINISTERIAL SALARIES *from 1 April 2008*

Ministers who are members of the House of Commons receive a parliamentary salary (£61,820) in addition to their ministerial salary.

Prime minister	£129,244
Cabinet minister (Commons)	£77,546
Cabinet minister (Lords)	£105,257
Minister of state (Commons)	£40,225
Minister of state (Lords)	£82,185
Parliamentary under-secretary (Commons)	£30,532
Parliamentary under-secretary (Lords)	£71,579

SPECIAL ADVISERS' SALARIES *from 1 April 2008*

Special advisers to government ministers are paid out of public funds; their salaries are negotiated individually, but are usually in the range of £38,862 to £102,918.

CIVIL SERVICE SALARIES *from 1 April 2008*

Senior Civil Servants	
Permanent secretary	£139,740–£273,250
Band 3	£99,960–£205,000
Band 2	£81,600–£160,000
Band 1A	£66,600–£127,000
Band 1	£57,300–£116,000

Staff are placed in pay bands according to their level of responsibility and taking account of other factors such as experience and marketability. Movement within and between bands is based on performance. Following the delegation of responsibility for pay and grading to government departments and agencies from 1 April 1996, it is no longer possible to show service-wide pay rates for staff outside the Senior Civil Service.

GOVERNMENT DEPARTMENTS

ATTORNEY-GENERAL'S OFFICE

Attorney-General's Office, 20 Victoria Street, London SW1H 0NF
T 020-7271 2492 F 020-7271 2434
E correspondenceunit@attorneygeneral.gsi.gov.uk
W www.attorneygeneral.gov.uk
Attorney-General's Chambers, Royal Courts of Justice, Belfast BT1 3JY
T 028-9054 6082 F 028-9054 6049

The law officers of the crown for England and Wales are the Attorney-General and the Solicitor-General. The Attorney-General, assisted by the Solicitor-General, is the chief legal adviser to the government and is also ultimately responsible for all crown litigation. She has overall responsibility for the work of the Law Officers' Departments (the Treasury Solicitor's Department, the Crown Prosecution Service, the Serious Fraud Office, the Revenue and Customs Prosecution Office, the Army Prosecuting Authority, HM Crown Prosecution Service Inspectorate and the Attorney-General's Office). She has a specific statutory duty to superintend the discharge of their duties by the Director of Public Prosecutions (who heads the Crown Prosecution Service) and the Director of the Serious Fraud Office. The Director of Public Prosecutions for Northern Ireland and the Crown Solicitor for Northern Ireland are also responsible to the Attorney-General for the performance of their functions. The Attorney-General has specific responsibilities for the enforcement of the criminal law and also performs certain public interest functions, eg protecting charities and appealing unduly lenient sentences. She also deals with questions of law arising in bills and with issues of legal policy.

Attorney-General, Rt. Hon. Baroness Scotland, QC
Private Secretary, W. Hart
Solicitor-General, V. Baird, QC, MP
Director-General, J. Jones
Director, Criminal Law, S. Patten

DEPARTMENT FOR BUSINESS, ENTERPRISE AND REGULATORY REFORM

1 Victoria Street, London SW1H 0ET
T 020-7215 5000 F 020-7215 0105
E enquiries@berr.gsi.gov.uk W www.berr.gov.uk

The Department for Business, Enterprise and Regulatory Reform (BERR) was established in June 2007 after the Department of Trade and Industry was disbanded. BERR promotes best practice in design and manufacture, and investment opportunities, and champions different industries' legitimate interests through policy and regulation. The department aims to create the conditions required for business success through competitive and flexible markets that provide value for businesses, consumers and employers. It is responsible for regulatory reform and works across government and the UK's regions to raise levels of UK productivity, and has joint responsibility – with the Department for International Development and the Foreign and Commonwealth Office respectively – for trade policy, and trade promotion and

inward investment. BERR also works closely with the newly established Department for Innovation, Universities and Skills.
Secretary of State for Business, Enterprise and Regulatory Reform, Rt. Hon. John Hutton, MP
Principal Private Secretary, Richard Abel
Senior Private Secretary, Catherine Capon
Private Secretaries, Tom Child; Melissa Perry; Simon Petrie
Parliamentary Private Secretary, Eric Joyce, MP
Special Advisers, John Williams; John Woodcock
Parliamentary Under-Secretary of State, Baroness Vadera *(Business and Competitiveness)*
Private Secretary, Faith Quigley
Parliamentary Private Secretary, vacant
Minister of State, Malcolm Wicks, MP *(Energy)*
Private Secretary, Fleur Ashton
Parliamentary Private Secretary, Dr Nick Palmer, MP
Minister of State, Lord Jones of Birmingham *(Trade and Investment)*
Private Secretary, Anna-Marie Durham
Parliamentary Private Secretary, Andy Slaughter, MP
Minister of State, Pat McFadden, MP *(Employment Relation and Postal Affairs)*
Private Secretary, Robert Porteous
Parliamentary Private Secretary, Jim McGovern, MP
Parliamentary Under-Secretary of State, Gareth Thomas, MP *(Trade and Consumer Affairs; also a minister with DfID)*
Private Secretary, Alan Dick
Permanent Secretary, Sir Brian Bender, KCB
Private Secretary, Jerome Glass
Head of Parliamentary Unit, Ian Webster

MANAGEMENT BOARD
Chair, Sir Brian Bender *(Permanent Secretary of State)*
Members, John Alty *(Fair Markets Group);* Andrew Cahn *(UK Trade and Industry);* Hilary Douglas *(Chief Operating Officer);* Mark Gibson *(Enterprise and Business Group);* Vicky Pryce *(Economics);* Willy Rickett *(Energy Group);* Rachel Sandby-Thomas *(Legal Services)*
Independent Members, Arnoud De Meyer; Roger Urwin; Dr Brian Woods-Scawen

BETTER REGULATION EXECUTIVE
1 Victoria Street, London SW1 0ET
T 020-7215 5000 **W** www.betterregulation.gov.uk

The Better Regulation Executive works with businesses and across government to minimise bureaucracy by reducing and simplifying regulation from the public, private and voluntary sectors.
Chair, William Sargent
Chief Executive, Jitinder Kohli

SHAREHOLDER EXECUTIVE
1 Victoria Street, London SW1H 0ET
T 020-7215 3909 **F** 020-7215 5336
W www.shareholderexecutive.gov.uk

The Shareholder Executive was established in September 2003 to improve the government's performance as a shareholder in government-owned businesses and to provide a source of corporate finance expertise within government; currently the executive's remit covers 27 businesses.
Chair, Philip Remnant
Chief Executive, Stephen Lovegrove

CABINET OFFICE

70 Whitehall, London SW1A 2AS
Switchboard 020-7276 3000 **T** 020-7276 1234
W www.cabinet-office.gov.uk

The Cabinet Office, alongside the Treasury, sits at the centre of the government. It has three core functions: to support the prime minister in defining and delivering the government's objectives; to support the cabinet in ensuring the coherence, quality and delivery of policy and operations across departments; and strengthening the Civil Service's capabilities in terms of organisation, leadership and skills. The department is headed by the Chancellor of the Duchy of Lancaster.
Prime Minister, First Lord of the Treasury and Minister for the Civil Service, Rt. Hon. Gordon Brown, MP
Principal Private Secretary to the Prime Minister, James Bowler
Chancellor of the Duchy of Lancaster and Minister for the Cabinet Office, Rt. Hon. Ed Miliband, MP
Parliamentary Private Secretary, Jeffrey Ennis, MP
Principal Private Secretary, Lee O'Rourke
Private Secretary, Louise Coward
Parliamentary Secretary, Phil Hope, MP
Assistant Private Secretaries, Gemma Lobb; Kate Wilson
Parliamentary Secretary, Tom Watson, MP
Private Secretary, Sarah Goulbourne
Secretary of the Cabinet and Head of the Home Civil Service, Sir Gus O'Donnell, KCB
Principal Private Secretary, Ciaran Martin
Private Secretary, Paul Rennie
Assistant Private Secretary, Jackie Fraser *(Diary)*
Permanent Secretary, Sir Richard Mottram, GCB *(Intelligence, Security and Resilience)*
Principal Private Secretary, Dominic Fagan
Private Secretary, Stephen Knight
Minister for the Olympics and London, Rt. Hon. Tessa Jowell, MP
Private Secretary, Alec Taylor
Parliamentary Private Secretary, John Mann, MP

The TRANSFORMATIONAL GOVERNMENT/ CABINET OFFICE MANAGEMENT DIRECTORATE comprises the Business Support Group, Cabinet Office Management, Change Team and the Transformational Government. It was established to provide overall technology leadership in three key areas of government: the transformation of public services for the benefit of citizens, businesses, taxpayers and front-line staff; the efficiency of the corporate services and infrastructure of government organisations; and the steps necessary to achieve the effective delivery of technology for government.

BUSINESS SUPPORT GROUP
Kirkland House, 22–26 Whitehall, London SW1A 2WH
T 020-7276 0530
Director-General, Strategic Finance and Operations, Roger Marsh

CABINET OFFICE MANAGEMENT
Admiralty Arch, The Mall, London SW1A 2WH
T 020-7276 3090
Director-General, Transformational Government and Cabinet Office Management, Alexis Cleveland

CHANGE TEAM
Kirkland House, 22–26 Whitehall, London SW1A 2WH
T 020-7276 2160
Director, Sarah Cox

TRANSFORMATIONAL GOVERNMENT
1 Horse Guards Road, London SW1A 2HQ
T 020-7276 3248
HM Government Chief Information Officer, John Suffolk

The CIVIL SERVICE CAPABILITY GROUP comprises Cabinet Office Human Resources, Performance and Change, Leadership and Talent, Workforce, Cabinet Office Shared Services, Governance and Stakeholders and the Capability Reviews team. The group is responsible for recruiting and developing staff and raising the capability of HR management throughout the civil service.
Director-General CSCG, Gill Rider

CABINET OFFICE HUMAN RESOURCES
Admiralty Arch South, The Mall, London SW1A 2WH
T 020-7276 6200
Director, Janette Durbin

PERFORMANCE AND CHANGE
Admiralty Arch, The Mall, London SW1A 2WH
T 020-7276 1462
Director, Peter Thomas

LEADERSHIP AND TALENT
Admiralty Arch, The Mall, London SW1A 2WH
T 020-7276 1171
Director, Helen Dudley

WORKFORCE
Admiralty Arch, The Mall, London SW1A 2WH
T 020-7276 1559
Director, Dusty Amroliwala

CABINET OFFICE SHARED SERVICES
Admiralty Arch, The Mall, London SW1A 2WH
T 020-7276 2088
Director, Janet Wilkes

GOVERNANCE AND STAKEHOLDERS
Admiralty Arch, The Mall, London SW1A 2WH
T 020-7276 1643
Director, Sue Jenkins

CAPABILITY REVIEWS
Admiralty Arch, The Mall, London SW1A 2WH
T 020-7270 1516
Director, Brian Etheridge

The DOMESTIC POLICY GROUP comprises the Ceremonial Secretariat, the Economic and Domestic Affairs Secretariat, the Office of the Third Sector, the Social Exclusion Task Force, the Strategy Unit and the European and Global Issues Secretariat.

CEREMONIAL SECRETARIAT
35 Great Smith Street, London SW1P 3BQ
T 020-7276 2777
Ceremonial Officer, Denis Brennan

ECONOMIC AND DOMESTIC AFFAIRS SECRETARIAT
Cabinet Office, 70 Whitehall, London SW1A 2WH
T 020-7276 0055
Director-General, Paul Britton, CB

OFFICE OF THE THIRD SECTOR
35 Great Smith Street, London SW1P 3BQ
T 020-7276 6400
Director-General, Campbell Robb

SOCIAL EXCLUSION TASK FORCE
Admiralty Arch, The Mall, London SW1A 2WH
T 020-7276 2323
Director, Naomi Eisenstadt

STRATEGY UNIT
Admiralty Arch, The Mall, London SW1A 2WH
T 020-7276 1881 W www.cabinetoffice.gov.uk/strategy
Director, Stephen Aldridge

EUROPEAN AND GLOBAL ISSUES SECRETARIAT
70 Whitehall, London SW1A 2WH
T 020-7276 1234
Prime Minister's International and European Policy Adviser, Jon Cunliffe

The COMMUNICATION AND INFORMATION GROUP comprises Cabinet Office Communications, Government Communication and the Histories, Openness and Records Unit.

CABINET OFFICE COMMUNICATIONS
22 Whitehall, London SW1A 2WH
T 020-7276 0079/2002
Director, Jenny Grey

GOVERNMENT COMMUNICATION
26 Whitehall, London SW1A 2WH
T 020-7276 2712 W www.comms.gov.uk
Permanent Secretary, vacant

HISTORIES, OPENNESS AND RECORDS UNIT
Admiralty Arch, The Mall, London SW1A 2WH
T 020-7276 6326
Departmental Records Officer and Adviser, Tessa Stirling, CBE

INTELLIGENCE, SECURITY AND RESILIENCE GROUP
70 Whitehall, London SW1A 2AS
W www.intelligence.gov.uk
The Prime Minister's Security Adviser and Head of Intelligence, Security and Resilience, Robert Hannigan

DIRECTORATE OF SECURITY AND INTELLIGENCE
26 Whitehall, London SW1A 2WH
Director, Chris Wright

CIVIL CONTINGENCIES SECRETARIAT
22 Whitehall, London SW1A 2WH
T 020-7276 5061
Director, Bruce Mann

EMERGENCY PLANNING COLLEGE
The Hawkhills, Easingwold, York YO61 3EG
T 01347-825006 W www.epcollege.gov.uk
Chief Executive, Michael Charlton-Weedy

COUNTER TERRORISM AND CRISIS MANAGEMENT TEAM
70 Whitehall, London SW1A 2AS
Deputy Director, Nick Gibbons

JOINT INTELLIGENCE ORGANISATION
70 Whitehall, London SW1A 2AS
W www.intelligence.gov.uk
Chair of the Joint Intelligence Committee and Head of Intelligence Assessment, Alex Allan

CENTRAL SPONSOR FOR INFORMATION ASSURANCE
2nd Floor, Cabinet Office, 26 Whitehall, London SW1A 2WH
T 020-7276 3108
W www.cabinetoffice.gov.uk/csia
Head, Roger Styles

FOREIGN AND DEFENCE POLICY SECRETARIAT
Cabinet Office, 70 Whitehall, London SW1A 2AS
T 020-7930 4433
Prime Minister's Foreign Policy Adviser and Head of Secretariat, Simon McDonald, CMG

PRIME MINISTER'S OFFICE
10 Downing Street, London SW1A 2AA
T 020-7930-4433
W www.number-10.gov.uk
Prime Minister, Rt. Hon Gordon Brown, MP
Parliamentary Private Secretary, Ian Austin, MP
Permanent Secretary, Jeremy Heywood, CB, CVO
Chief of Strategy and Principal Adviser, Stephen Carter
Principal Private Secretary, James Bowler
Director of Communications and the Prime Minister's Spokesman, Michael Ellam
Deputy Chief of Staff, Gavin Kelly
Director of Political Strategy, David Muir
Director of Government Relations, Sue Nye
Head of Policy Unit, Dan Corry
Adviser to the Prime Minister on Political Press Issues, Damian McBride
Head of International Economic Affairs, European and G8 Sherpa, Jon Cunliffe, CB
Head of Foreign and Defence Policy, Simon McDonald, CMG

CROSS GOVERNMENT UNITS in the Cabinet Office comprises the Committee on Standards in Public Life (*see* Public Bodies section), Independent Offices and the Office of the Parliamentary Counsel.

INDEPENDENT OFFICES

OFFICE OF THE COMMISSIONER FOR PUBLIC APPOINTMENTS (OCPA)
3rd Floor, 35 Great Smith Street, London SW1P 3BQ
T 020-7276 2625 F 020-7276 2633
E ocpa@gtnet.gov.uk W www.ocpa.gov.uk

The Commissioner for Public Appointments is responsible for monitoring, regulating and reporting on ministerial appointments to public bodies. The commissioner can investigate complaints about the way in which appointments were made or applicants treated.
Commissioner for Public Appointments, Janet Gaymer, CBE, QC
Secretary to the Commissioner and Head of the Independent Offices, Dr Richard Jarvis

OFFICE OF THE CIVIL SERVICE COMMISSIONERS (OCSC)
35 Great Smith Street, London SW1P 3BQ
T 020-7276 2617 W www.civilservicecommissioners.org

The Civil Service Commissioners are the custodians of the principle of selection on merit by fair and open competition; they publish a recruitment code and audit departments' and agencies' performance against it. When the most senior posts are opened to people from outside the service, the commissioners normally chair the recruitment process.
First Commissioner, Janet Paraskeva
Commissioners (part-time), Sir Michael Aaronson, CBE; Mark Addison; John MacAuslan; Dame Alexander Burslem, DBE; Janet Gaymer, CBE, QC; Prof. Christine Hallett; Ms Mary Jo Jacobi; Bernard Knight; Sir Neil McIntosh; Ms Elizabeth McMeikan; Anthea Millett, CBE; Ms Stella Pantelides; Ranjit Sondhi; Christopher Stephens; Libby Watkins

OFFICE OF THE PARLIAMENTARY COUNSEL
35 Whitehall, London SW1A 2AY
T 020-7210 2588 W www.parliamentary-counsel.gov.uk
First Parliamentary Counsel, Stephen Laws, CB
Chief Executive, Jim Barron, CBE

INTELLIGENCE AND SECURITY COMMITTEE SECRETARIAT
70 Whitehall, London SW1A 2AS
T 020-7276 1215 W www.cabinetoffice.gov.uk/intelligence
Head of Management Unit, Emma-Louise Avery

INTERNAL AUDIT SERVICE
4th Floor, Ashdown House, 123 Victoria Street, London SW1E 6DE
T 020-7944 6521
Head, Steve Simmonds

DEPARTMENT FOR CHILDREN, SCHOOLS AND FAMILIES

Sanctuary Buildings, Great Smith Street, London SW1P 3BT
Caxton House, Tothill Street, London SW1H 9NA
Castle View House, East Lane, Runcorn WA7 2GJ
Mowden Hall, Staindrop Road, Darlington DL3 9BG
Moorfoot, Sheffield S1 4PQ
T 0870-001 2345 Public Enquiries 0870-000 2288
F 01928-794248
E info@dcsf.gsi.gov.uk W www.dcsf.gov.uk

The Department for Children, Schools and Families (DCSF) was established in June 2007 in place of the Department for Education and Skills (DfES), in order to achieve better integrated children's services and improved educational standards; higher education and lifelong learning directorates moved to the new Department for Innovation, Universities and Skills.

The DCSF is responsible for everything affecting children and young people under the age of 19, including schools and relevant services. The department's objectives are to increase the number of children reaching expected standards; help children out of poverty; and re-engage disaffected young people. It also aims to respond to factors affecting children and families, such as demographic and socio-economic change, developing technology and increasing global competition.
Secretary of State for Children, Schools and Families, Rt. Hon. Ed Balls, MP
Principal Private Secretary, Sinead O'Sullivan
Private Secretary, Sophie Taylor
Special Advisers, Francine Bates; Alex Belardinelli
Parliamentary Private Secretary, Paul Clark, MP
Minister of State, Jim Knight, MP *(Schools and Learners)*
Private Secretary, Charles Deighton-Fox
Parliamentary Private Secretary, Madeline Moon, MP

Minister of State, Rt. Hon. Beverley Hughes, MP *(Children, Young People and Families)*
Private Secretary, Amy Buxton
Parliamentary Private Secretary, Christine Russell, MP
Parliamentary Under-Secretary of State, Lord Adonis *(Schools and Learners)*
Private Secretary, Samuel Cunningham
Parliamentary Under-Secretary of State, Kevin Brennan, MP *(Children, Young People and Families)*
Private Secretary, Nichola Vasey
Parliamentary Clerk, Deborah Lewis
Spokesperson in the House of Lords, Lord Adonis
Permanent Secretary, David Bell
Private Secretary, Lucy Andrew

MANAGEMENT BOARD
Chair, David Bell *(Permanent Secretary of State)*
Members, Philip Augar; Jon Coles *(Schools) (acting);* Jane Cooper *(Communications);* Tom Jeffery *(Children and Families);* Katherine Kerswell; Lesley Longstone *(Young People);* Jon Thompson *(Corporate Services)*

DEPARTMENT FOR COMMUNITIES AND LOCAL GOVERNMENT

Eland House, London SW1E 5DU
T 020-7944 4400 F 020-7944 9645
W www.communities.gov.uk

The Department for Communities and Local Government (DCLG) was formed in May 2006 with a remit to promote community cohesion and prevent extremism, as well as responsibility for housing, urban regeneration and planning. It unites the communities and civil renewal functions previously undertaken by the Home Office, with responsibility for regeneration, neighbourhood renewal and local government (previously held by the Office of the Deputy Prime Minister, which was abolished following a cabinet reshuffle in May 2006).

The DCLG also has responsibility for equality policy on race and faith (functions that were previously split between several government departments).

Secretary of State for the Department for Communities and Local Government, Minister for Women, Rt. Hon. Hazel Blears, MP
Private Secretary, Nick Dexter
Parliamentary Private Secretary, Robert Flello, MP
Minister of State, Rt. Hon. John Healey, MP *(Local Government)*
Private Secretary, Emily Arch
Parliamentary Private Secretary, Chris Mole, MP
Minister of State, Caroline Flint, MP *(Housing)*
Private Secretary, Mark Livesey
Parliamentary Private Secretary, Chris Ruane, MP
Parliamentary Under-Secretary of State, Parmjit Dhanda, MP
Private Secretary, Lee Burge
Parliamentary Under-Secretary of State, Baroness Andrews, OBE
Private Secretary, Alistair MacDonald
Parliamentary Under-Secretary of State, Iain Wright, MP
Private Secretary, Stella Michael
Permanent Secretary, Peter Housden
Private Secretary, Hulya Mustafa
Chief Scientist, Prof. Michael Kelly

MANAGEMENT BOARD
Chair, Peter Housden *(Permanent Secretary of State)*
Members, Christina Bienkowska *(Strategy and Performance);* Polly Cochrane; Peter Doyle; Mike Falvey *(HR and Business Change);* Debbie Hewitt; Richard McCarthy *(Housing and Planning);* Joe Montgomery *(Regions and Communities);* Hunada Nouss *(Finance and Corporate Services);* Susan Scholefield *(Cohesion and Resilience);* Rob Vincent; Sara Weir; Dame Jo Williams; Chris Wormald *(Local Government and Regeneration)*

DEPARTMENT FOR CULTURE, MEDIA AND SPORT

2–4 Cockspur Street, London SW1Y 5DH
T 020-7211 6200 F 020-7211 6032
E enquiries@culture.gov.uk W www.culture.gov.uk

The Department for Culture, Media and Sport (DCMS) was established in July 1997 and aims to improve the quality of life for all those in the UK through cultural and sporting activities while championing the tourism, creative and leisure industries. It is responsible for government policy relating to the arts, sport, the National Lottery, tourism, libraries, museums and galleries, broadcasting, creative industries – including film and the music industry – press freedom and regulation, licensing, gambling and the historic environment.

The department is also responsible for 61 public bodies that help deliver the department's strategic aims and objectives, the 2012 Olympic Games and Paralympic Games, the listing of historic buildings and scheduling of ancient monuments, the export licensing of cultural goods, and the management of the Government Art Collection and the Royal Parks (its sole executive agency). It has the responsibility for humanitarian assistance in the event of a disaster, as well as for the organisation of the annual Remembrance Day ceremony at the Cenotaph. In May 2005 the DCMS assumed responsibility for fashion design, advertising and the arts market from the then Department for Trade and Industry – now the Department for Business, Enterprise and Regulatory Reform – which it also works jointly with on design issues (including sponsorship of the Design Council) and on relations with the computer games and publishing industries.

Secretary of State for Culture, Media and Sport, Rt. Hon Andy Burnham, MP
Principal Private Secretary, Rita Patel
Special Advisers, Phil French; Jennifer Gerber
Parliamentary Private Secretary, Mary Creagh, MP
Minister of State, Rt. Hon. Margaret Hodge, MBE, MP *(Culture, Creative Industries and Tourism)*
Private Secretary, Ruth Evans
Parliamentary Private Secretary, Derek Wyatt, MP
Parliamentary Under-Secretary of State, Gerry Sutcliffe, MP *(Sport)*
Private Secretary, Graeme Brown
Permanent Secretary, Jonathan Stephens
Private Secretary, Sarah Taylor

MANAGEMENT BOARD
Chair, Jonathan Stephens *(Permanent Secretary of State)*
Members, Jeremy Beeton *(Government Olympic Executive);* Nicholas Holgate *(Corporate Strategy and Services);* Andrew Ramsay, CB *(Partnership and Programmes)*

MINISTRY OF DEFENCE

see Defence section

DEPARTMENT FOR ENVIRONMENT, FOOD AND RURAL AFFAIRS

Nobel House, 17 Smith Square, London SW1P 3JR
T 020-7238 3000 **Helpline** 0845-933 5577
F 020-7238 6591
E helpline@defra.gsi.gov.uk W www.defra.gov.uk

The Department for Environment, Food and Rural Affairs (DEFRA) is responsible for government policy on the environment, rural matters, farming and food production; its central aim is sustainable development. In association with the agriculture departments of the Scottish government, the National Assembly for Wales and the Northern Ireland Office, and with the Intervention Board, the department is responsible for negotiations in the EU on the common agricultural and fisheries policies, and for single European market questions relating to its responsibilities. Its remit includes international agricultural and food trade policy.

The department's five strategic priorities, published in *DEFRA's Five-Year Strategy: Delivering the Essentials of Life*, are climate change and energy; sustainable consumption and production; the protection of natural resources and the countryside; sustainable rural communities; and sustainable farming and food, including animal health and welfare. DEFRA is also the lead government department for emergencies in animal and plant diseases, flooding, food and water supply, dealing with the consequences of a chemical, biological, radiological or nuclear incident, and other threats to the environment.

Secretary of State for Environment, Food and Rural Affairs, Rt. Hon. Hilary Benn, MP
Principal Private Secretary, Rory O'Donnell
Private Secretaries, Rebecca Evernden; Anna Sanders; Amanda Small; Alex Thomas; Anne Voller
Parliamentary Private Secretaries, Nia Griffith, MP; Dr Ashok Kumar, MP
Minister of State, Phil Woolas, MP *(Environment)*
Senior Private Secretary, Neil Hornby
Private Secretaries, Claire Denniss; Robert Grant; Samantha Suares; Kathryn Wood
Minister of State, Rt. Hon. Lord Rooker *(Sustainable Food and Farming, and Animal Health)*
Senior Private Secretary, Rhian Mewis
Private Secretaries, William Boohan; Amelia Munn; Vincent Venturotti
Parliamentary Under-Secretary of State, Joan Ruddock, MP *(Climate Change, Biodiversity and Waste)*
Senior Private Secretary, Liz Kitchen
Private Secretaries, Rachel Dominey; Indy Gill; Martin Heffernan; David Miller
Parliamentary Under-Secretary of State, Jonathan Shaw, MP *(Marine, Landscape and Rural Affairs)*
Senior Private Secretary, Deborah Wells
Private Secretaries, Rob Davies; David Miller; Joe Speck; Craig Walker
Permanent Secretary, Helen Ghosh
Private Secretary, Jenny McClelland

MANAGEMENT BOARD

Chair, Helen Ghosh *(Permanent Secretary of State)*
Members, Gill Aitken *(Legal Services and Solicitor);* Mike Anderson *(Climate Change);* Poul Christensen; Alexis Cleveland; Bill Griffiths; Bill Stow *(Strategy and Evidence);* Peter Unwin *(Natural Environment);* Prof. Robert Watson *(Chief Scientific Adviser);* Ian Watt *(Finance);* Katrina Williams *(Food and Farming)*

FOREIGN AND COMMONWEALTH OFFICE

King Charles Street, London SW1A 2AH
T 020-7008 1500 W www.fco.gov.uk

The Foreign and Commonwealth Office (FCO) provides, through its staff in the UK and through its diplomatic missions abroad, the means of communication between the British government and other governments – and international governmental organisations – on all matters falling within the field of international relations.

It is responsible for alerting the British government to the implications of developments overseas; promoting British interests overseas; protecting British citizens abroad; explaining British policies to, and cultivating relationships with, governments overseas; the discharge of British responsibilities to the overseas territories; entry clearance UK visas (with the Home Office); and promoting British business overseas (jointly with the Department for Business, Enterprise and Regulatory Reform through UK Trade and Investment).

Secretary of State for Foreign and Commonwealth Affairs, Rt. Hon. David Miliband, MP
Principal Private Secretary, Matthew Gould
Special Advisers, Ravi Gurumurthy; Madlin Sadler; Sarah Schaefer
Parliamentary Private Secretary, Dan Norris, MP
Minister of State, Jim Murphy, MP *(Europe)*
Private Secretary, Nicholas Catsaras
Parliamentary Private Secretary, Neil Turner, MP
Minister of State, Dr Kim Howells, MP *(Middle East)*
Private Secretary, Scott Furssedonn
Parliamentary Private Secretary, John Robertson, MP
Minister of State, Lord Jones of Birmingham *(Trade and Investment)*
Minister of State, Lord Malloch-Brown, KCMG *(Africa, Asia and the UN)*
Private Secretary, Will Middleton
Parliamentary Private Secretary, Andy Slaughter, MP
Parliamentary Under-Secretary of State, Meg Munn, MP
Private Secretary, Alexandra Davidson
Permanent Under-Secretary of State and Head of HM Diplomatic Service, Sir Peter Ricketts, CMG
Private Secretary, Diane Sheard

MANAGEMENT BOARD

Group Chief Executive, UK Trade and Investment, Andrew Cahn
Members, Daniel Bethlehem *(Legal Adviser);* James Bevan *(Change and Delivery);* Nicola Brewer, CMG *(EU Policy);* Simon Fraser *(Europe and Globalisation);* Alistair Johnson; Mariat Leslie *(Defence/Intelligence);* Keith Luck *(Finance);* Mark Lyall Grant *(Political);* Alison Platt

GOVERNMENT EQUALITIES OFFICE

5th Floor, Eland House, Bressenden Place, London SW1E 5DU
T 020-7944 0601 E enquiries@geo.gsi.gov.uk
W www.equalities.gov.uk

The Government Equalities Office (GEO) was created in July 2007. The GEO is responsible for the government's overall strategy on equality, as well as on leading women's issues across government, and sponsoring the Equality and Human Rights Commission and Women's National Commission. The GEO reports to the Minister for Women and Equality.

Minister for Women and Equality, Rt. Hon. Harriet Harman, QC, MP *(Lord Privy Seal, Leader of the House of Commons and Labour Party Chair)*

Parliamentary Private Under-Secretary of State and Minister of the East of England, Barbara Follett, MP

SENIOR MANAGEMENT TEAM
Director-General, Jonathan Rees
Policy Director, Janice Shersby
Director, Corporate Services, Chris Bull
Deputy Director, Discrimination Law, Melanie Field
Head, Gender Equality Policy, Ann Keeling
Deputy Director, Equalities PSA and Strategy, Alison Rose

DEPARTMENT OF HEALTH

Richmond House, 79 Whitehall, London SW1A 2NS
T 020-7210 3000
W www.dh.gov.uk

The Department of Health is responsible for the provision of the National Health Service (NHS) in England and for social care. The department's aims are to support, protect, promote and improve the nation's health; to secure the provision of comprehensive, high-quality care for all those who need it, regardless of their ability to pay, where they live or their age; and to provide responsive adult social care for those who lack the support they need.

The Department of Health is responsible for setting health and social care policy in England. The department's work sets standards and drives modernisation across all areas of the NHS, social care and public health.

Secretary of State for Health, Rt. Hon. Alan Johnson, MP
Principal Private Secretary, Maeve Walsh
Parliamentary Private Secretary, Laura Moffat, MP
Minister of State, Ben Bradshaw, MP *(Health Services)*
Private Secretary, John Heine
Parliamentary Private Secretary, Rosie Cooper, MP
Minister of State, Rt. Hon. Dawn Primarolo, MP *(Public Health)*
Private Secretary, Sarah Kirby
Parliamentary Private Secretary, Helen Jones, MP
Parliamentary Under-Secretary of State, Prof. Lord Darzi, KBE
Private Secretary, Julia Scott
Parliamentary Under-Secretary of State, Ivan Lewis, MP *(Care Services)*
Private Secretary, Edward Scully
Parliamentary Under-Secretary of State, Ann Keen, MP *(Health)*
Private Secretary, Diane Sinclair
Parliamentary Clerk, Tim Elms

MANAGEMENT BOARD
Chair, Hugh Taylor, CB (*Permanent Secretary of State)*
Members, Julie Baddeley; David Behan, CBE *(Social Care, Local Government and Care Partnerships);* Prof. Sir Liam Donaldson, KB *(Chief Medical Officer);* Richard Douglas, CB *(Finance and Operations);* Derek Myers; David Nicholson, CBE *(NHS);* Mike Wheeler

NATIONAL CLINICAL DIRECTORS
Cancer, Prof. Mike Richards, CBE
Children, Young People and Community Services, Dr Sheila Shribman
Diabetes, Dr Rowan Hillson, MBE
Emergency Access, Prof. Sir George Alberti
Health and Work, Prof. Dame Carol Black
Heart Disease, Prof. Roger Boyle, CBE
Imaging, Dr Erika Denton
Renal Services, Dr Donal J. O'Donoghue
Learning Disabilities, vacant
Mental Health, Prof. Louis Appleby, CBE
Older People's Services, vacant
Pandemic Influenza Preparedness, Prof. Lindsey Davies
Patients and the Public, Joan Saddler, OBE
Primary Care, Dr David Colin-Thome
Transplants, Chris Rudge
Widening Participation in Learning, Prof. Bob Fryer, CBE

SOLICITOR'S OFFICE*
Solicitor, Richard Heaton
Director of DWP Legal Services, Greer Kerrigan, CB
Director of DH Legal Services, Frances Logan
* Also the solicitor's office for the Department for Work and Pensions

SPECIAL HEALTH AUTHORITIES
Health Protection Agency
W www.hpa.org.uk
Mental Health Act Commission
W www.mhac.org.uk
National Blood Service
W www.blood.co.uk
National Clinical Assessment Service
W www.ncas.nhs.uk
National Institute for Health and Clinical Excellence
W www.nice.org.uk
National Treatment Agency for Substance Misuse
W www.nta.nhs.uk
National Patient Safety Agency
W www.npsa.nhs.uk
NHS Appointments Commission
W www.appointments.org.uk
NHS Business Services Authority
W www.nhsbsa.nhs.uk
NHS Litigation Authority
W www.nhsla.com
UK Transplant
W www.uktransplant.org.uk

HOME OFFICE

2 Marsham Street, London SW1P 4DF
T 020-7035 4848 F 020-7035 4745
E public.enquiries@homeoffice.gsi.gov.uk
W www.homeoffice.gov.uk

The Home Office deals with those internal affairs in England and Wales which have not been assigned to other government departments. The Secretary of State for the Home Department is the link between the Queen and the public, and exercises certain powers on her behalf, including that of the royal pardon.

The Home Office aims to build a safe, just and tolerant society and to maintain and enhance public security and protection; to support and mobilise communities so that they are able to shape policy and improvement for their locality, overcome nuisance and anti-social behaviour, maintain and enhance social cohesion and enjoy their homes and public spaces peacefully; to deliver departmental policies and responsibilities fairly, effectively and efficiently; and to make the best use of resources. These objectives reflect the priorities of the government and the home secretary in areas of crime, citizenship and communities, namely to reduce crime and the fear of crime through visible, responsive and accountable policing; to reduce organised and international crime; to combat terrorism and other threats to national security; to ensure the effective delivery of justice; to reduce re-offending and protect the public; to reduce the availability and abuse of dangerous drugs; to regulate entry to, and settlement in, the UK in the interests of sustainable growth and social inclusion; and to support strong, active communities in which people of all races and backgrounds are valued and participate on equal terms.

The Home Office delivers these aims through the immigration services, its agencies and non-departmental public bodies, and by working with partners in private, public and voluntary sectors, individuals and communities. The home secretary is also the link between the UK government and the governments of the Channel Islands and the Isle of Man.

Secretary of State for the Home Department, Rt. Hon. Jacqui Smith, MP
Principal Private Secretary, Richard Westlake
Assistant Private Secretary, Gareth Edwards
Special Advisers, Susan Jackson; Andrew Lappin
Minister of State, Tony McNulty, MP *(Security, Counter-Terrorism and Policing Reform)*
Private Secretary, Neil Roberts
Minister of State, Liam Byrne, MP *(Borders, and Minister for the West Midlands)*
Private Secretary, Thomas Grieg
Parliamentary Under-Secretary of State, Lord West of Spithead, GCB, DSC *(Security and Counter-Terrorism)*
Private Secretary, Caroline Smith
Parliamentary Under-Secretary of State, Vernon Coaker, MP *(Crime Reduction)*
Private Secretary, Laura Ratcliffe
Parliamentary Under-Secretary of State, Meg Hillier, MP *(Identity)*
Private Secretary, Carol Jones
Permanent Secretary of State, Sir David Normington, KCB
Private Secretary, Isobel Arthur

MANAGEMENT BOARD
Chair, Sir David Normington, KCB *(Permanent Secretary of State)*
Members, Derrick Anderson; Yasmin Diamond *(Communications);* Charles Farr *(Office for Security and Counter Terrorism);* James Hall *(Identity and Passport Service);* John Heywood; Lin Homer, CB *(UK Border Agency);* Helen Kilpatrick *(Financial and Commercial);* Peter Makeham, CB *(Strategy and Reform);* Moira Wallace, OBE *(Crime Reduction and Community Safety Group);* Kevin White, CB *(Human Resources)*

OFFICE FOR CRIMINAL JUSTICE REFORM
Chief Executive, Jonathan Slater
Directors, Arwa'a Abdulla *(Policy and Process);* Catherine Lee *(Delivery and Communications) (acting)*

Note: The OCJR is a cross-departmental organisation, also reporting to the Ministry of Justice and the Office of the Attorney-General

DEPARTMENT FOR INNOVATION, UNIVERSITIES AND SKILLS

Kingsgate House, 66–74 Victoria Street, London SW1E 6SW
T 020-7215 5555 W www.dius.gov.uk

The Department for Innovation, Universities and Skills (DIUS) was established in June 2007 and brings together functions from the former Department for Trade and Industry – including responsibilities for science and innovation – with functions from the former Department for Education and Skills (further and higher education and skills).

The DIUS aims to sustain and develop a world-class research base; maximise its exploitation to support innovation across all sectors of the economy; increase and widen participation in higher education; raise participation and attainment by young people and adults in post-16 education and learning; reduce the skills gap amongst adults, particularly in terms of numeracy and literacy; and increase the supply of people in the fields of science, technology, engineering and mathematics.

Secretary of State for Innovation, Universities and Skills, Rt. Hon. John Denham, MP
Principal Private Secretary, Emran Mian
Private Secretaries, Charlotte Buckley; Catherine Perez
Parliamentary Private Secretary, Lyn Brown, MP
Minister of State, Ian Pearson, MP *(Science and Innovation)*
Private Secretary, Julian MacCormac
Parliamentary Private Secretary, Celia Barlow, MP
Minister of State, Bill Rammell, MP *(Lifelong Learning, Further and Higher Education)*
Private Secretary, Lisa Glover
Parliamentary Private Secretary, David Anderson, MP
Parliamentary Under-Secretary of State, David Lammy, MP *(Skills)*
Private Secretary, Robin Todd
Parliamentary Under-Secretary of State, Baroness Delyth Morgan *(Intellectual Property and Quality)*
Private Secretary, Kellie Hurst

MANAGEMENT BOARD
Chair, Ian Watmore *(Permanent Secretary of State)*
Members, Alan Aubrey; Prof. John Beddington *(Chief Scientific Adviser, Government Office for Science);* Bill Dickinson *(Finance and Corporate Services);* Zina Etheridge *(Strategy and Communications);* David Evans *(Innovation and International);* Julia King, CBE; Stephen Marston *(Further Education and Skills);* Dame Julie Mellor; Kristina Murrin; Shirley Pointer *(Human Resources);* Prof. Adrian Smith *(Science and Innovation);* Ruth Thompson *(Higher Education)*

DEPARTMENT FOR INTERNATIONAL DEVELOPMENT

1 Palace Street, London SW1 5HE
T 020-7023 0000 F 020-7023 0016
Abercrombie House, Eaglesham Road, East Kilbride, Glasgow G75 8EA
T 01355-844000 F 01355-844099
Public Enquiries 0845-300 4100
E enquiry@dfid.gov.uk W www.dfid.gov.uk

The Department for International Development (DFID) is responsible for promoting sustainable development and reducing poverty. The central focus of the government's policy, based on the 1997, 2000 and 2006 white papers on international development, is a commitment to the internationally agreed Millennium Development Goals, to be achieved by 2015. These seek to eradicate extreme poverty and hunger; achieve universal primary education; promote gender equality and empower women; reduce child mortality; improve maternal health; combat HIV/AIDS, malaria and other diseases; ensure environmental sustainability; and encourage a global partnership for development.

DFID's assistance is concentrated in the poorest countries of sub-Saharan Africa and Asia, but also contributes to poverty reduction and sustainable development in middle-income countries, including those in Latin America and Eastern Europe. The department works in partnership with governments committed to the

Millennium Development Goals, and with the private sector and the research community. It also works with multilateral institutions, including the World Bank, United Nations agencies and the European Commission. The department has headquarters in London and East Kilbride, offices in many developing countries, and staff based in British embassies and high commissions around the world.

Secretary of State for International Development, Rt. Hon. Douglas Alexander, MP
Principal Private Secretary, Matt Baugh
Private Secretary, Helen Winterton
Special Adviser, Anthony Vigor
Parliamentary Private Secretary, Kerry McCarthy, MP
Parliamentary Clerk, Jo Smith
Parliamentary Under-Secretary of State, Gareth R. Thomas, MP *(also a minister with BERR)*
Private Secretary, Alasdair Wardhaugh
Parliamentary Under-Secretary of State, Shahid Malik, MP
Private Secretary, Greg Hicks
Parliamentary Under-Secretary of State, Gillian Merron, MP
Private Secretary, Debbie Palmer
House of Lords Spokesperson, Baroness Amos
Liaison Peer, Baroness Whitaker
Whips, Bob Blizzard, MP *(Commons);* Baroness Royall *(Lords)*
Permanent Secretary, Minouche Shafik

MANAGEMENT BOARD

Members, Martin Dinham *(International);* Helen Ghosh; Bill Griffiths; Sue Owen *(Corporate Performance);* Mark Lowcock *(Country Programmes);* Andrew Steer *(Policy and Research)*

CDC GROUP

Cardinal Place, 80 Victoria Street SW1E 5JL
T 020-7484 7700 W www.cdcgroup.com

Founded in 1948, CDC is a government-owned fund of funds that provides capital to invest through third-party fund managers in private equity funds focused on emerging economies; it covers countries in Africa, Asia and Latin America. CDC is a public limited company with the Department for International Development as its 100 per cent shareholder.

Chair, Sir Malcolm Williamson
Chief Executive, Richard Laing

MINISTRY OF JUSTICE

Selborne House, 54 Victoria Street, London SW1E 6QW
T 020-7210 8500 E general.queries@justice.gsi.gov.uk
W www.justice.gov.uk

The Ministry of Justice (MoJ) was established in May 2007 and the responsibilities of the Department for Constitutional Affairs (DCA) were transferred to it. The MoJ's priorities are to protect the public; reduce reoffending; promote and provide access to justice; engender confidence in the justice system; uphold people's human rights, alongside their information and democratic rights; and to safeguard and modernise the constitution.

The MoJ incorporates the National Offender Management Service, which includes HM Prison Service and the National Probation Service, and the Office for Criminal Justice Reform (a cross-departmental organisation also reporting to the Home Office and the Office of the Attorney-General). In April 2006 the largest central government tribunals were incorporated into the MoJ (then, the DCA) as the Tribunals Service (*see* Tribunals section). The remit of the Lord Chancellor was also altered: he continues to be the government minister responsible to parliament for the judiciary and the courts system, but is no longer the head of the judiciary. The Lord Chief Justice has taken on the role of head of the judiciary and now performs many of the judicial functions formerly undertaken by the Lord Chancellor.

The MoJ established an independent Judicial Appointments Commission and related bodies, and retains its association with several associated departments, non-departmental public bodies and executive agencies, including the Northern Ireland Court Service, Her Majesty's Land Registry, the National Archives, the Legal Service Commission, and the Public Guardianship Office. The administrative functions of the Scotland Office and the Wales Office transferred to the MoJ in June 2003. Responsibilities for the maintenance of the relationship between Westminster and the devolved administrations in Edinburgh and Cardiff remain with the Secretary of State for Scotland and the Secretary of State for Wales respectively.

Secretary of State for Justice and Lord Chancellor, Rt. Hon. Jack Straw, MP
Principal Private Secretary, Alison Blackburne
Special Advisers, Mark Davies; Declan McHugh
Parliamentary Private Secretary, Mark Hendrick, MP
Minister of State, Rt. Hon. David Hanson, MP
Private Secretary, Philip Lawley
Parliamentary Private Secretary, Lynda Waltho, MP
Minister of State, Michael Wills, MP
Private Secretary, Joanna Burden
Parliamentary Private Secretary, Stephen Hesford, MP
Parliamentary Under-Secretary of State, Lord Hunt of Kings Heath, OBE
Private Secretary, Hugo Deadman
Parliamentary Under-Secretary of State, Bridget Prentice, MP
Private Secretary, Adam Rothapel
Parliamentary Under-Secretary of State, Maria Eagle, MP
Private Secretary, Dileeni Daniel-Selvaratnam
Permanent Secretary, Suma Chakrabarti
Private Secretary, Hannah Davenport
Parliamentary Clerk, Ann Nixon

CORPORATE MANAGEMENT BOARD

Chair, Suma Chakrabarti *(Permanent Secretary of State)*
Members, Ursula Brennan *(Corporate Performance);* Anne Bulford; Rowena Collins-Rice *(Democracy, Constitution and Law, Chief Legal Advisor);* Carolyn Downs; Helen Edwards, CBE *(Criminal Justice);* Peter Handcock, CBE *(Access to Justice);* David MacLeod; Marco Pierleoni *(Finance & Commercial);* Beverley Shears *(Corporate Human Resources);* Phil Wheatley *(National Offender Management Service)*

LORD CHANCELLOR'S DEPARTMENT

See Ministry of Justice

NORTHERN IRELAND OFFICE

11 Millbank, London SW1P 4PN
T 020-7210 3000
Castle Buildings, Stormont, Belfast BT4 3SG
T 028-9052 0700 E mail@nio.gov.uk
W www.nio.gov.uk

The Northern Ireland Office was established in 1972, when the Northern Ireland (Temporary Provisions) Act transferred the legislative and executive powers of the

Northern Ireland parliament and government to the UK parliament and a secretary of state.

The Northern Ireland Office is responsible primarily for security issues, law and order and prisons, and for matters relating to the political and constitutional future of the province. It also deals with international issues as they affect Northern Ireland.

Under the terms of the 1998 Good Friday Agreement, power was devolved to the Northern Ireland Assembly in 1999. The assembly took on responsibility for the relevant areas of work previously undertaken by the departments of the Northern Ireland Office, covering agriculture and rural development, the environment, regional development, social development, education, higher education, training and employment, enterprise, trade and investment, culture, arts and leisure, health, social services, public safety and finance and personnel. In October 2002 the Northern Ireland Assembly was suspended and Northern Ireland returned to direct rule, but despite repeated setbacks, devolution was restored on 8 May 2007. For further details, *see* Regional Government section.

Secretary of State for Northern Ireland, Rt. Hon. Shaun Woodward, MP
Parliamentary Private Secretary, Rob Marris, MP
Minister of State, Paul Goggins, MP
Permanent Secretary, Jonathan Phillips
Head of the Northern Ireland Civil Service, Nigel Hamilton

NORTHERN IRELAND INFORMATION SERVICE
Castle Buildings, Stormont Estate, Belfast BT4 3SG
T 028-9052 0700

OFFICE OF THE ADVOCATE-GENERAL FOR SCOTLAND

Dover House, Whitehall, London SW1A 2AU
T 020-7270 6713 **F** 020-7270 6813
Office of the Solicitor to the Advocate-General, Victoria Quay, Leith, Edinburgh EH6 6QQ
T 0131-244 1635 **F** 0131-244 1640
E privateoffice@advocategeneral.gsi.gov.uk
W www.oag.gov.uk

The Advocate-General for Scotland is one of the three law officers of the crown, alongside the Attorney-General and the Solicitor-General for England and Wales. He is the legal adviser to the UK government on Scottish law and is supported by staff in the Office of the Advocate-General for Scotland. The office is divided into the Legal Secretariat, based mainly in London, and the Office of the Solicitor to the Advocate-General, based in Edinburgh.

The post was created as a consequence of the constitutional changes set out in the Scotland Act 1998, which created a devolved Scottish parliament. The Lord Advocate and the Solicitor-General for Scotland then became part of the Scottish government and the Advocate-General took over their previous role as legal adviser to the government on Scots law. *See also* Regional Government section and Ministry of Justice.

Advocate-General for Scotland, Lord Davidson of Glen Clova, QC
Private Secretary, Chris Fawcett

OFFICE OF THE LEADER OF THE HOUSE OF COMMONS

26 Whitehall, London SW1A 2WH
T 020-7276 1005 **F** 020-7276 1006
E leader@commonsleader.x.gsi.gov.uk
W www.commonsleader.gov.uk

The Office of the Leader of the House of Commons is responsible for the arrangement of government business in the House of Commons and for planning and supervising the government's legislative programme. The Leader of the House of Commons upholds the rights and privileges of the house and acts as a spokesperson for the government as a whole.

The leader reports regularly to the cabinet on parliamentary business and the legislative programme. In her capacity as leader of the house, she is a member of the Public Accounts Commission and of the House of Commons Commission. She also chairs the cabinet committee on the legislative programme. As Lord Privy Seal, she is chair of the board of trustees of the Chevening Estate.

The Deputy Leader of the House of Commons supports the leader in handling the government's business in the house. She is responsible for monitoring MPs' and peers' correspondence and is a member of several committees, including the Ministerial Committee on the Law Commission.

Leader of the House of Commons and Lord Privy Seal, Rt. Hon. Harriet Harman, QC, MP
Principal Private Secretary, Stephen Hillcoat
Private Secretaries, Lise-Anne Boissiere; Mike Winter
Deputy Leader of the House of Commons, Helen Goodman, MP
Private Secretary, Paul Arnold

PRIVY COUNCIL OFFICE

2 Carlton Gardens, London SW1Y 5AA
T 020-7210 1033 **F** 020-7210 1071
W www.privy-council.gov.uk

The primary function of the office is to act as the secretariat to the Privy Council. It is responsible for the arrangements leading to the making of all royal proclamations and orders in council; for certain formalities connected with ministerial changes; for considering applications for the granting (or amendment) of royal charters; for the scrutiny and approval of by-laws and statutes of chartered institutions and of the governing instruments of universities and colleges; for approving use of the word 'university' in a company name; and for the appointment of high sheriffs and many crown and Privy Council appointments to governing bodies. Under the relevant acts, the office is responsible for the approval of certain regulations and rules made by the governing bodies of the medical and certain allied professions.

The Lord President of the Council is the ministerial head of the office and presides at meetings of the Privy Council, is a member of the cabinet and Leader of the House of Lords. She has no departmental portfolio but is a member of several cabinet committees, and supports the Lord Chancellor in his responsibility for the House of Lords reform. She is the Lords' spokesperson on equality and human rights issues, and is responsible to the prime minister for the organisation of government business in the house as well as repeating in the House of Lords statements made by the prime minister in the House of Commons. She also gives guidance to the house on matters of order and procedure. The Clerk of the Council is the administrative head of the Privy Council office.

Lord President of the Council (and Leader of the House of Lords), Baroness Ashton of Upholland, PC
Clerk of the Council, Judith Simpson
Head of Secretariat and Senior Clerk, Ceri King
Senior Clerks, Christopher Berry; Meriel McCullagh
Registrar of the Judicial Committee, Mary MacDonald

SCOTLAND OFFICE

Dover House, Whitehall, London SW1A 2AU
T 020-7270 6754 F 020-7270 6812
1 Melville Crescent, Edinburgh EH3 7HW
T 0131-244 9010 F 0131-244 9028
E scottish.secretary@scotland.gsi.gov.uk
W www.scotlandoffice.gov.uk

The Scotland Office is the department of the Secretary of State for Scotland which represents Scottish interests within the UK government in matters reserved to the UK parliament. The Secretary of State for Scotland also exercises certain specific functions in relation to devolution, including those provided for in the Scotland Act 1998; maintains the stability of the devolution settlement for Scotland; and pays grants to the Scottish Consolidated Fund and manages other financial transactions.

Reserved matters include the constitution, foreign affairs, defence, international development, the civil service, financial and economic matters, national security, immigration and nationality, misuse of drugs, trade and industry, various aspects of energy regulation (eg coal, electricity, oil, gas and nuclear energy), various aspects of transport, social security, employment, abortion, genetics, surrogacy, medicines, broadcasting and equal opportunities. Devolved matters include health and social work, education and training, local government and housing, justice and police, agriculture, forestry, fisheries, the environment, tourism, sports, heritage, economic development and internal transport. *See also* Regional Government section and Ministry of Justice.

Secretary of State for Scotland, Rt. Hon. Des Browne, MP
Private Secretary, Alasdair Smith
Parliamentary Private Secretary, Russell Brown, MP
Minister of State, David Cairns, MP
Private Secretary, Alasdair Smith
Parliamentary Private Secretary, Mike Lazarowicz, MP
Spokesperson in the House of Lords, Lord Davidson of Glen Clova

DEPARTMENT FOR TRANSPORT

Great Minster House, 76 Marsham Street, London SW1P 4DR
T 020-7944 8300 W www.dft.gov.uk

The Department for Transport (DfT) was established in May 2002 following the de-merger of the Department of Transport, Local Government and the Regions. The department's role is to oversee the delivery of a reliable, safe and secure transport system; to determine overall transport strategy and to manage relationships with the local, regional and private sector partners that deliver that strategy. Its main responsibilities are aviation, freight, health and safety, integrated and local transport, London Underground, maritime, mobility and inclusion, railways, roads and road safety, shipping and vehicles.

The department's work is focused on the following objectives: sustaining economic growth and productivity through reliable and efficient transport networks; improving the environmental performance of transport and tackling climate change; strengthening the safety and security of transport; and enhancing access to jobs, services and social networks, including for the most disadvantaged. The department funds provision and maintenance of infrastructure, subsidises services and fares on social grounds and sets regulatory standards, especially for safety, accessibility and environmental impact.

Secretary of State for Transport, Rt. Hon. Ruth Kelly, MP
Principal Private Secretary, Tim Figures
Minister of State, Rt. Hon. Rosie Winterton, MP
Private Secretary, Peter Lee
Parliamentary Under-Secretary of State, Tom Harris, MP
Private Secretary, Rachel Webbe
Parliamentary Under-Secretary of State, Jim Fitzpatrick, MP
Private Secretary, Eamonn Beirne
Permanent Secretary, Robert Devereux
Private Secretary, Victoria Robbe

MANAGEMENT BOARD
Chair, Robert Devereux *(Permanent Secretary of State)*
Members, Brian Collins *(Chief Scientific Adviser);* Richard Hatfield *(Safety, Service Delivery and Logistics);* Ann Hemingway; Bronwyn Hill *(City and Regional Networks Group);* Mike Mitchell *(National Networks);* Barbara Moorhouse *(Corporate Resources);* Christopher Muttukumaru *(Legal Services);* Simon Webb *(International Networks and Environment);* Deborah Williams

HM TREASURY

1 Horse Guards Road, London SW1A 2HQ
T 020-7270 4558 F 020-7270 4861
E public.enquiries@hm-treasury.gov.uk
W www.hm-treasury.gov.uk

HM Treasury is the country's economics and finance ministry, and is responsible for formulating and implementing the government's financial and economic policy. It aims to raise the rate of sustainable growth, boost prosperity, and provide the conditions necessary for universal economic and employment opportunities. The Office of the Lord High Treasurer has been continuously in commission for over 200 years. The Lord High Commissioners of HM Treasury are the First Lord of the Treasury (who is also the prime minister), the Chancellor of the Exchequer and five junior lords. This board of commissioners is assisted at present by the chief secretary, the parliamentary secretary (who is also the government chief whip in the House of Commons), the financial secretary, the economic secretary and the exchequer secretary. The prime minister as first lord is not primarily concerned with the day-to-day aspects of Treasury business; neither are the parliamentary secretary and the junior lords as government whips. Treasury business is managed by the Chancellor of the Exchequer and the other Treasury ministers, assisted by the permanent secretary.

The chief secretary is responsible for public expenditure, including spending reviews and strategic planning; in-year control; public sector pay and pensions; efficiency in public services; capital investment; and public service delivery and performance. He also has responsibility for the Treasury's interest in devolution, assists the Chancellor of the Exchequer where necessary on international and European issues, and oversees the integration of the tax and benefit system.

The financial secretary is the departmental minister for HM Revenue and Customs and the Valuation Office Agency and has strategic oversight of the UK tax system as a whole. She is the lead minister on European and international tax issues, and her responsibilities include the Finance Bill, the voluntary sector and charities, childcare issues and tax credits.

The exchequer secretary is a title only used occasionally, normally when the post of paymaster-general is allocated to a minister outside of the Treasury (as it is at present; Rt. Hon. Tessa Jowell, MP was appointed paymaster-general as Olympic minister within the Cabinet Office in June 2007). Her responsibilities include enterprise and productivity; competition and better regulation; science, innovation and skills policy; regional economic policy and environmental issues.

The economic secretary's responsibilities include financial services policy, including tax issues; personal savings policy; foreign exchange reserves and debt management policy; stamp duty land tax and real estate investment trusts; and EMU preparations.

Prime Minister and First Lord of the Treasury, Rt. Hon. Gordon Brown, MP
Chancellor of the Exchequer, Rt. Hon. Alistair Darling, MP
Principal Private Secretary, Dan Rosenfield
Private Secretaries, Gemma Dawson; Karen Braun Munzinger
Parliamentary Private Secretary, Ann Coffey, MP
Special Advisers, Catherine Macleod; Will McDonald *(special adviser to Yvette Cooper);* Sam White
Council of Economic Advisers, Andrew Maugham; David Pinto-Duchinsky; Geoffrey Spence
Chief Secretary to the Treasury, Rt. Hon. Yvette Cooper, MP
Private Secretary, Giles Thomson
Parliamentary Private Secretary, Angela C. Smith, MP
Financial Secretary to the Treasury, Rt. Hon. Jane Kennedy, MP
Private Secretary, Cerys Morgan
Parliamentary Private Secretary, David Wright, MP
Exchequer Secretary to the Treasury, Angela Eagle, MP
Private Secretary, Pedro Robel
Economic Secretary to the Treasury, Kitty Ussher, MP
Private Secretary, Simon Whitfield
Minister of State (jointly with the Home Office), Liam Byrne
Permanent Secretary to the Treasury, Nick Macpherson
Private Secretary, Amber Batool
Parliamentary Secretary to the Treasury and Government Chief Whip, Rt. Hon. Geoff Hoon, MP
Parliamentary Private Secretary, Sarah McCarthy-Fry, MP
Economic Adviser, Andrew Maugham
Lords Commissioners of HM Treasury (Whips), Alan Campbell, MP; Stephen McCabe, MP; Frank Roy, MP; Clarie Ward, MP; Dave Watts, MP
Assistant Whips, Bob Blizzard, MP; Tony Cunningham, MP; Wayne David, MP; Michael Foster, MP; Diana R. Johnson, MP; Sadiq Khan, MP; Siobhain McDonagh, MP; Alison Seabeck, MP; Mark Tami, MP

MANAGEMENT BOARD

Chair, Nick Macpherson *(Permanent Secretary of State)*
Members, John Kingman *(Public Services and Growth);* Mark Neale *(Budget, Tax and Welfare);* Stephen Pickford and Tom Scholar *(International and Finance);* Dave Ramsden *(Macroeconomic and Fiscal Policy);* Ray Shostak *(Director General, Performance Management);* Nigel Smith *(Office of Government Commerce)*

OFFICE OF GOVERNMENT COMMERCE (OGC)

1 Horse Guards Road, London SW1A 2HQ
T 0845-000 4999 E servicedesk@ogc.gsi.gov.uk
W www.ogc.gov.uk

The Office of Government Commerce was set up in April 2000. It is responsible for increasing the government's value for money by improving standards and capability in procurement, for example by commodities buying, delivering major capital projects, and maximising the effective use of 60 per cent of government spending and a £30bn property estate.

Chief Executive, Nigel Smith

WALES OFFICE

Gwydyr House, Whitehall, London SW1A 2ER
T 020-7270 0534
E walesoffice@walesoffice.gsi.gov.uk
W www.walesoffice.gov.uk

The Wales Office was established in 1999 when most of the powers of the Welsh Office were handed over to the National Assembly for Wales. It is the department of the Secretary of State for Wales, who is the key government figure liaising with the devolved government in Wales and who represents Welsh interests in the cabinet and parliament. The secretary of state has the right to attend and speak at sessions of the National Assembly (and must consult the assembly on the government's legislative programme). *See also* Regional Government section and Ministry of Justice.

Secretary of State for Wales, Rt. Hon. Paul Murphy, MP
Principal Private Secretary, Simon Morris
Parliamentary Under-Secretary, Huw Irranca-Davies, MP
Director of Office, Alan Cogbill

DEPARTMENT FOR WORK AND PENSIONS

Caxton House, Tothill Street, London SW1H 9NA
T 020-7962 8000 E enquiries@dwp.gsi.gov.uk
W www.dwp.gov.uk

The Department for Work and Pensions was formed in June 2001 from parts of the former Department of Social Security, the Department for Education and Employment and the Employment Service. The department helps unemployed people of working age into work, helps employers to fill their vacancies and provides financial support to people unable to help themselves, through back-to-work programmes. The department also administers the child support system, social security benefits and the social fund. In addition, the department has reciprocal social security arrangements with other countries.

In April 2002 the Benefits Agency and the Employment Service were replaced by the Jobcentre Plus network (responsible for helping to find jobs and paying benefits to people of working age), and the Pension Service which administers the Benefits Agency's pension-related services.

Secretary of State for Work and Pensions, Rt. Hon. James Purnell, MP
Principal Private Secretary, John Oliver
Private Secretaries, Helen Bache; Tom Fox; Zoe Rigden; Antonia Williams
Special Advisers, Matthew Burchell; Claire McCarthy
Parliamentary Private Secretary, Natascha Engel, MP
Minister of State, Rt. Hon. Stephen Timms, MP *(Employment and Welfare Reform)*
Private Secretary, Laura Timms
Parliamentary Private Secretary, vacant
Assistant Private Secretaries, Jessica Hodgson; Linda Reynolds
Minister of State, Mike O'Brien, MP *(Pensions Reform)*
Private Secretary, Jean-Paul Marks
Parliamentary Private Secretary, Jim Cunningham, MP
Assistant Private Secretaries, Michael Cordy; Helen Hutchings
Parliamentary Under-Secretary of State (Commons), James Plaskitt, MP
Private Secretary, Robin Gordon-Farleigh
Assistant Private Secretaries, Anahita Easton; Christopher Raitt
Parliamentary Under-Secretary of State (Lords), Lord McKenzie of Luton

Private Secretary, Sarah Kelly
Assistant Private Secretaries, Janet Smith; Maxine Thompson
Minister of State, Anne McGuire, MP *(Disabled People)*
Private Secretary, Lisa Pinnell
Assistant Private Secretaries, Kevin Green; Paul Warren
Parliamentary Under-Secretary of State, Barbara Follett, MP *(Equality)*
Permanent Secretary, Leigh Lewis
Private Secretaries, Phil Hall; Judith Tunstall; Lucy Wyatt

PENSIONS CLIENT DIRECTORATE
Director-General, Phil Wynn Owen

GROUP FINANCE DIRECTORATE
Director-General, John Codling

PROGRAMME AND SYSTEM DELIVERY
Director-General, Chief Information Officer, Joe Harley

HUMAN RESOURCES GROUP
Director-General (acting), Jane Saint

HEALTH, WORK AND WELLBEING DIRECTORATE
Director, Chief Medical Adviser, Chief Scientist, Dr Bill Gunnyeon
Deputy Director, Principal Scientific Adviser, Dr Peter Wright

LAW, GOVERNANCE AND SPECIAL POLICY GROUP
Director-General, Richard Heaton

COMMUNICATIONS NETWORK
Director, Sue Garrard

WORK, WELFARE AND EQUALITY GROUP
Director-General, Adam Sharples

EXECUTIVE AGENCIES

Executive agencies are well-defined business units that carry out services with a clear focus on delivering specific outputs within a framework of accountability to ministers. They can be set up or disbanded without legislation, and they are organisationally independent from the department they are answerable to. In the following list the agencies are shown in the accounts of their sponsor departments. Legally they act on behalf of the relevant secretary of state. Their chief executives also perform the role of accounting officers, which means they are responsible for the money spent by their organisations. Staff employed by agencies are civil servants.

CABINET OFFICE

COI (CENTRAL OFFICE OF INFORMATION)
Hercules Road, London SE1 7DU
T 020-7928 2345 F 020-7928 5037
W www.coi.gov.uk
The COI is the principal agency within government for the provision and procurement of marketing and communications services. Administrative responsibility for the COI rests with the minister for the Cabinet Office.
Chief Executive, A. Bishop
Deputy Chief Executive, P. Buchanan

MANAGEMENT BOARD
Members, G. Beasant; Ms A. Butler; M. Cross; I. Hamilton; G. Hooper; Ms E. Lochhead; N. Martinson; A. Wade; Mrs S. Whetton

ATTORNEY-GENERAL'S OFFICE

TREASURY SOLICITOR'S DEPARTMENT
1 Kemble Street, London WC2B 4TS
T 020-7210 3000 F 020-7210 3004
E thetreasurysolicitor@tsol.gsi.gov.uk
W www.tsol.gov.uk
The Treasury Solicitor's Department, which became an executive agency in 1996, provides legal services for many government departments and is answerable to the Attorney-General. Those departments without their own lawyers are provided with legal advice, and both they and other departments are provided with litigation services. The Treasury Solicitor is also the Queen's Proctor, and is responsible for collecting ownerless goods *(bona vacantia)* on behalf of the crown.
HM Procurator-General and Treasury Solicitor (Permanent Secretary), Paul Jenkins

BONA VACANTIA DIVISION
Head of Division (acting), Peter Loosley

CABINET OFFICE AND CENTRAL ADVISORY DIVISION
Head of Division, Peter Fish

DEPARTMENT OF CULTURE, MEDIA AND SPORT DIVISION
Legal Adviser, Patrick Kilgarriff

DEPARTMENT FOR CHILDREN, SCHOOLS AND FAMILIES DIVISION
Legal Adviser, Claire Johnston

EUROPEAN DIVISION
Head of Division, Frances Nash

HM TREASURY ADVISORY DIVISION
Legal Adviser, Stephen Parker

LITIGATION GROUP
Head of Division, Hugh Giles

DEPARTMENT FOR BUSINESS, ENTERPRISE AND REGULATORY REFORM

COMPANIES HOUSE
Crown Way, Cardiff CF14 3UZ
T 0870-333 3636 F 029-2038 0517
E enquiries@companieshouse.gov.uk
W www.companieshouse.gov.uk
Companies House incorporates companies, registers company documents and provides company information.
Registrar of Companies for England and Wales, Gareth Jones
Registrar of Companies for Scotland, Dorothy Blair

THE INSOLVENCY SERVICE
21 Bloomsbury Street, London WC1B 3QW
Insolvency Enquiry Line 0845-602 9848
Redundancy Enquiry Line 0845-145 0004
W www.insolvency.gov.uk
The role of the service includes administration and investigation of the affairs of bankrupts, partners and companies in compulsory liquidation; dealing with the disqualification of directors in all corporate failures; authorising and regulating the insolvency profession; providing banking and investment services for bankruptcy and liquidation estate funds; assessing and

paying statutory entitlement to redundancy payments when an employer cannot, or will not, pay its employees; and advising ministers on insolvency, redundancy and related issues.
Inspector-General and Chief Executive, Stephen Speed
Deputy Inspectors-General, Les Cramp; Graham Horne
Inspector of Companies, Robert Burns

DEPARTMENT FOR COMMUNITIES AND LOCAL GOVERNMENT

FIRE SERVICE COLLEGE

Moreton-in-Marsh, Gloucestershire GL56 0RH
T 01608-650831 F 01608-651788
W www.fireservicecollege.ac.uk
The Fire Service College provides fire-related training, both practical and theoretical, consultancy, and library and information services to the UK fire and rescue service, other UK public sector organisations, the private sector, and the international market. In addition to training, the college supports learning and development in the fire and rescue service through its Organisational Development Centre.
Chief Executive, Gill Newton

ORDNANCE SURVEY

Romsey Road, Southampton SO16 4GU
T 0845-605 0505 F 023-8079 2615
E customerservices@ordnancesurvey.co.uk
W www.ordnancesurvey.co.uk
Ordnance Survey is the national mapping agency for Great Britain. It is a government department and executive agency operating as a trading fund since 1999.
Director-General and Chief Executive, Vanessa Lawrence, CB

PLANNING INSPECTORATE

Temple Quay House, 2 The Square, Temple Quay, Bristol BS1 6PN
T 0117-372 6372
E enquiries@planning-inspectorate.gsi.gov.uk
Crown Buildings, Cathays Park, Cardiff CF10 3NQ
T 029-2082 3866 E wales@planning-inspectorate.gsi.gov.uk
W www.planning-inspectorate.gov.uk
The main work of the inspectorate consists of the processing of planning and enforcement appeals, and holding inquiries into local development plans and frameworks. It also deals with appeals against the decisions of local authorities on planning applications; appeals against local authority enforcement notices; listed building consent appeals; advertisement appeals; rights of way cases; and cases arising from the Environmental Protection and Water acts, the Transport and Works Act 1992 and other highways legislation.
Chief Executive, Katrine Sporle

THE QUEEN ELIZABETH II CONFERENCE CENTRE

Broad Sanctuary, London SW1P 3EE
T 020-7222 5000 F 020-7798 4200
E info@qeiicc.co.uk W www.qeiicc.co.uk
The centre provides secure conference facilities for national and international government and private sector use.
Chief Executive, Ernest Vincent

DEPARTMENT FOR CULTURE, MEDIA AND SPORT

THE ROYAL PARKS

The Old Police House, Hyde Park, London W2 2UH
T 020-7298 2000 F 020-7298 2005
E hq@royalparks.gsi.gov.uk W www.royalparks.org.uk
Royal Parks is responsible for maintaining and developing over 2,000 hectares (5,000 acres) of urban parkland contained within the eight royal parks in London: Bushy Park (with the Longford river); Green Park; Greenwich Park; Hyde Park; Kensington Gardens; Regent's Park (with Primrose Hill); Richmond Park and St James's Park.
Chief Executive, Mark Camley

DEPARTMENT FOR ENVIRONMENT, FOOD AND RURAL AFFAIRS

ANIMAL HEALTH

Corporate Centre, Block C, Government Buildings, Whittington Road, Worcester WR5 2LQ
T 01905-767111 F 01905-768854
E corporate-office@animalhealth.gsi.gov.uk
W www.defra.gov.uk/animalhealth
Animal Health is an executive agency that also works on behalf of the Welsh Assembly Government, the Scottish government and the Food Standards Agency. It is the government's delivery agent for ensuring the health and welfare of farmed animals. It is also responsible for the prevention, detection and management of diseases in animals. Animal Health's main responsibilities include the eradication of endemic disease; import and export certification; animal by-product regulation; preparedness for managing exotic animal diseases; and licensing the trade in endangered species for conservation purposes.
Chief Executive (interim), Prof. Steve Edwards

CENTRAL SCIENCE LABORATORY (CSL)

Sand Hutton, York YO41 1LZ
T 01904-462000 F 01904-462111
E science@csl.gov.uk W www.csl.gov.uk
The Central Science Laboratory specialises in the sciences underpinning sustainable land use, environmental protection and food safety. It provides a wide range of analytical, diagnostic and consultancy services to organisations in both the public and private sectors, designed to support the international land-based and food industries.
Chief Executive, Adrian Belton

CENTRE FOR ENVIRONMENT, FISHERIES AND AQUACULTURE SCIENCE (CEFAS)

Pakefield Road, Lowestoft, Suffolk NR33 0HT
T 01502-562244 F 01502-513865
W www.cefas.co.uk
Established in April 1997, the agency provides research and consultancy services in fisheries science and management, aquaculture, fish health and hygiene, environmental impact assessment, and environmental quality assessment.
Chief Executive, Richard Judge

GOVERNMENT DECONTAMINATION SERVICE

MoD Stafford, Beaconside, Stafford ST18 0AQ
T 0845-850 1323 F 01785-216363
E gds@gds.gsi.gov.uk W www.defra.gov.uk/gds
The Government Decontamination Service boosts the UK's capacity to resist and recover from deliberate and

accidental releases of chemical, biological, radiological and nuclear materials, and from major accidental releases of hazardous materials.
Chief Executive, Robert Bettley-Smith, FRICS

MARINE AND FISHERIES AGENCY
3–8 Whitehall Place, London SW1A 2HH
T 020-7270 8328 F 020-7270 8345
E info@mfa.gsi.gov.uk W www.mfa.gov.uk
The Marine and Fisheries Agency was established in October 2005 to coordinate for the first time the service delivery, inspection and enforcement of activities provided by the government to the fishing industry and other marine stakeholders in England and Wales.
Chief Executive, Nigel Gooding

VETERINARY LABORATORIES AGENCY
Woodham Lane, New Haw, Addlestone, Surrey KT15 3NB
T 01932-341111 F 01932-347046
E enquiries@vla.defra.gov.uk W www.vla.gov.uk
The Veterinary Laboratories Agency is a regional network of 16 veterinary laboratories and two surveillance centres, which provides all sectors of the animal health industry with animal disease surveillance, diagnostic services and veterinary scientific research.
Chief Executive (acting), C. Morrey

VETERINARY MEDICINES DIRECTORATE
Woodham Lane, New Haw, Addlestone, Surrey KT15 3LS
T 01932-336911 F 01932-336618
W www.vmd.gov.uk
The Veterinary Medicines Directorate is responsible for all aspects of the authorisation and control of veterinary medicines, including post-authorisation surveillance of residues in animals and animal products, and also for the provision of policy advice to ministers.
Chief Executive, Steve Dean

FOREIGN AND COMMONWEALTH OFFICE

FCO SERVICES
Hanslope Park, Milton Keynes MK19 7BH
T 01908-515789 E fco.serv@fco.gov.uk
W www.fcoservices.gov.uk
FCO Services was established in April 2006. It delivers a combination of secure business-to-business services to the FCO in the UK and at its missions overseas, other UK government departments and public bodies, friendly foreign governments and private sector organisations.

The Corps of Queen's Messengers, couriers of confidential and important documents, was transferred to FCO Services in 2006.
Chief Executive, Chris Moxey
Superintendent of the Corps of Queen's Messengers, Sqn. Ldr. J. S. Frizzell
Queen's Messengers, S. J. Addy; P. Allen; R. Allen; Maj. A. N. D. Bols; Maj. S. Cambridge; Maj. P. C. H. Dening-Smitherman; J. A. Hatfield; Sqn. Ldr. P. J. Hearn; Sqn. Ldr. A. Hill; W. Lisle; Maj. K. J. Rowbottom; Maj. J. H. Steele; R. T. Wilson

WILTON PARK CONFERENCE CENTRE
Wiston House, Steyning, W. Sussex BN44 3DZ
T 01903-815020 F 01903-816373
E admin@wiltonpark.org.uk W www.wiltonpark.org.uk
Wilton Park organises international affairs conferences and is hired out to government departments and commercial users.
Chief Executive, Donald Lamont

DEPARTMENT OF HEALTH

MEDICINES AND HEALTHCARE PRODUCTS REGULATORY AGENCY (MHRA)
Market Towers, 1 Nine Elms Lane, London SW8 5NQ
T 020-7084 2000 F 020-7084 2353
E info@mhra.gsi.gov.uk W www.mhra.gov.uk
The MHRA is responsible for protecting and promoting public and patient safety by ensuring that medicines, healthcare products and medical equipment meet appropriate standards of safety, quality, performance and effectiveness, and are used safely.
Chair, Prof. Sir Alasdair Breckenridge, CBE
Chief Executive, Prof. Kent Woods

NHS PURCHASING AND SUPPLY AGENCY
Premier House, 60 Caversham Road, Reading RG1 7EB
T 0118-980 8600 F 0118-980 8650
E pasa@pasa.nhs.uk W www.pasa.nhs.uk
The agency was established in April 2000 and is responsible for ensuring that the NHS makes the most effective use of its resources by getting the best value for money possible when purchasing goods and services. The agency advises ministers and government on policy and the strategic direction of procurement across the NHS.
Chief Operating Officer, John Cooper

HOME OFFICE

CRIMINAL RECORDS BUREAU
PO Box 110, Liverpool L69 3EF
T 0870-909 0811 W www.crb.gov.uk
The Criminal Records Bureau was launched in March 2002 and provides access to criminal record information to enable organisations in the public, private and voluntary sectors to make safer recruitment decisions by identifying candidates who may be unsuitable for certain work – especially that which involves children or vulnerable adults.
Chief Executive, Vincent Gaskell

HM PRISON SERVICE
see Prison Service section

IDENTITY AND PASSPORT SERVICE
Globe House, 89 Ecclestone Square, London SW1V 1PN
T Advice Line 0870-521 0410
E hqenquiries@ips.gsi.gov.uk W www.ips.gov.uk
The Identity and Passport Service was established in April 2006 and incorporates the UK Passport Service. Its role is to provide passport services and, in the future (as part of the National Identity Scheme), identity cards for British and foreign nationals resident in the UK.
Chief Executive and Registrar-General, James Hall

DEPARTMENT FOR INNOVATION, UNIVERSITIES AND SKILLS

NATIONAL WEIGHTS AND MEASURES LABORATORY
Stanton Avenue, Teddington, Middx TW11 0JZ
T 020-8943 7272 F 020-8943 7270
E info@nwml.gov.uk W www.nwml.gov.uk
The laboratory is responsible for ensuring all trade measurements are accurate, legal and fair to both buyer

and seller. It provides the following services: type approval; mass, length and volume calibration; ISO 9001 certification; metrology training; and consultancy. It is also responsible for the implementation of European directives on measuring instruments.
Chief Executive, Peter Mason

UK INTELLECTUAL PROPERTY OFFICE
Concept House, Cardiff Road, Newport NP10 8QQ
T 0845-950 0505 F 01633-814444
E enquiries@ipo.gov.uk W www.ipo.gov.uk
The UK Intellectual Property Office, formerly known as the Patent Office, was established in 1990 and became a trading fund in 1991. The office is responsible for intellectual property (IP) policy and operation in the UK, and aims to educate business, researchers and the public about the IP system; facilitate the appropriate protection and use of rights; design and provide commercial services to assist business use of the IP system; and create a domestic and international legal and political framework, which balances the interests of rights holders with the need for open competition and free markets.
Comptroller-General and Chief Executive, Ian Fletcher

MINISTRY OF JUSTICE

HER MAJESTY'S COURTS SERVICE
see Law Courts and Offices section

LAND REGISTRY
Lincoln's Inn Fields, London WC2A 3PH
T 020-7917 8888 F 020-7955 0110
E propertyinformationteam@landregistry.gsi.gov.uk
W www.landregistry.gov.uk
The registration of title to land was first introduced in England and Wales by the Land Registry Act 1862. Land Registry maintains and develops the Land Register for England and Wales, and is an executive agency and trading fund responsible to the Secretary of State for Justice. The Land Register has been open to public inspection since 1990.
Chief Land Registrar and Chief Executive, Peter Collis, CB
Deputy Chief Executive and Business Development Director, Ted Beardsall, CBE

NATIONAL ARCHIVES
Kew, Richmond, Surrey TW9 4DU
T 020-8876 3444 F 020-8878 8905
W www.nationalarchives.gov.uk
The National Archives, a government department and an executive agency reporting to the Secretary of State for Justice, was formed in April 2003 by bringing together the Public Record Office (founded in 1838) and the Historical Manuscripts Commission (founded in 1869).

The National Archives leads on record management policy with government, and provides access to government records at its sites in Kew and Islington and through digital resources available online. The National Archives also oversees information and archive management across the UK, setting standards and providing advice and support to raise the standards of information management. OPSI – with its copyright, legislation and official publishing roles – has operated from within the National Archives since October 2006.

The organisation administers the UK's public records system under the Public Records Acts of 1958 and 1967. The records it holds span 900 years – from the Domesday Book to the latest government papers to be released – and fill more than 160km (100 miles) of shelving.
Chief Executive, Ms Natalie Ceeney

OFFICE OF PUBLIC SECTOR INFORMATION
102 Petty France, London SW1H 9AJ
T 01603-723011 W www.opsi.gov.uk
The Office of Public Sector Information (OPSI) operates from within the National Archives as of October 2006, after previously being attached to the Cabinet Office. It is responsible for policy in relation to access and re-use of UK public sector information. The legal and statutory responsibilities of Her Majesty's Stationery Office (HMSO), in relation to statutory publishing and the management of crown copyright, operate from within the OPSI's wider remit.
Director/Controller, Carol Tullo

OFFICE OF THE PUBLIC GUARDIAN
Archway Tower, 2 Junction Road, London N19 5SZ
T 0845-330 2900 F 020-7664 7705
E customerservices@publicguardian.gsi.gov.uk
W www.publicguardian.gov.uk
The Office of the Public Guardian was established on 1 October 2007, in place of the Public Guardianship Office. It is responsible for providing services that support the financial, property, health and welfare matters of people lacking in the mental capacity to make decisions in a particular area. Capacity is assessed in accordance with the requirements set out in the Mental Capacity Act 2005.
Chief Executive and Public Guardian Designate, Martin John

TRIBUNALS SERVICE
see Tribunals section

NORTHERN IRELAND OFFICE

COMPENSATION AGENCY
Royston House, 34 Upper Queen Street, Belfast BT1 6FD
T 028-9024 9944 E comp-agency@nics.gov.uk
W www.compensationni.gov.uk
The Compensation Agency supports the victims of violent crime by providing compensation to those who sustain loss as a result of actions taken under emergency provisions legislation.
Chief Executive, Robert Crawford

FORENSIC SCIENCE NORTHERN IRELAND
151 Belfast Road, Carrickfergus, Co. Antrim BT38 8PL
T 028-9036 1888 F 028-9036 1900
E forensic.science@fsni.gov.uk W www.fsni.gov.uk
Forensic Science Northern Ireland aims to enhance the delivery of justice by providing scientific support and advice for the police and the legal profession, and training and analytical support for pathologists.
Chief Executive, Stanley Brown

NORTHERN IRELAND PRISON SERVICE
see Prison Service section

YOUTH JUSTICE AGENCY
Corporate Headquarters, 41–43 Waring Street, Belfast BT1 2DY
T 028-9031 6400 F 028-9031 6402/3
E info@yjani.gov.uk W www.youthjusticeagencyni.gov.uk
The Youth Justice Agency aims to prevent children committing criminal offences through provision of community-based services, youth conferencing services, attendance centres and secure custody.
Chief Executive, Bill Lockhart, OBE

DEPARTMENT FOR TRANSPORT

DRIVER AND VEHICLE LICENSING AGENCY (DVLA)
Longview Road, Swansea SA6 7JL
T 01792-782341 W www.dvla.gov.uk
The agency was established as an executive agency in 1990 and became a trading fund in 2004. It is responsible for registering and licensing drivers and vehicles, and for collection and enforcement of vehicle excise duty (some £4.9bn annually). The DVLA also maintains records of all those who are entitled to drive various types of vehicle (currently around 43 million people), all vehicles entitled to travel on public roads (currently 32 million), and drivers' endorsements, disqualifications and medical conditions.
Chief Executive, Noel Shanahan

DRIVING STANDARDS AGENCY
The Axis Building, 112 Upper Parliament Street, Nottingham NG1 6LP
T 0115-936 6666 F 0115-936 6573
E customer.services@dsa.gsi.gov.uk
W www.dsa.gov.uk
The agency is responsible for carrying out theory and practical driving tests for car drivers, motorcyclists, bus and lorry drivers, and for maintaining the registers of approved driving instructors and large goods vehicle instructors. It also supervises Compulsory Basic Training (CBT) for learner motorcyclists. There are two area offices, which manage over 400 practical driving test centres across Britain.
Chief Executive, Rosemary Thew

GOVERNMENT CAR AND DESPATCH AGENCY
46 Ponton Road, London SW8 5AX
T 020-7217 3839
W www.dft.gov.uk/gcda
The agency provides secure transport and mail distribution to government and the public sector.
Chief Executive, Roy Burke

HIGHWAYS AGENCY
123 Buckingham Palace Road, London SW1W 9HA
T 0845-955 6575 Information Line 0845-750 4030
E ha_info@highways.gsi.gov.uk W www.highways.gov.uk
The agency is responsible for delivering the Department for Transport's road programme and for operating, maintaining and improving the 7,138km (4,435 miles) of strategic road network in England on behalf of the Secretary of State for Transport (made up of motorways and trunk roads and valued at over £84bn).
Chief Executive, Graham Dalton

MARITIME AND COASTGUARD AGENCY
Spring Place, 105 Commercial Road, Southampton SO15 1EG
T 023-8032 9100 F 023-8032 9374
W www.mcga.gov.uk
The agency's aims are to prevent loss of life, continuously improve maritime safety and protect the marine environment.
Chief Executive, Peter Cardy
Chief Coastguard, Rod Johnson

VEHICLE CERTIFICATION AGENCY
1 Eastgate Office Centre, Eastgate Road, Bristol BS5 6XX
T 0117-952 4235 F 0117-952 4104
E enquiries@vca.gov.uk W www.vca.gov.uk
The agency is the UK authority responsible for ensuring that vehicles and vehicle parts have been designed and constructed to meet internationally agreed standards of safety and environmental protection.
Chief Executive, P. Markwick

VEHICLE AND OPERATOR SERVICES AGENCY
Berkeley House, Croydon Street, Bristol BS5 0DA
T 0117-954 3211 F 0117-954 3209
Enquiry Line 0870-606 0440
E enquiries@vosa.gov.uk W www.vosa.gov.uk
The Vehicle and Operator Services Agency was formed in April 2003 from the merger of the Vehicle Inspectorate and the Traffic Area Network. The agency works with the independent traffic commissioners to improve road safety and the environment; safeguard fair competition by promoting and enforcing compliance with commercial operator licensing requirements; process applications for licences to operate lorries and buses; register bus services; operate and administer testing schemes for all vehicles, including the supervision of the MOT testing scheme; enforce the law on vehicles to ensure that they comply with legal standards and regulations; enforce drivers' hours and licensing requirements; provide training and advice for commercial operators; and investigate vehicle accidents, defects and recalls.
Chief Executive, Stephen J. Tetlow, MBE

HM TREASURY

NATIONAL SAVINGS AND INVESTMENTS
375 Kensington High Street, London W14 8SD
T 020-7348 9200 F 020-7048 9698
E customerenquiries@nsandi.com
W www.nsandi.com
NS&I (National Savings and Investments) came into being in 1861 when the Palmerston government set up the Post Office Savings Bank, a savings scheme which aimed to encourage ordinary wage earners 'to provide for themselves against adversity and ill health'. NS&I was established as a government department in 1969. It became an executive agency of the Treasury in 1996 and is responsible for the design, marketing and administration of savings and investment products for personal savers and investors. It has approximately 27 million customers with over £85bn invested. *See also* Banking and Finance.
Chief Executive, Jane Platt

OGC BUYING SOLUTIONS
5th Floor, Royal Liver Building, Pier Head, Liverpool L3 1PE
T 0845-410 2222 F 0151-227 3315
W www.ogcbuyingsolutions.gov.uk
The agency provides a professional procurement service to government departments and other public bodies. From April 2000 it became an executive agency of the Office of Government Commerce in the Treasury.
Chief Executive, Alison Littley

ROYAL MINT
Llantrisant, Pontyclun CF72 8YT
T 01443-222111 F 01443-623178
E information.office@royalmint.gov.uk
W www.royalmint.gov.uk
The Royal Mint has operated as a trading fund since 1975, and was established as an executive agency in 1990.

The prime responsibility of the Royal Mint is the

provision of United Kingdom coinage, but it actively competes in world markets for a share of the available circulating coin business and about half of the coins and blanks it produces annually are exported. It also manufactures special proof and uncirculated quality coins in gold, silver and other metals; military and civil decorations and medals; commemorative and prize medals; and royal and official seals.
Master of the Mint, Chancellor of the Exchequer *(ex officio)*
Chief Executive, A. Stafford

UK DEBT MANAGEMENT OFFICE
Eastcheap Court, 11 Philpot Lane, London EC3M 8UD
T 0845-357 6500 F 0845-357 6509
W www.dmo.gov.uk
The UK Debt Management Office (DMO) was launched as an executive agency of HM Treasury in April 1998. The Chancellor of the Exchequer determines the policy and financial framework within which the DMO operates, but delegates operational decisions on debt and cash management and the day-to-day running of the office to the chief executive. The DMO's remit is to carry out the government's debt management policy of minimising financing costs over the long term, and to minimise the cost of offsetting the government's net cash flows over time, while operating at a level of risk approved by ministers in both cases. The DMO is also responsible for providing loans to local authorities through the Public Works Loan Board, and for managing the assets of certain public sector bodies through the Commissioners for the Reduction of the National Debt.
Chief Executive, Robert Stheeman

DEPARTMENT FOR WORK AND PENSIONS

CHILD SUPPORT AGENCY (CSA)
PO Box 55, Brierly Hill, West Midlands DY5 1YL
T 0845-713 3133 F 0845-713 8924
W www.csa.gov.uk
The CSA was set up in April 1993. It is responsible for the administration of the Child Support Act and for the assessment, collection and enforcement of maintenance payments. Government plans to establish a new organisation, the Child Maintenance and Enforcement Commission (CMEC), were outlined in the Child Maintenance White Paper; the new organisation will take over responsibility for the Child Support Agency's work in stages over a number of years from 2008.
Chief Executive of CSA and CMEC, Stephen Geraghty

JOBCENTRE PLUS
First Floor, Steel City House, West Street, Sheffield S1 2GQ
T 0845-606 0234 E contact-us@jobcentreplus.gsi.gov.uk
W www.jobcentreplus.gov.uk
Jobcentre Plus was formed in April 2002 following the merger of the Employment Service and some parts of the Benefits Agency. The agency administers claims for, and payment of, social security benefits to help people gain employment or improve their prospects for work, as well as helping employers to fill their vacancies.
Chief Executive, Lesley Strathie

THE PENSION, DISABILITY AND CARERS SERVICE
Room 204, Richmond House, 79 Whitehall, London SW1A 2NS
T 0113-307 8192
W www.thepensionservice.gov.uk, www.dwp.gov.uk/dcs
The Pension, Disability and Carers Service was formed in 2008 from the Pension Service and the Disability and Carers Service. The agency serves over 15 million customers in Great Britain and abroad and it employs over 16,000 staff. The service administers benefits including disability living allowance, state pension and winter fuel payments.
Chief Executive, Terry Moran

THE RENT SERVICE
5 Welbeck Street, London W1G 9YQ
T 020-7023 6000 F 020-7023 6222
E customer.services@therentservice.gov.uk
W www.therentservice.gov.uk
The Rent Service provides a rental valuation service to local authorities in England, supplying them with a range of valuations to assist them in settling claims for housing benefit. It also provides fair rent determinations for landlords and tenants under the provisions laid down in the Rent Act 1977. The service collects letting information for the Local Housing Allowance (LHA), introduced in April 2008, to ensure that the LHA is representative of the local market. The service will transfer its operational functions to the Valuation Office Agency in April 2009.
Chief Executive, Patrick Boyle

NON-MINISTERIAL GOVERNMENT DEPARTMENTS

CHARITY COMMISSION

PO Box 1227, Liverpool L69 3UG
T 0845-300 0218 E enquiries@charitycommission.gsi.gov.uk
W www.charitycommission.gov.uk
The Charity Commission for England and Wales is the government department whose aim is to give the public confidence in the integrity of charities. It also carries out the functions of the registration, monitoring and support of charities and the investigation of alleged wrongdoing. The commission maintains a computerised register of some 190,000 charities. It is accountable to the courts and, for its efficiency, to the home secretary. There are nine board members appointed by the Home Office for a fixed term and the commission has offices in London, Liverpool, Taunton and Newport.
Chair, Dame Suzi Leather
Chief Executive, Andrew Hind

CROWN ESTATE

16 New Burlington Place, London W1S 2HX
T 020-7851 5000 F 020-7851 5128
W www.thecrownestate.co.uk
The Crown Estate is valued at more than £5bn, and includes substantial blocks of urban property, primarily in London, almost 110,000 hectares (270,000 acres) of rural land, almost half of the foreshore, and the sea bed out to the 12 nautical mile territorial limit throughout the UK. The Crown Estate is part of the hereditary possessions of the sovereign 'in right of the crown', managed under the provisions of the Crown Estate Act 1961. The Crown Estate has a duty to maintain and enhance the capital value of estate and the income obtained from it. Under the terms of the act, the Crown Estate pays its revenue surplus to the Treasury every year.
Chair, Ian Grant, CBE
Chief Executive, Roger Bright

CROWN PROSECUTION SERVICE

50 Ludgate Hill, London EC4M 7EX
T 020-7796 8000 F 020-7796 8651
E enquiries@cps.gsi.gov.uk W www.cps.gov.uk

The Crown Prosecution Service (CPS) is the independent body responsible for prosecuting people in England and Wales. The CPS was established as a result of the Prosecution of Offences Act 1985. It works closely with the police to advise on lines of inquiry and to decide on appropriate charges and other disposals in all but minor cases. *See also* Law Courts and Offices.

Director of Public Prosecutions, Keir Starmer, QC
Chief Executive, Peter Lewis

EXPORT CREDITS GUARANTEE DEPARTMENT (ECGD)

PO Box 2200, 2 Exchange Tower, Harbour Exchange Square, London E14 9GS
T 020-7512 7000 F 020-7512 7649
E help@ecgd.gsi.gov.uk W www.ecgd.gov.uk

ECGD is the UK's official export credit agency and was established in 1919. A separate government department reporting to the Secretary of State for Business, Enterprise and Regulatory Reform, it has more than 80 years' experience of working closely with exporters, project sponsors, banks and buyers to help UK exporters of capital equipment and project-related goods and services. ECGD does this by providing help in arranging finance packages for buyers of UK goods by guaranteeing bank loans; insurance against non-payment to UK exporters; and overseas investment insurance – a facility that gives UK investors up to 15 years' insurance against political risks such as war, expropriation and restrictions on remittances.

Chief Executive and Accounting Officer, P. Crawford
Non-Executive Chair, G. Pimlott

FOOD STANDARDS AGENCY

Aviation House, 125 Kingsway, London WC2B 6NH
T 020-7276 8000 F 020-7276 8004
E helpline@foodstandards.gsi.gov.uk
W www.food.gov.uk

The FSA was established in April 2000 to protect public health from risks arising in connection with the consumption of food, and otherwise to protect the interests of consumers in relation to food. The agency has the general function of developing policy in these areas and provides information and advice to the government, other public bodies and consumers. It also sets standards for and monitors food law enforcement by local authorities. The agency is a UK-wide non-ministerial government body, led by a board which has been appointed to act in the public interest. It has executive offices in Scotland, Wales and Northern Ireland. It is advised by advisory committees on food safety matters of special interest to each of these areas.

Chair, Dame Deirdre Hutton, CBE
Deputy Chair, Dr Ian Reynolds
Chief Executive, Tim Smith

FOOD STANDARDS AGENCY NORTHERN IRELAND, 10C Clarendon Road, Belfast BT1 3BG T 028-9041 7700 E infofsani@foodstandards.gsi.gov.uk

FOOD STANDARDS AGENCY SCOTLAND, St Magnus House, 6th Floor, 25 Guild Street, Aberdeen AB11 6NJ T 01224-285100 E scotland@foodstandards.gsi.gov.uk

FOOD STANDARDS AGENCY WALES, 11th Floor, Southgate House, Wood Street, Cardiff CF10 1EW T 029-2067 8999 E wales@foodstandards.gsi.gov.uk

MEAT HYGIENE SERVICE

Kings Pool, Peasholme Green, York YO1 7PR
T 01904-455501 F 01904-455502
E mhs.enquiries@mhs.gov.uk

The Meat Hygiene Service was launched in April 1995 as an agency of the former Ministry of Agriculture, Fisheries and Food, and became an executive agency of the Food Standards Agency in April 2000. It protects public health and animal welfare at slaughter through veterinary supervision and meat inspection in approved fresh meat establishments in Great Britain.

Chief Executive, Steve McGrath

FORESTRY COMMISSION

Silvan House, 231 Corstorphine Road, Edinburgh EH12 7AT
T 0131-334 0303 F 0131-334 3047
E enquiries@forestry.gsi.gov.uk W www.forestry.gov.uk

The Forestry Commission is the government department responsible for forestry policy in Great Britain. It reports directly to forestry ministers (ie the Secretary of State for Environment, Food and Rural Affairs, the Scottish ministers and the National Assembly for Wales), to whom it is responsible for advice on forestry policy and for the implementation of that policy.

The commission's principal objectives are to protect Britain's forests and woodlands; expand Britain's forest area; enhance the economic value of forest resources; conserve and improve the biodiversity, landscape and cultural heritage of forests and woodlands; develop opportunities for woodland recreation; and increase public understanding of, and community participation in, forestry.

Chair (part-time), Rt. Hon. Lord Clark of Windermere
Director-General and Deputy Chair, T. Rollinson

FORESTRY COMMISSION ENGLAND, Great Eastern House, Tenison Road, Cambridge CB1 2DU T 01223-314546

FORESTRY COMMISSION SCOTLAND, Silvan House, 231 Corstorphine Road, Edinburgh EH12 7AT T 0131-334 0303

FORESTRY COMMISSION WALES, Victoria Terrace, Aberystwyth, Ceredigion SY23 2DQ T 0845-604 0845

NORTHERN RESEARCH STATION, Roslin, Midlothian EH25 9SY T 0131-445 2176

FOREST ENTERPRISE

Forest Enterprise England, 340 Bristol Business Park, Coldharbour Lane, Bristol BS16 1EJ
T 0117-906 6000 F 0117-931 2859
Forest Enterprise Scotland, 1 Highlander Way, Inverness Business and Retail Park, Inverness IV2 7GB
T 01463-232811 F 01463-243846

Forest Enterprise was established as an executive agency of the Forestry Commission in 1996 to manage the UK's forest estate; it ceased to exist as a single executive agency in March 2003, when three new agencies were created – one each for England, Wales and Scotland. Forest Enterprise Wales has since been wound up, with its responsibilities reabsorbed by the Forestry Commission.

The agencies in England and Scotland take their direction from their respective country governments but their basic remit is to provide environmental, social and economic benefits from the forests they manage.

Chief Executives, Simon Hodgson *(England);* Dr Hugh Insley *(Scotland)*

FOREST RESEARCH
Alice Holt Lodge, Farnham, Surrey GU10 4LH
T 01420-22255 F 01420-23653
E research.info@forestry.gsi.gov.uk
W www.forestresearch.gov.uk
Forest Research is also an executive agency of the Forestry Commission. Its objectives are to inform and support forestry's contribution to the development and delivery of the policies of the government and devolved administrations; to provide research, development and monitoring services relevant to UK forestry interests; and to transfer knowledge actively and appropriately.
Chief Executive, Dr James Pendlebury
Research Director, Dr Peter Freer-Smith

HM REVENUE AND CUSTOMS
Board of HM Revenue and Customs, 100 Parliament Street, London SW1A 2BQ
W www.hmrc.gov.uk
HMRC was formed following the integration of the Inland Revenue and HM Customs and Excise, which was made formal by parliament in April 2005. It administers, and advises the Chancellor of the Exchequer on, any matters connected with the following areas: income, corporation, capital gains, inheritance, insurance premium, stamp, land and petroleum revenue taxes; environmental taxes (climate change and aggregates levy, landfill tax); value added tax (VAT); customs duties and frontier protection; excise duties; National Insurance; tax credits, child benefit and the Child Trust Fund; enforcement of the minimum wage; and recovery of student loan repayments.
Chair, Mike Clasper

VALUATION OFFICE AGENCY
New Court, 48 Carey Street, London WC2A 2JE
T 020-7506 1700 F 020-7506 1998
E customerservices@voa.gsi.gov.uk W www.voa.gov.uk
Established in 1991, the Valuation Office is an executive agency of HM Revenue and Customs. It is responsible for compiling and maintaining the business rating and council tax valuation lists for England and Wales; valuing property throughout Great Britain for the purposes of taxes administered by the Inland Revenue; providing statutory and non-statutory property valuation services in England, Wales and Scotland; and giving policy advice to ministers on property valuation matters.
Chief Executive, Andrew Hudson

NATIONAL SCHOOL OF GOVERNMENT
Sunningdale Park, Larch Avenue, Ascot, Berks SL5 0QE
T 01344-634000 F 01344-634233
E customer.services@nationalschool.gsi.gov.uk
W www.nationalschool.gov.uk
The National School of Government became a separate non-ministerial department on 1 January 2007. It works both nationally and internationally to help government departments and public sector organisations build capacity in good governance and offer more effective, better value services.
Chair, Sir Brian Bender
Principal and Chief Executive, Robin Ryde

OFFICE OF FAIR TRADING (OFT)
Fleetbank House, 2–6 Salisbury Square, London EC4Y 8JX
T 020-7211 8000
E enquiries@oft.gsi.gov.uk W www.oft.gov.uk
The OFT is a non-ministerial government department established by statute in 1973, and it is the UK's consumer and competition authority. It encourages businesses to comply with competition and consumer law and to improve their trading practices through self-regulation. It acts decisively to stop hardcore or flagrant offenders, studies markets and recommends action where required, and empowers consumers with the knowledge and skills to make informed choices.
Chair, Philip Collins
Chief Executive Officer, John Fingleton

OFFICE OF GAS AND ELECTRICITY MARKETS (OFGEM)
9 Millbank, London SW1P 3GE
T 020-7901 7295 F 020-7901 7196
E consumeraffairs@ofgem.gov.uk W www.ofgem.gov.uk
OFGEM is the regulator for Britain's gas and electricity industries. Its role is to protect and advance the interests of consumers by promoting competition where possible, and through regulation only where necessary. OFGEM operates under the direction and governance of the Gas and Electricity Markets Authority, which makes all major decisions and sets policy priorities for OFGEM. OFGEM's powers are provided for under the Gas Act 1986 and the Electricity Act 1989, as amended by the Utilities Act 2000. It also has enforcement powers under the Competition Act 1998 and the Enterprise Act 2002.
Chair, Lord Mogg, KCMG
Chief Executive, Alistair Buchanan

OFFICE OF RAIL REGULATION
1 Kemble Street, London WC2B 4AN
T 020-7282 2000 F 020-7282 2040
E contact.cct@orr.gsi.gov.uk W www.rail-reg.gov.uk
The Office of the Rail Regulator was set up under the Railways Act 1993. It became the ORR in July 2004, under the provisions of the Railways and Transport Safety Act 2003. On 1 April 2006, in addition to its role as economic regulator, the ORR became the health and safety regulator for the rail industry. This transfer of responsibility from the Health and Safety Executive was given effect under the Railways Act 2005. The board and chair are appointed by the Secretary of State for Transport. The ORR's key roles are to ensure that Network Rail, the owner and operator of the national railway infrastructure (the track and signalling), manages the network efficiently and in a way that meets the needs of its users; to encourage continuous improvement in health and safety performance while securing compliance with relevant health and safety law, including taking enforcement action as necessary; and to develop policy and enhance relevant railway health and safety legislation. It is also responsible for licensing operators of railway assets, setting the terms for access by operators to the network and other railway facilities, and enforcing competition law in the rail sector.
Chair, Chris Bolt
Chief Executive, Bill Emery

OFFICE FOR STANDARDS IN EDUCATION, CHILDREN'S SERVICES AND SKILLS (OFSTED)
Royal Exchange Buildings, St Ann's Square, Manchester M2 7LA
T 0845-404040 E enquiries@ofsted.gov.uk
W www.ofsted.gov.uk
OFSTED was established under the Education (Schools

Act) 1992 and was relaunched on 1 April 2007 with a wider remit, bringing together four formerly separate inspectorates. It inspects and regulates care for children and young people, and inspects education and training for learners of all ages. *See also* The Education System.
HM Chief Inspector, Christine Gilbert, CBE
Chair, Zenna Atkins

POSTAL SERVICES COMMISSION (POSTCOMM)

Hercules House, 6 Hercules Road, London SE1 7DB
T 020-7593 2100 E info@psc.gov.uk
W www.psc.gov.uk

Postcomm is an independent regulator set up by the Postal Services Act 2000 to secure the universal postal service, improve postal services by introducing competition to the UK postal market, and ensure that postal operators, including Royal Mail, meet the needs of their customers throughout the UK. Postcomm also monitors – and reports to the Department for Business, Enterprise and Regulatory Reform – on the network of post offices in the UK.
Chair, Nigel Stapleton
Chief Executive, Sarah Chambers

REVENUE AND CUSTOMS PROSECUTIONS OFFICE (RCPO)

New Kings Beam House, 22 Upper Ground, London SE1 9BT
T 020-7147 7500 E enquiries@rcpo.gsi.gov.uk
W www.rcpo.gov.uk

The RCPO prosecutes major drug trafficking and tax fraud cases in the UK, currently at a rate of around 2,500 each year. It is an independent prosecuting authority and handles cases from HM Revenue and Customs and the Serious Organised Crime Agency. Prior to the establishment of the RCPO in April 2005, criminal prosecutions were handled separately by Customs and Excise and Inland Revenue Lawyers. The RCPO's director is appointed by the attorney-general.
Director, David Green, QC

SECURITY AND INTELLIGENCE SERVICES

GOVERNMENT COMMUNICATIONS HEADQUARTERS (GCHQ)

Hubble Road, Cheltenham GL51 0EX
T 01242-221491 F 01242-709054
E pressoffice@gchq.gsi.gov.uk W www.gchq.gov.uk

GCHQ produces signals intelligence in support of national security and the UK's economic wellbeing, and in the prevention or detection of serious crime. Additionally, GCHQ Communications-Electronics Security Group (CESG) is the national authority for information assurance, and provides advice and assistance to government departments, the armed forces and other national infrastructure bodies on the security of their communications and information systems. GCHQ was placed on a statutory footing by the Intelligence Services Act 1994 and is headed by a director who is directly accountable to the foreign secretary.
Director, Iain Lobban

SECRET INTELLIGENCE SERVICE (MI6)

PO Box 1300, London SE1 1BD
W www.mi6.gov.uk

The Secret Intelligence Service produces secret intelligence in support of the government's security, defence, foreign and economic policies. It was placed on a statutory footing by the Intelligence Services Act 1994 and is headed by a chief, known as 'C', who is directly accountable to the foreign secretary.
Chief, Sir J. M. Scarlett, KCMG, OBE

SECURITY SERVICE (MI5)

PO Box 3255, London SW1P 1AE
T 020-7930 9000
W www.mi5.gov.uk

The Security Service is responsible for security intelligence work against covertly organised threats to the UK. These include terrorism, espionage and the proliferation of weapons of mass destruction. The Security Service also provides security advice to a wide range of organisations to help reduce vulnerability to threats from individuals, groups or countries hostile to UK interests. The home secretary has parliamentary accountability for the Security Service.
Director-General, Jonathan Evans

SERIOUS FRAUD OFFICE

Elm House, 10–16 Elm Street, London WC1X 0BJ
T 020-7239 7272 F 020-7837 1173
E public.enquiries@sfo.gsi.gov.uk
W www.sfo.gov.uk

The Serious Fraud Office is an independent government department that investigates and prosecutes serious or complex fraud. It is part of the UK Criminal Justice System. The office is headed by a director who is appointed by and accountable to the Attorney-General, and has jurisdiction over England, Wales and Northern Ireland but not Scotland, the Isle of Man or the Channel Islands.
Director, Richard Alderman

UK STATISTICS AUTHORITY

Statistics House, Tredegar Park, Newport, Gwent NP10 8XG
E authority.enquiries@statistics.gov.uk
W www.statisticsauthority.gov.uk

The UK Statistics Authority was established on 1 April 2008 by the Statistics and Registration Service Act 2007 as an independent body operating at arm's length from the government. Its overall objective is to promote and safeguard the production and publication of official statistics and ensure their quality and comprehensiveness. The authority's main functions are the oversight of the Office for National Statistics; monitoring and reporting on all UK official statistics; and independent assessment of official statistics.

MANAGEMENT BOARD
Chair, Sir Michael Scholar, KCB
Board Members, Richard Alldritt *(Head of Assessment);* Karen Dunnell *(National Statistician);* Partha Dasgupta; Moira Gibb; Sir Alan Langlands *(ONS Director of Finance);* Prof. Steve Nickell; Prof David Rhind; Lord Rowe-Beddoe *(Deputy Chair, ONS);* Steve Newman

OFFICE FOR NATIONAL STATISTICS (ONS)

Cardiff Road, Newport NP10 8XG
T 0845-601 3034 E info@statistics.gov.uk
W www.statistics.gov.uk

The ONS was created in 1996 by the merger of the Central Statistical Office and the Office of Population Censuses and Surveys. On 1 April 2008 it became the executive office of the UK Statistics Authority. As part of these changes, the office's responsibility for the General Register Office transferred to the Identity and Passport Service of the Home Office.

The ONS is responsible for preparing, interpreting and publishing key statistics on the government, economy and society of the UK. Its key responsibilities include the provision of population estimates and projections and statistics on health and other demographic matters in England and Wales; the production of the UK National Accounts and other economic indicators; the organisation of population censuses in England and Wales and surveys for government departments and public bodies.
National Statistician and Director of ONS, Karen Dunnell

UK TRADE AND INVESTMENT

Kingsgate House, 66–74 Victoria Street, London SW1E 6SW
T 020-7215 8000 **W** www.uktradeinvest.gov.uk

UK Trade and Investment is a government organisation that helps UK-based companies succeed in international markets. It assists overseas companies to bring high quality investment to the UK economy.
Chief Executive, Andrew Cahn

WATER SERVICES REGULATION AUTHORITY (OFWAT)

Centre City Tower, 7 Hill Street, Birmingham B5 4UA
T 0121-625 1300 **F** 0121-625 1400
E enquiries@ofwat.gsi.gov.uk **W** www.ofwat.gov.uk

OFWAT succeeded the director-general of Water Services on 1 April 2006. It is the independent economic regulator of the water and sewerage companies in England and Wales. OFWAT's main duties are to ensure that the companies can finance and carry out the functions specified in the Water Industry Act 1991 and to protect the interests of water customers, by promoting value and safeguarding future water and sewerage services.
Chair, Philip Fletcher
Chief Executive, Regina Finn

PUBLIC BODIES

The following section is a listing of public bodies and selected other civil service organisations.

Whereas executive agencies are either part of a government department or are one in their own right (*see* Government Departments section), public bodies carry out their functions to a greater or lesser extent at arm's length from central government. Ministers are ultimately responsible to parliament for the activities of the public bodies sponsored by their department and in almost all cases (except where there is separate statutory provision) ministers make the appointments to their boards. Departments are responsible for funding and ensuring good governance of their public bodies.

The term 'public body' is a general one which includes public corporations, such as the BBC; NHS bodies; and non-departmental public bodies (NDPBs). There were 827 NDPBs sponsored by UK government departments as at 31 March 2008. This figure is made up of 203 executive NDPBs, 441 advisory NDPBs, 34 tribunal NDPBs and 149 independent monitoring boards. The following is not a complete list of these organisations.

ADJUDICATOR'S OFFICE

8th Floor, Euston Tower, 286 Euston Road, London NW1 3US
T 020-7667 1832 F 020-7667 1830
W www.adjudicatorsoffice.gov.uk

The Adjudicator's Office investigates complaints about the way HM Revenue and Customs, the Valuation Office Agency, the Office of the Public Guardian and the Insolvency Service have handled a person's affairs.
The Adjudicator, Dame Barbara Mills, DBE, QC

ADMINISTRATIVE JUSTICE AND TRIBUNALS COUNCIL

81 Chancery Lane, London WC2A 1BQ
T 020-7855 5200 F 020-7855 5201
E enquiries@ajtc.gsi.gov.uk
W www.ajtc.gov.uk

The Administrative Justice and Tribunals Council (AJTC) is a permanent standing advisory body set up under the Tribunals, Courts and Enforcement Act. It consists of 16 members appointed by the Lord Chancellor, Scottish and Welsh ministers. The Parliamentary Commissioner for Administration is an *ex officio* member of the council and of its Scottish and Welsh Committees.

The council keeps the administrative justice system under review, keeps the constitution working for those tribunals designated as being under AJTC oversight (in practice almost all statutory and administrative tribunals), and deals with some statutory inquiries. It is consulted by and advises government departments on a wide range of subjects relating to adjudicative procedures.
Chair, Rt. Hon. Lord Newton of Braintree, OBE
Members, The Parliamentary Commissioner *(ex officio),* Ann Abraham; Elizabeth Cameron; Sue Davis; Penny Letts, OBE; Prof. Alistair MacLeary; Bronwyn McKenna; Bernard Quoroll; Prof. Genevra Richardson, CBE; Dr Jonathan Spencer, CB; Dr Adrian V. Stokes, OBE; Pat Thomas, CBE; Brian Thompson; Prof. Sir Adrian Webb

WELSH COMMITTEE OF THE ADMINISTRATIVE JUSTICE AND TRIBUNALS COUNCIL
81 Chancery Lane, London WC2A 1BQ
T 020-7855 5200 F 020-7855 5201
E enquiries@ajtc.gsi.gov.uk
Chair, Prof. Sir Adrian Webb
Members, The Public Services Ombudsman for Wales *(ex officio),* Prof. Alice Brown; Elizabeth Cameron; Eileen MacDonald; Michael Menlowe

SCOTTISH COMMITTEE OF THE ADMINISTRATIVE JUSTICE AND TRIBUNALS COUNCIL
George House, 126 George Street, Edinburgh EH2 4HH
T 0131-271 4300 F 0131-271 4309
E scajtc@gtnet.gov.uk W www.ajtc.gov.uk
Chair, Prof. A. MacLeary
Members, The Parliamentary Commissioner for Administration *(ex officio)*; The Scottish Public Services Ombudsman *(ex officio)*; Lyndy Boyd; Elizabeth C. Cameron; Eileen MacDonald; Stephen Mannion; Michael Menlowe; Audrey Watson

ADVISORY, CONCILIATION AND ARBITRATION SERVICE (ACAS)

Brandon House, 180 Borough High Street, London SE1 1LW
T 020-7210 3613 Helpline 0845-747 4747
W www.acas.org.uk

The Advisory, Conciliation and Arbitration Service (ACAS) was set up under the Employment Protection Act 1975 (the provisions now being found in the Trade Union and Labour Relations (Consolidation) Act 1992).

ACAS is funded by the Department for Business, Enterprise and Regulatory Reform and overall guidance is provided by a council consisting of a full-time chair and part-time members from businesses, trade unions and independent sectors. The chair and members are appointed by the Secretary of State for Business, Enterprise and Regulatory Reform. ACAS aims to improve organisations and working life through better employment relations, to provide facilities for conciliation, mediation and arbitration as means of avoiding and resolving industrial disputes, and to provide advisory and information services on industrial relations matters to employers, employees and their representatives.

ACAS has 13 regional offices in Birmingham, Bury St Edmunds, Bristol, Cardiff, Fleet, Glasgow, Leeds, Liverpool, London, Manchester, Newcastle upon Tyne, Nottingham and Paddock Wood.
Chair, Ed Sweeney
Chief Executive, John Taylor

ADVISORY COUNCIL ON NATIONAL RECORDS AND ARCHIVES

The National Archives, Kew, Surrey TW9 4DU
T 020-8392 5377
W www.nationalarchives.gov.uk/advisorycouncil

The Advisory Council on National Records and Archives advises the Lord Chancellor on all matters relating to the preservation, use of, and access to historical manuscripts, records and archives of all kinds. The council meets four times a year, and its main task is to consider requests for the extended closure of public records, or from departments that want to keep records. The council encompasses the statutory Advisory Council on Public Records and the Advisory Council on Historic Manuscripts.
Chair, Rt. Hon. Sir Anthony Clarke *(Master of the Rolls)*

AGRICULTURE AND HORTICULTURE DEVELOPMENT BOARD

Area 2B, Nobel House, 17 Smith Square, London SW1P 3JR
T 020-7238 3079 E info@ahdb.org.uk W www.ahdb.org.uk

The Agriculture and Horticulture Development Board (AHDB) is a Non-Departmental Public Body established under the Agriculture and Horticulture development Board Order 2008. It became operational on 1 April 2008. AHDB raises levies via six sector organisations – cereals and oilseeds (HGCA), beef and lamb (EBLEX), horticulture (HDC), milk (DairyCo), pigs (BPEX), and potatoes (Potato Council) – the funds raised by each organisation are used for the benefit of that specific sector. The AHDB board consists of ten members: the chairs for each of the six sector organisations, and four independent members.
Chairman, John Bridge
Independent members, Chris Bones; John Bridge; Lorraine Clinton; Clare Dodgson
Sector members, Tim Bennett (DairyCo); Neil Bragg (HDC); John Cross (EBLEX); Dennis Heywood (Potato Council); Stewart Houston (BPEX); Jonathan Tipples (HGCA)
Chief executive (interim), Kevin Roberts

ANCIENT MONUMENTS BOARD FOR WALES (CADW)

Plas Carew, Unit 5–7 Cefn Coed, Parc Nantgarw, Cardiff CF15 7QQ
T 01443-336000 F 01443-336001
E cadw@wales.gsi.gov.uk W www.cadw.wales.gov.uk

The Ancient Monuments Advisory Board for Wales advises the Welsh Assembly Government on its statutory functions in respect of ancient monuments.
Chair, Richard Brewer
Members, Prof. Miranda Aldhouse-Green, FSA; Dr Nancy Edwards; Prof. Ralph Griffiths, DLITT; John Hilling; Christopher Musson, MBE, FSA; Dr Emma Plunkett Dillon; Dr Anthony Ward; Prof. Alasdair Whittle, FBA, DPHIL

ARCHITECTURE AND DESIGN SCOTLAND (A+DS)

Bakehouse Close, 146 Canongate, Edinburgh EH8 8DD
T 0131-556 6699 F 0131-556 6633
E info@ads.org.uk W www.ads.org.uk

Architecture and Design Scotland (A+DS) was established in 2005 by the Scottish government as the national champion for good architecture, design and planning in the built environment; it works with a wide range of organisations at national, regional and local levels. A+DS also assumed the independent design review and advisory role of the Royal Fine Art Commission for Scotland.
Chair, Raymond Young
Chief Executive, Sebastian Tombs

ARMED FORCES' PAY REVIEW BODY

6th Floor, Kingsgate House, 66–74 Victoria Street, London SW1E 6SW
T 020-7215 8534 W www.ome.uk.com

The Armed Forces' Pay Review Body was appointed in 1971. It advises the Prime Minister and the Secretary of State for Defence on the pay and allowances of members of naval, military and air forces of the crown.
Chair, Prof. David Greenaway
Members, Robert Burgin; Alison Gallico; Dr Peter Knight; Prof. Derek Leslie; Air Vice-Marshall Ian Stewart (retd), CB; Dr Anne Wright; Lord Young of Norwood Green

ARTS COUNCIL ENGLAND

14 Great Peter Street, London SW1P 3NQ
T 0845-300 6200 F 020-7973 6590
E enquiries@artscouncil.org.uk
W www.artscouncil.org.uk

Arts Council England is the national development agency for the arts in England, distributing public money from government and the National Lottery. Between 2006 and 2008 Arts Council England planned to invest £1.1bn of public funds in the arts in England. Arts Council grants are for individuals, arts organisations, national touring and other people who use the arts in their work.

In 2002, the Arts Council of England and nine regional arts boards joined together to form a single development organisation for the arts. The governing council's members and chair are appointed by the Secretary of State for Culture, Media and Sport usually for a term of four years, and meet approximately five times a year.
Chair, Prof. Sir Christopher Frayling
Members, Diran Adebayo; Janet Barnes; Tom Bloxham, MBE; Andrew Brewerton; Kentake Chinyelu-Hope; Felicity Harvest; Lady Hollick; Keith Khan; Sir Brian McMaster, CBE; Francois Matarasso; Elsie Owusu, OBE; Alice Rawsthorn; Dr Tom Shakespeare; Prof. Stuart Timperley; Dorothy Wilson
Chief Executive, Alan Davey

ARTS COUNCIL OF NORTHERN IRELAND

77 Malone Road, Belfast BT9 6AQ
T 028-9038 5200 F 028-9066 1715
E info@artscouncil-ni.org W www.artscouncil-ni.org

The Arts Council of Northern Ireland is the prime distributor of government funds in support of the arts in Northern Ireland. It is funded by the Department of Culture, Arts and Leisure and from National Lottery funds. In January 2007, the council launched a five-year plan which aims to increase arts funding from £6 to £10 per capita (an increase of approximately £20m for the period up to 2012).
Chair, Rosemary Kelly
Members, Eithne Benson; Kate Bond; Damien Coyle *(Vice-Chair)*; Raymond Fullerton; David Irvine; Anthony Kennedy; Bill Montgomery; Ian Montgomery; Sharon O'Connor; Joseph Rice; Paul Seawright; Brian Sore; Peter Spratt; Janine Walker
Chief Executive, Roisin McDonough

ARTS COUNCIL OF WALES

9 Museum Place, Cardiff CF10 3NX
T 029-2037 6500 F 029-2022 1447
E feedback@artswales.org.uk
W www.artswales.org.uk

The Arts Council of Wales was established in 1994 by royal charter and is the development body for the arts in Wales. It funds arts organisations with funding from the National Assembly for Wales and is the distributor of National Lottery funds to the arts in Wales. The grant for 2007–8 was £29.73m from the National Assembly and £9.85m from the National Lottery.

Chair, Prof. Dai Smith
Members, Simon Dancey; Maggie Hampton; John Metcalf; Robin Morrison; Christopher O'Neil; Dr Ian J. Rees; Clive Sefia; Ruth Till, MBE; David Vokes; Debbie Wilcox; Rhiannon Wyn Hughes, MBE
Chief Executive, Nick Capaldi

AUDIT COMMISSION

1st Floor, Millbank Tower, London SW1P 4HQ
T 0844-798 1212 F 0844-798 2945
E enquiries@audit-commission.gov.uk
W www.audit-commission.gov.uk

The Audit Commission was set up in 1983 and is an independent body responsible for ensuring that public money is spent economically, efficiently and effectively, to achieve high-quality local services for the public. Its remit covers around 11,000 bodies in England, which between them spend more than £180bn of public money each year. Its work covers local government, health, criminal justice organisations and public services.

The commission has a chair, a deputy chair and a board of up to 20 commissioners who are appointed by the Department of Communities and Local Government following consultation with key stakeholders.

Chair, Michael O'Higgins
Commissioners, Lord Adebowale; Steve Bundred; Jim Coulter; Dr Jennifer Dixon; Sheila Drew Smith; Cllr Stephen Houghton; Cllr Peter Jones; Sir Thomas Legg; Dame Denise Platt; Brian Pomeroy, CBE; Raj Rajagopal; Bharat Shah; Prof. Peter Smith; Jenny Watson; Cllr Chris White
Chief Executive, Steve Bundred

AUDIT SCOTLAND

110 George Street, Edinburgh EH2 4LH
T 0845-146 1010 F 0845-146 1009
E info@auditscotland.gov.uk W www.audit-scotland.gov.uk

Audit Scotland was set up on 1 April 2000 to provide services to the Accounts Commission and the Auditor-General for Scotland. Together they help to ensure that the Scottish government and public sector bodies in Scotland are held accountable for the proper, efficient and effective use of around £31bn of public funds.

Audit Scotland's work covers about 200 bodies including local authorities; police forces and fire rescue services; health boards; further education colleges; Scottish Water; the Scottish government; executive agencies such as the Prison Service and non-departmental public bodies such as Scottish Enterprise.

Audit Scotland carries out financial and regularity audits to ensure that public sector bodies adhere to the highest standards of financial management and governance. It also performs audits to ensure that these bodies achieve the best value for money. All of Audit Scotland's work in connection with local authorities, fire and police boards is carried out for the Accounts Commission; its other work is undertaken for the Auditor-General.

Auditor-General, R. W. Black
Chair of the Accounts Commission, J. Baillie

BANK OF ENGLAND

Threadneedle Street, London EC2R 8AH
T 020-7601 4444 F 020-7601 4771
E enquiries@bankofengland.co.uk
W www.bankofengland.co.uk

The Bank of England was incorporated in 1694 under royal charter. It is the banker of the government and it manages the issue of banknotes. Since 1997 it has been operationally independent and its Monetary Policy Committee has had responsibility for setting short-term interest rates to meet the government's inflation target. As the central reserve bank of the country, the Bank of England keeps the accounts of British banks, who maintain with it a proportion of their cash resources, and of most overseas central banks. The bank's core purposes are monetary stability and financial stability. Its responsibility for banking supervision was transferred to the Financial Services Authority in 1998.

Governor, M. A. King
Deputy Governors, Sir John Gieve, CB; Charles Bean
Non-Executive Directors, B. Barber; Roger Carr; Ms A. C. Fawcett, CBE; Hon. Peter Jay; Prof. Sir John Likierman; C. McCarthy; P. Myners; Sir Thomas Parker; Dr D. Potter, CBE; David Rhind; Susan Rice; A. Sarin; James Strachan; G. Wilkinson; Bob Wigley
Monetary Policy Committee, The Governor; the Deputy Governors; Mrs K. Barker; Prof. Tim Besley; D. Blanchflower; Spencer Dale; Dr Andrew Sentance; P. Tucker
Adviser to the Governor, Juliet Wheldon
Chief Cashier and Executive Director, Banking Services, A. Bailey
The Auditor, S. Brown

BIG LOTTERY FUND

1 Plough Place, London EC4A 1DE
T 020-7211 1800 F 020-7211 1750
Advice Line 0845-410 2030
E general.enquiries@biglotteryfund.org.uk
W www.biglotteryfund.org.uk

The Big Lottery Fund was launched in 2004, merging the New Opportunities Fund and the Lottery Charities Board (Community Fund). The fund is responsible for giving out half of the money for good causes raised by the National Lottery. The money is distributed to charitable, benevolent and philanthropic organisations in the voluntary and community sectors, as well as health, education and environmental projects. The Big Lottery Fund also assumed the Millennium Commission's role of supporting large-scale regenerative projects.

Chair, Prof. Sir Clive Booth
Vice-Chair, Anna Southall
Regional Chairs, Sanjay Dighe *(England)*; Breidge Gadd, CBE *(Northern Ireland)*; Alison Magee *(Scotland)*; Huw Vaughan *(Wales)*
General Members, Judith Donovan, CBE; Roland Doven, MBE; John Gartside, OBE; Esther O'Callaghan; Albert Tucker; Diana Whitworth

Chief Executive, Peter Wanless
Directors, Walter Rader *(Northern Ireland)*; Dharmendra Kanani *(Scotland)*; Ceri Doyle *(Wales)*

BOUNDARY COMMISSIONS

The commissions, established in 1944, are constituted under the Parliamentary Constituencies Act 1986 (as amended). The Speaker of the House of Commons is *ex officio* chair of all four commissions in the UK. Each of the four commissions is required by law to keep the parliamentary constituencies in their part of the UK under review (in the case of the Scottish Commission this includes constituencies for the Scottish parliament). The latest Boundary Commission report for England was laid before parliament in February 2007, and the proposals outlined will take effect at the next general election. The latest report from Northern Ireland was published in May 2006, from Wales in January 2005 and the most recent Scottish report on Westminster constituencies was completed in December 2004.

ENGLAND
1st Floor, 1 Myddelton Street, London EC1R 1UW
T 020-7014 2452 E bcomm.england@ons.gov.uk
W www.statistics.gov.uk/pbc/
Deputy Chair, Hon. Mr Justice Sullivan

WALES
1st Floor, Caradog House, 1–6 St Andrews Place, Cardiff CF10 3BE
T 029-2039 5031 F 029-2039 5250
E bcomm.wales@wales.gsi.gov.uk
W www.bcomm-wales.gov.uk
Deputy Chair, Hon. Justice Lloyd Jones

SCOTLAND
3 Drumsheugh Gardens, Edinburgh EH3 7QJ
T 0131-538 7510 F 0131-538 7511
E secretariat@bcomm-scotland.gov.uk
W www.bcomm-scotland.gov.uk
Deputy Chair, Hon. Lord McEwan

NORTHERN IRELAND
Forestview, Purdy's Lane, Newtownbreda, Belfast BT8 7AR
T 028-9069 4800 F 028-9069 4801
E bcni@belfast.org.uk W www.boundarycommission.org.uk
Deputy Chair, Hon. Mr Justice Coghlin

BRITISH BROADCASTING CORPORATION (BBC)

Television Centre, Wood Lane, London W12 7RJ
T 020-8743 8000 BBC **Information Line** 0870-010 0222
W www.bbc.co.uk

The BBC was incorporated under royal charter in 1926 as successor to the British Broadcasting Company Ltd. The BBC's current charter, which came into force on 1 January 2007 and extends to 31 December 2016, recognises the BBC's editorial independence and sets out its public purposes. The BBC Trust was formed under the new charter and replaces the Board of Governors; it sets the strategic direction of the BBC and has a duty to represent the interests of licence fee payers. The chair, vice-chair and other trustees are appointed by the Queen-in-Council. The BBC is financed by revenue from receiving licences for the home services and by grant-in-aid from parliament for the World Service (radio). *See also* Broadcasting.

BBC TRUST MEMBERS
Chair, Sir Michael Lyons
Vice-Chair, Chitra Bharucha
National Trustees, Alison Hastings *(England)*; Rotha Johnston *(Northern Ireland)*; Janet Lewis-Jones *(Wales)*; Jeremy Peat *(Scotland)*
Trustees, Diane Coyle; Dermot Gleeson; Patricia Hodgson; David Liddiment; Mehmuda Mian Pritchard; Richard Tait

EXECUTIVE BOARD
Director-General and Chair, Mark Thompson
Deputy Director-General, Mark Byford
Directors, Tim Davie *(Audio and Music)*; Jana Bennett *(Vision)*; *vacant (Marketing, Communications and Audiences)*; Erik Huggers *(Future Media and Technology)*; Stephen Kelly *(People)*; Zarin Patel *(Group Finance)*
Chief Executive, BBC Worldwide, John Smith
Chief Operating Officer, Caroline Thomson
Senior Independent Director, Marcus Agius
Non-Executive Directors, Dr Mike Lynch, OBE; David Robbie; Dr Samir Shah, OBE; Robert Webb, QC

STATION CONTROLLERS
BBC1, Jay Hunt
BBC2, Roly Keating
BBC3, Danny Cohen
BBC4, Janice Hadlow
BBC News Channel, Kevin Bakhurst
BBC Parliament, Peter Knowles
BBC Northern Ireland, Peter Johnston
BBC Scotland, Ken MacQuarrie
BBC Wales, Menna Richards
Radio 1, Andy Parfitt
Radio 2, Lesley Douglas
Radio 3, Roger Wright
Radio 4, Mark Damazer
Radio 5 Live, Adrian Van Klaveren

BRITISH COUNCIL

Bridgewater House, 58 Whitworth Street, Manchester M1 6BB
T 0161-957 7755 F 0161-957 7762
E general.enquiries@britishcouncil.org
W www.britishcouncil.org

The British Council was established in 1934, incorporated by royal charter in 1940 and granted a supplemental charter in 1993. It is an independent, non-political organisation which promotes Britain abroad and is the UK's international organisation for educational and cultural relations. The British Council is represented in 216 towns and cities in 109 countries. Turnover in 2006–7, including Foreign and Commonwealth Office grants and contracted money, was £551m.
Chair, Lord Kinnock, PC
Chief Executive, Martin Davidson, CMG

BRITISH FILM INSTITUTE (BFI)

21 Stephen Street, London W1T 1LN
T 020-7255 1444 W www.bfi.org.uk

The BFI, established in 1933, offers opportunities for people throughout the UK to experience, learn and discover more about the world of film and moving image culture. It incorporates the BFI National Archive, the BFI National Library, a range DVD releases, publications and educational materials (including the monthly *Sight and*

Sound magazine), BFI Southbank, BFI Distribution, the annual BFI London Film Festival as well as the BFI London Lesbian and Gay Film Festival, and the BFI IMAX cinema, and provides advice and support for regional cinemas and film festivals across the UK.
Chair, Greg Dyke
Director, Amanda Nevill

BRITISH LIBRARY

96 Euston Road, London NW1 2DB
T 020-7412 7332 F 020-7412 7340
E visitor-services@bl.uk W www.bl.uk

The British Library was established in 1973. It is the UK's national library and occupies a key position in the library and information network. It aims to serve scholarship, research, industry, commerce and all other major users of information. Its services are based on a collection of 150 million separate items, including books, journals, manuscripts, maps, stamps, music, patents, newspapers and sound recordings in all written and spoken languages. The library is now based at three sites: London (St Pancras and Colindale) and Boston Spa, W. Yorks. The library's sponsoring department is the Department for Culture, Media and Sport.

Access to the reading rooms at St Pancras is limited to holders of a British Library reader's pass; information about eligibility is available from the reader admissions office. The exhibition galleries and public areas are open to all, free of charge.

BRITISH LIBRARY BOARD
Chair, Sir Colin Lucas
Chief Executive and Deputy Chair, Mrs L. Brindley
Members, Ms D. Airey; H. Boyd-Carpenter, KCVO; R. S. Broadhurst, CBE; Prof. R. Burgess; Sir K. Calman; Ms S. Forbes, CBE; Prof. W. Hall, CBE; Ms E. Mackay, CB; Prof. K. McLuskie; S. Olswang; Dr G. W. Roberts; M. Semple, OBE

SCHOLARSHIP AND COLLECTIONS
Americas Collections, T 020-7412 7743
Asia, Pacific and Africa Collections, T 020-7412 7873
British and Irish Collections, T 020-7412 7538
British Library Newspapers, Colindale Avenue, London NW9 5HE T 020-7412 7353
British Library Sound Archive, T 020-7412 7676
Early Printed Collections, T 020-7412 7676
Map Library, T 020-7412 7702
Music Library, T 020-7412 7772
Philatelic Collections, T 020-7412 7635
Reader Information, T 020-7412 7676
West European Collections, T 020-7412 7572

OPERATIONS AND SERVICES
Permission Clearance, T 020-7412 7755
Research Services, T 020-7412 7797

SCIENCE, TECHNOLOGY AND INNOVATION
Business, T 020-7412 7454
National Preservation Office, T 020-7412 7612
Patents, T 020-7412 7919
Science and Technology, T 020-7412 7494/7288
Social Science, Law and Official Publications, T 020-7412 7536

BRITISH LIBRARY, BOSTON SPA
Boston Spa, Wetherby, W. Yorks LS23 7BQ
T 01937-546000

BRITISH MUSEUM

Great Russell Street, London WC1B 3DG
T 020-7323 8000 F 020-7323 8616
E information@britishmuseum.org
W www.britishmuseum.org

The British Museum houses the national collection of antiquities, ethnography, coins and paper money, medals, prints and drawings. The British Museum may be said to date from 1753, when parliament approved the holding of a public lottery to raise funds for the purchase of the collections of Sir Hans Sloane and the Harleian manuscripts, and for their proper housing and maintenance. The building (Montagu House) was opened in 1759. The existing buildings were erected between 1823 and the present day, and the original collection has increased to its current dimensions by gifts and purchases. Total government grant-in-aid for 2007–8 was £44.8m.

BOARD OF TRUSTEES
Appointed by the Sovereign, HRH The Duke of Gloucester, KG, GCVO
Appointed by the Prime Minister, Chief Emeka Anyaoku; Lord Broers; Sir Ronald Cohen; Prof. Sir Barry Cunliffe, CBE; Francis Finlay; Niall FitzGerald, KBE *(Chair)*; Val Gooding, OBE; Bonnie Greer; Penny Hugher; Baroness Kennedy; Richard Lambert; David Lindsell; Dr David Norgrove; Eric Salama
Appointed by the Trustees of the British Museum, Stephen Green; Lord Powell of Bayswater, KCMG; Sir John Tusa
Appointed by the Royal Society, Dr Olga Kennard; Ms Edmee P. Leventis
Appointed by the Royal Academy, Antony Gormley, OBE
Appointed by the British Academy, Sir Keith Thomas, FBA

OFFICERS
Director, Neil MacGregor
Deputy Director, Andrew Burnett
Director of Public Engagement, Joanna Mackle
Director of Marketing and Public Affairs, Gillian Marsh
Director of Administration, Chris Yates
Director of Visitor and Building Services, Stephen Gill
Heads of Departments, Xerxes Mazda *(Education)*; Zoe Hancock *(Planning and Projects)*; Carolyn Young *(Membership Development)*; Hannah Boulton *(Press)*; Jillian Marsh *(Marketing)*

KEEPERS
Keeper of Africa, Oceania and the Americas, Jonathan King
Keeper of Ancient Egypt and Sudan, Vivian Davies
Keeper of Ancient Near East Antiquities, Dr John Curtis
Keeper of Coins and Medals, Joe Cribb
Keeper of Department of Asia, Jan Stuart
Keeper of Greek and Roman Antiquities, Lesley Fitton
Keeper of Prehistory and Europe, Jonathan Williams
Keeper of Prints and Drawings, Antony Griffiths
Conservation, Documentation and Science, David Saunders

BRITISH PHARMACOPOEIA COMMISSION

Market Towers, 1 Nine Elms Lane, London SW8 5NQ
T 020-7084 2561 E bpcom@mhra.gsi.gov.uk
W www.pharmacopoeia.co.uk

The British Pharmacopoeia Commission sets standards for medicinal products used in human and veterinary medicines and is responsible for publication of the *British*

Pharmacopoeia (a publicly available statement of the standard that a product must meet throughout its shelf-life), the *British Pharmacopoeia (Veterinary)* and the *British Approved Names*. It has 16 members, including two lay members, who are appointed by the Appointments Commission (the body responsible for appointments to all of the Medicines Act advisory bodies).
Chair, Prof. A. D. Woolfson
Vice-Chair, V'lain Fenton-May
Secretary and Scientific Director, Dr M. G. Lee

BRITISH STANDARDS INSTITUTION

389 Chiswick High Road, London W4 4AL
T 020-8996 9001 F 020-8996 7001
E cservices@bsi-global.com W www.bsi-global.com

British Standards – a part of the BSI Group – was the world's first national standards-making body, established in 1901, and is the recognised authority in the UK for the preparation and publication of national standards, both for products and for the service sector. About 90 per cent of its standards work is internationally linked. British Standards are issued for voluntary adoption, though in some cases compliance with a British Standard is required by legislation. Industrial and consumer products and services certified as complying with the relevant British Standard and operating an assessed quality management system are eligible to carry BSI's certification trade mark, known as the 'Kitemark'.
Chair, Sir David John, KCMG
Chief Executive, Stevan Breeze

BRITISH WATERWAYS

64 Clarendon Road, Watford WD17 1DA
T 01923-201120 F 01923-201400
E enquiries.hq@britishwaterways.co.uk
W www.britishwaterways.co.uk

British Waterways conserves and manages the network of over 3,540km (2,200 miles) of canals and rivers in England, Scotland and Wales. Its sponsoring departments are the Department for Environment, Food and Rural Affairs in England and Wales, and the Enterprise, Transport and Lifelong Learning Department in Scotland.

Its responsibilities include maintaining the waterways and structures on and around them; looking after wildlife and the waterway environment; and ensuring that canals and rivers are safe and enjoyable places to visit.
Chair, Tony Hales
Vice-Chair, Dr Campbell Christie, CBE
Chief Executive, Robin Evans, FRICS

CENTRAL ARBITRATION COMMITTEE (CAC)

PO Box 51547, London SE1 1ZG
T 020-7904 2300 F 020-7904 2301
E enquiries@cac.gov.uk W www.cac.gov.uk

The CAC is a permanent independent body with statutory powers whose main function is to adjudicate on applications relating to the statutory recognition and de-recognition of trade unions for collective bargaining purposes, where such recognition or de-recognition cannot be agreed voluntarily. In addition, the CAC has a statutory role in determining disputes between trade unions and employers over the disclosure of information for collective bargaining purposes, and in resolving applications and complaints under the information and consultation regulations, and performs a similar role in relation to the legislation on the European Works Council, European companies, European cooperative societies and cross-border mergers. The CAC also provides voluntary arbitration in industrial disputes.

The committee consists of a chair and 11 deputy chairs, 29 members experienced as representatives of employers and 26 members experienced as representatives of workers. All members of the committee are appointed by the Secretary of State for Business, Enterprise and Regulatory Reform after consulting ACAS.
Chair, Sir Michael Burton
Chief Executive, Graeme Charles

CERTIFICATION OFFICE FOR TRADE UNIONS AND EMPLOYERS' ASSOCIATIONS

Brandon House, 180 Borough High Street, London SE1 1LW
T 020-7210 3734 F 020-7210 3612
E info@certoffice.org W www.certoffice.org

The Certification Office is an independent statutory authority. The certification officer is appointed by the Secretary of State for Business, Enterprise and Regulatory Reform and is responsible for maintaining a list of trade unions and employers' associations; ensuring compliance with statutory requirements; keeping annual returns from trade unions and employers' associations available for public inspection; determining complaints concerning trade union elections, certain ballots and certain breaches of trade union rules; for ensuring observance of statutory requirements governing mergers between trade unions and employers' associations; for overseeing the political funds and finances of trade unions and employers' associations; and for certifying the independence of trade unions.
Certification Officer, David Cockburn

SCOTLAND
69A George Street, Edinburgh EH2 2JG
T 0131-220 7660
Assistant Certification Officer for Scotland, Christine Stuart

CHURCH COMMISSIONERS

Church House, Great Smith Street, London SW1P 3AZ
T 020-7898 1000 F 020-7898 1131
E commissioners.enquiry@c-of-e.org
W www.cofe.anglican.org/about/churchcommissioners

The Church Commissioners were established in 1948 by the amalgamation of Queen Anne's Bounty (established 1704) and the Ecclesiastical Commissioners (established 1836). They are responsible for the management of some of the Church of England's assets, the income from which is predominantly used to help pay for the stipend and pension of the clergy and to support the church's work throughout the country. The commissioners own UK and global company shares, over 45,000ha (112,000 acres) of agricultural land, a residential estate in central London, and commercial property across Great Britain, plus an interest in overseas property via managed funds. They also carry out administrative duties in connection with pastoral reorganisation and closed churches.

The commissioners are: the Archbishops of Canterbury and of York; four bishops, three clergy and four lay persons elected by the respective houses of the General Synod; two deans elected by all the deans; three persons nominated by the Queen; three persons nominated by the

Archbishops of Canterbury and York; three persons nominated by the archbishops after consultation with others including the Lord Mayors of London and York and the vice-chancellors of the universities of Oxford and Cambridge; the First Lord of the Treasury; the Lord President of the Council; the home secretary; the Secretary of State for Culture, Media and Sport; and the Speakers of the House of Commons and the House of Lords.

CHURCH ESTATES COMMISSIONERS
First, A. Whittam Smith
Second, Sir Stuart Bell, MP
Third, T. E. H. Walker

OFFICERS
Secretary, A. C. Brown

ASSISTANT SECRETARIES
Chief Surveyor, J. Cannon
Chief Investments Manager, M. Chaloner
Pastoral and Redundant Churches, P. Lewis
Official Solicitor (acting), T. Crow

CIVIL AVIATION AUTHORITY (CAA)

CAA House, 45–59 Kingsway, London WC2B 6TE
T 020-7379 7311 E infoservices@caa.co.uk
W www.caa.co.uk

The CAA is the UK's specialist aviation regulator. Its responsibilities include ensuring that the aviation industry meets the highest technical and operational safety standards; preventing holidaymakers from being stranded abroad or losing money because of tour operator insolvency; planning and regulating all UK airspace; regulating airports, air traffic services and airlines; and providing advice on aviation policy from an economic standpoint. The government provides no direct funding; the CAA must meet its costs entirely from charges on those whom it regulates.
Chair, Sir Roy McNulty, CBE

COAL AUTHORITY

200 Lichfield Lane, Mansfield, Notts NG18 4RG
T 01623-637000 F 01623-622072
E thecoalauthority@coal.gov.uk W www.coal.gov.uk

The Coal Authority was established under the Coal Industry Act 1994 to manage certain functions previously undertaken by British Coal, including ownership of unworked coal. It is responsible for licensing coal mining operations and for providing information on coal reserves and past and future coal mining. It settles subsidence damage claims which are not the responsibility of licensed coal mining operators. It deals with the management and disposal of property, and with surface hazards such as abandoned coal mine shafts.
Chair, Dr Helen Mounsey
Chief Executive, Philip Lawrence

COMMISSION FOR ARCHITECTURE AND THE BUILT ENVIRONMENT (CABE)

1 Kemble Street, London WC2B 4AN
T 020-7070 6700 F 020-7070 6777
W www.cabe.org.uk

CABE was established in 1999 and is responsible for promoting the importance of high-quality architecture and urban design, and for encouraging the understanding of architecture through educational and regional initiatives. The commission offers free advice to local authorities, public sector clients and others embarking on building projects of any size or purpose. CABE has a board of 16 commissioners, appointed by the Secretary of State for Culture, Media and Sport for a maximum of two four-year terms.
Chair, John Sorrell, CBE
Chief Executive, Richard Simmons

COMMISSION FOR INTEGRATED TRANSPORT (CFIT)

2nd Floor, 55 Victoria Street, London SW1H 0EU
T 020-7944 8131 F 020-7944 8643
E cfit@dft.gsi.gov.uk W www.cfit.gov.uk

The CfIT was established in June 1999. Its role is to provide independent expert advice to the government in order to achieve a transport system that supports sustainable development. The CfIT also encourages best practice amongst local authorities and delivery agencies, and assesses both the impact of new technology on future policy options and transport policy initiatives from outside the UK. Members of the commission are appointed by the transport secretary.
Chair, Peter Hendy, CBE
Vice-Chairs, David Leeder; Dr Lynn Sloman

COMMISSION FOR RURAL COMMUNITIES

John Dower House, Crescent Place, Cheltenham GL50 3RA
T 01242-521381 E info@ruralcommunities.gov.uk
W www.ruralcommunities.gov.uk

The Commission for Rural Communities was established in October 2006; it was formerly an operating division of the now-defunct Countryside Agency. It is a statutory body under the Natural Environment and Rural Communities Act 2006 and it aims to provide well-informed, independent advice to government and to ensure that policies reflect the needs of people living and working in rural England, with a particular focus on tackling disadvantage. Its three key roles are to be a rural advocate, an expert adviser and an independent watchdog. The commission is funded by an annual grant from the Department for Environment, Food and Rural Affairs and commissioners are appointed by the secretary of state.
Chair and Rural Advocate, Dr Stuart Burgess
Commissioners, Prof. Sheena Asthana; Richard Burge; Dr Jim Cox, OBE; Norman Glass; Elinor Goodman; Alison McLean; Howard Petch, CBE; Prof. Mark Shucksmith; John Varley; Prof. Michael Winter, OBE
Chief Executive, Graham Garbutt

COMMITTEE ON STANDARDS IN PUBLIC LIFE

35 Great Smith Street, London SW1P 3BQ
T 020-7276 2595 F 020-7276 2585
E standards@evidence.x.gsi.gov.uk
W www.public-standards.gov.uk

The Committee on Standards in Public Life was set up in October 1994. It is a standing body whose chair and members are appointed by the prime minister; three members are nominated by the leaders of the three main

political parties. The committee's remit is to examine concerns about standards of conduct of all holders of public office, including arrangements relating to financial and commercial activities, and to make recommendations as to any changes in present arrangements which might be required to ensure the highest standards of propriety in public life. It is also charged with reviewing issues in relation to the funding of political parties. The committee does not investigate individual allegations of misconduct.
Chair, Sir Christopher Kelly, KCB
Members, Lloyd Clarke, QPM; Oliver Heald, MP; Dame Patricia Hodgson, DBE; Baroness Maddock; Rt. Hon. Alun Michael, MP; Sir Derek Morris; Dame Denise Platt; Dr Elizabeth Vallance; Dr Brian Woods-Scawen, CBE

COMMONWEALTH WAR GRAVES COMMISSION

2 Marlow Road, Maidenhead, Berks SL6 7DX
T 01628-634221 F 01628-771208
E casualty.enq@cwgc.org W www.cwgc.org

The Commonwealth War Graves Commission (formerly Imperial War Graves Commission) was founded by royal charter in 1917. It is responsible for the commemoration of around 1.7 million members of the forces of the Commonwealth who lost their lives in the two world wars. More than one million graves are maintained in 23,274 burial grounds throughout the world. Over three-quarters of a million men and women who have no known grave or who were cremated are commemorated by name on memorials built by the commission.

The funds of the commission are derived from the six participating governments, ie the UK, Canada, Australia, New Zealand, South Africa and India.
President, HRH The Duke of Kent, KG, GCMG, GCVO, ADC
Chair, Secretary of State for Defence (UK)
Vice-Chair, Adm. Sir Ian Garnett, KCB
Members, High Commissioners in London for Australia, Canada, South Africa, New Zealand and India; Lt.-Gen. Sir Alistair Irwin, KCB, CBE; Ian Henderson, CBE, FRICS; Sara Jones, CBE; Alan Meale, MP; Hon. Nicholas Soames, MP; Prof. Hew Strachan, FRSE; Sir Rob Young, GCMG
Director-General and Secretary to the Commission, R. E. Kellaway, CBE
Deputy Director-General, T. V. Reeves
Legal Adviser and Solicitor, G. C. Reddie

COMPETITION COMMISSION

Victoria House, Southampton Row, London WC1B 4AD
T 020-7271 0100
E info@cc.gsi.gov.uk W www.competition-commission.org.uk

The commission was established in 1948 as the Monopolies and Restrictive Practices Commission (later the Monopolies and Mergers Commission); it became the Competition Commission in April 1999 under the Competition Act 1998. The commission conducts in-depth inquiries into mergers, markets, and the regulation of major industries. Every inquiry the commission undertakes is in response to a reference made to it by another authority, usually the Office of Fair Trading. The commission has no power to conduct inquiries on its own initiative. The Enterprise Act 2002 introduced a new regime for the assessment of mergers and markets in the UK – in most related investigations the commission is responsible for making decisions on the competition questions and for making and implementing decisions on appropriate remedies.

The commission has a full-time chair and three deputy chairs. There are usually around 40 part-time commission members, who usually carry out investigations in groups of four or five after appointment by the chair. All are appointed by the Secretary of State for Business, Enterprise and Regulatory Reform for eight-year terms.
Chair, Peter Freeman
Deputy Chairs, Christopher Clarke; Dr Peter Davis; Diana Guy
Members, Jayne Almond; Prof. John Baillie; Christopher Bright; Laura Carstensen; Dr John Collings; Dr Diane Coyle; Prof. John Cubbin; Roger Davis; Carolan Dobson; Barbara Donoghue; Laurence Elks; Richard Farrant; Prof. Alan Gregory, FCMA; Ivar Grey; Prof. Alan Hamlin; Prof. Jonathan Haskel; Peter Hazell; Jill Hill; Richard Holroyd; Alexander Johnston; Ian Jones; Peter Jones; Prof. Bruce Lyons; Dame Barbara Mills, DBE, QC; Prof. Peter Moizer, FCA; Jeremy Peat; Christopher Smallwood; John Smith; Anthony Stern; Peter Stoddart, FCA; Prof. Sudi Sudarsanam; Richard Taylor; Robert Turgoose; Prof. Catherine Waddams; Steven Walzer; Prof. Michael Waterson; Jonathan Whiticar; Prof. Stephen Wilks, FCA; Fiona Woolf, CBE
Non-Executive Directors, Tony Foster; Dame Patricia Hodgson, DBE
Chief Executive and Secretary, Martin Stanley

COMPETITION SERVICE

Victoria House, Bloomsbury Place, London WC1A 2EB
T 020-7979 7979 F 020-7979 7978
E info@catribunal.org.uk W www.catribunal.org.uk

The Enterprise Act 2002 created the Competition Service, a non-departmental public body whose purpose is to fund and provide support services to the Competition Appeal Tribunal. Support services include everything necessary to facilitate the carrying out by the Competition Appeal Tribunal of its statutory functions such as administration, accommodation and office equipment.
Chief Executive, Charles Dhanowa

CONSUMER COUNCIL FOR WATER

Victoria Square House, Victoria Square, Birmingham B2 4AJ
T 0121-345 1000 F 0121-345 1001
E enquiries@ccwater.org.uk W www.ccwater.org.uk

The Consumer Council for Water was established in 2005 under the Water Act 2003 to represent consumers' interests in respect of price, service and value for money from their water and sewerage services, and to investigate complaints from customers about their water company. There are four regional committees in England and one in Wales.
Chair, Dame Yve Buckland, DBE

CORPORATION OF TRINITY HOUSE

Trinity House, Tower Hill, London EC3N 4DH
T 020-7481 6900 F 020-7480 7662
E enquiries@thls.org W www.trinityhouse.co.uk

The Corporation of Trinity House is the general lighthouse authority for England, Wales and the Channel Islands, and was granted its first charter by Henry VIII in 1514. Its remit is to assist the safe passage of a variety of vessels through some of the busiest sea-lanes in the world;

it does this by deploying and maintaining approximately 600 aids to navigation, ranging from lighthouses to a satellite navigation service. The corporation also has certain statutory jurisdiction over aids to navigation maintained by local harbour authorities and is responsible for marking or dispersing wrecks dangerous to navigation, except those occurring within port limits or wrecks of HM ships.

The statutory duties of Trinity House are funded by the General Lighthouse Fund, which is provided from light dues levied on ships calling at ports of the UK and the Republic of Ireland. The corporation is a deep-sea pilotage authority, authorised by the Secretary of State for Transport to license deep-sea pilots. In addition Trinity House is a charitable organisation that maintains a number of retirement homes for mariners and their dependants, funds a four-year training scheme for those seeking a career in the merchant navy, and also dispenses grants to a wide range of maritime charities. The charity work is wholly funded by its own activities.

The corporation is controlled by a board of Elder Brethren; a separate board controls the Lighthouse Service. The Elder Brethren also act as nautical assessors in marine cases in the Admiralty Division of the High Court.

ELDER BRETHREN

Master, HRH The Prince Philip, Duke of Edinburgh, KG, KT, PC

Deputy Master, Rear-Adm. Jeremy de Halpert, CB

Wardens, Cdre. Peter Melson, CBE, RN *(Rental)*; Capt. Duncan Glass *(Nether)*

Elder Brethren, HRH The Prince of Wales, KG, KT, GCB; HRH The Duke of York, KG, KCVO, ADC; HRH The Princess Royal, KG, KT, GCVO; Adm. Lord Boyce, GCB, OBE; Lord Browne of Madingley; Viscount Cobham; Capt. John Burton-Hall, RD; Lord Carrington, KG, GCMG, CH, PC; Lord Cuckney of Millbank; Capt. Sir Malcolm Edge, KCVO; Capt. Ian Gibb; Cdr. Sir Robin Gillett, Bt., GBE, RD; Lord Greenway; Lord Mackay of Clashfern, KT, PC; Capt. Peter Mason, CBE; Capt. David Orr; Douglas Potter; Capt. Nigel Pryke, MCIT, FNI; Capt. Derek Richards, RD, RNR; Cdr. Sir Miles Rivett-Carnac, RN; Lord Robertson of Port Ellen, KT, GCMG, PC; Rear-Adm. Sir Patrick Rowe, KCVO, CBE; Cdre. Jim Scorer; Sir Brian Shaw; Simon Sherard; Adm. Sir Jock Slater, GCB, LVO; Capt. David Smith, OBE, RN; Capt. David Squire, CBE, RFA; Cdre. Lord Sterling of Plaistow, CBE, GCVO, RNR; Capt. Colin Stewart, LVO; Sir Adrian Swire, AE; Capt. Sir Miles Wingate, KCVO; Capt. Thomas Woodfield, OBE; Capt. Richard Woodman

OFFICERS

Secretary, Peter Galloway

Director of Finance, Jerry Wedge

Director of Operations, Cdre. Jim Scorer

Director of Navigation, Capt. Duncan Glass

COUNTRYSIDE COUNCIL FOR WALES/CYNGOR CEFN GWLAD CYMRU

Maes-y-Ffynnon, Penrhosgarnedd, Bangor, Gwynedd LL57 2DW
T 0845-130 6229
E enquiries@ccw.gov.uk **W** www.ccw.gov.uk

The Countryside Council for Wales is the government's statutory adviser on sustaining natural beauty, wildlife and the opportunity for outdoor enjoyment in Wales and its inshore waters. It is funded by the National Assembly for Wales and accountable to the First Secretary, who appoints its members.

Chair, John Lloyd Jones, OBE

Chief Executive, Roger Thomas

COVENT GARDEN MARKET AUTHORITY

Covent House, New Covent Garden Market, London SW8 5NX
T 020-7720 2211 **F** 020-7622 5307
E info@cgma.gov.uk **W** www.cgma.gov.uk

The Covent Garden Market Authority is constituted under the Covent Garden Market Acts 1961 to 1977, the board being appointed by the Department of Environment, Food and Rural Affairs. The authority owns and operates the 22.7 hectare (56 acre) New Covent Garden Markets (fruit, vegetables, flowers), which have been trading at the site since 1974.

Chair (part-time), Rt. Hon. Baroness Dean of Thornton-le-Fylde

Chief Executive, Jan Lloyd

CRIMINAL CASES REVIEW COMMISSION

Alpha Tower, Suffolk Street Queensway, Birmingham B1 1TT
T 0121-633 1800 **F** 0121-633 1823
E info@ccrc.x.gsi.gov.uk **W** www.ccrc.gov.uk

The Criminal Cases Review Commission is an independent body set up under the Criminal Appeal Act 1995. It is a non-departmental public body reporting to parliament via the Lord Chancellor and Secretary of State for Justice. It is responsible for investigating possible miscarriages of justice in England, Wales and Northern Ireland, and deciding whether or not to refer cases back to an appeal court. Membership of the commission is by royal appointment; the senior executive staff are appointed by the commission.

Chair, Prof. Graham Zellick

Members, M. Allen; Ms P. Barrett; M. Emerton; J. England; Ms J. Goulding; D. Jessel; A. MacGregor, QC; I. Nicholl; E. Smith; J. Weeden

Principal Director, C. Albert

CRIMINAL INJURIES COMPENSATION AUTHORITY (CICA)

Tay House, 300 Bath Street, Glasgow G2 4LN
T 0800-358 3601
F 0141-331 2287
E enquiries@cica.gsi.gov.uk **W** www.cica.gov.uk

All applications for compensation for personal injury arising from crimes of violence in England, Scotland and Wales are dealt with at the above location (separate arrangements apply in Northern Ireland). Applications received up to 31 March 1996 are assessed on the basis of common law damages under the 1990 compensation scheme. Applications received on or after 1 April 1996 are assessed under a tariff-based scheme, made under the Criminal Injuries Compensation Act 1995, by the CICA. There is a separate avenue of appeal to the Criminal Injuries Compensation Appeals Panel (CICAP – *see* Tribunals section).

Chief Executive, Carole Oatway

CROFTERS COMMISSION

Castle Wynd, Inverness IV2 3EQ
T 01463-663450 F 01463-711820
E info@crofterscommission.org.uk
W www.crofterscommission.org.uk

The Crofters Commission, established in 1955 under the Crofters (Scotland) Act, is a government-funded organisation tasked with overseeing crofting legislation and developing crofting. It works with communities to regulate crofting and assist local development initiatives. It also advises Scottish ministers on crofting matters. The commission administers the Crofting Counties Agricultural Grants Scheme and the Crofters' Cattle Improvement Scheme. It also provides a free enquiry service.

Convenor, Drew Ratter
Chief Executive, Nick Reiter

DEER COMMISSION FOR SCOTLAND

Great Glen House, Leachkin Road, Inverness IV3 8NW
T 01463-725000 F 01463-725048
E enquiries@dcs.gov.uk W www.dcs.gov.uk

The Deer Commission for Scotland has the general functions of furthering the conservation and control of deer in Scotland. It has the statutory duty, with powers, to prevent damage to agriculture, forestry and the habitat by deer. It is funded by the Scottish government.

Chair (part-time), Prof. J. Milne, MBE
Director, N. Halfhide

DESIGN COUNCIL

34 Bow Street, London WC2E 7DL
T 020-7420 5200 F 020-7420 5300
E info@designcouncil.org.uk W www.designcouncil.org.uk

The Design Council is a campaigning organisation which works with partners in business, education and government to promote the effective use of good design; its aim is to make businesses more competitive and public services more effective. It is a registered charity with a royal charter and is funded jointly by grant-in-aid from the Department for Business, Enterprise and Regulatory Reform and the Department for Culture, Media and Sport; the secretaries of state of these two departments appoint the chair and members of the council.

Chair, Sir Michael Bichard
Chief Executive, David Kester

ENGLISH HERITAGE (HISTORIC BUILDINGS AND MONUMENTS COMMISSION FOR ENGLAND)

1 Waterhouse Square, 138–142 Holborn, London EC1N 2ST
T 020-7973 3000 F 020-7973 3001
W www.english-heritage.org.uk

English Heritage was established under the National Heritage Act 1983. On 1 April 1999 it merged with the Royal Commission on the Historical Monuments of England to become the new lead body for England's historic environment. It is sponsored by the Department for Culture, Media and Sport and its duties are to carry out and sponsor archaeological, architectural and scientific surveys and research designed to increase the understanding of England's past and its changing condition; to identify buildings, monuments and landscapes for protection whilst also offering expert advice, skills and grants to conserve these sites; to encourage town planners to make imaginative re-use of historic buildings to aid regeneration of the centres of cities, towns and villages; to manage and curate selected sites; and to curate and make publicly accessible the National Monuments Record, whose records of over one million historic sites and buildings, and extensive collections of photographs, maps, drawings and reports constitute the central database and archive of England's historic environment.

Chair, Lord Sandy Bruce-Lockhard
Commissioners, Maria Adebowale; Joyce Bridges, CBE; Prof. David Cannadine, DPHIL, LITT D, FBA; Manish Chande; Prof. Sir Barry Cunliffe, CBE; Gilly Drummond; Jane Grenville, FSA; Michael Jolly, CBE; Jane Kennedy; Earl of Leicester, CBE; Les Sparks, OBE, FRSA; Elizabeth Williamson, FSA
Chief Executive, Dr Simon Thurley

CUSTOMER SERVICES DEPARTMENT, PO Box 569, Swindon SN2 2YP T 0870-333 1181
E customers@english-heritage.org.uk
NATIONAL MONUMENTS RECORD CENTRE, Kemble Drive, Swindon SN2 2GZ T 01793-414600
F 01793-414606

ENVIRONMENT AGENCY

Rio House, Waterside Drive, Aztec West, Almondsbury, Bristol BS32 4UD
T 0870-850 6506 F 01709-312820
E enquiries@environment-agency.gov.uk
W www.environment-agency.gov.uk

The Environment Agency was established in 1996 under the Environment Act 1995 and is a non-departmental public body sponsored by the Department for Environment, Food and Rural Affairs and the National Assembly for Wales – around 60 per cent of the agency's funding is from the government, with the rest raised from various charging schemes. The agency is responsible for pollution prevention and control in England and Wales, and for the management and use of water resources, including flood defences, fisheries and navigation. It has head offices in London and Bristol, and eight regional offices.

THE BOARD
Chair, Lord Smith of Finsbury
Members, James Braithwaite, CBE; Andrew Brown; Peter Bye; Ted Cantle, CBE; John Edmonds; Prof. Ruth Hall; Richard Percy; Dr Lyndon Stanton; Cllr Kay Twitchen, OBE; Dr Malcolm Smith; Lady Warner, OBE; Lord Whitty
Chief Executive (acting), Paul Leinster

EQUALITY AND HUMAN RIGHTS COMMISSION

Arndale House, The Arndale Centre, Manchester M4 3AQ
T 0161-829 8100 Helpline 0845-604 6610 F 01925-884000
E info@equalityhumanrights.com
W www.equalityhumanrights.com

The Equality and Human Rights Commission is a statutory body, established under the Equality Act 2006 and launched in October 2007. It inherited the responsibilities of the Commission for Racial Equality, the Disability Rights Commission and the Equal Opportunities Commission. The Equality and Human

Rights Commission's purpose is to reduce inequality, eliminate discrimination, strengthen relations between people, and promote and protect human rights. It enforces equality legislation on age, disability and health, gender, race, religion and belief, sexual orientation or transgender status, and encourages compliance with the Human Rights Act 1998 throughout England, Wales and Scotland. The Secretary of State for Communities and Local Government appoints the chair and commissioners of the board.

Chair, Trevor Phillips
Deputy Chair, Baroness Prosser, OBE
Commissioners, Morag Alexander; Kay Allen; Baroness Campbell, DBE; Kay Carberry; Jeannie Drake, CBE; Joel Edwards; Baroness Greengross, OBE; Prof. Kay Hampton; Francesca Klug; Sir Bert Massie, CBE; Ziauddin Sardar; Maeve Sherlock, OBE; Ben Summerskill; Dr Neil Wooding
Chief Executive, Dr Nicola Brewer

EQUALITY COMMISSION FOR NORTHERN IRELAND

Equality House, 7–9 Shaftesbury Square, Belfast BT2 7DP
T 028-9050 0600 **F** 028-9024 8687
E information@equalityni.org **W** www.equalityni.org

The Equality Commission was set up in 1999 under the Northern Ireland Act 1998 and is responsible for promoting equality, keeping the relevant legislation under review, eliminating discrimination on the grounds of race, disability, sexual orientation, gender, religion and political opinion and for overseeing the statutory duty on public authorities to promote equality of opportunity.

Chief Commissioner, Bob Collins
Deputy Chief Commissioner, Anne O'Reilly
Chief Executive, Evelyn Collins, CBE

FOREIGN COMPENSATION COMMISSION (FCC)

Old Admiralty Building, London SW1A 2PA
T 020-7008 1321 **F** 020-7008 0160
W www.fcc.gov.uk

The FCC was set up by the Foreign Compensation Act 1950 primarily to distribute, under orders in council, funds received from other governments in accordance with agreements to pay compensation for expropriated British property and other losses sustained by British nationals. The FCC carries out both judicial and administrative functions, including the adjudication of claims by applicants and the investment and management of compensation funds. There are no active compensation programmes at present.

Chair, Dr John Barker

GAMBLING COMMISSION

Victoria Square House, Victoria Square, Birmingham B2 4BP
T 0121-230 6666 **F** 0121-233 6720
E info@gamblingcommission.gov.uk
W www.gamblingcommission.gov.uk

The Gambling Commission was established under the Gambling Act 2005, and took over the role previously occupied by the Gaming Board for Great Britain in regulating and licensing all commercial gambling – apart from spread betting and the National Lottery – ie casinos, bingo, remote gambling, gaming machines and lotteries. It also advises local and central government on related issues, and is responsible for the protection of children and the vulnerable from being exploited or harmed by gambling. The commission is sponsored by the Department for Culture, Media and Sport, with its work funded mainly by licence fees paid by the gambling industry.

Chair, Brian Pomeroy
Chief Executive, Jenny Williams

GOVERNMENT ACTUARY'S DEPARTMENT

Finlaison House, 15–17 Furnival Street, London EC4A 1AB
T 020-7211 2601 **F** 020-7211 2650
E enquiries@gad.gov.uk **W** www.gad.gov.uk

The Government Actuary's Department was established in 1919 and provides a consulting service to government departments, the public sector, and overseas governments. The actuaries advise on social security schemes and superannuation arrangements in the public sector at home and abroad, on population and other statistical studies, and on supervision of insurance companies and pension funds.

Government Actuary, T. J. Llanwarne
Deputy Government Actuary, A. I. Johnston
Chief Actuaries, E. I. Battersby; I. A. Boonin; J. Dunn; D. J. Hughes; S. R. Humphrey; K. Kneller; G. T. Russell

GOVERNMENT OFFICES FOR THE REGIONS

The nine Government Offices for the Regions (GOs) are the primary means by which a wide range of government policies are delivered in the English regions. The Government Offices bring together the activities and interests of ten 'sponsor' government departments: the Department for Communities and Local Government; the Department for Education and Skills; the Department of Trade and Industry; the Department for Environment, Food and Rural Affairs; the Home Office; the Department for Culture, Media and Sport; the Department for Work and Pensions; the Department for Transport; the Department of Health; and the Cabinet Office.

GOs contribute to the delivery of over 40 public service agreements (PSAs) on behalf of their sponsor departments. These PSAs cover a diverse range of tasks including regenerating communities, fighting crime, tackling housing needs, improving public health, raising standards in education and skills, tackling countryside issues, and reducing unemployment. GOs also manage European funds.

GOs directly manage the spending programmes of the government departments listed above. They oversee budgets and contracts delegated to regional organisations, as well as carrying out regulatory functions and sponsoring Regional Development Agencies. As part of central government, their role also includes providing a regional perspective to inform the development and evaluation of policy.

The Government Office Network comprises the nine regional Government Offices, and the Regional Coordination Unit.

REGIONAL COORDINATION UNIT

4th Floor, Eland House, Bressenden Place, London SW1E 5DU
T 020-7944 0702 **F** 020-7944 0759
W www.gos.gov.uk
Director-General, Joe Montgomery

Director, Brian Hackland
Deputy Directors, Elizabeth Whatmore *(Business Development)*; John Blundell and Clare Buchanan *(Directors Office)*; Vince Brady *(Human Resources)*; Julian Bowrey *(Strategy and Performance)*

EAST MIDLANDS
The Belgrave Centre, Stanley Place, Talbot Street, Nottingham NG1 5GG
T 0115-971 9971 F 0115-971 2404
E enquiries@goem.gsi.gov.uk
W www.goem.gov.uk
Regional Director, Jonathan Lindley

EAST OF ENGLAND
Eastbrook, Shaftesbury Road, Cambridge CB2 2DF
T 01223-372500 F 01223-372501
W www.go-east.gov.uk
Regional Director (interim), Andrea Young

LONDON
Riverwalk House, 157–161 Millbank, London SW1P 4RR
T 020-7217 3111 F 020-7217 3450
W www.gos.gov.uk/gol
Regional Director, Chris Hayes

NORTH EAST
Citygate, Gallowgate, Newcastle upon Tyne NE1 4WH
T 0191-201 3300 F 0191-202 3998
W www.go-ne.gov.uk
Regional Director, Jonathan Blackie

NORTH WEST
City Tower, Piccadilly Plaza, Manchester M1 4BE
T 0161-952 4000 F 0161-952 4099
W www.go-nw.gov.uk
Regional Director, Liz Meek

SOUTH EAST
Bridge House, 1 Walnut Tree Close, Guildford GU1 4GA
T 01483-882002 F 01483-882259
W www.go-se.gov.uk
Regional Director, Colin Byrne

SOUTH WEST
2 Rivergate, Temple Quay, Bristol BS1 6EH
T 0117-900 1700 F 0117-900 1900
W www.gosw.gov.uk
Regional Director, Jon Bright

WEST MIDLANDS
5 St Phillips Place, Colmore Row, Birmingham B3 2PW
T 0121-352 5050 F 0121-352 5194
E enquiries.team@gowm.gsi.gov.uk
W www.go-wm.gov.uk
Regional Director, Trudi Elliot

YORKSHIRE AND THE HUMBER
Lateral, 8 City Walk, Leeds LS11 9AT
T 0113-341 3000
E yhenquiries@goyh.gsi.gov.uk W www.goyh.gov.uk
Regional Director, Felicity Everiss

HEALTH AND SAFETY EXECUTIVE

London, Rose Court, 2 Southwark Bridge, London SE1 9HS
Liverpool, Redgrave Court, Merton Road, Bootle, Merseyside L20 7HS
T 0845-345 0055 F 0845-408 9566
E hse.infoline@natbrit.com W www.hse.gov.uk

The Health and Safety Commission (HSC) and the Health and Safety Executive (HSE) merged on 1 April 2008 to form a single national regulatory body responsible for promoting the cause of better health and safety at work.

HSE regulates all industrial and commercial sectors except operations in the air and at sea. This includes agriculture, construction, manufacturing, services, transport, mines, offshore oil and gas, nuclear, quarries and major hazard sites in chemicals and petrochemicals.

HSE is responsible for developing and enforcing health and safety law, providing guidance and advice, commissioning research, inspection including accident and ill-health investigation, developing standards and licensing or approving some work activities such as nuclear power and asbestos removal. HSE is a government agency sponsored by the Department for Work and Pensions.

Chair, Judith Hackitt, CBE
Board members, Sandy Blair; Danny Carrigan; Robin Dahlberg; Judith Donovan; David Gartside; Sayeed Khan; Hugh Robertson; Elizabeth Snape; John Spanswick
Chief Executive, Geoffrey Podger

HEALTH PROTECTION AGENCY (HPA)

7th Floor, Holborn Gate, 330 High Holborn, London WC1V 7PP
T 020-7759 2700 F 020-7759 2733
E webteam@hpa.org.uk W www.hpa.org.uk

The HPA was set up in 2003 and is responsible for providing an integrated approach to protecting public health through the provision of support and advice to the NHS, local authorities, emergency services, other NDPBs, the Department of Health and the devolved administrations.

The HPA works at local, regional, national and international levels to reduce the impact of infectious diseases and reduce exposure to chemicals, radiation and poisons, as well as ensuring a rapid response when hazards occur. The HPA provides services in Northern Ireland and works closely with the devolved administrations, so that there is a coordinated response to incidents, trends and outbreaks on a national level. Research and development projects conducted by HPA scientists are primarily concerned with new methods of treating illness and assessing exposure to chemicals or radiation, ie developing new vaccines and biomarkers of chemical exposure.

Chair, Sir William Stewart, DSc, FRS
Board Members, Dr Barbara Bannister, FRCP; Michael Beaumont, CBE, FCA; James T. Brown; Ian Cranston, FCA; Dr Paul Darragh, TD; Prof. Alan Maryon Davis; Prof. Charles Easmon, CBE; Prof. William Gelletly, OBE; Prof. Andrew Hall; Dr Vanessa Mayatt; John Wyn Owen, CB; Prof. Sandy Primrose
Chief Executive, Justin McCracken

HER MAJESTY'S OFFICERS OF ARMS

COLLEGE OF ARMS (HERALDS' COLLEGE)
Queen Victoria Street, London EC4V 4BT
T 020-7248 2762 F 020-7248 6448
E enquiries@college-of-arms.gov.uk
W www.college-of-arms.gov.uk

The Sovereign's Officers of Arms (Kings, Heralds and Pursuivants of Arms) were first incorporated by Richard III in 1484. The powers vested by the crown in the Earl Marshal (the Duke of Norfolk) with regard to state ceremonial are largely exercised through the college. The college is also the official repository of the arms and pedigrees of English, Welsh, Northern Irish and Commonwealth (except Canadian) families and their descendants, and its records include official copies of the records of the Ulster King of Arms, the originals of which remain in Dublin. The 13 officers of the college specialise in genealogical and heraldic work for their respective clients.

Arms have long been, and still are, granted by letters patent from the Kings of Arms. A right to arms can only be established by the registration in the official records of the College of Arms of a pedigree showing direct male line descent from an ancestor already appearing therein as being entitled to arms, or by making application through the College of Arms for a grant of arms. Grants are made to corporations as well as to individuals.
Earl Marshal, Duke of Norfolk

KINGS OF ARMS
Garter, P. L. Gwynn-Jones, CVO, FSA
Clarenceux, D. H. B. Chesshyre, CVO, FSA
Norroy and Ulster, T. Woodcock, LVO, FSA

HERALDS
Richmond (and Earl Marshal's Secretary), P. L. Dickinson, LVO
York, H. E. Paston-Bedingfeld
Chester, T. H. S. Duke
Lancaster, R. J. B. Noel
Windsor (and Registrar), W. G. Hunt, TD
Somerset, D. V. White

PURSUIVANTS
Rouge Dragon, C. E. A. Cheesman
Bluemantle, M. P. D. O'Donoghue

COURT OF THE LORD LYON
HM New Register House, Edinburgh EH1 3YT
T 0131-556 7255 **F** 0131-557 2148
W www.lyon-court.com

Her Majesty's Officers of Arms in Scotland are officers at the Court of the Lord Lyon (*see* Law Courts and Offices). In addition to ceremonial duties, officers may be consulted by members of the public on heraldic and genealogical matters in a professional capacity. The Lord Lyon is head of the Heraldic Executive and judge of the Court of the Lord Lyon.
Lord Lyon King of Arms, David Sellar, FSA SCOT

HERALDS
Albany, J. A. Spens, MVO, RD, WS
Rothesay, Sir Crispin Agnew of Lochnaw, Bt., QC
Ross, C. J. Burnett, FSA SCOT

PURSUIVANTS
Unicorn, Alastair Campbell of Airds
Carrick, Mrs C. G. W. Roads, MVO, FSA SCOT
Orkney Herald Extraordinary, Sir Malcolm Innes of Edingight, KCVO, WS
Angus Herald Extraordinary, R. O. Blair, LVO, WS
Lyon Clerk and Keeper of Records, Mrs C. G. W. Roads, MVO, FSA SCOT
Procurator-Fiscal, George Way of Plean, SSC
Herald Painter, Mrs Y. Holton
Macer, H. M. Love

HIGHLANDS AND ISLANDS ENTERPRISE

Cowan House, Inverness Retail and Business Park, Inverness IV2 7GF
T 01463-234171 **F** 01463-244469
E info@hient.co.uk **W** www.hie.co.uk

Highlands and Islands Enterprise (HIE) was set up under the Enterprise and New Towns (Scotland) Act 1991. Its role is to design, direct and deliver enterprise development, training and environmental and social projects and services. It focuses on helping high growth businesses, improving regional competitiveness and strengthening communities. HIE's budget for 2008–9 is £91.9m.
Chair, W. Roe
Chief Executive, I. J. R. S. Cumming

HISTORIC ENVIRONMENT ADVISORY COUNCIL FOR SCOTLAND

Longmore House, Salisbury Place, Edinburgh EH9 1SH
T 0131-668 8810 **F** 0131-668 8987
E heacs@scotland.gsi.gov.uk **W** www.heacs.org.uk

The Historic Environment Advisory Council for Scotland, established in 2003, is the advisory body set up to provide Scottish ministers with advice on issues affecting the historic environment and how the functions of the Scottish ministers may be exercised effectively for the benefit of said historic environment. In this context the historic environment means any or all structures and places in Scotland of historical, archaeological or architectural interest or importance.
Chair, Elizabeth Burns, CMG, OBE

HISTORIC ROYAL PALACES

Apartment 39A, Hampton Court Palace, Surrey KT8 9AU
T 0844-482 7777
E operators@hrp.org.uk **W** www.hrp.org.uk

Historic Royal Palaces was established in 1998 as a royal charter body with charitable status and is contracted by the Secretary of State for Culture, Media and Sport to manage the palaces on her behalf. The palaces – the Tower of London, Hampton Court Palace, the Banqueting House, Kensington Palace and Kew Palace – are owned by the Queen on behalf of the nation.

The organisation is governed by a board comprising a chair and ten non-executive trustees. The chief executive is accountable to the board of trustees and ultimately to parliament. Historic Royal Palaces receives no funding from the government or the crown.

TRUSTEES
Chair, Charles Mackay
Appointed by the Queen, Sir Trevor McDonald, OBE; Sir Adrian Montague; Sir Alan Reid, KCVO; Sir Hugh Roberts, KCVO, FSA
Appointed by the Secretary of State, Dawn Austwick, OBE; Bridget Cherry, OBE, FSA; Sue Farr; John Hamer; Malcolm Reading
Ex officio, Gen. Sir Roger Wheeler, GCB, CBE *(Constable of the Tower of London)*

OFFICERS
Chief Executive, Michael Day
Resident Governor, HM Tower of London, Maj.-Gen. Keith Cima

HORSERACE TOTALISATOR BOARD

Westgate House, Tote Park, Chapel Lane, Wigan WN3 4HS
T 0800-666 100
E customercare@totesport.com W www.totesport.com

The Horserace Totalisator Board (the Tote) was established by the Betting, Gaming and Lotteries Act 1963. Its function is to operate totalisators on approved racecourses in Great Britain, and it also provides on and off-course cash and credit offices. Under the Horserace Totalisator and Betting Levy Board Act 1972, it is further empowered to offer bets at starting price (or other bets at fixed odds) on any sporting event, and under the Horserace Totalisator Board Act 1997 to take bets on any event, except the National Lottery. The chair and members of the board are appointed by the Secretary of State for Culture, Media and Sport.

The government made a manifesto commitment March 2001 to sell the Tote to a racing trust to allow it to compete commercially. The necessary legislation for the privatisation of the Tote was passed in 2004 and the government announced on 5 March 2008 that it would look to sell the company on the open market.
Chair (interim), Sir Ian Good
Chief Executive, Trevor Beaumont

HOUSING CORPORATION

Maple House, 149 Tottenham Court Road, London W1T 7BN
T 0845-230 7000 F 020-7393 2111
E enquiries@housingcorp.gsx.gov.uk
W www.housingcorp.gov.uk

Established by parliament in 1964, the Housing Corporation funds new affordable housing and is the statutory regulator for housing associations. Under the Housing Act 1996, the corporation's regulatory role was widened to embrace new types of landlords, in particular local housing companies. The corporation is funded by the Department for Communities and Local Government; the £3.9bn programme of investment for 2006–8 was set to create 84,000 new affordable homes.
Chair, Peter Dixon
Chief Executive, Steve Douglas

HUMAN FERTILISATION AND EMBRYOLOGY AUTHORITY (HFEA)

21 Bloomsbury Street, London WC1B 3HF
T 020-7291 8200 F 020-7291 8201
E admin@hfea.gov.uk W www.hfea.gov.uk

The HFEA was established in 1991 under the Human Fertilisation and Embryology Act 1990. It is the UK's independent regulator tasked with overseeing safe and appropriate practice in fertility treatment and embryo research, including licensing and monitoring centres carrying out IVF, artificial insemination and human embryo research. HFEA also provides a range of detailed information for patients, professionals and government, and maintains a formal register of information about donors, fertility treatments and children born as a result of those treatments.
Chair, Prof. Lisa Jardine, CBE
Chief Executive (interim), Alan Dovan

HUMAN GENETICS COMMISSION

Area 605, Wellington House, 133–155 Waterloo Road, London SE1 8UG
T 020-7972 4351 F 020-7972 4300
E hgc@dh.gsi.gov.uk W www.hgc.gov.uk

The Human Genetics Commission was established in 1999, subsuming three previous advisory committees. Its remit is to give ministers strategic advice on how developments in human genetics will impact on people and healthcare, focusing in particular on the social and ethical implications.
Chair (acting), Sir John Sulston
Members, Prof. Emerita Brenda Almond; Prof. Stephen Bain; Dr Celia Brazell; Prof. Angus Clarke; Prof. Sarah Cunningham-Burley; Dr Paul Darragh; Dr Paul Debenham; Dr Frances Flinter; Ros Gardner; Prof. John Harris; Michael Harrison; Prof. Christopher Higgins; Prof. Lisa Jardine; Alastair Kent; Dr Rosemary Leonard; Alice Maynard; Lola Oni; Dr Christine Patch; Peter Sayers; Dr Rosalind Skinner; Dr Anita Thomas

HUMAN TISSUE AUTHORITY (HTA)

Ground Floor, Finlaison House, 15–17 Furnival Street, London EC4A 1AB
T 020-7211 3400 F 020-7211 3430
E enquiries@hta.gov.uk W www.hta.gov.uk

The HTA was established on 1 April 2005 under the Human Tissue Act 2004, and is sponsored and part-funded by the Department of Health. Its role is to inform the public and Secretary of State for Health about issues within its remit, which include the import, export, storage and use of human bodies and tissue for scheduled purposes, and disposal of human tissue following its use in medical treatment or for scheduled purposes. The HTA is the competent authority under the EU tissues and cells directive for regulating human tissue banking for transplant services.

The HTA also supersedes and extends the role that was previously performed by the now-defunct Unrelated Live Transplant Regulatory Authority (ULTRA) in setting out the circumstances in which live 'transplantable material' (from both related and unrelated donors) will be allowed.
Chair, Shirley Harrison
Chief Executive, Adrian McNeil

IMPERIAL WAR MUSEUM

Lambeth Road, London SE1 6HZ
T 020-7416 5000 F 020-7416 5374
E mail@iwm.org.uk W www.iwm.org.uk

The museum, founded in 1917, illustrates and records all aspects of the two world wars and other military operations involving Britain and the Commonwealth since 1914. It was opened in its present home, formerly Bethlem Royal Hospital, in 1936. The museum is a multi-branch organisation that also includes the Churchill Museum and Cabinet War Rooms in Whitehall; HMS *Belfast* in the Pool of London; Imperial War Museum Duxford in Cambridgeshire; and Imperial War Museum North in Trafford, Manchester.

The total grant-in-aid (including grants for special projects) for 2008–9 is £23.59m.

OFFICERS
Chair of Trustees, Air Chief Marshal Sir Peter Squire, GCB, DFC, AFC, DSc
Director-General, Sir Robert Crawford, CBE
Directors, Richard Ashton *(Imperial War Museum Duxford)*; Jon Card *(Secretary, Finance)*; Jim Forrester *(Imperial War Museum North)*; Angela Godwin *(Public Services)*; Brad King *(HMS Belfast)*; Phil Reed

(Churchill Museum and Cabinet War Rooms); Alan Stoneman *(Corporate Services)*; Mark Whitmore *(Collections)*

INDEPENDENT REVIEW SERVICE FOR THE SOCIAL FUND

4th Floor, Centre City Podium, 5 Hill Street, Birmingham B5 4UB
T 0121-606 2100 F 0121-606 2157
E sfc@irs-review.org.uk W www.irs-review.org.uk

The Social Fund Commissioner is appointed by the Secretary of State for Work and Pensions. The commissioner appoints Social Fund Inspectors, who provide an independent review for customers dissatisfied with decisions made in Jobcentre Plus offices throughout England, Scotland and Wales regarding the grants and loans available from the Discretionary Social Fund.
Social Fund Commissioner, Sir Richard Tilt

INDUSTRIAL INJURIES ADVISORY COUNCIL

6th Floor, The Adelphi, 1–11 John Adam Street, London WC2N 6HT
T 020-7962 8066 F 020-7712 2255
E iiac@dwp.gsi.gov.uk W www.iiac.org.uk

The Industrial Injuries Advisory Council was established under the Social Security Administration Act 1992, with statutory provisions governing its work set out in section 171 of the act. The council consists of 16 members appointed by the Secretary of State for Work and Pensions, and has three roles: to advise on the prescription of diseases; to advise on matters referred to the council by the secretary of state or proposals concerning the Industrial Injuries Disablement Benefit Scheme; and to advise on any other matter relating to industrial injuries benefit or its administration.
Chair, Prof. Keith Palmer

INFORMATION COMMISSIONER'S OFFICE

Wycliffe House, Water Lane, Wilmslow, Cheshire SK9 5AF
T 0845-630 6060 F 01625-524510
E mail@ico.gsi.gov.uk W www.ico.gov.uk

The Information Commissioner's Office is sponsored by the Ministry of Justice and oversees and enforces the Freedom of Information Act 2000 and the Data Protection Act 1998, with the objective of promoting public access to official information and protecting personal information.

The Data Protection Act 1998 sets out rules for the processing of personal information and applies to records held on computers and some paper files. It works in two ways: it dictates that those who record and use personal information (data controllers) must be open about how the information is used and must follow the eight principles of 'good information handling', and it gives individuals certain rights to access their personal information.

The Freedom of Information Act 2000 is designed to help end the culture of unnecessary secrecy and open up the inner workings of the public sector to citizens and businesses. Under the Freedom of Information Act, public authorities must produce a publication scheme that sets out what information the public authority is obliged to publish by law.

The Information Commissioner's Office also enforces and oversees the environmental information regulations, and the privacy and electronic communications regulations.

The Information Commissioner reports annually to parliament on the performance of his functions under the acts and has obligations to assess breaches of the acts.
Information Commissioner, Richard Thomas

INVESTIGATORY POWERS TRIBUNAL

PO Box 33220, London SW1H 9ZQ
T 020-7035 3711 W www.ipt-uk.com

The Investigatory Powers Tribunal replaced the Interception of Communications Tribunal, the Intelligence Services Tribunal, the Security Services Tribunal and the complaints function of the commissioner appointed under the Police Act 1997.

The Regulation of Investigatory Powers Act 2000 (RIPA) provides for a tribunal made up of senior members of the legal profession, independent of the government and appointed by the Queen, to consider all complaints against the intelligence services and those against public authorities in respect of powers covered by RIPA; and to consider proceedings brought under section 7 of the Human Rights Act 1998 against the intelligence services and law enforcement agencies in respect of these powers.
President, Rt. Hon. Lord Justice Mummery
Vice-President, Mr Justice Burton
Members, Sir Richard Gaskell; Sheriff Principal J. McInnes, QC; P. Scott, QC; R. Seabrook, QC
Tribunal Secretary, D. Payne

JOINT NATURE CONSERVATION COMMITTEE

Monkstone House, City Road, Peterborough PE1 1JY
T 01733-562626 F 01733-555948
E communications@jncc.gov.uk W www.jncc.gov.uk

The committee was established under the Environmental Protection Act 1990 and was reconstituted by the Natural Environment and Rural Communities Act 2006. It advises the government and others on UK and international nature conservation issues and disseminates knowledge on these subjects. It establishes common standards for the monitoring of nature conservation and research, and provides guidance to Natural England, Scottish Natural Heritage, the Council for Nature Conservation and the Countryside, and the Countryside Council for Wales.
Chair, Dr Peter Bridgewater
Deputy Chair, Prof. Lynda Warren

LAW COMMISSION

Conquest House, 37–38 John Street, London WC1N 2BQ
T 020-7453 1220 F 020-7453 1297
E chief.executive@lawcommission.gsi.gov.uk
W www.lawcom.gov.uk

The Law Commission was set up under the Law Commissions Act 1965, to make proposals to the government for the examination of the law in England and Wales and for its revision where it is unsuited for modern requirements, obscure, or otherwise unsatisfactory. It recommends to the Lord Chancellor programmes for the examination of different branches of the law and suggests whether the examination should be carried out by the commission itself or by some other body. The commission is also responsible for the

preparation of Consolidation and Statute Law (Repeals) Bills.
Chair, Hon. Mr Justice Etherton
Commissioners, E. J. Cooke; David Hertzell; Dr Jeremy Horder; Kenneth Parker, QC
Chief Executive (interim), W. Arnold

LEARNING AND SKILLS COUNCIL (LSC)

Cheylesmore House, Quinton Road, Coventry CV1 2WT
T 0870-900 6800 F 02476-823675
E info@lsc.gov.uk W www.lsc.gov.uk

The LSC was established in 2001 to replace the Further Education Funding and the Training and Enterprise Councils. It is a non-departmental public body responsible for the planning and funding of post-16 education in colleges, schools and training providers. Its remit is to ensure that high-quality post-16 provision is available to meet the needs of employers, individuals and communities. The LSC operates through a national office based in Coventry and also through local departments, which work to promote the equality of opportunity in the workplace; its budget for 2008–9 is £11.6bn.
Chair, Chris Banks, CBE
Chief Executive, Mark Haysom, CBE

LEGAL SERVICES COMMISSION

85 Gray's Inn Road, London WC1X 8TX
T 020-7759 0000
W www.legalservices.gov.uk,
www.communitylegaladvice.org.uk

The Legal Services Commission was created under the Access to Justice Act 1999 and replaced the Legal Aid Board in April 2000. It is a non-departmental public body which is sponsored by the Ministry of Justice.

The commission is responsible for two schemes. The Community Legal Service funds the delivery of civil legal and advice services, identifies priorities and unmet needs, and develops suppliers and services to meet those needs. The Criminal Defence Service provides free legal advice and representation for people involved in criminal investigations or proceedings.

The commission produces free information leaflets which are available from solicitors' and advisory offices, and from the commission's website.
Chief Executive, Carolyn Regan
Chair, vacant

MENTAL HEALTH ACT COMMISSION (MHAC)

Maid Marian House, 56 Hounds Gate, Nottingham NG1 6BG
T 0115-943 7100 F 0115-943 7101
E chiefexec@mhac.org.uk W www.mhac.org.uk

The MHAC was established in 1983. Its functions are to keep under review the operation of the Mental Health Act 1983; to visit and meet patients detained under the act; to investigate complaints falling within the commission's remit; to operate the 'consent to treatment' safeguards in the Mental Health Act; to publish a biennial report on its activities; to monitor the implementation of the code of practice; and to advise ministers.

The MHAC is comprised of approximately 100 part-time commission members, who are appointed by the Secretary of State for Health.
Chair, Prof. Lord Patel of Bradford
Vice-Chair, Deborah Jenkins, MBE
Chief Executive, Gemma Pearce

MUSEUM OF LONDON

150 London Wall, London EC2Y 5HN
T 0870-444 3852 F 0870-444 3853
E info@museumoflondon.org.uk
W www.museumoflondon.org.uk

The Museum of London illustrates the history of London from prehistoric times to the present day. It opened in 1976 and is based on the amalgamation of the former Guildhall Museum and London Museum. The museum is controlled by a board of governors, appointed (nine each) by the Greater London Authority (GLA) and the City of London Corporation. The museum is currently funded by grants from the GLA and the City of London Corporation. The total grant-in-aid for 2007–8 was £13.6m.
Chair of Board of Governors, Michael Cassidy, CBE
Director, Prof. Jack Lohman

MUSEUMS, LIBRARIES AND ARCHIVES COUNCIL (MLA)

1st Floor, Grosvenor House, 14 Bennetts Hill, Birmingham B2 5RS
T 0121-631 5800 F 0121-631 5825
E info@mla.gov.uk W www.mla.gov.uk

The MLA was launched in April 2000 and is the lead strategic agency for museums, libraries and archives. It works with nine regional agencies and is a non-departmental public body sponsored by the Department for Culture, Media and Sport. The MLA replaced the Museums and Galleries Commission (MGC) and the Library and Information Commission (LIC).
Chair, Mark Wood
Board Members, Geoffrey Bond, OBE; Sarah Carthew; Alex Cunningham; Nick Dodd; Yinnon Ezra, MBE; Helen Forde; John Hicks; Sir Geoffrey Holland; Glen Lawes; Prof. Sara Selwood; John Tarrant; Robert Wand
Chief Executive, Roy Clare

NATIONAL ARMY MUSEUM

Royal Hospital Road, London SW3 4HT
T 020-7730 0717
E info@national-army-museum.ac.uk
W www.national-army-museum.ac.uk

The National Army Museum was established by royal charter in 1960, and covers the history of five centuries of the British Army. It chronicles the campaigns and battles fought over this time as well as the social history and development of the Army, and its impact on Britain and the world. The museum houses a wide array of artefacts, paintings, photographs, uniforms and equipment.
Chair, General Sir Jack Deverell, KCB, OBE
Director, Dr Alan J. Guy

NATIONAL CONSUMER COUNCIL (NCC)

20 Grosvenor Gardens, London SW1W 0DH
T 020-7730 3469 F 020-7730 0191
E info@ncc.org.uk W www.ncc.org.uk

The NCC was set up by the government in 1975 to give an independent voice to consumers in the UK. Its role is to advocate the consumer interest to decision-makers in national and local government, industry and regulatory bodies, business and the professions. It does this through a combination of research and campaigning. The NCC is a non-profit-making company limited by guarantee and is

largely funded by grant-in-aid from the Department for Business, Enterprise and Regulatory Reform, and the Secretary of State for Business, Enterprise and Regulatory Reform appoints the chair and board members. The council is not a consumer advice or complaints body.
Chair, Lord Whitty
Chief Executive, Philip Cullam

NATIONAL ENDOWMENT FOR SCIENCE, TECHNOLOGY AND THE ARTS (NESTA)

1 Plough Place, London EC4A 1DE
T 020-7438 2500 F 020-7438 2501
E nesta@nesta.org.uk W www.nesta.org.uk

NESTA was established under the National Lottery Act 1998 with a £200m endowment from the proceeds of the National Lottery. Its endowment is presently over £300m. NESTA invests in early-stage companies, informs and shapes policy, and delivers practical programmes to enable others to solve future challenges.
Chair, Chris Powell
Chief Executive, Jonathan Kestenbaum

NATIONAL GALLERIES OF SCOTLAND

The Dean Gallery, 73 Belford Road, Edinburgh EH4 3DS
T 0131-624 6200 F 0131-623 7133
E enquiries@nationalgalleries.org W www.nationalgalleries.org

The National Galleries of Scotland comprise the National Gallery of Scotland, the Scottish National Portrait Gallery, the Scottish National Gallery of Modern Art, the Dean Gallery and the Royal Scottish Academy Building. There are also outstations at Paxton House, Berwickshire, and Duff House, Banffshire. Total government grant-in-aid for 2008–9 was forecast at £12.03m.

TRUSTEES
Chair, Sir Brian Ivory, CBE
Trustees, Ian Barr; Richard Burns; Herbert Coutts, MBE; James Dawney; Marc Ellington; James Knox; Ray Macfarlane; Alasdair Morton; Prof. Richard Thomson; Dr Ruth Wishart

OFFICERS
Director-General, John Leighton
Directors, M. Clarke *(National Gallery of Scotland)*; Dr Simon Groom *(Scottish National Gallery of Modern Art and Dean Gallery)*; J. Holloway *(Scottish National Portrait Gallery)*

NATIONAL GALLERY

Trafalgar Square, London WC2N 5DN
T 020-7747 2885 F 020-7747 2423
W www.nationalgallery.org.uk

The National Gallery, which houses a permanent collection of western European painting from the 13th to the 20th century, was founded in 1824, following a parliamentary grant of £60,000 for the purchase and exhibition of the Angerstein collection of pictures. The present site was first occupied in 1838; an extension to the north of the building with a public entrance in Orange Street was opened in 1975; the Sainsbury wing was opened in 1991; and the Getty Entrance opened off Trafalgar Square at the east end of the main building in 2004. Total government grant-in-aid for 2008–9 is £26.87m.

BOARD OF TRUSTEES
Chair, M. Getty
Trustees, S. Burke; Prof. D. Ekserdjian; J. Fenton; Lady Heseltine; Prof. Dame J. Higgins; M. Hintze; Lord Kerr of Kinlochard; Prof. M. King; P. Lankester; J. Lessore; Lady Normanby; R. Sondhi

OFFICERS
Director, Dr N. Penny
Director of Collections, Dr S. Foister
Director of Communications, C. Gough
Director of Conservation, M. H. Wyld, CBE
Director of Education, C. Wiggins
Director of Scientific Research, Dr A. Roy
Senior Curator, D. Jaffé

NATIONAL HERITAGE MEMORIAL FUND

7 Holbein Place, London SW1W 8NR
T 020-7591 6000 E enquire@hlf.org.uk
W www.nhmf.org.uk

The National Heritage Memorial Fund was set up under the National Heritage Act 1980 in memory of people who have given their lives for the United Kingdom. The fund provides grants to organisations based in the UK, mainly so they can buy items of outstanding interest and of importance to the national heritage. These must either be at risk or have a memorial character. The fund is administered by a chair and 14 trustees who are appointed by the prime minister.

The National Heritage Memorial Fund receives an annual grant from the Department for Culture, Media and Sport. Under the the National Lottery etc Act 1993 the trustees of the fund became responsible for the distribution of funds for both the National Heritage Memorial Fund and the Heritage Lottery Fund.
Chair, Jenny Abramsky
Head, Eilish McGuinness

NATIONAL LIBRARY OF SCOTLAND

George IV Bridge, Edinburgh EH1 1EW
T 0131-623 3700 F 0131-623 3701
E enquiries@nls.uk W www.nls.uk

The library, which was founded as the Advocates' Library in 1682, became the National Library of Scotland (NLS) in 1925. It is funded by the Scottish government. It contains about 14 million books and pamphlets, two million maps, 20,000 current periodicals, 350 newspaper titles and 120,000 manuscripts, including the recently acquired John Murray Archive. It has an unrivalled Scottish collection as well as online catalogues and digital resources which can be accessed through the NLS website.

Material can be consulted in the reading rooms, which are open to anyone with a valid reader's ticket.
Chair of the Trustees, Prof. Michael Anderson, OBE, FBA, FRSE
National Librarian and Secretary to the Trustees, M. Wade
Directors, C. Newton *(Collection Development)*; D. Campbell *(Corporate Services)*; G. Hunt *(Customer Services)*; T. Wishart *(Development)*; A. Miller *(Strategy and Communications)*

NATIONAL LIBRARY OF WALES/LLYFRGELL GENEDLAETHOL CYMRU

Aberystwyth SY23 3BU
T 01970-632800 **F** 01970-615709
E holi@llgc.org.uk **W** www.llgc.org.uk

The National Library of Wales was founded by royal charter in 1907, and is funded by the National Assembly for Wales. It contains about four million printed books, 40,000 manuscripts, four million deeds and documents, numerous maps, prints and drawings, and a sound and moving image collection. It specialises in manuscripts and books relating to Wales and the Celtic peoples. It is the repository for pre-1858 Welsh probate records, manorial records and tithe documents, and certain legal records. Admission is by reader's ticket to the reading rooms but entry to the exhibition programme is free.

President, Rt. Hon. Dafydd Wigley
Heads of Departments, G. Jenkins *(Collection Services)*; M. W. Mainwaring *(Corporate Services)*; Dr W. R. M. Griffiths *(Public Services)*
Librarian, A. M. W. Green

NATIONAL LOTTERY COMMISSION

101 Wigmore Street, London W1U 1QU
T 0845-712 5596 **F** 020-7016 3401
E publicaffairs@natlotcomm.gov.uk
W www.natlotcomm.gov.uk

The National Lottery Commission replaced the Office of the National Lottery (OFLOT) in 1999 under the National Lottery Act 1998. The commission is responsible for the granting, varying and enforcing of licences to run the National Lottery. It also runs the competition to award the next licence. Its duties are to ensure that the National Lottery is run with all due propriety, that the interests of players are protected, and, subject to these two objectives, that returns to the good causes are maximised. The commission does not have a role in the distribution of funds to good causes, this is undertaken by 16 distributors, visit www.lotteryfunding.org.uk for further information. Gaming and lotteries in the UK are officially regulated and may only be run by licensed operators or in licensed premises.

The Department of Culture, Media and Sport (DCMS) is responsible for gaming and lottery policy and laws. Empowered by the National Lottery Act 1993 (as amended), the DCMS directs the National Lottery Commission, who in turn regulates Camelot, the lottery operator. Camelot, a private company wholly owned by five shareholders, was granted a third licence to run the Lottery from 1 February 2009 for ten years.

Chair, Anne Wright, CBE
Chief Executive, Mark Harris

NATIONAL MARITIME MUSEUM

Park Row, Greenwich, London SE10 9NF
T 020-8858 4422 **F** 020-8312 6632
W www.nmm.ac.uk

Established in 1934, the National Maritime Museum provides information on the maritime history of Great Britain and is the largest institution of its kind in the world, with over two million items in its collections related to searfaring, navigation and astronomy. The museum is in three groups of buildings in Greenwich Park: the main building, the Queen's House (built by Inigo Jones, 1616–35) and the Royal Observatory (including Christopher Wren's Flamsteed House). In 1999 a £20m Heritage Lottery-supported project opened 16 new galleries in a glazed courtyard in the museum's west wing.

Director, Kevin Fewster
Chair, Lord Sterling of Plaistow, GCVO, CBE

NATIONAL MUSEUMS AND GALLERIES NORTHERN IRELAND

Botanic Gardens, Belfast BT9 5AB
T 028-9038 3000 **F** 028-9038 3006
W www.magni.org.uk

The organisation of National Museums and Galleries of Northern Ireland was established under the Museums and Galleries (Northern Ireland) Order in 1998 and includes the Ulster Museum with Armagh Museum, the Ulster Folk and Transport Museum, the Ulster American Folk Park and W5 at Odyssey (a wholly owned subsidiary).

Legislation requires National Museums and Galleries of Northern Ireland's board of trustees to care for, preserve and add to the collections; ensure that the collections are exhibited to the public; ensure that the significance of the collections is interpreted; and promote the awareness, appreciation and understanding of the public in relation to art, history and science, to the culture and way of life of the people and to the migration and settlement of people.

Chair, Margaret Elliott, CBE
Trustees, Linda Beers; Lt-Col. (retd) Reginald Harvey Bickers, OBE; Patricia Flanagan; Dan Harvey, OBE; Dame Geraldine Keegan; William Montgomery; Sean Neeson; Wendy Osborne, OBE; Thomas Shaw, CBE; Dr Alastair Walker
Chief Executive, Tim Cooke

NATIONAL MUSEUMS LIVERPOOL

127 Dale Street, Liverpool L2 2JH
T 0151-207 0001 **F** 0151-478 4790
W www.liverpoolmuseums.org.uk

The board of trustees of the National Museums Liverpool (formerly National Museums and Galleries on Merseyside) is responsible for the World Museum Liverpool, the Merseyside Maritime Museum, the Museum of Liverpool, the Lady Lever Art Gallery, the Walker Art Gallery, Sudley House, the National Conservation Centre and the International Slavery Museum. Total government grant-in-aid for 2007–8 was £21.5m.

Chair of the Board of Trustees, Loyd Grossman, OBE
Director, Dr David Fleming
Keeper of Art Galleries, R. King
Keeper, World Museum Liverpool, J. Millard
Keeper, Merseyside Maritime Museum, T. Tibbles
Keeper, Museum of Liverpool, J. Dugdale
Head of Collections Management, National Conservation Centre, Sally Ann Yates
Head of International Slavery Museum, Dr Richard Benjamin

NATIONAL MUSEUMS SCOTLAND

Chambers Street, Edinburgh EH1 1JF
T 0131-225 7534 **E** info@nms.ac.uk **W** www.nms.ac.uk

National Museums Scotland provides advice and expertise to the museums community across Scotland, and comprise the National Museum of Scotland, the National War Museum, the National Museum of Rural Life, the National

Museum of Flight, and the the National Museum of Costume. Total grant-in-aid funding from the Scottish government for 2008–9 is £21.078m.

Trustees are appointed by the Minister for Tourism, Culture and Sport for a term of four years, and may serve a second term.

Chair, Sir Angus Grossart, CBE, LLD, DLITT

Trustees, James Fiddes, OBE, FRICS; Lesley Hart, MBE; Michael Kirwan, FCA; Prof. Michael Lynch, FRSE, FSA (SCOT); Neena Mahal; Sir Neil McIntosh, CBE; Prof. Malcolm McLeod, CBE, FRSE; Prof. Stuart Monro, OBE; Ian Ritchie, CBE, FRENG, FRSE; Sir John Ward, CBE, FRSE, FRSA; Iain Watt

Director, Dr Gordon Rintoul

NATIONAL MUSEUM WALES – AMGUEDDFA CYMRU

Cathays Park, Cardiff CF10 3NP
T 029-2039 7951 F 029-2057 3321
E post@museumwales.ac.uk W www.museumwales.ac.uk

National Museum Wales – Amgueddfa Cymru aims to provide a complete illustration of the geology, mineralogy, zoology, botany, ethnography, archaeology, art, history and special industries of Wales. It is comprised of the National Museum Cardiff; St Fagans National History Museum; Big Pit – National Coal Museum, Blaenafon; the National Roman Legion Museum, Caerleon; the National Slate Museum, Llanberis; the National Wool Museum, Dre-fach Felindre; and the National Waterfront Museum, Swansea. Total funding from the Welsh Assembly government for 2007–8 was £24.7m.

President, Paul E. Loveluck, CBE

Vice-President, Elisabeth Elias

Director-General, Michael Houlihan

Trustees, Dr Haydn Edwards; Miriam Hazel Griffiths; Dr Iolo ap Gwynn; Prof. Colin L. Jones, OBE; Emeritus Prof. Richard G. W. Jones; Prof. J. W. Last, CBE; Christina Macaulay; Peter W. Morgan; Prof. Jonathan Osmond; Gareth Williams; H. R. C. Williams; Dr Brian Willott, CB; Rhiannon Wyn Hughes, MBE

NATIONAL PORTRAIT GALLERY

St Martin's Place, London WC2H 0HE
T 020-7306 0055 F 020-7306 0056
W www.npg.org.uk

The National Portrait Gallery was formed after a grant was made in 1856 to form a gallery of the portraits of the most eminent persons in British history. The present building was opened in 1896 and the Ondaatje Wing (including a new Balcony Gallery, Tudor Gallery, IT Gallery, lecture theatre and roof-top restaurant) opened in May 2000. There are three regional partnerships displaying portraits at Montacute House, Beningbrough Hall and Bodelwyddan Castle. Total government grant-in-aid for 2008–9 is £7.693m.

BOARD OF TRUSTEES

Chair, Prof. David Cannadine, FBA, FRSL

Trustees, Rt. Hon. Baroness Ashton of Upholland; Zeinab Badawi; Sir Nicholas Blake, QC; Prof. R. Boucher, CBE, FRENG; Marchioness of Douro, OBE; Amelia Fawcett, CBE; Flora Fraser; Sir Nicholas Grimshaw, CBE, PRA; Prof. Ludmilla Jordanova; David Mach, RA; Sir Christopher Ondaatje, CBE, OC; David Ross; Prof. Sara Selwood; Alexandra Shulman, OBE; Sir John Weston, KCMG

Director, Sandy Nairne

NATURAL ENGLAND

1 East Parade, Sheffield S1 2ET
T 0845-600 3078
E enquiries@naturalengland.org.uk
W www.naturalengland.org.uk

Natural England was established on 1 October 2006 after the Natural Environment and Rural Communities Act received royal assent in March 2006. The organisation encompasses three previous bodies: English Nature, the environmental land management elements of the Rural Development Service and the Countryside Agency's landscape, access and recreation division. It is responsible for enhancing biodiversity, landscapes and wildlife in rural, urban, coastal and marine areas; promoting access, recreation and public wellbeing; designating sites of special scientific interest, national parks and areas of outstanding natural beauty; managing national nature reserves; enforcing associated regulations; and contributing to the way natural resources are managed.

Chief Executive, Dr Helen Phillips

NATURAL HISTORY MUSEUM

Cromwell Road, London SW7 5BD
T 020-7942 5000 W www.nhm.ac.uk

The Natural History Museum originates from the natural history departments of the British Museum, which grew extensively during the 19th century; in 1860 it was agreed that the natural history collections should be separated from the British Museum's collections of books, manuscripts and antiquities. Part of the site of the 1862 International Exhibition in South Kensington was acquired for the new museum, and the museum opened to the public in 1881. In 1963 the Natural History Museum became completely independent with its own board of trustees. The Natural History Museum at Tring, bequeathed by the second Lord Rothschild, has formed part of the museum since 1937. The Geological Museum merged with the Natural History Museum in 1985. Total government grant-in-aid for 2007–8 was £43.4m.

Trustees, Daniel Alexander, QC; Prof. Sir Roy Anderson, FRS; Louise Charlton; Prof. David Drewry; Prof. Dianne Edwards, CBE, FRS; Prof Alex Halliday, FRS; Ian J. Henderson, CBE; Dr Derek Langslow, CBE; Prof. Jacquie McGlade; Prof Georgina Mace, CBE, FRS; Sir David Omand, GCB, KCB; *Chair,* Oliver Stocken

SENIOR STAFF

Director, Dr Michael Dixon
Director of Estates and Services, David Sanders
Director of Finance, Neil Greenwood
Director of Human Resources, Paul Brereton
Director, Natural History Museum at Tring, Teresa Wild
Director of Public Engagement Group, Sharon Ament
Director of Science, Richard Lane
Head of Audit and Review, David Thorpe
Head of Library and Information Services, Graham Higley
Keeper of Botany, Dr Johannes Vogel
Keeper of Entomology, Dr Malcolm Scoble
Keeper of Mineralogy, Dr Andy Fleet
Keeper of Palaeontology, Prof. Norman MacLeod
Keeper of Zoology, Prof. Phil Rainbow
Museum Manager, Ian Jenkinson

NHS PAY REVIEW BODY

6th Floor, Kingsgate House, 66–74 Victoria Street, London SW1E 6SW
T 020-7215 4453 F 020-7215 4445
W www.ome.uk.com

The Review Body for Nurses and Allied Health Professions was set up in 1983, and following the Agenda for Change in 2004 the body changed its name to the Review Body for Nursing and Other Health Professions. It was renamed the NHS Pay Review Body in July 2007 to recognise its broader staff remit. It advises the prime minister and the Secretary of State for Health, and ministers of the Scottish government, Welsh Assembly and Northern Ireland Assembly on the remuneration of nursing staff and other health professions employed in the National Health Service, which is currently over a million people.
Chair, Prof. Gillian Morris
Members, Philip Ashmore; Lucinda Bolton; Prof. Richard Disney; John Galbraith; Wilma MacPherson, CBE; Ian McKay; Sharon Whitlam

NORTHERN IRELAND HUMAN RIGHTS COMMISSION

Temple Court, 39 North Street, Belfast BT1 1NA
T 028-9024 3987 Textphone 028-9024 9066
F 028-9024 7844 E information@nihrc.org
W www.nihrc.org

The Northern Ireland Human Rights Commission was set up in March 1999. Its main functions are to keep under review the law and practice relating to human rights in Northern Ireland, to advise the government and to promote an awareness of human rights in Northern Ireland. It can also take cases to court. The members of the commission are appointed by the Secretary of State for Northern Ireland.
Chief Commissioner, Prof. Monica McWilliams
Commissioners, Jonathan Bell; Thomas Duncan; Prof. Colin Harvey; Alan Henry; Ann Hope; Colin Larkin; Eamonn O'Neill; Geraldine Rice; Lady Daphne Trimble
Chief Executive, Peter O'Neill

NORTHERN LIGHTHOUSE BOARD

84 George Street, Edinburgh EH2 3DA
T 0131-473 3100 F 0131-220 2093
E enquiries@nlb.org.uk W www.nlb.org.uk

The Northern Lighthouse Board is the general lighthouse authority for Scotland and the Isle of Man and owes its origin to an act of parliament passed in 1786. At present there are 19 commissioners who operate under the Merchant Shipping Act 1995.

The commissioners control 209 lighthouses, many lighted and unlighted buoys, a DGPS (differential global positioning system) station and an ELORAN (long-range navigation) system. *See also* Transport.
Chair, Capt. George Sutherland
Commissioners, Lord Advocate; Solicitor-General for Scotland; Lord Provosts of Edinburgh, Glasgow and Aberdeen; Convener of Highland Council; Convener of Argyll and Bute Council; Sheriffs-Principal of North Strathclyde, Tayside, Central and Fife, Grampian, Highlands and Islands, South Strathclyde, Dumfries and Galloway, Lothians and Borders and Glasgow and Strathkelvin; Capt. Mike Close Dr Andrew Cubie, CBE, FRSE; Robert Quayle; John Ross; Alistair Whyte
Chief Executive, Roger Lockwood, CB

OFFICE OF COMMUNICATIONS (OFCOM)

Riverside House, 2A Southwark Bridge Road, London SE1 9HA
T 0300-123 3000 F 0300-123 0811
E contact@ofcom.org.uk W www.ofcom.org.uk

OFCOM was established in 2003 under the Office of Communications Act 2002 as the independent regulator and competition authority for the UK communications industries with responsibility for television, radio, telecommunications and wireless communications services. It merged the functions of five regulatory bodies: the Independent Television Commission (ITC), the Broadcasting Standards Commission (BSC), the Office of Telecommunications (OFTEL), the Radio Authority (RAu) and the Radiocommunications Agency (RA).
Chief Executive, Ed Richards
Chair, David Currie
Deputy Chair, Philip Graf, CBE
Board Members, Millie Banerjee, CBE; Colette Bowe; Tim Gardham; Mike McTighe; Philip Rutnam

OFFICE OF MANPOWER ECONOMICS (OME)

6th Floor, Kingsgate House, 66–74 Victoria Street, London SW1E 6SW
T 020-7215 8253 F 020-7215 4445
W www.ome.uk.com

The OME was set up in 1971. It is an independent non-statutory organisation which is responsible for servicing independent review bodies which advise on the pay of various public service groups, the Police Negotiating Board and the Police Advisory Board for England and Wales. The OME is also responsible for servicing *ad hoc* bodies of inquiry and for undertaking research into pay and associated matters as requested by the government.
OME Director, Ian Jones
Director, National Health Service Pay Review Body Secretariat, Research and Analysis Group and OME Deputy Director, Margaret McEvoy
Director, Armed Forces' and Prison Service Secretariats, Christine Haworth
Director, Doctors and Dentists and Senior Salaries Secretariats, Keith Masson
Director, School Teachers', Police Negotiating Board and Police Advisory Board for England and Wales Secretariats, David Wilson

PARADES COMMISSION

Windsor House, 9–15 Bedford Street, Belfast BT2 7EL
T 028-9089 5900 F 028-9032 2988
E info@paradescommission.com
W www.paradescommission.org

The Parades Commission was set up under the Public Processions (Northern Ireland) Act 1998. Its function is to encourage and facilitate local accommodation on contentious parades; where this is not possible, the commission is empowered to make legal determinations about such parades, which may include imposing conditions on aspects of the notified parade (such as restrictions on routes/areas and exclusion of certain groups with a record of bad behaviour).

The chair and members are appointed by the Secretary of State for Northern Ireland; the membership must, as far as is practicable, be representative of the community in Northern Ireland.

Chair, Roger Poole
Vice-Chair, Anne Monaghan
Members, Kelly Andrews; Dr Joe Hendron; Vilma Patterson, MBE; Alison Scott-McKinley

PAROLE BOARD FOR ENGLAND AND WALES

Grenadier House, 99–105 Horseferry Road, London SW1P 2DX
T 0845-251 2220 F 0845-251 2221
W www.paroleboard.gov.uk

The Parole Board was established under the Criminal Justice Act 1967 and became an independent executive non-departmental public body under the Criminal Justice and Public Order Act 1994. It is the body that protects the public by making risk assessments about prisoners to decide who may safely be released into the community and who must remain in, or be returned to, custody. Board decisions are taken at two main types of panels of up to of three members: 'paper panels' for the vast majority of cases, or oral hearings for finely balanced decisions concerning prisoners serving life or on extended sentences.

Chair, Prof. Sir Duncan Nichol, CBE
Chief Executive, Christine Glenn

PAROLE BOARD FOR SCOTLAND

Saughton House, Broomhouse Drive, Edinburgh EH11 3XD
T 0131-244 8373 F 0131-244 6974
W www.scottishparoleboard.gov.uk

The board directs and advises the Scottish ministers on the release of prisoners on licence, and related matters.

Chair, Prof. Sandy Cameron
Vice-Chair, Sheriff Fiona Reith

PENSION PROTECTION FUND (PPF)

Knollys House, 17 Addiscombe Road, Croydon CR0 6SR
T 0845-600 2541 F 020-8633 4903
E information@ppf.gsi.gov.uk
W www.pensionprotectionfund.org.uk

The PPF became operational in 2005. It was established to pay compensation to members of eligible defined-benefit pension schemes where a qualifying insolvency event in relation to the employer occurs, or where there is a lack of sufficient assets in the pension scheme. The PPF is also responsible for the Fraud Compensation Fund (which provides compensation to occupational pension schemes that suffer a loss that can be attributed to dishonesty). The chair and board of the PPF are appointed by, and accountable to, the Secretary of State for Work and Pensions, and are responsible for paying compensation, calculating annual levies (which help fund the PPF), and setting and overseeing investment strategy.

Chair, Lawrence Churchill
Chief Executive, Partha Dasgupta

PENSIONS REGULATOR

Napier House, Trafalgar Place, Brighton BN1 4DW
T 0870-606 3636 F 0870-241 1144
E customersupport@thepensionsregulator.gov.uk
W www.thepensionsregulator.gov.uk

The Pensions Regulator was established in 2005 as the regulator of work-based pensions in the UK, replacing the Occupational Pensions Regulatory Authority (OPRA). It aims to protect the benefits of occupational and personal pension scheme members, promote good administration, and reduce the risk of situations leading to claims on the Pension Protection Fund. The regulator's approach is risk-based, focusing on education and enablement, with enforcement where appropriate. The regulator is able to collect detailed scheme information, issue improvement notices and third-party notices, disqualify trustees deemed unfit to carry out their duties, appoint independent trustees, direct pension schemes as to how to calculate their liabilities, and issue a contribution notice or financial support direction.

Chair, David Norgrove
Chief Executive, Tony Hobman

POLICE ADVISORY BOARD FOR ENGLAND AND WALES

6th Floor, Kingsgate House, 66–74 Victoria Street, London SW1E 6SW
T 020-7215 8101 F 020-7215 4445
W www.ome.uk.com

The Police Advisory Board for England and Wales was established in 1965 and provides advice to the home secretary on general questions affecting the police in England and Wales. It also considers draft regulations which the secretary of state proposes to make with respect to matters other than hours of duty, leave, pay and allowances or the issue, use and return of police clothing, personal equipment and other effects.

Independent Chair, John Randall
Independent Deputy Chair, Prof. Gillian Morris

POLICE NEGOTIATING BOARD (PNB)

6h Floor, Kingsgate House, 66–74 Victoria Street, London SW1E 6SW
T 020-7215 8101 F 020-7215 4445
W www.ome.uk.com

The PNB was established in 1980 to negotiate pay, allowances, hours of duty, leave and pensions of United Kingdom police officers and to make recommendations on these matters to the Secretary of State for Home Affairs, Northern Ireland secretary, and Scottish ministers.

Independent Chair, John Randall
Independent Deputy Chair, Prof. Gillian Morris

PRISON SERVICE PAY REVIEW BODY (PSPRB)

6th Floor, Kingsgate House, 66–74 Victoria Street, London SW1E 6SW
T 020-7215 8253 F 020-7215 4445
W www.ome.uk.com

The PSPRB was set up in 2001. It makes independent recommendations on the pay of prison governors, operational managers, prison officers and related grades for the Prison Service in England and Wales and for the Northern Ireland Prison Service.

Chair, Jerry Cope
Members, Dr Henrietta Campbell; Richard Childs, QPM; Bronwen Curtis; John Davies; Joseph Magee; Dr Peter Riach

REGIONAL DEVELOPMENT AGENCIES (RDAS)

Broadway House, Tothill Street, London SW1H 9NQ
T 020-7222 8180 F 020-7222 8182
E natsec@rda-secretariat.com
W www.englandsrdas.com

RDAs were established to help the English regions improve their relative economic performance and reduce social and economic disparities within and between regions. Their five statutory objectives are to further economic development and regeneration; to promote business efficiency and competitiveness; to promote employment; to enhance the development and application of skills relevant to employment; and to contribute to sustainable development. There are nine RDAs in England, and they are financed through a single fund provided by contributing government departments (BERR, DCSF, DIUS, DEFRA and DCMS). In 2007–8 the RDA's budget was £2.9bn, in 2008–9 it is £2.2bn.

RDA REGIONS

NORTH WEST: PO Box 37, Renaissance House, Centre Park, Warrington WA1 1XB T 01925-400100
Chair, Bryan Gray, MBE

YORKSHIRE: Victoria House, 2 Victoria Place, Leeds LS11 5AE T 0113-394 9600
Chair, Terry Hodgkinson

NORTH EAST: Stella House, Goldcrest Way, Newburn Riverside, Newcastle upon Tyne NE15 8NY T 0191-229 6200
Chair, Margaret Fay

WEST MIDLANDS: 3 Priestley Wharf, Holt Street, Aston Science Park, Birmingham B7 4BN T 0121-380 3500
Chair, Nick Paul

EAST MIDLANDS: Apex Court, City Link, Nottingham NG2 4LA T 0115-988 8300
Chair, Dr Bryan Jackson

EAST OF ENGLAND: The Business Centre, Station Road, Histon, Cambridge CB4 9LQ T 01223-713900
Chair, Richard Ellis

SOUTH WEST: Sterling House, Dix's Field, Exeter EX1 1QA T 01392-214747
Chair, Juliet Williams

LONDON: Palestra, 197 Blackfriars Road, London SE1 8AA T 020-7593 8700
Chair (interim), Harvey McGrath

SOUTH EAST: Cross Lanes, Guildford GU1 1YA T 01483-484200
Chair, Jim Braithwaite

REGISTRAR OF PUBLIC LENDING RIGHT

Richard House, Sorbonne Close, Stockton on Tees TS17 6DA
T 01642-604699 F 01642-615641
E authorservices@plr.uk.com W www.plr.uk.com

Under the Public Lending Right system, in operation since 1983, payment is made from public funds to authors whose books are lent out from public libraries. Payment is made once a year and the amount each author receives is proportionate to the number of times (established from a sample) that each registered book has been lent out during the previous year. The registrar of PLR, who is appointed by the Secretary of State for Culture, Media and Sport, compiles the register of authors and books. Authors resident in all EU countries are eligible to apply. (The term 'author' covers writers, illustrators, translators, and some editors/compilers.)

A payment of 5.98 pence was made in 2007–8 for each estimated loan of a registered book, up to a top limit of £6,600 for the books of any one registered author; the money for loans above this level is used to augment the remaining PLR payments. In 2008 the sum of £6.66m was paid out to 23,942 registered authors and assignees as the annual payment of PLR.
Registrar, Dr J. G. Parker
Chair of Advisory Committee, S. Brett

REVIEW BODY ON DOCTORS' AND DENTISTS' REMUNERATION

6th Floor, Kingsgate House, 66–74 Victoria Street, London SW1E 6SW
T 020-7215 8407 F 020-7215 4445
W www.ome.uk.com

The Review Body on Doctors' and Dentists' Remuneration was set up in 1971. It advises the prime minister,the Secretaries of State for Health, Scotland and Wales, and the Minister for Health, Northern Ireland on the remuneration of doctors and dentists taking any part in the National Health Service.
Chair, Ronald Amy, OBE
Members, Prof. John Beath; Dr Margaret Collingwood, TD; Katrina Easterling; David Grafton; Sally Smedley; Prof. Alasdair Smith; David Williamson

ROYAL AIR FORCE MUSEUM

Grahame Park Way, London NW9 5LL
T 020-8205 2266 F 020-8200 1751
E london@rafmuseum.org W www.rafmuseum.org

The museum has two sites, one at the former airfield at Hendon and the second at Cosford, in the West Midlands, both of which illustrate the development of aviation from before the Wright brothers to the present-day RAF with over 100 aircraft, as well as artefacts, aviation memorabilia, fine art and photographs. Total government grant-in-aid for 2006–7, provided by the Ministry of Defence, was £6.5m.
Director-General, Dr M. A. Fopp

ROYAL BOTANIC GARDEN EDINBURGH (RBGE)

20A Inverleith Row, Edinburgh EH3 5LR
T 0131-552 7171 F 0131-248 2901
W www.rbge.org.uk

The RBGE originated as the Physic Garden, established in 1670 beside the Palace of Holyroodhouse. The garden moved to its present 28-hectare site at Inverleith, Edinburgh, in 1821. There are also three regional gardens: Benmore Botanic Garden, near Dunoon, Argyll; Logan Botanic Garden, near Stranraer, Wigtownshire; and Dawyck Botanic Garden, near Stobo, Peeblesshire. Since 1986 RBGE has been administered by a board of trustees established under the National Heritage (Scotland) Act 1985. It receives an annual grant from the Scottish government's Rural and Environmental Research and Analysis Directorate.

The RBGE is an international centre for scientific research on plant diversity and for horticulture education and conservation. It has an extensive library, a herbarium

with almost three million preserved plant specimens, and over 15,000 species in the living collections.
Chair of the Board of Trustees, Sir George Mathewson, CBE, LLD, FRSE
Regius Keeper, Prof. Stephen Blackmore, FRSE

ROYAL BOTANIC GARDENS (RBG) KEW

Richmond, Surrey TW9 3AB
T 020-8332 5655 F 020-8332 5197
Wakehurst Place, Ardingly, W. Sussex RH17 6TN
T 01444-89000 F 01444-894069
E info@kew.org W www.kew.org

The Royal Botanic Gardens (RBG) Kew were originally laid out as a private garden for Kew House for George III's mother, Princess Augusta, in 1759. The gardens were much enlarged in the 19th century, notably by the inclusion of the grounds of the former Richmond Lodge. In 1965 the garden at Wakehurst Place was acquired; it is owned by the National Trust and managed by RBG Kew. Under the National Heritage Act 1983 a board of trustees was set up to administer the gardens, which in 1984 became an independent body supported by grant-in-aid from the Department of Environment, Food and Rural Affairs.

The functions of RBG Kew are to carry out research into plant sciences, to disseminate knowledge about plants and to provide the public with the opportunity to gain knowledge and enjoyment from the gardens' collections. There are extensive national reference collections of living and preserved plants and a comprehensive library and archive. The main emphasis is on plant conservation and biodiversity; Wakehurst Place houses the Millennium Seed Bank, which is the largest *ex situ* conservation project ever conceived – its aim is to acquire seed from ten per cent of Earth's wild plant species by 2010.

BOARD OF TRUSTEES
Chair, Lord Selborne
Members, Marcus Agius; Tanya Burman; Andrew Cahn; Richard Deverell; Prof. Jonathan Drori, CBE; Prof. Charles Godfray; Dr Sandy Harrison; Richard Lapthorne, CBE; Prof. Sir William Stewart
Director, Prof. Stephen Hopper

ROYAL COMMISSION ON ENVIRONMENTAL POLLUTION

Room 108, 55 Whitehall, c/o 3–8 Whitehall Place, London SW1A 2HH
T 020-7270 8159 F 020-7270 8303
E enquiries@rcep.org.uk W www.rcep.org.uk

The commission was set up in 1970 to advise on national and international matters concerning the pollution of the environment. The commission's advice is mainly in the form of reports which are the outcome of studies, the most recent of which relates to the urban environment. Members are appointed by the Queen on the advice of the prime minister.
Chair, Prof. Sir John Lawton, CBE, FRS
Members, Prof. Nicholas Cumpsty, FRENG; Prof. Michael H. Depledge; Dr Paul Ekins; Dr I. Graham-Bryce, CBE, FRSE; Prof. Stephen Holgate, FRCP; Prof. J. Jowell, QC; Prof. Peter Liss; Prof. Susan Owens, OBE; Prof. Judith Petts; Prof. S. Rayner; John Speirs, CBE, LVO; Prof. Janet Sprent, OBE, FRSE; Prof. Lynda Warren

ROYAL COMMISSION ON THE ANCIENT AND HISTORICAL MONUMENTS OF SCOTLAND

John Sinclair House, 16 Bernard Terrace, Edinburgh EH8 9NX
T 0131-662 1456 F 0131-662 1477
E info@rcahms.gov.uk W www.rcahms.gov.uk

The Royal Commission on the Ancient and Historical Monuments of Scotland (RCAHMS) was established by a royal warrant in 1908, which was revised in 1992, and is appointed to provide for the survey and recording of ancient and historical monuments connected with the culture, civilisation and conditions of life of the people in Scotland from the earliest times. It is funded by the Scottish government. More than 4.5 million items, including photographs, maps, drawings and documents, are available through the search room, and online databases provide access to 100,000 images and information on 275,000 buildings and sites. RCAHMS also looks after Scotland's national collection of historical aerial photography.
Chair, Prof. John Hume, OBE, FSA (SCOT)
Commissioners, Kate Byrne; Mark Hopton, FSA (SCOT); Prof. John Hunter, FSA, FSA (SCOT); Prof. Angus Macdonald, FSA (SCOT); Gordon Masterton; Prof. Christopher Morris, FSA, FRSE, FRSA; Dr Jane Murray, FSA (SCOT); Dr Stana Nenadic, FSA (SCOT)
Chief Executive, Diana Murray, FSA, FSA (SCOT)

ROYAL COMMISSION ON THE ANCIENT AND HISTORICAL MONUMENTS OF WALES

Crown Building, Plas Crug, Aberystwyth SY23 1NJ
T 01970-621200 F 01970-627701
E nmr.wales@rcahmw.gov.uk W www.rcahmw.gov.uk

The Royal Commission was established in 1908 and is currently empowered by a royal warrant of 2001 to survey, record, publish and maintain a database of ancient, historical and maritime sites and structures, and landscapes, in Wales. The commission is funded by the National Assembly for Wales and is also responsible for the National Monuments Record of Wales, which is open daily for public reference and has a public enquiry service. The commission is responsible for supplying archaeological information to Ordnance Survey, for the coordination of archaeological aerial photography in Wales, and for sponsorship of the regional Sites and Monuments Records.
Chair, Prof. Ralph A. Griffiths, DLITT, FRHISTS
Vice-Chair, Dr Llinos Smith, FRHISTS
Commissioners, Prof. Antony D. Carr, FSA, FRHISTS; Mrs A. Eastham; Neil Harries; John W. Lloyd, CB; Jonathan Matthews Hudson; John Newman, FSA; Henry Owen-John

ROYAL MAIL GROUP

148 Old Street, London EC1V 9HQ
T 020-7250 2888
W www.royalmailgroup.com

Crown services for the carriage of government dispatches were set up in about 1516. The conveyance of public correspondence began in 1635 and the mail service was made a parliamentary responsibility with the setting up of a Post Office in 1657. Telegraphs came under Post Office control in 1870 and the Post Office Telephone Service began in 1880. The National Girobank service of the Post

Office began in 1968. The Post Office ceased to be a government department in 1969 when responsibility for the running of the postal, telecommunications, giro and remittance services was transferred to a public authority of the same name.

The British Telecommunications Act 1981 separated the functions of the Post Office, making it solely responsible for postal services and Girobank. Girobank was privatised in 1990. The Postal Services Act 2000 turned the Post Office into a wholly owned public limited company establishing a regulatory regime under the Postal Service Commission. The Post Office Group changed its name to Consignia plc in March 2001 when its new corporate structure took effect; in November 2002 the name was changed to Royal Mail Group plc. As of 1 January 2006 the UK postal service market was fully liberalised, and any licensed operator is now able to deliver mail to businesses and residential customers.

The chair, chief executive and members of the board are appointed by the Secretary of State for Business, Enterprise and Regulatory Reform but responsibility for the running of Royal Mail Group as a whole rests with the board in its corporate capacity.

BOARD
Chair, Allan Leighton
Chief Executive (Royal Mail Group), Adam Crozier
Managing Director, Alan Cook, CBE *(Post Office Ltd)*
Members, Ian Duncan *(Group Finance Director)*; Mark Higson *(Managing Director of the Letters Business)*
Non-Executive Directors, David Fish; Richard Handover; Baroness Prosser, OBE; Helen Weir, CBE
Company Secretary, Jonathan Evans, OBE

ROYAL NAVAL MUSEUM

HM Naval Base (PP66), Portsmouth PO1 3NH
T 023-9272 7562 F 023-9272 7575
E info@royalnavalmuseum.org W www.royalnavalmuseum.org

The Royal Naval Museum is a non-departmental public body sponsored by the Ministry of Defence, and is a registered charity governed by a board of trustees. It is located in Portsmouth Historic Dockyard alongside Nelson's flagship, HMS *Victory*, and is housed in three buildings offering exhibitions on the Navy from the 18th century onwards. The museum aims to provide an effective and accessible repository for the heritage of the Navy, and to raise public awareness, and encourage scholarship and research into the history and achievements of the Royal Navy.
Chair, Adm. Sir Peter Abbott, GBE, KCB

SCHOOL TEACHERS' REVIEW BODY (STRB)

6th Floor, Kingsgate House, 66–74 Victoria Street, London SW1E 6SW
T 020-7215 8314 F 020-7215 4445
W www.ome.uk.com

The STRB was set up under the School Teachers' Pay and Conditions Act 1991. It is required to examine and report on such matters relating to the statutory conditions of employment of school teachers in England and Wales as may be referred to it by the education secretary.
Chair, Bill Cockburn, CBE, TD
Members, Jennifer Board; Monojit Chatterji; Dewi Jones; Elizabeth Kidd; Esmond Lindop; Bruce Warman; Anne Watts, CBE

SCIENCE MUSEUM

Exhibition Road, London SW7 2DD
T 0870-870 4868 E sciencem@sciencemuseum.org.uk
W www.sciencemuseum.org.uk

The Science Museum, part of the National Museum of Science & Industry (NMSI), houses the national collections of science, technology, industry and medicine. The museum began as the science collection of the South Kensington Museum and first opened in 1857. In 1883 it acquired the collections of the Patent Museum and in 1909 the science collections were transferred to the new Science Museum, leaving the art collections with the Victoria and Albert Museum. The Wellcome Wing was opened in July 2000.

Some of the museum's larger objects, ranging across aircraft, agricultural machinery, computing, mechanical engineering, and road and rail transport collections, are at Science Museum Swindon, Wilts. The NMSI also incorporates the National Railway Museum, York, the National Media Museum, Bradford, and Locomotion: the National Railway Museum at Shildon.

Total government grant-in-aid for 2007–8 was £38.5m.
Chair, Rt. Hon. Lord Waldegrave of North Hill
Trustees, Lady Chisholm; Sir Ron U. Cooke; Howard Covington; Lord Faulkner of Worcester; Dr Douglas Gurr; Lord Rees of Ludlow, FRS; Prof. Averil Macdonald; Sir Howard Newby, CBE; Dr Gill Samuels, CBE; Prof. Simon J. Schaffer; Dr Maggie Semple, OBE; Dr Tony Sewell; Martin G. Smith; Prof. Roderick A. Smith, FRENG; Janet Street-Porter; Christopher Swinson, OBE Sir William Wells; Michael G. Wilson, OBE
Director of NMSI, Martin J. Earwicker, FRENG
Director of Science Museum, Prof. Chris Rapley, CBE
Director of National Media Museum, Colin Philpott
Director of National Railway Museum, Andrew Scott, CBE

SCOTTISH ARTS COUNCIL

12 Manor Place, Edinburgh EH3 7DD
T 0131-226 6051 F 0131-225 9833
E help.desk@scottisharts.org.uk W www.scottisharts.org.uk

The Scottish Arts Council is the main arts development agency in Scotland. It is a non-departmental public body, accountable to the Scottish government. The Scottish Arts Council invests funds from the Scottish government and National Lottery and works with partners to support and develop artistic excellence and creativity throughout Scotland. The Scottish government have proposed the creation of a new body, Creative Scotland, that will inherit the existing functions and resources of the Scottish Arts Council and Scottish Screen.
Chair, Richard Holloway
Members, Dinah Caine; Donald Emslie; Steven Grimmond; Charles Lovatt; Ray Macfarlane *(Vice-Chair)*; Barbara McKissack; Jim McSharry; John Mulgrew; Rab Noakes; Ian Smith; Ben Twist
Chief Executive (acting), Jim Tough

SCOTTISH CRIMINAL CASES REVIEW COMMISSION

5th Floor, Portland House, 17 Renfield Street, Glasgow G2 5AH
T 0141-270 7030 F 0141-270 7040/23
E info@sccrc.org.uk W www.sccrc.org.uk

The commission is a non-departmental public body, funded by the Scottish Government Criminal Justice

Directorate, and established in April 1999. It assumed the role previously performed by the Secretary of State for Scotland to consider alleged miscarriages of justice in Scotland and refer cases meeting the relevant criteria to the High Court for determination. Members are appointed by the Queen on the recommendation of the First Minister; senior executive staff are appointed by the commission.

Chair, Very Revd Graham Forbes, CBE
Members, David Belfall; Graham Bell, QC; Prof. Brian Caddy; Stewart Campbell; Sir Gerald Gordon, CBE, QC; Gerard McClay
Chief Executive, Gerard Sinclair

SCOTTISH ENTERPRISE

5 Atlantic Quay, 150 Broomielaw, Glasgow G2 8LU
T 0141-248 2700 **Helpline** 0845-607 8787 F 0141-221 3217
W www.scottish-enterprise.com

Scottish Enterprise was established in 1991 and its purpose is to create jobs and prosperity for the people of Scotland. It is funded by the Scottish government and is responsible to the Scottish ministers. Working in partnership with the private and public sectors, Scottish Enterprise aims to further the development of Scotland's economy, to enhance the skills of the Scottish workforce and to promote Scotland's international competitiveness. Scottish Enterprise is concerned with attracting firms to Scotland and, through Scottish Development International, it helps Scottish companies to compete in world export markets.

Chair, Sir John Ward, CBE, FRSE, FRSA
Chief Executive, Jack Perry

SCOTTISH ENVIRONMENT PROTECTION AGENCY (SEPA)

Erskine Court, Castle Business Park, Stirling FK9 4TR
T 01786-457700 **Hotline** 0800-807060
F 01786-446885 E info@sepa.org.uk
W www.sepa.org.uk

SEPA was established in 1996 and is the public body responsible for environmental protection in Scotland. It regulates potential pollution to land, air and water; the storage, transport and disposal of controlled waste; and the safekeeping and disposal of radioactive materials. It does this within a complex legislative framework of acts of parliament, EC directives and regulations, granting licences to operations of industrial processes and waste disposal. SEPA also operates Floodline (T 0845-988 1188), a public service providing information on the possible risk of flooding 24 hours a day, 365 days a year.

Chair, David Sigsworth
Chief Executive, Campbell Gemmell
Directors, Colin Bayes *(Environmental Regulation and Improvement)*; Calum MacDonald *(Environmental and Organisational Development)*; Chris Spray *(Environmental Science)*

SCOTTISH LAW COMMISSION

140 Causewayside, Edinburgh EH9 1PR
T 0131-668 2131 F 0131-662 4900
E info@scotlawcom.gov.uk W www.scotlawcom.gov.uk

The Scottish Law Commission, established in 1965, keeps the law in Scotland under review and makes proposals for its development and reform. It is responsible to the Scottish ministers through the Scottish Government Justice Department.

Chair (part-time), Hon. Lord Drummond Young
Chief Executive, M. McMillan
Commissioners, Prof. G. L. Gretton; Prof. G. Maher, QC; Prof. J. M. Thomson; C. J. Tyre, QC

SCOTTISH LEGAL AID BOARD

44 Drumsheugh Gardens, Edinburgh EH3 7SW
T 0131-226 7061 **Helpline** 0845-122 8686
F 0131-220 4878
E general@slab.org.uk W www.slab.org.uk

The Scottish Legal Aid Board was set up under the Legal Aid (Scotland) Act 1986 to manage legal aid in Scotland. It reports to the Scottish government. Board members are appointed by Scottish ministers.

Chair, Iain A. Robertson, CBE
Members, Graham Bell, QC; Les Campbell; Joseph Hughes; Denise Loney; Paul McBride, QC; Susan McPhee; Ellen Morton; David Nicol; Elaine Rosie; Sheriff Kenneth Ross; Graham Watson
Chief Executive, Lindsay Montgomery

SCOTTISH NATURAL HERITAGE (SNH)

Great Glen House, Leachkin Road, Inverness IV3 8NW
T 01463-725000 F 01463-725067
E enquiries@snh.gov.uk W www.snh.org.uk

SNH was established in 1992 under the Natural Heritage (Scotland) Act 1991. It provides advice on nature conservation to all those whose activities affect wildlife, landforms and features of geological interest in Scotland, and seeks to develop and improve facilities for the enjoyment and understanding of the Scottish countryside. It is funded by the Scottish government.

Chair, Andrew Thin
Chief Executive, I. Jardine
Chief Scientific Adviser, C. Galbraith
Directors of Operations, J. Thomson *(Strategy and Communications)*; S. Davies *(North)*; R. Fairley *(South)*
Director of Corporate Services, J. Moore

SCOTTISH PRISONS COMPLAINTS COMMISSION

Government Buildings, Broomhouse Drive, Edinburgh EH11 3XD
T 0131-244 8423 F 0131-244 8430
E spcc@scotland.gsi.gov.uk
W www.scotland.gov.uk/topics/justice/prisons

The commission was established in 1994. It is an independent body to which prisoners in Scottish prisons can make applications in relation to any matter where they have failed to obtain satisfaction from the Scottish Prison Service's internal grievance procedures. Clinical judgements made by medical officers, matters which are the subject of legal proceedings and matters relating to sentence, conviction and parole decision-making are excluded from the commission's jurisdiction. The commissioner is appointed by the Scottish ministers.

Commissioner, Vaughan Barrett

SEAFISH INDUSTRY AUTHORITY

18 Logie Mill, Logie Green Road, Edinburgh EH7 4HS
T 0131-558 3331 F 0131-558 1442
E seafish@seafish.co.uk W www.seafish.org

Established under the Fisheries Act 1981, the authority works with all sectors of the UK seafood industry to satisfy consumers, raise standards, improve efficiency and secure a sustainable and profitable future. It is sponsored by the four UK fisheries departments, which appoint the board, and is funded by a levy on seafood.
Chair, Charles Howeson
Chief Executive, John Rutherford

SENIOR SALARIES REVIEW BODY

6th Floor, Kingsgate House, 66–74 Victoria Street, London SW1E 6SW
T 020-7215 8276 **F** 020-7215 4445
W www.ome.uk.com

The Senior Salaries Review Body (formerly the Top Salaries Review Body) was set up in 1971 to advise the prime minister on the remuneration of the judiciary, senior civil servants and senior officers of the armed forces. In 1993 its remit was extended to cover the pay, pensions and allowances of MPs, ministers and others whose pay is determined by the Ministerial and Other Salaries Act 1975, and also the allowances of peers. If asked, it advises on the pay of officers and members of the devolved parliament and assemblies.
Chair, Bill Cockburn, CBE, TD
Members, Mark Baker, CBE; Mary Galbraith; Prof. David Greenaway; Michael Langley; Jim McKenna; Mei Sim Lai, OBE; Sir Peter North, CBE, QC; Richard Pearson; Paul Williams

SERIOUS ORGANISED CRIME AGENCY (SOCA)

PO Box 8000, London SE11 5EN
T 020-7238 8000 **W** www.soca.gov.uk

SOCA was established in April 2006. It took over the functions of the National Criminal Intelligence Service and the National Crime Squad, as well as the role of HM Revenue and Customs in investigating drug trafficking and related criminal finance, and some of the functions of the UK Immigration Service in dealing with organised immigration crime. Its remit is to prevent and detect serious organised crime and to gather, store, analyse and disseminate information on crime. SOCA is also tasked with providing support to law enforcement partners. The Assets Recovery Agency merged with SOCA on 1 April 2008.

The Secretary of State for Home Affairs appoints the chair and director-general, may set SOCA strategies and will judge the success of its efforts. Grant-in-aid is provided by the Home Office and for 2008–9 is set provisionally at £442m in resource funding.
Chair, Sir Stephen Lander
Director-General, Bill Hughes
Directors, David Bolt *(Intelligence)*; Malcolm Cornberg *(Corporate Services)*; Paul Evans *(Intervention)*; Trevor Pearce *(Enforcement)*
Non-Executive Directors, Stephen Barrett; Elizabeth France; Ken Jarrold; Janet Paraskeva; Gen. Sir Roger Wheeler

STUDENT LOANS COMPANY LTD

100 Bothwell Street, Glasgow G2 7JD
T 0141-306 2000 **F** 0141-306 2005
W www.slc.co.uk

The Student Loans Company Ltd is wholly owned by the government. It administers the Student Loan Scheme (established in 1990) and the Income Contingent Loans Scheme (established in 1998), and provides loans to eligible students in higher education in the United Kingdom. In the region of £5.1bn of loans were distributed during the academic year to May 2008, of which £3bn was in maintenance loans. As at 31 March 2008 there were 2.7 million borrowers, and a total of £21.9bn of outstanding loans to be repaid.
Chair, Keith Bedell-Pearce
Chief Executive, Ralph Seymour-Jackson

TATE BRITAIN

Millbank, London SW1P 4RG
T 020-7887 8888
E visiting.britain@tate.org.uk **W** www.tate.org.uk

Tate Britain displays the national collection of British art from 1500 to the present day – with special attention and dedicated space given to Blake, Turner and Constable. The gallery opened in 1897, the cost of building (£80,000) being defrayed by Sir Henry Tate, who also contributed the nucleus of the present collection. The Turner wing was opened in 1910, and further galleries and a new sculpture hall followed in 1937. In 1979 a further extension was built, and the Clore Gallery was opened in 1987. The Centenary Development was opened in 2001.

There are four Tate galleries: Tate Britain and Tate Modern in London, Tate Liverpool and Tate St Ives; the entire Tate collection is available to view online.

BOARD OF TRUSTEES
Chair, Paul Myners, CBE
Trustees, Helen Alexander; Lord Browne; Sir Howard Davies; Jeremy Deller; David Ekserdjian; Anish Kapoor; Patricia Lankester; Franck Petitgas; Fiona Rae; Monisha Shah

OFFICERS
Director, Sir Nicholas Serota
Director, Tate Britain, Dr Stephen Deuchar
Director, Tate Liverpool, Dr Christoph Grunenberg
Director, Tate Modern, Vicente Todoli
Artistic Director, Tate St Ives, Martin Clark
Creative Director, Tate St Ives, Mark Osterfield

TATE MODERN

Bankside, London SE1 9TG
T 020-7887 8888 **E** visiting.modern@tate.org.uk
W www.tate.org.uk

Opened in May 2000, Tate Modern displays the Tate collection of international modern art dating from 1900 to the present day. It includes works by Dalí, Picasso, Matisse and Warhol as well as many contemporary works. It is housed in the former Bankside Power Station in London, which was redesigned by the Swiss architects Herzog and de Meuron.
Director, Vicente Todoli

TOURISM BODIES

Visit Britain, Visit Scotland, Visit Wales and the Northern Ireland Tourist Board are responsible for developing and marketing the tourist industry in their respective regions. Visit Wales is not listed here as it is part of the Welsh Assembly government, within the Department for Heritage, and not a public body.

VISIT BRITAIN
Thames Tower, Blacks Road, London W6 9EL T 020-8846 9000
W www.visitbritain.com
Chair, Christopher Rodrigues, CBE
Chief Executive, Tom Wright, CBE

VISIT SCOTLAND
94 Ocean Drive, Leith, Edinburgh EH6 6JH T 0131-472 2222
E generalenquiries@visitscotland.com
W www.visitscotland.com
Chair, Peter Lederer, CBE
Chief Executive, Philip Riddle, OBE

NORTHERN IRELAND TOURIST BOARD
St Anne's Court, 59 North Street, Belfast BT1 1NB
T 028-9023 1221 F 028-9024 0960 E info@nitb.com
W www.discovernorthernireland.com
Chair, Tom McGrath, CBE
Chief Executive, Alan Clarke

TRAINING AND DEVELOPMENT AGENCY (TDA)

151 Buckingham Palace Road, London SW1W 9SZ
T 020-7023 8000 E corporatecomms@tda.gov.uk
W www.tda.gov.uk, www.teach.gov.uk

The TDA was launched in September 2005 and took on the role, and expanded the remit of, the Teacher Training Agency. The TDA aims to attract able and committed people to teaching, concentrating specifically on subjects where teachers are in short supply; provide schools and their staff with good information on training and development opportunities; and ensure that new teachers enter schools with appropriate skills and knowledge, through working closely with providers of initial teacher training.
Chief Executive, Graham Holley

TRANSPORT FOR LONDON (TFL)

23rd Floor, Empress State Building, Empress Approach, London SW6 1TR
T 020-7222 5600
E enquire@tfl.gov.uk W www.tfl.gov.uk

TfL was formed in July 2000 as a functional body of the Greater London Authority and is responsible for the capital's transport system. Its role is to implement the Mayor of London's transport strategy and manage the transport services across London for which the mayor has responsibility.

As a result, TfL is responsible for London's buses, the Underground, the Docklands Light Railway (DLR) and the management of Croydon Tramlink and London River Services. It also runs Victoria Coach Station and London's Transport Museum, manages the Congestion Charging scheme and Low Emission Zone and regulates the city's taxis and private hire trade.
Chair, Boris Johnson
Commissioner, Peter Hendy

UK ATOMIC ENERGY AUTHORITY (UKAEA)

The Manor Court, Chilton,Oxon OX11 0RN
T 01235-431810 F 01235-431811
W www.ukaea.org.uk

The UKAEA was established by the Atomic Energy Authority Act 1954 and took over responsibility for the research and development of the civil nuclear power programme. The UKAEA is now responsible for the safe management and decommissioning of its radioactive plants and for leading the development of the Harwell Science and Innovation Campus. The UKAEA also undertakes the UK's contribution to the international fusion programme.
Chair, Lady Barbara Judge
Chief Executive, Norman Harrison

UK FILM COUNCIL

10 Little Portland Street, London W1W 7JG
T 020-7861 7861 F 020-7861 7862
E info@ukfilmcouncil.org.uk W www.ukfilmcouncil.org.uk

The council was created in April 2000 by the Department for Culture, Media and Sport. The council's board is comprised of 15 directors and has been established as a private company limited by guarantee, with an intention to move it to a statutory basis at a later stage. It invests grant-in-aid and National Lottery funds in film development and production, training, international development and export promotion, distribution and exhibition, and education.

UK Film Council International (formerly the British Film Commission) is part of the same organisation, and was originally established in 1991. Its remit is to attract inward investment by promoting the UK as an international production centre to the film and television industries and encouraging the use of British locations, services, facilities and personnel.
Chair, Stewart Till, CBE
Chief Executive, John Woodward
British Film Commissioner, Colin Brown

UNITED KINGDOM SPORTS COUNCIL (UK SPORT)

40 Bernard Street, London WC1N 1ST
T 020-7211 5100 F 020-7211 5246
E info@uksport.gov.uk W www.uksport.gov.uk

UK Sport was established by royal charter in 1996 and is accountable to parliament through the Department for Culture, Media and Sport. Its role is to lead the UK to sporting excellence by supporting winning athletes, world-class events, world-class standards and ethically fair and drug-free sport. UK Sport is responsible for managing and distributing public investment and is a statutory distributor of funds raised by the National Lottery. Government grant-in-aid for 2007–8 was £67.4m and national lottery funding was £49.5m.
Chair, Sue Campbell, CBE
Chief Executive, John Steele

VICTORIA AND ALBERT MUSEUM

Cromwell Road, London SW7 2RL
T 020-7942 2000 W www.vam.ac.uk

The Victoria and Albert Museum (V&A) is the national museum of fine and applied art and design. It descends directly from the Museum of Manufactures, which opened in Marlborough House in 1852 after the Great Exhibition of 1851. The museum was moved in 1857 to become part of the South Kensington Museum. It was renamed the Victoria and Albert Museum in 1899. It also houses the National Art Library and Print Room.

The museum administers the V&A Museum of Childhood at Bethnal Green, which was opened in 1872; the building is the most important surviving example of

the type of glass and iron construction used by Paxton for the Great Exhibition. Total government grant-in-aid for 2008–9 is £43.65m.
Chair, Paul Ruddock
Members, E. Davies, OBE; T. Dixon, OBE; Prof. Sir Christopher Frayling; Ms B. Jackson, CBE; Prof. Lisa Jardine, CBE; Rt. Hon. Sir Timothy Sainsbury; Dame Marjorie Scardino, DBE; S. Shah, OBE
Director of the V&A, M. Jones

WALLACE COLLECTION

Hertford House, Manchester Square, London W1U 3BN
T 020-7563 9500 F 020-7224 2155
E enquiries@wallacecollection.org
W www.wallacecollection.org

The Wallace Collection was bequeathed to the nation by the widow of Sir Richard Wallace, in 1897, and Hertford House was subsequently acquired by the government. The collection contains works by Titian and Rembrandt, and includes porcelain, furniture and an array of arms and armour. Total government grant-in-aid for 2007–8 was £4.89m.
Director, Rosalind Savill

WOMEN'S NATIONAL COMMISSION

Zones 4/G9, Eland House, Bressenden Place, London SW1E 5DU
T 020-7944 0585 F 020-7944 0583
E wnc@communities.gsi.gov.uk W www.thewnc.org.uk

The Women's National Commission was established in 1969 as an independent advisory committee to the government. It is an umbrella organisation representing women and women's organisations in the UK. Its remit is to ensure that the informed opinions of women are given their due weight in the deliberations of the government and in public debate on matters of public interest, including those of special interest to women. The commission is an advisory NDPB based within the Department for Communities and Local Government alongside the Women and Equality Unit.
Chair, Baroness Gould of Potternewton
Director (acting), Susan Green
Deputy Director, Daniel Barrow

REGIONAL GOVERNMENT

LONDON

GREATER LONDON AUTHORITY (GLA)

City Hall, The Queen's Walk, London SE1 2AA
T 020-7983 4100 E mayor@london.gov.uk
W www.london.gov.uk

On 7 May 1998 London voted in favour of the formation of the Greater London Authority (GLA). The first elections to the GLA took place on 4 May 2000 and the new authority took over its responsibilities on 3 July 2000. In July 2002 the GLA moved to one of London's most spectacular buildings, newly built on a brownfield site on the south bank of the Thames, adjacent to Tower Bridge. The third and last election to the GLA took place on 1 May 2008.

The structure and objectives of the GLA stem from its eight main areas of responsibility. These are transport, planning, economic development and regeneration, the environment, police, fire and emergency planning, culture and health. The bodies that coordinate these functions and report to the GLA are Transport for London (TfL), the London Development Agency (LDA), the Metropolitan Police Authority (MPA), and the London Fire and Emergency Planning Authority (LFEPA). The GLA also absorbed a number of other London bodies, such as the London Ecology Unit and the London Research Centre.

The GLA consists of a directly elected mayor, the Mayor of London, and a separately elected assembly, the London Assembly. The mayor has the key role of decision making, with the assembly performing the tasks of regulating and scrutinising these decisions. In addition, the GLA has around 600 permanent staff to support the activities of the mayor and the assembly, which are overseen by a head of paid service. The mayor may appoint two political advisers, though does not necessarily exercise this power, but he may not appoint the chief executive, the monitoring officer or the chief finance officer. These must be appointed by the assembly.

Every aspect of the assembly and its activities must be open to public scrutiny and therefore accountable. The assembly holds the mayor to account through scrutiny of his strategies, decisions and actions. This is carried out by direct questioning at assembly meetings and by conducting detailed investigations in committee.

People's Question Time gives Londoners the chance to question the mayor and the London Assembly about plans, priorities and policies for London. It is held twice a year in different areas of London.

The role of the mayor can be broken down into a number of key areas:

- to represent and promote London at home and abroad and speak up for Londoners
- to devise strategies and plans to tackle London-wide issues, such as crime, transport, housing and planning, environment, accountability, business and skills, public services, culture and arts, local government and the Olympic and Paralympic Games; and to set budgets for TfL, the LDA, the MPA and the LFEPA
- the mayor is chair of TfL and has the power to appoint the members of their board and those of the LDA; he also makes appointments to the police and fire authorities.
- with London's successful bid to host the 2012 Olympic and Paralympic Games, the previous mayor was the signatory to the contract with the International Olympic Committee undertaking that the games would be delivered

The role of the assembly can be broken down into a number of key areas:

- to check on and balance the mayor
- to scrutinise the mayor
- to have the power to amend the mayor's budget by a majority of two-thirds
- to have the power to summon the mayor, senior staff of the Authority and functional bodies
- to investigate issues of London-wide significance and make proposals to appropriate stakeholders
- to provide the deputy mayor and the members serving on the police, fire and emergency planning authorities with advice

Mayor, Boris Johnson
Deputy Mayors, Richard Barnes; Ian Clement (Government Relations); Kit Malthouse (Policing); Sir Simon Milton (Policy and Planning)
Chair of the London Assembly, Jennette Arnold
Deputy Chair of the Assembly, Darren Johnson

ELECTIONS AND THE VOTING SYSTEMS

The assembly is elected every four years at the same time as the mayor, and consists of 25 members. There is one member from each of the 14 GLA constituencies topped up with 11 London members who are representatives of political parties or individuals standing as independent candidates. The last election was on 1 May 2008.

Two distinct voting systems are used to appoint the existing mayor and the assembly. The mayor is elected using the supplementary vote system (SVS). With SVS, electors have two votes: one to give a first choice for mayor and one to give a second choice. Electors cannot vote twice for the same candidate. If one candidate gets more than half of all the first-choice votes, he or she becomes mayor. If no candidate gets more than half of the first-choice votes, the two candidates with the most first-choice votes remain in the election and all the other candidates drop out. The second-choice votes on the ballot papers of the candidates who drop out are then counted. Where these second-choice votes are for the two remaining candidates they are added to the first-choice votes these candidates already have. The candidate with the most first- and second-choice votes combined becomes the Mayor of London.

The assembly is appointed using the additional member system (AMS). Under AMS, electors have two votes. The first vote is for a constituency candidate. The second vote is for a party list or individual candidate contesting the London-wide assembly seats. The 14 constituency members are elected under the first-past-the-post system, the same system used in general and local elections. Electors vote for one candidate and the candidate with the most votes wins. The additional

(London) members are drawn from party lists or are independent candidates who stand as London members; they are chosen using a form of proportional representation.

The Greater London Returning Officer (GLRO) is the independent official responsible for running the election in London. He is supported in this by returning officers in each of the 14 London constituencies.

GLRO, Anthony Mayer

TRANSPORT FOR LONDON (TfL)

TfL is the integrated body responsible for London's transport system. Its role is to implement the mayor's transport strategy for London and manage transport services across the capital for which the mayor has responsibility. TfL is directed by a management board whose members are chosen for their understanding of transport matters and are appointed by the mayor, who chairs the board. TfL's role is:

- to manage the London Underground, buses, Croydon Tramlink and the Docklands Light Railway (DLR)
- to manage a network of main roads and all of London's traffic lights
- to regulate taxis and minicabs
- to run the London River Services, Victoria Coach Station and London's Transport Museum
- to help to coordinate the Dial-a-Ride and Taxicard schemes for door-to-door services for transport users with mobility problems
- to manage the North London railway (since autumn 2007)

The London Borough Councils maintain the role of highway and traffic authorities for 95 per cent of London's roads. A £5 congestion charge for motorists driving into central London between the hours of 7am and 6.30pm, Monday to Friday (excluding public holidays) was introduced on 17 February 2003, and was subsequently raised to £8 on 4 July 2005. On 19 February 2007, the charge zone roughly doubled in size after a westward expansion, and the time zone changed to finish earlier at 6pm.

TfL introduced a low emission zone for London on 4 February 2008. It consisted of a £200 daily charge for polluting vehicles that entered the zone, which covered most of Greater London. Lorries over 12 tonnes that did not meet emissions standards were the first to be affected. Charges for buses and coaches exceeding five tonnes began on 7 July 2008; further charges for other polluting vehicles are to be introduced by 2010.

Transport Commissioner for London, Peter Hendy

LONDON DEVELOPMENT AGENCY (LDA)

The LDA promotes economic development and regeneration. It is one of the nine regional development agencies set up around the country to perform this task. It is run by a board of 14 members appointed by the mayor. The key aspects of the LDA's role are:

- to further the economic development and regeneration of London
- to promote business efficiency, investment and competitiveness
- to promote employment
- to enhance the skills of local people
- to contribute to sustainable development

The London boroughs retain powers to promote economic development in their local areas.

Chair (interim), Harvey McGrath

THE ENVIRONMENT

The mayor is required to formulate strategies to tackle London's environmental issues including the quality of water, air and land; the use of energy and London's contribution to climate change targets; groundwater levels and traffic emissions; and municipal waste management.

METROPOLITAN POLICE AUTHORITY (MPA)

This body, which oversees the policing of London, consists of 23 members; 12 from the assembly, including the deputy mayor, four magistrates and seven independents. One of the independents is appointed directly by the home secretary. The role of the MPA is:

- to maintain an efficient and effective police force
- to secure best value in the delivery of policing services
- to publish an annual policing plan
- to set police targets and monitor performance
- to be part of the appointment, discipline and removal of senior officers
- to be responsible for the performance budget

The boundaries of the metropolitan police districts have been changed to be consistent with the 32 London boroughs. Areas beyond the GLA remit have been incorporated into the Surrey, Hertfordshire and Essex police areas. The City of London has its own police force.

Chair, Len Duvall

LONDON FIRE AND EMERGENCY PLANNING AUTHORITY (LFEPA)

In July 2000 the London Fire and Civil Defence Authority became the London Fire and Emergency Planning Authority. It consists of 17 members, 9 drawn from the assembly and 8 from the London boroughs. The role of the LFEPA is:

- to set the strategy for the provision of fire services
- to ensure that the fire brigade can meet all the normal requirements efficiently
- to ensure that effective arrangements are made for the fire brigade to receive emergency calls and deal with them promptly
- to ensure members of the fire brigade are properly trained and equipped
- to ensure that information useful to the development of the fire brigades is gathered
- to ensure arrangements for advice and guidance on fire protection are made

Chair, Brian Coleman

SALARIES *as at June 2008*	
Mayor	£137,579
Deputy Mayor	£90,954
Chair of the Assembly	£60,675
Assembly Members	£50,582
Assembly Members who are also MPs	£16,861

LONDON ASSEMBLY COMMITTEES

Chair, Audit Panel, Peter Hulme Cross
Chair, Budget Committee, John Biggs
Chair, Business Management and Administration Committee, Environment Committee, Darren Johnson
Chair, Confirmation Hearings Committee, vacant
Chair, Economic Development, Culture, Sport and Tourism Committee, Dee Doocey
Chair, Elections Review Committee, Brian Coleman
Chair, Health and Public Services Committee, Joanne McCartney
Chair, Planning and Spatial Development Committee, Tony Arbour

Chair, Standards Committee, Clare Lloyd-Jones
Chair, Transport Committee, Valerie Shawcross

GLA ORGANISATIONAL STRUCTURE

MAYOR'S OFFICE
Transport and Public Affairs (International and European Relations, London Stakeholders, Government and Parliamentary Liaison, Public Consultation, Public Affairs Publications, Events for London, Borough Liaison)
Business Planning and Regeneration
Economic and Business Policy (Private Sector, Strategic Evaluation Unit, Cultural Strategy)
Equalities and Policing
Environment
Tourism and Creative Industries (Cultural Strategy)
Advisers
London House (Brussels)
Administration Manager

MEDIA AND MARKETING
Mayor's Media Relations
Marketing
Public Liaison Unit
Communications Support Unit

FINANCE AND PERFORMANCE
Squares and Business Development Group
Strategic Finance and Performance
Financial Services
Economic Development and Transport

POLICY AND PARTNERSHIPS
Spatial Development Strategy
Planning Decisions
Architecture and Urbanism Unit
Environment
Olympics and Thames Gateway Unit
Housing and Homelessness
Policy Support (Health, Social Inclusion, Sustainable Development)
Business Support

SECRETARIAT
Assembly Support
Scrutiny and Investigation
Committee Services
External Relations

CORPORATE SERVICES
GLA Economics
Technology Group
Legal and Procurement
Human Resources
Information Services
Data Management
Business Support
Facilities Management

LONDON ASSEMBLY MEMBERS

as at 1 July 2008
Arbour, Tony, *C., South West,* Maj. 26,928
Arnold, Jennette, *Lab. North East,* Maj. 28,437
Bacon, Gareth, *C., London List*
Barnbrook, Richard, *BNP, London List*
Barnes, Richard, *C., Ealing and Hillingdon,* Maj. 28,638
Biggs, John, *Lab., City and East,* Maj. 31,553
Boff, Andrew, *C., London List*
Borwick, Victoria, *C., London List*
Cleverly, James, *C., Bexley and Bromley,* Maj. 75,237
Coleman, Brian, *C., Barnet and Camden,* Maj. 19,693
Doocey, Dee, *LD, London List*
Duvall, Len, *Lab., Greenwich and Lewisham,* Maj. 16,134
Evans, Roger, *C., Havering and Redbridge,* Maj. 43,025
Gavron, Nicky, *Lab., London List*
Johnson, Darren, *Green, London List*
Jones, Jenny, *Green, London List*
McCartney, Joanne, *Lab., Enfield and Haringey,* Maj. 1,402
Malthouse, Kit, *C., West Central,* Maj. 51,381
O'Connell, Stephen, *C., Croydon and Sutton,* Maj. 42,665
Pidgeon, Caroline, *LD, London List*
Qureshi, Murad, *Lab., London List*
Shah, Navin, *Lab., Brent and Harrow,* Maj. 1,649
Shawcross, Valerie, *Lab., Lambeth and Southwark,* Maj. 23,648
Tracey, Richard, *C., Merton and Wandsworth,* Maj. 26,293
Tuffrey, Michael, *LD, London List*

STATE OF THE PARTIES *as at 1 July 2008*

Party	*Seats*
Conservative (C.)	11
Labour (Lab.)	8
Liberal Democrats (LD)	3
Green	2
British National Party (BNP)	1

MAYORAL ELECTION RESULTS

as at 1 May 2008
E. 5,419,913 T. 2,456,990 (45.33%)
Change in turnout from 2004: + 8.38%
Good votes: 1st choice 2,415,952 (98.32%); 2nd choice 2,004,078 (82.94%)
Rejected votes: 1st choice 41,032 (1.67%); 2nd choice 412,054 (17.05%)

First	*Party*	*Votes*	*%*
Boris Johnson	C.	1,043,761	42.48
Ken Livingstone	Lab.	893,877	36.38
Brian Paddick	LD	236,685	9.63
Sian Berry	Green	77,374	3.15
Richard Barnbrook	BNP	69,710	2.84
Alan Craig	CPA	39,249	1.60
Gerard Batten	UKIP	24,222	0.91
Lindsey German	Left List	16,796	0.68
Matt O'Connor	Eng. Dem.	10,695	0.44
Winston McKenzie	Ind.	5,389	0.22

Second	*Party*	*Votes*	*%*
Brian Paddick	LD	641,412	26.11
Sian Berry	Green	331,727	13.50
Ken Livingstone	Lab.	303,198	12.34
Boris Johnson	C.	257,792	10.49
Richard Barnbrook	BNP	128,609	5.23
Gerard Batten	UKIP	113,651	4.63
Alan Craig	CPA	80,140	3.26
Matt O'Connor	Eng. Dem.	73,538	2.99
Winston McKenzie	Ind.	38,954	1.59
Lindsey German	Left List	35,057	1.43

LONDON ASSEMBLY ELECTION RESULTS

as at 1 May 2008

E. Electorate T. Turnout

See General Election Results for a list of party abbreviations

CONSTITUENCIES

BARNET AND CAMDEN

E. 376,818 T. 47.77%

Brian Coleman, C.	72,659
Nicky Gavron, Lab.	52,966
Nick Russell, LD	22,213
Miranda Dunn, Green	16,782
Magnus Nielsen, UKIP	3,678
Clement Adebayo, CPA	3,536
David Stevens, Eng. Dem.	2,146
Dave Hoefling, Left List	2,074
Graham Dare, Veritas	510

C. majority 19,693

BEXLEY AND BROMLEY

E. 407,003 T. 49.85%

James Cleverly, C.	105,162
Alex Heslop, Lab.	29,925
Tom Papworth, LD,	21,244
Paul Winnett, NF	11,288
Ann Garrett, Green	9,261
Mick Greenhough, UKIP	8,021
John Hemming-Clark, Ind.	6,684
Miranda Suit, CPA	4,408
Steven Uncles, Eng. Dem.	2,907
David Davis, Left List	1,050

C. majority 75,237

BRENT AND HARROW

E. 367,337 T. 43.10%

Navin Shah, Lab.	57,716
Bob Blackman, C.	56,067
James Allie, LD	19,299
Shahrar Ali, Green	10,129
Zena Sherman, CPA	4,180
Sunita Webb, UKIP	3,021
Pat McManus, Left List	2,287
Arvind Tailor, Eng. Dem.	2,150

Lab. majority 1,649

CITY AND EAST

E. 470,863 T. 39.79%

John Biggs, Lab.	63,635
Philip Briscoe, C.	32,082
Hanif Abdulmuhit, Respect	26,760
Robert Bailey, BNP	18,020
Rajonuddin Jalal, LD	13,724
Heather Finlay, Green	11,478
Thomas Conquest, CPA	7,306
Michael McGough, UKIP	3,078
Graham Kemp, NF	2,350
Michael Gavan, Left List	2,274
John Griffiths, Eng. Dem.	2,048
Julie Crawford, Ind.	701

Lab. majority 31,553

CROYDON AND SUTTON

E. 360,221 T. 48.99%

Stephen O'Connell, C.	76,477
Shafi Khan, Lab.	33,812
Abigail Lock, LD	32,335
David Pickles, UKIP	9,440
Shasha Khan, Green	8,969
David Campanale, CPA	6,910
Richard Castle, Eng. Dem.	4,186
Zana Hussain, Left List	1,361

C. majority 42,665

EALING AND HILLINGDON

E. 401,671 T. 44.05%

Richard Barnes, C.	74,710
Ranjit Dheer, Lab.	46,072
Nigel Bakhai, LD	18,004
Sarah Edwards, Green	12,606
Ian Edward, NF	7,939
Mary Boyle, CPA	5,100
Lynnda Robson, UKIP	4,465
Salvinder Dhillon, Left List	2,390
Sati Chaggar, Eng. Dem.	1,853

C. majority 28,638

ENFIELD AND HARINGEY

E. 351,536 T. 46.04%

Joanne McCartney, Lab.	52,665
Matthew Laban, C.	51,263
Monica Whyte, LD	23,550
Pete McAskie, Green	12,473
Segun Johnson, CPA	5,779
Sait Akgul, Left List	5,639
Brian Hall, UKIP	4,682
Teresa Cannon, Eng. Dem.	2,282

Lab. majority 1,402

GREENWICH AND LEWISHAM

E. 347,252 T. 42.98%

Len Duvall, Lab.	53,174
Andy Jennings, C.	37,040
Brian Robson, LD	18,174
Susan Luxton, Green	15,607
Tess Culnane, NF	8,509
Stephen Hammond, CPA	5,079
Arnold Tarling, UKIP	3,910
Jennifer Jones, Left List	2,045
Johanna Munilla, Eng. Dem.	1,716
Chris Flood, Soc. Alt.	1,587

Lab. majority 16,134

HAVERING AND REDBRIDGE

E. 369,407 T. 45.46%

Roger Evans, C.	78,493
Balvinder Saund, Lab.	35,468
Farrukh Islam, LD	12,443
Lawrence Webb, UKIP	12,203
Ashley Gunstock, Green	9,126
Leo Brookes, Eng. Dem.	6,487
Paula Warren, CPA	5,533
Dr Peter Thorogood, Ind.	3,450
Carole Vincent, Left List	1,473

C. majority 43,025

LAMBETH AND SOUTHWARK
E. 395,202 T. 42.09%

Valerie Shawcross, Lab.	60,601
Caroline Pidgeon, LD	36,953
Shirley Houghton, C.	32,835
Shane Collins, Green	18,011
Geoffrey Macharia, CPA	4,432
Jens Winton, UKIP	3,012
Katt Young, Left List	1,956
Janus Polenceus, Eng. Dem.	1,867
Jasmijn De Boo, Animals Count	1,828
Daniel Lambert, Socialist	1,588

Lab. majority 23,648

MERTON AND WANDSWORTH
E. 362,542 T. 47.16%

Richard Tracey, C.	75,103
Leonie Cooper, Lab.	48,810
Shas Sheehan, LD	17,187
Roy Vickery, Green	14,124
Strachan McDonald, UKIP	4,286
Ellen Greco, CPA	4,053
Steve Scott, Eng. Dem.	2,160
Kris Stewart, Left List	1,714

C. majority 26,293

NORTH EAST
E. 451,787 T. 43.80%

Jennette Arnold, Lab.	73,551
Alexander Ellis, C.	45,114
Meral Ece, LD	28,973
Aled Fisher, Green	28,845
Unjum Mirza, Left List	6,019
Nicholas Jones, UKIP	5,349
Maxine Hargreaves, CPA	5,323
John Dodds, Eng. Dem.	3,637

Lab. majority 28,437

SOUTH WEST
E. 415,092 T. 46.15%

Tony Arbour, C.	76,913
Stephen Knight, LD	49,985
Ansuya Sodha, Lab.	30,190
John Hunt, Green	12,774
Andrew Cripps, NF	4,754
Peter Dul, UKIP	3,779
Sue May, CPA	3,718
Andrew Constantine, Free England Party	2,908
Roger Cooper, Eng. Dem.	1,874
Tansy Hoskins, Left List	1,526

C. majority 26,928

WEST CENTRAL
E. 343,182 T. 48.48%

Kit Malthouse, C.	86,651
Murad Qureshi, Lab.	35,270
Julia Stephenson, Green	16,874
Merlene Emerson, LD	15,934
Paul Wiffen, UKIP	3,060
Alex Vaughan, Eng. Dem.	1,858
Explo Nani-Kofi, Left List	1,630
Abby Dharamsey, Ind.	962

C. majority 51,381

TOP-UP MEMBERS

BRITISH NATIONAL PARTY
Richard Barnbrook

CONSERVATIVE
Andrew Boff
Victoria Borwick
Gareth Bacon

GREEN PARTY
Darren Johnson
Jenny Jones

LABOUR
Nicky Gavron
Murad Qureshi

LIBERAL DEMOCRAT
Dee Doocey
Caroline Pidgeon
Michael Tuffrey

WALES

WELSH ASSEMBLY GOVERNMENT

Cathays Park, Cardiff CF10 3NQ
T 0845-010 3300 W http://new.wales.gov.uk

The Welsh Assembly Government is comprised of the first minister, deputy first minister, Welsh ministers, the counsel general (the chief legal adviser), and the deputy Welsh ministers. The 60 assembly members delegate their executive powers, including the implementation of policies and legislation, to the first minister – who is elected by the whole assembly and is therefore usually the leader of the largest political party. In turn, the first minister delegates responsibility for delivering the executive functions to Welsh ministers, who together form the cabinet.

The Welsh Assembly Government has responsibility over the following devolved areas: agriculture, fisheries, forestry and rural development; ancient monuments and historic buildings; culture; economic development; education and training; environment; fire and rescue services; food; health and health services; highways and transport; housing; local government; public administration; social welfare; sport and recreation; tourism; town and county planning; water and flood defence; and the Welsh language.

First Minister for Wales, Rt. Hon. Rhodri Morgan, AM
Deputy First Minister for Wales, and Minister for the Economy and Transport, Ieuan Wyn Jones, AM
Minister for Children, Education, Lifelong Learning and Skills, Jane Hutt, AM
Minister for Environment, Sustainability and Housing, Jane Davidson, AM
Minister for Finance and Public Service Delivery, Andrew Davies, AM
Minister for Health and Social Services, Edwina Hart, MBE, AM
Minister for Heritage, Alun Ffred Jones, AM
Minister for Rural Affairs, Elin Jones, AM
Minister for Social Justice and Local Government, Dr Brian Gibbons, AM
Deputy Minister for Housing, Jocelyn Davies, AM
Deputy Minister for Regeneration, Leighton Andrews, AM
Deputy Minister for Skills, John Griffiths, AM
Deputy Minister for Social Services, Gwenda Thomas, AM
Counsel General and Leader of the House, Carwyn Jones, AM
Clerk to the Assembly and Chief Executive of Assembly Commission, Claire Clancy

MANAGEMENT BOARD

Permanent Secretary, Dame Gillian Morgan
Director, Business Development, June Milligan
Director, Constitutional Affairs, Equality and Communication, Hugh Rawlings
Director, Corporate Information and Services, Dr Michael Harrington
Director, Economy and Transport, Gareth Hall
Director, Environment, Sustainability and Housing, Matthew Quinn
Director, Finance, Christine Daws
Director, Health and Social Services, Ann Lloyd
Director, Human Resources, Bernard Galton
Director, Legal Services, Jeff Godfrey
Director, Public Health and Health Professions, and Chief Medical Officer, Dr Tony Jewell
Director, Public Service and Performance, Richard Davies
Director, Rural Affairs and Heritage, Huw Brodie
Director, Social Justice and Local Government, Dr Emyr Roberts
Non-Executive Directors, Kathryn Bishop; Elan Cross Stephens; Adrian Webb

DEPARTMENTS

Children, Education, Lifelong Learning and Skills
Constitutional Affairs, Equality and Communication
Corporate Information and Services
Economy and Transport
Environment, Sustainability and Housing
Finance
Health and Social Services
Heritage
Human Resources
Legal Services
Public Health and Health Professions
Public Services and Performance
Rural Affairs
Social Justice and Local Government

EXECUTIVE AGENCIES

Planning Inspectorate
Welsh European Funding Office

PUBLIC SERVICES OMBUDSMAN FOR WALES

1 Ffordd yr Hen Gae, Pencoed CF35 5LJ
T 01656-641150 F 01656-641199
E ask@ombudsman-wales.org.uk
W www.ombudsman-wales.org.uk
Ombudsman, Peter Tyndall

ASSEMBLY COMMITTEES

Audit
Broadcasting
Business
Children and Young People
Communities and Culture
Enterprise and Learning
Equality of Opportunity
European and External Affairs
Finance
Health, Wellbeing and Local Government
Petitions
Standards of Conduct
Subordinate Legislation
Sustainability

ASSEMBLY COMMISSION

The Assembly Commission was created under the Government of Wales Act 2006. It is a corporate body which has responsibility for the provision of property, staff and services to support Assembly members. The commission is made up of three directorates, the Assembly Business directorate, the Legal Services directorate and the directorate of the Chief Operating Officer; all three are supported by a corporate unit and accountable to the chief executive. Membership of the Assembly Commission includes a presiding officer and four assembly members, with not more than one member (other than the presiding officer) from the same political group.

Presiding Officer, Lord Dafydd Elis-Thomas
Members, Lorraine Barrett; Peter Black; Chris Franks; William Graham
Chief Executive, Clare Clancy

NATIONAL ASSEMBLY FOR WALES

Cardiff Bay, Cardiff CF99 1NA
T 0845-010 5500 E webmaster@assemblywales.org
W www.assemblywales.org

In July 1997 the government announced plans to establish a National Assembly for Wales. In a referendum in September 1997 about 50 per cent of the electorate voted, of whom 50.3 per cent voted in favour of the assembly. Elections are held every four years and the first elections took place on 6 May 1999, the second on 1 May 2003 and the third on 3 May 2007.

Welsh Assembly members are elected using the additional member system. Voters are given two votes, one for a constituency member and one for a regional member. The constituency members are elected under the first-past-the-post system, also used to elect constituency members to the London Assembly. Four regional members in each of the five constituencies are then chosen from party lists or independent candidates using a form of proportional representation.

Until 2007 the National Assembly for Wales had responsibility in Wales for ministerial functions relating to health and personal social services; education; the Welsh language, arts and culture; local government; housing; water and sewerage; environmental protection; sport; agriculture and fisheries; forestry; land use, including town and country planning and conservation; roads; tourism; and European Union matters.

The Government of Wales Act 2006 introduced a radical change to the functions and status of the National Assembly for Wales. With effect from 25 May 2007 the act formally separated the National Assembly for Wales (the legislature – made up of 60 elected assembly members) and the Welsh Assembly Government (the executive – comprising the first minister, Welsh ministers, deputy Welsh ministers and the counsel general). It also made changes to the electoral process: candidates are no longer permitted to stand for both a constituency and on a regional list. The act enabled the National Assembly for Wales to formulate its own legislation (assembly measures) on devolved matters such as health, education, social services and local government; the assembly is given legislative competence (the legal authority to pass measures) on a case-by-case basis by the UK parliament.

The role of the National Assembly for Wales is to scrutinise and monitor the Welsh Assembly Government. It meets in the Senedd debating chamber. The 60 assembly members examine and approve assembly measures and approve certain items of subordinate legislation; approve budgets for the Welsh Assembly Government's programmes; hold Welsh ministers to account; and analyse and debate their decisions and policies.

Presiding Officer, Lord Dafydd Elis-Thomas, AM

SALARIES *as at 1 April 2008*	
First Minister*	£78,335
Minister/Presiding Officer*	£40,465
Deputy Presiding Officer*	£25,556
Assembly Members (AM)†	£50,692

* Also receives the assembly member salary

† Reduced by two-thirds if the member is already an MP or an MEP

MEMBERS OF THE NATIONAL ASSEMBLY FOR WALES

as at 4 June 2008

Andrews, Leighton, *Lab., Rhondda,* Maj. 6,215
Asghar, Mohammad, *PC, South Wales East region*
Barrett, Lorraine Jayne, *Lab., Cardiff S. and Penarth,* Maj. 2,754
Bates, Michael, *LD, Montgomeryshire,* Maj. 1,979
Black, Peter, *LD, South Wales West region*
Bourne, Prof. Nicholas, *C., Mid and West Wales region*
Burnham, Eleanor, *LD, North Wales region*
Burns, Angela, *C., Carmarthen West and South Pembrokeshire,* Maj. 98
Butler, Rosemary Janet Mair, *Lab., Newport W.,* Maj. 1,401
Cairns, Alun, *C., South Wales West region*
Chapman, Christine, *Lab., Cynon Valley,* Maj. 5,623
Cuthbert, Jeffrey, *Lab., Caerphilly,* Maj. 2,287
Davidson, Jane Elizabeth, *Lab., Pontypridd,* Maj. 3,347
Davies, Alun, *Lab., Mid and West Wales region*
Davies, Andrew David, *Lab., Swansea West,* Maj. 1,511
Davies, Andrew Robert, *C., South Wales Central region*
Davies, Jocelyn, *PC, South Wales East region*
Davies, Paul, *C., Preseli Pembrokeshire,* Maj. 3,205
Elis-Thomas, Lord Dafydd, *PC, Dwyfor Meirionnydd,* Maj. 8,868
Evans, Nerys, *PC, Mid and West Wales region*
Franks, Christopher, *PC, South Wales Central region*
German, Michael, *LD, South Wales East region*
Gibbons, Brian, *Lab., Aberavon,* Maj. 6,571
Graham, William, *C., South Wales East region*
Gregory, Janice, *Lab., Ogmore,* Maj. 7,900
Griffiths, Albert John, *Lab., Newport East,* Maj. 875
Griffiths, Lesley, *Lab., Wrexham,* Maj. 1,250
Hart, Edwina, *Lab., Gower,* Maj. 1,192
Hutt, Jane, *Lab., Vale of Glamorgan,* Maj. 83
Isherwood, Mark, *C., North Wales region*
James, Irene, *Lab., Islwyn,* Maj. 2,218
Jenkins, Bethan, *PC, South Wales West region*
Jones, Alun Ffred, *PC, Arfon,* Maj. 5,018
Jones, Carwyn Howell, *Lab., Bridgend,* Maj. 2,556
Jones, Elin, *PC, Ceredigion,* Maj. 3,955
Jones, Gareth, *PC, Aberconwy,* Maj. 1,693
Jones, Helen Mary, *PC, Llanelli,* Maj. 3,884
Jones, Margaret Ann (Ann), *Lab., Vale of Clwyd,* Maj. 92
Law, Trish, *Ind., Blaenau Gwent,* Maj. 5,357
Lewis, Huw, *Lab., Merthyr Tydfil and Rhymney,* Maj. 4,581
Lloyd, Dr David, *PC, South Wales West region*
Lloyd, Val, *Lab., Swansea East,* Maj. 4,961
Melding, David, *C., South Wales Central region*
Mewies, Sandra Elaine, *Lab., Delyn,* Maj. 511
Millar, Darren, *C., Clwyd West,* Maj. 1,596
Morgan, Hywel Rhodri, *Lab., Cardiff West,* Maj. 3,698
Morgan, Jonathan, *C., Cardiff North,* Maj. 4,844
Neagle, Lynne, *Lab., Torfaen,* Maj. 5,396
Ramsay, Nicholas, *C., Monmouth,* Maj. 8,469
Randerson, Jennifer Elizabeth, *LD, Cardiff C.,* Maj. 6,565
Ryder, Janet, *PC, North Wales region*
Sargeant, Carl, *Lab., Alyn and Deeside,* Maj. 3,362
Sinclair, Karen, *Lab., Clwyd South,* Maj. 1,119
Thomas, Gwenda, *Lab., Neath,* Maj. 1,944
Thomas, Rhodri, *PC, Carmarthen East and Dinefwr,* Maj. 8,469
Watson, Joyce, *Lab., Mid and West Wales region*
Williams, Brynle, *C., North Wales region*
Williams, Kirsty, *LD, Brecon and Radnorshire,* Maj. 5,354
Wood, Leanne, *PC, South Wales Central region*
Wyn Jones, Ieuan, *PC, Ynys Mon,* Maj. 4,392

STATE OF THE PARTIES *as at 4 June 2008*

	Constituency AMs	*Regional AMs*	*AM total*
Labour (Lab.)	23*	2	25*
Plaid Cymru (PC)	6*	8	14*
Conservative (C.)	5	7	12
Liberal Democrats (LD)	3	3	6
Others	1	0	1
The Presiding Officer	1	0	1
The Deputy Presiding Officer	1	0	1
Total	40	20	60

* Excludes the presiding officer (PC) and deputy presiding officer (Lab.), who have no party allegiance while in post

NATIONAL ASSEMBLY ELECTION RESULTS

as at 3 May 2007

E. Electorate T. Turnout

See General Election Results for a list of party abbreviations

CONSTITUENCIES

ABERAVON (S. WALES WEST)
E. 51,536 T. 20,528 (39.83%)

Brian Gibbons, Lab.	10,129
Linet Purcell, PC	3,558
Andrew Tutton, Neath Port Talbot Ratepayers Association	2,561
Daisy Meyland-Smith, C.	1,990
Claire Waller, LD	1,450
Captain Beany, Bean	840

Lab. majority 6,571 (32.01%)
4.82% swing Lab. to PC

ALYN AND DEESIDE (WALES N.)
E. 59,355 T. 21,095 (35.54%)

Carl Sargeant, Lab.	8,196
Will Gallagher, C.	4,834
Dennis Hutchinson, Ind.	3,241
Paul Brighton, LD	2,091
Dafydd Passe, PC	1,398
William Crawford, UKIP	1,335

Lab. majority 3,362 (15.94%)
3.66% swing Lab. to C.

BLAENAU GWENT (S. WALES EAST)
E. 52,816 T. 23,518 (44.53%)

Trish Law, Ind.	12,722
Keren Bender, Lab.	7,365
Gareth Lewis, LD	1,351
Natasha Asghar, PC	1,129
Bob Hayward, C.	951

Ind. majority 5,357 (22.78%)
46.5% swing Lab. to Ind.

BRECON AND RADNORSHIRE (WALES MID AND W.)
E. 55,428 T. 28,748 (51.87%)

Kirsty Williams, LD	15,006
Suzy Davies, C.	9,652
Neil Stone, Lab.	2,514
Arwel Lloyd, PC	1,576

LD majority 5,354 (18.62%)
0.58% swing LD to C.

BRIDGEND (S. WALES WEST)
E. 59,550 T. 24,552 (41.23%)

Carwyn Jones, Lab.	9,889
Emma Greenow, C.	7,333
Paul Warren, LD	3,730
Nicholas Thomas, PC	3,600

Lab. majority 2,556 (10.41%)
0.71% swing Lab. to C.

CAERNARFON (WALES N.)
E. 39,891 T. 19,573 (49.07%)

Alun Ffred Jones, PC	10,260
Martin Eaglestone, Lab.	5,242
Gerry Frobisher, C.	1,858
Mel ab Owain, LD	1,424
Elwyn Williams, UKIP	789

PC majority 5,018 (25.64%)
3.43% swing Lab. to PC

CAERPHILLY (S. WALES EAST)
E. 62,046 T. 26,922 (43.39%)

Jeff Cuthbert, Lab.	8,937
Lindsay Whittle, PC	7,000
Ron Davies, Ind.	6,071
Richard Foley, C.	3,227
Huw Price, LD	1,687

Lab. majority 1,937 (7.19%)
5.07% swing Lab. to PC

CARDIFF CENTRAL (S. WALES CENTRAL)
E. 62,202 T. 22,397 (36.01%)

Jenny Randerson, LD	11,462
Sue Lent, Lab.	4,897
Andrew Murphy, C.	3,137
Thomas Whitfield, PC	1,855
Frank Hughes, UKIP	1,046

LD majority 6,565 (29.31%)
2.71% swing LD to Lab.

CARDIFF NORTH (S. WALES CENTRAL)
E. 65,687 T. 33,702 (51.31%)

Jonathan Morgan, C.	15,253
Sophie Howe, Lab.	10,409
Ed Bridges, LD	4,287
Wyn Jones, PC	2,491
Dai Llewellyn, UKIP	1,262

C. majority 4,844 (14.37%)
8.16% swing Lab. to C.

CARDIFF SOUTH AND PENARTH (S. WALES CENTRAL)
E. 71,312 T. 26,728 (37.48%)

Lorraine Barrett, Lab.	10,106
Karen Robson, C.	7,352
Dominic Hannigan, LD	5,445
Jason Toby, PC	3,825

Lab. majority 2,754 (10.30%)
4.22% swing Lab. to C.

CARDIFF WEST (S. WALES CENTRAL)
E. 64,588 T. 26,889 (41.63%)

Rhodri Morgan, Lab.	10,390
Craig Williams, C.	6,692
Neil McEvoy, PC	5,719
Alison Goldsworthy, LD	4,088

Lab. majority 3,698 (13.75%)
8.77% swing Lab. to C.

CARMARTHEN EAST AND DINEFWR
(WALES MID AND W.)
E. 52,528 T. 29,269 (55.72%)

Rhodri Glyn Thomas, PC	15,655
Kevin Madge, Lab.	7,186
Henrietta Hensher, C.	4,676
Ian Walton, LD	1,752

PC majority 8,469 (28.94%)
5.85% swing Lab. to PC

CARMARTHEN WEST AND SOUTH PEMBROKESHIRE
(WALES MID AND W.)
E. 57,477 T. 28,568 (49.70%)

Angela Burns, C.	8,590
Christine Gwyther, Lab.	8,492
John Dixon, PC	8,340
John Gossage, LD	1,806
Malcolm Calver, Ind.	1,340

C. majority 98 (0.34%)
7.45% swing Lab. to C.

CEREDIGION (WALES MID AND W.)
E. 54,071 T. 30,108 (55.68%)

Elin Jones, PC	14,818
John Davies, LD	10,863
Trefor Jones, C.	2,369
Linda Grace, Lab.	1,530
Emyr Morgan, Ind.	528

PC majority 3,955 (13.14%)
2.20% swing PC to LD

CLWYD SOUTH (WALES N.)
E. 51,865 T. 19,498 (37.59%)

Karen Sinclair, Lab.	6,838
John Bell, C.	5,719
Nia Davies, PC	3,894
Frank Biggs, LD	1,838
David Rowlands, UKIP	1,209

Lab. majority 1,119 (5.74%)
6.04% swing Lab. to C.

CLWYD WEST (WALES N.)
E. 57,312 T. 26,205 (45.72%)

Darren Millar, C.	8,905
Alun Pugh, Lab.	7,309
Philip Edwards, PC	7,162
Simon Croft, LD	1,705
Warwick Nicholson, UKIP	1,124

C. majority 1,596 (6.09%)
4.13% swing Lab. to C.

CONWY (WALES N.)
E. 44,143 T. 20,699 (46.89%)

Gareth Jones, PC	7,983
Dylan Jones-Evans, C.	6,290
Denise Idris Jones, Lab.	4,508
Euron Hughes, LD	1,918

PC majority 1,693 (8.18%)
2.86% swing C. to PC

CYNON VALLEY (S. WALES CENTRAL)
E. 50,846 T. 19,517 (38.38%)

Christine Chapman, Lab.	11,058
Liz Walters, PC	5,435
Neill John, C.	2,024
Margaret Phelps, LD	1,000

Lab. majority 5,623 (28.81%)
7.16% swing Lab. to PC

DELYN (WALES N.)
E. 52,733 T. 21,668 (41.09%)

Sandy Mewies, Lab.	7,506
Antoinette Sandbach, C.	6,996
Meg Ellis, PC	3,179
Ian Matthews, LD	2,669
Derek Bigg, UKIP	1,318

Lab. majority 510 (2.35%)
3.63% swing Lab. to C.

GOWER (S. WALES WEST)
E. 61,520 T. 27,545 (44.77%)

Edwina Hart, Lab.	9,406
Byron Davis, C.	8,214
Darren Price, PC	5,106
Nick Tregoning, LD	2,924
Alex Lewis, UKIP	1,895

Lab. majority 1,192 (4.33%)
9.84% swing Lab. to C.

ISLWYN (S. WALES EAST)
E. 54,795 T. 23,564 (43.00%)

Irene James, Lab.	8,883
Kevin Etheridge, Ind.	6,665
Allan Pritchard, PC	5,084
Paul Williams, C.	1,797
Mark Maguire, LD	1,135

Lab. majority 2,218 (9.41%)
23.3% swing Lab. to Ind.

LLANELLI (WALES MID AND W.)
E. 56,154 T. 27,602 (49.15%)

Helen Mary Jones, PC	13,839
Catherine Thomas, Lab.	9,955
Andrew Morgan, C.	2,757
Jeremy Townsend, LD	1,051

PC majority 3,884 (14.07%)
7.08% swing Lab. to PC

MEIRIONNYDD NANT CONWY (WALES MID AND W.)
E. 46,718 T. 22,122 (47.35%)

Dafydd Elis-Thomas, PC	13,201
Mike Wood, C.	4,333
David Phillips, Lab.	2,749
Steve Churchman, LD	1,839

PC majority 8,868 (40.09%)
1.57% swing PC to C.

MERTHYR TYDFIL AND RHYMNEY (S. WALES EAST)
E. 54,025 T. 21,028 (38.92%)

Huw Lewis, Lab.	7,776
Amy Kitcher, LD	3,195
Clive Tovey, Ind.	2,622
Glyndwr Jones, PC	2,519
Jeff Edwards, Ind.	1,950
Giles Howard, C.	1,151
Jock Greer, Ind.	844
Vivienne Hadley, Ind.	809
Richard Williams, Ind.	162

Lab. majority 4,581 (21.79%)
15.77% swing Lab. to LD

MONMOUTH (S. WALES EAST)
E. 63,000 T. 29,565 (46.93%)

Nick Ramsay, C.	15,389
Richard Clark, Lab.	6,920
Jacqui Sullivan, LD	4,359
Jonathan Clark, PC	2,093
Ed Abrams, Eng. Dem.	804

C. majority 8,469 (28.65%)
0.99% swing C. to Lab.

MONTGOMERYSHIRE (WALES MID AND W.)
E. 48,377 T. 22,300 (46.10%)

Mick Bates, LD	8,704
Don Munford, C.	6,725
David Thomas, PC	3,076
Charles Lawson, UKIP	2,251
Rachel Maycock, Lab.	1,544

LD majority 1,979 (8.87%)
1.18% swing LD to C.

NEATH (S. WALES WEST)
E. 57,952 T. 25,200 (43.48%)

Gwenda Thomas, Lab.	10,934
Alun Llewelyn, PC	8,990
Andrew Sivertsen, C.	2,956
Sheila Waye, LD	2,320

Lab. majority 1,944 (7.71%)
7.29% swing Lab. to PC

NEWPORT EAST (S. WALES EAST)
E. 53,060 T. 19,906 (37.52%)

John Griffiths, Lab.	6,395
Ed Townsend, LD	5,520
Peter Fox, C.	4,512
Trefor Puw, PC	1,696
James Harris, Ind.	1,354
Mike Blundell, Eng. Dem.	429

Lab. majority 875 (4.40%)
12.00% swing Lab. to LD

NEWPORT WEST (S. WALES EAST)
E. 58,981 T. 23,659 (40.11%)

Rosemary Butler, Lab.	9,582
Matthew Evans, C.	8,181
Nigel Flanagan, LD	2,813
Brian Hancock, PC	2,449
Andrew Constantine, Eng. Dem.	634

Lab. majority 1,401 (5.92%)
5.79% swing Lab. to C.

OGMORE (S. WALES WEST)
E. 56,973 T. 22,766 (39.96%)

Janice Gregory, Lab.	11,761
Sian Caiach, PC	3,861
Norma Lloyd-Nesling, C.	2,663
Steve Smith, Ind.	2,337
Martin Plant, LD	2,144

Lab. majority 7,900 (34.70%)
2.65% swing Lab. to PC

PONTYPRIDD (S. WALES CENTRAL)
E. 57,512 T. 23,501 (40.86%)

Jane Davidson, Lab.	9,836
Michael Powell, LD	6,449
Richard Grigg, PC	4,181
Janice Charles, C.	3,035

Lab. majority 3,387 (14.41%)
11.08% swing Lab. to LD

PRESELI PEMBROKESHIRE (WALES MID AND W.)
E. 56,435 T. 28,720 (50.89%)

Paul Davies, C.	11,086
Tamsin Dunwoody, Lab.	7,881
John Osmond, PC	7,101
Hywel Davies, LD	2,652

C. majority 3,205 (11.16%)
8.52% swing Lab. to C.

RHONDDA (S. WALES CENTRAL)
E. 52,478 T. 22,107 (42.13%)

Leighton Andrews, Lab.	12,875
Jill Evans, PC	6,660
Karen Roberts, LD	1,441
Howard Parsons, C.	1,131

Lab. majority 6,215 (28.11%)
3.23% swing Lab. to PC

SWANSEA EAST (S. WALES WEST)
E. 59,186 T. 20,717 (35.00%)

Val Lloyd, Lab.	8,590
Helen Clarke, LD	3,629
Danny Bowles, PC	3,218
Bob Dowdle, C.	2,025
David Robinson, Ind.	1,618
Ray Welsby, Ind. Welsby	1,177
Gary Evans, Ind. Evans	460

Lab. majority 4,961 (23.95%)
0.49% swing LD to Lab.

SWANSEA WEST (S. WALES WEST)
E. 61,469 T. 22,879 (37.22%)

Andrew Davies, Lab.	7,393
Peter May, LD	5,882
Harri Davies, C.	4,379
Ian Titherington, PC	3,583
Richard Lewis, UKIP	1,642

Lab. majority 1,511 (6.60%)
5.75% swing Lab. to LD

TORFAEN (S. WALES EAST)
E. 62,592 T. 23,215 (37.09%)

Lynne Neagle, Lab.	9,921
Graham Smith, C.	4,525
Ian Williams, Ind.	3,348
Rhys ab Elis, PC	2,762
Patrick Legge, LD	2,659

Lab. majority 5,396 (23.24%)
6.18% swing Lab. to C.

VALE OF CLWYD (WALES N.)
E. 55,234 T. 22,275 (40.33%)

Ann Jones, Lab.	8,104
Matt Wright, C.	8,012
Mark Jones, PC	3,884
Mark Young, LD	2,275

Lab. majority 92 (0.41%)
7.40% swing Lab. to C.

VALE OF GLAMORGAN (S. WALES CENTRAL)
E. 68,856 T. 33,686 (48.92%)

Jane Hutt, Lab.	11,515
Gordon Kemp, C.	11,432
Barry Shaw, PC	4,671
Mark Hooper, LD	3,758
Kevin Mahoney, UKIP	2,310

Lab. majority 83 (0.25%)
4.02% swing Lab. to C.

WREXHAM (WALES N.)
E. 50,759 T. 19,567 (38.55%)

Lesley Griffiths, Lab.	5,633
John Marek, Ind.	4,383
Felicity Elphick, C.	3,372
Bruce Roberts, LD	3,268
Sion Aled Owen, PC	1,878
Peter Lewis, UKIP	1,033

Lab. majority 1,250 (6.39%)
6.0% swing Ind. to Lab.

YNYS MON (WALES N.)
E. 51,814 T. 26,820 (51.76%)

Ieuan Wyn Jones, PC	10,653
Peter Rogers, Ind.	6,261
Jonathan Austin, Lab.	4,681
James Roach, C.	3,480
Mandi Abrahams, LD	912
Francis Wykes, UKIP	833

PC majority 4,392 (16.38%)
10.5% swing PC to Ind.

REGIONS

MID AND WEST WALES
E. 427,188 T. 216,957 (50.79%)

PC	67,258	(31.00%)
C.	49,606	(22.86%)
Lab.	39,979	(18.43%)
LD	28,790	(13.27%)
Green	8,768	(4.04%)
UKIP	8,191	(3.78%)
BNP	6,389	(2.94%)
Soc. Lab.	2,196	(1.01%)
Ind.	1,598	(0.74%)
Welsh Christian Party	1,493	(0.69%)
Ind. Evans	1,108	(0.51%)
Comm. Brit.	666	(0.31%)
Veritas	502	(0.23%)
CPA	413	(0.19%)

PC majority 17,652 (8.14%)
1.16% swing PC to C. (2003 PC majority 5,423)

ADDITIONAL MEMBERS
Nick Bourne, *C.*
Alun Davies, *Lab.*
Joyce Watson, *Lab.*
Nerys Evans, *PC*

NORTH WALES
E. 463,106 T. 196,442 (42.42%)

Lab.	51,831	(26.38%)
PC	50,558	(25.74%)
C.	50,266	(25.59%)
LD	15,275	(7.78%)
BNP	9,986	(5.08%)
UKIP	8,015	(4.08%)
Green	5,660	(2.88%)
Soc. Lab.	2,209	(1.12%)
Welsh Christian Party	1,300	(0.66%)
Comm. Brit.	700	(0.36%)
CPA	642	(0.33%)

Lab. majority 1,273 (0.65%)
4.72% swing Lab. to PC (2003 Lab. majority 13,610)

ADDITIONAL MEMBERS
Brynle Williams, *C.*
Mark Isherwood, *C.*
Eleanor Burnham, *LD*
Janet Ryder, *PC*

SOUTH WALES CENTRAL
E. 493,481 T. 208,294 (42.21%)

Lab.	70,799	(33.99%)
C.	45,147	(21.67%)
PC	32,207	(15.46%)
LD	29,262	(14.05%)
BNP	7,889	(3.79%)
Green	7,831	(3.76%)
UKIP	7,645	(3.67%)
Welsh Christian Party	1,987	(0.95%)
Soc. Lab.	1,744	(0.84%)
Respect	1,079	(0.52%)
Soc. Alt.	838	(0.40%)
Comm. Brit.	817	(0.39%)
CPA	757	(0.36%)
Socialist Equality Party	292	(0.14%)

Lab. majority 25,652 (12.32%)
5.16% swing Lab. to C. (2003 Lab. majority 40,965)

ADDITIONAL MEMBERS
David Melding, *C.*
Andrew Davies, *C.*
Leanne Wood, *PC*
Chris Franks, *PC*

SOUTH WALES EAST
E. 461,315 T. 190,064 (41.20%)

Lab.	67,998	(35.78%)
C.	37,935	(19.96%)
PC	25,915	(13.63%)
LD	20,947	(11.02%)
BNP	8,940	(4.70%)
UKIP	8,725	(4.59%)
Green	5,414	(2.85%)
Ind.	4,876	(2.57%)
Soc. Lab.	3,693	(1.94%)
Welsh Christian Party	2,498	(1.31%)
Eng. Dem.	1,655	(0.87%)
Comm. Brit.	979	(0.52%)
CPA	489	(0.26%)

Lab. majority 30,063 (15.82%)
4.55% swing Lab. to C. (2003 Lab. majority 42,291)

ADDITIONAL MEMBERS
William Graham, *C.*
Michael German, *LD*
Jocelyn Davies, *PC*
Mohammed Asghar, *PC*

SOUTH WALES WEST
E. 408,186 T. 163,127 (39.96%)

Lab.	58,347	(35.77%)
PC	28,819	(17.67%)
C.	26,199	(16.06%)
LD	20,226	(12.40%)
BNP	8,993	(5.51%)
Green	6,130	(3.76%)
UKIP	5,914	(3.63%)
Soc. Lab.	2,367	(1.45%)
Welsh Christian Party	1,685	(1.03%)
Ind. James	1,186	(0.73%)
Soc. Alt.	1,027	(0.63%)
Respect	713	(0.44%)
Ind.	582	(0.36%)
Comm. Brit.	546	(0.33%)
CPA	393	(0.24%)

Lab. majority 29,528 (18.10%)
2.87% swing Lab. to PC (2003 Lab. majority 33,267)

ADDITIONAL MEMBERS
Alun Cairns, *C.*
Peter Black, *LD*
Bethan Jenkins, *PC*
Dai Lloyd, *PC*

SCOTLAND

SCOTTISH GOVERNMENT

St Andrew's House, Regent Road, Edinburgh EH1 3DG
T 0845-774 1741 **Enquiry Line** 0131-556 8400
F 01397-795001
E ceu@scotland.gsi.gov.uk **W** www.scotland.gov.uk

The Scottish government is the devolved government for Scotland. It is responsible for most of the issues of day-to-day concern to the people of Scotland, including health, education, justice, rural affairs and transport, and manages an annual budget of over £30bn.

The government was known as the Scottish executive when it was established in 1999, following the first elections to the Scottish parliament. The current administration was formed after elections in May 2007.

The government is led by a first minister who is nominated by the parliament and in turn appoints the other Scottish ministers who make up the cabinet.

Civil servants in Scotland are accountable to Scottish ministers, who are themselves accountable to the Scottish parliament.

CABINET

First Minister, Rt. Hon. Alex Salmond, MSP
Minister for EU, International and Culture, Linda Fabiani, MSP
Minister for Parliamentary Business, Bruce Crawford, MSP
Deputy First Minister and Cabinet Secretary for Health and Wellbeing, Nicola Sturgeon, MSP
Minister for Communities and Sport, Stewart Maxwell, MSP
Minister for Public Health, Shona Robison, MSP
Cabinet Secretary for Education and Lifelong Learning, Fiona Hyslop, MSP
Minister for Children and Early Years, Adam Ingram, MSP
Minister for Schools and Skills, Maureen Watt, MSP
Cabinet Secretary for Finance and Sustainable Growth, John Swinney, MSP
Minister for Enterprise, Energy and Tourism, Jim Mather, MSP
Minister for Transport, Infrastructure and Climate Change, Stewart Stevenson, MSP
Cabinet Secretary for Justice, Kenny MacAskill, MSP
Minister for Community Safety, Fergus Ewing, MSP
Cabinet Secretary for Rural Affairs and the Environment, Richard Lochhead, MSP
Minister for Environment, Michael Russell, MSP

LAW OFFICERS

Lord Advocate, Elish Angiolini, QC
Solicitor-General for Scotland, Frank Mulholland, QC

STRATEGIC BOARD

Permanent Secretary, Sir John Elvidge, KCB
Director-General, Economy, and Chief Economic Adviser, Dr Andrew Goudie
Director-General, Education, Philip Rycroft
Director-General, Environment, Richard Wakeford
Director-General, Finance and Corporate Services, Stella Manzie, CBE
Director-General, Health, and Chief Executive of NHS Scotland, Dr Kevin Woods
Director-General, Justice and Communities, Robert Gordon, CB
Non-Executive Directors, Prof. William Bound; David Fisher

CHANGE AND CORPORATE SERVICES

Saughton House, Broomhouse Drive, Edinburgh EH11 3XD
Director of Change and Corporate Services, Paul Gray

ECONOMY DEPARTMENT

Victoria Quay, Edinburgh EH6 6QQ
Directorates: Europe, External Affairs and Culture; Finance; Planning; Planning and Environmental Appeals; Public Service Reform; Scottish Development International; Scottish Procurement; Strategic Spending Review; Transport
Director-General and Chief Economic Adviser, Dr Andrew Goudie

EXECUTIVE AGENCIES

General Register Office of Scotland
Historic Scotland
National Archives of Scotland
Registers of Scotland
Scottish Public Pensions Agency
Scottish Water
Transport Scotland
Water Industry Commission

EDUCATION DEPARTMENT

Victoria Quay, Edinburgh EH6 6QQ
Directorates: Children, Young People and Social Care; Corporate Analytical Services; Enterprise, Energy and Tourism; General Group; Lifelong Learning; Office of the Chief Scientific Adviser; Schools
Director-General, Philip Rycroft

EXECUTIVE AGENCIES

HM Inspectorate of Education
Social Work Inspection Agency
Student Awards Agency for Scotland

ENVIRONMENT DEPARTMENT

Victoria Quay, Edinburgh EH6 6QQ
Directorates: Climate Change and Water Industry; DG Coordination – Environment; Environmental Quality; Greener Scotland; Marine; On the Ground; Rural and Environment Research and Analysis; Rural; Rural Payments and Inspections; State Veterinary Service
Director-General, Richard Wakeford

EXECUTIVE AGENCIES

Cairngorms National Park Authority
Crofters Commission
Deer Commission Scotland
Fisheries Research Service
Loch Lomond and Trossach National Park Authority
Royal Botanic Gardens
Scottish Agricultural Science Agency
Scottish Agricultural Wages Board
Scottish Environmental Protection Agency
Scottish Fisheries Protection Service
Scottish Natural Heritage

HEALTH DEPARTMENT

St Andrew's House, Regent Road, Edinburgh EH1 3DG
Directorates: E-Health; Health Delivery; Health Finance; Health Workforce; Healthcare Policy and Strategy; Primary and Community Care; Public Health and Wellbeing; Scottish Academy for Health Policy and Management
Director-General and Chief Executive of NHS Scotland, Dr Kevin Woods

EXECUTIVE AGENCIES
Mental Health Tribunal (Scotland)
Scottish Commission for the Regulation of Care

JUSTICE AND COMMUNITIES DEPARTMENT
St Andrew's House, Regent Road, Edinburgh EH1 3DG
Directorates: Civil and International Justice; Constitutional and Parliamentary Secretariat; Courts; Criminal Justice; DG Coordination – Justice; Housing and Regeneration; Judicial Appointments Board for Scotland; Office of the Scottish Parliamentary Counsel; Office of the Solicitor to the Scottish Government; OSSE Group A; OSSE Group B; OSSE Group C; Police and Community Safety
Director-General, Robert Gordon, CB

EXECUTIVE AGENCIES
Accountant in Bankruptcy
HM Inspector of Constabulary
HMC Inspector of Fire Rescue Service
HMC Inspector Prisons
Office of Scottish Charities Regulator
Parole Board for Scotland
Risk Management Authority
Scottish Charity Appeals Panel
Scottish Courts Service
Scottish Housing Regulator
Scottish Prison Service

CROWN OFFICE AND PROCURATOR FISCAL SERVICE
29 Chambers Street, Edinburgh EH1 1LD
T 0131-226 4962
Chief Executive and Crown Agent, Norman McFadyen

OFFICE OF THE PERMANENT SECRETARY
St Andrew's House, Regent Road, Edinburgh EH1 3DG
T 0131-244 4028 F 0131-244 2756
Permanent Secretary, Sir John Elvidge, KCB

AUDIT SCOTLAND
110 George Street, Edinburgh EH2 4LH
T 0845-146 1010 F 0845-146 1009
W www.audit-scotland.gov.uk
Auditor-General, Robert W. Black
Accounts Commission Chair, John Baillie

SCOTTISH PARLIAMENT

Edinburgh EH99 1SP
T 0131-348 5000 Textphone 0131-558 7676
F 0131-348 5601
E sp.info@scottish.parliament.uk
W www.scottish.parliament.uk

In July 1997 the government announced plans to establish a Scottish parliament. In a referendum on 11 September 1997 about 60 per cent of the electorate voted. Of those who voted, 74.3 per cent voted in favour of the parliament and 63.5 per cent in favour of it having tax-raising powers. Elections are held every four years. The first elections were held on 6 May 1999, when around 59 per cent of the electorate voted. The first meeting was held on 12 May 1999 and the Scottish parliament was officially opened on 1 July 1999 at the Assembly Hall, Edinburgh. A new building to house parliament was opened, in the presence of the Queen, at Holyrood on 9 October 2004. On 3 May 2007 the third elections to the Scottish parliament took place.

The Scottish parliament has 129 members (including the presiding officer), comprising 73 constituency members and 56 additional regional members, mainly from party lists. It can introduce primary legislation and has the power to raise or lower the basic rate of income tax by up to three pence in the pound. Members of the Scottish Parliament are elected using the additional member system, the same system used to elect London Assembly and Welsh Assembly members.

The areas for which the Scottish parliament is responsible include: education, health, law, environment, economic development, local government, housing, police, fire services, planning, financial assistance to industry, tourism, some transport, heritage and the arts, agriculture, forestry and food standards.

SALARIES *as at 1 November 2007*	
First Minister*	£78,359
Ministers*	£40,650
Lord Advocate*	£53,107
Solicitor-General for Scotland*	£38,402
Junior Ministers*	£25,462
MSPs†	£54,093
Presiding Officer*	£40,650
Deputy Presiding Officer*	£25,462

* In addition to the MSP salary
† Reduced by two-thirds if the member is already an MP or an MEP

MEMBERS OF THE SCOTTISH PARLIAMENT

as at 18 July 2008
Adam, Brian, *SNP, Aberdeen North,* Maj. 3,749
Ahmad, Bashir, *SNP, Glasgow region*
Aitken, Bill, *C., Glasgow region*
Alexander, Wendy, *Lab., Paisley North,* Maj. 5,113
Allan, Alasdair, *SNP, Western Isles,* Maj. 987
Baillie, Jackie, *Lab., Dumbarton,* Maj. 1,611
Baker, Claire, *Lab., Mid Scotland and Fife region*
Baker, Richard, *Lab., North East Scotland region*
Boyack, Sarah, *Lab., Edinburgh Central,* Maj. 1,193
Brankin, Rhona, *Lab., Midlothian,* Maj. 1,702
Brocklebank, Ted, *C., Mid Scotland and Fife region*
Brown, Gavin, *C., Lothians region*
Brown, Keith, *SNP, Ochil,* Maj. 490
Brown, Robert E., *LD, Glasgow region*
Brownlee, Derek, *C., South of Scotland region*
Butler, Bill, *Lab., Glasgow Anniesland,* Maj. 4,306
Campbell, Aileen, *SNP, South of Scotland region*
Carlaw, Jackson, *C., West of Scotland region*
Chisholm, Malcolm, *Lab., Edinburgh North and Leith,* Maj. 2,444
Coffey, Willie, *SNP, Kilmarnock and Loudon,* Maj. 1,342
Constance, Angela, *SNP, Livingston,* Maj. 870
Craigie, Cathie, *Lab., Cumbernauld and Kilsyth,* Maj. 2,079
Crawford, Bruce, *SNP, Stirling,* Maj. 620
Cunningham, Roseanna, *SNP, Perth,* Maj. 2,495
Curran, Margaret, *Lab., Glasgow Baillieston,* Maj. 3,934
Don, Nigel, *SNP, North East Scotland region*
Doris, Bob, *SNP, Glasgow region*
Eadie, Helen, *Lab., Dunfermline East,* Maj. 3,993
Ewing, Fergus, *SNP, Inverness East, Nairn and Lochaber,* Maj. 5,471
Fabiani, Linda, *SNP, Central Scotland region*
Ferguson, Patricia, *Lab., Glasgow Maryhill,* Maj. 2,310
Fergusson, Alex, *C., Galloway and Upper Nithsdale,* Maj. 3,333

Finnie, Ross, *LD, West of Scotland region*
FitzPatrick, Joe, *SNP, Dundee West,* Maj. 1,946
Foulkes, George, *Lab., Lothians region*
Fraser, Murdo, *C., Mid Scotland and Fife region*
Gibson, Kenneth, *SNP, Cunninghame North,* Maj. 48
Gibson, Rob, *SNP, Highlands and Islands region*
Gillon, Karen, *Lab., Clydesdale,* Maj. 2,893
Glen, Marlyn, *Lab., North East Scotland region*
Godman, Trish, *Lab., Renfrewshire West,* Maj. 2,178
Goldie, Annabel, *C., West of Scotland region*
Gordon, Charlie, *Lab., Glasgow Cathcart,* Maj. 2,189
Grahame, Christine, *SNP, South of Scotland region*
Grant, Rhoda, *Lab., Highlands and Islands region*
Gray, Iain, *Lab., East Lothian,* Maj. 2,448
Harper, Robin, *Scot. Green, Lothians region*
Harvie, Christopher, *SNP, Mid Scotland and Fife region*
Harvie, Patrick, *Scot. Green, Glasgow region*
Henry, Hugh, *Lab., Paisley South,* Maj. 4,230
Hepburn, Jamie, *SNP, Central Scotland region*
Hume, Jim, *LD, South of Scotland region*
Hyslop, Fiona, *SNP, Lothians region*
Ingram, Adam, *SNP, South of Scotland region*
Jamieson, Cathy, *Lab., Carrick, Cumnock and Doon Valley,* Maj. 3,986
Johnstone, Alex, *C., North East Scotland region*
Kelly, James, *Lab., Glasgow Rutherglen,* Maj. 4,378
Kerr, Andy, *Lab., East Kilbride,* Maj. 1,972
Kidd, Bill, *SNP, Glasgow region*
Lamont, Johann, *Lab., Glasgow Pollok,* Maj. 4,393
Lamont, John, *C., Roxburgh and Berwickshire,* Maj. 1,985
Livingstone, Marilyn, *Lab., Kirkcaldy,* Maj. 2,622
Lochhead, Richard, *SNP, Moray,* Maj. 7,924
MacAskill, Kenny, *SNP, Edinburgh East and Musselburgh,* Maj. 1,382
Macdonald, Lewis, *Lab., Aberdeen Central,* Maj. 382
MacDonald, Margo, *Ind., Lothians region*
Macintosh, Kenneth, *Lab., Eastwood,* Maj. 891
McArthur, Liam, *LD, Orkney,* Maj. 2,476
McAveety, Frank, *Lab., Glasgow Shettleston,* Maj. 2,881
McCabe, Tom, *Lab., Hamilton South,* Maj. 3,652
McConnell, Jack, *Lab., Motherwell and Wishaw,* Maj. 5,938
McGrigor, Jamie, *C., Highlands and Islands region*
McInnes, Alison, *LD, North East Scotland region*
McKee, Ian, *SNP, Lothians region*
McKelvie, Christina, *SNP, Central Scotland region*
McLetchie, David, *C., Edinburgh Pentlands,* Maj. 4,525
McMahon, Michael, *Lab., Hamilton North and Bellshill,* Maj. 4,865
McMillan, Stuart, *SNP, West of Scotland region*
McNeil, Duncan, *Lab., Greenock and Inverclyde,* Maj. 3,024
McNeill, Pauline, *Lab., Glasgow Kelvin,* Maj. 1,207
McNulty, Des, *Lab., Clydebank and Milngavie,* Maj. 3,179
Martin, Paul, *Lab., Glasgow Springburn,* Maj. 5,095
Marwick, Tricia, *SNP, Central Fife,* Maj. 1,166
Mather, Jim, *SNP, Argyll and Bute,* Maj. 815
Matheson, Michael, *SNP, Falkirk West,* Maj. 776
Maxwell, Stewart, *SNP, West of Scotland region*
Milne, Nanette, *C., North East Scotland region*
Mitchell, Margaret, *C., Central Scotland region*
Morgan, Alasdair, *SNP, South of Scotland region*
Mulligan, Mary, *Lab., Linlithgow,* Maj. 1,160
Munro, John F., *LD, Ross, Skye and Inverness West,* Maj. 3,486
Murray, Elaine, *Lab., Dumfries,* Maj. 2,839
Neil, Alex, *SNP, Central Scotland region*
O'Donnell, Hugh, *LD, Central Scotland region*
Oldfather, Irene, *Lab., Cunninghame South,* Maj. 2,168
Park, John, *Lab., Mid Scotland and Fife region*
Paterson, Gil, *SNP, West of Scotland region*
Peacock, Peter, *Lab., Highlands and Islands region*
Peattie, Cathy, *Lab., Falkirk East,* Maj. 1,872
Pringle, Mike, *LD, Edinburgh South,* Maj. 1,929
Purvis, Jeremy, *LD, Tweeddale, Ettrick and Lauderdale,* Maj. 598
Robison, Shona, *SNP, Dundee East,* Maj. 4,524
Rumbles, Mike, *LD, Aberdeenshire West and Kincardine,* Maj. 5,170
Russell, Michael, *SNP, South of Scotland region*
Salmond, Alex, *SNP, Gordon,* Maj. 2062
Scanlon, Mary, *C., Highlands and Islands region*
Scott, John, *C., Ayr,* Maj. 3,906
Scott, Tavish, *LD, Shetland,* Maj. 4,909
Simpson, Richard, *Lab., Mid Scotland and Fife region*
Smith, Elaine, *Lab., Coatbridge and Chryston,* Maj. 4,510
Smith, Elizabeth, *C., Mid Scotland and Fife region*
Smith, Iain, *LD, Fife North East,* Maj. 5,016
Smith, Margaret, *LD, Edinburgh West,* Maj. 5,886
Somerville, Shirley-Anne, *SNP, Lothians region**
Stephen, Nicol, *LD, Aberdeen South,* Maj. 2,732
Stevenson, Stewart, *SNP, Banff and Buchan,* Maj. 10,530
Stewart, David, *Lab., Highlands and Islands region*
Stone, Jamie, *LD, Caithness, Sutherland and Easter Ross,* Maj. 2,323
Sturgeon, Nicola, *SNP, Glasgow Govan,* Maj. 744
Swinney, John, *SNP, North Tayside,* Maj. 7,584
Thompson, Dave, *SNP, Highlands and Islands region*
Tolson, Jim, *LD, Dunfermline West,* Maj. 476
Watt, Maureen, *SNP, North East Scotland region*
Welsh, Andrew, *SNP, Angus,* Maj. 8,243
White, Sandra, *SNP, Glasgow region*
Whitefield, Karen, *Lab., Airdrie and Shotts,* Maj. 1,446
Whitton, David, *Lab., Strathkelvin and Bearsden,* Maj. 3,388
Wilson, Bill, *SNP, West of Scotland region*
Wilson, John, *SNP, Central Scotland region*

*Stefan Tymkewycz stepped down after his election to the Scottish parliament and was replaced by Shirley-Anne Somerville on 31 August 2007

STATE OF THE PARTIES *as at 18 July 2008*

	Constituency MSPs	*Regional MSPs*	*Total*
Scottish National Party (SNP)	21	26	47
Scottish Labour Party (Lab.)	37	9	46
Scottish Conservative and Unionist Party (C.)	3	13	16
Scottish Liberal Democrats (LD)	11	5	16
Scottish Green Party (Scot. Green)	0	2	2
Independent (Ind.)	0	1	1
Presiding Officer†	1	0	1
Total	73	56	129

† The presiding officer was elected as a constituency member for the Conservatives but has no party allegiance while in post

The Presiding Officer, Alex Fergusson, MSP
Deputy Presiding Officers, Trish Godman, MSP *(Lab.)*; Alasdair Morgan, MSP *(SNP)*

SCOTTISH PARLIAMENT ELECTION RESULTS

as at 3 May 2007

E. Electorate T. Turnout

See General Election Results for a list of party abbreviations

CONSTITUENCIES

ABERDEEN CENTRAL
(Scotland North East Region)
E. 46,588 T. 21,120 (45.33%)

Lewis Macdonald, Lab.	7,232
Karen Shirron, SNP	6,850
John Stewart, LD	4,693
Andrew Jones, C.	2,345

Lab. majority 382 (1.81%)
2.06% swing Lab. to SNP

ABERDEEN NORTH
(Scotland North East Region)
E. 51,507 T. 24,891 (48.33%)

Brian Adam, SNP	11,406
Elaine Thomson, Lab.	7,657
Steve Delaney, LD	3,836
Carol Garvie, C.	1,992

SNP majority 3,749 (15.06%)
6.62% swing Lab. to SNP

ABERDEEN SOUTH
(Scotland North East Region)
E. 56,700 T. 29,885 (52.71%)

Nicol Stephen, LD	10,843
Maureen Watt, SNP	8,111
Rami Okasha, Lab.	5,499
David Davidson, C.	5,432

LD majority 2,732 (9.14%)
11.21% swing LD to SNP

ABERDEENSHIRE WEST AND KINCARDINE
(Scotland North East Region)
E. 65,233 T. 34,823 (53.38%)

Mike Rumbles, LD	14,314
Dennis Robertson, SNP	9,144
Stewart Whyte, C.	8,604
James Noble, Lab.	2,761

LD majority 5,170 (14.85%)
8.48% swing LD to SNP

AIRDRIE AND SHOTTS
(Scotland Central Region)
E. 57,660 T. 27,160 (47.10%)

Karen Whitefield, Lab.	11,907
Sophia Coyle, SNP	10,461
Iain McGill, C.	2,370
Robert Gorrie, LD	1,452
Mev Brown, Scottish Voice	970

Lab. majority 1,446 (5.32%)
15.23% swing Lab. to SNP

ANGUS
(Scotland North East Region)
E. 61,362 T. 31,960 (52.08%)

Andrew Welsh, SNP	15,686
Alex Johnstone, C.	7,443
Doug Bradley, Lab.	5,032
Scott Rennie, LD	3,799

SNP majority 8,243 (25.79%)
1.67% swing C. to SNP

ARGYLL AND BUTE
(Highlands and Islands Region)
E. 48,846 T. 28,792 (58.94%)

Jim Mather, SNP	9,944
George Lyon, LD	9,129
Jamie McGrigor, C.	5,571
Mary Galbraith, Lab.	4,148

SNP majority 815 (2.83%)
9.17% swing LD to SNP

AYR
(Scotland South Region)
E. 55,034 T. 31,025 (56.37%)

John Scott, C.	12,619
John Duncan, Lab.	8,713
Iain White, SNP	7,952
Stuart Ritchie, LD	1,741

C. majority 3,906 (12.59%)
3.30% swing Lab. to C.

BANFF AND BUCHAN
(Scotland North East Region)
E. 56,324 T. 27,285 (48.44%)

Stewart Stevenson, SNP	16,031
Geordie Burnett-Stuart, C.	5,501
Kay Barnett, Lab.	3,136
Alison McInnes, LD	2,617

SNP majority 10,530 (38.59%)
3.30% swing C. to SNP

CAITHNESS, SUTHERLAND AND EASTER ROSS
(Highlands and Islands Region)
E. 41,789 T. 22,334 (53.44%)

Jamie Stone, LD	8,981
Rob Gibson, SNP	6,658
John McKendrick, Lab.	3,152
Donald MacDonald, C.	2,586
Gordon Campbell, Ind.	957

LD majority 2,323 (10.40%)
4.38% swing LD to SNP

CARRICK, CUMNOCK AND DOON VALLEY
(Scotland South Region)
E. 65,166 T. 33,785 (51.84%)

Cathy Jamieson, Lab.	14,350
Adam Ingram, SNP	10,364
Tony Lewis, C.	6,729
Paul McGreal, LD	1,409
Hugh Hill, Ind.	809
Ray Barry, Equal Parenting Alliance	124

Lab. majority 3,986 (11.80%)
9.61% swing Lab. to SNP

CLYDEBANK AND MILNGAVIE
(Scotland West Region)
E. 48,700 T. 26,765 (54.96%)

Des McNulty, Lab.	11,617
Gil Paterson, SNP	8,438
Murray Roxburgh, C.	3,544
Ashay Ghai, LD	3,166

Lab. majority 3,179 (11.88%)
2.61% swing Lab. to SNP

CLYDESDALE
(Scotland South Region)
E. 66,011 T. 33,332 (50.49%)

Karen Gillon, Lab.	13,835
Aileen Campbell, SNP	10,942
Colin McGavigan, C.	5,604
Fraser Grieve, LD	2,951

Lab. majority 2,893 (8.68%)
5.94% swing Lab. to SNP

COATBRIDGE AND CHRYSTON
(Scotland Central Region)
E. 54,423 T. 25,725 (47.27%)

Elaine Smith, Lab.	11,860
Frances McGlinchey, SNP	7,350
Ross Thomson, C.	2,305
Julie McAnulty, Ind.	1,843
Doreen Nisbet, LD	1,519
Gaille McCann, Scottish Voice	848

Lab. majority 4,510 (17.53%)
9.19% swing Lab. to SNP

CUMBERNAULD AND KILSYTH
(Scotland Central Region)
E. 49,197 T. 26,382 (53.63%)

Cathie Craigie, Lab.	12,672
Jamie Hepburn, SNP	10,593
Hugh O'Donnell, LD	1,670
Anne Harding, C.	1,447

Lab. majority 2,079 (7.88%)
2.87% swing SNP to Lab.

CUNNINGHAME NORTH
(Scotland West Region)
E. 55,925 T. 30,241 (54.07%)

Kenneth Gibson, SNP	9,295
Allan Wilson, Lab.	9,247
Philip Lardner, C.	5,466
Campbell Martin, Ind.	4,423
Lewis Hutton, LD	1,810

SNP majority 48 (0.16%)
5.99% swing Lab. to SNP

CUNNINGHAME SOUTH
(Scotland South Region)
E. 49,969 T. 23,422 (46.87%)

Irene Oldfather, Lab.	10,270
Duncan Ross, SNP	8,102
Pat McPhee, C.	3,073
Iain Dale, LD	1,977

Lab. majority 2,168 (9.26%)
8.71% swing Lab. to SNP

DUMBARTON
(Scotland West Region)
E. 54,023 T. 30,054 (55.63%)

Jackie Baillie, Lab.	11,635
Graeme McCormick, SNP	10,024
Brian Pope, C.	4,701
Alex Mackie, LD	3,385
John Black, Scottish Jacobite Party	309

Lab. majority 1,611 (5.36%)
8.79% swing Lab. to SNP

DUMFRIES
(Scotland South Region)
E. 53,518 T. 33,419 (62.44%)

Elaine Murray, Lab.	13,707
Murray Tosh, C.	10,868
Michael Russell, SNP	6,306
Lynne Hume, LD	2,538

Lab. majority 2,839 (8.50%)
2.54% swing C. to Lab.

DUNDEE EAST
(Scotland North East Region)
E. 53,804 T. 26,869 (49.94%)

Shona Robison, SNP	13,314
Iain Luke, Lab.	8,790
Chris Bustin, C.	2,976
Clive Sneddon, LD	1,789

SNP majority 4,524 (16.84%)
8.25% swing Lab. to SNP

DUNDEE WEST
(Scotland North East Region)
E. 49,711 T. 24,268 (48.82%)

Joe Fitzpatrick, SNP	10,955
Jill Shimi, Lab.	9,009
Michael Charlton, LD	2,517
Belinda Don, C.	1,787

SNP majority 1,946 (8.02%)
6.14% swing Lab. to SNP

DUNFERMLINE EAST
(Scotland Mid and Fife Region)
E. 51,115 T. 24,568 (48.06%)

Helen Eadie, Lab.	10,995
Ewan Dow, SNP	7,002
Graeme Brown, C.	3,718
Karen Utting, LD	2,853

Lab. majority 3,993 (16.25%)
7.62% swing Lab. to SNP

DUNFERMLINE WEST
(Scotland Mid and Fife Region)
E. 56,953 T. 29,525 (51.84%)

Jim Tolson, LD	9,952
Scott Barrie, Lab.	9,476
Len Woods, SNP	7,296
Peter Lyburn, C.	2,363
Susan Archibald, Scottish Voice	438

LD majority 476 (1.61%)
10.77% swing Lab. to LD

EAST KILBRIDE
(Scotland Central Region)
E. 66,935 T. 35,902 (53.64%)

Andy Kerr, Lab.	15,334
Linda Fabiani, SNP	13,362
Graham Simpson, C.	4,114
David Clark, LD	3,092

Lab. majority 1,972 (5.49%)
5.00% swing Lab. to SNP

EAST LOTHIAN
(Scotland South Region)
E. 61,378 T. 34,471 (56.16%)

Iain Gray, Lab.	12,219
Andrew Sharp, SNP	9,771
Judy Hayman, LD	6,249
Bill Stevenson, C.	6,232

Lab. majority 2,448 (7.10%)
10.08% swing Lab. to SNP

EASTWOOD
(Scotland West Region)
E. 67,347 T. 42,187 (62.64%)

Ken Macintosh, Lab.	15,099
Jackson Carlaw, C.	14,186
Stewart Maxwell, SNP	7,972
Gordon MacDonald, LD	3,603
Frank McGhee, Ind.	1,327

Lab. majority 913 (2.16%)
3.68% swing Lab. to C.

EDINBURGH CENTRAL
(Lothians Region)
E. 55,953 T. 29,396 (52.54%)

Sarah Boyack, Lab.	9,155
Siobhan Mathers, LD	7,962
Shirley-Anne Somerville, SNP	7,496
Fiona Houston, C.	4,783

Lab. majority 1,193 (4.06%)
2.73% swing Lab. to LD

EDINBURGH EAST AND MUSSELBURGH
(Lothians Region)
E. 56,578 T. 29,967 (52.97%)

Kenny MacAskill, SNP	11,209
Norman Murray, Lab.	9,827
Gillian Cole-Hamilton, LD	5,473
Christine Wright, C.	3,458

SNP majority 1,382 (4.61%)
12.91% swing Lab. to SNP

EDINBURGH NORTH AND LEITH
(Lothians Region)
E. 60,340 T. 31,685 (52.51%)

Malcolm Chisholm, Lab.	11,020
Mike Crockart, LD	8,576
Davie Hutchison, SNP	8,044
Iain Whyte, C.	4,045

Lab. majority 2,444 (7.71%)
6.92% swing Lab. to LD

EDINBURGH PENTLANDS
(Lothians Region)
E. 57,891 T. 34,377 (59.38%)

David McLetchie, C.	12,927
Sheila Gilmore, Lab.	8,402
Ian McKee, SNP	8,234
Simon Clark, LD	4,814

C. majority 4,525 (13.16%)
3.42% swing Lab. to C.

EDINBURGH SOUTH
(Lothians Region)
E. 57,621 T. 32,573 (56.53%)

Mike Pringle, LD	11,398
Donald Anderson, Lab.	9,469
Robert Holland, SNP	6,117
Gavin Brown, C.	5,589

LD majority 1,929 (5.92%)
2.71% swing Lab. to LD

EDINBURGH WEST
(Lothians Region)
E. 59,814 T. 34,752 (58.10%)

Margaret Smith, LD	13,677
Sheena Cleland, SNP	7,791
Gordon Lindhurst, C.	7,361
Richard Meade, Lab.	5,343
John Wilson, Ind.	580

LD majority 5,886 (16.94%)
7.00% swing LD to SNP

FALKIRK EAST
(Scotland Central Region)
E. 57,663 T. 30,333 (52.60%)

Cathy Peattie, Lab.	13,184
Annabelle Ewing, SNP	11,312
Scott Campbell, C.	3,701
Natalie Maver, LD	2,136

Lab. majority 1,872 (6.17%)
9.00% swing Lab. to SNP

FALKIRK WEST
(Scotland Central Region)
E. 56,254 T. 28,785 (51.17%)

Michael Matheson, SNP	12,068
Dennis Goldie, Lab.	11,292
Stephen O'Rourke, C.	2,887
Callum Chomczuk, LD	2,538

SNP majority 776 (2.70%)
1.13% swing Lab. to SNP

FIFE CENTRAL
(Scotland Mid and Fife Region)
E. 58,215 T. 26,965 (46.32%)

Tricia Marwick, SNP	11,920
Christine May, Lab.	10,754
Elizabeth Riches, LD	2,288
Maurice Golden, C.	2,003

SNP majority 1,166 (4.32%)
7.56% swing Lab. to SNP

FIFE NORTH EAST
(Scotland Mid and Fife Region)
E. 61,078 T. 31,552 (51.66%)

Iain Smith, LD	13,307
Ted Brocklebank, C.	8,291
Roderick Campbell, SNP	6,735
Kenny Young, Lab.	2,557
Tony Campbell, Ind.	662

LD majority 5,016 (15.90%)
0.68% swing LD to C.

GALLOWAY AND UPPER NITHSDALE
(Scotland South Region)
E. 52,583 T. 30,318 (57.66%)

Alex Fergusson, C.	13,387
Alasdair Morgan, SNP	10,054
Stephen Hodgson, Lab.	4,935
Alastair Cooper, LD	1,631
Sandy Richardson, Ind.	311

C. majority 3,333 (10.99%)
5.33% swing SNP to C.

GLASGOW ANNIESLAND
(Glasgow Region)
E. 48,344 T. 22,139 (45.79%)

Bill Butler, Lab.	10,483
Bill Kidd, SNP	6,177
Bill Aitken, C.	3,154
Danica Gilland, LD	2,325

Lab. majority 4,306 (19.45%)
4.38% swing Lab. to SNP

GLASGOW BAILLIESTON
(Glasgow Region)
E. 44,367 T. 17,272 (38.93%)

Margaret Curran, Lab.	9,141
Lachie McNeill, SNP	5,207
Richard Sullivan, C.	1,276
David Jackson, LD	1,060
George Hargreaves, Scottish Christian Party	588

Lab. majority 3,934 (22.78%)
5.52% swing Lab. to SNP

GLASGOW CATHCART
(Glasgow Region)
E. 47,822 T. 21,657 (45.29%)

Charlie Gordon, Lab.	8,476
James Dornan, SNP	6,287
David Smith, Ind.	2,911
Davena Rankin, C.	2,324
Shabnum Mustapha, LD	1,659

Lab. majority 2,189 (10.11%)
6.40% swing Lab. to SNP

GLASGOW GOVAN
(Glasgow Region)
E. 47,405 T. 21,521 (45.40%)

Nicola Sturgeon, SNP	9,010
Gordon Jackson, Lab.	8,266
Chris Young, LD	1,891
Martyn McIntyre, C.	1,680
Asif Nasir, Ind.	423
Elinor McKenzie, Comm. Brit.	251

SNP majority 744 (3.46%)
4.65% swing Lab. to SNP

GLASGOW KELVIN
(Glasgow Region)
E. 55,096 T. 23,500 (42.65%)

Pauline McNeill, Lab.	7,875
Sandra White, SNP	6,668
Martin Bartos, Green	2,971
Katy Gordon, LD	2,843
Brian Cooklin, C.	1,943
Niall Walker, Ind.	744
Isobel Macleod, Scottish Christian Party	456

Lab. majority 1,207 (5.14%)
4.88% swing Lab. to SNP

GLASGOW MARYHILL
(Glasgow Region)
E. 46,060 T. 16,564 (35.96%)

Patricia Ferguson, Lab.	7,955
Bob Doris, SNP	5,645
Kenn Elder, LD	1,936
Heather MacLeod, C.	1,028

Lab. majority 2,310 (13.95%)
7.74% swing Lab. to SNP

GLASGOW POLLOK
(Glasgow Region)
E. 47,189 T. 19,416 (41.15%)

Johann Lamont, Lab.	10,456
Chris Stephens, SNP	6,063
Gerald Michaluk, C.	1,460
Christine Gilmore, LD	1,437

Lab. majority 4,393 (22.63%)
0.85% swing Lab. to SNP

GLASGOW RUTHERGLEN
(Glasgow Region)
E. 50,005 T. 24,252 (48.50%)

James Kelly, Lab.	10,237
Margaret Park, SNP	5,857
Robert Brown, LD	5,516
Christina Harcus, C.	2,094
Tom Greig, Scottish Christian Party	548

Lab. majority 4,380 (18.06%)
6.43% swing Lab. to SNP

GLASGOW SHETTLESTON
(Glasgow Region)
E. 44,278 T. 14,801 (33.43%)

Frank McAveety, Lab.	7,574
John McLaughlin, SNP	4,693
Ross Renton, LD	1,182
William MacNair, C.	946
Bob Graham, Scottish Christian Party	406

Lab. majority 2,881 (19.46%)
9.45% swing Lab. to SNP

GLASGOW SPRINGBURN
(Glasgow Region)
E. 47,021 T. 17,612 (37.46%)

Paul Martin, Lab.	10,024
Anne McLaughlin, SNP	4,929
Katy McCloskey, LD	1,108
Gordon Wilson, C.	1,067
David Johnston, Scottish Christian Party	484

Lab. majority 5,095 (28.93%)
7.09% swing Lab. to SNP

GORDON
(Scotland North East Region)
E. 65,431 T. 35,363 (54.05%)

Alex Salmond, SNP	14,650
Nora Radcliffe, LD	12,588
Nanette Milne, C.	5,348
Neil Cardwell, Lab.	2,276
Donald Marr, Ind.	199
Dave Mathers, Ind.	185
Bob Ingram, Scottish Enterprise Party	117

SNP majority 2,062 (5.83%)
10.66% swing LD to SNP

GREENOCK AND INVERCLYDE
(Scotland West Region)
E. 44,646 T. 23,105 (51.75%)

Duncan McNeil, Lab.	10,035
Stuart McMillan, SNP	7,011
Ross Finnie, LD	3,893
Charles Ferguson, C.	2,166

Lab. majority 3,024 (13.09%)
6.37% swing Lab. to SNP

HAMILTON NORTH AND BELLSHILL
(Scotland Central Region)
E. 53,854 T. 25,366 (47.10%)

Michael McMahon, Lab.	12,334
Alex Neil, SNP	7,469
James Callander, C.	2,835
Douglas Herbison, LD	1,726
Joe Gorman, Scottish Voice	571
Gordon Weir, Ind.	431

Lab. majority 4,865 (19.18%)
6.75% swing Lab. to SNP

HAMILTON SOUTH
(Scotland Central Region)
E. 48,838 T. 23,211 (47.53%)

Tom McCabe, Lab.	10,280
Christina McKelvie, SNP	6,628
Margaret Mitchell, C.	2,929
Michael McGlynn, Ind.	1,764
John Oswald, LD	1,610

Lab. majority 3,652 (15.73%)
3.89% swing Lab. to SNP

INVERNESS EAST, NAIRN AND LOCHABER
(Highlands and Islands Region)
E. 71,609 T. 39,609 (55.31%)

Fergus Ewing, SNP	16,443
Craig Harrow, LD	10,972
Linda Stewart, Lab.	7,559
Jamie Halcro-Johnston, C.	4,635

SNP majority 5,471 (13.81%)
0.48% swing SNP to LD

KILMARNOCK AND LOUDOUN
(Scotland Central Region)
E. 60,753 T. 33,435 (55.03%)

Willie Coffey, SNP	14,297
Margaret Jamieson, Lab.	12,955
Janette McAlpine, C.	4,127
Ron Aitken, LD	2,056

SNP majority 1,342 (4.01%)
3.93% swing Lab. to SNP

KIRKCALDY
(Scotland Mid and Fife Region)
E. 50,761 T. 24,195 (47.66%)

Marilyn Livingstone, Lab.	10,627
Chris Harvie, SNP	8,005
Alice Soper, LD	3,361
David Potts, C.	2,202

Lab. majority 2,622 (10.84%)
5.58% swing Lab. to SNP

LINLITHGOW
(Lothians Region)
E. 56,175 T. 29,637 (52.76%)

Mary Mulligan, Lab.	12,715
Fiona Hyslop, SNP	11,565
Donald Cameron, C.	3,125
Martin Oliver, LD	2,232

Lab. majority 1,150 (3.88%)
1.62% swing Lab. to SNP

LIVINGSTON
(Lothians Region)
E. 66,348 T. 33,224 (50.08%)

Angela Constance, SNP	13,159
Bristow Muldoon, Lab.	12,289
Ernie Walker, Action to Save St John's Hospital	2,814
David Brown, C.	2,804
Evan Bell, LD	2,158

SNP majority 870 (2.62%)
7.31% swing Lab. to SNP

MIDLOTHIAN
(Lothians Region)
E. 48,395 T. 25,111 (51.89%)

Rhona Brankin, Lab.	10,671
Colin Beattie, SNP	8,969
Ross Laird, LD	2,704
P. J. Lewis, C.	2,269
George McCleery, Had Enough Party	498

Lab. majority 1,702 (6.78%)
8.37% swing Lab. to SNP

MORAY
(Highlands and Islands Region)
E. 60,959 T. 30,274 (49.66%)

Richard Lochhead, SNP	15,045
Mary Scanlon, C.	7,121
Lee Butcher, Lab.	4,580
Dominique Rommel, LD	3,528

SNP majority 7,924 (26.17%)
3.24% swing C. to SNP

MOTHERWELL AND WISHAW
(Scotland Central Region)
E. 53,875 T. 26,150 (48.54%)

Jack McConnell, Lab.	12,574
Marion Fellows, SNP	6,636
Diane Huddleston, C.	1,990
John Swinburne, SSCUP	1,702
Stuart Douglas, LD	1,570
Tom Selfridge, Scottish Christian Party	1,491
Richard Leat, Anti-Trident Party	187

Lab. majority 5,938 (22.71%)
6.88% swing Lab. to SNP

OCHIL
(Scotland Mid and Fife Region)
E. 58,104 T. 31,553 (54.30%)

Keith Brown, SNP	12,147
Brian Fearon, Lab.	11,657
George Murray, C.	4,284
Lorraine Caddell, LD	3,465

SNP majority 490 (1.55%)
0.29% swing Lab. to SNP

ORKNEY
(Highlands and Islands Region)
E. 16,195 T. 8,653 (53.43%)

Liam McArthur, LD	4,113
John Mowat, SNP	1,637
Helen Gardiner, C.	1,632
Iain MacDonald, Lab.	1,134
Barrie Johnson, Ind.	137

LD majority 2,476 (28.61%)
1.95% swing LD to SNP

PAISLEY NORTH
(Scotland West Region)
E. 44,081 T. 23,206 (52.64%)

Wendy Alexander, Lab.	12,111
Andy Doig, SNP	6,998
Malcolm MacAskill, C.	1,721
Angela McGarrigle, LD	1,570
Iain Hogg, SSP	525
John Plott, Ind.	281

Lab. majority 5,113 (22.03%)
1.31% swing SNP to Lab.

PAISLEY SOUTH
(Scotland West Region)
E. 49,175 T. 25,527 (51.91%)

Hugh Henry, Lab.	12,123
Fiona McLeod, SNP	7,893
Eileen McCartin, LD	3,434
Tom Begg, C.	2,077

Lab. majority 4,230 (16.57%)
3.38% swing SNP to Lab.

PERTH
(Scotland and Mid Fife Region)
E. 62,220 T. 34,862 (56.03%)

Roseanna Cunningham, SNP	13,751
Liz Smith, C.	11,256
Peter Barrett, LD	4,767
Doug Maughan, Lab.	4,513
Jim Fairlie, Free Scot.	575

SNP majority 2,495 (7.16%)
2.43% swing C. to SNP

RENFREWSHIRE WEST
(Scotland West Region)
E. 50,787 T. 29,129 (57.36%)

Trish Godman, Lab.	10,467
Annabel Goldie, C.	8,289
Bill Wilson, SNP	8,167
Simon Hutton, LD	2,206

Lab. majority 2,178 (7.48%)
1.22% swing Lab. to C.

ROSS, SKYE AND INVERNESS WEST
(Highlands and Islands Region)
E. 59,237 T. 31,719 (53.55%)

John Farquhar Munro, LD	13,501
Dave Thompson, SNP	10,015
Maureen Macmillan, Lab.	4,789
John Hodgson, C.	3,122
Iain Brodie, Scottish Enterprise Party	292

LD majority 3,486 (10.99%)
6.32% swing LD to SNP

ROXBURGH AND BERWICKSHIRE
(Scotland South Region)
E. 47,862 T. 25,680 (53.65%)

John Lamont, C.	10,556
Euan Robson, LD	8,571
Aileen Orr, SNP	4,127
Mary Lockhart, Lab.	2,108
Jesse Rae, No Description	318

C. majority 1,985 (7.73%)
9.40% swing LD to C.

SHETLAND
(Highlands and Islands Region)
E. 17,108 T. 9,795 (57.25%)

Tavish Scott, LD	6,531
Val Simpson, SNP	1,622
Mark Jones, C.	972
Scott Burnett, Lab.	670

LD majority 4,909 (50.12%)
11.99% swing SNP to LD

STIRLING
(Scotland and Mid Fife Region)
E. 52,864 T. 32,625 (61.71%)

Bruce Crawford, SNP	10,447
Sylvia Jackson, Lab.	9,827
Bob Dalrymple, C.	8,081
Alex Cole-Hamilton, LD	3,693
Liz Law, Peace Party	577

SNP majority 620 (1.90%)
9.41% swing Lab. to SNP

STRATHKELVIN AND BEARSDEN
(Scotland West Region)
E. 60,389 T. 36,595 (60.60%)

David Whitton, Lab.	11,396
Robin Easton, SNP	8,008
Jean Turner, Ind.	6,742
Stephanie Fraser, C.	5,178
Cathy McInnes, LD	4,658
Bob Handyside, Scottish Christian Party	613

Lab. majority 3,388 (9.26%)
3.91% swing Lab. to SNP

TAYSIDE NORTH
(Scotland Mid and Fife Region)
E. 62,133 T. 35,396 (56.97%)

John Swinney, SNP	18,281
Murdo Fraser, C.	10,697
Michael Marna, Lab.	3,243
James Taylor, LD	3,175

SNP majority 7,584 (21.43%)
3.96% swing C. to SNP

TWEEDDALE, ETTRICK AND LAUDERDALE
(Scotland South Region)
E. 53,588 T. 30,327 (56.59%)

Jeremy Purvis, LD	10,656
Christine Grahame, SNP	10,058
Derek Brownlee, C.	5,594
Catherine Maxwell-Stuart, Lab.	4,019

LD majority 598 (1.97%)
0.02% swing LD to SNP

WESTERN ISLES
(Highlands and Islands Region)
E. 22,051 T. 13,625 (61.79%)

Alasdair Allan, SNP	6,354
Alasdair Morrison, Lab.	5,667
Ruaraidh Ferguson, LD	852
Dave Petrie, C.	752

SNP majority 687 (5.04%)
5.43% swing Lab. to SNP

REGIONS

GLASGOW
E. 477,587 T. 206,618 (43.26%)
Lab. majority 23,006 (11.13%)

Lab.	78,838	(38.16%)
SNP	55,832	(27.02%)
LD	14,767	(7.15%)
C.	13,781	(6.67%)
Green	10,759	(5.21%)
Solidarity	8,525	(4.13%)
BNP	3,865	(1.87%)
SSCUP	3,703	(1.79%)
Scottish Christian Party	2,991	(1.45%)
Soc. Lab.	2,680	(1.30%)
CPA	2,626	(1.27%)
SSP	2,579	(1.25%)
Scottish Unionist Party	1,612	(0.78%)
Publican Party Smoking-Room in Pubs	952	(0.46%)
Ind. Shoaib	582	(0.28%)
Ind. Green	496	(0.24%)
UKIP	405	(0.20%)
Scottish Voice	389	(0.19%)
Ind. Nasir	317	(0.15%)
Scotland Against Crooked Lawyers	293	(0.14%)
Ind.	286	(0.14%)
Comm. Brit.	260	(0.13%)
Nine Per Cent Growth Party	80	(0.04%)

4.75% swing Lab. to SNP (2003 Lab. majority 42,146)

ADDITIONAL MEMBERS
Bill Aitken, *C.*
Robert Brown, *LD*
Bashir Ahmad, *SNP*
Sandra White, *SNP*
Bob Doris, *SNP*
Bill Kidd, *SNP*
Patrick Harvie, *Green*

HIGHLANDS AND ISLANDS
E. 337,794 T. 185,773 (55.00%)

SNP	63,979	(34.44%)
LD	37,001	(19.92%)
Lab.	32,952	(17.74%)
C.	23,334	(12.56%)
Green	8,602	(4.63%)
Scottish Christian Party	6,332	(3.41%)
SSCUP	3,841	(2.07%)
BNP	2,152	(1.16%)
Solidarity	1,833	(0.99%)
UKIP	1,287	(0.69%)
Soc. Lab.	1,027	(0.55%)
SSP	973	(0.52%)
Publican Party Smoking-Room in Pubs	914	(0.49%)
CPA	885	(0.48%)
Scottish Voice	450	(0.24%)
Scottish Enterprise Party	211	(0.11%)

SNP majority 26,978 (14.52%)
4.94% swing LD to SNP (2003 SNP majority 1,892)

ADDITIONAL MEMBERS
Mary Scanlon, *C.*
Jamie McGrigor, *C.*
Peter Peacock, *Lab.*
Rhoda Grant, *Lab.*
David Stewart, *Lab.*
Rob Gibson, *SNP*
Dave Thompson, *SNP*

LOTHIANS
E. 519,115 T. 287,039 (55.29%)

SNP	76,019	(26.48%)
Lab.	75,495	(26.30%)
C.	37,548	(13.08%)
LD	36,571	(12.74%)
Green	20,147	(7.02%)
Ind.	19,256	(6.71%)
SSCUP	4,176	(1.45%)
Solidarity	2,998	(1.04%)
BNP	2,637	(0.92%)
Soc. Lab.	2,190	(0.76%)
Scottish Christian Party	2,002	(0.70%)
SSP	1,994	(0.69%)
Publican Party Smoking-Room in Pubs	1,230	(0.43%)
Witchery Tour Party	867	(0.30%)
CPA	848	(0.30%)
UKIP	834	(0.29%)
Had Enough Party	670	(0.23%)
Scottish Voice	661	(0.23%)
Scotland Against Crooked Lawyers	322	(0.11%)
Ind. Scott	189	(0.07%)
Scottish Enterprise Party	183	(0.06%)
Ind. Wilson	129	(0.04%)
Ind. Thorp	73	(0.03%)

SNP majority 524 (0.18%)
4.22% swing Lab. to SNP (2003 Lab. majority 21,960)

ADDITIONAL MEMBERS
Gavin Brown, *C.*
George Foulkes, *Lab.*
Fiona Hyslop, *SNP*
Ian McKee, *SNP*
Stefan Tymkewycz, *SNP*
Robin Harper, *Green*
Margo MacDonald, *Ind.*

SCOTLAND CENTRAL
E. 559,452 T. 284,512 (50.86%)

Lab.	112,596	(39.58%)
SNP	89,210	(31.36%)
C.	24,253	(8.52%)
LD	14,648	(5.15%)
Green	7,204	(2.53%)
SSCUP	7,060	(2.48%)
Scottish Christian Party	5,575	(1.96%)
Solidarity	5,012	(1.76%)
CPA	4,617	(1.62%)
BNP	4,125	(1.45%)
Soc. Lab.	2,303	(0.81%)
SSP	2,188	(0.77%)
Scottish Voice	1,955	(0.69%)
Scottish Unionist Party	1,544	(0.54%)
Publican Party Smoking-Room in Pubs	1,500	(0.53%)
UKIP	722	(0.25%)

Lab. majority 23,386 (8.22%)
4.83% swing Lab. to SNP (2003 Lab. majority 47,044)

ADDITIONAL MEMBERS
Margaret Mitchell, *C.*
Hugh O'Donnell, *LD*
Alex Neil, *SNP*
Linda Fabiani, *SNP*
Jamie Hepburn, *SNP*
Christina McKelvie, *SNP*
John Wilson, *SNP*

SCOTLAND MID AND FIFE,
E. 513,443 T. 273,083 (53.19%)

SNP	90,090 (32.99%)
Lab.	71,922 (26.34%)
C.	44,341 (16.24%)
LD	36,195 (13.25%)
Green	10,318 (3.78%)
SSCUP	5,523 (2.02%)
BNP	2,620 (0.96%)
Solidarity	2,468 (0.90%)
Scottish Christian Party	1,698 (0.62%)
UKIP	1,587 (0.58%)
Soc. Lab.	1,523 (0.56%)
Publican Party Smoking-Room in Pubs	1,309 (0.48%)
SSP	1,116 (0.41%)
Scottish Voice	919 (0.34%)
CPA	790 (0.29%)
Free Scotland Party	664 (0.24%)

SNP majority 18,168 (6.65%)
4.45% swing Lab. to SNP (2003 Lab. majority 5,608)

ADDITIONAL MEMBERS
Murdo Fraser, *C.*
Liz Smith, *C.*
Ted Brocklebank, *C.*
John Park, *Lab.*
Claire Baker, *Lab.*
Richard Simpson, *Lab.*
Chris Harvie, *SNP*

SCOTLAND NORTH EAST
E. 506,660 T. 256,282 (50.58%)

SNP	105,265 (41.07%)
Lab.	52,125 (20.34%)
LD	40,934 (15.97%)
C.	37,666 (14.70%)
Green	8,148 (3.18%)
BNP	2,764 (1.08%)
Solidarity	2,004 (0.78%)
Scottish Christian Party	1,895 (0.74%)
CPA	1,173 (0.46%)
SSP	1,051 (0.41%)
UKIP	1,045 (0.41%)
SSCUP	930 (0.36%)
Scottish Voice	569 (0.22%)
Soc. Lab.	491 (0.19%)
Scottish Enterprise Party	222 (0.09%)

SNP majority 53,140 (20.73%)
6.82% swing Lab. to SNP (2003 SNP majority 17,274)

ADDITIONAL MEMBERS
Alex Johnstone, *C.*
Nanette Milne, *C.*
Richard Baker, *Lab.*
Marlyn Glen, *Lab.*
Alison McInnes, *LD*
Maureen Watt, *SNP*
Nigel Don, *SNP*

SCOTLAND SOUTH
E. 514,105 T. 276,910 (53.86%)

Lab.	79,762 (28.80%)
SNP	77,053 (27.83%)
C.	62,475 (22.56%)
LD	28,040 (10.13%)
Green	9,254 (3.34%)
SSCUP	5,335 (1.93%)
Solidarity	3,433 (1.24%)
BNP	3,212 (1.16%)
Scottish Christian Party	2,353 (0.85%)
Soc. Lab.	1,633 (0.59%)
UKIP	1,429 (0.52%)
SSP	1,114 (0.40%)
CPA	839 (0.30%)
Scottish Voice	490 (0.18%)
Ind.	488 (0.18%)

Lab. majority 2,709 (0.98%)
5.32% swing Lab. to SNP (2003 Lab. majority 15,128)

ADDITIONAL MEMBERS
Derek Brownlee, *C.*
Jim Hume, *LD*
Christine Grahame, *SNP*
Michael Russell, *SNP*
Adam Ingram, *SNP*
Alasdair Morgan, *SNP*
Aileen Campbell, *SNP*

SCOTLAND WEST
E. 475,073 T. 268,179 (56.45%)

Lab.	91,725 (34.20%)
SNP	75,953 (28.32%)
C.	40,637 (15.15%)
LD	22,515 (8.40%)
Green	8,152 (3.04%)
SSCUP	5,231 (1.95%)
Solidarity	4,774 (1.78%)
Scottish Christian Party	3,729 (1.39%)
BNP	3,241 (1.21%)
CPA	3,027 (1.13%)
Save Our NHS Group	2,682 (1.00%)
SSP	1,716 (0.64%)
Soc. Lab.	1,557 (0.58%)
Scottish Unionist Party	1,245 (0.46%)
UKIP	888 (0.33%)
Scottish Voice	522 (0.19%)
Scottish Jacobite Party	446 (0.17%)
Socialist Equality Party	139 (0.05%)

Lab. majority 15,772 (5.88%)
2.70% swing Lab. to SNP (2003 Lab. majority 12,351)

ADDITIONAL MEMBERS
Annabel Goldie, *C.*
Jackson Carlaw, *C.*
Ross Finnie, *LD*
Stewart Maxwell, *SNP*
Gil Paterson, *SNP*
Bill Wilson, *SNP*
Stuart McMillan, *SNP*

NORTHERN IRELAND

NORTHERN IRELAND EXECUTIVE

Stormont Castle, Stormont, Belfast BT4 3TT
T 028-9052 0700 **F** 028-9052 8195
W www.northernireland.gov.uk

The first minister and deputy first minister head the executive committee of ministers and, acting jointly, determine the total number of ministers in the executive. First and deputy first ministers are elected by Northern Ireland assembly members through a formula of parallel consent that requires a majority of designated unionists, a majority of designated nationalists and a majority of the whole assembly to vote in favour. The parties elected to the assembly select ministerial portfolios in proportion to party strengths using the d'Hondt nominating procedure.

The executive committee includes five DUP ministers, four SF ministers, two Ulster Unionist members, one Social Democratic and Labour Party minister alongside the first minister Peter Robinson, MLA of the DUP and the deputy first minister, Martin McGuinness, MLA, of SF.

EXECUTIVE COMMITTEE

First Minister, Rt. Hon. Peter Robinson, MP, MLA
Deputy First Minister, Martin McGuinness, MP, MLA
Junior Ministers, Gerry Kelly, MLA; Rt. Hon. Jeffrey Donaldson, MP, MLA
Minister for Agriculture and Rural Development, Michelle Gildernew, MP, MLA
Minister for Culture, Arts and Leisure, Gregory Campbell, MP, MLA
Minister for Education, Caitriona Ruane, MLA
Minister for Employment and Learning, Sir Reg Empey, MLA
Minister for Enterprise, Trade and Investment, Arlene Foster, MLA
Minister for Environment, Sammy Wilson, MP, MLA
Minister for Finance and Personnel, Nigel Dodds, OBE, MP, MLA
Minister for Health, Social Services and Public Safety, Michael McGimpsey, MLA
Minister for Regional Development, Conor Murphy, MP, MLA
Minister for Social Development, Margaret Ritchie, MLA

OFFICE OF THE FIRST MINISTER AND DEPUTY FIRST MINISTER

Stormont Castle, Stormont, Belfast BT4 3TT
T 028-9052 8400 **W** www.ofmdfmni.gov.uk

DEPARTMENT OF AGRICULTURE AND RURAL DEVELOPMENT

Dundonald House, Upper Newtownards Road, Belfast BT4 3SB
T 028-9052 4420 **W** www.dardni.gov.uk

EXECUTIVE AGENCIES
Forest Service
Rivers Agency

DEPARTMENT OF CULTURE, ARTS AND LEISURE

Interpoint, 20–24 York Street, Belfast BT15 1AQ
T 028-9025 8825 **W** www.dcalni.gov.uk

EXECUTIVE AGENCY
Public Record Office of Northern Ireland

DEPARTMENT OF EDUCATION

Rathgael House, Balloo Road, Bangor, Co. Down BT19 7PR
T 028-9127 9279 **W** www.deni.gov.uk

DEPARTMENT FOR EMPLOYMENT AND LEARNING

Adelaide House, 39–49 Adelaide Street, Belfast BT2 8FD
T 028-9025 7777 **W** www.delni.gov.uk

DEPARTMENT OF ENTERPRISE, TRADE AND INVESTMENT

Netherleigh, Massey Avenue, Belfast BT4 2JP **T** 028-9052 9900
W www.detini.gov.uk

EXECUTIVE AGENCIES
General Consumer Council for Northern Ireland
Health and Safety Executive
Invest Northern Ireland
Northern Ireland Tourist Board

DEPARTMENT OF THE ENVIRONMENT

Clarence Court, 10–18 Adelaide Street, Belfast BT2 8GB
T 028-9054 0540 **W** www.doeni.gov.uk

EXECUTIVE AGENCIES
Driver and Vehicle Agency (Northern Ireland)
Environment and Heritage Service
Planning Service

DEPARTMENT OF FINANCE AND PERSONNEL

Rathgael House, Balloo Road, Bangor BT19 7PR
T 028-9185 8111 **W** www.dfpni.gov.uk

EXECUTIVE AGENCIES
Northern Ireland Statistics and Research Agency*
Land and Property Services
* Incorporates Land Registers of Northern Ireland and Ordanance Survey of Northern Ireland

DEPARTMENT OF HEALTH, SOCIAL SERVICES AND PUBLIC SAFETY

Castle Buildings, Stormont, Belfast BT4 3SJ **T** 028-9052 0500
W www.dhsspsni.gov.uk

EXECUTIVE AGENCY
Northern Ireland Health and Social Services Estate Agency

DEPARTMENT FOR REGIONAL DEVELOPMENT

Clarence Court, 10–18 Adelaide Street, Belfast BT2 8GB
T 028-9054 0540 **W** www.drdni.gov.uk

EXECUTIVE AGENCY
Roads Agency

DEPARTMENT FOR SOCIAL DEVELOPMENT

Lighthouse Building, 1 Cromac Place, Gasworks Business Park, Ormeau Road, Belfast BT7 2JB **T** 028-9082 9028
W www.dsdni.gov.uk

EXECUTIVE AGENCY
Northern Ireland Housing Executive

NORTHERN IRELAND AUDIT OFFICE

106 University Street, Belfast BT7 1EU
T 028-9025 1000 **F** 028-9025 1106
E info@niauditoffice.gov.uk **W** www.niauditoffice.gov.uk
Comptroller and Auditor-General for Northern Ireland, J. M. Dowdall, CB

NORTHERN IRELAND AUTHORITY FOR UTILITY REGULATION
Queens House, 14 Queen Street, Belfast BT1 6ER
T 028-9031 1575 F 028-9031 1740
W http://ofreg.nics.gov.uk
Chair, Prof. Peter Matthews

NORTHERN IRELAND ASSEMBLY

Parliament Buildings, Stormont, Belfast BT4 3XX
T 028-9052 1333 F 028-9052 1961
W www.niassembly.gov.uk

The Northern Ireland Assembly was established as a result of the Belfast Agreement (also known as the Good Friday Agreement) in April 1998. The agreement was endorsed through a referendum held in May 1998 and subsequently given legal force through the Northern Ireland Act 1998.

The Northern Ireland Assembly has full legislative and executive authority for all matters that are the responsibility of the government's Northern Ireland departments – known as transferred matters. Excepted and reserved matters are defined in schedules 2 and 3 of the Northern Ireland Act 1998 and remain the responsibility of UK parliament.

The first assembly election occurred on 25 June 1998 and the 108 members elected met for the first time on 1 July 1998. Members of the Northern Ireland Assembly are elected by the single transferable vote system from 18 constituencies – six per constituency. Under the single transferable vote system every voter has a single vote that can be transferred from one candidate to another. Voters number their candidates in order of preference. Where candidates reach their quota of votes and are elected, surplus votes are transferred to other candidates according to the next preference on each voter's ballot slip. The candidate in each round with the fewest votes is eliminated and their surplus votes are redistributed according to the voter's next preference. The process is repeated until the required number of members are elected.

On 29 November 1999 the assembly appointed ten ministers as well as the chairs and deputy chairs for the ten statutory departmental committees. Devolution of powers to the Northern Ireland Assembly occurred on 2 December 1999, following several delays concerned with Sinn Fein's inclusion in the executive while Irish Republican Army (IRA) weapons were yet to be decommissioned.

Since the devolution of powers, the assembly has been suspended by the Secretary of State for Northern Ireland on four occasions. The first was between 11 February and 30 May 2000, with two 24-hour suspensions on 10 August and 22 September 2001 – all owing to a lack of progress in decommissioning. The final suspension took place on 14 October 2002 after unionists walked out of the executive following a police raid on Sinn Fein's office investigating alleged intelligence gathering.

The assembly was formally dissolved in April 2003 in anticipation of an election, which eventually took place on 26 November 2003. The results of the election changed the balance of power between the political parties, with an increase in the number of seats held by the Democratic Unionist Party (DUP) and Sinn Fein (SF), so that they became the largest parties. The assembly was restored to a state of suspension following the November election while political parties engaged in a review of the Belfast Agreement aimed at fully restoring the devolved institutions.

In July 2005 the leadership of the IRA formally ordered an end to its armed campaign; it authorised a representative to engage with the Independent International Commission on Decommissioning in order to verifiably put the arms beyond use. On 26 September 2005 General John de Chastelain, the chair of the commission, along with two independent church witnesses confirmed that the IRA's entire arsenal of weapons had been decommissioned.

Following the passing of the Northern Ireland Act 2006 the secretary of state created a non-legislative fixed-term assembly, whose membership consisted of the 108 members elected in the 2003 election. It first met on 15 May 2006 with the remit of making preparations for the restoration of devolved government; its discussions informed the next round of talks called by the British and Irish governments held at St Andrews. The St Andrews agreement of 13 October 2006 led to the establishment of the transitional assembly.

The Northern Ireland (St Andrews Agreement) Act 2006 set out a timetable to restore devolution, and also set the date for the third election to the assembly as 7 March 2007. The DUP and SF again had the largest number of Members of the Legislative Assembly (MLAs) elected, and although the initial restoration deadline of 26 March was missed, the leaders of the DUP and SF (Revd Dr Ian Paisley, MP, MLA and Gerry Adams, MLA, respectively) took part in a historic meeting and made a joint commitment to establish an executive committee in the assembly to which devolved powers were restored on 8 May 2007.

SALARIES *as at May 2008*

Assembly Member	£43,101

NORTHERN IRELAND ASSEMBLY MEMBERS

as at 8 May 2008

Adams, Gerry, *SF, West Belfast*
Anderson, Martina, *SF, Foyle*
Armstrong, Billy, *UUP, Mid Ulster*
Attwood, Alex, *SDLP, West Belfast*
Beggs, Roy, *UUP, East Antrim*
Boylan, Cathal, *SF, Newry and Armagh*
Bradley, Dominic, *SDLP, Newry and Armagh*
Bradley, Mary, *SDLP, Foyle*
Bradley, P. J., *SDLP, South Down*
Brady, Mickey, *SF, Newry and Armagh*
Bresland, Allan, *DUP, West Tyrone*
Brolly, Francie, *SF, East Londonderry*
Browne of Belmont, Lord, *DUP, East Belfast*
Buchanan, Thomas, *DUP, West Tyrone*
Burns, Thomas, *SDLP, South Antrim*
Burnside, David, *UUP, South Antrim*
Butler, Paul, *SF, Lagan Valley*
Campbell, Gregory, *DUP, East Londonderry*
Clarke, Trevor, *DUP, South Antrim*
Clarke, Willie, *SF, South Down*
Cobain, Fred, *UUP, North Belfast*
Coulter, Revd Dr Robert, *UUP, North Antrim*
Craig, Jonathan, *DUP, Lagan Valley*
Cree, Leslie, *UUP, North Down*
Dallat, John, *SDLP, East Londonderry*
Deeny, Dr Kieran, *Ind., West Tyrone*
Dodds, Nigel, *DUP, North Belfast*
Doherty, Pat, *SF, West Tyrone*
Donaldson, Jeffrey, *DUP, Lagan Valley*
Durkan, Mark, *SDLP, Foyle*

Easton, Alex, *DUP, North Down*
Elliot, Tom, *UUP, Fermanagh and South Tyrone*
Empey, Sir Reg, *UUP, East Belfast*
Farry, Stephen, *All., North Down*
Ford, David, *All., South Antrim*
Foster, Arlene, *DUP, Fermanagh and South Tyrone*
Gallagher, Tommy, *SDLP, Fermanagh and South Tyrone*
Gardiner, Samuel, *UUP, Upper Bann*
Gildernew, Michelle, *SF, Fermanagh and South Tyrone*
Hamilton, Simon, *DUP, Strangford*
Hanna, Carmel, *SDLP, South Belfast*
Hay, William, *DUP, Foyle*
Hilditch, David, *DUP, East Antrim*
Irwin, William, *DUP, Newry and Armagh*
Kelly, Dolores, *SDLP, Upper Bann*
Kelly, Gerry, *SF, North Belfast*
Kennedy, Danny, *UUP, Newry and Armagh*
Lo, Anna, *All., South Belfast*
Long, Naomi, *All., East Belfast*
Lunn, Trevor, *All., Lagan Valley*
Maginness, Alban, *SDLP, North Belfast*
Maskey, Alex, *SF, South Belfast*
Maskey, Paul, *SF, West Belfast*
McCallister, John, *UUP, South Down*
McCann, Fra, *SF, West Belfast*
McCann, Jennifer, *SF, West Belfast*
McCarthy, Kieran, *All., Strangford*
McCartney, Raymond, *SF, Foyle*
McCausland, Nelson, *DUP, North Belfast*
McClarty, David, *UUP, East Londonderry*
McCrea, Basil, *UUP, Lagan Valley*
McCrea, Ian, *DUP, Mid Ulster*
McCrea, Dr William, *DUP, South Antrim*
McDonnell, Dr Alasdair, *SDLP, South Belfast*
McElduff, Barry, *SF, West Tyrone*
McFarland, Alan, *UUP, North Down*
McGill, Claire, *SF, West Tyrone*
McGimpsey, Michael, *UUP, South Belfast*
McGlone, Patsy, *SDLP, Mid Ulster*
McGuinness, Martin, *SF, Mid Ulster*
***McHugh**, Gerry, *Ind., Fermanagh and South Tyrone*
McIlveen, Michelle, *DUP, Strangford*
McKay, Daithi, *SF, North Antrim*
McLaughlin, Mitchel, *SF, South Antrim*
McNarry, David, *UUP, Strangford*
McQuillan, Adrian, *DUP, East Londonderry*
Molloy, Francie, *SF, Mid Ulster*
Morrow, Lord, *DUP, Fermanagh and South Tyrone*
Moutray, Stephen, *DUP, Upper Bann*
Murphy, Conor, *SF, Newry and Armagh*
Neeson, Sean, *All., East Antrim*
Newton, Robin, *DUP, East Belfast*
Ni Chuilín, Caral, *SF, North Belfast*
O'Dowd, John, *SF, Upper Bann*
O'Loan, Declan, *SDLP, North Antrim*
O'Neill, Michelle, *SF, Mid Ulster*
Paisley, Revd Dr Ian, PC, *DUP, North Antrim*
Paisley, Ian Jr, *DUP, North Antrim*
Poots, Edwin, *DUP, Lagan Valley*
Purvis, Dawn, *PUP, East Belfast*
Ramsey, Pat, *SDLP, Foyle*
Ramsey, Sue, *SF, West Belfast*
Ritchie, Margaret, *SDLP, South Down*
Robinson, George, *DUP, East Londonderry*
Robinson, Iris, *DUP, Strangford*
Robinson, Ken, *UUP, East Antrim*
Robinson, Peter, *DUP, East Belfast*
†**Ross**, Alastair, *DUP, East Antrim*
Ruane, Caitriona, *SF, South Down*
Savage, George, *UUP, Upper Bann*
Shannon, Jim, *DUP, Strangford*
Simpson, David, *DUP, Upper Bann*
Spratt, Jimmy, *DUP, South Belfast*
Storey, Mervyn, *DUP, North Antrim*
Weir, Peter, *DUP, North Down*
Wells, Jim, *DUP, South Down*
Wilson, Brian, *Green, North Down*
Wilson, Sammy, *DUP, East Antrim*

* Gerry McHugh resigned from Sinn Fein on 30 November 2007 and now sits as an independent member

† George Dawson died on 7 May 2007 and was replaced by Alastair Ross, whose appointment was notified by the Chief Electoral Officer with effect from 14 May 2007

STATE OF THE PARTIES *as at May 2008*

Party	*Seats*
Democratic Unionist Party (DUP)	36
Sinn Fein (SF)	27
Ulster Unionist Party (UUP)	18
Social Democratic and Labour Party (SDLP)	16
Alliance Party (Alliance)	7
Independent (Ind.)	2
Progressive Unionist Party (PUP)	1
Green Party	1

NORTHERN IRELAND ASSEMBLY ELECTION RESULTS

as at 7 March 2007

E. Electorate T. Turnout
First = first-preference votes
Final = final total for that candidate, after all necessary transfers of lower-preference votes
R. = round
* = eliminated last
See General Election Results for a list of party abbreviations

ANTRIM EAST
E. 56,666 T. 30,293 (53.46%)

	First	*Final*	*Elected (R.)*
Sammy Wilson, DUP	6,755	6,755	First (1)
George Dawson, DUP	4,167	4,777	Second (2)
Sean Neeson, Alliance	3,114	5,191	Fourth (10)
Roy Beggs, UUP	3,076	5,115	Fifth (12)
David Hilditch, DUP	2,732	4,587	Third (3)
Ken Robinson, UUP	1,881	4,195	Sixth (13)
*Danny O'Connor, SDLP	1,769	3,298	
Stewart Dickson, Alliance	1,624		
Mark Dunn, UUP	1,617		
Oliver McMullan, SF	1,168		
Tom Robinson, UK Unionist Party	731		
Mark Bailey, Green	612		
John Anderson, Ind.	398		
Tim Lewis, C.	395		

ANTRIM NORTH
E. 72,814 T. 44,655 (61.33%)

	First	*Final*	*Elected (R.)*
Revd Ian Paisley, DUP	7,716	7,716	First (1)
Daithi McKay, SF	7,065	7,065	Second (1)
Ian Paisley Jr, DUP	6,106	7,264	Third (2)
Mervyn Storey, DUP	5,171	6,924	Fifth (8)

Revd Robert Coulter, UUP	5,047	6,579	Fourth (7)
Declan O'Loan, SDLP	3,281	6,498	Sixth (10)
*Deirdre Nelson, DUP	2,740	4,092	
Orla Black, SDLP	2,129		
Lyle Cubitt, UK Unionist Party	1,848		
Robert Swann, UUP	1,281		
Jayne Dunlop, Alliance	1,254		
Paul McGlinchey, Ind.	383		
James Gregg, Ind.	310		

ANTRIM SOUTH
E. 65,654 T. 38,481 (58.61%)

	First	*Final*	*Elected (R.)*
Mitchel McLaughlin, SF	6,313	6,313	First (1)
Revd William McCrea, DUP	6,023	6,023	Second (1)
David Ford, Alliance	5,007	5,495	Third (5)
David Burnside, UUP	4,507	6,926	Fourth (7)
Trevor Clarke, DUP	4,302	5,544	Fifth (8)
*Mel Lucas, DUP	2,840	4,429	
Thomas Burns, SDLP	2,721	5,396	Sixth (8)
Danny Kinahan, UUP	2,391		
Noreen McClelland, SDLP	1,526		
Stephen Nicholl, UUP	927		
Robert McCartney, UK Unionist Party	893		
Pete Whitcroft, Green	507		
Stephen O'Brien, C.	129		
Marcella Delaney, WP	89		

BELFAST EAST
E. 49,757 T. 29,873 (60.04%)

	First	*Final*	*Elected (R.)*
Peter Robinson, DUP	5,635	5,635	First (1)
Naomi Long, Alliance	5,585	5,585	Second (1)
Sir Reg Empey, UUP	4,139	4,620	Third (3)
Lord Wallace Browne, DUP	3,185	3,734	Fifth (10)
Dawn Purvis, Progressive Unionist Party	3,045	4,208	Fourth (10)
Robin Newton, DUP	2,335	3,517	Sixth (10)
*Michael Copeland, UUP	1,557	2,999	
Niall O'Donnghaile, SF	1,055		
Jim Rodgers, UUP	820		
Mary Muldoon, SDLP	816		
Steve Agnew, Green	653		
Glyn Chambers, C.	427		
Thomas Black, Socialist Party	225		
Joe Bell, WP	107		
Rainbow George, Make Politicians History	47		

BELFAST NORTH
E. 49,372 T. 30,067 (60.90%)

	First	*Final*	*Elected (R.)*
Nigel Dodds, DUP	6,973	6,973	First (1)
Gerry Kelly, SF	5,414	5,414	Second (1)
Caral Ni Chuilin, SF	3,680	4,587	Third (3)
Fred Cobain, UUP	2,498	3,967	Fifth (10)
Nelson McCausland, DUP	2,462	3,818	Sixth (10)
Alban Maginness, SDLP	2,212	4,830	Fourth (9)
Pat Convery, SDLP	1,868		
*William Humphrey, DUP	1,673	3,327	
Raymond McCord, Ind.	1,320		
Peter Emerson, Green	590		
Tommy McCullough, Alliance	486		
Robert McCartney, UK Unionist Party	360		
John Lavery, WP	139		
Rainbow George, Make Politicians History	40		

BELFAST SOUTH
E. 48,923 T. 30,533 (62.41%)

	First	*Final*	*Elected (R.)*
Jimmy Spratt, DUP	4,762	4,762	First (1)
Dr Alasdair McDonnell, SDLP	4,379	4,379	Second (1)
Alex Maskey, SF	3,996	4,167	Sixth (10)
Anna Lo, Alliance	3,829	4,415	Third (8)
Carmel Hanna, SDLP	3,748	4,262	Fifth (10)
Michael McGimpsey, UUP	2,647	4,927	Fourth (10)
*Christopher Stalford, DUP	2,035	3,275	
Dr Esmond Birnie, UUP	1,804		
Bob Stoker, UUP	1,122		
Brenda Cooke, Green	737		
Andrew Park, Progressive Unionist Party	410		
David Hoey, UK Unionist Party	298		
Jim Barbour, Socialist Party	248		
Paddy Lynn, WP	123		
Roger Lomas, C.	108		
Rainbow George, Make Politicians History	66		
Charles Smyth, Pro-Capitalism	22		
Geoffrey Wilson, Ind.	10		

BELFAST WEST
E. 50,792 T. 34,238 (67.41%)

	First	*Final*	*Elected (R.)*
Gerry Adams, SF	6,029	6,029	First (1)
Sue Ramsey, SF	4,715	5,267	Second (2)
Paul Maskey, SF	4,368	5,075	Third (6)
Jennifer McCann, SF	4,265	4,849	Fourth (6)
Fra McCann, SF	4,254	4,647	Sixth (6)
*Diane Dodds, DUP	3,661	4,166	
Alex Attwood, SDLP	3,036	4,779	Fifth (6)
Margaret Walsh, SDLP	1,074		
Sean Mitchell, People Before Profit	774		
Louis West, UUP	558		
John Lowry, WP	434		
Geraldine Taylor, Republican Sinn Fein	427		
Dan McGuinness, Alliance	127		
Rainbow George, Make Politicians History	68		

DOWN NORTH
E. 57,525 T. 30,930 (53.77%)

	First	*Final*	*Elected (R.)*
Alex Easton, DUP	4,946	4,946	First (1)
Peter Weir, DUP	3,376	4,380	Fifth (10)
Stephen Farry, Alliance	3,131	4,466	Second (8)
Leslie Cree, UUP	2,937	4,687	Third (10)
Brian Wilson, Green	2,839	4,572	Fourth (10)
Alan McFarland, UUP	2,245	3,986	Sixth (10)
*Alan Graham, DUP	2,147	3,255	
Marion Smith, UUP	2,098		
Robert McCartney, UK Unionist Party	1,806		
Brian Rowan, Ind.	1,194		
Alan Chambers, Ind.	1,129		
Liam Logan, SDLP	1,115		
James Leslie, C.	864		
Deaglan Page, SF	390		
Elaine Martin, Progressive Unionist Party	367		
Chris Carter, Ind.	123		

DOWN SOUTH
E. 71,704 T. 46,623 (65.02%)

	First	*Final*	*Elected (R.)*
Catriona Ruane, SF	6,334	6,676	First (7)
Margaret Ritchie, SDLP	5,838	6,945	Third (8)
P. J. Bradley, SDLP	5,652	6,650	Fourth (9)
Jim Wells, DUP	5,542	8,463	Fifth (10)
Willie Clarke, SF	5,138	7,382	Second (8)
John McCallister, UUP	4,447	7,721	Sixth (11)
*Michael Carr, SDLP	2,972	3,883	
Eamonn McConvey, SF	2,662		
William Burns, DUP	2,611		
Ciaran Mussen, Green	1,622		
Henry Reilly, UKIP	1,229		
David Griffin, Alliance	691		
Martin Cunningham, Ind.	434		
Nelson Wharton, UK Unionist Party	424		
Peter Bowles, C.	391		
Malachi Curran, Lab.	123		

FERMANAGH AND SOUTH TYRONE
E. 65,826 T. 46,845 (71.16%)

	First	*Final*	*Elected (R.)*
Arlene Foster, DUP	7,138	7,138	First (1)
Michelle Gildernew, SF	7,026	7,026	Second (1)
Tom Elliott, UUP	6,603	6,680	Third (2)
Gerry McHugh, SF	5,103	5,777	Sixth (8)
*Sean Lynch, SF	4,704	5,188	
Lord Morrow, DUP	4,700	7,014	Fifth (8)
Tommy Gallagher, SDLP	4,440	6,640	Fourth (7)
Kenny Donaldson, UUP	2,531		
Vincent Currie, SDLP	2,043		
Gerry McGeough, Ind.	814		
Allan Leonard, Alliance	521		
Michael McManus, Republican Sinn Fein	431		
Robert McCartney, UK Unionist Party	388		

FOYLE
E. 64,889 T. 41,455 (63.89%)

	First	*Final*	*Elected (R.)*
William Hay, DUP	6,960	6,960	First (1)
Mark Durkan, SDLP	6,401	6,401	Second (1)
Martina Anderson, SF	5,414	5,972	Third (6)
Raymond McCartney, SF	4,321	7,275	Fourth (8)
Pat Ramsey, SDLP	3,242	5,396	Fifth (10)
Lynn Fleming, SF	2,914		
Mary Bradley, SDLP	2,891	4,419	Sixth (10)
*Helen Quigley, SDLP	2,648	4,314	
Eamonn McCann, Socialist Environmental Alliance	2,045		
Peggy O'Hara, Ind.	1,789		
Peter Munce, UUP	1,755		
Adele Corry, Green	359		
Yvonne Boyle, Alliance	224		
Willie Frazer, Ind.	73		

LAGAN VALLEY
E. 70,101 T. 42,058 (60.00%)

	First	*Final*	*Elected (R.)*
Jeffrey Donaldson, DUP	9,793	9,793	First (1)
Paul Butler, SF	5,098	6,387	Second (6)
Basil McCrea, UUP	4,031	6,712	Third (7)
Trevor Lunn, Alliance	3,765	6,264	Fourth (7)
Jonathan Craig, DUP	3,471	6,147	Fifth (8)
Edwin Poots, DUP	3,457	5,386	Sixth (9)
*Paul Givan, DUP	3,377	4,728	
Marietta Farrell, SDLP	2,839		
Billy Bell, UUP	2,599		
Ronnie Crawford, UUP	1,147		
Michael Rogan, Green	922		
Robert McCartney, UK Unionist Party	853		
Neil Johnston, C.	387		
John Magee, WP	83		

LONDONDERRY EAST
E. 56,104 T. 34,180 (60.92%)

	First	*Final*	*Elected (R.)*
Gregory Campbell, DUP	6,845	6,845	First (1)
Francie Brolly, SF	4,476	5,003	Third (7)
George Robinson, DUP	3,991	4,869	Second (5)
David McClarty, UUP	2,875	4,409	Fifth (9)
Adrian McQuillan, DUP	2,650	4,074	Sixth (9)
John Dallat, SDLP	2,638	6,380	Fourth (8)
Billy Leonard, SF	2,321		
*Norman Hillis, UUP	2,054	3,195	
Orla Beattie, SDLP	1,797		
Barney Fitzpatrick, Alliance	1,401		
Edwin Stevenson, UUP	1,338		
Leslie Cubitt, UK Unionist Party	549		
Phillippe Moison, Green	521		
Michael McGonigle, Republican Sinn Fein	393		
Victor Christie, Ind.	73		

NEWRY AND ARMAGH
E. 70,823 T. 50,165 (70.83%)

	First	Final	Elected (R.)
Conor Murphy, SF	7,437	7,437	First (1)
Cathal Boylan, SF	7,105	7,105	Second (1)
Danny Kennedy, UUP	6,517	7,653	Fifth (5)
William Irwin, DUP	6,418	8,008	Fourth (5)
Mickey Brady, SF	6,337	7,514	Third (4)
Dominic Bradley, SDLP	5,318	6,311	Sixth (7)
*Sharon Haughey, SDLP	4,500	5,368	
Paul Berry, Ind.	2,317		
Davy Hyland, Ind.	2,188		
Willie Frazer, Ind.	605		
Arthur Morgan, Green	599		
Maire Hendron, Alliance	278		

STRANGFORD
E. 66,648 T. 36,340 (54.53%)

	First	Final	Elected (R.)
Iris Robinson, DUP	5,917	5,917	First (1)
Jim Shannon, DUP	4,788	5,178	Second (6)
Kieran McCarthy, Alliance	4,085	5,207	Third (9)
Simon Hamilton, DUP	3,889	4,998	Fifth (13)
David McNarry, UUP	3,709	6,036	Fourth (10)
Michelle McIlveen, DUP	3,468	4,579	Sixth (13)
*Joe Boyle, SDLP	3,068	4,548	
Angus Carson, UUP	2,128		
Dermot Kennedy, SF	1,089		
George Ennis, UK Unionist Party	872		
Stephanie Sim, Green	868		
Michael Henderson, UUP	675		
David Gregg, Ind.	650		
Bob Little, C.	508		
Cedric Wilson, Ind.	305		

TYRONE WEST
E. 58,367 T. 41,839 (71.68%)

	First	Final	Elected (R.)
Barry McElduff, SF	6,971	6,971	First (1)
Pat Doherty, SF	6,709	6,709	Second (1)
Clare McGill, SF	4,757	6,217	Third (3)
Tom Buchanan, DUP	4,625	6,208	Fourth (6)
Allan Bresland, DUP	4,244	5,543	Sixth (7)
Dr Kieran Deeny, Ind.	3,776	5,616	Fifth (7)
Derek Hussey, UUP	3,686		
*Josephine Deehan, SDLP	2,689	5,186	
Eugene McMenamin, SDLP	2,272		
Seamus Shiels, SDLP	1,057		
Joe O'Neill, Republican Sinn Fein	448		
Robert McCartney, UK Unionist Party	220		

ULSTER MID
E. 61,223 T. 44,728 (73.06%)

	First	Final	Elected (R.)
Martin McGuinness, SF	8,065	8,065	First (1)
Ian McCrea, DUP	7,608	7,608	Second (1)
Francie Molloy, SF	6,597	6,597	Third (1)
Michelle O'Neill, SF	6,432	6,432	Fourth (1)
Patsy McGlone, SDLP	4,976	6,430	Fifth (5)
Billy Armstrong, UUP	4,781	6,355	Sixth (7)
*Kate Lagan, SDLP	2,759	3,531	
Walter Millar, UK Unionist Party	1,210		
Ann Forde, DUP	1,021		
Brendan McLaughlin, Republican Sinn Fein	437		
Margaret Marshall, Alliance	221		
Harry Hutchinson, Ind.	170		

UPPER BANN
E. 70,716 T. 43,235 (61.14%)

	First	Final	Elected (R.)
John O'Dowd, SF	7,733	7,733	First (1)
David Simpson, DUP	6,828	6,828	Second (1)
Samuel Gardiner, UUP	5,135	7,265	Fourth (9)
Dolores Kelly, SDLP	4,689	6,191	Third (8)
Stephen Moutray, DUP	3,663	7,550	Fifth (11)
*Dessie Ward, SF	3,118	4,732	
Junior McCrum, DUP	2,975		
George Savage, UUP	2,167	5,998	Sixth (12)
Arnold Hatch, UUP	1,815		
David Calvert, No Description	1,332		
Helen Corry, Green	1,156		
Sheila McQuaid, Alliance	798		
Pat McAleenan, SDLP	761		
Barry Toman, Republican Sinn Fein	386		
David Fry, C.	248		
Suzanne Peeples, Ind.	78		

LOCAL GOVERNMENT

Major changes in local government were introduced in England and Wales in 1974 and in Scotland in 1975 by the Local Government Act 1972 and the Local Government (Scotland) Act 1973. Further significant alterations were made in England by the Local Government Acts of 1985, 1992 and 2000.

The structure in England was based on two tiers of local authorities (county councils and district councils) in the non-metropolitan areas; and a single tier of metropolitan councils in the six metropolitan areas of England and London borough councils in London.

Following reviews of the structure of local government in England by the Local Government Commission (now the Boundary Commission for England), 46 unitary (all-purpose) authorities were created between April 1995 and April 1998 to cover certain areas in the non-metropolitan counties. The remaining county areas continue to have two tiers of local authorities. The county and district councils in the Isle of Wight were replaced by a single unitary authority on 1 April 1995; the former counties of Avon, Cleveland, Humberside and Berkshire were replaced by unitary authorities; and Hereford and Worcester was replaced by a new county council for Worcestershire (with district councils) and a unitary authority for Herefordshire. In December 2007 the government announced that a further five county councils would become unitary authorities, replacing the current two-tier county/district system in Cornwall, Durham, Northumberland, Shropshire and Wiltshire by April 2009, subject to parliamentary approval. Subsequently the government announced the creation of two new unitary authorities for Bedfordshire (Bedford and Central Bedfordshire) and two new unitary authorities for Cheshire (Cheshire East and Cheshire West & Chester); in both, county and district councils would be abolished and their functions absorbed by the new unitary authorities.

The Local Government (Wales) Act 1994 and the Local Government etc (Scotland) Act 1994 abolished the two-tier structure in Wales and Scotland with effect from 1 April 1996, replacing it with a single tier of unitary authorities.

ELECTIONS

Local elections are normally held on the first Thursday in May. Generally, all British subjects, citizens of the Republic of Ireland, Commonwealth and other European Union citizens who are 18 years or over and resident on the qualifying date in the area for which the election is being held, are entitled to vote at local government elections. A register of electors is prepared and published annually by local electoral registration officers.

A returning officer has the overall responsibility for an election. Voting takes place at polling stations, arranged by the local authority and under the supervision of a presiding officer specially appointed for the purpose. Candidates, who are subject to various statutory qualifications and disqualifications designed to ensure that they are suitable to hold office, must be nominated by electors for the electoral area concerned.

In England, the Boundary Committee for England is responsible for carrying out periodic reviews of electoral arrangements and making recommendations to the Electoral Commission.

In Wales and Scotland these matters are the responsibility of the Local Government Boundary Commission for Wales and the Boundary Commission for Scotland respectively. The Local Government Act 2000 provided for the secretary of state to change the frequency and phasing of elections.

THE BOUNDARY COMMITTEE FOR ENGLAND, 1 Myddelton Street, London EC1R 1UW **T** 020-7014 2452 **E** bcomm.england@ons.gov.uk **W** www.statistics.gov.uk/pbc

LOCAL GOVERNMENT BOUNDARY COMMISSION FOR WALES, Caradog House, 1–6 St Andrew's Place, Cardiff CF10 3BE **T** 029-2039 5031 **E** lgbc.wales@wales.gsi.gov.uk **W** www.lgbc-wales.gov.uk

THE BOUNDARY COMMISSION FOR SCOTLAND, 3 Drumsheugh Gardens, Edinburgh EH3 7QJ **T** 0131-538 7510 **E** enquiries@scottishboundaries.gov.uk **W** www.bcomm-scotland.gov.uk

INTERNAL ORGANISATION

The council as a whole is the final decision-making body within any authority. Councils are free to a great extent to make their own internal organisational arrangements. The Local Government Act, given royal assent on 28 July 2000, allows councils to adopt one of three broad categories of a new constitution which include a separate executive.

These three categories are:

- A directly elected mayor with a cabinet selected by that mayor
- A cabinet, either elected by the council or appointed by its leader
- A directly elected mayor and council manager

Normally, questions of policy are settled by the full council, while the administration of the various services is the responsibility of committees of councillors. Day-to-day decisions are delegated to the council's officers, who act within the policies laid down by the councillors.

FINANCE

Local government in England, Wales and Scotland is financed from four sources: the council tax, non-domestic rates, government grants and income from fees and charges for services.

COUNCIL TAX

Under the Local Government Finance Act 1992, from 1 April 1993 the council tax replaced the community charge (which had been introduced in April 1989 in Scotland and April 1990 in England and Wales in place of domestic rates).

The council tax is a local tax levied by each local council. Liability for the council tax bill usually falls on the owner-occupier or tenant of a dwelling which is their sole or main residence. Council tax bills may be reduced because of the personal circumstances of people resident in a property, and there are discounts in the case of dwellings occupied by fewer than two adults.

In England, each county council, each district council and each police authority sets its own council tax rate. The district councils collect the combined council tax, and the county councils and police authorities claim their share from the district councils' collection funds. In Wales, each unitary authority and each police authority sets its own council tax rate. The unitary authorities collect the combined council tax and the police authorities claim their share from the funds. In Scotland, each local authority sets its own rate of council tax.

The tax relates to the value of the dwelling. In England and Scotland each dwelling is placed in one of eight valuation bands, ranging from A to H, based on the property's estimated market value as at 1 April 1991. In Wales there are nine bands, ranging from A to I, based on the estimated market value of property as at 1 April 2003.

The valuation bands and ranges of values in England, Wales and Scotland are:

England

A	Up to £40,000	E	£88,001–£120,000
B	£40,001–£52,000	F	£120,001–£160,000
C	£52,001–£68,000	G	£160,001–£320,000
D	£68,001–£88,000	H	Over £320,001

Wales

A	Up to £44,000	F	£162,001–£223,000
B	£44,001–£65,000	G	£223,001–£324,000
C	£65,001–£91,000	H	£324,001–£424,000
D	£91,001–£123,000	I	Over £424,001
E	£123,001–£162,000		

Scotland

A	Up to £27,000	E	£58,001–£80,000
B	£27,001–£35,000	F	£80,001–£106,000
C	£35,001–£45,000	G	£106,001–£212,000
D	£45,001–£58,000	H	Over £212,001

The council tax within a local area varies between the different bands according to proportions laid down by law. The charge attributable to each band as a proportion of the Band D charge set by the council is approximately:

A	67%	F	144%
B	78%	G	167%
C	89%	H	200%
D	100%	I	233%*
E	122%		

* Wales only

The average Band D council tax bill for each authority area is given in the tables on the following pages. There may be variations from the given figure within each district council area because of different parish or community precepts being levied.

NON-DOMESTIC RATES

Non-domestic (business) rates are collected by billing authorities; these are the district councils in those areas of England with two tiers of local government and unitary authorities in other parts of England, in Wales and in Scotland. In respect of England and Wales, the Local Government Finance Act 1988 provides for liability for rates to be assessed on the basis of a poundage (multiplier) tax on the rateable value of property (hereditaments). Separate multipliers are set by the Department for Communities and Local Government (DCLG) in England, the Welsh Assembly government and the Scottish government. Rates are collected by the billing authority for the area where a property is located. Rate income collected by billing authorities is paid into a national non-domestic rating (NNDR) pool and redistributed to individual authorities on the basis of the adult population figure as prescribed by the DCLG, the Welsh Assembly government or the Scottish government. The rates pools are maintained separately in England, Wales and Scotland. Actual payment of rates in certain cases is subject to transitional arrangements, to phase in the larger increases and reductions in rates resulting from the effects of the latest revaluation.

Rateable values for the 2005 rating lists came into effect on 1 April 2005. They are derived from the rental value of property as at 1 April 2003 and determined on certain statutory assumptions by the Valuation Office Agency in England and Wales, and by local area assessors in Scotland. New property which is added to the list, and significant changes to existing property, necessitate amendments to the rateable value on the same basis. Rating lists (valuation rolls in Scotland) remain in force until the next general revaluation. Such revaluations take place every five years, the next being in 2010.

Certain types of property are exempt from rates, eg agricultural land and buildings, certain businesses and some places of public religious worship. Charities and other non-profit-making organisations may receive full or partial relief. Since 1 April 2008 the owner or leaseholder of an empty commercial property in England and Wales is exempt from business rates for the first three months that the property is vacant (six months for an owner or leaseholder of an industrial property), after which they are charged the full amount. In Scotland, the owner or leaseholder of an empty commercial property is exempt from business rates for the first three months and entitled to a 50 per cent discount thereafter, except for some types of premises, such as factories, which are entirely exempt.

GOVERNMENT GRANTS

In addition to specific grants in support of revenue expenditure on particular services, central government pays a revenue support grant to local authorities. This grant is paid to each local authority so that if each authority spends at the level of its standard spending assessment, all authorities in the same class can set broadly the same council tax.

COMPLAINTS

ENGLAND

In England the Local Government Ombudsman investigates complaints of injustice arising from maladministration by local authorities and certain other bodies. The Local Government Ombudsman will not usually consider a complaint unless the local authority concerned has had an opportunity to investigate and reply to a complainant.

The Local Government Act 2000 established a Standards Board and an independent tribunal known as the Adjudication Panel for England. The Standards Board's main task is to ensure that standards of ethical conduct are maintained and to investigate any allegations that councillors have breached the council's code of conduct. At the end of the investigation, the case may be referred to either the relevant local authority's standards committee or the Adjudication Panel, which has a number of sanctions at its disposal, up to and including the disqualification of a member from holding office for five years. Unlike the ombudsmen, the Standards Board does not deal with issues of corporate maladministration nor seek to secure financial recompense for complainants.

Local Government Ombudsmen, Tony Redmond, Anne Seex, Jerry White

LOCAL GOVERNMENT OMBUDSMAN, PO Box 4771, Coventry CV4 0EH **T** 0845-602 1983 **W** www.lgo.org.uk
THE STANDARDS BOARD FOR ENGLAND, 4th Floor, Griffin House, 40 Lever Street, Manchester M1 1BB **T** 0161-817 5300 **W** www.standardsboard.gov.uk
THE ADJUDICATION PANEL FOR ENGLAND, 23 Victoria Avenue, Harrogate, North Yorkshire HG1 5RD **T** 01423-538783 **W** www.adjudicationpanel.co.uk

WALES

The office of Public Services Ombudsman for Wales came into force on 1 April 2006 incorporating the functions of the Local Government Ombudsman for Wales.

Public Service Ombudsman for Wales, Peter Tyndall
PUBLIC SERVICES OMBUDSMAN FOR WALES, 1 Ffordd yr Hen Gae, Pencoed CF35 5LJ **T** 01656-641150 **W** www.ombudsman-wales.org.uk

SCOTLAND

The Scottish Public Services Ombudsman is responsible for complaints regarding the maladaministration of local government in Scotland.

Scottish Public Services Ombudsman, Prof. Alice Brown
SCOTTISH PUBLIC SERVICES OMBUDSMAN, Freepost EH641, Edinburgh EH3 0BR **T** 0800-377 7330 **W** www.spso.org.uk

NORTHERN IRELAND

The Northern Ireland Commissioner for Complaints fulfils a similar function in Northern Ireland, investigating complaints about local authorities and certain public bodies. Complaints are made to the relevant local authority in the first instance but may also be made directly to the Commissioner.

Northern Ireland Commissioner for Complaints, Tom Frawley, CBE
NORTHERN IRELAND COMMISSIONER FOR COMPLAINTS, Freepost BEL 1478, Belfast BT1 6LR **T** 0800-343424 **W** www.ni-ombudsman.org.uk

THE QUEEN'S REPRESENTATIVES

The lord-lieutenant of a county is the permanent local representative of the Crown in that county. The appointment of lord-lieutenants is now regulated by the Lieutenancies Act 1997. They are appointed by the sovereign on the recommendation of the prime minister. The retirement age is 75. The office of lord-lieutenant dates from 1551, and its holder was originally responsible for maintaining order and for local defence in the county. The duties of the post include attending on royalty during official visits to the county, performing certain duties in connection with armed forces of the Crown (and in particular the reserve forces), and making presentations of honours and awards on behalf of the Crown. In England, Wales and Northern Ireland, the lord-lieutenant usually also holds the office of *Custos Rotulorum.* As such, he or she acts as head of the county's commission of the peace (which recommends the appointment of magistrates).

The office of sheriff (from the Old English shire-reeve) of a county was created in the tenth century. The sheriff was the special nominee of the sovereign, and the office reached the peak of its influence under the Norman kings. The Provisions of Oxford (1258) laid down a yearly tenure of office. Since the mid-16th century the office has been purely civil, with military duties taken over by the lord-lieutenant of the county. The sheriff (commonly known as 'high sheriff') attends on royalty during official visits to the county, acts as the returning officer during parliamentary elections in county constituencies, attends the opening ceremony when a high court judge goes on circuit, executes high court writs, and appoints under-sheriffs to act as deputies. The appointments and duties of the sheriffs in England and Wales are laid down by the Sheriffs Act 1887.

The serving high sheriff submits a list of names of possible future sheriffs to a tribunal which chooses three names to put to the sovereign. The tribunal nominates the high sheriff annually on 12 November and the sovereign picks the name of the sheriff to succeed in the following year. The term of office runs from 25 March to the following 24 March (the civil and legal year before 1752). No person may be chosen twice in three years if there is any other suitable person in the county.

CIVIC DIGNITIES

District councils in England may petition for a royal charter granting borough or 'city' status to the district. Local councils in Wales may petition for a royal charter granting county borough or 'city' status to the council.

In England and Wales the chairman of a borough or county borough council may be called a mayor, and the chair of a city council may be called a lord mayor if lord mayoralty has been conferred on that city. Parish councils in England and community councils in Wales may call themselves 'town councils', in which case their chair is the town mayor.

In Scotland the chair of a local council may be known as a convenor; a provost is the mayoral equivalent. The chair of the councils for the cities of Aberdeen, Dundee, Edinburgh and Glasgow are lord provosts.

ENGLAND

There are currently 34 counties, divided into 238 districts. In addition, there are 46 unitary authorities plus the Isles of Scilly and 36 metropolitan boroughs. Nine new unitary authorities are due to be created in April 2009 as part of a programme of local government reorganisation: five existing county councils will be given unitary status, abolishing the two-tier district/county system within these areas, and a further four unitaries will be created from the division of two existing county areas (Bedfordshire and Cheshire). The reorganisation will result in 27 counties; divided into 202 districts and 55 unitary authorities. The 36 metropolitan boroughs and the Isles of Scilly will remain the same.

The populations of most of the unitary authorities are in the range of 100,000 to 300,000. The district councils have populations broadly in the range of 60,000 to 100,000; some, however, have larger populations, because of the need to avoid dividing large towns, and some in mainly rural areas have smaller populations.

The main conurbations outside Greater London – Tyne and Wear, West Midlands, Merseyside, Greater Manchester, West Yorkshire and South Yorkshire – are divided into 36 metropolitan boroughs, most of which have a population of over 200,000.

There are also about 8,700 town and parish councils with a population coverage of around 17 million.

ELECTIONS

For districts, counties and for about 8,000 parishes, there are elected councils, consisting of directly elected councillors. The councillors elect one of their number as chair annually.

In general, councils can have whole council elections, elections by thirds or elections by halves. However all metropolitan authorities must hold elections by thirds. The electoral cycle of any new new unitary authorities would be specified in the appropriate statutory orders establishing them.

FUNCTIONS

In non-metropolitan areas, functions are divided between the districts and counties (those affecting the larger area or population are generally the responsibility of the county). The metropolitan and unitary councils, with the larger population in their areas, have wider functions than non-metropolitan councils. A few functions continue to be exercised over the larger area by joint bodies, made up of councillors from each district.

The allocation of functions is as follows:

County councils: education; strategic planning; traffic, transport and highways; fire service; consumer protection; refuse disposal; smallholdings; social care; libraries

District councils: local planning; housing; highways (maintenance of certain urban roads and off-street car parks); building regulations; environmental health; refuse collection; cemeteries and crematoria; collection of council tax and non-domestic rates

Unitary and metropolitan councils: their functions are all those listed above, except that the fire service is exercised by a joint body

Concurrently by county and district councils: recreation (parks, playing fields, swimming pools); museums; encouragement of the arts, tourism and industry

The Police and Magistrates Court Act 1994 set up police authorities in England and Wales separate from the local authorities.

PARISH COUNCILS

Parish or town councils are the most local tier of government in England. There are currently around 10,000 parishes in England, of which around 8,700 have councils served by approximately 70,000 councillors. Since 15 February 2008 local councils have been able to create new parish councils without seeking approval from the government. Around 80 per cent of parish councils represent populations of less than 2,500; parishes with no parish council can be grouped with neighbouring parishes under a common parish council. A parish council comprises at least five members, the number being fixed by the district council. Elections are held every four years, at the time of the election of the district councillor for the ward including the parish. Full parish councils must be formed for those parishes with more than 999 electors – below this number, parish meetings comprising the electors of the parish must be held at least twice a year.

Parish council functions include: allotments; encouragement of arts and crafts; community halls, recreational facilities (eg open spaces, swimming pools), cemeteries and crematoria; and many minor functions. They must also be given an opportunity to comment on planning applications. They may, like county and district councils, spend limited sums for the general benefit of the parish. They levy a precept on the district councils for their funds. Parish precepts for 2008–9 totalled £323m, an increase of 8.1 per cent on 2007–8.

REGIONAL ASSEMBLIES

Eight voluntary regional chambers were established for the East Midlands, the East of England, the North East, the North West, the South East, the South West, the West Midlands and Yorkshire and the Humber under the Regional Development Agencies Act 1998. The chambers operate within the same boundaries as the Regional Development Agencies.

The Regional Assemblies (Preparations) Act received royal assent on 8 May 2003, giving the chambers responsibility to act as regional planning bodies and to receive direct funding from central government for fulfilling this role.

The profile and number of assembly members varies from region to region but under guidance issued by the secretary of state, generally comprises 70 per cent elected local authority councillors and 30 per cent drawn from other sectors, including education, business, arts and culture, faith groups, community, voluntary and environmental organisations.

ROLE OF THE CHAMBERS

The government's *Sub-national Review of Economic Development and Regeneration* (July 2007) contained a number of recommendations for organising infrastructure at regional and local levels. In particular, regional assemblies in their current form are to be abolished by 2010, with responsibility for regional planning being passed to the regional development agencies. Local authorities will have a new statutory duty to assess local economic conditions and have a stronger role in the area's economic development. Currently all assemblies perform four core functions: acting as regional planning bodies and housing boards, advising the government and European institutions on matters of regional strategic and policy development and scrutinising the work of the Regional Development Agencies. They may also engage in other work according to regional circumstances and priorities. Principal areas of policy development include regional planning and transport, the environment, sustainable development, rural issues and equalities.

The English Regions Network (ERN) is the umbrella organisation for England's eight regional assemblies:

THE ENGLISH REGIONS NETWORK, c/o East of England Regional Assembly, Flempton House, Flempton, Bury St Edmonds, Suffolk IP28 6EG **E** info@ern.gov.uk **W** www.ern.gov.uk

FINANCE

The local government budget requirement (including parish precepts) for 2008–9 is £52.4bn; of this £24.8bn is to be raised through council tax, £20.5bn from redistributed business rates, £2.9bn from revenue support grant and £4.1bn from police grant.

In England, the average council tax per dwelling for 2008–9 is £1,146, up from £1,101 in 2007–8, an increase of 4 per cent. The average council tax for 2008–9 is £1,200 in shire areas, £1,199 in London and £952 in metropolitan areas. In England, the average council tax bill for a Band D dwelling (occupied by two adults, including parish precepts) for 2008–9 is £1,374, an average increase of 4 per cent from 2007–8. The average Band D council tax is £1,408 in shire areas, £1,328 in metropolitan areas and £1,292 in London. Since 2006–7 the London figure includes a levy to fund the 2012 Olympic Games which equates to a £20 a year increase on a Band D council tax.

The provisional amount estimated to be raised from national non-domestic rates from central and local lists is £20.5bn. The non-domestic rating multiplier for England for 2008–9 is 46.2p (45.8p for small businesses). The City of London is able to set a different multiplier from the rest of England; for 2008–9 this is 46.6p (46.2p for small businesses).

Under the Local Government and Housing Act 1989, local authorities have four main ways of paying for capital expenditure: borrowing and other forms of extended credit; capital grants from central government towards some types of capital expenditure; 'usable' capital receipts from the sale of land, houses and other assets; and revenue.

The amount of capital expenditure which a local authority can finance by borrowing (or other forms of credit) is effectively limited by the credit approvals issued to it by central government. Most credit approvals can be used for any kind of local authority capital expenditure; these are known as basic credit approvals. Others (supplementary credit approvals) can be used only for the kind of expenditure specified in the approval, and so are often given to fund particular projects or services.

Local authorities can use all capital receipts from the sale of property or assets for capital spending, except in the case of sales of council houses. Generally, the 'usable' part of a local authority's capital receipts consists of 25 per cent of receipts from the sale of council houses and 50 per cent of other housing assets such as shops or vacant land. The balance has to be set aside as provision for repaying debt and meeting other credit liabilities.

EXPENDITURE

Local authority budgeted net expenditure for 2008–9 is:

Service	*£ million*
Education	41,474
Highways and transport	6,099
Social care	19,460
Housing (excluding HRA)	2,483
Cultural, environment and planning	10,355
Police	12,245
Fire and rescue	2,364
Courts	69
Central services	3,704
Mandatory rent allowances	9,075
Mandatory rent rebates	671
Rent rebates granted to HRA tenants	3,757
Other services	320
Net current expenditure	112,077
Capital financing	3,572
Capital expenditure charged to revenue account	1,225
Council tax benefit	3,468
Discretionary non-domestic rate relief	28
Bad debt provision	35
Flood defence payments to Environment Agency	29
Pensions interest cost and expected return on pensions assets	3,782
Less interest receipts	(1,264)
Less specific grants outside AEF	(19,816)
Gross revenue expenditure	103,136
Less specific grants inside AEF	(42,123)
Less area based grant	(2,725)
Net revenue expenditure	58,288
Less appropriations from pensions reserves	(4,704)
Less appropriations from other revenue reserves	(1,194)
Less adjustments	(13)
BUDGET REQUIREMENT	52,403

HRA = Housing Revenue Account
AEF = aggregate external finance

LONDON

The Greater London Council was abolished in 1986 and London was divided into 32 borough councils, which have a status similar to the metropolitan borough councils in the rest of England, and the City of London Corporation.

In March 1998 the government announced proposals for a Greater London Authority (GLA) covering the area of the 32 London boroughs and the City of London, which would comprise a directly elected mayor and a 25-member assembly. A referendum was held in London on 7 May 1998; the turnout was approximately 34 per cent and 72 per cent of electors voted in favour of the GLA. A London mayor was elected on 4 May 2000 and the Authority assumed its responsibilities on 3 July 2000 (*see also* Regional Government).

The GLA is responsible for transport, economic development, strategic planning, culture, health, the environment, the police and fire and emergency planning. The separately elected assembly scrutinises the mayor's activities and approves plans and budgets. There are 14 constituency assembly members, each representing a separate area of London (each constituency is made up of two or three complete London boroughs). Eleven additional members, making up the total assembly complement of 25 members, are elected on a London-wide basis, either as independents or from party political lists on the basis of proportional representation.

LONDON BOROUGH COUNCILS

The London boroughs have whole council elections every four years, in the year immediately following the county council election year. The most recent elections took place on 4 May 2006.

The borough councils have responsibility for the following functions: building regulations, cemeteries and crematoria, consumer protection, education, youth employment, environmental health, electoral registration, food, drugs, housing, leisure services, libraries, local planning, local roads, museums, parking, recreation (parks, playing fields, swimming pools), refuse collection and street cleaning, social services, town planning, and traffic management.

CITY OF LONDON CORPORATION

The City of London Corporation is the local authority for the City of London. Its legal definition is the 'Mayor and Commonalty and Citizens of the City of London'. It is governed by the court of common council, which consists of the lord mayor, 25 other aldermen and 100 common councilmen. The lord mayor and two sheriffs are nominated annually by the City guilds (the livery companies) and elected by the court of aldermen. Aldermen and councilmen are elected from the 25 wards into which the City is divided; councilmen must stand for re-election annually. The council is a legislative assembly, and there are no political parties.

The corporation has the same functions as the London borough councils. In addition, it runs the City of London Police; is the health authority for the Port of London; has health control of animal imports throughout Greater London, including at Heathrow airport; owns and manages public open spaces throughout Greater London; runs the central criminal court; and runs Billingsgate, Smithfield and Spitalfields markets.

THE CITY GUILDS (LIVERY COMPANIES)

The livery companies of the City of London grew out of early medieval religious fraternities and began to emerge as trade and craft guilds, retaining their religious aspect, in the 12th century. From the early 14th century, only members of the trade and craft guilds could call themselves citizens of the City of London. The guilds began to be called livery companies, because of the distinctive livery worn by the most prosperous guild members on ceremonial occasions, in the late 15th century.

By the early 19th century the power of the companies within their trades had begun to wane, but those wearing the livery of a company continued to play an important role in the government of the City of London. Liverymen still have the right to nominate the lord mayor and sheriffs, and most members of the court of common council are liverymen.

WALES

The Local Government (Wales) Act 1994 abolished the two-tier structure of eight county and 37 district councils which had existed since 1974, and replaced it, from 1 April 1996, with 22 unitary authorities. The new authorities were elected in May 1995. Each unitary authority inherited all the functions of the previous county and district councils, except fire services (which are provided by three combined fire authorities, composed of representatives of the unitary authorities) and national parks (which are the responsibility of three independent national park authorities).

COMMUNITY COUNCILS

In Wales community councils are the equivalent of parishes in England. Unlike England, where many areas are not in any parish, communities have been established for the whole of Wales, approximately 865 communities in all. Community meetings may be convened as and when desired.

Community or town councils exist in 736 of the communities and further councils may be established at the request of a community meeting. Community councils have broadly the same range of powers as English parish councils. Community councillors are elected for a term of four years.

ELECTIONS

Elections take place every four years; the last elections took place in May 2008.

FINANCE

Total budgeted revenue expenditure for 2008–9 is £7bn, an increase of 3.6 per cent on 2007–8. Total budget requirement, which excludes expenditure financed by specific and special government grants and any use of reserves, is £5.4bn. This comprises revenue support grant of £3.1bn, support from the national non-domestic rate pool of £868m, police grant of £230m and £1.2bn to be raised through council tax. The non-domestic rating multiplier for Wales for 2008–9 is 46.6p. The average band D council tax levied in Wales for 2008–9 is £1,044, comprising unitary authorities £860, police authorities £160 and community councils £24.

EXPENDITURE

Local authority budgeted net revenue expenditure for 2008–9 is:

Service	*£ million*
Education	2,401
Social services	1,336
Council fund housing, including housing benefit	763
Local environmental services	384
Roads and transport	305
Libraries, culture, heritage, sport and recreation	270
Planning, economic and community development	108
Council tax collection	30
Debt financing costs: counties	311
Central administrative and other revenue expenditure	273
Police	643
Fire	142
National parks	17
Gross revenue expenditure	6,983
Less specific and special government grants	(1,545)
Net revenue expenditure	5,438
Less appropriations from reserves	(49)
BUDGET REQUIREMENT	5,389

SCOTLAND

The Local Government etc (Scotland) Act 1994 abolished the two-tier structure of nine regional and 53 district councils which had existed since 1975 and replaced it, from 1 April 1996, with 29 unitary authorities on the mainland; the three islands councils remained. The new authorities were elected in April 1995.

In July 1999 the Scottish parliament assumed responsibility for legislation on local government. The government had established a commission on local government and the Scottish parliament (the McIntosh Commission) to make recommendations on the relationship between local authorities and the Scottish parliament and on increasing local authorities' accountability.

The local government in Scotland bill was introduced to the Scottish parliament in May 2002. The bill focused on three integrated core elements:

- A power for local authorities to promote and improve the well-being of their area and/or persons in it
- Statutory underpinning for community planning through the introduction of a duty on local authorities and key partners, including police, health boards and enterprise agencies
- A duty to secure best value

ELECTIONS

The unitary authorities consist of directly elected councillors. The Scottish Local Government (Elections) Act 2002 moved elections from a three-year to a four-year cycle; the last elections took place in May 2007.

FUNCTIONS

The functions of the councils and islands councils are: education; social work; strategic planning; the provision of infrastructure such as roads; consumer protection; flood prevention; coast protection; valuation and rating; the police and fire services; civil defence; electoral registration; public transport; registration of births, deaths and marriages; housing; leisure and recreation; development and building control; environmental health; licensing; allotments; public conveniences; and the administration of district courts.

COMMUNITY COUNCILS

Scottish community councils differ from those in England and Wales. Their purpose as defined in statute is to ascertain and express the views of the communities they represent, and to take in the interests of their communities such action as appears to be expedient or practicable. Around 1,200 community councils have been established under schemes drawn up by local authorities in Scotland.

FINANCE

Budgeted total revenue support for 2008–9 is £10.1bn, comprising £7.3bn general revenue funding, non-domestic rate income of £2bn and ring-fenced grants of £764m. The non-domestic rate multiplier or poundage for 2008–9 is 45.8p. All non-domestic properties in with a rateable value of £15,000 or less may be eligible for a discount up to 80 per cent in the rate poundage. The average Band D council tax for 2008–9 is £1,149.

EXPENDITURE

The 2008–9 net expenditure budget estimates for local authorities in Scotland are:

Service	*£ million*
Education	4,611
Cultural and related services	591
Social work services	2,578
Police	1,125
Roads and transport	495
Environmental services	634
Fire	312
Planning and development services	193
Other	1,759
TOTAL	12,298

NORTHERN IRELAND

For the purpose of local government Northern Ireland has a system of 26 single-tier district councils.

ELECTIONS

Council members are elected for periods of four years at a time on the principle of proportional representation.

FUNCTIONS

The district councils have three main roles. These are:

Executive: responsibility for a wide range of local services including building regulations; community services; consumer protection; cultural facilities; environmental health; miscellaneous licensing and registration provisions, including dog control; litter prevention; recreational and social facilities; refuse collection and disposal; street cleaning; and tourist development

Representative: nominating representatives to sit as members of the various statutory bodies responsible for the administration of regional services such as drainage, education, fire, health and personal social services, housing, and libraries

Consultative: acting as the medium through which the views of local people are expressed on the operation in their area of other regional services – notably conservation (including water supply and sewerage services), planning and roads – provided by those departments of central government which have an obligation, statutory or otherwise, to consult the district councils about proposals affecting their areas

FINANCE

Local government in Northern Ireland is funded by a system of rates. The ratepayer receives a combined tax bill consisting of the regional rate and the district rate, which is set by each district council. The regional and district rates are both collected by the Land and Property Services Agency (formerly the Rate Collection Agency). The product of the district rates is paid over to each council whilst the product of the regional rate supports expenditure by the departments of the executive and assembly.

Since April 2007 domestic rates bills have been based on the capital value of a property, rather than the rental value. The capital value is defined as the price the property might reasonably be expected to realise had it been sold on the open market on 1 January 2005. Non-domestic rates bills are based on 2001 rental values.

Rate bills are calculated by multiplying the property's net annual rental value (NAV) (in the case of non-domestic property), or capital value (in the case of domestic property), by the regional and district rate poundages respectively.

For 2008–9 the overall average domestic poundage is 0.6424p compared to 0.6285p in 2007–8. The overall average non-domestic rate poundage in 2008–9 is 51.21p compared to 49.37p in 2007–8.

POLITICAL COMPOSITION OF LOCAL COUNCILS

as at May 2008

Abbreviations

All.	Alliance
BNP	British National Party
C.	Conservative
DUP	Democratic Unionist Party
Green	Green
Ind.	Independent
Ind. Un.	Independent Unionist
Lab.	Labour
LD	Liberal Democrat
Lib.	Liberal
O.	Other
PC	Plaid Cymru
R	Residents Associations/Ratepayers
SD	Social Democrat
SDLP	Social Democratic and Labour Party
SF	Sinn Fein
SNP	Scottish National Party
Soc.	Socialist
UUP	Ulster Unionist Party
v.	Vacant

Total number of seats is given in parentheses after council name.

ENGLAND

COUNTY COUNCILS

Bedfordshire (52)	C. 35; LD 9; Lab. 7; Ind. 1
Buckinghamshire (57)	C. 44; LD 11; Lab. 2
Cambridgeshire (69)	C. 43; LD 22; Lab. 4
Cheshire (51)	C. 24; Lab. 16; LD 8; Ind. 3
Cornwall (82)	LD 48; Ind. 19; C. 9; Lab. 5; Lib. 1
Cumbria (84)	Lab. 39; C. 32; LD 11; Ind. 2
Derbyshire (64)	Lab. 37; C. 15; LD 10; Ind. 1; v. 1
Devon (62)	LD 33; C. 23; Lab. 4; Ind. 2
Dorset (45)	C. 24; LD 16; Lab. 4; Ind. 1
Durham (126)	Lab. 67; LD 27; Ind. 22; C. 10
East Sussex (49)	C. 28; LD 13; Lab. 5; Ind. 1; O. 1; v. 1
Essex (75)	C. 50; Lab. 13; LD 8; Ind. 2; O. 2
Gloucestershire (63)	C. 33; LD 13; Lab. 12; O. 2; Ind. 1; R 1; v. 1
Hampshire (78)	C. 46; LD 28; Lab. 4
Hertfordshire (77)	C. 46; Lab. 16; LD 14; Green 1
Kent (84)	C. 57; Lab. 20; LD 6; Ind. 1
Lancashire (84)	Lab. 43; C. 31; LD 6; Ind. 2; Green 1; O. 1
Leicestershire (55)	C. 31; Lab. 13; LD 11
Lincolnshire (77)	C. 44; Lab. 20; LD 8; Ind. 3; O. 1; v. 1
Norfolk (84)	C. 47; Lab. 22; LD 13; Green 2
North Yorkshire (72)	C. 42; LD 19; Lab. 7; Ind. 4
Northamptonshire (73)	C. 45; Lab. 20; LD 8
Northumberland (67)	LD 26; C. 17; Lab. 17; Ind. 7
Nottinghamshire (67)	Lab. 36; C. 26; LD 5
Oxfordshire (74)	C. 44; LD 15; Lab. 8; Green 5; Ind. 2
Shropshire (48)	C. 27; LD 11; Lab. 9; v. 1
Somerset (58)	LD 29; C. 24; Lab. 4; O. 1
Staffordshire (62)	Lab. 32; C. 27; LD 2; Ind. 1
Suffolk (75)	C. 44; Lab. 18; LD 8; Ind. 5
Surrey (80)	C. 59; LD 12; R 7; Lab. 2
Warwickshire (62)	C. 28; Lab. 23; LD 10; Ind. 1
West Sussex (70)	C. 47; LD 16; Lab. 7
Wiltshire (49)	C. 30, LD 14; Lab. 3; Ind. 2
Worcestershire (57)	C. 29; Lab. 17; LD 8; Lib. 2; Ind. 1

DISTRICT COUNCILS

Adur (29)	C. 26; Ind. 2; LD 1
Allerdale (56)	O. 30; Lab. 21; Ind. 4; C. 1
Alnwick (30)	C. 12; LD 11; Ind. 4; Lab. 2; O. 1
Amber Valley (45)	C. 29; Lab. 14; BNP 2
Arun (56)	C. 42; LD 9; Lab. 3; Ind. 2
Ashfield (33)	LD 11; Lab. 9; Ind. 8; C. 3; O. 2
Ashford (43)	C. 28; LD 8; O. 3; Ind. 2; Lab. 2
Aylesbury Vale (59)	C. 37; LD 21; Ind. 1
Babergh (43)	C. 19; LD 16; Ind. 7; O. 1
Barrow-in-Furness (36)	C. 17; Lab. 8; Ind. 4; Soc. 4; O. 2; LD 1
Basildon (42)	C. 29; Lab. 10; LD 3
Basingstoke and Deane (60)	C. 35; LD 14; Lab. 9; Ind. 2
Bassetlaw (48)	C. 30; Lab. 16; Ind. 2
Bedford (54)	C. 20; LD 16; Lab. 11; Ind. 6; O. 1
Berwick-upon-Tweed (29)	LD 13; C. 9; Ind. 7
Blaby (39)	C. 28; LD 7; Lab. 4
Blyth Valley (50)	Lab. 29; LD 13; Ind. 5; C. 2; v. 1
Bolsover (37)	Lab. 27; Ind. 7; R 2; O. 1
Boston (32)	O. 25; C. 5; Ind. 2
Braintree (60)	C. 42; Lab. 9; R 5; Green 2; Ind. 1; LD 1
Breckland (54)	C. 48; Ind. 3; Lab. 3
Brentwood (37)	C. 28; LD 6; Lab. 2; Ind. 1
Bridgnorth (34)	Ind. 21; C. 6; LD 4; Lab. 2; O. 1
Broadland (47)	C. 35; LD 9; Ind. 3
Bromsgrove (39)	C. 27; Lab. 6; R 6
Broxbourne (38)	C. 35; Lab. 3
Broxtowe (44)	C. 16; LD 15; Lab. 10; Ind. 3
Burnley (45)	LD 23; Lab. 12; C. 6; BNP 4
Cambridge (42)	LD 27; Lab. 11; Ind. 2; C. 1; Green 1
Cannock Chase (41)	Lab. 15; LD 14; C. 12
Canterbury (50)	C. 29; LD 18; Lab. 2; v. 1
Caradon (42)	LD 21; Ind. 12; C. 9
Carlisle (52)	C. 21; Lab. 21; LD 7; Ind. 1; v. 2
Carrick (47)	C. 19; LD 18; Ind. 8; Lab. 1; O. 1
Castle Morpeth (33)	C. 12; LD 12; Lab. 6; Ind. 2; Green 1
Castle Point (41)	C. 25; Ind. 15; Lab. 1
Charnwood (52)	C. 32; Lab. 13; LD 5; BNP 1; Ind. 1
Chelmsford (57)	C. 31; LD 26
Cheltenham (40)	LD 20; C. 17; O. 3
Cherwell (50)	C. 44; Ind. 4; Lab. 2
Chester (60)	C. 33; Lab. 13; LD 13; Ind. 1
Chester-le-Street (34)	Lab. 26; Ind. 5; C. 2; LD 1
Chesterfield (48)	LD 38; Lab. 10

Chichester (48)	C. 33; LD 11; Ind. 3; v. 1
Chiltern (40)	C. 30; LD 9; Ind. 1
Chorley (47)	C. 28; Lab. 14; LD 3; Ind. 2
Christchurch (24)	C. 17; LD 4; Ind. 3
Colchester (60)	C. 27; LD 23; Lab. 7; Ind. 3
Congleton (48)	C. 25; LD 13; O. 6; Ind. 4
Copeland (51)	Lab. 31; C. 19; Ind. 1
Corby (29)	Lab. 16; C. 8; LD 5
Cotswolds (44)	C. 37; LD 5; Ind. 2
Craven (30)	C. 15; Ind. 10; LD 5;
Crawley (37)	C. 26; Lab. 9; LD 2
Crewe and Nantwich (56)	C. 28; Lab. 17; LD 6; O. 3; Ind. 2
Dacorum (51)	C. 44; LD 5; Lab. 2
Dartford (44)	C. 26; Lab. 12; R 6
Daventry (38)	C. 35; LD 2; Lab. 1
Derbyshire Dales (39)	C. 27; LD 8; Lab. 3; Ind. 1
Derwentside (55)	Lab. 29; Ind. 24; LD 2
Dover (45)	C. 28; Lab. 15; LD 2
Durham (50)	LD 27; Lab. 15; Ind. 8
Easington (51)	Lab. 46; Ind. 3; LD 2
East Cambridgeshire (39)	C. 24; LD 13; Ind. 2
East Devon (59)	C. 43; LD 10; Ind. 6
East Dorset (36)	C. 25; LD 11
East Hampshire (44)	C. 31; LD 13
East Hertfordshire (50)	C. 42; Ind. 4; LD 4
East Lindsey (60)	C. 27; Ind. 20; Lab. 8; LD 3; O. 2
East Northamptonshire (40)	C. 39; Ind. 1
East Staffordshire (39)	C. 24; Lab. 12; LD 2; Ind. 1
Eastbourne (27)	LD 20; C. 7
Eastleigh (44)	LD 38; C. 4; Lab. 2
Eden (38)	Ind. 20; C. 13; LD 5
Ellesmere Port and Neston (43)	Lab. 22; C. 17; Ind. 2; LD 2
Elmbridge (60)	C. 32; R 21; LD 7
Epping Forest (58)	C. 35; LD 9; R 6; BNP 4; Ind. 3; Lab. 1
Epsom and Ewell (38)	R 25; LD 11; C. 2
Erewash (51)	C. 30; Lab. 18; LD 2; Ind. 1
Exeter (40)	LD 13; C. 12; Lab. 11; Lib. 4
Fareham (31)	C. 22; LD 9
Fenland (40)	C. 39; Ind. 1
Forest Heath (27)	C. 20; LD 4; O. 2; Ind. 1
Forest of Dean (48)	C. 29; Ind. 9; Lab. 8; LD 2
Fylde (51)	C. 29; Ind. 14; R 3; O. 3; LD 2
Gedling (50)	C. 28; Lab. 9; LD 9; Ind. 4
Gloucester (36)	C. 17; LD 11; Lab. 8
Gosport (34)	C. 16; LD 14; Lab. 4
Gravesham (44)	C. 28; Lab. 16
Great Yarmouth (39)	C. 24; Lab. 15
Guildford (48)	C. 27; LD 21
Hambleton (44)	C. 39; Ind. 3; LD 2
Harborough (37)	C. 26; LD 11
Harlow (33)	C. 19; LD 8; Lab. 6
Harrogate (54)	C. 27; LD 21; Ind. 6
Hart (35)	C. 17; LD 10; O. 6; Ind. 2
Hastings (32)	C. 15; Lab 13; LD 3; Ind. 1
Havant (38)	C. 32; Lab 3; LD 3
Hertsmere (39)	C. 31; LD 5; Lab. 3
High Peak (43)	C. 24; Lab. 9; LD 6; Ind. 4
Hinckley and Bosworth (34)	LD 19; C. 13; Lab. 2
Horsham (44)	C. 30; LD 12; Ind. 2
Huntingdonshire (52)	C. 38; LD 12; Ind. 2
Hyndburn (35)	C. 18; Lab. 13; Ind. 4
Ipswich (48)	Lab. 21; C. 19; LD 8
Kennet (43)	C. 34; Ind. 9
Kerrier (44)	Ind. 24; LD 7; C. 6; O. 4; Lab. 2; Lib. 1
Kettering (36)	C. 28; Lab. 6; Ind. 2
King's Lynn and West Norfolk (62)	C. 52; Lab. 4; LD 4; Ind. 2
Lancaster (60)	Ind. 19; Lab. 13; Green 12; C. 11; LD 5
Lewes (41)	LD 22; C. 17; Ind. 2
Lichfield (56)	C. 44; Lab. 5; LD 4; Ind. 3
Lincoln City (33)	C. 18; Lab. 14; LD 1
Macclesfield (60)	C. 38; LD 12; Lab. 6; Ind. 2; R 2
Maidstone (55)	C. 29; LD 21; Ind. 5
Maldon (31)	C. 26; Ind. 5
Malvern Hills (38)	C. 29; LD 6; Ind. 2; Green 1
Mansfield (46)	Ind. 28; Lab. 13; LD 4; C. 1
Melton (28)	C. 20; Ind. 5; Lab. 3
Mendip (47)	C. 24; LD 22; O. 1
Mid Bedfordshire (53)	C. 38; LD 11; Ind. 4
Mid Devon (42)	C. 17; Ind. 15; LD 10
Mid Suffolk (40)	C. 22; LD 10; Ind. 4; Green 2; O. 2
Mid Sussex (54)	C. 29; LD 21; Lab. 1; v. 3
Mole Valley (41)	C. 22; LD 14; Ind. 3; O. 2
New Forest (60)	C. 45; LD 14; v. 1
Newark and Sherwood (46)	C. 25; Ind. 9; Lab. 6; LD 4; v. 2
Newcastle-under-Lyme (60)	C. 25; LD 19; Lab. 12; O. 4
North Cornwall (36)	Ind. 15; LD 14; C. 6; O. 1
North Devon (43)	C. 22; LD 17; Ind. 4
North Dorset (33)	C. 17; LD 13; Ind. 3
North East Derbyshire (53)	Lab. 27; C. 10; LD 8; Ind. 6; v. 2
North Hertfordshire (49)	C. 32; LD 9; Lab. 8
North Kesteven (43)	C. 25; Ind. 14; LD 4
North Norfolk (48)	LD 30; C. 16; Ind. 1; O. 1
North Shropshire (40)	C. 26; Ind. 12; Lab. 2
North Warwickshire (35)	C. 21; Lab. 14
North West Leicestershire (38)	C. 27; Lab. 5; LD 3; BNP 2; Ind. 1
North Wiltshire (54)	C. 39; LD 14; Lab. 1
Northampton (47)	LD 26; C. 15; Lab. 5; Ind. 1
Norwich (39)	Lab. 15; Green 13; LD 6; C. 5
Nuneaton and Bedworth (34)	C. 18; Lab. 14; BNP 2
Oadby and Wigston (26)	LD 21; C. 5
Oswestry (29)	C. 17; O. 6; LD 4; Ind. 2
Oxford (48)	Lab. 23; LD 16; Green 7; O. 2
Pendle (49)	LD 20; C. 16; Lab. 9; BNP 2; Ind. 1; O. 1
Penwith (35)	C. 17; LD 12; Ind. 5; Lab. 1
Preston (57)	Lab. 24; C. 21; LD 9; Ind. 2; O. 1
Purbeck (24)	C. 11; LD 11; Ind. 2
Redditch (29)	C. 15; Lab. 10; LD 3; BNP 1
Reigate and Banstead (51)	C. 39; R 6; LD 3; Ind. 2; Lab. 1
Restormel (45)	LD 20; Ind. 13; C. 10; O. 2
Ribble Valley (40)	C. 29; LD 10; Ind. 1
Richmondshire (34)	C. 17; O. 13; LD 3; Ind. 1
Rochford (39)	C. 33; LD 5; R 1
Rossendale (36)	C. 21; Lab. 11; LD 3; Ind. 1
Rother (38)	C. 27; LD 8; Ind. 2; v. 1
Rugby (48)	C. 27; Lab. 11; LD 10
Runnymede (42)	C. 36; Ind. 6

Rushcliffe (50)	C. 34; LD 11; Green 2; Lab. 2; Ind. 1
Rushmoor (42)	C. 29; LD 8; Lab. 5
Ryedale (30)	C. 14; LD 8; Ind. 5; Lib. 2; O. 1
St Albans (58)	LD 30; C. 22; Lab. 5; Ind. 1
St Edmundsbury (45)	C. 36; Lab. 3; LD 3; Ind. 2; O. 1
Salisbury (55)	C. 22; LD 19; Lab. 10; Ind. 4
Scarborough (50)	C. 22; Ind. 16; LD 6; Lab. 3; Green 2; O. 1
Sedgefield (50)	Lab. 30; Ind. 12; LD 6; C. 1; v. 1
Sedgemoor (50)	C. 36; Lab. 11; LD 3
Selby (41)	C. 29; Lab. 9; Ind. 3
Sevenoaks (54)	C. 41; LD 7; Lab. 5; Ind. 1
Shepway (46)	C. 35; LD 9; O. 2
Shrewsbury and Atcham (40)	C. 23; Lab. 10; LD 5; Ind. 1; v. 1
South Bedfordshire (50)	C. 34; LD 12; Lab. 4
South Bucks (40)	C. 36; Ind. 2; LD 2
South Cambridgeshire (57)	C. 32; LD 15; Ind. 9; Lab. 1
South Derbyshire (36)	C. 21; Lab. 14; Ind. 1
South Hams (40)	C. 27; LD 9; Ind. 3; O. 1
South Holland (37)	C. 25; Ind. 11; O. 1
South Kesteven (58)	C. 35; Ind. 15; LD 6; Lab. 2
South Lakeland (51)	LD 36; C. 14; Lab. 1
South Norfolk (46)	C. 39; LD 7
South Northamptonshire (42)	C. 35; Ind. 7
South Oxfordshire (48)	C. 38; LD 6; Ind. 2; Lab. 1; R 1
South Ribble (55)	C. 45; Lab. 8; LD 1; O. 1
South Shropshire (34)	C. 18; LD 11; Ind. 3; O. 2
South Somerset (60)	LD 38; C. 17; Ind. 5
South Staffordshire (49)	C. 42; Ind. 5; Lab. 1; LD 1
Spelthorne (39)	C. 31; LD 8
Stafford (59)	C. 40; Lab. 12; LD 5; Ind. 1; v. 1
Staffordshire Moorlands (56)	C. 35; LD 6; Lab. 5; R 5; Ind. 4; O. 1
Stevenage (39)	Lab. 30; C. 5; LD 3; O. 1
Stratford-on-Avon (53)	C. 32; LD 19; Ind. 2
Stroud (51)	C. 31; Lab. 7; Green 6; LD 5 Ind. 1; O. 1
Suffolk Coastal (55)	C. 44; LD 9; Ind. 1; Lab. 1
Surrey Heath (40)	C. 30; LD 7; Lab. 2; Ind. 1
Swale (47)	C. 27; Lab. 9; Ind. 6; LD 5
Tamworth (30)	C. 24; Lab. 5; Ind. 1
Tandridge (42)	C. 33; LD 8; Ind. 1
Taunton Deane (56)	LD 26; C. 25; Ind. 4; Lab. 1
Teesdale (32)	O. 15; Ind. 7; Lab. 6; C. 4
Teignbridge (46)	LD 21; C. 18; Ind. 7
Tendring (60)	C. 28; O. 15; Lab. 6; LD 6; Ind. 5
Test Valley (48)	C. 33; LD 15
Tewkesbury (38)	C. 19; LD 17; Ind. 2
Thanet (56)	C. 34; Lab. 19; Ind. 3
Three Rivers (48)	LD 31; C. 12; Lab. 4; BNP 1
Tonbridge and Malling (53)	C. 46; LD 7
Torridge (36)	C. 14; Ind. 13; LD 5; Lib. 4
Tunbridge Wells (48)	C. 44; LD 4
Tynedale (52)	C. 29; LD 9; Ind. 7; Lab. 7
Uttlesford (44)	C. 26; LD 15; Ind. 3
Vale of White Horse (51)	LD 33; C. 18
Vale Royal (57)	C. 26; Lab. 17; LD 11; O. 3
Wansbeck (45)	Lab. 27; C. 16; O. 2
Warwick (46)	C. 24; Lab. 9; LD 9; Ind. 4
Watford (37)	LD 28; C. 3; Green 3; Lab. 3
Waveney (48)	C. 30; Lab. 12; LD 3; Ind. 2; Green 1
Waverley (57)	C. 51; Ind. 3; LD 3
Wealden (55)	C. 34; LD 12; O. 6; Green 2; Ind. 1
Wear Valley (40)	Lab. 17; LD 16; Ind. 7
Wellingborough (36)	C. 29; Lab. 4; Ind. 2; v. 1
Welwyn and Hatfield (48)	C. 39; Lab. 5; LD 3; v. 1
West Devon (31)	C. 13; Ind. 10; LD 8
West Dorset (48)	C. 26; LD 16; Ind. 6
West Lancashire (54)	C. 35; Lab. 18; Ind. 1
West Lindsey (37)	LD 20; C. 16; Ind. 1
West Oxfordshire (49)	C. 40; LD 6; Ind. 2; Lab. 1
West Somerset (31)	Ind. 16; C. 13; Lab. 1; LD 1
West Wiltshire (44)	C. 26; LD 13; Ind. 2; O. 2; v. 1
Weymouth and Portland (36)	C. 16; LD 12; Ind. 4; Lab. 4
Winchester (57)	C. 29; LD 24; Ind. 3; Lab. 1
Woking (36)	C. 19; LD 17
Worcester (35)	C. 17; Lab. 13; LD 3; Ind. 2
Worthing (37)	C. 25; LD 12
Wychavon (45)	C. 35; LD 10
Wycombe (60)	C. 49; LD 6; Lab. 3; Ind. 2
Wyre (55)	C. 44; Lab. 8; Ind. 1; Lib. 1; v. 1
Wyre Forest (42)	C. 22; O. 10; Lib. 6; Lab. 2; LD 2

LONDON BOROUGH COUNCILS

Barking and Dagenham (51)	Lab. 37; BNP 12; C. 1; v. 1
Barnet (63)	C. 37; Lab. 20; LD 6
Bexley (63)	C. 54; Lab. 9
Brent (63)	LD 27; Lab. 20; C. 16
Bromley (60)	C. 49; LD 7; Lab. 4
Camden (54)	LD 22; Lab. 16; C. 13; Green 3
Croydon (70)	C. 44; Lab. 26
Ealing (69)	C. 43; Lab. 23; LD 3
Enfield (63)	C. 34; Lab. 27; O. 2
Greenwich (51)	Lab. 36; C. 13; LD 2
Hackney (57)	Lab. 45; C. 9; LD 2; Green 1
Hammersmith and Fulham (46)	C. 33; LD 13
Haringey (57)	Lab. 31; LD 26
Harrow (63)	C. 37; Lab. 24; LD 2
Havering (54)	C. 34; R 16; Lab. 2; BNP 1; O. 1
Hillingdon (65)	C. 44; Lab. 17; LD 2; Ind. 1; v. 1
Hounslow (60)	Lab. 24; C. 22; O. 6; LD 4; Ind. 4
Islington (48)	LD 24; Lab. 23; Green 1
Kensington and Chelsea (54)	C. 45; Lab. 9
Kingston upon Thames (48)	LD 25; C. 21; Lab. 1; Ind. 1
Lambeth (63)	Lab. 38; LD 18; C. 6; Green 1
Lewisham (55)	Lab. 26; LD 17; Green 6; C. 3; Soc. 2; Ind. 1
Merton (60)	C. 29; Lab. 27; R 3; Ind. 1
Newham (61)	Lab. 55; O. 6
Redbridge (63)	C. 33; Lab. 18; LD 10; BNP 1; Ind. 1; v. 1
Richmond upon Thames (54)	LD 35; C. 18; Ind. 1
Southwark (63)	Lab. 29; LD 27; C. 6; Green 1
Sutton (54)	LD 31; C. 21; Ind. 1; O. 1
Tower Hamlets (51)	Lab. 29; O. 10; C. 8; LD 4
Waltham Forest (60)	Lab. 25; LD 19; C. 15; v. 1
Wandsworth (60)	C. 51; Lab. 9
Westminster (60)	C. 48; Lab. 12

METROPOLITAN BOROUGHS

Barnsley (63)	Lab. 32; Ind. 22; C. 6; LD 1; O. 2
Birmingham (120)	C. 49; Lab. 36; LD 32; O. 3
Bolton (60)	Lab. 27; C. 23; LD 9; Ind. 1
Bradford (90)	Lab. 36; C. 35; LD 14; Green 3; BNP 2
Bury (51)	C. 26; Lab. 16; LD 9
Calderdale (51)	C. 21; LD 16; Lab. 9; Ind. 3; BNP 1; O. 1
Coventry (54)	C. 27; Lab. 24; Soc. 2; LD 1
Doncaster (64)	Lab. 26; Ind. 12; LD 12; C. 9; O. 5
Dudley (72)	C. 43; Lab. 26; LD 2; O. 1
Gateshead (66)	Lab. 41; LD 24; Lib. 1; v. 1
Kirklees (69)	C. 22; Lab. 21; LD 19; Green 4; BNP 2; Ind. 1
Knowsley (63)	Lab. 47; LD 16
Leeds (99)	Lab. 43; LD 24; C. 22; O. 5; Green 3; BNP 1; Ind. 1
Liverpool (90)	LD 46; Lab 39; Lib. 3; Green 2
Manchester (96)	Lab. 62; LD 33; C. 1
Newcastle-upon-Tyne (78)	LD 49; Lab. 29
North Tyneside (60)	C. 30; Lab. 21; LD 8; v. 1
Oldham (60)	LD. 30; Lab. 22; C. 7; Ind. 1
Rochdale (60)	LD 33; Lab. 18; C. 8; Ind. 1
Rotherham (63)	Lab. 50; C. 10; BNP 2; Ind. 1;
St Helens (48)	Lab. 23; LD 19; C. 6
Salford (60)	Lab. 36; C. 13; LD 9; Lib. 1; O. 1
Sandwell (72)	Lab. 49; C. 14; LD 5; Ind. 2; BNP 2
Sefton (66)	LD 27; Lab. 21; C. 18
Sheffield (84)	LD 45; Lab. 36; Green 3
Solihull (51)	C. 26; LD 18; Lab. 5; BNP 1; Green 1
South Tyneside (54)	Lab. 31; Ind. 10; O. 7; C. 3; LD 3
Stockport (63)	LD 36; C. 14; Lab. 10; Ind. 3
Sunderland (75)	Lab. 48; C. 22; Ind. 4; LD 1
Tameside (57)	Lab. 44; C. 10; Ind. 3
Trafford (63)	C. 39; Lab. 19; LD 5
Wakefield (63)	Lab. 32; C. 23; Ind. 6; LD 2
Walsall (60)	C. 33; Lab. 18; LD 6; Ind. 2; O. 1
Wigan (75)	Lab. 41; O. 11; C. 10; Ind. 8; LD 4; v. 1
Wirral (66)	C. 24; Lab. 21; LD 20; O. 1
Wolverhampton (60)	Lab. 28; C. 27; LD 5

UNITARY COUNCILS

Bath and North East Somerset (65)	LD 26; C. 31; Lab. 5; Ind. 2; O. 1
Blackburn with Darwen (64)	Lab. 27; C. 18; LD 11; Ind. 3; O. 5
Blackpool (42)	C. 26; Lab. 13; LD 3
Bournemouth (54)	C. 40; LD 7; Ind. 4; Lab. 3
Bracknell Forest (42)	C. 39; Lab. 3
Brighton and Hove (54)	C. 26; Lab. 13; Green 12; LD 2; Ind. 1
Bristol (70)	LD 31; Lab. 25; C. 13; Green 1
Darlington (53)	Lab. 29; C. 18; LD 5; Ind. 1
Derby (51)	LD 18; Lab. 17; C. 14; Ind. 2
East Riding of Yorkshire (67)	C. 46; LD 12; Ind. 4; Lab. 3; SD 1; O. 1
Halton (56)	Lab. 33; LD 14; C. 9
Hartlepool (48)	Lab. 23; Ind. 12; LD 6; C. 5; O. 2
Herefordshire (58)	C. 32; Ind. 13; LD 9; Lab. 2; O. 2
Isles of Scilly (21)*	O. 21
Isle of Wight (48)	C. 30; O. 9; Ind. 4; LD 3; Lab. 2
Kingston-upon-Hull (59)	LD 33; Lab. 19; C. 3; O. 3; Ind. 1
Leicester (54)	Lab. 38; C. 8; LD 6; Green 2
Luton (48)	Lab. 26; LD 17; C. 5
Medway (55)	C. 33; Lab. 13; LD 8; Ind. 1
Middlesbrough (49)	Lab. 28; Ind. 11; C. 6; Green 1; LD 1; O. 2
Milton Keynes (51)	LD 21; C. 20; Lab. 10
North East Lincolnshire (42)	LD 20; C. 16; Lab. 4; Ind. 2
North Lincolnshire (43)	Lab. 22; C. 18; Ind. 2; LD 1
North Somerset (61)	C. 46; Ind. 7; LD 5; Lab. 3
Nottingham (55)	Lab. 42; C. 7; LD 6
Peterborough (57)	C. 43; O. 9; LD 3; Lab. 2
Plymouth (57)	C. 37; Lab. 20
Poole (42)	C. 25; LD 17
Portsmouth (42)	C. 19; LD 19; Lab. 2; Ind. 2
Reading (46)	Lab. 19; C. 18; LD 8; Ind. 1
Redcar and Cleveland (59)	Lab. 28; LD 13; C. 11; Ind. 7
Rutland (26)	C. 19; Ind. 5; LD 2
Slough (41)	Lab. 22; C. 7; LD 3; Lib. 3; R 3; O. 3
South Gloucestershire (70)	C. 33; LD 28; Lab. 9
Southampton (48)	C. 26; Lab. 14; LD 8
Southend-on-Sea (51)	C. 27; LD 11; Ind. 7; Lab. 6
Stockton-on-Tees (56)	Lab. 22; Ind. 16; C. 13; LD 5
Stoke-on-Trent (60)	O. 26; Lab. 17; BNP 9; LD 5; Ind. 3
Swindon (59)	C. 43; Lab. 12; LD 3; Ind. 1
Telford and Wrekin (54)	C. 27; Lab. 18; Ind. 3; LD 3; O. 3
Thurrock (49)	C. 24; Lab. 22; Ind. 2; BNP 1
Torbay (36)	C. 23; LD 8; Ind. 3; O. 2
Warrington (57)	LD 28; Lab. 22; C. 7
West Berkshire (52)	C. 36; LD 16
Windsor and Maidenhead (57)	C. 36; LD 16; R 5
Wokingham (54)	C. 44; LD 10
York (47)	LD 20; Lab. 18; C. 7; Green 2

* Thirteen councillors are elected by the residents of the isle of St Mary's and two councillors each are elected by the residents of the four other islands (Bryher, St Martins, St Agnes and Tresco)

SHADOW UNITARY COUNCILS†

Cheshire East (81)	C. 59; LD 12; Lab. 6; O. 4
Cheshire West & Chester (72)	C. 55; Lab. 13; LD 4

† Established as part of a transitional arrangement: they will become unitary councils in April 2009 at which point the two-tier county/district system in these areas will be abolished. Until April 2009 council services continue to be the responsibility of the relevant county or district authority.

WALES

Blaenau Gwent (42)	Lab. 17; Ind. 16; O. 7; LD 2
Bridgend (54)	Lab. 27; LD 11; Ind. 9; C. 6; PC 1
Caerphilly (73)	Lab. 31; PC 32; Ind. 9; v. 1
Cardiff (75)	LD 35; C. 16; Lab. 13; PC 7; Ind. 3; v. 1
Carmarthenshire (74)	Ind. 31; PC 30; Lab. 11; O. 2

Ceredigion (42)	PC 19; Ind. 12; LD 9; Lab. 1; v. 1
Conwy (59)	C. 22; Ind. 13; PC 13; Lab. 7; LD 4
Denbighshire (47)	C. 18; Ind. 11; PC 8; Lab. 7; O. 3
Flintshire (70)	Ind. 26; Lab. 22; LD 12; C. 9; PC 1
Gwynedd (75)	PC 35; Ind. 18; O. 13; LD 5; Lab. 4
Merthyr Tydfil (33)	Ind. 16; Lab. 8; LD 6; O. 3
Monmouthshire (43)	C. 28; Lab. 7; LD 5; PC 3
Neath Port Talbot (64)	Lab. 37; PC 11; O. 9; LD 4; R 3
Newport (50)	Lab. 22; C. 17; LD 9; Ind. 1; PC 1
Pembrokeshire (60)	Ind. 38; C. 5; Lab. 5; PC 5; LD 3; O. 4
Powys (73)	O. 43; LD 15; C. 9; Lab. 4; Ind. 2
Rhondda Cynon Taff (75)	Lab. 44; PC 20; Ind. 6; LD 3; C. 1; v. 1
Swansea (72)	O. 38; Lab. 30; C. 4
Torfaen (44)	Lab. 18; Ind. 13; C. 5; O. 3; LD 2
Vale of Glamorgan (47)	C. 25; Lab. 13; PC 6; Ind. 3
Wrexham (52)	O. 28; Lab. 11; C. 5; Ind. 4; PC 4
Ynys Mon (Isle of Anglesey) (40)	O. 23; PC 8; Lab. 5; C. 2; LD 2

SCOTLAND

Aberdeen (43)	LD 15; SNP 13; Lab. 10; C. 4; Ind. 1
Aberdeenshire (68)	LD 24; SNP 22; C. 14; Ind. 8
Angus (29)	O. 15; SNP 13; Ind. 1
Argyll and Bute (36)	Ind. 15; SNP 10; LD 8; C. 3
Clackmannanshire (18)	Lab. 8; SNP 7; C. 1; Ind. 1; LD 1
Dumfries and Galloway (47)	C. 18; Lab. 14; SNP 10; LD 3; Ind. 2
Dundee (29)	SNP 13; Lab. 10; C. 3; LD 2; Ind. 1
East Ayrshire (32)	Lab. 14; SNP 14; C. 3; Ind. 1
East Dunbartonshire (24)	SNP 8; Lab. 6; C. 5; LD 3; Ind. 2
East Lothian (23)	Lab. 7; SNP 7; LD 6; C. 2; Ind. 1
East Renfrewshire (20)	C. 7; Lab. 7; SNP 3; Ind. 2; LD 1
Edinburgh (58)	LD 17; Lab. 15; SNP 12; C. 11; Green 3
Eilean Siar (Western Isles) (31)	Ind. 25; SNP 4; Lab. 2
Falkirk (32)	Lab. 14; SNP 13; Ind. 3; C. 2
Fife (78)	Lab. 24; SNP 23; LD 21; Ind. 5; C. 4; O. 2
Glasgow (79)	Lab. 46; SNP 22; Green 5; LD 5; C. 1
Highland (80)	Ind. 34; LD 21; SNP 17; Lab. 7; O. 1
Inverclyde (20)	Lab. 9; SNP 5; LD 4; C. 1; Ind. 1
Midlothian (18)	Lab. 9; SNP 6; LD 3
Moray (26)	Ind. 11; SNP 10; C. 3; Lab. 2
North Ayrshire (30)	Lab. 12; SNP 8; Ind. 5; C. 3; LD 2
North Lanarkshire (70)	Lab. 40; SNP 23; Ind. 4; C. 1; LD 1; O. 1
Orkney Islands (21)	Ind. 21
Perth and Kinross (41)	SNP 18; C. 12; LD 8; Lab. 3
Renfrewshire (40)	Lab. 17; SNP 17; LD 4; C. 2
Scottish Borders (34)	C. 11; LD 10; SNP 6; Ind. 5; O. 2
Shetland Islands (22)	O. 11; Ind. 11
South Ayrshire (30)	C. 12; Lab. 8; SNP 8; Ind. 2
South Lanarkshire (67)	Lab. 31; SNP 23; C. 8; Ind. 3; LD 2
Stirling (22)	Lab. 8; SNP 7; C. 4; LD 3
West Dunbartonshire (22)	Lab. 10; SNP 9; Ind. 2; Soc. 1
West Lothian (32)	Lab. 14; SNP 13; O. 3; C. 1; Ind. 1

NORTHERN IRELAND

Antrim (19)	DUP 5; UUP 5; SF 3; All. 2; SDLP 2; Ind. 1; O. 1
Ards (23)	DUP 11; UUP 6; All. 3; Ind. 2; SDLP 1
Armagh City (22)	DUP 6; SDLP 6; SF 5; UUP 5
Ballymena (24)	DUP 9; O. 6; UUP 4; Ind. 2; SDLP 2; SF 1
Ballymoney (16)	DUP 7; SF 3; SDLP 2; UUP 2; Ind. Un. 1; O. 1
Banbridge (17)	DUP 6; UUP 5; SDLP 3; All. 1; O. 1; SF 1
Belfast (51)	DUP 15; SF 14; SDLP 8; UUP 7; All. 4; O. 2; Ind. Un. 1
Carrickfergus (17)	DUP 8; UUP 4; All. 3; Ind. Un. 2
Castlereagh (23)	DUP 12; All. 4; UUP 4; SDLP 2; O. 1
Coleraine (22)	DUP 8; UUP 8; SDLP 3; All. 1; Ind. 1; SF 1
Cookstown (16)	SDLP 5; SF 5; DUP 3; UUP 3
Craigavon (26)	DUP 8; SF 6; UUP 6; Ind. 3; SDLP 3
Derry City (30)	SDLP 14; SF 10; DUP 5; UUP 1
Down (23)	SDLP 10; SF 5; DUP 3; UUP 3; C. 1; Green 1
Dungannon and South Tyrone (22)	SF 9; DUP 5; SDLP 4; UUP 4
Fermanagh (23)	SF 8; SDLP 5; UUP 5; DUP 4; Ind. 1
Larne (15)	DUP 4; UUP 4; All. 2; Ind. 2; SDLP 2; O. 1
Limavady (15)	SF 6; SDLP 3; DUP 2; O. 2; UUP 2
Lisburn (30)	DUP 12; UUP 7; SF 4; All. 3; SDLP 3; O. 1
Magherafelt (16)	SF 6; DUP 4; O. 2; SDLP 2; UUP 2
Moyle (15)	SF 4; DUP 3; Ind. 3; SDLP 3; UUP 2
Newry and Mourne (30)	SF 12; SDLP 9; DUP 2; Ind. 2; UUP 2; Green 1; O 2
Newtownabbey (25)	DUP 12; UUP 6; All. 3; Ind. Un. 1; O. 1; SDLP 1; SF 1
North Down (25)	DUP 8; UUP 8; All. 6; Ind. 2; Green 1
Omagh (21)	SF 10; DUP 3; SDLP 3; UUP 3; Ind. 2
Strabane (16)	SF 8; DUP 3; SDLP 2; UUP 2; Ind. 1

ENGLAND

The region of England lies between 55° 46′ and 49° 57′ 30″ N. latitude (from a few miles north of the mouth of the Tweed to the Lizard), and between 1° 46′ E. and 5° 43′ W. longitude (from Lowestoft to Land's End). England is bounded on the north by the Cheviot Hills; on the south by the English Channel; on the east by the Straits of Dover (Pas de Calais) and the North Sea; and on the west by the Atlantic Ocean, Wales and the Irish Sea. It has a total area of 130,432 sq. km (50,360 sq. miles): land 130,279 sq. km (50,301 sq. miles); inland water 153 sq. km (59 sq. miles).

POPULATION

The population at the 2001 census was 49,138,831. The average density of the population in 2001 was 377 persons per sq. km (976 per sq. mile).

FLAG

The flag of England is the cross of St George, a red cross on a white field (cross gules in a field argent). The cross of St George, the patron saint of England, has been used since the 13th century.

RELIEF

There is a marked division between the upland and lowland areas of England. In the extreme north the Cheviot Hills (highest point, the Cheviot, 815m/2,674ft) form a natural boundary with Scotland. Running south from the Cheviots, though divided from them by the Tyne Gap, is the Pennine range (highest point, Cross Fell, 893m/2,930ft), the main orological feature of the country. The Pennines culminate in the Peak District of Derbyshire (Kinder Scout, 636m/2,088ft). West of the Pennines are the Cumbrian mountains, which include Scafell Pike (978m/3,210ft), the highest peak in England, and to the east are the Yorkshire Moors, their highest point being Urra Moor (454m/1,490ft).

In the west, the foothills of the Welsh mountains extend into the bordering English counties of Shropshire (the Wrekin, 407m/1,334ft; Long Mynd, 516m/1,694ft) and Hereford and Worcester (the Malvern Hills – Worcestershire Beacon, 425m/1,394ft). Extensive areas of highland and moorland are also to be found in the south-western peninsula formed by Somerset, Devon and Cornwall, principally Exmoor (Dunkery Beacon, 519m/1,704ft), Dartmoor (High Willhays, 621m/2,038ft) and Bodmin Moor (Brown Willy, 420m/1,377ft). Ranges of low, undulating hills run across the south of the country, including the Cotswolds in the Midlands and south-west, the Chilterns to the north of London, and the North (Kent) and South (Sussex) Downs of the south-east coastal areas.

The lowlands of England lie in the Vale of York, East Anglia and the area around the Wash. The lowest-lying are the Cambridgeshire Fens in the valleys of the Great Ouse and the river Nene, which are below sea-level in places. Since the 17th century extensive drainage has brought much of the Fens under cultivation. The North Sea coast between the Thames and the Humber, low-lying and formed of sand and shingle for the most part, is subject to erosion and defences against further incursion have been built along many stretches.

HYDROGRAPHY

The Severn is the longest river in Great Britain, rising in the north-eastern slopes of Plynlimon (Wales) and entering England in Shropshire, with a total length of 354km (220 miles) from its source to its outflow into the Bristol Channel, where it receives the Bristol Avon on the east and the Wye on the west; its other tributaries are the Vyrnwy, Tern, Stour, Teme and Upper (or Warwickshire) Avon. The Severn is tidal below Gloucester, and a high bore or tidal wave sometimes reverses the flow as high as Tewkesbury (21.75km/13.5 miles above Gloucester). The scenery of the greater part of the river is very picturesque, and the Severn is a noted salmon river, with some of its tributaries being famous for trout. Navigation is assisted by the Gloucester and Berkeley Ship Canal (26km/16.25 miles), which admits vessels of 350 tons to Gloucester. The Severn Tunnel was begun in 1873 and completed in 1886 at a cost of £2m and after many difficulties caused by flooding. It is 7km (4 miles 628 yards) in length (of which 3.67km/2.25 miles are under the river). The Severn road bridge between Haysgate, Gwent, and Almondsbury, Glos, with a centre span of 988m (3,240ft), was opened in 1966.

The longest river wholly in England is the Thames, with a total length of 346km (215 miles) from its source in the Cotswold hills to the Nore, and is navigable by ocean-going ships to London Bridge. The Thames is tidal to Teddington (111km/69 miles from its mouth) and forms county boundaries almost throughout its course; on its banks are situated London, Windsor Castle, Eton College and Oxford University. Of the remaining English rivers, those flowing into the North Sea are the Tyne, Wear, Tees, Ouse and Trent from the Pennine Range, the Great Ouse (257km/160 miles), which rises in Northamptonshire, and the Orwell and Stour from the hills of East Anglia. Flowing into the English Channel are the Sussex Ouse from the Weald, the Itchen from the Hampshire Hills, and the Axe, Teign, Dart, Tamar and Exe from the Devonian hills. Flowing into the Irish Sea are the Mersey, Ribble and Eden from the western slopes of the Pennines and the Derwent from the Cumbrian mountains.

The English Lakes, notable for their picturesque scenery and poetic associations, lie in Cumbria's Lake District; the largest are Windermere (14.7 sq. km/5.7 sq. miles), Ullswater (8.8 sq. km/3.4 sq. miles) and Derwent Water (5.3 sq. km/2.0 sq. miles).

ISLANDS

The Isle of Wight is separated from Hampshire by the Solent. The capital, Newport, stands at the head of the estuary of the Medina, and Cowes (at the mouth) is the chief port. Other centres are Ryde, Sandown, Shanklin, Ventnor, Freshwater, Yarmouth, Totland Bay, Seaview and Bembridge.

Lundy (the name is derived from the Old Norse for 'puffin island'), 18km (11 miles) north-west of Hartland Point, Devon, is around 5km (3 miles) long and almost 1km (half a mile) wide on average, with a total area of around 452 hectares (1,116 acres), and a population of around 18. It became the property of the National Trust in 1969 and is now principally a bird sanctuary.

The Isles of Scilly comprise around 140 islands and

skerries (total area, 10 sq. km/6 sq. miles) situated 45 km (28 miles) south-west of Land's End in Cornwall. Only five are inhabited: St Mary's, St Agnes, Bryher, Tresco and St Martin's. The population at the 2001 census was 2,153. The entire group has been designated an Area of Outstanding Natural Beauty because of its unique flora and fauna. Tourism and the winter/spring flower trade for the home market form the basis of the economy of the islands. The island group is a recognised rural development area.

EARLY HISTORY

Archaeological evidence suggests that England has been inhabited since at least the Palaeolithic period, though the extent of the various Palaeolithic cultures was dependent upon the degree of glaciation. The succeeding Neolithic and Bronze Age cultures have left abundant remains throughout the country; the best-known of these are the henges and stone circles of Stonehenge (ten miles north of Salisbury, Wilts) and Avebury (Wilts), both of which are believed to have been of religious significance. In the latter part of the Bronze Age the Goidels, a people of the Celtic race, invaded the country and brought with them Celtic civilisation and dialects; as a result place names in England bear witness to the spread of the invasion across the whole region.

THE ROMAN CONQUEST

The Roman conquest of Gaul (57–50 BC) brought Britain into close contact with Roman civilisation, but although Julius Caesar raided the south of Britain in 55 and 54 BC, conquest was not undertaken until nearly 100 years later. In AD 43 the Emperor Claudius dispatched Aulus Plautius, with a well-equipped force of 40,000, and himself followed with reinforcements in the same year. Success was delayed by the resistance of Caratacus (Caractacus), the British leader from AD 48–51, who was finally captured and sent to Rome, and by a great revolt in AD 61 led by Boudicca (Boadicea), Queen of the Iceni, but the south of Britain was secured by AD 70, and Wales and the area north to the Tyne by about AD 80.

In AD 122, the Emperor Hadrian visited Britain and built a continuous rampart, since known as Hadrian's Wall, from Wallsend to Bowness (Tyne to Solway). The work was entrusted by the Emperor Hadrian to Aulus Platorius Nepos, legate of Britain from AD 122 to 126, and it was intended to form the northern frontier of the Roman Empire.

The Romans administered Britain as a province under a governor, with a well-defined system of local government, each Roman municipality ruling itself and its surrounding territory, while London was the centre of the road system and the seat of the financial officials of the Province of Britain. Colchester, Lincoln, York, Gloucester and St Albans stand on the sites of five Roman municipalities, and Wroxeter, Caerleon, Chester, Lincoln and York were at various times the sites of legionary fortresses. Well-preserved Roman towns have been uncovered at or near Silchester *(Calleva Atrebatum)*, ten miles south of Reading, Wroxeter *(Viroconium Cornoviorum)*, near Shrewsbury, and St Albans *(Verulamium)* in Hertfordshire.

Four main groups of roads radiated from London, and a fifth (the Fosse) ran obliquely from Lincoln through Leicester, Cirencester and Bath to Exeter. Of the four groups radiating from London, one ran south-east to Canterbury and the coast of Kent, a second to Silchester and thence to parts of western Britain and south Wales, a third (later known as Watling Street) ran through St Albans to Chester, with various branches, and the fourth reached Colchester, Lincoln, York and the eastern counties.

In the fourth century Britain was subjected to raids along the east coast by Saxon pirates, which led to the establishment of a system of coastal defences from the Wash to Southampton Water, with forts at Brancaster, Burgh Castle (Yarmouth), Walton (Felixstowe), Bradwell, Reculver, Richborough, Dover, Lympne, Pevensey and Porchester (Portsmouth). The Irish (Scoti) and Picts in the north were also becoming more aggressive and from around AD 350 incursions became more frequent and more formidable. As the Roman Empire came increasingly under attack towards the end of the fourth century, many troops were removed from Britain for service in other parts of the empire. The island was eventually cut off from Rome by the Teutonic conquest of Gaul, and with the withdrawal of the last Roman garrison early in the fifth century, the Romano-British were left to themselves.

SAXON SETTLEMENT

According to legend, the British King Vortigern called in the Saxons to defend his lands against the Picts. The Saxon chieftains Hengist and Horsa landed at Ebbsfleet, Kent, and established themselves in the Isle of Thanet, but the events during the one-and-a-half centuries between the final break with Rome and the re-establishment of Christianity are unclear. However, it would appear that over the course of this period the raids turned into large-scale settlement by invaders traditionally known as Angles (England north of the Wash and East Anglia), Saxons (Essex and southern England) and Jutes (Kent and the Weald), which pushed the Romano-British into the mountainous areas of the north and west. Celtic culture outside Wales and Cornwall survives only in topographical names. Various kingdoms established at this time attempted to claim overlordship of the whole country, hegemony finally being achieved by Wessex (with the capital at Winchester) in the ninth century. This century also saw the beginning of raids by the Vikings (Danes), which were resisted by Alfred the Great (871–899), who fixed a limit on the advance of Danish settlement by the Treaty of Wedmore (878), giving them the area north and east of Watling Street on the condition that they adopt Christianity.

In the tenth century the kings of Wessex recovered the whole of England from the Danes, but subsequent rulers were unable to resist a second wave of invaders. England paid tribute *(Danegeld)* for many years, and was invaded in 1013 by the Danes and ruled by Danish kings (including Cnut) from 1016 until 1042, when Edward the Confessor was recalled from exile in Normandy. On Edward's death in 1066 Harold Godwinson (brother-in-law of Edward and son of Earl Godwin of Wessex) was chosen to be King of England. After defeating (at Stamford Bridge, Yorkshire, 25 September) an invading army under Harald Hadraada, King of Norway (aided by the outlawed Earl Tostig of Northumbria, Harold's brother), Harold was himself defeated at the Battle of Hastings on 14 October 1066, and the Norman conquest secured the throne of England for Duke William of Normandy, a cousin of Edward the Confessor.

CHRISTIANITY

Christianity reached the Roman province of Britain from Gaul in the third century (or possibly earlier). Alban, traditionally Britain's first martyr, was put to death as a

Christian during the persecution of Diocletian (22 June 303) at his native town *Verulamium,* and the Bishops of *Londinium, Eboracum* (York), and *Lindum* (Lincoln) attended the Council of Arles in 314. However, the Anglo-Saxon invasions submerged the Christian religion in England until the sixth century: conversion was undertaken in the north from 563 by Celtic missionaries from Ireland led by St Columba, and in the south by a mission sent from Rome in 597 which was led by St Augustine, who became the first archbishop of Canterbury. England appears to have been converted again by the end of the seventh century and followed, after the Council of Whitby in 663, the practices of the Roman Church, which brought the kingdom into the mainstream of European thought and culture.

PRINCIPAL CITIES

There are 50 cities in England and space constraints prevent us from including profiles of them all. Below is a selection of England's principal cities with the date on which city status was conferred in parenthesis. Other cities are: Chichester (pre-1900), Derby (1977), Ely (pre-1900), Exeter (pre-1900), Gloucester (pre-1900), Hereford (pre-1900), Lancaster (1937), Lichfield (pre-1900), London (pre-1900), Peterborough (pre-1900), Plymouth (1928), Portsmouth (1926), Preston (2002), Ripon (pre-1900), Salford (1926), Sunderland (1992), Truro (pre-1900), Wakefield (pre-1900), Wells (pre-1900), Westminster (pre-1900), Wolverhampton (2000) and Worcester (pre-1900).

Certain cities have also been granted a lord mayoralty – this grant confers no additional powers or functions and is purely honorific. Cities with lord mayors are: Birmingham, Bradford, Bristol, Canterbury, Chester, Coventry, Exeter, Kingston-upon-Hull, Leeds, Leicester, Liverpool, London, Manchester, Newcastle-upon-Tyne, Norwich, Nottingham, Oxford, Plymouth, Portsmouth, Sheffield, Stoke-on-Trent, Westminster and York.

BATH (PRE-1900)

Bath stands on the River Avon between the Cotswold Hills to the north and the Mendips to the south. In the early 18th century, Bath became England's premier spa town where the rich and celebrated members of fashionable society gathered to 'take the waters' and enjoy the town's theatres and concert rooms. During this period the architect John Wood laid the foundations for a new Georgian city to be built using the honey-coloured stone for which Bath is famous today.

Contemporary Bath is a thriving tourist destination and remains a leading cultural, religious and historical centre with many art galleries and historic sites including the Pump Room (1790); the Royal Crescent (1767); the Circus (1754); the 18th-century Assembly Rooms (housing the Museum of Costume); Pulteney Bridge (1771); the Guildhall and the Abbey, now over 500 years old, which is built on the site of a Saxon monastery. In 2006 the Bath Thermae Spa was completed and the hot springs re-opened to the public for the first time since 1978; combining five historic spa buildings with contemporary architecture, it is the only spa in the UK to utilise naturally occurring thermal waters.

BIRMINGHAM (PRE-1900)

Birmingham is Britain's second largest city, with a population of over one million. The generally accepted derivation of 'Birmingham' is the *ham* (dwelling-place) of the *ing* (family) of *Beorma,* presumed to have been Saxon. During the Industrial Revolution the town grew into a major manufacturing centre and in 1889 was granted city status.

Recent developments include Millennium Point, which houses Thinktank, the Birmingham science museum, and Brindleyplace, a development of shops, offices and leisure facilities on a former industrial site clustered around canals. In 2003 the Bullring shopping centre was officially opened as part of the city's urban regeneration programme.

The principal buildings are the Town Hall (1834–50), the Council House (1879), Victoria Law Courts (1891), the University of Birmingham (1906–9), the 13th-century Church of St Martin-in-the-Bull-Ring (rebuilt 1873), the cathedral (formerly St Philip's Church) (1711), the Roman Catholic cathedral of St Chad (1839–41), the Assay Office (1773), the Rotunda (1964) and the National Exhibition Centre (1976). There is also the Birmingham Museum and Art Gallery which was founded in 1885 and is home to a collection of Pre-Raphaelite paintings.

BRADFORD (PRE-1900)

During the Industrial Revolution of the 18th and 19th centuries Bradford expanded rapidly, largely as a result of the thriving wool industry.

Bradford city centre has a host of buildings with historical and cultural interest, including City Hall, with its 19th-century Lord Mayor's rooms and Victorian law court; Bradford Cathedral; the Priestley, a theatre and arts centre originally established as the Bradford Civic Playhouse by J. B. Priestley and friends; the Colour Museum; the National Media Museum which houses seven floors of interactive displays and three cinemas; Piece Hall Yard which incorporates the Bradford Club, a Victorian Gothic style building dating from 1837, and the Peace Museum.

BRIGHTON AND HOVE (2000)

Brighton and Hove is situated on the south coast of England, around 96 km (60 miles) south of London. Originally a fishing village called Brighthelmstone, it was transformed into a fashionable seaside resort in the 18th century when Dr Richard Russell popularised the benefits of his 'sea-water cure'; as one of the closest beaches to London, Brighton began to attract wealthy visitors. One of these was the Prince Regent (the future King George IV), who first visited in 1783 and became so fond of the city that in 1807 he bought the former farmhouse he had been renting, and gradually turned it into Brighton's most recognisable building, the Royal Pavilion. The Pavilion is renowned for its Indo-Saracenic exterior, featuring minarets and an enormous central dome designed by John Nash, combined with the lavish chinoiserie of Frederick Crace's and Robert Jones' interiors.

Brighton and Hove's Regency heritage can also be seen in the numerous elegant squares and crescents designed by Amon Wilds and Augustin Busby that dominate the seafront.

Brighton and Hove is once again a fashionable resort, known for its cafe culture, lively nightlife and thriving gay scene.

BRISTOL (PRE-1900)

Bristol was a royal borough before the Norman conquest. The earliest form of the name is *Bricgstow.*

The principal buildings include the 12th-century

Cathedral with Norman chapter house and gateway; the 14th-century Church of St Mary Redcliffe; Wesley's Chapel, Broadmead; the Merchant Venturers' Almshouses; the Council House (1956); the Guildhall; the Exchange (erected from the designs of John Wood in 1743); Cabot Tower; the University and Clifton College. The Roman Catholic cathedral at Clifton was opened in 1973.

The Clifton Suspension Bridge, with a span of 214m (702ft) over the Avon, was projected by Isambard Kingdom Brunel in 1836 but was not completed until 1864. Brunel's SS *Great Britain,* the first ocean-going propeller-driven ship, now forms a museum at the Western Dockyard, from where she was originally launched in 1843. The docks themselves have been extensively restored and redeveloped; the 19th-century two-storey former tea warehouse is now the Arnolfini centre for contemporary arts, and an 18th-century sail loft houses the Architecture Centre. Behind the baroque-domed facade of the former 'E' Shed are shops, cafes, restaurants and the Watershed Media Centre, and on Princes Wharf disused transit sheds house the Industrial Museum.

CAMBRIDGE (1951)

Cambridge, a settlement far older than its ancient university, lies on the River Cam (or Granta). The city is a county town and regional headquarters. Its industries include technology research and development, and biotechnology. Among its open spaces are Jesus Green, Sheep's Green, Coe Fen, Parker's Piece, Christ's Pieces, the University Botanic Garden, and the 'Backs' – lawns and gardens through which the Cam winds behind the principal line of college buildings. Historical sites east of the Cam include King's Parade, Great St Mary's Church, Gibbs' Senate House and King's College Chapel.

University and college buildings provide the outstanding features of Cambridge's architecture but several churches (especially St Benet's, the oldest building in the city, and Holy Sepulchre or the Round Church) are also notable. The Guildhall (1937) stands on a site, of which at least part has held municipal buildings since 1224.

CANTERBURY (PRE-1900)

Canterbury, seat of the Archbishop of Canterbury, the primate of the Church of England, dates back to prehistoric times. It was the Roman *Durovernum Cantiacorum* and the Saxon *Cant-wara-byrig* (stronghold of the men of Kent). It was here in 597 that St Augustine began the conversion of the English to Christianity, when Ethelbert, King of Kent, was baptised.

Of the Benedictine St Augustine's Abbey, burial place of the Jutish Kings of Kent, only ruins remain. St Martin's Church, on the eastern outskirts of the city, is stated by Bede to have been the place of worship of Queen Bertha, the Christian wife of King Ethelbert, before the advent of St Augustine.

In 1170 the rivalry of Church and State culminated in the murder in Canterbury Cathedral, by Henry II's knights, of Archbishop Thomas Becket. His shrine became a great centre of pilgrimage, as described in Chaucer's *Canterbury Tales.* After the Reformation pilgrimages ceased, but the prosperity of the city was strengthened by an influx of Huguenot refugees, who introduced weaving. The poet and playwright Christopher Marlowe was born and raised in Canterbury (the city is home to the 1,000-seat Marlowe Theatre) and there are also literary associations with Defoe, Dickens, Joseph Conrad and Somerset Maugham.

The cathedral, its architecture ranging from the 11th to the 15th centuries, is famous worldwide. Visitors are attracted particularly to the Martyrdom, the Black Prince's Tomb, the Warriors' Chapel and the many examples of medieval stained glass.

The medieval city walls are built on Roman foundations and the 14th-century West Gate is one of the finest buildings of its kind in the country.

The Canterbury Arts Festival takes place at a variety of venues throughout the city each autumn.

CARLISLE (PRE-1900)

Carlisle is situated at the confluence of the rivers Eden and Caldew, 497km (309 miles) north-west of London and around 16km (10 miles) from the Scottish border. It was granted a charter in 1158.

The city stands at the western end of Hadrian's Wall and dates from the original Roman settlement of *Luguvalium.* Granted to Scotland in the tenth century, Carlisle is not included in the Domesday Book. William Rufus reclaimed the area in 1092 and the castle and city walls were built to guard Carlisle and the western border; the citadel is a Tudor addition to protect the south of the city. Border disputes were common until the problem of the Debateable Lands was settled in 1552. During the Civil War the city remained Royalist; in 1745 Carlisle was besieged for the last time by the Young Pretender (Bonnie Prince Charlie).

The cathedral, originally a 12th-century Augustinian priory, was enlarged in the 13th and 14th centuries after the diocese was created in 1133. To the south is a restored tithe barn and nearby the 18th-century church of St Cuthbert, the third to stand on a site dating from the seventh century.

Carlisle is the major shopping, commercial and agricultural centre for the area, and industries include the manufacture of metal goods, biscuits and textiles. However, the largest employer is the services sector, most notably in central and local government, retailing and transport. The city occupies an important position at the centre of a network of major roads, as a stage on the main west coast rail services, and with its own airport at Crosby-on-Eden.

CHESTER (PRE-1900)

Chester is situated on the River Dee. Its recorded history dates from the first century when the Romans founded the fortress of *Deva.* The city's name is derived from the Latin *castra* (a camp or encampment). During the Middle Ages, Chester was the principal port of north-west England but declined with the silting of the Dee estuary and competition from Liverpool. The city was also an important military centre, notably during Edward I's Welsh campaigns and the Elizabethan Irish campaigns. During the Civil War, Chester supported the King and was besieged from 1643 to 1646. Chester's first charter was granted *c.*1175 and the city was incorporated in 1506. The office of sheriff is the earliest created in the country (1120s), and in 1992 the mayor was granted the title of Lord Mayor, who also enjoys the title 'Admiral of the Dee'.

The city's architectural features include the city walls (an almost complete two-mile circuit), the unique 13th-century Rows (covered galleries above the street-level shops), the Victorian Gothic Town Hall (1869), the castle (rebuilt 1788 and 1822) and numerous half-timbered buildings. The cathedral was a Benedictine abbey until the Dissolution of the Monasteries.

Remaining monastic buildings include the chapter house, refectory and cloisters and there is a modern free-standing bell tower. The Norman church of St John the Baptist was a cathedral church in the early Middle Ages.

COVENTRY (PRE-1900)

Coventry is an important industrial centre, producing vehicles, machine tools, agricultural machinery, man-made fibres, aerospace components and telecommunications equipment. New investment has come from financial services, power transmission, professional services, leisure and education.

The city owes its beginning to Leofric, Earl of Mercia, and his wife Godiva who, in 1043, founded a Benedictine monastery. The guildhall of St Mary and three of the city's churches date from the 14th and 15th centuries, and 16th-century almshouses can still be seen. Coventry's first cathedral was destroyed during the Reformation, its second in the 1940 blitz (the walls and spire remain) and the new cathedral designed by Sir Basil Spence, consecrated in 1962, now draws numerous visitors.

Coventry is the home of the University of Warwick, Coventry University, Coventry Transport Museum, which specialises in British road transport, and the Skydome Arena.

DURHAM (PRE-1900)

The city of Durham is a major tourist attraction and its prominent Norman cathedral and castle are set high on a wooded peninsula overlooking the River Wear. The cathedral was founded as a shrine for the body of St Cuthbert in 995. The present building dates from 1093 and among its many treasures is the tomb of the Venerable Bede (673–735). Durham's prince bishops had unique powers up to 1836, being lay rulers as well as religious leaders. As a palatinate, Durham could have its own army, nobility, coinage and courts. The castle was the main seat of the prince bishops for nearly 800 years; it is now used as a college by the University of Durham. The university, founded in the early 19th century on the initiative of Bishop William Van Mildert, is England's third oldest.

Among other buildings of interest is the Guildhall in the Market Place which dates from the 14th century. Annual events include Durham's regatta in June (claimed to be the oldest rowing event in Britain) and the annual Gala (formerly Durham Miners' Gala) in July.

KINGSTON-UPON-HULL (PRE-1900)

Hull (officially Kingston-upon-Hull, so named by Edward I) lies at the junction of the River Hull with the Humber, 35km (22 miles) from the North Sea. It is one of the major seaports of the UK. The port provides a wide range of cargo services, including ro-ro and container traffic, and handles an estimated million passengers annually on daily sailings to Rotterdam and Zeebrugge. There is a variety of manufacturing and service industries. City status was accorded in 1897 and the office of mayor raised to the dignity of Lord Mayor in 1914.

The city, restored after heavy air raid damage during the Second World War, has good educational facilities with both the University of Hull and a campus of the University of Lincoln being within its boundaries. Hull is home to the world's only submarium, The Deep, a £45.5m project which opened in 2002, and the Kingston Communications Stadium, with a seating capacity for 25,000, which was also completed in 2002.

Tourism is a growing industry; the old town area has been renovated and includes museums, a marina and a shopping complex. Just west of the city is the Humber Bridge, the fifth-largest suspension bridge in the world.

LEEDS (PRE-1900)

Leeds, situated in the lower Aire Valley, is a junction for road, rail, canal and air services and an important commercial centre. It was first incorporated by Charles I in 1626. The earliest forms of the name are *Loidis* or *Ledes,* the origins of which are obscure.

The principal buildings are the Civic Hall (1933), the Town Hall (1858), the Municipal Buildings and Art Gallery (1884) with the Henry Moore Gallery (1982), the Corn Exchange (1863) and the University. The parish church (St Peter's) was rebuilt in 1841; the 17th-century St John's Church has a fine interior with a famous English Renaissance screen; the last remaining 18th-century church in the city is Holy Trinity in Boar Lane (1727). Kirkstall Abbey (about three miles from the centre of the city), founded by Henry de Lacy in 1152, is one of the most complete examples of a Cistercian house now remaining. Temple Newsam, birthplace of Lord Darnley and largely rebuilt by Sir Arthur Ingram *c.*1620, was acquired by the council in 1922. Adel Church, about five miles from the centre of the city, is a fine Norman structure. The Royal Armouries Museum forms part of a group of museums, including the Tower of London, which house the national collection of antique arms and armour.

LEICESTER (1919)

Leicester is situated in central England. The city was an important Roman settlement and also one of the five Viking boroughs of Danelaw. In 1485 Richard III was buried in Leicester following his death at the nearby Battle of Bosworth. In 1589 Queen Elizabeth I granted a charter to the city and the ancient title was confirmed by letters patent in 1919.

The textile industry was responsible for Leicester's early expansion and the city still maintains a strong manufacturing base. Cotton mills and factories are now undergoing extensive regeneration and are being converted into offices, apartments, bars and restaurants. The principal buildings include the two universities (the University of Leicester and De Montfort University), as well as the Town Hall, the 13th-century Guildhall, De Montfort Hall, Leicester Cathedral, the Jewry Wall (the UK's highest standing Roman wall), St Nicholas Church and St Mary de Castro church. The motte and Great Hall of Leicester can be seen from the castle gardens, situated next to the River Soar.

Leicester is now one of the UK's most ethnically diverse cities – home to the only Jain temple in the West and hosting the country's second-largest Caribbean carnival.

LINCOLN (PRE-1900)

Situated 64km (40 miles) inland on the River Witham, Lincoln derives its name from a contraction of *Lindum Colonia,* the settlement founded in AD 48 by the Romans to command the crossing of Ermine Street and Fosse Way. Sections of the third-century Roman city wall can be seen, including an extant gateway (Newport Arch), and excavations have discovered traces of a sewerage system unique in Britain. The Romans also drained the surrounding fenland and created a canal system, laying the foundations of Lincoln's agricultural prosperity and also the city's importance in the medieval wool trade as a port and staple town.

As one of the five boroughs of Danelaw, Lincoln was an important trading centre in the ninth and tenth centuries and prosperity from the wool trade lasted until the 14th century. This wealth enabled local merchants to build parish churches, of which three survive, and there are also remains of a 12th-century Jewish community (Jew's House and Court, Aaron's House). However, the removal of the staple to Boston in 1369 heralded a decline, from which the city only recovered fully in the 19th century, when improved fen drainage made Lincoln agriculturally important. Improved canal and rail links led to industrial development, mainly in the manufacture of machinery, components and engineering products.

The castle was built shortly after the Norman Conquest and is unusual in having two mounds; on one motte stands a keep (Lucy's Tower) added in the 12th century. It currently houses one of the four surviving copies of the Magna Carta. The cathedral was begun *c.*1073 when the first Norman bishop moved the see of Lindsey to Lincoln, but was mostly destroyed by fire and earthquake in the 12th century. Rebuilding was begun by St Hugh and completed over a century later. Other notable architectural features are the 12th-century High Bridge, the oldest in Britain still to carry buildings, and the Guildhall, situated above the 15th-century Stonebow gateway.

LIVERPOOL (PRE-1900)

Liverpool, on the north bank of the river Mersey, 5km (3 miles) from the Irish Sea, is the United Kingdom's foremost port for Atlantic trade. Tunnels link Liverpool with Birkenhead and Wallasey.

There are 2,100 acres of dockland on both sides of the river and the Gladstone and Royal Seaforth Docks can accommodate tanker-sized vessels. Liverpool Free Port was opened in 1984.

Liverpool was created a free borough in 1207 and a city in 1880. From the early 18th century it expanded rapidly with the growth of industrialisation and the transatlantic slave trade. Surviving buildings from this period include the Bluecoat Chambers (1717, formerly the Bluecoat School), the Town Hall (1754, rebuilt to the original design 1795), and buildings in Rodney Street, Canning Street and the suburbs. Notable from the 19th and 20th centuries are the Anglican cathedral, built from the designs of Sir Giles Gilbert Scott (the foundation stone was laid in 1904, but the building was only completed in 1980); the Catholic Metropolitan Cathedral (designed by Sir Frederick Gibberd, consecrated 1967) and St George's Hall (1842), regarded as one of the finest modern examples of classical architecture. The refurbished Albert Dock (designed by Jesse Hartley) contains the Merseyside Maritime Museum, the International Slavery Museum and the Tate Liverpool art gallery.

In 1852 an act was passed establishing a public library, museum and art gallery; as a result Liverpool had one of the first public libraries in the country. The Brown, Picton and Hornby libraries form one of the country's major collections. The Victoria Building of Liverpool University; the Royal Liver, Cunard and Mersey Docks & Harbour Company buildings at the Pier Head; the Municipal Buildings and the Philharmonic Hall are other examples of the city's fine architecture.

Six areas of Liverpool's maritime mercantile city were designated as UNESCO World Heritage Sites in 2004, and Liverpool was elected as the European Capital of Culture for 2008.

MANCHESTER (PRE-1900)

Manchester (the *Mamucium* of the Romans, who occupied it in AD 79) is a commercial and industrial centre engaged in the engineering, chemical, clothing, food processing and textile industries and in education. Banking, insurance and a growing leisure industry are among its prime commercial activities. The city is connected with the sea by the Manchester Ship Canal, opened in 1894, 57km (35.5 miles) long, and accommodating ships up to 15,000 tons.

The principal buildings are the Town Hall, erected in 1877 from the designs of Alfred Waterhouse, with a large extension of 1938; the Royal Exchange (1869, enlarged 1921); the Central Library (1934); Heaton Hall; the 17th-century Chetham Library; the Rylands Library (1900), which includes the Althorp collection; the university precinct; the 15th-century cathedral (formerly the parish church); the Manchester Central conference and exhibition centre and the Bridgewater Hall (1996) concert venue. Manchester is the home of the Hallé Orchestra, the Royal Northern College of Music, the Royal Exchange Theatre and numerous public art galleries.

To accommodate the Commonwealth Games held in the city in 2002, new sports facilities were built including a stadium, swimming pool complex and the National Cycling Centre.

The town received its first charter of incorporation in 1838 and was created a city in 1853.

NEWCASTLE UPON TYNE (PRE-1900)

Newcastle upon Tyne, on the north bank of the River Tyne, is 13km (8 miles) from the North Sea. A cathedral and university city, it is the administrative, commercial and cultural centre for north-east England and the principal port. It is an important manufacturing centre with a wide variety of industries.

The principal buildings include the Castle Keep (12th century), Black Gate (13th century), Blackfriars (13th century), West Walls (13th century), St Nicholas's Cathedral (15th century, fine lantern tower), St Andrew's Church (12th–14th century), St John's (14th–15th century), All Saints (1786 by Stephenson), St Mary's Roman Catholic Cathedral (1844), Trinity House (17th century), Sandhill (16th-century houses), Guildhall (Georgian), Grey Street (1834–9), Central Station (1846–50), Laing Art Gallery (1904), University of Newcastle Physics Building (1962) and Medical Building (1985), Civic Centre (1963) and the Central Library (1969). Open spaces include the Town Moor (927 acres) and Jesmond Dene. Ten bridges span the Tyne at Newcastle, including the tilting Millennium Bridge (2001), which links the city with Gateshead to the south.

The city's name is derived from the 'new castle' (1080) erected as a defence against the Scots. In 1400 it was made a county, and in 1882 a city.

NORWICH (PRE-1900)

Norwich grew from an early Anglo-Saxon settlement near the confluence of the rivers Yare and Wensum, and now serves as provincial capital for the predominantly agricultural region of East Anglia. The name is thought to relate to the most northerly of a group of Anglo-Saxon villages or *wics*. The city's first known charter was granted in 1158 by Henry II.

Norwich serves its surrounding area as a market town and commercial centre, with banking and insurance prominent among the city's businesses. From the 14th century until the Industrial Revolution, Norwich was the regional centre of the woollen industry, but now the biggest single industry is financial services and principal trades are engineering, printing, shoemaking, the production of chemicals and clothing, food processing and technology. Norwich is accessible to seagoing vessels by means of the River Yare, entered at Great Yarmouth, 32km (20 miles) to the east.

Among many historic buildings are the cathedral (completed in the 12th century and surmounted by a 15th-century spire 96m (315ft) in height); the keep of the Norman castle (now a museum and art gallery); the 15th-century flint-walled Guildhall; some thirty medieval parish churches; St Andrew's and Blackfriars' Halls; the Tudor houses preserved in Elm Hill and the Georgian Assembly House. The University of East Anglia is on the city's western boundary.

NOTTINGHAM (PRE-1900)

Nottingham stands on the River Trent. *Snotingaham* or *Notingeham,* literally the homestead of the people of Snot, is the Anglo-Saxon name for the Celtic settlement of *Tigguocobauc,* or the house of caves. In 878, Nottingham became one of the five boroughs of Danelaw. William the Conqueror ordered the construction of Nottingham Castle, while the town itself developed rapidly under Norman rule. Its laws and rights were later formally recognised by Henry II's charter in 1155. The castle became a favoured residence of King John. In 1642 King Charles I raised his personal standard at Nottingham Castle at the start of the Civil War.

Nottingham is home to Notts County FC (the world's oldest football league side), Nottingham Forest FC, Nottingham Racecourse, Trent Bridge cricket ground and the National Watersports Centre. The principal industries include textiles, pharmaceuticals, food manufacturing, engineering and telecommunications. There are two universities within the city boundaries.

Architecturally, Nottingham has a wealth of notable buildings, particularly those designed in the Victorian era by T. C. Hine and Watson Fothergill. The city council owns the castle, of Norman origin but restored in 1878, Wollaton Hall (1580–8), Newstead Abbey (home of Lord Byron), the Guildhall (1888) and Council House (1929). St Mary's, St Peter's and St Nicholas' churches are of interest, as is the Roman Catholic cathedral (Pugin, 1842–4). Nottingham was granted city status in 1897.

OXFORD (PRE-1900)

Oxford is a university city, an important industrial centre and a market town. Industry played a minor part in Oxford until the motor industry was established in 1912.

Oxford is known for its architecture, its oldest specimens being the reputedly Saxon tower of St Michael's Church, the remains of the Norman castle and city walls, and the Norman church at Iffley. It also has many Gothic buildings, such as the Divinity Schools, the Old Library at Merton College, William of Wykeham's New College, Magdalen and Christ Church colleges and many other college buildings. Later centuries are represented by the Laudian quadrangle at St John's College, the Renaissance Sheldonian Theatre by Wren, Trinity College Chapel, All Saints Church, Hawksmoor's mock-Gothic at All Souls College, and the 18th-century Queen's College. In addition to individual buildings, High Street and Radcliffe Square both form interesting architectural compositions. Most of the colleges have gardens, those of Magdalen, New College, St John's and Worcester being the largest.

The Oxford University Museum of Natural History, renowned for its spectacular neo-gothic architecture, houses the university's scientific collections of zoological, entomological and geological specimens and is attached to the neighbouring Pitt Rivers Museum which houses ethnographic and archaeological objects from around the world. The Ashmolean is the city's museum of art and archaeology and Modern Art Oxford hosts a programme of contemporary art exhibitions.

ST ALBANS (PRE-1900)

The origins of St Albans, situated on the River Ver, stem from the Roman town of *Verulamium.* Named after the first Christian martyr in Britain, who was executed there, St Albans has developed around the Norman abbey and cathedral church (consecrated 1115), built partly of materials from the old Roman city. The museums house Iron Age and Roman artefacts and the Roman theatre, unique in Britain, has a stage as opposed to an amphitheatre. Archaeological excavations in the city centre have revealed evidence of pre-Roman, Saxon and medieval occupation.

The town's significance grew to the extent that it was a signatory and venue for the drafting of the Magna Carta. It was also the scene of riots during the Peasants' Revolt, the French King John was imprisoned there after the Battle of Poitiers, and heavy fighting took place there during the Wars of the Roses.

Previously controlled by the Abbot, the town achieved a charter in 1553 and city status in 1877. The street market, first established in 1553, is still an important feature of the city, as are many hotels and inns, surviving from the days when St Albans was an important coach stop. Tourist attractions include historic churches and houses and a 15th-century clock tower.

The city is now home to a wide range of businesses, with special emphasis on information and legal services, and is home to the Royal National Rose Society.

SALISBURY (PRE-1900)

The history of Salisbury centres around the cathedral and cathedral close. The city evolved from an Iron Age camp a mile to the north of its current position which was strengthened by the Romans and called *Serviodunum.* The Normans built a castle and cathedral on the site and renamed it Sarum. In 1220 Bishop Richard Poore and the architect Elias de Derham decided to build a new Gothic style cathedral. The cathedral was completed 38 years later and a community known as New Sarum, now called Salisbury, grew around it. Originally the cathedral had a squat tower; the 123m (404ft) spire that makes the cathedral the tallest medieval structure in the world was added *c.*1315. A walled close with houses for the clergy was built around the cathedral; the Medieval Hall still stands today, alongside buildings dating from the 13th to the 20th century, including some designed by Sir Christopher Wren.

A prosperous wool and cloth trade allowed Salisbury to flourish until the 17th century. When the wool trade declined new crafts were established including cutlery, leather and basket work, saddlery, lacemaking, joinery and malting. By 1750 it had become an important road junction and coaching centre and in the Victorian era the railways enabled a new age of expansion and prosperity. Today Salisbury is a thriving tourist centre.

SHEFFIELD (PRE-1900)

Sheffield is situated at the junction of the Sheaf, Porter, Rivelin and Loxley valleys with the River Don and was created a city in 1893. Though its cutlery, silverware and plate have long been famous, Sheffield has other and now more important industries: special and alloy steels, engineering, tool-making, medical equipment and media-related industries (in its new cultural industries quarter). Sheffield has two universities and is an important research centre.

The parish church of St Peter and St Paul, founded in the 12th century, became the cathedral church of the Diocese of Sheffield in 1914. The Roman Catholic Cathedral Church of St Marie (founded 1847) was created a cathedral for the new diocese of Hallam in 1980. Parts of the present building date from *c.*1435. The principal buildings are the Town Hall (1897), the Cutlers' Hall (1832), City Hall (1932), Graves Art Gallery (1934), Mappin Art Gallery, the Crucible Theatre and the restored Lyceum theatre, which dates from 1897 and was reopened in 1990. Three major sporting and entertainment venues were opened between 1990 and 1991: Sheffield Arena, Don Valley Stadium and Pond's Forge. The Millennium Galleries opened in 2001.

SOUTHAMPTON (1964)

Southampton is a major seaport on the south coast of England, situated between the mouths of the Test and Itchen rivers. Southampton's natural deep-water harbour has made the area an important settlement since the Romans built the first port (known as *Clausentum*) in the first century, and Southampton's port has witnessed several important departures, including those of King Henry V in 1415 for the Battle of Agincourt, RMS *Titanic* in 1912, and the *Mayflower* in 1620.

The city's strategic importance, not only as a seaport but also as a centre for aircraft production, meant that it was heavily bombed during the Second World War; however, many historically significant structures remain, including the Wool House, dating from 1417 and now used as the Maritime Museum; parts of the Norman city walls which are among the most complete in the UK; the Bargate, which was originally the main gateway into the city; God's House Tower, now the Museum of Archaeology; St Michael's, the city's oldest church; and the Tudor Merchants Hall.

Home to the National Oceanography Centre, the international Southampton Boat Show and some of the country's principal watersports venues, Southampton's coastal setting and maritime history remain its main focus, but it also features extensive parks and a thriving entertainment scene.

STOKE-ON-TRENT (1925)

Stoke-on-Trent, standing on the River Trent and familiarly known as 'the potteries', is the main centre of employment for the population of north Staffordshire. The city is the largest clayware producer in the world (china, earthenware, sanitary goods, refractories, bricks and tiles) and also has a wide range of other manufacturing industries, including steel, chemicals, engineering and tyres. Extensive reconstruction has been carried out in recent years.

The city was formed by the federation of the separate municipal authorities of Tunstall, Burslem, Hanley, Stoke, Fenton, and Longton in 1910 and received its city status in 1925.

WINCHESTER (PRE-1900)

Winchester, the ancient capital of England, is situated on the River Itchen. The city is rich in architecture of all types, especially notable is the cathedral. Built in 1079–93 the cathedral exhibits examples of Norman, early English and Perpendicular styles and is the burial place of author Jane Austen. Winchester College, founded in 1382, is one of the country's most famous public schools, and the original building (1393) remains largely unaltered. St Cross Hospital, another great medieval foundation, lies one mile south of the city. The almshouses were founded in 1136 by Bishop Henry de Blois, and Cardinal Henry Beaufort added a new almshouse of 'Noble Poverty' in 1446. The chapel and dwellings are of great architectural interest, and visitors may still receive the 'Wayfarer's Dole' of bread and ale.

Excavations have done much to clarify the origins and development of Winchester. Part of the forum and several of the streets from the Roman town have been discovered. Excavations in the Cathedral Close have uncovered the entire site of the Anglo-Saxon cathedral (known as the Old Minster) and parts of the New Minster which was built by Alfred's son, Edward the Elder, and is the burial place of the Alfredian dynasty. The original burial place of St Swithun, before his remains were translated to a site in the present cathedral, was also uncovered.

Excavations in other parts of the city have thrown much light on Norman Winchester, notably on the site of the Royal Castle (adjacent to which the new Law Courts have been built) and in the grounds of Wolvesey Castle, where the great house built by Bishops Giffard and Henry de Blois in the 12th century has been uncovered. The Great Hall, built by Henry III between 1222 and 1236, survives and houses the Arthurian Round Table.

YORK (PRE-1900)

The city of York is an archiepiscopal seat. Its recorded history dates from AD 71, when the Roman Ninth Legion established a base under Petilius Cerealis that would later become the fortress of *Eburacum,* or *Eboracum.* In Anglo-Saxon times the city was the royal and ecclesiastical centre of Northumbria, and after capture by a Viking army in AD 866 it became the capital of the Viking kingdom of Jorvik. By the 14th century the city had become a great mercantile centre, mainly because of its control of the wool trade, and was used as the chief base against the Scots. Under the Tudors its fortunes declined, although Henry VIII made it the headquarters of the Council of the North. Excavations on many sites, including Coppergate, have greatly expanded knowledge of Roman, Viking and medieval urban life.

With its development as a railway centre in the 19th century the commercial life of York expanded, and today the city is home to the award-winning National Railway Museum. The principal industries are the manufacture of chocolate, scientific instruments and sugar.

The city is rich in examples of architecture of all periods. The earliest church was built in AD 627 and, from the 12th to 15th centuries, the present Minster was built in a succession of styles. Other examples within the city are the medieval city walls and gateways, churches and guildhalls. Domestic architecture includes the Georgian mansions of The Mount, Micklegate and Bootham.

LORD-LIEUTENANTS AND HIGH SHERIFFS

Area	*Lord-Lieutenant*	*High Sheriff (2008–9)*
Bedfordshire	S. Whitbread	Nazir Jessa
Berkshire	Hon. Mary Bayliss	Dr Carolyn Boulter
Bristol	Mary Prior, MBE	Prof. Richard Hodder-Williams
Buckinghamshire	Sir Henry Aubrey-Fletcher	Peter Thorogood
Cambridgeshire	Hugh Duberly, CBE	Judith Pearson
Cheshire	W. Bromley-Davenport	Alastair Stoddard
Cornwall	Lady Mary Holborow	Sir Ralph Vyvyan, Bt.
Cumbria	J. Cropper	Graham Lamont
Derbyshire	J. Bather	Lord Kerr
Devon	E. Dancer, CBE	Lady Clifford of Chudleigh
Dorset	Valerie Pitt-Rivers	John Raymond
Durham	Sir Paul Nicholson	Paul Towley
East Riding of Yorkshire	Hon. Susan Cunliffe-Lister	Michael Hall
East Sussex	Peter Field	Hugh Burnett, OBE
Essex	Lord Petre	Sarah Courage
Gloucestershire	Henry Elwes	Brian Thornton
Greater London	Sir David Brewer, CMG	Lady Vallance of Tummel
Greater Manchester	Warren Smith	Edith Conn, OBE
Hampshire	Mrs M. Fagan	Michael Campbell
Herefordshire	vacant	Lt.-Col. Michael Leigh
Hertfordshire	Countess of Verulam	Paul Cherry
Isle of Wight	Maj.-Gen. Martin White, CB, CBE	Alan Titchmarsh, MBE
Kent	Allan Willett, CMG	Richard Oldfield
Lancashire	Lord Shuttleworth	Col. Ewart Jolley
Leicestershire	Lady Gretton	David Wyrko, QPM
Lincolnshire	Anthony Worth	John Lockwood
Merseyside	Dame Lorna Fox Muirhead, DBE	Judith Greensmith
Norfolk	Richard Jewson	Viscountess Knollys, OBE
North Yorkshire	Lord Crathorne	Christopher Robson
Northamptonshire	Lady Juliet Townsend	Peter Ellwood, CBE
Northumberland	Sir John Riddell, CVO	Hon. Charles Beaumont
Nottinghamshire	Sir Andrew Buchanan, Bt.	Col. Roger Merryweather, TD
Oxfordshire	Tim Stevenson, OBE	Brig. Ian Inshaw
Rutland	Dr Laurence Howard, OBE	Thomas Cooper
Shropshire	A. Heber-Percy	Anne Gee, MBE
Somerset	Lady Gass	Anne Maw
South Yorkshire	David Moody	Dr Robert Bloomer, OBE
Staffordshire	J. Hawley, TD	Catherine Evans
Suffolk	Lord Tollemache	Diana Hunt
Surrey	Mrs S. Goad	Sally Varah
Tyne and Wear	N. Sherlock, OBE	John Squires, OBE
Warwickshire	M. Dunne	Anna Trye
West Midlands	Paul Sabapathy, CBE	Byron Head
West Sussex	vacant	Sir Richard Kleinwort, Bt.
West Yorkshire	Dr Ingrid Roscoe	Roger Bowers
Wiltshire	John Bush, OBE	Margaret Wilks
Worcestershire	M. Brinton	Lt.-Col. Michael Leigh

COUNTY COUNCILS

Council & Administrative Headquarters	*Telephone*	*Population**	*Council Tax†*	*Chief Executive*
Bedfordshire, Bedford	01234-363222	403,900	£1,123	Martin Reeves *(acting)*
Buckinghamshire, Aylesbury	01296-395000	487,400	£1,019	Chris Williams
Cambridgeshire, Cambridge	01223-717111	589,600	£979	Mike Parsons *(acting)*
Cheshire, Chester	0845-113 3311	686,300	£1,037	Jeremy Taylor
Cornwall, Truro	01872-322000	524,300	£1,018	Sheila Healy
Cumbria, Carlisle	01228-606060	496,200	£1,112	Peter Stybelski
Derbyshire, Matlock	01629-580000	754,100	£1,031	Nick Hodgson
Devon, Exeter	01392-382000	740,800	£1,064	Phil Norrey
Dorset, Dorchester	01305-221000	403,000	£1,096	David Jenkins
Durham, Durham	0191-383 3000	500,700	£1,024	John Richardson *(acting)*
East Sussex, Lewes	01273-481000	506,200	£1,089	Cheryl Miller, CBE
Essex, Chelmsford	0845-743 0430	1,361,200	£1,047	Joanna Killian
Gloucestershire, Gloucester	01452-425000	578,600	£1,036	Peter Bungard
Hampshire, Winchester	01962-841841	1,265,900	£999	Andrew Smith
Hertfordshire, Hertford	01992-555555	1,058,600	£1,081	Caroline Tapster
Kent, Maidstone	01622-671411	1,382,900	£1,002	Peter Gilroy, OBE
Lancashire, Preston	0545-053 0000	1,165,700	£1,077	Ged Fitzgerald
Leicestershire, Leicester	0116-232 3232	635,100	£1,008	John Sinnott
Lincolnshire, Lincoln	01522-552222	686,200	£1,022	Tony McArdle
Norfolk, Norwich	0844-800 8020	832,400	£1,092	David White
North Yorkshire, Northallerton	01609-780780	591,600	£988	John Marsden
Northamptonshire, Northampton	01604-236236	669,100	£956	Katherine Kerswell
Northumberland, Morpeth	01670-533000	309,900	£1,122	Jill Dixon
Nottinghamshire, Nottingham	0115-982 3823	769,100	£1,158	Nick Burrows
Oxfordshire, Oxford	01865-792422	632,000	£1,090	Joanna Simons
Shropshire, Shrewsbury	0845-678 9000	289,300	£1,019	Carolyn Downs
Somerset, Taunton	0845-345 9166	518,600	£1,000	Alan Jones
Staffordshire, Stafford	01785-223121	822,800	£985	Ron Hilton
Suffolk, Ipswich	0845-606 6067	702,000	£1,074	Andrea Hill
Surrey, Kingston upon Thames	0845-600 9009	1,085,200	£1,058	Richard Shaw
Warwickshire, Warwick	01926-410410	522,200	£1,086	Jim Graham
West Sussex, Chichester	01243-777100	770,800	£1,098	Mark Hammond
Wiltshire, Trowbridge	01225-713000	448,700	£1,021	Dr Keith Robinson
Worcestershire, Worcester	01905-763763	552,900	£985	Trish Haines

* *Source:* The Office of National Statistics – *Mid-2006 Population Estimates* (Crown copyright)

† Average 2008–9 Band D council tax in the county area exclusive of precepts for fire and police authorities. County councils claim their share of the combined council tax from the collection funds of the district authorities into whose area they fall. Average Band D council tax bills for the billing authority are given on the following pages

DISTRICT COUNCILS

District Council	*Telephone*	*Population**	*Council Tax†*	*Chief Executive*
Adur	01273-263000	60,300	£1,497	Ian Lowrie
Allerdale	01900-702702	94,300	£1,460	Gillian Bishop
Alnwick	01665-510505	32,000	£1,385	William Batey
Amber Valley	01773-570222	120,000	£1,421	Peter Carney
Arun	01903-737500	145,700	£1,435	Ian Sumnall
Ashfield	01623-450000	115,700	£1,534	Alan Mellor
Ashford	01233-637311	111,200	£1,338	David Hill
Aylesbury Vale	01296-585858	172,000	£1,409	Andrew Grant
Babergh	01473-822801	86,700	£1,413	Patricia Rockall
Barrow-in-Furness	01229-816300	71,800	£1,490	Tom Campbell
Basildon	01268-533333	168,600	£1,478	Bala Mahendran
Basingstoke and Deane	01256-844844	158,700	£1,307	Tony Curtis
Bassetlaw	01909-533533	111,400	£1,538	David Hunter
Bedford	01234-267422	154,700	£1,507	Shaun Field
Berwick-upon-Tweed	01289-330044	26,000	£1,391	Jane Pannell
Blaby	0116-275 0555	92,500	£1,414	Sandra Whiles
Blyth Valley	01670-542000	81,200	£1,352	Geoff Paul
Bolsover	01246-240000	73,900	£1,486	Wesley Lumley
Boston	01205-314200	58,300	£1,437	Michael Gallagher
Braintree	01376-552525	139,700	£1,417	Allan Reid
Breckland	01362-695333	128,300	£1,384	Trevor Holden
Brentwood	01277-312500	70,900	£1,404	Joanna Killian
Bridgnorth	01746-713100	51,800	£1,434	John Harmeston
Broadland	01603-431133	122,200	£1,431	Colin Bland
Bromsgrove	01527-881288	91,600	£1,416	Kevin Dicks
Broxbourne	01992-785555	88,900	£1,327	Mike Walker
Broxtowe	0115-917 7777	110,400	£1,541	Ruth Hyde
Burnley	01282-425011	88,000	£1,516	Steve Rumbelow
CAMBRIDGE CITY	01223-457000	117,900	£1,346	Rob Hammond
Cannock Chase	01543-462621	94,300	£1,415	Stephen Brown
CANTERBURY CITY	01227-862000	146,200	£1,372	Colin Carmichael
Caradon	01579-341000	83,300	£1,381	Byron Davies
CARLISLE CITY	01228-817000	103,300	£1,487	Maggie Mooney
Carrick	01872-224400	91,300	£1,379	John Winskill
Castle Morpeth	01670-535000	49,500	£1,426	Ken Dunbar
Castle Point	01268-882200	88,600	£1,452	David Marchant
Charnwood	01509-263151	162,400	£1,382	Brian Hayes
Chelmsford	01245-606606	162,800	£1,410	Steve Packham
Cheltenham	01242-262626	111,500	£1,406	Andrew North
Cherwell	01295-252535	137,400	£1,430	Mary Harpley
CHESTER CITY	01244-324324	119,700	£1,422	Chris Hardy
Chesterfield	01246-345345	100,500	£1,384	Huw Bowen
Chester-le-Street	0191-387 1919	53,200	£1,443	Roy Templeman
Chichester	01243-785166	108,900	£1,391	John Marsland
Chiltern	01494-729000	90,300	£1,420	Alan Goodrum
Chorley	01257-515151	103,700	£1,464	Donna Hall
Christchurch	01202-495000	45,000	£1,480	Michael Turvey
Colchester	01206-282222	170,800	£1,411	Adrian Pritchard
Congleton	01270-529529	92,400	£1,445	Glyn Chambers
Copeland	0845-054 8600	70,300	£1,476	Liam Murphy
Corby	01536-464000	54,800	£1,303	Chris Mallender
Cotswold	01285-623000	83,200	£1,409	Bob Austin
Craven	01756-700600	55,500	£1,424	Gill Dixon
Crawley	01293-438000	99,900	£1,409	Michael Coughlin
Crewe and Nantwich	01270-537777	115,800	£1,391	Paul Ancell
Dacorum	01442-228000	138,400	£1,385	Daniel Zammit
Dartford	01322-343434	89,900	£1,367	Graham Harris

* *Source:* ONS – *Mid-2006 Population Estimates* (Crown copyright)
† Average Band D council tax bill for 2008–9

District Council	*Telephone*	*Population**	*Council Tax†*	*Chief Executive*
Daventry	01327-871100	78,200	£1,313	Simon Bovey
Derbyshire Dales	01629-761100	69,800	£1,457	David Wheatcroft
Derwentside	01207-218000	86,500	£1,500	Mike Clark
Dover	01304-821199	106,400	£1,384	Nadeem Aziz
DURHAM CITY	0191-386 6111	92,200	£1,452	David Marrs
Easington	0191-527 0501	94,000	£1,587	Janet Johnson
East Cambridgeshire	01353-665555	79,600	£1,362	John Hill
East Devon	01395-516551	131,100	£1,418	Mark Williams
East Dorset	01202-886201	85,000	£1,529	Alan Breakwell
East Hampshire	01730-266551	110,100	£1,372	Will Godfrey
East Hertfordshire	01279-655261	132,600	£1,427	Anna Freimanis
East Lindsey	01507-601111	138,500	£1,391	Nigel Howells
East Northamptonshire	01832-742000	84,000	£1,308	David Oliver
East Staffordshire	01283-508000	107,700	£1,420	Jeanette McGarry
Eastbourne	01323-410000	94,900	£1,506	Martin Ray
Eastleigh	023-8068 8000	119,000	£1,371	Bernie Topham
Eden	01768-817817	51,700	£1,472	Kevin Douglas
Ellesmere Port and Neston	0151-356 6789	81,800	£1,413	Brenda Harvey
Elmbridge	01372-474474	129,500	£1,437	Robert Moran
Epping Forest	01992-564000	122,900	£1,427	Peter Haywood
Epsom and Ewell	01372-732000	69,600	£1,399	David Smith
Erewash	0115-907 2244	110,400	£1,409	Jeremy Jaroszek
EXETER CITY	01392-277888	119,600	£1,388	Philip Bostock
Fareham	01329-236100	108,400	£1,329	Alan Davies
Fenland	01354-654321	90,100	£1,436	Tim Pilsbury
Forest Heath	01638-719000	62,100	£1,416	David Burnip
Forest of Dean	01594-810000	81,700	£1,425	Tim Perrin
Fylde	01253-658658	75,700	£1,457	Phillip Woodward
Gedling	0115-901 3901	111,700	£1,516	Peter Murdock
GLOUCESTER CITY	01452-522232	113,200	£1,399	Julian Wain
Gosport	023-9258 4242	78,200	£1,391	Ian Lycett
Gravesham	01474-337000	97,400	£1,354	Glyn Thomson
Great Yarmouth	01493-856100	93,400	£1,416	Richard Packham
Guildford	01483-505050	133,100	£1,406	David Hill
Hambleton	0845-121 1555	86,300	£1,353	Peter Simpson
Harborough	01858-828282	81,300	£1,412	Sue Smith
Harlow	01279-446655	78,100	£1,473	Malcolm Morley
Harrogate	01423-500600	157,800	£1,460	Wallace Sampson
Hart	01252-622122	88,800	£1,389	Geoff Bonner
Hastings	0845-274 1066	86,100	£1,518	Roy Mawford
Havant	023-9247 4174	116,800	£1,378	Sandy Hopkins
Hertsmere	020-8207 2277	96,000	£1,393	Sajida Bijle *(acting)*
High Peak	0845-129 7777	92,000	£1,427	Simon Baker
Hinckley and Bosworth	01455-238141	103,800	£1,363	Steve Atkinson
Horsham	01403-215100	128,300	£1,396	Tom Crowley
Huntingdonshire	01480-388388	166,600	£1,371	David Monks
Hyndburn	01254-388111	82,200	£1,493	David Welsby
Ipswich	01473-432000	120,400	£1,516	James Hehir
Kennet	01380-724911	78,200	£1,408	Mark Boden
Kerrier	01209-614000	98,000	£1,380	Barry Manning
Kettering	01536-410333	87,900	£1,325	David Cook
King's Lynn and West Norfolk	01553-616200	142,300	£1,417	Ray Harding
LANCASTER CITY	01524-582000	143,000	£1,458	Mark Cullinan
Lewes	01273-471600	93,900	£1,541	John Crawford
Lichfield	01543-308000	96,700	£1,385	Nina Dawes
LINCOLN CITY	01522-881188	87,600	£1,479	Andrew Taylor
Macclesfield	01625-500500	150,600	£1,406	Vivienne Horton
Maidstone	01622-602000	142,800	£1,416	David Petford
Maldon	01621-854477	61,700	£1,434	Steve Watson
Malvern Hills	01684-862151	73,900	£1,395	Chris Bocock
Mansfield	01623-463463	99,900	£1,546	Ruth Marlow
Melton	01664-502502	48,900	£1,409	Lynn Aisbett
Mendip	01749-343399	108,300	£1,409	David Thomson
Mid Bedfordshire	08452-304040	132,200	£1,518	Jaki Salisbury
Mid Devon	01884-255255	74,500	£1,476	Gerald Hirsch
Mid Suffolk	01449-720711	92,000	£1,415	Andrew Good
Mid Sussex	01444-458166	129,100	£1,419	John Jory

District Council	*Telephone*	*Population**	*Council Tax†*	*Chief Executive*
Mole Valley	01306-885001	80,500	£1,394	Darren Mepham
New Forest	023-8028 5000	173,700	£1,402	David Yates
Newark and Sherwood	01636-650000	111,700	£1,592	Andrew Muter
Newcastle-under-Lyme	01782-717717	123,800	£1,392	Mark Barrow
North Cornwall	01208-893333	85,300	£1,391	Paul Masters *(acting)*
North Devon	01271-327711	91,500	£1,467	John Sunderland
North Dorset	01258-454111	66,700	£1,481	Elizabeth Goodall
North East Derbyshire	01246-231111	97,700	£1,482	Mrs Lee Adams
North Hertfordshire	01462-474000	121,500	£1,432	John Campbell
North Kesteven	01529-414155	103,200	£1,443	Ian Fytch
North Norfolk	01263-513811	100,600	£1,431	Philip Burton
North Shropshire	01939-232771	59,500	£1,464	vacant
North Warwickshire	01827-715341	62,300	£1,490	Jeremy Hutchinson
North West Leicestershire	01530-454545	89,600	£1,431	Christine Fisher
North Wiltshire	01249-706111	130,400	£1,444	Delwyn Burbidge
Northampton	01604-837837	200,100	£1,344	David Kennedy
NORWICH CITY	0844-980 3333	129,500	£1,483	Laura McGillivray
Nuneaton and Bedworth	02476-376376	120,700	£1,448	Christine Kerr
Oadby and Wigston	0116-288 8961	56,500	£1,411	Mark Hall
Oswestry	01691-671111	39,700	£1,496	Paul Shevlin
OXFORD CITY	01865-249811	149,100	£1,485	Peter Sloman
Pendle	01282-661661	90,100	£1,523	Stephen Barnes
Penwith	01736-362341	64,400	£1,327	Jim McKenna
PRESTON CITY	01772-906900	132,000	£1,516	Jim Carr
Purbeck	01929-556561	45,200	£1,512	Steve Mackenzie
Redditch	01527-64252	79,500	£1,414	Christopher Smith
Reigate and Banstead	01737-276000	129,800	£1,436	Nigel Clifford
Restormel	01726-223300	101,900	£1,341	Andrew Tremaine
Ribble Valley	01200-425111	57,800	£1,423	David Morris
Richmondshire	01748-829100	51,000	£1,443	Peter Simpson *(acting)*
Rochford	01702-546366	81,100	£1,450	Paul Warren
Rossendale	01706-217777	66,700	£1,522	Carolyn Wilkins
Rother	01424-787999	87,600	£1,492	Derek Stevens
Rugby	01788-533533	90,200	£1,433	Simon Warren
Runnymede	01932-838383	81,200	£1,373	Tim Williams
Rushcliffe	0115-981 9911	108,200	£1,537	Allen Graham
Rushmoor	01252-398398	88,700	£1,367	Andrew Lloyd
Ryedale	01653-600666	52,900	£1,442	Janet Waggott
ST ALBANS CITY	01727-866100	131,300	£1,423	Daniel Goodwin
St Edmundsbury	01284-763233	101,900	£1,430	vacant
SALISBURY CITY	01722-336272	115,300	£1,386	Manjeet Gill
Scarborough	01723-232323	108,300	£1,456	Jim Dillon
Sedgefield	01388-816166	87,700	£1,613	Brian Allen
Sedgemoor	0845-408 2540	111,000	£1,381	Mr Kerry Rickards
Selby	01757-705101	79,800	£1,433	Martin Connor
Sevenoaks	01732-227000	113,700	£1,423	Robin Hales
Shepway	01303-853000	99,600	£1,454	Alistair Stewart
Shrewsbury and Atcham	01743-281000	95,900	£1,425	Geraint Morgan
South Bedfordshire	01582-472222	117,000	£1,594	Jon Ruddick
South Bucks	01895-837200	63,700	£1,402	Chris Furness
South Cambridgeshire	08450-450500	135,400	£1,357	Greg Harlock
South Derbyshire	01283-221000	89,800	£1,403	Frank McArdle
South Hams	01803-861234	83,200	£1,440	David Incoll
South Holland	01775-761161	82,100	£1,432	Terry Huggins
South Kesteven	01476-406080	130,100	£1,413	Duncan Kerr
South Lakeland	01539-733333	104,800	£1,479	Peter Ridgway
South Norfolk	01508-533633	116,200	£1,450	Geoff Rivers
South Northamptonshire	0845-230 0226	88,800	£1,345	Jean Morgan
South Oxfordshire	01491-823000	128,100	£1,418	David Buckle
South Ribble	01772-421491	106,400	£1,477	Jean Hunter
South Shropshire	01584-813000	42,300	£1,505	Graham Biggs
South Somerset	01935-462462	156,700	£1,418	Philip Dolan
South Staffordshire	01902-696000	106,200	£1,352	Rolf Levesley
Spelthorne	01784-451499	90,500	£1,406	Roberto Tambini
Stafford	01785-619000	123,400	£1,373	Ian Thompson
Staffordshire Moorlands	01538-483483	95,300	£1,389	Simon Baker
Stevenage	01438-242242	79,300	£1,399	Peter Ollis

District Council	*Telephone*	*Population**	*Council Tax†*	*Chief Executive*
Stratford-on-Avon	01789-267575	116,100	£1,423	Paul Lankester
Stroud	01453-766321	110,300	£1,454	David Hagg
Suffolk Coastal	01394-383789	122,200	£1,401	Stephen Baker
Surrey Heath	01276-707100	82,400	£1,435	Michael Willis
Swale	01795-417330	128,500	£1,357	vacant
Tamworth	01827-709709	75,400	£1,354	David Weatherley
Tandridge	01883-722000	81,300	£1,438	Stephen Weigel
Taunton Deane	01823-356356	107,400	£1,363	Penny James
Teesdale	01833-690000	24,800	£1,476	Neil Stokell
Teignbridge	01626-361101	125,500	£1,448	Nicola Bulbeck
Tendring	01255-686868	144,600	£1,403	John Hawkins
Test Valley	01264-368000	113,600	£1,332	Roger Tetstall
Tewkesbury	01684-295010	78,800	£1,354	Bob Austin
Thanet	01843-577000	128,600	£1,402	Richard Samuel
Three Rivers	01923-776611	85,500	£1,407	Steven Halls
Tonbridge and Malling	01732-844522	113,900	£1,387	David Hughes
Torridge	01237-428700	64,200	£1,446	John van de Laarschot
Tunbridge Wells	01892-526121	104,600	£1,360	Sheila Wheeler
Tynedale	01434-652121	59,500	£1,399	Richard Robson
Uttlesford	01799-510510	71,400	£1,423	John Mitchell *(acting)*
Vale of White Horse	01235-520202	117,100	£1,392	Terry Stock
Vale Royal	01606-862862	126,000	£1,420	Anne Bingham-Holmes
Wansbeck	01670-532200	61,700	£1,371	Robert Stephenson
Warwick	01926-450000	132,900	£1,408	Chris Elliott
Watford	01923-226400	79,600	£1,469	Alastair Robertson
Waveney	01502-562111	116,800	£1,372	Stephen Baker
Waverley	01483-523333	116,800	£1,438	Mary Orton
Wealden	01323-443322	143,700	£1,532	Charles Lant
Wear Valley	01388-765555	62,300	£1,464	Gary Ridley
Wellingborough	01933-229777	75,500	£1,279	Lyn Martin-Bennison
Welwyn & Hatfield	01707-357000	105,500	£1,441	Michel Saminaden
West Devon	01822-813600	51,200	£1,502	David Incoll
West Dorset	01305-251010	96,200	£1,498	David Clarke
West Lancashire	01695-577177	109,800	£1,467	William Taylor
West Lindsey	01427-676676	86,500	£1,476	Duncan Sharkey
West Oxfordshire	01993-861000	100,200	£1,362	David Neudegg
West Somerset	01643-703704	35,300	£1,390	Adrian Dyer
West Wiltshire	01225-776655	124,800	£1,428	Ian Gallin
Weymouth and Portland	01305-838000	64,900	£1,568	Tom Grainger
WINCHESTER CITY	01962-840222	110,000	£1,372	Simon Eden
Woking	01483-755855	90,700	£1,437	Ray Morgan, OBE
WORCESTER CITY	01905-723471	93,400	£1,372	David Wareing
Worthing	01903-239999	98,700	£1,430	Ian Lowrie
Wychavon	01386-565000	116,300	£1,361	Jack Hegarty
Wycombe	01494-461000	161,300	£1,377	Ms Satterford
Wyre	01253-891000	110,400	£1,448	Jim Corry
Wyre Forest	01562-732928	98,200	£1,419	Walter Delin

Councils in CAPITAL LETTERS have city status

METROPOLITAN BOROUGH COUNCILS

Metropolitan Borough Councils	*Telephone*	*Population**	*Council Tax†*	*Chief Executive*
Barnsley	01226-770770	223,500	£1,330	Philip Coppard
BIRMINGHAM CITY	0121-303 9944	1,006,500	£1,213	Stephen Hughes
Bolton	01204-333333	262,400	£1,332	Sean Harriss
BRADFORD CITY	01274-432001	493,100	£1,237	Tony Reeves
Bury	0161-253 5000	182,900	£1,337	Mark Sanders
Calderdale	01422-357257	198,500	£1,398	Owen Williams
COVENTRY CITY	024-7683 3333	306,600	£1,386	Stella Manzie
Doncaster	01302-734444	290,300	£1,227	Paul Hart
Dudley	01384-812345	305,300	£1,198	Andrew Sparke
Gateshead	0191-433 3000	190,500	£1,525	Roger Kelly
Kirklees	01484-221000	398,200	£1,331	Rob Vincent
Knowsley	0151-489 6000	151,300	£1,350	Sheena Ramsey
LEEDS CITY	0113-234 8080	750,200	£1,244	Paul Rogerson
LIVERPOOL CITY	0151-233 3000	436,100	£1,446	Colin Hilton
MANCHESTER CITY	0161-234 5000	452,000	£1,272	Sir Howard Bernstein
NEWCASTLE UPON TYNE CITY	0191-232 8520	270,500	£1,449	Ian Stratford
North Tyneside	0191-643 2001	195,000	£1,415	Andrew Kerr
Oldham	0161-911 3000	219,600	£1,481	Andrew Kilburn
Rochdale	01706-647474	206,500	£1,371	Roger Ellis
Rotherham	01709-382121	253,300	£1,372	Mike Cuff
St Helens	01744-456000	177,600	£1,315	Carole Hudson
SALFORD CITY	0161-794 4711	218,000	£1,462	Barbara Spicer
Sandwell	0121-569 2200	287,600	£1,284	Allison Fraser
Sefton	0151-922 4040	277,400	£1,406	Graham Haywood
SHEFFIELD CITY	0114-272 6444	525,800	£1,425	John Mothersole
Solihull	0121-704 6000	203,000	£1,254	Mark Rogers *(acting)*
South Tyneside	0191-427 1717	151,000	£1,371	Irene Lucas
Stockport	0161-480 4949	280,600	£1,441	John Schultz
SUNDERLAND CITY	0191-553 1000	280,600	£1,289	Dave Smith *(acting)*
Tameside	0161-342 8355	214,400	£1,287	Janet Callender
Trafford	0161-912 1212	211,800	£1,211	David McNulty
WAKEFIELD CITY	01924-306090	321,200	£1,230	Joanne Roney
Walsall	01922-650000	254,500	£1,423	Paul Sheehan
Wigan	01942-244991	305,500	£1,310	Joyce Redfern
Wirral	0151-606 2000	311,200	£1,379	Stephen Maddox
WOLVERHAMPTON CITY	01902-556556	236,600	£1,412	Richard Carr

* *Source:* ONS – *Mid-2005 Population Estimates* (Crown copyright)

† Average Band D council tax bill for 2008–9

Councils in CAPITAL LETTERS have city status

UNITARY COUNCILS

Unitary Councils	*Telephone*	*Population**	*Council Tax†*	*Chief Executive*
Bath and North East Somerset	01225-477000	175,600	£1,373	John Everitt
Blackburn with Darwen	01254-585585	141,200	£1,417	Graham Burgess
Blackpool	01253-477477	142,700	£1,418	Peter Callow
Bournemouth	01202-451451	161,200	£1,396	Pam Donnellan
Bracknell Forest	01344-352000	112,200	£1,268	Timothy Wheadon
BRIGHTON AND HOVE CITY	01273-290000	251,400	£1,396	Alan McCarthy
BRISTOL CITY	0117-922 2000	410,500	£1,482	Jan Ormondroyd
Darlington	01325-380651	99,300	£1,339	Ada Burns
DERBY CITY	01332-293111	236,300	£1,277	Ray Cowlishaw
East Riding of Yorkshire	01482-887700	330,900	£1,422	Nigel Pearson
Halton	0151-424 2061	119,500	£1,279	David Parr
Hartlepool	01429-266522	91,100	£1,565	Paul Walker
Herefordshire	01432-260000	177,800	£1,399	C. Bull
Isle of Wight	01983-821000	138,500	£1,375	David Burbage *(acting)*
Isles of Scilly‡	01720-422537	2,100	£1,082	Philip Hygate
KINGSTON-UPON-HULL CITY	01482-609100	256,200	£1,293	Mr Kim Ryley
LEICESTER CITY	0116-254 9922	289,700	£1,324	Sheila Lock *(acting)*
Luton	01582-546000	186,800	£1,293	Kevin Crompton
Medway	01634-306000	251,700	£1,237	Neil Davies
Middlesbrough	01642-245432	138,400	£1,410	Jan Richmond
Milton Keynes	01908-691691	224,800	£1,312	Kate Page *(acting)*
North East Lincolnshire	01472-313131	158,900	£1,449	Elizabeth Jones *(acting)*
North Lincolnshire	01724-296296	159,000	£1,457	Simon Driver
North Somerset	01934-888888	201,400	£1,354	Graham Turner
NOTTINGHAM CITY	0115-915 5555	286,400	£1,463	Jane Todd
PETERBOROUGH CITY	01733-563141	163,300	£1,260	Gillian Beasley
PLYMOUTH CITY	01752-668000	248,100	£1,363	Barry Keel
Poole	01202-633633	136,900	£1,342	John McBride
PORTSMOUTH CITY	023-9282 2251	196,400	£1,289	David Williams
Reading	0118-939 0900	142,800	£1,410	Michael Coughlin
Redcar and Cleveland	0164-277 4774	139,500	£1,459	Amanda Skelton
Rutland	01572-722577	38,300	£1,606	Helen Briggs
Slough	01753-475111	119,500	£1,278	Ruth Bagley
South Gloucestershire	01454-868686	254,400	£1,434	Amanda Deeks
SOUTHAMPTON CITY	023-8022 3855	228,600	£1,368	Brad Roynon
Southend-on-Sea	01702-215000	159,900	£1,232	Robert Tinlin
Stockton-on-Tees	01642-393939	189,100	£1,391	George Garlick
STOKE-ON-TRENT CITY	01782-234567	239,700	£1,299	Steve Robinson
Swindon	01793-463000	186,600	£1,317	Gavin Jones
Telford and Wrekin	01952-202100	161,900	£1,352	Steve Wellings
Thurrock	01375-652652	148,900	£1,222	Angie Ridgwell
Torbay	01803-201201	133,200	£1,393	Elizabeth Raikes
Warrington	01925-444400	194,000	£1,286	Diana Terris
West Berkshire	01635-42400	148,800	£1,416	Nick Carter
Windsor and Maidenhead	01628-683800	138,800	£1,248	Ian Trenholm
Wokingham	0118-974 6000	153,800	£1,370	Susan Law
YORK CITY	01904-613161	191,800	£1,289	Bill McCarthy

* *Source:* ONS – *Mid-2006 Population Estimates* (Crown copyright)
† Average Band D council tax bill for 2008–9
‡ Under the Isles of Scilly Clause the council has additional functions to other unitary authorities and certain other functions are performed by Cornwall County Council for the benefit of the Isles of Scilly
Councils in CAPITAL LETTERS have city status

MAP OF COUNCILS IN ENGLAND

1 Hillingdon
2 Harrow
3 Barnet
4 Enfield
5 Waltham Forest
6 Redbridge
7 Barking and Dagenham
8 Havering
9 Ealing
10 Brent
11 Camden
12 Haringey
13 Islington
14 Hackney
15 Newham
16 Hounslow
17 Hammersmith and Fulham
18 Kensington and Chelsea
19 City of Westminster
20 City of London
21 Tower Hamlets
22 Richmond upon Thames
23 Wandsworth
24 Lambeth
25 Southwark
26 Lewisham
27 Greenwich
28 Bexley
29 Kingston upon Thames
30 Merton
31 Sutton
32 Croydon
33 Bromley

LONDON

THE CITY OF LONDON CORPORATION

The City of London is the historic centre at the heart of London known as 'the square mile' around which the vast metropolis has grown over the centuries. The City's residential population is roughly 9,000 and in addition, over 330,000 people work in the City. The civic government is carried on by the City of London Corporation through the Court of Common Council.

The City is an international financial and business centre, generating about £30bn a year for the British economy. It includes the head offices of the principal banks, insurance companies and mercantile houses, in addition to buildings ranging from the historic Roman Wall and the 15th-century Guildhall, to the massive splendour of St Paul's Cathedral and the architectural beauty of Wren's spires.

The City of London was described by Tacitus in AD 62 as 'a busy emporium for trade and traders'. Under the Romans it became an important administration centre and hub of the road system. Little is known of London in Saxon times, when it formed part of the kingdom of the East Saxons. In 886 Alfred recovered London from the Danes and reconstituted it a burgh under his son-in-law. In 1066 the citizens submitted to William the Conqueror who in 1067 granted them a charter, which is still preserved, establishing them in the rights and privileges they had hitherto enjoyed.

THE MAYORALTY

The mayoralty was probably established about 1189, the first mayor being Henry Fitz Ailwyn who filled the office for 23 years and was succeeded by Fitz Alan (1212–14). A new charter was granted by King John in 1215, directing the mayor to be chosen annually, which has been done ever since, though in early times the same individual often held the office more than once. A familiar instance is that of 'Whittington, thrice Lord Mayor of London' (in reality four times, 1397, 1398, 1406, 1419); and many modern cases have occurred. The earliest instance of the phrase 'lord mayor' in English is in 1414. It was used more generally in the latter part of the 15th century and became invariable from 1535 onwards. At Michaelmas the liverymen in Common Hall choose two aldermen who have served the office of sheriff for presentation to the Court of Aldermen, and one is chosen to be lord mayor for the following mayoral year.

LORD MAYOR'S DAY

The lord mayor of London was previously elected on the feast of St Simon and St Jude (28 October), and from the time of Edward I, at least, was presented to the King or to the Barons of the Exchequer on the following day, unless that day was a Sunday. The day of election was altered to 16 October in 1346, and after some further changes was fixed for Michaelmas Day in 1546, but the ceremonies of admittance and swearing-in of the lord mayor continued to take place on 28 and 29 October respectively until 1751. In 1752, at the reform of the calendar, the lord mayor was continued in office until 8 November, the 'new style' equivalent of 28 October. The lord mayor is now presented to the lord chief justice at the royal courts of justice on the second Saturday in November to make the final declaration of office, having been sworn in at Guildhall on the preceding day. The procession to the royal courts of justice is popularly known as the Lord Mayor's Show.

REPRESENTATIVES

Aldermen are mentioned in the 11th century and their office is of Saxon origin. They were elected annually between 1377 and 1394, when an act of parliament of Richard II directed them to be chosen for life.

The Common Council was, at an early date, substituted for a popular assembly called the *Folkmote*. At first only two representatives were sent from each ward, but now each of the City's 25 wards is represented by an alderman and at least two Common Councilmen (the number depending on the size of the ward).

OFFICERS

Sheriffs were Saxon officers; their predecessors were the *wic-reeves* and *portreeves* of London and Middlesex. At first they were officers of the Crown, and were named by the Barons of the Exchequer; but Henry I (in 1132) gave the citizens permission to choose their own Sheriffs, and the annual election of Sheriffs became fully operative under King John's charter of 1199. The citizens lost this privilege, as far as the election of the Sheriff of Middlesex was concerned, by the Local Government Act 1888; but the liverymen continue to choose two Sheriffs of the City of London, who are appointed on Midsummer Day and take office at Michaelmas.

The office of Chamberlain is an ancient one, the first contemporary record of which is 1237. The town clerk (or Common Clerk) is first mentioned in 1274.

ACTIVITIES

The work of the City of London Corporation is assigned to a number of committees which present reports to the Court of Common Council. These committees are: Barbican Centre; Barbican Residential; Board of Governors of the City of London Freeman's School, the City of London School, the City of London School for Girls, the Guildhall School of Music and Drama and the Museum of London; City Bridge Trust; City Lands and Bridge House Estates; Community and Children's Services; Court of Alderman; Court of Common Council; Education; Epping Forest and Commons; Establishment; Finance; Freedom Applications; Gresham (city side); Guildhall Improvement; Guildhall Yard East Building; Hampstead Heath Management; Joint Working Party of the Three Schools; Keats House Management; Libraries, Archives and Guildhall Art Gallery; Licensing; Livery; London Drug Policy Forum; Managers of West Ham Park; Markets; Open Spaces; Planning and Transportation; Police; Policy and Resources; Port Health and Environmental Services; Queen's Park and Highgate Wood Management and Standards Committees.

The City's estate, in the possession of which the City of London Corporation differs from other municipalities, is managed by the City Lands and Bridge House Estates Committee, the chairmanship of which carries with it the title of Chief Commoner.

The Honourable the Irish Society, which manages the City Corporation's estates in Ulster, consists of a governor and five other aldermen, the recorder, and 19 Common Councilmen, of whom one is elected deputy governor.

THE LORD MAYOR 2008–9

The Rt. Hon. the Lord Mayor, Ian Luder*
Private Secretary, Kay Brock
* Provisional at time of going to press

THE SHERIFFS 2008–9

George Gillon (Cordwainer); Alderman Roger Gifford (Cordwainer)

OFFICERS, ETC

Town Clerk, Chris Duffield
Chamberlain, Chris Bilsland
Chief Commoner (2008), John Barker
Clerk, The Honourable the Irish Society, C. Fisher

THE ALDERMEN

with office held and date of appointment to that office

Name and Ward	*CC*	*Ald.*	*Shff*	*Lord Mayor*
Lord Levene of Portsoken, KBE, *Aldgate*	1983	1984	1995	1998
Sir David Howard, Bt., *Cornhill*	1972	1986	1997	2000
Sir Michael Oliver, *Bishopsgate*	1980	1987	1997	2001
Sir Robert Finch, *Coleman Street*	–	1992	1999	2003
Sir Michael Savory, *Bread Street*	1980	1996	2001	2004
Sir David Brewer, *Bassishaw*	1992	1996	2002	2005
Sir John Stuttard, *Lime Street*	–	2001	2005	2006
Sir David Lewis, *Broad Street*	–	2001	2006	2007

All the above have passed the Civic Chair

Nicholas Anstee, *Aldersgate*	1987	1996	2003
Dr Andrew Parmley, *Vintry*	1992	2001	
Simon Walsh, *Farringdon Wt.*	1989	2000	
Robert Hall, *Farringdon Wn.*	1995	2002	
Alison Gowman, *Dowgate*	1991	2002	
Gordon Haines, *Queenhithe*	–	2004	
Roger Gifford, *Cordwainer*	–	2004	2008
David Mauleverer, *Walbrook*	–	2005	2001
Ian Luder, *Castle Baynard*	1998	2005	2007
Michael Bear, *Portsoken*	2003	2005	2007
David Wootton, *Langbourn*	2002	2005	
Alan Yarrow, *Bridge*	–	2007	
Jeffrey Evans, *Cheap*	–	2007	
Sir Paul Judge, *Tower*	–	2007	
Fiona Woolf, *Candlewick*	–	2007	
John White, *Billingsgate*	–	2008	
David Graves, *Cripplegate*	–	2008	

THE COMMON COUNCIL

Deputy: each Common Councilman so described serves as deputy to the alderman of her/his ward.

Abrahams, G. C. (2000)	*Farringdon Wt.*
Absalom, J. D. (1994)	*Farringdon Wt.*
Altman, L. P., CBE (1996)	*Cripplegate Wn.*
Ayers, K. E. (1996)	*Bassishaw*
Bain-Stewart, A. (2005)	*Farringdon Wn.*
Barker, *Deputy* J. A., OBE (1981)	*Cripplegate*
Barrow, D. (2007)	*Aldgate*
Bennett, J. A. (2005)	*Broad Street*
Bird, J. L., OBE (1977)	*Tower*
Boleat, M. J. (2002)	*Cordwainer*
Bradshaw, D. J. (1991)	*Cripplegate Wn.*
Brewster, J. W., OBE (1994)	*Bassishaw*
Burleigh, I. B. (2005)	*Portsoken*
Campbell-Taylor, Revd W. G. (2005)	*Portsoken*
Cassidy, *Deputy* M. J., CBE (1989)	*Coleman Street*
Catt, R. M. (2004)	*Castle Baynard*
Cenci Di Bello, Mrs P. J. (2004)	*Farringdon Wn.*
Chadwick, R. A. H. (1994)	*Tower*
Challis, N. K. (2005)	*Castle Baynard*
Chapman, J. D. (2006)	*Langbourn*
Cohen, Mrs C. M., OBE (1986)	*Lime Street*
Cotgrove, D. (1991)	*Lime Street*
Currie, *Deputy* Miss S. E. M. (1985)	*Cripplegate Wt.*
Day, M. J. (2005)	*Bishopsgate*
Dove, W. H., MBE (1993)	*Bishopsgate*
Duckworth, S. (2000)	*Bishopsgate*
Dudley, Revd Dr M. R. (2002)	*Aldersgate*
Duffield, R. W. (2004)	*Farringdon Wn.*
Eskenzi, *Deputy* A. N., CBE (1970)	*Farringdon Wn.*
Eve, *Deputy* R. A. (1980)	*Cheap*
Everett, K. M. (1984)	*Candlewick*
Farr, M. C. (1998)	*Walbrook*
Farrow, *Deputy* M. W. W. (1996)	*Farringdon Wt.*
FitzGerald, *Deputy* R. C. A. (1981)	*Bread Street*
Fraser, S. J. (1993)	*Coleman Street*
Fraser, *Deputy* W. B., OBE (1981)	*Vintry*
Fredericks, M. B. (2008)	*Tower*
Galloway, *Deputy* A. D., OBE (1981)	*Broad Street*
Gillon, G. M. F. (1995)	*Cordwainer*
Ginsburg, *Deputy* S. (1990)	*Bishopsgate*
Graves, A. C. (1985)	*Bishopsgate*
Haines, Revd S. D. (2005)	*Cornhill*
Halliday, *Deputy* Mrs P. A. (1992)	*Walbrook*
Hardwick, Dr P. B. (1987)	*Aldgate*
Harris, B. N. (2004)	*Bridge*
Henderson-Begg, M. (1977)	*Coleman Street*
Hilliard, N. R. M. (2005)	*Farringdon Wt.*
Hoffman, T. D. D. (2002)	*Vintry*
Holland, *Deputy* J., CBE (1972)	*Aldgate*
Hudson, M. (2007)	*Castle Baynard*
Hughes-Penney, R. C. (2004)	*Farringdon Wn.*
Hunt, W. G. (2004)	*Castle Baynard*
Jackson, L. St J. T. (1978)	*Bread Street*
James, Clare (2008)	*Farringdon Wn.*
Jones, H. L. M. (2004)	*Portsoken*
Kellett, Mrs M. W. F. (1986)	*Tower*
Kemp, D. L. (1984)	*Coleman Street*
King, *Deputy* A. J. N. (1999)	*Queenhithe*
Knowles, *Deputy* S. K. (1984)	*Candlewick*
Lawrence, *Deputy* G. A. (2002)	*Farringdon Wt.*
Leck, P. (1998)	*Aldersgate*
Lee, *Deputy* Revd Dr B. J. (2001)	*Portsoken*
Lord, C. E. (2001)	*Coleman Street*
McGuinness, *Deputy* C. S. (1997)	*Castle Baynard*
Malins, J. H., QC (1981)	*Farringdon Wt.*
Martinelli, *Deputy* P. J. (1994)	*Bassishaw*
Mayhew, J. P. (1996)	*Aldersgate*
Mead, Mrs W. (1997)	*Farringdon Wt.*
Mobsby, *Deputy* D. J. L. (1985)	*Billingsgate*
Mooney, B. D. F. (1998)	*Queenhithe*
Moys, Mrs S. D. (2001)	*Aldgate*
Nash, *Deputy* Mrs J. C., OBE (1983)	*Aldersgate*

Newman, Mrs P. B., CBE (1989)	*Aldersgate*
Nove, P. R., CBE (2004)	*Castle Baynard*
Owen, *Deputy* Mrs J., MBE (1975)	*Langbourn*
Owen-Ward, J. R. (1983)	*Bridge*
Page, M. (2002)	*Farringdon Wn.*
Pembroke, *Deputy* Mrs A. M. F. (1978)	*Cheap*
Pollard, J. H. G. (2002)	*Dowgate*
Price, E. E. (1996)	*Farringdon Wt.*
Pulman, *Deputy* G. A. G. (1983)	*Tower*
Punter, C. (1993)	*Cripplegate Wn.*
Quilter, S. D. (1998)	*Cripplegate Wt.*
Regan, R. D. (1998)	*Farringdon Wn.*
Robinson, Mrs D. C. (1989)	*Bishopsgate*
Roney, *Deputy* E. P. T., CBE (1974)	*Bishopsgate*
Scott, J. G. S. (1999)	*Broad Street*
Sherlock, *Deputy* M. R. C. (1992)	*Dowgate*
Simons, J. L. (2004)	*Castle Baynard*
Snyder, *Deputy* M. J. (1986)	*Cordwainer*
Spanner, J. H. (2001)	*Farringdon Wt.*
Starling, Mrs A. J. (2006)	*Cripplegate Wt.*
Stevenson, F. P. (1994)	*Cripplegate Wn.*
Thompson, D. J. (2004)	*Aldgate*
Tomlinson, J. (2004)	*Cripplegate Wt.*
Twogood, M. (2004)	*Farringdon Wt.*
Wang, *Deputy* Mrs C. A. M. (2004)	*Cornhill*
Welbank, J. M. (2005)	*Billingsgate*
Willoughby, *Deputy* P. J. (1985)	*Bishopsgate*

THE CITY GUILDS (LIVERY COMPANIES)

The constitution of the livery companies has been unchanged for centuries. There are three ranks of membership: freemen, liverymen and assistants. A person can become a freeman by patrimony (through a parent having been a freeman); by servitude (through having served an apprenticeship to a freeman); or by redemption (by purchase).

Election to the livery is the prerogative of the company, who can elect any of its freemen as liverymen. Assistants are usually elected from the livery and form a Court of Assistants which is the governing body of the company. The master (in some companies called the prime warden) is elected annually from the assistants.

The register for 2008–9 lists 24,636 liverymen of the guilds entitled to vote at elections at Common Hall.

The order of precedence, omitting extinct companies, is given in parentheses after the name of each company in the list below. In certain companies the election of Master or Prime Warden for the year does not take place until the autumn. In such cases the master or prime warden for 2007–8, rather than 2008–9, is given.

THE TWELVE GREAT COMPANIES
In order of civic precedence

MERCERS *(1)*. *Hall,* Mercers' Hall, Ironmonger Lane, London EC2V 8HE *Livery,* 247. *Clerk,* Menna McGregor *Master,* Daniel Hodson

GROCERS *(2)*. *Hall,* Grocers' Hall, Princes Street, London EC2R 8AD *Livery,* 349. *Clerk,* Brig. Robert Pridham, OBE *Master,* Robert Ringrofe

DRAPERS *(3)*. *Hall,* Drapers' Hall, Throgmorton Avenue, London EC2N 2DQ *Livery,* 310. *Clerk,* Rear-Adm. Alastair Ross, CB, CBE *Master,* David Addis

FISHMONGERS *(4)*. *Hall,* Fishmongers' Hall, London Bridge, London EC4R 9EL *Livery,* 348. *Clerk,* Keith Waters *Prime Warden,* Julian Cotterell

GOLDSMITHS *(5)*. *Hall,* Goldsmiths' Hall, Foster Lane, London EC2V 6BN *Livery,* 285. *Clerk,* R. Melly *Prime Warden,* G. Macdonald

MERCHANT TAYLORS *(6/7)*. *Hall,* Merchant Taylors' Hall, 30 Threadneedle Street, London EC2R 8JB *Livery,* 285. *Clerk,* Rear-Adm. Nicholas Harris, CB, MBE *Master,* Johny Armstrong

SKINNERS *(6/7)*. *Hall,* Skinners' Hall, 8 Dowgate Hill, London EC4R 2SP *Livery,* 400. *Clerk,* Maj.-Gen. Brian Plummer, CBE *Master,* Maj.-Gen. John Moore-Bick, CBE

HABERDASHERS *(8)*. *Hall,* Haberdashers' Hall, 18 West Smithfield, London EC1A 9HQ *Livery,* 300. *Clerk,* Rear-Adm. Richard Phillips, CB *Master,* G. Powell (from November 2008, subject to election)

SALTERS *(9)*. *Hall,* Salters' Hall, 4 Fore Street, London EC2Y 5DE *Livery,* 163. *Clerk,* Capt. D. Morris, RN *Master,* George Kirk

IRONMONGERS *(10)*. *Hall,* Ironmongers' Hall, 1 Shaftesbury Place, London EC2Y 8AA *Livery,* 133. *Clerk,* Col. Hamon Massey *Master,* R. Poulton

VINTNERS *(11)*. *Hall,* Vintners' Hall, Upper Thames Street, London EC4V 3BG *Livery,* 312. *Clerk,* Brig. Michael Smyth, OBE *Master,* M. Davies

CLOTHWORKERS *(12)*. *Hall,* Clothworkers' Hall, Dunster Court, Mincing Lane, London EC3R 7AH *Livery,* 228. *Clerk,* Andrew Blessley *Master,* J. West

OTHER CITY GUILDS
In alphabetical order

ACTUARIES *(91)*. 3rd Floor Cheapside House, 138 Cheapside, London EC2V 6BW *Livery,* 224. *Clerk,* David Johnson *Master,* Andrew Benke

AIR PILOTS AND AIR NAVIGATORS *(81)*. *Hall,* Cobham House, 9 Warwick Court, Gray's Inn, London WC1R 5DJ *Livery,* 600. *Clerk,* Paul Tacon *Grand Master,* HRH The Duke of York, KG, KCVO, ADC(P) *Master,* Air Cdre R. Peacock-Edwards, CBE, AFC

APOTHECARIES *(58)*. *Hall,* Apothecaries' Hall, 14 Black Friars Lane, London EC4V 6EJ *Livery,* 1,274. *Clerk,* A. Wallington-Smith *Master,* N. Wood, FRCS

ARBITRATORS *(93)*. 13 Hall Gardens, Colney Heath, St Albans, Herts AL4 0QF *Livery,* 175. *Clerk,* Gaye Duffy *Master,* Michael Stephens

ARMOURERS AND BRASIERS *(22)*. *Hall,* Armourers' Hall, 81 Coleman Street, London EC2R 5BJ *Livery,* 122. *Clerk,* Cdre Christopher Waite *Master,* Jonathan Haw

BAKERS *(19)*. *Hall,* Bakers' Hall, 9 Harp Lane, London EC3R 6DP *Livery,* 300. *Clerk,* John Tompkins *Master,* John Renshaw

BARBERS *(17)*. *Hall,* Barber-Surgeons' Hall, Monkwell Square, Wood Street, London EC2Y 5BL *Livery,* 210. *Clerk,* Col. Peter Durrant, MBE *Master,* A. Lewis

BASKETMAKERS *(52)*. Doric House, 108 Garstang Road West, Poulton le Fylde, Lancashire FY6 7SN *Livery,* 300. *Clerk,* Roger de Pilkyngton *Prime Warden,* Graham Lewinstein

BLACKSMITHS *(40)*. 48 Upwood Road, London SE12 8AN *Livery,* 235. *Clerk,* Christopher Jeal *Prime Warden,* Keith Gabriel

BOWYERS *(38)*. 5 Archer House, Vicarage Crescent, London SW11 3LF *Livery,* 93. *Clerk,* Richard Wilkinson *Master,* P. Marrow

BREWERS *(14)*. *Hall,* Brewers' Hall, Aldermanbury Square, London EC2V 7HR *Livery,* 180. *Clerk,* Brig. D. Ross, CBE *Master,* C. Brain

BRODERERS *(48)*. Ember House, 35–37 Creek Road, East Molesey, Surrey KT8 9BE *Livery*, 140. *Clerk*, Peter Crouch *Master*, William Bartholomew

BUILDERS MERCHANTS *(88)*. 4 College Hill, London EC4R 2RB *Livery*, 202. *Clerk*, T. Statham *Master*, John O' Carroll Bailey

BUTCHERS *(24)*. *Hall*, Butchers' Hall, 87 Bartholomew Close, London EC1A 7EB *Livery*, 633. *Clerk*, Cdre Anthony Morrow, CVO *Master*, Brian Wheatley

CARMEN *(77)*. Five Kings House, 1 Queen Street Place, London EC4R 1QS *Livery*, 500. *Clerk*, Walter Gill *Master*, Graham Westcott

CARPENTERS *(26)*. *Hall*, Carpenters' Hall, 1 Throgmorton Avenue, London EC2N 2JJ *Livery*, 184. *Clerk*, Tim Gregson *Master*, Michael Mathews

CHARTERED ACCOUNTANTS *(86)*. The Rustlings, Valley Close, Studham, Dunstable LU6 2QN *Livery*, 340. *Clerk*, Clifford Bygrave *Master*, Mrs E. Adams

CHARTERED ARCHITECTS *(98)*. 82A Muswell Hill Road, London N10 3JR *Livery*, 135. *Clerk*, David Cole-Adams *Master*, Ian Head

CHARTERED SECRETARIES AND ADMINISTRATORS *(87)*. 3rd Floor, Saddlers' House, 40 Gutter Lane, London EC2V 6BR *Livery*, 261. *Clerk*, Col. Michael Dudding, OBE, TD *Master*, Francis Spencer-Cotton

CHARTERED SURVEYORS *(85)*. 75 Meadway Drive, Horsell, Woking, Surrey GU21 4TF *Livery*, 345. *Clerk*, Amanda Jackson *Master*, Simon Kolesar

CLOCKMAKERS *(61)*. Salters' Hall, 4 Fore Street, London EC2Y 5DE *Livery*, 285. *Clerk*, Joe Buxton *Master*, Michael Sanderson, PHD

COACHMAKERS AND COACH-HARNESS MAKERS *(72)*. Elm Tree Cottage, Bottom House Farm Lane, Chalfont St Giles, Buckinghamshire HP8 4EE *Livery*, 400. *Clerk*, Gp Capt. Gerry Bunn, CBE *Master*, Michael Davis

CONSTRUCTORS *(99)*. Forge Farmhouse, Glassenbury, Cranbrook, Kent TN17 2QE *Livery*, 160. *Clerk*, Tim Nicholson *Master*, Roger Adcock

COOKS *(35)*. Coombe Ridge, Thursley Road, Churt, Farnham, Surrey GU10 2LQ *Livery*, 76. *Clerk*, Michael Thatcher, LLB *Master*, Hugh Thornton

COOPERS *(36)*. *Hall*, Coopers' Hall, 13 Devonshire Square, London EC2M 4TH *Livery*, 260. *Clerk*, Lt.-Col. Adrian Carroll *Master*, Hon. Judge B. Barker, QC

CORDWAINERS *(27)*. Clothworkers' Hall, Dunster Court, Mincing Lane, London EC3R 7AH *Livery*, 168. *Clerk*, John Miller *Master*, Richard Williams

CURRIERS *(29)*. Hedgerley, 10 The Leaze, Ashton Keynes, Wiltshire SN6 6PE *Livery*, 93. *Clerk*, Gp Capt. David Moss *Master*, Philip Linnell

CUTLERS *(18)*. *Hall*, Cutlers' Hall, Warwick Lane, London EC4M 7BR *Livery*, 100. *Clerk*, J. Allen *Master*, J. Pedder

DISTILLERS *(69)*. 1 The Sanctuary, Westminster, London SW1P 3JT *Livery*, 260. *Clerk*, C. Hughes *Master*, Derek Plant

DYERS *(13)*. *Hall*, Dyers' Hall, 10 Dowgate Hill, London EC4R 2ST *Livery*, 136. *Clerk*, Russell Vaizey *Prime Warden*, Ian Blair

ENGINEERS *(94)*. Wax Chandlers' Hall, 6 Gresham Street, London EC2V 7AD *Livery*, 340. *Clerk*, Air Vice-Marshal Graham Skinner, CBE *Master*, Anthony Roche, FRENG

ENVIRONMENTAL CLEANERS *(97)*. 6 Grange Meadows, Elmswell, Bury St Edmunds, Suffolk IP30 9GE *Livery*, 280. *Clerk*, Michael Bizley *Master*, Kenneth Marriott

FAN MAKERS *(76)*. Skinners' Hall, 8 Dowgate Hill, London EC4R 2SP *Livery*, 202. *Clerk*, Keith Patterson *Master*, W. Bryen

FARMERS *(80)*. *Hall*, The Farmers' and Fletchers' Hall, 3 Cloth Street, London EC1A 7LD *Livery*, 300. *Clerk*, Col. David King, OBE *Master*, Tom Copas

FARRIERS *(55)*. 19 Queen Street, Chipperfield, Kings Langley, Herts WD4 9BT *Livery*, 330. *Clerk*, Charlotte Clifford *Master*, C. Bettison

FELTMAKERS *(63)*. Post Cottage,Greywell, Hook, Hampshire RG29 1DA *Livery*, 171. *Clerk*, Maj. J. Coombs *Master*, N. Heal

FIREFIGHTERS *(103)*. The Insurance Hall, 20 Aldermanbury, London EC2V 7HY *Livery*, 80. *Clerk*, Martin Bonham *Master*, James Blott

FLETCHERS *(39)*. *Hall*, The Farmers' and Fletchers' Hall, 3 Cloth Street, London EC1A 7LD *Livery*, 143. *Clerk*, Capt. Michael Johnson, RN *Master*, Ian MacLellan

FOUNDERS *(33)*. *Hall*, Founders' Hall, 1 Cloth Fair, London EC1A 7JQ *Livery*, 155. *Clerk*, A. Gillett *Master*, R. Sichel

FRAMEWORK KNITTERS *(64)*. 86 Park Drive, Upminster, Essex RM14 3AS *Livery*, 215. *Clerk*, Alan Clark *Master*, Anthony Turner

FRUITERERS *(45)*. Chapelstones, 84 High Street, Codford St Mary, Warminster BA12 0ND *Livery*, 283. *Clerk*, Lt.-Col. L. French *Master*, E. Fraunfelter

FUELLERS *(95)*. 26 Merrick Square, London SE1 4JB *Livery*, 125. *Clerk*, Sir Anthony Reardon Smith, Bt. *Master*, Michael Husband

FURNITURE MAKERS *(83)*. *Hall*, Furniture Makers' Hall, 12 Austin Friars, London EC2N 2HE *Livery*, 284. *Clerk*, Mrs J. Wright *Master*, Ms M. Miller

GARDENERS *(66)*. 25 Luke Street, London EC2A 4AR *Livery*, 285. *Clerk*, Trevor Hines *Master*, Christine Cohen, OBE

GIRDLERS *(23)*. *Hall*, Girdlers' Hall, Basinghall Avenue, London EC2V 5DD *Livery*, 80. *Clerk*, Brig. I. Rees *Master*, I. Seaton

GLASS SELLERS *(71)*. 57 Witley Court, Coram Street, London WC1N 1HD *Livery*, 230. *Clerk*, Col. Audrey Smith *Master*, Robin Arculus

GLAZIERS AND PAINTERS OF GLASS *(53)*. *Hall*, Glaziers' Hall, 9 Montague Close, London SE1 9DD *Livery*, 270. *Clerk*, Alex Galloway, CVO *Master*, P. Doe

GLOVERS *(62)*. Oscar Court, 17A Tite Street, London SW3 4JR *Livery*, 250. *Clerk*, Carole Blackshaw *Master*, John Brown, CBE

GOLD AND SILVER WYRE DRAWERS *(74)*. Middleton House, Winterslow, Salisbury, Wiltshire SP5 1QR *Livery*, 305. *Clerk*, Cdr. R. House, RN *Master*, Timothy Waller

GUNMAKERS *(73)*. The Proof House, 48–50 Commercial Road, London E1 1LP *Livery*, 320. *Clerk*, Col. W. Chesshyre *Master*, C. Purdey

HACKNEY CARRIAGE DRIVERS *(104)*. 25 The Grove, Parkfield, Latimer, Buckinghamshire HP5 1UE *Livery*, 103. *Clerk*, Mary Whitworth *Master*, Andrew Overton

HORNERS *(54)*. c/o Clergy House, Hide Place, London SW1P 4NJ *Livery*, 225. *Clerk*, Raymond Layard *Master*, Michael Hart

INFORMATION TECHNOLOGISTS *(100)*. *Hall*, Information Technologists' Hall, 39A Bartholomew Close, London EC1A 7JN *Livery*, 287. *Clerk*, Michael Grant *Master*, David Morriss

INNHOLDERS *(32)*. *Hall*, Innholders' Hall, 30 College Street, London EC4R 2RH *Livery*, 154. *Clerk*, Dougal Bulger *Master*, Jeremy Pope, OBE

INSURERS *(92)*. The Hall, 20 Aldermanbury, London EC2V 7HY *Livery*, 380. *Clerk*, L. Walters *Master*, Michael Cooper-Mitchell

INTERNATIONAL BANKERS *(106)*. 12 Austin Friars, London EC2N 2HE *Livery*, 145. *Clerk*, Wg Cdr Tim Woods, BEM *Master*, Henry Angest

JOINERS AND CEILERS *(41)*. 75 Meadway Drive, Horsell, Woking, Surrey GU21 4TF *Livery*, 128. *Clerk*, Amanda Jackson *Master*, David Spencer-Phillips

LAUNDERERS *(89)*. *Hall*, Launderers' Hall, 9 Montague Close, London Bridge, London SE1 9DD *Livery*, 240. *Clerk*, Mrs J. Polek *Master*, Paul Woolfenden

LEATHERSELLERS *(15)*. *Hall*, Leathersellers' Hall, 15 St Helen's Place, London EC3A 6DQ *Livery*, 150. *Clerk*, Jonathan Cooke *Master*, Michael Binyon

LIGHTMONGERS *(96)*. Crown Wharf, 11A Coldharbour, Blackwall Reach, London E14 9NS *Livery*, 185. *Clerk*, Derek Wheatley *Master*, David Rowden

LORINERS *(57)*. Hampton House, High Street, East Grinstead, West Sussex RH19 3AW *Livery*, 344. *Clerk*, Peter Lusty *Master*, Christopher Giles

MAKERS OF PLAYING CARDS *(75)*. 256 St Davids Square, London E14 3WE *Livery*, 146. *Clerk*, David Barrett *Master*, Alderman J. White

MANAGEMENT CONSULTANTS *(105)*. Copperfield, The Ridgeway, Cranleigh GU6 7HR *Livery*, 148. *Clerk*, Lt.-Col. Dennis Hall *Master*, William Barnard

MARKETORS *(90)*. 13 Hall Gardens, Colney Heath, St Albans, Herts AL4 0QF *Livery*, 298. *Clerk*, Mrs G. Duffy *Master*, John Asher

MASONS *(30)*. 22 Cannon Hill, Southgate, London N14 6LG *Livery*, 160. *Clerk*, P. Clark *Master*, Fr. D. Mottershead

MASTER MARINERS *(78)*. *Hall*, HQS Wellington, Temple Stairs, Victoria Embankment, London WC2R 2PN *Livery*, 197. *Clerk*, Cdr. Rod Craig, RN *Master*, Capt. A. Davies

MUSICIANS *(50)*. 6th Floor, 2 London Wall Building, London EC2M 5PP *Livery*, 385. *Clerk*, Margaret Alford *Master*, Petronella Burnett-Brown

NEEDLEMAKERS *(65)*. PO Box 3682, Windsor, Berkshire SL4 3WR *Livery*, 200. *Clerk*, Philip Grant *Master*, Michael Cook

PAINTER-STAINERS *(28)*. *Hall*, Painters' Hall, 9 Little Trinity Lane, London EC4V 2AD *Livery*, 320. *Clerk*, Christopher Twyman *Master*, Richard Martin

PATTENMAKERS *(70)*. 3 The High Street, Sutton Valence, Kent ME17 3AG *Livery*, 200. *Clerk*, Col. R. Murfin, TD *Master*, Tim Watts

PAVIORS *(56)*. 3 Ridgemount Gardens, Enfield, Middx EN2 8QL *Livery*, 275. *Clerk*, John White *Master*, Christopher Laing

PEWTERERS *(16)*. *Hall*, Pewterers' Hall, Oat Lane, London EC2V 7DE *Livery*, 80. *Clerk*, Capt. Paddy Watson, RN *Master*, Christopher Peacock

PLAISTERERS *(46)*. *Hall*, Plaisterers' Hall, 1 London Wall, London EC2Y 5JU *Livery*, 210. *Clerk*, Hilary Machtus *Master*, Reginald Denby

PLUMBERS *(31)*. Wax Chandlers' Hall, 6 Gresham Street, London EC2V 7AD *Livery*, 360. *Clerk*, Lt.-Col. Anthony Paterson-Fox *Master*, Prof. R. Cartwright

POULTERS *(34)*. The Old Butchers, Station Road, Groombridge, Kent TN3 9QX *Livery*, 204. *Clerk*, Gwen Butcher *Master*, Alexander Glenny

SADDLERS *(25)*. *Hall*, Saddlers' Hall, 40 Gutter Lane, London EC2V 6BR *Livery*, 75. *Clerk*, Col. N. Lithgow, CBE *Master*, J. Godrich

SCIENTIFIC INSTRUMENT MAKERS *(84)*. 9 Montague Close, London SE1 9DD *Livery*, 210. *Clerk*, Neville Watson *Master*, Brian Lowings

SCRIVENERS *(44)*. HQS Wellington, Temple Stairs, Victoria Embankment, London WC2R 2PN *Livery*, 200. *Clerk*, Paul Elliott *Master*, William Kennair

SECURITY PROFESSIONALS *(108)*. 1 Wallis Mews, Guildford Road, Leatherhead, Surrey KT22 9DQ *Livery*, 292. *Clerk*, John Maddock *Master*, Simon Imbert

SHIPWRIGHTS *(59)*. Ironmongers Hall, Barbican, London EC2Y 8AA *Livery*, 446. *Clerk*, Rear-Adm. Derek Anthony, MBE *Prime Warden*, George Greenwood

SOLICITORS *(79)*. 4 College Hill, London EC4R 2RB *Livery*, 350. *Clerk*, Neil Cameron *Master*, Alexandra Marks

SPECTACLE MAKERS *(60)*. Apothecaries' Hall, Black Friars Lane, London EC4V 6EL *Livery*, 380. *Clerk*, Lt.-Col. John Salmon, OBE *Master*, J. Fried

STATIONERS AND NEWSPAPER MAKERS *(47)*. *Hall*, Stationers' Hall, Ave Maria Lane, London EC4M 7DD *Livery*, 454. *Clerk*, Brig. D. Sharp, AFC *Master*, N. Osborne

TALLOW CHANDLERS *(21)*. *Hall*, Tallow Chandlers' Hall, 4 Dowgate Hill, London EC4R 2SH *Livery*, 179. *Clerk*, Brig. R. Wilde, CBE *Master*, A. Travis

TAX ADVISERS *(107)*. 191 West End Road, Ruislip, Middlesex HA4 6LD *Freemen*, 129. *Clerk*, Paul Herbage *Master*, Richard Agutter

TIN PLATE WORKERS (ALIAS WIRE WORKERS) *(67)*. Highbanks, Ferry Road, Surlingham, Norwich, Norfolk NR14 7AR *Livery*, 220. *Clerk*, Michael Henderson-Begg *Master*, Roger Smaridge

TOBACCO PIPE MAKERS AND TOBACCO BLENDERS *(82)*. Green Meadow Island, Steep, Hampshire GU32 1AE *Livery*, 150. *Clerk*, Barbara Hines *Master*, Nigel Rich, CBE

TURNERS *(51)*. 182 Temple Chambers, Temple Avenue, London EC4Y 0HP *Livery*, 183. *Clerk*, Edward Windsor Clive *Master*, Col. R. Lucas

TYLERS AND BRICKLAYERS *(37)*. 30 Shelley Avenue, Tiptree CO5 0SF *Livery*, 151. *Clerk*, Barry Blumson *Master*, Ian Grimshaw

UPHOLDERS *(49)*. Hall in the Wood, 46 Quail Gardens, Selsdon Vale, Croydon CR2 8TF *Livery*, 213. *Clerk*, Jean Cody *Master*, Richard Nevard

WATER CONSERVATORS *(102)*. The Lark, 2 Bell Lane, Worlington, Bury St Edmunds, Suffolk IP28 8SE *Livery*, 210. *Clerk*, Ralph Riley *Master*, Prof. Lorna Walker

WAX CHANDLERS *(20)*. *Hall*, Wax Chandlers' Hall, 6 Gresham Street, London EC2V 7AD *Livery*, 130. *Clerk*, Richard Percival *Master*, Fianne Stanford

WEAVERS *(42)*. Saddlers' House, Gutter Lane, London EC2V 6BR *Livery*, 125. *Clerk*, John Snowdon *Upper Bailiff*, Freda Newcombe

WHEELWRIGHTS *(68)*. 7 Glengall Road, Bexleyheath, Kent DA7 4AL *Livery*, 218. *Clerk*, Brian François *Master*, David Wernick

WOOLMEN *(43)*. The Old Post Office, 56 Lower Way, Great Brickhill, Bucks MK17 9AG *Livery*, 141. *Clerk*, Gillian Wilson *Master*, Richard Hollis

WORLD TRADERS *(101)*. 13 Hall Gardens, Colney Heath, St. Albans, Hertfordshire AL4 0QF *Livery*, 210. *Clerk*, Mrs Gaye Duffy *Master*, Baroness Garden of Frognal

PARISH CLERKS *(No Livery*)*. Acreholt, 33 Medstead Road, Beech, Alton, Hampshire GU34 4AD *Members*, 95. *Clerk*, Lt.-Col. Brian Coombes *Master*, P. Kennerley

WATERMEN AND LIGHTERMEN *(No Livery*)*. *Hall*, Watermen's Hall, 16 St Mary-at-Hill, London EC3R 8EF *Craft Owning Freemen*, 408. *Clerk*, Colin Middlemiss *Master*, Richard Goddard

* Parish Clerks and Watermen and Lightermen have requested to remain with no livery

LONDON BOROUGH COUNCILS

Council	*Telephone*	*Population**	*Council Tax†*	*Chief Executive*
Barking and Dagenham	020-8592 4500	165,700	£1,326	Robert Whiteman
Barnet	020-8359 2000	328,600	£1,393	Leo Boland
Bexley	020-8303 7777	221,600	£1,399	Will Tuckley
Brent	020-8937 1234	271,400	£1,343	Gareth Daniel
Bromley	020-8464 3333	299,100	£1,263	Doug Patterson
Camden	020-7278 4444	227,500	£1,332	Moira Gibb, CBE
CITY OF LONDON CORPORATION	020-7606 3030	7,800	£923	Chris Duffield
Croydon	020-8686 4433	337,000	£1,406	Jon Rouse
Ealing	020-8825 5000	306,400	£1,370	Darra Singh
Enfield	020-8379 1000	285,300	£1,384	Rob Leak
Greenwich	020-8854 8888	222,600	£1,291	Mary Ney
Hackney	020-8356 5000	208,400	£1,308	Tim Shields
Hammersmith and Fulham	020-8748 3020	171,400	£1,173	Geoff Alltimes
Haringey	020-8489 0000	225,700	£1,471	Ita O'Donovan
Harrow	020-8863 5611	214,600	£1,462	Michael Lockwood
Havering	01708-434343	227,300	£1,483	Cheryl Coppell
Hillingdon	01895-250111	250,000	£1,423	Hugh Dunnachie *(acting)*
Hounslow	020-8583 2000	218,600	£1,400	Mark Gilks
Islington	020-7527 2000	185,500	£1,248	John Foster
Kensington and Chelsea	020-7937 5464	178,000	£1,068	Derek Myers
Kingston upon Thames	020-8547 5757	155,900	£1,580	Bruce McDonald
Lambeth	020-7926 1000	272,000	£1,235	Derrick Anderson
Lewisham	020-8314 6000	255,700	£1,327	Barry Quirk, CBE
Merton	020-8543 2222	197,700	£1,405	Ged Curran
Newham	020-8430 2000	248,400	£1,255	Joe Duckworth
Redbridge	020-8554 5000	251,900	£1,376	Roger Hampson
Richmond upon Thames	020-8891 1411	179,500	£1,544	Gillian Norton
Southwark	020-7525 5000	269,200	£1,222	Nicola Stanton
Sutton	020-8770 5000	184,400	£1,419	Paul Martin
Tower Hamlets	020-7364 5000	212,800	£1,175	Martin Smith
Waltham Forest	020-8496 3000	221,700	£1,441	Andrew Kilburn
Wandsworth	020-8871 6000	279,000	£687	Gerald Jones
WESTMINSTER	020-7641 6000	231,900	£688	Mike Moore

* *Source:* ONS – *Mid-2006 Population Estimates* (Crown copyright)
† Average Band D council tax bill for 2008–9
Councils in CAPITAL LETTERS have city status

WALES

Cymru

The principality of Wales (Cymru) occupies the extreme west of the central southern portion of the island of Great Britain, with a total area of 20,778 sq. km (8,022 sq. miles): land 20,733 sq. km (8,005 sq. miles); inland water 45 sq. km (17 sq. miles). It is bordered in the north by the Irish Sea, in the south by the Bristol Channel, in the east by the English counties of Cheshire West and Chester, Shropshire, Herefordshire and Gloucestershire, and in the west by St George's Channel.

Across the Menai Straits is Ynys Mon (Isle of Anglesey) (715 sq. km/276 sq. miles), communication with which is facilitated by the Menai Suspension Bridge (305m/1,000ft long) built by Telford in 1826, and by the Britannia Bridge (351m/1,151ft), a two-tier road and rail truss arch design, rebuilt in 1972 after a fire destroyed the original tubular railway bridge built by Stephenson in 1850. Holyhead harbour, on Holy Isle (north-west of Anglesey), provides ferry services to Dublin (113km/70 miles).

POPULATION

The population at the 2001 census was 2,903,085 (men 1,403,782; women 1,499,303). The average density of population in 2001 was 140 persons per sq. km (362 per sq. mile).

RELIEF

Wales is a country of extensive tracts of high plateau and shorter stretches of mountain ranges deeply dissected by river valleys. Lower-lying ground is largely confined to the coastal belt and the lower parts of the valleys. The highest mountains are those of Snowdonia in the north west (Snowdon, 1,085m/3,559ft), Berwyn (Aran Fawddwy, 906m/2,971ft), Cader Idris (Pen y Gadair, 892m/2,928ft), Dyfed (Plynlimon, 752m/2,467ft), and the Black Mountains, Brecon Beacons and Black Forest ranges in the south-east (Pen y Fan, 886m/2,906ft; Waun Fâch, 811m/2,660ft; Carmarthen Van, 802m/2,630ft).

HYDROGRAPHY

The principal river in Wales is the Severn, which flows from the slopes of Plynlimon to the English border. The Wye (209km/130 miles) also rises in the slopes of Plynlimon. The Usk (90km/56 miles) flows into the Bristol Channel through Gwent. The Dee (113km/70 miles) rises in Bala Lake and flows through the Vale of Llangollen, where an aqueduct (built by Telford in 1805) carries the Pontcysyllte branch of the Shropshire Union Canal across the valley. The estuary of the Dee is the navigable portion, it is 23km (14 miles) in length and about 8km (5 miles) in breadth. The Towy (109km/68 miles), Teifi (80km/50 miles), Taff (64km/40 miles), Dovey (48km/30 miles), Taf (40km/25 miles) and Conway (39km/24 miles) are wholly Welsh rivers.

The largest natural lake is Bala (Llyn Tegid) in Gwynedd, nearly 7km (4 miles) long and 1.6km (1 mile) wide. Lake Vyrnwy is an artificial reservoir, about the size of Bala, it forms the water supply of Liverpool; Birmingham's water is supplied from reservoirs in the Elan and Claerwen valleys.

WELSH LANGUAGE

According to the 2001 census results, the percentage of people aged three years and over who are able to speak Welsh is:

Blaenau Gwent	9.1	Neath Port Talbot	17.8
Bridgend	10.6	Newport	9.6
Caerphilly	10.9	Pembrokeshire	21.5
Cardiff	10.9	Powys	20.8
Carmarthenshire	50.1	Rhondda Cynon Taf	12.3
Ceredigion	51.8	Swansea	13.2
Conwy	29.2	Torfaen	10.7
Denbighshire	26.1	Vale of Glamorgan	11.1
Flintshire	14.1	Wrexham	14.4
Gwynedd	68.7	Ynys Mon (Isle of Anglesey)	59.8
Merthyr Tydfil	10.0		
Monmouthshire	9.0	*Total in Wales*	20.5

FLAG

The flag of Wales, the Red Dragon (Y Ddraig Goch), is a red dragon on a field divided white over green (per fess argent and vert a dragon passant gules). The flag was augmented in 1953 by a royal badge on a shield encircled with a riband bearing the words *Ddraig Goch Ddyry Cychwyn* and imperially crowned, but this augmented flag is rarely used.

EARLY HISTORY

The earliest inhabitants of whom there is any record appear to have been subdued or exterminated by the Goidels (a people of Celtic race) in the Bronze Age. A further invasion of Celtic Brythons and Belgae followed in the ensuing Iron Age. The Roman conquest of southern Britain and Wales was for some time successfully opposed by Caratacus (Caractacus or Caradog), chieftain of the Catuvellauni and son of Cunobelinus (Cymbeline). South-east Wales was subjugated and the legionary fortress at Caerleon-on-Usk established by around AD 75–7; the conquest of Wales was completed by Agricola around AD 78. Communications were opened up by the construction of military roads from Chester to Caerleon-on-Usk and Caerwent, and from Chester to Conwy (and thence to Carmarthen and Neath). Christianity was introduced in the fourth century, during the Roman occupation.

ANGLO-SAXON ATTACKS

The Anglo-Saxon invaders of southern Britain drove the Celts into the mountain stronghold of Wales, and into Strathclyde (Cumberland and south-west Scotland) and Cornwall, giving them the name of *Waelisc* (Welsh), meaning 'foreign'. The West Saxons' victory of Deorham (AD 577) isolated Wales from Cornwall and the battle of Chester (AD 613) cut off communication with Strathclyde and northern Britain. In the eighth century the boundaries of the Welsh were further restricted by the annexations of Offa, King of Mercia, and counter-attacks were largely prevented by the construction of an artificial boundary from the Dee to the Wye (Offa's Dyke).

In the ninth century Rhodri Mawr (844–878) united the country and successfully resisted further incursions of the Saxons by land and raids of Norse and Danish pirates by sea, but at his death his three provinces of Gwynedd (north), Powys (central) and Deheubarth (south) were divided among his three sons, Anarawd, Mervyn and Cadell. Cadell's son Hywel Dda ruled a large part of Wales and codified its laws but the provinces were not united again until the rule of Llewelyn ap Seisyllt (husband of the heiress of Gwynedd) from 1018 to 1023.

THE NORMAN CONQUEST

After the Norman conquest of England, William I created palatine counties along the Welsh frontier, and the Norman barons began to make encroachments into Welsh territory. The Welsh princes recovered many of their losses during the civil wars of Stephen's reign (1135–54), and in the early 13th century Owen Gruffydd, prince of Gwynedd, was the dominant figure in Wales. Under Llywelyn ap Iorwerth (1194–1240) the Welsh united in powerful resistance to English incursions and Llywelyn's privileges and *de facto* independence were recognised in the Magna Carta. His grandson, Llywelyn ap Gruffydd, was the last native prince; he was killed in 1282 during hostilities between the Welsh and English, allowing Edward I of England to establish his authority over the country. On 7 February 1301, Edward of Caernarvon, son of Edward I, was created Prince of Wales, a title subsequently borne by the eldest son of the sovereign.

Strong Welsh national feeling continued, expressed in the early 15th century in the rising led by Owain Glyndwr, but the situation was altered by the accession to the English throne in 1485 of Henry VII of the Welsh House of Tudor. Wales was politically annexed by England under the Act of Union of 1535, which extended English laws to the principality and gave it parliamentary representation for the first time.

EISTEDDFOD

The Welsh are a distinct nation, with a language and literature of their own; the national bardic festival (Eisteddfod), instituted by Prince Rhys ap Griffith in 1176, is still held annually.

PRINCIPAL CITIES

There are five cities in Wales (with date city status conferred): Bangor (pre-1900), Cardiff (1905), Newport (2002), St David's (1994) and Swansea (1969).

Cardiff and Swansea have also been granted Lord Mayoralities.

CARDIFF

Cardiff, at the mouth of the rivers Taff, Rhymney and Ely, is the capital city of Wales and at the 2001 census had a population of 305,353. The city has changed dramatically in recent years following the regeneration of Cardiff Bay and construction of a barrage, which has created a permanent freshwater lake and waterfront for the city. As the capital city, Cardiff is home to the National Assembly for Wales and is a major administrative, retail, business and cultural centre.

The city is home to many fine buildings including the City Hall, Cardiff Castle, Llandaff Cathedral, the National Museum of Wales, university buildings, law courts and the Temple of Peace and Health. The Millennium Stadium opened in 1999 and has hosted FA Cup finals and other high-profile English football matches since 2001.

SWANSEA

Swansea *(Abertawe)* is a seaport with a population of 223,293 at the 2001 census. The Gower peninsula was brought within the city boundary under local government reform in 1974.

The principal buildings are the Norman Castle (rebuilt *c*.1330), the Royal Institution of South Wales, founded in 1835 (including library), the University of Wales Swansea at Singleton and the Guildhall, containing Frank Brangwyn's British Empire panels. The Dylan Thomas Centre, formerly the old Guildhall, was restored in 1995. More recent buildings include the County Hall, the Maritime Quarter Marina, the Wales National Pool and the National Waterfront Museum.

Swansea was chartered by the Earl of Warwick (1158–84), and further charters were granted by King John, Henry III, Edward II, Edward III and James II, Oliver Cromwell and the Marcher Lord William de Breos. It was formally invested with city status in 1969 by HRH The Prince of Wales.

LORD-LIEUTENANTS AND HIGH SHERIFFS

Area	*Lord-Lieutenant*	*High Sheriff (2008–9)*
Clwyd	T. Jones, CBE	Stephen Cheshire
Dyfed	Hon. Robin Lewis, OBE	Claire Lewis
Gwent	S. Boyle	Judith Child
Gwynedd	Gruffydd Daniel	Peter Rogers
Mid Glamorgan	Kate Thomas	Anne Morgan
Powys	Hon. Mrs E. Legge-Bourke, LVO	Thomas Davis
S. Glamorgan	Dr Peter Beck, MD, FRCP	Brian Rees, OBE
W. Glamorgan	D. Byron Lewis	Pamela Spender

LOCAL COUNCILS

Council	*Administrative Headquarters*	*Telephone*	*Population**	*Council Tax†*	*Chief Executive*
Blaenau Gwent	Ebbw Vale	01495-350555	69,300	£1,264	Robin Morrison
Bridgend	Bridgend	01656-643643	132,600	£1,128	Dr Jo Farrar
Caerphilly	Hengoed	01443-815588	171,300	£1,029	Stewart Rosser
CARDIFF CITY	Cardiff	029-2087 2000	317,500	£984	Byron Davies
Carmarthenshire	Carmarthen	01267-234567	178,000	£1,074	Mark James
Ceredigion	Aberaeron	01545-570881	77,200	£1,017	Bronwen Morgan
Conwy	Conwy	01492-574000	111,300	£960	Derek Barker
Denbighshire	Ruthin	01824-706000	96,100	£1,162	Ian Miller
Flintshire	Mold	01352-752121	150,100	£1,043	Colin Everett
Gwynedd	Caernarfon	01286-672255	118,300	£1,102	Harry Thomas
Merthyr Tydfil	Merthyr Tydfil	01685-725000	55,500	£1,203	Alistair Neill
Monmouthshire	Cwmbran	01633-644644	87,900	£1,091	Colin Berg
Neath Port Talbot	Port Talbot	01639-763333	137,100	£1,243	Ken Sawyers
NEWPORT CITY	Newport	01633-656656	140,100	£886	Chris Freegard
Pembrokeshire	Haverfordwest	01437-764551	117,300	£829	Bryn Parry-Jones
Powys	Llandrindod Wells	01597-826000	131,100	£1,023	Mark Kerr
Rhondda Cynon Taff	Tonypandy	01443-424000	233,900	£1,157	Keith Griffiths
SWANSEA CITY	Swansea	01792-636000	227,100	£1,027	Paul Smith
Torfaen	Pontypool	01495-762200	91,000	£1,070	Alison Ward
Vale of Glamorgan	Barry	01446-700111	123,300	£1,003	John Maitland-Evans
Wrexham	Wrexham	01978-292000	131,000	£1,035	Isobel Garner
Ynys Mon (Isle of Anglesey)	Ynys Mon	01248-750057	68,900	£980	Derrick Jones

* *Source:* ONS – *Mid-2006 Population Estimates* (Crown copyright)
† Average Band D council tax bill 2008–9
Councils in CAPITAL LETTERS have city status

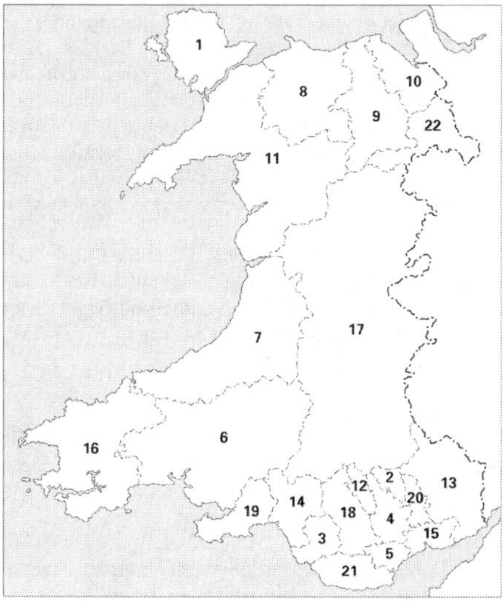

Key	*Council*	*Key*	*Council*
1	Anglesey (Ynys Mon)	12	Merthyr Tydfil
2	Blaenau Gwent	13	Monmouthshire
3	Bridgend	14	Neath Port Talbot
4	Caerphilly	15	Newport
5	Cardiff	16	Pembrokeshire
6	Carmarthenshire	17	Powys
7	Ceredigion	18	Rhondda, Cynon, Taff
8	Conwy	19	Swansea
9	Denbighshire	20	Torfaen
10	Flintshire	21	Vale of Glamorgan
11	Gwynedd	22	Wrexham

SCOTLAND

The Kingdom of Scotland occupies the northern portion of the main island of Great Britain and includes the Inner and Outer Hebrides, Orkney, Shetland and many other islands. It lies between 60° 51′ 30″ and 54° 38′ N. latitude and between 1° 45′ 32″ and 6° 14′ W. longitude, with England to the south, the Atlantic Ocean on the north and west, and the North Sea on the east.

The greatest length of the mainland (Cape Wrath to the Mull of Galloway) is 441km (274 miles), and the greatest breadth (Buchan Ness to Applecross) is 248km (154 miles). The customary measurement of the island of Great Britain is from the site of John o' Groats house, near Duncansby Head, Caithness, to Land's End, Cornwall, a total distance of 970km (603 miles) in a straight line and approximately 1,448km (900 miles) by road.

The total area of Scotland is 78,807 sq. km (30,427 sq. miles): land 77,907 sq. km (30,080 sq. miles), inland water 900 sq. km (347 sq. miles).

POPULATION

The population at the 2001 census was 5,062,011 (men 2,432,494; women 2,629,517). The average density of the population in 2001 was 64 persons per sq. km (166 per sq. mile).

RELIEF

There are three natural orographic divisions of Scotland. The southern uplands have their highest points in Merrick (843m/2,766ft), Rhinns of Kells (814m/2,669ft) and Cairnsmuir of Carsphairn (797m/2,614ft), in the west; and the Tweedsmuir Hills in the east (Broad Law 840m/2,756ft; Dollar Law 817m/2,682ft; Hartfell 808m/2,651ft).

The central lowlands, formed by the valleys of the Clyde, Forth and Tay, divide the southern uplands from the northern Highlands, which extend almost from the extreme north of the mainland to the central lowlands, and are divided into a northern and a southern system by the Great Glen.

The Grampian Mountains, which entirely cover the southern Highland area, include in the west Ben Nevis (1,343m/4,406ft), the highest point in the British Isles, and in the east the Cairngorm Mountains (Ben Macdui 1,309m/4,296ft; Braeriach 1,295m/4,248ft; Cairn Gorm 1,245m/4,084ft). The north-western Highland area contains the mountains of Wester and Easter Ross (Carn Eige 1,183m/3,880ft; Sgurr na Lapaich 1,151m/3,775ft).

Created, like the central lowlands, by a major geological fault, the Great Glen (97km/60 miles long) runs between Inverness and Fort William, and contains Loch Ness, Loch Oich and Loch Lochy. These are linked to each other and to the north-east and south-west coasts of Scotland by the Caledonian Canal, providing a navigable passage between the Moray Firth and the Inner Hebrides.

HYDROGRAPHY

The western coast is fragmented by peninsulas and islands, and indented by fjords (sea-lochs), the longest of which is Loch Fyne (68km/42 miles long) in Argyll. Although the east coast tends to be less fractured and lower, there are several great drowned inlets (firths), eg Firth of Forth, Firth of Tay and Moray Firth, as well as the Firth of Clyde in the west.

The lochs are the principal hydrographic feature. The largest in Scotland and in Britain is Loch Lomond (70 sq. km/27 sq. miles), in the Grampian valleys and the longest and deepest is Loch Ness (39km/24 miles long and 244m/800ft deep), in the Great Glen.

The longest river is the Tay (188km/117 miles), noted for its salmon. It flows into the North Sea, with Dundee on the estuary, which is spanned by the Tay Bridge (3,136m/10,289ft) opened in 1887 and the Tay Road Bridge (2,245m/7,365ft) opened in 1966. Other noted salmon rivers are the Dee (145km/90 miles) which flows into the North Sea at Aberdeen, and the Spey (177km/110 miles), the swiftest flowing river in the British Isles, which flows into Moray Firth. The Tweed, which gave its name to the woollen cloth produced along its banks, marks in the lower stretches of its 154km (96 mile) course the border between Scotland and England.

The most important river commercially is the Clyde (171km/106 miles), formed by the junction of the Daer and Portrail water, which flows through the city of Glasgow to the Firth of Clyde. During its course it passes over the picturesque Falls of Clyde, Bonnington Linn (9m/30ft), Corra Linn (26m/84ft), Dundaff Linn (3m/10ft) and Stonebyres Linn (24m/80ft), above and below Lanark. The Forth (106km/66 miles), upon which stands Edinburgh, the capital, is spanned by the Forth Railway Bridge (1890), which is 1,625m (5,330ft) long, and the Forth Road Bridge (1964), which has a total length of 1,876m (6,156ft) (over water) and a single span of 914m (3,000ft).

The highest waterfall in Scotland, and the British Isles, is Eas a'Chùal Aluinn with a total height of 201m (658ft), which falls from Glas Bheinn in Sutherland. The Falls of Glomach, on a head-stream of the Elchaig in Wester Ross, have a drop of 113m (370ft).

GAELIC LANGUAGE

According to the 2001 census, 1.2 per cent of the population of Scotland, mainly in Eilean Siar (Western Isles), were able to speak the Scottish form of Gaelic.

LOWLAND SCOTTISH LANGUAGE

Several regional lowland Scottish dialects, known variously as Scots, Scotch, Lallans or Doric, are widely spoken. The General Register Office (Scotland) estimated in 1996 that 1.5 million people, or 30 per cent of the population, are Scots speakers. A question on Scots was not included in the 2001 census.

FLAG

The flag of Scotland is known as the Saltire. It is a white diagonal cross on a blue field (saltire argent in a field azure) and represents St Andrew, the patron saint of Scotland.

THE SCOTTISH ISLANDS

ORKNEY

The Orkney Islands (total area 972 sq. km/376 sq. miles) lie about ten km (six miles) north of the mainland, separated from it by the Pentland Firth. Of the 90 islands and islets (holms and skerries) in the group, about one-third are inhabited.

The total population at the 2001 census was 19,245; the 2001 populations of the islands shown here include those of smaller islands forming part of the same council district.

Mainland, 15,339	Rousay, 267
Burray, 357	Sanday, 478
Eday, 121	Shapinsay, 300
Flotta, 81	South Ronaldsay, 854
Hoy, 392	Stronsay, 358
North Ronaldsay, 70	Westray, 563
Papa Westray, 65	

The islands are rich in prehistoric and Scandinavian remains, the most notable being the Stone Age village of Skara Brae, the burial chamber of Maes Howe, the many brochs (towers) and the 12th-century St Magnus Cathedral. Scapa Flow, between the Mainland and Hoy, was the war station of the British Grand Fleet from 1914 to 1919 and the scene of the scuttling of the surrendered German High Seas Fleet (21 June 1919).

Most of the islands are low-lying and fertile, and farming (principally beef cattle) is the main industry. Flotta, to the south of Scapa Flow, is the site of the oil terminal for the Piper, Claymore and Tartan fields in the North Sea.

The capital is Kirkwall (population 6,206) situated on Mainland.

SHETLAND

The Shetland Islands have a total area of 1,427 sq. km (551 sq. miles) and a population at the 2001 census of 21,988. They lie about 80km (50 miles) north of the Orkneys, with Fair Isle about half way between the two groups. Out Stack, off Muckle Flugga, 1.6km (one mile) north of Unst, is the most northerly part of the British Isles (60° 51′ 30″ N. lat.).

There are over 100 islands, of which 16 are inhabited. Populations at the 2001 census were:

Mainland, 17,575	Muckle Roe, 104
Bressay, 384	Trondra, 133
East Burra, 66	Unst, 720
Fair Isle, 69	West Burra, 784
Fetlar, 86	Whalsay, 1,034
Housay, 76	Yell, 957

Shetland's many archaeological sites include Jarlshof, Mousa and Clickhimin, and its long connection with Scandinavia has resulted in a strong Norse influence on its placenames and dialect.

Industries include fishing, knitwear and farming. In addition to the fishing fleet there are fish processing factories, and the traditional handknitting of Fair Isle and Unst is now supplemented with machine-knitted garments. Farming is mainly crofting, with sheep being raised on the moorland and hills of the islands. Latterly the islands have become a centre of the North Sea oil industry, with pipelines from the Brent and Ninian fields running to the terminal at Sullom Voe, the largest of its kind in Europe.

The capital is Lerwick (population 6,830) situated on Mainland. Lerwick is the main centre for supply services for offshore oil exploration and development.

THE HEBRIDES

Until the late 13th century the Hebrides included other Scottish islands in the Firth of Clyde, the peninsula of Kintyre (Argyll), the Isle of Man, and the (Irish) Isle of Rathlin. The origin of the name is probably the Greek *Eboudai,* latinised as *Hebudes* by Pliny, and corrupted to its present form. The Norwegian name *Sudreyjar* (Southern Islands) was latinised as *Sodorenses,* a name that survives in the Anglican bishopric of Sodor and Man.

There are over 500 islands and islets, of which about 100 are inhabited, though mountainous terrain and extensive peat bogs mean that only a fraction of the total area is under cultivation. Stone, Bronze and Iron Age settlement has left many remains, including those at Callanish on Lewis, and Norse colonisation influenced language, customs and placenames. Occupations include farming (mostly crofting and stock-raising), fishing and the manufacture of tweeds and other woollens. Tourism is also an important part of the economy.

The Inner Hebrides lie off the west coast of Scotland and are relatively close to the mainland. The largest and best-known is Skye (area 1,665 sq. km/643 sq. miles; pop. 9,251; chief town, Portree), which contains the Cuillin Hills (Sgurr Alasdair 993m/3,257ft); Bla Bheinn (928m/3,046ft); the Storr (719m/2,358ft) and the Red Hills (Beinn na Caillich 732m/2,403ft). Other islands in the Highland council area include Raasay (pop. 194), Rum, Eigg (pop. 131) and Muck.

Further south the Inner Hebridean islands include Arran (pop. 5,058) containing Goat Fell (874m/2,868ft); Coll and Tiree (pop. 934); Colonsay and Oronsay (pop. 113); Easdale (pop. 58); Gigha (pop. 110); Islay (area 608 sq. km/235 sq. miles; pop. 3,457); Jura (area 414 sq. km/160 sq. miles; pop. 188) with a range of hills culminating in the Paps of Jura (Beinn-an-Oir, 785m/2,576ft, and Beinn Chaolais, 755m/2,477ft); Lismore (pop. 146); Luing (pop. 220); and Mull (area 950 sq. km/367 sq. miles; pop. 2,696; chief town Tobermory) containing Ben More (967m/3,171ft).

The Outer Hebrides, separated from the mainland by the Minch, now form the Eilean Siar (Western Isles) council area (area 2,897 sq. km/1,119 sq. miles; pop. 26,502). The main islands are Lewis with Harris (area 1,994 sq. km/770 sq. miles, pop. 19,918), whose chief town, Stornoway, is the administrative headquarters; North Uist (pop. 1,320); South Uist (pop. 1,818); Benbecula (pop. 1,249) and Barra (pop. 1,078). Other inhabited islands include Bernera (233), Berneray (136), Eriskay (133), Grimsay (201), Scalpay (322) and Vatersay (94).

EARLY HISTORY

There is evidence of human settlement in Scotland dating from the third millennium BC, the earliest settlers being Middle Stone Age hunters and fishermen. Early in the second millennium BC, New Stone Age farmers began to cultivate crops and rear livestock; their settlements were on the west coast and in the north, and included Skara Brae and Maeshowe (Orkney). Settlement by the early Bronze Age 'Beaker Folk', so-called from the shape of their drinking vessels, in eastern Scotland dates from about 1800 BC. Further settlement is believed to have occurred from 700 BC onwards, as tribes were displaced from further south by new incursions from the Continent and the Roman invasions from AD 43.

Julius Agricola, the Roman governor of Britain AD 77–84, extended the Roman conquests in Britain by advancing into Caledonia, culminating with a victory at Mons Graupius, probably in AD 84; he was recalled to Rome shortly afterwards and his forward policy was not pursued. Hadrian's Wall, mostly completed by AD 30, marked the northern frontier of the Roman empire except for the period between about AD 144 and 190 when the frontier moved north to the Forth-Clyde isthmus and a turf wall, the Antonine Wall, was manned.

After the Roman withdrawal from Britain, there were centuries of warfare between the Picts, Scots, Britons, Angles and Vikings. The Picts, generally accepted to be descended from the indigenous Iron Age people of northern Scotland, occupied the area north of the Forth. The Scots, a Gaelic-speaking people of northern Ireland, colonised the area of Argyll and Bute (the kingdom of Dalriada) in the fifth century AD and then expanded eastwards and northwards. The Britons, speaking a Brythonic Celtic language, colonised Scotland from the south from the first century BC; they lost control of south-eastern Scotland (incorporated into the kingdom of Northumbria) to the Angles in the early seventh century but retained Strathclyde (south-western Scotland and Cumbria). Viking raids from the late eighth century were followed by Norse settlement in the western and northern isles, Argyll, Caithness and Sutherland from the mid-ninth century onwards.

UNIFICATION

The union of the areas which now comprise Scotland began in AD 843 when Kenneth mac Alpin, king of the Scots from *c.*834, also became king of the Picts, joining the two lands to form the kingdom of Alba (comprising Scotland north of a line between the Forth and Clyde rivers). Lothian, the eastern part of the area between the Forth and the Tweed, seems to have been leased to Kenneth II of Alba (reigned 971–995) by Edgar of England *c.*973, and Scottish possession was confirmed by Malcolm II's victory over a Northumbrian army at Carham *c.*1016. At about this time Malcolm II (reigned 1005–34) placed his grandson Duncan on the throne of the British kingdom of Strathclyde, bringing under Scots rule virtually all of what is now Scotland.

The Norse possessions were incorporated into the kingdom of Scotland from the 12th century onwards. An uprising in the mid-12th century drove the Norse from most of mainland Argyll. The Hebrides were ceded to Scotland by the treaty of Perth in 1266 after a Norwegian expedition in 1263 failed to maintain Norse authority over the islands. Orkney and Shetland fell to Scotland in 1468–9 as a pledge for the unpaid dowry of Margaret of Denmark, wife of James III, although Danish claims of suzerainty were relinquished only with the marriage of Anne of Denmark to James VI in 1590.

From the 11th century, there were frequent wars between Scotland and England over territory and the extent of England's political influence. The failure of the Scottish royal line with the death of Margaret of Norway in 1290 led to disputes over the throne which were resolved by the adjudication of Edward I of England. He awarded the throne to John Balliol in 1292 but Balliol's refusal to be a puppet king led to war. Balliol surrendered to Edward I in 1296 and Edward attempted to rule Scotland himself. Resistance to Scotland's loss of independence was led by William Wallace, who defeated the English at Stirling Bridge (1297), and Robert Bruce, crowned in 1306, who held most of Scotland by 1311 and routed Edward II's army at Bannockburn (1314). England recognised the independence of Scotland in the treaty of Northampton in 1328. Subsequent clashes include the disastrous battle of Flodden (1513) in which James IV and many of his nobles fell.

THE UNION

In 1603 James VI of Scotland succeeded Elizabeth I on the throne of England (his mother, Mary Queen of Scots, was the great-granddaughter of Henry VII), his successors reigning as sovereigns of Great Britain. Political union of the two countries did not occur until 1707.

THE JACOBITE REVOLTS

After the abdication (by flight) in 1688 of James VII and II, the crown devolved upon William III (grandson of Charles I) and Mary II (elder daughter of James VII and II). In 1689 Graham of Claverhouse roused the Highlands on behalf of James VII and II, but died after a military success at Killiecrankie.

After the death of Anne (younger daughter of James VII and II), the throne devolved upon George I (great-grandson of James VI and I). In 1715, armed risings on behalf of James Stuart (the Old Pretender, son of James VII and II) led to the indecisive battle of Sheriffmuir, and the Jacobite movement died down until 1745, when Charles Stuart (the Young Pretender) defeated the Royalist troops at Prestonpans and advanced to Derby (1746). From Derby, the adherents of 'James VIII and III' (the title claimed for his father by Charles Stuart) fell back on the defensive and were finally crushed at Culloden (16 April 1746) by an army led by by the Duke of Cumberland, son of George II.

PRINCIPAL CITIES

ABERDEEN

Aberdeen, 209km (130 miles) north-east of Edinburgh, received its charter as a Royal Burgh in 1124. Scotland's third largest city, Aberdeen lies between two rivers, the Dee and the Don, facing the North Sea; the city has a strong maritime history and is today a major centre for offshore oil exploration and production. It is also an ancient university town and distinguished research centre. Other industries include engineering, food processing, textiles, paper manufacturing and chemicals.

Places of interest include King's College, St Machar's Cathedral, Brig o' Balgownie, Duthie Park and Winter Gardens, Hazlehead Park, the Kirk of St Nicholas, Mercat Cross, Marischal College and Marischal Museum, Provost Skene's House, Aberdeen Art Gallery, Gordon Highlanders Museum, Satrosphere Science Centre, and Aberdeen Maritime Museum.

DUNDEE

The Royal Burgh of Dundee is situated on the north bank of the Tay estuary. The city's port and dock installations are important to the offshore oil industry and the airport also provides servicing facilities. Principal industries include textiles, biotechnology and digital media, lasers, printing, tyre manufacture, food processing, engineering and tourism.

The unique City Churches – three churches under one roof, together with the 15th-century St Mary's Tower –

are the most prominent architectural feature. Dundee is home to two historic ships: the Dundee-built RRS *Discovery* which took Capt. Scott to the Antarctic lies alongside Discovery Quay, and the frigate *Unicorn,* the only British-built wooden warship still afloat, is moored in Victoria Dock. Places of interest include Mills Public Observatory, the Tay road and rail bridges, Dundee Contemporary Arts centre, McManus Galleries, Claypotts Castle, Broughty Castle, Verdant Works (textile heritage centre) and the Sensation Science Centre.

EDINBURGH

Edinburgh is the capital city and seat of government in Scotland. The new Scottish parliament building designed by Enric Miralles was completed in 2004 and is open to visitors. The city is built on a group of hills and both the old and new towns are inscribed on the UNESCO World Cultural and Natural Heritage List for their cultural significance.

Other places of interest include the castle, which houses the Stone of Scone and also includes St Margaret's Chapel, the oldest building in Edinburgh, and near it, the Scottish National War Memorial; the Palace of Holyroodhouse, the Queen's official residence in Scotland; Parliament House, the present seat of the judicature; Princes Street; three universities (Edinburgh, Heriot-Watt, Napier); St Giles' Cathedral; St Mary's (Scottish Episcopal) Cathedral (Sir George Gilbert Scott); the General Register House (Robert Adam); the National and Signet libraries; the National Gallery of Scotland; the Royal Scottish Academy; the Scottish National Portrait Gallery and the Edinburgh International Conference Centre.

GLASGOW

Glasgow, a Royal Burgh, is Scotland's largest city and its principal commercial and industrial centre. The city occupies the north and south banks of the Clyde, formerly one of the chief commercial estuaries in the world. The main industries include engineering, electronics, finance, chemicals and printing. The city is also a key tourist and conference destination.

The chief buildings are the 13th-century Gothic cathedral, the university (Sir George Gilbert Scott), the City Chambers, the Royal Concert Hall, St Mungo Museum of Religious Life and Art, Pollok House, the School of Art (Charles Rennie Mackintosh), Kelvingrove Art Gallery and Museum, the Gallery of Modern Art, the Burrell Collection museum and the Mitchell Library. The city is home to the Royal Scottish National Orchestra, Scottish Opera, Scottish Ballet and BBC Scotland and Scottish Television (STV).

INVERNESS

Inverness was granted city status in 2000. The city's name is derived from the Gaelic for 'the mouth of the Ness', referring to the river on which it lies. Inverness is recorded as being at the junction of the old trade routes since AD 565. Today the city is the main administrative centre for the north of Scotland and is the capital of the Highlands. Tourism is one of the city's main industries.

Among the city's most notable buildings is Abertarff House, built in 1593 and the oldest secular building remaining in Inverness. Balnain House, built as a town house in 1726, is a fine example of early Georgian architecture. Once a hospital for Hanoverian soldiers after the battle of Culloden and as billets for the Royal Engineers when completing the first Ordnance Survey, today Balnain House is the National Trust for Scotland's regional HQ. The Old High Church, on St Michael's Mount, is the original parish church of Inverness and is built on the site of the earliest Christian church in the city. Parts of the church date back to the 14th century.

Stirling was granted city status in 2002. Aberdeen, Dundee, Edinburgh and Glasgow have also been granted Lord Mayoralty/Lord Provostship.

LORD-LIEUTENANTS

Title	*Name*
Aberdeen City*	Lord Provost Peter Stephen
Aberdeenshire	A. Farquharson, OBE
Angus	Mrs G. Osborne
Argyll and Bute	K. Mackinnon
Ayrshire and Arran	John Duncan, QPM
Banffshire	Clare Russell
Berwickshire	Maj. A. Trotter
Caithness	Miss M. Dunnett
Clackmannan	Mrs S. Cruickshank
Dumfries	Jean Tulloch
Dunbartonshire	vacant
Dundee City*	Lord Provost John Letford
East Lothian	W. Garth Morrison, CBE
Edinburgh City*	Rt. Hon. Lord Provost George Grubb
Eilean Siar (Western Isles)	A. Matheson, OBE
Fife	Mrs C. Dean
Glasgow City*	Rt. Hon. Lord Provost Robert Winter
Inverness	Donald Angus Cameron of Lochiel
Kincardineshire	Carol Kinghorn
Lanarkshire	G. Cox, MBE
Midlothian	Patrick Prenter, CBE
Moray	Grenville Shaw Johnston, OBE, TD
Nairn	Ewen Brodie of Lethan
Orkney	Dr Anthony Trickett, MBE
Perth and Kinross	Brig. Melville Jameson, CBE
Renfrewshire	Guy Clark
Ross and Cromarty	Janet Bowen
Roxburgh, Ettrick and Lauderdale	Hon. Capt. Gerald Maitland-Carew
Shetland	J. Scott
Stirling and Falkirk	Mrs M. McLachlan
Sutherland	Dr Monica Maitland Main
The Stewartry of Kirkcudbright	Lt.-Col. Sir Malcolm Walter Hugh Ross, GCVO, OBE
Tweeddale	Capt. D. Younger
West Lothian	Mrs I. Brydie, MBE
Wigtown	Marion Brewis

* The Lord Provosts of the four cities of Aberdeen, Dundee, Edinburgh and Glasgow are Lord-Lieutenants *ex officio* for those districts

LOCAL COUNCILS

Council	*Administrative Headquarters*	*Telephone*	*Population**	*Council Tax†*	*Chief Executive*
ABERDEEN	Aberdeen	01224-522000	206,900	£1,230	vacant
Aberdeenshire	Aberdeen	0845-404 0506	236,300	£1,141	Alan Campbell
Angus	Forfar	0845-277 7778	109,300	£1,072	David Sawers
Argyll and Bute	Lochgilphead	01546-602127	91,400	£1,178	Sally Reid
Clackmannanshire	Alloa	01259-452000	48,900	£1,148	Dave Jones
Dumfries and Galloway	Dumfries	01387-260000	148,000	£1,049	Philip Jones
DUNDEE	Dundee	01382-434000	142,200	£1,211	Alex Stephen
East Ayrshire	Kilmarnock	01563-576000	119,300	£1,189	Fiona Lees
East Dunbartonshire	Kirkintilloch	0845-045 4510	105,500	£1,142	Sue Bruce
East Lothian	Haddington	01620-827827	92,800	£1,118	Alan Blackie
East Renfrewshire	Giffnock	0141-577 3000	89,300	£1,126	Lorraine McMillan
EDINBURGH	Edinburgh	0131-200 2000	463,500	£1,169	Tom Aitchison, CBE
Eilean Siar (Western Isles)	Stornoway	01851-703773	26,400	£1,024	Malcolm Burr
Falkirk	Falkirk	01324-506070	149,700	£1,070	Mary Pitcaithly, OBE
Fife	Glenrothes	01592-414141	358,900	£1,118	Ronnie Hinds
GLASGOW	Glasgow	0141-287 2000	580,700	£1,213	George Black
Highland	Inverness	01463-702000	215,300	£1,163	Alistair Dodds
Inverclyde	Greenock	01475-717171	81,500	£1,198	John Mundell
Midlothian	Dalkeith	0131-270 7500	79,300	£1,210	Trevor Muir
Moray	Elgin	01343-543451	86,800	£1,135	Alastair Keddie
North Ayrshire	Irvine	0845-603 0590	135,500	£1,152	Ian Snodgrass
North Lanarkshire	Motherwell	01698-302222	323,800	£1,098	Gavin Whitefield
Orkney	Kirkwall	01856-873535	19,800	£1,037	Alistair Buchan
Perth and Kinross	Perth	01738-475000	140,200	£1,158	Bernadette Malone
Renfrewshire	Paisley	0141-842 5000	169,600	£1,165	David Martin
Scottish Borders	Melrose	01835-824000	110,200	£1,084	David Hume
Shetland	Lerwick	01595-693535	21,900	£1,053	Morgan Goodlad
South Ayrshire	Ayr	01292-612000	111,700	£1,154	David Anderson
South Lanarkshire	Hamilton	01698-454444	307,700	£1,101	Archie Strang
STIRLING	Stirling	0845-277 7000	87,800	£1,209	Keith Yates
West Dunbartonshire	Dumbarton	01389-737000	91,200	£1,163	David McMillan
West Lothian	Livingston	01506-775000	165,700	£1,128	Alex Linkston

* *Source:* ONS – *Mid-2006 Population Estimates* (Crown copyright)
† Average Band D council tax bill 2008–9
Councils in CAPITAL LETTERS have city status

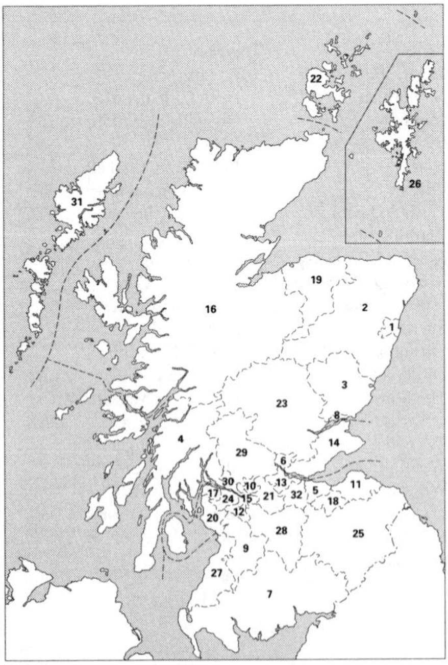

Key	*Council*	*Key*	*Council*
1	Aberdeen City	18	Midlothian
2	Aberdeenshire	19	Moray
3	Angus	20	North Ayrshire
4	Argyll and Bute	21	North Lanarkshire
5	City of Edinburgh	22	Orkney
6	Clackmannanshire	23	Perth and Kinross
7	Dumfries and Galloway	24	Renfrewshire
8	Dundee City	25	Scottish Borders
9	East Ayrshire	26	Shetland
10	East Dunbartonshire	27	South Ayrshire
11	East Lothian	28	South Lanarkshire
12	East Renfrewshire	29	Stirling
13	Falkirk	30	West Dunbartonshire
14	Fife	31	Western Isles (Eilean Siar)
15	Glasgow City	32	West Lothian
16	Highland		
17	Inverclyde		

NORTHERN IRELAND

Northern Ireland has a total area of 14,149 sq. km (5,463 sq. miles): land, 13,576 sq. km (5,242 sq. miles); inland water, 573 sq. km (221 sq. miles).

The population of Northern Ireland at the 2001 census was 1,685,267 (men 821,449; women 863,818). The average density of population in 2001 was 119 persons per sq. km (308 per sq. mile).

In 2001 the number of persons in the various religious denominations (expressed as percentages of the total population) were: Catholic, 40.26; Presbyterian, 20.69; Church of Ireland, 15.30; Methodist Church in Ireland, 3.51; other Christian (including Christian related) 6.07; other religions and philosophies, 0.3; no religion or religion not stated, 13.88.

FLAG

The official national flag of Northern Ireland is now the Union Flag. The flag formerly in use (a white, six-pointed star in the centre of a red cross on a white field, enclosing a red hand and surmounted by a crown) has not been used since.

PRINCIPAL CITIES

In addition to Belfast and Londonderry, three other places in Northern Ireland have been granted city status: Armagh (1994), Lisburn (2002) and Newry (2002).

BELFAST

Belfast, the administrative centre of Northern Ireland, is situated at the mouth of the River Lagan at its entrance to Belfast Lough. The city grew to be a great industrial centre, owing to its easy access by sea to Scottish coal and iron.

The principal buildings are of a relatively young age and include the parliament buildings at Stormont, the City Hall, Waterfront Hall, the Law Courts, the Public Library and the Museum and Art Gallery.

Belfast received its first charter of incorporation in 1613 and was created a city in 1888; the title of lord mayor was conferred in 1892.

LONDONDERRY

Londonderry (originally Derry) is situated on the River Foyle, and has important associations with the City of London. The Irish Society was created by the City of London in 1610, and under its royal charter of 1613 it fortified the city and was for a long time closely associated with its administration. Because of this connection the city was incorporated in 1613 under the new name of Londonderry.

The city is famous for the great siege of 1688–9, when for 105 days the town held out against the forces of James II. The city walls are still intact and form a circuit of 1.6 km (one mile) around the old city.

Interesting buildings are the Protestant cathedral of St Columb's (1633) and the Guildhall, reconstructed in 1912 and containing a number of beautiful stained glass windows, many of which were presented by the livery companies of London.

CONSTITUTIONAL HISTORY

Northern Ireland is subject to the same fundamental constitutional provisions which apply to the rest of the United Kingdom. It had its own parliament and government from 1921 to 1972, but after increasing civil unrest the Northern Ireland (Temporary Provisions) Act 1972 transferred the legislative and executive powers of the Northern Ireland parliament and government to the UK parliament and a secretary of state. The Northern Ireland Constitution Act 1973 provided for devolution in Northern Ireland through an assembly and executive, but a power-sharing executive formed by the Northern Ireland political parties in January 1974 collapsed in May 1974. Following the collapse of the power-sharing executive Northern Ireland returned to direct rule governance under the provisions of the Northern Ireland Act 1974, placing the Northern Ireland department under the direction and control of the Northern Ireland secretary.

In December 1993 the British and Irish governments published the Joint Declaration complementing their political talks, and making clear that any settlement would need to be founded on principles of democracy and consent. The declaration also stated that all democratically mandated parties could be involved in political talks as long as they permanently renounced paramilitary violence.

On 12 January 1998 the British and Irish governments issued a joint document, *Propositions on Heads of Agreement,* proposing the establishment of various new cross-border bodies; further proposals were presented on 27 January. A draft peace settlement was issued by the talks' chairman, US Senator George Mitchell, on 6 April 1998 but was rejected by the Unionists the following day. On 10 April agreement was reached between the British and Irish governments and the eight Northern Ireland political parties still involved in the talks (the Good Friday Agreement). The agreement provided for an elected Northern Ireland Assembly, a North/South Ministerial Council, and a British-Irish Council comprising representatives of the British, Irish, Channel Islands and Isle of Man governments and members of the new assemblies for Scotland, Wales and Northern Ireland. Further points included the abandonment of the Republic of Ireland's constitutional claim to Northern Ireland; the decommissioning of weapons; the release of paramilitary prisoners and changes in policing.

Referendums on the agreement were held in Northern Ireland and the Republic of Ireland on 22 May 1998. In Northern Ireland the turnout was 81 per cent, of which 71.12 per cent voted in favour of the agreement. In the Republic of Ireland, the turnout was about 55 per cent, of which 94.4 per cent voted in favour of both the agreement and the necessary constitutional change. In the UK, the Northern Ireland Act 1998, enshrining the provisions of the agreement, received royal assent in November 1998.

On 28 April 2003 the secretary of state again assumed responsibility for the direction of the Northern Ireland departments on the dissolution of the Northern Ireland

Assembly, following its initial suspension from midnight on 14 October 2002. In 2006, following the passing of the Northern Ireland Act, the secretary of state created a non-legislative fixed-term assembly which would cease to operate either when the political parties agreed to restore devolution, or on 24 November 2006 (whichever occurred first). In October 2006 a timetable to restore devolution was drawn up (St Andrews Agreement) and a transitional Northern Ireland Assembly was formed on 24 November. The transitional assembly was dissolved in January 2007 in preparation for elections to be held on 7 March; following the elections a power-sharing executive was formed and the new 108-member Northern Ireland Assembly became operational on 8 May 2007.
See also Regional Government.

FINANCE

Northern Ireland's expenditure is funded through the Northern Ireland Consolidated Fund (NICF). Up until devolution on 2 December 1999, the NICF was largely financed by Northern Ireland's attributed share of UK taxation and supplemented by a grant-in-aid. From devolution, these separate elements have been subsumed into a single block grant. The Northern Ireland Departmental Expenditure Limit for 2008–9 was set at £9,071m.

LORD-LIEUTENANTS AND HIGH SHERIFFS

County	*Lord-Lieutenant*	*Sheriff (2008)*
Antrim	Joan Christie	Lady Juliet Frazer
Armagh	The Earl of Caledon	Desmond Mitchell, MBE
Belfast City	Lady Carswell, OBE	Margaret McKenzie
Down	William Hall	Dr Alan Gillespie, CBE
Fermanagh	The Earl of Erne	Jonathan Styles
Londonderry	Denis Desmond, CBE	Patrick McGinnis
Londonderry City	Dr Donal Keegan, OBE	Eamon Gee
Tyrone	The Duke of Abercorn, KG	Robert Pollock, MBE

LOCAL COUNCILS

Council	*Telephone*	*Population**	*Chief Executive*
Antrim, Co. Down	028-9446 3113	51,500	David McCammick
Ards, Co. Down	028-9182 4000	76,200	Ashley Boreland
ARMAGH CITY, Co. Armagh	028-3752 9600	56,800	John Briggs
Ballymena, Co. Antrim	028-2566 0300	61,400	vacant
Ballymoney, Co. Antrim	028-2766 0200	29,200	John Dempsey
Banbridge, Co. Down	028-4066 0600	45,500	Liam Hannaway
BELFAST CITY, Co. Antrim and Co. Down	028-9032 0202	267,400	Peter McNaney
Carrickfergus, Co. Antrim	028-9335 8000	39,700	Alan Cardwell
Castlereagh, Co. Down	028-9046 4500	65,600	Adrian Donaldson
Coleraine, Co. Londonderry	028-7034 7034	56,700	Desi Wreath *(acting)*
Cookstown, Co. Tyrone	028-8676 2205	34,800	Michael McGuckin
Craigavon, Co. Armagh	028-3831 2400	86,800	Francis Rock
DERRY CITY, Co. Londonderry	028-7136 5151	107,900	John Meehan *(acting)*
Down, Co. Down	028-4461 0800	68,300	John McGrillen
Dungannon and South Tyrone, Co. Tyrone	028-8772 0300	52,300	Alan Burke/Iain Frazer *(acting)*
Fermanagh, Co. Fermanagh	028-6632 5050	60,600	Rodney Connor
Larne, Co. Antrim	028-2827 2313	31,300	Geraldine McGahey
Limavady, Co. Londonderry	028-7772 2226	34,300	Liam Flanigan
LISBURN CITY, Co. Antrim	028-9250 9250	112,900	Norman Davidson
Magherafelt, Co. Londonderry	028-7939 7979	42,400	John McLaughlin
Moyle, Co. Antrim	028-2076 2225	16,500	Richard Lewis
NEWRY and Mourne, Co. Down and Co. Armagh	028-3031 3031	93,400	Thomas McCall
Newtownabbey, Co. Antrim	028-9034 0000	81,200	Norman Dunn
North Down, Co. Down	028-9127 0371	78,700	Trevor Polley
Omagh, Co. Tyrone	028 8224 5321	51,000	Daniel McSorley
Strabane, Co. Tyrone	028-7138 2204	39,100	Philip Faithfull

* *Source:* ONS – *Mid-2006 Population Estimates* (Crown copyright)
Councils in CAPITAL LETTERS have city status

THE ISLE OF MAN

Ellan Vannin

The Isle of Man is an island situated in the Irish Sea, at latitude 54° 3′–54° 25′ N. and longitude 4° 18′–4° 47′ W., nearly equidistant from England, Scotland and Ireland. Although the early inhabitants were of Celtic origin, the Isle of Man was part of the Norwegian Kingdom of the Hebrides until 1266, when this was ceded to Scotland. Subsequently granted to the Stanleys (Earls of Derby) in the 15th century and later to the Dukes of Atholl, it was brought under the administration of the crown in 1765. The island forms the bishopric of Sodor and Man.

The total land area is 572 sq. km (221 sq. miles). The 2006 census showed a resident population of 80,058 (men, 39,523; women, 40,535). The main language in use is English. There are no remaining native speakers of Manx Gaelic but around 1,550 people are able to speak the language.

CAPITAL – ΨDouglas; population, 26,218 (2006). ΨCastletown (3,109) is the ancient capital; the other towns are ΨPeel (4,280) and ΨRamsey (7,309)

FLAG – A red flag charged with three conjoined armoured legs in white and gold

NATIONAL DAY – 5 July (Tynwald Day)

GOVERNMENT

The Isle of Man is a self-governing crown dependency, with its own parliamentary, legal and administrative system. The British government is responsible for international relations and defence. Under the UK Act of Accession, Protocol 3, the island's relationship with the European Union is limited to trade alone and does not extend to financial aid. The Lieutenant-Governor is the Queen's personal representative on the island.

The legislature, Tynwald, is the oldest parliament in the world in continuous existence. It has two branches: the Legislative Council and the House of Keys. The council consists of the President of Tynwald, the Bishop of Sodor and Man, the Attorney-General (who does not have a vote) and eight members elected by the House of Keys. The House of Keys has 24 members, elected by universal adult suffrage. The branches sit separately to consider legislation and sit together, as Tynwald Court, for most other parliamentary purposes.

The presiding officer of Tynwald Court is the President of Tynwald, elected by the members, who also presides over sittings of the Legislative Council. The presiding officer of the House of Keys is the Speaker, who is elected by members of the house.

The principal members of the Manx government are the chief minister and nine departmental ministers, who comprise the Council of Ministers.

Lieutenant-Governor, HE Vice-Adm. Sir Paul Haddacks, KCB
President of Tynwald, Hon. Noel Cringle
Speaker, House of Keys, Hon. Steve Rodan, SHK
The First Deemster and Clerk of the Rolls, John Kerruish
Clerk of Tynwald, Secretary to the House of Keys and Counsel to the Speaker, Roger Phillips
Clerk of the Legislative Council and Deputy Clerk of Tynwald, Jonathan King
Attorney-General, W. Corlett, QC
Chief Minister, Hon. Tony Brown, MHK
Chief Secretary, Mrs M. Williams

ECONOMY

Most of the income generated in the island is earned in the services sector with financial and professional services accounting for just over half of the national income. Tourism and manufacturing are also major generators of income whilst the island's other traditional industries of agriculture and fishing now play a smaller role in the economy. Under the terms of protocol 3, the island has tariff-free access to EU markets for its goods.

In May 2008 the island's unemployment rate was 1.3 per cent and inflation (RPI) was 5.6 per cent.

FINANCE

The budget for 2008–9 provides for net revenue expenditure of £566.5m. The principal sources of government revenue are taxes on income and expenditure. Income tax is payable at a rate of 10 per cent on the first £10,500 of taxable income for single resident individuals and 18 per cent on the balance, after personal allowances of £9,200. These bands are doubled for married couples. The rate of income tax for trading companies is zero per cent except for income from banking and land and property, which is taxed at 10 per cent. By agreement with the British government, the island keeps most of its rates of indirect taxation (VAT and duties) the same as those in the UK. However, VAT on tourist accommodation, property, repairs and renovations is charged at 5 per cent. A reciprocal agreement on national insurance benefits and pensions exists between the governments of the Isle of Man and the UK. Taxes are also charged on property (rates), but these are comparatively low.

The major government expenditure items are health, social security, social services and education, which account for 59 per cent of the government budget. The island makes an annual contribution to the UK for defence and other external services.

The island has a special relationship with the European Union and neither contributes money to nor receives funds from the EU budget.

Ψ = sea port

THE CHANNEL ISLANDS

The Channel Islands, situated off the north-west coast of France (at a distance of 16km (10 miles) at their closest point), are the only portions of the Dukedom of Normandy still belonging to the Crown, to which they have been attached since the Norman Conquest of 1066. They were the only British territory to come under German occupation during the Second World War, following invasion on 30 June and 1 July 1940. The islands were relieved by British forces on 9 May 1945, and 9 May (Liberation Day) is now observed as a bank and public holiday.

The islands consist of Jersey (11,630ha/28,717 acres), Guernsey (6,340ha/15,654 acres), and the dependencies of Guernsey: Alderney (795ha/1,962 acres), Brecqhou (30ha/74 acres), Great Sark (419ha/1,035 acres), Little Sark (97ha/239 acres), Herm (130ha/320 acres), Jethou (18ha/44 acres) and Lihou (15ha/38 acres) – a total of 19,474ha/48,083 acres, or 194 sq. km/75 sq. miles. The 2001 census showed the population of Jersey as 87,186; Guernsey, 59,807 and Alderney, 2,294. Sark did not complete the same census but a recent informal census gave its population figure as 591. The official languages are English and French. In country districts of Jersey and Guernsey and throughout Sark a Norman-French *patois* is also in use, though to a lesser extent.

GOVERNMENT

The islands are Crown dependencies with their own legislative assemblies (the States in Jersey, Guernsey and Alderney and the Chief Pleas in Sark), systems of local administration and law, and their own courts. Acts passed by the States require the sanction of the Queen-in-council. The British government is responsible for defence and international relations. The Channel Islands have trading rights only (not including financial aid) within the European Union.

In both Jersey and Guernsey bailiwicks the Lieutenant-Governor and Commander-in-Chief, who is appointed by the Crown, is the personal representative of the Queen and the channel of communication between the Crown (via the Privy Council) and the island's government.

Both Jersey and Guernsey have a ministerial system of government. In Jersey the executive comprises the Council of Ministers and consists of a chief minister and nine other ministers. The ministers are assisted by up to 13 assistant ministers. Members of the States who are not in the executive are able to sit on a number of scrutiny panels and the Public Accounts Committee to examine the policy of the executive and hold ministers to account. In Guernsey there is a Policy Council comprising a chief minister and ten departmental ministers. There are also five specialist committees, each led by a chair, responsible for public sector pay negotiations, parliamentary procedural matters and for scrutinising policy, finance and legislation.

Justice is administered by the royal courts of Jersey and Guernsey, each consisting of the bailiff and 12 elected jurats. The bailiffs of Jersey and Guernsey, appointed by the Crown, are presidents of the states and of the royal courts of their respective islands.

Each bailiwick constitutes a deanery under the jurisdiction of the Bishop of Winchester.

ECONOMY

A mild climate and good soil have led to the development of intensive systems of agriculture and horticulture, which form a significant part of the economy. Equally important are earnings from tourism and banking and finance: the low rates of income and corporation tax and the absence of death duties make the islands an important offshore financial centre. In addition, there is no VAT or equivalent tax in Guernsey and only small goods and services tax in Jersey (set at 3 per cent for three years from 6 May 2008).

Principal exports are agricultural produce and flowers; imports are chiefly machinery, manufactured goods, food, fuel and chemicals. Trade with the UK is regarded as internal.

British currency is legal tender in the Channel Islands but each bailiwick issues its own coins and notes (*see* Currency section). They also issue their own postage stamps; UK stamps are not valid.

JERSEY

Lieutenant-Governor and Commander-in-Chief of Jersey, HE Lt.-Gen. Andrew Peter Ridgway, CB, CBE, *apptd* 2006
Secretary and ADC, Lt.-Col. A. Woodrow, OBE, MC
Bailiff of Jersey, Sir Philip Bailhache
Deputy Bailiff, M. St J. Birt
Attorney-General, W. Bailhache, QC
Receiver-General, P. Lewin
Solicitor-General, Timothy Le Cocq, QC
Greffier of the States, M. de la Haye
States Treasurer, I. Black

FINANCE

	2006	*2007*
Revenue income	£732,557,000	£764,293,000
Revenue expenditure	£670,749,000	£691,143,000
Capital expenditure	£58,090,000	£52,393,000

CHIEF TOWN – ΨSt Helier, on the south coast
FLAG – A white field charged with a red saltire cross, and the arms of Jersey in the upper centre

GUERNSEY AND DEPENDENCIES

Lieutenant-Governor and Commander-in-Chief of the Bailiwick of Guernsey and its Dependencies, HE Vice-Adm. Sir Fabian Malbon, KBE, *apptd* 2005
Presiding Officer, Geoffrey Rowland
Deputy Presiding Officer, Richard Collas
HM Procureur and Receiver-General, John van Leuven, QC
HM Comptroller, Howard Roberts, QC
Chief Minister, Deputy Lyndon Trott
Chief Executive, Mike Brown

FINANCE

	2006	*2007*
Revenue	£325,098,105	£365,004,000
Expenditure	£294,612,476	£294,481,000

CHIEF TOWNS – ΨSt Peter Port, on the east coast of Guernsey; St Anne on Alderney
FLAG – White, bearing a red cross of St George, with a gold cross of Normandy overall in the centre

ALDERNEY
President of the States, Sir Norman Browse, OBE
Chief Executive, David Jeremiah, OBE, QC
Greffier, Sarah Kelly

SARK*
Seigneur of Sark, John Beaumont, OBE
Seneschal, Lt.-Col. R Guille, MBE
Greffier, Trevor Hamon

OTHER DEPENDENCIES
Herm and Lihou are owned by the States of Guernsey; Herm is leased. Jethou is leased by the Crown to the States of Guernsey and is sub-let by the States. Brecqhou is within the legislative and judicial territory of Sark.

* On 4 October 2006 the islanders of Sark voted in favour of establishing a 28-member elected assembly from December 2008. The Reform (Sark) Law 2008 and the Real Property (Transfer Tax, Charging and Related Provisions) (Sark) Law 2007 were given royal assent on 9 April 2008.

EUROPEAN PARLIAMENT

European parliament elections take place at five-yearly intervals; the first direct elections to the parliament were held in 1979. In mainland Britain, members of the European parliament (MEPs) were elected in all constituencies on a first-past-the-post basis until 1999, when a regional system of proportional representation was introduced; in Northern Ireland three MEPs have been elected by the single transferable vote system of proportional representation since 1979. From 1979 to 1994 the number of seats held by the UK in the European parliament was 81, which increased to 87 in the 1994 election and decreased to 78 (England 64, Wales 4, Scotland 7, Northern Ireland 3) following EU enlargement in 2004.

At the 2004 European parliament elections all UK MEPs were elected under a 'closed-list' regional system of proportional representation, with England being divided into nine regions and Scotland, Wales and Northern Ireland each constituting a region. Since June 2004 residents of Gibraltar vote in the South West region. Parties submitted a list of candidates for each region in their own order of preference. Voters voted for a party or an independent candidate, and the first seat in each region was allocated to the party or candidate with the highest number of votes. The rest of the seats in each region were then allocated broadly in proportion to each party's share of the vote. Each region returned the following number of members: East Midlands, 6; Eastern, 7; London, 9; North East, 3; North West, 9; South East, 10; South West, 7; West Midlands, 7; Yorkshire and the Humber, 6; Wales, 4; Northern Ireland, 3; Scotland, 7.

If a vacancy occurs due to the resignation or death of an MEP, it is filled by the next available person on that party's list. If an independent MEP resigns or dies, a by-election is held. Where an MEP leaves the party on whose list he/she was elected, there is no requirement to resign and he/she can remain in office until the next election.

British subjects and nationals of member states of the European Union are eligible for election to the European parliament provided they are 21 or over and not subject to disqualification. Since 1994, eligible citizens have had the right to vote in elections to the European parliament in the UK as long as they are entered on the electoral register.

MEPs currently receive a salary from the parliaments or governments of their respective member states, set at the level of the national parliamentary salary and subject to national taxation. British MEPs receive a salary of £61,820.

From 2009 a new MEP statute was due to take effect introducing the same salary for all MEPs at a rate of 38.5 per cent of the basic salary of a European court of justice judge.

The next elections to the European parliament will take place in June 2009. For further information visit the European parliament's website (W www.europarl.org.uk).

UK MEMBERS *as at June 2007*

* Denotes membership of the last European parliament
† Replacements since the last election
‡ Previously a member of UKIP
§ Previously a member of DUP
¶ Previously sat as a C.
** Previously a member of LD

§**Allister**, James (b. 1953), *NI, Northern Ireland*
Ashworth, Richard (b. 1947), *C., South East*
***Atkins**, Rt. Hon. Sir Robert (b. 1946), *C., North West*
***Attwooll**, Elspeth M. A. (b. 1943), *LD, Scotland*
Batten, Gerard (b. 1972), *UKIP, London*
***Beazley**, Christopher J. P. (b. 1952), *C., Eastern*
Bloom, Godfrey (b. 1949), *UKIP, Yorkshire and the Humber*
***Booth**, Graham (b. 1940), *UKIP, South West*
***Bowis**, John C., OBE (b. 1945), *C., London*
†**Bowles**, Sharon M. (b. 1953), *LD, South East*
***Bradbourn**, Philip, OBE (b. 1951), *C., West Midlands*
***Bushill-Matthews**, Philip (b. 1943), *C., West Midlands*
***Callanan**, Martin (b. 1961), *C., North East*
***Cashman**, Michael (b. 1950), *Lab., West Midlands*
***Chichester**, Giles B. (b. 1946), *C., South West*
Clark, Derek (b. 1933), *UKIP, East Midlands*
***Corbett**, Richard (b. 1955), *Lab., Yorkshire and the Humber*
***Davies**, Christopher G. (b. 1954), *LD, North West*
de Brún, Bairbre (b. 1954), *SF, Northern Ireland*
***Deva**, Niranjan J. A. (Nirj), FRSA (b. 1948), *C., South East*
***Dover**, Densmore (b. 1938), *C., North West*
***Duff**, Andrew N. (b. 1950), *LD, Eastern*
***Elles**, James E. M. (b. 1949), *C., South East*
***Evans**, Jillian R. (b. 1959), *PC, Wales*
***Evans**, Jonathan P., FRSA (b. 1950), *C., Wales*
***Evans**, Robert J. E. (b. 1956), *Lab., London*
***Farage**, Nigel P. (b. 1964), *UKIP, South East*
***Ford**, Glyn J. (b. 1950), *Lab., South West*
***Gill**, Neena (b. 1956), *Lab., West Midlands*
Hall, Fiona (b. 1955), *LD, North East*
*¶**Hannan**, Daniel J. (b. 1971), *NI, South East*
***Harbour**, Malcolm (b. 1947), *C., West Midlands*
***Heaton-Harris**, Christopher (b. 1967), *C., East Midlands*
*¶**Helmer**, Roger (b. 1944), *NI, East Midlands*
***Honeyball**, Mary (b. 1952), *Lab., London*
***Howitt**, Richard (b. 1961), *Lab., Eastern*
***Hudghton**, Ian (b. 1951), *SNP, Scotland*
***Hughes**, Stephen (b. 1952), *Lab., North East*
***Jackson**, Caroline F., DPHIL (b. 1946), *C., South West*
†**Kamall**, Syed S. (b. 1967), *C., London*
****Karim**, Sajjad (b. 1970), *C., North West*
‡**Kilroy-Silk**, Robert (b. 1942), *NI, East Midlands*
***Kinnock**, Glenys (b. 1944), *Lab., Wales*
***Kirkhope**, Timothy J. R. (b. 1945), *C., Yorkshire and the Humber*
Knapman, Roger (b. 1944), *UKIP, South West*
***Lambert**, Jean D. (b. 1950), *Green, London*
***Lucas**, Dr Caroline (b. 1960), *Green, South East*
***Ludford**, Baroness (b. 1951), *LD, London*
***Lynne**, Elizabeth (b. 1948), *LD, West Midlands*
***McAvan**, Linda (b. 1962), *Lab., Yorkshire and the Humber*
***McCarthy**, Arlene (b. 1960), *Lab., North West*
***McMillan-Scott**, Edward H. C. (b. 1949), *C., Yorkshire and the Humber*
***Martin**, David W. (b. 1954), *Lab., Scotland*
***Moraes**, Claude (b. 1965), *Lab., London*
***Morgan**, Eluned (b. 1967), *Lab., Wales*
‡**Mote**, Ashley (b. 1936), *NI, South East*

Nattrass, Mike (b. 1945), *UKIP, West Midlands*
*__Newton Dunn__, William F. (Bill) (b. 1941), *LD, East Midlands*
*__Nicholson__, James (b. 1945), *UUP, Northern Ireland*
*__Nicholson of Winterbourne__, Baroness (b. 1941), *LD, South East*
*__Parish__, Neil (b. 1956), *C., South West*
*__Purvis__, John R., CBE (b. 1938), *C., Scotland*
†**Simpson**, Brian (b. 1953), *Lab., North West*
*__Skinner__, Peter W. (b. 1959), *Lab., South East*
Smith, Alyn (b. 1973), *SNP, Scotland*
*__Stevenson__, Struan (b. 1948), *C., Scotland*
*__Stihler__, Catherine D. (b. 1973), *Lab., Scotland*
*__Sturdy__, Robert W. (b. 1944), *C., Eastern*
*__Sumberg__, David (b. 1941), *C., North West*
*__Tannock__, Dr Charles (b. 1957), *C., London*
*__Titford__, Jeffrey (b. 1933), *UKIP, Eastern*
*__Titley__, Gary (b. 1950), *Lab., North West,*
*__Van Orden__, Geoffrey (b. 1945), *C., Eastern*
*__Wallis__, Diana (b. 1954), *LD, Yorkshire and the Humber*
*__Watson__, Graham R. (b. 1956), *LD, South West*
Whittaker, John (b. 1945), *UKIP, North West*
†**Willmott**, Glenis (b. 1951), *Lab., East Midlands*
Wise, Tom (b. 1948), *UKIP, Eastern*

UK REGIONS *as at 10 June 2004 election*

Abbreviations

AGS	Alliance for Green Socialism
Common	The Common Good
ED	English Democrats
EFP	English Freedom Party
FW	Forward Wales
NI	Non-attached Members
OCV	Operation Christian Vote
Peace	Peace Party
PPBG	People's Party for Better Government
Respect	Respect – Unity Coalition
SEA	Socialist Environmental Alliance
Senior	Senior Citizens
Soc. All.	Socialist Alliance
SSP	Scottish Socialist Party
SWW	Scottish Wind Watch

For other abbreviations, *see* UK General Election Results

For detailed information on which areas of the country are covered by a particular region, please contact the Home Office.

EASTERN

(Bedfordshire, Cambridgeshire, Essex, Hertfordshire, Luton, Norfolk, Peterborough, Southend-on-Sea, Suffolk, Thurrock)

E. 4,137,210	T. 36.73%
C.	465,526 (30.8%)
UKIP	296,160 (19.6%)
Lab.	244,929 (16.2%)
LD	211,378 (14.0%)
Ind.	93,028 (6.2%)
Green	84,068 (5.6%)
BNP	65,557 (4.3%)
ED	26,807 (1.8%)
Respect	13,904 (0.9%)
Ind.	5,137 (0.3%)
ProLife	3,730 (0.3%)
C. majority	169,366

(June 1999, C. maj. 174,959)

MEMBERS ELECTED
*G. van Orden, *C.*
*J. Titford, *UKIP*
*R. Howitt, *Lab.*
*R. Sturdy, *C.*
A. Duff, *LD*
*C. Beazley, *C.*
T. Wise, *UKIP*

EAST MIDLANDS

(Derby, Derbyshire, Leicester, Leicestershire, Northamptonshire, Nottingham, Nottinghamshire, Rutland)

E. 3,220,019	T. 43.88%
C.	371,362 (26.4%)
UKIP	366,498 (26.1%)
Lab.	294,918 (21.0%)
LD	181,964 (12.9%)
BNP	91,860 (6.5%)
Green	76,633 (5.5%)
Respect	20,009 (1.4%)
Ind.	2,615 (0.2%)
Ind.	847 (0.1%)
C. majority	4,864

(June 1999, C. maj. 78,906)

MEMBERS ELECTED
*R. Helmer, *C.*
‡R. Kilroy-Silk, *NI*
*P. Whitehead, *Lab.*
*C. Heaton-Harris, *C.*
D. Clark, *UKIP*
*W. Newton Dunn, *LD*

LONDON

E. 5,054,957	T. 37.65%
C.	504,941 (26.5%)
Lab.	466,584 (24.5%)
LD	288,790 (15.2%)
UKIP	232,633 (12.2%)
Green	158,986 (8.4%)
Respect	91,175 (4.8%)
BNP	76,152 (4.0%)
CPA	45,038 (2.4%)
ED	15,945 (0.8%)
PPBG	5,205 (0.3%)
C. majority	38,357

(June 1999, Lab. maj. 26,477)

MEMBERS ELECTED
†S. Kamall, *C.*
*C. Moraes, *Lab.*
*Baroness Ludford, *LD*
*J. Bowis, *C.*
*M. Honeyball, *Lab.*
G. Batten, *UKIP*
*C. Tannock, *C.*
*J. Lambert, *Green*
*R. Evans, *Lab.*

NORTH EAST

(Co. Durham, Darlington, Hartlepool, Middlesbrough, Northumberland, Redcar and Cleveland, Stockton-on-Tees, Tyne and Wear)

E. 1,905,132	T. 41.54%
Lab.	266,057 (34.1%)
C.	144,969 (18.6%)
LD	138,791 (17.8%)
UKIP	94,887 (12.2%)
BNP	50,249 (6.4%)
Ind.	39,658 (5.1%)
Green	37,247 (4.8%)
Respect	8,633 (1.1%)
Lab. majority	121,088

(June 1999, Lab. maj. 57,000)

MEMBERS ELECTED
*S. Hughes, *Lab.*
*M. Callanan, *C.*
Ms F. Hall, *LD*

NORTHERN IRELAND

(Northern Ireland forms a three-member seat with a single transferable vote system)

E. 1,072,669	T. 51.72%
Jim Allister, *NI*	175,761 (31.9%)
Bairbre de Brún, *SF*	144,541 (26.3%)
Jim Nicholson, *UUP*	91,164 (16.6%)
Martin Morgan, *SDLP*	87,559 (15.9%)
John Gilliland, *Ind.*	36,270 (6.6%)
Eamonn McCann, *SEA*	9,172 (1.6%)
Lindsay Whitcroft, *Green*	4,810 (0.9%)

MEMBERS ELECTED
**J. Allister, *NI*
B. de Brún, *SF*
*J. Nicholson, *UUP*

NORTH WEST

(Blackburn-with-Darwen, Blackpool, Cheshire, Cumbria, Greater Manchester, Halton, Lancashire, Merseyside, Warrington)

E. 5,151,488	T. 41.46%
Lab.	576,388 (27.3%)
C.	509,446 (24.1%)
LD	335,063 (15.8%)
UKIP	257,158 (12.2%)
BNP	134,959 (6.4%)
Green	117,393 (5.6%)
Lib.	96,325 (4.6%)
ED	34,110 (1.6%)
Respect	24,636 (1.2%)
Country	11,283 (0.5%)
ProLife	10,084 (0.5%)
Ind.	8,318 (0.4%)
Lab. majority	66,942

(June 1999, C. maj. 9,516)

MEMBERS ELECTED
*G. Titley, *Lab.*
*D. Dover, *C.*
*C. Davies, *LD*
*A. McCarthy, *Lab.*
J. Whittaker, *UKIP*
*D. Sumberg, *C.*
*T. Wynn, *Lab.*
*Sir Robert Atkins, *C.*
S. Karim, *LD*

SCOTLAND

E. 3,839,952	T. 30.75%
Lab.	310,865 (26.4%)
SNP	231,505 (19.7%)
C.	209,028 (17.8%)
LD	154,178 (13.1%)
Green	79,695 (6.8%)
UKIP	78,828 (6.7%)
SSP	61,356 (5.2%)
OCV	21,056 (1.8%)
BNP	19,427 (1.6%)
SWW	7,255 (0.6%)
Ind.	3,624 (0.3%)
Lab. majority	79,360

(June 1999, Lab. maj. 14,962)

MEMBERS ELECTED
*D. Martin, *Lab.*
*I. Hudghton, *SNP*
*S. Stevenson, *C.*
*C. Stihler, *Lab.*
*E. Attwooll, *LD*
A. Smith, *SNP*
*J. Purvis, *C.*

SOUTH EAST

(Bracknell Forest, Brighton and Hove, Buckinghamshire, East Sussex, Hampshire, Isle of Wight, Kent, Medway, Milton Keynes, Oxfordshire, Portsmouth, Reading, Slough, Southampton, Surrey, West Berkshire, West Sussex, Windsor and Maidenhead, Wokingham)

E. 6,034,549	T. 36.78%
C.	776,370 (35.2%)
UKIP	431,111 (19.5%)
LD	338,342 (15.3%)
Lab.	301,398 (13.7%)
Green	173,351 (7.9%)
BNP	64,877 (2.9%)
Senior	42,681 (1.9%)
ED	29,126 (1.3%)
Respect	13,426 (0.9%)
Peace	12,572 (0.6%)
CPA	11,733 (0.5%)
ProLife	6,579 (0.3%)
Ind.	5,671 (0.3%)
C. majority	345,259

(June 1999, C. maj. 369,785)

MEMBERS ELECTED
*D. Hannan, *C.*
*N. Farage, *UKIP*
*N. Deva, *C.*
†S. Bowles, *LD*
*P. Skinner, *Lab.*
*J. Elles, *C.*
‡A. Mote, *NI*
R. Ashworth, *C.*
*Dr Caroline Lucas, *Green*
*Baroness Nicholson of Winterbourne, *LD*

SOUTH WEST

(Bath and North East Somerset, Bournemouth, Bristol, Cornwall, Devon, Dorset, Gloucestershire, North Somerset, South Gloucestershire, Swindon, Torbay, Wiltshire)

E. 3,845,210	T. 37.80%
C.	457,371 (31.6%)
UKIP	326,784 (22.5%)
LD	265,619 (18.3%)
Lab.	209,908 (14.5%)
Green	103,821 (7.2%)
BNP	43,653 (3.0%)
Country	30,824 (2.1%)
Respect	10,437 (0.7%)
C. majority	130,587

(June 1999, C. maj. 246,283)

MEMBERS ELECTED
*N. Parish, *C.*
G. Booth, *UKIP*
*G. Watson, *LD*
*Dr Caroline Jackson, *C.*
*G. Ford, *Lab.*
R. Knapman, *UKIP*
*G. Chichester, *C.*

WALES

E. 2,218,649	T. 41.86%
Lab.	297,810 (32.1%)
C.	177,771 (19.1%)
PC	159,888 (17.2%)
UKIP	96,677 (10.4%)
LD	96,116 (10.4%)
Green	32,761 (3.5%)
BNP	27,135 (2.9%)
FW	17,280 (1.9%)
Ch. D	6,821 (0.7%)
Respect	5,427 (0.6%)
Lab. majority	120,039

(June 1999, Lab. maj. 14,455)

MEMBERS ELECTED
*G. Kinnock, *Lab.*
*J. Evans, *C.*
*J. Evans, *PC*
*E. Morgan, *Lab.*

WEST MIDLANDS

(Herefordshire, Shropshire, Staffordshire, Stoke-on-Trent, Telford and Wrekin, Warwickshire, West Midlands Metropolitan area, Worcestershire)

E. 3,957,848	T. 36.63%
C.	392,937 (27.3%)
Lab.	336,613 (23.4%)
UKIP	251,366 (17.5%)
LD	197,479 (13.7%)
BNP	107,794 (7.5%)
Green	73,991 (5.2%)
Respect	34,704 (2.4%)
Pensioner	33,501 (2.3%)
Common	8,650 (0.6%)
C. majority	56,324

(June 1999, C. maj. 84,048)

MEMBERS ELECTED
*P. Bushill-Matthews, *C.*
*M. Cashman, *Lab.*
M. Nattrass, *UKIP*
*E. Lynne, *LD*
*P. Bradbourn, *C.*
*N. Gill, *Lab.*
*M. Harbour, *C.*

YORKSHIRE AND THE HUMBER

(East Riding of Yorkshire, Kingston-upon-Hull, North East Lincolnshire, North Lincolnshire, North Yorkshire, South Yorkshire, West Yorkshire, York)

E. 3,719,717	T. 42.93%
Lab.	413,213 (26.3%)
C.	387,369 (24.6%)
LD	244,607 (15.6%)
UKIP	228,666 (14.0%)
BNP	126,538 (8.0%)
Green	90,337 (5.7%)
Respect	29,865 (1.9%)
ED	24,068 (1.5%)
Ind.	14,762 (0.9%)
AGS	13,776 (0.9%)
Lab. majority	25,844

(June 1999, C. maj. 39,629)

MEMBERS ELECTED
*Linda McAvan, *Lab.*
*T. Kirkhope, *C.*
*D. Wallis, *LD*
G. Bloom, *UKIP*
*R. Corbett, *Lab.*
*E. McMillan-Scott, *C.*

LAW COURTS AND OFFICES

HIERARCHY OF ENGLISH COURTS

Court	*Courts it binds*	*Courts it follows*
European court of justice	The court making the preliminary reference	None
House of Lords	All English courts	None
Court of appeal	Divisional courts High court Crown court County courts Magistrates' courts	House of Lords
Divisional courts	High court Crown court County courts Magistrates' courts	House of Lords Court of appeal
High court	County courts Magistrates' courts	House of Lords Court of appeal Divisional courts
Crown court	None	House of Lords
County courts	None	Court of appeal
Magistrates' courts	None	Divisional courts High court

JUDICATURE OF ENGLAND AND WALES

The legal system in England and Wales is divided into criminal law and civil law. Criminal law is concerned with acts harmful to the community and the rules laid down by the state for the benefit of citizens, whereas civil law governs the relationships and transactions between individuals. Administrative law is a kind of civil law usually concerning the interaction of individuals and the state, and most cases are heard in tribunals specific to the subject (*see* Tribunals section). Scotland and Northern Ireland possess legal systems that differ from the system in England and Wales in law, judicial procedure and court structure, but retain the distinction between criminal and civil law.

The appellate committee of the House of Lords is the supreme judicial authority. It is the ultimate court of appeal for all courts in Great Britain and Northern Ireland (except criminal courts in Scotland) for all cases except those concerning the interpretation and application of European Community law, including preliminary rulings requested by British courts and tribunals, which are decided by the European court of justice (*see* European Union section). As a court of appeal the House of Lords consists of 12 Lords of Appeal in Ordinary (law lords); virtually all appeals concern the meaning of the law, rather than the evidence in a particular case.

Under the provisions of the Criminal Appeal Act 1995, a commission was set up to direct and supervise investigations into possible miscarriages of justice and to refer cases to the courts on the grounds of conviction and sentence; these functions were formerly the responsibility of the home secretary.

SUPREME COURT OF JUDICATURE

The supreme court of judicature comprises the high court of justice, the crown court and the court of appeal. The President of the Courts of England and Wales, a new title given to the Lord Chief Justice under the Constitutional Reform Act 2005, is the head of the judiciary.

The high court was created in 1875 and combined many previously separate courts. Sittings are held at the royal courts of justice in London or at about 120 district registries outside the capital. It is the superior civil court and is split into three divisions – the chancery division, the Queen's bench division and the family division – each of which is further divided. The chancery division is headed by the Chancellor of the High Court and is concerned mainly with equity, trusts, tax and bankruptcy, while also including two specialist courts, the patents court and the companies court. The Queen's bench division (QBD) is the largest of the three divisions, and is headed by its own president, who is also Head of Criminal Justice. It deals with common law (ie tort, contract, debt and personal injuries), some tax law, eg VAT tribunal appeals, and encompasses the admiralty court and the commercial court. The QBD also administers the technology and construction court. The family division was created in 1970 and is headed by its own president, who is also Head of Family Justice, and hears cases concerning divorce, access to and custody of children, and other family matters. The divisional court of the high court sits in the family and chancery divisions, and hears appeals from the magistrates' courts and county courts.

The crown court was set up in 1972 and sits at 92 centres throughout England and Wales. It deals with more serious (indictable) criminal offences, which are triable before a judge and jury, including treason, murder, rape, kidnapping, armed robbery and Official Secrets Act offences. It also handles cases transferred from the magistrates' courts where the magistrate decides his or her own power of sentence is inadequate, or where someone appeals against a magistrate's decision, or in a case that is triable 'either way' where the accused has chosen a jury trial. The crown court centres are divided into three tiers: high court judges, and sometimes circuit judges and recorders (part-time circuit judges), sit in first-tier centres and deal with the most serious (Class 1) criminal offences (eg murder, treason) and with some civil high court cases; the second-tier centres are presided over by high court judges, circuit judges or recorders and deal with Class 2 criminal offences (eg rape, manslaughter); third-tier courts deal with Class 3 criminal offences, with circuit judges or recorders presiding.

The court of appeal hears appeals against both fact and law, and was last restructured in 1966 when it replaced the court of criminal appeal. It is split into the civil division (which hears appeals from the high court, tribunals and in certain cases, the county courts) and the criminal division (which hears appeals from the crown court). Cases are heard by Lord Justices of Appeal if deemed suitable for reconsideration.

The Constitutional Reform Act 2005 instigated several key changes to the judiciary in England and Wales. These include the provision for the establishment of an independent supreme court, scheduled to open in October 2009; the reform of the post of Lord Chancellor, transferring its judicial functions to the President of the Courts of England and Wales; a duty on government ministers to uphold the independence of the judiciary by barring them from trying to influence judicial decisions through any special access to judges; the formation of a fully transparent and independent Judicial Appointments Commission that is responsible for selecting candidates to recommend for judicial appointment to the Secretary of State for Justice; and the creation of the post of Judicial Appointments and Conduct Ombudsman.

CRIMINAL CASES

In criminal matters the decision to prosecute (in the majority of cases) rests with the Crown Prosecution Service (CPS), which is the independent prosecuting body in England and Wales. The CPS is headed by the director of public prosecutions, who works under the superintendence of the Attorney-General. Certain categories of offence continue to require the Attorney-General's consent for prosecution.

Most minor criminal cases (summary offences) are dealt with in magistrates' courts, usually by a bench of three unpaid lay magistrates (justices of the peace) sitting without a jury and assisted on points of law and procedure by a legally trained clerk. There were 29,419 justices of the peace as at 1 April 2008. In busier courts a full-time, salaried and legally qualified 'district judge (magistrates' court)' – formerly known as a stipendiary judge – presides alone. There were 136 district judges (magistrates' courts) as at 1 April 2008. Magistrates' courts oversee the completion of 95 per cent of all criminal cases. Magistrates' courts also house some family proceedings courts (which deal with relationship breakdown and childcare cases) and youth courts. Cases of medium seriousness (known as 'offences triable either way') where the defendant pleads not guilty can be heard in the crown court for a trial by jury, if the defendant so chooses. Preliminary proceedings in a serious case to decide whether there is evidence to justify committal for trial in the crown court are dealt with in the magistrates' courts.

The 92 centres that the crown court sits in are divided into seven regions; a case is presided over by high court judges, circuit judges or recorders. There were 1,305 recorders as at 1 April 2008; they must sit a minimum of 15 days per year and are usually subject to a maximum of 30. A jury is present in all trials that are contested.

Appeals from magistrates' courts against sentence or conviction are made to the crown court, and appeals upon a point of law are made to the high court, which may ultimately be appealed to the House of Lords. Appeals from the crown court, either against sentence or conviction, are made to the court of appeal (criminal division), presided over by the Lord Chief Justice. Again, these appeals may be brought to the House of Lords if a point of law is contested, and if the house considers it is of sufficient importance.

CIVIL CASES

Most minor civil cases – including contract, tort (especially personal injuries), property, divorce and other family matters, bankruptcy etc – are dealt with by the county courts, of which there are 216 (*see* the Court Service website, W www.hmcourts-service.gov.uk, for further details). Cases are heard by circuit judges, recorders or district judges. For cases involving small claims (with certain exceptions, where the amount claimed is £5,000 or less) there are informal and simplified procedures designed to enable parties to present their cases themselves without recourse to lawyers. Where there are financial limits on county court jurisdiction, claims that exceed those limits may be tried in the county courts with the consent of the parties, subject to the court's agreement, or in certain circumstances on transfer from the high court. Outside London, bankruptcy proceedings can be heard in designated county courts. Magistrates' courts also deal with certain classes of civil case and committees of magistrates license public houses, clubs and betting shops. For the implementation of the Children Act 1989, a new structure of hearing centres was set up in 1991 for family proceedings cases, involving magistrates' courts (family proceedings courts), divorce county courts, family hearing centres and care centres.

Appeals in certain family matters heard in the family proceedings courts go to the family division of the high court. Appeals against decisions made in magistrates' courts are heard in the crown court. Appeals from county courts may be heard in the court of appeal (civil division), presided over by the Master of the Rolls, and may go on to the House of Lords.

CORONERS' COURTS

The coroners' courts investigate violent and unnatural deaths or sudden deaths where the cause is unknown. Doctors, the police, various public authorities or members of the public may bring cases before a local coroner (a senior lawyer or doctor), in order to determine whether further criminal investigation is necessary. Where a death is sudden and the cause is unknown, the coroner may order a post-mortem examination to determine the cause of death rather than hold an inquest in court. An inquest must be held however if a person died in a violent or unnatural way, or died in prison or other unusual circumstances. If the coroner suspects murder, manslaughter or infanticide, he or she must summon a jury.

HOUSE OF LORDS

AS FINAL COURT OF APPEAL

Senior Lord of Appeal in Ordinary (£211,000), Rt. Hon. Lord Phillips of Worth Matravers, 1938, *apptd* 2008

LORDS OF APPEAL IN ORDINARY *as at 13 June 2008* (each £203,800)
Style, The Rt. Hon. Lord/Lady–

Rt. Hon. Lord Hoffmann, *born* 1934, *apptd* 1995
Rt. Hon. Lord Hope of Craighead, *born* 1938, *apptd* 1996
Rt. Hon. Lord Saville of Newdigate, *born* 1936, *apptd* 1997
Rt. Hon. Lord Scott of Foscote, *born* 1934, *apptd* 2000
Rt. Hon. Lord Rodger of Earlsferry, *born* 1944, *apptd* 2001
Rt. Hon. Lord Walker of Gestingthorpe, *born* 1938, *apptd* 2002
Rt. Hon. Lady Hale of Richmond, *born* 1945, *apptd* 2004
Rt. Hon. Lord Carswell, *born* 1934, *apptd* 2004
Rt. Hon. Lord Brown of Eaton-under-Heywood, *born* 1937, *apptd* 2004
Rt. Hon. Lord Mance, *born* 1943, *apptd* 2005
Rt. Hon. Lord Neuberger of Abbotsbury, *born* 1948, *apptd* 2007

JUDICIAL OFFICE OF THE HOUSE OF LORDS
House of Lords, London SW1A 0PW T 020-7219 3111
Registrar, Clerk of the Parliaments

SENIOR JUDICIARY OF ENGLAND AND WALES

Lord Chief Justice of England and Wales (£236,300), Rt. Hon. Sir Igor Judge, *born* 1941, *apptd* 2008
Master of the Rolls and Head of Civil Justice (£211,000), Rt. Hon. Sir Anthony Clarke, *born* 1943, *apptd* 2005
President of the Queen's Bench Division and Head of Criminal Justice (£203,800), *vacant*
President of the Family Division and Head of Family Justice (£203,800), Rt. Hon. Sir Mark Potter, *born* 1937, *apptd* 2005
Chancellor of the High Court (£203,800), Rt. Hon. Sir Robert Morritt, CVO, *born* 1938, *apptd* 2000

SUPREME COURT OF JUDICATURE

COURT OF APPEAL
Master of the Rolls (£211,000), Rt. Hon. Sir Anthony Clarke, *born* 1943, *apptd* 2005
Secretary, Ms J. Sears
Clerk, Dawn Rollason

LORD JUSTICES OF APPEAL *as at 13 June 2008* (each £193,800)
Style, The Rt. Hon. Lord/Lady Justice [surname]

Rt. Hon. Sir Malcolm Pill, *born* 1938, *apptd* 1995
Rt. Hon. Sir Alan Ward, *born* 1938, *apptd* 1995
Rt. Hon. Sir Mathew Thorpe, *born* 1938, *apptd* 1995
Rt. Hon. Sir George Waller, *born* 1940, *apptd* 1996
Rt. Hon. Sir John Mummery, *born* 1938, *apptd* 1996
Rt. Hon. Sir Anthony May, *born* 1940, *apptd* 1997
Rt. Hon. Sir Simon Tuckey, *born* 1941, *apptd* 1998
Rt. Hon. Sir John Laws, *born* 1945, *apptd* 1999
Rt. Hon. Sir Stephen Sedley, *born* 1939, *apptd* 1999
Rt. Hon. Sir David Latham, *born* 1942, *apptd* 2000
Rt. Hon. Sir Bernard Rix, *born* 1944, *apptd* 2000
Rt. Hon. Dame Mary Arden, DBE, *born* 1947, *apptd* 2000
Rt. Hon. Sir David Keene, *born* 1941, *apptd* 2000
Rt. Hon. Sir John Dyson, *born* 1943, *apptd* 2001
Rt. Hon. Sir Andrew Longmore, *born* 1944, *apptd* 2001
Rt. Hon. Sir Robert Carnwath, CVO, *born* 1945, *apptd* 2002
Rt. Hon. Sir Scott Baker, *born* 1937, *apptd* 2002
Rt. Hon. Dame Janet Smith, DBE, *born* 1940, *apptd* 2002
Rt. Hon. Sir Roger Thomas, *born* 1947, *apptd* 2003
Rt. Hon. Sir Robin Jacob, *born* 1941, *apptd* 2003
Rt. Hon. Sir Nicholas Wall, *born* 1945, *apptd* 2004
Rt. Hon. Sir Maurice Kay, *born* 1942, *apptd* 2004
Rt. Hon. Sir Anthony Hooper, *born* 1937, *apptd* 2004
Rt. Hon. Sir William Gage, *born* 1938, *apptd* 2004
Rt. Hon. Sir Timothy Lloyd, *born* 1946, *apptd* 2005
Rt. Hon. Sir Martin Moore-Bick, *born* 1948, *apptd* 2005
Rt. Hon. Sir Nicholas Wilson, *born* 1945, *apptd* 2005
Rt. Hon. Sir Alan Moses, *born* 1945, *apptd* 2005
Rt. Hon. Sir Stephen Richards, *born* 1950, *apptd* 2005
Rt. Hon. Dame Heather Hallett, DBE, *born* 1949, *apptd* 2005
Rt. Hon. Sir Anthony Hughes, *born* 1948, *apptd* 2006
Rt. Hon. Sir Brian Leveson, *born* 1949, *apptd* 2006
Rt. Hon. Sir Lawrence Collins, *born* 1941, *apptd* 2007
Rt. Hon. Sir Roger Toulson, *born* 1946, *apptd* 2007
Rt. Hon. Sir Colin Rimer, *born* 1944, *apptd* 2007
Rt. Hon. Sir Stanley Burnton, *born* 1942, *apptd* 2007
Rt. Hon. Sir Rupert Jackson, *born* 1948, *apptd* 2008
Rt. Hon. Sir John Goldring, *born* 1944, *apptd* 2008

Ex Officio Judges, Lord Chief Justice of England and Wales; Master of the Rolls; President of the Queen's Bench Division; President of the Family Division; and Chancellor of the High Court

COURT OF APPEAL (CIVIL DIVISION)
Vice-President, Rt. Hon. Sir Mark Waller

COURT OF APPEAL (CRIMINAL DIVISION)
Vice-President, Rt. Hon. Sir David Latham
Judges, Lord Chief Justice of England and Wales; Master of the Rolls; Lord Justices of Appeal; and Judges of the High Court of Justice

COURTS-MARTIAL APPEAL COURT
Judges, Lord Chief Justice of England and Wales; Master of the Rolls; Lord Justices of Appeal; and Judges of the High Court of Justice

HIGH COURT OF JUSTICE

CHANCERY DIVISION
Chancellor of the High Court (£203,800), Rt. Hon. Sir Andrew Morritt, CVO, *born* 1938, *apptd* 2000
Secretary, Ms E. Harbert
Clerk, Sheila Glasgow

JUDGES *as at 13 June 2008* (each £170,200)
Style, The Hon. Mr/Mrs Justice [surname]

Hon. Sir John Lindsay, *born* 1935, *apptd* 1992
Hon. Sir Edward Evans-Lombe, *born* 1937, *apptd* 1993
Hon. Sir William Blackburne, *born* 1944, *apptd* 1993
Hon. Sir Nicholas Patten, *born* 1950, *apptd* 2000
Hon. Sir Terrence Etherton, *born* 1951, *apptd* 2001

Hon. Sir Peter Smith, *born* 1952, *apptd* 2002
Hon. Sir Kim Lewison, *born* 1952, *apptd* 2003
Hon. Sir David Richards, *born* 1951, *apptd* 2003
Hon. Sir George Mann, *born* 1951, *apptd* 2004
Hon. Sir Nicholas Warren, *born* 1949, *apptd* 2005
Hon. Sir David Kitchin, *born* 1955, *apptd* 2005
Hon. Sir Michael Briggs, *born* 1954, *apptd* 2006
Hon. Sir Launcelot Henderson, *born* 1951, *apptd* 2006
Hon. Sir Paul Morgan, *born* 1952, *apptd* 2007
Hon. Sir Alastair Norris, *born* 1950, *apptd* 2007
Hon. Sir Gerald Barling, *born* 1949, *apptd* 2007
Hon. Sir Christopher Floyd, *born* 1951, *apptd* 2007

The Chancery Division also includes three specialist courts: the companies court, the patents court and the bankruptcy court.

QUEEN'S BENCH DIVISION
Lord Chief Justice of England and Wales (£236,300), Rt. Hon. Sir Igor Judge, *born* 1941, *apptd* 2008
Secretary, Michèle Souris
Clerk, Helen Tyler
President (£203,800), vacant
Vice-President (£193,800), Rt. Hon. Sir Anthony May, *born* 1940, *apptd* 2002

JUDGES *as at 13 June 2008* (each £170,200)
Style, The Hon. Mr/Mrs Justice [surname]

Hon. Sir Stuart McKinnon, *born* 1938, *apptd* 1988
Hon. Sir John Forbes, *born* 1938, *apptd* 1993
Hon. Sir Andrew Collins, *born* 1942, *apptd* 1994
Hon. Sir Alexander Butterfield, *born* 1942, *apptd* 1995
Hon. Sir Robert Nelson, *born* 1942, *apptd* 1996
Hon. Sir David Eady, *born* 1943, *apptd* 1997
Hon. Sir Jeremy Sullivan, *born* 1945, *apptd* 1997
Hon. Sir David Penry-Davey, *born* 1942, *apptd* 1997
Hon. Sir David Steel, *born* 1943, *apptd* 1998
Hon. Sir Nicolas Bratza, *born* 1945, *apptd* 1998
Hon. Sir Michael Burton, *born* 1946, *apptd* 1998
Hon. Sir Patrick Elias, *born* 1947, *apptd* 1999
Hon. Sir Richard Aikens, *born* 1948, *apptd* 1999
Hon. Sir Stephen Silber, *born* 1944, *apptd* 1999
Hon. Dame Anne Rafferty, DBE, *born* 1950, *apptd* 2000
Hon. Sir Geoffrey Grigson, *born* 1944, *apptd* 2000
Hon. Sir Richard Henriques, *born* 1943, *apptd* 2000
Hon. Sir Stephen Tomlinson, *born* 1952, *apptd* 2000
Hon. Sir Andrew Smith, *born* 1947, *apptd* 2000
Hon. Sir Christopher Pitchford, *born* 1947, *apptd* 2000
Hon. Sir Duncan Ouseley, *born* 1950, *apptd* 2000
Hon. Sir Richard McCombe, *born* 1952, *apptd* 2001
Hon. Sir Raymond Jack, *born* 1942, *apptd* 2001
Hon. Sir Robert Owen, *born* 1944, *apptd* 2001
Hon. Sir Colin Mackay, *born* 1943, *apptd* 2001
Hon. Sir John Mitting, *born* 1947, *apptd* 2001
Hon. Sir Roderick Evans, *born* 1946, *apptd* 2001
Hon. Sir Nigel Davis, *born* 1951, *apptd* 2001
Hon. Sir Peter Gross, *born* 1952, *apptd* 2001
Hon. Sir Brian Keith, *born* 1944, *apptd* 2001
Hon. Sir Jeremy Cooke, *born* 1949, *apptd* 2001
Hon. Sir Richard Field, *born* 1947, *apptd* 2002
Hon. Sir Colman Treacy, *born* 1949, *apptd* 2002
Hon. Sir Peregrine Simon, *born* 1950, *apptd* 2002
Hon. Sir Roger Royce, *born* 1944, *apptd* 2002
Hon. Dame Laura Cox, DBE, *born* 1951, *apptd* 2002
Hon. Sir Adrian Fulford, *born* 1953, *apptd* 2002
Hon. Sir Jack Beatson, *born* 1948, *apptd* 2003
Hon. Sir Michael Tugendhat, *born* 1944, *apptd* 2003
Hon. Sir David Clarke, *born* 1942, *apptd* 2003
Hon. Dame Elizabeth Gloster, DBE, *born* 1949, *apptd* 2004
Hon. Sir David Bean, *born* 1954, *apptd* 2004
Hon. Sir Alan Wilkie, *born* 1947, *apptd* 2004
Hon. Dame Linda Dobbs, DBE, *born* 1951, *apptd* 2004
Hon. Sir Henry Hodge, OBE, *born* 1944, *apptd* 2004
Hon. Sir Paul Walker, *born* 1954, *apptd* 2004
Hon. Sir David Calvert-Smith, *born* 1945, *apptd* 2005
Hon. Sir Christopher Clarke, *born* 1947, *apptd* 2005
Hon. Sir Charles Openshaw, *born* 1947, *apptd* 2005
Hon. Dame Caroline Swift, DBE, *born* 1955, *apptd* 2005
Hon. Sir Brian Langstaff, *born* 1948, *apptd* 2005
Hon. Sir David Jones, *born* 1952, *apptd* 2005
Hon. Sir Vivian Ramsey, *born* 1950, *apptd* 2005
Hon. Sir Nicholas Underhill, *born* 1952, *apptd* 2006
Hon. Sir Stephen Irwin, *born* 1953, *apptd* 2006
Hon. Sir Nigel Teare, *born* 1952, *apptd* 2006
Hon. Sir Griffith Williams, *born* 1944, *apptd* 2007
Hon. Sir Wyn Williams, *born* 1951, *apptd* 2007
Hon. Sir Timothy King, *born* 1946, *apptd* 2007
Hon. Sir John Saunders, *born* 1959, *apptd* 2007
Hon. Sir Julian Flaux, *born* 1955, *apptd* 2007
Hon. Sir Nicholas Stadlen, *born* 1950, *apptd* 2007
Hon. Sir Robert Akenhead, *born* 1949, *apptd* 2007
Hon. Sir David Foskett, *born* 1949, *apptd* 2007
Hon. Sir Nicholas Blake, *born* 1949, *apptd* 2007
Hon. Sir Ross Cranston, *born* 1948, *apptd* 2007
Hon. Sir Peter Coulson, *born* 1958, *apptd* 2008
Hon. Sir David Maddison, *born* 1947, *apptd* 2008
Hon. Sir Richard Plender, *born* 1945, *apptd* 2008
Hon. Sir William Blair, *born* 1950, *apptd* 2008
Hon. Sir Alistair MacDuff, *born* 1945, *apptd* 2008
Hon. Sir Ian Burnett, *born* 1958, *apptd* 2008

The Queen's Bench Division also includes three specialist courts – the commercial court, the admiralty court and the administration court – and administers the technology and construction court.

FAMILY DIVISION
President (£203,800), Rt. Hon. Sir Mark Potter, *born* 1937, *apptd* 2005
Secretary, Mrs S. Leung
Clerk, John Curtis

JUDGES *as at 13 June 2008* (each £170,200)
Style, The Hon. Mr/Mrs Justice [surname]

Hon. Sir Jan Singer, *born* 1944, *apptd* 1993
Hon. Sir Hugh Bennett, *born* 1943, *apptd* 1995
Hon. Sir Edward Holman, *born* 1947, *apptd* 1995
Hon. Dame Mary Hogg, DBE, *born* 1947, *apptd* 1995
Hon. Sir Arthur Charles, *born* 1948, *apptd* 1998
Hon. Sir David Bodey, *born* 1947, *apptd* 1999
Hon. Dame Jill Black, DBE, *born* 1954, *apptd* 1999
Hon. Sir James Munby, *born* 1948, *apptd* 2000
Hon. Sir Paul Coleridge, *born* 1949, *apptd* 2000
Hon. Sir Mark Hedley, *born* 1946, *apptd* 2002
Hon. Dame Anna Pauffley, DBE, *born* 1956, *apptd* 2003
Hon. Sir Roderic Wood, *born* 1951, *apptd* 2004
Hon. Dame Florence Baron, DBE, *born* 1952, *apptd* 2004
Hon. Sir Ernest Ryder, *born* 1957, *apptd* 2004
Hon. Sir Andrew McFarlane, *born* 1954, *apptd* 2005
Hon. Dame Julia Macur, DBE, *born* 1957, *apptd* 2005
Hon. Sir Andrew Moylan, *born* 1953, *apptd* 2007
Hon. Dame Eleanor King, DBE, *born* 1957, *apptd* 2008
Hon. Dame Judith Parker, DBE, *born* 1950, *apptd* 2008

SUPREME COURT DEPARTMENTS AND OFFICES
Royal Courts of Justice, London WC2A 2LL
T 020-7947 6000

DIRECTOR'S OFFICE
T 020-7947 6159
Director, D. Thompson
Area Directors, L. Ladlow *(Court of Appeal)*; S. Fash *(High Court Group)*; H. Smith *(Probate Service)*
Managers, K. Richardson *(Finance)*; A. Monsarrat *(Regional Change and Performance)*

ADMIRALTY AND COMMERCIAL REGISTRY AND MARSHAL'S OFFICE
T 020-7947 6112
Registrar (£101,400), P. Miller
Admiralty Marshal and Court Manager, K. Houghton

BANKRUPTCY AND COMPANIES COURT
T 020-7947 6441
Chief Registrar (£126,400), S. Baister
Bankruptcy Registrars (£101,400), C. Derrett; G. W. Jaques; W. Nicholls; J. A. Simmonds
Court Manager, P. O'Brien

CENTRAL OFFICE OF THE SUPREME COURT
Senior Master of the Supreme Court (QBD), and Queen's Remembrancer (£126,400), S. D. Whitaker
Masters of the Supreme Court (QBD) (£101,400), P. G. A. Eyre; B. J. F. Fontaine; I. H. Foster; H. J. Leslie; P. Miller; G. H. Rose; J. G. G. Ungley; B. Yoxall
Court Manager, M. A. Brown

CHANCERY CHAMBERS
T 020-7947 6754
Chief Master of the Supreme Court (£126,400), J. I. Winegarten
Masters of the Supreme Court (£101,400), T. J. Bowles; N. W. Bragge; J. A. Moncaster; N. S. Price; P. R. Teverson
Court Manager, P. O'Brien

COURT OF APPEAL CIVIL DIVISION
T 020-7947 6916
Area Director (£101,400), L. Ladlow
Court Manager, Michael O'Neill

COURT OF APPEAL CRIMINAL DIVISION
T 020-7947 6011
Registrar (£101,400), R. A. Venne
Deputy Registrar, Ms P. A. Donnelly
Area Manager, Miss C. Brownbill

ADMINISTRATIVE OFFICE OF THE SUPREME COURT
T 020-7947 6655
Master of the Crown Office, and Queen's Coroner and Attorney (£101,400), R. A. Venne
Head of Crown Office, Mrs L. G. Knapman

EXAMINERS OF THE COURT
Empowered to take examination of witnesses in all divisions of the High Court.
Examiners, M. W. M. Chism; A. G. Dyer; A. W. Hughes; Mrs G. M. Keene; R. M. Planterose

SUPREME COURT COSTS OFFICE
T 020-7947 6423
Senior Costs Judge (£126,400), P. T. Hurst
Masters of the Supreme Court (£101,400), C. D. N. Campbell; A. Gordon-Saker; P. Haworth; J. E. O'Hare; P. R. Rogers; J. Simons; C. C. Wright
Court Manager, vacant

COURT OF PROTECTION
11th Floor, Archway Towers, 2 Junction Road, London N19 5SZ
T 0845-330 2900
Senior Judge (£126,400), D. Lush

ELECTION PETITIONS OFFICE
Room E19, Royal Courts of Justice, London WC2A 2LL
T 020-7947 7529

The office accepts petitions and deals with all matters relating to the questioning of parliamentary, European parliament and local government elections, and with applications for relief under the 'representation of the people' legislation.
Prescribed Officer (£126,400), S. D. Whitaker
Chief Clerk, M. Parker

OFFICE OF THE LORD CHANCELLOR'S VISITORS
11th Floor, Archway Towers, 2 Junction Road, London N19 5SZ
T 020-7664 7317

The Mental Capacity Act 2005 came into force on 1 October 2007, and it makes provision for two panels of court of protection visitors (special visitors or general visitors). At the time of going to press, no appointments had been made to either panel.

OFFICIAL RECEIVERS' DEPARTMENT
21 Bloomsbury Street, London WC1B 3QW
T 020-7637 1110
Chief Executive, S. Speed
Deputies, L. Gramp; G. Horn

OFFICIAL SOLICITOR'S DEPARTMENT
81 Chancery Lane, London WC2A 1DD
T 020-7911 7127
Official Solicitor to the Supreme Court, A. Pitblado
Deputy Official Solicitor, M. Maughan
Public Trustee, N. Crew

PRINCIPAL REGISTRY (FAMILY DIVISION)
First Avenue House, 42–49 High Holborn, London WC1V 6NP
T 020-7947 6000
Senior District Judge (£126,400), P. Waller
District Judges (£101,400), A. R. S. Bassett-Cross; M. C. Berry; Ms H. Black; Ms S. M. Bowman; Ms H. C. Bradley; G. C. Brasse; Ms P. Cushing; Ms K. E. Green; P. Greene; R. Harper; Ms H. MacGregor; K. Malik; C. Million; Ms D. Redgrave; Ms C. Reid; Ms L. D. Roberts; R. Robinson; Ms S. Walker; K. J. White
Area Director, London Civil and Family, L. Lennon
Head of Operations, London Family, J. Miller
Director for the Probate Service, H. Smith

DISTRICT PROBATE REGISTRARS
Probate Manager of London, K. Donnelly
Birmingham District, P. Walbeoff
Brighton District, K. Murphy
Bristol District, R. Joyce
Ipswich District, H. Whitby
Leeds District, A. Parry
Liverpool District, K. Clark-Rimmer
Manchester District, P. Burch

Newcastle District, C. Riley
Oxford District, R. D'Costa
Wales District, P. Curran
Winchester District, A. Butler

JUDGE ADVOCATES

The Judge Advocates are the officers in supreme control of the courts martial in the armed forces; historically, the Judge Advocate of the Fleet for the Royal Navy and the Judge Advocate-General for the Army and Royal Air Force. However, since 2004 the functions of the Judge Advocate of the Fleet have been largely delegated to the Judge Advocate-General. The two offices were amalgamated in 2008 under the Armed Forces Act 2006, and the role of Judge Advocate of the Fleet was completely transferred to the Judge Advocate General.

OFFICE OF THE JUDGE ADVOCATE-GENERAL OF THE FORCES
81 Chancery Lane, London WC2A IBQ
T 020-7218 8095
Judge Advocate-General (£136,500), His Hon. Judge Blackett
Vice-Judge Advocate-General (£119,000), Michael Hunter
Judge Advocates (£105,400)*, J. F. T. Bayliss; C. R. Burn; J. P. Camp; M. R. Elsom; R. D. Hill; A. J. B. McGrigor; R. C. C. Seymour
Style for Judge Advocates, Judge Advocate [surname]

* Salary includes £2,000 London salary lead and a London allowance of £2,000

HIGH COURT AND CROWN COURT CENTRES

First-tier centres deal with both civil and criminal cases and are served by high court and circuit judges. Second-tier centres deal with criminal cases only and are served by high court and circuit judges. Third-tier centres deal with criminal cases only and are served only by circuit judges.

LONDON REGION
First-tier – None
Second-tier – Central Criminal Court
Third-tier – Blackfriars, Harrow, Inner London Sessions House, Isleworth, Kingston, Snaresbrook, Southwark, Wood Green, Woolwich & Croydon
Regional Director, Kevin Pogson, 2nd Floor, Rose Court, 2 Southwark Bridge, London SE1 9HS T 020-7921 2010
Area Directors (London Crown), Sarah McAdam *(Central and South)*; Sandra Aston *(North and West)*
Area Director (London Civil and Family), Linda Lennon

The high court in Greater London sits at the Royal Courts of Justice.

MIDLAND REGION
First-tier – Birmingham, Lincoln, Nottingham, Stafford, Warwick
Second-tier – Leicester, Northampton, Shrewsbury, Worcester, Wolverhampton
Third-tier – Coventry, Derby, Hereford, Stoke-on-Trent
Regional Director, Alan Eccles, PO Box 11772, 6th Floor, Temple Court, Bull Street, Birmingham B4 6WF
T 0121-250 6162
Area Directors, Kelvin Launchbury *(Birmingham, Coventry, Solihull and Warwickshire)*; Peter Hammersley *(Black Country, Staffordshire and West Mercia)*; Mark Swales *(Derbyshire and Nottinghamshire)*; Richard Redgrave *(Leicestershire, Lincolnshire and Northamptonshire)*

NORTH-EAST REGION
First-tier – Leeds, Newcastle upon Tyne, Sheffield, Teesside
Second-tier – Bradford, York
Third-tier – Doncaster, Durham, Kingston-upon-Hull, Great Grimsby
Regional Director, S. Caven, 18th Floor, West Riding House, Albion Street, Leeds LS1 5AA T 0113-251 1200
Area Directors, Sheila Proudlock *(Cleveland, Durham and Northumbria)*; Paul Bradley *(South Yorkshire and Humber)*; Dyfed Foulkes *(North and West Yorkshire)*

NORTH-WEST REGION
First-tier – Carlisle, Chester, Liverpool, Manchester (Crown Square), Preston
Third-tier – Barrow-in-Furness, Bolton, Burnley, Knutsford, Lancaster, Manchester (Minshull Street), Warrington
Regional Director, Christine Mayer, PO Box 4237, Manchester M60 1TE T 0161-240 5800
Area Directors, Shaun McNally *(Cheshire and Merseyside)*; Gill Hague *(Cumbria and Lancashire)*; Richard Knott *(Greater Manchester)*

SOUTH-EAST REGION
First-tier – Cambridge, Chelmsford, Lewes, Norwich, Oxford
Second-tier – Ipswich, Luton, Maidstone, Reading, St Albans
Third-tier – Aylesbury, Basildon, Canterbury, Chichester, Croydon, Guildford, King's Lynn, Peterborough, Southend
Regional Director, Keith Budgen, 3rd Floor, Rose Court, 2 Southwark Bridge, London SE1 9HS
T 020-7921 2061
Area Directors, Mark Littlewood *(Bedfordshire, Essex and Hertfordshire)*; Dave Weston *(Kent)*; Pauline Cornford *(Norfolk, Suffolk and Cambridgeshire)*; Julia Eeles *(Sussex and Surrey)*; Jonathan Lane *(Thames Valley)*

SOUTH-WEST REGION
First-tier – Bristol, Exeter, Truro, Winchester
Second-tier – Dorchester & Weymouth, Gloucester, Plymouth
Third-tier – Barnstaple, Bournemouth, Newport (IoW), Portsmouth, Salisbury, Southampton, Swindon, Taunton
Regional Director, Peter Risk, 5th Floor, Greyfriars, Lewins Mead, Bristol BS1 2NR T 0117-910 3600
Area Directors, Rod White *(Avon and Somerset)*; David Gentry *(Devon and Cornwall)*; Rod Brummitt *(Dorset, Gloucestershire and Wiltshire)*; Simon Townley *(Hampshire and Isle of Wight)*

WALES REGION
First-tier – Caernarfon, Cardiff, Mold, Swansea
Second-tier – Carmarthen, Merthyr Tydfil, Newport, Welshpool
Third-tier – Dolgellau, Haverfordwest
Regional Director, Miss C. Pillman, Churchill House, Churchill Way, Cardiff CF10 2HH T 029-2067 8302
Area Directors, Luigi Strinati *(Mid and West Wales)*; Howard Lloyd *(North Wales)*; Alan Davies *(South-East Wales)*

CIRCUIT JUDGES

Circuit judges are barristers of at least seven years' standing or recorders of at least five years' standing. Circuit judges serve in the county courts and the crown court.

Style, His/Her Hon. Judge [surname]
Senior Presiding Judge, Rt. Hon. Lord Justice Leveson
Senior Circuit Judges, each £136,500
Circuit Judges at the Central Criminal Court, London (Old Bailey Judges), each £136,500
Circuit Judges, each £126,400

LONDON REGION
Presiding Judges, Hon. Mr Justice Bean; Hon. Mr Justice Calvert-Smith; Hon. Mr Justice Cooke; Hon. Mr Justice Gross

MIDLAND REGION
Presiding Judges, Hon. Mrs Justice Macur, DBE; Hon. Mr Justice Treacy

NORTH-EAST REGION
Presiding Judges, Hon. Mr Justice Simon; Hon. Mr Justice Wilkie

NORTH-WEST REGION
Presiding Judges, Hon. Mr Justice David Clarke; Hon. Mr Justice Irwin
Family Division Liaison Judge, Hon. Mr Justice Ryder

SOUTH-EAST REGION
Presiding Judges, Hon. Mr Justice Bean; Hon. Mr Justice Calvert-Smith; Hon. Mr Justice Cooke; Hon. Mr Justice Gross

SOUTH-WEST REGION
Presiding Judges, Hon. Mr Justice Owen; Hon. Mr Justice Royce

WALES REGION
Presiding Judges, Hon. Mr Justice Jones; Hon. Mr Justice Davis

DISTRICT JUDGES

District judges, formerly known as registrars of the court, are solicitors of at least seven years' standing and serve in county courts.

District Judges (each £101,400)

DISTRICT JUDGES (MAGISTRATES' COURTS)

District judges (magistrates' courts), formerly known as stipendiary magistrates, must be barristers or solicitors of at least seven years' standing (including at least two years' experience as a deputy district judge), and serve in magistrates' courts. All former provincial and metropolitan stipendiary magistrates can serve nationally within any district.

District Judges each £105,400 (salary includes £4,000 inner London weighting)

CROWN PROSECUTION SERVICE

50 Ludgate Hill, London EC4M 7EX
T 020-7796 8000 **E** enquiries@cps.gsi.gov.uk
W www.cps.gov.uk

The Crown Prosecution Service (CPS) is responsible for prosecuting cases investigated by the police in England and Wales, with the exception of cases conducted by the Serious Fraud Office and certain minor offences.

The CPS is headed by the director of public prosecutions (DPP), who works under the superintendence of the attorney-general. The service comprises a headquarters and 43 areas (including two head offices in London and York), with each area corresponding to a police area in England and Wales. Each area is headed by a chief crown prosecutor, supported by an area business manager.

Director of Public Prosecutions, Keir Starmer, QC
Chief Executive, Peter Lewis
Directors, Mike Kennedy *(Business Development)*; David Jones *(Business Information Systems)*; Sue Hemming *(Counter-Terrorism)*; Seamus Taylor *(Equality and Diversity)*; J. Graham *(Finance)*; Ros McCool *(Human Resources)*; Alison Saunders *(Organised Crime)*; Roger Daw *(Policy)*; C. Newell *(Principal Legal Adviser)*; Simon Clements *(Special Crime)*
Head of Strategic Communications, P. Teare

CPS AREAS ENGLAND

CPS DIRECT, 6th Floor, United House, Piccadilly, York YO1 9PQ **T** 01904-545400
Chief Crown Prosecutor, Martin Goldman

AVON AND SOMERSET, 2nd Floor, Froomsgate House, Rupert Street, Bristol BS1 2QJ **T** 0117-930 2800
Chief Crown Prosecutor, Barry Hughes

BEDFORDSHIRE, Sceptre House, 7–9 Castle Street, Luton LU1 3AJ **T** 01582-816600
Chief Crown Prosecutor, Richard Newcombe

CAMBRIDGESHIRE, Justinian House, Spitfire Close, Ermine Business Park, Huntingdon, Cambs PE29 6XY **T** 01480-825200
Chief Crown Prosecutor, Richard Crowley

CHESHIRE, 2nd Floor, Windsor House, Pepper Street, Chester CH1 1TD **T** 01244-408600
Chief Crown Prosecutor, Ian Rushton

CLEVELAND, 5 Linthorpe Road, Middlesbrough, Cleveland TS1 1TX **T** 01642-204500
Chief Crown Prosecutor, Gerry Wareham

CUMBRIA, 1st Floor, Stocklund House, Castle Street, Carlisle CA3 8SY **T** 01228-882900
Chief Crown Prosecutor, Claire Lindley

DERBYSHIRE, 7th Floor, St Peter's House, Gower Street, Derby DE1 1SB **T** 01332-614000
Chief Crown Prosecutor, Brian Gunn

DEVON AND CORNWALL, Hawkins House, Pynes Hill, Rydon Lane, Exeter EX2 5SS **T** 01392-288000
Chief Crown Prosecutor, Tracy Easton

DORSET, Ground Floor, Oxford House, Oxford Road, Bournemouth BH8 8HA **T** 01202-498700
Chief Crown Prosecutor (acting), Kate Brown

DURHAM, Elvet House, Hallgarth Street, Durham DH1 3AT **T** 0191-383 5800
Chief Crown Prosecutor, Chris Enzor

ESSEX, County House, 100 New London Road, Chelmsford CM2 0RG **T** 01245-455800
Chief Crown Prosecutor, Ken Caley

GLOUCESTERSHIRE, 2 Kimbrose Way, Gloucester GL1 2DB **T** 01452-872400
Chief Crown Prosecutor, Adrian Foster

GREATER MANCHESTER, PO Box 237, 8th Floor, Sunlight House, Quay Street, Manchester M60 3PS **T** 0161-827 4700
Chief Crown Prosecutor, John Holt

HAMPSHIRE AND ISLE OF WIGHT, 3rd Floor, Black Horse House, 8–10 Leigh Road, Eastleigh, Hants SO50 9FH **T** 023-8067 3800
Chief Crown Prosecutor, Nick Hawkins

HERTFORDSHIRE, Queen's House, 58 Victoria Street, St Albans, Herts AL1 3HZ T 01727-798700
Chief Crown Prosecutor, Charles Ingham
HUMBERSIDE, Citadel House, 58 High Street, Kingston-upon-Hull HU1 1QD T 01482-621000
Chief Crown Prosecutor, Barbara Petchey
KENT, Priory Gate, 29 Union Street, Maidstone ME14 1PT T 01622-356300
Chief Crown Prosecutor, Roger Coe-Salazar
LANCASHIRE, 2nd Floor Podium, Unicentre, Lord's Walk, Preston PR1 1OH T 01772-208100
Chief Crown Prosecutor, Robert Marshall
LEICESTERSHIRE, Princes Court, 34 York Road, Leicester LE1 5TU T 0116-204 6700
Chief Crown Prosecutor, Kate Carty
LINCOLNSHIRE, Crosstrend House, 10A Newport, Lincoln LN1 3DF T 01522-585900
Chief Crown Prosecutor, Jaswant Narwal
LONDON, 7th Floor, CPS HQ, 50 Ludgate Hill, London, EC4M 7EX T 020-7796 8000
Chief Crown Prosecutor, Dru Sharpling
MERSEYSIDE, 7th Floor (South), Royal Liver Building, Pier Head, Liverpool L3 1HN T 0151-239 6400
Chief Crown Prosecutor, Paul Whittaker
NORFOLK, Carmelite House, St James Court, Whitefriars, Norwich NR3 1SL T 01603-693000
Chief Crown Prosecutor, Peter Tidey
NORTH YORKSHIRE, Athena House, Kettlestring Lane, Clifton Moor, York YO30 4XF T 01904-731700
Chief Crown Prosecutor, Robert Turnbull
NORTHAMPTONSHIRE, Beaumont House, Cliftonville, Northampton NN1 5BE T 01604-823600
Chief Crown Prosecutor, Grace Ononiwu
NORTHUMBRIA, St Ann's Quay, 122 Quayside, Newcastle upon Tyne NE1 3BD T 0191-260 4200
Chief Crown Prosecutor, Nicola Reasbeck
NOTTINGHAMSHIRE, 2 King Edward Court, King Edward Street, Nottingham NG1 1EL T 0115-852 3300
Chief Crown Prosecutor, Judith Walker
SOUTH YORKSHIRE, Greenfield House, 32 Scotland Street, Sheffield S3 7DQ T 0114-229 8600
Chief Crown Prosecutor, Nigel Cowgill
STAFFORDSHIRE, Building 3, Etruria Valley Office Village, Etruria, Stoke-on-Trent ST1 5RU T 01782-664560
Chief Crown Prosecutor, Harry Ireland
SUFFOLK, 9th Floor, St Vincent's House, 1 Cutler Street, Ipswich IP1 1UL T 01473-282100
Chief Crown Prosecutor, Paula Abrahams
SURREY, Saxon House, 3 Onslow Street, Guildford, Surrey GU1 4YA T 01483-468200
Chief Crown Prosecutor, Portia Ragnauth
SUSSEX, City Gates, 185 Dyke Road, Brighton BN3 1TL T 01273-765600
Chief Crown Prosecutor, Mrs Sarah Jane Gallagher
THAMES VALLEY, Eaton Court, 112 Oxford Road, Reading RG1 7LL T 01189-513600
Chief Crown Prosecutor, Baljit Ubhey
WARWICKSHIRE, Rossmore House, 10 Newbold Terrace, Leamington Spa CV32 4EA T 01926-455000
Chief Crown Prosecutor, Mark Lynn
WEST MERCIA, Artillery House, Heritage Way, Droitwich, Worcester WR9 8YB T 01905-825000
Chief Crown Prosecutor, Colin Chapman
WEST MIDLANDS, Colmore Gate, 2 Colmore Row, Birmingham B3 2QA T 0121-262 1300
Chief Crown Prosecutor, David Blundell
WEST YORKSHIRE, Oxford House, Oxford Row, Leeds LS1 3BE T 0113-290 2700
Chief Crown Prosecutor, Neil Franklin
WILTSHIRE, 2nd Floor, Fox Talbot House, Bellinger Close, Malmesbury Road, Chippenham SN15 1BN T 01249-766100
Chief Crown Prosecutor, Karen Harrold

CPS AREAS WALES
DYFED POWYS, Heol Penlanffos, Tanerdy, Carmarthen, Dyfed SA31 2EZ T 01267-242100
Chief Crown Prosecutor, Jim Brisbane
GWENT, 6th Floor, Chartist Tower, Upper Dock Street, Newport, Gwent NP20 1DW T 01633-261100
Chief Crown Prosecutor, David Archer
NORTH WALES, Bromfield House, Ellice Way, Wrexham LL13 7YW T 01978-346000
Chief Crown Prosecutor, Ed Beltrami
SOUTH WALES, 20th Floor, Capital House, Greyfriars Road, Cardiff CF10 3PL T 029-2080 3905
Chief Crown Prosecutor, Christopher Woolley

HER MAJESTY'S COURTS SERVICE

4th Floor, 102 Petty France, London SW1H 9AJ
T 0845-456 8770 F 020-7189 2732
E customerserviceshq@hmcourts-service.gsi.gov.uk
W www.hmcourts-service.gov.uk

Her Majesty's Courts Service (HMCS) was launched on 1 April 2005, bringing together the Magistrates' Courts Service and the Court Service into a single organisation, and is responsible for the administration of the court of appeal, the high court, the crown court, the magistrates' courts and the county courts.. HMCS is an executive agency of the Ministry of Justice, and provides information on procedures and processes for the public, hearing lists, and address details for all relevant courts.
Chief Executive, Mrs Chris Mayer

JUDICIAL APPOINTMENTS COMMISSION

Steel House, 11 Tothill Street, London SW1H 9LJ
T 020-7210 1453 E enquiries@jac.gsi.gov.uk
W www.judicialappointments.gov.uk

The Judicial Appointments Commission was established as an independent non-departmental public body in April 2006 by the Constitutional Reform Act 2005. Its role is to select judicial office holders independently of government (a responsibility previously held by the Lord Chancellor). It has a statutory duty to encourage diversity in the range of persons available for selection and is sponsored by the Ministry of Justice and accountable to parliament through the Lord Chancellor. It is made up of 15 commissioners, including a chair.
Chair, Baroness Prashar, CBE
Commissioners, Dame Boreland-Kelly, DBE, FRSA; Dame Prof. Hazel Genn, DBE; Hon. Mr Justice Goldring; Rt. Hon. Lady Justice Hallett, DBE; Sir Geoffrey Inkin, OBE; Her Hon. Judge Kirkham; Edward Nally; Sara Nathan; Charles Newman; His Hon. Judge Pearl; Francis Plowden; Harriet Spicer; Jonathan Sumption, OBE, QC; Rt. Hon. Lord Justice Toulson
Chief Executive, Clare Pelham

DIRECTORATE OF JUDICIAL OFFICES

The Directorate of Judicial Offices for England and Wales (DJO) was established in April 2006 following the implementation of the Constitutional Reform Act 2005, and incorporates the Judicial Office, the Judicial Communications Office and the Judicial Studies Board. It provides the Lord Chief Justice and the judiciary with the support they need to fulfil the new responsibilities which transferred to the judiciary in April 2006. The DJO is funded by the Ministry of Justice, and although part of the directorate is based at the royal courts of justice (which is managed by HM Courts Service), the directorate works independently from government departments and agencies.

DIRECTOR'S OFFICE
T 020-7947 7598
Director, Debora Matthews
Director (interim), Steve Humphreys
Secretary, Sarah Welfoot

JUDICIAL OFFICE
T 020-7073 4858
Heads, Jonathan Creer *(Judicial HR Services)*; Amanda Jeffreys *(Planning and Governance)*
Secretary to the Judges' Council, Barbara Flaxman

JUDICIAL COMMUNICATIONS OFFICE
T 020-7073 4852
Head, Mike Wicksteed
Department Heads, Peter Farr *(Public Communications)*; Phillip Golding *(Corporate Communications)*

JUDICIAL STUDIES BOARD
Steel House, 11 Tothill Street, London SW1H 9LJ
T 020-7217 4708 W www.jsboard.co.uk
Executive Directors, Judith Killick; Maggy Pigott
Director of Studies, His Hon. Judge John Phillips, CBE
Heads, Mark Shore *(Corporate Services)*; Helen Baker *(Judicial Training)*; Lynne McGechie *(Magistrates' Training Unit and Senior Adviser)*; Judith Lennard *(Tribunals/Equal Treatment/Training Strategy)*

JUDICIAL COMMITTEE OF THE PRIVY COUNCIL

The Judicial Committee of the Privy Council is the final court of appeal for the United Kingdom overseas territories (*see* UK Overseas Territories section), crown dependencies and those independent Commonwealth countries which have retained this avenue of appeal (Antigua and Barbuda, Bahamas, Barbados, Belize, Brunei, Cook Islands and Niue, Dominica, Grenada, Jamaica, Kiribati, Mauritius, St Christopher and Nevis, St Lucia, St Vincent and the Grenadines, Trinidad and Tobago, and Tuvalu) and the sovereign base areas of Akrotiri and Dhekelia in Cyprus. The committee also hears appeals against pastoral schemes under the Pastoral Measure 1983, and deals with appeals from veterinary disciplinary bodies.

Under the devolution legislation enacted in 1998, the Judicial Committee of the Privy Council is the final arbiter in disputes as to the legal competence of matters done or proposed by the devolved legislative and executive authorities in Scotland, Wales and Northern Ireland.

In 2007 the Judicial Committee dealt with a total of 71 appeals and 33 petitions for special leave to appeal.

The members of the Judicial Committee are the Lords of Appeal in Ordinary, and other Privy Counsellors who hold or have held high judicial office in the United Kingdom or in certain designated courts of Commonwealth countries from which appeals are taken to committee.

JUDICIAL COMMITTEE OF THE PRIVY COUNCIL
Downing Street, London SW1A 2AJ T 020-7276 0483/5
Registrar of the Privy Council, Mary Macdonald
Group Manager, Jackie Lindsay

SCOTTISH JUDICATURE

Scotland has a legal system separate from, and differing greatly from, the English legal system in enacted law, judicial procedure and the structure of courts.

In Scotland the system of public prosecution is headed by the Lord Advocate and is independent of the police, who have no say in the decision to prosecute. The Lord Advocate, discharging his functions through the Crown Office in Edinburgh, is responsible for prosecutions in the high court, sheriff courts and district courts. Prosecutions in the high court are prepared by the Crown Office and conducted in court by one of the law officers, by an advocate-depute, or by a solicitor advocate. In the inferior courts the decision to prosecute is made and prosecution is preferred by procurators fiscal, who are lawyers and full-time civil servants subject to the directions of the Crown Office. A permanent legally qualified civil servant, known as the crown agent, is responsible for the running of the Crown Office and the organisation of the Procurator Fiscal Service, of which he or she is the head.

Scotland is divided into six sheriffdoms, each with a full-time sheriff principal. The sheriffdoms are further divided into sheriff court districts, each of which has a legally qualified resident sheriff or sheriffs, who are the judges of the court.

In criminal cases sheriffs principal and sheriffs have the same powers; sitting with a jury of 15 members, they may try more serious cases on indictment, or, sitting alone, may try lesser cases under summary procedure. Minor summary offences are dealt with in district courts which are administered by the district and the islands local government authorities and presided over by lay justices of the peace (of whom some 500 regularly sit in court) and, in Glasgow only, by stipendiary magistrates. Juvenile offenders (children under 16) may be brought before an informal children's hearing comprising three local lay people. The superior criminal court is the high court of justiciary which is both a trial and an appeal court. Cases on indictment are tried by a high court judge, sitting with a jury of 15, in Edinburgh and on circuit in other towns. Appeals from the lower courts against conviction or sentence are also heard by the high court, which sits as an appeal court only in Edinburgh. There is no further appeal to the House of Lords in criminal cases.

In civil cases the jurisdiction of the sheriff court extends to most kinds of action. Appeals against decisions of the sheriff may be made to the sheriff principal and thence to the court of session, or direct to the court of session, which sits only in Edinburgh. The court of session is divided into the inner and the outer house. The outer house is a court of first instance in which cases are heard by judges sitting singly, sometimes with a jury of 12. The inner house, itself subdivided into two divisions of equal status, is mainly an appeal court. Appeals may be made to the inner house from the outer house as well as from the sheriff court. An appeal may be made from the inner house to the House of Lords.

The judges of the court of session are the same as those of the high court of justiciary, with the Lord President of the court of session also holding the office of Lord Justice General in the high court. Senators of the College of Justice are Lords Commissioners of Justiciary as well as judges of the court of session. On appointment, a senator takes a judicial title, which is retained for life. Although styled The Hon./Rt. Hon. Lord, the senator is not a peer, although some judges are peers in their own right.

The office of coroner does not exist in Scotland. The local procurator fiscal inquires privately into sudden or suspicious deaths and may report findings to the crown agent. In some cases a fatal accident inquiry may be held before the sheriff.

COURT OF SESSION AND HIGH COURT OF JUSTICIARY

The Lord President and Lord Justice General (£211,000), Rt. Hon. Lord Hamilton, *born* 1942, *apptd* 2005
Private Secretary, A. Maxwell

INNER HOUSE
Lords of Session (each £193,800)

FIRST DIVISION
The Lord President

Rt. Hon. Lord Nimmo Smith (William Nimmo Smith), *born* 1942, *apptd* 1996
Rt. Hon. Lord Kingarth (Derek Emslie), *born* 1945, *apptd* 1997
Rt. Hon. Lord Eassie (Ronald Mackay), *born* 1945, *apptd* 2008
Rt. Hon. Lord Reed (Robert Reed), *born* 1956, *apptd* 2008

SECOND DIVISION
Lord Justice Clerk (£203,800), Rt. Hon. Lord Gill (Brian Gill), *born* 1942, *apptd* 2001
Rt. Hon. Lord Osborne (Kenneth Osborne), *born* 1937, *apptd* 1990
Rt. Hon. Lord Wheatley (John Wheatley), *born* 1941, *apptd* 2000
Rt. Hon. Lady Paton (Ann Paton), *born* 1952, *apptd* 2000
Rt. Hon. Lord Carloway (Colin Sutherland), *born* 1954, *apptd* 2008
Rt. Hon. Lord Clarke (Matthew Clarke), *born* 1947, *apptd* 2008

OUTER HOUSE
Lords of Session (each £170,200)
Rt. Hon. Lord Hardie (Andrew Hardie), *born* 1946, *apptd* 2000
Rt. Hon. Lord Mackay of Drumadoon (Donald Mackay), *born* 1946, *apptd* 2000
Hon. Lord McEwan (Robin McEwan), *born* 1943, *apptd* 2000
Hon. Lord Menzies (Duncan Menzies), *born* 1953, *apptd* 2001
Hon. Lord Drummond Young (James Drummond Young), *born* 1950, *apptd* 2001
Hon. Lord Emslie (Nigel Emslie), *born* 1947, *apptd* 2001
Hon. Lady Smith (Anne Smith), *born* 1955, *apptd* 2001
Hon. Lord Brodie (Philip Brodie), *born* 1950, *apptd* 2002
Hon. Lord Bracadale (Alastair Campbell), *born* 1949, *apptd* 2003
Hon. Lady Dorrian (Leona Dorrian), *born* 1959, *apptd* 2005
Hon. Lord Hodge (Patrick Hodge), *born* 1953, *apptd* 2005
Hon. Lord Macphail (Iain Macphail), *born* 1938, *apptd* 2005
Hon. Lord Glennie (Angus Glennie), *born* 1950, *apptd* 2005
Hon. Lord Kinclaven (Alexander F. Wylie), *born* 1951, *apptd* 2005
Hon. Lady Clark of Calton (Lynda Clark), *born* 1946, *apptd* 2006
Hon. Lord Turnbull (Alan Turnbull), *born* 1958, *apptd* 2006
Hon. Lord Brailsford (Sidney Brailsford), *born* 1954, *apptd* 2006
Hon. Lord Uist (Roderick Macdonald), *born* 1951, *apptd* 2006
Hon. Lord Malcolm (Colin M. Campbell), *born* 1953, *apptd* 2007
Hon. Lord Matthews (Hugh Matthews), *born* 1953, *apptd* 2007
Hon. Lord Woolman (Stephen Woolman), *born* 1953, *apptd* 2008

COURT OF SESSION AND HIGH COURT OF JUSTICIARY
Parliament House, Parliament Square, Edinburgh EH1 1HQ
T 0131-225 2595
Principal Clerk of Session and Justiciary, Graham Marwick
Deputy Principal Clerk of Justiciary, G. Prentice
Deputy Principal Clerk of Session and Principal Extractor, R. Cockburn
Depute in Charge of Offices of Court, Y. Anderson
Keeper of the Rolls, A. Moffat
Depute Clerks of Session and Justiciary, J. Atkinson; D. Bruton; A. Corr; D. Cullen; L. Curran; E. Dickson; W. Dunn; P. Fiddes; A. Finlayson; C. Fyffe; A. Hutchinson; T. Kell; A. Lynch; L. MacLachlan; D. MacLeod; R. MacPherson; A. McArdle; L. MacNamara; I. Martin; N. McGinley; A. McKay; D. Morrison; J. Moyes; R. Newlands; R. Phillips; C. Reid; C. Richardson; N. Robertson; C. Scott; B. Sinclair; A. Thompson; K. Todd; C. Truby; P. Weir

SHERIFF COURT OF CHANCERY
27 Chambers Street, Edinburgh EH1 1LB
T 0131-225 2525

The court deals with service of heirs and completion of title in relation to heritable property.
Sheriff Principal, Edward F. Bowen, QC

HM COMMISSARY OFFICE
27 Chambers Street, Edinburgh EH1 1LB
T 0131-225 2525

The office is responsible for issuing confirmation, a legal document entitling a person to execute a deceased person's will, and other related matters.
Commissary Clerk, David Fyfe

SCOTTISH LAND COURT
126 George Street, Edinburgh EH2 4HH
T 0131-271 4360

The court deals with disputes relating to agricultural and crofting land in Scotland.
Chair (£136,500), Hon. Lord McGhie (James McGhie), QC
Members, D. J. Houston; A. Macdonald *(part-time)*; J. A. Smith *(part-time)*
Principal Clerk, K. H. R. Graham, WS

SCOTTISH EXECUTIVE COURTS DIRECTORATE
Hayweight House, 23 Lauriston Street, Edinburgh EH3 9DQ
T 0131-229 9200

The Scottish Executive Courts Directorate is responsible for the provision of sufficient judges and sheriffs to meet the needs of the business of the supreme and sheriffs court in Scotland. It is also responsible for the efficient administration of a number of specialist courts and tribunals.
Deputy Director, J. L. Anderson

JUDICIAL APPOINTMENTS BOARD FOR SCOTLAND
9–10 St Andrew Square, Edinburgh EH2 2AF
T 0131-718 6045

The board's remit is to provide the first minister with a list of candidates recommended for appointment to the posts of senator of the court of session, sheriff principal, sheriff and part-time sheriff.
Chair, Sir Neil McIntosh, CBE

SCOTTISH COURT SERVICE
Hayweight House, 23 Lauriston Street, Edinburgh EH3 9DQ
T 0131-229 9200 W www.scotcourts.gov.uk

The Scottish Court Service is an executive agency within the Scottish Government Justice Department. It is responsible to the Scottish ministers for the provision of staff, courthouses and associated services for the supreme and sheriff courts.
Chief Executive, Eleanor Emberson

SHERIFFDOMS

SALARIES

Sheriff Principal	£136,500
Sheriff	£126,400

GLASGOW AND STRATHKELVIN
Sheriff Principal, James A. Taylor

GRAMPIAN, HIGHLAND AND ISLANDS
Sheriff Principal, Sir Stephen S. T. Young, Bt., QC

LOTHIAN AND BORDERS
Sheriff Principal, E. F. Bowen, QC

NORTH STRATHCLYDE
Sheriff Principal, B. A. Kerr, QC

SOUTH STRATHCLYDE, DUMFRIES AND GALLOWAY
Sheriff Principal, B. A. Lockhart

TAYSIDE, CENTRAL AND FIFE
Sheriff Principal, R. A. Dunlop, QC

STIPENDIARY MAGISTRATES

GLASGOW
R. B. Christie, *apptd* 1985; Mrs J. A. M. MacLean, *apptd* 1990

CROWN OFFICE AND PROCURATOR FISCAL SERVICE

CROWN OFFICE
25 Chambers Street, Edinburgh EH1 1LA
T 0131-226 2626 W www.crownoffice.gov.uk
Crown Agent, Norman McFadyen
Deputy Crown Agent, John Dunn

PROCURATORS FISCAL

SALARIES

Area Fiscals	£56,100–£160,000
District Procurator Fiscal	£46,000–£116,000

GRAMPIAN AREA
Area Procurator Fiscal, Ms A. Currie *(Aberdeen)*

HIGHLAND AND ISLANDS AREA
Area Procurator Fiscal, A. Laing *(Inverness)*

LANARKSHIRE AREA
Area Procurator Fiscal, Ms J. Cameron *(Hamilton)*

CENTRAL AREA
Area Procurator Fiscal, Mrs G. W. Watt *(Stirling)*

DUNDEE AREA
Area Procurator Fiscal, D. Howdle *(Dundee)*

FIFE AREA
Area Procurator Fiscal, C. Ritchie *(Kirkcaldy)*

LOTHIAN AND BORDERS AREA
Area Procurator Fiscal (interim), Ms L. Thomson *(Edinburgh)*

AYRSHIRE AREA
Area Procurator Fiscal, Ms M. Watson *(Kilmarnock)*

ARGYLL AND CLYDE AREA
Area Procurator Fiscal, J. Watt *(Paisley)*

DUMFRIES AND GALLOWAY AREA
Area Procurator Fiscal, T. Dysart *(Dumfries)*

GLASGOW AREA
Area Procurator Fiscal, Ms L. Thomson *(Glasgow)*

COURT OF THE LORD LYON

HM New Register House, Edinburgh EH1 3YT
T 0131-556 7255 F 0131-557 2148
W www.lyon-court.com

The Court of the Lord Lyon is the Scottish Court of Chivalry (including the genealogical jurisdiction of the *Ri-Sennachie* of Scotland's Celtic kings). The Lord Lyon King of Arms has jurisdiction, subject to appeal to the Court of Session and the House of Lords, in questions of heraldry and the right to bear arms. The court also administers the Scottish Public Register of All Arms and Bearings and the Public Register of All Genealogies.

Pedigrees are established by decrees of Lyon Court and by letters patent. As Royal Commissioner in Armory, the Lord Lyon grants patents of arms (which constitute the grantee and heirs noble in the Noblesse of Scotland) to virtuous and well-deserving Scotsmen and to petitioners (personal or corporate) in the Queen's overseas realms of Scottish connection, and also issues birthbrieves. For information on Her Majesty's Officers of Arms in Scotland, *see* the Court of the Lord Lyon in the Public Bodies section.
Lord Lyon King of Arms, David Sellar, FSA SCOT

NORTHERN IRELAND JUDICATURE

In Northern Ireland the legal system and the structure of courts closely resemble those of England and Wales; there are, however, often differences in enacted law.

The supreme court of judicature of Northern Ireland comprises the court of appeal, the high court of justice and the crown court. The practice and procedure of these courts is similar to that in England. The superior civil court is the high court of justice, from which an appeal lies to the Northern Ireland court of appeal; the House of Lords is the final civil appeal court.

The crown court, served by high court and county court judges, deals with criminal trials on indictment. Cases are heard before a judge and, except those involving offences specified under emergency legislation, a jury. Appeals from the crown court against conviction or sentence are heard by the Northern Ireland court of appeal; the House of Lords is the final court of appeal.

The decision to prosecute in cases tried on indictment and in summary cases of a serious nature rests in Northern Ireland with the director of public prosecutions, who is responsible to the attorney-general. Minor summary offences are prosecuted by the police.

Minor criminal offences are dealt with in magistrates' courts by a legally qualified resident magistrate and, where an offender is under the age of 17, by juvenile courts each consisting of a resident magistrate and two lay members specially qualified to deal with juveniles (at least one of whom must be a woman). On 1 July 2008 there were 759 justices of the peace in Northern Ireland. Appeals from magistrates' courts are heard by the county court, or by the court of appeal on a point of law or an issue as to jurisdiction.

Magistrates' courts in Northern Ireland can deal with certain classes of civil case but most minor civil cases are dealt with in county courts. Judgments of all civil courts are enforceable through a centralised procedure administered by the Enforcement of Judgments Office.

SUPREME COURT OF JUDICATURE

The Royal Courts of Justice, Belfast BT1 3JF
T 028-9023 5111
Lord Chief Justice of Northern Ireland (£211,000), Rt. Hon. Sir Brian Kerr, *born* 1948, *apptd* 2004
Principal Secretary, S. T. A. Rogers

LORD JUSTICES OF APPEAL (£193,800)
Style, The Rt. Hon. Lord Justice [surname]

Rt. Hon. Sir Malachy Higgins, *born* 1944, *apptd* 2007
Rt. Hon. Sir Paul Girvan, *born* 1948, *apptd* 2007
Rt. Hon. Sir Patrick Coghlin, *born* 1945, *apptd* 2008

PUISNE JUDGES (£170,200)
Style, The Hon. Mr Justice [surname]

Hon. Sir John Gillen, *born* 1947, *apptd* 1998
Hon. Sir Richard McLaughlin, *born* 1947, *apptd* 1999
Hon. Sir Ronald Weatherup, *born* 1947, *apptd* 2001
Hon. Sir Reginald Weir, *born* 1947, *apptd* 2003
Hon. Sir Declan Morgan, *born* 1952, *apptd* 2004
Hon. Sir Donnell Deeny, *born* 1950, *apptd* 2004
Hon. Sir Anthony Hart, *born* 1946, *apptd* 2005
Hon. Sir Seamus Treacy, *born* 1956, *apptd* 2007
Hon. Sir William Benjamin Synge Stephens, *born* 1954, *apptd* 2007

MASTERS OF THE SUPREME COURT (£101,400)
Master, Queen's Bench and Appeals, C. J. McCorry
Master, Office of Care and Protection, H. Wells
Master, Chancery and Probate, R. A. Ellison
Master, Matrimonial, C. W. G. Redpath
Master, Queen's Bench and Matrimonial, E. Bell
Master, Taxing Office, J. Baillie
Master, Bankruptcy, F. Kelly

OFFICIAL SOLICITOR
Official Solicitor to the Supreme Court of Northern Ireland, Miss B. M. Donnelly

COUNTY COURTS

JUDGES (£126,400)
Style, His/Her Hon. Judge [surname]

Judge Babington; Judge Finnegan; Judge Gibson, QC; Her Hon. Judge Kennedy; Judge Lockie; Judge Loughran; Judge Lynch; Judge McFarland; Judge McKay, QC; Judge McReynolds; Judge Markey, QC; Judge Martin *(Chief Social Security and Child Support Commissioner)*; Judge Philpott, QC; Judge Rodgers; Judge Smyth, QC

RECORDERS
Belfast (£147,420), Judge Burgess
Londonderry (£126,400), Judge Marrinan, QC

MAGISTRATES' COURTS

DISTRICT JUDGES (MAGISTRATES' COURTS) (£101,400)
There are 20 resident magistrates in Northern Ireland.

NORTHERN IRELAND COURT SERVICE
Windsor House, Bedford Street, Belfast BT2 7LT
T 028-9032 8594 W www.courtsni.gov.uk
Director, D. A. Laver

CROWN SOLICITOR'S OFFICE
PO Box 410, Royal Courts of Justice, Belfast BT1 3JY
T 028-9054 2555
Crown Solicitor, J. Conn

PUBLIC PROSECUTION SERVICE
93 Chichester Street, Belfast BT1 3TR
T 028-9089 7102 W www.ppsni.gov.uk
Director of Public Prosecutions, James Hamilton

TRIBUNALS

THE TRIBUNALS SERVICE

4 Abbey Orchard Street, London SW1P 2BS
T 020-3206 0644 E tscommsunit@tribunals.gsi.gov.uk
W www.tribunals.gov.uk

The Tribunals Service, launched in April 2006, is an executive agency within the Ministry of Justice that provides common administrative support to 21 central government tribunals (plus the Adjudicator to HM Land Registry and the Gender Recognition Panel, which are not technically tribunals). The service also aims to deliver greater consistency in practice and procedure, to ensure tribunals are manifestly independent from those whose decisions are being reviewed, and to provide increased access to information for the public.

A number of government tribunals are expected to join the Tribunals Service in the future and all new, non-devolved, central government tribunals will be established as part of the service.
Chief Executive, vacant

AGRICULTURAL LAND TRIBUNALS

c/o DEFRA, Nobel House, 17 Smith Square, London SW1P 3JR
T 0845-933 5577 E helpline@defra.gsi.gov.uk
W www.defra.gov.uk

Agricultural Land Tribunals settle disputes and other issues between agricultural landlords and tenants under the Agricultural Holdings Act 1986, and drainage disputes between neighbours under the Land Drainage Act 1991.

There are seven tribunals covering England and one covering Wales. For each tribunal the Lord Chancellor appoints a chair and one or more deputies (barristers or solicitors of at least seven years' standing). The Lord Chancellor also appoints lay members to three statutory panels: the 'landowners' panel, the 'farmers' panel and the 'drainage' panel.

Each tribunal is an independent statutory body with jurisdiction only within its own geographical area. A separate tribunal is constituted for each case, and consists of a chair and two lay members nominated by the chair.
Chairs (England), Shirley Evans; His Hon. Judge Machin; George Newsom; Paul de la Piquerie; His Hon. Robert Taylor; Nigel Thomas; Martin Wood
Chair (Wales), James Buxton

ASYLUM AND IMMIGRATION TRIBUNAL

PO Box 6987, Leicester LE1 6ZX
T 0845-600 0877 E customer.service@tribunals.gsi.gov.uk
W www.ait.gov.uk

The Asylum and Immigration Tribunal (AIT) is part of the Tribunals Service and hears appeals against decisions made by the Home Office; its powers are derived from the Immigration and Asylum Act 1999. This tribunal replaced the two-tiered Immigration Appellate Authority in 2005 by merging the Immigration Adjudicators and the Immigration Appeal Tribunal under Section 26 of the Asylum and Immigration (Treatment of Claimants, etc) Act 2004. Immigration judges are appointed by the Lord Chancellor and hear appeals against decisions to: refuse asylum under the Refugee Convention; refuse entry into the UK; refuse to issue or extend a visa; deport a person from the UK; or deprive a person of UK citizenship. An appeal against a decision will go before a hearing, where the appellant, his/her representative and a representative from the Home Office will attend before an immigration judge (or panel, sometimes including non-legal members) who will make a determination on whether the appeal should be allowed or dismissed. In certain circumstances, either side may apply for a reconsideration of the determination. Depending on how the appeal was heard (by a single immigration judge or by a panel) will dictate where any applications for reconsideration will be lodged.
President, Hon. Mr Justice Hodge, OBE
Deputy Presidents, Libby Arfon-Jones; Mark Ockelton

CARE STANDARDS TRIBUNAL

18 Pocock Street, London SE1 0BW
T 020-7960 0660 E cst@tribunals.gsi.gov.uk
W www.carestandardstribunal.gov.uk

The tribunal was established under the Protection of Children Act 1999 and considers appeals in relation to decisions made about the inclusion of individuals' names on the list of those considered unsuitable to work with children, restrictions from teaching and employment in schools/further education institutions, and the registration of independent schools. It also deals with general registration decisions made about care homes, children's homes, nurses' agencies, residential family centres and fostering agencies. The tribunal's president appoints the panels for each case and each appeal is heard by a legally qualified chair and two lay members with expertise in the field.
President, His Hon. Judge Pearl

CIVIL AVIATION AUTHORITY

CAA House, 45–59 Kingsway, London WC2B 6TE
T 020-7453 6162 E legal@caa.co.uk
W www.caa.co.uk

The Civil Aviation Authority (CAA) does not have a separate tribunal department as such, however for certain purposes the CAA must conform to tribunal requirements. For example, to deal with appeals against the refusal or revocation of aviation licences and certificates issued by the CAA, and the allocation of routes outside of the EU to airlines.

The chair and four non-executive members who may sit on panels for tribunal purposes are appointed by the Secretary of State for Transport.
Chair, Sir Roy McNulty, CBE

COMMONS COMMISSIONERS

Area 3C, Nobel House, 17 Smith Square, London SW1P 3JR
T 020-7238 6272 E commons.commissioners@defra.gsi.gov.uk

The Commons Commissioners are responsible for deciding disputes about boundaries, ownership or rights for common land arising under the Commons Registration Act 1965. They also enquire into the ownership of unclaimed common land and village greens. Commissioners must be barristers or solicitors of at least seven years' standing and are appointed by the Lord Chancellor.
Chief Commons Commissioner, Edward Cousins

COMPETITION APPEAL TRIBUNAL

Victoria House, Bloomsbury Place, London WC1A 2EB
T 020-7979 7979 E info@catribunal.org.uk
W www.catribunal.org.uk

The Competition Appeal Tribunal (CAT) is a specialist tribunal established to hear certain cases in the sphere of UK competition and economic regulatory law. It hears appeals against decisions of the Office of Fair Trading (OFT) and their sectoral regulators under the Competition Act 1998, and also decisions of the OFT, Secretary of State for Trade and Industry and Competition Commission under the merger control and market investigation provisions of the Enterprise Act 2002. The CAT also has jurisdiction under the Competition Act 1998 to award damages in respect of infringements of EC or UK competition law and to hear appeals against decisions of OFCOM under the Communications Act 2003.

Cases are heard before a panel consisting of three members: either the president or a member of the panel of chairmen and two ordinary members. The members of the panel of chairmen are judges of the Chancery Division of the high court and other senior lawyers. The ordinary members have expertise in law and/or related fields. The president and chairmen are appointed by the Lord Chancellor; the ordinary members are appointed by the secretary of state.

President, Hon. Mr Justice Barling

COPYRIGHT TRIBUNAL

Room 2G31, Concept House, Cardiff Road, Newport NP10 9FU
T 01633-811035 E copyright.tribunal@ipo.gov.uk
W www.ipo.gov.uk/copy/tribunal

The Copyright Tribunal resolves disputes over the terms and conditions of licences offered by, or licensing schemes operated by, collective licensing bodies in the copyright and related rights area. Its decisions are appealable to the high court on points of law only.

The chair and two deputy chairs are appointed by the Lord Chancellor. Up to eight ordinary members are appointed by the Secretary of State for Trade and Industry. The tribunal operates on a panel basis and its members have wide expertise in business, public administration, and the professions.

Chair, Judge Fysh, QC

CRIMINAL INJURIES COMPENSATION APPEALS PANEL

11th Floor, Cardinal Tower, Farringdon Road, London EC1M 3HS
T 020-7549 4600 E enquiries-cicap@tribunals.gsi.gov.uk
W www.cicap.gov.uk

The Criminal Injuries Compensation Appeals Panel determines appeals against review decisions made by the Criminal Injuries Compensation Authority on applications for compensation received from victims of crimes of violence. The chair and members of the panel are appointed by the Secretary of State for the Home Department. Each hearing panel consists of two or three members, one of whom will be a qualified lawyer.

Chair, Roger Goodier

EMPLOYMENT APPEAL TRIBUNAL

London Office: Audit House, 58 Victoria Embankment, London EC4Y 0DS T 020-7273 1041
Edinburgh Office: 52 Melville Street, Edinburgh EH3 7HF
T 0131-225 3963 W www.employmentappeals.gov.uk

The Employment Appeal Tribunal hears appeals (on points of law only) arising from decisions made by employment tribunals. Hearings are conducted by a judge, either alone or accompanied by two lay members who have practical experience in employment relations. Administrative support is provided by the Tribunals Service.

President, Hon. Mr Justice Elias
Registrar, Pauline Donleavy

EMPLOYMENT TRIBUNALS (ENGLAND AND WALES)

3rd Floor, Alexandra House, 14–22 The Parsonage, Manchester M3 2JA
T 0845-795 9775 W www.employmenttribunals.gov.uk

Employment Tribunals for England and Wales sit in 12 regions. The tribunals deal with matters of employment law, redundancy, dismissal, contract disputes, sexual, racial and disability discrimination and related areas of dispute which may arise in the workplace. A public register of judgments is held at 100 Southgate Street, Bury St Edmunds, Suffolk IP33 2AQ.

Chairs, who may be full-time or part-time, are legally qualified. They, along with the tribunal members, are appointed by the Ministry of Justice.

President, His Hon. Judge Meeran

EMPLOYMENT TRIBUNALS (SCOTLAND)

Central Office, Eagle Building, 215 Bothwell Street, Glasgow G2 7TS
T 0141-204 0730

Tribunals in Scotland have the same remit as those in England and Wales. Chairs are appointed by the Lord President of the Court of Session and lay members by the Secretary of State for Trade and Industry.

President, Colin Milne

FAMILY HEALTH SERVICES APPEAL AUTHORITY

30 Victoria Avenue, Harrogate HG1 5PR
T 01423-530280 E fhsau@nhsla.com W www.fhsaa.org.uk

The Family Health Services Appeal Authority (FHSAA) is completely independent of the Department of Health and considers appeals against the decisions of primary care trusts (PCTs), including appeals by GPs, dentists, pharmacists and opticians regarding action taken against them. The president allocates appeals and applications to panels normally consisting of a legal chair, a professional member and a lay member. The FHSAA's president and members are appointed by the Lord Chancellor.

President, Paul Kelly

FINANCIAL SERVICES AND MARKETS TRIBUNAL

15–19 Bedford Avenue, London WC1B 3AS
T 020-7612 9700 E fs&mt@tribunals.gsi.gov.uk
W www.financeandtaxtribunals.gov.uk

The Financial Services and Markets Tribunal hears cases arising from decisions issued by the Financial Services Authority against financial service providers, including banks, clearing houses, stockbrokers and mortgage advisers. The president, a panel of legally qualified chairs and a panel of lay members are all appointed by the Lord Chancellor.

President, Sir Stephen Oliver, QC

GENERAL COMMISSIONERS OF INCOME TAX

Selborne House, 54–60 Victoria Street, London SW1E 6QW
T 020-7210 0670

General commissioners of income tax operate under the Taxes Management Act 1970. They are unpaid judicial officers who sit in some 350 divisions throughout the UK to hear appeals against decisions by HM Revenue and Customs on a variety of taxation matters. The commissioners' jurisdiction was extended in 1999 to hear National Insurance appeals. The Lord Chancellor appoints general commissioners (except in Scotland, where they are appointed by the Scottish government). There are approximately 1,400 general commissioners appointed throughout the United Kingdom. In each division, commissioners appoint a clerk, who is normally legally qualified, who makes the administrative arrangements for appeal hearings and advises the commissioners on points of law and procedure. The Ministry of Justice pays the clerks' remuneration.

Appeals from the general commissioners are by way of case stated, on a point of law, to the high court (the court of session in Scotland or the court of appeal in Northern Ireland).

IMMIGRATION SERVICES TRIBUNAL

Procession House, 55 Ludgate Hill, London EC4M 7JW
T 020-7029 9790 **E** imset@tribunals.gsi.gov.uk
W www.immigrationservicestribunal.gov.uk

The Immigration Services Tribunal is an independent judicial body established in 2000 to provide a forum in which appeals against decisions of the Immigration Services Commissioner and complaints made by the Immigration Services Commissioner can be heard and determined. The cases exclusively concern people providing advice and representation services in connection with immigration matters.

The tribunal forms part of the Ministry of Justice. There is a president, who is the judicial head; other judicial members, who must be legally qualified; lay members, who must have substantial experience in immigration services or in the law and procedure relating to immigration; and a secretary, who is responsible for administration. The tribunal can sit anywhere in the UK.
President, His Hon. Judge Cripps

INDUSTRIAL TRIBUNALS AND THE FAIR EMPLOYMENT TRIBUNAL (NORTHERN IRELAND)

Long Bridge House, 20–24 Waring Street, Belfast BT1 2EB
T 028-9032 7666 **E** mail@employmenttribunalsni.org
W www.employmenttribunalsni.co.uk

The industrial tribunal system in Northern Ireland was set up in 1965 and has a similar remit to the employment tribunals in the rest of the UK. There is also a Fair Employment Tribunal, which hears and determines individual cases of alleged religious or political discrimination in employment. Employers can appeal to the Fair Employment Tribunal if they consider the directions of the Equality Commission to be unreasonable, inappropriate or unnecessary, and the Equality Commission can make application to the tribunal for the enforcement of undertakings or directions with which an employer has not complied.

The president, vice-president and chairs of the Industrial Tribunal and the Fair Employment Tribunal are appointed by the Lord Chancellor. The panel members to both the industrial tribunals and the Fair Employment Tribunal were appointed by the Department for Employment and Learning, but any future appointments will be made through a full public appointment process.
President of the Industrial Tribunals and the Fair Employment Tribunal, Eileen McBride

INFORMATION TRIBUNAL

Arnhem House Support Centre, PO Box 6987, Leicester LE1 6ZX
T 0845-6000 877 **E** informationtribunal@tribunals.gsi.gov.uk
W www.informationtribunal.gov.uk

The Information Tribunal determines appeals against notices issued by the Information Commissioner. The chair and deputy chair are appointed by the Lord Chancellor and must be legally qualified. Lay members are appointed by the Lord Chancellor to represent the interests of data users or data subjects. A tribunal consists of a chair and deputy chair sitting with two of the lay members. There is a separate panel of the tribunal which hears national security appeals; the chair of this panel is James Goudie, QC.
Chair, John Angel

LANDS TRIBUNAL

Procession House, 55 Ludgate Hill, London EC4M 7JW
T 020-7029 9780 **E** lands@tribunals.gsi.gov.uk
W www.landstribunal.gov.uk

The Lands Tribunal is an independent judicial body which determines questions relating to the valuation of land, rating appeals from valuation tribunals, appeals from leasehold valuation tribunals, the discharge or modification of restrictive covenants, and compulsory purchase compensation. The tribunal may also arbitrate under references by consent. The president and members are appointed by the Lord Chancellor. Cases are usually heard by a single member but they may sometimes be heard by two or three members.
President, G. R. Bartlett, QC

LANDS TRIBUNAL FOR SCOTLAND

George House, 126 George Street, Edinburgh EH2 4HH
T 0131-271 4350 **E** mailbox@lands-tribunal-scotland.org.uk
W www.lands-tribunal-scotland.org.uk

The Lands Tribunal for Scotland has much the same remit as the tribunal for England and Wales but also covers questions relating to tenants' rights to buy their homes under the Housing (Scotland) Act 1987. The president is appointed by the Lord President of the Court of Session.
President, Hon. Lord McGhie, QC

MENTAL HEALTH REVIEW TRIBUNALS

Secretariat: PO Box 8793, 5th Floor, Leicester LE1 8BN
T 0845-233 2022 **W** www.mhrt.org.uk

The Mental Health Review Tribunals are independent judicial bodies which review the cases of patients compulsorily detained under the provisions of the Mental Health Act 1983. They have the power to discharge the patient, to recommend leave of absence, to delay discharge, transfer to another hospital or that a guardianship order be made, to reclassify both restricted and unrestricted patients, and to recommend consideration of a supervision application. There are three tribunals in England and Wales, each headed by a regional chair who is appointed by the Lord Chancellor on a

part-time basis. Each tribunal is made up of at least three members, and must include a lawyer, who acts as president, a medical member and a lay member.
Liaison Judge, His Hon. Judge Sycamore

NATIONAL HEALTH SERVICE TRIBUNAL (SCOTLAND)

40 Craiglockhart Road North, Edinburgh EH14 1BT
T 0131-443 2575

The Scottish National Health Service Tribunal considers representations that the continued inclusion of a family health service practitioner (eg a doctor, dentist, optometrist or pharmacist on a health board's list would be prejudicial to the efficiency of the service concerned, by virtue either of fraudulent practices or unsatisfactory personal or professional conduct. If this is established, the tribunal has the power to disqualify practitioners from working in the NHS family health services. The tribunal sits when required and is composed of a chair, one lay member, and one practitioner member drawn from a representative professional panel. The chair is appointed by the Lord President of the Court of Session, and the lay member and the members of the professional panel are appointed by the Scottish ministers.
Chair, J. Michael D. Graham

NATIONAL PARKING ADJUDICATION SERVICE

Barlow House, Minshull Street, Manchester M1 3DZ
T 0161-242 5252 E info@trafficpenaltytribunal.gov.uk
W www.trafficpenaltytribunal.gov.uk

The Traffic Penalty Tribunal considers appeals from motorists against penalty charge notices issued by councils in England and Wales under the Road Traffic Act 1991 and the Traffic Management Act 2004, including appeals against bus lane contraventions. Parking adjudicators are appointed with the express consent of the Lord Chancellor and must be lawyers of five years' standing. Cases are decided by a single adjudicator, either in a postal, telephone or a personal hearing.
Head of Service, Louise Hutchinson

OFFICE OF THE SOCIAL SECURITY AND CHILD SUPPORT COMMISSIONERS

3rd Floor, Procession House, 55 Ludgate Hill, London EC4M 7JW
T 020-7029 9850 E osscsc@tribunals.gsi.gov.uk
George House, 126 George Street, Edinburgh EH2 4HH
T 0131-271 4310 E ossc@ossc-scotland.org.uk
W www.osscsc.gov.uk

Commissioners are the final statutory authority to decide appeals about points of law from Social Security and Child Support Appeals tribunals. They deal with cases about social security, tax credit, child support, housing benefit, council tax benefit and compensation recovery cases. They also decide appeals from Pensions Appeal Tribunals relating to war pensions and cases which have been referred to them under the Forfeiture Act 1982. The commissioners' jurisdiction covers England, Wales and Scotland. There are 18 commissioners, all of whom are qualified lawyers.
Chief Commissioner for Great Britain, His Hon. Judge Hickinbottom
Senior Commissioner for Scotland, D. J. May, QC

OFFICE OF THE SOCIAL SECURITY COMMISSIONERS AND CHILD SUPPORT COMMISSIONERS FOR NORTHERN IRELAND

Headline Building, 10–14 Victoria Street, Belfast BT1 3GG
T 028-9033 2344
E socialsecuritycommissioners@courtsni.gov.uk
W www.courtsni.gov.uk

The role of Northern Ireland Social Security Commissioners and Child Support Commissioners is similar to that of the commissioners in Great Britain; they also have jurisdiction to deal with questions arising under the Forfeiture (Northern Ireland) Order 1982. There are two commissioners for Northern Ireland.
Chief Commissioner, His Hon. Judge Martin, QC
Commissioner, Mrs M. F. Brown, LLB

PENSIONS APPEAL TRIBUNAL

Procession House, 55 Ludgate Hill, London EC4M 7JW
T 020-7029 9800 E pensions.appeal@tribunals.gsi.gov.uk
W www.pensionsappealtribunals.gov.uk

The Pensions Appeal Tribunals are independent from the Service Personnel and Veterans Agency and the Ministry of Defence, and deal with appeals concerning the two schemes that provide compensation for injuries sustained in the armed forces. Established in 1919, the war pensions scheme is applicable in respect of injuries that occurred before 5 April 2005. The tribunals adjudicate on entitlement to a war pension, the percentage at which the War Pensions Agency has assessed a disablement and whether an allowance is justified (ie for mobility needs). For injuries after that date, the armed forces compensation scheme applies, and tribunals decide on entitlement to and amount of the award. The tribunal members are appointed by the Secretary of State for Justice.
President, Dr H. M. G. Concannon, LLM

PENSIONS APPEAL TRIBUNALS FOR SCOTLAND
126 George Street, Edinburgh EH2 4HH
T 0131-271 4340 E info@patscotland.org.uk
W www.patscotland.org.uk
President, C. N. McEachran, QC

RESIDENTIAL PROPERTY TRIBUNAL SERVICE

10 Alfred Place, London WC1E 7LR
T 0845-600 3178 E rptscorporateunit@communities.gsi.gov.uk
W www.rpts.gov.uk

The Residential Property Tribunal Service provides members to sit on panels for the Rent Assessment Committees, Residential Property Tribunals and Leasehold Valuation Tribunals, and serves the private-rented and leasehold property market in England by resolving disputes between leaseholders, tenants and landlords. The president and chair are appointed by the Lord Chancellor and other members are appointed by the Department for Communities and Local Government and the Ministry of Justice.
Senior President, Siobhan McGrath

SOCIAL SECURITY AND CHILD SUPPORT APPEALS

4th Floor, 14 Grays Inn Road, Fox Court, London WC1X 8HN
T 020-3206 0644 W www.appeals-service.gov.uk

The Social Security and Child Support Appeals Tribunal arranges and hears appeals on a range of decisions, including those concerned with social security, child support, child tax credit, pensions credit, housing benefit, council tax benefit, vaccine damage, tax credits and compensation recovery.

Judicial authority rests with the president, while administrative responsibility is exercised by the Tribunals Service, which is an executive agency of the Ministry of Justice.

President, His Hon. Judge Harris

SOLICITORS' DISCIPLINARY TRIBUNAL

3rd Floor, Gate House, 1 Farringdon Street, London EC4M 7NS
T 020-7329 4808 E enquiries@solicitorsdt.com
W www.solicitorstribunal.org.uk

The Solicitors' Disciplinary Tribunal is an independent statutory body whose members are appointed by the Master of the Rolls. The tribunal considers applications made to it alleging either professional misconduct and/or a breach of the statutory rules by which solicitors are bound against an individually named solicitor, former solicitor, registered foreign lawyer, or solicitor's clerk. The tribunal has around 50 members, two thirds are solicitor members and one third are lay members. The president and solicitor members do not receive remuneration and lay members are remunerated by the Ministry of Justice.

President, A. Isaacs

SOLICITORS' DISCIPLINE TRIBUNAL (SCOTTISH)

Unit 3.5, The Granary Business Centre, Coal Road, Cuper, Fife KY15 5YQ
T 01334-659088 W www.ssdt.org.uk

The Scottish Solicitors' Discipline Tribunal is an independent statutory body with a panel of 22 members, 14 of whom are solicitors; members are appointed by the Lord President of the Court of Session. Its principal function is to consider complaints of misconduct against solicitors in Scotland.

Chair, A. Cockburn

SPECIAL COMMISSIONERS

15–19 Bedford Avenue, London WC1B 3AS
T 020-7612 9700 E sc@tribunals.gsi.gov.uk
W www.financeandtaxtribunals.gov.uk

The Special Commissioners is an independent body appointed by the Lord Chancellor to hear complex appeals against decisions of HM Revenue and Customs relating to direct tax matters.

Presiding Special Commissioner, Sir Stephen Oliver, QC

SPECIAL EDUCATIONAL NEEDS AND DISABILITY TRIBUNAL

Central Office, Procession House, 55 Ludgate Hill, London EC4M 7JW T 0870-241 2555
Darlington Office, Ground Floor, Mowden Hall, Staindrop Road DL3 9BG
E sendistqueries@tribunals.gsi.gov.uk W www.sendist.gov.uk

The Special Educational Needs and Disability Tribunal considers parents' appeals against the decisions of local education authorities (LEAs) about children's special educational needs and claims of disability discrimination in schools. Its president, chairs and specialist members are appointed by the Lord Chancellor.

President, Lady Rosemary Hughes

SPECIAL IMMIGRATION APPEALS COMMISSION

PO Box 36469, London EC4A 1WR
T 0845-600 0877 W www.siac.tribunals.gov.uk

The commission was set up under the Special Immigration Appeals Commission Act 1997. Its main function is to consider appeals against orders for deportations in cases which involve, in the main, considerations of national security or the public interest. The commission also hears appeals against decisions to deprive persons of citizenship status. Members are appointed by the Lord Chancellor.

Chair, Hon. Mr Justice Mitting

TRANSPORT TRIBUNAL

Procession House, 55 Ludgate Hill, London EC4M 7JW
T 020-7029 9780 E transport@tribunals.gsi.gov.uk
W www.transporttribunal.gov.uk

The Transport Tribunal has three jurisdictions: it hears appeals against decisions made by Traffic Commissioners at public inquiries, appeals against decisions of the Registrar of Approved Driving Instructors and is able to resolve disputes under the Postal Services Act 2000. The tribunal consists of a legally qualified president, other judicial members, and lay members. The president and legal members are appointed by the Lord Chancellor and the lay members by the transport secretary. Members of the Transport Tribunal also act as the London Service Permit Appeals Panel.

President, H. B. H. Carlisle, QC

VALUATION TRIBUNAL SERVICE

Chief Executive's Office, Block 1, Angel Square, 1 Torrens Street, London EC1V 1NY
T 020-7841 8700 W www.valuation-tribunals.gov.uk

The Valuation Tribunal Service (VTS) was created as a corporate body by the Local Government Finance Act 2003, and is responsible for providing or arranging the services required for the operation of valuation tribunals in England. The VTS board is comprised of a chair and members appointed by the secretary of state. There are 56 tribunals in England that hear appeals concerning council tax and non-domestic rating and land drainage rates. The VTS is funded by the Department for Communities and Local Government. A separate tribunal is constituted for each hearing, and consists of a chair and two or three other members. A clerk, who is a paid employee of the VTS, is present to advise on points of procedure and law. Members are appointed by a representative of the local authorities and the valuation tribunal president, and serve on a voluntary basis.

Chair, VTS Board, Anne Galbraith, OBE

VALUATION TRIBUNAL SERVICE FOR WALES

Governing Council of VTSW, Dinerth Road, Rhos on Sea, Colwyn Bay LL28 4UL
T 01492-546610 E northwales.vt@vto.gsx.gov.uk

The Valuation Tribunal Service for Wales (VTSW) was created under the Valuation Tribunals (Wales) Regulations

2005, and is responsible for providing or arranging the services required for the operation of the four tribunals in Wales. The governing council of the VTSW is comprised of four regional presidents, one of whom is elected director together with one member who is appointed by the National Assembly for Wales. The VTSW hear appeals concerning council tax and non-domestic rating, and land drainage rates in Wales. An individual tribunal, supported by a clerk, is constituted for each hearing and is normally serviced by three members, one of whom also chairs.
Chief Executive, J. C. Owen

VAT AND DUTIES TRIBUNALS

15–19 Bedford Avenue, London WC1B 3AS
T 020-7612 9700 E vatlon@tribunals.gsi.gov.uk
W www.financeandtaxtribunals.gov.uk

VAT and Duties Tribunals are independent and decide disputes between taxpayers and HM Revenue and Customs. In England and Wales, the president and chairs are appointed by the Lord Chancellor and members by the Treasury. Chairs in Scotland are appointed by the Lord President of the Court of Session.
President, Sir Stephen Oliver, QC
Vice-President, England and Wales, J. D. Demack
Vice-President, Scotland, T. G. Coutts, QC

TRIBUNAL CENTRES
EDINBURGH, 126 George Street, Edinburgh EH2 4HH T 0131-271 4330
LONDON, 15–19 Bedford Avenue, London WC1B 3AS T 020-7612 9700
MANCHESTER, Alexandra House, 14–22 The Parsonage, Manchester M3 2JA T 0161-833 5110

OMBUDSMAN SERVICES

The following section is a listing of selected ombudsman services. Ombudsmen are a free, independent and impartial means of resolving certain disputes outside of the courts. These disputes are, in the majority of cases, concerned with whether something has been badly or unfairly handled (for example due to delay, neglect, inefficiency or failure to follow proper procedures). Most ombudsman schemes are established by statute; they cover various public and private bodies and generally examine matters only after the relevant body has been given a reasonable opportunity to deal with the complaint.

After conducting an investigation an ombudsman will usually issue a written report, which normally suggests a resolution to the dispute and often includes recommendations concerning improvements to procedure.

BRITISH AND IRISH OMBUDSMAN ASSOCIATION (BIOA)

PO Box 308, Twickenham TW1 9BE
T 020-8894 9272 E secretary@bioa.org.uk
W www.bioa.org.uk

The BIOA was established in 1994 and exists to provide information for the public about ombudsmen and other complaint-handling services. An ombudsman scheme must meet four conditions to attain BIOA membership – independence from the organisations the ombudsman has the power to investigate, fairness, effectiveness and public accountability. Membership is open to ombudsmen schemes from the UK, Ireland, the Channel Islands, the Isle of Man and British overseas territories.

The following is a selection of organisations that are members of the BIOA.
Chair, Tony Redmond
Secretary, Ian Pattison

ASSEMBLY OMBUDSMAN FOR NORTHERN IRELAND AND NORTHERN IRELAND COMMISSIONER FOR COMPLAINTS

Progressive House, 33 Wellington Place, Belfast BT1 6HN
T 028-9023 3821 F 028-9023 4912
E ombudsman@ni-ombudsman.org.uk
W www.ni-ombudsman.org.uk

The ombudsman is appointed under legislation with powers to investigate complaints by people claiming to have sustained injustice in consequence of maladministration arising from action taken by a Northern Ireland government department, or any other public body within his remit. Staff are presently seconded from the Northern Ireland public sector.
Ombudsman, Tom Frawley
Deputy Ombudsman, J. MacQuarrie

EUROPEAN OMBUDSMAN

T (+33) (3) 8817 2313
E eo@ombudsman.europa.eu
W www.ombudsman.europa.eu

The European Ombudsman considers complaints from any EU citizen or any business, association or organisation with a registered office in the EU. It investigates reported instances of maladministration in the activities of the European Community institutions or bodies, for example contractual disputes, late payments and refusal of access to documents.
Ombudsman, P. Nikiforos Diamandouros

FINANCIAL OMBUDSMAN SERVICE

South Quay Plaza, 183 Marsh Wall, London E14 9SR
T 020-7964 1000 F 020-7964 1001
E complaint.info@financial-ombudsman.org.uk
W www.financial-ombudsman.org.uk

The Financial Ombudsman Service settles individual disputes between businesses providing financial services and their customers. The service examines complaints about most financial matters, including banking, insurance, mortgages, pensions, savings, loans and credit cards. *See also* Banking and Finance.
Chief Ombudsman, Walter Merricks, CBE
Chair, Sir Christopher Kelly, KCB

INDEPENDENT HOUSING OMBUDSMAN

81 Aldwych, London WC2B 4HN
T 020-7421 3800 F 020-7831 1942
E info@housing-ombudsman.org.uk
W www.housing-ombudsman.org.uk

The Housing Ombudsman Service, established in 1997, deals with complaints from residents concerning shortcomings in the way homes are managed by landlords and housing agents. The ombudsman has a statutory jurisdiction over all registered social landlords in England. Private and other landlords can join the service on a voluntary basis.
Ombudsman, Dr Mike Biles
Deputy Ombudsman, Rafael Runco

INDEPENDENT POLICE COMPLAINTS COMMISSION (IPCC)

90 High Holborn, London WC1V 6BH
T 0845-300 2002 F 020-7404 0430
E enquiries@ipcc.gsi.gov.uk W www.ipcc.gov.uk

The IPCC succeeded the Police Complaints Authority in 2004. It was established under the Police Reform Act 2002. The IPCC has teams of investigators headed by directors in each of its regions to assist with the supervision and management of some police investigations. They also carry out independent investigations into serious incidents or allegations of misconduct by persons serving with the police. The IPCC decides on appeals against complaints investigated by the police service. The IPCC also has responsibility for investigating complaints of serious incidents, including death or injury, made against staff of HM Revenue and Customs, the Serious Organised Crime Agency and the United Kingdom Border Agency. The 13 commissioners

of the IPCC must not previously have worked for the police.
Chair, Nick Hardwick
Deputy Chairs, Deborah Glass; Len Jackson
Chief Executive, Jane Furniss

LOCAL GOVERNMENT OMBUDSMAN

Advice Team, PO Box 4771, Coventry CV4 0EH
T 0845-602 1983 W www.lgo.org.uk

The Local Government Ombudsman deals with complaints of injustice arising from maladministration by local authorities and certain other bodies.

There are three ombudsmen in England, each with responsibility for different regions; they aim to provide satisfactory redress for complainants and better administration for the authorities. The ombudsmen investigate complaints about most council matters, including housing, planning, education, social services, consumer protection, drainage and council tax. *See also* Local Government.
Local Government Ombudsmen, Tony Redmond; Anne Seex; Jerry White

OFFICE OF THE LEGAL SERVICES OMBUDSMAN

3rd Floor, Sunlight House, Quay Street, Manchester M3 3JZ
T 0161-839 7262; 0845-601 0794 F 0161-832 5446
E lso@olso.gsi.gov.uk W www.olso.org

The Legal Services Ombudsman oversees the handling of complaints against solicitors, barristers, licensed conveyancers, legal executives and patent agents by their professional bodies. A complainant must first complain to the relevant professional body before raising the matter with the ombudsman, who will then investigate the way the complaint was dealt with. The ombudsman is independent of the legal profession and her services are free of charge, although she is unable to give legal advice.
Ombudsman, Zahida Manzoor, CBE
Operations Director, Gavin Brown

OFFICE OF THE PENSIONS OMBUDSMAN

6th Floor, 11 Belgrave Road, London SW1V 1RB
T 020-7834 9144 F 020-7821 0065
E enquiries@pensions-ombudsman.org.uk
W www.pensions-ombudsman.org.uk

The Pensions Ombudsman is appointed by the Secretary of State for Work and Pensions, under the Pension Schemes Act 1993 as amended by the Pensions Act 1995. He investigates and decides complaints and disputes about the way that personal and occupational pension schemes are run. As the Ombudsman for the Board of the Pension Protection Fund, he can deal with disputes about the decisions made by the board or the actions of their staff. He also deals with appeals against decisions made by the scheme manager under the Financial Assistance Scheme.
Pensions Ombudsman, Tony King

OMBUDSMAN FOR ESTATE AGENTS

Beckett House, 4 Bridge Street, Salisbury, Wiltshire SP1 2LX
T 01722-333306 F 01722-332296
E admin@oea.co.uk W www.oea.co.uk

The Ombudsman for Estate Agents was established in 1998 and provides a service for dealing with disputes between members of the National Association of Estate Agents and consumers who are actual or potential buyers or sellers of residential property in the UK.

Complaints the ombudsman consider include allegations of unfair treatment, maladministration and infringement of legal rights. The ombudsman's role is to resolve these complaints in full and final settlement and, where appropriate, make an award of financial compensation.
Ombudsman, Christopher Hamer

THE OMBUDSMAN SERVICE LTD (TOSL)

Wilderspool Park, Greenalls Avenue, Warrington WA4 6HL
W www.tosl.org.uk

TOSL is a not-for-profit private limited company that administers three ombudsman services – the Energy Supply Ombudsman, Otelo (the Office of the Telecommunications Ombudsman) and the Surveyors Ombudsman Service.

The Energy Supply Ombudsman resolves disputes between domestic customers (households) and their gas and electricity suppliers associated with billing and transfer issues.

Otelo deals with complaints from consumers concerning public communications providers (any company that provides an electronic communications network or service to members of the public or small businesses).

The Surveyors Ombudsman Service investigates complaints made about the service provided by chartered surveyors, for example a breach of legal obligations, avoidable delays, discourtesy or incompetence.
Chair, Peter Holland, CBE
Chief Ombudsman, Elizabeth France
Ombudsmen, Dr Richard Sills *(Energy)*; Ian Smith *(Surveyors)*; Andrew Walker *(Otelo)*

ENERGY SUPPLY OMBUDSMAN

PO Box 966, Warrington WA4 9DF
T 0845-055 0760 F 0845-055 0765
E enquiries@energy-ombudsman.org.uk
W www.energy-ombudsman.org.uk

OTELO

PO Box 730, Warrington WA4 6WU
T 0845-050 1614 F 0845-050 1615
E enquiries@otelo.org.uk W www.otelo.org.uk

SURVEYORS OMBUDSMAN SERVICE

PO Box 1021, Warrington WA4 9FE
T 0845-050 8181 F 0845-051 1213
E enquiries@surveyors-ombudsman.org.uk
W www.surveyors-ombudsman.org.uk

PARLIAMENTARY AND HEALTH SERVICE OMBUDSMAN

Millbank Tower, Millbank, London SW1P 4QP
T 0845-015 4033 F 020-7217 4000
E phso.enquiries@ombudsman.org.uk
W www.ombudsman.org.uk

The Parliamentary Ombudsman is independent of government and is an officer of parliament. She is responsible for investigating complaints referred to her by MPs from members of the public who claim to have sustained injustice in consequence of maladministration by or on behalf of government departments and certain non-departmental public bodies. In 1999 an additional 158 public bodies were brought within the jurisdiction of the Parliamentary Ombudsman. Certain types of action by government departments or bodies are excluded from investigation.

The Health Service Ombudsman for England is responsible for investigating complaints against National Health Service authorities and trusts that are not dealt with by those authorities to the satisfaction of the complainant. Complaints can be referred directly by the member of the public who claims to have sustained injustice or hardship in consequence of the failure in a service provided by a relevant body. The ombudsman's jurisdiction now covers complaints about family doctors, dentists, pharmacists and opticians, and complaints about actions resulting from clinical judgement.

The Health Service Ombudsman is also responsible for investigating complaints that information has been wrongly refused under the Code of Practice on Openness in the National Health Service 1995. The parliamentary and the health offices are presently held by the same person.

Parliamentary Ombudsman and Health Service Ombudsman, Ms A. Abraham

Deputy Parliamentary Commissioner, Ms T. Longdon

PRISONS AND PROBATION OMBUDSMAN FOR ENGLAND AND WALES

Ashley House, 2 Monck Street, London SW1P 2BQ
T 020-7035 2876 **F** 020-7035 2860
E mail@ppo.gsi.gov.uk **W** www.ppo.gov.uk

The ombudsman provides a free and independent complaints investigation service for prisoners, those held in immigration detention and those under probation supervision who have been unable to resolve their grievances with the Prison, Immigration and Probation Services. He also conducts independent investigations into the deaths of prisoners, residents of probation hostels and people detained by the immigration authorities.

Ombudsman, Stephen Shaw, CBE

PUBLIC SERVICES OMBUDSMAN FOR WALES

1 Ffordd yr Hen Gae, Pencoed CF35 5LJ
T 01656-641150 **F** 01656-641199
E ask@ombudsman-wales.org.uk
W www.ombudsman-wales.org.uk

The office of Public Services Ombudsman for Wales was established, with effect from 1 April 2006, by the Public Services Ombudsman (Wales) Act 2005. The ombudsman, who is appointed by the Queen, investigates complaints of injustice caused by maladministration or service failure by the National Assembly for Wales (and public bodies sponsored by the assembly); National Health Service bodies, including GPs; registered social landlords; local authorities, including community councils; fire and rescue authorities; police authorities; national park authorities; and countryside and environmental organisations. Free leaflets explaining the process of making a complaint are available from the ombudsman's office.

Ombudsman, Peter Tyndall

SCOTTISH PUBLIC SERVICES OMBUDSMAN

Freepost EH641, Edinburgh EH3 0BR
T 0800-377 7330 **F** 0800-377 7331
E ask@spso.org.uk **W** www.spso.org.uk

The Scottish Public Services Ombudsman was established in 2002. The ombudsman investigates complaints about Scottish government departments and agencies, councils, housing associations, the National Health Service (NHS) and other public bodies. The public bodies which the Scottish Public Services Ombudsman may consider investigating are contained in a list outlined in the Scottish Public Services Ombudsman Act 2002. The ombudsman's remit was extended in 2005 to cover Scotland's further education colleges and higher education institutions. Complaints considered by the ombudsman include complaints about poor service, failure to provide a service and administrative failure.

Scottish Public Services Ombudsman, Prof. Alice Brown

WATERWAYS OMBUDSMAN

PO Box 35, York YO60 6WW
T 01347-879075 **E** enquiries@waterways-ombudsman.org
W www.waterways-ombudsman.org

The Waterways Ombudsman considers complaints of maladministration or unfairness made against British Waterways or its subsidiaries, including British Waterways Marinas Limited. Complaints concerning the waterways responsibilities of the Environment Agency should be directed to the Parliamentary and Health Service Ombudsman.

Ombudsman, Hilary Bainbridge

THE POLICE SERVICE

There are 52 police forces in the United Kingdom: 43 in England and Wales, including the Metropolitan Police and the City of London Police, eight in Scotland and the Police Service of Northern Ireland. Most forces' areas are coterminous with one or more local authority areas. The Isle of Man, States of Jersey and Guernsey have their own forces responsible for policing in their respective islands and bailiwicks. The Serious Organised Crime Agency (SOCA) is responsible for the investigation of national and international serious organised crime.

Police authorities are independent bodies, responsible for the supervision of local policing. There are 43 police authorities in England and Wales, plus an additional one for British Transport Police. Most police authorities have 17 members, comprising nine local councillors, five independent members and three magistrates. Authorities which are responsible for larger areas may have more members, such as the Metropolitan Police Authority which has 23 members: 12 drawn from the London Assembly, seven independent members and four magistrates. The Corporation of London acts as the police authority for the City of London Police. In Scotland, six of the forces are maintained by joint police boards, made up of local councillors from each council in the force area; the other two constabularies (Dumfries & Galloway and Fife) are directly administered by their respective councils. The Northern Ireland Policing Board is an independent public body consisting of 19 political and independent members.

Police forces in England, Scotland and Wales are financed by central and local government grants and a precept on the council tax. The Police Service of Northern Ireland is wholly funded by central government. The police authorities, subject to the approval of the home secretary (in England and Wales), the Northern Ireland secretary and to regulations, are responsible for appointing the Chief Constable. In England and Wales the latter are responsible for the force's budget, levying the precept on the council tax, publishing annual policing plans and reports, setting local objectives, monitoring performance targets and appointing or dismissing senior officers. In Scotland the police authorities are responsible for setting the force's budget, providing the resources necessary to police the area adequately and appointing officers of the rank of Assistant Chief Constable and above. In Northern Ireland, the Northern Ireland Policing Board exercises similar functions.

The home secretary, the Northern Ireland secretary and the Scottish government are responsible for the organisation, administration and operation of the police service. They regulate police ranks, discipline, hours of duty and pay and allowances. All police forces are subject to inspection by HM Inspectors of Constabulary, who report to the home secretary, Scottish government or the Northern Ireland secretary.

COMPLAINTS

The Independent Police Complaints Commission (IPCC) has overall responsibility for the system of complaints against the police in England and Wales. Complaints can be made directly to the local police force or to the IPCC which will contact the police force concerned on the complainant's behalf. All complaints are reviewed by the police force. If the complaint is relatively minor, the police force will attempt to resolve it internally and an official investigation may not be required. Serious complaints are reported to the IPCC immediately and are formerly investigated by a senior officer. The Crown Prosecution Service then decides whether or not to bring criminal charges against the officer(s) involved. The IPCC has the power to initiate, carry out and oversee investigations and is also responsible for the way complaints are handled by local police forces. An officer who is dismissed, required to resign or reduced in rank, whether as a result of a complaint or not, may appeal to a police appeals tribunal established by the relevant police authority.

Under the Police, Public Order and Criminal Justice (Scotland) Act 2006, which came into force on 1 April 2007, the Police Complaints Commissioner for Scotland is responsible for providing independent scrutiny of the way Scottish police forces, authorities and policing agencies handle complaints from the public. The commissioner also has the power to direct police forces to re-examine any complaints which are not considered to have been dealt with satisfactorily. If there is a suggestion of criminal activity, the complaint is investigated by a procurator fiscal.

The Police Ombudsman for Northern Ireland provides an independent police complaints system for Northern Ireland, dealing with all stages of the complaints procedure. Complaints which cannot be resolved informally are investigated and the ombudsman recommends a suitable course of action to the Chief Constable of the Police Service of Northern Ireland or the Northern Ireland Policing Board based on the investigation's findings. The ombudsman may recommend that a police officer be prosecuted although the decision to prosecute a police officer rests with the Director of Public Prosecutions.

INDEPENDENT POLICE COMPLAINTS COMMISSION, T 0845-300 2002
E enquiries@ipcc.gsi.gov.uk W www.ipcc.gov.uk (*See* website for addresses of the regional offices.)

POLICE COMPLAINTS COMMISSIONER FOR SCOTLAND, PO Box 26300, Hamilton, ML3 3AR
T 0808-178 5577 E enquiries@pcc-scotland.org
W www.pcc-scotland.org
Police Complaints Commissioner for Scotland, Jim Martin

POLICE OMBUDSMAN FOR NORTHERN IRELAND, New Cathedral Buildings, St Anne's Square, 11 Church Street, Belfast BT1 1PG T 028-9082 8600
E info@policeombudsman.org
W www.policeombudsman.org
Police Ombudsman, Al Hutchinson

RATES OF PAY

London weighting of £2,106 per annum (from 1 July 2007) is awarded to all police officers working in London irrespective of their ranks and in addition to the salaries listed below:

BASIC RATES OF PAY *at 1 December 2007*

Chief Constables of Greater Manchester, Strathclyde and West Midlands*	£165,207–£168,006
Chief Constable*	£117,603–£156,807
Deputy Chief Constable*	£100,806–£128,808
Assistant Chief Constable and Commanders*	£84,003–£98,004
Chief Superintendent	£68,880–£72,807
Superintendent Range 2†	£66,045–£70,284
Superintendent	£57,681–£67,203
Chief Inspector‡§	£47,949 (£49,863)–£49,923 (£51,831)
Inspector‡§	£43,320 (£45,222)–£46,989 (£48,903)
Sergeant‡	£33,810–£37,998
Constable‡	£21,534–£33,810
Metropolitan Police	
Commissioner	£240,813
Deputy Commissioner	£198,807
City of London Police	
Commissioner	£148,977
Assistant Commissioner	£122,880
Police Service of Northern Ireland	
Chief Constable	£179,205
Deputy Chief Constable	£145,605

* Chief Officers may receive a bonus of at least five per cent of pensionable pay if their performance is deemed exceptional

† For Superintendents who were not promoted to the rank of Chief Superintendent on its re-introduction on 1 January 2002

‡ Officers who have been on the highest available salary for one year have access to a competence-related threshold payment of £1,122 per annum

§ London salary in parentheses (applicable only to officers in the Metropolitan and City of London police forces)

POLICE SERVICES

FORENSIC SCIENCE SERVICE

Headquarters: Trident Court, 2920 Solihull Parkway, Birmingham Business Park, Birmingham B37 7YN
T 0121-329 5200 W www.forensic.gov.uk

The Forensic Science Service (FSS) is a government-owned company which provides forensic science and technology services for UK police forces and other law enforcement agencies. Services are also available to defence lawyers and commercial companies. The FSS operates from 11 facilities across the UK.
Chief Executive, vacant
Chair, Bill Griffiths

NATIONAL EXTREMISM TACTICAL COORDINATION UNIT

PO Box 525, Huntingdon PE29 9AL
T 01480-425091 E mailbox@netcu.pnn.police.uk
W www.netcu.org.uk

The National Extremism Tactical Coordination Unit (NETCU) provides the police service of England and Wales and other law enforcement agencies with tactical advice and guidance on policing domestic extremism and associated criminality. The unit also supports organisations and companies that are the targets of domestic extremism campaigns. NETCU is funded by the Home Office, is accountable to the National Coordinator for Domestic Extremism and forms part of the Association of Chief Police Officers' Terrorism and Allied Matters business unit.
National Coordinator for Domestic Extremism, Anton Setchell

NATIONAL POLICING IMPROVEMENT AGENCY

4th Floor, 10–18 Victoria Street, London SW1H 0NN
T 020-7147 8200 W www.npia.police.uk

Established under the Police and Justice Act 2006 the National Policing Improvement Agency (NPIA) is a non-departmental public body sponsored and funded by the Home Office, with its executive leadership drawn from the police service. The NPIA is owned and governed by the board which comprises representatives of the Association of Chief Police Officers, the Association of Police Authorities and the Home Office, in addition to the chair, chief executive and two independent members. The board is responsible for agreeing the budget and setting the objectives for the NPIA.

The NPIA's remit is to ensure that agreed programmes of reforms are implemented and good practice is applied throughout the police service. It is also responsible for the procurement and deployment of information and communications technology systems to support and improve policing and is active in helping to recruit and train police personnel. The NPIA is charged with improving policing in England and Wales but it is also connected to policing bodies in Scotland and Northern Ireland and collaborates with them on some initiatives.
Chief Executive, Peter Neyroud, QPM
Chair, Peter Holland, CBE

NPIA MISSING PERSONS BUREAU

T 01256-602979 E missingpersonsbureau@npia.pnn.police.uk
W www.missingpersons.police.uk

The NPIA Missing Persons Bureau was launched in April 2008 within the National Policing Improvements Agency. The NPIA Missing Persons Bureau acts as the centre for the exchange of information connected with the search for missing persons nationally and internationally alongside the police and other related organisations. The unit focuses on cross-matching missing persons with unidentified persons or bodies by maintaining records, including a dental index of ante-mortem chartings of long-term missing persons and post-mortem chartings from unidentified bodies. The bureau also manages the missing children website (W www.missingkids.co.uk) and coordinates the child rescue alert services.

Information is supplied and collected for all persons who have been missing in the UK for over 14 days (or less where police deem appropriate), foreign nationals reported missing in the UK, UK nationals reported missing abroad and all unidentified bodies and persons found within the UK.

SERIOUS ORGANISED CRIME AGENCY

PO Box 8000, London SE11 5EN T 0800-528 0730
W www.soca.gov.uk

The Serious Organised Crime Agency (SOCA) is an executive non-departmental public body sponsored by, but operationally independent from, the Home Office. The agency was formed in April 2006 from the amalgamation of the National Crime Squad, National Criminal Intelligence Service, the part of HM Revenue and Customs responsible for dealing with drug trafficking and associated criminal finance and the part of the UK Immigration Service responsible for dealing with organised immigration crime.

SOCA broadly aims to apportion around 40 per cent of its operational effort in tackling primarily Class A drugs trafficking, around 25 per cent of its capabilities towards organised immigration crime, 10 per cent on individual and private sector fraud and 15 per cent to deal with other organised crime. SOCA works closely with other law enforcement agencies and organisations and the remaining 10 per cent of its capabilities is specifically set aside for assisting its law enforcement partners in achieving their objectives.

Chair, Sir Stephen Lander, KCB
Director-General, William Hughes, QPM

POLICE FORCES

ENGLAND*

Force	*Telephone*	*Strength*†	*Chief Constable*
Avon and Somerset	0845-456 7000	3,421	C. Port
Bedfordshire	01234-841212	1,217	Gillian Parker, QPM
Cambridgeshire	0845-456456	1,402	Julie Spence, OBE
Cheshire	01244-350000	2,292	P. Fahy, QPM
Cleveland	01642-326326	1,769	Sean Price, QPM
Cumbria	0845-330 0247	1,257	Craig Mackey
Derbyshire	0845-123 3333	2,072	M. Creedon
Devon and Cornwall	0845-277 7444	3,500	Stephen Otter
Dorset	01929-462727	1,490	M. Baker, QPM
Durham	0845-606 0365	1,733	T. Stoddart, QPM
Essex	01245-491491	3,476	R. Baker
Gloucestershire	0845-090 1234	1,351	Dr Timothy Brain, QPM
Greater Manchester	0161-872 5050	7,938	Dave Whatton *(acting)*
Hampshire	0845-045 4545	3,902	Paul Kernaghan, CBE, QPM
Hertfordshire	01707-354000	2,167	Frank Whiteley
Humberside	0845-606 0222	2,248	Tim Hollis, QPM
Kent	01622-690690	3,678	Michael Fuller, QPM
Lancashire	01772-614444	3,630	Stephen Finnigan, QPM
Leicestershire	0116-222 2222	2,244	Matt Baggott, CBE, QPM
Lincolnshire	01522-532222	1,236	Tony Lake, QPM
Merseyside	0151-709 6010	4,490	B. Hogan-Howe, QPM
North Yorkshire	0845-606 0247	1,580	Grahame Maxwell
Norfolk	0845-456 4567	1,558	Ian McPherson
Northamptonshire	0845-370 0700	1,347	Peter Maddison
Northumbria	01661-872555	4,031	M. Craik, QPM
Nottinghamshire	0115-967 0999	2,445	S. Green, QPM
South Yorkshire	0114-220 2020	3,252	M. Hughes, QPM
Staffordshire	0845-330 2010	2,362	Chris Sims, OBE
Suffolk	01473-613500	1,340	Simon Ash
Surrey	0845-125 2222	2,011	Robert Quick, QPM
Sussex	0845-607 0999	3,124	Martin Richards
Thames Valley	0845-850 5505	4,211	Sara Thornton, QPM
Warwickshire	01926-415000	1,042	Keith Bristow
West Mercia	0845-744 4888	2,515	Paul West, QPM
West Midlands	0845-113 5000	8,311	Sir Paul Scott-Lee, QPM
West Yorkshire	01924-375222	5,811	Sir Norman Bettison
Wiltshire	0845-408 7000	1,208	Brian Moore
WALES			
Dyfed-Powys	0845-330 2000	1,193	Ian Arundale
Gwent	01633-838111	1,492	Michael Tonge
North Wales	0845-607 1001	1,576	R. Brunstrom, QPM
South Wales	01656-655555	3,299	Barbara Wilding, CBE, QPM
SCOTLAND			
Central Scotland	01786-456000	827	Andew Cameron, CBE, QPM
Dumfries and Galloway	0845-600 5701	511	Patrick Shearer, QPM

Fife	0845-600 5702	1,073	Peter Wilson, QPM
Grampian	0845-600 5700	1,467	Colin McKerracher, QPM
Lothian and Borders	0131-311 3131	2,864	David Strang, QPM
Northern	01463-715555	732	Ian Latimer
Strathclyde	0141-532 2000	7,808	Stephen House, QPM
Tayside	01382-223200	1,184	John Vine, CBE, QPM
NORTHERN IRELAND			
Police Service of Northern Ireland	0845-600 8000	8,888	Sir Hugh Orde, OBE
ISLANDS			
Isle of Man	01624-631212	236	Mike Langdon, QPM
States of Jersey	01534-612612	245	Graham Power, QPM
Guernsey	01481-725111	177	G. Le Page

* For the City of London Police and the Metropolitan Police Service *see* London Forces
† Size of force as at February 2008
Source: R. Hazell & Co. *Police and Constabulary Almanac 2008*

LONDON FORCES

CITY OF LONDON POLICE

37 Wood Street, London EC2P 2NQ **T** 020-7601 2222
W www.cityoflondon.police.uk

Strength (February 2008), 858
Though small, the City of London has one of the most important financial centres in the world and the force has particular expertise in areas such as fraud investigation. The force has a wholly elected police authority, the police committee of the Corporation of London, which appoints the commissioner.
Commissioner, Mike Bowron, QPM
Assistant Commissioner, Frank Armstrong
Commander, Patrick Rice

METROPOLITAN POLICE SERVICE

New Scotland Yard, 8–10 Broadway, London SW1H 0BG
T 020-7230 1212 **W** www.met.police.uk

Strength (February 2008), 30,386
Commissioner, Sir Ian Blair, QPM
Deputy Commissioner, Paul Stephenson, QPM
The Metropolitan Police Service is divided into four main areas for operational purposes:

TERRITORIAL POLICING
Most of the day-to-day policing of London is carried out by 33 borough operational command units; 32 command units operate within the same boundaries as the London borough councils, plus there is an additional unit which is responsible for policing Heathrow airport.
Assistant Commissioner, Tim Godwin, OBE

SPECIALIST CRIME DIRECTORATE
The Specialist Crime Directorate's main areas of focus are dismantling organised criminal networks and seizing their assets; safeguarding children and young people from physical, sexual and emotional abuse; and the investigation and prevention of homicide.
Assistant Commissioner, John Yates, QPM

SPECIALIST OPERATIONS
Specialist Operations is divided into two commands:
- *Counter Terrorism Command* is responsible for the prevention and disruption of terrorist activity, domestic extremism and related offences both within London and nationally, providing an explosives disposal and chemical, biological, radiological and nuclear capability within London, assisting the security services in fulfilling their roles and providing a single point of contact for international partners in counter-terrorism matters
- *Protection Command* is responsible for the protection and security of high-profile persons, key public figures and official delegations in the UK and overseas. These include the current and former prime ministers, foreign dignitaries visiting the UK under the Vienna Convention, members of the British royal family and visiting European royal families, ambassadors, diplomats, MPs, peers and others where it is in the national interest or intelligence suggests protection is necessary

Assistant Commissioner, Andy Hayman, CBE, QPM

CENTRAL OPERATIONS
Central Operations consists of a number of specialised units with a broad range of policing functions which provide an integrated, community-focused service to London. Central Operations also has the remit for delivering the security arrangements for the 2012 London Olympic Games.
Assistant Commissioner, Tarique Ghaffur, CBE, QPM

SPECIALIST FORCES

BRITISH TRANSPORT POLICE

25–27 Camden Road, London NW1 9LN **T** 020-7830 8800
W www.btp.police.uk

Strength (February 2008), 2,781
British Transport Police is the national police force for the railways in England, Wales and Scotland, including the London Underground system, Docklands Light Railway, Glasgow Subway, Midland Metro Tram system and Croydon Tramlink. The chief constable reports to the British Transport Police Authority. The members of the authority are appointed by the transport secretary and include representatives from the rail industry as well as independent members. Officers are paid the same as other police forces.
Chief Constable, Ian Johnston, CBE, QPM
Deputy Chief Constable, Andy Trotter, OBE, QPM

CIVIL NUCLEAR CONSTABULARY

Building F6, Culham Science Centre, Abingdon, Oxfordshire OX14 3DB **T** 01235-466606 **W** www.cnc.police.uk

Strength (March 2008), 927

The Civil Nuclear Constabulary (CNC) operates under the strategic direction of the Department for Business Enterprise and Regulatory Reform. The CNC is a specialised armed force whose role is the protection of civil nuclear sites and nuclear materials. The constabulary is responsible for policing UK civil nuclear industry facilities and for escorting nuclear material between establishments within the UK and worldwide.

Chief Constable, Richard Thompson
Deputy Chief Constable, James Smith

MINISTRY OF DEFENCE POLICE

Ministry of Defence Police and Guarding Agency, Wethersfield, Braintree, Essex CM7 4AZ **T** 01371-854000

Strength (January 2008), 3,829

Part of the Ministry of Defence Police and Guarding Agency, the Ministry of Defence Police is a statutory civil police force with particular responsibility for the security and policing of the MoD environment. It contributes to the physical protection of property and personnel within its jurisdiction and provides a comprehensive police service to the MoD as a whole.

Chief Constable/Chief Executive, Steve Love
Deputy Chief Constable, David Ray, QPM

THE SPECIAL CONSTABULARY

The Special Constabulary is a force of trained volunteers who support and work with their local police force usually for a minimum of four hours a week. Special Constables are thoroughly grounded in the basic aspects of police work, such as self-defence, powers of arrest, common crimes and preparing evidence for court, before they can begin to carry out any police duties. Once they have completed their training, they have the same powers as a regular officer and wear a similar uniform. Information on the Special Constabulary can be found on the National Policing Improvement Agency website (**W** www.npia.police.uk).

STAFF ASSOCIATIONS

Police officers are not permitted to join a trade union or to take strike action. All ranks have their own staff associations.

ASSOCIATION OF CHIEF POLICE OFFICERS OF ENGLAND, WALES AND NORTHERN IRELAND, 10 Victoria Street, London SW1H 0NN **T** 020-7084 8950
Secretary, T. Flaherty

ENGLAND AND WALES

POLICE FEDERATION OF ENGLAND AND WALES, Federation House, Highbury Drive, Leatherhead, Surrey KT22 7UY **T** 01372-352000 **W** www.polfed.org
General Secretary, vacant

POLICE SUPERINTENDENTS' ASSOCIATION OF ENGLAND AND WALES, 67A Reading Road, Pangbourne, Reading RG8 7JD **T** 0118-984 4005 **E** enquiries@policesupers.com **W** www.policesupers.com
National Secretary, Chief Supt. Patrick Stayt

SCOTLAND

ASSOCIATION OF CHIEF POLICE OFFICERS IN SCOTLAND, 26 Holland Street, Glasgow G2 4NH **T** 0141-435 1230 **W** www.acpos.police.uk
General Secretary, Harry Bunch

ASSOCIATION OF SCOTTISH POLICE SUPERINTENDENTS, Secretariat, 173 Pitt Street, Glasgow G2 4JS **T** 0141-221 5796 **E** secretariat@scottishpolicesupers.org.uk **W** www.scottishpolicesupers.org.uk
General Secretary, Carol Forfar

SCOTTISH POLICE FEDERATION, 5 Woodside Place, Glasgow G3 7QF **T** 0141-332 5234 **W** www.spf.org.uk
General Secretary and Treasurer, Joe Grant

NORTHERN IRELAND

POLICE FEDERATION FOR NORTHERN IRELAND, 77–79 Garnerville Road, Belfast BT4 2NX **T** 028-9076 4200 **E** office.pfni@btconnect.com **W** www.policefed-ni.org.uk
Secretary, Stevie McCann

SUPERINTENDENTS' ASSOCIATION OF NORTHERN IRELAND, PSNI College, Garnerville Road, Belfast BT4 2NX **T** 028-9092 2201 **E** mail@psani.org **W** www.psani.org
Hon. Secretary, Supt. G. Thomson

THE PRISON SERVICE

The prison services in the United Kingdom are the responsibility of the Secretary of State for Justice, the Scottish Government Justice Department and the Secretary of State for Northern Ireland. The chief directors-general (chief executive in Scotland, director in Northern Ireland), officers of the Prison Service, the Scottish Prison Service and the Northern Ireland Prison Service are responsible for the day-to-day running of the system.

There are 140 prison establishments in England and Wales, 15 in Scotland* and three in Northern Ireland. Convicted prisoners are classified according to their assessed security risk and are housed in establishments appropriate to that level of security. There are no open prisons in Northern Ireland. Female prisoners are housed in women's establishments or in separate wings of mixed prisons. Remand prisoners are, where possible, housed separately from convicted prisoners. Offenders under the age of 21 are usually detained in a Young Offender Institution, which may be a separate establishment or part of a prison. Appellant and failed asylum seekers are held in Immigration Removal Centres, or in separate units of other prisons.

Eleven prisons are now run by the private sector, and in England, Wales and Scotland all escort services have been contracted out to private companies. In Scotland, one prison (Kilmarnock) was built and financed by the private sector and is being operated by private contractors.

There are independent prison inspectorates in England, Wales and Scotland which report annually on conditions and the treatment of prisoners. The Chief Inspector of Criminal Justice in Northern Ireland and HM Chief Inspector of Prisons for England and Wales perform an inspectorate role for prisons in Northern Ireland. Every prison establishment also has an independent monitoring board made up of local volunteers.

Any prisoner whose complaint is not satisfied by the internal complaints procedures may complain to the prisons ombudsman for England and Wales, the Scottish Prisons Complaints Commission or the prisoner ombudsman for Northern Ireland.

The 11 private sector prisons in England and Wales are the direct responsibility of the chief executive of the National Offender Management Service (NOMS). NOMS was created in January 2004, in order to integrate prisons and probation into a system whereby end-to-end management of offenders is provided; this is expected to reduce re-offending and cut the growth rate of the prison population. In May 2007 NOMS was amalgamated into the Ministry of Justice; in 2008 it was restructured with responsibilities for running HM Prison Service, overseeing the contracts of privately run prisons, managing probation performance and creating probation trusts. The prisons and probation inspectors, the prisons ombudsman and the independent monitoring boards report to the home secretary and to the secretary of state in Northern Ireland.

* A 16th prison, HMP Addiewell, is scheduled to open in Scotland in December 2008

PRISON STATISTICS

PRISON POPULATION (UK)
as at April 2008
The projected 'high scenario' prison population for 2014 in England and Wales is 101,900; the 'low scenario' is 88,800.

	Remand	*Sentenced*	*Other*
ENGLAND AND WALES			
Male	12,248	64,201	1,396
Female	862	3,517	95
Total	13,110	67,718	1,491
SCOTLAND*			
Male	1,373	5,446	—
Female	123	261	—
Total	1,496	5,707	—
N. IRELAND			
Male	445	990	5
Female	15	19	—
Total	460	1,009	5
UK TOTAL	15,066	74,434	1,496

* Figures for Scotland are an average for 2006–7
Sources: Home Office; Scottish Prison Service; Northern Ireland Prison Service

SENTENCED PRISON POPULATION BY SEX AND OFFENCE (ENGLAND AND WALES)
as at April 2008

	Male	*Female*
Violence against the person	17,863	775
Sexual offences	7,485	50
Burglary	7,690	197
Robbery	8,489	295
Theft, handling	3,395	433
Fraud and forgery	1,712	282
Drugs offences	9,792	1,024
Motoring offences	1,395	17
Other offences	6,092	423
Offence not recorded	192	13
*Total**	64,105	3,509

* Figures do not include civil (non-criminal) prisoners or fine defaulters
Source: Home Office – *Research Development Statistics*

SENTENCED POPULATION BY LENGTH OF SENTENCE (ENGLAND AND WALES)
as at April 2008

	Adults	*Young offenders*
Less than 12 months	6,456	2,074
12 months to less than 4 years	18,715	4,714
4 years to less than life	22,822	1,683
Life	10,227	833
*Total**	58,310	9,304

* Figures do not include civil (non-criminal) prisoners or fine defaulters
Source: Home Office – *Research Development Statistics*

AVERAGE DAILY SENTENCED POPULATION BY LENGTH OF SENTENCE 2006–7 (SCOTLAND)

	Adults	*Young offenders*
Less than 4 years	2,278	453
4 years or over (including life)	2,693	191
Total	4,971	645

Source: Scottish Prison Service – *Annual Report and Accounts 2006–7*

SUICIDES IN PRISON APRIL 2007–MARCH 2008 (ENGLAND AND WALES)

Men	78
Women	7
Total	85
Rate per 100,000 prisoners in custody	105.2

Source: NOMS, Safer Custody and Offender Policy Group

OPERATING COSTS OF PRISON SERVICE IN ENGLAND AND WALES 2007–8

Staff costs	£1,646,757,000
Other operating costs	£667,383,000
Operating income	(£256,169,000)
Net operating costs for the year	£2,057,971,000
Average cost per prisoner place	£29,561

Source: HM Prison Service – *Annual Report and Accounts 2007–8*

OPERATING COSTS OF SCOTTISH PRISON SERVICE 2007–8

Total income	£1,927,000
Total expenditure	£273,429,000
Staff costs	£132,329,000
Running costs	£111,692,000
Other current expenditure	£29,408,000
Operating cost	£271,502,000
Cost of capital charges	£21,874,000
Interest payable and similar charges	£13,000
Interest receivable	(£3,000)
Net operating cost	£293,386,000

Source: Scottish Prison Service – *Annual Report and Accounts 2007–8*

OPERATING COSTS OF NORTHERN IRELAND PRISON SERVICE 2007–8

Staff costs	£91,252,000
Net running costs	£20,849,000
Depreciation	£9,720,000
Finance charges	£6,966,000
Impairment of fixed assets	£0
Operating expenditure	£128,787,000
Other current expenditure	£6,977,000
Net operating costs for the year	£135,764,000

Source: Northern Ireland Prison Service – *Annual Report and Accounts 2007–8*

THE PRISON SERVICES

HM PRISON SERVICE

Cleland House, Page Street, London SW1P 4LN
T 0870-000 1397 E public.enquiries@hmps.gsi.gov.uk
W www.hmprisonservice.gov.uk

HM Prison Service became part of the National Offender Management Service on 1 April 2008 as part of the reorganisation of the Ministry of Justice.

SALARIES
from 1 April 2008

Senior Manager A	£60,442–£80,858
Senior Manager B	£55,528–£78,483
Senior Manager C	£53,357–£70,679
Senior Manager D	£44,589–£64,933
Manager E	£29,184–£44,894
Manager F	£26,280–£38,082
Manager G	£23,434–£31,351

THE NATIONAL OFFENDER MANAGEMENT SERVICE BOARD

Director-General (SCS), Phil Wheatley, CB
Chief Operating Officer (SCS), Michael Spurr
Director of Capacity Programme, Colin Allars
Director of Commissioning Operational Policy (SCS), Ian Poree
Director of Finance and Performance (SCS), Ann Beasley
Director of High Security Prisons (SCS), Steve Wagstaffe
Director of Human Resources (SCS), Robin Wilkinson
Director of Offender Health (SCS), Richard Bradshaw
Director of Probation, Roger Hill
Board Secretary and Head of Secretariat (SMB), Ken Everett
Legal Adviser, Andrew Dodsworth
Media Relations, Debbie Kirby
Race Equality Adviser, Beverley Thompson

AREA MANAGERS

Michelle Jaran-Howe *(Contracted Prisons);* Danny McAllister *(East Midlands);* Danny Adrian Smith *(Eastern);* Paul Carroll *(Kent and Sussex);* Nick Pascoe *(London);* Phil Copple *(North-East);* Ian Lockwood *(North-West);* Colin McConnell *(South Central);* Alan Scott *(South-West);* Yvonne Thomas *(Wales);* Sue McAllister *(West Midlands);* Tony Hassall *(Yorkshire and Humberside)*

PRISON ESTABLISHMENTS – ENGLAND AND WALES

POPULATION STATISTICS
as at 6 June 2008

Male prisoners	78,322
Female prisoners	4,469
Number of prisoners held in police cells under Operation Safeguard	0
Total	82,791
Useable operational capacity	83,171
Spaces available under Operation Safeguard*	400
Total	83,571
Number under home detention curfew supervision	2,417

* These vary from night to night and up to a 400-place ceiling

PRISON ESTABLISHMENTS KEY
* Women's establishment or establishment with units for women
† Remand Centre or establishment with units for remand prisoners
‡ Young Offender Institution or establishment with units for young offenders
§ Immigration Removal Centre or establishment with units for immigration detainees

as at April 2008

ACKLINGTON, nr. Morpeth, Northumberland NE65 9XF *Prisoners,* 875 *Governor,* Mick Lees
ALBANY, 55 Parkhurst Road, Newport, Isle of Wight PO30 5RS *Prisoners,* 556 *Governor,* Mel Jones
ALTCOURSE (private prison), Higher Lane, Fazakerley, Liverpool L9 7LH *Prisoners,* 1,255 *Director,* John McLaughlin
†‡ASHFIELD (private prison), Shortwood Road, Pucklechurch, Bristol BS16 9QJ *Prisoners,* 397 *Director,* Vicky O'Dea
ASHWELL, Oakham, Rutland, Leics LE15 7LF *Prisoners,* 548 *Governor (acting),* Ian Thomas
*‡ASKHAM GRANGE, Askham Richard, York YO23 3FT *Prisoners,* 97 *Governor,* Alec McCrystal
‡AYLESBURY, Bierton Road, Aylesbury, Bucks HP20 1EH *Prisoners,* 445 *Governor,* David Kennedy
BEDFORD, St Loyes Street, Bedford MK40 1HG *Prisoners,* 490 *Governor,* Frank Flynn
BELMARSH, Western Way, Thamesmead, London SE28 0EB *Prisoners,* 913 *Governor,* Claudia Sturt
BIRMINGHAM, Winson Green Road, Birmingham B18 4AS *Prisoners,* 1,453 *Governor,* James Shanley
BLAKENHURST, Hewell Lane, Redditch, Worcs B97 6QS *Prisoners,* 1,071 *Governor,* Terry Witton
BLANTYRE HOUSE, Horden, Goudhurst, Kent TN17 2NH *Prisoners,* 120 *Governor,* Jim Carmichael
BLUNDESTON, Lowestoft, Suffolk NR32 5BG *Prisoners,* 499 *Governor,* Sue Doolan
†‡BRINSFORD, New Road, Featherstone, Wolverhampton WV10 7PY *Prisoners,* 472 *Governor,* Pete Knapton
‡BRISTOL, 19 Cambridge Road, Horfield, Bristol BS7 8PS *Prisoners,* 607 *Governor,* Kenny Brown
‡BRIXTON, Jebb Avenue, London SW2 5XF *Prisoners,* 804 *Governor,* Paul McDowell
*†‡BROCKHILL, Hewell Lane, Redditch, Worcs B97 6RD *Prisoners,* 170 *Governor,* Alison Gomme
*BRONZEFIELD (private prison), Woodthorpe Road, Ashford, Middlesex TW15 3JZ *Prisoners,* 452 *Director,* Helga Swidenbank
BUCKLEY HALL, Buckley Hall Road, Rochdale, Lancs OL12 9DP *Prisoners,* 381 *Governor,* Mick Regan
BULLINGDON, PO Box 50, Bicester, Oxon OX25 1WD *Prisoners,* 994 *Governor,* Phil Taylor
‡BULLWOOD HALL, High Road, Hockley, Essex SS5 4TE *Prisoners,* 211 *Governor,* Roger Plant
CAMP HILL, Newport, Isle of Wight PO30 5PB *Prisoners,* 607 *Governor,* Ian Young
CANTERBURY, 46 Longport, Canterbury, Kent CT1 1PJ *Prisoners,* 299 *Governor,* Chris Bartlett
†CARDIFF, Knox Road, Cardiff CF24 0UG *Prisoners,* 764 *Governor,* Sian West
‡CASTINGTON, Morpeth, Northumberland NE65 9XG *Prisoners,* 370 *Governor,* Alex Tait
CHANNINGS WOOD, Denbury, Newton Abbott, Devon TQ12 6DW *Prisoners,* 720 *Governor,* Jeannine Hendrick
‡CHELMSFORD, 200 Springfield Road, Chelmsford, Essex CM2 6LQ *Prisoners,* 698 *Governor,* Rob Davis
COLDINGLEY, Shaftesbury Road, Bisley, Woking, Surrey GU24 9EX *Prisoners,* 386 *Governor,* John Robinson
‡COOKHAM WOOD, Rochester, Kent ME1 3LU *Prisoners,* 151 *Governor,* Helen Rinaldi
DARTMOOR, Princetown, Yelverton, Devon PL20 6RR *Prisoners,* 634 *Governor,* Serena Watts
‡DEERBOLT, Bowes Road, Barnard Castle, Co. Durham DL12 9BG *Prisoners,* 445 *Governor,* Jenny Mooney
‡DONCASTER (private prison), off North Bridge Road, Marshgate, Doncaster DN5 8UX *Prisoners,* 1,145 *Director,* Brian Anderson
†DORCHESTER, North Square, Dorchester, Dorset DT1 1JD *Prisoners,* 237 *Governor,* Tony Corcoran
DOVEGATE (private prison), Uttoxeter, Staffs ST14 8XR *Prisoners,* 834 *Director,* Wyn Jones
§DOVER, The Citadel, Western Heights, Dover, Kent CT17 9DR *Prisoners,* 299 *Governor,* Jim Carmichael
*DOWNVIEW, Sutton Lane, Sutton, Surrey SM2 5PD *Prisoners,* 345 *Governor,* Ian Murray
*‡DRAKE HALL, Eccleshall, Staffs ST21 6LQ *Prisoners,* 278 *Governor,* Bridie Oaks-Richards
DURHAM, Old Elvet, Durham DH1 3HU *Prisoners,* 924 *Governor,* Alan Tallentire
*‡EAST SUTTON PARK, Sutton Valence, Maidstone, Kent ME17 3DF *Prisoners,* 90 *Governor,* Jim Carmichael
*‡EASTWOOD PARK, Falfield, Wotton-under-Edge, Glos GL12 8DB *Prisoners,* 314 *Governor,* Tim Beeston
EDMUNDS HILL, Stradishall, Newmarket, Suffolk CB8 9YN *Prisoners,* 361 *Governor,* Norma Harrington
ELMLEY, Church Road, Eastchurch, Sheerness, Kent ME12 4DZ *Prisoners,* 990 *Governor,* Ed Tullet
ERLESTOKE, Devizes, Wilts SN10 5TU *Prisoners,* 456 *Governor,* Doug Moon
EVERTHORPE, Beck Road, Brough, E. Yorks HU15 1RB *Prisoners,* 670 *Governor,* Gary Monaghan
†‡EXETER, 30 New North Road, Exeter, Devon EX4 4EX *Prisoners,* 470 *Governor,* Mark Flinton
FEATHERSTONE, New Road, Featherstone, Wolverhampton WV10 7PU *Prisoners,* 684 *Governor,* Simon Cartwright
†‡FELTHAM, Bedfont Road, Feltham, Middx TW13 4ND *Prisoners,* 614 *Governor,* Cathy Robinson
FORD, Arundel, W. Sussex BN18 0BX *Prisoners,* 535 *Governor,* Fiona Radford
‡FOREST BANK (private prison), Agecroft Road, Pendlebury, Manchester M27 8FB *Prisoners,* 1,152 *Director,* Trevor Short
*FOSTON HALL, Foston, Derby DE65 5DN *Prisoners,* 254 *Governor,* Grey Riley-Smith
FRANKLAND, Brasside, Durham DH1 5YD *Prisoners,* 729 *Governor,* Bob Mullen
FULL SUTTON, York YO41 1PS *Prisoners,* 589 *Governor,* Steve Tilley
GARTH, Ulnes Walton Lane, Leyland, Preston PR26 8NE *Prisoners,* 812 *Governor,* Terry Williams
GARTREE, Gallow Field Road, Market Harborough, Leics LE16 7RP *Prisoners,* 566 *Governor,* Julia Morgan
†‡GLEN PARVA, 10 Tigers Road, Wigston, Leicester LE18 4TN *Prisoners,* 808 *Governor,* Nigel Smith
†‡GLOUCESTER, Barrack Square, Gloucester GL1 2JN *Prisoners,* 310 *Governor,* Mike Bolton
GRENDON, Grendon Underwood, Bucks HP18 0TL *Prisoners,* 522 *Governor,* Dr Peter Bennett
‡GUYS MARSH, Shaftesbury, Dorset SP7 0AH *Prisoners,* 571 *Governor,* Julia Killick
§HASLAR, 2 Dolphin Way, Gosport, Hampshire PO12 2AW *Prisoners,* 142 *Manager,* vacant

HAVERIGG, Millom, Cumbria LA18 4NA *Prisoners,* 626 *Governor,* Clive Chatterton
HEWELL GRANGE, Redditch, Worcs B97 6QQ *Prisoners,* 178 *Governor,* Alison Gomme
HIGH DOWN, High Down Lane, Sutton, Surrey SM2 5PJ *Prisoners,* 1,122 *Governor,* Peter Dawson
HIGHPOINT, Stradishall, Newmarket, Suffolk CB8 9YG *Prisoners,* 784 *Governor,* Dave Taylor
†‡HINDLEY, Gibson Street, Bickershaw, Wigan, Lancs WN2 5TH *Prisoners,* 498 *Governor,* Ray Hill
‡HOLLESLEY BAY, Woodbridge, Suffolk IP12 3JW *Prisoners,* 332 *Governor,* Declan Moore
*‡HOLLOWAY, Parkhurst Road, London N7 0NU *Prisoners,* 493 *Governor,* Sue Saunders
HOLME HOUSE, Holme House Road, Stockton-on-Tees TS18 2QU *Prisoners,* 997 *Governor,* Matt Spencer
‡HULL, Hedon Road, Hull HU9 5LS *Prisoners,* 1,024 *Governor,* Paul Foweather
‡HUNTERCOMBE, Nuffield, Henley-on-Thames, Oxon RG9 5SB *Prisoners,* 357 *Governor,* Kevin Leggett
KENNET, Parkbourn, Maghull, Liverpool, Merseyside L31 1HX *Prisoners,* 343 *Governor,* Derek Harrison
KINGSTON, 122 Milton Road, Portsmouth PO3 6AS *Prisoners,* 197 *Governor,* Ian Telfer
KIRKHAM, Freckleton Road, Kirkham, Preston, Lancs PR4 2RN *Prisoners,* 576 *Governor,* John Hewitson
KIRKLEVINGTON GRANGE, Yarm, Cleveland TS15 9PA *Prisoners,* 222 *Governor,* Alan Richer
LANCASTER, The Castle, Lancaster LA1 1YL *Prisoners,* 210 *Governor,* Peter Francis
†‡LANCASTER FARMS, Far Moor Lane, Stone Row Head, Off Quernmore Road, Lancaster LA1 3QZ *Prisoners,* 476 *Governor,* Paul Holland
LATCHMERE HOUSE, Church Road, Ham Common, Richmond, Surrey TW10 5HH *Prisoners,* 197 *Governor,* Steve Metcalf
LEEDS, 2 Gloucester Terrace, Stanningley Road, Leeds LS12 2TJ *Prisoners,* 995 *Governor,* Rob Kellet
LEICESTER, Welford Road, Leicester LE2 7AJ *Prisoners,* 367 *Governor,* Danny Mulligan
‡LEWES, Brighton Road, Lewes, E. Sussex BN7 1EA *Prisoners,* 631 *Governor,* Eoin McLennan-Murray
LEYHILL, Wotton-under-Edge, Glos GL12 8BT *Prisoners,* 495 *Governor,* Mick Bell
LINCOLN, Greetwell Road, Lincoln LN2 4BD *Prisoners,* 718 *Governor,* Michael Wood
§LINDHOLME, Bawtry Road, Hatfield Woodhouse, Doncaster DN7 6EE *Prisoners,* 1,083 *Governor,* Paul Kempster
LITTLEHEY, Perry, Huntingdon, Cambs PE28 0SR *Prisoners,* 714 *Governor,* David Taylor
LIVERPOOL, 68 Hornby Road, Liverpool L9 3DF *Prisoners,* 1,352 *Governor,* Alan Brown
LONG LARTIN, South Littleton, Evesham, Worcs WR11 8TZ *Prisoners,* 414 *Governor,* Ferdie Parker
*‡LOW NEWTON, Brasside, Durham DH1 5YA *Prisoners,* 300 *Governor,* Paddy Fox
LOWDHAM GRANGE (private prison), Lowdham, Notts NG14 7DA *Prisoners,* 676 *Director,* John Biggin
MAIDSTONE, 36 County Road, Maidstone, Kent ME14 1UZ *Prisoners,* 472 *Governor,* Steve O'Connell
MANCHESTER, 1 Southall Street, Manchester M60 9AH *Prisoners,* 1,216 *Governor,* Richard Vince
‡MOORLAND CLOSED, Bawtry Road, Hatfield Woodhouse, Doncaster DN7 6BW *Prisoners,* 766 *Governor,* Jacqui Tilley
‡MOORLAND OPEN, Thorne Road, Hatfield, Doncaster DN7 6EL *Prisoners,* 239 *Governor,* Jacqui Tilley
*MORTON HALL, Swinderby, Lincoln LN6 9PT *Prisoners,* 356 *Governor,* Susan Howard
THE MOUNT, Molyneaux Avenue, Bovingdon, Hemel Hempstead, Herts HP3 0NZ *Prisoners,* 752 *Governor,* Damian Evans
*‡NEW HALL, Dial Wood, Flockton, Wakefield, W. Yorks WF4 4XX *Prisoners,* 421 *Governor,* Gareth Sands
NORTH SEA CAMP, Freiston, Boston, Lincs PE22 0QX *Prisoners,* 309 *Governor,* Norman Warwick
‡NORTHALLERTON, East Road, Northallerton, N. Yorks DL6 1NW *Prisoners,* 243 *Governor,* Norman Griffin
‡NORWICH, Knox Road, Norwich, Norfolk NR1 4LU *Prisoners,* 547 *Governor,* Paul Baker
NOTTINGHAM, Perry Road, Sherwood, Nottingham NG5 3AG *Prisoners,* 545 *Governor,* Tom Wheatley
‡ONLEY, Willoughby, Rugby, Warks CV23 8AP *Prisoners,* 630 *Governor,* Robin Eldridge
†‡PARC (private prison), Heol Hopcyn John, Bridgend, S. Wales CF35 6AR *Prisoners,* 1,170 *Director,* Janet Wallsgrove
PARKHURST, Newport, Isle of Wight PO30 5NX *Prisoners,* 482 *Governor,* Carole Draper
‡PENTONVILLE, Caledonian Road, London N7 8TT *Prisoners,* 1,133 *Governor,* Nick Leader
*†PETERBOROUGH (private prison), Saville Road, Westfield, Peterborough PE3 7PD *Prisoners,* 359 *Director,* Mike Conway
‡PORTLAND, Easton, Portland, Dorset DT5 1DL *Prisoners,* 591 *Governor,* Steve Holland
‡PRESCOED, Coed-y-Paen, Pontypool, Monmouthshire NP4 0TB *Prisoners,* 405 *Governor,* David Ward
PRESTON, 2 Ribbleton Lane, Preston, Lancs PR1 5AB *Prisoners,* 725 *Governor,* vacant
RANBY, Retford, Notts DN22 8EU *Prisoners,* 1,083 *Governor,* Louise Taylor
†‡READING, Forbury Road, Reading, Berks RG1 3HY *Prisoners,* 260 *Governor,* Pauline Bryant
RISLEY, Warrington Road, Risley, Warrington, Cheshire WA3 6BP *Prisoners,* 1,086 *Governor,* Bob McColm
‡ROCHESTER, 1 Fort Road, Rochester, Kent ME1 3QS *Prisoners,* 389 *Governor,* John Wilson
RYE HILL (private prison), Willoughby, nr. Rugby, Warks CV23 8SZ *Prisoners,* 622 *Director,* Cathy James
*SEND, Ripley Road, Woking, Surrey GU23 7LJ *Prisoners,* 261 *Governor,* Ian Murray
SHEPTON MALLET, Cornhill, Shepton Mallet, Somerset BA4 5LU *Prisoners,* 183 *Governor,* Nick Evans
‡SHREWSBURY, The Dana, Shrewsbury, Shropshire SY1 2HR *Prisoners,* 315 *Governor,* Gerry Hendry
SPRING HILL, Grendon Underwood, nr. Aylesbury, Bucks HP18 0TL *Prisoners,* 314 *Governor,* Dr Peter Bennett
STAFFORD, 54 Gaol Road, Stafford ST16 3AW *Prisoners,* 678 *Governor,* Peter Small
STANDFORD HILL, Church Road, Eastchurch, Sheerness, Kent ME12 4AA *Prisoners,* 431 *Governor,* Andy Hudson
STOCKEN, Stocken Hall Road, Stretton, nr. Oakham, Leics LE15 7RD *Prisoners,* 774 *Governor,* Steve Turner
‡STOKE HEATH, Market Drayton, Shropshire TF9 2JL *Prisoners,* 647 *Governor,* Teresa Clarke
*‡STYAL, Wilmslow, Cheshire SK9 4HR *Prisoners,* 454 *Governor,* Steve Hall
SUDBURY, Ashbourne, Derbyshire DE6 5HW *Prisoners,* 559 *Governor,* Chris Davidson
SWALESIDE, Brabazon Road, Eastchurch, Isle of Sheppey, Kent ME12 4AX *Prisoners,* 770 *Governor,* Kieron Taylor
†‡SWANSEA, 200 Oystermouth Road, Swansea SA1 3SR *Prisoners,* 426 *Governor,* Andrea Whitfield

‡SWINFEN HALL, Lichfield, Staffs WS14 9QS *Prisoners,* 613 *Governor,* Tom Watson
‡THORN CROSS, Arley Road, Appleton Thorn, Warrington, Cheshire WA4 4RL *Prisoners,* 187 *Governor,* Derek Harrison
USK, 47 Maryport Street, Usk, Monmouthshire NP15 1XP *Prisoners,* 405 *Governor,* David Ward
THE VERNE, Portland, Dorset DT5 1EQ *Prisoners,* 575 *Governor,* Denise Hodder
WAKEFIELD, 5 Love Lane, Wakefield, West Yorks WF2 9AG *Prisoners,* 740 *Governor,* David Thompson
WANDSWORTH, PO Box 757, Heathfield Road, London SW18 3HS *Prisoners,* 1,474 *Governor,* Ian Mulholland
‡WARREN HILL, Hollesley, Woodbridge, Suffolk IP12 3JW *Prisoners,* 217 *Governor,* Roger Plant
WAYLAND, Griston, Thetford, Norfolk IP25 6RL *Prisoners,* 870 *Governor,* Richard Booty
WEALSTUN, Wetherby, W. Yorks LS23 7AZ *Prisoners,* 518 *Governor,* Amy Rice
WELLINGBOROUGH, Millers Park, Doddington Road, Wellingborough, Northants NN8 2NH *Prisoners,* 635 *Governor,* Peter Siddons
‡WERRINGTON, Stoke-on-Trent ST9 0DX *Prisoners,* 125 *Governor,* John Huntingdon
‡WETHERBY, York Road, Wetherby, W. Yorks LS22 5ED *Prisoners,* 355 *Governor,* Will Styles
WHATTON, 14 Cromwell Road, Whatton, Nottingham NG13 9FQ *Prisoners,* 817 *Governor,* Peter Wright
WHITEMOOR, Longhill Road, March, Cambs PE15 0PR *Prisoners,* 393 *Governor,* Steve Rodford
WINCHESTER, Romsey Road, Winchester SO22 5DF *Prisoners,* 547 *Governor,* Andy Lattimore
WOLDS (private prison), Everthorpe, Brough, E. Yorks HU15 2JZ *Prisoners,* 364 *Director,* Dave McDonnell
WOODHILL, Tattenhoe Street, Milton Keynes, Bucks MK4 4DA *Prisoners,* 823 *Governor,* Luke Serjeant
WORMWOOD SCRUBS, PO Box 757, Du Cane Road, London W12 0AE *Prisoners,* 1,273 *Governor,* Steve Metcalf
WYMOTT, Ulnes Walton Lane, Leyland, Preston PR26 8LW *Prisoners,* 1,067 *Governor,* Jayne Blake

SCOTTISH PRISON SERVICE (SPS)

Calton House, 5 Redheughs Rigg, Edinburgh EH12 9HW
T 0131-244 8747 **E** gaolinfo@sps.gov.uk
W www.sps.gov.uk

SALARIES 2008–9

Senior managers in the Scottish Prison Service, including governors and deputy governors of prisons, are paid across three pay bands:

Band I	£52,094–£64,900
Band H	£41,350–£53,777
Band G	£32,560–£44,715

SPS BOARD

Chief Executive, Mike Ewart
Directors, Rachel Gwyon *(Corporate Services);* Willie Pretswell *(Finance and Business Services);* Dr Andrew Fraser *(Health and Care);* Stephen Swan *(Human Resources, acting);* Eric Murch *(Partnerships and Commissioning);* Mike Duffy *(Prisons)*
Non-Executive Directors, Bill Carr; Eric Jackson; Elinor Smith

PRISON ESTABLISHMENTS

ABERDEEN, Craiginches, 4 Grampian Place, Aberdeen AB11 8FN *Prisoners,* 228 *Governor,* Audrey Mooney
†BARLINNIE, Glasgow G33 2QX *Prisoners,* 1,480 *Governor,* Bill McKinlay
CASTLE HUNTLY, Longforgan, Dundee DD2 5HL *Prisoners,* 278 *Governor,* Mike Inglis
*†‡CORNTON VALE, Cornton Road, Stirling FK9 5NU *Prisoners,* 346 *Governor,* Ian Gunn
†DUMFRIES, Terregles Street, Dumfries DG2 9AX *Prisoners,* 200 *Governor,* Martyn Bettel
†EDINBURGH, 33 Stenhouse Road, Edinburgh EH11 3LN *Prisoners,* 782 *Governor,* Nigel Ironside
GLENOCHIL, King O'Muir Road, Tullibody FK10 3AD *Prisoners,* 436 *Governor,* Dan Gunn
†‡GREENOCK, Gateside, Greenock PA16 9AH *Prisoners,* 310 *Governor,* Teresa Medhurst
*†INVERNESS, Porterfield, Inverness IV2 3HH *Prisoners,* 150 *Governor,* Eric Fairbairn
†‡KILMARNOCK (private prison), Bowhouse, Kilmarnock KA1 5AA *Prisoners,* 599 *Director,* Scott McNairn
NORANSIDE, Fern By Forfar, Angus DD8 3QY *Prisoners,* 161 *Governor,* Mike Inglis
†PERTH, 3 Edinburgh Road, Perth PH2 8AT *Prisoners,* 487 *Governor,* Kate Donegan
PETERHEAD, Aberdeenshire AB42 2YY *Prisoners,* 302 *Governor (acting),* Mike Hebden
†‡POLMONT, Falkirk FK2 0AB *Prisoners,* 611 *Governor,* Derek McGill
SHOTTS, Canthill Road, Lanarkshire ML7 4LE *Prisoners,* 515 *Governor (acting),* Malcolm McLennan

NORTHERN IRELAND PRISON SERVICE

Dundonald House, Upper Newtownards Road, Belfast BT4 3SU
T 028-9052 2922 **E** info@niprisonservice.gov.uk
W www.niprisonservice.gov.uk

SALARIES 2007–8

Governor 1	£69,009–£74,376
Governor 2	£62,766–£66,638
Governor 3	£54,312–£57,950
Governor 4	£47,232–£51,156
Governor 5	£41,487–£46,530

SENIOR STAFF

Director, Robin Masefield, CBE
Deputy Directors, Mark McGuckin *(Finance and Personnel);* Max Murray *(Operations);* Anne McCleary *(Services)*
Associate Director of Health and Healthcare, Philip McClements, OBE

PRISON ESTABLISHMENTS

*†‡HYDEBANK WOOD, Hospital Road, Belfast BT8 8NA *Prisoners,* 235 *Governor,* Austin Treacy
†§MAGHABERRY, Old Road, Ballinderry Upper, Lisburn, Co. Antrim BT28 2NF *Prisoners,* 806 *Governor,* Alan Longwell
MAGILLIGAN, Point Road, Limavady, Co. Londonderry BT49 0LR *Prisoners,* 433 *Governor,* Tom Woods

DEFENCE

The armed forces of the United Kingdom comprise the Royal Navy, the Army and the Royal Air Force (RAF). The Queen is Commander-in-Chief of all the armed forces. The Secretary of State for Defence is responsible for the formulation and content of defence policy and for providing the means by which it is conducted. The formal legal basis for the conduct of defence in the UK rests on a range of powers vested by statute and Letters Patent in the Defence Council, chaired by the Secretary of State for Defence. Beneath the ministers lies the top management of the Ministry of Defence (MoD), headed jointly by the Permanent Secretary and the Chief of Defence Staff. The Permanent Secretary is the government's principal civilian adviser on defence and has the primary responsibility for policy, finance, management and administration. He is also personally accountable to parliament for the expenditure of all public money allocated to defence purposes. The Chief of the Defence Staff is the professional head of the armed forces in the UK and the principal military adviser to the secretary of state and the government.

The Defence Management Board (DMB) is the executive board of the Defence Council. Chaired by the Permanent Secretary, it acts as the main executive board of the Ministry of Defence, providing senior level leadership and strategic management of defence.

The Central Staff, headed by the Vice-Chief of the Defence Staff and the Second Permanent Under-Secretary of State, is the policy core of the department. Defence Equipment and Support, headed by the Chief of Defence Material, is responsible for purchasing defence equipment and providing logistical support to the armed forces.

A permanent Joint Headquarters for the conduct of joint operations was set up at Northwood in 1996. The Joint Headquarters connects the policy and strategic functions of the MoD head office with the conduct of operations and is intended to strengthen the policy/executive division.

The UK pursues its defence and security policies through its membership of NATO (to which most of its armed forces are committed), the European Union, the Organisation for Security and Cooperation in Europe and the UN (*see* International Organisations section).

STRENGTH OF THE ARMED FORCES

	Royal Navy	*Army*	*RAF*	*All Services*
1975 strength	76,200	167,100	95,000	338,300
1990 strength	63,210	152,810	89,680	305,700
2001 strength	42,420	109,530	53,700	205,650
2002 strength	41,630	110,050	53,000	204,680
2003 strength	41,550	112,130	53,240	206,920
2004 strength	40,880	112,750	53,390	207,020
2005 strength	39,940	109,290	51,870	201,100
2006 strength	39,390	107,730	48,730	195,850
2007 strength	38,860	106,170*	45,370	190,400*
2008 strength	38,570*	105,090*	43,390*	187,060*

* provisional figures
Source: MoD Defence Analytical Services Agency *National Statistics* (Crown copyright)

SERVICE PERSONNEL BY RANK AND GENDER*

	Officers		*Other ranks*	
	Males	*Females*	*Males*	*Females*
All services	27,950	3,760	141,480	13,860
Royal Navy	6,780	700	28,110	2,980
Army	12,920	1,640	83,940	6,600
RAF	8,250	1,420	29,430	4,290

* provisional figures
Source: MoD Defence Analytical Services Agency *National Statistics* (Crown copyright)

UK regular forces include trained and untrained personnel and nursing services, but exclude Gurkhas, full-time reserve service personnel, mobilised reservists and naval activated reservists. As at 1 June 2008 these groups provisionally numbered:

All Gurkhas	3,840
Full-time reserve service	1,810
Mobilised reservists	
Army	1,460
RAF	150
Naval activated reservists	200

Source: MoD Defence Analytical Services Agency *National Statistics* (Crown copyright)

CIVILIAN PERSONNEL

1993 level	159,600
2000 level	121,300
2001 level	118,200
2002 level	110,100
2003 level	107,600
2004 level	108,990
2005 level	107,680
2006 level	102,970
2007 level	95,790
2008 level	88,690

Source: MoD Defence Analytical Services Agency *National Statistics* (Crown copyright)

UK REGULAR FORCES: DEATHS

In 2007 there were a total of 201 deaths among the UK regular armed forces, of which 27 were serving in the Royal Navy and Royal Marines, 143 in the Army and 31 in the RAF. The largest single cause of death was as a result of hostile action (killed in action and died of wounds), which accounted for 71 deaths (35 per cent of the total) in 2007. Land transport accidents accounted for 50 deaths (25 per cent) and other accidents accounted for a further 30 deaths (15 per cent). Suicides accounted for seven deaths or 3 per cent of the total.

NUMBER OF DEATHS AND MORTALITY RATES

	1998	*2001*	*2004*	*2006*	*2007*
Total number	165	142	169	190	201
Royal Navy	26	33	37	33	27
Army	97	80	95	110	143
RAF	42	29	37	47	31
Mortality rates per thousand					
Tri-service rate	0.78	0.69	0.81	0.96	1.05
Navy	0.62	0.79	0.92	0.84	0.69
Army	0.87	0.70	0.78	0.93	1.28
RAF	0.65	0.48	0.63	0.83	0.66

Source: MoD Defence Analytical Services Agency *National Statistics* (Crown copyright)

NUCLEAR FORCES

The Vanguard Class SSBN (ship submersible ballistic nuclear) provides the UK's strategic nuclear deterrent. Each Vanguard Class submarine is capable of carrying 16 Trident D5 missiles equipped with nuclear warheads.

There is a ballistic missile early warning system station at RAF Fylingdales in North Yorkshire.

ARMS CONTROL

The 1990 Conventional Armed Forces in Europe (CFE) treaty, which commits all NATO and former Warsaw Pact members to limiting their holdings of five major classes of conventional weapons, has been adapted to reflect the changed geo-strategic environment and negotiations continue for its implementation. The Open Skies Treaty, which the UK signed in 1992 and entered into force in 2002, allows for the overflight of States Parties by other States Parties using unarmed observation aircraft.

In 1968 the UK signed and ratified the Nuclear Non-Proliferation Treaty, which came into force in 1970 and was indefinitely and unconditionally extended in 1995. In 1996 the UK signed the Comprehensive Nuclear Test Ban Treaty and ratified it in 1998. The UK is a party to the 1972 Biological and Toxin Weapons Convention, which provides for a worldwide ban on biological weapons, and the 1993 Chemical Weapons Convention, which came into force in 1997 and provides for a verifiable worldwide ban on chemical weapons.

DEFENCE BUDGET DEPARTMENTAL EXPENDITURE LIMITS (DEL) *(£ billion)*

	Resource budget	*Capital budget*	*Total DEL*
2006–7 (outturn)	33.5	7.1	40.6
2007–8 (estimate)	36.7	8.1	44.8
2008–9 (projection)	33.6	7.9	41.5

Source: HM Treasury – *Budget 2008* (Crown copyright)

MINISTRY OF DEFENCE

Main Building, Whitehall, London SW1A 2HB
T 020-7218 9000 W www.mod.uk

Secretary of State for Defence, Rt. Hon. Des Browne, MP
Private Secretary, Paul Rimmer
Special Advisers, John McTernan; Alaina McDonald
Parliamentary Private Secretary, Dr Roberta Blackman-Woods, MP
Minister of State for the Armed Forces, Rt. Hon. Bob Ainsworth, MP
Private Secretary, Caroline Pucey
Parliamentary Private Secretary, Sharon Hodgson, MP
Parliamentary Under-Secretary of State and Minister for Defence Equipment and Support, Rt. Hon. Baroness Taylor of Bolton
Private Secretary, Rob Lingham
Under-Secretary of State for Defence and Minister for Veterans, Derek Twigg, MP
Private Secretary, Sue Pither

CHIEFS OF STAFF

Chief of the Defence Staff, Air Chief Marshal Sir Jock Stirrup, GCB, AFC, ADC
Vice Chief of the Defence Staff, Gen. Sir Timothy Granville-Chapman, GBE, KCB, CBE
First Sea Lord and Chief of the Naval Staff, Adm. Sir Jonathon Band, GCB, ADC
Assistant Chief of the Naval Staff, Rear-Adm. R. G. Cooling
Chief of the General Staff, Gen. Sir Richard Dannatt, KCB, CBE, MC
Assistant Chief of the General Staff, Maj.-Gen. S. Mayall
Chief of the Air Staff, Air Chief Marshal Sir Glenn Torpy, GCB, CBE, DSO
Assistant Chief of the Air Staff, Air Vice-Marshal T. Anderson, DSO

SENIOR OFFICIALS

Permanent Under-Secretary of State, Sir Bill Jeffrey, KCB
Second Permanent Under-Secretary of State, Sir Ian Andrews, CBE, TD
Chief of Defence Material, Gen. Sir Kevin O'Donoghue, KCB, CBE
Chief Scientific Adviser, Prof. Mark Welland, FRS, FRENG
Finance Director, Trevor Woolley, CB

THE DEFENCE COUNCIL

The Defence Council is the senior committee of the Ministry of Defence, and was established by royal prerogative under the Letters Patent in April 1964. The Letters Patent confer on the Defence Council the command over all of the armed forces and charge the council with such matters relating to the administration of the armed forces as the Secretary of State for Defence should direct them to execute. It is chaired by the Secretary of State for Defence and consists of the Minister of State for the Armed Forces, the Minister of State for Defence Equipment and Support, the Under-Secretary of State for Defence and the Minister for Veterans, the Chief of Defence Staff, the Permanent Under-Secretary of State, the First Sea Lord and Chief of the Naval Staff, the Chief of the General Staff, the Chief of the Air Staff, the Vice-Chief of Defence Staff, the Second Permanent Under-Secretary of State, the Chief Scientific Adviser, the Chief of Defence Material and the Finance Director.

CENTRAL STAFF

Vice-Chief of the Defence Staff, Gen. Sir Timothy Granville-Chapman, GBE, KCB, ADC
Second Permanent Under-Secretary of State, Sir Ian Andrews, CBE, TD

PERMANENT JOINT HQ

Chief of Joint Operations, Lt.-Gen. J. Houghton, CBE
Deputy Chief of Joint Operations, Maj.-Gen. J. Dutton, CBE

FLEET COMMAND

Commander-in-Chief Fleet, Adm. Sir Mark Stanhope, KCB, OBE
Deputy Commander-in-Chief Fleet, Vice-Adm. Paul Boissier, CB

NAVAL HOME COMMAND
Second Sea Lord and Commander-in-Chief Naval Home Command, Adm. Alan Massey, CBE, ADC
Chief of Staff to Second Sea Lord and Commander-in-Chief Naval Home Command, Rear-Adm. Michael Kimmons

LAND COMMAND
Commander-in-Chief Land Command, Gen. Sir David Richards, KCB, CBE, DSO
Chief of Staff Land Command, Maj.-Gen. J. Shaw, CBE

ADJUTANT-GENERAL'S COMMAND
Adjutant-General, Lt.-Gen. W. Rollo, CBE
Deputy Adjutant-General and Director-General Service Conditions (Army), Maj.-Gen. A. Gregory

AIR COMMAND
Commander-in-Chief Air Command, Air Chief Marshal Sir Clive Loader, KCB, OBE, ADC
Deputy Commander-in-Chief Operations, Air Marshal Iain McNicoll, CB, CBE
Deputy Commander-in-Chief Personnel, Air Marshal Stephen Dalton, CB

DEFENCE EQUIPMENT AND SUPPORT
Chief of Defence Material, Gen. Sir Kevin O'Donoghue, KCB, CBE
Chief Operating Officer, Dr Andrew Tyler
Chief of Corporate Services, T. Flesher
Chief of Material (Fleet), Vice-Adm. Trevor Soar, OBE
Chief of Material (Land), Lt.-Gen. R. Applegate, OBE
Chief of Material (Air), Air Marshal B. Thornton, CB

EXECUTIVE AGENCIES
DEFENCE SCIENCE AND TECHNOLOGY LABORATORY
Porton Down, Salisbury, Wiltshire SP4 0JQ T 01980-613121
E central-enquiries@dstl.gov.uk W www.dstl.gov.uk
Chief Executive, Martin Earwicker

DEFENCE STORAGE AND DISTRIBUTION AGENCY
Ploughley Road, Lower Arncott, Bicester, Oxon OX25 2LD
T 01869-259617 W www.dsda.org.uk
Chief Executive, Neil Firth

DEFENCE SUPPORT GROUP
Building 203, Monxton Road, Andover, Hampshire SP11 8HT
T 01264-383295 E info@dsg.mod.uk
Chief Executive, Archie Hughes

DEFENCE VETTING AGENCY
Building 107, Imphal Barracks, Fulford Road, York YO10 4AS
T 01904–662644 E dvacegm@land.mod.uk
Chief Executive, Jacky Ridley

MET OFFICE
E-2 WO61, Fitzroy Road, Exeter, Devon EX1 3PB
T 0870-900 0100 E enquiries@metoffice.gov.uk
W www.metoffice.gov.uk
Chief Executive, John Hirst

MINISTRY OF DEFENCE POLICE AND GUARDING AGENCY
Weathersfield, Braintree, Essex CM7 4AZ T 01371-854000
E mgsmdp@milnet.uk.net
Chief Constable, Steve Love

PEOPLE, PAY AND PENSIONS AGENCY
J Block Foxhill, Combe Down, Bath BA1 5AB T 0800-345 7772
E peopleservices@pppa.mod.uk
Chief Executive, David Ball

SERVICE CHILDREN'S EDUCATION
HQ UKSCE, Building 5, Military Complex, Wegberg BFPO 40
T (+49) (2161) 908 2291 W www.sceschools.com
Chief Executive, David Wadsworth

SERVICE PERSONNEL AND VETERANS AGENCY (SPVA)
JPAC Enquiry Centre, Main Point 465, Kentigern House, 65 Brown Street, Glasgow G2 8EX T 0800-085 3600 (service personnel enquiries) T 0800-169 2277 (veterans' enquiries)
Chief Executive, Rear-Adm. Trevor Spires

UK HYDROGRAPHIC OFFICE
Admiralty Way, Taunton, Somerset TA1 2DN T 01823-723366
E helpdesk@ukho.gov.uk W www.ukho.gov.uk
Chief Executive, Mike Robinson

ARMED FORCES TRAINING AND RECRUITMENT

In April 2006 the MoD removed agency status from three armed forces training agencies which now function as an integral part of their respective service.

Flag Officer Sea Training (FOST) is responsible for all Royal Navy and Royal Fleet Auxiliary training. FOST's International Defence Training provides the focal point for all aspects of naval training. Training is divided into five streams: Naval Core Training; Royal Marine; Submarine; Surface; Aviation.

The Army Recruiting and Training Division (ARTD) consists of a number of operating groups : Armour Centre; Army Staff Leadership School; Defence College of Aeronautical Engineering; Defence College of Communications and Information Systems; Defence College of Electro-Mechanical Engineering; Defence College of Intelligence; Defence College of Logistics; Defence College of Police and Guarding; Defence Medical Education and Training Agency; Initial Training Group; Recruiting Group; Royal Military Academy Sandhurst; Royal School of Artillery; Royal School of Military Engineering; School of Army Aviation and the School of Infantry.

The Royal Air Force No. 22 (Training) Group exists to recruit RAF personnel and provide trained specialist personnel to the armed forces as a whole, such as providing the army air corps with trained helicopter pilots. The group is split into eight areas: RAF College Cranwell and Director of Recruiting; the Directorate of Flying Training (DFT); the Directorate of Joint Technical Training (DJTT); the Air Cadet Organisation (ACO); Core Headquarters; the Defence College of Aeronautical Engineering (DCAE); the Defence College of Communications and Information Systems (DCCIS); the Defence College of Electro-Mechanical Engineering (DCEME).

USEFUL WEBSITES
W www.rncom.mod.uk
W www.army.mod.uk
W www.tgda.gov.uk

THE ROYAL NAVY

LORD HIGH ADMIRAL OF THE UNITED KINGDOM
HM The Queen

ADMIRALS OF THE FLEET
HRH The Prince Philip, Duke of Edinburgh, KG, KT, OM, GBE, AC, QSO, PC, *apptd* 1953
Sir Edward Ashmore, GCB, DSC, *apptd* 1977
Sir Henry Leach, GCB, *apptd* 1982
Sir Julian Oswald, GCB, *apptd* 1993
Sir Benjamin Bathurst, GCB, *apptd* 1995

ADMIRALS
(Former Chiefs or Vice Chiefs of Defence Staff and First Sea Lords who remain on the active list)

Slater, Sir Jock, GCB, LVO, *apptd* 1991
Boyce, Lord, GCB, OBE, *apptd* 1995
Abbott, Sir Peter, GBE, KCB, *apptd* 1995
Essenhigh, Sir Nigel, GCB, *apptd* 1998
West of Spithead, Lord, GCB, DSC, *apptd* 2000

ADMIRALS
Band, Sir Jonathon, KCB, ADC *(First Sea Lord and Chief of Naval Staff)*
Stanhope, Sir Mark, KCB, OBE *(Commander-in-Chief Fleet)*
HRH The Prince of Wales, KG, KT, GCB, OM, AK, QSO, PC, ADC

VICE-ADMIRALS
Dymock, Sir Anthony, KBE, CB *(UK Military Representative to NATO and the European Union)*
Boissier, (Robin) Paul, CB *(Deputy Commander-in-Chief Fleet and Chief Naval Warfare Officer)*
Soar, Trevor, OBE *(Chief of Material (Fleet) and Chief of Fleet Support to the Naval Board)*
Laurence, Timothy, CB, MVO *(Chief Executive Defence Estates)*
Wilkinson, Peter *(Deputy Chief of Defence Staff (Personnel))*
Massey, Alan, CBE, ADC *(Second Sea Lord and Commander-in-Chief Naval Home Command)*

REAR-ADMIRALS
HRH The Princess Royal, KG, KT, GCVO *(Chief Commandant for Women in the Royal Navy)*
Guild, Nigel, CB *(Director-General Capability (Carrier Strike) and Chief Naval Engineering Officer)*
Spires, Trevor *(Chief Executive Service Personnel and Veterans Agency)*
Wilcocks, Philip, CB, DSC *(Chief of Staff (Capability) to Commander-in-Chief Fleet, Rear-Adm. Surface Ships (Head of Fighting Arm))*
Lambert, Paul, CB *(Capability Manager (Precision Attack), Controller of the Navy)*
Cooke, David, MBE *(Cdr. (Operations) to Commander-in-Chief Fleet, Rear-Adm. Submarines (Head of Fighting Arm))*
Mathews, Andrew, CB *(Director-General Submarines)*
Ibbotson, Richard, CB, DSC *(Flag Officer Sea Training)*
Leaman, Richard, OBE *(Deputy Chief of Staff to the Supreme Allied Cdr. Transformation)*
Morisetti, Neil *(Commandant, Joint Services Command and Staff College)*
Rix, Anthony *(Chief of Staff to the Cdr. Allied Naval Forces Southern Europe)*
Zambellas, George, DSC *(Chief of Staff (Operations), Permanent Joint HQ)*
Cooling, Robert *(Assistant Chief of Naval Staff)*
Hussain, Amjad *(Director-General Weapons)*
Moncrieff, Ian *(National Hydrographer and Deputy Chief Executive UK Hydrographic Office)*
Johnstone-Burt, (Charles) Anthony, OBE (Cdr Joint Helicopter Command)
Snow, Christopher *(Deputy Cdr Striking Force NATO)*
Love, Robert, OBE *(Director-General Ships)*
Montgomery, Charles, CBE *(Naval Secretary and Chief of Staff (Personnel))*
Tibbitt, Ian *(Director-General Safety and Engineering)*
Richards, Alan *(Assistant Chief of Defence Staff (Policy))*
Charlier, Simon *(Chief of Staff (Aviation), Rear-Adm. Fleet Air Arm (Head of Fighting Arm))*
Jones, Philip *(Flag Officer Scotland, Northern England and Northern Ireland and Flag Officer Reserve Forces)*
Lister, Simon, OBE *(Senior Directing Staff (Navy), Royal College of Defence Studies)*

SURGEON REAR-ADMIRALS
Raffaelli, Philip, QHP *(Director-General Medical Operational Capability)*
Jarvis, Lionel *(Assistant Chief of Defence Staff (Health))*

ROYAL MARINES

CAPTAIN-GENERAL
HRH The Prince Philip, Duke of Edinburgh, KG, KT, OM, GBE, AC, QSO, PC

LIEUTENANT-GENERAL
Dutton, James, CBE *(Deputy Cdr International Security and Assistance Force)*

MAJOR-GENERALS
Rose, John, MBE *(Director-General Intelligence Collection)*
Robison, Garry *(Commandant-General Royal Marines)*
Thomas, Jeremy, DSO *(Senior British Military Adviser to US Central Command)*
Capewell, David, OBE *(Deputy Cdr. NATO Rapid Deployment Corps, Italy)*
Salmon, Andrew, OBE *(Cdr UK Amphibious Forces)*

The Royal Marines were formed in 1664 and are part of the Naval Service. Their primary purpose is to conduct amphibious and land warfare. The principal operational units are

- Three Commando Brigade, an amphibious all-arms brigade trained to operate in arduous environments (a core element of the UK's Joint Rapid Reaction Force). The commando units each have a strength of around 700 and are based in Taunton (40 Commando), Plymouth (42 Commando) and Arbroath (45 Commando)
- Fleet Protection Group, responsible for a wide range of tasks worldwide in support of the Royal Navy. The group is over 500 strong and is based at HM Naval Base Clyde on the west coast of Scotland
- Assault Group, responsible for landing craft training. Based at Poole, Dorset

The Royal Marines also provide detachments for warships and land-based naval parties as required.

ROYAL MARINES RESERVES (RMR)

The Royal Marines Reserve is a commando-trained volunteer force with the principal role, when mobilised, of supporting the Royal Marines. The RMR consists of approximately 600 trained ranks who are distributed between the five RMR centres in the UK. Approximately 10 per cent of the RMR are working with the regular corps on long-term attachments within all of the Royal Marines regular units.

OTHER PARTS OF THE NAVAL SERVICE

FLEET AIR ARM

The Fleet Air Arm (FAA) provides the Royal Navy with a multi-role aviation combat capability able to operate autonomously at short notice worldwide in all environments, over the sea and land. The FAA numbers some 6,200 people, which comprises 11.5 per cent of the total Royal Naval strength. It operates some 200 combat aircraft and more than 50 support/training aircraft.

ROYAL FLEET AUXILIARY SERVICE (RFA)

The Royal Fleet Auxiliary Service is a civilian-manned flotilla of 16 ships. Its primary role is to supply the Royal Navy at sea with fuel, ammunition, food and spares, enabling it to maintain operations away from its home ports. It also provides amphibious support and secure sea transport for Army units and their equipment and aviation support for the Royal Navy.

ROYAL NAVAL RESERVE (RNR)

The Royal Naval Reserve is an integral part of the Naval Service. It comprises up to 3,250 men and women who volunteer to train in their spare time to enable the Royal Navy to meet its operational commitments, at times of crisis or war.

The broad training requirements are set by the Royal Navy organisations responsible for the operational tasking of the respective branches; for most branches, training is conducted at one of the 13 RNR units across the UK. Basic training is provided at HMS Raleigh, Torpoint in Cornwall for ratings and at the Britannia Royal Naval College, Dartmouth in Devon for officers; both these and most other RNR courses are of two weeks duration or less.

QUEEN ALEXANDRA'S ROYAL NAVAL NURSING SERVICE

The first nursing sisters were appointed to naval hospitals in 1884 and the Queen Alexandra's Royal Naval Nursing Service (QARNNS) gained its current title in 1902. Nursing ratings were introduced in 1960 and men were integrated into the service in 1982; QARNNS recruits qualified nurses as both officers and ratings, and student nurse training can be undertaken in the service.

Patron, HRH Princess Alexandra, the Hon. Lady Ogilvy, KG, GCVO

Director of Naval Nursing Services and Matron-in-Chief, Capt. H. Allkins, QARNNS

HM FLEET

as at 1 June 2008

Submarines	
Vanguard Class	Vanguard, Vengeance, Victorious, Vigilant
Swiftsure Class	Sceptre, Superb
Trafalgar Class	Talent, Tireless, Torbay, Trafalgar, Trenchant, Triumph, Turbulent
Aircraft Carriers	Ark Royal, Illustrious, Invincible*
Amphibious Assault Ships	Ocean, Albion, Bulwark
Destroyers	
Type 42 Batch 2	Exeter, Liverpool, Nottingham, Southampton
Type 42 Batch 3	Edinburgh, Gloucester, Manchester, York
Frigates	
Type 22	Campbeltown, Chatham, Cornwall, Cumberland
Type 23	Argyll, Iron Duke, Kent, Lancaster, Monmouth, Montrose, Northumberland, Portland, Richmond, St Albans, Somerset, Sutherland, Westminster
Minehunters	
Hunt Class	Atherstone, Brocklesby, Cattistock, Chiddingfold, Hurworth, Ledbury, Middleton, Quorn
Sandown Class	Bangor, Blyth, Grimsby, Pembroke, Penzance, Ramsey, Shoreham, Walney
Patrol Class	
Archer Class P2000 Training Boats	Archer, Biter, Blazer, Charger, Dasher†, Example, Exploit, Explorer, Express, Puncher, Pursuer†, Raider, Ranger, Smiter, Tracker, Trumpeter
Gibraltar Squadron 16m	
Fast Patrol Class	Sabre, Scimitar
River Class Patrol Vessels	Mersey, Severn, Tyne, Clyde
Survey Vessels	
Ice Patrol Ship	Endurance
Ocean Survey Vessel	Scott
Coastal Survey Vessels	Gleaner, Roebuck
Multi-Role Survey Vessels	Echo, Enterprise

* HMS Invincible is currently being held at very low readiness

† HMS Dasher and HMS Pursuer form the Royal Navy Cyprus Squadron

ROYAL FLEET AUXILIARY

Landing Ship Dock (Auxiliary)	RFA Cardigan Bay, RFA Mounts Bay, RFA Largs Bay, RFA Lyme Bay
Wave Class	RFA Wave Knight, RFA Wave Ruler
Rover Class	RFA Black Rover, RFA Gold Rover
Leaf Class	RFA Orangeleaf, RFA Bayleaf
Fort Class	RFA Fort Austin, RFA Fort George, RFA Fort Rosalie, RFA Fort Victoria
Forward Repair Ship	RFA Diligence
Joint Casualty Treatment Ship/Maritime Afloat Training Capability	RFA Argus

THE ARMY

THE QUEEN

FIELD MARSHALS

HRH The Prince Philip, Duke of Edinburgh, KG, KT, OM, GBE, AC, QSO, PC, *apptd* 1953

Lord Bramall, KG, GCB, OBE, MC, *apptd* 1982

Lord Vincent of Coleshill, GBE, KCB, DSO, *apptd* 1991

Sir John Chapple, GCB, CBE, *apptd* 1992

HRH The Duke of Kent, KG, GCMG, GCVO, ADC, *apptd* 1993

Lord Inge, KG, GCB *apptd* 1994

FORMER CHIEFS OF STAFF

Gen. Lord Guthrie of Craigiebank, GCB, LVO, OBE, *apptd* 1992

Gen. Sir Roger Wheeler, GCB, CBE, *apptd* 1995

Gen. Sir Michael Walker, GCB, CMG, CBE, *apptd* 1997

Gen. Sir Mike Jackson, GCB, CBE, DSO, *apptd* 2000

GENERALS

Granville-Chapman, Sir Timothy, GBE, KCB, CBE *(Vice-Chief of the Defence Staff)*

O'Donoghue, Sir Kevin, KCB, CBE *(Chief of Defence Material, Defence Equipment and Support)*

Dannatt, Sir Richard, KCB, CBE, MC *(Chief of the General Staff)*

HRH The Prince of Wales, KG, KT, GCB, OM, AK, QSO, PC, ADC

McColl, Sir John, KCB, CBE, DSO *(Deputy Supreme Allied Cdr Europe)*

Richards, Sir David, KCB, CBE, DSO *(Commander-in-Chief Land Forces)*

LIEUTENANT-GENERALS

Houghton, J., CBE *(Chief of Joint Operations, Permanent Joint HQ (UK))*

Figgures, A., CBE *(Deputy Chief of the Defence Staff (Equipment Capability))*

Parker, N., CBE *(Cdr Regional Forces)*

Lamb, G., CMG, DSO, OBE *(Cdr Field Army)*

Lillywhite, L., MBE, QHS *(Surgeon General)*

Applegate, R., OBE *(Chief of Material (Land) and Quartermaster General)*

Leakey, A., CMG, CBE *(Director-General European Union Military Staff)*

Baxter, R., CBE *(Deputy Chief of the Defence Staff (Health))*

Rollo, W., CBE *(Adjutant-General)*

Pearson, P., CBE *(Deputy Cdr Allied Joint Force Command, Naples)*

Wall, P., CBE *(Deputy Chief of the Defence Staff (Commitments))*

Shirreff, A., CBE *(Cdr Allied Rapid Reaction Corps)*

Cooper, J., DSO, MBE *(Deputy Commanding General Multi National Force, Iraq and Senior British Military Representative (Iraq))*

Graham, A., CBE *(Director Defence Academy)*

Bill, D., CB *(UK Military Representative to NATO and the European Union)*

Riley, J., CB, DSO *(next appointment not yet announced)*

MAJOR-GENERALS

Howell, D., CB, OBE *(Director-General Army Legal Services)*

Roberts, Sir Sebastian, KCVO, OBE *(Senior Army Member, Royal College of Defence Studies)*

Whitley, A., CMG, CBE *(Senior British Loan Service Officer, Oman)*

Brown, C., CBE *(GOC Northern Ireland)*

Wilson, C., CBE *(Capability Manager (Battlespace Manoeuvre) and Master General of the Ordnance)*

Mans, M., CBE *(Military Secretary)*

White-Spunner, B., CBE *(GOC 3rd (UK) Division)*

Hawley, A., OBE, QHP *(Director-General Army Medical Services)*

Coward, G., CB, OBE *(Chief of Staff Joint Warfare Development, Permanent Joint HQ (UK))*

Everson, P., OBE *(GOC 4th Division)*

Newton, P., CBE *(Director-General Development Concepts and Doctrine)*

Gregory, A. *(Director-General Personnel)*

Melvin, R., OBE *(GOC UK Support Command, Germany)*

Mayall, S. *(Assistant Chief of the General Staff)*

Binns, G., CBE, DSO, MC *(GOC 1st (UK) Armoured Division)*

Von Bertele, M., OBE *(Chief Executive Defence Medical Education and Training Agency)*

Macklin, A. *(Armoured Fighting Vehicles Group Leader, Defence Equipment and Support)*

Berragan, G. *(Director-General Army Recruiting and Training)*

Shaw, J., CBE *(Chief of Staff HQ Land Forces)*

McDowall, D., MBE *(GOC 2nd Division)*

Lalor, S., TD *(Assistant Chief of the Defence Staff (Reserves and Cadets))*

Sykes, R. *(Defence Services Secretary)*

Page, J., OBE *(GOC 6th (UK) Division)*

Shouesmith, D. *(Assistant Chief of Defence Staff (Logistic Operations))*

Moore, W., CBE *(Director-General Logistics, Supply and Equipment (HQ Land Forces))*

Cubitt, W., CBE *(GOC London District and Maj.-Gen. Commanding The Household Division)*

Rutherford-Jones, D. *(Commandant Royal Military Academy Sandhurst)*

Rutledge, M., OBE *(GOC 5th Division)*

Brealey, B., *(GOC Theatre Troops)*

Bradshaw, A., OBE *(MoD)*

Hughes, C., CBE *(pending assignment)*

Inshaw, T., *(Director-General Training and Education)*

Boag, C., CBE *(Project HYPERION Team Leader)*

Kennett, A., CBE *(Director-General Training Support)*

Caplin, N. *(Kosovo Protection Corps Coordinator)*

Robbins, Ven. S., QHC *(Chaplain-General to HM Land Forces)*

Barrons, R., CBE *(Deputy Commanding Gen. Multi National Corps)*

Dale, I., CBE *(Director-General Land Equipment, Defence Equipment and Support)*

Gordon, J., CBE (Cdr British Forces Cyprus and Administrator of the Sovereign Base Areas of Akrotiri and Dhekelia)

CONSTITUTION OF THE ARMY

The army consists of the Regular Army, the Regular Reserve and the Territorial Army (TA). It is commanded by the Chief of the General Staff, who is the professional Head of Service and Chair of the Executive Committee of the Army Board, which provides overall strategic policy and direction to the commands. These are: Land Command, which comprises the Field Army, Regional Forces, the Joint Helicopter Command, the Theatre Troops and Land Support; and the Adjutant-General's Command, responsible for army personnel matters and education and training. The army is divided into functional arms and services, sub-divided into regiments and corps (listed below in order of precedence). The first phase of a major reform programme known as the Future Army Structure (FAS) was completed during 2008. The FAS incorporates changes in tactical doctrine, organisational structure, personnel terms and conditions of service and the introduction of new equipment. Under the first phase, the infantry was re-structured into large multi-battalion regiments, which involved amalgamations and changes in title for some regiments.

Further information in the public domain on the composition of the Army Board, Headquarters, Arms and Services, including addresses, can be obtained from the Army List, which is published annually by the Stationery Office and held in most public libraries. Members of the public can write for general information to Headquarters Adjutant General Secretariat, Trenchard Lines, Upavon, Wiltshire SN9 6BE. All enquiries with regard to records of serving personnel (Regular and Territorial Army) should be directed to The Army Personnel Centre Help Desk, Kentigern House, 65 Brown Street, Glasgow G2 8EX T 0141-224 2023/3303. Enquirers should note that the Army is governed in the release of personal information by various Acts of Parliament.

ORDER OF PRECEDENCE OF CORPS AND REGIMENTS OF THE BRITISH ARMY

ARMS

HOUSEHOLD CAVALRY
The Life Guards
The Blues and Royals (Royal Horse Guards and 1st Dragoons)

ROYAL HORSE ARTILLERY
(when on parade with their guns, the Royal Horse Artillery take precedence over the Household Cavalry)

ROYAL ARMOURED CORPS
1st the Queen's Dragoon Guards
The Royal Scots Dragoon Guards (Carabiniers and Greys)
The Royal Dragoon Guards
The Queen's Royal Hussars (The Queen's Own and Royal Irish)
9th/12th Royal Lancers (Prince of Wales')
The King's Royal Hussars
The Light Dragoons
The Queen's Royal Lancers
Royal Tank Regiment

ROYAL REGIMENT OF ARTILLERY
(with the exception of the Royal Horse Artillery (*see* above))

CORPS OF ROYAL ENGINEERS

ROYAL CORPS OF SIGNALS

REGIMENTS OF FOOT GUARDS
Grenadier Guards
Coldstream Guards
Scots Guards
Irish Guards
Welsh Guards

REGIMENTS OF INFANTRY
The Royal Regiment of Scotland
The Princess of Wales' Royal Regiment (Queen and Royal Hampshire's)
The Duke of Lancaster's Regiment (King's, Lancashire and Border)
The Royal Regiment of Fusiliers
The Royal Anglian Regiment
The Rifles
The Yorkshire Regiment
The Mercian Regiment
The Royal Welsh
The Royal Irish Regiment
The Parachute Regiment
The Royal Gurkha Rifles

SPECIAL AIR SERVICE

ARMY AIR CORPS

SERVICES

ROYAL ARMY CHAPLAINS' DEPARTMENT

THE ROYAL LOGISTIC CORPS

ROYAL ARMY MEDICAL CORPS

CORPS OF ROYAL ELECTRICAL AND MECHANICAL ENGINEERS

ADJUTANT-GENERAL'S CORPS

ROYAL ARMY VETERINARY CORPS

SMALL ARMS SCHOOL CORPS

ROYAL ARMY DENTAL CORPS

INTELLIGENCE CORPS

ARMY PHYSICAL TRAINING CORPS

QUEEN ALEXANDRA'S ROYAL ARMY NURSING CORPS

CORPS OF ARMY MUSIC

THE ROYAL MONMOUTHSHIRE ROYAL ENGINEERS (MILITIA) (TA)

THE HONOURABLE ARTILLERY COMPANY (TA)

REST OF THE TERRITORIAL ARMY (TA)

ARMY EQUIPMENT

Tanks	386
Challenger 2	386
Reconnaissance vehicles	475
Fuchs	11
Sabre	137
Scimitar	327
Reconnaissance aircraft	3
Armoured Infantry Fighting Vehicle	575
Armoured Personnel Carrier	2,718
Artillery pieces	877
Anti-tank missile	800+
Helicopters	299
Attack	166
Apache	67
Lynx	99
Observation	133
Gazelle	133
Unmanned aerial vehicle	192+
Surface-to-air missile	339+
Land radar	157
Miscellaneous boats/craft	4
Amphibious craft	4
Logistics and support vehicles	6

Source: Military Balance 2008

THE TERRITORIAL ARMY (TA)

The Territorial Army is part of the UK's reserve land forces and provides support to the regular army at home and overseas. The TA is divided into three types of unit: national, regional, and sponsored. TA soldiers serving in regional units complete a minimum of 27 days training a year, comprising some evenings, weekends and an annual two-week camp. National units normally specialise in a specific role or trade, such as logistics, IT, communications or medical services. Members of national units have a lower level of training commitment because of the travel involved and complete 19 days training a year, comprising two to three weekends and an annual two-week camp. As at 1 April 2008 the TA's total strength was 35,630 (the established liability is 42,000).

QUEEN ALEXANDRA'S ROYAL ARMY NURSING CORPS

The Queen Alexandra's Royal Army Nursing Corps (QARANC) was founded in 1902 as Queen Alexandra's Imperial Military Nursing Service and gained its present title in 1949. The QARANC has trained nurses for the register since 1950 and also trains and employs health care assistants to Level 2 NVQ, with the option to train to Level 3. The corps recruits qualified nurses as officers and other ranks and in 1992 male nurses already serving in the army were transferred to the QARANC.

Colonel-in-Chief, HRH The Countess of Wessex
Colonel Commandant, Brig. Jane Arigho, CBE

THE ROYAL AIR FORCE

THE QUEEN

MARSHAL OF THE ROYAL AIR FORCE
HRH The Prince Philip, Duke of Edinburgh, KG, KT, OM, GBE, AC, QSO, PC, *apptd* 1953

FORMER CHIEFS OF THE AIR STAFF

MARSHALS OF THE ROYAL AIR FORCE
Sir Michael Beetham, GCB, CBE, DFC, AFC, *apptd* 1982
Sir Keith Williamson, GCB, AFC, *apptd* 1985
Lord Craig of Radley, GCB, OBE, *apptd* 1988

AIR CHIEF MARSHALS
Sir Michael Graydon, GCB, CBE, *apptd* 1991
Sir Richard Johns, GCB, KCVO, OBE, *apptd* 1994
Sir Peter Squire, GCB, DFC, AFC *apptd* 1999

AIR RANK LIST

AIR CHIEF MARSHALS
Stirrup, Sir Jock, GCB, AFC, ADC *(Chief of the Defence Staff)*
Torpy, Sir Glenn, GCB, CBE, DSO, ADC *(Chief of the Air Staff)*
HRH The Prince of Wales, KG, KT, GCB, OM, AK, QSO, PC, ADC
Loader, Sir Clive, KCB, OBE, ADC *(Commander-in-Chief Air Command)*

AIR MARSHALS
Thornton, Sir Barry, KCB *(Chief of Material (Air) and Air Member for Material)*
Peach, S., CBE *(Chief of Defence Intelligence)*
McNicoll, I., CB, CBE *(Deputy Commander-in-Chief Operations, Air Command)*
Dalton, S., CB *(Deputy Commander-in-Chief Personnel and Air Member for Personnel, Air Command)*
Moran, C., OBE, MVO *(Deputy Cdr. Allied Joint Force Command, Brunssum)*
Walker, D., CBE, AFC *(Deputy Cdr. Allied Air Component Command, Ramstein)*

AIR VICE-MARSHALS
Maddox, N., CBE *(Chief of Staff (Operations) Air Command)*
Charles, R., CB *(Director RAF Legal Services)*
Ness, C. *(Director-General Combat (Air))*
Walker, D., OBE, MVO *(Master of the Royal Household)*
Ruddock, P., CBE *(Director-General Saudi Arabia Armed Forces Project)*
Leeson, K., CBE *(Assistant Chief of the Defence Staff (Resources and Plans)*
Nickols, C., CBE *(Assistant Chief of the Defence Staff (Operations), MoD)*
Harper, C., CBE *(Air Officer Commanding No. 1 Group)*
Walton, A., CBE *(Senior Directing Staff (Air), Royal College of Defence Studies)*
Mills, Revd P., QHC *(Director-General RAF Chaplaincy Services)*
Bryant, S., CBE *(Chief of Staff Personnel and Air Secretary)*
Pulford, A., CBE *(Assistant Chief of Defence Staff (Operations))*
Allan, R., OBE *(Director-General Information Systems and Services)*
Anderson, T., DSO *(Assistant Chief of the Air Staff)*
Routledge, M. *(Chief of Staff Strategy, Policy and Plans, Air Command)*
Kurth, N., CBE *(Chief of Staff (Support) Air Command)*
Garwood, R., CBE, DFC *(Air Officer Commanding No. 22 Training Group)*
Wiles, M. *(Director-General Joint Supply Chain)*
Dixon, C. *(Capability Manager (Information Superiority), Air Member for Equipment Capability)*
Evans, C., QHP *(Chief of Staff (Health) Air Command/Director-General RAF Medical Services)*
Hillier, S., CBE, DFC *(Air Officer Commanding No. 2 Group)*
Harwood, M., CBE *(Head of the British Defence Staff, USA)*

CONSTITUTION OF THE RAF

The RAF consists of a single command, Air Command, based at RAF High Wycombe. RAF Air Command was formed on 1 April 2007 from the amalgamation of Strike Command and Personnel and Training Command.

Air Command consists of three groups, each organised around specific operational duties. The Expeditionary Air Wings No. 1 Group is the coordinating organisation for the tactical fast-jet forces responsible for attack, offensive support and air defence operations. No. 2 Group provides air combat support including air transport and air to air refuelling; intelligence surveillance; targeting and reconnaissance; and force protection. No. 22 (Training) Group recruits personnel and provides trained specialist personnel to the RAF, as well as to the Royal Navy and the Army (*see also* Armed Forces Training and Recruitment).

RAF EQUIPMENT

Aircraft	
BAe 125	6
BAe 146	2
Dominie	9
Firefly	38
Globemaster	4
Harrier	78
Hawk	112
Hercules	43
Islander	2
Nimrod	18
Sentinel	5
Sentry	7
Super King Air (leased)	2
Tornado	205
Tristar	9
Tucano	95
Tutor	99
Typhoon	49
VC10	16
Helicopters	
Chinook	40
Griffin	16
Merlin	28
Puma	37
Sea King	25
Squirrel	31

Source: Military Balance 2008

ROYAL AUXILIARY AIR FORCE

The Auxiliary Air Force was formed in 1924 to train an elite corps of civilians to serve their country in flying squadrons in their spare time. In 1947 the force was awarded the prefix 'royal' in recognition of its distinguished war service and the Sovereign's Colour for the Royal Auxiliary Air Force (RAuxAF) was presented in 1989. The RAuxAF continues to recruit civilians who undertake military training in their spare time to support the Royal Air Force in times of emergency or war.

Air Commodore-in-Chief, HM The Queen

Honorary Inspector-General Royal Auxiliary Air Force, Air Vice-Marshal Barry Newton, CB, CVO, OBE

Inspector Royal Auxiliary Air Force, Gp Capt. Gary Bunkell, QVRM, AE, ADC

PRINCESS MARY'S ROYAL AIR FORCE NURSING SERVICE

The Princess Mary's Royal Air Force Nursing Service (PMRAFNS) was formed on 1 June 1918 as the Royal Air Force Nursing Service. In June 1923, His Majesty King George V gave his royal assent for the Royal Air Force Nursing Service to be known as the Princess Mary's Royal Air Force Nursing Service. Men were integrated into the PMRAFNS in 1980 and now serve as officers and other ranks.

Patron and Air Chief Commandant, HRH Princess Alexandra, The Hon. Lady Ogilvy, KG, GCVO

Director of Nursing Services and Matron-in-Chief, Gp Capt. W. B. Williams, RRC, QHN

SERVICE SALARIES

The following rates of pay apply from 1 April 2008.

The pay rates shown are for army personnel. The rates also apply to personnel of equivalent rank and pay band in the other services (*see* below for table of relative ranks).

Rank	*Annual salary*
SECOND LIEUTENANT	£23,475.24
LIEUTENANT	
On appointment	£28,216.32
After 1 year in rank	£28,962.48
After 2 years in rank	£29,704.32
After 3 years in rank	£30,442.56
After 4 years in rank	£31,188.36
CAPTAIN	
On appointment	£36,160.08
After 1 year in rank	£37,128.60
After 2 years in rank	£38,108.76
After 3 years in rank	£39,092.88
After 4 years in rank	£40,065.48
After 5 years in rank	£41,045.64
After 6 years in rank	£42,018.12
After 7 years in rank	£42,514.20
After 8 years in rank	£43,002.24
MAJOR	
On appointment	£45,548.64
After 1 year in rank	£46,673.40
After 2 years in rank	£47,790.12
After 3 years in rank	£48,922.68
After 4 years in rank	£50,043.72
After 5 years in rank	£51,176.16
After 6 years in rank	£52,300.92
After 7 years in rank	£53,421.72
After 8 years in rank	£54,550.56
LIEUTENANT-COLONEL	
On appointment	£63,927.36
After 1 year in rank	£64,774.80
After 2 years in rank	£65,614.32
After 3 years in rank	£66,454.32
After 4 years in rank	£67,293.84
After 5 years in rank	£71,158.56
After 6 years in rank	£72,107.52
After 7 years in rank	£73,065.00
After 8 years in rank	£74,022.60
COLONEL	
On appointment	£77,544.84
After 1 year in rank	£78,508.80
After 2 years in rank	£79,476.60
After 3 years in rank	£80,440.44
After 4 years in rank	£81,404.40
After 5 years in rank	£82,368.24
After 6 years in rank	£83,332.20
After 7 years in rank	£84,300.00
After 8 years in rank	£85,267.68
BRIGADIER	
On appointment	£92,536.56
After 1 year in rank	£93,473.40
After 2 years in rank	£94,410.24
After 3 years in rank	£95,343.12
After 4 years in rank	£96,287.76

PAY SYSTEM FOR SENIOR MILITARY OFFICERS

Revised pay rates effective from 1 April 2008 for all military officers of 2* rank and above (excluding medical and dental officers).

MAJOR-GENERAL (2*)	*Annual salary*
Scale 1	£98,198.52
Scale 2	£99,654.60
Scale 3	£101,580.60
Scale 4	£103,880.52
Scale 5	£106,180.56
Scale 6	£108,480.60
Scale 7	£110,778.60
LIEUTENANT-GENERAL (3*)	*Annual salary*
Scale 1	£115,576.56
Scale 2	£122,799.60
Scale 3	£130,022.52
Scale 4	£134,588.52
Scale 5	£139,156.56
Scale 6	£143,722.56
Scale 7	n/a
GENERAL (4*)	*Annual salary*
Scale 1	£154,700.04
Scale 2	£157,784.04
Scale 3	£160,938.96
Scale 4	£164,159.04
Scale 5	£167,439.96
Scale 6	£170,790.96
Scale 7	n/a

Field Marshal – appointments to this rank will not usually be made in peacetime. The salary for holders of the rank is equivalent to the salary of a 5-star General, a salary created only in times of war. In peacetime, the equivalent rank to Field Marshal is the Chief of the Defence Staff. From 1 April 2008, the annual salary range for the Chief of the Defence Staff is £222,358.68–£235,968.84.

OFFICERS COMMISSIONED FROM THE SENIOR RANKS

Rank	*Annual salary*
Level 15	£48,333.12
Level 14	£48,016.92
Level 13	£47,684.88
Level 12	£47,040.48
Level 11	£46,399.92
Level 10	£45,751.68
Level 9	£45,107.16
Level 8	£44,462.88
Level 7*	£43,658.40
Level 6	£43,162.32
Level 5	£42,658.44
Level 4†	£41,662.68
Level 3	£41,166.72
Level 2	£40,659.00
Level 1‡	£39,667.08

* Officers commissioned from the ranks with more than 15 years' service enter on level 7

† Officers commissioned from the ranks with between 12 and 15 years' service enter on level 4

‡ Officers commissioned from the ranks with less than 12 years' service enter on level 1

SOLDIERS' SALARIES

Under the Pay 2000 scheme, personnel are paid in either a high or low band in accordance with how their trade has been allocated to those bands at each rank. Pay is based on trade and rank, not on individual appointment, or in response to temporary changes in role.

Rates of pay effective from 1 April 2008 are:

Rank	*Lower Band*	*Higher Band*
PRIVATE		
Level 1	£16,226.76	£16,226.76
Level 2	£16,676.04	£17,492.16
Level 3	£17,125.20	£19,312.20
Level 4	£18,624.72	£20,765.04
LANCE CORPORAL (levels 5–7 also applicable to Privates)		
Level 5	£19,628.52	£22,959.72
Level 6	£20,448.72	£24,076.80
Level 7	£21,323.40	£25,181.88
Level 8	£22,299.72	£26,314.56
Level 9	£23,108.16	£27,599.28
CORPORAL		
Level 1	£25,181.88	£26,314.56
Level 2	£26,314.56	£27,599.28
Level 3	£27,599.28	£28,950.72
Level 4	£27,810.24	£29,626.20
Level 5	£28,029.00	£30,341.04
Level 6	£28,251.72	£30,969.72
Level 7	£28,458.48	£31,645.56

Rank	*Lower Band*	*Higher Band*
SERGEANT		
Level 1	£28,622.64	£31,239.24
Level 2	£29,372.52	£32,047.56
Level 3	£30,110.52	£32,860.08
Level 4	£30,415.20	£33,273.84
Level 5	£31,208.04	£33,922.32
Level 6	£32,285.76	£34,570.44
Level 7	£32,531.88	£35,218.80
STAFF SERGEANT		
Level 1	£31,684.56	£35,242.32
Level 2	£32,098.32	£36,093.60
Level 3	£33,141.12	£36,956.64
Level 4	£33,918.36	£37,811.88
WARRANT OFFICER II (levels 5–7 also applicable to Staff Sergeants)		
Level 5	£34,379.16	£38,671.20
Level 6	£35,933.52	£39,526.44
Level 7	£36,483.96	£40,096.68
Level 8	£36,956.64	£40,666.80
Level 9	£37,792.32	£41,248.80
WARRANT OFFICER I		
Level 1	£36,812.16	£40,131.60
Level 2	£37,526.88	£40,920.72
Level 3	£38,284.44	£41,623.68
Level 4	£39,042.12	£42,389.16
Level 5	£39,803.64	£43,146.84
Level 6	£40,920.72	£43,916.04
Level 7	£42,076.68	£44,587.80

RELATIVE RANK – ARMED FORCES

Royal Navy
1 Admiral of the Fleet
2 Admiral (Adm.)
3 Vice-Admiral (Vice-Adm.)
4 Rear-Admiral (Rear-Adm.)
5 Commodore (Cdre)
6 Captain (Capt.)
7 Commander (Cdr)
8 Lieutenant-Commander (Lt.-Cdr)
9 Lieutenant (Lt.)
10 Sub-Lieutenant (Sub-Lt.)
11 Acting Sub-Lieutenant (Acting Sub-Lt.)

Army
1 Field Marshal
2 General (Gen.)
3 Lieutenant-General (Lt.-Gen.)
4 Major-General (Maj.-Gen.)
5 Brigadier (Brig.)
6 Colonel (Col.)
7 Lieutenant-Colonel (Lt.-Col.)
8 Major (Maj.)
9 Captain (Capt.)
10 Lieutenant (Lt.)
11 Second Lieutenant (2nd Lt.)

Royal Air Force
1 Marshal of the RAF
2 Air Chief Marshal
3 Air Marshal
4 Air Vice-Marshal
5 Air Commodore (Air Cdre)
6 Group Captain (Gp Capt.)
7 Wing Commander (Wg Cdr)
8 Squadron Leader (Sqn Ldr)
9 Flight Lieutenant (Flt Lt)
10 Flying Officer (FO)
11 Pilot Officer (PO)

SERVICE RETIRED PAY

On compulsory retirement

Those who leave the services having served at least five years, but not long enough to qualify for the appropriate immediate pension, now qualify for a preserved pension and terminal grant, both of which are payable at age 60. The tax-free resettlement grants shown below are payable on release to those who qualify for a preserved pension and who have completed nine years' service from age 21 (officers) or 12 years from age 18 (other ranks).

The annual rates for army personnel are given. The rates also apply to personnel of equivalent rank in the other services, including the nursing services.

OFFICERS

Applicable to officers who give full pay service on the active list on or after 31 March 2008. Pensionable earnings for senior officers (*) is defined as the total amount of basic pay received during the year ending on the day prior to retirement, or the amount of basic pay received during any 12-month period within 3 years prior to retirement, whichever is the higher. Figures for senior officers are percentage rates of pensionable earnings on final salary arrangements on or after 31 March 2008.

No. of years reckonable service	*Capt. and below*	*Major*	*Lt.-Col.*	*Colonel*	*Brigadier*	*Major-General**	*Lieutenant-General**	*General**
16	£11,975	£14,262	£18,700	£22,651	£26,907	—	—	—
17	£12,527	£14,940	£19,656	£23,690	£27,956	—	—	—
18	£13,079	£15,617	£20,611	£24,729	£29,005	—	—	—
19	£13,631	£16,295	£21,567	£25,768	£30,054	—	—	—
20	£14,183	£16,972	£22,522	£26,807	£31,103	—	—	—
21	£14,735	£17,650	£23,478	£27,846	£32,152	—	—	—
22	£15,287	£18,327	£24,434	£28,885	£33,201	—	—	—
23	£15,839	£19,005	£25,389	£29,925	£34,250	—	—	—
24	£16,391	£19,682	£26,345	£30,964	£35,299	38.5%	—	—
25	£16,943	£20,360	£27,301	£32,003	£36,348	39.7%	—	—
26	£17,495	£21,037	£28,256	£33,042	£37,397	40.8%	—	—
27	£18,047	£21,715	£29,212	£34,081	£38,446	42.0%	42.0%	—
28	£18,599	£22,392	£30,167	£35,120	£39,495	43.1%	43.1%	—
29	£19,151	£23,070	£31,123	£36,159	£40,544	44.3%	44.3%	—
30	£19,703	£23,747	£32,079	£37,198	£41,593	45.4%	45.4%	45.4%
31	£20,255	£24,425	£33,034	£38,237	£42,642	46.6%	46.6%	46.6%
32	£20,806	£25,102	£33,990	£39,277	£43,691	47.7%	47.7%	47.7%
33	£21,358	£25,780	£34,945	£40,316	£44,740	48.9%	48.9%	48.9%
34	£21,910	£26,457	£35,901	£41,355	£45,789	50.0%	50.0%	50.0%

WARRANT OFFICERS, NCOS AND PRIVATES

(Applicable to soldiers who give full pay service on or after 31 March 2008)

No. of years reckonable service	*Below Corporal*	*Corporal*	*Sergeant*	*Staff Sergeant*	*Warrant Officer Level II*	*Warrant Officer Level I*
22	£7,087	£9,142	£10,023	£11,417	£12,189	£12,961
23	£7,334	£9,461	£10,373	£11,816	£12,614	£13,413
24	£7,582	£9,780	£10,722	£12,214	£13,040	£13,866
25	£7,829	£10,099	£11,072	£12,613	£13,465	£14,318
26	£8,076	£10,418	£11,422	£13,011	£13,891	£14,771
27	£8,324	£10,737	£11,772	£13,410	£14,316	£15,223
28	£8,571	£11,056	£12,122	£13,808	£14,742	£15,675
29	£8,819	£11,376	£12,472	£14,207	£15,167	£16,128
30	£9,066	£11,695	£12,821	£14,605	£15,593	£16,580
31	£9,313	£12,014	£13,171	£15,004	£16,018	£17,033
32	£9,561	£12,333	£13,521	£15,402	£16,444	£17,485
33	£9,808	£12,652	£13,871	£15,801	£16,869	£17,937
34	£10,055	£12,971	£14,221	£16,199	£17,294	£18,390
35	£10,303	£13,290	£14,571	£16,598	£17,720	£18,842
36	£10,550	£13,609	£14,921	£16,996	£18,145	£19,295
37	£10,797	£13,928	£15,270	£17,395	£18,571	£19,747

GRANTS AND GRATUITIES

Terminal grants are in each case three times the rate of retired pay or pension. There are special rates of retired pay for certain other ranks not shown above. Lower rates are payable in cases of voluntary retirement.

A gratuity of £4,070 is payable for officers with short service commissions for each year completed. Resettlement grants are £14,006 for officers and £9,573 for other ranks.

THE EDUCATION SYSTEM

Responsibility for education in England lies with the Secretaries of State for Children, Schools and Families (DCSF) and Innovation, Universities and Skills (DIUS); in Wales, with Welsh ministers; in Scotland, with Scottish ministers; and in Northern Ireland with the education minister and the minister for employment and learning.

EXPENDITURE

Most education expenditure is incurred by local authorities, which make their own expenditure decisions according to their needs. Expenditure for higher and further education in England and Scotland is met by the respective funding agencies; in Wales it is provided directly to post-16 providers.

The bulk of direct expenditure by the DIUS, the Welsh Assembly Government and the Scottish government is directed towards supporting post-16 education. Funding for higher education in universities and colleges is channelled through the Higher Education Funding Councils (HEFCs). Funding for research is distributed partly through the HEFCs and partly through Research Councils. Funding for further education, sixth form provision, work based learning and adult and community education is channelled through the funding councils for that sector, but in Wales is provided directly to post-16 providers through the Welsh Assembly Government's Department for Children, Education, Lifelong Learning and Skills (DCELLS). In addition, the DIUS currently funds student support for students who normally live in England and the Welsh Assembly Government is responsible for student support in Wales for students who normally live in Wales. The DCSF is responsible for the City Technology Colleges, the City College for the Technology of the Arts, and pays grants under the specialist schools programme in England. In Northern Ireland funding for higher and further education is provided by the Department for Employment and Learning. This department is also responsible for the provision of funding for student support.

LOCAL EDUCATION ADMINISTRATION

In England and Wales the school education service is administered by local authorities, which have day-to-day responsibility for providing state primary and secondary education and special schools. They are also responsible for securing early years education and special education for pupils in their area which can be in maintained and special schools or in non-local authority maintained schools and other settings. Local authorities share with the appropriate funding bodies (in Wales with the Assembly Government) the duty to provide adult education to meet local needs.

Unlike other services, where local authorities are financed largely from the council tax, since 2006–7 revenue funding for schools is provided through the Dedicated Schools Grant from the DCSF to each local authority. Funding for sixth forms is provided by the Learning and Skills Council in England, which is also responsible for funding further education. Capital funding is provided to schools and authorities through a combination of devolved, targeted and strategic programmes including the Building Schools for the Future and Academies programmes.

Authority-maintained schools usually manage their own budgets: the local authority allocates funds to schools, largely on the basis of pupil numbers, and the schools' governing bodies are responsible for overseeing spending and for most aspects of staffing, including appointments and dismissals. Local authorities have intervention powers to add additional governors, take back control of a school's budget or apply to the secretary of state to replace the governing body of a school with an interim executive board when a school is placed under special measures, is judged to require significant improvement or is causing concern and has not complied with a warning notice from the authority.

Funding support for statutory age school education in Wales is provided to local authorities through the revenue support grant – the block grant from the Welsh Assembly Government to support local authorities to deliver a wide range of services.

In Scotland there are three categories of school: publicly funded, grant aided and independent. The vast majority are publicly funded and the duty of providing education locally in Scotland rests with the education authorities. They are responsible for the construction of buildings, the employment of teachers and other staff, and the provision of equipment and materials.

Devolved school management is in place for all primary, secondary and special schools. From August 2007, parent councils replaced school boards. The new councils are designed to make parents more involved in their child's education.

Scotland has primary, secondary and special schools, of which there are 392 state-funded faith schools: 388 Catholic, one Jewish and three Episcopalian.

Education, with the exception of further and higher education, is administered locally in Northern Ireland by five education and library boards (ELBs), which fund controlled and maintained schools and whose costs are met in full by the Northern Ireland Executive. All grant-aided schools include elected parents and teachers on their boards of governors. All schools and colleges of further education have full responsibility for their own budgets, including staffing costs.

EDUCATION IN FIGURES

EXPENDITURE

UK EXPENDITURE ON EDUCATION AND TRAINING
(£m)

	2006–7 outturn	*2007–8 est*
Under-fives	4,101	4,400
Primary schools	19,958	21,343
Secondary schools	22,571	24,048
Post-secondary non-tertiary education	8,103	8,686
Tertiary education	10,356	11,467
Training	2,171	2,542
Other education and training	5,579	6,291
Total	72,839	78,777

Source: PESA 2008

UK MANAGED EXPENDITURE ON EDUCATION AND TRAINING *(percentage of GDP)*

	2005–6 outturn	*2006–7 outturn*	*2007–8 est*
Education and training	5.6	5.5	5.6
Education	5.4	5.3	5.4

Source: PESA 2008

UK MANAGED EXPENDITURE ON EDUCATION AND TRAINING *(£bn)*

1998–9	47.1	2003–4	63.3
1999–2000	48.6	2004–5	65.8
2000–1	52.2	2005–6	69.3
2001–2	56.9	2006–7	72.2
2002–3	58.6	2007–8 (est)	76.3
of which on education *(£bn)*			
1998–9	45.5	2003–4	61.2
1999–2000	47.0	2004–5	63.7
2000–1	50.5	2005–6	67.1
2001–2	55.2	2006–7	69.8
2002–3	56.6	2007–8 (est)	73.9

Source: PESA 2008

UK EXPENDITURE BY THE GOVERNMENT AND LOCAL AUTHORITIES (2006–7) *(£m)*

Local authorities	
Current	42,483
Capital	4,376
Total	46,859
Central government	
Current	18,818
Capital	477
Total	19,295
All public authorities	
Current	61,301
Capital	4,853
TOTAL	66,154

Source: PESA 2008

SCHOOLS AND PUPILS

PRE-SCHOOL EDUCATION (2007) *(percentage)*

	Public sector	*Private and voluntary*	*Total*
UK	64	35	99
England	62	39	101
Wales	85	—	85
Scotland	70	28	97
Northern Ireland	58	14	73

UK SCHOOLS BY CATEGORY (2006–7)

	England	*Wales*
Maintained nursery schools	448	31
Maintained primary and secondary schools	20,704	1,751
Community	12,838	1,475
Voluntary aided	4,285	162
Voluntary controlled	2,655	102
Foundation	926	12
Pupil referral units	448	41
Maintained special schools	1,006	44
Non-maintained special schools	72	—
City Technology Colleges and City Colleges for the Technology of the Arts	10	—
Academies	46	—
Independent schools	2,284	66
Total	25,018	1,933

Scotland	
Publicly funded schools	2,755
Primary	2,184
Secondary	381
Special	190
Independent	150
Primary	61
Secondary	55
Special	34
Total	2,905

Northern Ireland	
Grant-aided mainstream	
Nursery*	98
Primary	868
Secondary	226
grammar	69
other	157
Non-maintained mainstream	17
Special (maintained)	45†
Total	1,254

* Excludes voluntary and private pre-school education centres
† Figure includes three hospital schools

UK PUPILS IN THE MAINTAINED SECTOR (2006–7)

Nursery pupils	157,100
Primary pupils	4,921,900
Secondary pupils	3,941,600
Pupils in special schools	99,800
Pupils in pupil referral units	15,700
Total	9,136,100

SPECIAL NEEDS PUPILS (2006–7)

	Pupils with special educational needs	*Percentage of all pupils*
England	229,100	2.8
Wales	15,300	3.1
Scotland*	13,700	1.6
Northern Ireland	12,500	3.7
Total	270,600	2.8

*For Scotland, pupils with a record of needs or a coordinated support plan, including some who also had an individualised educational programme (IEP)

TEACHERS

FULL-TIME QUALIFIED TEACHERS (2005–6 est) *(thousands)*

	E&W	*Scotland*	*NI*	*UK*
Maintained nursery and primary schools	178.0	21.7	7.9	208.5
Maintained secondary schools	200	23.7	10.0	233.8
Non-maintained mainstream schools	54.5	2.6	0.1	57.2
All special schools	17.5	2.1	0.7	20.4
Total	451	50.1	18.7	519.8

UK PRIMARY SCHOOL PUPIL–TEACHER RATIOS*

	England	*Wales*	*Scotland*	*NI*
2004–5	22.5	20.7	17.6	20.0
2005–6	22.0	19.8	17.1	20.5
2006–7	21.8	19.9	16.3	20.8

*The average size of classes 'as taught' was 25.8 in 2006–7 (Figures refer to 'all classes' rather than 'one-teacher classes' only).

UK SECONDARY SCHOOLS (2006–7)

	England	*Wales*	*Scotland*	*NI*
No. of pupils	3,268,500	210,400	313,000	149,800
Average class size	21.3	20.4	—	—
Pupil-teacher ratio	16.5	16.6	12.0	14.5

POST-16 AND HIGHER EDUCATION

POST-16 STUDENTS (2005–6)

	Full-time	*Part-time*
UK	1,055,000	3,395,400
England	937,500	2,806,500
Wales	43,300	196,400
Scotland*	45,100	286,200
Northern Ireland	29,200	106,200

* Enrolments, not head count

HIGHER EDUCATION STUDENTS* (2006–7)

	Part-time	*Full-time*	*Total*
HE students	–	–	2,362,815
Postgraduate students	316,320	243,070	559,390
Undergraduate students	594,780	1,208,645	1,803,425

*includes UK, EU and non-EU students
Source: HESA 2008

UK HIGHER EDUCATION QUALIFICATIONS AWARDED (2006–7)

	Full-time	*Part-time*
First degrees	281,995	37,265
Higher degrees	93,125	35,265
Other postgraduate	39,790	34,040
Other graduate	51,280	78,290
Total	466,195	184,865

Source: HESA 2008

UK HIGHER EDUCATION INCOME BY SOURCE (2006–7)

	£ thousand	*Percentage of total*
Funding council grants	8,030,651	37.7
Tuition fees, education grants and contracts	5,413,985	25.4
Research grants and contracts	3,371,991	15.9
Endowment and investment	390,841	1.8
Other	4,077,385	19.2
Total	21,047,481	100

Source: HESA 2008

UK HIGHER EDUCATION EXPENDITURE (2006–7)

	£ thousand	*Percentage of total*
Staff costs	12,164,531	57.8
Other operating expenses	7,549,087	35.8
Depreciation	1,067,523	5.1
Interest payable	266,340	1.3
Total	21,047,481	100

Source: HESA 2008

Statistics are published by each of the home education departments and the Higher Education Statistics Agency (HESA) through press notices, bulletins and statistical volumes. These can be found on the following websites:
ENGLAND W www.dcsf.gov.uk
WALES W www.wales.gov.uk
SCOTLAND W www.scotland.gov.uk
NORTHERN IRELAND W www.deni.gov.uk
HESA W www.hesa.ac.uk

THE INSPECTORATE

ENGLAND

The Office for Standards in Education, Children's Services and Skills (OFSTED) was created on 1 April 2007. It has responsibility for the regulatory and inspection activities of the former Office for Standards in Education; inspection of adult learning and training formerly undertaken by the Adult Learning Inspectorate; the regulation and inspection of children's social care formerly undertaken by the Commission for Social Care Inspection; and the inspection of the Children and Family Court Advisory and Support Service formerly undertaken by Her Majesty's Inspectorate of Court Administration.

OFSTED is a non-ministerial government department whose executive head is Her Majesty's Chief Inspector of Education, Children's Services and Skills (HMCI). OFSTED is responsible for the registration and inspection of childcare, arrangements for social care and support of children and young people, and the inspection of all maintained and some independent schools. It is also responsible for the inspection of further education, all publicly funded adult education and training and some privately funded training provision, and the inspection of teacher training.

The inspection of the Children and Family Court Advisory and Support Service (CAFCASS) is also undertaken by OFSTED. Joint area reviews and annual performance assessments of local children's services provision continue to be led by OFSTED. The post of the Children's Rights Director (CRD) transferred to OFSTED from the Commission for Social Care Inspection on 1 April 2007.

The Education and Inspections Act that established the new OFSTED requires the inspectorate to promote improvement in the public services it inspects and regulates; ensure that these services focus on the interests of children, parents, learners and employers; and ensure that these services are efficient and effective. The act also established a board to provide strategic oversight of OFSTED. The non-executive board has a duty to have regard to the views of service users as well as a statutory purpose to encourage improvement.

WALES

HM Inspectorate for Education and Training in Wales (Estyn: Arolygiaeth Ei Mawrhydi dros Addysg a Hyfforddiant yng Nghymru) is responsible for inspecting early years provision in the non-maintained sector, primary schools, secondary schools, special schools (including independent special schools), pupil referral units, independent schools, further education, youth support services, local education authorities, initial teacher training, work-based learning, Careers Wales companies, the education, guidance and training elements of Workstep programmes and adult community based learning. Its remit from the Welsh ministers also includes providing advice on a wide range of education and training matters.

SCOTLAND

HM Inspectorate of Education (HMIE) is an executive agency of the Scottish government. HM Inspectors (HMIs) inspect or review and report on education in primary, secondary and special schools, further education institutions (under contract to the Scottish Further and Higher Education Funding Council), initial teacher education, community learning, care and welfare of pupils, the education functions of local authorities, prison education, children's services and in other contexts as necessary. They work in collaboration with the Care Commission in integrated inspection of pre-school education centres and residential schools, with Audit Scotland on the inspection of education authorities and on behalf of the Scottish Further and Higher Education Funding Council in the review of Scotland's 43 further education colleges.

The HMIs work in teams alongside lay members (who are volunteer members of the public) and associate assessors (who are practising teachers or senior educationalists seconded for the inspection). HMIE is led by the senior chief inspector, supported by six chief inspectors (five of whom head inspectorates) and twelve assistant chief inspectors. The Scottish Further and Higher Education Funding Council has a duty to ensure that provision is made for accessing and enhancing the quality of higher education provided and works on this with the Quality Assurance Agency for Higher Education (QAA).

NORTHERN IRELAND

Inspection is carried out in Northern Ireland by the Education and Training Inspectorate, which provides inspection services for the Department of Education Northern Ireland, the Department for Employment and Learning and the Department of Culture, Arts and Leisure. Schools are currently inspected once every five to seven years. In further education and training, survey inspections are carried out at least once every four years. In addition each educational institution is visited on a regular basis by a district inspector. The inspectorate provides evidence-based advice to ministers and departments to assist in the formulation of policies in education, training and youth.

SCHOOLS

Full-time education is compulsory in Great Britain for all children between five and 16 years and between four and 16 years in Northern Ireland. About 93 per cent of children in the United Kingdom receive free education from public funds and the rest attend fee-charging schools or are educated at home. Provision is being increased for pre-school children and many pupils remain at school after the minimum leaving age. No fees are charged in any publicly maintained school in England, Wales and Scotland. In Northern Ireland, fees may be charged in voluntary schools and are paid by pupils in preparatory departments of grammar schools, but pupils admitted to the secondary departments of grammar schools, unless they come from outside Northern Ireland, do not pay fees. Students under 19 years of age attending courses at further education colleges are not charged course fees.

ENGLAND AND WALES

There are two main types of school in England and Wales: schools maintained by the state, which charge no fees; and independent schools, which charge fees. Schools maintained by the state, with the exception of the academies and city technology colleges, which exist in England alone, are maintained by local authorities. Schools maintained by the state are classified as community, voluntary or foundation schools. Community schools are owned by local authorities and wholly funded by them (although sixth forms have separate funding arrangements). They are non-denominational and provide primary and secondary education. Schools in the voluntary category provide primary and secondary education and many have a particular religious ethos. Although the school buildings are in many cases provided by the voluntary body (known as the foundation), the authority financially maintains them.

There are two subdivisions in the voluntary category: *voluntary controlled* and *voluntary aided.* In the case of voluntary controlled schools, the authority bears all the costs. In voluntary aided schools, the governing body is responsible for capital expenditure on the buildings, perimeter walls and fences, playgrounds, furniture fixtures and fittings (including ICT), and the Secretary of State for Children, Schools and Families may pay a capital grant of up to 90 per cent of approved capital expenditure. The local authority is responsible for capital work to playing fields and for all revenue funding. Sixth forms have separate funding arrangements. The arrangements in Wales are similar but the rate of grant support is 85 per cent.

Foundation schools provide primary and secondary education. They can have a religious character, although most do not. They are funded by the local authority, and by the relevant funding bodies in respect of sixth form provision, although the land and buildings will be owned by a foundation or by the governors. The government's policy in England is to encourage community and voluntary controlled schools to become self-governing as foundation schools. The government is also encouraging schools to acquire foundations (known as trusts) as a means of forming permanent relationships with external partners.

Local authorities are required to provide the schools that they maintain with a delegated budget to cover their running costs. Authorities can retain funding of various centrally provided services, including transport and some special educational needs. The authority acts as admission authority for most community and some voluntary schools.

Academies (England only) are all-ability independent state schools with a mission to transform education where the status quo is sub-standard. They are established and managed by independent sponsors, and funded by the government at a level comparable to other local schools. No fees are paid by parents. There are currently 83 academies with a further 50 projected to open in September 2008. The DCSF is committed to establishing 400 academies with at least 240 open or in the pipeline by 2010.

City Technology Colleges (CTCs) and *City Colleges for the Technology of the Arts (CCTAs)* are found in England only, and are state-aided but independent of local authorities. Their aim is to widen the choice of secondary education in disadvantaged urban areas and to teach a broad curriculum with an emphasis on science, technology, business understanding and arts technologies. Capital costs are shared by government and business sponsors, and running costs are covered by a per capita grant from the DCSF. The government is now encouraging CTCs to convert to academies. To date ten have converted and a further two are considering converting with effect from September 2008. Two remaining CTCs and the one CCTA (the BRIT School, Croydon) currently have no plans to change their status.

Trust schools are foundation schools supported by a charitable foundation that shares the school's aspirations for their pupils and can support them in continuing improvement. As foundation schools they employ their own staff and set their own admissions arrangements. The trust holds the school's land and building and appoints govenors. Trust schools remain part of their local authority's group of maintained schools. The trust allows schools to build long-term relationships with partners such as businesses, charities, universities and other schools to help raise standards and widen opportunities for pupils. As of May 2008 there were 60 operating trust schools and over 280 schools working towards trust status.

SCHOOL MANAGEMENT INITIATIVES

Federations involve two or more schools in England combining their governing bodies or establishing a joint committee. This collaboration could entail sharing the curriculum, teaching resources, staff, ICT facilities, sports facilities or budgets. Federations can involve a mix of primary and secondary schools, and schools can form joint governance committees with FE colleges.

All publicly maintained schools have a *governing body*, usually made up of a number of parent and local community representatives, governors appointed by the authority if the school is local authority-maintained, the headteacher and other staff. Voluntary schools and some foundation schools have foundation governors who are generally appointed to protect the ethos of the school. Governing bodies are responsible for the overall conduct and policies of schools including their academic aims and objectives.

The *Specialist Schools Programme* is open to all maintained secondary schools in England, including special schools with secondary age pupils, that wish to develop a curriculum specialism in one of ten areas: arts, business and enterprise, engineering, humanities, languages, mathematics and computing, music, science, sport, and technology. A new specialism for Special Educational Needs (SEN) was also introduced in 2005. Specialist schools receive additional recurrent funding to support the targets within their plan. This is currently calculated at a rate of £129 per pupil per annum. In addition, they receive a one-off capital grant of £100,000 supplemented by sponsorship, to improve facilities. Specialist schools are expected to include sponsors, local businesses and/or employers on their governing bodies. In January 2008 there were around 2,890 designated specialist schools, representing over 88 per cent of England's total number of secondary schools. Re-designation to the programme is reviewed at the time the school has an OFSTED section 5 inspection, usually every three years. At this point, schools which meet certain prescribed criteria are also invited to take on extra roles under the High Performing Specialist School element of the programme.

Independent/State School Partnerships were launched in 1998 to encourage good practice for the benefit of both sectors. In the first nine years of the scheme more than 330 projects received joint funding of around £10m. In May 2008 the tenth round of partnerships was announced with 23 partnerships receiving over £4m over the next three years. The latest round has focused on support for gifted and talented young people, with activities centred on an increasing attainment in science, maths and modern foreign languages at GCSE, A-level and degree level, particularly from communities where aspirations are low.

The Leading Edge Partnership Programme is available to specialist schools which meet the High Performing Specialist Schools (HPSS) criteria. The programme is designed to enable groups of schools to work together to improve results at key stages 3 and 4, particularly amongst the lowest attaining pupils in the partnership. Schools in the programme are expected to develop solutions to challenges facing the education system and partnerships are expected to engage in opportunities to share practice, and learn from others through national events. There are currently over 200 such partnerships.

SCOTLAND

Education authority schools (known as publicly funded schools) are financed by local government, partly through revenue support grants from central government, and partly from local taxation. Devolved management from the local authority to the school is in place for more than 88 per cent of all school-level expenditure. A small number of grant-aided schools, mainly in the special sector, are conducted by boards of managers and receive grants direct from the Scottish government. Independent schools charge fees, receive no direct grant and are required to be registed with Scottish ministers and, like other schools, are subject to inspection by HMIE.

NORTHERN IRELAND

Controlled schools are managed by the education and library boards (ELBs) through boards of governors consisting of representatives of transferors (mainly the Protestant churches), parents, teachers and the ELB. Within the controlled sector there is a small number of integrated schools. There are also grant maintained integrated schools which are funded directly by the Department of Education.

Voluntary maintained schools are managed by boards of governors consisting of members nominated by trustees (mainly Roman Catholic) with representatives of teachers, parents and the ELB. Voluntary schools receive grants towards capital costs and running costs in whole or in part. A majority are entitled to capital grants at 100 per cent. Voluntary non-maintained schools are mainly voluntary grammar schools managed by boards of governors consisting of representatives of parents, teachers and, in most cases, the Department of Education and the ELB, as well as those appointed as provided in each school's scheme of management. Integrated schools exist to educate Protestant and Roman Catholic children, as well as those of other faiths and no faith, together. Latest figures show that there are currently 56 integrated schools, comprising 19 integrated second level colleges and 37 integrated primary schools.

There are a number of Irish-language schools and units, and in June 2008 there were 25 freestanding Irish-medium schools (23 of which received recurrent funding from the department) and 11 Irish-medium units attached to schools in the English language sector. Of the 23 schools, 22 are Irish-medium primary schools. There are also 3 Irish-medium nursery units.

THE STATE SYSTEM

SURE START

Sure Start is a programme in England designed to deliver the best start in life for every child. It aims to increase the availability of childcare; improve health, education and emotional development for young people; and support parents in their role. Children's centres providing integrated services for under-fives are being rolled out to communities, with the goal of opening 3,500 across England by 2010. Sure Start's remit is confined to the under-fives, but other programmes are targeted at older children, including as part of the extended schools initiative to ensure that accessible and affordable care is available for all children to at least age 14.

PRE-SCHOOL EDUCATION

Pre-school education is for children from 3 to 5 years of age. It is not compulsory, parents can take as little or as much of their entitlement as they choose, although a free place is available for every 3- and 4-year-old whose parents want one. In England all 3- and 4-year-olds are entitled to 12½ hours per week of free early education over 38 weeks of the year. Children are eligible from 1 January, 1 April or 1 September, following their third birthday. From September 2010 the free early education entitlement will increase from 12½ hours to 15 hours per week. Parents will be able to use their weekly entitlement for longer periods over a minimum of three days. Free places are funded by local authorities and are delivered by a range of providers in the maintained and non-maintained sectors – nursery schools; nursery classes in primary schools; private schools; private day nurseries; voluntary playgroups; pre-schools and registered childminders. In order to receive funding, providers should be working towards the early learning goals and other features of the foundation stage curriculum; they should be inspected on a regular basis by education inspectors appointed by OFSTED and meet any conditions set by the local authority.

Since September 2008 the foundation stage curriculum, Birth to Three Matters, and relevant elements of the national daycare standards will be consolidated into the Early Years Foundation Stage (EYFS). This is a single framework for the development, learning and care of all children in early years settings. The latest available data (January 2008) shows that around 95 per cent of 3-year-olds and virtually all 4-year-olds in England were receiving at least some free early education.

In Wales, a free part-time place in a maintained school or funded non-maintained setting is available for each child from the term following their third birthday. Non-maintained settings which are funded by local authorities to provide education are regularly inspected by the Care and Social Services Inspectorate for Wales and Estyn. From September 2008 the foundation phase framework for children's learning for 3 to 7-year-olds in Wales will be introduced on a four-year rolling programme.

In Scotland, councils have a duty to provide pre-school education for all 3- and 4-year-olds whose parents request one. In August 2007, the legal duty for provision increased to 475 hours of free pre-school education per year, although local authorities have the power to provide more if they choose. Most provision is delivered in daily 2.5 hour sessions, but alternative arrangements are possible. In Northern Ireland children who have reached the age of 4 on or before 1 July will commence primary school at the beginning of the September following. In Northern Ireland approximately 30 per cent of pre-school education takes place in voluntary/private sector playgroups funded by the Department of Education.

PRIMARY EDUCATION

Primary education begins at 5 years in Great Britain and 4 years in Northern Ireland. In England, Wales and Northern Ireland the transfer to secondary school is generally made at 11 years.

Primary schools consist mainly of infant schools for children aged 5 to 7, junior schools for those aged 7 to 11, and combined junior and infant schools for both age groups. First schools in some parts of England cater for ages 5 to 10 as the first stage of a three-tier system of first, middle and secondary schools. Unlike England, Scotland has only primary schools.

MIDDLE SCHOOLS

Middle schools take children from first schools, mostly in England, cover varying age ranges between 8 and 14 and usually lead on to comprehensive upper schools.

SECONDARY EDUCATION

Secondary schools are for children aged 11 to 16 and for those who choose to stay on to 18. At 16, many students prefer to move on to tertiary or sixth form colleges or into further education colleges or work-based training. Most secondary schools in England, Wales and Scotland are co-educational. The largest secondary schools have over 1,500 pupils and around 60 per cent of pupils in the United Kingdom are in schools which take over 1,000 pupils.

In England and Wales the main types of maintained secondary schools are comprehensive schools, whose admission arrangements are without reference to ability or aptitude; deemed middle schools (in England), for children aged between eight and 14 years who then move on to senior comprehensive schools at 12, 13 or 14; and (in England) grammar schools, with selective intake, providing an academic course from 11 to 16–18 years.

In Scotland all pupils in education authority secondary schools attend schools with a comprehensive intake. Most of these schools provide a full range of courses appropriate to all levels of ability from first to sixth year.

In Northern Ireland the process of selection (currently the 11-plus examination) is a key factor of the education system. Children are admitted to either grammar (42 per cent of pupils in 2007) or secondary schools (58 per cent of pupils in 2007) based on the grade they achieve in two tests taken during their seventh year at school when they are 10 or 11 years of age. Following a major review of post-primary education, which included research into the selective education system, extensive consultation and recommendations from the Post-Primary Review Working Group (Costello), Northern Ireland's education system was to embark on a process of major reform. However, following the restoration of the Northern Ireland Assembly a vote by the assembly will be required to end academic selection.

New arrangements for post-primary education, in particular the means by which pupils transfer from primary to post-primary schools, are being introduced. The minister for education announced in May 2008 key aspects of the arrangements to:

- End academic selection
- Introduce new post-primary admissions criteria
- Provide for informed selection at age 14

The proposals will be considered within the executive and assembly processes.

From 2013 the new post-primary arrangements will guarantee all pupils access to a much wider range of courses, with a minimum of 24 courses at key stage 4, and 27 at post-16. At least one third of the courses on offer will be general (academic) in nature, and at least one third will be (applied vocational/professional/technical). Legislation has been made to give effect to these changes and to enable schools to enter into collaborative arrangements with other schools, FE colleges or other providers.

SPECIAL EDUCATION

Wherever appropriate, taking parents' wishes into account, children with special educational needs are educated in ordinary schools, which are required to publish their policy for pupils with such needs. Schools and local authorities in England and Wales and ELBs in Northern Ireland are required to identify and secure provision for children with special educational needs and to involve the parents in decisions.

In Scotland, school placing is a matter of agreement between education authorities and parents. Parents have the right to say which school they want their child to attend, and a right of appeal where their wishes are not being met.

In Northern Ireland grant-aided special schools are funded by local ELBs and have partially delegated budgets. ELBs can also fund places in a small number of local independent schools, recognised by the Department of Education as providers of special education.

Maintained special schools are run by education authorities which pay all the costs of maintenance. All maintained schools must have a delegated budget. Non-maintained special schools are run by voluntary bodies; they may receive grants from central government for capital expenditure and for equipment but their current expenditure is met primarily from the fees charged to education authorities for pupils placed in the schools. Some independent schools provide education wholly or mainly for children with special educational needs.

Of all the pupils with statements of special educational needs (or a coordinated support plan of needs in Scotland) in 2006–7, 62 per cent were educated in mainstream schools.

ELECTIVE HOME EDUCATION

In England and Wales parents have the responsibility for their children's education, which they can fulfil either by sending children to school or, in a minority of cases, by educating at home. The education must be efficient and full-time, and suitable to the child's age, ability and aptitude and to any special educational needs the child may have. Parents have no legal obligation to notify the local authority that a child is being educated at home, but where a child is being taken out of school, they must notify the school that they are taking full responsibility for the child's education so that the child's name can be deleted from the school register. Is it then the school's duty to report this to the local authority. For children in special schools, parents must seek the consent of the local authority before taking steps to educate them outside the school system. Although home education is also legal in Scotland, different laws and guidance apply from those in England and Wales. There are no official figures on the numbers of pupils educated outside school.

THE CURRICULUM

ENGLAND

The national curriculum was introduced in England from 1988 for the period of compulsory schooling from 5 to 16. It is mandatory in all maintained schools. Following a review in 1999, a revised curriculum was introduced in schools from September 2000 extending the curriculum to include the foundation stage for children aged 3–5.

From September 2008 the Early Years Foundation Stage (EYFS) will be mandatory for all schools and nurseries in OFSTED-registered settings attended by children aged under 5. The EYFS brings together the existing national standards for daycare and childminding, Birth to Three Matters and curriculum guidance for the foundation stage.

The Childcare Act 2006 provides for the EYFS learning and development requirement to comprise three elements: the early learning goals, educational programmes and assessment arrangements. It sets out six areas covered by the early learning goals and educational programmes:

- Personal, social and emotional development
- Communication, language and literacy
- Problem solving, reasoning and numeracy
- Knowledge and understanding of the world
- Physical development
- Creative development

The Education Act 2002 extended the national curriculum to include the foundation stage. This act also established a single national assessment system called the foundation stage profile.

At key stages 1 and 2, the statutory subjects in the national curriculum are:

Core subjects	*Foundation subjects*
English	Design and Technology
Mathematics	Information and Communication Technology
Science	History
	Geography
	Art and Design
	Music
	Physical Education

At key stage 3 (11- to 14-year-olds) a modern foreign language and citizenship are introduced. At key stage 4 (14- to 16-year-olds) pupils are required to continue to study the core subjects, plus physical education, information and communication technology and citizenship. Careers, sex education are statutory subjects for all secondary pupils and work-related learning is compulsory for all pupils at key stage 4. In addition, schools must provide access for each key stage 4 pupil to a minimum of one course in the arts (art and design, music, dance, drama and media arts), one course in the humanities (history and geography), at least one modern foreign language and design and technology. Other subjects, such as classical languages are taught when the resources of individual schools permit. Religious education must be taught across all key stages. Parents have the right to withdraw their children from religious and sex education classes.

Statutory assessment takes place at the end of the EYFS and national tests and tasks take place in English and mathematics at the end of key stage 1 (7-year-olds), with the addition of science at the end of key stage 2 (11-year-olds). At key stage 1 the results of tasks and tests are not reported but are used to underpin teachers' overall assessment of pupils. At key stages 2 and 3 separate teacher assessments of pupils' progress are made to set alongside the test results. At key stage 4, the GCSE and vocational equivalents are the main form of assessment.

Each year the DCSF in England publishes four sets of achievement and attainment tables showing performance measures for every school and local authority based on results at key stages 2 and 3, GCSE, A-level and equivalent qualifications.

The Qualifications and Curriculum Authority (QCA) is a non-departmental public body that was established by the Education Act 1997. It is governed by a board whose members are appointed by the Secretary of State for Children, Schools and Families. QCA performs a wide range of functions in England, including monitoring and advising on the curriculum for young people of compulsory school age and developing associated assessments, tests and examinations. The QCA also has a statutory responsibility for regulating qualifications offered in schools, colleges and workplaces, a role that has now passed on an interim basis to the Office of the Qualifications and Examinations Regulator (OFQUAL) pending legislation to set up a permanent independent regulator (*see* below).

The National Assessment Agency (NAA) was launched in April 2004 by the then DfES to develop and deliver high quality national curriculum tests and supervise the delivery and modernisation of GCSE and A-level examinations. The NAA is a subsidiary of the QCA.

In April 2008 a new regulator of qualifications for England was created. The Office of the Qualifications and Examinations Regulator, known as OFQUAL, is responsible for ensuring that standards are maintained in all 14–19 qualifications and that different qualifications are more easily comparable. The government intends OFQUAL to become the sole regulator of 14–19 qualifications, but until this legislation is passed, it operates as part of QCA. Afterwards, the regulator will be accountable to parliament rather than to government ministers.

WALES

A national curriculum was introduced simultaneously in Wales and, although it is broadly similar to that of England, it has separate and distinctive characteristics which are reflected in the programmes of study where appropriate. Welsh is compulsory for pupils at all key stages, either as a first or as a second language. The curriculum has recently been revied for implementation from September 2008.

In July 2003 the minister announced that statutory testing would be removed for pupils in Wales at the end of key stage 2 from 2004–5 and from 2005–6 for key stage 3. Statutory teacher assessment remains and is being strengthened by moderation and accreditation arrangements. It is the only form of statutory assessment from key stages 1–3.

In 2006 ACCAC (the Qualifications, Curriculum and Assessment Authority for Wales or Awdurdod Cymwysterau, Cwricwlwm ac Asesu Cymru) merged with the Department of Training and Education, ELWa, Dysg and the Welsh Youth Agency to create the Department for Children, Education, Lifelong Learning and Skills.

SCOTLAND

The management and delivery of the curriculum in Scotland are not prescribed by statute but is the responsibility of education authorities and individual schools. Advice and guidance are provided by the Scottish government and Learning and Teaching Scotland, which also has a developmental role. Those bodies have produced guidelines on the structure of the curriculum. There are also guidelines on assessment across the whole curriculum and on reporting to parents.

National assessments for reading, writing and mathematics may be used as part of a range of evidence that teachers consider to arrive at judgements about pupils' levels of attainment. National assessments are carried out by the school when the teacher judges that a pupil has completed a level. Assessment for 5–14 year olds is done at six levels (A–F) and most pupils are expected to move from one level to the next at roughly 18-month to two-year intervals.

Provision is also made for teaching in Gaelic in many parts of Scotland and the number of pupils, from nursery to secondary, in Gaelic-medium education is growing.

For 16- to 18-year-olds, national qualifications, a unified framework of courses and awards which brings together both academic and vocational courses, was introduced in 1999. The Scottish Qualifications Authority awards the certificates.

Scotland is currently pursuing its biggest education reform for a generation in the shape of a major review of all aspects of the curriculum. *Curriculum for Excellence* – which aims to provide more professional autonomy for teachers, greater choice and opportunity for pupils and a single coherent curriculum for all children and young people aged 3–18 – will be fully implemented by 2009.

NORTHERN IRELAND

A revised statutory curriculum is being introduced on a phased basis from September 2007 to June 2010. The revised curriculum is less prescriptive in content to give schools greater flexibility to shape their teaching. It has a greater emphasis on developing skills, including the cross-curricular skills of communication, using mathematics and using ICT, along with thinking skills such as creativity, teamwork and problem solving. It also has a new area – known as personal development at primary level and learning for life and work at post-primary level – which includes employability, citizenship and personal development, to better prepare young people for all aspects of life and work. In addition to religious education, the revised curriculum is made up of areas of learning as set out below:

Primary	*Post-Primary*
The arts	Learning for life and work
Language and literacy	The arts
Mathematics and numeracy	Language and literacy
Personal development and mutual understanding	Mathematics and numeracy
	Modern languages
Physical education	Physical education
The world around us	Science and technology
	Environment and society

Key changes include the introduction of the new key stage known as the foundation stage, which covers years 1 and 2 of primary school. This is to allow a more appropriate learning style for the youngest pupils and to ease the transition from pre-school. At key stage 4, the statutory requirements have been significantly reduced in order to provide greater choice and flexibility for pupils. This will be counterbalanced by the entitlement framework, intended to be in place by 2013, which will guarantee pupils access to a wider range of academic and professional courses.

Revised assessment arrangements are also being introduced to support the revised curriculum. Diagnostic assessment of pupils in years 4 to 7 in literacy and numeracy will be carried out in the autumn term and will help teachers identify any particular strengths or weaknesses and inform teaching throughout the year. In the summer term, teachers will assess pupils in the cross-curricular skills of communication, using mathematics and using ICT, with reference to levels of progression, mapped to industry-recognised functional skills standards. This information will be reported to parents using a new pupil profile, which provides a standardised format for the annual school report to parents and will include information on a pupil's progress in the skills and areas of learning, their interests and strengths, and any focus for development. Pupils at key stage 4 and beyond will continue to be assessed through public examinations, including GCSEs and A-levels.

The Council for the Curriculum, Examinations and Assessment (CCEA) is a unique education body in the UK in that it combines the three functions of a curriculum advisory body, an awarding body and a qualifications regulatory body. It monitors and advises the Department of Education on all matters relating to the curriculum, assessment arrangements and examinations in grant-aided schools. It conducts GCSE, A- and AS-level examinations, pupil assessment at key stages 1, 2 and 3 and administers the transfer procedure tests. It also ensures that qualifications offered by awarding bodies in Northern Ireland are of an appropriate quality and standard.

INTERNATIONAL PRIMARY CURRICULUM

The International Primary Curriculum (IPC) is a comprehensive curriculum designed to improve learning and develop international awareness. The 226 schools in the UK which use the IPC are still required to follow the national curriculum but use the IPC as a tool to improve teaching and learning.

PUBLIC EXAMINATIONS AND QUALIFICATIONS

ENGLAND, WALES AND NORTHERN IRELAND

In 1988 a single system of examinations, the General Certificate of Secondary Education (GCSE) – usually taken after five years of secondary education – was introduced. The GCSE is the main method of assessing the performance of pupils on a subject-specific basis. The structure of the examination reflects national curriculum requirements where applicable. GCSE short-course qualifications are available in some subjects and comprise half the content of a full GCSE course. In September 2002 GCSEs in vocational subjects were introduced (known as applied GCSEs): art and design, business, engineering, health and social care, ICT, leisure and tourism, manufacturing, and science.

The GCSE differs from its predecessors in that there are syllabuses based on criteria covering course objectives, content and assessment methods; differentiated assessment (ie different papers or questions for different ranges of ability) and grade-related criteria (ie grades awarded on absolute rather than relative performance). The GCSE certificates are awarded on an eight-point scale, from A* to G. All GCSE syllabuses, assessments and grading procedures are monitored by qualification regulators for England, Wales and Northern Ireland (QCA, DCELLS and CCEA) to ensure that they conform to the national criteria. In England in 2007, 60.8 per cent of 15-year-olds (at the beginning of the academic year) gained at least five results at grade C or better at GCSE or equivalent (64 per cent in Northern Ireland), while 90 per cent achieved five or more at grade G or above.

Students are increasingly encouraged to continue their education post-16. For those who do so, in addition to the vocational qualifications outlined below, there are GCE (General Certificate of Education), AS (Advanced Subsidiary) and A (Advanced) Levels and the Advanced applied A-levels. Since September 2005 applied A-levels have AS/A2 units, bringing them into line with GCE A-levels. At the same time the formal distinction between GCEs and VCEs was dropped and both vocational and academic qualifications are now known as GCEs.

A-level courses usually last two years and have traditionally provided the foundation for entry to higher education. AS-level qualifications were introduced in September 2000 and represent the first half of a full A-level and are assessed accordingly. This new A-level qualification now consists of six units (three AS units and three A2 units). Students who go on to complete the full A-level will be assessed on their attainment in all six units, which may be taken either in stages or at the end of the course. From September 2008, revised A-level specifications have been introduced and most subjects reduced from six to four in order to reduce the burden of assessment. Applied A-levels will remain at six units. A-levels and AS-levels are marked on a six-point scale from A to E. An A* grade will be introduced to the grading of A-levels in 2010 to reward the most exceptional students.

An extended project will be introduced in September 2008. It will be a single piece of work requiring a high degree of planning, preparation, research and and autonomous working. Projects will differ by subject but will require research skills to explore a subject independently and in depth. It will be about the size of half an A-level.

VOCATIONAL QUALIFICATIONS

There are two broad categories of vocational qualifications: National Vocational Qualifications (NVQs), which demonstrate competence in a specific occupation (or aspect of an occupation), and vocationally related qualifications, which usually give a broader, more general preparation for an industry or wider occupational area. All vocational qualifications are based upon national occupational standards, which are designed by employers. Vocational qualifications are accredited into the national qualifications framework by the QCA at nine levels:

- Entry level
- Level 1 – Foundation Skills
- Level 2 – Operative/Semiskilled
- Level 3 – Technician/Craft/Skilled/Supervisory
- Level 4 – Technical/Middle Management
- Level 5 – Chartered/Professional/Senior Management
- Level 6 – Knowledge Based Professionals
- Level 7 – High Level Specialist Professional/Senior Professionals
- Level 8 – Leading Experts/Practitioners

General National Vocational Qualifications (GNVQs) have been replaced by vocational GCSEs (*see* above) while applied A-levels have replaced advanced GNVQs. They are available in different forms: the three-unit Advanced Subsidiary (equivalent to one GCE AS-level), the six-unit Advanced level (equivalent to one GCE A-level), and the 12-unit Double Award (equivalent to two GCE A-levels).

WELSH BACCALAUREATE

The Welsh Baccalaureate is a new qualification for 16–19 year olds that incorporates current approved qualifications like A-levels, GCSEs and NVQs and adds breadth and balance through a core programme of activities. It was piloted in 31 schools and colleges throughout Wales at both intermediate and advanced level between September

2003 and August 2007. Since September 2007, following a successful evaluation report, 75 centres have been approved to deliver the qualification as part of the post-16 roll-out and some 9,000 students are following WBQ courts in academic year 2007–8. In addition, the pilot has now been extended to include the development of a foundation level Welsh Baccalaureate since September 2006. This is being piloted in both pre- and post-16 settings.

SCOTLAND

Scotland has its own system of public examinations, and in 1999 a new system of national qualifications was introduced. Five levels of study are offered: Access, Intermediate 1, Intermediate 2, Higher and Advanced Higher. The new Higher course and Advanced Higher course are direct replacements for the old SCE Higher grade and the Certificate of Sixth Year Studies respectively. National qualifications are included on the Scottish Credit and Qualifications Framework (SCQF) (*see* below), with Access equating to levels 1 to 3, Intermediate 1 to level 4, Intermediate 2 to level 5, Higher to level 6 and Advanced Higher to level 7.

Skills for Work courses are available at Access 3, Intermediate1 and 2 and Higher level. These are practical courses designed to be an equivalent option to an existing qualification, such as Standard Grade, to help young people develop skills and knowledge in broad vocational areas, core skills, an understanding of the workplace, positive attitudes to learning and employability skills.

National courses consist of blocks of study called national units. A unit usually consists of around 40 hours of study and there are three units in a course. Unit awards demonstrate that a learner has achieved competence in a particular area of study. National course awards are graded by external assessment, which consists of an examination, coursework or performance, or a combination of two or more of these. National course awards also require candidates to pass all unit assessments of the course. A typical national course external assessment requires candidates to demonstrate long-term retention of knowledge, high levels of problem solving, integration of knowledge across a whole course and an ability to apply knowledge and skills in novel situations. The range of subjects has been expanded to include vocational qualifications.

A number of schools use the new national qualifications system for pupils in their fourth year of secondary education, but the majority of this lower age group still take the traditional Standard Grade examinations at the end of a two-year course.

A consultation on the next generation of national qualifications was launched in June 2008, taking views until the end of October 2008. This sets out the Scottish government's intention to review all national qualifications in the light of *Curriculum for Excellence.*

INTERNATIONAL BACCALAUREATE

The International Baccalaureate (IB) is a non-profit foundation that offers three programmes for students aged 3–19. Founded in 1968, the IB currently works with 2,319 schools and 617,000 students in 128 countries.

POST-16 EDUCATION

In the UK in 2005–6, 82 per cent of 16-year-olds and 69 per cent of 17-year-olds were in post-compulsory education, either at school or in further education. In 2006–7, there were 459 further education colleges in the UK of which 96 were sixth form colleges. In 2005–6, there were 60,000 full-time academic staff in further education institutions.

ENGLAND

The further education (FE) system provides a wide range of education and training opportunities for individuals from age 14 upwards and employers. Learning opportunities are provided at all levels from basic skills to higher education. The central policy aim is to build a further education system that provides the skills the economy needs to sustain quality of life and to contribute to the UK's international standing. The goal is to lead the world in skills development – with virtually all young people staying on in education and training to age 19, and half progressing to higher education; all adults having the support they need to improve their skills throughout life; and all employers seeing skills as key to their success.

In March 2006 the reform strategy *Further Education: Raising Skills, Improving Life Chances* was launched; it set out a programme of changes to deliver the above aims. Key aspects include:

- a new economic mission for FE
- providers of learning and skills to specialise to supply world class services
- an enhanced role for employers and learners in shaping development
- new entitlements to learning and support for those who most need it – free tuition for first level 3 for 19–25 year olds and learner accounts for adults on level 3 programmes
- a new strategy for raising quality, with intervention to eliminate poor quality provision
- public funding focused on delivery priorities
- less bureaucracy along with more autonomy for effective providers

The English FE system includes independent providers (voluntary and private sector) who offer a range of work-based and personal and community learning. Personal and community development learning takes place in a wide range of settings usually delivered via local authorities. Post-16 education and training (excluding Higher Education) in England is funded through the Learning and Skills Council (LSC).

WORK-BASED LEARNING

Apprenticeships are a way for learners to get practical experience while gaining nationally recognised qualifications. The LSC in England and the Welsh Assembly Government in Wales contribute towards the cost of the training and assessment. Apprenticeships normally last between one and three years (four in Wales) and there are two levels: apprenticeships and advanced apprenticeships at levels 2 and 3 respectively. Both of these lead to:

- National Vocational Qualifications (NVQs)
- Key Skills qualifications – transferable work-related skills such as IT and communication and problem solving
- Technical certificates – vocationally related qualifications that provide the basic knowledge of the NVQ

Currently over 180,000 young people start an apprenticeship each year in England, with similar programmes in place in Scotland, Northern Ireland and Wales.

> The government published *World Class Apprenticeships* in January 2008. This strategy sets out a major series of reforms over the next few years to strengthen and radically expand the programme, including establishing a new national apprenticeship service to run the programme in England.

Diplomas are new qualifications designed to give young people an alternative to traditional learning. Combining theoretical and applied learning, they aim provide a method that ensures that young people are both educated and employable. Pupils completing diplomas should have functional skills in English, Maths and ICT, and be able to apply these in work situations. Diploma Development Partnerships (DDPs) have been established to explore content development. These DDPs, led by Sector Skills Councils and including employers, higher education, school and college and awarding body representatives, specify the content of the diplomas. Awarding bodies will then develop the qualifications. The diplomas will be available in 14 lines of learning. The content for the first five lines (ICT, health and social care, engineering, creative and media and construction and the built environment) can be accessed via the QCA website. These qualifications have been available for teaching since September 2008. A further five diplomas, in business administration and finance, hair and beauty, hospitality and catering, land-based and environmental, and manufacturing will be available for teaching in 2009. The final four diplomas, in public services, sport and leisure, retail, and travel and tourism will be available in 2010. A new statutory entitlement will be in place for all 14–19 year olds from September 2013.

WALES

In Wales, the aims and makeup of the FE system are very similar to those outlined for England, although, as the education portfolio is devolved to the Welsh Assembly, the policy documents vary. Current thinking is outlined in *Skills That Work for Wales* which was published in July 2008 and is the Welsh response to the *Leitch Review of Skills in the UK*. The document sets out new approaches to funding; the transformation of the learning network; business support; and integrated skills and employment services delivered through a partnership between the Assembly Government and the Department for Work and Pensions.

SCOTLAND

Since autumn 2005, the Scottish Further and Higher Education Funding Council has been the statutory body responsible for funding Scotland's 46 further education colleges. The Scottish Qualifications Authority (SQA) is the statutory awarding body for qualifications in the national education and training system. It is both the main awarding body for qualifications for work including Scottish Vocational Qualifications (SVQs) and is also their accrediting body. The SQA is by statute required clearly to separate its awarding and accrediting functions.

There are three main qualification 'families' in Scottish further education: national qualifications; Higher national qualifications (HNC and HND); and SVQs. In addition to Standard Grade qualifications, national qualifications are available at five levels. Another feature of the qualifications system is the Scottish Group Award (SGA). SGAs are built up unit by unit and allow opportunity for credit transfer from other qualifications (such as Standard Grade or SVQ), providing a further option, especially for adult learners. SVQs are competence-based qualifications suitable for teaching in the workplace but they can also be taken in further education colleges. The Scottish Credit and Qualifications Framework includes qualifications across academic and vocational sectors. It comprises 12 levels, covering all mainstream qualifications from Access level in national qualifications to postgraduate qualifications, and including SVQs. In the academic year 2006–7 there were 468,155 student enrolments on vocational and non-vocational courses in further education colleges. Of this total, higher education courses accounted for 29 per cent of college activity.

NORTHERN IRELAND

All further education colleges are independent corporate bodies like their counterparts in the rest of the UK. Responsibility for the sector lies with the Department for Employment and Learning (DELNI), which funds the colleges directly. The colleges own their own property, are responsible for their own services and employ their own staff. The governing bodies of the colleges must include at least 50 per cent membership from those who are engaged or employed in business, industry, or any profession.

In August 2007 Northern Ireland's 16 further education colleges merged into six new area-based colleges. In 2006–7 there were 151,286 professional and technical enrolments across the six Northern Ireland FE colleges. Of these, 31,666 were full-time and 119,620 part-time. The majority of full-time enrolments are in the 16–19 age group, while most part-time students are over 19.

LEARNER SUPPORT

The *Education Maintenance Allowance* (EMA) is an income assessed allowance that supports 16–19-year-olds learning in England. The EMA consists of a weekly allowance of up to £30, plus bonus payments and is available to learners from households with an income of up to £30,810 and who enrol on a school programme. EMA is available for up to three years. In Wales, EMA consists of a weekly allowance of up to £30, plus periodic bonus payuments and is available to learners from low-income households who stay on in school or college.

Care2Learn is available in England to enable young parents under the age of 20, to return to learning after having a baby. The scheme is not income assessed and will pay up to £160 per week (£175 in London) to cover the costs of OFSTED registered childcare and travel, where the learner is taking part in a programme that is publicly-funded.

Parents aged 20 and over, who are attending a school sixth form or sixth form college may be eligible for support from the *Sixth Form College Childcare* scheme. This is an income assessed scheme that enables parents to return to learning by covering the costs of childcare at the same rates as C2L.

For adults (19 and over) in England similar discretionary learner support funds are available for the most disadvantaged students with the greatest need. These provide financial help with the costs of childcare, books, equipment and transport and residential funding. Funds are administered by colleges and other providers. The *adult learning grant* (ALG) provides low-skilled, low-income adults with support for the costs of learning. Up to £30 per week is paid during term time to adults (aged 19 and above) who are studying full time for their first full level 2 (5 GCSEs or equivalent) or first full level 3 qualification (2 A levels or equivalent). ALG is administered by the LSC and is available throughout England.

Dance and Drama Awards (DaDA) are scholarships funded by the LSC. They offer greatly reduced tuition fees, and income assessed support with living and learning costs, at some of the leading independent dance and drama schools in England. DaDA aim to ensure that access to training is based on potential to succeed in the profession and not ability to pay.

Residential Bursaries are available from 51 specialist residential colleges that offer courses not readily accessible elsewhere like agriculture, horticulture and art and design. Funding is allocated directly to the colleges by the LSC.

Discretionary Learner Support Funds are available to help students of age 16 and over with the costs associated with further education. They are distributed by the college and are targeted at those in greatest need.

For students over 18 in the UK who choose to fund their course themselves, *career development loans* are available from three high street banks. Loans of between £300 and £8,000 can be used to pay for the costs of vocational training courses. Interest on the loan is paid by the LSC while the student is completing the course. Eligible Welsh-domiciled students aged 19 years or over on further education courses, whether full-time or part-time (subject to a minimum contact requirement), receive a means-tested non-repayable assembly learning grant. Discretionary financial contingency funds are also available to all students suffering hardship and are administered by the institutions themselves. In addition, individual learning accounts are available in Wales, which provide adults with means-tested support of up to £200 to undertake a wide range of learning. Eligible Scottish-domiciled further education students can apply to their college for discretionary support in the form of bursaries. These can include allowances for maintenance, travel, study, dependants and additional support needs. College students receiving EMAs may also be eligible for the non-maintenance elements. Colleges administer discretionary funds specifically to help students with particular financial difficulties. They also have a childcare fund which is used to pay for registered childcare. Some colleges may offer different methods of childcare support and provision, for example on-site nurseries or childcare vouchers.

Full-time students over 19 years of age, resident in Northern Ireland and on certain vocational courses, may benefit from discretionary non-repayable further education bursaries. The bursaries are administered by the education and library boards. Support includes free tuition to all full-time students up to age 18 and to all full-time students over 18 undertaking a vocational course at level 3 or below. In addition, financial help is provided by colleges through a discretionary support fund for both full-time and part-time students whose access to and participation in further education is inhibited by financial considerations.

TEACHERS

ENGLAND AND WALES

All qualified teachers working in maintained primary, special and secondary schools, non-maintained special schools and pupil referral units are required to register with the General Teaching Council for England (GTCE) or the General Teaching Council for Wales (GTCW).

New entrants to the teaching profession in maintained primary and secondary schools are required to be graduates and to have qualified teacher status (QTS). QTS is achieved by successfully completing a course of initial teacher training, traditionally either a Bachelor of Education (BEd) degree, BA with QTS, BSc with QTS or the Postgraduate Certificate of Education (PGCE). New entrants are statutorily required to serve a three term (full-time, pro rata part-time) induction period during which they will have a structured programme of support. All initial teacher training has a strong element of practical school-based work, with student teachers spending significant periods of their training in the classroom.

In addition to the traditional routes, various employment-based routes to QTS have been developed. The Graduate Teacher Programme (GTP) is designed for mature, well-qualified people who can quickly take on teaching responsibilities and who need to earn a living while they train. Trainees are paid a salary and undergo up to a year of school-based training. The Registered Teacher Programme (RTP) is designed for people without a degree or formal teaching qualification but with at least two years of higher education; entrants are paid a salary and complete a degree while undergoing training for up to two years. For 2008–9 the RTP is only operating in England. Employment-based training routes account for about 15 per cent of all teacher training places in England; in Wales the GTP forms around 3 per cent of the total.

Teachers in further education (FE) are not required to have QTS, though roughly half have a teaching qualification and most have industrial, commercial or professional experience. Since July 2002, all new entrants to FE teaching in Wales are required to have, or to be working towards, a specified FE teaching qualification. A qualification for aspiring headteachers, the National Professional Qualification for Headship (NPQH), has been introduced. The National College for School Leadership administers this qualification and others and acts as a focus for development and support. In Wales, the NPQH and other headship programmes are administered by the Welsh Assembly Government and consideration is being given to establishing a similar scheme in respect of FE principals, in association with powers under the Education Act 2002 allowing the making of regulations requiring FE principals to have a specified qualification.

Eligible trainees on postgraduate initial teacher training (ITT) courses in England are entitled to a tax-free training bursary worth £4,000 (primary) and £6,000 (secondary). In Wales the respective figures are £2,200 and £4,200, plus a tuition grant of up to £1,890). Newly qualified teachers with a PGCE may also be eligible for a taxable 'golden hello' payment worth £5,000 after successfully completing the induction period. Those with a PGCE in modern languages, design and technology, music and religious education may receive £2,500. Details are available at W www.teach.gov.uk/funding.

In Wales a similar scheme operates, on a pilot basis, for those undertaking the full-time PGCE (FE) or PGCE (PcET). Eligible students receive a bursary of £6,000 (£7,000 for mathematics and science courses since September 2005), paid in instalments whilst studying. In England, other training awards may be available through the secondary shortage subject scheme (SSSS). This is an additional, means-tested hardship fund from the Training and Development Agency for Schools. The subjects currently included are: design and technology, geography, information technology, mathematics, modern languages, music, religious education and science.

In Wales, placement grants supported by the Higher Education Funding Council for Wales (HEFCW) provide £1,000 per funded student on undergraduate priority courses – the same subjects that attract the £4,000 training grant – and £600 to students on other undergraduate courses.

The Training and Development Agency for Schools (TDA) is the body responsible for attracting quality people to initial teacher training (ITT), funding universities, colleges and schools and for helping schools develop and train their staff. The TDA administers a returners' programme for qualified teachers who wish to refresh their skills before returning to the profession. Participants are entitled to a bursary of up to £150 a week to a total of £1,500 and additional childcare support. The TDA supports the sharing of good practice in teacher training, encourages schools to offer placements for trainee teachers, and funds training and assessment for higher level teaching assistant (HLTA) status. For more information about the TDA see W www.tda.gov.uk.

In Wales funding of ITT is undertaken by the HEFCW. On an integrated England and Wales basis the TDA also acts as a central source of information and advice on entry to teaching.

The General Teaching Council for England (GTCE), an independent professional council, acts as a disciplinary body dealing with cases of misconduct and incompetence in England. The GTCE also hears appeal hearings for registered teachers who have failed their induction year. In addition, it is responsible for promoting the profession and professional standards and for advising the secretary of state. The separate General Teaching Council for Wales (GTCW) fulfils a similar role in Wales and provides advice to the Welsh Assembly Government.

The Specialist Teacher Assistant scheme provides trained support to qualified teachers in the teaching of reading, writing and arithmetic to young pupils.

In January 2003 the DfES, Welsh Assembly Government, employers and teaching unions signed a national agreement, *Raising Standards and Tackling Workload,* setting out a three-year programme of reforms to provide more classroom support for teachers.

SCOTLAND

The General Teaching Council for Scotland (GTCS) advises central government on matters relating to teacher supply and the professional suitability of all teacher training courses. It is also the body responsible for disciplinary procedures in cases of professional misconduct. All teachers in maintained schools must be registered with the GTCS. Only graduates are accepted as entrants to the profession; primary school teachers undertake either a four-year vocational degree course or a one-year postgraduate course, while teachers of academic subjects in secondary schools undertake the latter. There is also a combined degree sometimes known as a concurrent degree.

The Scottish Qualification for Headship has been introduced for aspiring headteachers. Universities with specialist education departments provide both in-service and pre-service training for teachers. The universities are funded by the Scottish Higher Education Funding Council, which also sets intake levels for teacher education courses in line with guidance provided by the Scottish government.

NORTHERN IRELAND

All new entrants to teaching in grant-aided schools are graduates and hold an approved teaching qualification. A fully integrated programme of Initial Teacher Education (ITE), induction and early professional development as well as the Professional Qualification for Headship programme, is in place in Northern Ireland. ITE is provided by Queen's University, Belfast, University of Ulster, Stranmillis University College, St Mary's University College and the Open University (NI). The university colleges are concerned with teacher education mainly for the primary school sector and the universities mainly for the post-primary sector. The General Teaching Council for Northern Ireland (GTCNI) advises government on professional issues, maintains a register of professional teachers and acts as a disciplinary body.

SALARIES

Qualified teachers in England and Wales, other than the leadership group (which includes headteachers, deputy headteachers and advanced skills teachers) are paid on a six-point main pay scale. Teachers who demonstrate exceptional ability have the opportunity to be assessed against national standards and moving to the three point upper scale. An 'Excellent Teacher' scheme has been available to schools since September 2006. This allows eligible teachers to access a 'spot' salary. There are teaching and learning responsibility payments for specific posts, special needs work and recruitment and retention factors which may be awarded at the discretion of the relevant body, ie the governing body or the local authority. The advanced skills teacher grade was introduced to enhance prospects in the classroom for the most able teachers. Experienced teachers are assessed against national standards to move onto the upper pay scale, after which they receive performance-related pay increases. There is a statutory superannuation scheme. Teachers working in the London area are paid on separate pay scales. As at September 2008, salary scales for teachers in England and Wales are:

Headteacher	£40,494–£100,424
Excellent teachers	£37,672–£48,437
Advanced skills teacher	£35,794–£54,417
Classroom teacher (upper pay scale)	£32,660–£35,121
Classroom teacher (main pay scale)	£20,627–£30,148
Associate teachers	£15,113–£23,903
Inner London	
Headteacher	£47,265–£107,192
Excellent teachers	£37,672–£53,819
Advanced skills teacher	£42,559–£61,188
Classroom teacher (upper pay scale)	£37,672–£42,419
Classroom teacher (main pay scale)	£25,000–£34,768
Associate teachers	£19,007–£27,794

Teachers in Scotland are paid on a seven-point scale. The entry point is for newly qualified teachers undertaking their probationary year. Movement from the probationary point is dependent on achieving the standard for full registration. Additional allowances are payable under a range of circumstances, such as distant islands and remote schools. As at 1 April 2008, salary scales for teachers in Scotland were:

Headteacher/deputy headteacher	£40,290–£78,642
Principal teacher	£35,523–£45,846
Chartered teacher	£33,588–£39,942
Main grade	£20,472–£32,583

Teachers in Northern Ireland have broadly similar pay and working conditions as teachers in England and Wales, although negotiated through separate local negotiating machinery. There are a few exceptions to this, such as the lack of an advanced skills teacher grade. As at September 2007, salary scales for teachers in Northern Ireland are:

Principal	£39,525–£98,022
Vice-Principal	From £34,938
Classroom teacher	£20,133–£34,281

HIGHER EDUCATION

The term higher education is used to describe education above A-level, Higher and Advanced Higher Grade and their equivalent, which is provided in universities, colleges of higher education and in some FE colleges.

The main purposes of higher education are:

- to enable people to develop their capabilities and fulfil their potential, both personally and at work
- to advance knowledge and understanding through scholarship and research
- to contribute to an economically successful and culturally diverse nation

The government provides strategic direction to higher education in line with its policy commitments. Advice to government on matters relating to higher education and its use of funds is provided by the separate Higher Education Funding Councils for England and Wales, in Scotland by the Scottish Further and Higher Education Funding Council and by the Northern Ireland Higher Education Council. The former receive a block grant from central government which they allocate to the universities and colleges. In Northern Ireland the grant is allocated directly to institutions by the Department for Employment and Learning.

The Scottish Further and Higher Education Funding Council funds 19 institutions of higher education. There are 15 universities including the Open University in Scotland and there are also two specialist art colleges, a conservatoire, an agricultural college and the UHI Millennium Institute in the Highlands and Islands. The universities are broadly managed as described above and the remaining colleges are managed by independent governing bodies which include representatives of industrial, commercial, professional and educational interests.

In Northern Ireland higher education is provided in six regional further education colleges, the two universities and the two university colleges. These institutions offer a range of courses, including first and postgraduate degrees, PGCEs, undergraduate diplomas and certificates, foundation degrees, Higher National Diplomas and professional qualifications.

TYPES OF HIGHER EDUCATION INSTITUTION

The Further and Higher Education Act 1992 and parallel legislation in Scotland removed the distinction between higher education provided by the universities and that provided in England, Scotland and Wales by the former polytechnics and colleges of higher education. It allowed all polytechnics, and other higher education institutions which satisfy the necessary criteria, to award their own taught course and research degrees and to adopt the title of university. All the polytechnics and some colleges of higher education have since done so. The change of name does not affect the legal constitution of the institutions.

There are now 106 universities in the UK, up from the 48 which existed prior to the Further and Higher Education Acts 1992. Of the 106, 88 are in England (including the University of London, which has a federal structure), 13 in Wales, 14 in Scotland (including the Open University) and four (including two university colleges) in Northern Ireland. There are also 46 colleges of higher education in the UK, some of which are multidisciplinary while others specialise, for example, in initial teacher training. Some award their own degrees and qualifications, while others are validated by a university or a national body.

GOVERNANCE OF UNIVERSITIES AND COLLEGES

The pre-1992 universities each have their own system of internal governance but broad similarities exist. They are run by a council which is the executive governing body and is responsible for all the affairs of the university including appointments, promotions and bidding for and allocation of financial resources. At least half the members of the council are drawn from outside the university. Many of the council's functions are carried out through committees. The senate reports to the council and deals primarily with academic issues. It consists of the council and members elected from within the university. The 1992 Act, and the Education Reform Act 1988, set out the system of governance for universities which were formerly polytechnics or other higher education institutions and for the colleges of higher education. Each institution has an instrument and articles of government that are approved by the Privy Council. These post-1992 institutions are run by boards of governors, which are responsible for the mission, finances and all appointments. Much of the board's business is delegated to committees. In particular, there is usually an academic board that deals with all matters relating to teaching and research. Most of the newest universities to be created were originally established by trust deed and have become incorporated as companies limited by guarantee. Their memorandum and articles of association incorporate the instrument and articles of government and are subject to Privy Council approval.

OPEN UNIVERSITY AND THE UNIVERSITY FOR INDUSTRY

The non-residential Open University provides a modular programme of courses throughout the UK and most of Europe leading to first and higher degrees, diplomas and certificates. Students are taught through distance learning, using written and audio-visual materials and the internet, supported by tutorials and short residential courses. No qualifications are needed for entry at undergraduate level. In 2006–7 the Open University received £12.1m in public funding and there was a total of 164,000 undergraduate students, 18,000 postgraduate students and a further 32,000 students on programmes at other institutions validated by the university. More than 675,000 degrees, certificates and diplomas have been awarded since the university's first students started to study in 1971. Research across a wide range of disciplines feeds directly into the university's teaching. The university has five Centres of Research Excellence – in citizenship, identities and governance; comparative criminological research; computing; education and educational technology; and earth, planetary, space and astronomical research. In addition, it carries out internationally recognised research in geography, design, art history, music, history, literature, pure mathematics, statistics, materials engineering and biological sciences. The university's open content initative is making educational resources freely available on the internet, with learning support and collaboration tools to connect students and educators.

- the Open University is the UK's largest university, teaching 35 per cent of all part-time undergraduate students in the UK each year
- 35 per cent of new OU undergraduate students in the UK have fewer than two A-levels
- the most popular courses (for 2006–7) were an introduction to the social sciences (7,233 students); an introduction to the humanities (5,295); understanding health and social care (4,546); data, computing and information (4,010); and exploring psychology (3,923)
- the median age of new undergraduate level students is 32
- in 2006–7, more than 37,853 students received financial help in paying their fees.

The University for Industry (Ufi) Ltd operates learndirect and is the largest government-backed e-learning organisation in the world. Ufi aims to boost people's employability, by helping them gain skills and qualifications, as well as improve organisations' productivity and competitiveness. Through the national network of more than 840 learndirect centres in England and Wales, Ufi provides access and support to a range of services from taster activities to e-learning courses which are linked to qualifications. Since its launch in April 2000, more than 2.5 million learners have taken nearly 6.8 million learndirect courses.

ACADEMIC STAFF

Each university and college appoints its own academic staff. The Universities and Colleges Employers Association (UCEA) is the employers' association for subscribing universities and other higher education institutions in the UK. It provides a framework within which representatives of institutions receive guidance and discuss salaries, conditions of service, employee relations and all matters connected with the employment of staff and employees. The services of the UCEA include collective bargaining and an annual salary survey. Academic staff in higher education require no formal teaching qualification, however all new teaching staff are now expected to obtain a teaching qualification which meeets the requirements of the new professional standards. The Higher Education Academy leads, supports and informs the professional development and recognition of staff in higher education as well as promoting good practice and providing information, advice and resources; it has developed a professional standards framework in consulation with the sector. The Leadership Foundation for Higher Education provides a dedicated service of support and advice on leadership, governance and management for all the UK's HEIs.

In the academic year 2006–7 there were 169,995 academic staff in all higher education institutions in the UK, of which 113,685 were full-time.

As a result of the national framework agreement, staff working in higher education should be, since August 2006, paid on a single national pay scale, which is used as the basis for locally negotiated pay and grading structures. The framework sought to unify pay arrangements as well as address concerns about equal pay. Since October 2008 the 51-point national pay spine has ranged from £12,773 to £53,943.

COURSES

In the UK all universities and some colleges award their own degrees and other qualifications and may act as awarding and validating bodies for colleges. The power to award degrees is regulated by law and it is an offence to purport to award a UK degree unless authorised to do so. The Quality Assurance Agency for Higher Education advises government on applications for degree-awarding powers.

The Quality Assurance Agency for Higher Education (QAA) was established in 1997 and is an independent public body funded by subscriptions from UK universities and colleges of higher education, and through contracts with the main higher education funding bodies. Its principal role is to safeguard the standards of higher education qualifications and encourage improvements in quality where possible. It does this by working with universities and colleges to define standards for higher education, through a framework known as the academic infrastructure, which includes subject benchmark statements and code of practice. QAA also carries out reviews of higher education institutions against these standards and publishes their outcomes. It advises governments on applications for the grant of degree awarding powers, university title or designation as a higher education institution. QAA is governed by a board, which has overall responsibility for the conduct and strategic direction. The board has 15 members.

Facilities exist for full-time and part-time study, day release, sandwich or block release. Credit accumulation and transfer systems allow a student to achieve a final qualification by accumulating credits for courses of study successfully achieved, or even professional experience, over a period of time.

Higher education courses comprise: first degree and postgraduate (including research) degrees, there is also a variety of Higher Education Diplomas and Certificates, often studied part-time in Higher Education (DipHE); BTEC Higher National Diplomas (HND) and Higher National Certificates (HNC); and preparation for professional examinations.

The Foundation Degree, launched in 2001, is a two-year vocational higher education qualification, co-designed by employers, which forms either a self-contained qualification or a basis for further study leading to an honours degree or further professional qualifications.

Undergraduate courses lead to the title of Bachelor, Bachelor of Arts (BA) and Bachelor of Science (BSc) being the most common, except in certain Scottish universities where Master is sometimes used for a first degree in arts subjects. For a higher degree the titles are Master of Arts (MA), Master of Science (MSc) and the research degrees of Master of Philosophy (MPhil) and Doctor of Philosophy (PhD or, at a few universities, DPhil).

Most undergraduate courses at universities and colleges of higher education run for three years, but some take four years or longer. Postgraduate studies vary in length.

Post-experience short courses form a significant part of higher education provision, reflecting the demand for professional and technical training. An increasing proportion of these courses are co-funded by students and employers.

ADMISSIONS

The government's target is to increase participation in higher education to 50 per cent of 18- to 30-year-olds by 2010. Institutions suffer financial penalties if the number of students laid down for them by the funding councils is exceeded, but the individual university or college decides which students to accept. The formal entry requirements to most degree courses are two or more A-levels at grade E or above (or equivalent), and to HND courses one A-level (or equivalent). In practice, most offers of places require qualifications in excess of this, higher requirements usually reflecting the popularity of a course or institution. These requirements do not, however, exclude applications from students with a variety of non-GCSE qualifications or unquantified experience and skills.

For admission to a degree, DipHE or HND, potential students apply through UCAS, the organisation responsible for managing applications to higher education courses in the UK. UCAS operates an online application system and provides services to applicants, advisory services, schools, colleges and universities and facilitates and promotes access to higher education. Application services exist across a range of subject areas and for UK universities and colleges. More than 500,000 people wanting to study at a university or college of higher education use the service each year and 100,000 of them use the specialist services: the Graduate Teacher Training Registry (GTTR) and the Conservatoires UK Admissions Service (CUKAS). The Open University conducts its own admissions. Details of initial teacher training courses in Scotland can be obtained from those universities offering such courses, from Universities Scotland, and from the website created by the Scottish government to promote teaching: W www.teachinginscotland.com.

For admission as a postgraduate student, universities and colleges normally require a good first degree in a subject related to the proposed course of study or research. Applications can be made to individual institutions, except for teaching and social work. There is also now an alternative to applying to postgraduate courses; UKPASS is an online application service created by UCAS. It was set up in 2007 following demand from the higher education sector to have a centralised admissions service that would not only help institutions to monitor their applicants but would also enable them to get to know more about this particular group, which is the fastest growing sector of the UK higher education marketplace.

FEES AND GRANTS

FEES FOR FULL TIME STUDENTS IN 2008–9

The Higher Education Act 2004 introduced variable tuition fees for full time higher education courses at English and Welsh institutions, and these came into effect for courses starting in September 2006 or later. In Northern Ireland variable tuition fees were introduced under the Higher Education (Northern Ireland) Order 2005. Fees are capped at £3,000 subject only to inflationary increases until 2010. In the academic year 2007–8 the maximum an institution could charge new students was £3,070 a year, and in 2008–9 this rose to £3,145.

However, students who started their course before September 2006 would still be treated under the old student finance regime and make an annual contribution to their tuition fees depending on their own level of income and that of their household. In 2006 this was up to a maximum of £1,200 and in 2008 this could be up to £1,255.

From September 2006 no student – no matter when they started – has had to pay tuition fees before they start their course or whilst they are studying as student loans for tuition fees are available (*see* below). For current system students, these cover the full amount of any fees charged. For old system students, means-tested grants are also available.

Welsh Higher Education institutions also charge fees (up to £3,145 in 2008–9). Students who normally live in Wales (and EU students) and who study at a university or college in Wales are entitled to a fee grant up to a maximum of £1,890.

ENGLAND

The following table gives a brief breakdown of what help is available to full time higher education students in England in 2007–8:

Type of support	*Old system students**	*New system students†*
Student loan for tuition fees	Yes	Yes
Student loan for maintenance	Yes	Yes
Extra help for disabled students	Yes	Yes
Extra help for students with dependents	Yes	Yes
Help towards tuition fees	Yes	No
Higher education grant	Yes	No
Maintenance (or special support) grant	No	Yes
Access to learning fund (from institutions)	Yes	Yes

*Old system students are on higher education courses living in England who started (or are treated as starting) their course before September 2006

†New system students are on higher education courses which began in September 2006 or after

A maintenance grant of up to £2,765 to help with living costs is available to current system students only. Any amount due is assessed on income and does not have to be repaid. The full grant is available to students living with a household income lower than £17,910. Partial grants are available for household incomes up to £38,300. For students entitled to benefits, maintenance grants are replaced by a non-repayable special support grant which will not affect Department for Work and Pensions benefit entitlement.

REPAYMENT OF STUDENT LOANS

Repayment of both student loans for maintenance and student loans for tuition fees does not start until the April after the student has left their course and is earning more than £15,000 a year. Repayments are calculated at 9 per cent of income over the threshold of £15,000, so someone earning £18,000 would pay back around £5.19 a week. If income falls below the threshold, repayments cease until income rises above it again. Those who pay tax through PAYE have repayments deducted from their salaries, whilst the self-employed make repayments through their tax returns.

PART TIME HIGHER EDUCATION STUDENTS
Part-time higher education students on courses in England that are at least 50 per cent of an equivalent full-time course may be entitled to a grant towards their fees, and a grant towards their course costs. This help does not have to be repaid, and entitlement to the fee grant and the course grant depends on the student's income and that of their husband, wife or partner. Students who already have a degree cannot usually apply for this support.

For 2008–9, there are three different rates of fee grant depending on how intensive the course undertaken is:

Course intensity	*Maximum fee grant*
50–59 per cent of a full time course	£785
60–74 per cent of a full time course	£945
75 per cent or more of a full time course	£1,180

For 2008–9 the maximum course grant is £255 and does not depend on the intensity of the course. Students who receive the part-time grant for fees, but whose tuition fees are more than the amount of support available may be eligible for extra help from their institution. Part-time students with disabilities may be eligible for disabled students allowances.

WALES

From 2008, students who started after 2006 and 2007 have been charged a deferred flexible fee of up to £3,145. However, students who normally live in Wales and study at a university or college in Wales can apply for a fee grant of up to £1,845 a year which does not have to be repaid. This tuition fee grant is available regardless of family income and is paid directly to the place of study. Since September 2006 eligible full-time undergraduate students who live in Wales have not had to pay fees before starting their course or whilst they are studying. Instead, a student loan for fees can be taken out, which does not have to be repaid until the course is finished and earnings are over £15,000 a year.

Other aspects of Student Finance Wales student support arrangements for 2008 starters include:

- an assembly learning grant worth up to £2,835 for eligible students from low income households
- all eligible students can also apply for a student loan for maintenance of up to £6,480 to help with living costs

Students who normally live in Wales but choose to study elsewhere in the UK will be charged fees according to the fee regime of the country in which they study and that set by the institution. Student Finance Wales will provide a loan to defer this fee but students who live in Wales and are studying elsewhere in the UK will not be entitled to the fee grant.

Fee levels in Wales are the same for students who normally live elsewhere in the UK and began studying in Wales in the academic year 2006–7. However, these students are not eligible to receive Student Finance Wales services but will instead receive support from their home country. The Welsh national bursary began in Wales in the academic year 2007–8. Eligible students, regardless of where they live in the UK will receive a means tested bursary of a minimum around £310, which will be additional to other support received and will not be offset by any reductions in other forms of support.

SCOTLAND

The arrangements for Scottish students in Scotland from 2008 are as follows:

Tuition fees – contributions have been abolished for all eligible full-time Scottish domiciled and EU students studying in Scotland.

Student loans – living cost support is mainly provided through a means-tested student loan. An additional loan of £590 is available to young students from low-income backgrounds.

Bursaries – the young students' bursary (YSB) is available to young students from low-income backgrounds. It is non-repayable and reduces the level of debt which eligible students accrue during a course of study. In 2008–9 the maximum annual support provided through YSB is £2,575.

SUPPLEMENTARY GRANTS
Depending on eligibility, students in Scotland may also receive: the adult dependants grant; the lone parents grant; childcare fund support; travel costs and the disabled students allowance (consisting of the basic allowance, the special equipment allowance and non-medical personal help). Students who are experiencing particular financial difficulty can apply for assistance from their institution's discretionary funds.

NORTHERN IRELAND

The arrangements for Northern Ireland are very similar to those for England with these differences:

- the maintenance grant is worth up to £3,335
- the higher education bursary is up to £2,000
- the access to learning fund is known as the support fund in Northern Ireland and is allocated by central government directly to the institution

POSTGRADUATE AWARDS

In general, postgraduate students do not qualify for mandatory support (including student loans and tuition fee assistance). An exception to this is the PGCE.

Awards for postgraduate courses are the responsibility of the Research Councils, depending on the field of study. Research Councils are independent bodies and make their own decisions about expenditure on postgraduate support according to the resources available to them. The fact that a course lies within its remit does not oblige the Research Councils to support every or indeed any student applying for awards.

It is for institutions to decide the level of their fees. The government is raising the levels of award available to postgraduates under the competitive merit-based system provided by the Research Councils: the minimum PhD stipend will be £12,940 in 2008–9.

Targeted support is also available to meet particular needs: postgraduate students can apply through their colleges for discretionary help from the access to learning fund. Disabled students allowances are also available to eligible students undertaking postgraduate study.

There is support available to students in Scotland for postgraduate study through the Postgraduate Students' Allowances Scheme (PSAS), which is administered by the Student Awards Agency for Scotland (SAAS). Eligible students can apply for an award consisting of a means tested maintenance grant and payment of tuition fees. Courses supported under PSAS are generally nine-month-long, taught postgraduate diploma courses on largely vocational subjects. Awards from PSAS are discretionary, not mandatory, so there is no guarantee of an award at postgraduate level.

There is support available to students who wish to pursue postgraduate study in Northern Ireland (at either Queen's University of Belfast or University of Ulster). All students should apply to the university for an application form. Students should apply for a place on the course and for an award. As there are always more applicants than awards, not all applicants who secure a place on the courses will be successful in obtaining an award. *See also* Research Councils

LIFELONG LEARNING

In the UK, the duty of securing adult and continuing education leading to academic or vocational qualifications is statutory. The Learning and Skills Council (LSC) in England, the Welsh Assembly Government and the Scottish Funding Council are responsible for and fund those courses which take place in their sector and lead to academic and vocational qualifications, prepare students to undertake further or higher education courses, or confer basic skills; the Higher Education Funding Councils fund advanced courses of continuing education. Local authorities have the power, although not the duty, to provide those courses which do not fall within the remit of the funding bodies. In Northern Ireland the Department for Employment and Learning is responsible for the funding of the statutory further education sector.

In January 2006 Lord Leitch delivered his report into skills. This showed that England lags behind other major economies in terms of skills development and set out how the government can deliver its ambitions. The LSC is working together with the government to raise the nation's skills levels and increase the numbers of adults gaining Level 2 and higher qualifications. The LSC is responsible for funding and planning provision for apprenticeships, adult learning, offender learning and skills and leisure learning. It works closely with employers providing vocational education and work based learning. Twelve new national skills academies are due to be opened in 2008 in sectors including manufacturing, retail and financial services. The Train to Gain scheme provides employers with free and subsidised training for their employees and also provides them with independent advice and guidance via an impartial skills brokerage service. By 2020 the government aims to introduce more apprenticeships to deliver the Leitch ambition of 400,000 apprenticeships in England. In the summer of 2006, the LSC took over responsibility for offender learning across England. The LSC also provides several learner support funds.

Of the many voluntary bodies providing adult education, the biggest is the Workers' Educational Association (WEA), which operates throughout England and Scotland to provide over 14,000 courses each year, reaching more than 95,000 adults. The WEA is a charity supported by funding from the LSC in England, and by the Scottish government and local authorities in Scotland. Similar but separate organisations operate in Wales and Northern Ireland: Coleg Harlech WEA (covering North Wales), WEA South Wales and WEA Northern Ireland. The National Institute of Adult Continuing Education, has a broad remit to promote lifelong learning opportunities for adults.

Wales operates a range of programmes to support skills development, including the Workforce Development Programme, a flexible system of grants to meet part of the cost of training employees, an employers' pledge in association with Basic Skills Cymru, and the Wales Union Learning Fund. The new Wales skills strategy, Skills that Work for Wales, will be implemented from autumn 2008. Advice on its implementation, and on skills, employment and business development more generally, will be provided by the Wales Employment and Skills Board, the Chair of which is also a member of the UK Commission on Employment and Skills.

NIACE Dysgu Cymru, the Welsh committee, receives financial support from the Welsh Assembly and support in kind from local authorities, and advises government, voluntary bodies and education providers on adult continuing education and training matters in Wales. In Scotland, policy responsibility for community learning and development lies with Learning Connections and the Directorate General for Education of the Scottish government. Individual learning accounts (ILAs) are a Scottish government scheme that can pay for a wide range of learning activities with a variety of registered providers, including colleges and universities. ILA Scotland funding can be used by eligible learns to cover, either wholly or in part, the fee costs of learning. In Northern Ireland, responsibility for lifelong learning lies with the Department for Employment and Learning.

CONTACTS

APPRENTICESHIPS T 0800-015 0600
W www.apprenticeships.co.uk

COUNCIL FOR THE CURRICULUM EXAMINATIONS AND ASSESSMENT (NORTHERN IRELAND) T 028-9026 1200
W www.ccea.org.uk

DEPARTMENT FOR CHILDREN, SCHOOLS AND FAMILIES (ENGLAND) T 0870-000 2288
W www.dcsf.gov.uk

DEPARTMENT FOR EDUCATION NORTHERN IRELAND T 028-9127 9279 W www.deni.gov.uk

DEPARTMENT FOR EMPLOYMENT AND LEARNING NORTHERN IRELAND T 028 9025 7777
W www.delni.gov.uk

DEPARTMENT FOR INNOVATION, UNIVERSITIES AND SKILLS (ENGLAND) T 0870-001 0336
W www.dius.gov.uk

DIPLOMAS T 0870-000 2288 W www.dfes.gov.uk/14-19

EDUCATION DEPARTMENT, SCOTTISH GOVERNMENT T 0845-345 4745
W www.teachinginscotland.com

EDUCATION OTHERWISE T 0870-730 0074
W www.education-otherwise.org

EDUCATION AND TRAINING INSPECTORATE (NORTHERN IRELAND) T 028-9127 9726
W www.etini.gov.uk

EUROPEAN SOCIAL FUND W www.esf.gov.uk

GENERAL TEACHING COUNCIL FOR ENGLAND
T 08700-010 308 W www.gtce.org.uk

GENERAL TEACHING COUNCIL FOR NORTHERN IRELAND T 028-9033 3390 W www.gtcni.org.uk

GENERAL TEACHING COUNCIL FOR SCOTLAND
T 0131-314 6000 W www.gtcs.org.uk

GENERAL TEACHING COUNCIL FOR WALES
T 029-2055 0350 W www.gtcw.org.uk

HER MAJESTY'S CHIEF INSPECTOR OF EDUCATION AND TRAINING IN WALES
T 029-2044 6446 W www.estyn.gov.uk

HER MAJESTY'S INSPECTORATE OF EDUCATION IN SCOTLAND T 01506-600200 W www.hmie.gov.uk
HIGHER EDUCATION ACADEMY T 01904-717500 W www.heacademy.ac.uk
HIGHER EDUCATION FUNDING COUNCIL FOR ENGLAND T 0117-931 7317 W www.hefce.ac.uk
HIGHER EDUCATION FUNDING COUNCIL FOR WALES T 029-2076 1861 W www.hefcw.ac.uk
HIGHER EDUCATION STATISTICS AGENCY T 01242-255577 W www.hesa.ac.uk
HOME EDUCATION ADVISORY SERVICE T 01707-371854 W www.heas.org.uk
INTERNATIONAL BACCALAUREATE ORGANISATION T (+41) (22) 791 7740 W www.ibo.org
LEARNING AND SKILLS COUNCIL (ENGLAND) T 0845-019 4170 W www.lsc.gov.uk
LEARNING AND TEACHING SCOTLAND T 08700-100 297 W www.ltscotland.org.uk
NATIONAL ASSESSMENT AGENCY T 0870-0600 622 W www.naa.org.uk
NATIONAL INSTITUTE OF ADULT CONTINUING EDUCATION T 0116-204 4200 W www.niace.org.uk
OFFICE FOR STANDARDS IN EDUCATION, CHILDREN'S SERVICES AND SKILLS (ENGLAND) T 08456-404045 W www.ofsted.gov.uk
OPEN UNIVERSITY T 0870-333 4340 W www.open.ac.uk
PROFESSIONAL QUALIFICATION FOR HEADSHIP (NORTHERN IRELAND) T 028-9061 8121 W www.rtuni.org/pqhni.cfm
QUALITY ASSURANCE AGENCY T 0141-572 3420 W www.qaa.ac.uk
QUALIFICATIONS AND CURRICULUM AUTHORITY T 020-7509 5556 W www.qca.org.uk
SCOTTISH GOVERNMENT T 08457-741 741 W www.scotland.gov.uk
SCOTTISH FUNDING COUNCIL T 0131-313 6500 W www.sfc.ac.uk
SCOTTISH QUALIFICATION FOR HEADSHIP T 0131-651 6179 W www.sqh.ed.ac.uk
SCOTTISH QUALIFICATIONS AUTHORITY T 0845-279 1000 W www.sqa.org.uk
STUDENT AWARDS AGENCY FOR SCOTLAND T 0845-111 1711 W www.student-support-saas.gov.uk
STUDENT FINANCE DIRECT T 0845-607 7577 W www.studentsupportdirect.co.uk
STUDENT FINANCE WALES T 0845-602 8845 W www.studentfinancewales.co.uk
SURE START T 0870-000 2288 W www.surestart.gov.uk
TRAINING AND DEVELOPMENT AGENCY FOR SCHOOLS T 020-7023 8001 W www.tda.gov.uk
UCAS T 0871-468 0468 W www.ucas.com
UNIVERSITIES AND COLLEGES EMPLOYERS ASSOCIATION T 020-7383 2444 W www.ucea.ac.uk
UNIVERSITY FOR INDUSTRY T 0114-291 5000 W www.ufi.com
WELSH ASSEMBLY T 0845-010 5500 W www.wales.gov.uk
WORKERS' EDUCATION ASSOCIATION T 020-7426 3450 W www.wea.org.uk

UNIVERSITIES

The following is a list of universities, which are those institutions that have been granted degree awarding powers by either a royal charter, an act of parliament or have been granted permission to use the word 'university' (or 'university college') by the Privy Council. There are other recognised bodies in the UK with degree awarding powers, as well as institutions offering courses leading to a degree from a recognised body. Further information is available at W www.dius.gov.uk.

Student numbers represent the number of full-time and part-time students (including undergraduates and postgraduates) as at 2006–7.

Variable tuition fees or 'top-up-fees' were introduced for students starting courses in the 2006–7 academic year. Each university can now choose how much to charge students for tuition, up to a maximum of £3,145 for the 2008–9 academic year in England, Wales and Northern Ireland and £1,735 in Scotland (£2,760 for medicine). Students who started their course before 2006–7 are still charged according to the old system. For more information on tuition fees and student loans, *see* the Education System section.

Whether the fees apply varies depending on where the student is from. English and Northern Irish students pay top-up fees wherever they study in the UK; Welsh students pay variable fees in England, Scotland and Northern Ireland, but are entitled to a partial tuition fee grant if they remain in Wales or attend a course that is not available at any Welsh university; Scottish students only pay variable tuition fees in England, Wales and Northern Ireland. EU students pay fees as if they came from the country they are studying in (ie the lowest amount) and international students pay their university's international fees, which are typically much higher than variable fees.

RESEARCH ASSESSMENT EXERCISE

The research assessment exercise (RAE) gives a rating to each university department put forward for evaluation, based on the quality of its research. It is used to enable the higher education funding bodies to distribute public funds for research selectively on the basis of quality. Institutions conducting the best research receive a larger proportion of the available grant so that the infrastructure for the top level of research in the UK is protected and developed. The ratings run from the top score of 5* then down through 5, 4, 3a, 3b, 2 to 1 – the table below shows universities with a 5* by discipline. The next RAE is due at the end of 2008.

Subject	*Universities or university colleges*
Accounting and finance	LSE, Manchester
Archaeology	Cambridge, Oxford, Reading
Biological sciences	Bristol, Cambridge, Imperial, Leicester, Manchester, Newcastle, Sheffield, Dundee
Business and management	Lancaster, London Business School, Warwick
Chemistry	Bristol, Cambridge, Durham, Imperial, Oxford, UCL
Classics	Cambridge, King's, Oxford, UCL
Pre-clinical studies	Manchester, Sheffield

Subject	*Universities or university colleges*
Clinical (community based)	Bristol, Cambridge, King's, Oxford
Clinical (hospital based)	Cambridge, Edinburgh, Imperial, Oxford, UCL
Clinical laboratory sciences	Birmingham, Cambridge, Imperial, Newcastle, Oxford, Dundee
Communication and media studies	UEA, Goldsmiths
Computer science	Cambridge, Edinburgh, Imperial, Manchester, Southampton, York
Drama and performing arts	Bristol, Warwick
Economics	Essex, LSE, UCL, Warwick
Education	Bristol, Cardiff
Engineering (civil)	Bristol, Cardiff, Imperial, Southampton, Wales (Swansea)
Engineering (general)	Cambridge, Imperial, Oxford
English	Birkbeck, Cambridge, Durham, Leeds, Liverpool, Oxford, Reading, UCL, Warwick, York, Edinburgh, Glasgow, St Andrews, Cardiff
French	Aberdeen, Birmingham, Cambridge, Manchester, Oxford, RHUL
Geography	Bristol, Durham, Edinburgh, OU, RHUL, UCL
German, Dutch and Scandinavian	Birmingham, Cambridge, Edinburgh, Exeter, King's, Manchester, Nottingham, RHUL, UCL
History	Birkbeck, Cambridge, Durham, UEA, King's, LSE, SOAS, Oxford Brookes
Italian	Birmingham, Cambridge, Leeds, Oxford, Reading, UCL
Law	Cambridge, Durham, Keele, LSE, Oxford, Queen Mary, Southampton, UCL
Mathematics (pure)	Cambridge, Edinburgh, Imperial, Oxford
Mathematics (applied)	Bath, Bristol, Cambridge, Durham, Imperial, Warwick
Mathematics (statistics)	Bristol, Cambridge, Kent, Lancaster, Oxford, Warwick
Music	Birmingham, Cambridge, City, Manchester, Newcastle, Nottingham, Oxford, RHUL, Southampton
Other studies allied to medicine	Cardiff, Manchester, Surrey, Ulster
Pharmacology	Oxford, UCL
Philosophy	Cambridge, Edinburgh, King's, LSE, Oxford
Physics	Cambridge, Imperial, Lancaster, Oxford, Southampton
Politics	Essex, King's, Oxford, Sheffield, Wales (Aberystwyth)

Subject	*Universities or university colleges*
Psychology	Birmingham, Bristol, Cambridge, Cardiff, Newcastle, Oxford, Reading, UCL, York, Glasgow, St Andrews, Wales (Bangor)
Sociology	Essex, Goldsmiths, Lancaster, Loughborough, Manchester, Surrey
Sports-related subjects	Birmingham, LJM, Loughborough, Manchester, Glasgow
Theology and religious studies	Cardiff, Manchester, Nottingham, Oxford

FT = full time PT = part time

UNIVERSITY OF ABERDEEN (1495)
King's College, Aberdeen AB24 3FX T 01224-272000
W www.abdn.ac.uk
Students: 10,830 FT; 2,925 PT
Chancellor, Lord Wilson of Tillyorn, KT, GCMG, FRSE
Principal and Vice-Chancellor, Prof. C. Duncan Rice, FRSE
Academic Registrar, Dr Gillian Macintosh

UNIVERSITY OF ABERTAY DUNDEE (1994)
Bell Street, Dundee DD1 1HG T 01382-308000
W www.abertay.ac.uk
Students: 3,700 FT; 560 PT
Chancellor, The Rt. Hon. the Earl of Airlie, KT, GCVO
Vice-Chancellor, Prof. Bernard King, CBE, PHD
Academic Registrar, Dr Colin Fraser

ANGLIA RUSKIN UNIVERSITY (1992)
Rivermead Campus, Bishop Hall Lane, Chelmsford, Essex CM1 1SQ T 01245-493131 W www.anglia.ac.uk
Students: 10,700 FT; 8,800 PT
Chancellor, Lord Ashcroft, KCMG
Vice-Chancellor, Prof. Michael Thorne, FRSA
The Secretary and Clerk, Stephen Bennett

UNIVERSITY OF THE ARTS LONDON
(Formerly The London Institute (1986), University of the Arts London was formed in 2004)
65 Davies Street, London W1K 5DA T 020-7514 6000
W www.arts.ac.uk
Students: 20,835
Chancellor, Lord Stevenson of Coddenham, CBE
Rector, Sir Michael Bichard, KCB
University Secretary, Martin Prince

COLLEGES

CAMBERWELL COLLEGE OF ARTS (1898)
Peckham Road, London SE5 8UF T 020-7514 6302
W www.camberwell.arts.ac.uk
Head of College, Chris Wainwright

CENTRAL SAINT MARTINS COLLEGE OF ART & DESIGN (1854)
Southampton Row, London WC1B 4AP T 020-7514 7022
W www.csm.arts.ac.uk
Head of College, Jane Rapley, OBE

CHELSEA COLLEGE OF ART & DESIGN (1895)
Millbank, London SW1P 4RJ T 020-7514 7751
W www.chelsea.arts.ac.uk
Head of College, Chris Wainwright

LONDON COLLEGE OF COMMUNICATION (1894)
Elephant & Castle, London SE1 6SB T 020-7514 6500
W www.lcc.arts.ac.uk
Head of College (acting), Marilyn McMenemy

LONDON COLLEGE OF FASHION (1963)
20 John Princes Street, London W1G 0BJ T 020-7514 7500
W www.fashion.arts.ac.uk
Head of College, Dr Frances Corner

WIMBLEDON COLLEGE OF ART (1930)
Merton Hall Road, London SW19 3QA T 020-7514 9641
W www.wimbledon.arts.ac.uk
Head of College, Chris Wainwright

ASTON UNIVERSITY (1966)
Aston Triangle, Birmingham B4 7ET T 0121-204 3000
W www.aston.ac.uk
Students: 7,930 FT; 904 PT
Chancellor, Sir Michael Bett, CBE
Vice-Chancellor, Prof. Julia King, CBE, FRENG, FRSA
Registrar, Richard Middleton

UNIVERSITY OF BATH (1966)
Bath BA2 7AY T 01225-388388 W www.bath.ac.uk
Students: 10,493 FT; 2,530 PT
Chancellor, Lord Tugendhat
Vice-Chancellor, Prof. Glynis Breakwell, PHD, FRSA
University Secretary, Mark Humphriss

BATH SPA UNIVERSITY (2005)
Newton Park, Newton St Loe, Bath BA2 9BN T 01225-875875
W www.bathspa.ac.uk
Students: 4,774 FT; 1,947 PT
Vice-Chancellor, Prof. Frank Morgan
Academic Registrar, Christopher Ellicott

UNIVERSITY OF BEDFORDSHIRE (1993)
Park Square, Luton LU1 3JU T 01582-734111
W www.beds.ac.uk
Students: 10,250 FT; 5,641 PT
Chancellor, Sir Robin Biggam
Vice-Chancellor, Prof. Les Ebdon
Registrar, Prof. Jim Franklin

UNIVERSITY OF BIRMINGHAM (1900)
Edgbaston, Birmingham B15 2TT T 0121-414 3344
W www.bham.ac.uk
Students: 20,056 FT; 3,881 PT
Chancellor, Sir Dominic Cadbury
Vice-Chancellor, Prof. M. Sterling
Registrar and Secretary, Lee Sanders

BIRMINGHAM CITY UNIVERSITY (1992)
Perry Barr, Birmingham B42 2SU T 0121-331 5595
W www.bcu.ac.uk
Students: 14,654 FT; 8,336 PT
Chancellor, Lord Mayor of Birmingham, Councillor Randal Brew, OBE
Vice-Chancellor, Prof. David H. Tidmarsh
Registrar, Maxine Penlington

UNIVERSITY OF BOLTON (2005)
Deane Road, Bolton BL3 5AB T 01204-903903
W www.bolton.ac.uk
Students: 4,588 FT; 4,751 PT
Vice-Chancellor, Dr George Holmes

BOURNEMOUTH UNIVERSITY (1992)
Fern Barrow, Poole, Dorset BH12 5BB T 01202-524111
W www.bournemouth.ac.uk
Students: 12,460 FT; 5,415 PT
Chancellor, Lady Digby, DBE, DL
Vice-Chancellor, Prof. Paul Curran
Registrar, Noel Richardson

UNIVERSITY OF BRADFORD (1966)
Richmond Building, Richmond Road, Bradford, W. Yorks
BD7 1DP T 01274-232323 W www.brad.ac.uk
Students: 9,326 FT; 2,157 PT
Chancellor, Imran Khan
Vice-Chancellor, Prof. Mark Cleary
Registrar, Adrian Pearce

UNIVERSITY OF BRIGHTON (1992)
Mithras House, Lewes Road, Brighton BN2 4AT
T 01273-600900 W www.bton.ac.uk
Students: 13,127 FT; 5,835 PT
Chairman, Sir John Mogg
Vice-Chancellor, Prof. Julian M. Crampton
Registrar and Secretary, Christine E. Moon

UNIVERSITY OF BRISTOL (1909)
Senate House, Tyndall Avenue, Bristol BS8 1TH
T 0117-928 9000 W www.bristol.ac.uk
Students: 15,224 FT; 2,383 PT
Chancellor, Baroness Hale of Richmond, DBE, PC
Vice Chancellor, Prof. Eric Thomas
Registrar, Derek Pretty

BRUNEL UNIVERSITY (1966)
Uxbridge, Middx UB8 3PH T 01895-274000
W www.brunel.ac.uk
Students: 11,910 FT; 1,973 PT
Chancellor, Lord Wakeham, PC
Vice-Chancellor and Principal, Prof. C. Jenks
Secretary and Registrar, Susan Lapworth

UNIVERSITY OF BUCKINGHAM (1983)
Buckingham MK18 1EG T 01280-814080
W www.buckingham.ac.uk
Students: 799 FT; 68 PT
Chancellor, Sir Martin Jacomb
Vice-Chancellor, Terence Kealey, DPHIL
Registrar, Prof. Len Evans

BUCKINGHAMSHIRE NEW UNIVERSITY
High Wycombe Campus, Queen Alexander Road, High
Wycombe HP11 2JZ T 0800-0565 660
W www.bucks.ac.uk
Students: 5,395 FT; 3,900 PT
Vice-Chancellor, Dr. Ruth Farwell
Registrar, Hilary Garland

UNIVERSITY OF CAMBRIDGE (1209)
The Old Schools, Trinity Lane, Cambridge CB2 1TN
T 01223-337733 W www.cam.ac.uk
Students: 20,688 FT; 9,339 PT
Chancellor, HRH The Prince Philip, Duke of Edinburgh, KG, KT, OM, GBE, PC, FRS
Vice-Chancellor, Prof. Alison Richard (Newnham)
High Steward, Dame Bridget Ogilvie, DBE, FRS (Girton)
Deputy High Steward, Lord Richardson of Duntisbourne, KG, MBE, TD, PC (Gonville and Caius)
Commissary, Lord Mackay of Clashfern, KT, PC, FRSE (Trinity)
Pro-Vice-Chancellors, Prof. A. D. Cliff (Christ's); Prof. I. M. Leslie (Christ's); Prof. M. C. McKendrick (Girton); Prof. A. C. Minson (Wolfson); Dr K. B. Pretty (Homerton)
Proctors, Revd M. Guite (Girton); Dr P. Beattie (Corpus Christi)
Orator, Dr R. Thompson (Selwyn)
Registrary, Dr J. W. Nichols (Emmanuel)
Librarian, P. K. Fox (Selwyn)
Director of the Fitzwilliam Museum, Dr T. Potts
Academic Secretary, G. P. Allen (Wolfson)
Director of Finance, A. M. Reid (Wolfson)

COLLEGES AND HALLS *with dates of foundation*
CHRIST'S (1505)
Master, Prof. Frank Kelly, FRS
CHURCHILL (1960)
Master, Prof. Sir David Wallace, CBE, FRS
CLARE (1326)
Master, Prof. A. J. Badger
CLARE HALL (1966)
President, Prof. E. K. H. Salje, FRS
CORPUS CHRISTI (1352)
Master, Prof. S. Laing
DARWIN (1964)
Master, Prof. W. A. Brown, CBE
DOWNING (1800)
Master, Prof. B. J. Everitt, FRS
EMMANUEL (1584)
Master, Lord Wilson of Dinton, GCB
FITZWILLIAM (1966)
Master, Prof. R. D. Lethbridge
GIRTON (1869)
Master, Prof. Dame Marilyn Strathern, DBE, FBA
GONVILLE AND CAIUS (1348)
Master, Sir Christopher Hum, KCMG
HOMERTON (1824)
Principal, Dr K. B. Pretty
HUGHES HALL (1985)
President, Mrs S. Squire
JESUS (1496)
Master, Prof. R. Mair, FRS, FRENG
KING'S (1441)
Provost, Prof. T. R. Harrison
LUCY CAVENDISH (1965)
President, Dame Veronica Sutherland, DBE, CMG
MAGDALENE (1542)
Master, D. D. Robinson
MURRAY EDWARDS (1954)
President, Mrs A. M. Lonsdale, CBE
NEWNHAM (1871)
Principal, Dame Patricia Hodgson, DBE
PEMBROKE (1347)
Master, Sir Richard Dearlove, KCMG, OBE
PETERHOUSE (1284)
Master, Lord Wilson of Tillyorn, KT, GCMG, FRSE
QUEENS' (1448)
President, Prof. Lord Eatwell
ROBINSON (1977)
Warden, A. D. Yates
ST CATHARINE'S (1473)
Master, Prof. Dame Jean Thomas, DBE, FRS
ST EDMUND'S (1896)
Master, Prof. J. P. Luzio
ST JOHN'S (1511)
Master, Prof. C. Dobson, FRS
SELWYN (1882)
Master, Prof. R. J. Bowring

SIDNEY SUSSEX (1596)
Master, Prof. Dame Sandra Dawson, DBE
TRINITY (1546)
Master, Prof. Lord Rees of Ludlow, PRS
TRINITY HALL (1350)
Master, Prof. M. J. Daunton, FBA
WOLFSON (1965)
President, G. Johnson

CANTERBURY CHRIST CHURCH UNIVERSITY (2005)
North Holmes Road, Canterbury CT1 1QU **T** 01227-767700 **W** www.canterbury.ac.uk
Students: 7,855 FT; 7,089 PT
Chancellor, Most Revd Rowan Williams, PC, DPHIL
Vice-Chancellor and Principal, Prof. Michael Wright
Academic Registrar, Kevin Tomlinson

CARDIFF UNIVERSITY (1883)
Cardiff CF10 3XQ **T** 029-2087 4000 **W** www.cardiff.ac.uk
Students: 19,370 FT; 6,638 PT
President, Lord Kinnock, PC
Vice-Chancellor, Dr David Grant, CBE, FRENG
University Secretary, Dr Chris Turner

UNIVERSITY OF CENTRAL LANCASHIRE (1992)
Preston PR1 2HE **T** 01772-201201 **W** www.uclan.ac.uk
Students: 18,937 FT; 12,989 PT
Chancellor, Sir Richard Evans, CBE
Vice-Chancellor, Dr Malcolm McVicar

UNIVERSITY OF CHESTER (2005)
Parkgate Road, Chester CH1 4BJ **T** 01244-511000 **W** www.chester.ac.uk
Students: 8,156 FT; 2,614 PT
Chancellor, His Grace, The Duke of Westminster, KG, OBE, TD, DL
Vice-Chancellor and Principal, Prof. Tim Wheeler, DL
Director of Registry Services, Jonathan Moores

UNIVERSITY OF CHICHESTER (2005)
Bishop Otter Campus, College Lane, Chichester PO19 6PE **T** 01243-816000 **W** www.chi.ac.uk
Students: 3,525 FT; 1,556 PT
Vice-Chancellor, Dr Robin Baker

CITY UNIVERSITY (1966)
Northampton Square, London EC1V 0HB **T** 020-7040 5060 **W** www.city.ac.uk
Students: 13,801 FT; 10,500 PT
Pro-Chancellor, David Lewis, BT., DSC
Vice-Chancellor, Prof. Malcolm Gillies
Registrar, Eamon Martin

COVENTRY UNIVERSITY (1992)
Priory Street, Coventry CV1 5FB **T** 024-7688 7688 **W** www.coventry.ac.uk
Students: 12,112 FT; 5,363 PT
Chancellor, Sir John Egan
Vice-Chancellor, Prof. Madeleine Atkins, CBE
Academic Registrar and Secretary, Kate Quantrell

DE MONTFORT UNIVERSITY (1992)
The Gateway, Leicester LE1 9BH **T** 08459-454647 **W** www.dmu.ac.uk
Students: 14,342 FT; 5,038 PT
Chancellor, Lord Waheed Ali
Vice-Chancellor, Prof. Philip Tasker
Registrar, Eugene Critchlow

UNIVERSITY OF DERBY (1992)
Kedleston Road, Derby DE22 1GB **T** 01332-590500 **W** www.derby.ac.uk
Students: 14,871 FT; 10,603 PT
Chancellor, The Duke of Devonshire
Vice-Chancellor, Prof. John Coyne
Deputy Vice-Chancellor, June Hughes

UNIVERSITY OF DUNDEE (1967)
Nethergate, Dundee DD1 4HN **T** 01382-384000 **W** www.dundee.ac.uk
Students: 14,500 FT; 81,700 PT
Chancellor, Lord Narun Patel, FRSE
Vice-Chancellor, Sir Alan Langlands, FRSE
Secretary, Dr David Duncan

DURHAM UNIVERSITY (1832)
The University Office, Durham DH1 3HP **T** 0191-334 2000 **W** www.dur.ac.uk
Students: 13,421 FT; 1,636 PT
Chancellor, Bill Bryson
Vice-Chancellor and Warden, Prof. C. F. Higgins, FRSE, FRSA, FMEDSCI
Registrar and Secretary, L. Sanders

COLLEGES
COLLINGWOOD (1972)
Principal, Prof E. Corrigan, FRS
STEPHENSON (2001)
Principal, Prof. A. C. Darnell
GREY
Master, Prof. J. M. Chamberlain, DPHIL
HATFIELD (1846)
Master, Prof. T. P. Burt, DSC
JOHN SNOW (2001)
Principal, vacant
JOSEPHINE BUTLER (2006)
Principal, A. Simpson
ST AIDAN'S
Principal (acting), Susan F. Frenk, PHD
ST CHAD'S (1904)
Principal, Revd J. P. M. Cassidy, PHD
ST CUTHBERT'S SOCIETY (1888)
Principal, Prof. R. D. Boyne
ST HILD AND ST BEDE (1975)
Principal, vacant
ST JOHN'S (1909)
Principal, Revd D. Wilkinson, PHD
ST MARY'S
Principal, Prof. P. Gilmartin
TREVELYAN (1966)
Principal, Prof. H. M. Evans
UNIVERSITY (1832)
Master, Prof. M. E. Tucker
USHAW
President, Fr. J. Marsland
USTINOV
Principal, Penelope B. Wilson, DPHIL
VAN MILDERT (1965)
Master, Prof. P. O'Meara, DPHIL

UNIVERSITY OF EAST ANGLIA (1963)
Norwich NR4 7TJ **T** 01603-456161 **W** www.uea.ac.uk
Students: 11,028 FT; 3,826 PT
Chancellor, Sir Brandon Gough

Vice-Chancellor, Prof. Bill Macmillan
Academic Registrar, Brian Summers

UNIVERSITY OF EAST LONDON (1898)
University Way, London E16 2RD T 020-8223 3000
W www.uel.ac.uk
Students: 14,965 FT; 8,577 PT
Vice-Chancellor, Prof. Martin Everett
Deputy Vice-Chancellor, Nirmal Borkhataria
Registrar and Secretary, Alan Ingle

EDGE HILL UNIVERSITY (2006)
St Helens Road, Ormskirk, Lancs L39 4QP T 01695-575171
W www.edgehill.ac.uk
Students: 7,268 FT; 11,000 PT
Chancellor, Dr. Tanya Byron
Vice-Chancellor, Dr. John Cater
University Secretary, Lesley Munro

UNIVERSITY OF EDINBURGH (1583)
Old College, South Bridge, Edinburgh EH8 9YL T 0131-650 1000 W www.ed.ac.uk
Students: 21,419 FT; 3,724 PT
Chancellor, HRH The Prince Philip, Duke of Edinburgh, KG, KT, OM
Principal and Vice-Chancellor, Prof. Timothy O'Shea, FRSE
University Secretary, Melvyn Cornish

UNIVERSITY OF ESSEX (1965)
Wivenhoe Park, Colchester CO4 3SQ T 01206-873333
W www.essex.ac.uk
Students: 7,480 FT; 710 PT
Chancellor, Lord Phillips of Sudbury, OBE
Vice-Chancellor, Prof. Colin Riordan
Academic Registrar, Dr Tony Rich

UNIVERSITY OF EXETER (1955)
The Queen's Drive, Exeter EX4 4QJ T 01392-661000
W www.exeter.ac.uk
Students: 12,498 FT; 1,754 PT
Chancellor, Floella Benjamin, OBE
Vice Chancellor, Prof. Steve Smith
Registrar and Secretary, David Allen

UNIVERSITY OF GLAMORGAN (1992)
Pontypridd CF37 1DL T 0800-716925 W www.glam.ac.uk
Students: 11,670 FT; 9,876 PT
Chancellor, Lord Morris of Aberavon, KG, PC, QC
Vice-Chancellor, Prof. David Halton
Academic Registrar, John O'Shea

UNIVERSITY OF GLASGOW (1451)
Gilbert Scott Building, University Avenue, Glasgow G12 8QQ
T 0141-330 2000 W www.gla.ac.uk
Students: 18,059 FT; 6,041 PT
Chancellor, Prof. Sir Kenneth Calman, KCB, MD, FRCS
Vice-Chancellor, Sir Muir Russell, KCB, FRSE
Secretary of Court, David Newall

GLASGOW CALEDONIAN UNIVERSITY (1993)
City Campus, 70 Cowcaddens Road, Glasgow G4 0BA
T 0141-331 3000 W www.caledonian.ac.uk
Students: 11,603 FT; 4,009 PT
Chancellor, Lord Macdonald of Tradeston, PC, CBE
Vice-Chancellor and Principal, Prof. Pamela Gillies, FRSA
Registrar, Brendan Ferguson

UNIVERSITY OF GLOUCESTERSHIRE (2001)
The Park, Cheltenham GL50 2RH T 08707-210210
W www.glos.ac.uk
Students: 5,900 FT; 2,495 PT
Chancellor, Lord Carey of Clifton, PC
Vice-Chancellor, Prof. Patricia Broadfoot, CBE
Academic Registrar, Julie Thackray

UNIVERSITY OF GREENWICH (1992)
Old Royal Naval College, Park Row, Greenwich, London SE10 9LS T 020-8331 8000 W www.gre.ac.uk
Students: 15,162 FT; 9,681 PT
Chancellor, Lord Hart of Chilton
Vice-Chancellor, Baroness Blackstone
Secretary and Registrar, Linda Cording

HERIOT-WATT UNIVERSITY (1966)
Edinburgh EH14 4AS T 0131-449 5111 W www.hw.ac.uk
Students: 6,890 FT; 550 PT
Chancellor, Baroness Susan Greenfield, CBE, FRCP
Principal and Vice-Chancellor, Prof. Anton Muscatelli
Registrar, Kathy Patterson

UNIVERSITY OF HERTFORDSHIRE (1992)
College Lane, Hatfield, Herts AL10 9AB T 01707-284000
W www.herts.ac.uk
Students: 23,000
Chancellor, The Marquess of Salisbury, PC
Vice-Chancellor, Prof. Tim Wilson
Registrar, Philip Waters

UNIVERSITY OF HUDDERSFIELD (1992)
Queensgate, Huddersfield HD1 3DH T 01484-422288
W www.hud.ac.uk
Students: 12,218 FT; 7,489 PT
Chancellor, Patrick Stewart, OBE
Vice-Chancellor, Prof. Bob Cryan
Head of Registry, Kathy Sherlock

UNIVERSITY OF HULL (1927)
Cottingham Road, Hull HU6 7RX T 01482-466511
W www.hull.ac.uk
Students: 12,422 FT; 2,986 PT
Chancellor, Baroness Bottomley of Nettlestone, PC
Vice-Chancellor, Prof. David J. Drewry, FRSA
Quality Director, Registrar and Secretary, Frances Owen

IMPERIAL COLLEGE LONDON (1907)
South Kensington, London SW7 2AZ T 020-7589 5111
W www.imperial.ac.uk
Students: 12,129 FT; 895 PT
Rector, Sir Richard Sykes
Deputy Rector, Prof. Sir Leszek Borysiewicz
Academic Registrar, Vernon McClure

KEELE UNIVERSITY (1962)
Keele, Staffs ST5 5BG T 01782-621111 W www.keele.ac.uk
Students: 6,800 FT; 4,200 PT
Vice-Chancellor, Prof. Janet Finch, CBE
Registrar and Secretary, Helena Thorley

UNIVERSITY OF KENT (1965)
Canterbury, Kent CT2 7NZ T 01227-764000
W www.kent.ac.uk
Students: 12,908 FT; 3,247 PT
Chancellor, Prof. Sir Robert Worcester, KBE
Vice-Chancellor, Prof. Julia Goodfellow, CBE
Secretary of the Council, Karen Griffin

KINGSTON UNIVERSITY (1992)
River House, 53–57 High Street, Kingston upon Thames, Surrey KT1 1LQ **T** 020-8417 9000 **W** www.kingston.ac.uk
Students: 16,813 FT; 3,168 PT
Chancellor, Sir Peter Hall
Vice-Chancellor, Prof. Sir Peter Scott
Academic Registrar, Allison Stokes

UNIVERSITY OF LANCASTER (1964)
Bailrigg, Lancaster LA1 4YW **T** 01524-65201
W www.lancs.ac.uk
Students: 10,437 FT; 1,542 PT
Chancellor, Sir Christian Bonington, CBE
Vice-Chancellor, Prof. Paul Wellings
University Secretary, Fiona Aiken

UNIVERSITY OF LEEDS (1904)
Leeds LS2 9JT **T** 0113-243 1751 **W** www.leeds.ac.uk
Students: 26,352 FT; 4,111 PT
Chancellor, Lord Bragg, LLD, DLITT, DCL
Vice-Chancellor, Prof. Michael Arthur, DM, FRCP
Secretary, J. Roger Gair

LEEDS METROPOLITAN UNIVERSITY (1992)
Civic Quarter, Leeds LS1 3HE **T** 0113-283 2600
W www.leedsmet.ac.uk
Students: 14,911 FT; 2,484 PT
Chancellor, Brendan Foster, MBE
Vice-Chancellor, Prof. Simon Lee
Registrar, Stephen Denton

UNIVERSITY OF LEICESTER (1957)
University Road, Leicester LE1 7RH **T** 0116-252 2522
W www.le.ac.uk
Students: 10,045 FT; 9,330 PT
Chancellor, Sir Peter Williams, CBE, FRS, FRENG
Vice-Chancellor, Prof. Robert Burgess
Registrar, Dave Hall

UNIVERSITY OF LINCOLN (1992)
Brayford Pool, Lincoln LN6 7TS **T** 01522-882000
W www.lincoln.ac.uk
Students: 8,400 FT; 1,287 PT
Chancellor, Dame Elizabeth Esteve-Coll
Vice-Chancellor, Prof. David Chiddick
Registrar, Edmund Fitzpatrick

UNIVERSITY OF LIVERPOOL (1903)
Liverpool, Merseyside L69 7ZX **T** 0151-794 2000
W www.liv.ac.uk
Students: 15,015 FT; 3,294 PT
Chancellor, Lord Owen, CH, PC, FRCP
Vice-Chancellor, Sir Howard Newby, FRSA
Chief Operating Officer, Ron Calvert

LIVERPOOL HOPE UNIVERSITY (2005)
Hope Park, Liverpool L16 9JD **T** 0151-291 3000
W www.hope.ac.uk
Students: 5,124 FT; 2,328 PT
Chancellor, Baroness Caroline Cox
Vice-Chancellor, Prof. Gerald Pillay, FRSA
Registrar, Neil McLaughlin Cook

LIVERPOOL JOHN MOORES UNIVERSITY (1992)
Egerton Court, 2 Rodney Street, Liverpool L3 5UX **T** 0151-231 2121 **W** www.ljmu.ac.uk
Students: 15,995 FT; 8,405 PT
Chancellor, Dr. Brian May, CBE
Vice-Chancellor and Chief Executive, Prof. Michael Brown, CBE

UNIVERSITY OF LONDON (1836)
Senate House, Malet Street, London WC1E 7HU
T 020-7862 8000 **W** www.london.ac.uk
Chancellor, HRH the Princess Royal, KG, GCVO, FRS
Vice-Chancellor, Prof. Sir Graeme Davies, FRENG, FRSE
Pro-Chancellor, Lord Sutherland of Houndwood, KT, FBA
Director of Administration, Catherine Swarbrick

COLLEGES

BIRKBECK COLLEGE
Malet Street, London WC1E 7HX
Students: 715 FT; 17,740 PT
President, Prof J. E. Hobsbawm
Master, Prof. D. Latchman

CENTRAL SCHOOL OF SPEECH AND DRAMA
Embassy Theatre, Eton Avenue, London NW3 3HY
Students: 850 FT; 55 PT
President, Rt. Hon. Peter Mandleson
Principal, Prof. Gavin Henderson, CBE

COURTAULD INSTITUTE OF ART
North Block, Somerset House, Strand, London WC2R 0RN
Students: 395 FT; 60 PT
Director, Dr Deborah Swallow

GOLDSMITHS COLLEGE
Lewisham Way, New Cross, London SE14 6NW
Students: 5,700 FT; 1,745 PT
Warden, Prof. Geoffrey Crossick

HEYTHROP COLLEGE
Kensington Square, London W8 5HQ
Students: 365 FT; 485 PT
Principal, Revd Dr J. McDade, SJ, BD

INSTITUTE OF CANCER RESEARCH
Registered offices, 123 Old Brompton Road, London SW7 3RP
Chief Executive, Prof. P. Rigby

INSTITUTE OF EDUCATION
20 Bedford Way, London WC1H 0AL
Students: 190 FT; 11,520 PT
Director, Prof. G. Whitty

KING'S COLLEGE LONDON (includes Guy's, King's and St Thomas's Schools of Medicine, Dentistry and Biomedical Sciences)
Strand, London WC2R 2LS
Students: 15,905 FT; 5,920 PT
Principal, Prof. R. Trainor

LONDON BUSINESS SCHOOL
Sussex Place, Regent's Park, London NW1 4SU
Students: 870 FT; 620 PT (all postgraduate only)
Dean, Robin Buchanan

LONDON SCHOOL OF ECONOMICS AND POLITICAL SCIENCE
Houghton Street, London WC2A 2AE
Students: 8,020 FT; 1,010 PT
Director, Sir Howard Davies

LONDON SCHOOL OF HYGIENE AND TROPICAL MEDICINE
Keppel Street, London WC1E 7HT
Students: 660 FT; 485 PT (postgraduate only)
Dean, Prof. Sir Andrew Haines

QUEEN MARY (incorporating St Bartholomew's and the Royal London School of Medicine and Dentistry)
Mile End Road, London E1 4NS
Students: 11,300 FT; 1,280 PT
Principal, Prof. A. Smith, FRS

ROYAL ACADEMY OF MUSIC
Marylebone Road, London NW1 5HT
Students: 695 FT; 5 PT
Principal, Prof. Curtis Price, KBE

ROYAL HOLLOWAY
Egham Hill, Egham, Surrey TW20 0EX
Students: 8,620 FT; 4,200 PT
Principal, Prof. S. Hill, MPHIL

ROYAL VETERINARY COLLEGE
Royal College Street, London NW1 0TU
Students: 1,570 FT; 235 PT
Principal and Dean, Prof. Q. McKellar

ST GEORGE'S
Cranmer Terrace, London SW17 0RE
Students: 2,215 FT; 1,770 PT
Principal, Prof. Peter Kopelman, FRCGP

SCHOOL OF ORIENTAL AND AFRICAN STUDIES
Thornhaugh Street, Russell Square, London WC1H 0XG
Students: 3,825 FT; 905 PT
Director, Prof. Paul Webley

SCHOOL OF PHARMACY
29–39 Brunswick Square, London WC1N 1AX
Students: 850 FT; 535 PT
Dean, Prof. Anthony Smith

UNIVERSITY COLLEGE LONDON (including UCL Medical School)
Gower Street, London WC1E 6BT
Students: 16,125 FT; 3,265 PT
Provost and President, Prof. Malcolm Grant, CBE

INSTITUTES

UNIVERSITY OF LONDON INSTITUTE IN PARIS
9–11 rue de Constantine, 75340 Paris, Cedex 07
Director, Prof. Andrew Hussey

UNIVERSITY MARINE BIOLOGICAL STATION
Millport, Isle of Cumbrae KA28 0EG
Acting Director, Prof. J. Atkinson

SCHOOL OF ADVANCED STUDY
Senate House, Malet Street, London WC1E 7HU
Dean, Prof. Sir Roderick Floud

INSTITUTE OF ADVANCED LEGAL STUDIES
Charles Clore House, 17 Russell Square, London WC1B 5DR
Director, Prof. Avrom Sherr

INSTITUTE OF CLASSICAL STUDIES
Senate House, Malet Street, London WC1E 7HU
Director, Prof. M. Edwards

INSTITUTE OF COMMONWEALTH STUDIES
28 Russell Square, London WC1B 5DS
Director, Prof. R. Crook

INSTITUTE OF ENGLISH STUDIES
Senate House, Malet Street, London WC1E 7HU
Director, Prof. W. Gould

INSTITUTE OF GERMANIC AND ROMANCE STUDIES
Senate House, Malet Street, London WC1E 7HU
Director, Prof. Naomi Segal

INSTITUTE OF HISTORICAL RESEARCH
Senate House, Malet Street, London WC1E 7HU
Director, Prof. Derek Keene

INSTITUTE OF MUSICAL RESEARCH
Senate House, Malet Street, London WC1E 7HU
Director, Prof. Katharine Ellis

INSTITUTE OF PHILOSOPHY
Senate House, Malet Street, London WC1E 7HU
Director, Prof. Tim Crane

INSTITUTE FOR THE STUDY OF THE AMERICAS
31 Tavistock Square, London WC1H 9HA
Director, Prof. Maxine Molyneux

WARBURG INSTITUTE
Woburn Square, London WC1H 0AB
Director, Prof. C. Hope

DISTANCE LEARNING EXTERNAL PROGRAMME
Senate House, Malet Street, London WC1E 7HU
Director, J. M. McConnell
Dean, Prof. J. Kydd

LONDON METROPOLITAN UNIVERSITY (2002)
31 Jewry Street, London EC3N 2EY **T** 020-7423 0000
W www.londonmet.ac.uk
Students: 34,000 FT; 11,469 PT
Vice-Chancellor and Chief Executive, Brian Roper
Academic Registrar, Dr Ray Smith

LONDON SOUTH BANK UNIVERSITY (1992)
103 Borough Road, London SE1 0AA **T** 020-7815 7815
W www.lsbu.ac.uk
Students: 11,045 FT; 10,730 PT
Chancellor, Sir Trevor McDonald
Vice-Chancellor, Prof. Deian Hopkin, FRSA
Registrar, Dr Phil Cardew

LOUGHBOROUGH UNIVERSITY (1966)
Ashby Road, Loughborough, Leics LE11 3TU
T 01509-263171 **W** www.lboro.ac.uk
Students: 13,166 FT; 2,128 PT
Chancellor, Sir John Jennings, CBE, FRSE
Vice-Chancellor, Prof. Shirley Pearce, CBE
Chief Operating Officer, Will Spinks

UNIVERSITY OF MANCHESTER (2004)
Oxford Road, Manchester M13 9PL **T** 0161-306 6000
W www.manchester.ac.uk
Students: 34,458 FT; 3,729 PT
Co-Chancellors, Anna Ford and Sir Terry Leahy

President and Vice-Chancellor, Prof. Alan Gilbert
Registrar and Secretary, Albert McMenemy

MANCHESTER METROPOLITAN UNIVERSITY (1992)
All Saints, Manchester M15 6BH T 0161-247 2000
W www.mmu.ac.uk
Students: 26,417 FT; 6,328 PT
Chancellor, Dame Janet Smith, OBE, PC
Vice-Chancellor, Prof. John Brooks, DSC
Registrar, Gwyn Arnold

MIDDLESEX UNIVERSITY (1992)
North London Business Park, Oakleigh Road South, London N11 1QS T 020-8411 5555 W www.mdx.ac.uk
Students: 16,900 FT; 4,300 PT
Chancellor, Lord Sheppard of Didgemere, KT, KCVO
Vice-Chancellor, Prof. Michael Driscoll
Registrar, Colin Davis

NAPIER UNIVERSITY (1992)
Craighouse Road, Edinburgh EH10 5LG T 0845-260 6040
W www.napier.ac.uk
Students: 9,775 FT; 4,227 PT
Chancellor, Tim Waterstone
Principal and Vice-Chancellor, Prof. Joan Stringer, CBE
Registrar and Secretary, Dr Gerry Webber

UNIVERSITY OF NEWCASTLE UPON TYNE (1963)
6 Kensington Terrace, Newcastle upon Tyne NE1 7RU
T 0191-222 6000 W www.ncl.ac.uk
Students: 17,044 FT; 1,319 PT
Chancellor, Rt. Hon. Lord Patten of Barnes, CH, PC
Vice-Chancellor, Prof. Chris Brink, FRS, DPHIL
Registrar, Dr John Hogan

UNIVERSITY OF NORTHAMPTON (2005)
Park Campus, Boughton Green Road, Northampton NN2 7AL
T 01604-735500 W www.northampton.ac.uk
Students: 7,360 FT; 3,285 PT
Chancellor, Baroness Falkner
Vice-Chancellor, Ann Tate
Registrar, Jane Bunce

NORTHUMBRIA UNIVERSITY AT NEWCASTLE (1992)
Ellison Building, Ellison Place, Newcastle upon Tyne NE1 8ST
T 0191-232 6002 W www.northumbria.ac.uk
Students: 21,421 FT; 10,237 PT
Chancellor, Lord Stevens of Kirkwhelpington, QPM, FRSA
Vice-Chancellor, Prof. Andrew Wathey, FRENG
Registrar, Paul Kelly

UNIVERSITY OF NOTTINGHAM (1948)
King's Meadow Campus, Lenton Lane, Nottingham NG7 2NR
T 0115-951 5151 W www.nottingham.ac.uk
Students: 30,894 FT; 4,952 PT
Chancellor, Prof. Yang Fujia, LITTD
Vice Chancellor, Prof. Sir Colin Campbell
Registrar, Dr Paul Greatrix

NOTTINGHAM TRENT UNIVERSITY (1992)
Burton Street, Nottingham NG1 4BU T 0115-941 8418
W www.ntu.ac.uk
Students: 17,695 FT; 4,228 PT
Senior Pro-Vice-Chancellor, Peter Jones
Vice-Chancellor, Prof. Neil Gorman
Registrar, David Samson

OPEN UNIVERSITY (1969)
Walton Hall, Milton Keynes MK7 6AA T 01908-274066
W www.open.ac.uk
Students: 400 FT; 217,000 PT
Chancellor, Lord Puttnam
Vice-Chancellor, Prof. Brenda Gourley
Secretary, Fraser Woodburn

UNIVERSITY OF OXFORD (*c.*12th century)
University Offices, Wellington Square, Oxford OX1 2JD
T 01865-270000 W www.ox.ac.uk
Students: 18,675 FT; 1,318 PT
Chancellor, Lord Patten of Barnes, CH, PC (Balliol, St Antony's)
High Steward, Lord Rodger of Earlsferry (Balliol, New, St Hugh's)
Vice-Chancellor, Dr John Hood (All Souls, Templeton, Worcester)
Pro-Vice-Chancellors, Dame Fiona Caldicott (Somerville); Dr J. S. Dellandrea (Magdalen); Prof. E. A. Fallaize (St John's); Prof. E. G. McKendrick (Lady Margaret Hall); Prof. A. P. Monaco (Merton)
Registrar, Dr J. K. Maxton (University)
Secretary of the Faculties and Academic Registrar, M. D. Sibly (St Anne's)
Public Orator, R. H. A. Jenkyns
Director of University Library Services and Bodley's Librarian, Dr S. E. Thomas (Balliol)
Director of the Ashmolean Museum, Dr C. Brown (Worcester)
Keeper of Archives, S. Bailey
Director of Estates, Ms J. Wood
Director of Finance, G. F. B. Kerr

COLLEGES AND HALLS *with dates of foundation*
ALL SOULS (1438)
Warden, Prof. John Davis, FBA
BALLIOL (1263)
Master, Andrew Graham
BLACKFRIARS (1221)
Regent, Revd Richard Finn
BRASENOSE (1509)
Principal, Prof. Roger Cashmore, FRS
CAMPION HALL (1896)
Master, Revd Dr Peter l'Estrange
CHRIST CHURCH (1546)
Dean, Very Revd Christopher A. Lewis
CORPUS CHRISTI (1517)
President, Sir Tim Lankester, KCB
EXETER (1314)
Rector, Ms Frances Cairncross, CBE
GREEN TEMPLETON (2008)
President, Dr Colin Bundy
HARRIS MANCHESTER (1786)
Principal, Revd Ralph Waller
HERTFORD (1874)
Principal, Dr John Landers
JESUS (1571)
Principal, Lord Krebs, FRS
KEBLE (1868)
Warden, Prof. Averil Cameron, CBE, FBA
KELLOGG (1990)
President, Prof. Jonathan M. Michie
LADY MARGARET HALL (1878)
Principal, Dr Frances Lannon

LINACRE (1962)
Principal, Prof. Paul Slack, FBA
LINCOLN (1427)
Rector, Prof. Paul Langford, FBA
MAGDALEN (1458)
President, Prof. David Clary, FRS
MANSFIELD (1886)
Principal, Dr Diana Walford, FRCP
MERTON (1264)
Warden, Prof. Dame Jessica Rawson, CBE, FBA
NEW COLLEGE (1379)
Warden, Prof. Alan J. Ryan, FBA
NUFFIELD (1958)
Warden, Prof. Stephen Nickell, FBA
ORIEL (1326)
Provost, Sir Derek Morris
PEMBROKE (1624)
Master, Giles Henderson, CBE
QUEEN'S (1340)
Provost, Prof. Paul Madden, FRS
REGENT'S PARK (1820)
Principal, Revd Dr Robert Ellis
ST ANNE'S (1952)
Principal, Tim Gardam
ST ANTONY'S (1953)
Warden, Prof. Margaret MacMillan
ST BENET'S HALL (1897)
Master, Revd J. Felix Stephens
ST CATHERINE'S (1963)
Master, Prof. Roger Ainsworth
ST CROSS (1965)
Master, Prof. Andrew Goudie
ST EDMUND HALL (*c.*1278)
Principal, Prof. D. Mike Mingos, FRS
ST HILDA'S (1893)
Principal, Sheila Forbes, CBE
ST HUGH'S (1886)
Principal, Andrew Dilnot, CBE
ST JOHN'S (1555)
President, Sir Michael Scholar, KCB
ST PETER'S (1929)
Master, Prof. Bernard Silverman, FRS
ST STEPHEN'S HOUSE (1876)
Principal, Revd Dr Robin Ward
SOMERVILLE (1879)
Principal, Dame Fiona Caldicott, DBE, FRCP, FRCPSYCH
TRINITY (1554)
President, Sir Ivor Roberts, KCMG
UNIVERSITY (1249)
Master, Sir Ivor Crewe, GCB, CVO
WADHAM (1610)
Warden, Sir Neil Chalmers, CBE
WOLFSON (1966)
President, Prof. Hermione Lee, FBA, FRSL, CBE
WORCESTER (1714)
Provost, Richard Smethurst
WYCLIFFE HALL (1877)
Principal, Revd Dr Richard Turnbull

OXFORD BROOKES UNIVERSITY (1992)
Gipsy Lane, Oxford OX3 0BP T 01865-741111
W www.brookes.ac.uk
Students: 12,762 FT; 5,630 PT
Chancellor, Jon Snow
Vice-Chancellor, Prof. Janet Beer
Academic Registrar, Stephen Marshall

UNIVERSITY OF THE WEST OF SCOTLAND (1992)
Paisley PA1 2BE T 0141-848 3000 W www.uws.ac.uk
Students: 9,726 FT; 10,573 PT
Chancellor, Sir Robert Smith, FSA
Principal and Vice-Chancellor, Prof. Seamus McDaid
Secretary, Kenneth Alexander

UNIVERSITY OF PLYMOUTH (1992)
Drake Circus, Plymouth PL4 8AA T 01752-600600
W www.plymouth.ac.uk
Students: 19, 639 FT; 14,042 PT
Vice-Chancellor and Chief Executive, Prof. Wendy Purcell, LLD
Academic Registrar and Secretary, Jane Hopkinson

UNIVERSITY OF PORTSMOUTH (1992)
6–8, Hampshire Terrace, Portsmouth PO1 2RY
T 023-9284 8484 W www.port.ac.uk
Students: 16,500 FT; 2,240 PT
Chancellor, Sheila Hancock, OBE
Vice-Chancellor, Prof. John Craven
Academic Registrar, Andy Rees

QUEEN MARGARET UNIVERSITY (2007)
Queen Margaret University Drive, Musselburgh, Edinburgh
EH21 6UU T 0131-474 0000 W www.qmu.ac.uk
Students: 5,655 FT; 1,928 PT
Chancellor, Sir Tom Farmer, CBE, KCSG
Principal and Vice Chancellor, Prof. Anthony Cohen, FRSE
Academic Registrar, Irene Hynd

QUEEN'S UNIVERSITY BELFAST (1908)
University Road, Belfast BT7 1NN T 028-9024 5133
W www.qub.ac.uk
Students: 15,480 FT; 7,370 PT
Chancellor, Senator George Mitchell
Vice-Chancellor, Prof. Peter Gregson, FRENG
Registrar, James O'Kane

UNIVERSITY OF READING (1926)
Whiteknights, PO Box 217, Reading RG6 6AH
T 0118-987 5123 W www.reading.ac.uk
Students: 11,338 FT; 6,454 PT
Chancellor, John Madejski, OBE
Vice-Chancellor, Prof. Gordon Marshall, CBE, FBA
Director of Academic Services, Dr Richard Nesser

ROBERT GORDON UNIVERSITY (1992)
Schoolhill, Aberdeen AB10 1FR T 01224-262000
W www.rgu.ac.uk
Students: 9,250 FT; 4,600 PT
Chancellor, Sir Ian Wood, CBE
Vice-Chancellor, Prof. R. Michael Pittilo
Academic Registrar, Hilary Douglas

ROEHAMPTON UNIVERSITY (2004)
Erasmus House, Roehampton Lane, London SW15 5PU
T 020-8392 3000 W www.roehampton.ac.uk
Students: 7,160 FT; 1,370 PT
Chancellor, John Simpson, CBE
Vice-Chancellor, Prof. Paul O'Prey
Academic Secretary, Andrew Skinner

ROYAL COLLEGE OF ART (1967)
Kensington Gore, London SW7 2EU T 020-7590 4444
W www.rca.ac.uk
Students: 830 FT; 40 PT (postgraduate only)

Provost, Sir Terence Conran
Rector and Vice-Provost, Prof. Sir Christopher Frayling
Registrar, Alan Selby

ROYAL COLLEGE OF MUSIC (1882)
Prince Consort Road, London SW7 2BS **T** 020-7589 3643
W www.rcm.ac.uk
Students: 600 FT; 20 PT
President, HRH The Prince of Wales, KG, KT, GCB
Vice-Chancellor, Prof. Colin Lawson, DMUS, FRCM
Director of Operations, Kevin Porter

UNIVERSITY OF ST ANDREWS (1413)
College Gate, St Andrews, Fife KY16 9AJ **T** 01334-476161
W www.st-andrews.ac.uk
Students: 7,410 FT; 1,555 PT
Chancellor, Sir Menzies Campbell, CBE, QC, MP
Principal and Vice-Chancellor, Dr Brian Lang
Registrar, Lorraine Fraser

UNIVERSITY OF SALFORD (1967)
Salford, Greater Manchester M5 4WT **T** 0161-295 5000
W www.salford.ac.uk
Students: 14,937 FT; 4,369 PT
Chancellor, Prof. Sir Martin Harris
Vice-Chancellor, Prof. Michael Harloe
Registrar, Dr Adrian Graves

UNIVERSITY OF SHEFFIELD (1905)
Western Bank, Sheffield S10 2TN **T** 0114-222 2000
W www.shef.ac.uk
Students: 20,535 FT; 3,379 PT
Chancellor, Sir Peter Middleton, GCB
Vice-Chancellor, Prof. Keith Burnett, CBE, DPHIL, FRS
Registrar and Secretary, Dr D. E. Fletcher

SHEFFIELD HALLAM UNIVERSITY (1992)
City Campus, Howard Street, Sheffield S1 1WB
T 0114-225 5555 **W** www.shu.ac.uk
Students: 19,720 FT; 9,680 PT
Chancellor, Prof. Lord Winston, DSc, FRCOG, FRCP
Vice-Chancellor, Prof. Philip Jones, LLB, LLM
Secretary and Registrar, Elizabeth Winders

UNIVERSITY OF SOUTHAMPTON (1952)
Building 37, Highfield, Southampton SO17 1BJ
T 023-8059 5000 **W** www.soton.ac.uk
Students: 15,585 FT; 2,486 PT
Chancellor, Sir John Parker
Vice-Chancellor, Prof. William A. Wakeham
Registrar and Chief Operating Officer, Simon Higman

SOUTHAMPTON SOLENT UNIVERSITY (2005)
East Park Terrace, Southampton SO14 0YN **T** 023-8031 9000
W www.solent.ac.uk
Students: 9,155 FT; 1,688 PT
Chancellor, Admiral the Lord West of Spithead, GCB, DSC
Vice-Chancellor, Prof. Van Gore
Dean of Academic Standards, Dr Ann Read

STAFFORDSHIRE UNIVERSITY (1992)
Federation House, Stoke-on-Trent, Staffs ST4 2DE
T 01782-294000 **W** www.staffs.ac.uk
Students: 9,801 FT; 6,568 PT
Chancellor, Lord Morris of Handsworth
Vice-Chancellor, Prof. Christine E. King, CBE
University Secretary, Ken Sproston

UNIVERSITY OF STIRLING (1967)
Stirling FK9 4LA **T** 01786-473171 **W** www.stir.ac.uk
Students: 7,170 FT; 2,270 PT
Chancellor, Dame Diana Rigg, OBE
Vice-Chancellor, Prof. Christine Hallett, FRSE
Registrar, Joanna Morrow

UNIVERSITY OF STRATHCLYDE (1964)
16 Richmond Street, Glasgow G1 1XQ **T** 0141-552 4400
W www.strath.ac.uk
Students: 13,760 FT; 1,490 PT
Chancellor, Rt. Hon. Lord Hope of Craighead, FRSE
Vice-Chancellor and Principal, Prof. Andrew Hamnett, DPHIL, FRSC, FRSE
Secretary, Dr Peter West, OBE

UNIVERSITY OF SUNDERLAND (1992)
Edinburgh Building, Chester Road, Sunderland SR1 3SD
T 0191-515 2000 **W** www.sunderland.ac.uk
Students: 11,000 FT; 8,000 PT
Chancellor, Steve Cram, MBE
Vice-Chancellor, Prof. Peter Fidler
Registrar, Beatrice Ollerenshaw

UNIVERSITY OF SURREY (1966)
Guildford, Surrey GU2 7XH **T** 01483-300800
W www.surrey.ac.uk
Students: 9,495 FT; 2,694 PT
Chancellor, HRH the Duke of Kent, KG, GCMG, GCVO
Vice-Chancellor, Prof. Christopher Snowden, FRS, FRENG
Registrar, P. Henry, TD

UNIVERSITY OF SUSSEX (1961)
Sussex House, Falmer, Brighton BN1 9RH **T** 01273-606755
W www.sussex.ac.uk
Students: 11,459
Chancellor, Lord Attenborough, CBE
Vice-Chancellor, Prof. Michael Farthing
Academic Registrar, Dr Philip Harvey

UNIVERSITY OF TEESSIDE (1992)
Middlesbrough, Tees Valley TS1 3BA **T** 01642-218121
W www.tees.ac.uk
Students: 9,769 FT; 13,884 PT
Chancellor, Lord Sawyer
Vice-Chancellor and Chief Executive, Prof. Graham Henderson
University Secretary and Clerk to Governors, Morgan McClintock

THAMES VALLEY UNIVERSITY (1992)
St Mary's Road, Ealing, London W5 5RF **T** 020-8579 5000
W www.tvu.ac.uk
Students: 20,985 FT; 24,001 PT
Chancellor, Lord Karan Bilimoria, CBE
Vice-Chancellor, Prof. Peter John
Registrar, Chris Broomfield

UNIVERSITY OF ULSTER (1984)
Cromore Road, Coleraine, Co. Londonderry BT52 1SA
T 0870-040 0700 **W** www.ulster.ac.uk
Students: 16,250 FT; 7,011 PT
Chancellor, Sir Richard Nichols
Vice-Chancellor, Prof. Richard Barnett
Registrar, Norma Cameron

UNIVERSITY OF WALES (1893)
King Edward VII Avenue, Cathays Park, Cardiff CF10 3NS
T 029-2037 6999 W www.wales.ac.uk
Chancellor, HRH The Prince of Wales, KG, KT, GCB
Senior Vice-Chancellor, Prof. R. M. Clement, FRSA

ACCREDITED INSTITUTIONS

ABERYSTWYTH UNIVERSITY
Old College, King Street, Aberystwyth SY23 2AX
T 01970-623111
Students: 7,160 FT; 3,860 PT
Vice-Chancellor, Prof. N. G. Lloyd

BANGOR UNIVERSITY
Gwynedd LL57 2DG T 01248-351151
Students: 6,920 FT; 3,140 PT
Vice-Chancellor, Prof. R. M. Jones

UNIVERSITY OF WALES, LAMPETER
Lampeter SA48 7ED T 01570-422351
Students: 1,365 FT; 7,780 PT
Vice-Chancellor, Prof. R. A. Pearce

UNIVERSITY OF WALES, NEWPORT
Caerleon Campus, PO Box 179, Newport NP6 1YG
T 01633-430088
Students: 3,425 FT; 5,950 PT
Vice-Chancellor, Dr P. Noyes

SWANSEA UNIVERSITY
Singleton Park SA2 8PP T 01792-205678
Students: 9,610 FT; 4,210 PT
Vice-Chancellor, Prof. R. B. Davies

UNIVERSITY OF WALES INSTITUTE, CARDIFF
Llandaff Centre, Western Avenue, Cardiff CF5 2SG
T 029-2041 6070
Students: 7,555 FT; 2,435 PT
Vice-Chancellor, Prof. A. J. Chapman

NORTH EAST WALES INSTITUTE OF HIGHER EDUCATION
Plas Coch, Mold Road, Wrexham LL11 2AW T 01978-290666
Students: 2,651 FT; 4,520 PT
Principal, Prof. M. Scott

SWANSEA METROPOLITAN UNIVERSITY
Mount Pleasant, Swansea SA1 6ED T 01792-481000
Students: 6,620 FT; 1,980 PT
Principal, Prof. D. Warner

TRINITY COLLEGE, CARMARTHEN
Carmarthen SA31 3EP T 01267-676767
Students: 1,405 FT; 995 PT
Principal, Dr M. Hughes

UNIVERSITY OF WARWICK (1965)
Coventry CV4 7AL T 024-7652 3523 W www.warwick.ac.uk
Students: 13,979 FT; 4,233 PT
Chancellor, Richard Lambert
Vice-Chancellor, Prof. Nigel Thrift
Registrar, Jon Baldwin Press Officer

UNIVERSITY OF WESTMINSTER (1992)
309 Regent Street, London W1B 2UW T 020-7911 5000
W www.wmin.ac.uk
Students: 14,460 FT; 10,250 PT
Chancellor, Lord Paul
Vice-Chancellor and Rector, Prof. Geoffrey Petts
Academic Registrar, Evelyne Rugg

UNIVERSITY OF THE WEST OF ENGLAND (1992)
Frenchay Campus, Coldharbour Lane, Bristol BS16 1QY
T 0117-965 6261 W www.uwe.ac.uk
Students: 20,206 FT; 7,470 PT
Chancellor, Baroness Elizabeth Butler-Sloss, GBE, PC
Vice-Chancellor, Prof. Stephen West, KB, CBE
Registrar, Tessa Harrison

UNIVERSITY OF WINCHESTER (2005)
Winchester SO22 4NR T 01962-841515
W www.winchester.ac.uk
Students: 3,339 FT; 1,961 PT
Chancellor, Mary Fagan
Vice-Chancellor, Prof. Joy Carter
Registrar, Lyn Black

UNIVERSITY OF WOLVERHAMPTON (1992)
Wulfruna Street, Wolverhampton WV1 1SB T 01902-321000
W www.wlv.ac.uk
Students: 13,247 FT; 7,162 PT
Chancellor, Lord Paul
Vice-Chancellor, Prof. Caroline Gipps
Registrar, Paul Travill

UNIVERSITY OF WORCESTER (2005)
Henwick Grove, Worcester WR2 6AJ T 01905-855000
W www.worcester.ac.uk
Students: 5,090 FT; 3,207 PT
Chancellor, HRH The Duke of Gloucester, KG, GCVO
Vice-Chancellor and Chief Executive, Prof. David Green
Registrar and Secretary, John Ryan

UNIVERSITY OF YORK (1963)
Heslington, York YO10 5DD T 01904-430000
W www.york.ac.uk
Students: 8,267 FT; 901 PT
Chancellor, Greg Dyke
Vice-Chancellor, Prof. Brian Cantor, FRENG, FIM, FRMS
Registrar, Sally Neocosmos

YORK ST JOHN UNIVERSITY (2006)
Lord Mayor's Walk, York YO31 7EX T 01904-624624
W www.yorksj.ac.uk
Students: 4,106 FT; 1,511 PT
Chancellor, Dr John Sentamu
Vice-Chancellor, Diane Willcocks
Registrar, Pauline Aldous

PROFESSIONAL EDUCATION

The organisations selected below provide specialist training, conduct examinations or are responsible for maintaining a register of those with professional qualifications in their sector, thereby controlling entry into a profession.

EU RECOGNITION

It is possible for those with professional qualifications obtained in the UK to have these recognised in other European countries. Further information can be obtained online (W www.dcfs.gov.uk/europeopen) or from:

DEPARTMENT FOR INNOVATION, UNIVERSITIES AND SKILLS Kingsgate House, 66-74 Victoria Street, London SW1E 6SW T 020-7215 5555 E info@dius.gsi.gov.uk

ACCOUNTANCY

Salary range: £20,000–£35,000 rising to £50,000–£100,000 in senior posts

Many chartered accountancy trainees are graduates, and entry to the profession is open to graduates of all disciplines. It is also possible to train as a chartered accountant with good A-level results as some training contracts are available to school-leavers. The undergraduate degree is followed by a three-year training contract with an approved employer culminating in professional exams provided by the Institute of Chartered Accountants in England and Wales (ICAEW), the Institute of Chartered Accountants of Scotland (ICAS) or the Institute of Chartered Accountants in Ireland (ICAI). Success in the examination and membership of one of the institutes allows the use of the designation 'chartered accountant' and the letters ACA or CA.

The training route for chartered certified accountants is similar to that of chartered accountants and is taken by students in a range of business sectors and countries. The Association of Chartered Certified Accountants (ACCA) qualification involves up to 14 examinations and a minimum of three years of relevant supervised experience. Chartered certified accountants can use the designatory letters ACCA.

Chartered management accountants focus on accounting for businesses, and most do not work in accountancy practices but in industry, commerce, not-for-profit and public sector organisations. Graduates who have not studied a business or accounting undergraduate degree must gain the Chartered Institute of Management Accountants (CIMA) Certificate in Business Accounting (formerly known as the foundation level) before studying for the CIMA Professional Qualification. The qualification requires three years of practical experience combined with nine examinations and a pass in the Institute's Test of Professional Competence in Management Accounting (TOPCIMA).

Chartered public finance accountants usually work for public bodies, but they can also work in the private sector. To gain chartered public finance accountant status (CPFA), trainees must complete the three parts of the Chartered Institute of Public Finance and Accountancy (CIPFA) Professional Accountancy Qualification (PAQ), which takes approximately three years. The first stage is the certificate level, which leads to affiliate membership of CIPFA, the second is the diploma level which leads to associate membership, and finally completion of the Final Test of Professional Competence leads to full membership of CIPFA.

ASSOCIATION OF CHARTERED CERTIFIED ACCOUNTANTS (ACCA) 29 Lincoln's Inn Fields, London WC2A 3EE T 020-7059 5000 E info@accaglobal.com W www.accaglobal.com
Chief Executive, Helen Brand

CHARTERED INSTITUTE OF MANAGEMENT ACCOUNTANTS (CIMA) 26 Chapter Street, London SW1P 4NP T 020-7663 5441 W www.cimaglobal.com
Chief Executive, Charles Tilley

CHARTERED INSTITUTE OF PUBLIC FINANCE AND ACCOUNTANCY (CIPFA) 3 Robert Street, London WC2N 6RL T 030-7543 5600 E corporate@cipfa.org W www.cipfa.org.uk
Chief Executive, Steve Freer

INSTITUTE OF CHARTERED ACCOUNTANTS IN ENGLAND AND WALES (ICAEW) Chartered Accountants' Hall, PO Box 433, London EC2P 2BJ T 020-7920 8100 W www.icaew.com
Chief Executive, Michael Izza

INSTITUTE OF CHARTERED ACCOUNTANTS IN IRELAND (ICAI) The Linenhall, 32–38 Linenhall Street, Belfast BT2 8BG T 028-9032 1600 E ca@icai.ie W www.icai.ie
Chief Executive, Pat Costello

INSTITUTE OF CHARTERED ACCOUNTANTS OF SCOTLAND (ICAS) CA House, 21 Haymarket Yards, Edinburgh EH12 5BH T 0131-347 0100 E enquiries@icas.org.uk W www.icas.org.uk
Chief Executive, Anton Colella

ACTUARIAL SCIENCE

Salary range: £25,000–35,000 for graduate trainees; £45,000–£56,000 after qualification; up to £100,000 for senior roles

Actuaries apply financial and statistical theories to solve business problems. These problems usually involve analysing future financial events in order to assess investment risks for businesses. The UK actuarial profession is controlled by the Institute of Actuaries in London and the Faculty of Actuaries in Edinburgh (operating together as 'the actuarial profession'). The faculty and institute together develop actuarial techniques and set examinations, professional codes and disciplinary standards. UK qualified actuaries may be fellows of either organisation. On average, it takes five years to qualify as an actuary; examinations are held twice a year, and applicants to the profession must also have completed three years of actuarial work experience before gaining fellowship.

The Financial Reporting Council (FRC) is the unified independent regulator for corporate reporting, auditing, actuarial practice, corporate governance and the professionalism of accountants and actuaries. The FRC's Board for Actuarial Standards sets and maintains technical actuarial standards independently of the profession while the Professional Oversight Board of the FRC oversees the regulation of the actuarial profession by its members. The Accountancy and Actuarial Discipline Board operates an investigation and discipline scheme in relation to members of the profession who raise issues affecting UK public interest.

FACULTY OF ACTUARIES Maclaurin House, 18 Dublin Street, Edinburgh EH1 3PP T 0131-240 1300
E faculty@actuaries.org.uk W www.actuaries.org.uk
Secretary, Richard Maconachie

FINANCIAL REPORTING COUNCIL (FRC) 5th Floor, Aldwych House, 71–91 Aldwych, London WC2B 4HN
T 020-7492 2300 W www.frc.org.uk
Chief Executive, Paul Boyle

INSTITUTE OF ACTUARIES Staple Inn Hall, High Holborn, London WC1V 7QJ T 020-7632 2100
E institute@actuaries.org.uk W www.actuaries.org.uk
Chief Executive, Caroline Instance

ARCHITECTURE

Salary range: £17,000–£34,000; project architect and senior roles £36,000–£80,000

It takes a minimum of seven years to become an architect, involving three stages: a three-year first degree, a two-year second degree or diploma and two years of professional experience followed by the successful completion of a professional practice examination.

The Architects Registration Board (ARB) is the independent regulator for the profession. It was set up by an act of parliament in 1997 and is responsible for maintaining the register of UK architects, prescribing qualifications that lead to registration as an architect, investigating complaints about the conduct and competence of architects, and ensuring only those who are registered with ARB use the title of 'architect'. It is only following registration with ARB that an architect can apply for chartered membership of the Royal Institute of British Architects (RIBA). RIBA, the UK body for architecture and the architectural profession received its royal charter in 1837 and recognises courses at 40 UK and 57 overseas schools of architecture for exemption from their own examinations. RIBA provides support and training for its members in the form of training, technical services and events and sets standards for the education of architects.

The Chartered Institute of Architectural Technologists is the qualifying body for chartered architectural technologists (MCIAT) and architectural technicians (TCIAT).

ARCHITECTS REGISTRATION BOARD (ARB)
8 Weymouth Street, London W1W 5BU T 020-7580 5861
E info@arb.org.uk W www.arb.org.uk
Registrar and Chief Executive, Alison Carr

CHARTERED INSTITUTE OF ARCHITECTURAL TECHNOLOGISTS 397 City Road, London EC1V 1NH
T 020-7278 2206 E info@ciat.org.uk W www.ciat.org.uk
Chief Executive, Francesca Berriman

ROYAL INSTITUTE OF BRITISH ARCHITECTS (RIBA) 66 Portland Place, London W1B 1AD
T 020-7580 5533 E info@inst.riba.org W www.riba.org
Chief Executive, Richard Hastilow, CBE

ENGINEERING

Salary range:
Civil/structural engineer £22,000–£63,000
Electrical engineer £33,000–£42,000
Chemical engineer £23,000 (new graduates); £47,000–£62,000 with experience; up to £150,000 at senior levels

The Engineering Council UK (ECUK) sets standards of professional competence and ethics for engineers, technologists and technicians, and regulates the profession through the 35 institutions (Licensed Members) listed below who are licensed to put suitably qualified members on the ECUK's Register of Engineers. All candidates for registration as Chartered Engineer, Incorporated Engineer or Engineering Technician must satisfy the competence standards set by ECUK and be members of the appropriate institution. Applicants must show that they have a satisfactory educational base, have undergone approved professional development, and, at interview, must demonstrate their professional competence against specific criteria.

ENGINEERING COUNCIL UK, 246 High Holborn, London WC1V 7EX T 020-3206 0500 E info@engc.org.uk
W www.engc.org.uk
Chief Executive Officer, Andrew Ramsay

LICENSED MEMBERS

BRITISH COMPUTER SOCIETY
W www.bcs.org.uk

BRITISH INSTITUTE OF NON-DESTRUCTIVE TESTING
W www.bindt.org

CHARTERED INSTITUTON OF BUILDING SERVICES ENGINEERS W www.cibse.org

CHARTERED INSTITUTION OF WATER AND ENVIRONMENTAL MANAGEMENT
W www.ciwem.org.uk

ENERGY INSTITUTE
W www.energyinst.org.uk

INSTITUTE OF ACOUSTICS
W www.ioa.org.uk

INSTITUTE OF CAST METALS ENGINEERS
W www.icme.org.uk

INSTITUTE OF HEALTHCARE ENGINEERING AND ESTATE MANAGEMENT W www.iheem.org.uk

INSTITUTE OF HIGHWAY INCORPORATED ENGINEERS
W www.ihie.org.uk

INSTITUTE OF MARINE ENGINEERING, SCIENCE AND TECHNOLOGY W www.imarest.org

INSTITUTE OF MATERIALS, MINERALS AND MINING
W www.iom3.org

INSTITUTE OF MEASUREMENT AND CONTROL
W www.instmc.org.uk

INSTITUTE OF THE MOTOR INDUSTRY
W www.motor.org.uk

INSTITUTE OF PHYSICS
W www.iop.org

INSTITUTE OF PHYSICS AND ENGINEERING IN MEDICINE W www.ipem.ac.uk

INSTITUTE OF PLUMBING AND HEATING ENGINEERING W www.iphe.org.uk

INSTITUTION OF AGRICULTURAL ENGINEERS
W www.iagre.org

INSTITUTION OF CHEMICAL ENGINEERS
W www.icheme.org

INSTITUTION OF CIVIL ENGINEERS
W www.ice.org.uk

INSTITUTION OF ENGINEERING DESIGNERS
W www.ied.org.uk

INSTITUTION OF ENGINEERING AND TECHNOLOGY
W www.theiet.org
INSTITUTION OF FIRE ENGINEERS
W www.ife.org.uk
INSITITUTION OF GAS ENGINEERS AND MANAGERS
W www.igem.org.uk
INSTITUTION OF HIGHWAYS AND TRANSPORTATION
W www.iht.org
INSTITUTION OF LIGHTING ENGINEERS
W www.ile.co.uk
INSTITUTION OF MECHANICAL ENGINEERS
W www.imeche.org.uk
INSTITUTION OF NUCLEAR ENGINEERS
W www.inuce.org.uk
INSITITUTION OF RAILWAY SIGNAL ENGINEERS
W www.irse.org
INSTITUTION OF ROYAL ENGINEERS
W www.instre.org
INSTITUTION OF STRUCTURAL ENGINEERS
W www.istructe.org.uk
INSTITUTION OF WATER OFFICERS
W www.iwo.org.uk
ROYAL AERONAUTICAL SOCIETY
W www.raes.org.uk
ROYAL INSTITUTION OF NAVAL ARCHITECTS
W www.rina.org.uk
SOCIETY OF ENVIRONMENTAL ENGINEERS
W www.environmental.org.uk
SOCIETY OF OPERATIONS ENGINEERS
W www.soe.org.uk
WELDING INSTITUTE
W www.twi.co.uk

HEALTHCARE

CHIROPRACTIC

Salary range: £22,000–£25,000 starting salary; with own practice up to £70,000

Chiropractic specialises in the diagnosis and treatment of conditions caused by problems with joints, ligaments, tendons and nerves of the body. The General Chiropractic Council (GCC) is the statutory regulatory body for chiropractors and its role and remit is defined in the Chiropractors Act 1994. The GCC sets the criteria for the recognition of chiropractic degrees and for standards of proficiency and conduct. Details of the institutions offering degree programmes are available on the GCC website (*see* below). It is illegal for anyone in the UK to use the title 'chiropractor' unless registered with the GCC.

The British Chiropractic Association, McTimoney Chiropractic Association, Scottish Chiropractic Association and the United Chiropractic Association are representative bodies for the profession and are sources of further information about chiropractic.

BRITISH CHIROPRACTIC ASSOCIATION 59 Castle Street, Reading RG1 7SN T 0118-950 5950
E enquiries@chiropractic-uk.co.uk
Executive Director, Sue Wakefield

GENERAL CHIROPRACTIC COUNCIL 44 Wicklow Street, London WC1X 9HL T 020-7713 5155
E enquiries@gcc-uk.org W www.gcc-uk.org
Chief Executive, Margaret Coats

MCTIMONEY CHIROPRACTIC ASSOCIATION
Crowmarsh Gifford, Wallingford OX10 8DJ T 01491-829211
E admin@mctimoney-chiropractic.org
W www.mctimoney-chiropractic.org
Chair, Christina Cunliffe

SCOTTISH CHIROPRACTIC ASSOCIATION Laigh Hatton Farm, Old Greenock Road, Bishopton, Renfrewshire PA7 5BP T 01505-863151 E admin@sca-chiropractic.org
W www.sca-chiropractic.org
Chief Executive, Morag Cairns

UNITED CHIROPRACTIC ASSOCIATION 17 Fore Street, Ivybridge PL21 9AB T 01752-896223
E admin@united-chiropractic.org
W www.united-chiropractic.org
Secretary, Melissa Sandford

DENTISTRY

Salary range: £28,000–£80,000

The General Dental Council (GDC) is the organisation that regulates dental professionals in the United Kingdom. All dentists, dental hygienists, dental therapists, clinical dental technicians and orthodontic therapists must be registered with the GDC to work in the UK, whether they work in the NHS, in private practice or any other form of practice. From July 2008 by law all dental nurses and technicians will need to be registered with the GDC.

There are various different routes to qualify for registration, including holding a degree or licentiate in dental surgery from a UK university or Royal Surgical College; completing the GDC's qualifying examination; or holding a relevant European Economic Area or overseas diploma. The GDC works to set standards of dental practice, behaviour and education, and helps to protect patients by hearing complaints and taking action against professionals where necessary.

The British Dental Association is a membership organisation that provides dentists with professional and educational services. It has over 18,000 qualified members and over 3,500 student members.

BRITISH DENTAL ASSOCIATION 64 Wimpole Street, London W1G 8YS T 020-7935 0875 E enquiries@bda.org
W www.bda.org
Chief Executive, Peter Ward

GENERAL DENTAL COUNCIL 37 Wimpole Street, London W1G 8DQ T 020-7887 3800
E information@gdc-uk.org W www.gdc-uk.org
Chief Executive, Duncan Rudkin

MEDICINE

Salary range: GP £50,000–£120,000

The General Medical Council (GMC) sets the standards for basic medical education; this covers undergraduate study (usually five years) and the first year of training after graduation. Subsequent training is regulated by the Postgraduate Medical Education and Training Board (PMETB). The first two years of training after graduation are collectively called the 'foundation programme'.

All doctors must be registered with the GMC, which is responsible for protecting the public by setting standards for professional practice, overseeing medical education, keeping a register of qualified doctors and taking action where a doctor's fitness to practise is in doubt. Doctors are eligible for full registration upon successful completion of the first year of training after graduation.

Following the foundation programme, many doctors undertake specialist training (provided by the colleges and faculties listed below) to become either a consultant or a GP. Once specialist training has been completed, doctors are awarded the Certificate of Completion of Training (CCT) and are eligible to be placed on either the GMC's specialist register or its GP register. The responsibility for awarding CCTs lies with the PMETB.

GENERAL MEDICAL COUNCIL (GMC) 350 Euston Road, London NW1 3JN T 0845-357 8001 E gmc@gmc-uk.org W www.gmc-uk.org
Chief Executive, Finlay Scott

POSTGRADUATE MEDICAL EDUCATION AND TRAINING BOARD (PMETB) Hercules House, Hercules Road, London SE1 7DU T 020-7160 6100 E info@pmetb.org.uk W www.pmetb.org.uk
Chief Executive, Paul Streets

SOCIETY OF APOTHECARIES OF LONDON Black Friars Lane, London EC4V 6EJ T 020-7236 1189 E clerk@apothecaries.org W www.apothecaries.org
Clerk, N. L. Wood

SPECIALIST TRAINING COLLEGES AND FACULTIES

COLLEGE OF EMERGENCY MEDICINE W www.collemergencymed.ac.uk

FACULTY OF PHARMACEUTICAL MEDICINE W www.fpm.org.uk

FACULTY OF PUBLIC HEALTH W www.fphm.org.uk

ROYAL COLLEGE OF ANAESTHETISTS W www.rcoa.ac.uk

ROYAL COLLEGE OF GENERAL PRACTITIONERS W www.rcgp.org.uk

ROYAL COLLEGE OF OBSTETRICIANS AND GYNAECOLOGISTS W www.rcog.org.uk

ROYAL COLLEGE OF OPTHALMOLOGISTS W www.rcophth.ac.uk

ROYAL COLLEGE OF PAEDIATRICS AND CHILD HEALTH W www.rcpch.ac.uk

ROYAL COLLEGE OF PATHOLOGISTS W www.rcpath.org

ROYAL COLLEGE OF PHYSICIANS OF LONDON W www.rcplondon.ac.uk

ROYAL COLLEGE OF PHYSICIANS AND SURGEONS OF GLASGOW W www.rcpsg.ac.uk

ROYAL COLLEGE OF PHYSICIANS OF EDINBURGH W www.rcpe.ac.uk

ROYAL COLLEGE OF PSYCHIATRISTS W www.rcpsych.ac.uk

ROYAL COLLEGE OF RADIOLOGISTS W www.rcr.ac.uk

ROYAL COLLEGE OF SURGEONS OF EDINBURGH W www.rcsed.ac.uk

ROYAL COLLEGE OF SURGEONS OF ENGLAND W www.rcseng.ac.uk

MEDICINE, SUPPLEMENTARY PROFESSIONS

The standard of professional education for arts therapists, biomedical scientists, chiropodists and podiatrists, clinical scientists, dietitians, occupational therapists, operating department practitioners, orthoptists, paramedics, physiotherapists, prosthetists and orthotists, radiographers, and speech and language therapists is regulated by the Health Professions Council (HPC), who only register those practitioners who meet certain standards of training, performance and conduct. Other than biomedical science and clinical science, all the professions listed below are described by the NHS as 'allied health professions'. The HPC currently registers over 170,000 professionals.

HEALTH PROFESSIONS COUNCIL Park House, 184 Kennington Park Road, London SE11 4BU T 020-7582 0866 E info@hpc-uk.org W www.hpc-uk.org
Chief Executive and Registrar, Marc Seale

ART, DRAMA AND MUSIC THERAPIES
Salary range: £23,000 rising to £28,000–£42,000 in senior posts

An art, drama or music therapist encourages people to express their feelings and emotions through art, such as painting and drawing, drama or music. A postgraduate qualification in the relevant therapy is required. Details of accredited training programmes in the UK can be obtained from the following organisations:

ASSOCIATION OF PROFESSIONAL MUSIC THERAPISTS 61 Church Hill Road, East Barnet, Herts EN4 8SY T 020-8440 4153 E apmtoffice@aol.com W www.apmt.org
Administrator, Louise Karena

BRITISH ASSOCIATION OF ART THERAPISTS 24–27 White Lion Street, London N1 9PD T 020-7686 4216 E info@baat.org W www.baat.org
Chief Executive, Val Huet

BRITISH ASSOCIATION OF DRAMA THERAPISTS Waverley, Battledown Approach, Cheltenham, Gloucestershire GL52 6RE T 01242-235 5155 E enquiries@badth.org.uk W www.badth.org.uk
Chair, Madeleine Andersen-Warren

BIOMEDICAL SCIENCES
Salary range: £20,000–60,000

Biomedical scientists analyse specimens from patients in order to assist with doctors' diagnoses. Qualifications from higher education establishments and training in medical laboratories are required for membership of the Institute of Biomedical Science, which sets the professional standards of competence for practitioners.

INSTITUTE OF BIOMEDICAL SCIENCE 12 Coldbath Square, London EC1R 5HL T 020-7713 0214 E mail@ibms.org W www.ibms.org
Chief Executive, Alan Potter

CHIROPODY AND PODIATRY
Salary range: £19,000–£31,000

Chiropodists and podiatrists assess, diagnose and treat problems of the lower leg and foot. The Society of Chiropodists and Podiatrists is the professional body and trade union, and qualifications granted and degrees recognised by the society are approved by the Health Professions Council (HPC). HPC registration is required in order to use the titles chiropodist and podiatrist.

SOCIETY OF CHIROPODISTS AND PODIATRISTS 1 Fellmonger's Path, Tower Bridge Road, London SE1 3LY T 020-7234 8620 E enq@scpod.org W www.feetforlife.org
Chief Executive, Joanna Brown

CLINICAL SCIENCE
Salary range: £23,000–£70,000

Clinical scientists conduct tests in laboratories in order to diagnose and manage disease. The Association of Clinical Scientists is responsible for setting the criteria for competence of applicants to the HPC's register and to present a Certificate of Attainment to candidates following a successful assessment. This certificate will allow direct registration with the HPC.

ASSOCIATION OF CLINICAL SCIENTISTS c/o Association for Clinical Biochemistry, 130–132 Tooley Street, London SE1 2TU T 020-7940 8960 E info@assclinsci.org W www.assclinsci.org
Chair, Neil Lewis

DIETETICS
Salary range: £19,000–£36,000

Dietitians advise patients on how to improve their health and counter specific health problems by eating a healthy diet. The British Dietetic Association, established in 1936, is the professional association for dietitians. Full membership is open to UK registered dietitians, who must also be registered with the Health Professions Council.

BRITISH DIETETIC ASSOCIATION 5th Floor, Charles House, 148–149 Great Charles Street Queensway, Birmingham B3 3HT **T** 0121-200 8080 **E** info@bda.uk.com **W** www.bda.uk.com
Chief Executive, Andy Burman

OCCUPATIONAL THERAPY
Salary range: £19,000–£36,000; up to £50,000 in consultancy posts

Occupational therapists work with people who have physical, mental and/or social problems, either from birth or as a result of accident, illness or ageing, and aim to make them as independent as possible. The professional qualification and eligibility for registration may be obtained upon successful completion of a validated course in any of the educational institutions approved by the College of Occupational Therapists, which is the professional body for occupational therapy in the UK. The courses are normally degree-level courses based in higher education institutions.

COLLEGE OF OCCUPATIONAL THERAPISTS 106–114 Borough High Street, London SE1 1LB **T** 020-7357 6480 **W** www.cot.org.uk
Chief Executive, Julia Scott

ORTHOPTICS
Salary range: £19,000–£25,000 rising to £31,000–£50,000 in senior posts

Orthoptists undertake the diagnosis and treatment of all types of squint and other anomalies of binocular vision, working in close collaboration with ophthalmologists. The professional body is the British and Irish Orthoptic Society and training is at degree level.

BRITISH AND IRISH ORTHOPTIC SOCIETY Tavistock House North, Tavistock Square, London WC1H 9HX **T** 020-7387 7992 **W** www.orthoptics.org.uk
Chair, Rosemary Auld

PARAMEDICAL SERVICES
Salary range: £19,000–£25,000

Paramedics deal with accidents and emergencies, assessing patients and carrying out any specialist treatment and care needed in the first instance. The body that represents ambulance professionals is the British Paramedic Association.

BRITISH PARAMEDIC ASSOCIATION 28 Wilfred Street, Derby DE23 8GF **T** 01332-746356 **E** exec.bpa@britishparamedic.org **W** www.britishparamedic.org
Chief Executive, Roland Furber

PHYSIOTHERAPY
Salary range: £19,000–£25,000 for junior roles; up to £36,000 as advanced clinician; up to £50,000 as senior manager; up to £88,000 for consultancy roles

Physiotherapists are concerned with movement and function and deal with problems arising from injury, illness and ageing. Full-time three- or four-year degree courses are available at over 30 higher education institutions in the UK. Information about courses leading to state registration is available from the Chartered Society of Physiotherapy.

CHARTERED SOCIETY OF PHYSIOTHERAPY 14 Bedford Row, London WC1R 4ED **T** 020-7306 6666 **W** www.csp.org.uk
Chief Executive, Phil Gray

PROSTHETICS AND ORTHOTICS
Salary range: £18,000 on qualification, rising to £35,000 with experience

Prosthetists provide artificial limbs, while orthotists provide devices to support or control a part of the body. It is necessary to obtain an honours degree to become a prosthetist or orthotist. Training is centred at the universities of Salford and Strathclyde.

BRITISH ASSOCIATION OF PROSTHETISTS AND ORTHOTISTS Sir James Clark Building, Abbey Mill Business Centre, Paisley PA1 1TJ **T** 0141-561 7217 **E** enquiries@bapo.com **W** www.bapo.org
Chair, Steve Mottram

RADIOGRAPHY
Salary range: starting at £19,000; up to £50,000 at consultant level

In order to practise both diagnostic and therapeutic radiography in the UK, it is necessary to have successfully completed a course of education and training recognised by the Privy Council. Such courses are offered by universities throughout the UK and lead to the award of a degree in radiography. Further information is available from the Society and College of Radiographers.

SOCIETY AND COLLEGE OF RADIOGRAPHERS 207 Providence Square, Mill Street, London SE1 2EW **T** 020-7740 7200 **E** info@sor.org **W** www.sor.org
Chief Executive, Richard Evans

SPEECH AND LANGUAGE THERAPY
Salary range: £18,500 rising upwards of £33,000 in senior roles

Speech and language therapists (SLTs) work with people with speech, voice and swallowing problems. The Royal College of Speech and Language Therapists is the professional body for speech and language therapists and support workers. Alongside the Health Professions Council, it accredits education and training courses leading to qualification.

ROYAL COLLEGE OF SPEECH AND LANGUAGE THERAPISTS 2 White Hart Yard, London SE1 1NX **T** 020-7378 1200 **E** info@rcslt.org **W** www.rcslt.org
Chief Executive, Kamini Gadhok

NURSING
Salary range: £19,000 starting salary; £25,000–£30,000 with experience; rising to £60,000 in senior positions

In order to practice in the UK all nurses and midwives must be registered with the Nursing and Midwifery Council (NMC). The NMC is a statutory regulatory body that establishes and maintains standards of education, training, conduct and performance for nursing and midwifery. Courses leading to registration are at a minimum of diploma in higher education, although some are offered at degree level and all are a minimum of three years if undertaken full-time. The NMC approves programmes run jointly by higher education institutions with their healthcare service partners who offer clinical placements. The nursing part of the register has four fields of practice: adult, children's, learning disability and mental health nursing. During the first year of a nursing course, the common foundation programme, students have experience of the first four fields of practice. In addition those studying to become adult nurses have experience of nursing in relation to medicine, surgery, maternity care and nursing in the home. The NMC also sets standards for programmes leading to registration as a midwife and a range of post-registration courses including specialist practice programmes, nurse prescribing and those for teachers of nursing and midwifery. The NMC has a part of the register for specialist community public health nurses and approves programmes for health visitors, occupational health nurses and school nurses.

The Royal College of Nursing is the largest professional union for nursing in the UK, representing qualified nurses, healthcare assistants and nursing students in the NHS and the private sector.

NURSING AND MIDWIFERY COUNCIL 23 Portland Place, London W18 1PZ T 020-7637 7181
E communications@nmc-uk.org W www.nmc-uk.org
Chief Executive and Registrar, Sarah Thewlis

ROYAL COLLEGE OF NURSING 20 Cavendish Square, London W1G 0RN T 020-740 3333 W www.rcn.org.uk
Chief Executive and General Secretary, Dr Peter Carter

OPTOMETRY AND DISPENSING OPTICS

Salary range:
Optometrist £20,000–£50,000 (up to £73,000 for consultant posts)
Dispensing Optician £20,000–£40,000

There are various routes to qualification as a dispensing optician. Qualification takes three years in total, and can be completed by combining a distance learning course or day release while working as a trainee under the supervision of a qualified and registered optician. Alternatively, students can do a two-year full-time course followed by one year of supervised practice with a qualified and registered optician. Training must be done at a training establishment approved by the regulatory body – the General Optical Council (GOC). There are six training establishments which are approved by the GOC: the Association of British Dispensing Opticians (ABDO), Anglia Ruskin University, Bradford College, the City and Islington College, City University and Glasgow Caledonian University. All routes are concluded by ABDO examinations, successful completion of which leads to registration with the GOC, which is compulsory for all practising dispensing opticians. After qualifying as a dispensing optician and completing training to fit contact lenses, students have the option to take a career progression course at the University of Bradford that allows them to graduate with a degree in optometry in one calendar year.

Optometrists must obtain an undergraduate optometry degree from one of the eight institutions approved by the GOC (Anglia Ruskin University, Aston University, the University of Bradford, Cardiff University, City University, Glasgow Caledonian University, the University of Manchester and the University of Ulster). Following graduation, trainees must complete a year of supervised salaried training with a registered optometrist during which they must successfully complete the assessments within the scheme for registration set by the College of Optometrists. As with dispensing opticians, optometrists must then register with the GOC in order to practise.

ASSOCIATION OF BRITISH DISPENSING OPTICIANS 199 Gloucester Terrace W2 6LD
T 020-7298 5100 E general@abdo.org.uk
W www.abdo.org.uk
General Secretary, Sir Anthony Garrett, CBE

COLLEGE OF OPTOMETRISTS 42 Craven Street, London WC2N 5NG T 020-7839 6000
E optometry@college-optometrists.org
W www.college-optometrists.org
Chief Executive, Bryony Pawinska

GENERAL OPTICAL COUNCIL (GOC) 1 Harley Street, London W1G 8DJ T 020-7580 3898 E goc@optical.org
W www.optical.org
Acting Chief Executive and Registrar, Dian Taylor

OSTEOPATHY

Salary Range: £16,000–£65,000

Osteopathy is a way of detecting and treating damage in areas of the body such as muscles, ligaments, nerves and joints. Osteopathy is a statutorily self-regulated healthcare profession. The General Osteopathic Council (GOsC) maintains a register of those entitled to practise osteopathy in the UK. It is a criminal offence for anyone to describe themselves as an osteopath unless they are registered with the GOsC.

To gain entry to the register, applicants must hold a recognised qualification from an osteopathic education institute accredited by the GOsC; this involves a four to five year honours degree programme combined with clinical training.

GENERAL OSTEOPATHIC COUNCIL Osteopathy House, 176 Tower Bridge Road, London SE1 3LU
T 020-7357 6655 E info@osteopathy.org.uk
W www.osteopathy.org.uk
Chief Executive and Registrar, Evlynne Gilvarry

PHARMACY

Salary range: £20,000–£60,000

Pharmacists are involved in the preparation and use of medicines, from the discovery of their active ingredients to their use by patients. Pharmacists also monitor the effects of medicines, both for patient care and for research purposes.

The Royal Pharmaceutical Society of Great Britain (RPSGB) is the regulatory and professional body for pharmacists in England, Scotland and Wales. It has a statutory duty to maintain the registers of pharmacists and pharmacy premises. The Pharmaceutical Society of Northern Ireland (PSNI) performs the same role in Northern Ireland. In order to register, students must complete a four-year degree in pharmacy that is accredited by either the RPSGB or the PSNI followed by one year of pre-registration training at an approved pharmacy, and must then pass an entrance examination. The RPSGB is working towards the demerger of its regulatory and professional roles that would result in the creation of a new General Pharmaceutical Council and a new professional body by 2010.

PHARMACEUTICAL SOCIETY OF NORTHERN IRELAND 7 3 University Street, Belfast BT7 1HL
T 02890-326927 E mail@psni.org.uk W www.psni.org.uk
Director, Trevor Patterson

ROYAL PHARMACEUTICAL SOCIETY OF GREAT BRITAIN (RPSGB) 1 Lambeth High Street, London SE1 7JN T 020-7735 9141 E enquiries@rpsgb.org
W www.rpsgb.org
Chief Executive and Registrar, Jeremy Holmes

PSYCHOLOGY

Salary range: £25,000 rising to £50,000 with experience; up to £80,000+ in senior posts

Psychologists can work in a range of settings including prisons, schools and hospitals as well as businesses. The UK psychological profession is represented by the British Psychological Society (BPS), which has more than 45,000 members. It accredits undergraduate and postgraduate qualifications in psychology, and offers support to members through continuing professional development. The Association of Educational Psychologists (AEP) represents the interests of educational psychologists, while the British Association for Counselling and Psychotherapy (BACP) sets educational standards and provides professional support to those psychologists working in psychotherapy or counselling-related roles. The BPS website provides more information on the different specialisations that may be pursued by psychologists.

BRITISH PSYCHOLOGICAL SOCIETY (BPS)
St Andrews House, 48 Princess Road East, Leicester LE1 7DR T 0116-254 9568 E enquiries@bps.org.uk
W www.bps.org.uk
President, Dr Elizabeth Campbell

ASSOCIATION OF EDUCATIONAL PSYCHOLOGISTS (AEP) 26 The Avenue, Durham DH1 4ED T 0191-384 9512 W www.aep.org.uk
General Secretary, Charles Ward

BRITISH ASSOCIATION FOR COUNSELLING AND PSYCHOTHERAPY (BACP) BACP House, 15 St John's Business Park, Lutterworth, Leicestershire LE17 4HB
T 01455-883300 E bacp@bacp.co.uk W www.bacp.co.uk
President, Cary Cooper CBE

INFORMATION MANAGEMENT

Salary range: £20,000–£25,000 (newly qualified); £50,000+ in senior positions

The Chartered Institute of Library and Information Professionals (CILIP) is the professional body for librarians, information specialists and knowledge managers. CILIP accredits undergraduate and postgraduate courses in librarianship and information science (for a full list of accredited courses see the CILIP website). The Association for Information Management also provides training and advice on a wide range of topics relating to information professionals.

ASSOCIATION FOR INFORMATION MANAGEMENT (ASLIB) Holywell Centre, 1 Phipp Street, London EC2A 4PS T 020-7613 3031
E aslib@aslib.com W www.aslib.co.uk
Chief Executive, Roger Bowes

CHARTERED INSTITUTE OF LIBRARY AND INFORMATION PROFESSIONALS (CILIP)
7 Ridgmount Street, London WC1E 7AE T 020-7255 0500
E info@cilip.org.uk W www.cilip.org.uk
President, Bruce Madge

LAW

There are two types of practising lawyers: barristers and solicitors. Solicitors tend to work as a group in firms, and can be approached directly by individuals. They advise on a variety of legal issues and must decide the most appropriate course of action, if any. Barristers, on the other hand, are usually self-employed. If a solicitor believes that a barrister is required, he or she will instruct one on behalf of the client; the client will not have contact with the barrister without the solicitor being present.

When specialist expertise is needed, barristers give opinions on complex matters of law, and when clients require representation in the higher courts (crown courts, high courts, the court of appeal and the House of Lords), barristers provide a specialist advocacy service. However, solicitors – who represent their clients in the lower courts such as tribunals, magistrates' courts and county courts – can also apply for advocacy rights in the higher courts instead of briefing a barrister.

THE BAR

Salary range: £70,000–£200,000+

The governing body of the Bar of England and Wales is the General Council of the Bar, also known as the Bar Council. Since January 2006, the regulatory functions of the Bar Council (including regulating the education and training requirements for those wishing to enter the profession) have been undertaken by the Bar Standards Board.

In the first (or 'academic') stage of training, aspiring barristers must obtain a law degree of a good standard (at least second class). Alternatively, a non-law degree (at least second class) followed by a one-year full-time or two-year part-time Graduate Diploma in Law (PgDL).

The second (vocational) stage is the completion of the Bar Vocational Course (BVC), which is available at eight validated institutions in the UK and must be applied for around one year in advance (W www.bvconline.co.uk). All barristers must join one of the four Inns of Court prior to commencing the BVC.

Students are 'called to the Bar' by their Inn after completion of the vocational stage, but cannot practise as a barrister until completion of the third stage, which is called 'pupillage'. Call to the Bar does not entitle a person to practise as a barrister – successful completion of pupillage is now a pre-requisite. Pupillage lasts for two six-month periods: the 'non-practising six' and the 'practising six'. The former consists of shadowing an experienced barrister, while the latter involves appearing in court as a barrister.

Admission to the Bar of Northern Ireland is controlled by the Honorable Society of the Inn of Court of Northern Ireland; admission as an Advocate to the Scottish Bar is through the Faculty of Advocates.

BAR STANDARDS BOARD The Bar Council, 289–293 High Holborn, London WC1V 7HZ T 020-7611 1444
W www.barstandardsboard.org.uk
Director, Mandie Lavin

FACULTY OF ADVOCATES Parliament House, Edinburgh EH1 1RF T 0131-226 5071
W www.advocates.org.uk
Chief Executive Officer, Tony Parker

GENERAL COUNCIL OF THE BAR 289–293 High Holborn, London WC1V 7HZ T 020-7242 0082
E contactus@barcouncil.org.uk W www.barcouncil.org.uk
Chief Executive, David Hobart

GENERAL COUNCIL OF THE BAR OF NORTHERN IRELAND The Bar Library, 91 Chichester Street, Belfast BT1 3JQ T 028-9056 2349
E chief.executive@barcouncil-ni.org.uk
W www.barlibrary.com
Chief Executive, Brendan Garland

HONOURABLE SOCIETY OF THE INN OF COURT OF NORTHERN IRELAND The Under-Treasurer's Office, Room 1–3, Royal Courts of Justice, Belfast BT1 3JF
T 028-9072 4699
Under-Treasurer, J. W. Wilson QC

THE INNS OF COURT

HONOURABLE SOCIETY OF GRAY'S INN 8 South Square, London WC1R 5ET T 020-7458 7800
W www.graysinn.org.uk
Under-Treasurer, Brig. Anthony Faith, CBE

HONOURABLE SOCIETY OF LINCOLN'S INN Treasury Office, Lincoln's Inn, London WC2A 3TL
T 020-7405 1393 E mail@lincolnsinn.org.uk
W www.lincolnsinn.org.uk
Under-Treasurer, Col. D. Hills, MBE

HONOURABLE SOCIETY OF THE INNER TEMPLE Inner Temple, London EC4Y 7HL T 020-7797 8250
E enquiries@innertemple.org.uk
W www.innertemple.org.uk
Sub-Treasurer, Patrick Maddams

HONOURABLE SOCIETY OF THE MIDDLE TEMPLE Middle Temple Lane, London EC4Y 9AT T 020-7427 4800
E studentenquiries@middletemple.org.uk
W www.middletemple.org.uk
Under-Treasurer, Air Cdre Peter Hilling

SOLICITORS

Salary range: £30,000–£90,000

Graduates from any discipline can train to be a solicitor; however, if the undergraduate degree is not in law, a one-year conversion course (either the Common Professional Examination (CPE) or the Graduate Diploma in Law (GDL)) must be completed. The next stage, and the beginning of the vocational phase, is the Legal Practice Course (LPC), which takes one year and is obligatory for both law and non-law graduates. The LPC provides professional instruction for prospective solicitors and can be completed on a full-time or part-time basis. Trainee solicitors then enter the final stage, which is a paid period of supervised work that lasts two years for full-time contracts. The employer that provides the training contract must be authorised by the Solicitors Regulation Authority (SRA) (the regulatory body of the Law Society of England and Wales), the Law Society of Scotland, or the Law Society of Northern Ireland. The SRA also monitors the training contract to ensure that it provides the trainee with the necessary expertise to qualify as a solicitor.

Conveyancers are specialist property lawyers, dealing with the legal processes involved in transferring buildings, land and associated finances from one owner to another. This was the sole responsibility of solicitors until 1987 but under current legislation it is now possible for others to train as conveyancers.

COUNCIL FOR LICENSED CONVEYANCERS 16–17 Glebe Road, Chelmsford, Essex CM1 1QG T 01245-349599
W www.conveyancer.org.uk

THE LAW SOCIETY OF ENGLAND AND WALES The Law Society's Hall, 113 Chancery Lane, London WC2A 1PL
T 020-7242 1222 E enquiries@lawsociety.org.uk
W www.lawsociety.org.uk
Chief Executive, Des Hudson

LAW SOCIETY OF NORTHERN IRELAND 40 Linenhall Street, Belfast BT2 8BA T 028-9023 1614
E info@lawsoc-ni.org W www.lawsoc-ni.org
Chief Executive and Secretary, Alan Hunter

LAW SOCIETY OF SCOTLAND 26 Drumsheugh Gardens, Edinburgh EH3 7YR T 0131-226 7411
E lawscot@lawscot.org.uk W www.lawscot.org.uk
Chief Executive, vacant

SOLICITORS REGULATION AUTHORITY Ipsley Court, Berrington Close, Redditch, Worcs B98 0TD
T 0870-606 2555 E info.services@sra.org.uk
W www.sra.org.uk
Chair, Peter Williamson

SURVEYING

Salary range: £38,000 in junior posts; £50,000+ in senior roles

The Royal Institution of Chartered Surveyors (RICS) is the professional body that represents and regulates property professionals including land surveyors, valuers, auctioneers, quantity surveyors and project managers. Entry to the institution, following completion of a RICS-accredited degree, is through completion of the Assessment of Professional Competence (APC), which involves a period of practical training concluded by a final assessment of competence. Entry as a technical surveyor requires completion of the Assessment of Technical Competence (ATC), which mirrors the format of the APC. The different levels of RICS membership are MRICS (member) or FRICS (fellow) for chartered surveyors, and TechRICS for technical surveyors.

Relevant courses can also be accredited by the Chartered Institute of Building (CIOB), which represents managers working in a range of construction disciplines; CIOB offers four levels of membership to those who satisfy its requirements: FCIOB (fellow), MCIOB (member), ICIOB (incorporated) and ACIOB (associate).

CHARTERED INSTITUTE OF BUILDING Englemere, King's Ride, Ascot SL5 7TB T 01344-630700
E reception@ciob.org.uk W www.ciob.org.uk
Chief Executive, Chris Blythe

ROYAL INSTITUTION OF CHARTERED SURVEYORS (RICS) 12 Great George Street, Parliament Square, London SW1P 3AD T 0870-333 1600
E contactrics@rics.org W www.rics.org
Chief Executive, Louis Armstrong

TEACHING

(*See also* Education)

Salary range: £20,000–£41,000; headteacher £45,000–£90,000

The General Teaching Councils for England, Northern Ireland, Scotland and Wales maintain registers of qualified teachers in their respective countries, and registration is a legal requirement in order to teach in local authority schools. The Graduate Teacher Training Registry (GTTR) processes applications for entry to postgraduate teaching courses in England, Wales and Scotland.

Further information on how to become a teacher in England and Wales is available on the Training and

Development Agency for Schools website (*see* below). Personal advice is available from the Teaching Information Line (T 0845-600 0991; T 0845-600 0992 for Welsh speakers). Details on courses in Scotland can be obtained from universities and the GTTR. Details of the courses in Northern Ireland can be obtained from individual universities and the Department of Education for Northern Ireland.

The College of Teachers, under the terms of its royal charter, provides professional qualifications and membership to teachers and those involved in education in the UK and overseas.

DEPARTMENT OF EDUCATION NORTHERN IRELAND Rathgael House, Balloo Road, Bangor BT19 7PR T 028-9127 9279 E mail@deni.gov.uk W www.deni.gov.uk
Permanent Secretary, Will Haire

GENERAL TEACHING COUNCIL FOR ENGLAND Whittington House, 19–30 Alfred Place, London WC1E 7EA T 0870-001 0308 E info@gtce.org.uk W www.gtce.org.uk
Chief Executive, Keith Bartley

GENERAL TEACHING COUNCIL FOR NORTHERN IRELAND 4th Floor, Albany House, 73–75 Great Victoria Street, Belfast BT2 7AF T 028-9033 3390 E info@gtcni.org.uk W www.gtcni.org.uk
Chairperson, Sally McKee

GENERAL TEACHING COUNCIL FOR SCOTLAND Clerwood House, 96 Clermiston Road, Edinburgh EH12 6UT T 0131-314 6000 E gtcs@gtcs.org.uk W www.gtcs.org.uk
Chief Executive, vacant

GENERAL TEACHING COUNCIL FOR WALES 4th Floor, Southgate House, Wood Street, Cardiff CF10 1EW T 029-2055 0350 E information@gtcw.org.uk W www.gtcw.org.uk
Chief Executive, Gary Brace

GRADUATE TEACHER TRAINING REGISTRY Rosehill, New Barn Lane, Cheltenham GL52 3LZ T 0871-468 0469 E enquiries@gttr.ac.uk W www.gttr.ac.uk
Chief Executive, Anthony McClaran

THE COLLEGE OF TEACHERS Institute of Education, 20 Bedford Way, London WC1H 0AL T 020-7911 5536 E enquiries@cot.ac.uk W www.cot.ac.uk
President, Prof. Geof Whitty, FRSA

TRAINING AND DEVELOPMENT AGENCY FOR SCHOOLS 151 Buckingham Palace Road, London SW1W 9SZ T 020-7023 8001 W www.tda.gov.uk
Chief Executive, Graham Holley

VETERINARY MEDICINE

Salary range: veterinary surgeons £30,000–£50,000

The regulatory body for veterinary surgeons in the UK is the Royal College of Veterinary Surgeons (RCVS), which keeps the register of those entitled to practise veterinary medicine as well as the list of qualified veterinary nurses. Holders of recognised degrees from any of the six UK university veterinary schools or from certain EU or overseas universities are entitled to be registered, and holders of certain other degrees may take a statutory membership examination. The UK's veterinary schools are located at the University of Bristol, the University of Cambridge, the University of Edinburgh, the University of Glasgow, the University of Liverpool and the Royal Veterinary College in London; all veterinary degrees last for five years except that offered at Cambridge, which lasts for six. A new course at the University of Nottingham is undergoing approval in time for its first veterinary graduates in 2011.

The British Veterinary Association is the professional body representing veterinary surgeons. The British Veterinary Nursing Association is the professional body representing veterinary nurses.

BRITISH VETERINARY ASSOCIATION 7 Mansfield Street, London W1G 9NQ T 020-7636 6541 E bvahq@bva.co.uk W www.bva.co.uk
Secretary General, Henrietta Alderman

BRITISH VETERINARY NURSING ASSOCIATION 82 Greenway Business Centre, Harlow Business Park, Harlow CM19 5QE T 01279-408644 E bvna@bvna.co.uk W www.bvna.org.uk

ROYAL COLLEGE OF VETERINARY SURGEONS Belgravia House, 62–64 Horseferry Road, London SW1P 2AF T 020-7222 2001 E admin@rcvs.org.uk W www.rcvs.org.uk
Registrar, Jane Hern

INDEPENDENT SCHOOLS

Independent schools (non-maintained mainstream schools) charge fees and are owned and managed under special trusts, with profits being used for the benefit of the schools concerned. In 2006–7 there were 2,542 non-maintained mainstream schools (of which 46 were academies) in the United Kingdom, educating over 670,000 pupils, or approximately 7 per cent of the total school-age population. The approximate number of pupils at non-maintained mainstream schools in 2006–7 was:

UK	670,700
England	630,800
Wales	9,700
Scotland	29,400
Northern Ireland	800

The Independent Schools Council (ISC), formed in 1974, acts on behalf of the eight independent schools' associations which constitute it. These associations are:

Association of Governing Bodies of Independent Schools (AGBIS)
Council of British International Schools (COBIS)
Girls' Schools Association (GSA)
Headmasters' & Headmistresses' Conference (HMC)
Independent Association of Prep Schools (IAPS)
Independent Schools Association (ISA)
Independent Schools' Bursars Association (ISBA)
Society of Headmasters & Headmistresses of Independent Schools (SHMIS)

There were 509,093 pupils being educated in 1,276 Independent Schools Council (ISC) accredited schools in 2007. Most of the schools outside ISC membership are likely to be privately owned. The Independent Schools Inspectorate (ISI) was demerged from ISC with effect from 1 January 2008 and is legally and operationally independent of ISC. ISI works as an accredited inspectorate of schools in ISC membership under a framework agreed with the DCSF. A school must pass an ISI accreditation inspection to qualify for membership of an association within ISC.

In 2007 at GCSE 57.4 per cent of all exams taken by independent school candidates achieve either an A* or A grade (compared to the national average of 19.5 per cent), and at A-level 76.1 per cent of entries were awarded an A or B grade (national average, 49.7 per cent). In 2007 over 125,000 pupils at ISC schools received help with their fees in the form of bursaries and scholarships from the schools. These cost the schools over £300m.

INDEPENDENT SCHOOLS COUNCIL
St Vincent House, 30 Orange Street, London WC2H 7HH
T 020-7766 7070 **W** www.isc.co.uk

The list of schools below was compiled from the *Independent Schools Yearbook 2008–9* (ed. Judy Mott, published by A&C Black) which includes schools whose heads are members of one of the ISC's five headteachers' associations. Further details are available online (**W** www.isyb.co.uk).

The fees shown below represent the upper limits payable during 2008–9 (fees noted with an * are for 2007–8) for UK pupils who do not qualify for any reduction; scholarships and bursaries are available at many of the schools listed.

School	*Web Address*	*Termly fees Day*	*Board*	*Head*
ENGLAND				
Abbey Gate College, Cheshire	www.abbeygatecollege.co.uk	£3,046	–	Mrs L. M. Horner
The Abbey School, Berks	www.theabbey.co.uk	£3,660	–	Mrs B. Stanley
Abbots Bromley School for Girls, Staffs	www.abbotsbromley.staffs.sch.uk	£4,200	£8,340	Mrs P. J. Woodhouse
Abbot's Hill School, Herts	www.abbotshill.herts.sch.uk	£4,330	–	Mrs K. Lewis
Abbotsholme School, Derbys	www.abbotsholme.com	£5,450	£8,000	S. Fairclough
Abingdon School, Oxon	www.abingdon.org.uk	£4,250	£8,320	M. Turner
Ackworth School, W. Yorks	www.ackworthschool.com	£3,628	£5,939	P. J. Simpson
Aldenham School, Herts	www.aldenham.com	£5,584	£8,117	J. C. Fowler
Alderley Edge School for Girls, Cheshire	www.aesg.info	£2,759	–	Mrs K. Mills
Alleyn's School, London SE22	www.alleyns.org.uk	£4,332	–	C. Diggory
Amberfield School, Suffolk	www.amberfield.suffolk.sch.uk	£3,075	–	Mrs L. Ingram
Ampleforth College, N. Yorks	www.ampleforthcollege.york.sch.uk	£5,245	£8,575	Revd. C. G. Everitt
Ardingly College, W. Sussex	www.ardingly.com	£6,150	£8,200	P. Green
Arnold School, Lancs	www.arnoldschool.com	£2,778	–	B. M. Hughes
Arts Educational School, Herts	www.aes-tring.com	£6,570	£8,950	S. Anderson
Ashford School, Kent	www.ashfordschool.co.uk	£4,368	£7,941	M. Buchanan
Ashville College, N. Yorks	www.ashville.co.uk	£3,445	£6,760	A. A. P. Fleck
Austin Friars St Monica's School, Cumbria	www.austinfriars.cumbria.sch.uk	£3,418	–	C. J. Lumb
Bablake School, W. Midlands	www.bablake.com	£2,793	–	J. W. Watson
Badminton School, Bristol	www.badminton.bristol.sch.uk	£4,790	£8,510	Mrs J. A. Scarrow
Bancroft's School, Essex	www.bancrofts.essex.sch.uk	£3,850	–	Mrs M. E. Ireland

Barnard Castle School, Co. Durham	www.barnardcastleschool.org.uk	£3,332	£5,758	D. H. Ewart
Batley Grammar School, W. Yorks	www.batleygrammar.co.uk	£2,769	–	Mrs B. P. Tullie
Battle Abbey School, E. Sussex	www.battleabbeyschool.com	£4,200	£6,930	R. C. Clark
Bearwood College, Berks	www.bearwoodcollege.co.uk	£4,930	£8,460	S. G. G. Aiano
Bedales School, Hants	www.bedales.org.uk	£6,992	£8,888	K. J. Budge
Bedford High School for Girls, Beds	www.bedfordhigh.co.uk	£3,537	£6,628	Mrs J. A. Eldridge
Bedford Modern School, Beds	www.bedmod.co.uk	£3,469	–	S. Smith
Bedford School, Beds	www.bedfordschool.org.uk	£4,789	£7,536	J. S. Moule
Bedstone College, Shrops	www.bedstone.org	£3,730	£6,750	M. S. Symonds
Beechwood Sacred Heart School, Kent	www.beechwood.org.uk	£4,315	£7,315	N. Beesley
Benenden School, Kent	www.benenden.kent.sch.uk	–	£9,180	Mrs C. M. Oulton
Berkhamsted Collegiate School, Herts	www.berkhamstedcollegiateschool.org.uk	£4,947	£7,816	M. S. Steed
Bethany School, Kent	www.bethanyschool.org.uk	£4,590	£6,959	N. D. B. Dorey
Birkdale School, S. Yorks	www.birkdaleschool.org.uk	£3,248	–	R. J. Court
Birkenhead High School, Merseyside	www.gdst.net/birkenheadhigh	£2,966	–	Mrs C. H. Evans
Birkenhead School, Merseyside	www.birkenheadschool.co.uk	£2,909	–	D. J. Clark
Bishop's Stortford College, Herts	www.bishops-stortford-college.herts.sch.uk	£4,517	£6,281	J. G. Trotman
Blackheath High School, London SE3	www.blackheathhighschool.gdst.net	£3,700	–	Mrs E. A. Laws
Bloxham School, Oxon	www.bloxhamschool.com	£5,455	£8,305	M. E. Allbrook
Blundell's School, Devon	www.blundells.org	£5,215	£8,085	I. R. Davenport
Bolton School Boys' Division	www.boltonschool.org/seniorboys	£2,930	–	P. J. Britton
Bolton School Girls' Division	www.boltonschool.org/seniorgirls	£2,930	–	Mrs G. Richards
Bootham School, N. Yorks	www.boothamschool.com	£4,530	£7,250	J. F. J. Taylor
Box Hill School, Surrey	www.boxhillschool.com	£4,300	£7,250	M. Eagers
Bradfield College, Berks	www.bradfieldcollege.org.uk	£6,960	£8,700	P. J. M. Roberts
Bradford Girls' Grammar School, W. Yorks	www.bggs.com	£3,511	–	Mrs L. J. Warrington
Bradford Grammar School, W. Yorks	www.bradfordgrammar.com	£3,176*	–	S. R. Davidson
Brentwood School, Essex	www.brentwoodschool.co.uk	£4,271	£7,535	D. I. Davies
Brighton and Hove High School, E. Sussex	www.gdst.net/bhhs	£2,966	–	K. Roberts
Brighton College, E. Sussex	www.brightoncollege.net	£5,510	£8,540	R. J. Cairns
Brigidine School Windsor, Berks	www.brigidine.org.uk	£4,155	–	Mrs E. Robinson
Bristol Grammar School, Bristol	www.bristolgrammarschool.co.uk	£3,280	–	R. I. MacKinnon
Bromley High School, Kent	www.bromleyhigh.gdst.net	£3,700	–	Mrs L. Duggleby
Bromsgrove School, Worcs	www.bromsgrove-school.co.uk	£3,950	£7,740	C. J. Edwards
Bruton School for Girls, Somerset	www.brutonschool.co.uk	£3,857	£6,207	J. Burrough
Bryanston School, Dorset	www.bryanston.co.uk	£7,196	£8,995	Ms S. J. Thomas
Burgess Hill School for Girls, W. Sussex	www.burgesshill-school.com	£4,000	£6,950	Mrs A. Aughwane
Bury Grammar School Boys, Lancs	www.bgsboys.co.uk	£2,566	–	Revd. S. C. Harvey
Bury Grammar School Girls, Lancs	www.bgsg.bury.sch.uk	£2,566	–	Mrs R. Georghiou
Canford School, Dorset	www.canford.com	£6,675	£8,560	J. D. Lever
Casterton School, Lancs	www.castertonschool.co.uk	£4,315	£7,211	P. McLaughlin
Caterham School, Surrey	www.caterhamschool.co.uk	£4,298	£8,018	J. P. Thomas
Central Newcastle High School	www.newcastlehigh.gdst.net	£2,966	–	Mrs H. J. French
Channing School, London N6	www.channing.co.uk	£4,130	–	Mrs B. Elliott
Charterhouse, Surrey	www.charterhouse.org.uk	£7,572	£9,160	Revd J. S. Witheridge
Cheadle Hulme School, Cheshire	www.cheadlehulmeschool.co.uk	£2,876	–	P. V. Dixon
Cheltenham College, Glos	www.cheltcoll.gloucs.sch.uk/cc	£6,875	£9,175	J. S. Richardson
The Cheltenham Ladies' College	www.cheltladiescollege.org	£5,710	£8,503	Mrs V. Tuck
Chetham's School of Music, Manchester	www.chethams.com	sliding scale		Mrs C. Hickman
Chetwynde School, Cumbria	www.chetwynde.co.uk	£2,332	–	Mrs I. Nixon
Chigwell School, Essex	www.chigwell-school.org	£4,529	£6,537	M. E. Punt
Christ's Hospital School, W. Sussex	www.christs-hospital.org.uk	–	£6,814	J. Franklin
Churcher's College, Hants	www.churcherscollege.com	£3,450	–	S. H. L. Williams

City of London Freemen's School, Surrey	www.clfs.surrey.sch.uk	£4,560	£7,257	P. MacDonald
City of London School, London	www.clsb.org.uk	£4,089	–	D. R. Levin
City of London School for Girls, London EC2	www.clsg.org.uk	£4,125	–	Miss D. Vernon
Claremont Fan Court School, Surrey	www.claremont-school.co.uk	£4,072	–	Mrs P. B. Farrar
Clayesmore School, Dorset	www.clayesmore.com	£6,193	£8,464	M. G. Cooke
Clifton College, Bristol	www.cliftoncollegeuk.com	£5,795	£8,590	M. J. Moore
Clifton High School, Bristol	www.cliftonhigh.bristol.sch.uk	£3,200	£5,220	Mrs C. Culligan
Cobham Hall, Kent	www.cobhamhall.com	£4,400	£8,300	P. Mitchell
Cokethorpe School, Oxon	www.cokethorpe.org.uk	£4,495	–	D. J. Ettinger
Colfe's School, London SE12	www.colfes.com	£3,927	–	R. F. Russell
Colston's School, Bristol	www.colstons.bristol.sch.uk	£3,090	£6,200	P. T. Fraser
Combe Bank School, Kent	www.combebank.kent.sch.uk	£4,450	–	Mrs R. Martin
Concord College, Shrops	www.concordcollegeuk.com	£3,476	£7,316	N. G. Hawkins
Cranford House School, Oxon	www.cranfordhouse.oxon.sch.uk	£3,950	–	Mrs C. Hamilton
Cranleigh School, Surrey	www.cranleigh.org	£7,075	£8,680	G. Waller
Croydon High School, Surrey	www.gdst.net/croydonhigh	£3,700	–	Z. M. Braganza
Culford School, Suffolk	www.culford.co.uk	£4,840	£7,600	J. F. Johnson-Munday
Dame Alice Harpur School, Beds	www.dahs.co.uk	£3,293	–	Mrs J. Berry
Dame Allan's Boys' School, Tyne and Wear	www.dameallans.co.uk	£2,894	–	Dr J. R. Hind
Dame Allan's Girls' School, Tyne and Wear	www.dameallans.co.uk	£2,894	–	Dr J. R. Hind
Dauntsey's School, Wilts	www.dauntseys.wilts.sch.uk	£4,715	£7,950	S. Roberts
Dean Close School, Glos	www.deanclose.org.uk	£6,160	£8,720	Revd T. M. Hastie-Smith
Denstone College, Staffs	www.denstonecollege.org	£3,610	£5,735	D. M. Derbys
Derby High School, Derbys	www.derbyhigh.derby.sch.uk	£2,910	–	C. T. Callaghan
Dodderhill School, Worcs	www.dodderhill.co.uk	£2,900	–	Mrs J. M. Mumby
Dover College, Kent	www.dovercollege.org.uk	£3,760	£7,622	S. Jones
d'Overbroeck's College, Oxon	www.doverbroecks.com	£3,850	£6,625	S. Cohen
Downe House, Berks	www.downehouse.net	£6,570	£9,075	E. McKendrick
Downside, Somerset	www.downside.co.uk	£3,975	£7,406*	D. Maidlow Davis
Duke of York's Royal Military School, Kent	www.doyrms.mod.uk	–	£2,911	C. H. Johnson
Dulwich College, London SE21	www.dulwich.org.uk	£4,392	£8,844	G. G. Able
Dunottar School, Surrey	www.dunottar.surrey.sch.uk	£3,750	–	Mrs J. Hellier
Co. Durham High School for Girls, Co. Durham	www.dhsfg.org.uk	£2,980	–	Mrs A. J. Templeman
Co. Durham School, Co. Durham	www.durhamschool.co.uk	£4,666	£6,663	D. R. Best
Eastbourne College, E. Sussex	www.eastbourne-college.co.uk	£5,435	£8,210	S. P. Davies
Edgbaston High School	www.edgbastonhigh.co.uk	£2,810	–	Dr R. A. Weeks
Ellesmere College, Shrops	www.ellesmere.com	£4,636	£7,384	B. J. Wignall
Eltham College, London SE9	www.eltham-college.org.uk	£3,875	–	P. J. Henderson
Emanuel School, London SW11	www.emanuel.org.uk	£4,410	–	M. D. Hanley-Browne
Epsom College, Surrey	www.epsomcollege.org.uk	£6,124	£8,965	S. R. Borthwick
Eton College, Berks	www.etoncollege.com	–	£9,360	A. R. M. Little
Ewell Castle School, Surrey	www.ewellcastle.co.uk	£3,550	–	A. J. Tibble
Exeter School, Devon	www.exeterschool.org.uk	£3,100	–	R. Griffin
Farlington School, W. Sussex	www.farlingtonschool.net	£4,196	£6,673	Mrs J. Goyer
Farnborough Hill, Hants	www.farnborough-hill.org.uk	£3,280	–	Mrs S. Buckle
Farringtons School, Kent	www.farringtons.org.uk	£3,610	£6,600	Mrs C. James
Felsted School, Essex	www.felsted.org	£5,848	£7,813	Dr M. J. Walker
Forest School, London E17	www.forest.org.uk	£4,135	–	A. G. Boggis
Framlingham College, Suffolk	www.framlingham.suffolk.sch.uk	£4,686	£7,291	Mrs G. M. Randall
Francis Holland School, London NW1	www.francisholland.org	£4,300	–	Mrs V. M. Durham
Francis Holland School, London SW1	www.fhs-sw1.org.uk	£4,385	–	Miss S. J. Pattenden
Frensham Heights, Surrey	www.frensham-heights.org.uk	£5,100	£7,560	A. Fisher
Friends' School, Essex	www.friends.org.uk	£4,265	£6,640	G. Wigley
Fulneck School, W. Yorks	www.fulneckschool.co.uk	£3,165	£5,790	T. Kernohan
Gateways School, W. Yorks	www.gatewayschool.co.uk	£3,093	–	Mrs D. Davidson
Giggleswick School, N. Yorks	www.giggleswickschool.co.uk	£5,615	£8,203	G. P. Boult

The Godolphin and Latymer School, London W6	www.godolphinandlatymer.com	£4,490	–	Miss M. Rudland
The Godolphin School, Wilts	www.godolphin.org	£5,093	£7,397	Miss M. J. Horsburgh
The Grange School, Cheshire	www.grange.org.uk	£2,695	–	C. P. Jeffery
Greenacre School for Girls, Surrey	www.greenacre.surrey.sch.uk	£3,595	–	Mrs P. M. Wood
Grenville College, Devon	www.grenvillecollege.co.uk	£3,525	£6,885	A. Waters
Gresham's School, Norfolk	www.greshams.com	£6,180	£8,050	P. D. John
Guildford High School, Surrey	www.guildfordhigh.surrey.sch.uk	£3,872	–	Mrs F. J. Boulton
The Haberdashers' Aske's Boys' School, Herts	www.habsboys.org.uk	£4,285	–	P. B. Hamilton
Haberdashers' Aske's School for Girls, Herts	www.habsgirls.org.uk	£3,562	–	Mrs E. Radice
Haileybury, Herts	www.haileybury.com	£6,335	£8,435	S. A. Westley
Halliford School, Middx	www.hallifordschool.co.uk	£3,400	–	P. V. Cottam
Hampshire Collegiate School	www.hampshirecs.org.uk	£4,003	£6,623	D. F. Chapman
Hampton School, Middx	www.hamptonschool.org.uk	£4,290	–	B. R. Martin
Harrogate Ladies' College	www.hlc.org.uk	£4,150	£7,060	G. F. Hazell
Harrow School, Middx	www.harrowschool.org.uk	–	£9,335	B. J. Lenon
Headington School, Oxon	www.headington.org	£4,050	£7,775	Mrs A. Coutts
Heathfield St Mary's, Berks	www.heathfieldstmarys.com	–	£8,698	M. McSwiggan
Heathfield School, Middx	www.heathfield.gdst.net	£3,700	–	Miss C. M. Juett
Hereford Cathedral School	www.hcsch.org	£3,336	–	P. A. Smith
Hethersett Old Hall School, Norfolk	www.hohs.co.uk	£3,525	£6,595	S. G. Crump
Highclare School, W. Midlands	www.highclareschool.co.uk	£3,050	–	Mrs M. Viles
Highgate School, London N6	www.highgateschool.org.uk	£4,730	–	A. S. Pettitt
Hipperholme Grammar School Foundation, W. Yorks	www.hipperholmegrammar.org.uk	£2,665*	–	Dr J. Scarth
Hollygirt School, Notts	www.hollygirt.co.uk	£2,760	–	Mrs P. S. Hutley
Holy Trinity School, Worcs	www.holytrinity.co.uk	£2,865	–	Mrs Y. Wilkinson
Hull Collegiate School, E. Yorks	www.hullcollegiateschool.co.uk	£2,898	–	R. Haworth
Hurstpierpoint College, W. Sussex	www.hppc.co.uk	£5,785	£7,725	T. J. Manly
Hymers College, E. Yorks	www.hymerscollege.co.uk	£2,640	–	D. C. Elstone
Immanuel College, Herts	www.immanuelcollege.co.uk	£4,068	–	P. Skelker
Ipswich High School, Suffolk	www.ipswichhighschool.co.uk	£2,966	–	Ms E. Purves
Ipswich School, Suffolk	www.ipswich.suffolk.sch.uk	£3,451	£6,053	I. G. Galbraith
James Allen's Girls' School, London SE22	www.jags.org.uk	£4,095	–	Mrs M. Gibbs
The John Lyon School, Middx	www.johnlyon.org	£4,215	–	K. J. Riley
Kelly College, Devon	www.kellycollege.com	£4,450	£7,800	Dr G. R. W. Hawley
Kent College, Kent	www.kentcollege.com	£4,729	£7,647	D. J. Lamper
Kent College Pembury, Kent	www.kent-college.co.uk	£4,862	£6,027	Mrs S. A. Huang
Kimbolton School, Cambs	www.kimbolton.cambs.sch.uk	£3,755	£6,220	J. Belbin
King Edward VI High School for Girls, W. Midlands	www.kehs.org.uk	£3,000	–	Miss S. H. Evans
King Edward VI School, Hants	www.kes.hants.sch.uk	£3,495	–	A. J. Thould
King Edward VII and Queen Mary School, Lancs	www.keqms.co.uk	£2,600	–	R. J. Karling
King Edward's School, Somerset	www.kesbath.com	£3,420	–	M. Boden
King Edward's School, W. Midlands	www.kes.bham.sch.uk	£2,990	–	J. A. Claughton
King Edward's School, Surrey	www.kesw.surrey.sch.uk	£5,380	£7,490	P. Kerr Fulton-Peebles
King Henry VIII School, W. Midlands	www.khviii.com	£2,793	–	G. Fisher
King William's College, IOM	www.kwc.im	£5,553	£8,088	Dr S. J. Welch
Kingham Hill School, Oxon	www.kingham-hill.oxon.sch.uk	£5,080	£7,560	M. J. Morris
King's College School, London SW19	www.kcs.org.uk	£5,150	–	A. D. Halls
King's College, Somerset	www.kings-taunton.co.uk	£5,070	£7,795	R. R. Biggs
King's High School, Warks	www.kingshighwarwick.co.uk	£3,042	–	Mrs E. Surber
King's School, Somerset	www.kingsbruton.com	£5,808	£7,997	N. M. Lashbrook
The King's School, Canterbury, Kent	www.kings-school.co.uk	£6,805	£9,210	N. Clements
The King's School, Chester, Cheshire	www.kingschester.co.uk	£3,154	–	C. D. Ramsey

The King's School, Cambs	www.kingsschoolely.co.uk	£5,190	£7,510	S. E. Freestone
The King's School, Glos	www.thekingsschool.co.uk	£4,780	–	A. K. J. Macnaughton
The King's School, Macclesfield, Cheshire	www.kingsmac.co.uk	£2,785	–	S. Coyne
King's School, Rochester, Kent	www.kings-school-rochester.co.uk	£5,030	£8,460	Dr I. R. Walker
The King's School, Tyne and Wear	www.kings-tynemouth.org.uk	£2,951	–	P. J. S. Cantwell
The King's School, Worcs	www.ksw.org.uk	£3,408	–	T. H. Keyes
The Kingsley School, Warks	www.thekingsleyschool.com	£3,160	–	Mrs C. A. Mannion Watson
Kingston Grammar School, Surrey	www.kgs.org.uk	£4,343	–	C. D. Baxter
Kingswood School, Somerset	www.kingswood.bath.sch.uk	£3,475	£7,749	S. A. Morris
Kirkham Grammar School, Lancs	www.kirkhamgrammar.co.uk	£2,720	£4,935	D. R. Walker
The Lady Eleanor Holles School, Middx	www.lehs.org.uk	£4,180	–	Mrs G. Low
Lancing College, W. Sussex	www.lancingcollege.co.uk	£5,950	£8,570	J. W. J. Gillespie
Langley School, Norfolk	www.langleyschool.co.uk	£3,275	£6,660	D. K. Findlay
Latymer Upper School, London W6	www.latymer-upper.org	£4,490	–	P. J. Winter
Lavant House, W. Sussex	www.lavanthouse.org.uk	£3,995	£6,285	Mrs M. Scott
The Grammar School at Leeds, W. Yorks	www.gsal.org.uk	£3,198	–	M. Bailey
Leicester Grammar School, Leics	www.leicestergrammar.org.uk	£3,040	–	C. P. M. King
Leicester High School for Girls	www.leicesterhigh.co.uk	£2,900	–	Mrs J. Burns
Leighton Park School, Berks	www.leightonpark.com	£5,300	£8,085	J. H. Dunston
Leweston School, Dorset	www.leweston.co.uk	£4,765	£7,345	A. J. F. Aylward
The Leys School, Cambs	www.theleys.net	£5,210	£7,980	M. Slater
The Licensed Victuallers' School, Berks	www.lvs.ascot.sch.uk	£4,060	£7,245	G. Best
Lincoln Minster School, Lincs	www.lincolnminsterschool.co.uk	£3,323	£6,289	C. Rickart
Liverpool College, Merseyside	www.liverpoolcollege.org.uk	£2,865	–	H. van Mourik Broekman
Lodge School, Surrey	www.lodgeschool.co.uk	£3,725	–	P. A. Maynard
Longridge Towers School, Northumberland	www.lts.org.uk	£3,160	£6,630	A. E. Clemit
Lord Wandsworth College, Hants	www.lordwandsworth.org	£5,618	£7,918	I. G. Power
Loughborough Grammar School, Leics	www.lesgrammar.org	£3,126	£5,604	P. B. Fisher
Loughborough High School	www.leshigh.org	£2,913	–	B. A. O'Connor
Luckley–Oakfield School, Berks	www.luckley.wokingham.sch.uk	£4,101	£6,988	Miss V. A. Davis
Magdalen College School, Oxon	www.mcsoxford.org	£3,856	–	T. R. Hands
Malvern College, Worcs	www.malcol.org	£5,899	£9,211	A. R. Clark
Malvern St James, Worcs	www.malvernstjames.co.uk	£4,405	£8,710	Mrs R. Hayes
The Manchester Grammar School	www.mgs.org	£2,992	–	C. Ray
Manchester High School for Girls	www.manchesterhigh.co.uk	£2,878	–	Mrs C. Lee-Jones
Manor House School, Surrey	www.manorhouseschool.org	£3,970	–	Miss Z. Axton
The Marist Senior School, Berks	www.themaristschools.com	£3,220	–	K. McCloskey
Marlborough College, Wilts	www.marlboroughcollege.org	£6,930	£9,230	N. A. Sampson
Marymount International School, Surrey	www.marymountlondon.com	£5,648	£9,643	Sr Kathleen Fagan
The Maynard School, Devon	www.maynard.co.uk	£3,155	–	Dr D. West
Merchant Taylors' Boys' School, Merseyside	www.merchanttaylors.com	£2,727	–	D. H. I. Cook
Merchant Taylors' Girls' School, Merseyside	www.merchanttaylors.com	£2,727	–	Mrs L. A. Robinson
Merchant Taylors' School, Middx	www.mtsn.org.uk	£4,760	–	S. N. Wright
Mill Hill School, London NW7	www.millhill.org.uk	£5,067	£8,006	Dr D. Luckett
Millfield, Somerset	www.millfieldschool.com	£5,940	£8,700	C. Considine
Milton Abbey School, Dorset	www.miltonabbey.co.uk	£6,800	£9,060	W. J. Hughes-D'Aeth
Moira House Girls School, E. Sussex	www.moirahouse.co.uk	£4,370	£7,530	Mrs L. Watson
Monkton Senior, Somerset	www.monktoncombeschool.com	£5,524	£8,178	R. P. Backhouse
More House School, London SW1	www.morehouse.org.uk	£4,255	–	R. Carlysle
Moreton Hall, Shrops	www.moretonhall.org	£6,400	£7,950*	J. Forster
Mount St Mary's College, Derbys	www.msmcollege.com	£3,260	£6,230	L. E. McKell
The Mount School, London NW7	www.mountschool.com	£3,375	–	Mrs J. K. Jackson

The Mount School, N. Yorks	www.mountschoolyork.co.uk	£4,400	£6,840	Mrs D. J. Gant
New Hall School, Essex	www.newhallschool.co.uk	£4,820	£7,270	Mrs K. Jeffrey
Newcastle-under-Lyme School	www.nuls.org.uk	£2,747	–	N. A. Rugg
The Newcastle upon Tyne Church High School, Tyne and Wear	www.churchhigh.com	£3,073	–	Mrs J. Gatenby
North Cestrian Grammar School, Cheshire	www.ncgs.co.uk	£2,490	–	D. G. Vanstone
North London Collegiate School, Middx	www.nlcs.org.uk	£3,975	–	Mrs B. McCabe
Northampton High School	www.gdst.net/northamptonhigh	£3,169	–	Mrs S. A. Dixon
Northamptonshire Grammar School, Northants	www.ngs-school.com	£3,532	–	N. R. Toone
Northwood College, Middx	www.northwoodcollege.co.uk	£3,791	–	Mrs R. Mercer
Norwich High School, Norfolk	www.gdst.net/norwich	£2,966	–	Mrs V. C. Bidwell
Norwich School, Norfolk	www.norwich-school.org.uk	£3,506	–	J. B. Hawkins
Notre Dame Senior School, Surrey	www.notredame.co.uk	£3,710	–	Mrs B. Williams
Notting Hill and Ealing High School, London W13	www.nhehs.gdst.net	£3,700	–	Ms L. Hunt
Nottingham Girls' High School, Notts	www.gdst.net/nottinghamgirlshigh	£2,966	–	Mrs S. Gorham
Nottingham High School, Notts	www.nottinghamhigh.co.uk	£3,358	–	K. D. Fear
Oakham School, Rutland	www.oakham.rutland.sch.uk	£4,990	£8,350	Dr J. A. F. Spence
Ockbrook School, Derbys	www.ockbrook.derby.sch.uk	£2,940	£5,440	Mrs A. M. Steele
The Old Palace School of John Whitgift, Surrey	www.oldpalace.croydon.sch.uk	£3,286	–	Ms J. Harris
Oldham Hulme Grammar Schools, Lancs	www.hulme-grammar.oldham.sch.uk	£2,622	–	Dr P. G. Neeson
The Oratory School, Berks	www.oratory.co.uk	£5,935	£8,215	C. I. Dytor
Oswestry School, Shrops	www.oswestryschool.org.uk	£3,965	£6,745	P. D. Stockdale
Oundle School, Northants	www.oundleschool.org.uk	£5,505	£8,450	C. M. P. Bush
Our Lady of Sion School, W. Sussex	www.sionschool.org.uk	£3,050	–	M. Scullion
Our Lady's Abingdon Senior School, Oxon	www.olab.org.uk	£3,185	–	Mrs L. Renwick
Oxford High School, Oxon	www.gdst.net/oxfordhigh	£2,966	–	Miss O. S. Lusk
Padworth College, Berks	www.padworth.com	£3,000	£6,950	Mrs L. Melhuish
Palmers Green High School, London N21	www.pghs.co.uk	£3,400	–	Mrs C. Edmundson
Pangbourne College, Berks	www.pangbournecollege.com	£5,457	£7,780*	T. J. C. Garnier
The Perse School for Girls and the Stephen Perse Sixth Form College, Cambs	www.perse.cambs.sch.uk	£4,035	–	Miss P. M. Kelleher
The Perse Upper School, Cambs	www.perse.co.uk	£4,123	–	E. C. Elliott
Peterborough High School, Cambs	www.peterboroughhigh.co.uk	£3,497	£6,457	A. Meadows
Pipers Corner School, Bucks	www.piperscorner.co.uk	£3,975	£6,550	H. J. Ness-Gifford
Plymouth College, Devon	www.plymouthcollege.com	£3,720	£7,060	S. J. Wormleighton
Pocklington School, E. Yorks	www.pocklingtonschool.com	£3,517	£6,297	M. E. Ronan
Polam Hall School, Co. Durham	www.polamhall.com	£3,520	£6,570	Miss M. Green
Portland Place School, London	www.portland-place.co.uk	£4,495	–	R. Walker
The Portsmouth Grammar School, Hants	www.pgs.org.uk	£3,630	–	J. E. Priory
Portsmouth High School, Hants	www.gdst.net/portsmouthhigh	£2,966	–	Mrs J. Clough
The Princess Helena College, Herts	www.phc.herts.sch.uk	£5,080	£7,335	Mrs J-A. Duncan
Princethorpe College, Warks	www.wcisf.co.uk	£2,815	–	J. M. Shinkwin
Prior Park College, Somerset	www.priorparkschools.co.uk	£3,706	£7,446	R. G. G. Mercer
Prior's Field, Surrey	www.priorsfieldschool.com	£4,420	£7,150	J. A. Roseblade
The Purcell School, Herts	www.purcell-school.org	£7,709	£9,859	P. Crook
Putney High School, London SW15	www.gdst.net/putneyhigh	£3,700	–	Dr D. V. Lodge
Queen Anne's School, Berks	www.qas.org.uk	£5,560	£8,195	Mrs J. Harrington
Queen Elizabeth Grammar School, W. Yorks	www.wgsf.org.uk	£3,033	–	M. R. Gibbons
Queen Elizabeth's Grammar School, Lancs	www.qegs.blackburn.sch.uk	£2,943	–	S. A. Corns
Queen Elizabeth's Hospital, Bristol	www.qehbristol.co.uk	£3,184	–	S. W. Holliday

Queen Margaret's School, N. Yorks	www.queenmargaretsschool.co.uk	£4,787	£7,555	G. A. H. Chapman
Queen Mary's School, N. Yorks	www.queenmarys.org	£4,350	£5,665	R. A. McKenzie Johnston
Queen's College, London, London	www.qcl.org.uk	£4,370	–	M. M. Connell
Queen's College, Somerset	www.queenscollege.org.uk	£4,435	£6,915	C. J. Alcock
Queen's Gate School, London SW7	www.queensgate.org.uk	£4,485	–	Mrs R. M. Kamaryc
The Queen's School, Cheshire	www.queens.cheshire.sch.uk	£3,140	–	Mrs C. M. Buckley
Queenswood, Herts	www.queenswood.org	£6,560	£8,495	Mrs P. C. Edgar
Radley College, Oxon	www.radley.org.uk	£8,820	–	A. W. McPhail
Ratcliffe College, Leics	www.ratcliffecollege.com	£4,166	£6,282	P. Farrar
The Read School, N. Yorks	www.readschool.co.uk	£2,746	£5,884	R. A. Hadfield
Reading Blue Coat School, Berks	www.blue-coat.reading.sch.uk	£3,780	–	M. J. Windsor
The Red Maids' School, Bristol	www.redmaids.bristol.sch.uk	£3,005	–	Mrs I. Tobias
Redland High School for Girls, Bristol	www.redland.bristol.sch.uk	£2,960	–	Mrs C. P. Bateson
Reed's School, Surrey	www.reeds.surrey.sch.uk	£5,883	£7,717	D. W. Jarrett
Reigate Grammar School, Surrey	www.reigategrammar.org	£4,286	–	D. S. Thomas
Rendcomb College, Glos	www.rendcombcollege.co.uk	£5,655	£7,582	G. Holden
Repton School, Derbys	www.repton.org.uk	£6,215	£8,375	R. A. Holroyd
Rishworth School, W. Yorks	www.rishworth-school.co.uk	£3,195	£6,120	R. A. Baker
Roedean School, E. Sussex	www.roedean.co.uk	£5,250	£9,050	Mrs C. Shaw
Rossall School, Lancs	www.rossallschool.org.uk	£4,315	£8,830	Dr S. C.Winkley
The Royal Grammar School, Surrey	www.rgs-guildford.co.uk	£4,033	–	J. M. Cox
Royal Grammar School, Tyne and Wear	www.rgs.newcastle.sch.uk	£2,933	–	B. Trafford
RGS Worcester and The Alice Ottley School, Worcs	www.rgsao.org	£3,012	–	A. R. Rattue
The Royal High School, Bath, Somerset	www.gdst.net/royalhighbath	£2,966	£5,815	J. Graham-Brown
The Royal Hospital School, Suffolk	www.royalhospitalschool.org	£3,507	£6,556	H. W. Blackett
The Royal Masonic School for Girls, Herts	www.royalmasonic.herts.sch.uk	£4,260	£6,640	Mrs D. Rose
Royal Russell School, Surrey	www.royalrussell.co.uk	£4,230	£8,370	J. R. Jennings
Royal School Hampstead, London	www.royalschoolhampstead.net	£3,200	£6,360	J. Ebner-Landy
The Royal Wolverhampton School, W. Midlands	www.theroyalschool.co.uk	£3,730	£7,420	S. M. Bailey
Rugby School, Warks	www.rugbyschool.net	£5,510	£8,845	P. S. J. Derham
Ryde School with Upper Chine, IOW	www.rydeschool.org.uk	£3,015	£6,165	Dr N. J. England
Rye St Antony School, Oxon	www.ryestantony.co.uk	£3,550	£5,950	Miss A. M. Jones
St Albans High School, Herts	www.sahs.org.uk	£3,705	–	Ms J. Pain
St Albans School, Herts	www.st-albans.herts.sch.uk	£4,135	–	A. R. Grant
St Andrew's School, Beds	www.standrewsschoolbedford.com	£3,185	–	S. P. Skehan
St Bede's College, Manchester	www.stbedescollege.co.uk	£2,665	–	M. L. Barber
St Bede's Senior School, E. Sussex	www.stbedesschool.org	£4,785	£7,780	S. Cole
St Bees School, Cumbria	www.st-bees-school.org	£4,624	£7,715	P. J. Capes
St Benedict's School, London W5	www.stbenedictsealing.org.uk	£3,820	–	C. J. Cleugh
St Catherine's School, Surrey	www.stcatherines.info	£4,155	£6,840	Mrs A. M. Phillips
St Catherine's School, Middx	www.stcatherineschool.co.uk	£3,355	–	Sr P. A. Thomas
St Christopher School, Herts	www.stchris.co.uk	£4,500	£7,900	R. Palmer
St Columba's College, Herts	www.stcolumbascollege.net	£3,339	–	D. Buxton
St David's School, Middx	www.stdavidsschool.com	£3,888	£7,201	Mrs T. Smith
St Dominic's Priory School, Staffs	www.st-dominics.co.uk	£2,736	–	Mrs P. Adamson
St Dominic's School, Staffs	www.stdominicsschool.co.uk	£3,250	–	Mrs S. White
St Dunstan's College, London SE6	www.stdunstans.org.uk	£4,058	–	Mrs J. D. Davies
St Edmund's College, Herts	www.stedmundscollege.org	£4,450	£7,220	C. P. Long
St Edmund's School, Kent	www.stedmunds.org.uk	£5,178	£8,019	J. M. Gladwin
St Edward's, Oxford, Oxon	www.stedwards.oxon.sch.uk	£7,203	£9,005	A. F. Trotman
St Edward's School, Glos	www.stedwards.co.uk	£3,708	–	A. J. Nash
Saint Felix School, Suffolk	www.stfelix.co.uk	£3,995	£6,995	D. A. T. Ward
St Francis' College, Herts	www.st-francis.herts.sch.uk	£3,505	£6,895	Miss M. Hegarty
St Gabriel's School, Berks	www.st-gabriels.w-berks.sch.uk	£3,830	–	A. Jones
St George's College, Surrey	www.st-georges-college.co.uk	£4,455	–	J. A. Peake
St George's School, W. Midlands	www.sgse.co.uk	£3,100	–	Miss H. Phillips

St George's School, Berks	www.stgeorges-ascot.org.uk	£5,480	£8,450	Mrs C. L. Jordan
The School of St Helen and St Katharine, Oxon	www.shsk.org.uk	£3,395	–	Miss R. Edbrooke
St Helen's School for Girls, Middx	www.sthn.co.uk	£3,985	–	Mrs M. Morris
St James Independent School for Senior Boys, London W14	www.stjamesschools.co.uk	£3,700	–	D. Boddy
St James Senior Girls' School, London W14	www.stjamesschools.co.uk	£3,700	–	Mrs L. Hyde
St John's College, Hants	www.stjohnscollege.co.uk	£2,750	£6,050	N. W. Thorne
St John's School, Surrey	www.stjohnsleatherhead.co.uk	£5,790	£7,960	N. J. R. Haddock
St Joseph's College, Suffolk	www.stjos.co.uk	£3,535	£6,115	Mrs S. Grant
St Joseph's Convent School, Berks	www.st-josephs.reading.sch.uk	£3,500	–	Mrs M. Sheridan
St Lawrence College, Kent	www.slcuk.com	£4,547	£7,764	Revd M. Aitken
St Leonards–Mayfield School, E. Sussex	www.stlm.e-sussex.sch.uk	£4,995	£7,520	Miss A. M. Beary
St Margaret's School, Herts	www.stmargaretsbushey.org.uk	£4,080	£7,345	Mrs L. Crighton
St Margaret's School, Devon	www.stmargarets-school.co.uk	£3,000	–	Mrs S. Cooper
St Martha's Senior School, Herts	www.st-marthas.org.uk	£2,825	–	J. Sheridan
Saint Martin's, W. Midlands	www.saintmartins-school.com	£3,110	–	Mrs J. Carwithen
St Mary's College, Merseyside	www.stmaryscrosby.co.uk	£2,687	–	M. Kennedy
St Mary's Hall, E. Sussex	www.stmaryshall.co.uk	£4,203	£6,939	Mrs S. M. Meek
St Mary's School Ascot, Berks	www.st-marys-ascot.co.uk	£6,310	£8,870	Mrs M. Breen
St Mary's School, Wilts	www.stmaryscalne.org	£6,300	£8,800	Mrs H. Wright
St Mary's School, Cambs	www.stmaryscambridge.co.uk	£3,875	£7,770	Miss C. F. Avery
St Mary's School, Essex	www.stmaryscolchester.org.uk	£2,870	–	Mrs H. Vipond
St Mary's School, Bucks	www.stmarysschool.co.uk	£3,825	–	Mrs F. A. Balcombe
St Mary's School, Dorset	www.st-marys-shaftesbury.co.uk	£4,990	–	R. James
St Mary's, Worcs	www.stmarys.org.uk	£3,105	–	Mrs S. K. Cookson
St Nicholas' School, Hants	www.st-nicholas.hants.sch.uk	£3,346	–	A. V. Whatmough
St Paul's Girls' School, London W6	www.spgs.org	£4,841	–	Ms C. M. Farr
St Paul's School, London SW13	www.stpaulsschool.org.uk	£5,507	£8,163	G. M. Stephen
St Peter's School, N. Yorks	www.st-peters.york.sch.uk	£4,450	£7,165	R. I. Smyth
St Swithun's School, Hants	www.stswithuns.com	£4,640	£7,650	Dr H. L. Harvey
St Teresa's School, Surrey	www.stteresasschool.com	£4,290	£6,935	Mrs L. Falconer
Scarborough College, N. Yorks	www.scarboroughcollege.co.uk	£3,478	£5,786	T. L. Kirkup
Seaford College, W. Sussex	www.seaford.org	£4,950	£7,560	T. J. Mullins
Sedbergh School, Cumbria	www.sedberghschool.org	£4,950	£8,250	C. H. Hirst
Sevenoaks School, Kent	www.sevenoaksschool.org	£5,312	£8,518	Mrs C. L. Ricks
Shebbear College, Devon	www.shebbearcollege.co.uk	£3,176	£5,904	R. S. Barnes
Sheffield High School, S. Yorks	www.sheffieldhighschool.org.uk	£2,966	–	V. A. Dunsford
Sherborne Girls, Dorset	www.sherborne.com	£6,400	£8,800	Mrs J. Dwyer
Sherborne School, Dorset	www.sherborne.org	£7,175	£8,860	S. F. Eliot
Shiplake College, Oxon	www.shiplake.org.uk	£5,171	£7,666	A. G. S. Davies
Shrewsbury High School, Shrops	www.gdst.net/shrewsburyhigh	£2,966	–	Mrs M. Cass
Shrewsbury School, Shrops	www.shrewsbury.org.uk	£6,110	£8,705	J. W. R. Goulding
Sibford School, Oxon	www.sibford.oxon.sch.uk	£3,556	£6,909	M. Goodwin
Sidcot School, Somerset	www.sidcot.org.uk	£3,950	£6,600	J. Walmsley
Silcoates School, W. Yorks	www.silcoates.com	£3,656	–	D. S. Wideman
Sir William Perkins's School, Surrey	www.swps.org.uk	£3,652	–	Mrs S. D. Cooke
Solihull School, W. Midlands	www.solsch.org.uk	£3,083	–	P. J. Griffiths
South Hampstead High School, London NW3	www.gdst.net/shhs	£3,700	–	Mrs J. E. Stephen
Stafford Grammar School, Staffs	www.stafford-grammar.co.uk	£2,839	–	M. R. Darley
Stamford High School, Lincs	www.ses.lincs.sch.uk	£3,616	£6,768	Dr P. R. Mason
Stamford School, Lincs	www.ses.lincs.sch.uk	£3,616	£6,768	S. C. Roberts
Stanbridge Earls School, Hants	www.stanbridgeearls.co.uk	£5,910	£7,870	G. P. Link
Stockport Grammar School, Cheshire	www.stockportgrammar.co.uk	£2,742	–	A. H. Chicken
Stonar School, Wilts	www.stonarschool.com	£3,220	£6,860	Mrs S. Shayler
Stonyhurst College, Lancs	www.stonyhurst.ac.uk	£4,714	£8,064	A. R. Johnson
Stover School, Devon	www.stover.co.uk	£2,775	£6,495	Mrs S. Bradley
Stowe School, Bucks	www.stowe.co.uk	£6,620	£8,950	A. K. Wallersteiner
Streatham and Clapham High School, London SW16	www.gdst.net/streathamhigh	£3,700	–	Mrs S. Mitchell
Sunderland High School, Tyne and Wear	www.sunderlandhigh.co.uk	£2,494*	–	Dr A. Slater

Surbiton High School, Surrey	www.surbitonhigh.com	£3,703	–	Ms E. A. Haydon
Sutton High School, Surrey	www.gdst.net/suttonhigh	£3,700	–	S. J. Callaghan
Sutton Valence School, Kent	www.svs.org.uk	£5,260	£8,320	J. S. Davies
Sydenham High School, London SE26	www.gdst.net/sydenhamhigh	£3,700	–	Mrs K. E. Pullen
Talbot Heath, Dorset	www.talbotheath.org.uk	£3,231	£5,381	Mrs C. Dipple
Taunton School, Somerset	www.tauntonschool.co.uk	£4,700	£7,530	Dr J. H. Newton
Teesside High School, Cleveland	www.teessidehigh.co.uk	£3,333	–	T. A. Packer
Tettenhall College, W. Midlands	www.tettenhallcollege.co.uk	£3,712	£6,513	P. C. Bodkin
Thetford Grammar School, Norfolk	www.thetgram.norfolk.sch.uk	£3,173	–	G. J. Price
Thornton College, Bucks	www.thorntoncollege.com	£3,130	£5,150	A. T. Williams
Thorpe House School, Norfolk	www.thorpehouseschool.com	£2,480	–	A. Todd
Tonbridge School, Kent	www.tonbridge-school.co.uk	£6,970	£9,380	T. H. P. Haynes
Tormead School, Surrey	www.tormeadschool.org.uk	£3,745	–	Mrs S. E. Marks
Trent College, Notts	www.trentcollege.net	£4,159	£5,194	Mrs G. Dixon
Trinity School, Surrey	www.trinity-school.org	£3,758	–	M. J. Bishop
Truro High School for Girls, Cornwall	www.trurohigh.co.uk	£3,250	£6,125	M. A. McDowell
Truro School, Cornwall	www.truroschool.com	£3,360	£6,460	P. K. Smith
Tudor Hall, Oxon	www.tudorhallschool.com	£5,112	£7,865	Miss W. Griffiths
University College School, London NW3	www.ucs.org.uk	£4,850	–	K. J. Co. Durham
Uppingham School, Rutland	www.uppingham.co.uk	£6,146	£8,780	R. Harman
Wakefield Girls' High School, W. Yorks	www.wgsf.org.uk	£3,033	–	Mrs P. A. Langham
Walthamstow Hall, Kent	www.walthamstow-hall.co.uk	£4,570	–	Mrs J. Milner
Warminster School, Wilts	www.warminsterschool.org.uk	£6,880	£4,028	M. J. Priestley
Warwick School, Warks	www.warwickschool.org	£3,230	£6,892	E. B. Halse
Wellingborough School, Northants	www.wellingboroughschool.org	£3,668	–	G. R. Bowe
Wellington College, Berks	www.wellingtoncollege.org.uk	£6,725	£8,975	A. F. Seldon
Wellington School, Somerset	www.wellington-school.org.uk	£3,365	£5,983	M. S. Reader
Wells Cathedral School, Somerset	www.wells-cathedral-school.com	£4,461	£7,457	E. C. Cairncross
Wentworth College, Dorset	www.wentworthcollege.com	£3,645	£5,975	Miss S. Coe
West Buckland School, Devon	www.westbuckland.devon.sch.uk	£3,600	£6,225	J. F. Vick
Westfield School, Tyne and Wear	www.westfield.newcastle.sch.uk	£3,067	–	Mrs M. Farndale
Westholme School, Lancs	www.westholmeschool.com	£2,510	–	Mrs L. Croston
Westminster School, London SW1	www.westminster.org.uk	£6,888	£9,172	M. S. Spurr
Westonbirt, Glos	www.westonbirt.gloucs.sch.uk	£5,760	£8,300	Mrs M. Henderson
Whitgift School, Surrey	www.whitgift.co.uk	£4,272	–	C. A. Barnett
Wimbledon High School, London	www.gdst.net/wimbledon	£3,700	–	Mrs H. Hanbury
Winchester College, Hants	www.winchestercollege.org	£8,825	£9,290	R. D. Townsend
Windermere St Anne's School, Cumbria	www.wsaschool.com	£4,170	£7,466	A. Graham
Wisbech Grammar School, Cambs	www.wgs.cambs.sch.uk	£3,200	–	N. J. G. Hammond
Withington Girls' School, Manchester	www.withington.manchester.sch.uk	£2,850	–	Mrs J. D. Pickering
Woldingham School, Surrey	www.woldinghamschool.co.uk	£4,995	£8,290	Mrs J. Triffitt
Wolverhampton Grammar School, W. Midlands	www.wgs.org.uk	£3,425	–	J. V. Darby
Woodbridge School, Suffolk	www.woodbridge.suffolk.sch.uk	£3,998	£7,064	S. H. Cole
Woodhouse Grove School, W. Yorks	www.woodhousegrove.co.uk	£3,220	£6,255	D. C. Humphreys
Worksop College, Notts	www.worksopcollege.notts.sch.uk	£4,870	£7,185	R. A. Collard
Worth School, W. Sussex	www.worthschool.co.uk	£5,935	£8,012	G. G. Carminati
Wrekin College, Shrops	www.wrekincollege.com	£4,630	£7,645	S. G. Drew
Wychwood School, Oxon	www.wychwood-school.org.uk	£3,475	£5,650	Mrs S. Wingfield Digby
Wycliffe College, Glos	www.wycliffe.co.uk	£7,215	£9,335	Mrs M. E. Burnet Ward
Wycombe Abbey School, Bucks	www.wycombeabbey.com	£6,825	£9,100	Mrs P. E. Davies
Wykeham House School, Hants	www.wykehamhouse.com	£2,995	–	Mrs L. R. Clarke
Yarm School, Cleveland	www.yarmschool.org	£3,167	–	D. M. Dunn
The Yehudi Menuhin School, Surrey	www.yehudimenuhinschool.co.uk	sliding scale		N. Chisholm

WALES

Christ College, Brecon	www.christcollegebrecon.com	£4,405	£6,810	Mrs E. Taylor
Haberdashers' Monmouth School for Girls, Monmouth	www.habs-monmouth.org	£3,676	£6,505	Mrs H. Davy
Howell's School, Denbigh	www.howells.org	£3,700	£6,050	Miss R. Hodgson
Howell's School Llandaff, Cardiff	www.gdst.net/howells-llandaff	£2,985	–	Mrs S. Davis
Llandovery College, Llandovery	www.llandoverycollege.com	£4,270	£6,313	I. M. Hunt
Monmouth School, Monmouth	www.habs-monmouth.org	£3,735	£6,289	S. G. Connors
Rougemont School, Newport	www.rougemontschool.co.uk	£3,080	–	Dr J. Tribbick
Ruthin School, Ruthin	www.ruthinschool.co.uk	£3,500	£6,500	J. S. Rowlands
Rydal Penrhos School, Colwyn Bay	www.rydal-penrhos.com	£3,540	£7,740	P. A. Lee-Browne
St David's College, Llandudno	www.stdavidscollege.co.uk	£5,070	£7,555	C. Condrup

NORTHERN IRELAND

Bangor Grammar School, Bangor	www.bangorgrammarschool.org.uk	–	–	S. D. Connolly
Belfast Royal Academy, Belfast	www.belfastroyalacademy.com	£43	–	
Campbell College, Belfast	www.campbellcollege.co.uk	£1,990	£7,900	J. A. Piggot
Coleraine Academical Institution	www.coleraineai.com	£43*	–	D. R. Carruthers
Foyle and Londonderry College, Londonderry	www.foylenet.org/foyleandlondonderry	£40*	–	W. J. Magill
Methodist College, Belfast	www.methody.org	£6,410	£8,360	J. S. W. Naismith
Portora Royal School, Enniskillen	www.portoraroyal.co.uk	£42*	–	J. N. Morton
The Royal Belfast Academical Institution, Belfast	www.rbai.org.uk	£253*	–	Miss J. Williamson
The Royal School Dungannon, Dungannon	www.royaldungannon.com	£45	£5,750	P. D. Hewitt

SCOTLAND

Dollar Academy, Dollar	www.dollaracademy.org.uk	£3,030	£3,885	J. S. Robertson
The High School of Dundee	www.highschoolofdundee.co.uk	£3,047	–	Dr J. D. Halliday
The Edinburgh Academy	www.edinburghacademy.org.uk	£3,360	–	M. G. Longmore
Fettes College, Edinburgh	www.fettes.com	£5,946	£8,166	M. C. B. Spens
George Heriot's School, Edinburgh	www.george-heriots.com	£2,937	–	A. G. Hector
George Watson's College, Edinburgh	www.gwc.org.uk	£2,952	–	G. Edwards
The Glasgow Academy, Glasgow	www.theglasgowacademy.org.uk	£2,766	–	P. J. Brodie
The High School of Glasgow	www.glasgowhigh.com	£2,961	–	C. D. R. Mair
Glenalmond College, Perth	www.glenalmondcollege.co.uk	£5,640	£8,270	G. C. Woods
Hutchesons' Grammar School	www.hutchesons.org	£2,803	–	Dr K. M. Greig
Kelvinside Academy, Glasgow	www.kelvinsideacademy.org.uk	£3,098	–	J. L. Broadfoot
Kilgraston, Bridge of Earn	www.kilgraston.com	£4,275	£7,295	M. Farmer
Lomond School, Helensburgh	www.lomond-school.org	£2,805	£3,195	A. D. Macdonald
Loretto School, Edinburgh	www.loretto.com	£5,540	£8,150	P. A. Hogan
The Mary Erskine School, Edinburgh	www.esms.edin.sch.uk	£2,830	£5,646	J. N. D. Gray
Merchiston Castle School, Edinburgh	www.merchiston.co.uk	£5,735	£7,920	A. R. Hunter
Morrison's Academy, Crieff	www.morrisonsacademy.org	£2,991	–	G. S. H. Pengelley
Robert Gordon's College, Aberdeen	www.rgc.aberdeen.sch.uk	£2,983	–	H. Ouston
St Aloysius' College, Glasgow	www.staloysius.org	£2,670	–	J. Stoer
St Columba's School, Kilmacolm	www.st-columbas.org	£2,827	–	D. G. Girdwood
St George's School for Girls, Edinburgh	www.st-georges.edin.sch.uk	£3,370	£6,710	Dr J. McClure
St Margaret's School for Girls, Aberdeen	www.st-margaret.aberdeen.sch.uk	£3,023	–	Mrs A. Everest
St Margaret's School, Edinburgh	www.st-margarets.edin.sch.uk	£3,179	£6,683	Mrs E. M. Davis
Stewart's Melville College, Edinburgh	www.esms.edin.sch.uk	£2,830	£5,646	J. N. D. Gray
Strathallan School, Perth	www.strathallan.co.uk	£5,320	£7,840	B. K. Thompson

CHANNEL ISLANDS

Elizabeth College, Guernsey	www.elizcoll.org	£2,311	–	N. D. Argent
The Ladies' College, Guernsey	www.ladiescollege.sch.gg	£1,988	–	Ms J. Riches
Victoria College, Jersey	www.vcj.sch.je	£1,320	–	R. G. Cook

NATIONAL ACADEMIES OF SCHOLARSHIP

The national academies are self-governing bodies whose members are elected as a result of achievement and distinction in the academy's field. Within their discipline, the academies provide advice, support education and exceptional scholars, stimulate debate, promote UK research worldwide and collaborate with international counterparts.

In addition to income from donations, membership contributions, trading and investments, the English academies receive grant-in-aid funding from the science budget, administered by the Department for Innovation, Universities and Skills*; the allocations for the year 2008–9 are as follows:

	£ thousand
Royal Society	43,360
British Academy	22,540
Royal Academy of Engineering	10,279

Source: DIUS – Science Budget Allocations 2008–9 to 2010–11

* The Academy of Medical Sciences receives grant-in-aid funding from the Department of Health. It was allocated £1.75m spread over five years from 2004.

ACADEMY OF MEDICAL SCIENCES (1998)

10 Carlton House Terrace, London SW1Y 5AH
T 020-7969 5288
W www.acmedsci.ac.uk

The Academy of Medical Sciences was established in 1998 to promote advances in medical science and to ensure these are converted into healthcare benefits for society.

The academy campaigns for the development, protection and promotion of careers for academics in the biomedical sciences and encourages good practice in training and development.

The academy is independent and self-governing and receives funding from a variety of sources including the fellowship, charitable donations, government and industry.

Fellows are elected from a broad range of medical sciences: biomedical, clinical and population based. The academy includes in its remit vetinary medicine, dentistry, nursing, medical law, economics, sociology and ethics. Elections are from nominations put forward by existing fellows.

At June 2008 there were 920 fellows and 24 honorary fellows.

President, Prof. Sir John Bell, FRS, PMedSci
Vice-Presidents, Sir Michael Rutter, CBE, FRS, FMedSci; Prof. Ronald Laskey, FRS, FMedSci
Executive Director, Mary Manning

BRITISH ACADEMY (1902)

10 Carlton House Terrace, London SW1Y 5AH
T 020-7969 5200
W www.britac.ac.uk

The British Academy is an independent, self-governing learned society for the promotion of the humanities and social sciences. It supports advanced academic research and is a channel for the government's support of research in those disciplines.

The fellows are scholars who have attained distinction in one of the branches of study that the academy exists to promote. Candidates must be nominated by existing fellows. There are 770 ordinary fellows, 15 honorary fellows and 306 corresponding fellows overseas.

President, Baroness O'Neill, FBA
Chief Executive, Dr R. Jackson

ROYAL ACADEMY OF ENGINEERING (1976)

3 Carlton House Terrace, London SW1Y 5DG
T 020-7766 0600 W www.raeng.org.uk

The Royal Academy of Engineering was established as the Fellowship of Engineering in 1976. It was granted a royal charter in 1983 and its present title in 1992. It is an independent, self-governing body whose object is the pursuit, encouragement and maintenance of excellence in the whole field of engineering, in order to promote the advancement of science, art and practice of engineering for the benefit of the public.

Election to the fellowship is by invitation only, from nominations supported by the body of fellows. At May 2008 there were 1,383 fellows. The Duke of Edinburgh is the senior fellow and the Duke of Kent is a royal fellow.

President, Lord Browne of Madingley, FRENG, FRS
Senior Vice-President, Prof. W. Hall, CBE, FRENG
Chief Executive, P. D. Greenish, CBE

ROYAL SOCIETY (1660)

6–9 Carlton House Terrace, London SW1Y 5AG
T 020-7451 2500
W www.royalsociety.org

The Royal Society is an independent academy promoting the natural and applied sciences. Founded in 1660, the society has three roles, as the UK academy of science, as a learned society and as a funding agency. It is an independent, self-governing body under a royal charter, promoting and advancing all fields of physical and biological sciences, of mathematics and engineering, medical and agricultural sciences and their application.

Fellows are elected for their contributions to science, both in fundamental research resulting in greater understanding, and also in leading and directing scientific and technological progress in industry and research establishments. A maximum of 44 new fellows, who must be citizens or residents of the British Commonwealth countries or Ireland, may be elected annually.

Up to eight foreign members, who are selected from those not eligible to become fellows because of citizenship or residency, are elected annually for their contributions to science.

One honorary fellow may be elected each year from those not eligible for election as fellows or foreign members. There are approximately 1,400 fellows and foreign members covering all scientific disciplines.

President, Prof. Lord Rees of Ludlow, PRS
Executive Secretary, S. Cox, CVO

ROYAL SOCIETY OF EDINBURGH (1783)

22–26 George Street, Edinburgh EH2 2PQ
T 0131-240 5000
W www.royalsoced.org.uk

The Royal Society of Edinburgh (RSE) is an educational charity and Scotland's National Academy of Science and Letters. An independent body with charitable status, its multidisciplinary membership of around 1,500 fellows represents a knowledge resource for the people of Scotland. Granted its royal charter in 1783 for the 'advancement of learning and useful knowledge', the society organises conferences, debates and lectures; conducts independent inquiries; facilitates international collaboration and showcases the country's research and development capabilities; provides educational activities for primary and secondary school students and awards prizes and medals. The society also awards over £1.7m annually to Scotland's top researchers and entrepreneurs working in Scotland.

At May 2008 there were 1,503 fellows.

President, Sir Michael Atiyah, OM, PPRS, FRSE
Vice-Presidents, Prof. Tariq Durrani, OBE, FRENG, FRSE; Prof. Janet McDonald, FRSE; Lord Patel, FRSE
General Secretary, Prof. Geoffrey Boulton, OBE, FRS, FRSE

PRIVATELY FUNDED ARTS ACADEMIES

The Royal Academy and the Royal Scottish Academy support the visual arts community in the UK, hold educational events and promote interest in the arts. They are entirely privately funded through contributions by 'friends' (regular donors who receive benefits such as free entry, previews and magazines), bequests, corporate donations and exhibitions.

ROYAL ACADEMY OF ARTS (1768)

Burlington House, Piccadilly, London W1J 0BD
T 020-7300 8000
W www.royalacademy.org.uk

The Royal Academy of Arts is an independent, self-governing society devoted to the encouragement and promotion of the fine arts.

Membership of the academy is limited to 80 academicians, all being painters, engravers, sculptors or architects. Candidates are nominated and elected by the existing academicians. There is also a limited class of honorary academicians, of whom as of June 2008 there were 20.

President, Sir Nicholas Grimshaw, PRA
Secretary and Chief Executive, Charles Saumarez Smith

ROYAL SCOTTISH ACADEMY (1838)

The Mound, Edinburgh EH2 2EL
T 0131-225 6671
W www.royalscottishacademy.org

Founded in 1826 and granted a Royal Charter in 1838, The Royal Scottish Academy is an independent institution led by prominent Scottish artists and architects. It promotes and supports the visual arts through an ongoing exhibitions programme, related educational events and through a series of awards, bursaries and scholarships for artists at all stages of their careers.

Members are elected from the disciplines of art and architecture and elections are from nominations put forward by the existing membership. At mid-2008 there were 30 honorary members and 104 members.

President, Prof. Bill Scott, PRSA
Secretary, Arthur Watson, RSA

RESEARCH COUNCILS

The government funds basic and applied civil science research, mostly through seven research councils, which are established under royal charter and supported by the Department for Innovation, Universities and Skills (DIUS). The councils support research and training in universities and other higher education establishments. The science budget, administered by the DIUS, contributes to public sector investment in research, with funding from other government departments (including higher education funding) and regional development making up the remaining investment. The councils also receive income for research commissioned by government departments and the private sector, in addition to income from charitable sources. The annual science budget will rise from £3.54bn in 2008–9 to almost £4bn in 2010–11.

The government science budget for 2008–9 includes the following allocations:

	£ thousand
Arts and Humanities Research Council	103,492
Biotechnology and Biological Sciences Research Council	427,000
Economic and Social Research Council	164,924
Engineering and Physical Sciences Research Council	795,057
Medical Research Council	605,538
Natural Environment Research Council	392,150
Science and Technology Facilities Council	623,641
Higher Education Innovation Fund	85,000
Capital Investment Fund	135,000

Source: DIUS – *Science Budget Allocations 2008–9 to 2010–11*

ALCOHOL EDUCATION AND RESEARCH COUNCIL

Room 178, Queen Anne Business Centre, 28 Broadway, London SW1H 9JX **T** 020-7340 9502 **F** 020-7340 9505
W www.aerc.org.uk

The AERC was established by act of parliament in 1982 to administer the Alcohol Education and Research Fund. The government fund is used in UK education and research projects to develop new ways to help those with drinking problems. The AERC funds up to five research projects of around £50,000 every year and awards a number of small research grants up to a maximum of £5,000. The AERC aims to increase awareness of alcohol issues, to reduce alcohol-related harm and to encourage best practice.
Chair, Prof. Robin Davidson
Director, Prof. Ray Hodgson

ARTS AND HUMANITIES RESEARCH COUNCIL

Whitefriars, Lewins Mead, Bristol BS1 2AE
T 0117-987 6500 **W** www.ahrc.ac.uk

Launched in April 2005 as the successor organisation to the Arts and Humanities Research Board, the AHRC provides approximately £100m from the government to fund postgraduate training and research in the arts and humanities, encompassing disciplines such as English literature, history, modern languages, archaeology, music and drama. In any one year, the AHRC makes approximately 700 research awards and around 1,000 postgraduate awards. Awards are made after a rigorous peer review process, to ensure the quality of applications.
Chair, Prof. Sir Alan Wilson
Chief Executive, Prof. Philip Esler

BIOTECHNOLOGY AND BIOLOGICAL SCIENCES RESEARCH COUNCIL

Polaris House, North Star Avenue, Swindon SN2 1UH
T 01793-413200

Established by royal charter in 1994, the BBSRC funds basic and strategic biological research in order to advance UK expertise on the understanding and exploitation of biological systems. It funds research into how all living organisms function and behave. To deliver its mission, the BBSRC supports research and training in universities and research centres throughout the UK, including the institutes listed below.
Chair, Dr P. Ringose
Chief Executive (interim), Steve Visscher

INSTITUTES

BABRAHAM INSTITUTE, Babraham Hall, Babraham, Cambridge CB2 4AT **T** 01223-496000
Director, Prof. Michael Wakelam

IAH PIRBRIGHT LABORATORY, Ash Road, Pirbright, Woking, Surrey GU24 0NF **T** 01483-232441
Head, Dr John Anderson

INSTITUTE FOR ANIMAL HEALTH, Compton Laboratory, Compton, Newbury, Berks RG20 7NN
T 01635-578411
Director, Prof. M. Shirley

INSTITUTE OF FOOD RESEARCH, Norwich Research Park, Colney Lane, Norwich NR4 7UA **T** 01603-255000
Director, Prof. D. White

JOHN INNES CENTRE, Norwich Research Park, Colney, Norwich NR4 7UH **T** 01603-450000
Director, Prof. C. Lamb

NORTH WYKE RESEARCH, Okehampton, Devon EX20 2SB
T 01837-883500
Head, Prof. Les Firbank

ROTHAMSTED RESEARCH, Rothamsted, Harpenden, Herts AL5 2JQ **T** 01582-763133
Director, Prof. I. R. Crute

ROTHAMSTED RESEARCH, BROOM'S BARN RESEARCH STATION, Higham, Bury St. Edmunds, Suffolk IP28 6NP
T 01284-812200
Director, Bill Clark

ECONOMIC AND SOCIAL RESEARCH COUNCIL

Polaris House, North Star Avenue, Swindon SN2 1UJ
T 01793-413000
E comms@esrc.ac.uk **W** www.esrcsocietytoday.ac.uk

The purpose of the ESRC is to promote and support research and postgraduate training in the social sciences.

It also provides advice, disseminates knowledge and promotes public understanding in these areas.
Chair, Lord A. Turner
Chief Executive, Prof. I. Diamond

RESEARCH CENTRES
CENTRE FOR ANALYSIS OF RISK AND REGULATION, London School of Economics and Political Science, Houghton Street, London WC2A 2AE T 020-7955 6577
Director, Prof. B. Hutter
CENTRE FOR BUSINESS RELATIONSHIPS, ACCOUNTABILITY, SUSTAINABILITY AND SOCIETY, University of Cardiff, 55 Park Place, Cardiff CF10 3AT T 029-2087 6582
Director, Prof. K. Peattie
CENTRE FOR COMPETITION POLICY, University of East Anglia, Norwich NR4 7TJ T 01603-593715
Director, Prof. C. Waddams
CENTRE FOR ECONOMIC LEARNING AND SOCIAL EVOLUTION, University College, Gordon Street, London WC1H 0AN T 020-7679 4565
Director, Prof. M. Armstrong
CENTRE FOR ECONOMIC PERFORMANCE, London School of Economics and Political Science, Houghton Street, London WC2A 2AE T 020-7955 7048
Director, Prof. J. Van Reenen
CENTRE FOR MARKET AND PUBLIC ORGANISATION, University of Bristol, Bristol BS8 1TN T 0117-928 8436
Director, Prof. S. Burgess
CENTRE FOR MICROECONOMIC ANALYSIS OF PUBLIC POLICY, Institute for Fiscal Studies, 7 Ridgmount Street, London WC1E 7AE T 020-7291 4800
Director, Prof. R. Blundell
CENTRE ON MIGRATION, POLICY AND SOCIETY, University of Oxford, Oxford OX2 6QS T 01865-274711
Director (acting), Nicholas Van Hear
CENTRE FOR RESEARCH ON SOCIO-CULTURAL CHANGE, University of Manchester, Manchester M13 9PL T 0161-275 8985
Directors, Prof. M. Savage; Prof. K. Williams
CENTRE FOR SOCIAL, TECHNOLOGICAL AND ENVIRONMENTAL PATHWAYS TO SUSTAINABILITY, Institute of Development Studies, Brighton BN1 9RE T 01273-606261
Director, Prof. M. Leach
DEAFNESS, COGNITION AND LANGUAGE, 49 Gordon Square, London WC1H OPD T 020-7679 4200
Director, Prof. Bencie Woll
ELECTRICITY POLICY RESEARCH GROUP, University of Cambridge, Trumpinton Street CB2 1AG T 01223-335246
Director, Prof. D. Newbery
LANGUAGE-BASED AREA STUDIES CENTRES, T 01793-413089
Directors, Dr Frank Pieke; Prof. Robert Hillenbrand; Dr Robin Azelwood; Dr Richard Berry; Prof. Victor King
RESEARCH CENTRE ON MICRO-SOCIAL CHANGE, University of Essex, Colchester, Essex CO4 3SQ T 01206-872957
Director, Prof. S. Pudney
RESEARCH GROUP ON LIFESTYLES, VALUES AND ENVIRONMENT, University of Surrey, Guildford, Surrey GU2 1AG T 01793-413061
Director, Prof. T. Jackson
SUSSEX ENERGY GROUP, The Freeman Centre, University of Sussex, Brighton BN1 9QE T 01273-876584
Director, Prof. G. MacKerron

ENGINEERING AND PHYSICAL SCIENCES RESEARCH COUNCIL

Polaris House, North Star Avenue, Swindon SN2 1ET
T 01793-444000, **Helpline** 01793-444100
W www.epsrc.ac.uk

The EPSRC is the UK government's main funding agency for research and training in engineering and the physical sciences in universities and other organisations throughout the UK. It also provides advice, disseminates knowledge and promotes public understanding in these areas.
Chair, John Armitt, CBE, FRENG
Chief Executive, Prof. David Delpy, FRS

HEALTH PROTECTION AGENCY

7th Floor, Holborn Gate, 330 High Holborn, London WC1V 7PP
T 020-7759 2700 F 020-7759 2733 E webteam@hpa.org.uk
W www.hpa.org.uk

The Health Protection Agency is a Special Health Authority, established in 2003 (merged with the National Radiological Protection Board in 2005), it gives advice to the public, health authorities and the government. It works to reduce the impact of infectious diseases and exposure to chemicals, poisons and radiation at local, national and regional levels and in emergency situations. The agency researches new ways to combat illness and to assess exposure to chemicals and radiation to determine whether treatment is needed.
Chairman, Sir William Stewart
Chief Executive, Justin McCracken

RESEARCH CENTRES
CENTRE FOR INFECTIONS, 61 Colindale Avenue, London NW9 5EQ T 020-8200 4400
Director, Prof. Peter Borriello
CENTRE FOR EMERGENCY PREPAREDNESS AND RESPONSE Porton Down, Salisbury, SP4 0JG T 01980-612100
Director, Dr Stephen Chatfield
CENTRE FOR RADIATION, CHEMICAL AND ENVIRONMENTAL HAZARDS, Chilton, Didcot OX11 0RQ T 01235-831600
Director, Dr Roger Cox

MEDICAL RESEARCH COUNCIL

20 Park Crescent, London W1B 1AL T 020-7636 5422
W www.mrc.ac.uk

The purpose of the MRC is to promote medical and related biological research. The council employs its own research staff and funds research by other institutions and individuals, complementing the research resources of the universities and hospitals.

Chair, Sir John Chisholm
Chief Executive, Sir Leszek Borysiewicz
Chair, Neurosciences and Mental Health Board, Prof. C. Kennard
Chair, Molecular and Cellular Medicine Board, Prof. P. Luzio
Chair, Infections and Immunity Board, Prof. D. Smith
Chair, Population and Systems Medicine Board, Prof. S. Holgate

MRC UNITS AND CENTRES

Anatomical Neuropharmacology Unit
W mrcanu.pharm.ox.ac.uk

Biostatistics Unit
W www.mrc-bsu.cam.ac.uk

Cambridge Behavioural and Clinical Neuroscience Institute
W www.psychol.cam.ac.uk/bcni

Cancer Cell Unit
W www.hutchison-mrc.cam.ac.uk

Cell Biology Unit
W www.ucl.ac.uk/lmcb

Centre for Developmental and Biomedical Genetics
W cdbg.shef.ac.uk

Centre for Developmental Neurobiology at King's College London
W www.kcl.ac.uk/depsta/biomedical/mrc

Centre for Neurodegenerative Research
W cnr.iop.kcl.ac.uk

Centre for Nutritional Epidemiology in Cancer Prevention and Survival
W www.srl.cam.ac.uk

Centre for Protein Engineering
W www.mrc-cpe.cam.ac.uk

Centre for Regenerative Medicine
W www.scrm.ed.ac.uk

Clinical Sciences Centre
W www.csc.mrc.ac.uk

Clinical Trials Unit
W www.ctu.mrc.ac.uk

Cognition and Brain Sciences Unit
W www.mrc-cbu.cam.ac.uk

Collaborative Centre for Human Nutrition Research
W www.mrc-hnr.cam.ac.uk

Dunn Human Nutrition Unit
W www.mrc-dunn.cam.ac.uk

Epidemiology Resource Centre
W www.mrc.soton.ac.uk

Epidemiology Unit
W www.mrc-epid.cam.ac.uk

Functional Genomics Unit
W www.mrcfgu.ox.ac.uk

Human Genetics Unit
W www.hgu.mrc.ac.uk

Human Immunology Unit
T 01865-222336

Human Reproductive Sciences Unit
W www.hrsu.mrc.ac.uk

Institute of Hearing Research
W www.ihr.mrc.ac.uk

Laboratories, the Gambia
W www.mrc.gm

Laboratory of Molecular Biology
W www2.mrc-lmb.cam.ac.uk

Mammalian Genetics Unit
W www.mgu.har.mrc.ac.uk

Molecular Haemotology Unit
W www.imm.ox.ac.uk/groups/mrc_molhaem

MRC/Asthma UK Centre in Allergic Mechanisms of Asthma
T 020-7188 1943

MRC/Cancer Research UK/BHF Clinical Trial Service Unit & Epidemiological Studies Unit
W www.ctsu.ox.ac.uk

MRC General Practice Research Framework
W www.gprf.mrc.ac.uk

MRC Radiation Oncology and Biology Initiative
W www.rob.ox.ac.uk

MRC/UCL Centre for Medical Molecular Virology
T 020-7504 9343

MRC Unit for Lifelong Health and Ageing
W www.nhsd.mrc.ac.uk

MRC/University of Birmingham Centre for Immune Regulation
W www.bham.ac.uk/mrcbcir

MRC/University of Edinburgh Centre for Inflammation Research
W www.cir.med.ed.ac.uk

MRC/University of Sussex Centre in Genome Damage and Stability
W www.sussex.ac.uk/gdsc

National Institute for Medical Research
W www.nimr.mrc.ac.uk

Prion Unit
W www.prion.ucl.ac.uk

Protein Phosphorylation Unit
W www.dundee.ac.uk/lifesciences/mrcppu

Social and Public Health Sciences Unit
W www.msoc-mrc.gla.ac.uk

Social, Genetic and Developmental Psychiatry Research Centre
T 020-7848 0871

Centre for Stem Cell Biology and Medicine
W www.stemcells.cam.ac.uk

MRC/University of Bristol Centre for Synaptic Plasticity
W www.bris.ac.uk/depts/synaptic

Toxicology Unit
W www.le.ac.uk/mrctox

MRC/UVRIUganda Research Unit on AIDS
T (+256) (41) 320272

Virology Unit
W www.mrcvu.gla.ac.uk

NATIONAL PHYSICAL LABORATORY

Hampton Road, Teddington, Middx TW11 0LW
T 020-8977 3222 F 020-8943 6458 E enquiry@npl.co.uk
W www.npl.co.uk

The NPL was established in 1900 and is the UK's national standards laboratory. It develops, maintains and disseminates national measurement standards for physical quantities such as mass, length, time, temperature, voltage, force and pressure. It also conducts underpinning research on engineering materials and information technology, and disseminates good measurement practice. It is government-owned but contractor-operated.
Managing Director, S. McQuillan

NATURAL ENVIRONMENT RESEARCH COUNCIL

Polaris House, North Star Avenue, Swindon SN2 1EU
T 01793-411500 W www.nerc.ac.uk

The NERC funds and carries out impartial scientific research in the sciences relating to natural environment. Its work covers the full range of atmospheric, earth, biological, terrestrial and aquatic sciences, from the depths of the oceans to the upper atmosphere. Its mission is to gather and apply knowledge, create understanding and predict the behaviour of the natural environment and its resources.
Chair, Edmund Wallis
Chief Executive, Prof. Alan Thorpe

RESEARCH CENTRES

BRITISH ANTARCTIC SURVEY, High Cross, Madingley Road, Cambridge CB3 0ET T 01223-221400
Director, Prof. Nick Owens

BRITISH GEOLOGICAL SURVEY, Kingsley Dunham Centre, Keyworth, Nottingham NG12 5GG
T 0115-936 3100
Executive Director, Dr John Ludden

CENTRE FOR ECOLOGY AND HYDROLOGY, Maclean Building, Benson Lane, Crowmarsh Gifford, Wallingford OX10 8BB T 01491-838800
Director, Prof. Patricia Nuttall, OBE

PROUDMAN OCEANOGRAPHIC LABORATORY, Joseph Proudman Building, 6 Brownlow Street, Liverpool L3 5DA T 0151-795 4800
Director, Prof. Andrew Willmott

COLLABORATIVE CENTRES

CENTRE FOR OBSERVATION OF AIR-SEA INTERACTIONS AND FLUXES, Plymouth Marine Laboratory, Prospect Place, Plymouth PL1 3DH
T 01752-633429
Director, Prof. Jim Aiken

CENTRE FOR OBSERVATION AND MODELLING OF EARTHQUAKES AND TECTONICS, Department of Earth Sciences, University of Oxford, Parks Road, Oxford OX1 3PR
T 01865-272030
Director, Prof. Barry Parsons

CENTRE FOR POLAR OBSERVATION AND MODELLING, Department of Space and Climate Physics, Pearson Building, University College London, Gower Street, London WC1E 6BT T 020-7679 3031
Director, Prof. Duncan Wingham

CENTRE FOR POPULATION BIOLOGY, Imperial College London, Silwood Park Campus, Ascot SL5 7PY
T 020-7594 2475
Director, Prof. Georgina Mace, FRS

CLIMATE AND LAND SURFACE SYSTEMS INTERACTION CENTRE, School of Engineering, Computer Science and Mathematics, Harrison Building, North Park Road, University of Exeter EX4 4QF
T 01792-295144
Director, Prof. Peter Cox

DATA ASSIMILATION RESEARCH CENTRE, Department of Meteorology, University of Reading, PO Box 243, Earley Gate, Reading RG6 6BB
T 0118-378 6728
Director, Prof. Alan O'Neill

ENVIRONMENTAL SYSTEMS SCIENCE CENTRE, PO Box 238, University of Reading, Harry Pitt Building, 3 Earley Gate, Reading RG6 6AL
T 0118-378 8741
Director, Prof. Robert Gurney, OBE

NATIONAL INSTITUTE FOR ENVIRONMENTAL E-SCIENCE, Department of Earth Sciences, University of Cambridge, Downing Street, Cambridge CB2 3EQ
T 01223-764917
Director, Dr Martin Dove

NATIONAL OCEANOGRAPHY CENTRE, SOUTHAMPTON, University of Southampton, Waterfront Campus, European Way, Southampton SO14 3ZH T 023-8059 6666
Director, Prof. Ed Hill

NATIONAL CENTRES FOR ATMOSPHERIC SCIENCE, School of Earth and Environment, University of Leeds LS2 9JT T 0113-343 5158
Director, Prof. Stephen Mobbs

NCAS GLOBAL COMPOSITION AND CLIMATE RESEARCH, Department of Chemistry, University of Cambridge, Lensfield Road, Cambridge CB2 1EW
T 01223-336473
Director, Prof. John Pyle, FRS

NCAS BRITISH ATMOSPHERIC DATA CENTRE, Rutherford Appleton Laboratory, Chilton, Didcot OX11 0QX
T 01235-446432
Director, Dr Bryan Lawrence

NCAS-CLIMATE, Department of Meteorology, University of Reading, PO Box 243, Earley Gate, Reading RG6 6BB
T 0118-378 8424
Director, Prof. Julia Slingo

NCAS DISTRIBUTED INSTITUTE FOR ATMOSPHERIC COMPOSITION, School of Chemistry, University of Leeds, Leeds LS2 9JT
T 0113-343 6450
Director, Alasdair Lewis

NCAS FACILITY FOR AIRBORNE ATMOSPHERIC MEASUREMENTS, Building 125, Cranfield University, Cranfield, Bedford MK43 0AL T 01234-754411
Head of Facility, Prof. Stephen Mills

NCAS UNIVERSITIES FACILITY FOR ATMOSPHERIC MEASUREMENTS, School of Earth and Environment, University of Leeds, Leeds LS2 9JT
T 0113-343 6408
Director, Dr Alan Blyth

NCAS UNIVERSITIES WEATHER RESEARCH NETWORK, Department of Meteorology, University of Reading, PO Box 243, Earley Gate, Reading RG6 6BB
T 0118-378 8957
Director, vacant

NERC CENTRE FOR TERRESTRIAL CARBON DYNAMICS, University of Sheffield, Hicks Building, Hounsfield Road, Sheffield S3 7RH T 0114-222 3803
Director, Prof. Shaun Quegan

PLYMOUTH MARINE LABORATORY, Prospect Place, Plymouth PL1 3DH T 01752-633100
Director, Dr Peter Claridge

SCOTTISH ASSOCIATION FOR MARINE SCIENCE, Dunstaffnage Marine Laboratory, Oban PA37 1QA
T 01631-559000
Director, Prof. Graham Shimmield

SEA MAMMAL RESEARCH UNIT, Gatty Marine Laboratory, University of St Andrews, St Andrews KY16 8LB
T 01334-462630
Director, Prof. Ian Boyd

TYNDALL CENTRE FOR CLIMATE CHANGE RESEARCH, School of Environmental Sciences, University of East Anglia, Norwich, Norfolk NR4 7TJ T 01603-593900
Executive Director, Prof. Andrew Watkinson

SCIENCE AND TECHNOLOGY FACILITIES COUNCIL

Polaris House, North Star Avenue, Swindon SN2 1SZ
T 01793-442000 F 01793-442002 W www.scitech.ac.uk

Formed by royal charter on 1 April 2007, through the merger of the Council for the Central Laboratory of the Research Councils and the Particle Physics and Astronomy Research Council, the STFC is a non-departmental public body reporting to the Department for Innovation, Universities and Skills.

The STFC invests in large national and international research facilities, whilst delivering science, technology and expertise for the UK. The council is involved in research projects including the Diamond Light Source Synchrotron and the Large Hadron Collider, and develops new areas of science and technology. The EPSRC has transferred its responsibility for nuclear physics to the STFC.

Chair, Peter Warry
Chief Executive, Prof. Keith Mason

CHILBOLTON OBSERVATORY, Chilbolton, Stockbridge, Hampshire SO20 6BJ T 01264-860391
DARESBURY LABORATORY, Daresbury Science and Innovation Campus, Warrington WA4 4AD T 01925-603000
RUTHERFORD APPLETON LABORATORY, Harwell Science and Innovation Campus, Didcot OX11 0QX T 01235-445000
UK ASTRONOMY TECHNOLOGY CENTRE, Royal Observatory, Edinburgh, Blackford Hill, Edinburgh EH9 3HJ T 0131-668 8100

RESEARCH AND TECHNOLOGY ORGANISATIONS

Over 30 industrial and technological research bodies are members of the Association of Independent Research and Technology Organisations Limited (AIRTO). Members' activities span a wide range of disciplines from life sciences to engineering. Their work includes basic research, development and design of innovative products or processes, instrumentation testing and certification, and technology and management consultancy. AIRTO publishes a directory to help clients identify the organisations that might be able to assist them. For a full list of members, *see* AIRTO's website.

AIRTO LTD, c/o CCFRA, Station Road, Chipping Campden, Glos GL55 6LD T 01386-842247
E airto@campden.co.uk W www.airto.co.uk
President, Prof. R. Brook, OBE, FRENG

HEALTH

NATIONAL HEALTH SERVICE

The National Health Service (NHS) came into being on 5 July 1948 under the National Health Service Act 1946, covering England and Wales and, under separate legislation, Scotland and Northern Ireland. The NHS is now administered by the Secretary of State for Health (in England), the Welsh Assembly Government, the Scottish government and the Secretary of State for Northern Ireland.

The function of the NHS is to provide a comprehensive health service designed to secure improvement in the physical and mental health of the people and to prevent, diagnose and treat illness. It was founded on the principle that treatment should be provided according to clinical need rather than ability to pay, and should be free at the point of delivery.

Hospital, mental, dental, nursing, ophthalmic and ambulance services and facilities for the care of expectant and nursing mothers and young children are provided by the NHS to meet all reasonable requirements. Rehabilitation services such as occupational therapy, physiotherapy, speech therapy and surgical and medical appliances are supplied where appropriate. Specialists and consultants who work in NHS hospitals can also engage in private practice, including the treatment of their private patients in NHS hospitals.

STRUCTURE

The structure of the NHS remained relatively stable for the first 30 years of its existence. In 1974, a three-tier management structure comprising regional health authorities, area health authorities and district management teams was introduced in England, and the NHS became responsible for community health services. In 1979 area health authorities were abolished and district management teams were replaced by district health authorities.

The National Health Service and Community Care Act 1990 provided for more streamlined regional health authorities and district health authorities, and for the establishment of family health services authorities (FHSA) and NHS trusts. The concept of the 'internal market' was introduced into health care, whereby care was provided through NHS contracts where health authorities or boards and GP fundholders (the purchasers) were responsible for buying health care from hospitals, non-fundholding GPs, community services and ambulance services (the providers). The Act also paved the way for the community care reforms, which were introduced in April 1993, and changed the way care is administered for older people, the mentally ill, the physically disabled and people with learning disabilities.

ENGLAND

Regional health authorities in England were abolished in April 1996 and replaced by eight regional offices which, together with the headquarters in Leeds, formed the NHS executive (which has since been merged with the Department of Health). In April 2002, as an interim arrangement, the eight regional offices were replaced by four directorates of health and social care (DHSC). In April 2003, the DHSCs were abolished.

HEALTH AUTHORITIES

In April 1996 the district health authorities and family health service authorities were merged to form 100 unified health authorities (HAs) in England. In April 2002, 28 new health authorities were formed from the existing HAs. In October 2002, as part of the new arrangements set out in the NHS Reform and Health Care Professions Act 2002, these new health authorities were renamed strategic health authorities. The whole of England is now split into 10 strategic health authorities (SHAs) each of which is divided into various types of trusts that take responsibilty for running different NHS services locally. The different types of trusts comprise acute trusts and foundation trusts (which are responsible for the management of NHS hospitals), ambulance trusts, care trusts, mental health trusts and primary care trusts. SHAs are charged with improving and monitoring the performance of the trusts in their area.

PRIMARY CARE TRUSTS

The first 17 primary care trusts (PCTs) became operational on 1 April 2000 and there are now around 150 PCTs in England. PCTs were created to give primary care professionals greater control over how resources are best used to benefit patients. PCTs are free-standing statutory bodies responsible for securing the provision of services and integrating health and social care locally. PCTs receive most of their funding directly from the Department of Health and can use this to purchase hospital and other services from NHS trusts and other healthcare providers. They are also responsible for making payments to independent primary care contractors such as GPs and dentists.

Each PCT is overseen by a board, typically comprising a chair; at least five non-executive directors who are appointed by the Appointments Commission; at least five executive members, including the chief executive, finance director and director of public health; and at least two members of the PCT's professional executive committee (PEC), which is made up of health professionals. Clinical expertise is provided by the PEC with representation from local GPs, nurses, other health professionals and social services. The board concentrates on the overall strategies for the trust and ensures the trust meets its statutory, financial and legal obligations.

ACUTE TRUSTS AND FOUNDATION TRUSTS

Hospitals are managed by acute trusts that are responsible for the quality of hospital health care and for spending funds efficiently.

First introduced in April 2004, there are now 92 foundation trusts in England. NHS foundation trusts are NHS hospitals, but have their own accountability and governance systems, which function outside of the Department of Health's framework, giving them greater freedom to run their own affairs. NHS foundation trusts treat patients according to NHS principles and standards and are inspected by the Healthcare Commission.

STRATEGIC HEALTH AUTHORITIES

EAST OF ENGLAND, Victoria House, Capital Park, Fulbourn, Cambridge CB21 5XB T 01223-597500 W www.eoe.nhs.uk
Chief Executive, Neil McKay

EAST MIDLANDS, Octavia House, Bostocks Lane, Sandiacre, Nottingham NG10 5QG T 0115-968 4444 W www.eastmidlands.nhs.uk
Chief Executive, Barbara Hakin

LONDON, 4th Floor Southside, 105 Victoria Street, London SW1E 6QT T 020-7932 3700 W www.london.nhs.uk
Chief Executive, Ruth Carnall, CBE

NORTH EAST, Riverside House, Goldcrest Way, Newcastle upon Tyne NE15 8NY T 0191-210 6400 W www.northeast.nhs.uk
Chief Executive, Ian Dalton

NORTH WEST, Gateway House, Piccadilly South, Manchester M60 7LP T 0161-236 9456 W www.northwest.nhs.uk
Chief Executive, Mike Farrar, CBE

SOUTH CENTRAL, Newbury Business Park, London Road, Newbury, Berks RG14 2PZ T 01635-275500 W www.southcentral.nhs.uk
Chief Executive, Jim Easton

SOUTH EAST, York House, 18–20 Masetts Road, Horley, Surrey RH6 7DE, T 01293-778899 W www.southeastcoast.nhs.uk
Chief Executive, Candy Morris

SOUTH WEST, South West House, Blackbrook Park Avenue, Taunton, Somerset TA1 7PX T 01823-361000 W www.southwest.nhs.uk
Chief Executive, Sir Ian Carruthers, OBE

WEST MIDLANDS, St Chad's Court, 213 Hagley Road, Edgbaston, Birmingham B16 9RG T 0845-155 1022 W www.westmidlands.nhs.uk
Chief Executive, Cynthia Bower

YORKSHIRE AND THE HUMBER, Blenheim House, Duncombe Street, Leeds LS1 4PL T 0113-295 2000 W www.yorkshireandhumber.nhs.uk
Chief Executive, Margaret Edwards

Contact details for PCTs and other NHS trusts in England can be found on the NHS Choices website (W www.nhs.uk).

WALES

LOCAL HEALTH BOARDS AND COMMUNITY HEALTH COUNCILS

In Wales there were five HAs which replaced the former 17 HAs and FHSAs in April 1996. The HAs set up 22 local health groups (LHGs), coterminous with local authority areas (*see* Local Government section), which began work in April 1999. Originally they advised HAs, but in March 2003 the five HAs were abolished and the LHGs, were renamed local health boards (LHB) and took up a role similar to PCTs, assuming responsibility for commissioning services and devising strategies for improving health. They also integrate the delivery of primary and community care. Each local health board has a governing body made up of local doctors, a nurse, other health professionals, members of the local authority and voluntary organisations and others to represent the interests of patients. There is also a small executive team to take action on decisions and provide services for the public. There are also 19 community health councils (CHCs).

SPECIALISED SERVICES AND PUBLIC HEALTH

Although LHBs plan and fund most hospital and family health services there are a few specialised services which are overseen at national level. These services are the responsibility of the Health Commission Wales (specialised services), which was set up in April 2003. The National Public Health Service for Wales also gives advice and guidance to LHBs on a range of issues such as communicable disease protection and control as well as childhood immunisation.

NHS TRUSTS AND HOSPITALS

There are nine NHS trusts in Wales, including one all-Wales ambulance trust. Between them, the trusts are responsible for managing 117 hospitals.

REGIONAL OFFICES

There are three regional offices of the Welsh Assembly Government for mid and west Wales, north Wales and south-east Wales. The regional offices support coordination at local level between LHBs, local authorities and NHS trusts. They have a specific role in ensuring that Welsh Assembly Government initiatives are carried out. Contact details for the LHBs, community health councils, NHS trusts and all other NHS national and local services in Wales are available in the *NHS Wales Directory* on the NHS Wales website (W www.wales.nhs.uk).

SCOTLAND

In Scotland, the Scottish Government Health Department leads the central management of the NHS, heading a Management Executive, which oversees the work of 14 area health boards responsible for all health services in their area. On 31 March 2006 Argyll and Clyde health board was dissolved and the administrative boundaries for the Greater Glasgow and Highland health boards were changed to allow them to take responsibility for managing the delivery of health services in relevant parts of the Argyll and Clyde area. Greater Glasgow health board took responsibility for healthcare services in Inverclyde, Renfrewshire, West Dunbartonshire and East Renfrewshire and was re-named the Greater Glasgow and Clyde health board. Highland health board took responsibility for healthcare services in Argyll and Bute.

HEALTH BOARDS

AYRSHIRE AND ARRAN, Eglinton House, Ailsa Hospital, Dalmellington Road, Ayr KA6 6AB T 01292-513600 W www.nhsayrshireandarran.com

BORDERS, Newstead, Melrose TD6 9DB T 01896-825500 W www.nhsborders.org.uk

DUMFRIES AND GALLOWAY, Mid North, Crichton Hall, Dumfries DG1 4TG T 01387-272702 W www.nhsdg.scot.nhs.uk

FIFE, Hayfield House, Hayfield Road, Kirkcaldy, Fife KY2 5AH T 01592-643355 W www.nhsfife.scot.nhs.uk

FORTH VALLEY, Carseview House, Castle Business Park, Stirling FK9 4SW T 01786-463031 W www.nhsforthvalley.com

GRAMPIAN, Summerfield House, 2 Eday Road, Aberdeen AB15 6RE T 0845-456 6000 W www.nhsgrampian.org

GREATER GLASGOW AND CLYDE, Dalian House, 350 St Vincent Street, Glasgow G3 8YZ T 0141-201 4444 W www.nhsggc.org.uk

HIGHLAND, Assynt House, Beechwood Park, Inverness IV2 3BW T 01463-717123 W www.nhshighland.scot.nhs.uk

LANARKSHIRE, 14 Beckford Street, Hamilton, Lanarkshire ML3 0TA T 01698-281313 W www.nhslanarkshire.org.uk

LOTHIAN, Deaconess House, 148 Pleasance, Edinburgh EH8 9RS T 0131-536 9000 W www.nhslothian.scot.nhs.uk
ORKNEY, Garden House, New Scapa Road, Kirkwall, Orkney KW15 1BQ T 01856-888000 W www.ohb.scot.nhs.uk
SHETLAND, Brevik House, South Road, Lerwick ZE1 0TG T 01595-743060 W www.shb.scot.nhs.uk
TAYSIDE, Kings Cross, Clepington Road, Dundee DD3 8EA T 01382-818479 W www.nhstayside.scot.nhs.uk
WESTERN ISLES, 37 South Beach Street, Stornoway, Isle of Lewis HS1 2BB T 01851-702997 W www.wihb.scot.nhs.uk

NORTHERN IRELAND

In Northern Ireland there are four health and social services boards responsible for commissioning services to meet the needs of their respective populations. They are also responsible for assessing the needs of that population, establishing objectives and developing policies and priorities to meet these objectives.

EASTERN, Champion House, 12–22 Linenhall Street, Belfast BT2 8BS T 028-9032 1313 W www.ehssb.n-i.nhs.uk
NORTHERN, County Hall, 182 Galgorm Road, Ballymena BT42 1QB T 028-2531 1000 W www.nhssb.n-i.nhs.uk
SOUTHERN, Tower Hill, Armagh BT61 9DR T 028-3741 0041 W www.shssb.org
WESTERN, 15 Gransha Park, Clooney Road, Londonderry BT47 6FN T 028-7186 0086 W www.whssb.n-i.nhs.uk

THE NHS PLAN

In July 2000 the government launched the NHS Plan, a ten-year strategy to modernise the health service. In June 2004 it also launched the NHS Improvement Plan, which set out the next stage of NHS reform, moving the focus from access to services towards the broader issues of public health and chronic disease management. The core aims are to sustain increased levels of investment in the NHS and to continue to focus on the improvements outlined in the NHS Plan, while delivering greater levels of choice and information to patients. In July 2004, the Department of Health published *National Standards, Local Action: Health and Social Care Standards and Planning Framework 2005/6–2007/8,* which cut the number of national targets that NHS providers must comply with from 62 to 20. These national targets, which cover areas such as waiting times for accident and emergency treatment, have become national core standards which all providers of care must maintain from April 2005. Alongside this, NHS providers have been given power to set more locally relevant targets.

In June 2008 the Department of Health published *High Quality Care for All,* the final report of the next stage review. The report emphasised that there would be more choice for patients such as care plans for those with long-term conditions and the right for patients to choose care providers, including GPs. The report also stated that there would be increased investment in wellbeing and prevention services. In addition there was to be no new centrally imposed targets, instead service providers would be able to initiate and make changes to improve the quality of care for patients.

FINANCE

The NHS is still funded mainly through general taxation, although in recent years more reliance has been placed on the NHS element of national insurance contributions, patient charges and other sources of income.

The budgeted departmental expenditure limit for the NHS in England was set at £97.1bn for 2008–9. Expenditure for the NHS in Wales, Scotland and Northern Ireland is set by the devolved governments.

PRIVATE FINANCE INITIATIVE

The Private Finance Initiative (PFI) was launched in 1992, and involves the private sector in designing, building, financing and operating new hospitals and primary care premises, which are then leased to the NHS. Partnerships for Health, a public-private venture between the Department of Health and Partnerships UK plc was established in September 2001. Its role was to support the development of NHS Local Improvement Finance Trusts (LIFT) by implementing a standard approach to procurement as well as providing some equity. LIFTs were set up as limited companies with the local NHS Partnerships for Health and the private sector as shareholders to build and refurbish primary care premises, which the schemes own and then rent to GPs on a lease basis (as well as other parties such as chemists, opticians, dentists etc).

As at the end of 2007, there were 49 approved LIFT projects in England; of these, 45 had reached financial close. Forty-two of these schemes now have buildings open to patients. The total capital cost of all LIFT schemes at the end of 2007 was £1,311.39m.

EMPLOYEES AND SALARIES

NHS HEALTH SERVICE STAFF (GREAT BRITAIN)

Full-time equivalent

All hospital, community and public health medical staff	92,670
All hospital and community dental staff	3,466
Nursing and midwifery staff	485,289
General medical practitioners	40,634
General dental practitioners	2,301
Ophthalmic medical practitioners	439
Ophthalmic opticians	10,228

Source: ONS – *Annual Abstract of Statistics 2008* (Crown copyright)

SALARIES

Many general practitioners (GPs) are self-employed and hold contracts, either on their own or as part of a partnership, with their local primary care trust. The profit of GPs varies according to the services they provide for their patients and the way they choose to provide these services. Most contracted GPs would expect to earn between £80,000 and £120,000. The pay range for salaried GPs employed directly by primary care trusts for 2008–9 is £52,462–£79,167, dependent on, among other factors, length of service and experience. Most NHS dentists are self-employed contractors. A new contract for dentists was introduced on 1 April 2006 which provides dentists with an annual income in return for carrying out an agreed amount, or units, of work. An NHS-contracted dentist can typically expect to earn between £60,000 and £120,000. A salaried dentist employed directly by a PCT earns between £36,000 and £78,000.

BASIC SALARIES FOR HOSPITAL MEDICAL AND DENTAL STAFF*
from 1 April 2008

Consultant (2003 contract)	£73,403–£98,962
Consultant (pre-2003 contract)	£60,944–£79,001
Specialist Registrar	£30,231–£45,562
Speciality Registrar (full)	£28,976–£45,562
Speciality Registrar (fixed term)	£28,976–£38,336
Senior House Officer	£27,116–£37,755
House Officer	£21,862–£24,591

* These figures do not include merit awards, discretionary points or banding supplements

NURSES
From 1 December 2004 a new pay system *Agenda for Change* was introduced throughout the UK for all NHS staff with the exception of medical and dental staff, doctors in public health medicine and the community health service. Nurses' salaries are incorporated in the *Agenda for Change* nine pay band structure, which provides additional payments for flexible working such as providing out-of-hours services, working weekends and nights and being 'on-call'.

SALARIES FOR NURSES AND MIDWIVES

Nurse/Midwife Consultant	£37,106–£64,118
Modern Matron	£37,106–£44,527
Nurse advanced/team manager	£29,091–£38,352
Midwife higher level	£29,091–£38,352
Nurse specialist/team leader	£24,103–£32,653
Hospital/Community Midwife	£24,103–£32,653
Registered Nurse/entry level Midwife	£20,225–£26,123

HEALTH SERVICES

PRIMARY CARE

Primary care comprises the services provided by general practitioners, community health centres, pharmacies, dental surgeries and opticians. Primary nursing care includes the work carried out by practice nurses, community nurses, community midwives and health visitors.

PRIMARY MEDICAL SERVICES
In England, primary medical services are the responsibility of primary care trusts (PCT) who contract with healthcare providers – GPs, dentists, pharmacists etc – to provide the service to the NHS.

In Wales, responsibility for primary medical services rests with local health boards (LHB), in Scotland with the 14 health boards and in Northern Ireland with the four health and social services boards.

Any vocationally trained doctor may provide general or personal medical services. GPs may also have private fee-paying patients, but not if that patient is already an NHS patient on that doctor's patient list.

A person who is ordinarily resident in the UK is eligible to register with a GP (or PMS provider) for free primary care treatment. Should a patient have difficulty in registering with a doctor, he or she should contact the local PCT for help. When a person is away from home he/she can still access primary care treatment from a GP if they ask to be treated as a temporary resident. In an emergency any doctor in the service will give treatment and advice.

GPs or PCTs are responsible for the care of their patients 24 hours a day, seven days a week, but can fulfil the terms of their contract by delegating or transferring responsibility for out-of-hours (OOH) care to an accredited provider.

Increasingly, some secondary care services, such as minor operations and consultations, can be provided in a primary care setting. The number of such practitioners is growing.

In addition there are around 90 NHS walk-in centres throughout England. Usually open seven days a week, from early in the morning until late in the evening, they are nurse-led and provide treatment for minor ailments and injuries, health information and self-help advice.

HEALTH COSTS
Some people are exempt from, or entitled to help with, health costs such as prescription charges, ophthalmic and dental costs, and in some cases help towards travel costs to and from hospital.

The following list is intended as a general guide to those who may be entitled to help, or who are exempt from some of the charges relating to the above:

- children under 16 and young people in full time education who are under 19
- people aged 60 or over
- pregnant women and women who have had a baby in the last 12 months
- people, or their partners, who are in receipt of income support and/or income-based jobseeker's allowance
- people in receipt of the pension credit guarantee credit
- people with a specified medical condition or disability who have a valid exemption certificate
- diagnosed glaucoma patients, people who have been advised by an ophthalmologist that they are at risk of glaucoma and people aged 40 or over who have an immediate family member who is a diagnosed glaucoma patient
- diagnosed diabetic patients
- NHS in-patients
- NHS out-patients for all prescribed contraceptives, medication given at a hospital, NHS walk-in centre, personally administered by a GP or supplied at a hospital or primary care trust clinic for the treatment of a sexually transmissable infection
- patients of the Community Dental Service or an out-patient of the NHS Hospital Dental Service
- people registered blind or partially sighted
- people who need complex lenses
- war pensioners whose treatment/prescription is for their accepted disablement and who have a valid exemption certificate
- people who are entitled to, or named on, a valid NHS tax credit exemption or HC2 certificate

People in other circumstances may also be eligible for help; *see* booklet HC12 (England) and HCS2 (Scotland) for further information.

WALES
On 1 April 2007 all prescription charges (including those for medical supports and appliances and wigs) for people living in Wales were abolished. The above guide still applies for NHS dental and optical charges although all people aged under 25 living in Wales are also entitled to free dental examinations.

PHARMACEUTICAL SERVICES

Patients may obtain medicines and appliances under the NHS from any pharmacy whose owner has entered into arrangements with the PCT to provide this service. There are also some suppliers who only provide special appliances. In rural areas, where access to a pharmacy may be difficult, patients may be able to obtain medicines, etc, from a dispensing doctor.

In England, a charge of £7.10 is payable for each item supplied (except for contraceptives for which there is no charge), unless the patient is exempt and the declaration on the back of the prescription form is completed. Prepayment certificates (£27.85 valid for three months, £102.50 valid for a year) may be purchased by those patients not entitled to exemption who require frequent prescriptions.

Since 1 April 2008 prescription charges in Scotland have been different from England; a charge of £5 is payable for each item supplied and prepayment certificates are available for four months (£17.00) and 12 months (£48.00).

In Northern Ireland the health minister announced on 2 April that prescription charges would be frozen at 2007–8 levels while a review of prescription charges is carried out; a charge of £6.85 is payable for each indvidual item supplied and prepayment cartificates cost £35.85 for four months and £98.70 for 12 months). In Wales NHS prescription charges were abolished on 1 April 2007.

DENTAL SERVICES

Dentists, like doctors, may take part in the NHS and also have private patients. Dentists are responsible to the local health provider in whose areas they provide services. Patients may go to any dentist who is taking part in the NHS and is willing to accept them. On 1 April 2006 the charging system for NHS dentistry in England and Wales was changed. There is now a three-tier payment system based on the individual course of treatment required.

COURSE OF TREATMENT COSTS 2008–9

	England/Wales
Examination, diagnosis, preventive care (A)* (eg x-rays, scale and polish)	£16.20/£12.00
A+ basic additional treatment (eg fillings and extractions)	£44.60/£39.00
A+ all other treatment (eg more complex procedures such as crowns, dentures etc)	£198.00/£177.00

* Urgent and out-of-hours treatment will also be charged at this payment tier

The cost of individual treatment plan should be known prior to treatment and some dental practices may require payment in advance. There is no charge for writing a prescription or removing stitches and only one charge is payable for each course of treatment even if more than one visit to the dentist is required. If additional treatment is required within two months of visiting the dentist and this is covered by the course of treatment most recently paid for (eg payment was made for the second tier of treatment but an additional filling is required) then this will be provided free of charge.

SCOTLAND AND NORTHERN IRELAND

Scotland and Northern Ireland have yet to simplify their charging systems, NHS dental patients pay 80 per cent of the cost of the individual items of treatment provided up to a maximum of £384. Patients in Scotland are entitled to free basic and extensive examinations.

GENERAL OPHTHALMIC SERVICES

General ophthalmic services are administered by local health providers. Testing of sight may be carried out by any ophthalmic medical practitioner or ophthalmic optician (optometrist). The optician must give the prescription to the patient, who can take this to any supplier of glasses to have them dispensed. Only registered opticians can supply glasses to children and to people registered as blind or partially sighted.

Free eyesight tests and help towards the cost are available to people in certain circumstances. Help is also available for the purchase of glasses or contact lenses (*see* Health Costs section). In Scotland eye examinations, which include a sight test, are free to all. Help is also available for the purchase of glasses or contact lenses to those entitled to help with health costs in the same way it is available to those in England and Wales.

CHILD HEALTH SERVICES

Pre-school services at GP surgeries or child health clinics provide regular monitoring of children's physical, mental and emotional health and development and advise parents on their children's health and welfare.

NHS DIRECT AND NHS 24

NHS Direct is a 24-hour nurse-led advice telephone service for England and Wales. It provides medical advice as well as directing people to the appropriate part of the NHS for treatment if necessary (T 0845-4647).

NHS 24 provides an equivalent service for Scotland (T 0845-424 2424).

SECONDARY CARE AND OTHER SERVICES

HOSPITALS

NHS hospitals provide acute and specialist care services, treating conditions which normally cannot be dealt with by primary care specialists, and provide for medical emergencies.

NUMBER OF BEDS 2006

	Average daily	
	available beds	*occupation of beds*
England	167,000	141,000
Wales	14,000	11,000
Scotland	27,400	22,100
Northern Ireland	8,049	6,697

OUT-PATIENT ACTIVITY 2006

	New cases	*Total attendances*
England*	13,370,000	44,768,000
Wales	813,000	2,933,000
Scotland	2,763,000	6,083,000
Northern Ireland	1,081,000	2,233,000

* 2004 figures

Source: ONS – *Annual Abstract of Statistics 2008* (Crown copyright)

HOSPITAL CHARGES

Acute or foundation trusts can provide hospital accommodation in single rooms or small wards, if not required for patients who need privacy for medical reasons. The patient is still an NHS patient, but there may be a charge for these additional facilities. Acute or foundation trusts can charge for certain patient services that are considered to be additional treatments over and above the normal hospital service provision. There is no blanket policy to cover this and each case is considered in the light of the patient's clinical need. However, if an item or service is considered to be an integral part of a patient's treatment by their clinician, then a charge should not be made.

In some NHS hospitals, accommodation and services are available for the treatment of private patients where it does not interfere with care for NHS patients. Income generated by treating private patients is then put back into local NHS services. Private patients undertake to pay the full costs of medical treatment, accommodation, medication and other related services. Charges for private patients are set locally.

WAITING LISTS

England

Under the charter *Your Guide to the NHS,* patients were guaranteed admission within 18 months of being placed on a waiting list. In July 2004 a new target, of an 18 week maximum wait from start time (ie seeing a GP) to treatment, was set to be achieved by 2008. Known as the referral to treatment (RTT) pathway, monthly data is published on the NHS 18-weeks website (W www.18weeks.nhs.uk). In May 2008 the number of patients who completed their RTT pathway totalled 278,141; of which 89 per cent were seen within 18 weeks compared with 53 per cent in May 2007.

Wales

In Wales the number of patients waiting for in-patient or day case treatment totalled 50,960 on 31 May 2008, a decrease from 62,011 at the end of May 2007; of these, 41,078 had been waiting up to 14 weeks, 9,671 had been waiting between 14 and 22 weeks and 211 over 22 weeks. The number of patients waiting for a first outpatient appointment totalled 157,646 at the end of May 2008, compared with 170,782 at the end of May 2007; of these, 112,008 had been waiting up to 10 weeks, 45,409 had been waiting between 10 and 22 weeks and 47 over 22 weeks.

Scotland

In Scotland the national standard is for inpatients and day cases to be admitted for treatment within 18 weeks of being placed on the waiting list from 31 December 2007 (this will be reduced to 15 weeks from 31 March 2009. At the 31 March 2008 62,604 patients were on the list; of these, 40 had been waiting over 18 weeks and 1,992 had been waiting over 15 weeks.

Northern Ireland

In 2007 the health minister set new targets to ensure that by March 2008 no patient will wait more than 13 weeks for a first outpatient appointment and no more than 21 weeks for inpatient or day-case treatment. The number of people waiting for a first outpatient appointment at the end of March 2008 was 72,957, of these, 59 had been waiting over 13 weeks. The number of people waiting for inpatient treatment at the end of March 2008 was 36,994, of these, 56 had been waiting for more than 21 weeks.

AMBULANCE SERVICE

The NHS provides emergency ambulance services free of charge via the 999 emergency telephone service. Air ambulances, provided through local charities and partially funded by the NHS, are used throughout the UK. They assist with cases where access may be difficult or heavy traffic could hinder road progress. Non-emergency ambulance services are provided free of charge to patients who are deemed to require them on medical grounds.

Since 1 April 2001 all services have had a system of call prioritisation. The prioritisation procedures require all emergency calls to be classified as either immediately life threatening (category A) or other emergency (category B). Services are expected to reach 75 per cent of Category A (life threatening) calls within eight minutes and 95 per cent of category B calls within 19 minutes.

BLOOD SERVICES

There are four national bodies which coordinate the blood donor programme in the UK. Donors give blood at local centres on a voluntary basis.

NATIONAL BLOOD SERVICE, Oak House, Reeds Crescent, Watford, Herts WD24 4QN T 0845-771 1711 W www.blood.co.uk

WELSH BLOOD SERVICE, Ely Valley Road, Talbot Green, Pontyclun CF72 9WB T 01443-622000 W www.welsh-blood.org.uk

SCOTTISH NATIONAL BLOOD TRANSFUSION SERVICE, 21 Ellen's Glen Road, Edinburgh EH17 7QT T 0131-536 5700 W www.scotblood.co.uk

NORTHERN IRELAND BLOOD TRANSFUSION SERVICE, Belfast City Hospital Complex, Lisburn Road, Belfast BT9 7TS T 028-9032 1414 W www.nibts.org

HOSPICES

Hospice or palliative care may be available for patients with life-threatening illnesses. It may be provided at the patient's home or in a voluntary or NHS hospice or in hospital, and is intended to ensure the best possible quality of life for the patient during their illness, and to provide help and support to both the patient and the patient's family. The National Council for Palliative Care coordinates NHS and voluntary services in England, Wales and Northern Ireland; the Scottish Partnership for Palliative Care performs the same function in Scotland.

NATIONAL COUNCIL FOR PALLIATIVE CARE, The Fitzpatrick Building, 188–194 York Way, London N7 9AS T 020-7697 1520 W www.ncpc.org.uk

SCOTTISH PARTNERSHIP FOR PALLIATIVE CARE, 1A Cambridge Street, Edinburgh EH1 2DY T 0131-229 0538 W www.palliativecarescotland.org.uk

NHS CHARTERS

The original Patient's Charter was published in 1991 and came into force in 1992; an expanded version was published in 1995. The charter set out the rights of patients in relation to the standards of service they should expect to receive at all times and standards of service that the NHS aimed to provide.

The Patient's Charter was replaced nationally in 2001 with *Your Guide to the NHS,* which provided information on how to get treatment and gave specific details on minimum standards for patients, targets for the NHS and improvements in the NHS Plan. It also detailed what patients had a right to expect from the NHS and what is expected from patients.

Information for patients about all aspects of the NHS has now been reorganised and is available on the NHS Choices website (W www.nhs.uk).

A proposed NHS constitution was published on 30 June 2008; a consultation on its contents and how to put it into practice is currently underway.

COMPLAINTS

Firstly, an attempt must be made to resolve the complaint at a local level directly with the healthcare provider concerned. Patient advice and liaison services (PALS) have been established for every NHS and primary care trust in England. PALS are not part of the complaints procedure itself, but can give advice on local complaints procedure, or resolve concerns informally. Secondly, if the case is not resolved locally, an independent review can be requested by the Healthcare Commission in England or by the relevant health and social services board in Northern Ireland. As a final resort, complainants may approach the Health Service Ombudsman in England, the Scottish Public Services Ombudsman, Public Services Ombudsman for Wales or the Commissioner for Complaints in Northern Ireland.

RECIPROCAL ARRANGEMENTS

The European Health Insurance Card (EHIC) allows UK residents access to state-provided healthcare that may become necessary while temporarily travelling in all European Economic Area countries and Switzerland either free of charge or at a reduced cost. A card is free, valid for up to five years and should be obtained before travelling. Applications can be made by telephone (T 0845-606 2030), online (W www.ehic.org.uk) or by post (a form is available from the post office).

The UK also has bilateral agreements with several other countries, including Australia and New Zealand, for the free provision of urgent medical treatment.

European Economic Area nationals visiting the UK and visitors from other countries with which the UK has bilateral health care agreements are entitled to receive emergency health care on the NHS on the same terms as it is available to UK residents.

SOCIAL WELFARE

SOCIAL SERVICES

The Secretary of State for Health (in England), the National Assembly of Wales, the Scottish government and the Secretary of State for Northern Ireland are responsible, under the Local Authority Social Services Act 1970, for the provision of social services for older people, disabled people, families and children, and those with mental disorders. Personal social services are administered by local authorities according to policies, with standards set by central and devolved government. Each authority has a director and a committee responsible for the social services functions placed upon them. Local authorities provide, enable and commission care after assessing the needs of their population. The private and voluntary sectors also play an important role in the delivery of social services, and an estimated six million people in the UK provide substantial regular care for a member of their family.

Under the Health and Social Care (Community Health and Standards) Act 2003 the Commission for Social Care Inspection (CSCI) was established in April 2004. The CSCI was established as a single, regulatory authority, to ensure that local authority, private and voluntary care services throughout England are run in accordance with the national minimum standards and regulations that have been set by the government through a system of inspections and self-assessment. In April 2007 the Office for Standards in Education, Children's Services and Skills (OFSTED) was made responsible for inspecting and regulating all care services for children and young people in England; the CSCI is now only responsible for all adult social care services. Both OFSTED and the CSCI collate information on local care services and make this information available to the public.

The Care and Social Services Inspectorate Wales (CSSIW), an operationally independent part of the Welsh Assembly Government, is reponsible for the regulation and inspection of all social care services in Wales and the Scottish Commission for the Regulation of Care (the Care Commission), established in April 2002 under the Regulation of Care (Scotland) Act 2001, is the independent care services regulator for Scotland. The Department of Health, Social Services and Public Safety is responsible for social care services in Northern Ireland.

COMMISSION FOR SOCIAL CARE INSPECTION (CSCI), 33 Greycoat Street, London SW1P 2QF
T 020-7979 2000 E enquiries@csci.gsi.gov.uk
W www.csci.org.uk

OFFICE FOR STANDARDS IN EDUCATION, CHILDREN'S SERVICES AND SKILLS (OFSTED), Royal Exchange Buildings, St Ann's Square, Manchester M2 7LA T 0845-640 4045 E enquiries@ofsted.gov.uk
W www.ofsted.gov.uk

CARE AND SOCIAL SERVICES INSPECTORATE WALES (CSSIW), Cathays Park, Cardiff CF10 3NQ
T 01443-848450 E cssiw@wales.gsi.gov.uk
W www.cssiw.org.uk

SCOTTISH COMMISSION FOR THE REGULATION OF CARE, Compass House, 11 Riverside Drive, Dundee DD1 4NY T 01382-207100
E enquiries@carecommission.com
W www.carecommission.com

DEPARTMENT OF HEALTH, SOCIAL SERVICES AND PUBLIC SAFETY, Castle Buildings, Stormont, Belfast BT4 3SJ T 028-9052 0500 W www.dhsspsni.gov.uk

STAFF

Total Social Services Staff (England)	279,400
Home help service	31,700
Field social workers	40,100
Day care establishments staff	27,300
Residential care staff	46,400

Source: ONS – *Annual Abstract of Statistics 2008* (Crown copyright)

OLDER PEOPLE

Services for older people are designed to enable them to remain living in their own homes for as long as possible. Local authority services include advice, domestic help, meals in the home, alterations to the home to aid mobility, emergency alarm systems, day and/or night attendants, laundry services and the provision of day centres and recreational facilities. Charges may be made for these services. Respite care may also be provided in order to allow carers temporary relief from their responsibilities.

Local authorities and the private sector also provide 'sheltered housing' for older people, sometimes with resident wardens.

If an older person is admitted to a residential home, charges are made according to a means test; if the person cannot afford to pay, the costs are met by the local authority.

DISABLED PEOPLE

Services for disabled people are designed to enable them to remain living in their own homes wherever possible. Local authority services include advice, adaptations to the home, meals in the home, help with personal care, occupational therapy, educational facilities and recreational facilities. Respite care may also be provided in order to allow carers temporary relief from their responsibilities.

Special housing may be available for disabled people who can live independently, and residential accommodation for those who cannot.

FAMILIES AND CHILDREN

Local authorities are required to provide services aimed at safeguarding the welfare of children in need and, wherever possible, allowing them to be brought up by their families. Services include advice, counselling, help in the home and the provision of family centres. Many authorities also provide short-term refuge accommodation for women and children.

DAY CARE

In allocating day care places to children, local authorities give priority to children with special needs, whether in terms of their health, learning abilities or social needs. Since September 2001 OFSTED has been responsible for the regulation and registration of all early years childcare and education provision in England (previously the responsibility of the local authorities). All day care and childminding services which care for children under eight years of age for more than two hours a day must register with OFSTED and are inspected at least every two years. As at 30 June 2008 there were 1,553,100 registered childcare places and 100,600 registered childcare providers in England.

CHILD PROTECTION

Children considered to be at risk of physical injury, neglect or sexual abuse are placed on the local authority's child protection register. Local authority social services staff, schools, health visitors and other agencies work together to prevent and detect cases of abuse. In England as at 31 March 2007 there were 27,900 children on child protection registers, of these, 12,500 were at risk of neglect, 3,500 of physical abuse, 2,000 of sexual abuse and 7,100 of emotional abuse. At 31 March 2007 there were 2,295 children on child protection registers in Wales, 2,593 in Scotland and 1,639 in Northern Ireland*.

LOCAL AUTHORITY CARE

Local authorities are required to provide accommodation for children who have no parents or guardians or whose parents or guardians are unable or unwilling to care for them. A family proceedings court may also issue a care order where a child is being neglected or abused, or is not attending school; the court must be satisfied that this would positively contribute to the well-being of the child.

The welfare of children in local authority care must be properly safeguarded. Children may be placed with foster families, who receive payments to cover the expenses of caring for the child or children, or in residential care.

Children's homes may be run by the local authority or by the private or voluntary sectors; all homes are subject to inspection procedures. In England as at 31 March 2007, 60,000 children were in the care of local authorities, of these, 42,300 were in foster placements. In Wales 4,640 children were being looked after by local authorities on 31 March 2007, 14,060 in Scotland and 2,436 children in Northern Ireland.*

ADOPTION

Local authorities are required to provide an adoption service, either directly or via approved voluntary societies.

PEOPLE WITH LEARNING DISABILITIES

Services for people with learning disabilities are designed to enable them to remain living in the community wherever possible. Local authority services include short-term care, support in the home, the provision of day care centres, and help with other activities outside the home. Residential care is provided for the severely or profoundly disabled.

MENTALLY ILL PEOPLE

Under the care programme approach, mentally ill people should be assessed by specialist services, receive a care plan and a key worker should be appointed for each patient. Regular reviews of the person's progress should be conducted. Local authorities provide help and advice to mentally ill people and their families, and places in day centres and social centres. Social workers can apply for a mentally disturbed person to be compulsorily detained in hospital. Where appropriate, mentally ill people are provided with accommodation in special hospitals, local authority accommodation, or at homes run by private or voluntary organisations. Patients who have been discharged from hospitals may be placed on a supervision register.

* 2006 figures for Northern Ireland

NATIONAL INSURANCE

The National Insurance (NI) scheme operates under the Social Security Contributions and Benefits Act 1992 and the Social Security Administration Act 1992, and orders and regulations made thereunder. The scheme is financed by contributions payable by earners, employers and others (*see* below). Money collected under the scheme is used to finance the National Insurance Fund (from which contributory benefits are paid) and to contribute to the cost of the National Health Service.

NATIONAL INSURANCE FUND

Estimated receipts, payments and statement of balances of the National Insurance Fund for 2008–9:

Receipts	*£ million*
Net national insurance contributions	80,930
Compensation from the Consolidated Fund for statutory sick, maternity, paternity and adoption pay recoveries	1,910
Income from investments	2,267
State scheme premiums	74
Other receipts	55
TOTAL RECEIPTS	85,236

Payments	*£ million*
Benefits	
At present rates	66,992
Increase due to proposed rate changes	2,663
Personal and stakeholder pensions contracted-out rebates	2,167
Age-related rebates for contracted-out money purchase schemes	212
Administration costs	1,528
Redundancy fund payments	249
Transfer to Northern Ireland	505
Other payments	42
TOTAL PAYMENTS	74,358

Balances	*£ million*
Opening balance	46,069
Excess of receipts over payments	10,878
BALANCE AT END OF YEAR	56,947

CONTRIBUTIONS

There are six classes of National Insurance contributions (NICs):

Class 1	paid by employees and their employers
Class 1A	paid by employers who provide employees with certain benefits in kind for private use, such as company cars
Class 1B	paid by employers who enter into a pay as you earn (PAYE) settlement agreement with HM Revenue and Customs
Class 2	paid by self-employed people
Class 3	voluntary contributions paid to protect entitlement to the state pension for those who do not pay enough NI contributions in another class
Class 4	paid by the self-employed on their taxable profits over a set limit. These are normally paid by self-employed people in addition to class 2 contributions. Class 4 contributions do not count towards benefits.

The lower and upper earnings limits and the percentage rates referred to below apply from April 2008 to April 2009.

CLASS 1

Class 1 contributions are paid where a person:

- is an employed earner (employee), office holder (eg company director) or employed under a contract of service in Great Britain or Northern Ireland
- is 16 or over and under state pension age
- earns at or above the earnings threshold of £100.00 per week (including overtime pay, bonus, commission, etc, without deduction of superannuation contributions)

Class 1 contributions are made up of primary and secondary contributions. Primary contributions are those paid by the employee and these are deducted from earnings by the employer. Since 6 April 2001 the employee's and employer's earnings thresholds have been the same and are referred to as the earnings threshold. Primary contributions are not paid on earnings below the earnings threshold of £105.00 per week. However, between the lower earnings limit of £90.00 per week and the earnings threshold of £105.00 per week, NI contributions are treated as having been paid to protect the benefit entitlement position of lower earners. Contributions are payable at the rate of 11 per cent on earnings between the earnings threshold and the upper earnings limit of £770.00 per week (9.4 per cent for contracted-out employment). Above the upper earnings limit 1 per cent is payable.

Some married women or widows pay a reduced rate of 4.85 per cent on earnings between the earnings threshold and upper earnings limits and 1 per cent above this. It is no longer possible to elect to pay the reduced rate but those who had reduced liability before 12 May 1977 may retain it for as long as certain conditions are met. *See* leaflet *Married Women Paying Reduced Rate National Insurance Contributions (NICs).*

Secondary contributions are paid by employers of employed earners at the rate of 12.8 per cent on all earnings above the earnings threshold of £105.00 per week. There is no upper earnings limit for employers' contributions. Employers operating contracted-out salary related schemes pay reduced contributions of 9.1 per cent; those with contracted-out money-purchase schemes pay 11.4 per cent. The contracted-out rate applies only to that portion of earnings between the earnings threshold and the upper earnings limits. Employers' contributions below and above those respective limits are assessed at the appropriate not contracted-out rate.

CLASS 2

Class 2 contributions are paid where a person is self-employed and is 16 or over and under state pension age. Contributions are paid at a flat rate of £2.30 per week regardless of the amount earned. However, those with earnings of less than £4,825 a year can apply for small earnings exception, eg exemption from liability to pay class 2 contributions. Those granted exemption from class 2 contributions may pay class 2 or class 3 contributions voluntarily. Self-employed earners (whether or not they pay class 2 contributions) may also be liable to pay class 4 contributions based on profits. There are special rules for those who are concurrently employed and self-employed.

Married women and widows can no longer choose not to pay class 2 contributions but those who elected not to pay class 2 contributions before 12 May 1977 may retain the right for as long as certain conditions are met.

Class 2 contributions are collected by the national insurance contributions department of HM Revenue and Customs (HMRC), by direct debit or quarterly bills. *See* leaflet CA04.

CLASS 3

Class 3 contributions are voluntary flat-rate contributions of £8.10 per week payable by persons over the age of 16 who would otherwise be unable to qualify for retirement pension and certain other benefits because they have an insufficient record of class 1 or class 2 contributions. This may include those who are not working, those not liable for class 1 or class 2 contributions or those excepted from class 2 contributions. Married women and widows who on or before 11 May 1977 elected not to pay class 1 (full rate) or class 2 contributions cannot pay class 3 contributions while they retain this right. Class 3 contributions are collected by HMRC by quarterly bills or direct debit. *See* leaflet CA04.

CLASS 4

Self-employed people whose profits and gains are over £5,435 a year pay class 4 contributions in addition to class 2 contributions. This applies to self-employed earners over 16 and under the state pension age. Class 4 contributions are calculated at 8 per cent of annual profits or gains between £5,435 and £40,040 and 1 per cent above. Class 4 contributions are assessed and collected by HMRC. It is possible, in some circumstances, to apply for exceptions from liability to pay class 4 contributions or to have the amount of contribution reduced.

PENSIONS

Many people will qualify for a state pension; however, there are further pension choices available, such as personal and stakeholder pensions. There are also other non-pension savings and investment options. The following section provides background information on existing pension schemes.

STATE PENSION SCHEME

The state pension scheme consists of:

- basic state pension
- additional state pension

People may be able to get both or either when they reach state pension age and meet the qualifying conditions.

The state pension does not have to be claimed at state pension age, people can delay claiming it to earn extra weekly state pension or a lump sum payment.

Basic State Pension

The amount of basic state pension paid is dependent on the number of 'qualifying years' a person has established during their working life. In 2008–9, the full basic state pension is £90.70 a week and the minimum basic state pension is £22.68 a week *(see also* Benefits, State Pension: Categories A and B).

Qualifying Years

A 'qualifying year' is a tax year in which a person has enough earnings on which they have paid, are treated as having paid, or have been credited with national insurance (NI) contributions (*see* National Insurance Credits section). By state pension age, a person needs to have one qualifying year from NI contributions paid or from NI contributions treated as being paid to be eligible for any basic state pension. The number of qualifying years can be reduced if a person qualifies for home responsibilities protection (*see* below).

National Insurance Credits

Those in receipt of carer's allowance, working tax credit (with a disability element), jobseeker's allowance, incapacity benefit, statutory sick pay or statutory maternity pay may have class 1 NI contributions credited to them. Persons undertaking certain training courses or jury service or who have been wrongly imprisoned for a conviction which is quashed on appeal may also get class 1 NI credits for each week they receive benefit or fulfil certain conditions. Class 1 credits are also available to men for the tax years in which they reach age 60 up to age 64, if they are not liable to pay contributions. Class 1 NI credits count toward all future contributory benefits. A class 3 NI credit for basic state pension and bereavement benefit purposes is awarded, where required, for each week the working tax credit (without a disability element) has been received. Class 3 credits are also awarded automatically to young people aged 16 to 18 if they have not paid enough contributions to gain a qualifying year. However, a state pension will not be paid based on a record of NI credits alone.

Working Life

Working life is counted from the start of the tax year in which a person reaches 16 to the end of the tax year before the one in which they reach state pension age: for men this is normally 49 years and for women this varies between 44 and 49 years depending on their birth date (*see* State Pension Age). To get the full rate (100 per cent) basic state pension a person must normally have qualifying years for about 90 per cent of their working life. To get the minimum basic state pension (25 per cent) a person will normally need ten or eleven qualifying years.

State Pension Age

State pension age is:

- 65 for men
- 60 for women born on or before 5 April 1950
- 65 for women born on or after 6 April 1955

Women born between 6 April 1950 and 5 April 1955 will have a state pension age between 60 and 65 depending on their date of birth. Further information can be obtained from the online state pension calculator (W www.thepensionservice.gov.uk/resourcecentre/state pensioncalc.asp).

Using the NI Contribution Record of Another Person to Claim a State Pension

Married women who are not entitled to a state pension on their own NI contributions may get a basic state pension calculated using their husband's NI contribution record. A basic state pension may be paid of up to 60 per cent of the husband's entitlement (up to £54.35 a week in 2008–9). From 6 April 2010, married men and civil partners will be able to claim a basic state pension based on their wife or civil partner's NI contributions if better than one based on their own record and if their wife or civil partner was born after 6 April 1950. A state pension is also payable to widows, widowers, surviving civil partners, and people who are divorced or whose civil partnership has been dissolved, based on their late or ex-spouse's/civil partner's NI contributions.

Non-contributory State Pensions

A non-contributory state pension may be payable to those aged 80 or over who live in England, Scotland or Wales, and have done so for a total of ten years or more for any continuous period in the 20 years after their 60th birthday, if they are not entitled to another category of state pension, or are entitled to one below the rate of £54.35 a week in 2008–9 (*see also* Benefits, State Pension: Category D).

Graduated Retirement Benefit

Graduated Retirement Benefit (GRB) is based on the amount of graduated NI contributions paid into the GRB scheme between April 1961 and April 1975.

Home Responsibilities Protection

It is possible for people who have a low income or are unable to work because they care for children or a sick or disabled person at home to reduce the number of qualifying years required. This is called home responsibilities protection (HRP) and can be given for any tax year since April 1978; the number of years for which HRP is given is deducted from the number of qualifying years needed. HRP may, in some cases, also qualify the recipient for additional state pension. Since April 2003, HRP has also been available to approved foster carers.

Additional State Pension

The amount of additional state pension paid depends on the amount of earnings a person has, or is treated as having, between the lower and upper earnings limits for each complete tax year between 6 April 1978 (when the scheme started) and the tax year before they reach state pension age. The right to additional state pension does not depend on the person's right to basic state pension.

From 1978 to 2002, additional state pension was called the State Earnings-Related Pension Scheme (SERPS). SERPS covered all earnings by employees from 6 April 1978 to 5 April 1997 on which standard rate class 1 NI contributions had been paid, and earnings between 6 April 1997 and 5 April 2002 if the standard rate class 1 NI contributions had been contracted-in.

In 2002, SERPS was reformed through the state second pension, by improving the pension available to low and moderate earners and extending access to certain carers and people with long-term illness or disability. If earnings on which class 1 NI contributions have been paid or can be treated as paid are above the annual NI lower earnings limit (£4,680 for 2008–9) but below the statutory low earnings threshold (£13,500 for 2008–9), the state second pension regards this as earnings of £13,500 and it is treated as equivalent. Certain carers and people with long-term illness and disability will be considered as having earned at the low earnings threshold for each complete tax year since 2002–3 even if they do not work at all, or earn less than the annual NI lower earnings limit.

The amount of additional state pension paid also depends on when a person reaches state pension age; changes phased in from 6 April 1999 mean that pensions are calculated differently from that date.

Inheritance
Men or women widowed before 6 October 2002 can inherit all of their late spouse's SERPS pension. From 6 October 2002, the maximum percentage of SERPS pension that a person can inherit from a late spouse or civil partner depends on their late spouse or civil partner's date of birth:

Maximum SERPS entitlement	*d.o.b (men)*	*d.o.b (women)*
100%	5/10/37 or earlier	5/10/42 or earlier
90%	6/10/37 to 5/10/39	6/10/42 to 5/10/44
80%	6/10/39 to 5/10/41	6/10/44 to 5/10/46
70%	6/10/41 to 5/10/43	6/10/46 to 5/10/48
60%	6/10/43 to 5/10/45	6/10/48 to 5/7/50
50%	6/10/45 or later	6/7/50 or later

The maximum state second pension a person can inherit from a late spouse or civil partner is 50 per cent.

Pension Forecasts
The Pension, Disability and Carers Service provides a state pension forecasting.
T 0845-300 0168 **W** www.thepensionservice.gov.uk

PRIVATE PENSION SCHEMES

Contracted-Out Appropriate Personal Pension Schemes (including Appropriate Stakeholder Pension Schemes)
Since July 1988 an employee has been able to start a personal pension which, if it meets certain conditions, can be used in place of the additional state pension. These pensions are known as appropriate personal pensions (APPs) and employees who use them in place of the additional state pension are said to be 'contracted-out' of the state scheme.

At the end of the tax year HM Revenue and Customs pays an age-related rebate on contracted-out employees NI contributions together with tax relief on the employee's share of the rebate directly into the scheme to be invested on behalf of the employee. These payments are known as 'minimum contributions'.

Age-related rebates are intended to provide benefits broadly equivalent to those given up in the additional state pension. At retirement, a contracted-out deduction will be made from additional state pension accrued from 6 April 1978 to 5 April 1997.

Contracted-Out Salary-Related (COSR) Scheme
- these schemes (also known as contracted-out defined benefit (DB) schemes) provide a pension related to earnings and the length of pensionable service
- any notional additional state pension built up from 6 April 1978 to 5 April 1997 will be reduced by the amount of guaranteed minimum pension (GMP) accrued during that period (the contracted-out deduction)
- from 6 April 1997 these schemes no longer provide a GMP. Instead, as a condition of contracting out they have to satisfy a reference scheme test to ensure that the benefits provided are at least as good as a prescribed standard
- when someone contracts out of the additional state pension through a COSR scheme, both the scheme member and the employer, pay a reduced rate of NI contributions (known as the contracted-out rebate) to compensate for the additional state pension given up

Contracted-Out Money Purchase (COMP) Scheme
- these schemes (also known as contracted-out defined contribution (DC) schemes) provide a pension based on the value of the fund at retirement, ie the money paid in, along with the investment return
- the part of the COMP fund derived from protected rights (rights made up mainly from the contracted-out rebate and its investment return) is intended to provide benefits broadly equivalent to those given up in the additional state pension
- a contracted-out deduction, which may be more or less than that part of the pension derived from the protected rights, will be made from any notional additional pension built up from 6 April 1988 to 5 April 1997
- as with a COSR scheme, when someone contracts out of the additional state pension through a COMP scheme, both the scheme member and the employer pay a reduced rate of NI contributions (the contracted-out rebate) to compensate for the state pension given up. In addition, at the end of each tax year, HM Revenue and Customs pays an additional age-related rebate direct to the scheme for investment on behalf of the employee

Contracted-Out Mixed Benefit (COMB) Scheme
A mixed benefit scheme is a single scheme with both a salary related section and a money purchase section. Scheme rules set out which section individual employees may join and the circumstances (if any), in which members may move between sections. Each section must satisfy the respective contracting-out conditions for COSR and COMP schemes.

For more information on contracted-out pension schemes *see* the Department for Work and Pensions' leaflet PM7 *Contracting out of State Second Pension – Your Guide.*

STAKEHOLDER PENSION SCHEMES
Introduced in 2001, stakeholder pensions are available to everyone but are principally for moderate earners who do

not have access to a good value company pension scheme. Stakeholder pensions must meet a number of minimum standards to make sure they are flexible, portable and annual management charges are capped. The minimum contribution is £20.

As with personal pensions it is possible to invest up to £3,600 (including tax relief) into stakeholder pensions each year without evidence of earnings. Contributions can be made on someone else's behalf, for example, a non-working partner.

Stakeholder pensions can also be used by employees to contract out of the additional state pension. For more information *see* Contracted-Out Appropriate Personal Pension Schemes (including Appropriate Stakeholder Pension Schemes).

COMPLAINTS

The Pensions Advisory Service provides information and guidance to members of the public, on state, company, personal and stakeholder schemes. They also help any member of the public who has a problem, complaint or dispute with their occupational or personal pensions.

There are two bodies for pension complaints. The Financial Ombudsman Service deals with complaints which predominantly concern the sale and/or marketing of occupational, stakeholder and personal pensions. The Pensions Ombudsman deals with complaints which predominantly concern the management (after sale or marketing) of occupational, stakeholder and personal pensions.

The Pensions Regulator is the UK regulator for work-based pension schemes; it concentrates its resources on schemes where there is the greatest risk to the security of members' benefits, promotes good administration practice for all work-based schemes and works with trustees, employers and professional advisers to put things right when necessary.

WAR PENSIONS AND THE ARMED FORCES COMPENSATION SCHEME

The Service Personnel and Veterans Agency (SPVA), formerly the Veterans Agency, is an executive agency of the Ministry of Defence. SPVA was formed on 1 April 2007 from the former Armed Services Personnel Administration Agency and the Veterans Agency to provide services to both serving personnel and veterans.

SPVA is responsible for the administration of the war pensions scheme and the armed forces compensation scheme (AFCS) to members of the armed forces in respect of disablement or death due to service. There is also a scheme for civilians and civil defence workers in respect of the Second World War, and other schemes for groups such as merchant seamen and Polish armed forces who served under British command during the Second World War. The agency is also responsible for the administration of the armed forces pension scheme, which provides occupational pensions for ex-service personnel *(see* Defence).

THE WAR PENSIONS SCHEME

War disablement pension is awarded for the disabling effects of any injury, wound or disease which was the result of, or was aggravated by, conditions of service in the armed forces prior to 6 April 2005. Claims are only considered once the person has left the armed forces. The amount of pension paid depends on the severity of disablement, which is assessed by comparing the health of the claimant with that of a healthy person of the same age and sex. The person's earning capacity or occupation are not taken into account in this assessment. A pension is awarded if the person has a disablement of 20 per cent or more and a lump sum is usually payable to those with a disablement of less than 20 per cent. No award is made for noise-induced sensorineural hearing loss where the assessment of disablement is less than 20 per cent.

A pension is payable to war widows, widowers and surviving civil partners where the spouse's or civil partner's death was due to, or hastened by, service in the armed forces, prior to 6 April 2005, or where the spouse or civil partner was in receipt of a war disablement pension constant attendance allowance (or would have been if not in hospital) at the time of death. A pension is also payable to widows, widowers or surviving civil partners if the spouse or civil partner was receiving the war disablement pension at the 80 per cent rate or higher in conjunction with unemployability supplement at the time of death. War widows, widowers and surviving civil partners receive a standard rank-related rate, but a lower weekly rate is payable to war widows, widowers and surviving civil partners of personnel below the rank of Major who are under the age of 40, without children and capable of maintaining themselves. This is increased to the standard rate at age 40. Allowances are paid for children (in addition to child benefit) and adult dependants. An age allowance is automatically given when the widow, widower or surviving civil partner reaches 65 and increased at ages 70 and 80.

Pensioners living overseas receive the same pension rates as those living in the UK. All war disablement pensions and allowances and pensions for war widows, widowers and surviving civil partners are tax-free in the UK; this does not always apply in overseas countries due to different tax laws.

SUPPLEMENTARY ALLOWANCES

A number of supplementary allowances may be awarded to a war pensioner which are intended to meet various needs which may result from disablement or death and take account of its particular effect on the pensioner, pensioner's spouse or civil partner. The principal supplementary allowances are unemployability supplement, allowance for lowered standard of occupation and constant attendance allowance. Others include exceptionally severe disablement allowance, severe disablement occupational allowance, treatment allowance, mobility supplement, comforts allowance, clothing allowance, age allowance and widow/widower/surviving civil partner's age allowance. Rent and children's allowances are also available on pensions for war widows, widowers and surviving civil partners.

ARMED FORCES COMPENSATION SCHEME

The armed forces compensation scheme (AFCS) became effective on 6 April 2005 and covers all regular (including Gurkhas) and reserve personnel whose injury, ill health or death is caused by service on or after 6 April 2005. Ex-members of the armed forces who served prior to this date or who are in receipt of any pension under the war pensions scheme will continue to receive their pension and any associated benefits in the normal way. The new scheme affects only those who served after 6 April 2005.

The AFCS provides compensation where service in the armed forces is the only or main cause of injury, illness or death. Compensation can also be paid in certain exceptional circumstances to off-duty personnel, for example, to victims of a terrorist attack targeted due to their position in the armed forces. Under the terms of the scheme a lump sum is payable to service or ex-service personnel based on a 15-level tariff, graduated according to the seriousness of the condition. A guaranteed income payment (GIP), payable for life, is received by those who could be expected to experience a serious loss of earning capability. A GIP will also be paid to surviving spouses, civil partners and unmarried partners who meet certain criteria. GIP is calculated by multiplying the pensionable pay of the service person by a factor which depends on the age of the person's last birthday. The younger the person, the higher the factor, because there are more years to normal retirement age.

DEPARTMENT FOR WORK AND PENSIONS BENEFITS

Most benefits are paid in addition to those in receipt of payments under the AFCS and the war pensions scheme, but may be affected by any supplementary allowances in payment. Any state pension for which a war widow, widower or surviving civil partner qualifies for on their own NI contribution record can be paid in addition to monies received under the war pensions scheme.

CLAIMS AND QUESTIONS

Further information on the war pensions scheme, the armed forces compensation scheme and the nearest War Pensioners' Welfare Office can be obtained from the Service Personnel and Veterans Agency by telephone (**T** 0800-169 2277, if calling from the UK or, if living overseas, **T** (+44) (125) 386-6043).

SERVICE PERSONNEL AND VETERANS AGENCY,
Norcross, Blackpool FY5 3WP
E veterans.help@spva.gsi.gov.uk
W www.veterans-uk.info

TAX CREDITS

Tax credits are administered by HM Revenue and Customs and are awarded for up to 12 months, although they can be adjusted during the year to reflect changes in income or circumstances.

WORKING TAX CREDIT

Working tax credit is a payment from the government to support people on low incomes. It may be claimed by anyone over the age of 16 working 16 hours a week or more who meets one or more of the following conditions:

- is responsible for a child under 16 or a young person under 20 who is in relevant education or training or is registered for work, education or training with an approved body
- has a disability that puts them at a disadvantage in getting a job
- is aged 50 or over and returning to work after a period on benefits
- is aged 25 or over and works 30 or more hours a week

The system makes assumptions based on the national minimum wage and the number of hours worked per week. An annual income of £8,775 represents the 2008–9 income of an adult working 30 hours a week at the national minimum wage: six months at the 2007–8 rate of £5.52 per hour and six months at the rate of £5.73 per hour (national minimum wage from October 2008).

WORKING TAX CREDIT 2008–9

Annual Income/Status	*Tax Credit per annum*
£5,000*	
Single	–
Couple	–
Single adult with a disability	£4,205
£8,775†	
Single	£1,620
Couple	£3,390
Single adult with a disability	£4,025
£10,000	
Single	£1,140
Couple	£2,910
Single adult with a disability	£3,545
£15,000	
Single	–
Couple	£960
Single adult with a disability	£1,595

* Those with incomes of £5,000 a year are assumed to work part-time (working between 16 and 30 hours a week).

† Income of £8,775 represents the income of an adult working 30 hours per week at the national minimum wage rate (*see* above for explanation). In families with an income of £8,775 a year or more, at least one adult is assumed to be working 30 or more hours a week.

CHILDCARE

In families with children where a lone parent or both partners in a couple work for at least 16 hours a week, or where one partner works and the other is disabled, the family is entitled to the childcare element of working tax credit. This payment can contribute up to 80 per cent of childcare costs up to a maximum of £175 a week for one child and up to £300 a week for two or more children. Families can only claim if they use an approved or registered childcare provider.

CHILD TAX CREDIT

Child tax credit combines all income-related support for children and is paid direct to the main carer. The credit is made up of a main 'family' payment with additional payments for each extra child in the household, for children with a disability and an extra payment for children who are severely disabled. Child tax credit is available to households where:

- there is at least one dependant under 16
- there is at least one dependant under 20 who is in relevant education or training or is registered for work, education or training with an approved body

CHILD TAX CREDIT AND WORKING TAX CREDIT 2008–9 *(£ per year)*

	One Child		*Two Children*	
Annual Income	*No Childcare*	*Maximum Childcare*	*No Childcare*	*Maximum Childcare*
0	2,635	2,635	4,720	4,720
5,000*	6,205	13,505	8,295	20,810
8,775*	6,025	13,325	8,115	20,630
10,000†	5,545	12,845	7,635	20,150
15,000	3,595	10,895	5,685	18,200
20,000	1,645	8,945	3,735	16,250
25,000	545	6,995	1,785	14,300
30,000	545	5,045	545	12,350
35,000	545	3,095	545	10,400
40,000	545	1,145	545	8,450
45,000	545	545	545	6,500
50,000	545	545	545	4,550
60,000	–	–	–	650
65,000	–	–	–	230
70,000	–	–	–	–

* At income levels of £5,000 and £8,775 awards are shown for lone parents. At an income level of £5,000 the award is shown for a lone parent working part-time (between 16 and 30 hours a week). At an income level of £8,775 the award is shown for a lone parent working 30 hours a week.

† At an income level of £10,000 awards are shown for two parents working part-time (between 16 and 30 hours per week)

BENEFITS

The following is intended as a general guide to the benefits system. Conditions of entitlement and benefit rates change annually and all prospective claimants should check exact entitlements and rates of benefit directly with their local Jobcentre Plus office, pension centre or online (W www.direct.gov.uk). Leaflets relating to the various benefits and contribution conditions for different benefits are available from local Jobcentre Plus offices; leaflet BRA5DWP *Social Security Benefit Rates* is a general guide to benefit rates and contributions.

CONTRIBUTORY BENEFITS

Entitlement to contributory benefits depends on national insurance contribution conditions being satisfied either by the claimant or by someone on the claimant's behalf (depending on the kind of benefit). The class or classes of national insurance contribution relevant to each benefit are:

Jobseeker's allowance (contribution-based)	Class 1
Incapacity benefit	Class 1 or 2
Employment and Support Allowance (contributory)	Class 1 or 2
Widow's benefit and bereavement benefit	Class 1, 2 or 3
State pensions, categories A and B	Class 1, 2 or 3

The system of contribution conditions relates to yearly levels of earnings on which national insurance (NI) contributions have been paid.

JOBSEEKER'S ALLOWANCE

Jobseeker's allowance (JSA) replaced unemployment benefit and income support for unemployed people under state pension age from 7 October 1996. There are two routes of entitlement. Contribution-based JSA is paid at a personal rate (ie additional benefit for dependants is not paid) to those who have made sufficient NI contributions in two particular tax years. Savings and partner's earnings are not taken into account and payment can be made for up to six months. Rates of JSA correspond to income support rates.

Claims are made through Jobcentre Plus. A person wishing to claim JSA must generally be unemployed or working on average less than 16 hours a week, capable of work and available for any work which he or she can reasonably be expected to do, usually for at least 40 hours per week. The claimant must agree and sign a 'jobseeker's agreement', which will set out his or her plans to find work, and must actively seek work. If the claimant refuses work or training the benefit may be sanctioned for between one and 26 weeks.

A person will be sanctioned from JSA for up to 26 weeks if he or she has left a job voluntarily without just cause or through misconduct. In these circumstances, it may be possible to receive hardship payments, particularly where the claimant or the claimant's family is vulnerable, eg if sick or pregnant, or with children or caring responsibilities. *See* leaflet JSAL5 *(JSA – Helping You Back to Work)*.

Weekly Rates from April 2008

Person under 18	£47.95
Person aged 18–24	£47.95
Person aged 25 to state pension age*	£60.50

* Since October 2003 people aged between 60 and state pension age can choose to claim pension credits instead of JSA.

INCAPACITY BENEFIT

Employment and support allowance replaced incapacity benefit for new claimants from 27 October 2008. Those claiming incapacity benefit prior to this date will continue to receive it for as long as they qualify. There are three rates of incapacity benefit:

- short-term lower rate for the first 28 weeks of sickness
- short-term higher rate from weeks 29 to 52
- long-term rate from week 53 onwards

The terminally ill and those entitled to the highest rate care component of disability living allowance are paid the long-term rate after 28 weeks. Incapacity benefit is taxable after 28 weeks.

Two rates of age addition are paid, with long-term benefit based on the claimant's age when incapacity started. The higher rate is payable where incapacity for work commenced before the age of 35, and the lower rate where incapacity commenced before the age of 45.

Increases are made for claimants over the age of 60 and for adult dependants caring for children. Dependent children are provided for through the child tax credit system.

There are two medical tests of incapacity: the 'own occupation' test and the 'personal capability' assessment. Those who worked before becoming incapable of working are assessed, for the first 28 weeks of incapacity, on their ability to do their own job. After 28 weeks (or from the start of incapacity for those who were not working) claimants are assessed on their ability to carry out a range of work-related activities. *See* leaflets IB1 and IB214. Incapacity benefit claimants (excluding people who are severely disabled and those who are terminally ill) are invited back for work-focused interviews at intervals of not longer than three years. The interviews do not include medical tests, but if the claimant is due for a medical test around the same time, their local office will aim to schedule both together.

Weekly Rates from April 2008
Short-term incapacity benefit

Person under state pension age	
Lower rate	£63.75
Higher rate	£75.40
Increase for adult dependant	£39.40
Person over state pension age	
Lower rate	£81.10
Higher rate	£85.40
Increase for adult dependant	£48.65

Long-term incapacity benefit

Person under state pension age	£84.50
Increase for adult dependant	£48.65
Age addition – lower rate	£8.90
Age addition – higher rate	£17.75

EMPLOYMENT AND SUPPORT ALLOWANCE

From 27 October 2008, employment and support allowance (ESA) replaces incapacity benefit and income support paid on the grounds of incapacity or disability. The new benefit consists of two strands, contribution-based benefit and income-related benefit, so that people no longer need to make two claims for benefit in order to gain their full entitlement. Contributory ESA is available to those who have limited capability for work but cannot get statutory sick pay from their employer. Those over pensionable age are not entitled to ESA. Apart from those who qualify under the special provisions for people incapacitated in youth, entitlement to contributory

ESA is based on a person's NI contribution record. In order to qualify for contributory ESA, two contribution conditions, based on the last three years before the tax year in which benefit is claimed, must be satisfied. The amount of contributory ESA payable may be reduced where the person receives more than a specified amount of occupational or personal pension. Contributory ESA is paid only in respect of the person claiming the benefit – there are no additional amounts for dependants.

At the outset, new claimants are paid a basic allowance (the same rate as jobseeker's allowance) for 13 weeks while their medical condition is assessed and a work capability assessment is conducted. Following the completion of the assessment phase those claimants capable of engaging in work-related activities will receive a work-related activity component on top of the basic rate. The work-related activity component can be subject to sanctions if the claimant does not engage in the conditionality requirements without good reason. The maximum sanction is equal to the value of the work-related activity component of the benefit.

Those with the most severe health conditions or disabilities will receive the support component, which is more than the work-related activity component. Claimants in receipt of the support component are not required to engage in work-related activities, although they can volunteer to do so or undertake permitted work if their condition allows.

Weekly Rates from 27 October 2008

ESA plus work-related activity component	£84.50
ESA plus support component	
Lower rate	£89.50
Higher rate	£102.10

BEREAVEMENT BENEFITS

Bereavement benefits replaced widow's benefit on 9 April 2001. Those claiming widow's benefit before this date will continue to receive it under the old scheme for as long as they qualify. The new system provides bereavement benefits for widows, widowers and, from 5 December 2005, surviving civil partners (providing that their deceased spouse or civil partner paid NI contributions). The new system offers benefits in three forms:

- *Bereavement payment* – may be received by a man or woman who is under the state pension age at the time of their spouse or civil partner's death, or whose husband, wife or civil partner was not entitled to a category A retirement pension when he or she died. It is a single tax-free lump sum of £2,000 payable immediately on widowhood or loss of a civil partner
- *Widowed parent's allowance* – a taxable benefit payable to the surviving partner if he or she is entitled or treated as entitled to child benefit, or to a widow if she is expecting her husband's baby at the time of his death
- *Bereavement allowance* – a taxable weekly benefit paid for 52 weeks after the spouse or civil partner's death. If aged over 55 and under state pension age the full allowance is payable, if aged between 45 and 54 a percentage of the full rate is paid. A widow, widower or surviving civil partner may receive this allowance if his or her widowed parent's allowance ends before 52 weeks.

It is not possible to receive widowed parent's allowance and bereavement allowance at the same time. Bereavement benefits and widow's benefit, in any form, cease upon remarriage or a new civil partnership or are suspended during a period of cohabitation as partners without being legally married or in a civil partnership. *(See* leaflets *What to do after a death in England and Wales* or *What to do after a death in Scotland).*

Weekly Rates from April 2008

Bereavement payment (lump sum)	£2,000
Widowed parent's allowance (or widowed mother's allowance)	£90.70
Bereavement allowance (or widow's pension), full entitlement (aged 55 and over at time of spouse's or civil partner's death)	£90.70

Amount of bereavement allowance (or widow's pension) by age of widow/widower or surviving civil partner at spouse's or civil partner's death:

aged 54	£84.35
aged 53	£78.00
aged 52	£71.65
aged 51	£65.30
aged 50	£58.96
aged 49	£52.61
aged 48	£46.26
aged 47	£39.91
aged 46	£33.56
aged 45	£27.21

STATE PENSION: CATEGORIES A AND B

Category A pension is payable for life to men and women who reach state pension age, who satisfy the contributions conditions and who claim for it. Category B pension is payable for life to married women, widows, widowers and surviving civil partners and is based on their wife, husband or civil partner's contributions. It is payable to a married woman only when both the wife and husband have both reached state pension age and claimed their state pension (from 6 April 2010 it will no longer be a condition that the husband has actually claimed his state pension). From 6 April 2010 a married man and civil partner will be able to qualify for a category B pension from their wife's or civil partner's contributions providing the wife or civil partner were born on or after 6 April 1950. Category B pension is also payable to widows, widowers and surviving civil partners who are bereaved before state pension age if they were previously entitled to widowed parent's allowance or bereavement allowance based on their late spouse's or civil partner's NI contributions. Widows who are bereaved when over state pension age can qualify for a category B pension regardless of the age of their husband when he died, although at present, it is only paid to widowers and civil partners bereaved over state pension age if their wife or civil partner had reached state pension age when they died. Widowers or surviving civil partners who reach state pension age on or after 6 April 2010 will be able to get a category B pension on the same terms as widows.

Where a person is entitled to both a category A and category B pension then they can be combined to give a composite pension, but this cannot be more than the full rate pension. Where a person is entitled to more than one category A or category B pension then only one can be paid. In such cases the person can choose which to get; if no choice is made, the most favourable one is paid.

A person may defer claiming their pension beyond state pension age. In doing so they may earn increments which will increase the weekly amount paid by one per cent per five weeks of deferral (equivalent to 10.4 per cent/year) when they claim their state pension. If a person delays claiming for at least 12 months they are given the option of a one-off taxable lump sum, instead of a pension increase, based on the weekly pension deferred, plus interest of at least 2 per cent above the Bank of England base rate. If a married man defers his category A pension, his wife cannot claim a category B pension on his contributions but she may earn increments on her state pension during this time. A woman can defer her category B pension, and earn increments, even if her husband is claiming his category A pension.

An increase is paid for an adult dependant, providing the dependant's earnings do not exceed the rate of Jobseeker's Allowance for a single person and the couple are living together. If the couple are not living together an increase is payable if the dependant's earnings are not above £52.30. Provision for children is made through child tax credits. An age addition of 25p per week is payable with a state pension if a pensioner is aged 80 or over.

Since 1989 pensioners have been allowed to have unlimited earnings without affecting their state pension.

Weekly Rates from April 2008

Category A or B pension for a single person	£90.70
Category B pension (married women)	£54.35
Increase for adult dependant	£54.35
Age addition at age 80	£0.25

GRADUATED RETIREMENT BENEFIT

Graduated NI contributions were first payable from April 1961 and were calculated as a percentage of earnings between certain bands. The graduated retirement benefit scheme existed until April 1975, however, it is still paid in addition to any state pension to those who made the relevant contributions. A person will receive graduated retirement benefit based on their own contributions, even if not entitled to a basic state pension. Widows, widowers and surviving civil partners may inherit half of their deceased spouse's or civil partner's entitlement, but none that the deceased spouse or civil partner may have been eligible for from a former spouse or civil partner.

Graduated retirement benefit is calculated using a weekly rate for each 'unit' of graduated contributions paid by the employee (half a unit or more counts as a whole unit); the rate varies from person to person. A unit of graduated retirement benefit can be calculated by adding together all graduated contributions and dividing by 7.5 (men) or 9 (women). If a person defers making a claim beyond state pension age, they may earn an increase or a one-off lump sum payment in respect of their deferred graduated retirement benefit; calculated in the same way as for the category A or B state pension.

NON-CONTRIBUTORY BENEFITS

These benefits are paid from general taxation and are not dependent on NI contributions.

JOBSEEKER'S ALLOWANCE (INCOME-BASED)

Those who do not qualify for contribution-based jobseeker's allowance (JSA(c)), those who have exhausted their entitlement to contribution-based JSA or those for whom contribution-based JSA provides insufficient income may qualify for income-based JSA. The amount paid depends on age, whether they are single or a couple, number of dependants and amount of income and savings. Income-based JSA is comprised of three parts:

- a personal allowance for the jobseeker and his/her partner*
- premiums for people with special needs
- amounts for housing costs

* Since April 2003, child dependants have been provided for through the child tax credit system, although an increase in JSA for dependent children is still available for existing claimants.

The rules of entitlement are the same as for contribution-based JSA.

If one person in a couple was born after 28 October 1957 and neither person in the couple has responsibility for a child or children, then the couple will have to make a joint claim for JSA if they wish to receive income-based JSA.

Weekly Rates from April 2008

Person under 18	£47.95
Person aged 18–24	£47.95
Person aged 25 to state pension age	£60.50
Couple with one or both under 18*	£47.95–£59.15
Couple aged 18 to state pension age	£94.95
Lone parents*	£47.95–£60.50
Dependent children (from birth to the day before 20th birthday)	£52.59
Family premium	£16.75

* depending on circumstances

MATERNITY ALLOWANCE

Maternity allowance (MA) is a benefit available for pregnant women who cannot get statutory maternity pay (SMP) from their employer or have been employed/self-employed during or close to their pregnancy. In order to qualify for payment, a woman must have been employed and/or self-employed for at least 26 weeks in the 66 week period up to and including the week before the baby is due (test period). These weeks do not have to be in a row and any part weeks worked will count towards the 26 weeks. She must also have average weekly earning of at least £30 (maternity allowance threshold) over any 13 weeks of the woman's choice within the test period.

Self-employed women who pay class 2 NI contributions or who hold a small earnings exception certificate are deemed to have enough earnings to qualify for MA.

A woman can choose to start receiving MA from the 11th week before the week in which the baby is due (if she stops work before then) up to the day following the day of birth. The exact date MA starts will depend on when the woman stops work to have her baby or if the baby is born before she stops work. However, where the woman is absent from work wholly or partly due to her pregnancy in the four weeks before the week the baby is due to be born, MA will start the day following the first day of absence from work. MA is paid for a maximum of 39 weeks.

For more information *see* leaflet NI17A *A Guide to Maternity Benefits* available on the Department for Work and Pensions website (W www.dwp.gov.uk/advisers/ni17a/).

Weekly Rates from April 2008

Standard rate	£117.18 or 90 per cent of the women's average weekly earnings if less than £117.18
Increase for adult dependant	£39.40

CHILD BENEFIT

Child benefit is payable for virtually all children aged under 16 and for those aged 16 and 17 if they are in relevant education or training or are registered for work, education or training with an approved body.

Weekly Rates from April 2008

Eldest/only child	£18.80
Each subsequent child	£12.55

GUARDIAN'S ALLOWANCE

Guardian's allowance is payable to a person who is bringing up a child or young person because the child's parents have died, or in some circumstances, where only one parent has died. To receive the allowance the person must be in receipt of child benefit for the child or young person, although they do not have to be the child's legal guardian.

Weekly Rate from April 2008

Each child	£13.45

CARER'S ALLOWANCE

Carer's allowance (CA) is a benefit payable to people who spend at least 35 hours per week caring for a severely disabled person. To qualify for CA a person must be caring for someone in receipt of one of the following benefits:

- the middle or highest rate of disability living allowance care component
- either rate of attendance allowance
- constant attendance allowance, paid at not less than the normal maximum rate or basic (full-day) rate, under the industrial injuries or war pension schemes

See leaflet CAA5DCS.

Weekly Rates from April 2008

Carer's allowance	£50.55
Increase for dependent adult	£30.20

SEVERE DISABLEMENT ALLOWANCE

Since April 2001 severe disablement allowance (SDA) has not been available to new claimants. Those claiming SDA before that date will continue to receive it for as long as they qualify.

Weekly Rates from April 2008

Basic rate	£51.05
Age related addition*:	
Under 40	£17.75
40–49	£11.40
50–59	£5.70

* The age addition applies to the age when incapacity began

ATTENDANCE ALLOWANCE

This may be payable to disabled people who claim after the age of 65 and who need a lot of care or supervision because of physical or mental disability, and who have needed help for a period of at least six months. Attendance allowance has two rates: the lower rate is for day or night care, and the higher rate is for day and night care. People not expected to live for more than six months because of a progressive disease can receive the highest rate of attendance allowance straight away. *See* leaflet *Attendance Allowance.*

Weekly Rates from April 2008

Higher rate	£67.00
Lower rate	£44.85

DISABILITY LIVING ALLOWANCE

This may be payable to disabled people who claim before the age of 65 who have personal care and/or mobility needs because of an illness or disability for a period of at least three months and are likely to have those needs for a further six months or more. The allowance has two components: the care component, which has three rates, and the mobility component, which has two rates. The rates depend on the care and mobility needs of the claimant. People not expected to live for more than six months because of a progressive disease will automatically receive the highest rate of the care component. *See* leaflets *Disability Living Allowance* and *Disability Living Allowance for Children.*

Weekly Rates from April 2008

Care component	
Higher rate	£67.00
Middle rate	£44.85
Lowest rate	£17.75
Mobility component	
Higher rate	£46.75
Lower rate	£17.75

STATE PENSION: CATEGORY D

Category D pension is provided for people aged 80 and over if they are not entitled to another category of pension or are entitled to a state pension that is less than the category D rate. The person must also normally live in Great Britain and have done so for a continuous period of ten years within any 20-year period since their 60th birthday.

Weekly Rates from April 2008

Single person	£54.35
Age addition to State Pension at age 80	£0.25

INCOME SUPPORT

Income support is a benefit for those aged 16 and over whose income is below a certain level. It can be paid to people who are not expected to sign on as unemployed (income support for unemployed people was replaced by jobseeker's allowance in October 1996) and who are:

- incapable of work due to sickness or disability
- bringing up children alone
- looking after a person who has a disability
- registered blind

Pension credit replaced income support for people aged 60 or over on 6 October 2003. Some people who are not in the above categories may also be able to claim income support.

Income support is also payable to people who work fewer than 16 hours a week on average (or 24 hours for a partner). Some people can claim income support if they work longer hours.

Income support is not payable if the claimant, or claimant and partner, have capital or savings in excess of £16,000. For capital and savings in excess of £6,000, a deduction of £1 a week is made for every £250 or part of £250 held. Different limits apply to people permanently in residential care and nursing homes: the upper limit is £16,000 and deductions apply for capital in excess of £10,000.

Sums payable depend on fixed allowances laid down by law for people in different circumstances. If both partners are eligible for income support, either may claim it for the couple. People receiving income support may be able to receive housing benefit, help with mortgage or home loan interest and help with healthcare. They may also be eligible for help with exceptional expenses from the Social Fund. Special rates may apply to some people living in residential care or nursing homes. Leaflet IS20 (only available online) gives a detailed explanation of income support.

In October 1998 the government's voluntary *New Deal for Lone Parents* programme became available throughout the UK. All lone parents receiving income support are assigned a personal adviser at a Jobcentre who will provide guidance and support with a view to enabling the claimant to find work.

INCOME SUPPORT PREMIUMS

Income support premiums are additional weekly payments for those with special needs. People qualifying for more than one premium will normally only receive the highest single premium for which they qualify. However, family premium, disabled child premium, severe disability premium and carer premium are payable in addition to other premiums.

People with children may qualify for:

- the family premium if they have at least one child (a higher rate is paid to lone parents whose claim was made prior to 6 April 1998)
- the disabled child premium if they have a child who receives disability living allowance or is registered blind

Carers may qualify for:

- the carer premium if they or their partner are in receipt of carer's allowance

Long-term sick or disabled people may qualify for:

- the disability premium if they or their partner are receiving certain benefits because they are disabled or cannot work; are registered blind; or if the claimant has been incapable of work or receiving statutory sick pay for at least 364 days (196 days if the person is terminally ill), including periods of incapacity separated by eight weeks or less
- the severe disability premium if the person lives alone and receives attendance allowance or the middle or higher rate of disability living allowance care component and no one receives carer's allowance for caring for that person. This premium is also available to couples where both partners meet the above conditions

WEEKLY RATES OF INCOME SUPPORT
from April 2008

Single person	
under 18	£47.95
aged 18–24	£47.95
aged 25 and over	£60.50
aged under 18 and a single parent	£47.95
aged 18 and over and a single parent	£60.15
Couples	
Both under 18	£47.95
Both under 18 with responsibility for a child	£72.35
One under 18, one aged 18-24	£47.95
One under 18, one aged 25+	£60.50
Both aged 18+	£94.95
Dependent children	£52.59
Premiums	
Family premium	£16.75
Family (lone parent) premium	£16.75
Disabled child premium	£48.72
Carer premium	£27.75
Disability premium	
Single person	£25.85
Couples	£36.85
Enhanced disability premium	
Single person	£12.60
Couples	£18.15
Enhanced disabled child premium	£19.60
Severe disability premium	
Lower rate (single person and some couples)	£50.35
Higher rate (couples)	£100.70

PENSION CREDIT

Pension credit was introduced on 6 October 2003 and replaced income support for those aged 60 and over.

There are two elements to pension credit:

THE GUARANTEE CREDIT

The guarantee credit provides a guaranteed minimum income, with additional elements for people who have:

- eligible housing costs
- severe disabilities
- caring responsibilities

Income from state pension, private pensions, earnings and certain benefits are taken into account when calculating the guarantee credit. For savings and capital in excess of £6,000 (£10,000 for people living in residential care and nursing homes); £1 for every £500 or part of £500 held is taken into account as income when working out entitlement to pension credit.

People receiving the guarantee credit element of pension credit will be able to receive housing benefit, council tax benefit and help with healthcare costs.

THE SAVINGS CREDIT

Single people aged 65 or over (and couples where one member is 65 or over) may be entitled to a savings credit which will reward pensioners who have made modest provision towards their retirement. The savings credit is calculated by taking into account any qualifying income above the savings credit threshold. For 2008–9 the threshold is £91.20 for single people and £145.80 for couples. The savings credit gives pensioners a cash addition calculated at 60p for every pound of qualifying income they have between the savings credit threshold and the guarantee credit. After this, the maximum reward will be reduced by 40p for every pound of income above the guarantee level. The maximum savings credit is £19.71 per week (£26.13 a week for couples).

Income that qualifies towards the savings credit includes state pensions, earnings, second pensions and capital above £6,000.

Some people will be entitled to the guarantee credit, some to the savings credit and some to both.

Where only the savings credit is in payment, people need to claim standard housing benefit or council tax benefit. Although local authorities take any savings credit into account in the housing benefit or council tax benefit assessment, for people aged 65 and over housing benefit or council tax benefit is enhanced to ensure that gains in pension credit are not depleted.

WEEKLY RATES OF PENSION CREDIT
from April 2008

Standard minimum guarantee	
Single	£124.05
Couple	£189.35
Additional amount for severe disability	
Single	£50.35
Couple (one qualifies)	£50.35
Couple (both qualify)	£100.70
Additional amount for carers	£27.75

HOUSING BENEFIT
Housing benefit is designed to help people with rent (including rent for accommodation in guesthouses, lodgings or hostels). It does not cover mortgage payments. The amount of benefit paid depends on:

- the income of the claimant, and partner if there is one, including earned income, unearned income (any other income including some other benefits) and savings
- number of dependants
- certain extra needs of the claimant, partner or any dependants
- number and gross income of people sharing the home who are not dependent on the claimant
- how much rent is paid

Housing benefit is not payable if the claimant, or claimant and partner, have savings in excess of £16,000. The amount of benefit is affected if savings held exceed £6,000 (£10,000 for people living in residential care and nursing homes). Housing benefit is not paid for meals, fuel or certain service charges that may be included in the rent. Deductions are also made for most non-dependants who live in the same accommodation as the claimant (and their partner).

The maximum amount of benefit (which is not necessarily the same as the amount of rent paid) may be paid where the claimant is in receipt of income support, income-based jobseeker's allowance, the guarantee element of pension credit or where the claimant's income is less than the amount allowed for their needs. Any income over that allowed for their needs will mean that their benefit is reduced. *See* leaflets HBA5DWP and RR2 (only available online).

LOCAL HOUSING ALLOWANCE
Local housing allowance (LHA), which was rolled out nationally from 7 April 2008, is a new way of calculating the rent element of housing benefit based on the area in which a customer lives and household size. It affects customers in the deregulated private rented sector who make a new claim for housing benefit or existing customers who move address. LHA ensures that tenants in similar circumstances in the same area receive the same amount of financial support for their housing costs. It does not affect the way a customer's income or capital is taken into account. LHA is paid to the tenant rather than the landlord in most circumstances and tenants are able to keep any excess benefit up to a maximum of £15 per week that is over and above the cost of their rent. If their rent is higher than their LHA entitlement they must make up the difference from other sources of income.

COUNCIL TAX BENEFIT
Nearly all the rules which apply to housing benefit apply to council tax benefit, which helps people on low incomes to pay council tax bills. The amount payable depends on how much council tax is paid and who lives with the claimant. The benefit may be available to those receiving income support, income-based jobseeker's allowance, the guarantee element of pension credit or to those whose income is less than that allowed for their needs. Any income over that allowed for their needs will mean that their council tax benefit is reduced. Deductions are made for non-dependants.

The maximum amount that is payable for those living in properties in council tax bands A to E is 100 per cent of the claimant's council tax liability. This also applies to those living in properties in bands F to H who were in receipt of the benefit at 31 March 1998 if they have remained in the same property.

If a person shares a home with one or more adults (not their partner) who are on a low income, it may be possible to claim a second adult rebate. Those who are entitled to both council tax benefit and second adult rebate will be awarded whichever is the greater. Second adult rebate may be claimed by those not in receipt of or eligible for council tax benefit.

THE SOCIAL FUND

REGULATED PAYMENTS
Sure Start Maternity Grant
Sure start maternity grant (SSMG) is a one-off payment of £500 to help people on low incomes pay for essential items for new babies that are expected, born, adopted, the subject of a parental order (following a surrogate birth) or, in certain circumstances, the subject of a residency order. SSMG can be claimed any time from the 29th week of pregnancy up to three months after the birth, adoption or date of parental or residency order. Those eligible are people in receipt of income support, income-based jobseeker's allowance, pension credit, child tax credit at a rate higher than the family element or working tax credit where a disability or severe disability element is in payment.

Funeral Payments
Payable to help cover the necessary cost of burial or cremation, a new burial plot with an exclusive right of burial (where burial is chosen), certain other expenses, and up to £700 for any other funeral expenses, such as the funeral director's fees, the coffin or flowers. Those eligible are people receiving income support, income-based jobseeker's allowance, pension credit, child tax credit at a higher rate than the family element, working tax credit where a disability or severe disability element is in payment, council tax benefit or housing benefit who have good reason for taking responsibility for the funeral expenses. These payments are recoverable from any estate of the deceased.

Cold Weather Payments
A payment of £8.50 when the average temperature is recorded at or forecast to be 0°C or below over seven consecutive days in the qualifying person's area. Payments are made to people on pension credit, income support and those on income-based jobseeker's allowance who have a child who is disabled or under the age of five, or whose benefit includes a pensioner or disability premium. Payments are made automatically and do not have to be repaid.

Winter Fuel Payments
For winter 2008–9 the winter fuel payment is £250 for households with someone aged 60–79 and £400 for households with someone aged 80 or over. The majority

of eligible people are paid automatically before Christmas, although a few need to claim. Payments do not have to be repaid.

DISCRETIONARY PAYMENTS

Community Care Grants

These are intended to help people on income support, income-based jobseeker's allowance, in receipt of pension credit, or receiving payments on account of such benefits (or those likely to receive these benefits on leaving residential or institutional accommodation) to live as independently as possible in the community; ease exceptional pressures on families; care for a prisoner or young offender released on temporary licence; help people set up home as part of a resettlement programme and/or assist with certain travelling expenses. They do not have to be repaid.

Budgeting Loans

These are interest-free loans to people who have been receiving income support, income-based jobseeker's allowance, pension credit or payments on account of such benefits for at least 26 weeks, for intermittent expenses that may be difficult to budget for.

Crisis Loans

These are interest-free loans to anyone, whether receiving benefits or not, who is without resources in an emergency or due to a disaster, where there is no other means of preventing serious damage or serious risk to their or their family members' health or safety.

SAVINGS

Savings over £500 (£1,000 for people aged 60 or over) are taken into account for community care grants and savings of £1,000 (£2,000 for people aged 60 or over) are taken into account for budgeting loans. All savings are taken into account for crisis loans. Savings are not taken into account for sure start maternity grant, funeral payments, cold weather or winter fuel payments.

INDUSTRIAL INJURIES AND DISABLEMENT BENEFITS

The Industrial Injuries Scheme, administered under the Social Security Contributions and Benefits Act 1992, provides a range of benefits designed to compensate for disablement resulting from an industrial accident (ie an accident arising out of and in the course of an earner's employment) or from a prescribed disease due to the nature of a person's employment. Those who are self-employed are not covered by this scheme.

INDUSTRIAL INJURIES DISABLEMENT BENEFIT

A person must be at least 14 per cent disabled (except for certain respiratory diseases) and 20 per cent for occupational deafness in order to qualify for this benefit. The amount paid depends on the degree of disablement:

- those assessed as 14–19 per cent disabled are paid at the 20 per cent rate
- those with disablement of over 20 per cent will have the percentage rounded up or down to the nearest 10 per cent, eg a disablement of 44 per cent will be paid at the 40 per cent rate while a disablement of 45 per cent will be paid at the 50 per cent rate

Except for certain respiratory diseases which are paid immediately, benefit is payable 15 weeks (90 days) after the date of the accident or onset of the disease (subject to backdating limits) and may be payable for a limited period or for life. The benefit is payable whether the person works or not and those who are incapable of work are entitled to draw statutory sick pay or incapacity benefit in addition to industrial injuries disablement benefit. It may also be possible to claim the following allowances:

- reduced earnings allowance for those who are unable to return to their regular work or work of the same standard and who had their accident (or whose disease started) before 1 October 1990. At state pension age this is converted to retirement allowance
- constant attendance allowance for those with a disablement of 100 per cent who need constant care. There are four rates of allowance depending on how much care the person needs
- exceptionally severe disablement allowance for those who are entitled to constant care attendance allowance at one of the higher rates and who need constant care permanently

See leaflet DWP 1004.

*Weekly Rates of Benefit from April 2008**

Degree of disablement:	
100 per cent	£136.80
90	£123.12
80	£109.44
70	£95.76
60	£82.08
50	£68.40
40	£54.72
30	£41.04
20	£27.36
Unemployability supplement	£84.50
Addition for adult dependant (subject to earnings rule)	£48.65
Reduced earnings allowance (maximum)	£54.72
Retirement allowance (maximum)	£13.68
Constant attendance allowance (normal maximum rate)	£54.80
Exceptionally severe disablement allowance	£54.80

* There is a weekly benefit for those under 18 with no dependants which is set at a lower rate

OTHER BENEFITS

People who are disabled because of an accident or disease that was the result of work that they did before 5 July 1948 are not entitled to industrial injuries disablement benefit. They may, however, be entitled to payment under the Workmen's Compensation Scheme or the Pneumoconiosis, Byssinosis and Miscellaneous Diseases Benefit Scheme. *See* leaflet GL23. People who suffer from certain industrial diseases caused by dust, or their dependants, can make a claim for an additional payment under the Pneumoconiosis etc (Workers' Compensation) Act 1979 if they are unable to get damages from the employer who caused or contributed to the disease.

Diffuse Mesothelioma

It is the government's intention to extend the coverage of compensation to sufferers of Diffuse Mesothelioma who have been exposed to asbestos in the UK but are unable to claim compensation from other sources. The scheme will offer a single lump sum payment to the sufferer, based on the sufferer's age. The government aims to introduce the scheme by the end of 2008.

CLAIMS AND QUESTIONS

Entitlement to benefit and regulated Social Fund payments is determined by a decision maker on behalf of the Secretary of State for the Department for Work and Pensions. A claimant who is dissatisfied with that decision can ask for an explanation. He or she can dispute the decision by applying to have it revised or, in particular circumstances, superseded. The claimant can go to the Appeals Service where the case will be heard by an independent tribunal. There is a further right of appeal to a social security commissioner against the tribunal's decision but this is on a point of law only and leave to appeal must first be obtained.

Decisions on claims and applications for housing benefit and council tax benefit are made by local authorities. The explanation, dispute and appeals process is the same as for other benefits. *See* leaflets GL24DWP and NI260DMA.

All decisions on applications to the discretionary Social Fund are made by Jobcentre Plus Social Fund decision makers. Applicants can ask for a review of the decision within 28 days of the date on the decision letter. The Social Fund review officer will review the case and there is a further right of review by an independent Social Fund inspector.

EMPLOYER PAYMENTS

STATUTORY MATERNITY PAY

Employers pay statutory maternity pay (SMP) to pregnant women who have been employed by them full or part-time continuously for at least 26 weeks into the 15th week before the week the baby is due, and whose earnings on average at least equal the lower earnings limit applied to NI contributions (£90 per week from April 2008). SMP can be paid for a maximum period of up to 39 weeks. If the qualifying conditions are met women will receive a payment of 90 per cent of their average earnings for the first six weeks, followed by 33 weeks at £117.18 or 90 per cent of the woman's average weekly earnings if this is less than £117.18. SMP can be paid, at the earliest, 11 weeks before the week in which the baby is due, up to the day following the birth. Women can decide when they wish their maternity leave and pay to start and can work until the baby is born. However, where the woman is absent from work wholly or partly due to her pregnancy in the four weeks before the week the baby is due to be born, SMP will start the day following the first day of absence from work.

Employers are reimbursed for 92 per cent of the SMP they pay. Small employers with annual gross NI payments of £45,000 or less recover 100 per cent of the SMP paid out plus 4.5 per cent in compensation for the secondary NI contributions paid on SMP.

For more information *see* leaflet NI7A *A Guide to Maternity Benefits* available on the Department for Work and Pensions website (W www.dwp.gov.uk/advisers/ni17a/).

STATUTORY PATERNITY PAY

Employers pay statutory paternity pay (SPP) to employees who are taking leave when a child is born or placed for adoption. To qualify the employee must:

- have responsibility for the child's upbringing
- be the biological father of the child (or the child's adopter), or the spouse/civil partner/partner of the mother or adopter
- be taking time off work to care for the child and/or support the mother or adopter
- have been employed by the same employer for at least 26 weeks ending with the 15th week before the baby is due (or the week in which the adopter is notified of having been matched with a child)
- continue working for the employer up to the child's birth (or placement for adoption)
- have earnings on average at least equal to the lower earnings limit applied to NI contributions (£90 per week from April 2008)

Employees who meet these conditions receive payment of £117.18 or 90 per cent of the employee's average weekly earnings if this is less than £117.18. The employee can choose to be paid for one or two consecutive weeks. The earliest the SPP period can begin is the date of the child's birth or placement for adoption. The SPP period must be completed within eight weeks of that date. SPP is not payable for any week in which the employee works. Employers are reimbursed in the same way as for statutory maternity pay. More information is available online at
(W www.direct.gov.uk/workandparents
W www.businesslink.gov.uk/employingpeople).

STATUTORY ADOPTION PAY

Employers pay statutory adoption pay (SAP) to employees taking adoption leave from their employers. To qualify for SAP the employee must:

- be newly matched with a child by an adoption agency
- have been employed by the same employer for at least 26 weeks ending the week in which they have been notified of being matched with a child
- have earnings at least equal to the lower earnings limit applied to NI contributions (£90 per week from April 2008)

Employees who meet these conditions receive payment of £117.18 or 90 per cent of their average weekly earnings if this is less than £117.18 for up to 39 weeks. The earliest SAP can be paid from is two weeks before the expected date of placement, the latest it can start is the date of the child's placement. Where a couple adopt a child, only one of them may receive SAP, the other may be able to receive statutory paternity pay (SPP) if they meet the eligibility criteria. Employers are reimbursed in the same way as for statutory maternity pay. More information is available online at
(W www.direct.gov.uk/workandparents
W www.businesslink.gov.uk/employingpeople).

STATUTORY SICK PAY

Employers pay statutory sick pay (SSP) for up to a maximum of 28 weeks to any employee incapable of work for four or more consecutive days. Employees must have done some work under their contract of service and have average weekly earnings, in a specified period, at or above the point at which earnings become relevant for NI purposes (£90 from April 2008). SSP is a daily payment and is usually paid for the days that an employee would normally work, these days are known a qualifying days. SSP is not paid for the first three qualifying days in a period of sickness. SSP is paid at £75.40 per week and is subject to PAYE and NI contributions. Employees who cannot obtain SSP may be able to claim incapacity benefit. Employers may be able to recover some SSP costs. More information is available online at
W www.direct.gov.uk.

THE WATER INDUSTRY

Water services in England and Wales are provided by private companies. In Scotland there is a single authority, Scottish Water, that is answerable to the Scottish government, and in Northern Ireland all services are provided by the Water Service, which remains in the public sector as an executive agency within Northern Ireland's Department for Regional Development. In the UK the water industry provides services to over 20 million properties and has an annual turnover of £7bn. It also manages assets that include over 2,500 water and 9,000 sewerage treatment plants, 1,000 reservoirs and over 700,000km of water mains and sewers.

ENGLAND AND WALES

The water industry supplies around 18,000 million litres of water every day. In 2002 water companies in England and Wales carried out around 2.9 million tests on drinking water samples, of which 99.87 per cent met all British and European standards. In England and Wales the Secretary of State for Environment, Food and Rural Affairs and the National Assembly for Wales have overall responsibility for water policy and oversee environmental standards for the water industry.

Water UK is the industry association that represents all UK water and wastewater service suppliers at national and European level and is funded directly by its members who are the service suppliers for England, Scotland, Wales and Northern Ireland; every member has a seat on the Water UK Council.

WATER UK, 1 Queen Anne's Gate, London SW1H 9BT T 020-7344 1844 W www.water.org.uk
Chief Executive, Pamela Taylor

WATER SERVICE COMPANIES
(members of Water UK)

ANGLIAN WATER SERVICES LTD, Customer Services, PO Box 770, Lincoln LN5 7WX T 08457-145145 W www.anglianwater.co.uk

BOURNEMOUTH & WEST HAMPSHIRE WATER PLC, George Jessel House, Francis Avenue, Bournemouth, Dorset BH11 8NX T 01202-590059 W www.bwhwater.co.uk

BRISTOL WATER PLC, PO Box 218, Bridgwater Road, Bristol BS99 7AU T 0117-966 5881 W www.bristolwater.co.uk

CAMBRIDGE WATER PLC, 90 Fulbourn Road, Cambridge CB1 9JN T 01223-706050 W www.cambridge-water.co.uk

CHOLDERTON & DISTRICT WATER COMPANY, Estate Office, Cholderton, Salisbury, Wiltshire SP4 0DR T 01980-629203 W www.choldertonwater.co.uk

DEE VALLEY WATER PLC, Packsaddle, Wrexham Road, Rhostyllen, Wrexham LL14 4EH T 01978-846946 W www.deevalleygroup.com

DWR CYMRU (WELSH WATER), Pentwyn Road, Nelson, Treharris, Mid Glamorgan CF46 6LY T 0800-052 0145 W www.dwrcymru.co.uk

ESSEX & SUFFOLK WATER PLC (subsidiary of Northumbrian Water Ltd), Hall Street, Chelmsford, Essex CM2 0HH T 0845-782 0999 W www.eswater.co.uk

FOLKESTONE & DOVER WATER SERVICES LTD, Cherry Garden Lane, Folkestone, Kent CT19 4QB T 0845-888 5888 W www.fdws.co.uk

NORTHUMBRIAN WATER LTD, Abbey Road, Pity Me, Durham DH1 5FJ T 0870-608 4820 W www.nwl.co.uk

PORTSMOUTH WATER PLC, PO Box 8, West Street, Havant, Hampshire PO9 1LG T 023-9249 9888 W www.portsmouthwater.co.uk

SEVERN TRENT PLC, 2297 Coventry Road, Birmingham B26 3PU T 0121-722 4000 W www.severntrent.com

SOUTH EAST WATER LTD, Rocfort Road, Snodland, Kent ME6 5AH T 0845-301 0845 W www.southeastwater.co.uk

SOUTH STAFFORDSHIRE WATER PLC, PO Box 63, Walsall WS2 7PJ T 0845-607 0456 W www.south-staffs-water.co.uk

SOUTH WEST WATER LTD, Peninsula House, Rydon Lane, Exeter EX2 7HS T 0800-169 1144 W www.swwater.co.uk

SOUTHERN WATER, Southern House, Yeoman Road, Worthing, W. Sussex BN13 3NX T 0845-278 0845 W www.southernwater.co.uk

SUTTON AND EAST SURREY WATER PLC, London Road, Redhill, Surrey RH1 1LJ T 01737-772000 W www.waterplc.com

TENDRING HUNDRED WATER SERVICES LTD, Mill Hill, Manningtree, Essex CO11 2AZ T 01206-399333 W www.thws.co.uk

THAMES WATER UTILITIES LTD, PO Box 436, Swindon SN38 ITU T 0845-920 800 W www.thameswater.com

THREE VALLEYS WATER PLC, PO Box 48, Bishops Rise, Hatfield, Hertfordshire AL10 9HL T 01707-268111 W www.3valleys.co.uk

UNITED UTILITIES WATER PLC, Haweswater House, Lingley Mere Business Park, Lingley Green Avenue, Great Sankey, Warrington WA5 3LP T 01925-237000 W www.unitedutilities.com

WESSEX WATER SERVICES LTD, Claverton Down Road, Bath BA2 7WW T 01225-526000 W wessexwater.co.uk

YORKSHIRE WATER SERVICES LTD, PO Box 52, Bradford BD3 7YD T 0845-124 2424 W www.yorkshirewater.com

ISLAND WATER AUTHORITIES
(not members of Water UK)

COUNCIL OF THE ISLES OF SCILLY, Town Hall, St Mary's, Isles of Scilly TR21 0LW T 01720-422537 W www.scilly.gov.uk

ISLE OF MAN WATER AUTHORITY, Tromode Road, Douglas, Isle of Man IM2 5PA T 01624-695949 W www.gov.im/water

JERSEY WATER, PO Box 69, Mulcaster House, Westmount Road, St. Helier, Jersey JE4 9PN T 01534-707300 W www.jerseywater.je

STATES OF GUERNSEY WATER BOARD, PO Box 30, South Esplanade, St Peter Port, Guernsey GY1 3AS T 01481-724552 W www.gov.gg

WATER SUPPLY AND CONSUMPTION 2006–7

	Supply		*Consumption*			
	Supply from Treatment Works (megalitres/day)	*Total Leakage (megalitres/day)*	*Household (litres/head/day) Unmetered*	*Household (litres/head/day) Metered*	*Non-household (litres/property/day) Unmetered*	*Non-household (litres/property/day) Metered*
WATER AND SEWERAGE COMPANIES						
Anglian	1,156	202	156	137	207	2,929
Dwr Cymru	860	210	157	127	456	2,228
Northumbrian	716	146	151	140	810	3,431
Severn Trent	1,953	524	146	117	853	2,154
South West	447	83	164	139	1,120	1,560
Southern	552	82	149	136	681	2,467
Thames	2,643	790	157	143	877	3,024
United Utilities	1,898	468	144	122	750	2,687
Wessex	363	72	154	138	3,220	2,146
Yorkshire	1,285	294	152	136	133	2,727
Total	11,871	2,871	—	—	—	—
Average	—	—	153	133	911	2,535
WATER ONLY COMPANIES						
Total	3,123	548	—	—	—	—
Average	—	—	158	133	753	2,512

Source: OFWAT

REGULATORY BODIES

The Water Services Regulation Authority (OFWAT) was established under the Water Industry Act 1991 and is the independent economic regulator of the water and sewerage companies in England and Wales. Overall responsibility for water policy and overseeing environmental standards for the water industry lies with DEFRA and the Welsh Assembly. OFWAT's main duties are to ensure that the companies can finance and carry out their statutory functions and to protect the interests of water customers. OFWAT is a non-ministerial government department headed by a board following a change in legislation introduced by the Water Act 2003.

Under the Competition Act 1998, from 1 March 2000 the Competition Appeal Tribunal has heard appeals against the regulator's decisions regarding anti-competitive agreements and abuse of a dominant position in the marketplace. The Water Act 2003 placed a new duty on OFWAT to contribute to the achievement of sustainable development.

The Environment Agency was set up by the Environment Act 1995 as a non-departmental public body and is sponsored largely by DEFRA and the Welsh Assembly. The Environment Agency has statutory duties and powers in relation to water resources, pollution control, flood defence, fisheries, recreation, conservation and navigation in England and Wales. They are also responsible for issuing permits, licences, consents and registrations such as industrial licences to extract water and fishing licences.

The Drinking Water Inspectorate (DWI) is the drinking water quality regulator for England and Wales, responsible for assessing the quality of the drinking water supplied by the water companies and investigating any incidents affecting drinking water quality, initiating prosecution where necessary. The DWI also provides scientific advice on drinking water policy issues to DEFRA and the Welsh Assembly.

OFWAT, Centre City Tower, 7 Hill Street, Birmingham B5 4UA
T 0121-625 1300 E enquiries@ofwat.gsi.gov.uk
W www.ofwat.gov.uk
Chairman, Philip Fletcher
Chief Executive, Regina Finn

METHODS OF CHARGING

In England and Wales, most domestic customers still pay for domestic water supply and sewerage services through charges based on the rateable value of their property. Overall, companies expect about 35 per cent of household customers in England and Wales to have metered supplies in 2008–9. Industrial and most commercial customers are charged according to consumption.

Under the Water Industry Act 1999, water companies can continue basing their charges on the old rateable value of property. Domestic customers can continue paying on an unmeasured basis unless they choose to pay according to consumption. After having a meter installed (which is free of charge), a customer can revert to unmeasured charging within 12 months. Domestic, school and hospital customers cannot be disconnected for non-payment.

Price limits for the period 2005–10 were set by OFWAT in December 2004.

The average increase in prices for 2008–9 is 5.8 per cent, which includes inflation of 4.3 per cent. Average bills for water services range from £90 for Portsmouth Water to £204 for South West Water, with an overall average of £157. The average sewerage bill costs £174, ranging from £115 for Thames water up to £293 for South West Water.

SCOTLAND

Overall responsibility for national water policy in Scotland rests with the Scottish ministers. Until the Local Government (Scotland) Act 1994, water supply and sewerage services were local authority responsibilities. The Central Scotland Water Development Board had the function of developing new sources of water supply for the purpose of providing water in bulk to water authorities whose limits of supply were within the board's area. Under the act, three new public water authorities, covering the north, east and west of Scotland respectively, took over the provision of water and sewerage services from April 1996. The Central Scotland Water Development Board was then abolished. The act also established the Scottish Water and Sewerage Customers Council representing consumer interests. It monitored the performance of the authorities; approved charges schemes; investigated complaints; and advised the secretary of state. The Water Industry Act 1999, whose Scottish provisions were accepted by the Scottish government, abolished the Scottish Water and Sewerage Customers Council and replaced it in November 1999 with a Water Industry Commissioner.

The Water Industry (Scotland) Act 2002 resulted from the Scottish government's proposal that a single authority was better placed than three separate authorities to harmonise changes across the Scottish water industry. In 2002 the three existing water authorities (East of Scotland Water, North of Scotland Water and West of Scotland Water) merged to form Scottish Water. Scottish Water is a public sector company, structured and managed like a private company, but remains answerable to the Scottish parliament. Scottish Water is regulated by the Water Industry Commissioner for Scotland, the Scottish Environment Protection Agency (SEPA), and the Drinking Water Quality Regulator for Scotland. The Water Industry Commissioner is responsible for regulating all aspects of economic and customer service performance, including water and sewerage charges. SEPA is responsible for environmental issues, including controlling pollution and promoting the cleanliness of Scotland's rivers, lochs and coastal waters.

METHODS OF CHARGING

Scottish Water sets charges for domestic and non-domestic water and sewerage provision through charges schemes which are regulated by the Water Industries Commissioner for Scotland. In February 2004 the harmonisation of all household charges across the country was completed following the merger of the separate authorities under Scottish Water.

SCOTTISH WATER, PO Box 8855, Edinburgh EH10 6YQ
T 0845-601 8855 W www.scottishwater.co.uk

SCOTTISH ENVIRONMENT PROTECTION AGENCY, Erskine Court, Castle Business Park, Stirling FK9 4TR T 01786-457700 W www.sepa.org.uk

WATER INDUSTRY COMMISSIONER FOR SCOTLAND, Ochil House, Springkerse Business Park, Stirling FK7 7XE T 01786-430200
W www.watercommissioner.co.uk

NORTHERN IRELAND

In Northern Ireland ministerial responsibility for water services lies with the minister of the Department for Regional Development. The Water Service, which is an executive agency of the Department for Regional Development, is responsible for policy and coordination with regard to supply, distribution and cleanliness of water, and the provision and maintenance of sewerage services.

The Water Service comprises four divisions: Eastern, Northern, Western and Southern. The main divisional offices are based in Belfast, Ballymena, Londonderry and Craigavon.

METHODS OF CHARGING

The Water Service is currently funded from public funds and direct charges. The department's policy is to meter all properties that are not exclusively domestic. They are, however, granted an allowance of 200 cubic metres per annum to reflect domestic usage, known as the domestic usage allowance. Customers are charged only for water used in excess of this allowance together with a standing charge, which is intended to cover the costs of meter provision, maintenance, reading and billing. This allowance is not granted if rates are not paid on the property. Traders operating from de-rated, rate exempt or rate rebated premises are required to pay for the treatment and disposal of trade effluent which they discharge into the public sewer. From April 2008, sewerage charges were introduced for all non-domestic customers in Northern Ireland connected to the public sewers.

Water and sewerage services in Northern Ireland became self-financed in 2006. Under new legislation domestic customers are charged directly for water and sewerage services, currently a proportion of the rates paid on domestic properties. Following a public consultation document *The Reform of the Water and Sewerage Services In Northern Ireland* the initial conclusion from the Department for Regional Development was that the new domestic charge would include a fixed element and a variable element, the latter determined by property value or consumption.

NORTHERN IRELAND WATER SERVICE, PO Box 126, Belfast BT1 9DJ T 08457-440088 W www.waterni.gov.uk

ENERGY

The main primary sources of energy in Britain are oil, natural gas, coal, nuclear power and water power. The main secondary sources (ie sources derived from the primary sources) are electricity, coke and smokeless fuels and petroleum products. The Department for Environment, Food and Rural Affairs (DEFRA) is responsible for promoting energy efficiency.

INDIGENOUS PRODUCTION OF PRIMARY FUELS
Million tonnes of oil equivalent

	2007
Coal	10.7
Primary oils	84.2
Natural gas	72.1
Primary electricity	14.9
Renewable and waste	4.0
Total	185.9

Source: Department for Business, Enterprise and Regulatory Reform

INLAND ENERGY CONSUMPTION BY PRIMARY FUEL
Million tonnes of oil equivalent, seasonally adjusted

	2007
Coal	40.8
Petroleum	75.6
Natural gas	90.0
Nuclear electricity	14.0
Hydro electricity	0.9
Net Imports	0.4
Renewables and waste	4.4
Total	226.0

Source: Department for Business, Enterprise and Regulatory Reform

TRADE IN FUELS AND RELATED MATERIALS (2007)

	Quantity, million tonnes of oil equivalent	*Value £m*
Imports		
Coal and other solid fuel	30.0	2,072
Crude petroleum	48.3	11,682
Petroleum products	40.6	12,205
Natural gas	29.1	2,883
Electricity	0.7	240
Total	148.7	29,082
Exports		
Coal and other solid fuel	0.5	65
Crude petroleum	50.1	12,299
Petroleum products	34.4	9,150
Natural gas	10.6	996
Electricity	0.3	108
Total	95.9	22,618

Source: HM Customs & Excise

OIL

Until the 1960s Britain imported almost all its oil supplies. In 1969 oil was discovered in the Arbroath field of the UK Continental Shelf (UKCS). The first oilfield to be brought into production was the Argyll field in 1975, and since the mid-1970s Britain has been a major producer of crude oil.

Licences for exploration and production are granted to companies by the Department for Business, Enterprise and Regulatory Reform; the leading British oil companies are BP and Shell. At the end of 2004, 565 seaward production licences and 101 onshore petroleum exploration and development licences had been awarded, and there were a total of 264 offshore oil and gas fields in production. The UK has nine refineries at present producing approximately 82 million tonnes of oil products a year. To date, the UK has produced around 37 billion barrels of oil equivalent (boe). It is estimated that there is 16 to 25 billion barrels remaining to be produced. Total production from the UKCS peaked in 1999 and is now declining; estimates have suggested that production could fall from today's figure of 3 million boe per day to around 1 million by 2020, although with further investment the rate of decline may be slowed. Royalties are payable on fields approved before April 1982 and petroleum revenue tax is levied on fields approved between 1975 and March 1993.

DRILLING ACTIVITY (2007)
by number of wells started

	Offshore	*Onshore*
Exploration	34	8
Appraisal	77	7
Development	166	15

Source: Department for Business, Enterprise and Regulatory Reform

INDIGENOUS PRODUCTION AND REFINERY RECEIPTS
Thousand tonnes

	2006	*2007*
Indigenous production	76,578	76,832
Crude oil	69,665	70,357
NGLs*	6,913	6,475
Refinery receipts	75,844	75,707

* Natural Gas Liquids: condensates and petroleum gases derived at onshore treatment plants

Source: Department for Business, Enterprise and Regulatory Reform

DELIVERIES OF PETROLEUM PRODUCTS FOR INLAND CONSUMPTION BY ENERGY USE
Thousand tonnes

	2006	*2007*
Industry	6,348	6,218
Transport	53,457	53,571
Domestic	2,927	2,594
Other	1,399	1,376
Total	64,131	63,759

Source: Department for Business, Enterprise and Regulatory Reform

COAL

Coal has been mined in Britain for centuries and the availability of coal was crucial to the industrial revolution of the 18th and 19th centuries. Mines were in private ownership until 1947 when they were nationalised and came under the management of the National Coal Board, later the British Coal Corporation. The corporation held a monopoly on coal production until 1994 when the industry was restructured. Under the Coal Industry Act 1994, the Coal Authority was established to take over ownership of coal reserves and to issue licences to private mining companies. The Coal Authority was also given the responsibility of dealing with the physical legacy of mining, eg subsidence damage claims, and is responsible for holding and making available all existing records. It also publishes current data on the coal industry.

The mines owned by the British Coal Corporation were sold as five separate businesses in 1994 and coal production is now undertaken entirely in the private sector. Coal output was around 50 million tonnes a year in 1994 but has since declined to below 17 million tonnes. As at 31 March 2008 there were seven large and ten small underground mines as well as 31 surface mines in the UK.

The main consumer of coal in the UK is the electricity supply industry. Coal still supplies a third of the UK's electricity needs but as indigenous production has declined, imports have risen to make up the shortfall. An energy white paper, published in 2003, had four policy goals, one of which was to cut carbon dioxide emissions by 60 per cent by 2050. This recognised that for a low-carbon economy the development of cleaner coal technologies is required. In November 2005 the government announced an energy policy review and published a report in July 2006. This was the foundation for a further energy white paper published in May 2007 which set out the government's international and domestic energy strategy to meet the long-term challenges posed by climate change to ensure secure, clean and affordable energy. Coal continues to play an important role in the future generating mix, but there is a need to tackle carbon emissions through the introduction of abatement technologies and, in the long term, the introduction of carbon capture and storage (CCS).

In November 2007 the government launched a competition to support a commercial scale demonstration of the full chain of CCS on a coal-fired power station. CCS attempts to mitigate the effects of global warming by capturing the carbon dioxide emissions from power stations that burn fossil fuels, preventing the gas from being released into the atmosphere, storing it in underground geological formations. This will be one of the first projects of its kind in the world, with the aim to demonstrate the possibilities of CCS by 2014.

There are concerns, however, about the continued importance of coal in the UK's energy mix. The potential construction of Britain's first coal-fired station in 30 years at Kingsnorth in Kent has raised concern from environmental groups who questioned the government's commitment to reducing greenhouse gas emissions.

INLAND COAL USE
Thousand tonnes

	2006	*2007*
Fuel producers		
Electricity generators	57,363	52,558
Heat generation	457	456
Coke manufacture	5,929	5,933
Blast furnaces	1,121	1,242
†Other conversion industries	276	245
Final consumption		
Industry	1,704	1,759
Domestic	561	648
Public administration	20	14
Commerce	6	6
Agriculture	5	4

† Mainly recycled products
Source: Department for Business, Enterprise and Regulatory Reform

COAL PRODUCTION AND FOREIGN TRADE
Thousand tonnes

	2006	*2007*
Deep-mined	9,444	7,674
Opencast	8,635	8,866
Imports	50,529	43,365
Exports	–443	–521
Total supply	67,341*	62,866*
TOTAL	67,450	62,872

* Includes an estimate for slurry and stock change
Source: Department for Business, Enterprise and Regulatory Reform

GAS

From the late 18th century gas in Britain was produced from coal. In the 1960s town gas began to be produced from oil-based feedstocks using imported oil. In 1965 gas was discovered in the North Sea in the West Sole field, which became the first gasfield in production in 1967, and from the late 1960s natural gas began to replace town gas. From October 1998 Britain was connected to the continental European gas system via a pipeline from Bacton, Norfolk to Zeebrugge, Belgium. Gas is transported through 275,000km of mains pipeline including 6,400km of high-pressure gas pipelines owned and operated in the UK by National Grid Gas plc.

The gas industry in Britain was nationalised in 1949 and operated as the Gas Council. The Gas Council was replaced by the British Gas Corporation in 1972 and the industry became more centralised. The British Gas Corporation was privatised in 1986 as British Gas plc. In 1993 the Monopolies and Mergers Commission found that British Gas' integrated business in Great Britain as a gas trader and the owner of the gas transportation system could operate against the public interest. In February 1997, British Gas demerged its trading arm to become two separate companies, BG plc and Centrica plc. BG Group, as the company is now known, is an international natural gas company whose principal business is finding and developing gas reserves and building gas markets. Its core operations are located in the UK, South America, Egypt, Trinidad and Tobago, Kazakhstan and India. Centrica runs the trading and services operations under the British Gas brand name in Great Britain. In October

2000 BG demerged its pipeline business, Transco, which became part of Lattice Group, finally merging with the National Grid Group in 2002 to become National Grid Transco plc.

In July 2005 National Grid Transco plc changed its name to National Grid plc and Transco plc became National Grid Gas plc. In the same year National Grid Gas also completed the sale of four of its eight gas distribution networks. The distribution networks transport gas at lower pressures, which eventually supply the consumers such as domestic customers. The Scotland and south-east of England networks were sold to Scotia Gas Networks. The Wales and south-west network was sold to Wales & West Utilities and the network in the north-east to Northern Gas Networks. This was the biggest change in the corporate structure of gas infrastructure since privatisation in 1986.

Competition was gradually introduced into the industrial gas market from 1986. Supply of gas to the domestic market was opened to companies other than British Gas, starting in April 1996 with a pilot project in the West Country and Wales, with the rest of the UK following soon after. Since competition was introduced in domestic retail of gas, around half of Britain's 20 million gas customers have changed their supplier.

Declines in UK indigenous gas production and increasing demand led to the UK becoming a net importer of gas once more in 2004. In 2007, imports rose by 39 per cent. Until 2004 the UK was entirely self-sufficient in terms of gas consumption, but it is estimated that by 2010 half of the total will come from elsewhere. A report from Centrica predicted that gas bills could rise by up to 60 per cent in the next few years if oil prices remain high and the UK continues to become more reliant on imports.

BG GROUP PLC, Thames Valley Park, Reading RG6 1PT
T 0118-935 3222 W www.bg-group.com
Chair, Sir Robert Wilson
Chief Executive, Frank Chapman

CENTRICA PLC, Millstream, Maidenhead Road, Windsor, Berkshire SL4 5GD T 01753-494000 W www.centrica.co.uk
Chair, Roger Carr
Chief Executive, Sam Laidlaw

NATIONAL GRID TRANSCO PLC, 1–3 Strand, London WC2N 5EH T 020-7004 3000 W www.ngtgroup.com
Chair, Sir John Parker
Deputy Group Chief Executive, Steve Holliday

UK GAS CONSUMPTION BY INDUSTRY
GWh

	2005	*2006*
Iron and steel industry	8,410	8,172
Other industries	144,615	135,594
Domestic	384,009	364,555
Public administration	50,317	48,853
Agriculture	2,261	2,013
Miscellaneous	20,156	20,079
Total gas consumption	1,092,482	1,035,101

Source: Annual Abstract of Statistics 2008 (Crown copyright)

ELECTRICITY

The first power station in Britain generating electricity for public supply began operating in 1882. In the 1930s a national transmission grid was developed and it was reconstructed and extended in the 1950s and 1960s. Power stations were operated by the Central Electricity Generating Board.

Under the Electricity Act 1989, 12 regional electricity companies, responsible for the distribution of electricity from the national grid to consumers, were formed from the former area electricity boards in England and Wales. Four companies were formed from the Central Electricity Generating Board: three generating companies (National Power plc, Nuclear Electric plc and Powergen plc) and the National Grid Company plc, which owned and operated the transmission system in England and Wales. National Power and Powergen were floated on the stock market in 1991.

National Power was demerged in October 2000 to form two separate companies: International Power plc and Innogy plc, which manages the bulk of National Power's UK assets. Nuclear Electric was split into two parts in 1996: British Energy (*see* Nuclear Energy) and Magnox Electric, which owns the magnox nuclear reactors in the public sector. Magnox was integrated into British Nuclear Fuels (BNFL) in 1998.

The National Grid Company was floated on the stock market in 1995 and formed a new holding company, National Grid Group. National Grid Group completed a merger with Lattice in 2002 to form National Grid Transco, a public limited company. National Grid Transco has since undergone a series of name changes (*see* Gas).

Following privatisation, generators and suppliers in England and Wales traded via the Electricity Pool. A competitive wholesale trading market known as NETA (New Electricity Trading Arrangements) replaced the Electricity Pool in March 2001, which was extended to include Scotland via the British Electricity Transmissions and Trading Arrangements (BETTA) in 2005. As part of BETTA, National Grid became the system operator for all transmission. The introduction of competition into the domestic electricity market was completed in May 1999. With the gas market also open, most suppliers now offer their customers both gas and electricity. Since competition was introduced, around half of Britain's 26 million electricity customers have switched their supplier.

In Scotland, three new companies were formed under the Electricity Act 1989: Scottish Power plc and Scottish Hydro-Electric plc, which were responsible for generation, transmission, distribution and supply; and Scottish Nuclear Ltd. Scottish Power and Scottish Hydro-Electric were floated on the stock market in 1991. Scottish Hydro-Electric merged with Southern Electric in 1998 to become Scottish and Southern Energy plc. Scottish Nuclear was incorporated into British Energy in 1996. BETTA opened the Scottish market to the same competition that had applied in England and Wales.

In Northern Ireland, Northern Ireland Electricity plc was set up in 1993 under a 1991 Order in Council. In 1993 it was floated on the stock market and in 1998 it became part of the Viridian Group and is responsible for distribution and supply.

On 30 September 2003 the Electricity Association, the industry's main trade association, was replaced with three separate trade bodies:

ASSOCIATION OF ELECTRICITY PRODUCERS, 1st Floor, 17 Waterloo Place, London SW1Y 4AR T 020-7930 9390 W www.aepuk.com
ENERGY NETWORKS ASSOCIATION, 18 Stanhope Place, London W2 2HH T 020-7706 5100 W www.energynetworks.org
ENERGY RETAIL ASSOCIATION, 4th Floor, 17 Waterloo Place, London SW1Y 4AR T 020-7930 9175 W www.energy-retail.org.uk

ELECTRICITY GENERATION, SUPPLY AND CONSUMPTION
GWh

	2005	*2006*
Electricity generated		
Conventional thermal and other*	140,399	157,382
Combined cycle gas turbine stations	130,689	118,495
Nuclear stations	81,618	75,451
Hydroelectric stations		
Natural flow	3,826	3,727
Pumped storage	2,930	3,853
Renewables other than hydro	2,746	2,750
Major power producers: total	362,212	361,657
Other generators	36,160	36,670
Electricity used on works: total	17,872	18,566
Electricity supplied (gross)		
Conventional thermal and other*	133,407	148,868
Combined cycle gas turbine stations	128,179	116,398
Nuclear stations	75,173	69,237
Hydroelectric stations		
Natural flow	3,821	3,714
Pumped storage	2,776	3,722
Renewables other than hydro	2,592	2,645
Major power producers: total	345,947	344,584
Other generators total	34,522	35,175
Electricity used in pumping	3,707	4,918
Electricity consumed		
Fuel industries	8,275	7,896
Final users total	345,542	343,464
Industrial sector	119,206	116,988
Domestic sector	116,811	116,449
Other sectors	109,525	110,027
Total	376,793	374,841

* Includes electricity supplied by gas turbines, oil engines and plants producing electricity from renewable resources other than hydro

Source: Annual Abstract of Statistics 2008 (Crown copyright)

GAS AND ELECTRICITY SUPPLIERS

With the gas and electricity markets open, most suppliers offer their customers both services. The majority of gas/electricity companies have become part of larger multi-utility companies, often operating internationally. The following list comprises a selection of suppliers offering gas and electricity. Organisations in italics are subsidiaries of the companies listed in capital letters directly above.

ENGLAND, SCOTLAND AND WALES
CE ELECTRIC UK, W www.ce-electricuk.com
Northern Electric Distribution Ltd, Manor House, Station Road, New Penshaw, Houghton-le-Spring DH4 7LA T 0845-070 7172
Yorkshire Electricity Distribution, Manor House, Station Road, New Penshaw, Houghton-le-Spring DH4 7LA T 0845-602 4454
CENTRICA PLC, Millstream, Maidenhead Road, Windsor, Berkshire SL4 5GD T 01753-494000 W www.centrica.com
British Gas/Scottish Gas, PO Box 3055, Eastbourne BN21 9FE T 0845-955 5200 W www.house.co.uk
EDF ENERGY, 40 Grosvenor Place, Victoria, London SW1X 7EN T 0800-096 9000 W www.edfenergy.com
E.ON, Westwood Way, Westwood Business Park, Coventry, CV4 8LG T 024-7642 4000 W www.eon-uk.com
NPOWER, PO Box 93, Peterlee SR8 2XX T 0800-389 2388 W www.npower.com
SCOTTISH AND SOUTHERN ENERGY PLC, Inveralmond House, 200 Dunkeld Road, Perth PH1 3AQ T 01738-456000 W www.scottish-southern.co.uk
Scottish Hydro Electric, PO Box 7506, Perth PH1 3QR T 0845-300 2141 W www.hydro.co.uk
Southern Electric, PO Box 7506, Perth PH1 3QR T 0845-744 4555 W www.southern-electric.co.uk
SWALEC, PO Box 7506, Perth PH1 3QR T 0800-052 5252 W www.swalec.co.uk
SCOTTISHPOWER, New Alderton House, Dove Wynd, Bellshill, ML4 3FF T 0845-270 6543 W www.scottishpower.co.uk

NORTHERN IRELAND
VIRIDIAN GROUP PLC, 120 Malone Road, Belfast BT9 5HT T 028-9066 8416 W www.viridiangroup.co.uk
Energia, Energia House, 62 Newforge Lane, Belfast BT9 5NF T 028-9068 5900 W www.viridianenergia.co.uk
Northern Ireland Electricity, 120 Malone Road, Belfast BT9 5HT T 08457-643643 W www.nie.co.uk

REGULATION OF THE GAS AND ELECTRICITY INDUSTRIES

The Office of the Gas and Electricity Markets (OFGEM) regulates the gas and electricity industries in Great Britain. It was formed in 1999 by the merger of the Office of Gas Supply and the Office of Electricity Regulation. OFGEM's overriding aim is to protect and promote the interests of all gas and electricity customers by promoting competition and regulating monopolies. It is governed by an authority and its powers are provided for under the Gas Act 1986, the Electricity Act 1989 and the Utilities Act 2000. Energywatch is the independent gas and electricity watchdog, set up in November 2000 through the Utility Act to protect and promote the interests of gas and electricity consumers. In October 2008 Energywatch will be merged with Postwatch and the National Consumer Council to form a new advocacy body.

THE OFFICE OF THE GAS AND ELECTRICTY MARKETS (OFGEM), 9 Millbank, London SW1 3GE T 020-7901 7000 W www.ofgem.gov.uk
ENERGYWATCH, 8th Floor, Percy House, Percy Street, Newcastle upon Tyne NE1 4PW T 0845-906 0708 W www.energywatch.org.uk

NUCLEAR POWER

Nuclear reactors began to supply electricity to the national grid in 1956; nuclear power is generated in the UK at six magnox reactors, seven advanced gas-cooled reactors (AGR) and one pressurised water reactor (PWR), Sizewell 'B' in Suffolk. In 1989 nuclear stations were withdrawn from privatisation. In 1996 Nuclear Electric Ltd and Scottish Nuclear Ltd became operating subsidiaries of British Energy and the magnox stations were transferred to Nuclear Electric which became Magnox Electric, later part of British Nuclear Fuels Ltd.

British Energy manages eight nuclear power stations (seven AGRs and one PWR) and generates around one-fifth of the UK's electricity.

In April 2005 the responsibility for the decommissioning of civil nuclear reactors and other nuclear facilities used in research and development was handed by the UK Atomic Energy Authority (UKAEA) to a new body, the Nuclear Decommissioning Authority (NDA). The NDA is a non-departmental public body, funded mainly by the Department for Business, Enterprise and Regulatory Reform. UK Nirex, which was set up by the nuclear generating companies with the agreement of the government, is responsible for the disposal of intermediate and some low-level nuclear waste. The UKAEA now operates on a private contractor basis and is currently decommissioning the nuclear power stations at Dounreay, Harwell, Windscale, Withrin and the JET facilities at Culham.

SAFETY AND REGULATION

The Nuclear Safety Directorate of the Health and Safety Executive is the nuclear industry's regulator. Operations at all UK nuclear power stations are governed by a site licence which is issued under the Nuclear Installations Act. The Nuclear Installations Inspectorate (NII) monitors compliance and has the jurisdiction to close down a reactor if the terms of the licence are breached. BERR is responsible for security at all the UK's nuclear power stations which are policed by the Civil Nuclear Constabulary, a specialised armed force created in April 2005.

THE NUCLEAR DILEMMA

Despite a 2007 high court ruling that described a government consultation supporting an expansion of nuclear energy as 'misleading' and 'seriously flawed', the government has continued with plans to build a new generation of nuclear power stations. The 2008 Energy Bill paved the way for the construction of up to ten new nuclear power stations by 2020.

There are a number of factors which have affected the government's backing of nuclear power: domestic gas supplies are running low; oil and gas prices are high; carbon emissions must be cut to comply with EU legislation and meet global climate change targets; and a number of coal-fired power stations that fail to meet clean air requirements are due to be closed. The government has long foreseen an energy gap in the country's future generating capacity due to the decommissioning of current nuclear stations and the necessity of cutting back on fossil fuels.

- Nuclear power provided 15 per cent of the world's electricity production in 2007.
- In 2007, 16 countries relied on nuclear energy to supply at least 25 per cent of their electricity; it generated 16 per cent of electricity in the UK and almost 77 per cent in France.

Nuclear power has a number of advantages: reactors emit virtually no carbon dioxide, uranium prices have remained steady for decades and supply does not depend on agreements with unstable foreign regimes. However, the advantages of low emissions are countered by the high costs of construction and there are difficulties in disposing of nuclear waste. Currently, the only method is to store it securely until it has slowly decayed to safe levels. Finally, public distrust persists with the risk of nuclear terrorism and images of disasters such as Chernobyl difficult to forget, despite the advances in safety technology.

RENEWABLE SOURCES

Renewable sources of energy principally include biofuels, hydro, wind and solar. Renewable sources produced over 5.1 million tonnes of oil equivalent for primary energy usage in 2007; of this, about 4.1 million tonnes was used to generate electricity and 0.7 million tonnes to generate heat. In 2007, the UK generated 5 per cent of its total energy production from renewable sources, up by 0.5 percent from 2006 and renewable energy use grew by 8.4 percent in 2007, over five times the level of usage recorded in 1990.

The government's principal mechanism for developing renewable energy sources are Non-Fossil Fuel Obligation Renewables Orders. Under the terms of the orders, regional electricity companies are required to buy specified amounts of electricity from non-fossil fuel sources. The Renewables Obligation (RO) aims to increase the contribution of electricity from renewables in the UK, so that 9.1 per cent of licensed UK electricity sales should be from renewable sources eligible for the RO by 2009, and 15.4 per cent should be eligible by 2016. In 2007 renewables accounted for 4.9 per cent of sales on an RO basis, a rise on the 2006 figure of 4.4 percent.

A renewables obligation has been in place in England and Wales since April 2002 to give incentives to generators to supply progressively higher levels of renewable energy over time. These measures included exempting renewable energy sources from the climate change levy, capital grants, enhanced research funding and regional planning to meet renewables targets. The government approved an EU-wide agreement in March 2007 to generate 20 per cent of energy production from renewable sources by 2020. It has since negotiated down the national share in this target to 15 per cent of energy production by 2020 (and 10 per cent by 2010), a figure many believe optimistic. Other impediments to the expansion of renewable energy production include planning restrictions, rising raw material prices, and the possible redirection of funds to develop nuclear energy sources.

RENEWABLE ENERGY SOURCES (2007)

	Percentage
Biofuels and wastes	81.8
Landfill gas	29.9
Sewage gas	4.3
Wood combustion	8.5
Co-firing	12.4
Waste combustion	10.1
Other biofuels	16.7
Hydro	8.5
Large-scale	7.6
Small-scale	0.9
Wind	8.8
Geothermal and active solar heating	0.9
Total	100

Source: Department for Business, Enterprise and Regulatory Reform

TRANSPORT

CIVIL AVIATION

Since the privatisation of British Airways in 1987, UK airlines have been operated entirely by the private sector. In 2007, total capacity of British airlines amounted to 54 billion tonne km, of which 41 billion tonne km was on scheduled services. British airlines carried around 131 million passengers, 102 million on scheduled services and 29 million on charter flights. Overall, passenger traffic grew by 2.4 per cent. Traffic at the five main London airports grew by 2 per cent over 2007 and regional airlines saw a growth of 2.9 per cent, largely due to the expansion of 'no-frills' airlines. Leading British airlines include BMI, British Airways, EasyJet, First Choice Airways, Monarch, My Travel Airways, Thomas Cook Airlines, Thomsonfly and Virgin Atlantic. Irish airline Ryanair also operates frequent flights from Britain.

There are around 141 licensed civil aerodromes in Britain, with Heathrow and Gatwick handling the highest volume of passengers. BAA plc owns and operates seven major airports: Heathrow, Gatwick, Stansted, Southampton, Glasgow, Edinburgh and Aberdeen, which between them handle about 62 per cent of air passengers and a high percentage of air cargo traffic in Britain. Other airports are controlled by local authorities or private companies.

The Civil Aviation Authority (CAA), an independent statutory body, is responsible for the regulation of UK airlines. This includes economic and airspace regulation, air safety, consumer protection and environmental research and consultancy. All commercial airline companies must be granted an air operator's certificate, which is issued by the CAA to operators meeting the required safety standards. The CAA issues airport safety licences, which must be obtained by any airport used for public transport and training flights. All British-registered aircraft must be granted an airworthiness certificate, and the CAA issues professional licences to pilots, flight crew, ground engineers and air traffic controllers. The CAA also manages the Air Travel Organiser's Licence (ATOL), the UK's principal travel protection scheme. The CAA's costs are met entirely from charges on those whom it regulates; there is no direct government funding of the CAA's work.

The Transport Act, passed by parliament on 29 November 2000, separated the CAA from its subsidiary, National Air Traffic Services (NATS), which provides air traffic control services to aircraft flying in UK airspace and over the eastern part of the North Atlantic. In March 2001 the Airline Group, a consortium of seven UK airlines (British Airways, BMI, Virgin Atlantic, Britannia, Monarch, EasyJet and Airtours), was selected by the government as its strategic partner for NATS. Financial restructuring of NATS was completed in March 2003 with additional equity investment of £65m each from BAA and the government. The new structure enabled NATS to begin a ten-year £1bn investment programme, to increase its flight handling capability to three million flights per annum by 2010. NATS is a public private partnership between the Airline Group, which holds 42 per cent of the shares; NATS staff, who hold 5 per cent; BAA, which holds 4 per cent, and the government, which holds 49 per cent and a golden share. In 2007 NATS handled a total of 2,470,940 flights, an increase of 3.6 per cent on 2006.

AIR PASSENGERS 2007

All UK Airports: Total	240,721,773
Aberdeen (BAA)	3,411,140
Barra (HIAL)*	10,415
Belfast City	2,186,867
Belfast International	5,236,055
Benbecula (HIAL)*	34,992
Biggin Hill†	–
Birmingham	9,134,055
Blackpool	557,636
Bournemouth	1,083,379
Bristol	5,883,856
Cambridge	2,151
Campbeltown (HIAL)*	8,901
Cardiff	2,093,507
City of Derry (Eglinton)	427,586
Coventry	598,916
Doncaster Sheffield	1,074,373
Dundee	65,419
Durham Tees Valley	733,676
Edinburgh (BAA)	9,037,200
Exeter	1,012,493
Gatwick (BAA)	35,165,404
Glasgow (BAA)	8,726,087
Gloucestershire	5,324
Hawarden (Chester)†	–
Heathrow (BAA)	67,852,387
Humberside	465,872
Inverness (HIAL)*	697,480
Islay (HIAL)*	28,406
Isle of Man	753,359
Isles of Scilly (St Mary's)	130,778
Isles of Scilly (Tresco)	40,730
Kent International	15,556
Kirkwall (HIAL)*	131,903
Lands End (St Just)	28,278
Leeds Bradford	2,859,858
Lerwick (Tingwall)	5,059
Liverpool	5,463,234
London City	2,912,123
Luton	9,919,361
Lydd	2,696
Manchester	21,891,723
Newcastle	5,623,607
Newquay	352,548
Norwich	699,359
Nottingham East Midlands International	5,406,504
Penzance Heliport	115,998
Plymouth	78,156
Prestwick	2,420,709
Scatsta	252,894
Shoreham	8,026
Southampton (BAA)	1,965,422
Southend	49,311
Stansted (BAA)	23,759,250
Stornoway (HIAL)*	126,203

Sumburgh (HIAL)*	146,960
Tiree (HIAL)*	7,807
Wick (HIAL)*	20,784
Channel Islands Airports: Total	2,511,842
Alderney	79,087
Guernsey	886,736
Jersey	1,546,019

* Highlands and Islands Airports Ltd (HIAL)
† Figure not supplied by airport
Source: Civil Aviation Authority

CAA, CAA House, 45–59 Kingsway, London WC2B 6TE T 020-7379 7311 W www.caa.co.uk
BAA, 130 Wilton Road, London SW1V 1LQ T 020-8745 9800 W www.baa.com

Gatwick Airport	T 0870-000 2468
Heathrow Airport	T 0870-000 0123
Southampton Airport	T 0870-040 0009
Stansted Airport	T 0870-000 0303
Aberdeen Airport	T 0870-040 0006
Edinburgh Airport	T 0870-040 0007
Glasgow Airport	T 0870-040 0008

BMI, Donington Hall, Castle Donington, Derby DE74 2SB T 01332-854000 W www.flybmi.com
BRITISH AIRWAYS, PO Box 365, Waterside, Harmondsworth UB7 0GB T 0844-493 0787 W www.britishairways.com
EASYJET, Hangar 89, London Luton Airport LU2 9PF T 0871-244 2366 W www.easyjet.com
FIRST CHOICE AIRWAYS, Diamond House, Peel Cross Road, Salford, Manchester M5 4DT T 0871-664 0144 W www.firstchoice.co.uk
MONARCH, Prospect House, Prospect Way, London Luton Airport LU2 9NU T 0870-040 5040 W www.flymonarch.com
THOMAS COOK AIRLINES, Thomas Cook Business Park, Coningsby Road, Peterborough PE3 8SB T 0844-855 0515 W www.thomascookairlines.com
THOMSONFLY, Columbus House, Westwood Way, Westwood Business Park, Coventry CV4 8TT T 0871-231 4869 W www.thomsonfly.com
VIRGIN ATLANTIC, The Office, Crawley, Sussex RH10 9NU T 01293-562345 W www.virgin-atlantic.com

RAILWAYS

The railway network in Britain was developed by private companies in the 19th century. In 1948 the main railway companies were nationalised and were run by a public authority, the British Transport Commission. The commission was replaced by the British Railways Board in 1963, operating as British Rail. On 1 April 1994, responsibility for managing the track and railway infrastructure passed to a newly formed company, Railtrack plc. In October 2001 Railtrack was put into administration under the Railways Act 1993 and Ernst and Young was appointed as administrator. In October 2002 Railtrack was taken out of administration and replaced by the not-for-profit company Network Rail. The British Railways Board continued as operator of all train services until 1996–7, when they were sold or franchised to the private sector.

The Strategic Rail Authority (SRA) was created to provide strategic leadership to the rail industry and formally came into being on 1 February 2001 following the passing of the Transport Act 2000. In January 2002 it published its first strategic plan, setting out the strategic priorities for Britain's railways over the next ten years. In addition to its coordinating role, the SRA was responsible for allocating government funding to the railways and awarding and monitoring the franchises for operating rail services.

On 15 July 2004 the transport secretary announced a new structure for the rail industry in the white paper *The Future of Rail.* These proposals were implemented under the Railways Act 2005, which abolished the Strategic Rail Authority, passing most of its functions to the Department for Transport; established the Rail Passengers Council (RPC) as a single national body, dissolving the regional committees; and gave devolved governments in Scotland and Wales more say in decisions at a local level. In addition, responsibility for railway safety regulation was transferred to the Office of Rail Regulation from the Health and Safety Executive.

OFFICE OF RAIL REGULATION

The Office of Rail Regulation (ORR) was established on 5 July 2004 by the Railways and Transport Safety Act 2003, replacing the Office of the Rail Regulator. As the railway industry's economic and safety regulator, the ORR's principal function is to regulate Network Rail's stewardship of the national network. The ORR also licenses operators of railway assets, approves agreements for access by operators to track, stations and light maintenance depots, and enforces domestic competition law. The ORR is led by a board appointed by the Secretary of State for Transport, under the chairmanship of Chris Bolt. Mr Bolt also fulfils the role of International Rail Regulator (IRR), a statutory office separate from the ORR, which licenses both the operation of certain international rail services in the European Economic Area and access to railway infrastructure in Great Britain for the purpose of operating international services.

SERVICES

For privatisation, under the Railways Act 1993, domestic passenger services were divided into 25 train operating units, which were franchised to private sector operators via a competitive tendering process. The train operators formed the Association of Train Operating Companies (ATOC) to act as the official voice of the passenger rail industry and provide its members with a range of services enabling them to comply with conditions imposed on them through their franchise agreements and operating licences.

As at June 2008 there were 27 passenger train operating companies (TOCs): Arriva Trains Wales; c2c; Chiltern Railways; CrossCountry; East Midlands Trains; Eurostar; First Capital Connect; First Great Western; First ScotRail; First Transpennine Express; Gatwick Express; Grand Central; Heathrow Connect; Heathrow Express; Hull Trains; Island Line (Isle of Wight); London Midland; London Overground; Merseyrail; National Express East Anglia; National Express East Coast; Northern Rail; South West Trains; Southeastern; Southern; Virgin Trains and Wrexham and Shropshire.

Network Rail publishes a national timetable which contains details of rail services operated over the UK network and sea ferry services which provide connections with Ireland, the Isle of Man, the Isle of Wight, the Channel Islands and some European destinations.

The national rail enquiries service offers information about train times and fares for any part of the country,

Transport for London (TfL) provides London-specific travel information for all modes of travel and Eurostar provides information for international channel tunnel rail services:

NATIONAL RAIL ENQUIRIES
T 08457-484950 W www.nationalrail.co.uk
TRANSPORT FOR LONDON
T 020-7222 1234 W www.tfl.gov.uk
EUROSTAR
T 08705-186 186 W www.eurostar.com

PASSENGER FOCUS AND LONDON TRAVELWATCH

Passenger Focus is the operating name of the Rail Passengers' Council, a single national consumer body for rail, which is funded by the Department for Transport but whose independence is guaranteed by an act of parliament. Rail Users' Consultative Committees were set up under the Railways Act 1993 to protect the interests of users of the services and facilities provided on Britain's rail network. The Transport Act 2000 changed their name to Rail Passenger Committees (RPCs) and brought the committees under the overall sponsorship of the Strategic Rail Authority. There were eight RPCs nationwide, one for each of the six English regions and one each for Scotland and Wales. Under the Railways Act 2005, the eight regional committees were disbanded in June 2005 and their functions and duties transferred to the Rail Passengers' Council, the Strategic Rail Authority was abolished and sponsorship for the Rail Passengers' Council transferred to the Department for Transport.

Established in July 2000, London TravelWatch is the operating name of the official watchdog organisation representing the interests of transport users in and around the capital. Officially known as the London Transport Users' Committee, it is sponsored and funded by the London Assembly and is independent of the transport operators. London TravelWatch represents users of buses, the Underground, river and rail services in and around London, including Eurostar and Heathrow Express, Croydon Tramlink and the Docklands Light Railway. The interests of pedestrians, cyclists and motorists are also represented, as are those of taxi users.

FREIGHT

Rail freight services are provided by a small number of companies. On privatisation, British Rail's bulk freight operations were sold to English, Welsh and Scottish Railways (EWS). There are currently eight freight operating companies licensed to provide services for moving goods by rail: Advenza Freight; Direct Rail Services; EWS; Fastline; FM Rail; Freightliner; GB Railfreight and the West Coast Railway Company. The Department for Transport announced in June 2007 that £44m worth of funding would be awarded via the Rail Environmental Benefit Procurement Scheme over three years in order to encourage the movement of freight on rail that would otherwise be transported by road.

NETWORK RAIL

Network Rail is responsible for the tracks, bridges, tunnels, level crossings, viaducts and 18 main stations that form Britain's rail network. In addition to providing the timetables for the passenger and freight operators, Network Rail is also responsible for all the signalling and electrical control equipment needed to operate the rail network and for monitoring and reporting performance across the industry.

Network Rail is a private company run as a commercial business; it is directly accountable to its members and regulated by the ORR. The members have similar rights to those of shareholders in a public company except they do not receive dividends or share capital and thereby have no financial or economic interest in Network Rail. All of Network Rail's profits are reinvested into maintaining and upgrading the rail infrastructure.

ASSOCIATION OF TRAIN OPERATING COMPANIES, 3rd Floor, 40 Bernard Street, London WC1N 1BY T 020-7841 8000 W www.atoc.org
LONDON TRAVELWATCH, 6 Middle Street, London EC1A 7JA T 020-7505 9000 W www.londontravelwatch.org.uk
NETWORK RAIL, 40 Melton Street, London NW1 2EE T 020-7557 8000 W www.networkrail.co.uk
OFFICE OF RAIL REGULATION, 1 Kemble Street, London WC2B 4AN T 020-7282 2000 W www.rail-reg.gov.uk
PASSENGER FOCUS, Freepost (RRRE-ETTC-LEET), PO Box 4257, Manchester M60 3AR T 0845-3022 022 W www.passengerfocus.org.uk

RAIL SAFETY

On 1 April 2006 responsibility for health and safety policy and enforcement on the railways transferred from the Health and Safety Executive to the Office of Rail Regulation (ORR).

In 2007 a total of 32 passengers, railway staff and other members of the public were fatally injured in all rail incidents, compared with 21 in 2006.

ACCIDENTS ON RAILWAYS

	2006	*2007*
Train incidents	1,061	1,006
Train incident fatalities	1	5
Passengers	0	1
Railway employees	0	0
Others	1	4
Train incident injuries	43	111
Passengers	20	94
Railway staff	19	13
Others	4	4

TRESPASSERS, SUICIDES AND ATTEMPTED SUICIDES 2007*

Fatalities	270
Injuries	122

* Includes all incidents on rail (network rail, London Underground and other rail systems, such as trams). Fatality data is subject to change pending the outcome of Coroners' inquests
Source: ORR – *Railway Safety Statistical Report 2007*

OTHER RAIL SYSTEMS

Responsibility for the London Underground passed from the government to the Mayor and Transport for London on 15 July 2003, with a public-private partnership (PPP) already in place. Plans for a public-private partnership for London Underground were pushed through by the government in February 2002 despite opposition from the Mayor of London and a range of transport organisations. Under the PPP, long-term contracts with private companies were estimated to enable around £16bn to be invested in renewing and upgrading the Underground's infrastructure over 15 years.

Responsibility for stations, trains, operations, signalling and safety remains in the public sector. In 2006–7 there were 1,040 million passenger journeys on the London Underground, an increase of 7.2 per cent on the previous year.

Britain has nine other light rail, tram or underground systems: Blackpool Corporation Trams, Croydon Tramlink, Docklands Light Railway (DLR), Glasgow Subway, Manchester Metrolink, Nottingham Express Transit (NET), Stagecoach Supertram in Sheffield, Tyne and Wear Metro and West Midlands Metro.

Light rail and metro systems in Great Britain contributed to the growth in public transport, with 192 million passenger journeys in 2006–7, an increase of 8.6 per cent on the previous year. In England there were 179 million passenger journeys in 2006–7, compared with 124 million in 2000–1. The government's ten-year Transport Plan target is to double light rail use in England (measured by number of passenger journeys) by 2010 compared to 2000 levels.

THE CHANNEL TUNNEL

The earliest recorded scheme for a submarine transport connection between Britain and France was in 1802. Tunnelling began simultaneously on both sides of the Channel three times: in 1881, in the early 1970s, and on 1 December 1987, when construction workers bored the first of the three tunnels which form the Channel Tunnel. Engineers 'holed through' the first tunnel (the service tunnel) on 1 December 1990 and tunnelling was completed in June 1991. The tunnel was officially inaugurated by the Queen and President Mitterrand of France on 6 May 1994.

The submarine link comprises two rail tunnels, each carrying trains in one direction, which measure 7.6m (24.93ft) in diameter. Between them lies a smaller service tunnel, measuring 4.8m (15.75ft) in diameter. The service tunnel is linked to the rail tunnels by 130 cross-passages for maintenance and safety purposes. The tunnels are 50km (31 miles) long, 38km (24 miles) of which is under the seabed at an average depth of 40m (132ft). The rail terminals are situated at Folkestone and Calais, and the tunnels go underground at Shakespeare Cliff, Dover, and Sangatte, west of Calais.

RAIL LINKS

The British Channel Tunnel Rail Link route runs from Folkestone to St Pancras station, London, with intermediate stations at Ashford and Ebbsfleet in Kent.

Construction of the rail link was financed by the private sector with a substantial government contribution. A private sector consortium, London and Continental Railways Ltd (LCR), comprising Union Railways and the UK operator of Eurostar, owns the rail link and was responsible for its design and construction. The rail link was constructed in two phases: phase one, from the Channel Tunnel to Fawkham Junction, Kent, began in October 1998 and opened to fare-paying passengers on 28 September 2003; phase two, from Southfleet Junction to St Pancras, was completed in November 2007.

Infrastructure developments in France have been completed and there are direct services from the UK to Avignon, Calais, Disneyland Paris, Lille and Paris. High-speed trains run from Lille to the south of France.

Eurostar, the high speed passenger train service, connects London with Paris in 2 hours 15 minutes, Brussels in 1 hour 51 minutes and Lille in 1 hour 20 minutes. There are Eurostar terminals at London St Pancras, Ashford and Ebbsfleet in Kent, Paris Gare Du Nord, Brussels-South and Lille in France.

ROADS

HIGHWAY AUTHORITIES

The powers and responsibilities of highway authorities in England and Wales are set out in the Highways Act 1980; for Scotland there is separate legislation.

Responsibility for trunk road motorways and other trunk roads in Great Britain rests in England with the Secretary of State for Transport, in Scotland with the Scottish government, and in Wales with the Welsh assembly. The costs of construction, improvement and maintenance are paid for by central government in England and by the Welsh assembly government in Wales. The highway authority for non-trunk roads in England, Wales and Scotland is, in general, the local authority in whose area the roads lie. With the establishment of the Greater London Authority in July 2000, Transport for London became the highway authority for roads in London.

In Northern Ireland the Department of Regional Development is the statutory road authority responsible for public roads and their maintenance and construction; the Roads Service executive agency carries out these functions on behalf of the department.

FINANCE

In England all aspects of trunk road and motorway funding are provided directly by the government to the Highways Agency, which operates, maintains and improves a network of motorways and trunk roads over 7,138km (4,435 miles) long, on behalf of the secretary of state. Since 2001 the length of the network that the Highways Agency is responsible for has been decreasing due to a policy of de-trunking, which transfers responsibility for non-core roads to local authorities. For the financial year 2008–9 the Highways Agency's total planned expenditure is £6,937m: £896m for maintenance, £1,070m for major improvements and revenue support for private investment, £413m for existing network improvements and technology and the remainder for other programmes and administration costs.

Government support for local authority capital expenditure on roads and other transport infrastructure is provided through grant and credit approvals as part of the Local Transport Plan (LTP). Local authorities bid for resources on the basis of a five-year programme built around delivering integrated transport strategies. As well as covering the structural maintenance of local roads and the construction of major new road schemes, LTP funding also includes smaller-scale safety and traffic management measures with associated improvements for public transport, cyclists and pedestrians.

For the financial year 2008–9, planned expenditure in the form of LTP funding for local authorities is £1,746m: £703m for road maintenance, £578m for small-scale integrated transport measures and £465m for new and existing major projects.

Total expenditure by the Welsh assembly government on trunk roads, motorways, rail, bus and other transport services (including grants to local authorities) in 2007–8 was over £590m. Planned expenditure for 2008–9 is also estimated to be around £590m.

Since 1 July 1999 all decisions on Scottish transport expenditure have been devolved to the Scottish government. Total expenditure on motorways and trunk roads in Scotland during 2007–8 was £902m, including depreciation and cost of capital charge. Planned expenditure for 2008–9 is £930m.

In Northern Ireland total expenditure by the Roads Service on all roads in 2007–8 was £121.4m, with £92.1m spent on trunk roads and motorways. Planned expenditure for 2008–9 is £158.8m, with £145.8m allocated for trunk roads and motorways.

The Transport Act 2000 gave English and Welsh local authorities (outside London) powers to introduce road-user charging or workplace parking levy schemes. The act requires that the net revenue raised is used to improve local transport services and facilities for at least ten years. The aim is to reduce congestion and encourage greater use of alternative modes of transport. Schemes developed by local authorities require government approval. The government's 2000 *Ten Year Plan for Transport* assumed that eight large road user charging schemes and 12 large workplace parking levy schemes will be developed by 2010. The UK's first toll road, the M6 Toll, opened in December 2003 and runs for 43.5km (27 miles) around Birmingham from junction 3a to junction 11a on the M6.

Charging schemes in London are allowed under the 1999 Greater London Authority Act. The Central London Congestion Charge Scheme began on 17 February 2003 (*see also* Regional Government).

ROAD LENGTHS 2006
Kilometres

	England	*Wales*	*Scotland*	*Great Britain*
Motorways	3,007	141	407	3,555
Dual carriageway	6,569	553	783	7,905
Single carriageway	25,680	3,621	9,549	38,850
B roads	19,719	3,014	7,426	30,159
C roads	64,372	9,791	10,336	84,499
Unclassified roads	184,741	17,177	31,465	233,383
Total	304,088	34,297	59,966	398,351

Source: Department for Transport

FREIGHT TRANSPORT BY ROAD (GREAT BRITAIN) 2006

GOODS MOVED	
By mode of working (billion tonne kilometres)	
All modes	156
Own account	44
Public haulage	112
By gross weight of vehicle (billion tonne kilometres)	
All vehicles	156
3.5–25 tonnes	16
Over 25 tonnes	139
GOODS LIFTED	
By mode of working (million tonnes)	
All modes	1,810
Own account	686
Public haulage	1,123
By gross weight of vehicle (million tonnes)	
All vehicles	1,810
3.5–25 tonnes	257
Over 25 tonnes	1,553

Source: Department for Transport

ROAD TRAFFIC BY TYPE OF VEHICLE (GREAT BRITAIN) 2006
Million vehicle kilometres

All motor vehicles	506,400
Cars and taxis	402,400
Motorcycles	5,200
Buses and coaches	5,400
Light vans	64,300
Other goods vehicles	29,100
Pedal cycles	4,600

Source: Department for Transport

BUSES

The majority of bus services outside London – some 83 per cent – are provided on a commercial basis by private operators. Local authorities have powers to subsidise services where needs are not being met by a commercial service.

The Transport Act 2000 outlines a ten-year transport plan intended to promote bus use, through agreements between local authorities and bus operators, and to improve the standard and efficiency of services. Funding for many new services has been made available through the rural bus grants and urban bus challenge schemes. In addition, the Bus Service Operators Grant (BSOG) is paid directly to bus operators by the government and reinburses the major part of the excise duty paid on the fuel used in operating locally registered bus services. In 2006–7 BSOG amounted to £454m.

Since April 2008 people aged 60 and over and disabled people who qualify under the categories listed in the Transport Act 2000 have been able to travel for free on any local bus across England after 9.30am Monday to Friday and all day at weekends and bank holidays. Local authorities recompense operators for the reduced fare revenue. A similar scheme operates in Wales, although there is no time restriction. In Scotland, people aged 60 and over and disabled people have been able to travel for free on any local or long-distance bus anywhere in Scotland since April 2006.

In London, Transport for London (TfL) has overall responsibility for setting routes, service standards and fares for the bus network. Almost all routes are competitively tendered to commercial operators.

In Northern Ireland, passenger transport services are provided by Ulsterbus and Metro (formerly Citybus), two wholly owned subsidiaries of the Northern Ireland Transport Holding Company. Along with Northern Ireland Railways, Ulsterbus and Metro operate under the brand name of Translink and are publicly owned. Ulsterbus is responsible for virtually all bus services in Northern Ireland except Belfast city services, which are operated by Metro.

BUS PASSENGER JOURNEYS 2006–7 (GREAT BRITAIN)
No. of journeys (millions)

England	4,371
London	1,993
Wales	119
Scotland	482
Total	4,972

Source: Department for Transport

TAXIS AND PRIVATE HIRE VEHICLES

A taxi is a public transport vehicle with fewer than nine passenger seats, which is licensed to 'ply for hire'. This distinguishes taxis from private hire vehicles which must be booked in advance through an operator. In London, taxis and private hire vehicles are licensed by the Public Carriage Office (PCO), part of TfL. Outside of London, local authorities are responsible for the licensing of taxis and private hire vehicles operational in their respective administrative areas. At the end of March 2007 there were 68,906 taxis and 128,802 licensed private hire vehicles in England, of these, 21,596 taxis and 44,363 private hire vehicles were licensed by the PCO in London.

ROAD SAFETY

In March 2000, the government published a new road safety strategy, *Tomorrow's Roads – Safer for Everyone,* which set new casualty reduction targets for 2010. The new targets include a 40 per cent reduction in the overall number of people killed or seriously injured in road accidents, a 50 per cent reduction in the number of children killed or seriously injured and a 10 per cent reduction in the slight casualty rate (per 100 million vehicle kilometres), all compared with the average for 1994–8.

There were 247,780 reported casualties on roads in Great Britain in 2007, 4 per cent less than in 2006. Child casualties fell by 7 per cent with 121 child fatalities, a decrease of 28 per cent compared to 2006 figures. Car user casualties decreased by 6 per cent on the 2006 level to 161,433 and fatalities decreased by 11 per cent to 1,431. Pedestrian casualties were 30,191 in 2007, 3 per cent less than 2006, while pedestrian deaths were 5 per cent lower compared to 2006 at 644. Compared to 2006, pedal cyclist casualties remained the same at 16,195, although the number of pedal cyclists killed on British roads decreased by 7 per cent to 136.

ROAD ACCIDENT CASUALTIES 2007

	Fatal	*Serious*	*Slight*	*All Severities*
Average for 1994–8	3,578	44,078	272,272	319,928
England	2,499	24,221	192,744	219,464
Wales	162	1,241	10,868	12,271
Scotland	282	2,315	13,448	16,045
Great Britain	2,943	27,777	217,060	247,780

Source: Department for Transport

ROAD ACCIDENT CASUALTIES

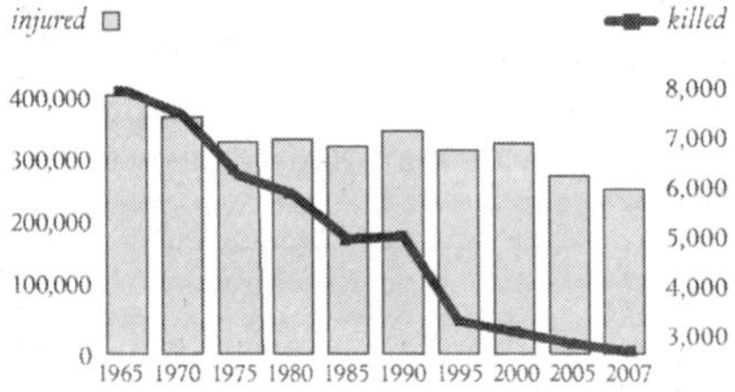

Source: Department for Transport

DRIVING LICENCES

It is necessary to hold a valid full licence in order to drive unaccompanied on public roads in the UK. Learner drivers must obtain a provisional driving licence before starting to learn to drive and must then pass theory and practical tests to obtain a full driving licence.

There are separate tests for driving motorcycles, cars, passenger-carrying vehicles (PCVs) and large goods vehicles (LGVs). Drivers must hold full car entitlement before they can apply for PCV or LGV entitlements.

The Driver and Vehicle Licensing Agency (DVLA) ceased the issue of paper licences in March 2000, however, those currently in circulation will remain valid until they expire or the details on them change. The photocard driving licence was introduced to comply with the second EC directive on driving licences. This requires a photograph of the driver to be included on all UK licences issued from July 2001.

To apply for a first photocard driving licence, individuals are required to complete the form *Application for a Driving Licence* (D1).

The minimum age for driving motor cars, light goods vehicles up to 3.5 tonnes and motorcycles is 17 (moped, 16). Since June 1997, drivers who collect six or more penalty points within two years of qualifying lose their licence and are required to take another test. All forms and leaflets including *What You Need to Know About Driving Licences* (D100), are available from post offices, DVLA local offices and online (W www.dvla.gov.uk or W www.direct.gov.uk).

The DVLA is responsible for issuing driving licences, registering and licensing vehicles, and collecting excise duty in Great Britain. Driver and Vehicle Licensing Northern Ireland (DVLNI), part of the Driver and Vehicle Agency (DVA), has similar responsibilities in Northern Ireland.

DRIVING LICENCE FEES*
valid from February 2008 to March 2009

Provisional licence	
Car, motorcycle or moped	£50.00
Bus or lorry	Free
After disqualification until passing re-test	Free
Changing a provisional licence to a full licence	Free
Renewal	
At age 70 and over	Free
For medical reasons	Free
Bus or lorry licence	Free
After disqualification	£65.00
After disqualification for some drink driving offences†	£90.00
After revocation	£50.00
Renewing the photo on the licence	£17.50
Replacing a lost or stolen licence	£17.50
Adding an entitlement to a full licence	Free
Removing expired endorsements	
from a photocard licence	£17.50
from a paper licence (while exchanging it for a photocard licence)	£17.50
Exchanging	
a paper licence for a photocard licence	£17.50
a photocard for a photocard licence	£17.50
a full GB licence for a full Northern Ireland licence	Free
a full GB licence for a full EC/EEA or other foreign licence (including Channel Islands and Isle of Man)	Free
a full EC/EEA or other foreign licence (including Channel Islands and Isle of Man) for a full GB licence	£50.00

Change of name or address (existing licence must be surrendered)	Free

* If the application involves two separate fees only the higher fee is payable
† For an alcohol-related offence where the DVLA needed to arrange medical enquiries

DRIVING TESTS

The Driving Standards Agency (DSA) is responsible for carrying out driving tests and approving driving instructors in Great Britain. Driver and Vehicle Testing, part of the Driver and Vehicle Agency, is responsible for testing drivers and vehicles in Northern Ireland.

DRIVING TESTS TAKEN AND PASSED
April 2007–March 2008

	Number Taken	*Percentage Passed*
Practical Test		
Car	1,769,860	44
Motorcycle	87,962	67
Large goods vehicle	70,766	46
Passenger-carrying vehicle	10,331	50
Theory Test		
Car	1,451,379	65
Motorcycle	94,180	78
Large goods vehicle	41,486	73
Passenger-carrying vehicle	9,141	70

Source: DSA

The theory and practical driving tests can be booked with a postal application, online (W www.dsa.gov.uk or W www.direct.gov.uk) or by phone (theory test T 0870-010 1372, practical test T 0300-200 1122).

DRIVING TEST FEES (WEEKDAY/EVENING* AND WEEKEND)
from April 2008

Theory tests	
Car and motorcycle	£30.00
Lorry and bus	£32.00
Practical tests	
Car	£56.50/£67.00
Tractors and other specialist vehicles	£56.50/£67.00
Motorcycle	£60.00/£70.00
Lorry and bus	£105.00/£125.00
Car and trailer	£105.00/£125.00
Extended tests for disqualified drivers	
Car	£113.00/£134.00
Motorcycle	£120.00/£140.00

* After 4.30pm

VEHICLE LICENCES

Registration and first licensing of vehicles is through local offices of the DVLA in Swansea. Local facilities for relicensing are available at any post office which deals with vehicle licensing. Applicants will need to take their vehicle registration document (V5C) or, if this is not available, the applicant must complete form V62. Postal applications can be made to the post offices shown in the V100 booklet, which also provides guidance on registering and licensing vehicles. All forms and booklets are available at post offices, DVLA local offices and online (W www.dvla.gov.uk or W www.direct.gov.uk).

MOTOR VEHICLES LICENSED 2007 (GREAT BRITAIN)

	Thousands
All cars	28,228
Motorcycles	1,263
Light goods vehicles	3,187
Heavy goods vehicles	528
Buses and coaches	181
Other vehicles*	570
Total	33,957

* Includes rear diggers, lift trucks, rollers, ambulances, taxis, three wheelers and agricultural vehicles
Source: Department for Transport

VEHICLE EXCISE DUTY

Details of the present duties chargeable on motor vehicles are available at DVLA local offices, post offices and online (W www.dvla.gov.uk or W www.direct.gov.uk). The Vehicle Excise and Registration Act 1994 provides *inter alia* that any vehicle kept on a public road but not used on roads is chargeable to excise duty as if it were in use. All non-commercial vehicles constructed before 1 January 1973 are exempt from vehicle excise duty. Any vehicle licensed on or after 31 January 1998, not in use and not kept on public roads must be registered as SORN (Statutory Off Road Notification) to be exempted from vehicle excise duty. From 1 January 2004 the registered keeper of a vehicle remains responsible for taxing a vehicle or making a SORN declaration until that liability is formally transferred to a new keeper.

RATES OF DUTY *from March 2008*

	12 months *rate £*	6 months *rate £*
Light goods vehicles registered before 1 March 2001		
Under 1,549cc	120.00	66.00
Over 1,549cc	185.00	101.75
Light goods vehicles registered on or after 1 March 2001	180.00	99.00
Euro 4 light goods vehicles registered between 1 March 2003 and 31 December 2006	120.00	66.00
Motorcycles (with or without sidecar)		
Not over 150cc	15.00	–
151–400cc	33.00	–
401–600cc	48.00	–
600cc+	66.00	36.30
Tricycles		
Not over 150cc	15.00	–
All others	66.00	36.30
*Buses**		
Seating 10–17	165.00	90.75
Seating 18–36	220.00	121.00
Seating 37–61	330.00	181.50
Seating 62+	500.00	275.00

* Seating capacity includes driver. The 12-months rate for all buses with reduced pollution is £165.00 and the 6-months rate is £90.75.

RATES OF DUTY
Cars registered on or after 1 March 2001

Band	CO_2 Emissions (g/km)	Petrol and Diesel Car 12 months	6 months	Alternative Fuel Car 12 months	6 months
A	Up to 100	–	–	–	–
B	101–120	£35.00	–	£15.00	–
C	121–150	£120.00	£66.00	£100.00	£55.00
D	151–165	£145.00	£79.75	£125.00	£68.75
E	166–185	£170.00	£93.50	£150.00	£82.50
F	185+	£210.00	£115.50	£195.00	£107.25
Cars registered on or after 23 March 2006					
G	225+	£400.00	£220.00	£385.00	£211.75

MOT TESTING
Cars, motorcycles, motor caravans, light goods and dual-purpose vehicles more than three years old must be covered by a current MOT test certificate. However, some vehicles (ie minibuses, ambulances and taxis) may require a certificate at one year old. All certificates must be renewed annually. The MOT testing scheme is administered by the Vehicle and Operator Services Agency (VOSA) on behalf of the Secretary of State for Transport.

A fee is payable to MOT testing stations, which must be authorised to carry out tests. The current maximum fees are:

For cars, private hire and public service vehicles (all up to eight passenger seats), motor caravans, dual purpose vehicles, ambulances and taxis	£53.10
For motorcycles	£27.15
For motorcycles with sidecar	£34.65
For three-wheeled vehicles	£34.65
Private passenger vehicles and ambulances with*:	
9–12 passenger seats	£55.50 (£62.00)
13–16 passenger seats	£57.65 (£78.00)
16+ passenger seats	£78.15 (£120.70)
Goods vehicles (3,000–3,500kg)	£56.75

* Figures in parentheses include seatbelt installation check

SHIPPING AND PORTS

Sea trade has always played a central role in Britain's economy. By the 17th century Britain had built up a substantial merchant fleet and by the early 20th century it dominated the world shipping industry. Until the late 1990s the size and tonnage of the UK-registered trading fleet had been steadily declining. In December 1998 the government published *British Shipping: Charting a New Course,* which outlined strategies to promote the long-term interests of British shipping. By the end of 2007 the number of ships in the UK fleet had increased by 71 per cent whilst gross tonnage had more than quadrupled. The UK-flagged merchant fleet now constitutes 1.3 per cent of the world fleet in terms of vessels and 1.7 per cent in terms of gross tonnage.

Freight is carried by liner and bulk services, almost all scheduled liner services being containerised. About 95 per cent by weight of Britain's overseas trade is carried by sea; this amounts to 75 per cent of its total value. Passengers and vehicles are carried by roll-on, roll-off ferries, hovercraft, hydrofoils and high-speed catamarans. There were around 45 million ferry passengers in 2007, of whom 24 million travelled internationally.

Lloyd's of London provides the most comprehensive shipping intelligence service in the world. *Lloyd's Shipping Index,* published daily, lists some 25,000 ocean-going vessels and gives the latest known report of each.

PORTS
There are more than 650 ports in Great Britain for which statutory harbour powers have been granted. Of these about 120 are commercially significant ports. In 2007* the largest ports in terms of freight tonnage were Grimsby and Immingham (66.2 million tonnes), London (52.7 million tonnes), Tees and Hartlepool (49.8 million tonnes), Southampton (43.3 million tonnes), Forth (36.7 million tonnes), Milford Haven (35.5 million tonnes), Liverpool (32.3 million tonnes), Felixstowe (25.7 million tonnes), Dover (25.1 million tonnes) and Sullom Voe (16.6 million tonnes). Belfast is the principal freight port in Northern Ireland.

Broadly speaking, ports are owned and operated by private companies, local authorities or trusts. The largest operator is Associated British Ports which owns 21 ports. Provisional port traffic results show that 581.1 million tonnes were handled by UK ports in 2007, a decrease of 0.5 per cent on the previous year's figure of 584 million tonnes.

* Provisional data

MARINE SAFETY
The Maritime and Coastguard Agency is an executive agency of the Department for Transport. Working closely with the shipping industry and the public its aims are to:

- reduce accidents and accident related deaths within UK search and rescue waters and coastline
- reduce accidents and accident related deaths from UK registered merchant ships and fishing vessels
- reduce the number of incidents of pollution from shipping activities in the UK pollution control zone

HM Coastguard maintains a 24-hour search and rescue response and coordination capability for the whole of the UK coast and the internationally agreed search and rescue region. HM Coastguard is responsible for mobilising and organising resources in response to people in distress at sea, or at risk of injury or death on the UK's cliffs or shoreline. There are around 500 full-time coastguards who staff marine rescue coordination centres and a further 3,000 voluntary coastguard rescue officers who staff the 401 coastguard rescue teams. In 2007 HM Coastguard rescued approximately 4,500 people whose life was at risk and gave assistance to around 23,000 more people.

Locations hazardous to shipping in coastal waters are marked by lighthouses and other lights and buoys. The lighthouse authorities are the Corporation of Trinity House (for England, Wales and the Channel Islands), the Northern Lighthouse Board (for Scotland and the Isle of Man), and the Commissioners of Irish Lights (for Northern Ireland and the Republic of Ireland). Trinity House maintains 69 lighthouses, 10 light vessels/floats, 412 buoys, 19 beacons, 48 radar beacons and seven DGPS (Differential Global Positioning System) stations*. The Northern Lighthouse Board maintains 209 lighthouses, 163 buoys, 37 beacons, 26 radar beacons, nine AIS (automatic identification system) stations, four DGPS stations and one LORAN (long-range navigation) station; and Irish Lights looks after 80 lighthouses, 149 buoys, 47 beacons, 22 radar beacons, three DGPS stations, two LANBYs (large automatic navigational buoys) and one light float.

Harbour authorities are responsible for pilotage within their harbour areas; and the Ports Act 1991 provides for the transfer of lights and buoys to harbour authorities where these are used for mainly local navigation.

* DGPS is a satellite-based navigation system

UK-OWNED TRADING VESSELS
100 gross tons and over, as at end 2006

Type of vessel	*No.*	*Gross tonnage*
Liquid	173	4,676,000
Dry bulk	60	2,614,000
Specialised carrier	26	596,000
Container	91	4,254,000
Ro-Ro	133	1,343,000
Other general cargo	179	972,000
Passenger	47	921,000
All trading vessels	709	15,376,000
of which registered in the UK	402	6,657,000

Source: Department for Transport

UK SEA PASSENGER MOVEMENTS 2007

Type of journey	*No. of passenger movements**
International†	23,668,000
Domestic	3,640,000

* Passengers are included at both departure and arrival if their journeys begin and end at a UK seaport
† Routes to Belgium, Denmark, Faroe Islands, Finland, France, Germany, Ireland, the Netherlands, Norway, Spain and Sweden
Source: Department for Transport

MARINECALL WEATHER FORECAST SERVICE

Marinecall offers a wide range of inshore, offshore and European forecasts from the Met Office which include gale and strong wind warnings, the general situation, wind speed and direction, probability and strength of gusts, developing weather conditions, visibility and sea state. Information is provided by various means including telephone, fax, SMS etc. Marinecall 10-day forecasts contain a 48-hour inshore/offshore sea area summary, followed by a 1–5 day forecast for the local sea area, 6–10 day national forecast and an outlook for the month ahead. In addition fax forecasts provide a synopic chart. Other services such as area specific, current weather reports and 48-hour forecasts are also available.

MARINECALL 10-DAY FORECAST

	By Phone	By Fax
INSHORE AREA	09068-500+	09065-300+
Cape Wrath – Rattray Head	451	251
Rattray Head – Berwick	452	252
Berwick – Whitby	453	253
Whitby – Gibraltar Point	454	254
Gibraltar Point – North Foreland	455	255
North Foreland – Selsey Bill	456	256
Selsey Bill – Lyme Regis	457	257
Lyme Regis – Hartland Point	458	258
Hartland Point – St David's Head	459	259
St David's Head – Great Ormes Head	460	260
Great Ormes Head – Mull of Galloway	461	261
Mull of Galloway – Mull of Kintyre	462	262
Mull of Kintyre – Ardnamurchan	463	263
Ardnamurchan – Cape Wrath	464	264
Lough Foyle – Carlingford Lough	465	265
Channel Islands	432	–
OFFSHORE AREA		
English Channel	992	270
Southern North Sea	991	271
Irish Sea	954	273
Biscay	953	274
North-west Scotland	955	275
Northern North Sea	985	276

Marinecall by UK land-line is charged at 60p per minute and Marinecall by fax at £1.50 per minute. Calls from mobiles may be subject to network operator surcharges. Subscription packages are available.

UK SHIPPING FORECAST AREAS

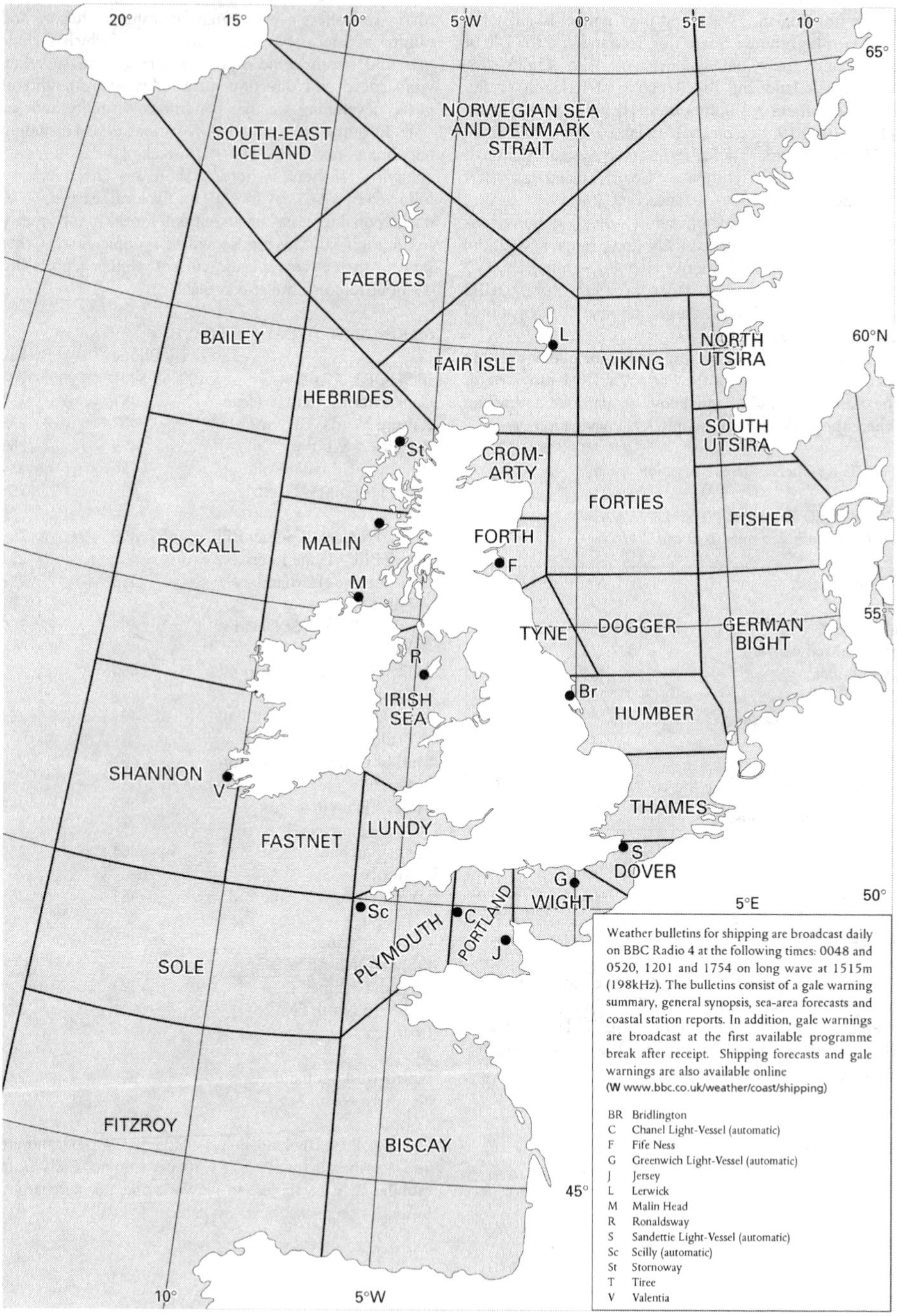

Weather bulletins for shipping are broadcast daily on BBC Radio 4 at the following times: 0048 and 0520, 1201 and 1754 on long wave at 1515m (198kHz). The bulletins consist of a gale warning summary, general synopsis, sea-area forecasts and coastal station reports. In addition, gale warnings are broadcast at the first available programme break after receipt. Shipping forecasts and gale warnings are also available online
(**W** www.bbc.co.uk/weather/coast/shipping)

BR Bridlington
C Chanel Light-Vessel (automatic)
F Fife Ness
G Greenwich Light-Vessel (automatic)
J Jersey
L Lerwick
M Malin Head
R Ronaldsway
S Sandettie Light-Vessel (automatic)
Sc Scilly (automatic)
St Stornoway
T Tiree
V Valentia

RELIGION IN THE UK

The 2001 census included a voluntary question on religion for the first time (although the question had been included in previous censuses in Northern Ireland); 92 per cent of people chose to answer the question. In the UK, 71.6 per cent of people in Britain identified themselves as Christian (42.1 million people). After Christianity, the next most prevalent faith was Islam with 2.7 per cent describing their religion as Muslim (1.6 million people). The next largest religious groups were Hindus (559,000), followed by Sikhs (336,000), Jews (267,000), Buddhists (152,000) and people from other religions (179,000). Together, these groups accounted for less than 3 per cent of the total UK population. People in Northern Ireland were most likely to say that they identified with a religion (86 per cent) compared with 77 per cent in England and Wales and 67 per cent in Scotland. The English counties with the highest proportion of Christians are Durham, Merseyside and Cumbria, each with 82 per cent or more; in Wales it is Ynys Mon (Isle of Anglesey) (79 per cent). London has the highest proportion of Muslims (8.5 per cent), Hindus (4.1 per cent), Jews (2.1 per cent), Buddhists (0.8 per cent) and people of other religions (0.5 per cent). Around 16 per cent of the UK population stated they had no religion. The districts with the highest proportions of people with no religion were Norwich, Brighton and Hove and Cambridge, all with over 25 per cent. This category included those who identified themselves as agnostics, atheists, heathens and Jedi Knights.

CENSUS 2001 RESULTS — RELIGIONS IN THE UK

	thousands	*per cent*
Christian	42,079	71.6
Buddhist	152	0.3
Hindu	559	1.0
Jewish	267	0.5
Muslim	1,591	2.7
Sikh	336	0.6
Other religion	179	0.3
All religions	45,163	76.8
No religion	9,104	15.5
Not stated	4,289	7.3
All no religion/not stated	13,626	23.2
TOTAL	58,789	100

Source: Census 2001

INTER-CHURCH AND INTER-FAITH COOPERATION

The main umbrella body for the Christian churches in the UK is Churches Together in Britain and Ireland. There are also ecumenical bodies in each of the constituent countries of the UK: Churches Together in England, Action of Churches Together in Scotland, CYTUN (Churches Together in Wales), and the Irish Council of Churches. The Free Churches Group (formerly the Free Churches Council), which is closely associated with Churches Together in England, represents most of the free churches in England and Wales, and the Evangelical Alliance represents evangelical Christians.

The Inter Faith Network for the United Kingdom promotes cooperation between faiths, and the Council of Christians and Jews works to improve relations between the two religions. Churches Together in Britain and Ireland also has a commission on inter-faith relations.

ACTION OF CHURCHES TOGETHER IN SCOTLAND, Inglewood House, Alloa FK10 2HU T 01259-216980 E ecumenical@acts-scotland.org W www.acts-scotland.org
General Secretary, Brother Stephen Smyth

CHURCHES TOGETHER IN BRITAIN AND IRELAND, 3rd Floor, Bastille Court, 2 Paris Gardens, London SE1 8ND T 020-7654 7254 E info@ctbi.org.uk W www.ctbi.org.uk
General Secretary, Revd Bob Fyffe

CHURCHES TOGETHER IN ENGLAND, 27 Tavistock Square, London WC1H 9HH T 020-7529 8131 E office@cte.org.uk W www.churches-together.net
General Secretary, David Cornick

COUNCIL OF CHRISTIANS AND JEWS, 1st Floor, Camelford House, 87–89 Albert Embankment, London SE1 7TP T 020-7820 0090 E cjrelations@ccj.org.uk W www.ccj.org.uk
Chief Executive, David Gifford

CYTUN (CHURCHES TOGETHER IN WALES), 58 Richmond Road, Cardiff CF24 3UR T 029-2046 4204 E post@scytun.org.uk W www.cytun.org.uk
Chief Executive, Revd Aled Edwards, OBE

EVANGELICAL ALLIANCE, 186 Kennington Park Road, London SE11 4BT T 020-7207 2100 E info@eauk.org W www.eauk.org
General Director, Joel Edwards

FREE CHURCHES GROUP, 27 Tavistock Square, London WC1H 9HH T 020-7529 8131 E freechurch@cte.org.uk
Executive Secretary, Revd Mark Fisher

INTER-FAITH NETWORK FOR THE UK, 8A Lower Grosvenor Place, London SW1W 0EN T 020-7931 7766 E ifnet@interfaith.org.uk W www.interfaith.org.uk
Director, Dr Harriet Crabtree

IRISH COUNCIL OF CHURCHES, Inter-Church Centre, 48 Elmwood Avenue, Belfast BT9 6AZ T 028-9066 3145 E info@irishchurches.org W www.irishchurches.org
General Secretary, Michael Earle

CHRISTIANITY

Christianity is a monotheistic faith based on the person and teachings of Jesus Christ, and all Christian denominations claim his authority. Central to its teaching is the concept of God and his son Jesus Christ, who was crucified and resurrected in order to enable mankind to attain salvation.

The Jewish scriptures predicted the coming of a *Messiah,* an 'anointed one', who would bring salvation. To Christians, Jesus of Nazareth, a Jewish rabbi (teacher) who was born in Palestine, was the promised Messiah. Jesus' birth, teachings, crucifixion and subsequent resurrection are recorded in the *Gospels,* which, together with other scriptures that summarise Christian belief, form the *New Testament.* This, together with the Hebrew scriptures – entitled the *Old Testament* by Christians – makes up the Bible, the sacred texts of Christianity.

BELIEFS

Christians believe that sin distanced mankind from God, and that Jesus was the son of God, sent to redeem mankind from sin by his death. In addition, many believe that Jesus will return again at some future date, triumph over evil and establish a kingdom on earth, thus inaugurating a new age. The Gospel assures Christians that those who believe in Jesus and obey his teachings will be forgiven their sins and will be resurrected from the dead.

PRACTICES

Christian practices vary widely between different Christian churches, but prayer, charity and giving (for the maintenance of the church buildings, for the work of the church, and to the poor and needy) are common to all. In addition, certain days of observance, ie the *Sabbath, Easter* and *Christmas,* are celebrated by most Christians. The Orthodox, Roman Catholic and Anglican churches celebrate many more days of observance, based on saints and significant events in the life of Jesus. The belief in sacraments, physical signs believed to have been ordained by Jesus Christ to symbolise and convey spiritual gifts, varies greatly between Christian denominations; *baptism* and the *Eucharist* are practised by most Christians. Baptism, symbolising repentance and faith in Jesus, is an act marking entry into the Christian community; the Eucharist, the ritual re-enactment of the Last Supper, Jesus' final meal with his disciples, is also practised by most denominations. Other sacraments, such as anointing the sick; the laying on of hands to symbolise the passing on of the office of priesthood or to heal the sick and speaking in tongues, where it is believed that the person is possessed by the Holy Spirit, are less common. In denominations where infant baptism is practised, confirmation (where the person repeats the commitments made for him or her at infancy) is common. Matrimony and the ordination of priests are also widely believed to be sacraments. Many Protestants regard only baptism and the Eucharist to be sacraments; the Quakers and the Salvation Army reject the use of sacraments.

Most Christians believe that God actively guides the church.

THE EARLY CHURCH

The Apostles were Jesus' first converts and are recognised by Christians as the founders of the Christian community. The new faith spread rapidly throughout the eastern provinces of the Roman Empire. Early Christianity was subjected to great persecution until AD 313, when Emperor Constantine's Edict of Toleration confirmed its right to exist and it was established as the religion of the Roman Empire in AD 381.

The Christian faith was slowly formulated in the first millennium of the Christian era. Between AD 325 and 787 there were seven Oecumenical Councils at which bishops from the entire Christian world assembled to resolve various doctrinal disputes. The estrangement between East and West began after Constantine moved the centre of the Roman Empire from Rome to Constantinople, and it grew after the division of the Roman Empire into eastern and western halves. Linguistic and cultural differences between Greek East and Latin West served to encourage separate ecclesiastical developments which became pronounced in the tenth and early 11th centuries.

Administration of the church was divided between five ancient patriarchates: Rome and all the West, Constantinople (the imperial city – the 'New Rome'), Jerusalem and all of Palestine, Antioch and all the East and Alexandria and all of Africa. Of these, only Rome was in the Latin West and after the schism in 1054, Rome developed a structure of authority centralised on the Papacy, while the Orthodox East maintained the style of localised administration.

Papal authority over the doctrine and jurisdiction of the church in Western Europe was unrivalled after the split with the Eastern Orthodox Church until the Protestant Reformation in the 16th century.

CHRISTIANITY IN BRITAIN

An English church already existed when Pope Gregory sent Augustine to evangelise the English in AD 596. Conflicts between Church and State during the Middle Ages culminated in the Act of Supremacy in 1534, which repudiated papal supremacy and declared King Henry VIII to be the supreme head of the church in England. Since 1559 the English monarch has been termed the Supreme Governor of the Church of England.

In 1560 the jurisdiction of the Roman Catholic Church in Scotland was abolished and the first assembly of the Church of Scotland ratified the Confession of Faith, drawn up by a committee led by John Knox. In 1592 parliament passed an act guaranteeing the liberties of the church and its Presbyterian government. King James VI (James I of England) and later Stuart monarchs attempted to reintroduce episcopacy, but a Presbyterian church was finally restored in 1690 and secured by the Act of Settlement (1690) and the Act of Union (1707).

PORVOO DECLARATION

The Porvoo Declaration was drawn up by representatives of the British and Irish Anglican churches and the Nordic and Baltic Lutheran churches and was approved by the General Synod of the Church of England in July 1995. Churches that approve the declaration regard baptised members of each other's churches as members of their own, and allow free interchange of episcopally ordained ministers within the rules of each church.

NON-CHRISTIAN RELIGIONS AND BELIEFS

BAHA'I FAITH

Mirza Husayn-'Ali, known as *Baha'u'llah* (Glory of God) was born in Iran in 1817 and became a follower of the *Bab,* a religious reformer and prophet who was imprisoned for his beliefs and executed on the grounds of heresy in 1850. Baha'u'llah was himself imprisoned in 1852, and in 1853 he had a vision that he was the 'promised one' foretold by the Bab. He was exiled after his release from prison and eventually arrived in Acre, now in Israel, where he continued to compose the Baha'i sacred scriptures. He died in 1892 and was succeeded by his son, Abdu'l-Baha, as spiritual leader, under whose guidance the faith spread to Europe and North America. He was followed by Shoghi Effendi, his grandson, who translated many of Baha'u'llah's works into English. Upon his death in 1957, a democratic system of leadership was brought into operation.

The Baha'i faith espouses the unity and relativity of religious truth and teaches that there is only one God, whose will has been revealed to mankind by a series of messengers, such as Zoroaster, Abraham, Moses, Buddha, Krishna, Christ, Muhammad, the Bab and Baha'u'llah, who were seen as the founders of separate religions, but whose common purpose was to bring God's message to mankind. It teaches that all races and both sexes are equal and deserving of equal opportunities and treatment, that education is a fundamental right and encourages a fair distribution of wealth. In addition, the faith exhorts mankind to establish a world federal system to promote peace and tolerance.

A feast is held every 19 days, which consists of prayer and readings of Baha'i scriptures, consultation on community business, and social activities. Music, food and beverages usually accompany the proceedings. There is no clergy; each local community elects a local assembly, which coordinates community activities, enrols new members, counsels and assists members in need, and conducts Baha'i marriages and funerals. A national assembly is elected annually by locally elected delegates, and every five years the national spiritual assemblies meet together to elect the Universal House of Justice, the supreme international governing body of the Baha'i Faith. Worldwide there are over 13,000 local spiritual assemblies; there are around five million members residing in about 235 countries, of which 179 have national organisations.

THE BAHA'I OFFICE OF PUBLIC INFORMATION, 27 Rutland Gate, London SW7 1PD **T** 020-7584 2566 **E** nsa@bahai.org.uk **W** www.bahai.org.uk
Secretary of the National Spiritual Assembly, Dr Kishan Manocha
Secretary for External Affairs, Robert Weinberg

BUDDHISM

Buddhism originated in what is now the Bihar area of northern India in the teachings of Siddhartha Gautama, who became the *Buddha* (Enlightened One). The Buddhist era is dated from his passing away 45 years after his enlightenment; the year 2009 is 2552 by the Buddhist reckoning.

Fundamental to Buddhism is the concept of rebirth, whereby each life carries with it the consequences of the conduct of earlier lives (known as the law of *karma*) and this cycle of death and rebirth is broken only when the state of *nirvana* has been reached. Buddhism steers a middle path between belief in personal continuity and the belief that death results in total extinction.

While doctrine does not have a pivotal position in Buddhism, a statement of four 'Noble Truths' is common to all its schools and varieties. These are: suffering is inescapable in even the most fortunate of existences; craving is the root cause of suffering; abandonment of the selfish mindset is the way to end suffering; and bodily and mental discipline, accompanied by the cultivation of wisdom and compassion, provides the spiritual path ('Noble Eightfold Path') to accomplish this. Buddhists deny the idea of a creator and prefer to emphasise the practical aspects of moral and spiritual development.

The schools of Buddhism can be broadly divided into three: *Theravada,* the generally monastic-led tradition practised in Sri Lanka and South-East Asia; *Mahayana,* the philosophical and popular traditions of the Far East; and *Esoteric,* the Tantric-derived traditions found in Tibet and Mongolia and, to a lesser extent, China and Japan. The extensive Theravada scriptures are contained in the *Pali Canon,* which dates in its written form from the first century BC. Mahayana and Esoteric schools have Sanskrit-derived translations of these plus many more additional scriptures as well as exegetical material.

In the East the new and full moons and the lunar quarter days were (and to a certain extent, still are) significant in determining the religious calendar. Most private homes contain a shrine where offerings, worship and other spiritual practices (such as meditation, chanting or mantra recitation) take place on a daily basis. Buddhist festivals vary according to local traditions within the different schools and there is very little uniformity – even in commemorating the birth, enlightenment and death of the Buddha.

There is no governing authority for Buddhism in the UK. Communities representing all schools of Buddhism operate independently. The Buddhist Society was established in 1924; it runs courses, lectures and meditation groups, and publishes books about Buddhism. The Network of Buddhist Organisations was founded in 1993 to promote fellowship and dialogue between Buddhist organisations and to facilitate cooperation in matters of common interest.

There are estimated to be at least 300 million Buddhists worldwide. Of the 152,000 Buddhists in the UK (according to the 2001 census), 60,000 are white British (the majority are converts), 36,000 Chinese, 15,000 Asian and 36,000 'other ethnic'.

THE BUDDHIST SOCIETY, 58 Eccleston Square, London SW1V 1PH **T** 020-7834 5858 **E** info@thebuddhistsociety.org **W** www.thebuddhistsociety.org

FRIENDS OF THE WESTERN BUDDHIST ORDER, The London Buddhist Centre, 51 Roman Road, London E2 0HU **T** 0845-458 4716 **E** info@lbc.org.uk **W** www.lbc.org.uk

THE NETWORK OF BUDDHIST ORGANISATIONS, 6 Tyne Road, Bishopston, Bristol BS7 8EE **T** 0845-345 8978 **E** secretary@nbo.org.uk **W** www.nbo.org.uk

TIBET HOUSE TRUST, Tibet House, 1 Culworth Street, London NW8 7AF **T** 020-7722 5378 **E** secretary@tibet-house-trust.co.uk **W** www.tibet-house-trust.co.uk

SOKA GAKKAI INTERNATIONAL (UK), Taplow Court Grand Cultural Centre, Taplow, Berkshire SL6 0ER **T** 01628-773163 **W** www.sgi-uk.org

HINDUISM

Hinduism has no historical founder but had become highly developed in India by *c.*2500 BC. Its adherents originally called themselves Aryans; Muslim invaders first called the Aryans 'Hindus' (derived from 'Sindhu', the name of the river Indus) in the eighth century.

Most Hindus hold that *satya* (truthfulness), honesty, sincerity and devotion to God are essential for good living. They believe in one supreme spirit *(Brahman),* and in the transmigration of *atman* (the soul). Most Hindus accept the doctrine of *karma* (consequences of actions), the concept of *samsara* (successive lives) and the possibility of all atmans achieving *moksha* (liberation from samsara) through *jnana* (knowledge), *yoga* (meditation), *karma* (work or action) and *bhakti* (devotion).

Most Hindus offer worship to *murtis* (images of deities) representing different incarnations or aspects of Brahman, and follow their *dharma* (religious and social duty) according to the traditions of their *varna* (social class), *ashrama* (stage in life), *jaiti* (caste) and *kula* (family).

Hinduism's sacred texts are divided into *shruti* ('that which is heard'), including the *Vedas,* and *smriti* ('that which is remembered'), including the *Ramayana,* the *Mahabharata,* the *Puranas* (ancient myths), and the sacred law books. Most Hindus recognise the authority of the *Vedas,* the oldest holy books, and accept the philosophical teachings of the *Upanishads*, the *Vedanta Sutras* and the *Bhagavad-Gita*.

Hindus believe Brahman to be omniscient, omnipotent, limitless and all-pervading. Brahman is usually worshipped in its deity form. Brahma, Vishnu and Shiva are the most important deities or aspects of Brahman worshipped by Hindus; their respective consorts are Saraswati, Lakshmi and Durga or Parvati, also known as Shakti. There are believed to have been ten *avatars* (incarnations) of Vishnu, of whom the most important are Rama and Krishna. Other popular gods are Ganesha, Hanuman and Subrahmanyam. All Hindu gods are seen as aspects of the supreme spirit (Brahman), not as competing deities.

Orthodox Hindus revere all gods and goddesses equally, but there are many denominations, including the Hare-Krishna movement (ISKCon), the Arya Samaj and the Swaminarayan Hindu mission, in which worship is concentrated on one deity. The *guru* (spiritual teacher) is seen as the source of spiritual guidance.

Hinduism does not have a centrally trained and ordained priesthood. The pronouncements of the *shankaracharyas* (heads of monasteries) of Shringeri, Puri, Dwarka and Badrinath are heeded by the orthodox but may be ignored by the various sects.

The commonest form of worship is *puja*, in which water, flowers, food, fruit, incense and light are offered to the deity. Puja may be done either in a home shrine or a *mandir* (temple). Many British Hindus celebrate *samskars* (purification rites), for example to name a baby, the sacred thread (an initiation ceremony), marriage and cremation.

The largest communities of Hindus in Britain are in Leicester, London, Birmingham and Bradford, and developed as a result of immigration from India, eastern Africa and Sri Lanka.

There are an estimated 800 million Hindus worldwide; there are around 559,000 adherents, according to the 2001 UK census, and over 140 temples in the UK.

ARYA SAMAJ LONDON, 69A Argyle Road, London W13 0LY T 020-8991 1732
E aryasamajlondon@yahoo.co.uk
General Secretary, Amrit Lal Bhardwaj

BHARATIYA VIDYA BHAVAN, Institute of Indian Art and Culture, 4A Castletown Road, London W14 9HE
T 020-7381 3086 E info@bhavan.net W www.bhavan.net
Executive Director, Dr M. N. Nandakumara

INTERNATIONAL SOCIETY FOR KRISHNA CONSCIOUSNESS (ISKCON), Bhaktivedanta Manor, Dharam Marg, Hilfield Lane, Aldenham, Watford, Herts WD25 8EZ T 01923-851000
E bhaktivendanta.manor@pamho.net
W www.krishnatemple.com
Temple President, Gauri das

NATIONAL COUNCIL OF HINDU TEMPLES (UK), Shree Sanatan Mandir, 84 Weymouth Street, Leicester LE4 6FQ T 0116-266 1402 E info@nchtuk.org
W www.nchtuk.org
General Secretary, Sanjay Jagatia

SWAMINARAYAN HINDU MISSION (SHRI SWAMINARAYAN MANDIR), 105–119 Brentfield Road, London NW10 8LD T 020-8965 2651
E info@mandir.org W www.mandir.org

HUMANISM

Humanism traces its roots back to ancient times, with Indian, Chinese, Greek and Roman philosophers expressing Humanist ideas some 2,500 years ago. Confucius, the Chinese philosopher who lived *c*.500 BC, believed that religious observances should be replaced with moral values as the basis of social and political order and that 'the true way' is based on reason and humanity. He also stressed the importance of benevolence and respect for others, and believed that the individual situation should be considered rather than the global application of traditional rules.

Humanists believe that there is no God or other supernatural being, that humans have only one life (Humanists do not believe in an after-life or reincarnation) and that humans can live ethical and fulfilling lives without religious beliefs through a moral code derived from a shared history, personal experience and thought. There are no sacred Humanist texts. Particular emphasis is placed on science as the only reliable source of knowledge of the universe. Many Humanists recognise a need for ceremonies to mark important occasions in life and the British Humanist Association has a network of celebrants who are trained and accredited to conduct baby namings, weddings and funerals. The British Humanist Association's campaigns for a secular society (a society based on freedom of religious or non-religious belief with no privileges for any particular set of beliefs) are based on equality and human rights. The association also campaigns for inclusive schools that meet the needs of all parents and pupils, regardless of their religious or non-religious beliefs.

BRITISH HUMANIST ASSOCIATION, 1 Gower Street, London WC1E 6HD T 020-7079 3580 F 020-7079 3588
E info@humanism.org.uk W www.humanism.org.uk
Chief Executive, Hanne Stinson

ISLAM

Islam (which means 'peace arising from submission to the will of Allah' in Arabic) is a monotheistic religion which was taught in Arabia by the Prophet Muhammad, who was born in Mecca (Al-Makkah) in 570 AD. Islam spread to Egypt, north Africa, Spain and the borders of China in the century following the Prophet's death, and is now the predominant religion in Indonesia, the near and Middle East, northern and parts of western Africa, Pakistan, Bangladesh, Malaysia and some of the former Soviet republics. There are also large Muslim communities in other countries.

For Muslims (adherents of Islam), there is one God *(Allah)*, who holds absolute power. Muslims believe that Allah's commands were revealed to mankind through the prophets, who include Abraham, Moses and Jesus, but that Allah's message was gradually corrupted until revealed finally and in perfect form to Muhammad through the angel *Jibril* (Gabriel) over a period of 23 years. This last, incorruptible message is said to have been recorded in the *Qur'an* (Koran), which contains 114 divisions called *surahs*, each made up of *ayahs* of various lengths, and is held to be the essence of all previous scriptures. The *Ahadith* are the records of the Prophet Muhammad's deeds and sayings (the *Sunnah*) as practised and recounted by his immediate followers. A culture and a system of law and theology gradually developed to form a distinctive Islamic civilisation. Islam makes no distinction between sacred and worldly affairs and provides rules for every aspect of human life. The *Shariah* is the sacred law of Islam based primarily upon prescriptions derived from the *Qur'an* and the *Sunnah* of the Prophet.

The 'five pillars of Islam' are *shahadah* (a declaration of faith in the oneness and supremacy of Allah and the messengership of Muhammad); *salat* (formal prayer, to be performed five times a day facing the *Ka'bah* (the most sacred shrine in the holy city of Mecca)); *zakat* (welfare due, paid annually on all savings at the rate of 2.5 per cent); *sawm* (fasting during the month of Ramadan from dawn until sunset); and *hajj* (pilgrimage to Mecca made once in a lifetime if the believer is financially and physically able). Some Muslims would add *jihad* as the sixth pillar (striving for the cause of good and resistance to evil).

Two main groups developed among Muslims. *Sunni* Muslims accept the legitimacy of Muhammad's first four *caliphs* (successors as head of the Muslim community) and of the authority of the Muslim community as a whole. About 90 per cent of Muslims are Sunni Muslims.

Shi'ites recognise only Muhammad's son-in-law Ali as his rightful successor and the *Imams* (descendants of Ali, not to be confused with *imams,* who are prayer leaders or religious teachers) as the principal legitimate religious authority. The largest group within Shi'ism is *Twelver Shi'ism,* which has been the official school of law and theology in Iran since the 16th century; other subsects include the *Ismailis,* the *Druze* and the *Alawis,* the latter two differing considerably from the main body of Muslims. The *Ibadis* of Oman are neither Sunni nor Shia, deriving from the strictly observant *Khariji* (Seceeders). There is no organised priesthood, but learned men such as imams, *ulama,* and *ayatollahs* are accorded great respect. The *Sufis* are the mystics of Islam. Mosques are centres for worship and teaching and also for social and welfare activities.

Islam was first recorded in western Europe in the eighth century AD when 800 years of Muslim rule began in Spain. Later, Islam spread to eastern Europe. More recently, Muslims came to Europe from Africa, the Middle East and Asia in the late 19th century. Both the Sunni and Shi'a traditions are represented in Britain, but the majority of Muslims in Britain adhere to Sunni Islam. Efforts to establish a representative national body for Muslims in Britain resulted in the founding, in 1997, of the Muslim Council of Britain. In addition, there are many other Muslim organisations in the UK. There are around 1,200 million Muslims worldwide, with nearly two million adherents and about 1,650 mosques in the UK.

IMAMS AND MOSQUES COUNCIL, 20–22 Creffield Road, London W5 3RP T 020-8992 6636
E msraza@muslimcollege.ac.uk
Director, Moulana M. S. Raza

ISLAMIC CULTURAL CENTRE – THE LONDON CENTRAL MOSQUE, 146 Park Road, London NW8 7RG
T 020-7725 2213 E info@iccuk.org W www.iccuk.org
Director, Dr Ahmad Al-Dubayan

MUSLIM COUNCIL OF BRITAIN, PO Box 57330, London E1 2WJ T 0845-262 6786 E admin@mcb.org.uk
W www.mcb.org.uk
Secretary-General, Dr Muhammad Abdul Bari

MUSLIM WORLD LEAGUE LONDON, 46 Goodge Street, London W1T 4LU T 020-7636 7568
Director, Abdul Aziz al-Harbi

UNION OF MUSLIM ORGANISATIONS OF THE UK AND EIRE, 109 Campden Hill Road, London W8 7TL
T 020-7221 6608
Secretary-General, Dr Syed A. Pasha

JAINISM

Jainism traces its history to Vardhamana Jnatriputra, known as *Tirthankara Mahavira* (the Great Hero) whose traditional dates were 599–527 BC. Jains believe he was the last of a series of 24 *Jinas* (those who overcome all passions and desires) or *Tirthankaras* (those who show a way across the ocean of life) stretching back to remote antiquity. Born to a noble family in north-eastern India (the state of Bihar), he renounced the world for the life of a wandering ascetic and after 12 years of austerity and meditation he attained enlightenment. He then preached his message until, at the age of 72, he left the mortal world and achieved total liberation *(moksha)* from the cycle of death and rebirth.

Jains declare that the Hindu rituals of transferring merit are not acceptable as each living being is responsible for its own actions. They recognise some of the minor deities of the Hindu pantheon, but the supreme objects of worship are the Tirthankaras. The pious Jain does not ask favours from the Tirthankaras, but seeks to emulate their example in his or her own life.

Jains believe that the universe is eternal and self-subsisting, that there is no omnipotent creator God ruling it and the destiny of the individual is in his or her own hands. *Karma,* the fruit of past actions, is believed to determine the place of every living being and rebirth may be in the heavens, on earth as a human, an animal or other lower being, or in the hells. The ultimate goal of existence for Jains is *moksha,* a state of perfect knowledge and tranquility for each individual soul, which can be achieved only by gaining enlightenment.

The Jainist path to liberation is defined by the three jewels: *Samyak Darshan* (right perception), *Samyak Jnana* (right knowledge) and *Samyak Charitra* (right conduct). Of the five fundamental precepts of the Jains, *Ahimsa* (non-injury to any form of being, in any mode: thought, speech or action) is the first and foremost, and was popularised by Gandhi as *Ahimsa paramo dharma* (non-violence is the supreme religion).

The largest population of Jains can be found in India but there are approximately 30,000 Jains in Britain, sizeable communities in North America, East Africa, Australia and smaller groups in many other countries.

INSTITUTE OF JAINOLOGY, Unit 18, Silicon Business Centre, 28 Wadsworth Road, Perivale, Greenford, Middx UB6 7JZ T 020-8997 2300 E enquiries@jainology.org
W www.jainology.org
Hon. Secretary, Dr Harshad Sanghrajka

JUDAISM

Judaism is the oldest monotheistic faith. The primary text of Judaism is the Hebrew bible or *Tanakh,* which records how the descendants of Abraham were led by Moses out of their slavery in Egypt to Mount Sinai where God's law *(Torah)* was revealed to them as the chosen people. The *Talmud,* which consists of commentaries on the *Mishnah* (the first text of rabbinical Judaism), is also held to be authoritative, and may be divided into two main categories: the *halakah* (dealing with legal and ritual matters) and the *aggadah* (dealing with theological and ethical matters not directly concerned with the regulation of conduct). The *midrash* comprises rabbinic writings containing biblical interpretations in the spirit of the aggadah. The halakah has become a source of division: orthodox Jews regard Jewish law as derived from God and therefore unalterable; progressive Jews seek to interpret it in the light of contemporary considerations; and conservative Jews aim to maintain most of the traditional rituals but to allow changes in accordance with tradition. Reconstructionist Judaism, a 20th-century movement, regards Judaism as a culture rather than a theological system and accepts all forms of Jewish practice.

The family is the basic unit of Jewish ritual, with the synagogue playing an important role as the centre for public worship and religious study. A synagogue is led by a group of laymen who are elected to office. The Rabbi is primarily a teacher and spiritual guide. The Sabbath is the central religious observance. Most British Jews are descendants of either the *Ashkenazim* of central and eastern Europe or the *Sephardim* of Spain, Portugal and the Middle East.

The Chief Rabbi of the United Hebrew Congregations of the Commonwealth is appointed by a Chief Rabbinate Conference, and is the rabbinical authority of the mainstream Orthodox sector of the Ashkenazi Jewish community, the largest body of which is the United Synagogue. His formal ecclesiastical authority is not recognised by the Reform Synagogues of Great Britain (the largest progressive group), the Union of Liberal and Progressive Synagogues, the Sephardi community or the Assembly of Masorti Synagogues. He is, however, generally recognised both outside the Jewish community and within it as the public religious representative of the totality of British Jewry. The Chief Rabbi is President of the London *Beth Din* (Court of Judgement), a rabbinic court. The *Dayanim* (Assessors) adjudicate in disputes or on matters of Jewish law and tradition; they also oversee dietary law administration, marriage, divorce and issues of personal status.

The Board of Deputies of British Jews, established in 1760, is the representative body of British Jewry. The basis of representation is through the election of deputies by synagogues and communal organisations. It protects and promotes interests of British Jewry, acts as the central voice of the community and seeks to counter anti-Jewish discrimination and anti-Semitic activities.

There are over 12.5 million Jews worldwide; in Great Britain and Ireland there are an estimated 285,000 adherents, around 435 rabbis and ministers and about 365 synagogues. Of these, approximately 190 congregations and about 175 rabbis and ministers are under the jurisdiction of the Chief Rabbi; 100 orthodox congregations have a more independent status; and 80 congregations are outside the jurisdiction of the Chief Rabbi.

OFFICE OF THE CHIEF RABBI, Adler House, 735 High Road, London N12 0US T 020-8343 6301 F 020-8343 6310 E info@chiefrabbi.org W www.chiefrabbi.org
Chief Rabbi, Sir Jonathan Sacks

BETH DIN (COURT OF THE CHIEF RABBI), 735 High Road, London N12 0US T 020-8343 6270
E info@bethdin.org.uk W www.theus.org.uk
Registrar, David Frei
Dayanim, Rabbi Chanoch Ehrentreu *(Consultant Dayan);* Menachem Gelley *(Senior Dayan);* Ivan Binstock; Yonason Abraham; Shmuel Simons

ASSEMBLY OF MASORTI SYNAGOGUES, Alexander House, 3 Shakespeare Road, London N3 1XE
T 020-8349 6650 E enquiries@masorti.org.uk
W www.masorti.org.uk
Executive Director, Michael Gluckman

BOARD OF DEPUTIES OF BRITISH JEWS, 6 Bloomsbury Square, London WC1A 2LP
T 020-7543 5400 F 020-7543 0010 E info@bod.org.uk
W www.bod.org.uk
President, Henry Grunwald, QC

FEDERATION OF SYNAGOGUES, 65 Watford Way, London NW4 3AQ T 020-8202 2263
E info@federationofsynagogues.com
W www.federationofsynagogues.com
President, Alan Finlay
Chief Executive, Dr Eli Kienwald

LIBERAL JUDAISM, The Montagu Centre, 21 Maple Street, London W1T 4BE T 020-7580 1663
E montagu@liberaljudaism.org W www.liberaljudaism.org
Chief Executive, Rabbi Danny Rich

THE MOVEMENT FOR REFORM JUDAISM, The Sternberg Centre for Judaism, 80 East End Road, London N3 2SY T 020-8349 5640 E admin@reformjudaism.org.uk
W www.reformjudaism.org.uk
Head of Movement, Rabbi Dr Tony Bayfield

SPANISH AND PORTUGUESE JEWS' CONGREGATION, 2 Ashworth Road, London W9 1JY
T 020-7289 2573 E howardmiller@spsyn.org.uk
W www.sandp.org
Chief Executive, Howard Miller

UNION OF ORTHODOX HEBREW CONGREGATIONS, 140 Stamford Hill, London N16 6QT
T 020-8802 6226 F 020-8809 6590
President, Rabbi Dovid Frand
Executive Coordinator, Chanoch Kesselman
Secretary, Chayim Schneck

UNITED SYNAGOGUE HEAD OFFICE, Adler House, 735 High Road, London N12 0US T 020-8343 8989
F 020-8343 6262 E info@unitedsynagogue.org.uk
W www.theus.org.uk
Chief Executive (interim), Stuart Taylor

PAGANISM

Paganism draws on the ideas of the Celtic people of pre-Roman Europe and is closely linked to Druidism. The first historical record of Druidry comes from classical Greek and Roman writers of the third century BC, who noted the existence of Druids among a people called the Keltoi who inhabited central and southern Europe. The word druid may derive from the Indo-European 'dreo-vid', meaning 'one who knows the truth'. In practice it was probably understood to mean something like 'wise-one' or 'philosopher-priest'.

Paganism is a pantheistic nature-worshipping religion which incorporates beliefs and ritual practices from ancient times. Pagans place much emphasis on the natural world and the ongoing cycle of life and death is central to their beliefs. Most Pagans believe that they are part of nature and not separate from, or superior to it, and seek to live in a way that minimises harm to the natural environment (the word Pagan derives from the Latin *Paganus,* meaning 'rural'). Paganism strongly emphasises the equality of the sexes, with women playing a prominent role in the modern Pagan movement and goddess worship featuring in most ceremonies. Paganism cannot be defined by any principal beliefs because it is shaped by each individual's experiences.

The Pagan Federation was founded in 1971 to provide information on Paganism, campaigns on issues which affect Paganism and provides support to members of the Pagan community. Within the UK the Pagan Federation is divided into 13 districts each with a district manager, regional and local coordinators. Local meetings are called 'moots' and take place in private homes, pubs or coffee bars. The Pagan Federation publishes a quarterly journal, *Pagan Dawn,* formerly *The Wiccan* (founded in 1968). The federation also publishes other material, arranges members-only and public events and maintains personal contact by letter with individual members and the wider Pagan community. An annual conference is held at the end of each November and there are regional gatherings throughout the year.

THE PAGAN FEDERATION, BM Box 7097, London WC1N 3XX T 0798-603 4387 E secretary@paganfed.org
W www.paganfed.org
President, Lindsey Heffern
Secretary, Pam Gardner

SIKHISM

The Sikh religion dates from the birth of Guru Nanak in the Punjab in 1469. 'Guru' means teacher but in Sikh tradition has come to represent the divine presence of God giving inner spiritual guidance. Nanak's role as the human vessel of the divine guru was passed on to nine successors, the last of whom (Guru Gobind Singh) died in 1708. The immortal guru is now held to reside in the sacred scripture, Guru Granth Sahib, and so to be present in all Sikh gatherings.

Guru Nanak taught that there is one God and that different religions are like different roads leading to the same destination. He condemned religious conflict, ritualism and caste prejudices. The fifth Guru, Guru Arjan Dev, largely compiled the Sikh Holy scripture, a collection of hymns *(gurbani)* known as the *Adi Granth.* It includes the writings of the first five gurus and the ninth guru, and selected writings of Hindu and Muslim saints whose views are in accord with the gurus' teachings. Guru Arjan Dev also built the Golden Temple at Amritsar, the centre of Sikhism. The tenth guru, Guru Gobind Singh, passed on the guruship to the sacred scripture, *Guru Granth Sahib* and founded the *Khalsa,* an order intended to fight against tyranny and injustice. Male initiates to the order added 'Singh' to their given names and women added 'Kaur'. Guru Gobind Singh also made the wearing of five symbols obligatory: *kaccha* (a special undergarment), *kara* (a steel bangle), *kirpan* (a small sword), *kesh* (long unshorn hair, and consequently the wearing of a turban) and *kangha* (a comb). These practices are still compulsory for those Sikhs who are initiated into the Khalsa (the *Amritdharis*). Those who do not seek initiation are known as *Sehajdharis.*

There are no professional priests in Sikhism; anyone with a reasonable proficiency in the Punjabi language can conduct a service. Worship can be offered individually or communally, and in a private house or a *gurdwara* (temple). Sikhs are forbidden to eat meat prepared by ritual slaughter; they are also asked to abstain from smoking, alcohol and other intoxicants. Such abstention is compulsory for the Amritdharis.

There are about 20 million Sikhs worldwide and, according to the 2001 census, there are 336,000 adherents in the UK. Every gurdwara manages its own affairs; there is no central body in the UK. The Sikh Missionary Society provides an information service.

SIKH MISSIONARY SOCIETY UK, 10 Featherstone Road, Southall, Middx UB2 5AA T 020-8574 1902
E info@sikhmissionarysociety.org
W www.sikhmissionarysociety.org
Hon. General Secretary, Surinder Singh Purewal, MBE

ZOROASTRIANISM

Zoroastrians are followers of the Iranian prophet Spitaman Zarathushtra (or Zoroaster in its hellenised form) who lived *c.*1200 BC. Zoroastrians were persecuted in Iran following the Arab invasion of Persia in the seventh century AD and a group (who are known as Parsis) migrated to India in the eighth century AD to avoid harassment and persecution. Zarathushtra's words are recorded in five poems called the *Gathas,* which, together with other scriptures, forms the *Avesta.*

Zoroastrianism teaches that there is one God, *Ahura Mazda* (the Wise Lord), and that all creation stems ultimately from God; the Gathas teach that human beings have free will, are responsible for their own actions and can choose between good and evil. It is believed that choosing *Asha* (truth or righteousness), with the aid of *Vohu Manah* (good mind), leads to happiness for the individual and society, whereas choosing evil leads to unhappiness and conflict. The *Gathas* also encourage hard work, good deeds and charitable acts. Zoroastrians believe that after death the immortal soul is judged by God, and is then sent to paradise or hell, where it will stay until the end of time to be resurrected for the final judgement.

In Zoroastrian places of worship, an urn containing fire is the central feature; the fire symbolises purity, light and truth and is a visible symbol of the *Fravashi* or *Farohar,* the presence of Ahura Mazda in every human being. Zoroastrians respect nature and much importance is attached to cultivating land and protecting air, earth and water.

The Zoroastrian Trust Funds of Europe is the main body for Zorastrians in the UK. Founded in 1861 as the Religious Funds of the Zorastrians of Europe, it disseminates information on the Zoroastrian faith, provides a place of worship and maintains separate burial grounds for Zoroastrians. It also holds religious and social functions and provides assistance to Zoroastrians as considered necessary, including the provision of loans and grants to students of Zoroastrianism.

There are approximately 140,000 Zoroastrians worldwide, of which around 7,000 reside in Britain, mainly in London and the South East.

ZOROASTRIAN TRUST FUNDS OF EUROPE, Zoroastrian Centre, 440 Alexandra Avenue, Harrow, Middx HA2 9TL T 020-8866 0765 E secretary@ztfe.com
W www.ztfe.com
President, Paurushasp B. Jila

CHURCHES

There are two established (ie state) churches in the United Kingdom: the Church of England and the Church of Scotland. There are no established churches in Wales or Northern Ireland, though the Church in Wales, the Scottish Episcopal Church and the Church of Ireland are members of the Anglican Communion.

CHURCH OF ENGLAND

The Church of England is the established (ie national) church in England and is organised locally into dioceses and parishes. It traces its life back to the first coming of Christianity to England. Its position is defined by the ancient creeds of the church and by the 39 Articles of Religion (1571), the Book of Common Prayer (1662) and the Ordinal. The Church of England is thus both catholic and reformed. It is the mother church of the Anglican Communion.

THE ANGLICAN COMMUNION

The Anglican Communion consists of 38 independent provincial or national Christian churches throughout the world, many of which are in Commonwealth countries and originate from missionary activity by the Church of England. Every ten years all the bishops in the Communion meet at the Lambeth Conference, convened by the Archbishop of Canterbury. The conference has no policy-making authority but is an important forum for discussing and forming consensus around issues of common concern. The Anglican Consultative Council was formed following a resolution of the 1968 Lambeth Conference which discerned the need for more frequent and representative contact than was possible through a once-a-decade conference of bishops. The council came into being in 1969 and meets every two to three years to liaise between the member churches and provinces of the Anglican Communion.

There are about 70 million Anglicans organised into 500 dioceses and 64,000 individual congregations worldwide.

STRUCTURE

The Church of England is divided into the two provinces of Canterbury and York, each under an archbishop. The two provinces are subdivided into 44 dioceses.

Legislative provision for the Church of England is made by the General Synod, established in 1970. It also discusses and expresses opinion on any other matter of religious or public interest. The General Synod has 467 members in total, divided between three houses: the House of Bishops, the House of Clergy and the House of Laity. It is presided over jointly by the Archbishops of Canterbury and York and normally meets twice a year. The synod has the power, delegated by parliament, to frame statute law (known as a 'measure') on any matter concerning the Church of England. A measure must be laid before both houses of parliament, who may accept or reject it but cannot amend it. Once accepted the measure is submitted for royal assent and then has the full force of law. In addition to the General Synod, there are synods at diocesan level.

The Archbishops' Council was established in January 1999. Its creation was the result of changes to the Church of England's national structure proposed in 1995 and subsequently approved by the synod and parliament. The council's purpose, set out in the National Institutions Measure 1998, is 'to coordinate, promote and further the work and mission of the Church of England'. It reports to the General Synod. The Archbishops' Council comprises the Archbishops of Canterbury and York, *ex officio,* the prolocutors elected by the convocations of Canterbury and York, the chair and vice-chair of the House of Laity, elected by that house, two bishops, two clergy and two lay persons elected by their respective houses of the General Synod, and up to six persons appointed jointly by the two archbishops with the approval of the General Synod.

There are also a number of national boards, councils and other bodies working on matters such as social responsibility, mission, Christian unity and education which report to the General Synod through the Archbishops' Council.

GENERAL SYNOD OF THE CHURCH OF ENGLAND, Church House, Great Smith Street, London SW1P 3NZ T 020-7898 1000
Joint Presidents, Archbishops of Canterbury and York
HOUSE OF BISHOPS: *Chair,* Archbishop of Canterbury; *Vice-Chair,* Archbishop of York
HOUSE OF CLERGY: *Chairs (alternating),* Ven. Norman Russell; Canon Glyn Webster
HOUSE OF LAITY: *Chair,* Dr Christina Baxter; *Vice-Chair,* Dr Philip Giddings
ARCHBISHOPS' COUNCIL, Church House, Great Smith Street, London SW1P 3NZ T 020-7898 1000
Joint Presidents, Archbishops of Canterbury and York; *Secretary-General,* William Fittall

THE ORDINATION OF WOMEN

The canon making it possible for women to be ordained to the priesthood was promulgated in the General Synod in February 1994 and the first 32 women priests were ordained on 12 March 1994.

MEMBERSHIP

In 2006, 138,400 people were baptised, the Church of England had an electoral roll membership of 1.3 million, and each week about 1.3 million people attended services. As at December 2007 there were over 16,000 churches and places of worship; 357 dignitaries (including bishops, archdeacons and cathedral clergy); 7,723 full-time parochial stipendiary clergy; 337 full-time non parochial stipendiary clergy; 1,569 chaplains etc; 387 lay workers and Church Army evangelists; 7,962 licensed readers and 2,382 readers with permission to officiate and active emeriti; and approximately 4,600 active retired ordained clergy.

	Full-time Diocesan Clergy 2007 Male	Female	Electoral Roll Membership 2006
Bath and Wells	170	41	39,500
Birmingham	133	43	19,100
Blackburn	181	18	35,800
Bradford	82	15	12,100
Bristol	104	26	17,000
Canterbury	115	25	22,900
Carlisle	117	25	21,800
Chelmsford	321	70	51,100
Chester	205	40	49,400
Chichester	284	18	56,700
Coventry	97	18	17,300
Derby	130	26	20,600
Durham	154	38	23,500
Ely	111	32	18,500
Europe	107	12	10,800
Exeter	196	29	32,100
Gloucester	113	25	22,500
Guildford	144	28	30,500
Hereford	69	25	18,100
Leicester	104	31	17,900
Lichfield	254	47	48,200
Lincoln	148	38	27,400
Liverpool	161	47	29,300
London	444	73	63,800
Manchester	200	49	35,700
Newcastle	109	29	17,000
Norwich	157	38	23,600
Oxford	284	87	57,900
Peterborough	124	28	19,000
Portsmouth	93	14	18,500
Ripon and Leeds	92	34	17,700
Rochester	185	35	31,600
St Albans	197	61	42,100
St Edmundsbury and Ipswich	114	25	25,200
Salisbury	166	42	43,600
Sheffield	126	35	20,600
Sodor and Man	16	1	2,800
Southwark	270	80	46,200
Southwell and Nottingham	113	38	19,500
Truro	91	18	17,500
Wakefield	112	39	21,600
Winchester	185	20	41,200
Worcester	111	33	20,400
York	191	47	37,900
Total	6,880	1,543	1,265,500

STIPENDS 2008–9*

Archbishop of Canterbury	£68,740
Archbishop of York	£58,920
Bishop of London	£54,010
Other diocesan bishops	£37,320
Suffragan bishops	£30,440
Assistant bishops (full-time)	£29,460
Deans	£30,440
Archdeacons (recommended)	£29,460
Residentiary canons	£23,570
Incumbents and clergy of similar status	£21,600†

* Rates are for those appointed on or after 1 April 2004, transitional arrangements are in place for those appointed prior to this date.

† National Stipend Benchmark (adjusted regionally to reflect variations in the cost of living)

CANTERBURY

104TH ARCHBISHOP AND PRIMATE OF ALL ENGLAND

Most Revd and Rt. Hon. Rowan Williams, *cons.* 1992, *apptd* 2002; Lambeth Palace, London SE1 7JU
Signs Rowan Cantuar:

BISHOPS SUFFRAGAN

Dover, Rt. Revd Stephen Venner, *cons. 1994, apptd* 1999; Upway, St Martin's Hill, Canterbury, Kent CT1 1PR

Maidstone, Rt. Revd Graham Cray, *cons.* 2001, *apptd* 2001; Bishop's House, Pett Lane, Charing, Ashford, Kent TN27 0DL

Ebbsfleet, Rt. Revd Andrew Burnham, *cons.* 2000, *apptd* 2000 (provincial episcopal visitor); Bishop's House, Dry Sandford, Abingdon, Oxon OX13 6JP

Richborough, Rt. Revd Keith Newton, *cons.* 2002, *apptd* 2002 (provincial episcopal visitor); 6 Mellis Gardens, Woodford Green, Essex IG8 0BH

DEAN

Very Revd Robert Willis, *apptd* 2001

Organist, D. Flood, FRCO, *apptd* 1988

ARCHDEACONS

Canterbury, Ven. Sheila Watson, *apptd* 2007
Maidstone, Ven. Philip Down, *apptd* 2002

Vicar-General of Province and Diocese, Chancellor Sheila Cameron, QC
Commissary-General, His Hon. Richard Walker
Joint Registrars of the Province, Canon John Rees; Stephen Slack
Diocesan Registrar and Legal Adviser, Richard Sturt
Diocesan Secretary, Julian Hills, Diocesan House, Lady Wootton's Green, Canterbury CT1 1NQ **T** 01227-459401

YORK

97TH ARCHBISHOP AND PRIMATE OF ENGLAND

Most Revd and Rt. Hon. Dr John Sentamu, *cons.* 1996, *trans.* 2005; Bishopthorpe, York YO23 2GE
Signs Sentamu Ebor:

BISHOPS SUFFRAGAN

Beverley, Rt. Revd Martyn Jarrett (provincial episcopal visitor), *cons.* 1994, *apptd* 2000; 3 North Lane, Roundhay, Leeds LS8 2QJ

Hull, Rt. Revd Richard Frith, *cons.* 1998, *apptd* 1998; Hullen House, Woodfield Lane, Hessle, Hull HU13 0ES

Selby, Rt. Revd Martin Wallace, *cons.* 2003, *apptd* 2003; Bishop's House, Barton le Street, Malton, York YO17 6PL

Whitby, Rt. Revd Robert Ladds, *cons.* 1999, *apptd* 1999; 60 West Green, Stokesley, Middlesbrough TS9 5BD

DEAN

Very Revd Keith Jones, *apptd* 2004

Master of the Music, Philip Moore, FRCO, *apptd* 1983

ARCHDEACONS

Cleveland, Ven. Paul Ferguson, *apptd* 2001
East Riding, Ven. David Butterfield, *apptd* 2006
York, Ven. Richard Seed, *apptd* 1999

Chancellor of the Diocese, Revd Peter Collier, QC, *apptd* 2006
Registrar and Legal Secretary, Lionel Lennox
Diocesan Secretary, Peter Warry, Diocesan House, Aviator Court, Clifton Moor, York YO30 4WJ **T** 01904-699500

LONDON *(Canterbury)*
132ND BISHOP
Rt. Revd and Rt. Hon Richard Chartres, *cons.* 1992, *apptd* 1995; The Old Deanery, Dean's Court, London EC4V 5AA
Signs Richard Londin:

AREA BISHOPS
Edmonton, Rt. Revd Peter Wheatley, *cons.* 1999, *apptd* 1999; 27 Thurlow Road, London NW3 5PP
Kensington, vacant
Stepney, Rt. Revd Canon Stephen Oliver, *cons.* 2003, *apptd* 2003; 63 Coborn Road, London E3 2DB
Willesden, Rt. Revd Peter Broadbent, *cons.* 2001, *apptd* 2001; 173 Willesden Lane, London NW6 7YN

BISHOP SUFFRAGAN
Fulham, Rt. Revd John Broadhurst, *cons.* 1996, *apptd* 1996; 26 Canonbury Park South, London N1 2FN

DEAN OF ST PAUL'S
Rt. Revd Graeme Knowles, *apptd* 2007

Organist, Andrew Carwood, *apptd* 2007

ARCHDEACONS
Charing Cross, Ven. Dr William Jacob, *apptd* 1996
Hackney, Ven. Lyle Dennen, *apptd* 1999
Hampstead, Ven. Michael Lawson, *apptd* 1999
London, Ven. Peter Delaney, *apptd* 1999
Middlesex, Ven. Stephen Welch, *apptd* 2006
Northolt, Ven. Rachel Treweek, *apptd* 2006

Chancellor, Nigel Seed, QC, *apptd* 2002
Registrar and Legal Secretary, Paul Morris
Diocesan Secretary, Keith Robinson, London Diocesan House, 36 Causton Street, London SW1P 4AU T 020-7932 1226

DURHAM *(York)*
71ST BISHOP
Rt. Revd Dr N. Thomas Wright, *cons.* 2003, *apptd* 2003; Auckland Castle, Bishop Auckland DL14 7NR
Signs Thomas Dunelm:

BISHOP SUFFRAGAN
Jarrow, Rt. Revd Mark Bryant, *cons.* 2007, *apptd* 2007; Bishop's House, Ivy Lane, Low Fell, Gateshead NE9 6QD

DEAN
Very Revd Michael Sadgrove, *apptd* 2003

Organist, James Lancelot, FRCO, *apptd* 1985

ARCHDEACONS
Auckland, Ven. Nicholas Barker, *apptd* 2007
Durham, Ven. Ian Jagger, *apptd* 2006
Sunderland, Ven. Stuart Bain, *apptd* 2002

Chancellor, The Worshipful Revd Dr Rupert Bursell, QC, *apptd* 1989
Registrar and Legal Secretary, Hilary Monckton-Milnes
Diocesan Secretary, Ian Boothroyd, Diocesan Office, Auckland Castle, Bishop Auckland, Co. Durham DL14 7QJ T 01388-604515

WINCHESTER *(Canterbury)*
96TH BISHOP
Rt. Revd Michael C. Scott-Joynt, *cons.* 1987, *trans.* 1995: Wolvesey, Winchester SO23 9ND
Signs Michael Winton:

BISHOPS SUFFRAGAN
Basingstoke, Rt. Revd Trevor Willmott, *cons.* 2002, *apptd* 2002; Bishopswood End, Kingswood Rise, Four Marks, Alton, Hants GU34 5BD
Southampton, Rt. Revd Paul Butler, *cons.* 2004, *apptd* 2004; Ham House, The Crescent, Romsey SO51 7NG

DEAN
Very Revd James Atwell, *apptd* 2005
Dean of Jersey (A Peculiar), Very Revd Robert Key, *apptd* 2005
Dean of Guernsey (A Peculiar), Very Revd Paul Mellor, *apptd* 2003
Director of Music, Andrew Lumsden, *apptd* 2002

ARCHDEACONS
Bournemouth, Ven. Adrian Harbidge, *apptd* 1998
Winchester, vacant

Chancellor, Christopher Clark, *apptd* 1993
Registrar and Legal Secretary, Peter White
Diocesan Secretary, Andrew Howard, Church House, 9 The Close, Winchester, Hants SO23 9LS T 01962-624742

BATH AND WELLS *(Canterbury)*
78TH BISHOP
Rt. Revd Peter Price, *cons.* 1997, *apptd* 2002; The Palace, Wells BA5 2PD
Signs Peter Bath & Wells

BISHOP SUFFRAGAN
Taunton, Rt. Revd Peter Maurice, *cons.* 2006, *apptd* 2006; The Palace, Wells BA5 2PD

DEAN
Very Revd John Clarke, *apptd* 2004

Organist, Matthew Owens, *apptd* 2005

ARCHDEACONS
Bath, Ven. Andrew Piggott, *apptd* 2005
Taunton, Ven. John Reed, *apptd* 1999
Wells, Ven. Nicola Sullivan, *apptd* 2006

Chancellor, Timothy Briden, *apptd* 1993
Registrar and Legal Secretary, Tim Berry
Diocesan Secretary, Nicholas Denison, The Old Deanery, Wells, Somerset BA5 2UG T 01749-670777

BIRMINGHAM *(Canterbury)*
8TH BISHOP
Rt. Revd David Urquhart, *cons.* 2000, *apptd* 2006; Bishop's Croft, Old Church Road, Harborne, Birmingham B17 0BG
Signs David Birmingham:

BISHOP SUFFRAGAN
Aston, vacant

DEAN
Very Revd Bob Wilkes, *apptd* 2006

Organist, Marcus Huxley, FRCO, *apptd* 1986

ARCHDEACONS
Aston, Ven. Dr Brian Russell, *apptd* 2005
Birmingham, Ven. Hayward Osborne, *apptd* 2001

Chancellor, His Hon. Judge Martin Cardinal, *apptd* 2005
Registrar and Legal Secretary, Hugh Carslake

Diocesan Secretary, Jim Drennan, 175 Harborne Park Road, Harborne, Birmingham B17 0BH T 0121-426 0400

BLACKBURN *(York)*
8TH BISHOP
Rt. Revd Nicholas Reade, *apptd* 2003, *cons.* March 2004; Bishop's House, Ribchester Road, Blackburn BB1 9EF
Signs Nicholas Blackburn

BISHOPS SUFFRAGAN
Burnley, Rt. Revd John Goddard, *cons.* 2000, *apptd* 2000; Dean House, 449 Padiham Road, Burnley BB12 6TE
Lancaster, Rt. Revd Geoffrey Pearson, *cons.* 2006, *apptd* 2006; The Vicarage, Whinney Brow Lane, Shireshead, Forton, Preston PR3 0AE

DEAN
Very Revd Christopher Armstrong, *apptd* 2001

Organist, Richard Tanner, *apptd* 1998

ARCHDEACONS
Blackburn, Ven. John Hawley, *apptd* 2002
Lancaster, Ven. Peter Ballard, *apptd* 2006

Chancellor, John Bullimore, *apptd* 1990
Registrar and Legal Secretary, Thomas Hoyle
Diocesan Secretary, Graeme Pollard, Diocesan Office, Cathedral Close, Blackburn BB1 5AA T 01254-503070

BRADFORD *(York)*
9TH BISHOP
Rt. Revd David James, *apptd* 2002; Bishopscroft, Ashwell Road, Heaton, Bradford BD9 4AU
Signs David Bradford

DEAN
Very Revd Dr David Ison, *apptd* 2005

Organist, Andrew Teague, FRCO, *apptd* 2003

ARCHDEACONS
Bradford, Ven. David Lee, *apptd* 2004
Craven, Ven. Paul Slater, *apptd* 2005

Chancellor, John de G. Walford, *apptd* 1999
Registrar and Legal Secretary, Peter Foskett
Diocesan Secretary, Malcolm Halliday, Kadugli House, Elmsley Street, Steeton, Keighley BD20 6SE T 01535-650555

BRISTOL *(Canterbury)*
55TH BISHOP
Rt. Revd Michael Hill, *cons.* 1998, *apptd* 2003; Wethered House, 11 The Avenue, Clifton, Bristol BS8 3HG
Signs Michael Bristol

BISHOP SUFFRAGAN
Swindon, Rt. Revd Dr Lee Rayfield, *cons.* 2005, *apptd* 2005; Mark House, Field Rise, Swindon, Wiltshire, SN1 4HP

DEAN
Very Revd Robert W. Grimley, *apptd* 1997

Organist and Director of Music, Mark Lee, *apptd* 1998

ARCHDEACONS
Bristol, Ven. Tim McClure, *apptd* 1999
Malmesbury, Ven. Alan Hawker, *apptd* 1998

Chancellor, Dr James Behrens, *apptd* 2005
Registrar and Legal Secretary, Tim Berry
Diocesan Secretary, Lesley Farrall, Diocesan Church House, 23 Great George Street, Bristol BS1 5QZ T 0117-906 0100

CARLISLE *(York)*
66TH BISHOP
Rt. Revd Graham Dow, *cons.* 1985, *apptd* 2000; Rose Castle, Dalston, Carlisle CA5 7BZ
Signs Graham Carlisle:

BISHOP SUFFRAGAN
Penrith, Rt. Revd James Newcome, *cons.* 2002, *apptd* 2002; Holm Croft, Castle Road, Kendal, Cumbria LA9 7AU

DEAN
Very Revd Mark Boyling, *apptd* 2004

Organist, Jeremy Suter, FRCO, *apptd* 1991

ARCHDEACONS
Carlisle, vacant
West Cumberland, Ven. Colin Hill, *apptd* 2004
Westmorland and Furness, Ven. George Howe, *apptd* 2000

Chancellor, Geoffrey Tattersall, QC, *apptd* 2003
Registrar and Legal Secretary, Jane Lowdon
Diocesan Secretary, Derek Hurton, Church House, West Walls, Carlisle CA3 8UE T 01228-522573

CHELMSFORD *(Canterbury)*
9TH BISHOP
Rt. Revd John Warren Gladwin, *cons.* 1994, *apptd* 2003, *trans.* 2004; Bishopscourt, Margaretting, Ingatestone CM4 0HD
Signs John Chelmsford

BISHOPS SUFFRAGAN
Barking, Rt. Revd David Hawkins, *cons.* 2002, *apptd* 2003; Barking Lodge, Verulam Avenue, London, E17 8ES
Bradwell, Rt. Revd Dr Laurence Green, *cons.* 1993, *apptd* 1993; Bishop's House, Orsett Road, Horndon-on-the-Hill, Stanford-le-Hope, Essex SS17 8NS
Colchester, Rt. Revd Christopher Morgan, *cons.* 2001, *apptd* 2001; 1 Fitzwalter Road, Colchester, Essex CO3 3SS

DEAN
Very Revd Peter S. M. Judd, *apptd* 1997

Master of Music, Peter Nardone, *apptd* 2000

ARCHDEACONS
Colchester, Ven. Annette Cooper, *apptd* 2004
Harlow, Ven. Peter Taylor, *apptd* 1996
Southend, Ven. David Lowman, *apptd* 2001
West Ham, Ven. Elwin Cockett, *apptd* 2007

Chancellor, George Pulman, QC, *apptd* 2001
Registrar and Legal Secretary, Brian Hood
Chief Executive, Steven Webb, 53 New Street, Chelmsford, Essex CM1 1AT T 01245-294400

CHESTER *(York)*
40TH BISHOP
Rt. Revd Peter R. Forster, PHD, *cons.* 1996, *apptd* 1996; Bishop's House, Chester CH1 2JD
Signs Peter Cestr:

BISHOPS SUFFRAGAN
Birkenhead, Rt. Revd Keith Sinclair, *cons.* 2007, *apptd* 2007; Bishop's Lodge, 67 Bidston Road, Prenton CH43 6TR

Stockport, Rt. Revd Robert Atwell, *cons.* 2008, *apptd* 2008; Bishop's Lodge, Back Lane, Dunham Town, Altrincham WA14 4SG

DEAN
Very Revd Dr Gordon McPhate, *apptd* 2002

Organist and Director of Music, Philip Rushforth, FRCO, *apptd* 2008

ARCHDEACONS
Chester, Ven. Donald Allister, *apptd* 2002
Macclesfield, Ven. Richard Gillings, *apptd* 1994

Chancellor, His Hon. Judge Turner, QC, *apptd* 1998
Registrar and Legal Secretary, Helen McFall
Diocesan Secretary, Dr John Mason, Church House, Lower Lane, Aldford, Chester CH3 6HP T 01244-620444

CHICHESTER *(Canterbury)*
102ND BISHOP
Rt. Revd John Hind, *cons.* 1991, *apptd* 2001; The Palace, Chichester PO19 1PY
Signs John Cicestr:

BISHOPS SUFFRAGAN
Horsham, Rt. Revd Lindsay Urwin, *cons.* 1993, *apptd* 1993; Bishop's House, 21 Guildford Road, Horsham, W. Sussex RH12 1LU
Lewes, Rt. Revd Wallace Benn, *cons.* 1997, *apptd* 1997; Bishop's Lodge, 16A Prideaux Road, Eastbourne, E. Sussex BN21 2NB

DEAN
Very Revd Nicholas Frayling, *apptd* 2002

Organist, Sarah Baldock, *apptd* 2007

ARCHDEACONS
Chichester, Ven. Douglas McKittrick, *apptd* 2002
Horsham, Ven. Roger Combes, *apptd* 2003
Lewes and Hastings, Ven. Philip Jones, *apptd* 2005

Chancellor, Mark Hill
Registrar and Legal Secretary, John Stapleton
Diocesan Secretary, Jonathan Prichard, Diocesan Church House, 211 New Church Road, Hove, E. Sussex BN3 4ED T 01273-421021

COVENTRY *(Canterbury)*
9TH BISHOP
Rt. Revd Christopher Cocksworth, *cons.* 2008, *apptd* 2008; The Bishop's House, 23 Davenport Road, Coventry CV5 6PW
Signs Christopher Coventry

BISHOP SUFFRAGAN
Warwick, Rt. Revd John Stroyan, *cons.* 2005, *apptd* 2005; Warwick House, 139 Kenilworth Road, Coventry CV4 7AP

DEAN
Very Revd John Irvine, *apptd* 2001

Director of Music, Mr Kerry Beaumont, *apptd* 2006

ARCHDEACONS
Coventry, Ven. Ian Watson, *apptd* 2007
Warwick, Ven. Michael Paget-Wilkes, *apptd* 1990

Chancellor, Sir William Gage, *apptd* 1980
Registrar and Legal Secretary, David Dumbleton
Diocesan Secretary, Simon Lloyd, Cathedral & Diocesan Offices, 1 Hilltop, Coventry CV1 5AB
T 024-7652 1200

DERBY *(Canterbury)*
7TH BISHOP
Rt. Revd Alastair Redfern, *cons.* 1997, *apptd* 2005; Bishop's House, 6 King Street, Duffield, Belper, Derbyshire, DE56 4EU
Signs Alastair Derby

BISHOP SUFFRAGAN
Repton, Rt. Revd Humphrey Southern, *cons.* 2007, *apptd* 2007; Repton House, Lea, Matlock, Derbys DE4 5JP

DEAN
Very Revd Dr Jeffrey Cuttell, *apptd* 2008

Organist, Peter Gould, *apptd* 1982

ARCHDEACONS
Chesterfield, Ven. David Garnett, *apptd* 1996
Derby, Ven. Christopher Cunliffe, *apptd* 2006

Chancellor, His Hon. Judge John Bullimore, *apptd* 1981
Registrar and Legal Secretary, Mrs Nadine Waldron
Diocesan Secretary, Bob Carey, Derby Church House, Full Street, Derby DE1 3DR T 01332-388650

ELY *(Canterbury)*
68TH BISHOP
Rt. Revd Dr Anthony Russell, *cons.* 1988, *apptd* 2000; The Bishop's House, Ely, Cambs CB7 4DW
Signs Anthony Ely

BISHOP SUFFRAGAN
Huntingdon, Rt. Revd David Thomson, DPHIL, *cons.* 2008, *apptd* 2008; 14 Lynn Road, Ely, Cambs CB6 1DA

DEAN
Very Revd Dr Michael Chandler, *apptd* 2003

Director of Music, Paul Trepte, FRCO, *apptd* 1991

ARCHDEACONS
Cambridge, Ven. John Beer, *apptd* 2004
Huntingdon and Wisbech, Ven. Hugh McCurdy, *apptd 2005*

Chancellor, The Hon. Mr Justice Gage, QC
Registrar, Peter Beesley
Diocesan Secretary, Dr Matthew Lavis, Bishop Woodford House, Barton Road, Ely, Cambs CB7 4DX
T 01353-652701

EXETER *(Canterbury)*
70TH BISHOP
Rt. Revd Michael Langrish, *cons.* 1993, *apptd* 2000; The Palace, Exeter, EX1 1HY
Signs Michael Exon:

BISHOPS SUFFRAGAN
Crediton, Rt. Revd Robert Evens, *cons.* 2004, *apptd* 2004; 32 The Avenue, Tiverton EX16 4HW
Plymouth, Rt. Revd John Ford, *cons.* 2006, *apptd* 2005; 31 Riverside Walk, Tamerton Foliot, Plymouth PL5 4AQ

DEAN
Very Revd Jonathan Meyrick, *apptd* 2005

Director of Music, Andrew Millington, *apptd* 1999

ARCHDEACONS
Barnstaple, Ven. David Gunn-Johnson, *apptd* 2003
Exeter, Ven. Penny Driver, *apptd* 2006
Plymouth, Ven. Tony Wilds, *apptd* 2001
Totnes, Ven. John Rawlings, *apptd* 2006

Chancellor, Hon. Sir Andrew McFarlane
Registrar and Legal Secretary, M. Follett
Diocesan Secretary, Mark Beedell, The Old Deanery, The Cloisters, Exeter EX1 1HS **T** 01392-272686

GIBRALTAR IN EUROPE *(Canterbury)*
BISHOP
Rt. Revd Dr Geoffrey Rowell, *cons.* 1994, *apptd* 2001; Bishop's Lodge, Church Road, Worth, Crawley, West Sussex RH10 7RT

BISHOP SUFFRAGAN
In Europe, Rt. Revd David Hamid, *cons.* 2002, *apptd* 2002; 14 Tufton Street, London SW1P 3QZ
Dean, Cathedral Church of the Holy Trinity, Gibraltar, Very Revd Alan Woods
Chancellor, Pro-Cathedral of St Paul, Valletta, Malta, Canon Thomas Mendel
Chancellor, Pro-Cathedral of the Holy Trinity, Brussels, Belgium, Canon Dr Robert Innes

ARCHDEACONS
Eastern, Ven. Patrick Curran
North-West Europe, Ven. John de Wit
France, Ven. Kenneth Letts
Gibraltar, Ven. David Sutch
Italy, Ven. Arthur Siddall
Scandinavia and Germany, vacant
Switzerland, Ven. Arthur Siddall

Chancellor, Mark Hill
Registrar and Legal Secretary, vacant
Diocesan Secretary, Adrian Mumford, 14 Tufton Street, London SW1P 3QZ **T** 020-7898 1155

GLOUCESTER *(Canterbury)*
40TH BISHOP
Rt. Revd Michael Perham, *cons.* 2004, *apptd* 2004; Bishopscourt, Pitt Street, Gloucester GL1 2BQ
Signs Michael Gloucestr

BISHOP SUFFRAGAN
Tewkesbury, Rt. Revd John S. Went, *cons.* 1995, *apptd* 1995; Bishop's House, Staverton, Cheltenham GL51 0TW

DEAN
Very Revd Nicholas Bury, *apptd* 1997

Director of Music, Adrian Partington, *apptd* 2007

ARCHDEACONS
Cheltenham, Ven. Hedley Ringrose, *apptd* 1998
Gloucester, Ven. Geoffrey Sidaway, *apptd* 2000

Chancellor and Vicar-General, June Rodgers, *apptd* 1990
Registrar and Legal Secretary, Chris Peak
Diocesan Secretary, Dr Kevin Brown, Church House, College Green, Gloucester GL1 2LY **T** 01452-410022

GUILDFORD *(Canterbury)*
9TH BISHOP
Rt. Revd Christopher Hill, *cons.* 1996, *apptd* 2004; Willow Grange, Woking Road, Guildford GU4 7QS
Signs Christopher Guildford

BISHOP SUFFRAGAN
Dorking, Rt. Revd Ian Brackley, *cons.* 1996, *apptd* 1995; Dayspring, 13 Pilgrims Way, Guildford GU4 8AD

DEAN
Very Revd Victor Stock, *apptd* 2002

Organist, Katherine Dienes-Williams, *apptd* 2007

ARCHDEACONS
Dorking, Ven. Julian Henderson, *apptd* 2005
Surrey, Ven. Stuart Beake, *apptd* 2005

Chancellor, Andrew Jordan
Registrar and Legal Secretary, Peter Beesley
Diocesan Secretary, Stephen Marriott, Diocesan House, Quarry Street, Guildford GU1 3AG **T** 01483-571826

HEREFORD *(Canterbury)*
104TH BISHOP
Rt. Revd Anthony Priddis, *cons.* 1996, *apptd* 2004; The Bishop's House, Hereford HR4 9BN
Signs Anthony Hereford

BISHOP SUFFRAGAN
Ludlow, Rt. Revd Michael Wrenford Hooper, *cons.* 2002, *apptd* 2002; Bishop's House, Corvedale Road, Craven Arms, Shropshire SY7 9BT

DEAN
Very Revd Michael Tavinor, *apptd* 2002

Organist, Geraint Bowen, FRCO, *apptd* 2001

ARCHDEACONS
Hereford, Ven. Malcom Colmer, *apptd* 2005
Ludlow, Rt. Revd Michael Hooper, *apptd* 2002

Chancellor, Roger Kaye
Registrar and Legal Secretary, Peter Beesley
Diocesan Secretary, John Clark, The Palace, Hereford HR4 9BL **T** 01432-373300

LEICESTER *(Canterbury)*
6TH BISHOP
Rt. Revd Timothy J. Stevens, *cons.* 1995, *apptd* 1999; Bishop's Lodge, 10 Springfield Road, Leicester LE2 3BD
Signs Timothy Leicester

DEAN
Very Revd Vivienne F. Faull, *apptd* 2000

Master of Music, Jonathan Gregory, *apptd* 1994

ARCHDEACONS
Leicester, Ven. Richard Atkinson, *apptd* 2002
Loughborough, Ven. Paul Hackwood, *apptd* 2005

Chancellor, Dr James Behrens
Registrar and Legal Secretary, Trevor Kirkman
Diocesan Secretary, Jane Easton, Church House, 3–5 St Martin's East, Leicester LE1 5FX **T** 0116-248 7400

LICHFIELD *(Canterbury)*
98TH BISHOP
Rt. Revd Jonathan Gledhill, *cons.* 1996, *apptd* 2003; Bishop's House, The Close, Lichfield WS13 7LG
Signs Jonathan Lichfield

BISHOPS SUFFRAGAN
Shrewsbury, Rt. Revd Dr Alan Smith, *cons.* 2001, *apptd* 2002; 68 London Road, Shrewsbury SY2 6PG

Stafford, Rt. Revd A. Gordon Mursell, *cons.* 2005, *apptd* 2005; Ash Garth, 6 Broughton Crescent, Barlaston, Stoke on Trent ST12 9DD
Wolverhampton, Rt. Revd Clive Gregory, *cons.* 2007, *apptd* 2007; 61 Richmond Road, Wolverhampton WV3 9JH

DEAN
Very Revd Adrian Dorber, *apptd* 2005

Organist, Philip Scriven, *apptd* 2002

ARCHDEACONS
Lichfield, Ven. Christopher Liley, *apptd* 2001
Salop, Ven. John Hall, *apptd* 1998
Stoke-on-Trent, Ven. Godfrey Owen Stone, *apptd* 2002
Walsall, Revd Robert Jackson, *apptd* 2004

Chancellor, His Hon. Judge Marten Coates
Registrar and Legal Secretary, N. Blackie
Diocesan Secretary, D. R. Taylor, St Mary's House, The Close, Lichfield, Staffs WS13 7LD T 01543-306030

LINCOLN *(Canterbury)*

71ST BISHOP
Rt. Revd Dr John Saxbee, *cons.* 1994, *apptd* 2002; Bishop's House, Eastgate, Lincoln LN2 1QQ
Signs John Lincoln

BISHOPS SUFFRAGAN
Grantham, Rt. Revd Dr Timothy Ellis, *cons.* 2006, *apptd* 2006; Saxonwell Vicarage, Church Street, Long Bennington, Newark NG23 5ES
Grimsby, Rt. Revd David D. J. Rossdale, *cons.* 2000, *apptd* 2000; Bishop's House, Church Lane, Irby-upon-Humber, Grimsby DN37 7JR

DEAN
Very Revd Philip Buckler, *apptd* 2007

Director of Music, A. Prentice, *apptd* 2003

ARCHDEACONS
Lincoln, vacant
Lindsey and Stow, Ven. Jane Sinclair, *apptd* 2007

Chancellor, Mark Bishop, QC, *apptd* 2007
Registrar and Legal Secretary, Caroline Mockford, *apptd* 2008
Diocesan Secretary, Max Manin, The Old Palace, Lincoln LN2 1PU T 01522-504050

LIVERPOOL *(York)*

7TH BISHOP
Rt. Revd James Jones, *cons.* 1994, *apptd* 1998; Bishop's Lodge, Woolton Park, Liverpool L25 6DT
Signs James Liverpool

BISHOP SUFFRAGAN
Warrington, Rt. Revd David Jennings, *cons.* 2000, *apptd* 2000; 34 Central Avenue, Eccleston Park, Prescot, Merseyside L34 2QP

DEAN
Very Revd Justin Welby, *apptd* 2007

Director of Music, David Poulter, *apptd* 2008

ARCHDEACONS
Liverpool, Ven. Richard Panter, *apptd* 2002
Warrington, Ven. Peter Bradley, *apptd* 2001

Chancellor, Hon. Sir Mark Hedley
Registrar and Legal Secretary, Roger Arden
Diocesan Secretary, Mike Eastwood, St James House, 20 St James Street, Liverpool L1 7BY T 0151-709 9722

MANCHESTER *(York)*

11TH BISHOP
Rt. Revd Nigel McCulloch, *cons.* 1986, *apptd* 2002, *trans.* 2002; Bishopscourt, Bury New Road, Manchester M7 4LE
Signs Nigel Manchester

BISHOPS SUFFRAGAN
Bolton, Rt. Revd Christopher Edmondson, *cons.* 2008, *apptd* 2008; Bishop's Lodge, Walkden Road, Worsley, Manchester M28 2WH
Hulme, Rt. Revd Stephen Lowe, *cons.* 1999, *apptd* 1999; 14 Moorgate Avenue, Withington, Manchester M20 1HE
Middleton, Rt. Revd Mark Davies, *cons.* 2008, *apptd* 2008; The Hollies, Manchester Road, Rochdale OL11 3QY

DEAN
Revd Rogers Govender, *apptd* 2006

Organist, Christopher Stokes, *apptd* 1992

ARCHDEACONS
Bolton, Ven. John Applegate, *apptd* 2002
Manchester, Ven. Andrew Ballard, *apptd* 2005
Rochdale, Cherry Vann, *apptd* 2008

Chancellor, G. Tattersall
Registrar and Legal Secretary, Jane Monks
Diocesan Secretary, John Beck, Diocesan Church House, 90 Deansgate, Manchester M3 2GH T 0161-828 1400

NEWCASTLE *(York)*

11TH BISHOP
Rt. Revd J. Martin Wharton, *cons.* 1992, *apptd* 1997; Bishop's House, 29 Moor Road South, Gosforth, Newcastle upon Tyne NE3 1PA
Signs Martin Newcastle

ASSISTANT BISHOP
Rt. Revd Paul Richardson, *cons.* 1987, *apptd* 1999

DEAN
Very Revd Christopher C. Dalliston, *apptd* 2003

Director of Music, Scott Farrell, *apptd* 2002

ARCHDEACONS
Lindisfarne, Ven. Dr Peter Robinson, *apptd* 2008
Northumberland, Ven. Geoffrey Miller, *apptd* 2004

Chancellor, Prof. David McClean, *apptd* 1998
Registrar and Legal Secretary, Jane Lowdon
Diocesan Secretary, Philip Davies, Church House, St John's Terrace, North Shields NE29 6HS T 0191-270 4100

NORWICH *(Canterbury)*

71ST BISHOP
Rt. Revd Graham R. James, *cons.* 1993, *apptd* 2000; Bishop's House, Norwich NR3 1SB
Signs Graham Norvic:

BISHOPS SUFFRAGAN
Lynn, Rt. Revd James Langstaff, *cons.* 2004, *apptd* 2004; The Old Vicarage, Castle Acre, King's Lynn PE32 2AA
Thetford, Rt. Revd David J. Atkinson, *cons.* 2001, *apptd* 2001; The Red House, 53 Norwich Road, Stoke Holy Cross, Norwich NR14 8AB

DEAN
Very Revd Graham Smith, *apptd* 2004

Master of Music, David Lowe, *apptd* 2007

ARCHDEACONS
Lynn, Ven. Martin Gray, *apptd* 1999
Norfolk, Ven. David Hayden, *apptd* 2002
Norwich, Ven. Jan McFarlane, *apptd* 2008

Chancellor, His Hon. Judge Paul Downes, *apptd* 2007
Registrar and Legal Secretary, Ian Mayers
Diocesan Secretary, Revd Canon Richard Bowett, Diocesan House, 109 Dereham Road, Easton, Norwich, Norfolk NR9 5ES T 01603-880853

OXFORD *(Canterbury)*

42ND BISHOP
Rt. Revd John Pritchard, *cons.* 2002, *apptd* 2007; Diocesan Church House, North Hinksey Lane, Oxford OX2 0NB
Signs John Oxon:

AREA BISHOPS
Buckingham, Rt. Revd Dr Alan Wilson, *cons.* 2003, *apptd* 2003; Sheridan, Grimms Hill, Great Missenden, Bucks HP16 9BD
Dorchester, Rt. Revd Colin Fletcher, *cons.* 2000, *apptd* 2000; Arran House, Sandy Lane, Yarnton, Oxon OX5 1PB
Reading, Rt. Revd Stephen Cottrell, *cons.* 2004, *apptd* 2004; Bishop's House, Tidmarsh Lane, Tidmarsh, Reading RG8 8HA

DEAN OF CHRIST CHURCH
Very Revd Dr Christopher Lewis, *apptd* 2003

Organist, Dr Stephen Darlington, FRCO, *apptd* 1985

ARCHDEACONS
Berkshire, Ven. Norman Russell, *apptd* 1998
Buckingham, Ven. Karen Gorham, *apptd* 2007
Oxford, Ven. Julian Hubbard, *apptd* 2005

Chancellor, Revd Dr Rupert Bursell, *apptd* 2001
Registrars and Legal Secretaries, Dr F. E. Robson and Revd. Canon John Rees
Diocesan Secretary, Rosemary Pearce, Diocesan Church House, North Hinksey, Oxford OX2 0NB T 01865-208202

PETERBOROUGH *(Canterbury)*

37TH BISHOP
Rt. Revd Ian P. M. Cundy, *cons.* 1992, *apptd* 1996; Bishop's Lodging, The Palace, Peterborough PE1 1YA
Signs Ian Petriburg:

BISHOP SUFFRAGAN
Brixworth, Rt. Revd Frank White, *cons.* 2002, *apptd* 2002; 4 The Avenue, Dallington, Northampton NN1 4RZ

DEAN
Very Revd Charles Taylor, *apptd* 2007

Organist, Andrew Reid, *apptd* 2004

ARCHDEACONS
Northampton, Ven. Christine Allsopp, *apptd* 2005
Oakham, Ven. David Painter, *apptd* 2000

Chancellor, David Pittaway, QC, *apptd* 2005
Registrar and Legal Secretary, Revd Canon Raymond Hemingray
Diocesan Secretary, Canon Richard Pestell, Diocesan Office, The Palace, Peterborough PE1 1YB T 01733-887000

PORTSMOUTH *(Canterbury)*

8TH BISHOP
Rt. Revd Dr Kenneth Stevenson, *cons.* 1995, *apptd* 1995; Bishopsgrove, 26 Osborn Road, Fareham, Hants PO16 7DQ
Signs Kenneth Portsmouth

DEAN
Very Revd David Brindley, *apptd* 2002

Organist, David Price, *apptd* 1996

ARCHDEACONS
Isle of Wight, Ven. Caroline Baston, *apptd* 2006
Portsdown, Ven. Trevor Reader, *apptd* 2006
The Meon, Ven. Peter Hancock, *apptd* 1999

Chancellor, C. Clark, QC
Registrar and Legal Secretary, Hilary Tyler
Diocesan Secretary, Wendy Kennedy, Diocesan Offices, 1st Floor, Peninsular House, Wharf Road, Portsmouth PO2 8HB T 023-9289 9664

RIPON AND LEEDS *(York)*

12TH BISHOP
Rt. Revd John Packer, *cons.* 1996, *apptd* 2000; Bishop Mount, Ripon HG4 5DP
Signs John Ripon and Leeds

BISHOP SUFFRAGAN
Knaresborough, Rt. Revd James Bell, *cons.* 2004, *apptd* 2004; Thistledown, Main Street, Exelby, Bedale DL8 2HD

DEAN
Revd Keith Jukes, *apptd* 2007

Director of Music, Andrew Bryden, *apptd* 2003

ARCHDEACONS
Leeds, Ven. Peter Burrows, *apptd* 2005
Richmond, Ven. Janet Henderson, *apptd* 2007

Chancellor, His Hon. Judge Grenfell, *apptd* 1992
Registrars and Legal Secretaries, Christopher Tunnard; Nichola Harding
Diocesan Secretary, Philip Arundel, Diocesan Office, St Mary's Street, Leeds LS9 7DP T 0113-200 0540

ROCHESTER *(Canterbury)*

106TH BISHOP
Rt. Revd Dr Michael Nazir-Ali, *cons.* 1984, *apptd* 1994; Bishopscourt, Rochester ME1 1TS
Signs Michael Roffen:

BISHOP SUFFRAGAN
Tonbridge, Rt. Revd Dr Brian C. Castle, *cons.* 2002, *apptd* 2002; Bishop's Lodge, 48 St Botolph's Road, Sevenoaks TN13 3AG

DEAN
Very Revd Adrian Newman, *apptd* 2004

Director of Music, Scott Farrell, *apptd* 2008

ARCHDEACONS
Bromley, Ven. Paul Wright, *apptd* 2003
Rochester, Ven. Peter Lock, *apptd* 2000
Tonbridge, Ven. Clive Mansell, *apptd* 2002

Chancellor, John Gallagher, *apptd* 2006
Registrar and Legal Secretary, Owen Carew-Jones
Diocesan Secretary, Canon Louise Gilbert, St Nicholas Church, Boley Hill, Rochester ME1 1SL T 01634-560000

ST ALBANS *(Canterbury)*

9TH BISHOP

Rt. Revd Christopher W. Herbert, *cons.* 1995, *apptd* 1995; Abbey Gate House, St Albans AL3 4HD
Signs Christopher St Albans

BISHOPS SUFFRAGAN

Bedford, Rt. Revd Richard N. Inwood, *cons.* 2003, *apptd* 2003; Bishop's Lodge, Bedford Road, Cardington, Bedford MK44 3SS
Hertford, Rt. Revd Christopher R. J. Foster, *cons.* 2001, *apptd* 2001; Hertford House, Abbey Mill Lane, St Albans AL3 4HE

DEAN

Very Revd Dr Jeffrey John, *apptd* 2004

Organist, Andrew Lucas, *apptd* 1998

ARCHDEACONS

Bedford, Ven. Paul Hughes, *apptd* 2004
Hertford, Ven. Trevor Jones, *apptd* 1997
St Albans, Ven. Jonathan Smith, *apptd* 2008

Chancellor, Roger Kaye, *apptd* 2002
Registrar and Legal Secretary, David Cheetham
Diocesan Secretary, Susan Pope, Holywell Lodge, 41 Holywell Hill, St Albans AL1 1HE T 01727-854532

ST EDMUNDSBURY AND IPSWICH *(Canterbury)*

10TH BISHOP

Rt. Revd Nigel Stock, *cons.* 2000, *apptd* 2007; Bishop's House, 4 Park Road, Ipswich IP1 3ST
Signs Nigel St Edmundsbury and Ipswich

BISHOP SUFFRAGAN

Dunwich, Rt. Revd Clive Young, *cons.* 1999, *apptd* 1999; 28 Westerfield Road, Ipswich IP4 2UJ

DEAN

Very Revd Neil Collings, *apptd* 2006

Director of Music, James Thomas, *apptd* 1997

ARCHDEACONS

Ipswich, vacant
Sudbury, Ven. David Brierley, *apptd* 2006
Suffolk, Ven. Geoffrey Arrand, *apptd* 1994

Chancellor, The Hon. Mr Justice Blofeld, *apptd* 1974
Registrar and Legal Secretary, James Hall
Diocesan Secretary, Nicholas Edgell, Diocesan Office, St Nicholas Centre, 4 Cutler Street, Ipswich IP1 1UQ T 01473-298500

SALISBURY *(Canterbury)*

77TH BISHOP

Rt. Revd Dr David S. Stancliffe, *cons.* 1993, *apptd* 1993; South Canonry, The Close, Salisbury SP1 2ER
Signs David Sarum

BISHOPS SUFFRAGAN

Ramsbury, Rt. Revd Stephen Conway, *cons.* 2006, *apptd* 2006; Southbroom House, London Road, Devizes, Wiltshire SN10 1LT
Sherborne, vacant

DEAN

Very Revd June Osborne, *apptd* 2004

Organist, David Halls, *apptd* 2005

ARCHDEACONS

Dorset, Ven. Alistair Magowan, *apptd* 2000
Sherborne, Ven. Paul Taylor, *apptd* 2004
Wilts, Ven. John Wraw, *apptd* 2004
Sarum, Ven. Alan Jeans, *apptd* 2003

Chancellor, His Hon. Judge Samuel Wiggs, *apptd* 1997
Registrar and Legal Secretary, Andrew Johnson
Diocesan Secretary, Lucinda Herklots, Church House, Crane Street, Salisbury SP1 2QB T 01722-411922

SHEFFIELD *(York)*

7TH BISHOP

vacant

BISHOP SUFFRAGAN

Doncaster, Rt. Revd Cyril Guy Ashton, *cons.* 2000, *apptd* 2000; Bishop's House, 3 Farrington Court, Wickersley, Rotherham S66 1JQ

DEAN

Very Revd Peter Bradley, *apptd* 2003

Master of Music, Neil Taylor, *apptd* 1997

ARCHDEACONS

Doncaster, Ven. Robert Fitzharris, *apptd* 2001
Sheffield and Rotherham, Ven. Richard Blackburn, *apptd* 1999

Chancellor, Prof. David McClean, *apptd* 1992
Registrar and Legal Secretary, Andrew Vidler
Diocesan Secretary, Malcolm Fair, Diocesan Church House, 95–99 Effingham Street, Rotherham S65 1BL T 01709-309100

SODOR AND MAN *(York)*

81ST BISHOP

Rt. Revd Robert Paterson, *cons.* 2008, *apptd* 2008; The Bishop's House, The Falls, Tromode Road, Douglas, Isle of Man IM4 4PZ

ARCHDEACON OF MAN

Ven. Brian Smith, *apptd* 2005
Vicar-General and Chancellor, Clare Faulds
Registrar, Jonathan Kewley
Diocesan Secretary, D. Robertson, 2 North Shore Road, Ramsey, Isle of Man IM8 3DF T 01624-816538

SOUTHWARK *(Canterbury)*

9TH BISHOP

Rt. Revd Dr Tom F. Butler, *cons.* 1985, *apptd* 1998; Bishop's House, 38 Tooting Bec Gardens, London SW16 1QZ
Signs Thomas Southwark

AREA BISHOPS

Croydon, Rt. Revd Nicholas Baines, *cons.* 2003, *apptd* 2003; St Matthew's House, 100 George Street, Croydon, Surrey CR0 1PE
Kingston upon Thames, Rt. Revd Richard Cheetham, *cons.* 2002, *apptd* 2002; Kingston Episcopal Area Office, St Cecilia's, Sutherland Grove, London SW18 5JR
Woolwich, Rt. Revd Christopher Chessun, *cons.* 2005, *apptd* 2005; Diocesan Office (*see* below)

DEAN

Very Revd Colin B. Slee, OBE, *apptd* 1994

Organist, Peter Wright, FRCO, *apptd* 1989

ARCHDEACONS
Croydon, Ven. Tony Davies, *apptd* 1994
Lambeth, Ven. Christopher Skilton, *apptd* 2003
Lewisham, Ven. Christine Hardman, *apptd* 2001
Reigate, Ven. Daniel Kajumba, *apptd* 2001
Southwark, Ven. Dr Michael Ipgrave, *apptd* 2004
Wandsworth, Ven. Stephen Roberts, *apptd* 2005

Chancellor, Charles George, QC
Registrar and Legal Secretary, Paul Morris
Diocesan Secretary, Simon Parton, Trinity House, 4 Chapel Court, Borough High Street, London SE1 1HW T 020-7939 9400

SOUTHWELL AND NOTTINGHAM *(York)*

10TH BISHOP
Rt. Revd George H. Cassidy, *cons.* 1999, *apptd* 1999; Bishop's Manor, Southwell NG25 0JR
Signs George Southwell

BISHOP SUFFRAGAN
Sherwood, Rt. Revd Anthony Porter, *cons.* 2006, *apptd* 2006; Dunham House, 8 Westgate, Southwell NG25 0JL

DEAN
Very Revd John Guille, *apptd* 2007

Organist, Paul Hale, *apptd* 1989

ARCHDEACONS
Newark, Ven. Nigel Peyton, *apptd* 1999
Nottingham, Ven. Peter Hill, *apptd* 2007

Chancellor, Linda Box, *apptd* 2005
Registrar and Legal Secretary, Christopher Hodson
Diocesan Secretary, Dunham House, Westgate, Southwell, Notts NG25 0JL T 01636-817204

TRURO *(Canterbury)*

15TH BISHOP
Rt. Revd Tim Thornton, *cons.* 2001, *apptd* 2009; Lis Escop, Truro TR3 6QQ
Signs Tim Truro

BISHOP SUFFRAGAN
St Germans, Rt. Revd Royden Screech, *cons.* 2000, *apptd* 2000; Royden Screech, 32 Falmouth Road, Truro, Cornwall TR1 2HX

DEAN
Very Revd Dr Christopher Hardwick, *apptd* 2005

Organist, Chris Gray, *apptd* 2008

ARCHDEACONS
Cornwall, Ven. Roger Bush, *apptd* 2006
Bodmin, Ven. Clive Cohen, *apptd* 2000

Chancellor, Timothy Briden, *apptd* 1998
Registrar and Legal Secretary, Martin Follett
Diocesan Secretary, Sheri Sturgess, Diocesan House, Kenwyn, Truro TR1 1JQ T 01872-274351

WAKEFIELD *(York)*

12TH BISHOP
Rt. Revd Stephen Platten, *cons.* 2003, *apptd* 2003; Bishop's Lodge, Woodthorpe Lane, Wakefield WF2 6JL
Signs Stephen Wakefield

BISHOP SUFFRAGAN
Pontefract, Rt. Revd Anthony William Robinson, *cons.* 2003, *apptd* 2002; Pontefract House, 181A Manygates Lane, Wakefield WF2 7DR

DEAN
Very Revd Jonathan Greener, *apptd* 2007

Organist, Jonathan Bielby, FRCO, *apptd* 1972

ARCHDEACONS
Halifax, Ven. Robert Freeman, *apptd* 2003
Pontefract, Peter Townley, *apptd* 2008

Chancellor, Paul Downes, *apptd* 2006
Registrar and Legal Secretaries, Julian Gill; Julia Wilding
Diocesan Secretary, Ashley Ellis, Church House, 1 South Parade, Wakefield WF1 1LP T 01924-371802

WORCESTER *(Canterbury)*

113TH BISHOP
Rt. Revd Dr John Inge, *cons.* 2003, *apptd* 2007; The Bishop's Office, The Old Palace, Deansway, Worcester WR1 2JE
Signs John Wigorn

SUFFRAGAN BISHOP
Dudley, Rt. Revd Dr David S. Walker, *cons.* 2000, *apptd* 2000; The Bishop's House, Bishop's Walk, Cradley Heath B64 7JF

DEAN
Very Revd Peter Atkinson, *apptd* 2006

Organist, Dr Adrian Lucas, *apptd* 1996

ARCHDEACONS
Dudley, Ven. Fred Trethewey, *apptd* 2001
Worcester, vacant

Chancellor, Charles Mynors, *apptd* 1999
Registrar and Legal Secretary, Michael Huskinson
Diocesan Secretary, Robert Higham, The Old Palace, Deansway, Worcester WR1 2JE T 01905-20537

ROYAL PECULIARS

WESTMINSTER
The Collegiate Church of St Peter
Dean, Very Revd Dr John Hall
Sub Dean and Archdeacon, Canon Robert Wright, *apptd* 2005
Chapter Clerk and Receiver-General, Sir Stephen Lamport, KCVO, Chapter Office, 20 Dean's Yard, London SW1P 3PA
Organist, James O'Donnell, *apptd* 1999
Registrar, Stuart Holmes, MVO
Legal Secretary, Christopher Vyse, *apptd* 2000

WINDSOR
The Queen's Free Chapel of St George within Her Castle of Windsor
Dean, Rt. Revd David Conner, *apptd* 1998
Chapter Clerk, Charlotte Manley, LVO, OBE, *apptd* 2003; Chapter Office, The Cloisters, Windsor Castle, Windsor, Berks SL4 1NJ
Director of Music, Timothy Byram-Wigfield, *apptd* 2004

OTHER ANGLICAN CHURCHES

THE CHURCH IN WALES

The Anglican Church was the established church in Wales from the 16th century until 1920, when the estrangement of the majority of Welsh people from Anglicanism resulted in disestablishment. Since then the Church in Wales has been an autonomous province consisting of six sees. The bishops are elected by an electoral college comprising elected lay and clerical members, who also elect one of the diocesan bishops as Archbishop of Wales.

The legislative body of the Church in Wales is the Governing Body, which has 143 members divided between the three orders of bishops, clergy and laity. Its president is the Archbishop of Wales and it meets twice annually. Its decisions are binding upon all members of the church. The church's property and finances are the responsibility of the Representative Body. There are about 68,700 members of the Church in Wales, with 555 stipendiary clergy and 977 parishes.

THE GOVERNING BODY OF THE CHURCH IN WALES, 39 Cathedral Road, Cardiff CF11 9XF T 029-2034 8200 *Lay Secretary,* John Shirley

12th ARCHBISHOP OF WALES, Most Revd Dr Barry Morgan (Bishop of Llandaff), *elected* 2003 *Signs* Barry Cambrensis

BISHOPS

Bangor (81st), vacant; Ty'r Esgob, Bangor, Gwynedd LL57 2SS *Stipendiary clergy,* 48

Llandaff (102nd), Most Revd Dr Barry Morgan (*also* Archbishop of Wales), *b.* 1947, *cons.* 1993, *trans.* 1999; Llys Esgob, The Cathedral Green, Llandaff, Cardiff CF5 2YE *Signs* Barry Cambrensis. *Stipendiary clergy,* 143

Monmouth (9th), Rt. Revd Dominic Walker, *b.* 1948, *cons.* 1997, *elected* 2003; Bishopstow, Stow Hill, Newport NP20 4EA *Signs* Dominic Monmouth. *Stipendiary clergy,* 90

St Asaph (74th), Rt. Revd John Davies, *b.* 1943, *cons.* 1999, *elected* 1999; Esgobty, Upper Denbigh Road, St Asaph, Denbighshire LL17 0TW *Signs* John St Asaph. *Stipendiary clergy,* 102

St David's (128th), vacant. *Stipendiary clergy,* 126

Swansea and Brecon (9th), Rt. Revd John Davies, *b.* 1953, *cons.* 2008, *elected* 2008; Ely Tower, Castle Square, Brecon, Powys LD3 9DB *Signs* John Swansea & Brecon. *Stipendiary clergy,* 71

The stipend for a diocesan bishop of the Church in Wales is £36,792 a year for 2008–9.

SCOTTISH EPISCOPAL CHURCH

The Scottish Episcopal Church was founded after the Act of Settlement (1690) established the presbyterian nature of the Church of Scotland. The Scottish Episcopal Church is a member of the worldwide Anglican Communion. The governing authority is the General Synod, an elected body of 140 members which meets once a year. The bishop who convenes and presides at meetings of the General Synod is called the 'primus' and is elected by his fellow bishops.

In 2007 there were 40,860 members of the Scottish Episcopal Church, of whom 27,622 were communicants. There are seven bishops, approximately 518 serving clergy, and 319 churches and places of worship.

THE GENERAL SYNOD OF THE SCOTTISH EPISCOPAL CHURCH, 21 Grosvenor Crescent, Edinburgh EH12 5EE T 0131-225 6357 W www.scotland-anglican.org *Secretary-General,* J. F. Stuart

PRIMUS OF THE SCOTTISH EPISCOPAL CHURCH, Most Revd Dr Idris Jones (Bishop of Glasgow and Galloway), *elected* 2006

BISHOPS

Aberdeen and Orkney, Rt. Revd Dr Bob Gillies, *b.* 1951, *cons.* 2007, *elected* 2007. *Clergy,* 54

Argyll and the Isles, Rt. Revd Martin Shaw, *b.* 1944, *cons.* 2004, *elected* 2004. *Clergy* 22

Brechin, Rt. Revd Dr John Mantle, *b.* 1946, *cons.* 2005, *elected* 2005. *Clergy,* 35

Edinburgh, Rt. Revd Brian Smith, *b.* 1943, *cons.* 1993, *elected* 2001. *Clergy,* 162

Glasgow and Galloway, Most Revd Dr Idris Jones, *b.* 1943, *cons.* 1998, *elected* 1998. *Clergy,* 99

Moray, Ross and Caithness, Rt. Revd Mark Strange, *b.* 1961, *cons.* 2007, *elected* 2007. *Clergy,* 31

St Andrews, Dunkeld and Dunblane, Rt. Revd David Chillingworth, *b.* 1951, *cons.* 2005, *elected* 2005. *Clergy,* 86

The minimum stipend of a diocesan bishop of the Scottish Episcopal Church for 2008 is £32,400 (ie 1.5 times the standard clergy stipend of £21,600).

CHURCH OF IRELAND

The Anglican Church was the established church in Ireland from the 16th century but never secured the allegiance of the majority and was disestablished in 1871. The Church of Ireland is divided into the provinces of Armagh and Dublin, each under an archbishop. The provinces are subdivided into 12 dioceses.

The legislative body is the General Synod, which has 660 members in total, divided between the House of Bishops and the House of Representatives. The Archbishop of Armagh is elected by the House of Bishops; other episcopal elections are made by an electoral college.

There are about 400,000 members of the Church of Ireland, with two archbishops, ten bishops, about 600 clergy and about 1,100 churches and places of worship.

CENTRAL OFFICE, Church of Ireland House, Church Avenue, Rathmines, Dublin 6 T (+353) (1) 497 8422 *Chief Officer and Secretary of the Representative Church Body,* D. C. Reardon

PROVINCE OF ARMAGH

Archbishop of Armagh, Primate of all Ireland and Metropolitan, Most Revd Alan Harper, OBE, *b.* 1944, *cons.* 2002, *trans.* 2007. *Clergy,* 55

BISHOPS

Clogher, Rt. Revd Michael Jackson, PHD, DPHIL, *b.* 1956, *cons.* 2002, *apptd* 2002. *Clergy,* 32

Connor, Rt. Revd Alan Abernethy, *b.* 1957, *cons.* 2007, *apptd* 2007. *Clergy,* 106

Derry and Raphoe, Rt. Revd Kenneth Good, *b.* 1952, *cons.* 2002, *apptd* 2002. *Clergy,* 51

Down and Dromore, Rt. Revd Harold Miller, *b.* 1950, *cons.* 1997, *apptd* 1997. *Clergy,* 116

Kilmore, Elphin and Ardagh, Rt. Revd Kenneth Clarke, *b.* 1949, *cons.* 2001, *apptd* 2001. *Clergy,* 21

Tuam, Killala and Achonry, Rt. Revd Richard Henderson, DPHIL, *b.* 1957, *cons.* 1998, *apptd* 1998. *Clergy,* 13

PROVINCE OF DUBLIN
Archbishop of Dublin, Bishop of Glendalough, Primate of Ireland and Metropolitan, Most Revd John R. W. Neill, *b.* 1945, *apptd* 2002. *Clergy,* 86

BISHOPS
Cashel and Ossory, Rt. Revd Michael Burrows, *b.* 1961, *cons.* 2006, *apptd* 2006. *Clergy,* 42
Cork, Cloyne and Ross, Rt. Revd W. Paul Colton, *b.* 1960, *cons.* 1999, *apptd* 1999. *Clergy,* 30
Limerick and Killaloe, Rt. Revd Trevor Williams, *b.* 1948, *cons.* 2008. *Clergy,* 19
Meath and Kildare, Most Revd Richard Clarke, PHD, *b.* 1949, *cons.* 1996, *apptd* 1996. *Clergy,* 26

OVERSEAS

PRIMATES
Primate and Presiding Bishop of Aotearoa, New Zealand and Polynesia, Most Revd William Brown Turei
Primate of Australia, Most Revd Phillip Aspinall
Primate of Brazil, Most Revd Maurício Araújo de Andrade
Archbishop of the Province of Burundi, Most Revd Bernard Ntahoturi
Archbishop and Primate of Canada, Most Revd Frederick Hiltz
Archbishop of the Province of Central Africa, Most Revd Eston Dickson Pembamoyo
Primate of the Central Region of America, Most Revd Martin de Jesus Barahona
Archbishop of the Province of Congo, Most Revd Dr Dirokpa Balufuga Fidèle
Primate of the Province of Hong Kong Sheng Kung Hui, Most Revd Paul Kwong
Archbishop of the Province of the Indian Ocean, Most Revd Gerald James Ernest
Primate of Japan (Nippon Sei Ko Kai), Most Revd Nathaniel Makoto Uematsu
President-Bishop of Jerusalem and the Middle East, Most Revd Dr Mouneer Hanna Anis
Archbishop of the Province of Kenya, Most Revd Benjamin M. P. Nzimbi
Archbishop of the Province of Korea, Most Revd Francis Kyung Jo Park
Archbishop of the Province of Melanesia, Most Revd Sir Ellison Leslie Pogo, KBE
Archbishop of Mexico, Most Revd Carlos Touche-Porter
Archbishop of the Province of Myanmar, Most Revd Stephen Than Myint Oo
Archbishop of the Province of Nigeria, Most Revd Peter Akinola
Archbishop of Papua New Guinea, Most Revd James Ayong
Prime Bishop of the Philippines, Most Revd Ignacio Capuyan Soliba
Archbishop of the Province of Rwanda, Most Revd Emmanuel Musaba Kolini
Primate of the Province of South East Asia, Most Revd Dr John Chew
Metropolitan of the Province of Southern Africa, Most Revd Thabo Cecil Makgoba
Presiding Bishop of the Southern Cone of America, Most Revd Gregory James Venables
Archbishop of the Province of the Sudan, Most Revd Daniel Deng Bul Yak
Archbishop of the Province of Tanzania, Most Revd Valentino Mokiwa
Archbishop of the Province of Uganda, Most Revd Henry Luke Orombi
Presiding Bishop and Primate of the USA, Most Revd Katharine Jefferts Schori
Archbishop of the Province of West Africa, Most Revd Justice Ofei Akrofi
Archbishop of the Province of the West Indies, Most Revd Drexel Wellington Gomez

OTHER CHURCHES AND EXTRA-PROVINCIAL DIOCESES
Anglican Church of Bermuda, extra-provincial to Canterbury
Bishop, Rt. Revd Ewen Ratteray
Church of Ceylon, extra-provincial to Canterbury
Bishop of Colombo, Rt. Revd Duleep de Chickera
Bishop of Kurunagala, Rt. Revd Kumara Illangasinghe
Episcopal Church of Cuba, Rt. Revd Miguel Tamayo *(interim)*
Falkland Islands, extra-provincial to Canterbury
Episcopal Commissary, Rt. Revd Stephen Venner (Bishop of Dover)
Lusitanian Church (Portuguese Episcopal Church), extra-provincial to Canterbury
Bishop, Rt. Revd Fernando Soares
Reformed Episcopal Church of Spain, extra-provincial to Canterbury
Bishop, Rt. Revd Carlos López-Lozano

MODERATION OF CHURCHES IN FULL COMMUNION WITH THE ANGLICAN COMMUNION
Church of Bangladesh, Rt. Revd Paul Sishir Sarkar
Church of North India, Most Revd Joel Vidyasagar Mal
Church of South India, Most Revd John Wilson Gladstone
Church of Pakistan, Rt. Revd Dr Alexander John Malik

CHURCH OF SCOTLAND

The Church of Scotland is the established (ie national) church of Scotland. The church is reformed in doctrine, and presbyterian in constitution, ie based on a hierarchy of councils of ministers and elders and, since 1990, of members of a diaconate. At local level the Kirk Session consists of the parish minister and ruling elders. At district level the presbyteries, of which there are 44 in Britain, consist of all the ministers in the district, one ruling elder from each congregation, and those members of the diaconate who qualify for membership. The General Assembly is the supreme authority, and is presided over by a Moderator chosen annually by the Assembly. The sovereign, if not present in person, is represented by a Lord High Commissioner who is appointed each year by the Crown.

The Church of Scotland has about 489,118 members, 984 ministers and 1,179 churches. There are about 21 ministers and other personnel working overseas.

Lord High Commissioner (2008–9), Rt. Hon. George Reid
Moderator of the General Assembly (2008–9), Rt. Revd David Lunan
Principal Clerk, Very Revd Dr F. Macdonald
Depute Clerk, Revd. Dr M. MacLean
Procurator, L. Dunlop
Law Agent and Solicitor of the Church, Mrs J. Wilson
Parliamentary Agent, I. McCulloch *(London)*
General Treasurer, I. Grimmond
Secretary, Church and Society Council, Revd Ewan Aitken

CHURCH OFFICE, 121 George Street, Edinburgh EH2 4YN
T 0131-225 5722

PRESBYTERIES AND CLERKS
Edinburgh, Revd G. White
West Lothian, Revd D. Shaw
Lothian, J. McCulloch
Melrose and Peebles, Jack Stewart
Duns, Roger Dodd
Jedburgh, Revd W. Frank Campbell
Annandale and Eskdale, Revd C. Haston
Dumfries and Kirkcudbright, Revd G. Savage
Wigtown and Stranraer, Revd D. Dutton
Ayr, Revd J. Crichton
Irvine and Kilmarnock, Revd C. Brockie
Ardrossan, Revd J. Mackay
Lanark, Revd J. Cutler
Greenock and Paisley, Revd A. Ward
Glasgow, Revd Dr A. Kerr
Hamilton, Revd S. Paterson
Dumbarton, Revd C. Caskie
Argyll, I. Maclagan
Falkirk, Revd J. O'Brien
Stirling, Dorothy Kinloch
Dunfermline, Revd E. Kenny
Kirkcaldy, Rosemary Frew
St Andrews, Revd J. Redpath
Dunkeld and Meigle, Revd J. Russell
Perth, Revd D. Main
Dundee, Revd J. Wilson
Angus, Revd M. Bicket
Aberdeen, Revd George Cowie and Revd John Ferguson
Kincardine and Deeside, Revd Hugh Conkey
Gordon, Revd Euan Glen
Buchan, George Berstan
Moray, Revd Hugh Smith
Abernethy, Revd J. MacEwan
Inverness, Revd A. Younger
Lochaber, Revd D. Anderson
Ross, Revd T. McWilliam
Sutherland, Revd J. Goskirk
Caithness, J. Houston
Lochcarron-Skye, Revd A. MacArthur
Uist, Revd M. Smith
Lewis, Revd T. Sinclair
Orkney, Revd T. Hunt
Shetland, Revd C. Greig
England, Revd Scott Brown
Europe, Revd J. Cowie

The stipends for ministers in the Church of Scotland in 2008 range from £22,239–£29,526, depending on length of service. In addition, congregations can make extra payments.

ROMAN CATHOLIC CHURCH

The Roman Catholic Church is one worldwide Christian church acknowledging as its head the Bishop of Rome, known as the Pope (Father). He leads a communion of followers of Christ, who believe they continue his presence in the world as servants of faith, hope and love to all society. The Pope is held to be the successor of St Peter and thus invested with the power which was entrusted to St Peter by Jesus Christ. A direct line of succession is therefore claimed from the earliest Christian communities. With the fall of the Roman Empire the Pope also became an important political leader. His territory is now limited to the 0.44 sq. km (0.17 sq. miles) of the Vatican City State, created to provide some independence to the Pope from Italy and other nations.

The Pope exercises spiritual authority over the church with the advice and assistance of the Sacred College of Cardinals, the supreme council of the church. He is also advised by bishops in communion with him, by a group of officers which form the Roman Curia and by his ambassadors, called Apostolic Nuncios, who liaise with the Bishops' Conference in each country.

Those members of the College of Cardinals who are under the age of 80 elect a successor of the Pope following his death. The assembly of the cardinals called to the Vatican for the election of a new Pope is known as the conclave. In complete seclusion the cardinals vote by a secret ballot; a two-thirds majority is necessary before the vote can be accepted as final. When a cardinal receives the necessary number of votes, the Dean of the Sacred College formally asks him if he will accept election and the name by which he wishes to be known. On his acceptance of the office of Supreme Pontiff, the conclave is dissolved and the first Cardinal Deacon announces the election to the assembled crowd in St Peter's Square.

The number of cardinals was fixed at 70 by Pope Sixtus V in 1586 but has been steadily increased since the pontificate of John XXIII and at the end of March 2005 stood at 183, plus one cardinal 'in pectore' (their name kept secret by the Pope for fear of persecution). At the end of March 2005, 117 of the 183 cardinals were cardinal electors, who took part in the election of Pope Benedict XVI, following the death of Pope John Paul II in April 2005.

The Pope has full legislative, judicial and administrative power over the whole church. He is aided in his administration by the curia, which is made up of a number of departments. The Secretariat of State is the central office for carrying out the Pope's instructions and is presided over by the Cardinal Secretary of State. It maintains relations with the departments of the curia, with the episcopate, with the representatives of the Holy See in various countries, governments and private persons. The congregations and pontifical councils are the Pope's ministries and include departments such as the Congregation for the Doctrine of Faith, whose field of competence concerns faith and morals; the Congregation for the Clergy and the Congregation for the Evangelisation of Peoples, the Pontifical Council for the Family and the Pontifical Council for the Promotion of Christian Unity.

The Vatican State does not have diplomatic representatives. The Holy See, composed of the Pope and those who help him in his mission for the church, is recognised by the Conventions of Vienna as an international moral body. The representatives of the Holy See are known as Apostolic Nuncios. Where representation is only to the local churches and not to the government of a country, the papal representative is known as an apostolic delegate. The Roman Catholic Church has an estimated 840 million adherents under the care of some 2,500 diocesan bishops worldwide.

SOVEREIGN PONTIFF
His Holiness Pope Benedict XVI (Joseph Ratzinger), *born* Bavaria, Germany, 16 April 1927; *ordained priest* 1951; *appointed Archbishop* (of Munich), March 1977; *created Cardinal* June 1977; *assumed pontificate* 19 April 2005

SECRETARIAT OF STATE
Secretary of State, HE Cardinal Tarcisio Bertone
First Section (General Affairs), Most Revd Fernando Filoni (Titular Archbishop of Volturno)
Second Section (Relations with Other States), Most Revd Dominique Mamberti (Titular Archbishop of Sagona)

BISHOPS' CONFERENCE
The Catholic Church in England and Wales consists of a total of 22 dioceses. The Bishops' Conference, which coordinates common activity, includes the diocesan bishops, the Apostolic Exarch of the Ukrainians, the Bishop of the Forces and the auxiliary bishops. The conference is headed by the president (HE Cardinal Cormac Murphy-O'Connor, Archbishop of Westminster) and vice-president (The Most Revd Patrick Kelly, Archbishop of Liverpool). There are six departments, each with an episcopal chair: the Department for Christian Life and Worship (the Bishop of Leeds), the Department for Dialogue and Unity (the Archbishop of Southwark), the Department for Catholic Education and Formation (the Archbishop of Birmingham), the Department for Christian Responsibility and Citizenship (the Archbishop of Cardiff), the Department for International Affairs (the Bishop of Portsmouth) and the Department for Evangelisation and Catechesis (the Bishop of Nottingham).

The Bishops' Conference Standing Committee is made up of two directly elected bishops in addition to the Metropolitan Archbishops and chairs from each of the above departments. The committee has general responsibility for continuity of policy between the plenary sessions of the conference, preparing the conference agenda and implementing its decisions.

The administration of the Bishops' Conference is funded by a levy on each diocese, according to income. A general secretariat in London coordinates and supervises the Bishops' Conference administration activities. There are also other agencies and consultative bodies affiliated to the conference.

The Bishops' Conference of Scotland is the permanently constituted assembly of the bishops of Scotland. The conference is headed by the president (HE Cardinal Keith Patrick O'Brien, Archbishop of St. Andrews and Edinburgh). The conference establishes various agencies which have an advisory function in relation to the conference. The more important of these agencies are called commissions and each one has a bishop president who, with the other members of the commissions, are appointed by the conference.

The Irish Episcopal Conference has as its president Cardinal Sean Brady of Armagh. Its membership comprises all the archbishops and bishops of Ireland and it appoints various commissions to assist it in its work. There are three types of commissions: (a) those made up of lay and clerical members chosen for their skills and experience, and staffed by full-time expert secretariats; (b) commissions whose members are selected from existing institutions and whose services are supplied on a part-time basis; and (c) commissions of bishops only.

The Catholic Church in the UK has an estimated 1,595,105 mass attendees, 6,147 priests and 4,583 churches.

Bishops' Conferences secretariats:
ENGLAND AND WALES, 39 Eccleston Square, London SW1V 1BX T 020-7630 8220 F 020-7901 4821
E secretariat@cbcew.org.uk W www.catholicchurch.org.uk
General Secretary, Mgr Andrew Summersgill
SCOTLAND, 64 Aitken Street, Airdrie, Lanarkshire ML6 6LT
T 01236-764061 E gensec@bpsconfscot.com
General Secretary, Revd Paul Conroy
IRELAND, Columba Centre, Maynooth, County Kildare
T (+353) (1) 505 3000 W www.catholiccommunications.ie
Secretary, Most Revd William Lee (Bishop of Waterford and Lismore)
Executive Secretary, Revd Aidan O'Boyle

GREAT BRITAIN

APOSTOLIC NUNCIO TO GREAT BRITAIN
Most Revd Faustino Sainz Muñoz, 54 Parkside, London SW19 5NE T 020-8944 7189

ENGLAND AND WALES
THE MOST REVD ARCHBISHOPS
Westminster, HE Cardinal Cormac Murphy-O'Connor, *cons.* 1977, *apptd* 2000 *Auxiliaries,* George Stack, *cons.* 2001; Bernard Longley, *cons.* 2003; Alan Hopes, *cons.* 2003; John Arnold, *cons.* 2006. *Clergy,* 690. *Archbishop's Residence,* Archbishop's House, Ambrosden Avenue, London SW1P 1QJ T 020-7798 9033
Birmingham, Vincent Nichols, *cons.* 1992, *apptd* 2000 *Auxiliaries,* Philip Pargeter, *cons.* 1990; David McGough, *cons.* 2005; William Kenney, *cons.* 1987. *Clergy,* 443. *Archbishop's Residence,* Archbishop's House, 8 Shadwell Street, Birmingham B4 6EY T 0121-236 9090
Cardiff, Peter Smith, *cons.* 1995, *apptd* 2001. *Clergy,* 96. *Archbishop's Residence,* Archbishop's House, 41–43 Cathedral Road, Cardiff CF11 9HD T 029-2022 0411
Liverpool, Patrick Kelly, *cons.* 1984, *apptd* 1996 *Auxiliary,* Thomas Williams, *cons.* 2003. *Clergy,* 466. *Diocesan Curia,* Archdiocese of Liverpool, Centre for Evangelisation, Croxteth Drive, Sefton Park, Liverpool L17 1AA T 0151-522 1000
Southwark, Kevin McDonald, *cons.* 2001, *apptd* 2003 *Auxiliaries,* John Hine, *cons.* 2001; Patrick Lynch, *cons.* 2006; Paul Hendricks, *cons.* 2006. *Clergy,* 570. *Diocesan Curia,* Archbishop's House, 150 St George's Road, London SE1 6HX T 020-7928 5592

THE RT. REVD BISHOPS
Arundel and Brighton, Kieran Conry, *cons.* 2001, *apptd* 2001. *Clergy,* 102. *Diocesan Curia,* Bishop's House, The Upper Drive, Hove, E. Sussex BN3 6NB T 01273-506387
Brentwood, Thomas McMahon, *cons.* 1980, *apptd* 1980. *Clergy,* 121. *Bishop's Office,* Cathedral House, Ingrave Road, Brentwood, Essex CM15 8AT T 01277-232266
Clifton, Declan Lang, *cons.* 2001, *apptd* 2001. *Clergy,* 251. *Bishop's House,* St Ambrose, North Road, Leigh Woods, Bristol BS8 3PW T 0117-973 3072
East Anglia, Michael Evans, *cons* 2003, *apptd* 2003. *Clergy,* 129. *Diocesan Curia,* The White House, 21 Upgate, Poringland, Norwich NR14 7SH T 01508-492202
Hallam, John Rawsthorne, *cons.* 1981, *apptd* 1997. *Clergy,* 75. *Bishop's House,* 75 Norfolk Road, Sheffield S2 2SZ T 0114-278 7988
Hexham and Newcastle, vacant. *Clergy,* 211. *Diocesan Curia,* Bishop's House, East Denton Hall, 800 West Road, Newcastle upon Tyne NE5 2BJ T 0191-228 0003
Lancaster, Patrick O'Donoghue, *cons.* 1993, *apptd* 2001. *Clergy,* 248. *Bishop's Residence,* Bishop's Apartment, Cathedral House, Balmoral Road, Lancaster LA1 3BT T 01524-596050
Leeds, Arthur Roche, *cons.* 2001, *apptd* 2004. *Clergy,* 193. *Diocesan Curia,* Hinsley Hall, 62 Headingley Lane, Leeds LS6 2BX T 0113-261 8022

Menevia (Wales), Mark Jabalé, *cons.* 2001, *apptd* 2001. *Clergy,* 60. *Diocesan Curia,* 27 Convent Street, Swansea SA1 2BX T 01792-644017

Middlesbrough, Terence Drainey, *cons.* 2008, *apptd* 2007. *Clergy,* 102. *Diocesan Curia,* 50A The Avenue, Linthorpe, Middlesbrough TS5 6QT T 01642-850505

Northampton, Peter Doyle, *Clergy,* 178. *Diocesan Curia,* Bishop's House, Marriott Street, Northampton NN2 6AW T 01604-715635

Nottingham, Malcolm McMahon, *cons.* 2000, *apptd* 2000. *Clergy,* 162. *Bishop's House,* 27 Cavendish Road East, The Park, Nottingham NG7 1BB T 0115-947 4786

Plymouth, Christopher Budd, *cons.* 1986, *apptd* 1985. *Clergy,* 130. *Bishop's Residence,* Bishop's House, 31 Wyndham Street West, Plymouth PL1 5RZ T 01752-224414

Portsmouth, Crispian Hollis, *cons.* 1987, *apptd* 1989. *Clergy,* 282. *Bishop's Residence,* Bishop's House, Edinburgh Road, Portsmouth, Hants PO1 3HG T 023-9282 0894

Salford, Terence Brain, *cons.* 1991, *apptd* 1997. *Clergy,* 387. *Diocesan Curia,* 5 Gerald Road, Pendleton, Salford M6 6DL T 0161-736 1421

Shrewsbury, Brian Noble, *cons.* 1995, *apptd* 1995. *Clergy* 141. *Diocesan Curia,* 2 Park Road South, Prenton, Wirral CH43 4UX T 0151-652 9855

Wrexham (Wales), Edwin Regan, *cons.*1994, *apptd* 1994. *Clergy,* 45. *Diocesan Curia,* Bishop's House, Sontley Road, Wrexham LL13 7EW T 01978-262726

SCOTLAND

THE MOST REVD ARCHBISHOPS

St Andrews and Edinburgh, HE Cardinal Keith Patrick O'Brien, *cons.* 1985, *apptd* 1985, *elevated* 2003. *Clergy,* 170. *Diocesan Office,* 100 Strathearn Road, Edinburgh EH9 1BB T 0131-623 8900

Glasgow, Mario Joseph Conti, *cons.* 1977, *apptd* 2002. *Clergy,* 225. *Diocesan Curia,* 196 Clyde Street, Glasgow G1 4JY T 0141-226 5898

THE RT. REVD BISHOPS

Aberdeen, Peter Moran, *cons.* 2003, *apptd* 2003. *Clergy,* 43. *Diocesan Curia,* Bishop's House, 3 Queen's Cross, Aberdeen AB15 4XU T 01224-319154

Argyll and the Isles, Ian Murray, *cons.* 1999, *apptd* 1999. *Clergy,* 32. *Bishop's House,* Esplanade, Oban, Argyll PA34 5AB T 01631-571395

Dunkeld, Vincent Logan, *cons.* 1981. *Clergy,* 43. *Diocesan Curia,* 24–28 Lawside Road, Dundee DD3 6XY T 01382-225453

Galloway, John Cunningham, *cons.* 2004, *apptd* 2004. *Clergy* 56. *Diocesan Curia,* Candida Casa, 8 Corsehill Road, Ayr KA7 2ST T 01292-266750

Motherwell, Joseph Devine, *cons.* 1977, *apptd* 1983. *Clergy,* 123. *Diocesan Curia,* Coursington Road, Motherwell ML1 1PP T 01698-269114

Paisley, Philip Tartaglia, *cons.* 2005, *apptd* 2005. *Clergy,* 83. *Diocesan Curia,* Diocesan Centre, Cathedral Precincts, Incle Street, Paisley PA1 1HR T 0141-847 6130

BISHOPRIC OF THE FORCES

Rt. Revd Thomas Matthew Burns, *cons.* 2002, *apptd* 2002. *Administration,* RC Bishopric of the Forces, Wellington House, St Omer Barracks, Thornhill Road, Aldershot, Hants GU11 2BG T 01252-348234

IRELAND

There is one hierarchy for the whole of Ireland. Several of the dioceses have territory partly in the Republic of Ireland and partly in Northern Ireland.

APOSTOLIC NUNCIO TO IRELAND

HE Most Revd Giuseppe Leanza (Titular Archbishop of Lilybaeum), 183 Navan Road, Dublin 7 T (+353) (1) 838 0577 F (+353) (1) 838 0276

THE MOST REVD ARCHBISHOPS

Armagh, Seán Brady (*also* Primate of all Ireland), *cons.* 1995, *apptd* 1996. *Archbishop Emeritus,* HE Cardinal Cahal Daly, *cons.* 1967, *elevated* 1991. *Auxiliary Bishop,* Most Revd Gerard Clifford, *cons.* 1991. *Clergy,* 165. *Bishop's Residence,* Ara Coeli, Armagh BT61 7QY T 028-3752 2045

Cashel and Emly, Dermot Clifford, *cons.* 1986, *apptd* 1988. *Clergy,* 103. *Archbishop's House,* Thurles, Co. Tipperary T (+353) (504) 21512

Dublin, Diarmuid Martin, *cons.* 1999, *apptd Coadjutor Archbishop* 2003, *succeeded as Archbishop* 2004. *Emeritus Archbishop,* HE Cardinal Desmond Connell, *cons.* 1988, *elevated* 2001. *Auxiliaries,* Eamonn Walsh, *cons.* 1990; Fiachra O'Ceallaigh, *cons* 1994; Raymond Field, *cons.* 1997. *Clergy,* 994. *Communications Office,* Archbishop's House, Drumcondra, Dublin 9 T (+353) (1) 836 0723

Tuam, Michael Neary, *cons.* 1992, *apptd* 1995. *Clergy,* 141. *Archbishop's Residence,* Archbishop's House, Tuam, Co. Galway T (+353) (93) 24166

THE RT. REVD BISHOPS

Achonry, Brendan Kelly, *cons.* 2008, *apptd* 2007. *Clergy,* 53. *Diocesan Office,* Bishop's House, St Nathy's, Edmondstown, Ballaghaderreen, Co. Roscommon T (+353) (94) 986 0021

Ardagh and Clonmacnois, Colm O'Reilly, *cons.* 1983, *apptd* 1983. *Clergy,* 65. *Diocesan Office,* Ballinalee Road, Longford, Co. Longford T (+353) (43) 46432

Clogher, Joseph Duffy, *cons.* 1979, *apptd* 1979. *Clergy,* 74. *Bishop's Residence,* Bishop's House, Monaghan T (+353) (47) 81019

Clonfert, John Kirby, *cons.* 1988, *apptd* 1988. *Clergy,* 43. *Bishop's Residence,* St Brendan's, Coorheen, Loughrea, Co. Galway T (+353) (91) 841560

Cloyne, John Magee, *cons.* 1987, *apptd* 1987. *Clergy,* 144. *Diocesan Centre,* Cobh, Co. Cork T (+353) (21) 481 1430

Cork and Ross, John Buckley, *cons.* 1984, *apptd* 1998. *Clergy,* 136. *Diocesan Office,* Cork and Ross Offices, Redemption Road, Cork T (+353) (21) 430 1717

Derry, Seamus Hegarty, *cons.* 1982, *apptd* 1994. *Auxiliary,* Francis Lagan, *cons.* 1988. *Clergy,* 130. *Bishop's House,* St Eugene's Cathedral, Derry BT48 9YG T 028-7126 2894

Down and Connor, Noel Treanor, *cons.* 2008, *apptd* 2008. *Auxiliaries,* Anthony Farquhar, *cons.* 1983; Donal McKeown, *cons.* 2001. *Clergy,* 240. *Bishop's Residence,* Lisbreen, 73 Somerton Road, Belfast, Co. Antrim BT15 4DE T 028-9077 6185

Dromore, John McAreavey, *cons.* 1999, *apptd* 1999. *Clergy,* 43. *Bishop's Residence,* Bishop's House, 44 Armagh Road, Newry, Co. Down BT35 6PN T 028-3026 2444

Elphin, Christopher Jones, *cons.* 1994, *apptd* 1994. *Clergy,* 70. *Bishop's Residence,* St Mary's, Sligo T (+353) (71) 916 2670

Ferns, Denis Brennan, *cons.* 2006, *apptd* 2006. *Clergy,* 123. *Bishop's Residence,* Bishop's House, Summerhill, Wexford T (+353) (53) 912 2177

Galway, Kilmacduagh and Kilfenora, Martin Drennan, *cons.* 1997, *apptd* 2005. *Clergy,* 78. *Bishop's Residence,*

Mount Saint Mary's, Taylor's Hill, Galway
T (+353) (91) 563566

Kerry, William Murphy, *cons.* 1995, *apptd* 1995. *Clergy,* 124. *Bishop's Residence,* Bishop's House, Killarney, Co. Kerry T (+353) (64) 31168

Kildare and Leighlin, James Moriarty, *cons.* 1991, *apptd* 2002. *Clergy,* 110. *Bishop's Residence,* Bishop's House, Dublin Road, Carlow T (+353) (59) 917 6725

Killala, John Fleming, *cons.* 2002, *apptd* 2002. *Clergy,* 54. *Bishop's Residence,* Bishop's House, Ballina, Co. Mayo T (+353) (96) 21518

Killaloe, William Walsh, *cons.* 1994, *apptd* 1994. *Clergy,* 130. *Diocesan Office,* Westbourne, Ennis, Co. Clare T (+353) (65) 682 8638

Kilmore, Leo O'Reilly, *cons.* 1997, *apptd* 1998. *Clergy,* 90. *Bishop's Residence,* Bishop's House, Cullies, Co. Cavan T (+353) (49) 433 1496

Limerick, Donal Murray, *cons.* 1982, *apptd* 1996. *Clergy,* 109. *Diocesan Office,* Social Service Centre, Henry Street, Limerick T (+353) (61) 315856

Meath, Michael Smith, *cons.* 1984, *apptd* 1990. *Clergy,* 141. *Bishop's House,* Dublin Road, Mullingar, Co. Westmeath T (+353) (44) 934 8841

Ossory, Séamus Freeman, *cons.* 2007, *apptd* 2007. *Clergy,* 79. *Bishop's Residence,* Sion House, Kilkenny T (+353) (56) 776 2448

Raphoe, Philip Boyce, *cons.* 1995, *apptd* 1995. *Clergy,* 82. *Bishop's Residence,* Ard Adhamhnáin, Letterkenny, Co. Donegal T (+353) (74) 912 1208

Waterford and Lismore, William Lee, *cons.* 1993, *apptd* 1993. *Clergy,* 114. *Bishop's House,* John's Hill, Waterford T (+353) (51) 874463

OTHER CHURCHES IN THE UK

AFRICAN AND AFRO-CARIBBEAN CHURCHES

There are more than 160 Christian churches or groups of African or Afro-Caribbean origin in the UK. These include the Apostolic Faith Church, the Cherubim and Seraphim Church, the New Testament Church Assembly, the New Testament Church of God, the Wesleyan Holiness Church and the Aladura Churches. The Afro-West Indian United Council of Churches and the Council of African and Afro-Caribbean Churches UK (which was initiated as the Council of African and Allied Churches in 1979) are the media through which the member churches can work jointly to provide services they cannot easily provide individually.

There are about 341 adherents of African and Afro-Caribbean churches in the UK. The Council of African and Afro-Caribbean Churches UK has about 17,000 members, 250 ministers and 125 congregations.

There are also numerous African and Caribbean Pentecostal churches and ministries which are members of the African Caribbean Evangelical Alliance.

COUNCIL OF AFRICAN AND AFRO-CARIBBEAN CHURCHES UK, 31 Norton House, Sidney Road, London SW9 0UJ T 020-7274 5589 E olu_abiola@lineone.net
Chair, HG Most Revd Father Olu A. Abiola

ASSOCIATED PRESBYTERIAN CHURCHES OF SCOTLAND

The Associated Presbyterian Churches came into being in 1989 as a result of a division within the Free Presbyterian Church of Scotland. Following two controversial disciplinary cases, the culmination of deepening differences within the church, a presbytery was formed calling itself the Associated Presbyterian Churches which has around 600 members, 9 ministers and 15 churches.

ASSOCIATED PRESBYTERIAN CHURCHES OF SCOTLAND, APC Manse, Polvinster Road, Oban PA34 5TN T 01631-567076 E archibald.mcphail@virgin.net W www.apchurches.org
Moderator of Presbytery, Kenneth MacLean
Clerk of Presbytery, Revd Archibald McPhail

BAPTIST CHURCH

Baptists trace their origins to John Smyth, who in 1609 in Amsterdam reinstituted the baptism of conscious believers as the basis of the fellowship of a gathered church. Members of Smyth's church established the first Baptist church in England in 1612. They came to be known as 'General' Baptists and their theology was Arminian, whereas a later group of Calvinists who adopted the baptism of believers came to be known as 'Particular' Baptists. The two sections of the Baptists were united into one body, the Baptist Union of Great Britain and Ireland, in 1891. In 1988 the title was changed to the Baptist Union of Great Britain.

Baptists emphasise the complete autonomy of the local church, although individual churches are linked in various kinds of associations. There are international bodies (such as the Baptist World Alliance) and national bodies, but some Baptist churches belong to neither. However, in Great Britain the majority of churches and associations belong to the Baptist Union of Great Britain. There are also Baptist Unions in Wales, Scotland and Ireland which are much smaller than the Baptist Union of Great Britain, and there is some overlap of membership.

There are currently some 140,529 members, 2,078 ministers and 2,150 churches associated with the Baptist Union of Great Britain. The Baptist Union of Great Britain is one of the founder members of the European Baptist Federation (1948) and the Baptist World Alliance (1905) which represents nearly 150,000 churches and over 40 million members worldwide.

In the Baptist Union of Scotland there are 13,418 members, 140 pastors and 173 churches.

In the Baptist Union of Wales (Undeb Bedyddwyr Cymru) there are 15,941 members, 96 pastors and 449 churches, including those in England.

BAPTIST UNION OF GREAT BRITAIN, Baptist House, PO Box 44, 129 Broadway, Didcot, Oxon OX11 8RT T 01235-517700 E info@baptist.org.uk W www.baptist.org.uk
General Secretary, Revd Jonathan Edwards

BAPTIST UNION OF SCOTLAND, 14 Aytoun Road, Glasgow G41 5RT T 0141-423 6169 F 0141-424 1422 E director@scottishbaptist.org.uk
General Director, Revd William Slack

BAPTIST UNION OF WALES, Y Llwyfan, Trinity College, College Road, Carmarthen SA31 3EQ T 01267-245660 W www.buw.org.uk
President of the English Assembly (2008–9), Revd Peter Richards
President of the Welsh Assembly (2008–9), Gwenallt Rees
General Secretary of the Baptist Union of Wales, Revd Peter Thomas

THE BRETHREN

The Brethren was founded in Dublin in 1827–8. It rejected denominationalism and clericalism and based itself on the structures and practices of the early church. Many groups sprang up and that at Plymouth became the best known, which resulted in the designation by others as Plymouth Brethren.

Early worship had a prescribed form but quickly assumed an unstructured, non-liturgical format. There were services devoted to worship, usually involving the breaking of bread, and separate preaching meetings. There is no salaried ministry.

A theological dispute led in 1848 to schism between the Open Brethren and the Closed or Exclusive Brethren, each branch later suffering further divisions.

Open Brethren churches are completely independent, but freely cooperate with each other. Open Brethren churches are run by appointed elders. Exclusive Brethren churches believe in a universal fellowship between congregations. They do not have elders, but appoint respected members of their congregation to perform certain administrative functions.

The Brethren are established throughout the UK, Ireland, Europe, India, Africa and Australasia. In the UK there are an estimated 71,415 members, 1,268 assembly halls and around 207 full-time workers who perform administrative functions. There are a few publishing houses which publish Brethren related literature. Chapter Two is the main supplier of such literature in the UK and also has a Brethren history archive which is available for use by appointment.

CHAPTER TWO, Conduit Mews, London SE18 7AP
T 020-8316 5389 W www.chaptertwobooks.org.uk

CONGREGATIONAL FEDERATION

The Congregational Federation was founded by members of Congregational churches in England and Wales who did not join the United Reformed Church in 1972. There are also churches in Scotland and France affiliated to the federation. The federation exists to encourage congregations of believers to worship in free assembly, but it has no authority over them and emphasises their right to independence and self-governance.

The federation has 9,151 members, 80 accredited ministers and 295 churches in England, Wales and Scotland.

CONGREGATIONAL FEDERATION, 8 Castle Gate, Nottingham NG1 7AS T 0115-911 1460
E admin@congregational.org.uk
W www.congregational.org.uk
President of the Federation (2008–9), Revd Wayne Hawkins
General Secretary, Revd M. Heaney

FELLOWSHIP OF INDEPENDENT EVANGELICAL CHURCHES

The Fellowship of Independent Evangelical Churches was founded by Revd E. J. Poole-Connor (1872–1962) in 1922. In 1923 the fellowship published its first register of non-denominational pastors, evangelists and congregations who had accepted the doctrinal basis for the fellowship.

Members of the fellowship have two primary convictions, firstly to defend the evangelical faith, and secondly that evangelicalism is the bond that unites the fellowship, rather than forms of worship or church government.

The Fellowship of Independent Evangelical Churches exists to promote the welfare of non-denominational Bible churches and to give expression to the fundamental doctrines of evangelical Christianity. It supports individual churches by gathering and disseminating information and resources, advising churches on current theological, moral, social and practical issues and seeking to uphold the quality and integrity of church leaders through the Pastors' Association.

More than 490 churches are linked through the fellowship, which has 11 regions covering the whole of the UK. There are more than 330 pastors and approximately 35,000 people worship in fellowship churches every Sunday.

FELLOWSHIP OF INDEPENDENT EVANGELICAL CHURCHES, 39 The Point, Market Harborough, Leics LE16 7QU T 01858-434540 E admin@fiec.org.uk
W www.fiec.org.uk
President, Revd Rupert Bentley-Taylor
General Secretary, Richard Underwood

FREE CHURCH OF ENGLAND

The Free Church of England, otherwise called the Reformed Episcopal Church, is an independent church, constituted according to the historic faith, tradition and practice of the Church of England. Its roots lie in the 18th century, but most of its growth took place from the 1840s onwards, as clergy and congregations joined it from the established church in protest against the Oxford Movement. The historic episcopate was conferred on the English church in 1876 through bishops of the Reformed Episcopal Church (which had broken away from the Protestant Episcopal Church in the USA in 1873). A branch of the Reformed Episcopal Church was founded in the UK and this merged with the Free Church of England in 1927 to create the present church.

Worship is according to the *Book of Common Prayer* and some modern liturgy is permissable. Only men are ordained to the orders of deacon, presbyter and bishop.

The Free Church of England has around 1,290 members, 29 congregations and around 44 ministers, now mainly confined to England. It also has a few members in New Zealand and one congregation in St Petersburg, Russia.

THE FREE CHURCH OF ENGLAND, 329 Wolverhampton Road West, Willenhall WV13 2RL
T 01902-607335 W www.fcofe.org.uk
General Secretary, Rt. Revd Paul Hunt

FREE CHURCH OF SCOTLAND

The Free Church of Scotland was formed in 1843 when over 400 ministers withdrew from the Church of Scotland as a result of interference in the internal affairs of the church by the civil authorities. In 1900, all but 26 ministers joined with others to form the United Free Church (most of which rejoined the Church of Scotland in 1929). In 1904 the remaining 26 ministers were recognised by the House of Lords as continuing the Free Church of Scotland.

The church maintains strict adherence to the Westminster Confession of Faith (1648) and accepts the Bible as the sole rule of faith and conduct. Its general assembly meets annually. It also has links with reformed churches overseas. The Free Church of Scotland has about 12,000 members, 90 ministers and 100 congregations.

FREE CHURCH OF SCOTLAND, 15 North Bank Street, The Mound, Edinburgh EH1 2LS T 0131-226 5286
E offices@freechurchofscotland.org.uk
Chief Administrative Officer, R. M. Morrison

FREE PRESBYTERIAN CHURCH OF SCOTLAND

The Free Presbyterian Church of Scotland was formed in 1893 by two ministers of the Free Church of Scotland who refused to accept a Declaratory Act passed by the Free Church General Assembly in 1892. The Free Presbyterian Church of Scotland is Calvinistic in doctrine and emphasises observance of the Sabbath. It adheres strictly to the Westminster Confession of Faith of 1648.

The church has about 3,000 members in Scotland and about 4,000 in overseas congregations. It has 20 ministers and 50 churches in the UK.

FREE PRESBYTERIAN CHURCH OF SCOTLAND, 133 Woodlands Road, Glasgow G3 6LE T 0141-332 9283
Moderator 2008–9, Revd W. Weale
Clerk of the Synod, Revd John MacLeod

HOLY APOSTOLIC CATHOLIC ASSYRIAN CHURCH OF THE EAST

The Holy Apostolic Catholic Assyrian Church of the East traces its beginnings to the middle of the first century. It spread from Upper Mesopotamia throughout the territories of the Persian Empire. The Assyrian Church of the East became theologically separated from the rest of the Christian community following the Council of Ephesus in 431. The church is headed by the Catholicos Patriarch and is episcopal in government. The liturgical language is Syriac (Aramaic). The Assyrian Church of the East and the Roman Catholic Church agreed a common Christological declaration in 1994 and a process of dialogue between the Assyrian Church of the East and the Chaldean Catholic Church, which is in communion with Rome but shares the Syriac liturgy, was instituted in 1996.

The church has about 400,000 members in the Middle East, India, Europe, North America and Australasia. In the UK there are around 6,290 members, two congregations and 11 priests.

The church in Great Britain forms part of the diocese of Europe under Mar Odisho Oraham.

HOLY APOSTOLIC CATHOLIC ASSYRIAN CHURCH OF THE EAST, 66 Montague Road, London W7 3PQ T 020-8579 7259
Representative in Great Britain, Very Revd Younan Y. Younan

INDEPENDENT METHODIST CHURCHES

The Independent Methodist Churches were formed in 1805 and remained independent when the Methodist Church in Great Britain was formed in 1932. They are mainly concentrated in the industrial areas of the north of England.

The churches are Methodist in doctrine but their organisation is congregational. All the churches are members of the Independent Methodist Connexion of Churches. The controlling body of the Connexion is the Annual Meeting, to which churches send delegates. The Connexional President is elected annually. Between annual meetings the affairs of the Connexion are handled by departmental committees. Ministers are appointed by the churches and trained through the Connexion. The ministry is open to both men and women and is unpaid.

There are 1,900 members, 86 ministers and 87 churches in Great Britain.

INDEPENDENT METHODIST RESOURCE CENTRE, Fleet Street, Pemberton, Wigan, WN5 0DS T 01942-223526 E resourcecentre@imcgb.org.uk W www.imcgb.org.uk
President, Ken Irwin
General Secretary, William Gabb

LUTHERAN CHURCH

Lutheranism is based on the teachings of Martin Luther, the German leader of the Protestant Reformation. The authority of the scriptures is held to be supreme over church tradition. The teachings of Lutheranism are explained in detail in 16th-century confessional writings, particularly the Augsburg Confession. Lutheranism is one of the largest Protestant denominations and it is particularly strong in northern Europe and the USA. Some Lutheran churches are episcopal, while others have a synodal form of organisation; unity is based on doctrine rather than structure. Most Lutheran churches are members of the Lutheran World Federation, based in Geneva.

Lutheran services in Great Britain are held in 18 languages to serve members of different nationalities. Services usually follow ancient liturgies. English-language congregations are members either of the Lutheran Church in Great Britain or of the Evangelical Lutheran Church of England. The Lutheran Church in Great Britain and other Lutheran churches in Britain are members of the Lutheran Council of Great Britain, which represents them and coordinates their common work.

There are over 70 million Lutherans worldwide; in Great Britain there are about 100,000 members, 50 clergy and 100 congregations.

THE LUTHERAN COUNCIL OF GREAT BRITAIN, 30 Thanet Street, London WC1H 9QH T 020-7554 2900 F 020-7383 3081 E enquiries@lutheran.org.uk W www.lutheran.org.uk
General Secretary, Revd Thomas Bruch

METHODIST CHURCH

The Methodist movement started in England in 1729 when the Revd John Wesley, an Anglican priest, and his brother Charles met with others in Oxford and resolved to conduct their lives and study by 'rule and method'. In 1739 the Wesleys began evangelistic preaching and the first Methodist chapel was founded in Bristol in the same year. In 1744 the first annual conference was held, at which the Articles of Religion were drawn up. Doctrinal emphases included repentance, faith, the assurance of salvation, social concern and the priesthood of all believers. After John Wesley's death in 1791 the Methodists withdrew from the established church to form the Methodist Church. Methodists gradually drifted into many groups, but in 1932 the Wesleyan Methodist Church, the United Methodist Church and the Primitive Methodist Church united to form the Methodist Church of Great Britain.

The governing body of the Methodist Church is the conference. The conference is held in June each year and consists of three parts: the diaconal, ministerial and representative sessions. In addition, there are 32 district synods whose purpose is to decide policy for the district and be the link between the conference and the circuits. The circuit is the basic structure of the Methodist Church and is usually formed from the local churches in a defined area; a number of circuits make up each district. There are over 60 million Methodists worldwide; in Great Britain there are 286,319 members, 1,995 ministers and 5,626 churches.

THE METHODIST CHURCH OF GREAT BRITAIN, Methodist Church House, 25 Marylebone Road, London NW1 5JR T 020-7486 5502 W www.methodist.org.uk
President of the Conference (2008–9), Revd Stephen Poxon
Vice-President of the Conference (2008–9), David Walton
Secretary of the Conference, Revd David Deeks

IRELAND
The Methodist Church in Ireland is autonomous but has close links with British Methodism. It has a community roll of 53,668, 15,502 members, 230 ministers, 218 lay preachers and 220 churches.
METHODIST CHURCH IN IRELAND, 1 Fountainville Avenue, Belfast BT9 6AN T 028-9032 4554
E secretary@irishmethodist.org W www.irishmethodist.org
President (2008–9), Revd Aian Ferguson
Secretary, Revd Donald Ker

ORTHODOX CHURCHES

EASTERN ORTHODOX CHURCH
The Eastern (or Byzantine) Orthodox Church is a communion of self-governing Christian churches that recognises the honorary primacy of the Oecumenical Patriarch of Constantinople.

The position of Orthodox Christians is that the faith was fully defined during the period of the Oecumenical Councils. In doctrine it is strongly trinitarian, and stresses the mystery and importance of the sacraments. It is episcopal in government. The structure of the Orthodox Christian year differs from that of western churches.

Orthodox Christians throughout the world are estimated to number about 300 million; there are 291,690 in the UK.

GREEK ORTHODOX CHURCH (PATRIARCHATE OF ANTIOCH)
There are 16 parishes in the UK. The Diocese of Western and Central Europe is led by HE Metropolitan John (Yazigi).
PATRIARCHATE OF ANTIOCH IN THE UK, St George's Cathedral, 1A Redhill Street, London NW1 4BG
T 020-7383 0403 E fr.s.gholam@antiochgreekorth.co.uk
W www.antiochgreekorth.co.uk
Priest, Fr. Samir Gholam

GREEK ORTHODOX CHURCH (PATRIARCHATE OF CONSTANTINOPLE)
The presence of Greek Orthodox Christians in Britain dates back at least to 1677 when Archbishop Joseph Geogirenes of Samos fled from Turkish persecution and came to London. The present Greek cathedral in Moscow Road, Bayswater, was opened for public worship in 1879 and the Diocese of Thyateira and Great Britain was established in 1922. There are now 120 parishes and other communities (including monasteries) in the UK, served by five bishops, 106 clergy, nine cathedrals and about 94 churches.
THE PATRIARCHATE OF CONSTANTINOPLE IN GREAT BRITAIN, Thyateira House, 5 Craven Hill, London W2 3EN
T 020-7723 4787 F 020-7224 9301 E mail@thyateira.org.uk
W www.thyateira.org.uk
Archbishop, Gregorios of Thyateira and Great Britain

RUSSIAN ORTHODOX CHURCH
The records of Russian Orthodox Church activities in Britain date from the visit to England of Tsar Peter I in the early 18th century. Clergy were sent from Russia to serve the chapel established to minister to the staff of the Imperial Russian Embassy in London.

In 2007, after an 80-year division, the Russian Orthodox Church Outside Russia agreed to become an autonomous part of the Russian Orthodox Church, Patriarchate of Moscow. The reunification agreement was signed by Patriarch Alexy II, Patriarch of the Russian Orthodox Church and Metropolitan Laurus, leader of the Russian Orthodox Church Outside Russia on 17 May at a ceremony at Christ the Saviour Cathedral in Moscow.

The diocese of Sourozh is the diocese of the Russian Orthodox Church in Great Britain and Ireland and is led by Bishop Elisey of Sourozh.
DIOCESE OF SOUROZH, Diocesan Office, Cathedral of the Dormition and All Saints, 67 Ennismore Gardens, London SW7 1NH T 020-7584 0096 W www.sourozh.org
Diocesan Bishop, Rt. Revd Elisey (Ganaba) of Sourozh
Assistant Diocesan Bishop, Most Revd Anatoly (Kuznetsov) of Kerch

SERBIAN ORTHODOX CHURCH (PATRIARCHATE OF SERBIA)
There are around 40,000 members in the UK served by 11 clergy. The Patriarchate of Serbia is represented by Bishop Dositej of Great Britain and Scandinavia.
SERBIAN ORTHODOX CHURCH IN GREAT BRITAIN, Saint Sava, 89 Lancaster Road, London W11 1QQ
T 020-7727 8367 E crkva@spclondon.org
W www.spclondon.org
Representative, Very Revd Milun Kostic

OTHER NATIONALITIES
The Patriarchates of Romania and Bulgaria (Diocese of Western Europe) have memberships estimated at 16,000 and 1,600 respectively, while the Georgian Orthodox Church has around 400 members. The Belarusian (membership estimated at 2,300) and Latvian (membership of around 110) Orthodox churches are part of the Patriarchate of Constantinople.

ORIENTAL ORTHODOX CHURCHES
The term 'Oriental Orthodox Churches' is now generally used to describe a group of six ancient eastern churches which reject the Christological definition of the Council of Chalcedon (AD 451) and use Christological terms in different ways from the Eastern Orthodox Church. There are estimated to be around 50 million members worldwide of the Oriental Orthodox Churches and about 18,319 in the UK.

ARMENIAN ORTHODOX CHURCH (PATRIARCHATE OF ETCHMIADZIN)
The Armenian Orthodox Church is led by HH Karekin II, Catholicos of All Armenians. Bishop Nathan Hovhannisian is the Primate of the Armenian Church of Great Britain and President of the Armenian Community and Church Council.
ARMENIAN CHURCH OF GREAT BRITAIN, The Armenian Vicarage, Iverna Gardens, London W8 6TP T 020-7937 0152
E arajnortaran@aol.com W www.accc.org.uk
Primate, Bishop Nathan Hovhannisian

COPTIC ORTHODOX CHURCH
The Coptic Orthodox Church is led by HH Pope Shenouda III and is represented in Great Britain by Bishop Angaelos at the Coptic Orthodox Cathedral of St George at the Coptic Orthodox Church Centre. The

Coptic Orthodox Church is the largest Oriental Orthodox community in Great Britain.

COPTIC ORTHODOX CHURCH CENTRE, Shephalbury Manor, Broadhall Way, Stevenage, Herts SG2 8RH
T 01438-745232 E info@copticcentre.com
W www.copticcentre.com
Bishop, Bishop Angaelos

BRITISH ORTHODOX CHURCH

The British Orthodox Church is canonically part of the Coptic Orthodox Patriarchate of Alexandria. As it ministers to British people all its services are in English.

THE BRITISH ORTHODOX CHURCH, 10 Heathwood Gardens, Charlton, London SE7 8EP T 020-8854 3090
E boc@nildram.co.uk W www.britishorthodox.org
Metropolitan, Abba Seraphim

INDIAN ORTHODOX CHURCH

The Indian Orthodox Church, also known as the Malankara Orthodox Church, is part of the Diocese of Europe, UK and Canada. The church in Great Britain can be contacted via Fr. Abraham Thomas.

INDIAN ORTHODOX CHURCH, St Gregorios Indian Orthodox Church, Cranfield Road, Brockley, London SE4 1UF T 020-8691 9456 E vicar@indian-orthodox.co.uk
W www.indian-orthodox.co.uk
Vicar, Revd Fr. Abraham Thomas

SYRIAN ORTHODOX CHURCH

The Patriarchate Vicariate of the Syrian Orthodox Church in the United Kingdom is represented by HE Athanasius Toma Dawod.

SYRIAN ORTHODOX CHURCH IN THE UK, 5 Canning Road, Croydon CR0 6QA T 020-8654 7531
E enquiry@syrianorthodoxchurch.net
W www.syrianorthodoxchurch.net
Patriarchal Vicar, HE Athanasius Toma Dawod

PENTECOSTAL CHURCHES

Pentecostalism is inspired by the descent of the Holy Spirit upon the apostles at Pentecost. The movement began in Los Angeles, USA, in 1906 and is characterised by baptism with the Holy Spirit, divine healing, speaking in tongues (glossolalia), and a literal interpretation of the scriptures.

The Pentecostal movement in Britain dates from 1907. Initially, groups of Pentecostalists were led by laymen and did not organise formally. However, in 1915 the Elim Foursquare Gospel Alliance (more usually called the Elim Pentecostal Church) was founded in Ireland by George Jeffreys and currently has about 550 churches, 68,500 adherents and 650 accredited ministers. In 1924 about 70 independent assemblies formed a fellowship, the Assemblies of God in Great Britain and Ireland, which now incorporates around 600 churches and is known as the Assemblies of God Incorporated.

The Apostolic Church grew out of the 1904–5 revivals in South Wales and was established in 1916. The Apostolic has around 109 churches, 5,400 adherents and 103 ministers in the UK. The New Testament Church of God was established in England in 1953 and has about 121 congregations, around 25,810 menbers and 305 ministers across England and Wales. In recent years many aspects of Pentecostalism have been adopted by the growing charismatic movement within the Roman Catholic, Protestant and Eastern Orthodox churches. There are about 105 million Pentecostalists worldwide, with about 301,135 adherents in the UK.

THE APOSTOLIC CHURCH, International Administration Offices, PO Box 389, Swansea SA7 9LA T 01792-790300
E admin@apostolic-church.org
National Leader, Warren Jones

THE ASSEMBLIES OF GOD INCORPORATED, PO Box 7634, Nottingham NG11 6ZY T 0115-921 7272
E info@aog.org.uk W www.aog.org.uk

THE ELIM PENTECOSTAL CHURCH, PO Box 38, Cheltenham, Glos GL50 3HN T 01242-519904
E info@elimhq.net W www.elim.org.uk
General Superintendent, Revd John Glass

THE NEW TESTAMENT CHURCH OF GOD, 3 Cheyne Walk, Northampton NN1 5PT T 01604-824222
E bigmove@ntcg.org.uk W www.ntcg.org.uk
Administrative Bishop, Eric Brown

PRESBYTERIAN CHURCH IN IRELAND

The Presbyterian Church in Ireland is reformed in doctrine and presbyterian in constitution. Presbyterianism was established in Ireland as a result of the Ulster plantation in the early 17th century when English and Scottish Protestants settled in the north of Ireland.

There are 21 presbyteries under the chief court known as the general assembly. The general assembly meets annually and is presided over by a moderator who is elected for one year. The ongoing work of the church is undertaken by 15 boards under which there are specialist committees.

There are around 225,900 members of Irish presbyterians churches in the UK, forming 606 congregations.

THE PRESBYTERIAN CHURCH IN IRELAND, Church House, Belfast BT1 6DW T 028-9032 2284
E info@presbyterianireland.org
W www.presbyterianireland.org
Moderator (2008–9), Revd Dr Donald Patton
Clerk of Assembly and General Secretary, Revd Dr Donald Watts

PRESBYTERIAN CHURCH OF WALES

The Presbyterian Church of Wales or Calvinistic Methodist Church of Wales is Calvinistic in doctrine and presbyterian in constitution. It was formed in 1811 when Welsh Calvinists severed the relationship with the established church by ordaining their own ministers. It secured its own confession of faith in 1823 and a Constitutional Deed in 1826, and since 1864 the General Assembly has met annually, presided over by a moderator elected for a year. The doctrine and constitutional structure of the Presbyterian Church of Wales was confirmed by act of parliament in 1931–2.

The Church has 31,677 members, 68 ministers and 714 congregations.

THE PRESBYTERIAN CHURCH OF WALES, Tabernacle Chapel, 81 Merthyr Road, Whitchurch, Cardiff CF14 1DD
T 029-2062 7465 E swyddfa.office@ebcpcw.org.uk
W www.ebcpcw.org.uk
Moderator (2008–9), Revd Haydn Thomas
General Secretary, Revd Ifan Roberts

RELIGIOUS SOCIETY OF FRIENDS (QUAKERS)

Quakerism is a religious denomination which was founded in the 17th century by George Fox and others in an attempt to revive what they saw as the original 'primitive Christianity'. The movement, at first called Friends of the Truth, started in the Midlands, Yorkshire and north-west England, but there are now Quakers all over Britain and in 36 countries around the world. The colony of Pennsylvania, founded by William Penn, was originally Quaker.

Emphasis is placed on the experience of God in daily life rather than on sacraments or religious occasions. There is no church calendar. Worship is largely silent and there are no appointed ministers; the responsibility for conducting a meeting is shared equally among those present. Religious tolerance and social reform have always been important to Quakers, together with a commitment to peace and non-violence in resolving disputes.

There are more than 25,300 'friends' or Quakers in Great Britain. There are about 500 places where Quaker meetings are held, many of them Quaker-owned Friends Meeting Houses. The Britain Yearly Meeting is the name given to the central organisation of Quakers in Britain.

THE RELIGIOUS SOCIETY OF FRIENDS (QUAKERS) IN BRITAIN, Friends House, 173–177 Euston Road, London NW1 2BJ T 020-7663 1000
E enquiries@quaker.org.uk W www.quaker.org.uk
Recording Clerk, Gillian Ashmore

SALVATION ARMY

The Salvation Army is an international Christian organisation working in 111 countries worldwide. As a church and registered charity, the Salvation Army is funded through donations from its members, the general public and, where appropriate, government grants.

The Salvation Army was founded by a Methodist minister, William Booth, in the East End of London in 1865, and now has 776 local church and community centres, 59 residential centres for the homeless, 17 elderly care centres and six substance misuse centres. It also runs a clothing recycling programme, charity shops, a prison visiting service and a family tracing service. In 1878 it adopted a quasi-military command structure intended to inspire and regulate its endeavours and to reflect its view that the church was engaged in spiritual warfare. There are 45,164 members and around 1,371 ministers in the UK. Salvationists emphasise evangelism and the provision of social welfare.

UK TERRITORIAL HEADQUARTERS, 101 Newington Causeway, London SE1 6BN T 0845-634 0101
E info@salvationarmy.org.uk W www.salvationarmy.org.uk
UK Territorial Commander, Commissioner John Matear

SEVENTH-DAY ADVENTIST CHURCH

The Seventh-day Adventist Church was founded in 1863 in the USA and the first church in the UK was established in 1886. It is a worldwide Christian church with 14.75 million members worshipping in 121,564 congregrations in 202 countries. Slightly more than 70 per cent of all Seventh-day Adventists live in Africa, the Caribbean and Central and South America. In the UK there are 28,110 members worshipping in 279 churches and companies.

The beliefs and practices of the church are rooted in the Bible and are summarised under 28 core beliefs. The mission of the church is to proclaim to all people the everlasting gospel of the three angels' messages of Revelation 14:6–12, leading them to accept Jesus as their personal saviour and to prepare for his imminent return.

The world church is divided administratively into 13 divisions, each made up of 'unions' of churches. The British Isles headquarters is known as the British Union Conference of Seventh-day Adventists.

BRITISH UNION CONFERENCE OF SEVENTH-DAY ADVENTISTS, Stanborough Park, Watford WD25 9JZ
T 01923-672251 W www.adventist.org.uk
President, Don McFarlane

THE (SWEDENBORGIAN) NEW CHURCH

The New Church is based on the teachings of the 18th century Swedish scientist and theologian Emanuel Swedenborg (1688–1772), who believed that Jesus Christ appeared to him and instructed him to reveal the spiritual meaning of the Bible. He claimed to have visions of the spiritual world, including heaven and hell, and conversations with angels and spirits. He published several theological works, including descriptions of the spiritual world and a Bible commentary.

The second coming of Jesus Christ is believed to have already taken place and is still taking place, being not an actual physical reappearance of Christ, but rather his return in spirit. It is also believed that concurrent with our life on earth is life in a parallel spiritual world, of which we are usually unconscious until death. There are around 30,000 Swedenborgians worldwide, with 8,470 members, 25 Churches and 11 ministers in the UK.

THE GENERAL CONFERENCE OF THE NEW CHURCH, Swedenborg House, 20 Bloomsbury Way, London WC1A 2TH T 0845-686 0086
E enquiries@generalconference.org.uk
W www.generalconference.org.uk
Chief Executive, Michael Hindley

UNDEB YR ANNIBYNWYR CYMRAEG

Undeb Yr Annibynwyr Cymraeg, the Union of Welsh Independents, was formed in 1872 and is a voluntary association of Welsh Congregational churches and personal members. It is mainly Welsh-speaking. Congregationalism in Wales dates back to 1639 when the first Welsh Congregational church was opened in Gwent. Member churches are traditionally Calvinistic in doctrine, although a wide range of interpretations are permitted, and congregationalist in organisation. Each church has complete independence in the government and administration of its affairs.

The Union has 28,892 members, 98 ministers and 449 member churches.

UNDEB YR ANNIBYNWYR CYMRAEG, 5 Axis Court, Riverside Business Park, Swansea Vale, Swansea SA7 0AJ
T 01792-795888 E undeb@annibynwyr.org
W www.annibynwyr.org
President of the Union (2008–9), Margaret Jones
General Secretary, Revd Dr Geraint Tudur

UNITED REFORMED CHURCH

The United Reformed Church (URC) was first formed by the union of most of the Congregational churches in England and Wales with the Presbyterian Church of England in 1972. Congregationalism dates from the mid-16th century. It is Calvinistic in doctrine, and its followers form independent self-governing congregations bound under God by covenant, a principle laid down in the writings of Robert Browne (1550–1633). From the late 16th century the movement was driven underground by persecution, but the cause was defended at the Westminster Assembly in 1643 and the Savoy Declaration of 1658 laid down its principles. Congregational churches formed county associations for mutual support and in 1832 these associations merged to form the Congregational Union of England and Wales.

Presbyterianism in England also dates from the mid 16th century, and was Calvinistic and evangelical in its doctrine. It was governed by a hierarchy of courts.

In the 1960s there was close cooperation locally and nationally between congregational and presbyterian churches. This led to union negotiations and a Scheme of

Union, supported by act of parliament in 1972. In 1981 a further unification took place, with the Reformed Association of Churches of Christ becoming part of the URC. In 2000 a third union took place, with the Congregational Union of Scotland. In its basis the United Reformed Church reflects local church initiative and responsibility with a conciliar pattern of oversight.

The United Reformed Church is divided into 13 synods, each with a synod moderator. There are around 1,620 congregations which serve around 75,000 adults and 70,000 children and young people. There are around 750 serving ministers.

The General Assembly is the central body, and comprises around 400 representatives, mainly appointed by the synods, of which half are lay persons and half are ministers. From 2010 the General Assembly will meet biennially to elect two moderators, both lay and ordained, who will then become the public representatives of the URC. This will replace the current arrangement where one lay or ordained moderator is elected annually by the General Assembly. As a transitional arrangement the moderator will remain in office for two years from 2008.

UNITED REFORMED CHURCH, 86 Tavistock Place, London WC1H 9RT T 020-7916 2020 E urc@urc.org.uk W www.urc.org.uk
Moderator of the General Assembly (2008–2010), Revd John Marsh
General Secretary, Revd Roberta Rominger

WESLEYAN REFORM UNION

The Wesleyan Reform Union was founded by Methodists who left or were expelled from Wesleyan Methodism in 1849 following a period of internal conflict. Its doctrine is conservative evangelical and its organisation is congregational, each church having complete independence in the government and administration of its affairs. The union has 1,625 members, 18 ministers, 112 lay preachers and 98 churches.

THE WESLEYAN REFORM UNION, Wesleyan Reform Church House, 123 Queen Street, Sheffield S1 2DU T 0114-272 1938 E admin@thewru.co.uk W www.thewru.com
President (2008–9), Revd Geoffrey Clark
General Secretary, Revd Colin Braithwaite

NON-TRINITARIAN CHURCHES

CHRISTADELPHIAN

Christadelphians believe that the Bible is the word of God and that it reveals both God's dealings with mankind in the past and his plans for the future. These plans centre on the work of Jesus Christ, who it is believed will return to Earth to establish God's kingdom. Christadelphians have existed since the 1850s, beginning in the USA through the work of an Englishman, Dr John Thomas.

THE CHRISTADELPHIAN, 404 Shaftmoor Lane, Hall Green, Birmingham B28 8SZ T 0121-777 6328 F 0121-778 5024 E enquiries@thechristadelphian.com W www.thechristadelphian.com

CHURCH OF CHRIST, SCIENTIST

The Church of Christ, Scientist was founded by Mary Baker Eddy in the USA in 1879 to 'reinstate primitive Christianity and its lost element of healing'. Christian Science teaches the need for spiritual regeneration and salvation from sin, but is best known for its reliance on prayer alone in the healing of sickness. Adherents believe that such healing is the result of divine laws, or divine science, and is in direct line with that practised by Jesus Christ (revered, not as God, but as the son of God) and by the early Christian church.

The denomination consists of The First Church of Christ, Scientist, in Boston, Massachusetts, USA (the 'mother church') and its branch churches in almost 80 countries worldwide. The Bible and Mary Baker Eddy's book, *Science and Health with Key to the Scriptures,* are used for daily spiritual guidance and healing by all members and are read at services; there are no clergy. Those engaged in full-time healing are called Christian Science practitioners, of whom there are 1,500 worldwide. The church also publishes *The Christian Science Monitor.*

No membership figures are available, since Mary Baker Eddy felt that numbers are no measure of spiritual vitality and ruled that such statistics should not be published. There are almost 2,000 branch churches worldwide, including over 100 in the UK.

CHRISTIAN SCIENCE COMMITTEE ON PUBLICATION, Unit T10, Tideway Yard, 125 Mortlake High Street, London SW14 8SN T 020-8150 0245 E londoncs@csps.com W www.christianscience.com
District Manager for the UK and the Republic of Ireland, Tony Lobl

CHURCH OF JESUS CHRIST OF LATTER-DAY SAINTS

The Church of Jesus Christ of Latter-Day Saints (often referred to as 'Mormons') was founded in New York State, USA, in 1830, and came to Britain in 1837. The oldest continuous congregation of the church is in Preston, Lancashire.

Mormons are Christians who claim to belong to the 'restored church' of Jesus Christ. They believe that true Christianity died when the last original apostle died, but that it was given back to the world by God and Christ through Joseph Smith, the church's founder and first president. They accept and use the Bible as scripture, but believe in continuing revelation from God and use additional scriptures, including *The Book of Mormon: Another Testament of Jesus Christ.* The importance of the family is central to the church's beliefs and practices. Church members set aside Monday evenings as family home evenings when Christian family values are taught. Polygamy was formally discontinued in 1890.

The church has no paid ministry: local congregations are headed by a leader chosen from amongst their number. The world governing body, based in Utah, USA, is led by a president, believed to be the chosen prophet, and his two counsellors. There are more than 13 million members worldwide, with over 190,000 adherents and 411 congregations in the UK.

CHURCH OF JESUS CHRIST OF LATTER-DAY SAINTS, British Headquarters, 751 Warwick Road, Solihull, W. Midlands B91 3DQ T 0121-712 1200 W www.lds.org.uk

JEHOVAH'S WITNESSES

The movement now known as Jehovah's Witnesses grew from a Bible study group formed by Charles Taze Russell in 1872 in Pennsylvania, USA. In 1896 it adopted the name of the Watch Tower Bible and Tract Society, and in 1931 its members became known as Jehovah's Witnesses.

Jehovah's (God's) Witnesses believe in the Bible as the word of God, and consider it to be inspired and historically accurate. They take the scriptures literally, except where there are obvious indications that they are figurative or symbolic, and reject the doctrine of the Trinity. Witnesses also believe that the earth will remain forever and that all those approved of by Jehovah will have eternal life on a cleansed and beautified earth; only 144,000 will go to heaven to rule with Christ. They believe that the second coming of Christ began in 1914 and his thousand-year reign on earth is imminent, and that armageddon (a final battle in which evil will be defeated) will precede Christ's rule of peace. They refuse to take part in military service and do not accept blood transfusions.

The nine-member world governing body is based in New York, USA. There is no paid ministry, but each congregation has elders assigned to look after various duties and every Witness is assigned homes to visit in their congregation. There are over 6.9 million Jehovah's Witnesses worldwide, with 130,000 Witnesses in the UK organised into more than 1,500 congregations.

BRITISH ISLES HEADQUARTERS, Watch Tower House, The Ridgeway, London NW7 1RN **T** 020-8906 2211
E opi@uk.jw.org **W** www.watchtower.org

UNITARIAN AND FREE CHRISTIAN CHURCHES

Unitarianism has its historical roots in the Judaeo-Christian tradition but rejects the deity of Christ and the doctrine of the Trinity. It allows the individual to embrace insights from all the world's faiths and philosophies, as there is no fixed creed. It is accepted that beliefs may evolve in the light of personal experience.

Unitarian communities first became established in Poland and Transylvania in the 16th century. The first avowedly Unitarian place of worship in the British Isles opened in London in 1774. The General Assembly of Unitarian and Free Christian Churches came into existence in 1928 as the result of the amalgamation of two earlier organisations.

There are about 4,400 Unitarians in Great Britain and Ireland and about 72 Unitarian ministers. Nearly 200 self-governing congregations and fellowship groups, including a small number overseas, are members of the General Assembly.

GENERAL ASSEMBLY OF UNITARIAN AND FREE CHRISTIAN CHURCHES, Essex Hall, 1–6 Essex Street, London WC2R 3HY **T** 020-7240 2384
E info@unitarian.org.uk **W** www.unitarian.org.uk
Chief Executive, Revd Steve Dick

COMMUNICATIONS

TELECOMMUNICATIONS

In 1984 the Telecommunications Act set the framework for a competitive market for telecommunications by abolishing British Telecom's (BT) exclusive right to provide services. In the early 1990s the market was opened up and a number of new national public telecommunications operators (PTOs) were given licences. This ended the duopoly that had existed in the 1980s when only BT and Mercury were licensed to provide fixed line telecoms networks in the UK.

Four EU directives covering framework, authorisation, access and interconnection and universal services were agreed in March 2002 with the aim of further developing a pro-competitive regulatory structure. These directives were provided for in the Communications Act which came into force in July 2003. Under the act licences are no longer required for providing communications networks or services in the UK. All persons providing such networks and services are subject to 'general conditions of entitlement', which constitute a set of rules they are obliged to comply.

Mobile network technology has improved dramatically since the launch in 1985 of the first-generation 900MHz analogue GSM service (known as TACS), which offered little or no data capability. In 1992 Vodafone launched a new digital global system for mobile communications (GSM) network, usually referred to as 2G or second generation. This technology used digital encoding and allowed voice and low-speed data communications. 2G technology was later extended to 2.5G, allowing additional features such as an enhanced data transfer rate.

RECENT DEVELOPMENTS

The four GSM operators, namely Vodafone, O2, T-Mobile and Orange, were joined in March 2003 by the first 3G operator, '3' (Hutchison 3UK). Vodafone, Orange and T-Mobile all launched their own third generation (3G) services in 2004, and O2 in February 2005. 3G offers far greater capability in data transmission and services.

Technological developments have merged the previously distinct areas of television, internet and telephony. In 2005, operators introduced live streaming television over 3G networks, with deals struck between broadcasters and mobile operators. In May 2005 Orange became the first operator in the UK to launch a mobile television service. Rival operators have since introduced similar services.

The government is also encouraging the use of Wi-Fi (wireless fidelity). Deregulation has allowed public network operators to use certain parts of the spectrum, which are exempt from licensing for wireless LAN (Wi-Fi) type systems. Initially only personal use was permitted in these bands, but this has now been expanded to a full commercial service. There are an estimated 14,500 'hotspots' throughout the UK, of which 1,500 are in London.

FIXED LINE COMMUNICATIONS

In the year to December 2006 customers spent £9.5bn on fixed line telephony and the number of fixed exchange lines stood at 33.6 million. The number of fixed lines fell by 1.4 per cent in 2006 compared with 2005. Due to Local Loop Unbundling, which enables operators to connect directly to the consumer using BT lines and then add their own equipment to offer broadband and other services, there was a two per cent increase in the market share for alternative fixed network operators in 2006.

Excluding corporate connections, at the end of 2006 there were 16.6 million internet connections in the UK, a one million increase from 2005. In addition to overall growth in internet penetration there was also a large-scale migration from narrowband to broadband access, with the total number of residential and small/medium business broadband connections reaching 13 million.

TOTAL TELECOMS CONNECTIONS
millions

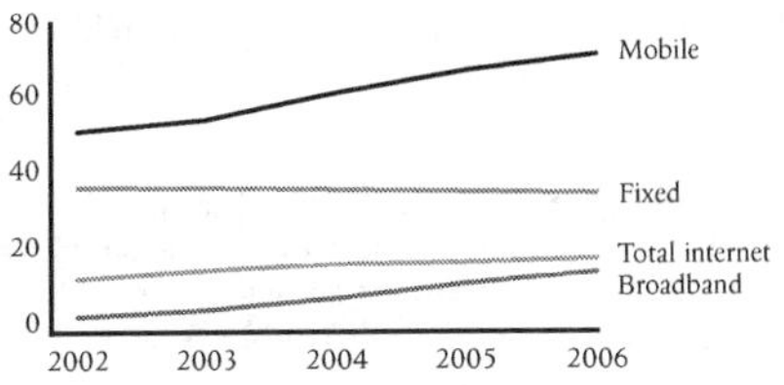

Source: OFCOM *The Communications Market 2007*

MOBILE COMMUNICATIONS

In *The Communications Market 2007* report, UK regulator OFCOM revealed that year-on-year growth in mobile revenues continued during 2006, with income from users totalling £13.9bn and representing 36 per cent of all retail telecoms revenue. At the end of 2006 there were 69.7 million active mobile connections in the UK, exceeding the size of the UK population. This is due to the number of people having more than one mobile subscription, either for a second mobile phone or a substitute wireless device such as a Blackberry.

MOBILE SUBSCRIPTIONS BY NETWORK
Active subscriptions, millions

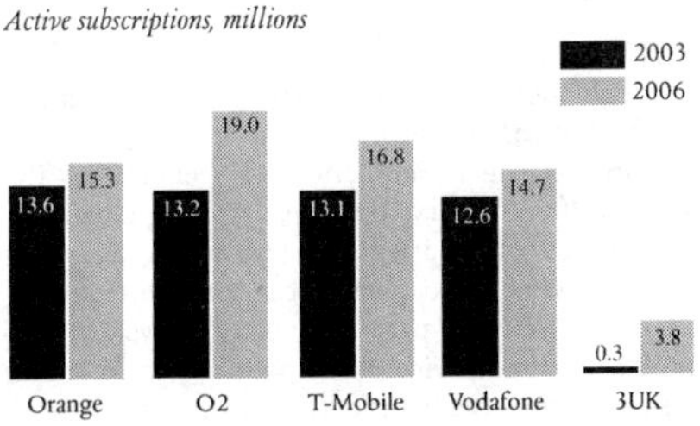

Source: OFCOM *The Communications Market 2007*

With various technologies converging, the structure of the mobile communications industry is becoming increasingly complex, but it can be divided into two types of players: network operators, such as Vodafone and Orange, who own the infrastructure, set tariffs and bill customers; and mobile virtual network operators (MVNOs), who lease network capacity from the operators.

MOBILE SUBSCRIPTIONS

There are two basic types of mobile subscription: contracts and pre-pay or 'pay-as-you-go'. The proportion of contract to pay-as-you-go customers in the UK has remained relatively constant over the last few years. At the end of 2006 there were 24.4 million active contract subscribers and 45.3 million pre-pay customers.

HEALTH

In 1999 the Independent Expert Group on Mobile Phones (IEGMP) was established to examine the possible effects of mobile phones, base stations and transmitters on health. The main findings of the IEGMP's report *Mobile Phones and Health,* published in May 2000, found that:

- exposure to radio frequency radiation below guideline levels did not cause adverse health effects to the general population
- the use of mobile phones by drivers of any vehicle can increase the chance of accidents
- the widespread use of mobile phones by children for non-essential calls should be discouraged because if there are unrecognised adverse health effects children may be more vulnerable
- there is no general risk to the health of people living near to base stations on the basis that exposures are expected to be much lower than guidelines set by the International Commission on Non-Ionising Radiation Protection

As part of its response to the research recommendations contained in the IEGMP's report, the government set up the Mobile Telecommunications Health and Research (MTHR) programme in 2001 to undertake independent research into the possible health risks from mobile telephone technology. The MTHR programme published its report in September 2007 concluding that neither mobile phones nor base stations have been found to be associated with any biological or adverse health effects. The full report can be found on the MTHR website (**W** www.mthr.org.uk).

The Health Protection Agency is the main body responsible for providing advice and information on the effects of exposure from mobile phones and base stations. Detailed information about the typical levels of exposure from mobile phones and to those who live near base stations can be found on its website (**W** www.hpa.org.uk).

SAFETY WHILE DRIVING

Under legislation that came into effect in December 2003 it is illegal for drivers to use a hand-held mobile phone while driving. Since February 2007, under the Road Safety Act 2006, the fixed penalty for using a hand-held mobile device while driving is £60 and three penalty points. The same fixed penalty can also be issued to a driver for not having proper control of a vehicle while using a hands-free device. If the police or driver chooses to take the case to court rather than issue or accept a fixed penalty notice, the maximum fine is £1,000 for car drivers and £2,500 for drivers of vans, lorries, buses and coaches.

REGULATION

Formed in 2003, OFCOM is an independent body responsible for the regulation of the UK's communications industry – for setting market controls and ensuring that the industry players do not behave in an anti-competitive manner. OFCOM inherited all the duties of the former communications and broadcasting regulators, OFTEL and the Radiocommunications Agency in addition to the duties enacted in the provisions laid down in the Communications Act 2003. Competition in the communications market is also regulated by the Office of Fair Trading, although OFCOM takes the lead in competition investigations in the UK market. The Competition Appeal Tribunal hears appeals against OFCOM's decisions and price-related appeals are referred to the Competition Commission.

CONTACTS

DEPARTMENT FOR BUSINESS, ENTERPRISE AND REGULATORY REFORM, 1 Victoria Street, London SW1V 0ET **T** 020-7215 5000 **W** www.berr.gov.uk

OFCOM, Riverside House, 2A Southwark Bridge Road, London SE1 9HA **T** 020-7981 3000 **W** www.ofcom.org.uk

POSTAL SERVICES

The Royal Mail Group plc operates Parcelforce Worldwide, Post Office and Royal Mail, which combined handle around 84 million items of mail each day. The Postal Services Commission (Postcomm), an independent regulator accountable to parliament, oversees postal operations in the UK. It is responsible for the smooth introduction of competition into postal services, and the market was opened to full competition in January 2006. All postal operators, including Royal Mail, are licensed by Postcomm; the licence requires the operators to ensure that the mail they handle is always secure and to maintain certain standards. Postwatch is the consumer organisation responsible for postal services and takes up complaints on behalf of consumers against any licensed provider of postal services. In October 2008 Postwatch is due to be merged with Energywatch as part of National Consumer Council plans to form a new, enhanced consumer representation and advocacy body.

POSTCOMM, Hercules House, 6 Hercules Road, London SE1 7DB **T** 020-7593 2100 **W** www.psc.gov.uk

POSTWATCH, Freepost, Postwatch **T** 08456-013265 **W** www.postwatch.co.uk

PRICING IN PROPORTION

In August 2006 Royal Mail introduced a new pricing system, whereby the pricing of mail depends upon its size as well as its weight. The system is designed to rebalance postage prices to reflect the fact that larger, bulkier items cost more to handle than smaller, lighter ones. There are three basic categories of correspondence:

LETTER

Length up to 240mm, *width* up to 165mm, *thickness* up to 5mm, *weight* up to 100g, eg most cards, postcards and bills

LARGE LETTER

Length up to 353mm, *width* up to 250mm, *thickness* up to 25mm, *weight* up to 750g, eg most A4 documents, CDs and magazines

PACKET

Length over 353mm, *width* over 250mm, *thickness* over

25mm, *weight* over 750g, eg VHS cassettes, books, prints and posters in cylindrical packaging

INLAND POSTAL SERVICES

Below are details of a number of popular postal services along with prices correct as at April 2008.

INLAND POST RATES

Format	*Maximum weight*	*First class*	*Second class*†
Letter*	100g	£0.36	£0.27
Large letter	100g	£0.52	£0.42
	250g	£0.78	£0.66
	500g	£1.08	£0.90
	750g	£1.57	£1.31
Packet	100g	£1.14	£0.95
	250g	£1.45	£1.24
	500g	£1.94	£1.63
	750g	£2.51	£2.08
	1,000g	£3.08	£2.49

* Includes postcards

† First class post is normally delivered on the following working day and second class within three working days

UK PARCEL RATES

Maximum weight	*Standard tariff**
2kg	£4.20
4kg	£6.85
6kg	£9.30
8kg	£11.40
10kg	£12.24
20kg	£14.26

* Standard parcels are normally delivered within three to five working days

OVERSEAS POSTAL SERVICES

Royal Mail divides the world into two zones: **Europe** (Albania, Andorra, Armenia, Austria, Azerbaijan, Azores, Balearic Islands, Belarus, Belgium, Bosnia and Hercegovina, Bulgaria, Canary Islands, Corsica, Croatia, Cyprus, Czech Republic, Denmark, Estonia, Faroe Islands, Finland, France, Georgia, Germany, Gibraltar, Greece, Greenland, Hungary, Iceland, Ireland, Italy, Kazakhstan, Kosovo, Kyrgyzstan, Latvia, Liechtenstein, Lithuania, Luxembourg, Macedonia, Madeira, Malta, Moldova, Monaco, Montenegro, the Netherlands, Norway, Poland, Portugal, Romania, Russian Federation, San Marino, Serbia, Slovakia, Slovenia, Spain, Sweden, Switzerland, Tajikistan, Turkey, Turkmenistan, Ukraine, Uzbekistan, Vatican City State) and **Rest of the World 1** (all countries that are not listed under Europe)

OVERSEAS SURFACE MAIL RATES*

Letters

Maximum weight	*Standard tariff*	*Maximum weight*	*Standard tariff*
20g†	£0.48	450g	£4.36
60g	£0.82	500g	£4.81
100g	£1.16	750g	£7.07
150g	£1.63	1,000g	£9.32
200g	£2.09	1,250g	£11.58
250g	£2.55	1,500g	£13.84
300g	£3.45	1,750g	£16.03
350g	£3.91	2,000g	£18.18
400g	£4.81		

* Letters and postcards to Europe are sent by Airmail

† Includes postcards

Small packets and printed papers

Maximum weight	*Standard tariff*	*Maximum weight*	*Standard tariff*
100g	£0.81	450g	£2.73
150g	£1.09	500g	£3.00
200g	£1.37	750g	£4.37
250g	£1.64	1,000g	£5.73
300g	£1.91	1,500g	£8.46
350g	£2.18	2,000g*	£11.09
400g	£2.46		

* Maximum weight. For printed papers only: add £0.26 for each additional 50g up to a maximum weight of 5kg

AIRMAIL LETTERS

Europe

Maximum weight	*Standard tariff*	*Maximum weight*	*Standard tariff*
20g*	£0.50	300g	£3.47
40g	£0.72	320g	£3.66
60g	£0.94	340g	£3.85
80g	£1.14	360g	£4.04
100g	£1.36	380g	£4.23
120g	£1.58	400g	£4.42
140g	£1.80	420g	£4.61
160g	£2.02	440g	£4.80
180g	£2.24	460g	£4.99
200g	£2.44	480g	£5.18
220g	£2.64	500g	£5.37
240g	£2.85	1,000g	£9.12
260g	£3.06	2,000g	£15.62
280g	£3.26		

* Includes postcards

Rest of the World

Maximum weight	*Standard tariff*
Postcards	£0.56
20g	£0.81
40g	£1.22
60g	£1.64
80g	£2.08
100g	£2.52
500g	£10.50
1,000g	£17.50
2,000g	£30.00

Note that there are different rates for small packets and printed matter. *See* W www.royalmail.com for further details.

SPECIAL DELIVERY SERVICES

SPECIAL DELIVERY NEXT DAY

A guaranteed next working day delivery service by 1pm to 99 per cent of the UK for first class letters and packets (maximum item weight is 10kg). Prices start at £4.60. There is also a service which guarantees delivery by 9am (maximum item weight is 2kg). Prices start at £10.30.

INTERNATIONAL SIGNED FOR AND AIRSURE

Express airmail services (maximum weight 2kg) that include £34 compensation in case of loss or damage. The fee for International Signed For is £3.50 plus airmail postage. The fee for Airsure is £4.20 plus airmail postage.

RECORDED SIGNED FOR

Provides a record of posting and delivery of letters and ensures a signature on delivery. This service is recommended for items of little or no monetary value. All packets must be handed to the post office and a receipt issued as proof of posting. The charge is 72p plus the standard first or second class postage with up to £36 compensation in case of loss or damage.

OTHER SERVICES

BUSINESS SERVICES

A range of postal services are available to businesses including business collection, freepost, business reply services, business packaging for special deliveries and international bulk mailing options.

COMPENSATION

Compensation for loss or damage to an item sent varies according to the service used to send the item.

PASSPORT APPLICATIONS

Around 2,000 post offices process passport applications. To find out your nearest office, and for further information, *see* W www.postoffice.co.uk.

TRACK AND TRACE

This online service, accessible from www.royalmail.com and www.postoffice.co.uk, enables customers to track the progress of items sent using the special delivery services listed above.

REDIRECTION

A printed form obtainable from the Post Office or from www.royalmail.com must be signed by the person to whom the letters are to be addressed. A fee is payable for each different surname on the application form. The charges are: one month, £7.35 (abroad via airmail, £14.85); three months, £16.15 (£32.30); six months, £24.90 (£49.80); 12 months, £37.40 (£74.75).

KEEPSAFE

Mail is held for up to two months while the addressee is away and is delivered when the addressee returns. Prices start at £8.50 for 17 days. Perishable items are returned to the sender. Recorded items are held for a week before being returned to the sender, and Special Delivery items for three weeks beyond the keepsafe expiry date.

POST OFFICE BOX

A PO Box provides a short and memorable alternative address. Mail is held at a local delivery office until the addressee is ready to collect it. A PO Box costs £48.80 for six months or £60.15 for a year.

CONTACTS

Royal Mail general enquiries
T 08457-740740 W www.royalmail.com
Royal Mail business enquiries
T 08457-950950
Postcode enquiry line
T 0906-302 1222 / 08457-111222
Parcelforce Worldwide
T 08708-501150 W www.parcelforce.com
Post Office enquiries
T 08457-223344 W www.postoffice.co.uk

INTERNATIONAL DIRECT DIALLING

When dialling add two zeros before the IDD code, followed by the area code and the telephone number. Also add two zeros before the IDD code when dialling into the UK unless otherwise indicated. Calls to Midway Island, Tristan da Cunha and Wake Island must be made by calling the international operator on 155.

* No extra zeros should be added
† Varies depending on area and/or carrier

	IDD from UK	*IDD to UK*
Afghanistan	93	44
Albania	355	44
Algeria	213	44
American Samoa	1 684	011 44*
Andorra	376	44
Angola	244	44
Anguilla	1 264	011 44*
Antigua and Barbuda	1 268	011 44*
Argentina	54	44
Armenia	374	44
Aruba	297	44
Ascension Island	247	44
Australia	61	11 44
Austria	43	44
Azerbaijan	994	810 44*
Azores	351	44
Bahamas	1 242	011 44*
Bahrain	973	44
Bangladesh	880	44
Barbados	1 246	011 44*
Belarus	375	810 44*
Belgium	32	44
Belize	501	44
Benin	229	44
Bermuda	1 441	011 44*
Bhutan	975	44
Bolivia	591	10 44† 11 44† 12 44† 13 44†
Bosnia and Hercegovina	387	44
Botswana	267	44
Brazil	55	14 44† 15 44† 21 44† 23 44† 31 44†
British Virgin Islands	1 284	011 44*
Brunei	673	44
Bulgaria	359	44
Burkina Faso	226	44
Burundi	257	44
Cambodia	855	1 44
Cameroon	237	44
Canada	1	011 44*
Cape Verde	238	0 44*
Cayman Islands	1 345	011 44*
Central African Republic	236	19 44*
Chad	235	15 44*
Chile	56	44
China	86	44
Colombia	57	9 44*
The Comoros	269	44
Congo, Dem. Rep. of	243	44
Congo, Rep. of	242	44
Cook Islands	682	44

Costa Rica	506	44
Côte d'Ivoire	225	44
Croatia	385	44
Cuba	53	119 44*
Cyprus	357	44
Czech Rep.	420	44
Denmark	45	44
Djibouti	253	44
Dominica	1 767	011 44*
Dominican Rep.	1 809 1 829	011 44*
East Timor	670	44
Ecuador	593	44
Egypt	20	44
El Salvador	503	44
Equatorial Guinea	240	44
Eritrea	291	44
Estonia	372	44
Ethiopia	251	44
Falkland Islands	500	44
Faeroe Islands	298	44
Fiji	679	44
Finland	358	990 44*†
France	33	44
French Guiana	594	44
French Polynesia	689	44
Gabon	241	44
The Gambia	220	44
Georgia	995	810 44*
Germany	49	44
Ghana	233	44
Gibraltar	350	44
Greece	30	44
Greenland	299	44
Grenada	1 473	011 44*
Guadeloupe	590	44
Guam	1 671	011 44*
Guatemala	502	44
Guinea	224	44
Guinea-Bissau	245	44
Guyana	592	1 44
Haiti	509	44
Honduras	504	44
Hong Kong	852	1 44
Hungary	36	44
Iceland	354	44
India	91	44
Indonesia	62	1 44† 7 44†
Iran	98	44
Iraq	964	44
Ireland	353	44
Israel	972	44†
Italy	39	44
Jamaica	1 876	011 44*
Japan	81	1 44† 010 44† 41 44† 61 44†
Jordan	962	44†
Kazakhstan	7	810 44*
Kenya	254	44
Kiribati	686	44
Korea, Dem. People's Rep. of	850	44
Korea, Republic of	82	1 44† 2 44†
Kuwait	965	44
Kyrgyzstan	996	144
Laos	856	14 44*
Latvia	371	44
Lebanon	961	44
Lesotho	266	44
Liberia	231	44
Libya	218	44
Liechtenstein	423	44
Lithuania	370	44
Luxembourg	352	44
Macao	853	44
Macedonia	389	44
Madagascar	261	44
Madeira	351	44
Malawi	265	44
Malaysia	60	44
Maldives	960	44
Mali	223	44
Malta	356	44
Marshall Islands	692	011 44*
Martinique	596	44
Mauritania	222	44
Mauritius	230	44
Mayotte	269	10 44*
Mexico	52	98 44*
Micronesia, Federated States of	691	011 44*
Moldova	373	44
Monaco	377	44
Mongolia	976	1 44
Montenegro	382	44
Montserrat	1 664	011 44*
Morocco	212	44
Mozambique	258	44
Myanmar	95	44
Namibia	264	44
Nauru	674	44
Nepal	977	44
The Netherlands	31	44
Netherlands Antilles	599	44
New Caledonia	687	44
New Zealand	64	44
Nicaragua	505	44
Niger	227	44
Nigeria	234	9 44
Niue	683	44
Norfolk Island	672	44
Northern Mariana Islands	1 670	011 44*
Norway	47	44
Oman	968	44
Pakistan	92	44
Palau	680	011 44*
Panama	507	44
Papua New Guinea	675	05 44*
Paraguay	595	2 44
Peru	51	44
The Philippines	63	44
Poland	48	44
Portugal	351	44
Puerto Rico	1 787 1 939	011 44*
Qatar	974	44
Réunion	262	44
Romania	40	44
Russian Federation	7	810 44*
Rwanda	250	44

St Christopher and Nevis	1 869	011 44*
St Helena	290	44
St Lucia	1 758	011 44*
St Pierre and Miquelon	508	44
St Vincent and the Grenadines	1 784	011 44*
Samoa	685	0 44*
San Marino	378	44
Sao Tome and Principe	239	44
Saudi Arabia	966	44
Senegal	221	44
Serbia	381	44
Seychelles	248	44
Sierra Leone	232	44
Singapore	65	1 44
Slovakia	421	44
Slovenia	386	44
Solomon Islands	677	44
Somalia	252	44
South Africa	27	44
Spain	34	44
Sri Lanka	94	44
Sudan	249	44
Suriname	597	44
Swaziland	268	44
Sweden	46	44
Switzerland	41	44
Syria	963	44
Taiwan	886	2 44
Tajikistan	992	810 44*
Tanzania	255	0 44
Thailand	66	1 44
Togo	228	44
Tokelau	690	44
Tonga	676	44
Trinidad and Tobago	1 868	011 44*
Tunisia	216	44
Turkey	90	44
Turkmenistan	993	810 44*
Turks and Caicos Islands	1 649	011 44*
Tuvalu	688	44
Uganda	256	0 44
Ukraine	380	810 44*
United Arab Emirates	971	44
United States of America	1	011 44*
Uruguay	598	44
Uzbekistan	998	810 44*
Vanuatu	678	44
Vatican City State	39	44
Venezuela	58	44
Vietnam	84	44
Virgin Islands	1 340	011 44*
Yemen	967	44
Zambia	260	44
Zimbabwe	263	44

INFORMATION TECHNOLOGY

INTERNET TRENDS

There can be no doubt that the popularity of the internet continues to rise. Affordability combined with wider regional access to broadband meant that half of UK households were subscribed to broadband services in 2008. In addition, the advent of Web 2.0, a second-generation internet platform, has enabled users to reach higher quality content in a different way – streaming videos, downloading music and uploading photographs; these are all services that dial-up modem users cannot use effectively.

TOP 10 BROADBAND SUBSCRIBERS BY COUNTRY

Country	*2006*	*2007*
1. USA	58,355,000	72,914,000
2. China	51,723,000	66,464,000
3. Japan	25,882,000	28,426,000
4. Germany	14,863,000	19,965,000
5. UK	13,372,000	15,679,000
6. France	12,703,000	15,551,000
7. South Korea	14,043,000	14,710,000
8. Italy	8,748,000	10,861,000
9. Canada	7,723,000	8,659,000
10. Spain	6,643,000	8,035,000

Source: www.point-topic.com

The popularity of social networking and ease of uploading user-generated content have led to a new culture of sharing public and private lives online, no doubt helped by a wave of sharing websites such as Flickr (photographs), YouTube (videos) and Last.FM (music recommendations). Social networking sites such as Myspace, Facebook and Bebo have millions of international members and are in the top ten UK's most popular websites, leading some analysts to the conclusion that online friendships are replacing real life interaction.

Spending online is rising and Ebay and Amazon continue to be favoured online shopping destinations. Over £4bn was spent each month by UK surfers in 2007 and this figure is likely to rise as new security measures are introduced.

Web office applications are expected to be another growth area as they are beginning to merge with desktop applications. Google's Docs (word processing), Adobe Photoshop Express (image editor) and BaseCamp (project management) are all web-based applications accessable for free via any internet browser.

- In 2007 17 per cent of people accessing the internet in the UK created a profile on a social networking site
- 90 per cent of UK music singles sales came from digital downloads
- Internet take-up is highest among the young, but 'silver surfers' are the most active, spending an average of almost 42 hours online every month
- In 2007 the highest level of internet access was in the South West and London, the lowest in Yorkshire and the Humber, the North East and Northern Ireland

Sources: Oxford Internet Institute, OFCOM Communications Report 2007, Office of National Statistics

THE YEAR IN TECHNOLOGY

EVEN THE ROYALS ARE DOING IT

Not to be outdone by the rest of the UK, on 23 December 2007 the royal household launched its own channel on video-sharing website YouTube, aptly titled the Royal Channel. Showcasing both modern and archived footage of royal life, the Queen helped kick off the channel with her 2007 Christmas broadcast. The channel has already received over a million views and is continuing to draw attention from fans around the world.

ONE LAPTOP PER CHILD BECOMES REALITY

The one laptop per child project, which aims to provide children in third-world countries with $100 laptops, finally delivered results in December 2007. The first batch of green and white laptops—called the XO—was shipped. Containing a high-resolution screen, wireless capability, web camera and open source software, the laptops were highly desired by both the technorati and the general public. Despite the high interest, the XO was not made available to the public except for a two-week period in November 2007 through a 'Give One, Get One' program. The initiative enabled people in America and Canada to purchase two machines: one to be given to a child in a developing country and the other shipped to the purchaser.

POLITICAL NETIZENS

Countries with an active policy of media censorship found it more difficult to quell the voices of dissent as indicated by last year's uprisings in Myanmar and Tibet. Despite being able to block traditional forms of media such as newspapers, television and radio, authorities have been unsuccessful at stopping activist blogs, photographs and video (usually taken with mobile phones) from being transmitted over the internet. Human rights violations were particularly highlighted in China, leading to much media coverage and high-profile Hollywood protests against the country's role as host of the 2008 summer Olympics in Beijing.

DOWNLOADING NEW MUSIC LEGALLY

In a climate of rampant illegal music downloading, several high-profile music artists decided to try a new business model—giving away their music for free. In October 2007 UK music act Radiohead released its latest album *In Rainbows* on the internet, giving fans the option to pay whatever they wanted, even if this meant paying nothing. It was reported that 1.2 million downloads were sold on the day of the album's release and the group's frontman Thom Yorke commented that the profits made from the internet release outstripped combined profits from the group's previous albums. American band Nine inch Nails followed suit, reputedly earning $750,000 (£375,000) in just 2 days, also exceeding the total amount earned by selling CDs in music shops.

	July	*October*	*January*	*April*
1.	Camelot	Avril	Jewsons	chihuahua
2.	Dermalogica	PSP Themes	Zoom airlines	John Terry
3.	Hulk Hogan	Capital FM	Orange	marathon
4.	Wonder woman	Berlin	Virgin	ringworm
5.	CAD	Pokemon	NHS Careers	arabic keyboard
6.	Body shop	Sky Scanner	Jimmy Choo	tea
7.	Leicester	Boots.com	M and M Direct	Antarctica
8.	Europe	Charity Commission	iPlayer	wedding shoes
9.	widgets	Aldo	Sharm el Sheikh	World War I
10.	Scarborough	cocker spaniel	divorce	Evanescence

Source: Google zeitgeist

WHAT ARE WE SEARCHING?

Every month Google compiles a list of key words whose popularity has increased the most in comparison with the previous month. Above is a list of these search terms for four months of the year in review (2007–8).

BBC IPLAYER

In December 2007 the BBC launched a website and media player that enabled its viewers to access and download BBC television programmes directly to their computers. The BBC was criticised for its digital rights management software, as it only allowed to watch programmes on authorised devices, which deleted these recordings after a set period of time. Compared with VCRs, which allowed viewers to keep programmes for as long as they wanted, this introduced an unnecessary expense for UK licence payers.

INTERNET UNDER WATER

In five separate incidents in early 2008, up to 75 per cent of internet services were lost in Bahrain, Egypt, India, Kuwait, Oman, Pakistan, Qatar, Saudi Arabia and the United Arab Emirates as a result of underwater cable lines being severed. Originally thought to be acts of sabotage, the severed cables were ultimately blamed on ship anchors. In certain areas of the world, up to 90 per cent of internet services are delivered via undersea cables.

POPULAR WEBSITES OF 2008

Bbc.co.uk: Latest news, sport, travel, finance and weather from the BBC

Bebo.com: School and college social network, like MySpace and Facebook

Ebay.co.uk: Online auction site

Facebook.com: A social networking website allowing members to upload photos and share links and videos

Google.com: A search engine enabling users to search the web, Usenet and images. Features include page ranking, caching and translating results

Google.co.uk: A UK-specific version of the pre-eminent search engine offering a choice of UK pages or world results

Live.com: A search engine from Microsoft

Myspace.com: A social networking website allowing users to create private communities and share photos, music and videos

Yahoo.com: A search engine offering personalised content, free email and chatrooms

Youtube.com: A video-sharing website used to watch and share videos through websites, mobile devices and email

A SHORT HISTORY OF THE INTERNET

Prior to the advent of the internet, computers tended to be connected together by hardware and protocols that were specific to each particular connection. Typically, links were point-to-point (physically established between the two computers). In 1969 ARPANET was formed by the US department of defence to establish a way for the computer capability of the military to be dispersed so that no single centre was critical to the operation of the network as a whole. This was achieved by interconnecting computers both directly and by way of other intermediary computers; thus if one computer was destroyed, other pathways of communication could be established. These interconnections, when drawn, appeared as a net or web. ARPANET was extended to non-military users such as universities early in the 1970s, with initial international links appearing in 1972.

The introduction of domain names (eg www.whitakersalmanack.com) in 1984 offered an easier means of using the web. Prior to domain names, IP addresses (eg 192.168.1.100) were used for accessing destination computers. However, before 1989 the internet was still primarily limited to government agencies, the military, academic and research organisations and some big businesses.

In 1989, what most people perceive as 'the internet' was born. It was effectively invented at CERN (the European Particle Physics Laboratory) by Tim Berners-Lee as a way for scientists to share information by placing it in a prescribed format on a server. Initially text only, development of computer capability allowed the inclusion of images.

The internet is effectively a very large network of computers, connected through various telecommunications links. Millions of routers (*see* Glossary) around the world link together massive networks of computers to form a backbone to the internet. Most home and business users will connect up to an ISP (internet service provider) via a telephone or a digital line. ISPs have their own routers, which all the lines connect to. The internet 'traffic' is then routed to another (often larger) telecommunications company, which is also connected by fibre-optic lines to other such companies across the globe. Websites are stored on servers that are designed for hosting, running a special program that 'serves' up the content.

As use of technology has increased, the downloading of music, pictures and video from the internet has become faster and more practical. Analogue media, such as music stored on a tape, or a painting, loses quality in reproduction. Digital media on the other hand can be copied flawlessly between computers, as it is the simple process of replicating a string of zeros and ones.

The Data Protection Act 1984 (revised 1998) was

introduced to ensure the correct and proper handling of personal and sensitive data held on computer databases. During the 1980s computer hacking was still not illegal, but the number of serious computer attacks was rapidly increasing. Failed attempts to prosecute these hackers brought about the Computer Misuse Act, passed in 1990 to protect computer systems from unauthorised access. Copyright law has also been amended to encompass the concept of 'digital property' and include criminal sanctions for breaching the copyright of protected music, video, books, software and website material.

DEVELOPMENT OF COMPUTERS

The abacus was the first true calculating machine and was probably invented in China around 500 BC. The invention of the first mechanical calculating machine in 1623 is credited to Wilhelm Schickard, a friend of the astronomer Johannes Kepler. Unfortunately there are no surviving examples of this machine, so the machine built by French scientist and philosopher Blaise Pascal between 1642 and 1645 tends to be credited as the first true mechanical calculator. This was a device that used cogs and wheels to perform addition and subtraction over eight columns of digits. In 1673 Gottfried Leibniz invented an improved calculator that could be used to multiply, divide and find square roots.

The next significant step towards the modern computer occurred in 1804 when Joseph-Marie Jacquard invented an automated loom. Patterns in cloth woven on the loom were dictated by a series of punchcards. This was the first time that data had been stored on cards and then processed in a machine.

The closest ancestors of the modern computer are the Difference Engine and the Analytical Engine devised by mathematician Charles Babbage 30 years after the Jacquard Loom. The Difference Engine, a clockwork-like mechanism, designed to compute mathematical tables, was abandoned by Babbage in the 1840s due to the limitations of the technology of the period and a lack of funds. Unlike the Difference Engine, the Analytical Engine was designed as a general-purpose tool capable of storing information. Babbage's work relied heavily on mechanics and physical machinery and it was not until the 20th-century invention of the electrical vacuum tube, and then the transistor, that computers became a feasible means of solving problems.

FIRST GENERATION

War has played a significant role in the development of the computer. In 1943, during the Second World War, British and American scientists started work on electro-mechanical computers. Colossus, a British effort, was specifically developed to crack German coding ciphers, whilst the US machine, Harvard Mark I, was developed as a more general-purpose electro-mechanical programmable computer (partly intended for atom bomb research). Regarded as early 'first generation' computers, these machines primarily comprised wired circuits and vacuum tubes. Punched cards and paper tape were largely employed as the input, output and main storage systems. In 1946 ENIAC (Electronic Numerical Integrator and Computer) was completed at the University of Pennsylvania, USA. Capable of carrying out 100,000 calculations a second, it was remarkable for its day despite weighing 30 tons.

SECOND GENERATION

Similar to light bulbs, vacuum tubes (more commonly known as 'valves') were prone to failure, requiring tedious checks to resolve problems (ENIAC alone contained 18,000 vacuum valves). In 1947 the transistor was invented, initially to replace vacuum tubes used in amplifiers. Performing the same role as a vacuum tube but less prone to failure, smaller and more efficient, the transistor allowed smaller 'second generation' computers to be developed throughout the 1950s and early 1960s.

THIRD GENERATION

In 1958 Jack St Claire Kilby, of Texas Instruments, invented the first integrated circuit (or 'microchip'). Six months later Robert Noyce of Fairchild Semiconductors independently produced a similar integrated circuit. A microchip is comprised of a large number of transistors and other components fabricated from a wafer ('chip') of silicon, interconnected by a surface film of conductive material rather than by wires. By reducing distance between components, savings are made in both size and electricity. In 1963 the first 'third generation' computers based on microchip technology appeared.

FOURTH GENERATION

In 1971 Intel produced the first 'microprocessor', heralding a 'fourth generation' of computers. The Intel 4004 (capable of 60,000 instructions per second) grouped much of the processing functions onto a single microchip. Around the same time, Intel invented the RAM (random access memory) chip, which grouped significant amounts of memory onto a single chip. Supercomputers and mainframes, utilising scores of microprocessors, had terrific power, capable of 150 million instructions per second. Developments such as multi-layer circuits, and the use of copper instead of gold in microchips, yielded improvements in size and performance through miniaturisation. The size of the transistor was scaled down from thumb size to far smaller than the thickness of a human hair, allowing for greater density and thus exponentially increasing the total power of the computer.

NEXT GENERATION

Most modern computers are still regarded as 'fourth generation' as they use essentially the same technology, albeit highly miniaturised. Gordon Moore, co-founder of Intel, observed in 1965 that the number of transistors per square inch had doubled every 12 months since the inception of the integrated circuit. The widely recognised current definition of the so-called 'Moore's Law' is that the number of transistors on a microprocessor doubles every 18 months and is likely to do so for the next few decades. Moore underestimated the improvement in microprocessing power that has occurred since then – microprocessing 'clock' speeds are now measured in mega- and even gigahertz.

Processor	*Clock speed*	*Year of launch*
Intel 80286	8MHz	1982
Intel 80386	16MHz	1985
Intel 80486	25Mhz	1989
Intel Pentium	60MHz	1993
Intel Pentium II	350MHz	1997
Intel Pentium 4	1,500MHz	2000

There are many technological paradigms currently in research that could shape the next generation of computers. The future of computer technology could for example be dependent on the physics of light. Already used extensively in the computer industry for high-speed communications, light offers future possibilities for both calculation and storage. Another strong candidate is the use of quantum computing, where data is not held in bits (zeros and ones) but 'qubits' that, when combined, can hold a greater magnitude of information. Next generation computers may also utilise technology such as neural interfaces, joining the human central nervous system to a computer input and output system. Nanotechnology, a new manufacturing technology that works on a molecular level, is fast becoming a major subject of research. Continuing miniaturisation in computer architecture has a great deal of scope to advance many areas of science, such as medicine, robotics and materials. Theorised applications in medicine include the ability to produce cell-like structures that combat certain diseases or even destroy cancerous cells. Nanorobotics also presents the ability to construct devices that can regenerate when damaged, particularly useful in space exploration. With the current high investment in research, nanotechnology seems likely to become one of the next technological revolutions.

GLOSSARY OF TERMS

The following is a selected list of modern computing terms. It is by no means exhaustive but is intended to cover those that the average computer user might encounter.

ADSL: Asymmetric Digital Subscriber Line – high-speed internet connection, four or more times faster than a modem, but using the same standard cables as a regular telephone. Faster at downloading than uploading.

AJAX: Asynchronous JavaScript and XML – a more interactive way of including content in a web page achieved by exchanging small amounts of data with the server behind the scenes, so that an entire web page does not have to be reloaded each time the user makes a change.

BANDWIDTH: Determines how much data can be sent through a connection. Usually measured in bits-per-second (bps). A full page of English text is about 16,000 bits. A fast modem can move about 57,000bps. Full-motion, full-screen video would require roughly 10,000,000bps, depending on compression.

BLOG: A blog (short for web log) is an online personal journal that is frequently updated and intended to be read by the public. Blogs generally represent the personality of the author and may include philosophy, commentary on the internet and other social issues and links to favourite websites. Blogs are kept by 'bloggers' and are commonly available as RSS feeds.

BLUETOOTH: Standard for short-range (10m) wireless connectivity between devices such as laptops, mobile phones and printers to interact without cables. Bluetooth can presently operate at speeds of up to 2Mbps.

BROADBAND: Generic term to describe high-speed internet-using technologies such as ISDN, ADSL etc as opposed to narrowband connections via modem.

BROWSER: Typically referring to a 'web browser' program that allows a computer user to view web page content on their computer, eg Microsoft Explorer, Netscape Navigator, AOL or Safari.

COOKIE: A piece of information sent by a web server to a web browser which is then saved and sent back to the server whenever the browser makes requests from the server. Cookies contain information such as login, registration or online 'shopping cart' data, user preferences, etc and are usually set to expire after a predetermined length of time.

CSS: Cascading Style Sheet – a standard for specifying the appearance of text. It provides a single 'library' of styles that are used throughout a large number of related documents. A CSS file might specify for example that all numbered lists are to appear in italics.

DOMAIN: A set of words or letters, separated by dots, used to identify an internet server, eg www.whitakersalmanack.co.uk, where 'www' denotes a web (http) server, 'whitakersalmanack' denotes the organisation name, 'co' denotes that the organisation is a company and 'uk' indicates United Kingdom. (For a complete list of country suffixes *see* Internet Domain Names section.)

EXTRANET: An extranet is a secure and private subset of the internet, typically used for exchanging information and services within a specific group.

FILE SERVER: A computer on a network that stores files which users can access from other computers on the network. Popular modern systems include Microsoft Windows, UNIX, Novell NetWare, and MacOS Server.

FIREWALL: Computer or device to protect a network from security risks posed by the internet. Just as a firewall protects parts of a building from a fire raging on the other side, a network firewall stops risks posed by the internet from egressing into a private network.

FTP: File Transfer Protocol – an internet protocol enabling exchange of files with a remote server.

GPRS: General Packet Radio Services – a service for continuous wireless communication over the internet from mobile phones and computers. GPRS tends to be charged for by volume of information transferred rather than by time, which allows a more economic continuous connection compared with direct dial over a modem.

HIT: A single request from a web browser for a single item from a web server; thus in order for a web browser to display a page that contains three graphics, four 'hits' would occur at the server: one for the HTML page, and one for each of the three graphics. The number of hits on a website is not synonymous with the number of distinct visitors.

HTML: HyperText Mark-up Language – a small programming language used to denote or mark-up how an internet page should be presented to a user from an HTTP server via a web browser. HTML is an evolving standard that has grown greatly from its first version to accommodate new types of web content and features provided by the different web browsers (eg Netscape and Internet Explorer).

HTTP: HyperText Transfer Protocol – an internet protocol whereby a web server sends web pages, images and files to a web browser.

INTRANET: Subset of the internet, using internet protocols over a local area network, common today for publishing information and services within an organisation.

JAVA: a high-level, object-orientated computer language developed by Sun Microsystems, especially designed for use via the web.

META TAG: A type of HTML tag that contains information not normally displayed to the user. Meta tags are typically used to include information for search engines to help them categorise a page.

MODEM: Modulator-Demodulator – a device that modulates digital signals from a computer into analogue signals for transmission over a standard telephone line, and demodulates an incoming analogue signal and converts it to a digital signal for the computer.

MP3: A popular format for compressing audio information for transmission over the internet for later playback on personal computers, music players and other devices.

MPEG: Motion Picture Encoding Group – popular format standard for compressing video and audio information for transmission over the internet for later playback on personal computers and on hand-held devices.

OPEN CONTENT: Copyrighted information that is made available by the owner to the general public under licence terms that allow reuse of the material, often with the requirement that the reuser grant the public the same rights to the modified version. Information that is in the 'public domain' might also be considered a form of open content.

OPEN-SOURCE: A computer program that has its source-code (the instructions that make up a program) freely available for viewing and modification is said to be open-source.

PDF: Portable Document Format – a file format designed to enable printing and viewing of documents with all their formatting (typefaces, images, layout, etc) appearing the same regardless of the operating system used. The PDF format is based on the widely used Postscript document-description language. Both PDF and Postscript were developed by the Adobe Corporation.

PODCASTING: A form of audio and video broadcasting using the internet. The word is a portmanteau of 'iPod' and broadcasting, though podcasting does not require the use of an iPod. A podcaster creates a list of files and makes it available in the RSS 2.0 format. The list can then be obtained using various podcast 'retriever' software which makes the files available to digital devices (including, but not limited to, iPods) where users may then listen or watch at their convenience.

RAM: Random Access Memory – the main memory that is used by a computer to store temporary data (while accessing or altering individual storage locations) that is lost when the computer is turned off.

ROUTER: Where multiple networks are joined together, a router acts like a fast sorting office, examining the destination address of each information packet and passing or routing it to the appropriate network in the most efficient manner.

RSS: Rich Site Summary or RDF Site Summary or Real Simple Syndication – a commonly used protocol for syndication and sharing of content, originally developed to facilitate the syndication of news articles, now widely used to share the contents of blogs. Mashups are often made using RSS feeds.

SERVER: A node on a network that provides service to the terminals on the network. These computers have higher hardware specifications, ie more resources and greater speed, in order to handle large amounts of data.

SPAM: A term used for unsolicited, generally junk, email. To spam someone is to send them (multiple) junk emails. Junk email is becoming a major issue with some estimates suggesting that spam is becoming more prevalent than legitimate email. Most spam contains offers of pornography, get-rich schemes, prescription drugs, low-cost finance or discount goods or services. Many legislatures around the globe are taking steps to ban or regulate spam.

TAG: As a noun, a tag is a basic element of the languages used to create web pages (HTML) and similar languages such as XML.

TCP/IP: Transmission Control Protocol/Internet Protocol – the lifeblood of the internet, TCP/IP defines how information and requests generated by all other protocols are transmitted over the internet. Information on the internet is chopped up into small chunks or packets which are addressed with a destination and origination address. It sometimes happens that a packet gets lost and TCP/IP dictates how such a loss is handled.

USB: Universal Serial Bus – standard for connecting serial devices such as scanners, digital cameras, keyboards, modems and printers to computers. With USB, speeds of 10Mbps and higher are possible.

URL: Uniform Resource Locator – address of an internet file accessible on the internet, eg http://www.whitakersalmanack.com

USER-GENERATED CONTENT (UGC): Refers to various media content produced or primarily influenced by end-users, as opposed to traditional media producers such as licensed broadcasters and production companies. These forms of media include digital video, blogging, podcasting, mobile phone photography and wikis.

VIRUS: A computer program or script written for the express purpose of replicating itself onto as many machines as possible (much like its biological namesake), often with negative side effects to the host computer and computer network. Such effects vary from harmless screen messages to corruption of document integrity, network overload or the compromising of data security or privacy. Historically transmitted slowly by floppy disk and over networks within offices, the prevalence of email means viruses can spread globally within minutes.

VOIP: Voice Over IP – various technologies used to make telephone calls over IP networks, especially the internet. Just as modems allow computers to connect to the internet over regular telephone lines, VOIP technology allows humans to talk over internet connections. Costs for VOIP calls can be much lower than for traditional telephone calls. Because the IP networks are packet-switched, this allows for vastly different ways of handling connections and more efficient use of network resources.

VPN: Virtual Private Network – usually refers to a network parts of which are connected using the public internet, but the data sent across the internet is encrypted, so the entire network is 'virtually' private.

WAP: Wireless Application Protocol – a set of standards to define how portable devices connected via radio waves (such as mobile phones) can access internet services.

WEBDAV: Web-based Distributed Authoring and Versioning – a set of extensions to the HTTP protocol that allows multiple users not only to read but also to add, delete and change documents residing on a web server.

WEB 2.0: Generally refers to a second generation of services available on the web that lets people collaborate and share information online. In contrast to the first generation, Web 2.0 gives users an experience closer to desktop applications than traditional static web pages. The term was popularised as the name for a series of web development conferences that started in October 2004. Web 2.0 applications often use a combination of techniques including AJAX and web syndication. They also allow for mass publishing (web-based social software).

WI-FI: Industry brand name for the increasingly popular high frequency wireless local area Ethernet networking technology. Wi-Fi is also a popular term for a form of wireless data communication.

WIKI: Software that allows users to freely create and edit web page's content using any web browser. Theoretically this encourages democratic use of the internet and promotes content composition by non-technical users.

WLAN: Wireless Local Area Network – a network where information is transferred by radio frequency rather than wires between computers and base stations. As radio waves can pass through objects such as walls, it is becoming increasingly important for WLANs to be secured by encryption against unauthorised access.

XHTML: eXtensible HyperText Mark-up Language – essentially HTML expressed as valid XML. XHTML is intended to be used for the same purpose as HTML (creating web pages) but is much more strictly defined, which makes it easier to create software that can read, edit and check it for errors. XHTML is expected to eventually replace HTML.

XML: eXtensible Mark-up Language – similar to HTML but more powerful, XML allows information to be encoded or tagged in a manner that is both human and computer readable. The advent of XML has greatly simplified the exchange of information between many formerly incompatible systems.

INTERNET DOMAIN NAMES

Internet top-level domains names are two-letter codes that appear at the end of a website address to identify its country of origin. Websites that use a country code top-level domain must be registered with the individual country or dependent territory. The list below is of active domain names for countries only.

ad	Andorra
ae	United Arab Emirates
af	Afghanistan
ag	Antigua and Barbuda
al	Albania
am	Armenia
ao	Angola
aq	The Antarctic
ar	Argentina
at	Austria
au	Australia
az	Azerbaijan
ba	Bosnia and Hercegovina
bb	Barbados
bd	Bangladesh
be	Belgium
bf	Burkina Faso
bg	Bulgaria
bh	Bahrain
bi	Burundi
bj	Benin
bn	Brunei
bo	Bolivia
br	Brazil
bs	The Bahamas
bt	Bhutan
bw	Botswana
by	Belarus
bz	Belize
ca	Canada
cd	Congo, Dem. Republic of
cf	Central African Republic
cg	Congo, Republic of
ch	Switzerland
ci	Côte d'Ivoire
cl	Chile
cm	Cameroon
cn	China
co	Colombia
cr	Costa Rica
cu	Cuba
cv	Cape Verde
cy	Cyprus
cz	Czech Republic
de	Germany
dj	Djibouti
dk	Denmark
dm	Dominica
do	Dominican Republic
dz	Algeria
ec	Ecuador
ee	Estonia
eg	Egypt
er	Eritrea
es	Spain
et	Ethiopia
eu	European Union
fi	Finland
fj	Fiji
fm	Micronesia, Federated States of
fr	France
ga	Gabon
gd	Grenada
ge	Georgia
gh	Ghana
gm	The Gambia
gn	Guinea
gq	Equatorial Guinea
gr	Greece
gt	Guatemala
gw	Guinea-Bissau
gy	Guyana
hn	Honduras
hr	Croatia
ht	Haiti
hu	Hungary
id	Indonesia
ie	Ireland
il	Israel
in	India
iq	Iraq
ir	Iran
is	Iceland
it	Italy
jm	Jamaica
jo	Jordan
jp	Japan
ke	Kenya
kg	Kyrgyzstan
kh	Cambodia
ki	Kiribati
km	The Comoros
kn	St Christopher and Nevis
kr	Korea, Republic of
kw	Kuwait
kz	Kazakhstan
la	Laos
lb	Lebanon
lc	St Lucia
li	Liechtenstein
lk	Sri Lanka
lr	Liberia
ls	Lesotho
lt	Lithuania
lu	Luxembourg
lv	Latvia
ly	Libya
ma	Morocco
mc	Monaco
md	Moldova
mg	Madagascar
mh	Marshall Islands
mk	Macedonia
ml	Mali
mm	Myanmar
mn	Mongolia
mr	Mauritania
mt	Malta
mu	Mauritius
mv	Maldives
mw	Malawi
mx	Mexico
my	Malaysia
mz	Mozambique
na	Namibia
ne	Niger
ng	Nigeria
ni	Nicaragua
nl	The Netherlands

no	Norway
np	Nepal
nr	Nauru
nz	New Zealand
om	Oman
pa	Panama
pe	Peru
pg	Papua New Guinea
ph	The Philippines
pk	Pakistan
pl	Poland
pt	Portugal
pw	Palau
py	Paraguay
qa	Qatar
ro	Romania
ru	Russian Federation
rw	Rwanda
sa	Saudi Arabia
sb	Solomon Islands
sc	Seychelles
sd	Sudan
se	Sweden
sg	Singapore
si	Slovenia
sk	Slovakia
sl	Sierra Leone
sm	San Marino
sn	Senegal
so	Somalia
sr	Suriname
st	São Tomé and Príncipe
sv	El Salvador
sy	Syria
sz	Swaziland
td	Chad
tg	Togo
th	Thailand
tj	Tajikistan
tl	East Timor
tm	Turkmenistan
tn	Tunisia
to	Tonga
tp	East Timor*
tr	Turkey
tt	Trinidad and Tobago
tv	Tuvalu
tw	Taiwan
tz	Tanzania
ua	Ukraine
ug	Uganda
uk	United Kingdom
us	United States of America
uy	Uruguay
uz	Uzbekistan
va	Vatican City State (Holy See)
vc	St Vincent and the Grenadines
ve	Venezuela
vn	Vietnam
vu	Vanuatu
ws	Samoa
ye	Yemen
yu	Montenegro; Serbia†
za	South Africa
zm	Zambia
zw	Zimbabwe

* No new registrations are being accepted for the code .tp, which is active but being phased out in favour of .tl

† Montenegro and Serbia have been assigned new codes, .me and .rs. They are not yet active as of April 2008

Note: North Korea has no internet country code top-level domain, but .kp is reserved for the country

THE ENVIRONMENT

Over the past 20 years, the production of ozone-layer damaging chemicals has been cut by 95 per cent, a greenhouse gas emission reduction treaty and carbon trading have been established and much legislation has been put in place. But there are persistent and intractable problems that remain unresolved, according the UN environment programme's *Global Environment Outlook (GEO-4)* report, which assessed the current state of the global atmosphere, land, water and biodiversity and evaluated the changes since 1987.

There is now visible and unequivocal evidence for climate change. Global average temperatures have risen by 0.7 per cent since 1906 and 0.2 per cent in the past 25 years. The second half of the 20th century was the warmest period in the northern hemisphere for 1,300 years, according to another UN report, *Climate Change 2007*. Extreme weather events have become more frequent and regional climate patterns are changing. Heat waves and variations in storm tracks and precipitation can now be traced back to climate change caused by human activity.

If the average temperature rises this century by more than 2°C above pre-industrial levels (current estimates vary between 1.8 and 4°C) major, irreversible damage is thought likely, such as thawing of the Arctic permafrost, which would release large quantities of methane gas into the atmosphere. Other environmental concerns include biodiversity, marine ecosystems, land and water resources, air pollution and health.

According to the European Environment Agency, past legislation has worked. Water and air have been cleaned up, ozone-depleting substances have been phased out, and waste recycling has risen. UK government indicators show fewer air pollution emissions, more waste recycling and better local environmental quality compared to 1999. However, these success stories are being undermined by changes in personal consumption patterns. Areas showing deterioration since 1999 include aviation emissions of greenhouse gases, fossil fuels used in electricity generation, and urban ozone generation. Europeans are living longer and more live alone, putting greater demands on living space. They travel further and more often and are consuming natural resources at twice the world's average rate.

Transport is the fastest growing contributor to greenhouse gas emissions and is expected to continue to be for the foreseeable future. It is currently responsible for 21 per cent of total greenhouse gas emissions with passenger cars alone accounting for 12 per cent of EU carbon dioxide emissions. Between 1990 and 2003, passenger transport volumes in Europe grew by 20 per cent and carbon dioxide emissions from road transport rose by 26 per cent between 1990 and 2004. Air transport grew by 96 per cent with emissions from aviation growing by 86 per cent between 1990 and 2004.

This has prompted the EU to propose legislation to reduce the carbon dioxide emissions of new cars to 120g per kilometre by 2012. In 2004 average emissions were 160g per kilometre. Interest in biofuels is also increasing. Since April 2008 fuel suppliers have had to ensure that 2.5 per cent of fuel comes from renewable sources (rising to 5 per cent from 2010). Biodiesel is the most common biofuel in Europe, while ethanol is the most common worldwide. Biofuels have numerous benefits, including reducing fossil fuel use, decreasing greenhouse gas emissions and promoting rural development. But there are also downsides including higher prices for food crops, such as corn and wheat, pressure on farmland biodiversity, soil erosion and deforestation. With these issues in mind, world governments are preferring and supporting sustainable biofuel production. Any rewards under the EU biofuel rules after 2011 will only be given for biofuels that meet sustainability standards.

Attention is increasingly turning to individuals and to what they can do to reduce their carbon footprint. This is a measure of the amount of carbon dioxide emitted through the burning of fossil fuels as part of a person's daily life or, in the case of an organisation, as part of its everyday operations. More than 40 per cent of the UK's carbon dioxide emissions come from people's home and travel. In the EU households are responsible for 16 per cent of the greenhouse gas emissions with 70 per cent of energy used for home heating, 14 per cent for heating water and 12 per cent for lighting and appliances.

The UK's carbon footprint is 648 million tonnes of carbon dioxide per annum, according to the Carbon Trust. This means the average Briton's annual carbon footprint is 10.92 tonnes of carbon dioxide, whereas the average American generates 20 tonnes of carbon dioxide each year. Initiatives aimed at individuals are being launched, such as the UK's 'We're in This Together' campaign that aims to provide people with practical solutions to help reduce their household emissions by one tonne over three years.

SELECTED UK TARGETS

AIR QUALITY AND ATMOSPHERE

- Reduce carbon dioxide emissions to 26–32 per cent below 1990 levels by 2020, and by 60 per cent by 2050
- UK to reduce greenhouse gas emissions by 12.5 per cent below 1990 levels by 2008–12

WASTE

- Recycle or compost 40 per cent of household waste by 2010, 45 per cent by 2015 and 50 per cent by 2020
- Reduce amount of household waste not re-used, recycled or composted by 45 per cent from 22.2 million tonnes in 2000 to 12.2 million tonnes by 2020.
- Reduce biodegradable municipal waste sent to landfill to 75 per cent of 1995 levels by 2010, 50 per cent by 2013 and 35 per cent by 2020
- Recycle or compost 55 per cent of municipal waste in Scotland by 2020

ENERGY

- Provide 10 per cent of UK electricity from renewable sources by 2010 and 20 per cent by 2020
- Scotland to generate 31 per cent of electricity by 2011 from renewable sources, rising to 50 per cent by 2020

EUROPEAN UNION MEASURES

Environmental policies are developed at several levels: international conventions and protocols, European directives, and national legislation and strategies. The EU is developing a set of policies – the sixth environment action programme; the Cardiff Process (which aims to integrate environmental concerns into other policies); and the EU sustainable development strategy – that form the framework for more detailed strategies. EU environmental legislation is based around the principle that the polluter pays.

The first environment action programme began in the 1970s. The sixth, *Environment 2010: Our Future, Our Choice,* was adopted in January 2001 and is the cornerstone of EU policy. It focuses on four topics: climate change, nature and biodiversity, environment and health, and natural resources and waste.

The EC is also diversifying the methods it uses, in particular to include market-based instruments such as environmental taxes and voluntary measures. These are increasingly being used across Europe, such as the emissions trading scheme for greenhouse gas emissions.

A new directive on energy taxation will enable countries to offer companies tax breaks in return for lowered emissions. It also taxes energy sources, particularly focusing on efficiency. Taxing energy consumption and selling the right to emit greenhouse gases both follow the polluter pays principle and some European countries are already taxing pollution in a variety of ways: Denmark and Finland tax tyres, Denmark and Italy tax plastic bags, while France taxes paper and cardboard.

SUSTAINABLE DEVELOPMENT

The environmental agenda has become part of a wider move to address sustainability that incorporates social, environmental and economic development. During the World Summit on Sustainable Development, held in Johannesburg in 2002, governments agreed on a series of commitments in five priority areas: water and sanitation, energy, health, agriculture and biodiversity. Targets and timetables approved included halving the number of people who lack access to clean water or proper sanitation by 2015, and reducing biodiversity loss by 2010. Following the summit, the United Nations Commission on Sustainable Development agreed its programme for the next 15 years. In addition, 2005–15 has been named as the 'Water for Life' decade.

The EU's latest sustainable development strategy, launched in 2005, focuses on climate change and clean energy; public health threats; social exclusion, demography and migration; management of natural resources; sustainable transport and global poverty and development. These challenges are related and there are established links between them, eg the use of renewable energy and climate change, or climate change and poverty.

The UK also has a sustainable development strategy, *Securing the Future,* alongside a framework for sustainable development across the UK, *Our Future – Different Paths,* shared between the government, the devolved administrations and the Northern Ireland Office. The Scottish Executive's vision, priorities and indicators for sustainable development are set out in *Choosing our Future,* while the Welsh National Assembly has the *Sustainable Development Action Plan 2004–2007.*

CLIMATE CHANGE AND AIR POLLUTION

Temperature in central England has risen by approximately 1°C since the 1970s, with 2006 being the warmest year on record. Severe wind storms have become more frequent over the past few decades, but not above that seen in the 1920s. The sea level around the UK rose by 1mm/year in the 20th century, although the rate for the 1990s and 2000s is higher than this. The government's response to climate change has been driven by the UN framework convention on climate change. This is a binding agreement that aims to reduce the risks of global warming by limiting greenhouse gas emissions.

Progress towards the convention's targets is assessed at regular conferences. At Kyoto in 1997, the Kyoto protocol was adopted. It covers the six main greenhouse gases – carbon dioxide, methane, nitrous oxide, hydrofluorocarbons (HFCs), perfluorocarbons (PFCs) and sulphur hexafluoride. Under the protocol, industrialised countries agreed to legally binding targets for cutting emissions of greenhouse gases by 5.2 per cent below 1990 levels by 2008–12. The protocol entered into force in February 2005 after it was ratified by Russia. The USA has stated that it will not ratify the treaty and Australia originally also refused to ratify but has now done so.

The latest data from member states shows that the 15 pre-2004 member states can meet, and possibly overachieve, the Kyoto target to reduce greenhouse gas emissions to 8 per cent below 1990 levels, if all the measures in the pipeline are implemented. Existing policies will yield a 4 per cent reduction. Planned but not yet implemented policies will reduce emissions by a further 3.9 per cent. Kyoto mechanisms will yield another 2.5 per cent, while carbon sinks and forest planting will contribute an extra 0.9 per cent reduction. All new member states that have a Kyoto target are also on track to meet it.

The latest provisional figures show that the UK has already achieved its Kyoto target: in 2007 greenhouse gas emissions were 2 per cent lower than in 2006, as a result of fuel switching from coal to natural gas for electricity generation and lower fossil fuel consumption by households and industry. Final figures for 2006 show that emissions were 16.4 per cent below 1990 levels, and 20.7 per cent below when the effect of the EU emissions trading scheme is taken into account, against the Kyoto target of 12.5 per cent. Emissions were down 0.5 per cent on 2005, while the economy grew by 2.9 per cent – meaning the UK is continuing to break the link between economic growth and emissions. Household and business sector emissions fell by 4 per cent and 1.6 per cent, respectively. But energy supply and transport emissions increased by 1.5 per cent and 1.3 per cent.

The government has a climate change bill which, together with an accompanying strategy, sets out a framework to transform the UK into a low-carbon economy. The bill proposes a legally binding target of a 60 per cent reduction in carbon dioxide emissions below 1990 levels by 2050, with the possibility that this could be tightened to 80 per cent, and an interim target of a reduction of 26–32 per cent by 2020. It also proposes five-year carbon budgets.

The UK also has an environmental transformation fund to bring forward the development of new low-carbon energy and energy-efficient technologies with a budget of

£400m until 2011. An international element, with £800m in funding, focuses on poverty reduction, environment protection and helping developing countries to tackle climate change.

Existing measures to tackle climate change in the UK are covered by the climate change programme, launched in March 2006. The measures to reduce emissions target every sector of the economy and include: a stricter emissions cap for industry; measures to encourage the uptake of biofuels in petrol; tighter building regulations; measures to improve household energy efficiency; a renewed emphasis on encouraging and enabling the general public, businesses and public authorities to help achieve the government's targets; and increased levels of microgeneration.

Scotland needs to save 1.7 million tonnes of carbon by 2010 to contribute to UK commitments. In the first year of its climate change programme, Scotland increased investment in renewable technology and met its renewable energy target for 2010 ahead of schedule.

The UK also has a voluntary greenhouse gas emissions trading scheme that allows businesses to buy or sell emission allowances to meet emission targets. A study into emissions trading for individuals in the UK concluded that a personal carbon allowance and trading scheme has the potential to achieve emissions savings in a fairer way than carbon taxes. This would involve setting an overall emission cap and dividing emissions rights equally across the population. These carbon credits would then be surrendered when buying fuel, transport or energy. Those who need more would buy them from those who can emit less than their quota. The government is now looking at whether or not a personal carbon allowance is a realistic and workable option.

The EC has a mandatory emissions trading scheme at company level for carbon dioxide in the European Union. The companies covered by the scheme account for almost half of the EU's total carbon dioxide emissions. From 2012, the scheme will include airlines. Emissions from all domestic and international flights that arrive at, or depart from, EU airports will be covered. Rises in ticket prices are expected to be modest. The EU has also indicated its willingness to link the scheme to trading schemes in other countries.

The EC has begun to place a greater emphasis on adaptation to climate change with working groups looking at carbon dioxide capture and geological storage; impacts and adaptation; aviation; and carbon dioxide and cars. It says that global emissions will not be reduced by more than half by 2050 unless carbon capture and storage is used. It expects these technologies to make a major contribution, particularly after 2020. The EC has set out proposals and options for keeping climate change to manageable levels in *Limiting Global Climate Change to 2 degree Celsius.* This is part of a package of measures to establish a new energy policy for Europe. It also contributes to the international discussions on a future global agreement to combat climate change after 2012, when the Kyoto emissions targets expire. An EC impact assessment predicts investment in a low-carbon economy will require about 0.5 per cent of global GDP over the period 2013–20, compared with the Stern Review's estimate that uncontrolled climate change will cost 5–20 per cent of GDP in the longer term. The EU's priority is to get a comprehensive international agreement on climate change by the end of 2009, as agreed at the Bali UNFCCC meeting in 2007.

WASTE

Waste policy in the UK follows a number of principles: the waste hierarchy of reduce, reuse, recycle, dispose; the proximity principle of disposing of waste close to its generation; and national self-sufficiency.

EU directives play an important role in driving UK policy, particularly regarding commercial and industrial waste. Its European integrated products policy aims to internalise the environmental costs of products throughout their life cycle using market forces, by focusing on eco-design and incentives to ensure increased demand for greener products. The EU is addressing greater responsibility for end-of-life products through a series of directives on packaging waste, vehicles, waste electrical and electronic equipment, and batteries, while the EC is revising its waste framework directive to simplify legislation, implement a more effective waste prevention policy and encourage reuse and recycling.

The UK generates about 335 million tonnes of waste each year, of which household waste accounts for 9 per cent. The proportion of household waste recycled or composted in the UK has been steadily increasing to 32 per cent in the year to June 2007, compared to 26.7 per cent in 2005–6. Scotland recycled 24.4 per cent of municipal waste in 2005–6, up from 17.3 per cent in the previous year.

RECYCLING HABITS
kilogrammes per head per year

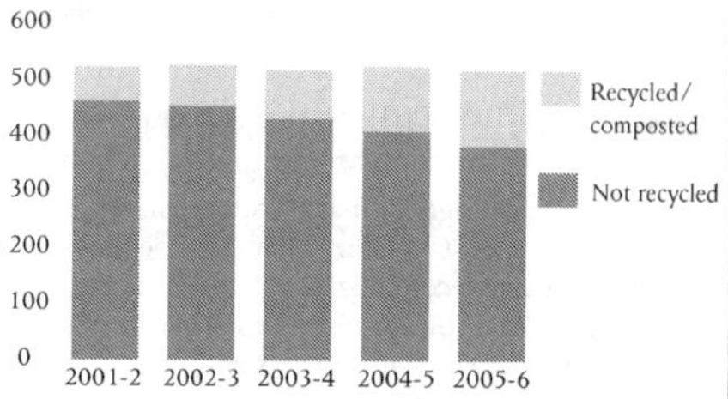

Source: DEFRA

The UK is still behind some other European countries. The Netherlands and Austria recycle or compost around 60 per cent of their municipal waste, while Belgium and Germany recycle and compost about half. Greece, however, still landfills over 90 per cent of its waste.

The UK government's new waste strategy, launched in 2007, includes decoupling waste growth from economic growth, putting more emphasis on prevention and reuse; landfilling less non-municipal waste, and investing in the infrastructure needed to divert waste from landfill.

WATER

Water quality targets are set at both EU and UK level for drinking water sources, wastewater discharges, rivers, coastal water and bathing water. The aim is achieve 'good water status' throughout the EU by 2015. The EC has launched WISE (Water Information System for Europe), an interactive internet tool which allows users to monitor water quality in their neighbourhood and provides access to water data and other information.

Bathing water quality results for 2007 show that all but two of the 561 coastal bathing areas in the UK met the

EU directive's minimum requirements, compared to two-thirds in 1988, while over three-quarters met the tighter standard. These figures show a great improvement since the early 1990s, when less than a third of England's beaches complied with the toughest standards. Scotland has a new bathing waters strategy to raise standards to meet the European directive. In 2006, 71 per cent of UK rivers were of good biological quality, compared with 67 per cent in 2000.

ENERGY

Energy used in the home is responsible for 25 per cent of the UK's carbon dioxide emissions. The UK has four energy policy goals set out in the new energy bill – cutting carbon dioxide emissions by 60 per cent by 2050 with real progress by 2020, maintaining reliable energy supplies, promoting competitive energy markets, and ensuring homes are adequately and affordably heated.

In terms of renewable energy, the UK has a target to increase the contribution of renewables to 10 per cent of electricity by 2010, with an aspiration to reach 20 per cent by 2020. Renewables capacity is increasing: in 2006 it accounted for 4.7 per cent of electricity generated, an increase of 7.5 per cent on 2005. Hydropower is the UK's largest renewable source, with a capacity of 4,244MW, while wind power capacity is 2,437MW and photovoltaic capacity is 3,390kW.

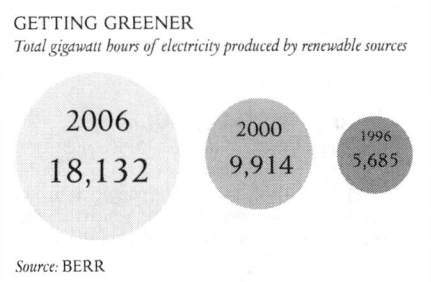

GETTING GREENER

Total gigawatt hours of electricity produced by renewable sources

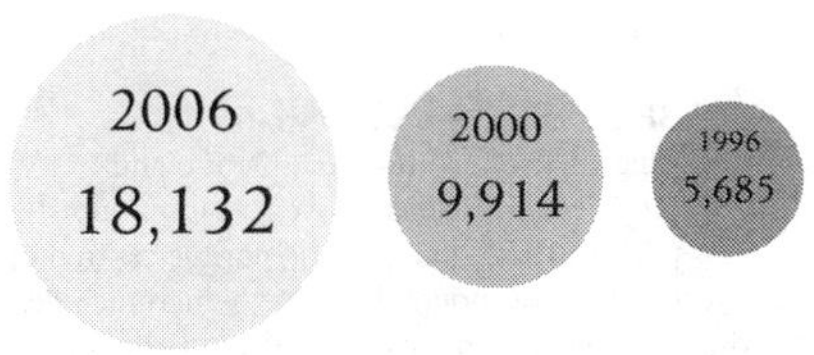

Source: BERR

The EC has also adopted a number of targets. These are to reduce greenhouse gas emissions from developed countries by 30 per cent by 2020 (the EU has committed to cutting its own emissions by 20 per cent but will increase this reduction to 30 per cent under a global agreement); to improve energy efficiency by 20 per cent by 2020; and to increase the level of biofuels in transport fuel to 10 per cent by 2020.

A new eco-design directive will set efficiency standards for household items such as boilers, computers and washing machines, as well as commercial equipment and component parts.

The EU's renewables directive aims to increase the EU's share of electricity produced from renewable energy sources to 21 per cent by 2010 (up from 15.2 per cent in 2001). In 2004 13.7 per cent of EU electricity was from renewables. Most of this was from hydropower (70 per cent), followed by biomass (15 per cent) and wind (13 per cent).

Worldwide, wind energy has the largest share of investment and is growing at 25–30 per cent annually,

ALTERNATIVE ENERGY

Gigawatt hours generated

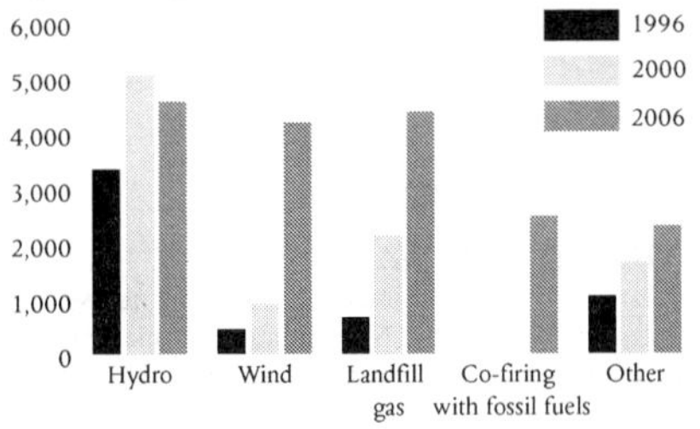

Source: BERR

accounting for 90GW of electricity in 2007. Grid-tied solar photovoltaic technology is growing at 50–60 per cent per year and accounts for 8GW.

ENVIRONMENT AND HEALTH

Particulate matter in the air, noise and ground-level ozone damage the health of thousands of people every year. Pollutants, including pesticides, endocrine disruptors, dioxins and PCBs persist in the environment and not enough is known about their long-term effect on health. There are also concerns about the effects of electromagnetic fields on human health and the potential risks associated with nanotechnology are unclear.

Concerns about pollution's impact on health are addressed in the Environment and Health Action Plan 2004–10 that proposes closer co-operation between the health, environment and research areas. It builds on an assessment of the current knowledge in the areas of integrated monitoring of dioxins and PCBs, heavy metals and endocrine disrupters; childhood cancer, neurodevelopmental disorders and respiratory health; and human biomonitoring, environment and health indicators; and research needs.

A new chemicals policy, under which industry will have to provide information on the effects of chemicals on human health and the environment, as well as on safe ways of handling them, has also been set up.

CONTACTS

DEPARTMENT OF ENVIRONMENT, FOOD AND RURAL AFFAIRS, Eastbury House, 30–34 Albert Embankment, London SE1 7TL **T** 08459-335577 **W** www.defra.gov.uk

ENVIRONMENT AGENCY, Rio House, Almonsbury, Bristol BS32 4UD **T** 08708-506506 **W** www.environment-agency.gov.uk

EUROPEAN ENVIRONMENT AGENCY, Kongens Nytorv 6, DK-1050 Copenhagen K, Denmark **T** +45 3336 7100 **W** www.eea.europa.eu

ROYAL COMMISSION ON ENVIRONMENTAL POLLUTION, Third Floor, The Sanctuary, London SW1P 3JS **T** 020-7799 8970 **W** www.rcep.org.uk

SCOTTISH GOVERNMENT, ENVIRONMENT AND RURAL AFFAIRS DEPARTMENT, Pentland House, 47 Robb's Loan, Edinburgh EH14 1TY **T** 0131-556 8400 **W** www.scotland.gov.uk

CONSERVATION AND HERITAGE

NATIONAL PARKS

ENGLAND AND WALES

There are now eight national parks in England and three in Wales. In addition, the Norfolk and Suffolk Broads are considered to have equivalent status to a national park. Under the provisions of the National Parks and Access to the Countryside Act 1949, as clarified by the Natural Environment and Rural Communities Act 2006, areas designated as national parks have a statutory requirement to conserve and protect scenic landscapes from inappropriate development and to provide access to the land for public enjoyment.

Natural England is the statutory body which has the power to designate national parks in England, and the Countryside Council for Wales is responsible for national parks in Wales. Designations in England are confirmed by the Secretary of State for Environment, Food and Rural Affairs and those in Wales by the National Assembly for Wales. The designation of a national park does not affect the ownership of the land or remove the rights of the local community. The majority of the land in the national parks is owned by private landowners (74 per cent) or by bodies such as the National Trust (7 per cent) and the Forestry Commission (7 per cent). The national park authorities own only around 2 per cent of the land.

The Environment Act 1995 replaced the existing national park boards and committees with free-standing national park authorities (NPAs). NPAs are the sole local planning authorities for their areas and as such influence land use and development, and deal with planning applications. Their duties include conserving and enhancing the natural beauty, wildlife and cultural heritage of the parks; promoting opportunities for public understanding and enjoyment; and fostering the economic and social well-being of the communities within national parks. The NPAs publish management plans as statements of their policies and appoint their own officers and staff.

The Broads Authority was established under the Norfolk and Suffolk Broads Act 1998 and meets the requirement for the authority to have a navigation function in addition to a regard for the needs of agriculture, forestry and the economic and social interests of those who live or work in the Broads.

MEMBERSHIP

Membership of English NPAs comprises local authority appointees, members directly appointed by the environment secretary of state and members appointed by him after a consultation with local parishes. Under the Natural Environment and Rural Communities Act 2006 every district, county or unitary authority with land in a national park is entitled to appoint at least one member unless it chooses to opt out. The total number of local authority and parish members must exceed the number of national members. Since 1 April 2007 all NPAs have 22 members, except for the Peak District which has 30.

The Broads Authority has 21 members: nine appointed by the constituent local authorities, two appointed by the Navigation Committee and ten appointed by the Secretary of State. The Secretary of State's appointees include at least three which are appointed after consultation with representatives of boating interests and at least two which are appointed after consultation with representatives of landowning and farming interests.

In Wales two-thirds of NPA members are appointed by the constituent local authorities and one-third by the Welsh Assembly Government, advised by the Countryside Council for Wales.

FUNDING

The English NPAs and the Broads Authority are funded by central government. In the financial year 2008–9 a core grant totalling £46m was allocated between the authorities.

In Wales, national parks are funded via a grant from the National Assembly. National park grant for 2008–9 amounted to £11.65m; comprising £11.15m in revenue grant (on which the three Welsh NPAs can levy a further third of their monies from their constituent local authorities) and an additional £500,000 non levyable capital grant.

All NPAs and the Broads Authority can take advantage of grants from other bodies including lottery and European grants.

The national parks (with date designation confirmed) are:

BRECON BEACONS (1957), Powys (66 per cent)/Carmarthenshire/Rhondda, Cynon and Taff/Merthyr Tydfil/Blaenau Gwent/Monmouthshire, 1,344 sq. km/519 sq. miles – The park is centred on the Brecon Beacons mountain range, which includes the three highest mountains in southern Britain (Pen y Fan, Corn Du and Cribyn), but also includes the valley of the rivers Usk and Wye, the Black Mountains to the east and the Black Mountain to the west. There are information centres at the national park visitor centre at Libanus (near Brecon), Abergavenny, Llandovery, Pontneddfechan and Craig-y-nos Country Park.
National Park Authority, Plas y Ffynnon, Cambrian Way, Brecon, Powys LD3 7HP T 01874-624437
E enquiries@breconbeacons.org
W www.breconbeacons.org
Chief Executive, Christopher Gledhill

BROADS (1989), Norfolk/Suffolk, 303 sq. km/117 sq. miles – The Broads are located between Norwich and Great Yarmouth on the flood plains of the six rivers flowing through the area to the sea. The area is one of fens, winding waterways, woodland and marsh. The 60 or so broads are man-made, and many are connected to the rivers by dykes, providing over 200km of navigable waterways. There are information centres at Beccles, Hoveton, Potter Heigham, Ranworth, Whitlingham and Toad Hole Cottage at How Hill.
Broads Authority, 18 Colegate, Norwich NR3 1BQ
T 01603-610734 E broads@broads-authority.gov.uk
W www.broads-authority.gov.uk
Chief Executive, Dr John Packman

DARTMOOR (1951), Devon, 954 sq. km/368 sq. miles – The park consists of moorland and rocky granite tors, and is rich in prehistoric remains. There are information

centres at Haytor, Newbridge, Princetown (main visitor centre) and Postbridge.
National Park Authority, Parke, Bovey Tracey, Devon TQ13 9JQ **T** 01626-832093 **E** hq@dartmoor-npa.gov.uk **W** www.dartmoor-npa.gov.uk
Chief Executive, Kevin Bishop, PHD

EXMOOR (1954), Somerset (71 per cent)/Devon, 693 sq. km/267 sq. miles – Exmoor is a moorland plateau inhabited by wild Exmoor ponies and red deer. There are many ancient remains and burial mounds. There are national park centres at Dunster, Dulverton and Lynmouth.
National Park Authority, Exmoor House, Dulverton, Somerset TA22 9HL **T** 01398-323665 **E** info@exmoor-nationalpark.gov.uk **W** www.exmoor-nationalpark.gov.uk
Chief Executive/National Park Officer, Dr Nigel Stone

LAKE DISTRICT (1951), Cumbria, 2,292 sq. km/885 sq. miles – The Lake District includes England's highest mountains (Scafell Pike, Helvellyn and Skiddaw) but it is most famous for its glaciated lakes. There are national park information centres at Bowness Bay, Keswick, Glenridding and a visitor centre at Brockhole, Windermere.
National Park Authority, Murley Moss, Oxenholme Road, Kendal, Cumbria LA9 7RL **T** 01539-724555 **E** hq@lake-district.gov.uk **W** www.lake-district.gov.uk
National Park Officer, Richard Leafe

NEW FOREST (2005), Hampshire, 567 sq. km/219 sq. miles – The forest has been protected since 1079 when it was declared a royal hunting forest. The area consists of forest, ancient woodland and heathland. Much of the forest is managed by the Forestry Commission, which provides several campsites. The main villages are Brockenhurst, Burley and Lyndhurst, which has a visitor centre.
National Park Authority, South Efford House, Milford Road, Lymington, Hants SO41 0JD **T** 01590-646600 **E** enquiries@newforestnpa.gov.uk **W** www.newforestnpa.gov.uk
Chief Executive, Lindsay Cornish

NORTH YORK MOORS (1952), North Yorkshire (96 per cent)/Redcar and Cleveland, 1,432 sq. km/554 sq. miles – The park consists of woodland and moorland, and includes the Hambleton Hills and the Cleveland Way. There are information centres at Danby, Sutton Bank and at the Old Coastguard Station in Robin Hood's Bay.
National Park Authority, The Old Vicarage, Bondgate, Helmsley, York YO6 5BP **T** 01439-770657 **E** info@northyorkshiremoors-npa.gov.uk **W** www.visitnorthyorkshiremoors.co.uk
Chief Executive/National Park Officer, Andrew Wilson

NORTHUMBERLAND (1956), Northumberland, 1,049 sq. km/405 sq. miles – The park is an area of hill country stretching from Hadrian's Wall to the Scottish border. There are information centres at Ingram, Once Brewed and Rothbury.
National Park Authority, Eastburn, South Park, Hexham, Northumberland NE46 1BS **T** 01434-605555 **E** enquires@nnpa.org.uk **W** www.northumberlandnationalpark.org.uk
Chief Executive, Tony Gates

PEAK DISTRICT (1951), Derbyshire (64 per cent)/Staffordshire/South Yorkshire/Cheshire/West Yorkshire/Greater Manchester, 1,438 sq. km/555 sq. miles – The Peak District includes the gritstone moors of the 'Dark Peak' and the limestone dales of the 'White Peak'. There are information centres at Bakewell, Castleton, Edale and Upper Derwent.
National Park Authority, Aldern House, Baslow Road, Bakewell, Derbyshire DE45 1AE **T** 01629-816200 **E** customer.service@peakdistrict.gov.uk **W** www.peakdistrict.gov.uk
Chief Executive, Jim Dixon

PEMBROKESHIRE COAST (1952 and 1995), Pembrokeshire, 620 sq. km/240 sq. miles – The park includes cliffs, moorland and a number of islands, including Skomer. There are information centres at St David's, Newport and Tenby.
National Park Authority, Llanion Park, Pembroke Dock, Pembrokeshire SA72 6DY **T** 0845-345 7275 **E** info@pembrokeshirecoast.org.uk **W** www.pcnpa.org.uk
Chief Executive (National Park Officer), Nic Wheeler

SNOWDONIA/ERYRI (1951), Gwynedd/Conwy, 2,132 sq. km/823 sq. miles – Snowdonia is an area of deep valleys and rugged mountains. There are information centres at Aberdyfi, Beddgelert, Betws y Coed, Blaenau Ffestiniog, Dolgellau and Harlech.
National Park Authority, Penrhyndeudraeth, Gwynedd LL48 6LF **T** 01766-770274 **E** parc@snowdonia-npa.gov.uk **W** www.snowdonia-npa.gov.uk
Chief Executive, Aneurin Phillips

YORKSHIRE DALES (1954), North Yorkshire (88 per cent)/Cumbria, 1,762 sq. km/680 sq. miles – The Yorkshire Dales is composed primarily of limestone overlaid in places by millstone grit. The three peaks of Ingleborough, Whernside and Pen-y-Ghent are within the park. There are information centres at Grassington, Hawes, Aysgarth Falls, Malham and Reeth.
National Park Authority, Yoredale, Bainbridge, Leyburn, N. Yorks DL8 3EL **T** 0870-166-6333 **E** info@yorkshiredales.org.uk **W** www.yorkshiredales.org.uk
Chief Executive, David Butterworth

THE SOUTH DOWNS

In 1999 the Countryside Agency began the process of designating the South Downs (within the Sussex Downs and East Hampshire areas of outstanding natural beauty) as a national park. A designation order for a South Downs national park was submitted by the Countryside Agency to the secretary of state on 27 January 2003. In February 2006 the designation process was indefinitely postponed following a high court judgement (the 'Meyrick' judgement) regarding part of the 2005 New Forest designation which changed the way in which criteria for national park status had generally been understood. The Department for Environment, Food and Rural Affairs (DEFRA) clarified the national parks legislation through the Natural Environment and Rural Communities Act 2006 and the South Downs designation process was restarted in March 2007.

THE SOUTH DOWNS, West Sussex/Hampshire, 1,637 sq. km/632 sq. miles – The South Downs contains a diversity of natural habitats, including flower-studded chalk grassland, ancient woodland, flood meadow, lowland heath and rare chalk heathland.
South Downs Joint Committee, Victorian Barn, Victorian Business Centre, Ford Lane, Ford, Arundel, W. Sussex BN18 0EF **T** 01243-558700 **E** comms@southdowns-aonb.gov.uk **W** www.southdowns.gov.uk
South Downs Officer, Martin Beaton

SCOTLAND

On 9 August 2000 the national parks (Scotland) bill received royal assent, giving parliament the ability to create national parks in Scotland. The first two Scottish national parks became operational in 2002 and 2003 respectively. The Act gives Scottish parks wider powers than in England and Wales, including statutory responsibilities for the economy and rural communities. The board of each Scottish NPA consists of 25 members, of which five are directly elected by a postal ballot of the local electorate. The remaining 20 members, ten of which are nominated by the constituent local authorities, are chosen by the Scottish ministers. In Scotland, the national parks are central government bodies and wholly funded by the Scottish government. Funding for 2008–9 totals £12.3m.

CAIRNGORMS (2003), Morayshire, 3,800 sq. km/1,466 sq. miles – The Cairngorms national park is the largest in the UK. It displays a vast collection of landforms and includes four of Scotland's highest mountains.
National Park Authority, 14 The Square, Grantown-on-Spey, Morayshire PH26 3HG T 01479-873535
E enquiries@cairngorms.co.uk W www.cairngorms.co.uk
Chief Executive, Jane Hope

LOCH LOMOND AND THE TROSSACHS (2002), Argyll and Bute/Perth and Kinross/Stirling/West Dunbartonshire, 1,865 sq. km/720 sq. miles – The park boundaries encompass lochs, rivers, forests, 20 mountains above 3,000ft including Ben More and a further 20 mountains between 2,500ft and 3,000ft.
National Park Authority, Carrochan, Carrochan Road, Balloch G83 8EG T 01389-722600
E info@lochlomond-trossachs.org
W www.lochlomond-trossachs.org
Chief Executive, Fiona Logan

NORTHERN IRELAND

There is a power to designate national parks in Northern Ireland under the Nature Conservation and Amenity Lands Order (Northern Ireland) 1985, but there are currently no national parks in Northern Ireland.

AREAS OF OUTSTANDING NATURAL BEAUTY

ENGLAND AND WALES

Under the National Parks and Access to the Countryside Act 1949, provision was made for the designation of areas of outstanding natural beauty (AONBs). Natural England is responsible for AONBs in England and the Countryside Council for Wales for the Welsh AONBs. Designations in England are confirmed by the Secretary of State for Environment, Food and Rural Affairs and those in Wales by the National Assembly for Wales. The Countryside and Rights of Way (CROW) Act 2000 placed greater responsibility on local authorities to protect AONBs and made it a statutory duty for relevant authorities to produce a management plan for their AONB area. The CROW Act also provided for the creation of conservation boards for larger and more complex AONBs. The first two conservation boards for the Cotswolds and Chilterns AONBs were established in July 2004.

The primary objective of the AONB designation is to conserve and enhance the natural beauty of the area. Where an AONB has a conservation board, it has the additional purpose of increasing public understanding and enjoyment of the special qualities of the area; the board has greater weight should there be a conflict of interests between the two. In addition, the board is also required to foster the economic and social well-being of the local communities but without incurring significant expenditure in doing so. Overall responsibility for AONBs lies with the relevant local authorities or conservation board. To coordinate planning and management responsibilities between local authorities in whose area they fall, AONBs are overseen by a joint advisory committee (or similar body) which includes representatives from the local authorities, landowners, farmers, residents and conservation and recreation groups. Core funding for AONBs is provided by central government through Natural England and the Countryside Council for Wales.

The 40 Areas of Outstanding Natural Beauty (with date designation confirmed) are:

ARNSIDE AND SILVERDALE (1972), Cumbria/Lancashire, 75 sq. km/29 sq. miles
BLACKDOWN HILLS (1991), Devon/Somerset, 370 sq. km/143 sq. miles
CANNOCK CHASE (1958), Staffordshire, 68 sq. km/26 sq. miles
CHICHESTER HARBOUR (1964), Hampshire/West Sussex, 74 sq. km/29 sq. miles
CHILTERNS (1965; extended 1990), Bedfordshire/Buckinghamshire/Herefordshire/Oxfordshire, 833 sq. km/322 sq. miles
CLWYDIAN RANGE (1985), Denbighshire/Flintshire, 157 sq. km/61 sq. miles
CORNWALL (1959; Camel Estuary 1983), 958 sq. km/370 sq. miles
COTSWOLDS (1966; extended 1990), Gloucestershire/Oxfordshire/Warwickshire/Wiltshire/Worcestershire, 2,038 sq. km/787 sq. miles
CRANBORNE CHASE AND WEST WILTSHIRE DOWNS (1983), Dorset/Hampshire/Somerset/Wiltshire, 983 sq. km/380 sq. miles
DEDHAM VALE (1970; extended 1978, 1991), Essex/Suffolk, 90 sq. km/35 sq. miles
DORSET (1959), Dorset/Somerset, 1,129 sq. km/436 sq. miles
EAST DEVON (1963), 268 sq. km/103 sq. miles
EAST HAMPSHIRE (1962), 383 sq. km/148 sq. miles
FOREST OF BOWLAND (1964), Lancashire/North Yorkshire, 802 sq. km/310 sq. miles
GOWER (1956), Swansea, 188 sq. km/73 sq. miles
HIGH WEALD (1983), East Sussex/Kent/Surrey/West Sussex, 1,460 sq. km/564 sq. miles
HOWARDIAN HILLS (1987), North Yorkshire, 204 sq. km/79 sq. miles
ISLE OF WIGHT (1963), 189 sq. km/73 sq. miles
ISLES OF SCILLY (1976), 16 sq. km/6 sq. miles
KENT DOWNS (1968), 878 sq. km/339 sq. miles
LINCOLNSHIRE WOLDS (1973), 558 sq. km/215 sq. miles
LLEYN (1957), Gwynedd, 161 sq. km/62 sq. miles
MALVERN HILLS (1959), Gloucestershire/Worcestershire, 150 sq. km/58 sq. miles
MENDIP HILLS (1972; extended 1989), Somerset, 198 sq. km/76 sq. miles
NIDDERDALE (1994), North Yorkshire, 603 sq. km/233 sq. miles
NORFOLK COAST (1968), 451 sq. km/174 sq. miles
NORTH DEVON (1960), 171 sq. km/66 sq. miles

NORTH PENNINES (1988), Cumbria/Durham/North Yorkshire/Northumberland, 1,983 sq. km/766 sq. miles
NORTH WESSEX DOWNS (1972), Hampshire/Oxfordshire/Wiltshire, 1,730 sq. km/668 sq. miles
NORTHUMBERLAND COAST (1958), 135 sq. km/52 sq. miles
QUANTOCK HILLS (1957), Somerset, 99 sq. km/38 sq. miles
SHROPSHIRE HILLS (1959), 804 sq. km/310 sq. miles
SOLWAY COAST (1964), Cumbria, 115 sq. km/44 sq. miles
SOUTH DEVON (1960), 337 sq. km/130 sq. miles
SUFFOLK COAST AND HEATHS (1970), 403 sq. km/156 sq. miles
SURREY HILLS (1958), 419 sq. km/162 sq. miles
SUSSEX DOWNS (1966), 983 sq. km/379 sq. miles
TAMAR VALLEY (1995), Cornwall/Devon, 195 sq. km/75 sq. miles
WYE VALLEY (1971), Gloucestershire/Herefordshire/Monmouthshire, 326 sq. km/126 sq. miles
YNYS MON (ISLE OF ANGLESEY) (1967), 221 sq. km/85 sq. miles

NORTHERN IRELAND

The Department of the Environment for Northern Ireland, with advice from the Council for Nature Conservation and the Countryside, designates Areas of Outstanding Natural Beauty in Northern Ireland. At present there are nine and these cover a total area of 2,849 sq. km (1,100 sq. miles). Dates given are those of designation.

ANTRIM COAST AND GLENS (1988), Co. Antrim, 706 sq. km/272 sq. miles
BINEVENAGH (2006), Co. Londonderry, 166 sq. km/64 sq. miles
CAUSEWAY COAST (1989), Co. Antrim, 42 sq. km/16 sq. miles
LAGAN VALLEY (1965), Co. Down, 21 sq. km/8 sq. miles
LECALE COAST (1967), Co. Down, 31 sq. km/12 sq. miles
MOURNE (1986), Co. Down, 570 sq. km/220 sq. miles
RING OF GULLION (1991), Co. Armagh, 154 sq. km/59 sq. miles
SPERRIN (1968; extended 2008), Co. Tyrone/Co. Londonderry, 1,185 sq. km/457 sq. miles
STRANGFORD LOUGH (1972), Co. Down, 186 sq. km/72 sq. miles

NATIONAL SCENIC AREAS

In Scotland, national scenic areas have a broadly equivalent status to AONBs. Scottish Natural Heritage recognises areas of national scenic significance. At the end of June 2007 there were 40, covering a total area of 1,001,800 hectares (2,475,443 acres).

Development within national scenic areas is dealt with by local authorities, who are required to consult Scottish Natural Heritage concerning certain categories of development. Disagreements between Scottish Natural Heritage and local authorities are referred to the Scottish government. Land management uses can also be modified in the interest of scenic conservation.

ASSYNT-COIGACH, Highland, 90,200 ha/222,884 acres
BEN NEVIS AND GLEN COE, Highland, 101,600 ha/251,053 acres
CAIRNGORM MOUNTAINS, Highland/Aberdeenshire/Moray, 67,200 ha/166,051 acres
CUILLIN HILLS, Highland, 21,900 ha/54,115 acres
DEESIDE AND LOCHNAGAR, Aberdeenshire, 40,000 ha/98,840 acres
DORNOCH FIRTH, Highland, 7,500 ha/18,532 acres
EAST STEWARTRY COAST, Dumfries and Galloway, 4,500 ha/11,119 acres
EILDON AND LEADERFOOT, Borders, 3,600 ha/8,896 acres
FLEET VALLEY, Dumfries and Galloway, 5,300 ha/13,096 acres
GLEN AFFRIC, Highland, 19,300 ha/47,690 acres
GLEN STRATHFARRAR, Highland, 3,800 ha/9,390 acres
HOY AND WEST MAINLAND, Orkney Islands, 14,800 ha/36,571 acres
JURA, Argyll and Bute, 21,800 ha/53,868 acres
KINTAIL, Highland, 15,500 ha/38,300 acres
KNAPDALE, Argyll and Bute, 19,800 ha/48,926 acres
KNOYDART, Highland, 39,500 ha/97,604 acres
KYLE OF TONGUE, Highland, 18,500 ha/45,713 acres
KYLES OF BUTE, Argyll and Bute, 4,400 ha/10,872 acres
LOCH NA KEAL, Mull, Argyll and Bute, 12,700 ha/31,382 acres
LOCH LOMOND, Argyll and Bute, 27,400 ha/67,705 acres
LOCH RANNOCH AND GLEN LYON, Perthshire and Kinross, 48,400 ha/119,596 acres
LOCH SHIEL, Highland, 13,400 ha/33,111 acres
LOCH TUMMEL, Perthshire and Kinross, 9,200 ha/22,733 acres
LYNN OF LORN, Argyll and Bute, 4,800 ha/11,861 acres
MORAR, MOIDART AND ARDNAMURCHAN, Highland, 13,500 ha/33,358 acres
NITH ESTUARY, Dumfries and Galloway, 9,300 ha/22,980 acres
NORTH ARRAN, North Ayrshire, 23,800 ha/58,810 acres
NORTH-WEST SUTHERLAND, Highland, 20,500 ha/50,655 acres
RIVER EARN, Perthshire and Kinross, 3,000 ha/7,413 acres
RIVER TAY, Perthshire and Kinross, 5,600 ha/13,838 acres
ST KILDA, Eilean Siar (Western Isles), 900 ha/2,224 acres
SCARBA, LUNGA AND THE GARVELLACHS, Argyll and Bute, 1,900 ha/4,695 acres
SHETLAND, Shetland Isles, 11,600 ha/28,664 acres
SMALL ISLANDS, Highland, 15,500 ha/38,300 acres
SOUTH LEWIS, HARRIS AND NORTH UIST, Eilean Siar (Western Isles), 109,600 ha/270,822 acres
SOUTH UIST MACHAIR, Eilean Siar (Western Isles), 6,100 ha/15,073 acres
THE TROSSACHS, Stirling, 4,600 ha/11,367 acres
TROTTERNISH, Highland, 5,000 ha/12,355 acres
UPPER TWEEDDALE, Borders, 10,500 ha/25,945 acres
WESTER ROSS, Highland, 145,300 ha/359,036 acres

THE NATIONAL FOREST

The National Forest is being planted across 517 sq. km (200 sq. miles) of Derbyshire, Leicestershire and Staffordshire. Seven million trees, of mixed species but mainly broadleaved, covering over 5,400 hectares (13,300 acres) have been planted. The aim is to eventually cover about one-third of the designated area.

The project was developed in 1992–5 by the Countryside Commission and is now run by the National Forest Company, which was established in April 1995. The National Forest Company is responsible for the delivery of the government-approved National Forest Strategy and is funded by the DEFRA.

NATIONAL FOREST COMPANY, Enterprise Glade, Bath Lane, Moira, Swadlincote, Derbyshire DE12 6BD
T 01283-551211 E enquiries@nationalforest.org
W www.nationalforest.org
Chief Executive, Sophie Churchill

SITES OF SPECIAL SCIENTIFIC INTEREST

Site of special scientific interest (SSSI) is a legal notification applied to land in England, Scotland or Wales which Natural England (NE) (formerly English Nature), Scottish Natural Heritage (SNH) or the Countryside Council for Wales (CCW) identifies as being of special interest because of its flora, fauna, geological, geomorphological or physiographical features. In some cases, SSSIs are managed as nature reserves.

NE, SNH and CCW must notify the designation of an SSSI to the local planning authority, every owner/occupier of the land, and the environment secretary, the Scottish ministers or the National Assembly for Wales. Forestry and agricultural departments and a number of other interested parties are also formally notified.

Objections to the notification of an SSSI can be made and ultimately considered at a full meeting of the Council of NE or CCW. In Scotland an objection will be dealt with by the main board of SNH or an appropriate subgroup, depending on the nature of the objection. Unresolved objections on scientific grounds from those with a legal interest in the land must be referred to the Advisory Committee on SSSI.

The protection of these sites depends on the cooperation of individual landowners and occupiers. Owner/occupiers must consult NE, SNH or CCW and gain written consent before they can undertake certain listed activities on the site. Funds are available through management agreements and grants to assist owners and occupiers in conserving sites' interests. Sites can also be protected by management schemes, management notices and other enforcement mechanisms. As a last resort a site can be purchased.

The number and area of SSSIs in Britain as at May 2008 was:

	Number	*Hectares*	*Acres*
England	4,114	1,076,983	2,661,258
Scotland	1,455	1,039,005	2,567,346
Wales	1,018	264,773	654,281

NORTHERN IRELAND

In Northern Ireland 257 Areas of Special Scientific Interest (ASSIs) have been declared by the Department of the Environment for Northern Ireland.

NATIONAL NATURE RESERVES

National nature reserves are defined in the National Parks and Access to the Countryside Act 1949 as modified by the Natural Environment and Rural Communities Act 2006. National nature reserves may be managed solely for the purpose of conservation, or for both the purposes of conservation and recreation, providing this does not compromise the conservation purpose.

Natural England (NE), Scottish Natural Heritage (SNH) or the Countryside Council for Wales (CCW) can declare as a national nature reserve land which is held and managed as a nature reserve under an agreement; land held and managed by NE, SNH or CCW; or land held and managed as a nature reserve by an approved body. NE, SNH or CCW can make by-laws to protect reserves from undesirable activities; these are subject to confirmation by the Secretary of State for Environment, Food and Rural Affairs, the National Assembly for Wales or the Scottish ministers in Scotland.

The number and area of national nature reserves in Britain as at May 2008 was:

	Number	*Hectares*	*Acres*
England	222	93,103	230,057
Scotland	66	140,245	346,541
Wales	69	24,307	60,066

NORTHERN IRELAND

Nature reserves are established and managed by the Department of the Environment for Northern Ireland, with advice from the Council for Nature Conservation and the Countryside. Nature reserves are declared under the Nature Conservation and Amenity Lands (Northern Ireland) order 1985; to date, 47 nature reserves have been declared.

LOCAL NATURE RESERVES

Local nature reserves are defined in the National Parks and Access to the Countryside Act 1949 (as amended by the Natural Environment and Rural Communities Act 2006) as land designated for the study and preservation of flora and fauna, or of geological or physiographical features. Local nature reserves also have a statutory obligation to provide opportunities for the enjoyment of nature or open air recreation, providing this does not compromise the conservation purpose of the reserve. Local authorities in England, Scotland and Wales have power to acquire, declare and manage reserves in consultation with Natural England, Scottish Natural Heritage and the Countryside Council for Wales. There is similar legislation in Northern Ireland where the consulting organisation is the Environment and Heritage Service.

Any organisation, such as water companies, educational trusts, local amenity groups and charitable nature conservation bodies, such as wildlife trusts, may manage local nature reserves, provided that a local authority has a legal interest in the land. This means that the local authority must either own it, lease it or have a management agreement with the landowner.

The number and area of designated local nature reserves in Britain as at May 2008 was:

	Number	*Hectares*	*Acres*
England	1,382	35,000	86,450
Scotland	51	9,888	24,433
Wales	74	5,049	12,477

FOREST NATURE RESERVES

The Forestry Commission is the government department responsible for forestry policy throughout Great Britain. Forestry is a devolved matter, with the separate Forestry Commissions for England, Scotland and Wales reporting directly to their appropriate minister. The Forestry Commission in each country is led by a director who is also a member of the GB Board of Commissioners. As at March 2008, Forestry Commission-managed woodland amounted to around 760,000 hectares: 202,000 hectares in England, 106,000 hectares in Wales and 452,000 hectares in Scotland.

NORTHERN IRELAND

There are 34 forest nature reserves in Northern Ireland, covering 1,512 hectares (3,736 acres). They are designated and administered by the Forest Service, an agency of the Department of Agriculture and Rural Development for Northern Ireland. There are also 16 national nature reserves on Forest Service-owned property.

MARINE NATURE RESERVES

The Secretary of State for Environment, Food and Rural Affairs, the National Assembly for Wales and the Scottish government have the power to designate marine nature reserves. Natural England, Scottish Natural Heritage and the Countryside Council for Wales select and manage these reserves. Marine nature reserves may be established in Northern Ireland under a 1985 Order.

Marine nature reserves provide protection for marine flora and fauna, and geological and physiographical features on land covered by tidal waters or parts of the sea in or adjacent to the UK. Reserves also provide opportunities for study and research.

The three statutory marine nature reserves are:

LUNDY (1986), Bristol Channel
SKOMER (1990), Dyfed
STRANGFORD LOUGH (1995), Northern Ireland

WORLD HERITAGE SITES

The Convention Concerning the Protection of the World Cultural and Natural Heritage was adopted by the United Nations Educational Scientific and Cultural Organisation (UNESCO) in 1972 and ratified by the UK in 1984. As at 30 November 2007 185 states were party to the convention. The convention provides for the identification, protection and conservation of cultural and natural sites of outstanding universal value.

Cultural sites may be:

- monuments
- groups of buildings
- sites of historic, aesthetic, archaeological, scientific, ethnologic or anthropologic value
- historic areas of towns
- 'cultural landscapes', ie sites whose characteristics are marked by significant interactions between human populations and their natural environment

Natural sites may be:

- those with remarkable physical, biological or geological formations
- those with outstanding universal value from the point of view of science, conservation or natural beauty
- the habitat of threatened species and plants

Governments which are party to the convention nominate sites in their country for inclusion in the World Cultural and Natural Heritage List. Nominations are considered by the World Heritage Committee, an inter-governmental committee composed of 21 representatives of the parties to the convention. The committee is advised by the International Council on Monuments and Sites (ICOMOS), the International Centre for the Study of the Preservation and Restoration of Cultural Property (ICCROM) and the World Conservation Union (IUCN). ICOMOS evaluates and reports on proposed cultural and mixed sites, ICCROM provides expert advice and training on how to conserve and restore cultural property and IUCN provides technical evaluations of natural heritage sites and reports on the state of conservation of listed sites. The Department for Culture, Media and Sport represents the UK government in matters relating to the convention.

A prerequisite for inclusion in the World Cultural and Natural Heritage List is the existence of an effective legal protection system in the country in which the site is situated (eg listing, conservation areas and planning controls in the UK) and a detailed management plan to ensure the conservation of the site. Inclusion in the list does not confer any greater degree of protection on the site than that offered by the national protection framework.

If a site is considered to be in serious danger of decay or damage, the committee may add it to a complementary list, the World Heritage in Danger List. Sites on this list may benefit from particular attention or emergency measures.

Financial support for the conservation of sites on the World Cultural and Natural Heritage List is provided by the World Heritage Fund. This is administered by the World Heritage Committee, which determines the financial and technical aid to be allocated. The fund's income is derived from compulsory and voluntary contributions from the states party to the convention and from private donations.

DESIGNATED SITES

As at 10 July 2008, following the 32nd session of the World Heritage Committee, 878 sites were inscribed on the World Cultural and Natural Heritage List. Of these, 24 are in the United Kingdom and three in British overseas territories; 22 are listed for their cultural significance (†), four for their natural significance (*) and one for both cultural and natural significance. The year in which sites were designated appears in parentheses. In 2005 Hadrian's Wall, a World Heritage Site in its own right since 1987, was joined by the upper German-Raetian Limes to form the first section of a trans-national world heritage site, Frontiers of the Roman Empire.

UNITED KINGDOM

†Bath – the city (1987)
†Blaenarvon industrial landscape, Wales (2000)
†Blenheim Palace and Park, Oxfordshire (1987)
†Canterbury Cathedral, St Augustine's Abbey, St Martin's Church, Kent (1988)
†Castle and town walls of King Edward I, north Wales – Beaumaris, Caernarfon Castle, Conwy Castle, Harlech Castle, Ynys Mon (Isle of Anglesey) (1986)
†Cornwall and west Devon mining landscape (2006)
†Derwent Valley Mills, Derbyshire (2001)
*Dorset and east Devon coast (2001)
†Durham Cathedral and Castle (1986)
†Edinburgh old and new towns (1995)
†Frontiers of the Roman Empire, Hadrian's Wall, northern England (1987, 2005)
*Giant's Causeway and Causeway coast, Co. Antrim (1986)
†Greenwich, London – maritime Greenwich, including the Royal Naval College, Old Royal Observatory, Queen's House, town centre (1997)
†Heart of Neolithic Orkney (1999)
†Ironbridge Gorge, Shropshire – the world's first iron bridge and other early industrial sites (1986)
†Liverpool – six areas of the maritime mercantile city (2004)
†New Lanark, South Lanarkshire, Scotland (2001)
†Royal Botanic Gardens, Kew (2003)
†*St Kilda, Eilean Siar (Western Isles) (1986)
†Saltaire, West Yorkshire (2001)
†Stonehenge, Avebury and related megalithic sites, Wiltshire (1986)
†Studley Royal Park, Fountains Abbey, St Mary's Church, N. Yorkshire (1986)
†Tower of London (1988)
†Westminster Abbey, Palace of Westminster, St Margaret's Church, London (1987)

BRITISH OVERSEAS TERRITORIES

*Henderson Island, Pitcairn Islands, South Pacific Ocean (1988)
*Gough Island and Inaccessible Island (part of Tristan da Cunha), South Atlantic Ocean (1995)
†St George town and related fortifications, Bermuda (2000)

WORLD HERITAGE CENTRE, UNESCO, 7 Place de Fontenoy, 75352 Paris 07 SP, France
W http://whc.unesco.org

CONSERVATION OF WILDLIFE AND HABITATS

The UK is party to a number of international conventions.

BERN CONVENTION

The 1979 Bern Convention on the Conservation of European Wildlife and Natural Habitats came into force in the UK in June 1982. Currently there are 47 contracting parties and a number of other states attend meetings as observers.

The aims are to conserve wild flora and fauna and their natural habitats, especially where this requires the cooperation of several countries, and to promote such cooperation. The convention gives particular emphasis to endangered and vulnerable species.

All parties to the convention must promote national conservation policies and take account of the conservation of wild flora and fauna when setting planning and development policies. Reports on contracting parties' conservation policies must be submitted to the standing committee every four years.

SECRETARIAT OF THE BERN CONVENTION STANDING COMMITTEE, Council of Europe, 67075 Strasbourg-Cedex, France **T** (+33) (3) 8841 2000 **W** www.coe.int

BIODIVERSITY

The UK ratified the Convention on Biological Diversity in June 1994. As at July 2008 there were 191 parties to the convention.

The objectives are the conservation of biological diversity, the sustainable use of its components and the fair and equitable sharing of the benefits arising out of the use of genetic resources. There are seven thematic work programmes addressing agricultural biodiversity, marine and coastal biodiversity and the biodiversity of inland waters, dry and sub-humid lands, islands, mountains and forests. The Conference of the Parties to the Convention on Biological Diversity adopted a supplementary agreement to the convention known as the Cartagena Protocol on Biosafety on 29 January 2000. The protocol seeks to protect biological diversity from potential risks that may be posed by introducing modified living organisms, resulting from biotechnology, into the environment. As at July 2008, 147 countries were party to the protocol; the UK joined on 17 February 2004.

The UK Biodiversity Action Plan (UKBAP) is the UK government's response to the Convention on Biological Diversity and constitutes a record of UK biological resources and a detailed plan for their protection. UKBAP currently consists of 391 species action plans, 47 habitat action plans and 174 local biodiversity plans. In August 2007 the UK list of priority species and habitats was approved; it includes 1,149 species and 65 habitats. Conservation action plans for these species and habitats are expected to be completed by the end of 2008. The UK Biodiversity Partnership Standing Committee guides and supports the UK Biodiversity Partnership in implementing UKBAP; it also coordinates between the four UK country groups which form the partnership and are responsible for implementing UKBAP at a national level. In addition, the UK Biodiversity Partnership includes two support groups: the Biodiversity Research Advisory Group and the Biodiversity Reporting and Information Group.

BIODIVERSITY POLICY UNIT, Zone 1/07, Temple Quay House, 2 The Square, Temple Quay, Bristol BS1 6PN **T** 0845-933 5577 **W** www.ukbap.org.uk

BONN CONVENTION

The 1979 Convention on Conservation of Migratory Species of Wild Animals (also known as CMS or Bonn Convention) came into force in the UK in October 1979. As at 1 March 2008, 108 countries were party to the convention.

It requires the protection of listed endangered migratory species and encourages international agreements covering these and other threatened species. International agreements can range from legally binding treaties to less formal memorandums of understanding.

Six agreements have been concluded to date under the convention. They aim to conserve seals in the Wadden Sea; bat populations in Europe; small cetaceans of the Baltic and North Seas; African-Eurasian migratory waterbirds; cetaceans of the Mediterranean Sea, Black Sea and contiguous Atlantic area; and albatrosses and petrels. A further 14 memorandums of understanding have been agreed for the Siberian crane, slender-billed curlews, marine turtles of the Atlantic coast of Africa, Indian Ocean and South-East Asia, the middle-European population of the great bustard, bukhara deer, aquatic warblers, West African populations of the African elephant, the saiga antelope, cetaceans of the Pacific Islands, dugongs (large marine mammals), Mediterranean monk seals, the ruddy-headed goose and grassland birds.

UNEP/CMS SECRETARIAT, United Nations Premises, Hermann-Ehlers-Str. 10, 53113 Bonn, Germany **T** (+49) (228) 815 2426 **E** secretariat@cms.int **W** www.cms.int

CITES

The 1973 Convention on International Trade in Endangered Species of Wild Fauna and Flora (CITES) is an agreement between governments to ensure that international trade in specimens of wild animals and plants does not threaten their survival. The UK became party to the convention in July 1975 and there are currently 173 member countries. Countries party to the convention ban commercial international trade in an agreed list of endangered species and regulate and monitor trade in other species that might become endangered. The convention accords varying degrees of protection to more than 30,000 species of animals and plants whether they are traded as live specimens or as products derived from them, such as fur coats and dried herbs.

The Conference of the Parties to CITES meets every two to three years to review the convention's implementation. The Wildlife Species Conservation Division at the Department for Environment, Food and Rural Affairs in Bristol (*see* address above) carries out the government's responsibilities under CITES.

CITES SECRETARIAT, International Environment House, Chemin des Anémones, CH-1219 Châtelaine, Geneva, Switzerland **T** (+41) (22) 917 8139/8140 **E** info@cites.org **W** www.cites.org

EUROPEAN WILDLIFE TRADE REGULATION

The Council (EC) Regulation on the Protection of Species of Wild Fauna and Flora by Regulating Trade Therein came into force in the UK on 1 June 1997. It is intended to standardise wildlife trade regulations across Europe and to improve the application of CITES.

RAMSAR CONVENTION

The 1971 Ramsar Convention on Wetlands of International Importance especially as Waterfowl Habitat entered into force in the UK in May 1976. As at June 2008, 158 countries were party to the convention.

The aim of the convention is the conservation and wise use of wetlands and their resources. Governments that are party to the convention must designate wetlands and include wetland conservation considerations in their land-use planning. 1,743 wetland sites, totalling 161 million hectares, have been designated for inclusion in the list of wetlands of international importance. The UK currently has 166 designated sites covering 917,988 hectares. The member countries meet every three years to assess the progress of the convention and the next meeting is scheduled for November 2008.

The UK has set targets under the Ramsar Strategic Plan, 2003–8. Progress towards these is monitored by the UK Ramsar Committee, known as the Joint Working Party. The UK and the Republic of Ireland have established a formal protocol to ensure common monitoring standards for waterbirds in the two countries.

RAMSAR CONVENTION SECRETARIAT, rue Mauverney 28, CH-1196 Gland, Switzerland
T (+41) (22) 999 0170 W www.ramsar.org

UK LEGISLATION

The Wildlife and Countryside Act 1981 gives legal protection to a wide range of wild animals and plants. Every five years the statutory nature conservation agencies (Natural England, Countryside Council for Wales and Scottish Natural Heritage) are required to review schedules 5 (animals, other than birds) and 8 (plants) of the Wildlife and Countryside Act 1981. They make recommendations to the Secretary of State for Environment, Food and Rural Affairs, the National Assembly for Wales and the Scottish government for changes to these schedules. The most recent variation of schedule 5 for England came into effect in February 2008 (the fourth quinquennial review recommended no changes schedule 8, the fifth is currently underway).

Under section 9 of the act it is an offence to kill, injure, take, possess or sell (whether alive or dead) any wild animal included in schedule 5 of the act and to disturb its place of shelter and protection or to destroy that place. However certain species listed on schedule 5 are protected against some, but not all, of these activities.

Under section 13 of the act it is illegal without a licence to pick, uproot, sell or destroy plants listed in schedule 8. Since January 2001, under the Countryside and Rights of Way Act 2000, persons found guilty of an offence under part 1 of the Wildlife and Countryside Act 1981 face a maximum penalty of up to £5,000 and/or up to six months custodial sentence per specimen.

BIRDS

The act lays down a close season for birds (listed on Schedule 2, part 1) from 1 February to 31 August inclusive, each year. Exceptions to these dates are made for:

Capercaillie and (except Scotland) Woodcock – 1 February to 30 September
Snipe – 1 February to 11 August
Birds listed on schedule 2, part 1 (below high water mark) (*see* below) – 21 February to 31 August
Wild duck and wild geese, in or over any area below the high-water mark of ordinary spring tides – 21 February to 31 August
Birds listed on schedule 2, part 1, which may be killed or taken outside the close season are: capercaillie; coot; certain wild duck (gadwall, goldeneye, mallard, pintail, pochard, shoveler, teal, tufted duck, wigeon); certain wild geese (Canada, greylag, pink-footed, white-fronted (in England and Wales only)); golden plover; moorhen; snipe; and woodcock.

Section 16 of the 1981 act allows licences to be issued on either an individual or general basis, to allow the killing, taking and sale of certain birds for specified reasons such as public health and safety. All other wild birds are fully protected by law throughout the year.

ANIMALS PROTECTED BY SCHEDULE 5

Adder *(Vipera berus)**
Allis Shad *(Alosa alosa)**
Anemone, Ivell's Sea *(Edwardsia ivelli)*
Anemone, Starlet Sea *(Nematosella vectensis)*
Bat, Horseshoe, all species *(Rhinolophidae)*
Bat, Typical, all species *(Vespertilionidae)*
Beetle *(Hypebaeus flavipes)*
Beetle, Lesser Silver Water *(Hydrochara caraboides)*
Beetle, Mire Pill *(Curimopsis nigrita)**
Beetle, Rainbow Leaf *(Chrysolina cerealis)*
Beetle, Spangled Water *(Graphoderus zonatus)*
Beetle, Stag *(Lucanus cervus)**
Beetle, Violet Click *(Limoniscus violaceus)*
Beetle, Water *(Paracymus aeneus)*
Burbot *(Lota lota)*
Butterfly, Adonis Blue *(Lysandra bellargus)*
Butterfly, Black Hairstreak *(Strymonidia pruni)*
Butterfly, Brown Hairstreak *(Thecla betulae)*
Butterfly, Chalkhill Blue *(Lysandra coridon)*
Butterfly, Chequered Skipper *(Carterocephalus palaemon)*
Butterfly, Duke of Burgundy Fritillary *(Hamearis lucina)*
Butterfly, Glanville Fritillary *(Melitaea cinxia)*
Butterfly, Heath Fritillary *(Mellicta athalia* or *Melitaea athalia)*
Butterfly, High Brown Fritillary *(Argynnis adippe)*
Butterfly, Large Blue *(Maculinea arion)*
Butterfly, Large Copper *(Lycaena dispar)*
Butterfly, Large Heath *(Coenonympha tullia)*
Butterfly, Large Tortoiseshell *(Nymphalis polychloros)*
Butterfly, Lulworth Skipper *(Thymelicus acteon)*
Butterfly, Marsh Fritillary *(Eurodryas aurinia)*
Butterfly, Mountain Ringlet *(Erebia epiphron)*
Butterfly, Northern Brown Argus *(Aricia artaxerxes)*
Butterfly, Pearl-bordered Fritillary *(Boloria euphrosyne)*
Butterfly, Purple Emperor *(Apatura iris)*
Butterfly, Silver Spotted Skipper *(Hesperia comma)*
Butterfly, Silver-studded Blue *(Plebejus argus)*
Butterfly, Small Blue *(Cupido minimus)*
Butterfly, Swallowtail *(Papilio machaon)*
Butterfly, White Letter Hairstreak *(Stymonida w-album)*
Butterfly, Wood White *(Leptidea sinapis)*
Cat, Wild *(Felis silvestris)*
Cicada, New Forest *(Cicadetta montana)*
Crayfish, Atlantic Stream *(Austropotomobius pallipes)**
Cricket, Field *(Gryllus campestris)*

Cricket, Mole *(Gryllotalpa gryllotalpa)*
Damselfly, Southern *(Coenagrion mercuriale)*
Dolphin, all species *(Cetacea)*
Dormouse *(Muscardinus avellanarius)*
Dragonfly, Norfolk Aeshna *(Aeshna isosceles)*
Frog, Common *(Rana temporaria)**
Goby, Couch's *(Gobius couchii)*
Goby, Giant *(Gobius cobitis)*
Grasshopper, Wart-biter *(Decticus verrucivorus)*
Hatchet Shell, Northern *(Thyasira gouldi)*
Hydroid, Marine *(Clavopsella navis)*
Lagoon Snail *(Paludinella littorina)*
Lagoon Snail, De Folin's *(Caecum armoricum)*
Lagoon Worm, Tentacled *(Alkmaria romijni)*
Leech, Medicinal *(Hirudo medicinalis)*
Lizard, Sand *(Lacerta agilis)*
Lizard, Viviparous *(Lacerta vivipara)**
Marten, Pine *(Martes martes)*
Moth, Barberry Carpet *(Pareulype berberata)*
Moth, Black-veined *(Siona lineata* or *Idaea lineata)*
Moth, Essex Emerald *(Thetidia smaragdaria)*
Moth, Fiery Clearwing *(Bembecia chrysidiformis)*
Moth, Fisher's Estuarine *(Gortyna borelii)*
Moth, New Forest Burnet *(Zygaena viciae)*
Moth, Reddish Buff *(Acosmetia caliginosa)*
Moth, Sussex Emerald *(Thalera fimbrialis)*
Mussel, Fan *(Atrina fragilis)**
Mussel, Freshwater Pearl *(Margaritifera margaritifera)*
Newt, Great Crested (or Warty) *(Triturus cristatus)*
Newt, Palmate *(Triturus helveticus)**
Newt, Smooth *(Triturus vulgaris)**
Otter, Common *(Lutra lutra)*
Porpoise, all species *(Cetacea)*
Sandworm, Lagoon *(Armandia cirrhosa)*
Sea Fan, Pink *(Eunicella verrucosa)**
Sea Slug, Lagoon *(Tenellia adspersa)*
Sea-mat, Trembling *(Victorella pavida)*
Seahorse, Short Snouted (England only) *(Hippocampus hippocampus)*
Seahorse, Spiny (England only) *(Hippocampus guttulatus)*
Shad, Twaite *(alosa fallax)**
Shark, Angel (England only) *(Squatina squatina)**
Shark, Basking *(Cetorhinus maximus)*
Shrimp, Fairy *(Chirocephalus diaphanus)*
Shrimp, Lagoon Sand *(Gammarus insensibilis)*
Shrimp, Tadpole *(Triops cancriformis)*
Slow-worm *(Anguis fragilis)**
Snail, Glutinous *(Myxas glutinosa)*
Snail, Roman (England only) *(Helix pomatia)**
Snail, Sandbowl *(Catinella arenaria)*
Snake, Grass *(Natrix natrix* or *Natrix helvetica)**
Snake, Smooth *(Coronella austriaca)*
Spider, Fen Raft *(Dolomedes plantarius)*
Spider, Ladybird *(Eresus niger)*
Squirrel, Red *(Sciurus vulgaris)*
Sturgeon *(Acipenser sturio)*
Toad, Common *(Bufo bufo)**
Toad, Natterjack *(Bufo calamita)*
Turtle, Marine, all species *(Dermochelyidae* and *Cheloniidae)*
Vendace *(Coregonus albula)*
Vole, Water *(Arvicola terrestris)*
Walrus *(Odobenus rosmarus)*
Whale, all species *(Cetacea)*
Whitefish *(Coregonus lavaretus)*

* These species are protected against some, but not all, of the activities listed under section 9 of the Wildlife and Countryside Act 1981

PLANTS PROTECTED BY SCHEDULE 8
Adder's Tongue, Least *(Ophioglossum lusitanicum)*
Alison, Small *(Alyssum alyssoides)*
Anomodon, Long-leaved *(Anomodon longifolius)*
Beech-lichen, New Forest *(Enterographa elaborata)*
Blackwort *(Southbya nigrella)*
Bluebell *(Hyacinthoides non-scripta)**
Bolete, Royal *(Boletus regius)*
Broomrape, Bedstraw *(Orobanche caryophyllacea)*
Broomrape, Oxtongue *(Orobanche loricata)*
Broomrape, Thistle *(Orobanche reticulata)*
Cabbage, Lundy *(Rhynchosinapis wrightii)*
Calamint, Wood *(Calamintha sylvatica)*
Caloplaca, Snow *(Caloplaca nivalis)*
Catapyrenium, Tree *(Catapyrenium psoromoides)*
Catchfly, Alpine *(Lychnis alpina)*
Catillaria, Laurer's *(Catellaria laureri)*
Centaury, Slender *(Centaurium tenuiflorum)*
Cinquefoil, Rock *(Potentilla rupestris)*
Cladonia, Convoluted *(Cladonia convoluta)*
Cladonia, Upright Mountain *(Cladonia stricta)*
Clary, Meadow *(Salvia pratensis)*
Club-rush, Triangular *(Scirpus triquetrus)*
Colt's-foot, Purple *(Homogyne alpina)*
Cotoneaster, Wild *(Cotoneaster integerrimus)*
Cottongrass, Slender *(Eriophorum gracile)*
Cow-wheat, Field *(Melampyrum arvense)*
Crocus, Sand *(Romulea columnae)*
Crystalwort, Lizard *(Riccia bifurca)*
Cudweed, Broad-leaved *(Filago pyramidata)*
Cudweed, Jersey *(Gnaphalium luteoalbum)*
Cudweed, Red-tipped *(Filago lutescens)*
Cut-grass *(Leersia oryzoides)*
Diapensia *(Diapensia lapponica)*
Dock, Shore *(Rumex rupestris)*
Earwort, Marsh *(Jamesoniella undulifolia)*
Eryngo, Field *(Eryngium campestre)*
Fern, Dickie's Bladder *(Cystopteris dickieana)*
Fern, Killarney *(Trichomanes speciosum)*
Flapwort, Norfolk *(Leiocolea rutheana)*
Fleabane, Alpine *(Erigeron borealis)*
Fleabane, Small *(Pulicaria vulgaris)*
Fleawort, South Stack *(Tephroseris integrifolia ssp maritima)*
Frostwort, Pointed *(Gymnomitrion apiculatum)*
Fungus, Hedgehog *(Hericium erinaceum)*
Galingale, Brown *(Cyperus fuscus)*
Gentian, Alpine *(Gentiana nivalis)*
Gentian, Dune *(Gentianella uliginosa)*
Gentian, Early *(Gentianella anglica)*
Gentian, Fringed *(Gentianella ciliata)*
Gentian, Spring *(Gentiana verna)*
Germander, Cut-leaved *(Teucrium botrys)*
Germander, Water *(Teucrium scordium)*
Gladiolus, Wild *(Gladiolus illyricus)*
Goblin Lights *(Catolechia wahlenbergii)*
Goosefoot, Stinking *(Chenopodium vulvaria)*
Grass-poly *(Lythrum hyssopifolia)*
Grimmia, Blunt-leaved *(Grimmia unicolor)*
Gyalecta, Elm *(Gyalecta ulmi)*
Hare's-ear, Sickle-leaved *(Bupleurum falcatum)*
Hare's-ear, Small *(Bupleurum baldense)*
Hawk's-beard, Stinking *(Crepis foetida)*
Hawkweed, Northroe *(Hieracium northroense)*
Hawkweed, Shetland *(Hieracium zetlandicum)*
Hawkweed, Weak-leaved *(Hieracium attenuatifolium)*
Heath, Blue *(Phyllodoce caerulea)*
Helleborine, Red *(Cephalanthera rubra)*
Helleborine, Young's *(Epipactis youngiana)*

Horsetail, Branched *(Equisetum ramosissimum)*
Hound's-tongue, Green *(Cynoglossum germanicum)*
Knawel, Perennial *(Scleranthus perennis)*
Knotgrass, Sea *(Polygonum maritimum)*
Lady's-slipper *(Cypripedium calceolus)*
Lecanactis, Churchyard *(Lecanactis hemisphaerica)*
Lecanora, Tarn *(Lecanora archariana)*
Lecidea, Copper *(Lecidea inops)*
Leek, Round-headed *(Allium sphaerocephalon)*
Lettuce, Least *(Lactuca saligna)*
Lichen, Arctic Kidney *(Nephroma arcticum)*
Lichen, Ciliate Strap *(Heterodermia leucomelos)*
Lichen, Coralloid Rosette *(Heterodermia propagulifera)*
Lichen, Ear-lobed Dog *(Peltigera lepidophora)*
Lichen, Forked Hair *(Bryoria furcellata)*
Lichen, Golden Hair *(Teloschistes flavicans)*
Lichen, Orange-fruited Elm *(Caloplaca luteoalba)*
Lichen, River Jelly *(Collema dichotomum)*
Lichen, Scaly Breck *(Squamarina lentigera)*
Lichen, Stary Breck *(Buellia asterella)*
Lily, Snowdon *(Lloydia serotina)*
Liverwort, Lindenberg's Leafy *(Adelanthus lindenbergianus)*
Marsh-mallow, Rough *(Althaea hirsuta)*
Marshwort, Creeping *(Apium repens)*
Milk-parsley, Cambridge *(Selinum carvifolia)*
Moss, Alpine Copper *(Mielichoferia mielichoferi)*
Moss, Baltic Bog *(Sphagnum balticum)*
Moss, Blue Dew *(Saelania glaucescens)*
Moss, Blunt-leaved Bristle *(Orthotrichum obtusifolium)*
Moss, Bright Green Cave *(Cyclodictyon laetevirens)*
Moss, Cordate Beard *(Barbula cordata)*
Moss, Cornish Path *(Ditrichum cornubicum)*
Moss, Derbyshire Feather *(Thamnobryum angustifolium)*
Moss, Dune Thread *(Bryum mamillatum)*
Moss, Flamingo *(Desmatodon cernuus)*
Moss, Glaucous Beard *(Barbula glauca)*
Moss, Green Shield *(Buxbaumia viridis)*
Moss, Hair Silk *(Plagiothecium piliferum)*
Moss, Knothole *(Zygodon forsteri)*
Moss, Large Yellow Feather *(Scorpidium turgescens)*
Moss, Millimetre *(Micromitrium tenerum)*
Moss, Multi-fruited River *(Cryphaea lamyana)*
Moss, Nowell's Limestone *(Zygodon gracilis)*
Moss, Polar Feather *(Hygrohypnum polare)*
Moss, Rigid Apple *(Bartramia stricta)*
Moss, Round-leaved Feather *(Rhyncostegium rotundifolium)*
Moss, Schleicher's Thread *(Bryum schleicheri)*
Moss, Slender Green Feather *(Drepanocladus vernicosus)*
Moss, Triangular Pygmy *(Acaulon triquetrum)*
Moss, Vaucher's Feather *(Hypnum vaucheri)*
Mudwort, Welsh *(Limosella austeralis)*
Naiad, Holly-leaved *(Najas marina)*
Naiad, Slender *(Najas flexilis)*
Orache, Stalked *(Halimione pedunculata)*
Orchid, Early Spider *(Ophrys sphegodes)*
Orchid, Fen *(Liparis loeselii)*
Orchid, Ghost *(Epipogium aphyllum)*
Orchid, Lapland Marsh *(Dactylorhiza lapponica)*
Orchid, Late Spider *(Ophrys fuciflora)*
Orchid, Lizard *(Himantoglossum hircinum)*
Orchid, Military *(Orchis militaris)*
Orchid, Monkey *(Orchis simia)*
Pannaria, Caledonia *(Panneria ignobilis)*
Parmelia, New Forest *(Parmelia minarum)*
Parmentaria, Oil Stain *(Parmentaria chilensis)*
Pear, Plymouth *(Pyrus cordata)*
Penny-cress, Perfoliate *(Thlaspi perfoliatum)*
Pennyroyal *(Mentha pulegium)*
Pertusaria, Alpine Moss *(Pertusaria bryontha)*
Petalwort *(Petallophyllum ralfsi)*
Physcia, Southern Grey *(Physcia tribacioides)*
Pigmyweed *(Crassula aquatica)*
Pine, Ground *(Ajuga chamaepitys)*
Pink, Cheddar *(Dianthus gratianopolitanus)*
Pink, Childing *(Petroraghia nanteuilii)*
Pink, Deptford (England and Wales only) *(Dianthus armeria)*
Polypore, Oak *(Buglossoporus pulvinus)*
Pseudocyphellaria, Ragged *(Pseudocyphellaria lacerata)*
Psora, Rusty Alpine *(Psora rubiformis)*
Puffball, Sandy Stilt *(Battarraea phalloides)*
Ragwort, Fen *(Senecio paludosus)*
Ramping-fumitory, Martin's *(Fumaria martinii)*
Rampion, Spiked *(Phyteuma spicatum)*
Restharrow, Small *(Ononis reclinata)*
Rock-cress, Alpine *(Arabis alpina)*
Rock-cress, Bristol *(Arabis stricta)*
Rustwort, Western *(Marsupella profunda)*
Sandwort, Norwegian *(Arenaria norvegica)*
Sandwort, Teesdale *(Minuartia stricta)*
Saxifrage, Drooping *(Saxifraga cernua)*
Saxifrage, Tufted *(Saxifraga cespitosa)*
Saxifrage, Yellow Marsh *(Saxifrage hirulus)*
Solenopsora, Serpentine *(Solenopsora liparina)*
Solomon's-seal, Whorled *(Polygonatum verticillatum)*
Sow-thistle, Alpine *(Cicerbita alpina)*
Spearwort, Adder's-tongue *(Ranunculus ophioglossifolius)*
Speedwell, Fingered *(Veronica triphyllos)*
Speedwell, Spiked *(Veronica spicata)*
Spike-rush, Dwarf *(Eleocharis parvula)*
Star-of-Bethlehem, Early *(Gagea bohemica)*
Starfruit *(Damasonium alisma)*
Stonewort, Bearded *(Chara canescens)*
Stonewort, Foxtail *(Lamprothamnium papulosum)*
Strapwort *(Corrigiola litoralis)*
Sulphur-tresses, Alpine *(Alectoria ochroleuca)*
Threadmoss, Long-leaved *(Bryum neodamense)*
Turpswort *(Geocalyx graveolens)*
Violet, Fen *(Viola persicifolia)*
Viper's-grass *(Scorzonera humilis)*
Water-plantain, Floating *(Luronium natans)*
Water-plantain, Ribbon-leaved *(Alisma gramineum)*
Wood-sedge, Starved *(Carex depauperata)*
Woodsia, Alpine *(Woodsia alpina)*
Woodsia, Oblong *(Woodsia ilvenis)*
Wormwood, Field *(Artemisia campestris)*
Woundwort, Downy *(Stachys germanica)*
Woundwort, Limestone *(Stachys alpina)*
Yellow-rattle, Greater *(Rhinanthus serotinus)*

* Protected against some, but not all, of the activities listed under section 13 of the Wildlife and Countryside Act 1981

THE YEAR IN REVIEW

Matthew Saunders

RECENT REFORM AND LEGISLATION

On 2 April 2008 the heritage protection bill was published. It heralded the most radical transformation in the legislation protecting historic buildings and sites in England and Wales since listing was first introduced in 1947.

The existing separation between listing (of buildings), scheduling (of archaeological sites) and registration (of historic gardens and battlefields) is to be abolished in favour of a single unified Heritage Register. They are to be called heritage assets, eligible for protection following identification of 'special historic, archaeological, architectural or artistic interest'. Virtually anything within reason could be on the register, whether an earthwork, a building, a garden, a cave, machinery or a vehicle, vessel or aircraft. The compilation would be entrusted to English Heritage in England and CADW (the Welsh history buildings agency) and the Welsh Assembly in Wales. Registration would be preceded by consultations and could be followed by an appeal. In order to preclude preemptive demolition, there would be procedures for interim protection while, to reduce the likelihood of a shock spot listing, Certificates of No Intention to Register would take the place of the present Certificates of Immunity from Listing.

Open spaces, such as historic parks and gardens, would continue to be protected informally but works of demolition, extension and alteration impinging on character would require heritage asset consent, which would be administered by the local planning authority. The planning authorities have to be seen to receive and take into account expert advice in respect of such applications although, in parallel with the provisions of the concurrent planning bill, there would be a new provision for internal reviews by councillors of decisions on heritage asset consent taken by officers.

For the first time, the bill also introduces public access to all publicly owned registered heritage structures 'where appropriate and practicable'. There is to be a new statutory duty on local planning authorities to create and maintain an historic environment record for their particular area (although in Wales it would be outsourced, probably to existing Welsh archaeological trusts). District councils would also be encouraged, but not obliged, to prepare inventories of locally listed buildings.

The existing ecclesiastical exemption – which provides for work on listed places of worship to be decided through the internal procedures of the Church of England, the Church in Wales, the Roman Catholic Church, the United Reformed Church, the Methodists and the Baptists – is to be widened to include the estimated 16,700 listed structures such as churchyard monuments, crosses, charnel houses, lychgates and boundary walls that exist in the grounds of church buildings. The novel concept of the heritage management agreement would provide a framework for the supervision of change in large complexes such as country house estates, hospitals and universities and should reduce bureaucratic pressure in those areas.

The government promised to introduce further clauses to the bill which would allow English Heritage and Welsh ministers to offer loans alongside grants and to tighten up control over total and partial demolition within conservation areas. The 1992 court case which permitted planning authorities to agree to development in conservation areas which did not actively harm them (as opposed to enhance) would be reversed. In an associated step, the planning bill abolished conservation area consent and merged it with the requirement to seek planning permission. The impact assessment, published at the same time as the bill, estimated the total cost of the reform at £6.52m with monetised benefits in return of £4.8m. The costs, including extra funding to local authorities, were estimated elsewhere at around £400,000 per annum, offset by the saving of eight civil service jobs. The annual cost in England of the appeals was put at £26,192. The bill, further explained on the English Heritage website, is expected to be implemented by 2010.

In 2007–8 other government moves were modest by comparison, particularly in a tight round for public spending. The comprehensive spending review of autumn 2007 found English Heritage a further £11m over three years bucking a recent history of budget cuts. In the equivalent period there was a further £100,000 for the Churches Conservation Trust, and the earlier promise to double the annual allocation to the National Heritage Memorial Fund to £10m was fulfilled. The government also pledged £45m for regeneration projects within historic coastal resorts.

THE PLIGHT OF LISTED CHURCHES

There are more Grade I-listed places of worship than any other type of building and there were important developments in 2007–8 in the protection and appreciation of churches, chapels and cathedrals. The National Churches Trust (NCT) became the new name for the Historic Churches Preservation Trust. The NCT multiplied its roles, giving as much stress to advocacy – raising the profile of the historic church – as its pre-existing function as the largest single provider of private grants towards repair. It also promises to create a national churches photographic archive and to promote county historic churches trusts, where they are either new or non-existent.

In a parallel move, December 2007 saw the launch of a new forum based within Heritage Link to highlight the plight of historic places of worship. The principal funders appear to be listening in that the Heritage Lottery Fund (HLF) and English Heritage pledged to carry forward their joint scheme offering grants to places of worship in use with an HLF budget for 2008–9 of £18m. The allocation for cathedrals seemed modest by comparison, the English Heritage joint scheme with the Wolfson Foundation spent just £2.1m in 2007–8 on 25 grants. The HLF can be much more bountiful. In 2007–8 grants of £4,012,000 went to Hereford Cathedral and £9,254,000 to York Minster. CADW became the first state agency to offer micro grants of up to £500 per building, to encourage maintenance and minor repair. Its 'Spring Clean' programme, launched in 2008 with a budget of

£80,000 was allocated within six weeks. In a similar vein, the Church Buildings Maintenance website in Scotland, launched in 2007, offered basic, and occasionally advanced, information on how to look after all manner of places of worship.

Unfortunately, there were devastating fires at the historic churches of Radford Semele and St Barnabas, Erdington, both in Warwickshire. Major churches such as the parish church in Brighton, St Peter's by Sir Charles Barry, were closed and others of equal importance (St John the Evangelist at Broughton in Salford, Greater Manchester) came close. The major complex by E. W. Pugin in Worcestershire, Stanbrook Abbey, was closed down and placed on the market. The Bishop of Worcester moved out of Hartlebury Castle in the same county where his predecessors had been in continual occupation since *c.*1260, leaving the future of this major historic building in doubt.

However, safe homes were found for several redundant churches. The Grade I listed medieval church at Kingston Buci, near Brighton, passed to the Churches Conservation Trust, as did St Leonard's at Linley in Shropshire, consecrated in 1138. Three churches (Penllech and Llanfihangel Rogiet in Wales and Llancillo in Herefordshire) passed to the Friends of Friendless Churches, whilst the Welsh Religious Buildings Trust, which deals with non-Anglican buildings, took into care the early 19th-century chapel at Llwynrhydowen in Ceredigion.

NEW FUNDING FOUND

The National Heritage Memorial Fund (NHMF), set up to rescue the pre-eminent for public collections, contributed £7m to the most spectacular saving of Dumfries House in Ayrshire. Its contribution was, however, dwarfed by that of £20m through the charities foundation of the Prince of Wales. The house, the work of the Adam Brothers, was expected to open to the public late in 2008 under the aegis of an independent trust. The NHMF also found a grant to guarantee public ownership of the collection of art dealer Anthony d'Offay. A grant of up to £1.95m from the same source helped to save Turner's *The Blue Rigi* for the Tate, while lesser sums guaranteed the version of the execution warrant of Mary Queen of Scots made for the Earl of Kent, and the important archive belonging to the former prime minister Henry Addington.

The HLF, which shares the same trustees as the NHMF but distributes the proceeds of the Lottery rather than taxpayers' money, launched its third strategic plan, for 2008–13, in the spring of 2008. At its height the HLF was able to distribute £330m a year. For 2008–9 its budget had been reduced to £220m a year with £180m per annum for the remainder of the five-year period. This is partially explained by the diversion of Lottery resources to pay for the 2012 Olympics. The highly influential chairmanship of Dame Liz Forgan came to an end in October 2008 when she was succeeded by Jenny Abramsky, CBE, formerly of the BBC.

HLF grants in 2007–8 were dominated by two ships. In May 2007 one of the world's most famous ships, the *Cutty Sark,* was gutted by fire halfway through a conservation campaign to which the HLF had already contributed £13m. Faced with such an icon in distress, HLF offered a further £10m. At the same meeting, an initial allocation of £19.1m was made to Henry VIII's great flagship, the *Mary Rose,* to rehouse it within a spectacular new building designed by Wilkinson Eyre. Other major grants offered in the year included to Clitheroe Castle, Lancashire (£1.8m); Agatha Christie's Greenway House, near Brixham in Devon (£800,000); Epping Forest (£4.7m); the creation of the first ever local museum at Barnsley, South Yorkshire (£2.6m); the Great Fen Project, Cambridgeshire (£8.9m) to allow the local Wildlife Trust to reclaim this last great expanse of fenland; the City Variety Music Hall, Leeds (£3m); Tudor House, Southampton (£3.5m); St James's Priory Church, Bristol (£3.2m); and the garden and house by Lutyens at Great Dixter in Sussex (£3.7m).

As a result of HLF grants a number of major sites and attractions opened or reopened in 2007–8, among them the Royal Festival Hall; the Museum at Wollaton Hall in Nottinghamshire; the John Rylands Library in Manchester; the International Slavery Gallery in Albert Dock, Liverpool; the London Transport Museum; Cusworth Hall, near Doncaster, now housing the Museum of South Yorkshire Life; England's oldest public park at Birkenhead on the Wirral; Birmingham Town Hall; Wentworth Castle, South Yorkshire; the Monastery of St Francis, Gorton in Manchester; the Royal Hall, Harrogate; Leeds City Museum based in the former Leeds Institute; the Darnley Mausoleum at Cobham in Kent; St Martin-in-the-Fields, Trafalgar Square; Hastings Museum; the new Visitor Centre at Cardiff Castle; Torre Abbey, Torquay in Devon; and the Bluecoat School, Liverpool.

Other new attractions unconnected with HLF included Port Eliot in Cornwall, a country house which opened to the public for the first time in 2008, and the reopening of the great Charles Barry gardens at Trentham in Staffordshire. Plans were announced for a new museum at Chichester and another in celebration of the Axminster Carpet in Devon.

However, the future looked bleak for other institutions. The Livesey Museum, dedicated to children in London's Old Kent Road, closed its doors, while a similar threat hovered over the Bass Museum on the history of malting in Burton-upon-Trent, and the Textile Conservation Centre at Southampton.

NEW INFORMATION RESOURCES

After several years in gestation, English Heritage published its *Conservation Principles: Policies and Guidance* in spring 2008, which attempted to set down for the first time its philosophical codes with the hope that this will be adopted by outside parties. The document laid down a 'family' of heritage values including the evidential, the historical, the aesthetic and the communal.

Two important websites – Images of England and the Listed Building System – were launched; access is through the Heritage Gateway website (W www.heritagegateway.org.uk). In the same year the Theatres Trust launched a new online learning resource, Exploring Theatres, offering the best collection hitherto on historic theatres.

HISTORIC BUILDINGS AND MONUMENTS

ENGLAND

Under the Planning (Listed Buildings and Conservation Areas) Act 1990, the Secretary of State for Culture, Media and Sport has a statutory duty to compile lists of buildings or groups of buildings in England which are of special architectural or historic interest. Under the Ancient Monuments and Archaeological Areas Act 1979 as amended by the National Heritage Act 1983, the secretary of state is also responsible for compiling a schedule of ancient monuments. Decisions are taken on the advice of English Heritage. On 1 April 2005 responsibility for the administration of the listing system was transferred from the secretary of state to English Heritage. This marked the start of a programme of changes designed to increase the involvement and awareness of the property owner and make the listing process more straightforward and more accountable.

LISTED BUILDINGS

Listed buildings are classified into Grade I, Grade II* and Grade II. There are currently around 373,200 individual listed buildings in England, of which approximately 92 per cent are Grade II listed. Almost all pre-1700 buildings are listed, as are most buildings of 1700 to 1840. English Heritage carries out thematic surveys of particular types of buildings with a view to making recommendations for listing, and members of the public may propose a building for consideration. The main purpose of listing is to ensure that care is taken in deciding the future of a building. No changes which affect the architectural or historic character of a listed building can be made without listed building consent (in addition to planning permission where relevant). Applications for listed building consent are normally dealt with by the local planning authority, although English Heritage is always consulted about proposals affecting Grade I and Grade II* properties. It is a criminal offence to demolish a listed building, or alter it in such a way as to affect its character, without consent.

SCHEDULED MONUMENTS

There are currently around 22,400 scheduled monuments in England. English Heritage is carrying out a Monuments Protection Programme assessing archaeological sites with a view to making recommendations for scheduling, and members of the public may propose a monument for consideration. All monuments proposed for scheduling are considered to be of national importance. Where buildings are both scheduled and listed, ancient monuments legislation takes precedence. The main purpose of scheduling a monument is to preserve it for the future and to protect it from damage, destruction or any unnecessary interference. Once a monument has been scheduled, scheduled monument consent is required before any works can be carried out. The scope of the control is more extensive and more detailed than that applied to listed buildings, but certain minor works, as detailed in the Ancient Monuments (Class Consents) Order 1994, may be carried out without consent. It is a criminal offence to carry out unauthorised work to scheduled monuments.

WALES

Under the Planning (Listed Buildings and Conservation Areas) Act 1990 and the Ancient Monuments and Archaeological Areas Act 1979, the National Assembly for Wales is responsible for listing buildings and scheduling monuments in Wales on the advice of Cadw (the Welsh Assembly's historic environment division), the Historic Buildings Advisory Council for Wales, the Ancient Monuments Advisory Board for Wales and the Royal Commission on the Ancient and Historical Monuments of Wales (RCAHMW). The criteria for evaluating buildings are similar to those in England and the same listing system is used. There are approximately 29,900 listed buildings and approximately 4,000 scheduled monuments in Wales.

SCOTLAND

Under the Planning (Listed Buildings and Conservation Areas) (Scotland) Act 1997 and the Ancient Monuments and Archaeological Areas Act 1979, Scottish ministers are responsible for listing buildings and scheduling monuments in Scotland on the advice of Historic Scotland, the Historic Environment Advisory Council for Scotland (HEACS) and the Royal Commission on the Ancient and Historical Monuments of Scotland (RCAHMS). The criteria for evaluating buildings are similar to those in England but an A, B, C(S) categorisation is used. There are approximately 47,000 listed buildings and 8,000 scheduled monuments in Scotland.

NORTHERN IRELAND

Under the Planning (Northern Ireland) Order 1991 and the Historic Monuments and Archaeological Objects (Northern Ireland) Order 1995, the Department of the Environment of the Northern Ireland Executive is responsible for listing buildings and scheduling monuments in Northern Ireland on the advice of the Environment and Heritage Service, the Historic Buildings Council for Northern Ireland and the Historic Monuments Council for Northern Ireland. The criteria for evaluating buildings are similar to those in England but an A, B+, B1 and B2 categorisation is used. There are approximately 8,200 listed buildings and 1,758 scheduled monuments in Northern Ireland.

ENGLAND

For more information on any of the English Heritage properties listed below, the official website is www.english-heritage.org.uk

For more information on any of the National Trust properties listed below, the official website is www.nationaltrust.org.uk

(EH) English Heritage property
(NT) National Trust property

A LA RONDE (NT), Exmouth, Devon EX8 5BD
T 01395-265514
Unique 16-sided house completed *c.*1796

ALNWICK CASTLE, Alnwick, Northumberland NE66 1NQ
T 01665-510777 W www.alnwickcastle.com
Seat of the Dukes of Northumberland since 1309; Italian Renaissance-style interior; gardens with spectacular water features

ALTHORP, Northants NN7 4HQ T 01604-770107
W www.althorp.com
Spencer family seat; Diana, Princess of Wales memorabilia

ANGLESEY ABBEY (NT), Lode, Cambs CB25 9EJ
T 01223-810080
House built *c.*1600; houses many paintings and a unique clock collection; gardens and Lode Mill

APSLEY HOUSE (EH), London W1J 7NT T 020-7499 5676
Built by Robert Adam 1771–8, home of the Dukes of Wellington since 1817 and known as 'No. 1 London'; collection of fine and decorative arts

ARUNDEL CASTLE, Arundel, W. Sussex BN18 9AB
T 01903-882173 W www.arundelcastle.org
Castle dating from the Norman Conquest; seat of the Dukes of Norfolk

AVEBURY (NT), Wilts SN8 1RF T 01672-539250
Remains of stone circles constructed 4,000 years ago surrounding the later village of Avebury

BANQUETING HOUSE, Whitehall, London SW1A 2ER
T 0844-482 7777 W www.hrp.org.uk
Designed by Inigo Jones; ceiling paintings by Rubens; site of the execution of Charles I

BASILDON PARK (NT), Reading, Berks RG8 9NR
T 0118-984 3040
Palladian mansion built in 1776–83 by John Carr

BATTLE ABBEY (EH), Battle, E. Sussex TN33 0AD
T 01424-775705
Remains of the abbey founded by William the Conqueror on the site of the Battle of Hastings

BEAULIEU, Brockenhurst, Hants SO42 7ZN T 01590-612345
W www.beaulieu.co.uk
House and gardens; Beaulieu Abbey and exhibition of monastic life; National Motor Museum

BEESTON CASTLE (EH), Cheshire CW6 9TX
T 01829-260464
13th-century inner ward with gatehouse and towers, and remains of outer ward built by Ranulf, sixth Earl of Chester

BELTON HOUSE (NT), Grantham, Lincs NG32 2LS
T 01476-566116
17th-century house; formal gardens in landscaped park

BELVOIR CASTLE, Grantham, Leics NG32 1PE
T 01476-871000 W www.belvoircastle.com
Seat of the Dukes of Rutland; 19th-century Gothic-style castle

BERKELEY CASTLE, Glos GL13 9BQ T 01453-810332
W www.berkeley-castle.com
Completed 1153; site of the murder of Edward II (1327)

BLENHEIM PALACE, Woodstock, Oxon OX20 1PX
T 0870-060 2080 W www.blenheimpalace.com
Seat of the Dukes of Marlborough and Winston Churchill's birthplace; designed by Vanbrugh

BLICKLING HALL (NT), Blickling, Norfolk NR11 6NF
T 01263-738030
Jacobean house with state rooms; temple and 18th-century orangery

BODIAM CASTLE (NT), Bodiam, E. Sussex TN32 5UA
T 01580-830196
Well-preserved medieval moated castle built in 1385

BOLSOVER CASTLE (EH), Bolsover, Derbys S44 6PR
T 01246-822844
17th-century buildings on site of medieval castle

BOSCOBEL HOUSE (EH), Bishops Wood, Shrops ST19 9AR T 01902-850244
Timber-framed 17th-century hunting lodge; refuge of fugitive Charles II

BOUGHTON HOUSE, Kettering, Northants NN14 1BJ
T 01536-515731 W www.boughtonhouse.org.uk
A 17th-century house with French-style additions; home of the Dukes of Buccleuch and Queensbury

BOWOOD HOUSE, Calne, Wilts SN11 0LZ
T 01249-812102 W www.bowood-house.co.uk
An 18th-century house in Capability Brown park, with lake, temple and arboretum

BROADLANDS, Romsey, Hants SO51 9ZD T 01794-505010
W www.broadlands.net
Palladian mansion in Capability Brown park; Mountbatten exhibition

BRONTË PARSONAGE, Haworth, W. Yorks BD22 8DR
T 01535-642323 W www.bronte.org.uk
Home of the Brontë sisters; museum and memorabilia

BUCKFAST ABBEY, Buckfastleigh, Devon TQ11 0EE
T 01364-645550 W www.buckfast.org.uk
Benedictine monastery on medieval foundations

BUCKINGHAM PALACE, London SW1A 1AA
T 020-7766 7300 W www.royal.gov.uk
Purchased by George III in 1761, and the Sovereign's official London residence since 1837; 18 state rooms, including the Throne Room, and Picture Gallery

BUCKLAND ABBEY (NT), Yelverton, Devon PL20 6EY
T 01822-853607
13th-century Cistercian monastery; home of Sir Francis Drake

BURGHLEY HOUSE, Stamford, Lincs PE9 3JY
T 01780-752451 W www.burghley.co.uk
Late Elizabethan house built by William Cecil, first Lord Burghley

CALKE ABBEY (NT), Ticknall, Derbys DE73 7LE
T 01332-863822
Baroque 18th-century mansion

CARISBROOKE CASTLE (EH), Newport, Isle of Wight PO30 1XY T 01983-522107
W www.carisbrookecastlemuseum.org.uk
Norman castle; museum; prison of Charles I 1647–8

CARLISLE CASTLE (EH), Carlisle, Cumbria CA3 8UR
T 01228-591922
Medieval castle; prison of Mary Queen of Scots

CARLYLE'S HOUSE (NT), Cheyne Row, London SW3 5HL
T 020-7352 7087
Home of Thomas Carlyle

CASTLE ACRE PRIORY (EH), Swaffham, Norfolk PE32 2XD T 01760-755394
Remains include 12th-century church and prior's lodgings

CASTLE DROGO (NT), Drewsteignton, Devon EX6 6PB
T 01647-433306
Granite castle designed by Lutyens
CASTLE HOWARD, N. Yorks YO60 7DA T 01653-648444
W www.castlehoward.co.uk
Designed by Vanbrugh 1699–1726; mausoleum designed by Hawksmoor
CASTLE RISING CASTLE (EH), King's Lynn, Norfolk PE31 6AH T 01553-631330
12th-century keep in a massive earthwork with gatehouse and bridge
CHARTWELL (NT), Westerham, Kent TN16 1PS
T 01732-868381
Home of Sir Winston Churchill
CHATSWORTH, Bakewell, Derbys DE45 1PP
T 01246-565300 W www.chatsworth.org
Tudor mansion in magnificent parkland
CHESTERS ROMAN FORT (EH), Chollerford, Northumberland NE46 4EU T 01434-681379
Roman cavalry fort built to guard Hadrian's Wall
CHYSAUSTER ANCIENT VILLAGE (EH), Penzance, Cornwall TR20 8XA T 07831-757934
Remains of Celtic settlement; eight stone-walled homesteads
CLIFFORD'S TOWER (EH), York YO1 9SA
T 01904-646940
13th-century tower built on a mound; remains of a castle built by William the Conqueror
CLIVEDEN (NT), Taplow, Berks SL6 0JA
T 01628-605069
Former home of the Astors, now a hotel set in garden and woodland
CORBRIDGE ROMAN SITE (EH), Corbridge, Northumberland NE45 5NT T 01434-632349
Excavated central area of a Roman town and successive military bases
CORFE CASTLE (NT), Wareham, Dorset BH20 5EZ
T 01929-481294
Ruined former royal castle dating from the 11th century
CROFT CASTLE (NT), Herefordshire HR6 9PW
T 01568-780246
Pre-Conquest border castle with Georgian-Gothic interior
DEAL CASTLE (EH), Deal, Kent CT41 7BA
T 01304-372762
Largest of the coastal defence forts built by Henry VIII
DICKENS HOUSE, Doughty Street, London WC1N 2LX
T 020-7405 2127 W www.dickensmuseum.com
House occupied by Dickens 1837–9; manuscripts, furniture and portraits
DOVE COTTAGE, Grasmere, Cumbria LA22 9SH
T 01539-435544 W www.wordsworth.org.uk
Wordsworth's home 1799–1808; museum
DOVER CASTLE (EH), Dover, Kent CT16 1HU
T 01304-211067
Castle with Roman, Saxon and Norman features; wartime operations rooms
DR JOHNSON'S HOUSE, Gough Square, London EC4A 3DE T 020-7353 3745 W www.drjohnsonshouse.org
Home of Samuel Johnson 1748–59
DUNSTANBURGH CASTLE (EH), Craster, nr Alnwick, Northumberland NE66 3TT T 01665-576231
14th-century castle ruins on a cliff with a substantial gatehouse-keep
ELTHAM PALACE (EH), Eltham, London SE9 5QE
T 020-8294 2548
Combines an Art Deco country house and remains of medieval palace set in moated gardens
FARLEIGH HUNGERFORD CASTLE (EH), Somerset BA2 7RS T 01225-754026
Late 14th-century castle with two courts; chapel with tomb of Sir Thomas Hungerford
FARNHAM CASTLE KEEP (EH), Farnham, Surrey GA9 0JA T 01252-713393
Large 12th-century castle keep with motte and bailey wall
FOUNTAINS ABBEY (NT), nr Ripon, N. Yorks HG4 3DY
T 01765-608888 W www.fountainsabbey.org.uk
Deer park; St Mary's Church; ruined Cistercian monastery; Georgian water garden
FRAMLINGHAM CASTLE (EH), Woodbridge, Suffolk IP13 9BP T 01728-724189
Castle (*c.*1200) with high curtain walls enclosing an almshouse (1639)
FURNESS ABBEY (EH), Barrow-in-Furness, Cumbria LA13 0PJ T 01229-823420
Remains of church and cloister buildings founded in 1123
GLASTONBURY ABBEY, Glastonbury, Somerset BA6 9EL T 01458-832267
W www.glastonburyabbey.com
Ruins of a 12th-century abbey rebuilt after fire; site of an early Christian settlement
GOODRICH CASTLE (EH), Ross-on-Wye, Herefordshire HR9 6HY T 01600-890538
Remains of 13th-century castle with 12th-century keep
GREENWICH, London SE10 9NF T 020-8858 4422
W www.rog.nmm.ac.uk
Former Royal Observatory (founded 1675) housing the time ball and zero meridian of longitude; the Queen's House, designed for Queen Anne, wife of James I, by Inigo Jones; Painted Hall and Chapel (Royal Naval College)
GRIMES GRAVES (EH), Brandon, Norfolk IP26 5DE
T 01842-810656
Neolithic flint mines; one shaft can be descended
GUILDHALL, London EC2P 2EJ T 020-7606 3030
W www.cityoflondon.gov.uk
Centre of civic government of the City built *c.*1441; facade built 1788–9
HADDON HALL, Bakewell, Derbys DE45 1LA
T 01629-812855 W www.haddonhall.co.uk
Well-preserved 12th-century manor house
HAILES ABBEY (EH), Cheltenham, Glos GL54 5PB
T 01242-602398
Ruins of a 13th-century Cistercian monastery
HAM HOUSE (NT), Richmond-upon-Thames, Surrey TW10 7RS T 020-8940 1950
Stuart house with lavish interiors and formal gardens
HAMPTON COURT PALACE, East Molesey, Surrey KT8 9AU T 0844-482 7777 W www.hrp.org.uk
16th-century palace with additions by Wren; gardens with maze; Tudor tennis court
HARDWICK HALL (NT), Chesterfield, Derbys S44 5QJ
T 01246-850430
Built 1591–7 for Bess of Hardwick
HARDY'S COTTAGE (NT), Higher Bockhampton, Dorset DT2 8QJ T 01297-561900
Birthplace and home of Thomas Hardy
HAREWOOD HOUSE, Harewood, W. Yorks LS17 9LG
T 0113-218 1010 W www.harewood.org
18th-century house designed by John Carr and Robert Adam; park by Capability Brown

HATFIELD HOUSE, Hatfield, Herts AL9 5NQ
T 01707-287010 W www.hatfield-house.co.uk
Jacobean house built by Robert Cecil; surviving wing of Royal Palace of Hatfield (*c.*1485)

HELMSLEY CASTLE (EH), Helmsley, N. Yorks YO62 5AB
T 01439-770442
12th-century keep and curtain wall with 16th-century buildings; spectacular earthwork defences

HEVER CASTLE, nr Edenbridge, Kent TN8 7NG
T 01732-865224 W www.hever-castle.co.uk
13th-century double-moated castle; childhood home of Anne Boleyn

HOLKER HALL, Cumbria LA11 7PL T 01539-558328
W www.holker-hall.co.uk
Former home of the Dukes of Devonshire; award-winning gardens

HOLKHAM HALL, Wells-next-the-Sea, Norfolk NR23 1AB
T 01328-710227 W www.holkham.co.uk
Palladian mansion; notable fine art collection

HOUSESTEADS ROMAN FORT (EH), Hexham, Northumberland NE47 6NN T 01434-344363
Excavated infantry fort on Hadrian's Wall with museum

HUGHENDEN MANOR (NT), High Wycombe, Bucks HP14 4LA T 01494-755573
Home of Disraeli; small formal garden

JANE AUSTEN'S HOUSE, Chawton, Hants GU34 1SD T 01420-83262
W www.jane-austens-house-museum.org.uk
Jane Austen's home from 1809 to 1817

KEDLESTON HALL (NT), Derbys DE22 5JH
T 01332-842191
Classical Palladian mansion built 1759–65; complete Robert Adam interiors

KELMSCOTT MANOR, nr Lechlade, Glos GL7 3HJ
T 01367-252486 W www.kelmscottmanor.org.uk
Summer home of William Morris, with products of Morris and Co.

KENILWORTH CASTLE (EH), Kenilworth, Warks CV8 1NE
T 01926-864152
Largest castle ruin in England

KENSINGTON PALACE, Kensington Gardens, London W8 4PX T 0870-751 5170 W www.hrp.org.uk
Built in 1605 and enlarged by Wren; birthplace of Queen Victoria; Royal Ceremonial Dress Collection

KENWOOD HOUSE (EH), Hampstead Lane, London NW3 7JR T 020-8348 1286
Adam villa housing the Iveagh bequest of paintings and furniture

KEW PALACE, Richmond-upon-Thames, Surrey TW9 3AB
T 0870-751 5179 W www.hrp.org.uk
Includes Queen Charlotte's Cottage, used by King George III and family as a summerhouse

KINGSTON LACY (NT), Wimborne Minster, Dorset BH21 4EA T 01202-883402
17th-century house with 19th-century alterations; important art collection

KNEBWORTH HOUSE, Knebworth, Herts SG3 6PY
T 01438-812661 W www.knebworthhouse.com
Tudor manor house concealed by 19th-century Gothic decoration; Lutyens gardens

KNOLE (NT), Sevenoaks, Kent TN15 0RP T 01732-462100
House dating from 1456 set in parkland; fine art collection; birthplace of Vita Sackville-West

LAMBETH PALACE, London SE1 7JU T 020-7898 1200
W www.archbishopofcanterbury.org
Official residence of the Archbishop of Canterbury; partly dating from the 12th century

LANERCOST PRIORY (EH), Brampton, Cumbria CA8 2HQ T 01697-73030
The nave of the Augustinian priory church, *c.*1166, is still used; remains of other claustral buildings

LANHYDROCK (NT), Bodmin, Cornwall PL30 5AD
T 01208-265950
House dating from the 17th century; 50 rooms, including kitchen and nursery

LEEDS CASTLE, nr Maidstone, Kent ME17 1PL
T 01622-765400 W www.leeds-castle.com
Castle dating from 9th century, on two islands in lake

LEVENS HALL, Kendal, Cumbria LA8 0PD T 01539-560321
W www.levenshall.co.uk
Elizabethan house with unique topiary garden (1694); steam engine collection

LINCOLN CASTLE, Lincoln, Lincs LN1 3AA
T 01522-511068 W www.lincolnshire.gov.uk
Built by William the Conqueror in 1068

LINDISFARNE PRIORY (EH), Holy Island, Northumberland TD15 2RX T 01289-389200
Founded in AD 635; re-established in the 12th century as a Benedictine priory, now ruined

LITTLE MORETON HALL (NT), Congleton, Cheshire CW12 4SD T 01260-272018
Timber-framed moated Tudor manor house with knot garden

LONGLEAT HOUSE, Warminster, Wilts BA12 7NW
T 01985-844400 W www.longleat.co.uk
Elizabethan house in Italian Renaissance style; safari park

LULLINGSTONE ROMAN VILLA (EH), Eynsford, Kent DA4 0JA T 01322-863467
Large villa occupied for much of the Roman period; fine mosaics

MANSION HOUSE, London EC4N 8BH
W www.cityoflondon.gov.uk
The official residence of the Lord Mayor of London

MARBLE HILL HOUSE (EH), Twickenham, Middx TW1 2NL T 020-8892 5115
English Palladian villa with Georgian paintings and furniture

MICHELHAM PRIORY, Hailsham, E. Sussex BN27 3QS
T 01323-844224 W www.sussexpast.co.uk
Tudor house built onto an Augustinian priory

MIDDLEHAM CASTLE (EH), Leyburn, N. Yorks DL8 4QJ
T 01969-623899
12th-century keep within later fortifications; childhood home of Richard III

MONTACUTE HOUSE (NT), Montacute, Somerset TA15 6XP T 01935-823289
Elizabethan house with National Portrait Gallery collection of portraits from the period

MOUNT GRACE PRIORY (EH), Northallerton, N. Yorks DL6 3JG T 01609-883494
Carthusian priory with remains of monastic buildings

NETLEY ABBEY (EH), Hants T 02392-378291
Remains of Cistercian abbey; used as house in Tudor period

OLD SARUM (EH), Salisbury, Wilts SP1 3SD
T 01722-335398
Earthworks enclosing remains of Norman castle and cathedral

ORFORD CASTLE (EH), Orford, Suffolk IP12 2ND
T 01394-450472
Circular keep of *c.*1170 and remains of coastal defence castle built by Henry II

OSBORNE HOUSE (EH), East Cowes, Isle of Wight PO32 6JX T 01983-200022
Queen Victoria's seaside residence
OSTERLEY PARK (NT), Isleworth, Middx TW7 4RB T 020-8232 5050 W www.osterleypark.org.uk
Elizabethan mansion set in parkland
PENDENNIS CASTLE (EH), Falmouth, Cornwall TR11 4LP T 01326-316594
Well-preserved 16th-century coastal defence castle
PENSHURST PLACE, Penshurst, Kent TN11 8DG T 01892-870307 W www.penshurstplace.com
House with medieval Baron's Hall and 14th-century gardens
PETWORTH HOUSE (NT), Petworth, W. Sussex GU28 0AE T 01798-342207
Late 17th-century house set in Capability Brown landscaped deer park
PEVENSEY CASTLE (EH), Pevensey, E. Sussex BN24 5LE T 01323-762604
Walls of a 4th-century Roman fort; remains of an 11th-century castle
PEVERIL CASTLE (EH), Castleton, Derbys S33 8WQ T 01433-620613
12th-century castle defended on two sides by precipitous rocks
POLESDEN LACEY (NT), nr Dorking, Surrey RH5 6BD T 01372-452048
Regency villa remodelled in the Edwardian era; fine paintings and furnishings
PORTCHESTER CASTLE (EH), Portchester, Hants PO16 9QW T 02392-378291
Walls of a late Roman fort enclosing a Norman keep and an Augustinian priory church
POWDERHAM CASTLE, Kenton, Devon EX6 8JQ T 01626-890243 W www.powderham.co.uk
Medieval castle with 18th- and 19th-century alterations; historic home of the Earl of Devon
RABY CASTLE, Staindrop, Co. Durham DL2 3AH T 01833-660202 W www.rabycastle.com
14th-century castle with walled gardens
RAGLEY HALL, Alcester, Warks B49 5NJ T 01789-762090 W www.ragleyhall.com
17th-century house with gardens, park and lake
RICHBOROUGH ROMAN FORT (EH), Richborough, Kent CT13 9JW T 01304-612013
Landing-site of the Claudian invasion in AD 43
RICHMOND CASTLE (EH), Richmond, N. Yorks DL10 4QW T 01748-822493
12th-century keep with 11th-century curtain wall
RIEVAULX ABBEY (EH), nr Helmsley, N. Yorks YO62 5LB T 01439-798228
Remains of a Cistercian abbey founded *c.*1132
ROCHESTER CASTLE (EH), Rochester, Kent ME1 1SW T 01634-402276
11th-century castle partly on the Roman city wall, with a square keep of *c.*1130
ROCKINGHAM CASTLE, Market Harborough, Leics LE16 8TH T 01536-770240 W www.rockinghamcastle.com
Built by William the Conqueror
ROYAL PAVILION, Brighton BN1 1EE T 01273-290900 W www.royalpavilion.org.uk
Palace of George IV, in Chinese style with Indian exterior and Regency gardens
RUFFORD OLD HALL (NT), nr Ormskirk, Lancs L40 1SG T 01704-821254
16th-century hall with unique screen
ST AUGUSTINE'S ABBEY (EH), Canterbury, Kent CT1 1TF T 01227-767345
Remains of Benedictine monastery founded AD 597
ST MAWES CASTLE (EH), St Mawes, Cornwall TR2 3AA T 01326-270526
Coastal defence castle built by Henry VIII
ST MICHAEL'S MOUNT (NT), Cornwall TR17 0HS T 01736-710507
12th-century castle with later additions, off the coast at Marazion
SANDRINGHAM, Norfolk PE35 6EN T 01553-612908 W www.sandringhamestate.co.uk
The Queen's private residence; a neo-Jacobean house built in 1870
SCARBOROUGH CASTLE (EH), Scarborough, N. Yorks YO11 1HY T 01723-372451
Remains of 12th-century keep and curtain walls
SHERBORNE CASTLE, Sherborne, Dorset DT9 3PY T 01935-813182 W www.sherbornecastle.com
16th-century castle built by Sir Walter Raleigh set in landscaped gardens
SHUGBOROUGH ESTATE (NT), Milford, Staffs ST17 0XB T 01889-881388
House set in 18th-century park with monuments, temples and pavilions in the Greek Revival style; arboretum; seat of the Earls of Lichfield
SKIPTON CASTLE, Skipton, N. Yorks BD23 1AW T 01756-792442 W www.skiptoncastle.co.uk
D-shaped castle, six round towers and inner courtyard
SMALLHYTHE PLACE (NT), Tenterden, Kent TN30 7NG T 01580-762334
Half-timbered 16th-century house; home of Ellen Terry 1899–1928; the Barn Theatre
STANFORD HALL, Lutterworth, Leics LE17 6DH T 01788-860250 W www.stanfordhall.co.uk
William and Mary house with Stuart portraits; motorcycle museum
STONEHENGE (EH), nr Amesbury, Wilts SP4 7DE T 0870-333 1181
Prehistoric monument consisting of concentric stone circles surrounded by a ditch and bank
STONOR PARK, Henley-on-Thames, Oxon RG9 6HF T 01491-638587 W www.stonor.com
Medieval house with Georgian facade; centre of Roman Catholicism after the Reformation
STOURHEAD (NT), Stourton, Wilts BA12 6QD T 01747-841152
English 18th-century Palladian mansion with famous gardens
STRATFIELD SAYE HOUSE, Hants RG7 2BZ T 01256-882882 W www.stratfield-saye.co.uk
House built 1630–40; home of the Dukes of Wellington since 1817
STRATFORD-UPON-AVON, Warks T 01789-204016 W www.shakespeare.org.uk
Shakespeare's Birthplace Trust with Shakespeare Centre; Anne Hathaway's Cottage, home of Shakespeare's wife; Mary Arden's House, home of Shakespeare's mother; grammar school attended by Shakespeare; Holy Trinity Church, where Shakespeare is buried; Royal Shakespeare Theatre (burnt down 1926, rebuilt 1932) and Swan Theatre (opened 1986)
SUDELEY CASTLE, Winchcombe, Glos GL54 5JD T 01242-602308 W www.sudeleycastle.co.uk
Castle built in 1442; restored in the 19th century
SULGRAVE MANOR, nr Banbury, Oxon OX17 2SD T 01295-760205 W www.sulgravemanor.org.uk
Home of George Washington's family

SYON HOUSE, Brentford, Middx TW8 8JF T 020-8560 0881 W www.syonpark.co.uk
Built on the site of a former monastery; Adam interior; Capability Brown park

TILBURY FORT (EH), Tilbury, Essex RM18 7NR T 01375-858489
17th-century coastal fort

TINTAGEL CASTLE (EH), Tintagel, Cornwall PL34 0HE T 01840-770328
13th-century cliff-top castle and Dark Age settlement site; linked with Arthurian legend

TOWER OF LONDON, London EC3N 4AB T 0870-756 6060 W www.hrp.org.uk
Royal palace and fortress begun by William the Conqueror in 1078; houses the Crown Jewels

TRERICE (NT), nr Newquay, Cornwall TR8 4PG T 01637-875404
Elizabethan manor house

TYNEMOUTH PRIORY AND CASTLE (EH), Tyne and Wear NE30 4BZ T 0191-257 1090
Remains of a Benedictine priory, founded *c.*1090, on Saxon monastic site

UPPARK (NT), South Harting, W. Sussex GU31 5QR T 01730-825415
Late 17th-century house, completely restored after fire; Fetherstonhaugh art collection

WALMER CASTLE (EH), Walmer, Kent CT14 7LJ T 01304-364288
One of Henry VIII's coastal defence castles, now the residence of the Lord Warden of the Cinque Ports

WALTHAM ABBEY (EH), Waltham Abbey, Essex EN9 1DJ T 01992-702200
Ruined abbey including 14th-century gatehouse and bridge, refounded by Harold II

WARKWORTH CASTLE (EH), Warkworth, Northumberland NE65 0UJ T 01665-711423
14th-century keep amidst earlier ruins, with hermitage upstream

WARWICK CASTLE, Warwick, Warks CV34 4QU T 0870-442 2000 W www.warwick-castle.co.uk
Medieval castle with Madame Tussaud's waxworks, in Capability Brown park

WHITBY ABBEY (EH), Whitby, N. Yorks YO22 4JT T 01947-603568
Remains of Norman church on the site of a monastery founded in AD 657

WILTON HOUSE, nr Salisbury, Wilts SP2 0BJ T 01722-746714 W www.wiltonhouse.co.uk
17th-century house on the site of a Tudor house and ninth-century nunnery

WINDSOR CASTLE, Windsor, Berks SL4 1NJ T 020-7766 7304 W www.royal.gov.uk
Official residence of the Queen; oldest royal residence still in regular use; largest inhabited castle in the world. Also St George's Chapel

WOBURN ABBEY, Woburn, Beds MK17 9WA T 01525-290333 W www.woburnabbey.co.uk
Built on the site of a Cistercian abbey; seat of the Dukes of Bedford; important art collection; antiques centre

WROXETER ROMAN CITY (EH), nr Shrewsbury, Shropshire SY5 6PH T 01743-761330
Second-century public baths and part of the forum of the Roman town of Viroconium

WALES

For more information on any of the Cadw properties listed below, the official website is www.cadw.wales.gov.uk

For more information on any of the National Trust properties listed below, the official website is www.nationaltrust.org.uk

(C) Property of Cadw: Welsh Historic Monuments
(NT) National Trust property

BEAUMARIS CASTLE (C), Anglesey LL58 8AP T 01248-810361
Concentrically planned castle, still virtually intact

CAERLEON ROMAN BATHS AND AMPHITHEATRE (C), Newport NP18 1AE T 01633-422518
Rare example of a legionary bath-house and late first-century arena surrounded by bank for spectators

CAERNARFON CASTLE (C), Gwynedd LL55 2AY T 01286-677617 W www.caernarfon.com
Castle built between 1283 and 1330, initially for King Edward I of England; setting for the investiture of Prince Charles in 1969

CAERPHILLY CASTLE (C), Caerphilly CF83 1JD T 029-2088 3143
Concentrically-planned castle (*c.*1270) notable for its scale and use of water defences

CARDIFF CASTLE, Cardiff CF10 3RB T 029-2087 8100 W www.cardiffcastle.com
Castle built on the site of a Roman fort; spectacular towers and rich interior

CASTELL COCH (C), Tongwynlais, Cardiff CF15 7JS T 029-2081 0101
'Fairytale castle' rebuilt 1875–90 on medieval foundations

CHEPSTOW CASTLE (C), Monmouthshire NP16 5EZ T 01291-624065
Rectangular keep amid extensive fortifications; developed throughout the Middle Ages

CONWY CASTLE (C), Gwynedd LL32 8AY T 01492-592358
Built for Edward I, 1283–7, on a narrow rocky outcrop

CRICCIETH CASTLE (C), Gwynedd LL55 0DP T 01766-522227
Native Welsh 13th-century castle, altered by Edward I and Edward II

DENBIGH CASTLE (C), Denbighshire LL16 3NB T 01745-813385
Remains of the castle (begun 1282), including triple-towered gatehouse

HARLECH CASTLE (C), Gwynedd LL46 2YH T 01766-780552
Well-preserved Edwardian castle, constructed 1283–90, on an outcrop above the former shoreline

PEMBROKE CASTLE, Dyfed SA71 4LA T 01646-684585 W www.pembrokecastle.co.uk
Castle founded in 1093; Great Tower built in the late 12th century; birthplace of King Henry VII

PENRHYN CASTLE (NT), Bangor, Gwynedd LL57 4HN T 01248-353084
Neo-Norman castle built in the 19th-century; railway museum; private art collection

PORTMEIRION, Gwynedd LL48 6ER T 01766-770228 W www.portmeirion-village.com
Village in Italianate style built by Clough Williams-Ellis

POWIS CASTLE (NT), Welshpool, Powys SY21 8RF T 01938-551929
Medieval castle with interior in variety of styles; 17th-century gardens; Clive of India museum

RAGLAN CASTLE (C), Monmouthshire NP15 2BT T 01291-690228
Remains of 15th-century castle with moated hexagonal keep

ST DAVIDS BISHOP'S PALACE (C), Dyfed SA62 6PE T 01437-720517
Remains of residence of Bishops of St Davids built 1328–47

TINTERN ABBEY (C), nr Chepstow, Monmouthshire NP16 6SE T 01291-689251
Remains of 13th-century church and conventual buildings of a 12th-century Cistercian monastery

TRETOWER COURT AND CASTLE (C), nr Crickhowell, Powys NP8 1RF T 01874-730279
Medieval house rebuilt in the 15th century, with remains of 12th-century castle nearby

SCOTLAND

For more information on any of the Historic Scotland properties listed below, the official website is www.historic-scotland.gov.uk

For more information on any of the National Trust for Scotland properties listed below, the official website is www.nts.org.uk

(HS) Historic Scotland property
(NTS) National Trust for Scotland property

ABBOTSFORD HOUSE, Melrose, Roxburghshire TD6 9BQ T 01896-752043 W www.scottsabbotsford.co.uk
Home of Sir Walter Scott

ANTONINE WALL, between the Clyde and the Forth
Built around AD 142; consists of ditch, turf rampart, road and forts at regular intervals

BALMORAL CASTLE, Ballater, Aberdeenshire AB35 5TB T 01339-742534 W www.balmoralcastle.com
Baronial-style castle built for Victoria and Albert; the Queen's private residence

BLACK HOUSE, ARNOL (HS), Lewis, Western Isles HS2 9DB T 01851-710395
Traditional Lewis thatched house

BLAIR CASTLE, Blair Atholl, Perthshire PH18 5TL T 01796-481207 W www.blair-castle.co.uk
Mid-18th-century mansion with 13th-century tower; seat of the Dukes and Earls of Atholl

BONAWE IRON FURNACE (HS), Taynuilt, Argyll PA35 1JQ T 01866-822432
Charcoal-fuelled ironworks founded in 1753

BOWHILL, Selkirkshire TD7 5ET T 01750-22204
Seat of the Dukes of Buccleuch and Queensberry; fine collection of paintings, including portrait miniatures

BROUGH OF BIRSAY (HS), Orkney KW17 2NH T 01856-721205
Remains of Norse and Pictish village on the tidal island of Birsay

CAERLAVEROCK CASTLE (HS), Glencaple, Dumfriesshire DG1 4RU T 01387-770244
Triangular 13th-century castle with classical Renaissance additions

CAIRNPAPPLE HILL (HS), Torphichen, West Lothian T 01506-634622
Neolithic and Bronze Age ceremonial site and burial chambers

CALANAIS STANDING STONES (HS), Lewis, Western Isles HS2 9DY T 01851-621422
Standing stones in a cross-shaped setting, dating from *c.* 3000 BC

CATERTHUNS (BROWN AND WHITE) (HS), Menmuir, nr Brechin, Angus T 0131-668 8800
Two large Iron Age hill forts

CAWDOR CASTLE, Nairn, Moray IV12 5RD T 01667-404401 W www.cawdorcastle.com
14th-century keep with 15th- and 17th-century additions

CLAVA CAIRNS (HS), nr Inverness, Inverness-shire T 01667-460232
Bronze Age cemetery complex of cairns and standing stones

CRATHES CASTLE (NTS), nr Banchory, Aberdeenshire AB31 5QJ T 08444-932166
16th-century baronial castle in woodland, fields and gardens

CULZEAN CASTLE (NTS), Maybole, Ayrshire KA19 8LE T 08444-932149 W www.culzeanexperience.org
18th-century Adam castle with oval staircase and circular saloon

DRYBURGH ABBEY (HS), nr Melrose, Roxburghshire TD6 0RQ T 01835-822381
12th-century abbey containing tomb of Sir Walter Scott

DUNVEGAN CASTLE, Skye IV55 8WF T 01470-521206 W www.dunvegancastle.com
13th-century castle with later additions; home of the chiefs of the Clan MacLeod; trips to seal colony

EDINBURGH CASTLE (HS) EH1 2NG T 0131-225 9846
Includes the Scottish Crown Jewels, Scottish National War Memorial, Scottish United Services Museum and historic apartments

EDZELL CASTLE (HS), nr Brechin, Angus DD9 7UE T 01356-648631
16th-century tower house on medieval foundations; walled garden

EILEAN DONAN CASTLE, Dornie, Ross and Cromarty IV40 8DX T 01599-555202 W www.eileandonancastle.com
13th-century castle with Jacobite relics at the meeting point of three sea lochs

ELGIN CATHEDRAL (HS), Moray IV30 1EL T 01343-547171
13th-century cathedral and chapterhouse

FLOORS CASTLE, Kelso, Roxburghshire TD5 7SF T 01573-223333 W www.floorscastle.com
Largest inhabited castle in Scotland; seat of the Dukes of Roxburghe; built 1721 by William Adam

FORT GEORGE (HS), Ardersier, Inverness-shire IV2 7TD T 01667-460232
18th-century fort, still a working army barracks

GLAMIS CASTLE, Forfar, Angus DD8 1RJ T 01307-840393 W www.glamis-castle.co.uk
Seat of the Lyon family (later Earls of Strathmore and Kinghorne) since 1372

GLASGOW CATHEDRAL (HS), Lanarkshire G4 0QZ T 0141-552 6891 W www.glasgowcathedral.org.uk
Medieval cathedral with elaborately vaulted crypt

GLENELG BROCHS (HS), Shielbridge, Ross and Cromarty T 01667-460232
Two broch towers (Dun Telve and Dun Troddan) with well-preserved structural features

HOPETOUN HOUSE, South Queensferry, W. Lothian EH30 9SL T 0131-331 2451 W www.hopetounhouse.com
House designed by Sir William Bruce, enlarged by William Adam, built 1699

HUNTLY CASTLE (HS), Aberdeenshire AB54 4SH T 01466-793191
Ruin of a 16th- and 17th-century baronial residence

INVERARAY CASTLE, Argyll PA32 8XE T 01499-302203
W www.inveraray-castle.com
Gothic-style 18th-century castle; seat of the Dukes of Argyll

IONA ABBEY (HS), Iona, Inner Hebrides PA76 6SQ
T 01681-700512
Monastery founded by St Columba in AD 563

JARLSHOF (HS), Sumburgh Head, Shetland ZE3 9JN
T 01950-460112
Prehistoric and Norse settlement

JEDBURGH ABBEY (HS), Scottish Borders TD8 6JQ
T 01835-863925
Romanesque and early Gothic church founded *c.*1138

KELSO ABBEY (HS), Kelso, Scottish Borders TD5 7JD
Remains of great abbey church founded 1128

KISIMUL CASTLE (HS), Castlebay, Barra, Western Isles
T 01871-810313
Medieval home of the Clan MacNeil

LINLITHGOW PALACE (HS), Kirkgate, Linlithgow, W. Lothian EH49 7AL T 01506-842896
Ruin of royal palace in park setting; birthplace of James V and Mary, Queen of Scots

MAES HOWE (HS), Stenness, Orkney KW16 3HA
T 01856-761606
Neolithic chambered tomb

MEIGLE SCULPTURED STONES (HS), Meigle, Perthshire PH12 8SB T 01828-640612
Twenty-six carved stones dating from the 8th to the 10th centuries

MELROSE ABBEY (HS), Melrose, Roxburghshire TD6 9LG
T 01896-822562
Ruin of Cistercian abbey founded *c.*1136 by David I

MOUSA BROCH (HS), Island of Mousa, Shetland
T 01856-841815
Finest surviving Iron Age broch tower

NEW ABBEY CORN MILL (HS), Dumfriesshire DG2 8BX
T 01387-850260
Working water-powered mill; operates in summer months

PALACE OF HOLYROODHOUSE, Edinburgh EH8 8DX
T 0131-556 5100 W www.royal.gov.uk
The Queen's official Scottish residence; main part of the palace built 1671–9

RING O' BRODGAR (HS), nr Stromness, Orkney
T 01856-841815
Neolithic circle of upright stones with an enclosing ditch

ROSSLYN CHAPEL, Roslin, Midlothian EH25 9PU
T 0131-440 2159 W www.rosslynchapel.org.uk
Historic church with unique stone carvings

RUTHWELL CROSS (HS), Ruthwell, Dumfriesshire
T 01387-870249
Seventh-century Anglian cross

ST ANDREWS CASTLE AND CATHEDRAL (HS), Fife KY16 9QL T 01334-477196 (castle); 01334-472563 (cathedral)
Ruins of 13th-century castle and remains of the largest cathedral in Scotland

SCONE PALACE, Perth, Perthshire PH2 6BD
T 01738-552300 W www.scone-palace.net
House built 1802–13 on the site of a medieval palace

SKARA BRAE (HS), nr Stromness, Orkney KW16 3LR
T 01856-841815
Stone Age village with adjacent replica house

SMAILHOLM TOWER (HS), nr Kelso, Roxburghshire TD5 7PG T 01573-460365
Well-preserved 15th-century tower-house

STIRLING CASTLE (HS), Stirlingshire FK8 1EJ
T 01786-450000
Great Hall and gatehouse of James IV, palace of James V, Chapel Royal remodelled by James VI

TANTALLON CASTLE (HS), North Berwick, E. Lothian EH39 5PN T 01620-892727
Fortification with earthwork defences; and a 14th-century curtain wall with towers

THREAVE CASTLE (HS), Castle Douglas, Kirkcudbrightshire T 07711-223101
Late 14th-century tower on an island; accessible only by boat

URQUHART CASTLE (HS), Drumnadrochit, Inverness-shire IV63 6XJ T 01456-450551
13th-century castle remains on the banks of Loch Ness

NORTHERN IRELAND

For the Northern Ireland Environment and Heritage Service, the official website is www.ehsni.gov.uk

For more information on any of the National Trust properties listed below, the official website is www.nationaltrust.org.uk

(EHS) Property in the care of the Northern Ireland Environment and Heritage Service
(NT) National Trust property

CARRICKFERGUS CASTLE (EHS), Carrickfergus, Co. Antrim BT38 7BG T 028-9335 1273
Castle begun in 1180 and garrisoned until 1928

CASTLE COOLE (NT), Enniskillen, Co. Fermanagh BT74 6JY T 028-6632 2690
18th-century mansion by James Wyatt in parkland

CASTLE WARD (NT), Strangford, Co. Down BT30 7LS
T 028-4488 1204
18th-century house with Classical and Gothic facades

DEVENISH ISLAND (EHS), nr Enniskillen, Co. Fermanagh T 028-9054 6518
Island monastery founded in the sixth century by St Molaise

DOWNHILL DEMESNE (NT), Castlerock, Co. Londonderry BT51 4RP T 028-2073 1582
Ruins of palatial house in landscaped estate including Mussenden Temple

DUNLUCE CASTLE (EHS), Bushmills, Co. Antrim BT57 8UY T 028-2073 1938
Ruins of 16th-century stronghold of the McDonnells

FLORENCE COURT (NT), Enniskillen, Co. Fermanagh BT92 1DB T 028-6634 8249
Mid-18th-century house with Rococo decoration

GREY ABBEY (EHS), Greyabbey, Co. Down BT22 2NQ
T 028-9054 6552
Substantial remains of a Cistercian abbey founded in 1193

HILLSBOROUGH FORT (EHS), Hillsborough, Co. Down BT26 6AG T 028-9054 3095
Square keep built in 1650

MOUNT STEWART (NT), Newtownards, Co. Down BT22 2AD T 028-4278 8387
18th century house; childhood home of Lord Castlereagh; Temple of the Winds

NENDRUM MONASTERY (EHS), Mahee Island, Co. Down T 028-9181 1491
Island monastery founded in the fifth century by St Machaoi

TULLY CASTLE (EHS), Co. Fermanagh T 028-9054 6552
Fortified house and bawn built in 1613

WHITE ISLAND (EHS), Co. Fermanagh
Tenth-century monastery; 12th-century church featuring stone figures dating from the sixth century

MUSEUMS AND GALLERIES

There are approximately 2,500 museums and galleries in the United Kingdom. Around 1,860 are accredited by the Museums, Libraries and Archives Council (MLA), which indicates that they have an appropriate constitution, are soundly financed, have adequate collection management standards and public services, and have access to professional curatorial advice. Applications for accreditation are assessed by either the relevant regional agency in England; Museums, Archives, Libraries, Wales (CyMAL); the Scottish Museums Council or the Northern Ireland Museums Council.

The following is a selection of museums and art galleries in the United Kingdom. Opening hours and admission charges vary. Further information about museums and galleries in the UK is available from the Museums Association (W www.museumsassociation.org T 020-7426 6910).

W www.24hourmuseum.org.uk is the UK's national virtual museum and includes a database of all the museums and galleries in the UK.

ENGLAND

* England's national museums and galleries, which receive government funding directly from the DCMS. These institutions are deemed to have collections of national importance, and the government is able to call upon their staff for expert advice

BARNARD CASTLE
The Bowes Museum, Co. Durham DL12 8NP T 01833-690606 W www.thebowesmuseum.org.uk
European art from the late medieval period to the 19th century; music and costume galleries; English period rooms from Elizabeth I to Victoria; local archaeology

BATH
American Museum, Claverton Manor BA2 7BD T 01225-460503 W www.americanmuseum.org
American decorative arts from the 17th to 19th century; American heritage exhibition
Fashion Museum, Bennett Street BA1 2QH T 01225-477173 W www.fashionmuseum.co.uk
Fashion from the 18th century to the present day
Roman Baths Museum, Pump Room, Stall Street BA1 1LZ T 01225-477785 W www.romanbaths.co.uk
Museum adjoins the remains of a Roman baths and temple complex
Victoria Art Gallery, Bridge Street BA2 4AT T 01225-477233 W www.victoriagal.org.uk
European Old Masters and British art since the 15th century

BEAMISH
The North of England Open Air Museum, Co. Durham DH9 0RG T 0191-370 4000 W www.beamish.org.uk
Recreated northern town from the early 1800s and 1900s

BEAULIEU
National Motor Museum, Hants SO42 7ZN T 01590-612345 W www.beaulieu.co.uk
Displays of over 250 vehicles dating from 1895 to the present day

BIRMINGHAM
Aston Hall, Trinity Road B6 6JD T 0121-327 0062 W www.bmag.org.uk
Jacobean House containing paintings, furniture and tapestries from the 17th to 19th century
Barber Institute of Fine Arts, University of Birmingham, Edgbaston B15 2TS T 0121-414 7333 W www.barber.org.uk
Fine arts, including Old Masters
Birmingham Museum and Art Gallery, Chamberlain Square B3 3DH T 0121-303 2834 W www.bmag.org.uk
Includes notable collection of Pre-Raphaelite art
Museum of the Jewellery Quarter, Vyse Street, Hockley B18 6HA T 0121-554 3598 W www.bmag.org.uk
Built around a real jewellery workshop

BOVINGTON
Tank Museum, BH20 6JG T 01929-405096 W www.tankmuseum.co.uk
Collection of 300 tanks from the earliest days of tank warfare to the present

BRADFORD
Bradford Industrial Museum and Horses at Work, Moorside Road, Eccleshill BD2 3HP T 01274-435900 W www.bradfordmuseums.org
Engineering, textiles, transport and social history exhibits, including recreated back-to-back cottages, shire horses and horse tram-rides
Cartwright Hall Art Gallery, Lister Park BD9 4NS T 01274-431212 W www.bradfordmuseums.org
British 19th- and 20th-century fine art
**National Media Museum,* Princes Way BD1 1NQ T 0870-7010200 W www.nationalmediamuseum.org.uk
Photography, film and television interactive exhibits; features the UK's first IMAX cinema and the only public Cinerama screen in the world

BRIGHTON
Booth Museum of Natural History, Dyke Road BN1 5AA T 01273-292777 W www.booth.virtualmuseum.info
Zoology, botany and geology collections; British birds in recreated habitats
Brighton Museum and Art Gallery, Royal Pavilion Gardens BN1 1EE T 01273-292882 W www.brighton.virtualmuseum.info
Includes fine art and design, fashion, non-Western art, Brighton history

BRISTOL
Arnolfini, Narrow Quay BS1 4QA T 0117-917 2300 W www.arnolfini.org.uk
Contemporary visual arts, dance, performance, music, talks and workshops
Blaise Castle House Museum, Henbury BS10 7QS T 0117-903 9818 W www.bristol-city.gov.uk/museums
Agricultural and social history collections in an 18th-century mansion
City Museum and Art Gallery, Queen's Road BS8 1RL T 0117-922 3571 W www.bristol-city.gov.uk/museums
Includes fine and decorative art, oriental art, Egyptology and Bristol ceramics and paintings

CAMBRIDGE
Fitzwilliam Museum, Trumpington Street CB2 1RB T 01223-332900 W www.fitzmuseum.cam.ac.uk

Antiquities, fine and applied arts, clocks, ceramics, manuscripts, furniture, sculpture, coins and medals
**Imperial War Museum Duxford,* Duxford CB22 4QR T 01223-835000 W http://duxford.iwm.org.uk
Displays of military and civil aircraft, tanks, guns and naval exhibits
Sedgwick Museum of Earth Sciences, Downing Street CB2 3EQ T 01223-333456 W www.sedgwickmuseum.org
Extensive geological collection
University Museum of Archaeology and Anthropology, Downing Street CB2 3DZ T 01223-333516 W http://museum.archanth.cam.uk
Archaeology and anthropology from all parts of the world
University Museum of Zoology, Downing Street CB2 3EJ T 01223-336600 W www.zoo.cam.ac.uk
Extensive zoological collection
Whipple Museum of the History of Science, Free School Lane CB2 3RH T 01223-330906 W www.hps.cam.ac.uk/whipple
Scientific instruments from the 14th century to the present

CARLISLE
Tullie House Museum and Art Gallery, Castle Street CA3 8TP T 01228-618718 W www.tulliehouse.co.uk
Prehistoric archaeology, Hadrian's Wall, Viking and medieval Cumbria, and the social history of Carlisle; also British 19th- and 20th-century art and English porcelain

CHATHAM
Dickens World, Leviathan Way ME4 4LL T 01634-890421 W www.dickensworld.co.uk
Theme park based on the life, books and era of Charles Dickens
The Historic Dockyard, ME4 4TZ T 01634-823800 W www.chdt.org.uk
Maritime attractions including HMS *Cavalier,* the UK's last Second World War destroyer
Royal Engineers Museum of Military Engineering, Prince Arthur Road, Gillingham ME4 4UG T 01634-822839 W www.remuseum.org.uk
Regimental history, ethnography, decorative art and photography

CHELTENHAM
Art Gallery and Museum, Clarence Street GL50 3JT T 01242-237431 W www.cheltenhammuseum.org.uk
Paintings, arts and crafts

CHESTER
Grosvenor Museum, Grosvenor Street CH1 2DD T 01244-402008 W www.chester.gov.uk
Roman collections, natural history, art, Chester silver, local history and costume

CHICHESTER
Weald and Downland Open Air Museum, Singleton PO18 0EU T 01243-811363 W www.wealddown.co.uk
Rebuilt vernacular buildings from south-east England; includes medieval houses, agricultural and rural craft buildings and a working watermill

COLCHESTER
Colchester Castle Museum, Castle Park CO1 1TJ T 01206-282939 W www.colchestermuseums.org.uk
Largest Norman keep in Europe standing on foundations of the Roman Temple of Claudius; tours of the Roman vaults, castle walls and chapel

COVENTRY
Coventry Transport Museum, Hales Street CV1 1PN T 024-7623 4270 W www.transport-museum.com
Hundreds of motor vehicles and bicycles
Herbert Art Gallery and Museum, Jordan Well CV1 5QP T 024-7683 2386 W www.theherbert.org
Local history, archaeology and industry, and fine and decorative art

DERBY
Derby Museum and Art Gallery, The Strand DE1 1BS T 01332-716659 W www.derby.gov.uk/
Includes paintings by Joseph Wright of Derby and Derby porcelain
Pickford's House Museum, Friar Gate DE1 1DA T 01332-255363 W www.derby.gov.uk/
Georgian town house by architect Joseph Pickford; museum of Georgian life and costume
The Silk Mill, Derby's Museum of Industry and History, Full Street DE1 3AF T 01332-255308 W www.derby.gov.uk/
Rolls-Royce aero engine collection and railway engineering gallery; on the site of two silk mills built in the early 1700s

DEVIZES – *Wiltshire Heritage Museum,* Long Street SN10 1NS T 01380-727369 W www.wiltshireheritage.org.uk
Natural and local history, art gallery, archaeological finds from Bronze Age, Iron Age, Roman and Saxon sites

DORCHESTER
Dorset County Museum, High West Street DT1 1XA T 01305-262735 W www.dorsetcountymuseum.org
Includes a collection of Thomas Hardy's manuscripts, books, notebooks and drawings; local history

DOVER
Dover Museum, Market Square CT16 1PB T 01304-201066 W www.dovermuseum.co.uk
Contains Dover Bronze Age Boat Gallery and archaeological finds from Bronze Age, Roman and Saxon sites

GATESHEAD
Baltic Centre for Contemporary Art, South Shore Road NE8 3BA T 0191-478 1810 W www.balticmill.com
Contemporary art exhibitions and events
Shipley Art Gallery, Prince Consort Road NE8 4JB T 0191-477 1495 W www.twmuseums.org.uk/shipley
Contemporary crafts

GAYDON
Heritage Motor Centre, Banbury Road, Warks CV35 0BJ T 01926-641188 W www.heritage-motor-centre.co.uk
History of British motor industry from 1895 to present; classic vehicles; engineering gallery; Corgi and Lucas collections

GLOUCESTER
National Waterways Museum, Gloucester Docks GL1 2EH T 01452-318200 W www.nwm.org.uk
Two-hundred-year history of Britain's canals and inland waterways

GOSPORT
Royal Navy Submarine Museum, Haslar Jetty Road, Hants PO12 2AS T 023-9252 9217 W www.rnsubmus.co.uk
Underwater warfare, including the submarine *Alliance;* first Royal Navy submarine

GRASMERE
Dove Cottage and the *Wordsworth Museum,* Cumbria LA22 9SH T 01539-435544 W www.wordsworth.org.uk
William Wordsworth's home and garden

HULL
Ferens Art Gallery, Queen Victoria Square HU1 3RA T 01482-300300 W www.hullcc.gov.uk
European art, especially Dutch 17th-century paintings, British portraits from 17th to 20th century, and marine paintings

Hull Maritime Museum, Queen Victoria Square HU1 3DX
T 01482-300300 W www.hullcc.gov.uk
Whaling, fishing and navigation exhibits

HUNTINGDON

The Cromwell Museum, Grammar School Walk PE29 3LF
T 01480-375830 W www.cambridgeshire.gov.uk/cromwell
Portraits and memorabilia relating to Oliver Cromwell

IPSWICH

Christchurch Mansion and *Wolsey Art Gallery,* Christchurch Park IP4 2BE T 01473-433554 W www.ipswich.gov.uk
Tudor house with paintings by Gainsborough, Constable and other Suffolk artists; furniture and 18th-century ceramics; temporary exhibitions

LEEDS

Armley Mills, Leeds Industrial Museum, Canal Road, Armley LS12 2QF T 0113-263 7861
W www.leeds.gov.uk/armleymills
World's largest woollen mill, now a museum for textiles, clothing and engine manufacture in the area

Leeds City Art Gallery, The Headrow LS1 3AA
T 0113-247 8256 W www.leeds.gov.uk/artgallery
British and European paintings including English watercolours; modern sculpture; Henry Moore gallery; print room

Lotherton Hall, Aberford LS25 3EB T 0113-281 3259
W www.leeds.gov.uk/lothertonhall
Costume, ceramics and furniture collections in furnished Edwardian house; deer park and bird garden

**Royal Armouries Museum,* Armouries Drive LS10 1LT
T 0113-220 1916 W www.royalarmouries.org
National collection of arms and armour from BC to present; demonstrations of foot combat in museum's five galleries; falconry and mounted combat in the tiltyard

Temple Newsam, LS15 0AE T 0113-264 5535
W www.leeds.gov.uk/templenewsam
Old Masters and 17th- and 18th-century decorative art in furnished Jacobean/Tudor house

LEICESTER

Jewry Wall Museum, St Nicholas Circle LE1 4LB
T 0116-225 4971 W www.leicester.gov.uk
Archaeology; Roman Jewry Wall and baths; mosaics

New Walk Museum and Art Gallery, New Walk LE1 7EA
T 0116-255 4900 W www.leicester.gov.uk
Natural history and geology; ancient Egypt gallery; European art and decorative arts

LINCOLN

Museum of Lincolnshire Life, Burton Road LN1 3LY
T 01522-528448 W www.lincolnshire.gov.uk
Social history and agricultural collection

The Collection, Danes Terrace LN2 1LP T 01522-550990
W www.thecollection.lincoln.museum
Artefacts from the Stone Age to the Viking and Medieval eras; adjacent art gallery with decorative and contemporary visual arts

LIVERPOOL

**Lady Lever Art Gallery,* Wirral CH62 5EQ T 0151-478 4136
W www.liverpoolmuseums.org.uk/ladylever
Paintings, furniture and porcelain

**Merseyside Maritime Museum,* Albert Dock L3 4AQ
T 0151-478 4499
W www.liverpoolmuseums.org.uk/maritime
Floating exhibits, working displays and craft demonstrations; incorporates *HM Customs and Excise National Museum*

* *Sudley House,* Mossley Hill Road L18 8BX T 0151-724 3245
W www.liverpoolmuseums.org.uk/sudley
Late 18th- and 19th-century paintings in former shipowner's home

**Tate Liverpool,* Albert Dock L3 4BB T 0151-702 7400
W www.tate.org.uk/liverpool
Twentieth-century paintings and sculpture

**Walker Art Gallery,* William Brown Street L3 8EL
T 0151-478 4199 W www.liverpoolmuseums.org.uk/walker
Paintings from the 14th to 20th century

**World Museum Liverpool,* William Brown Street L3 8EN
T 0151-478 4393 W www.liverpoolmuseums.org.uk/wml
Includes Egyptian mummies, weapons and classical sculpture; planetarium, aquarium, vivarium and natural history centre

LONDON: GALLERIES

Barbican Art Gallery, Barbican Centre, Silk Street EC2Y 8DS
T 020-7638 4141 W www.barbican.org.uk
Temporary exhibitions

Courtauld Institute of Art Gallery, Somerset House, Strand WC2R 0RN T 020-7872 0220 W www.courtauld.ac.uk
Impressionist and post-impressionist paintings

Dulwich Picture Gallery, Gallery Road, Dulwich Village SE21 7AD T 020-8693 5254
W www.dulwichpicturegallery.org.uk
England's first public art gallery; designed by Sir John Soane to house 17th- and 18th-century paintings

Hayward Gallery, Belvedere Road SE1 8XZ T 020-7960 5226
W www.southbankcentre.co.uk
Temporary exhibitions

**National Gallery,* Trafalgar Square WC2N 5DN
T 020-7747 2885 W www.nationalgallery.org.uk
Western painting from the 13th to 20th century; early Renaissance collection in the Sainsbury Wing

**National Portrait Gallery,* St Martin's Place WC2H 0HE
T 020-7306 0055 W www.npg.org.uk
Portraits of eminent people in British history

Percival David Foundation of Chinese Art, Gordon Square WC1H 0PD T 020-7387 3909
Chinese ceramics from 10th to 18th century

Photographers' Gallery, Great Newport Street WC2H 7HY
T 020-7831 1772 W www.photonet.org.uk
Temporary exhibitions

The Queen's Gallery, Buckingham Palace SW1A 1AA
T 020-7766 7301 W www.royal.gov.uk
Art from the Royal Collection

Royal Academy of Arts, Burlington House, Piccadilly W1J 0BD
T 020-7300 8000 W www.royalacademy.org.uk
British art since 1750 and temporary exhibitions; annual Summer Exhibition

Saatchi Gallery, Sloane Square SW3 4RY T 020-7823 2363
W www.saatchi-gallery.co.uk
Contemporary art including paintings, photographs, sculpture and installations

Serpentine Gallery, Kensington Gardens W2 3XA
T 020-7402 6075 W www.serpentinegallery.org
Temporary exhibitions of British and international contemporary art

**Tate Britain,* Millbank SW1P 4RG T 020-7887 8888
W www.tate.org.uk/britain
British painting and 20th-century painting and sculpture

**Tate Modern,* Bankside SE1 9TG T 020-7887 8888
W www.tate.org.uk/modern
International modern art from 1900 to the present

**Wallace Collection,* Manchester Square W1U 3BN
T 020-7563 9500 W www.wallacecollection.org
Paintings and drawings, French 18th-century furniture, armour, porcelain, clocks and sculpture

Whitechapel Art Gallery, Whitechapel High Street E1 7QX
T 020-7522 7888 W www.whitechapel.org
Temporary exhibitions of modern art

LONDON: MUSEUMS

Bank of England Museum, Threadneedle Street EC2R 8AH (entrance on Bartholomew Lane) T 020-7601 5545 W www.bankofengland.co.uk/museum
History of the Bank of England since 1694

**British Museum,* Great Russell Street WC1B 3DG T 020-7323 8000 W www.thebritishmuseum.ac.uk
Antiquities, coins, medals, prints and drawings; temporary exhibitions

**Cabinet War Rooms,* King Charles Street SW1A 2AQ T 020-7930 6961 W cwr.iwm.org.uk
Underground rooms used by Churchill and the government during the Second World War

Cutty Sark, Greenwich SE10 9HT T 020-8858 2698 W www.cuttysark.org.uk
Damaged by fire in May 2007; temporary exhibition next to the ship while closed

Design Museum, Shad Thames SE1 2YD T 0870-833 9955 W www.designmuseum.org
The development of design and the mass-production of consumer objects

Firepower, the Royal Artillery Museum, Royal Arsenal, Woolwich SE18 6ST T 020-8855 7755 W www.firepower.org.uk
The history and development of artillery over the last 700 years including the collections of the Royal Regiment of Artillery

Geffrye Museum, Kingsland Road E2 8EA T 020-7739 9893 W www.geffrye-museum.org.uk
English urban domestic interiors from 1600 to present day; also paintings, furniture, decorative arts, walled herb garden and period garden rooms

**HMS Belfast,* Morgan's Lane, Tooley Street SE1 2JH T 020-7940 6300 W http://hmsbelfast.iwm.org.uk
Life on a Second World War cruiser

Horniman Museum, London Road SE23 3PQ T 020-8699 1872 W www.horniman.ac.uk
Museum of anthropology, musical instruments and natural history; aquarium; reference library; sunken, water and flower gardens

**Imperial War Museum,* Lambeth Road SE1 6HZ T 020-7416 5320 W http://london.iwm.org.uk
All aspects of the two world wars and other military operations involving Britain and the Commonwealth since 1914

London Metropolitan Archives, Northampton Road EC1R 0HB T 020-7332 3820 W www.cityoflondon.gov.uk
Material on the history of London and its people dating 1067–2006

London Transport Museum, Covent Garden Piazza WC2E 7BB T 020-7379 6344 W www.ltmuseum.co.uk
Vehicles, photographs and graphic art relating to the history of transport in London

MCC Museum, Lord's, St John's Wood NW8 8QN T 020-7616 8656 W www.lords.org
Cricket museum; conducted tours by appointment

**Museum in Docklands,* West India Quay, Hertsmere Road E14 4AL T 0870-444 3857 W www.museumindocklands.org.uk
Explores the story of London's river, port and people over 2,000 years, from Roman times through to the recent regeneration of London's Docklands

**Museum of Childhood at Bethnal Green* (V&A), Cambridge Heath Road E2 9PA T 020-8983 5200 W www.museumofchildhood.org.uk
Toys, games and exhibits relating to the social history of childhood

Museum of Garden History, Lambeth Palace Road SE1 7LB T 020-7401 8865 W www.museumgardenhistory.org
History and development of gardens and gardening; recreated 17th-century garden

**Museum of London,* London Wall EC2Y 5HN T 0870-444 3852 W www.museumoflondon.org.uk
History of London from prehistoric times to present day

National Army Museum, Royal Hospital Road SW3 4HT T 020-7730 0717 W www.national-army-museum.ac.uk
Five-hundred-year history of the British soldier; exhibits include model of the Battle of Waterloo and recreated First World War trench

**National Maritime Museum,* Greenwich SE10 9NF T 020-8858 4422 W www.nmm.ac.uk
Maritime history of Britain; collections include globes, clocks, telescopes and paintings; comprises the main building, the Royal Observatory and the Queen's House

**Natural History Museum,* Cromwell Road SW7 5BD T 020-7942 5000 W www.nhm.ac.uk
Natural history collections

Petrie Museum of Egyptian Archaeology, University College London, Malet Place WC1E 6BT T 020-7679 2884 W www.petrie.ucl.ac.uk
Egyptian archaeology collection

Royal Air Force Museum, Hendon NW9 5LL T 020-8205 2266 W www.rafmuseum.org.uk
Aviation from before the Wright brothers to the present-day RAF; features more than 90 full-size aircraft

Royal Mews, Buckingham Palace SW1A 1AA T 020-7766 7302 W www.royal.gov.uk
State vehicles, including the Queen's gold state coach; home to the Queen's horses

**Science Museum,* Exhibition Road SW7 2DD T 0870 870 4868 W www.sciencemuseum.org.uk
Science, technology, industry and medicine collections; children's interactive gallery; IMAX cinema

Shakespeare's Globe Exhibition, Bankside SE1 9DT T 020-7902 1400 W www.shakespeares-globe.org
Recreation of Elizabethan theatre using 16th-century techniques; includes a tour of the theatre

**Sir John Soane's Museum,* Lincoln's Inn Fields WC2A 3BP T 020-7405 2107 W www.soane.org
Art and antiquities collected by Soane throughout his lifetime; house designed by Soane

Tower Bridge Experience, SE1 2UP T 020-7403 3761 W www.towerbridge.org.uk
History of the bridge and display of Victorian steam machinery; panoramic views from walkways

**Victoria and Albert Museum,* Cromwell Road SW7 2RL T 020-7942 2000 W www.vam.ac.uk
Includes National Art Library and Print Room; fine and applied art and design; furniture, glass, textiles, theatre and dress collections

Wimbledon Lawn Tennis Museum, Church Road SW19 5AE T 020-8946 6131 W www.wimbledon.org/museum
Tennis trophies, fashion and memorabilia; view of Centre Court

MALTON

Eden Camp, N. Yorks YO17 6RT T 01653 697777 W www.edencamp.co.uk
Restored POW camp and Second World War memorabilia

MANCHESTER

Gallery of Costume, Platt Hall, Rusholme M14 5LL T 0161-224 5217 W www.manchestergalleries.org
Exhibits from the 17th century to the present day

**Imperial War Museum North,* Trafford Wharf, Trafford Park M17 1TZ T 0161-836 4000 W http://north.iwm.org.uk
History of war in the 20th and 21st centuries
Manchester Art Gallery, Mosley Street M2 3JL
T 0161-235 8888 W www.manchestergalleries.org
Six centuries of European fine and decorative art
Manchester Museum, Oxford Road M13 9PL T 0161-275 2634
W www.museum.manchester.ac.uk
Collections include archaeology, decorative arts, Egyptology, natural history and zoology
**Museum of Science and Industry,* Liverpool Road, Castlefield M3 4FP T 0161-832 2244 W www.msim.org.uk
On site of world's oldest passenger railway station; galleries relating to space, energy, power, transport, aviation, textiles and social history
Whitworth Art Gallery, Oxford Road M15 6ER
T 0161-275 7450 W www.whitworth.manchester.ac.uk
Watercolours, drawings, prints, textiles, wallpapers and British art

MILTON KEYNES

Bletchley Park National Codes Centre, Bucks MK3 6EB
T 01908-640404 W www.bletchleypark.org.uk
Home of British codebreaking during the Second World War; Enigma machine; computer museum; wartime toys and memorabilia

MONKWEARMOUTH

Monkwearmouth Station Museum, North Bridge Street, Sunderland SR5 1AP T 0191-567 7075
W www.twmuseums.org.uk/monkwearmouth
Victorian train station; interactive galleries

NEWCASTLE UPON TYNE

Discovery Museum, Blandford Square NE1 4JA
T 0191-232 6789 W www.twmuseums.org.uk/discovery
Science and industry, local history, fashion; Tyneside's maritime history; *Turbinia* (first steam-driven vessel) gallery
Laing Art Gallery, New Bridge Street NE1 8AG
T 0191-232 7734 W www.twmuseums.org.uk/laing
18th- and 19th-century collection, watercolour gallery

NEWMARKET

National Horseracing Museum, High Street CB8 8JH
T 01638-667333 W www.nhrm.co.uk
Horseracing simulator, temporary exhibitions and tours of local trainers' yards and studs

NORTH SHIELDS

Stephenson Railway Museum, Middle Engine Lane NE29 8DX
T 0191-200 7146 W www.twmuseums.org.uk/stephenson
Locomotive engines and rolling stock

NOTTINGHAM

Brewhouse Yard Museum, Castle Boulevard NG7 1FB
T 0115-915 3600 W www.nottinghamcity.gov.uk
Social history from the 17th to 20th century
Castle Museum and Art Gallery, Friar Lane NG1 6EL
T 0115-915 3700 W www.nottinghamcity.gov.uk
Paintings, ceramics, silver and glass; history of Nottingham
Industrial Museum, Wollaton Park, Wollaton NG8 2AE
T 0115-915 3900 W www.nottinghamcity.gov.uk
Lacemaking machinery, steam engines and transport exhibits
Natural History Museum, Wollaton Hall, Wollaton NG8 2AE
T 0115-915 3900 W www.nottinghamcity.gov.uk
Local natural history and wildlife dioramas

OXFORD

Ashmolean Museum, Beaumont Street OX1 2PH
T 01865-278000 W www.ashmolean.org
European and oriental fine and applied arts, archaeology, Egyptology and numismatics
Modern Art Oxford, Pembroke Street OX1 1BP
T 01865-722733 W www.modernartoxford.org.uk
Temporary exhibitions
Museum of the History of Science, Broad Street OX1 3AZ
T 01865-277280 W www.mhs.ox.ac.uk
Displays include early scientific instruments, chemical apparatus, clocks and watches
Oxford University Museum of Natural History, Parks Road OX1 3PW T 01865-272950 W www.oum.ox.ac.uk
Entomology, geology, mineralogy and zoology. Closed for redevelopment due to re-open spring 2009
Pitt Rivers Museum, South Parks Road OX1 3PP
T 01865-270927 W www.prm.ox.ac.uk
Ethnographic and archaeological artefacts

PLYMOUTH

City Museum and Art Gallery, Drake Circus PL4 8AJ
T 01752-304774 W www.plymouthmuseum.gov.uk
Local and natural history; ceramics; silver; Old Masters; temporary exhibitions

PORTSMOUTH

Charles Dickens Birthplace, Old Commercial Road PO1 4QL
T 023-9282 7261 W www.charlesdickensbirthplace.co.uk
Dickens memorabilia
D-Day Museum, Clarence Esplanade, Southsea PO5 3NT
T 023-9282 7261 W www.ddaymuseum.co.uk
Includes the Overlord embroidery
Portsmouth Historic Dockyard, HM Naval Base PO1 3LJ
T 023-9283 9766 W www.historicdockyard.co.uk
Incorporates the *Royal Naval Museum* (PO1 3NH T 023-9272 7562 W www.royalnavalmuseum.org), HMS *Victory* (PO1 3NH T 023-9286 1533 W www.hms-victory.com), *HMS Warrior* (PO1 3QX T 023-9277 8600 W www.hmswarrior.org), the *Mary Rose* (PO1 3LX T 023-9281 2931 W www.maryrose.org) and *Action Stations* (PO1 3LJ T 023-9289 3316 W www.actionstations.org)
History of the Royal Navy and of the dockyard; warships and technology spanning 500 years

PRESTON

Harris Museum and Art Gallery, Market Square PR1 2PP
T 01772-258248 W www.harrismuseum.org.uk
British art since the 18th century; ceramics, glass, costume and local history; contemporary exhibitions
National Football Museum, Sir Tom Finney Way PR1 6PA
T 01772-908442 W www.nationalfootballmuseum.com
Home to the FIFA, FA and Football League collections on long-term loan

ST ALBANS

Verulamium Museum, St Michael's Street AL3 4SW
T 01727-751810 W www.stalbansmuseums.org.uk
Remains of Iron Age settlement and the third-largest city in Roman Britain; exhibits include Roman wall plasters, jewellery, mosaics and room reconstructions

ST IVES

**Tate St Ives,* Porthmeor Beach, Cornwall TR26 1TG
T 01736-796226 W www.tate.org.uk/stives
Modern art, much by artists associated with St Ives; includes the Barbara Hepworth Museum and Sculpture Garden

SALISBURY

Salisbury & South Wiltshire Museum, The Close SP1 2EN
T 01722-332151 W www.salisburymuseum.org.uk
Archaeology collection

SHEFFIELD

Graves Art Gallery, Surrey Street S1 1XZ T 0114-278 2600
W www.sheffieldgalleries.org.uk
20th-century British art, Grice Collection of Chinese ivories

Millennium Galleries, Arundel Gate S1 2PP T 0114-278 2600 W www.sheffieldgalleries.org.uk
Incorporates four different galleries: the Special Exhibition Gallery, the Craft and Design Gallery, the Metalwork Gallery and the Ruskin Gallery, which houses John Ruskin's collection of paintings, drawings, books and medieval manuscripts
Weston Park Museum, Western Bank S10 2TP T 0114-278 2600 W www.sheffieldgalleries.org.uk
World history for families
SOUTHAMPTON
City Art Gallery, Commercial Road SO14 7LP T 023-8083 2277 W www.southampton.gov.uk/art
Fine art collection spanning six centuries of European art
God's House Tower Museum of Archaeology, Winkle Street SO14 2NY T 023-8063 5904 W www.southampton.gov.uk
Roman, Saxon and medieval archaeology
Maritime Museum, Town Quay Road SO14 2NY T 023-8063 5904 W www.southampton.gov.uk
Southampton maritime history
SOUTH SHIELDS
Arbeia Roman Fort, Baring Street NE33 2BB T 0191-456 1369 W www.twmuseums.org.uk/arbeia
Excavated ruins; reconstructions of original buildings
South Shields Museum and Art Gallery, Ocean Road NE33 2JA T 0191-456 8740 W www.twmuseums.org.uk/southshields
South Tyneside history; interactive art gallery
STOKE-ON-TRENT
Etruria Industrial Museum, Lower Bedford Street ST4 7AF T 01782-233144 W www.stoke.gov.uk/museums
Britain's sole surviving steam-powered potter's mill
Gladstone Pottery Museum, Longton ST3 1PQ T 01782-237777 W www.stoke.gov.uk/museums
A working Victorian pottery
Potteries Museum and Art Gallery, Hanley ST1 3DW T 01782-232323 W www.stoke.gov.uk/museums
Pottery, china and porcelain collections and a Mark XVI Spitfire
SUNDERLAND
Sunderland Museum & Winter Gardens, Burdon Road SR1 1PP T 0191-553 2323 W www.twmuseums.org.uk/sunderland
Fine and decorative art, local history and gardens
TELFORD
Ironbridge Gorge Museums, TF8 7DQ T 01952-884391 W www.ironbridge.org.uk
World's first iron bridge; Blists Hill (late Victorian working town); Museum of Iron; Jackfield Tile Museum; Coalport China Museum; Tar Tunnel; Broseley Pipeworks
WAKEFIELD
National Coal Mining Museum for England, Overton WF4 4RH T 01924-848806 W www.ncm.org.uk
Includes underground tours of one of Britain's oldest working mines
Yorkshire Sculpture Park, West Bretton WF4 4LG T 01924-832631 W www.ysp.co.uk
Open-air sculpture gallery including works by Moore, Hepworth, Frink and others in 202 hectares (500 acres) of parkland
WEYBRIDGE
Brooklands Museum, KT13 0QN T 01932-857381 W www.brooklandsmuseum.com
Birthplace of British motorsport; world's first purpose-built motor racing circuit
WILMSLOW
Quarry Bank Mill, Styal SK9 4LA T 01625-527468 W www.nationaltrust.org.uk
Working mill owned by the National Trust illustrating history of cotton industry; costumed guides at restored Apprentice House
WINCHESTER
INTECH, Telegraph Way, Hampshire SO21 1HX T 01962-863791 W www.intech-uk.com
Interactive science centre and planetarium
WORCESTER
City Museum and Art Gallery, Foregate Street WR1 1DT T 01905-25371 W www.worcestercitymuseums.org.uk
Includes a military museum, 19th-century chemist shop and changing art exhibitions
Museum of Worcester Porcelain, Severn Street WR1 2NE T 01905-746000 W www.worcesterporcelainmuseum.org.uk
Worcester porcelain from 1751 to the present day. Also the *Royal Worcester Visitor Centre* (W www.royalworcester.co.uk)
WROUGHTON
**Science Museum*, Wilts SN4 9LT T 01793-846200 W www.sciencemuseum.org.uk
Aircraft displays and some of the Science Museum's transport and agricultural collection
YEOVIL
Fleet Air Arm Museum, Royal Naval Air Station, Yeovilton, Somerset BA22 8HT T 01935-840565 W www.fleetairarm.com
History of naval aviation; historic aircraft, including Concorde 002
YORK
Beningbrough Hall, Beningbrough YO30 1DD T 01904-472027 W www.nationaltrust.org.uk
18th-century house with portraits from the National Portrait Gallery
Jorvik – The Viking City, Coppergate YO1 9WT T 01904-543400 W www.jorvik-viking-centre.co.uk
Reconstruction of Viking York based on archaeological evidence
**National Railway Museum*, Leeman Road YO26 4XJ T 0844-815 3139 W www.nrm.org.uk
Includes locomotives, rolling stock and carriages
York Castle Museum, Eye of York YO1 9RY T 01904-687687 W www.yorkcastlemuseum.org.uk
Reconstructed streets and rooms; costume and military collections
York Art Gallery, Exhibition Square YO1 7EW T 01904-687687 W www.yorkartgallery.org.uk
European and British painting spanning seven centuries; modern pottery; decorative arts
Yorkshire Museum & Gardens, Museum Gardens YO1 7FR T 01904-687687 W www.yorkshiremuseum.org.uk
Yorkshire life from Roman to medieval times; geology and biology; York observatory

WALES

* Members of National Museum Wales, a public body that receives its funding through grant-in-aid from the Welsh Assembly

BLAENAFON
**Big Pit National Coal Museum*, Torfaen NP4 9XP T 01495-790311 W www.museumwales.ac.uk
Colliery with underground tour

BODELWYDDAN
Bodelwyddan Castle, Denbighshire LL18 5YA T 01745-584060 W www.bodelwyddan-castle.co.uk
Portraits from the National Portrait Gallery; furniture from the Victoria and Albert Museum; sculptures from the Royal Academy

CAERLEON
**National Roman Legion Museum,* NP18 1AE T 01633-423134 W www.museumwales.ac.uk
Material from the site of the Roman fortress of Isca and its suburbs

CARDIFF
**National Museum Cardiff,* Cathays Park CF10 3NP T 029-2039 7951 W www.museumwales.ac.uk
Includes natural sciences, archaeology and Impressionist paintings
**St Fagans: National History Museum,* St Fagans CF5 6XB T 029-2057 3500 W www.museumwales.ac.uk
Open-air museum with re-erected buildings, agricultural equipment and costume

DRE-FACH FELINDRE
**National Wool Museum,* nr Llandysul SA44 5UP T 01559-370929 W www.museumwales.ac.uk
Exhibitions, a working woollen mill and craft workshops

LLANBERIS
**National Slate Museum,* Gwynedd LL55 4TY T 01286-870630 W www.museumwales.ac.uk
Former slate quarry with original machinery and plant; slate crafts demonstrations; working waterwheel

LLANDRINDOD WELLS
National Cycle Collection, Automobile Palace, Temple Street LD1 5DL T 01597-825531 W www.cyclemuseum.org.uk
Over 200 bicycles on display, from 1819 to the present day

SWANSEA
Glynn Vivian Art Gallery, Alexandra Road SA1 5DZ T 01792-516900 W www.swansea.gov.uk/glynnvivian
Paintings, ceramics, Swansea pottery and porcelain, clocks, glass and Welsh art
**National Waterfront Museum,* Oystermouth Road SA1 3RD T 01792-638950 W www.museumwales.ac.uk
Wales during the Industrial Revolution
Swansea Museum, Victoria Road SA1 1SN T 01792-653763 W www.swansea.gov.uk/swanseamuseum
Archaeology, social history, Swansea pottery

SCOTLAND

* Members of National Museums of Scotland or National Galleries of Scotland, which are non-departmental public bodies funded by, and accountable to, the Scottish government

ABERDEEN
Aberdeen Art Gallery, Schoolhill AB10 1FQ T 01224-523700 W www.aagm.co.uk
Impressionists, Scottish Colourists, decorative art and modern art
Aberdeen Maritime Museum, Shiprow AB11 5BY T 01224-337700 W www.aagm.co.uk
Maritime history, including shipbuilding and North Sea oil

DUMFRIES
National Museum of Costume, New Abbey DG2 8HQ T 01387-850375 W www.nms.ac.uk/costume
History of fashion from the 1850s to the 1950s

EDINBURGH
Britannia, Leith EH6 6JJ T 0131-555 5566 W www.royalyachtbritannia.co.uk
Former royal yacht with royal barge and royal family picture gallery
City Art Centre, Market Street EH1 1DE T 0131-529 3993 W www.cac.org.uk
Scottish late 19th and 20th century art and temporary exhibitions
**Dean Gallery,* Belford Road EH4 3DS T 0131-624 6200 W www.nationalgalleries.org
Dada, Surrealism and sculpture – particularly works by Sir Eduardo Paolozzi
Museum of Childhood, High Street EH1 1TG T 0131-529 4142 W www.cac.org.uk
Toys, games, clothes and exhibits relating to the social history of childhood
Museum of Edinburgh, Canongate EH8 8DD T 0131-529 4143 W www.cac.org.uk
Local history, silver, glass and Scottish pottery
**Museum of Flight,* East Fortune Airfield, East Lothian EH39 5LF T 01620-897240 W www.nms.ac.uk/flight
Display of aircraft
**Museum of Scotland,* Chambers Street EH1 1JF T 0131-225 7534 W www.nms.ac.uk/scotland
Scottish history from prehistoric times to the present
**National Gallery of Scotland,* The Mound EH2 2EL T 0131-624 6200 W www.nationalgalleries.org
Paintings, drawings and prints from the early Renaissance to the end of the 19th century
**National War Museum of Scotland,* Edinburgh Castle EH1 2NG T 0131-247 4413 W www.nms.ac.uk/war
History of Scottish military and conflicts
**Royal Museum,* Chambers Street EH1 1JF T 0131-247 4422 W www.nms.ac.uk
Decorative arts, natural history, science and industry; part of the museum will be closed from spring 2008
**Scottish National Gallery of Modern Art,* Belford Road EH4 3DR T 0131-624 6200 W www.nationalgalleries.org
20th-century painting, sculpture and graphic art
**Scottish National Portrait Gallery,* Queen Street EH2 1JD T 0131-624 6200 W www.nationalgalleries.org
Portraits of eminent people in Scottish history; the national collection of photography
The Writers' Museum, Lawnmarket EH1 2PA T 0131-529 4901 W www.cac.org.uk
Robert Louis Stevenson, Walter Scott and Robert Burns exhibits

FORT WILLIAM
West Highland Museum, Cameron Square PH33 6AJ T 01397-702169 W www.westhighlandmuseum.org.uk
Includes tartan collections and exhibits relating to 1745 uprising

GLASGOW
Burrell Collection, Pollokshaws Road G43 1AT T 0141-287 2550 W www.glasgowmuseums.com
Paintings, textiles, furniture, ceramics, stained glass and silver from classical times to the 19th century
Gallery of Modern Art, Royal Exchange Square G1 3AH T 0141-229 1996 W www.glasgowmuseums.com
Collection of contemporary Scottish and world art
Hunterian Museum & Art Gallery, University of Glasgow G12 8QQ T 0141-330 4221 W www.hunterian.gla.ac.uk
Rennie Mackintosh and Whistler collections; Old Masters; Scottish paintings; archaeology; medicine; zoology

Kelvingrove Art Gallery & Museum, Argyle Street G3 8AG
T 0141-287 2699 W www.glasgowmuseums.com
Includes Old Masters, 19th-century French paintings and armour collection

Museum of Piping, McPhater Street G4 0HW
T 0141-353 0220 W www.thepipingcentre.co.uk
The history and origins of bagpiping

**Museum of Rural Life,* East Kilbride G76 9HR
T 0131-247 4377 W www.nms.ac.uk
History of rural life and work

Museum of Transport, Bunhouse Road G3 8DP
T 0141-287 2720 W www.glasgowmuseums.com
Includes a reproduction of a 1938 Glasgow street, cars since the 1930s, trams and a Glasgow subway station

People's Palace and Winter Gardens, Glasgow Green G40 1AT
T 0141-271 2962 W www.glasgowmuseums.com
History of Glasgow since 1750

St Mungo Museum of Religious Life and Art, Castle Street G4 0RH T 0141-553 2557 W www.glasgowmuseums.com
Explores universal themes through objects from all the main world religions

NORTHERN IRELAND

* Members of National Museums Northern Ireland, a non-departmental public body of the Northern Ireland Office

ARMAGH

**Armagh County Museum,* The Mall East BT61 9BE
T 028-3752 3070 W www.armaghcountymuseum.org.uk
Local history; archaeology; crafts

BELFAST

**W5,* Odyssey, Queen's Quay BT3 9QQ T 028-9046 7700 W www.w5online.co.uk
Interactive science and technology centre

HOLYWOOD

**Ulster Folk and Transport Museum,* Cultra, Co. Down BT18 0EU T 028-9042 8428 W www.uftm.org.uk
Open-air museum with original buildings from Ulster town and rural life *c.*1900; indoor galleries including Irish rail and road transport and *Titanic* exhibitions

LONDONDERRY

The Tower Museum, Union Hall Place BT48 6LU
T 028-7137 2411 W www.derrycity.gov.uk/museums
Tells the story of Ireland through the history of Londonderry

OMAGH

**Ulster American Folk Park,* Castletown, Co. Tyrone BT78 5QY
T 028-8224 3292 W www.folkpark.com
Open-air museum telling the story of Ulster's emigrants to America; restored or recreated dwellings and workshops; ship and dockside gallery

SIGHTS OF LONDON

For historic buildings, museums and galleries in London, *see* the Historic Buildings and Monuments and Museums and Galleries sections.

BRIDGES

The bridges over the Thames in London, from east to west, are:

Queen Elizabeth II Bridge (2,872m/9,423ft), engineer: William Halcrow and partners, opened 1991

Tower Bridge (268m/880ft by 18m/60ft), architect: Horace Jones, engineer: John Wolfe Barry, opened 1894

London Bridge (262m/860ft by 32m/105ft), original 13th-century stone bridge rebuilt and opened 1831 (engineer: John Rennie), reconstructed in Arizona when current London Bridge opened 1973 (architect: Lord Holford, engineer: Mott, Hay and Anderson)

Cannon Street Railway Bridge (261m/855ft), engineers: John Hawkshaw and John Wolfe Barry, originally named the Alexandra Bridge, opened 1866; renovated 1979–82

Southwark Bridge (244m/800ft by 17m/55ft), engineer: John Rennie, opened 1819; rebuilt 1912–21 (architect: Ernest George, engineer: Mott, Hay and Anderson)

Millennium Bridge (325m/1,066ft by 5m/15ft), architect: Foster and Partners, engineer: Ove Arup and Partners, opened 2000; reopened after modification 2002

Blackfriars Railway Bridge (284m/933ft), engineers: John Wolfe Barry and Henri Marc Brunel, opened 1886

(*London, Chatham and Dover Railway Bridge* (234m/933ft), engineer: Joseph Cubitt, opened in 1864; only the columns remain, the rest of the structure was removed in 1985)

Blackfriars Bridge (294m/963ft by 32m/105ft), engineer: Robert Mylne, opened 1769; rebuilt 1869 (engineer: Joseph Cubitt); widened 1909

Waterloo Bridge (366m/1,200ft by 24m/80ft), engineer: John Rennie, opened 1817; rebuilt 1945 (architect: Sir Giles Gilbert Scott, engineer: Rendel, Palmer and Triton)

Golden Jubilee Bridges (325m/1,066ft by 4.7m/15ft), architect: Lifschutz Davidson, engineer: WSP Group, opened 2002; commonly known as the Hungerford Footbridges

Hungerford Railway Bridge (366m/1,200ft), engineer: Isambard Kingdom Brunel, suspension bridge opened 1845; present railway bridge opened 1864 (engineer: John Hawkshaw); widened in 1886

Westminster Bridge (228m/748ft by 26m/85ft), engineer: Charles Labelye, opened 1750; rebuilt 1862 (architect: Charles Barry, engineer: Thomas Page)

Lambeth Bridge (237m/776ft by 18m/60ft), engineer: Peter W. Barlow, original suspension bridge opened 1862; current structure opened 1932 (architect: Reginald Blomfield, engineer: George W. Humphreys)

Vauxhall Bridge (231m/759ft by 24m/80ft), engineer: James Walker, opened 1816; redesigned and opened 1906 (architect: William Edward Riley, engineers: Alexander Binnie and Maurice Fitzmaurice)

Grosvenor Railway Bridge (213m/700ft), engineer: John Fowler, opened 1860; rebuilt 1965; also known as the Victoria Railway Bridge

Chelsea Bridge (213m/698ft by 25m/83ft), original suspension bridge opened 1858 (engineer: Thomas Page); rebuilt 1937 (architects: George Topham Forrest and E. P. Wheeler, engineer: Rendel, Palmer and Triton)

Albert Bridge (216m/710ft, by 12m/40ft) engineer: Rowland M. Ordish, opened 1873; restructured 1884 (engineer: Joseph Bazalgette); strengthened 1971–3

Battersea Bridge (204m/670ft by 17m/55ft), engineer: Henry Holland, opened 1771; rebuilt 1890 (engineer: Joseph Bazalgette)

Battersea Railway Bridge (204m/670ft), engineer: William Baker, opened 1863

Wandsworth Bridge (189m/619ft by 18m/60ft), engineer: Julian Tolmé, opened 1873; rebuilt 1940 (architect: E. P. Wheeler, engineer: T. Peirson Frank)

Putney Railway Bridge (229m/750ft), engineers: W. H. Thomas and William Jacomb, opened 1889; also known as the Fulham Railway Bridge or the Iron Bridge – it has no official name

Putney Bridge (213m/700ft by 23m/74ft), architect: Jacob Ackworth, original wooden bridge opened 1729; current granite structure completed in 1886 (engineer: Joseph Bazalgette)

Hammersmith Bridge (210m/688ft by 10m/33ft), engineer: William Tierney Clarke; the first suspension bridge in London, originally built 1827; rebuilt 1887 (engineer: Joseph Bazalgette)

Barnes Railway Bridge (also footbridge, 110m/360ft), engineer: Joseph Locke, opened 1849; rebuilt 1895 (engineers: London and South Western Railway); the original structure stands unused

Chiswick Bridge (137m/450ft by 21m/70ft), architect: Herbert Baker, engineer: Alfred Dryland, opened 1933

Kew Railway Bridge (175m/575ft), engineer: W. R. Galbraith, opened 1869

Kew Bridge (110m/360ft by 17m/56ft), engineer: Robert Tunstall, original timber bridge built 1759; replaced by a Portland stone structure in 1789 (engineer: James Paine); current granite bridge renamed King Edward VII Bridge in 1903, but still known as Kew Bridge (engineers: John Wolfe Barry and Cuthbert Brereton)

Richmond Lock (91m/300ft by 11m/36ft), engineer: F. G. M. Stoney, lock and footbridge opened 1894

Twickenham Bridge (85m/280ft by 21m/70ft), architect: Maxwell Ayrton, engineer: Alfred Dryland, opened 1933

Richmond Railway Bridge (91m/300ft), engineer: Joseph Locke, opened 1848; rebuilt 1906–8 (engineer: J. W. Jacomb-Hood)

Richmond Bridge (85m/280ft by 10m/36ft), architect: James Paine, engineer: Kenton Couse, built 1777; widened 1939

Teddington Lock (198m/650ft), engineer: G. Pooley, two footbridges opened 1889; marks the end of the tidal reach of the Thames

Kingston Railway Bridge, architects: J. E. Errington and W. R. Galbraith, engineer: Thomas Brassey, opened 1863

Kingston Bridge (116m/382ft), engineer: Edward Lapidge,

built 1825–8; widened 1911–14 (engineers: Basil Mott and David Hay) and 1999–2001

Hampton Court Bridge, engineers: Samuel Stevens and Benjamin Ludgator, built 1753; replaced by iron bridge 1865; present bridge opened 1933 (architect: Edwin Lutyens, engineer: W. P. Robinson)

CEMETERIES

In 1832, in response to the overcrowding of burial grounds in London, the government authorised the establishment of seven non-denominational cemeteries that would encircle the city. These large cemeteries, known as the 'magnificent seven', were seen by many Victorian families as places in which to demonstrate their wealth and stature, and as a result there are some highly ornate graves and tombs.

THE MAGNIFICENT SEVEN

Abney Park, Stamford Hill, N16 (13 hectares/32 acres), established 1840; tomb of General Booth, founder of the Salvation Army, and memorials to many nonconformists and dissenters

Brompton, Old Brompton Road, SW10 (16 hectares/40 acres), established 1840; graves of Sir Henry Cole, Emmeline Pankhurst, John Wisden

Highgate, Swains Lane, N6 (15 hectares/38 acres), established 1839; graves of Douglas Adams, George Eliot, Michael Faraday, Karl Marx, Christina Rossetti and Radclyffe Hall; western side only accessible as part of a guided tour

Kensal Green, Harrow Road, W10 (31.5 hectares/79 acres), established 1832; tombs of William Makepeace Thackeray, Anthony Trollope, Sydney Smith, Wilkie Collins, Tom Hood, George Cruikshank, Leigh Hunt, Isambard Kingdom Brunel and Charles Kemble

Nunhead, Linden Grove, SE15 (21 hectares/52 acres), established 1840; closed in 1969, subsequently restored and opened for burials

Tower Hamlets, Southern Grove, E3 (11 hectares/27 acres), established 1841; bombed heavily during the Second World War and closed to burials in 1966; now a nature reserve

West Norwood Cemetery and Crematorium, Norwood High Street, SE27 (17 hectares/42 acres), established 1837; tombs of Sir Henry Bessemer, Mrs Beeton, Sir Henry Tate and Joseph Whitaker *(Whitaker's Almanack)*

OTHER CEMETERIES

Bunhill Fields, City Road, EC1 (1.6 hectares/4 acres), 17th-century nonconformist burial ground containing the graves of William Blake, John Bunyan and Daniel Defoe

City of London Cemetery and Crematorium, Aldersbrook Road, E12 (81 hectares/200 acres), established 1856

Golders Green Crematorium, Hoop Lane, NW11 (5 hectares/12 acres), established 1902; retains the ashes of Kingsley Amis, Peter Sellers, Marc Bolan, Sigmund Freud, Ivor Novello, Bram Stoker, H. G. Wells, Anna Pavlova and Joe Orton

Hampstead, Fortune Green Road, NW6 (10.5 hectares/26 acres), established 1876; graves of Kate Greenaway, Lord Lister, Marie Lloyd

MARKETS

Billingsgate (fish), a market site for over 1,000 years, with the Lower Thames Street site dating from 1876; moved to the Isle of Dogs (Trafalgar Way, E14) in 1982; owned and run by the Corporation of London

Borough, Southwark Street, SE1 (vegetables, fruit, flowers, etc), established on present site in 1756; privately owned and run

Camden Lock, NW1 (second-hand clothing, jewellery, alternative fashion, crafts), established in 1973

Columbia Road, E2 (flowers), dates from 19th century; became dedicated flower market in the 20th century

Covent Garden (vegetables, fruit, flowers, etc), established in 1670 under a charter of Charles II; owned and run by the Covent Garden Market Authority, whose board is appointed by DEFRA; moved in 1974 to Nine Elms, SW8

Leadenhall, Leadenhall Street, EC3 (meat, poultry, fish, etc), site of market since 14th century; present hall built 1881; owned and run by the Corporation of London

Petticoat Lane, Middlesex Street, E1, a market has existed on the site for over 500 years, now a Sunday morning market selling almost anything

Portobello Road, W11, originally for herbs and horse-trading from 1870; became famous for antiques after the closure of the Caledonian Market in 1948

Smithfield, EC1 (meat, poultry), built 1866–8, refurbished 1993–4; the site of St Bartholomew's Fair from 12th to 19th century; owned and run by the Corporation of London

New Spitalfields, E10 (vegetables, fruit, etc), established 1682, modernised 1928, moved out of the City to Leyton in 1991

Old Spitalfields, E1, continues to trade on the original Spitalfields site on Commercial Street, selling arts, crafts, books, clothes, organic food and antiques on Sundays

MONUMENTS

CENOTAPH

Whitehall, SW1. The Cenotaph (from the Greek meaning 'empty tomb') was built to commemorate 'The Glorious Dead' and is a memorial to all ranks of the sea, land and air forces who gave their lives in the service of the Empire during the First World War. Designed by Sir Edwin Lutyens and constructed in plaster as a temporary memorial in 1919, it was replaced by a permanent structure of Portland stone and unveiled by George V on 11 November 1920, Armistice Day. An additional inscription was made in 1946 to commemorate those who gave their lives in the Second World War.

FOURTH PLINTH

Trafalgar Square, WC2. The fourth plinth (1841) was designed for an equestrian statue that was never built due to lack of funds. From 1999 temporary works have been displayed on the plinth including *Ecce Homo* (Mark Wallinger), *Regardless of History* (Bill Woodrow), *Monument* (Rachel Whiteread), and *Alison Lapper Pregnant* (Marc Quinn). *Model for a Hotel* by Thomas Schütte was installed in 2007.

LONDON MONUMENT

(Commonly called the Monument), Monument Street, EC3. Built to designs by Sir Christopher Wren and Robert Hooke between 1671 and 1677, the Monument commemorates the Great Fire of London, which broke out in Pudding Lane on 2 September 1666. The fluted Doric column is 36.6m (120ft) high, the moulded cylinder above the balcony supporting a flaming vase of gilt bronze is an additional 12.8m

(42ft), and the column is based on a square plinth 12.2m (40ft) high (with fine carvings on the west face), making a total height of 61.6m (202ft) – the tallest isolated stone column in the world, with views of London from a gallery at the top (311 steps).

OTHER MONUMENTS

(sculptor's name in parentheses):

Viscount Alanbrooke (Roberts-Jones), Whitehall
Albert Memorial (Scott), Kensington Gore
Battle of Britain (Day), Victoria Embankment
Beatty (Wheeler), Trafalgar Square
Belgian Gratitude (setting by Blomfield, statue by Rousseau), Victoria Embankment
Boadicea (or Boudicca), *Queen of the Iceni* (Thornycroft), Westminster Bridge
Brunel (Marochetti), Victoria Embankment
Burghers of Calais (Rodin), Victoria Tower Gardens, Westminster
Burns (Steell), Embankment Gardens
Canada Memorial (Granche), Green Park
Carlyle (Boehm), Chelsea Embankment
Cavalry (Jones), Hyde Park
Edith Cavell (Frampton), St Martin's Place
Charles I (Le Sueur), Trafalgar Square
Charles II (Gibbons), Royal Hospital, Chelsea
Churchill (Roberts-Jones), Parliament Square
Cleopatra's Needle (20.9m/68.5ft high, *c.*1500BC, erected in 1878; the sphinxes are Victorian), Thames Embankment
Clive (Tweed), King Charles Street
Captain Cook (Brock), The Mall
Oliver Cromwell (Thornycroft), outside Westminster Hall
Cunningham (Belsky), Trafalgar Square
Gen. Charles de Gaulle (Conner), Carlton Gardens
Disraeli, Earl of Beaconsfield (Raggi), Parliament Square
Lord Dowding (Winter), Strand
Duke of Cambridge (Jones), Whitehall
Duke of York (37.8m/124ft column, with statue by Westmacott), Carlton House Terrace
Edward VII (Mackennal), Waterloo Place
Elizabeth I (Kerwin, 1586, oldest outdoor statue in London; from Ludgate), Fleet Street
Eros (Shaftesbury Memorial) (Gilbert), Piccadilly Circus
Marechal/Marshall Foch (Mallisard, copy of one in Cassel, France), Grosvenor Gardens
Charles James Fox (Westmacott), Bloomsbury Square
George III (Cotes Wyatt), Cockspur Street
George IV (Chantrey), Trafalgar Square
George V (Reid Dick and Scott), Old Palace Yard
George VI (Macmillan), Carlton Gardens
Gladstone (Thornycroft), Strand
Guards' (Crimea) (Bell), Waterloo Place
Guards Division (Ledward, figures, Bradshaw, cenotaph), Horse Guards' Parade
Haig (Hardiman), Whitehall
Sir Arthur (Bomber) Harris (Winter), Strand
Gen. Henry Havelock (Behnes), Trafalgar Square
Irving (Brock), north side of National Portrait Gallery
James II (Gibbons), Trafalgar Square
Jellicoe (Macmillan), Trafalgar Square
Samuel Johnson (Fitzgerald), opposite St Clement Danes
Kitchener (Tweed), Horse Guards' Parade
Abraham Lincoln (Saint-Gaudens, copy of one in Chicago), Parliament Square
Mandela (Walters), Parliament Square
Milton (Montford), St Giles, Cripplegate
Mountbatten (Belsky), Foreign Office Green
Gen. Charles James Napier (Adams), Trafalgar Square
Nelson (Railton), Trafalgar Square, with Landseer's lions (cast from guns recovered from the wreck of the *Royal George*)
Florence Nightingale (Walker), Waterloo Place
Palmerston (Woolner), Parliament Square
Peel (Noble), Parliament Square
Pitt (Chantrey), Hanover Square
Portal (Nemon), Embankment Gardens
Prince Albert (Bacon), Holborn Circus
Queen Elizabeth Gate (Lund and Wynne), Hyde Park Corner
Raleigh (Macmillan), Greenwich
Richard I (Coeur de Lion) (Marochetti), Old Palace Yard
Roberts (Bates), Horse Guards' Parade
Royal Air Force (Blomfield), Victoria Embankment
Franklin D. Roosevelt (Reid Dick), Grosvenor Square
Royal Artillery (Great War) (Jagger and Pearson), Hyde Park Corner
Royal Artillery (South Africa) (Colton), The Mall; *Captain Scott* (Lady Scott), Waterloo Place; *Shackleton* (Jagger), Kensington Gore
Shakespeare (Fontana, copy of one by Scheemakers in Westminster Abbey), Leicester Square
Smuts (Epstein), Parliament Square
Sullivan (Goscombe John), Victoria Embankment
Trenchard (Macmillan), Victoria Embankment
Victoria Memorial (Webb and Brock), in front of Buckingham Palace
Raoul Wallenberg (Jackson), Great Cumberland Place
George Washington (Houdon copy), Trafalgar Square
Wellington (Boehm), Hyde Park Corner
Wellington (Chantrey), outside Royal Exchange
John Wesley (Adams Acton), City Road
Westminster School (Crimea) (Scott), Broad Sanctuary
William III (Bacon), St James's Square
Wolseley (Goscombe John), Horse Guards' Parade

PARKS, GARDENS AND OPEN SPACES

CORPORATION OF LONDON OPEN SPACES

W www.cityoflondon.gov.uk

Ashtead Common (200 hectares/500 acres), Surrey
Burnham Beeches and *Fleet Wood* (220 hectares/540 acres), Bucks. Purchased by the Corporation for the benefit of the public in 1880, Fleet Wood (26 hectares/65 acres) being presented in 1921
Coulsdon Common (51 hectares/127 acres), Surrey
Epping Forest (2,428 hectares/6,000 acres), Essex. Purchased by the Corporation and opened to the public in 1882. The present forest is 19.3km (12 miles) long by around 3km (2 miles) wide, approximately one-tenth of its original area
Farthing Downs and New Hill (95 hectares/235 acres), Surrey
Hampstead Heath (319 hectares/791 acres), NW3 Including Golders Hill (15 hectares/36 acres) and Parliament Hill (110 hectares/271 acres)
Highgate Wood (28 hectares/70 acres), N6/N10
Kenley Common (56 hectares/139 acres), Surrey
Queen's Park (12 hectares/30 acres), NW6
Riddlesdown (43 hectares/107 acres), Surrey
Spring Park (21 hectares/51 acres), Kent
West Ham Park (31 hectares/77 acres), E15
West Wickham Common (10 hectares/26 acres), Kent
Woodredon and Warlies Park Estate (299 hectares/740 acres), Waltham Abbey

Also over 150 smaller open spaces within the City of London, including *Finsbury Circus* and *St Dunstan-in-the-East*

OTHER PARKS AND GARDENS

CHELSEA PHYSIC GARDEN, 66 Royal Hospital Road, SW3 4HS T 020-7352 5646 W www.chelseaphysicgarden.co.uk A garden of general botanical research and education, maintaining a wide range of rare and unusual plants; established in 1673 by the Society of Apothecaries

HAMPTON COURT PARK AND GARDENS (303.5 hectares/750 acres), Surrey KT8 9AU T 0844-482 7777 W www.hrp.org.uk Also known as Home Park, the park lies beyond the palace's formal gardens. It contains a herd of deer and a 1,000-year-old oak tree from the original park

ROYAL PARKS

W www.royalparks.gov.uk

Bushy Park (445 hectares/1,099 acres), Middx. Adjoins Hampton Court; contains avenue of horse-chestnuts enclosed in a fourfold avenue of limes planted by William III

Green Park (19 hectares/47 acres), W1 Between Piccadilly and St James's Park, with Constitution Hill leading to Hyde Park Corner

Greenwich Park (74 hectares/183 acres), SE10

Hyde Park (142 hectares/350 acres), W1/W2 From Park Lane to Kensington Gardens and incorporating the Serpentine lake, Apsley House, the Achilles Statue, Rotten Row and the Ladies' Mile; fine gateway at Hyde Park Corner. To the north-east is Marble Arch, originally erected by George IV at the entrance to Buckingham Palace and re-erected in the present position in 1851

Kensington Gardens (111 hectares/275 acres), W2/W8 From the western boundary of Hyde Park to Kensington Palace; contains the Albert Memorial, Serpentine Gallery and Peter Pan statue

Kew, Royal Botanic Gardens (120 hectares/300 acres), Richmond, Surrey TW9 3AB T 020-8332 5655 W www.kew.org Officially inscribed on the UNESCO list of World Heritage Sites

Regent's Park and *Primrose Hill* (197 hectares/487 acres), NW1 From Marylebone Road to Primrose Hill surrounded by the Outer Circle; divided by the Broad Walk leading to the Zoological Gardens

Richmond Park (1,000 hectares/2,500 acres), Surrey. Designated a National Nature Reserve, a Site of Special Scientific Interest and a Special Area of Conservation

St James's Park (23 hectares/58 acres), SW1 From Whitehall to Buckingham Palace; ornamental lake of 4.9 hectares (12 acres); the Mall leads from Admiralty Arch to Buckingham Palace, Birdcage Walk from Storey's Gate to Buckingham Palace

PLACES OF HISTORICAL AND CULTURAL INTEREST

1 Canada Square
Canary Wharf, E14 5DY T 020-7418 2000
W www.canarywharf.com
Also known as 'Canary Wharf', the steel and glass skyscraper is the tallest structure in London and the tallest habitable building in the UK

30 St Mary Axe
EC3A 8EP W www.30stmaryaxe.com
Completed in 2004 and commonly known as the 'Gherkin', it is the second-tallest building in the City of London

Alexandra Palace
Alexandra Palace Way, Wood Green, N22 7AY
T 020-8365 2121 W www.alexandrapalace.com
The Victorian palace was severely damaged by fire in 1980 but was restored, and reopened in 1988. Alexandra Palace now provides modern facilities for exhibitions, conferences, banquets and leisure activities. There is an ice rink, a boating lake, the Phoenix Bar and a conservation area

Barbican Centre
Silk Street, EC2Y 8DS T 020-7638 4141
W www.barbican.org.uk
Owned, funded and managed by the Corporation of London, the Barbican Centre opened in 1982 and houses the Barbican Theatre, a studio theatre called The Pit and the Barbican Hall; it is also home to the London Symphony Orchestra. There are three cinemas, seven conference rooms, two art galleries, a sculpture court, a lending library, trade and banqueting facilities, a conservatory, shops, restaurants, cafes and bars

Central Criminal Court
Old Bailey, EC4M 7EH T 020-7248 3277
W www.cityoflondon.gov.uk
The highest criminal court in the UK, the 'Old Bailey' was built in 1907 on the site of the old Newgate Prison. Trials held there have included those of Oscar Wilde, Dr Crippen and the Yorkshire Ripper

Charterhouse
Charterhouse Square, EC1M 6AN T 020-7253 9503
A Carthusian monastery from 1371 to 1537, purchased in 1611 by Thomas Sutton, who endowed it as a residence for aged men 'of gentle birth' and a school for poor scholars (removed to Godalming in 1872)

Downing Street, SW1
Number 10 Downing Street is the official town residence of the Prime Minister, number 11 of the Chancellor of the Exchequer and number 12 is the office of the Government Whips. The street was named after Sir George Downing, Bt., soldier and diplomat, who was MP for Morpeth from 1660 to 1684

George Inn
Borough High Street, SE1 1NH T 020-7407 2056
W www.nationaltrust.org.uk
The last galleried inn in London, built in 1677. Now owned by the National Trust and run as an ordinary public house

GREENWICH, SE10

Royal Naval College T 020-8269 4747
W www.greenwichfoundation.org.uk
The building was the Greenwich Hospital until 1869. It was built by Charles II, largely from designs by John Webb, and by Queen Mary II and William III, from designs by Wren. It stands on the site of an ancient abbey, a royal house and Greenwich Palace, which was constructed by Henry VII. Henry VIII, Mary I and Elizabeth I were born in the royal palace and Edward VI died there

Greenwich Park (74 hectares/183 acres), SE10
T 020-8858 2608 W www.royalparks.gov.uk
Enclosed by Humphrey, Duke of Gloucester, and laid out by Charles II from the designs of Le Nôtre. On a hill in Greenwich Park is the *Royal Observatory* (founded 1675). Its buildings are now managed by the *National Maritime Museum,* T 020-8858 4422 W www.nmm.ac.uk and the earliest building is named Flamsteed House, after John Flamsteed (1646–1719), the first Astronomer Royal

The Cutty Sark, T 020-8858 2698, W www.cuttysark.org.uk
The last of the famous tea clippers, it was moved into a specially constructed dry dock in 1954 and opened to the public in 1957

Horse Guards, Whitehall, SW1
Archway and offices built about 1753. The changing of the guard takes place daily at 11am (10am on Sundays) and the inspection at 4pm. Only those with the Queen's permission may drive through the gates and archway into *Horse Guards' Parade,* where the colour is 'trooped' on the Queen's official birthday

HOUSES OF PARLIAMENT

House of Commons, Westminster, SW1A 0AA T 020-7219 4272 E hcinfo@parliament.uk W www.parliament.uk

House of Lords, Westminster, SW1A 0PW T 020-7219 3107 E hlinfo@parliament.uk W www.parliament.uk
The royal palace of Westminster, originally built by Edward the Confessor, was the normal meeting place of Parliament from about 1340. St Stephen's Chapel was used from about 1550 for the meetings of the House of Commons, which had previously been held in the Chapter House or Refectory of Westminster Abbey. The House of Lords met in an apartment of the royal palace. The fire of 1834 destroyed much of the palace, and the present Houses of Parliament were erected on the site from the designs of Sir Charles Barry and Augustus Welby Pugin between 1840 and 1867. The chamber of the House of Commons was destroyed by bombing in 1941, and a new chamber designed by Sir Giles Gilbert Scott was used for the first time in 1950. *Westminster Hall and the Crypt Chapel* was the only part of the old palace of Westminster to survive the fire of 1834. It was built by William II from 1097 to 1099 and altered by Richard II between 1394 and 1399. The hammerbeam roof of carved oak dates from 1396–8. The Hall was the scene of the trial of Charles I. *The Victoria Tower* of the House of Lords is 98.5m (323ft) high, and when Parliament is sitting, the Union flag flies by day from its flagstaff. *The Clock Tower* of the House of Commons is 96.3m (316ft) high and contains 'Big Ben', the hour bell said to be named after Sir Benjamin Hall, First Commissioner of Works when the original bell was cast in 1856. This bell, which weighed 16 tons 11 cwt, was found to be cracked in 1857. The present bell (13.5 tons) is a recasting of the original and was first brought into use in 1859. The dials of the clock are 7m (23ft) in diameter, the hands being 2.7m (9ft) and 4.3m (14ft) long (including balance piece). A light is displayed from the Clock Tower at night when parliament is sitting.

During session, tours of the Houses of Parliament are only available to UK residents who have made advance arrangements through an MP or peer. Overseas visitors are no longer provided with permits to tour the Houses of Parliament during session, although they can tour during the summer opening and attend debates for both houses in the Strangers' Galleries. During the summer recess tickets for tours of the Houses of Parliament can be booked by telephone (T 0870-906 3773) or bought on site at the ticket office on Abingdon Green opposite Parliament and the Victoria Tower Gardens. The Strangers' Gallery of the House of Commons is open to the public when the house is sitting. To acquire tickets in advance UK residents should write to their local MP and overseas visitors should apply to their embassy or high commission in the UK for a permit. If none of these arrangements have been made, visitors should join the public queue outside St Stephen's Entrance, where there is also a queue for entry to the House of Lords Gallery.

INNS OF COURT

The Inns of Court are ancient unincorporated bodies of lawyers which for more than five centuries have had the power to call to the Bar those of their members who have qualified for the rank or degree of Barrister-at-Law. There are four Inns of Court as well as many lesser inns

Lincoln's Inn, Chancery Lane/Lincoln's Inn Fields, WC2A 3TL T 020-7405 1393 W www.lincolnsinn.org.uk
The most ancient of the inns with records dating back to 1422. The hall and library buildings are of 1845, although the library is first mentioned in 1474; the old hall (late 15th century) and the chapel were rebuilt *c.*1619–23

Inner Temple, King's Bench Walk, EC4Y 7HL T 020-7797 8250 W www.innertemple.org.uk

Middle Temple, Middle Temple Lane, EC4Y 9AT T 020-7427 4800 W www.middletemple.org.uk
Records for the Middle and Inner Temple date back to the beginning of the 16th century. The site was originally occupied by the Order of Knights Templar *c.*1160–1312. The two inns have separate halls thought to have been formed *c.*1350. The division between the two societies was formalised in 1732 with Temple Church and the Masters House remaining in common. The Inner Temple Garden is normally open to the public on weekdays between 12.30pm and 3pm

Temple Church, EC4Y 7BB T 020-7353 8559 W www.templechurch.com
The nave forms one of five remaining round churches in England

Gray's Inn, South Square, WC1R 5ET T 020-7458 7800 W www.graysinn.info
Founded early 14th century; Hall 1556–8
No other 'Inns' are active, but there are remains of *Staple Inn,* a gabled front on Holborn (opposite Gray's Inn Road). *Clement's Inn* (near St Clement Danes Church), *Clifford's Inn,* Fleet Street, and *Thavies Inn,* Holborn Circus, are all rebuilt. *Serjeants' Inn,* Fleet Street, and another (demolished 1910) of the same name in Chancery Lane, were composed of Serjeants-at-Law, the last of whom died in 1922

Institute of Contemporary Arts
The Mall, SW1Y 5AH T 020-7930 3647 W www.ica.org.uk
Exhibitions of modern art in the fields of film, theatre, new media and the visual arts

Lloyd's
Lime Street, EC3M 7HA T 020-7327 1000 W www.lloyds.com
International insurance market which evolved during the 17th century from Lloyd's Coffee House. The present building was opened for business in May 1986, and houses the Lutine Bell. Underwriting is on three floors with a total area of 10,591 sq. m (114,000 sq. ft). The Lloyd's building is not open to the general public

London Central Mosque and the Islamic Cultural Centre
Park Road, NW8 7RG T 020-7724 3363 W www.iccuk.org
The focus for London's Muslims; established in 1944 but not completed until 1977, the mosque can accommodate about 5,000 worshippers; guided tours are available

London Eye
South Bank, SE1 7PB T 0870-990 0600
W www.londoneye.com

Opened in March 2000 as London's millennium landmark, this 450ft observation wheel is the capital's fourth-largest structure. The wheel provides a 30-minute ride offering panoramic views of the capital

London Zoo

Regent's Park, NW1 4RY **T** 020-7722 3333

W www.londonzoo.org

Madame Tussauds

Marylebone Road, NW1 5LR **T** 0870-999 0046

W www.madame-tussauds.co.uk

Waxwork exhibition

Marlborough House

Pall Mall, SW1Y 5HX **T** 020-7747 6491

W www.thecommonwealth.org

Built by Wren for the first Duke of Marlborough and completed in 1711, the house reverted to the Crown in 1835. In 1863 it became the London house of the Prince of Wales and was the London home of Queen Mary until her death in 1953. In 1959 Marlborough House was given by the Queen as the headquarters for the Commonwealth Secretariat and it was opened as such in 1965. The Queen's Chapel, Marlborough Gate, was begun in 1623 from the designs of Inigo Jones for the Infanta Maria of Spain, and completed for Queen Henrietta Maria. Marlborough House is not open to the public

Port of London

Port of London Authority, Bakers' Hall, 7 Harp Lane, EC3R 6LB **T** 01474-562200 **W** www.portoflondon.co.uk

The Port of London covers the tidal section of the River Thames from Teddington to the seaward limit (the outer Tongue buoy and the Sunk light vessel), a distance of 150km. The governing body is the Port of London Authority (PLA). Cargo is handled at privately operated riverside terminals between Fulham and Canvey Island, including the enclosed dock at Tilbury, 40km below London Bridge. Passenger vessels and cruise liners can be handled at moorings at Greenwich, Tower Bridge and Tilbury

Roman Remains

The city wall of Roman *Londinium* was largely rebuilt during the medieval period but sections may be seen near the White Tower in the Tower of London; at Tower Hill; at Coopers' Row; at All Hallows, London Wall, its vestry being built on the remains of a semi-circular Roman bastion; at St Alphage, London Wall, showing a succession of building repairs from the Roman until the late medieval period; and at St Giles, Cripplegate. Sections of the great forum and basilica, more than 165m^2, have been encountered during excavations in the area of Leadenhall, Gracechurch Street and Lombard Street. Traces of Roman activity along the river include a massive riverside wall built in the late Roman period, and a succession of Roman timber quays along Lower and Upper Thames Street. Finds from these sites can be seen at the Museum of London

Other major buildings are the amphitheatre at Guildhall, remains of bath-buildings in Upper and Lower Thames Street, and the temple of Mithras in Walbrook.

Royal Albert Hall

Kensington Gore, SW7 2AP **T** 020-7589 8212

W www.royalalberthall.com

The elliptical hall, one of the largest in the world, was completed in 1871; since 1941 it has been the venue each summer for the Promenade Concerts founded in 1895 by Sir Henry Wood. Other events include pop and classical music concerts, dance, opera, sporting events, conferences and banquets

Royal Courts of Justice

Strand, WC2A 2LL **T** 020-7947 6000

W www.hmcourts-service.gov.uk

Victorian Gothic building that is home to the High Court. Visitors are free to watch proceedings

Royal Hospital, Chelsea

Royal Hospital Road, SW3 4SR **T** 020-7881 5200

W www.chelsea-pensioners.co.uk

Founded by Charles II in 1682, and built by Wren; opened in 1692 for old and disabled soldiers. The extensive grounds include the former Ranelagh Gardens and are the venue for the Chelsea Flower Show each May

Royal Opera House

Covent Garden, WC2E 9DD **T** 020-7240 1200

W www.royaloperahouse.org

Home of The Royal Ballet (1931) and The Royal Opera (1946). The Royal Opera House is the third theatre to be built on the site, opening 1858; the first was opened in 1732

St James's Palace

Pall Mall, SW1A 1BQ **T** 020-7930 4832 **W** www.royal.gov.uk

Built by Henry VIII, only the Gatehouse and Presence Chamber remain; later alterations were made by Wren and Kent. Representatives of foreign powers are still accredited 'to the Court of St James's'. *Clarence House* (1825), the official London residence of the Prince of Wales and his sons, stands within the St James's Palace estate

St Paul's Cathedral

St Paul's Churchyard, EC4M 8AD **T** 020-7236 4128

E chapter@stpaulscathedral.org.uk **W** www.stpauls.co.uk

Built 1675–1710. The cross on the dome is 111m (365ft) above ground level, the inner cupola 66.4 m (218ft) above the floor. 'Great Paul' in the south-west tower weighs nearly 17 tons. The organ by Father Smith (enlarged by Willis and rebuilt by Mander) is in a case carved by Grinling Gibbons, who also carved the choir stalls

Somerset House

Strand, WC2R 1LA **T** 020 7845 4600

W www.somersethouse.org.uk

The river facade (183m/600ft long) was built in 1776–1801 from the designs of Sir William Chambers; the eastern extension, which houses part of King's College, was built by Smirke in 1829–35. Somerset House was the property of Lord Protector Somerset, at whose attainder in 1552 the palace passed to the Crown, and it was a royal residence until 1692. Somerset House has recently undergone extensive renovation and is home to the Gilbert Collection, Embankment Galleries and the Courtauld Institute Gallery. Open-air concerts and ice-skating (Dec–Jan) are held in the courtyard

SOUTH BANK, SE1

Arts complex on the south bank of the River Thames which consists of:

The *Royal Festival Hall* **T** 0871-663 2500

W www.southbankcentre.co.uk

Opened in 1951 for the Festival of Britain, adjacent are the 917-seat *Queen Elizabeth Hall,* the *Purcell Room,* and the *Hayward Gallery.*

BFI Southbank **T** 020-7255 1444 **W** www.bfi.org.uk

Opened in 1952 and is administered by the British Film Institute, has three auditoria showing over 1,000 films a year. The London Film Festival is held here every November. There is also an IMAX cinema with 477 seats

The *Royal National Theatre,* T 020-7452 3000

W www.nationaltheatre.org.uk

Opened in 1976 and stages classical, modern, new and neglected plays in its three auditoria: the Olivier, the Lyttelton and the Cottesloe theatres

Southwark Cathedral

London Bridge, SE1 9DA T 020-7367 6700

E cathedral@southwark.anglican.org

W www.southwark.anglican.org/cathedral

Mainly 13th century, but the nave is largely rebuilt. The tomb of John Gower (1330–1408) is between the Bunyan and Chaucer memorial windows in the north aisle; Shakespeare's effigy, backed by a view of Southwark and the Globe Theatre, is in the south aisle; the tomb of Bishop Andrewes (died 1626) is near the screen. The Lady Chapel was the scene of the consistory courts of the reign of Mary (Gardiner and Bonner) and is still used as a consistory court. John Harvard, after whom Harvard University is named, was baptised here in 1607, and the chapel by the north choir aisle is his memorial chapel.

Thames Embankments

Sir Joseph Bazalgette (1819–91) constructed the *Victoria Embankment,* on the north side from Westminster to Blackfriars for the Metropolitan Board of Works, 1864–70; (the seats, of which the supports of some are a kneeling camel, laden with spicery, and of others a winged sphinx, were presented by the Grocers' Company and by W. H. Smith, MP, in 1874); the *Albert Embankment,* on the south side from Westminster Bridge to Vauxhall, 1866–9, and the the Chelsea Embankment, 1871–4. The total cost exceeded £2m. Bazalgette also inaugurated the London main drainage system, 1858–65. A medallion *(Flumini vincula posuit)* has been placed on a pier of the *Victoria Embankment* to commemorate the engineer

Thames Flood Barrier

W www.environment-agency.gov.uk

Officially opened in May 1984, though first used in February 1983, the barrier consists of ten rising sector gates which span approximately 570 yards from bank to bank of the Thames at Woolwich Reach. When not in use the gates lie horizontally, allowing shipping to navigate the river normally; when the barrier is closed, the gates turn through 90 degrees to stand vertically more than 50 feet above the river bed. The barrier took eight years to complete and can be raised within about 30 minutes

Westminster Abbey

Broad Sanctuary, SW1P 3PA T 0207-222 5152

E info@westminster-abbey.org

W www.westminster-abbey.org

Founded as a Benedictine monastery over 1,000 years ago, the church was rebuilt by Edward the Confessor in 1065 and again by Henry III in the 13th century. The abbey is the resting place for monarchs including Edward I, Henry III, Henry V, Henry VII, Elizabeth I, Mary I and Mary Queen of Scots, and has been the setting of coronations since that of William the Conqueror in 1066. In Poets' Corner there are memorials to many literary figures, and many scientists and musicians are also remembered here. The grave of the Unknown Warrior is to be found in the nave

Westminster Cathedral

Francis Street, SW1P 1QW T 020-7798 9055

W www.westminstercathedral.org.uk

Roman Catholic cathedral built 1895–1903 from the designs of J. F. Bentley. The campanile is 284 feet high

LONDON THEATRES

Adelphi Theatre, Strand, WC2R 0NS T 020-7344 0055 ⊖ Charing Cross

Aldwych Theatre, Aldwych, WC2B 4DF T 020-7379 3367 ⊖ Covent Garden/Holborn

Almeida Theatre, Almeida Street, N1 1TA T 020-7359 4404 ⊖ Angel/Highbury & Islington

Apollo Theatre, Shaftesbury Avenue, W1D 7EZ T 0870-890 1101 ⊖ Piccadilly Circus

Apollo Victoria Theatre, Wilton Road, SW1 1LL T 0207-834 6318 ⊖ Victoria

Barbican Theatre, Barbican Centre, EC2Y 8DS T 020-7638 8891 ⊖ Barbican/Moorgate

Cambridge Theatre, Earlham Street, WC2 9HU T 0870-890 1102 ⊖ Covent Garden/Leicester Square

Chelsea Theatre, World's End Place, SW10 0DR T 020-7352 1967 ⊖ Sloane Square

Comedy Theatre, Panton Street, SW1Y 4DN T 0870-060 6637 ⊖ Leicester Square/Piccadilly Circus

Criterion Theatre, Jermyn Street, SW1Y 4XA T 0844-847 1778 ⊖ Piccadilly Circus

Dominion Theatre, Tottenham Court Road, W1T 7AQ T 020-7927 0900 ⊖ Tottenham Court Road

Donmar Warehouse, Earlham Street, WC2H 9LX T 0870-060 6624 ⊖ Covent Garden

Duchess Theatre, Catherine Street, WC2B 5LA T 020-7494 5075 ⊖ Covent Garden

Duke Of York's Theatre, St Martin's Lane, WC2N 4BG T 0870-060 6623 ⊖ Leicester Square/Piccadilly Circus

Fortune Theatre, Russell Street, WC2B 5HH T 0870-060 6626 ⊖ Covent Garden

Garrick Theatre, Charing Cross Road, WC2H 0HH T 020-7520 5690 ⊖ Charing Cross/Leicester Square

Gielgud Theatre, Shaftesbury Avenue, W1D 6AR T 0844-482 5138 ⊖ Piccadilly Circus

Globe Theatre, New Globe Walk, SE1 9DT T 020-7902 1400 ⊖ Mansion House

Hackney Empire, Mare Street, E8 1EJ T 020-8985 2424 ⊖ Bethnal Green

Her Majesty's Theatre, Haymarket, SW1Y 4QL T 020-7494 5400 ⊖ Piccadilly Circus

Jermyn Street Theatre, Jermyn Street, SW1Y 6ST T 020-7287 2875 ⊖ Piccadilly Circus

London Coliseum, St Martin's Lane, WC2N 4ES T 020-7836 0111 ⊖ Charing Cross

London Palladium, Argyll Street, W1F 7TF T 020-7494 5020 ⊖ Oxford Circus

Lyceum Theatre, Wellington Street, WC2E 7RQ T 0870-243 9000 ⊖ Covent Garden

Lyric Theatre,Shaftesbury Avenue, W1D 7ES T 0870-040 0082 ⊖ Piccadilly Circus

Lyric Theatre Hammersmith, King Street, W6 0QL T 0871-221 1729 ⊖ Hammersmith

National Theatre, South Bank, SE1 9PX T 020-7452 3000 ⊖ Waterloo

New Ambassadors Theatre, West Street, WC2H 9ND T 0870-060 6627 ⊖ Leicester Square

New London Theatre, Drury Lane, WC2B 5PW T 020-7242 9802 ⊖ Holborn

Noël Coward (formerly Albery), St Martin's Lane, WC2N 4AA T 0844-482 5138 ⊖ Leicester Square

Novello Theatre, Aldwych, WC2B 4LD T 020-7759 9640 ⊖ Charing Cross

Old Vic Theatre, The Cut, SE1 8NB T 0870-060 6628 ⊖ Waterloo
Palace Theatre, Shaftesbury Avenue, W1V 8AY T 0870-895 5579 ⊖ Leicester Square/Piccadilly Circus
Phoenix Theatre, Charing Cross Road, WC2H 0JP T 0870-060 6629 ⊖ Tottenham Court Road
Piccadilly Theatre, Denman Street, W1D 7DY T 0870-060 6630 ⊖ Piccadilly Circus
Playhouse Theatre, Northumberland Avenue, WC2N 5DE T 0870-060 6631 ⊖ Embankment
Prince Edward Theatre, Old Compton Street, W1D 4HS T 020-7447 5459 ⊖ Leicester Square
Prince of Wales Theatre, Coventry Street, W1D 6AS T 0844-482 5115 ⊖ Piccadilly Circus
Queen's Theatre, Shaftesbury Avenue, W1D 6BA T 020-7395 5243 ⊖ Piccadilly Circus
Royal Albert Hall, Kensington Gore, SW7 2AP T 020-7589 8212 ⊖ South Kensington
Royal Court Theatre, Sloane Square, SW1W 8AS T 020-7565 5000 ⊖ Sloane Square
Royal Festival Hall, South Bank SE1 8XX T 0871-663 2500 ⊖ Waterloo
Sadler's Wells, Rosebery Avenue, EC1R 4TN T 020-7863 8198 ⊖ Angel
St Martin's Theatre, West Street, WC2H 9NZ T 0870-162 8787 ⊖ Leicester Square
Savoy Theatre, Strand, WC2R 0ET T 0870-164 8787 ⊖ Charing Cross
Shaftesbury Theatre, Shaftesbury Avenue, WC2H 8DP T 020-7379 5399 ⊖ Holborn/Tottenham Court Road
Soho Theatre,Dean Street, W1D 3NE T 020-7287 5060 ⊖ Tottenham Court Road
Southwark Playhouse, Shipwright Yard, SE1 2TF T 0844-847 1656 ⊖ Southwark
Theatre Royal Drury Lane, Catherine Street, WC2B 5JF T 020-7494 5000 ⊖ Covent Garden
Theatre Royal Haymarket, Haymarket, SW1Y 4HT T 020-7930 8890 ⊖ Piccadilly Circus
Trafalgar Studios, Whitehall, SW1A 2DY T 0870-060 6632 ⊖ Charing Cross/Embankment
Tricycle Theatre, Kilburn High Road, NW6 7JR T 020-7372 6611 ⊖ Kilburn
Vaudeville Theatre, Strand, WC2R 0NH T 0870-890 0511 ⊖ Charing Cross
Venue Theatre, Leicester Place, WC2H 7BP T 020-7734 6004 ⊖ Leicester Square
Victoria Palace Theatre, Victoria Street, SW1E 5EA T 0870-895 5577 ⊖ Victoria
Wyndham's Theatre, Charing Cross Road, WC2H 0DA T 0870-060 6633 ⊖ Leicester Square
Young Vic, The Cut, SE1 8LZ T 020-7922 2922 ⊖ Waterloo

HALLMARKS

Hallmarks are the symbols stamped on gold, silver or platinum articles to indicate that they have been tested at an official Assay Office and that they conform to one of the legal standards. The marking of gold and silver articles to identify the maker was instituted in England in 1363 under a statute of Edward III. In 1478 the Assay Office in Goldsmiths' Hall was established and all gold and silversmiths were required to bring their wares to be date-marked by the Hall, hence the term 'hallmarked'.

With certain exceptions, all gold, silver or platinum articles are required by law to be hallmarked before they are offered for sale. Current hallmarking requirements come under the UK Hallmarking Act 1973 and subsequent amendments. The act is built around the principle of description, where it is an offence for any person to apply to an unhallmarked article a description indicating that it is wholly or partly made of gold, silver or platinum. There is an exemption by weight: compulsory hallmarks are not needed on gold under 1g, silver under 7.78g and platinum under 0.5g. Also, some descriptions, such as rolled gold and gold plate, are permissible. The four assay offices at London, Birmingham, Sheffield and Edinburgh operate under the act.

MODERN HALLMARKS

Since January 1999, UK hallmarks have consisted of three compulsory symbols – the sponsor's mark, the millesimal fineness (purity) mark and the assay office mark. Traditional marks such as the year date letter, the Britannia for 958 silver, the lion passant for 925 silver (lion rampant in Scotland) and the orb for 950 platinum may be added voluntarily. The distinction between UK and foreign articles has been removed, and more finenesses are now legal, reflecting the more common finenesses elsewhere in Europe.

SPONSOR'S MARK

Instituted in England in 1363, the sponsor's mark was originally a device such as a bird or fleur-de-lis. Now it consists of a combination of at least two initials (usually a shortened form of the manufacturer's name) and a shield design. The London Assay Office offers 45 standard shield designs but other designs are possible by arrangement.

MILLESIMAL FINENESS MARK

The millesimal fineness (purity) mark indicates the number of parts per thousand of pure metal in the alloy. The current finenesses allowed in the UK are:

Gold	999	
	990	
	916.6	(22 carat)
	750	(18 carat)
	585	(14 carat)
	375	(9 carat)
Silver	999	
	958.4	(Britannia)
	925	(sterling)
	800	
Platinum	999	
	950	
	900	
	850	

ASSAY OFFICE MARK

This mark identifies the particular assay office at which the article was tested and marked. The British assay offices are:

LONDON, Goldsmiths' Hall, Gutter Lane, London EC2V 8AQ T 020-7606 8971 W www.thegoldsmiths.co.uk

BIRMINGHAM, PO Box 151, Newhall Street, Birmingham B3 1SB T 0121-236 6951 W www.theassayoffice.co.uk

SHEFFIELD, Guardians' Hall, 137 Portobello Street, Sheffield S1 4DS T 0114-275 5111 W www.assayoffice.co.uk

EDINBURGH, Goldsmiths' Hall, 24a Broughton Street, Edinburgh EH1 3RH T 0131-556 1144 W www.assayofficescotland.com

Assay offices formerly existed in other towns, eg Chester, Exeter, Glasgow, Newcastle, Norwich and York, each having its own distinguishing mark.

DATE LETTER

The date letter shows the year in which an article was assayed and hallmarked. Each alphabetical cycle has a distinctive style of lettering or shape of shield. The date letters were different at the various assay offices and the particular office must be established from the assay office mark before reference is made to tables of date letters. Date letter marks became voluntary from 1 January 1999.

The table which follows shows one specimen shield and letter used by the London Assay Office on silver articles for each alphabetical cycle from 1498. The same letters are found on gold articles but the surrounding shield may differ. Until 1 January 1975 two calendar years are given for each specimen date letter as the letter changed annually in May on St Dunstan's Day (the patron saint of silversmiths). Since 1 January 1975, each date letter has indicated a calendar year from January to December and each office has used the same style of date letter and shield for all articles:

LONDON (GOLDSMITHS' HALL) DATE LETTERS FROM 1498

	from	*to*
	1498–9	1517–8
	1518–9	1537–8
	1538–9	1557–8
	1558–9	1577–8
	1578–9	1597–8
	1598–9	1617–8
	1618–9	1637–8
	1638–9	1657–8
	1658–9	1677–8
	1678–9	1696–7
	1697	1715–6
	1716–7	1735–6
	1736–7	1738–9
	1739–40	1755–6
	1756–7	1775–6
	1776–7	1795–6
	1796–7	1815–6
	1816–7	1835–6
	1836–7	1855–6
	1856–7	1875–6
	1876–7 [A to M square shield, N to Z as shown]	1895–6
	1896–7	1915–6
	1916–7	1935–6
	1936–7	1955–6
	1956–7	1974
	1975	1999
	2000	

OTHER MARKS

FOREIGN GOODS

Foreign goods imported into the UK are required to be hallmarked before sale, unless they already bear a convention mark (*see* below) or a hallmark struck by an independent assay office in the European Economic Area which is deemed to be equivalent to a UK hallmark.

The following are the assay office marks used for gold until the end of 1998. For silver and platinum the symbols remain the same but the shields differ in shape.

CONVENTION HALLMARKS

Special marks at authorised assay offices of the signatory countries of the International Convention on Hallmarking (Austria, the Czech Republic, Denmark, Finland, Hungary, Ireland, Latvia, Lithuania, the Netherlands, Norway, Poland, Portugal, Sweden, Switzerland, UK and Ukraine) are legally recognised in the United Kingdom as approved hallmarks. These consist of a sponsor's mark, a common control mark, a fineness mark (arabic numerals showing the standard in parts per thousand), and an assay office mark. There is no date letter.

The common control marks are:

GOLD SILVER PLATINUM

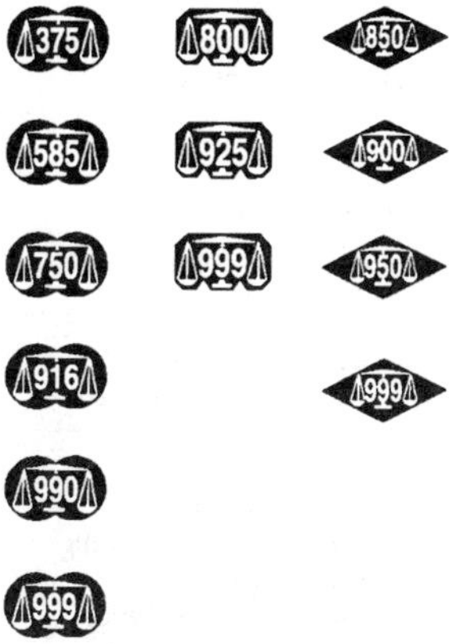

COMMEMORATIVE MARKS

There are other marks to commemorate special events: the silver jubilee of King George V and Queen Mary in 1935, the coronation of Queen Elizabeth II in 1953, and her silver jubilee in 1977. During 1999 and 2000 there was a voluntary additional Millennium Mark. A mark to commemorate the golden jubilee of Queen Elizabeth II was available during 2002.

BRITISH CURRENCY

The unit of currency is the pound sterling (£) of 100 pence. The decimal system was introduced on 15 February 1971.

COIN

Gold Coins
One hundred pounds £100*
Fifty pounds £50*
Twenty-five pounds £25*
Ten pounds £10*
Five pounds £5
Two pounds £2
Sovereign £1
Half-sovereign 50p

Silver Coins
(Britannia coins)*
Two pounds £2
One pound £1
Fifty pence 50p
Twenty pence 20p

Maundy Money†
Fourpence 4p
Threepence 3p
Twopence 2p
Penny 1p

Bi-colour Coins‡
Two pounds £2

Nickel-Brass Coins
Two pounds £2 (pre-1997)§
One pound £1

Cupro-Nickel Coins
Crown £5 (since 1990)§
Fifty pence 50p
Crown 25p (pre-1990)§
Twenty pence 20p
Ten pence 10p
Five pence 5p

Bronze Coins
Two pence 2p
One penny 1p

Copper-plated Steel Coins¶
Two pence 2p
One penny 1p

* Britannia coins: gold bullion coins introduced 1987; silver coins introduced 1997
† Gifts of special money distributed by the sovereign annually on Maundy Thursday to the number of elderly poor men and women corresponding to the sovereign's own age
‡ Cupro-nickel centre and nickel-brass outer ring
§ Commemorative coins; not intended for general circulation
¶ Since September 1992, although in 1998 the 2p was struck in both copper-plated steel and bronze

GOLD COIN

Gold ceased to circulate during the First World War. Since then controls on buying, selling and holding gold coin have been imposed at various times but have subsequently been revoked. Under the Exchange Control (Gold Coins Exemption) Order 1979, gold coins may now be imported and exported without restriction, except gold coins which are more than 50 years old and valued at a sum in excess of £8,000; these cannot be exported without specific authorisation from the Department for Business, Enterprise and Regulatory Reform.

Value Added Taxation on the sale of gold coins was revoked in 2000.

SILVER COIN

Prior to 1920 silver coins were struck from sterling silver, an alloy of which 925 parts in 1,000 were silver. In 1920 the proportion of silver was reduced to 500 parts. Since 1947 all 'silver' coins, except Maundy money, have been struck from cupro-nickel, an alloy of 75 parts copper and 25 parts nickel, except for the 20p, composed of 84 parts copper, 16 parts nickel. Maundy coins continue to be struck from sterling silver.

BRONZE COIN

Bronze, introduced in 1860 to replace copper, is an alloy of 97 consisting mainly of copper with small amounts of zinc and tin. Bronze was replaced by copper-plated steel in September 1992 with the exception of 1998 when the 2p was made in both copper-plated steel and bronze.

LEGAL TENDER

Gold (dated 1838 onwards, if not below least current weight)	to any amount
£5 (Crown since 1990)*	to any amount
£2	to any amount
£1	to any amount
50p	up to £10
25p (Crown pre-1990)*	up to £10
20p	up to £10
10p	up to £5
5p	up to £5
2p	up to 20p
1p	up to 20p

* Redeemable at the Post Office

The £1 coin was introduced in 1983 to replace the £1 note. The following coins have ceased to be legal tender:

Farthing	31 Dec 1960
Halfpenny (½d)	31 Jul 1969
Half-crown	31 Dec 1969
Threepence	31 Aug 1971
Penny (1d)	31 Aug 1971
Sixpence	30 Jun 1980
Halfpenny (½p)	31 Dec 1984
Old 5 pence	31 Dec 1990
Old 10 pence	30 Jun 1993
Old 50 pence	28 Feb 1998

The Channel Islands and the Isle of Man issue their own coinage, which are legal tender only in the island of issue.

	Metal	*Standard weight (g)*	*Standard diameter (mm)*
1p	bronze	3.56	20.3
1p	copper-plated steel	3.56	20.3
2p	bronze	7.13	25.9
2p	copper-plated steel	7.13	25.9
5p	cupro-nickel	3.25	18.0
10p	cupro-nickel	6.5	24.5
20p	cupro-nickel	5.0	21.4
25p Crown	cupro-nickel	28.28	38.6
50p	cupro-nickel	8.00	27.3
£1	nickel-brass	9.5	22.5
£2	nickel-brass	15.98	28.4
£2	cupro-nickel, nickel-brass	12.00	28.4
£5 Crown	cupro-nickel	28.28	38.6

The 'remedy' is the amount of variation from standard permitted in weight and fineness of coins when first issued from the Royal Mint.

THE TRIAL OF THE PYX
The Trial of the Pyx is the examination by a jury to ascertain that coins made by the Royal Mint, which have been set aside in the pyx (or box), are of the proper weight, diameter and composition required by law. The trial is held annually, presided over by the Queen's Remembrancer, with a jury of freemen of the Company of Goldsmiths.

BANKNOTES

Bank of England notes are currently issued in denominations of £5, £10, £20 and £50 for the amount of the fiduciary note issue, and are legal tender in England and Wales. No £1 notes have been issued since 1984 and in March 1998 the outstanding notes were written off in accordance with the provision of the Currency Act 1983.

The current E series of notes was introduced from June 1990, replacing the D series (*see* below). A new-style £20 note, the first in series F, was introduced on 13 March 2007. The historical figures portrayed in these series are:

£5	May 2002–date	Elizabeth Fry
£5	Jun 1990–2003	George Stephenson*
£10	Nov 2000–date	Charles Darwin*
£10	Apr 1992–2003	Charles Dickens*
£20	Mar 2007–date	Adam Smith
£20	Jun 1999–date	Sir Edward Elgar
£20	Jun 1991–2001	Michael Faraday*
£50	Apr 1994–date	Sir John Houblon

* These notes have been withdrawn from circulation: George Stephenson on 21 Nov 2003; Charles Dickens on 31 Jul 2003; Michael Faraday on 28 Feb 2001

NOTE CIRCULATION
Note circulation is highest at the two peak spending periods of the year, around Christmas and during the summer holiday period.

The value of notes in circulation (£million) at the end of February 2007 and 2008 was:

	2007	*2008*
£5	1,100	1,242
£10	5,886	6,115
£20	23,740	25,648
£50	6,705	7,526
Other notes*	1,108	4,447
TOTAL	38,449	44,978

* Includes higher value notes used internally in the Bank of England, eg as cover for the note issues of banks in Scotland and Northern Ireland in excess of their permitted issue

LEGAL TENDER
Banknotes which are no longer legal tender are payable when presented at the head office of the Bank of England in London.

The white notes for £10, £20, £50, £100, £500 and £1,000, which were issued until April 1943, ceased to be legal tender in May 1945, and the white £5 note in March 1946.

The white £5 note issued between October 1945 and September 1956, the £5 notes issued between 1957 and 1963 (bearing a portrait of Britannia) and the first series to bear a portrait of the queen, issued between 1963 and 1971, ceased to be legal tender in March 1961, June 1967 and September 1973 respectively.

The series of £1 notes issued during the years 1928 to 1960 and the 10 shilling notes issued from 1928 to 1961 (those without the royal portrait) ceased to be legal tender in May and October 1962 respectively. The £1 note first issued in March 1960 (bearing on the back a representation of Britannia) and the £10 note first issued in February 1964 (bearing a lion on the back), both bearing a portrait of the Queen on the front, ceased to be legal tender in June 1979. The £1 note first issued in 1978 ceased to be legal tender on 11 March 1988. The 10 shilling note was replaced by the 50p coin in October 1969, and ceased to be legal tender on 21 November 1970.

The D series of banknotes was introduced from 1970 and ceased to be legal tender from the dates shown below. The predominant identifying feature of each note was the portrayal on the back of a prominent figure from British history:

£1	Feb 1978–Mar 1988	Sir Isaac Newton
£5	Nov 1971–Nov 1991	Duke of Wellington
£10	Feb 1975–May 1994	Florence Nightingale
£20	Jul 1970–Mar 1993	William Shakespeare
£50	Mar 1981–Sep 1996	Sir Christopher Wren

The £1 coin was introduced on 21 April 1983 to replace the £1 note.

OTHER BANKNOTES
Scotland – Banknotes are issued by three Scottish banks. The Royal Bank of Scotland issues notes for £1, £5, £10, £20, £50 and £100. Bank of Scotland and the Clydesdale Bank issue notes for £5, £10, £20, £50 and £100. Scottish notes are not legal tender in the UK but they are an authorised currency.

Northern Ireland – Banknotes are issued by four banks in Northern Ireland. The Bank of Ireland, the Northern Bank and the Ulster Bank issue notes for £5, £10, £20, £50 and £100. The First Trust Bank issues notes for £10, £20, £50 and £100. Northern Ireland notes are not legal tender in Northern Ireland but they circulate widely and enjoy a status comparable to that of Bank of England notes.

Channel Islands – The States of Guernsey issues its own currency notes and coinage. The notes are for £1, £5, £10, £20 and £50, and the coins are for 1p, 2p, 5p, 10p, 20p, 50p, £1, £2 and £5. The States of Jersey issues its own currency notes and coinage. The notes are for £1, £5, £10, £20 and £50, and the coins are for 1p, 2p, 5p, 10p, 20p, 50p, £1 and £2.

The Isle of Man – The Isle of Man government issues notes for £1, £5, £10, £20 and £50. Although these notes are only legal tender in the Isle of Man, they are accepted at face value in branches of the clearing banks in the UK. The Isle of Man issues coins for 1p, 2p, 5p, 10p, 20p, 50p, £1, £2 and £5.

Although none of the series of notes specified above is legal tender in the UK, they are generally accepted by banks irrespective of their place of issue. At one time banks made a commission charge for handling Scottish and Irish notes but this was abolished some years ago.

BANKING AND PERSONAL FINANCE

There are two main types of deposit-taking institutions: banks and building societies, although National Savings and Investments also provides savings products. Banks and building societies are supervised by the Financial Services Authority and National Savings and Investments is accountable to the Treasury. As a result of the conversion of several building societies into banks in the 1990s, the size of the banking sector, which was already substantially greater than the non-bank deposit-taking sector, increased further.

The main institutions within the British banking system are the Bank of England (the central bank), retail banks, investment banks and overseas banks. In its role as the central bank, the Bank of England acts as banker to the government and as a note-issuing authority; it also oversees the efficient functioning of payment and settlement systems.

Since May 1997, the Bank of England has had operational responsibility for monetary policy. At monthly meetings of its monetary policy committee the bank sets the interest rate at which it will lend to the money markets.

OFFICIAL INTEREST RATES 2003–8

6 November 2003	3.75%
5 February 2004	4.00%
6 May 2004	4.25%
10 June 2004	4.50%
5 August 2004	4.75%
4 August 2005	4.50%
3 August 2006	4.75%
9 November 2006	5.00%
11 January 2007	5.25%
10 May 2007	5.50%
5 July 2007	5.75%
6 December 2007	5.50%
7 February 2008	5.25%
10 April 2008	5.00%

RETAIL BANKING

Retail banks offer a wide variety of financial services to individuals and companies, including current and deposit accounts, loan and overdraft facilities, automated teller (cash dispenser) machines, cheque guarantee cards, credit and debit cards, investment services, pensions, insurance and mortgages. All banks offer telephone and internet banking facilities in addition to traditional branch services.

The Financial Ombudsman Service provides independent and impartial arbitration in disputes between banks and their customers (*see* Financial Services Regulation).

PAYMENT CLEARINGS

The Association for Payment Clearing Services (APACS) is the UK trade association for payments and for those institutions that deliver payment services to customers. It is also the banking industry's voice on payment issues regarding plastic cards, card fraud, cheques, electronic payments and cash. Membership of APACS is open to any member of a payment scheme which is widely used or significant in the UK. As at April 2008 APACS had 31 members, comprising the major banks, one building society and Royal Mail Group.

There are three separate companies which manage the majority of payment clearings in the UK (and which are contactable through APACS):

- BACS Payment Schemes Ltd manages the schemes under which electronic payments are made, processing direct debits, direct credits and standing orders
- CHAPS Ltd provides electronic same-day clearing for sterling and euro payments
- Cheque and Credit Clearing Company Ltd oversees the clearing of cheques and paper credits in Great Britain

APACS, Mercury House, Triton Court, 14 Finsbury Square, London EC2A 1LQ **T** 020-7711 6200 **W** www.apacs.org.uk

MAJOR RETAIL BANKS' FINANCIAL RESULTS 2007

Bank group	*Profit before taxation £ million*	*Profit after taxation £ million*	*Total assets £ million*
Abbey	1,110	822	199,372
Alliance and Leicester	399	296	78,955
Barclays	7,076	5,095	1,227,361
HBOS	5,474	4,109	666,947
HSBC	12,167	10,279	1,183,048
Lloyds TSB	4,000	3,321	353,346
Northern Rock*	(168)	(199)	109,321
RBS Group	9,900	7,712	1,900,519

* On 17 February 2008 the Chancellor of the Exchequer announced the decision to take Northern Rock into temporary public ownership; the ordinary, preference and foundation shares of Northern Rock were transferred to the Treasury Solicitor on 22 February 2008.

GLOSSARY OF FINANCIAL TERMS

AER (ANNUAL EQUIVALENT RATE) – A notional rate quoted on savings and investment products which demonstrates the return on interest, when compounded and paid annually.

APR (ANNUAL PERCENTAGE RATE) – Calculates the total amount of interest payable over the whole term of a product (such as investment or loan), allowing consumers to compare rival products on a like-for-like basis. Companies offering loans, credit cards, mortgages or overdrafts are required by law to provide the APR rate. Where typical APR is shown, it refers to the company's typical borrower and so is given as a best example; rate and costs may vary depending on individual circumstances.

ANNUITY – A type of insurance policy that provides regular income in exchange for a lump sum. Everyone who has a pension and has built up a lump sum with their provider must buy an annuity by the time they reach 75. The annuity can be bought from a company other than the existing pension provider.

ASU – Accident, sickness and unemployment insurance taken out by a borrower to protect against being unable to work for these reasons. The policy will usually pay a percentage of the normal monthly mortgage repayment if the borrower is unable to work.

ATM (AUTOMATED TELLER MACHINE) – Commonly referred to as cash machines. Users can access their bank accounts using a card for simple transactions such as withdrawing and depositing cash. Some banks and independent ATM deployers charge for transactions.

BANKER'S DRAFT – A cheque drawn on a bank against a cash deposit. Considered to be a secure way of receiving money in instances where a cheque could 'bounce' or where it is not desirable to receive cash.

BASE RATE – The minimum rate at which banks are prepared to lend money. This acts as a benchmark for all other interest rates.

BASIS POINT – Unit of measure (usually one-hundredth of a percentage point) used to express movements in interest rates, foreign rates or bond yields.

BUY-TO-LET – The purchase of a residential property for the sole purpose of letting to a tenant. Not all lenders provide mortgage finance for this purpose. Buy-to-let mortgages typically require at least a 15–25 per cent deposit and the loan agreed is based on a combination of the borrower's income in addition to the rental value of the property. Because of the higher risks involved in letting property, buy-to-let mortgages are more expensive.

CAPITAL GAIN/LOSS – Increase/decrease in the value of a capital asset when it is sold or transferred compared to its initial worth.

CAPPED RATE MORTGAGE – The interest rate applied to a loan is guaranteed not to rise above a certain rate for a set period of time; the rate can therefore fall but will not rise above the capped rate. The level at which the cap is fixed is usually higher than for a fixed rate mortgage for a comparable period of time. The lender normally imposes early redemption penalties within the first few years.

CASH CARD – Issued by banks and building societies for withdrawing cash from ATMs.

CHARGE CARD – Charge cards, eg American Express and Diners Club, can be used in a similar way to credit cards but the debt must be settled in full each month.

CHIP AND PIN CARD – A credit/debit card which incorporates an embedded chip containing unique owner details. When used with a PIN number, such cards offer greater security as they are less prone to fraud. Since 14 February 2006, most card transactions in the UK have required the use of a chip and pin card.

CREDIT CARD – Normally issued with a credit limit, credit cards can be used for purchases until the limit is reached. There is normally an interest-free period on the outstanding balance of up to 56 days. Charges can be avoided if the balance is paid off in full within the interest-free period. Alternatively part of the balance can be paid and in most cases there is a minimum amount set by the issuer (normally a percentage of the outstanding balance) which must be paid on a monthly basis. Some card issuers charge an annual fee and most issuers belong to a least one major credit card network, eg Mastercard or Visa.

CREDIT RATING – Overall credit worthiness of a borrower based on information from a credit reference agency, such as Experian or Equifax, which holds details of credit agreements, payment records, county court judgements etc for all adults in the UK. This information is supplied to lenders who use it in their credit scoring or underwriting systems to calculate the risk of granting a loan to an individual and the probability that it will be repaid. Each lender sets their own criteria for credit worthiness and may accept or reject a credit application based on an individual's credit rating.

CRITICAL ILLNESS COVER – Insurance that covers borrowers against critical illnesses such as stroke, heart attack or cancer and is designed to protect mortgage or other loan payments.

DEBIT CARD – Debit cards were introduced on a large scale in the UK in the mid-1980s, replacing cash and cheques to purchase goods and services. They can be used to withdraw cash from ATMs in the UK and abroad and may also function as a cheque guarantee card. Funds are automatically withdrawn from an individual's bank account after making a purchase and no interest is charged.

DISCOUNTED MORTGAGE – Discounted mortgages guarantee an interest rate set at a margin below the standard variable rate for a period of time. The discounted rate will move up or down with the standard variable rate, but the payment rate will retain the agreed differential below the standard variable rate. The lender normally imposes early redemption penalties within the first few years.

EARLY REDEMPTION PENALTY – *see* Redemption Penalty

ENDOWMENT MORTGAGE – Only the interest on a property loan is paid back to the lender each month as long as an endowment life insurance policy is taken out for an agreed amount of time, typically 25 years. When the policy matures the lender will take repayment of the money owed on the property loan and any surplus goes to the policyholder. If the endowment policy shows a shortfall on projected returns, the policy holder must make further provision to pay off the mortgage.

EQUITY – When applied to real estate, equity is the difference between the value of a property and the amount outstanding on any loan secured against it. Negative equity occurs when the loan is greater than the market value of the property.

FIXED RATE MORTGAGE – A repayment mortgage

where the interest rate on the loan is fixed for a set amount of time, normally a period of between one and ten years. The interest rate does not vary with changes to the base rate resulting in the monthly mortgage payment remaining the same for the duration of the fixed period. The lender normally imposes early redemption penalties within the first few years.

INTEREST ONLY MORTGAGE – Only interest is paid by the borrower and capital remains constant for the term of the loan. The onus is on the borrower to make provision to repay the capital at the end of the term. This is usually achieved through an investment vehicle such as an endowment policy or pension.

ISA – The individual savings account is a means by which investors can save and invest without paying any tax on the proceeds. Money can be invested across three investment elements: cash, stocks and shares and life insurance products. There are limits on the amount that can be invested during any given tax year.

LOAN TO VALUE – This is the ratio between the size of a mortgage loan sought and the mortgage lender's valuation. On a loan of £55,000, for example, on a property valued at £100,000 the loan to value is 55 per cent. This means that there is sufficient equity in the property for the lender to be reassured that if interest or capital repayments were stopped, it could sell the property and recoup the money owed. Fewer options are available to borrowers requiring high LTV.

MIG (MORTGAGE INDEMNITY GUARANTEE) – An insurance policy designed to protect the lender against loss in the event of the borrower defaulting or ceasing to repay a mortgage. It offers no protection to the borrower. Not all lenders charge MIG premiums.

ONLINE BANKING – Also known as internet or e-banking, where a range of banking transactions from paying bills, transferring funds to arranging overdrafts can be carried out online.

PERSONAL PENSION PLAN (PPP) – Designed for the self-employed or those in non-pensionable employment. Contributions made to a PPP are exempt from tax and the retirement age may be selected at any time from age 50 to 75. Up to 25 per cent of the pension fund may be taken as a tax-free cash sum on retirement.

PHISHING – A fraudulent attempt to obtain bank account details and security codes through an email. The email purports to come from a *bona fide* bank or building society and attempts to steer the recipient, usually under the pretext that the banking institution is updating its security arrangements, to a website which requests personal details.

PIN (PERSONAL IDENTIFICATION NUMBER) – A PIN is issued alongside a cash card to allow the user to access a bank account via an ATM. PINs are also issued with smart, credit and debit cards and, since 14 February 2006, have been requested in the majority of shops and restaurants as a further security measure when making a purchase.

PORTABLE MORTGAGE – A mortgage product that can be transferred to a different property in the event of a house move. Preferable where early redemption penalties are charged.

REDEMPTION PENALTY – A charge levied for paying off a loan, debt balance or mortgage before a date agreed with the lender.

REPAYMENT MORTGAGE – In contrast to the interest only mortgage, the monthly repayment includes an element of the capital sum borrowed in addition to the interest charged.

SELF-CERTIFICATION – Several lenders allow borrowers to self-certify their income. This type of scheme is useful to the self-employed who may not have accounts available or any other person who has difficulty proving their regular income.

SHARE – A share is a divided-up unit of the value of a company. If a company is worth £100 million, and there are 50 million shares in issue, then each share is worth £2 (usually listed as pence). As the overall value of the company fluctuates so does the share price.

SMART CARD – A new generation of cashless payment system. They carry more information than debit cards including mortgage and health details and a fixed number of units of real money. The card is used in conjunction with a PIN and once the money on the card is spent, it must be loaded again by transferring money to it from a bank account via an ATM or telephone.

TELEPHONE BANKING – Banking facilities which can be accessed via the telephone.

UNIT TRUST – A 'pooled' fund of assets, usually shares, owned by a number of individuals. Managed by professional, authorised fund-management groups, unit trusts have traditionally delivered better returns than average cash deposits, but do rise and fall in value as their underlying investment varies in value.

WITH-PROFITS – Usually applies to pensions, endowments, savings schemes or bonds. The intention is to smooth out the rises and falls in the stock market for the benefit of the investor. Actuaries working for the insurance company, or fund managers, hold back some profits in good years in order to make up the difference in years when shares perform badly.

VARIABLE RATE MORTGAGE – Repayment mortgages where the interest rate set by the lender increases or decreases in relation to the base interest rate which can result in fluctuating monthly repayments.

FINANCIAL SERVICES REGULATION

FINANCIAL SERVICES AUTHORITY

The FSA has been the single regulator for financial services in the UK since 1 December 2001, when the Financial Services and Markets Act 2000 (FSMA) came into force. The FSA's aim is to promote efficient, orderly and fair financial markets and help retail consumers to receive a fair deal.

The FSA is required to pursue four statutory objectives:
- maintaining market confidence
- raising public awareness
- protecting consumers
- reducing financial crime

The legislation also requires the FSA to have regard to the following principles while carrying out its general functions:
- using its resources in an economic and efficient way
- the responsibilities of regulated firms' own management
- being proportionate in imposing burdens or restrictions on the industry
- facilitating innovation
- the international character of financial services and the competitive position of the United Kingdom
- not impeding or distorting competition unnecessarily

ORGANISATION AND STRUCTURE

The FSA is a company limited by guarantee and financed by levies on the industry. It receives no funds from the public purse. It is accountable to treasury ministers and, through them, to parliament. The FSA must report annually on the achievement of its statutory objectives to the Treasury, which is required to lay the report before parliament. The FSA's budgeted costs for 2008–9 are £323m.

FSA REGISTER

The FSA register is a public record of financial services firms, individuals and other bodies who come under the FSA's regulatory jurisdiction as defined in the FSMA. The register has information on all authorised firms currently doing business in the UK. It includes firms that are UK registered as well as those authorised in other European economic area states that conduct business in the UK. Each entry outlines exactly what regulated activities the firm or individual is authorised to carry out.

FINANCIAL SERVICES AUTHORITY, 25 The North Colonnade, Canary Wharf, London E14 5HS **T** 020-7066 1000
Helpline 0845-606 1234 **W** www.fsa.gov.uk
Chair, Sir Callum McCarthy
Chief Executive, Hector Sants

COMPENSATION

Created under the FSMA, the Financial Services Compensation Scheme (FSCS) is the UK's statutory fund of last resort for customers of authorised financial services firms. It provides compensation if a firm authorised by the FSA is unable, or likely to be unable, to pay claims against it. In general this is when a firm has stopped trading and has insufficient assets to meet claims, or is in insolvency. The FSCS covers deposits, insurance policies, insurance broking (for business on or after 14 January 2005), investment business and mortgage advice and arranging (for business on or after 31 October 2004). The FSCS is independent of the FSA, with separate staff and premises. However, the FSA appoints the board of the FSCS and sets its guidelines. The FSCS is funded by levies on authorised firms.

The Pension Protection Fund (PPF) is a statutory fund established under the Pensions Act 2004 and became operational on 6 April 2005. The fund was set up to pay compensation to members of eligible defined benefit pension schemes, where there is a qualifying insolvency event in relation to the employer and where there are insufficient assets in the pension scheme to cover PPF levels of compensation. Compulsory annual levies are charged on all eligible schemes to help fund the PPF, in addition to investment of PPF assets.

FINANCIAL SERVICES COMPENSATION SCHEME, 7th Floor, Lloyds Chambers, Portsoken Street, London E1 8BN
T 020-7892 7300 **E** enquiries@fscs.org.uk
W www.fscs.org.uk
Chair, David Hall
Chief Executive, Loretta Minghella

PENSION PROTECTION FUND, Knollys House, 17 Addiscombe Road, Croydon, Surrey CR0 6SR **T** 0845-600 2541
E information@ppf.gsi.gov.uk
W www.pensionprotectionfund.org.uk
Chair, Lawrence Churchill
Chief Executive, Partha Dasgupta

DESIGNATED PROFESSIONAL BODIES

Professional firms are exempt from requiring direct regulation by the FSA if they carry out only certain restricted activities that arise out of, or are complementary to, the provision of professional services, such as arranging the sale of shares on the instructions of executors or trustees, or providing services to small, private companies. These firms are, however, supervised by designated professional bodies (DPBs). There are a number of safeguards to protect consumers dealing with firms that do not require direct regulation. These arrangements include:
- the FSA's power to ban a specific firm from taking advantage of the exemption and to restrict the regulated activities permitted to the firms
- rules which require professional firms to ensure that their clients are aware that they are not authorised persons
- a requirement for the DPBs to supervise and regulate the firms and inform the FSA on how the professional firms carry on their regulated activities

See Professional Education section for the following:
Association of Chartered Certified Accountants
Council for Licensed Conveyancers
Institute of Actuaries
Institute of Chartered Accountants in England and Wales

Institute of Chartered Accountants in Ireland
Institute of Chartered Accountants of Scotland
Law Society of England and Wales
Law Society of Northern Ireland
Law Society of Scotland
Royal Institution of Chartered Surveyors

RECOGNISED INVESTMENT EXCHANGES

The FSA currently supervises seven recognised investment exchanges (RIEs) in the UK; under the FSMA, recognition confers an exemption from the need to be authorised to carry out regulated activities in the UK. The RIEs are organised markets on which member firms can trade investments such as equities and derivatives. As a regulator the FSA must focus on the impact of changes brought about by the continued growth in electronic trading by exchanges and other organisations. Issues such as how these changes affect market quality, reliability and access are important and the FSA works with the exchanges to ensure that new systems meet regulatory requirements. The RIEs are listed with their year of recognition in parentheses:

EUROPEAN DERIVATIVES EXCHANGE (EDX) LONDON (2003), 10 Paternoster Square, London EC4M 7LS **T** 020-7797 1000 **W** www.londonstockexchange.com/edx (*see also* London Stock Exchange)

INTERCONTINENTAL EXCHANGE (ICE) FUTURES EUROPE (2001)*, International House, 1 St Katharine's Way, London E1W 1UY **T** 020-7265 3648 **W** www.theice.com

LONDON INTERNATIONAL FINANCIAL FUTURES (LIFFE) ADMINISTRATION AND MANAGEMENT (2001), Cannon Bridge House, 1 Cousin Lane, London EC4R 3XX **T** 020-7623 0444 **W** www.liffe.com

LONDON METAL EXCHANGE (2001), 56 Leadenhall Street, London EC3A 2BJ **T** 020-7264 5555 **W** www.lme.co.uk

LONDON STOCK EXCHANGE (LSE) (2001), 10 Paternoster Square, London EC4M 7LS **T** 020-7797 1000 **W** www.londonstockexchange.com

PLUS MARKETS (2007), Standon House, 21 Mansell Street, London E1 8AA **T** 020-7553 2000 **W** www.plusmarketsgroup.com

SWISS EXCHANGE (SWX) EUROPE (2001), 34th Floor, One Canada Square, Canary Wharf, London E14 5AA **T** 020-7864 4310 **W** www.swxeurope.com

RECOGNISED CLEARING HOUSES

The FSA is also responsible for recognising and supervising recognised clearing houses (RCHs), which organise the settlement of transactions on recognised investment exchanges. There are currently four RCHs in the UK:

CLEAR EUROPE (2008), International House, 1 St Katharine's Way, London E1 1UY **T** 020-7265 3648

EUROCLEAR UK AND IRELAND (2001), Watling House, 33 Cannon Street, London EC4M 5SB **T** 020-7849 0000 **W** www.euroclear.com

EUROPEAN CENTRAL COUNTERPARTY (2008), Broadgate West, 1 Snowdon Street, London EC2A 2DQ **T** 020-7650 1401 **W** www.euroccp.co.uk

LONDON CLEARING HOUSE (LCH) CLEARNET (2001), Aldgate House, 33 Aldgate High Street, London EC3N 1EA **T** 020-7426 7000 **W** www.lchclearnet.com

OMBUDSMAN SCHEMES

The Financial Ombudsman Service was set up by the Financial Services and Markets Act 2000 to provide consumers with a free, independent service for resolving disputes with authorised financial firms. The Financial Ombudsman Service can consider complaints about most financial matters including: banking; credit cards and store cards; financial advice; hire purchase and pawnbroking; insurance; loans and credit; mortgages; pensions; savings and investments; stocks, shares, unit trusts and bonds.

Complainants must first complain to the firm involved. They do not have to accept the ombudsman's decision and are free to go to court if they wish, but if a decision is accepted, it is binding for both the complainant and the firm.

The Pensions Ombudsman can investigate and decide complaints and disputes about the way that occupational and personal pension schemes are administered and managed. The Pensions Ombudsman is also the Ombudsman for the board of the Pension Protection Fund (PPF) and as such can deal with disputes regarding decisions made by the board or the actions of PPF staff.

FINANCIAL OMBUDSMAN SERVICE, South Quay Plaza, 183 Marsh Wall, London E14 9SR **Helpline** 0845-080 1800 **T** 020-7964 1000
E complaint.info@financial-ombudsman.org.uk
W www.financial-ombudsman.org.uk
Chief Ombudsman, Walter Merricks, CBE
Principal Ombudsmen, Tony Boorman; David Thomas

PENSIONS OMBUDSMAN, 11 Belgrave Road, London SW1V 1RB **T** 020-7834 9144 **E** enquiries@pensions-ombudsman.org.uk **W** www.pensions-ombudsman.org.uk
Pensions Ombudsman/Pension Protection Fund Ombudsman, Tony King
Deputy Pensions Ombudsman/Pension Protection Fund Ombudsman, Charlie Gordon

PANEL ON TAKEOVERS AND MERGERS

The Panel on Takeovers and Mergers is an independent body, established in 1968, whose main functions are to issue and administer the City code on takeovers and mergers. Its principal objective is to ensure equality of treatment and opportunity for all shareholders in takeover bids and mergers.

The panel comprises up to 34 members drawn from major financial and business institutions. The chair, deputy chair and up to 20 independent members are nominated by the panel's own nomination committee. The remaining members are nominated by professional bodies representing the banking, insurance, investment, pension and accountancy industries and the CBI.

PANEL ON TAKEOVERS AND MERGERS, 10 Paternoster Square, London EC4M 7DY **T** 020-7382 9026
W www.thetakeoverpanel.org.uk
Chair, Peter Scott, QC

NATIONAL SAVINGS AND INVESTMENTS

NS&I (National Savings and Investments) is an executive agency of HM Treasury and one of the UK's largest financial providers, with 28 million customers and over £84bn invested. NS&I offers savings and investment products to personal savers and investors and the money is used to manage the national debt. When people invest in National Savings and Investments they are lending money to the government which pays them interest or prizes in return. All products are financially secure because they are guaranteed by HM Treasury.

TAX-FREE PRODUCTS

SAVINGS CERTIFICATES

Index-Linked Saving Certificates
Otherwise known as inflation-beating savings, index-linked saving certificates are fixed rate investments that pay tax-free returns guaranteed to be above inflation. They are available in three- and five-year terms and are sold in issues. The minimum investment for each issue is £100 and the maximum £15,000.

Fixed Interest Saving Certificates
Fixed interest saving certificates are fixed rate investments that pay tax-free returns. They are available in two- and five-year terms and are sold in issues for which the minimum investment is £100 and the maximum £15,000.

PREMIUM BONDS

Introduced in 1956, premium bonds enable savers to enter a regular draw for tax-free prizes, while retaining the right to get their money back. A sum equivalent to interest on each bond is put into a prize fund and distributed by monthly prize draws. The prizes are drawn by ERNIE (electronic random number indicator equipment) and are free of all UK income tax and capital gains tax. Two £1m jackpots are drawn each month.

Bonds are in units of £1, with a minimum purchase of £100; above this, purchases must be in multiples of £10, up to a maximum holding limit of £30,000 per person. Bonds become eligible for prizes once they have been held for one clear calendar month following the month of purchase. Each £1 unit can win only one prize per draw, but it will be awarded the highest for which it is drawn. Bonds remain eligible for prizes until they are repaid.

The scheme offers a facility to reinvest prize wins automatically. Upon completion of an automatic prize reinvestment mandate, holders receive new bonds which are immediately eligible for future prize draws. Bonds can only be held in the name of an individual and not by organisations.

As at March 2008, 169.30 million prizes totalling £10.9bn had been distributed since the first prize draw in 1957.

CHILDREN'S BONUS BONDS

Children's bonus bonds were introduced in 1991. The bonds are sold in five-year issues at multiples of £25. For each issue the minimum holding is £25 and the maximum holding is £3,000 per child. They can be bought for any child under 16, but must be held by a parent or guardian. All returns are totally exempt from UK income tax and a bonus is payable if the bond is held for the full five years.

OTHER PRODUCTS

GUARANTEED EQUITY BONDS

Guaranteed equity bonds are five-year investments where the returns are linked to the performance of the FTSE-100 index with a guarantee that the original capital invested will be returned even if the FTSE-100 index fell over the five years. They are sold in limited issues with a minimum investment of £1,000 and a maximum of £1m. The returns are subject to income tax on maturity, unless they are held in a self-invested pension plan (SIPP).

SAVINGS AND INVESTMENT ACCOUNTS

The easy access savings account was launched in January 2004 replacing the ordinary account (also known as the Post Office savings account). The easy access savings account offers access to savings via Post Office counters, an ATM card, telephone and online. It can be opened with a minimum balance of £100 and has a maximum limit of £2m (£4m jointly). The interest is paid without deduction of tax at source.

The investment account is a passbook account which pays tiered rates of interest. It can be opened with a minimum balance of £20 and has a maximum limit of £100,000. The interest is paid without deduction of tax at source.

Since April 1999 NS&I has offered cash individual savings accounts (ISAs). A cash ISA can be opened online, by post, telephone and in post offices with a minimum investment of £10. A direct ISA was launched in April 2006 which can be opened and managed by telephone and online with a minimum investment of £1,000. Interest for both ISAs is calculated daily and is free of tax.

INCOME BONDS

NS&I income bonds were introduced in 1982. They are suitable for those who want to receive regular monthly payments of interest while preserving the full cash value of their capital. The bonds are sold in multiples of £500. The minimum holding is £500 and the maximum £1m (sole or joint holding). A variable rate of interest is calculated on a day-to-day basis and paid monthly. Interest is taxable but is paid without deduction of tax at source.

GUARANTEED INCOME BONDS

Guaranteed income bonds were introduced in February 2008. They are designed for those who want to receive regular monthly payments of interest while preserving the full cash value of their capital. The minimum holding is £500 and the maximum £1m, including any amount held in guaranteed growth bonds and fixed rate savings bonds (the latter was closed to new investment in 2008). A fixed rate of interest is calculated on a day-to-day basis and paid monthly on these bonds. Interest is taxable and tax is deducted at source.

GUARANTEED GROWTH BONDS

Guaranteed growth bonds were introduced in February 2008. They are suitable for those who want to receive regular monthly payments of interest while preserving the full cash value of their capital. The minimum holding is £500 and the maximum £1m, including any amount held in guaranteed income bonds and fixed rate savings bonds (the latter was closed to new investment in 2008). A fixed rate of interest is calculated on a day-to-day basis and is paid annually on the anniversary of the date of investment. Interest is taxable and tax is deducted at source.

FURTHER INFORMATION

Further information can be obtained online (W www.nsandi.com), by telephone (T 0845-964 5000) or at Post Office counters.

NATIONAL DEBT

The decision to transfer monetary policy to the Bank of England in 1997 while HM Treasury retained control of fiscal matters led to the creation of the UK Debt Management Office (DMO) as an executive agency of HM Treasury. In April 2000 exchequer cash management was transferred to the DMO which assumed responsibility for issuing Treasury bills (very short-dated securities) and gilts. The national debt also includes the liabilities of National Savings and Investments and other public sector debt and foreign currency. In 2002 the operations of the long-standing statutory functions of the Public Works Loan Board, which lends capital to local authorities, and the Commissioners for the Reduction of National Debt, which manages the investment portfolios of certain public funds, were integrated within the DMO. (*See also* Government Departments.)

THE LONDON STOCK EXCHANGE

The London Stock Exchange serves the needs of industry and investors by providing facilities for raising capital and a central marketplace for securities trading. This marketplace covers government stocks (called gilts), UK and overseas company shares (called equities and fixed interest stocks), and other instruments such as covered warrants and exchange traded funds (ETFs).

Firms trading on the London Stock Exchange buy and sell shares on behalf of the public, as well as institutions such as pension funds or insurance companies. In return for transacting the deal, the broker will charge a commission, which is usually based upon the value of the transaction. The market makers, or wholesalers, in each security do not charge a commission for their services, but will quote the broker two prices, a price at which they will buy and a price at which they will sell. It is the middle of these two prices which is published in lists of share prices in newspapers.

HISTORY

The London Stock Exchange is one of the world's oldest stock exchanges dating back more than 300 years when it began in the coffee houses of 17th-century London.

'BIG BANG'

In March 1986 the London Stock Exchange opened its doors for the first time to overseas and corporate membership, allowing banks, insurance companies and overseas securities houses to become members of the exchange and to buy existing member firms. On 27 October 1986 further reforms took place which became known as 'big bang':

- the abolition of scales of minimum commissions, allowing clients to negotiate freely with their brokers about the charge for their services
- the abolition of the separation of member firms into brokers and jobbers: all firms are now broker/dealers able to operate in a dual capacity
- the introduction of the Stock Exchange automated quotations system (SEAQ) which moved dealing away from face-to-face trading on the market floor to being conducted via telephone and later electronically, with the launch of the stock exchange electronic trading service (SETS) in 1997
- individual members ceased to have voting rights
- the London Stock Exchange became a private limited company under the Companies Act 1985

RECENT DEVELOPMENTS

The London Stock exchange became demutualised in 2000 and listed on its own main market in 2001 in order to allow further commercialisation.

In 2003 the London Stock Exchange created EDX London (European derivatives exchange), a recognised investment exchange for international equity derivatives, and on 1 October 2007 the exchange merged with the Italian stock exchange Borsa Italiana.

PRIMARY MARKETS

The London Stock Exchange enables companies to raise capital for development and growth through the issue of securities. For a company entering the market for the first time there is a choice of four exchange markets, depending upon the size, history and requirements of the company:

- the main market
- the Alternative Investment Market (AIM), established in June 1995, enables small, young and growing companies to raise capital, widen their investor base and have their shares traded on a regulated market without the expense of a full London Stock Exchange listing. Many companies use AIM as a stepping-stone to a full listing
- the Professional Securities Market (PSM), established in July 2005, provides a solution to issuers who want to list their debt securities, convertible securities or depository receipts in London without having to re-state their financial information to conform with international financial reporting standards
- the Specialist Fund Market (SFM), established in November 2007, is the exchange's market for highly specialised investment entities that wish to target institutional, professional and highly knowledgeable investors

Once admitted, all companies are obliged to keep their shareholders informed of their progress, making announcements of a price-sensitive nature through a primary information provider approved by the FSA.

At 31 December 2007 there were 3,307 companies listed on the London Stock Exchange: 1,239 main market UK-listed, with an equity market value of £1,932.5bn; 341 main market internationally listed, with an equity market value of £2,293.4bn; 1,694 listed on AIM, with a market value of £97.6bn; 31 listed on PSM; and two companies listed on the Specialist Fund Market.

REGULATION

The Financial Services Authority (FSA) has overall responsibility for regulating the UK's financial industry under the provisions of the Financial Services and Markets Act 2000. The Act compels business to be conducted through a recognised investment exchange (RIE). The London Stock Exchange is an authorised RIE.

LONDON STOCK EXCHANGE, 10 Paternoster Square, London EC4M 7LS T 020-7797 1000
W www.londonstockexchange.com
Chair, Chris Gibson-Smith
Chief Executive, Dame Clara Furse, DBE

INSURANCE

AUTHORISATION AND REGULATION OF INSURANCE COMPANIES

Since 2001, the Financial Services Authority (FSA) has been the authorising, enforcement, supervisory and rule-making body of insurers. Since 2005, this has also included insurance brokers.

The FSA's powers are primarily conferred by the Financial Services and Markets Act 2000, which unified the previous sectoral arrangements and regulators.

AUTHORISATION

The FSA's role is to ensure that firms to which it grants authorisation satisfy the necessary financial criteria, that the senior management of the company are 'fit and proper persons' and that unauthorised firms are not permitted to trade. This part of the FSA's role was previously undertaken by HM Treasury under the Insurance Companies Act 1982, which was repealed when the Financial Services and Markets Act came fully into force. At the end of 2007 there were over 1,000 insurance organisations and friendly societies with authorisation from the FSA to transact one or more classes of insurance business in the UK. However, the single European insurance market, established in 1994, gave insurers authorised in any other European Union country automatic UK authorisation without further formality. This means a potential market of over 5,000 insurers.

REGULATION

All life insurers, general insurers, re-insurers, insurance and reinsurance brokers, financial advisers and composite firms are statutorily regulated. This is achieved through the formulation (after consultation) by the FSA of rules and guidance for regulated organisations. The FSA is also responsible for consumer education and the reduction of financial crime, particularly money laundering.

FINANCIAL SERVICES AUTHORITY, 25 The North Colonnade, London E14 5HS T 020-7066 1000 W www.fsa.gov.uk

COMPLAINTS

Disputes between policyholders and insurers can be referred to the Financial Ombudsman Service (FOS). Policyholders with a complaint against their financial services provider must firstly take the matter to the highest level within the company. Thereafter, if it remains unresolved and it involves an amount below £100,000, they can refer, free of charge, to the Ombudsman Bureau, which examines the facts of a complaint and delivers a decision binding on the provider (but not the policyholder). Small businesses with a turnover of up to £1m also have access to the scheme. The Financial Ombudsman Service also covers other areas of the financial services industry including banks, building societies and investment firms. In 2007 the FOS handled 123,089 complaints about financial services companies.

FINANCIAL SERVICES OMBUDSMAN SERVICE, South Quay Plaza, 183 Marsh Wall, London E14 9SR T 020-7964 1000 F 020-7964 1002 W www.financial-ombudsman.org.uk
Chief Ombudsman, Walter Merricks

ASSOCIATION OF BRITISH INSURERS

Over 90 per cent of the domestic business of UK insurance companies is transacted by the 360 members of the Association of British Insurers (ABI). ABI is a trade association which protects and promotes the interests of all its insurance company members. Only insurers authorised in EU countries are eligible for membership. Brokers, intermediaries, financial advisers and claims handlers may not join ABI but may have their own trade associations.

ASSOCIATION OF BRITISH INSURERS (ABI), 51 Gresham Street, London EC2V 7HQ W www.abi.org.uk
Chair, Archie Kane
Director-General, Stephen Haddrill

BALANCE OF PAYMENTS

The financial services industry contributes 8.5 per cent to the UK's gross domestic product (GDP). In 2006 insurance companies' net exports recovered to £3.5bn, after falling to £1.6bn in 2004.

TAKEOVERS AND MERGERS

2007 saw the battle between Standard Life and Pearl Group to take over the closed fund specialist Resolution Group. Initially, the Resolution board backed the cash and shares offer from Standard Life, but less than an hour after its final offer, Standard Life was outbid by Pearl and withdrew from the race.

GENERAL INSURANCE

Climate change and its consequences have been an issue of concern to general insurers for a number of years, but 2007 would have put an end to any doubts insurers might have had about the validity of the claims they received. The year began with storms and floods in January, while September saw a series of tornados across the UK. These disasters were dwarfed by the very serious flooding of June and July. The latest estimate for the total cost of the 180,000 claims for that period now amounts to £3bn. 130,000 were domestic claims, 30,000 commercial and 20,000 motor. By the end of 2007 insurers had settled about 60 per cent of the domestic claims although many of the outstanding cases were simply waiting for buildings to dry out before repairs could be completed. By April 2008 97.5 per cent of domestic claimants were expected to have returned to their homes. Inevitably, the subject of premium increases and availability of future cover remains a vital issue. At present, insurers have an agreement with the UK government (dating back to 1953) to continue to offer flood cover as long as the UK's flood defences are adequately maintained. While the announcement at the beginning of July that the government was increasing spending on flood defences to £800m a year, insurers are still concerned that more needs to be done if the agreement is to be maintained. In September 2007 the industry unveiled an initiative called ClimateWise (W www.climatewise.org.uk) – planned before the storms of June and July – to become more actively involved in the climate change debate and work to reduce its effects.

The fight against fraud has also been an ongoing issue for some years. In May 2008 the ABI announced that insurance fraud was costing £1.6bn per year. This adds nearly £40 per year to the premiums paid by honest policyholders. The new Insurance Fraud Bureau (W www.insurancefraudbureau.org) began to record some successes during 2007 but more needs to be done, particularly in the co-ordination of police forces

In October 2007 the House of Lords gave a judgment that sufferers of a disease known as pleural plaques – small fibrous disks on the inside of the chest – could not claim compensation from their employers' insurers as the disease has no effect on health or ability to work, produces no symptoms and does not cause other asbestos-related diseases. The insurers' satisfaction at this outcome was short-lived, however, as the Scottish government immediately announced it planned to legislate to overturn this ruling. Despite an increase in weather damage claims of over 400 per cent, continued losses on the motor account and rises (although very much smaller) in business interruption and theft claims costs, the general insurance industry still managed an overall underwriting profit of £1.6bn and a trading profit (which takes into account the profits on investments) of £6.7bn. Not so surprising were the small falls recorded in the costs of fire and domestic subsidence claims.

LONDON INSURANCE MARKET

The London Insurance Market is a unique wholesale marketplace and a distinct, separate sector of the UK insurance and reinsurance industry. It is the world's leading market for internationally traded insurance and reinsurance, its business comprising mainly overseas non-life large and high-exposure risks. The market is centred on the City of London, which provides the required financial, banking, legal and other support services. Around 57 per cent of London market business is transacted at Lloyd's, 37 through insurance companies and the remainder through protection and indemnity clubs. In 2006 the market had a written gross premium income of over £24bn. Around 150 Lloyd's brokers service the market.

The trade association for the international insurers and reinsurers writing primarily non-marine insurance and all classes of reinsurance business in the London market is the International Underwriting Association (IUA).

INTERNATIONAL UNDERWRITING ASSOCIATION, London Underwriting Centre, 3 Mincing Lane, London EC3R 7DD
W www.iua.co.uk

BRITISH INSURANCE COMPANIES

The following insurance company figures refer to members and certain non-members of the ABI.

WORLDWIDE GENERAL BUSINESS UNDERWRITING RESULTS *(£m)*

	2005			*2006*		
	UK	*Overseas*	*Total*	*UK*	*Overseas*	*Total*
Motor						
Premiums	10,397	3,412	13,809	10,277	3,289	13,566
Profit (loss)	(191)	221	30	(204)	3	(201)
Percentage of premiums	1.8	6.5	0.2	2.0	0.1	1.5
Non-motor						
Premiums	20,146	6,054	26,200	20,144	6,681	26,825
Profit (loss)	1,340	612	1,952	1,685	218	1,903
Percentage of premiums	6.7	10.1	47.5	8.4	3.3	7.1

CLAIMS STATISTICS *(£m)*

	2003	*2004*	*2005*	*2006*	*2007*
Theft	630	512	475	517	525
Fire	1,067	812	1,128	1,139	1,102
Weather	610	424	735	475	2,459
Domestic subsidence	390	199	225	302	162
Business interruption	92	108	267	168	320
Total	2,738	2,052	2,851	2,601	4,568

NET PREMIUM INCOME BY SECTOR 2006 *(£m)*

	UK	*Overseas*
Motor	10,277	3,289
Non-motor	20,144	6,681
Marine, aviation and transport	343	245
Reinsurance	267	98
Total general business	31,031	10,313
Ordinary long-term	122,735	28,870
Industrial long-term	247	–
Total long-term business	122,982	28,870

WORLDWIDE GENERAL BUSINESS TRADING RESULTS *(£m)*

	2005	*2006*
Net written premiums	42,129	41,440
Underwriting results	1,805	1,624
Investment income	6,213	5,118
Overall trading profit	8,017	6,742
Profit as percentage of premium income	19.0	16.3

LLOYD'S OF LONDON

Lloyd's of London is an international market for almost all types of general insurance. Lloyd's currently has a capacity to accept insurance premiums of around £15.95bn. Much of this business comes from outside Great Britain and makes a valuable contribution to the balance of payments.

A policy is underwritten at Lloyd's by a mixture of private and corporate members, corporate members having been admitted for the first time in 1992. Specialist underwriters accept insurance risks at Lloyd's on behalf of members (referred to as 'Names') grouped in syndicates. There are currently 72 syndicates of varying sizes, each managed by an underwriting agent approved by the Council of Lloyd's.

Members divide into three categories: corporate organisations, individuals who have no limit to their liability for losses, and those who have an agreed limit. Corporate members represent 84% of the market's capacity, individuals with unlimited liability represent 7 per cent with the remaining 9 per cent being individuals with a limited liability (known as NameCos).

Lloyd's is incorporated by an act of parliament (Lloyd's Acts 1871 onwards) and is governed by an 18-person council, made up of six working, six external and six nominated members. The structure immediately below this changed when, in 2002, Lloyd's members voted at an extraordinary general meeting to implement a new franchise system for the market with the aim of improving profitability. The first move was the introduction of a new governance structure, replacing the Lloyd's Market Board and the Lloyd's Regulatory Board with a new 11-person Lloyd's Franchise Board. Four main committees report to this new board.

The corporation is a non-profit making body chiefly financed by its members' subscriptions. It provides the premises, administrative staff and services enabling Lloyd's underwriting syndicates to conduct their business. It does not, however, assume corporate liability for the risks accepted by its members. Individual members are responsible to the full extent of their personal means for their underwriting affairs unless they have converted to limited liability companies.

Lloyd's syndicates have no direct contact with the public. All business is transacted through insurance brokers accredited by the Corporation of Lloyd's. In addition, non-Lloyd's brokers in the UK, when guaranteed by Lloyd's brokers, are able to deal directly with Lloyd's motor syndicates, a facility which has made the Lloyd's market more accessible to the insuring public.

The FSA has ultimate responsibility for the regulation of the Lloyd's market. However, in situations where Lloyd's internal regulatory and compensation arrangements are more far-reaching – as for example with the Lloyd's Central Fund which safeguards claim payments to policyholders – the regulatory role is delegated to the Council of Lloyd's.

Lloyd's also provides the most comprehensive shipping intelligence service in the world. The shipping and other information received from Lloyd's agents, shipowners, news agencies and other sources throughout the world is collated and distributed to the media as well as to the maritime and commercial sectors in general. *Lloyd's List* is London's oldest daily newspaper and contains news of general commercial interest as well as shipping information. It has been independent of Lloyd's since a management buy-out in 1992. *Lloyd's Shipping Index*, published weekly, lists some 23,000 ocean-going merchant vessels in alphabetical order and gives the latest known report of each.

DEVELOPMENTS IN 2007

The Lloyd's market recorded a pre-tax profit in 2007 of £3,846m (up 5 per cent from £3,662m in 2006). These results reflect the international nature of much of Lloyd's business. While the insurance companies were hit by heavy losses caused by the UK flooding in June and July 2007, Lloyd's, with its more international client base, escaped reasonably unscathed as the level of catastrophes in the rest of the world remained low. These results may have been a contributing factor to the continued rise in the number of syndicates operating at Lloyd's. Inevitably, this increased capacity and profitability brings fears of a softening of the market with some rate reductions (or maintenance of current levels) already in evidence.

LLOYD'S OF LONDON, One Lime Street, London EC3M 7HA
T 020-7327 1000 W www.lloydsoflondon.co.uk
Chair, Lord Levene of Portsoken
Chief Executive, Richard Ward

LLOYD'S MEMBERSHIP

	2006	*2007*
Individual	1,124	907
Corporate	1,017	1,155

TOTAL MARKET CAPACITY *(£m)*

	2006	*2007*
Individual (unlimited liability)	1,124	1,127
Individual (limited liability)	927	1,449
Corporate	12,427	13,524
Total	14,788	16,100

LLOYD'S SEGMENTAL RESULTS 2007 *(£m)*

	Gross premiums written	*Net earned premium*	*Result*
Reinsurance	5,453	4,312	790
Casualty	3,809	2,975	408
Property	3,364	2,805	205
Marine	1,226	1,010	127
Motor	983	866	14
Energy	1,019	774	206
Aviation	464	323	50
Life	46	30	3
Total from syndicate operations	16,366	13,095	1,803

LIFE AND LONG-TERM INSURANCE AND PENSIONS

Work on a number of life and pensions issues continued throughout 2007 but very little seemed to have been completed. Uppermost on the agenda is the reform of pensions. Discussions and consultations on this issue have been ongoing for some years and although the pensions bill was published in December, a lot remains to be done. The proposal is for the introduction in 2012 of a new form of pension – the personal account. In September 2007 the government appointed Paul Myners to chair the Delivery Authority charged with the task of introducing the account. The main challenge for this new authority will be to ensure that the accounts complement rather than compete with existing pension provision and attract people at the lower end of the income scale. With UK personal debt now at around £1.4 trillion and the worsening economic climate, encouraging further saving is becoming increasingly difficult.

With adverse publicity and poor investment returns the endowment insurance market has seen a major decline in recent years. In its place the industry has attempted to encourage and promote the benefits of protection insurances like term or whole-life policies and income and payment protection cover. This may prove an uphill struggle particularly as the Financial Ombudsman Service highlighted payment protection policies as one of its main reasons for complaint.

The way that life and long-term insurances are sold came under the spotlight in 2007 with the Financial Services Authority's retail distribution review. This review will cover all aspects of the buying process, including qualifications of the sales staff and how they are paid (by commission from the premium or a straight fee). At present, financial advisers either have to be independent intermediaries – representing the whole market – or be 'tied' to one insurance company. It is thought the review will also look at the possibility of a third status where the adviser represents a small number of insurers. The final report is expected in the autumn of 2008.

The Northern Rock crisis did not have a direct effect of the insurance industry (except for those insurance companies who were investors in the bank) but it has raised concerns that as bank deposits are competing with insurance and other investment related products, the actions of the government may distort the savings market. Although premium income for regular premium products showed a small fall, single premium business for both life insurances and pensions continued to rise. The largest increase was for individual single premium pensions, which more than doubled to just under £25bn.

PAYMENTS TO POLICYHOLDERS *(£m)*

	2005	*2006*
Payments to UK policyholders	108,848	141,361
Payments to overseas policyholders	13,447	17,487
Total	122,295	158,848

WORLDWIDE LONG-TERM PREMIUM INCOME *(£m)*

	2002	*2003*	*2004*	*2005*	*2006*
UK Life Insurance					
Regular Premium	12,015	11,777	10,507	10,542	9,407
Single Premium	23,731	17,010	20,516	25,421	31,206
Total	35,746	28,787	31,023	36,032	40,613
Individual Pensions					
Regular Premium	8,547	8,059	8,973	7,910	8,283
Single Premium	19,443	14,278	12,036	11,631	24,833
Total	27,990	22,337	21,009	19,601	33,116
Other Pensions					
Regular Premium	3,744	4,239	4,183	4,761	5,843
Single Premium	26,682	29,052	25,836	34,838	38,554
Total	30,426	*33,291*	30,019	39,539	44,397
Other (eg Income protection, Annuities)	1,922	5,502	4,994	4,400	4,856
TOTAL UK PREMIUM INCOME	96,084	89,917	87,045	99,503	122,982
Overseas Premium Income					
Regular Premium	7,436	7,958	7,692	8,171	8,024
Single Premium	17,833	14,464	16,075	16,814	20,756
Total	25,269	22,422	23,767	24,985	28,780
TOTAL WORLDWIDE PREMIUM INCOME	121,353	112,339	110,812	124,488	151,762

PRIVATE MEDICAL INSURANCE

	2003	*2004*	*2005*	*2006*	*2007*
Number of people covered (thousand)	6,080	5,820	5,820	5,879	6,004
Corporate	4,207	4,084	4,125	4,188	4,341
Personal	1,873	1,736	1,695	1,691	1,663
Gross Earned Premiums (£m)	2,816	2,855	2,942	3,070	3,241
Corporate	1,394	1,433	1,493	1,561	1,696
Personal	1,422	1,422	1,449	1,509	1,545
Gross Claims Incurred (£m)	2,203	2,188	2,255	2,376	2,501

INVESTMENTS OF INSURANCE COMPANIES 2006

Investment of funds	*Long-term business (£m)*	*General business (£m)*
Index-linked British government securities	44,222	841
Non-index-linked British government securities	121,380	10,645
Other UK public sector debt securities	32,501	695
Overseas government, provincial and municipal securities	38,128	10,041
Debentures, loan shares, preference and guaranteed stocks and shares		
UK	131,207	11,342
Overseas	125,928	15,436
Ordinary stocks and shares UK	337,095	8,199
Overseas	182,989	3,440
Unit trusts		
Equities	137,359	3,909
Fixed interest	30,728	767
Loans secured on property	20,391	4,582
Real property and ground rents	78,504	1,771
Other invested assets	87,169	40,652
Total invested assets	1,367,600	112,319
NET INVESTMENT INCOME	56,411	5,118

NEW BUSINESS

	2003	*2004*	*2005*	*2006*	*2007*
New regular premiums					
Investment and savings	186	109	117	92	88
Individual protection	1,117	977	1,046	1,033	1,040
Group protection	273	385	387	311	318
Individual pension	1,859	1,864	2,127	3,024	3,273
Group pension	862	802	766	753	821
Offshore business	n/a	n/a	26	22	21
TOTAL REGULAR	4,297	4,137	4,469	5,235	5,561
New single premiums					
Investments and savings	16,372	20,150	24,121	30,540	38,795
Individual protection	1,264	1,606	1,698	1,634	1,486
Individual pensions	10,551	10,621	12,164	18,758	22,165
Retirement income products	9,208	9,022	9,307	12,157	14,061
Occupational pensions	5,760	4,385	6,544	10,796	10,969
Offshore business	n/a	n/a	4,804	7,150	7,930
TOTAL SINGLE	43,155	45,784	58,638	81,034	95,406

ECONOMIC STATISTICS

All data is for the UK unless otherwise stated.

ABBREVIATIONS

AAS	*Annual Abstract of Statistics*
ST	*Social Trends*

THE BUDGET (2008)

GOVERNMENT RECEIPTS

£ billion

	Outturn 2006–7	*Estimate 2007–8*	*Projection 2008–9*
HM Revenue and Customs (HMRC)			
Income tax (gross of tax credits)	147.8	155.6	160.2
Income tax credits	(4.4)	(4.7)	(5.2)
National insurance contributions (NIC)	87.3	97.4	104.6
Value added tax	77.4	80.5	83.8
Corporation tax[1]	44.8	47.0	51.9
Corporation tax credits[2]	(0.5)	(0.6)	(0.6)
Petroleum revenue tax	2.2	1.7	1.7
Fuel duties	23.6	24.9	25.7
Capital gains tax	3.8	4.8	5.0
Inheritance tax	3.6	3.9	3.2
Stamp duties	13.4	14.3	13.5
Tobacco duties	8.1	8.1	7.6
Spirits duties	2.3	2.3	2.3
Wine duties	2.4	2.6	2.9
Beer and cider duties	3.3	3.3	3.4
Betting and gaming duties	1.4	1.5	1.5
Air passenger duty	1.0	2.0	2.1
Insurance premium tax	2.3	2.3	2.4
Landfill tax	0.8	0.9	1.1
Climate change levy	0.7	0.7	0.7
Aggregates levy	0.3	0.3	0.4
Customs duties and levies	2.3	2.4	2.5
TOTAL HMRC	423.6	451.2	470.5
Vehicle excise duties	5.1	5.6	6.1
Business rates	21.0	21.8	23.7
Council tax[3]	22.2	23.7	24.9
Other taxes and royalties[4]	13.9	14.7	15.7
NET TAXES AND NIC[5]	485.8	517.1	541.0
Accruals adjustments on taxes	5.0	1.4	2.0
Less own resources contribution to European Commission (EC) budget	(4.6)	(5.0)	(4.7)
Less private company corporation tax payments	(0.3)	(0.2)	(0.2)
Tax credits adjustment[6]	0.6	0.6	0.7
Interest and dividends	6.3	7.9	7.0
Other receipts[7]	26.9	28.1	29.4
CURRENT RECEIPTS	519.7	549.9	575.2
North Sea revenues[8]	9.0	7.7	9.9

1 National accounts measure: gross of enhanced and payable tax credits
2 Includes enhanced company tax credits
3 Council tax figures are projections based on stylised assumptions and are not government forecasts as increases are determined annually by local authorities
4 Includes VAT refunds and money paid into the National Lottery Distribution Fund
5 Includes VAT and 'traditional own resources' contributions to EC budget
6 Tax credits which are scored as negative tax in the calculation of net taxes and NIC but expenditure in the national accounts
7 Includes gross operating surplus, rent and business rate payments by local authorities
8 Consists of North Sea corporation tax and petroleum revenue tax

Source: HM Treasury – *Budget 2008* (Crown copyright)

GOVERNMENT EXPENDITURE

The 1998 Economic and Fiscal Strategy Report introduced changes to the public expenditure control regime. Three-year departmental expenditure limits (DELs) now apply to most government departments. Spending which cannot easily be subject to three-year planning is reviewed annually in the budget as annually managed expenditure (AME). Current and capital expenditure are treated separately.

DEPARTMENTAL EXPENDITURE LIMITS *£ billion*

	Outturn 2006–7	*Estimate 2007–8*	*Projection 2008–9*
Resource DEL			
Children, Schools and Families	42.1	44.9	46.9
Health	80.4	89.2	94.0
of which NHS England	78.5	87.1	92.5
Transport	6.9	6.8	6.4
Innovation, Universities and Skills	14.0	15.5	16.4
Communities	3.6	4.2	4.3
Local Government	22.5	22.7	24.7
Home Office	8.3	8.7	9.1
Justice	8.4	8.9	9.3
Law Officers' Departments	0.7	0.7	0.7
Defence	33.5	36.7	33.6
Foreign and Commonwealth Office	1.8	1.9	1.8
International Development	4.2	4.6	4.9
Business, Enterprise and Regulatory Reform	2.2	2.9	2.4
Environment, Food and Rural Affairs	3.1	3.1	2.9
Culture, Media and Sport	1.5	1.7	1.6
Work and Pensions	7.9	8.1	8.0
Scotland	22.4	23.8	24.4
Wales	11.7	12.5	13.0
Northern Ireland Executive	7.2	7.6	8.1

Northern Ireland Office	1.2	1.4	1.2
Chancellor's departments	5.0	4.8	4.8
Cabinet Office	1.7	1.9	2.1
Independent bodies	0.7	0.8	0.9
Modernisation funding	0.0	0.0	0.5
Reserve	0.0	0.0	2.3
Allowance for shortfall	0.0	(0.4)	0.0
TOTAL RESOURCE DEL	291.2	313.2	324.3
Capital DEL			
Children, Schools and Families	4.1	5.5	6.0
Health	3.2	3.6	4.7
of which NHS England	3.1	3.3	4.6
Transport	6.5	7.1	7.3
Innovation, Universities and Skills	1.9	2.0	2.0
Communities	5.4	6.1	7.0
Local Government	0.2	0.0	0.1
Home Office	0.6	0.8	0.9
Justice	0.5	1.0	0.7
Law Officers' Departments	0.0	0.0	0.0
Defence	7.1	8.1	7.9
Foreign and Commonwealth Office	0.2	0.2	0.2
International Development	0.8	0.7	0.9
Business, Enterprise and Regulatory Reform	1.2	1.1	1.2
Environment, Food and Rural Affairs	0.9	0.9	1.0
Culture, Media and Sport	0.3	0.5	1.0
Work and Pensions	0.2	0.1	0.1
Scotland	3.0	3.5	3.2
Wales	1.3	1.5	1.6
Northern Ireland Executive	0.8	1.0	1.0
Northern Ireland Office	0.1	0.0	0.1
Chancellor's departments	0.3	0.3	0.3
Cabinet Office	0.3	0.4	0.4
Independent bodies	0.1	0.1	0.1
Reserve	0.0	0.0	0.7
Allowance for shortfall	0.0	(0.7)	0.0
TOTAL CAPITAL DEL	38.9	43.9	48.1
Less depreciation	(10.0)	(11.8)	(11.5)
TOTAL DEL	320.1	345.3	360.9

Source: HM Treasury – *Budget 2008* (Crown copyright)

ANNUALLY MANAGED EXPENDITURE *£ billion*

	Outturn 2006–7	*Estimate 2007–8*	*Projection 2008–9*
Resource AME			
Social security benefits[1]	131.3	138.5	146.4
Tax credits[1]	16.3	17.1	19.0
Net public service pensions[2]	1.2	2.3	2.9
National Lottery	0.7	0.9	0.9
BBC domestic services	3.3	3.3	3.5
Other departmental expenditure	3.2	2.9	2.0
Net expenditure transfers to EU institutions[3]	4.7	5.4	5.5
Locally-financed expenditure[4]	23.4	24.7	25.7
Central government gross debt interest	27.6	29.9	30.3
AME margin	0.0	0.0	0.9
Accounting adjustments	4.1	1.9	5.1
TOTAL RESOURCE AME	215.9	227.0	242.0
Capital AME			
National Lottery	0.7	0.8	0.6
Locally-financed expenditure[4]	4.7	4.2	4.6
Public corporations' own-financed capital expenditure	5.4	4.7	5.2
Other capital expenditure	(0.2)	(0.3)	0.6
AME margin	0.0	0.0	0.1
Accounting adjustments	(6.8)	(7.1)	(7.6)
TOTAL CAPITAL AME	3.8	2.3	3.4

[1] Child allowances in income support and jobseeker's allowance are included under tax credits
[2] Reported on a national accounts basis
[3] AME spending component only
[4] This expenditure is mainly financed by council tax revenues
Source: HM Treasury – *Budget 2008* (Crown copyright)

EMPLOYMENT

DISTRIBUTION OF THE WORKFORCE

Claimant count	863,900
Workforce jobs	31,536,000
HM forces	197,000
Self-employment jobs	4,216,000
Employees jobs	27,068,000
Government-supported trainees	55,000

Source: ONS – *AAS 2008* (Crown copyright)

EMPLOYMENT

	Thousands	
Age	*Male*	*Female*
16–17	241	277
18–24	1,925	1,690
25–34	3,458	2,826
35–49	5,880	5,140
50–64(m)/59(f)	3,876	2,627
65+(m)/60+(f)	403	808
All aged 16+	15,785	13,369

m = male, f = female
Source: ONS – *AAS 2008* (Crown copyright)

UNEMPLOYMENT

	Thousands	
Age	*Male*	*Female*
16–17	109	87
18–24	313	209
25–34	160	142
35–49	205	185
50–64(m)/59(f)	151	72
65+(m)/60+(f)	13	15
All aged 16+	951	710

Source: ONS – *AAS 2008* (Crown copyright)

DURATION OF UNEMPLOYMENT

	Thousands
All unemployed	1,661
Duration of unemployment	
Less than 6 months	1,000
6 months–1 year	265
1 year +	396
1 year + as percentage of total	23.8

Source: ONS – *AAS 2008* (Crown copyright)

AVERAGE EARNINGS AND HOURS OF FULL-TIME EMPLOYEES

	All	*Male*	*Female*
Average weekly earnings (£)	549.9	606.1	462.8
Average hours	39.4	40.7	37.4
Average hourly earnings (£)			
Including overtime	13.96	14.90	12.38
Excluding overtime	14.00	14.98	12.40

Source: ONS – *AAS 2008* (Crown copyright)

LABOUR DISPUTES BY DURATION

Under 5 days	126
5–10 days	19
10–20 days	10
20–30 days	1
30–50 days	2
50+ days	–

Source: ONS – *AAS 2008* (Crown copyright)

WORKING DAYS LOST THROUGH LABOUR DISPUTES BY INDUSTRY

Mining, quarrying, electricity, gas and water	12,000
Manufacturing	18,000
Construction	15,000
Transport, storage and communications	41,000
Public administration and defence	627,000
Education	31,000
Health and social work	5,000
Other community, social and personal services	2,000
All other industries and services	5,000

Source: ONS – *AAS 2008* (Crown copyright)

TRADE UNIONS

Year	*No. of unions*	*Total membership*
1998	238	7,851,904
1999	237	7,897,519
2000	226	7,779,393
2001	216	7,750,990
2002	210	7,735,983
2003	206	7,559,062
2004	193	7,473,000
2005	192	7,602,842

Source: ONS – *AAS 2008* (Crown copyright)

TRADE

TRADE IN GOODS — *£ million*

	Exports	*Imports*	*Balance*
1997	171,923	184,265	(12,342)
1998	164,056	185,869	(21,813)
1999	166,166	195,217	(29,051)
2000	187,936	220,912	(32,976)
2001	189,093	230,305	(41,212)
2002	186,524	234,229	(47,705)
2003	188,320	236,927	(48,607)
2004	190,877	251,770	(60,893)
2005	211,608	280,397	(68,789)
2006	243,631	321,186	(77,555)
2007	220,857	308,506	(87,649)

Source: ONS – *AAS 2008* (Crown copyright)

BALANCE OF PAYMENTS

Current Account	*£ million*
Trade in goods and services	
Trade in goods	(87,649)
Trade in services	38,450
Total trade in goods and services	(49,199)
Income	
Compensation of employees	(622)
Investment income	5,902
Total income	5,280
Current transfers	
Central government	(10,031)
Other sectors	(3,845)
Total current transfers	(13,876)
TOTAL (CURRENT BALANCE)	(57,795)

Source: ONS – *AAS 2008* (Crown copyright)

HOUSEHOLD INCOME AND EXPENDITURE

HOUSEHOLD EXPENDITURE — *£ per week*

	Socio-economic classification				
	Managerial and professional	*Intermediate occupation*	*Routine and manual*	*Never worked and long-term unemployed*[1]	*All households*[2]
Food and non-alcoholic drinks	56.70	49.49	45.99	38.05	46.89
Alcoholic drinks, tobacco and narcotics	12.86	12.69	13.11	8.79	11.12
Clothing and footwear	35.25	25.45	22.44	25.98	23.24
Housing (net)[3], fuel and power	56.04	51.83	50.03	63.51	47.56
Household goods and services	44.99	32.49	24.99	16.43	30.26
Health	7.32	4.31	4.52	1.37	5.87
Transport	100.81	70.18	52.49	41.76	62.03
Communication[4]	14.81	14.69	12.13	11.72	11.75
Recreation and culture	82.65	67.35	54.46	31.95	58.48
Education	15.84	5.24	2.58	15.85	7.22
Restaurants and hotels	59.44	41.48	35.51	28.65	37.88
Miscellaneous goods and services	53.61	39.87	33.04	16.91	36.01
Other expenditure	136.07	98.74	66.74	22.15	77.59
Total expenditure	676.37	513.81	418.01	323.11	455.89

1 Includes households where the reference person is a student
2 Includes retired households and others that are not classified
3 Excludes mortgage interest payments and council tax (domestic rates in Northern Ireland) which are included in 'other expenditure'
4 Includes mobile phone equipment and services

Source: ONS – *ST 2008* (Crown copyright)

AVERAGE ANNUAL HOUSEHOLD INCOME

Number of households in the UK	24,799
Original income (before state benefits)	£28,224
Gross income (after state benefits)	£32,779
Disposable income	£26,039
Post-tax income	£21,277

Source: ONS – *AAS 2008* (Crown copyright)

AVERAGE WEEKLY HOUSEHOLD INCOME BY SOURCE

	Amount £	*Percentage of total*
Wages and salaries	£432.40	67
Self-employment	£56.20	9
Investments	£21.20	3
Annuities and pensions (other than social security benefits)	£45.40	7
Social security benefits	£79.90	12
Other sources	£6.60	1
Total	£641.90	100

Source: ONS – *AAS 2008* (Crown copyright)

SATISFACTION WITH STANDARD OF LIVING (ENGLAND)

	Percentages
Very satisfied	30
Fairly satisfied	55
Neither satisfied nor dissatisfied	9
Fairly dissatisfied	5
Very dissatisfied	1

Source: ONS – *ST 2008* (Crown copyright)

AVERAGE DWELLING PRICES BY REGION

UK AVERAGE HOUSE PRICE
by region, 2006

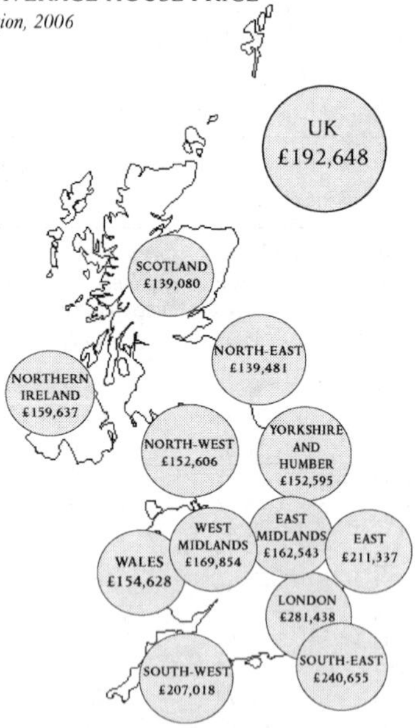

Source: ONS - *ST 2008* (Crown copyright)

NUMBER OF TAXPAYERS BY ANNUAL INCOME[1]

	Number of taxpayers (thousands)
£5,225[2]–£7,499	2,460
£7,500–£9,999	3,630
£10,000–£14,999	6,380
£15,000–£19,999	4,890
£20,000–£29,999	6,670
£30,000–£49,999	5,220
£50,000–£99,999	1,750
£100,000–£199,999	418
£200,000–£499,999	123
£500,000–£999,999	22
£1,000,000+	8
All incomes	31,600

[1] Includes investment income
[2] Basic personal tax-free allowance for 2007–8 (*see* Taxation)
Source: ONS – *ST 2008* (Crown copyright)

HOUSEHOLD OWNERSHIP OF SELECTED DURABLE GOODS

	2000	*2006*
		Percentages
Car	72	76
One	44	44
Two	22	26
Three+	6	6
Central heating, full or partial	91	95
Washing machine	92	96
Fridge/freezer or deep freezer	94	97
Dishwasher	25	38
Telephone	93	91
Mobile phone	47	80
Home computer	44	67
DVD player/video recorder	87	83
Digital television service*	40	71
Internet connection	32	59

* Includes digital, satellite and cable receivers
Source: ONS – *AAS 2008* (Crown copyright)

SAVINGS AND DEBT

HOUSEHOLD SAVINGS *(per cent)*

Economic status of family unit	*No savings*	*Less than £1,500*	*£1,500–£9,999*	*£10,000–£19,999*	*£20,000+*	*All families (=100%) thousands*
Self-employed	22	23	28	10	16	2,307
Single or couple, both in full-time work	31	26	26	8	9	9,010
Couple, one in full-time work, one in part-time work	20	24	28	11	16	2,923
Couple, one in full-time work, one not working	27	22	24	11	15	2,445
One or more in part-time work	42	23	17	6	12	3,262
Head or spouse aged 60+	25	16	26	11	21	8,523
Head or spouse unemployed	75	15	7	1	1	1,065
Head or spouse sick or disabled	71	17	7	2	3	2,116
Other family units	65	17	10	2	5	1,666
All families	35	21	23	8	13	33,317

Source: ONS – *ST 2008* (Crown copyright)

DEBT

Type of unsecured debt	*Percentage of adults with this debt*	*Average amount outstanding*
Credit card	19	£2,284
Personal loan	16	£7,751
Car loan	9	£5,769
Catalogue	6	£220
Student loan company	5	£6,973
Family and friends	3	£2,875
Storecard	3	£471
Social fund loan	2	£484
Money lender	1	£1,336
Store loan	1	£1,201
Rent arrears	1	£682

Source: ONS – *ST 2008* (Crown copyright)

COST OF LIVING AND INFLATION RATES

The first cost of living index to be calculated took July 1914 as 100 and was based on the pattern of expenditure of working-class families in 1914. The cost of living index was superseded in 1947 by the general index of retail prices (RPI), although the older term is still popularly applied.

The Harmonised Index of Consumer Prices (HICP) was introduced in 1997 to enable comparisons within the European Union using an agreed methodology. In 2003 the National Statistician renamed the HICP as the Consumer Prices Index (CPI) to reflect its role as the main target measure of inflation for macroeconomic purposes. The RPI and indices based on it will continue to be published alongside the CPI. Pensions, benefits and index-linked gilts continue to be calculated with reference to RPI or its derivatives.

CPI AND RPI

The RPI and CPI measure the changes month by month in the average level of prices of goods and services purchased by households in the UK. The indices are compiled using a selection of around 650 goods and services, and the prices charged for these items are collected at regular intervals at about 150 locations throughout the country. The Office for National Statistics (ONS) reviews the components of the indices once every year to reflect changes in consumer preferences and the establishment of new products. The table below shows changes made by the ONS to the CPI 'shopping basket' in 2008.

CPI excludes a number of items that are included in RPI, mainly related to housing such as council tax and a range of owner-occupier housing costs, such as mortgage payments. The CPI covers all private households, whereas RPI excludes the top 4 per cent by income and pensioner households who derive at least three-quarters of their income from state benefits. The two indices use different methodologies to combine the prices of goods and services, which means that since 1996 the CPI inflation measure is less than the RPI inflation measure.

INFLATION RATE

The twelve-monthly percentage change in the 'all items' index of the RPI or CPI is referred to as the rate of inflation. As the most familiar measure of inflation, RPI is often referred to as the 'headline rate of inflation'. CPI is the main measure of inflation for macroeconomic purposes and forms the basis for the government's inflation target, which is currently 2 per cent. The percentage change in prices between any two months/years can be obtained using the following formula:

$$\frac{\text{Later date RPI/CPI} - \text{Earlier date RPI/CPI}}{\text{Earlier date RPI/CPI}} \times 100$$

eg to find the CPI rate of inflation for 2006, using the annual averages for 2005 and 2006:

$$\frac{102.3 - 100.0}{100.0} \times 100 = 2.3$$

From 14 February 2006 the reference year for CPI was re-based to 2005=100 to improve price comparison clarity across the EU. None of the underlying data, from which the re-referenced series was calculated, was revised. Historical rates of change (such as annual inflation

'SHOPPING BASKET' OF GOODS AND SERVICES

Changes to the CPI* 2008 basket of goods and services include:

Goods and Services Group	*Removed items*	*New items*
Alcoholic beverages	lager stubbies	bottled lager (4.3 to 7.5 per cent)
Audio-visual equipment	35mm camera film; CD single (top 40); TV repair	non-chart CD album; portable digital storage device
Catering services	–	muffin
Food	frozen vegetarian ready meal	peppers; small-type oranges
Furniture, furnishings and carpets	washable carpet	
Household appliances	microwave oven	
Non-alcoholic beverages	–	pure fruit smoothies
Recreation and culture	–	livery charges
Transport	steering lock device	–
Miscellaneous	–	flower bouquet (next-day delivery)

* RPI goods and services are grouped together under different classifications

figures), calculated from the re-based rounded index levels, were revised due to the effect of rounding. The CPI rate of inflation figure given in the table below may differ by plus or minus 0.1 percentage points from the figure calculated by the above equation. The change of reference period and revision due to rounding does not apply to the RPI which remains unchanged.

The RPI and CPI figures are published by the Office for National Statistics on either the second or third Tuesday of each month in an Indices bulletin and electronically on the National Statistics website (W www.statistics.gov.uk).

PURCHASING POWER OF THE POUND

Changes in the internal purchasing power of the pound may be defined as the 'inverse' of changes in the level of prices: when prices go up, the amount which can be purchased with a given sum of money goes down. To find the purchasing power of the pound in one month or year, given that it was 100p in a previous month or year, the calculation would be:

$$100p \times \frac{\text{Earlier month/year RPI}}{\text{Later month/year RPI}}$$

Thus, if the purchasing power of the pound is taken to be 100p in 1975, the comparable purchasing power in 2000 would be:

$$100p \times \frac{34.2}{170.3} = 20.1p$$

For longer term comparisons, it has been the practice to use an index which has been constructed by linking together the RPI for the period 1962 to date; an index derived from the consumers expenditure deflator for the period from 1938 to 1962; and the pre-war 'cost of living' index for the period 1914 to 1938. This long-term index enables the internal purchasing power of the pound to be calculated for any year from 1914 onwards. It should be noted that these figures can only be approximate.

	Annual average RPI (1987 = 100)	*Purchasing power of £ (1998 = 1.00)*	*Annual average CPI (2005 = 100)**	*Rate of inflation (RPI/CPI)*
1914	2.8	58.18		
1915	3.5	46.54		
1920	7.0	23.27		
1925	5.0	32.58		
1930	4.5	36.20		
1935	4.0	40.72		
1938	4.4	37.02		
There are no official figures for 1939–45				
1946	7.4	22.01		
1950	9.0	18.10		
1955	11.2	14.54		
1960	12.6	12.93		
1965	14.8	11.00		
1970	18.5	8.80		
1975	34.2	4.76		
1980	66.8	2.44	18.0	
1985	94.6	1.72	6.1	
1990	126.1	1.29	71.5	9.5/7.0
1995	149.1	1.09	86.0	3.5/2.6
1998	162.9	1.0	91.1	3.4/1.6
2000	170.3	0.96	93.1	3.0/0.8
2005	192.0	0.85	100	2.8/2.1
2006	198.1	0.82	102.3	3.2/2.3
2007	206.6	0.79	104.7	4.3/2.4

* In accordance with an EU Commission regulation all published CPI figures were re-based to 2005 = 100 with effect from 14 February 2006, replacing the 1996 = 100 series

TAXATION

The government raises money to pay for public services such as education, health and the social security system through tax. Each year the Chancellor of the Exchequer's budget sets out how much it will cost to provide these services and how much tax is therefore needed to pay for them. HM Revenue and Customs (HMRC) is the government department that collects it. There are several different types of tax. The varieties that individuals may have to pay include income tax payable on earnings, pensions, state benefits, savings and investments; capital gains tax (CGT) payable on the disposal of certain assets; inheritance tax (IHT) payable on estates upon death and certain lifetime gifts; stamp duty payable when purchasing property and shares; and value added tax (VAT) payable on goods and services plus certain other duties such as fuel duty on petrol and excise duty on alcohol and tobacco. Government funds are also raised from companies and small businesses through corporation tax.

HELP AND INFORMATION ON TAXATION

For detailed information on any aspect of taxation individuals may contact their local tax office or enquiry centre. The HMRC website (W www.hmrc.gov.uk) provides wide-ranging information online. All HMRC forms, leaflets and guides are listed on, and can be downloaded from, the website or ordered by telephone. A list of all HMRC telephone helplines and order lines can also be found on the website. Those most relevant to topics covered in this section on taxation have been included at pertinent points throughout. Information on taxation is also available in the Money, Tax and Benefits section of the government's public information website for individuals, W www.direct.gov.uk, and the Taxes, Returns and Payroll section of the equivalent information website for companies, W www.businesslink.gov.uk.

INCOME TAX

Income tax is a tax on different sorts of income. Not all types of income are taxable, however, and individuals are only taxed on their 'taxable income' above a certain level. Even then, there are other reliefs and allowances that can reduce or, in some cases, cancel out an individual's income tax bill.

An individual's taxable income is assessed each tax year, starting on 6 April one year and ending on 5 April the following year. The following information relates specifically to the year of assessment 2008–9 ending on 5 April 2009 and has only limited application to earlier years. Changes due to come into operation at a later date are briefly mentioned where information is available. Types of income that are taxable include:

- earnings from employment or self-employment
- most pensions income including state, company and personal pensions
- interest on most savings
- income (dividends) from shares
- income from property
- income received from a trust
- certain state benefits
- an individual's share of any joint income

There are certain sorts of income on which individuals never pay tax. These are ignored altogether when working out how much income tax an individual may need to pay. Types of income that are not taxable include:

- certain state benefits and tax credits such as working tax credit, child tax credit, pension credit, attendance allowance, disability living allowance, income support, housing benefit and the first 28 weeks of incapacity benefit
- winter fuel payments
- income from tax-free National Savings and Investments, such as savings certificates
- interest and terminal bonuses under Save As You Earn schemes
- interest, dividends and other income from various tax-free investments, notably individual savings accounts (ISAs)
- premium bond, national lottery and gambling prizes

PERSONAL ALLOWANCE

Every individual resident in the UK for tax purposes has a 'personal allowance'. This is an amount of taxable income an individual is allowed to earn or receive each year tax-free. This tax year (2008–9) the basic personal allowance or tax-free amount is £6,035. Unusually, this amount was announced on 13 May 2008 replacing the basic personal allowance of £5,435 previously announced in the 2008 March budget – *see* below. Individuals may be entitled to a higher personal allowance if they are 65 or over. Income tax is only due on an individual's taxable income that is above his or her tax-free allowance. Husbands and wives are taxed separately, with each entitled to his or her personal allowance. Each spouse may obtain other allowances and reliefs where the required conditions are satisfied.

The amount of personal allowance depends on an individual's age on 5 April 2008 and, if he or she is 65 or over, the total income received from all taxable sources. There are three age-related levels of personal allowance – *see* table below. If an individual becomes 65 or 75 during the year to 5 April 2008, he or she is entitled to the allowance for that age group.

If an individual's income is over the 'income limit', then the age-related allowance reduces by half the amount (£1 for every £2) he or she has over that limit, until the basic rate allowance is reached. For a 66-year-old with an income of £22,200 (£400 over the limit), for example, the age-related allowance would reduce by £200 to £21,600.

Individuals always receive the basic allowance, whatever the level of their income. The age-related allowances for 2008–9 have been increased significantly – by £1,180 over indexation – as part of the personal tax system modernisation announced in the 2007 budget. This increase means that in 2008–9 no-one aged 65 or over need pay tax on income of up to £173 a week and as a result has removed 580,000 pensioners from paying income tax, according to the government. The government has also announced that the personal allowance for those aged 75 and over will increase to £10,000 in 2010–11 meaning that no pensioner aged 75 or over will pay any tax until their annual income reaches £10,000.

LEVELS OF PERSONAL ALLOWANCE FOR 2008–9

	Personal allowance	*Income limit*
Age under 65	£6,035	none
Age 65–74	£9,030	£21,800
Age 75 and over	£9,180	£21,800

BLIND PERSON'S ALLOWANCE

If an individual is registered blind or is unable to perform any work for which eyesight is essential, he or she can claim blind person's allowance, an extra amount of tax-free income added to the personal allowance. In 2008–9 the blind person's allowance is £1,800. It is the same for everyone who can claim it, whatever his or her age or level of income. If an individual is married or in a civil partnership and cannot use all of his or her blind person's allowance because of insufficient income, the unused part of the allowance can be passed to the spouse or civil partner.

Other deductible allowances and reliefs that have the effect of reducing an income tax bill are available to taxpayers in certain circumstances and will be explained in more detail later in this section.

CALCULATING INCOME TAX DUE

Individuals' liability to pay income tax is determined by establishing their level of taxable income for the year. For married couples and civil partners income must be allocated between the couple by reference to the individual who is beneficially entitled to that income. Where income arises from jointly held assets, it is normally apportioned equally between the partners. If, however, the beneficial interests in jointly held assets are not equal, in most cases couples can make a special declaration to have income apportioned by reference to the actual interests in that income.

To work out an individual's liability for tax, his or her taxable income must be allocated between three different types: earned income (excluding income from savings and dividends); income from savings; and company dividends from shares and other equity-based investments.

After the tax-free allowance plus any deductible allowances and reliefs have been taken into account, the amount of tax an individual pays is calculated using different tax rates and a series of tax bands. The tax band applies to an individual's income after tax allowances and any reliefs have been taken into account. Individuals are not taxed on all of their income.

As part of the government's ongoing programme of reform to the UK tax and benefit system, there are some significant changes to income tax rates for 2008–9. The basic rate of income tax has been reduced from 22 per cent to 20 per cent. At the same time, the 10 per cent starting rate has been removed for earned income and pensions. This change creates a simpler structure of two rates: a 20 pence (in the pound) basic rate and a 40 pence (in the pound) higher rate.

Note that the 10 per cent starting rate continues to be available for savings income only, with a limit of £2,320. If an individual's taxable non-savings income is above this £2,320 limit then the 10 per cent savings rate is not applicable.

The abolition of the 10 per cent starting rate of tax, which came into effect on 6 April 2008, meant that certain groups of tax payers, including many low-paid individuals, would actually be worse off as a result of the change. An estimated 5.3 million families were affected. Consequently, on 13 May 2008, the Chancellor of the Exchequer Alistair Darling announced a rescue package which meant that 4.2 million households would receive as much – or more than – they had originally lost through the abolition of the 10 per cent rate, while the remaining 1.1 million households would see their loss at least halved.

In an unprecedented change to the rules after the start of a tax year, the Chancellor increased the 2008–9 basic personal allowance for anyone under 65 to £6,035, an increase of £600 from the £5,435 previously announced in the budget, and reduced the threshold at which individuals start to pay higher rate tax by £600.

The point at which individuals start to pay higher rate income tax is sometimes called the 'higher rate threshold'. It is the total of the personal allowance and the basic rate limit. In order to reduce the higher rate threshold as announced by the Chancellor, the basic rate limit was reduced by £1,200 from the £36,000 previously announced in the budget to £34,800. This made the 2008–9 threshold for higher rate tax £40,835 instead of the previous £41,435. As a result of the changes all 22 million basic rate taxpayers would gain an additional £120 in the 2008–9 tax year while higher rate taxpayers would see no difference in the amount of tax they paid for 2008–9.

INCOME TAX RATES FOR 2008–9

Band	*Earned*	*Band*	*Savings*	*Dividends*
£0–£34,800	20%	£0–£2,320*	10%	10%
£34,800+	40%	£2,320–£34,800	20%	10%
		£34,800+	40%	32.5%

*If an individual's taxable non-savings income is above £2,320 the 20 per cent tax band applies to savings income from £0–£34,800

The first calculation is applied to earned income which includes income from employment or self-employment, most pension income and rental income plus the value of a wide range of employee fringe benefits such as company cars, living accommodation and private medical insurance (for more information on fringe benefits, *see* later section on payment of income tax). In working out the amount of an individual's net taxable earnings, all expenses incurred 'wholly, exclusively and necessarily' in the performance of his or her work duties, together with the cost of business travel, may be deducted. Fees and subscriptions to certain professional bodies may also be deducted. Redundancy payments and other sums paid on the termination of an employment are assessable to income tax, but the first £30,000 is normally tax-free provided the payment is not linked with the recipient's retirement or performance.

The first £34,800 of taxable income remaining after the tax-free allowance plus any deductible allowances and reliefs have been taken into account is taxed at the new basic rate of 20 per cent. Any excess over £34,800 is taxed at the higher rate of 40 per cent.

Savings and dividend income is added to an individual's other taxable income and taxed last. This means that tax on these sorts of income is based on an individual's highest income tax band.

SAVINGS INCOME

The second calculation is applied to any income from savings received by an individual. The appropriate rate at which it must be taxed is determined by adding income from savings to an individual's other taxable income, excluding dividends.

There is a new 10 per cent starting rate for savings income only, with a limit of £2,320. If an individual's taxable non-savings income is above this limit then the 10 per cent savings rate is not applicable. Savings income that falls above the £2,320 band but within the £34,800 basic rate band is taxable at 20 per cent. Savings income that falls above the £34,800 band is taxable at 40 per cent. If savings income falls on both sides of a tax band, the relevant amounts are taxed at the rates for each tax band.

Most savings income, such as interest paid on bank and building society accounts, already has tax at a rate of 20 per cent deducted from it 'at source' – that is, before it is paid out to individuals. This is confirmed by the entry 'net interest' on bank and building society statements.

Higher rate taxpayers whose income is sufficient to pay 40 per cent tax on their savings income must let their tax office know what savings income they have received so that the extra tax they owe can be collected.

Non taxpayers – that is, individuals, including most children, whose taxable income is less than their tax allowances – can register to have their savings interest paid 'gross' without any tax being deducted from it at source. To do this, they must complete form R85, available at all banks and building societies. Parents or guardians need to fill in this form on behalf of those under 16.

Non taxpayers who have already had tax deducted from their savings interest can claim it back from HMRC by filling in form R40. For help or information about registering to get interest paid tax-free or to claim tax back on savings interest, individuals may call a dedicated savings helpline on T 0845-980 0645. Further information is available in the leaflet *IR111: Bank and building society interest – Are you paying tax when you don't need to?*

DIVIDEND INCOME

The third and final income tax calculation is on UK dividends, which means income from shares in UK companies and other share-based investments including unit trusts and open-ended investment companies (OEICs).

Tax on dividends is paid at different rates from tax on savings income and there are two different rates. The rate an individual pays depends on whether his or her overall taxable income (after allowances) falls within or above the basic rate income tax limit, which is £34,800 for the 2008–9 tax year. All dividend income that falls within this limit is taxable at 10 per cent while any that falls above is taxable at 32.5 per cent.

When dividends are paid, a voucher is sent that shows the dividend paid and the amount of associated 'tax credit'. Companies pay dividends out of profits on which they have already paid or are due to pay tax. The tax credit takes account of this and is available to the shareholder to offset against any income tax that may be due on their dividend income. The dividend paid represents 90 per cent of their dividend income. The remaining 10 per cent is made up of the tax credit. In other words the tax credit represents 10 per cent of the dividend income.

Individuals who pay tax at the basic rate have no tax to pay on their dividend income because the tax liability is 10 per cent – the same amount as the tax credit. Higher rate taxpayers pay a total of 32.5 per cent tax on dividend income that falls above the £34,800 basic rate income tax limit, but because the first 10 per cent of the tax due on their dividend income is already covered by the tax credit, in practice they owe only 22.5 per cent.

Non taxpayers cannot claim the 10 per cent tax credit. This is because income tax has not been deducted from the dividends paid to them. The view is that they have simply been given a 10 per cent credit against any income tax due.

If there is significant change to an individual's savings or other income, whatever his or her current tax bracket, it is the individual's responsibility to contact the relevant tax office immediately, even if he or she does not normally complete a tax return. This enables the tax office to work out whether extra or less tax should be paid.

INDIVIDUAL SAVINGS ACCOUNTS (ISA)

There is a small selection of savings and investment products that are tax-free, meaning that there is no tax to pay on any income they generate in the form of interest or dividends nor on any increase in the value of the capital invested. Their tax-efficient status has been granted by the government in order to give people an incentive to save more. For this reason there are usually limits and restrictions on the amount of money that an individual may invest in such savings and investments. Individual savings accounts (ISAs) are the best known among tax-efficient savings and investments. They were introduced in 1999 to replace other similar schemes called PEPs and TESSAs. Individuals can use an ISA to save cash, or invest in stocks and shares. Changes have been made to the ISA rules taking effect from April 2008 which simplify an individual's options. These reforms have removed the distinction between what were previously known as maxi and mini ISAs.

From 6 April 2008 an individual may save up to £7,200 each tax year in an ISA and receive all profits free of tax provided that they are UK residents and are over 18 (over 16 for cash ISAs). An ISA must be in an individual's name and cannot be held jointly with another person.

Individuals may invest in two separate ISAs each tax year; a cash ISA and a stocks and shares ISA (an umbrella term covering investments in unit trusts, company shares, bonds, investment-type life insurance and so on). Up to £3,600 of an individual's ISA allowance may be saved in one cash ISA with one provider. The remainder of the £7,200 can be invested in one stocks and shares ISA with either the same or a different provider.

Under the new rules mini cash ISAs, TESSA-only ISAs (TOISAs) and the cash component of a maxi ISA automatically become cash ISAs. Similarly, mini stocks and shares ISAs and the stocks and shares component of a maxi ISA automatically become stocks and shares ISAs. All Personal Equity Plans (PEPs) also automatically become stocks and shares ISAs.

ISA savers now have the option to transfer some or all of the money they have saved in previous tax years in cash ISAs to their stocks and shares ISA without affecting their annual ISA investment allowance. They may also choose to transfer all the money they have saved to date in a cash ISA in the current tax year to a stocks and shares ISA. However, the rules do not allow the reverse; that is, the transfer of monies saved in a stocks and shares ISA to a cash ISA.

Further details are available via HMRC's ISA helpline on T 0845-604 1701.

DEDUCTIBLE ALLOWANCES AND RELIEF

Income taxpayers may be entitled to certain tax-deductible allowances and reliefs as well as their personal allowances. Examples include the married couple's allowance and maintenance payments relief, both of which are explained below. Unlike the tax-free allowances, these are not amounts of income that an individual can receive tax-free but amounts by which their tax bill can be reduced.

MARRIED COUPLE'S ALLOWANCE

A married couple's allowance (MCA) is available to taxpayers who are married or are in a civil partnership only where one or other partner was born before 6 April 1935. Eligible couples can start to claim the MCA from the year of marriage or civil partnership registration.

The MCA is restricted to give relief at a fixed rate of 10 per cent which means that, unlike the personal allowance, it is not income that can be received without paying tax. Instead, it reduces an individual's tax bill by up to a fixed amount calculated as 10 per cent of the amount of the allowance to which they are entitled.

In 2008–9 there are two different levels of MCA:

- £6,535 at 10 per cent – if either partner was born before 6 April 1935 but is aged under 75. This is worth up to £653.50 off their tax bill
- £6,625 at 10 per cent – if either partner is aged 75 or over. This is worth up to £662.50 off their tax bill

The MCA is made up of two parts: a minimum amount (£2,540 in 2008–9); and a second amount dependent on the age bracket of the individual or his or her partner. For a couple where one or other was born before 6 April 1935 but is under 75, this second amount is £3,995. Where one or the other is aged 75 or over, it is £4,085.

For married couples, the minimum amount will always be due whatever the level of the husband's income. The age-related amount can be reduced if the husband's income exceeds certain limits. Whatever the level of the allowance, it is normally reduced in the year of marriage to take account of the months elapsed before the marriage.

The husband will normally receive the allowance but the couple can jointly decide which of them will get the minimum amount of the allowance. Alternatively, they can decide to have the minimum amount of the allowance split equally between them. They must inform their tax office of their decision by completing form 18 before the start of the new tax year in which they want the decision to become effective. Once this is done, the change will apply until the couple decides to alter it, so there is no need to complete a new form every year. If there is no such decision, the husband will normally get the allowance. The remaining part of the allowance due because of age must go to the husband unless he does not have sufficient income to use it.

If an individual does not have enough income to use all his or her share of the married couple's allowance, the tax office can transfer the unused part of it to his or her spouse or civil partner.

Like the personal allowance, the MCA can be gradually reduced at the rate of £1 of the allowance for every £2 of income above the income limit (£21,800 in 2008–9). The amount of MCA can only be affected by the husband's income, and it only starts to be affected if his personal allowance has already been reduced back to the basic level for people under 65. The wife's income never affects the amount of the MCA. It does not matter whether all or part of the minimum amount of the allowance has been transferred to her. Whatever the level of the husband's income, the MCA can never be reduced below a minimum level. In 2008–9 this minimum amount is £2,540 at 10 per cent.

The same system of allowance allocation applies to civil partners based on the income of the highest earner. *See* leaflets *FS1 (MCA): Married couple's allowance restrictions*; and *REV BN 28: Tax and civil partners.*

MAINTENANCE PAYMENTS RELIEF

An allowance is available to reduce an individual's tax bill for maintenance payments he or she makes to his or her ex spouse or former civil partner in certain circumstances. To be eligible one or other partner must have been born before 6 April 1935; the couple must be legally separated or divorced; the maintenance payments being made must be under a court order; and the payments must be for the maintenance of an ex spouse or former civil partner (provided he or she is not now remarried or in a new civil partnership) or for children who are under 21. For this tax year 2008–9, this allowance enables individuals to reduce their tax bill by the lower of 10 per cent of £2,540 (maximum £254) or 10 per cent of the amount actually paid in maintenance payments. To claim maintenance payments relief individuals should contact their tax office and request form 41.

CHARITABLE DONATIONS

A number of charitable donations qualify for tax relief. Individuals can increase the value of regular or one-off charitable gifts, however small, by using the Gift Aid scheme that allows charities or Community Amateur Sports Clubs (CASCs) to reclaim basic rate tax relief on donations they receive.

The basic rate of income tax went down from 22 per cent to 20 per cent from 6 April 2008. This was expected to result in a reduction in revenue from Gift Aid donations for charities and CASCs. With a 22 per cent rate, each £100 donated via the scheme is worth £128 to the recipient but with a 20 per cent rate, each £100 gift is worth just £125.

However, it was announced in the 2008 budget that charities and CASCs would be able to claim 'transitional relief' for at least three years (2008–9, 2009–10 and 2010–11) funded by the government, allowing them to retain the 22 per cent relief rate. It therefore remains the case that, until at least 5 April 2011, for every £10 a donor gives using the Gift Aid scheme, the charity or CASC actually receives £12.82 once it reclaims the transitional tax relief at a rate of 22 per cent.

The transitional provision means that where Gift Aid donations are made by basic rate taxpayers, the 22 per cent reclaimable is preserved without an impact on the donor. In the case of higher rate taxpayers the overall effect of the provision is beneficial. Higher rate relief continues to be given in relation to the difference between the basic and higher rates of income tax which means that from April 2008 the higher rate tax relief claimed by the donor increased from 18 per cent to 20 per cent (being the difference between the unchanged 40 per cent higher rate and the new 20 per cent basic rate). Non taxpayers should not use Gift Aid.

For employees or those in receipt of an occupational

pension, a tax-efficient way of making regular donations to charities is to make them straight from a salary or pension before income tax is deducted under the Payroll Giving scheme. This effectively reduces the cost of giving for donors which may allow them to give more. For example, it costs a basic-rate taxpayer only £8 in take-home pay to give £10 to charity from their pre-tax pay and where a donor pays higher rate tax at 40 per cent that same donation of £10 costs the taxpayer just £6. Anyone who pays tax through PAYE can give to any charity of their choosing in this way, providing his or her employer or pension provider offers a payroll giving scheme, and there is no limit to the amount individuals can donate.

TAX RELIEF ON PENSION CONTRIBUTIONS

Pensions are long-term investments designed to help ensure that people have enough income in retirement. The government encourages individuals to save towards a pension by offering tax relief on their contributions. The tax relief given is based on the basic rate of income tax which went down from 22 per cent to 20 per cent from April 6 2008. The basic rate change has had no effect on individuals whose contributions to a company pension scheme are taken from their gross salary before tax is deducted. For individuals who make payments into a pension from their net (after-tax) salary, however, the basic rate reduction from 22 per cent to 20 per cent means that the amount of tax relief given on their pension contributions has gone down by 2 per cent in 2008–9. This means that individuals who contribute from their net salary to a pension scheme, whether it be an individual personal pension, a group personal pension or a group SIPP (self-invested personal pension), need to pay more in contributions from 2008–9 to achieve the same amount in their pension fund once tax relief is applied as previously.

For each pound individuals contribute to their pension from net salary, the pension provider claims tax back from the government at the basic rate and reinvests it on behalf of the individual into the scheme. In 2007–8, with a basic rate of 22 per cent, this meant a taxpayer had to pay in £78 to end up with £100 in their pension fund. From 2008–9, however, with a basic rate of 20 per cent, a taxpayer needs to contribute £80 to achieve the same £100 in their fund.

Regular savers who wish to be in the same position as prior to the tax change need to increase to their net contributions by 2.5 per cent. For example, an individual who was contributing £150 a month from their net salary into a personal pension prior to the tax change (with 22 per cent basic rate relief) needs to increase their monthly contribution to £153.84 in order to achieve the same grossed-up sum (£192.30) going into their pension fund once 20 per cent basic rate relief is applied.

Higher rate taxpayers get 40 per cent tax relief on money they put into a pension. On contributions made from net salary, the first 20 per cent is claimed back from HMRC by the pension scheme in the same way as for a lower rate taxpayer. It is then up to individuals to claim back the other 20 per cent from their tax office, either when they fill in their annual tax return or by letter.

The most that non taxpayers can pay into a pension is £2,880 a year; since they receive basic rate 20 per cent tax relief on this sum, the government effectively tops up their contribution to make it £3,600 which is the current universal pension allowance. (In 2007–8 non-taxpayers had only to put £2,808 into a pension to end up with £3,600 because of the higher 22 per cent rate of tax relief available). Such pension contributions may be made on behalf of a non taxpayer by another individual. A parent may contribute to a pension on behalf of a child, for example, or a husband on behalf of a non-taxpaying wife.

Until April 2006 there were various restrictions – based on age and salary – limiting the amounts an individual could save and get tax relief on in personal and company pension schemes. But on 6 April 2006 a new, simplified pensions regime came into effect that included the introduction of just one, more generous annual allowance applied to all types of pension scheme.

In any one tax year, individuals can get tax relief on pension contributions of 100 per cent of their annual earnings, irrespective of age, up to a maximum 'annual allowance' (£235,000 for 2008–9). Everyone now also has a 'lifetime allowance' (£1.65m for 2008–9) which means taxpayers can save up to a total of £1.65m in their pension fund and still get tax relief at their highest income tax rate on all their contributions. Individuals may pay concurrently into as many different types of pension as they wish and get tax relief on all their contributions, provided they do not exceed the annual allowance.

For information and leaflets on pensions and tax relief, contact the government's Pensions Service on T 0845-606 0265 or visit W www.thepensionservice.gov.uk. Another useful source of information and advice is The Pensions Advisory Service (TPAS), an independent voluntary organisation grant-aided by the Department for Work and Pensions at W www.pensionsadvisoryservice.org.uk. Its Pensions Helpline is on T 0845-601 2923.

PAYMENT OF INCOME TAX

Employees have their income tax deducted from their wages throughout the year by their employer who sends it on to HMRC. Those in receipt of a company pension have their due tax deducted in the same way by their pension provider. This system of collecting income tax is known as 'pay as you earn' (PAYE).

BENEFITS IN KIND

The PAYE system is also used to collect tax on certain fringe benefits or 'benefits in kind' that employees or directors receive from their employer but that are not included in their salary cheque or wages. These include company cars, private medical insurance paid for by the employer or cheap or free loans from the employer. Some fringe benefits are tax-free, including employer-paid contributions into an employee's pension fund, cheap or free canteen meals, works buses, in-house sports facilities, reasonable relocation expenses, provision of a mobile phone, workplace nursery places provided for the children of employees, and certain other employer-supported childcare up to £55 per week.

For taxable fringe benefits tax is paid on the 'taxable value' of the benefit. The way this is worked out depends on whether or not the benefit is given to a director or 'higher-paid' employee defined as an individual earning £8,500 gross or more per year, including the value of his or her taxable fringe benefits. Company directors normally count as higher-paid, however much they earn.

Employers submit returns for individual employees to the tax office on the form P11D, with details of any fringe benefits they have been given. Employees should get a copy of this form by 6 July following the end of the tax year and must enter the value of the fringe benefits they have received on their tax return for the relevant year, even if tax has already been paid on them under PAYE. Fringe benefits may be taxed under PAYE by being offset against personal tax allowances in an individual's PAYE code. Otherwise tax will be collected after the end of the tax year by the issue of an assessment on the fringe benefits.

SELF-ASSESSMENT

Individuals who are not on PAYE, notably the self-employed, need to complete a self-assessment tax return each year, in paper form or online at the HMRC website (W www.hmrc.gov.uk), and pay any income tax owed in twice-yearly instalments. Some individuals with more complex tax affairs such as those who earn money from rents or investments above a certain level may also need to fill out a self-assessment return, even if they are on PAYE. HMRC uses the figures supplied on the tax return to work out the individual's tax bill, or they can choose to work it out themselves. It is called 'self-assessment' because individuals are responsible for making sure the details they provide are correct.

Tax returns are usually sent out in early April, following the end of the tax year to which they apply. They may also go out at other times, for example if an individual wants to claim an allowance or repayment or to register for self-assessment for the first time.

Individuals with simple tax affairs, or with self-employment or rental income of less than £15,000, receive a short four-page return. Those with more complex affairs must fill out a full return that has 12 core pages plus extra pages, depending on the sorts of income received.

Central to the self-assessment system is the requirement for individuals to contact their tax office if they do not receive a self-assessment return but think they should or if their financial circumstances change. Individuals have six months from when the tax year ends to report any new income, for example. If an individual becomes self-employed, they have three months after the calendar month in which they began self-employed work to let HMRC know. This can be done by telephoning the helpline number for the newly self-employed on T 08459-154515.

TAX RETURN FILING AND PAYMENT DEADLINES

There are also key deadlines for filing (sending in) completed tax returns and paying the tax due. Failure to do so can incur penalties, interest charges and surcharges. The deadlines are more generous for individuals who do not want to calculate the tax due themselves and file their tax return online.

KEY FILING DATES FOR SELF-ASSESSMENT RETURNS ISSUED ON OR AFTER 6 APRIL 2008*

Date	*Why the deadline is important*
31 Oct	Deadline for filing paper returns for tax year ended the previous 5 April. Late filing incurs an automatic £100 penalty. This deadline applies whether the taxpayer calculates his or her own tax liability or whether he or she wants HMRC to calculate it on their behalf.
31 Jan	Deadline for online filing of returns received by the previous 31 October. Late filing incurs an automatic £100 penalty.
29 Dec	Where a taxpayer's agent (eg an accountant) submits his or her tax return via electronic lodgement service (ELS), it must be sent back by this date if the taxpayer wants HMRC to collect tax through his or her tax code (if possible) where the amount owed is less than £2,000.
30 Dec	Where a taxpayer files the return online, he or she must do so by this date if HMRC is to collect tax through his or her tax code (if possible) where the amount owed is less than £2,000. Otherwise it can be filed up to 31 January.

* New filing dates for paper and online self assessment tax returns have been introduced applying to tax returns issued on or after 6 April 2008 relating to the tax year 2007–8 and subsequent years. For paper returns, the deadline has been reduced from 31 January to 31 October (for tax year 2007–8 that will be 31 October 2008). For returns filed online, the date remains at 31 January (for tax year 2007–8 that will be 31 January 2009).

KEY SELF-ASSESSMENT DATES

Date	*What payments or penalties are due?*
31 Jan	If a tax return was sent by the previous 31 October, this is the deadline for paying the balance of any tax owed – the 'balancing payment'. for paying the balance of any tax owed – the 'balancing payment'. HMRC will charge daily interest after this date until it receives the payment. It is also the date by which a taxpayer must make any first 'payment on account' for the current tax year. For example on 31 January 2009 a taxpayer will have to pay both the balancing payment for the year 2007–8 and the first payment on account for 2008–9.
28 Feb	If the balancing payment is not paid by 31 January, there is an automatic 5 per cent surcharge incurred on top of the amount outstanding. This is in addition to any interest payments.
31 Jul	The deadline for making a second payment on account for tax owing for the preceding tax year. If tax is still owed that was due by the previous 31 January, there is a second automatic 5 per cent surcharge levied on top of the amount owed.

TAX CREDITS

Child tax credit and working tax credit are paid to qualifying individuals. Although the title of both credits incorporates the word 'tax', neither affects the amount of income tax payable or repayable. Both are forms of social security benefits. *See* the Social Welfare section.

CAPITAL GAINS TAX

Capital gains tax (CGT) is a tax on capital 'gains'. A gain is an increase in value. When an individual disposes of an asset – that is, something he or she owns such as shares, land or buildings – by selling it or giving it away, CGT may have to be paid on the gain or profit. An individual is potentially chargeable to CGT on gains that accrue from disposals made during a year of tax assessment.

A number of changes to simplify the capital gains tax regime were announced in the 2007 pre-budget to take effect for disposals made on or after 6 April 2008. The following information relates to the year of assessment

2008–9 ending on 5 April 2009 and incorporates these changes. It therefore has only limited relevance to earlier years.

Liability extends to individuals who are either resident or ordinarily resident in the UK for the tax year, but special rules apply where a person permanently leaves the UK or comes to this country for the purpose of acquiring residence. Non-residents are not usually liable to CGT unless they carry on a business in the UK through a branch or agency. However, individuals who left the UK after 16 March 1998 and who have been resident or ordinarily resident in at least four of the seven years preceding departure may remain liable to CGT unless they reside overseas over a period of five complete tax years. Exceptions to this may apply where there is a disposal of assets acquired in the period of absence. Individuals should consult their tax office for details, which are available in leaflet *IR20: Residents and non-residents: Liability to tax in the United Kingdom.*

CAPITAL GAINS CHARGEABLE TO CGT

Typically, individuals have made a gain if they sell an asset for more than they paid for it. It is the gain that is taxed, not the amount the individual receives for the asset. For example, a man buys shares for £1,000 and later sells them for £3,000. He has made a gain of £2,000 (£3,000 less £1,000). If someone gives an asset away, the gain will be based on the difference between what the asset was worth when originally acquired compared with its worth at the time of disposal. The same is true when an asset is sold for less than its full worth in order to give away part of the value. For example, a woman buys a property for £120,000 and three years later, when the property's market value has risen to £180,000, she gives it to her son. The son may pay nothing for the property or pay less than its true worth, eg £100,000. Either way, she has made a gain of £60,000 (£180,000 less £120,000).

If an individual disposes of an asset he or she received as a gift, the gain is worked out according to the market value of the asset when it was received. For example, a man gives his sister a painting worth £8,000. She pays nothing for it. Later she sells the painting for £10,000. For CGT purposes, she is treated as making a gain of £2,000 (£10,000 less £8,000). If an individual inherits an asset, the estate of the person who died does not pay CGT at the time. If the inheritor later disposes of the asset, the gain is worked out by looking at the market value at the time of the death. For example, a woman acquires some shares for £5,000 and leaves them to her niece when she dies. No CGT is payable at the time of death when the shares are worth £8,000. Later the niece sells the shares for £10,000. She has made a gain of £2,000 (£10,000 less £8,000).

Individuals may also have to pay CGT if they dispose of part of an asset or exchange one asset for another. Similarly, CGT may be payable if an individual receives a capital sum of money from an asset without disposing of it, for example where he or she receives compensation when an asset is damaged.

Assets that may lead to a CGT charge when they are disposed of include:

- shares in a company
- units in a unit trust
- land and buildings (though not normally an individual's main home – *see* 'disposal of a home' section for details)
- higher value jewellery, paintings, antiques and other personal effects assets used in business such as goodwill

EXEMPT GAINS

Certain kinds of assets do not give rise to a chargeable gain when they are disposed of. Assets exempt from CGT include:

- an individual's private car
- an individual's main home, provided certain conditions are met
- tax-free investments such as assets held in an individual savings account (ISA)
- UK government gilts or 'bonds'
- personal belongings including jewellery, paintings, antiques individually worth £6,000 or less
- cash in sterling or foreign currency held for an individual or his/her family's own personal use
- betting, lottery or pools winnings
- personal injury compensation

DISPOSAL OF A HOME: PRIVATE RESIDENCE RELIEF

Individuals do not have to pay CGT when they sell their main home if all the following conditions are met:

- they bought it and made any expenditure on it, primarily for use as their home rather than with a view to making a profit
- the property was their only home throughout the period they owned it (ignoring the last three years of ownership)
- the property was actually used as their home all the time that they owned it and, throughout the period, it was not used for any purpose other than as a home for the individual, his or her family and no more than one lodger
- the garden and area of grounds sold with the property does not exceed 5,000 sq. m (1.24 acres) including the site of the property

Even if all these conditions are not met, individuals may still be entitled to CGT relief when they sell the home. They may, for example, qualify for relief if they lived away from home temporarily while working abroad. Married couples or couples in a civil partnership may have relief from CGT on only one home. There is a special exception, however, where the spouse or partner each had a qualifying home before marriage or civil partnership and both live together in one of these homes after marriage or civil partnership and sell the other. Provided that it is sold within three years of marriage or the civil partnership, they may not have to pay any CGT (subject to the normal rules for this relief). If they sell it after more than three years it may qualify for partial relief. There are special rules on divorce and separation. Further details are available in HMRC help sheet *IR283: Private residence relief.*

Certain other kinds of disposal similarly do not give rise to a chargeable gain. For example, individuals who are married or in a civil partnership and who live together may sell or give assets to their spouse or civil partner without having to pay CGT. Individuals may not, however, give or sell assets cheaply to their children without having to consider CGT. There is no CGT to pay on assets given to a registered charity. See HMRC help sheet *IR178: Giving shares and securities to charity.*

CALCULATING CGT

CGT is worked out for each tax year and is charged on the total of an individual's taxable gains after taking into account certain costs and reliefs that can reduce or defer chargeable gains, allowable losses made on assets to which CGT normally applies and an annual exempt (tax-free) amount that applies to every individual. If the total of an individual's net gains in a tax year is less than the annual exempt amount (AEA), the individual will not have to pay CGT. For the tax year 2008–9 the AEA is £9,600. If an individual's net gains are more than the AEA, they pay CGT on the excess. Should any part of the exemption remain unused, this cannot be carried forward to a future year. A smaller exemption amount (£4,800 for 2008–9) applies to most trusts.

There are certain reliefs available that may eliminate, reduce or defer CGT, though several reliefs previously available were withdrawn from April 2008 as part of the government's simplification of the CGT regime as explained further below. Some reliefs are available to many people while others are available only in special circumstances. Some reliefs are given automatically while others are given only if they are claimed. Some of the costs of buying, selling and improving assets may be deducted from total gains when working out an individual's chargeable gain.

RATES OF TAX

The net gains remaining, if any, calculated after deduction of costs, taking into account all CGT reliefs and subtracting the annual exemption, incur liability to capital gains tax. The rate of CGT individuals pay used to depend on their overall income and their consequent top rate of income tax. Under the new regime however, for disposals made on or after 6 April 2008, individuals and trustees pay a single rate of charge to CGT at 18 per cent.

CGT for 2008–9 falls due for payment in full on 31 January 2010. If payment is delayed, interest or surcharges may be imposed. A husband and wife or registered civil partners who live together are separately assessed to CGT. Each partner must independently calculate his or her gains and losses with each entitled to the AEA of £9,600 for 2008–9.

VALUATION OF ASSETS

The disposal proceeds – that is the amount received as consideration for the disposal of an asset – are the sum used to establish the gain or loss once certain allowable costs have been deducted. In most cases this is straightforward because the disposal proceeds are the amount actually received for disposing of the asset. This may include cash payable now or in the future and the value of any asset received in exchange for the asset disposed of. However, in certain circumstances, the disposal proceeds may not accurately reflect the value of the asset and the individual may be treated as disposing of an asset for an amount other than the actual amount (if any) that they received. This applies, in particular, where an asset is transferred as a gift or sold for a price known to be below market value. Disposal proceeds in such transactions are deemed to be equal to the market value of the asset at the time it was disposed of rather than the actual amount (if any) received for it.

Market value represents the price that an asset might reasonably be expected to fetch upon sale in the open market. In the case of unquoted shares or securities, it is to be assumed that the hypothetical purchaser in the open market would have available all the information that a prudent prospective purchaser of shares or securities might reasonably require if that person were proposing to purchase them from a willing vendor by private treaty and at arm's length. The market value of unquoted shares or securities will often be established following negotiations with the specialist HM Revenue and Customs Shares & Assets Valuation department. The valuation of land and interests in land in the UK is dealt with by District Valuer Services, part of the Valuation Office Agency. Special rules apply to determine the market value of shares quoted on the London Stock Exchange.

ALLOWABLE COSTS

When working out a chargeable gain, once the actual or notional disposal proceeds have been determined, five kinds of allowable costs may be deducted. There is a general rule that no costs that could be taken into account when working out income or losses for income tax purposes may be deducted. Subject to this, allowable costs are:

- acquisition costs – the actual amount spent on acquiring the asset or, in certain circumstances, the equivalent market value
- incidental costs of acquiring the asset such as fees paid for professional advice, valuation costs, stamp duty and advertising costs to find a seller
- enhancement costs – incurred for the purpose of enhancing the value of the asset (not including normal maintenance and repair costs)
- expenditure on defending or establishing a person's rights over the asset
- incidental costs of disposing of the asset such as fees paid for professional advice, valuation costs, stamp duty and advertising costs to find a buyer

If an individual disposes of part of his or her interest in an asset, or part of a holding of shares of the same class in the same company, or part of a holding of units in the same unit trust, he or she can deduct part of the allowable costs of the asset or holding when working out the chargeable gain. Allowable costs may also be reduced by some reliefs.

INDEXATION ALLOWANCE AND TAPER RELIEF (BOTH ABOLISHED)

For many years an indexation allowance could be inserted when calculating a gain on the disposal of an asset. It was largely replaced by taper relief in 1998 (*see* below). Indexation allowance has now been totally withdrawn. For disposals on or after 6 April 2008 indexation allowance is no longer available in computing the gain arising.

Taper relief was introduced with effect from 6 April 1998 to replace the former indexation allowance and was extended substantially in the years following its introduction. It came into effect for disposals on or after 6 April 1998 and could be used to reduce the amount of the gain chargeable to CGT. The amount of relief available depended on the length of time an asset had been held since that date and whether the asset was classified as a business or non-business asset for taper relief purposes. Taper relief was available to individuals, partnerships, estates and trusts but could not be claimed by companies to whom other tax rules applied.

Taper relief has now been abolished. For disposals on or after 6 April 2008 taper relief is no longer available (even if assets were held before this date) and the chargeable gain is liable to tax at the new rate of 18 per cent, subject to the deduction of allowable losses, any other reliefs and the AEA.

ENTREPRENEURS' RELIEF

In January 2008, the government announced a new relief – entrepreneurs' relief – from CGT for gains arising on the disposal of a business. The announcement came after complaints that the new 18 per cent CGT flat rate would mean small business owners paying almost twice as much tax as before when they sold their businesses and that the change could deter entrepreneurs from starting new UK businesses. The new relief took effect from 6 April 2008 alongside the CGT reform programme.

Entrepreneurs' relief is available in respect of gains made on the disposal of all or part of a business (including professions and vocations, but not including a property letting business other than furnished holiday lettings), or of gains made on disposals of assets following the cessation of a business by certain individuals who were involved in running the business. The relief also applies to gains on disposals of shares and securities in a trading company (or the holding company of a trading group) provided that the individual making the disposal has been an officer or employee of the company, or of a company in the same group of companies, and owns at least 5 per cent of the ordinary share capital of the company.

The relief reduces gains liable to CGT (at the single 18 per cent rate) by 4/9ths, resulting in an effective 10 per cent rate (5/9ths × 18 per cent). It is available for gains of up to £1m on disposals of a business by an individual. The first £1m of gains that qualify for relief are charged to CGT at the effective rate of 10 per cent. Gains in excess of £1m are charged at the normal 18 per cent rate. An individual is able to make claims for relief on more than one occasion up to a lifetime total of £1m of gains qualifying for relief.

Where an individual qualifies for entrepreneurs' relief on a disposal of shares or securities, relief is also available in respect of any 'associated disposal' of an asset which was used in the company's (or group's) business. For example, if a company director who owns the premises from which the company carries on its business sells the premises at the same time as he sells his shares in the company, the sale of the premises may count as an associated disposal and any gain may attract entrepreneurs' relief. The relief due on an associated disposal is restricted where the asset in question was not wholly in business use throughout the period it was owned. A similar rule allows relief on an associated disposal by a member of a partnership who is entitled to relief on disposal of his or her interest in the assets of the partnership.

Certain trustees may also benefit from entrepreneurs' relief on gains on assets used in a business.

BUSINESS ASSET ROLL-OVER RELIEF

A capital gain on the disposal of certain types of asset used in a person's business may be deferred or 'rolled over' if the proceeds are reinvested in new qualifying trading assets. The gain is deducted from the base cost of the new asset and only becomes chargeable to CGT on the eventual disposal of that replacement asset unless a further roll-over situation then develops. Full relief is available if all the proceeds from the original asset (the old asset) are reinvested in the qualifying replacement asset (the new asset). If only part of the proceeds is reinvested, the difference represents an immediately chargeable gain. If the amount not reinvested is greater than the gain, no roll-over relief is due.

Relief is only available if the acquisition of the new asset takes place within a period commencing 12 months before, and ending three years after, the disposal of the old asset. However, HMRC may extend this time limit at their discretion where there is a clear intention to acquire a replacement asset. The most common types of business assets that qualify for roll-over relief are land, buildings occupied and used for the purposes of trade, fixed plant and machinery. Assets used for the commercial letting of furnished holiday accommodation qualify if certain conditions are satisfied. Roll-over relief is also available where shares in a company are transferred to trustees administering an employees' share incentive plan for the benefit of persons employed by that company.

GIFTS HOLD-OVER RELIEF

The gift of an asset is treated as a disposal made for a consideration equal to market value, with a corresponding acquisition by the transferee at an identical value. In the case of gifts made by individuals and a limited range of trustees to a transferee resident in the UK, a form of hold-over relief may be available. This relief, which must be claimed, in effect enables liability for CGT to be deferred and passed to the person to whom the gift is made. Relief is limited to the transfer of certain assets including the following:

- gifts of assets used for the purposes of a business carried on by the donor or his or her personal company
- gifts of shares in trading companies that are not listed on a stock exchange
- gifts of shares or securities in the donor's personal trading company
- gifts of agricultural land and buildings that would qualify for inheritance tax agricultural property relief
- gifts that are chargeable transfers for inheritance tax purposes
- certain types of gifts that are specifically exempted from inheritance tax

Hold-over relief is automatically due on certain sorts of gifts including gifts to charities and community amateur sports clubs and gifts of works of art where certain undertakings have been given. There are certain rules to prevent gifts hold-over relief being used for tax-avoidance purposes. For example, restrictions may apply where an individual gifts assets to trustees administering a trust in which the individual retains an interest or the assets transferred comprise a dwelling-house. Subject to these exceptions, the effect of a valid claim for hold-over relief is similar to that following a claim for roll-over relief on the disposal of business assets. Adjustments may be necessary where some consideration (less than market value) is given for a gift or where a gifted asset has not been used for business purposes throughout the period of ownership.

OTHER CGT RELIEFS

Enterprise investment scheme (EIS) deferral relief allows the deferral of gains on the disposal of an asset when an individual subscribes for shares in an EIS company. Similarly, venture capital trust (VCT) deferral relief allows the deferral of gains on the disposal of an asset when an individual subscribes for shares in a VCT. For detailed information on these schemes and for more general guidance on CGT, see the capital gains tax pages on the HMRC website (W www.hmrc.gov.uk/cgt/index.htm#4).

INHERITANCE TAX

Inheritance tax (IHT) is a tax on the value of a person's estate on death and on certain gifts made by an individual during his or her lifetime, usually payable within six months of death. Broadly speaking, a person's estate is everything he or she owned at the time of death including property, possessions, money and investments, less his or her debts. Not everyone pays IHT. It only applies if the taxable value of an estate is above the current inheritance tax threshold. If an estate, including any assets held in trust and gifts made within seven years of death, is less than the threshold, no IHT will be due. See table for the lower threshold limit, known as the nil rate band.

2006–7	£285,000
2007–8	£300,000
2008–9	£312,000
2009–10	£325,000
2010–11	£350,000

An important change introduced in the 2007 autumn pre-budget report now means that a claim can be made to transfer any unused IHT nil-rate band on a person's death to the estate of their surviving spouse or civil partner if he or she dies on or after 9 October 2007. This applies where the IHT nil-rate band of the first deceased spouse or civil partner was not fully used in calculating the IHT liability of their estate. When the surviving spouse or civil partner dies, the unused amount may be added to their own nil-rate band (*see* below for details).

IHT used to be something only very wealthy individuals needed to consider. This is no longer the case. A dramatic rise in house prices over recent years coupled with the fact that the IHT threshold has not kept pace with house price inflation means that the estates of an increasing number of 'ordinary' taxpayers, who would not consider themselves wealthy, are now becoming liable for IHT purely because of the value of their home. However, there are a number of ways that individuals – while still alive – can legally reduce the IHT bill that will apply to their estates on death. Several valuable IHT exemptions are available (explained further below) which allow individuals to pass on assets during their lifetime or in their will without any IHT being due. IHT forms and information leaflets can be downloaded from the HMRC website (W www.hmrc.gov.uk). The main guide is entitled *HMRC Inheritance Tax: Customer Guide.* Paper versions and further help are available from the IHT & Probate Helpline on T 0845-302 0900.

DOMICILE

Liability to IHT depends on an individual's domicile at the time of any gift or on death. Domicile is a complex legal concept and what follows explains some of the main issues. An individual is domiciled in the country where he or she has a permanent home. Domicile is different from nationality or residence, and an individual can only have one domicile at any given time.

A 'domicile of origin' is normally acquired from the individual's father on birth, though this may not be the country in which he or she is born. For example, a child born in Germany while his or her father is working there, but whose permanent home is in the UK, will have the UK as his or her domicile of origin. Until a person legally changes his or her domicile, it will be the same as that of the person on whom they are legally dependent.

Individuals can legally acquire a new domicile – a 'domicile of choice' – from the age of 16 by leaving the current country of domicile and settling in another country and providing strong evidence of intention to live there permanently or indefinitely. Women who were married before 1974 acquired their husband's domicile and still retain it until they legally acquire a new domicile.

For IHT purposes, there is a concept of 'deemed domicile'. This means that even if a person is not domiciled in the UK under general law, he or she is treated as domiciled in the UK at the time of a transfer (ie at the time of a lifetime gift or on death) if he or she (a) was domiciled in the UK within the three years immediately before the transfer, or (b) was 'resident' in the UK in at least 17 of the 20 income tax years of assessment ending with the year in which a transfer is made. Where a person is domiciled, or treated as domiciled, in the UK at the time of a gift or on death, the location of assets is immaterial and full liability to IHT arises. A non-UK domiciled individual is also liable to IHT but only on chargeable property in the UK. The assets of husband and wife and registered civil partners are not merged for IHT purposes, except that the IHT value of assets owned by one spouse or civil partner may be affected if the other also owns similar assets (eg shares in the same company or a share in their jointly-owned house). Each spouse or partner is treated as a separate individual entitled to receive the benefit of his or her exemptions, reliefs and rates of tax.

IHT EXEMPTIONS

There are some important exemptions that allow individuals to legally pass assets on to others, both before and after their death – without being subject to IHT.

Exempt beneficiaries

Assets can be given away to certain people and organisations without any IHT having to be paid. These gifts, which are exempt whether individuals make them during their lifetime or in their will, include gifts to:

- a husband, wife or civil partner, even if the couple is legally separated (but not if they are divorced or the civil partnership has dissolved), as long as both partners have a permanent home in the UK. Note that gifts to an unmarried partner or a partner with whom the donor has not formed a civil partnership are not exempt
- UK charities
- some national institutions, including national museums, universities and the National Trust
- UK political parties

Annual exemption

The first £3,000 of gifts made each tax year by each individual is exempt from IHT. If this exemption is not used, or not wholly used in any year, the balance may be carried forward to the following year only. A couple, therefore, may give away a total of £6,000 per tax year between them or £12,000 if they haven't used their previous year's annual exemptions.

Wedding gifts/civil partnership ceremony gifts

Some gifts are exempt from IHT because of the type of gift or reason for making it. Wedding or civil partnership ceremony gifts made to either of the couple are exempt from IHT up to certain amounts:

- gifts by a parent, £5,000
- gifts by a grandparent or other relative, £2,500
- gifts by anyone else, £1,000

The gift must be made on or shortly before the date of the wedding or civil partnership ceremony. If the ceremony is called off and the gift is still made, this exemption will not apply.

Small gifts
An individual can make small gifts, up to the value of £250, to any number of people in any one tax year without them being liable for IHT. However, a larger sum such as £500 cannot be given and exemption claimed for the first £250. In addition, this exemption cannot be used with any other exemption when giving to the same person. For example, a parent cannot combine a 'small gifts exemption' with a 'wedding/civil partnership ceremony gift exemption' to give a child £5,250 when he or she gets married or forms a civil partnership. Neither may an individual combine a 'small gifts exemption' with the 'annual exemption' to give someone £3,250. Note that it is possible to use the 'annual exemption' with any other exemption, such as the 'wedding/civil partnership ceremony gift exemption'. For example, if a child marries or forms a civil partnership, the parent can give him or her a total IHT-free gift of £8,000 by combining £5,000 under the wedding/civil partnership gift exemption and £3,000 under the annual exemption.

Normal expenditure
Any gifts made out of individuals' after-tax income (not capital) are exempt from IHT if they are part of their normal expenditure and do not result in a fall in their standard of living. These can include regular payments to someone, such as an allowance or gifts for Christmas or a birthday and regular premiums paid on a life insurance policy for someone else.

Maintenance gifts
An individual can make IHT-free maintenance payments to his or her spouse or registered civil partner, ex-spouse or former civil partner, relatives dependent because of old age or infirmity, and children (including adopted children and step-children) who are under 18 or in full-time education.

POTENTIALLY EXEMPT TRANSFERS
If an individual makes a gift to either another individual or certain types of trust and it is not covered by one of the above exemptions, it is known as a 'potentially exempt transfer' (PET). A PET is only free of IHT on two strict conditions: (a) the gift must be made at least seven years before the donor's death. If the donor does not survive seven years after making the gift, it will be liable for IHT and (b) the gift must be made as a true gift with no strings attached (technically known as a 'gift with reservation of benefit'). This means that the donor must give up all rights to the gift and stop benefiting from it in any way.

If a gift is made and the donor does retain some benefit from it then it will still count as part of his or her estate no matter how long he or she lives after making it. For example, a father could make a lifetime gift of his home to his child. HMRC would not accept this as a true gift, however, if the father continued to live in the home (unless he paid his child a full commercial rent to do so) because he would be considered to still have a material interest in the gifted home. Its value, therefore, would still be liable for IHT.

In some circumstances a gift with strings attached might give rise to an income tax charge on the donor based on the value of the benefit he or she retains. In this case the donor can choose whether to pay the income tax or have the gift treated as a gift with reservation.

CHARGEABLE TRANSFERS
Any remaining lifetime gifts that are not (potentially or otherwise) exempt transfers are chargeable transfers or 'chargeable gifts', meaning that they incur liability to IHT. Chargeable transfers comprise mainly gifts to or from companies and gifts to particular types of trust called discretionary trusts. There is an immediate claim for IHT on chargeable gifts, and additional tax may be payable if the donor dies within seven years of making a chargeable gift.

DEATH
Immediately before the time of death an individual is deemed to make a transfer of value. This transfer will comprise the value of assets forming part of the deceased's estate after subtracting most liabilities. Any exempt transfers may be excluded such as transfers for the benefit of a surviving spouse or civil partner, and charities. Death may also trigger three additional liabilities:

- a PET made within the seven years before the death loses its potential status and becomes chargeable to IHT
- the value of gifts made with reservation may incur liability if any benefit was enjoyed within the seven years before the death
- additional tax may become payable for chargeable lifetime transfers made within the seven years before the death

The 'personal representative' (the person nominated to handle the affairs of the deceased person) arranges to value the estate and pay any IHT that is due. One or more personal representatives can be nominated in a person's will, in which case they are known as the 'executors'. If a person dies without leaving a will a court can nominate the personal representative, who is then known as the 'administrator'. Valuing the deceased person's estate is one of the first things his or her personal representative needs to do. The representative will not normally be able to take over management of the estate (called 'applying for probate') until all or some of any IHT that is due has been paid.

VALUATIONS
When valuing a deceased person's estate all assets (property, possessions and money) owned at the time of death and certain assets given away during the seven years before death must be included. The valuation must accurately reflect what those assets would reasonably fetch in the open market at the date of death. The value of all of the assets that the deceased owned should include:

- his or her share of any assets owned jointly with someone else, for example a house owned with a partner
- any assets that are held in a trust, from which the deceased had the right to benefit
- any assets given away, but in which he or she kept an interest (gifts with reservation)
- PETs given away within the last seven years

Most estate assets can be valued quite easily, for example money in bank accounts or stocks and shares. In other instances the help of a professional valuer may be needed. Advice on how to value different assets including joint or trust assets is available at W www.hmrc.gov.uk. When valuing an estate, special relief is made available for certain assets. The two main reliefs are business relief and agricultural property relief outlined below. Once all assets have been valued, the next step is to deduct from the total assets everything that the deceased person owed such as unpaid bills, outstanding mortgages and other loans plus their funeral expenses. The value of all of the assets, less the deductible debts, is their estate. IHT is only payable on any value above £312,000 for the tax year 2008–9 at the current rate of 40 per cent.

RELIEF FOR SELECTED ASSETS

Agricultural Property

Relief from IHT is available on the agricultural value of agricultural property that is transferred. Agricultural property generally includes land or pasture used in the growing of crops or intensive rearing of animals for food consumption. It can also include farmhouses and farm cottages. The agricultural property can be owner-occupied or let. Relief is only due if the transferor has owned the property and it has been occupied for agricultural purposes for a minimum period.

The chargeable value transferred, either on a lifetime gift or on death, must be determined. This value may then be reduced by a percentage. Under current rates, a 100 per cent deduction will be available if the transferor retained vacant possession or could have obtained that possession within a period of 12 months following the transfer. In other cases, notably including land let to tenants, a lower deduction of 50 per cent is usually available. However, this lower deduction may be increased to 100 per cent if the letting was made after 31 August 1995.

To qualify for the relief, the agricultural property must either have been occupied by the transferor for the purposes of agriculture throughout a two-year period ending on the date of the transfer, or have been owned by the transferor throughout a period of seven years ending on that date and also occupied for agricultural purposes.

Business Relief

Business relief is available on transfers of certain types of business and of business assets if they qualify as relevant business property and the transferor has owned them for a minimum period. The relief can be claimed for transfers made during the person's lifetime and on death and on chargeable occasions arising on relevant business property held in trust. Where the chargeable value transferred is attributable to relevant business property, the business relief reduces that value by a percentage. Business relief may be claimed on relevant business property including:

- a business or an interest in a business such as a partnership
- unquoted shares and securities
- shares or securities of a quoted company which themselves or with other listed shares or securities give the transferor control of a company
- any land, buildings, plant or machinery owned by a partner or controlling shareholder and used wholly or mainly in the business of the partnership or company immediately before the transfer; this applies only if the partnership interest or shareholding would itself, if it were transferred, qualify for business relief
- any land, buildings, machinery or plant that were used wholly or mainly for the purpose of a business carried on by the transferor

If an asset qualifies for business relief, the rates at which it is currently allowed are as follows:

A business or interest in a business	100%
A holding of shares in an unquoted company	100%
Control holding of shares in a quoted company (more than 50 per cent of the voting rights)	50%
Land, buildings or plant and machinery used in a business of which the deceased was a partner at the date of death or used by a company controlled by the deceased	50%
Land, buildings, plant and machinery held in a trust where the deceased had the right to benefit from the trust and the asset was used in a business carried on by the deceased	50%

It is a general requirement that the property must have been retained for a period of two years before the transfer or death, and restrictions may be necessary if the property has not been used wholly for business purposes. The same property cannot obtain both business property relief and the relief available for agricultural property.

CALCULATION OF TAX PAYABLE

The calculation of IHT payable adopts the use of a cumulative or 'running' total. Looking back seven years from the death the chargeable value of gifts in that period is added to the total value of the estate at death. The gifts will use up all or part of the inheritance tax threshold (the 'nil-rate band' above which IHT becomes payable) first.

Lifetime Chargeable Transfers

The value transferred by lifetime chargeable transfers must be added to the seven-year running total to calculate whether any IHT is due. If the nil-rate band is exceeded, tax will be imposed on the excess at the rate of 20 per cent. However, if the donor dies within a period of seven years from the date of the chargeable lifetime transfer, additional tax may be due. This is calculated by applying tax at the full rate of 40 per cent in substitution for the rate of 20 per cent previously used. The amount of tax is then reduced to a percentage by applying tapering relief. This percentage is governed by the number of years from the date of the lifetime gift to the date of death, as follows:

PERIOD OF YEARS BEFORE DEATH

Not more than 3	100%
More than 3 but not more than 4	80%
More than 4 but not more than 5	60%
More than 5 but not more than 6	40%
More than 6 but not more than 7	20%

Should this exercise produce liability greater than that previously paid at the 20 per cent rate on the lifetime transfer, additional tax, representing the difference, must be paid. Where the calculation shows an amount falling below tax paid on the lifetime transfer, no additional liability can arise nor will the shortfall become repayable.

Tapering relief is, of course, only available if the calculation discloses a liability to IHT. There is no liability if the lifetime transfer falls within the nil rate band.

Potentially Exempt Transfers

Where a PET loses immunity from liability to IHT because the donor dies within seven years of making the transfer, the value transferred enters into the running total. Any liability to IHT will be calculated by applying the full rate of 40 per cent, reduced to the percentage governed by tapering relief if the original transfer occurred more than three years before death. Again, liability to IHT can only arise if the nil-rate band is exceeded.

Death

On death, IHT is due on the value of the deceased's estate plus the running total of gifts made in the seven years before death if they come to more than the nil-rate band. IHT is then charged at the full rate of 40 per cent on the amount in excess of the nil-rate band.

Settled Property and Trusts

Trusts are special legal arrangements that can be used by individuals to control how their assets are distributed to their beneficiaries and minimise their IHT liability. Complex rules apply to establish IHT liability on settled property which includes property held in trust, and individuals are advised to take expert legal advice when setting up trusts.

RATES OF TAX

Previously there were several rates of IHT that progressively increased as the value transferred grew in size. However, since 1988 there have been only three rates:

- a nil rate
- a lifetime rate of 20 per cent
- a full rate of 40 per cent

The nil-rate band usually changes on an annual basis, and for events taking place after 5 April 2008 applies to the first £312,000. Any excess over this level is taxable at 20 per cent or 40 per cent as the case may be. The IHT threshold will be increased to £325,000 for 2009–10 and £350,000 for 2010–11.

TRANSFER OF NIL-RATE BAND

Transfers of property between spouses or civil partners are generally exempt from IHT. This means that someone who dies leaving some or all of their property to their spouse or civil partner may not have fully used up their nil-rate band. Under new rules introduced in autumn 2007, any nil-rate band unused on the first death can be used when the surviving spouse or civil partner dies. A transfer of unused nil-rate band from a deceased spouse or civil partner (no matter what the date of their death) may be made to the estate of their surviving spouse or civil partner who dies on or after 9 October 2007.

Where a valid claim to transfer unused nil-rate band is made, the nil-rate band that is available when the surviving spouse or civil partner dies is increased by the proportion of the nil-rate band unused on the first death. For example, if on the first death the chargeable estate is £150,000 and the nil-rate band is £300,000, 50 per cent of the nil-rate band would be unused. If the nil-rate band when the survivor dies is £325,000, then that would be increased by 50 per cent to £487,500. The amount of the nil-rate band that can be transferred does not depend on the value of the first spouse or civil partner's estate. Whatever proportion of the nil-rate band is unused on the first death is available for transfer to the survivor.

The amount of additional nil-rate band that can be accumulated by any one surviving spouse or civil partner is limited to the value of the nil-rate band in force at the time of their death. This may be relevant, for example, where a person dies having survived more than one spouse or civil partner.

Where the new rules have effect, personal representatives will not have to claim for unused nil-rate band to be transferred at the time of the first death. Any claims for transfer of unused nil-rate band amounts are made by the personal representatives of the estate of the second spouse or civil partner to die when they make an IHT return.

Detailed guidance on how to transfer the nil-rate band can be found on the HMRC website.

PAYMENT OF TAX

IHT is normally due six months after the end of the month in which the death occurs or the chargeable transaction takes place. This is referred to as the 'due date'. Tax on some assets such as business property, certain shares and securities and land and buildings (including the deceased person's home) can be deferred and paid in equal instalments over ten years, though interest will be charged in most cases. If IHT is due on lifetime gifts and transfers, the person or transferee who received the gift or assets is normally liable to pay the IHT, though any IHT already paid at the time of a transfer into a trust or company will be taken into account. If tax owed is not paid by the due date, interest is charged on any unpaid IHT, no matter what caused the delay in payment.

CORPORATION TAX

Corporation tax is a tax on a company's profits, including all its income and gains. This tax is payable by UK resident companies and by non-resident companies carrying on a trade in the UK through a permanent establishment. The following comments are confined to companies resident in the UK. The word 'company' is also used to include:

- members' clubs, societies and associations
- trade associations
- housing associations
- groups of individuals carrying on a business but not as a partnership (for example, cooperatives)

A company's taxable income is charged by reference to income or gains arising in its 'accounting period', which is normally 12 months long. In some circumstances accounting periods can be shorter than 12 months, but never longer. The accounting period is also normally the period for which a company's accounts are drawn up, but the two periods do not have to coincide.

If a company is liable to pay corporation tax on its profits, several things must be done. HMRC must be informed that the company exists and is liable for tax. A self-assessment company tax return plus full accounts and calculation of tax liability must be filed by the statutory filing date, normally 12 months after the end of the accounting period. Companies have to work out their own tax liability and have to pay their tax without prior assessment by HMRC. Records of all company expenditure and income must be kept in order to work out the tax liability correctly. Companies are liable to penalties if they fail to carry out these obligations.

Measures to reform the business tax system were announced in the 2007 budget with a staged introduction over the next few years. The major elements of the reform package apply from 2008–9.

Extensive corporation tax information is available on the HMRC website and companies may file their company tax returns online at the HMRC's corporation tax online service at W www.hmrc.gov.uk/ctsa/ct-online.htm.

RATE OF TAX

The rate of corporation tax is fixed for a financial year starting on 1 April and ending on the following 31 March. If a company's accounting period does not coincide with the financial year, its profits must be apportioned between the financial years and the tax rates for each financial year applied to those profits. The corporation tax liability is the total tax for both financial years.

The main rate of corporation tax for 2008–9 has gone down to 28 per cent. It was 30 per cent for the preceding nine years. North Sea oil and gas ring fence activities however retain a main corporation tax rate of 30 per cent.

SMALL COMPANIES' RATE

Where the profits of a company do not exceed stated limits, corporation tax becomes payable at the small companies' rate. It is the amount of profits and not the size of the company that governs the application of the small companies' rate.

For each of the three financial years ending on 31 March 2000, 31 March 2001 and 31 March 2002 the small companies' rate was 20 per cent. It was then reduced to 19 per cent for ensuing years but increased once again to 20 per cent from April 2007 when it was announced that there would be staged increases in the small companies' rate. It went up from 20 per cent to 21 per cent from April 2008 and will go up again to 22 per cent from April 2009. (North Sea oil and gas ring fence activities will retain a small companies' rate of 19 per cent).

A company can make profits of up to £300,000 without losing the benefit of the small companies' rate. If, however, its profits exceed £300,000 but fall below £1,500,000, then marginal small companies' rate relief applies to ease the transition. The effect of marginal relief is that the average rate of corporation tax imposed on all profits steadily increases from the lower small companies' rate of 21 per cent to the main rate of 28 per cent, with tax being imposed on profits in the margin at an increased rate. HMRC has produced an easy-to-use corporation tax marginal relief rate calculator on its website at W www.hmrc.gov.uk/calcs/mrr.htm.

Where a change in the rate of tax is introduced and the accounting period of a company overlaps 31 March, profits must be apportioned to establish the appropriate rate for each part of those profits.

The lower limit of £300,000 and the upper limit of £1,500,000 apply to a period of 12 months and must be proportionately reduced for shorter periods. Some restriction in the small companies' rate and the marginal rate may be necessary if there are two or more associated companies, namely companies under common control. From 1 April 2006 a previous corporation tax 'starting rate' of zero for very small companies and a 19 per cent non-corporate distribution rate (NCDR), which could apply to company profits distributed to persons who were not companies, were replaced with a single banding for small companies.

CORPORATION TAX ON PROFITS

£ per year	*2007–8*	*2008–9*
£0–£300,000	20%	21%
£300,001–£1,500,000	Marginal relief	Marginal relief
£1,500,000 or more	30%	28%

CAPITAL ALLOWANCES

Businesses can claim tax allowances, called capital allowances, on certain purchases or investments. This means that a proportion of these costs can be deducted from a business' taxable profits and reduce its tax bill. Capital allowances are currently available on plant and machinery, buildings and research and development. The amount of the allowance depends on what is being claimed for. As part of the staged business tax reform package announced in the 2007 budget, changes to the capital allowances regime are being introduced. Most of the changes took effect from April 2008.

Detailed information on capital allowances is available from the Enhanced Capital Allowances website (W www.eca.gov.uk).

PAYMENT OF TAX

Corporation tax liabilities are normally due and payable in a single lump sum not later than nine months and one day after the end of the accounting period. For 'large' companies – those with profits over £1.5m which pay corporation tax at the main rate – there is a requirement to pay corporation tax in four quarterly instalments. Where a company is a member of a group, the profits of the entire group must be merged to establish whether the company is large.

CAPITAL GAINS

Chargeable gains arising to a company are calculated in a manner similar to that used for individuals. However, companies are not entitled to the CGT annual exemption of £9,600. Companies do not suffer capital gains tax on chargeable gains but incur liability to corporation tax instead. Tax is due on the full chargeable gain of an accounting period after subtracting relief for losses, if any.

GROUPS OF COMPANIES

Each company within a group is separately charged to corporation tax on profits, gains and income. However, where one group member realises a loss for which special rules apply, other than a capital loss, a claim may be made to offset the deficiency against profits of some other member of the same group. The transfer of capital assets from one member of a group to a fellow member will usually incur no liability to tax on chargeable gains.

SPORTS CLUBS

Though corporation tax is payable by unincorporated associations including most clubs, a substantial exemption from liability to corporation tax, introduced in April 2002, is available to qualifying registered community amateur sports clubs (CASCs). Sports clubs that are registered as CASCs are exempt from liability to corporation tax on:

- profits from trading where the turnover of the trade is less than £30,000 in a 12-month period (limit was £15,000 prior to 1 April 2004)
- income from property where gross rental income is less than £20,000 in a 12-month period (limit was £10,000 prior to 1 April 2004)
- bank and building society interest received
- chargeable gains

All of the exemptions depend upon the club having been a registered CASC for the whole of the relevant accounting period and the income or gains being used only for qualifying purposes. If the club has only been a registered CASC for part of an accounting period the exemption amounts of £30,000 (for trading) and £20,000 (for income from property) are reduced proportionately. Only interest and gains received after the club is registered are exempted.

Among other advantages available to registered clubs is that donations may be received under the Gift Aid arrangements. Charities are also generally exempt from corporation tax where they operate through a company structure.

VALUE ADDED TAX

Value added tax (VAT) is a tax on consumer expenditure charged when an individual buys goods and services in the European Union including the UK. It is normally included in the sale price of goods and services and paid at the point of purchase. Each EU country has its own rate of VAT. From a business point of view, VAT is charged on most business transactions involving the supply of goods and services by a registered trader in the UK and Isle of Man. It is also charged on goods, and some services, imported from places outside the EU and on goods and some services coming into the UK from the other EU countries. VAT is administered by HM Revenue and Customs. A wide range of information on VAT, including VAT forms, is available online (W www.hmrc.gov.uk). HMRC runs a national advice service enquiry line dealing with all general queries about taxes and duties including VAT on T 0845-010 9000.

RATES OF TAX

There are three rates of VAT in the UK. The standard rate – currently 17.5 per cent – is payable on most goods and services in the UK. The reduced rate – currently 5 per cent – is payable on certain goods and services including, for example, domestic fuel and power, children's car seats, women's sanitary products, contraceptive products and the installation of energy-saving materials such as wall insulation and solar panels. The 5 per cent rate was also introduced on 'over the counter' sales of smoking cessation products from 1 July 2007 to take effect alongside the introduction of the ban on smoking in public places in England. Since 1 January 2008 renovations and alterations to residential properties that have been empty for at least two years have been eligible for the 5 pre cent rate. A zero, or nil, rate applies to certain items including, for example, children's clothes, books, newspapers, most food and drink, and drugs and aids for disabled people. There are numerous exceptions to the zero-rated categories however. While most food and drink is zero-rated, items including ice creams, chocolates, sweets, potato crisps and alcoholic drinks are not. Neither are drinks or items sold for consumption in a restaurant or cafe. 'Takeaway' cold items such as sandwiches are zero-rated, while takeaway hot foods like fish and chips are not.

REGISTRATION

All traders, including professional persons and companies, must register for VAT if they are making 'taxable supplies' of a value exceeding stated limits. All goods and services that are VAT-rated are defined as 'taxable supplies' including zero-rated items which must be included when calculating the total value of a trader's taxable supplies – his or her 'taxable turnover'. The limits that govern mandatory registration are amended periodically.

From 1 April 2008, an unregistered trader must register for VAT if:

- at the end of any month the total value of his or her taxable turnover (not just profit) for the past 12 months or less is more than the current VAT threshold of £67,000 – *and*
- at any time he or she has reasonable grounds to expect that his or her taxable turnover will be more than the current registration threshold of £67,000 in the next thirty days alone

To register for VAT, form VAT 1 must be completed and sent to HMRC within 30 days of any of the above. Traders who do not register at the correct time can be fined. Traders must charge VAT on their taxable supplies from the date they first need to be registered. Traders who only supply zero-rated goods may not have to register for VAT even if their taxable turnover goes above the registration threshold. However, a trader in this position must inform HMRC first and apply to be 'exempt from registration'. A trader whose taxable turnover does not reach the mandatory registration limit may choose to register for VAT voluntarily if what he or she does counts as a business for VAT purposes. This step may be thought advisable to recover input tax (*see* below) or to compete with other registered traders. Registered traders may submit an application for deregistration if their taxable turnover subsequently falls. An application for deregistration can be made if the taxable turnover for the year beginning on the application date is not expected to exceed £65,000.

INPUT TAX

Registered traders suffer input tax when buying in goods or services for the purposes of their business. It is the VAT that traders pay out to their suppliers on goods and services coming *in* to their business. Relief can usually be obtained for input tax suffered, either by setting that tax against output tax due or by repayment. Most items of input tax can be relieved in this manner. Where a registered trader makes both exempt supplies and taxable supplies to his customers or clients, there may be some restriction in the amount of input tax that can be recovered.

OUTPUT TAX

When making a taxable supply of goods or services, registered traders must account for output tax, if any, on the value of that supply. Output tax is the term used to describe the VAT on the goods and services that they supply or sell – the VAT on supplies going *out* of the business and collected from customers on each sale made.

Usually the price charged by the registered trader will be increased by adding VAT, but failure to make the required addition will not remove liability to account for output tax. The liability to account for output tax, and also relief for input tax, may be affected where a trader is using a special second-hand goods scheme.

EXEMPT SUPPLIES

VAT is not chargeable on certain goods and services because the law deems them 'exempt' from VAT. These include the provision of burial and cremation facilities, insurance, loans of money, certain types of education and training and some property transactions. The granting of a lease to occupy land or the sale of land will usually comprise an exempt supply, for example, but there are numerous exceptions. Exempt supplies do not enter into the calculation of taxable turnover that governs liability to mandatory registration (*see* above). Such supplies made by a registered trader may, however, limit the amount of input tax that can be relieved. It is for this reason that the exemption may be useful.

COLLECTION OF TAX

Registered traders submit VAT returns for accounting periods usually of three months in duration, but arrangements can be made to submit returns on a monthly basis. Very large traders must account for tax on a monthly basis, but this does not affect the three-monthly return. The return will show both the output tax due for supplies made by the trader in the accounting period and also the input tax for which relief is claimed. If the output tax exceeds input tax the balance must be remitted with the VAT return. Where input tax suffered exceeds the output tax due, the registered trader may claim recovery of the excess from HMRC.

This basis for collecting tax explains the structure of VAT. Where supplies are made between registered traders the supplier will account for an amount of tax that will usually be identical to the tax recovered by the person to whom the supply is made. However, where the supply is made to a person who is not a registered trader there can be no recovery of input tax and it is on this person that the final burden of VAT eventually falls. Where goods are acquired by a UK trader from a supplier within the EU, the trader must also account for the tax due on acquisition. There are a number of simplified arrangements to make VAT accounting easier for businesses, particularly small businesses, and there is advice on the HMRC website about how to choose the most appropriate scheme for a business:

Cash accounting

This scheme allows businesses to only pay VAT on the basis of payments received from their customers rather than on invoice dates or time of supply. It can therefore be useful for businesses with cash flow problems that cannot pay their VAT as a result. Businesses may use the cash accounting scheme if taxable turnover is under £1,350,000. There is no need to apply for the scheme – eligible businesses may start using it at the beginning of a new tax period. If a trader opts to use this scheme, he or she can do so until the taxable turnover reaches £1,600,000.

Annual accounting

If taxable turnover is under £1,350,000 a year, the trader may join the annual accounting scheme which allows them to make monthly or quarterly instalments during the year based on an estimate of their total annual VAT bill. At the end of the year they submit a single return and any balance due. The advantages of this scheme for businesses are easier budgeting and cash flow planning because fixed payments are spread regularly throughout the year. Once a trader has joined the annual accounting scheme, membership may continue until the annual taxable turnover reaches £1,600,000.

Flat rate scheme

Introduced in the 2002 budget, this scheme allows small businesses with an annual taxable turnover under £150,000 excluding VAT (£187,500 including VAT) to save on administration by paying VAT as a set flat percentage of their annual turnover instead of accounting internally for VAT on each individual 'in and out'. The percentage rate used is governed by the trade sector into which the business falls. The scheme can no longer be used once VAT-inclusive turnover exceeds £225,000.

Retail schemes

There are special schemes that offer retailers an alternative if it is impractical for them to issue invoices for a large number of supplies direct to the public. These schemes include a provision to claim relief from VAT on bad debts where goods or services are supplied to a customer who does not pay for them.

VAT FACT SUMMARY
from 1 April 2008

Standard rate	17.5%
Reduced rate	5%
Registration (last 12 months or next 30 days)	£67,000
Deregistration (next 12 months under)	£65,000
Cash accounting scheme – up to	£1,350,000
Flat rate scheme – up to	£150,000*
Annual accounting scheme – up to	£1,350,000

* Excluding VAT

STAMP DUTY

For the majority of people, contact with stamp duty arises when they buy a property. Stamp duty is payable by the buyer as a way of raising revenue for the government based on the purchase price of a property, stocks and shares. This section aims to provide a broad overview of stamp duty as it may affect the average person.

STAMP DUTY LAND TAX

Stamp duty land tax was introduced on 1 December 2003 and covers the purchase of houses, flats and other land, buildings and certain leases in the UK.

Before 1 December 2003 property purchasers had to submit documents providing all details of the purchase to the Stamp Office for 'stamping'. The purchaser's solicitor or licensed conveyancer would then send the stamped documentation to the appropriate land registry to register ownership of the property. Under stamp duty land tax, purchasers do not have to send documents for stamping. Instead, a land transaction return form SDLT1, which contains all information regarding the purchase that is relevant to HMRC, is signed by the purchaser. Buyers of property are responsible for completing the land transaction return and payment of stamp duty, though the solicitor or licensed conveyancer acting for them in a land transaction will normally complete the relevant paperwork. Once HMRC has received the completed land transaction return and the payment of any stamp duty due, a certificate will be issued that enables a solicitor or licensed conveyancer to register the property in the new owner's name at the Land Registry.

The threshold for notification of residential property went up from £1,000 to £40,000 on 12 March 2008. This means that taxpayers entering into a transaction involving residential or non-residential property where the chargeable consideration is less than £40,000 no longer need to notify HMRC about the transaction.

RATES OF STAMP DUTY LAND TAX

The following table shows the rates of stamp duty that apply on a property purchase price. A change in 2005, welcomed by many first-time buyers, was the doubling of the threshold from £60,000 to £120,000, below which no stamp duty is payable on residential property purchases. The new threshold took effect from 17 March 2005. This was increased again to £125,000 from 23 March 2006:

Purchase price	*Rate of tax (% of purchase price)*
£125,000 or less*	0%
£125,001 to £250,000	1%
£250,001 to £500,000	3%
£500,001 or more	4%

* For transactions of non-residential land and property, the zero per cent rate applies for purchases of up to £150,000. A 1 per cent rate is payable for transactions of £150,001–£250,000; thereafter, rates are as per residential property transactions. The zero per cent band for residential property transactions in certain designated disadvantaged areas is £150,000. A full list of these areas can be found at W www.hmrc.gov.uk

From 3 September 2008, the chancellor raised the stamp duty threshold to £175,000 for a year to assist first-time buyers.

When assessing how much stamp duty is payable, the entire purchase price must be taken into account so the relevant stamp duty rate is paid on the whole sum, not just on the amount over each tax threshold. For example, on a property bought for £250,000, 1 per cent – £2,500 – is payable in stamp duty. On a property bought for £250,001, however, 3 per cent of the whole price – £7,500 – is payable.

RELIEF FOR NEW ZERO CARBON HOMES

A new relief from stamp duty land tax was introduced on 1 October 2007 for the vast majority of new 'zero carbon' homes in the UK. The relief is time limited for five years and therefore expires on 30 September 2012. Qualifying criteria for the relief require zero carbon emissions from all energy use in the home over a year. To achieve this, the fabric of the home is required to reach a very high energy efficiency standard and to be able to provide onsite renewable heat and power. New homes which are liable to stamp duty land tax on the first sale are eligible to qualify. The relief provides complete removal of stamp duty liabilities for all homes up to a purchase price of £500,000. Where the purchase price is in excess of £500,000 then the stamp duty liability is reduced by £15,000. The balance of the stamp duty is due in the normal way. Relief is not available on second and subsequent sales of new zero carbon homes.

FIXTURES AND CHATTELS

As well as buying a property a purchaser may buy items inside the property. Some things inside a property are, in law, part of the land. These are called 'fixtures'. Examples are fitted kitchen units and bathroom suites. Because these fixtures are part of the land, any price paid for them must be taken into account for stamp duty purposes. Other things inside a property are not part of the land. These are called 'chattels'. Examples are free-standing cookers, curtains and fitted carpets. The purchase of chattels is not chargeable to stamp duty. However, where both a property and chattels are purchased, the amount shown on the land transaction return as the purchase price of the property must be a 'just and reasonable' apportionment of the total amount paid. As with other entries on the form, the purchaser is responsible for the accuracy of this information. HMRC pays especial attention to residential property purchases just below stamp duty thresholds to prevent arrangements between buyer and seller to hand over cash so that the purchase price on paper looks lower or to pay unreasonably high amounts to buy chattels.

STAMP DUTY RESERVE TAX

Stamp duty or stamp duty reserve tax (SDRT) is payable at the rate of 0.5 per cent when shares are purchased. Stamp duty is payable when the shares are transferred using a stock transfer form, whereas SDRT is payable on 'paperless' share transactions where the shares are transferred electronically without using a stock transfer form. Most share transactions nowadays are paperless and settled by stockbrokers through CREST (the electronic settlement and registration system). SDRT therefore now accounts for the majority of taxation collected on share transactions effected through the London Stock Exchange.

The flat rate of 0.5 per cent is based on the amount paid for the shares, not what they are worth. If, for example, shares are bought for £2,000, £10 SDRT is payable, whatever the value of the shares themselves. If shares are transferred for free, no SDRT is payable.

A higher rate of 1.5 per cent is payable if shares are transferred into a 'depositary receipt scheme' or a 'clearance service'. These are special arrangements where the shares are held by a third party.

CREST automatically deducts the SDRT and sends it to the HMRC. A stockbroker will settle up with CREST for the cost of the shares and the SDRT and then bill the purchaser for these and the broker's fees. If shares are not purchased through CREST, the stamp duty must be paid by the purchaser to HMRC.

UK stamp duty or SDRT is not payable on the purchase of foreign shares, though there may be foreign taxes to pay. SDRT is already accounted for in the price paid for units in unit trusts or shares in open-ended investment companies.

HELP AND INFORMATION

Further information on stamp duty land tax is available via the stamp taxes helpline on T 0845-603 0135 (open 8.30am to 5.00pm Monday to Friday) or the HMRC website (W www.hmrc.gov.uk), where a stamp duty calculator for both shares and land and property can be found. For buyers wishing to undertake their own conveyancing, copies of the land transaction return (SDLT1) and guidance notes (SDLT6) can be obtained by calling T 0845-302 1472.

LEGAL NOTES

These notes outline certain aspects of the law as they might affect the average person. They are intended only as a broad guideline and are by no means definitive. The law is constantly changing so expert advice should always be taken. In some cases, sources of further information are given in these notes.

It is always advisable to consult a solicitor without delay. Anyone who does not have a solicitor already can contact the following for assistance in finding one: Citizens Advice Bureau (W www.nacab.org.uk), the Community Legal Service (W www.legalservices.gov.uk), the Law Society of England and Wales For assistance in Scotland, contact the Scottish Citizens Advice Bureau (W www.cas.org.uk) or the Law Society of Scotland.

The community legal service fund and legal aid and assistance schemes exist to make the help of a lawyer available to those who would not otherwise be able to afford one. Entitlement depends on an individual's means but a solicitor or Citizens Advice Bureau will be able to advise about entitlement.

LAW SOCIETY OF ENGLAND AND WALES
113 Chancery Lane, London WC2A 1PL T 020-7242 1222 W www.lawsociety.co.uk

LAW SOCIETY OF SCOTLAND
26 Drumsheugh Gardens, Edinburgh EH3 7YR T 0131-1226 7411 W www.lawscot.org.uk

ABORTION

Abortion is governed by the Abortion Act 1967. This act is currently under review by the Common Select Committee on science and technology. The provisions below are accurate at the time of writing.

Under the provisions of the Abortion Act 1967, a legally induced abortion must be:

- performed by a registered medical practitioner
- carried out in an NHS hospital or other approved premises
- certified by two registered medical practitioners as justified on one or more of the following grounds:
  (a) that the pregnancy has not exceeded its twenty-fourth week and that the continuance of the pregnancy would involve risk, greater than if the pregnancy were terminated, of injury to the physical or mental health of the pregnant woman or any existing children of her family
  (b) that the termination is necessary to prevent grave permanent injury to the physical or mental health of the pregnant woman
  (c) that the continuance of the pregnancy would involve risk to the life of the pregnant woman, greater than if the pregnancy were terminated
  (d) that there is a substantial risk that if the child were born it would suffer from such physical or mental abnormalities as to be seriously handicapped.

In determining whether the continuance of a pregnancy would involve such risk of injury to health as is mentioned in grounds (a) or (b), account may be taken of the pregnant woman's actual or reasonably foreseeable environment.

The requirements relating to the opinion of two registered medical practitioners and to the performance of the abortion at an NHS hospital or other approved place cease to apply in circumstances where a registered medical practitioner is of the opinion, formed in good faith, that a termination is immediately necessary to save the life, or to prevent grave permanent injury to the physical or mental health, of the pregnant woman.

The provisions of the Abortion Act 1967 do not apply to Northern Ireland, where abortion is not legal.

Further information and advice can be obtained from:

FAMILY PLANNING ASSOCIATION (UK)
50 Featherstone Street, London EC1Y 8QU T 0845 122 8690 W www.fpa.org.uk

FAMILY PLANNING ASSOCIATION (SCOTLAND)
Unit 10, Firhill Business Centre, 76 Firhill Road, Glasgow G20 7BA T 0141-576 5088 W www.fpa.org.uk

FAMILY PLANNING ASSOCIATION (NORTHERN IRELAND)
3rd Floor, Ascot House, 24–31 Shaftsbury Square, Belfast BT2 7DB T 0845-122 8687 W www.fpa.org.uk
3rd Floor, 67 Carlisle Road, Derry BT48 6JL T 028-7126 0016 W www.fpa.org.uk

BRITISH PREGNANCY ADVISORY SERVICE (BPAS)
T 08457-304030 W www.bpas.org

ADOPTION OF CHILDREN

The Adoption and Children Act 2002 reforms the framework for domestic and intercountry adoption in England and Wales and some parts of it extend to Scotland and Northern Ireland.

WHO MAY APPLY FOR AN ADOPTION ORDER

A couple (whether married or two people living as partners in an enduring family relationship) may apply for an adoption order where both of them are over 21 or where one is only 18 but the natural parent and the other is 21. An adoption order may be made for one applicant where that person is 21 and: a) the court is satisfied that person is the partner of a parent of the person to be adopted; or b) they are not married and are not civil partners; or c) married or in a civil partnership but they are separated from their spouse or civil partner and living apart with the separation likely to be permanent; or d) their spouse/civil partner is either unable to be found, or their spouse/civil partner is incapable by reason of ill-health of making an application. There are certain qualifying conditions an applicant must meet eg residency in the British Isles.

ARRANGING AN ADOPTION

Adoptions may generally only be arranged by an adoption agency or by way of an order from the high court; breach of the restrictions on who may arrange an adoption would constitute a criminal offence. When deciding whether a child should be placed for adoption, the court or adoption agency must consider all the factors set out in the 'welfare checklist'. These factors include amongst other things the child's wishes, needs and any harm which the child has suffered or is likely to suffer, and the interest of the child is paramount. The parents must consent to the adoption, although the need for consent can be dispensed with by the court.

ADOPTION ORDER

Once an adoption has been arranged, a court order is necessary to make it legal; this may be obtained from the high court, county court or magistrates court (including family proceedings court). An adoption order may not be given unless the court is either satisfied that the consent of the child's natural parents (or guardians) has correctly been given or that consent should be dispensed with, eg where the parent or guardian cannot be found or is incapable of giving consent or where the welfare of the child so demands.

An adoption order has the effect of extinguishing the parental responsibility that a person other than the adopters (or adopter) has for the child, although where an order is made on the application of the partner of the parent, that parent keeps parental responsibility. This means that once adopted the child has the same status as a child born to the adoptive parents and will be treated as such for the purposes of intestate succession, National Insurance, child benefit etc. In addition the child may lose rights to the estates of those losing their parental responsibility.

REGISTRATION AND CERTIFICATES

All adoption orders made in England and Wales are required to be registered in the Adopted Children Register which also contains particulars of children adopted under registrable foreign adoptions. The General Register Office keeps this register from which certificates may be obtained in a similar way to birth certificates. The General Register Office also has equivalents in Scotland and Northern Ireland.

TRACING NATURAL PARENTS OR CHILDREN WHO HAVE BEEN ADOPTED

An adult adopted person may apply to the Registrar-General to obtain a certified copy of his/her birth certificate. For those adopted before 12 November 1975 it is obligatory to receive counselling services before this information is given. In any event, adoption agencies and adoption support agencies should provide services to adopted persons to assist them in obtaining information about their adoption and facilitate contact with their relatives. There is an Adoption Contact Register which provides a safe and confidential way for birth parents and other relatives to assure an adopted person that contact would be welcome. The BAAF (*see* below) can provide addresses of organisations which offer advice, information and counselling to adopted people, adoptive parents and people who have had their children adopted. Further information can be obtained from:

BRITISH ASSOCIATION FOR ADOPTION AND FOSTERING (BAAF)
Saffron House, 6–10 Kirkby Street, London EC1N 8TS
T 020-7421 2600 **W** www.baaf.org.uk

SCOTLAND

The relevant legislation is the Adoption (Scotland) Act 1978 (as amended by the Children Act 1995 and the Adoption and Children (Scotland) Act 2007) and the provisions are similar to those described above. In Scotland, petitions for adoption are made to the sheriff court or the court of session. The 2007 Act is expected to come into force in March 2009. It will repeal the 1978 Act, save for Part IV and will further amend the Children (Scotland) Act 1995.

Further information can be obtained from:

BRITISH ASSOCIATION FOR ADOPTION AND FOSTERING (BAAF)
BAAF Scottish Centre, 40 Shandwick Place, Edinburgh EH2 4RT
T 0131-220 4749

SCOTTISH ADOPTION ADVICE SERVICE
16 Sandyford Place, Glasgow G3 7NB **T** 0141-339 0772

BIRTHS (REGISTRATION)

It is the duty of the parents of a child born in England or Wales to register the birth within 42 days of the date of birth at the register office in the district in which the baby was born. If it is inconvenient to go to the district where the birth took place, the information for the registration may be given to a registrar in another district. Failure to register the birth within 42 days without reasonable cause may leave the parents liable to a penalty. If a birth has not been registered within 12 months of its occurrence it is possible for the late registration of the birth to be authorised by the Registrar-General, provided certain requirements can be met.

If the parents of the child were married to each other at the time of the birth (or conception), either parent may register the birth. If the parents were not married to each other at the time of the child's birth (or conception), the father's particulars may be entered in the register only where he attends the register office with the mother and they sign the birth register together. Where an unmarried parent is unable to attend the register office either parent may submit to the registrar a statutory declaration acknowledging the father's paternity (this form may be obtained from any registrar in England or Wales); alternatively a parental responsibility agreement or appropriate court order may be produced to the registrar.

If the parents do not register the birth of their child the following people may do so:

- the occupier of the house or hospital where the child was born
- a person who was present at the birth
- a person who is responsible for the child

Upon registration of the birth a short certificate is issued.

BIRTHS ABROAD

There are certain countries where birth registrations may be made for British subjects overseas. The British consul or high commission may register the births and issue certificates which are then sent to the General Register Office. If a birth is registered by the British consul or high commission, the registration would show the person's claim to British citizenship, British dependent territories citizenship or British overseas citizenship.

SCOTLAND

In Scotland the birth of a child must be registered within 21 days at the register office of either the district in which the baby was born or the district in which the mother was resident at the time of the birth.

If the child is born, either in or out of Scotland, on a ship, aircraft or land vehicle that ends its journey at any place in Scotland, the child, in most cases, will be registered as if born in that place.

CERTIFICATES OF BIRTHS, DEATHS OR MARRIAGES

Certificates of births, deaths or marriages that have taken place in England and Wales since 1837 can be obtained from the General Register Office or the Family Records Centre.

Certificates of births, marriages and deaths may be obtained in the following ways:

- by post, telephone, fax or online (details of which may be obtained by calling T 0845-603 7788 or visiting W www.gro.gov.uk)
- locally from the register office where the event was originally registered

Marriage or death certificates may be obtained from the minister of the church in which the marriage or funeral took place. Any register office can advise about the best way to obtain certificates.

The fees for certificates are:

Online application:

- full certificate of birth, marriage, death or adoption, £10.00
- full certificate of birth, marriage, death or adoption with GRO reference supplied, £7.00

By postal/phone/fax application:

- full certificate of birth, marriage, death or adoption, £11.50
- full certificate of birth, marriage, death or adoption with GRO reference supplied, £8.50
- extra copies of the same birth, marriage or death certificate issued at the same time, £7.00

A priority service is also available with certificates despatched on the working day following receipt of your application at an additional cost. Visit W www.gro.gov.uk or call T 0845-603 7788 for further information.

Indexes prepared from the registers are available for searching by the public at the Family Records Centre in London or at a Superintendent Registrar's Office; indexes at the latter relate only to births, deaths and marriages which occurred in that registration district. There is no charge for searching the indexes in the Public Search Room at the Family Records Centre but a general search fee is charged for searches at a Superintendent Registrar's Office. A fee is charged for verifying index references against the records.

The Society of Genealogists has many records of baptisms, marriages and deaths prior to 1837.

SCOTLAND

Certificates of births, deaths or marriages that have taken place in Scotland since 1855 can be obtained from the General Register Office for Scotland or from the appropriate local registrar:

- each extract or abbreviated certificate of birth, death, marriage, civil partnership or adoption within the year of registration, £8.50
- extract or abbreviated certificate of birth, death, marriage, civil partnership or adoption outwith the current year of registration, £13.50

A priority service for response within 24 hours is available for an additional fee.

The General Register Office for Scotland also keeps the Register of Divorces (including decrees of declaration of nullity of marriage), and holds parish registers dating from before 1855.

Fee for each particular search is:

- personal application: £8.00
- postal, telephone or fax order: £13.00

A priority service for a response within 24 hours is available for an additional fee of £10.00

General search in the indexes to the statutory registers and parochial registers, per day or part thereof:

- full or part day search pass: £10.00
- quarterly search pass: £440.00
- annual search pass: £1,250.00

Online searching is also available. For more information, visit W www.scotlandspeople.gov.uk Further information can be obtained from:

THE GENERAL REGISTER OFFICE
General Register Office, Trafalgar Road, Southport PR8 2HH
T 0845-603 7788 W www.gro.gov.uk

FAMILY RECORDS CENTRE
1 Myddelton Street, London EC1R 1UW

THE GENERAL REGISTER OFFICE FOR SCOTLAND
New Register House, 3 West Register Street, Edinburgh EH1 3YT
T 0131-334 0380 W www.gro-scotland.gov.uk

THE SOCIETY OF GENEALOGISTS
14 Charterhouse Buildings, Goswell Road, London EC1M 7BA
T 020-7251 8799

BRITISH CITIZENSHIP

Almost everyone who was a citizen of the UK and colonies and had a right of abode in the UK prior to the British Nationality Act 1981 became British citizens when the act came into force. British citizens have the right to live permanently in the UK and are free to leave and re-enter the UK at any time.

A person born on or after 1 January 1983 in the UK (including, for this purpose, the Channel Islands and the Isle of Man) is entitled to British citizenship if he/she falls into one of the following categories:

- he/she has a parent who is a British citizen
- he/she has a parent who is settled in the UK
- he/she is a newborn infant found abandoned in the UK
- his/her parents subsequently settle in the UK or become British citizens and an application is made before he/she is 18
- he/she lives in the UK for the first ten years of his/her life and is not absent for more than 90 days in each of those years
- he/she is adopted in the UK and one of the adopters is a British citizen
- if he/she has always been stateless and lives in the UK for a period of five years before his/her 22nd birthday

A person born outside the UK may acquire British citizenship if he/she falls into one of the following categories:

- he/she has a parent who is a British citizen otherwise than by descent, eg a parent who was born in the UK
- he/she has a parent who is a British citizen serving the crown overseas
- the home secretary consents to his/her registration while he/she is a minor
- he/she is a British dependent territories citizen, a British overseas citizen, a British subject or a British protected person and has been lawfully resident in the UK for five years
- he/she is a British dependent territories citizen who

acquired that citizenship from a connection with Gibraltar
- he/she is adopted or naturalised

Where parents are married, the status of either may confer citizenship on their child. If a child is illegitimate, the status of the mother determines the child's citizenship.

Under the 1981 act, Commonwealth citizens and citizens of the Republic of Ireland were entitled to registration as British citizens before 1 January 1988. In 1983, citizens of the Falkland Islands were granted British citizenship.

Renunciation of British citizenship must be registered with the home secretary and will be revoked if no new citizenship or nationality is acquired within six months. If the renunciation was required in order to retain or acquire another citizenship or nationality, the citizenship may be reacquired once. The secretary of state may deprive a person of a citizenship status if he or she is satisfied that the person has done anything seriously prejudicial to the vital interests of the United Kingdom, or a British overseas territory, unless making the order would have the effect of rendering a person stateless. A person may also be deprived of a citizenship status which results from his registration or naturalisation if the secretary of state is satisfied that the registration or naturalisation was obtained by means of fraud, false representation or concealment of a material fact.

BRITISH DEPENDENT TERRITORIES CITIZENSHIP

Under the 1981 act, this type of citizenship was conferred on citizens of the UK and colonies by birth, naturalisation or registration in British dependent territories. British dependent territories citizens may be entitled to registration as British citizens on completion of five years' legal residence in the UK.

On 1 July 1997 citizens of Hong Kong who did not qualify to register as British citizens under the British Nationality (Hong Kong) Act 1990 lost their British dependent territories citizenship on the handover of sovereignty to China; they may, however, have applied to register as British nationals (overseas).

BRITISH OVERSEAS CITIZENSHIP

Under the 1981 act, as amended by the British Overseas Territories Act 2002, this type of citizenship was conferred on any UK and colonies citizens who did not qualify for British citizenship or citizenship of the British dependent territories. British overseas citizenship may be acquired by the wife, civil partner and minor children of a British overseas citizen in certain circumstances. British overseas citizens may be entitled to registration as British citizens on completion of five years' legal residence in the UK.

RESIDUAL CATEGORIES

British subjects, British protected persons and British nationals (overseas) may be entitled to registration as British citizens on completion of five years' legal residence in the UK.

Citizens of the Republic of Ireland who were also British subjects before 1 January 1949 can retain that status if they fulfil certain conditions.

EUROPEAN UNION CITIZENSHIP

British citizens (including Gibraltarians who are registered as such) are also EU citizens and are entitled to travel freely to other EU countries to work, study, reside and set up a business. EU citizens have the same rights with respect to the United Kingdom.

NATURALISATION

Naturalisation is granted at the discretion of the home secretary. The basic requirements are five years' residence (three years if the applicant is married to, or is the civil partner of a British citizen), good character, adequate knowledge of the English, Welsh or Scottish Gaelic language, passing the UK citizenship test and an intention to reside permanently in the UK.

STATUS OF ALIENS

Aliens may not hold public office or vote in Britain and they may not own a British ship or aircraft. Citizens of the Republic of Ireland are not deemed to be aliens. Certain provisions of the Immigration and Asylum Act 1999 make provision about immigration and asylum and about procedures in connection with marriage by superintendent registrar's certificate.

CONSUMER LAW

SALE OF GOODS

A sale of goods contract is the most common type of contract. It is governed by the Sale of Goods Act 1979 (as amended by the Sale and Supply of Goods Act 1994). The act provides protection for buyers by implying terms into every sale of goods contract. These terms include:
- an implied term that the seller will pass good title to the buyer (unless the seller agrees to transfer only such title as he has)
- where the seller sells goods by reference to a description, an implied term that the goods will match that description and, where the sale is by sample and description, it will not be sufficient that the bulk of the goods corresponds with the sample if the goods do not also correspond with the description
- where goods are sold by a business seller, an implied term that the goods will be of satisfactory quality if they meet the standard that a reasonable person would regard as satisfactory, taking into account any description of the goods, the price, and all other relevant circumstances. The quality of the goods includes their state and condition, relevant aspects being whether they are fit for the purposes for which such goods are commonly supplied, their appearance and finish, freedom from minor defects and their safety and durability. This term will not be implied, however, if a buyer has examined the goods and should have noticed the defect or if the seller specifically drew the buyer's attention to the defect
- where goods are sold by a business seller, an implied term that the goods are reasonably fit for any purpose made known to the seller by the buyer (either expressly or by implication), unless it is shown that the buyer does not rely on the seller's judgement, or it is not reasonable for him/her to do so
- where goods are sold by sample, implied terms that the bulk of the sample will correspond with the sample in quality, and that the goods are free from any defect rendering them unsatisfactory which would have been apparent on a reasonable examination of the sample

Some of the above terms can be excluded from contracts by the seller. The seller's right to do this is, however, restricted by the Unfair Contract Terms Act 1977. The act offers more protection to a buyer who 'deals as a consumer', (that is where the seller is selling in the course of a business, the goods are of a type ordinarily bought for private use and the goods are bought by a buyer who is not a business buyer, though not allowing any liability for breach of the implied terms described above to be excluded). In a sale by auction or competitive tender, a buyer never deals as consumer. Also, a seller can never exclude the implied term as to title mentioned above.

HIRE-PURCHASE AGREEMENTS
Terms similar to those implied in contracts of sales of goods are implied into contracts of hire-purchase, under the Supply of Goods (Implied Terms) Act 1973. The 1977 act limits the exclusion of these implied terms as before.

SUPPLY OF GOODS AND SERVICES
Under the Supply of Goods and Services Act 1982, similar terms are also implied in other types of contract under which ownership of goods passes, eg a contract for 'work and materials' such as supplying new parts while servicing a car, and contracts for the hire of goods (though not hire-purchase agreements). These types of contracts have additional implied terms:

- that the supplier will use reasonable care and skill in carrying out the service
- that the supplier will carry out the service in a reasonable time (unless the time has been agreed)
- that the supplier will make a reasonable charge (unless the charge has already been agreed)

The 1977 act limits the exclusion of these implied terms in a similar manner as before.

UNFAIR TERMS
The Unfair Terms in Consumer Contracts Regulations 1999 apply to contracts between business sellers (or suppliers of goods and services) and consumers. Where the terms have not been individually negotiated, ie where the terms were drafted in advance so that the consumer was unable to influence those terms, there will be an unfair term where a term operates to the detriment of the consumer (ie carries a significant imbalance in the parties' rights and obligations arising under the contract). An unfair term does not bind the consumer but the contract will continue to bind the parties if it is capable of existing without the unfair term. The regulations contain a non-exhaustive list of terms which are regarded as unfair. Whether a term is regarded as fair or not will depend on many factors, including the nature of the goods or services, the surrounding circumstances (such as the bargaining strength of both parties) and the other terms in the contract.

TRADE DESCRIPTIONS
It is a criminal offence under the Trade Descriptions Act 1968 for a business seller to apply a false trade description of goods or to supply or offer to supply any goods to which a false description has been applied. A 'trade description' includes descriptions of quality, size, composition, fitness for purpose, performance, method of manufacture, and place and date of manufacture of the goods.

FAIR TRADING
The Fair Trading Act 1973 is designed to protect the consumer. It provides for the appointment of a Director-General of Fair Trading, one of whose duties is to review commercial activities in the UK relating to the supply of goods and services to consumers. An example of a practice which has been prohibited by a reference made under this act is that of business sellers posing in advertisements as private sellers.

CONSUMER PROTECTION
Under the Consumer Protection Act 1987, producers of goods are liable for any injury, death or damage to private property exceeding £275 caused by a defect in their product (subject to certain defences).

The Consumer Protection (Cancellation of Contracts Concluded Away from Business Premises) Regulations 1987 allow consumers a seven-day period in which to cancel contracts for the supply of goods and services, where the contracts were made during an unsolicited visit by a trader to the consumer's home or workplace. A contract will not be enforceable at all in this situation unless the trader has written to the consumer to notify them of the right to cancel within seven days.

Consumers are also afforded protection under the Consumer Protection (Distance Selling) Regulations 2000 in relation to cancellation periods, for example.

CONSUMER CREDIT
In matters relating to the provision of credit (or the supply of goods on hire or hire-purchase), consumers are also protected by the Consumer Credit Act 1974 (as amended by the Consumer Credit Act 2006). Under this act a licence, issued by the Director-General of Fair Trading, is required to conduct a consumer credit or consumer hire business or an ancillary credit business. Any 'fit' person as defined within the act may apply to the Director-General of Fair Trading for a licence, which is normally renewable after five years. A licence is not necessary if only exempt agreements are involved. The provisions of the act only apply to 'regulated' agreements, ie those that are with individuals or partnerships, those that are not exempt (certain local authority and building society loans will be exempt). Sole traders, unincorporated associations and partnerships with three or fewer partners entering consumer credit agreements for business purposes are protected when the value of the credit does not exceed £25,000. Individuals entering consumer credit agreements for personal purposes are protected by the act irrespective of the value of the credit. Provisions include:

- the terms of the regulated agreement can be altered by the creditor, provided the agreement gives him/her the right to do so; in such cases the debtor must be given proper notice of this
- in order for a creditor to enforce a regulated agreement, the agreement must comply with certain formalities and must be properly executed. The debtor must also be given specified information by the creditor or his/her broker or agent during the negotiations which take place before the signing of the agreement. The agreement must state certain information such as the amount of credit, the annual interest rate, and the amount and timing of repayments
- if an agreement is signed other than at the creditor's (or credit broker's or negotiator's) place of business and oral representations were made in the debtor's presence during discussions pre-agreement, the debtor has a right to cancel the agreement. Time for cancellation expires five clear days after the debtor receives a second copy of the agreement. The agreement must inform the debtor of his right to cancel and how to cancel
- if the debtor is in arrears (or otherwise in breach of the agreement), the creditor must serve a default notice before taking any action such as repossessing the goods
- if the agreement is a hire-purchase or conditional sale

agreement, the creditor cannot repossess the goods without a court order if the debtor has paid one third of the total price of the goods
- in agreements where the debtor is required to make grossly exorbitant payments or where the agreement grossly contravenes the ordinary principles of fair trading, the debtor may request that the court alter or set aside some of the terms of the agreement. The agreement can also be reopened during enforcement proceedings by the court itself

Where a credit reference agency has been used to check the debtor's financial standing, the creditor must give the agency's name to the debtor, who is entitled to see the agency's file on him. A fee of £1 is payable to the agency.

SCOTLAND

The legislation governing the sale and supply of goods applies to Scotland as follows:
- the Sale of Goods Act 1979 applies with some modifications and it has been amended by the Sale and Supply of Goods Act 1994
- the Supply of Goods (Implied Terms) Act 1973 applies
- the Supply of Goods and Services Act 1982 does not extend to Scotland but some of its provisions were introduced by the Sale and Supply of Goods Act 1994
- only Parts II and III of the Unfair Contract Terms Act 1977 apply
- the Trade Descriptions Act 1968 applies with minor modifications
- the Consumer Credit Act 1974 applies
- the Consumer Protection Act 1987 applies
- the General Product Safety Regulations 2005 apply
- the Unfair Terms in Consumer Contracts Regulations 1999 apply
- the Unfair Terms in Consumer Contracts (Amendment) Regulations 2001 apply
- the Consumer Protection (Distance Selling) Regulations 2000 apply
- the Sale and Supply of Goods to Consumers Regulations 2002 apply

PROCEEDINGS AGAINST THE CROWN

Until 1947, proceedings against the crown were generally possible only by a procedure known as a petition of right, which put the litigant at a considerable disadvantage. The Crown Proceedings Act 1947 placed the crown (not the sovereign in his/her private capacity, but as the embodiment of the state) largely in the same position as a private individual. The act did not however, extinguish or limit the crown's prerogative or statutory powers, and it granted immunity to HM ships and aircraft. It also left certain crown privileges unaffected. The act largely abolished the special procedures which previously applied to civil proceedings by and against the crown. Civil proceedings may be instituted against the appropriate government department or if there is doubt regarding which is the appropriate department, then against the attorney-general.

In Scotland proceedings against the crown founded on breach of contract could be taken before the 1947 act and no special procedures applied. The crown could, however, claim certain special pleas. The 1947 act applies in part to Scotland and brings the practice of the two countries as closely together as the different legal systems permit. As a result of the Scotland Act 1998 actions against government departments should be raised against the Lord Advocate or the advocate-general. Actions should be raised against the Lord Advocate where the department involved administers a devolved matter. Devolved matters include agriculture, education, housing, local government, health and justice. Actions should be raised against the advocate-general where the department is dealing with a reserved matter. Reserved matters include defence, foreign affairs and social security.

DEATHS

WHEN A DEATH OCCURS

If the death (including stillbirth) was expected, the doctor who attended the deceased during their final illness should be contacted. If the death was sudden or unexpected, the family doctor (if known) and police should be contacted. If the cause of death is quite clear the doctor will provide:
- a medical certificate that shows the cause of death
- a formal notice that states that the doctor has signed the medical certificate and that explains how to get the death registered

If the death was known to be caused by a natural illness but the doctor wishes to know more about the cause of death, he/she may ask the relatives for permission to carry out a post–mortem examination.

In England and Wales a coroner is responsible for investigating deaths occurring in the following circumstances:
- where there is no doctor who can issue a medical certificate of cause of death
- when no doctor has treated the deceased during his or her last illness or when the doctor attending the patient did not see him or her within 14 days before death, or after death
- when the death occurred during an operation or before recovery from the effect of an anaesthetic
- when the death was sudden and unexplained or attended by suspicious circumstances
- when the death might be due to an industrial injury or disease, or to accident, violence, neglect or abortion, attended by suspicious circumstances
- the death occurred in prison or in police custody

The doctor will write on the formal notice that the death has been referred to the coroner; if the post-mortem shows that death was due to natural causes, the coroner may issue a notification which gives the cause of death so that the death can be registered. If the cause of death was violent or unnatural, the coroner is obliged to hold an inquest.

In Scotland the office of coroner does not exist. The local procurator fiscal inquires into sudden or suspicious deaths. A fatal accident inquiry will be held before the sheriff where the death has resulted from an accident during the course of the employment of the person who has died, or where the person who has died was in legal custody, or where the Lord Advocate deems it in the public interest that an inquiry be held.

REGISTERING A DEATH

In England and Wales the death must be registered by the registrar of births and deaths for the district in which it occurred; details can be obtained from the doctor or local council, or at a post office or police station. Information concerning a death can be given before any registrar of births and deaths in England and Wales. The registrar will pass the relevant details to the registrar for the district where the death occurred, who will then register the death.

In England and Wales the death must normally be registered within five days; in Scotland it must be registered within eight days. If the death has been referred to the coroner/local procurator fiscal it cannot be registered until the registrar has received authority from the coroner/local procurator fiscal to do so. Failure to register a death involves a penalty in England and Wales and may lead to a court decree being granted by a sheriff in Scotland.

If the death occurred at a house or hospital, the death may be registered by:

- any relative of the deceased
- any person present at the death
- the occupier or any inmate of the house or hospital if he/she knew of the occurrence of the death
- any person making the funeral arrangements
- in Scotland, the deceased's executor or legal representative

For deaths that took place elsewhere, the death may be registered by:

- any relative of the deceased
- someone present at the death
- someone who found the body
- a person in charge of the body
- any person making the funeral arrangements

The majority of deaths are registered by a relative of the deceased. The registrar would normally allow one of the other listed persons to register the death only if there were no relatives available.

The person registering the death should take the medical certificate of the cause of death with them; it is also useful, though not essential, to take the deceased's birth and marriage certificates, NHS medical card (if possible), pension documents and life assurance details. The details given to the registrar must be absolutely correct, otherwise it may be difficult to change them later. The person registering the death should check the entry very carefully before it is signed. The registrar will issue a certificate for burial or cremation, a certificate of registration of death and a certificate for social security benefits – all free of charge. A death certificate is a certified copy of the entry in the death register; these can be provided on payment of a fee and may be required for the following purposes:

- the will
- bank and building society accounts
- savings bank certificates and premium bonds
- insurance policies
- pension claims

If the death occurred abroad or on a foreign ship or aircraft, the death should be registered according to the local regulations of the relevant country and a death certificate should be obtained. The death can also be registered with the British consul in that country and a record will be kept at the General Register Office. This avoids the expense of bringing the body back.

After 12 months (three months in Scotland) of death or the finding of a dead body, no death can be registered without the consent of the registrar-general.

BURIAL AND CREMATION

In most circumstances in England and Wales a certificate for burial or cremation must be obtained from the registrar before the burial or cremation can take place. If the death has been referred to the coroner, an order for burial or a certificate for cremation must be obtained. In Scotland a body may be buried (but not cremated) before the death is registered.

Funeral costs can normally be repaid out of the deceased's estate and will be given priority over any other claims. If the deceased has left a will it may contain directions concerning the funeral; however, these directions need not be followed by the executor.

The deceased's papers should also indicate whether a grave space had already been arranged. This information will be contained in a document known as a 'Deed of Grant'. Most town churchyards and many suburban churchyards are no longer open for burial because they are full. Most cemeteries are non-denominational and may be owned by local authorities or private companies; fees vary.

If the body is to be cremated, an application form, two cremation certificates (for which there is a charge) or a certificate for cremation if the death was referred to the coroner, and a certificate signed by the medical referee must be completed in addition to the certificate for burial or cremation (the form is not required if the coroner has issued a certificate for cremation). All the forms are available from the funeral director or crematorium. Most crematoria are run by local authorities; the fees usually include the medical referee's fee and the use of the chapel. Ashes may be scattered, buried in a churchyard or cemetery, or kept.

The registrar must be notified of the date, place and means of disposal of the body within 96 hours (England and Wales) or three days (Scotland).

If the death occurred abroad or on a foreign ship or aircraft, a local burial or cremation may be arranged. If the body is to be brought back to England or Wales, a death certificate from the relevant country or an authorisation for the removal of the body from the country of death from the coroner or relevant authority will be required. To arrange a funeral in England or Wales, an authenticated translation of a foreign death certificate or a death certificate issued in Scotland or Northern Ireland which must show the cause of death, is needed, together with a certificate of no liability to register from the registrar in England and Wales in whose sub-district it is intended to bury or cremate the body. If it is intended to cremate the body, a cremation order will be required from the Home Office or a certificate for cremation.

Further information can be obtained from:

THE GENERAL REGISTER OFFICE
General Register Office, Trafalgar Road, Southport PR8 2HH
T 0845-603 7788 W www.gro.gov.uk

THE GENERAL REGISTER OFFICE FOR SCOTLAND
New Register House, 3 West Register Street, Edinburgh EH1 3YT
T 0131-314 4452

DIVORCE AND RELATED MATTERS

There are three types of matrimonial suit: annulment of marriage, judicial separation and divorce. To obtain an annulment, judicial separation or divorce in England and Wales (provided a European Union court (except Denmark) has jurisdiction) the one commencing the proceedings (the petitioner) and the one defending the proceedings (the respondent) must be habitually resident in England and Wales; or the petitioner and the respondent must have last been habitually resident in England and Wales and one of them must continue to reside there; or the respondent must be habitually resident in England and Wales; or the petitioner must have been habitually resident in England and Wales throughout the period of at least one year ending with the start of proceedings; or the petitioner must be domiciled in England and Wales and must have been habitually resident in England and Wales throughout the period of at least six months, ending with the start of the proceedings; or both parties must be domiciled in England and Wales. If no European Union court (except Denmark) has jurisdiction, one or both parties must be domiciled in England and Wales. All cases are commenced in a divorce county court or in the Principal Registry in London. If a suit is defended, it may be transferred to the high court.

NULLITY OF MARRIAGE

Various circumstances have the potential to render a marriage void or voidable in nullity proceedings including: if there has been wilful non-consummation of the marriage; one partner has a venereal disease at the time of the marriage and the other did not know about it; the female partner was pregnant at the time of the marriage with another person's child and the male partner did not know of the pregnancy; the parties were within prohibited degrees of consanguinity, affinity or adoption; the parties were not male and female; either of the parties was already married or had entered a civil partnership; either of the parties was under the age of 16; the formalities of the marriage were defective, eg the marriage did not take place in an authorised building and both parties knew of the defect.

SEPARATION

A couple may enter into a private agreement to separate by consent without getting divorced but for the agreement to be valid it must be followed by an immediate separation; a solicitor should be contacted.

Another form of separation is judicial separation. Judicial separation does not dissolve a marriage and it is not necessary to prove that the marriage has irretrievably broken down. Either party can petition for a judicial separation at any time; the grounds listed below as grounds for divorce are also grounds for judicial separation. To petition for judicial separation, the parties do not have to prove that they have been married for 12 months or more.

A financial settlement between spouses in a separation agreement or which accompanies a judicial separation is not binding on the court and will not necessarily be upheld by the court after the commencement of divorce proceedings.

DIVORCE

Neither party can petition for divorce until at least one year after the date of the marriage. The sole ground for divorce is the irretrievable breakdown of the marriage; this must be proved on one or more of the following facts:

- the respondent has committed adultery and the petitioner finds it intolerable to live with him/her; however, the petitioner cannot rely on an act of adultery by the respondent if they have lived together as husband and wife for more than six months after the discovery of the adultery
- the respondent has behaved in such a way that the petitioner cannot reasonably be expected to continue living with him/her
- the respondent has deserted the petitioner for two years immediately before the petition
- the petitioner and the respondent have lived separately for two years immediately before the petition and the respondent consents to the divorce
- the petitioner and the respondent have lived separately for five years immediately before the petition

A total period of less than six months during which the parties have resumed living together is disregarded in determining whether the prescribed period of separation or desertion has been continuous (but may not be included as part of the period of separation).

The Matrimonial Causes Act 1973 requires the solicitor for the petitioner to certify whether the possibility of a reconciliation has been discussed with the petitioner.

THE DECREE NISI

A decree nisi does not dissolve or annul the marriage, but must be obtained before a divorce or annulment can take place.

Where the suit is undefended, the evidence normally takes the form of a sworn written statement made by the petitioner which is considered by a district judge. If the judge is satisfied that the petitioner has proved the contents of the petition, a date will be set for the pronouncement of the decree nisi in open court: neither party need attend.

If the suit is defended, the petition will be heard in open court with parties giving oral evidence.

THE DECREE ABSOLUTE

The decree nisi is capable of being made absolute on the application of the petitioner six weeks after the decree nisi. If the petitioner does not apply, the respondent must wait for a further three months before application may be made. In exceptional circumstances the granting of the decree absolute may be delayed, for example if matters regarding children are not capable of resolution. A decree absolute is unlikely to be applied for until the financial matters have been resolved. The decree absolute dissolves or annuls the marriage. Where the couple have been married in accordance with Jewish or other religious usages, the court may require them to produce a declaration that they have taken such steps as are required to dissolve the marriage in accordance with those usages before the decree absolute is issued.

MAINTENANCE

Either party may be liable to pay maintenance to a spouse or former spouse. If there are any children of the marriage, both parties have a legal responsibility to support them financially if they can afford to do so.

The courts are responsible for assessing maintenance for a spouse or former spouse, taking into account each party's income and essential outgoings and other aspects of the case. The court also deals with any maintenance for a child that has been treated by the spouses as a child of the family, such as a step-child.

In February 2006, the Secretary of State for Work and Pensions announced a dual approach to the reform of child maintenance – £120 million of investment in a three year Operational Improvement Plan to stabilise and improve the performance of the Child Support Agency, and a fundamental review of the child maintenance system, led by Sir David Henshaw.

The Government responded to Sir David Henshaw's recommendations in July 2006, published a White Paper in December 2006, and introduced the Child Maintenance and Other Payments Bill into Parliament in June 2007.

This Bill proposes wide-ranging changes to the system, including the establishment of a new Commission as a statutory body, to replace the CSA. To maximise the number of effective child maintenance agreements in place – whether private or statutory – the Commission will ensure parents take responsibility for providing financial support for their children, providing support for setting up arrangements, and delivering a new statutory system with improvement assessment, collection and enforcement processes. The changes are currently being considered by Parliament.

At the time of writing the CSA is still responsible for assessing the maintenance that non-resident parents shall pay for their natural or adopted children (whether or not a marriage has taken place).

The CSA accepts applications only when all the people involved are habitually resident in the UK; the courts will continue to deal with cases where one of the individuals lives abroad. The CSA deals with all new cases unless it is agreed by the spouses that the court may grant an order for child support (but even in agreed jurisdiction cases one parent may give the other 14 months' notice to have the case dealt with by the CSA).

A formula is used to work out how much child maintenance is payable under CSA jurisdiction. The formula requires the non-resident parent to pay 15 per cent net of post-tax, national insurance and pension contributions for one child, 20 per cent for two and 25 per cent for more than two. An earnings cap of £104,000 net a year applies. The parent with care's income is not taken into account. Deductions are applied for staying contact and for further children in the non-resident parent's household. In court jurisdiction cases, the CSA formula is adopted as a guideline only.

Some cases involving unusual circumstances are treated as special cases and the assessment is modified, and in some cases the court retains jurisdiction (for educational costs and high income cases, for example). Where there is financial need (eg because of disability or continual education) maintenance may be ordered by the court for children even beyond the age of 18.

CSA maintenance is reviewed automatically every two years. Either parent can report a change of circumstances and request a review at any time. An independent complaints examiner for the CSA has been appointed.

If the non-resident parent does not pay CSA maintenance, the CSA may make an order for payments to be deducted directly from his/her salary; if all other methods fail, the CSA may take court action to enforce payment.

OTHER FINANCIAL RELIEF

Unlike in some other jurisdictions, there is no algebraic formula for division of assets on divorce. The courts must exercise their powers so as to achieve an outcome which is fair between the parties. In determining what is 'fair' the court must have regard to all the circumstances of the case, first consideration being given to the welfare of any minor child(ren) of the family. Beyond this, the court must have particular regard to a prescribed list of statutory factors, being:

- the income, earning capacity, property and other financial resources which each of the parties to the marriage has or is likely to have in the foreseeable future, including in the case of earning capacity, any increase in that capacity which it would, in the opinion of the court, be reasonable to expect a party to the marriage to take steps to acquire
- the financial needs, obligations and responsibilities which each of the parties to the marriage has or is likely to have in the foreseeable future
- the standard of living enjoyed by the family before the breakdown of the marriage
- the age of each party to the marriage and the duration of the marriage
- any physical or mental disability of either of the parties to the marriage
- the contribution which each of the parties has made or is likely in the foreseeable future to make to the welfare of the family, including any contribution by looking after the home or caring for the family
- the conduct of each of the parties, if that conduct is such that it would, in the opinion of the court, be inequitable to disregard it
- in the case of proceedings for divorce or nullity of marriage, the value to each of the parties to the marriage of any benefit (for example a pension) which by reason of the dissolution of the marriage that party will lose the chance of acquiring.

The court also has a duty to consider making an order which will settle once and for all the parties financial responsibilities towards each other. This is known as a financial 'clean break'. Where a clean break is not possible, the court will combine provision of capital via a lump sum and/or property adjustment order and/or pension sharing/attachment order with an ongoing income order, known as maintenance (alimony).

Maintenance can be for a 'term' (ie for a limited period only) or it can be for the joint lives of the parties. In some cases, the courts use nominal maintenance to leave a party's income claims open. It is possible for either party to apply to court to vary the amount or duration of the maintenance at a future date.

Prior to 2000, in considering the above factors, the courts considered the 'reasonable financial requirements' of the applicant, usually the wife, and treated this as determinative of the extent of the applicant's award. In the landmark case of *White v White* in 2000 the House of Lords re-evaluated the court's approach to dividing assets on divorce. The law lords enunciated three key principles. Firstly, the outcome has to be as fair as possible in all the circumstances with each party being entitled to a fair share of the available property. Secondly, in seeking to achieve a fair outcome there is no space for discriminating between the breadwinner and the homemaker in their respective roles. Thirdly, having considered all the circumstances of the case, and the statutory checklist, the judge should consider his view against the 'yardstick of equality of division'.

More recently, the law lords have offered further guidance as to how to achieve a fair division of assets on divorce in the cases of *Miller* and *McFarlane*. In determining fairness, the court must now consider three strands or principles, being each party's respective needs, the possibility of compensating the financially weaker party for any 'relationship' generated disadvantage, which will be relevant where one party has given up a career, and 'equal sharing' of family assets, which is applicable as much to short marriages as to long marriages, and which will apply unless there is good reason to the contrary.

In the recent 'huge money' divorce case of *Charman* the presumption of 50:50 in assessing financial awards on divorce emerged undamaged. Those with trust interests must be aware that the court will ignore the trust structure if it takes the view that the assets will be made available to the party on request. The court acknowledged that London is increasingly perceived as 'the divorce capital of the world' and given that wealthy couples tend to have connections with more than one country, 'forum shopping' and securing the most advantageous jurisdiction for a divorce will be of critical importance in many cases.

In assessing whether there is a good reason to depart from the concept of equal sharing, the court will consider the nature of property and whether the property was acquired during the marriage otherwise than by inheritance or gift, known as matrimonial property, such as the matrimonial home, or other property to which the other spouse has not contributed. Whilst the yardstick of equality will apply to matrimonial assets to give full effect to the sharing entitlement, it will apply less readily to non-matrimonial assets, particularly in short marriages.

Additionally, conduct and special contributions will be relevant in assessing whether there should be a departure from equality, but only in exceptional cases, where such conduct or contribution is 'gross and obvious'.

At the time of writing, the Law Commission had published its report on the Marital Property Agreements project, which will examine the status and enforceability of agreements made between spouses or civil partners (or those contemplating marriage or civil partnership) concerning their property or finances. This project is due to commence in late 2009 with a report and draft Bill expected in late 2012.

COHABITING COUPLES

Rights of unmarried couples are not the same as for married couples. Agreements, whether express or inferred by conduct, often determine interest in money and property. Reliance upon inferences is problematic, therefore it is advisable to consider entering into a contract, or 'cohabitation agreement', which establishes how money and property should be divided in the event of a relationship breakdown. This area of the law is still developing. In July 2007, the Law Commission published its report to Parliament, recommending a scheme to provide remedies for eligible candidates. In the absence of further law in this area, cohabitation agreements are governed by the general principles of contract law.

CIVIL PARTNERSHIP

The Civil Partnership Act 2004 came into force on 5 December 2005; it has UK-wide status. Same-sex couples, by registering as civil partners, are able to gain legal recognition of their relationship and thereby obtain rights and obligations broadly equivalent to those of married couples. These rights and responsibilities include a duty to provide reasonable maintenance for your civil partner and any children of the family, equitable treatment in respect of life assurance and pension benefits, recognition under intestacy rules and domestic violence protection. In addition, inheritance tax is waived as with married couples and there is a right of succession for tenancy. A civil partnership which has irretrievably broken down may be dissolved by the court on the application of either civil partner. The irretrievable breakdown of the partnership must be proved on one of four facts. These facts are the same as those for divorce (*see* above), save for a civil partner may not seek dissolution of the partnership on the basis of the other's adultery.

DOMESTIC VIOLENCE

The Domestic Violence, Crime and Victims Act 2004 is intended to provide greater protection for victims of domestic violence. If one spouse has been subjected to violence at the hands of the other, it is possible to obtain an order from court to restrain further violence and if necessary to have the other spouse excluded from the home. Such orders also apply to civil partnerships and cohabiting couples (including same sex couples), and may also apply to a range of other relationships including parents and children and, to a lesser extent, non-cohabiting couples.

SCOTLAND

Although some provisions are similar to those for England and Wales, there is separate legislation for Scotland covering nullity of marriage, judicial separation, divorce and ancillary matters. The principal legislation in relation to family law in Scotland is the Family Law (Scotland) Act 1985. The Family Law (Scotland) Act 2006 came in to force on 4 May 2006, and introduced reforms to various aspects of Scottish family law. The following is confined to major points on which the law in Scotland differs from that of England and Wales.

An action for judicial separation or divorce may be raised in the court of session; it may also be raised in the sheriff court if either party was resident in the sheriffdom for 40 days immediately before the date of the action or for 40 days ending not more than 40 days before the date of the action. The fee for starting a divorce petition in the sheriff court is £92.

The grounds for raising an action of divorce in Scotland have been subject to reform in terms of the 2006 act. The current grounds for divorce are:

- the defender has committed adultery. When adultery is cited as proof that the marriage has broken down irretrievably, it is not necessary in Scotland to prove that it is also intolerable for the pursuer to live with the defender
- the defender's behaviour is such that the pursuer cannot reasonably be expected to cohabit with the defender
- there has been no cohabitation between the parties for one year prior to the raising of the action for divorce, and the defender consents to the granting of decree of divorce
- there has been no cohabitation between the parties for two years prior to the raising of the action for divorce

The previously available ground of desertion has been abolished by the 2006 act.

A simplified procedure for 'do-it-yourself divorce' was introduced in 1983 for certain divorces. If the action is based on one or two years' separation and will not be opposed, and if there are no children under 16 and no financial claims, and there is no sign that the applicant's spouse is unable to manage his or her affairs through mental illness or handicap, the applicant can write directly to the local sheriff court or to the court of session for the appropriate forms to enable him or her to proceed. The fee is £70, unless the applicant receives income support, family credit or legal advice and assistance, in which case there is no fee.

Where a divorce action has been raised, it may be sisted or put on hold for a variety of reasons. In all actions for divorce an extract decree, which brings the marriage to an end, will be made available 14 days after the divorce has been granted. Unlike in England, there is no decree nisi, only a final decree of divorce. Parties must ensure that all financial issues have been resolved prior to divorce, as it is not possible to seek further financial provision after divorce has been granted.

FINANCIAL PROVISION

In relation to financial provision on divorce, the first, and most important, principle is fair sharing of the matrimonial property. In terms of Scots law matrimonial property is defined as all property acquired by either spouse from the date of marriage up to the date of separation. Property acquired before the marriage is not deemed to be matrimonial unless it was acquired for use by the parties as a family home or as furniture for that home. Property acquired after the date of separation is not matrimonial property. Any property acquired by either of the parties by way of gift or inheritance during the marriage is excluded and does not form part of the matrimonial property.

When considering whether to make an award of financial provision a court shall also take account of any economic advantage derived by either party to the marriage as a result of contributions, financial or otherwise, by the other, and of any economic disadvantage suffered by either party for the benefit of the other party. The court must also ensure that the economic burden of caring for a child under the age of 16 is shared fairly between the parties.

A court can also consider making an order requiring one party to pay the other party a periodical allowance for a certain period of time following divorce. Such an order may be appropriate in cases where there is insufficient capital to effect a fair sharing of the matrimonial property. Orders for periodical allowance are uncommon, as courts will favour a 'clean break' where possible.

CHILDREN
The court has the power to award a residence order in respect of any children of the marriage or to make an order regulating the child's contact with the non-resident parent. The court will only make such orders if it is deemed better for the child to do so than to make no order at all, and the welfare of the children is of paramount importance. The fact that a spouse has caused the breakdown of the marriage does not in itself preclude him/her from being awarded residence.

NULLITY
An action for 'declaration of nullity' can be brought if someone with a legitimate interest is able to show that the marriage is void or voidable. The action can only be brought in the court of session. Although the grounds on which a marriage may be void or voidable are similar to those on which a marriage can be declared invalid in England, there are some differences. Where a spouse is capable of sexual intercourse but refuses to consummate the marriage, this is not a ground for nullity in Scots law, though it could be a ground for divorce. Where a spouse was suffering from venereal disease at the time of marriage and the other spouse did not know, this is not a ground for nullity in Scots law, neither is the fact that a wife was pregnant by another man at the time of marriage without the knowledge of her husband.

COHABITING COUPLES
The law in Scotland now provides certain financial and property rights for cohabiting couples in terms of the Family Law (Scotland) Act 2006, or 'the 2006 act'. The relevant 2006 act provisions do not place cohabitants in Scotland on an equal footing with married couples or civil partners, but provide some rights for cohabitants in the event that the relationship is terminated by separation or death. The provisions relate to couples who cease to cohabit after 4 May 2006.

The legislation provides for a presumption that any contents of the home shared by the cohabitants are owned in equal shares. A former cohabitant can also seek financial provision on termination of the relationship in the form of a capital payment if they can successfully demonstrate that they have been financially disadvantaged, and that conversely the other cohabitant has been financially advantaged, as a consequence of contributions made (financial or otherwise). Such a claim must be made no later than one year after the day on which the cohabitants cease to cohabit.

The 2006 act also provides that a cohabitant may make a claim on their partner's estate in the event of that partner's death, providing that there is no will. A claim of this nature must be made no later than six months after the date of the partner's death.

Further information can be obtained from:

THE PRINCIPAL REGISTRY
First Avenue House, 42–49 High Holborn, London WC2V 6NP

THE COURT OF SESSION
Parliament House, Parliament Square, Edinburgh EH1 1RQ
T 0131-225 2595

THE CHILD SUPPORT AGENCY
National Enquiry Line 08457-133133 W www.csa.gov.uk

EMPLOYMENT LAW

PAY AND CONDITIONS
The Employment Rights Act 1996 consolidates the statutory provisions relating to employees' rights. Employers must give each employee employed for one month or more a written statement containing the following information:

- names of employer and employee
- date when employment began and the date on which the employee's period of *continuous* employment began (taking into account any employment with a previous employer which counts towards that period)
- remuneration and intervals at which it will be paid
- job title or description of job
- hours and place(s) of work
- holiday entitlement and holiday pay
- provisions concerning incapacity for work due to sickness and injury, including provisions for sick pay
- details of pension scheme(s)
- length of notice period that employer and employee need to give to terminate employment
- if the employment is not intended to be permanent, the period for which it is expected to continue or, if it is for a fixed term, the end date of the contract
- details of any collective agreement which affects the terms of employment
- details of disciplinary and grievance procedures
- if the employee is to work outside the UK for more than one month, the period of such work and the currency in which payment is made
- a note stating whether a contracting out certificate is in force

This must be given to the employee within two months of the start of their employment. The Working Time Regulations 1998, the National Minimum Wage Act 1998, the Employment Rights (Dispute Resolution) Act 1998 and the Employment Relations Act 1999 now supplement the 1996 act. If the employer does not provide the written statement within two months then the employee can complain to an employment tribunal, which can specify the information that the employer should have given. The Employment Act 2002 provides that when, in the context of an employee's successful tribunal claim, the employer is also found to have been in breach of the duty to provide the written statement at the time proceedings were commenced, the tribunal must award the employee two weeks' pay, and may award four weeks' pay, unless it is unjust or inequitable to do so.

FLEXIBLE WORKING

The Employment Act 2002 (and regulations made under it) gives employees who are responsible for the upbringing of a child the right to apply for a flexible working pattern for the purpose of caring for that child. The right was extended to carers of adults in 2006. If an application under the act is rejected, it is open to the employee to complain to an employment tribunal.

SICK PAY

Employees absent from work through illness or injury are entitled to receive Statutory Sick Pay (SSP) from the employer for a maximum period of 28 weeks in any three-year period. Where average earnings (before deductions such as tax and National Insurance) are £87 a week or more, the standard rate of SSP is £72.55 per week.

MATERNITY AND PARENTAL RIGHTS

Under the Employment Relations Act 1999, the Employment Act 2002 and the Maternity and Parental Leave Regulations 1999 (as amended in 2002 and 2006), both men and women are entitled to take leave when they become a parent. Women are protected from discrimination, detriment or dismissal by reason of their pregnancy. Men are protected from suffering a detriment or dismissal for taking paternity or parental leave.

All women are entitled to a maximum period of maternity leave of 52 weeks. This comprises 26 weeks' ordinary maternity leave, followed immediately by 26 weeks' additional maternity leave. A woman who takes ordinary maternity leave normally has the right to return to the job in which she was employed before her absence. If she takes additional maternity leave, she is entitled to return to the same job or, if that is not reasonably practicable, to another job that is suitable and appropriate for her to do.

A woman will qualify for Statutory Maternity Pay (SMP), which is payable for up to 39 weeks, if she has been continuously employed for not less than 26 weeks at the beginning of the 14th week before the expected week of childbirth. The first six weeks of SMP are paid at 90 per cent of the employee's average weekly earnings, and the remaining 33 weeks are paid at the rate of £122.75 per week, or 90 per cent of weekly earnings, whichever is lower.

Employees are entitled to adoption leave and adoption pay subject to fulfillment of criteria similar (but not identical) to those in relation to maternity leave and pay. Where a couple is adopting a child, one may take adoption leave, and the other may take paternity leave.

Certain employees are entitled to paternity leave on the birth or adoption of a child. To be eligible, the employee must be the child's father, or the partner of the mother or adopter, and meet other conditions. One of those conditions is that they must have been continuously employed for not less than 26 weeks at the beginning of the 14th week before the expected week of childbirth (or, in the case of adoptions, 26 weeks ending with the week in which notification of the adoption match is given). The employee may take either one week's leave, or two consecutive weeks' leave. This leave may be taken at any time between the date of the child's birth (or placement of adoption) and 56 days later. During paternity leave, most employees will be entitled to Statutory Paternity Pay, which is paid at the same rate as the second stage rate of SMP (ie £122.75 per week or 90 per cent of weekly earnings, whichever is lower).

Any employee with one year's service who has, or expects to have, responsibility for a child may take parental leave to care for the child. Each parent is entitled to a total of 13 weeks' parental leave for each of their children (or 18 weeks if the child is disabled) but this leave must be taken (at the rate of no more than four weeks per year, and in blocks of whole weeks only) before the child's fifth birthday (or 18th birthday if the child is disabled).

In May 2007 the government issued a consultation paper on certain proposed modifications to statutory paternity leave and pay. The proposed scheme would allow a father to take some of the mother's statutory maternity leave (and pay) where the mother wants to return to work before the end of her ordinary or additional maternity leave entitlement. At the time of writing the consultation is still underway.

SUNDAY TRADING

The Sunday Trading Act 1994 allows shops to open on Sunday for serving retail customers. The Employment Rights Act 1996 gives shop workers and betting workers the right not to be dismissed, selected for redundancy or to suffer any detriment (such as the denial of overtime, promotion or training) if they refuse to work on Sundays. This does not apply to those who, under their contracts, are employed to work on Sundays.

TERMINATION OF EMPLOYMENT

An employee may be dismissed without notice if guilty of gross misconduct but in other cases a period of notice must be given by the employer. The minimum periods of notice specified in the Employment Rights Act 1996 are:

- one week if the employee has been continuously employed for one month or more but for less than two years
- two weeks if the employee has been continuously employed for at least two years
- a week is added for every additional complete year of continuous employment up to 12 years (making the maximum statutory notice period 12 weeks after 12 years' continuous employment)
- longer periods apply if these are specified in the contract of employment

If an employee is dismissed with less notice than he/she is entitled to by statute, or under their contract if longer, he/she will have a wrongful dismissal claim (unless the employer paid the employee in lieu of notice in accordance with a contractual provision entitling it to do so). This claim for wrongful dismissal can be brought by the employee either in the court system or the employment tribunal, but if brought in the tribunal the maximum amount that can be awarded is £25,000. This claim can also be brought by an employee whose fixed-term contract has been terminated prematurely, and without justification, by the employer.

REDUNDANCY

An employee dismissed because of redundancy may be entitled to redundancy pay. This applies if:

- the employee has at least two years' continuous service

- the employee is dismissed by the employer (this can include cases of voluntary redundancy)
- dismissal is due to redundancy. Redundancy can mean closure of the entire business, closure of a particular site of the business, or a reduction in the need for employees to carry out work of a particular kind (eg as a result of over-manning or a reduction in work).

An employee may not be entitled to a redundancy payment if offered a suitable alternative job by the same employer. The amount of statutory redundancy pay depends on the length of service, age, and their earnings, subject to a weekly maximum of (currently) £310. The maximum payment that can be awarded is £9,300. The redundancy payment is guaranteed by the State in cases where the employer becomes insolvent (subject to the conditions above).

UNFAIR DISMISSAL

Complaints of unfair dismissal are dealt with by an employment tribunal. Any employee with one year's continuous service (subject to exceptions, including in relation to whistleblowers – *see* below) can make a complaint to the tribunal. At the tribunal, it is for the employer to prove that the dismissal was due to one or more of the following six potentially fair reasons:

- the employee's capability or qualifications for the job he/she was employed to do
- the employee's conduct
- redundancy
- retirement
- a legal restriction preventing the continuation of the employee's contract
- some other substantial reason

If the employer succeeds in showing this, the tribunal must then decide whether the employer acted reasonably in dismissing the employee for that reason. If the employee is found to have been unfairly dismissed, the tribunal can order that he/she be reinstated, re-engaged or compensated. Any person believing that they may have been unfairly dismissed should contact their local Citizens Advice Bureau or seek legal advice. A claim must be brought within three months of the date of termination of employment.

The normal maximum compensatory award for unfair dismissal is £60,600 (as at 1 February 2007). Where an employer has failed to follow the statutory dismissal procedures which came into force on 1 October 2004, the tribunal must usually increase the compensatory award by 10 per cent and it may increase by up to 50 per cent.

WHISTLEBLOWING

Under the whistleblowing legislation (Public Interest Disclosure Act 1998, which inserted provisions into the Employment Rights Act 1996) dismissal of an employee is automatically unfair if the reason or principal reason for the dismissal is that the employee has made a protected disclosure. The legislation also makes it unlawful to subject workers (a broad category that includes employees and certain other individuals, such as agency workers) who have made a protected disclosure to any detriment on the ground that they have done so.

For a disclosure to qualify for protection, the claimant must show that he has disclosed information, which in his reasonable belief tends to show one or more of the following six categories of wrongdoing:

- criminal offences
- breach of any legal obligation
- miscarriages of justice
- danger to the health and safety of any individual
- damage to the environment
- the deliberate concealing of information about any of the above

The malpractices can be past, present, prospective or merely alleged.

A qualifying disclosure will only be protected if the manner of the disclosure fulfills certain conditions, including being made in good faith and being made to a defined category of persons, which varies according to the type of disclosure.

Any whistleblower claim in the employment tribunal must normally be brought within three months of the date of dismissal or other act leading to a detriment.

An individual does not need to have been working with the employer for any particular period of time to be able to bring such a claim and compensation is uncapped (and can include an amount for injury to feelings).

DISCRIMINATION

Discrimination in employment on the grounds of sex (including gender reassignment), sexual orientation, race, colour, nationality, ethnic or national origins, religion or belief, married status, age or (subject to wide exceptions) disability is unlawful. Discrimination legislation generally covers direct discrimination, indirect discrimination, harassment and victimisation. Only in limited circumstances can such discrimination be justified (rendering it lawful).

An individual does not need to be employed for any particular period of time to be able to claim discrimination, and discrimination compensation is uncapped (and can include an amount for injury to feelings). These features distinguish the discrimination laws from, for example, the unfair dismissal laws.

The following legislation applies to those employed in Great Britain but not to employees in Northern Ireland or (subject to EC exceptions) to those who work mainly abroad:

- the Equal Pay Act 1970 (as amended) entitles men and women to equality in matters related to their contracts of employment
- the Sex Discrimination Act 1975 (as amended) makes it unlawful to discriminate on the grounds of sex or marital/civil partner status. This covers all aspects of employment (including advertising for recruits, terms offered, opportunities for promotion and training, and dismissal procedures) and protects job applicants, employees and other types of worker, as well as ex-workers
- the Race Relations Act 1976 gives individuals the right not to be discriminated against on the grounds of race, colour, nationality, or ethnic or national origins. It applies to all aspects of employment
- the Disability Discrimination Act 1995 makes discrimination against a disabled person in all aspects of employment unlawful. In certain circumstances, the employer may show that the less favourable treatment is justified. The act also imposes a duty on employers to make 'reasonable adjustments' to the arrangements and physical features of the workplace if these place disabled people at a substantial disadvantage compared with those who are not disabled. The definition of a 'disabled person' is wide and now includes people diagnosed with HIV, cancer and multiple sclerosis. Since early 2007 there has been a new positive duty on

public bodies to promote equality of opportunity for disabled people

- the Employment Equality (Religion or Belief) Regulations 2003 make discrimination against a person on the grounds of religion or belief, in all aspects of employment, unlawful
- the Employment Equality (Sexual Orientation) Regulations 2003 make discrimination against an individual on the grounds of sexual orientation, in all aspects of employment, unlawful
- The Employment Equality (Age) Regulations 2006 outlaw age discrimination in the workplace. This legislation is having profound implications for employers' policies and practices and has required major changes to selection procedures, recruitment policies, terms and conditions, benefits, dismissals and retirements

The Equal Opportunities Commission, the Commission for Racial Equality and the Disability Rights Commission (which will soon all be merged into the new Commission for Equality and Human Rights) have, as part of their roles, the function of eliminating such discrimination in the workplace, and can provide further information and assistance.

In Northern Ireland similar provisions exist but are contained in separate legislation (although the Disability Discrimination Act does extend to Northern Ireland).

In Northern Ireland there is one combined body working towards equality and eliminating discrimination, the Equality Commission for Northern Ireland.

WORKING TIME

The Working Time Regulations 1998 impose rules that limit working hours and provide for rest breaks and holidays. The regulations apply to workers and so cover not only employees but also other individuals who undertake to perform personally any work or services (eg freelancers). The regulations are complex and subject to various exceptions and qualifications but the basic provisions relating to adult day workers are as follows:

No worker is permitted to work more than an average of 48 hours per week (unless they opt out of this limit), and a worker is entitled to the following breaks:

- 11 consecutive hours' rest in every 24-hour period
- an uninterrupted rest period of at least 24 hours in each 7 day period (in addition to the daily rest period)
- 20 minutes' rest break provided that the working day is longer than 6 hours
- 4 weeks' paid annual leave (this is to increase to 4.8 weeks (24 days full-time) on 1 October 2007 and 5.6 weeks (28 days full-time) on 1 April 2009). 5.6 weeks equates to 4 weeks plus public holidays

There are specific provisions relating to night work and young workers (ie those over school leaving age but under 18).

HUMAN RIGHTS

On 2 October 2000 the Human Rights Act 1998 came into force. This act incorporates the European Convention on Human Rights into the law of the United Kingdom. The main principles of the act are as follows:

- all legislation must be interpreted and given effect by the courts as compatible with the Convention so far as it is possible to do so. Before the second reading of a new bill the minister responsible for the bill must provide a statement regarding the compatibility of the bill with the Human Rights Act
- subordinate legislation (eg statutory instruments) which are incompatible with the Convention can be struck down by the courts
- primary legislation (eg acts of parliament) which is incompatible with the Convention cannot be struck down by a court, but the higher courts can make a declaration of incompatibility which is a signal to parliament to change the law
- all public authorities (including courts and tribunals) must not act in a way which is incompatible with the Convention
- individuals whose Convention rights have been infringed by a public authority may bring proceedings against that authority, but the act is not intended to create new rights as between individuals

The main human rights protected by the Convention are the right to life (article 2); protection from torture and inhuman or degrading treatment (article 3); protection from slavery or forced labour (article 4); the right to liberty and security of the person (article 5); the right to a fair trial (article 6); the right not to be subject to retrospective criminal offences (article 7); the right to respect for private and family life (article 8); freedom of thought, conscience and religion (article 9); freedom of expression (article 10); freedom of peaceful association and assembly (article 11); the right to marry and found a family (article 12); protection from discrimination (article 14); the right to property (article 1 Protocol No.1); the right to education (article 2 Protocol No.1); and the right to free election (article 3 Protocol No.1). Most of the Convention rights are subject to limitations which deem the breach of the right acceptable on the basis it is 'necessary in a democratic society'.

PARENTAL RESPONSIBILITY

The Children Act 1989 gives the mother parental responsibility for the child. There are different rules for unmarried fathers obtaining parental responsibility depending on whether the child was born before or after 1 December 2003. For babies born after 1 December 2003, unmarried fathers can get parental responsibility by: (a) registering the child's birth jointly with the mother at the time of birth or (b) re-registering the birth if you are the natural father or (c) marrying the mother of their child or (d) by obtaining a parental responsibility order from the court or (e) registering with the court for parental responsibility. The Adoption and Children Act 2002 also makes provision for a father who is not married to the child's mother to acquire parental responsibility for the child if he becomes registered as the child's father. The consent of a father without parental responsibility is not required for adoption. However, adoption agencies and local authorities must be careful to establish if possible the identity of the father, as the father then has an opportunity to apply for parental responsibility within the proceedings.

In Scotland, the relevant legislation is the Children (Scotland) Act 1995, which also gives the mother parental responsibility for her child whether or not she is married to the child's father. A father who is married to the mother, either at the time of the child's conception or subsequently, will also have automatic parental rights. Section 23 of the 2006 act provides that an unmarried father will obtain automatic parental responsibilities and rights if he is registered as the father on the child's birth certificate. For unmarried fathers who are not named on the birth certificate, or whose children were born before the 2006 act came into force, it is possible to acquire parental responsibilities and rights by applying to the court or by entering into a parental responsibilities and rights agreement with the mother. The father of any child, regardless of parental rights, has a duty to aliment that child until he/she is 18 (25 if the child is still at an educational establishment).

LEGITIMATION
Under the Legitimacy Act 1976, an illegitimate person automatically becomes legitimate when his/her parents marry. This applies even where one of the parents was married to a third person at the time of the birth. In such cases it is necessary to re-register the birth of the child. In Scotland, the status of illegitimacy has finally been abolished by section 21 of the 2006 act. The Law Reform Act 1987 reformed the law so as to remove so far as possible the legal disadvantages of illegitimacy.

JURY SERVICE

In England and Wales a person charged with more serious criminal offences and more complex civil cases is entitled to be tried by jury. No such right exists in Scotland, although more serious offences are heard before a jury. In England and Wales there are 12 members of a jury in a criminal case and eight members in a civil case. In Scotland there are 12 members of a jury in a civil case in the court of session (the civil jury being confined to the court of session and a restricted number of actions), and 15 in a criminal trial in the high court of justiciary. Jurors are normally asked to serve for ten working days, although jurors selected for longer cases are expected to sit for the duration of the trial.

Every 'registered' parliamentary or local government elector between the ages of 18 and 70 who has lived in the UK (including, for this purpose, the Channel Islands and the Isle of Man) for any period of at least five years since reaching the age of 13 is qualified to serve on a jury unless he/she is 'mentally disordered' or disqualified.

Those disqualified from jury service include:

- those who have at any time been sentenced by a court in the UK (including, for this purpose, the Channel Islands and the Isle of Man) to a term of imprisonment or youth custody of five years or more
- those who have been imprisoned or detained for public protection
- those who have within the previous ten years served any part of a sentence of imprisonment, youth custody or detention, been detained in a young offenders' institution, received a suspended sentence of imprisonment or order for detention, or received a community service order
- those who are on bail in criminal proceedings

The court has the discretion to excuse a juror from service, or defer the date of service, if the juror can show there is good reason why he/she should be excused from attending or good reason why his attendance should be deferred. It is an offence to fail to attend when summoned or to make false representations in an attempt to evade service. The defendant can object to any juror if he/she can show cause.

A juror may claim travelling expenses, a subsistence allowance and an allowance for other financial loss (eg loss of earnings or benefits, fees paid to carers or child-minders) up to a stated limit. It is a contempt of court for a juror to disclose what happened in the jury room even after the trial is over. A jury's verdict need not be unanimous. In criminal proceedings the agreement of ten jurors will suffice (when there are at least 11 jurors remaining). In civil proceedings the agreement of seven jurors will suffice. However the court must be satisfied that the jury had reasonable time to consider its verdict based on the nature and complexity of the case. In criminal proceedings this must be no less than two hours.

SCOTLAND

Qualification criteria for jury service in Scotland are similar to those in England and Wales, except that the maximum age for a juror is 65, members of the judiciary are ineligible for ten years after ceasing to hold their post, and others concerned with the administration of justice are only eligible for service five years after ceasing to hold office. Certain persons who have the right to be excused include full-time members of the medical, dental, nursing, veterinary and pharmaceutical professions, full-time members of the armed forces, ministers of religion, persons who have served on a jury within the previous five years, members of the Scottish parliament, members of the Scottish government and junior Scottish ministers. Those convicted of a serious crime are automatically disqualified. Those who are incapable by reason of a mental disorder may also be excused. The maximum fine for a person serving on a jury knowing himself/herself to be ineligible is £1,000. The maximum fine for failing to attend without good cause is also £1,000.

Further information can be obtained from:

THE COURT SERVICE
Southside, 105 Victoria Street, London SW1E 6QT
T 020-7210 2266

SCOTTISH COURTS SERVICE
Courts of Session, Parliament House, Parliament Square, Edinburgh EH1 1RQ T 0131-225 2595

THE CLERK OF JUSTICIARY
High Court of Justiciary, Lawnmarket, Edinburgh EH2 2NS
T 0131-240 6900

LANDLORD AND TENANT

RESIDENTIAL LETTINGS
The provisions outlined here apply only where the tenant lives in a separate dwelling from the landlord and where the dwelling is the tenant's only or main home. It does not apply to licensees such as lodgers, guests or service occupiers.

The 1996 Housing Act radically changed certain aspects of the legislation referred to below; in particular, the grant of assured and assured shorthold tenancies under the Housing Act 1988.

ASSURED SHORTHOLD TENANCIES
If a tenancy was granted on or after 15 January 1989 and before 28 February 1997, the tenant would have an assured tenancy unless the landlord served notice under section 20 in the prescribed form prior to the commencement of the tenancy, stating that the tenancy is to be an assured shorthold tenancy and the tenancy is for a minimum fixed term period of six months (*see* below). An assured tenancy gives that tenant greater rights of security. The tenant could, for example, stay in possession of the dwelling for as long as the tenant observed the terms of the tenancy. The landlord cannot obtain

possession from such a tenant unless the landlord can establish a specific ground for possession (set out in the Housing Act 1988) and obtains a court order. The rent payable is that agreed with the landlord at the start of the tenancy. The landlord has the right to increase the rent annually by serving a notice. If that happens the tenant can apply to have the rent fixed by the rent assessment committee of the local authority. The tenant or the landlord may request that the committee sets the rent in line with open market rents for that type of property.

Under the Housing Act 1996, all new lettings entered into on or after 28 February 1997 (for whatever term) will be assured shorthold tenancies unless the landlord serves a notice stating that the tenancy is not to be an assured shorthold tenancy. This means that the landlord is entitled to possession at the end of the tenancy provided he serves a notice under section 21 Housing Act 1988 and commences the proceedings in accordance with the correct procedure. The landlord must obtain a court order, however, to obtain possession if the tenant refuses to vacate at the end of the tenancy. If the tenancy is an assured shorthold tenancy, the court must grant the order. For both assured and assured shorthold tenancies, if the tenant is more than eight weeks in arrears, the landlord can serve notice and, if the tenant is still in arrears at the date of the hearing, the court must make an order for possession.

REGULATED TENANCIES

Before the Housing Act 1988 came into force (15 January 1989) there were regulated tenancies; some are still in existence and are protected by the Rent Act 1977. Under this act it is possible for the landlord or the tenant to apply to the local rent officer to have a 'fair' rent registered. The fair rent is then the maximum rent payable.

SECURE TENANCIES

Secure tenancies are generally given to tenants of local authorities, housing associations (before 15 January 1989) and certain other bodies. This gives the tenant security of tenure unless the terms of the agreement are broken by the tenant and it is reasonable to make an order for possession. Those with secure tenancies may have the right to buy their property. In practice this right is generally only available to council tenants.

AGRICULTURAL PROPERTY

Tenancies in agricultural properties are governed by the Agricultural Holdings Act 1986, the Agricultural Tenancies Act 1995 (both amended by the Regulatory Reform (Agricultural Tenancies) (England and Wales) Order 2006) and the Rent (Agriculture) Act 1976, which give similar protections to those described above, eg security of tenure, right to compensation for disturbance, etc. The Agricultural Holdings (Scotland) Act 1991 along with Agricultural Holdings (Scotland) Act 2003 apply similar provisions to Scotland.

EVICTION

The Protection from Eviction Act 1977 (as amended by the Housing Act 1988) sets out the procedure a landlord must follow in order to obtain possession of property. It is unlawful for a landlord to evict a tenant otherwise than in accordance with the law. For common law tenancies and for Rent Act tenants a Notice to Quit in the prescribed form giving 28 days is required. For secure and assured tenancies a Notice Seeking Possession must be served. It is unlawful for the landlord to evict a person by putting their belongings onto the street, by changing the locks and so on. It is also unlawful for a landlord to harass a tenant in any way in order to persuade him/her to give up the tenancy. The tenant may be able to obtain an injunction to restrain the actions of the landlord and get back into the property and be awarded damages.

LANDLORD RESPONSIBILITIES

Under the Landlord and Tenant Act 1985, where the term of the lease is less than seven years, the landlord is responsible for maintaining the structure and exterior of the property, for sanitation, for heating and hot water, and all installations for the supply of water, gas and electricity.

LEASEHOLDERS

Strictly speaking, leaseholders have bought a long lease rather than a property and in certain limited circumstances the landlord can end the tenancy. Under the Leasehold Reform Act 1967 (as amended by the Housing Acts 1969, 1974 and 1980), leaseholders of houses may have the right to buy the freehold or to take an extended lease for a term of 50 years. This applies to leases where the term of the lease is over 21 years and where the leaseholder has occupied the house as his/her main residence for the last two years, or for a total of two years over the last ten.

The Leasehold Reform, Housing and Urban Development Act came into force in 1993 and allows the leaseholders of flats in certain circumstances to buy the freehold of the building in which they live.

Responsibility for maintenance of the structure, exterior and interior of the building should be set out in the lease. Usually the upkeep of the interior of his/her part of the property is the responsibility of the leaseholder, and responsibility for the structure, exterior and common interior areas is shared between the freeholder and the leaseholder(s).

If leaseholders are in any way dissatisfied with treatment from their landlord or with charges made in respect of lease extensions, they are entitled to have their situation evaluated by the Leasehold Valuation Tribunal.

The Commonhold and Leasehold Reform Act 2002 makes provision for the freehold estate in land to be registered as commonhold land and for the legal interest in the land to be vested in a 'commonhold association' ie a private limited company.

BUSINESS LETTINGS

The Landlord and Tenant acts 1927 and 1954 (as amended) give security of tenure to the tenants of most business premises. The landlord can only evict the tenant on one of the grounds laid down in the 1954 act, and in some cases where the landlord repossesses the property the tenant may be entitled to compensation.

SCOTLAND

In Scotland assured and short assured tenancies exist for lettings after 2 January 1989 and are similar to assured tenancies in England and Wales. The relevant legislation is the Housing (Scotland) Act 1988.

Most tenancies created before 2 January 1989 were regulated tenancies and the Rent (Scotland) Act 1984 still applies where these exist. The act defines, among other things, the circumstances in which a landlord can increase the rent when improvements are made to the property. The provisions of the Rent Act do not apply to tenancies where the landlord is the Crown, a local authority or a housing corporation.

The Housing (Scotland) Acts of 1987 and 2001 relate to local authority responsibilities for housing, the right to buy, and local authority secured tenancies. The provisions are broadly similar to England and Wales.

In Scotland, business premises are not controlled by statute to the same extent as in England and Wales, although the Tenancy of Shops (Scotland) Act 1949 gives some security to tenants of shops. Tenants of shops can apply to the sheriff, within 21 days of being served a notice to quit, for a renewal of tenancy if threatened with eviction. This application may be dismissed on various grounds including where the landlord has offered to sell the property to the tenant at an agreed price or, in the absence of agreement as to price, at a price fixed by a single arbiter appointed by the parties or the sheriff. The act extends to properties where the Crown or government departments are the landlords or the tenants.

Under the Leases Act 1449 the landlord's successors (either purchasers or creditors) are bound by the agreement made with any tenants so long as the following conditions are met:

- the lease, if for more than one year, must be in writing
- there must be a rent
- there must be a term of expiry
- the tenant must have entered into possession
- the subjects of the lease must be land
- the landlord, if owner, must be the proprietor with a recorded title, ie the title deeds are recorded in the Register of Sasines or registered in the Land Register

The Antisocial Behaviour (Scotland) Act 2001 provides that all landlords letting property in Scotland must register with the local authority in which the let property is situated. It is a criminal offence to fail to do this. Exceptions apply to holiday lets, owner-occupied accommodation and agricultural holdings. The act applies to partnerships, trusts and companies as well as to individuals.

LEGAL AID

The Access to Justice Act 1999 has transformed what used to be known as the Legal Aid system. The Legal Aid Board has been replaced by the Legal Services Commission, which is responsible for the development and administration of two legal funding schemes in England and Wales, namely the Criminal Defence Service and the Community Legal Service fund. The Criminal Defence Service assists people who are under police investigation or facing criminal charges. The Community Legal Service is designed to increase access to legal information and advice by involving a much wider network of funders and providers in giving publicly funded legal services. In Scotland, provision of legal aid is governed by the Legal Aid (Scotland) Act 1986 and administered by the Scottish Legal Aid Board.

LEGAL SERVICES COMMISSION

(85 Gray's Inn Road, London WC1X 8TX **T** 020-7759 0000 **W** www.legalservices.gov.uk)

CIVIL LEGAL AID

From 1 January 2000, only organisations (such as solicitors or Citizens Advice Bureaux) with a contract with the Legal Services Commission have been able to give initial help in any civil matter. Moreover, from that date decisions about funding were devolved from the Legal Services Commission to contracted organisations in relation to any level of publicly funded service in family and immigration cases. For other types of case, applications for public funding are made through a solicitor (or other contracted legal services providers) in much the same way as the former Legal Aid. On 1 April 2001 the so-called civil contracting scheme was extended to cover all levels of service for all types of cases.

Under the new civil funding scheme there are broadly seven levels of service available:

- legal help
- help at court
- general family help
- legal representation – either investigative help or full representation
- help with mediation
- family mediation
- such other services as authorised by specific orders

ELIGIBILITY

Eligibility for funding from the Community Legal Service depends broadly on five factors:

- the level of service sought (*see* above)
- whether the applicant qualifies financially
- the merits of the applicant's case
- a costs-benefits analysis (if the costs are likely to outweigh any benefit that might be gained from the proceedings, funding may be refused)
- whether there is any public interest in the case being litigated (ie whether the case has a wider public interest beyond that of the parties involved – for example, a human rights case)

The limits on capital and income above which a person is not entitled to public funding vary with the type of service sought.

CONTRIBUTIONS

Some of those who qualify for Community Legal Service funding will have to contribute towards their legal costs. Contributions must be paid by anyone who has a disposable income or disposable capital exceeding a prescribed amount. The rules relating to applicable contributions are complex and detailed information can be obtained from the Legal Services Commission.

STATUTORY CHARGE

A statutory charge is made if a person keeps or gains money or property in a case for which they have received legal aid. This means that the amount paid by the Community Legal Service fund on their behalf is deducted from the amount that the person receives. This does not apply if the court has ordered that the costs be paid by the other party (unless the amount paid by the other party does not cover all of the costs). In certain circumstances, the Legal Services Commission may waive or postpone payment.

CONTINGENCY OR CONDITIONAL FEES

This system was introduced by the Courts and Legal Services Act 1990. It offers legal representation on a 'no win, no fee' basis. It provides an alternative form of assistance, especially for those cases which are ineligible for funding by the Community Legal Service. The main area for such work is in the field of personal injuries.

Not all solicitors offer such a scheme and different solicitors may well have different terms. The effect of the agreement is that solicitors will not make any charges until the case is concluded successfully. If a case is won then the losing party will usually have to pay towards costs, with the winning party contributing around one third.

SCOTLAND
Civil legal aid is available for cases in the following:
- the sheriff courts
- the court of session
- the House of Lords
- the lands valuation appeal court
- the Scottish land court
- the Lands Tribunal for Scotland
- the Employment Appeal Tribunals
- the Judicial Committee of the Privy Council
- the Proscribed Organisations Appeal Commissioner
- proceedings before the Social Security Commissioners
- proceedings before the Child Support Commissioners

Civil legal aid is not available for defamation actions, small claims or simplified divorce procedures or petitions by a debtor for his own sequestration.

Eligibility for civil legal aid is assessed in a similar way to that in England and Wales, though the financial limits differ in some respects and are as follows:
- a person is eligible and will not have to pay a contribution if his yearly disposable income is £3,156 or less and disposable capital is £7,147 or less
- if disposable income exceeds £10,306, the person is not eligible for legal aid
- if disposable income is between £3,156 and £10,306, contributions are payable
- if disposable capital exceeds £11,847, the person is not eligible for legal aid
- if disposable capital is between £7,147 and £11,847, contributions are payable
- those receiving income support or income-related job seeker's allowance qualify automatically

CRIMINAL LEGAL AID

The Legal Services Commission provides defendants facing criminal charges with free legal representation if they pass a merits test and a means test.

Criminal legal aid covers the cost of preparing a case and legal representation in criminal proceedings. It is also available for appeals against verdicts or sentences in magistrates' courts, the crown court or the court of appeal. It is not available for bringing a private prosecution in a criminal court.

If granted criminal legal aid, either the person may choose their own solicitor or the court will assign one. Contributions to the legal costs may be required if the case proceeds to the crown court. The rules relating to applicable contributions are complex and detailed information can be obtained from the Legal Services Commission.

DUTY SOLICITORS
The Legal Aid Act 1988 also provides free advice and assistance to anyone questioned by the police (whether under arrest or helping the police with their enquiries). No means test or contributions are required for this.

SCOTLAND
Legal advice and assistance operates in a similar way in Scotland. A person is eligible:
- if disposable income does not exceed £223 a week. If disposable income is between £91 and £223 a week, contributions are payable
- if disposable capital does not exceed £1,561 (if the person has dependent relatives, the savings allowance is higher)
- if receiving income support or income-related job seeker's allowance they qualify automatically provided they have no savings over the limit

The procedure for application for criminal legal aid depends on the circumstances of each case. In solemn cases (more serious cases, such as murder) heard before a jury, a person is automatically entitled to criminal legal aid until they are given bail or placed in custody. Thereafter, it is for the court to decide whether to grant legal aid. The court will do this if the person accused cannot meet the expenses of the case without undue hardship on him or his dependants. In less serious cases the procedure depends on whether the person is in custody:
- anyone taken into custody has the right to free legal aid from the duty solicitor up to and including the first court appearance
- if the person is not in custody and wishes to plead guilty, they are not entitled to criminal legal aid but may be entitled to legal advice and assistance, including assistance by way of representation
- if the person is not in custody and wishes to plead not guilty, they can apply for criminal legal aid. This must be done within 14 days of the first court appearance at which they made the plea

The criteria used to assess whether or not criminal legal aid should be granted is similar to the criteria for England and Wales. When meeting with your solicitor, take evidence of your financial position such as details of savings, bank statements, pay slips, pension book or benefits book.
Further information can be obtained from:

THE SCOTTISH LEGAL AID BOARD
44 Drumsheugh Gardens, Edinburgh EH3 7SW
T 0131-226 7061 W www.slab.org.uk

MARRIAGE

Any two persons may marry provided that:
- they are at least 16 years old on the day of the marriage (in England and Wales persons under the age of 18 must generally obtain the consent of their parents; if consent is refused an appeal may be made to the high court, the county court or a court of summary jurisdiction)
- they are not related to one another in a way which would prevent their marrying
- they are unmarried (a person who has already been married must produce documentary evidence that the previous marriage has been ended by death, divorce or annulment)
- they are not of the same sex (though same sex couples can register a civil partnership instead)
- they are capable of understanding the nature of a marriage ceremony and of consenting to marriage

The marriage may be valid in England and Wales and void by the law of the domicile of both or either of the parties. The parties should check the marriage will be recognised as valid in their home country if either is not a British citizen.

DEGREES OF RELATIONSHIP
A marriage between persons within the prohibited degrees of consanguinity, affinity or adoption is void.

A man may not marry his mother, daughter, grandmother, granddaughter, sister, aunt, niece, great-grandmother, adoptive mother, former adoptive mother, adopted daughter or former adopted daughter.

A woman may not marry her father, son, grandfather, grandson, brother, uncle, nephew, great-grandfather, adoptive father, former adoptive father, adopted son or former adopted son. Under the Marriage Act 1983, some exceptions to the law permit a man or a woman to marry certain step-relatives or in-laws.

ENGLAND AND WALES

TYPES OF MARRIAGE CEREMONY

It is possible to marry by either religious or civil ceremony. A religious ceremony can take place at a church or chapel of the Church of England or the Church in Wales, or at any other place of worship which has been formally registered by the Registrar-General.

A civil ceremony can take place at a register office, a registered building or any other premises approved by the local authority.

An application for an approved premises licence must be made by the owners or trustees of the building concerned; it cannot be made by the prospective marriage couple. Approved premises must be regularly open to the public so that the marriage can be witnessed; the venue must be deemed to be a permanent and immovable structure. Open-air ceremonies are prohibited.

Non-Anglican marriages may also be solemnised following the issue of a Registrar-General's licence in unregistered premises where one of the parties is seriously ill, is not expected to recover, and cannot be moved to registered premises. Detained and housebound persons may be married at their place of residence.

MARRIAGE IN THE CHURCH OF ENGLAND OR THE CHURCH IN WALES

Marriage by banns

The marriage must take place in a parish in which one of the parties lives, or in a church in another parish if it is the usual place of worship of either or both of the parties. The banns must be called in the parish in which the marriage is to take place on three Sundays before the day of the ceremony; if either or both of the parties lives in a different parish the banns must also be called there. After three months the banns are no longer valid. The minister will not perform the marriage unless he or she is satisfied that the banns have been properly called.

Marriage by common licence

The vicar who is to conduct the marriage will arrange for a common licence to be issued by the diocesan bishop; this dispenses with the necessity for banns. One of the parties must have lived in the parish for 15 days immediately before the issuing of the licence or must usually worship at the church. Eligibility requirements vary from diocese to diocese, but it is not normally required that the parties should have been baptised. The licence is valid for three months.

Marriage by special licence

A special licence is granted by the Archbishop of Canterbury in special circumstances for the marriage to take place at any place, with or without previous residence in the parish, or at any time. Application must be made to the registrar of the Faculty Office (1 The Sanctuary, London SW1P 3JT T 020-7222 5381).

Marriage by certificate

The marriage can be conducted on the authority of the superintendent registrar's certificate, provided that the vicar's consent is obtained (there is no obligation upon the vicar to accept the certificate). One of the parties must live in the parish or must usually worship at the church.

MARRIAGE BY OTHER RELIGIOUS CEREMONY

One of the parties must normally live in the registration district where the marriage is to take place. In addition to giving notice to the superintendent registrar it may also be necessary to book a registrar to be present at the ceremony.

CIVIL MARRIAGE

A marriage may be solemnised at any register office, registered building or approved premises in England and Wales. The superintendent registrar of the district should be contacted, and, if the marriage is to take place at approved premises, the necessary arrangements at the venue must also be made.

NOTICE OF MARRIAGE

Unless it is to take place by banns or under common or special licence in the Church of England or the Church in Wales, a notice of the marriage must be given in person to the superintendent registrar. Notice of marriage may be given in the following ways:

- by certificate. Both parties must have lived in a registration district in England or Wales for at least seven days immediately before giving notice at the local register office. If they live in different registration districts, notice must be given in both districts. The marriage can take place in any register office or other approved premises in England and Wales no sooner than 16 days after notice has been given, when the superintendent registrar issues a certificate.
- by licence (often known as 'special licence'). One of the parties must have lived in a registration district in England or Wales for at least 15 days before giving notice at the register office; the other party need only be a resident of, or be physically in, England and Wales on the day notice is given. The marriage can take place one clear day (other than a Sunday, Christmas Day or Good Friday) after notice has been given.

A notice of marriage is valid for 12 months, unless it is for the marriage of a detained or housebound person, when it will usually only be accepted within three months of publication. Notice for marriages taking place within the Church of England or Church of Wales should also only be valid within three months of publication. It should be possible to make an advance (provisional) booking 12 months before the ceremony. In this case it is still necessary to give formal notice three months before the marriage. When giving notice of the marriage it is necessary to produce official proof, if relevant, that any previous marriage has ended in divorce or death by producing a decree absolute or death certificate; it is also necessary to provide proof of age, identity and nationality for each of the parties, for example, with a passport. If either party is under 18 years old, evidence of consent by their parent or guardian is required. There are special procedures for those wishing to get married in the UK that are subject to immigration control; the register office will be able to advise on these.

SOLEMNISATION OF THE MARRIAGE

On the day of the wedding there must be at least two other people present who are prepared to act as witnesses and sign the marriage register. A registrar of marriages must be present at a marriage in a register office or at approved premises, but an authorised person may act in the capacity of registrar in a registered building.

If the marriage takes place at approved premises, the room must be separate from any other activity on the premises at the time of the ceremony, and no food or drink can be sold or consumed in the room during the ceremony or for one hour beforehand.

The marriage must be solemnised between 8am and 6pm, with open doors. At some time during the ceremony the parties must make a declaration that they know of no legal impediment to the marriage and they must also say the contracting words; the declaratory and contracting words may vary according to the form of service. A civil marriage cannot contain any religious aspects, but it may be possible for non-religious music and/or readings to be included. It may also be possible to embellish the marriage vows taken by the couple.

CIVIL FEES

Marriage at a Register Office

By superintendent registrar's certificate, £30 per person for the notice of the marriage (which is not refundable if the marriage does not in fact take place) and £40 for the ceremony at the register office.

Marriage on Approved Premises

By superintendent registrar's certificate, £30 per person for the ceremony at the register office.

An additional fee will also be payable for the superintendent registrar's and registrar's attendance at the marriage. This is set locally by the local authority responsible. A further charge is likely to be made by the owners of the building for the use of the premises. For marriages taking place in a religious building other than the Church of England or Church of Wales, an additional fee of £47 is payable for the registrar's attendance at the marriage unless an 'Authorised Person' appointed by the trustees of the building has agreed to register the marriage. Additional fees may be charged by the trustees of the building for the wedding and by the person who performs the ceremony.

ECCLESIASTICAL FEES

(Church of England and Church in Wales*)

Marriage by banns

For publication of banns, £19

For certificate of banns issued at time of publication, £12.00

For marriage service, £240

Marriage by common licence

Fee for licence, £70

Marriage by special licence

Fee for licence, £140

* These fees are revised from 1 April each calendar year. Some may not apply to the Church in Wales

SCOTLAND

REGULAR MARRIAGES

A regular marriage is one which is celebrated by a minister of religion or authorised registrar or other celebrant. Each of the parties must complete a marriage notice form and return it to the district registrar for the area in which they are to be married, irrespective of where they live, within the three month period prior to the date of the marriage and not later than 15 days prior to that date. The district registrar must then enter the date of receipt and certain details in a marriage book kept for this purpose, and must also enter the names of the parties and the proposed date of marriage in a list which is displayed in a conspicuous place at the registration office until the date of the marriage has passed. All persons wishing to enter into a regular marriage in Scotland must follow the same preliminary procedure regardless of whether they intend to have a religious or civil ceremony. Before the marriage ceremony takes place any person may submit an objection in writing to the district registrar.

A marriage schedule, which is prepared by the registrar, will be issued to one or both of the parties in person up to seven days before a religious marriage; for a civil marriage the schedule will be available at the ceremony. The schedule must be handed to the celebrant before the ceremony starts; it must be signed immediately after the wedding and the marriage must be registered within three days.

The authority to conduct a religious marriage is deemed to be vested in the authorised celebrant rather than the building in which it takes place; open-air religious ceremonies are therefore permissible in Scotland.

From 10 June 2002 it has been possible, under the Marriage (Scotland) Act 2002, for venues or couples to apply to the local council for a licence to allow a civil ceremony to take place at a venue other than a registration office. To obtain further information, a venue or couple should contact the district registrar in the area they wish to marry. A list of licensed venues is also available on the General Registers of Scotland website (W www.gro-scotland.gov.uk).

MARRIAGE BY COHABITATION WITH HABIT AND REPUTE

Prior to the enactment of the 2006 act, if two people had lived together constantly as husband and wife and were generally held to be such by the neighbourhood and among their friends and relations, a presumption could arise from which marriage could be inferred. Before such a marriage could be registered, however, a decree of declarator of marriage had to be obtained from the court of session. Section 3 of the 2006 act provides that it will no longer be possible for a marriage to be constituted by cohabitation with habit and repute, but it will still be possible for couples whose period of cohabitation began before commencement of the 2006 act to seek a declarator under the old rule of law.

CIVIL FEES

The fee for submitting a notice of marriage to the district registrar is £26 per person. Solemnisation of a civil marriage costs £46.50, whilst the extract of the entry in the register of marriages attracts a fee of £8.50. The costs of religious marriage ceremonies can vary.

Further information can be obtained from:

THE GENERAL REGISTER OFFICE
Trafalgar Road, Southport PR8 2HH
T 0845-603 7788 W www.gro.gov.uk

THE GENERAL REGISTER OFFICE FOR SCOTLAND
New Register House, 3 West Register Street, Edinburgh EH1 3YT
T 0131-314 4452

TOWN AND COUNTRY PLANNING

The planning system can help to protect the environment and assist individuals in assessing their land rights. There are a number of acts governing the development of land and buildings in England and Wales and advice should always be sought from a Citizens Advice Bureau or local planning authority before undertaking building works on any land or to property. If development takes place which requires planning permission without permission being given, enforcement action may take place and the situation may need to be rectified.

PLANNING PERMISSION

Planning permission is needed if the work involves:

- making a material change in use, such as dividing off part of the house so that it can be used as a separate home or dividing off part of the house for commercial use, eg for a workshop
- going against the terms of the original planning permission, eg there may be a restriction on fences in front gardens on an open-plan estate
- building, engineering for mining, except for the permissions below
- new or wider access to a main road
- additions or extensions to flats or maisonettes

Planning permission is not needed to carry out internal alterations or work which does not affect the external appearance of the building, and are not works for making good damage or works begun after 5 December 1968 for the alteration of a building by providing additional space in it underground.

There are certain types of development for which the Secretary of State for the Environment, Food and Rural Affairs has granted general permissions (permitted development rights). These include:

- house extensions and additions (including conservatories, loft conversions, garages and dormer windows). Up to 10 per cent or up to 50 cubic metres (whichever is the greater) can be added to the original house for terraced houses or houses on land designated as an area of outstanding natural beauty or in a conservation area. Up to 15 per cent or 70 cubic metres (whichever is the greater) to other kinds of houses. The maximum that can be added to any house is 115 cubic metres
- buildings such as garden sheds and greenhouses so long as they are no more than 3 metres high (or 4 metres if the roof is ridged), are no nearer to a highway than the house or 20 metres (whichever is nearer), and at least half the ground around the house remains uncovered by buildings
- adding a porch with a ground area of less than 3 square metres and that is less than 3 metres in height and not within 2 metres of any boundary of the curtilage of the dwelling house with a highway
- putting up fences, walls and gates of under 1 metre in height if next to a road and under 2 metres elsewhere
- laying patios, paths or driveways for domestic use

However, before carrying out any of the above permitted developments you should contact your local authority to find out whether the general permission has been modified in your area.

OTHER RESTRICTIONS

It may be necessary to obtain other types of permissions before carrying out any development. These permissions are separate from planning permission and apply regardless of whether or not planning permission is needed, eg:

- building regulations will probably apply if a new building is to be erected, if an existing one is to be altered or extended, or if the work involves building over a drain or sewer. The building control department of the local authority will advise on this
- any alterations to a listed building or the grounds of a listed building must be approved by the local authority. Listing will include not only the main building but everything in the curtilage of the building
- local authority approval is necessary if a building (or, in some circumstances, gates, walls, fences or railings) in a conservation area is to be demolished; each local authority keeps a register of all local buildings that are in conservation areas
- many trees are protected by tree preservation orders and must not be pruned or taken down without local authority consent
- bats and many other species are protected, and Natural England, the Countryside Council for Wales or Scottish National Heritage must be notified before any work is carried out that will affect the habitat of protected species, eg timber treatment, renovation or extensions of lofts
- any development in areas designated as a national park, an area of outstanding national beauty, a national scenic area or in the Norfolk or Suffolk Broads is subject to greater restrictions. The local planning authority will advise or refer enquirers to the relevant authority

The local authority should be contacted if a planning permission is required. There may also be restriction on development contained in the title to the property which should be considered when works are planned.

VOTERS' QUALIFICATIONS

Those entitled to vote at parliamentary, and local government elections are those who are:

- on the electoral roll
- aged 18 years or older
- British citizens, Commonwealth citizens or citizens of the Irish Republic who are resident in the UK
- In Northern Ireland electors must have been resident in Northern Ireland during the whole of the three-month period prior to the relevant date

British citizens resident abroad are entitled to vote for 15 years after leaving Britain, as overseas electors in parliamentary and EU elections in the constituency in which they were last resident. Members of the armed forces, Crown servants and employees of the British Council who are overseas and their spouses are entitled to vote regardless of how long they have been abroad. British citizens who had never been registered as an elector in the UK are not eligible to register as an overseas voter unless they left the UK before they were 18, providing they left the country no more than 15 years ago.

The main categories of people who are not entitled to vote at general elections are:

- sitting peers in the House of Lords
- convicted persons detained in pursuance of their sentences (though remand prisoners, unconvicted prisoners and civil prisoners can vote if on the electoral register)
- those convicted within the previous five years of corrupt or illegal election practices
- EU citizens (who may only vote in EU and local government elections)

Under the Representation of the Peoples Act 2000, several new groups of people are permitted to vote for the first time. These include: people who live on barges; people in mental health hospitals (other than those with criminal convictions) and homeless people who have made a 'declaration of local connection'.

REGISTERING TO VOTE

Voters must be entered on an electoral register. The Electoral Registration Officer (ERO) for each council area is responsible for preparing and publishing the register for his area by 1 December each year. Names may be added to the register to reflect changes in people's circumstances as they occur and each month during December to August, the ERO publishes a list of alterations to the published register.

A registration form is sent to all households in the autumn of each year and the householder is required to provide details of all occupants who are eligible to vote, including ones who will reach their 18th birthday in the year covered by the register. Anyone failing to supply information to the ERO when requested, or supplying false information, may be fined. Application forms and more information are available from the Electoral Commission on W www.electoralcommision.org.uk.

VOTING

Voting is not compulsory in the UK. Those who wish to vote do so in person at the allotted polling station. Postal votes are now available to anyone on request. Those who will be away at the time of the election, those who will not be able to attend in person due to physical incapacity or the nature of their occupation, and those who have changed address during the period for which the register is valid, may apply for a postal vote or nominate a proxy to vote for them. Overseas electors who wish to vote must do so by proxy.

Further information can be obtained from the local authority's ERO in England and Wales or the electoral registration office in Scotland, or the Chief Electoral Officer in Northern Ireland.

WILLS

In a will a person leaves instructions as to the disposal of their property after they die. A will is also used to appoint executors (who will administer the estate), give directions as to the disposal of the body, appoint guardians for children and, for larger estates, can operate to reduce the level of inheritance tax. It is best to have a will drawn up by a solicitor, but if a solicitor is not employed the following points must be taken into account:

- if possible the will must not be prepared on behalf of another person by someone who is to benefit from it or who is a close relative of a major beneficiary
- the language used must be clear and unambiguous and it is better to avoid the use of legal terms where the same thing can be expressed in plain language
- it is better to rewrite the whole document if a mistake is made. If necessary, alterations can be made by striking through the words with a pen, and the signature or initials of the testator and the witnesses must be put in the margin opposite the alteration. No alteration of any kind should be made after the will has been executed
- if the person later wishes to change the will or part of it, it is better to write a new will revoking the old. The use of codicils (documents written as supplements or containing modifications to the will) should be left to a solicitor
- the will should be typed or printed, or if handwritten be legible and preferably in ink. Commercial will forms can be obtained from some stationers

The form of a will varies to suit different cases – a solicitor will be able to advise as to wording, however, 'DIY' will-writing kits can be purchased from good stationery shops and many banks offer a will-writing service.

LAPSED LEGATEES

If a person who has been left property in a will dies before the person who made the will, the gift fails and will pass to the person entitled to everything not otherwise disposed of (the residuary estate).

If the person left the residuary estate dies before the person who made the will, their share will generally pass to the closest relative(s) of the person who made the will (as in intestacy), unless the will names a beneficiary such as a charity who will take as a 'long stop' if this gift is unable to take effect for any reason. It is always better to draw up a new will if a beneficiary predeceases the person who made the will.

EXECUTORS

It is usual to appoint two executors, although one is sufficient. No more than four persons can deal with the estate of the person who has died. The name and address of each executor should be given in full (the addresses are not essential but including them adds clarity to the document). Executors should be 18 years of age or over. An executor may be a beneficiary of the will.

WITNESSES

A person who is a beneficiary of a will, or the spouse of a beneficiary at the time the will is signed, must not act as a witness or else he/she will be unable to take his/her gift. Husband and wife can both act as witnesses provided neither benefits from the will.

It is better that a person does not act as an executor and as a witness, as he/she can take no benefit under a will to which he/she is witness. The identity of the witnesses should be made as explicit as possible.

EXECUTION OF A WILL

The person making the will should sign his/her name at the foot of the document, in the presence of the two witnesses. The witnesses must then sign their names while the person making the will looks on. If this procedure is not adhered to, the will will be considered invalid. There are certain exceptional circumstances where these rules are relaxed, eg where the person may be too ill to sign.

CAPACITY TO MAKE A WILL

Anyone aged 18 or over can make a will. However, if there is any suspicion that the person making the will is not, through reasons of infirmity or age, fully in command of his/her faculties, it is advisable to arrange for a medical practitioner to examine the person making the will at the time it is to be executed (to verify his/her mental capacity and to record that medical opinion in writing), and to ask the examining practitioner to act as a witness. If a person is not mentally able to make a will, the court may do this for him/her by virtue of the Mental Health Act 1983.

REVOCATION

A will may be revoked or cancelled in a number of ways:

- a later will revokes an earlier one if it says so; otherwise the earlier will is by implication revoked by the later one to the extent that it contradicts or repeats the earlier one
- a will is also revoked if the physical document on which it is written is destroyed by the person whose will it is. There must be an intention to revoke the will

and it may not be sufficient to obliterate the will with a pen
- a will is revoked when the person marries or forms a civil partnership, unless it is clear from the will that the person intended the will to stand after the marriage or civil partnership
- where a marriage or civil partnership ends in divorce or dissolution or is annulled or declared void, gifts to the spouse or civil partner and the appointment of the spouse or civil partner as executor fail unless the will says that this is not to happen. A former spouse or civil partner is treated as having predeceased the testator. A separation does not change the effect of a married person's will.

PROBATE AND LETTERS OF ADMINISTRATION

Probate is granted to the executors named in a will and once granted, the executors are obliged to carry out the instructions of the will. Letters of administration are granted where no executor is named in a will or is willing or able to act or where there is no will or no valid will; this gives a person, often the next of kin, similar powers and duties to those of an executor.

Applications for probate or for letters of administration can be made to the Principal Registry of the Family Division, to a district probate registry or to a probate sub-registry. Applicants will need the following documents: the Probate Application Form: the original will (if any); a certificate of death; oath for executors or administrators; and the appropriate tax form (an 'IHT 205' if no inheritance tax is owed; otherwise an 'IHT 200'). Certain property, up to the value of £5,000, may be disposed of without a grant of probate or letters of administration.

WHERE TO FIND A PROVED WILL

Since 1858 wills which have been proved, that is wills on which probate or letters of administration have been granted, must have been proved at the Principal Registry of the Family Division or at a district probate registry. The Lord Chancellor has power to direct where the original documents are kept but most are filed where they were proved and may be inspected there and a copy obtained. The Principal Registry also holds copies of all wills proved at district probate registries and these may be inspected at First Avenue House, High Holborn. An index of all grants, both of probate and of letters of administration, is compiled by the Principal Registry and may be seen either at the Principal Registry or at a district probate registry.

It is also possible to discover when a grant of probate or letters of administration is issued by requesting a standing search. In response to a request and for a small fee, a district probate registry will supply the names and addresses of executors or administrators and the registry in which the grant was made, of any grant in the estate of a specified person made in the previous 12 months or following six months. This is useful for applicants who may be beneficiaries to a will but who have lost contact with the deceased and for creditors of the deceased.

INTESTACY

Intestacy occurs when someone dies without leaving a will or leaves a will which is invalid or which does not take effect for some reason. Intestacy can be partial, for instance, if there is a will which disposes of some but not all of the testator's property. In such cases the person's estate (property, possessions, other assets following the payment of debts) passes to certain members of the family. The relevant legislation is the Administration of Estates Act 1925, as amended by various legislation including the Intestates Estates Act 1952, the Law Reform (Succession) Act 1995, and the Trusts of Land and Appointment of Trustees Act 1996 and Orders made thereunder. Some of the provisions of this legislation are described below. If a will has been written that disposes of only part of a person's property, these rules apply to the part which is undisposed of.

If the person (intestate) leaves a spouse or a civil partner who survives for 28 days and children (legitimate, illegitimate and adopted children and other descendants), the estate is divided as follows:
- the spouse or civil partner takes the 'personal chattels' (household articles, including cars, but nothing used for business purposes), £125,000 tax-free (with interest payable at six per cent from the time of the death until payment) and a life interest in half of the rest of the estate (which can be capitalised by the spouse or civil partner if he/she wishes)
- the rest of the estate goes to the children*

If the person leaves a spouse or civil partner who survives for 28 days but no children:
- the spouse or civil partner takes the personal chattels, £200,000 tax-free (interest payable as before) and full ownership of half of the rest of the estate
- the other half of the rest of the estate goes to the parents (equally, if both alive) or, if none, to the brothers and sisters of the whole blood*
- if there are no parents or brothers or sisters of the whole blood or their children, the spouse or civil partner takes the whole estate

If there is no surviving spouse or civil partner, the estate is distributed among those who survive the intestate as follows:
- to surviving children*, but if none to
- parents (equally, if both alive), but if none to
- brothers and sisters of the whole blood* (including issue of deceased ones), but if none to
- brothers and sisters of the half blood* (including issue of deceased ones), but if none to
- grandparents (equally, if more than one), but if none to
- aunts and uncles of the whole blood*, but if none to
- aunts and uncles of the half blood*, but if none to
- the crown, Duchy of Lancaster or the Duke of Cornwall (*bona vacantia*)

* To inherit, a member of these groups must survive the intestate and attain the age of 18, or marry under that age. If they die under the age of 18 (unless married under that age), their share goes to others, if any, in the same group. If any member of these groups predeceases the intestate leaving children, their share is divided equally among their children.

In England and Wales the provisions of the Inheritance (Provision for Family and Dependants) Act 1975 may allow other people to claim provision from the deceased's assets. This act also applies to cases where a will has been made and allows a person to apply to the court if they feel that the will or rules of intestacy or both do not make adequate provision for them. The court can order payment from the deceased's assets or the transfer of property from them if the applicant's claim is accepted. The application must be made within six months of the grant of probate or letters of administration and the following people can make an application:
- the spouse or civil partner

- a former spouse or civil partner who has not remarried or formed a subsequent civil partnership
- a child of the deceased
- someone treated as a child of the deceased's family
- someone maintained by the deceased
- someone who has cohabited for two years before the death in the same household as the deceased and as the husband or wife or civil partner of the deceased

SCOTLAND

In Scotland any person over 12 and of sound mind can make a will. The person making the will can only freely dispose of the heritage and what is known as the 'dead's part' of the estate because:

- the spouse or civil partner has the right to inherit one-third of the moveable estate if there are children or other descendants, and one-half of it if there are not
- children are entitled to one-third of the moveable estate if there is a surviving spouse or civil partner, and one-half of it if there is not

The remaining portion is the dead's part, and legacies and bequests are payable from this. Debts are payable out of the whole estate before any division.

From August 1995, wills no longer needed to be 'holographed' and it is now only necessary to have one witness. The person making the will still needs to sign each page. It is better that the will is not witnessed by a beneficiary although the attestation would still be sound and the beneficiary would not have to relinquish the gift.

Subsequent marriage or civil partnership does not revoke a will but the birth of a child who is not provided for may do so. A will may be revoked by a subsequent will, either expressly or by implication, but in so far as the two can be read together both have effect. If a subsequent will is revoked, the earlier will is revived.

Wills may be registered in the sheriff court Books of the Sheriffdom in which the deceased lived or in the Books of Council and Session at the Registers of Scotland.

CONFIRMATION

Confirmation (the Scottish equivalent of probate) is obtained in the sheriff court of the sheriffdom in which the deceased was resident at the time of death. Executives are either 'nominate' (named by the deceased in the will) or 'dative' (appointed by the court in cases where no executor is named in a will or in cases of intestacy). Applicants for confirmation must first provide an inventory of the deceased's estate and a schedule of debts, with an affidavit. In estates under £30,000 gross, confirmation can be obtained under a simplified procedure at reduced fees, with no need for a solicitor. The local sheriff clerk's office can provide assistance.

Further information can be obtained from:

PRINCIPAL REGISTRY (FAMILY DIVISION)
First Avenue House, 42–49 High Holborn, London WC2V 6NP
T 020-7947 6980

REGISTERS OF SCOTLAND
Meadowbank House, 153 London Road, Edinburgh EH8 7AU
T 0131-659 6111

INTESTACY

The rules of distribution are contained in the Succession (Scotland) Act 1964 and are extended to include civil partners by the Civil Partnership Act 2004.

A surviving spouse or civil partner is entitled to 'prior rights'. This means that the spouse or civil partner has the right to inherit:

- the matrimonial or family home up to a value of £300,000, or one matrimonial or family home if there is more than one, or, in certain circumstances, the value of the home
- the furnishings and contents of that home, up to the value of £24,000
- a cash sum of £42,000 if the deceased left children or other descendants, or £75,000 if not

These figures are increased from time to time by regulations.

Once prior rights have been satisfied legal rights are settled. Legal rights are:

Jus relicti(ae) and rights under the section 131 of the Civil Partnership Act 2004 – the right of a surviving spouse or civil partner to one-half of the net moveable estate, after satisfaction of prior rights, if there are no surviving children; if there are surviving children, the spouse or civil partner is entitled to one-third of the net moveable estate

Legitim and rights under the section 131 of the Civil Partnership Act 2004 – the right of surviving children to one-half of the net moveable estate if there is no surviving spouse or civil partner; if there is a surviving spouse or civil partner, the children are entitled to one-third of the net moveable estate after the satisfaction of prior rights

Where there is no surviving spouse, civil partner or children, half of the estate is taken by the parents and half by the brothers and sisters. Failing that, the lines of succession, in general, are:

- to descendants
- if no descendants, then to collaterals (ie brothers and sisters) and parents
- surviving spouse or civil partner
- if no collaterals, parents, spouse or civil partner, then to ascendants collaterals (ie aunts and uncles), and so on in an ascending scale
- if all lines of succession fail, the estate passes to the crown. Relatives of the whole blood are preferred to relatives of the half blood. The right of representation, ie the right of the issue of a person who would have succeeded if he/she had survived the intestate, also applies

INTELLECTUAL PROPERTY

Intellectual property is a broad term covering a number of legal rights provided by the government to help people protect their creative works and encourage further innovation. By using these legal rights people can own the things they create and control the way in which others use their innovations. Intellectual property owners can take legal action to stop others using their intellectual property, they can license their intellectual property to others or they can sell it on. Different types of intellectual property utilise different forms of protection including copyright, designs, patents and trademarks which are all covered below in more detail.

COPYRIGHT

Copyright protects all original literary, dramatic, musical and artistic works (including photographs, maps and plans), published editions of works, computer programs, sound recordings, films (including video and DVD) and broadcasts (including cable, radio, satellite broadcasts, and transmissions on the internet). Under copyright the creators of these works can control the various ways in which their material may be exploited, the rights broadly covering copying, adapting, issuing (including renting and lending) copies to the public, performing in public, and broadcasting the material. The transfer of copyright works to formats accessible to visually impaired persons without infringement of copyright was enacted in 2002.

Copyright protection in the United Kingdom is automatic and there is no official registration system. Steps can be taken by the work's creator to provide evidence that he/she had the work at a particular time (eg by depositing a copy with a bank or solicitor). The main legislation is the Copyright, Designs and Patents Act 1988, which has been amended by other acts and by statutory instrument to take account of EU directives. As a result of an EU directive effective from January 1996, the term of copyright protection for literary, dramatic, musical and artistic works lasts for 70 years after the death of the author. For film copyright lasts for 70 years after the death of the director, authors of the screenplay and dialogue or the composer of any music specially created for the film. Sound recordings are protected for 50 years after their publication, and broadcasts for 50 years from the end of the year in which the first broadcast/transmission was made. Published editions remain under copyright protection for 25 years from the end of the year in which the edition was published.

The main international treaties protecting copyright are the Berne Convention for the Protection of Literary and Artistic Works (administered by the World Intellectual Property Organisation (WIPO)), the Rome Convention for the Protection of Performers, Producers of Phonograms and Broadcasting Organisations (administered jointly by UNESCO and the International Labour Organisation), and the Universal Copyright Convention (developed by UNESCO); the UK is a signatory to these conventions. Copyright material created by UK nationals or residents is protected in each country that is a member of the conventions by the national law of that country. A list of participating countries may be obtained from the UK Intellectual Property Office.

Two treaties which strengthen and update international standards of protection, particularly in relation to new technologies, were agreed in December 1996: the WIPO copyright treaty, and the WIPO performance and phonograms treaty. In May 2001 the European Union passed a new directive (which in 2003 became law in the UK) aimed at harmonising copyright law throughout the EU to take account of the internet and other technologies. More information can be found online (W www.ipo.gov.uk).

LICENSING

Use of copyright material without seeking permission in each instance may be permitted under 'blanket' licences available from copyright licensing agencies. The International Federation of Reproduction Rights Organisations facilitates agreements between its member licensing agencies and on behalf of its members with organisations such as the WIPO, UNESCO, the European Union and the Council of Europe.

DESIGN PROTECTION

Design protection covers the outward appearance of an article and in the UK takes two forms: registered design and design right, which are not mutually exclusive. Registered design protects the aesthetic appearance of an article, including shape, configuration, pattern or ornament, although artistic works such as sculptures are excluded, being generally protected by copyright. In order to qualify for protection, a design must be new and materially different from earlier UK published designs. The owner of the design must apply to the UK Intellectual Property Office. Initial registration lasts for five years and can be extended in five-year increments to a maximum of 25 years. The current legislation is the Registered Designs Act 1949 which has been amended several times, most recently by the Registered Designs Regulations 2003.

UK applicants wishing to protect their designs in the EU can do so by applying for a Registered Community Design with the Office of Harmonisation in the Internal Market. Outside the EU separate applications must be made in each country in which protection is sought.

Design right is an automatic right which applies to the shape or configuration of articles and does not require registration. Unlike registered design, two-dimensional designs do not qualify for protection but designs of semiconductor chips (topographies) are protected by design right. Designs must be original and non-commonplace. The term of design right is ten years from first marketing of the design and the right is effective only in the UK. The current legislation is Part 3 of the Copyright, Designs and Patents Act 1988, amended on 9 December 2001 to incorporate the European designs directive.

PATENTS

A patent is a document issued by the UK Intellectual Property Office relating to an invention and giving the proprietor the right for a limited period to stop others from making, using or selling the invention without the inventor's permission. In return the patentee pays a fee to cover the costs of processing the patent and publicly discloses details of the invention.

To qualify for a patent an invention must be new, must exhibit an inventive step, and must be capable of industrial application. The patent is valid for a maximum of 20 years from the date on which the application was filed, subject to payment of annual fees from the end of the fourth year.

The UK Intellectual Property Office, established in 1852, is responsible for ensuring that all stages of an application comply with the Patents Act 1977, and that the invention meets the criteria for a patent.

The WIPO is responsible for administering many of the international conventions on intellectual property. The Patent Cooperation Treaty allows inventors to file a single application for patent rights in some or all of the contracting states. This application is searched by an International Searching Authority and published by the International Bureau of WIPO. It may also be the subject of an (optional) international preliminary examination. Applicants must then deal directly with the patent offices in the countries where they are seeking patent rights. The European Patent Convention allows inventors to obtain patent rights in all the contracting states by filing a single application with the European Patent Office. More information can be found online (**W** www.ipo.gov.uk).

RESEARCH DISCLOSURES

Research disclosures are publicly disclosed details of inventions. Once published, an invention is considered no longer novel and becomes prior art. Publishing a disclosure is significantly cheaper than applying for a patent, however unlike a patent, it does not entitle the author to exclusive rights to use or license the invention. Instead, research disclosures are primarily published to ensure the inventor freedom to use the invention. This works because publishing legally prevents other parties from patenting the disclosed innovation and in the UK, patent law dictates that by disclosing, even the inventor relinquishes their right to a patent.

In theory, publishing details of an invention anywhere should be enough to make a research disclosure. However to be effective a research disclosure needs to be published in a location which patent examiners will include in their prior art searches. To ensure global legal precedent it must be included in a publication with a recognised date stamp and made publicly available across the world.

The *Research Disclosure* journal established in 1960, published by KMP Ltd, is the primary publisher of research disclosures. It is the only disclosure service recognised by the Patent Cooperation Treaty as a mandatory search resource which must be consulted by the international search authorities. More information can be found online (**W** www.researchdisclosure.com).

TRADE MARKS

Trade marks are a means of identification, whether a word or device or a combination of both, a logo, or the shape of goods or their packaging, which enable traders to make their goods or services readily distinguishable from those supplied by other traders. Registration prevents other traders using the same or similar trade marks for similar products or services for which the mark is registered.

In the UK trade marks are registered at the UK Intellectual Property Office. In order to qualify for registration a mark must be capable of distinguishing its proprietor's goods or services from those of other undertakings; it should be non-deceptive, should not be contrary to law or morality and should not be similar or identical to any earlier marks for the same or similar goods or services. The relevant current legislation is the Trade Marks Act 1994.

It is possible to obtain an international trade mark registration, effective in 80 countries, under the Madrid Agreement or the Madrid Protocol, to which the UK is party. British companies can obtain international trade mark registration through a single application to the WIPO in those countries party to the protocol.

EC trade mark regulation is now in force and is administered by the Office for Harmonisation in the Internal Market (Trade Marks and Designs) in Alicante, Spain. The office registers EC trade marks, which are valid throughout the European Union. The national registration of trade marks in member states continues in parallel with EC trade mark standards.

DOMAIN NAMES

A domain name is a name by which a company or organisation is known on the internet and is a shorthand way of identifying a company's website. A domain name has to be registered separately from a trade mark. Although there are many registrars prepared to register domain names, each country has a central registry to store unique names and addresses used on the internet. A list of accredited registrars can be found online (**W** www.icann.org).

CONTACTS

THE UK INTELLECTUAL PROPERTY OFFICE, Cardiff Road, Newport NP10 8QQ **T** 0845-950 0505 **W** www.ipo.gov.uk

COPYRIGHT LICENSING AGENCY LTD, 90 Tottenham Court Road, London W1T 0LP **T** 020-7631 5555 **W** www.cla.co.uk

EUROPEAN PATENT OFFICE, Headquarters, Erhardtstrasse 27, D-8000, Munich 2, Germany **T** (+49) 892 3990 **W** www.epo.org

WORLD INTELLECTUAL PROPERTY ORGANISATION, 34 chemin des Colombettes, CH-1211 Geneva 20, Switzerland **T** (+41) 22 338 9111 **W** www.wipo.int

BROADCASTING

CROSS-MEDIA OWNERSHIP

The rules surrounding cross-media ownership were overhauled as part of the 2003 Communications Act. The act simplified and relaxed existing rules to encourage dispersion of ownership and new market entry while preventing the most influential media in any community being controlled by too narrow a range of interests. However, transfers and mergers are not solely subject to examination on competition grounds by the competition authorities. The secretary of state has a broad remit to decide if a transaction is permissible and can intervene on public interest grounds (relating both to newspapers and cross-media criteria, if broadcasting interests are also involved). The Office of Communications (OFCOM) has an advisory role in this context. Government and parliamentary assurances were given that any intervention into local newspaper transfers would be rare and exceptional.

REGULATION

OFCOM is the regulator for the communication industries in the UK and has responsibility for television, radio, telecommunications and wireless communications services. It replaced the Broadcasting Standards Commission, the Independent Television Commission, the Radio Authority, the Radio Communications Agency and OFTEL. OFCOM is required to report annually to parliament and exists to further the interests of consumers by balancing choice and competition with the duty to foster plurality; protect viewers and listeners and promote cultural diversity in the media; and to ensure full and fair competition between communications providers.

OFFICE OF COMMUNICATIONS (OFCOM)
Riverside House, 2A Southwark Bridge Road, London SE1 9HA
T 020-7981 3000 E enquiries@ofcom.org.uk
W www.ofcom.org.uk
Chief Executive, Ed Richards

COMPLAINTS

Under the Communications Act 2003 OFCOM's licensees are obliged to adhere to the provisions of its codes (including advertising, programme standards, fairness, privacy and sponsorship). Complainants should contact the broadcaster in the first instance (details can be found on OFCOM's website); however, if the complainant wishes the complaint to be considered by OFCOM, it will do so. Complaints should be made within a reasonable time as broadcasters are only required to keep recordings for the following periods of time: radio, 42 days; television, 90 days; and cable and satellite, 60 days. OFCOM can fine a broadcaster, revoke a licence or take programmes off the air.

TELEVISION

There are six major television broadcasters operating in the UK. Four of these – the BBC, ITV, Channel 4 and Five – are free-to-air analogue terrestrial networks. BSky B and Virgin Media Television provide satellite television services.

The BBC is the oldest broadcaster in the world. The corporation began a London-only television service from Alexandra Palace in 1936 and achieved nationwide coverage 15 years later. A second station, BBC Two, was launched in 1964. The BBC's digital services comprise BBC Three, BBC Four, BBC News 24 and BBC Parliament; the children's channels, CBeebies and CBBC; and the interactive channel BBCi. The services are funded by the licence fee. The corporation also has a commercial arm, BBC Worldwide, which was formed in 1994 and exists to maximise the value of the BBC's programme and publishing assets for the benefit of the licence payer. Its businesses include international programming distribution, magazines, other licensed products, live events and media monitoring.

The ITV (Independent Television) network was set up on a regional basis in 1955 to provide competition for the BBC. It comprised a number of independent licensees, the majority of which have now merged to form ITV plc. The network generates funds through broadcasting television advertisements. Its flagship analogue channel was renamed ITV1 in 2001 as part of a rebranding exercise to coincide with the creation of a number of digital-only channels. These now include ITV2, ITV3, ITV4, ITV Play and CiTV. ITV Network Centre is wholly owned by the ITV companies and undertakes commissioning and scheduling of programmes shown across the ITV network and, as with the other terrestrial channels, 25 per cent of programmes must come from independent producers.

Channel 4 and S4C were launched in 1982 to provide programmes with a distinctive character that appeal to interests not catered for by ITV. Although state-owned, Channel 4 receives no public funding and is financed by commercial activities, including advertising. S4C's digital service, S4C Digidol broadcasts entirely in the Welsh language. Channel 4 has expanded to create the digital stations E4, More4 and Film4.

Channel 5 (later renamed Five) began broadcasting in 1997. Despite initial problems with coverage, it now reaches about 80 per cent of the population. Digital stations Five US and Five Life (later renamed Fiver) were launched in October 2006.

BSkyB was formed after the merger in 1990 of Sky Television and British Sky Broadcasting. The company operates a satellite television service and has around 40 television channels, including Sky One and the Sky Sports and Sky Movies ranges. It is part-owned by Rupert Murdoch's News Corporation. Sky Digital was launched in 1998 and offers access to 530 channels. With the 2005 acquisition of Easynet, an internet access provider and network operator, BSkyB now offers voice over IP (VoIP) telephony, video on demand and internet-based TV. With a special box, Sky+ allows viewers to pause and rewind live TV and record up to 40 hours of programming. Virgin Television runs a similar service called Virgin On Demand.

Virgin Media Television was founded in February 2007 as the television production arm of Virgin Media. It was previously known as NTL:Telewest. It owns a number of channels available via satellite, digital and cable platforms, including Bravo, Trouble and Living and runs a single branded channel, Virgin 1.

TRENDS IN PEAK TIME CHANNEL OUTPUT

- BBC One's schedule has the highest proportion of news (20 per cent) and the most variation across programme genre of the main free-to-air channels
- Over 60 per cent of BBC Two's programme output falls under the categories of current affairs, factual, religion and arts
- Drama and soaps (47 per cent) and entertainment (19 per cent) dominate the ITV schedule
- Channel 4 shows a high proportion of news and factual programming (50 per cent of programmes fit into news, current affairs, factual, arts or religion categories)
- Five shows a higher proportion of films than the other public-service channels, which account for 19 per cent of its peak time output

Source: OFCOM Public Service Broadcasting Annual Report 2008

TOP TV OF 2007

Audience size by channel, millions

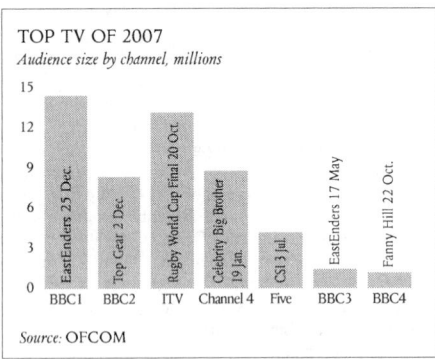

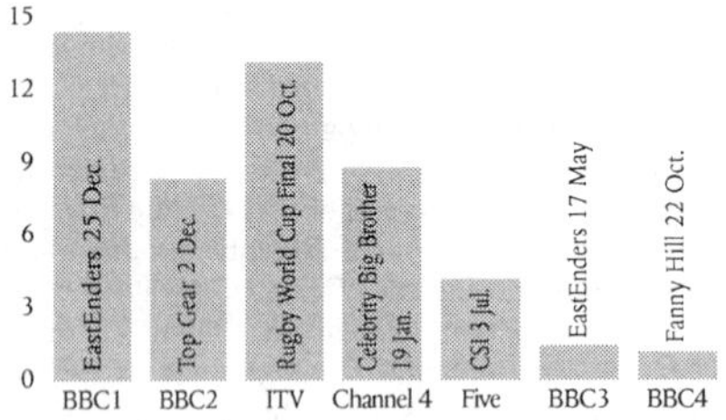

Source: OFCOM

THE TELEVISION LICENCE

In the United Kingdom and its dependencies, a television licence is required to receive any publicly broadcast television service, regardless of its source, including commercial, satellite and cable programming.

The TV licence is classified as a tax, therefore non-payment is a criminal offence. A fine of up to £1,000 can be imposed on those successfully prosecuted. The Broadcasting Act 1990 made the BBC responsible for licence administration. TV Licensing is the name of the agent contracted to collect the licence fee on behalf of the BBC. Total licence fee income for 2006 was £3,124.8m. In 2008 an annual colour television licence cost £139.50 and a black and white licence £47. Concessions are available for the elderly and the disabled. Further details can be found at W www.tvlicensing.co.uk/information

DIGITAL TELEVISION

Digital broadcasting has dramatically increased the number and reception quality of television channels. Sound and pictures are converted into a digital format and compressed, using as few bits as possible to convey the information on a digital signal. This technique enables several television channels to be carried in the space used by the current analogue signals to carry one channel. Digital signals can be received by standard aerials using Freeview (*see* below), satellite dishes or cable. The signals are decoded and turned back into sound and pictures by either a set-top box or a decoder built into the television set (iDTV). A basic package of channels is available without charge and services are also offered by cable and satellite companies.

The Broadcasting Act 1996 provided for the licensing of 20 or more digital terrestrial television channels (on six frequency channels or 'multiplexes'). The first digital services went on air in autumn 1998.

In June 2002, following the collapse of ITV Digital, the digital terrestrial television licence was awarded to a consortium made up of the BBC, BSkyB and transmitter company Crown Castle by the Independent Television Commission. Freeview, a new digital network, was launched on 30 October 2002. Freeview offers around 30 digital channels and requires the purchase of a set-top box, but is subsequently free of charge.

By April 2008, 87 per cent of British homes had access to multi-channel TV. Freeview, cable and satellite channels now account for over a third of all TV viewing. The digital channels combined have a greater share of viewing than any of the five main channels and continue to increase this lead.

DIGITAL SWITCHOVER

The digital switchover involves the turning off of the analogue terrestrial transmissions network that has been in place since the 1930s and replacing it with an all-digital terrestrial network. Viewers who receive television through an aerial will need to upgrade their sets with a set-top box (typically costing between £20 and £100) or use integrated digital television (iDTV), cable or satellite digital services. The switchover will take place between 2008 and 2012. The old analogue frequencies are likely to be sold to mobile telephone companies. For more information, *see* W www.digitaluk.co.uk.

Region	*Expected switchover date*
Border	2008–9
West Country, Granada	2009
Wales	2009–10
West, STV North	2010
STV Central	2010–11
Central, Yorkshire, Anglia	2011
Meridian, London, Tyne Tees, Ulster	2012

Source: Digital UK

RECENT DEVELOPMENTS

The advent of digital television has coincided with the emergence of the internet as a viable alternative means of watching TV. Channel 4's 4oD (4 On Demand) service allows viewers to revisit and download programmes from the previous 28 days and access an archive of older footage using their PC. The BBC launched its iPlayer on Christmas Day 2007; viewers are now able to watch programmes broadcast in the previous seven days via the streaming option or download and store programmes for up to 30 days on their computer. A new integrated service, launched in June 2008, allows viewers to access BBC radio programmes in addition to televisual output. Eventually, the iPlayer will be offered through Freeview and satellite. ITV has a similar service called Catch Up, and Five's service is called Demand Five. Online streaming of TV has been a major success, especially with a younger demographic. In May 2008 alone, there were over 21.8m requests to view shows on iPlayer alone—around 700,000 requests a day.

High Definition (HD) TV is the latest development in

TV picture quality, providing more vibrant colours, greater detail and picture clarity in addition to improved sound quality. While a standard television picture is made up of 576 lines of pixels, an HD television screen uses either 720 or 1,080 lines. Sky Digital, ITV and the BBC all provide HD channels, with a growing number becoming available. To access HD channels, viewers need an 'HD Ready' TV set and HD TV decoder available through satellite services or a cable connection. It is expected that up to four HD channels will become available through Freeview from 2009.

ESTIMATED AUDIENCE SHARE

						Percentage of all homes
	1982	*1987*	*1992*	*1997*	*2002*	*2007*
BBC One	38.0	38.0	34.0	30.8	26.2	22.0
BBC Two	12.0	12.0	10.0	11.6	11.4	8.5
ITV1	50.0	42.0	41.0	32.9	24.1	19.2
Channel 4	—	8.0	10.0	10.6	10.0	8.6
Five	—	—	—	2.3	6.3	5.1
Others	—	—	5.0	11.8	22.1	36.5

Source: BARB

CONTACTS

THE BRITISH BROADCASTING CORPORATION

BBC TV Centre, Wood Lane, London W12 7RJ **T** 020-8743 8000 **W** www.bbc.co.uk

Chair, Sir Michael Lyons

BBC Worldwide Ltd, Woodlands, 80 Wood Lane, London W12 0TT **T** 020-8433 2000 **W** www.bbcworldwide.com

INDEPENDENT TELEVISION NETWORK

ITV Network Centre/ITV Association, 200 Gray's Inn Road, London WC1V 8HF **T** 020-7843 8000 **W** www.itv.com

Chair, Michael Grade

INDEPENDENT TELEVISION NETWORK REGIONS AND COMPANIES

Anglia (eastern England), Anglia House, Rose Lane, Norwich NR1 3JG **T** 01603-615151 **W** www.itvlocal.com/anglia

Border (Borders and the Isle of Man), Television Centre, Carlisle CA1 3NT **T** 01228-525101 **W** www.itvlocal.com/border

Central (east, west and south Midlands), Gas Street, Birmingham B1 2JT **T** 0870-600 6766 **W** www.itvlocal.com/central

Channel (Channel Islands), The Television Centre, St Helier, Jersey JE1 3ZD **T** 01534-816816 **W** www.channelonline.tv

Granada (north-west England), Quay Street, Manchester M60 9EA **T** 0161-832 7211 **W** www.itvlocal.com/granada

London (London), London Television Centre, Upper Ground, London SE1 9LT **T** 020-7620 1620 **W** www.itvlocal.com/london

Meridian (south and south-east England), Solent Business Park, Whiteley, Hants PO15 7PA **T** 01489-442000 **W** www.itvlocal.com/meridian

STV (Scotland), 200 Renfield Street, Glasgow G2 3PR **T** 0141-300 3000 **W** www.stv.tv

Tyne Tees (north-east England), Television House, The Watermark, Gateshead, Tyne and Wear NE11 9SZ **T** 0191-404 8700 **W** www.itvlocal.com/tynetees

Ulster (Northern Ireland), Havelock House, Belfast BT7 1EB **T** 02890-328122 **W** www4.u.tv

Wales, The Television Centre, Culverhouse Cross, Cardiff CF5 6XJ **T** 029-2059 0590 **W** www.itvlocal.com/wales

West, Television Centre, Bath Road, Bristol BS4 3HG **T** 0117-972 2722 **W** www.itvlocal.com/west

Westcountry (south-west England), Langage Science Park, Western Wood Way, Plymouth PL7 5BQ **T** 01752-333333 **W** www.itvlocal.com/westcountry

Yorkshire (Yorkshire), 96–104 Kirkstall Road, Leeds LS3 1JS **T** 0113-243 8283 **W** www.itvlocal.com/yorkshire

OTHER TELEVISION COMPANIES

Channel 4 Television, 124 Horseferry Road, London SW1P 2TX **T** 020-7396 4444 **W** www.channel4.com

Five Broadcasting Ltd, 22 Long Acre, London WC2E 9LY **T** 020-7421 7270 **W** www.five.tv

GMTV, The London Television Centre, Upper Ground, London SE1 9TT **T** 020-7827 7000 **W** www.gm.tv

Owned by ITV and Disney, with 75 per cent and 25 per cent respectively, GMTV provides breakfast television and sells its own advertising.

Independent Television News, 200 Gray's Inn Road, London WC1X 8XZ **T** 020-7833 3000 **W** www.itn.co.uk

Sianel Pedwar Cymru (S4C), Parc Ty Glas, Llanishen, Cardiff CF14 5DU **T** 0870-600 4141 **W** www.s4c.co.uk

S4C schedules Welsh language and some Channel 4 programmes.

Teletext Ltd, Building 10, Chiswick Park, 566 Chiswick High Road, London W4 5TS **T** 020-8323 5000 **W** www.teletext.co.uk

Provides teletext services for the ITV companies and Channel 4 and offers holiday, car rental and mobile telecom services.

DIRECT BROADCASTING BY SATELLITE TELEVISION

British Sky Broadcasting Group, Grant Way, Isleworth, Middx TW7 5QD **T** 020-7705 3000 **W** www.sky.com

Chair, James Murdoch

Virgin Media Television, 160 Great Portland Street, London W1W 5QA **T** 020-7299 5000 **W** www.virginmediatv.co.uk

Chair, Jim Mooney

RADIO

ESTIMATED AUDIENCE SHARE

			Percentage
	Jan–Mar 2006	*Jan–Mar 2007*	*Jan-Mar 2008*
BBC Radio 1	9.1	10.1	10.0
BBC Radio 2	16.0	15.8	16.0
BBC Radio 3	1.3	1.2	1.2
BBC Radio 4	11.7	12.2	12.0
BBC Radio Five Live	4.6	4.2	4.6
Five Live Sports Extra	0.1	0.1	0.2
6 Music	0.2	0.3	0.3
BBC7	0.3	0.4	0.4
Asian Network	0.2	0.2	0.3
1Xtra	0.2	0.2	0.3
BBC Local/Regional	11.1	10.6	9.6
BBC World Service	0.6	0.7	0.7
All BBC	55.4	56.0	55.5
All independent	42.6	42.1	42.4
All national independent	10.5	10.7	11.2
All local independent	32.2	31.4	31.2
Other	2.0	1.8	2.1

Source: RAJAR/Ipsos-MORI

UK domestic radio services are broadcast across three wavebands: FM, medium wave and long wave (used by

BBC Radio 4). In the UK the FM waveband extends in frequency from 87.5MHz to 108MHz and the medium waveband from 531kHz to 1602kHz. A number of radio stations are now being broadcast in both analogue and digital as well as a growing number in digital alone. As at March 2008, the BBC Radio network controlled nearly 56 per cent of the listening market (*see* BBC Radio section), with the independent sector (*see* Independent Radio section) holding 42 per cent.

DIGITAL RADIO

DAB (Digital Audio Broadcasting) allows more services to be broadcast to a higher technical quality and provides the data facility for text and pictures. It improves the robustness of high fidelity radio services, especially compared with current FM and AM radio transmissions. It was developed in a collaborative research project under the pan-European Eureka 147 initiative and has been adopted as a world standard by the International Telecommunication Union for new digital radio systems. The frequencies allocated for terrestrial digital radio in the UK are 174 to 239MHz. More spectrum (in the 'L-Band' range: 1452–1490MHz) was introduced in 2007.

It is necessary to possess a digital radio set in order to receive digital broadcasts. Digital radios are available is several different forms: as standalone portable units, hi-fi stacks, car radios and PC cards, and inbuilt within a mobile phone. Newer DAB radios allow the listener to rewind, pause and record broadcasts and can be uploaded to a computer using a USB cable. Some portable sets now combine MP3 playback with DAB. An alternative method is to listen to digital radio through television sets via Freeview, cable or satellite.

The possibility of a switchover to entirely digital radio services remains uncertain. Although increasing, the number of people listening to digital radio remains relatively low. In November 2007 the government launched the Digital Radio Working Group, which is looking at strategies to ensure the future of digital radio and at potential switchover timetables.

LICENSING

The Broadcasting Act 1996 provided for the licensing of digital radio services (on multiplexes, where a number of stations share one frequency to transmit their services). To allocate the multiplexes, OFCOM advertises licences for which interested parties can bid. Once the licence has been awarded, the new owner seeks out services to broadcast on the multiplex. In 2007, 4 Digital group was awarded a new multiplex licence, the second commercial multiplex after Digital One, which already operates eight services. The new multiplex is to incorporate Channel 4 digital radio stations, although launch dates for the various channels are uncertain. The BBC has a separate national multiplex for its services. There are local multiplexes around the country, each broadcasting an average of seven services, plus the local BBC station. There are also several regional multiplexes covering a wider area and broadcasting up to 11 services each.

INNOVATIONS

As with television, the opportunities offered by digital services and the internet have made important changes to radio. The internet offers a number of advantages compared to other digital platforms such as DAB including a higher sound quality, a greater range of channel availability and flexibility in listening opportunity. Listeners can tune in to the majority of radio stations live on the internet or listen again online for seven days after broadcast. DAB radio does not allow the same interactivity as the data is only able to travel one-way from broadcaster to listener, unlike the internet which allows a two-way flow of information.

Since 2005 increasing numbers of radio stations offer all or part of their programmes as downloadable files, known as podcasts, to listen to on computers or mobile devices such as mp3 players or phones. Podcasting technology allows listeners to subscribe in order to automatically receive the latest episodes of regularly transmitted programmes as soon as they become available.

The relationship between a radio presenter and his or her audience is also undergoing change. The quantity and easy availability of music on the internet has led to the creation of shows dedicated entirely to music sent in by listeners. Another new development in internet-based radio has been personalised radio stations, such as last.fm. Personalised stations log what music is being listened to (online) and what is skipped and, based on the choices made, plays tracks it predicts the user will like. WiFi technology is also making changes to radio-listening behaviour. WiFi internet radios and media adaptors (which plug into a hi-fi) mean that people are not limited to listening to internet radio stations, podcasts, or on-demand programmes solely when using their computer.

BBC RADIO

BBC Radio broadcasts network services to the UK, Isle of Man and the Channel Islands. There is also a tier of national services in Wales, Scotland and Northern Ireland and 40 local radio stations in England and the Channel Islands. In Wales and Scotland there are also dedicated language services in Welsh and Gaelic respectively. The frequency allocated for digital BBC broadcasts is 225.648MHz.

Broadcasting House, Portland Place, London W1A 1AA
T 020-7580 4468

BBC NETWORK RADIO STATIONS

Radio 1 (contemporary pop music and entertainment news) – 24 hours a day, *frequencies:* 97–99 FM and digital

Radio 2 (popular music, entertainment, comedy and the arts) – 24 hours a day, *frequencies:* 88–91 FM and digital

Radio 3 (classical music, classic drama, documentaries and features) – 24 hours a day, *frequencies:* 90–93 FM and digital

Radio 4 (news, documentaries, drama, entertainment and cricket on long wave in season) – 5.20am–1am daily, with BBC World Service overnight, *frequencies:* 92–95 FM and 198 LW and digital

Radio Five Live (news and sport) – 24 hours a day, *frequencies:* 693/909 MW and digital

Five Live Sports Extra (live sport) – schedule varies, digital only

6 Music (contemporary and classic pop and rock music) – 24 hours a day, digital only

BBC7 (comedy, drama and children's) – 24 hours a day, digital only

Asian Network (news, music and sport) – 24 hours a day Friday and Saturday; 5am–1am Sunday–Thursday, with Radio Five Live overnight, *frequencies:* various MW frequencies in Midlands and digital

1Xtra (urban music: drum & bass, garage, hip hop, R&B) – 24 hours a day, digital only

BBC NATIONAL RADIO STATIONS

Radio Cymru (Welsh-language), *frequencies:* digital; 93.6–96.8 FM and 103.5–105 FM, coverage 97%
Radio Foyle, frequency: digital (tv-only); 792 AM and 93.1 MW
Radio Nan Gaidheal (Gaelic service), *frequencies:* digital; 103.5–105 FM plus 990 MW, coverage 90%
Radio Scotland, frequencies: digital; 810/585 MW and 92.4–94.7 FM, coverage 99%. Local programmes for: Highlands and Islands; North East; Borders; South West; Orkney; and Shetland
Radio Ulster, frequencies: digital; 1341 MW and 92.4–95.4 FM, coverage 96%. Local programmes on Radio Foyle
Radio Wales, frequencies: digital; 882 MW and 93.9–95.9 FM, coverage 97%

BBC LOCAL RADIO STATIONS

There are 41 local stations serving England and the Channel Islands:
Berkshire, PO Box 1044, Reading RG4 8FH T 0118-946 4200 *Frequencies:* 94.6/95.4/104.1/104.4 FM and DAB
Bristol, Whiteladies Road, Bristol BS8 2LR T 0117-974 2211 *Frequencies:* 94.9/104.6/103.6 FM and 1548 AM and DAB
Cambridgeshire, 104 Hills Road, Cambridge CB2 1LQ T 01223-259696 *Frequencies:* 95.7/96 FM
Cleveland, Broadcasting House, Newport Road, Middlesbrough TS1 5DG T 01642-225211 *Frequency:* 95 FM and DAB
Cornwall, Phoenix Wharf, Truro TR1 1UA T 01872-275421 *Frequencies:* 95.2/103.9 FM and DAB
Coventry and Warwickshire, Priory Place, Coventry CV1 5SQ T 024-7655 1000 *Frequencies:* 94.8/104/103.7 FM and DAB
Cumbria, Annetwell Street, Carlisle CA3 8BB T 01228-592444 *Frequencies:* 95.6/96.1/104.1 FM
Derby, 56 St Helen's Street, Derby DE1 3HY T 01332-361111 *Frequencies:* 95.3/96.0/104.5 FM, 1116 AM
Devon, Broadcasting House, Seymour Road, Plymouth PL3 5BD T 01752-260323 *Frequencies:* 94.8/95.7/95.8/96.0/103.4/104.3 FM and DAB
Essex, PO Box 765, Chelmsford CM2 9XB T 01245-616000 *Frequencies:* 95.3/103.5 FM and DAB
Gloucestershire, London Road, Gloucester GL1 1SW T 01452-308585 *Frequencies:* 95.0/95.8/104.7 FM, 1413 AM
Guernsey, Broadcasting House, Bulwer Avenue, St Sampson's GY2 4LA T 01481-200600 *Frequencies:* 93.2/99 FM, 1116 MW
Hereford and Worcester, Hylton Road, Worcester WR2 5WW T 01905-748485 *Frequencies:* 94.7/104.0/104.4/104.6 FM, 738/1584 MW
Humberside, Queen's Court, Hull HU1 3RH T 01482-323232 *Frequency:* 95.9 FM, 1485 AM and DAB
Jersey, 18 Parade Road, St Helier JE2 3PL T 01534-837228 *Frequency:* 88.8 FM and DAB
Kent, The Great Hall, Mount Pleasant, Tunbridge Wells TN1 1QQ T 01892-670000 *Frequencies:* 96.7/97.6/104.2 FM, 774 AM
Lancashire, 20–26 Darwen Street, Blackburn BB2 2EA T 01254-262411 *Frequencies:* 95.5/103.9/104.5 FM and DAB
Leeds, 2 St Peter's Square, Leeds LS9 8AH T 0113-244 2131 *Frequencies:* 92.4/95.3 FM, 774 AM and DAB
Leicester, 9 St Nicholas Place, Leicester LE1 5LB T 0116-251 6688 *Frequency:* 104.9 FM and DAB
Lincolnshire, PO Box 219, Newport, Lincoln LN1 3XY T 01522-511411 *Frequencies:* 94.9/104.7 FM, 1368 AM and DAB
London, PO Box 949, Marylebone High Street, London W1A 6FL T 020-7224 2424 *Frequency:* 94.9 FM and DAB
Manchester, PO Box 27, Oxford Road, Manchester M60 1SJ T 0161-200 2020 *Frequencies:* 95.1 FM and DAB
Merseyside, PO Box 95.8, Liverpool L69 1ZJ T 0151-708 5500 *Frequencies:* 95.8 FM, 1485 AM and DAB
Newcastle, Broadcasting Centre, Barrack Road, Newcastle upon Tyne NE99 1RN T 0191-232 4141 *Frequencies:* 95.4/96.0 FM, 1458 AM and DAB
Norfolk, The Forum, Millennium Plain, Norwich NR2 1BH T 01603-617411 *Frequencies:* 95.1/95.6/104.4 FM and DAB
Northampton, Broadcasting House, Abington Street, Northampton NN1 2BH T 01604-239100 *Frequencies:* 103.6/104.2 FM
Nottingham, London Road, Nottingham NG2 4UU T 0115-955 0500 *Frequencies:* 95.5/103.8 FM and DAB
Oxford, 269 Banbury Road, Oxford OX2 7DW T 08459-311 444 *Frequency:* 95.2 FM
Sheffield, 54 Shoreham Street, Sheffield S1 4RS T 0114-273 1177 *Frequencies:* 88.6/94.7/104.1 FM and DAB
Shropshire, 2–4 Boscobel Drive, Harlescott, Shrewsbury SY1 3TT T 01743-248484 *Frequency:* 96 FM and DAB
Solent, Havelock Road, Southampton SO14 7PU T 023-8063 1311 *Frequencies:* 96.1/103.8 FM
Somerset Sound, Broadcasting House, Park Street, Taunton TA1 4DA T 01823-323956 *Frequency:* 95.5 FM,1566 AM
Southern Counties, Broadcasting House, Queens Road, Brighton, East Sussex BN1 3XB T 08459-570057 *Frequencies:* 95–95.3/104–104.8 FM, 1161/1368/1485 AM and DAB
Stoke, Cheapside, Hanley, Stoke-on-Trent ST1 1JJ T 01782-208080 *Frequencies:* 94.6/104.1 FM and DAB
Suffolk, Broadcasting House, St Matthew's Street, Ipswich IP1 3EP T 01473-250000 *Frequencies:* 95.5/95.9/103.9/104.6 FM
Swindon, Broadcasting House, 56–58 Prospect Place, Swindon SN1 3RW T 01793-513626 *Frequency:* 103.6 FM and DAB
Tees, Broadcasting House, Newport Road, Middlesborough TS1 5DJ T 01642-225211 *Frequency:* 95 FM and DAB
Three Counties, 1 Hastings Street, Luton LU1 5XL T 01582-637400 *Frequencies:* 94.7/95.5/98.0/103.8/104.5 FM, 630/1161 AM
Wiltshire, Broadcasting House, 56–58 Prospect Place, Swindon SN1 3RW T 01793-513626 *Frequencies:* 103.5/104.3/104.9 FM and DAB
WM (West Midlands), The Mailbox,102–108 Wharfside Street, Birmingham B1 1AY T 0121-567 6000 *Frequency:* 95.6 FM and DAB
York, 20 Bootham Row, York YO30 7BR T 01904-641351 *Frequencies:* 95.5/103.7/104.3 FM

BBC WORLD SERVICE

The BBC World Service broadcasts to an estimated weekly audience of 182 million worldwide, in 32 languages including English, and is now available in 154 capital cities. It no longer broadcasts in Dutch, French for Europe, German, Hebrew, Italian, Japanese or Malay because it was found that most speakers of these languages preferred to listen to the English broadcasts. In 2006 services in ten languages (Bulgarian, Croatian, Czech, Greek, Hungarian, Kazakh, Polish, Slovak, Slovene, and Thai) were terminated to provide funding for a new Arabic television channel, which was launched in March 2008. In August 2008 the BBC's Romanian World Service broadcasts were discontinued after 68 years. The BBC World Service website offers interactive news services in English, Arabic, Chinese, Hindi, Persian, Portuguese for Brazil, Russian, Spanish and Urdu with audiostreaming available in 32 languages.

LANGUAGES
Albanian, Arabic, Azeri, Bengali, Burmese, Caribbean-English, Cantonese, French for Africa, Hausa, Hindi, Indonesian, Kinyarwanda/Kirundi, Kyrgyz, Macedonian, Mandarin, Nepali, Pashto, Persian, Portuguese for Brazil, Russian, Serbian, Sinhala, Somali, Spanish, Swahili, Tamil, Turkish, Ukrainian, Urdu, Uzbek and Vietnamese.

UK frequencies: 648 MW in southern England and overnight on BBC Radio 4, BBC Radio Ulster, BBC Radio Wales or the Asian Network.

BBC Learning English teaches English worldwide through radio, television and a wide range of published and online courses.
BBC Monitoring tracks the global media for the latest news reports emerging around the world.
BBC World Service Trust is a registered charity established in 1999 by BBC World Service. It promotes development through the innovative use of the media in the developing world. The trust presently works in over 40 countries worldwide, tackling health, education and good governance.
BBC WORLD SERVICE, Bush House, Strand, London WC2B 4PH T 020-7557 2462

INDEPENDENT RADIO

Until 1973, the BBC had a legal monopoly on radio broadcasting in the UK. During this time, the corporation's only competition came from pirate stations located abroad, such as Radio Luxembourg. Christopher Chataway, Minister for Post and Telecommunications in Edward Heath's government, changed this by creating the first licences for commercial radio stations. The Independent Broadcasting Authority (IBA) awarded the first of these licences to the London Broadcasting Company (LBC) to provide London's news and information service. LBC was followed by Capital Radio, to offer the city's entertainment service, Radio Clyde in Glasgow and BRMB in Birmingham.

The IBA was dissolved when the Broadcasting Act of 1990 de-regulated broadcasting, to be succeeded by the less rigid Radio Authority (RA). The RA began advertising new licences for the development of independent radio in January 1991. It awarded national and local radio, satellite and cable services licences, and long-term restricted service licences for stations serving non-commercial establishments such as hospitals and universities. The first national commercial digital multiplex licence was awarded in October 1998 and a number of local digital multiplex licences followed.

At the end of 2003 the RA was replaced by OFCOM, which now carries out the licensing administration.

The RadioCentre was formed in July 2006 as a result of the merger between the Radio Advertising Bureau (RAB) and the Commercial Radio Companies Association (CRCA), the former non-profit trade body for commercial radio companies in the United Kingdom, to operate essentially as a union for commercial radio stations. It is possible to listen to 93 per cent of independent radio stations online, while 48 per cent can be listened to on DAB radios.

THE RADIOCENTRE, 77 Shaftesbury Avenue, London W1D 5DU T 020-7306 2603 W www.radiocentre.org
Chief Executive, Andrew Harrison

INDEPENDENT NATIONAL RADIO STATIONS

Absolute 1215, 1 Golden Square, London W1F 9DJ T 020-7434 1215 – 24 hours a day, *Frequencies:* 1197/1215/1233/1242/1260 AM and DAB
Classic FM, 30 Leicester Square, London WC2H 7LA T 020-7343 9000 – 24 hours a day, *Frequencies:* 100–102 FM and DAB
Talk Sport, 18 Hatfields, London SE1 8DJ T 020-7959 7800 – 24 hours a day, *Frequencies:* 1053/1071/1089/1107 AM and DAB

INDEPENDENT LOCAL RADIO STATIONS ENGLAND

2BR, Lomeshaye Business Village, Nelson, Lancs BB9 7DR T 01282-690000 *Frequency:* 99.8 FM
2CR FM, 5–7 Southcote Road, Bournemouth BH1 3LR T 01202-234900 *Frequency:* 102.3 FM and DAB
2-Ten FM, PO Box 2020, Reading, Berks RG31 7FG T 0118-945 4400 *Frequencies:* 97.0/102.9/103.4 FM and DAB
3FM, 45 Victoria Street, Douglas, IOM IM1 3RS T 01624-616333 *Frequencies:* 104–106 FM
3TR FM, Riverside Studios, Warminster, Wilts BA12 9HQ T 01985-211111 *Frequency:* 107.5 FM
95.8 Capital Radio, 30 Leicester Square, London WC2H 7LA T 020-7766 6000 *Frequency:* 95.8 FM and DAB
96 Trent FM, Maid Marian Way, Nottingham NG1 6JR T 0115-873 1500 *Frequencies:* 96.2/96.5 FM and DAB
96.2 The Revolution, Sarah Moor Studios, Henshaw Street, Oldham OL1 3JF T 0161-621 6500 *Frequency:* 96.2 FM
96.2 Touch FM, Watch Close, Spon Street, Coventry CV1 3LN T 024-7652 5656 *Frequency:* 96.2 FM
96.3 Radio Aire, 51 Burley Road, Leeds LS3 1LR T 0113-283 5500 *Frequency:* 96.3 FM
96.4 FM BRMB, Nine Brindleyplace, 4 Oozells Square, Birmingham B1 2DJ T 0121-566 5200 *Frequency:* 96.4 FM
96.4 Eagle Radio, Dolphin House, North Street, Guildford, Surrey GU1 4AA T 01483-300964 *Frequency:* 96.4 FM
96.9 Chiltern FM, 5 Abbey Court, Fraser Road, Priory Business Park, Bedford MK44 3WH T 01234-235010 *Frequency:* 96.9 FM
96.9 Viking FM, The Boathouse, Commercial Road, Hull, E. Yorks HU1 2SG T 01482-325141 *Frequency:* 96.9 FM and DAB
97 FM Plymouth Sound, Earl's Acre, Plymouth PL3 4HX T 01752-275600 *Frequencies:* 96.6/97 FM and DAB
97.2 Stray FM, The Hamlet, Hornbeam Park Avenue, Harrogate HG2 8RE T 01423-522972 *Frequency:* 97.2 FM
97.4 Rock FM, PO Box 974, St. Paul's Square, Preston, Lancs PR1 1YE T 01772-477700 *Frequency:* 97.4 FM and DAB
97.6 Chiltern FM, Chiltern Road, Dunstable LU6 1HQ T 01582-676200 *Frequency:* 97.6 FM
99.9 Radio Norwich, Stanton House, 29 Yarmouth Road, Norwich NR7 0SA T 0845-365 6999 *Frequency:* 99.9 FM
100–102 Century FM, Century House, PO Box 100,

Gateshead NE8 2YY T 0191-490 3600 *Frequencies:* 96.2/94.6/100.7/101.8 FM and DAB

100.7 Heart FM, 1 The Square, 111 Broad Street, Birmingham B15 1AS T 0121-695 0000 *Frequency:* 100.7 FM

102 Touch FM, The Guard House Studios, Banbury Road, Stratford-upon-Avon, Warwickshire CV37 7HX T 01789-262636 *Frequency:* 102.0 FM

102.2 Smooth FM, 26–27 Castlereagh Street, London W1H 5DL T 020-7706 4100 *Frequency:* 102.2 FM

102.4 Wish FM, Orrell Lodge, Orrell Road, Wigan, Lancs WN5 8HJ T 01942-761024 *Frequency:* 102.4 FM

102.7 Hereward FM, PO Box 225, Queensgate Centre, Peterborough PE1 1XJ T 01733-460460 *Frequency:* 102.7 FM and DAB

102.7 Mercury FM, 9 The Stanley Centre, Kelvin Way, Crawley, W. Sussex RH10 9SE T 01293-519161 *Frequencies:* 97.5/102.7 FM

103.2 Alpha FM, Radio House, 11 Woodland Road, Darlington, Co Durham DL3 7BJ T 01325-255552 *Frequency:* 103.2 FM

103.2 Power FM, Radio House, Whittle Avenue, Segensworth West, Fareham, Hants PO15 5SH T 01489-587610 *Frequency:* 103.2 FM

103.4 Sun FM, PO Box 1034, Sunderland, Tyne and Wear SR5 2YL T 0191-548 1034 *Frequency:* 103.4 FM

105.4 Century FM, Laser House, Waterfront Quays, Manchester M50 3XW T 0161-662 4701 *Frequency:* 105.4 FM

107 The Bee, 8 Dalton Court, Darwen, Lancs BB3 0DG T 01254-778000 *Frequency:* 107 FM

107.2 Dream FM, The Brooks, Winchester, Hampshire, SO23 8FT T 01962-841071 *Frequency:* 107.2 FM

107.2 The Wyre, Foley House, 123 Stourport Road, Kidderminster DY11 7BW T 01562-641072 *Frequency:* 107.2 FM

107.4 Telford FM, c/o The Shropshire Star, Waterloo Road, Ketley TF1 5HU T 01952-280011 *Frequency:* 107.4 FM

107.4 The Quay, Media House, Tipner Wharf, Twyford Avenue, Portsmouth PO2 8PE T 023-9236 4141 *Frequency:* 107.4 FM

107.5 Sovereign Radio, 14 St Mary's Walk, Hailsham, E. Sussex BN27 1AF T 01323-442700 *Frequency:* 107.5 FM

107.6 FM Juice Liverpool, 27 Fleet Street, Liverpool L1 4AR T 0151-707 3107 *Frequency:* 107.6 FM

107.6 Touch Banbury, Unit 9a, Manor Park, Banbury, Oxfordshire OX16 3TB T 0129-566 1076 *Frequency:* 107.6 FM

107.7 Splash FM, The Guildbourne Centre, Worthing, W. Sussex BN11 1LZ T 01903-233005 *Frequency:* 107.7 FM

107.7 The Wolf, 2nd Floor, Mander House, Wolverhampton WV1 3NB T 01902-571070 *Frequency:* 107.7 FM

107.8 Arrow FM, Priory Meadow Centre, Hastings, E. Sussex TN34 1PJ T 01424-461177 *Frequency:* 107.8 FM

107.8 Radio Jackie, 110–112 Tolworth Broadway, Surbiton, Surrey KT6 7JD T 020-8288 1300 *Frequency:* 107.8 FM

107.9 Dune FM, The Power Station, Victoria Way, Southport, Merseyside PR8 1RR T 01704-502500 *Frequency:* 107.9 FM

107.9 Pennine FM, The Old Stable Block, Lockwood Park, Huddersfield HD1 3UR T 01484-321107 *Frequency:* 107.9 FM

1548 AM Capital Gold, 30 Leicester Square, London WC2H 7LA T 020-7054 8000 *Frequency:* 1548 AM

Abbey FM, 22A Duke Street, Barrow-in-Furness, Cumbria LA14 1HU T 01229-845880 *Frequency:* 107.3 FM

Absolute Radio Classic Rock, 1 Golden Square, London W1F 9DJ T 020-7434 1215 *Frequency:* digital only

Absolute Radio London, 1 Golden Square, London W1F 9DJ T 020-7434 1215 *Frequency:* 105.8 FM

Absolute Radio Xtreme, 1 Golden Square, London W1F 9DJ T 020-7434 1215 *Frequency:* digital only

The Arrow, 1 The Square, 111 Broad Street, Birmingham, West Midlands B15 1AS T 0121-695 0000 *Frequency:* DAB only

Asian Sound Radio, Globe House, Southall Street, Manchester M3 1LG T 0161-288 1000 *Frequencies:* 963/1377 AM and DAB

Atlantic FM, Unit 10, Wheal Kitty Workshops, St Agnes, Cornwall TR5 0RD T 01872-554400 *Frequencies:* 105.0/107.0 FM

Bath FM, Station House, Ashley Avenue, Lower Weston, Bath BA1 3DS T 01225-471571 *Frequency:* 107.9 FM

The Bay, PO Box 969, St George's Quay, Lancaster LA1 3LD T 0871-200 0747 *Frequencies:* 96.9/102.3/103.2 FM

The Beach, PO Box 1034, Lowestoft, Suffolk NR32 2TL T 0845-345 1035 *Frequencies:* 97.4/103.4 FM and DAB

Beacon Radio, 267 Tettenhall Road, Wolverhampton WV6 0DE T 01902-461300 *Frequencies:* 97.2/103.1 FM and DAB

Big L, 1–3 Colmore Crescent, Moseley, Birmingham B13 9SJ T 0121-449 5051 *Frequency:* 1395 AM

Bright 106.4, 11A The Market Place Shopping Centre, Burgess Hill, W. Sussex RH15 9NP T 01444-248127 *Frequency:* 106.4 FM

Brighton's Juice 107.2, 170 North Street, Brighton BN1 1EA T 01273-386107 *Frequency:* 107.2 FM and DAB

BRMB, Nine Brindleyplace, 4 Oozells Square, Birmingham B1 2DJ T 0121-566 5200 *Frequency:* 96.4 FM and DAB

Brunel FM, The Lime Kiln Studios, Lime Kiln, Wooton Bassett SN4 7HF T 01793-853777 *Frequency:* 107.7 FM

Central Radio, 18 Hatfields, London SE1 8DJ T 01772-702020 *Frequencies:* 96.3/106.5 FM

CFM (Carlisle and West Cumbria), PO Box 964, Carlisle, Cumbria CA1 3NG T 01228-818964 *Frequencies:* 96.4/102.5 FM (Carlisle); 102.2/103.4 FM (west Cumbria)

Cheshire's 106.9 Silk FM, Radio House, Bridge Street, Macclesfield, Cheshire SK11 6DJ T 01625-268000 *Frequency:* 106.9 FM

Choice 96.9/107.1 FM, 30 Leicester Square, London WC2H 7LA T 020-7766 6810 *Frequency:* 96.9/107.1 FM and DAB

Classic Hits (954/1530), PO Box 262, Worcester WR6 5ZE T 01905-740600 *Frequencies:* 954/1530 AM

Club Asia, Asia House, 227–247 Gascoigne Road, Barking, Essex IG11 7LN T 020-8594 6662 *Frequencies:* 963/972 AM

Compass FM, 26A Wellowgate, Grimsby, Lincs DN32 0RA T 01472-346666 *Frequency:* 96.4 FM

Connect FM, 2nd Floor, 5 Church Street, Peterborough PE1 1XB T 0844-800 1769 *Frequencies:* 97.2/107.4 FM

County Sound Radio 1566 AM, Dolphin House, North Street, Guildford, Surrey GU1 4AA T 01483-300964 *Frequency:* 1566 AM

Dearne FM, Unit 7, Network Centre, Zenith Park, Whaley Road, Barnsley S75 1HT T 01226-321733 *Frequencies:* 97.1/102.0 FM

Dee 106.3, 2 Chantry Court, Chester CH1 4QN T 01244-391000 *Frequency:* 106.3 FM

Delta FM, Tindle House, High Street, Bordon, Hants GU35 0AY T 01420-473473 *Frequencies:* 97.1/101.6/101.8/102.0 FM

Dream 100 FM, Northgate House, St Peter's Street, Colchester, Essex CO1 1HT T 01206-764466 *Frequency:* 100.2 FM

Dream 107.7 FM, 12 Bentalls Shopping Centre, Colchester Road, Heybridge, Maldon, Essex CM9 4GD T 0845-365 1078 *Frequency:* 107.7 FM

Easy Radio London (1035), Radio House, Merrick Road, Southall, Middlesex UB2 4AU T 020-8574 6666 *Frequency:* 1035 AM and DAB

Energy FM, 100 Market Street, Douglas, IOM IM1 2PH T 01624-611936 *Frequencies:* 91.2 FM (Laxey); 93.4 FM (north Isle of Man); 98.4 FM (Ramsey); 98.6 FM
Essex FM, Radio House, 31, Glebe House, Chelmsford, Essex CM1 1QG T 01245-524500 *Frequencies:* 96.3/97.5/102.6 FM and DAB
Fen Radio 107.5, 5 Church Mews, Wisbech, Cambridgeshire PE13 1HL T 01945-467107 *Frequency:* 107.5 FM
Fire 107.6 FM, The Picture House, 307 Holden Hurst Road, Bournemouth, Dorset BH8 8BX T 01202-318100 *Frequency:* 107.6 FM
Fosseway Radio, Suite 1, 1 Castle Street, Hinckley, Leics LE10 1DA T 01455-614151 *Frequency:* 107.9 FM
Fox FM, Brush House, Pony Road, Oxford OX4 2XR T 01865-871000 *Frequencies:* 97.4/102.6 FM
Fresh Radio, Firth Mill, Firth Street, Skipton, N. Yorks BD23 2PT T 01756-799991 *Frequencies:* 936/1413/1431 AM
Galaxy Birmingham, 1 The Square, 111 Broad Street, Birmingham, West Midlands B15 1AS T 0121-695 0000 *Frequency:* 102.2 FM and DAB
Galaxy Manchester, 5th Floor, The Triangle, Hanging Ditch, Manchester M4 3TR T 0161-279 0300 *Frequency:* 102.0 FM and DAB
Galaxy North East, Kingfisher Way, Silverlink Business Park, Wallsend, Tyne and Wear NE28 9NX T 0191-206 8000 *Frequencies:* 105.3/105.6/105.8/106.4 FM and DAB
Galaxy Yorkshire, Joseph's Well, Hanover Walk, Leeds LS3 1AB T 0113-213 0105 *Frequencies:* 105.1/105.6/105.8 FM and DAB
GaydarRadio 6th Floor, Queens House, 2 Holly Road, Twickenham, Middlesex TW1 4EG T 020-8744 1287 *Frequency:* digital
Gemini FM, Hawthorn House, Exeter Business Park, Exeter EX1 3QS T 01392-444444 *Frequencies:* 96.4/97.0/103.0 FM and DAB
Gold (Berkshire and North Hampshire), The Chase, Calcot, Reading, Berks RG3 7RB T 0118-945 4400 *Frequencies:* 1431/1485 AM and DAB
Gold (Birmingham), Nine Brindleyplace, 4 Oozells Square, Birmingham B1 2DJ T 0121-245 5000 *Frequency:* 1152 AM and DAB
Gold (Bristol and Bath), PO Box 2000, One Passage Street, Bristol BS99 7SN T 0117-984 3200 *Frequency:* 1260 AM and DAB
Gold (Cambridgeshire), PO Box 225, Queensgate Centre, Peterborough, Cambridge PE1 1XJ T 01733-460460 *Frequency:* 1332 AM and DAB
Gold (Devon), Hawthorn House, Exeter Business Park, Exeter EX1 3QS T 01392-444444 *Frequencies:* 666/954 AM and DAB
Gold (Dorset and Hampshire), 5–7 Southcote Road, Bournemouth, Dorset BH1 3LR T 01202-234900 *Frequency:* 828 AM and DAB
Gold (East Midlands), Chapel Quarter, Maid Marian Way, Nottingham NG1 6JR T 01245-524549 *Frequencies:* 1359/1431 AM and DAB
Gold (Essex), 31 Glebe Road, Chelmsford, Essex CM1 1QG T 01245 524549 *Frequencies:* 1359/1431 AM and DAB
Gold (Gloucester and Cheltenham), Bridge Studios, Eastgate Centre, Gloucester GL1 1SS T 01452-572400 *Frequency:* 774 AM and DAB
Gold (Hampshire), Radio House, Whittle Avenue, Segensworth West, Farnham, Hants PO15 5SH T 01489-587610 *Frequencies:* 1170/1557 AM and DAB
Gold (Herts, Beds and Bucks), Chiltern Road, Dunstable, Beds LU6 1HQ T 01582-676200 *Frequencies:* 792/828 AM and DAB
Gold (Kent), Radio House, John Wilson Business Park, Whitstable, Kent CT5 3QX T 01227-772004 *Frequencies:* 603/1242 AM and DAB
Gold (London), 30 Leicester Square, London WC2H 7LA T 020-7054 8000 *Frequency:* 1548 AM and DAB
Gold (Manchester), Laser House, Waterfront Quays, Manchester M5 2XW T 0161-662 4700 *Frequency:* 1458 AM and DAB
Gold (Norfolk), St George's Plain, 47–49 Colegate, Norwich NR3 1DB T 01603-630621 *Frequency:* 1152 AM and DAB
Gold (Northamptonshire), 19–21 St Edmunds Road, Northampton NN1 5DY T 01604-795600 *Frequency:* 1557 AM and DAB
Gold (Plymouth), Earl's Acre, Plymouth PL3 4HX T 01752-275600 *Frequency:* 1152 AM and DAB
Gold (Suffolk), Alpha Business Park, 6–12 White House Road, Ipswich IP1 5LT T 01473-461000 *Frequency:* 1170/1251 AM and DAB
Gold (Sussex), Radio House, PO Box 2000, Brighton BN41 2SS T 01273-430111 *Frequencies:* 945/1323 AM and DAB
Gold (Sussex and Surrey), 9 The Stanley Centre, Kelvin Way, Crawley, W. Sussex RH10 9SE T 01293-519161 *Frequency:* 1521 AM and DAB
Gold (Warwickshire), Hertford Place, Coventry CV1 3TT T 024-7686 8200 *Frequency:* 1359 AM and DAB
Gold (Wiltshire), 1st Floor, Chiseldon House, Stonehill Green, Westlea, Swindon, Wilts SN5 7HB T 01793-663000 *Frequencies:* 936/1161 AM and DAB
Gold (Wolverhampton and Shropshire), 267 Tettenhall Road, Wolverhampton WV6 0DQ T 01902-461200 *Frequencies:* 990/1017 AM and DAB
GWR FM (Bristol and Bath), PO Box 2000, One Passage Street, Bristol BS99 7SN T 0117-984 3200 *Frequencies:* 96.3/103.0 FM and DAB
GWR FM (Swindon and West Wiltshire), Chiseldon House, Stonehill Green, Westlea, Swindon, Wilts SN5 7HB T 01793-842600 *Frequencies:* 96.5/97.2/102.2 FM and DAB
Hallam FM, Radio House, 900 Herries Road, Sheffield S6 1RH T 0114-209 1000 *Frequencies:* 97.4/102.9/103.4 FM and DAB
Heart 106, City Link, Nottingham NG2 4NG T 0115-910 6100 *Frequency:* 106 FM and DAB
Heart 106.2, The Chrysalis Building, Bramley Road, London W10 6SP T 020-7468 1062 *Frequency:* 106.2 FM and DAB
Hertbeat FM, The Pump House, Knebworth Park, Herts SG3 6HQ T 01438-810900 *Frequencies:* 106.7/106.9 FM
Hertfordshire's Mercury (96.6), Unit 5, The Metro Centre, Dwight Road, Watford WD18 9UP T 01923-205470 *Frequency:* 96.6 FM
High Peak Radio, The Studios, Smithbrook Close, Chapel-en-le-Frith, High Peak, Derbys SK23 0QD T 01298-813144 *Frequencies:* 103.3/106.4 FM
Horizon Radio, 14 Vincent Avenue, Crownhill, Milton Keynes MK8 0AB, T 01908-269111 *Frequency:* 103.3 FM
Imagine FM, Regent House, Heaton Lane, Stockport, Cheshire, SK4 1BX T 0161-609 1400 *Frequency:* 104.9 FM
Invicta FM, Radio House, John Wilson Business Park, Whitstable, Kent CT5 3QX T 01227-772004 *Frequencies:* 95.9/96.1/97.0/102.8/103.1 FM and DAB
Isle of Wight Radio, Dodnor Park, Newport, IOW PO30 5XE T 01983-822557 *Frequencies:* 102.0/107.0 FM
Ivel FM, The Studios, Middle Street, Yeovil, Somerset BA20 1DJ T 01935-848488 *Frequency:* 105.6/106.6 FM
Jack FM, 270 Woodstock Road, Oxford OX2 7NW T 01865-315980 *Frequency:* 106 FM
KCR FM, Paramount Studios, Paramount Business Park, Wilson Road, Liverpool L36 6AW T 0151-949 5510 *Frequency:* 106.7 FM

Kerrang! 105.2 FM, Kerrang House, 20 Lionel Street, Birmingham B3 1AQ T 0845-053 1052 *Frequency:* 105.2 FM and DAB

Kestrel FM, 2nd Floor, Paddington House, Festival Place, Basingstoke, Hants RG21 7LJ T 01256-694000 *Frequency:* 107.6 FM

Key 103, Castle Quay, Castlefield, Manchester M15 4PR T 0161-288 5000 *Frequency:* 103.0 FM and DAB

Kick FM, The Studios, 42 Bone Lane, Newbury, Berks RG14 5SD T 01635-841600 *Frequencies:* 105.6/107.4 FM

Kismat, Radio House, Bridge Road, Southall, Middx UB2 4AT T 020-8574 6666 *Frequency:* 1035 AM and DAB

Kiss 100 FM, Mappin House, 4 Winsley Street, London W1W 8HF T 020-7975 8100 *Frequency:* 100.0 FM and DAB

Kiss 101 FM, 26 Baldwin Street, Bristol BS1 1SE T 0117-901 0101 *Frequency:* 97.2/101.0 FM and DAB

Kiss FM 105–108, 26 Baldwin Street, Bristol BS1 1SE T 0117-901 0101 *Frequencies:* 105.6/106.1/106.4/107.7 FM and DAB

KL.FM 96.7, 18 Blackfriars Street, King's Lynn, Norfolk PE30 1NN T 01553-772777 *Frequency:* 96.7 FM

KMFM for Ashford, Express House, 34–36 North Street, Ashford, Kent TN24 8JR T 01233-623232 *Frequency:* 107.7 FM

KMFM for Canterbury, 9 St George's Place, Canterbury, Kent CT1 1UU T 01227-475950 *Frequency:* 106.0 FM

KMFM for Maidstone, 6–8 Mill Street, Maidstone, Kent ME15 6XH T 01622-662500 *Frequency:* 105.5 FM

KMFM for Medway, Medway House, Ginsbury Close, Sir Thomas Longley Road, Medway City Estate, Strood, Rochester, Kent ME2 4DU T 01634-711079 *Frequencies:* 100.4/107.9 FM

KMFM for Shepway and White Cliffs Country, 93–95 Sandgate Road, Folkestone, Kent CT20 2BQ T 01303-220303 *Frequencies:* 96.4/106.8 FM

KMFM for Thanet, 183 Northdown Road, Cliftonville, Margate, Kent CT9 2TA T 01843-220222 *Frequency:* 107.2 FM

KMFM for West Kent, 1 East Street, Tonbridge, Kent TN9 1AR T 01732-369200 *Frequencies:* 96.2/101.6 FM

Lakeland Radio, Unit 4, Lakelands Food Park, Plumgarths, Crook Road, Kendal, Cumbria LA8 8QJ T 01539-737380 *Frequencies:* 100.1/100.8 FM

Lantern FM, Unit 2B, Lauder Lane, Roundswell Business Park, Barnstaple EX31 3TA T 01271-366350 *Frequencies:* 96.2/97.3 FM

LBC 97.3 FM, The Chrysalis Building, 13 Bramley Road, London W10 6SP T 020-7314 7300 *Frequency:* 97.3 FM and DAB

LBC News 1152 AM, The Chrysalis Building, 13 Bramley Road, London W10 6SP T 020-7314 7308 *Frequency:* 1152 AM and DAB

Leicester Sound, 6 Dominus Way, Meridian Business Park, Leicester LE19 1RP T 0116-256 1300 *Frequency:* 105.4 FM and DAB

Lincs FM, Witham Park, Waterside South, Lincoln LN5 7JN T 01522-549900 *Frequencies:* 96.7/102.2/97.6 FM and DAB

Lite FM, 2nd Floor, 5 Church Street, Peterborough PE1 1XB T 01733-898106 *Frequency:* 106.8/96.4 FM

London Greek Radio, LGR House, 437 High Road, London N12 0AP T 020-8349 6950 *Frequency:* 103.3 FM

London Turkish Radio, 185B High Road, Wood Green, London N22 6BA T 020-8881 0606 *Frequency:* 1584 AM

Magic 105.4 FM, Mappin House, 4 Winsley Street, London W1W 8HF T 020-7182 8000 *Frequency:* 105.4 FM and DAB

Magic 828, 51 Burley Road, Leeds LS3 1LR T 0113-283 5500 *Frequency:* 828 AM and DAB

Magic 999, St Paul's Square, Preston, Lancs PR1 1YE T 01772-477700 *Frequency:* 999 AM and DAB

Magic 1152 (Tyne & Wear), 55 Degrees North, Pilgrim Street, Newcastle upon Tyne NE1 6BF T 0191-230 6100 *Frequency:* 1152 AM and DAB

Magic 1161 AM, Commercial Road, Hull, E. Yorks HU1 2SG T 01482-325141 *Frequency:* 1161 AM and DAB

Magic 1170, Radio House, Yale Crescent, Thornaby, Stockton-on-Tees TS17 6AA T 01642-888222 *Frequency:* 1170 AM and DAB

Magic 1548 AM, St John's Beacon, 1 Houghton Street, Liverpool L1 1RL T 0151-472 6800 *Frequency:* 1548 AM and DAB

Magic AM, Radio House, 900 Herries Road, Sheffield S6 1RH T 0114-209 1000 *Frequencies:* 990/1305/1548 AM and DAB

Manchester's Magic 1152, Castle Quay, Castlefield, Manchester M1 4AW T 0161-288 5000 *Frequency:* 1152 AM and DAB

Mansfield 103.2 FM, The Media Suite, Brunts Business Centre, Samuel Brunts Way, Mansfield, Notts NG18 2AH T 01623-646666 *Frequency:* 103.2 FM

Manx Radio, PO Box 1368, Broadcasting House, Douglas, IOM IM99 1SW T 01624-682600 *Frequencies:* 89.0/97.2/103.7 FM, 1368 AM

Mercia FM, Hertford Place, Coventry CV1 3TT T 024-7686 8200 *Frequencies:* 97.0/102.9 FM and DAB

Mercury FM, 9 The Stanley Centre, Kelvin Way, Crawley, West Sussex RH10 9SE T 01293-519161 *Frequency:* 97.5/102.7 FM

Metro Radio, 55 Degrees North, Pilgrim Street, Newcastle upon Tyne NE99 1BB T 0191-230 6100 *Frequencies:* 97.1/102.6/103.0/103.2 FM and DAB

Minster FM, PO Box 123, Dunnington, York YO1 5ZX T 01904-488888 *Frequencies:* 102.3/104.7 FM

Mix 96, Friars Square Studios, 11 Bourbon Street, Aylesbury, Bucks HP20 2PZ T 01296-399396 *Frequency:* 96.2 FM

Mix 107, 11 Duke Street, High Wycombe, Bucks HP13 6EE T 01494-446611 *Frequencies:* 107.4/107.7 FM

NME, B2 Blue Fin Building, 110 Southwark Street, London SE1 0SU T 0207-922 1991 *Frequency:* digital only

North Norfolk Radio, The Studio, Breck Farm, Stody, Norfolk NR24 2ER T 01263-860808 *Frequencies:* 96.2/103.2 FM

Northants 96, 19–21 St Edmunds Road, Northampton NN1 5DY T 01604-795600 *Frequency:* 96.6 FM

Oak 107, 7 Waldron Court, Prince William Road, Loughborough, Leics LE11 5GD T 01509-211711 *Frequency:* 107.0 FM

Ocean FM, Radio House, Whittle Avenue, Segensworth West, Fareham, Hants PO15 5SH T 01489-587610 *Frequencies:* 96.7/97.5 FM and DAB

Orchard FM, Haygrove House, Shoreditch Road, Taunton, Somerset TA3 7BT T 01823-338448 *Frequencies:* 96.5/97.1/102.6 FM

Original 106, Roman Landing, Kingsway, Southampton SO14 1BN T 023-8038 4100 *Frequency:* 106 FM

Original 106.5, County Gates, Ashton Road, Bristol BS3 2JH T 0117-996 1065 *Frequency:* 106.5 FM

Oxford's FM 1079, 270 Woodstock Road, Oxford OX2 7NW T 0845-444 1079 *Frequency:* 107.9 FM

Palm (105.5), Marble Court, Lymington Road, Torquay TQ1 4FB T 01803-321 055 *Frequency:* 105.5 FM

Passion Radio, Guildbourne Centre, Worthing, West Sussex BN11 1LZ T 08707-444703 *Frequency:* digital only

Peak 107 FM, Radio House, Foxwood Road, Chesterfield,

Derbys S41 9RF T 01246-269107 *Frequencies:* 102.0/107.4 FM

Pirate FM, Carn Brea Studios, Wilson Way, Redruth, Cornwall TR15 3XX T 01209-314400 *Frequencies:* 102.2/102.8 FM and DAB

Planet Rock, 30 Leicester Square, London WC2H 7LA T 020-7766 6810 *Frequency:* digital only

Plymouth Sound, Earls Acre, Plymouth PL3 4HX T 01752-275600 *Frequencies:* 96.6/97 FM and DAB

Polish Radio London 91.8, Unit 6, King Street Cloisters, Clifton Walk, London W6 0GY T 020-8846 3619 *Frequency:* 91.8 FM and DAB

Power FM Radio House, Whittle Avenue, Segensworth West, Fareham, Hampshire PO15 5SH T 01489-587610 *Frequency:* 103.2 FM and DAB

Premier Christian Radio, 22 Chapter Street, London SW1P 4NP T 020-7316 1300 *Frequencies:* 1305/1332/1413 AM and DAB

Pulse Classic Gold, Forster Square, Bradford, W. Yorks BD1 5NE T 01274-203040 *Frequencies:* 1278/1530 AM

The Pulse of West Yorkshire, Forster Square, Bradford, W. Yorks BD1 5NE T 01274-203040 *Frequencies:* 97.5/102.5 FM and DAB

Q103 FM, Enterprise House, The Vision Park, Chivers Way, Histon, Cambridge CB4 9WW T 01223-235255 *Frequencies:* 97.4/103.0 FM and DAB

Quay 102.4 FM, Harbour Studios, The Esplanade, Watchet, Somerset TA23 0AJ T 01984-634900 *Frequencies:* 100.8/102.4 FM

Radio Broadland 102.4, St George's Plain, 47–49 Colegate, Norwich NR3 1DB T 01603-630621 *Frequency:* 102.4 FM and DAB

Radio City 96.7, St John's Beacon, 1 Houghton Street, Liverpool L1 1RL T 0151-472 6800 *Frequency:* 96.7 FM and DAB

Radio Hampshire, The Friends Provident St Mary's Stadium, Britannia Road, Southampton SO14 5FP T 02380-330300 *Frequency:* 107.8 FM and DAB

Radio Wave 96.5 FM, 965 Mowbray Drive, Blackpool, Lancs FY3 7JR T 01253-304965 *Frequency:* 96.5 FM

Radio XL 1296 AM, KMS House, Bradford Street, Birmingham B12 0JD T 0121-753 5353 *Frequency:* 1296 AM

Ram FM, 35/36 Irongate, Derby DE1 3GA T 01332-324000 *Frequency:* 102.8 FM

Reading 107 FM, Radio House, Madejski Stadium, Reading, Berks RG2 0FN T 0118-986 2555 *Frequency:* 107.0 FM

Real Radio (Yorkshire), 1 Sterling Court, Capitol Park, Leeds WF3 1EL T 0113-238 1114 *Frequencies:* 106.2/107.6/107.7 FM and DAB

Ridings FM, 2 Thornes Office Park, Monckton Road, Wakefield WF2 7AN T 01924-367177 *Frequency:* 106.8 FM and DAB

Rother FM, Aspen Court, Bessemer Way, Rotherham S60 1FB T 01709-369991 *Frequency:* 96.1 FM

Rugby FM, Suites 4–6, Dunsmore Business Centre, Spring Street, Rugby, Warks CV21 3HH T 01788-541100 *Frequency:* 107.1 FM

Rutland Radio, 40 Melton Road, Oakham, Rutland, Leics LE15 6AY T 01572-757868 *Frequencies:* 97.4/107.2 FM

Sabras Radio, Radio House, 63 Melton Road, Leicester LE4 6PN T 0116-261 0666 *Frequency:* 1260 AM and DAB

The Saint, The Friends Provident, St. Mary's Stadium, Britannia Road, Southampton SO14 5FP T 023-8033 0300 *Frequency:* 107.8 FM

The Severn, Abbey Studios, 13-14 Abbey Foregate, Shrewsbury SY2 6AE T 01743-284940 *Frequencies:* 106.5/ 107.1 FM

Severn Sound, Bridge Studios, Eastgate Centre, Gloucester GL1 1SS T 01452-572400 *Frequencies:* 102.4/103.0 FM

SGR Colchester, Abbeygate Two, 9 Whitewell Road, Colchester, Essex CO2 7DE T 01206-575859 *Frequency:* 96.1 FM

SGR-FM, Alpha Business Park, 6–12 White House Road, Ipswich, Suffolk IP1 5LT T 01473-461000 *Frequencies:* 96.4/97.1 FM

Signal 1, Stoke Road, Stoke-on-Trent ST4 2SR T 01782-441300 *Frequencies:* 96.4/96.9/102.6 FM and DAB

Signal 2, Stoke Road, Stoke-on-Trent ST4 2SR T 01782-441300 *Frequency:* 1170 AM and DAB

Smooth Radio, PO Box 5050, London SW1E 6ZR T 08700-707766 *Frequency:* digital only

Smooth 95.7/107.7, Church Street, Gateshead NE8 2YY T 0845-401 0975 *Frequencies:* 95.7FM /107.7 FM

Smooth 100.4, 8 Exchange Quay, Manchester M5 3EJ T 0845-050 1004 *Frequency:* 100.4 FM

Smooth 105.7, 3rd Floor, Crown House, Beaufort Court 123 Hagley Road, Birmingham B16 8LD T 0121-452 1057 *Frequency:* 105.7 FM

Smooth 106.6, Saga Radio House, Unit 2, Alder Court, Rennie Hogg Road, Riverside, Retail Park, Nottingham NG2 1RX T 0115-986 1066 *Frequencies:* 101.4/106.6 FM

South FM, 2–6 Basildon Road, Abbey Wood, London SE2 0EW T 020-8311 3112 *Frequency:* 107.3 FM

Southend Radio 105.1, Western Esplanade, Southend-on-Sea, Essex SS1 1EE T 01702-455070 *Frequency:* 105.1 FM

South Hams Radio, Unit 1G, South Hams Business Park, Churchstow, Kingsbridge, Devon TQ7 3QH T 01548-854595 *Frequency:* 100.5/100.8/101.2/101.9 FM

Southern FM, PO Box 2000, Franklin Road, Brighton BN41 2SS T 01273-430111 *Frequencies:* 102.4/103.5 FM and DAB

Spectrum Radio, 4 Ingate Place, Battersea, London SW8 3NS T 020-7627 4433 *Frequency:* 558 AM and DAB

Spire FM, City Hall Studios, Malthouse Lane, Salisbury, Wilts SP2 7QQ T 01722-416644 *Frequency:* 102.0 FM

Spirit FM, 9/10 Dukes Court, Bognor Road, Chichester, W. Sussex PO19 8FX T 01243-773600 *Frequencies:* 96.6/102.3 FM

Star 106.6, The Observatory, Slough, Berks SL1 1LH T 01753-551066 *Frequency:* 106.6 FM

Star Radio in Bristol, Bristol Evening Post Building, Temple Way, Bristol BS99 7HD T 0117-910 6600 *Frequency:* 107.2 FM

Star Radio in Cambridge, 20 Mercers Row, Cambridge CB5 8HY T 01223-305107 *Frequencies:* 107.1/107.9 FM

Star Radio in Cheltenham, Cheltenham Film Studios, 1st Floor, West Suite, Arle Court, Cheltenham, Glos GL51 6PN T 01242-699555 *Frequency:* 107.5 FM

Star Radio in Somerset, 11 Beaconsfield Road, Weston-super-Mare BS23 1YE T 01934-624455 *Frequency:* 107.7 FM

Star Radio in Stroud, Brunel Mall, London Road, Stroud GL5 2BP T 01453-767369 *Frequencies:* 107.3/107.9 FM

Sunrise FM, Sunrise House, 55 Leeds Road, Little Germany, Bradford BD1 5AF T 01274-735043 *Frequency:* 103.2 FM and DAB

Sunrise Radio, Sunrise House, Sunrise Road, Southall, Middx UB2 4AT T 020-8574 6666 *Frequency:* 1458 AM and DAB

Telford FM, c/o The Shropshire Star, Waterloo Road, Ketley TF1 5HU T 01952-280011 *Frequency:* 107.4 FM

Ten 17, Latton Bush Centre, Southern Way, Harlow, Essex CM18 7BB T 01279-431017 *Frequency:* 101.7 FM

TFM, Radio House, Yale Crescent, Thornaby, Stockton-on-Tees TS17 6AA T 01642-888222 *Frequency:* 96.6 FM and DAB

Time 106.6, The Observatory, Slough, Berkshire SL1 1LH T 01753-551066 *Frequency:* 106.6 FM

Time 106.8, 2–6 Basildon Road, Abbey Wood, London SE2 0EW T 020-8311 3112 *Frequency:* 106.8 FM

Time 107.5, 7th Floor, Lambourne House, 7 Western Road, Romford, Essex RM1 3LD T 01708-731 643 *Frequency:* 107.5 FM

Tower FM, The Mill, Brownlow Way, Bolton BL1 2RA T 01204-387000 *Frequency:* 107.4 FM

Town FM, First Floor, Radio House Prion Court, Great Blakenham, Ipswich, Suffolk IP6 0LW T 0845-365 1102 *Frequency:* 102.0 FM

Touch FM, 5/6 Aldergate, Tamworth, Staffordshire B79 7DJ T 01827-318000 *Frequencies:* 101.6/ 102.4 FM and DAB

Trax FM (Bassetlaw), White Hart Yard, Bridge Street, Worksop, Notts S80 1HR T 01909-500611 *Frequency:* 107.9 FM and DAB

Trax FM (Doncaster), 5 Sidings Court, White Rose Way, Doncaster DN4 5NU T 01302-341166 *Frequency:* 107.1 FM and DAB

Vale FM, Longmead Studios, Shaftesbury, Dorset SP7 8QQ T 01747-855711 *Frequencies:* 96.6/97.4 FM

Wave 105 FM, 5 Manor Court, Barnes Wallis Road, Segensworth East, Fareham, Hampshire PO15 5TH T 01489-481050 *Frequencies:* 105.2/105.8 FM and DAB

Wessex FM, Radio House, Trinity Street, Dorchester, Dorset DT1 1DJ T 01305-250333 *Frequencies:* 96.0/97.2 FM

Wirral's Buzz 97.1 FM, Pacific Road Arts Centre, Pacific Road, Birkenhead CH41 1LJ T 0151-650 1700 *Frequency:* 97.1 FM

Wire FM, Warrington Business Park, Long Lane, Warrington WA2 8TX T 01925-445545 *Frequency:* 107.2 FM

Wyvern FM, First Floor, Kirkham House, John Comyn Drive, Worcester WR3 7NS T 01905-545500 *Frequencies:* 96.7/97.6/102.8 FM

XFM Manchester, Laser House, Waterfront Quay, Salford Quays, Manchester M50 3XW T 0161-662 4701 *Frequency:* 97.7 FM and DAB

XFM UK, 30 Leicester Square, London WC2H 7LA T 020-7054 8000 *Frequency:* 104.9 FM and DAB

Yorkshire Coast Radio (Bridlington), Unit 2B, Newchase Business Centre, Hopper Hill Road, Scarborough, N.Yorks YO11 3YS T 01723-581700 *Frequency:* 102.4 FM

Yorkshire Coast Radio (Scarborough), Unit 2B, Newchase Business Centre, Hopper Hill Road, Scarborough, N. Yorks YO11 3YS T 01723-581700 *Frequencies:* 96.2/103.1 FM

Yorkshire Radio, PO Box 197, Elland Road, Leeds LS11 1AZ T 0113-367 6117 *Frequency:* digital

Zee Radio, 4 Ingate Place, Battersea, SW8 4NS T 020-7501 1524 *Frequencies:* 558 AM and DAB

WALES

96.4 FM The Wave, PO Box 964, Victoria Road, Gowerton, Swansea SA4 3AB T 01792-511964 *Frequency:* 96.4 FM and DAB

97.1 Radio Carmarthenshire, PO Box 971, Llanelli, Carmarthenshire SA15 1YH T 0845-355 0570 *Frequencies:* 97.1/97.5 FM

97.5 Scarlet FM, PO Box 971, Llanelli, Carmarthenshire SA15 1YH T 0845-890 7000 *Frequency:* 97.5 FM

102.5 Radio Pembrokeshire, Unit 14, The Old School Estate, Station Road, Narberth, Pembrokeshire SA67 7DU T 01834-869384 *Frequencies:* 102.5/107.5 FM

106.3 Bridge FM, PO Box 1063, Bridgend CF35 6WF T 0845-890 4000 *Frequency:* 106.3 FM

Afan FM, AquaDome, Hollywood Park, Princess Margaret Way, Port Talbot SA12 6QW T 0845-467 1079 *Frequency:* 107.9 FM

Champion FM 103, Llys-Y-Dderwen, Parc Menai, Bangor, Gwynedd LL55 4BN T 01248-673400 *Frequency:* 103.0 FM

Coast 96.3, PO Box 963, Bangor LL57 4ZR T 01248-673272 *Frequency:* 96.3 FM

Gold (North Wales and Cheshire), Mold Road, Gwersyllt, Wrexham LL11 4AF T 01978-752202 *Frequency:* 1260 AM and DAB

Gold (South Wales), Red Dragon Centre, Atlantic Wharf, Cardiff CF10 4DJ T 029-2066 2066 *Frequencies:* 1305/1359 AM and DAB

MFM Marcher Sound 103.4, The Studios, Mold Road, Gwersyllt, Wrexham LL11 4AF T 01978-752200 *Frequency:* 103.4 FM

Nation Radio Box 10, Wellfield Road, Cardiff CF24 3DG T 0845-025 1000 *Frequencies:* 106.8/107.3 FM and DAB

Radio Ceredigion, Yr Hen Ysgol Gymraeg, Aberystwyth, Ceredigion, SY23 1LF T 01970-627999 *Frequencies:* 96.6/97.4/103.3/FM

Radio Maldwyn, The Studios, The Park, Newtown, Powys SY16 2NZ T 01686-623555 *Frequency:* 756 AM

Real Radio (Wales), Unit 1, Ty-Nant Court, Ty-Nant Road, Morganstown, Cardiff CF15 8LW T 029-2031 5100 *Frequencies:* 105.2/105.4/105.7/105.9/106/106.2 FM and DAB

Red Dragon FM, Atlantic Wharf, Cardiff CF10 4DJ T 029-2066 2066 *Frequencies:* 97.4/103.2 FM and DAB

Swansea Bay Radio Newby House, Neath Abbey Industrial Estate, Neath SA10 7DR T 0845-8904000 *Frequency:* 102.1 FM

Swansea Sound, Victoria Road, Gowerton, Swansea SA4 3AB T 01792-511170 *Frequency:* 1170 AM and DAB

Valleys Radio, PO Box 1116, Ebbw Vale, Gwent NP23 8XW T 01495-301116 *Frequencies:* 999/1116 AM

SCOTLAND

Argyll FM, 27–29 Longrow, Campbelltown, Argyll PA28 8ER T 01586-551800 *Frequencies:* 106.5/107.1/107.7 FM

Central 103.1 FM, 201–203 High Street, Falkirk FK1 1DU T 01324-611164 *Frequency:* 103.1 FM

Clyde 1, Clydebank Business Park, Clydebank, Glasgow G81 2RX T 0141-565 2200 *Frequencies:* 97/102.5/103.3 FM and DAB

Clyde 2, Clydebank Business Park, Clydebank, Glasgow G81 2RX T 0141-565 2200 *Frequency:* 1152 AM and DAB

Cuillin FM, Stormyhill Road, Portree, Isle of Skye IV51 9DY T 01478-611234 *Frequency:* 106.2 FM

Forth One, Forth House, Forth Street, Edinburgh EH1 3LE T 0131-556 9255 *Frequencies:* 97.3/97.6/102.2 FM and DAB

Forth 2, Forth House, Forth Street, Edinburgh EH1 3LE T 0131-556 9255 *Frequency:* 1548 AM and DAB

Heartland FM, Atholl Curling Rink, Lower Oakfield, Pitlochry, Perthshire PH16 5HQ T 01796-474040 *Frequency:* 97.5 FM

Isles FM, PO Box 333, Stornoway, Isle of Lewis HS1 2PU T 01851-703333 *Frequency:* 103.0 FM

Kingdom FM, Haig House, Haig Business Park, Balgonie Road, Markinch, Fife KY7 6AQ T 01592-753753 *Frequencies:* 95.2/96.1/96.6/105.4/106.3 FM

Lanarkshire's L107, Media Corp House, 2 Caird Park, Hamilton, Lanarkshire ML3 0EU T 01698-303420 *Frequencies:* 107.5/107.9 FM

Lochbroom FM, Radio House, Mill Street, Ullapool, Ross-shire IV26 2UN T 01854-613131 *Frequencies:* 96.8/102.2 FM

Moray Firth Radio (MFR), Scorguie Place, Inverness IV3 8UJ T 01463-224433 *Frequencies:* 97.4 FM, 1107 AM and DAB

NECR, The Shed, School Road, Kintore, Iveruie, Aberdeenshire AB51 0US T 01467-632909 *Frequencies:* 97.1/101.9/102.1/102.6/103.2/106.4 FM

Nevis Radio, Ben Nevis Estate, Claggan, Fort William PH33 6PR T 01397-700007 *Frequencies:* 96.6/97.0/102.3/102.4 FM

Northsound 1, Abbotswell Road, West Tullos, Aberdeen AB12 3AJ T 01224-337000 *Frequencies:* 96.9/97.6/103.0 FM and DAB

Northsound 2, Abbotswell Road, West Tullos, Aberdeen AB12 3AJ T 01224-337000 *Frequency:* 1035 AM and DAB

Oban FM, 132 George Street, Oban, Argyll PA34 5NT T 01631-570057 *Frequency:* 103.3 FM

Original 106, Craigshaw Road, West Tullos, Aberdeen AB12 3AR T 01224-294860 *Frequency:* 106 FM

Radio Borders, Tweedside Park, Galashiels TD1 3TD T 01896-759444 *Frequencies:* 96.8/97.5/103.1/103.4 FM

Real Radio (Scotland), Parkway Court, Glasgow Business Park, Glasgow G69 6GA T 0141-781 1011 *Frequencies:* 100.3/101.1 FM and DAB

RNA FM, Rosemount Road, Arbroath, Angus DD11 2AT T 01241-879660 *Frequencies:* 100.3 /101.1 FM

Rock Radio, Unit 1130, Glasgow Business Park, Glasgow G69 6GA T 0141-4781 1010 *Frequency:* 96.3 FM and DAB

SIBC, Market Street, Lerwick, Shetland ZE1 0JN T 01595-695299 *Frequencies:* 96.2/102.2 FM

Smooth 105.2, Glasgow Business Park, Baillieston, Glasgow G69 6GA T 0141-781 1010 *Frequency:* 105.2 FM

South West Sound FM, Unit 40, The Loreburne Centre, High St, Dumfries DG1 4DA T 01387-250999 *Frequencies:* 96.5/97.0/103.0 FM

Talk 107, 9 South Gyle Crescent, Edinburgh EH12 9EB T 0131-316 3107 *Frequency:* 107.0 FM and DAB

Tay AM, 6 North Isla Street, Dundee DD3 7JQ T 01382-200800 *Frequencies:* 1161/1584 AM and DAB

Tay FM, 6 North Isla Street, Dundee DD3 7JQ T 01382-200800 *Frequencies:* 96.4/102.8 FM and DAB

Two Lochs Radio, Gairloch, Ross-shire IV21 2BQ T 0870-741 4657 *Frequencies:* 106.0/106.6 FM

UCA, University Campus Ayr, Beech Grove, Ayr, S. Ayrshire KA8 0SR T 01292-886385 *Frequency:* 87.7 FM and DAB

Wave 102, 8 South Tay Street, Dundee DD1 1PA T 01382-901000 *Frequency:* 102.0 FM and DAB

Waves Radio, 7 Blackhouse Circle, Blackhouse Industrial Estate, Peterhead, Aberdeenshire AB42 1BW T 01779-491012 *Frequency:* 101.2 FM and DAB

West FM, Radio House, 54A Holmston Road, Ayr KA7 3BE T 01292-283662 *Frequencies:* 96.7/97.5 FM and DAB

West Sound AM, Radio House, 54A Holmston Road, Ayr KA7 3BE T 01292-283662 *Frequency:* 1035 AM and DAB

XFM Scotland, Four Winds Pavilion, Pacific Quay, Glasgow G51 1EB T 0141-566 6106 *Frequencies:* 105.7/106.1 FM and DAB

Yourradio, Pioneer Park Studios, Unit 3, 80 Castlegreen Street, Dumbarton G82 1JB T 01389-734444 *Frequencies:* 103.0 FM (Dumbarton), 106.9 FM (Helensburgh)

NORTHERN IRELAND

Citybeat 96.7 FM, 2nd Floor, Arena Building, 85 Ormeau Road, Belfast, Antrim BT7 1SH T 028-9023 4967 *Frequency:* 96.7 FM and DAB

Cool FM, PO Box 974, Belfast BT1 1RT T 028-9181 7181 *Frequency:* 97.4 FM and DAB

Downtown Radio, Newtownards, Co. Down BT23 4ES T 028-9181 5555 *Frequencies:* 96.4 FM (Limavady); 96.6 FM (Enniskillen); 97.1 FM (Larne); 102.3 FM (Ballymena); 102.4 FM (Londonderry) and DAB

Q97.2 FM, 24 Cloyfin Road, Coleraine, Co. Londonderry BT52 2NU T 028-7035 9100 *Frequency:* 97.2 FM

Q101.2 West FM, 42A Market Street, Omagh, Co. Tyrone BT78 1EH T 028-8224 5777 *Frequency:* 101.2 FM

Q102.9 FM, The Riverview Suite, 87 Rossdowney Road, Waterside, Londonderry BT47 5SU T 028-7134 4449/346666 *Frequency:* 102.9 FM

Seven FM, 1 Millenium Park, Woodside Industrial Estate, Woodside Road, Ballymena, Co Antrim BT42 4QJ T 028-2564 8777 *Frequency:* 107.0 FM

Six FM, 2C Park Avenue, Cookstown, Co. Tyrone BT80 5AH T 028-8675 8696 *Frequencies:* 106.0/107.2 FM

U105, Ulster Television plc, Unit 105, Havelock House Ormeau Road, Belfast BT7 1EB T 028 9033 2105 *Frequency:* 105.8 FM

CHANNEL ISLANDS

Channel 103 FM, 6 Tunnell Street, St Helier, Jersey JE2 4LU T 01534-888103 *Frequency:* 103.7 FM

Island FM, 12 Westerbrook, St Sampsons, Guernsey GY2 4QQ T 01481-242000 *Frequencies:* 93.7/104.7 FM

THE PRESS

The newspaper and periodical press in the UK is large and diverse, catering for a wide variety of views and interests. There is no state control or censorship of the press; however, it is subject to the laws on publication, and the Press Complaints Commission (PCC) was set up by the industry as a means of self-regulation.

The press is not state-subsidised and receives few tax concessions. The income of most newspapers and periodicals is derived largely from sales and from advertising; the press is the largest advertising medium in Britain.

SELF-REGULATION

The PCC was founded by the newspaper and magazine industry in January 1991 to replace the Press Council (established in 1953). It is a voluntary, non-statutory body set up to operate the press' self-regulation system following the Calcutt report in 1990 on privacy and related matters, when the industry feared that failure to regulate itself might lead to statutory regulation of the press. The performance of the PCC was reviewed after 18 months of operation (the *Calcutt Review of Press Self-Regulation,* presented to parliament in January 1993) to determine whether statutory measures were required. No proposals for replacing the self-regulation system have been made to date. The commission is funded by the industry through the Press Standards Board of Finance.

COMPLAINTS

The PCC's aims are to consider, adjudicate, conciliate, and resolve complaints of unfair treatment by the press; and to ensure that the press maintains the highest professional standards and shows respect for generally recognised freedoms, including freedom of expression, the public's right to know, and the right of the press to operate free from improper pressure. The commission judges newspaper and magazine conduct by a code of practice drafted by editors, agreed by the industry and ratified by the commission.

The PCC has three classes of members: the chairman, public members and press members. Although a number of the commision's members are newspaper or magazine editors, the majority of the 17 members have no connection with the press in order to ensure that the PCC maintains independence from the newspaper industry. The PCC received a total of 4,340 complaints in 2007, rising by 70 per cent since 1996.

PRESS COMPLAINTS COMMISSION
Halton House, 20–23 Holborn, London EC1N 2JD
T 020-7831 0022 F 020-7831 0025
E complaints@pcc.org.uk
W www.pcc.org.uk
Chair, Sir Christopher Meyer, KCMG

NEWSPAPERS

Newspapers are mostly financially independent of any political party, though most adopt a political stance in their editorial comments, usually reflecting proprietorial influence. Ownership of the national and regional daily newspapers is concentrated in the hands of large corporations whose interests cover publishing and communications, although *The Guardian* and *The Observer* are owned by the *Scott Trust,* formed in 1936 to protect the financial and editorial independence of *The Guardian* in perpetuity. The rules on cross-media ownership, as amended by the Broadcasting Act 1996, which limited the extent to which newspaper organisations may become involved in broadcasting, have been relaxed by the Communications Act 2003: newspapers with over 20 per cent share of national circulation may own national and/or local radio licences.

There are around 15 daily and 15 Sunday national papers and several hundred local papers that are published daily, weekly or twice-weekly. Scotland, Wales and Northern Ireland all have at least one daily and one Sunday national paper.

UK CIRCULATION

National Daily Newspapers	*June 2007*	*June 2008*
The Sun	2,852,952	2,884,987
Daily Mail	2,123,008	2,042,453
Daily Mirror	1,433,954	1,340,535
The Daily Telegraph	841,555	813,346
Daily Express	720,386	694,260
Daily Star	666,343	606,331
The Times	597,899	576,444
Daily Record	389,152	374,595
The Guardian	314,519	302,636
The Independent	188,986	176,785
Financial Times	136,697	131,807
The Herald	69,218	63,949
The Scotsman	56,979	51,361

National Sunday Newspapers	*June 2007*	*June 2008*
News of the World	3,021,301	2,908,392
The Mail on Sunday	2,033,504	1,947,444
Sunday Mirror	1,312,198	1,243,042
The Sunday Times	1,008,168	983,767
Sunday Express	668,997	625,193
The People	669,056	580,948
The Sunday Telegraph	620,255	598,493
Sunday Mail	486,534	459,465
Sunday Post	411,317	383,122
The Observer	401,959	386,140
Daily Star Sunday	320,383	304,927
The Independent on Sunday	204,138	162,832
Sunday Sport	97,281	78,576
Scotland on Sunday	72,815	66,918
Sunday Herald	53,964	45,450

Source: Audit Bureau of Circulations Ltd.

Newspapers are usually published in either broadsheet or smaller, tabloid format. The 'quality' daily papers, ie those providing detailed coverage of a wide range of public matters, have traditionally used a broadsheet format, while the tabloid papers typically take a more populist approach and are more illustrated. In 2004 this correlation between format and content was abandoned when three traditionally broadsheet newspapers, *The Times, The Independent* and *The Scotsman,* switched to tabloid-sized editions, while *The Guardian* launched a new 'Berliner' format in September 2005. In October 2005 *The Independent on Sunday* became the first Sunday broadsheet to be published in the tabloid (or 'compact') size, and *The Observer,* like its daily counterpart *The Guardian,* began publishing in the Berliner format in January 2006.

NATIONAL DAILY NEWSPAPERS

DAILY EXPRESS
Northern & Shell Building, 10 Lower Thames Street, London EC4R 6EN **T** 0871-434 1010 **W** www.express.co.uk
Editor, Peter Hill

DAILY MAIL
Northcliffe House, 2 Derry Street, London W8 5TT
T 020-7938 6000 **W** www.dailymail.co.uk
Editor, Paul Dacre

DAILY MIRROR
1 Canada Square, Canary Wharf, London E14 5AP
T 020-7293 3000 **W** www.mirror.co.uk
Editor, Richard Wallace

DAILY RECORD
1 Central Quay, Glasgow G3 8DA **T** 0141-309 3000
W www.record-mail.co.uk/rm
Editor, Bruce Waddell

DAILY SPORT
19 Great Ancoats Street, Manchester M60 4BT
T 0161-236 4466 **W** www.dailysport.co.uk
Editor, Michael McLiheney

DAILY STAR
Express Newspapers, Northern & Shell Building, 10 Lower Thames Street, London EC3R 6EN **T** 0871-434 1010
W www.dailystar.co.uk
Editor, Dawn Neesom

THE DAILY TELEGRAPH
111 Buckingham Palace Road, London SW1W 0DT
T 020-7931 2000 **W** www.telegraph.co.uk
Editor, William Lewis

FINANCIAL TIMES
1 Southwark Bridge, London SE1 9HL **T** 020-7873 3000
W www.ft.com
Editor, Lionel Barber

THE GUARDIAN
119 Farringdon Road, London EC1R 3ER **T** 020-7278 2332
W www.guardian.co.uk
Editor, Alan Rusbridger

THE HERALD
Herald & Times Group, 200 Renfield Street, Glasgow G2 3QB
T 0141-302 7000 **W** www.theherald.co.uk
Editor, Charles McGhee

THE INDEPENDENT
Independent House, 191 Marsh Wall, London E14 9RS
T 020-7005 2000 **W** www.independent.co.uk
Editor, Simon Kelner

MORNING STAR
People's Press Printing Society Ltd, William Rust House, 52 Beachy Road, London E3 2NS **T** 020-8510 0815
W www.morningstaronline.co.uk
Editor, John Haylett

THE SCOTSMAN
Barclay House, 108 Holyrood Road, Edinburgh EH8 8AS
T 0131-620 8620 **W** www.scotsman.com
Editor, Mike Gilson

THE SUN
News Group Newspapers Ltd, 1 Virginia Street, London E1 9XP **T** 020-7782 4000 **W** www.the-sun.co.uk
Editor, Rebekah Wade

THE TIMES
1 Pennington Street, London E98 1TT **T** 020-7782 5000
W www.timesonline.co.uk
Editor, James Harding

WEEKLY NEWSPAPERS

DAILY STAR SUNDAY
Express Newspapers, The Northern and Shell Building, 10 Lower Thames Street, London EC3R 6EN **T** 0871-434 1010
W www.dailystarsunday.co.uk
Editor, Gareth Morgan

INDEPENDENT ON SUNDAY
Independent House, 191 Marsh Wall, London E14 9RS
T 020-7005 2000 **W** www.independent.co.uk
Editor, John Mullin, *Editor-at-Large,* Janet Street-Porter

THE MAIL ON SUNDAY
Northcliffe House, 2 Derry Street, London W8 5TS
T 020-7938 6000 **W** www.mailonsunday.co.uk
Editor, Peter Wright

NEWS OF THE WORLD
1 Virginia Street, London E98 1NW **T** 020-7782 4000
W www.newsoftheworld.co.uk
Editor, Colin Myler

THE OBSERVER
3–7 Herbal Hill, London EC1R 5EJ **T** 020-7278 2332
W www.observer.co.uk
Editor, John Mulholland

THE PEOPLE
1 Canada Square, Canary Wharf, London E14 5AP
T 020-7293 3000 **W** www.people.co.uk
Editor, Lloyd Embley

SCOTLAND ON SUNDAY
108 Holyrood Road, Edinburgh EH8 8AS **T** 0131-620 8620
W www.scotlandonsunday.co.uk
Editor, Les Snowdon

SUNDAY EXPRESS
The Nothern & Shell Building, 10 Lower Thames Street, London EC3R 6EN **T** 08714-341010 **W** www.express.co.uk
Editor, Martin Townsend

SUNDAY HERALD
200 Renfield Street, Glasgow G2 3QB **T** 0141-302 7800
W www.sundayherald.com
Editor, Richard Walker

SUNDAY MAIL
1 Central Quay, Glasgow G3 8DA **T** 0141-309 3000
W www.sundaymail.co.uk
Editor, Alan Rennie

SUNDAY MIRROR
One Canada Square, Canary Wharf, London E14 5AP
T 020-7293 3000 **W** www.sundaymirror.co.uk
Editor, Tina Weaver

THE SUNDAY POST
144 Port Dundas Road, Glasgow G4 0HZ **T** 0141-332 9933
W www.sundaypost.com
Editor, David Pollington

THE SUNDAY TELEGRAPH
111 Buckingham Palace Road, London SW1W 0DT
T 020-7931 2000 **W** www.telegraph.co.uk
Editor, Ian MacGregor

THE SUNDAY TIMES
1 Pennington Street, London E98 1ST **T** 020-7782 5000
W www.timesonline.co.uk
Editor, John Witherow

WALES ON SUNDAY
Thomson House, Havelock Street, Cardiff CF10 1XR
T 029-2058 3583 **W** www.icwales.co.uk
Editor, Tim Gordon

REGIONAL DAILY NEWSPAPERS

EAST ANGLIA

CAMBRIDGE EVENING NEWS
Winship Road, Milton, Cambs. CB24 6PP **T** 01223-434437
W www.cambridge-news.co.uk
Editor, Murray Morse

EAST ANGLIAN DAILY TIMES
30 Lower Brook Street, Ipswich, Suffolk IP4 1AN
T 01473-230023 **W** www.eadt.co.uk
Editor, Terry Hunt

EASTERN DAILY PRESS
Prospect House, Rouen Road, Norwich NR1 1RE
T 01603-628311 **W** www.edp24.co.uk
Editor, Peter Franzen, OBE

EVENING STAR
Archant Regional, Press House, 30 Lower Brook Street, Ipswich, Suffolk IP4 1AN **T** 01473-230023
W www.eveningstar.co.uk
Editor, Jess Gallagher

EVENING TELEGRAPH
Telegraph House, 57 Priesgate, Peterborough PE1 1JW
T 01733-555111 **W** www.peterboroughtoday.co.uk
Editor, Rebecca Stephens

NORWICH EVENING NEWS
Prospect House, Rouen Road, Norwich NR1 1RE
T 01603-628311 **W** www.eveningnews24.co.uk
Editor, James Foster

EAST MIDLANDS

BURTON MAIL
65–68 High Street, Burton on Trent DE14 1LE
T 01283-512345 **W** www.burtonmail.co.uk
Editor, Paul Hazeldine

EVENING TELEGRAPH
Northcliffe House, Meadow Road, Derby DE1 2BH
T 01332-291111 **W** www.thisisderbyshire.co.uk
Editor, Steve Hall

THE LEICESTER MERCURY
St George Street, Leicester LE1 9FQ **T** 0116-251 2512
W www.thisisleicestershire.co.uk
Editor, Nick Carter

LINCOLNSHIRE DAILY ECHO
Brayford Wharf East, Lincoln, LN5 7AT **T** 01522-820000
W www.thisislincolnshire.co.uk
Editor, Jon Grubb

NORTHAMPTON CHRONICLE & ECHO
Upper Mounts, Northampton NN1 3HR **T** 01604-467000
Editor, David Summers

NOTTINGHAM EVENING POST
Castle Wharf House, Nottingham NG1 7EU
T 0115-948 2000 **W** www.thisisnottingham.co.uk
Editor, Malcolm Pheby

LONDON

EVENING STANDARD
Northcliffe House, 2 Derry Street, London W8 5TT
T 020-7938 6000 **W** www.thisislondon.com
Editor, Veronica Wadley

LONDON LITE
Northcliffe House, 2 Derry Street, London W8 5TT
T 020-7938 6000 **W** www.thelondonlite.co.uk
Editor, Martin Clarke

THE LONDON PAPER
1 Pennington Street, London E98 1BD
T 020-7782 5000 **W** www.thelondonpaper.com
Editor, Stefano Hatfield

METRO
Northcliffe House, 2 Derry Street, London W8 5TT
T 020-7651 5200 **W** www.metro.co.uk
Editor, Kenny Campbell

NORTH EAST

EVENING CHRONICLE
Groat Market, Newcastle upon Tyne NE1 1ED
T 0191-232 7500 **W** www.chroniclelive.co.uk
Editor, Paul Robertson

EVENING GAZETTE
Borough Road, 105–111 Middlesbrough TS1 3AZ
T 01642-245401 **W** www.gazettelive.co.uk
Editor, Sue Giles

HARTLEPOOL MAIL
Northeast Press Ltd, New Clarence House, Wesley Square, Hartlepool TS24 8BX **T** 01429-239333
W www.hartlepoolmail.co.uk, www.peterleemail.co.uk
Editor, Joy Yates

THE JOURNAL
Groat Market, Newcastle upon Tyne NE1 1ED
T 0191-232 7500 **W** www.icnewcastle.co.uk
Editor, Brian Aitken

THE NORTHERN ECHO
Priestgate, Darlington, Co. Durham DL1 1NF
T 01325-381313 **W** www.thenorthernecho.co.uk
Editor, Peter Barron

THE SHIELDS GAZETTE
Chapter Row, South Shields, Tyne & Wear NE33 1BL
T 0191-427 4800 **W** www.shieldsgazette.com
Editor, John Szymanski

SUNDERLAND ECHO
Echo House, Pennywell, Sunderland, Tyne & Wear SR4 9ER
T 0191-501 5800 **W** www.sunderlandecho.com
Editor, Rob Lawson

NORTH WEST

THE BLACKPOOL GAZETTE
Avroe House, Avroe Crescent, Blackpool Business Park, Squires Gate, Blackpool FY4 2DP **T** 01253-400888
W www.blackpoolgazette.co.uk
Editor, David Helliwell

THE BOLTON NEWS
Newspaper House, Churchgate, Bolton, Lancs. BL1 1DE
T 01204- 522345 **W** www.theboltonnews.co.uk
Editor-in-Chief, Ian Savage

LANCASHIRE EVENING POST
Oliver's Place, Preston PR2 9ZA **T** 01772-254841
W www.lep.co.uk
Editor, Simon Reynolds

LANCASHIRE TELEGRAPH
Newspaper House, High Street, Blackburn, Lancs. BB1 1HT
T 01254-678678 **W** www.thisislancashire.co.uk
Editor, Kevin Young

LIVERPOOL DAILY POST
PO Box 48, Old Hall Street, Liverpool L69 3EB
T 0151-227 2000 **W** www.liverpooldailypost.co.uk
Editor, Mark Thomas

LIVERPOOL ECHO
PO Box 48, Old Hall Street, Liverpool L69 3EB
T 0151-227 2000 **W** www.liverpoolecho.co.uk
Editor, Alastair Machray

MANCHESTER EVENING NEWS
1 Scott Place, Manchester M3 3RN **T** 0161-832 7200
W www.manchestereveningnews.co.uk
Editor, Paul Horrocks

NEWS AND STAR
CN Group, Newspaper House, Dalston Road, Carlisle CA2 5UA T 01228-612600 W www.news-and-star.co.uk
Editor, Neil Hodgkinson

NORTH-WEST EVENING MAIL
Newspaper House, Abbey Road, Barrow-in-Furness, Cumbria LA14 5QS T 01229-840150 W www.nwemail.co.uk
Editor, Jonathan Lee

OLDHAM EVENING CHRONICLE
PO Box 47, Union Street, Oldham, Lanashire OL1 1EQ T 0161-633 2121 W www.oldham-chronicle.co.uk
Editor, Jim Williams

SOUTH

THE ARGUS
Argus House, Crowhurst Road, Hollingbury, Brighton BN1 8AR T 01273-544544 W www.theargus.co.uk
Editor, Michael Beard

ECHO
Newspaper House, Chester Hall Lane, Basildon, Essex SS14 3BL T 01268-522792 W www.echo-news.co.uk
Editor, Martin McNeill

MEDWAY MESSENGER
Medway House, Ginsbury Close, Sir Thomas Longley Road, Medway City Estate, Strood, Kent ME2 2DU T 01634-227800 W www.medwaymessenger.co.uk
Editor, David Jones

THE NEWS, PORTSMOUTH
The News Centre, Hilsea, Portsmouth PO2 9SX T 023-9266 4488 W www.thenews.co.uk
Editor, Mark Waldron

OXFORD MAIL
Newspaper House, Osney Mead, Oxford OX2 0EJ T 01865-425262 W www.oxfordmail.net
Editor, Simon O'Neill

READING EVENING POST
8 Tessa Road, Reading, Berks. RG1 8NS T 0118-918 3000 W www.getreading.co.uk
Editor, Andy Murrill

SOUTHERN DAILY ECHO
Newspaper House, Test Lane, Redbridge, Southampton SO16 9JX T 023-8042 4777 W www.dailyecho.co.uk
Editor, Ian Murray

SWINDON ADVERTISER
100 Victoria Road, Old Town, Swindon SN1 3BE T 01793-528144 W www.swindonadvertiser.co.uk
Editor, David King

SOUTH WEST

THE CITIZEN
1 Clarence Parade, Cheltenham GL50 3NY T 01242-271900 W www.nng.co.uk
Editor, Ian Mean

DAILY ECHO
Richmond Hill, Bournemouth BH2 6HH T 01202-554601 W www.bournemouthecho.co.uk
Editor, Neal Butterworth

DORSET ECHO
Fleet House, Hampshire Road, Weymouth, Dorset DT4 9XD T 01305-830930 W www.dorsetecho.co.uk
Editor, David Murdock

EVENING POST
Temple Way, Bristol BS99 7HD T 0117-934 3000 W www.thisisbristol.co.uk
Editor, Mike Norton

EXPRESS & ECHO
Heron Road, Sowton, Exeter EX2 7NF T 01392-442211 W www.thisisexeter.co.uk
Editor, Marc Astley

GLOUCESTERSHIRE ECHO
1 Clarence Parade, Cheltenham, Glos. GL50 3NY T 01242-271900 W www.thisisgloucestershire.co.uk
Editor, Anita Syvret

THE HERALD
17 Brest Road, Derriford Business Park, Plymouth PL6 5AA T 01752-765500 W www.thisisplymouth.co.uk
Editor, Bill Martin

HERALD EXPRESS
Harmsworth House, Barton Hill Road, Torquay, Devon TQ2 8JN T 01803-676000 W www.thisissouthdevon.co.uk
Editor, Andy Phelan

WESTERN DAILY PRESS
Temple Way, Bristol BS99 7HD T 0117-934 3000 W www.westerndailypress.co.uk
Editor, Andy Wright

WESTERN MORNING NEWS
17 Brest Road, Derriford, Plymouth PL6 5AA T 01752-765500 W www.westernmorningnews.co.uk
Editor, Alan Qualtrough

WEST MIDLANDS

BIRMINGHAM MAIL
PO Box 78, Weaman Street, Birmingham B4 6AY T 0121-236 3366 W www.birminghammail.net
Editor, Steve Dyson

THE BIRMINGHAM POST
PO Box 78, Weaman Street, Birmingham B4 6AT T 0121-236 3366 W www.birminghampost.net
Editor, Mark Reeves

COVENTRY TELEGRAPH
Corporation Street, Coventry CV1 1FP T 024-7663 3633 W www.iccoventry.co.uk
Editor, Alan Kirby

EXPRESS & STAR
Queen Street, Wolverhampton WV1 1ES T 01902-313131 W www.expressandstar.com
Editor, Adrian Faber

THE SENTINEL
Sentinel House, Etruria, Stoke-on-Trent ST1 5SS T 01782-602525 W www.thisisthesentinel.co.uk
Editor, Michael Sassi

SHROPSHIRE STAR
Waterloo Road, Ketley, Telford TF1 5HU T 01952-242424 W www.shropshirestar.com
Editor, Sarah Jane Smith

WORCESTER NEWS
Berrows House, Hylton Road, Worcester WR2 5JX T 01905-742244 W www.worcesternews.co.uk
Editor, Kevin Ward

YORKSHIRE AND HUMBERSIDE

EVENING COURIER
PO Box 19, King Cross Street, Halifax HX1 2SF T 01422-260200 W www.halifaxcourier.co.uk
Editor, John Furbisher

GRIMSBY TELEGRAPH
80 Cleethorpe Road, Grimsby, North East Lincolnshire DN31 3EH T 01472-360360 W www.thisisgrimsby.co.uk
Editor, Michelle Lalor

THE HUDDERSFIELD DAILY EXAMINER
Trinity Mirror Huddersfield Ltd, PO Box A26, Queen Street South, Huddersfield HD1 2TD T 01484-430000 W www.examiner.co.uk
Editor, Roy Wright

HULL DAILY MAIL
Blundell's Corner, Beverley Road, Hull HU3 1XS T 01482-327111 W www.thisishullandeastriding.co.uk
Editor, John Meehan

LINCOLNSHIRE ECHO
Brayford Wharf East, Lincoln LN5 7AT **T** 01522-820000
W www.thisislincolnshire.co.uk
Editor, Jon Grubb

THE PRESS
PO Box 29, 76–86 Walmgate, York YO1 9YN
T 01904-653051 **W** www.yorkpress.co.uk
Editor, Kevin Booth

SCARBOROUGH EVENING NEWS
17–23 Aberdeen Walk, Scarborough, North Yorkshire
YO11 1BB **T** 01723-363636
W www.scarborougheveningnews.co.uk
Editor, Ed Asquith

THE STAR
York Street, Sheffield S1 1PU **T** 0114-276 7676
W www.thestar.co.uk
Editor, Alan Powell

TELEGRAPH & ARGUS
Hall Ings, Bradford BD1 1JR **T** 01274-729511
W www.thetelegraphandargus.co.uk
Editor, Perry Austin-Clarke

YORKSHIRE EVENING POST
PO Box 168, Wellington Street, Leeds LS1 1RF
T 0113-2432701 **W** www.ypn.co.uk
Editor, Paul Napier

YORKSHIRE POST
Wellington Street, Leeds LS1 1RF **T** 0113-243 2701
W www.yorkshirepost.co.uk
Editor, Peter Charlton

SCOTLAND

THE COURIER
D.C. Thomson & Co. Ltd, 80 Kingsway East, Dundee DD4 8SL
T 01382-223131 **W** www.thecourier.co.uk
Editor, Bill Hutcheon

DUNDEE EVENING TELEGRAPH AND POST
80 Kingsway East, Dundee DD4 8SL **T** 01382-223131
W www.eveningtelegraph.co.uk
Editor, Gordon Wishart

EVENING EXPRESS
Aberdeen Journals Ltd, PO Box 43, Lang Stracht, Mastrick,
Aberdeen AB15 6DF **T** 01224-690222
W www.thisisaberdeen.co.uk
Editor, Damian Bates

EVENING NEWS
108 Holyrood Road, Edinburgh EH8 8AS **T** 0131-620 8620
W www.edinburghnews.com
Editor, John McLellan

GLASGOW EVENING TIMES
200 Renfield Street, Glasgow G2 3QB **T** 0141-302 7000
W www.eveningtimes.co.uk
Editor, Donald Martin

INVERNESS COURIER
New Century House, Stadium Road, Inverness IV1 1FF
T 01463-732222 **W** www.inverness-courier.co.uk
Editor, Robert Taylor

PAISLEY DAILY EXPRESS
Scottish and Universal Newspapers Ltd, 14 New Street,
Paisley, Renfrewshire PA1 1YA **T** 0141-887 7911
W www.insidescotland.co.uk
Editor, Anne Dalrymple

THE PRESS AND JOURNAL
Lang Stracht, Aberdeen AB15 6DF **T** 01224-690222
W www.pressandjournal.co.uk
Editor, Derek Tucker

WALES

EVENING LEADER
NWN Media Ltd, Mold Business Park, Wrexham Road, Mold,
Flintshire CH7 1XY **T** 01352-707707
W www.eveningleader.co.uk
Editor, Barrie Jones

SOUTH WALES ARGUS
Cardiff Road, Maesglas, Newport, Gwent NP20 3QN
T 01633-777219 **W** www.southwalesargus.co.uk
Editor, Gerry Keighley

SOUTH WALES ECHO
Thomson House, Havelock Street, Cardiff CF10 1XR
T 029-2058 3622 **W** www.icwales.co.uk
Editor, Mike Hill

SOUTH WALES EVENING POST
PO Box 14, Adelaide Street, Swansea SA1 1QT
T 01792-510000 **W** www.thisissouthwales.co.uk
Editor, Spencer Feeney

WESTERN MAIL
Thomson House, Havelock Street, Cardiff CF10 1XR
T 029-2058 3583 **W** www.icwales.co.uk
Editor, Alan Edmunds

NORTHERN IRELAND

BELFAST TELEGRAPH
124–144 Royal Avenue, Belfast BT1 1EB **T** 028-9026 4000
W www.belfasttelegraph.co.uk
Editor, Martin Lindsay

IRISH NEWS
113–117 Donegall Street, Belfast BT1 2GE **T** 028-9032 2226
W www.irishnews.com
Editor, Noel Doran

NEWS LETTER
2 Esky Drive, Portadown, Craigaron, Belfast BT63 5WD
T 028-3839 3939 **W** www.newsletter.co.uk
Editor, Darwin Templeton

CHANNEL ISLANDS

GUERNSEY PRESS AND STAR
PO Box 57, Braye Road, Vale, Guernsey GY1 3BW
T 01481-240240 **W** www.guernseypress.com
Editor, Richard Digard

JERSEY EVENING POST
PO Box 582, Five Oaks, St Saviour, Jersey JE4 8XQ
T 01534-611611 **W** www.thisisjersey.com
Editor, Chris Bright

PERIODICALS

ACCOUNTANCY AGE
VNU Business Publications, VNU House, 32–34 Broadwick
Street, London W1A 2HG **T** 020-7316 9236
W www.accountancyage.com
Editor, Gavin Hinks

AESTHETICA MAGAZINE
PO Box 371, York YO23 1WL **T** 01904-527560
W www.aestheticamagazine.com
Editor, Cherie Federico

AFRICA CONFIDENTIAL
Asempa Ltd, 73 Farringdon Road, London EC1M 3JQ
T 020-7831 3511 **W** www.africa-confidential.com
Editor, Patrick Smith

AMBIT
17 Priory Gardens, London N6 5QY **T** 020-8340 3566
W www.ambitmagazine.co.uk
Editor, Martin Bax

THE ARCHITECTURAL REVIEW
EMAP Construct, Greater London House, Hampstead Road, London NW1 7EJ **T** 020-7728 4591 **W** www.arplus.com
Editor, Paul Finch

ARCHITECTURE TODAY
161 Rosebery Avenue, London EC1R 4QX **T** 020-7837 0143 **W** www.architecturetoday.co.uk
Editor, Ian Latham

ARENA
Mappin House, 4 Winsley Street, London W1W 8HF **T** 020-7182 8000 **W** www.arenamagazine.co.uk
Editor, Giles Hattersley

ART REVIEW
1 Sekforde Street, 23–24 Smithfield Street, London EC1R 0BE **T** 020-7107 2760 **W** www.artreview.com
Editor, Mark Rappolt

ATTITUDE
Ground Floor, 211 Old Street, London EC1V 9NR **T** 020-7608 6500 **W** www.attitude.co.uk
Editor, Adam Mattera

THE BEANO
D.C. Thomson & Co. Ltd, Albert Square, Dundee DD1 9QJ **T** 01382-223131 **W** www.beanotown.com
Editor, Alan Digby

THE BIG ISSUE
1–5 Wandsworth Road, London SW8 2LN **T** 020-7526 3200 **W** www.bigissue.com
Editor, John Bird

BIRDWATCH
The Chocolate Factory, 5 Clarendon Road, London N22 6XJ **T** 020-8881 0550 **W** www.birdwatch.co.uk
Editor, Dominic Mitchell

BIZARRE
30 Cleveland Street, London W1T 4JD **T** 020-7907 6000 **W** www.bizarremag.com
Editor, David McComb

THE BOOKSELLER
5th Floor, Endeavour House, 189 Shaftesbury Avenue, London WC2H 8TJ **T** 020-7420 6006 **W** www.thebookseller.com
Editor, Neill Denny

BRITISH CHESS MAGAZINE
44 Baker Street, London W1U 7RT **T** 020-7486 8222 **W** www.bcmchess.co.uk
Editor, John Saunders

BRITISH DEAF NEWS
c/o AG Associates, 16 Hurstway, Fulwood, Preston, Lancs PR2 9TT **T** 02476-550936 (text) **W** www.bda.org.uk
Editor, Alison Gudgeon

THE BRITISH JOURNAL OF PHOTOGRAPHY
32–34 Broadwick Street, London W1A 2HG **T** 020-7316 9000 **W** www.bjp-online.com
Editor, Simon Bainbridge

BRITISH JOURNALISM REVIEW
Sage Publications, 1 Oliver's Yard, 55 City Road, London EC1Y 1SP **T** 020-7324 8500 **W** www.bjr.org.uk
Editor, Bill Hagerty

BRITISH MEDICAL JOURNAL
BMJ Publishing Group, BMA House, Tavistock Square, London WC1H 9JR **T** 020-7387 4499 **W** www.bmj.com
Editor, Dr Fiona Godlee

THE BUSINESS
22 Old Queen Street, London SW1H 9HP **T** 020-7961 0200 **W** www.thebusiness.co.uk
Editor, Martin Vander Weyer

CLASSIC CARS
Media House, Lynchwood, Peterborough Business Park, Peterborough PE2 6EA **T** 01733-468582 **W** www.classiccarsmagazine.co.uk
Editor, Phil Bell

CLASSICAL MUSIC
Rhinegold Publishing Ltd, 241 Shaftesbury Avenue, London WC2H 8TF **T** 020-7333 1742 **W** www.rhinegold.co.uk
Editor, Keith Clarke

CLASSICS MONTHLY
30 Monmouth Street, Bath BA1 2BW **T** 01225-442244
Editor, Gary Stretton

CLIMB MAGAZINE
PO Box 21, Buxton, Derbyshire SK17 9BR **T** 01298-72801 **W** www.climbmagazine.com
Editor, Neil Pearsons

COIN NEWS
Orchard House, Duchy Road, Heathpark, Honiton, Devon EX14 1YD **T** 01404-46972 **W** www.tokenpublishing.com
Editor, John W. Mussell

COMPANY
72 Broadwick Street, London W1V 2BP **T** 020-7439 5000 **W** www.company.co.uk
Editor, Victoria White

CONDÉ NAST TRAVELLER
Hanover Square, London W1S 1JU **T** 020-7499 9080 **W** www.cntraveller.com
Editor, Sarah Miller

CONTEMPORARY REVIEW
PO Box 1242, Oxford OX1 4FJ **T** 01865-201529
Editor, Dr Richard Mullen

COSMOPOLITAN
72 Broadwick Street, London W1F 9EP **T** 020-7439 5000
Editor, Louise Court

COUNTRY LIFE
The Blue Fin Building, 110 Southwark Street, London SE1 0SU **T** 020-3148 5000 **W** www.countrylife.co.uk
Editor, Mark Hedges

COUNTRY LIVING
National Magazine House, 72 Broadwick Street, London W1F 9EP **T** 020-7439 5000 **W** www.countryliving.co.uk
Editor, Susy Smith

CYCLING WEEKLY
Leon House, 233 High Street, Croydon CR9 1HZ **T** 020-8726 8463 **W** www.cyclingweekly.co.uk
Editor, Robert Garbutt

DANCING TIMES
45–47 Clerkenwell Green, London EC1R 0EB **T** 020-7250 3006 **W** www.dancing-times.co.uk
Editor, Mary Clarke

DARTS WORLD
World Magazines Ltd, 81 Selwood Road, Croydon CR0 7JW **T** 020-8650 6580 **W** www.dartsworld.com
Editor, Tony Wood

DISABILITY NOW
6 Market Road, London N7 9PW **T** 020-7619 7323 **W** www.disabilitynow.org.uk
Editor, Ian Macrae

EASTERN EYE
Ethnic Media Group, Unit 2, 65 Whitechapel Road, London E1 1DU **T** 020-7650 2000 **W** www.easterneyeonline.co.uk
Editor, Hamant Verma

THE ECOLOGIST
Unit 102, Lana House Studios, 116–118 Commercial Street, London E1 6NF **T** 020-7422 8100 **W** www.theecologist.org
Editor, Pat Thomas

THE ECONOMIST
25 St James's Street, London SW1A 1HG **T** 020-7830 7000 **W** www.economist.com
Editor, John Micklethwait

ELLE
64 North Row, London W1K 7LL **T** 020-7150 7000 **W** www.elleuk.com
Editor, Lorraine Candy

EMPIRE
Mappin House, 4 Winsley Street, London W1W 8HF **T** 020-7182 8000 **W** www.empireonline.com
Editor, Mark Dinning

THE ENGINEER
St Giles House, 50 Poland Street, London W1F 7AX **T** 020-7970 4000 **W** www.theengineer.com
Editor, Andrew Lee

ESQUIRE
National Magazine House, 72 Broadwick Street, London W1F 9EP **T** 020-7439 5000 **W** www.esquire.co.uk
Editor, Jeremy Langmead

ESSENTIALS
The Blue Fin Building, 110 Southwark Street, London SE1 0SU **T** 020-3148 7211
Editor, Julie Barton-Breck

FAMILY HISTORY MONTHLY
Unit 101, 140 Wales Farm Road, London W3 6UG **T** 0208-752 8157
Editor, Sarah Warwick

FARMERS WEEKLY
Quadrant House, The Quadrant, Sutton, Surrey SM2 5AS **T** 020-8652 4911 **W** www.fwi.co.uk
Editor, Jane King

FHM
Mappin House, 4 Winsley Street, London W1W 8HF **T** 020-7182 8028 **W** www.fhm.com
Editor, Anthony Naguera

THE FIELD
The Blue Fin Building, 110 Southwark Street, London SE1 0SU **T** 020-3148 5000 **W** www.thefield.co.uk
Editor, Jonathan Young

FILM REVIEW
Visual Imagination Ltd, 9 Blades Court, Deodar Road, London SW15 2NU **T** 020-8875 1520 **W** www.visimag.com
Editor, Nikki Baughan

FORTEAN TIMES
Box 2409, London NW5 4NP **T** 020-7907 6235 **W** www.forteantimes.com
Editor, David Sutton

FORTNIGHT
11 University Road, Belfast BT7 1NA **T** 028-9023 2353 **W** www.fortnight.org
Editor, Rudie Goldsmith

FOURFOURTWO
Haymarket, Teddington Studios, Broom Road, Teddington, Middlesex TW11 9BE **T** 020-8267 5061 **W** www.fourfourtwo.com
Editor, Hugh Sleight

GAY TIMES – GT
Spectrum House, 32–34 Gordon House Road, London NW5 1LP **T** 020-7424 7400 **W** www.gaytimes.co.uk
Editor, Joseph Galliano

GEOGRAPHICAL JOURNAL
Royal Geographical Society, 1 Kensington Gore, London SW7 2AR **T** 020-7591 3026
Editor, Prof. John Briggs

GOLF MONTHLY
The Blue Fin Building, 110 Southwark Street, London SE1 0SU **T** 020-3148 4530 **W** www.golf-monthly.co.uk
Editor, Michael Harris

GOOD HOUSEKEEPING
72 Broadwick Street, London W1F 9EP **T** 020-7439 5000 **W** www.natmags.co.uk
Editor, Louise Chunn

GQ
Vogue House, Hanover Square, London W1S 1JU **T** 020-7499 9080 **W** www.gq-magazine.co.uk
Editor, Dylan Jones

GRANTA
12 Addison Avenue, London W11 4QR **T** 020-7605 1360 **W** www.granta.com
Editor, Jason Cowley

GRAZIA
Endeavour House, 189 Shaftesbury Avenue, London WC2H 8JG **W** www.graziamagazine.co.uk
Editor, Jane Bruton

GREEN FUTURES
Overseas House, 19–23 Ironmonger Row, London EC1V 3QN **W** www.greenfutures.org.uk
Editor, Roger East

THE GROWER
174 Hammersmith Road, London W6 7JP **T** 020-8267 4977 **W** www.growermagazine.com
Editor, Kate Lowe

GUITARIST
30 Monmouth Street, Bath BA1 2BW **T** 01225-442244 **W** www.futurenet.co.uk
Editor, Michael Leonard

HARPER'S BAZAAR
National Magazine House, 72 Broadwick Street, London W1F 9EP **T** 020-7439 5000 **W** www.natmags.co.uk
Editor, Lucy Yeomans

HEALTH & FITNESS MAGAZINE
2 Balcombe Street, London NW1 6NW **T** 020-7042 4000 **W** www.healthandfitnessonline.co.uk
Editor, Mary Comber

HEAT
Endeavour House, 189 Shaftesbury Avenue, London WC2H 8JG **T** 020-7859 8657 **W** www.heatworld.com
Editor, Julian Linley

HELLO!
Wellington House, 69–71 Upper Ground, London SE1 9PQ **T** 020-7667 8700
Editor, Kay Goddard

HISTORY TODAY
20 Old Compton Street, London W1D 4TW **T** 020-7534 8000 **W** www.historytoday.com
Editor, Peter Furtado

HOMES AND GARDENS
The Blue Fin Building, 110 Southwark Street, London SE1 0SU **T** 020-3148 5000 **W** www.homesandgardens.com
Editor, Deborah Barker

HOUSE & GARDEN
Vogue House, Hanover Square, London W1S 1JU **T** 020-7499 9080
Editor, Susan Crewe

HOUSE BEAUTIFUL
72 Broadwick Street, London W1F 9EP **T** 020-7439 5000 **W** www.allaboutyou.com/housebeautiful
Editor, Julia Goodwin

HORSE & HOUND
9th Floor, The Blue Fin Building, 110 Southwark Street, London SE1 0SU T 020-3148 4562
W www.horseandhound.co.uk
Editor, Lucy Higginson

IN STYLE
The Blue Fin Building, 110 Southwark Street, London SE1 0SU T 020-3148 5000 W www.instyle.com
Editor, Trish Halpin

INSIDE SOAP
64 North Row, London W1K 7LL T 020-7750 7570
W www.insidesoap.co.uk
Editor, Steven Murphy

THE IRISH POST
1st Floor, West Wing, 26–28 Hammersmith Grove, London W6 7HA T 020-8741 0649 W www.irishpost.co.uk
Editor, Jon Myles

JAZZ JOURNAL INTERNATIONAL
3 & 3A Forest Road, Loughton, Essex IG10 1DR
T 020-8532 0456
Editor, Janet Cook

JEWISH CHRONICLE
25 Furnival Street, London EC4A 1JT T 020-7415 1500
W www.thejc.com
Editor, David Rowan

KERRANG!
Mappin House, London W1W 8HF T 020-7436 1515
W www.kerrang.com
Editor, Paul Brannigan

THE LADY
39–40 Bedford Street, London WC2E 9ER T 020-7379 4717
W www.lady.co.uk
Editor, Arline Usden

LANCET
32 Jamestown Road, London NW1 7BY T 020-7424 4910
W www.thelancet.com
Editor, Dr Richard Horton

THE LAWYER
50 Poland Street, London W1V 4AX T 020-7970 4000
W www.thelawyer.com
Editor, Catrin Griffiths

THE LITERARY REVIEW
44 Lexington Street, London W1F 0LW T 020-7437 9392
W www.literaryreview.co.uk
Editor, Nancy Sladek

THE LONDON MAGAZINE
70 Wargrave Avenue, London N15 6UB T 020-8400 5882
W www.thelondonmagazine.net
Editor, Sebastian Barker

LONDON REVIEW OF BOOKS
28 Little Russell Street, London WC1A 2HN T 020-7209 1101
W www.lrb.co.uk
Editor, Mary-Kay Wilmers

MARIE CLAIRE
7th Floor, The Blue Fin Building, 110 Southwark Street, London SE1 0SU T 020-3148 7513
W www.marieclaire.co.uk
Editor, Marie O'Riordan

MEDIA WEEK
Haymarket Publishing Ltd, 174 Hammersmith Road, London W6 7JP T 020-8267 8026
Editor, Steve Barrett

MEN'S HEALTH
33 Broadwick Street, London W1F 9EP T 020-7339 4400
W www.menshealth.co.uk
Editor, Morgan Rees

MIXMAG
90–92 Pentonville Road, London N1 9HS T 020-7520 8625
W www.mixmag.net
Editor, Andrew Harrison

MOJO
Mappin House, 4 Winsley Street, London W1W 8HF
T 020-7436 1515 W www.mojo4music.com
Editor, Phil Alexander

MONEYWISE
Standon House, 21 Mansell Street, London E1 8AA
T 020-7680 3600 W www.moneywise.co.uk
Editor, Emma-Lou Montgomery

MORE
Endeavour House, 189 Shaftesbury Avenue, London WC2H 8JG T 020-7208 3165 W www.moremagazine.co.uk
Editor, Lisa Smosarski

MOTHER & BABY
Endeavour House, 189 Shaftsbury Avenue, London WC2H 8JG T 020-7347 1869
W www.motherandbabymagazine.com
Editor, Elena Dalrymple

MOTOR CYCLE NEWS
Peterborough Business Park, Lynchwood, Peterborough PE2 6EA T 01733-468000 W www.motorcyclenews.com
Editor, Marc Potter

MUSIC WEEK
1st Floor, Ludgate House, 245 Blackfriars Road, London SE1 9UR W www.musicweek.com
Editor, Paul Williams

THE NATIONAL TRUST MAGAZINE
Heelis, Kemble Drive, Swindon SN2 2NA T 01793-817400
W www.nationaltrust.org.uk
Editor, Sue Herdman

NATURE
Macmillan Magazines Ltd, The Macmillan Building, 4 Crinan Street, London N1 9XW T 020-7833 4000
W www.nature.com/nature
Editor, Philip Campbell

NEW HUMANIST
1 Gower Street, London WC1E 6HD T 020-7436 1151
W www.newhumanist.org.uk
Editor, Caspar Melville

NEW INTERNATIONALIST
55 Rectory Road, Oxford OX4 1BW T 01865-811400
W www.newint.org
Editors, Vanessa Baird, David Ransom, Chris Brazier, Jess Worth, Wayne Ellwood, Adam Ma'anit, Dinyar Godrej

NEW MUSICAL EXPRESS (NME)
IPC Ignite, The Blue Fin Building, 110 Southwark Street, London SE1 0SU T 020-3148 5000
Editor, Conor McNicholas

NEW NATION
Technology Centre, 65 Whitehchapel Road, London E1 1DU
T 020-7650 2000 W www.ethnicmedia.co.uk
Editor, Lester Holloway

NEW SCIENTIST
Lacon House, 84 Theobalds Road, London WC1X 8NS
T 020-7611 1200 W www.newscientist.com
Editor, Jeremy Webb

NEW STATESMAN
3rd Floor, 52 Grosvenor Gardens, London SW1W 0AU
T 020-7730 3444 W www.newstatesman.com
Acting Editor, Sue Matthias

NURSING TIMES
Greater London House, Hampstead Road, London NW1 7EJ
T 020-7728 5000
Editor, Rachel Downey

NUTS
King's Reach Tower, Stamford Street, London SE1 9LS
T 020-7261 5660 W www.nutsmag.co.uk
Editor, Dominic Smith

OK!
Northern & Shell Building, 10 Lower Thames Street, London EC3R 6EN T 0871-434 1010 W www.okmagazine.org
Editor, Lisa Byrne

THE OLDIE
65 Newman Street, London W1T 3EG T 020-7436 8801
W www.theoldie.co.uk
Editor, Richard Ingrams

ORGANIC GARDENING
22B Hayburn Crescent, Glasgow G11 5AY T 0141-357 5537
W www.organicgardeningmagazine.co.uk
Editor, Gaby Bartai

PC ADVISOR
99 Gray's Inn Road, London WC1X 8TY T 020-7071 3615
W www.pcadvisor.co.uk
Editor, Paul Trotter

PC ANSWERS
Future Publishing Ltd, 30 Monmouth Street, Bath BA1 2BW
T 01225-442244 W www.futurenet.co.uk
Editor, Nick Veitch

PEACE NEWS
5 Caledonian Road, London N1 9DY T 020-7278 3344
W www.peacenews.info
Editors Milan Rai, Emily Johns

PEOPLE'S FRIEND
80 Kingsway East, Dundee DD4 8SL T 01382-223131
Editor, Angela Gilchrist

THE PHOTOGRAPHER
The British Institute of Professional Photography, 18 Dove Close, Bishops Stortford CM23 4JD T 01279-503871
W www.bipp.com
Editor, Steve Hynes

POETRY LONDON
81 Lambeth Walk, London SE11 6DX T 020-7735 8880
W www.poetrylondon.co.uk
Editors, Maurice Riordan, Scott Verner, Martha Kapos

POETRY REVIEW
22 Betterton Street, London WC2H 9BX T 020-7420 9883
W www.poetrysociety.org.uk
Editor, Fiona Sampson

POLICE REVIEW
Jane's Information Group, 180 Wardour Street, London W1F 8FY T 020-8276 4701 W www.policereview.com
Editor, Chris Herbert

THE POLITICAL QUARTERLY
9600 Garsington Road, Oxford OX4 2DQ T 01865-776868
W www.blackwellpublishing.com
Editors, Andrew Gamble, Tony Wright MP

PONY MAGAZINE
Headley House, Headley Road, Grayshott, Surrey GU26 6TU
T 01428-601020
Editor, Janet Rising

PRACTICAL PARENTING
Magicalia Publishing, Berwick House, 8–10 Knoll Rise, Orpington BR6 0EL T 01689-899200
W www.practicalparenting.co.uk
Editor, Susie Boone

PRESS GAZETTE
Wilmington Business Information, 8 Shepardess Walk, London N1 5LB T 020-7324 2385
W www.pressgazette.co.uk
Editor, Dominic Ponsford

PRIMA
72 Broadwick Street, London W1F 9EP T 020-7439 5000
Editor, Maire Fahey

PRIVATE EYE
6 Carlisle Street, London W1D 3BN T 020-7437 4017
W www.private-eye.co.uk
Editor, Ian Hislop

PROSPECT MAGAZINE
2 Bloomsbury Place, London WC1A 2QA T 020-7255 1281
W www.prospect-magazine.co.uk
Editor, David Goodhart

PUBLISHING NEWS
7 John Street, London WC1N 2ES T 0870-870 2345
W www.publishingnews.co.uk
Editor, Liz Thomson

PULSE
Ludgate House, 245 Blackfriars Road, London SE1 9UY
T 020-7921 8102 W www.pulsetoday.co.uk
Editor, Jo Haynes

Q MAGAZINE
Mappin House, 4 Winsley Street, London W1W 8HF
T 020-7182 8000 W www.q4music.com
Editor, Paul Rees

RA MAGAZINE
Royal Academy of Arts, Burlington House, Piccadilly, London W1J 0BD T 020-7300 5820 W www.ramagazine.org.uk
Editor, Sarah Greenberg

RADIO TIMES
BBC Worldwide Ltd, 80 Wood Lane, London W12 0TT
T 020-8433 3400 W www.radiotimes.com
Editor, Gill Hudson

RAILWAY MAGAZINE
The Blue Fin Building, 110 Southwark Street, London SE1 0SU T 020-3148 5000
Editor, Nick Pigott

READER'S DIGEST
The Reader's Digest Association Ltd, 11 Westferry Circus, Canary Wharf, London E14 4HE T 020-7715 8000
W www.readersdigest.co.uk
Editor, Katherine Walker

RED
64 North Row, London W1K 7LL T 020-7150 7000
W www.redmagazine.co.uk
Editor, Sam Baker

RED PEPPER
1B Waterlow Road, London N19 5NJ
W www.redpepper.org.uk
Co-Editors, Hilary Wainwright, Oscar Reyes

RESTAURANT MAGAZINE
6th Floor, 103 Regent Street, London W1B 4HL
T 020-7534 3756 W www.restaurantmagazine.co.uk
Editor, Paul Wootton

RUGBY WORLD
9th Floor, The Blue Fin Building, 110 Southwark Street, London SE1 0SU T 020-3148 4700 W www.rugbyworld.com
Editor, Paul Morgan

RUNNER'S WORLD
Natmag Rodale Ltd, 33 Broadwick Street, London W1F 0DG
T 020-7339 4400 W www.runnersworld.co.uk
Editor, Andy Dixon

SAGA MAGAZINE
The Saga Building, Enbrook Park, Sandgate, Folkestone, Kent CT20 3SE T 01303-771523
Editor, Katy Bravery

SCOTTISH HOME AND COUNTRY
42 Heriot Row, Edinburgh EH3 6ES T 0131-225 1724
W www.swri.org.uk
Editor, Liz Ferguson

SCREEN INTERNATIONAL
Greater London House, 1 Hampstead Road, London NW1 7EJ
T 020-7728 5630 W www.screendaily.com
Editor, Michael Gubbins

SEWING WORLD
Traplet House, Pendragon Close, Malvern WR14 1GA
T 01684-588500 W www.sewingworldmagazine.com
Editor, Wendy Gardiner

SHOOTING TIMES AND COUNTRY MAGAZINE
The Blue Fin Building, 110 Southwark Street, London
SE1 0SU T 020-3148 5000 W www.shootingtimes.co.uk
Editor, Camilla Clark

SIGHT AND SOUND
BFI, 21 Stephen Street, London W1T 1LN T 020-7255 1444
W www.bfi.org.uk/sightandsound
Editor, Nick James

THE SKIER AND THE SNOWBOARDER MAGAZINE
PO Box 386, Sevenoaks, Kent TN13 1AQ T 0845-3108303
W www.ski.co.uk/skimag
Editor, Frank Baldwin

SNOOKER SCENE
Hayley Green Court, 130 Hagley Road, Halesowen, West
Midlands B63 1DY T 0121-585 9188
W www.snookerscene.com
Editor, Clive Everton

SOLICITORS JOURNAL
Waterlow Professional Publishing, 6–14 Underwood Street,
London N1 7JQ T 020-7549 8670
W www.solicitorsjournal.com
Editor, Jean-Yves Gilg

THE SPECTATOR
22 Old Queen Street, London SW1H 9HP T 020-7961 0200
W www.spectator.co.uk
Editor, Matthew d'Ancona

SPIRIT & DESTINY
H. Bauer Publishing, Academic House, 24–28 Oval Road,
London NW1 7DT T 020-7241 8000
W www.spiritanddestiny.co.uk
Editor, Rhiannon Powell

THE STAGE
Stage House, 47 Bermondsey Street, London SE1 3XT
T 020-7403 1818 W www.thestage.co.uk
Editor, Brian Attwood

STUFF
Haymarket Ltd, Teddington Studios, Broom Road,
Teddington, Middlesex TW11 9BE T 020-8267 5036
W www.stuff.tv
Editor, Fraser Macdonald

THE TABLET
1 King Street Cloisters, Clifton Walk, London W6 0QZ
T 020-8748 8484 W www.thetablet.co.uk
Editor, Catherine Pepinster

TAKE A BREAK
H. Bauer Publishing Ltd, Academic House, 24–28 Oval Road,
London NW1 7DT T 020-7241 8000 W www.bauer.com
Editor, John Dale

TATLER
Vogue House, Hanover Square, London W1S 1JU
T 020-7499 9080 W www.tatler.co.uk
Editor, Geordie Greig

THE TEACHER
National Union of Teachers, Hamilton House, Mabledon
Place, London WC1H 9BD T 020-7380 4708
Editor, Elyssa Campbell-Barr

THIRD WAY
13–17 Long Lane, London EC1A 9PN T 020-7776 1072
W www.thirdway.org.uk
Editor, Simon Jones

TIME OUT
Universal House, 251 Tottenham Court Road, London
W1T 7AB T 020-7813 3000 W www.timeout.com
Editor, Gordon Thomson

THE TIMES EDUCATIONAL SUPPLEMENT (TES)
26 Red Lion Square, London WC1R 4HQ T 020-3194 3300
W www.tes.co.uk
Editor, Gerard Kelly

THE TIMES LITERARY SUPPLEMENT (TLS)
Times House, 1 Pennington Street, London E98 1BS
T 020-7782 5000 W www.thetls.co.uk
Editor, Peter Stothard

TOTAL FILM
Future Publishing, 2 Balcombe Street, London NW1 6NW
T 020-7042 4000 W www.totalfilm.com
Editor, Nev Pierce

TRAVELLER
Wexas Ltd, 45 Brompton Road, London SW3 1DE
T 020-7589 0500 W www.traveller.org.uk
Editor, Amy Sohanpaul

TRIBUNE
9 Arkwright Road, London NW3 6AN T 020-7433 6410
W www.tribunemagazine.co.uk
Editor, Chris McLaughlin

TV TIMES MAGAZINE
The Blue Fin Building, 110 Southwark Street, London
SE1 0SU T 020-3148 5615 W www.tvtimes.co.uk
Editor, Ian Abbott

VANITY FAIR
The Condé Nast Publications Ltd, Vogue House, Hanover
Square, London W1S 1JU T 020-7499 9080
W www.vanityfair.co.uk
Editor, Graydon Carter

VIZ
Dennis Publishing, 30 Cleveland Street, London W1T 4JD
T 020-7907 6000 W www.viz.co.uk
Editor, Richard Downey

VOGUE
Vogue House, Hanover Square, London W1S 1JU
T 020-7499 9080 W www.vogue.co.uk
Editor, Alexandra Shulman

WALK
The Ramblers' Association, 2nd Floor, Camelford House,
87–90 Albert Embankment, London SE1 7TW
T 020-7339 8500 W www.ramblers.org.uk
Editor, Dominic Bates

WALLPAPER
The Blue Fin Building, 110 Southwark Street, London
SE1 0SU T 020-3148 5000 W www.wallpaper.com
Editor, Tony Chambers

WANDERLUST
PO Box 1832, Windsor SL4 1YT T 01753-620426
W www.wanderlust.co.uk
Editor, Dan Linstead

WATERWAYS WORLD
151 Station Street, Burton-on-Trent DE14 1BG
T 01283-742950 W www.waterwaysworld.com
Editor, Richard Fairhurst

WEDDING MAGAZINE
l6th Floor, The Blue Fin Building, 110 Southwark Street,
London SE1 0SU T 020-3148 7790
W www.weddingmagazine.co.uk
Editor, Catherine Westwood

WEIGHT WATCHERS MAGAZINE
River Publishing Ltd, Victory House, 14 Leicester Place,
London WC2H 7BZ T 020-7306 0304
W www.weightwatchers.co.uk
Editor, Mary Frances

WHAT CAR?
Haymarket Motoring Magazines Ltd, Teddington Studios, Broom Road, Teddington, Middlesex TW11 9BE
T 020-8267 5688 **W** www.whatcar.com
Editor, Steve Fowler

THE WISDEN CRICKETER
4th Floor, 46 Loman Street, London SE1 0EH
T 020-7921 9195 **W** www.cricinfo.com
Editor, John Stern

WOMAN'S OWN
The Blue Fin Building, 110 Southwark Street, London SE1 0SU **T** 020-3148 5000
Editor, Karen Livermore

THE WORD
90–92 Pentonville Road, London N1 9HS **T** 020-7520 8625
W www.wordmagazine.co.uk
Editor, Mark Ellen

WORLD SOCCER
The Blue Fin Building, 110 Southwark Street, London SE1 0SU **T** 020-3148 5000 **W** www.worldsoccer.com
Editor, Gavin Hamilton

THE WORLD TODAY
Chatham House, 10 St James's Square, London SW1Y 4LE
T 020-7957 5700 **W** www.theworldtoday.org
Editor, Alison Coulridge

YACHTING MONTHLY
The Blue Fin Building, 110 Southwark Street, London SE1 0SU **T** 020-3148 4872 **W** www.yachtingmonthly.com
Editor, Paul Gelder

YOGA & HEALTH
PO Box 16969, London E1W 1FY **T** 020-7480 5456
W www.yogaandhealthmag.com
Editor, Jane Sill

YOUNG WRITER
5th Floor, 31–32 Park Row, Leeds LS1 5JD **T** 0113-2002929
W www.youngwriter.org
Editor, Jonathan Telfer

ZEST
National Magazine House, 72 Broadwick Street, London W1F 9EP **T** 020-7439 5000 **W** www.zest.co.uk
Editor, Alison Pylkkänen

ZOO
Mappin House, 4 Winsley Street, London W1W 8HF
T 020-7182 8355 **W** www.zootoday.co.uk
Editor, Ben Todd

BOOK PUBLISHERS

This is a selection of UK publishers and is not an exhaustive list. For more information refer to *Writers' and Artists' Year Book*, published by A&C Black.

ANDERSEN PRESS LTD
20 Vauxhall Bridge Road, London SW1V 2SA T 020-7840 8701
W www.andersenpress.co.uk
Children's books. Founded 1976

ANVIL PRESS POETRY
Neptune House, 70 Royal Hill, London SE10 8RF
T 020-8469 3033 W www.anvilpresspoetry.com
Poetry. Founded 1968

ARCADIA BOOKS LTD
15–16 Nassau Street, London W1W 7AB T 020-7436 9898
W www.arcadiabooks.co.uk
Original fiction, fiction in translation, autobiography, biography, travel, gender studies, gay books. Founded 1996

BERG PUBLISHERS
1st Floor, Angel Court, 81 St Clements Street, Oxford OX4 1AW
T 01865-245104 W www.bergpublishers.com
Social anthropology, cultural studies, dress and fashion studies, European history. Founded 1983

A&C BLACK PUBLISHERS LTD
36 Soho Square, London W1D 3QY T 020-7758 0200
W www.acblack.com
Children's and educational books, art and craft, drama, ornithology, reference, sport, theatre, books for writers, dictionaries. Founded 1807

BLOOMSBURY PUBLISHING PLC
36 Soho Square, London W1D 3QY T 020-7494 2111
W www.bloomsbury.com
Fiction, biography, illustrated, travel, children's, trade paperbacks and mass market paperbacks. Founded 1986

BOYDELL & BREWER LTD
PO Box 9, Woodbridge, Suffolk IP12 3DF T 01394-610600
W www.boydell.co.uk
Medieval studies, history, maritime history, literature, archaeology, art history, music. Founded 1969

MARION BOYARS PUBLISHERS LTD
24 Lacy Road, London SW15 1NL T 020-8788 9522
W www.marionboyars.co.uk
Literary fiction, film, memoirs, travel, cultural studies, jazz, music, cookery. Founded 1975

THE BRITISH LIBRARY PUBLICATIONS
Publishing Office, The British Library, 96 Euston Road, London NW1 2DB T 020-7412 7469 W www.bl.uk
Arts, bibliography, music, maps, oriental, manuscript studies, history, literature. Founded 1979

CAMBRIDGE UNIVERSITY PRESS
The Edinburgh Building, Shaftesbury Road, Cambridge CB2 8RU
T 01223-312393 W www.cambridge.org
Academic and reference books and journals. Founded 1534

CANONGATE BOOKS LTD
14 High Street, Edinburgh EH1 1TE T 0131-557 5111
W www.canongate.net
Adult general non-fiction and fiction. Founded 1973

JONATHAN CAPE
The Random House Group, 20 Vauxhall Bridge Road, London SW1V 2SA T 020-7840 8400 W www.randomhouse.co.uk
Poetry

CHAMBERS HARRAP PUBLISHERS LTD
7 Hopetoun Crescent, Edinburgh EH7 4AY T 0131-556 5929
W www.chambersharrap.co.uk
English language and bilingual dictionaries, reference, word games, writing guides, puzzles

JAMES CLARKE & CO. LTD
PO Box 60, Cambridge CB1 2NT T 01223-350865
W www.lutterworth.com
Theology, academic, reference books. Founded 1859

THE CONTINUUM INTERNATIONAL PUBLISHING GROUP LTD
The Tower Building, 11 York Road, London SE1 7NX
T 020-7922 0880 W www.continuumbooks.com
Serious non-fiction and reference works

JAMES CURREY LTD
73 Botley Road, Oxford OX2 0BS T 01865-244111
W www.jamescurrey.co.uk
Academic studies of Africa and the third world: history, anthropology, archaeology, economics, agriculture, politics, literary criticism, sociology. Founded 1985

GERALD DUCKWORTH & CO. LTD
First Floor, 90–93 Cowcross Street, London EC1M 6BF
T 020-7490 7300 W www.ducknet.co.uk
Academic and reference. Founded 1898

EARTHSCAN
8–12 Camden High Street, London NW1 0JH T 020-7387 8558
W www.earthscan.co.uk
Academic and professional, including sustainable development, climate and energy

EDINBURGH UNIVERSITY PRESS
22 George Square, Edinburgh EH8 9LF T 0131-650 4218
W www.eup.ed.ac.uk
Academic books and journals

EGMONT BOOKS
3rd Floor, Beaumont House, Avonmore Road, London W14 8TS
T 020-7605 6600 W www.egmont.co.uk
Children's books. Founded 1878

ELSEVIER LTD (BUTTERWORTH HEINEMANN)
Linacre House, Jordan Hill, Oxford OX2 8DP T (01865) 310366
W www.bh.com
Science, technology and health sciences

FABER AND FABER LTD
3 Queen Square, London WC1N 3AU **T** 020-7465 0045
W www.faber.co.uk
General fiction and non-fiction, children's fiction and non-fiction, drama, film, music, poetry

FABIAN SOCIETY
11 Dartmouth Street, London SW1H 9BN **T** 020-7227 4900
W www.fabians.org.uk
Current affairs, political thought, economics, education, environment, foreign affairs, social policy. Founded 1884

SAMUEL FRENCH LTD
52 Fitzroy Street, London W1T 5JR **T** 020-7387 9373, 020-7255 4300 **W** www.samuelfrench-london.co.uk
Plays. Founded 1830

GRANTA PUBLICATIONS
12 Addison Avenue, London W11 4QR **T** 020-7605 1360
W www.granta.com
History, literary fiction, memoir, political non-fiction. Founded 1982

HACHETTE LIVRE UK LTD
338 Euston Road, London NW1 3BH
T 020-7873 6000 **W** www.hachettelivre.co.uk
Fiction and non-fiction

HARLEQUIN MILLS & BOON LTD
Eton House, 18–24 Paradise Road, Richmond, Surrey TW9 1SR
T 020-8288 2800 **W** www.millsandboon.co.uk
Romance. Founded 1908

HEADLINE PUBLISHING GROUP
338 Euston Road, London NW1 3BH **T** 020-7873 6000
W www.headline.co.uk
Autobiography, biography, fiction, hobbies, TV

HARPERCOLLINS PUBLISHERS
77–85 Fulham Palace Road, London W6 8JB **T** 020-8741 7070
W www.harpercollins.co.uk
Biographies, celebrity memoirs, dictionaries, fiction, history, maps, popular science and reference. Founded 1819

HODDER & STOUGHTON
338 Euston Road, London NW1 3BH **T** 020-7873 6000
W www.hodder.co.uk
Autobiography, biography, fiction, humour, lifestyle, travel

LONELY PLANET PUBLICATIONS
2nd Floor, 186 City Road, London EC1V 2NT **T** 020-7106 2100
W www.lonelyplanet.com
Travel guides

MACMILLAN PUBLISHERS LTD
The Macmillan Building, 4 Crinan Street, London N1 9XW
T 020-7833 4000 **W** www.macmillan.com
Primary and secondary education, academic, fiction and non-fiction

MERRELL PUBLISHERS LTD
81 Southwark Street, London SE1 0HX **T** 020-7928 8880
W www.merrellpublishers.com
Visual culture

METHUEN PUBLISHING LTD
8 Artillery Row, London SW1P 1RZ **T** 020-7798 1600
W www.methuen.co.uk
Literary fiction and non-fiction

JOHN MURRAY
338 Euston Road, London NW1 3BH **T** 020-7873 6000
W www.johnmurray.co.uk
Fiction and non-fiction: travel, history, entertainment, reference, biography and memoir

MICHELIN MAPS AND GUIDES
Hannay House, 39 Clarendon Road, Watford, Herts. WD17 1JA
T 01923-205240 **W** www.michelin.co.uk/travel
Tourist guides, maps and atlases, hotel and restaurant guides

NEW HOLLAND PUBLISHERS (UK) LTD
Garfield House, 86–88 Edgware Road, London W2 2EA
T 020-7724 7773 **W** www.newhollandpublishers.com
Illustrated non-fiction books

OBERON BOOKS
521 Caledonian Road, London N7 9RH **T** 020-7607 3637
W www.oberonbooks.com
New and classic play texts, programme texts and general theatre and performing arts books. Founded 1986

OMNIBUS PRESS/MUSIC SALES LTD
14–15 Berners Street, London W1T 3LJ **T** 020-7612 7400
W www.omnibuspress.com
Rock music biographies, general music books. Founded 1976

ONEWORLD CLASSICS/CALDER PUBLICATIONS
243–253 Lower Mortlake Road, Richmond, Surrey TW9 2LL
T 020-8948 9550 **W** www.oneworldclassics.com
European, international and British fiction and plays, art, literary, music and social criticism, biography and autobiography, essays, humanities and social sciences

ONEWORLD PUBLICATIONS
185 Banbury Road, Oxford OX2 7AR **T** 01865-310597
W www.oneworld-publications.com
Religion, philosophy, history, psychology, self-help, popular science. Founded 1986.

THE ORION PUBLISHING GROUP LTD
Orion House, 5 Upper St Martin's Lane, London WC2H 9EA
T 020-7240 3444 **W** www.orionbooks.co.uk
Fiction, non-fiction and audio

OXFORD UNIVERSITY PRESS
Great Clarendon Street, Oxford OX2 6DP **T** 01865-556767
W www.oup.com
Academic, dictionaries, literature, reference. Founded 1478

PENGUIN GROUP (UK)
80 Strand, London WC2R 0RL **T** 020-7010 3000
W www.penguin.co.uk
Biography, children's, current affairs, fiction, history, humour, literature, politics, sport, travel

PHAIDON PRESS LTD
Regent's Wharf, All Saints Street, London N1 9PA
T 020-7843 1000 **W** www.phaidon.com
Visual arts, lifestyle and culture

continued on page 634

PUBLISHERS' FAMILY TREE

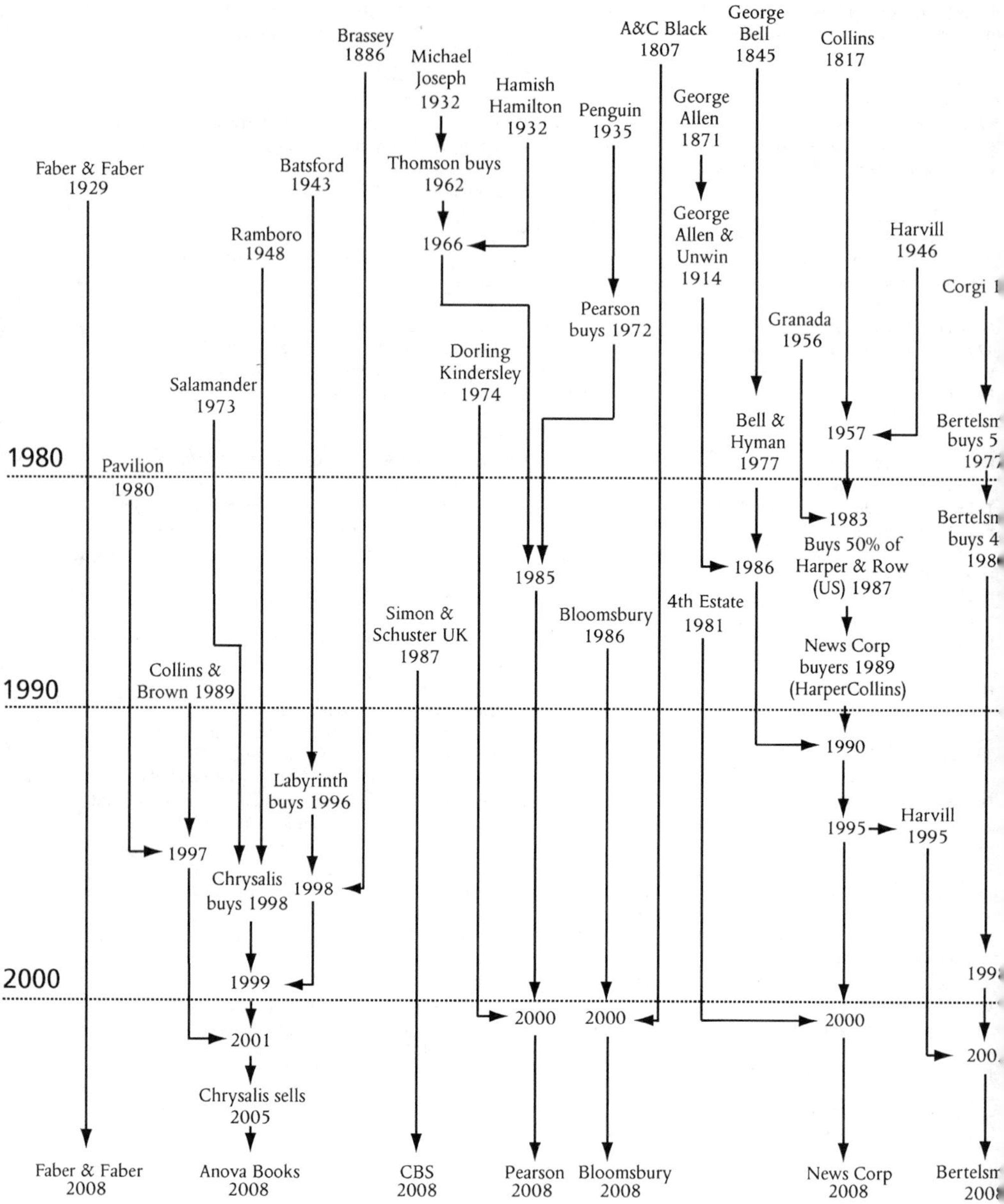

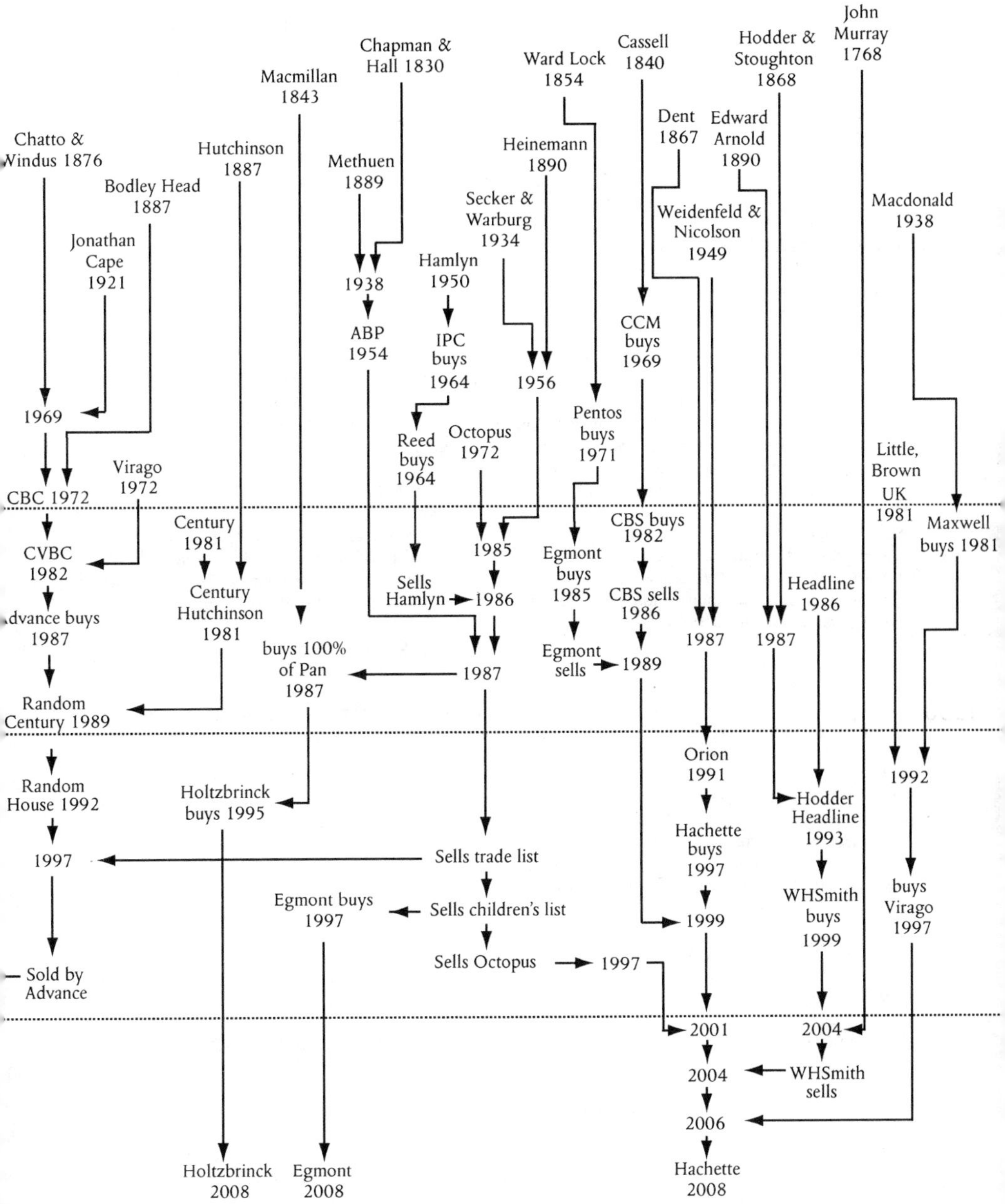
Chatto & Windus 1876
Bodley Head 1887
Jonathan Cape 1921
Hutchinson 1887
Macmillan 1843
Chapman & Hall 1830
Methuen 1889
Ward Lock 1854
Cassell 1840
Hodder & Stoughton 1868
John Murray 1768
Dent 1867
Edward Arnold 1890
Heinemann 1890
Secker & Warburg 1934
Hamlyn 1950
Weidenfeld & Nicolson 1949
Macdonald 1938
1938
ABP 1954
IPC buys 1964
1956
CCM buys 1969
1969
Reed buys 1964
Octopus 1972
Pentos buys 1971
Little, Brown UK 1981
Virago 1972
CBC 1972
Century 1981
CBS buys 1982
Maxwell buys 1981
CVBC 1982
1985
Egmont buys 1985
Sells Hamlyn
1986
CBS sells 1986
Headline 1986
Century Hutchinson 1981
dvance buys 1987
buys 100% of Pan 1987
1987
Egmont sells
1989
1987
1987
Random Century 1989
Orion 1991
1992
Random House 1992
Holtzbrinck buys 1995
Hodder Headline 1993
1997
Sells trade list
Hachette buys 1997
Egmont buys 1997
Sells children's list
WHSmith buys 1999
buys Virago 1997
1999
Sold by Advance
Sells Octopus
1997
2001
2004
2004
WHSmith sells
2006
Holtzbrinck 2008
Egmont 2008
Hachette 2008

PLUTO PRESS
345 Archway Road, London N6 5AA **T** 020-8348 2724
W www.plutobooks.com
Politics, anthropology, development, media, cultural

POLITY PRESS
65 Bridge Street, Cambridge CB2 1UR **T** 01223-324315
W www.polity.co.uk
Anthropology, history, literary theory, media and cultural studies, philosophy, politics, social and political theory, sociology, philosophy. Founded 1983

THE RANDOM HOUSE GROUP LTD
20 Vauxhall Bridge Road, London SW1V 2SA **T** 020-7840 8400
W www.randomhouse.co.uk
Bestselling fiction, lifestyle, non-fiction, children's books

THE READER'S DIGEST ASSOCIATION LTD
11 Westferry Circus, Canary Wharf, London E14 4HE
T 020-7715 8000 **W** www.readersdigest.co.uk
Condensed and series books, DIY, computers, puzzles, gardening, medical, handicrafts, law, touring guides, encyclopedias, dictionaries, nature, folklore, atlases, cookery, music

SCHOLASTIC LTD
Euston House, 24 Eversholt Street, London NW1 1DB
T 020-7756 7761 **W** www.scholastic.co.uk
Children's fiction and non-fiction and education for primary schools. Founded 1964

SIMON & SCHUSTER UK LTD
Africa House, 64–78 Kingsway, London WC2B 6AH
T 020-7316 1900 **W** www.simonsays.co.uk
Commercial and literary fiction; general and serious non-fiction

SPRINGER-VERLAG LONDON LTD
Ashbourne House, The Guildway, Old Portsmouth Road, Guildford GU3 1LP **T** 01483-734666 **W** www.springer.com
Medicine, computing, engineering, astronomy, mathematics, chemistry, biosciences. Founded 1972

SWEET & MAXWELL
100 Avenue Road, London NW3 3PF **T** 020-7393 7000
W www.sweetandmaxwell.co.uk
Law. Founded 1799

TANGO BOOKS LTD
PO Box 32595, London W4 5YD **T** 020-8996 9970
W www.tangobooks.co.uk
Novelty children's fiction and non-fiction books

TAYLOR AND FRANCIS GROUP
2 and 4 Park Square, Milton Park, Abingdon, Oxon OX14 4RN
T 020-7017 6000 **W** www.tandf.co.uk
Academic and reference books

THAMES & HUDSON LTD
181A High Holborn, London WC1V 7QX **T** 020-78455000
W www.thamesandhudson.com
Illustrated non-fiction

THINK BOOKS
Think Publishing Ltd, The Pall Mall Deposit, 124–128 Barlby Road, London W10 6BL **T** 020-8962 3020
W www.thinkpublishing.co.uk
Specialises in books on the outdoors, gardening and wildlife. Founded 2005

TSO (THE STATIONERY OFFICE)
Head office St Crispins, Duke Street, Norwich NR3 1PD
T 0870-600 5522 **W** www.tso.co.uk
Business, current affairs, directories, driving guides, professional, reference

USBORNE PUBLISHING LTD
Usborne House, 83–85 Saffron Hill, London EC1N 8RT
T 020-7430 2800 **W** www.usborne.com
Children's books. Founded 1973

V&A PUBLISHING
V&A Museum, South Kensington, London SW7 2RL
T 020-7942 2966 **W** www.vandabooks.com
Popular and scholarly books on fine and decorative arts, architecture, contemporary design, fashion and photography. Founded 1980

VERSO LTD
6 Meard Street, London W1F 0EG **T** 020-7437 3546
W www.versobooks.com
Current affairs, politics, sociology, economics, history, philosophy, cultural studies. Founded 1970

UNIVERSITY OF WALES PRESS
10 Columbus Walk, Brigantine Place, Cardiff CF10 4UP
T 029-2049 6899 **W** www.wales.ac.uk/press
Academic and educational (Welsh and English). Founded 1922

WILEY-BLACKWELL
9600 Garsington Road, Oxford OX4 2DQ **T** 01865-776868
W www.blackwellpublishing.com
Medicine, veterinary medicine, dentistry, nursing and allied health, science

WORDSWORTH EDITIONS LTD
8B East Street, Ware, Herts SG12 9HJ **T** 01920-465167
W www.wordsworth-editions.com
Reprints of classic books. Founded 1987

YALE UNIVERSITY PRESS LONDON
47 Bedford Square, London WC1B 3DP **T** 020-7079 4900
W www.yalebooks.co.uk
Art, architecture, history, economics, political science, religion, history of science, biography, current affairs and music. Founded 1961

EMPLOYERS' AND TRADE ASSOCIATIONS

Most national employers' associations are members of the Confederation of British Industry (CBI).

CBI

Centre Point, 103 New Oxford Street, London WC1A 1DU
T 020-7379 7400 W www.cbi.org.uk

The CBI was founded in 1965 and is an independent non-party political body financed by industry and commerce. It exists primarily to ensure that the government understands the intentions, needs and problems of British business. It is the recognised spokesman for the business viewpoint and is consulted as such by the government.

The CBI speaks for some 240,000 businesses that together employ approximately one-third of the private sector workforce. Member companies, which decide all policy positions, include 80 of the FTSE 100 index, some 200,000 small and medium-size firms, more than 20,000 manufacturers and over 150 sectoral associations.

The governing body of the CBI is the chairmen's committee, which meets four times a year in London under the chairmanship of the president. It is assisted by 16 expert standing committees which advise on the main aspects of policy. There are 12 regional councils and offices, covering the administrative regions of England, Wales, Scotland and Northern Ireland. There are also offices in Beijing, Brussels and Washington.
President, Martin Broughton

WALES: 2 Caspian Point, Caspian Way, Cardiff Bay, Cardiff CF10 4DQ T 029-2045 3710
Regional Director, David Rosser

SCOTLAND: 16 Robertson Street, Glasgow G2 8DS T 0141-222 2184
Regional Director, Ian McMillan

NORTHERN IRELAND: Scottish Amicable Building, 11 Donegall Square, Belfast BT1 5JE T 028-9032 6658
Regional Director, Nigel Smyth

ASSOCIATIONS

ADVERTISING ASSOCIATION 7th Floor North, Artillery House, 11–19 Artillery Row, London SW1P 1RT T 020-7340 1100 E aa@adassoc.org.uk W www.adassoc.org.uk
Chief Executive, Baroness Peta Buscombe

ASSOCIATION OF BRITISH INSURERS 51 Gresham Street, London EC2V 7HQ T 020-7600 3333 E info@abi.org.uk W www.abi.org.uk
Director-General, Stephen Haddrill

BLC LEATHER TECHNOLOGY CENTRE LTD Leather Trade House, Kings Park Road, Moulton Park, Northampton NN3 6JD T 01604-679999 E info@blcleathertech.com W www.blcleathertech.com
Sales Director, Adam Hughes

BRITISH APPAREL AND TEXTILE CONFEDERATION 5 Portland Place, London W1B 1PW T 020-7636 7788 E batc@dial.pipex.com W www.apparel-textiles.co.uk
Director-General, John Wilson, OBE

BRITISH BANKERS' ASSOCIATION Pinners Hall, 105–108 Old Broad Street, London EC2N 1EX T 020-7216 8800 E info@bba.org.uk W www.bba.org.uk
Chief Executive, Angela Knight

BRITISH BEER AND PUB ASSOCIATION Market Towers, 1 Nine Elms Lane, London SW8 5NQ T 020-7627 9191 E web@beerandpub.com W www.beerandpub.com
Chief Executive, Rob Hayward, OBE

BRITISH CLOTHING INDUSTRY ASSOCIATION LTD 5 Portland Place, London W1B 1PW T 020-7636 7788 E bcia@dial.pipex.com *Director,* John Wilson, OBE

BRITISH ELECTROTECHNICAL AND ALLIED MANUFACTURERS' ASSOCIATION (BEAMA) Westminster Tower, 3 Albert Embankment, London SE1 7SL T 020-7793 3000 E info@beama.org.uk W www.beama.org.uk
Chief Executive Officer, David Dossett

BRITISH MARINE FEDERATION Marine House, Thorpe Lea Road, Egham TW20 8BF T 01784-473377 E info@britishmarine.co.uk W www.britishmarine.co.uk
Chief Executive, Rob Stevens, CB

BRITISH OFFICE SUPPLIES AND SERVICES (BOSS) FEDERATION 29–34 Farringdon Point, Farringdon Road EC1M 3LF T 0845-450 1565 E info@bossfederation.co.uk W www.bossfederation.co.uk
General Manager, Philippa Morrell

BRITISH PHONOGRAPHIC INDUSTRY Riverside Building, County Hall, Westminster Bridge Road, London SE1 7JA T 020–7803 1300 E general@bpi.co.uk W www.bpi@co.uk *Chief Executive,* Geoff Taylor

BRITISH PLASTICS FEDERATION 6 Bath Place, Rivington Street, London EC2A 3JE T 020-7457 5000 E bpf@bpf.co.uk W www.bpf.co.uk
Director-General, Peter Davis, OBE

BRITISH PORTS ASSOCIATION Africa House, 64–78 Kingsway, London WC2B 6AH T 020-7242 1200 E info@britishports.org.uk W www.britishports.org.uk
Director, David Whitehead

BRITISH PRINTING INDUSTRIES FEDERATION Farringdon Point, 29–35 Farringdon Road, London EC1M 3JF T 0870-240 4085 E info@bpif.org.uk W www.britishprint.com
Chief Executive, Michael Johnson

BRITISH PROPERTY FEDERATION 7th Floor, 1 Warwick Row, London SW1E 5ER T 020-7828 0111 E info@bpf.org.uk W www.bpf.org.uk
Chief Executive, Liz Peace

BRITISH RETAIL CONSORTIUM 2nd Floor, 21 Dartmouth Street, London SW1H 9BP T 020-7854 8900 E info@brc.org.uk W www.brc.org.uk
Director-General, Stephen Robertson

BRITISH TYRE MANUFACTURERS' ASSOCIATION LTD 6 Bath Place, Rivington Street, London EC2A 3JE T 020-7457 5040 E mail@btmauk.com W www.btmauk.com *Chief Executive,* John Dorken

CHAMBER OF SHIPPING LTD Carthusian Court, 12 Carthusian Street, London EC1M 6EZ T 020-7417 2800 E postmaster@british-shipping.org W www.british-shipping.org
Director-General, Mark Brownrigg

CHEMICAL INDUSTRIES ASSOCIATION Kings Buildings, Smith Square, London SW1P 3JJ T 020-7834 3399 E enquiries@cia.org.uk W www.cia.org.uk *Chief Executive,* Steve Elliott

CONFEDERATION OF PAPER INDUSTRIES 1 Rivenhall Road, Swindon SN5 7BD T 01793-889600 E cpi@paper.org.uk W www.paper.org.uk
Director-General, Dr Martin Oldman

CONFEDERATION OF PASSENGER TRANSPORT UK Drury House, 34–43 Russell Street, London WC2B 5HA **T** 020-7240 3131 **E** admin@cpt-uk.org **W** www.cpt-uk.org *Chief Executive,* Simon Posner

CONSTRUCTION CONFEDERATION 55 Tufton Street, London SW1P 3QL **T** 0870-898 9090 **E** enquiries@thecc.org.uk **W** www.thecc.org.uk *Chief Executive,* Stephen Ratcliffe

CONSTRUCTION PRODUCTS ASSOCIATION 26 Store Street, London WC1E 7BT **T** 020-7323 3770 **E** enquiries@constructionproducts.org.uk **W** www.constructionproducts.org.uk *Chief Executive,* Michael Ankers, FRSA

DAIRY UK 93 Baker Street, London W1U 6QQ **T** 020-7486 7244 **E** info@dairyuk.org **W** www.dairyuk.org *Director-General,* J. Begg

ENGINEERING EMPLOYERS' FEDERATION (EEF) Broadway House, Tothill Street, London SW1H 9NQ **T** 020-7222 7777 **E** enquiries@eef-fed.org.uk **W** www.eef.org.uk *Director-General,* Martin Temple, CBE

FEDERATION OF BAKERS 6 Catherine Street, London WC2B 5JW **T** 020-7420 7190 **E** info@bakersfederation.org.uk **W** www.bakersfederation.org.uk *Director,* Gordon Polson

FEDERATION OF MASTER BUILDERS Gordon Fisher House, 14–15 Great James Street, London WC1N 3DP **T** 020-7242 7583 **E** central@fmb.org.uk **W** www.fmb.org.uk *Director-General,* Richard Diment

FEDERATION OF SPORTS AND PLAY ASSOCIATIONS Federation House, Stoneleigh Park, CV8 2RF **T** 024-7641 4999 **E** admin@sportsandplay.com **W** www.sportsandplay.com *Managing Director,* Jane Montgomery

FINANCE AND LEASING ASSOCIATION 2nd Floor, Imperial House, 15–19 Kingsway, London WC2B 6UN **T** 020-7836 6511 **E** info@fla.org.uk **W** www.fla.org.uk *Director-General,* Stephen Sklaroff

FOOD AND DRINK FEDERATION 6 Catherine Street, London WC2B 5JJ **T** 020-7836 2460 **E** generalenquiries@fdf.org.uk **W** www.fdf.org.uk *Director-General,* Melanie Leech

FREIGHT TRANSPORT ASSOCIATION LTD Hermes House, St John's Road, Tunbridge Wells TN4 9UZ **T** 01892-526171 **E** enquiries@fta.co.uk **W** www.fta.co.uk *Chief Executive,* Theo de Pencier

INSTITUTE OF CHARTERED FORESTERS 59 George Street, Edinburgh EH2 2JG **T** 0131-240 1425 **E** icf@charteredforesters.org **W** www.charteredforesters.org *Executive Director,* Shireen Chambers

KNITTING INDUSTRIES' FEDERATION LTD 12 Beaumanor Road, Leicester LE4 5QA **T** 0116-266 3332 **E** directorate@knitfed.co.uk *Director,* Anne Carvell

LEATHER PRODUCERS' ASSOCIATION 8 Queensberry Road, Kettering NN15 7HL **T** 01536-483668 **E** jakopo@btinternet.com *National Secretary,* Jack Purvis

MANAGEMENT CONSULTANCIES ASSOCIATION 60 Trafalgar Square, London WC2N 5DS **T** 020-7321 3990 **E** mca@mca.org.uk **W** www.mca.org.uk *Chief Executive,* Peter Hill

NATIONAL ASSOCIATION OF BRITISH MARKET AUTHORITIES (NABMA) The Guildhall, Oswestry SY11 1PZ **T** 01691–680713 **E** nabma@nabma.com **W** www.nabma.com *Chief Executive,* Graham Wilson

NATIONAL FARMERS' UNION (NFU) Stoneleigh Park, Stoneleigh CV8 2TZ **T** 024-7685 8500 **E** nfu@nfuonline.com **W** www.nfuonline.com *Director-General,* Richard Macdonald

NATIONAL FEDERATION OF RETAIL NEWSAGENTS Yeoman House, Sekforde Street, London EC1R 0HF **T** 020-7253 4225 **E** service@nfrnonline.com **W** www.nfrnonline.com *General Manager,* Paul Chambers

NATIONAL LANDLORDS ASSOCIATION 3rd floor, 22–26 Albert Embankment, London SE1 7TJ **T** 020-7840 8900 **E** info@landlords.org.uk **W** www.landlords.org.uk *Chair,* David Salusbury

NATIONAL MARKET TRADERS' FEDERATION Hampton House, Hawshaw Lane, Hoyland, Barnsley S74 0HA **T** 01226-749021 **E** enquiries@nmtf.co.uk **W** www.nmtf.co.uk *Chief Executive Officer,* Joe Harrison

NEWSPAPER PUBLISHERS ASSOCIATION LTD St Andrews House, 18–20 St Andrews Street, London EC4A 3AY **T** 020-7632 7430 *Director,* David Newell

NEWSPAPER SOCIETY St Andrews House, 18–20 St Andrews Street, London EC4A 3AY **T** 020-7632 7400 **E** ns@newspapersoc.org.uk **W** www.newspapersoc.org.uk *Director,* David Newell

OIL AND GAS UK Second Floor, 232–242 Vauxhall Bridge Road, London SW1V 1AY **T** 020-7802 2400 **E** info@oilandgasuk.co.uk **W** www.oilandgasuk.co.uk *Chief Executive,* Malcolm Webb

PUBLISHERS ASSOCIATION 29B Montague Street, London WC1B 5BW **T** 020-7691 9191 **E** mail@publishers.org.uk **W** www.publishers.org.uk *Chief Executive,* Simon Juden

RADIOCENTRE 77 Shaftesbury Avenue, London W1D 5DU **T** 020-7306 2603 **E** info@radiocentre.org **W** www.radiocentre.org *Chief Executive,* Andrew Harrison

ROAD HAULAGE ASSOCIATION LTD Roadway House, 35 Monument Hill, Weybridge KT13 8RN **T** 01932-841515 **E** weybridge@rha.net **W** www.rha.net *Chief Executive,* Roger King

SOCIETY OF BRITISH AEROSPACE COMPANIES LTD Salamanca Square, 9 Albert Embankment, London SE1 7SP **T** 020-7091 4500 **E** post@sbac.co.uk **W** www.sbac.co.uk *Chief Executive,* Ian Godden

SOCIETY OF MOTOR MANUFACTURERS AND TRADERS LTD Forbes House, Halkin Street, London SW1X 7DS **T** 020-7235 7000 **W** www.smmt.co.uk *Chief Executive,* Paul Everitt

TIMBER TRADE FEDERATION The Building Centre, 26 Store Street, London WC1E 7BT **T** 020-3205 0067 **E** ttf@ttf.co.uk **W** www.ttf.co.uk *Chief Executive,* John White

TRADE MARKS, PATENTS & DESIGNS FEDERATION Fifth Floor, 63–66 Hatton Gardens, London EC1N 8LE **T** 020-7242 3923 **E** admin@tmpdf.org.uk **W** www.tmpdf.org.uk *President,* Tim Frain

UK PETROLEUM INDUSTRY ASSOCIATION LTD Quality House, Quality Court, London WC2A 1HP **T** 020-7269 7600 **E** info@ukpia.com **W** www.ukpia.com *Director-General,* Chris Hunt

ULSTER FARMERS' UNION 475 Antrim Road, Belfast BT15 3DA **T** 028-9037 0222 **E** info@ufuhq.com **W** www.ufuni.org *Chief Executive,* Clarke Black

TRADE UNIONS

A trade union is an organisation of workers formed (historically) for the purpose of collective bargaining over pay and working conditions. Today, trade unions may also provide legal and financial advice, sickness benefits and education facilities to their members. Legally any employee has the right to join a trade union, but not all employers recognise all or any trade unions. Conversely an employee also has the right not to join a trade union, in particular since the practice of a 'closed shop' system, where all employees have to join the employer's preferred union, is no longer permitted. Below is a list of key dates in the development of British trade unionist movement.

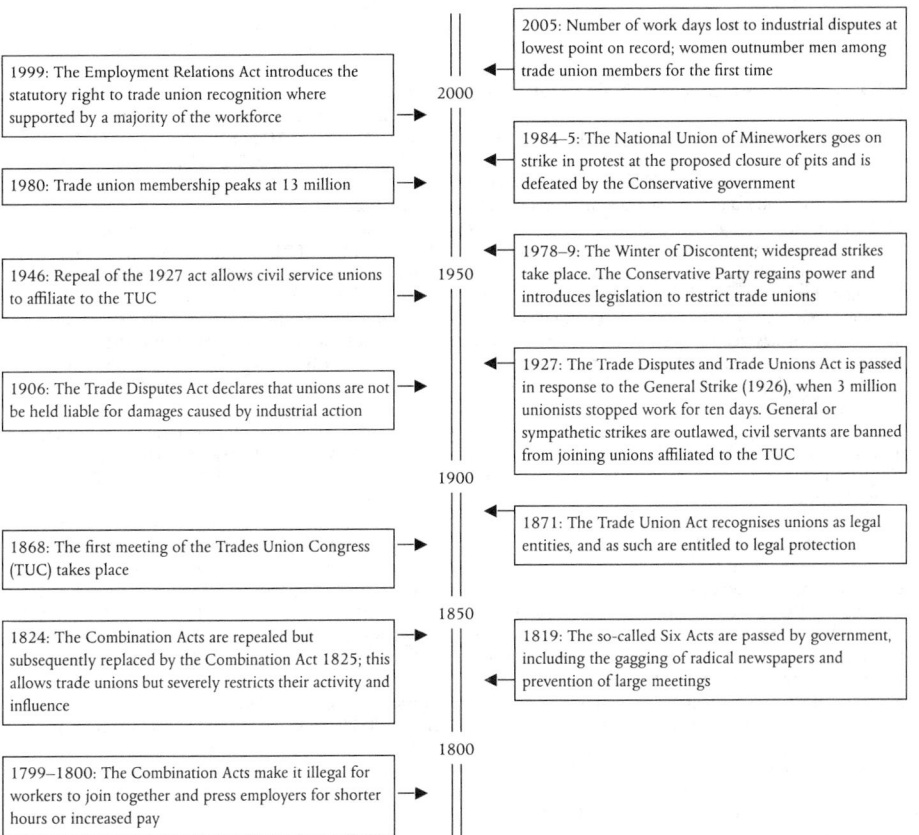

2005: Number of work days lost to industrial disputes at lowest point on record; women outnumber men among trade union members for the first time

2000

1999: The Employment Relations Act introduces the statutory right to trade union recognition where supported by a majority of the workforce

1984–5: The National Union of Mineworkers goes on strike in protest at the proposed closure of pits and is defeated by the Conservative government

1980: Trade union membership peaks at 13 million

1978–9: The Winter of Discontent; widespread strikes take place. The Conservative Party regains power and introduces legislation to restrict trade unions

1950

1946: Repeal of the 1927 act allows civil service unions to affiliate to the TUC

1927: The Trade Disputes and Trade Unions Act is passed in response to the General Strike (1926), when 3 million unionists stopped work for ten days. General or sympathetic strikes are outlawed, civil servants are banned from joining unions affiliated to the TUC

1906: The Trade Disputes Act declares that unions are not be held liable for damages caused by industrial action

1900

1871: The Trade Union Act recognises unions as legal entities, and as such are entitled to legal protection

1868: The first meeting of the Trades Union Congress (TUC) takes place

1850

1824: The Combination Acts are repealed but subsequently replaced by the Combination Act 1825; this allows trade unions but severely restricts their activity and influence

1819: The so-called Six Acts are passed by government, including the gagging of radical newspapers and prevention of large meetings

1800

1799–1800: The Combination Acts make it illegal for workers to join together and press employers for shorter hours or increased pay

THE CENTRAL ARBITRATION COMMITTEE

PO Box 51547, London SE1 1ZG **T** 020-7904 2300
F 020-7904 2301 **E** enquiries@cac.gov.uk **W** www.cac.gov.uk

The Central Arbitration Committee's main role is concerned with requests for trade union recognition and de-recognition under the statutory procedures of Schedule A1 of the Employment Rights Act 1999. It also determines disclosure of information complaints under the Trade Union and Labour Relations (Consolidation) Act 1992, considers applications and complaints under the Information and Consultation Regulations 2004, and performs a similar role in relation to European works councils, European companies, European cooperative societies and cross mergers. It also provides voluntary arbitration in industrial disputes.

Chair, Sir Michael Burton
Chief Executive, Graeme Charles

TRADES UNION CONGRESS (TUC)

Congress House, 23–28 Great Russell Street, London WC1B 3LS **T** 020-7636 4030
E info@tuc.org.uk **W** www.tuc.org.uk

The Trades Union Congress, founded in 1868, is an independent association of trade unions. The TUC promotes the rights and welfare of those in work and helps the unemployed. It helps its member unions promote membership in new areas and industries, and campaigns for rights at work for all employees, including part-time and temporary workers, whether union members or not. TUC representatives sit on many public bodies at national and international level such as government, political parties, employers and the European Union.

The governing body of the TUC is the annual congress. Between congresses, business is conducted by a general council, which meets five times a year, and an executive committee, which meets monthly. The full-time staff is headed by the general secretary who is elected by congress and is a permanent member of the general council.

There are 58 affiliated unions, with a total membership of nearly 6,500,000.

President (2007–8), Dave Prentis
General Secretary, Brendan Barber

SCOTTISH TRADES UNION CONGRESS (STUC)

333 Woodlands Road, Glasgow G3 6NG **T** 0141-337 8100
E info@stuc.org.uk **W** www.stuc.org.uk

The congress was formed in 1897 and acts as a national centre for the trade union movement in Scotland. The STUC promotes the rights to welfare of those in work and helps the unemployed. It helps its member unions to promote membership in new areas and industries, and campaigns for rights at work for all employees, including part-time temporary workers, whether union members or not. It also makes representations to government and employers. In March 2008 it consisted of 37 unions with a total membership of 644,674 and 22 directly affiliated trades councils.

The annual congress in April elects a 36-member general council on the basis of six sections.

Chair, Phil McGarry
General Secretary, Grahame Smith

WALES TUC

1 Cathedral Road, Cardiff CF11 9SD **T** 029-2034 7010
E wtuc@tuc.org.uk **W** www.wtuc.org.uk

The Wales TUC was established in 1974 to ensure that the role of the TUC was effectively undertaken in Wales. Its structure reflects the four economic regions of Wales and matches the regional committee areas of the National Assembly of Wales. The regional committees oversee the delivery of Wales TUC policy and campaigns in the relevant regions, and liaise with local government, training organisations and regional economic development bodies. The Wales TUC seeks to reduce unemployment, increase the levels of skill and pay, and eliminate discrimination.

The governing body of Wales TUC is the conference, which meets annually in May and elects a general council (usually of around 50 people) which oversees the work of the TUC throughout the year.

There are over 50 affiliated unions, with a total membership of around 500,000.

President, Ruth Jones
General Secretary, Felicity Williams

TUC-AFFILIATED UNIONS

As at April 2008

ACCORD Simmons House, 46 Old Bath Road, Charvil RG10 9QR **T** 0118-934 1808 **E** info@accordhq.org **W** www.accord-myunion.org
General Secretary, Ged Nichols *Membership:* 30,098

ACM (ASSOCIATION FOR COLLEGE MANAGEMENT) 35 The Point, Market Harborough LE16 7QU **T** 01858-461110 **E** admin@acm.uk.com **W** www.acm.uk.com
General Secretary, Peter Pendle *Membership:* 3,882

ADVANCE (FORMERLY ANGU) 2nd Floor, 16–17 High Street, Tring HP23 5AH **T** 01442-891122 **E** info@advance-union.org **W** www.advance-union.org
General Secretary, Linda Rolph *Membership:* 6,783

AEP (ASSOCIATION OF EDUCATIONAL PSYCHOLOGISTS) Unit 4, The Riverside Centre, Frankland Lane, Durham DH1 5TA **T** 0191-384 9512 **E** sao@aep.org.uk **W** www.aep.org.uk
General Secretary, Charles Ward *Membership:* 3,222

AFA COUNCIL 7 (ASSOCIATION OF FLIGHT ATTENDANTS) United Airlines Cargo Centre, Shoreham Road East, Heathrow Airport TW6 3UA **T** 020-8276 6723 **E** afalhr@unitedafa.org **W** www.afalhr.org.uk
President, Saad Bhatkar *Membership:* 585

ASLEF (ASSOCIATED SOCIETY OF LOCOMOTIVE ENGINEERS AND FIREMEN) 9 Arkwright Road, London NW3 6AB **T** 020-7317 8600 **E** info@aslef.org.uk **W** www.aslef.org.uk
General Secretary, Keith Norman *Membership:* 19,000

ASPECT (FORMERLY NAEIAC) Woolley Hall, Woolley WF4 2JR **T** 01226-383428 **E** info@aspect.org.uk **W** www.aspect.org.uk
General Secretary, John Chowcat *Membership:* 4,000

ATL (ASSOCIATION OF TEACHERS AND LECTURERS) 7 Northumberland Street, London WC2N 5RD **T** 020-7930 6441 **E** info@atl.org.uk **W** www.atl.org.uk
General Secretary, Mary Bousted *Membership:* 158,846

BACM-TEAM (BRITISH ASSOCIATION OF COLLIERY MANAGEMENT – TECHNICAL, ENERGY AND ADMINISTRATIVE MANAGEMENT) Danom House, 6A South Parade, Doncaster DN1 2DY **T** 01302-815551 **E** enquiries@bacmteam.org.uk **W** www.bacmteam.org.uk
General Secretary, Patrick Carragher *Membership:* 2,751

BALPA (BRITISH AIR LINE PILOTS' ASSOCIATION) BALPA House, 5 Heathrow Boulevard, 278 Bath Road, West Drayton UB7 0DQ **T** 020-8476 4000 **E** balpa@balpa.org **W** www.balpa.org
Chair, Ian Saunders *Membership:* 11,000

BDA (BRITISH DIETETIC ASSOCIATION) 5th Floor, Charles House, 148–149 Great Charles Street, Birmingham B3 3HT **T** 0121-200 8080 **E** info@bda.uk.com **W** www.bda.uk.com
Chief Executive, Andy Burman *Membership:* 5,000

BECTU (BROADCASTING, ENTERTAINMENT, CINEMATOGRAPH AND THEATRE UNION) 373–377 Clapham Road, London SW9 9BT **T** 020-7346 0900 **E** info@bectu.org.uk **W** www.bectu.org.uk
General Secretary, Gerry Morrissey *Membership:* 26,200

BFAWU (BAKERS, FOOD AND ALLIED WORKERS' UNION) Stanborough House, Great North Road, Stanborough, Welwyn Garden City AL8 7TA **T** 01707-260150 **E** info@bfawu.org **W** www.bfawu.org
General Secretary, Joe Marino *Membership:* 24,000

BIOS (BRITISH AND IRISH ORTHOPTIC SOCIETY) Tavistock House North, Tavistock Square, London WC1H 9HX **T** 020-7387 7992 **E** bios@orthoptics.org.uk **W** www.orthoptics.org.uk
Executive Officer, Rosie Auld *Membership:* 1,000

BSU (BRITANNIA STAFF UNION) Court Lodge, Leonard Street, Leek ST13 5JP **T** 01538-399627

E staff.union@britannia.co.uk W www.britanniasu.org.uk
General Secretary, John Stoddard *Membership:* 3,400

CDNA (COMMUNITY AND DISTRICT NURSING ASSOCIATION) Thames Valley University, 18–22 Bond Street, London W5 5AA T 020-8231 0180 E info@cdnaonline.org W www.cdnaonline.org
Chief Executive, Anne Duffy *Membership:* 3,000

COMMUNITY Swinton House, 324 Gray's Inn Road, London WC1X 8DD T 020-7239 1200 E info@community-tu.org W www.community-tu.org
General Secretary, Michael Leahy, OBE *Membership:* 70,000

CONNECT (THE UNION FOR PROFESSIONALS IN COMMUNICATIONS) 30 St George's Road, London SW19 4BD T 020-8971 6000 E union@connectuk.org W www.connectuk.org
General Secretary, A. Askew *Membership:* 19,700

CSMTS (CARD SETTING MACHINE TENTERS' SOCIETY) 48 Scar End Lane, Staincliffe, Dewsbury WF13 4NY T 01924-400206
General Secretary, Anthony John Moorhouse *Membership:* 80

CSP (CHARTERED SOCIETY OF PHYSIOTHERAPY) 14 Bedford Row, London WC1R 4ED T 020-7306 6666 E enquiries@csp.org.uk W www.csp.org.uk
Chief Executive, Phil Gray *Membership:* 48,000

CWU (COMMUNICATION WORKERS UNION) 150 The Broadway, Wimbledon, London SW19 1RX T 020-8971 7200 E info@cwu.org W www.cwu.org
General Secretary, W. Hayes *Membership:* 238,395

DGSU (DERBYSHIRE GROUP STAFF UNION) The Lodge, Duffield Hall, DE56 1AG T 01332-844396 E deirdre.smith@dgsu.org.uk W www.dgsu.org.uk
Chair, Deirdre Smith *Membership:* 500

DSA (DIAGEO STAFF ASSOCIATION) Sun Works Cottage, Park Royal Brewery, London NW10 7RR T 020-8978 6069 E diageo.staff.association@diageo.com
Chair, Tara Kelly *Membership:* 400

EIS (EDUCATIONAL INSTITUTE OF SCOTLAND) 46 Moray Place, Edinburgh EH3 6BH T 0131-225 6244 E enquiries@eis.org.uk W www.eis.org.uk
General Secretary, Ronald A. Smith *Membership:* 59,000

EQUITY Guild House, Upper St Martin's Lane, London WC2H 9EG T 020-7379 6000 E info@equity.org.uk W www.equity.org.uk
General Secretary, Christine Payne *Membership:* 35,527

FBU (FIRE BRIGADES UNION) Bradley House, 68 Coombe Road, Kingston upon Thames KT2 7AE T 020-8541 1765 E office@fbu.org.uk W www.fbu.org.uk
President, Mick Shaw *Membership:* 47,000

FDA 8 Leake Street, London SE1 7NN T 020-7401 5555 E info@fda.org.uk W www.fda.org.uk
General Secretary, Jonathan Baume *Membership:* 18,569

GMB 22–24 Worple Road, London SW19 4DD T 020-8947 3131 E info@gmb.org.uk W www.gmb.org.uk
General Secretary, Paul Kenny *Membership:* 601,536

HCSA (HOSPITAL CONSULTANTS' AND SPECIALISTS' ASSOCIATION) 1 Kingsclere Road, Overton, Basingstoke RG25 3JA T 01256-771777 E conspec@hcsa.com W www.hcsa.com
Chief Executive, Stephen Campion *Membership:* 3,100

MU (MUSICIANS' UNION) 60–62 Clapham Road, London SW9 0JJ T 020-7582 5566 E info@musiciansunion.org.uk W www.musiciansunion.org.uk
General Secretary, John F. Smith *Membership:* 32,000

NACODS (NATIONAL ASSOCIATION OF COLLIERY OVERMEN, DEPUTIES AND SHOTFIRERS) Wadsworth House, 130–132 Doncaster Road, Barnsley S70 1TP T 01226-203743 E natnacods@aol.com W www.nacods.co.uk
General Secretary, Rowland Soar *Membership:* 400

NACO (NATIONAL ASSOCIATION OF COOPERATIVE OFFICIALS) 6A Clarendon Place, Hyde SK14 2QZ T 0161-351 7900 E ndb@nacoco-op.org W www.naco.coop
President, Roger Davies *Membership:* 2,165

NAPO (TRADE UNION AND PROFESSIONAL ASSOCIATION FOR FAMILY COURT AND PROBATION STAFF) 4 Chivalry Road, London SW11 1HT T 020-7223 4887 E info@napo.org.uk W www.napo.org.uk
General Secretary, Judy McKnight *Membership:* 9,000

NASUWT (NATIONAL ASSOCIATION OF SCHOOLMASTERS/UNION OF WOMEN TEACHERS) Hillscourt Education Centre, Rose Hill, Rednal, Birmingham B45 8RS T 0121-453 6150 E nasuwt@mail.nasuwt.org.uk W www.nasuwt.org.uk
General Secretary, Ms Chris Keates *Membership:* 265,202

NAUTILUS UK Oceanair House, 750–760 High Road, Leytonstone, London E11 3BB T 020-8989 6677 E enquiries@nautilusuk.org W www.nautilusuk.org
General Secretary, Brian Orrell *Membership:* 19,000

NGSU (NATIONWIDE GROUP STAFF UNION) Middleton Farmhouse, 37 Main Road, Middleton Cheney OX17 2QT T 01295-710767 E ngsu@ngsu.org.uk W www.ngsu.org.uk
President, Bill Blumsom *Membership:* 13,884

NUJ (NATIONAL UNION OF JOURNALISTS) Headland House, 308–312 Gray's Inn Road, London WC1X 8DP T 020-7278 7916 E info@nuj.org.uk W www.nuj.org.uk
General Secretary, Jeremy Dear *Membership:* 37,964

NUM (NATIONAL UNION OF MINEWORKERS) Miners' Offices, 2 Huddersfield Road, Barnsley S70 2LS T 01226-215555 E chris.kitchen@num.org.uk W www.num.org.uk
President, I. Lavery *Membership:* 2,000

NUT (NATIONAL UNION OF TEACHERS) Hamilton House, Mabledon Place, London WC1H 9BD T 020-7388 6191 W www.teachers.org.uk
General Secretary (acting), Christine Blower *Membership:* 292,045

PCS (PUBLIC AND COMMERCIAL SERVICES UNION) 160 Falcon Road, London SW11 2LN T 020-7924 2727 E editor@pcs.org.uk W www.pcs.org.uk
General Secretary, Mark Serwotka *Membership:* 320,000

PFA (PROFESSIONAL FOOTBALLERS' ASSOCIATION) 20 Oxford Court, Bishopsgate, Manchester M2 3WQ T 0161-236 0575 E info@thepfa.co.uk W www.givemefootball.com
Chief Executive, Gordon Taylor *Membership:* 3,694

POA (PRISON OFFICERS' ASSOCIATION) Cronin House, 245 Church Street, London N9 9HW T 020-8803 0255 E general@poauk.org.uk W www.poauk.org.uk
General Secretary, Brian Caton *Membership:* 36,179

PROSPECT New Prospect House, 8 Leake Street, London SE1 7NN T 020-7902 6600 E enquiries@prospect.org.uk W www.prospect.org.uk
President, Graeme Henderson *Membership:* 102,015

RMT (NATIONAL UNION OF RAIL, MARITIME AND TRANSPORT WORKERS) Unity House, 39 Chalton Street, London NW1 1JD T 020-7387 4771 E info@rmt.org.uk W www.rmt.org.uk
General Secretary, Bob Crow *Membership:* 75,000

SCP (SOCIETY OF CHIROPODISTS AND PODIATRISTS) 1 Fellmonger's Path, Tower Bridge Road, London SE1 3LY T 020-7234 8620 E enq@scpod.org W www.feetforlife.org
Chief Executive, Joanna Brown *Membership:* 10,000

SKISA (SKIPTON STAFF ASSOCIATION) 1 Providence Place, Skipton BD23 2HN T 01756-692000 E brian.mcdaid@hml.co.uk
Chair, Brian McDaid *Membership:* 1,400

SOR (SOCIETY OF RADIOGRAPHERS) 207 Providence Square, Mill Street, London SE1 2EW T 020-7740 7200 E info@sor.org W www.sor.org
Chief Executive, Richard Evans *Membership:* 22,516

TSSA (TRANSPORT SALARIED STAFFS' ASSOCIATION) Walkden House, 10 Melton Street, London NW1 2EJ T 020-7387 2101 E enquiries@tssa.org.uk W www.tssa.org.uk
President, Andy Bain *Membership:* 33,000

UBAC (UNION FOR BRADFORD AND BINGLEY STAFF AND STAFF IN ASSOCIATED COMPANIES) H13 PO Box 88, Croft Road, Crossflatts BB16 2UA T 07721-978154 E ubac@bbg.co.uk
General Secretary, David Matthews
Membership: 1,415

UCAC (UNDEB CENEDLAETHOL ATHRAWON CYMRU) (NATIONAL UNION OF THE TEACHERS OF WALES) Pen Roc, Rhodfa'r Môr, Aberystwyth SY23 2AZ T 01970-639950 E ucac@athrawon.com W www.athrawon.com
General Secretary, Gruff Hughes *Membership:* 4,000

UCATT (UNION OF CONSTRUCTION, ALLIED TRADES AND TECHNICIANS) UCATT House, 177 Abbeville Road, London SW4 9RL T 020-7622 2442 E info@ucatt.org.uk W www.ucatt.org.uk
General Secretary, Alan Ritchie *Membership:* 120,000

UCU (UNIVERSITY AND COLLEGE UNION) 27 Britannia Street, London WC1X 9JP T 020-7837 3636 E hq@ucu.org.uk W www.ucu.org.uk
President, Sasha Callaghan *Membership:* 120,000

UNISON 1 Mabledon Place, London WC1H 9AJ T 0845-355 0845 W www.unison.org.uk
General Secretary, Dave Prentis *Membership:* 1,400,000

UNITE (FORMERLY AMICUS AND T&G)* 35 King Street, London WC2E 8JG T 0845-850 4242 E enquiries@amicustheunion.org W www.unitetheunion.org
General Secretaries, Derek Simpson; Tony Woodley
Membership: 2,500,000

UNITY Hillcrest House, Garth Street, Hanley, Stoke-on-Trent ST1 2AB T 01782-272755 E contact@unitytheunion.org.uk W www.unitytheunion.org.uk
General Secretary, Geoff Bagnall *Membership:* 6,376

URTU (UNITED ROAD TRANSPORT UNION) 76 High Lane, Chorlton-cum-Hardy, Manchester M21 9EF T 0800-526639 E info@urtu.com W www.urtu.com
General Secretary, Robert Monks *Membership:* 16,500

USDAW (UNION OF SHOP, DISTRIBUTIVE AND ALLIED WORKERS) 188 Wilmslow Road, Manchester M14 6LJ T 0161-224 2804 E enquiries@usdaw.org.uk W www.usdaw.org.uk
General Secretary, John Hannett *Membership:* 360,029

WRITERS' GUILD OF GREAT BRITAIN (WGGB) 15 Britannia Street, London WC1X 9JN T 020-7833 0777 E admin@writersguild.org.uk W www.writersguild.org.uk
President, David Edgar *Membership:* 2,300

YORKSHIRE INDEPENDENT STAFF ASSOCIATION (YISA) c/o Yorkshire Building Society, Yorkshire House, Yorkshire Drive, Rooley Lane, Bradford BD5 8LJ T 01274-472453 E kmwatson@ybs.co.uk
General Secretary, Karen Watson *Membership:* 1,400

* Formed from the amalgamation of Amicus and T&G; an 18-month transitional period began on 1 May 2007. At the time of going to press, Unite had agreed an accord with United Steeworkers (of the USA) to begin preparations for the creation of the first transatlantic trade union, which will represent over 3.4 million members in the UK, Ireland, USA and Canada

NON-AFFILIATED UNIONS

As at April 2008

ASCL (ASSOCIATION OF SCHOOL AND COLLEGE LEADERS) 130 Regent Road, Leicester LE1 7PG T 0116-299 1122 E info@ascl.org.uk W www.ascl.org.uk
General Secretary, Dr J. E. Dunford, OBE
Membership: 13,700

BDA (BRITISH DENTAL ASSOCIATION) 64 Wimpole Street, London W1G 8YS T 020-7935 0875 E enquiries@bda.org W www.bda.org
President, Dr Joseph Rich *Membership:* 23,000

CIOJ (CHARTERED INSTITUTE OF JOURNALISTS) 2 Dock Offices, Surrey Quays Road, London SE16 2XU T 020-7252 1187 E memberservices@cioj.co.uk W www.cioj.co.uk
General Secretary, Dominic Cooper *Membership:* 2,000

NAHT (NATIONAL ASSOCIATION OF HEAD TEACHERS) 1 Heath Square, Boltro Road, Haywards Heath RH16 1BL T 01444-472472 E info@naht.org.uk W www.naht.org.uk
General Secretary, Mick Brookes *Membership:* 28,125

NSEAD (NATIONAL SOCIETY FOR EDUCATION IN ART AND DESIGN) The Gatehouse, Corsham Court, Corsham SN13 0BZ T 01249-714825 E bookshop@nsead.org W www.nsead.org
General Secretary, Dr John Steers *Membership:* 2,500

PGA (PRISON GOVERNORS ASSOCIATION) Room 217, Cleland House, Page Street, London SW1P 4LN T 020-7217 8591 E paddy.scriven@hmps.gsi.gov.uk
General Secretary, Paddy Scriven *Membership:* 1,270

RBA (RETAIL BOOK ASSOCIATION) 22 Borough Fields Shopping Centre, Wootton Bassett, Swindon SN4 7AX T 01793-841414 E info@the-rba.org W www.the-rba.org
President, David Pickles *Membership:* 4,300

RCM (ROYAL COLLEGE OF MIDWIVES) 15 Mansfield Street, London W1G 9NH T 020-7312 3535 E info@rcm.org.uk W www.rcm.org.uk
General Secretary, Dame Karlene Davis, DBE
Membership: 37,000

SOCIETY OF AUTHORS 84 Drayton Gardens, London SW10 9SB T 020-7373 6642 E info@societyofauthors.org W www.societyofauthors.org
General Secretary, Mark Le Fanu, OBE
Membership: 8,500

SSTA (SCOTTISH SECONDARY TEACHERS' ASSOCIATION) West End House, 14 West End Place, Edinburgh EH11 2ED T 0131-313 7300 E info@ssta.org.uk W www.ssta.org.uk
General Secretary, David Eaglesham
Membership: 10,500

SPORTS BODIES

SPORTS COUNCILS

CENTRAL COUNCIL OF PHYSICAL RECREATION Burwood House, 14–16 Caxton Street, London SW1H 0QT T 020-7976 3900 E info@ccpr.org.uk W www.ccpr.org.uk
Chief Executive Officer, Tim Lamb

SPORT ENGLAND 3rd Floor, Victoria House, Bloomsbury Square, London WC1B 4SE T 0845-850 8508 E info@sportengland.org W www.sportengland.org
Chief Executive, Jennie Price

SPORTSCOTLAND Caledonia House, South Gyle, Edinburgh EH12 9DQ T 0131-317 7200 E library@sportscotland.org.uk W www.sportscotland.org.uk
Chief Executive, Stewart Harris

SPORTS COUNCIL FOR NORTHERN IRELAND House of Sport, 2A Upper Malone Road, Belfast BT9 5LA T 028-9038 1222 E info@sportni.net W www.sportni.net
Chief Executive, Eamonn McCartan

SPORTS COUNCIL FOR WALES Sophia Gardens, Cardiff CF11 9SW T 0845-045 0904 E scw@scw.co.uk W www.sports-council-wales.org.uk
Chief Executive, Dr Huw Jones

UK SPORT 40 Bernard Street, London WC1N 1ST T 020-7211 5100 E info@uksport.gov.uk W www.uksport.gov.uk
Chief Executive, John Steele

AMERICAN FOOTBALL

BRITISH AMERICAN FOOTBALL ASSOCIATION West House, Hedley on the Hill, Stocksfield NE43 7SW T 01661-843179 E chairman@bafa.org.uk W www.bafa.org.uk
Chair, Gary Marshall

ANGLING

NATIONAL FEDERATION OF ANGLERS National Water Sports Centre, Adbolton Lane, Holme Pierrepoint, Nottingham NG12 2LU T 0115-981 3535 E office@nfadirect.com W www.nfadirect.com
Chief Executive Officer, Paul Baggaley

ARCHERY

GRAND NATIONAL ARCHERY SOCIETY Lilleshall National Sports Centre, Newport TF10 9AT T 01952-677888 E enquiries@gnas.org W www.gnas.org
Chief Executive, David Sherratt

ASSOCIATION FOOTBALL

FOOTBALL ASSOCIATION 25 Soho Square, London W1D 4FA T 020-7745 4545 W www.thefa.com
Chief Executive, Brian Barwick

FOOTBALL ASSOCIATION OF WALES 11–12 Neptune Court, Vanguard Way, Cardiff CF24 5PJ T 029-2043 5830 E info@faw.org.uk W www.faw.org.uk
Secretary-General, David G. Collins

FOOTBALL LEAGUE 30 Gloucester Place, London W1U 8FL T 0844-463 1888 E fl@football-league.co.uk W www.football-league.co.uk
Chief Operating Officer, A. G. Williamson

IRISH FOOTBALL ASSOCIATION 20 Windsor Avenue, Belfast BT9 6EG T 028-9066 9458 E info@irishfa.com W www.irishfa.com
Chief Executive, Howard J. C. Wells

IRISH PREMIER LEAGUE Benmore House, Unit 2, 343–353 Lisburn Road, Belfast BT9 7EN T 028-9066 9559 E enquiries@irishpremierleague.com W www.irishpremierleague.com
Secretary, Craig Stanfield

SCOTTISH FOOTBALL ASSOCIATION Hampden Park, Glasgow G42 9AY T 0141-616 6000 E info@scottishfa.co.uk W www.scottishfa.co.uk
Chief Executive, Gordon Smith

SCOTTISH FOOTBALL LEAGUE The National Stadium, Hampden Park, Glasgow G42 9EB T 0141-620 4160 E info@scottishfootballleague.com W www.scottishfootballleague.com
Chief Executive, David A. Longmuir

ATHLETICS

ATHLETICS NORTHERN IRELAND Athletics House, Old Coach Road, Belfast BT9 5PR T 028-9060 2707 E info@niathletics.org W www.niathletics.org
Chair, David Seaton, MBE

SCOTTISH ATHLETICS 9A South Gyle Crescent, South Gyle, Edinburgh EH12 9EB T 0131-539 7320 E admin@scottishathletics.org.uk W www.scottishathletics.org.uk
Chief Executive, Geoff Wightman

UK ATHLETICS Athletics House, Central Boulevard, Blythe Valley Park, Solihull B90 8AJ T 0121-713 8400 E information@ukathletics.org.uk W www.ukathletics.net
Chief Executive, Niels de Vos

WELSH ATHLETICS Cardiff Athletics Stadium, Leckwith Road, Cardiff CF11 8AZ T 029-2064 4870 E office@welshathletics.org W www.welshathletics.org
Chief Executive Officer, Matt Newman

BADMINTON

BADMINTON ENGLAND National Badminton Centre, Milton Keynes MK8 9LA T 01908-268400 E enquiries@badmintonengland.co.uk W www.badmintonengland.co.uk
Chief Executive, Adrian Christy

BADMINTON SCOTLAND Cockburn Centre, 40 Bogmoor Place, Glasgow G51 4QT T 0141-445 1218 E enquiries@badmintonscotland.org.uk W www.badmintonscotland.org.uk
Chief Executive, Anne Smillie

WELSH BADMINTON UNION Unit E4, South Point Industrial Estate, Foreshore Road, Cardiff CF10 4SP T 029-2049 7225 E wbu@welshbadminton.net W www.welshbadminton.net
Chair, Robert Hall

BASEBALL

BASEBALLSOFTBALL UK Ariel House, 74A Charlotte Street, London W1T 4QJ T 020-7453 7055 W www.baseballsoftballuk.com
Head of Operations, Jenny Fromer

BASKETBALL

BASKETBALL SCOTLAND Caledonia House, South Gyle, Edinburgh EH12 9DQ T 0131-317 7260 E enquiries@basketball-scotland.com W www.basketball-scotland.com
Chief Executive Officer, Kevin Pringle

ENGLAND BASKETBALL EIS Sheffield, Coleridge Road, Sheffield S9 5DA T 0870-774 4225 E info@englandbasketball.co.uk W www.englandbasketball.com
Chief Executive, Keith Mair

BILLIARDS AND SNOOKER

WORLD LADIES BILLIARDS AND SNOOKER ASSOCIATION Richmond Lodge, 231 Ramnoth Road, Wisbech, PE13 2SN T 01945-588598 E admin@worldladiessnooker.co.uk W www.worldladiessnooker.co.uk
Chair, Mandy Fisher

WORLD SNOOKER 2nd Floor, Albert House, 111–117 Victoria Street, Bristol BS1 6AX T 0117-317 8200 E enq@worldsnooker.com W www.worldsnooker.com
Chair, Sir Rodney Walker

BOBSLEIGH AND LUGE

BRITISH BOB SKELETON ASSOCIATION 4–10 Barttelot Road, Horsham RH12 1DQ T 01403-221844 E hq@bobteamgb.org W www.bobteamgb.org
Chair, Bruce Ropner

BRITISH BOBSLEIGH ASSOCIATION 4–10 Barttelot Road, Horsham RH12 1DQ T 01403-221844 E hq@bobteamgb.org W www.bobteamgb.org
Chair, Bruce Ropner

GREAT BRITAIN LUGE ASSOCIATION 61 West Malvern Road, Malvern, Worcs WR14 4NF T 01684-576604 E markaluge@hotmail.com W www.gbla.org.uk
Chief Executive, Lt.-Col Mark Armstrong

BOWLS

BOWLS ENGLAND Lyndhurst Road, Worthing BN11 2AZ T 01903-820222 E ebaqueries@bowlsengland.com W www.bowlsengland.com
Chief Executive, A. Allcock, MBE

BRITISH ISLES BOWLS COUNCIL 23 Leysland Avenue, Countesthorpe LE8 5XX T 0116-277 3234 E michaelswatland@btinternet.com W www.britishislesbowls.com
Hon. Secretary, Michael Swatland

ENGLISH INDOOR BOWLING ASSOCIATION David Cornwell House, Bowling Green, Leicester Road, Melton Mowbray LE13 0FA T 01664-481900 E enquiries@eiba.co.uk W www.eiba.co.uk
President, T. G. Day

ENGLISH WOMEN'S INDOOR BOWLING ASSOCIATION 3 Moulton Business Park, Scirocco Close, Northampton NN3 6AP T 01604-494163 E ewiba@btconnect.com W www.ewiba.com
National Secretary, Tricia Thomas

BOXING

AMATEUR BOXING ASSOCIATION OF ENGLAND English Institute of Sport, Coleridge Road, Sheffield S9 5DA T 0114-223 5654 E info@abae.org.uk W www.abae.co.uk
Chief Executive, Paul King

BRITISH BOXING BOARD OF CONTROL The Old Library, Trinity Street, Cardiff CF10 1BH T 029-2036 7000 E info@bbbofc.com W www.bbbofc.com
Chair, Charles Giles

CANOEING

BRITISH CANOE UNION 18 Market Place, Bingham, Nottingham NG13 8AP T 0845-370 9500 E info@bcu.org.uk W www.bcu.org.uk
Chair, Brian Chapman

CHESS

ENGLISH CHESS FEDERATION The Watch Oak, Chain Lane, Battle TN33 0YD T 01424-775222 E office@englishchess.org.uk W www.englishchess.org.uk
President, Gerry Walsh

CRICKET

ENGLAND AND WALES CRICKET BOARD Lord's Cricket Ground, London NW8 8QZ T 020-7432 1200 E reception@ecb.co.uk W www.ecb.co.uk
Chief Executive, David Collier

MCC Lord's Cricket Ground, St John's Wood, London NW8 8QN T 020-7616 8500 E communications@mcc.org.uk W www.lords.org
Secretary and Chief Executive, Keith Bradshaw

CROQUET

CROQUET ASSOCIATION Cheltenham Croquet Club, Old Bath Road, Cheltenham GL53 7DF T 01242-242318 E caoffice@croquet.org.uk W www.croquet.org.uk
President, Bernard Neal

CURLING

BRITISH CURLING ASSOCIATION 51 Atholl Road, Pitlochry, Perthshire PH16 5BU T 01463-242922 E info@britishcurling.co.uk W www.britishcurling.co.uk
Chair, Chris L. Hildrey

ROYAL CALEDONIAN CURLING CLUB Cairnie House, Avenue K, Ingliston Showground, Newbridge EH28 8NB T 0131-333 3003 E office@royalcaledoniancurlingclub.org W www.royalcaledoniancurlingclub.org
President, Alistair J. McCabe

CYCLING

BRITISH CYCLING FEDERATION National Cycling Centre, Stuart Street, Manchester M11 4DQ T 0870-871 2000 E info@britishcycling.org.uk W www.britishcycling.org.uk
Chief Executive, Peter King

CYCLING TIME TRIALS 77 Arlington Drive, Pennington, Leigh WN7 3QP T 01942-603976 E phil.heaton@cyclingtimetrials.org.uk W www.cyclingtimetrials.org.uk
Chair, Peter McGrath

DARTS

BRITISH DARTS ORGANISATION 2 Pages Lane, Muswell Hill, London N10 1PS T 020-8883 5544 E britishdartsorg@btconnect.com W www.bdodarts.com
Chair, Dave Alderman

EQUESTRIANISM

BRITISH EQUESTRIAN FEDERATION Stoneleigh Park, Kenilworth CV8 2RH T 024-7669 8871 E info@bef.co.uk W www.bef.co.uk
Chief Executive, Andrew Finding

BRITISH EVENTING Stoneleigh Park, Kenilworth CV8 2RN T 024-7669 8856 E info@britisheventing.com W www.britisheventing.com
Business Director, Terry Bailey

ETON FIVES

ETON FIVES ASSOCIATION 3 Bourchier Close, Sevenoaks TN13 1PD T 01732-458775 E efa@etonfives.co.uk W www.etonfives.co.uk
Chair, Richard Barber, OBE

FENCING

BRITISH FENCING ASSOCIATION 1 Baron's Gate, 33–35 Rothschild Road, London W4 5HT T 020-8742 3032 E enquiries@britishfencing.com W www.britishfencing.com
Chief Executive Officer, Piers Martin

GLIDING

BRITISH GLIDING ASSOCIATION 3rd Floor, Kimberley House, Vaughan Way, Leicester LE1 4SE T 0116-253 1051 E office@gliding.co.uk W www.gliding.co.uk
Chief Executive, Pete Stratten

GOLF

LADIES' GOLF UNION The Scores, St Andrews KY16 9AT T 01334-475811 E info@lgu.org W www.lgu.org
Chief Executive, Shona Malcolm

THE ROYAL AND ANCIENT GOLF CLUB OF ST ANDREWS Golf Place, St Andrews KY16 9JD T 01334-460000 E thesecretary@randagc.org W www.randa.org
Secretary, Peter Dawson

GYMNASTICS

BRITISH GYMNASTICS Ford Hall, Lilleshall National Sports Centre, Newport TF10 9NB T 0845-129 7129 E information@british-gymnastics.org W www.british-gymnastics.org
Chief Executive, Brian Stocks

HANDBALL

BRITISH HANDBALL ASSOCIATION 40 Newchurch Road, Rawtenstall, Rossendale BB4 7QX T 01706-229354 E office@britishhandball.com W http://britishhandball.worldhandball.com
Chair, Stevie Neilson

HOCKEY

ENGLAND HOCKEY The National Hockey Stadium, Silbury Boulevard, Milton Keynes MK9 1HA T 01908-544644 E info@englandhockey.org W www.englandhockey.co.uk
Executive Chair, Philip Kimberley

SCOTTISH HOCKEY UNION 589 Lanark Road, Edinburgh EH14 5DA T 0131-453 9070 E info@scottish-hockey.org.uk W www.scottish-hockey.org.uk
Chief Executive, Brent Deans

WELSH HOCKEY UNION Severn House, Station Terrace, Ely, Cardiff CF5 4AA T 029-2057 3940 E info@welsh-hockey.co.uk W www.welsh-hockey.co.uk
Chief Executive, Mike Leatt

HORSERACING

BRITISH HORSERACING AUTHORITY 151 Shaftesbury Avenue, London WC2H 8AL T 020-7152 0000 E info@britishhorseracing.com W www.britishhorseracing.com
Chair, Nick Coward

THE JOCKEY CLUB 151 Shaftesbury Avenue, London WC2H 8AL T 020-7189 3800 E info@thejockeyclub.co.uk W www.thejockeyclub.co.uk
Senior Steward, Julian Richmond-Watson

ICE HOCKEY

ICE HOCKEY UK 19 Heather Avenue, Rise Park, Romford RM1 4SL T 07917-194264 E ihukoffice@yahoo.co.uk W www.icehockeyuk.co.uk
Chair, Bob Wilkinson

ICE SKATING

NATIONAL ICE SKATING ASSOCIATION OF THE UK National Ice Centre, Lower Parliament Street, Nottingham NG1 1LA T 0115-988 8060 E info@iceskating.org.uk W www.iceskating.org.uk
Chief Executive, Keith Horton

LACROSSE

ENGLISH LACROSSE ASSOCIATION Belle Vue Athletics Centre, Pink Bank Lane, Manchester M12 5GL T 0161-227 3626 E info@englishlacrosse.co.uk W www.englishlacrosse.co.uk
Chief Executive Officer, David Shuttleworth

LAWN TENNIS

LAWN TENNIS ASSOCIATION 100 Priory Lane, London SW15 5JQ T 020-8487 7000 E info@lta.org.uk W www.lta.org.uk
Chief Executive, Roger Draper

MARTIAL ARTS

BRITISH JUDO ASSOCIATION Suite B, Loughborough Technology Park, Epinal Way, Loughborough LE11 3GE T 01509-631670 E bja@britishjudo.org.uk W www.britishjudo.org.uk
Chief Executive, Scott McCarthy

BRITISH TAEKWONDO COUNCIL Yiewsley Leisure Centre, Otterfield Road, West Drayton UB7 8PE T 01895-427359 E admin@tkdcouncil.com W www.britishtaekwondocouncil.org
Chair, M. Prewett

MARTIAL ARTS DEVELOPMENT COMMISSION PO Box 416, Wembley HA0 3WD T 0870-770 0461 E office@madec.org W www.madec.org
Chair, Richard Thomas

MODERN PENTATHLON

PENTATHLON GB Norwood House, University of Bath, Claverton Down, Bath BA2 7AY T 01225-386808 E enquiries@pentathlongb.org W www.pentathlongb.org
Chief Executive, Peter Hart

MOTOR SPORTS

AUTO-CYCLE UNION ACU House, Wood Street, Rugby CV21 2YX T 01788-566400 E admin@acu.org.uk W www.acu.org.uk
General Secretary, Gary Thompson, MBE

MOTORCYCLE CIRCUIT RACING CONTROL BOARD Motorsport Vision Racing, Brands Hatch Circuit, Fawkham, Longfield, Kent DA3 8NG T 01474-875296 E bsb@msvracing.co.uk W www.mcrcb-events.co.uk
General Manager, Doug Barnfield

MOTORCYCLE GREAT BRITAIN ACU House, Wood Street, Rugby CV21 2YX T 01788-566400 E admin@acu.org.uk W www.acu.org.uk
General Secretary, Gary Thompson, MBE, BEM

MOTOR SPORTS ASSOCIATION Motor Sports House, Riverside Park, Colnbrook SL3 0HG T 01753-765000 W www.msauk.org
Chief Executive, Colin Hilton

SCOTTISH AUTO CYCLE UNION 28 West Main Street, Uphall EH52 5DW T 01506-858354 E office@sacu.co.uk W www.sacu.co.uk
President, Andy Russell

MOUNTAINEERING

BRITISH MOUNTAINEERING COUNCIL 177–179 Burton Road, Manchester M20 2BB T 0161-445 6111 E office@thebmc.co.uk W www.thebmc.co.uk
Chief Executive, Dave Turnbull

MULTI-SPORTS BODIES

BRITISH OLYMPIC ASSOCIATION 1 Wandsworth Plain, London SW18 1EH T 020-8871 2677 E boa@boa.org.uk W www.olympics.org.uk
Chief Executive, Simon Clegg, CBE

BRITISH UNIVERSITIES SPORTS ASSOCIATION 20–24 Kings Bench Street, London SE1 0QX T 020-7633 5080 E office@busa.org.uk W www.busa.org.uk
Chief Executive, Jenny Brown

COMMONWEALTH GAMES COUNCIL FOR ENGLAND PO Box 36288, London SE19 2YY T 020-8676 3543 E info@cgce.co.uk W www.cgce.co.uk
Chief Executive, Ann Hogbin, CBE

COMMONWEALTH GAMES FEDERATION Second Floor, 138 Piccadilly, London W1J 7NR T 020-7491 8801 E info@thecgf.com W www.thecgf.com
Chief Executive Officer, Michael Hooper

NETBALL

ALL ENGLAND NETBALL ASSOCIATION Netball House, 9 Paynes Park, Hitchin SG5 1EH T 01462-442344 E info@englandnetball.co.uk W www.englandnetball.co.uk
Chief Executive, Paul Clark

NETBALL NORTHERN IRELAND House of Sport, Upper Malone Road, Belfast BT9 5LA T 028-9038 3806 E netballni@houseofsport.net
President, Denise Prue

NETBALL SCOTLAND Suite 196, Second Floor, Central Chambers, 93 Hope Street, Glasgow G2 6LD T 0141-572 0114 E tellus@netballscotland.com W www.netballscotland.com
Chair, Brian McKelvie

WELSH NETBALL ASSOCIATION Second Floor, 33–35 Cathedral Rd, Cardiff CF11 9HB T 029-2023 7048 E welshnetball@welshnetball.com W www.welshnetball.co.uk
Chief Executive Officer, Mrs S. J. Holvey

ORIENTEERING

BRITISH ORIENTEERING FEDERATION 8A Stancliffe House, Whitworth Road, Darley Dale, Matlock DE4 2HJ T 01629-734042 E info@britishorienteering.org.uk W www.britishorienteering.org.uk
Chief Executive, Mike Hamilton

POLO

THE HURLINGHAM POLO ASSOCIATION Manor Farm, Little Coxwell, Faringdon SN7 7LW T 01367-242828 E enquiries@hpa-polo.co.uk W www.hpa-polo.co.uk
Chief Executive, David Wood

RACKETS AND REAL TENNIS

TENNIS AND RACKETS ASSOCIATION c/o The Queen's Club, Palliser Road, London W14 9EQ T 020-7386 3447/8 E office@tennis-rackets.net W www.tennisandrackets.com
Chief Executive, J. D. Wyatt

ROWING

AMATEUR ROWING ASSOCIATION The Priory, 6 Lower Mall, London W6 9DJ T 020-8237 6700 E info@ara-rowing.org W www.ara-rowing.org
National Manager, Rosemary Napp

HENLEY ROYAL REGATTA Regatta Headquarters, Henley-on-Thames RG9 2LY T 01491-572153 W www.hrr.co.uk
Secretary, D. G. M. Grist

RUGBY FIVES

THE RUGBY FIVES ASSOCIATION 32 Ashbourne Grove, East Dulwich, London SE22 8RL T 020-7627 8303 E andy.pringle@mac.com W www.rfa.org.uk
General Secretary, Andy Pringle

RUGBY LEAGUE

BRITISH AMATEUR RUGBY LEAGUE ASSOCIATION West Yorkshire House, 4 New North Parade, Huddersfield HD1 5JP T 01484-544131 E info@barla.org.uk W www.barla.org.uk
Chair, Spen Allison

THE RUGBY FOOTBALL LEAGUE Red Hall, Red Hall Lane, Leeds LS17 8NB T 0844-477 7113 E enquiries@rfl.uk.com W www.therfl.co.uk
Executive Chair, Richard Lewis

RUGBY UNION

IRISH RUGBY FOOTBALL UNION 10–12 Lansdowne Road, Dublin 4 T (+353) 1647 3800 E info@irishrugby.ie W www.irishrugby.ie
Chief Executive, P. R. Browne

RUGBY FOOTBALL UNION Rugby House, Rugby Road, Twickenham TW1 1DS T 0870-405 2000 E reception@rfu.com W www.rfu.com
Chief Executive, Frances Baron

RUGBY FOOTBALL UNION FOR WOMEN Rugby House, Rugby Road, Twickenham TW1 1DS T 020-8831 7996 E rfuw@therfu.com W www.rfu.com
Managing Director, Rosie Williams

SCOTTISH RUGBY UNION Murrayfield, Roseburn Street, Edinburgh EH12 5PJ T 0131-346 5000 E feedback@sru.org.uk W www.scottishrugby.org
Chief Executive, Gordon McKie

SCOTTISH WOMEN'S RUGBY UNION Scottish Rugby Union, Murrayfield, Edinburgh EH12 5PJ T 0131-346 5000 E women@sru.org.uk W www.scottishrugby.org
Chair, Sandra Kinnear

WELSH RUGBY UNION Westgate Terrace, Millennium Stadium, Westgate Street, Cardiff CF10 1NS T 0870-013 8600 E info@wru.co.uk W www.wru.co.uk
Chief Executive, Roger Lewis

SHOOTING

BRITISH SHOOTING Edmonton House, Bisley Camp, Brookwood, Woking GU24 0NP T 01483-486948 E admin@gbtsf.org.uk W www.britishshooting.org.uk
Chair, P. J. Boakes

CLAY PIGEON SHOOTING ASSOCIATION Edmonton House, Bisley Camp, Brookwood, Woking GU24 0NP T 01483-485400 E info@cpsa.co.uk W www.cpsa.co.uk
National Director and Chair, Terry Bobbett

NATIONAL RIFLE ASSOCIATION Bisley, Brookwood, Woking GU24 0PB T 01483-797777 E info@nra.org.uk W www.nra.org.uk
Chair, Bill Richards

NATIONAL SMALL-BORE RIFLE ASSOCIATION Lord Robert's Centre, Bisley Camp, Brookwood, Woking GU24 0NP T 01483-485505 E info@nsra.co.uk W www.nsra.co.uk
Chair (acting), Ken Nash

SKIING AND SNOWBOARDING

SNOWSPORT GB Hillend, Biggar Road, Midlothian EH10 7EF T 0131-445 7676 E info@snowsportgb.com W www.snowsportgb.com
Chief Executive, Mark Simmers

SNOWSPORT SCOTLAND Hillend, Biggar Road, Midlothian, EH10 7EF T 0131-445 4151 E info@snowsportscotland.org W www.snowsportscotland.org
Chief Executive, Jane Harvey

SPEEDWAY

BRITISH SPEEDWAY PROMOTERS' ASSOCIATION ACU House, Wood Street, Rugby CV21 2YX T 01788-560648 E office@britishspeedway.plus.com W www.british-speedway.co.uk
Chair, Peter Toogood

SQUASH

ENGLAND SQUASH National Squash Centre, Rowsley Street, Manchester M11 3FF T 0161-231 4499 E enquiries@englandsquash.com W www.englandsquash.com
Chief Executive, Nick Rider

SCOTTISH SQUASH Caledonia House, 1 Redheughs Rigg, South Gyle, Edinburgh EH12 9DQ T 0131-317 7343 E info@scottishsquash.org W www.scottishsquash.org
Chief Operating Officer, Kim Atkinson

SQUASH WALES St Mellons Country Club, St Mellons, Cardiff CF3 2XR T 01633-681646 E squashwales@squashwales.co.uk W www.squashwales.co.uk
Chair, Phil Brailey

SUB-AQUA

BRITISH SUB-AQUA CLUB Telford's Quay, South Pier Road, Ellesmere Port CH65 4FL T 0151-350 6200 E postmaster@bsac.com W www.bsac.com
Chief Executive, Mary Elizabeth Tetley

SWIMMING

AMATEUR SWIMMING ASSOCIATION Harold Fern House, Derby Square, Loughborough LE11 5AL T 01509-618700 E customerservices@swimming.org W www.britishswimming.org
Chief Executive, D. Sparkes

SCOTTISH SWIMMING National Swimming Academy, University of Stirling, Stirling FK9 4LA T 01786-466520 E info@scottishswimming.com W www.scottishswimming.com
Chair, Maureen Campbell

SWIM WALES Wales National Pool, Sketty Lane, Swansea SA2 8QG T 01792-513636 E secretary@welshasa.co.uk W www.welshasa.co.uk
Chief Executive, Robert James

TABLE TENNIS

ENGLISH TABLE TENNIS ASSOCIATION Queensbury House, Havelock Road, Hastings TN34 1HF T 01424-722525 E admin@etta.co.uk W www.etta.co.uk
Chief Executive, R. Yule

TABLE TENNIS ASSOCIATION OF WALES 8 Hopkins Close, Thornbury, Bristol BS35 2PX T 01454-417491 E ttaw@btinternet.com W www.ttaw.co.uk
Chair, Kim Johnson

TABLE TENNIS SCOTLAND Caledonia House, South Gyle, Edinburgh EH12 9DQ T 0131-317 8077 E sarah.moffat@ttscotland.com W www.ttscotland.com
Chair, Jonathan Whitaker

TRIATHLON

BRITISH TRIATHLON PO Box 25, Loughborough LE11 3WX T 01509-226161 E info@britishtriathlon.org W www.britishtriathlon.org
Chief Executive, Zara Hyde Peters

VOLLEYBALL

ENGLISH VOLLEYBALL ASSOCIATION Suite B, Loughborough Technology Centre, Epinal Way, Loughborough LE11 3GE T 01509-631699 E info@volleyballengland.org W www.volleyballengland.org
President, Richard Callicott

NORTHERN IRELAND VOLLEYBALL ASSOCIATION UUJ Sports Centre, Shore Road, Newtonabbey BT37 0QB T 028-9036 6373 E mark@nivb.com W www.nivb.com
General Secretary, Mark Fulton

SCOTTISH VOLLEYBALL ASSOCIATION 48 The Pleasance, Edinburgh EH8 9TJ T 0131-556 4633 E info@scottishvolleyball.org W www.scottishvolleyball.org
Chair, Margaret Ann Fleming

WALKING

RACE WALKING ASSOCIATION Hufflers, Heard's Lane, Shenfield, Brentwood CM15 0SF T 01277-220687 E racewalkingassociation@btinternet.com W www.racewalkingassociation.btinternet.co.uk
Hon. General Secretary, Peter Cassidy

WATER SKIING

BRITISH WATER SKI FEDERATION The Tower, Thorpe Road, Chertsey, Surrey KT16 8PH T 01932-570885 E info@bwsf.co.uk W www.britishwaterski.org.uk
Executive Officer, Patrick Donovan

WEIGHTLIFTING

BRITISH WEIGHTLIFTERS ASSOCIATION (BWLA) Lilleshall National Sports Centre, Nr. Newport TF10 9AT T 01952-604201 E lorraine.fleming@bwla.co.uk W www.bwla.co.uk
Chair, Bill Barton

WRESTLING

BRITISH WRESTLING ASSOCIATION 12 Westwood Lane, Chesterfield S43 1PA T 01246-236443 E admin@britishwrestling.org W www.britishwrestling.org
Chair, Malcolm Morley

YACHTING

ROYAL YACHTING ASSOCIATION RYA House, Ensign Way, Hamble, Southampton SO31 4YA T 0845-345 0400 E info@rya.org.uk W www.rya.org.uk
Chief Executive, Rod Carr, OBE

CLUBS

Originally called gentlemen's clubs, these organisations are permanent institutions with a fixed clubhouse, which usually includes restaurants, bars, a library and overnight accommodation. Members are fee-paying and typically vetted for their suitability.

Gentlemen's clubs were created for males of the English upper class and grew out of the seventeenth-century fashion for coffee houses which enjoyed enormous popularity, despite opposition from Charles II, who believed they encouraged the spreading of royal disaffection. The first of the London clubs – White's – was founded in 1693 by Francesco Bianco in St James's Street, in the area that quickly became known as 'clubland' (*see* map below). Membership to the first of the clubs was a matter of hereditary privilege or special favour, a deliberately exclusionary measure which prompted an enormous growth in the number of clubs throughout the nineteenth century, fed by a burgeoning and aspirational middle class.

At the turn of the twentieth century, there were more than 200 gentlemen's clubs in London alone, half of which had been founded since 1870. Inevitably, this level of competition could not be sustained, particularly given the number of men killed in two world wars. Financial restrictions necessitated greater provision for women and the relaxation of the social qualifications needed for membership. Nevertheless, waiting lists still exist for the leading clubs and a recommendation from at least one current member is almost always required to join.

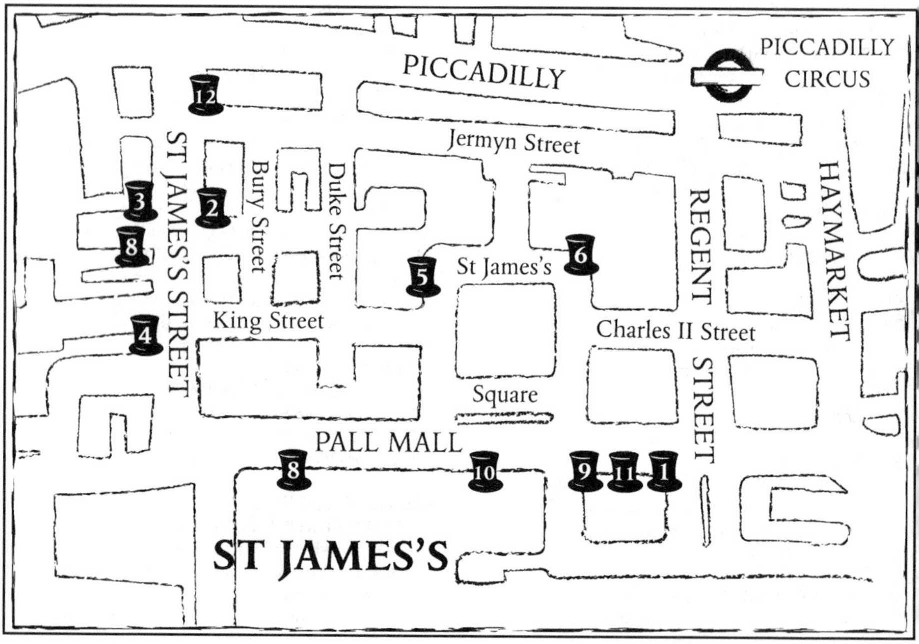

1 Athenaeum
2 Boodle's
3 Brooks's
4 Carlton and National clubs
5 East India Club
6 Naval and Military Club
7 Oxford and Cambridge Club
8 Pratt's
9 Reform Club
10 Royal Automobile Club
11 Travellers Club
12 White's

* Men only † Women only

ARMY AND NAVY CLUB (1837), 36 Pall Mall, London SW1Y 5JN T 020-7930 9721
E secretary@therag.co.uk W www.armynavyclub.co.uk
Chief Executive and Secretary, Cdr. J. A. Holt, MBE, RN

ARTS CLUB (1863), 40 Dover Street, London W1S 4NP
T 020-7499 8581 E secretary@theartsclub.co.uk
W www.theartsclub.co.uk
Secretary, Brian Clivaz
Former members: Charles Dickens, Algernon Charles Swinburne, Ivan Turgenev

ATHENAEUM (1824), 107 Pall Mall, London SW1Y 5ER
T 020-7930 4843 E library@hellenist.org.uk
Secretary, J. H. Ford
Former members: Matthew Arnold, Michael Faraday, Anthony Trollope

ATHENAEUM (1797), Church Alley, Liverpool L1 3DD
T 0151-709 7770 E info@theathenaeum.org.uk
W www.theathenaeum.org.uk
Honorary Secretary, David Gee

AUTHORS' CLUB (1892), 40 Dover Street, London W1S 4NP T 020-7408 5092 W www.theauthorsclub.co.uk
Secretary, Anna Drybala
Former members: E. M. Forster, Jerome K. Jerome, George Meredith

BATH AND COUNTY CLUB (1858), Queen's Parade, Bath BA1 2NJ T 01225-423732
E secretary@bathandcountyclub.com
W www.bathandcountyclub.com
President, Sir Alec Morris, KBE, CB

BEEFSTEAK CLUB* (1876), 9 Irving Street, London WC2H 7AH T 020-7930 5722 E beefsteakclub@tiscali.co.uk
Secretary, Maria Hibbert
Former members: John Betjeman, Rudyard Kipling, Harold Macmillan

BOODLE'S (1762), 28 St James's Street, London SW1A 1HJ T 020-7930 7166 E secretary@boodles.org
Secretary, Andrew Phillips
Former members: Winston Churchill, Ian Fleming

BROOKS'S* (1764), St James's Street, London SW1A 1LN T 020-7493 4411 E secretary@brooksclub.org
Secretary, G. Snell
Former members: Edward Gibbon, Roy Jenkins, William Pitt

BUCK'S CLUB* (1919), 18 Clifford Street, London W1S 3RF T 020-7734 2337 E secretary@bucksclub.co.uk
Secretary, Maj. Rupert Lendrum

CALEDONIAN CLUB (1891), 9 Halkin Street, London SW1X 7DR T 020-7235 5162 E admin@caledonianclub.com
W www.caledonianclub.com
Secretary, P. Varney

CANNING CLUB (1910), 4 St James's Square, London SW1Y 4JU T 020-7827 5730
E canningclub@navalandmilitaryclub.co.uk
Secretary, Emma Whitehouse

CARLTON CLUB (1832), 69 St James's Street, London SW1A 1PJ T 020-7493 1164 E info@carltonclub.co.uk
W www.carltonclub.co.uk
Secretary, Jonathan Orr-Ewing
Former members: Stanley Baldwin, Benjamin Disraeli, William Gladstone

CAVALRY AND GUARDS CLUB (1890), 127 Piccadilly, London W1J 7PX T 020-7499 1261
E secretary@cavgds.co.uk W www.cavgds.co.uk
Secretary, D. Cowdery

CHELSEA ARTS CLUB (1891), 143 Old Church Street, London SW3 6EB T 020-7376 3311
E secretary@chelseaartsclub.com
W www.chelseaartsclub.com
Secretary, D. Winterbottom

CITY LIVERY CLUB (1914), 38 St. Mary Axe, London EC3A 8EX T 020-7369 1672
E postbox@cityliveryclub.com
W www.cityliveryclub.com
Hon. Secretary, P. Herbage

CITY OF LONDON CLUB* (1832), 19 Old Broad Street, London EC2N 1DS T 020-7588 7991
E secretary@cityoflondonclub.com
W www.cityoflondonclub.com
Secretary, Ian Faul
Former member: Robert Peel

CITY UNIVERSITY CLUB (1895), 50 Cornhill, London EC3V 3PD T 020-7626 8571
E secretary@cityuniversityclub.co.uk
W www.cityuniversityclub.co.uk
Secretary, Miss R. C. Graham

THE COBDEN CLUB (1996), 170-172 Kensal Road, London W10 5BN T 020-8960 4222
E info@thecobden.co.uk W www.thecobden.co.uk
Membership Secretary, Lesley Young

THE COMMONWEALTH CLUB (1868), 25 Northumberland Avenue, London WC2N 5AP
T 020-7766 9200 E info@rcsint.org W www.rcsint.org
Membership Secretary, Jamie Gould

DEN NORSKE KLUB LTD (1887), In & Out, 4 St James's Square, London SW1Y 4JU T 020-7839 6242
W www.dennorskeklub.co.uk
Secretary, Jenifer Andersen

DURHAM COUNTY CLUB (1890), 52 Old Elvet, Durham DH1 3HN T 0191-384 8156
Hon. Secretary, S. Smith

EAST INDIA CLUB* (1849), 16 St James's Square, London SW1Y 4LH T 020-7930 1000
E secretary@eastindiaclub.co.uk
W www.eastindiaclub.co.uk
Secretary, A. Bray

FARMERS CLUB (1842), 3 Whitehall Court, London SW1A 2EL T 020-7930 3557
E reception@thefarmersclub.com
W www.thefarmersclub.com
Secretary, Air Cdre Stephen Skinner

FOX CLUB 46 Clarges Street, London W1J 7ER
T 020-7495 3656 E gerry@foxclublondon.com
W www.foxclublondon.com
Secretary, Bethan Seaton

FREWEN CLUB* (1869), 98 St Aldate's, Oxford OX1 1BT T 01865-243816
Hon. General Secretary, M. J. Dean

GARRICK CLUB* (1831), 15 Garrick Street, London WC2E 9AY T 020-7379 6478 E office@garrickclub.co.uk
W www.garrickclub.co.uk
Secretary, Olaf Born
Former members: Charles Dickens, Henry Irving, William Thackeray

GROUCHO CLUB (1985), 45 Dean Street, London W1D 4QB T 020-7439 4685 E info@thegrouchoclub.com
W www.thegrouchoclub.com
Secretary, Miriam Brown

THE HURLINGHAM CLUB (1869), Ranelagh Gardens, London SW6 3PR T 020-7736 8411
Chief Executive, Rear-Adm. Niall Kilgour, CB
Former member: King Edward VII

LONDON PRESS CLUB (1882), St Bride Institute, 14 Bride Lane, London EC4Y 8EQ T 020-7353 7086
E info@londonpressclub.co.uk
W www.londonpressclub.co.uk
Secretary, Peter Durrant
Former members: Edgar Wallace, Lord Astor, Lord Rothermere

NATIONAL CLUB* (1845), c/o The Carlton Club, 69 St James's Street, London SW1A 1PJ T 01225-480606
W www.thenationalclub.org.uk
Hon. Secretary, The Revd James Paice
Former member: Lord Coggan

NATIONAL LIBERAL CLUB (1882), Whitehall Place, London SW1A 2HE T 020-7930 9871 W www.nlc.org.uk
Secretary, S. J. Roberts
Former members: Ramsey MacDonald, George Bernard Shaw, H. G. Wells

NAVAL AND MILITARY CLUB (1862), 4 St James's Square, London SW1Y 4JU T 020-7827 5757
E club@navalandmilitaryclub.co.uk

W www.navalandmilitaryclub.co.uk
Secretary, Ian Gregory
THE NEW CLUB (1874), 2 Montpellier Parade, Cheltenham GL50 1UD T 01242-541121
E secretary@thenewclub.co.uk
W www.thenewclub.co.uk
Hon. Secretary, Peter Chadwick
THE NEW CLUB (1787), 86 Princes Street, Edinburgh EH2 2BB T 0131-226 4881 E info@newclub.co.uk
W www.newclub.co.uk
Secretary, Brig. C. D. M. Ritchie, CBE
Former members: Walter Scott, Alec Douglas-Home
NEW CAVENDISH CLUB (1920), 44 Great Cumberland Place, London W1H 7BS T 020-7723 0391
E info@newcavendishclub.co.uk
W www.newcavendishclub.co.uk
Chair, Christine Bird
NORTHERN COUNTIES CLUB (1829), 11 Hood Street, Newcastle upon Tyne NE1 6LH T 0191-232 2744
E secretary@northerncountiesclub.co.uk
W www.northerncountiesclub.co.uk
General Manager, D. J. Devennie
ORIENTAL CLUB (1824), Stratford House, Stratford Place, London W1C 1ES T 020-7629 5126
W www.orientalclub.org.uk
Secretary, Capt. D. M. Swain, RN
OXFORD AND CAMBRIDGE CLUB (1836), 71 Pall Mall, London SW1Y 5HD T 020-7930 5151
E club@oandc.uk.com
W www.oxfordandcambridgeclub.co.uk
Secretary, Alistair E. Telfer
Former members: Clement Attlee, William Gladstone, Duke of Wellington
PORTLAND CLUB (1816), 69 Brook Street, London W1Y 4ER T 020-7499 1523
Secretary, J. Burns, CBE
PRATT'S CLUB* (1841), 14 Park Place, London SW1A 1LP T 020-7493 0397 E secretary@prattsclub.org
Secretary, Graham Snell
Former member: Winston Churchill
REFORM CLUB (1836), 104–105 Pall Mall, London SW1Y 5EW T 020-7930 9374
E generaloffice@reformclub.com W www.reformclub.com
Secretary, M. D. B. McKerchar
Former members: Isambard Kingdom Brunel, Guy Burgess, Henry James
ROYAL AIR FORCE CLUB (1918), 128 Piccadilly, London W1J 7PY T 020-7399 1000 E admin@rafclub.org.uk
W www.rafclub.org.uk
Secretary, P. N. Owen
ROYAL ANGLO-BELGIAN CLUB (1955), 60 Knightsbridge, London SW1X 7LF T 020-7235 2121
E membership@ra-bc.com W www.ra-bc.com
Chairman, Michel Vanhoonacker
ROYAL AUTOMOBILE CLUB (1897), Pall Mall Clubhouse, 89 Pall Mall, London SW1Y 5HS
T 020-7930 2345 W www.royalautomobileclub.co.uk
Secretary, A. I. G. Kennedy, CB, CBE
Former members: Winston Churchill, Charles Rolls
ROYAL NORTHERN & UNIVERSITY CLUB (1854), 9 Albyn Place, Aberdeen AB1 1YE
T 01224-583292 W www.rnuc.org.uk
Secretary, Rosemary Black
ROYAL OVER-SEAS LEAGUE (1910), Over-Seas House, Park Place, St James's Street, London SW1A 1LR
T 020-7408 0214 E info@rosl.org.uk W www.rosl.org.uk
Director-General, R. F. Newell, LVO
ST STEPHEN'S CLUB (1870), 34 Queen Anne's Gate, London SW1H 9AB T 020-7222 1382
E info@ststephensclub.co.uk W www.ststephensclub.co.uk
Secretary, Bernard Moray
Former member: Benjamin Disraeli
SAVAGE CLUB* (1857), 1 Whitehall Place, London SW1A 2HD T 020-7930 8118 E info@savageclub.com
W www.savageclub.com
Hon. Secretary, vacant
Former members: Edward Elgar, Alexander Fleming, Dylan Thomas, Harry Secombe, Mark Twain, Peter Ustinov
SAVILE CLUB* (1868), 69 Brook Street, London W1K 4ER T 020-7629 5462 W www.savileclub.co.uk
Secretary, Julian Malone-Lee
Former members: Max Beerbohm, Thomas Hardy, Robert Louis Stevenson
SCOTTISH ARTS CLUB (1872), 24 Rutland Square, Edinburgh EH1 2BW T 0131-229 8157
E scottishartsclub@btconnect.com
W www.scottishartsclub.co.uk
Manager, Deirdre Nicholson
SLOANE CLUB (1976), Lower Sloane Street, London SW1W 8BS T 020-7730 9131 W www.sloaneclub.co.uk
Secretary, Fran Bremner
SOHO HOUSE 40 Greek Street, London W1D 4EB
T 020-7734 5188 W www.sohohouse.com (1995),
THREE ALBION PLACE (1849), 3 Albion Place, Leeds LS1 6JL T 0113-388 2800 E info@3albionplace.com
W www.3albionplace.com
Sales Manager, Maragaret Hirst
TRAVELLERS CLUB* (1819), 106 Pall Mall, London SW1Y 5EP T 020-7930 8688
E secretary@thetravellersclub.org.uk
W www.thetravellersclub.org.uk
Secretary, David Broadhead
Former members: Arthur Balfour, Alec Douglas-Home, Anthony Powell
TURF CLUB (1868), 5 Carlton House Terrace, London SW1Y 5AQ T 020-7930 8555 E mail@turfclub.co.uk
Secretary, Lt.-Col. O. R. StJ. Breakwell, MBE
ULSTER REFORM CLUB (1885), 4 Royal Avenue, Belfast BT1 1DA T 028-9032 3411
E info@ulsterreformclub.com W www.ulsterreformclub.com
General Manager, A. W. Graham
UNIVERSITY WOMEN'S CLUB† (1886), 2 Audley Square, London W1K 1DB T 020-7499 2268
E uwc@uwc-london.com
W www.universitywomensclub.com
Secretary, Ms S. McCue
THE VICTORIA CLUB (1853), 8 Beresford Street, St Helier JE2 4WN T 01534-723381
E victoriaclub@jerseymail.co.uk
W www.victoriaclubjersey.com
Manager, Martyn Styles
VINCENT'S (1863), 1A King Edward Street, Oxford OX1 4HS T 01865-722984 E vin5oxford@yahoo.co.uk
W www.vincents.org
Secretary, Simon Ackroyd
Former members: Roger Bannister, King Edward VIII
WESTERN CLUB (1825), 32 Royal Exchange Square, Glasgow G1 3AB T 0141-221 2016
E secretary@westernclub.co.uk W www.westernclub.co.uk
Secretary, Douglas Gifford
WHITE'S* (1693), 37–38 St James's Street, London SW1A 1JG T 020-7493 6671
Secretary, D. A. Anderson
Former members: Beau Brummel, Horace Walpole, Evelyn Waugh

SOCIETIES AND INSTITUTIONS

ABBEYFIELD SOCIETY (1956), Abbeyfield House, 53 Victoria Street, St Albans AL1 3UW **T** 01727-857536 **E** post@abbeyfield.com **W** www.abbeyfield.com
Chief Executive, Paul Allen

ACTION FOR BLIND PEOPLE (1857), 14–16 Verney Road, London SE16 3DZ **T** 0800-915 4666 **W** www.actionforblindpeople.org.uk
Chief Executive, Stephen Remington

ACTION MEDICAL RESEARCH (1952), Vincent House, Horsham RH12 2DP **T** 01403-210406 **E** info@action.org.uk **W** www.action.org.uk
Chief Executive, Simon Moore

ACTORS' BENEVOLENT FUND (1882), 6 Adam Street, London WC2N 6AD **T** 020-7836 6378 **E** office@abf.org.uk **W** www.actorsbenevolentfund.co.uk
General Secretary, Willie Bicket

ACTORS' CHARITABLE TRUST (1896), Africa House, 64–78 Kingsway, London WC2B 6BD **T** 020-7636 7868 **E** robert@tactactors.org **W** www.tactactors.org
General Secretary, Robert Ashby

ADAM SMITH INSTITUTE (1977), 23 Great Smith Street, London SW1P 3BL **T** 020-7222 4995 **E** info@adamsmith.org **W** www.adamsmith.org
President, Dr Madsen Pirie

ADVERTISING STANDARDS AUTHORITY (1962), Mid City Place, 71 High Holborn, London WC1V 6QT **T** 020-7492 2222 **E** enquiries@asa.org.uk **W** www.asa.org.uk
Director-General, Christopher Graham

AGE CONCERN (1940), Astral House, 1268 London Road, London SW16 4ER **T** 020-8765 7200, **Freephone** 0800-009 966 **W** www.ageconcern.org.uk
Director-General, Gordon Lishman, CBE

AGE CONCERN CYMRU, Ty John Pathy, 13–14 Neptune Court, Vanguard Way, Cardiff CF24 5PJ **T** 029-2043 1555 **E** enquiries@accymru.org.uk **W** www.accymru.org.uk
Director, R. W. Taylor

AGE CONCERN SCOTLAND (1943), Causewayside House, 160 Causewayside, Edinburgh EH9 1PR **T** 0845-125 9732 **E** enquiries@acscot.org.uk **W** www.ageconcernscotland.org.uk
Chair, Ian Kennedy

AGRICULTURAL ENGINEERS ASSOCIATION (1875), Samuelson House, Paxton Road, Orton Centre, Peterborough PE2 5LT **T** 08456-448748 **E** ceo@aea.uk.com **W** www.aea.uk.com
Chief Executive Officer, Roger Lane-Nott

ALCOHOLICS ANONYMOUS (1947), PO Box 1, 10 Toft Green, York YO1 7NJ **T** 01904-644026, **Helpline** 0845-769 7555 **E** help@alcoholics-anonymous.org.uk **W** www.alcoholics-anonymous.org.uk
General Secretary, Ann Napier

ALEXANDRA ROSE DAY (1912), 5 Mead Lane, Farnham GU9 7DY **T** 01252-726171 **E** enquiries@alexandraroseday.org.uk **W** www.alexandraroseday.org.uk
Operations Director, Diana le Clercq

ALZHEIMER'S SOCIETY (1979), Devon House, 58 St Katharine's Way, London E1W 1JX **T** 020-7423 3500 **E** info@alzheimers.org.uk **W** www.alzheimers.org.uk
Chief Executive, Neil Hunt

AMNESTY INTERNATIONAL UNITED KINGDOM (1961), The Human Rights Action Centre, 17–25 New Inn Yard, London EC2A 3EA **T** 020-7033 1500 **E** information@amnesty.org.uk **W** www.amnesty.org.uk
UK Director, Kate Allen

AMREF UK (1957), Clifford's Inn, Fetter Lane, London EC4A 1BZ **T** 020-7269 5520 **E** info@amrefuk.org **W** www.amref.org/uk
Chief Executive, Jo Ensor

ANCIENT MONUMENTS SOCIETY (1924), St Ann's Vestry Hall, 2 Church Entry, London EC4V 5HB **T** 020-7236 3934 **E** office@ancientmonumentssociety.org.uk **W** www.ancientmonumentssociety.org.uk
Secretary, M. J. Saunders, MBE

ANGLO-BELGIAN SOCIETY (1982), 5 Hartley Close, Bickley BR1 2TP **T** 020-8467 8442 **E** secretary@anglo-belgiansoc.com **W** www.anglo-belgiansoc.com
Chair, David Colvin CMG

ANGLO-DANISH SOCIETY (1924), 6 Keats Avenue, Littleover, Derby DE23 4ED **T** 01332-517160 **E** info@anglo-danishsociety.org.uk **W** www.anglo-danishsociety.org.uk
Chair, Simon Freeman

ANIMAL CONCERN (1876), PO Box 5178, Dumbarton G82 5YJ **T** 01389-841639 **E** animals@jfrobins.force9.co.uk **W** www.animalconcern.com
Secretary, John F Robins

ANIMAL HEALTH TRUST (1942), Lanwades Park, Kentford, Newmarket CB8 7UU **T** 01638-751000 **E** info@aht.org.uk **W** www.aht.org.uk
Chief Executive Officer, Dr Peter Webbon

ANTHROPOSOPHICAL SOCIETY IN GREAT BRITAIN (1923), Rudolf Steiner House, 35 Park Road, London NW1 6XT T 020-7723 4400 E rsh-office@anth.org.uk W www.rsh.anth.org.uk
General Secretaries, Ann Druitt & Philip Martyn

ANTI-SLAVERY INTERNATIONAL (1839), Thomas Clarkson House, The Stableyard, Broomgrove Road, London SW9 9TL T 020-7501 8920 E antislavery@antislavery.org W www.antislavery.org
Director, Aidan McQuade

ARCHITECTS BENEVOLENT SOCIETY (1850), 43 Portland Place, London W1B 1QH T 020-7580 2823 E help@absnet.org.uk W www.absnet.org.uk
Company Secretary, Keith Robinson

ARCHITECTURAL HERITAGE FUND (1976), Alhambra House, 27–31 Charing Cross Road, London WC2H 0AU T 020-7925 0199 E ahf@ahfund.org.uk W www.ahfund.org.uk
Chief Executive, I. Lush

ARLIS/UK AND IRELAND (1969), The National Art Library, V&A South Kensington, Cromwell Road, London SW7 2RL T 020-7942 2317 E arlis@vam.ac.uk W www.arlis.org.uk
Chair, Vanessa Crane

ART FUND (1903), Millais House, 7 Cromwell Place, London SW7 2JN T 020-7225 4800 E info@artfund.org W www.artfund.org
Director, David Barrie

ARTHRITIS CARE (1947), 18 Stephenson Way, London NW1 2HD T 020-7380 6500 E helplines@arthritiscare.org.uk W www.arthritiscare.org.uk
Chief Executive, Neil Betteridge

ASLIB (1924), Holywell Centre, 1 Phipp Street, London EC2A 4PS T 020-7613 3031 E aslib@aslib.com W www.aslib.co.uk
Managing Director, Roger Bowes

ASSOCIATION FOR CONSULTANCY AND ENGINEERING, Alliance House, 12 Caxton Street, London SW1H 0QL T 020-7222 6557 E consult@acenet.co.uk W www.acenet.co.uk
Chief Executive, Nelson Ogunshakin

ASSOCIATION FOR LANGUAGE LEARNING (1990), University of Leicester, University Road, Leicester LE7 7RH T 0116-229 7453 E info@all-languages.org.uk W www.all-languages.org.uk
President, Helen Myers

ASSOCIATION FOR SCIENCE EDUCATION (1901), College Lane, Hatfield AL10 9AA T 01707-283000 E info@ase.org.uk W www.ase.org.uk
Chief Executive, Dr Derek Bell

ASSOCIATION FOR THE PROTECTION OF RURAL SCOTLAND (1926), 3rd Floor, Gladstone's Land, 483 Lawnmarket, Edinburgh EH1 2NT T 0131-225 7012 E info@ruralscotland.org W www.ruralscotland.org
Director, vacant

ASSOCIATION OF ACCOUNTING TECHNICIANS (1980), 140 Aldersgate Street, London EC1A 4HY T 0845-863 0800 E aat@aat.org.uk W www.aat.org.uk
Chief Executive, Jane Scott Paul

ASSOCIATION OF ANAESTHETISTS OF GREAT BRITAIN AND IRELAND (1932), 21 Portland Place, London W1B 1PY T 020-7631 1650 E info@aagbi.org W www.aagbi.org
President, Dr Richard Birks

ASSOCIATION OF BRITISH DISPENSING OPTICIANS (1925), 199 Gloucester Terrace, London W2 6LD T 020-7298 5100 E general@abdo.org.uk W www.abdo.org.uk
General Secretary, Sir Anthony Garrett, CBE

ASSOCIATION OF BRITISH INSURERS (1985), 51 Gresham Street, London EC2V 7HQ T 020-7600 3333 E info@abi.org.uk W www.abi.org.uk
Director-General, Stephen Haddrill

ASSOCIATION OF BRITISH TRAVEL AGENTS (1950), 68–71 Newman Street, London W1T 3AH T 020-7637 2444 E abta@abta.co.uk W www.abta.com
Chief Executive, Mark Tanzer

ASSOCIATION OF BUILDING ENGINEERS (1925), Lutyens House, Billing Brook Road, Weston Favell, Northampton NN3 8NW T 01604-404121 E building.engineers@abe.org.uk W www.abe.org.uk
Chief Executive, D. Gibson

ASSOCIATION OF BUSINESS RECOVERY PROFESSIONALS (1990), 8th Floor, 120 Aldersgate Street, London EC1A 4JQ T 020-7566 4200 E association@r3.org.uk W www.r3.org.uk
Chief Operating Officer, Graham Rumney

ASSOCIATION OF CHARTERED CERTIFIED ACCOUNTANTS (1904), 29 Lincoln's Inn Fields, London WC2A 3EE T 0141-582 2000 E info@accaglobal.com W www.accaglobal.com
Chief Executive, Allen Blewitt

ASSOCIATION OF CONSULTING SCIENTISTS (1958), 5 Willow Heights, Cradley Heath B64 7PL T 0121-602-3515 E sg@sgconsult.co.uk W www.consultingscientists.co.uk
Secretary, Dr Stuart Guy

ASSOCIATION OF CONVENIENCE STORES LTD (1995), Federation House, 17 Farnborough Street, Farnborough GU14 8AG T 01252-515001 E acs@acs.org.uk W www.acs.org.uk
Chief Executive, James Lowman

ASSOCIATION OF CORPORATE TREASURERS (1979), 51 Moorgate, London EC2R 6BH T 020-7847 2540 E enquiries@treasurers.org W www.treasurers.org
Chief Executive, Richard Raeburn

ASSOCIATION OF COUNCIL SECRETARIES AND SOLICITORS (1996), 4 Sutton Court Lawns, Sutton Poyntz, Weymouth DT3 6LH T 01305-836328 W www.acses.org.uk
President, David Carter

ASSOCIATION OF COUNTY CHIEF EXECUTIVES (1974), Chief Executive's Office, Shire Hall, Castle Hill CB3 0AP T 01233 717111
Hon. Secretary, Mark Lloyd

ASSOCIATION OF DIRECTORS OF CHILDREN'S SERVICES (2007), Ellen Wilkinson Building, Devas Street, University of Manchester, Oxford Road, Manchester M13 9PL
T 0161-275 8810 E info@adcs.org.uk
W www.adcs.org.uk
Executive Director, Chris Waterman

ASSOCIATION OF DRAINAGE AUTHORITIES (1937), 12 Cranes Drive, Surbiton KT5 8AL
T 020-8399 7350 E admin@ada.org.uk
W www.ada.org.uk
Chief Executive, Jean Venables, OBE FRENG

ASSOCIATION OF FRIENDLY SOCIETIES (1995), PO Box 21, Altrincham, Cheshire WA14 4PD
T 0161-952 5051 E info@afs.org.uk W www.afs.org.uk
General Secretary, Martin Shaw

ASSOCIATION OF GENEALOGISTS AND RESEARCHERS IN ARCHIVES (1968), 29 Badgers Close, Horsham RH12 5RU E agra@agra.org.uk
W www.agra.org.uk
Company Secretary, David R. Young

ASSOCIATION OF ROYAL NAVY OFFICERS (1920), 70 Porchester Terrace, London W2 3TP
T 020-7402 5231 E osec@arno.org.uk
W www.arno.org.uk
Secretary, Cdr. W. K. Ridley

ASTHMA UK (1989), Summit House, 70 Wilson Street, London EC2A 2DB T 020-7786 4900 E info@asthma.org.uk
W www.asthma.org.uk
Chief Executive, Neil Churchill

AUDIT BUREAU OF CIRCULATIONS LTD (1931), Saxon House, 211 High Street, Berkhamsted HP4 1AD
T 01442-870800 E abcpost@abc.co.uk
W www.abc.org.uk
Chief Executive, Chris Boyd

AUTOMOBILE ASSOCIATION (1905), Fanum House, Basingstoke RG21 4EA T 0800-085 2721
E customer.services@theaa.com W www.theaa.com
Chief Executive, Andrew Strong

BALTIC AIR CHARTER ASSOCIATION (1949), The Baltic Exchange, 38 St Mary Axe, London EC3R 8BH
T 020-7623 5501 E baca@balticexchange.com
W www.baca.org.uk
Chair, Markham Jackson

BALTIC EXCHANGE (1744), 38 St Mary Axe, London EC3A 8BH T 020-7623 5501
E enquiries@balticexchange.com
W www.balticexchange.com
Chief Executive, Jeremy Penn

BALTIC EXCHANGE CHARITABLE SOCIETY (1978), 20 St Dunstans Hill, London EC3R 8HL
T 020-7283 6090
Secretary, R. J. M. Butler

BAR ASSOCIATION FOR LOCAL GOVERNMENT AND THE PUBLIC SERVICE (1945), c/o Birmingham City Council, Ingleby House, 11–14 Cannon Street, Birmingham B2 5EN T 0121-303 9991
E chairman@balgps.org.uk W www.balgps.org.uk
Chair, M. F. N. Ahmad

BARNARDO'S (1866), Tanners Lane, Barkingside, Ilford IG6 1QG T 020-8550 8822
E information@barnardos.org.uk W www.barnardos.org.uk
Chief Executive, Martin Narey

BARRISTERS' BENEVOLENT ASSOCIATION (1873), 14 Gray's Inn Square, London WC1R 5JP
T 020-7242 4761 E enquiries@the-bba.com
W www.the-bba.com
Director, Janet South

BEAT, Wensum House, 103 Prince of Wales Road, Norwich NR1 1DW T 0870-770 3256,
Helpline 0845-634 1414, **Youthline** 0845-634 7650
E info@b-eat.co.uk W www.b-eat.co.uk
Chief Executive, Mrs Susan Ringwood

BEVIN BOYS ASSOCIATION (1989), 1 Rundlestone Court, Poundbury, Dorchester DT1 3TN T 01305-261269
Chairman, Warwick Taylor, MBE

BIBLIOGRAPHICAL SOCIETY (1892), c/o University of London, Institute of English Studies, Senate House, Malet Street, London WC1E 7HU T 020-7862 8679
E admin@bibsoc.org.uk W www.bibsoc.org.uk
Hon. Secretary, M. L. Ford

BIRMINGHAM AND WARWICKSHIRE ARCHAEOLOGICAL SOCIETY (1870), c/o Birmingham and Midland Institute, Margaret Street, Birmingham B3 3BS
W www.birminghamandwarwickshirearchaeologicalsociety.co.uk
President, Dr D. Hooke

BLUE CROSS (1897), Shilton Road, Burford OX18 4PF
T 01993-822651 E info@bluecross.org.uk
W www.thebluecross.org.uk
Chief Executive, John Rutter

BOOK AID INTERNATIONAL (1954), 39–41 Coldharbour Lane, London SE5 9NR T 020-7733 3577
E info@bookaid.org W www.bookaid.org
Director, Clive Nettleton

BOOKSELLERS ASSOCIATION OF THE UK & IRELAND LTD (1895), Minster House, 272 Vauxhall Bridge Road, London SW1V 1BA T 020-7802 0802
E mail@booksellers.org.uk W www.booksellers.org.uk
Chief Executive, T. E. Godfray

BOOKTRUST (1926), Book House, 45 East Hill, London SW18 2QZ T 020-8516 2977
E query@booktrust.org.uk W www.booktrust.org.uk
Director, Vivian Bird

BOTANICAL SOCIETY OF SCOTLAND (1836), c/o Royal Botanic Garden Edinburgh, 20A Inverleith Row, Edinburgh EH3 5LR T 0131-552 7171
W www.botsocscot.org.uk
Hon. General Secretary, Dr M. P. Cochrane

BOTANICAL SOCIETY OF THE BRITISH ISLES (1836), c/o Department of Botany, The Natural History Museum, Cromwell Road, London SW7 5BD T 020-7942 5002 E coordinator@bsbi.org.uk W www.bsbi.org.uk
Director of Research and Development, K. Walker

BOYS' BRIGADE (1883), Felden Lodge, Felden, Hemel Hempstead HP3 0BL T 01442-231681 E enquiries@boys-brigade.org.uk W www.boys-brigade.org.uk
Brigade Secretary, Steven Dickinson

BRISTOL AND GLOUCESTERSHIRE ARCHAEOLOGICAL SOCIETY (1876), Stonehatch, Oakridge Lynch, Stroud GL6 7NR T 01285-760460 E john@loosleyj.freeserve.co.uk W www.bgas.org.uk
Hon. General Secretary, John Loosley

BRITISH AND FOREIGN BIBLE SOCIETY (1804), Stonehill Green, Westlea, Swindon SN5 7DG T 01793-418222 E contactus@biblesociety.org.uk W www.biblesociety.org.uk
Chief Executive, James Catford

BRITISH ANTIQUE DEALERS' ASSOCIATION (1918), 20 Rutland Gate, London SW7 1BD T 020-7589 4128 E info@bada.org W www.bada.org
Secretary-General, Mrs E. J. Dean

BRITISH ASSOCIATION FOR EARLY CHILDHOOD EDUCATION (1923), 136 Cavell Street, London E1 2JA T 020-7539 5400 E office@early-education.org.uk W www.early-education.org.uk
Chief Executive, Anne Nelson

BRITISH ASSOCIATION FOR LOCAL HISTORY, PO Box 6549, Somersal Herbert DE6 5WH T 01283-585947 E mail@balh.co.uk W www.balh.co.uk

BRITISH ASSOCIATION OF COMMUNICATORS IN BUSINESS (1949), Suite GA2, Oak House, Woodlands Business Park, Breckland, Linford Wood West MK14 6EY T 01908-313755 E enquiries@cib.uk.com W www.cib.uk.com
Chief Executive, Kathie Jones

BRITISH ASSOCIATION OF SOCIAL WORKERS (1970), 16 Kent Street, Birmingham B5 6RD T 0121-622 3911 W www.basw.co.uk
Director, I. Johnston

BRITISH ASTRONOMICAL ASSOCIATION (1890), Burlington House, Piccadilly, London W1J 0DU T 020-7734 4145 E office@britastro.org W www.britastro.org
President, Roger Pickard

BRITISH BEEKEEPERS' ASSOCIATION (1874), National Beekeeping Centre, Stoneleigh Park, Kenilworth CV8 2LG T 024-7669 6679 E bbka@britishbeekeepers.com W www.britishbeekeepers.com
General Secretary, Martin Tovey

BRITISH BOARD OF FILM CLASSIFICATION (1912), 3 Soho Square, London W1D 3HD T 020-7440 1570 E contact_the_bbfc@bbfc.co.uk W www.bbfc.co.uk
Director, David Cooke

BRITISH CHAMBERS OF COMMERCE, 65 Petty France, St James Park, London SW1H 9EU T 020-7654 5800 E info@britishchambers.org.uk W www.chamberonline.co.uk
Director-General, David Frost

BRITISH COMPUTER SOCIETY (1957), 1st Floor, Block D, North Star House, North Star Avenue SN2 1FA T 01793-417417 E bcs@hq.bcs.org.uk W www.bcs.org
Chief Executive, David Clarke

BRITISH DEAF ASSOCIATION (1890), 1–3 Worship Street, London EC2A 2AB T 02476-550936 E midlands@bda.org.uk W www.bda.org.uk
Executive Chair, Francis P. Murphy

BRITISH DENTAL ASSOCIATION (1880), 64 Wimpole Street, London W1G 8YS T 020-7935 0875 E enquiries@bda.org W www.bda.org
Chief Executive, Peter Ward

BRITISH EXPERTISE (1965), One Westminster Palace Gardens, 1–7 Artillery Row, London SW1P 1RJ T 020-7222 3651 E mail@britishexpertise.org W www.britishexpertise.org
Chief Executive, G. Hand

BRITISH FALSE MEMORY SOCIETY (1993), Bradford on Avon BA15 1NF T 01225-868682 E bfms@bfms.org.uk W www.bfms.org.uk
Director, M. Greenhalgh

BRITISH FEDERATION OF WOMEN GRADUATES (1907), 4 Mandeville Courtyard, 142 Battersea Park Road, London SW11 4NB T 020-7498 8037 E hq@bfwg.org.uk W www.bfwg.org.uk
President, Elizabeth M. E. Poskitt

BRITISH HEALTH CARE ASSOCIATION (1930), Unit 8, Cherry Hall Road, Noth Kettering Business Park, Kettering NN14 1UE T 01536-519960 E steve.fritz@bhcaservices.co.uk W www.bhca.org.uk
Chief Executive, Stephen Fritz

BRITISH HEART FOUNDATION (1961), 14 Fitzhardinge Street, London W1H 6DH T 020-7935 0185 E internet@bhf.org.uk W www.bhf.org.uk
Director-General, Peter Hollins

BRITISH HEDGEHOG PRESERVATION SOCIETY (1982), Hedgehog House, Dhustone, Ludlow SY8 3PL T 01584-890801 E info@britishhedgehogs.org.uk W www.britishhedgehogs.org.uk
Chief Executive, Fay Vass

BRITISH HERPETOLOGICAL SOCIETY (1947), c/o The Zoological Society of London, Regent's Park, London NW1 4RY T 01674-671676 E enquiries@thebhs.org W www.thebhs.org
President, Prof. Trevor J. C. Beebee

BRITISH HOROLOGICAL INSTITUTE (1858), Upton Hall, Upton, Newark NG23 5TE **T** 01636-813795 **E** info@bhi.co.uk **W** www.bhi.co.uk

BRITISH HORSE SOCIETY (1947), Stoneleigh Deer Park, Stareton Lane, Kenilworth CV8 2XZ **T** 0844-848 1666 **E** enquiry@bhs.org.uk **W** www.bhs.org.uk
Chief Executive, Graham Cory

BRITISH HOSPITALITY ASSOCIATION, Queens House, 55–56 Lincoln's Inn Fields, London WC2A 3BH **T** 0845-880 7744 **E** info@bha.org.uk **W** www.bha.org.uk
Chief Executive, Robert Cotton, OBE

BRITISH HUMANIST ASSOCIATION (1896), 1 Gower Street, London WC1E 6HD **T** 020-7079 3580 **E** info@humanism.org.uk **W** www.humanism.org.uk
Chief Executive, Hanne Stinson

BRITISH INSTITUTE IN EASTERN AFRICA (1959), 10 Carlton House Terrace, London SW1Y 5AH **T** 020-7969 5201 **E** biea@britac.ac.uk **W** www.biea.ac.uk
Director, Dr Justin Willis

BRITISH INSTITUTE OF GRAPHOLOGISTS (1983), PO Box 3060, Gerrards Cross, SL9 9XP **T** 01753-891241 **E** contact@britishgraphology.org **W** www.britishgraphology.org
Chair, John Beck

BRITISH INSTITUTE OF PROFESSIONAL PHOTOGRAPHY (1901), 1 Prebendal Court, Oxford Road, Aylesbury HP19 8EY **T** 01296-718350 **E** info@bipp.com **W** www.bipp.com
Chief Executive Officer, Chris Harper

BRITISH INTERPLANETARY SOCIETY (1933), 27–29 South Lambeth Road, London SW8 1SZ **T** 020-7735 3160 **E** mail@bis-spaceflight.com **W** www.bis-spaceflight.com
Executive Secretary, Suszann Parry

BRITISH-ISRAEL-WORLD FEDERATION (1919), 121 Low Etherley, Bishop Auckland, Co Durham DL14 0HA **T** 01388-834395 **E** admin@britishisrael.co.uk **W** www.britishisrael.co.uk
President, M. A. Clark

BRITISH LUNG FOUNDATION (1985), 73–75 Goswell Road, London EC1V 7ER **T** 08458-505020 **E** enquiries@blf-uk.org **W** www.lunguk.org
Chief Executive, Dame Helena Shovelton, DBE

BRITISH MANAGEMENT DATA FOUNDATION (1979), Highfield, Longridge, Sheepscombe GL6 7QU **T** 01452-812837 **E** bmdfstroud@aol.com **W** www.bmdf.co.uk; www.eurotreaties.com
Director, Anthony Cowgill, MBE

BRITISH MEDICAL ASSOCIATION (1832), BMA House, Tavistock Square, London WC1H 9JP **T** 020-7387 4499 **W** www.bma.org.uk
Chief Executive, Tony Bourne

BRITISH MENSA LTD (1946), St John's House, St John's Square, Wolverhampton WV2 4AH **T** 01902-772771 **E** enquiries@mensa.org.uk **W** www.mensa.org.uk
Chief Executive and Company Secretary, John Stevenage

BRITISH MUSIC HALL SOCIETY (1963), 'Meander', 361 Watford Road, Chiswell Green, St Albans AL2 3DB **T** 01727-768878 **W** www.music-hall-society.com
President, Roy Hudd

BRITISH MUSIC INFORMATION CENTRE (1967), 1st Floor, British Music House, 26, Berners Street, London W1T 3LR **T** 020-7580 3869 **E** info@bmic.co.uk **W** www.bmic.co.uk
Director, Matthew Greenall

BRITISH NATURALISTS' ASSOCIATION (1905), 1 Bracken Mews, London E4 7UT **E** info@bna-naturalists.org **W** www.bna-naturalists.org
Hon. Membership Secretary, Yvonne Griffiths

BRITISH NUCLEAR ENERGY SOCIETY (1962), 1 Great George Street, London SW1P 3AA **T** 020-8698 1500 **E** admin@inuce.org.uk **W** www.bnes.org.uk
Secretary, Mark Askew

BRITISH NUTRITION FOUNDATION (1967), High Holborn House, 52–54 High Holborn, London WC1V 6RQ **T** 020-7404 6504 **E** postbox@nutrition.org.uk **W** www.nutrition.org.uk
Director-General, Prof. J. L. Buttriss, PHD

BRITISH PHARMACOLOGICAL SOCIETY (1931), 16 Angel Gate, City Road, London EC1V 2PT **T** 020-7417 0110 **E** ks@bps.ac.uk **W** www.bps.ac.uk
President, Jeff Aronson

BRITISH POLIO FELLOWSHIP (1939), Eagle Office Centre, The Runway, South Ruislip HA4 6SE **T** 0800-018 0586 **E** info@britishpolio.org.uk **W** www.britishpolio.org.uk
Chief Executive, Graham Ball

BRITISH PSYCHOLOGICAL SOCIETY (1901), St Andrews House, 48 Princess Road East, Leicester LE1 7DR **T** 0116-254 9568 **E** enquiry@bps.org.uk **W** www.bps.org.uk
President, Elizabeth Campbell

BRITISH RED CROSS (1870), 44 Moorfields, London EC2Y 9AL **T** 0844-871 1111 **E** information@redcross.org.uk **W** www.redcross.org.uk
Chief Executive, Sir Nicholas Young

BRITISH TRUST FOR ORNITHOLOGY (1933), The Nunnery, Thetford IP24 2PU **T** 01842-750050 **E** info@bto.org **W** www.bto.org
Director, Dr Andy Clements

BRITISH UNION FOR THE ABOLITION OF VIVISECTION (1898), 16A Crane Grove, London N7 8NN **T** 020-7700 4888 **E** info@buav.org **W** www.buav.org
Chief Executive (acting), Lindsey Lavender

BRITISH VETERINARY ASSOCIATION (1883), 7 Mansfield Street, London W1G 9NQ **T** 020-7636 6541 **E** bvahq@bva.co.uk **W** www.bva.co.uk
Secretary General, Henrietta Alderman

BTBS THE BOOK TRADE CHARITY (1837), The Foyle Centre, The Retreat, Kings Langley WD4 8LT T 01923-263128
E btbs@booktradecharity.demon.co.uk
W www.booktradecharity.demon.co.uk
Chief Executive, David Hicks

BUCKINGHAMSHIRE ARCHAEOLOGICAL SOCIETY (1847), County Museum, Church Street, Aylesbury HP20 2QP
T 01296-387341 E bucksas@buckscc.gov.uk
W www.bucksas.org.uk
Hon. Secretary, Maureen Brown

BUILDING SOCIETIES ASSOCIATION (1869), York House, 23 Kingsway, London WC2B 6UJ
T 020-7520 5900 E information@bsa.org.uk
W www.bsa.org.uk
Director-General, A. Coles

CAFOD (CATHOLIC FUND FOR OVERSEAS DEVELOPMENT) (1962), Romero Close, Stockwell Road, London SW9 9TY
T 020-7733 7900 E cafod@cafod.org.uk
W www.cafod.org.uk
Director, Chris Bain

CALOUSTE GULBENKIAN FOUNDATION (1956), 98 Portland Place, London W1B 1ET
T 020-7636 5313 E info@gulbenkian.org.uk
W www.gulbenkian.org.uk
Director, Andrew Barnett

CAMBRIAN ARCHAEOLOGICAL ASSOCIATION (1847), Halfway House, Pont y Pandy, Bangor LL57 3DG
T 01248-364865 W www.cambrians.org.uk
General Secretary, Rev M. Coombe

CAMBRIDGE ANTIQUARIAN SOCIETY (1840), 21 High Street, West Wickham, Cambridge CB21 4RY
E secretary@camantsoc.org W www.camantsoc.org
Hon. Secretary, Janet Morris

CAMPAIGN FOR COURTESY (1986), 240 Tolworth Rise South, Surbiton, Surrey KT5 9NB T 020-8330 3707
E peter.foot1@btinternet.com
W www.campaignforcourtesy.org
Chairman, Peter G. Foot

CAMPAIGN FOR FREEDOM OF INFORMATION (1984), Suite 102, 16 Baldwins Gardens, London EC1N 7RJ
T 020-7831 7477 E admin@cfoi.demon.co.uk
W www.cfoi.org.uk
Director, Maurice Frankel

CAMPAIGN FOR NUCLEAR DISARMAMENT (1958), 162 Holloway Road, London N7 8DQ
T 020-7700 2393 E enquiries@cnduk.org
W www.cnduk.org
Chair, Kate Hudson

CAMPAIGN FOR THE PROTECTION OF RURAL WALES (1928), Ty Gwyn, 31 High Street, Welshpool SY21 7YD T 01938-552525 E info@cprwmail.org.uk
W www.cprw.org.uk
Director, Peter Ogden

CANADA-UNITED KINGDOM CHAMBER OF COMMERCE (1921), 38 Grosvenor Street, London W1K 4DP T 020-7258 6578 E info@canada-uk.org
W www.canada-uk.org
Executive Director, Nigel Bacon

CANCER RESEARCH UK, (2002), PO Box 123, Lincoln's Inn Fields, London WC2A 3PX T 020-7242 0200
W www.cancerresearchuk.org
Chief Executive, Harpal Kumar

CARERS UK (1965), 32–36 Loman Street, Southwark, London SE1 0EE T 020-7922 8000 E info@carersuk.org
W www.carersuk.org
Chief Executive, Imelda Redmond

CARNEGIE UNITED KINGDOM TRUST (1913), Andrew Carnegie House, Pittencrieff Street, Dunfermline KY12 8AW T 01383-721445 E info@carnegieuk.org
W www.carnegieuktrust.org.uk
Chief Executive, C. McConnell

CATHEDRALS FABRIC COMMISSION FOR ENGLAND (1991), Church House, Great Smith Street, London SW1P 3NZ T 020-7898 1863
E enquiries@ccb.c-of-e.org.uk
Secretary (acting), Maggie Goodall

CATHOLIC TRUTH SOCIETY (1868), 40–46 Harleyford Road, London SE11 5AY T 020-7640 0042
E info@cts-online.org.uk W www.cts-online.org.uk
General Secretary, Fergal Martin

CATHOLIC UNION OF GREAT BRITAIN (1872), St Maximillian Kolbe House, 63 Jeddo Road, London W12 9EE T 020-8749 1321 E info@catholicunion.org
W www.catholicunion.org
President, Lord Brennan, QC

CENTRAL AND CECIL HOUSING TRUST (1927), 266 Waterloo Road, London, Richmond SE1 8RQ
T 020-7922 5300 E enquiries@ccht.org.uk
W www.ccht.org.uk
Chief Executive, Dorry McLaughlin

CENTRAL COUNCIL OF CHURCH BELL RINGERS (1891), The Cottage, School Hill, Warnham, Horsham RH12 3QN T 01403-269743 W www.cccbr.org.uk
Hon. Secretary, Ian H. Oram

CENTREPOINT (1969), Central House, 25 Clamperdown Street, London E1 8DZ T 0845-466 3400
E info@centrepoint.org W www.centrepoint.org.uk
Chief Executive, Anthony Lawton

CHARITIES AID FOUNDATION (1924), 25 Kings Hill Avenue, West Malling ME19 4TA T 01732-520000
E enquiries@cafonline.org W www.cafonline.org
Chief Executive, John Low, FRSA

CHARTERED INSTITUTE OF ARBITRATORS (1915), International Arbitration and Mediation Centre, 12–14 Bloomsbury Square, London WC1A 2LP
T 020-7421 7444 E info@arbitrators.org
W www.arbitrators.org
Director-General, Michael Forbes Smith

CHARTERED INSTITUTE OF ENVIRONMENTAL HEALTH (1883), Chadwick Court, 15 Hatfields, London SE1 8DJ T 020-7928 6006 E information@cieh.org W www.cieh.org
Chief Executive, G. Jukes

CHARTERED INSTITUTE OF JOURNALISTS (1890), 2 Dock Offices, Surrey Quays Road, London SE16 2XU T 020-7252 1187 E memberservices@cioj.co.uk W www.cioj.co.uk
General Secretary, Dominic Cooper

CHARTERED INSTITUTE OF LINGUISTS (1910), Saxon House, 48 Southwark Street, London SE1 1UN T 020-7940 3100 E info@iol.org.uk W www.iol.org.uk
Chief Executive, D. John Hammond

CHARTERED INSTITUTE OF PURCHASING AND SUPPLY (1932), Easton House, Easton on the Hill, Stamford PE9 3NZ T 01780-756777 E info@cips.org W www.cips.org
Chief Executive, Simon Sperryn

CHARTERED INSTITUTE OF TAXATION (1930), 12 Upper Belgrave Street, London SW1X 8BB T 020-7235 9381 E post@ciot.org.uk W www.tax.org.uk
Secretary-General, R. A. Dommett

CHARTERED INSTITUTION OF BUILDING SERVICES ENGINEERS (1898), Delta House, 222 Balham High Road, London SW12 9BS T 020-8675 5211 E enquiries@cibse.org W www.cibse.org
Chief Executive, Stephen Matthews

CHARTERED INSURANCE INSTITUTE (1897), 42-48 High Road, South Woodford, London E18 2JP T 020-8989 8464 E customer.serv@cii.co.uk W www.cii.co.uk
Chief Executive, Dr A. Scott

CHARTERED MANAGEMENT INSTITUTE (1947), Management House, Cottingham Road, Corby NN17 1TT T 01536-204222 E enquiries@managers.org.uk W www.managers.org.uk
Chief Executive, Ruth Spellman

CHATHAM HOUSE (1920), Chatham House, 10 St James's Square, London SW1Y 4LE T 020-7957 5700 E contact@chathamhouse.org.uk W www.chathamhouse.org.uk
Director, Dr Robin Niblett

CHILDREN 1ST (1884), 83 Whitehouse Loan, Edinburgh EH9 1AT T 0131-446 2300 E info@children1st.org.uk W www.children1st.org.uk
Chief Executive, Anne Houston

CHILDREN'S SOCIETY (1881), Edward Rudolf House, Margery Street, London WC1X 0JL T 0845-300 1128 E supporteraction@childrenssociety.org.uk W www.childrenssociety.org.uk
Chief Executive, Bob Reitemeier

CHRISTIAN AID (1945), 35 Lower Marsh, London SE1 7RL T 020-7620 4444 E info@christian-aid.org W www.christianaid.org.uk
Director, Dr Daljeep Mukarji

CHRISTIAN AID SCOTLAND (1945), Pentagon Centre, 36 Washington Street, Glasgow G3 8AZ T 0141-221 7475 E info@christian-aid.org W www.christianaid.org.uk
National Secretary for Scotland, Gavin McLellan

CHRISTIAN EDUCATION, 1020 Bristol Road, Selly Oak, Birmingham B29 6LB T 0121-472 4242 E enquiries@christianeducation.org.uk W www.christianeducation.org.uk
Chief Executive, Peter Fishpool

CHURCHILL CENTRE UK (1968), PO Box 1915, Quarley, Andover SP10 9EE T 01264-889627 E ndege@tiscali.co.uk W www.winstonchurchill.org
UK Chairman, P. H. Courtenay

CHURCHILL SOCIETY – LONDON (1990), Ivy House, 18 Grove Lane, Ipswich IP4 1NR T 01473-413533 E dutysecretary@churchill-society-london.org.uk W www.churchill-society-london.org.uk
General Secretary, J. H. Rogers

CHURCH LADS' AND CHURCH GIRLS' BRIGADE (1891), 2 Barnsley Road, Wath-upon-Dearne, Rotherham S63 6PY T 01709-876535 E brigadesecretary@clcgb.org.uk W www.clcgb.org.uk
Brigade Secretary, A. Millward

CHURCH MISSION SOCIETY (1799), 99 Watlington Road, Oxford OX4 6B2 T 0845-620 1799 E info@cms-uk.org W www.cms-uk.org
General Secretary, Revd Canon T. Dakin

CHURCH MONUMENTS SOCIETY (1979), Moor View, Exbourne EX20 3SA T 01837-851483 E churchmonuments@aol.com W www.churchmonumentssociety.org
Secretary, Dr Amy Harris

CHURCH UNION (1859), Faith House, 7 Tufton Street, London SW1P 3QN T 01371-830132 E secretary@churchunion.co.uk W www.churchunion.co.uk
Chair, David Llewelyn Morgan

CITIZENS ADVICE (1939), Myddelton House, 115–123 Pentonville Road, London N1 9LZ T 020-7833 2181 W www.citizensadvice.org.uk
Chief Executive, D. Harker

CITY BUSINESS LIBRARY (1970), Corporation of London, 1 Brewers' Hall Garden, London EC2V 5BX T 020-7332 1812 E cbl@cityoflondon.gov.uk W www.cityoflondon.gov.uk/citybusinesslibrary
Business Librarian, Goretti Considine

CITY OF COVENTRY FREEMEN'S GUILD (1946), 1 Trossachs Road, Coventry CV5 7BJ T 024-7646 3203 W www.coventryfreemensguild.co.uk
Hon. Clerk, George Wilkinson

CIVIC TRUST (1957), Essex Hall, 1–6 Essex Street, London WC2R 3HU T 020-7539 7900 E info@civictrust.org.uk W www.civictrust.org.uk
Managing Director, Peter Bembridge

CLASSICAL ASSOCIATION (1903), Senate House, Malet Street, London WC1E 7HU T 020-7862 8706 E office@classicalassociation.org W www.classicalassociation.org
Secretary, Clare Roberts

COLLEGE OF OPTOMETRISTS (1980), 42 Craven Street, London WC2N 5NG T 020-7839 6000 E optometry@college-optometrists.org W www.college-optometrists.org
Chief Executive, Bryony Pawinska

COMMONWEALTH SOCIETY FOR THE DEAF 'SOUND SEEKERS' (1959), 34 Buckingham Palace Road, London SW1W 0RE T 020-7233 5700 E sound.seekers@btinternet.com W www.sound-seekers.org.uk
Chief Executive, Gary Williams

CONSUMERS' ASSOCIATION (1957), 2 Marylebone Road, London NW1 4DF T 020-7770 7000 E which@which.co.uk W www.which.co.uk
Chief Executive, Peter Vicary-Smith

CONTEMPORARY APPLIED ARTS (1948), 2 Percy Street, London W1T 1DD T 020-7436 2344 E sales@caa.org.uk W www.caa.org.uk
Director, Sarah Edwards

COOPERATIVE GROUP (CWS) LTD. (1863), PO Box 53, New Century House, Manchester M60 4ES T 0161-834 1212 W www.co-op.co.uk
Chief Executive, Peter Marks

COOPERATIVE PARTY (1917), 77 Weston Street, London SE1 3SD T 020-7367 4150 E mail@party.coop W www.party.coop
General Secretary, Michael Stephenson

COOPERATIVES UK, Holyoake House, Hanover Street, Manchester M60 0AS T 0161-246 2900 E info@cooperatives-uk.coop W www.cooperatives-uk.coop
Chief Executive, Dame Pauline Green

CORAM FAMILY (1739), 49 Mecklenburgh Square, London WC1N 2QA T 020-7520 0300 E reception@coram.org.uk W www.coram.org.uk
Chief Executive, Dr Carol Homden

CORPORATION OF CHURCH HOUSE (1888), Church House, Great Smith Street, London SW1P 3AZ T 020-7898 1000 E info@churchhouse.org.uk W www.churchhouse.org.uk
Secretary, Colin D. L. Menzies

COUNCIL FOR AWARDS OF ROYAL AGRICULTURAL SOCIETIES, 23 Queen's Road, Ryde, PO33 3BG T 01626-873159 E john@wibbs.fsnet.co.uk
Hon. Secretary, Dr John Wibberley

COUNCIL FOR BRITISH ARCHAEOLOGY (1944), St Mary's House, 66 Bootham, York YO30 7BZ T 01904-671417 E info@britarch.ac.uk W www.britarch.ac.uk
Director, Dr M. Heyworth

COUNCIL FOR THE CARE OF CHURCHES (1921), Church House, Great Smith Street, London SW1P 3NZ T 020-7898 1866 E enquiries@ccb.c-of-e.org.uk
Secretary (acting), Stephen Bowler

COUNCIL FOR WORLD MISSION (1977), Ipalo House, 32–34 Great Peter Street, London SW1P 2DB T 020-7222 4214 E council@cwmission.org.uk W www.cwmission.org.uk
General Secretary, Revd Dr D. van der Water

COUNCIL OF CHRISTIANS AND JEWS (1942), 1st Floor, Camelford House, 87-89 Albert Embankment, London SE1 7TP T 020-7820 0090 E cjrelations@ccj.org.uk W www.ccj.org.uk
Chief Executive, David Gifford

COUNCIL OF UNIVERSITY CLASSICAL DEPARTMENTS (1972), Faculty of Classics, Sidgwick Avenue, Cambridge CB3 9DA T 01223-335158 E ro225@cam.ac.uk W www.rhul.ac.uk/classics/cucd
Chair, Prof Robin G. Osborne, FBA

COUNSEL AND CARE (1954), Twyman House, 16 Bonny Street, London NW1 9PG T 020-7241 8555 E advice@counselandcare.org.uk W www.counselandcare.org.uk
Chief Executive, Stephen Burke

COUNTRY HOUSES FOUNDATION (2005), The Manor, Hasely Business Centre, Warwick CV35 7LS T 0845-402 4102 E info@countryhousesfoundation.org.uk W www.countryhousesfoundation.org.uk
Chief Executive, David Price

COUNTRY LAND & BUSINESS ASSOCIATION (1907), 16 Belgrave Square, London SW1X 8PQ T 020-7235 0511 E mail@cla.org.uk W www.cla.org.uk
President, Sir Henry Aubrey-Fletcher

COUNTRYSIDE ALLIANCE (1997), Old Town Hall, 367 Kennington Road, London SE11 4PT T 020-7840 9200 E info@countryside-alliance.org W www.countryside-alliance.org.uk
Chief Executive, Simon Hart

CPRE (CAMPAIGN TO PROTECT RURAL ENGLAND) (1926), 128 Southwark Street, London SE1 0SW T 020-7981 2800 E info@cpre.org.uk W www.cpre.org.uk
Chief Executive, Shaun Spiers

CRAFTS COUNCIL (1971), 44A Pentonville Road, London N1 9BY T 020-7278 7700 E reference@craftscouncil.org.uk W www.craftscouncil.org.uk
Chief Executive, Rosy Greenlees

CRISIS UK (1967), 66 Commercial Street, London E1 6LT T 0870-011 3335 E enquiries@crisis.org.uk W www.crisis.org.uk
Chief Executive, Leslie Morphy

CRUSE BEREAVEMENT CARE (1959), PO Box 800, Richmond TW9 1RG T 020-8939 9530 E info@cruse.org.uk W www.cruse.org.uk
Chief Executive, Debbie Kerslake

CTC (THE UK'S NATIONAL CYCLISTS' ORGANISATION) (1878), Parklands, Railton Road, Guildford GU2 9JX 0870-873 0060 **E** cycling@ctc.org.uk **W** www.ctc.org.uk
Director, Kevin Mayne

CYSTIC FIBROSIS TRUST (1964), 11 London Road, Bromley BR1 1BY **T** 020-8464 7211 **E** enquiries@cftrust.org.uk **W** www.cftrust.org.uk
Chief Executive, Rosie Barnes

DATA (DESIGN AND TECHNOLOGY ASSOCIATION), 16 Wellesbourne House, Walton Road, Wellesbourne CV35 9JB **T** 01789-470007 **E** info@data.org.uk **W** www.data.org.uk
Chief Executive, Richard Green

DAY ONE CHRISTIAN MINISTRIES (1831), Ryelands Road, Leominster HR6 8NZ **T** 01568-613740 **E** sales@dayone.co.uk **W** www.dayone.co.uk
General Secretary, John Roberts

DEMOS, Third Floor, Magdalen House, 136 Tooley Street, London SE1 2TU **T** 0845-458 5949 **E** hello@demos.co.uk **W** www.demos.co.uk
Director, Catherine Fieschi

DIABETES UK (1934), Macleod House, 10 Parkway, London NW1 7AA **T** 020-7424 1000 **E** info@diabetes.org.uk **W** www.diabetes.org.uk
Chief Executive, Douglas Smallwood

DIANA, PRINCESS OF WALES MEMORIAL FUND (1997), County Hall, Westminster Bridge Road, London SE1 7PB **T** 020-7902 5500 **E** memorial.fund@memfund.org.uk **W** www.theworkcontinues.org
Chief Executive, Dr Astrid Bonfield

DITCHLEY FOUNDATION (1958), Ditchley Park, Enstone, Chipping Norton OX7 4ER **T** 01608-677346 **E** mail@ditchley.co.uk **W** www.ditchley.co.uk
Director, Sir Jeremy Greenstock, GCMG

DOWN'S SYNDROME ASSOCIATION (1970), The Langdon Down Centre, 2A Langdon Park, Teddington TW11 9PS **T** 0845-230 0372 **E** info@downs-syndrome.org.uk **W** www.downs-syndrome.org.uk
Chief Executive Officer, Mrs C. Boys

DUKE OF EDINBURGH'S AWARD (1956), Gulliver House, Madeira Walk, Windsor SL4 1EU **T** 01753-727400 **E** info@theaward.org **W** www.theaward.org
Chief Executive, Peter Westgarth

DYSLEXIA ACTION (2006), Park House, Wick Road, Egham TW20 0HH **T** 01784-222300 **E** info@dyslexiaaction.org.uk **W** www.dyslexiaaction.org.uk
Chief Executive, Shirley Cramer

EAST OF ENGLAND AGRICULTURAL SOCIETY (1797), East of England Showground, Peterborough PE2 6XE **T** 01733-234451 **E** info@eastofengland.org.uk **W** www.eastofengland.org.uk
Chief Executive, Andrew Mercer

ECCLESIOLOGICAL SOCIETY (1879), 38 Rosebery Avenue, New Malden KT3 4JS **E** info@ecclsoc.org **W** www.ecclsoc.org
Chair, Trevor Cooper

EGYPT EXPLORATION SOCIETY (1882), 3 Doughty Mews, London WC1N 2PG **T** 020-7242 1880 **W** www.ees.ac.uk
Secretary-General, Dr Patricia Spencer

ELECTORAL REFORM SOCIETY (1884), 6 Chancel Street, London SE1 0UU **T** 020-7928 1622 **E** ers@electoral-reform.org.uk **W** www.electoral-reform.org.uk
Chief Executive, Dr Ken Ritchie

ELGAR FOUNDATION (1935), The Elgar Birthplace Museum, Lower Broadheath, Worcester WR2 6RH **T** 01905-333224 **E** birthplace@elgarmuseum.org **W** www.elgarmuseum.org
Museum Director, Catherine Sloan

ELGAR SOCIETY (1951), 17 Earlsfield Road, London SW18 8DB **T** 020-8870 3205 **E** info@elgar.org **W** www.elgar.org
Chair, Andrew Neill

ENABLE SCOTLAND (1954), 6th Floor, 7 Buchanan Street, Glasgow G1 3HL **T** 0141-226 4541 **E** enable@enable.org.uk **W** www.enable.org.uk
Chief Executive, Norman Dunning

ENGLISH ASSOCIATION (1906), University of Leicester, University Road, Leicester LE1 7RH **T** 0116-252 3982 **E** engassoc@le.ac.uk **W** www.le.ac.uk/engassoc
Chief Executive, Ms H. Lucas

ENGLISH CHESS FEDERATION (1904), The Watch Oak, Chain Lane, Battle TN33 0YD **T** 01424-775222 **E** office@englishchess.org.uk **W** www.englishchess.org.uk
Chief Executive, Martin Regan

ENGLISH FOLK DANCE AND SONG SOCIETY (1932), Cecil Sharp House, 2 Regent's Park Road, London NW1 7AY **T** 020-7485 2206 **E** info@efdss.org **W** www.efdss.org
Chief Executive, K. Spicer

ENGLISH-SPEAKING UNION OF THE COMMONWEALTH (1918), Dartmouth House, 37 Charles Street, London W1J 5ED **T** 020-7529 1550 **E** esu@esu.org **W** www.esu.org
Director-General, Mrs V. Mitchell, OBE

ENVIRONMENT COUNCIL (1970), 212 High Holborn, London WC1V 7BF **T** 020-7836 2626 **E** info@envcouncil.org.uk **W** www.the-environment-council.org.uk
Chief Executive, Mike King

EPILEPSY ACTION (1950), New Anstey House, Gate Way Drive, Yeadon, Leeds LS19 7XY **T** 0113-210 8800 **E** helpline@epilepsy.org.uk **W** www.epilepsy.org.uk
Chief Executive, P. Lee

ESPERANTO ASSOCIATION OF BRITAIN (1976), Esperanto House, Station Road, Barlaston, Stoke-on-Trent ST12 9DE T 0845-230 1887 E eab@esperanto-gb.org W www.esperanto-gb.org
President, Prof. John Wells

EVANGELICAL LIBRARY, 78A Chiltern Street, London W1U 5HB T 020-7935 6997 E stlibrary@zen.co.uk W www.elib.org.uk
Librarian, S. J. Taylor

EX-SERVICES MENTAL WELFARE SOCIETY (1919), Tyrwhitt House, Oaklawn Road, Leatherhead, KT22 0BX T 01372-841600 E contactus@combatstress.org.uk W www.combatstress.org.uk
Chairman, Maj.-Gen. Peter Currie, CB

FACULTY OF ACTUARIES (1856), 18 Dublin Street, Edinburgh EH1 3PP T 0131-240 1300 E faculty@actuaries.org.uk W www.actuaries.org.uk
Secretary, Richard Maconachie

FAIR ISLE BIRD OBSERVATORY TRUST (1948), Fair Isle Bird Observatory, Fair Isle ZE2 9JU T 01595-760258 E fairisle.birdobs@zetnet.co.uk W www.fairislebirdobs.co.uk
Administrator, H. Shaw

FAITH AND THOUGHT (1865), 15 The Drive, Harlow CM20 3QD E revjdbuxton@sky.com W www.faithandthought.org.uk
President, Sir John Houghton, FRS

FAMILY WELFARE ASSOCIATION (1869), 501–505 Kingsland Road, London E8 4AU T 020-7254 6251 E fwa.headoffice@fwa.org.uk W www.fwa.org.uk
Chief Executive, Helen Dent

FAUNA AND FLORA INTERNATIONAL (1903), Great Eastern House, Tenison Road, Cambridge CB1 2TT T 01223-571000 E info@fauna-flora.org W www.fauna-flora.org
Chief Executive, Mark Rose

FEDERATION OF FAMILY HISTORY SOCIETIES (1974), PO Box 8857, Lutterworth LE17 9BJ T 01455-203133 E info@ffhs.org.uk W www.ffhs.org.uk
Administrator, Philippa McCray

FIELDS IN TRUST (1925), 2d Woodstock Studios, 3b Woodstock Grove, London W12 8LE T 020-8735 3850 E info@fieldsintrust.org W www.fieldsintrust.org
Director, Alison Moore-Gwyn

FIELD STUDIES COUNCIL (1943), Preston Montford, Montford Bridge, Shrewsbury SY4 1HW T 01743-852100 E fsc.headoffice@field-studies-council.org W www.field-studies-council.org
Chief Executive, A. D. Thomas

FIRE FIGHTERS CHARITY (1943), Second Floor, Copenhagen Court, 32 New Street, Basingstoke RG21 7DT T 01256-366566 E info@firefighterscharity.org.uk W www.firefighterscharity.org.uk
Chief Executive, Roy Lawrenson

FIRE PROTECTION ASSOCIATION (1946), London Road, Moreton in Marsh, Glos GL56 0RH T 01608-812500 E fpa@thefpa.co.uk W www.thefpa.co.uk
Managing Director, Jonathan O'Neill

FLAG INSTITUTE (1971), 38 Hill Street, Mayfair, London W1J 5NS E membership@flaginstitute.org W www.flaginstitute.org
President, Capt. Malcolm Farrow, OBE, FFI, RN

FLEET AIR ARM OFFICERS' ASSOCIATION (1957), 4 St James's Square, London SW1Y 4JU T 020-7930 7722 E faaoa@fleetairarmoa.org W www.fleetairarmoa.org
Chair, Rear-Adm. S. Lidbetter

FOOD FROM BRITAIN, 4th Floor, Manning House, 22 Carlisle Place, London SW1P 1JA T 020-7233 5111 E info@foodfrombritain.co.uk W www.foodfrombritain.com
Chief Executive (interim), John Adams

FOREIGN PRESS ASSOCIATION IN LONDON (1888), 11 Carlton House Terrace, London SW1Y 5AJ T 020-7930 0445 E secretariat@foreign-press.org.uk W www.foreign-press.org.uk
General Manager, B. Jenner

FORENSIC SCIENCE SOCIETY (1959), Clarke House, 18A Mount Parade, Harrogate HG1 1BX T 01423-506068 W www.forensic-science-society.org.uk
President, Brian W. J. Rankin

FOUNDATION FOR SPORT AND THE ARTS (1991), Wolton House, 55 Charnock Road, Walton L67 1AA T 0151-259 5505 E contact@thefsa.net W www.thefsa.net
Secretary, R. Boardley

FOUNDATION FOR THE STUDY OF INFANT DEATHS (1971), Artillery House, 11–19 Artillery Row, London SW1P 1RT T 020-7222 8001 E office@fsid.org.uk W www.fsid.org.uk
Director, Mrs J. Epstein

FPA (1930), 50 Featherstone Street, London EC1Y 8QU T 020-7608 5240 E library&information@fpa.org.uk W www.fpa.org.uk
Chief Executive, Ms June Bentley

FRANCO-BRITISH SOCIETY (1924), 2 Dovedale Studios, 465 Battersea Park Road, London SW11 4LR T 020 7924 3511 E execsec@francobritishsociety.org.uk W www.francobritishsociety.org.uk
Executive Secretary, Mrs Kate Brayn

FRIENDS OF CATHEDRAL MUSIC (1956), 21 Bradford Road, Trowbridge BA14 9AL T 0845-644 3721 E info@fcm.org.uk W www.fcm.org.uk
Secretary, Roger Bishton

FRIENDS OF FRIENDLESS CHURCHES (1957), St Ann's Vestry Hall, 2 Church Entry, London EC4V 5HB T 020-7236 3934 E office@friendsoffriendlesschurches.org.uk W www.friendsoffriendlesschurches.org.uk
Hon. Director, Matthew Saunders, MBE

FRIENDS OF THE BODLEIAN (1925), Bodleian Library, Oxford OX1 3BG **T** 01865-277234 **E** fob@bodley.ox.ac.uk **W** www.bodley.ox.ac.uk/friends
Chairman, Prof. Jon Stallworthy

FRIENDS OF THE EARTH SCOTLAND (1978), Thorn House, 5 Rose Street, Edinburgh EH2 2PR **T** 0131-243 2700 **E** info@foe-scotland.org.uk **W** www.foe-scotland.org.uk
Chief Executive Officer, Duncan McLaren

FRIENDS OF THE NATIONAL LIBRARIES (1931), c/o Department of Manuscripts, The British Library, 96 Euston Road, London NW1 2DB **T** 020-7412 7559 **W** www.friendsofnationallibraries.org.uk
Chairman, Lord Egremont, FRSL

FURNITURE HISTORY SOCIETY (1964), 1 Mercedes Cottages, St John's Road, Haywards Heath RH16 4EH **T** 01444-413845 **E** furniturehistorysociety@hotmail.com **W** www.furniturehistorysociety.org
Membership Secretary, Dr Brian Austen

GALLIPOLI ASSOCIATION (1969), Earleydene Orchard, Earleydene, Ascot SL5 9JY **T** 01344-626523 **E** webmaster@gallipoli-association.org **W** www.gallipoli-association.org
Hon. Secretary, J. C. Watson Smith

GAME AND WILDLIFE CONSERVATION TRUST (1969), Fordingbridge SP6 1EF **T** 01425-652381 **E** info@gct.org.uk **W** www.gct.org.uk
Chief Executive, Teresa Dent

GARDEN HISTORY SOCIETY (1965), 70 Cowcross Street, London EC1M 6EJ **T** 020-7608 2409 **E** enquiries@gardenhistorysociety.org **W** www.gardenhistorysociety.org
Chair, Dr Colin Treen

GEMMOLOGICAL ASSOCIATION AND GEM TESTING LABORATORY OF GREAT BRITAIN (1931), 27 Greville Street (Saffron Hill entrance), London EC1N 8TN **T** 020-7404 3334 **E** information@gem-a.com **W** www.gem-a.com
Chief Executive Officer, Dr Jack Ogden

GENERAL DENTAL COUNCIL (1956), 37 Wimpole Street, London W1G 8DQ **T** 020-7887 3800 **E** information@gdc-uk.org **W** www.gdc-uk.org
Chief Executive & Registrar, Duncan Rudkin

GENERAL MEDICAL COUNCIL (1858), Regent's Place, 350 Euston Road, London NW1 3JN **T** 0845-357 8001 **E** gmc@gmc-uk.org **W** www.gmc-uk.org
Chief Executive, Finlay Scott

GENERAL OPTICAL COUNCIL (1959), 41 Harley Street, London W1G 8DJ **T** 020-7580 3898 **E** goc@optical.org **W** www.optical.org
Chief Executive and Registrar, P. C. Coe

GENERAL OSTEOPATHIC COUNCIL (1997), Osteopathy House, 176 Tower Bridge Road, London SE1 3LU **T** 020-7357 6655 **E** info@osteopathy.org.uk **W** www.osteopathy.org.uk
Chief Executive and Registrar, Evlynne Gilvarry

GEOGRAPHICAL ASSOCIATION (1893), 160 Solly Street, Sheffield S1 4BF **T** 0114-296 0088 **E** info@geography.org.uk **W** www.geography.org.uk
Chief Executive, David Lambert

GEOLOGICAL SOCIETY OF LONDON (1807), Burlington House, Piccadilly, London W1J 0BG **T** 020-7434 9944 **E** enquiries@geolsoc.org.uk **W** www.geolsoc.org.uk
Executive Secretary, E. Nickless

GEOLOGISTS' ASSOCIATION (1858), Burlington House, Piccadilly, London W1J 0DU **T** 020-7434 9298 **E** geol.assoc@btinternet.com **W** www.geologistsassociation.org.uk
Executive Secretary, Sarah Stafford

GEORGIAN GROUP (1937), 6 Fitzroy Square, London W1T 5DX **T** 0871-750 2936 **E** info@georgiangroup.org.uk **W** www.georgiangroup.org.uk
Secretary, Robert Bargery

GIRLGUIDING UK (1910), 17–19 Buckingham Palace Road, London SW1W 0PT **T** 020-7834 6242 **E** chq@girlguiding.org.uk **W** www.girlguiding.org.uk
Chief Guide, Liz Burnley

GIRLS' BRIGADE ENGLAND AND WALES, PO Box 196, 129 The Broadway, Didcot OX11 8XN **T** 01235-510425 **E** admin@girlsbrigadeew.org.uk **W** www.girlsbrigadeew.org.uk
National Director, Ruth Gilson

GIRLS' VENTURE CORPS AIR CADETS (1964), 1 Bawtry Gate, Sheffield, S9 1WD **T** 0114-2448405 **E** gvcac@toucansurf.com **W** www.gvcac.org.uk
Corps Director, Mrs Brenda Layne, MBE

GLASGOW CHAMBER OF COMMERCE (1783), 30 George Square, Glasgow G2 1EQ **T** 0141-204 2121 **E** chamber@glasgowchamber.org **W** www.glasgowchamber.org
Chief Executive, Richard Cairns

GREEK INSTITUTE (1969), 34 Bush Hill Road, London N21 2DS **T** 020-8360 7968 **E** info@greekinstitute.co.uk **W** www.greekinstitute.co.uk
Director, Dr K. Tofallis

GREENPEACE UK (1979), Canonbury Villas, London N1 2PN **T** 020-7865 8100 **E** info@uk.greenpeace.org **W** www.greenpeace.org.uk
Executive Director, John Sauven

GUIDE DOGS FOR THE BLIND ASSOCIATION (1934), Hillfields, Burghfield Common, Reading RG7 3YG **T** 0118-983 5555 **E** guidedogs@guidedogs.org.uk **W** www.guidedogs.org.uk
Chief Executive, Bridget Warr

GURKHA WELFARE TRUST (1969), PO Box 18215, 2nd Floor, 1 Old Street, London EC1V 9XB **T** 01722-323955 **E** staffassistant@gwt.org.uk **W** www.gwt.org.uk
Chief Executive, Colonel William Shuttlewood, OBE

HAIG HOMES (1929), Alban Dobson House, Green Lane, Morden SM4 5NS T 020-8685 5777
E haig@haighomes.org.uk W www.haighomes.org.uk
Chief Executive, Maj.-Gen. P. V. R. Besgrove, CBE

HAKLUYT SOCIETY (1846), c/o Map Library, The British Library, 96 Euston Road, London NW1 2DB
T 01428-641850 E office@hakluyt.com
W www.hakluyt.com
President, Richard M. Bateman

HALIFAX ANTIQUARIAN SOCIETY (1900), Treetops, Copley Lane, Halifax HX3 0TJ
T 01422-346088 W www.halifaxhistory.org.uk
Hon. Secretary, J. H. Patchett

HANSARD SOCIETY FOR PARLIAMENTARY GOVERNMENT (1944), 40–43 Chancery Lane, London WC2A 1JA T 020-7438 1222 E hansard@hansard.lse.ac.uk
W www.hansardsociety.org.uk
Chief Executive, Fiona Booth

HAWICK ARCHAEOLOGICAL SOCIETY (1856), 8 Melgund Place, Hawick TD9 9HY T 01450-376220
E info@airchieoliver.co.uk W www.airchieoliver.co.uk
Hon. Secretary, Gerald M. Graham

HEARING CONCERN (1947), 95 Grays Inn Road, London WC1X 8TX T 020-7440 9871
E info@hearingconcern.org.uk
W www.hearingconcern.org.uk
Chief Executive, Damian Barry

HELP THE AGED (1961), 207–221 Pentonville Road, London N1 9UZ T 020-7278 1114
E info@helptheaged.org.uk W www.helptheaged.org.uk
Director-General, C. M. Lake, CBE

HERALDRY SOCIETY (1947), PO Box 772, Guildford GU3 3ZX T 01483-237373
E memsec@theheraldrysociety.com
W www.theheraldrysociety.com
Honorary Secretary, Melvyn Jeremiah

HIGH SHERIFFS' ASSOCIATION OF ENGLAND & WALES (1971), Heritage House, PO Box 21, Baldock SG6 3ZQ T 01462-896688 E secretary@highsheriffs.com
W www.highsheriffs.com
Chair, Patrick Dent, DL

HISPANIC AND LUSO BRAZILIAN COUNCIL (1943), Canning House, 2 Belgrave Square, London SW1X 8PJ T 020-7235 2303
E enquiries@canninghouse.com W www.canninghouse.com
Director, Veronica Scott

HISTORICAL ASSOCIATION (1906), 59A Kennington Park Road, London SE11 4JH T 020-7735 3901
E enquiry@history.org.uk W www.history.org.uk
Chief Executive, Rebecca Sullivan

HISTORIC HOUSES ASSOCIATION (1973), 2 Chester Street, London SW1X 7BB T 020-7259 5688
E info@hha.org.uk W www.hha.org.uk
Director-General, Nick Way

HONOURABLE SOCIETY OF CYMMRODORION (1751), 30 Eastcastle Street, London W1W 8DJ T 020-7631 0502
E aelodau1751we@yahoo.co.uk
W www.cymmrodorion1751.org.uk
Hon. Secretary, Jon Parry

HOSTELLING INTERNATIONAL NORTHERN IRELAND (1931), 22–32 Donegall Road, Belfast BT12 5JN T 028-9032 4733 E info@hini.org.uk
W www.hini.org.uk
Hon. Secretary, Kevin Butler

HUGUENOT SOCIETY OF GREAT BRITAIN AND IRELAND (1885), The Huguenot Library, University College, Gower Street, London WC1E 6BT
T 020-7679 5199 E secretary@huguenotsociety.org.uk
W www.huguenotsociety.org.uk
Hon. Secretary, Barbara Julien

HUMANE RESEARCH TRUST (1962), Brook House, 29 Bramhall Lane South, Bramhall, Stockport SK7 2DN
T 0161-439 8041 E info@humaneresearch.org.uk
W www.humaneresearch.org.uk
Chair, K. Cholerton

HYMN SOCIETY OF GREAT BRITAIN AND IRELAND (1936), 99 Barton Road, Lancaster LA1 4EN
T 01524-66740 E robcanham@haystacks.fsnet.co.uk
W www.hymnsocietygbi.org.uk
Hon. Secretary, Revd Robert A. Canham

INCORPORATED SOCIETY OF MUSICIANS (1882), 10 Stratford Place, London W1C 1AA
T 020-7629 4413 E membership@ism.org W www.ism.org
Chief Executive, Deborah Annetts

INDEPENDENTAGE (1863), 6 Avonmore Road, London W14 8RL T 020-7605 4200
E charity@independentage.org.uk
W www.independentage.org.uk
Chief Executive, Janet Morrison

INDEPENDENT SCHOOLS' BURSARS ASSOCIATION (1932), Unit 11–12, Manor Farm, Cliddesden RG25 2JB T 01256-330369
E office@theisba.org.uk W www.theisba.org.uk
General Secretary, Jonathan Cook

INDEPENDENT SCHOOLS COUNCIL (1998), St Vincent House, 30 Orange Street, London WC2H 7HH T 020-7766 7070 E office@isc.co.uk
W www.isc.co.uk
Chief Executive, Christopher Parry, CBE

INDUSTRY AND PARLIAMENT TRUST (1977), Suite 101, 3 Whitehall Court, London SW1A 2EL
T 020-7839 9400 E admin@ipt.org.uk W www.ipt.org.uk
Chief Executive, Sally Muggeridge

INSTITUTE FOR COMPLEMENTARY MEDICINE (1982), Unit 25, Tavern Quay Business Centre, Sweden Gate, London SE16 7TX T 020-7231 5855
E info@i-c-m.org.uk W www.i-c-m.org.uk
Director, Frances Fewell

INSTITUTE OF ACOUSTICS (1974), 77A St Peter's Street, St Albans AL1 3BN **T** 01727-848195 **E** ioa@ioa.org.uk **W** www.ioa.org.uk
Chief Executive, Kevin Macan-Lind

INSTITUTE OF ADMINISTRATIVE MANAGEMENT (1915), 6 Graphite Square, Vauxhall Walk, London SE11 5EE **T** 020-7091 2600 **E** info@instam.org **W** www.instam.org
Chief Executive, Jenny Hewell

INSTITUTE OF BIOLOGY (1950), 9 Red Lion Court, London EC4A 3EF **T** 020-7936 5900 **E** info@iob.org **W** www.iob.org
Chief Executive, Prof. A. D. B. Malcolm

INSTITUTE OF BREWING AND DISTILLING (1886), 33 Clarges Street, London W1J 7EE **T** 020-7499 8144 **E** enquiries@ibd.org.uk **W** www.ibd.org.uk
Executive Director, Simon Jackson

INSTITUTE OF BRITISH ORGAN BUILDING (1995), 13 Ryefields, Thurston, Bury St Edmunds IP31 3TD **T** 01359-233433 **E** administrator@ibo.co.uk **W** www.ibo.co.uk
President, Katherine Venning

INSTITUTE OF CANCER RESEARCH (1909), 123 Old Brompton Road, London SW7 3RP **T** 020-7352 8133 **W** www.icr.ac.uk
Chief Executive, Prof. Peter Rigby

INSTITUTE OF CAST METAL ENGINEERS (1904), National Metalforming Centre, 47 Birmingham Road, West Bromwich B70 6PY **T** 0121-601 6979 **E** info@icme.org.uk **W** www.icme.org.uk
Manager, Dr Pam Murrell

INSTITUTE OF CHARTERED ACCOUNTANTS IN ENGLAND AND WALES (1880), PO Box 433, Moorgate Place, London EC2P 2BJ **T** 020-7920 8100 **W** www.icaew.com
Chief Executive, Michael Izza

INSTITUTE OF CHARTERED SECRETARIES AND ADMINISTRATORS (1891), 16 Park Crescent, London W1B 1AH **T** 020-7580 4741 **E** info@icsa.co.uk **W** www.icsa.org.uk
Chief Executive, Roger Dickinson

INSTITUTE OF CHARTERED SHIPBROKERS (1911), 85 Gracechurch Street, London EC3V 0AA **T** 020-7623 1111 **E** info@ics.org.uk **W** www.ics.org.uk
Director, Alan Phillips

INSTITUTE OF DIRECTORS (1903), 116 Pall Mall, London SW1Y 5ED **T** 020-7766 8866 **E** enquiries@iod.com **W** www.iod.com
Chief Operating Officer, A. Main Wilson

INSTITUTE OF ECONOMIC AFFAIRS (1955), 2 Lord North Street, London SW1P 3LB **T** 020-7799 8900 **E** iea@iea.org.uk **W** www.iea.org.uk
Director-General, John Blundell

INSTITUTE OF FIELD ARCHAEOLOGISTS (1982), School of Human and Environmental Science, Whiteknights, University of Reading, PO Box 227 RG6 6AB **T** 0118-378 6446 **E** admin@archaeologists.net **W** www.archaeologists.net
Chief Executive, Peter Hinton

INSTITUTE OF FINANCIAL ACCOUNTANTS (1916), Burford House, 44 London Road, Sevenoaks TN13 1AS **T** 01732-458080 **E** mail@ifa.org.uk **W** www.ifa.org.uk
Chief Executive, David Woodgate

INSTITUTE OF FOOD SCIENCE AND TECHNOLOGY (1964), 5 Cambridge Court, 210 Shepherd's Bush Road, London W6 7NJ **T** 020-7603 6316 **E** info@ifst.org **W** www.ifst.org
Chief Executive, Helen G. Wild

INSTITUTE OF HEALTHCARE MANAGEMENT, 18–21 Morley Street, London SE1 7QZ **T** 020-7620 1030 **E** enquiries@ihm.org.uk **W** www.ihm.org.uk
Chief Executive, Susan Hodgetts

INSTITUTE OF HEALTH PROMOTION AND EDUCATION, School of Dentistry, University of Manchester, Higher Cambridge Street, Manchester M15 6FH **T** 0161-275 6610 **E** honsec@ihpe.org.uk **W** www.ihpe.org.uk
Hon. Secretary, Prof. A. S. Blinkhorn

INSTITUTE OF HERALDIC AND GENEALOGICAL STUDIES (1961), 79–82 Northgate, Canterbury CT1 1BA **T** 01227-768664 **E** ihgs@ihgs.ac.uk **W** www.ihgs.ac.uk
Principal, C. R. Humphery-Smith

INSTITUTE OF MANAGEMENT SERVICES (1941), Brooke House, 24 Dam Street, Lichfield WS13 6AA **T** 01543-266 909 **E** admin@ims-stowe.fsnet.co.uk **W** www.ims-productivity.com

INSTITUTE OF MASTERS OF WINE (1953), Mapfre House, 2/3 Philpot Lane, London EC3M 8AN **T** 020-7621 2830 **W** www.masters-of-wine.org
Executive Director, Siobhan Turner

INSTITUTE OF MATERIALS, MINERALS AND MINING (2002), 1 Carlton House Terrace, London SW1Y 5DB **T** 020-7451 7300 **E** admin@iom3.org **W** www.iom3.org
Chief Executive, Dr Bernie Rickinson

INSTITUTE OF MATHEMATICS AND ITS APPLICATIONS (1964), Catherine Richards House, 16 Nelson Street, Southend-on-Sea SS1 1EF **T** 01702-354020 **E** post@ima.org.uk **W** www.ima.org.uk
Executive Director, David Youdan

INSTITUTE OF THE MOTOR INDUSTRY (1920), Fanshaws, Brickendon, Hertford SG13 8PQ **T** 01992-511521 **E** imi@motor.org.uk **W** www.motor.org.uk
Chief Executive, Sarah Sillars

INSTITUTION OF CIVIL ENGINEERS (1818), 1 Great George Street, London SW1P 3AA T 020-7222 7722 W www.ice.org.uk
Director-General, Tom Foulkes

INSTITUTION OF ENGINEERING AND TECHNOLOGY (1871), Michael Faraday House, Stevenage SG1 2AY T 01438-313311 E postmaster@iet.org.uk W www.theiet.org
Chief Executive, Robin McGill

INSTITUTION OF GAS ENGINEERS & MANAGERS (1862), Charnwood Wing, Holywell Park, Ashby Road, Loughborough LE11 3GH T 01509-282728 E general@igem.org.uk W www.igem.org.uk
Chief Executive, J. Williams

INSTITUTION OF MECHANICAL ENGINEERS (1847), 1 Birdcage Walk, London SW1H 9JJ T 020-7222 7899 E enquiries@imeche.org W www.imeche.org
Chief Executive, Ruth Spellman, OBE

INSTITUTION OF OCCUPATIONAL SAFETY AND HEALTH (1945), The Grange, Highfield Drive, Wigston LE18 1NN T 0116-257 3100 E techinfo@iosh.co.uk W www.iosh.co.uk
Chief Executive, R. W. H. Strange

INTERCONTINENTAL CHURCH SOCIETY (1823), 1 Athena Drive, Tachbrook Park CV34 6NL T 01926-430347 E enquiries@ics-uk.org W www.ics-uk.org
Communications Manager, David Healey

INTERNATIONAL AFRICAN INSTITUTE (1926), SOAS, Thornhaugh Street, Russell Square, London WC1H 0XG T 020-7898 4420 E iai@soas.ac.uk W www.internationalafricaninstitute.org
Hon. Director, Prof. Philip Burnham

INTERNATIONAL INSTITUTE FOR CONSERVATION OF HISTORIC AND ARTISTIC WORKS (1950), 6 Buckingham Street, London WC2N 6BA T 020-7839 5975 E iic@iconservation.org W www.iiconservation.org
Secretary-General, David Leigh

INTERNATIONAL PEN (1921), Brownlow House, 50–51 High Holborn, London WC1V 6ER T 020-7405 0338 E info@internationalpen.org.uk W www.internationalpen.org.uk
Executive Director, Caroline McCormick

INTERNATIONAL STUDENTS HOUSE (1962), 1 Park Crescent, Regent's Park, London W1B 1SH T 020-7631 8300 E info@ish.org.uk W www.ish.org.uk
Executive Director, Peter Anwyl

INTERNATIONAL TREE FOUNDATION (1924), Sandy Lane, Crawley Down RH10 4HS T 01342-717300 E info@internationaltreefoundation.org W www.internationaltreefoundation.org
Company Secretary, Lyn Baylis

INTERSERVE (1852), 5-6 Walker Avenue, Wolverton Hill MK12 5TW T 01908-552700 E enquiries@isewi.org W www.interserveonline.org.uk
National Director, Steve Bell

IRAN SOCIETY (1935), 2 Belgrave Square, London SW1X 8PJ T 020-7235 5122 E info@iransociety.org W www.iransociety.org
Chair, Hugh Arbuthnott, CMG

ISCO (1973), St George's House, Knoll Road, Camberley GU15 3SY T 01276-687525 W www.isco.org.uk
Director of Operations, Chris Marley

ISLE OF WIGHT NATURAL HISTORY AND ARCHAEOLOGICAL SOCIETY (1919), Salisbury Gardens, Dudley Road, Ventnor PO38 1EJ T 01983-855385 W www.iwnhas.org
President, Mrs J. Jones

JAPAN SOCIETY (1891), Swire House, 59 Buckingham Gate, London SW1E 6AJ T 020-7828 6330 E info@japansociety.org.uk W www.japansociety.org.uk
Director, Heidi Potter

JOHN STUART MILL INSTITUTE (1992), 1 Whitehall Place, London SW1A 2HE T 01973-752473 E jsmi@cyberstar.uk.com W www.jsmillinstitute.org.uk
Convenor, Dr Alan Butt Philip

JOURNALISTS' CHARITY (1864), Dickens House, 35 Wathen Road, Dorking RH4 1JY T 01306-887511 E enquiries@journalistscharity.org.uk W www.journalistscharity.org.uk
Director, David Ilott

JUSTICE (1957), 59 Carter Lane, London EC4V 5AQ T 020-7329 5100 E admin@justice.org.uk W www.justice.org.uk
Director, Roger Smith

KING'S FUND (1897), 11–13 Cavendish Square, London W1G 0AN T 020-7307 2400 E library@kingsfund.org.uk W www.kingsfund.org.uk
Chief Executive, Niall Dickson

KIPLING SOCIETY (1927), 6 Clifton Road, London W9 1SS T 020-7286 0194 E jane@keskar.fsworld.co.uk W www.kipling.org.uk
Hon. Secretary, Jane Keskar

LCIA (LONDON COURT OF INTERNATIONAL ARBITRATION) (1892), 70 Fleet Street, London EC4Y 1EU T 020-7936 7007 E lcia@lcia.org W www.lcia.org
Director-General, Adrian Winstanley

LEAGUE OF THE HELPING HAND (1908), PO Box 2548, Henfield, BN5 9WS T 01273-493551 E secretary@lhh.org.uk W www.lhh.org.uk
Executive Secretary, Moira Parrott

LEPROSY MISSION, ENGLAND, WALES, THE CHANNEL ISLANDS AND THE ISLE OF MAN (1874), Goldhay Way, Orton Goldhay, Peterborough PE2 5GZ T 01733-370505 E post@tlmew.org.uk W www.leprosymission.org.uk
National Director, Rupert Haydock

LEUKAEMIA RESEARCH FUND (1960), 43 Great Ormond Street, London WC1N 3JJ T 020-7405 0101 E info@lrf.org.uk W www.lrf.org.uk
Chief Executive, Cathy Gilman

LINNEAN SOCIETY OF LONDON (1788), Burlington House, Piccadilly, London W1J 0BF T 020-7434 4479 E info@linnean.org W www.linnean.org
Executive Secretary (acting), Ms Gina Douglas

LIONS CLUBS INTERNATIONAL (BRITISH ISLES AND IRELAND) (1950), 257 Alcester Road South, Kings Heath, Birmingham B14 6DT T 0121-441 4544 E lionsmd105@lineone.net W www.lions.org.uk
Office Manager, Mrs J. Davis

LISTENING BOOKS (1959), 12 Lant Street, London SE1 1QH T 020-7407 9417 E info@listening-books.org.uk W www.listening-books.org.uk
Director, Bill Dee

LLOYD'S OF LONDON, One Lime Street, London EC3M 7HA T 020-7327 6930 W www.lloyds.com
Chief Executive Officer, Richard Ward

LOCAL GOVERNMENT ASSOCIATION (1997), Local Government House, Smith Square, London SW1P 3HZ T 020-7664 3000 E info@lga.gov.uk W www.lga.gov.uk
Chief Executive, Paul Coen

LONDON AND MIDDLESEX ARCHAEOLOGICAL SOCIETY (1855), c/o Museum of London, 150 London Wall, London EC2Y 5HN T 020-7814 5734 W www.lamas.org.uk
Hon. Secretary, Jackie Keily

LONDON CATALYST (1873), 45 Westminster Bridge Road, London SE1 7JB T 020-7021 4204 E london.catalyst@peabody.org.uk W www.londoncatalyst.org.uk
Director, Victor Willmott, OBE

LONDON CITY MISSION (1835), 175 Tower Bridge Road, London SE1 2AH T 020-7407 7585 W www.lcm.org.uk
Chief Executive, Revd Dr John Nicholls

LONDON COLLEGE OF OSTEOPATHIC MEDICINE, 8–10 Boston Place, London NW1 6QH T 020-7262 1128 (1946), E steve.gregory@lcom.uk W www.lcom.org.uk
Clinic Manager, Anne Dalby

LONDON COUNCILS (2000), 59½ Southwark Street, London SE1 0AL T 020-7934 9999 E info@londoncouncils.gov.uk W www.londoncouncils.gov.uk
Chief Executive, John O'Brien

LONDON LIBRARY (1841), 14 St James's Square, London SW1Y 4LG T 020-7930 7705 E membership@londonlibrary.co.uk W www.londonlibrary.co.uk
Librarian, Inez T. P. A. Lynn

MACMILLAN CANCER SUPPORT (1911), 89 Albert Embankment, London SE1 7UQ T 0808-808 2020 E cancerline@macmillan.org.uk W www.macmillan.org.uk
Chief Executive, Ciarán Devane

MAGISTRATES' ASSOCIATION (1920), 28 Fitzroy Square, London W1T 6DD T 020-7387 2353 E secretariat@magistrates-association.org.uk W www.magistrates-association.org.uk
Chief Executive and Secretary, Sally Dickinson

MAKING MUSIC, THE NATIONAL FEDERATION OF MUSIC SOCIETIES (1935), 2–4 Great Eastern Street, London EC2A 3NW T 0870-903 3780 E info@makingmusic.org.uk W www.makingmusic.org.uk
Chief Executive, Robin Osterley

MANORIAL SOCIETY OF GREAT BRITAIN (1906), 104 Kennington Road, London SE11 6RE T 020-7735 6633 W www.msgb.co.uk
Chairman, Robert Smith

MARIE CURIE CANCER CARE (1948), 89 Albert Embankment, London SE1 7TP T 020-7599 7777 W www.mariecurie.org.uk
Chief Executive, Thomas Hughes-Hallett

MARINE BIOLOGICAL ASSOCIATION OF THE UK (1884), Citadel Hill, Plymouth PL1 2PB T 01752-633207 E sec@mba.ac.uk W www.mba.ac.uk
President (interim), Sir Neil Chalmers

MARINE SOCIETY AND SEA CADETS, 202 Lambeth Road, London SE1 7JW T 020-7654 7000 E info@ms-sc.org W www.ms-sc.org
Chief Executive Officer, Michael J. Cornish

MARRIAGE CARE (1946), 1 Blythe Mews, Blythe Road, London W14 0NW T 020-7371 1341 E info@marriagecare.org.uk W www.marriagecare.org.uk
Chief Executive, Terry Prendergast

MATHEMATICAL ASSOCIATION, 259 London Road, Leicester LE2 3BE T 0116-221 0013 (1871), E office@m-a.org.uk W www.m-a.org.uk
Chief Executive, Peter Hill

MDF THE BIPOLAR ORGANISATION (1983), Castle Works, 21 St George's Road, London SE1 6ES T 08456-340540 E mdf@mdf.org.uk W www.mdf.org.uk
Charity Manager, Jon Rodriguez

ME ASSOCIATION (1976), 7 Apollo Office Court, Radclive Road, Gawcott MK18 4DF T 0870-444 8233 E meconnect@meassociation.org.uk W www.meassociation.org.uk
Chair, Neil Riley

MEDIAWATCH-UK (1965), 3 Willow House, Kennington Road, Ashford TN24 0NR T 01233-633936 E info@mediawatchuk.org W www.mediawatchuk.org
Director, John C. Beyer

MEDICAL WOMEN'S FEDERATION (1917), Tavistock House North, Tavistock Square, London WC1H 9HX T 020-7387 7765 E admin.mwf@btconnect.com W www.medicalwomensfederation.org.uk
President, Dr Helen Goodyear

MENCAP (ROYAL MENCAP SOCIETY) (1946), Canon Lodge, Canon Street, Taunton TA1 1SW T 020-7454 0454 E information@mencap.org.uk W www.mencap.org.uk
Chief Executive, Jo Williams, CBE

MERCHANT NAVY WELFARE BOARD (1948), 30 Palmerston Road, Southampton SO14 1LL T 023-8033 7799 E enquiries@mnwb.org.uk W www.mnwb.org
Chief Executive, Capt. D. A. Parsons

MIDDLE EAST ASSOCIATION (1961), Bury House, 33 Bury Street, London SW1Y 6AX T 020-7839 2137 E info@the-mea.co.uk W www.the-mea.co.uk
Director-General, Michael Thomas

MIGRAINE ACTION ASSOCIATION (1958), 27 East Street, LE1 6NB T 0116-275 8317 E info@migraine.org.uk W www.migraine.org.uk
Director, Ms Lee Tomkins

MILITARY HISTORICAL SOCIETY (1948), National Army Museum, Royal Hospital Road, London SW3 4HT T 01252-621056 E m.h.s@hotmail.co.uk W www.militaryhistsoc.plus.com
Chairman, Tim Wright

MIND (NATIONAL ASSOCIATION FOR MENTAL HEALTH) (1946), 15–19 Broadway, London E15 4BQ T 020-8519 2122, Infoline 0845-766 0163 E contact@mind.org.uk W www.mind.org.uk
Chief Executive, Paul Farmer

MISSING PEOPLE (1993), PO Box 28908, London SW14 72U T 020-8392 4590 E info@missingpeople.org.uk W www.missingpeople.org.uk
Chief Executive, Paul Tuohy

MISSION TO SEAFARERS (1856), St Michael Paternoster Royal, College Hill, London EC4R 2RL T 020-7248 5202 E general@missiontoseafarers.org W www.missiontoseafarers.org
Secretary-General, The Revd Canon Bill Christianson

MULTIPLE SCLEROSIS SOCIETY (1953), MS National Centre, 372 Edgware Road, Staples Corner, London NW2 6ND T 020-8438 0700 E info@mssociety.org.uk W www.mssociety.org.uk
Chief Executive, Simon Gillespie

MUSEUMS ASSOCIATION (1889), 24 Calvin Street, London E1 6NW T 020-7426 6910 E info@museumsassociation.org W www.museumsassociation.org
Director, Mark Taylor

NABS, 47–50 Margaret Street, London W1W 8SB T 020-7462 3150 E nabs@nabs.org.uk W www.nabs.org.uk
Chief Executive (interim), Carole Butler

NATIONAL AIDS TRUST (1987), New City Cloisters, 196 Old Street, London EC1V 9FR T 020-7814 6767 E info@nat.org.uk W www.nat.org.uk
Chief Executive, Deborah Jack

NATIONAL ASSOCIATION FOR COLITIS AND CROHN'S DISEASE, 4 Beaumont House, Sutton Road, St Albans AL1 5HH T 01727-830038, Information Line 01727-844296 E nacc@nacc.org.uk W www.nacc.org.uk
Director, Richard Driscoll

NATIONAL ASSOCIATION FOR GIFTED CHILDREN (1967), Suite 14, Challenge House, Bletchley, Milton Keynes MK3 6DP T 0845-450 0295 E amazingchildren@nagcbritain.org.uk W www.nagcbritain.org.uk
Chief Executive, Denise Yates

NATIONAL ASSOCIATION OF CLUBS FOR YOUNG PEOPLE (1925), 371 Kennington Lane, London SE11 5QY T 020-7793 0787 E office@clubsforyoungpeople.org.uk W www.clubsforyoungpeople.org.uk
Chief Executive, Simon Antrobus

NATIONAL CAMPAIGN FOR THE ARTS LTD (1985), 1 Kingly Street, London W1B 5PA T 020-7287 3777 E nca@artscampaign.org.uk W www.artscampaign.org.uk
Director, Louise de Winter

NATIONAL CATTLE ASSOCIATION (DAIRY) (1998), Brick House, Risbury, Leominster HR6 0NQ T 01568-760632 E timbrigstocke@hotmail.com
Executive Secretary, Tim Brigstocke

NATIONAL CHILDBIRTH TRUST (1956), Alexandra House, Oldham Terrace, London W3 6NH T 0870-770 3236 E enquiries@national-childbirth-trust.co.uk W www.nctpregnancyandbabycare.co.uk
Chief Executive, Ms B. Phipps

NATIONAL COUNCIL OF WOMEN OF GREAT BRITAIN (1895), 72 Victoria Road, Darlington DL1 5JG T 01325-367375 E info@ncwgb.org W www.ncwgb.org
President, Monica Hall

NATIONAL EXTENSION COLLEGE (1963), Michael Young Centre, Purbeck Road, Cambridge CB2 2HN T 01223-400200 E info@nec.ac.uk W www.nec.ac.uk
Chief Executive, Alison West

NATIONAL FOUNDATION FOR EDUCATIONAL RESEARCH IN ENGLAND AND WALES (1946), The Mere, Upton Park, Slough SL1 2DQ T 01753-574123 E enquiries@nfer.ac.uk W www.nfer.ac.uk
Chief Executive, Sue Rossiter

NATIONAL GARDENS SCHEME CHARITABLE TRUST (1927), Hatchlands Park, East Clandon, Guildford GU4 7RT T 01483-211535 E ngs@ngs.org.uk W www.ngs.org.uk
Chief Executive, Julia Grant

NATIONAL LANDLORDS ASSOCIATION, 3rd floor, 22–26 Albert Embankment, London SE1 7TJ T 020-7840 8900 E info@landlords.org.uk W www.landlords.org.uk
Chair, David Salusbury

NATIONAL OPERATIC AND DRAMATIC ASSOCIATION (1899), NODA House, 55–60 Lincoln Road, Peterborough PE1 2RZ **T** 0870-770 2480 **E** everyone@noda.org.uk **W** www.noda.org.uk
Chief Executive, M. Pemberton

NATIONAL OSTEOPOROSIS SOCIETY (1986), Camerton, Bath BA2 0PJ **T** 01761-471771 **E** info@nos.org.uk **W** www.nos.org.uk
Chief Executive, Claire Severgnini

NATIONAL SECULAR SOCIETY (1866), 25 Red Lion Square, London WC1R 4RL **T** 020-7404 3126 **E** enquiries@secularism.org.uk **W** www.secularism.org.uk
Executive Director, K. P. Wood

NATIONAL SOCIETY FOR EPILEPSY (1892), Chesham Lane, Chalfont St Peter SL9 0RJ **T** 01494-601300 **Helpline,** 01494-601400 **W** www.epilepsynse.org.uk
Chief Executive, Graham Faulkner

NATIONAL SOCIETY FOR PROMOTING RELIGIOUS EDUCATION (1811), Church House, Great Smith Street, London SW1P 3AZ **T** 020-7898 1499 **E** info@natsoc.c-of-e.org.uk **W** www.natsoc.org.uk
General Secretary, Revd Jan Ainsworth

NATIONAL TRUST (1895), Heelis, Kemble Drive, Swindon SN2 2NA **T** 0844-800 1895 **E** enquiries@thenationaltrust.org.uk **W** www.nationaltrust.org.uk
Director-General, Fiona Reynolds

NATIONAL TRUST FOR SCOTLAND (1931), Wemyss House, 28 Charlotte Square, Edinburgh EH2 4ET **T** 0844-493 2100 **E** information@nts.org.uk **W** www.nts.org.uk
Chief Executive, Mark Adderley

NATIONAL UNION OF STUDENTS (1922), 2nd Floor, Centro 3, 19 Mandela Street, London NW1 0DU **T** 0871-221 8221 **E** nusuk@nus.org.uk **W** www.nus.org.uk
President, Matt Hyde

NCH (1869), 85 Highbury Park, London N5 1UD **T** 020-7704 7000 **W** www.nch.org.uk
Chief Executive, Clare Tickell

NEWCOMEN SOCIETY (1920), The Science Museum, London SW7 2DD **T** 020-7371 4445 **E** office@newcomen.com **W** www.newcomen.com
Executive Secretary, Dick Swann

NHS CONFEDERATION (1997), 29 Bressenden Place, London SW1E 5DD **T** 020-7074 3200 **W** www.nhsconfed.org
Chair, Bryan Stoten

NORFOLK AND NORWICH ARCHAEOLOGICAL SOCIETY (1846), 77 High Road, Gorleston, Great Yarmouth NR31 0PB **T** 01603-661270 **W** www.nnas.info
Hon. Secretary, Margaret Gooch

NORTHERN IRELAND TOURIST BOARD (1948), St Anne's Court, 59 North Street, Belfast BT1 1NB **T** 028-9023 1221 **E** pcu@nitb.com **W** www.nitb.com
Chief Executive, Alan Clarke

NOTARIES SOCIETY (1882), PO Box 266 Melton, Woodbridge IP12 1WX **T** 01394-380436 **E** admin@thenotariessociety.org.uk **W** www.thenotariessociety.org.uk
Secretary, C. J. Vaughan

NSPCC (NATIONAL SOCIETY FOR THE PREVENTION OF CRUELTY TO CHILDREN) (1884), Weston House, 42 Curtain Road, London EC2A 3NH **T** 020-7825 2500 **E** info@nspcc.org.uk **W** www.nspcc.org.uk
Director and Chief Executive, Dame Mary Marsh

NUFFIELD FOUNDATION (1943), 28 Bedford Square, London WC1B 3JS **T** 020-7631 0566 **W** www.nuffieldfoundation.org **E** cporter@nuffieldfoundation.org
Director, A. Tomei

NUFFIELD TRUST (1940), 59 New Cavendish Street, London W1G 7LP **T** 020-7631 8450 **E** info@nuffieldtrust.org.uk **W** www.nuffieldtrust.org.uk
Director, Dr Jennifer Dixon

NURSE AID (1917), PO Box 223, Evesham WR11 4WB **T** 01386-446023 **E** admin@nurseaid.org.uk **W** www.nurseaid.org.uk
Director, Mrs A. M. Barnard

NURSING AND MIDWIFERY COUNCIL (2002), 23 Portland Place, London W1B 1PZ **T** 020-7637 7181 **W** www.nmc-uk.org
Chief Executive, Sarah Thewlis

OFFICERS' ASSOCIATION (1919), Mountbarron House, 6–20 Elizabeth Street, London SW1W 9RB **T** 0845-873 7140 **E** om@oaed.org.uk **W** www.officersassociation.com
General Secretary, Maj.-Gen. J. C. B. Sutherell, CBE

OPEN SPACES SOCIETY (1865), 25A Bell Street, Henley-on-Thames RG9 2BA **T** 01491-573535 **E** hq@oss.org.uk **W** www.oss.org.uk
General Secretary, Kate Ashbrook

OPSIS (1992), c/o Queen Alexandra College, Court Oak Road, Birmingham B17 9TG **T** 0121-428 5037 **E** enquiries@opsis.org.uk **W** www.opsis.org.uk
Chief Executive, Mike Brace, OBE

ORDERS AND MEDALS RESEARCH SOCIETY (1942), PO Box 1233, High Wycombe HP11 9BW **T** 01494-441207 **E** generalsecretary@omrs.org **W** www.omrs.org.uk
General Secretary, P. M. R. Helmore

OVERSEAS DEVELOPMENT INSTITUTE (1960), 111 Westminster Bridge Road, London SE1 7JD **T** 020-7922 0300 **E** odi@odi.org.uk **W** www.odi.org.uk
Director, S. Maxwell

OVERSEAS SERVICE PENSIONERS' ASSOCIATION (1960), 138 High Street, Tonbridge TN9 1AX **T** 01732-363836 **E** mail@ospa.org.uk **W** www.ospa.org.uk
Secretary, D. F. B. Le Breton, CBE

OXFAM GREAT BRITAIN (1942), Oxfam House, John Smith Drive, Oxford OX4 2JY T 0870-333 2700 W www.oxfam.org.uk
Director, Barbara Stocking, CBE

OXFORD PRESERVATION TRUST (1927), 10 Turn Again Lane, St Ebbes, Oxford OX1 1QL T 01865-242918 E info@oxfordpreservation.org.uk W www.oxfordpreservation.org.uk
Director, Debbie Dance

OXFORDSHIRE ARCHITECTURAL AND HISTORICAL SOCIETY (1839), 7A Burford Road, Chipping Norton OX7 5EB T 01608-641352 E secretary@oahs.org.uk W www.oahs.org.uk
Hon. Secretary, A. Lang

OXFORD UNIVERSITY SOCIETY (1932), University Offices, Wellington Square, Oxford OX1 2JD T 01865-611610 E enquiries@ousoc.ox.ac.uk W www.alumni.ox.ac.uk
Secretary, Lady Nancy Kenny

PALAEONTOLOGICAL ASSOCIATION (1957), c/o Department of Earth Sciences, The University, South Road, Durham DH1 3LE T 01970-687107 E palass@palass.org W www.palass.org
Chief Executive, Dr T. J. Palmer

PARLIAMENTARY AND SCIENTIFIC COMMITTEE (1939), 3 Birdcage Walk, Westminster, London SW1H 9JJ T 020-7222 7085 E secretariat@pandsctte.demon.co.uk W www.scienceinparliament.org.uk
Scientific Secretary, Prof. Peter Simpson

PENSIONS ADVISORY SERVICE (1983), 11 Belgrave Road, London SW1V 1RB T 0845-601 2923 E enquiries@pensionsadvisoryservice.org.uk W www.pensionsadvisoryservice.org.uk
Chief Executive, M. McLean, OBE

PILGRIMS OF GREAT BRITAIN (1902), Allington Castle, Maidstone ME16 0NB T 01622-606404 E sec@pilgrimsociety.org
Chair, Sir Robert Worcester, KBE, DL

PLAIN ENGLISH CAMPAIGN (1979), PO Box 3, New Mills, High Peak SK22 4QP T 01663-744409 E info@plainenglish.co.uk W www.plainenglish.co.uk
Director, Ms C. Maher

POETRY SOCIETY (1909), 22 Betterton Street, London WC2H 9BX T 020-7420 9880 E info@poetrysociety.org.uk W www.poetrysociety.org.uk
Director, Jules Mann

POWYSLAND CLUB (1867), Cartref, 14 Berriew Road, Welshpool SY21 7SS T 01938-552161 W www.powyslandclub.co.uk
Hon. Secretary, Revd Roger L. Brown

PRE-SCHOOL LEARNING ALLIANCE (1961), The Fitzpatrick Building, 188 York Way, London N7 9AD T 020-7697 2500 E info@pre-school.org.uk W www.pre-school.org.uk
Chief Executive, Steve Alexander

PRINCESS ROYAL TRUST FOR CARERS (1991), Unit 14, Bourne Court, Southend Road, Woodford Green IG8 8HD T 0844 800 4361 E info@carers.org W www.carers.org
Chairman, Ian Robertson

PRINCE'S TRUST (1976), 18 Park Square East, London NW1 4LH T 0800-842842 E webinfops@princes-trust.org.uk W www.princes-trust.org.uk
Chief Executive, M. Milburn

PRISONERS ABROAD (1978), 89–93 Fonthill Road, London N4 3JH T 020-7561 6820 E info@prisonersabroad.org.uk W www.prisonersabroad.org.uk
Chief Executive, Pauline Crowe

PRIVATE LIBRARIES ASSOCIATION (1956), Ravelston, South View Road, Pinner HA5 3YD E dchambers@aol.com W http://plabooks.org
Chairman of the Council, David Chambers

PROFESSIONAL FOOTBALLERS' ASSOCIATION (1907), 20 Oxford Court, Bishopsgate, Manchester M2 3WQ T 0161-236 0575 E info@thepfa.co.uk W www.givemefootball.com
Chief Executive, Gordon Taylor, OBE

PROSTATE UK (1994), 10 Northfields Prospect, Putney Bridge Road, London SW18 1PE T 020-8877 5840 E info@prostateuk.org W www.prostateuk.org
Chief Executive, Brig. John Anderson

QUAKER PEACE AND SOCIAL WITNESS, Friends House, 173–177 Euston Road, London NW1 2BJ T 020-7663 1000 E qpsw@quaker.org.uk W www.quaker.org.uk
General Secretary, Kevin Franz

QUEEN ELIZABETH'S FOUNDATION FOR DISABLED PEOPLE (1934), Leatherhead Court, Leatherhead KT22 0BN T 01372-841100 E info@qef.org.uk W www.qef.org.uk
Chief Executive, Cynthia Robinson

QUEEN'S NURSING INSTITUTE (1887), 3 Albemarle Way, London EC1V 4RQ T 020-7549 1400 E mail@qni.org.uk W www.qni.org.uk
Director, Rosemary Cook

QUEEN VICTORIA CLERGY FUND (1897), Church House, Great Smith Street, London SW1P 3AZ T 020-7898 1000 E info@churchhouse.org.uk
Chief Executive, Colin Menzies

QUIT (1926), 4th Floor, 211 Old Street, London EC1V 9NR T 020-7251 1551 E info@quit.org.uk W www.quit.org.uk
Chief Executive, Steve Crone

RADAR (ROYAL ASSOCIATION FOR DISABILITY AND REHABILITATION) (1977), 12 City Forum, 250 City Road, London EC1V 8AF T 020-7250 3222 E radar@radar.org.uk W www.radar.org.uk
Chair, Phil Friend, OBE

RAILWAY AND CANAL HISTORICAL SOCIETY (1954), 3 West Court, West Street, Oxford OX2 0NP
T 01865-240514 E secretary@rchs.org.uk
W www.rchs.org.uk
Hon. Secretary, M. Searle

REFUGEE COUNCIL (1981), 240–250 Ferndale Road, London SW9 8BB T 020-7346 6700
E info@refugeecouncil.org.uk
W www.refugeecouncil.org.uk
Chief Executive, Donna Covey

REGIONAL STUDIES ASSOCIATION (1965), PO Box 2058, Seaford BN25 4QU
T 01323-899698 E info@rsa-ls.ac.uk
W www.regional-studies-assoc.ac.uk
Chief Executive, Sally Hardy

RELATE (1938), Premier House, Carolina Court, Lakeside, Doncaster DN4 5RA T 0300-100 1234
E enquiries@relate.org.uk W www.relate.org.uk

RESEARCH DEFENCE SOCIETY (1908), 25 Shaftesbury Avenue, London W1D 7EG
T 020-7287 2818 E info@rds-net.org.uk
W www.rds-net.org.uk
Executive Director, Dr S. Festing

RETHINK (1972), 5th Floor, Royal London House, 22–25 Finsbury Square, London EC2A 1DX
T 0845-456 0455 E info@rethink.org
W www.rethink.org
Chief Executive, Paul Jenkins

RETIRED NURSES' NATIONAL HOME (1934), Riverside Avenue, Bournemouth BH7 7EE
T 01202-396418 E rnnhoffice@btconnect.com
W www.rnnh.co.uk
Chair, Mrs S. Young

RNIB NATIONAL LIBRARY SERVICE (1868), Far Cromwell Road, Bredbury, Stockport SK6 2SG
T 0845-762 6843 E cservices@rnib.org.uk
W www.rnib.org.uk/reading
Head of National Library Service, Helen Brazier

RNIB (ROYAL NATIONAL INSTITUTE OF THE BLIND) (1868), 105 Judd Street, London WC1H 9NE
T 020-7388 1266, Helpline 0845-766 9999
E helpline@rnib.org.uk W www.rnib.org.uk
Chief Executive, Lesley-Anne Alexander

RNID (1911), 19–23 Featherstone Street, London EC1Y 8SL T 020-7296 8000, Textphone 020-7296 8001
E informationline@rnid.org.uk W www.rnid.org.uk
Chief Executive, Jackie Ballard

ROADS AND ROAD TRANSPORT HISTORY ASSOCIATION (1992), c/o Kithead Trust, De Salis Drive, Hampton Lovett, Droitwich WR9 0QE
E enquiries@rrtha.org.uk W www.rrtha.org.uk
Chair, Grahame Boyes

ROTARY INTERNATIONAL IN GREAT BRITAIN AND IRELAND (1922), Kinwarton Road, Alcester B49 6PB T 01789-765411 E secretary@ribi.org
W www.rotary-ribi.org
Secretary, Annemarie Harte

ROYAL AERONAUTICAL SOCIETY (1866), 4 Hamilton Place, London W1J 7BQ T 020-7670 4300
W www.raes.org.uk
Chief Executive, Keith Mans

ROYAL AIR FORCE BENEVOLENT FUND (1919), 67 Portland Place, London W1B 1AR T 0800-169 2942
E info@rafbf.org.uk W www.rafbf.org
Controller, Air Marshal Sir Robert Wright, KBE, AFC

ROYAL AIR FORCES ASSOCIATION (1943), 117½ Loughborough Road, Leicester LE4 5ND
T 0116-266 5224 E enquiries@rafa.org.uk
W www.rafa.org.uk
Secretary-General, E. Jarron

ROYAL ARTILLERY ASSOCIATION (1920), Artillery House, Artillery Centre, Larkhill, Salisbury SP4 8QT T 01980-845895
E AC-RHQRA-RACF-RAA-GenSecPA@mod.uk
W www.theraa.co.uk
General Secretary, Lt.-Col. I. A. Vere Nicoll, MBE

ROYAL ASSOCIATION FOR DEAF PEOPLE (1841), 18 Westside Centre, London Road, Stanway CO3 8PH T 0845-668 2525 E info@royaldeaf.org.uk
W www.royaldeaf.org.uk
Chief Executive, Tom Fenton

ROYAL ASSOCIATION OF BRITISH DAIRY FARMERS (1876), Dairy House, Unit 31, Stoneleigh Deer Park, Stareton, Kenilworth CV8 2LY
T 0845-458 2711 E office@rabdf.co.uk
W www.rabdf.co.uk
Chief Executive, N. Everington

ROYAL BIRMINGHAM SOCIETY OF ARTISTS (1814), 4 Brook Street, Birmingham B3 1SA
T 0121-236 4353 E secretary@rbsa.org.uk
W www.rbsa.org.uk
Gallery Director, Marie Considine

ROYAL BRITISH LEGION (1921), 48 Pall Mall, London SW1Y 5JY T 0845-7725 725
E info@britishlegion.org.uk W www.britishlegion.org.uk
Director-General, Chris Simpkins

ROYAL BRITISH LEGION SCOTLAND (1921), New Haig House, Logie Green Road, Edinburgh EH7 4HR
E admin@rblscotland.org W www.rblscotland.org
General Secretary, Douglas Mackenzie

ROYAL CALEDONIAN SCHOOLS TRUST (1815), Unit 75, WENTA Business Park, Colne Way, Watford WD24 7ND T 01923-215 350 E admin@rsct.org.uk
W www.rsct.org.uk
Chief Executive, John Horsfield

ROYAL CAMBRIAN ACADEMY (1882), Crown Lane, Conwy LL32 8AN T 01492-593413
E rca@rcaconwy.org W www.rcaconwy.org
President, Maurice Cockrill

ROYAL CELTIC SOCIETY (1820), 23 Rutland Street, Edinburgh EH1 2RN T 0131-228 6449
E gcameron@stuartandstuart.co.uk
W www.royalcelticsociety.org.uk
Secretary, J. Gordon Cameron, WS

ROYAL COLLEGE OF OBSTETRICIANS AND GYNAECOLOGISTS (1929), 27 Sussex Place, Regent's Park, London NW1 4RG T 020-7772 6200 W www.rcog.org.uk
Chief Executive, Helen Moffatt

ROYAL COLLEGE OF PHYSICIANS (1518), 11 St Andrews Place, Regent's Park, London NW1 4LE T 020-7935 1174 E infocentre@rcplondon.ac.uk W www.rcplondon.ac.uk
Chief Executive, M. T. Else

ROYAL COLLEGE OF PSYCHIATRISTS (1841), 17 Belgrave Square, London SW1X 8PG T 020-7235 2351 E rcpsych@rcpsych.ac.uk W www.rcpsych.ac.uk
President, Vanessa Cameron

ROYAL COLLEGE OF RADIOLOGISTS (1975), 38 Portland Place, London W1B 1JQ T 020-7636 4432 E enquiries@rcr.ac.uk W www.rcr.ac.uk
Chief Executive, A. Hall

ROYAL COLLEGE OF SURGEONS OF ENGLAND (1800), 35–43 Lincoln's Inn Fields, London WC2A 3PE T 020-7405 3474 W www.rcseng.ac.uk
Executive General Manager, David Munn

ROYAL COLLEGE OF VETERINARY SURGEONS (1844), Belgravia House, 62–64 Horseferry Road, London SW1P 2AF T 020-7222 2001 E admin@rcvs.org.uk W www.rcvs.org.uk
Registrar, Miss J. C. Hern

ROYAL COMMISSION FOR THE EXHIBITION OF 1851 (1850), 453 Sherfield Building, Imperial College SW7 2AZ T 020-7594 8790 E royalcom1851@imperial.ac.uk W www.royalcommission1851.org.uk
Chairman, Sir Alan Rudge, CBE, FRENG, FRS

ROYAL COMMONWEALTH EX-SERVICES LEAGUE (1921), 48 Pall Mall, London SW1Y 5JG T 020-7973 7263 W www.commonwealthveterans.org.uk

ROYAL GEOGRAPHICAL SOCIETY (with the INSTITUTE OF BRITISH GEOGRAPHERS) (1830), 1 Kensington Gore, London SW7 2AR T 020-7591 3000 E enquiries@rgs.org W www.rgs.org
Director, Dr R. Gardner, CBE

ROYAL HISTORICAL SOCIETY (1868), University College London, Gower Street, London WC1E 6BT T 020-7387 7532 E royalhistsoc@ucl.ac.uk W www.royalhistoricalsociety.org
President, Prof. Martin Daunton

ROYAL HORTICULTURAL SOCIETY (1804), 80 Vincent Square, London SW1P 2PE T 0845-260 5000 E info@rhs.org.uk W www.rhs.org.uk
Director-General, Inga Grimsey

ROYAL HOSPITAL FOR NEURO-DISABILITY (1854), West Hill, Putney, London SW15 3SW T 020-8780 4500 E info@rhn.org.uk W www.rhn.org.uk
Chief Executive, Peter Franklyn

ROYAL HUMANE SOCIETY (1774), Brettenham House, Lancaster Place, London WC2E 7EP T 020-7836 8155 E info@royalhumanesociety.org.uk W www.royalhumanesociety.org.uk
Secretary, Dick Wilkinson, TD

ROYAL INSTITUTE OF BRITISH ARCHITECTS (1837), 66 Portland Place, London W1B 1AD T 020-7580 5533 E info@inst.riba.org W www.architecture.com
Chief Executive, Richard Hastilow, CBE

ROYAL INSTITUTE OF NAVIGATION (1947), 1 Kensington Gore, London SW7 2AT T 020-7591 3130 E info@rin.org.uk W www.rin.org.uk
Director, Gp Capt. D. W. Broughton, MBE

ROYAL INSTITUTION OF CHARTERED SURVEYORS (1868), 12 Great George Street, Parliament Square, London SW1P 3AD T 020-7222 7000 E contactrics@rics.org W www.rics.org
Chief Executive, J. H. A. J. Armstrong

ROYAL INSTITUTION OF GREAT BRITAIN (1799), 21 Albemarle Street, London W1S 4BS T 020-7409 2992 E ri@ri.ac.uk W www.rigb.org
Director, Baroness Greenfield, CBE

ROYAL INSTITUTION OF NAVAL ARCHITECTS (1860), 10 Upper Belgrave Street, London SW1X 8BQ T 020-7235 4622 E hq@rina.org.uk W www.rina.org.uk
Chief Executive, T. Blakeley

ROYAL NATIONAL COLLEGE FOR THE BLIND (1872), College Road, Hereford HR1 1EB T 01432-265725 E info@rncb.ac.uk W www.rncb.ac.uk
Principal, Mrs C. Steadman

ROYAL NATIONAL LIFEBOAT INSTITUTION (1824), West Quay Road, Poole BH15 1HZ T 0845-122 6999 E info@rnli.org.uk W www.rnli.org.uk
Chief Executive, Andrew Freemantle, CBE

ROYAL NAVAL ASSOCIATION (1949), 82 Chelsea Manor Street, London SW3 5QJ T 020-7352 6764 E rna@netcomuk.co.uk W www.royal-naval-association.co.uk
President, Vice-Adm. John McAnally, CB, LVO

ROYAL NAVAL BENEVOLENT SOCIETY FOR OFFICERS (1739), 70 Porchester Terrace, London W2 3TP T 020-7402 5231 E rnbso@arno.org.uk
Chair, Rear-Adm. D. J. Anthony, MBE

ROYAL PHILATELIC SOCIETY LONDON (1869), 41 Devonshire Place, London W1G 6JY T 020-7486 1044 E secretary@rpsl.org.uk W www.rpsl.org.uk
President, S. J. Sacher, CBE

ROYAL PHILHARMONIC SOCIETY (1813), 10 Stratford Place, London W1C 1BA T 020-7491 8110 E admin@royalphilharmonicsociety.org.uk W www.royalphilharmonicsociety.org.uk
Chair, Graham Sheffield

ROYAL SCHOOL OF CHURCH MUSIC (1927), 19 The Close, Salisbury SP1 2EB T 01722-424848 E enquiries@rscm.com W www.rscm.com
Director-General, Lindsay Gray

ROYAL SCHOOL OF NEEDLEWORK (1872), Apartment 12A, Hampton Court Palace KT8 9AU T 020-3166 6932 E enquiries@royal-needlework.org.uk W www.royal-needlework.org.uk
Principal, Dr Susan Kay-Williams

ROYAL SOCIETY (1660), 6–9 Carlton House Terrace, London SW1Y 5AG T 020-7451 2500 E info@royalsociety.org W www.royalsociety.org
Executive Secretary, Stephen Cox, CVO

ROYAL SOCIETY FOR ASIAN AFFAIRS (1901), 2 Belgrave Square, London SW1X 8PJ T 020-7235 5122 E sec@rsaa.org.uk W www.rsaa.org.uk
Chairman of Council, Sir Harold Walker, KCMG

ROYAL SOCIETY FOR THE PREVENTION OF ACCIDENTS (1917), RoSPA House, Edgbaston Park, 353 Bristol Road, Birmingham B5 7ST T 0121-248 2000 E help@rospa.com W www.rospa.com
Chief Executive, Tom Mullarkey, MBE

ROYAL SOCIETY FOR THE PREVENTION OF CRUELTY TO ANIMALS (1824), Wilberforce Way, Horsham RH13 9RS T 0300-123 4555 W www.rspca.org.uk
Director-General, Mark Watts

ROYAL SOCIETY FOR THE PROTECTION OF BIRDS (1889), The Lodge, Sandy SG19 2DL T 01767-680551 W www.rspb.org.uk
Chief Executive, G. R. Wynne

ROYAL SOCIETY OF MEDICINE (1805), 1 Wimpole Street, London W1G 0AE T 020-7290 2900 E membership@rsm.ac.uk W www.rsm.ac.uk
Chief Executive, Ian Balmer

ROYAL SOCIETY OF MINIATURE PAINTERS, SCULPTORS AND GRAVERS (1895), 3 Briar Walk, London SW15 6UD T 020-8785 2338 E info@royal-miniature-society.org.uk W www.royal-miniature-society.org.uk
Executive Secretary, Phyllis Rennell

ROYAL SOCIETY OF MUSICIANS OF GREAT BRITAIN (1738), 10 Stratford Place, London W1C 1BA T 020-7629 6137 W www.royalsocietyofmusicians.co.uk
Secretary, Mrs M. Gibb

ROYAL SOCIETY OF ST GEORGE (1894), 127 Sandgate Road, Folkstone CT20 2BH T 01303-241795 E info@rssg.u-net.com W www.royalsocietyofstgeorge.com
Chair, James E. Newton

ROYAL SOCIETY OF TROPICAL MEDICINE AND HYGIENE (1907), 50 Bedford Square, London WC1B 3DP T 020-7580 2127 E mail@rstmh.org W www.rstmh.org
Hon. Secretaries, Prof. G. Pasvol; Dr J. R. Stothard

ROYAL STAR AND GARTER HOMES FOR DISABLED EX-SERVICE MEN AND WOMEN (1916), Richmond Hill, Richmond TW10 6RR T 020-8439 8000 E generalenquiries@starandgarter.org W www.starandgarter.org
Chief Executive, Lynn McDougall

ROYAL THEATRICAL FUND (1839), 11 Garrick Street, London WC2E 9AR T 020-7836 3322 E admin@trtf.com W www.trtf.com
President, Sir Donald Sinden, CBE, FRSA

ROYAL WATERCOLOUR SOCIETY (1804), Bankside Gallery, 48 Hopton Street, London SE1 9JH T 020-7928 7521 E info@banksidegallery.com W www.royalwatercoloursociety.co.uk
President, Richard Sorrell

ROYAL ZOOLOGICAL SOCIETY OF SCOTLAND (1909), Edinburgh Zoo, 134 Corstorphine Road, Edinburgh EH12 6TS T 0131-334 9171 E info@rzss.org.uk W www.edinburghzoo.org.uk
Chief Executive, David Windmill

RSABI (1897), The Rural Centre, West Mains of Ingliston, Newbridge, Edinburgh EH28 8LT T 0131-472 4166 E rsabi@rsabi.org.uk W www.rsabi.org.uk
Chief Executive, Dr Maurice S Hankey

ST ALBANS AND HERTFORDSHIRE ARCHITECTURAL AND ARCHAEOLOGICAL SOCIETY (1845), 24 Monks Horton Way, St Albans AL1 4HA T 01727-851734 E admin@stalbanshistory.org W www.stalbanshistory.org
Secretary, B. R. Hanlon

ST DUNSTAN'S (1915), 12–14 Harcourt Street, London W1H 4HD T 020-7723 5021 E enquiries@st-dunstans.org.uk W www.st-dunstans.org.uk
Chief Executive, Robert Leader

ST JOHN AMBULANCE (1877), 27 St John's Lane, London EC1M 4BU T 020-7324 4000 E info@sja.org.uk W www.sja.org.uk
Chief Executive, Sue Killen

SALTIRE SOCIETY (1936), 9 Fountain Close, 22 High Street, Edinburgh EH1 1TF T 0131-556 1836 E saltire@saltiresociety.org.uk W www.saltiresociety.org.uk
Administrator, Mrs K. Munro

SAMARITANS (1953), The Upper Mill, Kingston Road, Ewell KT17 2AF T 020-8394 8300 E admin@samaritans.org W www.samaritans.org
Chief Executive, Dominic Rudd

SANE (1986), 1st Floor, Cityside House, 40 Adler Street, London E1 1EE T 020-7375 1002, Helpline 0845-767 8000 E info@sane.org.uk W www.sane.org.uk
Chief Executive, Ms M. Wallace, MBE

SAVE BRITAIN'S HERITAGE (1975), 70 Cowcross Street, London EC1M 6EJ T 020-7253 3500 E save@btinternet.com W www.savebritainsheritage.org
President, Marcus Binney, OBE

SAVE THE CHILDREN UK (1919), 1 St. John's Lane, London EC1M 4AR T 020-7012 6400 E supporter.care@savethechildren.org.uk W www.savethechildren.org.uk
Chief Executive, Jasmine Whitbread

SCHOOL LIBRARY ASSOCIATION (1937), Unit 2, Lotmead Business Village, Lotmead Farm, Wanborough, nr Swindon SN4 0UY T 01793-791787 E info@sla.org.uk W www.sla.org.uk
Chief Executive, Ms K. Lemaire

SCHOOL OF PUBLIC POLICY (1996), University College London, 29 Tavistock Square, London WC1H 9QU T 020-7679 4999 E spp@ucl.ac.uk W www.ucl.ac.uk/spp
Director, Prof. Richard Bellamy

SCOPE (1952), 6 Market Road, London N7 9PW T 020-7619 7100, **Helpline** 0808-800 3333 E response@scope.org.uk W www.scope.org.uk
Chair, Alice Maynard

SCOTTISH ASSOCIATION FOR MARINE SCIENCE (1884), Dunstaffnage Marine Laboratory, Oban, Argyll PA37 1QA T 01631-559000 E info@sams.ac.uk W www.sams.ac.uk
Director, Laurence Mee

SCOTTISH COUNCIL FOR VOLUNTARY ORGANISATIONS (1943), Mansfield Traquair Centre, 15 Mansfield Place, Edinburgh EH3 6BB T 0131-556 3882 E enquiries@scvo.org.uk W www.scvo.org.uk
Chief Executive, M. Sime

SCOTTISH NATIONAL WAR MEMORIAL (1927), The Castle, Edinburgh EH1 2YT T 0131-226 7393 E info@snwm.org W www.snwm.org
Secretary to the Trustees, Lt.-Col. I. Shepherd

SCOTTISH NATURAL HISTORY LIBRARY (1970), Foremount House, Kilbarchan PA10 2EZ T 01505-702419
Director, Dr J. A. Gibson

SCOTTISH RURAL PROPERTY AND BUSINESS ASSOCIATION, Stuart House, Eskmills Business Park, Musselburgh EH21 7PB T 0131-653 5400 E info@srpba.com W www.srpba.com
Chief Executive, Douglas McAdam

SCOTTISH SOCIETY FOR THE PREVENTION OF CRUELTY TO ANIMALS (1839), Braehead Mains, 603 Queensferry Road, Edinburgh EH4 6EA T 0131-339 0222 W www.scottishspca.org
Chief Executive, Stuart Earley

SCOTTISH SOCIETY FOR THE PROTECTION OF WILD BIRDS (1927), Foremount House, Kilbarchan PA10 2EZ T 01505-702419
Hon. Secretary, Dr J. A. Gibson

SCOTTISH WILDLIFE TRUST (1964), Cramond House, Cramond Glebe Road, Edinburgh EH4 6NS T 0131-312 7765 E enquiries@swt.org.uk W www.swt.org.uk
Chief Executive, Simon Milne

SCOUT ASSOCIATION (1907), Gilwell Park, Chingford, London E4 7QW T 020-8443 7100 E scout.association@scout.org.uk W www.scouts.org.uk
Chief Executive, D. M. Twine, CBE

SEEABILITY (1799), SeeAbility House, Hook Road, Epsom KT19 8SQ T 01372-755000 E enquiries@seeability.org W www.seeability.org
Chief Executive, D. Scott-Ralphs

SELDEN SOCIETY (1887), School of Law, Queen Mary, Mile End Road, London E1 4NS T 020-7882 5136 E selden-society@qmul.ac.uk W www.selden-society.qmul.ac.uk
Secretary, V. Tunkel

SENSE (THE NATIONAL DEAFBLIND AND RUBELLA ASSOCIATION) (1955), 101 Pentonville Road, London N1 9LG T 0845-127 0060 E enquiries@sense.org.uk W www.sense.org.uk
Chief Executive, A. Best

SHELTER (NATIONAL CAMPAIGN FOR HOMELESS PEOPLE), 88 Old Street, London EC1V 9HU T 0845-458 4590, **Helpline** 0808-800 4444 E info@shelter.org.uk W www.shelter.org.uk
Director, Adam Sampson

SHIRE HORSE SOCIETY (1878), East of England Showground, Peterborough PE2 6XE T 01733-234451 E info@shire-horse.org.uk W www.shire-horse.org.uk
Chief Executive Officer, Andrew Mercer

SIGHTSAVERS INTERNATIONAL (ROYAL COMMONWEALTH SOCIETY FOR THE BLIND) (1950), Grosvenor Hall, Bolnore Road, Haywards Heath RH16 4BX T 01444-446600 E info@sightsavers.org W www.sightsavers.org.uk
Chief Executive, Dr Caroline Harper, OBE

SIR OSWALD STOLL FOUNDATION (1916), 446 Fulham Road, London SW6 1DT T 020-7385 2110 E info@oswaldstoll.org.uk W www.oswaldstoll.org.uk
Chief Executive, R. C. Brunwin

SOCIÉTÉ JERSIAISE (1873), 7 Pier Road, St Helier JE2 4XW T 01534-758314 E societe@societe-jersiaise.org W www.societe-jersiaise.org
Executive Director, Mrs P. Syvret

SOCIETY FOR NAUTICAL RESEARCH (1910), 6 Ashmeadow Road, Arnside, via Carnforth LA5 0AE T 01524-761616 E honsec@snr.org.uk W www.snr.org.uk
Hon. Secretary, Peter Winterbottom

SOCIETY FOR PROMOTING CHRISTIAN KNOWLEDGE (1698), 36 Causton Street, London SW1P 4ST T 020-7592 3900 E spck@spck.org.uk W www.spck.org.uk
General Secretary, Simon Kingston

SOCIETY FOR PSYCHICAL RESEARCH (1882), 49 Marloes Road, London W8 6LA T 020-7937 8984 W www.spr.ac.uk
Secretary, Peter Johnson

SOCIETY FOR THE PROMOTION OF ROMAN STUDIES (1910), Senate House, Malet Street, London WC1E 7HU T 020-7862 8727 E office@romansociety.org W www.romansociety.org
Secretary, Dr Fiona Haarer

SOCIETY FOR THE PROTECTION OF UNBORN CHILDREN (1967), 3 Whitacre Mews, London SE11 4AB T 020-7091 7091 E information@spuc.org.uk W www.spuc.org.uk
National Director, John Smeaton

SOCIETY OF ANTIQUARIES OF NEWCASTLE UPON TYNE (1813), The Black Gate, Castle Garth, Newcastle upon Tyne NE1 1RQ T 0191-261 5390 E admin@newcastle-antiquaries.org.uk W www.newcastle-antiquaries.org.uk
Hon. Secretary, Dr N. Hodgson

SOCIETY OF ARCHIVISTS (1947), Prioryfield House, 20 Canon Street, Taunton TA1 1SW T 01823-327030 E societyofarchivists@archives.org.uk W www.archives.org.uk
Executive Director, J. Chambers

SOCIETY OF AUTHORS (1884), 84 Drayton Gardens, London SW10 9SB T 020-7373 6642 E info@societyofauthors.org W www.societyofauthors.org
General Secretary, Mark Le Fanu, OBE

SOCIETY OF BOTANICAL ARTISTS (1985), 1 Knapp Cottages, Wyke, Gillingham SP8 4NQ T 01747-825718 E pam@soc-botanical-artists.org W www.soc-botanical-artists.org
Executive Secretary, Pam Henderson

SOCIETY OF COUNTY TREASURERS, Warwickshire County Council, PO Box 3, Shire Hall, Warwick CV34 4RH T 01926-412003 E davidclarketr@warwickshire.gov.uk W www.warwickshire.gov.uk
Hon. Secretary, David Clarke

SOCIETY OF EDITORS, University Centre, Granta Place, Mill Lane, Cambridge CB2 1RU T 01223-304080 E info@societyofeditors.org W www.societyofeditors.co.uk
Executive Director, Bob Satchwell

SOCIETY OF GENEALOGISTS (1911 and 1999), 14 Charterhouse Buildings, Goswell Road, London EC1M 7BA T 020-7251 8799 E librarian@sog.org.uk W www.sog.org.uk
Chief Executive, June Perrin

SOCIETY OF INDEXERS (1957), Woodbourn Business Centre, 10 Jessell Street, Sheffield S9 3HY T 0114-244 9561 E admin@indexers.org.uk W www.indexers.org.uk
Chair, Sue Lightfoot

SOCIETY OF LEGAL SCHOLARS (1908), School of Law, Southampton University, Southampton SO17 1BJ T 023-8059 4039 E s.j.thomson@soton.ac.uk W www.legalscholars.ac.uk
Hon. Secretary, Prof. Stephen Bailey

SOCIETY OF LOCAL AUTHORITY CHIEF EXECUTIVES AND SENIOR MANAGERS, Hope House, 45 Great Peter Street, London SW1P 3LT T 0845-601 0649 E hope.house@solace.org.uk W www.solace.org.uk
Director-General, David Clark

SOCIETY OF SCHOOLMASTERS AND SCHOOLMISTRESSES (1798), c/o L. I. Baggott, SGBI Office, Queen Mary House, Manor Park Road, Chistlehurst BR7 5PY T 020-8468 7997 E sgbi@sgbi.freeserve.co.uk
Secretary (acting), Laurence Baggott, FCA

SOCIETY OF SOLICITORS IN THE SUPREME COURT OF SCOTLAND (1784), SSC Library, Parliament House, 11 Parliament Square, Edinburgh EH1 1RF T 0131-225 6268 E enquiries@ssclibrary.co.uk W www.ssclibrary.co.uk
Secretary, I. L. S. Balfour

SOCIETY OF WOMEN ARTISTS (1855), 1 Knapp Cottages, Wyke, Gillingham SP8 4NQ T 01747-825718 E pamhenderson@dsl.pipex.com W www.society-women-artists.org.uk
Executive Secretary, Pam Henderson

SOCIETY OF WRITERS TO HM SIGNET (1594), The Signet Library, Parliament Square, Edinburgh EH1 1RF T 0131-220 3249 E enquiries@wssociety.co.uk W www.wssociety.co.uk
Chief Executive, Robert Pirrie

SOIL ASSOCIATION (1946), South Plaza, Marlborough Street, Bristol BS1 3NX T 0117-314 5000 E info@soilassociation.org W www.soilassociation.org
Director, Patrick Holden

SOMERSET ARCHAEOLOGICAL AND NATURAL HISTORY SOCIETY (1849), Taunton Castle, Taunton TA1 4AA T 01823-272429 E office@sanhs.org W www.sanhs.org
Chairman, Dr Pat Hill-Cottingham

SOUTH AMERICAN MISSION SOCIETY (1844), Allen Gardiner Cottage, Pembury Road, Tunbridge Wells TN2 3QU T 01892-538647 E finsec@samsgb.org W www.samsgb.org
General Secretary (interim), Bill Lattimer

SOUTH WALES INSTITUTE OF ENGINEERS (1857/2007), Suite 2, Bay Chambers, West Bute Street, Cardiff CF10 5BB T 0292-063 0561 E cherry.cronly@swieet2007.org.uk W www.swieet2007.org.uk
Hon. Secretary, D. M. Morgan

SPURGEONS (1867), 74 Wellingborough Road, Rushden NN10 9TY T 01933-412412 E info@spurgeons.org W www.spurgeons.org
Chief Executive, T. Jeffrey

STANDING COUNCIL OF THE BARONETAGE (1903), Forestside, Martin's Corner, Hambledon, Waterlooville PO7 4RA T 023-9263 2672 E secretary@baronetage.org W www.baronetage.org
Chair, Sir Ian Lowson, BT, OSTJ

SURREY ARCHAEOLOGICAL SOCIETY (1854), Castle Arch, Guildford GU1 3SX **T** 01483-532454 **E** info@surreyarchaeology.org.uk **W** www.surreyarchaeology.org.uk
Hon. Secretary, David Calow

SUSSEX ARCHAEOLOGICAL SOCIETY (1846), Bull House, 92 High Street, Lewes BN7 1XH **T** 01273-486260 **E** admin@sussexpast.co.uk **W** www.sussexpast.co.uk
Chief Executive, J. Manley

SUZY LAMPLUGH TRUST (1986), National Centre for Personal Safety, 20 Albert Embankment, London SE1 7TJ **T** 020-7091 0014 **E** info@suzylamplugh.org **W** www.suzylamplugh.org
Chief Executive, Steven Gauge

SWEDENBORG SOCIETY (1810), 20–21 Bloomsbury Way, London WC1A 2TH **T** 020-7405 7986 **E** swed.soc@netmatters.co.uk **W** www.swedenborg.org.uk
Secretary, Richard Lines

TAVISTOCK INSTITUTE (1947), 30 Tabernacle Street, London EC2A 4UE **T** 020-7417 0407 **W** www.tavinstitute.org
Director, Phil Swann

TERRENCE HIGGINS TRUST (1982), 314–320 Gray's Inn Road, London WC1X 8DP **T** 0845-122 1200 **E** info@tht.org.uk **W** www.tht.org.uk
Chief Executive, Nick Partridge

THEATRES TRUST (1976), 22 Charing Cross Road, London WC2H 0QL **T** 020-7836 8591 **E** info@theatrestrust.org.uk **W** www.theatrestrust.org.uk
Director, Mhora Samuel

THORESBY SOCIETY (1889), Claremont, 23 Clarendon Road, Leeds LS2 9NZ **T** 0113-247 0704 **E** president@thoresby.org.uk **W** www.thoresby.org.uk
President, C. J. Morgan

TOGETHER: WORKING FOR WELLBEING (1879), 12 Old Street, London EC1V 9BE **T** 020-7780 7300 **E** contactus@together-uk.org **W** www.together-uk.org
Chief Executive, Liz Felton

TOWN AND COUNTRY PLANNING ASSOCIATION (1899), 17 Carlton House Terrace, London SW1Y 5AS **T** 020-7930 8903 **W** www.tcpa.org.uk
Chief Executive, Gideon Amos

TOWNSWOMEN'S GUILDS, Chamber of Commerce House, 75 Harborne Road, Birmingham B15 3DA **T** 0121-326 0400 **E** tghq@townswomen.org.uk **W** www.townswomen.org.uk
National Secretary, Mrs D. Calvert

TRADING STANDARDS INSTITUTE (1881), 1 Sylvan Court, Sylvan Way, Southfields Business Park, Basildon SS15 6TH **T** 0845-608 9400 **E** institute@tsi.org.uk **W** www.tsi.org.uk
Chief Executive, Ron Gainsford

TURNER SOCIETY (1975), BCM Box Turner, London WC1N 3XX **W** www.turnersociety.org.uk
Chair, Eric Shanes

UK YOUTH (1911), 26 Rosebery Avenue, London EC1R 4SX **T** 020-7242 4045 **E** info@ukyouth.org.uk **W** www.ukyouth.org.uk
Chief Executive, John Bateman, OBE

UNITED GRAND LODGE OF ENGLAND (1717), Freemasons' Hall, Great Queen Street, London WC2B 5AZ **T** 020-7831 9811 **E** ugle@ugle.org.uk **W** www.ugle.org.uk
Grand Master, HRH The Duke of Kent, KG, GCMG, GCVO

UNITED KINGDOM RESERVE FORCES ASSOCIATION (1972), Holderness House, 51–61 Clifton Street, London EC2A 4EY **T** 020-7426 8361 **E** co-rfa@co.rfca.mod.uk **W** www.ukrfa.org
President, Air Vice-Marshal B. H. Newton, CB, CVO, OBE

UNITED NATIONS ASSOCIATION OF GREAT BRITAIN AND NORTHERN IRELAND (1945), 3 Whitehall Court, London SW1A 2EL **T** 020-7766 3444 **W** www.una.org.uk
Executive Director, Sam Daws

UNITED REFORMED CHURCH HISTORY SOCIETY (1972), Westminster College, Madingley Road, Cambridge CB3 0AA **T** 01223-741300 **E** mt212@cam.ac.uk
Hon. Secretary, Revd E. J. Brown

UNIVERSITIES FEDERATION FOR ANIMAL WELFARE (1926), The Old School, Brewhouse Hill, Wheathampstead AL4 8AN **T** 01582-831818 **E** ufaw@ufaw.org.uk **W** www.ufaw.org.uk
Chief Executive and Scientific Director, Dr J. K. Kirkwood

UNIVERSITIES UK (2000), Woburn House, 20 Tavistock Square, London WC1H 9HQ **T** 020-7419 4111 **E** info@universitiesuk.ac.uk **W** www.universitiesuk.ac.uk
Chief Executive, Baroness Warwick

VEGAN SOCIETY (1944), Donald Watson House, 21 Hylton Street, Hockley B18 6HJ **T** 0845-458 8244 **E** info@vegansociety.com **W** www.vegansociety.com
General Managers, Dave Palmer and Rosamund Raha

VEGETARIAN SOCIETY OF THE UNITED KINGDOM LTD (1847), Parkdale, Dunham Road, Altrincham, Cheshire WA14 4QG **T** 0161-925 2000 **E** info@vegsoc.org **W** www.vegsoc.org
Chief Executive, Dr Annette Pinner

VERNACULAR ARCHITECTURE GROUP (1952), 'Ashley', Willows Green, Chelmsford CM3 1QD **T** 01245-361408 **W** www.vag.org.uk
Hon. Secretary, Mrs B. A. Watkin

VICTIM SUPPORT CENTRE (1979), National Centre, Cranmer House, 39 Brixton Road, London SW9 6DZ **T** 020-7735 9166 **E** contact@victimsupport.org.uk **W** www.victimsupport.org.uk
Chief Executive, Gillian Guy

VICTIM SUPPORT SCOTLAND (1985), 15–23 Hardwell Close, Edinburgh EH8 9RX T 0131-668 4486 E info@victimsupport.org.uk W www.victimsupport.org
Chief Executive, D. McKenna

VICTORIA CROSS AND GEORGE CROSS ASSOCIATION (1956), Horse Guards, Whitehall, London SW1A 2AX T 020-7930 3506
Secretary, Mrs D. Grahame, OBE, MVO

VICTORIAN SOCIETY (1958), 1 Priory Gardens, Bedford Park, London W4 1TT T 020-8994 1019 E admin@victoriansociety.org.uk W www.victoriansociety.org.uk
Director, Dr Ian Dungavell

VISITSCOTLAND (1969), Ocean Point One Building, 94, Ocean Drive, Edinburgh EH6 6JH T 0131-472 222 E info@visitscotland.com W www.visitscotland.com
Chief Executive, Philip Riddle

VSO (VOLUNTARY SERVICE OVERSEAS) (1958), 317 Putney Bridge Road, London SW15 2PN T 020-8780 7500 E enquiry@vso.org.uk W www.vso.org.uk
Chief Executive, Mark Goldring

WELLBEING OF WOMEN (1965), 27 Sussex Place, Regent's Park, London NW1 4SP T 020-7772 6400 E wellbeingofwomen@rcog.org.uk W www.wellbeingofwomen.org.uk
Directors, Liz Campbell

WESLEY HISTORICAL SOCIETY (1893), 7 Haugh Shaw Road, Halifax, West Yorkshire HX1 3AH T 01422-250780 E johnahargreaves@blueyonder.co.uk W www.wesleyhistoricalsociety.org.uk
General Secretary, Dr John A. Hargreaves, PHD, FSA

WESTMINSTER FOUNDATION FOR DEMOCRACY (1992), Artillery House, 11–19 Artillery Row, London SW1P 1RT T 020-7799 1311 E wfd@wfd.org W www.wfd.org
Chief Executive, David French

WILDFOWL AND WETLANDS TRUST (1946), Slimbridge GL2 7BT T 01453-891900 E info.slimbridge@wwt.org.uk W www.wwt.org.uk
Chief Executive, M. Spray

WILLIAM MORRIS SOCIETY AND KELMSCOTT FELLOWSHIP (1955), Kelmscott House, 26 Upper Mall, London W6 9TA T 020-8741 3735 E william.morris@care4free.net W www.morrissociety.org
Hon. Secretary, P. Bennett

WILTSHIRE ARCHAEOLOGICAL AND NATURAL HISTORY SOCIETY (1853), Wiltshire Heritage Museum, 41 Long Street, Devizes SN10 1NS T 01380-727369 E wanhs@wiltshireheritage.org.uk W www.wiltshireheritage.org.uk
Director, David Dawson

WINE AND SPIRIT TRADE ASSOCIATION (1824), International Wine and Spirit Centre, 39–45 Bermondsey Street, London SE1 3XF T 020-7089 3877 E info@wsta.co.uk W www.wsta.co.uk
Chief Executive, J. Beadles

WOMEN'S ENGINEERING SOCIETY (1919), c/o The IEE, Michael Faraday House, Six Hills Way, Stevenage SG1 2AY T 01438-765506 E info@wes.org.uk W www.wes.org.uk
President, Grazyna Whapshott

WOMEN'S ROYAL NAVAL SERVICE BENEVOLENT TRUST (1941), 311 Twyford Avenue, Portsmouth PO2 8RN T 023-9265 5301 E wrnsbt@care4free.net
General Secretary, Mrs Sarah Ayton

WOODLAND TRUST (1972), Autumn Park, Dysart Road, Grantham NG31 6LL T 01476-581111 E enquiries@woodlandtrust.org.uk W www.woodlandtrust.org.uk
Chief Executive, Sue Holden

WORCESTERSHIRE ARCHAEOLOGICAL SOCIETY (1854), 26 Albert Park Road, Malvern WR14 1HN T 01299-250416 E museum@worcestershire.gov.uk W www.communigate.co.uk/worcs
Hon. Secretary, Dr J. W. Dunleavey

WORKING FAMILIES (2003), 1–3 Berry Street, London EC1V 0AA T 020-7253 7243 E office@workingfamilies.org.uk W www.workingfamilies.org.uk
Chief Executive, Sarah Jackson

WRVS (1938), Garden House, Milton Hill, Abingdon OX13 6AD T 01235-442900 E enquiries@wrvs.org.uk W www.wrvs.org.uk
Chief Executive, Lynne Berry

YORKSHIRE ARCHAEOLOGICAL SOCIETY (1863), Claremont, 23 Clarendon Road, Leeds LS2 9NZ T 0113-245 7910 W www.yas.org.uk
General Secretary, M. J. Heron

YOUNG MEN'S CHRISTIAN ASSOCIATION (1844), National Council of YMCAs, 640 Forest Road, London E17 3DZ T 0845-873 6633 E enquiries@ymca.org.uk W www.ymca.org.uk
National Secretary, Angela Sarkis

YOUNG WOMEN'S CHRISTIAN ASSOCIATION ENGLAND & WALES (1855), Clarendon House, 52 Cornmarket Street, Oxford OX1 3EJ T 01865-304200 E info@ywca.org.uk W www.ywca.org.uk
Chief Executive, Gill Tishler

YOUTH HOSTELS ASSOCIATION (ENGLAND & WALES) (1930), Trevelyan House, Dimple Road, Matlock DE4 3YH T 01629-592600 E customerservices@yha.org.uk W www.yha.org.uk
Chief Executive, Roger Clarke

ZOOLOGICAL SOCIETY OF LONDON (1826), Regent's Park, London NW1 4RY T 020-7722 3333 W www.zsl.org
Director-General, Ralph Armond, FRS

THE WORLD

THE WORLD IN FIGURES

THE NORTH AND SOUTH POLES

AIR DISTANCES FROM LONDON

TIME ZONES

CURRENCIES AND EXCHANGE RATES

TRAVEL OVERSEAS

EUROPEAN UNION

INTERNATIONAL ORGANISATIONS

COUNTRIES OF THE WORLD A–Z

UK OVERSEAS TERRITORIES

THE WORLD IN FIGURES

THE EARTH

The shape of the Earth is that of an oblate spheroid or solid of revolution whose meridian sections are ellipses, whilst the sections at right angles are circles.

DIMENSIONS

Equatorial diameter = 12,756.27km (7,926.38 miles)
Polar diameter = 12,713.50km (7,899.80 miles)
Equatorial circumference = 40,075.01km (24,901.46 miles)
Polar circumference = 40,007.86km (24,859.73 miles)
Mass = 5,974,000,000,000,000,000,000 tonnes (5.879×10^{21} tons)

The equatorial circumference is divided into 360 degrees of longitude, which is measured in degrees, minutes and seconds east or west of the Greenwich meridian (0°) to 180°, the meridian 180° E. coinciding with 180° W. This dateline was internationally ratified on 13 October 1884. The position of the dateline has been modified on occasions, most recently on 1 January 1995 when it was moved to the east of Kiribati. *See also* Astronomy.

Distance north and south of the equator is measured in degrees, minutes and seconds of latitude. The equator is 0°, the North Pole is 90°N. and the South Pole is 90°S. The tropics lie at 23° 27′ N. (Tropic of Cancer) and 23° 27′ S. (Tropic of Capricorn). The Arctic Circle lies at 66° 33′ N. and the Antarctic Circle at 66° 33′ S. (Note the tropics and the Arctic and Antarctic circles are affected by the slow decrease in obliquity of the ecliptic, of about 0.47 arcseconds per year. The effect of this is that the Arctic and Antarctic circles are currently moving towards their respective poles by about 14m per annum, while the tropics move towards the equator by the same amount.)

AREA, ETC

The surface area of the Earth is 510,069,120km² (196,938,800 miles²), of which the water area is 70.92 per cent and the land area is 29.08 per cent.

The radial velocity on the Earth's surface at the equator is 1,669.79km per hour (1,037.56mph). The Earth's mean velocity in its orbit around the Sun is 107,229km per hour (66,629mph). The Earth's mean distance from the Sun is 149,597,870km (92,955,807 miles).

OCEANS

AREA

	km²	*miles²*
Pacific	155,557,000	59,270,000
Atlantic	76,762,000	29,638,000
Indian	68,556,000	26,467,000
Southern	20,327,000	7,848,300
Arctic	14,056,000	5,427,000

The equator divides the Pacific into the North and South Pacific and the Atlantic into the North and South Atlantic. In 2000 the International Hydrographic Organisation approved the description of the 20,327,000km² (7,848,300 miles²) of circum-Antarctic waters up to 60°S. as the Southern Ocean – a seventh ocean.

GREATEST OCEAN DEPTHS

Greatest depth	*Location*	*metres*	*feet*
Mariana Trench*	Pacific	10,911	35,798
Puerto Rico Trench	Atlantic	8,605	28,232
South Sandwich Trench	Southern	7,235	23,737
Java (Sunda) Trench	Indian	7,125	23,376
Molloy Deep	Arctic	5,680	18,400

* On 23 January 1960, Jacques Piccard (Swiss) and Don Walsh (USA) descended in the bathyscaphe *Trieste* to the floor of the Mariana Trench, a depth later calculated as 10,916m (25,831ft). The current depth was calculated by the Japanese remote-controlled probe *Kaiko* on 24 March 1995.

SEAS

LARGEST BY AREA

	km²	*miles²*
South China	2,974,600	1,148,500
Caribbean	2,515,900	971,400
Mediterranean	2,509,900	969,100
Bering	2,261,000	873,000
Gulf of Mexico	1,507,600	582,100
Okhotsk	1,392,000	537,500
Japan	1,012,900	391,100
Hudson Bay	730,100	281,900
East China	664,600	256,600
Andaman	564,880	218,100
Black Sea	507,900	196,100
Red Sea	453,000	174,900
North Sea	427,100	164,900

GREATEST DEPTHS

	metres	*feet*
Caribbean	8,605	28,232
East China (Ryu Kyu Trench)	7,507	24,629
South China	7,258	23,812
Mediterranean (Ionian Basin)	5,150	16,896
Andaman	4,267	14,000
Bering	3,936	12,913
Gulf of Mexico	3,504	11,496
Okhotsk	3,365	11,040
Japan	3,053	10,016
Red Sea	2,266	7,434
Black Sea	2,212	7,257
North Sea	439	1,440

THE CONTINENTS

There are six geographic continents, although America is often divided politically into North and Central America, and South America, making seven.

AFRICA is surrounded by sea except for the narrow isthmus of Suez in the north-east, through which was cut the Suez Canal (opened 17 November 1869). Its extreme longitudes are 17° 20′ W. at Cape Verde, Senegal, and 51° 24′ E. at Raas Xaafunn, Somalia. The extreme latitudes are 37° 20′ N. at Cape Blanc, Tunisia, and 34° 50′ S. at Cape Agulhas, South Africa, about 7,081km (4,400 miles) apart. The Equator passes across Gabon, Republic of Congo, Uganda, Kenya and Somalia in the middle of the continent.

NORTH AMERICA, including Mexico, is surrounded by ocean except in the south, where the isthmian states of Central America link North America with South America. Its extreme longitudes are 168° 5′ W. at Cape Prince of Wales, Alaska, and 55° 40′ W. at Cape Charles, Newfoundland. The extreme continental latitudes are the tip of the Boothia peninsula, NW Territories, Canada (71° 51′ N.) and 14° 22′ N. in southern Mexico near La Victoria, Guatemala.

SOUTH AMERICA lies mostly in the southern hemisphere, the equator passing across Ecuador, Colombia and Brazil in the north of the continent. It is surrounded by ocean except where it is joined to Central America in the north by the narrow isthmus through which was cut the Panama Canal (opened 15 August 1914). Its extreme longitudes are 34° 47′ W. at Cape Branco in Brazil and 81° 20′ W. at Punta Pariña, Peru. The extreme continental latitudes are 12° 25′ N. at Punta Gallinas, Colombia, and 53° 54′ S. at the southernmost tip of Peninsula de Brunswick, Chile. Cape Horn, on Cape Island, Chile, lies in 55° 59′ S.

ANTARCTICA lies almost entirely within the Antarctic Circle (66° 33′ S.) and is the largest of the world's glaciated areas. Ninety-eight per cent of the continent is permanently covered in ice. The ice amounts to some 30 million km^3 (7.2 million miles^3) and represents more than 70 per cent of the world's fresh water. The ice sheet is on average 1.6km (1 mile) thick; if it were to melt, the world's seas would rise by more than 60m (197ft). The environment is too hostile for unsupported human habitation.

ASIA is the largest continent and occupies 29.6 per cent of the world's land surface. The extreme longitudes are 26° 05′ E. at Baba Buran, Turkey, and 169° 40′ W. at Mys Dezhneva (East Cape), Russia, a distance of about 9,656km (6,000 miles). Its extreme northern latitude is 77° 45′ N. at Mys Chelyuskin, Russia, and it extends over 8,046km (5,000 miles) south to Tanjong Piai, Malaysia.

AUSTRALIA is the smallest of the continents and lies in the southern hemisphere. It is entirely surrounded by ocean. Its extreme longitudes are 113° 11′ E. at Steep Point, Western Australia, and 153° 11′ E. at Cape Byron, New South Wales. The extreme latitudes are 10° 42′ S. at Cape York, Queensland, and 39°S. at South East Point, Tasmania. Australia, together with New Zealand (Australasia), Papua New Guinea and the Pacific Islands, comprises Oceania.

EUROPE, including European Russia, is the smallest continent in the northern hemisphere. Its extreme latitudes are 71° 11′ N. at Nord Kapp in Norway, and 36° 23′ N. at Akra Tainaron (Matapas) in southern Greece, a distance of about 3,862km (2,400 miles). Its breadth from Cabo Carvoeiro in Portugal (9° 34′ W.) in the west to the Kara River, north of the Urals (66° 30′ E.) in the east is about 5,310km (3,300 miles). The division between Europe and Asia is generally regarded as the watershed of the Ural Mountains; down the Ural river to Atyrau, Kazakhstan; across the Caspian Sea to Apsheronskiy Poluostrov, near Baku; along the watershed of the Caucasus Mountains to Anapa and then across the Black Sea to the Bosporus in Turkey; across the Sea of Marmara to Canakkale Bogazi (Dardanelles).

Continent	*Area*	
	km^2	miles^2
Asia	43,998,000	16,988,000
America*	41,918,000	16,185,000
Africa	29,800,000	11,506,000
Antarctica	13,209,000	5,100,000
Europe†	9,699,000	3,745,000
Australia	7,618,493	2,941,526

* North and Central America has an area of 24,255,000km^2 (9,365,000 miles^2)

† Includes 5,571,000km^2 (2,151,000 miles^2) of former USSR territory, including the Baltic states, Belarus, Moldova, Ukraine and the part of Russia west of the Ural Mountains and Kazakhstan west of the Ural river. European Turkey (24,378km^2/9,412 miles^2) comprises territory to the west and north of the Bosporus and the Dardanelles

GLACIATED AREAS

It is estimated that 14,800,000km^2 (5,712,800 miles^2) or 10 per cent of the world's land surface is permanently covered with ice. Glacial retreat and thinning occurs where glaciers melt faster than they are created. The phenomenon has been observed since the mid-19th century but has accelerated since about 1980 as a result of global warming. It is most notable in the Antarctic: a 2005 report by the American Association for the Advancement of Science indicated that 87 per cent of the continent's 244 marine glaciers have retreated over the past 50 years. The largest glacier is the 515km (320 miles) long Lambert-Fisher Ice Passage, Mac Robertson Land, Eastern Antarctica.

Location	*Area*	
	km^2	miles^2
South Polar regions	13,830,000	5,340,000
North Polar regions (incl. Greenland)	1,965,000	758,500
Alaska-Canada	58,800	22,700
Asia	37,800	14,600
South America	11,900	4,600
Europe	10,700	4,128
New Zealand	1,015	391
Africa	238	92

PENINSULAS

Peninsula	*Area*	
	km^2	miles^2
Arabian	3,250,000	1,250,000
Southern Indian	2,072,000	800,000
Alaskan	1,500,000	580,000
Labradorian	1,300,000	500,000
Scandinavian	800,300	309,000
Iberian	584,000	225,500

LARGEST ISLANDS

Island and ocean	*Area*	
	km^2	miles^2
Greenland (Kalaallit Nunaat), Arctic	2,175,500	840,000
New Guinea, Pacific	792,500	306,000
Borneo, Pacific	725,450	280,100
Madagascar, Indian	587,041	226,674
Baffin Island, Arctic	507,451	195,928
Sumatra, Indian	427,350	165,000
Honshu, Pacific	227,413	87,805
Great Britain, Atlantic*	218,077	84,200
Victoria Island, Arctic	217,292	83,897
Ellesmere Island, Arctic	196,236	75,767

* Mainland only

LARGEST DESERTS

Desert and location	*Area (approx)*	
	km^2	miles^2
Sahara, N. Africa	9,000,000	3,500,000
Gobi, Mongolia/China	1,300,000	500,000
Arabian (Eastern) Desert, Egypt	1,000,000	385,000
Kalahari Desert, Botswana/Namibia/S. Africa	570,000	220,000
Great Victoria, Australia	350,000	135,000
Taklimakan Shamo, Mongolia/China	320,000	125,000
Kara Kum, Turkmenistan*	310,000	120,000
Great Sandy, Australia	270,000	100,000
Thar Desert, India/Pakistan	260,000	100,000
Somali Desert, Somalia	260,000	100,000

* Together with the Kyzyl Kum 259,000km^2 (100,000 miles^2) known as the Turkestan Desert

DEEPEST DEPRESSIONS

Depression and location	*Maximum depth below sea level*	
	metres	feet
Dead Sea, Jordan/Israel	408	1,338
Lake Assal, Djibouti	156	511
Turfan Depression, Sinkiang, China	153	505
Qattara Depression, Egypt	132	436
Mangyshlak peninsula, Kazakhstan	131	433
Danakil Depression, Ethiopia	116	383
Death Valley, California, USA	86	282
Salton Sink, California, USA	71	235
West of Ustyurt plateau, Kazakhstan	70	230
Prikaspiyskaya Nizmennost', Russia/Kazakhstan	67	220
Lake Sarykamysh, Uzbekistan/Turkmenistan	45	148
El Faiyum, Egypt	44	147
Peninsula Valdes, Chubut, Argentina	40	131
Lake Eyre, South Australia	16	52

The world's largest exposed depression is the Prikaspiyskaya Nizmennost' covering the hinterland of the northern third of the Caspian Sea, which is itself 28m (92ft) below sea level.

Western Antarctica and central Greenland largely comprise crypto-depressions under ice burdens. The Antarctic Bentley subglacial trench has a bedrock 2,538m (8,326ft) below sea level. In Greenland (lat. 73° N., long. 39° W.) the bedrock is 365m (1,197ft) below sea level.

Nearly one quarter of the area of the Netherlands lies marginally below sea-level, an area of more than 10,000km^2 (3,860 miles^2).

No part of the Maldives is higher than 2.4m (8ft) and nowhere in Lesotho is lower than 1,381m (4,531ft).

CAVES

DEEPEST CAVES

The world's deepest cave was discovered in January 2001 by a team of Ukrainian cave explorers in the Arabikskaya system in the western Caucasus mountains of Georgia. It is a branch of the Voronya or 'Crow's Cave'.

Cave system/location	*Depth*	
	metres	feet
Krubera (Voronya), Georgia	2,191	7,188
Illyuzia-Mezhonnogo-Snezhnaya, Georgia	1,753	5,751
Lamprechtsofen Vogelschacht, Austria	1,632	5,354
Gouffre Mirolda, France	1,626	5,335
Réseau Jean Bernard, France	1,602	5,256
Torca del Cerro del Cuevon/Torca de las Saxifragas, Spain	1,589	5,213
Sarma, Georgia	1,543	5,062
Shakta Vyacheslav, Georgia	1,508	4,947
Sima de la Cornisa (Torca Magali), Spain	1,507	4,944
Cehi 2, Slovenia	1,502	4,928
Sistema Cheve (Cuicateco), Mexico	1,484	4,868
Sistema Huautla, Mexico	1,475	4,839

LONGEST CAVE SYSTEMS

Cave system/location	*Total known length*	
	km	miles
Mammoth Cave System, USA	590.6	367
Jewel Cave, USA	225.4	140
Optimisticheskaya, Ukraine	215.0	133
Wind Cave, USA	205.6	128
Lechuguilla Cave, USA	198.6	123
Hölloch, Switzerland	194.2	121
Fisher Ridge System, USA	177.3	110
Sistema Ox Bel Ha, Mexico (submerged)	169.9	106
Sistema Sac Actun, Mexico (submerged)	157.3	98
Siebenhengste-hohgant, Switzerland	154.0	96
Gua Air Jernih, Malaysia	151.4	94

LONGEST MOUNTAIN RANGES

Range and location	*Length*	
	km	miles
Cordillera de Los Andes, South America	7,200	4,500
Rocky Mountains, North America	4,800	3,000
Himalaya-Karakoram-Hindu Kush, Central Asia	3,850	2,400
Great Dividing Range, Australia	3,620	2,250
Trans-Antarctic Mts, Antarctica	3,540	2,200
Atlantic Coast Range, Brazil	3,050	1,900
West Sumatran-Javan Range, Indonesia	2,900	1,800
Aleutian Range, Alaska and N.W. Pacific	2,650	1,650
Tien Shan, Central Asia	2,250	1,400
Central New Guinea Range, Papua New Guinea	2,010	1,250

HIGHEST MOUNTAINS

The world's twelve 8,000m (26,247ft) mountains (with five subsidiary peaks) are all in the Himalaya-Karakoram-Hindu Kush ranges.

Mountain (first ascent)	*Height*	
	metres	feet
Mt Everest* (Qomolangma) (29 May 1953)	8,850	29,035
K2 (Qogir)† (31 July 1954)	8,611	28,251
Kangchenjunga (25 May 1955)	8,597	28,208
Lhotse I (18 May 1956)	8,510	27,923
Makalu I (15 May 1955)	8,480	27,824
Lhotse Shar (II) (12 May 1979)	8,400	27,560
Dhaulagiri I (13 May 1960)	8,171	26,810
Manaslu I (Kutang I) (9 May 1956)	8,156	26,760
Cho Oyu (19 October 1954)	8,153	26,750
Nanga Parbat (Diamir) (3 July 1953)	8,125	26,660

* Named after Sir George Everest (1790–1866), Surveyor-General of India 1830–43, in 1863. He pronounced his name Eve-rest

† Formerly named after Col. Henry Haversham Godwin-Austen (1834–1923), who worked on the Trigonometrical Survey of India, which established the heights of the Himalayan peaks, including Everest

The culminating summits in the other major mountain ranges are:

Mountain, by range or country	*Height*	
	metres	feet
Pik Pobedy, Tien Shan	7,439	24,406
Cerro Aconcagua, Cordillera de Los Andes	6,960	22,834
Mt McKinley (S. Peak), Alaska Range	6,194	20,320
Kilimanjaro (Kibo), Tanzania	5,894	19,340
Hkakabo Razi, Myanmar	5,881	19,296
Citlaltépetl (Orizaba), Mexico	5,655	18,555
El'brus, (W. Peak), Caucasus	5,642	18,510
Vinson Massif, Antarctica	4,897	16,066
Puncak Jaya, Central New Guinea Range	4,884	16,023
Mt Blanc, Alps	4,807	15,771

HIGHEST ACTIVE VOLCANOES

Although it displays fumarolic activity, emitting steam and gas, no major eruption has ever been observed of the world's highest volcano and second highest peak in the western hemisphere, the 6,893m (22,615ft) Ojos del Salado, in the Andes on the Argentina/Chile border.

Volcano and location (most recent activity)	*Height*	
	metres	feet
Volcan Llullaillaco, Andes, Argentina/Chile (1877)	6,723	22,057
Volcan Guallatiri, Andes, Chile (1960)	6,069	19,882
Cotopaxi, Andes, Ecuador (1904)	5,897	19,347
Tupungatito, Andes, Chile (1987)	5,640	18,504
Lascar, Andes, Chile (2006)	5,591	18,346
Popocatepetl, Mexico (2006)	5,465	17,930
Nevado del Ruiz, Colombia (1991)	5,321	17,457
Sangay, Andes, Ecuador (2007)	5,188	17,021
Irruputuncu, Chile (1995)	5,163	16,939
Klyuchevskaya Sopka, Kamchatka peninsula, Russia (2005)	4,835	15,863

LAKES

LARGEST LAKES

The areas of some of the lakes listed are subject to seasonal variation. The most voluminous lakes are the Caspian Sea (saline) with 78,700km³ (18, 880 miles³) and Baikal (fresh water) with 23,000km³ (5,518 miles³). Baikal is also the world's deepest lake (*see* below). It is estimated that it contains as much water as the entire Great Lakes system – more than 20 per cent of the world's fresh water and some 90 per cent of all the fresh water in Russia.

The Aral was once the fifth largest in the world, with an area of 68,000km² (26,255 miles²), but since the 1960s many of its feeder rivers have been diverted for irrigation, as a result of which its area shrank to 17,160km² (6,626 miles²). Its salinity was almost three times that of seawater, and severe pollution led to the extinction of many aquatic species. Since the construction of the Kok-Aral dam (2005), water levels are rising again, especially in the north.

Lake and location	*Area*		*Length*	
	km²	miles²	km	miles
Caspian Sea, Iran/Azerbaijan/Russia/Turkmenistan/Kazakhstan	371,000	143,000	1,171	728
Michigan–Huron, USA/Canada*	117,610	45,300	1,010	627
Superior, Canada/USA	82,100	31,700	563	350
Victoria, Uganda/Tanzania/Kenya	69,500	26,828	362	225
Tanganyika, Dem. Rep. of Congo/Tanzania/Zambia/Burundi	32,900	12,665	725	450
Great Bear, Canada	31,328	12,096	309	192
Baykal (Baikal), Russia†	30,500	11,776	620	385
Malawi (Nyasa), Tanzania/Malawi/Mozambique	28,900	11,150	580	360
Great Slave, Canada	28,570	11,031	480	298
Erie, Canada/USA	25,670	9,910	388	241

* Lakes Michigan and Huron may be regarded as lobes of the same lake. The Michigan lobe has an area of 57,750km² (22,300 miles²) and the Huron lobe an area of 59,570km² (23,000 miles²)

† World's deepest lake (1,637m/5,371ft)

UNITED KINGDOM (BY COUNTRY)

Lake and location	*Area*		*Length*	
	km²	miles²	km	miles
Lough Neagh, Northern Ireland	381.73	147.39	28.90	18.00
Loch Lomond, Scotland	71.12	27.46	36.44	22.64
Windermere, England	14.74	5.69	16.90	10.50
Lake Vyrnwy, Wales (artificial)	4.53	1.75	7.56	4.70
Llyn Tegid (Bala), Wales (natural)	4.38	1.69	5.80	3.65

LARGEST MANMADE LAKES

*Dam/lake**	*Volume*	
	km³	miles³
Owen Falls, Uganda/Kenya/Tanzania (1954)	204.80	49.13
Bratskoye, Russia (1967)	169.27	40.61
Nasser, Egypt (1970)	168.90	40.52

Kariba, Zimbabwe/Zambia (1959)	160.30	38.46
Volta, Ghana (1965)	148.00	35.51
Manicouagan (Daniel Johnson dam), Canada (1968)	141.85	34.03
Guri (Raul Leoni), Venezuela (1986)	136.30	33.11
Krasnoyarskoye, Russia (1967)	73.30	17.58
Wadi-Tatar, Iraq (1967)	72.80	17.46
Williston (W. A. C. Bennett dam), Canada (1967)	70.31	16.87

* Formed as a result of dam construction

DEEPEST LAKES

Lake and location	*Greatest depth*	
	metres	feet
Baikal, Russia	1,637	5,371
Tanganyika, Burundi/Tanzania/Dem. Rep. of Congo/Zambia	1,470	4,825
Caspian Sea, Azerbaijan/Iran/Kazakhstan/Russia/Turkmenistan	1,025	3,363
Malawi, Malawi/Mozambique/Tanzania	706	2,316
Issyk Kul, Kyrgyzstan	702	2,303
Great Slave, Canada	614	2,015
Danau Toba, Indonesia	590	1,936
Hornindalsvastnet, Norway	514	1,686
Sarezskoye Ozero, Tajikistan	505	1,657
Tahoe, USA	501	1,645
Lago Argentina, Argentina	500	1,640
Lac Kivu, Rwanda/Dem. Rep. of Congo	480	1,574
Quesnel, Canada	475	1,558

LONGEST RIVERS

River, source and outflow	*Length*	
	km	miles
Nile (Bahr-el-Nil), R. Luvironza, Burundi–E. Mediterranean Sea	6,725	4,180
Amazon (Amazonas), Lago Villafro, Peru–S. Atlantic Ocean	6,448	4,007
Yangtze-Kiang (Chang Jiang), Kunlun Mts, W. China–Yellow Sea	6,380	3,964
Mississippi-Missouri-Red Rock, Montana–Gulf of Mexico	5,970	3,710
Yenisey-Angara, W. Mongolia–Kara Sea	5,536	3,440
Huang He (Yellow River), Bayan Har Shan range, Central China–Yellow Sea	5,463	3,395
Ob'-Irtysh, W. Mongolia–Kara Sea	5,410	3,362
Zaire (Congo), R. Lualaba, Dem. Rep. of Congo-Zambia–S. Atlantic Ocean	4,665	2,900
Amur-Argun, R. Argun, Khingan Mts, N. China–Sea of Okhotsk	4,416	2,744
Lena-Kirenga, R. Kirenga, W. of Lake Baikal–Laptev Sea, Arctic Ocean	4,400	2,734

BRITISH ISLES

River, source and outflow	*Length*	
	km	miles
Shannon, Co. Cavan, Rep. of Ireland–Atlantic Ocean	386	240
Severn, Powys, Wales–Bristol Channel	354	220
Thames, Gloucestershire, England–North Sea	346	215
Tay, Perthshire, Scotland–North Sea	188	117
Clyde, Lanarkshire, Scotland–Firth of Clyde	158	98.5
Tweed, Scottish Borders–North Sea	155	96.5
Bann (Upper and Lower), Co. Down, N. Ireland–Atlantic Ocean	122	76

WATERFALLS

GREATEST BY HEIGHT

Waterfall, river and location	*Total drop*		*Greatest single leap*	
	metres	feet	metres	feet
Salto Angel, Carrao Auyan Tepui, Venezuela	979	3,212	807	2,648
Tugela, Tugela, S. Africa (5 leaps)	948	3,110	410	1,350
Ramnefjellsfossen, Jostedal Glacier, Norway	800	2,625	600	1,970
Mongefossen, Monge, Norway	773	2,535	—	—
Gocta, Cocahuayco, Peru	771	2,531	—	—
Mutarazi, Mutarazi, Zimbabwe	762	2,499	479	1,572
Yosemite, Yosemite Creek, USA	739	2,425	435	1,430
Østre Mardola Foss, Mardals, Norway*	655	2,149	296	974
Tyssestrengene, Tysso, Norway*	646	2,120	289	948
Cuquenan, Arabopo, Venezuela	610	2,000	—	—

* Volume much affected by hydroelectric harnessing

BRITISH ISLES, BY HEIGHT

Waterfall, river and location	*Total drop*	
	metres	feet
Eas a' Chual Aluinn, Glas Bheinn, Sutherland, Scotland	200	656
Powerscourt Falls, Dargle, Co. Wicklow, Rep. of Ireland	121	398
Pistyll-y-Llyn, Powys/Dyfed border, Wales (cascades)	91	300
Pistyll Rhyadr, Clwyd/Powys border, Wales (single leap)	71.5	235
Cauldron Snout, Tees, Cumbria/Durham, England (cascades)	61	200

GREATEST BY VOLUME

*Waterfall, river and location**	*Mean annual flow* m^3/sec
Khone, Mekong, Laos	11,610
Para, Caura, Venezuela	3,540
Paulo Afonso, Sao Francisco, Brazil	2,832
Niagara (Horseshoe), Niagara/Lake Erie–Lake Ontario, Canada	2,407
Salto de Iguaçu, Parana, Argentina/Brazil	1,746
Victoria (Mosi-oa-Tunya), Zambezi, Zimbabwe/Zambia	1,088
Virginia, Nahanni, Canada	1,000

Sivasamudram, Kaveri (Cauvery), India	934
Kongou, Ivindo, Gabon	900
Williamette, Williamette, Oregon, USA	874

* Excludes waterfalls that have been submerged as a result of dam construction or consist of rapids or cascades with individual vertical drops of less than 6m (20ft)

DAMS

TALLEST DAMS

Dam and location	*Height*	
	metres	feet
Rogun, Tajikistan	335	1,098
Nurek, Tajikistan	300	984
Grande Dixence, Switzerland	285	935
Longtan, China	285	935
Inguri, Georgia	272	892
Borucu, Costa Rica	267	876
Vaiont, Italy	262	859
Manuel M. Torres, Mexico	261	856
Tehri, India	261	856

GREATEST VOLUME* DAMS

Dam and location	*Volume*	
	thousand m^3	thousand yd^3
Three Gorges, China†	39,300,000	51,402,459
Syncrude Tailings, Canada (1992)	540,000	706,293
Chapetón , Argentina†	296,200	387,415
Pati, Argentina (1990)	238,180	311,528
New Cornelia Tailings, USA (1973)	209,500	274,016
Tarbela, Pakistan (1976)	121,720	159,204
Kambaratinsk, Kyrgyzstan†	112,200	146,752
Fort Peck, USA (1937)	96,050	125,629
Lower Usuma, Nigeria (1990)	93,049	121,703
Cipasang, Indonesia†	90,000	117,716

* Of material used in construction (earth, rocks, concrete, etc)
† Under construction

TALLEST ...

All heights are in accordance with the Council on Tall Buildings and Urban Habitat's regulations, which measure from the ground level of the main entrance to the architectural tip of the building and include spires but not antennae, signage or flag poles.

INHABITED BUILDINGS*

Building and location	*Height*	
	metres	feet
Burj Dubai, Dubai, UAE (2008)	819	2,686
Taipei 101, Taipei, Taiwan (2003)	509	1,671
Federation Tower, Moscow, Russia (2009)	506	1,660
SWFC, Shanghai, China (2008)	492	1,613
ICC, Hong Kong, China (2008)	484	1,588
Petronas Towers I and II, Kuala Lumpur, Malaysia (1998)	452	1,482
Greenland Square Zifeng Tower, Nangjing, China (2008)	450	1,475
Sears Tower, Chicago, USA (1974)†	442	1,450
Jin Mao, Shanghai, China (1998)	420	1,378
Trump Tower, Chicago, USA (2008)	415	1,360
Princess Tower, Dubai, UAE (2009)	414	1,357
Two International Finance Centre, Hong Kong, China (2003)	412	1,352
Al Hamra Tower, Kuwait (2009)	412	1,352

* The two World Trade Center towers, One (1972) 110 storeys, 417m (1,368ft) or 521m (1,716ft) with TV antennae; and Two (1973) 110 storeys, 415m (1,362ft), were destroyed by two terrorist-hijacked aircraft on 11 September 2001
† With TV antennae, 520m (1,707ft)

STRUCTURES

Structure and location	*Height*	
	metres	feet
Warszawa Radio Mast, Konstantynow, Poland (1974)*	646	2,120
KVLY (formerly KTHI)-TV Mast, North Dakota (guyed), USA (1963)†	629	2,063
Indosat Telkom Tower, Jakarta, Indonesia	558	1,831
CN Tower, Toronto, Canada (1975)	555	1,822
Ostankino Tower, Moscow, Russia (1967)	540	1,772

* Collapsed during renovation, August 1991. New structure planned on site at Solkajawski
† The USA has eight other guyed TV towers above 555m (1,822ft)

TWIN TOWERS

Structure and location	*Storeys*	*Height*	
		metres	feet
Petronas Towers, Kuala Lumpur, Malaysia (1997)	96	452	1,482
Guangzhou IFC, Guangzhou, China (2009)	104	437	1,433
The Cullinan, Hong Kong, China (2008)	68	270	885
Al Kazim Towers, Dubai, UAE (2008)	53	265	870
Grand Gateway, Shanghai, China (2005)	52	262	860
Dual Towers, Manama, Bahrain (2007)	53	260	855
Abraj Al Bait Towers, Mecca, Saudi Arabia (2008)	55	260	855
Al Fattan Towers, Dubai, UAE (2006)	60	245	802
Destroyed			
World Trade Center One, New York City, USA (1972)	110	417	1,368
World Trade Center Two, New York City, USA (1973)	110	415	1,362

CHURCHES

Structure and location	*Height*	
	metres	feet
Sagrada Família, Barcelona, Spain (2026*)	170	558
Ulm Cathedral, Ulm, Germany (1890)	162	530
Notre-Dame Cathedral, Rouen, France (1876)	158	518
Cologne Cathedral, Cologne, Germany (1880)	157	516
Our Lady of Peace Basilica, Yamoussoukro, Côte d'Ivoire (1990)	149	489
St Nicholas Church, Hamburg, Germany (1847)	147	482
Notre-Dame Cathedral, Strasbourg, France (1439)	144	472

Queen of Peace Shrine and Basilica, Lichen, Poland (2002)		140	459
Basilica of St Peter, Rome, Italy (1626)		138	452
St Stephen's Cathedral, Vienna, Austria (1570)		137	448

* Projected completion date

The Chicago Methodist Temple, Chicago, USA (completed 1924) is 173m (568ft) high, but is sited atop a 25-storey, 100m (328ft) building. Salisbury Cathedral (1521), at 123m (404ft), is the UK's tallest religious building. St Paul's Cathedral, London, and Liverpool Anglican Cathedral are the only others in the UK over 100m (328ft) tall.

TALLEST STRUCTURES — A CHRONOLOGY

Structure and location	*Year*	*Height*	
		metres	feet
Djoser's Step Pyramid, Saqqara, Egypt	c.2650 BC	61	200
Pyramid of Meidum, Egypt	c.2600 BC	92	302
Snefru's Bent Pyramid, Dahshur, Egypt	c.2600 BC	102	336
Red Pyramid, Dahshur, Egypt	c.2590 BC	105	345
Great Pyramid, Giza, Egypt*	c.2580 BC	146	479
Liuhe (Six Harmonies) Pagoda, Hangzhou, China†	AD 970	150	492
Lincoln Cathedral, Lincoln, England‡	1311–1400	160	525
St Paul's Cathedral, London, England§ℂ	1315	149	489
St Olaf's Church, Tallinn, Estonia**	1438–1519	159	522
St Mary's Church, Stralsund, Germany§	1384–1478	151	495
Notre-Dame, Strasbourg, France§	1439	143	469
St Nicholas Church, Hamburg, Germany§	1847	147	482
Rouen Cathedral, Rouen, France	1876	148	485
Cologne Cathedral, Cologne, Germany	1880	157	515
Washington Monument, Washington DC, USA	1884	169	555
Eiffel Tower, Paris, France	1889	300	984
Chrysler Building, New York, USA	1930	319	1,046
Empire State Building, New York, USA	1930	381	1,250
KWTV Mast, Oklahoma City, USA	1954	479	1,572
KOBR-TV Tower, Caprock, USA	1960	490	1,608
KFVS TV Mast, Egypt Mills, USA	1960	511	1,677
Nexstar Broadcasting Tower Vivian, Vivian, USA	1961	534	1,752
KVLY (formerly KTHI)-TV Mast, Blanchard, USA§	1963	629	2,063
Warszawa Radio Mast, Konstantynow, Poland††	1974	646	2,118
Burj Dubai, Dubai, UAE	2009	819	2,686

* Later reduced through loss of topstone to 137m (449ft)
† Destroyed in 1121
‡ Destroyed in 1549
§ The collapse of taller structures enabled these runners-up to gain or re-gain the status of 'world's tallest'
ℂ Destroyed in 1561
** Spire burned down in 1625; renovated in 1931 to present height of 123m (403ft)
†† Collapsed in 1991 during renovation

BRIDGES

The longest stretch of bridgings of any kind is that carrying the Interstate 55 and Interstate 10 highways at Manchac, Louisiana, USA (1979), on twin concrete trestles over 55.21km (34.31 miles). The 'floating' bridging at Evergreen Point, Seattle, Washington, USA (1963), is 3,839m (12,596ft) long, of which 2,310m (7,578ft) floats.

LONGEST SUSPENSION SPANS

Bridge and location	*Length*	
	metres	feet
Akashi-Kaikyo, Japan (1998)	1,990	6,529
Xihoumen, China (2008)	1,650	5,413
Storebaelt East Bridge, Denmark (1998)	1,624	5,328
Runyang (Yangtze), China (2005)	1,490	4,888
Humber Estuary, England (1981)	1,410	4,626
Jiangyin (Yangtze), China (1999)	1,385	4,544
Tsing Ma, Hong Kong, China (1997)	1,377	4,518
Verrazano Narrows, USA (1964)	1,298	4,260
Golden Gate, USA (1937)	1,280	4,200
Yangluo, China (2007)	1,280	4,200

LONGEST CANTILEVER SPANS

Bridge and location	*Length*	
	metres	feet
Pont de Québec (rail-road), St Lawrence, Canada (1917)	548.6	1,800
Firth of Forth (rail), Scotland (two spans of 1,710ft each) (1890)	521.2	1,710
Minato (Nanko), Japan (1974)	510.0	1,673
Commodore John Barry, USA (1974)	494.3	1,622
Greater New Orleans, USA (I 1958, II 1988)*	480.0	1,575
Howrah (rail-road), India (1936–43)	457.2	1,500
Veterans Memorial, USA (1995)	445.0	1,460
Transbay, USA (1936)	426.7	1,400
Horace Wilkinson, USA (1969)	376.0	1,235
Tappan Zee, USA (1955)	369.0	1,212

* Jointly known as Crescent City Connection

LONGEST STEEL ARCH SPANS

Bridge and location	*Length*	
	metres	feet
Chaotianmen, China (2008)	552.0	1,811
New River Gorge, USA (1977)	518.0	1,700
Bayonne (Kill van Kull), USA (1931)	510.5	1,675
Sydney Harbour, Australia (1932)	502.9	1,650
Chenab, India (due in 2008)	480.0	1,575
Wushan, China (2005)	460.0	1,509

Caiyuanba, China (2005)	420.0	1,378
Fremont, USA (1973)	382.0	1,253
Zdakov, Czech Republic (1967)	380.0	1,247
Numata River Gorge, Japan (2007)	380.0	1,247

TALLEST BRIDGE TOWERS

Bridge and location	*Height*	
	metres	feet
Millau, France (2004)	343	1,125
Akashi-Kaikyo, Japan (1998)	298	978
Stonecutters, Hong Kong, China (2008)	298	978
East Bridge, Great Belt Fixed Link, Denmark (1997)	254	833
Golden Gate, USA (1937)	227	754
Tatara, Japan (1999)	226	741
Jambatan Pulau Pinang, Malaysia (1985)	225	739
Le Ponte de Normandie, France (1994)	215	705
Verrazano Narrows, USA (1964)	211	692
Tsing Ma, China (1997)	206	675

LONGEST VEHICULAR TUNNELS

Tunnel and location	*Length*	
	km	miles
*Seikan (rail), Tsugaru Channel, Japan (1988)	53.85	33.46
*Channel tunnel, (rail) Cheriton, Kent, UK–Sangatte, Calais, France (1994)	50.45	31.35
Moscow metro, Serpukhovsko–Timiryazevskaya line, Moscow, Russia (1983)	38.90	24.17
Lötschberg (rail), Switzerland (2007)	34.58	21.49
Guadarrama (rail), Spain (2007)	28.38	17.63
Northern Line tube, East Finchley–Morden, London (1939)	27.84	17.30
Iwate-Ichinoe (rail), Japan (2002)	25.81	16.03
Laerdal–Aurland Road Link, Norway (2000)	24.51	15.22
*Oshimizu (rail), Honshu, Japan (1982)	22.17	13.78
Simplon II (rail), Brigue, Switzerland–Iselle, Italy (1922)	19.82	12.31

* Sub-aqueous

The longest non-vehicular tunnelling in the world is the Delaware Aqueduct in New York State, USA, constructed in 1937–44 to a length of 168.9km (105 miles).

St Gotthard (rail) tunnel in Switzerland will be 57.07km (35.46 miles) long when completed in 2010.

BRITISH RAIL TUNNELS

	Length	
	km	miles
Severn, Bristol—Newport	6.88	4.28
Totley, Manchester—Sheffield	5.70	3.54
Standedge, Manchester—Huddersfield	4.89	3.04
Sodbury, Swindon—Bristol	4.06	2.53
Strood, Medway, Kent	3.61	2.24
Disley, Stockport—Sheffield	3.54	2.20
Ffestiniog, Llandudno—Blaenau Ffestiniog	3.53	2.19
Bramhope, Leeds—Harrogate	3.44	2.14
Cowburn, Manchester—Sheffield	3.39	2.10

The longest road tunnel in Britain is the Mersey Queensway Tunnel (1934), 3.42km (2 miles 228 yards) long. The longest canal tunnel, at Standedge, W. Yorks, is 5.03km/3.13 miles long; it was completed in 1811, closed in 1944 and reopened in 2001.

LONGEST SHIP CANALS

Canal	*Length*		*Min. depth*	
	km	miles	metres	feet
White Sea–Baltic (formerly Stalin) (1933), of which canalised river 51.5km (32 miles)	235	146.02	5.0	16.5
Rhine–Main–Danube, Germany (1992)	171	106.25	4.0	13.1
*Suez (1869), links Red and Mediterranean Seas	162	100.60	12.9	42.3
V. I. Lenin Volga–Don, Russia (1952), links Black and Caspian Seas	100	62.20	3.6	11.8
Kiel (or North Sea), Germany (1895), links North and Baltic Seas	98	60.90	13.7	45.0
*Houston, USA (1940), links inland city with Gulf of Mexico	91	56.70	10.4	34.0
Alphonse XIII, Spain (1926), gives Seville access to Atlantic Ocean	85	53.00	7.6	25.0
Panama (1914), links Pacific Ocean and Caribbean Sea; lake chain, 78.9km (49 miles) dug	82	50.71	12.5	41.0
Danube–Black Sea, Romania (1984)	64.4	40.02	7.0	23.0
Manchester Ship, UK (1894), links city with Irish Channel	64	39.70	8.5	28.0
Welland (1932), circumvents Niagara Falls and Rapids	43.5	27.00	8.8	29.0
Brussels (Rupel Sea), Belgium (1922), renders Brussels an inland port	32	19.80	6.4	21.0

* Has no locks

The first section of China's Grand Canal, running 1,782km (1,107 miles) from Beijing to Hangzhou, was opened in AD 610 and completed in 1283. Today it is limited to 2,000-tonne vessels.

The St Lawrence Seaway comprises the Beauharnois, Welland and Welland Bypass and Seaway 54-59 canals, and allows access to Duluth, Minnesota, USA via the Great Lakes from the Atlantic end of Canada's Gulf of St Lawrence, a distance of 3,769km (2,342 miles). The St Lawrence Canal, completed in 1959, is 293km (182 miles) long.

THE NORTH AND SOUTH POLES

THE ARCTIC

The Arctic is a region around the Earth's north pole; it includes the ice-covered Arctic Ocean, parts of Canada, the USA, Greenland, Iceland, Finland, Norway, Sweden and Russia. The area is commonly defined as lying north of the line of latitude known as Arctic Circle (running at 66° 33′N) or inside the 10°C July isotherm, which roughly marks the edge of the habitat where trees can grow.

The climate is harsh, with temperatures in the winter months as low as −40°C, though more typical is a range between −25°C and 0°C. There is very little daylight or precipitation. In the summer months, temperatures vary between 0°C and 10°C, along with continuous daylight and damp, foggy conditions. The Arctic is rarely as cold as the Antarctic as there is water, not land, underneath the Arctic ice. The water is warmer than the air above it causing heat to rise and moderating the cold. The polar icepack is, on average, around 3m thick and the extent of the ice doubles between summer and winter.

The polar bear is the region's apex predator and feeds on a diet of seals, walruses and whales. Other native species include varieties of caribou, lemming, wolf, hare and fox. Vegetation is limited to tundra consisting of around 1,700 species of low-lying shrubs, herbs, lichens and mosses, which become less abundant closer to the pole.

THE NORTH WEST PASSAGE

In 1494 King Henry VII commissioned an Anglicised Italian, John Cabot, to discover a route around the northern tip of what would become America, but he never progressed beyond Newfoundland. Numerous other explorers – whose names now litter the geography of north-east Canada – attempted the mission, but were also unsuccessful. The passage was finally navigated by Norwegian Roald Amundsen in 1906, although the shallow waterways he encountered ensured that the route held little commercial potential.

The extent of Arctic sea-ice has become a key measure of climate change in the region. Scientists have demonstrated beyond doubt that the amount of ice in the Arctic is falling year on year, and predictions of an entirely ice-free region range from 2015 to 2100. The rate at which the ice melts grows exponentially: the white ice reflects sunlight back into space while the dark seas absorb its heat, causing the sea temperature to rise and melt the surrounding ice. The current lowest extent was recorded on 16 September 2007, when the amount of ice was 41 per cent below the 1978–2000 average summer medium.

For the first time since records began (1978), the Northwest Passage was declared open and ice-free in 2007. The possibility of economies benefiting from climate change remains an uneasy subject but the option of new trade routes has forced governments to reconsider their respective positions on the region. Under current UN legislation, no-one owns the pole or the ocean surrounding it and Arctic countries are limited to an economic zone of 200 nautical miles from their coastline. This law is currently being challenged by Russia, which planted a flag in the seabed below the pole in August 2007 to symbolise its claim to the ridge extending across much of the Arctic as an extension of the Eurasian continent – and therefore part of Russia. Norway and Denmark have also lodged appeals to the UN.

THE ANTARCTIC

The Antarctic is generally defined as the area lying within the Antarctic Convergence, the zone where cold northward-flowing Antarctic sea water sinks below warmer southward-flowing water. This zone is approximately at latitude 50°S. in the Atlantic Ocean and latitude 55°–62°S. in the Pacific Ocean. The continent itself lies almost entirely within the Antarctic Circle, an area of around 13,209,000 sq. km, 99.4 per cent of which is permanently ice-covered. The average thickness of the ice is 2,450m but in places exceeds 4,500m. The ice amounts to some 30 million cubic km and represents almost 70 per cent of the world's fresh water and 90 per cent of the world's ice. Much of the sea freezes in winter, forming fast ice which breaks up in summer and drifts north as pack ice.

FLORA AND FAUNA

The only land animals to survive on the Antarctic continent are tiny insects and mites, with nematodes, rotifers and tardigrades in the mosses. The largest land animal is the *Belgica antarctica*, a flightless midge just 12mm in size. The snow petrel is one of only three birds that breed exclusively in Antarctica and have been seen at the South Pole. Large numbers of seals, penguins and other sea-birds go ashore to breed in the summer; the emperor penguin is the only species that breeds ashore throughout the winter. By contrast, the Antarctic seas abound with life; recent expeditions identified over 700 previously unknown species. Krill, which congregates in large schools containing millions of organisms, is the centre of the Antarctic ecosystem and provides a diet for whales (including killer, humpback and blue whales), a number of species of seal, penguins, albatrosses and other smaller birds. Four species of albatross breed in South Georgia during the summer, but their numbers are in serious decline due to the effects of longline fishing in the Southern Ocean region.

With almost all of the Antarctic continent permanently covered in ice, only a small number of flowering plants, ferns and clubmosses survive. Most of these are found on the sub-Antarctic islands, while only two species (a grass and a pearlwort) extend south of 60°S. Antarctic vegetation is dominated by lichens and mosses, with a few liverworts, algae and fungi surviving in the cracks and pore spaces of sandstone and granite rocks. The 1978 Antarctic Conservation Act introduced new measures to maintain the balance of the ecosystem in the face of rising numbers of human visits. The introduction of alien plant and animal species is illegal, as is the extraction of indigenous species.

HISTORY AND DISCOVERY

The idea of Antarctica is much older than the proof of the continent's existence. The belief in *Terra Australis*, a vast southern continent to balance the northern lands of Europe, Asia and North Africa, originated with Aristotle and was commonly found on world maps until the end of the eighteenth century. The size of this land was corrected after the explorer James Cook circumnavigated the globe in 1774. He travelled from New Zealand to the Cape of Good Hope (via Tierra del Fuego) at a high southern latitude (between 53° and 60°), confirming that any landmass must be confined to the polar regions.

The date of the first sighting of Antarctica is unclear. In 1820 three separate expeditions, from the UK, the USA and Russia each claimed to have seen the continent within days of each other and the argument has never been settled. The golden age of Antarctic exploration was prompted by the discovery of the magnetic North Pole in 1831, but it was not until the beginning of the twentieth century that real progress was made. James Clark Ross was the first to identify the approximate location of the South Pole, but he was unable to reach it. British explorers Robert Scott in 1901–4 and Ernest Shackleton in 1907–9 got closer, but it was not until Norwegian adventurer Roald Amundsen pioneered a new route, through the Axel Heiberg Glacier, that the pole was reached in December 1911. Scott's second attempt was also successful, but he arrived a month later. Infamously, he and all his team perished on their return journey.

CLIMATE AND TERRAIN

Antarctica is the highest, coldest and driest continent on Earth with average coastal temperatures ranging from just above freezing in the summer (December–February) to −20°C (−4°F) in the winter. Conditions on the interior plateau are more severe with katabatic (gravity-driven) winds and frequent cyclonic storms pushing average winter temperatures down to −65°C (−85°F). The Vostok research station holds the current record for the lowest surface temperature ever recorded on earth at −89.5°C (−129°F). Elevation extremes range from 4,897m (Vinson Massif) at the highest point to −2,555m (Bentley Subglacial Trench) at the lowest.

CLIMATE CHANGE

Unlike in the Arctic, where there has been a significant and visible decline in the levels of sea ice, there have been only negligible changes in equivalent levels in the Antarctic. However, a number of other important changes to the ecosystem have been observed. The British Antarctic Survey have found that the west coast of the Antarctic Peninsula has become one of the fastest-warming areas on the planet, with annual mean temperatures rising by nearly 3°C in the last 50 years. This is approximately ten times the mean rate of global warming. Curiously, the temperatures recorded by the Amundsen-Scott station at the South Pole actually show a recent cooling. The precise cause of this is unknown, but scientists have proposed that the warming of the seas in the surrounding ocean has produced more precipitation, which has cooled the centre when it falls as snow.

This change in climate has already affected the continent's wildlife. The number of Adelie penguins – a species well adapted to sea ice conditions – has fallen, replaced by open-water species such as the chinstrap penguin. Similarly, there has been a substantial fall in the recorded levels of krill because of the reduction in sea ice that provides protection from predators.

The climate is evidently changing, but as yet, it cannot be conclusively proven that these changes are a result of human activity rather than natural variability. However, the collapse of the Larsen B ice shelf in 2002 indicates some human impact – records show it has been stable for much of the previous 10,000 years. Recent warm temperatures are exceptional within this context, making natural deviation alone unlikely.

ANTARCTIC LAW

The Antarctic treaty was signed on 1 December 1959 when 12 states (Argentina, Australia, Belgium, Chile, France, Japan, New Zealand, Norway, South Africa, the Soviet Union, the UK and the USA) pledged themselves to promote scientific and technical cooperation unhampered by politics. The signatories agreed to establish free use of the Antarctic continent for peaceful scientific purposes; freeze all territorial claims and disputes in the Antarctic; ban all military activities in the area; and prohibit nuclear explosions and the disposal of radioactive waste. The Antarctic treaty was defined as covering areas south of latitude 60° S., excluding the high seas but including the ice shelves, and came into force in 1961. The treaty provides that any member of the UN can accede to it. It has since been signed by a further 34 states. In 1998 an extension to the treaty came into effect, placing a 50-year ban on mining, oil exploration and mineral extraction in Antarctica. Furthermore, all tourists, explorers and expeditions now need permission to enter the Antarctic.

SCIENTIFIC RESEARCH

There are 20 nations with permanently manned research stations in Antarctica:

Country	*Number of research stations*
Argentina	6
Russian Federation	5
Australia	3
Chile	3
USA	3
China	2
France	2
UK	2

Brazil, Germany, India, Italy (shared with France), Japan, New Zealand, Norway, Poland, Republic of Korea, South Africa, Ukraine and Uruguay each have a single station.

POPULATION AND TOURISM

Antarctica has no indigenous inhabitants, although the continent maintains a population of tourists, scientists and research workers which peaks in the summer months, at approximately 3,500.

Antarctic tourism is a growth industry. The first *Lonely Planet* guide to Antarctica was published in 1996 and ship-borne cruises now depart from Argentina, Chile, Australia and New Zealand, lasting from two days to several weeks. The continent has also become a popular venue for extreme sports enthusiasts: it is now possible to sky-dive, ski, ride a motorbike and fly a helicopter across the continent, whilst the huts built by Scott and Shackleton are also popular attractions. The Antarctic and

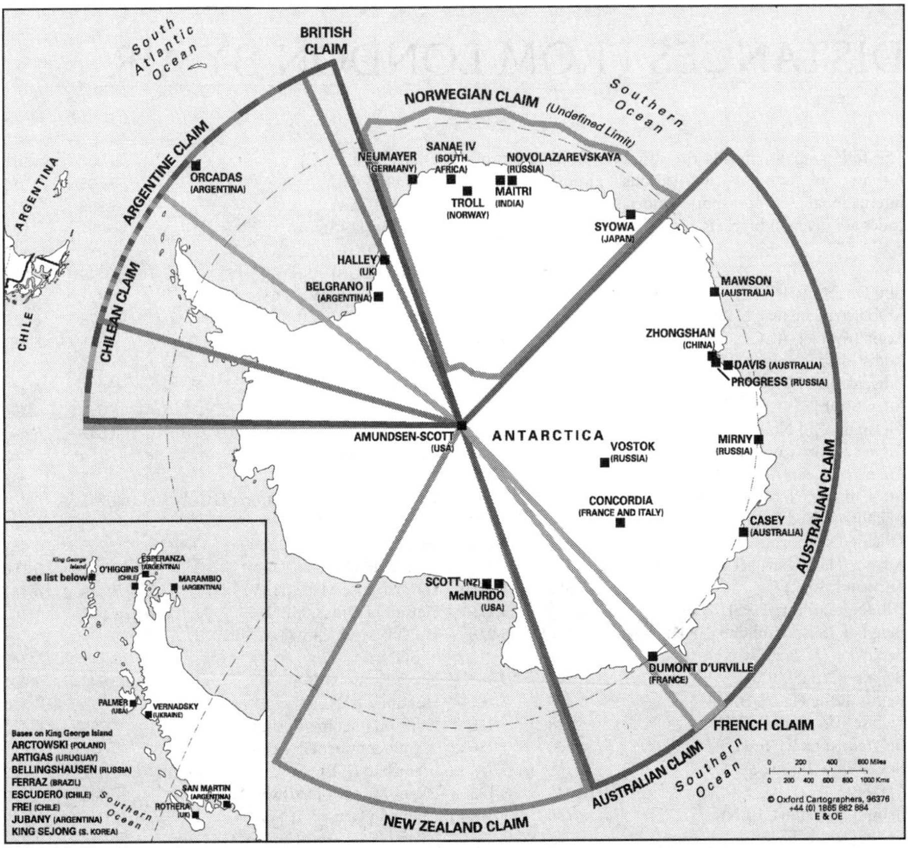

Southern Ocean Coalition recorded 4,698 tourists in the 1990–1 summer season, rising to over 28,000 by 2005–6.

In 1991 the International Association of Antarctica Tour Operators was founded with the objective of providing a self-regulating code of conduct for all operators to follow, but membership is not yet compulsory, raising fears about the environmental damage a booming tourist industry could create.

INTERNATIONAL POLAR YEAR

The first International Polar Year (IPY) since 1957 began on 1 March 2007. IPY is a large collaborative scientific programme focused on both the Arctic and Antarctic. The 'year' actually spans two full seasonal cycles on both poles, and so runs until March 2009. Four 'urgencies' have been identified for particular study in this period: the effects of changing levels of snow and ice within the polar regions; their tangential influence on the wider world; the changes facing northern communities and the further discovery and understanding of life under ice.

THE BRITISH ANTARCTIC SURVEY

The British Antarctic Survey (BAS) is part of the Natural Environment Research Council and carries out the majority of Britain's scientific research in Antarctica. Over 400 staff are employed by BAS and the organisation supports five research stations, two of which are staffed throughout the winter months. See the BAS website (W www.bas.ac.uk) for further information.

DISTANCES FROM LONDON BY AIR

The following list details the distances from Heathrow Airport in London to various airports abroad. International Air Transport Association (IATA) airport codes are given in brackets.

To	*Km*	*Miles*
Abu Dhabi (AUH)	5,512	3,425
Acapulco (Gen. Juan N Alvarez, ACA)	9,177	5,702
Accra (Kotoka, ACC)	5,097	3,167
Addis Ababa (Bole, ADD)	5,915	3,675
Adelaide (ADL)	16,283	10,111
Aden (ADE)	5,907	3,670
Alexandria (El Nohza, ALY)	3,350	2,082
Algiers (Houari Boumedienne, ALG)	1,666	1,035
Amman (Queen Alia, AMM)	3,681	2,287
Amsterdam (Schiphol, AMS)	370	230
Anchorage (Ted Stevens, ANC)	7,196	4,472
Ankara (Esenboga, ESB)	2,848	1,770
Atlanta (Hartsfield-Jackson, ATL)	6,756	4,198
Auckland (AKL)	18,353	11,404
Bali (Ngurah Rai, DPS)	12,518	7,779
Bangkok (Suvarnabhumi, BKK)	9,540	5,928
Barcelona (El Prat, BCN)	1,146	712
Beijing (Capital, PEK)	8,148	5,063
Beirut (Rafic Hariri, BEY)	3,478	2,161
Belfast (Aldergrove, BFS)	524	325
Belgrade (Nikola Tesla, BEG)	1,700	1,056
Belize City (Philip Goldson, BZE)	8,340	5,182
Benghazi (Benina, BEN)	2,734	1,699
Berlin (Tegel, TXL)	947	588
Bogotá (El Dorado, BOG)	8,468	5,262
Boston (Logan, BOS)	5,239	3,255
Brasília (Presidente Juscelino Kubitschek, BSB)	8,775	5,452
Bratislava (M. R. Stefanik, BTS)	1,315	817
Brazzaville (Maya Maya, BZV)	6,368	3,957
Bridgetown (Grantley Adams, BGI)	6,748	4,193
Brisbane (BNE)	16,533	10,273
Brussels (BRU)	349	217
Bucharest (Henri Coanda, OTP)	2,103	1,307
Budapest (Ferihegy, BUD)	1,486	923
Buenos Aires-Ezeiza (Ministro Pistarini, EZE)	11,129	6,915
Cairo (CAI)	3,531	2,194
Calgary (YYC)	7,012	4,357
Canberra (CBR)	16,999	10,563
Cape Town (CPT)	9,675	6,011
Caracas (Simón Bolívar, CCS)	7,466	4,639
Casablanca (Mohammed V, CMN)	2,092	1,300
Chennai/Madras (Meenambakkam, MAA)	8,229	5,113
Chicago (O'Hare, ORD)	6,343	3,941
Cologne/Bonn (Konrad Adenauer, CGN)	533	331
Colombo (Bandaranaike, CMB)	8,708	5,411
Copenhagen (CPH)	978	608
Dallas-Fort Worth (DFW)	7,622	4,736
Damascus (DAM)	3,577	2,223
Dar es Salaam (DAR)	7,502	4,662
Darwin (DRW)	13,861	8,613
Denver (DEN)	7,492	4,655
Dhaka (Zia, DAC)	8,008	4,976
Doha (DOH)	5,235	3,253
Douala (DLA)	5,356	3,328
Dresden (DRS)	987	613
Dubai (DXB)	5,494	3,414
Dublin (DUB)	449	279
Dubrovnik (DBV)	1,727	1,073
Dundee (DND)	579	359
Durban (DUR)	9,555	5,937
Düsseldorf (DUS)	500	310
Edmonton (YEG)	6,805	4,229
Frankfurt (FRA)	653	406
Gaborone (Sir Seretse Khama, GBE)	8,842	5,494
Geneva (GVA)	754	468
Glasgow (GLA)	555	345
Guatemala City (La Aurora, GUA)	8,745	5,435
Hamburg (HAM)	745	463
Hannover (HAJ)	703	437
Harare (HRE)	8,298	5,156
Havana (José Martí, HAV)	7,479	4,647
Helsinki (Vantaa, HEL)	1,847	1,147
Ho Chi Minh City (Tan Son Nhat, SGN)	10,211	6,345
Hong Kong (HKG)	9,640	5,990
Honolulu (HNL)	11,619	7,220
Houston (George Bush Intercontinental, IAH)	7,759	4,821
Islamabad (ISB)	6,062	3,767
Isle of Man (Ronaldsway, IOM)	403	250
Istanbul (Ataturk, IST)	2,510	1,560
Jakarta (Soekarno-Hatta, CGK)	11,712	7,277
Jeddah (King Abdulaziz, JED)	4,743	2,947
Johannesburg (OR Tambo, JNB)	9,068	5,634
Kabul (Khwaja Rawash, KBL)	5,726	3,558
Karachi (Jinnah, KHI)	6,334	3,935
Kathmandu (Tribhuvan, KTM)	7,354	4,570
Khartoum (KRT)	4,943	3,071
Kiev (Boryspil, KBP)	2,184	1,357
Kigali (KGL)	6,600	4,101
Kilimanjaro (JRO)	7,055	4,384
Kingston, Jamaica (Norman Manley, KIN)	7,513	4,668
Kinshasa (N'Djili, FIH)	6,387	3,969
Kolkata/Calcutta (Netaji Subhas Chandra Bose, CCU)	7,979	4,958
Kraków (John Paul II, KRK)	1,425	886
Kuala Lumpur (KUL)	10,552	6,557
Kuwait (KWI)	4,671	2,903
Lagos (Murtala Muhammed, LOS)	5,000	3,107
Larnaca (LCA)	3,276	2,036
Las Palmas (Gran Canaria, LPA)	2,897	1,800
Lisbon (Portela, LIS)	1,564	972
Ljubljana (Brnik, LJU)	1,233	767
Lomé-Tokoin (Gnassingbe Eyadema, LFW)	5,036	3,129
Los Angeles (LAX)	8,753	5,439
Luanda (Quatro de Fevereiro, LAD)	6,830	4,243
Lusaka (LUN)	7,933	4,929
Luxor (LXR)	3,999	2,485
Lyon-Bron (LYN)	750	466
Madrid (Barajas, MAD)	1,244	773
Málaga (AGP)	1,675	1,041

Malé (MLE)	8,533	5,302
Malmö-Sturup (MMX)	1,017	632
Malta (Luqa, MLA)	2,100	1,305
Manila (Ninoy Aquino, MNL)	10,758	6,685
Maputo (MPM)	9,184	5,707
Marrakech-Menara (RAK)	2,292	1,424
Marseille (Provence, MRS)	988	614
Melbourne (Tullamarine, MEL)	16,897	10,499
Memphis (MEM)	7,005	4,353
Menorca (Mahon, MAH)	1,339	832
Mexico City (Benito Juarez, MEX)	8,899	5,529
Miami (MIA)	7,104	4,414
Milan (Malpensa, MXP)	979	609
Minneapolis-St Paul (MSP)	6,439	4,001
Minsk (Minsk 2, MSQ)	1,893	1,176
Mombasa (Moi, MBA)	7,236	4,497
Montego Bay (Sangster, MBJ)	7,544	4,687
Montevideo (Carrasco, MVD)	11,010	6,841
Montréal (Pierre Elliott Trudeau, YUL)	5,213	3,239
Moscow (Sheremetyevo, SVO)	2,506	1,557
Mumbai/Bombay (Chhatrapati Shivaji, BOM)	7,207	4,478
Munich (Franz Josef Strauss, MUC)	940	584
Muscat (MCT)	5,828	3,621
Naples-Capodichino (NAP)	1,628	1,011
Nassau (Lynden Pindling, NAS)	6,973	4,333
Natal (Augusto Severo, NAT)	7,180	4,462
N'Djamena (NDJ)	4,588	2,851
Newark (Liberty, EWR)	5,558	3,454
New Delhi (Indira Gandhi, DEL)	6,727	4,180
New York (John F. Kennedy, JFK)	5,536	3,440
Nice (Côte d'Azur, NCE)	1,039	645
Novosibirsk (Tolmachevo, OVB)	5,216	3,241
Orlando (MCO)	6,954	4,321
Osaka (Itami, ITM)	9,498	5,901
Oslo (Gardermoen, OSL)	1,206	749
Ostend-Bruges (OST)	232	144
Ottawa (Macdonald-Cartier, YOW)	5,344	3,321
Ouagadougou (OUA)	4,348	2,702
Palma de Mallorca (PMI)	1,347	836
Panama City (Tocumen, PTY)	8,448	5,249
Paris (Charles de Gaulle, CDG)	346	215
Penang (PEN)	10,277	6,386
Perth, Australia (PER)	14,497	9,008
Philadelphia (PHL)	5,686	3,533
Pisa (Galileo Galilei, PSA)	1,184	736
Port of Spain (Piarco, POS)	7,088	4,404
Prague (Ruzyne, PRG)	1,043	649
Québec (Jean Lesage, YQB)	4,979	3,093
Quito (Mariscal Sucre, UIO)	9,188	5,709
Rabat (Sale, RBA)	2,001	1,243
Rangoon/Yangon (RGN)	8,984	5,582
Reykjavik (Keflavik, KEF)	1,895	1,177
Rhodes (Diagoras, RHO)	2,805	1,743
Riga (RIX)	1,695	1,054
Rimini (Federico Fellini, RMI)	1,275	793
Rio de Janeiro-Galeao (Antonio Carlos Jobim, GIG)	9,245	5,745
Riyadh (King Khaled, RUH)	4,936	3,067
Rome (Fiumicino, FCO)	1,441	895
St Lucia (Hewanorra, UVF)	6,785	4,216
St Petersburg (Pulkovo, LED)	2,114	1,314
Salt Lake City (SLC)	7,806	4,850
Salzburg (W. A. Mozart, SZG)	1,048	651
San Diego (Lindbergh Field, SAN)	8,802	5,469
San Francisco (SFO)	8,610	5,351
Sao Paulo (Congonhas, CGH)	9,483	5,892
Sarajevo (SJJ)	1,636	1,017
Seoul (Gimpo, SEL)	8,863	5,507
Seychelles (SEZ)	8,169	5,076
Shannon (SNN)	594	369
Shetland Islands (Sumburgh, LSI)	936	582
Singapore (Changi, SIN)	10,873	6,756
Skopje (Alexander the Great, SKP)	1,963	1,220
Sofia (Vrazhdebna, SOF)	2,038	1,266
Split-Kastela (SPU)	1,530	951
Stockholm (Arlanda, ARN)	1,461	908
Strasbourg (Entzheim, SXB)	663	412
Stuttgart (STR)	754	469
Suva (Nausori, SUV)	16,285	10,119
Sydney (Kingsford Smith, SYD)	17,008	10,568
Tahiti (Faa'a, PPT)	15,361	9,545
Taipei (Taiwan Taoyuan, TPE)	9,775	6,074
Tbilisi (TBS)	3,571	2,219
Tehran (Imam Khomeini, IKA)	4,411	2,741*
Tel Aviv (Ben Gurion, TLV)	3,585	2,227
Thessaloniki (Makedonia, SKG)	2,164	1,345
Tokyo (Narita, NRT)	9,585	5,956
Toronto (Pearson, YYZ)	5,704	3,544
Treviso (St Angelo, TSF)	1,130	703
Tripoli (TIP)	2,362	1,468
Trondheim (Vaernes, TRD)	1,490	926
Tunis-Carthage (TUN)	1,830	1,137
Turin (Sandro Pertini, TRN)	917	570
Ulaanbaatar (Buyant Uhaa, ULN)	6,984	4,340
Vancouver (YVR)	7,574	4,707
Venice (Marco Polo, VCE)	1,150	715
Vienna (VIE)	1,272	790
Vladivostok (VVO)	8,526	5,298
Warsaw (Frederic Chopin, WAW)	1,468	912
Washington (Dulles, IAD)	5,898	3,665
Wellington (WLG)	18,817	11,692
Zagreb (Pleso, ZAG)	1,365	848
Zürich-Kloten (ZRH)	787	490

* International flights transferred to Imam Khomeini airport in 2007. Distances currently listed are for the old international airport, Mehrabad.

TIME ZONES

Standard time differences from the Greenwich meridian

+ hours ahead of GMT
– hours behind GMT
* may vary from standard time at some part of the year (Summer Time or Daylight Saving Time)
† some areas may keep another time zone
h hours
m minutes

	h	*m*
Afghanistan	+ 4	30
*Albania	+ 1	
Algeria	+ 1	
*Andorra	+ 1	
Angola	+ 1	
Antigua and Barbuda	– 4	
*†Argentina	– 3	
*Armenia	+ 4	
*Australia		
*ACT, NSW (except Broken Hill area), Tas, Vic, Whitsunday Islands	+10	
Northern Territory	+ 9	30
Queensland	+10	
*South Australia	+ 9	30
*Western Australia	+ 8	
Christmas Island (Indian Ocean)	+ 7	
Cocos (Keeling) Islands	+ 6	30
Norfolk Island	+11	30
*Austria	+ 1	
*Azerbaijan	+ 4	
*Bahamas	– 5	
Bahrain	+ 3	
Bangladesh	+ 6	
Barbados	– 4	
*Belarus	+ 2	
*Belgium	+ 1	
Belize	– 6	
Benin	+ 1	
Bhutan	+ 6	
Bolivia	– 4	
*Bosnia and Hercegovina	+ 1	
Botswana	+ 2	
*Brazil		
central states	– 4	
N. and N. E. coastal states	– 2	
*S. and E. coastal states, including Brasilia	– 3	
Fernando de Noronha Island	– 2	
Brunei	+ 8	
*Bulgaria	+ 2	
Burkina Faso	0	
Burundi	+ 2	
Cambodia	+ 7	
Cameroon	+ 1	
*Canada		
*Alberta	– 7	
*†British Columbia	– 8	
*Manitoba	– 6	
*New Brunswick	– 4	
*†Newfoundland	– 3	30
*†Northwest Territories	– 7	
*Nova Scotia	– 4	
*Nunavut		
central	– 6	
eastern	– 5	
mountain	– 7	
*Ontario		
east of 90° W.	– 5	
west of 90° W.	– 6	
*Prince Edward Island	– 4	
*Québec		
east of 63° W.	– 4	
*west of 63° W.	– 5	
*†Saskatchewan	– 6	
*Yukon	– 8	
Cape Verde	– 1	
Central African Republic	+ 1	
Chad	+ 1	
*Chile	– 4	
China (inc. Hong Kong and Macao)	+ 8	
Colombia	– 5	
The Comoros	+ 3	
Congo, Dem. Rep. of		
Haut-Zaire, Kasai, Kivu, Shaba	+ 2	
Kinshasa, Mbandaka	+ 1	
Congo, Republic of	+ 1	
Costa Rica	– 6	
Côte d'Ivoire	0	
*Croatia	+ 1	
*Cuba	– 5	
*Cyprus	+ 2	
*Czech Republic	+ 1	
*Denmark	+ 1	
*Faeroe Islands	0	
*Greenland	– 3	
Danmarks Havn, Mesters Vig	0	
*Scoresby Sund	– 1	
*Thule area	– 4	
Djibouti	+ 3	
Dominica	– 4	
Dominican Republic	– 4	
East Timor	+ 9	
Ecuador	– 5	
Galápagos Islands	– 6	
*Egypt	+ 2	
El Salvador	– 6	
Equatorial Guinea	+ 1	
Eritrea	+ 3	
*Estonia	+ 2	
Ethiopia	+ 3	
Fiji	+ 12	
*Finland	+ 2	
*France	+ 1	
French Guiana	– 3	
French Polynesia	–10	
Guadeloupe	– 4	
Marquesas Islands	– 9	30
Martinique	– 4	
New Caledonia	+11	
Réunion	+ 4	
*St Pierre and Miquelon	– 3	
Wallis and Futuna	+12	
Gabon	+ 1	
The Gambia	0	
Georgia	+ 4	
*Germany	+ 1	
Ghana	0	
*Greece	+ 2	
Grenada	– 4	
Guatemala	– 6	
Guinea	0	
Guinea-Bissau	0	
Guyana	– 4	
*Haiti	– 5	
Honduras	– 6	
*Hungary	+ 1	
Iceland	0	
India	+ 5	30
Indonesia		
Java, Kalimantan (west and central), Madura, Sumatra	+ 7	
Bali, Flores, Kalimantan (south and east), Lombok, Sulawesi, Sumbawa, West Timor	+ 8	
Irian Jaya, Maluku	+ 9	
*Iran	+ 3	30
Iraq	+ 3	
*Ireland, Republic of	0	
*Israel	+ 2	
*Italy	+ 1	
Jamaica	– 5	
Japan	+ 9	
*Jordan	+ 2	
Kazakhstan		
western	+ 5	
eastern	+ 6	
Kenya	+ 3	
Kiribati	+12	
Line Islands	+14	
Phoenix Islands	+13	
Korea, Dem. People's Rep. of	+ 9	
Korea, Republic of	+ 9	
Kuwait	+ 3	
Kyrgyzstan	+ 6	
Laos	+ 7	
*Latvia	+ 2	
*Lebanon	+ 2	

	h	*m*
Lesotho	+ 2	
Liberia	0	
Libya	+ 2	
*Liechtenstein	+ 1	
*Lithuania	+ 2	
*Luxembourg	+ 1	
*Macedonia	+ 1	
Madagascar	+ 3	
Malawi	+ 2	
Malaysia	+ 8	
Maldives	+ 5	
Mali	0	
*Malta	+ 1	
Marshall Islands	+12	
Mauritania	0	
*Mauritius	+ 4	
*Mexico	− 6	
*Nayarit, Sinaloa, S. Baja California	− 7	
*N. Baja California	− 8	
Sonora	− 7	
Micronesia, Fed. States of		
Chuuk, Yap	+10	
Kosrae, Pingelap, Pohnpei	+11	
*Moldova	+ 2	
*Monaco	+ 1	
†Mongolia	+ 8	
*Montenegro	+ 1	
*Morocco	0	
Mozambique	+ 2	
Myanmar	+ 6	30
*Namibia	+ 1	
Nauru	+12	
Nepal	+ 5	45
*The Netherlands	+ 1	
Aruba	− 4	
Netherlands Antilles	− 4	
*New Zealand	+12	
Cook Islands	−10	
Niue	−11	
Tokelau Island	−10	
Nicaragua	− 6	
Niger	+ 1	
Nigeria	+ 1	
*Norway	+ 1	
*Svalbard, Jan Mayen	+ 1	
Oman	+ 4	
*Pakistan	+ 5	
Palau	+ 9	
Panama	− 5	
Papua New Guinea	+10	
*Paraguay	− 4	
Peru	− 5	
The Philippines	+ 8	
*Poland	+ 1	
*Portugal	0	
*Azores	− 1	
*Madeira	0	
Qatar	+ 3	
*Romania	+ 2	
*Russia		
Zone 1	+ 2	
Zone 2	+ 3	
Zone 3	+ 4	
Zone 4	+ 5	
Zone 5	+ 6	
Zone 6	+ 7	
Zone 7	+ 8	
Zone 8	+ 9	
Zone 9	+10	
Zone 10	+11	
Zone 11	+12	
Rwanda	+ 2	
St Christopher and Nevis	− 4	
St Lucia	− 4	
St Vincent and the Grenadines	− 4	
Samoa	−11	
*San Marino	+ 1	
São Tomé and Príncipe	0	
Saudi Arabia	+ 3	
Senegal	0	
*Serbia	+ 1	
Seychelles	+ 4	
Sierra Leone	0	
Singapore	+ 8	
*Slovakia	+ 1	
*Slovenia	+ 1	
Solomon Islands	+11	
Somalia	+ 3	
South Africa	+ 2	
*Spain	+ 1	
*Canary Islands	0	
Sri Lanka	+ 5	30
Sudan	+ 3	
Suriname	− 3	
Swaziland	+ 2	
*Sweden	+ 1	
*Switzerland	+ 1	
*Syria	+ 2	
Taiwan	+ 8	
Tajikistan	+ 5	
Tanzania	+ 3	
Thailand	+ 7	
Togo	0	
Tonga	+13	
Trinidad and Tobago	− 4	
*Tunisia	+ 1	
*Turkey	+ 2	
Turkmenistan	+ 5	
Tuvalu	+12	
Uganda	+ 3	
*Ukraine	+ 2	
United Arab Emirates	+ 4	
*United Kingdom	0	
Anguilla	− 4	
*Bermuda	− 4	
†British Antarctic Territory	− 3	
British Indian Ocean Territory	+ 5	
British Virgin Islands	− 4	
Cayman Islands	− 5	
*Falkland Islands	− 4	
*Gibraltar	+ 1	
Montserrat	− 4	
Pitcairn Islands	− 8	
St Helena and Dependencies	0	
South Georgia Islands	− 2	
*Turks and Caicos Islands	− 5	
*United States of America		
*Alaska	− 9	
Aleutian Islands, east of 169° 30′ W.	− 9	
Aleutian Islands, west of 169° 30′ W.	−10	
*central time	− 6	
*eastern time	− 5	
Guam	+10	
Hawaii	−10	
*mountain time	− 7	
Northern Mariana Islands	+10	
*Pacific time	− 8	
Puerto Rico	− 4	
Samoa, American	−11	
Virgin Islands	− 4	
*Uruguay	− 3	
Uzbekistan	+ 5	
Vanuatu	+11	
*Vatican City State	+ 1	
Venezuela	− 4	30
Vietnam	+ 7	
Yemen	+ 3	
Zambia	+ 2	
Zimbabwe	+ 2	

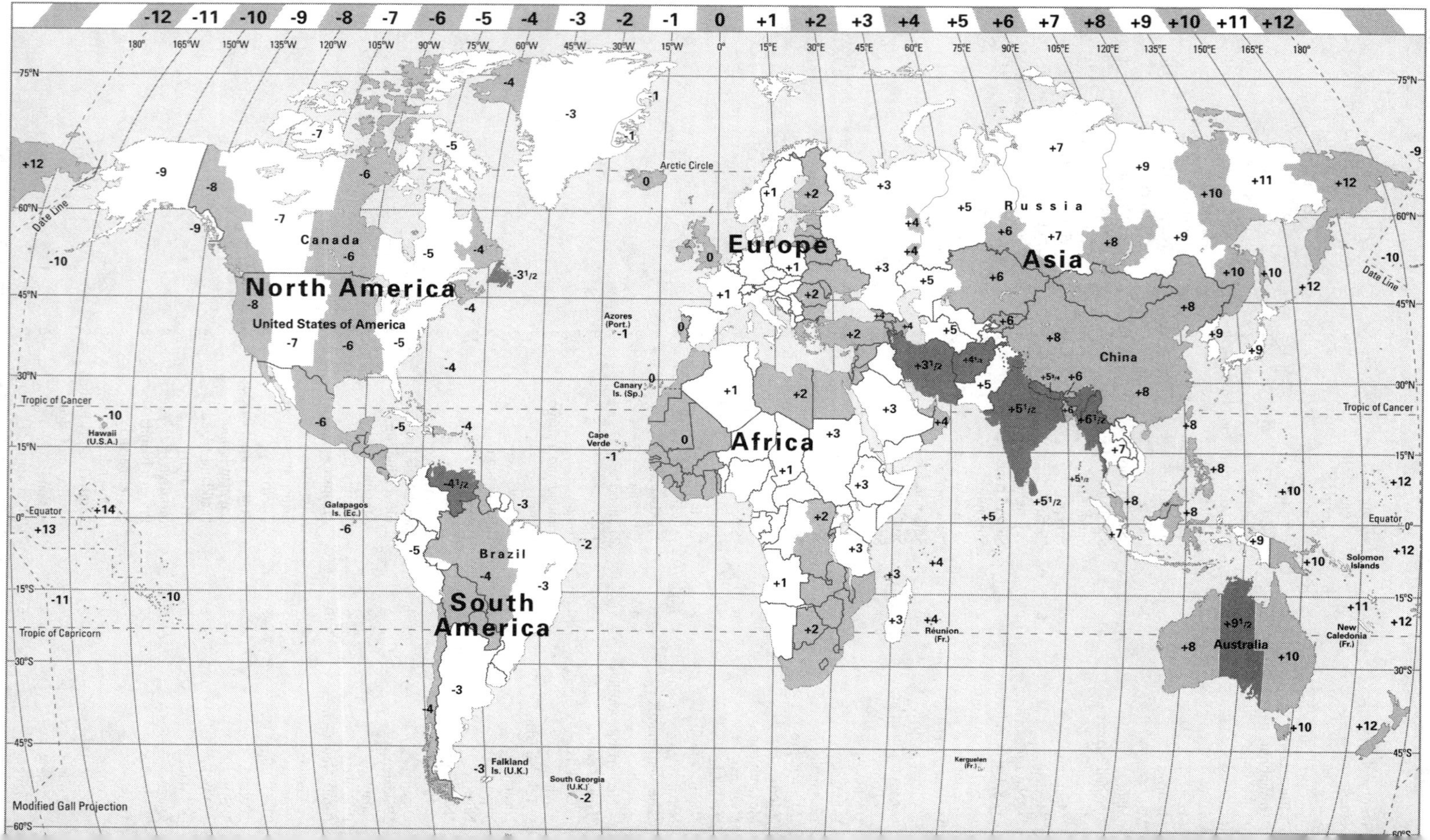
-12 -11 -10 -9 -8 -7 -6 -5 -4 -3 -2 -1 0 +1 +2 +3 +4 +5 +6 +7 +8 +9 +10 +11 +12
North America
Canada
United States of America
South America
Brazil
Europe
Africa
Asia
Russia
China
Australia
Arctic Circle
Tropic of Cancer
Equator
Tropic of Capricorn
Date Line
Hawaii (U.S.A.)
Galapagos Is. (Ec.)
Azores (Port.)
Canary Is. (Sp.)
Cape Verde
Falkland Is. (U.K.)
South Georgia (U.K.)
Réunion (Fr.)
Kerguelen (Fr.)
Solomon Islands
New Caledonia (Fr.)
Modified Gall Projection

CURRENCIES AND EXCHANGE RATES

Average rate against £1 sterling on 31 March 2008

COUNTRY/TERRITORY	CURRENCY	VALUE
Afghanistan	Afghani (Af) of 100 puls	Af 76.80
Albania	Lek (Lk) of 100 qindarka	Lk 154.73
Algeria	Algerian dinar (DA) of 100 centimes	DA 129.58
American Samoa	Currency is that of the USA	US$1.99
Andorra	Euro (€) of 100 cents	€1.25
Angola	Readjusted kwanza (Krzl) of 100 centimos	Kzrl 149.19
Anguilla	East Caribbean dollar (EC$) of 100 cents	EC$5.37
Antigua and Barbuda	East Caribbean dollar (EC$) of 100 cents	EC$5.37
Argentina	Peso of 100 centavos	Pesos 6.29
Armenia	Dram of 100 luma	Dram 614.64
Aruba	Aruban guilder	Guilder 3.56
Ascension Island	Currency is that of St Helena	—
Australia	Australian dollar ($A) of 100 cents	$A2.18
Austria	Euro (€) of 100 cents	€1.25
Azerbaijan	New manat of 100 gopik	New manat 1.66
The Bahamas	Bahamian dollar (B$) of 100 cents	B$1.99
Bahrain	Bahraini dinar (BD) of 1,000 fils	BD 0.75
Bangladesh	Taka (Tk) of 100 poisha	Tk 136.30
Barbados	Barbados dollar (BD$) of 100 cents	BD$3.98
Belarus	Belarusian rouble of 100 kopeks	BYR 4,267.16
Belgium	Euro (€) of 100 cents	€1.25
Belize	Belize dollar (BZ$) of 100 cents	BZ$3.92
Benin	Franc CFA of 100 centimes	Francs 822.77
Bermuda	Bermuda dollar of 100 cents	$1.99
Bhutan	Ngultrum of 100 chetrum (Indian currency is also legal tender)	Ngultrum 79.74
Bolivia	Boliviano ($b) of 100 centavos	$b14.85
Bosnia and Hercegovina	Convertible mark of 100 fenings	Mark 2.45
Botswana	Pula (P) of 100 thebe	P 13.20
Brazil	Real of 100 centavos	Real 3.48
Brunei	Brunei dollar (B$) of 100 sen	B$2.74
Bulgaria	Lev of 100 stotinki	Leva 2.45
Burkina Faso	Franc CFA of 100 centimes	Francs 822.77
Burundi	Burundi franc of 100 centimes	Francs 2,341.58
Cambodia	Riel of 100 sen	Riel 7,849.31
Cameroon	Franc CFA of 100 centimes	Francs 822.77
Canada	Canadian dollar (C$) 100 cents	C$2.04
Cape Verde	Escudo Caboverdiano of 100 centavos	Esc 141.29
Cayman Islands	Cayman Islands dollar (CI$) of 100 cents	CI$1.63
Central African Republic	Franc CFA of 100 centimes	Francs 822.77
Chad	Franc CFA of 100 centimes	Francs 822.77
Chile	Chilean peso of 100 centavos	Pesos 868.24
China	Renminbi yuan of 10 jiao or 100 fen	Yuan 13.94
Colombia	Colombian peso of 100 centavos	Pesos 3,640.80
The Comoros	Comorian franc (KMF) of 100 centimes	Francs 617.07
Congo, Rep. of	Franc CFA of 100 centimes	Francs 822.77
Congo, Dem. Rep. of	Congolese franc of 100 cents	CFr 1,096.11
Cook Islands	Currency is that of New Zealand	NZ$2.53
Costa Rica	Costa Rican colón (C) of 100 céntimos	C983.13
Côte d'Ivoire	Franc CFA of 100 centimes	Francs 822.77
Croatia	Kuna of 100 lipa	Kuna 9.12
Cuba	Cuban peso of 100 centavos	Pesos 1.99
Cyprus	Euro (€) of 100 cents	€1.25
Czech Republic	Koruna (Kcs) of 100 haleru	Kcs 31.62
Denmark	Danish krone of 100 ore	Kroner 9.35
Djibouti	Djibouti franc of 100 centimes	Francs 349.48
Dominica	East Caribbean dollar (EC$) of 100 cents	EC$5.37
Dominican Republic	Dominican Republic peso (RD$) of 100 centavos	RD$67.38
East Timor	Currency is that of the USA	US$1.99

Ecuador	Currency is that of the USA (formerly sucre of 100 centavos)	US$1.99
Egypt	Egyptian pound (£E) of 100 piastres or 1,000 millièmes	£E10.83
El Salvador	Currency is that of USA	US$1.99
Equatorial Guinea	Franc CFA of 100 centimes	Francs 822.77
Eritrea	Nakfa of 100 cents	Nakfa 30.01
Estonia	Kroon of 100 senti	Kroons 19.63
Ethiopia	Ethiopian birr (EB) of 100 cents	EB 18.96
Faeroe Islands	Currency is that of Denmark	Kroner 9.35
Falkland Islands	Falkland pound of 100 pence	—
Fiji	Fiji dollar (F$) of 100 cents	F$2.97
Finland	Euro (€) of 100 cents	€1.25
France	Euro (€) of 100 cents	€1.25
French Guiana	Euro (€) of 100 cents	€1.25
French Polynesia	Franc CFP of 100 centimes	Francs 149.58
Gabon	Franc CFA of 100 centimes	Francs 822.77
Gambia	Dalasi (D) of 100 butut	D 39.00
Georgia	Lari of 100 tetri	Lari 2.91
Germany	Euro (€) of 100 cents	€1.25
Ghana	Cedi of 100 pesewas	Cedi 1.96
Gibraltar	Gibraltar pound of 100 pence	—
Greece	Euro (€) of 100 cents	€1.25
Greenland	Currency is that of Denmark	Kroner 9.35
Grenada	East Caribbean dollar (EC$) of 100 cents	EC$5.37
Guadeloupe	Euro (€) of 100 cents	€1.25
Guam	Currency is that of the USA	US$1.99
Guatemala	Quetzal (Q) of 100 centavos	Q 15.11
Guinea	Guinea franc of 100 centimes	Francs 8,685.14
Guinea-Bissau	Franc CFA of 100 centimes	Francs 9822.77
Guyana	Guyana dollar (G$) of 100 cents	G$398.52
Haiti	Gourde of 100 centimes	Gourdes 75.82
Honduras	Lempira of 100 centavos	Lempiras 37.56
Hong Kong	Hong Kong (HK$) of 100 cents	HK$15.47
Hungary	Forint of 100 filler	Forints 326.12
Iceland	Icelandic krona (Kr) of 100 aurar	Kr 150.46
India	Indian rupee (Rs) of 100 paise	Rs 79.74
Indonesia	Rupiah (Rp) of 100 sen	Rp 18,294.94
Iran	Iranian rial of 100 dinar	Rials 18,250.22
Iraq	New Iraqi dinar (NID) of 1,000 fils	NID 1,882.1
Ireland, Republic of	Euro (€) of 100 cents	€1.25
Israel	Shekel of 100 agora	Shekels 7.02
Italy	Euro (€) of 100 cents	€1.25
Jamaica	Jamaican dollar (J$) of 100 cents	J$141.24
Japan	Yen of 100 sen	Yen 197.84
Jordan	Jordanian dinar (JD) of 10 dirhams	JD 1.41
Kazakhstan	Tenge of 100 tiyn	Tenge 239.87
Kenya	Kenyan shilling (Ksh) of 100 cents	Ksh 124.72
Kiribati	Currency is that of Australia	$A2.18
Korea, Dem. People's Rep. of	Won of 100 chon	Won 284.92
Korea, Republic of	Won of 100 jeon	Won 1,968.32
Kuwait	Kuwaiti dinar (KD) of 1,000 fils	KD 0.53
Kyrgyzstan	Som of 100 tyiyn	Som 72.44
Laos	Kip (K) of 100 att	K 17,380.99
Latvia	Lats of 100 santims	Lats 0.88
Lebanon	Lebanese pound (L£) of of 100 piastres	L£3,005.10
Lesotho	Loti (M) of 100 lisente	M 16.15
Liberia	Liberian dollar (L$) of 100 cents	L$124.00
Libya	Libyan dinar (LD) of 1,000 dirhams	LD 2.37
Liechtenstein	Currency is that of Switzerland	Francs 1.97
Lithuania	Litas of 100 centas	Litas 4.33
Luxembourg	Euro (€) of 100 cents	€1.25
Macao	Pataca of 100 avos	Pataca 15.93
Macedonia	Denar of 100 deni	Den 77.25
Madagascar	Ariary of 5 iraimbilanja	MGA 3,317.14
Malawi	Kwacha (K) of 100 tambala	MK 279.20
Malaysia	Malaysian dollar (ringgit) (M$) of 100 sen	M$6.36
Maldives	Rufiyaa of 100 laaris	Rufiyaa 25.44
Mali	Franc CFA of 100 centimes	Francs 822.77

Malta	Euro (€) of 100 cents	€1.25
Marshall Islands	Currency is that of the USA	US$1.99
Martinique	Currency is that of France	€1.25
Mauritania	Ouguiya (UM) of 5 khoums	UM 482.97
Mauritius	Mauritius rupee of 100 cents	Rs 51.28
Mayotte	Currency is that of France	€1.25
Mexico	Peso of 100 centavos	Pesos 21.20
Micronesia, Federated States of	Currency is that of the USA	US$1.99
Moldova	Moldovan leu of 100 bani	MDL 20.91
Monaco	Euro (€) of 100 cents	€1.25
Mongolia	Tugrik of 100 mongo	Tugriks 2,321.00
Montenegro	Euro (€) of 100 cents	€1.25
Montserrat	East Caribbean dollar (EC$) of 100 cents	EC$5.37
Morocco	Dirham (DH) of 100 centimes	DH 14.41
Mozambique	New metical (MT) of 100 centavos	MT 48.53
Myanmar	Kyat (K) of 100 pyas	K 12.81
Namibia	Namibian dollar of 100 cents	$16.15
Nauru	Currency is that of Australia	$A2.18
Nepal	Nepalese rupee of 100 paisa	Rs 127.58
The Netherlands	Euro (€) of 100 cents	€1.25
Netherlands Antilles	Netherlands Antilles guilder of 100 cents	Guilders 3.56
New Caledonia	Franc CFP of 100 centimes	Francs 149.58
New Zealand	New Zealand dollar (NZ$) of 100 cents	NZ$2.53
Nicaragua	Córdoba (C$) of 100 centavos	C$38.03
Niger	Franc CFA of 100 centimes	Francs 822.77
Nigeria	Naira (N) of 100 kobo	N 232.67
Niue	Currency is that of New Zealand	NZ$2.53
Norfolk Island	Currency is that of Australia	$A2.18
Northern Mariana Islands	Currency is that of the USA	US$1.99
Norway	Krone of 100 ore	Kroner 10.10
Oman	Rial Omani (OR) of 1,000 baisas	OR 0.77
Pakistan	Pakistan rupee of 100 paisa	Rs 124.61
Palau	Currency is that of the USA	US$1.99
Panama	Balboa of 100 centésimos (US notes are in circulation)	Balboa 1.99
Papua New Guinea	Kina (K) of 100 toea	K 5.43
Paraguay	Guarani (Gs) of 100 céntimos	Gs 8,620.79
Peru	New Sol of 100 centimos	New Sol 5.45
The Philippines	Philippine peso (P) of 100 centavos	P 83.02
Pitcairn Islands	Currency is that of New Zealand	NZ$2.53
Poland	Zloty of 100 groszy	Zlotych 4.41
Portugal	Euro (€) of 100 cents	€1.25
Puerto Rico	Currency is that of the USA	US$1.99
Qatar	Qatar riyal of 100 dirhams	Riyals 7.23
Réunion	Currency is that of France	€1.25
Romania	New leu of 100 bani	Lei 4.68
Russian Federation	Rouble of 100 kopeks	Rbl 46.60
Rwanda	Rwanda franc of 100 centimes	Francs 1,081.4
St Christopher and Nevis	East Caribbean dollar (EC$) of 100 cents	EC$5.37
St Helena	St Helena pound (£) of 100 pence	—
St Lucia	East Caribbean dollar (EC$) of 100 cents	EC$5.37
St Pierre and Miquelon	Currency is that of France	€1.25
St Vincent and the Grenadines	East Caribbean dollar (EC$) of 100 cents	EC$5.37
Samoa	Tala (S$) of 100 sene	S$4.96
San Marino	Euro (€) of 100 cents	€1.25
Sao Tome and Princípe	Dobra of 100 centimos	Dobra 28,890.06
Saudi Arabia	Saudi riyal (SR) of 100 halala	SR 7.46
Senegal	Franc CFA of 100 centimes	Francs 822.77
Serbia	New dinar of 100 paras	New dinars 103.38
Seychelles	Seychelles rupee of 100 cents	Rs 15.93
Sierra Leone	Leone (Le) of 100 cents	Le 5,904.79
Singapore	Singapore dollar (S$) of 100 cents (fully interchangeable with Brunei currency)	S$2.74
Slovakia	Koruna (Sk) of 100 halierov	Kcs 40.73
Slovenia	Euro (€) of 100 cents	€1.25
Solomon Islands	Solomon Islands dollar (SI$) of 100 cents	SI$14.59
Somalia	Somali shilling of 100 cents	Shillings 2,690.22
South Africa	Rand (R) of 100 cents	R 16.15
Spain	Euro (€) of 100 cents	€1.25

Sri Lanka	Sri Lankan rupee of 100 cents	Rs 214.25
Sudan	Sudanese pound of 100 piastres	SDG 4.03
Suriname	Surinam dollar of 100 cents	Dollar 5.46
Swaziland	Lilangeni (E) of 100 cents (South African currency is also in circulation)	E 16.15
Sweden	Swedish krona of 100 ore	Kronor 11.79
Switzerland	Swiss franc of 100 rappen (or centimes)	Francs 1.97
Syria	Syrian pound (S£) of 100 piastres	S£102.11
Taiwan	New Taiwan dollar (NT$) of 100 cents	NT$60.38
Tajikistan	Somoni (TJS) of 100 dirams	Somoni 6.88
Tanzania	Tanzanian shilling of 100 cents	Shillings 2,434.69
Thailand	Baht of 100 satang	Baht 62.58
Togo	Franc CFA of 100 centimes	Francs 822.77
Tokelau	Currency is that of New Zealand	NZ$2.53
Tonga	Pa'anga (T$) of 100 seniti	T$3.57
Trinidad and Tobago	Trinidad and Tobago dollar (TT$) of 100 cents	TT$12.57
Tristan da Cunha	Currency is that of the UK	—
Tunisia	Tunisian dinar of 1,000 millimes	Dinars 2.28
Turkey	New Turkish lira (TL) of 100 kurus	TL 2.66
Turkmenistan	Manat of 100 tennesi	Manat 10,405.29
Turks and Caicos Islands	Currency is that of the USA	US$1.99
Tuvalu	Currency is that of Australia	$A2.18
Uganda	Uganda shilling of 100 cents	Shillings 3,368.82
Ukraine	Hryvna of 100 kopiykas	UAH 9.93
United Arab Emirates	UAE dirham (Dh) of 100 fils	Dirham 7.30
United States of America	US dollar (US$) of 100 cents	US$1.99
Uruguay	Uruguayan peso of 100 centésimos	Pesos 40.79
Uzbekistan	Sum of 100 tiyin	Sum 2,583.81
Vanuatu	Vatu	Vatu 191.99
Vatican City State	Euro (€) of 100 cents	€1.25
Venezuela	Bolívar fuerte (Bs. F) of 100 céntimos	Bs. F 4.27
Vietnam	Dong of 10 hao or 100 xu	Dong 32,018.63
Virgin Islands, British	Currency is that of the USA (£ sterling and EC$ also circulate)	US$1.99
Virgin Islands, US	Currency is that of the USA	US$1.99
Wallis and Futuna Islands	Franc CFP of 100 centimes	Francs 149.58
Yemen	Riyal of 100 fils	Riyals 395.41
Zambia	Kwacha (K) of 100 ngwee	K 7,274.25
Zimbabwe	Zimbabwe dollar (Z$) of 100 cents	Z$59,625

Source: WM/Reuters Closing Spot Rates

TRAVEL OVERSEAS

PASSPORT REGULATIONS

Application forms for United Kingdom passports can be obtained from the UK Identity and Passport Service's (IPS) general telephone enquiry line or website, regional passport offices, or from main post offices.
UK IDENTITY AND PASSPORT SERVICE
T 0870-521 0410 W www.ips.gov.uk/passport

REGIONAL OFFICES
- Hampton House, 47–53 High Street, Belfast BT1 2QS
- Millburngate House, Durham DH97 1PA
- 3 Northgate, 96 Milton Street, Cowcaddens, Glasgow G4 0BT
- 101 Old Hall Street, Liverpool L3 9BD
- Globe House, 89 Eccleston Square, London SW1V 1PN
- Olympia House, Upper Dock Street, Newport, Gwent NP20 1XA
- Aragon Court, Northminster Road, Peterborough PE1 1QG

The passport offices are open Monday–Saturday on an appointment-only basis (appointments should be arranged by calling the central telephone number listed above). For an additional fee, passport offices provide either a guaranteed same-day service (for renewals and minor amendments only) or a one-week fast-track service (all except new adult applications).

Standard postal applications are processed within three weeks. The completed application form should be posted, with the appropriate supporting documents and fee, to the regional passport office indicated on the addressed envelope which is provided with each application form. Accompanying cheques and postal orders should be crossed and made payable to 'Identity and Passport Service' or to 'Post Office Ltd' when using the Check & Send service. For online applications, the completed online form will be printed out by the Passport Office and posted to the applicant for them to sign and return. After the paper copy has been received, online applications are also returned within three weeks.

Applications can also be submitted through Check & Send outlets at selected main post offices, who, for a small handling charge, will forward the application form to the relevant regional passport office after having checked that it has been completed correctly and has the appropriate documents attached. Applications through partners take a minimum of two weeks.

A passport cannot be issued or extended on behalf of a person already abroad; such persons should apply to the nearest British High Commission or Consulate.
UK passports are granted to:
- British citizens
- British dependent territories citizens
- British nationals (overseas)
- British overseas territories citizens
- British subjects
- British protected persons

UK passports are generally available for travel to all countries. The possession of a passport does not, however, exempt the holder from compliance with any immigration regulations in force in British or foreign countries, or from the necessity of obtaining a visa where required (*see* below for a list of countries for which UK citizens require a visa).

Biometric passports were introduced in 2006. The new design and security features, including a chip containing the biometrics (the facial image and biographical data of the holder), will render the passport more secure against forgery and aid border controls.

ADULTS

A passport granted to a person over 16 will normally be valid for ten years. Thereafter, or if at any time the passport contains no further space for visas, a new passport must be obtained.

The issue of passports including details of the holder's spouse has been discontinued, but existing family passports may be used until expiry. A spouse who is included in a family passport cannot travel on the passport without the holder.

British nationals born on or before 2 September 1929 are eligible for a free standard passport.

CHILDREN

Since 5 October 1998 all children under the age of 16 are required to have their own passport. This is primarily to help prevent child abductions. The passports are initially valid for five years, but can be renewed for a further five years at the end of this period.

Children included in their parents' passports when the new regulations came into force are not affected and can continue to travel on them until they reach the age of 16 or the passport expires or is amended.

COUNTERSIGNATURES

A countersignature is only needed if the application is for a first passport or to replace a lost, stolen or missing passport, though a countersignature is also needed for renewals if the applicant's appearance has significantly changed and the photograph in their previous passport is unrecognisable. The signatory must be willing to enter their own passport number on to the form. The list of acceptable countersignatories includes: MP; justice of the peace; minister of religion; a professionally qualified person (eg doctor, engineer, lawyer, teacher); bank officer; military officer; established civil servant; police officer; or a person of similar standing who has known the applicant for at least two years, and who is either a British citizen, British dependent territories citizen, British national (overseas), British overseas territories citizen, British subject or a citizen of a Commonwealth country. A relative or partner must not countersign the application.

If the application is for a child under the age of 16, the countersignature should be by someone of relevant standing who has known the parent or person with parental responsibility who signs the declaration of consent, rather than the child.

PHOTOGRAPHS

Two identical, unmounted, recent colour photographs of the applicant must be sent. These photographs should measure 45mm by 35mm, be printed on normal thin photographic paper and should be taken full face against a white background. The photo must show the applicant's full face, looking straight at the camera, with a neutral expression and with their mouth closed. The person who countersigns the application form should certify one photograph as a true likeness of the applicant.

DOCUMENTATION

The applicant's birth certificate or previous British passport, and other documents in support of the statements made in the application, must be produced at the time of applying. Details of which documents are required are set out in the notes accompanying the application form.

If the passport applicant is a British national by naturalisation or registration, the certificate proving this must be produced with the application, unless the applicant holds a previous British passport issued after registration or naturalisation.

INTERVIEWS

Interviews for adults applying for their first passport (not including those who held their own passport as a child) were introduced on 1 June 2007 to combat passport fraud and forgery. After applying for a passport, applicants will be sent a letter asking them to book an interview at one of the 68 offices in the UK. Interviews last for approximately 30 minutes and applicants are asked to confirm facts about themselves that someone attempting to steal their identity would not know. The IPS recommends that new applicants now allow six weeks to receive their passport and there is no one-week fast-track service for first adult passports.

48-PAGE PASSPORTS

The 48-page passport is intended to meet the needs of frequent travellers who fill standard passports well before the validity has expired. It is valid for ten years but is not available for children.

PASSPORT FEES*	
First adult passport	£72
First child passport	£46
Renewal or amendment of adult passport	£72
Renewal or amendment of child passport	£46
48-page passport	£85

* Standard postal applications only. A charge is added for applications made in person at a partner office in the UK, currently £7 for Check & Send at a post office.

HEALTH ADVICE

Health Advice for Travellers, published by the Department of Health, contains information on health precautions, reciprocal health agreements with other countries and immunisation. It is available online, from some travel agents, local post offices or the Department of Health, Richmond House, 79 Whitehall, London SW1A 2NS
T 020-7210 4850 E dhmail@dh.gsi.gov.uk
W www.dh.gov.uk/travellers

IMMUNISATION

In very general terms immunisation against typhoid, polio and hepatitis A should be considered for all countries with lower standards of hygiene and sanitation. Protection against malaria, in the form of tablets, as well as measures to avoid mosquito bites, is advised for visits to malarious areas.

Immunisation against yellow fever is compulsory for entry into some countries, either for all travellers or for those arriving from a yellow fever-infected area, and is recommended for all travellers to infected areas.

A doctor should be consulted, preferably at least eight weeks before departure, and will advise travellers and arrange vaccinations. Most doctors will charge a fee for a course of vaccinations. If children will be travelling outside Europe, North America, Australia and New Zealand, the doctor should be informed, especially if they have not completed their full course of childhood immunisation. As a precaution, it is also recommended that all travellers are up to date with their tetanus and diptheria inoculations.

Country-by-country guidance is set out on the website W www.fitfortravel.scot.nhs.uk. Healthcare professionals can obtain information about immunisation recommendations from the Department of Health publication *Health Information for Overseas Travel* or from:

HEALTH PROTECTION AGENCY, 7th Floor, Holborn Gate, 330 High Holborn, London WC1V 7PP
T 020-7759 2700 E webteam@hpa.org.uk W www.hpa.org.uk

SCOTTISH GOVERNMENT HEALTH DEPARTMENT, St Andrew's House, Edinburgh EH1 3DG
T 0131-556 8400 W www.scotland.gov.uk

HEALTH PROTECTION SCOTLAND, Clifton House, Clifton Place, Glasgow G3 7LN
T 0141-300 1100 E hpsenquiries@hps.scot.nhs.uk
W www.hps.scot.nhs.uk

DEPARTMENT OF HEALTH, SOCIAL SERVICES AND PUBLIC SAFETY, Castle Buildings, Stormont, Belfast BT4 3SJ
T 028-9052 0500 E webmaster@dhsspsni.gov.uk
W www.dhsspsni.gov.uk

NATIONAL TRAVEL HEALTH NETWORK AND CENTRE (NaTHNaC), Hospital for Tropical Diseases, Mortimer Market Centre, Capper Street, London WC1E 6JB
T 0845-155 8000
W www.nathnac.org/travel

MEDICAL TREATMENT ABROAD

Details of free or reduced cost emergency medical treatment when visiting European countries, and countries with which the UK has reciprocal health arrangements, are set out in *Health Advice for Travellers* and on the DOH website (W www.dh.gov.uk/travellers). They also contain guidance on applying for the European Health Insurance Card (EHIC), which was introduced in September 2005 as a replacement for the E111 form. EHIC entitles people to urgent medical treatment in the European Economic Area (EEA) and Switzerland. The booklet and website also explain changes to entitlement and the claims process.

For countries where the UK has no healthcare agreements, including Canada, the USA, India, the Far East, Africa and Latin America, it is advisable to take out medical insurance. A certain amount of insurance is also needed in countries with which the UK has healthcare agreements.

VISA REQUIREMENTS

The countries listed below require British citizens to hold a valid visa before arrival. The list only includes countries with diplomatic representation in the UK (*see* Countries of the World section for other foreign embassy contact details). It is advisable to check specific visa requirements with the appropriate embassy before making final travel arrangements.

Afghanistan, Algeria, Angola, Armenia, Australia, Azerbaijan, Bangladesh, Belarus, Benin, Burkina Faso, Cambodia, Cameroon, Cape Verde, Central African Republic, Chad, China, Dem. Rep. of Congo, Rep. of Congo, Côte d'Ivoire, Cuba, Djibouti, Egypt, Equatorial Guinea, Eritrea, Ethiopia, Gabon, Ghana, Guinea, Guinea-Bissau, India, Indonesia, Iran, Iraq, Kazakhstan, Dem. People's Republic of Korea, Kyrgyzstan, Laos, Liberia, Libya, Mali, Mauritania, Mongolia, Mozambique, Myanmar, Nauru, Nepal, Niger, Nigeria, Pakistan, Russian Federation, Sao Tome and Príncipe, Saudi Arabia, Sierra Leone, Somalia, Sudan, Suriname, Syria, Tajikistan, Tanzania, Togo, Turkmenistan, Uganda, Uzbekistan, Venezuela (only for entry over land or by sea), Vietnam, Yemen, Zambia, Zimbabwe.

Residents of the following countries must hold a valid visa for every entry to the UK:

Afghanistan, Albania, Algeria, Angola, Armenia, Azerbaijan, Bahrain, Bangladesh, Belarus, Benin, Bhutan, Burkina Faso, Burundi, Cambodia, Cameroon, Cape Verde, Central African Republic, Chad, China, Colombia, Comoros, Dem. Rep. of Congo, Rep. of Congo, Côte d'Ivoire, Cuba, Djibouti, Dominican Republic, Egypt, Equatorial Guinea, Eritrea, Ethiopia, Fiji, Gabon, Gambia, Georgia, Ghana, Guinea, Guinea-Bissau, Guyana, Haiti, India, Indonesia, Iran, Iraq, Jamaica, Jordan, Kazakhstan, Kenya, Dem. People's Republic of Korea, Kuwait, Kyrgyzstan, Laos, Lebanon, Liberia, Libya, Macedonia, Madagascar, Malawi, Mali, Mauritania, Moldova, Mongolia, Montenegro, Morocco, Mozambique, Myanmar, Nepal, Niger, Nigeria, Oman, Pakistan, Peru, Philippines, Qatar, Russian Federation, Rwanda, Sao Tome and Príncipe, Saudi Arabia, Senegal, Serbia, Sierra Leone, Somalia, Sri Lanka, Sudan, Suriname, Syria, Taiwan, Tajikistan, Tanzania, Thailand, Togo, Tunisia, Turkey, Turkmenistan, Uganda, Ukraine, United Arab Emirates, Uzbekistan, Vietnam, Yemen, Zambia, Zimbabwe.

BAGGAGE RESTRICTIONS

The maximum size for items of hand luggage is 56cm × 45cm × 35cm per bag, including wheels, handles and external pockets. From 7 January 2008, the airports below allow passengers to take more than one item into the aircraft cabin. Other airports in the UK still have a one bag restriction in place, and individual airlines may operate their own policies.

Passengers are allowed to carry small amounts of liquids as cabin baggage. These must be in containers not greater then 100ml, and placed in a single, transparent resealable bag which must not exceed one litre in capacity. Liquids are classified as drinks, make-up such as mascara or lipstick, sprays, pastes and gels. Medicines that are larger than 100ml must be accompanied by relevant documentation, such as a doctor's letter, and passengers may be asked to taste liquid medicines or test them on the skin. Liquid baby food or milk can be taken on board but may have to be tasted by the adult. One lighter is permitted as cabin baggage; this must be carried in the clear bag or separately for the duration of the flight and not placed in the main hand luggage bag.

Sharp items must not be carried in hand luggage; any essential items should be placed in a bag in the hold. Prohibited sharp items include knives, scissors, razor blades, cutlery, tools, hiking poles and hypodermic needles. Other prohibited items include party poppers, crackers and non-safety matches.

The amount passengers can check into the hold is determined by each airline. The airline will usually set a 'free baggage allowance' according to the number of items and the weight of each item; if this is exceeded there is normally an excess baggage charge. See W www.dft.gov.uk for more information on baggage restrictions.

THE EUROPEAN UNION

MEMBER STATE	ACCESSION DATE	POPULATION (2007)	COUNCIL VOTES	EP SEATS
Austria	1 Jan 1995	8,298,923	10	18
Belgium	1 Jan 1958	10,584,534	12	24
Bulgaria	1 Jan 2007	7,679,290	10	18
Cyprus	1 May 2004	778,537	4	6
Czech Republic	1 May 2004	10,287,189	12	24
Denmark	1 Jan 1973	5,447,084	7	14
Estonia	1 May 2004	1,342,409	4	6
Finland	1 Jan 1995	5,276,955	7	14
France	1 Jan 1958	63,392,140	29	78
Germany	1 Jan 1958	82,310,995	29	99
Greece	1 Jan 1981	11,170,957	12	24
Hungary	1 May 2004	10,066,158	12	24
Ireland	1 Jan 1973	4,314,634	7	13
Italy	1 Jan 1958	59,131,287	29	78
Latvia	1 May 2004	2,281,305	4	9
Lithuania	1 May 2004	3,384,879	7	13
Luxembourg	1 Jan 1958	476,187	4	6
Malta	1 May 2004	406,020	3	5
The Netherlands	1 Jan 1958	16,357,992	13	27
Poland	1 May 2004	38,125,479	27	54
Portugal	1 Jan 1986	10,599,095	12	24
Romania	1 Jan 2007	21,565,119	14	35
Slovakia	1 May 2004	5,393,637	7	14
Slovenia	1 May 2004	2,010,377	4	7
Spain	1 Jan 1986	44,474,631	27	54
Sweden	1 Jan 1995	9,113,257	10	19
UK	1 Jan 1973	60,798,438	29	78

Source: Eurostat

CHRONOLOGY

1950 Robert Schuman (French foreign minister) proposes that France and West Germany pool their coal and steel industries under a supranational authority (Schuman Plan)
1951 Paris treaty, signed by France, West Germany, Belgium, Italy, Luxembourg and the Netherlands, establishes the European Coal and Steel Community (ECSC)
1952 ECSC treaty enters into force
1957 Treaty of Rome, signed by the six ECSC member countries, establishes the European Economic Community (EEC) and the European Atomic Energy Authority (EURATOM). Treaty aims to create a customs union; remove obstacles to free movement of capital, goods, people and services; establish common external trade policy and common agricultural and fisheries policies; coordinate economic policies; harmonise social policies; promote cooperation in nuclear research
1958 EEC and EURATOM begin operation. Joint parliament and Court of Justice established for all three communities, and the Commission, Council of Ministers, Economic and Social Committee and Investment Bank for the EEC established
1962 Common Agricultural Policy (CAP) agreed
1967 EEC, ECSC and EURATOM merge to form the European Communities (EC), with a single Council of Ministers and Commission
1968 EEC customs union completed
Implementation of CAP completed
1974 Regular heads of governments summits begin
1975 'Own resources' funding of EC budget introduced
UK renegotiates its terms of accession
European Regional Development Fund created
1979 European Monetary System (EMS) comes into operation
First direct elections to European Parliament
1984 Fontainebleau summit settles UK annual budget rebate and agrees first major CAP reform
1986 Single European Act (SEA) signed
European Political Cooperation (EPC) established
1988 Second major CAP reform
1991 Maastricht treaty agreed
1992 Single internal market programme completed
1993 The exchange rate mechanism (ERM) of the EMS effectively suspended
Maastricht treaty enters into force, establishing the European Union (EU)
1994 European Economic Area (EEA) agreement comes into operation
Norway rejects EU membership in referendum
1997 Amsterdam treaty agreed
1998 11 states chosen to enter first round of European Monetary Union (EMU)
1999 Euro launched
Amsterdam treaty enters into force
2000 Treaty of Nice agreed
ECSC treaty expires following transfer of coal and steel sectors to the treaty of Rome
2004 Cyprus, Czech Republic, Estonia, Hungary, Latvia, Lithuania, Malta, Poland, Slovakia and Slovenia become members of the EU
The European constitution is signed in Rome
2005 France and the Netherlands reject the European constitution
2007 Bulgaria and Romania become members of the EU. The EU celebrates its 50th birthday.
EU leaders agree on a new reform treaty to replace the constitution of 2004, later named the treaty of Lisbon. At the time of going to press, the treaty was expected to be ratified by the end of 2008 and in force by 1 January 2009

LEGISLATIVE PROCESS

The core of the EU policy-making process is a dialogue between the European Commission, which initiates and implements policy, and the Council of Ministers, which takes policy decisions. An increasing degree of democratic control is exercised by the European Parliament.

The original legislative process is known as the consultative procedure. The commission drafts a proposal which it submits to the council and to the parliament. The council then consults the Economic and Social Committee (ESC), the parliament and the Committee of the Regions; the parliament may request that amendments are made. With or without these amendments, the proposal is then adopted by the council and becomes law.

Under the Single European Act (SEA), the role of the parliament was strengthened by the introduction of the cooperation procedure. The parliament now has a second reading of proposals in some fields, and after this reading its rejection of a proposal can only be overturned by a unanimous decision of the council. The Maastricht treaty extended the scope of the cooperation procedure, which was applied to single market laws and harmonisation, trans-European networks, development policy, the social fund, and some aspects of transport, environment, research, social policy and competition policy.

The SEA introduced the assent procedure, whereby an absolute majority of the parliament must vote to approve laws in certain fields before they are passed. Issues covered by the assent procedure include foreign treaties, accession treaties, international agreements with budgetary implications, citizenship, residence rights, the CAP, and regional and structural funds.

The Maastricht treaty introduced the co-decision procedure; if, after the parliament's second reading of a proposal, the council and parliament fail to agree, a conciliation committee of the two will reach a compromise. If a compromise is not reached, the parliament can reject the legislation by the vote of an absolute majority of its members. The Amsterdam treaty extended the co-decision procedure to all areas covered by qualified majority voting, with the exception of measures related to European Monetary Union (EMU).

The council issues the following legislation:

- regulations, which are binding in their entirety and directly applicable to all member states; they do not need to be incorporated into national law to come into effect
- directives, which are less specific, binding as to the result to be achieved but leaving the method of implementation open to member states; a directive thus has no force until it is incorporated into national law
- decisions, which are also binding but are addressed solely to one or more member states or individuals in a member state
- recommendations
- opinions, which are merely persuasive

The council also has certain budgetary powers, including the power to reject the budget as a whole and to increase expenditure or redistribute money within sectors. However, the final decision on whether the budget should be adopted or rejected lies with the parliament.

The council may delegate legislative powers to the commission. These consist of implementing powers and technical updating of existing legislation.

The European Central Bank has legislative powers within its field of competence. The commission also has limited legislative powers, where it has been delegated the power to implement or revise legislation by the council.

EUROPEAN CONSTITUTION AND TREATY OF LISBON

The European constitution was established in 2004, and was intended to replace all earlier treaties with a single text designed to suit the needs of an expanded European Union. However, the constitution was abandoned in 2005 after it was rejected in referendums in France and the Netherlands.

After a period of reflection, the treaty of Lisbon was drawn up to replace the European constitution and was signed by leaders of the 27 EU member states in December 2007. It amends, rather than replaces, the existing treaties. As with the constitution, governments of EU member states must ratify the treaty of Lisbon before it can enter into force, scheduled for 1 January 2009. Ireland, the only country to hold a referendum on the treaty, voted against ratification on 12 June 2008. At the time of going to press, all other countries were continuing with the ratification process and 19 member states had endorsed the treaty.

The treaty of Lisbon contains many of the changes that the constitution attempted to introduce; for example, a politician will be chosen as president of the European Council for a 2.5 year term, replacing the current system whereby the presidency rotates between countries every six months. In addition, a new post (high representative of the Union for foreign affairs and security policy) will be created in order to strengthen coherence in external action and raise the EU's profile on the world stage; from 2014, a smaller European Commission will be introduced, with fewer commissioners than there are member states; a limit of 751 members in the European Parliament; the introduction of qualified majority voting in the Council of Ministers; and the removal of national vetoes in a number of areas.

RECENT LEGISLATION

MAASTRICHT TREATY

Agreed in Maastricht, the Netherlands, in 1991, the treaty came into effect in November 1993 following ratification by the member states. Three pillars formed its basis:

- the European Community (removing Economic from its name) with its established institutions and decision-making processes
- a common foreign and security policy (*see* below) with the Western European Union as the potential defence component of the EU
- cooperation in justice and home affairs, with the Council of Ministers coordinating policies on asylum, immigration, conditions of entry, cross-border crime, drug trafficking and terrorism

The treaty established a common European citizenship for nationals of all member states and introduced the principle of subsidiarity, whereby decisions are taken at the most appropriate level (national, regional or local). It extended EC competency into the areas of environmental and industrial policies, consumer affairs, health, and education and training, and extended qualified majority voting in the Council of Ministers to some areas which had previously required a unanimous vote. The powers of the European Parliament over the budget and over the European Commission were also enhanced, and a co-decision procedure enabled the parliament to override decisions made by the council in certain policy areas. A separate protocol to the Maastricht treaty on social policy was agreed by 11 states and was incorporated into the Amsterdam treaty in 1997 following adoption by the UK.

COMMON FOREIGN AND SECURITY POLICY

The common foreign and security policy (CFSP) was created as a pillar of the EU by the Maastricht treaty (*see* above). It adopted the machinery of the European political cooperation framework, which it replaced, and was charged with providing a forum for member states and EU institutions to consult on foreign affairs.

The CFSP system is headed by the Council of the European Union, which provides general lines of policy. Specific policy decisions are taken by the Council of Foreign Ministers, which meets at least four times a year to determine areas for joint action. The high representative of the CFSP initiates action, manages the CFSP and represents it abroad. The Council of Ministers is supported by the Political Committee, which meets monthly, or within 48 hours if there is a crisis, to prepare for ministerial discussions. A group of correspondents, designated diplomats in each member's foreign ministry, provides day-to-day contact.

As part of the CFSP the EU also created a European security and defence policy (ESDP) with the potential, if agreed later on, for creating a common defence structure. In the recent past, ESDP missions have been deployed in the former Yugoslavia, Lebanon and the Democratic Republic of Congo. The member states agreed at the Helsinki summit in 1999 to establish a capability for military crisis-management operations, known as the rapid reaction force, which would have a credible intervention capability and be able to undertake peacemaking missions independently of NATO. The force was declared operational at the Laeken summit in 2001.

The Amsterdam treaty introduced qualified majority voting for foreign affairs and created a high representative on CFSP to act as a spokesperson. It also established a new planning and early warning unit to monitor international developments and provide the opportunity for the EU to react to these developments with a cohesive response. The unit consists of specialists from the member states, the council and the commission, as well as from the Western European Union (WEU).

SCHENGEN AGREEMENT

The Schengen agreement was signed by France, Germany, Belgium, Luxembourg and the Netherlands in 1985. The agreement committed the five states to abolishing internal border controls, erecting external frontiers against illegal immigrants, drug traffickers, terrorists and organised crime, and implementing the Schengen Information System to enable police stations and consular agents from Schengen member states to access data on specific individuals or vehicles and objects which are lost or stolen.

Subsequently signed by Spain and Portugal, the

agreement was ratified by the seven signatory states and entered into force in March 1995 with the removal of internal frontier, passport, customs and immigration controls. Provisional agreement was reached in 1995 between the signatory states and the Nordic Union on a merger of the two frontier-free zones – Denmark, Finland and Sweden in 1996 and Iceland and Norway in 2001. Italy and Austria became full members of the agreement in 1998; Greece in 2000; and the Czech Republic, Estonia, Hungary, Lithuania, Latvia, Malta, Poland, Slovakia and Slovenia in 2007. The UK and the Republic of Ireland have not signed the agreement and are only partial participants, since their border controls have been maintained. At the time of going to press, Switzerland was expected to gain full membership imminently but there is no date set for Cyprus, Bulgaria or Romania to join.

The Schengen agreement originated as an intergovernmental agreement but became part of the EU following the signing of the Amsterdam treaty. A second generation Schengen Information System (SIS II), which will cater for the newest member states, is under development, but with delays due to legal and technical problems.

AMSTERDAM TREATY

The treaties of Rome and Maastricht were amended through the Amsterdam treaty, which was signed in 1997 and came into effect on 1 May 1999. It extended the scope of qualified majority voting and the powers of the European parliament. It also included a formal commitment to fundamental human rights, gave additional powers to the European Court of Justice and provided for the reform of the CFSP.

ENLARGEMENT AND EXTERNAL RELATIONS

The procedure for accession to the EU is laid down in the treaty of Rome; states must be stable European democracies governed by the rule of law with free-market economies. A membership application is studied by the European Commission, which produces an 'opinion'. If the opinion is positive, negotiations may be opened leading to an accession treaty that must be approved by all member state governments and parliaments, the European Parliament, and the applicant state's government and parliament.

Cyprus, the Czech Republic, Estonia, Hungary, Latvia, Lithuania, Malta, Poland, Slovakia and Slovenia became full members of the EU on 1 May 2004. Bulgaria and Romania joined the EU on 1 January 2007. The European Council recalled the offer of an accession partnership to Turkey in 2002, following the commission's conclusion that Turkey did not yet fully meet the required political criteria. However, at its December 2004 meeting in Brussels, the council decided that Turkey sufficiently met the Copenhagen political criteria, and accession negotiations began in October 2005. Accession talks with Croatia, originally due to start in March 2005 but postponed due to the lack of full cooperation with the UN war crimes tribunal, began in October 2005. Macedonia was granted candidate status in December 2005.

The EU has several types of agreements with other European and non-European states. Association agreements include a commitment to EU financial aid and to eventual membership; such an agreement has been signed with Turkey (1963). Partnership and cooperation agreements (PCAs) are legal frameworks, based on the respect of democratic principles and human rights, setting out the political, economic and trade relationship between the EU and its partner countries. Each PCA is a ten-year bilateral treaty signed and ratified by the EU and the individual state. Agreements have been implemented with Russia (1997), Ukraine and Moldova (1998), Armenia, Azerbaijan, Georgia, Kazakhstan, Kyrgyzstan and Uzbekistan (1999). PCAs have also been signed with Belarus (1995), Turkmenistan (1998) and Tajikistan (2004) but are not yet in force. In 2003 the PCA council summit decreed to strengthen EU cooperation with the Russian Federation by establishing a permanent partnership council (PPC). At the council's first meeting in April 2004 a protocol was signed, extending the PCA with the Russian Federation to the ten new member states of the EU; the agreement currently in place also covers Romania and Bulgaria. A trade and cooperation agreement with Mongolia entered into force in 1993, intended to foster trade and economic relations; the agreement also included a commitment to protect human rights. The European neighbourhood policy was developed in 2004 and applies to the enlarged EU's immediate neighbours. It aims to strengthen stability and security through economic integration and deeper political relationships based on a mutual commitment to common values (democracy, human rights, rule of law, good governance and market economy).

A stabilisation and association agreement (SAA) – which is tailored towards the western Balkan states and is similar to the earlier Europe agreements held with previous candidate countries, in that it provides the contractual framework for relations that will lead to accession to the EU – entered into force with Montenegro in March 2007, Croatia in February 2005, and with Macedonia in April 2004. SAA negotiations were launched with Bosnia and Hercegovina in November 2005, Serbia in October 2005, and Kosovo in November 2006; the SAA with Albania was signed in June 2006 and will enter into force following its ratification.

TREATY OF NICE

The treaty of Nice was signed in 2001 and came into effect in 2003. It aims to enable the EU to accommodate up to 13 new member states, and extends qualified majority voting to 30 further articles of the treaties that previously required unanimity. The weighting of votes in the EU Council was altered from 1 January 2005 in preparation for the new member states. To obtain a qualified majority, a decision requires a specified number of votes (to be reviewed following each accession); the decision has to be approved by a majority of member states and represent at least 62 per cent of the total population of the EU. The treaty also set the number of MEPs that both existing and new member states would have following enlargement.

The Maastricht treaty established the right of groups of member states to work together without requiring the participation of all members (enhanced cooperation); the treaty of Nice removes the right of individual member states to veto the launch of enhanced cooperation.

The European Commission has been limited to one member per member state since 2005, with a maximum of 27 commissioners; a rotation system is to be introduced once EU membership exceeds 27 states. The treaty also adds to the powers of the president of the commission and amends the rules of operation of the Court of Justice.

ECONOMY

COMMUNITY BUDGET

The principles of funding the European Community budget were established by the treaty of Rome and remain, with modifications, to this day. There is a legally binding limit on the overall level of resources (known as 'own resources') that the community can raise from its member states; this limit is defined as a percentage of gross national product (GNP). Budget revenue and expenditure must balance, and there is therefore no deficit financing. The 'own resources' decision, which came into effect in 1975 and has been regularly updated, states that there are four sources of community funding under which each member state makes contributions: levies charged on agricultural imports into the community from non-member states; customs duties on imports from non-member states; contributions based on member states' shares of a notional community-harmonised VAT base; and contributions based on member states' shares of community GNP. The latter is the budget-balancing item and covers the difference between total expenditure and the revenue from the other three sources.

The framework budget for 2007–13 (formally known as the Financial Perspective) was completed at the end of the UK's presidency of the EU in December 2005. A figure of €862.36bn (£682.21bn) was agreed, which is equal to 1.045 per cent of the EU's combined gross national income.

From 1984 up until 2005, the UK had received an annual rebate equivalent to 66 per cent of the difference between UK contributions to the budget and its receipts. This was introduced to compensate the UK for disproportionate contributions caused by its high share of agricultural and non-agricultural imports from non-member states and its relatively small receipts from the Common Agricultural Policy, the most important portion of community expenditure. Before the budget for 2007–13 was finalised, the UK conceded €10.5bn (£8.3bn) (approximately 20 per cent) of its rebate over the six-year period, in return for a wide-ranging review of EU spending, due to be held in 2008–9.

BUDGET 2008

	*Billion euro**
Sustainable growth	58.0
Natural resources	55.0
Global activities	7.3
Freedom, security and justice	0.7
Citizenship	0.6
Administration	7.3
Compensations to new EU countries	0.2
Total	129.1

Source: Office for Official Publications of the European Communities

* 1 euro = £0.79 as at 9 May 2008

SINGLE MARKET

Even after the removal of tariffs and quotas between member states in the 1970s and 1980s, the EC was still separated into a number of national markets by a series of non-tariff barriers. It was to overcome these internal barriers to trade that the concept of the single market was developed. The measures to be undertaken were codified in the commission's 1985 white paper on completing the internal market.

The white paper included articles removing obstacles distorting the internal market: the elimination of frontier controls; the mutual recognition of professional qualifications; the harmonisation of product specifications, largely by the mutual recognition of national standards; open tendering for public procurement contracts; the free movement of capital; the harmonisation of VAT and excise duties; and the reduction of state aid to particular industries. The Single European Act (SEA) aided the completion of the single market by changing the legislative process within the EC, particularly with the introduction of qualified majority voting in the Council of Ministers for some policy areas, and the introduction of the assent procedure in the European parliament. The SEA also extends EC competence into the fields of technology, the environment, regional policy, monetary policy and external policy. The single market came into effect on 1 January 1993, though full implementation of the elimination of frontier controls and the harmonisation of taxes have been repeatedly delayed. A fundamental review of the single market was completed in 2007, which resulted in an operational set of initiatives intended to modernise single market policy.

EUROPEAN ECONOMIC AREA

The EC single market programme spurred European non-member states to open negotiations with the EC on preferential access for their goods, services, labour and capital to the single market. Principal among these states were European Free Trade Association (EFTA) members who opened negotiations on extending the single market to EFTA by the formation of the European Economic Area (EEA), encompassing all 19 EC and EFTA states. Agreement was reached in 1992, but the operation of the EEA was delayed by its rejection in a Swiss referendum, necessitating an additional protocol agreed by the remaining 18 states. The EEA came into effect in 1994 after ratification by 17 member states (Liechtenstein joined in 1995 after adapting its customs union with Switzerland).

Austria, Finland and Sweden joined the EU on 1 January 1995, leaving only Norway, Iceland and Liechtenstein as the non-EU EEA members. Under the EEA agreement, the three states are to adopt the EU's *acquis communautaire,* apart from in the fields of agriculture, fisheries, and coal and steel.

The EEA is controlled by regular ministerial meetings and by a joint EU-EFTA committee which extends relevant EU legislation to EEA states. Apart from single market measures, there is cooperation in several areas, including education, civil protection, research and development, consumer policy and tourism. An EFTA Court of Justice has been established in Luxembourg and an EFTA surveillance authority in Brussels to supervise the implementation of the EEA Agreement.

The EEA Enlargement Agreement came into force on 1 May 2004, which allowed the simultaneous expansion of both the EU and the EEA without disruption of the internal market. A similar process took place to ensure that Bulgaria and Romania could become contracting parties to the EEA upon joining the EU in 2007.

EUROPEAN MONETARY SYSTEM AND THE SINGLE CURRENCY

The European Monetary System (EMS) began operation in March 1979 with three main purposes. The first was to establish monetary stability in Europe, initially in exchange rates between EC member state currencies through the Exchange Rate Mechanism (ERM), and in the longer term to be part of a wider stabilisation process, overcoming inflation and budget and trade deficits. The second purpose was to overcome the constraints resulting from the interdependence of EC economies, and the third was to aid the long-term process of European monetary integration.

The Maastricht treaty set in motion timetables for achieving economic and monetary union (EMU) and a single currency (the euro). At the Brussels summit in May 1998, 11 member states were judged to fulfil or be close to fulfilling the necessary convergence criteria for participation in the first stage of EMU: Austria, Belgium, Finland, France, Germany, Ireland, Italy, Luxembourg, the Netherlands, Portugal and Spain. The criteria were:

- the budget deficit should be 3 per cent or less of gross domestic product (GDP)
- total national debt must not exceed 60 per cent of GDP
- inflation should be no more than 1.5 per cent above the average rate of the three best performing economies in the EU
- long-term interest rates should be no more than 2 per cent above the average of the three best performing economies in the EU in the previous 12 months
- applicants must have been members of the ERM for two years without having realigned or devalued their currency

Under the terms of a stability and growth pact agreed in Dublin in December 1996, penalties may be imposed on EMU members with high budget deficits. Governments with deficits exceeding 3 per cent of GDP will receive a warning and will be obliged to pay up to 0.5 per cent of their GDP into a fund after ten months. This will become a fine if the budget deficit is not rectified within two years. A member state with negative growth will be allowed to apply for an exemption from the fine in 'exceptional circumstances', eg a recession whereby GDP had fallen by 0.75 per cent or more during one year.

On 1 January 1999 the qualifying member states adopted the euro at irrevocably fixed exchange rates, the European Central Bank (ECB) took charge of the single monetary policy, and the euro replaced the ecu on a one-for-one basis.

In 2000 Greece was judged to have fulfilled the criteria for participation and adopted the euro on 1 January 2001. Referendums on the adoption of the euro have been held in Denmark and Sweden, but participation was rejected. In June 2003 Britain announced that the euro would not be adopted at present on the grounds that the country was not economically ready to join the single currency, though a future joining of the eurozone was not ruled out.

The euro is now the legal currency in the participating states. Notes and coins were introduced on 1 January 2002 and circulated alongside national currencies for a period of up to two months, after which time national notes and coins ceased to be legal tender. The new EU member states are expected to adopt the euro when the necessary economic conditions have been met; Slovenia joined the eurozone on 1 January 2007, Cyprus and Malta on 1 January 2008, and at the time of going to press, Slovakia was due to join on 1 January 2009.

The ECB meets twice a month to set the following month's monetary policy applicable to the countries participating in the euro. Its governing council has 21 members, being the six members of the ECB's executive board and the 15 governors of the national central banks of the participating states.

COMMON AGRICULTURAL POLICY

The Common Agricultural Policy (CAP) was established to increase agricultural production, provide a fair standard of living for farmers and ensure the availability of food at reasonable prices. This aim was achieved by a number of mechanisms, including import levies, intervention purchase and export subsidies.

These measures stimulated production but also placed increasing demands on the EC budget, which were exacerbated by the increase in EC members and yields enlarged by technological innovation; CAP now accounts for over 40 per cent of EC expenditure. To surmount these problems reforms were agreed in 1984, 1988, 1992, 1997, 1999 and 2003.

REFORMS

The 1984 reforms created the system of co-responsibility levies: farm payments to the EC by volume of product sold. This system was supplemented by national quotas for particular products, such as milk. The 1988 reforms emphasised 'set-aside', whereby farmers are given direct grants to take land out of production as a means of reducing surpluses. The set-aside reforms were extended in 1993 for another five years and to every farm in the EC. The 1999 reforms further reduced surpluses of cereals, beef and milk by cutting the intervention prices by up to 20 per cent and compensating producers by making area payments. Under the reforms, CAP rules were also simplified, eliminating inconsistencies between policies.

In June 2003, EU farm ministers adopted a fundamental reform of the CAP, which included the following provisions:

- a single farm payment for EU farmers, independent of production
- payment to be linked to the respect of environmental, food safety, animal and plant health and animal welfare standards, and the requirement to keep all farmland in good condition
- a strengthened rural development policy with more EU money to help farmers meet EU production standards (begun in 2005)
- a reduction in direct payments for bigger farms
- a mechanism for financial discipline to ensure that the farm budget fixed until 2013 is not exceeded

The single farm payment entered into force in 2005. The ten EU members that joined in 2004 were also given access to a special €5.8bn (£3.9bn) three-year funding package. The 2007–13 EU budget stipulated that no extra money would be made available to pay farm subsidies to Romania and Bulgaria.

A CAP 'health check' was carried out in 2008 and resulted in a set of proposals intended to further modernise and streamline EU agricultural policy, and to allow farmers to follow market signals by breaking the link between direct payments and production. These include abolishing the requirement for farmers to leave ten per cent of their arable land fallow; a gradual increase in milk quotas before their abolition in 2015 and a general reduction in market intervention.

THE UK AND THE EU IN 2008

- The constitution and treaty of Lisbon: Prime Minister Gordon Brown ruled out a public vote on the treaty of Lisbon (the successor to the rejected European

constitution), stating that it did not alter the UK constitution. At the time of going to press, the bill to ratify the treaty was being passed through the House of Lords.
- Immigration: findings released by the Institute for Public Policy Research showed that around half of the migrants from Eastern Europe that arrived in the UK after the EU expansion in 2004 (one million) have already returned to their home countries.
- Metric and imperial measurements: the EC's industry commissioner ruled in May 2007 that EU plans to enforce metrication by 2009 had been shelved; imperial weights and measures can be displayed indefinitely alongside metric measurements.
- The environment: the UK is committed to targets agreed by the EU in March 2007 to cut greenhouse gas emissions by 20 per cent by 2020 (compared to 1990 levels) and to generate 20 per cent of energy from renewable sources by 2020. (*see also* Environment)
- The UK's rebate: in April 2007 the Treasury began implementing the reduction in the UK's rebate from the EU budget that was agreed in December 2005, comprising a 20 per cent concession of the rebate (approximately €10.5bn (£7.1bn)) over a six-year period.

INSTITUTIONS

EUROPEAN PARLIAMENT

E eplondon@europarl.europa.eu W www.europarl.europa.eu

The European parliament (EP) originated as the common assembly of the ECSC, acquiring its present name in 1962. The parliament now comprises 785 seats. Members (MEPs), initially appointed from the membership of national parliaments, have been directly elected at five-year intervals since 1979. Elections to the parliament are held on differing bases throughout the EC; British MPs have been elected by a regional list system of proportional representation since June 1999. The most recent elections were held in June 2004, and the next elections are due to be held in June 2009.

MEPs serve on committees which scrutinise draft EC legislation and the activities of the European Commission. A minimum of 12 plenary sessions a year are held in Strasbourg and six additional shorter plenary sessions a year are held in Brussels; committees meet in Brussels, and the secretariat's headquarters is in Luxembourg.

The influence of the EP has gradually expanded within the EU since the Single European Act of 1985, which introduced the cooperation procedure; the Maastricht treaty, which extended the cooperation procedure and introduced the co-decision procedure (*see* Legislative Process); and the Amsterdam treaty, which effectively extended co-decision to all areas except economic and monetary union, and taxation. Parliament has general powers of supervision over the European Commission, and powers of consultation and co-decision with the Council of Ministers; it votes to approve a newly appointed commission and can dismiss it at any time by a two-thirds majority. Under the Maastricht treaty it has the right to be consulted on the appointment of the new commission, and can also veto its appointment. The EP can reject the EU budget as a whole, alter non-compulsory expenditure not specified in the EU primary legislation, and can question the commission's management of the budget and call in the court of auditors. Although the EP cannot directly initiate legislation, its reports can spur the commission into action. In accordance with the Maastricht treaty the EP appoints the European Ombudsman, to provide citizens with redress against maladministration by EU institutions.

The EP's organisation is deliberately biased in favour of multinational political groupings; recognition of a political grouping in the parliament entitles it to offices, funding, representation on committees and influence in debates and legislation. A political group must be comprised of a minimum of 19 MEPs elected in at least six member states. For a list of UK MEPs, *see* European Parliament section.

PARLIAMENT, Allée du Printemps, BP 1024/F, F-67070 Strasbourg Cedex, France
T (+33) (3) 8817 4001 F (+33) (3) 8817 5184
Wiertzstraat, Postbus 1047, B-1047 Brussels, Belgium
T (+32) (2) 284 2111 F (+32) (2) 284 6974

SECRETARIAT, Centre Européen, Plateau du Kirchberg, BP 1601, L-2929 Luxembourg
T (+352) 43001 F (+352) 4300 29393/29292
President, Hans-Gert Poettering (Germany)

OMBUDSMAN, 1 Avenue du Président Robert Schuman, CS 30403, F-67001, Strasbourg Cedex, France
E euro-ombudsman@europarl.europa.eu
W www.euro-ombudsman.europa.eu
Ombudsman, Nikiforos Diamandouros (Greece)

EUROPEAN PARLIAMENT UK OFFICE
2 Queen Anne's Gate, London SW1H 9AA
E eplondon@europarl.europa.eu W www.europarl.org.uk

EUROPEAN PARLIAMENT OFFICE IN SCOTLAND
The Tun, Holyrood Road, Edinburgh EH8 8PJ
E epedinburgh@europarl.europa.eu

COUNCIL OF THE EUROPEAN UNION

Rue de la Loi, 175 B-1048 Brussels, Belgium
W www.consilium.europa.eu

The Council of the European Union (Council of Ministers) is the main decision-making body of the European Union, and formally comprises the foreign ministers of the member states but in practice the ministers attending depend on the subject under discussion. It passes laws, usually legislating jointly with the European parliament; it coordinates the broad economic policies of the member states; it defines and implements the EU's common foreign and security policy; it concludes agreements between the EU and other states or international organisations; and it coordinates the actions of member states in the area of police and judicial cooperation. Council decisions are taken by qualified majority vote (in which members' votes are weighted), by a simple majority, or by unanimity.

Unanimity votes are taken on sensitive issues such as taxation and constitutional matters; in preparation for an expanded EU, the Amsterdam treaty extended areas where qualified majority votes may be taken, to areas such as single market laws and harmonisation, environment policy, health and safety, transport policy, overseas aid, research and development, culture, consumer protection, education and training, the development of a single currency and some aspects of social policy. Member states have weighted votes in the council loosely proportional to their relative population sizes (*see* introductory table), with a total of 345 votes. The acts of the council can take the form of regulations, directives, decisions, common actions or common positions, recommendations or opinions. The council can also adopt conclusions, declarations or resolutions. The number of votes each member state can cast is set by treaties. The treaties also define cases in which a simple majority, qualified majority or unanimity are required. A qualified majority will be reached if the following two conditions are met:

- a majority of member states approve (in some cases a two-thirds majority)
- a minimum of 255 votes is cast in favour of the proposal, ie 73.9 per cent of the total (roughly the same share as under the previous system)

In addition, a member state may ask for confirmation that the votes in favour represent at least 62 per cent of the total population of the EU. If this is found not to be the case, the decision will not be adopted.

The treaty of Nice agreed amendments to the treaties in relation to the size and composition of the European Commission, the weighting of votes and the extension of qualified majority voting in the Council of Ministers and other issues relating to the treaty of Amsterdam. The extension of qualified majority voting to external border controls, the EU budget, the composition of the European courts and certain committees, visa rules and structural funds, was also agreed.

The European Council, comprising the heads of state or government of the member states and the president of the European Commission, meets twice a year to provide overall policy direction. The presidency of the European Council is held in rotation for six-month periods, setting the agenda for and chairing all council meetings, and a summit is held in the country holding the presidency at the end of its period in office. The holders of the presidency for the years 2008–9 are:
2008 Jan–Jun, Slovenia
2008 Jul–Dec, France
2009 Jan–Jun, Czech Republic
2009 Jul–Dec, Sweden

GENERAL SECRETARIAT OF THE COUNCIL OF THE EUROPEAN UNION
Wetstraat 175, B-1048 Brussels, Belgium
W www.consilium.europa.eu
Secretary-General of the Council of the European Union and High Representative for the Common Foreign and Security Policy, Javier Solana (Spain)
Deputy Secretary-General of the Council of the European Union, Pierre de Boissieu (France)

OFFICE OF THE UNITED KINGDOM PERMANENT REPRESENTATIVE TO THE EUROPEAN UNION
Ave d'Auderghem 10, B-1040 Brussels, Belgium
E ukrep@fco.gov.uk
Ambassador and UK Permanent Representative, Kim Darroch, CMG, *apptd* 2007

EUROPEAN COMMISSION
Wetstraat 200, rue de la Loi, B-1049 Brussels, Belgium

The European Commission consists of 27 commissioners, one per member state. The members of the commission are appointed for five-year renewable terms by the agreement of the member states; the terms run concurrently with the terms of the European parliament. The president and the other commissioners are nominated by the governments of the member states, and, under the terms of the Nice treaty, the appointments are approved by the European parliament. The commissioners pledge sole allegiance to the EC. The commission initiates and implements EC legislation and is the guardian of the EC treaties. It is the exponent of community-wide interests rather than the national preoccupations of the council. Each commissioner is supported by advisers and oversees the departments assigned to them, known as directorates-general and services. Each directorate-general is headed by a director-general.

President José Manuel Barroso was nominated by the governments of the member states on 29 June 2004, and the European parliament confirmed his appointment with a secret ballot vote on 22 July 2004. He announced the finalised commission on 4 November 2004, which officially took office on 22 November.

The commission has a total staff of around 24,000 permanent civil servants.

COMMISSIONERS *as at May 2007*
President, José Manuel Barroso (Portugal)
Vice-President, Administrative Affairs, Audit and Anti-Fraud, Siim Kallas (Estonia)
Vice-President, Enterprise and Industry, Günter Verheugen (Germany)
Vice-President, Institutional Relations and Communication Strategy, Margot Wallstrom (Sweden)
Vice-President, Justice, Freedom and Security, Franco Frattini (Italy)
Vice-President, Transport, Jacques Barrot (France)
Agriculture and Rural Development, Mariann Fischer Boel (Denmark)
Competition, Neelie Kroes (Netherlands)
Consumer Protection, Meglena Kuneva (Bulgaria)
Development and Humanitarian Aid, Louis Michel (Belgium)
Economic and Monetary Affairs, Joaquin Almunia (Spain)
Education, Training, Culture and Youth, Jan Figel (Slovakia)
Employment, Social Affairs and Equal Opportunities, Vladimir Spidla (Czech Republic)
Energy, Andris Piebalgs (Latvia)
Enlargement, Olli Rehn (Finland)
Environment, Stavros Dimas (Greece)
External Relations and European Neighbourhood Policy, Benita Ferrero-Waldner (Austria)
Financial Programming and Budget, Dalia Grybauskaite (Lithuania)
Fisheries and Maritime Affairs, Joe Borg (Malta)
Health, Androula Vassiliou (Cyprus)
Information, Society and Media, Viviane Reding (Luxembourg)
Internal Market and Services, Charlie McCreevy (Ireland)
Multilingualism, Leonard Orban (Romania)
Regional Policy, Danuta Hübner (Poland)
Science and Research, Janez Potocnik (Slovenia)
Taxation and Customs Union, Laszlo Kovacs (Hungary)
Trade, Peter Mandelson (UK)

COURT OF JUSTICE OF THE EUROPEAN COMMUNITIES
Boulevard Konrad Adenauer, Kirchberg, L–2925 Luxembourg
W www.curia.europa.eu

The Court of Justice is common to the two European Communities. It exists to safeguard the law in the interpretation and application of the community treaties, to decide on the legality of decisions of the Council of Ministers or the European Commission, and to determine infringements of the treaties. Cases may be brought to it by the member states, the community institutions, firms or individuals. Its decisions are directly binding in the member countries, and the Maastricht treaty enhanced the court's powers by permitting it to impose fines on member states. The 27 judges and eight advocates-general of the court are appointed for renewable six-year terms by the member governments in concert. During 2007, 580 new cases were lodged at the court and 570 cases were concluded.

President, Vassilios Skouris (Greece)
First Advocate-General, Luis Miguel Poiares Pessoa Maduro (Portugal)

COURT OF FIRST INSTANCE

Palais de la Cour de Justice, Boulevard Konrad Adenauer, Kirchberg, L-2925 Luxembourg

Established under powers conferred by the Single European Act, the Court of First Instance has jurisdiction to hear and determine all actions brought by natural or legal persons, and all direct actions except those reserved for the court of justice. It is composed of 27 judges, appointed for renewable six-year terms by the governments of the member states. During 2007, 522 new cases were lodged at the court and 397 cases were concluded.

President, Marc Jaeger (Luxembourg)

EUROPEAN COURT OF AUDITORS

12 rue Alcide de Gasperi, L–1615 Luxembourg
E euraud@eca.europa.eu W www.eca.europa.eu

The European Court of Auditors, established in 1977, examines the accounts of all revenue and expenditure of the European Communities and community bodies. It evaluates whether all revenue has been received and all expenditure incurred in a lawful and regular manner and in accordance with the principles of sound financial management. The court issues an annual report and a statement of assurance as to the reliability of the accounts and the legality and regularity of the underlying transactions. It also publishes special reports on specific topics and delivers opinions on financial matters. The court has one member from each member state appointed for a six-year term by the Council of Ministers following consultation with the European parliament.

President, Vitor Caldeira (Portugal)

FINANCIAL BODIES

EUROPEAN CENTRAL BANK

Kaiserstrasse 29, D-60311 Frankfurt am Main, Germany
E info@ecb.int W www.ecb.int

The European Central Bank (ECB), which superseded the European Monetary Institute, became fully operational on 1 January 1999 and defines and implements the single monetary policy for the euro area. The ECB's main task is to maintain the euro's purchasing power and price stability in the 15 EU countries that have introduced the currency since 1999. Its governing bodies are the executive board, the governing council and the general council. The executive board consists of the president, the vice-president and four other members. All members are appointed by the governments of the states participating in the single currency, at the level of heads of state and government. The governing council, the main decision-making body of the ECB, comprises the six members of the executive board and the governors of the national central banks of the 15 euro area states. The general council comprises the president and vice-president and the 27 governors of the national central banks, the other members of the executive board being entitled to participate but not to vote. The ECB is independent of national governments and of all other EU institutions.

President, Jean-Claude Trichet (France)
Vice-President, Lucas Papademos (Greece)

EUROPEAN INVESTMENT BANK

100 Boulevard Konrad Adenauer, L-2950 Luxembourg
E info@eib.org W www.eib.org

The European Investment Bank (EIB) was set up in 1958 under the terms of the treaty of Rome and is the financing arm of the European Union. The EIB's main activity is to provide long-term loans in support of investments undertaken by private or public promoters, for projects furthering European integration. Six key operational areas have been set out in the bank's corporate operational plan for 2008–2010: cohesion and convergence; development of trans-European networks of transport and energy; environmental protection and sustainable communities; implementation of the Innovation 2010 initiative; support for small and medium-sized enterprises; and sustainable, competitive and secure energy.

The EIB also operates outside the EU, in support of EU development and cooperation policies in partner countries including the enlargement area of Europe (both candidate and potential candidate countries), the Mediterranean, Russia and the Southern Caucasus, Africa, the Caribbean and the Pacific, Asia and Latin America.

The EIB assesses and selects the projects it finances independently and never finances over 50 per cent of the total cost of a project. Each EIB-financed project must be financially, technically and environmentally viable.

The bank is not dependent on the EU budget, and raises its own resources on the capital markets. It is the biggest supranational bond issuer and lender in the world with an AAA credit rating. In 2007 it borrowed €55bn and lent a total of €47.8bn, of which €41bn was lent within the EU.

The shareholders of the EIB are the 27 member states, whose ministers of economy and finance constitute its board of governors. This body lays down general directives on the credit policy of the bank and appoints members to the board of directors. The board of directors consists of 27 members nominated by the member states, and one by the European Commission. It takes decisions on the granting and raising of loans and the fixing of interest rates. A management committee, composed of the bank's president and eight vice-presidents and also appointed by the board of governors, is responsible for the day-to-day operations of the bank.

President, Philippe Maystadt (Belgium)

ADVISORY BODIES

COMMITTEE OF THE REGIONS

Bâtiment Jacques Delors, rue Belliard 99–101, B-1040 Brussels, Belgium
E pressecdr@cor.europa.eu W www.cor.europa.eu

The Committee of the Regions (CoR) was established in 1994 and is the political assembly which provides local and regional authorities with a voice within the European

Union. The EU treaties oblige the European Commission and Council of Ministers to consult the Committee of the Regions whenever new proposals are made in areas which have repercussions at regional or local level. The CoR issues opinions on proposals for EU laws, which directly affect local and regional authorities. It can also draw up opinions on its own initiative, which enables it to put issues on the EU agenda, as well as resolutions on topical political issues.

The committee has 344 full members and the same number of alternate members. They are proposed by the member states to the Council of Ministers, which appoints them for a four-year renewable term of office. Members must hold a regional or local authority electoral mandate or be politically accountable to an elected assembly. They participate in the work of six specialist commissions which are responsible for drafting the CoR's opinions and resolutions on a wide range of topics.

President, Luc Van den Brande (Belgium)
Secretary-General, Gerhard Stahl (Germany)

EUROPEAN ECONOMIC AND SOCIAL COMMITTEE

Rue Belliard 99, B-1040 Brussels, Belgium
W www.eesc.europa.eu

The European Economic and Social Committee (EESC) is an advisory and consultative body, which has 344 members appointed by the governments of the 27 member states for a four-year renewable term (this will increase to a five-year term once the treaty of Lisbon has entered into force). It is divided into three groups: employers, workers, and other interest groups such as consumers, farmers and the self-employed. Every two years (2.5 years after the treaty of Lisbon is in effect) the EESC elects a bureau made up of 39 members, and a president and two vice-presidents chosen from each of the three groups in rotation. The EESC issues opinions on draft EC legislation and can bring matters to the attention of the commission, council and parliament. The EESC's competencies have increased as a result of revisions to the treaty of Rome, and the treaty of Nice formally recognised the importance of the opinions of the EU's economic and social partners.

President, Dimitris Dimitriadis (Greece)

AGENCIES

EUROPEAN ENVIRONMENT AGENCY

Kongens Nytorv 6, DK–1050 Copenhagen K, Denmark
T (+45) 3336 7100 W www.eea.europa.eu

The European Environment Agency (EEA) aims to support sustainable development and to help achieve significant and measurable improvement in Europe's environment, through the provision of information to policy-making agents and the public. The EEA has been operational since 1994, and now has 32 member countries. It is a European Union body but is open to non-EU countries that share its objectives. The management board consists of representatives of the member countries, two representatives of the European Commission and two representatives designated by the European parliament.

Chair, Lars-Erik Liljelund (Sweden)

EUROPEAN JUDICIAL COOPERATION UNIT (EUROJUST)

Maanweg 174, 2516 AB The Hague, The Netherlands
E info@eurojust.europa.eu W www.eurojust.europa.eu

The European Union's Judicial Cooperation Unit (Eurojust) was established in 2002 with the aim of enhancing the development of Europe-wide cooperation in criminal justice cases involving serious cross-border and organised crime. Eurojust improves cooperation between the authorities of member states, in particular by facilitating the execution of international mutual legal assistance and through the implementation of extradition requests; it is the first permanent network of judicial authorities to be established anywhere in the world. It is a key interlocutor with the European Parliament, the Council of Ministers and the European Commission.

The college of Eurojust is composed of 27 national members, one nominated by each member state. The national members are experienced prosecutors or judges.

President of the College, José Luís Lopes da Mota (Portugal)

EUROPEAN POLICE OFFICE (EUROPOL)

PO Box 90850, NL-2509 LW, The Hague, The Netherlands
E info@europol.europa.eu W www.europol.europa.eu

The European Police Office (Europol) came into being on 1 October 1998 and assumed its full powers on 1 July 1999. It superseded the Europol Drugs Unit and exists to improve police cooperation between member states and to combat terrorism, illicit traffic in drugs and other serious forms of organised international crime. It is ultimately responsible to the Council of Ministers. Each member state has a national unit to liaise with Europol, and the units send at least one liaison officer to represent its interests at Europol headquarters. Europol maintains a computerised information system, designed to facilitate the exchange of information between member states, and it has a management board comprising one senior representative from each member state. All Europol activities are monitored by an independent joint supervisory body to ensure that the rights of the individual are upheld.

Director, Max-Peter Ratzel (Germany)

EUROPEAN COMMUNITY INFORMATION

EUROPEAN COMMISSION REPRESENTATION

ENGLAND, 8 Storey's Gate, London SW1P 3AT T 020-7973 1992
WALES, 2 Caspian Point, Caspian Way, Cardiff CF10 4QQ T 029-208 95020
SCOTLAND, 9 Alva Street, Edinburgh EH2 4PH T 0131-225 2058
NORTHERN IRELAND, Windsor House, 9–15 Bedford Street, Belfast BT2 7EG T 028-9024 0708

EUROPEAN COMMISSION DELEGATIONS

AUSTRALIA, 18 Arkana Street, Yarralumla, ACT 2600, Canberra
CANADA, 45 O'Connor Street, Suite 1900, Ottawa, Ontario K1P 1A4
USA, 2300 M Street, NW Washington DC 20037
UK OFFICE OF THE EUROPEAN PARLIAMENT, 2 Queen Anne's Gate, London SW1H 9AA T 020-7227 4300

EUROPEAN PARLIAMENT

POLITICAL GROUPINGS
as at June 2008

	EPP-ED	PES	ALDE	GUE/NGL	Green/EFA	UEN	Ind-Dem	Others	Total
Austria	6	7	1	–	2	–	–	2	18
Belgium	6	7	6	–	2	–	–	3	24
Bulgaria	5	5	5	–	–	–	–	3	18
Cyprus	3	–	1	2	–	–	–	–	6
Czech Republic	14	2	–	6	–	–	1	1	24
Denmark	1	5	4	1	1	1	1	–	14
Estonia	1	3	2	–	–	–	–	–	6
Finland	4	3	5	1	1	–	–	–	14
France	18	31	10	3	6	–	3	7	78
Germany	49	23	7	7	13	–	–	–	99
Greece	11	8	–	4	–	–	1	–	24
Hungary	13	9	2	–	–	–	–	–	24
Ireland	5	1	1	1	–	4	1	–	13
Italy	24	15	14	7	2	13		3	78
Latvia	3	–	1	–	1	4	–	–	9
Lithuania	2	2	7	–	–	2	–	–	13
Luxembourg	3	1	1	–	1	–	–	–	6
Malta	2	3	–	–	–	–	–	–	5
The Netherlands	7	7	5	2	4	–	2	–	27
Poland	15	9	5	–	–	20	3	2	54
Portugal	9	12	–	3	–	–	–	–	24
Romania	18	10	6	–	1	–	–	–	35
Slovakia	8	3	–	–	–	–	–	3	14
Slovenia	4	1	2	–	–	–	–	–	7
Spain	24	24	2	1	3	–	–	–	54
Sweden	6	5	3	2	1	–	2	–	19
UK	27	19	11	1	5	–	10	5	78
Total	288	215	101	41	43	44	24	29	785

EPP-ED – European People's Party and European Democrats
W www.epp-ed.eu

PES – Party of European Socialists
W www.socialistgroup.eu

ALDE – Alliance of Liberals and Democrats for Europe
W www.alde.eu

GUE/NGL – Confederal Group of the European United Left/Nordic Green Left
W www.guengl.eu

Green/EFA – Greens/European Free Alliance
W www.greens-efa.org

UEN – Union for Europe of the Nations
W www.uengroup.org

Ind-Dem – Independence/Democracy Group
W www.indemgroup.org

INTERNATIONAL ORGANISATIONS

International organisations are intergovernmental organisations, whose membership can only include either sovereign states or other international organisations. They are subject to international law and are capable of entering into agreements among themselves or with states. They do not include private non-governmental organisations with an international scope. International organisations are usually established by a treaty providing them with legal recognition, which distinguishes them from collections of states such as the G8.

AFRICAN UNION

PO Box 3243, Addis Ababa, Ethiopia
T (+251) (1) 1551 7700 E webmaster@africa-union.org
W www.africa-union.org

The African Union (AU), was launched in 2002 as a successor to the amalgamated Organisation of African Unity and the African Economic Community. It currently has 53 members, representing every African country except Morocco, which left the AU in 1984 in protest at the Saharan Arab Democratic Republic, representing Western Sahara, being admitted as a member. The AU aims to further African unity and solidarity, to coordinate political, economic, social and defence policies, and eventually, to create an African single currency.

Chief AU governing organs include the assembly of heads of state or government, which coordinates the organisation's policies; the executive council, composed of ministers from member states; the African Commission, which is the AU secretariat and consists of ten commissioners, each with a separate portfolio; the peace and security council, modelled on that of the UN and capable of military intervention, and the pan-African parliament, established in 2004 to debate and advise heads of state.

Substantial budgetary arrears due to delays in the payment of national contributions have led to the AU continually facing difficulties in furthering its aims. Since 2004, the AU has deployed a peacekeeping force in the Darfur region of Sudan. The number of troops has steadily grown but has not been able to contain the violence. In December 2007, the AU force was amalgamated into a joint UN–AU operation (UNAMID) with a target strength of 26,000 personnel.
Chair, Jakaya Kikwete (Tanzania)

ANDEAN COMMUNITY

General Secretariat, Paseo de la Republica 3895, esq. Aramburs, San Isidro, Lima 27, Peru
T (+51) (1) 411 1400 E contacto@comunidadandina.org
W www.comunidadandina.org

The Andean Community began operating formally on 21 November 1969 with the establishment of its commission and was known as the Andean Pact until 1996. It comprises four member states – Bolivia, Colombia, Ecuador and Peru – and the bodies of the Andean Integrated System (AIS). Mexico and Panama hold observer status, while Argentina, Brazil, Chile, Paraguay and Uruguay are associated states.

The organisation's objectives are to facilitate economic growth, boost job availability and assist the creation of a Latin American common market. It also aims to reduce the differences in development that exist between the member states. It seeks to achieve its objectives through a programme of complete trade liberalisation, a common external tariff, the reduction of border controls, the coordination of national legislation and the promotion of industrial, agricultural and technological development.

The general secretariat of the Andean Community is its executive body, responsible for administration and dispute resolution. The general secretariat operates under the direction of the secretary-general, who is elected by the Andean council of foreign ministers (ACFM). It can propose decisions or suggestions to the ACFM. It also manages the integration process, ensures that community commitments are fulfilled and maintains relations with the member countries and the executive bodies of other international organisations.

The Andean presidential council is the highest-level body of the AIS and comprises the presidents of the member states. Its responsibilities include setting new policies, evaluating the integration process and communicating with other bodies. The chairmanship is rotated among the members of the council each calendar year.

In 2001, the organisation introduced Andean passports for member states and in 2005 created a policy of free flow of persons, enabling citizens to travel throughout the area without requiring a visa.
Secretary-General, Freddy Ehlers (Ecuador)

ARAB MAGHREB UNION

14 rue Zalagh, Agdal, Rabat, Morocco
T (+212) (3) 767 1274 E sg.uma@maghrebarabe.org
W www.maghrebarabe.org

The treaty establishing the Arab Maghreb Union (AMU) was signed on 17 February 1989 by the heads of state of the five member states: Algeria, Libya, Mauritania, Morocco and Tunisia. The AMU aims to strengthen ties between the member countries by developing agriculture and commerce, introducing the free circulation of goods and services, and establishing joint projects and economic cooperation programmes.

Decisions must be unanimous and are made by a council of heads of state briefed by a council of foreign affairs ministers. A consultative assembly – consisting of 30 representatives from each member state – is based in Algiers, the secretariat is in Rabat, and the court of justice, with two judges from each country, operates in Nouakchott, Mauritania.
Secretary-General, Habib Ben Yahia (Tunisia)

ARCTIC COUNCIL

Polarmiljosenteret, 9296 Tromso, Norway T (+47) 7775 0140
W www.arctic-council.org

The Arctic Council was founded in 1996 in Ottawa, Canada, and is a regional forum for socio-economic development and scientific research within the Arctic region. It comprises eight states: Canada, Denmark (including Greenland and the Faeroe Islands), Finland, Iceland, Norway, Russia, Sweden and the USA. A further six organisations representing indigenous peoples are granted permanent participatory status and include the Saami Council, Inuit Circumpolar Conference and the Arctic Athabaskan Council. Five states (France, Germany, the Netherlands, Poland and the UK) have observer status.

Decisions within the Arctic Council are taken at biennial ministerial meetings attended by foreign ministers or designates of the member states. The chairmanship of the council and secretariat also rotate on a biennial basis. Between these meetings, the operation of the council is administered by the Committee of Senior Arctic Officials.

The main scientific work of the Arctic Council is carried out in six working groups, each focusing on specific issues such as the monitoring and prevention of pollution, climate change, biodiversity and public health.

Chair, Norway (until March 2009), Denmark (2009–11)

ASIA COOPERATION DIALOGUE

E acd@mfa.go.th W www.acddialogue.com

The Asia Cooperation Dialogue (ACD) was initiated by former Thailand prime minister, Thaksin Shinawatra, and inaugurated in June 2002. It currently has 30 members.

Its purpose is to provide a continent-wide forum to assist development in every Asian nation, with the ultimate goal to create an Asian community capable of equal interaction with the rest of the world. It aims to achieve these objectives through promoting interdependence among Asian countries, improving quality of life and expanding the continent's trade and financial markets.

Representatives from each of the member states (typically foreign ministers) meet annually to discuss ACD developments, issues of regional cooperation and methods of enhancing Asian unity. In addition, ministers also meet following the annual UN general assembly to update policy and project progress.

ASIAN-AFRICAN LEGAL CONSULTATIVE ORGANISATION

E-66, Vasant Marg, Vasant Vihar, 110057 New Delhi, India T (+91) (11) 2615 2251
E mail@aalco.org W www.aalco.int

The Asian-African Legal Consultative Organisation (AALCO), founded as a result of the Bandung Conference of 1955, was previously known as both the Asian Legal Consultative Committee and the Asian-African Legal Consultative Committee before its name was changed again in 2001. It was initally established as a non permanent committee for a five-year term which was repeatedly extended until 1981, when its was granted permanent status. It has 48 member states.

The functions of the AALCO include serving as an advisory body to its member states in the field of international law, operating as a forum for common concerns among its members and making recommendations to governments and other international organisations.

Representatives from member states meet for the annual session which is hosted on a rotational basis and is attended by members of government, observers from other organisations and members of the International Court of Justice and International Law Commission.

The secretariat is located in New Delhi and is responsible for the day-to-day functioning of the organisation. It is headed by a secretary-general, elected to a three-year term. Other infrastructure includes four regional arbitration centres in Egypt, Iran, Malaysia and Nigeria.

Secretary-General, Dr Wafik Z. Kamil (Egypt)

ASIAN DEVELOPMENT BANK

PO Box 789, 0980 Manila, The Philippines
T (+632) 632 4444 W www.adb.org

The Asian Development Bank (ADB) was founded in 1966 and is a multilateral financial institution dedicated to reducing poverty in Asia and the Pacific. It has 67 member countries from across the world. The ADB extends loans, equity investments and technical assistance to governments and public and private enterprises in its member countries and promotes the investment of public and private capital for development. The bank's programmes prioritise economic growth, human development, good governance, environmental protection, private sector growth and regional cooperation.

The ADB is controlled by its board of governors, which consists of a representative from each of the member states. Its powers are delegated to a board of directors which is responsible for administration and policy review.

The ADB raises funds through members' contributions and issuing bonds on the world's capital markets. In 2006, the ADB provided loans totalling US$10,100m (£5,107m) and technical assistance costing US$243.4m (£123.1m).

President, Haruhiko Kuroda (Japan)

ASIA-PACIFIC ECONOMIC COOPERATION

35 Heng Mui Keng Terrace, Singapore 119616
T (+65) 6891 9600 E info@apec.org W www.apec.org

Asia-Pacific Economic Cooperation (APEC) is an economic forum for Pacific Rim countries to discuss regional economy, cooperation, trade and investment. APEC was founded in 1989 in response to the growing interdependence among Asia-Pacific economies. The 1994 Declaration of Common Resolve envisaged a free trade zone, to be established by 2010 in industrialised economies and by 2020 in developing member economies. Its 21 members define and fund work programmes for APEC's four committees, 11 working groups and other task forces.

APEC's chairmanship rotates annually among member states and the chair is responsible for hosting the annual ministerial meeting of foreign affairs and trade ministers. The permanent secretariat, based in Singapore, is responsible for implementing policy.

Executive-Director, HE Juan Carlos Capuñay (Peru)

ASSOCIATION OF SOUTH-EAST ASIAN NATIONS

Jalan Sisingamangaraja 70a, Jakarta 12110, Indonesia
T (+62) (21) 726 2991/724 3372 E public@aseansec.org
W www.aseansec.org

The Association of South-East Asian Nations (ASEAN) is a geo-political and economic organisation formed in 1967 with the aim of accelerating economic growth, social progress and cultural development, and ensuring regional stability. It currently has ten member states.

The ASEAN summit, an annual meeting of the heads of government, is the organisation's highest authority. The ASEAN ministerial meeting is an annual meeting of foreign ministers of member states and is responsible for the formulation of policy guidelines and the coordination of ASEAN's activities. The ASEAN economic ministers meet annually to coordinate economic policy.

An ASEAN free trade area was implemented in 2003, while a common preferential tariff was introduced in 1993. At the ASEAN summit in 1995, a south-east Asia nuclear weapon-free zone was declared. In November 2007 members signed a charter committing the organisation to the promotion of democracy and the establishment of a regional human rights body.

The secretary-general of ASEAN is appointed on merit by the heads of government and can initiate, advise, coordinate and implement ASEAN activities. In addition to the ASEAN secretariat based in Jakarta, each member state has a national secretariat in its foreign ministry which organises and implements activities at national level.

Secretary-General, Dr Surin Pitsuwan (Thailand)

BALTIC ASSEMBLY

Room 616, 2 Citadeles Street, Riga, LV-1010, Latvia
T (+371) 6722 5178 E baltasam@baltasam.org
W www.baltasam.org

Established in November 1991, the Baltic Assembly (BA) is an international organisation for cooperation between the parliaments of Estonia, Latvia and Lithuania. Each member state appoints between 12 and 20 parliamentarians to the assembly, including a head and deputy head of the national delegation. The political allegiances of the appointments reflect party proportions in each of the domestic parliaments. The BA holds two sessions per year in each of the member states in rotation. In addition, there are permanent and *ad hoc* committees. The Baltic council of ministers, which comprises the heads of government and ministers of the member states, meets with the BA once a year and promotes intergovernmental and regional cooperation between the Baltic states; the joint sessions are known as the Baltic council.

President, Erika Zommere (Latvia)

CAB INTERNATIONAL

Nosworthy Way, Wallingford, Oxon OX10 8DE
T 01491-832111 E enquiries@cabi.org W www.cabi.org

Founded in 1930, CAB International (CABI) (formerly the Commonwealth Agricultural Bureau) is a non-profit organisation specialising in scientific knowledge to assist sustainable development, with an emphasis on agriculture, forestry and natural resources and the needs of developing countries. The organisation consists of 40 countries and five British overseas territories; each is represented on an executive council. A governing board provides guidance on policy issues.

CABI has two divisions: bioscience and publishing. They undertake research and provide consultancy aimed at raising agricultural productivity, conserving biological resources, protecting the environment and controlling disease. Any country is eligible to apply for membership. Applications are by invitation from existing members and are authorised by a head of state or delegated authority.

Chief Executive Officer, Dr Trevor Nicholls (UK)

CARIBBEAN COMMUNITY AND COMMON MARKET

PO Box 10827, Georgetown, Guyana
T (+592) 222 001 0075 E info@caricom.org
W www.caricom.org

The Caribbean Community and Common Market (CARICOM) was established in 1973 with the signing of the Treaty of Chaguaramas. The objectives of CARICOM are to improve member states' working and living standards, boost employment levels, promote economic development and competitiveness, coordinate foreign and economic policies and enhance cooperation in the delivery of services such as health and education.

The supreme organ is the conference of heads of government, which determines policy and resolves conflict. The community council of ministers consists of ministers of government assigned to CARICOM affairs and is responsible for economic and strategic planning. The principal administrative arm is the secretariat, based in Guyana. The Bureau of the Conference of Heads of Government is the executive body; it comprises the chairman of the conference, the outgoing chair and the secretary-general, who are all authorised to initiate proposals and to secure the implementation of decisions. In addition, there are four ministerial councils dealing with trade and economic development, foreign and community relations, human and social development, and finance and planning.

In 2005, Suriname became the first country to issue CARICOM passports. Seven other member states have introduced them since.

CARICOM has 15 member states and five associate members.

Secretary-General, Edwin W. Carrington (Trinidad and Tobago)

THE COMMONWEALTH

The Commonwealth is a voluntary association of 53 sovereign and independent states together with their associated states and dependencies. All of the states were formerly part of the British Empire or League of Nations (later the UN) mandated territories, except for Mozambique which was admitted as a unique case because of its history of cooperation with neighbouring Commonwealth nations.

The status and relationship of member nations were first defined by the inter-imperial relations committee of the 1926 Imperial Conference, when the six existing dominions (Australia, Canada, the Irish Free State, Newfoundland, New Zealand and South Africa) were described as 'autonomous communities within the British Empire, equal in status, in no way subordinate one to another in any aspect of their domestic or external affairs, though united by a common allegiance to the Crown and freely associated as members of the British Commonwealth of Nations'. This formula was given legal substance by the Statute of Westminster 1931.

This concept of a group of countries owing allegiance to a single crown changed in 1949 when India decided to become a republic. Her continued membership of the Commonwealth was agreed by the other members on the basis of her 'acceptance of the monarch as the symbol of the free association of its independent member nations and as such the head of the Commonwealth'. This enabled subsequent new republics to join the association. Member nations agreed at the time of the accession of Queen Elizabeth II to recognise Her Majesty as the new head of the Commonwealth. However, the position is not vested in the British Crown.

THE MODERN COMMONWEALTH

As the UK's former colonies joined, after India and Pakistan in 1947, the Commonwealth was transformed from a grouping of all-white dominions into a multiracial association of equal nations. It increasingly focused on promoting development and racial equality. South Africa withdrew in 1961 when it became clear that its reapplication for membership on becoming a republic would be rejected over its policy of apartheid.

The new goals of advocating democracy, the rule of law, good government and social justice were enshrined in the Harare Commonwealth Declaration (1991), which formed the basis of new membership guide-lines agreed in Cyprus in 1993. Following the adoption of measures at the New Zealand summit in 1995 against serious or persistent violations of these principles, Nigeria was suspended in 1995 and Sierra Leone was suspended in 1997 for anti-democratic behaviour. Sierra Leone's suspension was revoked the following year when a legitimate government was returned to power. Similarly, Nigeria's suspension was lifted in 1999, the day a newly elected civilian president took office. A heads of government meeting in 1997 established a set of economic principles for the Commonwealth, promoting economic growth whilst protecting smaller member states from the negative effects of globalisation. Zimbabwe was suspended from the councils of the Commonwealth in March 2002 and, in 2003, the Zimbabwean government officially confirmed its departure from the association. Following President Pervez Musharraf's imposition of emergency rule in Pakistan in November 2007, the country was briefly suspended from the Commonwealth's councils. The suspension was lifted after successful democratic elections in February 2008.

MEMBERSHIP

Membership of the Commonwealth involves acceptance of the association's basic principles and is subject to the approval of existing members. There are 53 members at present, of which 16 have Queen Elizabeth II as head of state, 31 are republics and six have national monarchies. (The date of joining the Commonwealth is shown in parentheses.)

*Antigua and Barbuda (1981)
*Australia (1931)
*The Bahamas (1973)
Bangladesh (1972)
*Barbados (1966)
*Belize (1981)
Botswana (1966)
Brunei (1984)
Cameroon (1995)
*Canada (1931)
Cyprus (1961)
Dominica (1978)
§Fiji (1970)
The Gambia (1965)
Ghana (1957)
*Grenada (1974)
Guyana (1966)
India (1947)
*Jamaica (1962)
Kenya (1963)
Kiribati (1979)
Lesotho (1966)
Malawi (1964)
Malaysia (1957)
Maldives (1982)
Malta (1964)
Mauritius (1968)
Mozambique (1995)
Namibia (1990)
†Nauru (1968)
New Zealand (1931)
Nigeria (1960)
Pakistan (1947)
*Papua New Guinea (1975)
*St Kitts and Nevis (1983)
*St Lucia (1979)
*St Vincent and the Grenadines (1979)
Samoa (1970)
Seychelles (1976)
Sierra Leone (1961)
Singapore (1965)
*Solomon Islands (1978)
South Africa (1931)
Sri Lanka (1948)
Swaziland (1968)
Tanzania (1961)
Tonga (1970)
Trinidad and Tobago (1962)
‡Tuvalu (1978)
Uganda (1962)
*United Kingdom
Vanuatu (1980)
Zambia (1964)

* Realms of Queen Elizabeth II
† Nauru is a special member
‡ Originally a special member due to its small size, small economy and limited involvement in international affairs, Tuvalu became a full member in September 2000
§ Currently suspended from the Commonwealth

COUNTRIES WHICH HAVE LEFT THE COMMONWEALTH

Republic of Ireland (1949)
Pakistan (1972, rejoined 1989; suspended 1999, suspension lifted 2004; suspended 2007, suspension lifted 2008)
South Africa (1961, rejoined 1994)
Zimbabwe (2003)

In each of the realms where Queen Elizabeth II is head of state (except for the UK), she is personally represented by a governor-general, who holds in all essential respects the same position in relation to the administration of public affairs in the realm as is held by Her Majesty in the UK. The governor-general is appointed by the Queen on the advice of the government of the state concerned.

INTERGOVERNMENTAL AND OTHER LINKS

The main forum for consultation is the Commonwealth heads of government meetings, held biennially to discuss international developments and to consider cooperation among members. Decisions are reached by consensus, and the views of the meeting are set out in a communiqué. There are also annual meetings of finance ministers and frequent meetings of ministers and officials in other fields, such as education, health, gender and youth affairs. Intergovernmental links are complemented by the activities of some 80 Commonwealth non-governmental organisations linking professionals, sportsmen and sportswomen, and interest groups, forming a people's Commonwealth. The Commonwealth Games take place every four years.

Assistance to other Commonwealth countries normally has priority in the bilateral aid programmes of the association's developed members (Australia, Canada, New Zealand and the United Kingdom), who direct about 30 per cent of their aid to other member countries. Developing Commonwealth nations also assist their poorer partners, and many Commonwealth voluntary organisations promote development.

COMMONWEALTH SECRETARIAT

The Commonwealth has a secretariat, established in 1965 in London, which is funded by member governments. This is the main agency for multilateral communication between member governments on issues relating to the Commonwealth as a whole. It promotes consultation and cooperation, disseminates information on matters of common concern, organises meetings including the biennial summits, coordinates Commonwealth activities, and provides technical assistance for economic and social development through the Commonwealth fund for technical cooperation.

The Commonwealth foundation was established by Commonwealth governments in 1966 as an autonomous body with a board of governors representing Commonwealth governments that fund the foundation. It promotes and funds exchanges and other activities aimed at strengthening the skills and effectiveness of professionals and non-governmental organisations. It also promotes culture, rural development, social welfare and the role of women.

COMMONWEALTH SECRETARIAT, Marlborough House, Pall Mall, London SW1Y 5HX **T** 020-7747 6500 **E** info@commonwealth.int **W** www.thecommonwealth.org
Secretary-General, Kamalesh Sharma (India)

COMMONWEALTH FOUNDATION, Marlborough House, Pall Mall, London SW1Y 5HY **T** 020-7930 3783 **E** geninfo@commonwealth.int **W** www.commonwealthfoundation.com
Chair, Prof. Guido de Marco (Malta)

COMMONWEALTH INSTITUTE, New Zealand House, 80 Haymarket, London SW1Y 4TQ **T** 020-7024 9822 **E** information@commonwealth-institute.org.uk **W** www.commonwealth.org.uk

COMMONWEALTH OF INDEPENDENT STATES

Ul. Kirova 17, Minsk 220030, Belarus
T (+375) (17) 222 3559 **E** postmaster@cis.minsk.by
W www.cis.minsk.by

The Commonwealth of Independent States (CIS) is a multilateral grouping of 12 former Soviet republics. It was formed in 1991 and its charter was signed by seven states in 1993. The CIS acts as a coordinating mechanism for foreign, defence and economic policies and as a forum for addressing problems arising from the break-up of the USSR. These matters are addressed in more than 70 inter-state, intergovernmental coordinating and consultative statutory bodies.

The two supreme CIS organs are the council of heads of state, which meets twice a year, and the council of heads of government. The executive committee, based in Minsk and Moscow, provides administrative support. There are also numerous ministerial, parliamentary, economic and security councils.

On becoming members of the CIS, the member states agreed to recognise their existing borders, respect one another's territorial integrity and reject the use of military force or coercion to settle disputes. A treaty on collective security was signed in 1992 by six states and a joint peacemaking force, to intervene in CIS conflicts, was agreed upon by nine states. Russia concluded bilateral and multilateral agreements with other CIS states under the supervision of the council of heads of collective security (established 1993). These were gradually upgraded into CIS agreements under the umbrella of the collective security treaty, enabling Russia to station troops in eight of the other 11 CIS states (not Moldova, Turkmenistan or Ukraine), and giving Russian forces *de facto* control of virtually all of the former USSR's external borders. Only Ukraine and Moldova remained outside the defence cooperation framework and did not sign the treaty. In 1999, Azerbaijan, Georgia and Uzbekistan withdrew from the treaty and formed a new defensive grouping with Moldova and Ukraine.

In 1991, 11 republics signed a treaty forming an economic community. Members agreed to refrain from economic actions that would damage each other and to coordinate economic and monetary policies. A coordinating consultative committee, an economic arbitration court and an inter-state bank were established. A single monetary unit, the rouble, was originally agreed upon by all member states, and the members recognised that the basis of recovery for their economies was private ownership, free enterprise and competition.

The 11 CIS members who signed the Establishment of an Economic Union treaty in September 1993 (Ukraine is an associate member of the economic union) committed themselves to a common economic space with free movement of goods, services, capital and labour. Belarus, Kazakhstan, Kyrgyzstan and Russia signed a treaty on the establishment of a customs union in 1996; the treaty was later signed by Tajikistan. In 2000, the presidents of the five countries approved a treaty establishing the Eurasian Economic Community and in 2006, Russia, Belarus and Kazakhstan announced the formation of a customs union.
Executive Secretary, Sergey Lebedev (Russian Federation)

COOPERATION COUNCIL FOR THE ARAB STATES OF THE GULF

PO Box 7153, Riyadh 11-462, Saudi Arabia
T (+966) (1) 482 7777 **W** www.gcc-sg.org

The Cooperation Council for the Arab States of the Gulf, or Gulf Cooperation Council (GCC), as it is informally known, was established on 25 May 1981. Its main objectives are increasing coordination and integration, harmonising economic, commercial, educational and social policies and promoting scientific and technical innovation among its member states. It also aims to establish a common currency by 2010. The GCC has six members: Bahrain, Kuwait, Oman, Qatar, Saudi Arabia and the United Arab Emirates.

The highest authority of the GCC is the supreme council, whose presidency rotates among members' heads of states. It holds one regular session every year, but extraordinary sessions may be convened if necessary.

The ministerial council, which ordinarily meets every three months, consists of the foreign ministers of the member states or other delegated ministers. It is authorised to propose policies and recommendations and ensure that resolutions are implemented.
Secretary-General, Abdul-Rahman bin Hamad al-Attiyah (Qatar)

COUNCIL OF EUROPE

Avenue de l'Europe, F-67075 Strasbourg, France
T (+33) (3) 8841 2000 **W** www.coe.int

The Council of Europe was founded in 1949. Its aim is to achieve greater unity between its members, to safeguard their European heritage and to facilitate their progress in economic, social, cultural, educational, scientific, legal and administrative matters, and to further pluralist democracy, human rights and fundamental freedoms. It has 47 members.

The organs are the committee of ministers, consisting of the foreign ministers of member countries, and the parliamentary assembly of 318 members (and 318 substitutes), elected or chosen by the national parliaments of member countries in proportion to the relative strength of political parties.

The committee of ministers is the executive organ. The majority of its conclusions take the form of international agreements (known as European conventions) or recommendations to governments. Decisions of the ministers may also be embodied in partial agreements to which a limited number of member governments are party.

One of the principal achievements of the Council of Europe is the European Convention on Human Rights (1950) under which the European Commission and the European Court of Human Rights was established. They merged in 1993. The reorganised European Court of Human Rights sits in chambers of seven judges, or exceptionally, as a grand chamber of 17 judges. Litigants must exhaust legal processes in their own country prior to bringing cases before the court.

Among other conventions and agreements are the European Social Charter, the European Cultural Convention, the European Code of Social Security, the European Convention on the Protection of National Minorities, and conventions on extradition, the legal status of migrant workers, torture prevention, conservation and the transfer of sentenced prisoners. Most recently, the specialised bodies of the Venice Commission and Demosthenes have been set up to assist in developing legislative, administrative and constitutional reforms in Central and Eastern Europe.

Non-member states take part in certain Council of Europe activities, such as educational, cultural and sports activities on a regular or *ad hoc* basis. The council's ordinary budget for 2008 totalled €279.7m (£220m).
Secretary-General, Rt. Hon. Terry Davis (UK)

COUNCIL OF THE BALTIC SEA STATES

PO Box 2010, Stromsborg, S-103 11 Stockholm, Sweden
T (+46) 8440 1920 **E** cbss@cbss.org **W** www.cbss.org

The Council of the Baltic Sea States was established in 1992 with the aim of creating a regional forum to increase cooperation and coordination among the states which border on the Baltic Sea. The organisation focuses on assisting new democratic institutions, economic and technical development, humanitarian aid and health, energy and environmental issues, cultural programmes, education, tourism, transportation and communication. It currently has 12 members (11 countries and the European Commission) while a further seven countries (including the UK and the USA) hold observer status.

The council consists of the foreign ministers of each member state and a member of the European Commission. Chairmanship of the council rotates on an annual basis, and the annual session is held in the country currently in the chair. The foreign minister of the presiding country is responsible for coordinating activities between the sessions. Since 1998 a permanent international secretariat has been established in Stockholm, Sweden.
Chair, Denmark (2008–9)

ECONOMIC COMMUNITY OF WEST AFRICAN STATES

Secretariat Building, 101 Yakubu Gowon Crescent, PMB 401, Abuja, Nigeria
T (+234) (9) 314 7647 **E** info@ecowas.int **W** www.ecowas.int

The Economic Community of West African States (ECOWAS) was founded in 1975 and came into operation in 1977. It aims to prevent and control regional conflicts and promote the cultural, economic and social development of West Africa through mutual cooperation.

The supreme authority of ECOWAS is vested in the annual summit of heads of government of all 15 member states. A council of ministers meets biannually to monitor the organisation and make recommendations to the summit. ECOWAS operates through a secretariat, headed by the executive secretary. The ECOWAS parliament was inaugurated in November 2000 and judges for the court of justice were sworn in in January 2001.

Five member states of ECOWAS (The Gambia, Ghana, Guinea, Nigeria and Sierra Leone) have announced plans to introduce the Eco as a single common currency on 1 December 2009. Eight other states currently use the CFA franc. These currencies are planned to eventually be amalgamated. An ECOWAS travel certificate is operational in seven countries and a common passport in a separate three.

An ECOWAS peacekeeping force has been involved in attempts to restore peace in Liberia (1990–6), in Guinea-Bissau (1998–9) and in Sierra Leone (1997–9).
Executive Secretary, Dr Mohamed ibn Chambas (Ghana)

EUROPEAN BANK FOR RECONSTRUCTION AND DEVELOPMENT

One Exchange Square, London EC2A 2JN
T 020-7338 6000 **W** www.ebrd.com

The European Bank for Reconstruction and Development (EBRD), established in 1991, is an international institution, whose membership comprises 61 member states, the European Community and the European Investment Bank.

The aim of EBRD is to build market economies and democracies in 29 countries across the world. EBRD provides project financing for banks, industries and businesses. It also works with publicly owned companies to support privatisation, restructuring state-owned firms and improving public services.

The main forms of EBRD financing are loans, equity investments and guarantees. No more than 40 per cent of the EBRD's investment can be made in state-owned concerns. The EBRD pays particular attention to strengthening the financial sector and to promoting small and medium-sized enterprises. It works in cooperation with national governments, private companies, and international organisations such as the OECD, the IMF, the World Bank and the UN specialised agencies. The EBRD is also able to borrow on world capital markets.

In 2007, the EBRD invested €5.6bn (£4.5bn) and made a net profit of €1.9bn (£1.5bn).

The highest authority is the board of governors; each member appoints one governor and one alternate. The governors delegate most powers to a 23-member board of directors; the directors are responsible for the EBRD's operations and budget, and are elected by the governors for three-year terms. The governors also elect the president of the board of directors, who acts as the bank's president for a four-year term.
President, Jean Lemierre (France)

EUROPEAN FREE TRADE ASSOCIATION

9–11 rue de Varembé, CH-1211 Geneva 20, Switzerland
T (+41) (22) 332 2626 **E** mail.gva@efta.int **W** www.efta.int

The European Free Trade Association (EFTA) was established in 1960 by Austria, Denmark, Norway, Portugal, Sweden, Switzerland and the UK, and was subsequently joined by Finland, Iceland and Liechtenstein. Six members have left to join the European Union: Denmark and the UK (1972), Portugal (1985), Austria, Finland and Sweden (1995). The existing members are Iceland, Liechtenstein, Norway and Switzerland.

The first objective of EFTA was to establish free trade in industrial products between members; this was achieved in 1966. Its second objective was the creation of a single market in Western Europe and in 1972 EFTA signed free trade agreements with the EC covering trade in industrial goods. The remaining tariffs on industrial products were abolished in 1977 and the Luxembourg Declaration on broader cooperation between EFTA and the EC was signed in 1984.

An agreement on the creation of the European Economic Area (EEA), an extension of the EC single market to the EFTA states, was signed in 1992 and entered into force in January 1994. Switzerland rejected EEA membership in a referendum in 1992 and Liechtenstein joined in May 1995 after adapting its customs union with Switzerland.

Since 2002, free trade area agreements have been signed between the EFTA states and Canada, Chile, Egypt, Lebanon, the Republic of Korea, Singapore, the Southern African Customs Union (SACU) and Tunisia. With these agreements, the EFTA states will have concluded free trade agreements with states and territories representing a population of 3840 million, in addition to the free trade relations with the EU. Negotiations on free trade agreements with Algeria, Columbia, the Gulf Cooperation Council and Thailand are ongoing.

The EFTA council is the principal organ. It meets regularly at the level of ambassadors to the EFTA secretariat in Geneva.

Secretary-General, Kare Bryn (Norway)

EUROPEAN ORGANISATION FOR NUCLEAR RESEARCH (CERN)

CH-1211 Geneva 23, Switzerland
T (+41) (22) 767 6111 E cern.reception@cern.ch
W www.cern.ch

The convention establishing the European Organisation for Nuclear Research (CERN) came into force in 1954. CERN promotes European collaboration in high-energy physics with scientific goals and no military implication. It has 20 member states and eight members with observer status, including the European Commission and UNESCO.

The council, which is the highest policy-making body, comprises two delegates from each member state and is chaired by the president, who is elected by the council in session. The council also elects a director-general, who is responsible for the internal organisation of CERN. The director-general heads a workforce of approximately 2,500, including physicists, craftsmen, technicians and administrative staff. At present nearly 9,000 physicists use CERN's facilities.

Tim Berners-Lee developed the World Wide Web whilst working at CERN in 1990.

Director-General, Dr Robert Aymar (France), Dr Rolf-Dieter Heuer (Germany) (from 2009)

EUROPEAN SPACE AGENCY

8–10 rue Mario Nikis, F-75738 Paris Cedex 15, France
T (+33) (1) 5369 7155 W www.esa.int

The European Space Agency (ESA) was created in 1975 by the merger of the European Space Research Organisation and the European Launcher Development Organisation. Its aims include the advancement of space research and technology and the implementation of European space policy. ESA has 17 member states and one cooperating state. ESA's mandatory activities are funded by contributions from all member states and calculated in accordance with each country's gross national income. In 2008, ESA's budget amounted to around €3,000m (£2,421m).

The agency is directed by a council composed of the representatives of the member states; its chief officer is the director-general who is elected by the council every four years. ESA has liaison offices in Belgium, the United States of America and Russia, while a launch base is stationed in French Guiana.

Director-General, Jean-Jacques Dordain (France)

EUROPEAN UNION

See European Union section

FOOD AND AGRICULTURE ORGANISATION OF THE UNITED NATIONS

Viale delle Terme di Caracalla, 00153 Rome, Italy
T (+39) (06) 57051 E fao-hq@fao.org W www.fao.org

The Food and Agriculture Organisation (FAO) is a specialised UN agency, established in 1945. It assists rural populations by raising levels of nutrition and living standards, and by encouraging greater efficiency in food production and distribution. It analyses and publishes information on agriculture and natural resources. The FAO also advises governments on national agricultural policy and planning through its investment centre and collaboration with the World Bank and other financial institutions. The FAO's field programme covers a range of activities, including strengthening crop production, rural and livestock development and conservation.

The FAO's top priorities are sustainable agriculture, rural development and food security. The organisation monitors potential famine areas, channels emergency aid from governments and other agencies, assists in rehabilitation, and responds to urgent or unforeseen requests for technical assistance.

The FAO has 193 members (192 states plus the European Community). It is governed by a biennial conference of its members which sets a programme and budget. The budget for 2008–9 was US$929.8m (£471.4m), funded by member countries in proportion to their gross national income. The FAO is also funded by the UN development programme, donor governments and other institutions.

The conference elects a director-general and a 49-member council which governs between conferences. The regular and field programmes are administered by a secretariat, headed by the director-general. Five regional, 11 sub-regional and 73 national offices help administer the field programme.

Director-General, Jacques Diouf (Senegal)

INTERNATIONAL ATOMIC ENERGY AGENCY

Vienna International Centre, Wagramer Strasse 5, PO Box 100, A-1400 Vienna, Austria
T (+43) (1) 26000 E official.mail@iaea.org W www.iaea.org

The International Atomic Energy Agency (IAEA) was established in 1957. It is an intergovernmental organisation that reports to, but is not a specialised agency of, the UN.

The IAEA aims to enhance the contribution of atomic energy to peace, health and prosperity. It does not advocate the use of atomic energy for military purposes. It establishes atomic energy safety standards and offers services to its member states for the safe operation of their nuclear facilities and for radiation protection. It is the focal point for international conventions on the early notification of a nuclear accident, accident assistance, civil liability for nuclear damage, physical protection of nuclear material, and the safety of spent fuel and radioactive waste management. The IAEA also encourages research and training in nuclear power. It is additionally charged with drawing up safeguards and verifying their use in accordance with several international nuclear weapons treaties.

The IAEA has 144 members that meet annually in a general conference. The conference decides policy, a programme and a budget – €290m (£230m) in 2008 – as well as electing a director-general and a 35-member board of governors. The board meets four times a year to formulate policy which is implemented by the secretariat.

Director-General, Mohamed ElBaradei (Egypt)

INTERNATIONAL CIVIL AVIATION ORGANISATION

999 University Street, Montréal, Québec, Canada H3C 5H7
T (+1) (514) 954 8219 E icaohq@icao.int W www.icao.int

The International Civil Aviation Organisation (ICAO) was founded with the signing of the Chicago Convention on International Civil Aviation in 1944 and became a specialised agency of the UN in 1947. It sets international technical standards and regulations for aviation safety, security and efficiency, as well as environmental protection.

ICAO has 190 members and is governed by an assembly. A council of 36 members is elected, which represents leading air transport nations as well as less developed countries. The council elects the president, appoints the secretary-general and supervises the organisation through subsidiary committees, serviced by a secretariat.

President of the Council, Roberto Kobeh González (Mexico)

INTERNATIONAL CONFEDERATION OF FREE TRADE UNIONS

5 Boulevard du Roi Albert II, Bus 1, B-1210 Brussels, Belgium
T (+32) (2) 224 0211 E internetpo@icftu.org W www.icftu.org

The International Confederation of Free Trade Unions (ICFTU) was created in 1949. It aims to establish, maintain and promote free trade unions, and to promote peace with economic security and social justice. In April 2008, the ICFTU had 155 million members in 241 affiliated organisations in 156 countries and territories.

The congress, the supreme authority of the ICFTU, is composed of delegates from the affiliated trade union organisations. The congress elects an executive board of 53 members, including five nominated by the women's committee and one by the youth committee. The board establishes the budget and receives suggestions and proposals from affiliates, as well as acting on behalf of the confederation. The congress also elects the general secretary. A steering committee of 17 members of the executive board plus the general secretary and the president meet twice a year to oversee ICFTU financial matters.

General Secretary, Guy Ryder (UK)

INTERNATIONAL CRIMINAL POLICE ORGANISATION (INTERPOL)

200 Quai Charles de Gaulle, F-69006 Lyon, France
E compr@interpol.int W www.interpol.int

Interpol was set up in 1923 to establish an international criminal records office and to harmonise extradition procedures. In 2007, the organisation comprised 186 member states. Interpol's aims are to promote cooperation between criminal police authorities and to support government agencies concerned with combating crime, while respecting national sovereignty. It is financed by annual contributions from the governments of member states.

Interpol's policy is decided by the general assembly which meets annually and is composed of delegates appointed by the member states. The 13-member executive committee is elected by the general assembly from the member states' delegates and is chaired by the president, who has a four-year term of office. The permanent administrative organ is the general secretariat, headed by the secretary-general, who is appointed by the general assembly.

Secretary-General, Ronald K. Noble (USA)

INTERNATIONAL ENERGY AGENCY

9 rue de la Fédération, F-75739 Paris, France
T (+33) (1) 4057 6500/01 E info@iea.org W www.iea.org

The International Energy Agency (IEA), founded in 1974, is an autonomous agency within the framework of the Organisation for Economic Cooperation and Development (OECD). The IEA's objectives include the improvement of energy cooperation worldwide, development of alternative energy sources and the promotion of relations between oil producing and oil consuming countries. The IEA also maintains an emergency system to alleviate the effects of severe oil supply disruptions.

The main decision-making body is the governing board, composed of senior energy officials from member countries. The IEA secretariat, with a staff of energy experts, carries out the work of the governing board and its subordinate bodies. The executive director is appointed by the board. The IEA has 27 member states.

Executive Director, Nobuo Tanaka (Japan)

INTERNATIONAL FRANCOPHONE ORGANISATION

Cabinet du Secrétaire général, 28 rue de Bourgogne, F-75007 Paris, France
T (+33) (1) 4411 1250 W www.francophonie.org

The International Francophone Organisation (known as La Francophonie) is an intergovernmental organisation founded in 1970 by 21 French-speaking countries. It aims to prevent conflict and promote development and cooperation, represent its member states internationally and promote French culture and language.

The conference of heads of state and heads of government of countries using French as a common language, also known as the Francophone summit, takes place biennially. Other institutions include the ministerial conference, the permanent council and the secretariat.

The ministerial conference, which consists of the foreign ministers or the ministers responsible for Francophone affairs of each member state, implements decisions made at the summits and puts forward prospective new members. The permanent council, which is chaired by the secretary-general and consists of representatives of the member states, oversees the execution of decisions made by the ministerial conference, allocates funds, and reviews and approves projects.

La Francophonie has 55 members, two associate member states and 13 observers.

Secretary-General, Abdou Diouf (Senegal)

INTERNATIONAL FUND FOR AGRICULTURAL DEVELOPMENT

44 Via Paolo di Dono, 00142 Rome, Italy
T (+39) (06) 54591 E ifad@ifad.org W www.ifad.org

The International Fund for Agricultural Development (IFAD) began operations as a UN specialised agency in 1978. It aims to mobilise funds for agricultural and rural projects in developing countries, provide employment and additional income for poor farmers, reduce malnutrition and improve food security systems.

IFAD has 165 members and membership is divided into three lists: List A (OECD countries), List B (OPEC countries), and List C (developing countries) which is subdivided into C1 (Africa), C2 (Europe, Asia and the Pacific) and C3 (Latin America and the Caribbean). All powers are vested in a governing council of all member countries. It elects an 18-member executive board responsible for IFAD's operations. The council meets annually and elects a president who is also chair of the board. The president serves a four-year term that can be renewed once.

Since its establishment, IFAD has committed more than $10bn (£5bn) in loans for 766 approved projects and programmes.

President, Lennart Bage (Sweden)

INTERNATIONAL HYDROGRAPHIC ORGANISATION

International Hydrographic Organisation, 4 Quai Antoine 1er, B.P. 445, 98011, Monaco
T (+377) 9310 8100 E info@ihb.mc W www.iho.shom.fr

The International Hydrographic Organisation began its activity in 1921 with 19 member states and, at the invitation of H.S.H. Prince Albert I, was provided with headquarters in the Principality of Monaco. In 1970, its name was changed from the International Hydrographic Bureau. The IHO is an intergovernmental organisation that has a purely consultative role and aims to support safety in international navigation and set policy for marine conservation. The IHO has a membership of 80 states that meet at five-yearly conferences to set policy, approve budget, review progress and adopt programmes of work. Each member is represented at these conferences by their most senior hydrographer. All member states have an opportunity to initiate new proposals for IHO consideration. Outside of its membership, the IHO acts to promote hydrography and facilitate the exchange of technology with developing countries. It is also the source that defines the boundaries between seas and oceans.

President, Vice-Adm. Alexandros Maratos (Greece)

INTERNATIONAL LABOUR ORGANISATION

4 route des Morillons, CH-1211 Geneva 22, Switzerland
T (+41) (22) 799 6111 E ilo@ilo.org W www.ilo.org

The International Labour Organisation (ILO) was established in 1919 as an autonomous body of the League of Nations and became the UN's first specialised agency in 1946. The ILO aims to increase employment, improve working conditions and living standards and encourage democratic development.

It sets minimum international labour standards through the drafting of international conventions. Member countries are obliged to submit these to their domestic authorities for ratification, and thus undertake to bring their domestic legislation in line with the conventions. Members must report to the ILO periodically on how these regulations are being implemented. The ILO is also a principal resource centre for information, analysis and guidance on labour and employment.

The ILO has 181 members and is composed of the International Labour Conference, the governing body and the International Labour Office. The conference of members meets annually, and is attended by national delegations. It adopts international labour conventions and recommendations, provides a forum for discussion of world employment and social issues and approves the ILO's programme and budget.

The 56-member governing body is composed of 28 government, 14 worker and 14 employer members and acts as the ILO's executive council. Ten governments, including the UK, hold permanent seats on the governing body because of their industrial importance. There are also various regional conferences and advisory committees. The ILO acts as a secretariat and as a centre for operations, publishing and research.

Director-General, Juan Somavia (Chile)

INTERNATIONAL MARITIME ORGANISATION

4 Albert Embankment, London SE1 7SR
T 020-7735 7611 E media@imo.org W www.imo.org

Originally called the Inter-Governmental Maritime Consultative Organisation, the International Maritime Organisation (IMO) was established as a UN specialised agency in 1948. Owing to delays in treaty ratification it did not commence operations until 1958.

The IMO fosters intergovernmental cooperation in technical matters relating to international shipping, particularly regarding safety and security at sea, efficiency in navigation and protecting the marine environment from pollution caused by shipping. The IMO is responsible for convening maritime conferences and drafting marine conventions. It also provides technical aid to countries wishing to develop their activities at sea.

In 2008, the IMO had 167 members and three associate members. It is governed by an assembly comprising delegates of all its members. It meets biennially to formulate policy, set a budget (£49.8m for 2008–9), to vote on specific recommendations on pollution, maritime safety and security, and to elect the council. The council, which meets twice a year, fulfils the functions of the assembly between sessions and appoints a secretary-general. It consists of 40 members: ten from the world's largest shipping nations, ten from the nations

most dependent on seaborne trade, and 20 other members to ensure a fair geographical representation. The IMO acts as the secretariat for the London Convention (1972) which regulates the disposal of land-generated waste at sea.
Secretary-General, Efthimios E. Mitropoulos (Greece)

INTERNATIONAL MONETARY FUND

700 19th Street NW, Washington DC 20431, USA
T (+1) (202) 623 7300 **E** publicaffairs@imf.org **W** www.imf.org

The International Monetary Fund (IMF) was established at the UN Monetary and Financial Conference at Bretton Woods, New Hampshire, in 1944. Its articles of agreement entered into force in 1945 and it began operations in 1947.

The IMF exists to promote international monetary cooperation, the expansion of world trade and exchange stability. It advises members on their economic and financial policies; promotes policy coordination among the major industrial countries; and gives technical assistance in central banking, balance of payments accounting, taxation and other financial matters. The IMF serves as a forum for members to discuss monetary policy issues and seeks the balanced growth of international trade. It has 185 members.

Upon joining the IMF, a member is assigned a quota, based on the member's relative standing in the world economy and its balance of payments position. The quota determines the member's capital subscription to the fund, access to IMF resources, voting power and share in the allocation of special drawing rights (SDRs). Quotas are reviewed every five years and adjusted accordingly, although a broader set of reforms are set to be introduced to reflect the growing role of developing countries in the world economy. The SDR, an international reserve asset issued by the IMF, is calculated daily on a basket of usable currencies and is the IMF's unit of account; on 25 April 2007, 1 SDR equalled US$1.62 (£0.81). SDRs are allocated at intervals to supplement members' reserves and thereby improve international financial liquidity. Total quotas as at March 2007 were US$357bn (£179bn).

The IMF is not a bank and does not lend money; it provides temporary financial assistance by selling a member's SDRs or other members' currencies in exchange for the member's own currency. The member can then use the purchased currency to alleviate its balance of payments difficulties. IMF financial resources derive primarily from members' capital subscriptions, which are equivalent to their quotas. In addition, the IMF is authorised to borrow from official lenders. It may also draw on a line of credit of SDR18.5bn from various countries under the so-called general arrangements to borrow (GAB). Periodic charges are also levied on financial assistance. In March 2008, total outstanding IMF credits amounted to US$16.1bn (£8.1bn).

The IMF supports long-term efforts at economic reform and transformation as well as medium-term programmes under the extended fund facility, which runs for three to four years and is aimed at overcoming balance of payments difficulties stemming from macroeconomic and structural problems. Members experiencing a temporary balance of payments shortfall have access to the compensatory and contingency financing facility.

The IMF is headed by a board of governors, comprising representatives of all members, which meets annually. The governors delegate powers to 24 executive directors, who are appointed or elected by member countries. The executive directors operate the fund on a daily basis under a managing director, whom they elect.
Managing Director, Dominique Strauss-Kahn (France)

INTERNATIONAL ORGANISATION FOR MIGRATION

17 route des Morillons, CH-1211 Geneva 19, Switzerland
T (+41) 22717 9111 **E** info@iom.int **W** www.iom.int

The International Organisation for Migration (IOM) was founded in 1951 to resettle European displaced persons and refugees. During the 1960s and 1970s the IOM developed links with the United Nations High Commissioner for Refugees (UNHCR) and began a programme of assistance and reintegration outside of Europe. There are currently 122 member states and 18 observer countries. Internally, the IOM is led by a director-general who is elected for a five-year term. The director-general's office has the constitutional authority to manage the organisation, carry out the activities within its mandate and develop current policies, procedures and strategies. The office of the inspector-general (OIG) incorporates the functions of evaluation, internal audit and assessment of projects. The OIG is also involved in investigations within the formal complaints procedure.

The role of the IOM has recently expanded to cover migration health services, counter-trafficking measures, emergency and post-crises management and assisted voluntary returns.
Director-General, Brunson McKinley (USA)

INTERNATIONAL RED CROSS AND RED CRESCENT MOVEMENT

19 avenue de la Paix, CH-1202 Geneva, Switzerland
T (+41) 2273 46001 **W** www.icrc.org

The International Red Cross and Red Crescent Movement is composed of three elements – the International Committee of the Red Cross, the International Federation of Red Cross and Red Crescent Societies, and the national Red Cross and Red Crescent societies.

The International Committee of the Red Cross (ICRC), the organisation's founding body, was formed in 1863. It aims to negotiate between warring factions and to protect and assist victims of armed conflict. It also seeks to ensure the application of the Geneva Conventions regarding prisoners of war and detainees.

The International Federation of Red Cross and Red Crescent Societies was founded in 1919 to assist the humanitarian activities of national societies, coordinate their relief operations for victims of natural disasters and care for refugees outside areas of conflict. There are Red Cross and Red Crescent societies in 185 countries, with a total membership of over 250 million.

The international conference of the Red Cross and Red Crescent meets every four years, bringing together delegates of the ICRC, the International Federation and the national societies, as well as representatives of nations bound by the Geneva Conventions.
President, Jakob Kellenberger (Switzerland)

INTERNATIONAL TELECOMMUNICATION UNION

Place des Nations, CH-1211 Geneva 20, Switzerland
T (+41) (22) 730 5111 **E** itumail@itu.int **W** www.itu.int

The International Telecommunication Union (ITU) was founded in Paris in 1865 as the International

Telegraph Union and became a UN specialised agency in 1947.

ITU is an intergovernmental organisation for the development of telecommunications and the harmonisation of national telecommunication policies. It comprises 191 member states and some 650 sector members and 100 associates who represent public and private organisations involved in telecommunications. Its mission is to promote the development of information and communication technologies, and to offer technical assistance to developing countries.

ITU operates initiatives aimed at promoting the growth and expansion of electronic commerce. These include a programme of strategic workshops; the adoption of international regulations, treaties and technical standards to foster global interactivity; and the provision of policy advice and technical assistance. ITU also organises worldwide and regional exhibitions and forums to exchange ideas, knowledge and technology.

Secretary-General, Hamadoun Touré (Mali)

INTERNATIONAL WHALING COMMISSION

The Red House, 135 Station Road, Impington, Cambridge CB24 9NP **T** 01223-233971

E secretariat@iwcoffice.org **W** www.iwcoffice.org

The International Whaling Commission (IWC) was set up under the International Convention for the Regulation of Whaling, signed in Washington DC in 1946. It has 79 member states as of April 2008. The purpose of the IWC is to provide for the conservation of whale stocks, enabling the development of the whaling industry. The organisation reviews and revises the schedule to the convention which sets limits for when and where whaling can take place, coordinates and funds whale research and publishes and promotes scientific studies.

The IWC has four main committees, responsible for scientific, technical, conservation and finance matters. There are further sub-committees concerned with aboriginal subsistence whaling, infractions and working groups involved with whale-killing methods and animal welfare issues.

Chair, Dr William Hogarth (USA)

LATIN UNION

131 rue du Bac, F-75007 Paris, France

T (+33) (1) 4549 6060 **E** ulsg@unilat.org **W** www.unilat.org

The Latin Union is an international organisation whose member states use a Romance language. It was created in 1954 with the signing of a constituent agreement in Madrid and has existed as a functioning institution since 1983. The aims of the organisation are to protect, project and promote the common heritage and to unify identities of the Latin and Latin-influenced world. It has 37 member states and 3 members with observer status.

The congress is the senior body of the organisation. It consists of representatives from each of the member states and meets every two years. It is responsible for approving the budget and setting the agenda for the Union's activities. The executive council is made up of representatives from 12 member states who are elected for a four-year term by congress. The general secretariat is directed by a secretary-general who is elected by congress and instructed to implement policy.

The official languages of the Latin Union are French, Italian, Portuguese, Spanish and Romanian, though the latter is not used as a working language.

Secretary-General, Bernardino Osio

LEAGUE OF ARAB STATES

Maidan Al-Tahrir, Cairo, Egypt

T (+20) (2) 575 0511 **W** www.arableagueonline.org

The League of Arab States was founded in 1945 to protect the independence and sovereignty of its member states, supervise the affairs and interests of Arab countries and promote the process of integration among them. The organisation has 22 member states. The League itself has observer status at the United Nations.

The heads of member states meet annually at the Arab League summit, while foreign ministers convene every six months as part of the Arab League council. Member states participate in various specialised agencies which develop specific areas of cooperation between Arab states. These include: the Arab Organisation for Mineral Resources; the Arab Monetary Fund; the Arab Satellite Communications Organisation; the Arab Academy of Maritime Transport; the Arab Bank for Economic Development in Africa; the Arab League Educational, Cultural and Scientific Organisation and the Council of Arab Economic Unity.

Secretary-General, Amre Moussa (Egypt)

MERCOSUR

Luis Piera 1992, piso 1, 11200-Montevideo, Uruguay

T (+598) (2) 412 9024 **E** secretaria@mercosur.org.uy

W www.mercosur.org.uy

In 1988, Brazil and Argentina signed an integration, cooperation and development treaty which aimed to create a common market between the two countries within ten years, eliminating all tariff barriers and harmonising macroeconomic policies. The agreement was to be open to other Latin American countries. Paraguay and Uruguay expressed their interest and MERCOSUR (the Southern Common Market) was created by the treaty of Asunción, which was signed by the four countries on 26 March 1991. Venezuela became the fifth member in 2006. Five other countries have associate member status.

The Common Market Council (CMC) is the highest-level agency of MERCOSUR, with authority to conduct its policy and responsibility for compliance with the treaty of Asunción. The CMC comprises ministers of foreign affairs and economic ministers of the member states and meets at least once a year.

The Common Market Group is the executive body of MERCOSUR and is coordinated by the foreign ministries of the member states. Its function is to implement decisions made by the CMC and resolve disputes. It can establish subgroups to work on particular issues and comprises four permanent members and four substitutes from each country. Other bodies include a joint parliamentary committee, a trade commission and a socio-economic advisory forum.

In 2005, Argentina, Brazil, Paraguay and Uruguay became associate members of the Andean Community, reciprocating MERCOSUR's action to grant associate membership to all Andean Community nations. In December 2005, the Columbian president ratified a free trade agreement with MERCOSUR giving Columbian products preferential access to MERCOSUR countries.

President, Carlos Alvarez (Argentina)

NORDIC COUNCIL

Store Strandstraede 18, DK-1255 Copenhagen, Denmark T (+45) 3396 0400
E nordisk-rad@norden.org W www.norden.org

The Nordic Council was established in March 1952 as an advisory body on economic and social cooperation, comprising of parliamentary delegates from Denmark, Iceland, Norway and Sweden. It was subsequently joined by Finland (1956), and representatives from the Faroes (1970), the Aland Islands (1970), and Greenland (1984).

Cooperation is regulated by the treaty of Helsinki signed in 1962. This was amended in 1971 to create a Nordic council of ministers, which discusses all matters except defence and foreign affairs. Decisions of the council of ministers, which are taken by consensus, are binding, although if ratification by member parliaments is required, decisions only become effective following parliamentary approval. The council of ministers is advised by the Nordic Council, to which it reports annually. There are ministers for Nordic cooperation in every member government.

The Nordic Council comprises 87 voting delegates nominated from member parliaments and about 80 non-voting government representatives. It meets at least once a year in plenary sessions. The full council chooses a 13-member praesidium, which conducts business between sessions. A secretariat, headed by a secretary-general provides administrative support. The presidency and chairmanship of the Nordic Council rotate between the five countries but the same country never holds the presidency and chair of both organisations for the same year.
President, Erkki Tuomioja (Finland)

NORTH AMERICAN FREE TRADE AGREEMENT

NAFTA Secretariat, Canadian Section, 90 Sparks Street, Suite 705, Ottawa, Ontario K1P 5B4, Canada
T (+1) (613) 992 9388 E canada@nafta-sec-alena.org

NAFTA Secretariat, Mexican Section, Blvd. Adolfo López Mateos 3025, 2° Piso, Col. Héroes de Padierna, C.P. 10700, Mexico, D.F. T (+52) (55) 629 9630
E mexico@nafta-sec-alena.org

NAFTA Secretariat, US Section, Room 2061, 14th Street and Constitution Avenue, NW, Washington DC, 20230, USA
T (+1) (202) 482 5438 E usa@nafta-sec-alena.org
W www.nafta-sec-alena.org

The leaders of Canada, Mexico and the USA signed the North American Free Trade Agreement (NAFTA) on 17 December 1992 in their respective capitals; it came into force in January 1994 after being ratified by the legislatures of the three member states.

NAFTA aims to eliminate barriers to trade in goods and services, promote fair competition within the free trade area, protect and enforce intellectual property rights and create a framework for further cooperation. To achieve these aims, import tariffs and quotas are being removed, with the aim of achieving a free trade zone by 2008 at the latest.

The NAFTA secretariat is composed of Canadian, Mexican and US sections. It is responsible for administering the dispute settlement provisions of the agreement, providing assistance to the Free Trade Commission and support for various committees and working groups, and facilitating the operation of the agreement.

NORTH ATLANTIC TREATY ORGANISATION

Blvd Leopold III, Brussels B-1110, Belgium
T (+32) (2) 707 4111 E natodoc@hq.nato.int W www.nato.int

NATO is the structural framework for a political and military alliance designed to provide common security for its members through cooperation and consultation in political, military and economic as well as scientific and other non-military fields.

The North Atlantic treaty (treaty of Washington) was signed in 1949 by Belgium, Canada, Denmark, France, Iceland, Italy, Luxembourg, the Netherlands, Norway, Portugal, the UK and the USA. Greece and Turkey acceded to the treaty in 1952, the Federal Republic of Germany in 1955 (the reunited Germany acceded in October 1990), Spain in 1982, and the Czech Republic, Hungary and Poland in 1999. Bulgaria, Estonia, Latvia, Lithuania, Romania, Slovakia and Slovenia signed membership protocols in March 2003 and officially joined the North Atlantic Treaty Organisation (NATO) in March 2004.

STRUCTURE

The North Atlantic council (NAC), chaired by the secretary-general, is the highest authority of the alliance and is composed of permanent representatives of the 26 member countries. It meets at ministerial level (foreign and/or defence ministers) at least twice a year. The permanent representatives (ambassadors) head national delegations of advisers and experts. The defence planning committee (DPC) and the nuclear planning group (NPG) are composed of representatives of all member countries except France (which does not participate in NATO's integrated military structure). Both the DPC and the NPG also meet at ministerial level at least twice a year. The NATO secretary-general chairs the council, the DPC and the NPG. Much of the NAC policy is prepared and drafted by the senior political committee, a group of deputy permanent representatives and policy advisers.

The senior military authority in NATO, under the council and DPC, is the military committee, composed of the chief of defence staffs of each member country except Iceland, which has no military forces and is represented by a civilian. The military committee, which is assisted by an integrated international military staff, also meets in permanent session with permanent military representatives and is responsible for making recommendations to the council and DPC on measures considered necessary for the common defence of the NATO area and for supplying guidance on military matters to the NATO strategic commanders. The chair of the military committee, elected for a period of two to three years, represents the committee on the council.

The alliance's military command structure is divided between two functional strategic commands. The strategic commanders have responsibility for all NATO military operations (allied command operations or ACO) and for the further transformation of the alliance's military forces and capabilities (allied command transformation or ACT). There is also a regional planning group for Canada and the USA. The headquarters of ACO is at Mons, Belgium, and comes under the command of the Supreme Allied Commander Europe (SACEUR). The headquarters of ACT is at Norfolk, Virginia, USA, and is under the command of the Supreme Allied Commander, Transformation.

POST COLD WAR DEVELOPMENTS

The Euro-Atlantic partnership council (EAPC) was established in 1997 to develop closer security links with Eastern European and former Soviet states. Replacing the North Atlantic cooperation council (NACC) as the first institutional framework for cooperation between NATO member countries and former adversaries from Central and Eastern Europe, the EAPC focuses on defence planning, defence industry conversion, defence management and force structuring, and the democratic concepts of civilian-military relations. Its membership comprises the 26 NATO members and Albania, Armenia, Austria, Azerbaijan, Belarus, Bosnia and Hercegovina, Croatia, Finland, Georgia, Ireland, Kazakhstan, Kyrgyzstan, Macedonia, Malta, Moldova, Montenegro, Russia, Serbia, Sweden, Switzerland, Tajikistan, Turkmenistan, Ukraine and Uzbekistan. The EAPC provides the multilateral, political framework for the partnership for peace programme (PFP) in which each of its member countries participates. The PFP is the basis for practical, bilateral security cooperation between NATO and individual partner countries in the fields of defence planning and budgeting, military exercises and civil emergency operations. It also works to improve interoperability between the forces of partner and member countries to enable them to undertake joint operations and has provided the context for cooperation by many of the partner countries in NATO-led peacekeeping and peace-support operations in Bosnia and Hercegovina, Kosovo and Afghanistan.

NATO and Russia committed themselves to helping build a stable, secure and undivided continent on the basis of partnership and mutual interest, when they signed the 1997 Founding Act on mutual relations, cooperation and security, which provided for the creation of a NATO-Russia permanent joint council (PJC). In May 2002 it was replaced by the NATO-Russia council which brought together the 27 participating countries for consultation and practical cooperation in fields of common interest and endeavour on the basis of equality. The NRC meets every month at ambassadorial level and twice each year at ministerial level to address issues of common concern such as the threat of global terrorism and bilateral programmes in other areas of security such as defence reform, search and rescue, and civil emergency planning. NATO and Ukraine pursue an annual programme of cooperation and consultation following the signing of a NATO-Ukraine charter in 1997. NATO's Mediterranean dialogue, launched in 1994, aims to improve trust and understanding of NATO's goals and objectives among the countries of the southern Mediterranean area: Algeria, Egypt, Israel, Jordan, Mauritania, Morocco and Tunisia.

At its summit meeting in 2004, the alliance launched the Istanbul cooperation initiative, inviting contacts and cooperation with interested countries in the broader Middle East region.

The development of a European security and defence identity, which would strengthen NATO's European pillar, was agreed at the 1999 NATO summit meeting in Washington. Since then further developments have served to strengthen cooperation between NATO and the European Union and to establish a strategic partnership. This has led *inter alia* to the transfer of responsibility from NATO to the European Union, for continuing peace-support operations in the Former Yugoslav Republic of Macedonia and in Bosnia and Hercegovina, in accordance with special arrangements providing for NATO support for EU-led military operations of this kind.

At the Washington summit a defence capabilities initiative was also launched. It aims to improve defence interoperability among NATO forces to ensure the effectiveness of future multinational operations. At the 2002 Prague summit, further measures to improve capabilities were taken on the basis of a new capabilities commitment, in which member countries agreed to specific targets and time frames for improvements. A military concept for defence against terrorism was also agreed, and additional initiatives taken in the areas of nuclear, biological and chemical weapons defence, and protection against cyber attacks. A missile defence feasibility study was initiated. The NATO response force, a rapid-reaction unit comprising land, sea and air special forces was officially launched at the Prague summit and became fully operational (approx. 25,000 troops) in 2006.

AFGHANISTAN

From January 2001, following the establishment of the Afghan Transitional Authority, an international security assistance force (ISAF) was created on the basis of a UN mandate to provide the security needed to allow infrastructure reconstruction and create a stable democratic government. A number of NATO member countries took on responsibility on a six-monthly rotational basis for the leadership of this force. In 2002, NATO began providing support for ISAF at the request of the lead nations and, in August 2003, assumed full responsibility for the leadership of ISAF. In accordance with decisions taken at the Istanbul summit meeting in June 2004, and at the request of President Karzai, ISAF extended its authority from the capital, Kabul, to provide security assistance for almost 50 per cent of the country. In 2008, there were approximately 47,000 ISAF troops serving in Afghanistan from 40 NATO and non-NATO countries.

IRAQ

Following a summit meeting in Istanbul in 2004, NATO agreed to establish an Iraq training mission. This included the foundation of a joint staff college that was tasked with the training of Iraqi army officers and other senior defence staff. It is estimated that around 900 officers have graduated from the centre since its opening at Ar-Rustamiyah, near Baghdad, in September 2005. In 2007, NATO also launched a two-year training course for the Iraqi police, under the supervision of an Italian Carabinieri unit.

Secretary-General and Chair of the North Atlantic Council, of the DPC and of the NPG, Jaap de Hoop Scheffer (The Netherlands)

ORGANISATION FOR ECONOMIC COOPERATION AND DEVELOPMENT

2 rue André-Pascal, F-75775 Paris, France
T (+33) (1) 4524 8200 **E** webmaster@oecd.org
W www.oecd.org

The Organisation for Economic Cooperation and Development (OECD) was formed in 1961 to replace the Organisation for European Economic Cooperation. It is the instrument for international cooperation among industrialised member countries on economic and social policies. Its objectives are to assist its member governments in creating policies designed to achieve high, sustained economic growth and maintaining financial stability; to contribute to world trade on a multilateral basis and to stimulate members' aid to developing countries. OECD has 30 members, the vast majority in Europe. The European Commission is involved in the work of the OECD but is not a member of the organisation.

The council is the supreme body of the organisation. It is composed of one representative for each member country and meets at permanent representative level under the chairmanship of the secretary-general, and at ministerial level (usually once a year) under the chair of a minister, elected annually. Decisions and recommendations are adopted by the unanimous agreement of all members. Most of the OECD's work is undertaken in over 150 specialised committees and working parties. These are serviced by an international secretariat headed by a secretary-general.

In May 2006, OECD revealed it is considering expansion, with a number of countries interested in gaining membership. Before this can take place, a new method for calculating member funding is required. Funding is currently divided according to a member states' economy and population size, but many of the proposed members may struggle to fund their participation.

Secretary-General, Angel Gurria (Mexico)

ORGANISATION FOR SECURITY AND COOPERATION IN EUROPE

6 Wallnerstrasse, 1010 Vienna, Austria
T (+43) (1) 5143 66000 E info@osce.org W www.osce.org

The Organisation for Security and Cooperation in Europe (OSCE) was launched in 1975 as the Conference on Security and Cooperation in Europe (CSCE) under the Helsinki Final Act. This established agreements between NATO members, Warsaw Pact members, and neutral and non-aligned European countries covering security, cooperation and human rights. It was renamed in 1995.

The Charter of Paris for a New Europe, signed in November 1990, committed members to support multiparty democracy, free-market economics, the rule of law and human rights. The signatories also agreed to regular meetings of heads of government, ministers and officials. The first CSCE summit was held in Helsinki in December 1992, at which the Helsinki Document was adopted. This declared the CSCE to be a regional organisation under the UN charter and defined the structures of the organisation.

Three structures have been established: the ministerial council, which comprises the foreign ministers of participating states and meets at least once a year; the permanent council, which is the main regular body for political consulation, meeting weekly in Vienna; and the forum for security cooperation, also meeting weekly. The chairmanship of the OSCE rotates annually and the post of chair-in-office is held by the foreign minister of a participating state.

The OSCE is also underpinned by four permanent institutions: a secretariat (Vienna); an office for democratic institutions and human rights (Warsaw), which is charged with furthering human rights, democracy and the rule of law; an office of the high commissioner on national minorities (The Hague), which identifies ethnic tensions that might endanger peace and promotes their resolution; and a representative on freedom of the media (Vienna), which is responsible for assisting governments in the furthering of free, independent and pluralistic media.

The OSCE has 19 field missions in Europe, the Caucasus and Central Asia. Since 1996, the OSCE has observed more than 150 elections and supervised all elections in Bosnia and Hercegovina between 1996 and 2000 and in Kosovo between 2000 and 2004. In 1999, the charter on European security committed the OSCE to cooperating with other organisations and institutions concerned with the promotion of security within the OSCE area. The OSCE has 56 participating states and in 2008 its budget was €164m (£128m).

Chair, Finland (2008)
Chair-in-office, Alexander Stubb (Finland)

ORGANISATION OF AMERICAN STATES

17th Street and Constitution Avenue, NW, Washington DC 20006, USA T (+1) (202) 458 3000
E multimedia@oas.org W www.oas.org

Originally founded in 1890 for largely commercial purposes, the Organisation of American States (OAS) adopted its present name and charter in 1948. The charter entered into force in 1951 and was amended in 1967, 1985 and 1996; the 1992 Protocol of Washington, which gives the OAS the right to suspend a member state whose democratically elected government is overturned by force, was ratified in 1997. OAS has 35 member states. Cuba remains a member but has been excluded from participation since 1962. The European Union and 59 non-American states have permanent observer status.

The OAS aims to strengthen the peace and security of the continent; to promote and consolidate representative democracy; to prevent possible causes of difficulties and to ensure the peaceful resolution of disputes among member states; to seek the resolution of political, judicial and economic problems that may arise among them; to promote their economic, social and cultural development; and to achieve an effective limitation of conventional weapons.

The declaration of principles and the plan of action resulting from the 1994 Miami summit and signed by all the members except Cuba, envisage the establishment of a free trade area, in which barriers to trade and investment will be progressively eliminated.

Policy is determined by the annual general assembly, which is the supreme authority and elects the secretary-general for a five-year term. The meeting of consultation of ministers of foreign affairs considers urgent problems on an *ad hoc* basis. The permanent council, comprising one representative from each member state, promotes friendly relations, acts as an intermediary in case of disputes arising between states and oversees the general secretariat, the main administrative body. The inter-American council for integral development was created in 1996 by the ratification of the protocol of Managua to promote sustainable development.

Secretary-General, Jose Miguel Insulza (Chile)

ORGANISATION OF ARAB PETROLEUM EXPORTING COUNTRIES

PO Box 20501, Safat 13066, Kuwait
T (+965) 495 9000 E oapec@oapecorg.org
W www.oapecorg.org

The Organisation of Arab Petroleum Exporting Countries (OAPEC) was founded in 1968. Its objectives are to promote cooperation in economic activities, safeguard members' interests, unite efforts to ensure the flow of oil to consumer markets, and create a favourable climate for the investment of capital and expertise. OAPEC has 11 member states, although Tunisia's membership has been inactive since 1987.

The ministerial council is composed of oil ministers from the member countries and meets twice a year to determine policy and approve the budgets and accounts of the general secretariat and the judicial tribunal. The judicial tribunal is composed of seven part-time judges who rule on disputes between member countries and between countries and oil companies. The executive organ of OAPEC is the general secretariat.

The members are Algeria, Bahrain, Egypt, Iraq, Kuwait, Libya, Qatar, Saudi Arabia, Syria and the United Arab Emirates.

Secretary-General, Abbas Ali Nagi (Kuwait)

ORGANISATION OF THE BLACK SEA ECONOMIC COOPERATION

Sakip Sabanci Caddesi, Musir Fuad Pasa Yalisi, Eski Tersane, 34460 Istanbul, Turkey **T** (+90) (212) 229 6330/6335
E info@bsec-organization.org **W** www.bsec-organization.org

The Black Sea Economic Cooperation (BSEC) resulted from the Istanbul Summit Declaration and the adoption of the Bosporus Statement on 25 June 1992. BSEC acquired a permanent secretariat in 1994. A charter was inaugurated to found the Organisation of the Black Sea Economic Cooperation in May 1999, following the Yalta Summit of the heads of state or government in June 1998. It has 12 member states.

The organisation aims to promote closer political and economic cooperation between the countries in the Black Sea region and to foster security, regional initiatives, social justice, economic liberty and respect for human rights.

The council of the ministers of foreign affairs is the highest decision-making authority and meets twice--yearly. The meetings rotate among the member states and the chair is the foreign minister of the state in which the meeting is held. There is also a committee of senior officials and 16 working groups, which deal with specific areas of cooperation.

Chair, Albania

ORGANISATION OF THE ISLAMIC CONFERENCE

PO Box 178, Jeddah 21411, Saudi Arabia
T (+966) (2) 690 0001 **E** cabinet@oic-oci.org
W www.oic-oci.org

The Organisation of the Islamic Conference (OIC) was established in 1969 with the purpose of promoting solidarity and cooperation between Islamic countries. It also has the specific aims of coordinating efforts to safeguard Muslim holy places, supporting the formation of a Palestinian state, coordinating the views of member states in international forums such as the UN, and improving cooperation in the fields of economics, culture and science.

The OIC has three main bodies, the summit of the heads of state, the conference of foreign ministers and the general secretariat which is headed by a secretary-general, elected by the conference of foreign ministers for a once-renewable five-year term.

In addition to this structure, the OIC has several subsidiary bodies, institutions, and standing committees. These include the international Islamic court of justice; the Islamic Solidarity Fund, to aid Islamic institutions in member countries; the Islamic Development Bank, to finance development projects in poorer member states and the Islamic Educational, Scientific and Cultural Organisation.

The achievement of the OIC's aims has often been prevented by political rivalry and conflicts between member states, such as the Iran-Iraq war and the Iraqi invasion of Kuwait. Egypt's membership was suspended from 1979 to 1984 because of its peace treaty with Israel. Saudi Arabia, the main source of funding, exercises great influence within the OIC. Since 1991, the OIC has become more united and has spoken out in protest of violence against Muslims in India, the Occupied Territories and Bosnia-Hercegovina. From 1993 to 1995 the OIC coordinated the offering of troops to the UN by Muslim states to protect Muslim areas of Bosnia-Hercegovina.

The organisation has 57 members (56 sovereign Muslim states in Africa, the Middle East, central and south-east Asia and Europe, plus the Palestine Authority) and five observer states.

Secretary-General, Prof. Ekmeleddin Ihsanoglu (Turkey)

ORGANISATION OF THE PETROLEUM EXPORTING COUNTRIES

Obere Donaustrasse 93, A-1020 Vienna, Austria
T (+43) (1) 2111 2279 **E** prid@opec.org **W** www.opec.org

The Organisation of the Petroleum Exporting Countries (OPEC) was created in 1960 as a permanent intergovernmental organisation with the principal aims of unifying and coordinating the petroleum policies of its members, determining ways of protecting their interests, and ensuring the stabilisation of prices in international oil markets. Since 1982, OPEC has attempted to impose overall production limits and production quotas to maintain stable oil prices.

The supreme authority is the conference of ministers of oil, mining and energy of member countries, which meets at least twice a year. The board of governors, nominated by member countries, directs the management of OPEC and implements conference resolutions. The secretariat carries out executive functions under the direction of the board of governors.

OPEC's 13 member countries hold about three-quarters of the world's oil reserves and, in 2007, OPEC accounted for around 45 per cent of the world's oil production.

Secretary-General, Abdalla Salem El-Badri (Libya)

PACIFIC ISLANDS FORUM

Secretariat, Private Mail Bag, Suva, Fiji
T (+679) 331 2600 **E** info@forumsec.org.fj
W www.forumsec.org.fj

The Pacific Islands Forum (PIF), formerly the South Pacific Forum, was established in 1971 and represents heads of governments of 16 independent and self-governing Pacific island countries. It aims to foster cooperation between its governments and to represent the interests of the region in international organisations. The PIF meets annually, following which a dialogue is conducted at ministerial level with 12 forum partners.

The PIF secretariat comprises divisions dealing with

development and economic policy, trade and investment, political and international affairs and services, and is responsible for implementing Forum decisions.

In 2006, French Polynesia and New Caledonia became associate members. Tokelau, Wallis and Futuna and East Timor, the Commonwealth and the Asia Development Bank currently hold observer status.

Secretary-General, Gregory Lawrence Urwin (Australia)

PARTNERS IN POPULATION AND DEVELOPMENT

IPH Building, Mohakhali, 1212 Dhaka, Bangladesh
T (+88) (2) 988 1882 **E** partners@ppdsec.org
W www.partners-popdev.org

Partners in Population and Development (PPD) is an inter-governmental organisation launched at the UN International Conference on Population and Development in Cairo in 1994. It has 21 member states. PPD is dedicated to forming partnerships between and among individuals, organisations and the governments of developing countries. It provides a platform for its members to share successful experiences in education, migration, sexual health and combating infant mortality.

PPD is controlled by a board of directors consisting of a single representative from each member state. The responsibilities of the board include setting policy, promoting cooperation among members and providing advice to the secretariat. The secretariat is based in Dhaka, Bangladesh, and is mandated to serve as the administrative centre of the organisation. It ensures policies are implemented and identifies new areas for collaboration. PPD also has an international advisory committee consisting mainly of scientists who advise the board and secretariat of current trends in population, development and reproductive health.

PPD is a permanent observer at the United Nations.

Chair, HE Zhang Weqing (China)

SECRETARIAT OF THE PACIFIC COMMUNITY

BP D5, 98848 Nouméa Cedex, 95 Promenade Roger Laroque, New Caledonia **T** (+687) 262 000
E spc@spc.int **W** www.spc.int

The Secretariat of the Pacific Community (SPC) (formerly the South Pacific Commission) was established in 1947 by Australia, France, the Netherlands, New Zealand, the UK and the USA with the aim of promoting the economic and social stability of the islands in the region. The community now numbers 26 member states and territories: the four remaining founder states (the Netherlands and the UK have withdrawn) and the other 22 states and territories of Melanesia, Micronesia and Polynesia.

The SPC is a technical assistance agency with programmes in marine and land development and social resources. The governing body is the conference of the Pacific community.

Director-General, Dr Jimmie Rodgers (Solomon Islands)

SHANGHAI COOPERATION ORGANISATION

41 Liangmaqiao Road, Chaoyang District, 100600 Beijing, China **T** (+86) (10) 6532 9807
E sco@sectsco.org **W** www.sectsco.org

The Shanghai Cooperation Organisation (SCO) is a permanent inter-governmental organisation. It was established in 1996 as the Shanghai Five, when China, Kazakhstan, Kyrgyzstan, Russia and Tajikistan signed an agreement on cooperating to resolve disputes along the former Sino-Soviet border. It was renamed in 2001 when Uzbekistan became an official member.

The main principle of the SCO is strengthening cooperation among member states across a range of fields, including politics, economics, culture, energy, transportation, environment protection and tourism. The organisation encourages regional peace, security and stability, and the pursuit of democracy.

The council of heads of states meets annually and is the organisation's supreme body responsible for policy. The council of heads of governments also holds annual meetings to discuss cooperation strategies and approve budget. The SCO has two permanent bodies, a secretariat based in Beijing and a regional anti-terrorist structure in Tashkent. The secretary-general and the director of the executive committee are appointed by the council of heads of state for a period of three years.

Since 2005, Iran, Mongolia and Pakistan have applied for full membership and India has gained observer status. In the same year, the SCO announced it would prioritise joint energy projects, including developments in the oil and gas sectors, the exploration of new hydrocarbon reserves and joint use of water resources. The creation of an inter-bank SCO council was also agreed in order to fund future joint projects.

Secretary-General, Bolat Nurgaliev (Kazakhstan)

SOUTH ASIAN ASSOCIATION FOR REGIONAL COOPERATION

PO Box 4222, Tridevi Marg, Kathmandu, Nepal
T (+977) (1) 422 1785/6350 **E** saarc@saarc-sec.org
W www.saarc-sec.org

The South Asian Association for Regional Cooperation (SAARC) was established in 1985 by Bangladesh, Bhutan, India, the Maldives, Nepal, Pakistan and Sri Lanka. Its primary objective is the acceleration of economic and social development in member states through collective action in agreed areas of cooperation. These include agricultural and environmental development, science and technology and transport and communications.

A SAARC preferential trading arrangement, which is designed to reduce tariffs on trade between SAARC member states, was signed in 1993 and entered into force in 1995. A committee of experts was established in 1998 to draft a comprehensive treaty to create a South Asian free trade area. Agreement was reached in 2002 to work towards the establishment of a South Asian economic union.

The highest authority rests with the heads of state or government of each member state. The council of ministers, which meets twice a year, is made up of the foreign ministers of member states and is responsible for formulating policy. The standing committee is composed of the foreign secretaries of the member states and monitors and coordinates SAARC programmes; it meets twice a year. Technical committees are assigned to individual areas of SAARC's activities. Its secretariat monitors, facilitates and promotes SAARC's activities and serves as a channel of communication between the association and other regional and intergovernmental institutions.

In 2005, as the only country in South Asia not to be a member of SAARC, Iran declared its wish to join and has since become an observer member, along with Japan,

South Korea, USA and the EU. In 2007, Afghanistan was admitted as SAARC's eighth member state.
Secretary-General, HE Dr Sheel Kant Sharma (India)

SOUTHERN AFRICAN DEVELOPMENT COMMUNITY

Private Bag 0095, Gaborone, Botswana
T (+267) 395 1863 **E** registry@sadc.int **W** www.sadc.int

The Southern African Development Community (SADC) was formed in 1992 by the members of its predecessor, the Southern African Development Coordination Conference. The latter was founded in 1980 to harmonise economic development among the countries in southern Africa and reduce their dependence on South Africa. The SADC now comprises 14 countries, including South Africa, and works on a regional basis to increase economic integration and regional security.

It aims to evolve common political values, promote development and economic growth, regional security, sustainable development and the interdependence of member states, maximise production and strengthen and consolidate the historical, social and cultural links among the peoples of the region.
Executive Secretary, Tomaz Augusto Salomao (Mozambique)

UNITED NATIONS

UN Plaza, New York, NY 10017, USA
T (+1) (212) 963 1234 **W** www.un.org

The United Nations (UN) is an intergovernmental organisation dedicated through signature of the UN charter to the maintenance of international peace and security and the solution of economic, social and political problems through international cooperation.

The UN was founded as a successor to the League of Nations and inherited many of its procedures and institutions. The name United Nations was first used in the Washington Declaration 1942 to describe the 26 states that had allied to fight the Axis powers. The UN charter developed from discussions at the Moscow conference of the foreign ministers of China, the Soviet Union, the UK and the USA in 1943. Further progress was made at Dumbarton Oaks, Washington, in 1944 during talks involving the same states. The role of the security council was formulated at the Yalta conference in 1945. The charter was formally drawn up and signed by 50 allied nations at the San Francisco conference between April and June 1945. Following ratification the UN came into effect on 24 October 1945, which is celebrated annually as United Nations Day. The UN flag is light blue with the UN emblem centred in white.

The principal organs of the UN are the general assembly, the security council, the economic and social council, the secretariat and the international court of justice. The economic and social council is an auxiliary, charged with assisting and advising the general assembly and security council. The official languages used are Arabic, Chinese, English, French, Russian and Spanish. Deliberations at the international court of justice are in English and French only.

MEMBERSHIP

Membership is open to all countries which accept the charter and its principle of peaceful co-existence. New members are admitted by the general assembly on the recommendation of the security council. The original membership of 51 states has grown to 192 *(see opposite)*.

OBSERVERS

Permanent observer status is held by the Holy See. The Palestine Authority has special observer status.

THE GENERAL ASSEMBLY

UN Plaza, New York, NY 10017, USA

The general assembly is the main deliberative organ of the UN. It consists of all members, each entitled to five representatives but having only one vote. The annual session begins on the third Tuesday of September, when the president is elected, and usually continues until mid-December. Special sessions are held on specific issues and emergency special sessions can be called within 24 hours.

The assembly is empowered to discuss any matter within the scope of the charter, except when it is under consideration by the security council, and to make recommendations. Under the peace resolution, adopted in 1950, the assembly may also take action to maintain international peace and security when the security council fails to do so because of a lack of unanimity of its permanent members. Important decisions, such as those on peace and security, the election of officers, the budget, etc, need a two-thirds majority. Others need a simple majority. The assembly has effective power only over the internal operations of the UN itself; external recommendations are not legally binding.

The work of the general assembly is divided among a number of committees, on each of which every member has the right to be represented. Subjects include human rights, the use of torture, peacemaking, assisting developing countries and discrimination. In addition, the general assembly appoints *ad hoc* committees to consider more specific issues. All committees consider items referred to them by the assembly and recommend draft resolutions to its plenary meeting.

The assembly is assisted by a number of functional committees. The general committee coordinates its proceedings and operations, while the credentials committee verifies the representatives. There are also two standing committees, the advisory committee on administration and budgetary questions and the committee on contributions, which suggests the scale of members' payments to the UN.
President of the General Assembly, HE Srgjan Kerim (Macedonia)

SPECIALISED BODIES

The assembly has created a large number of specialised bodies, some of which are supervised jointly with the economic and social council. They are supported by UN and voluntary contributions from governments, non-governmental organisations and individuals. These organisations include:

CONFERENCE ON DISARMAMENT

Palais des Nations, CH-1211 Geneva 10, Switzerland

The Conference on Disarmament (CD) was established in 1979 as the single multilateral disarmament negotiating forum of the international community. Originally comprising 40 member states, the CD has expanded to 65 members. The non-proliferation of nuclear weapons treaty entered into force on 5 March 1970 and has so far been

Members of the UN

Afghanistan
Albania
Algeria
Andorra
Angola
Antigua and Barbuda
Argentina*
Armenia
Australia*
Austria
Azerbaijan
Bahamas
Bahrain
Bangladesh
Barbados
Belarus*
Belgium*
Belize
Benin
Bhutan
Bolivia*
Bosnia and Hercegovina
Botswana
Brazil*
Brunei
Bulgaria
Burkina Faso
Burundi
Cambodia
Cameroon
Canada*
Cape Verde
Central African Republic
Chad
Chile*
China*
Colombia*
Comoros
Congo, Republic of the
Costa Rica*
Côte d'Ivoire
Croatia
Cuba*
Cyprus
Czech Republic
Congo, Dem. Rep of the
Denmark*
Djibouti
Dominica
Dominican Republic*
East Timor
Ecuador*
Egypt*
El Salvador*
Equatorial Guinea
Eritrea
Estonia
Ethiopia*
Fiji
Finland
France*
Gabon
The Gambia
Georgia
Germany
Ghana
Greece*
Grenada
Guatemala*
Guinea
Guinea-Bissau
Guyana
Haiti*
Honduras*
Hungary
Iceland
India*
Indonesia
Iran*
Iraq*
Ireland
Israel
Italy
Jamaica
Japan
Jordan
Kazakhstan
Kenya
Kiribati
Korea, Dem. People's Rep. of
Korea, Rep. of
Kuwait
Kyrgyzstan
Laos
Latvia
Lebanon*
Lesotho
Liberia*
Libya
Liechtenstein
Lithuania
Luxembourg*
FYR Macedonia
Madagascar
Malawi
Malaysia
Maldives
Mali
Malta
Marshall Islands
Mauritania
Mauritius
Mexico*
Micronesia, Federated States of
Moldova
Monaco
Mongolia
Montenegro
Morocco
Mozambique
Myanmar
Namibia
Nauru
Nepal
The Netherlands*
New Zealand*
Nicaragua*
Niger
Nigeria
Norway*
Oman
Pakistan
Palau
Panama*
Papua New Guinea
Paraguay*
Peru*
The Philippines*
Poland*
Portugal
Qatar
Romania
Russian Federation*
Rwanda
St Kitts and Nevis
St Lucia
St Vincent and the Grenadines
Samoa
San Marino
São Tomé and Princípe
Saudi Arabia*
Senegal
Serbia
Seychelles
Sierra Leone
Singapore
Slovakia
Slovenia
Solomon Islands
Somalia
South Africa*
Spain
Sri Lanka
Sudan
Suriname
Swaziland
Sweden
Switzerland
Syria
Tajikistan
Tanzania
Thailand
Togo
Tonga
Trinidad and Tobago
Tunisia
Turkey*
Turkmenistan
Tuvalu
Uganda
Ukraine*
United Arab Emirates
United Kingdom*
United States of America*
Uruguay*
Uzbekistan
Vanuatu
Venezuela
Vietnam
Yemen
Zambia
Zimbabwe

*Original member (ie from 1945). Czechoslovakia, Yugoslavia and the USSR were all original members until their dissolution.

ratified by 188 states. A chemical weapons convention was agreed in Paris in 1993 and came into force in April 1997 after being ratified by 87 countries. It bans the use, production, stockpiling and transfer of all chemical weapons. All US and Russian weapons must be destroyed within 15 years of the convention entering into force and all other states' weapons must be destroyed within ten years.

UNITED NATIONS CHILDREN'S FUND (UNICEF)
3 UN Plaza, New York, NY 10017, USA **T** (+1) 212 326 7000
W www.unicef.org

Established in 1947 to assist children and mothers in the immediate post-war period, UNICEF now concentrates on developing countries. It provides primary healthcare and health education. In particular, UNICEF conducts programmes in oral hydration, immunisation against leading diseases, child growth monitoring and the encouragement of breast-feeding. Its operations are often conducted alongside the World Health Organisation.

UNITED NATIONS DEVELOPMENT PROGRAMME (UNDP)
1 UN Plaza, New York, NY 10017, USA **T** (+1) 212 906 5000
W www.undp.org

Established in 1966 from the merger of the UN expanded programme of technical assistance and the UN special fund, UNDP is the central funding agency for economic and social development projects around the world. Much of its annual expenditure is channelled through UN specialised agencies, governments and non-governmental organisations.

UNITED NATIONS HIGH COMMISSIONER FOR REFUGEES (UNHCR)
Case Postale 2500, CH-1211 Geneve 2 Depot, Switzerland
T (+41) 22 739 8111 W www.unhcr.org

Established in 1951 to protect the rights and interests of refugees, UNHCR organises emergency relief and longer-term solutions, such as voluntary repatriation, local integration or resettlement.

UNITED NATIONS RELIEF AND WORKS AGENCY FOR PALESTINE REFUGEES IN THE NEAR EAST (UNRWA)
HQ Gaza PO Box 140157, Amman 11814, Jordan
T (+972) 8 677 7333 W www.unrwa.org

Established in 1949 to bring relief to the Palestinians displaced by the Arab-Israeli conflict. The UN general assembly has repeatedly voted every three years to extend the mandate of the UNRWA, most recently until June 2011.

UNITED NATIONS HUMAN RIGHTS COUNCIL (UNHRC)
Palais des Nations, CH-1211 Geneva 10, Switzerland
T (+22) 917 9000 E infodesk@ohchr.org W www.ohchr.org

The UNHRC is a 47-member council, established in 2006, replacing the United Nations Commission on Human Rights (UNCHR). The UNHRC has a mandate to secure respect for, and prevent violations of human rights by engaging in dialogue with governments and international organisations. It is also responsible for the coordination of all UN human rights activities and reports to, and is directly elected by, the general assembly.

THE SECURITY COUNCIL
UN Plaza, New York, NY 10017, USA
T (+41) (22) 917 9000 W www.un.org/docs/sc

The security council is the senior arm of the UN and has the primary responsibility for maintaining world peace and security. It consists of 15 members, each with one representative and one vote. There are five permanent members – China, France, Russia, the UK and the USA – and ten non-permanent members. Each of the non-permanent members is elected for a two-year term by a two-thirds majority of the general assembly and is ineligible for immediate re-election. Five of the elective seats are allocated to Africa and Asia, one to eastern Europe, two to Latin America and two to western Europe and remaining countries. Procedural questions are determined by a majority vote. Other matters require a majority inclusive of the votes of the permanent members; they thus have a right of veto. The abstention of a permanent member does not constitute a veto. The presidency rotates each month by state in (English) alphabetical order. Parties in a dispute, other non-members and individuals can be invited to participate in security council debates but are not permitted to vote.

The security council is empowered to settle or adjudicate in disputes or situations which threaten international peace and security. It can adopt political, economic and military measures to achieve this end. Any matter considered to be a threat to or breach of the peace or an act of aggression can be brought to the security council's attention by any member state or by the secretary-general. The charter envisaged members placing at the disposal of the security council armed forces and other facilities which would be coordinated by the military staff committee, composed of military representatives of the five permanent members. The security council is also supported by a committee of experts, to advise on procedural and technical matters, and a committee on admission of new members.

Owing to superpower disunity, the security council has rarely played the decisive role set out in the charter; the military staff committee was effectively suspended from 1948 until 1990, when a meeting was convened during the Gulf crisis on the formation and control of UN-supervised armed forces. In 1992, heads of government laid plans to transform the UN in light of the changed post-Cold War world. The secretary-general produced *An Agenda for Peace,* a report which centred on the establishment of a UN army composed of national contingents on permanent standby, as envisaged at the time of the UN's formation. However, enthusiasm for UN intervention waned in the rest of the decade after a problematic mission in Somalia during which 42 UN personnel were killed. The security council has since been criticised for its failure to intervene in subsequent conflicts, including the genocide in Rwanda and the ongoing situation in Darfur.

The security council also has the power to elect judges to the international court of justice and to recommend to the general assembly the election of a secretary-general.

PEACEKEEPING FORCES
The security council has established a number of peacekeeping forces since its foundation, comprising contingents provided mainly by neutral and non-aligned UN members. As at 2008, current operations were:

Continent	*UN Code*	*Year implemented*	*Personnel deployed*
Africa			
Western Sahara	MINURSO	1991	491
Democratic Republic of the Congo	MONUC	1999	22,000
Ethiopia and Eritrea	UNMEE	2000	909
Liberia	UNMIL	2003	15,277
Côte d'Ivoire	UNOCI	2004	10,489
Sudan	UNMIS	2005	13,398
Darfur, Sudan	UNAMID	2007	10,302
Central African Republic and Chad	MINURCAT	2007	133
The Americas			
Haiti	MINUSTAH	2004	10,849
Asia			
India and Pakistan	UNMOGIP	1949	117
East Timor	UNMIT	2006	2,837
Europe			
Cyprus	UNFICYP	1964	1,083
Georgia	UNOMIG	1993	435
Kosovo	UNMIK	1999	4,537
Middle East			
Egypt, Israel, Jordan, Lebanon and Syria	UNTSO	1948	377
Israel and Syria	UNDOF	1978	1,187
Lebanon	UNIFIL	1974	13,249

TOP FIVE CONTRIBUTORS TO UN PEACEKEEPING MISSIONS (*as at* May 2008)

Country	*Number of Troops*
Pakistan	10,629
Bangladesh	9,047
India	8,964
Nigeria	5,415
Nepal	3,667

Source: UN Department of Public Information

INTERNATIONAL CRIMINAL TRIBUNAL FOR THE FORMER YUGOSLAVIA
Churchill Plein 1, NL-2517 JW The Hague, The Netherlands
T (+31) 7051 25000 W www.un.org/icty

In February 1993, the security council voted to establish the International Criminal Tribunal for the Former Yugoslavia (ICTFY) a war crimes tribunal to hear cases covering grave breaches of the Geneva Conventions and crimes against humanity during the Balkans conflict of the 1990s. The court was inaugurated in November 1993 in The Hague with 11 judges elected by the UN general assembly from 11 states, divided into two trial chambers of three judges each and an appeal chamber of the remaining five. The court is unable to force suspects to stand trial but is empowered to pass verdicts in the absence of suspects and can put suspects under an 'act of accusation' which prevents them from leaving their own country. As well as running and managing a detention unit based at The Hague and a witness protection and assistance programme, the ICTFY also has powers to interview witnesses and seize evidence. The total budget for 2006–7 was US$276m (£138m) and 1137 staff representing 82 nations are currently employed by the tribunal.
President, Fausto Pocar (Italy)

INTERNATIONAL CRIMINAL TRIBUNAL FOR RWANDA
Churchill Plein 1, NL-2517 JW The Hague, The Netherlands
T (+31) 7051 25027 E ictr-press@un.org W http://69.94.11.53

Following serious violations of humanitarian law in Rwanda, the UN security council created the International Criminal Tribunal for Rwanda on 8 November 1994. The purpose of this measure was to contribute to the process of national reconciliation in Rwanda and to the maintenance of peace in the region. The tribunal was established for the prosecution of persons responsible for genocide and other serious violations of international humanitarian law committed in the territory of Rwanda between 1 January 1994 and 31 December 1994. It may also deal with the prosecution of Rwandan citizens responsible for genocide and other such violations of international law committed in the territory of neighbouring states during the same period. The total budget for 2006–7 was US$270m and 1,042 staff representing 85 nations are currently employed by the tribunal.
President, Judge Charles Michael Dennis Byron (St Christopher and Nevis)

UNITED NATIONS MONITORING, VERIFICATION AND INSPECTION COMMISSION (UNMOVIC)
ALCOA Building, 866 United Nations Plaza, Room A-610, 48th St., New York, NY 10017, USA
T (+1) (212) 963 3022 E info@unmovic.org
W www.unmovic.org

The United Nations Monitoring, Verification and Inspection Commission (UNMOVIC), was created by UN Security Council Resolution 1284, adopted in December 1999.

UNMOVIC is mandated to verify Iraq's compliance with its obligation not to possess or acquire weapons of mass destruction (biological or chemical, together with ballistic missiles with a target distance of more than 150km), to destroy all research, development and production facilities and to desist from the future development or acquisition of such weapons. It also operates a monitoring and verification programme to ensure that prohibited items and programmes are not reactivated.

In January 2003, chief weapons inspector Dr Hans Blix stated that Iraq had failed to disarm, greatly strengthening the American and British case for war. US president George W. Bush presented the deadline of 17 March 2003 for Iraq to disarm and despite no UN support, began air strikes against Baghdad on 19 March. In a report covering March to May 2003, Blix stated that the commission had at no point during the inspections in Iraq found evidence of the continuation or resumption of programmes of weapons of mass destruction or significant quantity of proscribed items – whether pre-1991 or after. He stressed that this did not mean that such items could not exist as there remained long lists of unaccounted items.

Following the adoption of Resolution 1762 on 29 June 2007, the UN security council terminated the mandate of UNMOVIC.
Executive Chair (acting), Demetrius Perricos (Greece)

THE ECONOMIC AND SOCIAL COUNCIL
UN Plaza, New York, NY 10017, USA
E ecosocinfo@un.org W www.un.org/ecosoc

The economic and social council is responsible under the general assembly for the economic and social work of the UN and for the coordination of the activities of the 14 specialised agencies and other UN bodies. It makes reports and recommendations on economic, social, cultural, educational, health and related matters, often in consultation with non-governmental organisations, passing the reports to the general assembly and other UN bodies. It also drafts conventions for submission to the assembly and calls conferences on matters within its remit.

The council consists of 54 members, 18 of whom are elected annually by the general assembly for a three-year term. Each has one vote and can be immediately re-elected on retirement. A president is elected annually and is also eligible for re-election. One substantive session is held annually and decisions are reached by a simple majority vote of those present.

The council has established a number of standing committees on particular issues and several commissions. Commissions include statistical, human rights, social development, sustainable development, status of women, crime prevention and criminal justice, narcotic drugs, science and technology for development and population; and regional economic commissions.
President, HE Leo Merores (Haiti)

THE SECRETARIAT
UN Plaza, New York, NY 10017, USA

The secretariat services the other UN organs and is headed by a secretary-general elected by a majority vote of the general assembly on the recommendation of the security council. He is assisted by an international staff, chosen to represent the international character of the organisation. The secretary-general is charged with bringing to the attention of the security council any matter which he considers poses a threat to international peace and security. He may also bring other matters to the attention of the general assembly and other UN bodies and may be entrusted by them with additional duties. As chief administrator to the UN, the secretary-general is present in person or via representatives at all meetings of the other five main organs of the UN. He may also act as an impartial mediator in disputes between member states.

The power and influence of the secretary-general has been determined largely by the character of the office-holder and by the state of relations between the superpowers. The thaw in these relations since the mid-1980s has increased the effectiveness of the UN, particularly in its attempts to intervene in international disputes. It helped to end the Iran-Iraq War and sponsored peace in Central America. Following Iraq's invasion of Kuwait in 1990, the UN took its first collective security action since the Korean War. Conflicts in Cyprus, East Timor, Libya, Nigeria and Western Sahara have been successfully prevented from escalating or spreading during the administration of Kofi Annan. However, the UN was heavily criticised for its failure to act in the Rwandan genocide of 1994 and its inability to halt the continuing conflict in Darfur, while the invasion of Iraq by the USA and UK in 2003 without a UN mandate showed the organisation can be bypassed.

Secretary-General, Ban Ki-moon (South Korea)
Deputy Secretary-General, Asha-Rose Migiro (Tanzania)

FORMER SECRETARIES-GENERAL	
1946–53	Trygve Lie (Norway)
1953–61	Dag Hammarskjöld (Sweden)
1961–71	U Thant (Burma)
1971–81	Kurt Waldheim (Austria)
1981–91	Javier Pérez de Cuéllar (Peru)
1991–96	Boutros Boutros-Ghali (Egypt)
1997–2006	Kofi Annan (Ghana)

UK MISSION TO THE UN
1 Dag Hammarskjöld Plaza, 885 Second Avenue, New York, NY 10017, USA
T (+1) (212) 745 9200 E uk@un.int W www.ukun.org
Permanent Representative to the United Nations and Representative on the Security Council, Sir John Sawers, *apptd* 2007

UK MISSION TO THE OFFICE OF THE UN AND OTHER INTERNATIONAL ORGANISATIONS IN GENEVA
58 Avenue Louis Casai, 1216 Cointrin GE Geneva, Switzerland
T (+41) (22) 918 2300 E geneva_un@fco.gov.uk
Permanent UK Representative, Peter Gooderham, *apptd* 2008

UK MISSION TO THE UN IN VIENNA
Jaurčsgasse 12, A-1030 Vienna, Austria
Permanent UK Representative, HE Simon Smith, *apptd* 2007

REGIONAL UN INFORMATION CENTRE
Block C2, Level 7, 155 rue de la Loi, Wetstraat 155, Brussels 1040, Belgium
T (+32) 2287 8484 E info@unric.org W www.unric.org

THE INTERNATIONAL COURT OF JUSTICE
The Peace Palace, NL-2517 KJ, The Hague, The Netherlands

The international court of justice is the principal judicial organ of the UN. The statute of the court is an integral part of the UN charter and all members of the UN are *ipso facto* parties to it. The court is composed of 15 judges, elected by both the general assembly and the security council for nine-year terms which are renewable. Judges may deliberate over cases in which their country is involved. If no judge on the bench is from a country which is a party to a dispute under consideration, that party may designate a judge to participate *ad hoc* in that particular deliberation. If any party to a case fails to adhere to the judgement of the court, the other party may have recourse to the security council.

President, Rosalyn Higgins (UK)
Vice-President, Awn Shawkat al-Khasawneh (Jordan)
Judges, Shi Jiuyong (China); Ronny Abraham (France); Bruno Simma (Germany); Hisashi Owada (Japan); Raymond Ranjeva (Madagascar); Bernado Sepulveda-Amor (Mexico); Mohamed Bennouna (Morocco); Kenneth Keith (New Zealand); Leonid Skotnikov (Russian Federation); Abdul G. Koroma (Sierra Leone); Peter Tomka (Slovakia); Thomas Buergenthal (USA); Gonzalo Parra-Aranguren (Venezuela)

UNITED NATIONS EDUCATIONAL, SCIENTIFIC AND CULTURAL ORGANISATION

7 place de Fontenoy, F-75352 Paris, France
T (+33) (01) 4568 1000 E bpi@unesco.org W www.unesco.org

The United Nations Educational, Scientific and Cultural Organisation (UNESCO) was established in 1946. It promotes collaboration among its member states in education, science, culture and communication. It aims to further a universal respect for human rights, justice and the rule of law, without distinction of race, sex, language or religion, in accordance with the UN charter.

UNESCO runs a number of programmes to improve education and extend access to it. It provides assistance to ensure the free flow of information and its wider dissemination without any obstacle to freedom of expression, and to maintain cultural heritage in the face of development. It fosters research and study in social and environmental sciences. The UNESCO world heritage list includes more than 800 cultural and natural sites.

UNESCO has 193 member states and six associate members. The general conference, consisting of representatives of all the members, meets biennially to decide the programme and the budget. It elects the 58-member executive board, which supervises operations, and appoints a director-general who heads a secretariat responsible for carrying out the organisation's programmes. In most member states national commissions liaise with UNESCO to execute its policies.

Director-General, Koichiro Matsuura (Japan)

UNITED NATIONS INDUSTRIAL DEVELOPMENT ORGANISATION

Vienna International Centre, Wagramerstrasse 5, PO Box 300, A-1400 Vienna, Austria
T (+43) (1) 260 260 E unido@unido.org W www.unido.org

The United Nations Industrial Development Organisation (UNIDO) was established in 1966 by the UN general assembly to act as the central coordinating body for industrial activities within the UN. It became a UN specialised agency in 1985. UNIDO aims to help countries with developing and transitional economies by increasing the productivity and competitiveness of their agricultural industries.

UNIDO has 172 members. It is funded by regular and operational budgets, together with contributions for technical cooperation activities. The regular budget is derived from member states' contributions. Technical cooperation is funded mainly through voluntary contributions from donor countries and institutions and by intergovernmental and non-governmental organisations. A general conference of all the members meets biennially to discuss strategy and policy, approve the budget – €381.6m (£308m) in 2008–9 – and elect the director-general. The industrial development board is composed of representatives from 53 member states and reviews the work programme and the budget, which is prepared by the programme and budget committee of 27 member states.

Director-General, Kandeh K. Yumkella (Sierra Leone)

UNIVERSAL POSTAL UNION

4 Weltpoststrasse 4, CH-3000 Bern 15, Switzerland
T (+41) (31) 350 3111 E info@upu.int W www.upu.int

The Universal Postal Union (UPU) was established by the treaty of Bern 1874, taking effect from 1875, and became a UN specialised agency in 1948. The UPU exists to form and regulate a single postal territory of all member countries for the reciprocal exchange of correspondence without discrimination. With a total of 191 members, it also assists and advises on the improvement of postal services.

The universal postal congress is the UPU's supreme authority and meets every four years. The council of administration meets annually to ensure continuity between congresses, to investigate regulatory developments and broad policy issues, to approve the budget and to examine proposed treaty changes. The consultative committee, set up in 2004 and consisting of customers, suppliers and printers, represents the interests of the wider international postal sector and provides a forum for dialogue between postal industry stakeholders. The three UPU bodies are served by the international bureau, a secretariat headed by a director-general.

Funding is provided by members according to a scale of contributions drawn up by the congress. The council of administration sets the budget which amounts to approximately SFr35m (£14.5m) per year.

Director-General, Edouard Dayan (France)

UNREPRESENTED NATIONS AND PEOPLES ORGANISATION

PO Box 85878, 2508 CN, The Hague, The Netherlands
T (+31) (70) 364 6504 E unpo@unpo.org W www.unpo.org

The Unrepresented Nations and Peoples Organisation (UNPO) was founded in 1991 to offer an international forum for occupied nations, indigenous peoples and national minorities who are not represented in other international organisations.

The UNPO does not aim to represent these nations and peoples, but rather to assist and empower them to represent themselves more effectively, and provides professional services and facilities as well as education and training in the fields of diplomacy, international and human rights law, democratic processes, institution building, conflict management and resolution, and environmental protection.

Participation is open to all nations and peoples who are inadequately represented at the UN and who declare allegiance to five principles relating to the right of self-determination of all peoples: human rights, democracy, non-violence and the rejection of terrorism, and protection of the natural environment. Applicants must show that they constitute a nation or people and that the organisation applying for membership is representative of that nation or people.

As at April 2008, there were 70 full members.

General Secretary, Marino Busdachin (Italy)

WESTERN EUROPEAN UNION

15 rue de l'Association, 1000 Brussels, Belgium
T (+32) (2) 500 4412 E secretariatgeneral@weu.int
W www.weu.int

Western European Union (WEU) is a defence and security organisation. It began as the Brussels Treaty Organisation (BTO) and was formed in 1948 by Belgium, France, Luxembourg, the Netherlands and the UK. The BTO was designed to provide collective self-defence and economic and social collaboration amongst its signatories. It was modified to become the WEU in 1954 with the admission of West Germany and Italy.

In 1991, the EU Maastricht Treaty committed the European Community to the establishment of a common foreign and security policy. The WEU was designated as the future defence component of the European Union and member states of the EU who were not already members of the WEU were invited to join or become observers. In 1992, the WEU's role as the common security dimension of the EU was enhanced when WEU ministers signed a declaration with remaining European NATO members to give them various forms of WEU membership.

A council of ministers (foreign and defence) meets biannually in the presiding country and from 1999 the sequence of WEU presidencies has been harmonised with those of the EU. A council of the member states' permanent representatives meets in Brussels. It is chaired by the secretary-general and serviced by the secretariat.

In 1999, NATO and the EU decided to establish a direct relationship; the EU committed itself to ensuring that it was able to take decisions on conflict prevention and crisis management and NATO agreed to give the EU access to its collective assets and capabilities for operations in which NATO as a whole was not engaged. The WEU's crisis management functions were transferred to the EU in 2001.

The WEU currently has ten member states, six associate members, five observers and a further seven countries are associate partners.

Presidency, France (2008), Germany, Greece (2009)
Secretary-General, Javier Solana Madariaga (Spain)

WORLD BANK GROUP

1818 H Street NW, Washington DC 20433, USA
T (+1) (202) 473 1000 E pic@worldbank.org
W www.worldbank.org

The World Bank Group was founded in 1944 and is one of the world's largest sources of development assistance. It has 185 members. Originally directed towards post-war reconstruction in Europe, the bank subsequently turned owards assisting less-developed countries and is currently working in more than 100. It works with government agencies, non-governmental organisations and the private ector to formulate assistance strategies. Its local offices mplement the bank's programme in each country.

The World Bank is owned by the governments of member countries and its capital is subscribed by its members. It finances its lending primarily from borrowing n world capital markets, and derives a substantial contribution to its resources from its retained earnings and the repayment of loans. The interest rate on its loans is calculated in relation to its cost of borrowing. Loans generally have a grace period of five years and are repayable within 20 years.

The World Bank Group consists of two institutions and three affiliates. The International Bank for Reconstruction and Development (IBRD) provides loans and development assistance to middle-income countries and creditworthy poorer countries (total loans for 2007 US$12.8bn (£6.4bn)). The International Development Association (IDA) performs the same function as the World Bank but primarily to less-developed countries and on terms that bear less heavily on their balance of payments than IBRD loans (total loans for 2007 US$11.9bn (£5.9bn)).

The three affiliates are the International Finance Corporation (IFC), which has 179 members and promotes private sector investment in developing member countries by mobilising domestic and foreign capital; the Multilateral Investment Guarantee Agency (MIGA), which promotes foreign direct investment in developing states by providing guarantees to potential investors and advisory services to developing member countries; and the International Centre for Settlement of Investment Disputes, which has 155 members (known as contracting states) and provides facilities for resolving disputes between foreign investors and their host countries.

The IBRD and its affiliates are financially and legally distinct but share headquarters. The IBRD is headed by a board of governors, consisting of one governor and one alternate governor appointed by each member country. Twenty-four executive directors exercise all powers of the World Bank except those reserved to the board of governors. The president, elected by the executive directors, conducts the business of the bank, assisted by an international staff. Membership in both the IFC and the IDA is open to all IBRD countries. The IDA is administered by the same staff as the bank; the IFC has its own personnel but draws on the IBRD for administrative and other support. All share the same president.

President, Robert Zoellick (USA)

WORLD CUSTOMS ORGANISATION

rue de Marche 30, B-1210, Brussels, Belgium
T (+32) 2209 9211 E information@wcoomd.org
W www.wcoomd.org

The World Customs Organisation (WCO) is an independent body that works to enhance the effectiveness and efficiency of customs administrations worldwide. By developing a harmonised commodity description and coding system, the WCO introduced a universal goods classification and revenue collection method. The WCO also administers the WTO valuation agreement.

With 172 member governments that process more than 98 per cent of international trade, the WCO is organised into a forum where each member has one representative and one vote. The WCO is directed by the council and a policy commission. Locally recruited staff are used to provide secretarial, translation, interpretation and general support services.

Secretary-General, Michel Danet (France)

WORLD HEALTH ORGANISATION

Avenue Appia 20, 1211 Geneva 27, Switzerland
T (+41) (22) 791 2111 E info@who.int W www.who.int

The UN International Health Conference, held in 1946, established the World Health Organisation (WHO) as a UN specialised agency, with effect from 1948. It is dedicated to attaining the highest possible level of health for all. It collaborates with member governments, UN agencies and other bodies to improve health standards, control communicable diseases and promote all aspects of family and environmental health. It seeks to raise the standards of health teaching and training, and promotes research through collaborating with research centres worldwide.

WHO has 193 members and is governed by the annual assembly of members which sets policy, approves the budget, appoints a director-general, and adopts health conventions and regulations. It also elects 34 members who designate one expert to serve on the executive board. The board effects the programme, suggests initiatives and is empowered to deal with emergencies. A secretariat, headed by the director-general, supervises the activities of six regional offices.

Director-General, Dr Margaret Chan (China)

WORLD INTELLECTUAL PROPERTY ORGANISATION

PO Box 18, CH-1211, Geneva 20, Switzerland
T (+41) (22) 338 9111 E information.centre@wipo.int
W www.wipo.int

The World Intellectual Property Organisation (WIPO) was established in 1967 by the Stockholm Convention, which entered into force in 1970. WIPO administers 24 treaties that deal with different legal and administrative aspects of intellectual property, notably the Paris Convention for the protection of industrial property and the Bern Convention for the protection of literary and artistic works. WIPO became a UN specialised agency in 1974.

Intellectual property falls into two main branches: industrial property (inventions, trademarks, industrial designs and geographical indications) and copyright (literary, musical, photographic, audiovisual and artistic works, etc). WIPO assists creative intellectual activity and facilitates technology transfer, particularly to developing countries.

WIPO's mission is to promote the protection of intellectual property rights worldwide. The organisation's activities fall into three broad categories, namely, the progressive development of interational intellectual property law, assistance to developing countries and services which facilitate the process of obtaining intellectual property rights in multiple countries.

WIPO had 184 members as at May 2008. The biennial session of all its governing bodies sets policy, a programme and a budget. A separate agency, the International Union for the Protection of New Varieties of Plants, established by convention in 1961, is linked to WIPO and has 65 members.

Director-General, Dr Kamil Idris (Sudan)

WORLD METEOROLOGICAL ORGANISATION

7 bis, avenue de la Paix, PO Box 2300, CH-1211 Geneva 2, Switzerland **T** (+41) (22) 730 8111
E wmo@wmo.int **W** www.wmo.int

The World Meteorological Organisation (WMO) was established in 1950 and became a UN specialised agency in 1951, succeeding the International Meteorological Organisation founded in 1873. It facilitates cooperation in the establishment of networks for making, processing and exchanging meteorological, climatological, hydrological and geophysical observations. It also fosters collaboration between meteorological and hydrological services, and furthers the application of meteorology to aviation, shipping, environment, water problems, agriculture and the mitigation of natural disasters.

In March 2008, the WMO had 182 member states and six member territories. Six regional associations are responsible for the coordination of activities within their own regions. There are also eight technical commissions, which study meteorological and hydrological problems, establish methodology and procedures, and make recommendations to the executive council and the congress. The supreme authority is the world meteorological congress, which meets every four years to determine general policy and set the budget (SFr269.8m (£136m) for 2008–11). It also elects 31 members of the 37-member executive council which supervises the implementation of congress decisions, initiates studies and makes recommendations on matters needing international action. The secretariat is headed by a secretary-general, appointed by the congress.

Secretary-General, Michel Jarraud (France)

WORLD TOURISM ORGANISATION

Capitán Haya 42, 28020 Madrid, Spain
T (+34) 9156 78100 **E** omt@unwto.org **W** www.unwto.org

Originally formed in 1925 as the International Congress of Official Tour Associations, the World Tourism Organisation (UNWTO) was officially launched in 1975 to act as an executing agency of the United Nations Development Programme. Primarily concerned with developing public and private sector partnerships, the UNWTO also promotes the global code of ethics for tourism, a framework of policy aimed at tour operators, governments, labour organisations and travellers. There are 153 member states and seven associate member states.

The general assembly is the principal gathering of the UNWTO and meets every two years in order to approve policy and budget. Every four years, the assembly elects a secretary-general. The executive council is UNWTO's governing board and meets twice a year to ensure the organisation adheres to policy and budget. It is composed of 30 members of the general assembly. As host country of UNWTO's headquarters, Spain has a permanent seat on the executive council.

Secretary-General, Francesco Frangialli (France)

WORLD TRADE ORGANISATION

Centre William Rappard, 154 rue de Lausanne, CH-1211 Geneva 21, Switzerland **T** (+41) (22) 739 5111
E enquiries@wto.org **W** www.wto.org

The World Trade Organisation was established on 1 January 1995 as the successor to the General Agreement on Tariffs and Trade (GATT).

GATT was dedicated to the expansion of non-discriminatory international trade and progressively extended free trade via 'rounds' of multilateral negotiations. The final act of the Uruguay round was signed by trade ministers from the 128 GATT negotiating states and the EU in Marrakesh, Morocco, in 1994. The implementation of the Uruguay round measures in 2002 resulted in a reduction on duties on manufactured goods from 40 per cent in the 1940s to 3 per cent. New talks on agriculture and services began in 2000 and were incorporated into a broader agenda launched at the 2001 ministerial conference in Doha, Qatar.

The WTO is the legal and institutional foundation of the multilateral trading system. It provides the contractual obligations determining how governments frame and implement trade policy and provides the forum for the debate, negotiation and adjudication of trade problems. The WTO's principal aims are to liberalise world trade and place it on a secure basis, and it seeks to achieve this through a combination of an agreed set of trade rules and market access agreements and further trade liberalisation negotiations. The WTO also administers and implements multilateral agreements in fields such as agriculture, textiles and clothing, services, government procurement, rules of origin and intellectual property.

The highest authority of the WTO is the ministerial conference composed of all members, which meets at least once every two years. The general council meets as required and acts on behalf of the ministerial conference in regard to the regular working of the WTO. The general council also convenes in two particular forms: as the dispute settlement body, dealing with disagreements between members arising from the Uruguay round final act; and as the trade policy review body, conducting regular reviews of the trade policies of members. A secretariat of 625 staff headed by a director-general services WTO bodies and provides trade performance and trade policy analysis.

As at May 2008, there were 151 WTO members and 32 observers. The WTO budget for 2007 was SFr182m (£87m), with members' contributions calculated on the basis of their share of the total trade conducted by WTO members. The official languages of the WTO are English, French and Spanish.

Director-General, Pascal Lamy (France)

COUNTRIES OF THE WORLD A–Z

DEFINITIONS AND ABBREVIATIONS

est = estimate
(m) = male; (f) = female
BIRTH RATE – figures are per 1,000 population. The birth rate is usually the dominant factor in determining the rate of population growth. It depends on both the level of fertility and the age structure of the population
CPI SCORE – the perception of the degree of corruption as seen by business people and country analysts; ranging between 10 (highly clean) and 0 (highly corrupt)
DEATH PENALTY:
abolitionist for all crimes – countries whose laws do not provide for the death penalty for any crime
abolitionist in practice – countries which retain the death penalty for ordinary crimes such as murder but can be considered abolitionist in practice, in that they have not executed anyone during the last decade, are believed to have a policy against carrying out executions or countries that have made a commitment against the death penalty
abolitionist for ordinary crimes only – countries whose laws provide for the death penalty only for exceptional crimes such as those under military law or committed in exceptional circumstances
retentionist – countries that retain the death penalty for ordinary crimes
GROSS ENROLMENT RATIO – the ratio of total enrolment, regardless of age, to the total population of the relevant age group expressed as a percentage; this figure can be above 100 per cent where, for example, there are a greater number of children are attending classes designed for six-year-olds than there are six-year-olds in the country, due to some children starting school late or skipping a year
GROSS NATIONAL INCOME (GNI) – the total incomes earned by a country's residents, regardless of where the assets are located; the second figure is GNI divided by the population to give a per capita figure
FOREIGN DIRECT INVESTMENT (FDI) – the net inflows of investment to acquire a lasting management interest in an enterprise operating in a foreign economy to that of the investor
HEALTH EXPENDITURE – where a period of years is given (eg 2000–5), data is for the most recent year available
HIV/AIDS ADULT PREVALENCE – estimate of the percentage of the total adult population (aged 15–49) living with HIV/AIDS
INFANT MORTALITY RATE – averages for male and female infants under one year old and per 1,000 live births
LIFE EXPECTANCY – averages for men and women aged between 15 and 49 years
MORTALITY RATE – figures are per 1,000 population. This indicator is significantly affected by age distribution, and most countries will eventually show a rise in the overall death rate, in spite of continued decline in mortality at all ages, as declining fertility results in an ageing population
PARAMILITARIES – not included in the total military personnel figure for each country
POPULATION BELOW POVERTY LINE – although strict definitions of poverty vary considerably between nations, this figure most commonly represents the percentage of the adult population whose income is under US$1 per day
TOTAL EXTERNAL DEBT – the total public and private debt owed to nonresidents repayable in foreign currency, goods, or services

AFGHANISTAN

Jomhuri-ye Eslami-ye Afghanestan – Islamic Republic of Afghanistan

Area – 647,500 sq. km
Capital – Kabul; population, 3,277,000 (2007 est)
Major cities – Herat, Jalalabad, Kandahar, Mazar-e-Sharif
Currency – Afghani (Af) of 100 puls
Population – 31,889,923 rising at 2.63 per cent per year (2007 est); Pashtun (42 per cent), Tajik (27 per cent), Hazara (9 per cent), Uzbek (9 per cent), Aimak (4 per cent), Turkmen (3 per cent), Baloch (2 per cent) (est)
Religion – Islam (99 per cent) (est). The majority of the population practises Sunni Islam
Language – Dari, Pashto (both official), Uzbek, Turkmen
Urban population – 24.3 per cent (2005 est)
Median age (years) – 17.6 (2007 est)
National anthem – 'Milli Tharana' ['National Anthem']
National day – 19 August (Independence Day)
Life expectancy (years) – 43.77 (2007 est)
Mortality rate – 19.96 (2007 est)
Birth rate – 46.21 (2007 est)
Infant mortality rate – 157.43 (2007 est)
Death penalty – Retained
CPI score – 1.8 (2007)
Population below poverty line – 53 per cent (2003)

CLIMATE AND TERRAIN

Mountains, chief among which are the Hindu Kush, cover three-quarters of the landlocked country, with plains in the north and south-west. Elevation extremes range from 7,485m at the highest point (Nowshak, in the Hindu Kush) to 258m at the lowest (Amu Dar'ya). There are three great river basins, the Amu Dar'ya (Oxus), Helmand and Kabul. Natural hazards are flooding, drought and earthquakes. The climate is arid to semi-arid, with extreme temperatures. Summers are hot and dry and the winters cold with heavy snowfalls, particularly in the northern mountains. Annual rainfall varies between 101mm and 406mm per year. The temperatures in Kabul average −8°C to 2°C in January and 16°C to 33°C in July.

HISTORY AND POLITICS

Afghanistan first became a nation in 1747 under Ahmad Shah Durrani. Britain and Russia vied for influence over the country in the 19th and early 20th centuries, but it remained independent. The monarchy was overthrown in 1973 and a republic was declared. After a coup in 1978, a communist government took power, and Muslim guerrilla (mujahidin) resistance began. The government was overthrown in a further coup in 1979 that prompted an invasion by the Soviet Union, which installed a pro-Soviet government. The mujahidin, with US backing, fought against Soviet forces, which withdrew in 1989, and against Afghan government forces until the government collapsed in 1992. Mujahidin forces overran Kabul and declared an Islamic state. However, factionalism led to constant civil conflict until the rise of the Taliban, which, between 1994–8, extended its power across more than 90 per cent of the country and imposed strict Shariah law.

The Taliban allowed the al-Qaida network to base terrorist training camps in Afghanistan, and its refusal to hand over leaders after the 11 September 2001 terrorist attacks on the USA led to the regime's overthrow by a US-led international coalition and the Northern Alliance, a grouping of the four main mujahidin factions. A multi-ethnic interim government under Hamid Karzai was installed in December 2001 and, following a *Loya Jirga* (tribal council) in 2002, a transitional government was installed until presidential and parliamentary elections were held in 2004 and 2005.

The government's control of areas outside Kabul is tenuous and dependent on the presence of foreign troops. The vacuum has given rise to local infighting, and instability continues due to violent opposition by drug producers and traffickers to drug-eradication programmes. In some provinces, in the south and east in particular, Taliban-inspired violence against government forces and foreign troops has risen since 2005.

In 2004 Hamid Karzai was elected president for a five-year term with 55.4 per cent of the vote. Elections to the lower house of the legislature and to the provincial seats in the upper house were held in September 2005 and the new legislature was inaugurated in December. A new government was approved by the legislature in spring 2006.

POLITICAL SYSTEM

Under the 2004 constitution, the executive president, who is directly elected for a five-year term, appoints the government, subject to the approval of the lower house of the legislature. The bicameral legislature, the *Jirga*, comprises a lower house, the *Wolesi Jirga* (House of the People), and the *Meshrano Jirga* (House of Elders). The *Wolesi Jirga* has 249 members directly elected for a five-year term; ten seats are reserved for the Kuchi ethnic group and at least 65 seats for women. The *Meshrano Jirga* has 102 members: 34 indirectly elected by provincial councils for a three-year term; 34 indirectly elected by district councils for a four-year term; and 34 appointed by the president for a five-year term. There are no formal political parties at present.

HEAD OF STATE

President, Hamid Karzai, *elected* 9 October 2004, *sworn in* 7 December 2004
First Vice-President, Ahmad Zia Massood
Vice-President, Karim Khalili

SELECTED GOVERNMENT MEMBERS *as at May 2008*

Defence, Gen. Abdul Raheem Wardak
Foreign Affairs, Rangeen Dadfar Spanta
Finance, Anwar-ul Haq Ahadi
Interior, Ahmad Moqbel Zarar

EMBASSY OF THE ISLAMIC REPUBLIC OF AFGHANISTAN

31 Prince's Gate, London SW7 1QQ
T 020-7589 8891
Ambassador Extraordinary and Plenipotentiary, HE Dr Mohammad Rahim Sherzoy, *apptd* 2007

BRITISH EMBASSY

PO Box 334, 15th Street, Roundabout Wazir Akbar Khan, Kabul
T (+93) (70) 102 000 E britishembassy.kabul@fco.gov.uk
W www.britishembassy.gov.uk/afghanistan
Ambassador Extraordinary and Plenipotentiary, HE Sir Sherard Cowper-Coles, KCMG, LVO, *apptd* 2007

BRITISH COUNCIL

House 15–17, Kart-e-Parwan, Kabul
T (+93) (70) 000 0102 E info.afghanistan@britishcouncil.org
W www.britishcouncil.org/afghanistan
Director, Malcolm Jardine

DEFENCE

The Afghan Transitional Administration plans to bolster security through the establishment of a national army and police force recruited from all the different tribes and ethnicities. The current army has a strength of 35,000 troops, with a planned expansion to 50,000. NATO's International Security Assistance Force currently has 41,000 troops in Afghanistan.
Military expenditure – US$161m (2007)

ECONOMY AND TRADE

The economy, devastated by 30 years of constant conflict, is improving with international assistance (over US$24bn pledged since 2002), agricultural recovery and service sector growth. Reconstruction is hampered by continuing conflict, criminal activity, corruption and the government's inability to impose its authority nationwide. Industrial development and trade are hindered by the inadequacies of the transport and energy infrastructure, and living conditions are poor for the majority of the population. The eradication of the illegal opium trade and the search for oil and gas in the northern region are two major long-term objectives.

Most of the labour force is engaged in agriculture, which has seen a huge expansion in opium production, from 185 tonnes in 2001 to 4,475 tonnes in 2005. Production has continued to increase and may account for 60 per cent of total national output. Less lucrative agricultural products are wheat, fruit, nuts, wool, meat, sheepskins and lambskins. Natural gas, coal and copper are exploited. Other industries include the manufacture of silk and wool, handwoven carpets, soap, furniture, shoes and fertilisers. These agricultural and manufactured products are the main exports. Imports are chiefly capital goods, food, textiles and petroleum products. The main trading partners are India and Pakistan.
GNI – US$19,000m (2002); US$700 per capita (2002)
Annual average growth of GDP – 7.5 per cent (2007 est)
Inflation rate – 16.3 per cent (2005 est)

Unemployment – 40 per cent (2005 est)
Total external debt – US$8,000m (2004)
Imports – US$1,300m (2001)
Exports – US$1,200m (2001)

BALANCE OF PAYMENTS
Trade – US$850m deficit (2006)
Current Account – US$444m deficit (2006)

Trade with UK	*2006*	*2007*
Imports from UK	£22,428,000	£41,429,673
Exports to UK	£10,605,000	£638,261

COMMUNICATIONS

There are two international airports, at Kabul and Kandahar, and a further four major and 16 smaller regional airports servicing internal flights. The Amu Dar'ya river makes up most of the 1,200km of inland waterways and carries barge traffic; the main river ports are Kheyrabad and Shir Khan. There is no railway system, although there are railheads on the Pakistan border and a railway is under construction from Mashhad, in Iran, to Herat. Much of the road system is in total disrepair, although many of the highways from Kabul to Kandahar and Herat have been reconstructed. The fixed-line telephone network is very limited in extent (280,000 main lines in 2006), and connections are exceeded by mobile phone distribution (2.5m subscribers in 2006), as the major cities now have coverage.

EDUCATION AND HEALTH

Education is free and nominally compulsory, elementary schools having been established in most centres. In 2002, schools reopened to 1.5 million children, many of whom had not received schooling for six years under the Taliban.
Gross enrolment ratio (percentage of relevant age group) – primary 87 per cent; secondary 16 per cent; tertiary 1 per cent (2005 est)
Health expenditure (per capita) – US$14 (2004)
Hospital beds (per 1,000 people) – 0.4 (2000–5)

MEDIA AND CULTURE

The media was severely restricted under the Taliban, which banned television broadcasting. However, in late 2001 Radio Afghanistan returned to the air in Kabul after the Taliban deserted the capital, and within days Kabul TV also began broadcasting. Relays of foreign radio stations are available in Kabul, including the BBC, Radio France Internationale, Deutsche Welle, US-funded broadcasts from Radio Free Afghanistan and the Voice of America, and Radio Azadi run by the International Security Assistance Force. Local radio stations include Radio Afghanistan, Erat Radio Khilid Kabul and Arman FM. Private television stations have sprung up since 2001 and five networks now challenge the state-run TV Afghanistan. Content is limited by Islamic law. The press now enjoys considerable freedom of expression, although print runs are small. Titles include *Hewad*, *Anis* and the Northern Alliance organ *Payam-e Mojahed*.

Due to prolonged conflict in the region, much of the cultural heritage has been destroyed. During the civil war the Kabul Museum was looted, and treasures such as the Kunduz Hoard (silver Greek-style coins) were stolen. This was followed during the Taliban regime by systematic iconoclasm, most notably of the giant Bamiyan Buddhas, carved by Buddhist monks in the fourth to sixth centuries, which were demolished in March 2001.

ALBANIA

Republika e Shqiperise – Republic of Albania

Area – 28,748 sq. km
Capital – Tirana; population, 406,000 (2007 est)
Major towns – Durres, Elbasan
Currency – Lek (Lk) of 100 qindarka
Population – 3,600,523 rising at 0.53 per cent per year (2007 est); Albanian (95 per cent), Greek (3 per cent) (est)
Religion – Islam (65 per cent), Albanian Orthodox (20 per cent), Roman Catholicism (10 per cent) (est)
Language – Albanian (official), Greek, Vlach, Romani, Slavic dialects
Population density – 116 per sq. km (2006)
Urban population – 45 per cent (2005 est)
Median age (years) – 29.2 (2007 est)
National anthem – 'Hymni i Flamurit' ['Hymn to the Flag']
National day – 28 November (Independence Day)
Life expectancy (years) – 77.6 (2007 est)
Mortality rate – 5.33 (2007 est)
Birth rate – 15.16 (2007 est)
Infant mortality rate – 20.02 (2007 est)
Death penalty – Abolished for all crimes (since 2007)
CPI score – 2.9 (2007)
Population below poverty line – 25 per cent (2004 est)

CLIMATE AND TERRAIN

Much of the country is mountainous, with the highest point at 2,764m (Maja e Korabit), and nearly half is covered by forest. The lowest point of elevation is 0m (Adriatic Sea). The climate is Mediterranean with frequent thunderstorms. The average daily temperature ranges from 2°C in January to 31°C in July.

HISTORY AND POLITICS

Albania was under Turkish suzerainty from 1468 until 1912, when independence was declared. After a period of unrest, a republic was declared in 1925 and in 1928 a monarchy. The king went into exile in 1939 when the country was occupied by the Italians; Albania was liberated in 1944. Elections in 1945 resulted in a communist-controlled assembly; the king was deposed *in absentia* and a republic declared in 1946.

From 1946 to 1990 Albania was a one-party, communist state, and isolated from outside influence, particularly after breaking with the USSR in 1961 and China in 1978. Gradual moves towards democratic reform and westernisation began in the late 1980s, and between 1990 and 1992 democratic elections took place, the communists losing power in 1992. Economic decline and food shortages led to rioting in the early 1990s, and rioting broke out again in 1997 following the collapse of several investment schemes, with anti-government protests nationwide. The country experienced further political and economic pressure in 1999 when Serbian attacks on ethnic Albanians in Kosovo caused over 400,000 people to take refuge in Albania. The government supported NATO's moves to deal with the crisis and by the end of 1999 nearly all the refugees had left Albania.

Talks with the EU on an association agreement began in 2003 and, following progress on political and economic reform, a stabilisation and association agreement was signed in 2006.

In the 2005 general election, the Democratic Party (PD) defeated the Socialist Party in polls, the results of which were disputed; the PD leader Sali Berisha was appointed prime minister at the head of a four-party coalition government in September after re-runs in a number of constituencies. Bamir Topi, of the PD, was elected president in July 2007 in the fourth round of voting.

POLITICAL SYSTEM

Under the 1998 constitution, the president is indirectly elected by the legislature for a five-year term, renewable only once. The unicameral legislature, the People's Assembly, has 140 members directly elected for a four-year term. The president appoints the prime minister, who must be approved by the People's Assembly. The Assembly elects the council of ministers.

HEAD OF STATE

President, Bamir Topi, *elected by the People's Assembly* 20 July 2007, *took office* 24 July 2007

SELECTED GOVERNMENT MEMBERS *as at May 2008*

Prime Minister, Sali Berisha
Deputy Prime Minister, Gazemend Oketa
Foreign Affairs, Lulzim Basha
Defence, Gazmend Oketa
Interior, Bujar Nishani
Finance, Ritvan Bode

EMBASSY OF THE REPUBLIC OF ALBANIA

2nd Floor, 24 Buckingham Gate, London SW1E 6LB
T 020-7828 8898 E embassy.london@mfa.gov.al
W www.albanianembassy.co.uk
Ambassador Extraordinary and Plenipotentiary, HE Zef Mazi, *apptd* 2007

BRITISH EMBASSY

Rruga Skenderbeg 12, Tirana
T (+355) (4) 234 973 W www.uk.al
Ambassador Extraordinary and Plenipotentiary, HE Fraser Wilson, MBE, *apptd* 2006

BRITISH COUNCIL

Rruga Perlat Rexhepi, Pallati 197 Ana, Tirana
T (+355) (4) 240 856/7 W www.britishcouncil.org/albania
Director, Joan Barry

DEFENCE

The army has 40 main battle tanks and 123 armoured personnel carriers. The navy has 31 patrol and coastal combatant vessels at two bases, Durrës and Vlore. The air force has 13 helicopters.

Military budget – US$208m (2007)
Military personnel – 11,020: army 6,200, navy 1,100, air force 1,370, joint staff 2,350; paramilitary 500
Conscription duration – 12 months

ECONOMY AND TRADE

Albania is one of the poorest countries in Europe. The communist isolationist policy left a dilapidated energy and transport infrastructure, antiquated equipment and practices, and widespread corruption. After years of liberalisation measures, the economy is showing signs of sustained growth and inflation is under control. Nevertheless, the economy is still heavily dependent on the US$600–800m (£300–400m) a year remitted by nationals working abroad and overseas aid of about US$350m (£175m), primarily from the EU. The problems with infrastructure and corruption have deterred foreign investment, and tackling these is a government priority. The opening of a new thermal power plant should relieve energy shortages.

Agriculture accounts for 58 per cent of employment but only 21.7 per cent of GDP. The main crops are wheat, maize, vegetables, fruit, sugar beet and livestock products. The principal industries are food processing, textiles and clothing, timber, oil, cement, chemicals, mining (base metals) and hydro-electric power.

Trade is mainly with neighbouring countries. Exports include textiles and footwear, crude oil, minerals (bitumen, chrome, nickel, copper), tobacco, fruit and vegetables. Imports include machinery and equipment, foodstuffs, textiles and chemicals.

GNI – US$9,300m; US$2,930 per capita (2006)
Annual average growth of GDP – 5 per cent (2007 est)
Inflation rate – 3 per cent (2007 est)
Unemployment – 13 per cent (2007 est)
Total external debt – US$1,550m (2004)
Imports – US$3,100m (2006)
Exports – US$800m (2006)

BALANCE OF PAYMENTS

Trade – US$2,261m deficit (2006)
Current Account – US$535m deficit (2006)

Trade with UK	*2006*	*2007*
Imports from UK	£17,149,000	£18,359,973
Exports to UK	£1,559,000	£2,535,991

EDUCATION AND HEALTH

Literacy rate – 98.7 per cent (2004 est)
Gross enrolment ratio (percentage of relevant age group) – primary 105 per cent; secondary 77 per cent; tertiary 19 per cent (2006 est)
Health expenditure (per capita) – US$169 (2005)
Hospital beds (per 1,000 people) – 3.0 (2000–6)

MEDIA

The public broadcaster Albanian Radio and TV (RTSh) faces increasing competition from around 75 private television channels, many of which were established less than ten years ago. There are approximately 30 private radio stations. Political parties, trade unions, religious groups and state bodies are prohibited from owning private television and radio stations but can own newspapers.

ALGERIA

Al-Jumhuriyah al-Jaza'iriyah ad Dimuqratiyah ash Sha'biyah – People's Democratic Republic of Algeria

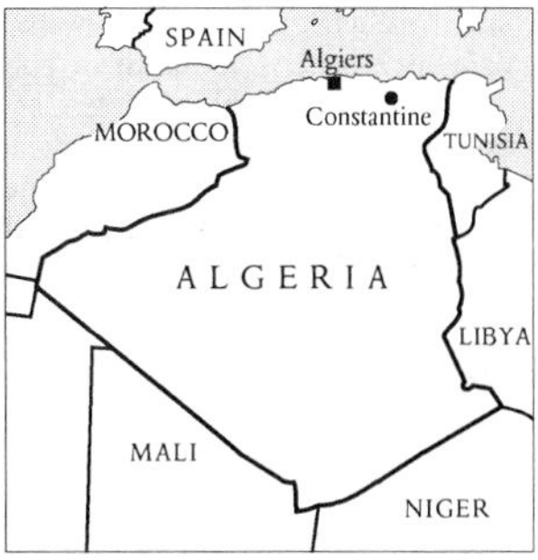

Area – 2,381,740 sq. km
Capital – Algiers (El Djazair, Al Jaza'ir); population, 3,354,000 (2007 est). It is one of the principal ports of the Mediterranean
Major cities – Al Jilfah, Batna, Constantine (Qacentina), Oran (Wahran)
Currency – Algerian dinar (DA) of 100 centimes
Population – 33,333,216, rising at 1.22 per cent per year (2007 est); Arab-Berber (99 per cent) (est)
Religion – Islam (99 per cent) (est)
Language – Arabic (official), French, Berber dialects
Population density – 14 per sq. km (2006)
Urban population – 60 per cent (2005 est)
Median age (years) – 25.5 (2007 est)
National anthem – 'Kassaman' ['We Pledge']
National day – 1 November (Revolution Day)
Life expectancy (years) – 73.52 (2007 est)
Mortality rate – 4.62 (2007 est)
Birth rate – 17.11 (2007 est)
Infant mortality rate – 28.78 (2007 est)
Death penalty – Retained, but not used
CPI score – 3.0 (2007)
Population below poverty line – 25 per cent (2005 est)

CLIMATE AND TERRAIN

Algeria, the second largest country in Africa after Sudan, is dominated by the Sahara desert, which covers 80 per cent of its territory. The eastern part of the Atlas mountain range crosses the north of the country, separating the coastal plain, where the majority of the population lives, from the desert plateaux of the interior. The mountains are subject to earthquakes, flooding and mudslides during the rainy season (November to March). The highest point of elevation is 3,003m (Tahat) and the lowest is –40m (Chott Melrhir). Algeria has mild, wet winters and hot, dry summers. The climate is drier along the coastline, while the high plateaux experience cold winters.

HISTORY AND POLITICS

Algeria was a Roman province that came under Arabic and Islamic influence from the eighth century, and was part of the Ottoman Empire from the 16th century until its annexation by France in 1830. It gained its independence in 1962 following an eight-year guerrilla war by the socialist Front de Libération Nationale (FLN). Ben Bella was elected president in 1963, but was deposed in 1965 by Col. Houari Boumedienne, who was formally elected president in 1976, when the FLN became the only permitted political party.

A new constitution agreed by referendum in 1988 moved Algeria towards pluralism. However, the 1991 legislative elections were abandoned in anticipation of the success of the opposition Islamic Salvation Front (FIS), which had campaigned on a radical Islamist platform. The FIS was banned in 1991, triggering civil unrest and conflict between Islamic groups (the FIS-backed Islamic Salvation Army and the more extreme Armed Islamic Group) and the military. A state of emergency was declared in 1992 and the country suffered an insurgency that claimed an estimated 100,000 lives. The level of violence has fallen since 1999, when the newly elected president Abdelaziz Bouteflika initiated a policy of reconciliation with the Islamists, and his 'charter for peace and reconciliation' was approved by referendum in 2005. In 2006 a second amnesty for militants was supported by the FIS leadership, but since 2006 a group allying itself to al-Qaida has carried out a number of bombings.

Another divisive issue is the ethnic Berber population's campaign since 2001 for greater political and cultural recognition. Following occasionally violent demonstrations and a Berber boycott of the 2002 and 2004 elections, negotiations led to an agreement in 2005 that promised greater government investment in the Berber-populated Kabylie region and greater recognition for the Berber language Tamazight. The Berber protests also reflected a more widespread discontent with social conditions and living standards among the population.

In 2004, Bouteflika was elected for a second term as president with 85 per cent of the vote. In the 2007 legislative election, the National Liberation Front gained the highest number of seats. The elections were blighted by violence, a low turnout and a high number of spoilt ballots, suggesting widespread political disaffection.

POLITICAL SYSTEM

The president is directly elected for a five-year term. The bicameral Barlaman comprises a lower house, the National People's Assembly, with 389 members, directly elected for a five-year term. The Council of the Nation has 144 members; one-third are appointed by the president, and two-thirds are indirectly elected for six-year terms, of whom half are re-elected every three years. Although Algeria is no longer a one-party state, parties based on religion, including the FIS, are banned under the constitution.

HEAD OF STATE

President, Defence, Abdelaziz Bouteflika, *elected* 15 April 1999, *re-elected* April 2004

SELECTED GOVERMENT MEMBERS *as at May 2008*

Prime Minister, Abdelaziz Belkhadem
Finance, Karim Djoudi
Foreign Affairs, Mourad Medelci
Interior, Noureddine Yazid Zerhouni

ALGERIAN EMBASSY

54 Holland Park, London W11 3RS
T 020-7221 7800 E info@algerianembassy.org.uk
W www.algerianembassy.org.uk
Ambassador Extraordinary and Plenipotentiary, HE Mohamed Salah Dembri, *apptd* 2005

BRITISH EMBASSY

7th Floor, Hilton Hotel Alger, Pins Maritimes, Palais des Expositions, El Mohammadia, Algiers

T (+213) (21) 230 068 W www.britishembassy.gov.uk/algeria
Ambassador Extraordinary and Plenipotentiary, HE Andrew Henderson, *apptd* 2006

BRITISH COUNCIL
12 rue Slimane Amirate, Hydra, Algiers
T (+213) (21) 480 947 E john.mitchell@britishcouncil.org
Director, John Mitchell

DEFENCE

The army has 895 main battle tanks, 1,040 armoured infantry fighting vehicles and 750 armoured personnel carriers. The navy has 2 submarines, 3 frigates and 20 patrol and coastal vessels. There are bases at Mers el Kebir, Algiers, Annaba and Jijel. The air force has 141 combat aircraft and 33 armed helicopters.
Military budget – US$3,690m (2007)
Military personnel – 147,000: army 127,000, navy 6,000, air force 14,000; paramilitary 187,200
Conscription duration – 18 months

ECONOMY AND TRADE

In 1994 the government embarked on the liberalisation of the centrally planned economy, and in 1997 initiated a privatisation programme. These reforms, combined with recent high oil prices, have resulted in trade surpluses, record foreign exchange reserves and the reduction of foreign debt. However, diversification away from the energy sector and development of the banking system and infrastructure are progressing slowly because of the difficulty of attracting foreign and internal investment, often deterred by corruption and bureaucratic resistance, and the economic buoyancy has had little impact on the social ills of poverty and high unemployment.

Algeria has substantial oil and gas reserves and the hydrocarbon industry accounts for nearly 60 per cent of government revenue, 30 per cent of GDP and over 95 per cent of export earnings. Services provide 30.9 per cent of GDP, industry 61 per cent and agriculture 8.1 per cent. Industries other than oil and gas production and processing include mining, electrical goods, food processing and light industries.

Algeria's main trading partners are the USA, France, Italy and Spain. The chief imports are capital goods, foodstuffs and consumer goods.
GNI – US$101,200m; US$3,030 per capita (2006)
Annual average growth of GDP – 4.6 per cent (2007 est)
Inflation rate – 4.6 per cent (2007 est)
Unemployment – 14.1 per cent (2007 est)
Total external debt – US$3,358m (2007 est)
Imports – US$21,000m (2006)
Exports – US$52,800m (2006)

BALANCE OF PAYMENTS
Trade – US$33,730m surplus (2006)
Current Account – US$28,950m surplus (2006)

Trade with UK	*2006*	*2007*
Imports from UK	£167,225,000	£168,962,079
Exports to UK	£962,297,000	£910,532,175

EDUCATION AND HEALTH

Literacy rate – 69.8 per cent (2004 est)
Gross enrolment ratio (percentage of relevant age group) – primary 110 per cent; secondary 83 per cent; tertiary 22 per cent (2006 est)
Health expenditure (per capita) – US$108 (2005)
Hospital beds (per 1,000 people) – 1.7 (2000–6)

MEDIA

The state controls the television (Entreprise Nationale de Télévision) and radio stations (Radio-Télévision Algérienne), but domestic satellite dishes are used by the population to receive French and European channels, some of which actively target Algerian viewers. There are five main daily newspapers, all of them published in French. There is no direct censorship but laws permit prison terms and fines for insulting or defaming the president, MPs, judges and the army. Daily newspapers mark the anniversary of the introduction of these laws with a day of suspended production.

ANDORRA

Principat d'Andorra – Principality of Andorra

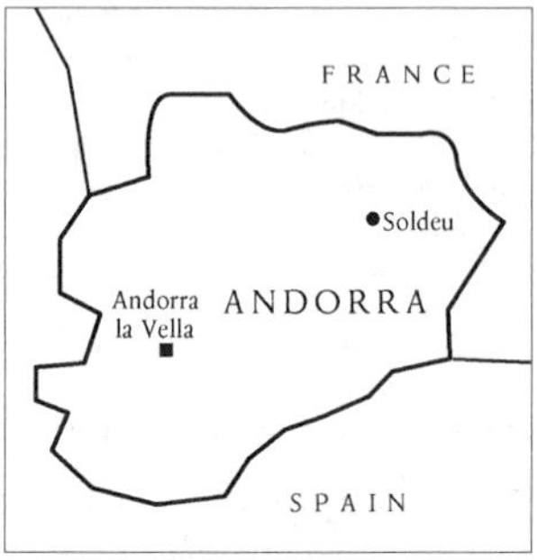

Area – 468 sq. km
Capital – Andorra la Vella; population, 24,000 (2007 est)
Major cities – Encamp, Les Escaldes
Currency – Euro (€) of 100 cents
Population – 71,822, rising at 0.84 per cent per year (2007 est); Spanish (43 per cent), Andorran (33 per cent), Portuguese (11 per cent), French (7 per cent) (est)
Religion – Roman Catholicism (90 per cent) (est)
Language – Catalan (official), French, Castilian, Portuguese
Population density – 142 per sq. km (2006)
Urban population – 91.3 per cent (2005 est)
Median age (years) – 41.5 years (2007 est)
National anthem – 'El Gran Carlemany' ['The Great Charlemagne']
National day – 8 September (Our Lady of Meritxell Day)
Life expectancy (years) – 83.52 (2007 est)
Mortality rate – 6.45 (2007 est)
Birth rate – 8.45 (2007 est)
Infant mortality rate – 4.03 (2007 est)
Death penalty – Abolished for all crimes (since 1990)

CLIMATE AND TERRAIN

Located between the French and Spanish borders, Andorra is a landlocked country of dramatic mountains interspersed by narrow valleys. A third of the country is classified as forest. The highest point of elevation is 2,946m (Coma Pedrosa) and the lowest is 840m (Riu Runer). The climate is alpine, with heavy snowfall in winter and warm summers. The average temperature ranges from −1 to 6°C in January to 12 to 26°C in July.

HISTORY AND POLITICS

Liberated from Muslim rule by Charlemagne in 803, Andorra is a small, neutral principality that was formed by a *paréage* (a type of feudal treaty) in 1278 and since then has owed dual allegiance to two co-princes, the Spanish

Bishop of Urgel and the head of state of France. Andorra became an independent democratic parliamentary co-principality in 1993. The first elections under the new constitution were held in 1993, and on 20 January 1994 the first sovereign government of Andorra took office. The country subsequently formalised its links with the EU and joined the UN and the Council of Europe.

In the 2005 legislative election the governing Liberal Party of Andorra (PLA) won half the seats, and Albert Pintat of the PLA became president of the executive council.

POLITICAL SYSTEM

Under the 1993 constitution, the two co-princes remain heads of state, represented in Andorra by the permanent delegates (the Spanish vicar-general of the diocese of Urgel and the French prefect of the Pyrénées Orientales department at Perpignan), but their powers now relate solely to relations with France and Spain. The constitution established an independent judiciary and allows Andorra to conduct its own foreign policy, while its people may now join political parties and trade unions.

Andorra has a unicameral legislature, the *Consell General de las Valls* (General Council of the Valleys), whose 28 members are directly elected for a four-year term by proportional representation. The council appoints the president of the Executive Council, who designates government members.

Permanent French Delegate, Emmanuelle Mignon
Permanent Episcopal Delegate, Nemesi Marqués Oste

SELECTED GOVERNMENT MEMBERS *as at May 2007*
President of the Executive Council, Albert Pintat Santolária
Finance, Ferran Mirapeix Lucas
Foreign Affairs, Meritxell Mateu Pi
Justice and Interior, Antoni Riberygua Sasplugas

EMBASSY OF THE PRINCIPALITY OF ANDORRA
63 Westover Road, London SW18 2RF T 020-8874 4806
Ambassador Extraordinary and Plenipotentiary, Maria Rosa Picart de Francis, *apptd* 2007

BRITISH CONSULATE-GENERAL
Ambassador, HE Stephen Wright, *apptd* 2007, resident at Madrid, Spain

ECONOMY AND TRADE

The economy is largely based on tourism, especially skiing (80 per cent of GDP, with 11 million visitors annually), banking and commerce (due in part to the principality's tax-free status), tobacco products, forestry, furniture-making and sheep-farming. Andorra has been a member of the EU customs union since 1991.

Annual average growth of GDP – 3.5 per cent (2005 est)
Inflation rate – 3.2 per cent (2005)

Trade with UK	*2006*	*2007*
Imports from UK	£7,349,000	£6,626,479
Exports to UK	£165,000	£114,202

COMMUNICATIONS

There are 269km of roads but no railways, airports or waterways. A road into Andorra from Spain is open all year round, and that from France is closed only occasionally in winter. Mobile telephones are nearly twice as widespread as fixed-line connections.

MEDIA

The Andorran media is heavily influenced by France and Spain and Andorrans have access to broadcasts from both countries. There are two radio stations in Andorra, one is privately owned and one is operated by the government (Radio Andorra), as well as a state-owned television channel and two major daily newspapers *(Diari d'Andorra and El Periodic).*

ANGOLA

Republica de Angola – Republic of Angola

Area – 1,246,700 sq. km
Capital – Luanda; population, 4,000,000 (2007 est)
Major cities – Cabinda, Huambo, Lubango
Currency – Readjusted kwanza (Kzrl) of 100 centimos
Population – 12,263,596, rising at 2.18 per cent per year (2007 est); Ovimbundu (37 per cent), Kimbundu (25 per cent), Bakongo (13 per cent) (est)
Religion – The majority of the population follows Christianity with Roman Catholicism the largest denomination. A small portion of the rural population practises animism or indigenous religions
Language – Portuguese (official), Bantu
Population density – 13 per sq. km (2006)
Urban population – 37.2 per cent (2005 est)
Median age (years) – 17.9 (2007 est)
National anthem – 'Angola Avante' ['Forward Angola']
National day – 11 November (Independence Day)
Life expectancy (years) – 37.63 (2007 est)
Mortality rate – 24.81 (2007 est)
Birth rate – 45.51 (2007 est)
Infant mortality rate – 184.44 (2007 est)
HIV/AIDS adult prevalence – 3.2 per cent (2005 est)
Death penalty – Abolished for all crimes (since 1992)
CPI score – 2.2 (2007)
Population below poverty line – 70 per cent (2003 est)
Literacy rate – 66.8 per cent (2004 est)
Gross enrolment ratio (percentage of relevant age group) – secondary 19 per cent (2002); tertiary 3 per cent (2006 est)
Health expenditure (per capita) – US$36 (2005)

CLIMATE AND TERRAIN

The land rises from a narrow coastal plain to a large interior plateau. On the plateau rise the Cunene, Cubango and Cuanza rivers and the headwaters of tributaries of the Zambezi and Congo rivers, although some of these are dry except in the rainy season, when flooding may occur. The south is desert. The highest point of elevation is 2,620m (Morro de Moco) and the lowest is 0m (Atlantic Ocean). The climate is tropical in the north, with a cool, dry season from May to October and a hot, rainy season from November to April, and sub-tropical in the south and along the coast to Luanda.

HISTORY AND POLITICS

A Portuguese colony was established in the region in the 15th century and its territory expanded over the centuries, the current boundaries being defined in the 19th century. An anti-colonial war began in 1961, and Angola became independent on 11 November 1975. Shortly afterwards, civil war broke out between the Popular Movement for the Liberation of Angola (MPLA) government and two factions, the National Union for the Total Independence of Angola (UNITA) led by Jonas Savimbi, and the Front for the Liberation of Angola (FNLA). The FNLA ceased operations in the 1980s and foreign support for the MPLA and UNITA was withdrawn after 1988, but the civil war between the government and UNITA continued. A peace agreement in 1991 was followed by multiparty elections in 1992 but UNITA refused to accept the results and fighting resumed. Another peace agreement (the Lusaka protocol) was signed in 1994 but UNITA appeared not to comply with its provisions and UN peacekeeping forces were deployed.

In 1997 a government of national reconciliation was formed under the power-sharing provisions of the Lusaka protocol. Although a nominal participant, UNITA prevented the restoration of central state administration in key areas. In spite of UN intervention, fighting continued until 2002, when, following the death of Jonas Savimbi in February, UNITA and the government signed a formal ceasefire agreement in April and pledged to adhere to the 1994 peace agreement. UNITA gradually demobilised its forces and transformed itself into a political party, electing Isaias Samakuva as leader in 2003.

Voter registration began in 2004 in preparation for elections in 2006, but was not completed until 2007 because of the inaccessibility of many parts of the country, causing the elections to be delayed repeatedly. Legislative elections were scheduled for 5–6 September 2008, with a presidential election in 2009.

SECESSION

In the northern enclave of Cabinda, separatists have fought for independence since the mid-1970s. Following the end of the civil war, the government stepped up its military campaign against the separatists, destroying their military capability by 2004, although it was accused of serious infringements of human rights. A truce in 2006 led to talks and a peace agreement signed by most of the separatist groups, although one remaining faction continues its attacks.

POLITICAL SYSTEM

The 1975 constitution has been heavily amended, notably in 1991, when a multiparty system was adopted and the MPLA, formerly a Marxist-Leninist party, ceased to be the sole legal party. The executive president is directly elected for a five-year term and appoints the council of ministers. The unicameral National Assembly has 223 members, directly elected for a four-year term. Neither presidential nor legislative elections have been held since 1992; in 1996 and in 2000, the National Assembly adopted a constitutional amendment extending its own mandate.

HEAD OF STATE

President, Jose Eduardo dos Santos, *re-elected* 30 September 1992

SELECTED GOVERNMENT MEMBERS *as at May 2008*

Prime Minister, Interior, Fernando da Piedade Dias dos Santos
Deputy Prime Minister, Aguinaldo Jaime
Defence, Gen. Kundi Pahiama
Finance, Jose Pedro de Morais
Foreign Affairs, Joao Bernardo de Miranda
Interior, Gen. Roberto Leal Monteiro

EMBASSY OF THE REPUBLIC OF ANGOLA

22 Dorset Street, London W1U 6QY
T 020-7299 9850 E embassy@angola.org.uk
Ambassador Extraordinary and Plenipotentiary, HE Ana Maria Teles Carreira, *apptd* 2005

BRITISH EMBASSY

Rua Diogo Cao 4 (Caixa Postal 1244), Luanda
T (+244) (22) 233 4582 W www.britishembassy.gov.uk/angola
Ambassador Extraordinary and Plenipotentiary, HE Patricia Phillips, *apptd* 2007

DEFENCE

The army has an estimated 300 main battle tanks, 250 armoured infantry fighting vehicles and 170 armoured personnel carriers. The navy is based at Luanda and has 9 patrol and coastal combatant vessels. The air force has 90 combat aircraft and 16 armed helicopters.
Military budget – US$2,290m (2007)
Military personnel – 107,000: army 100,000, navy 1,000, air force 6,000; paramilitary 10,000

ECONOMY AND TRADE

Since the civil war ended, the government has made progress towards liberalising the economy and stabilising the exchange rate. Inflation has been brought down from 325 per cent in 2000 to 12.5 per cent in 2007. This progress has been possible due to high economic growth driven by the post-war increase in oil production (further buoyed by a high global price) and developments in agriculture. However, widespread corruption means that most of the population has seen little benefit and 70 per cent remained below the poverty line in 2003.

Angola and the Cabinda enclave are rich in natural resources that include oil, diamonds, gold, uranium and other minerals, forests and fisheries. The main industries involve extracting and processing oil (oil production and related activities account for about 85 per cent of GDP), gems, metals and other minerals, forestry, fishing and the manufacture of cement, metal products, tobacco products and textiles, and ship repair. Agriculture is mostly at subsistence level, although coffee, sisal and cotton are exported. Production has risen but the country still imports much of its food; expansion is hampered by unexploded landmines and damaged infrastructure in areas affected by the civil war. Angola generates sufficient hydroelectric power to supply 75 per cent of its energy needs at present and plans to increase capacity both for domestic use and for export.

The main trading partners are the USA, China, Portugal and South Korea. The principal exports are crude oil, diamonds, refined petroleum products, gas, agricultural products and timber. The main imports are machinery and electrical equipment, vehicles and spare parts, medicines, foodstuffs, textiles and military goods.
GNI – US$32,700m; US$1,970 per capita (2006)
Annual average growth of GDP – 16.3 per cent (2007 est)
Inflation rate – 12.5 per cent (2007 est)
Total external debt – US$8,835m (2007 est)
Exports – US$35,100m (2006)

BALANCE OF PAYMENTS
Trade – US$26,935 surplus (2006)
Current Account – US$10,538m surplus (2006)

Trade with UK	*2006*	*2007*
Imports from UK	£206,322,000	£273,498,643
Exports to UK	£16,037,000	£154,539,594

COMMUNICATIONS

The conflict of the past 30 years has left the road and rail systems in extremely poor condition. Land transport difficulties are compounded by the many uncleared landmines and security problems. Reconstruction began in 2005 with foreign aid, especially from China, and several projects were completed in 2006. There are 51,429km of roads, 5,349km of which are surfaced, and 2,761km of railway. Most internal travel takes place by air between the country's 232 airports. The main ports are Luanda, Lobito and Benguela. The fixed-line telephone system is poor, with fewer than one fixed line per 100 people; mobile phone use is growing rapidly and was about 19 per 100 people in 2006.

MEDIA

Angola's only news agency (Angop), the country's biggest broadcaster, Televisao Popular de Angola (TPA), and the country's only daily newspaper *(Jornal de Angola)* are all government-owned and rarely outspoken although freedom of speech is enshrined in the constitution. There are several commercial radio stations and private newspapers, one private television station, and some subscription services (operated by Multichoice Angola) that include Brazilian and Portuguese channels. The private media is liable to harassment.

ANTIGUA AND BARBUDA

State of Antigua and Barbuda

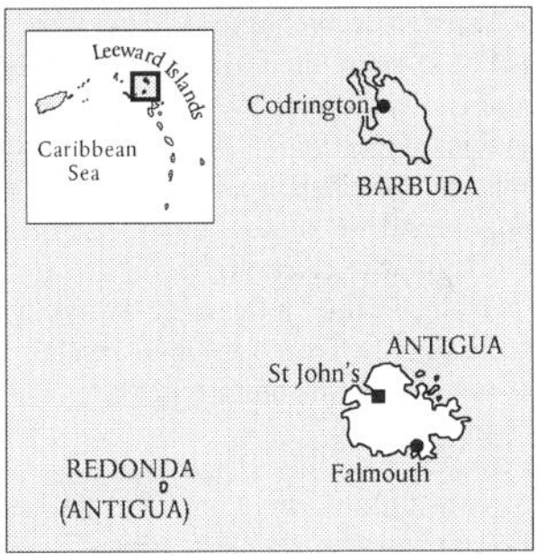

Area – 443 sq. km; Antigua 279 sq. km; Barbuda 160 sq. km; Redonda 1.2 sq. km
Capital – St John's; population, 26,000 (2007 est)
Currency – East Caribbean dollar (EC$) of 100 cents
Population – 69,481 rising at 0.53 per cent per year (2007 est)
Religion – Christianity (74 per cent), Rastafarianism (1 per cent) (est). Around 5 per cent of the population is atheist
Language – English (official)
Population density – 191 per sq. km (2006)
Urban population – 38.4 per cent (2005 est)
Median age (years) – 30.3 (2007 est)
National anthem – 'Fair Antigua, We Salute Thee'
National day – 1 November (Independence Day)
Life expectancy (years) – 72.42 (2007 est)
Mortality rate – 5.31 (2007 est)
Birth rate – 16.62 (2007 est)
Infant mortality rate – 18.26 (2007 est)
Death penalty – Retained

CLIMATE AND TERRAIN

Antigua is part of the Leeward Islands in the eastern Caribbean. It is distinguished from the rest of the Leeward Islands by an absence of high hills and forest, and has a drier climate than most of the West Indies. The elevation extremes range from 402m at the highest point (Boggy Peak) to 0m sea level (Caribbean Sea).

Barbuda is 48km away from Antigua. It is a very flat coral island with a large lagoon. Both of the islands lie within the hurricane belt and are subject to tropical storms and hurricanes between June and November.

HISTORY AND POLITICS

Antigua was discovered by Columbus in 1493. Colonised by the English in 1632, it was granted to Lord Willoughby by Charles II. Barbuda was colonised from Antigua in 1661. Administered as part of the Leeward Islands Federation from 1871 to 1956, it became internally self-governing in 1967 and fully independent on 1 November 1981.

The Antigua Labour Party, which had been in office since 1976, was defeated in the 2004 election by the United Progressive Party, which took office under Baldwin Spencer.

POLITICAL SYSTEM
The head of state is the British monarch, represented by the governor-general. The bicameral parliament comprises a senate of 17 appointed members and a House of Representatives of 17 directly elected members; both chambers serve a five-year term.
Governor-General, HE Louise Lake-Tack, *apptd* 2007

SELECTED GOVERNMENT MEMBERS *as at May 2008*
Prime Minister, Foreign Affairs and Foreign Trade, National Security, Barbuda Affairs, Ecclesiastical Affairs, Winston Baldwin Spencer
Deputy Prime Minister, Public Works, Transport, Wilmoth Daniel
Minister of Finance and Economy, Leon Errol Cort

HIGH COMMISSION FOR ANTIGUA AND BARBUDA
2nd Floor, 45 Crawford Place, London W1H 4LP
T 020-7258 0070 E enquiries@antigua-barbuda.com
W www.antigua-barbuda.com
High Commissioner, HE Dr Carl Roberts, *apptd* 2004

BRITISH HIGH COMMISSION
High Commissioner, HE Duncan Taylor, *apptd* 2005, resident at Bridgetown, Barbados

DEFENCE

The navy has 3 patrol and coastal combatant vessels at a base at St Johns.
Military budget – US$14m (2007 est)
Military personnel – 170: army 125, navy 45 (combined Antigua and Barbuda Defence Force)

ECONOMY AND TRADE

Antigua is one of the Caribbean's more prosperous nations. The economy is largely based on tourism and

related services (contributing more than half of GDP), construction and light manufacturing. To reduce its dependence on tourism, the government has encouraged the establishment of internet gambling sites. Agricultural production includes livestock, sea island cotton, mixed market gardening and fishing, mostly for local consumption.
GNI – US$929m; US$11,050 per capita (2006)
Annual average growth of GDP – 3.8 per cent (2007 est)
Inflation rate – 2.8 per cent (2007 est)
Unemployment – 11 per cent (2001 est)
Total external debt – US$359.8m (2006)

BALANCE OF PAYMENTS
Trade – US$490m deficit (2006)
Current Account – US$162m deficit (2006)

Trade with UK	*2006*	*2007*
Imports from UK	£30,816,000	£25,754,268
Exports to UK	£5,517,000	£8,606,008

MEDIA AND CULTURE

Many of the television and radio stations are owned or controlled by the Antigua Labour Party. Antigua's first independent radio station, Observer Radio, began broadcasting in 2001.

Antiguan culture is dominated by cricket and the country has produced several of the sport's most illustrious names. Batsman Viv Richards (*b.* 1952) and Richie Richardson (*b.* 1962) both captained the West Indian team, while Curtly Ambrose (*b.* 1963) is one of only ten bowlers to have taken 400 Test wickets.

ARGENTINA

República Argentina – Argentine Republic

Area – 2,766,890 sq. km
Capital – Buenos Aires; population, 12,795,000 (2007)
Major cities – Córdoba, La Plata, Mar del Plata, Mendoza, Rosario, Salta, San Miguel de Tucumán, Santa Fé
Currency – Peso of 100 centavos
Population – 40,301,927 rising at 0.94 per cent per year (2007 est)
Religion – Roman Catholicism (70 per cent), Protestantism (9 per cent), Islam (1 per cent) (est)
Language – Spanish (official), English, Italian, French, German
Population density – 14 per sq. km (2006)
Urban population – 90.6 per cent (2005 est)
Median age (years) – 29.9 (2007 est)
National anthem – 'Marcha de la Patria' ['March of the Fatherland']
National day – 25 May (Revolution Day)
Life expectancy (years) – 76.32 (2007 est)
Mortality rate – 7.55 (2007 est)
Birth rate – 16.53 (2007 est)
Infant mortality rate – 14.29 (2007 est)
Death penalty – Retained for certain crimes
CPI score – 2.9 (2007)
Population below poverty line – 38.5 per cent (2005)

CLIMATE AND TERRAIN

The Andes mountain range runs the full length of Argentina, on the country's western border with Chile and is an area prone to earthquakes. East of the Andes, the north of the country is mostly subtropical forest and savanna, the east is rich, grassy pampas, and the southern Patagonian plateau has an arid, desert-like terrain. The highest point of elevation is 6,960m (Cerro Aconcagua) and the lowest is −105m (Laguna del Carbon). Temperatures range from subtropical to subantarctic, with an average annual temperature of 16°C.

HISTORY AND POLITICS

The estuary of La Plata was discovered in 1515 by Juan Díaz de Solís and the region was subsequently colonised by the Spanish. Spain ruled the territory from the 16th century until 1810. In 1816, after a long campaign of liberation, independence was declared by the congress of Tucumán and during the following century, power swung between conservative and liberal factions, and between civil and military regimes.

A 1943 coup introduced a period of military rule before Juan Domingo Perón became president in 1946, establishing an authoritarian regime. His overthrow in 1955 instigated 18 years of political instability until 1973, when he was recalled from exile. Perón died within a year and was succeeded by his widow, vice-president Maria Estela Martínez de Perón. A coup led to the establishment of a military junta in 1976 which conducted a campaign known as the 'dirty war' in which over 8,000 people are alleged to have disappeared. The failure of Argentina's attempt to annex the Falkland Islands in 1982 discredited the junta and led to the restoration of civilian rule in 1983.

The presidential election in October 2007 was won in the first round by Cristina Fernandez de Kirchner, wife of the outgoing president Néstor Kirchner. Following the simultaneous legislative elections, the largest party in each chamber remained the Judicialist Party, a Peronist grouping including the Front for Liberty and the Front for Victory, the party of the incoming president.

POLITICAL SYSTEM

The 1853 constitution was amended in 1994. The executive president is directly elected for a four-year term, renewable only once. The bicameral National Congress consists of a 72-member senate (three members for each province and three for Buenos Aires) and a 257-member Chamber of Deputies. Deputies are directly elected for a four-year term, with half of the seats renewable every two years. Senators are directly elected for a six-year term, with one-third of seats renewable every two years.

HEAD OF STATE
President, Cristina Fernandez de Kirchner, *sworn in* 10 December 2008
Vice-President, Julio Cobos

SELECTED GOVERNMENT MEMBERS *as at May 2008*
Cabinet Chief, Alberto Fernández

Defence, Nilda Garré
Economy, Carlos Fernandez
Foreign Relations, International Trade and Worship, Jorge Taiana
Interior, Florencio Randazzo

EMBASSY OF THE ARGENTINE REPUBLIC
65 Brook Street, London W1K 4AH
T 020-7318 1300 E info@argentine-embassy-uk.org
W www.argentine-embassy-uk.org
Ambassador Extraordinary and Plenipotentiary, HE Federico Mirré, *apptd* 2003

BRITISH EMBASSY
Dr Luis Agote 2412/52 (Casilla de Correo 2050),
1425 Buenos Aires
T (+54) (11) 4808 2200
W www.britishembassy.gov.uk/argentina
Ambassador Extraordinary and Plenipotentiary, HE Dr John Hughes, *apptd* 2004

BRITISH COUNCIL
4th Floor, Marcelo T. de Alvear 590, C1058AAF Buenos Aires
T (+54) (11) 4114 8600 W www.britishcouncil.org/argentina
Director, Martin Fryer

FEDERAL STRUCTURE
The republic is divided into 22 provinces, each with an elected governor and legislature, the federal district of Buenos Aires, which has an elected mayor and autonomous government, and the national territory of Tierra del Fuego.

DEFENCE

The army has 213 main battle tanks, 123 armoured infantry fighting vehicles and 413 armoured personnel carriers. The navy has 3 submarines, 5 destroyers, 9 frigates, 15 patrol and coastal vessels and 28 combat aircraft. There are bases at Ushuaio, Mar del Plata, Buenos Aires, Puerto Belgrano and Zarate. The air force has 119 combat aircraft.
Military budget – US$2,050m (2007)
Military personnel – 76,000: army 41,400, navy 20,000, air force 14,600; paramilitary 31,240

ECONOMY AND TRADE

The economy has been turned around since the economic collapse of 2001–2. Argentina has experienced strong growth since 2003, restructuring its defaulted debt in 2005 and repaying its IMF loan in 2006. The government budget is in surplus, exports are strong, and public debt, unemployment and the percentage of the population living below the poverty line are all gradually falling. Rising inflation and excessive demand for energy remain problems.

The country is rich in natural resources, particularly lead, zinc, tin, copper, iron ore, manganese, uranium, oil and coal. The fertile pampas supports a strong and export-orientated agricultural sector; the main crops are cereals, oil-bearing seeds, fruit, tea, tobacco and livestock products, especially beef, mutton and wool.

The main industrial activities are food processing (meat-packing, flour-milling, sugar-refining, wine production) and the production of motor vehicles, consumer durables, textiles, chemicals, petrochemicals, printing, metallurgy and steel.

The main trading partners are Brazil, USA, China and Chile. The principal exports include edible oils, fuel and energy, cereals and motor vehicles. The major imports are machinery, motor vehicles, petrol and natural gas, chemicals and plastics.
GNI – US$201,400m; US$5,150 per capita (2006)
Annual average growth of GDP – 8.5 per cent (2007 est)
Inflation rate – 8.5 per cent (2007 est)
Unemployment – 8.9 per cent (2007 est)
Total external debt – US$118,000m (2007)
Imports – US$34,000m (2006)
Exports – US$47,000m (2006)

BALANCE OF PAYMENTS
Trade – US$12,411m surplus (2006)
Current Account – US$5,413m surplus (2006)

Trade with UK	*2006*	*2007*
Imports from UK	£216,078,000	£226,534,918
Exports to UK	£359,126,000	£429,020,748

COMMUNICATIONS

The road and rail networks are extensive in the north and centre of the country; in Patagonia, roads are fewer and there are no railways. The 31,902km of railway is state owned. The combined national and provincial road network totals approximately 229,144km, of which 68,809km are surfaced. A US$20bn (£10bn) programme of road-building and upgrading of existing road, rail and air infrastructure began in 2000. The main form of internal long-distance travel is by air and there are over 1,000 airports and airfields; the principal airports are at Buenos Aires, Cordoba, Salta and Rio Gallegos. There are many ports on the long coastline and the 11,000km of inland waterways formed by the major rivers; Buenos Aires, Ensenada (La Plata) and Bahia Blanca are the main seaports. The telecommunications system has modernised rapidly since the market was opened to competition and foreign investment in 1998. Fixed-line telephone density was nearly 25 per 100 people in 2006, while the rapid rise in mobile phone use reached 80 per 100 people.

EDUCATION AND HEALTH

Since 2007 education is compulsory until the age of 18.
Literacy rate – 97.2 per cent (2004 est)
Gross enrolment ratio (percentage of relevant age group) – primary 113 per cent; secondary 86 per cent; tertiary 65 per cent (2006 est)
Health expenditure (per capita) – US$484 (2005)
Hospital beds (per 1,000 people) – 4.1 (2000–6)

MEDIA AND CULTURE

The media is well developed, with over 150 daily newspapers (published in both English and Spanish), including seven major dailies published in Buenos Aires. There are hundreds of commercial radio stations (many unlicensed), over 40 television stations and widespread access to cable television.

The culture is primarily Latin American but has strong European influences due to the country's large Italian and Spanish populations. Argentina's most notable writer is Jorge Luis Borges (1899–1986) whose short stories belong within the magical realist movement. The world's first animated films were made in Argentina by Quirino Cristani (1896–1984) and the country's film-making pedigree has been maintained by the success of composer Lalo Schiffrin (*b.* 1932).

Argentina has historically been a successful sporting country. Its football team is a double World Cup winner and has held the Copa America trophy 14 times. Two of football's greatest entertainers, Alfredo di Stefano (*b.* 1926) and Diego Maradona (*b.* 1960), are Argentinian. Juan Michael Fangio's (1911–95) record of five Formula One World Championships stood for 45 years until 2003.

ARGENTINE ANTARCTIC TERRITORY

The Argentine Antarctic Territory consists of the Antarctic Peninsula and a triangular section extending to the South Pole, defined as the area between 25°W and 74° W and 60°S. This overlaps with both Britain's and Chile's claim areas (*see also* The North and South Poles). Administratively, the territory is a department of the province of Tierra del Fuego, Antarctica, and South Atlantic Islands. The population varies from 150 to 300 people, all of whom are scientific researchers.

ARMENIA

Hayastani Hanrapetut'yun – Republic of Armenia

Area – 29,800 sq. km
Capital – Yerevan; population, 1,102,000 (2007 est)
Major cities – Gyumri, Vanadzor
Currency – Dram of 100 luma
Population – 2,971,650, falling at 0.13 per cent per year (2007 est); Armenian (97.9 per cent), Kurdish (1.3 per cent). The Armenian diaspora numbers some 5,300,000
Religion – Christianity (Armenian Church) (90 per cent) (est). Armenia adopted Christianity as its official religion in AD 301, the first state in the world to do so
Language – Armenian, Yezidi, Russian
Population density – 107 per sq. km (2006)
Urban population – 64.1 per cent (2005 est)
Median age (years) – 30.8 (2007 est)
National anthem – 'Mer Hayrenik' ['Our Fatherland']
National day – 21 September (Independence Day)
Life expectancy (years) – 72.12 (2007 est)
Mortality rate – 8.29 (2007 est)
Birth rate – 12.34 (2007 est)
Infant mortality rate – 21.69 (2007 est)
Death penalty – Abolished for all crimes (since 2003)
CPI score – 3.0 (2007)
Population below poverty line – 26.5 per cent (2004 est)

CLIMATE AND TERRAIN

A landlocked country lying between the Black and Caspian seas, Armenia lies in the south-western part of the Caucasus region. It is very mountainous, consisting of several vast tablelands surrounded by ridges. The elevation extremes range from 4,090m at the highest point (Aragats Lerrnagagat) to 400m at the lowest (Debed river). The climate is continental, dry and cold, but the Ararat valley has a long, hot and dry summer. Armenia is in an active seismic zone, and the north of the country suffered an earthquake in 1988 that left an estimated 50,000 people dead.

HISTORY AND POLITICS

Armenia was first unified in 95 BC but was divided between the Persian and Byzantine empires in AD 387 and then conquered in the 11th century by the Seljuk Turks and the Mongols. In the 16th century most of Armenia was incorporated into the Ottoman Empire. In 1639 the country was divided again, the most easterly areas, now the Republic of Armenia, becoming part of the Persian Empire. In 1828 eastern Armenia became part of the Russian Empire while western Armenia remained under Ottoman rule. The Ottomans launched pogroms against the Armenians from 1894 onwards, and from 1915 to 1918 deported or killed over 1,500,000.

Armenia declared its independence on 28 May 1918, but was crushed and divided between Turkish and Soviet forces in 1920, with the area under Soviet control proclaimed a Soviet Socialist Republic. The Soviet government was overthrown by a nationalist revolt in 1921 but reinstated by the Red Army a few months later. In early 1922 Armenia acceded to the USSR.

An Armenian nationalist movement gained power in national elections in mid-1990. In a referendum in 1991, 99 per cent of the electorate voted for independence, which was declared on 21 September 1991. In 1992, a state of emergency was declared as a result of a worsening economic situation and the dispute with Azerbaijan over Nagorny-Karabakh. Prime Minister Vazgen Sarkisian and six other politicians were shot dead in the national assembly during an attempted coup in 1999.

In the 2007 legislative election, the Republican Party of Armenia (HHK) remained the largest party in the legislature, with 65 seats, and its leader Serzh Sarkisian, prime minister since March 2007, continued in office at the head of a four-party coalition government. Sarkisian won the February 2008 presidential election in the first round with 52.9 per cent of the vote; protests by opposition supporters continued for some weeks, causing a state of emergency to be declared in March. After his inauguration President Sarkisian nominated Tigran Sargsyan as prime minister.

FOREIGN RELATIONS

A longstanding dispute with Azerbaijan over the predominantly Armenian-populated Azeri enclave of Nagorny-Karabakh escalated in 1992 into war, when ethnic Armenian Nagorno-Karabakh forces, supported by Armenia, breached Azerbaijan's defences to form a land bridge to Armenia. By the end of summer 1992, all of Nagorny-Karabakh was under Armenian control, and by the end of 1993 all Azeri territory that separated Nagorny-Karabakh from Armenia and all mountainous Azeri territory around Nagorny-Karabakh was under the control of the Armenians. Armenia claims this territory as historically native land arbitrarily given to Azerbaijan by Stalin in 1921–2. A ceasefire agreement between Armenia, Azerbaijan and Nagorny-Karabakh was reached in 1994, but talks mediated by the Organisation for Security and Cooperation in Europe have failed to make any progress towards a peaceful resolution.

POLITICAL SYSTEM

The 1995 constitution was amended by referendum in 2005. The president is directly elected for a five-year term, renewable only once. The unicameral *Azgayin Joghov* (National Assembly) has 131 members who are directly elected for a four-year term.

HEAD OF STATE
President, Serzh Sarkisian, *elected* 19 February 2008, *inaugurated* 9 April 2008

SELECTED GOVERNMENT MEMBERS *as at May 2008*
Prime Minister, Tigran Sargsyan
Deputy Prime Minister, Armen Gevorgian
Defence, Seyran Ohanian
Economy, Nerses Yeritsian
Foreign Affairs, Eduard Nalbandian

EMBASSY OF THE REPUBLIC OF ARMENIA
25A Cheniston Gardens, London W8 6TG
T 020-7938 5435 E armemb@armenianembassyuk.com
Ambassador Extraordinary and Plenipotentiary, HE Dr Vahe Gabrielyan, *apptd* 2003

BRITISH EMBASSY
34 Baghramyan Avenue, Yerevan 375019
T (+374) (10) 264 301 W www.britishembassy.gov.uk/armenia
Ambassador Extraordinary and Plenipotentiary, HE Anthony Cantor, *apptd* 2006

BRITISH COUNCIL
c/o The British Embassy
T (+374) (56) 9923 W www.britishcouncil.org/armenia
Manager, Arevik Saribekyan

DEFENCE

The army has 110 main battle tanks, 104 armoured infantry fighting vehicles and 136 armoured personnel carriers. The air force has 16 combat aircraft and 8 armed helicopters.

Russia maintains 3,170 army personnel in Armenia. An agreement on military cooperation with Russia was signed in 1996 which paved the way for joint military exercises. A protocol was also signed on the establishment of coalition troops in Transcaucasia and the planned use of Russian and Armenian armed forces as part of coalition troops in cases of mutual interest. In 2001 Russian president Vladimir Putin signed a federal law relating to an agreement between the Russian Federation and the Republic of Armenia on the joint planning of the use of troops in the interests of joint security provision. This stipulates measures to prevent the use by third countries of the territory of Armenia for purposes that may inflict damage on Russian national interests.
Military budget – US$295m (2007)
Military personnel – 42,080: army 38,945, air force 3,135; paramilitary 4,748
Conscription duration – 24 months

ECONOMY AND TRADE

The economy experienced a severe decline following the break-up of the USSR in 1991, adding to existing problems arising from the 1988 earthquake and subsequently exacerbated by the trade embargos imposed by Azerbaijan and Turkey over the Nagorny-Karabakh conflict, both of which are still in place. An economic liberalisation programme initiated in 1994 has brought some stability and sustained high growth rates, although poverty is still widespread, resulting in high levels of emigration by younger adults.

Armenia has a strong agricultural sector, although this is in need of modernisation. It produces fruit, vegetables and livestock as cash crops, and grain. There are large mineral deposits, including copper ore and molybdenum. Industry is diversified and most small and medium-sized enterprises are now privatised. The main activities are diamond-processing, the production of industrial machinery, vehicles, textiles and clothing, chemicals, instruments, microelectronics, jewellery, software development and food processing. The constraining energy shortages of the mid-1990s were overcome by reopening the nuclear power plant at Metsamor. This has enabled Armenia to become an energy exporter, but there is international pressure to close the plant because of the earthquake risks in the area.

The trade deficit is partly offset by international aid and remittances from citizens working abroad. The main trading partners are Russia, EU countries, Israel, the USA and neighbouring states. Principal exports are diamonds, foodstuffs, mineral products and energy. The main imports are natural gas, petrol, tobacco products, foodstuffs and diamonds.
GNI – US$5,800m; US$1,920 per capita (2006)
Annual average growth of GDP – 10.5 per cent (2007 est)
Inflation rate – 4.5 per cent (2007 est)
Unemployment – 7.4 per cent (2006 est)
Total external debt – US$2,261m (2007)
Imports – US$2,190m (2006)
Exports – US$1,000m (2006)

BALANCE OF PAYMENTS
Trade – US$1,190m deficit (2006)
Current Account – US$115m deficit (2006)

Trade with UK	*2006*	*2007*
Imports from UK	£11,084,000	£11,774,319
Exports to UK	£2,622,000	£485,462

EDUCATION AND HEALTH

State education is free and compulsory for all children aged seven to 14. Children attend primary school for three years, until the age of nine, then progress on to secondary school for five years, until the age of 14. At the end of intermediate school a certificate of basic education is awarded. Senior secondary school may be attended for two years from the ages of 14 to 16.
Literacy rate – 99.4 per cent (2004 est)
Gross enrolment ratio (percentage of relevant age group) – primary 98 per cent; secondary 90 per cent; tertiary 32 per cent (2006 est)
Health expenditure (per capita) – US$88 (2005)
Hospital beds (per 1,000 people) – 4.5 (2000–6)

MEDIA

Armenia has more than 40 private television stations, which operate alongside two public networks. The main Russian television channels are also available. Television and radio are both controlled by the state and all print and broadcast media are obliged to register with the ministry of justice. Censorship is banned under a 2004 media law, but journalists have been imprisoned for libel and defamation offences. Newspapers have limited influence, often due to small print runs, and tend to be owned by wealthy individuals and political parties.

AUSTRALIA

Commonwealth of Australia

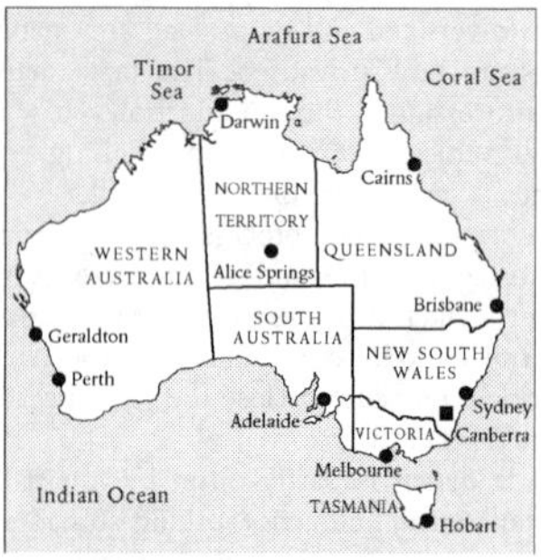

Area – 7,686,850 sq. km
Capital – Canberra, in the Australian Capital Territory; population, 378,000 (2007 est). It has been the seat of government since 1927
Major cities – Adelaide, Brisbane, Melbourne, Perth, Sydney
Currency – Australian dollar ($A) of 100 cents
Population – 20,434,176 rising at 0.82 per cent per year (2007 est)
Religion – Roman Catholicism (26 per cent), other Christian denominations (38 per cent), Buddhism (2 per cent), Islam (2 per cent) (est); 19 per cent is estimated to be atheist
Language – English (official), Chinese, Italian
Population density – 3 per sq. km (2006)
Urban population – 92.7 per cent (2005 est)
Median age (years) – 37.1 (2007 est)
National anthem – 'Advance Australia Fair'
National day – 26 January (Australia Day)
Life expectancy (years) – 80.62 (2007 est)
Mortality rate – 7.56 (2007 est)
Birth rate – 12.02 (2007 est)
Infant mortality rate – 4.57 (2007 est)
Death penalty – Abolished for all crimes (since 1985)
CPI score – 8.6 (2007)

CLIMATE AND TERRAIN

Australia is a continent, the world's sixth-largest country and home to a wide variety of landscapes and weather conditions. The interior is dominated by hot deserts and is only thinly populated. The eastern and south-eastern coastlines are the most densely populated areas and feature mountains, flat golden beaches and rainforests. The highest point of elevation is 2,229m (Mt Kosciuszko) and the lowest is –15m (Lake Eyre). The summer begins in December, the winter in June, the spring in September and the autumn in March. Average temperatures range from 0°C to 34°C.

HISTORY AND POLITICS

The Aboriginals are thought to have arrived in Australia from south-east Asia *c.*40,000 years ago. Europeans first discovered Australia in the 17th century. Its eastern coast was claimed by Capt. James Cook on behalf of Britain in 1770 and became a penal colony; Tasmania, Western Australia, South Australia, Victoria and Queensland were established as colonies between 1825 and 1859. The individual colonies became self-governing from the 1850s onwards and were federated as the Commonwealth of Australia on 1 January 1901, at which time Australia gained dominion status within the British Empire. Australia became independent within the British Commonwealth under the 1931 Statute of Westminster. Following a referendum in 1967, the Aboriginal population was granted full political rights. In 1986, the Australia Act was passed, which abolished the remaining legislative, executive and judicial links to the UK while retaining the British monarch as head of state. In 1998, the Constitutional Convention voted to hold a national referendum on whether to sever constitutional links with the British monarchy, but the referendum in 1999 on the proposal to make Australia a republic was defeated, with 45.3 per cent voting in favour and 54.7 per cent against.

The Liberal Party/National Party coalition government, in power since 1996, was defeated in the 2007 general election by the Australian Labor Party, which won 83 out of the 150 seats in the house of representatives and 32 of the 76 seats in the senate. The ALP leader, Kevin Rudd, became prime minister and reversed many of the previous government's policies, signing the Kyoto protocol on climate change, apologising for past abuses of Aborigines and ending the detention of asylum seekers in small Pacific island states.

POLITICAL SYSTEM

The Commonwealth of Australia is a federation of six states and two territories. The constitution defines the powers of the federal government, and residuary legislative power remains with the states. Executive power is vested in the British monarch, who is represented by the governor-general, assisted by a federal government.

Parliament consists of Queen Elizabeth II, the senate and the House of Representatives. The constitution provides that the number of members of the House of Representatives shall be proportionate to the population of each state, with a minimum of five members for each

STATES AND TERRITORIES

	Area (sq. km)	*Population (2007 est)*	*Capital*	*Governor (2008)*
Australian Capital Territory (ACT)	2,349	340,300	Canberra	–
New South Wales (NSW)	801,349	6,908,900	Sydney	Prof. Marie Bashir, AC
Northern Territory (NT)	1,352,158	216,500	Darwin*	Ian Pauling, QC†
Queensland (Qld)	1,734,157	4,201,100	Brisbane	Quentin Bryce, AC
South Australia (SA)	985,335	1,588,500	Adelaide	Rear Adm. Kevin Scarce, AC, MBE
Tasmania (Tas.)	67,914	494,500	Hobart	William Cox, AC
Victoria (Vic.)	227,594	5,226,400	Melbourne	David de Kretser, AC
Western Australia (WA)	2,534,483	2,118,500	Perth	Ken Michael, AC

* Seat of administration † Administrator

state, and that the number of senators shall be, as nearly as practicable, half the number of representatives. There are currently 150 members, including two members for the Northern Territory and two for the Australian Capital Territory; they are directly elected for a three-year term. There are 76 senators, each of the six states returning 12 senators, and the Australian Capital Territory and the Northern Territory two each. Senators are elected for six years by universal suffrage, half the members retiring every third year, except in the Australian Capital Territory and the Northern Territory, where members are elected for a three-year term.
Governor-General, Quentin Bryce, *apptd* 2007

SELECTED GOVERNMENT MEMBERS *as at May 2008*
Prime Minister, Kevin Rudd
Deputy Prime Minister, Julia Gillard
Defence, Joel Fitzgibbon
Foreign Affairs, Stephen Smith
Treasurer, Wayne Swan

AUSTRALIAN HIGH COMMISSION
Australia House, Strand, London WC2B 4LA
T 020-7379 4334 W www.uk.embassy.gov.au
High Commissioner, HE Hon. Richard Alston, *apptd* 2005

BRITISH HIGH COMMISSION
Commonwealth Avenue, Yarralumla, Canberra, ACT 2600
T (+61) (2) 6270 6666 E bhc.canberra@uk.emb.gov.au
W www.uk.emb.gov.au
High Commissioner, HE Helen Liddell, *apptd* 2005

BRITISH COUNCIL
Suite 403, 203–233 New South Head Road, Edgecliff, NSW 2027
T (+61) (2) 9326 2022 W www.britishcouncil.org.au
Director, Christopher Wade

FEDERAL STRUCTURE
Each state has its own constitution, executive, legislature and judicature. Executive authority is vested in a governor (appointed by the Crown), assisted by a council of ministers or executive council. Each state has a legislative council and a legislative assembly or house of assembly, which are elected for four-year terms, except Queensland, the Northern Territory and Australian Capital Territory, which have legislative assemblies only.

DEFENCE

The army has 172 main battle tanks, 299 armoured infantry fighting vehicles, 487 armoured personnel carriers and 22 armed helicopters. The navy has 6 submarines, 12 frigates, 11 patrol and coastal vessels and 46 armed helicopters. There are bases at Sydney, Stirling, Cairns, Darwin, Flinders, Jervis Bay and Nowra. The air force has 120 combat aircraft.
Military expenditure – US$17,200m (2006)
Military personnel – 51,293: army 25,259, navy 12,784, air force 13,250

ECONOMY AND TRADE

Australia has a highly diversified and internationally competitive free-market economy that has seen sustained strong growth since the early 1990s. The expansion was based on the economic reforms of the 1980s, low inflation, high export prices for raw materials and agricultural products, a property boom and growing trade links with China. Although the economy remains robust, the trade deficit has grown in recent years because of high import levels and a strong currency, while agricultural output, a key export sector, dropped by about 20 per cent in 2006 owing to the worst drought in a century. The service sector contributes 70.7 per cent of GDP and employs 75.2 per cent of the workforce; industry accounts for 25.6 per cent of GDP and 21.2 per cent of labour; and agriculture contributes 3.7 per cent of GDP and employs 3.6 per cent of the workforce.

A wide range of crops can be grown owing to the diversity of climatic and soil conditions, although most are confined to specific regions. Scant or erratic rainfall, limited scope for irrigation and unsuitable soils or topography have restricted intensive agriculture, although wheat is a major export and sugar cane and fruit are important crops. Cattle and sheep ranching is widespread, providing meat, meat derivatives, wool and dairy products.

Significant natural resources include bauxite, coal, copper, diamonds, gold, iron ore, lead, mineral salts, nickel, silver, tin, tungsten, uranium, zinc, oil and natural gas. The main industrial activities are mining, the production of industrial and transport equipment, chemicals and steel, and food processing. Production and processing of hydrocarbons are expected to increase once the exploitation of oil and gas fields in the Timor Sea begins.

Over the past 20 years, the focus of Australia's trade, like its foreign policy, has shifted from Europe to Asia and the Pacific region. It is a leading member of the Asia-Pacific Economic Co-operation forum and is negotiating free-trade agreements with China and the ASEAN countries. Major trading partners include Japan, China, USA, South Korea, Singapore, India and New Zealand. The chief exports are coal, iron ore, gold, meat, wool, alumina, wheat, machinery and transport equipment. The main imports are machinery and transport equipment, computers, office and telecommunications equipment, crude oil and petroleum products.
GNI – US$742,300m; US$35,860 per capita (2006)
Annual average growth of GDP – 4.2 per cent (2007 est)
Inflation rate – 2.4 per cent (2007 est)
Unemployment – 4.7 per cent (2007 est)
Total external debt – US$757,900m (2007)
Imports – US$139,000m (2006)
Exports – US$123,000m (2006)

BALANCE OF PAYMENTS
Trade – US$15,960m deficit (2006)
Current Account – US$41,690m deficit (2006)

Trade with UK	*2006*	*2007*
Imports from UK	£2,420,322,000	£2,512,796,170
Exports to UK	£2,141,266,000	£2,228,205,041

COMMUNICATIONS

Most long-distance internal travel is by air or road. There are 461 airports and airfields. Road and rail networks are concentrated in the more densely populated areas of the east and south, and around Perth in the west. Elsewhere, roads are more usual than railways, and both skirt the deserts of the interior, apart from a few transcontinental routes. There are six government-owned railway systems, and in 2006 there was a total of 38,550km of railway track. Most heavy freight is moved by road trains (trucks hauling two or three trailers) which measure up to 45m in length. There are 810,641km of roads. The 11 major ports and terminals include all the state capitals except Hobart, and there are private mining ports at Gove and Groote Eylandt in the Northern Territory. Mobile telephone distribution has grown rapidly to about 19.7 million in 2006, exceeding fixed-line usage. There were around 15.3 million internet users in 2006.

EDUCATION AND HEALTH

Education is administered by the state and is compulsory between the ages of six and 15 (16 in Tasmania). It is available at government schools controlled by the state education department and at private or independent schools, some of which are denominational.

Gross enrolment ratio (percentage of relevant age group) – primary 104 per cent; secondary 149 per cent; tertiary 73 per cent (2006 est)

Health expenditure (per capita) – US$3,181 (2005)

Hospital beds (per 1,000 people) – 4.0 (2000–6)

MEDIA

Australia's leading newspapers are *The Sydney Morning Herald, Herald Sun, The Australian* and *The Daily Telegraph*. There is an established tradition of public service broadcasting (via the Australian Broadcasting Corporation and the Special Broadcasting Service) and of commercial television (Seven Network, Nine Network, Ten Network). Commercial broadcasters are required to transmit a minimum percentage of Australian programming. Media tycoon Rupert Murdoch owns News Corporation and a considerable subscription-based television empire.

CULTURE

Indigenous Aboriginal culture was superseded on colonisation by European culture and latterly by influences from the USA, but the country has also been successful in exporting modern aspects of its culture. Australia's most decorated authors are Nobel Prize winner Patrick White (1912–90) and double Booker Prize winner Peter Carey (*b.* 1943). Germaine Greer (*b.* 1939) and Clive James (*b.* 1939) are respected cultural commentators.

The country's cinema enjoyed a renaissance in the 1980s, with acclamation for both art-house and mass-market films, such as the *Mad Max* and *Crocodile Dundee* franchises. Director Baz Luhrmann (*b.* 1962) and actors Russell Crowe (*b.* 1964) and Nicole Kidman (*b.* 1967) are established figures in Hollywood. Soap operas *Neighbours* and *Home and Away* and the programmes of naturalist Steve Irwin (1962–2006) are broadcast internationally.

Sport is an integral part of the culture. Australian rules football and cricket are the country's most popular sports and it takes part at international level in most major team sports, in addition to producing individual participants such as swimmer Ian Thorpe (*b.* 1982), athlete Cathy Freeman (*b.* 1973) and tennis players Rod Laver (*b.* 1938) and Roy Emerson (*b.* 1936).

EXTERNAL TERRITORIES

ASHMORE AND CARTIER ISLANDS

Ashmore Islands (known as Middle, East and West Islands) and Cartier Island are situated in the Indian Ocean 320km off Australia's north-west coast. There is a nature reserve on Ashmore Reef and a marine reserve around Cartier Island. The islands became an Australian territory in 1933, and are administered through the Attorney-General's Department.

THE AUSTRALIAN ANTARCTIC TERRITORY

The Australian Antarctic Territory was established in 1933 and comprises all the islands and territories, other than Adélie Land, that are situated south of latitude 60° S. and lying between 160° E. longitude and 45° E. longitude. The territory is administered by the Antarctic Division of the Department of the Environment, Water, Heritage and the Arts (*see also* The North and South Poles).

CHRISTMAS ISLAND

Area – 135 sq. km

Population – 1,402 (2007 est)

Christmas Island is situated in the Indian Ocean about 1,565km north-west of Northwest Cape in Western Australia. The island was annexed by Britain in 1888, but sovereignty was transferred to Australia in 1958 and the island is administered through the Attorney-General's Department. The Shire of Christmas Island (SOCI) is responsible for municipal functions and services on the island; it has nine members directly elected for a four-year term. The main industry is phosphate mining; the government sector and tourism also provide employment. A space satellite launching facility is currently being built on the island for the Asia Pacific Space Centre.

COCOS (KEELING) ISLANDS

Area – 14 sq. km

Population – 596 (2007 est)

The Cocos (Keeling) Islands are two separate atolls (North Keeling Island and, 24km to the south, the main atoll) comprising 27 small coral islands, situated in the Indian Ocean, about 2,950km north-west of Perth. The main islands of the southern atoll are West Island (about 9km in length); Home Island, where 80 per cent of the population lives, including most of the Cocos Malay community; Direction Island; Horsburgh Island and South Island.

The islands were declared a British possession in 1857, and became an Australian territory in 1955. All land in the islands was granted to George Clunies-Ross and his heirs by Queen Victoria in 1886. The Australian government purchased most of the Clunies-Ross land and property in 1978, and the remainder in 1984 and 1993. The land is held in trust for the residents, with the local government body, the Shire of the Cocos (Keeling) Islands, as trustee. In 1984 the Cocos community, in a UN-supervised Act of Self-Determination, voted to integrate with Australia. The islands are administered through the Attorney-General's Department. The seven-member Shire of Cocos (Keeling) Islands is responsible for municipal functions and services. The government sector is the main employer; coconuts are the only cash crop.

CORAL SEA ISLANDS TERRITORY

The Coral Sea Islands Territory lies east of Queensland between the Great Barrier Reef and longitude 156° 06′ E., and between latitudes 12° and 24° S. It comprises scattered islands, spread over a sea area of 780,000 sq. km. The islands are formed mainly of coral and sand, and most are extremely small. There is a manned meteorological station on Willis Island but the remaining islands are uninhabited. The Territory was established in 1969 and is administered through the Attorney-General's Department.

HEARD ISLAND AND MCDONALD ISLANDS

The Territory of Heard Island and the McDonald Islands, about 4,100km south-west of Perth, comprises all the islands and rocks lying between 52° 30′ and 53° 30′ S. latitude and 72° and 74° 30′ E. longitude. The subantarctic islands were discovered in the 1850s and transferred from British to Australian administration in 1947; they are now administered by the Antarctic Division of the Department of the Environment, Water, Heritage and the Arts.

NORFOLK ISLAND

Area – 34.6 sq. km
Population – 2,114 (2007 est)
Seat of government – Kingston
National day – 8 June (Bounty Day)

Norfolk Island is situated in the South Pacific Ocean, about 1,600km north-east of Sydney. It is around 8km long by 5km wide. The climate is mild and subtropical. Discovered by Captain Cook in 1774, the island served as a penal colony from 1788 to 1814 and from 1825 to 1855. In 1856, 194 descendants of the *Bounty* mutineers accepted an invitation to leave Pitcairn and settle on Norfolk Island.

The island has had a substantial degree of internal self-government since 1979, when the nine-member legislative assembly was established. The Administrator represents the federal government and reports to the Attorney-General. The Australian government intended to change the governance arrangements, on the grounds of financial unsustainability. This was dropped in late 2006 after the island's assembly committed to generating more revenue and promoting tourism, on which the economy is heavily dependent.

AUSTRIA

Republik Österreich – Republic of Austria

Area – 83,870 sq. km
Capital – Vienna; population, 2,315,000 (2007 est)
Major cities – Graz, Innsbruck, Klagenfurt, Linz, Salzburg
Currency – Euro (€) of 100 cents
Population – 8,199,783 rising at 0.08 per cent per year (2007 est); Austrians (91.1 per cent), former Yugoslavs (4 per cent), Turks (1.6 per cent)
Religion – Roman Catholicism (74 per cent), Protestantism (5 per cent), Islam (4 per cent) (est). It is estimated 12 per cent of the population is atheist
Language – German (official nationwide), Slovene, Croatian, Hungarian (each official in different regions), Turkish, Serbian
Population density – 100 per sq. km (2006)
Urban population – 65.8 per cent (2005 est)
Median age (years) – 41.3 (2007 est)
National anthem – 'Land der Berge, Land am Strome' ['Land of Mountains, Land on the River']
National day – 26 October
Life expectancy (years) – 79.21 (2007 est)
Mortality rate – 9.84 (2007 est)
Birth rate – 8.69 (2007 est)
Infant mortality rate – 4.54 (2007 est)
Death penalty – Abolished for all crimes (since 1968)
CPI score – 8.1 (2007)
Population below poverty line – 5.9 per cent (2004)

CLIMATE AND TERRAIN

The north and east of the landlocked country feature rolling hills in the river Danube basin, while the west and south contain the Austrian Alps, famous as a winter sports destination. The highest point of elevation is 3,798m (Grossglockner) and the lowest is 115m (Lake Neusiedl). Around 47 per cent of the land area is forested. There is a temperate climate, with temperature averages ranging from 2°C in January to 20°C in July.

HISTORY AND POLITICS

The Austrian state dates back to the eighth century AD when Charlemagne conquered the territory, which had been settled from the sixth century onwards by Germanic tribes, and founded the *Ostmark,* the eastern march of the Holy Roman Empire. It became a duchy and in 1282 passed to the Habsburg dynasty, which established an empire that united much of central Europe, including present-day Austria and Hungary. Hegemony was lost to Prussia in the 19th century, when growing Hungarian nationalism also led to the establishment of the dual monarchy of Austria-Hungary. The assassination of the heir to the throne in 1914 triggered the First World War, towards the end of which the Austro-Hungarian Empire collapsed, and most of the German-speaking lands became the Republic of Austria in November 1918. In March 1938, Austria was incorporated into Nazi Germany (the *Anschluss*) under the name *Ostmark.* After the Second World War, the Republic of Austria was reconstituted within its 1937 frontiers and a freely elected government took office in December 1945. The country was divided into four zones, each occupied by the UK, USA, USSR or France, while Vienna was jointly occupied by the four powers.

In 1955 the occupying powers withdrew, recognising Austria as a sovereign, independent and democratic state with the same frontiers as on 1 January 1938. Austria joined the EU in 1995 and its national assembly ratified the EU constitution in 2005.

The 2004 presidential election was won by Heinz Fischer of the Social Democrats (SPÖ). In the 2006 legislative elections, the Social Democrats (SPÖ) became the largest party but without an outright majority. After weeks of negotiations, it formed a coalition with the Austrian People's Party (ÖVP), but the alliance lasted less than two years after the OVP withdrew in July 2008. A general election was scheduled for September 2008.

POLITICAL SYSTEM

Under the 1955 constitution, the federal president is directly elected for a six-year term, renewable only once. There is a bicameral legislature, the *Parlament,* consisting of the *Nationalrat* (National Council), which has 183 members directly elected for a four-year term, and the

Bundesrat (Federal Council), which has 62 members elected for terms of various lengths by the provincial assemblies. There is a 4 per cent qualification for parliamentary representation. Some powers may only be exercised by both houses acting together as the *Bundesversammlung* (Federal Assembly). The executive is headed by the federal chancellor, who is appointed by the president.

HEAD OF STATE
Federal President, Heinz Fischer, *took office* 8 July 2004

SELECTED GOVERNMENT MEMBERS *as at May 2008*
Chancellor, Alfred Gusenbauer
Vice-Chancellor, Finance, Wilhelm Molterer
Defence, Norbert Darabos
Foreign Affairs, Ursula Plassnik
Interior, Maria Fekter

EMBASSY OF AUSTRIA
18 Belgrave Mews West, London SW1X 8HU
T 020-7344 3250 E london-ob@bmeia.gv.at
W www.bmeia.gv.at/london
Ambassador Extraordinary and Plenipotentiary, HE Gabriele Matzner-Holzer, *apptd* 2005

BRITISH EMBASSY
Jaurèsgasse 10, 1030 Vienna
T (+43) (1) 716 130 E britem@netway.at
W www.britishembassy.at
Ambassador Extraordinary and Plenipotentiary, HE Simon Smith *apptd* 2007

BRITISH COUNCIL
Siebensterngasse 21, 1070 Vienna
T (+43) (1) 533 2616 W www.britishcouncil.org/austria
Regional Director, Terry Toney

FEDERAL STRUCTURE
There are nine provinces: Burgenland, Carinthia, Lower Austria, Salzburg, Styria, Tirol, Upper Austria, Vienna and Vorarlberg. Each has its own assembly and government.

DEFENCE
The army has 114 main battle tanks, 112 armoured infantry fighting vehicles and 458 armoured personnel carriers. The air force has 41 combat aircraft.
Military budget – US$3,210m (2007)
Military personnel – 39,600: army 32,900, air force 6,700
Conscription duration – 6 months (9–10 months for officers, NCOs and specialists)

ECONOMY AND TRADE
Austria has a well-developed free-market economy which is closely linked to other EU states. Its proximity to the new EU members in central, east and south-east Europe makes for strong commercial links with those countries and is also an attraction for foreign investors. Rates of growth have been low in recent years, reflecting the trend for Europe as a whole, and small budget deficits occurred in 2006 and 2007 owing to reductions in taxes.

The services sector contributes most to GDP (67 per cent in 2007), followed by industry (30.4 per cent) and the small but highly developed agricultural sector (1.6 per cent). The main industries include construction, manufacturing of machinery, vehicles and parts, food processing, timber and wood processing, production of metals and metal goods, chemicals, paper and cardboard and communications equipment, and tourism.

The main trading partners are other EU states, the USA and Switzerland. Principal exports include the goods produced by the main industries, iron and steel, and textiles. The main imports are machinery and equipment, motor vehicles, chemical products, metal goods, oil and oil products, and foodstuffs.
GNI – US$329,200m; US$39,750 per capita (2006)
Annual average growth of GDP – 3.3 per cent (2007 est)
Inflation rate – 1.9 per cent (2007 est)
Unemployment – 4.3 per cent (2007 est)
Total external debt – US$752,500m (2007)
Imports – US$134,300m (2006)
Exports – US$134,100m (2006)

BALANCE OF PAYMENTS
Trade – US$188m deficit (2006)
Current Account – US$7,927m surplus (2006)

Trade with UK	*2006*	*2007*
Imports from UK	£1,615,600,000	£1,357,438,956
Exports to UK	£2,369,100,000	£2,453,970,909

COMMUNICATIONS
Although landlocked, Austria is strategically located in central Europe because of the navigability of the Danube and the presence of traversable passes over the Alps. Of the 425km of waterways, 358km are navigable and there is considerable trade through the Danube ports (Vienna, Krems, Enns, Linz) from both local and foreign shipping. There are 133,718km of roads and a network of 1,677km of *Autobahn* between major cities that also links up with German and Italian networks. The railways are state-owned and comprised 6,383km of track in 2006. The main airports are at Vienna, Graz, Innsbruck, Klagenfurt, Linz and Salzburg. Mobile telephone distribution was over 9 million in 2006, and there were 4.2 million internet users.

EDUCATION AND HEALTH
Education is free and compulsory between the ages of six and 15.
Gross enrolment ratio (percentage of relevant age group) – primary 102 per cent; secondary 102 per cent; tertiary 49 per cent (2006 est)
Health expenditure (per capita) – US$3,788 (2005)
Hospital beds (per 1,000 people) – 7.7 (2000–6)

MEDIA
The public broadcaster Österreichischer Rundfunk (ÖRF) dominated Austrian television and radio for many years, but the number of private broadcasters is now increasing. By contrast, Austria's print media is largely privately owned. There are five main daily titles, including *Der Standard* and *Neue Kronenzeitung*.

CULTURE
During the 18th, 19th and 20th centuries Vienna was one of Europe's greatest cultural centres. Musicians included Haydn (1732–1809), Mozart (1756–91), Beethoven (1770–1827), Mahler (1860–1911), Schoenberg (1874–1951) and the Strauss family. The late 19th century produced the writers Rilke (1875–1926) and Robert Musil (1880–1942), while notable scientists included Erwin Schrödinger (1887–1961), who contributed to the development of quantum mechanics, and Gregor Mendel (1822–1884), whose experiments with pea plants are

widely believed to be the beginning of modern genetics.

In art, the symbolist paintings of Gustav Klimt (1862–1918) are among the most recognisable of Art Nouveau and director Fritz Lang (1890–1976) produced two of the earliest film classics: *Metropolis* (1927) and *M* (1931).

AZERBAIJAN

Azerbaycan Respublikasi – Republic of Azerbaijan

Area – 86,600 sq. km
Capital – Baku (Baki); population, 1,892,000 (2007 est)
Major cities – Ganca, Sumqayit
Currency – New Manat of 100 gopik
Population – 8,120,247 rising at 0.69 per cent per year (2007 est); Azeri (90.6 per cent), Dagestani (2.2 per cent), Russian (1.8 per cent), Armenian (1.5 per cent). There are more Azeris in Iran than in Azerbaijan
Religion – Islam (96 per cent) (est)
Language – Azeri (official), Lezgi, Russian, Armenian
Population density – 103 per sq. km (2006)
Urban population – 49.9 per cent (2005 est)
Median age – 27.6 years (2007 est)
National anthem – 'Azerbaijan Marsi' ['March of Azerbaijan']
National day – 28 May (Founding of the Democratic Republic of Azerbaijan)
Life expectancy – 65.96 (2007 est)
Mortality rate – 8.35 (2007 est)
Birth rate – 17.47 (2007 est)
Infant mortality rate – 58.31 (2007 est)
Death penalty – Abolished for all crimes (since 1998)
CPI score – 2.1 (2007)
Population below poverty line – 24 per cent (2005 est)

CLIMATE AND TERRAIN

Azerbaijan lies on the western shore of the Caspian Sea, in the eastern part of the Caucasus region. The north-east of the country is taken up by the south-eastern end of the main Caucasus ridge, its south-western part by the smaller Caucasus hills and its south-eastern corner by the spurs of the Talysh Ridge. Central Azerbaijan lies in a depression irrigated by the river Kura and the lower reaches of its tributary the Araks. The highest point of elevation is 4,485m (Bazarduzu Dagi) while the lowest is −28m (Caspian Sea). Azerbaijan has a continental climate.

HISTORY AND POLITICS

The Turkic Azeri people formed an independent state in the first century BC. This was invaded in the seventh century AD by Muslim Arabs, who introduced Islam and secured the region as a province of the Muslim caliphate. Azerbaijan was invaded by Persia in the 16th century. The country was divided during the Russo-Persian wars of the early 19th century, the northern portion (present-day Azerbaijan) becoming part of the Russian Empire and the southern portion remaining Persian and subsequently Iranian.

In 1918 the Azerbaijan Democratic Republic was established. It was subsequently overthrown by communists and Azerbaijan acceded to the USSR in 1922.

In 1990, the Azeri Popular Front took power from the local communist party and declared independence from the Soviet Union. Soviet troops restored the communist regime, which declared Azerbaijan's independence in August 1991 after the failed coup in Moscow. The president, elected in 1992, was overthrown in a coup in 1993 and replaced by Heydar Aliyev, the former communist party leader, who retained power despite a number of coup attempts in the mid-1990s. Aliyev won the presidential election in 1998, but withdrew from the 2003 presidential race owing to health problems (he subsequently died in December 2003) and endorsed the campaign of his son, Ilham, who was successfully elected. His regime has proven to be as authoritarian as that of his father. The 2005 legislative election was won by the ruling New Azerbaijan Party by a large margin; as with all other presidential and legislative elections since independence, external monitors judged that the poll failed to meet international democratic standards. A presidential election was due in October 2008.

SECESSION

In 1988 the predominantly Armenian-populated region of Nagorny-Karabakh attempted to secede and unite with Armenia, leading to conflict between the separatists and Soviet Azeri forces. This escalated in 1992, when Nagorno-Karabakh forces, with Armenian support, breached Azeri defences to form a land bridge between the enclave and Armenia, before going on to capture all the Azeri territory between Nagorny-Karabakh and Armenia. Although Azeri forces pushed back the Nagorno-Karabakh forces in early 1994, about 16 per cent of Azeri territory remains in separatist control, and Azerbaijan has had to absorb over half a million Azeris displaced from the territory. A ceasefire was agreed in 1994, and has held despite occasional infringements. Peace talks mediated by the OSCE have failed to make any progress towards a peaceful resolution.

POLITICAL SYSTEM

The 1995 constitution was amended in 2002. The executive president is directly elected for a five-year term; under the 1995 constitution, this was not renewable but a 2002 referendum allowed this proviso to be waived. Legislative power is vested in the unicameral *Milli Majlis* (National Assembly), which has 125 members directly elected for a five-year term. The president appoints the prime minister and the cabinet.

HEAD OF STATE
President, Ilham Aliyev, *assumed office* 31 October 2003

SELECTED GOVERNMENT MEMBERS *as at May 2008*
Prime Minister, Artur Rasizade
First Deputy Prime Ministers, Abbas Abbasov; Yagub Abdulla Eyyubov
Deputy Prime Ministers, Elchin Efendiyev; Ali Hasanov; Abid Sarifov
Defence, Col.-Gen. Safar Abiyev

Finance, Samir Sharifov
Foreign Affairs, Elmar Muharram Mammadyarov

EMBASSY OF THE REPUBLIC OF AZERBAIJAN
4 Kensington Court, London W8 5DL
T 020-7938 3412 E azembuk@btconnect.com
Ambassador Extraordinary and Plenipotentiary, HE Fakhraddin Gurbanov, *apptd* 2007

BRITISH EMBASSY
45 Khagani Street, 1000 Baku
T (+994) (12) 497 51 88 E office@britemb.baku.az
W www.britishembassy.az
Ambassador Extraordinary and Plenipotentiary, HE Carolyn Browne, *apptd* 2007

BRITISH COUNCIL
1 Vali Mammadov Street, Icheri Sheher, Baku AZ1000
T (+994) (12) 497 1593/497 2013
W www.britishcouncil.org/azerbaijan
Director, Andy Williams

DEFENCE

The army has 220 main battle tanks, 127 armoured infantry fighting vehicles and 468 armoured personnel carriers. The navy is based at Baku, with a share of the former Soviet Caspian Fleet Flotilla, comprising six patrol and coastal vessels. The air force has 47 combat aircraft and 15 armed helicopters.
Military budget – US$936m (2007)
Military personnel – 66,740: army 56,840, navy 2,000, air force 7,900; paramilitary 15,000
Conscription duration – 17 months, but can be extended for ground forces

ECONOMY AND TRADE

Azerbaijan is making the transition from a command to a market economy, but the slow progress is exacerbated by its failure to attract foreign investment in sectors other than energy, widespread corruption and rising inflation. The economy is dominated by oil and natural gas extraction and related industries, centred in Baku and Sumgait, and exploited through co-production deals with foreign companies; production began in 2006 and is expected to double the current GDP by 2010. Oil pipelines (2,436km) link the Azeri oilfields to Black Sea ports in Russia and Georgia, and to the Turkish port of Ceyhan.

Although agriculture contributes only 6 per cent of GDP, it employs over 40 per cent of the workforce. The main crops are cotton, cereals, rice, fruit, vegetables, tea, tobacco and livestock. Around 90 per cent of agricultural land has now been privatised. Industry produces oil, natural gas, petroleum products, oilfield equipment, steel, iron ore, cement, chemicals, petrochemicals and textiles.

Russia and other former Soviet republics are increasingly being replaced as trade partners by Turkey, Iran and various European countries. Oil and gas constitute 90 per cent of exports, which also include machinery, cotton and foodstuffs. Principal imports are machinery and equipment, oil products, foodstuffs, metals and chemicals.
GNI – US$15,600m; US$1,840 per capita (2006)
Annual average growth of GDP – 31 per cent (2007 est)
Inflation rate – 16 per cent (2007 est)
Unemployment – 8.5 per cent (2005 est)
Total external debt – US$2,022m (2007 est)
Imports – US$5,300m (2006)
Exports – US$6,400m (2006)

BALANCE OF PAYMENTS
Trade – US$1,105m surplus (2006)
Current Account – US$3,708m surplus (2006)

Trade with UK	*2006*	*2007*
Imports from UK	£474,844,000	£240,078,535
Exports to UK	£232,950,000	£109,278,007

COMMUNICATIONS

There are 2,122km of railway track, about half of it electrified, and over 59,000km of roads, though only half are paved. Moscow has agreed to provide US$300m (£150m) for the construction of the Azeri section of the north-south highway between northern and central Europe and the Gulf states. There are 27 airports, of which three (at Baku, Ganca and Naxcivan) accept international flights, with another two being extended to do so. Baku is the main port. There are ferry links to Turkmenistan.

The telephone system needs modernising and expanding but is a state-owned monopoly so change is slow. Mobile telephone distribution is growing rapidly and in 2006 was 40 per 100 people, compared to 15 main lines per 100 people. There were 829,000 internet users in 2006.

EDUCATION AND HEALTH

Education up to university level is free.
Literacy rate – 98.8 per cent (2004 est)
Gross enrolment ratio (percentage of relevant age group) – primary 96 per cent; secondary 83 per cent; tertiary 15 per cent (2006 est)
Health expenditure (per capita) – US$62 (2005)
Hospital beds (per 1,000 people) – 8.2 (2000–6)

MEDIA

The state runs press, television and radio but there is a growing private sector, boosted by the issue of five new regional television licences in 2002. Media outlets critical of the government have been subjected to harassment, despite the guarantee of freedom of speech in the constitution. As a requirement of the country's membership of the Council of Europe, a public television and radio service, iTV, was launched in 2005.

THE BAHAMAS

Commonwealth of the Bahamas

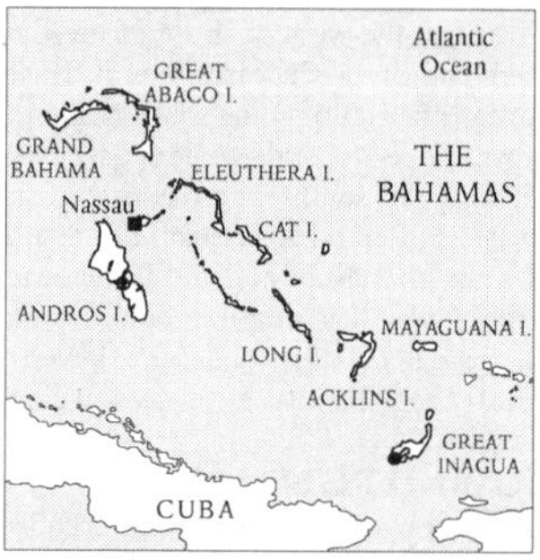

Area – 13,940 sq. km
Capital – Nassau; population, 240,000 (2007 est)
Currency – Bahamian dollar (B$) of 100 cents

Population – 305,655 rising at 0.6 per cent per year (2007 est)
Religion – Protestantism (72 per cent), Roman Catholicism (14 per cent) (est)
Language – English (official), Creole
Population density – 33 per sq. km (2006)
Urban population – 90 per cent (2005 est)
Median age (years) – 28.1 (2007 est)
National anthem – 'March on, Bahamaland'
National day – 10 July (Independence Day)
Life expectancy (years) – 65.66 (2007 est)
Mortality rate – 9.13 (2007 est)
Birth rate – 17.3 (2007 est)
Infant mortality rate – 24.17 (2007 est)
HIV/AIDS adult prevalence – 2.8 per cent (2005 est)
Death penalty – Retained
Population below poverty line – 9.3 per cent (2004)

CLIMATE AND TERRAIN

The Bahamas extend in a chain running from the coast of Florida in the north-west almost to Hispaniola in the south-east. The group consists of more than 700 islands and 2,400 cays, all low-lying. The highest point is 63m at Mount Alvernia on Cat Island and the lowest 0m at the Atlantic Ocean. The principal islands include: Abaco, Acklins, Andros, Berry Islands, Bimini, Cat Island, Crooked Island, Eleuthera, Exuma, Grand Bahama, Harbour Island, Inagua, Long Island, Mayaguana, New Providence (on which the capital, Nassau, is located), Ragged Island, Rum Cay, San Salvador and Spanish Wells. The 14 major islands are inhabited, as are a few of the smaller islands. The climate is semitropical. The hurricane season is June to November.

HISTORY AND POLITICS

The Bahamas was discovered by Columbus in 1492, settled by the British in the 17th century and became a crown colony in 1717. Taken over in 1782 by the Spanish, the islands were restored to Britain by the treaty of Versailles in 1783. The Bahamas became self-governing in 1964 and gained their independence on 10 July 1973.

The Progressive Liberal Party (PLP) held power for 25 years until the Free National Movement (FNM) won an absolute majority in the 1992 general election. Power has subsequently alternated between the two parties, and the PLP was defeated in the 2007 legislative election, which the FNM won with 23 seats.

POLITICAL SYSTEM

The head of state is the British monarch, who is represented by a governor-general. The bicameral parliament has a Senate of 16 appointed members and a House of Assembly of 41 members; both chambers serve for a five-year term.
Governor-General, Arthur Dion Hanna, *apptd* 2006

SELECTED GOVERNMENT MEMBERS *as at May 2008*

Prime Minister, Finance, Hubert Ingraham
Deputy Prime Minister, Foreign Affairs, Brent Symonette
National Security and Immigration, Tommy Turnquest
Attorney-General, Claire Hepburn

HIGH COMMISSION OF THE COMMONWEALTH OF THE BAHAMAS

10 Chesterfield Street, London W1J 5JL
T 020-7408 4488 E information@bahamashclondon.net
High Commissioner, HE Basil O'Brien, CMG, *apptd* 1999

BRITISH HIGH COMMISSION

High Commissioner, Jeremy Michael Cresswell, *apptd* 2005, resident in Kingston, Jamaica

DEFENCE

The Royal Bahamian Defence Force has 14 patrol and coastal combatant vessels.
Military budget – US$45m (2007 est)
Military personnel – 860

ECONOMY AND TRADE

The Bahamas have enjoyed sustained economic growth in recent decades owing to the development of tourism and offshore financial services. The services sector contributes 90 per cent of GDP and employs about 55 per cent of the labour force. The lack of diversification makes the economy vulnerable to fluctuations in these sectors, and the growth rate slowed in the period 2000–3, when the tightening of financial regulations caused a number of international businesses to relocate elsewhere, and because of fewer visitors from the USA (over 80 per cent of all visitors) since 2001.

Manufacturing and agriculture account for 10 per cent of GDP and employment. Agricultural production is mainly of fresh vegetables, fruit, meat and eggs. Mineral reserves are exploited to produce aragonite and salt for export. Other industrial products include cement, rum, pharmaceuticals, steel pipes and the provision of oil trans-shipment services.

The main trading partners are the USA, Spain, Brazil and Poland. The chief exports are mineral products and salt, animal products, rum, chemicals, fruit and vegetables. Imports are chiefly machinery and transport equipment, manufactured articles, chemicals, fuel, foodstuffs and livestock.
GNI – US$4,700m (2003); US$15,110 per capita (2003)
Annual average growth of GDP – 2.8 per cent (2007 est)
Inflation rate – 2.4 per cent (2007 est)
Unemployment – 7.6 per cent (2006 est)
Total external debt – US$342.6m (2004 est)
Imports – US$2,400m (2006)
Exports – US$700m (2006)

BALANCE OF PAYMENTS

Trade – US$1,726m deficit (2006)
Current Account – US$1,578m deficit (2006)

Trade with UK	*2006*	*2007*
Imports from UK	£61,671,000	£18,488,470
Exports to UK	£74,381,000	£5,008,490

COMMUNICATIONS

The main ports are Nassau (New Providence), Freeport and South Riding Point (Grand Bahama). International air services are operated from Andros, Chubb Cay, Eleuthera, Exuma, Grand Bahama and New Providence. More than 60 smaller airports and landing strips facilitate services between the islands, mainly provided by Bahamasair, the national carrier. The Bahamas have some 2,693km of roads, 1,546km of which are paved. There are no railways.

BAHRAIN

Mamlakat al-Bahrayn – Kingdom of Bahrain

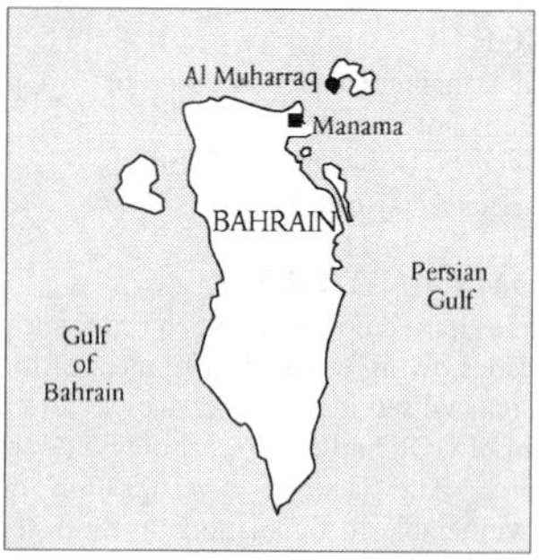

Area – 665 sq. km
Capital – Manama; population, 157,000 (2007 est)
Major towns – Al Muharraq, Ar Rifa
Currency – Bahraini dinar (BD) of 1,000 fils
Population – 708,573 rising at 1.39 per cent per year (2007 est); Bahraini (62.4 per cent). The rest of the population consists of an expatriate minority, including large numbers of Europeans and South Asians
Religion – The vast majority of the population practises Islam
Language – Arabic (official), English, Farsi, Urdu
Population density – 1,041 per sq. km (2006)
Urban population – 90.2 per cent (2005 est)
Median age (years) – 29.7 (2007 est)
National anthem – 'Bahrainona' ['Our Bahrain']
National day – 16 December
Life expectancy (years) – 74.68 (2007 est)
Mortality rate – 4.21 (2007 est)
Birth rate – 17.53 (2007 est)
Infant mortality rate – 16.18 (2007 est)
Death penalty – Retained
CPI score – 5.0 (2007)
Literacy rate – 87.7 per cent (2004 est)

CLIMATE AND TERRAIN

Bahrain consists of a group of 33 low-lying islands situated approximately halfway down the Gulf, some 32km off the east coast of Saudi Arabia. The largest of these, Bahrain Island, is about 48km long and 16km wide at its broadest. The capital, Manama, is situated on the north shore. The elevation extremes range from 122m at the highest point (Jabal ad Dukhan) to 0m at sea level. The climate is hot and humid, with average temperatures ranging from 20°C to 40°C and little rainfall.

HISTORY AND POLITICS

Bahrain was ruled by Persia (Iran) from 1602 until it was ousted in 1783 by the al-Khalifa family, who remain in power. It was under British political control from 1820 until 1971, when it became fully independent. In 1975 the legislature was suspended and the emir assumed virtually absolute power after clashes between the Sunni and Shia communities. Moves to return to democratic rule were made only in response to civil agitation from the 1990s onwards, and a 40-member consultative council, the *Majlis al-Shura,* was appointed in 1996; this is an advisory body with no legislative powers. A new constitution was introduced in 2002 and established Bahrain as a kingdom and a constitutional monarchy and legalised elections and political parties. There is a continuing campaign for political reform, including greater powers for the legislature.

The legislative election in 2002, the first since 1973, was boycotted by Shia opposition groups, but in the 2006 election, a radical Shia group won 17 of the 40 seats. Although some Shia ministers were appointed, the majority of the cabinet are Sunnis.

POLITICAL SYSTEM

Under the 2002 constitution, the country became a constitutional hereditary monarchy with the king as head of state. The king appoints the cabinet. There is a bicameral legislature national assembly consisting of a lower house, *Majlis al-Nuwab* (Council of representatives), and an upper house, *Majlis al-Shura* (Consultative council). The former has 40 members directly elected for a four-year term and the 40 members of the upper house are appointed by the king for a four-year term. The 2002 constitution granted women the right to vote.

HEAD OF STATE

HH The King of Bahrain, C.-in -C. of the Armed Forces, Shaikh Hamad bin Isa al-Khalifa, KCMG *succeeded as amir* 6 March 1999, *proclaimed king* 14 Feburary 2002
Crown Prince, Chair of the National Economic Development Council, Shaikh Salman bin Hamad al-Khalifa

SELECTED GOVERNMENT MEMBERS *as at May 2008*

Prime Minister, HH Shaikh Khalifa bin Salman al-Khalifa
Deputy Prime Ministers, Shaikh Mohammed bin Mubarak al-Khalifa; Shaikh Ali bin Khalifa al-Khalifa; Jawad bin Salem al Oraied
Foreign Affairs, Shaikh Khalid bin Ahmed bin Mohammed al-Khalifa
Defence, Shaikh Mohammad bin Abdullah al-Khalifa
Finance, Shaikh Ahmed bin Mohammed al-Khalifa
Interior, Lt.-Gen. Shaikh Rashid bin Abdulla bin Ahmed al-Khalifa

EMBASSY OF THE KINGDOM OF BAHRAIN

30 Belgrave Square, London SW1X 8QB
T 020-7201 9170 E information@bahrainembassy.co.uk
Ambassador Extraordinary and Plenipotentiary, HE Shaikh Khalifa bin Abdullah bin Mohamed al-Khalifa, *apptd* 2007

BRITISH EMBASSY

PO Box 114, 21 Government Avenue, Manama 306
T (+973) 1757 4100 E britemb@batelco.com.bh
W www.ukembassy.gov.bh
Ambassador Extraordinary and Plenipotentiary, HE James Bowden, *apptd* 2007

BRITISH COUNCIL

PO Box 452, AMA Centre, 146 Shaikh Salman Highway, Manama 356
T (+973) 17 261 555 W www.britishcouncil.org/bahrain
Director, Sandra Hamrouni

DEFENCE

The army has 180 main battle tanks, 25 armoured infantry fighting vehicles and 235 armoured personnel carriers. The navy, based at Mina Salman, has 1 frigate and 8 patrol and coastal vessels. The air force has 33 combat aircraft and 24 armed helicopters.
Military budget – US$539m (2007)
Military personnel – 8,200: army 6,000, navy 700, air force 1,500; paramilitary 11,260

ECONOMY AND TRADE

Bahrain was one of the first Gulf states to discover oil, in the 1930s, but reserves and production are lower than neighbouring countries and so it has sought to diversify its economy, developing particularly as an offshore financial centre and tourist destination. Petroleum production and refining accounted for an estimated 11 per cent of GDP, 70 per cent of government revenue and 60 per cent of total exports in 2005. Other industries include petrochemicals, aluminium smelting and ship repair. The main trading partners are Saudi Arabia, Japan and the USA.

GNI – US$14,022m; US$19,350 per capita (2006)
Annual average growth of GDP – 6.6 per cent (2007 est)
Inflation rate – 3.5 per cent (2007 est)
Unemployment – 15 per cent (2005 est)
Total external debt – US$7,692m (2007 est)
Imports – US$8,900m (2006)
Exports – US$11,600m (2006)

BALANCE OF PAYMENTS
Trade – US$2,618m surplus (2006)
Current Account – US$2,112m surplus (2006)

Trade with UK	*2006*	*2007*
Imports from UK	£263,644,000	£216,963,540
Exports to UK	£164,485,000	£99,740,649

COMMUNICATIONS

Bahrain International airport is one of the main air traffic centres of the Gulf; it is the headquarters of Gulf Air, and a stopping point for other airlines on routes between Europe and Australia and the Far East. A 25km causeway links Bahrain to Saudi Arabia; construction of its continuation, linking Bahrain to Qatar, was approved in 2005. Of the 3,498km of road, 2,768km is paved. There are no railways. The main ports and terminals are Mina' Salman and Sitrah. Mobile telephone distribution is close to 100 per cent.

MEDIA

Domestic television and radio is run by the state-controlled Bahrain Radio and Television Corporation (BRTC). The country's first private radio station, Sawt al-Ghad, was launched in 2005, but was closed down by the government a year later due to alleged irregularities. Bahrain has a free press but self-censorship is widely practised. There are four main daily newspapers, two of which are published in English.

BANGLADESH

Gana Prajatantri Banladesh – People's Republic of Bangladesh

Area – 144,000 sq. km
Capital – Dhaka; population, 13,485,000 (2007 est)
Major cities – Chittagong, Gazipur, Khulna, Narayanganj
Currency – Taka (Tk) of 100 paisa
Population – 150,448,339 rising at 2.06 per cent per year (2007 est); Bengali (98 per cent) (est)
Religion – Islam (88 per cent), Hinduism (10 per cent) (est). The majority of the population practises Sunni Islam
Language – Bengali (official), English
Population density – 1,198 per sq. km (2006)
Urban population – 25 per cent (2005 est)
Median age (years) – 22.5 (2007 est)
National anthem – 'Amar Shonar Bangla' ['My Golden Bengal']
National day – 26 March (Independence Day)
Life expectancy (years) – 62.84 (2007 est)
Mortality rate – 8.13 (2007 est)
Birth rate – 29.36 (2007 est)
Infant mortality rate – 59.12 (2007 est)
Death penalty – Retained
CPI score – 2.0 (2007)
Population below poverty line – 45 per cent (2004 est)

CLIMATE AND TERRAIN

Although hilly in the south-east and north-east, over 75 per cent of the country is less than 3m above sea-level; the highest elevation is 1,230m (Keokradong) and the lowest 0m at the Indian Ocean. The south-west forms the delta of the Ganges (Padma) and Brahmaputra (Jamuna) rivers on the Bay of Bengal, the largest estuarine delta in the world; with annual rainfall of over 2,500mm, about one third of the country floods each year during the monsoon season. The climate is tropical: hot, wet and extremely humid during the summer, and mild and dry during the winter.

HISTORY AND POLITICS

In British India, Bangladesh was the region of East Bengal and the Sylhet district of Assam. On independence in 1947, these territories acceded to Pakistan, forming East Pakistan. Tensions between East and West Pakistan (separated by over 1,600km) caused the east to seek autonomy; fighting in 1970 developed into civil war in 1971. After several months and with the support of India, Bangladesh achieved independence from Pakistan on 16 December 1971.

The late 1970s and 1980s were marked by political instability, with a number of coups and attempted coups, the assassination of President Mujibar Rahman in 1975 and President Zia in 1981, and long periods of government under martial law (1975–8, 1982–6) or a state of emergency (1987–8, 2007–). Mass anti-government protests forced the resignation in 1990 of Gen. Ershad (assumed power in 1982, elected president in 1986); and the Bangladesh Nationalist Party (BNP) won the subsequent parliamentary elections. In 1991 a constitutional amendment returned Bangladesh to parliamentary government.

Parliamentary government has remained in place since this date, despite a number of boycotts of parliament. The governments have been formed, or coalition governments have been led, by one of the two main parties: the BNP, led by Khaleda Zia (widow of President Zia), in 1991–6 and 2001–6; and the Awami League, led by Sheikh Hasina Wajed (daughter of President Mujibar Rahman), in 1996–2001.

The BNP-led four-party government headed by

Khaleda Zia stepped down in 2006 when its term of office expired. Following violent protests over the choice of a caretaker government and the impartiality of election preparations, President Iajuddin Ahmed assumed the leadership of a caretaker administration until the January 2007 legislative election. However, these elections were postponed and a state of emergency declared because of continuing protests and the opposition parties' threat to boycott the election unless electoral reforms were implemented. Fakhruddin Ahmed took over from the president as head of the caretaker administration, which launched an anti-corruption drive against politicians and bureaucrats. A number of party leaders, including Sheikh Hasina, were arrested in April 2007 on charges relating to the 2006 violence, and Khaleda Zia was placed under virtual house arrest. President Ahmed's term of office expired in September 2007 but he has continued in the post until a new parliament is convened and elects his successor. The government has promised elections by the end of 2008.

POLITICAL SYSTEM

The head of state is the president, elected by the legislature for a five-year term. The unicameral parliament, *Jatiya Sangsad,* has 345 members directly elected for a five-year term; under a 2004 constitutional amendment, 45 seats are reserved for women. The president appoints the prime minister and the cabinet, on the advice of the prime minister.

HEAD OF STATE
President, Iajuddin Ahmed, *elected* 6 September 2002

SELECTED GOVERNMENT MEMBERS *as at May 2008*
Chief Adviser for the Caretaker Government, Establishment, Election Commission, Fakhruddin Ahmed
Finance and Planning, Mirza Azizul Islam
Foreign Affairs, Iftekhar Ahmed Chowdhury
Law, Justice and Parliamentary Affairs, A. F. Hassan Arif

HIGH COMMISSION FOR THE PEOPLE'S REPUBLIC OF BANGLADESH
28 Queen's Gate, London SW7 5JA
T 020-7584 0081 E bhclondon@btconnect.com
W www.bhclondon.org.uk
High Commissioner, HE Shafi U Ahmed, *apptd* 2007

BRITISH HIGH COMMISSION
PO Box 6079, United Nations Road, Baridhara, Dhaka 1212
T (+880) (2) 882 2705 E dhaka.consular@fco.gov.uk
W www.ukinbangladesh.org
High Commissioner, HE Anwar Choudhury, *apptd* 2004

BRITISH COUNCIL
PO Box 161, 5 Fuller Road, Dhaka 1000
T (+880) (2) 861 8905 W www.britishcouncil.org/bangladesh
Director, Dr June Rollinson

DEFENCE

The army has 210 main battle tanks and 180 armoured personnel carriers. The navy has 4 frigates and 38 patrol and coastal vessels. There are bases at Chittagong, Dhaka, Kaptai, Khulna and Mangla. The air force has 76 combat aircraft.
Military expenditure – US$938m (2006)
Military personnel – 150,000: army 120,000, navy 16,000, air force 14,000; paramilitaries 63,910

ECONOMY AND TRADE

Bangladesh is a poor country, dependent on foreign aid and with nearly half its population living below the poverty line. Many migrate to the Gulf states and south-east Asia to find work and their remittances, worth about US$4bn (£2bn) a year, and garment exports are the mainstay of the economy. These have fuelled the steady annual growth of 5–6 per cent in recent years. However, the many state-owned enterprises are inefficient and there is an apparent lack of political will to address this problem, or to speed up other economic reforms because of political infighting, corruption and the opposition of vested interests.

The service and industrial sectors account for 52.3 per cent and 28.7 per cent of GDP respectively. Although the smallest contributor to GDP, agriculture is the primary occupation of over 60 per cent of the workforce. The chief industries are based on processing agricultural products such as cotton, jute, tea and sugar, the manufacture of garments, newsprint, cement and fertiliser, fishing and light engineering. Most exports are to the USA and EU countries; imports come mainly from China, India and other Asian countries.
GNI – US$70,500m; US$450 per capita (2006)
Annual average growth of GDP – 6 per cent (2007 est)
Inflation rate – 8.8 per cent (2007 est)
Unemployment – 2.5 per cent (2007 est)
Total external debt – US$20,250m (2007 est)
Imports – US$15,000m (2006)
Exports – US$9,100m (2006)

BALANCE OF PAYMENTS
Trade – US$5,861m deficit (2006)
Current Account – US$762m surplus (2006)

Trade with UK	*2006*	*2007*
Imports from UK	£75,995,000	£60,682,976
Exports to UK	£746,179,000	£718,051,455

COMMUNICATIONS

The principal seaports are Chittagong and Mongla. A state enterprise, the Bangladesh Shipping Corporation, operates the Bangladesh merchant fleet. The 8,370km of internal waterways are a key element of the transport infrastructure, although reduced to 5,200km in the dry season. There are three international airports (at Dhaka, Chittagong and Sylhet) and five domestic airports, with a sixth under construction. The international airline, Bangladesh Biman, provides international and internal flights. There are 2,768km of rail track, and rail links with India. The country's 239,226km of roads includes only 22,726km which are paved. The telephone network is limited, with fewer than 1 main line per 100 people, and has been overtaken by mobile telephone distribution, which had achieved a density of 13 per 100 people by 2006.

EDUCATION AND HEALTH

Primary education is compulsory and free, but attendance is variable.
Literacy rate – 41.1 per cent (2004 est)
Gross enrolment ratio (percentage of relevant age group) – primary 103 per cent; secondary 44 per cent; tertiary 6 per cent (2006 est)
Health expenditure (per capita) – US$12 (2005)
Hospital beds (per 1,000 people) – 0.3 (2000–6)

MEDIA

The main broadcasters (Radio Bangladesh and Bangladesh Television) are state-owned and subject to censorship. The main commercial stations are ATN Bangla TV and Channel i, but their influence is limited to urban areas. The four main newspapers are *The Daily Star, Dainik Ittefaq, Daily Prothom Alo* and *The New Nation.* The constitution promises press freedom, but journalists are regularly subjected to harassment.

BARBADOS

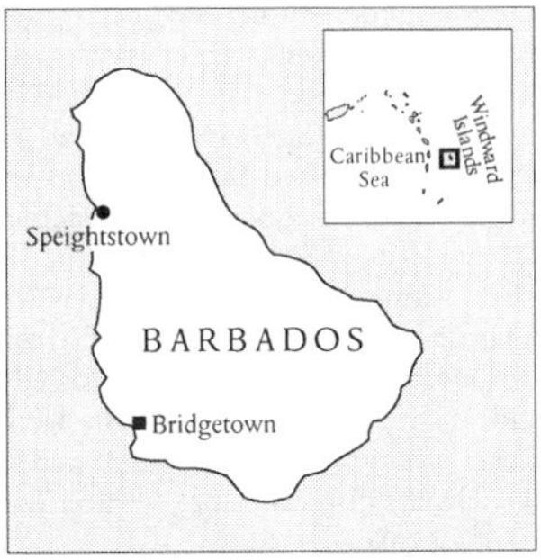

Area – 431 sq. km
Capital – Bridgetown, in the parish of St Michael; population, 116,000 (2007)
Currency – Barbados dollar (BD$) of 100 cents
Population – 280,946, rising at 0.37 per cent per year (2007 est)
Religion – Protestantism (36 per cent), Roman Catholicism (3 per cent), Islam (1 per cent) (est)
Language – English (official)
Population density – 681 per sq. km (2006)
Urban population – 52.9 per cent (2005)
Median age (years) – 35 (2007 est)
National anthem – 'In Plenty and in Time of Need'
National day – 30 November (Independence Day)
Life expectancy (years) – 73 (2007 est)
Mortality rate – 8.61 (2007 est)
Birth rate – 12.61 (2007 est)
Infant mortality rate – 11.55 (2007 est)
HIV/AIDS adult prevalence rate – 1.2 per cent (2005 est)
Death penalty – Retained
CPI score – 6.9 (2007)

CLIMATE AND TERRAIN

Barbados is the most easterly of the Caribbean islands. The land rises in a series of terraced tablelands, and elevation extremes range from 336m (Mt Hillaby) at the highest point to 0m (Atlantic Ocean) at the lowest. The climate is tropical with a wet season from June to October, and the island is subject to occasional hurricanes.

HISTORY AND POLITICS

The first inhabitants of Barbados were Amerindian nomads from South America who arrived on the islands *c.*350 AD. Arawak Indians and then Caribs followed. The island was uninhabited when settled by the British in 1627 and was a crown colony from 1652, achieving self-government in 1961. It became an independent state within the Commonwealth on 30 November 1966.

Since independence, power has alternated between the two main political parties, the Barbados Labour Party (BLP) and the Democratic Labour Party (DLP). In the January 2008 general election the BLP was defeated by the DLP, which won 20 of the 30 seats and took office under David Thompson.

POLITICAL SYSTEM

The head of state is the British sovereign, represented by the governor-general. The bicameral parliament consists of a senate and a House of Assembly. The former comprises 21 senators appointed by the governor-general for a five-year term, of whom 12 are appointed on the advice of the prime minister, two on the advice of the leader of the opposition and seven at the governor-general's discretion to represent religious, economic and social interests. The House of Assembly comprises 30 members directly elected for a five-year term.

There are 11 administrative areas (parishes): St Michael, Christ Church, St Andrew, St George, St James, St John, St Joseph, St Lucy, St Peter, St Philip and St Thomas.

Governor-General, HE Sir Clifford Husbands, GCMG, KA, *apptd* June 1996

SELECTED GOVERNMENT MEMBERS *as at May 2008*

Prime Minister, Economy, Finance, David Thompson
Attorney-General, Home Affairs, Freundel Stuart
Foreign Affairs, Christopher Sinckler

BARBADOS HIGH COMMISSION

1 Great Russell Street, London WC1B 3ND
T 020-7631 4975 E london@foreign.gov.bb
High Commissioner, HE Edwin Pollard, OBE, *apptd* 2003

BRITISH HIGH COMMISSION

PO Box 676, Lower Collymore Rock, Bridgetown
T (+1) (246) 430 7800 E britishhc@sunbeach.net
W www.britishhighcommission.gov.uk/barbados
High Commissioner, HE Duncan Taylor, *apptd* 2005

DEFENCE

The navy has 9 patrol and coastal combatant vessels located at Bridgetown.
Military budget – US$22.5m (2006 est)
Military personnel – 610: army 500, navy 110

ECONOMY AND TRADE

Historically, Barbados' chief products were sugar, rum and molasses. Since independence, tourism, offshore finance and information services, and light industry (especially assembling components for re-export) have become of greater significance. The main trading partners are the USA, Trinidad and Tobago and the UK. Chief exports are manufactured goods, sugar and molasses, rum, other food and beverages, chemicals and electronic components.
GNI – US$2,500m (2003); US$9,270 per capita (2003)
Annual average growth of GDP – 4 per cent (2007 est)
Inflation rate – 5.5 per cent (2007 est)
Unemployment – 10.7 per cent (2003 est)
Total external debt – US$668m (2003)
Imports – US$1,590m (2006)
Exports – US$390m (2006)

BALANCE OF PAYMENTS

Trade – US$1,201m deficit (2006)
Current Account – US$278m deficit (2006)

Trade with UK	*2006*	*2007*
Imports from UK	£46,989,000	£49,226,587
Exports to UK	£19,865,000	£20,018,890

COMMUNICATIONS

Barbados has around 1,600km of roads, all of which are surfaced. The Grantley Adams International airport is situated at Seawell, 19km from Bridgetown, and is a hub for connections to other Caribbean islands. Bridgetown, the only port of entry, has a deep-water harbour with berths for eight ships; there are also four tanker terminals. Mobile phone ownership is high, at 206,200 in 2005.

EDUCATION

Education is free in government schools at primary (ages four to 11) and secondary (ages 11 to 18) levels.
Literacy rate – 99.7 per cent (2004 est)

MEDIA

Barbados has two daily newspapers, both privately-owned. The sole television station is run by the government-owned Caribbean Broadcasting Corporation. There are both public and privately owned radio stations. The media air a range of views and are free to criticise the authorities.

BELARUS

Respublika Byelarus – Republic of Belarus

Area – 207,600 sq. km
Capital – Minsk (the administrative centre of the CIS); population, 1,805,000 (2007 est)
Major cities – Brest, Homyel', Hrodna, Mahilyow, Vicebsk
Currency – Belarusian rouble of 100 kopeks
Population – 9,724,723 falling at 0.41 per cent per year (2007 est); Belarusian (81.2 per cent), Russian (11.4 per cent), Polish (3.9 per cent), Ukrainian (2.4 per cent)
Religion – Orthodox Christianity (40 per cent), Roman Catholicism (7 per cent) (est). Up to 50 per cent of the population has no religious affiliation
Language – Belarusian, Russian (both official)
Population density – 47 per sq. km (2006)
Urban population – 71.6 per cent (2005 est)
Median age (years) – 38.2 (2007 est)
National anthem – 'My Belarusy' ['We, the Belarusians']
National day – 3 July (Independence Day)
Life expectancy (years) – 70.05 (2007 est)
Mortality rate – 13.98 (2007 est)
Birth rate – 9.5 (2007 est)
Infant mortality rate – 6.63 (2007 est)
Death penalty – Retained
CPI score – 2.1 (2007)
Population below poverty line – 27.1 per cent (2003 est)

CLIMATE AND TERRAIN

Belarus is a landlocked country in eastern Europe, and was formerly part of the USSR. Much of the land is a plain, with many lakes, forests, swamps and marshy areas. Its main rivers are the upper reaches of the Dnieper, the Nyoman and the Western Dvina. Elevation extremes range from 346m (Dzyarzhynskaya Hara) at the highest point to 90m (Nyoman river) at the lowest. The climate is continental, with cold winters and relatively cool and rainy summers.

HISTORY AND POLITICS

The area was absorbed into Lithuania in the 13th century, and came under Polish rule from the 1570s, but following the partitions of Poland in the late 18th century it came under the control of the expanding Russian Empire. It was the site of fierce fighting during the First World War, but its brief period of independence ended, after a war over the territory, in partition between Poland and the USSR. The Polish territory was largely regained after the Second World War, which devastated Belarus; 25 per cent of the population was killed and thousands were deported.

Belarus declared its independence from the USSR after a failed coup in Moscow in 1991. Stanislav Shuskevich became Belarusian leader at the head of a coalition of Communists and Democrats, but he was forced to resign in 1994 and was replaced by Gen. Mecheslav Grib who pursued closer political, economic and trade relations with Russia. The 1994 presidential election was won by Alexander Lukashenko.

President Lukashenko has opposed privatisation and economic liberalisation since the late 1990s, precipitating economic collapse and public unrest. His regime has become increasingly repressive, with many allegations of human rights abuses, particularly concerning the imprisonment or disappearance of opposition leaders and the violent suppression of public demonstrations. The EU and USA have imposed sanctions several times in recent years because of the regime's poor human rights record and obstructiveness towards international election monitors. Elections between 2000–6 were condemned as neither free nor fair by opposition groups and international observers. In the 2004 legislative election, opposition parties failed to win any seats; in the 2006 presidential election, President Lukashenko was returned with 82.6 per cent of the vote. Popular protests at the outcome of these polls and subsequent public expressions of opposition to the regime were suppressed by the police. The next legislative election is scheduled for October 2008.

FOREIGN RELATIONS

Belarus was a founder member of the Commonwealth of Independent States (CIS) in 1991. President Lukashenko, who opposed the break-up of the Soviet Union, has sought closer relations with Russia. In 1997 a treaty was signed with Russia providing for closer political and economic integration, and in 1999 the two countries signed a treaty on the creation of a union state, which committed them to eventually becoming a confederal state. However, there has been little real progress towards integration, and Russia has increasingly condemned Belarus' poor economic development.

POLITICAL SYSTEM

Under the 1994 constitution, the president is directly elected for a five-year term; this was renewable only once until a 2004 constitutional amendment removed the two-term limit. The president may appoint half the members of the constitutional court and the electoral commission. The legislature is the bicameral national assembly, comprising a 110-member House of Representatives (lower chamber), directly elected for a four-year term, and a Council of the Republic, which has 56 members elected by regional *soviets* (councils) and other members appointed by the president, for a four-year term.

President Lukashenko's term of office was extended by two years by referendum in 1996, when his powers were increased at the expense of the legislature, and again in 1997.

HEAD OF STATE
President, Alexander Lukashenko, *elected* 10 July 1994, *re-elected* September 2001, March 2006

SELECTED GOVERNMENT MEMBERS *as at May 2008*
Prime Minister, Sergei Sidorsky
First Deputy Prime Minister, Vladimir Semashko
Deputy Prime Ministers, Alexander Kosinets; Vasiliy B. Dolgolev; Andrei Kobyakov *(Economy)*; Ivan Bambiza; Vasiliy Gapeev; Viktar Bura
Finance, Nikolai Korbut
Foreign Affairs, Sergei Martynov

EMBASSY OF THE REPUBLIC OF BELARUS
6 Kensington Court, London W8 5DL
T 020-7937 3288 E uk@belembassy.org
W www.uk.belembassy.org
Ambassador Extraordinary and Plenipotentiary, HE Aleksandr Mikhnevich, *apptd* 2006

BRITISH EMBASSY
37 Karl Marx Street, 220030 Minsk
T (+375) (172) 105 920 E britinfo@nsys.by
W www.britishembassy.gov.uk/belarus
Ambassador Extraordinary and Plenipotentiary, HE Brian Bennett, *apptd* 2002

DEFENCE

The army has 1,586 main battle tanks, 1,588 armoured infantry fighting vehicles and 916 armoured personnel carriers. The air force has 175 combat aircraft and 50 armed helicopters.
Military budget – US$525m (2007)
Military personnel – 72,940: army 29,600, joint staff 25,170, air force 18,170; paramilitary 110,000
Conscription duration – 9–12 months

ECONOMY AND TRADE

Although very prosperous under the Soviet regime, the country experienced a dramatic economic decline after independence and over a quarter of the population lives below the poverty line. Since 1994, President Lukashenko has resisted structural reform of the economy and reimposed state control of prices and currency exchange rates. Some privatised businesses have been renationalised, and the small private sector is subject to pressure and intervention by the state, circumstances which continue to discourage foreign investment. Recent years have seen steady economic growth, largely based on the re-export at market prices of heavily discounted oil from Russia. This revenue stream will be reduced in future by a sharp increase in oil and gas prices from early 2007 (increasing to world prices by 2011), Russia's introduction of an export duty on oil shipped to Belarus, and Belarus' obligation to share with Russia its duties on re-exported oil.

Industrial output has grown faster than the economy as a whole. The main activities are the manufacture of machinery and equipment, vehicles, domestic appliances, chemicals and textiles. These commodities, along with oil, mineral products, metals and foodstuffs, form the main exports and the main imports. The main trading partner is Russia.
GNI – US$33,800m; US$3,470 per capita (2006)
Average annual growth of GDP – 6.9 per cent (2007 est)
Inflation rate – 8.3 per cent (2007 est)
Unemployment – 1.6 per cent (2005)
Total external debt – US$9,272m (2007)
Imports – US$22,000m (2006)
Exports – US$20,000m (2006)

BALANCE OF PAYMENTS
Trade – US$2,618m deficit (2006)
Current Account – US$1,512m deficit (2006)

Trade with UK	*2006*	*2007*
Imports from UK	£62,763,000	£66,793,369
Exports to UK	£726,243,000	£589,498,319

COMMUNICATIONS

Belarus has an extensive 2,500km canal and river system but its use is limited by shallowness or location. There is an international airport at Minsk and seven other major domestic airports, plus over 70 smaller airports and airfields. Most of the 93,310km of roads are surfaced but many are in bad repair. There are 5,512km of railways. The telephone system is state-operated; the network is being modernised but is not extensive in rural areas. Land-line connections (3.3 million in 2006) are exceeded by mobile phone distribution (5.9 million). There were 5.5 million internet users in 2006.

EDUCATION AND HEALTH

The education system comprises pre-school, general secondary, out-of-school, vocational training and trade schools, secondary specialised and higher education. General secondary education begins at the age of six.
Literacy rate – 99.6 per cent (2004 est)
Gross enrolment ratio (percentage of relevant age group) – primary 96 per cent; secondary 96 per cent; tertiary 66 per cent (2006 est)
Health expenditure (per capita) – US$204 (2005)
Hospital beds (per 1,000 people) – 11.1 (2000–6)

MEDIA

A Soviet-era attitude to press freedom remains; the government controls media content and the appointment of senior editors in the print and broadcast media. State-run newspapers and television channels receive large subsidies and support government policies, while opposition publications are frequently subjected to harassment. The most popular privately owned newspaper is *Belorusskaya Delovaya Gazeta.* The Belarusian National State Teleradio Company operates domestic radio and TV channels. Radio Baltic Waves (Baltijos Bangos) is a private broadcaster that targets Belarusian audiences but operates from Vilnius in Lithuania.

BELGIUM

Koninkrijk Belgie/Royaume de Belgique/Königreich Belgien – Kingdom of Belgium

Area – 30,528 sq. km
Capital – Brussels; population, 1,743,000 (2007 est)
Major cities – Antwerp, Bruges, Charleroi, Ghent, Liège
Currency – Euro (€) of 100 cents
Population – 10,392,226 rising at 0.12 per cent per year (2007 est); Fleming (58 per cent), Walloon (31 per cent) (est)
Religion – Roman Catholicism (57 per cent), Islam (4 per cent) (est). In addition, 9 per cent of the population is estimated to be laic (belonging to a non-confessional philosophical organisation) and 9 per cent atheist
Language – Dutch, French, German (all official)
Population density – 349 per sq. km (2006)
Urban population – 97.3 per cent (2005 est)
Median age (years) – 41.1 (2007 est)
National anthem – 'La Brabançonne' ['The Song of Brabant']
National day – 21 July (Ascension of King Leopold I, 1831)
Life expectancy (years) – 78.92 (2007 est)
Mortality rate – 10.32 (2007 est)
Birth rate – 10.29 (2007 est)
Infant mortality rate – 4.56 (2007 est)
Death penalty – Abolished for all crimes (since 1996)
CPI score – 7.1 (2007)
Population below poverty line – 15 per cent (2007 est)

CLIMATE AND TERRAIN

There are two distinct regions; the west is generally low-lying and fertile, while the east, the tableland of the Ardennes, is more rugged with poorer soil. Elevation extremes range from sea level on the North Sea coast to 694m at the highest point (Signal de Botrange). The polders near the coast, which are protected by dykes against floods, cover an area of 499 sq. km. The principal rivers are the Schelde and the Meuse (Maas). Average temperatures range from 2°C in January to 18°C in July.

HISTORY AND POLITICS

Part of the Roman Empire until the second century, it was invaded Germanic tribes and then became part of the Frankish Empire until much of the area was absorbed by the duchy of Burgundy from 1385. It was under the rule of the Spanish Habsburgs from 1477 until 1713 and the Austrian Habsburgs until 1794, when the area was conquered and held by Revolutionary France. After the collapse of the Napoleonic regime in 1814, it united with the kingdom of the Netherlands. The Belgian Revolution in 1830 led to the declaration of independence on 14 October 1830, and in 1831 the country became a constitutional monarchy. In the 20th century Belgium was invaded and occupied by Germany in both world wars; Eupen and Malmédy were ceded to Belgium by Germany under the Versailles treaty of 1919.

Tensions between the Flemings (Flemish speakers in the north of the country) and the Walloons (French speakers in the south) caused political instability in the post-war period, and several governments collapsed. Inter-communal disputes led in 1980 to the establishment of regional assemblies, and in 1989 the country adopted a federal constitution. Belgium was a founder member of the EU in 1957 and joined the eurozone in 2002. In 2005, the federal parliament approved the EU constitution.

After the 2003 general election, liberal and socialist parties held the majority of seats in the chamber of representatives and Guy Verhofstadt, prime minister since 1999, formed a new liberal-socialist coalition government. This coalition was defeated in the June 2007 election, in which the Christian Democrats won the most seats but not an outright majority. Negotiations for a new coalition lasted until February 2008, and a new five-party government led by the Christian Democrats took office the following month. After the country's Dutch and French-speaking parties failed to agree on a plan for regional devolution, Prime Minister Yves Leterme attempted to resign in July 2008.

POLITICAL SYSTEM

Belgium is a constitutional monarchy with a bicameral legislature (the Federal Chambers) consisting of a senate and a Chamber of Representatives. The latter has 150 members, directly elected by proportional representation for a four-year term. The senate has 71 members, who serve a four-year term; 40 are directly elected and the rest are co-opted by the elected members.

Amendments to the constitution since 1968 have devolved power to the regions. The national government retains competence only in foreign and defence policies, the national budget and monetary policy, social security, and the judicial, legal and penal systems.

HEAD OF STATE

HM The King of the Belgians, King Albert II, *born* 6 June 1934; *acceded* 9 August 1993
Heir, HRH Prince Philippe Léopold Louis Marie, *born* 15 April 1960

SELECTED GOVERNMENT MEMBERS *as at May 2008*

Prime Minister, Yves Leterme
Deputy Prime Ministers, Didier Reynders *(Finance);* Patrick Dewael *(Interior);* Laurette Onkelinx; Jo Vandeurzen *(Justice);* Joelle Milquet
Foreign Affairs, Karel De Gucht
Defence, Pieter De Crem

EMBASSY OF BELGIUM

17 Grosvenor Crescent, London SW1X 7EE
T 020-7470 3700 E london@diplobel.be
W www.diplomatie.be/london
Ambassador Extraordinary and Plenipotentiary, HE Jean-Michel Veranneman de Watervliet, *apptd* 2006

BRITISH EMBASSY

rue d'Arlon 85, 1040 Brussels
T (+32) (2) 287 6211 W www.british-embassy.be
Ambassador Extraordinary and Plenipotentiary, HE Dr Rachel Aronn, *apptd* 2007

BRITISH COUNCIL
Leopold Plaza, Rue de Trône 108/Troonstraat 108, 1050 Brussels
T (+32) (2) 227 0840 W www.britishcouncil.org/belgium
Regional Director, Stephen Roman

FEDERAL STRUCTURE
There are three communities: Flemish, Francophone and Germanophone. Each community has its own assembly, which elects the community government. At this level, Flanders is covered by the Flemish community assembly; most of Wallonia is covered by the Francophone community assembly, and areas of Wallonia lying in the German-speaking communities of Eupen and Malmédy are covered by the Germanophone community assembly; Brussels is covered by a joint community commission of the Flemish and Francophone community assemblies.

At regional level, Belgium is divided into the three regions of Wallonia, Brussels and Flanders. Each region has its own directly elected assembly and government.

The ten provinces of Belgium are: Antwerp, East Flanders, Flemish Brabant, Hainaut, Liege, Limburg, Luxembourg, Namur, Walloon Brabant and West Flanders. In addition, 589 communes form the lowest level of local government.

Minister-President of the Brussels Capital Government, Charles Picqué
Minister-President of the Flemish Community and Flemish Region, Kris Peeters
Minister-President of the Walloon Region and of the French Community, Rudy Demotte
Minister-President of the German-speaking Community, Karl-Heinz Lambertz

DEFENCE

The army has 40 main battle tanks, 95 armoured infantry fighting vehicles and 224 armoured personnel carriers. The navy is based at Zeebrugge and Ostend and has 2 frigates and 1 patrol and coastal vessel. The air force has 71 combat aircraft and 6 air bases.

The headquarters of NATO, Supreme Headquarters Allied Powers Europe, and the Western European Union Military Planning Cell are in Belgium; 1,367 US personnel (EUCOM) are stationed in the country.

Military expenditure – US$4,420 million (2006)
Military personnel – 39,690: army 12,571, navy 1,605, air force 7,470, medical and joint services 18,044

ECONOMY AND TRADE

Belgium has a free-market economy with highly diversified industrial and commercial sectors. With no natural resources except coal (production of which has now ceased), industry is based largely on the processing of imported raw materials for export. This makes the economy dependent on the state of world markets, and rates of growth have recently been low. Principal industries are engineering and metal products, vehicle assembly, transport equipment, scientific instruments, food processing and beverages, chemicals, base metals, textiles, glass, petroleum and diamonds.

Industry accounts for about one quarter of GDP and one quarter of employment. There is a large service sector, largely owing to the location in Brussels of EU institutions, NATO headquarters and a number of other international organisations. The service sector accounts for nearly three-quarters of GDP and the same proportion of employment. There is a small agricultural sector (1 per cent of GDP and 2 per cent of employment). The government has succeeded in balancing the budget recently but public debt is high (86 per cent of GDP in 2007).

About 75 per cent of trade is with other EU states, especially Germany, France and the Netherlands. External trade statistics relate to Luxembourg as well as Belgium as the two countries formed an economic union in 1921.

GNI – US$405,400m; US$38,460 per capita (2006)
Annual average growth of GDP – 2.7 per cent (2007 est)
Inflation rate – 1.7 per cent (2007 est)
Unemployment – 7.6 per cent (2007 est)
Total external debt – US$1,313,000m (2007)
Imports – US$354,000m (2006)
Exports – US$369,000m (2006)

BALANCE OF PAYMENTS
Trade – US$15,030m surplus (2006)
Current Account – US$10,588m surplus (2006)

Trade with UK	*2006*	*2007*
Imports from UK	£12,751,800,000	£11,728,937,125
Exports to UK	£13,863,900,000	£14,708,661,171

COMMUNICATIONS

There are 2,043km of inland waterways, of which 1,528km are in regular commercial use; ship canals link Ostend and Zeebrugge with Bruges and Ghent, Ghent with Terneuzen in the Netherlands, Brussels with Charleroi and Willebroek Rupel, and Liège with Antwerp. The rivers Meuse (Maas), Sambre and Schelde form an integral part of the network. The main seaports are Antwerp, Ghent, Ostend and Zeebrugge, with inland ports at Brussels and Liège. The major airports are at Antwerp, Brussels, Liège and Ostend. The rail system is run by Belgian National Railways and at 3,536km the network is one of the densest in the world. There are 150,567km of roads, including 1,747km of motorways. Mobile phone ownership was 9.7 million in 2006, representing over 90 per cent of the population, and in 2005 there were nearly 5 million internet users.

EDUCATION AND HEALTH

Nursery schools provide free education for children from two-and-a-half to six years of age. There are over 4,000 primary schools (six to 12 years) and more than 1,000 secondary schools offering a general academic education, slightly over half of which are free institutions (predominantly Roman Catholic and subsidised by the state) and the remainder state-run institutions. The official school-leaving age is 18.

Gross enrolment ratio (percentage of relevant age group) – primary 102 per cent; secondary 109 per cent; tertiary 62 per cent (2006 est)
Health expenditure (per capita) – US$3,451 (2005)
Hospital beds (per 1,000 people) – 5.3 (2000–6)

MEDIA AND CULTURE

The media reflects the multilingual nature of the population. There are two broadcasting authorities with programming priorities in radio, TV and external broadcasting. RTBF is the French-language broadcaster. VRT is the Flemish broadcaster. There are also French and Flemish commercial television channels and Belgischer Rundfunk (BRF), a German-language radio broadcaster. Cable television is popular, with 95 per cent of the population subscribing to domestic and foreign channels. A small number of media groups own and run the main news publications.

Belgium has contributed a number of significant names to art, including Peter Paul Rubens (1577–1640), who commands a room of his own in the Louvre, Pieter Bruegel, the Elder (*c.*1525–69) and Anthony van Dyck (1599–1641). Notable modern artists include James Ensor (1860–1949) and surrealist René Magritte (1898–1967), and those behind comic characters Tintin (Hergé) and the Smurfs (Peyo). The prolific novelist Georges Simenon (1903–89) achieved notable success writing in French. The country's chocolate and beer are considered to be among the world's finest. Six of the seven Trappist breweries are based in Belgium, as is the world's largest brewery, InBev, producers of Stella Artois and Leffe.

BELIZE

Area – 22,966 sq. km
Capital – Belmopan; population, 16,000 (2007 est)
Major towns – Belize City (the former capital), Orange Walk, San Ignacio
Currency – Belize dollar (BZ$) of 100 cents. The Belize dollar is tied to the US dollar
Population – 294,385 rising at 2.26 per cent per year (2007 est); *mestizo* (48.7 per cent), Creole (24.9 per cent), Maya (10.6 per cent), Garifuna (6.1 per cent) (est)
Religion – Roman Catholicism (50 per cent), other Christian denominations (25 per cent) (est). Around 10 per cent of the population has no religious affiliation
Language – English (official), Spanish, Mayan, Creole, Garifuna, German
Population density – 13 per sq. km (2006)
Urban population – 48.6 per cent (2005 est)
Median age (years) – 19.9 (2007 est)
National anthem – 'Land of the Free'
National day – 21 September (Independence Day)
Life expectancy (years) – 68.25 (2007 est)
Mortality rate – 5.76 (2007 est)
Birth rate – 28.34 (2007 est)
Infant mortality rate – 24.38 (2007 est)
HIV/AIDS adult prevalence rate – 2.1 per cent (2005 est)
Death penalty – Retained
CPI score – 3.0 (2007)
Population below poverty line – 33.5 per cent (2002 est)

CLIMATE AND TERRAIN

Belize comprises a large coastal plain, swamps in the north, fertile land in the south, and the Maya Mountains. The highest point of elevation is 1,160m (Victoria Peak), the lowest is at 0m (Caribbean Sea). The climate is subtropical but is cooled by trade winds. There are frequent hurricanes (the hurricane season is June to November). Belize's inner coastal waters are protected by the world's second-largest barrier reef.

HISTORY AND POLITICS

Numerous ruins in the area indicate that Belize was heavily populated by the Maya. The first British settlement was established in 1638 but was subject to repeated attacks by the Spanish, who claimed sovereignty until their defeat by the British navy and settlers in 1798. In 1862 the area was recognised by Britain as a colony and called British Honduras. The colony became self-governing in 1964. In 1973 it was renamed Belize, and it was granted independence on 21 September 1981.

Since independence, power has alternated between the two main politicial parties, the People's United Party (PUP) and the United Democratic Party (UDP). The PUP, in power since 1998, lost the legislative election in February 2008 to the UDP, which won an overwhelming majority of seats and took office under Dean Barrow.

FOREIGN RELATIONS

There is a longstanding territorial dispute with Guatemala, which claims half of the territory of Belize. In 2002 Belize and Guatemala agreed a draft settlement brokered by the the Organisation of American States, but Guatemala rejected the terms of the settlement in 2003.

POLITICAL SYSTEM

Under the 1981 constitution, the head of state is the British sovereign, represented by a governor-general. There is a bicameral national assembly, comprising a house of representatives (29 members directly elected for a five-year term) and a senate (13 members appointed by the governor-general, including six on the advice of the prime minister, three on the advice of the opposition leader, and one each representing various sectors of society). The prime minister is appointed by the governor-general and is responsible to the legislature.
Governor-General, HE Sir Colville Young, GCMG, *apptd* 17 November 1993

SELECTED GOVERNMENT MEMBERS *as at May 2008*
Prime Minister, Finance, Dean Barrow
Deputy Prime Minister, Gaspar Vega
Attorney-General, Foreign Affairs, Wilfred Elrington

BELIZE HIGH COMMISSION
3rd Floor, 45 Crawford Place, London W1H 4LP
T 020-7723 3603 E bzhc-lon@btconnect.com
W www.belizehighcommission.com
High Commissioner, HE Lawrence Sylvester, *apptd* 2006

BRITISH HIGH COMMISSION
PO Box 91, Belmopan
T (+501) 822 2146 E brithicom@btl.net
W www.britishhighbze.com
High Commissioner, HE Alan Jones, *apptd* 2004

DEFENCE

Military budget – US$18m (2007 est)
Military personnel – 1,050 (all army)

ECONOMY AND TRADE

The economy has grown steadily since 1999, although the rate of growth has slowed slightly in recent years. This is partly owing to the downturn in tourism, which now dominates the economy. The government introduced an austerity budget in 2005 to deal with the budget and trade deficits and the high level of foreign debt, which was restructured in 2007. About one-third of the population lives below the poverty line.

The services sector, primarily tourism, accounts for around 65 per cent of GDP; industry contributes about

13.7 per cent, and agriculture and fisheries contribute about 21.3 per cent. The main industries apart from tourism are garment manufacturing and food processing, construction and oil production; commercial exploitation of oil reserves began in 2006. The main crops are also major export items: sugar, bananas, citrus fruits and juice, fish products, molasses and timber (mostly mahogany). The UK and the USA account for over 66 per cent of export revenue. Imports are primarily machinery and transport equipment, manufactured goods, fuel, chemicals, pharmaceuticals, food, beverages and tobacco.
GNI – US$1,114m; US$3,740 per capita (2006)
Annual average growth of GDP – 3 per cent (2007)
Inflation rate – 2.8 per cent (2007 est)
Unemployment – 9.4 per cent (2006)
Total external debt – US$1,200m (2005 est)
Imports – US$680m (2006)
Exports – US$270m (2006)

BALANCE OF PAYMENTS
Trade – US$410m deficit (2006)
Current Account – US$27m deficit (2006)

Trade with UK	*2006*	*2007*
Imports from UK	£8,244,000	£11,679,178
Exports to UK	£86,503,000	£38,772,929

COMMUNICATIONS

Although there are 825km of waterways, these are only accessible to small craft. The main port is Belize City, which has deep water quays. There are about 17 major airports and airfields, including the international airport is at Belize City. There are 2,872km of roads, but no railway system. Mobile phone distribution has reached a density of about 40 per 100 people, exceeding land-line connections of 12 per 100 people.

EDUCATION

Education is free and compulsory for nine years. The government maintains some schools but most are run by churches.
Literacy rate – 76.9 per cent (2004 est)

MEDIA

The government-operated radio service was privatised in 1998 and there is now a variety of commercial radio stations. There are no daily newspapers but there are a number of privately owned weekly news publications. There are three main television stations (Channels 5, 7 and 9), all of which are commercial.

BENIN

République du Bénin – Republic of Benin

Area – 112,620 sq. km
Capital – Porto Novo; population, 257,000 (2007 est)
Major cities – Abomey-Calavi, Cotonou, Djougou, Parakou
Currency – Franc CFA of 100 centimes
Population – 8,078,314 rising at 2.67 per cent per year (2007 est); Fon (39.2 per cent), Adja (15.2 per cent), Yoruba (12.3 per cent), Bariba (9.2 per cent), Fula (7 per cent), Ottmari (6.1 per cent), Yoa-Lopka (4 per cent), Denda (2.5 per cent)
Religion – Roman Catholicism (27 per cent), Islam (24 per cent). Among the most commonly practised indigenous religions is voodoo, which originated in this region of Africa.
Language – French (official), Fon, Yoruba
Population density – 79 per sq. km (2006)
Urban population – 46.1 per cent (2005 est)
Median age (years) – 17.7 (2007 est)
National anthem – 'L'Aube Nouvelle' ['The Dawn of a New Day']
National day – 1 August
Life expectancy – 53.44 (2007 est)
Mortality rate – 11.94 (2007 est)
Birth rate – 38.1 (2007 est)
Infant mortality rate – 77.85 (2007 est)
HIV/AIDS adult prevalence – 1.6 per cent (2005 est)
Death penalty – Retained, but not used
CPI score – 2.7 (2007)
Population below poverty line – 33 per cent (2001 est)
Literacy rate – 33.6 per cent (2004 est)
Gross enrolment ratio (percentage of relevant age group) – primary 96 per cent; secondary 32 per cent (2006 est)
Health expenditure (per capita) – US$28 (2005)
Hospital beds (per 1,000 people) – 0.5 (2000–6)

CLIMATE AND TERRAIN

Benin has a short coastline of 124km on the Gulf of Guinea but extends northwards inland for about 700km. The coast is a sandbar backed by lagoons that are fed by rivers. Elevation extremes range from 658m (Mt Sokbaro) at the highest point to 0m (Atlantic Ocean) at the lowest. Benin has a tropical climate.

HISTORY AND POLITICS

Dahomey, on the site of modern-day Benin, was a west African kingdom founded in the 11th and 12th centuries that rose to prominence during the 15th and 16th centuries. The first Europeans to visit the country were the Portuguese in 1472. Slavery became the region's primary trade, hence the area's historical name of the Slave Coast.

After a war between the French and the Dahomey kingdom in 1892–4, the French established a protectorate and this was incorporated into the federation of French West Africa in 1899. Dahomey became an independent republic within the French Community in 1958; full independence was proclaimed on 1 August 1960. Between 1960 and 1972 there was acute political instability, with frequent switches from civil to military rule and regional ethnic conflicts, until a coup d'état in 1972 brought to power a Marxist-Leninist military government headed by Lt.-Col. Mathieu Kérékou. The name of the country was changed to Benin in 1975.

The country became more stable and moved gradually towards democratic government; civil rule was restored in 1977 (though Kérékou remained president), Marxist-Leninism was abandoned in 1989 for economic liberalisation, a pluralistic constitution was adopted in 1990, and legislative and presidential elections were held in 1991. The transition to fully democratic government was effected smoothly and has operated successfully, making Benin one of the most stable countries in Africa.

The 2006 presidential election was won in the second round by Yayi Boni, an independent candidate, who received 74.5 per cent of the vote. In the 2007 legislative election, the Cauri Forces for an Emerging Benin party, which supports the president, won the most seats.

POLITICAL SYSTEM
Under the 1990 constitution, the executive president is directly elected for a five-year term. The unicameral National Assembly has 83 members, directly elected for a four-year term. The president appoints and chairs the council of ministers.

HEAD OF STATE
President and Head of the Armed Forces, Yayi Boni, *elected* 19 March 2006

SELECTED GOVERNMENT MEMBERS *as at May 2008*
Foreign Affairs, Moussa Okanla
Defence, Issifou Kogui N'douro
Economy, Soule Mana Lawani
Interior, Security, Gen. Felix Hessou

EMBASSY OF THE REPUBLIC OF BENIN
87 Avenue Victor Hugo, F-75116 Paris, France
T (+33) (1) 4500 9882 E ambassade.benin@gofornet.com
Ambassador Extraordinary and Plenipotentiary, HE Edgar-Yves Monnou, *apptd* 2004

BRITISH AMBASSADOR
HE Richard Gozney, *apptd* 2004, resident at Abuja, Nigeria

DEFENCE
The army has 18 light tanks. The navy has 2 patrol and coastal combatant vessels.
Military budget – US$57m (2007 est)
Military personnel – 4,750: army 4,300, navy 100, air force 350; paramilitary 2,500
Conscription duration – 18 months

ECONOMY AND TRADE
The economy is underdeveloped, with over a third of the population below the poverty line, and Benin has a high trade deficit and massive foreign debt. Economic restructuring to meet the criteria of international aid donors secured a US$460m (£230m) debt reduction package in 2000, G8 debt relief in 2005 and a US$307m (£153m) grant in 2006. Economic growth has been steady since 2000 but its effects have been outweighed by even more rapid population growth. Expansion plans include the development of tourism, new agricultural products and food processing systems and information and communications technology, and attracting more foreign investment. Privatisation of industries, including utilities, began in 2001.

Agriculture is mostly at subsistence level and contributes 33.2 per cent to GDP, declining recently as industry (14.5 per cent) and services (52.3 per cent) have developed. The main cash crops are cotton, cashew nuts, shea butter, palm products and seafood, and the principal industrial activities are textiles and food processing. The main trading partners are China (20.9 per cent of exports; 46.6 per cent of imports), Indonesia, France, India, Thailand, Netherlands and neighbouring countries, to which textiles and some of the cash crops are exported.
GNI – US$4,700m; US$530 per capita (2006)
Annual average growth of GDP – 4.5 per cent (2007 est)
Inflation rate – 2.5 per cent (2007 est)
Total external debt – US$1,600m (2000)
Imports – US$990m (2006)
Exports – US$570m (2006)

BALANCE OF PAYMENTS
Trade – US$420m deficit (2006)
Current Account – US$296m deficit (2006)

Trade with UK	*2006*	*2007*
Imports from UK	£37,644,000	£42,720,342
Exports to UK	£291,000	£104,658

MEDIA
The media in Benin is mostly free of interference. Free speech is guaranteed by the constitution, although journalists are wary of stringent libel laws. There are over 50 newspapers and periodicals, including five daily newspapers, four of which are privately-owned. The state runs a single television station and there are a handful of other commercial broadcasters. Radio stations are also a mixture of state, commercial and local.

BHUTAN

Druk Gyalkhap – Kingdom of Bhutan

Area – 47,000 sq. km
Capital – Thimphu; population, 83,000 (2007 est)
Major cities – Geylegphug, Phuentsholing
Currency – Ngultrum of 100 chetrum (Indian currency is also legal tender)
Population – 2,327,849 rising at 2.08 per cent per year (2007 est); Bhote (50 per cent), ethnic Nepalese (35 per cent), indigenous or migrant tribes (15 per cent) (est)
Religion – Buddhism (66 per cent), Hinduism (25 per cent) (est)
Language – Dzongkha, English (both official)
Population density – 14 per sq. km (2006)
Urban population – 9.1 per cent (2005 est)
Median age (years) – 20.5 (2007 est)
National anthem – 'Druk Tsendhen' ['The Thunder Dragon Kingdom']
National day – 17 December
Life expectancy (years) – 55.17 (2007 est)
Mortality rate – 12.46 (2007 est)
Birth rate – 33.28 (2007 est)
Infant mortality rate – 96.37 (2007 est)

Death penalty – Abolished for all crimes (since 2004)
CPI score – 5.0 (2007)
Population below poverty line – 31.7 per cent (2003)

CLIMATE AND TERRAIN

Bhutan is a landlocked Himalayan country lying between China and India. There is a mountainous northern region which is infertile and sparsely populated, a central zone of upland valleys, where most of the population and cultivated land is found, and densely forested foothills in the south, which are mainly inhabited by Nepalese settlers and indigenous tribespeople. Extremes of elevation range from 7,553m (K'ula Kangri) at the highest point to 97m (Drangme Chhu) at the lowest. The climate is determined by altitude and average temperatures range from 4°C in January to 17°C in July. There is heavy annual rainfall of around 1,000mm in the central valleys and 5,000mm in the south.

HISTORY AND POLITICS

Bhutan's remoteness limited outside contact until modern times, although it signed a treaty of cooperation with Britain in 1774. A trade treaty was signed with Britain in 1865 after Britain had annexed the south of the country. A 1910 treaty placed foreign relations under the guidance of the British government in India, and in 1949 Bhutan signed a similar treaty with India under which it is guided by India in its external relations; a 2007 agreement revising this relationship gave Bhutan more say over its foreign and defence policies. It has its own diplomatic representatives and is a member of the UN.

Although the country has opened up since the 1970s, the monarchy has taken measures to preserve its indigenous culture, language and the environment, including compulsory national dress and restrictions on tourism. The emphasis on the majority culture, together with the granting of citizenship only to Nepalis settled in Bhutan before 1958, led to tension with the sizeable Nepali minority which resulted in an exodus to Nepal, where they remain living in refugee camps. In 2001 Bhutan and Nepal began an agreed process of refugee repatriation but progress is slow.

Bhutan's transition from an absolute monarchy to a democracy began in the 1950s, with the establishment of an elected legislature in 1953, and the transfer of powers from the king to the legislature in 1969 and 1989. The king endorsed a draft constitution in 2005, and the legislature elected in spring 2008 is expected to debate the draft constitution before a referendum is held to confirm it. King Jigme Singye Wangchuk abdicated in December 2006 in favour of the Crown Prince.

The elections to the National Assembly in March 2008 resulted in an overwhelming majority for the pro-monarchy Bhutan Harmony Party (DPT), which won 45 of the 47 seats; the DPT leader, Jigme Thinley, was appointed prime minister and formed a government. Concern about the implications of such a large majority led to popular demonstrations calling for the restoration of absolute monarchy.

POLITICAL SYSTEM

Bhutan has no formal constitution until the 2005 draft constitution is confirmed. The head of state is the hereditary monarch, whose position is confirmed by a two-thirds majority in a vote in the legislature every three years. The draft constitution introduces a bicameral legislature comprising a National Assembly with 47 directly elected members and a National Council with 25 members, 20 directly elected and five appointed by the king. Both chambers serve a five-year term. The cabinet is nominated by the king and approved by the National Assembly; members serve for a five-year term.

HEAD OF STATE

HM The King of Bhutan, Jigme Khesar Namgyal Wangchuk, *born* 21 February 1980, *acceded* 14 December 2006

SELECTED GOVERNMENT MEMBERS *as at May 2008*

Prime Minister, Jigme Thinley
Finance, Wangdi Norbu
Foreign Affairs, Ugyen Tshering
Home and Cultural Affairs, Minjur Dorji

HONORARY CONSULATE

2 Windacres, Warren Road, Guildford GU1 2HG
T 01483-538189 E mrutland@aol.com
Honorary Consul, Michael R. Rutland

ECONOMY AND TRADE

The economy is based on industry (37 per cent of GDP in 2005), and agriculture (25 per cent of GDP). The services sector is growing, accounting for 38 per cent of GDP. Agriculture and animal husbandry engage around 63 per cent of the workforce in what is largely a self-sufficient rural society, although the country's mountainous topography and 60 per cent forest cover limit the area under cultivation. The principal food crops are rice, cereals, vegetables and fruit. Bhutan is the world's largest producer of cardamom, which forms its principal export to countries other than India.

Industries include mining (limestone, gypsum, dolomite, graphite, coal), cement, chemicals, food processing, distilling and forestry. Tourism and postage stamps are increasingly important sources of foreign exchange. Principal exports are electricity (to India), cardamom, gypsum, timber, handicrafts, cement, fruit, precious stones and spices; main imports are fuel and lubricants, grain, aircraft, machinery and parts, vehicles, fabrics and rice.

GNI – US$928m; US$1,430 per capita (2006)
Annual average growth of GDP – 8.8 per cent (2005 est)
Inflation rate – 5.5 per cent (2005 est)
Unemployment – 2.5 per cent (2004)
Total external debt – US$593m (2004)
Imports – US$300m (2006)
Exports – US$400m (2006)

BALANCE OF PAYMENTS

Trade – US$30m surplus (2006)
Current Account – US$29m deficit (2006)

Trade with UK	*2006*	*2007*
Imports from UK	£513,000	£1,003,678
Exports to UK	£58,000	£57,850

MEDIA

Television was introduced as recently as 1999 owing to fears that outside influences would undermine the country's culture and institutions. Services are controlled by the state-run Bhutan Broadcasting Service (BBS). Radio broadcasting was introduced in 1973 and internet access in 1999. Media freedom is heavily restricted by the government, ensuring there are no private broadcasters, although cable TV relays from India are very popular.

BOLIVIA

República de Bolivia – Republic of Bolivia

Area – 1,098,580 sq. km
Capital – La Paz, the seat of government; population, 1,590,000 (2007 est). Sucre is the legal centre and seat of the judiciary.
Major cities – Cochabamba, El Alto, Oruro, Santa Cruz, Sucre
Currency – Boliviano ($b) of 100 centavos
Population – 9,119,152 rising at 1.42 per cent per year (2007 est); Quechua (30 per cent), *mestizo* (30 per cent), Aymara (25 per cent) (est)
Religion – Roman Catholicism (78 per cent), Protestantism (16 per cent), other Christian denominations (3 per cent) (est)
Language – Spanish, Quechua, Aymara (all official)
Population density – 9 per sq. km (2006)
Urban population – 64.4 per cent (2005 est)
Median age (years) – 22.2 (2007 est)
National anthem – 'Himno Nacional de la República de Bolivia' ['National Anthem of the Republic of Bolivia']
National day – 6 August (Independence Day)
Life expectancy (years) – 66.19 (2007 est)
Mortality rate – 7.44 (2007 est)
Birth rate – 22.82 (2007 est)
Infant mortality rate – 50.43 (2007 est)
Death penalty – Retained for certain crimes
CPI score – 2.9 (2007)
Population below poverty line – 60 per cent (2006 est)

CLIMATE AND TERRAIN

A landlocked country, Bolivia's chief topographical feature is its great central plateau. Over 800km in length and at an average altitude of 3,750m above sea level, this plateau lies between the two great chains of the Andes, which traverse the country from south to north. Elevation extremes range from 6,542m (Nevado Sajama) at the highest point to 90m (Rio Paraguay) at the lowest. The land falls from the Andean ridges in the west through forested foothills to the plains of the north and east. These are drained by the principal rivers, the Itenez, Beni, Mamore and Madre de Dios. The wet season is November to March. There is an average temperature of 26°C in most of the country but the south is prone to droughts, while temperatures become subpolar at an altitude of 500m.

HISTORY AND POLITICS

The area of present-day Bolivia was assimilated into the Inca Empire in 1450. The Inca Empire was conquered by the Spanish in 1525. Bolivia won its independence from Spain in 1825 after a war of liberation led by Simón Bolívar (1783–1830), from whom the country derives its name. Much territory was lost after wars with neighbouring countries, including a devastating defeat in the Chaco War (1932–5) against Paraguay.

Bolivia was ruled by military juntas from 1936 to 1952 and from 1964 to 1982, when civilian rule was restored amid worsening economic conditions as the tin market collapsed and inflation rose dramatically. Austerity measures introduced in 1983 succeeded over the next decade in curbing inflation and attracting foreign investment, but the measures widened social divisions and created great social unrest. The unrest centred on coca crop eradication programmes, which were essential to attract overseas aid but caused economic hardship amongst the poor, and plans to exploit and export natural gas. Civil unrest over the latter resulted in the resignations of two successive presidents: Gonzalo Sánchez de Lozada in 2002 (after only three months in office) and his successor Carlos Mesa in 2005.

Evo Morales, the country's first indigenous president and a former coca growers' leader, has dealt with these issues by renationalising the energy industry and promising to relax restrictions on coca cultivation and seek alternative uses for the crop. There are plans to renationalise other industries, including utilities. A draft constitution containing provisions that would give greater political power to the indigenous population has been strongly opposed, especially by the wealthier regions in the east of the country, and several regions voted for greater autonomy in May and June 2008. The opposition-dominated senate passed a bill requiring a recall referendum on the mandates of the president, vice-president and nine regional governors; it was held on 10 August but only two of the governors lost their seats.

President Morales, leader of the Movement Towards Socialism (MAS), took office in 2006 after winning the 2005 presidential elections. In the simultaneous legislative elections, the MAS won an outright majority in the lower chamber of the legislature but the Social and Democratic Power party became the largest party in the upper chamber.

POLITICAL SYSTEM

The 1967 constitution was revised in 1994. It provides for an executive president who is directly elected for a five-year term, which is not renewable; the president is chosen by the legislature if no candidate wins the majority of the vote. The bicameral National Congress consists of a 27-member senate and a 130-member Chamber of Deputies; members of both chambers are directly elected for a five-year term.

An assembly was elected in June 2006 to consider a new constitution. In May 2008 the first of two referendums on a new draft constitution intended to give greater political power to the indigenous population was postponed for logistical reasons.

HEAD OF STATE

President, Evo Morales Ayma, *elected* 18 December 2005, *sworn in* 22 January 2006
President of the Senate; Vice-President, Alvaro Garcia Linera

SELECTED GOVERNMENT MEMBERS *as at May 2008*

Defence, Walker Rodriguez San Miguel
Finance, Luis Alberto Arce Catacora
Foreign Affairs, David Choquehuanca Cespedes
Interior, Alfredo Rada Velez

BOLIVIAN EMBASSY
106 Eaton Square, London SW1W 9AD
T 020-7235 2257 E bolivianembassy@yahoo.co.uk
W www.boembassy-london.com
Ambassador Extraordinary and Plenipotentiary, HE Maria Beatriz Souviron, *apptd* 2006

BRITISH EMBASSY
PO Box 694, Avenida Arce 2732, La Paz
T (+591) (2) 243 2397 E ppa@megalink.com
Ambassador Extraordinary and Plenipotentiary, HE Nigel Baker, MVO, *apptd* 2007

DEFENCE

The army has 54 light tanks and 115 armoured personnel carriers. The navy has 54 patrol and coastal vessels at 12 bases. The air force has 33 combat aircraft and 15 armed helicopters.

Military budget – US$166m (2007)
Military personnel – 46,100: army 34,800, navy 4,800, air force 6,500; paramilitary 37,100

ECONOMY AND TRADE

The country is one of the poorest and least developed in South America. Economic reform from 1983 turned around the 1980s economic crisis, creating steady growth in the 1990s, although this has slowed since 1999. Despite this growth, over 60 per cent of the population lives below the poverty line. Debt cancellation by the G8 countries and international institutions, and budget and trade surpluses have relieved fiscal pressures on the government, but foreign investment has dropped as a result of the renationalisation of the energy industry.

Mining (principally for zinc, tin and gold) and smelting, natural gas and oil production and agriculture are the principal industries. The export of natural gas has contributed to higher economic growth since 2003; production in 2006 was 12,740m cubic metres, of which 10,580m cubic metres was exported.

In 1996 Bolivia joined MERCOSUR, which aims to create a free trade zone. Bolivia's main trading partners are other South American countries, particularly Brazil and Argentina, and the USA. Principal exports are natural gas, soya beans and soya products, crude oil, zinc ore and tin. The main imports are petroleum products, plastics, paper, aircraft and aircraft parts, processed food, vehicles and insecticides.

GNI – US$10,300m; US$1,100 per capita (2006)
Annual average growth of GDP – 4 per cent (2007 est)
Inflation rate – 12 per cent (2007 est)
Unemployment – 8 per cent (2006)
Total external debt – US$3,800m (2007 est)
Imports – US$2,800m (2006)
Exports – US$3,900m (2006)

BALANCE OF PAYMENTS
Trade – US$1,044m surplus (2006)
Current Account – US$1,312m surplus (2006)

Trade with UK	*2006*	*2007*
Imports from UK	£6,081,000	£7,351,089
Exports to UK	£10,170,000	£7,777,991

COMMUNICATIONS

Although landlocked, Bolivia has 10,000km of commercially navigable waterways, with an inland port on the river Paraguay at the border with Brazil. It has free port privileges at seaports in Argentina, Brazil, Chile and Paraguay, and a lease on a free-trade zone at the Peruvian port of Ilo. Bolivia has 1,061 airports and airfields, including four international airports serving the major cities. The 3,504km of railways form an eastern network and an Andean network; plans to link the two were initiated in 2004, and the link would complete a transcontinental railway line between the Brazilian and Chilean coasts. Of the 62,479km of roads, fewer than 4,000km are surfaced. The land-line telephone system is largely confined to the cities. Mobile phone use is growing rapidly.

EDUCATION AND HEALTH

Elementary education is compulsory and free from the ages of seven to 14.

Literacy rate – 86.5 per cent (2004 est)
Gross enrolment ratio (percentage of relevant age group) – primary 109 per cent; secondary 82 per cent; tertiary 41 per cent (2006 est)
Health expenditure (per capita) – US$71 (2005)
Hospital beds (per 1,000 people) – 1.0 (2000–6)

MEDIA

Radio is the most important news medium owing to low literacy levels, particularly in rural areas. The media is largely privately owned and operated. Journalists practise self-censorship, avoiding sensitive topics such as drug-trafficking and political corruption. There are six daily newspapers, each with limited influence. Television is mostly commercial, with only one government-run channel.

BOSNIA AND HERCEGOVINA

Bosna i Hercegovina – Bosnia and Hercegovina

Area – 51,129 sq. km
Capital – Sarajevo; population, 376,000 (2007 est)
Major towns – Banja Luka, Bosanski Samac, Mostar, Tuzla, Zenica
Currency – Convertible mark of 100 fenings
Population – 4,552,198 rising at 1 per cent per year (2007 est); Bosniak (48 per cent), Serb (37.1 per cent), Croat (14.3 per cent) (est)
Religion – Islam (40 per cent), Orthodox Christianity (31 per cent), Roman Catholicism (15 per cent), Protestantism (4 per cent) (est)
Language – Bosnian, Croatian, Serbian (all official)
Population density – 77 per sq. km (2006)
Urban population – 45.3 per cent (2005 est)
Median age (years) – 38.9 (2007 est)

National anthem – 'Drzavna Himna Bosne i Hercegovine' ['National Anthem of Bosnia and Hercegovina']
National day – 25 November
Life expectancy (years) – 78.17 (2007 est)
Mortality rate – 8.42 (2007 est)
Birth rate – 8.8 (2007 est)
Infant mortality rate – 9.58 (2007 est)
Death penalty – Abolished for all crimes (since 2001)
CPI score – 3.3 (2007)
Population below poverty line – 25 per cent (2004 est)
Literacy rate – 94.6 per cent (2004 est)
Health expenditure (per capita) – US$243 (2005)
Hospital beds (per 1,000 people) – 3.0 (2000–6)

CLIMATE AND TERRAIN

The country lies in the Balkan peninsula and includes the Dinaric Alps in the west. The mountainous centre is split by gorges, while the north is lower-lying, falling to the valley of the river Sava, which forms the northern border with Croatia. There is 20km of Adriatic coastline. The highest point of elevation is 2,386m (Maglic), the lowest point is 0m (Adriatic Sea). Average temperatures in Sarajevo range from 0°C in January to 25°C in July.

HISTORY AND POLITICS

The country was settled by Slavs in the seventh century and conquered by the Ottoman Turks in 1463. Ruled by the Turks for over 400 years, the country came under Austro-Hungarian control in 1878. The assassination of Franz Ferdinand, the heir to the Austro-Hungarian throne, by Gavrilo Princip, an ethnic Serb, precipitated the First World War, after which Bosnia-Hercegovina became part of the Kingdom of Serbs, Croats and Slovenes (renamed Yugoslavia in 1929). It was occupied by German and Axis forces between 1941 and 1945. At the end of the war, Bosnia-Hercegovina became part of the Socialist Federal Republic of Yugoslavia, which collapsed in 1991–2 following the secession of Slovenia and Croatia in 1991.

In October 1991 the government of Bosnia-Hercegovina outlined plans for a referendum on independence. In response, the Serbian Democratic Party, led by Radovan Karadzic, pulled out of the coalition government and declared a separate Serb republic, comprising predominantly Serb regions within Bosnia. The referendum, though boycotted by Bosnian Serbs, showed 99.43 per cent in favour and independence was declared on 5 March 1992. Despite the turnout failing to match the two-thirds required by the constitution to make the result legal, Bosnia-Hercegovina was recognised as an independent state and granted UN membership in May 1992.

In March 1992 Bosnian Serb militia supported by Federal Yugoslav Army (JNA) forces began a military campaign in eastern Bosnia, expelling Muslim (Bosniak) and Croat inhabitants. The military firepower of the JNA ensured 70 per cent of the country fell to the Bosnian Serbs by May. The Serbs also instituted a blockade of Sarajevo, which led to the deployment of a UN protection force whose role was quickly expanded to provide protection throughout the country.

Meanwhile, the government of Bosnia-Hercegovina splintered further as the Croatian Democratic Union proclaimed the Croatian Republic of Herceg-Bosnia in western and northern areas with a predominantly Croat population. Tensions between the Bosniaks and the Croats were aggravated by the 1993 joint UN-EC plan (the Vance-Owen plan), which proposed to divide the country into ten autonomous areas on ethnic lines, and further conflicts broke out. The Bosniak-Croat conflict was officially ended by the Washington agreement in 1994, and the two forces then united against the Serbs.

The Vance-Owen plan was also rejected by the Serbs. In July 1995 Bosnian Serb forces under Ratko Mladic moved into the UN-designated safe area of Srebrenica and killed 8,000 Bosniak men, in an event later deemed genocide by the International Criminal Tribunal for the Former Yugoslavia. In August NATO intervened in the siege of Sarajevo following months of bloodshed. A sustained bombing campaign was launched against Serb forces, the impact of which forced the Serb leader Slobodan Milosevic to participate in negotiation of the Dayton agreement, which brought the war to an end in December 1995. It is estimated 100,000 died between 1992 and 1995.

The Dayton agreement preserved Bosnia as a single state with an almost equal division of territory between two self-governing entities, the Federation of Bosnia-Hercegovina (Bosniak/Croat) and the Republic of Serbia (Bosnian Serbs), with a national government, presidency and democratically elected institutions. Since 1995 international peacekeeping duties have been undertaken by, successively, the UN (1995), NATO (1995–2005) and the EU (2005–). The country signed a stabilisation and association agreement with the EU – commonly believed to be a significant step towards full membership – in July 2008.

The latest legislative and collective presidental elections were held in 2006. In the federal legislature, the largest party remained the Bosniak-dominated Party for Democratic Action (SDA). It became a partner in a coalition government with four other parties under the premiership of Nikola Spiric. The SDA also retained its majority in the Federation of Bosnia and Hercegovina and formed a new government under Nedzad Brankovic. In the Republika Srpska, the Alliance of Independent Social Democrats won the most seats and formed a government under Milorad Dodik. Milan Jelic, elected president of Republika Srpska in 2006, died in September 2007; Rajko Kuzmanovic was elected to replace him in December. The 2007 presidential election in the Bosniak-Croat Federation was won by Borjana Kristo.

POLITICAL SYSTEM

Under the Dayton Peace Accord, the Bosnian republican (national) government is responsible for foreign affairs, currency, citizenship and immigration. The head of state is a collective presidency comprising a representative from each of the three ethnic groups, all directly elected for a four-year term; the chairmanship of the presidency rotates among its members every eight months. Legislative authority is vested in the bicameral Parliamentary Assembly of Bosnia and Hercegovina, comprising a House of Peoples and a House of Representatives. Both houses have four-year terms. The House of Peoples has 15 members, ten from the Federation and five from the Republika Srpska, who are selected by the House of Representatives. The House of Representatives has 42 members who are directly elected to the two constituent chambers, the Chamber of Deputies of the Federation, which has 28 members, and the Chamber of Deputies of the Republika Srpska, which has 14 members.

In the Bosniac-Croat Federation, the president and vice-president are elected by the Bosniac and Croat members of the House of Peoples for a four-year term; a second vice-president is elected to represent the Serb population. There is a bicameral Assembly comprising a

58-member House of Peoples elected on an ethnic basis and a House of Representatives with 98 directly elected members.

In the Republika Srpska, the president is directly elected for a four-year term. There is a unicameral people's assembly with 83 members directly elected for a four-year term.

There is a national council of ministers and each of the entities also has its own executive. All appointments to the executives are in consultation with the UN High Representative and may be vetoed by him.

REPUBLIC OF BOSNIA AND HERCEGOVINA
HEADS OF STATE
Presidency Members, Nebojsa Radmanovic, Zeljko Komsic, Haris Silajdzic

SELECTED GOVERNMENT MEMBERS *as at May 2008*
Prime Minister, European Integration, Nikola Spiric
Deputy Prime Ministers, Dragan Vrankic *(Finance)*; Tarik Sadovic *(Security)*
Foreign Affairs, Sven Alkalaj
Defence, Selmo Cikotic

OFFICE OF THE UN HIGH REPRESENTATIVE / EU SPECIAL REPRESENTATIVE
UN High Representative, Miroslav Lajcak, *apptd* 2007

EMBASSY OF BOSNIA AND HERCEGOVINA
5–7 Lexham Gardens, London W8 5JJ
T 020-7373 0867 E embassy@bhembassy.co.uk
W www.bhembassy.co.uk
Ambassador Extraordinary and Plenipotentiary, HE Dr Tanja Milasinovic, *apptd* 2005

BRITISH EMBASSY
Tina Ujevica 8, 71000 Sarajevo
T (+387) (33) 282 200 E britemb@bih.net.ba
W www.britishembassy.ba
Ambassador Extraordinary and Plenipotentiary, HE Matthew Rycroft, CBE, *apptd* 2005

BRITISH COUNCIL
Ljubljanska 9, 71000 Sarajevo
T (+387) (33) 250 220 W www.britishcouncil.org/bih
Director, Michael Moore

FEDERATION OF BOSNIA AND HERCEGOVINA
HEAD
President, Borjana Kristo
Vice-Presidents, Mirsad Kebo, Spomenka Micic

SELECTED GOVERNMENT MEMBERS *as at may 2008*
Prime Minister, Nedzad Brankovic
Deputy Prime Ministers, Gavrilo Grahovac *(Culture and Sport)*; Vjekoslav Bevanda *(Finance)*
Interior, Muhidin Alic
Defence, Marina Pendes

REPUBLIKA SRPSKA
HEAD
President, Rajko Kuzmanovic
Vice-Presidents, Adil Osmanovic; Davor Cordas

SELECTED GOVERNMENT MEMBERS *as at may 2008*
Prime Minister, Milorad Dodik
Economic Affairs, Jasna Brkic
Interior, Stanislav Cadjo

DEFENCE

A reform process completed in 2006 united the separate armies of the Republika Sprska and the Federation of Bosnia Hercegovina into a single entity. The armed forces have 325 main battle tanks, 132 armoured infantry fighting vehicles and 193 armoured personnel carriers. The air wing has 17 combat capable aircraft.
Military budget – US$142m (2006)
Military personnel – 9,047: armed forces 9,007, State Joint Operational Command 21, State Joint Staff 19

ECONOMY AND TRADE

When the civil war broke out, the structure of the economy (dominated by state-owned industries, mainly of a military nature) still reflected the central planning of the Communist era. Industrial recovery after the war has been hampered by this lack of diversity and commercial potential. Privatisation of industry has been slow, and although most agriculture is now in the private sector, it suffers from inefficiency. The economic growth rate has improved in recent years but government spending is high, there is a considerable trade deficit and high unemployment. Unofficial economic activity could represent output equivalent to half of the official GDP. The difficulties inherent in tackling these problems is exacerbated by the uneasy relations and reluctant co-operation between the different national and local political and administrative entities.

Most agricultural products are for domestic consumption and foodstuffs also have to be imported. The main industrial activities include mining (metals, minerals and coal), production of steel, textiles, tobacco products, wooden furniture and domestic appliances, assembly of vehicles, tanks and aircraft, and oil refining. The country has enough hydroelectric power for its needs and is an exporter of electricity, but an importer of natural gas. The main trading partners are Croatia, Italy, Slovenia, Germany and other EU states. Principal exports are metals, clothing and wood products, and the main imports are machinery and equipment, chemicals, fuels and foodstuffs.
GNI – US$12,700m; US$3,230 per capita (2006)
Annual average growth of GDP – 5.5 per cent (2007 est)
Inflation rate – 1.5 per cent (2007 est)
Unemployment – 45.5 per cent (2004 est)
Total external debt – US$7,057m (2007 est)

BALANCE OF PAYMENTS
Trade – US$1,823m deficit (2006)
Current Account – US$1,025m deficit (2006)

Trade with UK	*2006*	*2007*
Imports from UK	£18,905,000	£19,699,344
Exports to UK	£7,933,000	£7,709,795

COMMUNICATIONS

Although the country has 20km of coastline on the Adriatic Sea, there are no seaports. There are four river ports on the river Sava, which is navigable by shipping but its use is limited. The 28 airports and airfields include international airports at Sarajevo, Banja Luka, Mostar and Tuzla. There are 608km of railways and 21,846km of roads, 11,425km of which are paved. The telephone network needs modernising and expanding. Mobile phone subscribers, at 1.1 million in 2006, are double the number of main-line subscribers.

MEDIA

Since the 1995 peace accord, efforts have been made to reintroduce a balanced press that crosses ethnic divides. These efforts have not been entirely successful because of the pressure placed on the media by governments and political parties. A national broadcasting service is being developed under the aegis of the Office of the High Representative. There are more than 200 commercial television and radio stations, but development has slowed due to a weak advertising market.

BOTSWANA

Republic of Botswana

Area – 600,370 sq. km
Capital – Gaborone; population, 224,000 (2007 est)
Major cities – Francistown, Molepolole, Selebi-Phikwe
Currency – Pula (P) of 100 thebe
Population – 1,815,508 rising at 1.5 per cent per year (2007 est); Tswana (79 per cent), Kalanga (11 per cent), Basarwa (3 per cent) (est)
Religion – Christianity (70 per cent) (est), around 20 per cent espouse no religion
Language – English (official), Setswana, Kalanga, Sekgalagadi
Population density – 3 per sq. km (2006)
Urban population – 52.5 per cent (2005 est)
Median age (years) – 20.9 (2007 est)
National anthem – 'Fatshe Leno La Rona' ['Blessed be This Noble Land']
National day – 30 September (Botswana Day)
Life expectancy (years) – 50.58 (2007 est)
Mortality rate – 13.63 (2007 est)
Birth rate – 23.17 (2007 est)
Infant mortality rate – 43.97 (2007 est)
HIV/AIDS adult prevalence – 23.6 per cent (2005)
Death penalty – Retained
CPI score – 5.4 (2007)
Population below poverty line – 30.3 per cent (2003)

CLIMATE AND TERRAIN

A landlocked country in southern Africa, Botswana lies on an undulating plateau. The Kalahari desert covers about three-quarters of the country, in the south and west. To the east, streams run into the Marico, Notwani and Limpopo rivers. In the north lies a flat region comprising the Makgadikgadi salt pans and the swampland of the Okavango delta. Elevation extremes range from 1,489m (Tsodilo Hills) at the highest point to 513m (junction of the Limpopo and Shashe rivers) at the lowest. The climate is subtropical in the north, arid in the south and west, and temperate in the east. Average temperatures range from 26°C in January to 13°C in July.

HISTORY AND POLITICS

The Tswana people were dominant in the area from the 17th century. In 1885, at the request of indigenous chiefs fearing invasion by the Boers, Britain formally took control of Bechuanaland, and the northern part of the territory was declared the Bechuanaland Protectorate, while land to the south of the Molopo river became British Bechuanaland, which was later incorporated into the Cape Colony. In 1964, the British Protectorate of Bechuanaland became self-governing, and on 30 September 1966 it became an independent republic under the name Botswana. Since independence, Botswana has been stable and relatively prosperous owing to the diamond mining industry. There is a high level of HIV/AIDS among the population and although an advanced treatment programme in place since 2001 is reducing the level of infection, the country faces serious demographic and social problems.

The 2004 general election was won by the Botswana Democratic Party, with 51.7 per cent of the vote. In the presidential election the following day, Festus Mogae was re-elected for a second term. President Mogae stood down in April 2008, having completed two terms of office, and was succeeded by the vice-president, Lt.-Gen. Ian Khama, son of the country's first president.

POLITICAL SYSTEM

Under the 1966 constitution, the executive president is elected by the legislature for a five-year term, renewable only once. He appoints the vice-president and the cabinet. The unicameral National Assembly has 57 members directly elected for a five-year term, plus a variable number of co-opted members (currently four). A 15-member House of Chiefs advises on tribal matters and constitutional changes.

HEAD OF STATE

President, C.-in-C. of the Armed Forces, HE Lt.-Gen. Ian Khama, *sworn in* 1 April 2008
Vice-President, Lt.-Gen. Mompati Merafhe

SELECTED GOVERNMENT MEMBERS *as at May 2008*

Finance and Development Planning, Baledzi Gaolathe
Foreign Affairs, Phandu Skelemani
Home Affairs, Charles Tibone
Defence, Dikgakgamatso Seretse

BOTSWANA HIGH COMMISSION

6 Stratford Place, London W1C 1AY
T 020-7499 0031 E bohico@govbw.com
High Commissioner, HE Roy Blackbeard, *apptd* 1998

BRITISH HIGH COMMISSION

Private Bag 0023, Gaborone
T (+267) 395 2841 E bhc@botsnet.bw
W www.britishhighcommission.gov.uk/botswana
High Commissioner, HE Francis Martin, *apptd* 2005

BRITISH COUNCIL

PO Box 439, British High Commission Building, Queen's Road, The Mall, Gaborone
T (+267) 395 3602 W www.britishcouncil.org/botswana
Director, Stephen Forbes

DEFENCE

The army has 55 light tanks and 156 armoured personnel carriers. The air wing has 31 combat capable aircraft.

Military budget – US$283m (2007 est)

Military personnel – 9,000: army 8,500, air force 500; paramilitary 1,500

ECONOMY AND TRADE

Botswana has been relatively prosperous since independence because of its mining industry, political stability and sound economic management. Despite this, about 30 per cent of the population lives below the poverty line and there are high levels of unemployment. Longer-term problems are the impact of the high levels of HIV/AIDS among the workforce, and the levelling off of diamond production, which currently accounts for 70–80 per cent of export earnings. The government has sought to reduce the economy's dependence on the diamond industry by diversifying; safari tourism and financial services in particular have grown in recent years, and the services sector now contributes 46.9 per cent of GDP. The industrial sector contributes 51.5 per cent of GDP, of which 36 per cent is from mining diamonds, copper, nickel, salt, soda ash, potash and coal. Agriculture is predominantly pastoral and accounts for 1.6 per cent of GDP. Cattle-rearing represents over 80 per cent of agricultural production.

The main trading partners are European and other southern African countries. Principal exports are diamonds, copper, nickel, soda ash, meat and textiles. The main imports are foodstuffs, machinery, electrical goods, transport equipment, textiles, energy and fuel.

GNI – US$10,400m; US$5,570 per capita (2006)

Annual average growth of GDP – 4.7 per cent (2007 est)

Inflation rate – 7.2 per cent (2007 est)

Unemployment – 23.8 per cent (2004)

Total external debt – US$513m (2007 est)

Imports – US$3,150mm (2006)

Exports – US$4,600m (2006)

BALANCE OF PAYMENTS

Trade – US$1,450m surplus (2006)

Current Account – US$1,947m surplus (2006)

Trade with UK	*2006*	*2007*
Imports from UK	£13,942,000	£20,403,880
Exports to UK	£1,204,906,000	£1,611,473,008

COMMUNICATIONS

Because of its landlocked position, Botswana's trade is dependent on its international rail and road links. The only railway line is the link from Zimbabwe to South Africa, which passes through eastern Botswana. There are 24,355km of roads, of which 8,914km are paved. These include a highway connecting all the main towns and district capitals. The network links at the borders with the road networks of South Africa and Namibia. A major link is the 595km Trans-Kalahari Highway, completed in 1998, which connects Botswana with Namibia's capital (Windhoek) and its port of Walvis Bay. There are over 80 airports and airfields, including the international airport at Gaborone. The land-line telephone system is limited in extent and connections have declined in recent years, while mobile phone distribution is growing rapidly; there were about 60 mobile phones per 100 people in 2006.

EDUCATION AND HEALTH

Botswana does not have a compulsory education policy. Many children receive ten years of education, though the government announced in 2004 that efforts would be made to increase this to 12 years (seven years of primary education, three years of junior secondary, and two years of senior secondary).

Literacy rate – 78.9 per cent (2004 est)

Gross enrolment ratio (percentage of relevant age group) – primary 108 per cent; secondary 75 per cent; tertiary 5 per cent (2006 est)

Health expenditure (per capita) – US$362 (2005)

Hospital beds (per 1,000 people) – 2.2 (2000–6)

MEDIA

Botswana has a good record on press transparency, though newspaper circulation is almost entirely limited to urban areas. In rural communities radio is the most important news medium; there are state-run and private commercial stations, and programmes are broadcast in both English and Setswana. State-run television (Botswana Television) was established in 2000.

BRAZIL

República Federativa do Brasil – Federative Republic of Brazil

Area – 8,511,965 sq. km

Capital – Brasilia; population, 3,599,000 (2007 est)

Major cities – Belo Horizonte, Fortaleza, Rio de Janeiro (the former capital), Salvador, Sao Paulo

Currency – Real of 100 centavos

Population – 190,010,647 rising at 1.01 per cent per year (2007 est)

Religion – Roman Catholicism (74 per cent), Protestantism (15 per cent) (est)

Language – Portuguese (official), English, French, Spanish

Population density – 22 per sq. km (2006)

Urban population – 84.2 per cent (2005 est)

Median age (years) – 28.6 (2007 est)

National anthem – 'Hino Nacional Brasileiro' ['Brazilian National Anthem']

National day – 7 September (Independence Day)

Life expectancy (years) – 72.24 (2007 est)

Mortality rate – 6.19 (2007 est)

Birth rate – 16.3 (2007 est)

Infant mortality rate – 27.62 (2007 est)

Death penalty – Retained for certain crimes

CPI score – 3.5 (2007)

Population below poverty line – 31 per cent (2005)

CLIMATE AND TERRAIN

Brazil is South America's biggest country, taking up almost half of the continent. There are five distinct topographical areas: the Amazon basin (north and west, taking up nearly a third of the country), the river Plate basin (south), the Guyanan Highlands (north of the Amazon), the Brazilian Highlands (south of the Amazon), and the coastal strip. Brazil is mostly tropical, with the equator passing through the north and the Tropic of Capricorn through the south-east. It is the location of the world's biggest rainforest. The Amazon basin sees annual rainfall of up to 2,000mm a year and there is no dry season (average temperature 17°C). The north-east is the driest area of the country and can experience long periods of drought (average temperature 40°C). The southern states have a seasonal temperate climate (the average temperature is between 17°C and 19°C). Elevation extremes range from 3,014m (Pico da Neblina) at the highest point to 0m (Atlantic Ocean) at the lowest.

HISTORY AND POLITICS

Brazil was claimed by the Portuguese navigator Pedro lvares Cabral in 1500 and colonised by Portugal in the early 16th century, becoming a viceroyalty in 1572. During the Napoleonic Wars the Portuguese court transferred to Brazil. In 1822 it became an independent monarchy under Pedro I, son of King Joao VI of Portugal. In 1889, Pedro II was dethroned in a coup, and a republic was proclaimed in 1891. Brazil was a dictatorship from 1930 to 1945 and under military rule from 1964 to 1985, when civilian rule was restored after several years of gradual democratisation. Governments since then have faced difficult economic conditions, and exploitation of the Amazon basin has attracted controversy because it threatens the environmentally important rainforest.

In the 2006 legislative election, the Party of the Brazilian Democratic Movement (PMDB) became the largest party in the chamber of deputies and increased its seats in the senate, although the largest party in that house was the Liberal Front Party. President Luis ('Lula') da Silva of the Workers' Party (PT) was elected to a second term in the simultaneous presidential election. After the elections, the coalition government, dominated by the PT and including the PMDB, continued in office.

POLITICAL SYSTEM

Under the 1988 constitution, the executive president is directly elected for a four-year term; in 1997 the constitution was amended to allow the president to stand for a second term. The National Congress consists of an 81-member federal senate (three senators per state, directly elected for an eight-year term) and a 513-member Chamber of Deputies which is directly elected every four years; the number of deputies per state depends upon the state's population.

The republic's 26 states each has a governor and a legislative assembly with a four-year term.

HEAD OF STATE

President, Luis Inacio 'Lula' da Silva, *sworn in* 1 January 2003, *re-elected* October 2006
Vice-President, Jose Alencar Gomes da Silva

SELECTED GOVERNMENT MEMBERS *as at May 2008*

Defence, Nelson Jobim
Foreign Affairs, Celso Amorim
Finance, Guido Mantega
Attorney-General, Jose Antonio Dias Toffoli

EMBASSY OF BRAZIL

32 Green Street, London W1K 7AT
T 020-7399 9000 E infolondres@brazil.org.uk
W www.brazil.org.uk
Ambassador Extraordinary and Plenipotentiary, HE José Maurício Bustani, *apptd* 2003

BRITISH EMBASSY

Setor de Embaixadas Sul, Quadra 801, Conjunto K, 70408, Brasília DF
T (+55) (61) 3325 2710 E contact@uk.org.br
W www.uk.org.br
Ambassador Extraordinary and Plenipotentiary, HE Alan Charlton, CMG, *apptd* 2008

BRITISH COUNCIL

Edificio Centro Empresarial Varig, SCN Quadra 04, Bloco B, Torre Oeste Conjunto 202, 70710-926 Brasília DF
T (+55) (61) 2106 7500 W www.britishcouncil.org.br
Director, David Cordingley

FEDERAL STRUCTURE

The Federative Republic of Brazil is composed of the federal district in which the capital lies and 26 states: Acre, Alagoas, Amapa, Amazonas, Bahia, Ceará, Distrito Federal, Espirito Santo, Goias, Maranhao, Mato Grosso, Mato Grosso do Sul, Minas Gerais, Para, Paraiba, Parana, Pernambuco, Piaui, Rio de Janeiro Rio Grande de Norte, Rio Grande de Sul, Rondonia, Roraima, Santa Catarina, Sao Paulo, Sergipe and Tocantins.

DEFENCE

The army has 224 main battle tanks, 803 armoured personnel carriers and 63 armed helicopters. The navy is equipped with 5 submarines, 1 aircraft carrier, 4 corvettes, 10 frigates and 33 patrol and coastal vessels. Naval aviation consists of 18 combat aircraft and 25 armed helicopters; the Marines have 17 light tanks and 50 armoured personnel carriers. The air force has 309 combat aircraft.
Military budget – US$21,600m (2007)
Military personnel – 367,901: army 238,200, navy 62,261, air force 67,440
Conscription duration – 12 months (can extend to 18)

ECONOMY AND TRADE

Historically subject to severe boom and bust cycles, the economy was stabilised by reforms in the 1990s that included privatisation and the removal of trade barriers. Tight fiscal management, IMF programmes, a growth in output and an expanding export base have produced steady growth in recent years, and Brazil's economy has a growing international significance. Public debt and foreign debt are being reduced, but poverty is still widespread.

The country is rich in mineral deposits, including iron ore (hematite), bauxite, gold, manganese, nickel, platinum and uranium. It also produces oil, natural gas and hydroelectricity, although it is a net importer of all three. Brazil is the world's largest producer of coffee; the other main agricultural products being soya beans, wheat, rice, maize, sugar cane, cocoa, citrus fruits and beef. The expansion of agriculture and forestry threaten the rainforest, despite recent governments' attempts to prevent further depredations by loggers and farmers. Tourism is a growing industry. In 2007 services generated 64 per cent of GDP, industry 30.8 per cent and agriculture 5.1 per cent.

The main trading partners are the USA, Argentina, China and Germany. Principal exports are transport equipment, iron ore, soya beans, footwear, coffee and vehicles. The main imports are machinery, electrical and transport equipment, chemicals, fuel, vehicle parts and electronics.
GNI – US$892,600m; US$4,710 per capita (2006)
Annual average growth of GDP – 4.9 per cent (2007 est)
Inflation rate – 4.1 per cent (2007 est)
Unemployment – 9.8 per cent (2007 est)
Total external debt – US$230,300m (2007)
Imports – US$96,000m (2006)
Exports – US$138,000m (2006)

BALANCE OF PAYMENTS
Trade – US$41,955m surplus (2006)
Current Account – US$13,621m surplus (2006)

Trade with UK	*2006*	*2007*
Imports from UK	£920,759,000	£1,078,046,447
Exports to UK	£1,931,748,000	£2,073,405,615

COMMUNICATIONS
The 1,751,868km road network and 29,252km rail network are concentrated in the more densely populated south and east of the country. The railways are used primarily for transporting minerals to the ports; most passenger and freight traffic is on the roads. The Trans-Amazonian Highway connects the Amazon region with the rest of the country, although being unpaved it is often impassable in the rainy season. In remote regions, transport is primarily by air or water, utilising the 50,000km of navigable waterways and the 4,263 airports and airfields; international flights operate to the major cities. Rio de Janeiro and Santos are the two leading seaports but there are also another 14 fully equipped ports. The land-line telephone system is extensive. Mobile phone distribution has grown rapidly to 99.9 million in 2006. In the same year, there were 42.6 million internet users.

EDUCATION AND HEALTH
The education system includes both public and private institutions. Public education is free at all levels. Brazil has 42 million students (2002) and 30.5 million of these are enrolled in primary education.
Literacy rate – 88.4 per cent (2004 est)
Gross enrolment ratio (percentage of relevant age group) – primary 140 per cent; secondary 106 per cent; tertiary 24 per cent (2006 est)
Health expenditure (per capita) – US$371 (2005)
Hospital beds (per 1,000 people) – 2.6 (2000–6)

MEDIA AND CULTURE
Brazilian television is South America's biggest media industry, with Brazilian-made soap operas, game shows and dramas exported all over the world. There are thousands of radio stations and hundreds of television channels. Globo, Brazil's most successful broadcasting conglomerate, dominates the market and owns television and radio networks, newspapers and subscription television stations. The country is heavily promoting digital television and aims to cut off the analogue signal in 2016.

Paolo Coelho (*b.* 1947) is Brazil's most commercially successful author and his novel *The Alchemist* is estimated to have sold 50 million copies worldwide. The film industry is currently thriving, with two directors, Walter Salles *(The Motorcycle Diaries)* and Fernando Meirelles *(City of God)*, achieving international recognition.

Football is central to contemporary Brazil. The country has produced some of the world's most technically gifted players, including Pele (*b.* 1940), Zico (*b.* 1953) and Ronaldinho (*b.* 1980). The yellow jersey of the national team is widely recognised due to a record five World Cup victories.

BRUNEI

Negara Brunei Darussalam – Sultanate of Brunei Darussalam

Area – 5,770 sq. km
Capital – Bandar Seri Begawan; population, 22,000 (2007 est)
Major towns – Kampong Ayer, Kuala Belait, Seria, Tutong
Currency – Brunei dollar (B$) of 100 sen (fully interchangeable with Singapore currency)
Population – 374,577 rising at 1.81 per cent per year (2007 est); Malay (67 per cent), Chinese (15 per cent) (est)
Religion – Islam (45 per cent), Buddhism (2 per cent), Christianity (1 per cent) (est)
Language – Malay (official), English, Chinese
Population density – 72 per sq. km (2006)
Urban population – 77.6 per cent (2005 est)
Median age (years) – 27.2 (2007 est)
National anthem – 'Allah Peliharakan Sultan' ['God Bless the Sultan']
National day – 23 February
Life expectancy (years) – 75.3 (2007 est)
Mortality rate – 3.26 (2007 est)
Birth rate – 18.56 (2007 est)
Infant mortality rate – 13.12 (2007 est)
Death penalty – Retained, but not used

CLIMATE AND TERRAIN
The country lies in the north-east of the island of Borneo and is divided in two by the Limbang river valley in Sarawak (Malaysia). The terrain is mostly rainforest (75 per cent), with extensive mangrove swamps along the coastal plain. There are mountains on the border with Sarawak. Elevation extremes range from 1,850m (Bukit Pagon) at the highest point to 0m (South China Sea) at the lowest. The climate is tropical, with high levels of humidity and an average daily temperature of between 24°C and 30°C.

HISTORY AND POLITICS
Formerly a powerful Muslim sultanate that controlled Borneo and parts of the Philippines, Brunei was reduced

to its present size by the mid-19th century and became a British protectorate in 1888. In 1963 the sultanate chose to remain a British dependency rather than joining the Federation of Malaysia, and on 1 January 1984 Brunei gained full independence from Britain.

The first written constitution was promulgated in 1959, but in 1962 the legislative election was annulled after it was won by a party that sought to remove the sultan; a state of emergency was declared and the sultan has ruled by decree since. A ministerial system of government was introduced in 1984. Some political liberalisation and modernisation has taken place since 2004, when the legislature was reopened with 21 members appointed by the sultan. The constitution has been amended to allow 15 members to be elected in future but no date has been set for a legislative election.

POLITICAL SYSTEM
The 1959 constitution vests supreme executive authority in the sultan, who presides over and is advised by a privy council, a religious council and a council of cabinet ministers. The 21-member appointed legislative council was reconvened in 2004 and passed constitutional amendments that will increase its size to 45 members, one-third of whom will be directly elected. There are now three legal political groupings.

HEAD OF STATE
HM The Sultan of Brunei, Defence, Prime Minister, Finance, HM Sir Hassanal Bolkiah, GCB, *acceded* 1967, *crowned* 1 August 1968
HM Crown Prince, Senior Minister in the Prime Minister's Office, Prince Al-Muhtadee Billah

SELECTED GOVERNMENT MEMBERS *as at May 2008*
Foreign Affairs, Prince Mohamed Bolkiah
Home Affairs, Pehin Dato Adanan Yussof

BRUNEI DARUSSALAM HIGH COMMISSION
19–20 Belgrave Square, London SW1X 8PG
T 020-7581 0521 E bhcl@brunei-high-commission.co.uk
High Commissioner, HE Pengiran Dato Maidin Hashim, *apptd* 2006

BRITISH HIGH COMMISSION
PO Box 2197, Bandar Seri Begawan 8674
T (+673) (2) 222 231 E brithc@brunet.bn
W www.britishhighcommission.gov.uk/brunei
High Commissioner, John Saville, *apptd* 2005

DEFENCE
The army has 20 light tanks and 39 armoured personnel carriers. The navy has 6 patrol and coastal vessels. The air force has 5 support helicopters. There are 110 UK troops currently stationed in Brunei.
Military budget – US$355m (2007)
Military personnel – 7,000: army 4,900, navy 1,000, air force 1,100; paramilitaries 2,250

ECONOMY AND TRADE
The economy is based on the production of oil and natural gas and the income from overseas investments. Royalties and taxes from these operations form the bulk of government revenue and have enabled the construction of free health, education and welfare services. However, oil and gas reserves are declining and Brunei is diversifying its economy, developing financial services and tourism.

In 2005 agriculture accounted for 1 per cent of GDP, industry accounted for 72 per cent and services for 27 per cent. The main trading partners are other countries in the Pacific Rim region and the UK. Principal exports are crude oil, natural gas, refined products and clothing. The main imports are machinery and transport equipment, manufactured goods, foodstuffs (over 80 per cent of domestic requirements is imported) and chemicals.
GNI – US$10,287m; US$26,930m per capita (2006)
Annual average growth of GDP – 0.4 per cent (2005 est)
Inflation rate – 1.1 per cent (2005)
Unemployment – 4 per cent (2006)

BALANCE OF PAYMENTS
Trade – US$3,149m surplus (2006)
Current Account – US$6,462m surplus (2006)

Trade with UK	*2006*	*2007*
Imports from UK	£79,306,000	£866,778,981
Exports to UK	£75,319,000	£61,790,827

COMMUNICATIONS
There are five ports, at Kuala Belait, Muara and Tanjong Salirong, and terminals at Lumut and Seria. Seria is the location of one of Brunei's two airports, the other being the international airport at Bandar Seri Begawan. The 209km of waterways is navigable only by shallow craft. There is a road network of 3,650km, most of which is paved, but no railway service. The telephone system is extensive and modern. Mobile phone distribution is very high.

EDUCATION
All levels of education are free. Children undertake seven years of primary education, three of lower secondary and two years of upper secondary which can be in a secondary school, a vocational school or technical college.
Literacy rate – 92.7 per cent (2004 est)

MEDIA
The media is privately owned but very tightly controlled; laws against reporting 'false news' carry heavy punishments, and criticism of the government is therefore rare. The only broadcast media organisation, Radio Television Brunei (RTB), is state-owned and controlled. It broadcasts television in Malay and English and radio in Malay, English, Mandarin Chinese and Gurkhali. Internet access is mostly unrestricted.

BULGARIA

Republika Balgariya – Republic of Bulgaria

Area – 110,910 sq. km
Capital – Sofia; population, 1,185,000 (2007 est)
Major cities – Burgas, Plovdiv, Varna
Currency – Lev of 100 stotinki
Population – 7,322,858 falling at 0.84 per cent per year (2007 est); Bulgarian (83.9 per cent), Turkish (9.4 per cent), Romani (4.7 per cent)
Religion – Orthodox Christianity (85 per cent), Islam (13 per cent) (est)
Language – Bulgarian (official), Turkish, Romani
Population density – 71 per sq. km (2006)
Urban population – 70.5 per cent (2005 est)
Median age (years) – 40.9 (2007 est)
National anthem – 'Mila Rodino' ['Dear Native Land']
National day – 3 March (Liberation Day)
Life expectancy (years) – 72.57 (2007 est)
Mortality rate – 14.28 (2007 est)
Birth rate – 9.62 (2007 est)
Infant mortality rate – 19.16 (2007 est)
Death penalty – Abolished for all crimes (since 1998)
CPI score – 4.1 (2007)
Population below poverty line – 14.1 per cent (2003 est)

CLIMATE AND TERRAIN

The country is dominated by mountains: the Balkan Mountains cross the country from west to east, averaging 2,000m in height; and the Rhodope Mountains in the south-west climb to almost 3,000m. Elevation extremes range from 2,925m (Musala) at the highest point to 0m (Black Sea) at the lowest. The lowland plains of the north and south-east are in the basins of the main rivers: the Danube in the north, which forms much of the border with Romania, and the Maritsa, which divides the Balkan and Rhodope Mountains, and follows the Black Sea coast. The climate is transitional between that of the Mediterranean and of the southern plains of Russia. Temperatures in Sofia range from 0°C in January to 25°C in July.

HISTORY AND POLITICS

Bulgarians are descended from Slavs who came to the area of modern-day Bulgaria in the fifth century AD. The Bulgarian state can trace its foundation back to AD 680. Bulgaria was part of the Ottoman Empire from 1390 until 1877, when Turkish rule was brought to an end with the aid of Russia. A principality of Bulgaria was created by the Treaty of Berlin in 1878, and in 1908 the country was declared an independent kingdom.

Bulgaria was allied with Germany in both world wars and was occupied in 1944 by the Soviet Union. A coup d'état in September 1944 gave power to the Fatherland Front, a coalition of Communists, Agrarians and Social Democrats, which came to be dominated by the Communists. A referendum in 1946 led to the abolition of the monarchy and the establishment of a republic dominated by the Communist Party (BCP), which in 1947 resulted in a one-party state and a centralised economy. From the mid-1980s cautious reforms were introduced in line with the Soviet policies of *perestroika* and *glasnost,* and Bulgaria became a multiparty democracy in 1990. Political and economic liberalisation progressed slowly in the early 1990s, causing economic difficulties and political unrest. The political volatility had calmed by the late 1990s, when more radical economic reforms were introduced. Since then progress has been sufficient for Bulgaria to become a member of the EU in 2007.

In the 2005 general election, the Coalition for Bulgaria (led by the Bulgarian Socialist Party) won the most seats but not an outright majority. After a month of negotiation, the BSP leader Sergei Stanishev succeeded in forming a coalition government with the National Movement for Simeon II and the Turkish Movement for Rights and Freedoms. Georgi Parvanov, president since 2002, was elected to a second term of office in 2006.

POLITICAL SYSTEM

Under the 1991 constitution, the president is directly elected for a five-year term, renewable once only. The head of government is the prime minister, who is appointed by the president, and is usually the leader of the largest party in the legislature. There is a unicameral National Assembly of 240 members who are directly elected for a four-year term.

HEAD OF STATE

President, Georgi Parvanov, *elected* 18 November 2001, *re-elected* 29 October 2006
Vice-President, Angel Marin

SELECTED GOVERNMENT MEMBERS *as at May 2008*

Prime Minister, Sergey Stanishev
Deputy Prime Ministers, Emel Etem; Ivailo Kalfin *(Foreign Affairs);* Daniel Vulchev; Meglena Plougchieva
Defence, Nikolai Tsonev
Finance, Plamen Oresharski
Internal Affairs, Mihail Mikov

EMBASSY OF THE REPUBLIC OF BULGARIA
186–188 Queen's Gate, London SW7 5HL
T 0870-060 2350 E info@bulgarianembassy.org.uk
W www.bulgarianembassy.org.uk
Ambassador Extraordinary and Plenipotentiary, HE Dr Lachezar Matev, *apptd* 2005

BRITISH EMBASSY
9 Moskovska Street, Sofia 1000
T (+359) (2) 933 9222 E britembsof@mbox.cit.bg
W www.british-embassy.bg
Ambassador Extraordinary and Plenipotentiary, HE Steve Williams, *apptd* 2007

BRITISH COUNCIL
7 Krakra Street, 1504 Sofia
T (+359) 2942 4344 W www.britishcouncil.org/bulgaria
Director, Tony Buckby

DEFENCE

The army has 1,474 main battle tanks, 214 armoured infantry fighting vehicles and 2,409 armoured personnel carriers. The navy has 1 submarine, 2 frigates, 19 patrol and coastal vessels, and 6 armed helicopters. There are bases at Atya, Blachik, Vidin, Sozopol, Burgas and Varna. The air force has 80 combat aircraft and 18 armed helicopters.
Military expenditure – US$703m (2006)
Military personnel – 40,747: army 18,773, navy 4,100, air force 9,344, central staff 8,530; paramilitary 34,000
Conscription duration – 9 months

ECONOMY AND TRADE

The government adopted radical economic reforms in 1996 and the economy has achieved stability and steady growth over the past decade. This was reinforced by the imposition of a fixed exchange rate against the Deutsche Mark in 1997 (the currency is now fixed against the euro).

As a result, foreign investment has grown, although administrative corruption and organised crime remain potential deterrents. Despite economic growth and responsible fiscal management, the current account is in deficit, inflation is rising and living standards are still low.

Natural resources include copper, lead, zinc, other minerals, coal and timber. Fertile arable land produces crops that include vegetables, fruit, tobacco, wine, wheat, barley, sunflowers and livestock. About 8 per cent of the workforce is engaged in agriculture, which accounted for 8.1 per cent of GDP in 2007. Industries include energy generation, food processing, beverages, tobacco, machinery and equipment, base metals, chemicals, mining and oil refining. Tourism is growing. One of the main exports is electricity generated at the controversial Kozloduy nuclear power plant. Bulgaria has decommissioned two reactors in response to EU concerns about safety.

The main trading partners are EU countries and Turkey. Principal exports are clothing and footwear, iron and steel, machinery and equipment, and fuels. The main imports are predominantly raw materials for the industrial sector.

GNI – US$30,700m; US$3,990 per capita (2006)
Annual average growth of GDP – 6.1 per cent (2007 est)
Inflation rate – 7.8 per cent (2007 est)
Unemployment – 8 per cent (2007 est)
Total external debt – US$29,290m (2007)
Imports – US$23,000m (2006)
Exports – US$15,000m (2006)

BALANCE OF PAYMENTS
Trade – US$8,168m deficit (2006)
Current Account – US$4,940m deficit (2006)

Trade with UK	*2006*	*2007*
Imports from UK	£224,343,000	£202,236,117
Exports to UK	£197,643,000	£233,233,660

COMMUNICATIONS

The main ports are Burgas, Varna and Nesebur on the Black Sea. There are 470km of waterways, and inland ports include Vidin, Lom and Ruse on the river Danube. The main airports are at Sofia, Plovdiv, Burgas and Varna. There are 4,294km of railways and 44,033km of roads, including 333km of motorways. The telephone system is extensive but needs modernising. Mobile phone distribution is high, at 8.2 million in 2006. There were 2.4 million main lines in use in 2006, and 1.8 million internet users.

EDUCATION AND HEALTH

Education is free and compulsory for children from six to 16 years.

Literacy rate – 98.2 per cent (2004 est)
Gross enrolment ratio (percentage of relevant age group) – primary 102 per cent; secondary 105 per cent; tertiary 44 per cent (2006 est)
Health expenditure (per capita) – US$272 (2005)
Hospital beds (per 1,000 people) – 6.4 (2000–6)

MEDIA AND CULTURE

In 1996 Bulgaria gave national radio and television the status of public services and granted them independence. The first national commercial channels were launched in 2003.

Bulgaria is still a country in transition; some rural areas are virtually unchanged since the Communist era, while urban centres are now radically Western in character and outlook. Bulgaria's Roman and Byzantine ruins are culturally significant, as are its churches and monasteries. Notable Bulgarian writers include Stoyan Mikhaylovski (1856–1927) and Iordan Iovkov (1884–1938).

BURKINA FASO

Area – 274,200 sq. km
Capital – Ouagadougou; population, 1,149,000 (2007 est)
Major city – Bobo-Dioulasso
Currency – Franc CFA of 100 centimes
Population – 14,326,203 rising at 3 per cent per year (2007 est)
Religion – Islam (60 per cent), indigenous religions (24 per cent), Roman Catholicism (17 per cent) (est). Atheism is virtually non-existent
Language – French (official)
Population density – 52 per sq. km (2006)
Urban population – 18.6 per cent (2005 est)
Median age (years) – 16.5 (2007 est)
National anthem – 'Une Seule Nuit' ['One Single Night']
National day – 11 December (Republic Day)
Life expectancy – 49.21 (2007 est)
Mortality rate – 15.31 (2007 est)
Birth rate – 45.28 (2007 est)
Infant mortality rate – 89.79 (2007 est)
HIV/AIDS adult prevalence – 2 per cent (2005 est)
Death penalty – Retained, but not used
CPI score – 2.9 (2007)
Population below poverty line – 46.4 per cent (2003)

CLIMATE AND TERRAIN

Burkina Faso is a landlocked state occupying a plateau in west Africa. There are wooded savannahs in the south and the north is semi-desert. Elevation extremes range from 749m (Tena Kourou) at the highest point to 200m (Mouhoun river) at the lowest. The wet season is from June to October and the dry season from December to May; there are recurring droughts. Average temperatures range from 24°C in January to 28°C in July.

HISTORY AND POLITICS

Burkina Faso (Upper Volta until 1983) was part of the Mossi Empire in the 18th and 19th centuries. It was annexed by France in 1896 and between 1932 and 1947 was administered as part of the colony of the Ivory Coast. In 1947 its original borders were reconstituted, and in 1958 became autonomous within the French

Community; full independence was achieved on 5 August 1960.

In the three decades after independence there were several military coups, the latest of which, in 1987, brought to power Capt. Blaise Compaoré. Military rule ended in 1991 when a new constitution was adopted, and multiparty elections were held in 1992. Despite the constitutional restriction on the number of terms a president may serve, President Compaoré was re-elected for a third term in 2005. The 2007 legislative election was won by the governing Congress for Democracy and Progress (CDP) with a large overall majority.

POLITICAL SYSTEM
Under the 1991 constitution, the president is directly elected; in 2000 the presidential term was reduced from seven to five years, renewable only once. The unicameral National Assembly has 111 deputies, who are directly elected for a five-year term. Executive power is jointly vested in the president and the council of ministers, both responsible to the legislature.

HEAD OF STATE
President, Capt. Blaise Compaoré, *assumed office* 1987, *elected* 1991, *re-elected* 1998, 2005

SELECTED GOVERNMENT MEMBERS *as at May 2008*
Prime Minister, Tertius Zongo
Defence, Yero Boli
Finance, Jean-Baptiste Compaoré
Foreign Affairs, Col. Djibril Yipeme Bassole

EMBASSY OF THE REPUBLIC OF BURKINA FASO
16 Place Guy d'Arezzo, 1180 Brussels, B-1180, Belgium
T (+32) (2) 345 9912 E ambassade.burkina@skynet.be
W www.ambassadeduburkina.be
Ambassador Extraordinary and Plenipotentiary, HE Kadré Désiré Ouedraogo, *apptd* 2001

BRITISH HIGH COMMISSIONER
Dr Nicholas Westcott, CMG, *apptd* 2007, resident at Accra, Ghana

DEFENCE
The army has 13 armoured personnel carriers. The air force has 5 combat capable aircraft and 2 armed helicopters.
Military budget – US$101m (2007 est)
Military personnel – 10,800: army 6,400, air force 200, Gendarmerie 4,200; Paramilitary 250

ECONOMY AND TRADE
Despite economic reforms introduced in the 1990s and international aid, the country is very poor, with a high level of foreign debt and 46 per cent of the population below the poverty line; rising food prices sparked violent protests in spring 2008. Around 90 per cent of the population is engaged in subsistence agriculture, which is vulnerable to the harsh climatic conditions, while the economy is heavily dependent on cotton exports and therefore exposed to the vagaries of global price fluctuations. The situation in neighbouring Cote d'Ivoire continues to harm trade and industry.

Agriculture contributes 29.4 per cent of GDP; the principal cash crop apart from cotton is livestock. Although there are few natural resources, small quantities of gold are mined. The processing of cotton and other agricultural products, gold mining and manufacturing of beverages, soap, cigarettes and textiles are the main industries, contributing 19 per cent to GDP. Services account for 51.7 per cent of GDP. The main trading partners are China, Côte d'Ivoire, France and Singapore. Principal exports are cotton, livestock and gold. The chief imports are capital goods, foodstuffs and fuel.
GNI – US$6,300m; US$440 per capita (2006)
Annual average growth of GDP – 5.6 per cent (2007 est)
Inflation rate – 1.2 per cent (2007 est)
Total external debt – US$1,330m (2007)
Imports – US$1,450m (2006)
Exports – US$430m (2006)

BALANCE OF PAYMENTS
Trade – US$1,020m deficit (2006)
Current Account – US$585m deficit (2006)

Trade with UK	*2006*	*2007*
Imports from UK	£2,730,000	£3,859,104
Exports to UK	£540,000	£1,187,261

COMMUNICATIONS
There are over 30 airports and airfields; the two main airports are at Ouagadougou, which receives international flights, and Bobo Dioulasso. There are 15,272km of roads, of which 4,766km are surfaced; an estimated 60 per cent of the country's villages are further than 3km from a main road, and the predominantly unpaved roads are often impassable during the wet season. There is 622km of railway track in operation. Fixed-line telephone connections are fewer than one per 100 people; mobile phone distribution is growing rapidly, with over 1 million subscribers in 2006.

EDUCATION AND HEALTH
Literacy rate – 12.8 per cent (2004 est)
Gross enrolment ratio (percentage of relevant age group) – primary 60 per cent; secondary 15 per cent; tertiary 2 per cent (2006 est)
Health expenditure (per capita) – US$27 (2005)
Hospital beds (per 1,000 people) – 1.4 (2002)

MEDIA
Radio is the country's most popular medium. Tens of private and community radio stations and several private television channels operate alongside state-run equivalents. All media outlets are government regulated but some dissent is still expressed.

BURUNDI

République du Burundi – Republic of Burundi

Area – 27,830 sq. km
Capital – Bujumbura; population, 429,000 (2007 est)
Currency – Burundi franc of 100 centimes
Population – 8,390,505 rising at 3.59 per cent per year (2007 est); Hutu (85 per cent), Tutsi (14 per cent), Twa (1 per cent) (est)
Religion – Roman Catholicism (62 per cent), indigenous beliefs (23 per cent), Islam (10 per cent) (est). The remainder of the population belongs to other Christian denominations or has no religious affiliation
Language – Kirundi, French (both official), Swahili
Population density – 318 per sq. km (2006)
Urban population – 10.6 per cent (2005 est)
Median age (years) – 16.7 (2007 est)
National day – 1 July (Independence Day)
National anthem – 'Burundi Bwacu' ['Our Burundi']
Mortality rate – 13.17 (2007 est)
Birth rate – 41.97 (2007 est)
Infant mortality rate – 61.93 (2007 est)
Life expectancy – 51.29 (2007 est)
HIV/AIDS adult prevalence – 3.1 per cent (2005 est)
Death penalty – Retained
CPI score – 2.5 (2007)
Population below poverty line – 68 per cent (2002 est)
Literacy rate – 58.9 per cent (2004 est)
Gross enrolment ratio (percentage of relevant age group) – primary 103 per cent; secondary 14 per cent; tertiary 2 per cent (2006 est)
Health expenditure (per capita) – US$3 (2005)
Hospital beds (per 1,000 people) – 0.7 (2000–6)

CLIMATE AND TERRAIN

The landlocked country lies across the Nile–Congo watershed in central Africa. A hilly interior rises 1,500m to the country's highest point at 2,670m (Heha) and falls to a plateau in the east. The river Ruzizi forms part of the north-western border with the Democratic Republic of the Congo, along with Lake Tanganyika (the lowest elevation in the country at 772m) in the south-west. The climate is equatorial. The dry season lasts from June to September. The average daily temperature is 23°C.

HISTORY AND POLITICS

From the 16th century the area was ruled by Tutsi kings who dominated a predominantly Hutu population. Germany annexed the area in 1890 and included it in German East Africa, which after the First World War was administered by Belgium. In 1946 it was joined with Rwanda as a UN Trust Territory but broke the union when it became independent as a constitutional monarchy on 1 July 1962. The monarchy was overthrown in 1966 and the country became a republic and a one-party state.

The majority of the population remains Hutu but after independence, political and military power tended to lie with the Tutsi minority, leading to intercommunal tensions that have often resulted in ethnic conflict. The first multiparty elections in 1993 ended Tutsi political dominance with the election of a Hutu president, Melchior Ndadaye, and a Hutu majority in the legislature. Ndadaye was killed shortly afterwards in a coup by the Tutsi-dominated army; although the coup was suppressed, inter-racial fighting left more than 100,000 dead. The following year Nadadaye's successor, Cyprien Ntaryamira (also a Hutu), was killed when the plane in which he was travelling with the Rwandan president was shot down. These deaths sparked off fierce ethnic conflict which degenerated into a civil war that lasted over a decade.

Two years of talks between Burundi's many political parties resulted in a peace accord at Arusha (Tanzania) in July 2000; the accord was ratified by the transitional assembly in November. In October 2001 a transitional constitution was adopted and institutions set up; legislative elections took place in July 2005. The National Council for the Defence of Democracy–Forces for the Defence of Democracy (CNDD–FDD), a Hutu party, won a majority of seats in both chambers of the legislature. Pierre Nkurunziz of the CNDD-FDD was elected president by members of the newly elected legislature in August 2005. A government was formed of a coalition of six parties dominated by the CNDD-FDD; one party, Frodebu, withdrew in 2006.

Between 2000 and 2006, the government signed ceasefire agreements with most of the rebel groups, and in February 2007 the UN ended its peacekeeping mission and redirected its operations to helping with reconstruction. However, the ceasefire with the FLN rebel group, signed in 2006, has not held and there was fighting between the FLN and the army around the capital in spring 2008.

POLITICAL SYSTEM

Under the 2005 constitution, the executive president is directly elected for a five-year term, renewable only once; this provision will come into effect for future elections, President Nkurunziza having been elected by the legislature in 2005.

The bicameral *Parlement* comprises the National Assembly and the senate; members of both serve a five-year term. The former has 100 directly elected members, three co-opted members from the Twa ethnic group, and up to 21 members (currently 15) co-opted to ensure a 60 per cent Hutu and 40 per cent Tutsi split and that 30 per cent of the total are women. The senate has 49 members: 34 directly elected members (one Hutu and one Tutsi from each province); three co-opted Twa members; all former presidents (currently four); and enough women (currently eight) to make the number of women senators up to 30 per cent of the total. The constitution also specifies the proportion of Hutu, Tutsi and female members of the council of ministers.

HEAD OF STATE

President, Pierre Nkurunziza, *sworn in* 26 August 2005
First Vice-President, Yves Sahinguvu
Second Vice-President, Gabriel Ntisezerana

SELECTED GOVERNMENT MEMBERS *as at May 2008*

Defence, Maj.–Gen. Germain Niyoyankana
Finance, Clotilde Nizigama
Interior, Venant Kamana

EMBASSY OF THE REPUBLIC OF BURUNDI

46 Sq. Marie Louise, 1000 Brussels, Belgium
T (+32) (2) 230 4535 E ambassade.burundi@skynet.be
W www.ambassade-burundi.be
Ambassador Extraordinary and Plenipotentiary, HE Laurent Kavakure, *apptd* 2006

BRITISH AMBASSADOR

HE Nicholas Cannon, OBE, *apptd* 2008, resident at Kigali, Rwanda

DEFENCE

The army has 47 armoured personnel carriers. The air wing has 2 combat capable aircraft and 2 armed helicopters.

Military budget – US$46m (2007 est)
Military personnel – army 35,000 (including air wing 200); paramilitary 31,050

ECONOMY AND TRADE

Economic activity has increased since fighting ended, but reform and reconstruction are hampered by a lack of administrative capacity and a poorly educated workforce. At present, exports of coffee and tea account for over 90 per cent of foreign exchange earnings, leaving the economy vulnerable to the effects of global price fluctuations and weather conditions. Agriculture employed over 90 per cent of the workforce in 2002, accounting for 44.9 per cent of GDP in 2006 and producing the main exports: coffee, tea, sugar, cotton and hides. Industry is relatively small-scale and employs only 2.3 per cent of the workforce but contributes 20.9 per cent of GDP. The main activities are light manufacturing, food processing, the assembly of imported components and public sector construction. The service sector contributes 34.1 per cent of GDP and employs 4.1 per cent of the workforce. Most trade is with Switzerland, the UK, Saudi Arabia, Pakistan, Kenya and Japan, but is constrained by the poor transport infrastructure and limited connections with neighbouring countries and the coast.

GNI – US$800m; US$100 per capita (2006)
Annual average growth of GDP – 5.5 per cent (2007 est)
Inflation rate – 7 per cent (2007 est)
Total external debt – US$1,200m (2003)
Imports – US$430m (2006)
Exports – US$60m (2006)

BALANCE OF PAYMENTS
Trade – US$372m deficit (2006)
Current Account – US$132m deficit (2006)

Trade with UK	*2006*	*2007*
Imports from UK	£1,085,000	£1,121,286
Exports to UK	£688,000	£608,341

COMMUNICATIONS

There are no railways at present, but in late 2006 a feasibility study was planned into the possibility of including Burundi in a project to expand the rail network in this region of central Africa to facilitate trade. Movement is currently either by water, on Lake Tanganyika, by road or by air. Bujumbura is the only port, the location of the only airport with a surfaced runway, and the main focus of the limited road network of 12,322km, only 1,286km of which is paved. The telephone system is rudimentary and limited. Mobile phone distribution is growing but was still less than two per 100 people.

MEDIA

La Radiodiffusion et Télévision Nationale du Burundi (RTNB) is the main TV station and is government-controlled. Low literacy levels mean that the dominant news medium is radio. Radio Burundi (RTNB) broadcasts in Kirundi, Swahili, French and English and is state-controlled. There are several opposition newspapers published sporadically due to government interference.

CAMBODIA

Preahreacheanachakr Kampuchea – Kingdom of Cambodia

Area – 181,040 sq. km
Capital – Phnom Penh; population, 1,466,000 (2007 est)
Major towns – Battambang, Siem Reap, Sihanoukville
Currency – Riel of 100 sen
Population – 13,995,904 rising at 1.73 per cent per year (2007 est); Khmer (90 per cent), Vietnamese (5 per cent), Chinese (1 per cent) (est)
Religion – Buddhism (93 per cent), Islam (3 per cent), Christianity (2 per cent) (est)
Language – Khmer (official), French, English
Population density – 80 per sq. km (2006)
Urban population – 19.7 per cent (2005 est)
Median age (years) – 21.3 (2007 est)
National anthem – 'Nokoreach' ['Royal Kingdom']
National day – 9 November (Independence Day)
Life expectancy (years) – 61.29 (2007 est)
Mortality rate – 8.24 (2007 est)
Birth rate – 25.53 (2007 est)
Infant mortality rate – 58.45 (2007 est)
HIV/AIDS adult prevalence – 1.5 per cent (2005 est)
Death penalty – Abolished for all crimes (since 1989)
CPI score – 2.0 (2007)
Population below poverty line – 35 per cent (2004)
Literacy rate – 73.6 per cent (2004 est)
Gross enrolment ratio (percentage of relevant age group) – primary 122 per cent; secondary 38 per cent; tertiary 5 per cent (2006 est)
Health expenditure (per capita) – US$29 (2005)
Hospital beds (per 1,000 people) – 0.6 (2000–6)

CLIMATE AND TERRAIN

Cambodia is a mostly flat country, apart from the Cardamom Mountains in the south-west and the uplands of the north-east. Dominated by the Mekong river, Cambodia is also home to Tonle Sap, the largest lake in south-east Asia. The highest point of elevation is at 1,810m (Phnum Aoral) while the lowest is 0m (Gulf of Thailand). The monsoon season is from May to November. Temperatures range from 25°C in January to 32°C in July.

HISTORY AND POLITICS

Although the Khmer people have inhabited the region for almost 2,000 years, the Khmer kingdom was at its strongest during the 11th century, its territory covering modern-day Laos, Thailand and Vietnam. The kingdom lost power and territory from 1432 onwards.

Cambodia became a French protectorate in 1863 and part of Indochina in 1887. It became an associate state within the French Union in 1949, and gained full independence in 1953 as the Kingdom of Cambodia. From the late 1960s there was a growing insurgency led by the Khmer Rouge, and in 1970 the monarchy was overthrown in a right-wing coup and the country was renamed the Khmer Republic. Fighting throughout the country involved forces from North and South Vietnam and the USA. In 1975, Phnom Penh fell to the North Vietnamese-backed Khmer Rouge. During Khmer Rouge rule under Pol Pot (1975–8), extreme Marxist policies were brutally implemented and famine, disease and maltreatment caused the deaths of an estimated 2.5 million people. In 1978, Vietnamese troops invaded Cambodia and in 1979 established a government in Phnom Penh. Fighting continued between the Vietnamese-backed government and guerrilla resistance from the Khmer Rouge and Prince Sihanouk's nationalist forces until the Vietnamese withdrawal in 1987–9.

Under a UN peace plan agreed in 1991, multiparty elections were held in 1993, a new constitution was adopted and Prince Sihanouk was elected king. The premiership was shared between the two main parties, the Cambodian People's Party (CPP), headed by Hun Sen and other former leaders of the Vietnamese-backed regime, and Funcinpec, formed by supporters of the king and led by Prince Ranariddh. Ranariddh was ousted as co-prime minister in 1997 in an effective coup by Hun Sen, who became the sole prime minister. The CPP won the 1998, 2003 and 2008 elections but without the two-thirds majority needed to form a government on its own, and the coalition with Funcinpec has continued.

King Sihanouk abdicated in October 2004 and was succeeded by one of his sons, Prince Norodom Sihamoni.

INSURGENCIES

The Khmer Rouge was outlawed in 1994 but continued with guerrilla warfare until 1996, when it was weakened by internal divisions. Pol Pot was seized in 1997 and died in captivity in 1998. The remaining Khmer Rouge soldiers surrendered in 1999. The trials of former leaders of the Khmer Rouge regime for atrocities committed during its rule began before an international tribunal in 2007.

POLITICAL SYSTEM

Under the 1993 constitution, Cambodia is a pluralist liberal democracy with a hereditary constitutional monarchy. Executive power rests with the government, with the king having the power only to make appointments and declare a state of emergency, in consultation with the government. Legislative power is vested in the bicameral parliament, comprising the National Assembly, which has 123 members directly elected for a five-year term, and the senate, which has 57 members elected for a six-year term; and commune councils, two members appointed by the king and two appointed by the National Assembly.

HEAD OF STATE

HM The King of Cambodia, Supreme Commander of the Cambodian National Armed Forces, Norodom Sihamoni, *elected by the Council of the Throne* 29 October 2004

President of the National Assembly, Heng Samrin

SELECTED GOVERNMENT MEMBERS *as at May 2008*

Prime Minister, Hun Sen

Deputy Prime Ministers, Hor Namhong *(Foreign Affairs),* Sar Kheng *(Interior),* Gen. Tea Banh *(Defence),* Sok An; Lu Lay-sreng; Gen. Nhoek Bunchhai; Kong Sam-ol; Keo Puth Rasmey; Bin Chhin

ROYAL EMBASSY OF CAMBODIA

64 Brondesbury Park, London NW6 7AT

T 020-8451 7850 E cambodianembassy@btconnect.com

W www.cambodianembassy.org.uk

Ambassador Extraordinary and Plenipotentiary, HE Hor Nambora, *apptd* 2004

BRITISH EMBASSY

29 Street 75, Phnom Penh

T (+855) (23) 427 124 E britemb@bigpond.com.kh

W www.britishembassy.gov.uk/cambodia

Ambassador Extraordinary and Plenipotentiary, HE David Reader, *apptd* 2005

DEFENCE

The army has 150 main battle tanks, 70 armoured infantry fighting vehicles and 190 armoured personnel carriers. The navy has 10 patrol and coastal vessels with bases at Phnom Penh and Ream. The air force has 24 combat aircraft.

Military budget – US$139m (2007)

Military personnel – 124,300: army 75,000, navy 2,800, air force 1,500, provincial forces 45,000; paramilitaries 67,000

ECONOMY AND TRADE

Since the Khmer Rouge insurgency ended in 1999 the government has made progress with economic reform and development. But the country remains very poor, with 40 per cent of the population below the poverty line and an absence of basic infrastructure in rural areas. The demographic imbalance (over half the population is under 21), lack of education and lack of vocational skills also pose serious problems. Economic growth has been driven by the expansion of garment manufacturing and tourism, and the discovery of oil and gas deposits in territorial waters promises additional revenue once exploitation begins. Recent international aid has been made conditional on the government tackling the widespread corruption.

The industrial sector and tourism are growing more rapidly than the economy as a whole; the service sector contributes 43 per cent of GDP, industry 26 per cent and agriculture 31 per cent. Agriculture still employs over 75 per cent of the workforce; the main crops are rice, rubber, maize, vegetables, cashew nuts and tapioca. The main industrial activities are tourism, garment and textiles manufacturing, processing of agricultural and forestry products, fishing and mining gemstones. Exports go mostly to the USA, Hong Kong and Europe; imports come mainly from other countries in the region.

GNI – US$7,000m; US$490 per capita (2006)

Annual average growth of GDP – 8.5 per cent (2007 est)

Inflation rate – 4.4 per cent (2007 est)

Unemployment – 2.5 per cent (2000)

Total external debt – US$3,980m (2007 est)

Imports – US$1,000m (2005)

Exports – US$1,000m (2005)

BALANCE OF PAYMENTS

Trade – US$576m surplus (2006)

Current Account – US$146m deficit (2006)

Trade with UK	*2006*	*2007*
Imports from UK	£2,646,000	£2,566,655
Exports to UK	£91,805,000	£99,223,390

COMMUNICATIONS

There are 2,400km of navigable waterways, mostly on the Mekong river, and ships of up to 2,500 tons can sail as far as Phnom Penh all year round. The deep-water port at Sihanoukville (Kompong Som) on the Gulf of Thailand can receive ships of up to 10,000 tons. The port is linked to Phnom Penh by a modern highway. The main airports are at Phnom Penh, Angkor and Sihanoukville, the latter two having been upgraded to deal with the increasing tourist traffic. The country has about 38,257km of roads, although only 2,406km are surfaced and most are in a state of disrepair. There are two railway lines, one from Phnom Penh to the Thai border, the other from Phnom Penh to Kampot and Sihanoukville.

Land-line and mobile telephone systems operate in the cities and major towns, and mobile phone distribution is expanding rapidly in rural areas.

MEDIA

Much of the media is owned by political parties but the prime minister, Hun Sen, has expressed his support for press freedom. The state broadcaster is National Television of Cambodia (TVK) and there are five other major commercial and privately owned channels. There are no restrictions on the ownership and use of private satellite dishes, and foreign radio is also easily received and widely accessed.

CAMEROON

République du Cameroun – Republic of Cameroon

Area – 475,440 sq. km
Capital – Yaoundé; population, 1,611,000 (2007 est)
Major cities – Bamenda, Douala, Garoua, Maroua
Currency – Franc CFA of 100 centimes
Population – 18,060,382 rising at 2.24 per cent per year (2007 est); Cameroon Highlanders (31 per cent), Equatorial Bantu (19 per cent), Kirdi (11 per cent), Fulani (10 per cent), North-western Bantu (8 per cent), Eastern Nigritic (7 per cent) (est)
Religion – Christianity (40 per cent), indigenous religions (40 per cent), Islam (20 per cent) (est)
Language – English, French (official)
Population density – 39 per sq. km (2006)
Urban population – 52.9 per cent (2005 est)
Median age (years) – 18.9 (2007 est)
National anthem – 'Chant de Ralliement' ['Rallying Song']
National day – 20 May (Republic Day)
Life expectancy (years) – 52.86 (2007 est)
Mortality rate – 12.66 (2007 est)
Birth rate – 35.07 (2007 est)
Infant mortality rate – 65.84 (2007 est)
HIV/AIDS adult prevalence – 4.9 per cent (2005 est)
Death penalty – Retained
CPI score – 2.4 (2007)
Population below poverty line – 48 per cent (2000 est)
Literacy rate – 67.9 per cent (2004 est)
Gross enrolment ratio (percentage of relevant age group) – primary 106 per cent; secondary 41 per cent; tertiary 7 per cent (2006 est)
Health expenditure (per capita) – US$49 (2005)

CLIMATE AND TERRAIN

There are three main geographic zones: desert plains in the north (the Lake Chad basin), mountains and savannah plateau in the central region, and tropical rainforests in the south and east. Elevation extremes range from 4,095m (Mt Cameroun) at the highest point to 0m (Atlantic Ocean) at the lowest. The wet season runs from June to September in the north and from May to November in the south.

HISTORY AND POLITICS

The Bakas (Pygmies) and Bantu speakers of the Cameroonian highlands were probably the country's earliest inhabitants. Cameroon was explored by the Portuguese from 1472 and later by Spanish, Dutch and English traders. The Fulani people of the western Sahel conquered northern Cameroon between the 1770s and the early 1800s.

The German protectorate of Kamerun was established in 1884. After the First World War it was divided into the League of Nations-mandated territories (later UN trusteeships) of East (French) and West (British) Cameroon. On 1 January 1960 East Cameroon became independent as the Republic of Cameroon. This was joined on 1 October 1961 by the southern part of West Cameroon after a plebiscite held under the auspices of the UN; the northern part voted to join Nigeria. Cameroon became a federal republic with separate state governments; the federal system was abolished in 1972. From 1972 to 1992, the country was ruled by one party, the Cameroon People's Democratic Movement (RDPC), with Paul Biya as president from 1982.

Economic decline in 1990 provoked widespread civil unrest and agitation for political pluralism. In the 1992 multiparty elections, the ruling RDPC won the legislative election, and Paul Biya the presidential. The result was challenged by the opposition, which alleged vote-rigging; similar allegations have been made after all subsequent elections, to the extent that in 1997 the opposition boycotted the presidential election altogether. In 2004 Paul Biya was returned to office with 70.8 per cent of the vote. In the 2007 legislative election, the RDCP retained its overwhelming majority in the legislature, although by-elections are still awaited for 17 seats where the original results were annulled because of suspected fraud. Protests at food and fuel costs in February 2008 developed into anti-government protests that were violently suppressed.

INTERNATIONAL RELATIONS

A long-running dispute with Nigeria over the oil-rich Bakassi peninsula was referred to the international court of justice and in 2002 the court ruled in favour of Cameroon. In August 2006, the peninsula was officially handed over to Cameroon.

Cameroon joined the Commonwealth in 1995, becoming the first member that had never been entirely under British rule at any point in its history.

POLITICAL SYSTEM
The 1972 constitution was amended in 1990 to enable a return to multiparty rule. It was amended again in 1996 to extend the president's term of office and to provide for the establishment of a second legislative chamber, but this has not yet been implemented.

The president is directly elected for a seven-year term, and appoints the prime minister and cabinet; presidents were limited to serving two terms of office but this restriction was removed in 2008 to allow President Biya to stand again in 2011. The unicameral National Assembly has 180 members, directly elected for a five-year term.

President, Paul Biya, *took power* 6 November 1982, *elected* 14 January 1984, *re-elected* 1988, 1992, 1997, 2004

SELECTED GOVERNMENT MEMBERS *as at May 2008*
Prime Minister, Ephraim Inoni
Deputy Prime Ministers, Ali Amadou; Jean Nkuete
Economy, Louis Paul Motaze
Foreign Affairs, Henri Ayissi Eyebe

HIGH COMMISSION FOR THE REPUBLIC OF CAMEROON
84 Holland Park, London W11 3SB
T 020-7727 0771 E hicom@cameroonhicom.co.uk
W www.cameroonhicom.co.uk
High Commissioner, HE Samuel Libock Mbei, *apptd* 1995

BRITISH HIGH COMMISSION
PO Box 547, Avenue Winston Churchill, Yaoundé
T (+237) (2) 220 545 E bhc.yaounde@fco.gov.uk
W www.britcam.org
High Commissioner, HE Syd Maddicott, *apptd* 2006

BRITISH COUNCIL
Immeuble Christo, Avenue Charles de Gaulle, BP 818, Yaoundé
T (+237) (2) 211 696/203 172
W www.britishcouncil.org/cameroon
Director, Paul Scott

DEFENCE
The army has 22 armoured infantry fighting vehicles and 33 armoured personnel carriers. The navy has 11 patrol and coastal combatant vessels at 3 bases. The air force has 15 combat capable aircraft and 7 armed helicopters.
Military budget – US$324m (2007 est)
Military personnel – 14,100: army 12,500, navy 1,300, air force 300; paramilitary 9,000

ECONOMY AND TRADE
Cameroon's political stability and natural resources such as oil and timber have enabled agricultural, industrial and infrastructure development. But progress is hampered by a large and top-heavy public sector and endemic corruption. Recent IMF funding has been conditional on the implementation of greater transparency and privatisation.

Agriculture contributes 44.3 per cent to GDP, industry 15.9 per cent and services 39.8 per cent. About 70 per cent of the workforce is engaged in agriculture. The main industrial activity is oil production and refining. Revenue is also earned from the oil pipeline passing through the country from Chad. The main trading partners are EU countries, Nigeria, the USA, South Korea and China. Principal exports are crude oil and petroleum products, timber, cocoa, aluminium, coffee and cotton. Imports are chiefly machinery, electrical equipment, transport equipment, fuel and foodstuffs.
GNI – US$18,100m; US$990 per capita (2006)
Annual average growth of GDP – 3.2 per cent (2007 est)
Inflation rate – 2 per cent (2007 est)
Unemployment – 30 per cent (2001 est)
Total external debt – US$2,449m (2007 est)
Imports – US$3,200m (2006)
Exports – US$3,800m (2006)

BALANCE OF PAYMENTS
Trade – US$600m surplus (2006)
Current Account – US$118m surplus (2006)

Trade with UK	*2005*	*2006*
Imports from UK	£26,066,000	£22,828,000
Exports to UK	£176,431,000	£70,500,000

COMMUNICATIONS
The main seaports are at Douala and the Limboh terminal. Some inland navigation is also possible on the river Benue. There are 45 airports and airfields; of these, the main ones are at Yaoundé, Douala and Garoua. The 50,000km of roads include 5,000km of surfaced roads linking the main population centres. A rail network of 987km links the coast with the capital and the central highlands.

The telephone service is very restricted, with fewer than one fixed line per 100 people in 2005. Mobile phone distribution is growing steadily and there were 14 per 100 people in 2005.

MEDIA
The government controls the media via the state-run Cameroon Radio-Television Corporation (CRTV), which operates national television and radio networks as well as provincial stations. Newspapers are also subject to government control. The first private television station, TV Max, was launched in 2001. Dozens of private radio stations were set up following a liberalisation of telecommunications in 2000.

CANADA

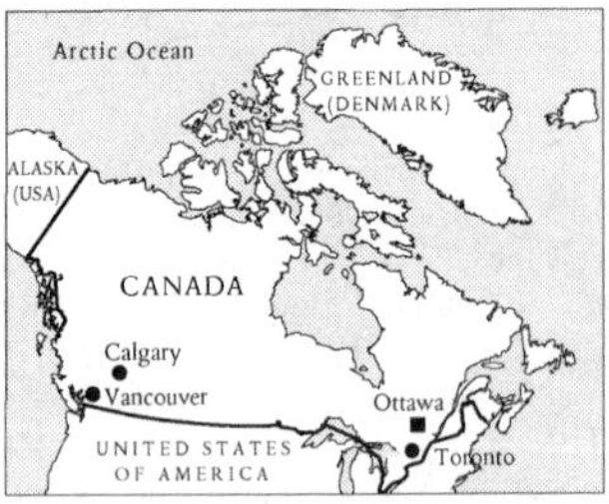

Area – 9,984,670 sq. km
Capital – Ottawa; population, 1,145,000 (2007 est)
Major cities – Calgary, Edmonton, Hamilton, Montréal, Québec, Toronto, Vancouver, Winnipeg
Currency – Canadian dollar (C$) of 100 cents
Population – 33,390,141 rising at 0.87 per cent per year (2007 est)
Religion – Roman Catholicism (44 per cent), Protestantism (29 per cent), Islam (2 per cent), Judaism (1 per cent), Buddhism (1 per cent), Hinduism (1 per cent), Sikhism (1 per cent) (est)
Language – English, French (official)

Population density – 4 per sq. km (2006)
Urban population – 81.1 per cent (2005 est)
Median age (years) – 39.1 (2007 est)
National anthem – 'O Canada'
National day – 1 July (Canada Day)
Life expectancy (years) – 80.34 (2007 est)
Mortality rate – 7.86 (2007 est)
Birth rate – 10.75 (2007 est)
Infant mortality rate – 4.63 (2007 est)
Death penalty – Abolished for all crimes (since 1998)
CPI score – 8.7 (2007)

CLIMATE AND TERRAIN

Canada occupies the entire northern part of the North American continent except for Alaska. The most southerly point is Middle Island in Lake Erie. The six main geographic divisions are: the Appalachian-Acadian region; the Canadian Shield, which comprises more than half the country; the St Lawrence-Great Lakes lowland; the interior plains; the Cordilleran region and the Arctic archipelago. Elevation extremes range from 5,959m (Mt Logan) at the highest point to 0m (Atlantic Ocean) at the lowest. The climate of the eastern and central portions presents greater extremes than in corresponding latitudes in Europe, but the climate is milder in the south-western part of the prairie region and the southern parts of the Pacific slope. The tornado season is May to September, peaking in June and early July in Ontario, Alberta, Québec, Saskatchewan and Manitoba through to Thunder Bay. The interior of British Columbia and western New Brunswick are also tornado zones.

HISTORY AND POLITICS

St John's, Newfoundland, was established as a shore base for English fisheries in 1504 and claimed for England in 1583. The French explored the St Lawrence Seaway from the 1530s, and founded Québec in 1608. The Hudson's Bay Company, founded in 1670, was significant in exploring and opening up the interior. From the 17th century the territory was a pawn in the power struggles of the main colonial powers. Britain gained large areas of the country under the treaty of Utrecht (1713), and after the Seven Years' War, the treaty of Paris (1763) awarded almost all of France's North American possessions to Britain. The American War of Independence caused many British loyalists to migrate to southern Canada, exacerbating existing tensions between British and French colonists. In the mid-19th century, Canadian territory still under Hudson's Bay Company control was brought under government control.

The British North America Act of 1867 formed a dominion under the name of Canada, comprising four provinces – Ontario, Québec, New Brunswick and Nova Scotia. To this federation the other provinces and territories were subsequently admitted: Manitoba and Northwest Territories (1870), British Columbia (1871), Prince Edward Island (1873), Yukon (1898), Alberta and Saskatchewan (1905) and Newfoundland (1949). In 1982, the constitution was patriated (severed from the British parliament).

In 1985, following French-Canadian separatist agitation, the federal prime minister and the provincial premiers concluded the Meech Lake accord which provided for Québec to be recognised as a distinct society within Canada. However, two provincial legislatures withheld approval and the accord did not come into force. A referendum in Québec calling for sovereignty and a new political and economic partnership was defeated in 1995, and support for independence has declined. In 1997, Québec was recognised as having a 'unique character' by leaders of the other provinces and territories, and in 2006 the federal parliament passed a motion recognising the Québecois as a nation within a united Canada.

An autonomous territory for the Inuit people, Nunavut ('our land'), was created by partitioning the Northwest Territories and was inaugurated on 1 April 1999.

A parliamentary vote of no confidence ended 12 years of Liberal government in 2005. A snap general election was won by the Conservative Party of Canada with 124 seats; the Liberal party won 103 seats, the Bloc Quebecois 51 seats and the New Democratic Party 29 seats. The Conservative Party formed a minority government under Stephen Harper.

POLITICAL SYSTEM

Under the 1982 constitution, the head of state is the British monarch, represented by a governor-general appointed on the advice of the Canadian prime minister.

The bicameral parliament consists of a senate and a House of Commons. The senate comprises 105 members, appointed by the governor-general on the recommendation of the prime minister, the seats being distributed between the various provinces. The House of Commons has 308 members, directly elected for a five-year term; from 2009 the term will be fixed at four years. Representation is proportional to the population of each province.

GOVERNOR-GENERAL
Governor-General, HE Michaëlle Jean

SELECTED GOVERNMENT MEMBERS *as at May 2008*
Prime Minister, Stephen Harper
Finance, James Michael Flaherty
Defence, Peter Gordon MacKay

CANADIAN HIGH COMMISSION
Macdonald House, 1 Grosvenor Square, London W1K 4AB
T 020-7258 6600 E ldn@international.gc.ca
W www.london.gc.ca
High Commissioner, HE James R. Wright, *apptd* 2006

BRITISH HIGH COMMISSION
80 Elgin Street, Ottawa, Ontario K1P 5K7
T (+1) (613) 237 1530 E bhc@fco.gov.uk
W www.britainincanada.org
High Commissioner, HE Anthony Cary, CMG, *apptd* 2007

BRITISH COUNCIL
c/o British High Commission
T (+1) (613) 364 6233/6236 W www.britishcouncil.org/canada
Director, Martin Rose

DEFENCE

The Canadian armed forces are unified and organised into three functional commands: land force command, maritime command and air command.

The army (land forces) has 86 main battle tanks and 1,321 armoured personnel carriers. The navy (maritime forces) has 4 submarines, 3 destroyers, 12 frigates and 12 patrol and coastal vessels. There are bases at Esquimalt, Halifax, Ottawa and Québec City. The air force has 107 combat aircraft.

Military expenditure – US$14,950m (2006)
Military personnel – 64,000: army 33,300, navy 11,100, air force 19,600

FEDERAL STRUCTURE

Provinces or Territories (with official contractions)	*Population (2006)*	*Capital*	*Lieutenant-Governor*	*Premier*
Alberta (AB)	3,375,763	Edmonton	Normie Kwong	Ed Stelmach
British Columbia (BC)	4,310,452	Victoria	Steven Point	Gordon Campbell
Manitoba (MB)	1,177,765	Winnipeg	John Harvard	Gary Doer
New Brunswick (NB)	749,168	Fredericton	Herménégilde Chiasson	Shawn Graham
Newfoundland and Labrador (NF)	509,677	St John's	John Crosbie	Danny Williams
Northwest Territories (NT)	41,861	Yellowknife	†Tony Whitford	Floyd Roland
Nova Scotia (NS)	934,405	Halifax	Mayann E. Francis	Rodney MacDonald
§Nunavut (NT)	30,782	Iqaluit	†Ann Meekitjuk Hanson	Paul Okalik
Ontario (ON)	12,686,952	Toronto	David Onley	Dalton McGinley
Prince Edward Island (PE)	138,519	Charlottetown	Barbara Hagerman	Robert Ghiz
Québec (QC)	7,651,531	Québec	Pierre Duchesne	Jean Charest
Saskatchewan (SK)	985,386	Regina	Gordon Barnhart	Brad Wall
Yukon Territory (YT)	31,229	Whitehorse	†Geraldine Van Bibber	Dennis Fentie

† Commissioner
§ Nunavut was created in 1999 from the Northwest Territories

ECONOMY AND TRADE

Canada has a highly developed, industrialised and diversified market economy, which developed in the second half of the 20th century when mining, manufacturing and services transformed it from a predominantly rural to an industrial economy. Abundant natural resources, a skilled workforce and modern equipment provide a solid basis for further strong growth. Tight management of government finances has resulted in balanced budgets since the late 1990s, and free-trade agreements with the USA in 1989 and 1994 have stimulated trade.

Canada's wealth of natural resources make it the world's largest exporter of timber, pulp and newsprint (nearly half the land is forested), and it is one of the world's largest exporters of minerals, particularly uranium (of which it is the world's largest single producer) and diamonds (of which it is the world's third largest producer). About 5.3 per cent of the land area is farmed, of which 4.6 per cent is under cultivation, mostly in the prairie region of western Canada. The country is one of the world's leading food producers, particularly of wheat, barley, oilseed, tobacco, fruit, vegetables and dairy products. The fishing industry is also significant but has declined in recent years because of the restrictions introduced to protect stocks after decades of overfishing. Oil, natural gas and hydroelectricity production is high enough for Canada to be a net exporter of energy. The shrinking of the Arctic ice cap is opening up access to offshore oil and gas reserves, new fishing grounds and shipping routes in the region. The government has development plans for the area but the assertion of its sovereignty has attracted criticism from other Arctic countries and is complicated by the lack of international agreement on countries' territorial claims.

In 2007, the services sector contributed 69.1 per cent of GDP, industry 28.8 per cent and agriculture 2.1 per cent. Finance and real estate generated most revenue in the services sector, and tourism is growing.

The USA is the main trading partner, taking 82 per cent of exports and providing 55 per cent of imports. The main exports are motor vehicles and parts, industrial machinery, aircraft, telecommunications equipment, chemicals, plastics, fertilisers, forestry products, energy products (including crude oil, natural gas and electricity) and aluminium.

GNI – US$1,196,600m; US$36,650 per capita (2006)
Annual average growth of GDP – 2.5 per cent (2007 est)
Inflation rate – 2.1 per cent (2007 est)
Unemployment – 6 per cent (2007 est)
Total external debt – US$758,600m (2007)
Imports – US$358,000m (2006)
Exports – US$390,000m (2006)

BALANCE OF PAYMENTS
Trade – US$31,880m surplus (2006)
Current Account – US$20,792m surplus (2006)

Trade with UK	*2006*	*2007*
Imports from UK	£3,863,464,000	£3,287,138,613
Exports to UK	£5,040,027,000	£5,867,765,994

COMMUNICATIONS

Canada has coastline on three oceans, the Atlantic, the Arctic and the Pacific. In addition, the Great Lakes/St Lawrence Seaway system, the world's longest inland waterway, provides ocean-going shipping with access to the North American interior. There are over 300 ports, the most significant of which are Vancouver and Prince Rupert on the Pacific coast and Montréal, Halifax, Port Cartier, Sept-Iles/Pointe Noire, Saint John and Québec in the east. Most deep-water ports are open all year, and Churchill, on Hudson's Bay, is ice-free for longer periods now as a result of global warming.

There are over 300 airports, of which 26 serve national and provincial capitals and other major cities. The national carriers are Air Canada and Canadian Airlines International. The 48,068km railway network transports over 270 million tonnes of freight a year; the main service providers are Canadian National Railways and Canadian Pacific Railways, which also own several US lines. There are 1.04 million km of roads. The 7,300km Trans-Canadian Highway links all ten provinces.

The telephone system has 21 million main lines in use. There were 19 million mobile phone subscribers in 2006, and 22 million internet users in 2005.

EDUCATION AND HEALTH

Education is under the control of the provincial governments, the cost of the publicly controlled schools being met by local taxation and aided by provincial grants. Education is compulsory between the ages of six and 15 or seven and 16.

Gross enrolment ratio (percentage of relevant age group) – primary 100 per cent; secondary 117 per cent; tertiary 62 per cent (2006 est)

Health expenditure (per capita) – US$3,430 (2005)
Hospital beds (per 1,000 people) – 3.6 (2000–6)

MEDIA

The public broadcaster, the Canadian Broadcasting Corporation (CBC), was established in the 1930s and transmits programmes in English and French. Société Radio Canada is the French-language public broadcast service. There are several commercial television channels. The CBC also operates four radio networks, and television channels and radio services for indigenous peoples in the north of the country. There are around 2,000 licensed radio stations. The broadcasting regulator enforces quotas of Canadian material (30–35 per cent) on Canadian radio and television.

CULTURE

Canadian culture was originally influenced by the British and French heritage of its settlers, but is now dominated by the neighbouring USA. Canada has produced a long list of actors, directors and comedians who have achieved success in film and television, including Jim Carrey (*b.* 1962), David Cronenberg (*b.* 1943), Mike Myers (*b.* 1963) and the Sutherlands, Donald (*b.* 1935) and Kiefer (*b.* 1966).

The country is also one of the world's largest exporters of popular music. Leonard Cohen (*b.* 1934), Joni Mitchell (*b.* 1943), Neil Young (*b.* 1945), and Céline Dion (*b.* 1968) are all internationally successful, while the Montreal International Jazz Festival is the largest of its kind in the world. Among Canada's many award-winning writers are Nobel laureate Saul Bellow (1915–2005), the Booker prize winner Margaret Atwood (*b.* 1939) and Carol Shields (1935–2003), who won the Pulitzer.

CAPE VERDE

Republica de Cabo Verde – Republic of Cape Verde

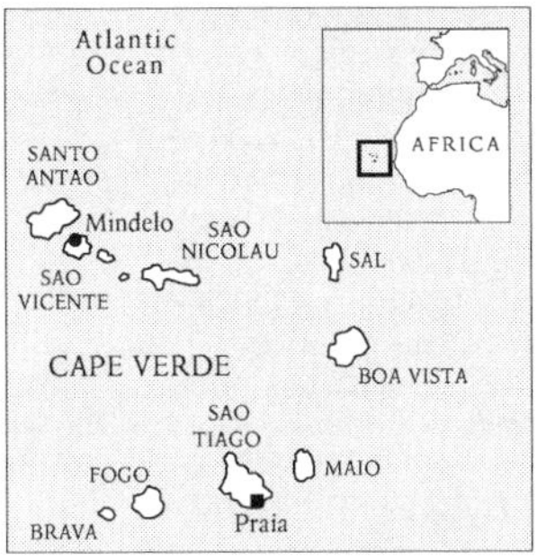

Area – 4,033 sq. km. Comprises the Windward Islands (Santo Antao, Sao Vicente, Santa Luzia, Sao Nicolau, Boa Vista and Sal) and Leeward Islands (Maio, Sao Tiago, Fogo and Brava)
Capital – Praia, on Sao Tiago; population, 125,000 (2007)
Major town – Mindelo
Currency – Escudo Caboverdiano of 100 centavos
Population – 423,613 rising at 0.61 per cent per year (2007 est)
Religion – Roman Catholicism (85 per cent) (est). Less than 1 per cent is atheist
Language – Creole (official), Portuguese, French
Population density – 129 per sq. km (2006)
Urban population – 57.6 per cent (2005 est)
Median age (years) – 20.2 (2007 est)
National anthem – 'Cantico da Liberdade' ['Song of Liberty']
National day – 5 July (Independence Day)
Life expectancy – 71.02 (2007 est)
Mortality rate – 6.5 (2007 est)
Birth rate – 24.4 (2007 est)
Infant mortality rate – 45.27 (2007 est)
Death penalty – Abolished for all crimes (since 1981)
CPI score – 4.9 (2007)
Population living below poverty line – 30 per cent (2000)
Literacy rate – 75.7 per cent (2004)

CLIMATE AND TERRAIN

The republic consists of a group of islands of volcanic origin lying 600km off the west African coast. Elevation extremes range from 2,829m (Mt Fogo) at the highest point to 0m (Atlantic Ocean) at the lowest. The climate is hot and dry.

HISTORY AND POLITICS

The islands were uninhabited when they were first discovered and colonised *c.*1460 by Portugal. Administered with Portuguese Guinea until 1879, they became an overseas province in 1951. The country achieved independence on 5 July 1975 after a campaign by the African Party for the Independence of Guinea Bissau and Cape Verde (PAIGC).

The republic was a one-party state under the African Party for the Independence of Cape Verde (PAICV) until 1990. Multiparty elections in 1991 were won by the opposition Movement for Democracy (MPD), and the MPD candidate Antonio Mascarenhas Monteiro was elected president. The MPD and President Monteiro served two terms until the 2001 legislative elections returned the PAICV to power, and its candidate, Pedro Pires, narrowly won the second round of the presidential election. In the 2006 elections, the PAICV retained its overall majority in the national assembly with 41 seats, and President Pires was re-elected with 51 per cent of the vote.

POLITICAL SYSTEM

Under the 1992 constitution, the president is directly elected for a five-year term. There is a unicameral National Assembly with 72 members directly elected for a five-year term. The prime minister appoints the council of ministers.

HEAD OF STATE
President, Pedro Pires, *elected* 25 February 2001, *re-elected* 12 February 2006

SELECTED GOVERNMENT MEMBERS *as at May 2008*
Prime Minister, Jose Maria Neves
Economy, Joao Pereira Silva
Finance and Planning, Cristina Duarte
Foreign Affairs, Victor Borges
Defence, Christina Fontes Lima

EMBASSY OF THE REPUBLIC OF CAPE VERDE
Avenue Jeane 29, 1050 Brussels, Belgium
T (+32) (2) 643 6270
Ambassador Extraordinary and Plenipotentiary, HE Fernando Jorge Wahnon Ferreira, *apptd* 2007

BRITISH AMBASSADOR
HE Christopher Trott, *apptd* 2007, resident at Dakar, Senegal

DEFENCE

The coast guard has 2 patrol and coastal combatant vessels.
Military budget – US$8.1m (2007 est)
Military personnel – 1,200: army 1,000, coast guard 100, air force 100

ECONOMY AND TRADE

The islands have few natural resources, little fresh water and are subject to periods of prolonged drought. The economy is dependent on foreign aid; reforms are intended to attract foreign investment to finance diversification and develop the private sector. The expatriate population is larger than the resident one and remittances are equivalent to over 20 per cent of GDP. The service sector dominates, with commerce, tourism, transport and public services accounting for 73.9 per cent of GDP in 2007. Industry contributed 16.9 per cent and agriculture 9.3 per cent; fishing resources are not fully exploited.

The main industries are the production of food, beverages, garments and footwear, fishing and fish processing, salt mining and ship repair. The main trading partners are Portugal, Spain and other EU and African countries. Exports are footwear, garments, fish and hides. Imports include foodstuffs (over 80 per cent of food is imported), industrial products, transport equipment and fuels.
GNI – US$1,105m; US$2,130 per capita (2006)
Annual average growth of GDP – 7 per cent (2007 est)
Inflation rate – 3 per cent (2007 est)
Unemployment – 21 per cent (2000 est)
Total external debt – US$325m (2002)
Imports – US$540m (2006)
Exports – US$20m (2006)

BALANCE OF PAYMENTS
Trade – US$522m deficit (2006)
Current Account – US$60m deficit (2006)

Trade with UK	*2005*	*2006*
Imports from UK	£4,345,000	£4,121,000
Exports to UK	£538,000	£635,000

COMMUNICATIONS

The main ports are Praia, Mindelo and Tarrafal. Ferry services operate between the islands. There are eight operational airports, including international airports at Praia and on Sal, and regular internal flights between the islands. The national carrier, Cape Verde Airlines, is being privatised. The islands have no railways. There are over 5,000km of roads; most of these are paved with cobbles but a programme to resurface the roads with asphalt began in 2007.

Since privatisation in 1995 the telephone system has been modernised and extends to all the islands. Mobile phone services were introduced in 1998 and there were 108,900 subscribers in 2006.

MEDIA

Freedom of the media is guaranteed in the constitution and this is generally upheld. There is a growing private sector in both print and broadcast journalism, but the majority of the media is state-run. Portuguese African services and Radio France Internationale are both available, as are a range of Portuguese and Brazilian newspapers.

CENTRAL AFRICAN REPUBLIC

République Centrafricaine – Central African Republic

Area – 622,984 sq. km
Capital – Bangui; population, 672,000 (2007 est)
Major cities – Berbérati, Bimbo
Currency – Franc CFA of 100 centimes
Population – 4,369,038 rising at 1.51 per cent per year (2007 est); Baya (33 per cent), Banda (27 per cent), Mandjia (13 per cent), Sara (10 per cent), Mboum (7 per ent), M'Baka (4 per cent), Yakoma (4 per cent) (est)
Religion – Christianity (80 per cent), Islam (10 per cent) (est). Some also practise animism, although these beliefs are often integrated into Christian and Muslim worship
Language – French (official), Sangho
Population density – 7 per sq. km (2006)
Urban population – 43.8 per cent (2005 est)
Median age (years) – 18.5 (2007 est)
National anthem – 'La Renaissance' ['The Revival']
National day – 1 December (Republic Day)
Life expectancy – 43.74 (2007 est)
Mortality rate – 18.46 (2007 est)
Birth rate – 33.52 (2007 est)
Infant mortality rate – 83.97 (2007 est)
HIV/AIDS adult prevalence – 10 per cent (2005 est)
Death penalty – Abolitionist in practice
CPI score – 2.0 (2007)
Literacy rate – 48.6 per cent (2004 est)
Gross enrolment ratio (percentage of relevant age group) – primary 61 per cent; tertiary 1 per cent (2006 est)
Health expenditure (per capita) – US$13 (2005)

CLIMATE AND TERRAIN

This landlocked central African state lies on a plateau between the Chad and Congo river basins, with hills in the north-east and the west. The main river is the Oubangui, which is the lowest point of elevation (335m). The highest is Mount Ngaoui (1,420m). The climate is tropical with a wet season in the north from June to September and in the south from May to October. The north can reach a temperature of 40°C between February and May and the humidity can be extreme. The south has a more equatorial climate.

HISTORY AND POLITICS

The area was annexed by France in the 1880s and the colony of Ubanghi Chari became part of French

Equatorial Africa. In 1958 it elected to remain within the French Community and adopted the title of the Central African Republic. The country became fully independent on 17 August 1960. Since independence it has been politically unstable, experiencing several coups. Jean-Bedel Bokassa, who took power in 1966, proclaimed himself emperor in 1976 and renamed the country the Central African Empire. In 1979 Bokassa was deposed in a bloodless coup and the country reverted to a republic. Gen. André Kolingba seized power in 1981 and instituted military rule until 1985, when a civilian-dominated cabinet was appointed. The country was a one-party state from 1986 until 1993, when political pluralism and a civilian government were restored. The government was overthrown in a 2003 coup led led by Gen. François Bozizé, who declared himself president and appointed a transitional government until elections were held in 2005.

There has been an insurgency in the north since 2003, causing thousands to seek refuge from the violence in Chad and Cameroon. The government signed a peace accord with one rebel group in February 2007, but the north is unstable and not fully under government control.

In the 2005 elections, Gen. Bozizé was elected president in the second round of voting. The National Convergence–Kwa Na Kwa, which supports the president, won most seats in the legislature and became the main party in a coalition government that included seven parties and a number of independents.

POLITICAL SYSTEM
Under the 2004 constitution, the president is elected for a five-year term, renewable only once. There is a unicameral National Assembly, which has 105 members, directly elected for a five-year term. The prime minister is appointed by the president and appoints the ministers.

HEAD OF STATE
President, Defence, Gen. François Bozizé, *took power* 15 March 2003

SELECTED GOVERNMENT MEMBERS *as at May 2008*
Prime Minister, Finance and Budget, Faustin Archange Touadera
Foreign Affairs, Dieudonné Kombo Yaya
Interior, Gen. Raymond Paul Ndougou

EMBASSY OF THE CENTRAL AFRICAN REPUBLIC
30 rue des Perchamps, 75016, Paris
T (+33) (1) 4224 4256
Ambassador Extraordinary and Plenipotentiary, vacant

BRITISH AMBASSADOR
HE Syd Maddicott, *apptd* 2006, resident at Yaoundé, Cameroon

DEFENCE
The army has 3 main battle tanks, 39 armoured personnel carriers and 9 patrol and coastal combatant vessels.
Military budget – US$18m (2007 est)
Military personnel – 3,150: army 2,000, air force 150, Gendarmerie 1,000
Conscription duration – 24 months

ECONOMY AND TRADE
The economy is largely undeveloped owing to decades of instability and misrule. Development is still hindered by political factionalism, a landlocked location, poor transport infrastructure, an unskilled workforce and corruption. The country is dependent on international aid. Natural resources include diamonds, gold, uranium, timber and oil; diamond and gold mining and forestry are among the main industrial activities but the economy still rests on agriculture, which accounts for over 50 per cent of GDP. Most production is at subsistence level but cotton, coffee and tobacco form the main exports along with diamonds and timber. The main imports are food, textiles, fuels and machinery. Trade is mainly with EU countries, the USA, Cameroon and Indonesia.
GNI – US$1,500m; US$350 per capita (2006)
Annual average growth of GDP – 4 per cent (2007 est)
Inflation rate – 4 per cent (2007 est)
Unemployment – 8 per cent (2001 est)
Total external debt – US$1,153m (2007 est)
Imports – US$210m (2006)
Exports – US$120m (2006)

BALANCE OF PAYMENTS
Trade – US$90m deficit (2006)
Current Account – US$40m deficit (2006)

Trade with UK	*2005*	*2006*
Imports from UK	£508,000	£626,000
Exports to UK	£161,000	£100,000

COMMUNICATIONS
The infrastructure is poor, with no railway system and little of the 23,810km road network is surfaced, making many roads unusable in the wet season. There are 2,800km of waterways, mostly on the Oubangui and Sangha rivers, which are navigable all year and are used for passenger and freight transport. The principal airport is at Bangui, and there are about 50 other airports and airfields. The telephone system had 12,000 main lines in use in 2006. Mobile phone distribution is much more widespread, at 100,000 in 2006.

MEDIA
The most balanced media output is from the UN-sponsored radio broadcaster Radio Ndeke Luka. The other radio and television stations are operated by the state via Télévision Centrafricaine (TVCA). There are a number of privately owned newspapers but relatively low literacy levels mean that they have little influence. Legislation passed in 2004 abolished prison terms for press offences.

CHAD

République du Tchad – Republic of Chad

Area – 1,284,000 sq. km
Capital – N'Djaména; population, 989,000 (2007 est)
Major cities – Abéché, Moundou, Sarh
Currency – Franc CFA of 100 centimes
Population – 9,885,661 rising at 2.32 per cent per year (2007 est)
Religion – Islam (54 per cent), Christianity (33 per cent) (est). Most Muslims adhere to a moderate branch of mystical Islam known locally as Tijaniyah (Sufism), which incorporates some indigenous religious elements
Language – French, Arabic (official), Sara
Population density – 8 per sq. km (2006)
Urban population – 25.8 per cent (2005 est)
Median age (years) – 16.3 (2007 est)
National anthem – 'La' Tchadienne'
National day – 11 August (Independence Day)
Life expectancy– 47.2 (2007 est)
Mortality rate – 16.69 (2007 est)
Birth rate – 42.35 (2007 est)
Infant mortality rate – 102.07 (2007 est)
HIV/AIDS adult prevalence – 3.1 per cent (2005 est)
Death penalty – Retained
CPI score – 1.8 (2007)
Population living below poverty line – 80 per cent (2001 est)
Literacy rate – 25.5 per cent (2004 est)
Gross enrolment ratio (percentage of relevant age group) – primary 76 per cent; secondary 15 per cent; tertiary 1 per cent (2006 est)
Health expenditure (per capita) – US$22 (2005)
Hospital beds (per 1,000 people) – 0.4 (2000–6)

CLIMATE AND TERRAIN

The population of this landlocked country is concentrated in the fertile lowlands of the south, away from the arid central and northern desert areas. The highest point of elevation is 3,415m (Emi Koussi) and the lowest is at 160m (the Djourab depression). The north is almost rainless, the south is tropical and the central plain is hot and dry with a wet season from June to September.

HISTORY AND POLITICS

Chad was colonised by France from the 1890s and became part of French Equatorial Africa. It became self-governing after the Second World War and fully independent on 11 August 1960. Since independence the country has been politically unstable due to tension between the Muslim Arab north and the Christian and animist African south; different factions have attracted support from Libya and France. After a number of coups in the 1960s and 1970s, fighting led to civil war. In 1982 French-supported rebels captured the capital and formed a government under Hissène Habré, but fighting with Libyan-backed factions continued until a ceasefire was agreed in 1987 by all three countries. Habré was deposed in 1990 in a Libyan-backed coup led by Idriss Déby. Under Déby, there has been a gradual move towards democracy. A new constitution establishing a unified, democratic state was introduced in 1996, but despite a decade of greater political stability, violence continues, with insurgencies and refugee problems. Déby's regime was nearly overthrown by rebels in 2006, and again in 2008.

Déby won the first multiparty presidential election in 1996 and was re-elected in 2001 and 2006, despite doubts over the integrity of the polls. The 2002 legislative election was won by Déby's Patriotic Salvation Movement (MPS). The election due in April 2006 was postponed until 2007, and then, after negotiations with the main opposition parties, until 2009.

INSURGENCIES

There are armed insurgencies in the north and in the east, although one rebel group, the United Front for Change, signed a peace agreement with the government in December 2006. The east of the country has also been destabilised by the overspill of fighting from Sudan's Darfur region, with incursions by militias to attack the estimated 200,000 Sudanese refugees taking shelter in Chad. States of emergency were declared in the north and east in October 2007, and the UN and EU have authorised the deployment of a joint peacekeeping force to protect refugees from Darfur.

POLITICAL SYSTEM

The 1996 constitution was amended in 2005 to remove the limit on the number of terms a president may serve. The president is directly elected for a five-year term. The unicameral National Assembly of 155 members is directly elected for a four-year term. The prime minister is appointed by the president.

HEAD OF STATE

President, Idriss Déby, *took power* December 1990, *elected* 3 July 1996, *re-elected* 2001, 2006

SELECTED GOVERNMENT MEMBERS *as at May 2008*

Prime Minister, Youssouf Saleh Abbas
Economy, Ousmane Matar Breme
Finance, Abakar Mallah Mourcha
Foreign Affairs, Moussa Faki Mahamat
Interior, Ahmat Mahamat Bachir
Defence, Gen. Kamougue Wadal Abdelkader

EMBASSY OF THE REPUBLIC OF CHAD

Boulevard Lambermont 52, 1030 Brussels, Belgium
T (+32) (2) 215 1975 E ambassade.tchad@chello.be

Ambassador Extraordinary and Plenipotentiary, HE Ahmat Abderaman Hagger, *apptd* 2006

BRITISH AMBASSADOR

HE Syd Maddicott, *apptd* 2006, resident at Yaoundé, Cameroon

DEFENCE

The army has 60 main battle tanks, 9 armoured infantry fighting vehicles and 20 armoured infantry fighting vehicles. The air force has 4 combat capable aircraft and 2 armed helicopters.
Military budget – US$72m (2007 est)
Military personnel – 25,350: army 17,000–20,000, air force 350, Republican Guard 5,000; paramilitary 9,500

ECONOMY AND TRADE

Economic development has been limited by political instability, a landlocked location and poor transport infrastructure. About 80 per cent of the workforce is occupied in subsistence agriculture, herding and fishing, which contribute about 22 per cent of GDP. The main development, funded by foreign investment and international aid, is the exploitation of oil deposits in the Doba basin in the south, which came into production in 2003; the oil is exported via a pipeline through Cameroon. The use of the oil revenue is subject to restrictions imposed by the World Bank. The government's failure to comply with these led the World Bank to freeze the account and suspend loans in 2006; the government is now close to insolvency.

Chad's main trading partners are the USA, France, Cameroon and China. Principal exports are oil, cattle, cotton and gum arabic. The main imports are machinery and transport equipment, industrial goods, food and textiles.

GNI – US$4,700m; US$450 per capita (2006)
Annual average growth of GDP – –1.3 per cent (2007 est)
Inflation rate – 4 per cent (2007 est)
Total external debt – US$1,600m (2005 est)
Imports – US$1,200m (2006)
Exports – US$3,750m (2006)

BALANCE OF PAYMENTS
Trade – US$2,550m surplus (2006)
Current Account – US$600m deficit (2006)

Trade with UK	*2006*	*2007*
Imports from UK	£3,063,000	£5,981,268
Exports to UK	£243,000	£868,937

COMMUNICATIONS

There are over 4,000km of waterways, although only 2,000km is navigable all year round. Of the 33,400km of roads, only 267km are surfaced, so many are unusable in the wet season. The principal airport is at N'Djaména and there are 50 other airports and airfields. There are no railways. The telephone system is primitive; mobile phone distribution is growing rapidly.

MEDIA

Low levels of literacy make radio the most important news medium. Radiodiffusion Nationale Tchadienne is the state-controlled radio station. There are private radio stations but they are closely monitored by the government. There is only one television station, Télétchad, and it is state-owned and controlled. Privately owned opposition newspapers circulate in the capital.

CHILE

República de Chile – Republic of Chile

Area – 756,950 sq. km
Capital – Santiago; population, 5,720,000 (2007 est)
Major cities – Antofagasta, Puente Alto, San Bernado, Temuco, Valparaíso, Viña del Mar
Currency – Chilean peso of 100 centavos
Population – 16,284,741 rising at 0.92 per cent per year (2007 est)
Religion – Roman Catholicism (70 per cent), other Christian denominations (16 per cent) (est). An estimated 8 per cent of the population is atheist
Language – Spanish (official)
Population density – 22 per sq. km (2006)
Urban population – 87.7 per cent (2005 est)
Median age (years) – 30.7 (2007 est)
National anthem – 'Himno Nacional de Chile' ['National Anthem of Chile']
National day – 18 September (Independence Day)
Life expectancy (years) – 76.96 (2007 est)
Mortality rate – 5.87 (2007 est)
Birth rate – 15.03 (2006 est)
Infant mortality rate – 8.36 (2007 est)
Death penalty – Retained for certain crimes
CPI score – 7.0 (2007)
Population living below poverty line – 18.2 per cent (2005)

CLIMATE AND TERRAIN

Chile lies between the shores of the South Pacific Ocean and the Andes (1,524m to 4,572m above sea level), extending 4,480km, from the arid north around Arica to Cape Horn; the average breadth, north of 41°, is 160km. The Atacama desert lies in the north. In the central zone there is a fertile valley between the Andes and the low coastal range of mountains, with a Mediterranean climate. The south is cool, with high rainfall. Elevation extremes range from 6,880m (Nevado Ojos del Salado) at the highest point to 0m (Pacific Ocean) at the lowest.

HISTORY AND POLITICS

Chile was discovered by Spanish adventurers in the 16th century and remained under Spanish rule until 1810, when the first autonomous government was established. Full independence was consolidated in 1818 after a revolutionary war.

A military coup in 1973 overthrew the Marxist president Salvador Allende. General Augusto Pinochet, who led the coup, assumed the presidency and retained the office until elections were held in 1989, beginning the transition to full democracy. Between 1998 and his death in 2006, a number of unsuccessful attempts were made to bring Gen. Pinochet to trial for human rights atrocities committed during his time in office.

In the 2005 legislative elections, the ruling Coalition of Parties for Democracy (CPD) won an overall majority in the both chambers of the legislature, although the CPD lost control of the upper house in early 2008 after several senators defected. The CPD candidate, Michelle Bachelet, became the country's first female president in 2006 after winning the second round of the presidential election.

POLITICAL SYSTEM

The 1981 constitution was amended in 1989 and 2005. The executive president is directly elected for a four-year term that is not renewable. The bicameral National Congress, comprises a senate of 38 members elected for an eight-year term (half renewed every four years) and a Chamber of Deputies of 118 members directly elected for a four-year term.

HEAD OF STATE
President, Michelle Bachelet, *elected* 15 January 2006, *sworn in* 11 March 2006

SELECTED GOVERNMENT MEMBERS *as at May 2008*
Defence, José Goñi Carrasco
Economy, Hugo Lavados
Finance, Andrés Velasco
Foreign Affairs, Alejandro Foxley
Interior, Edmundo Perez Yoma

EMBASSY OF CHILE
12 Devonshire Street, London W1G 7DS
T 020-7580 6392 E embachile@embachile.co.uk
Ambassador Extraordinary and Plenipotentiary, HE Rafael Moreno, *apptd* 2006

BRITISH EMBASSY
PO Box 72-D, Av. El Bosque Norte 0125, Santiago 9
T (+56) (2) 370 4100 E chancery.santiago@fco.gov.uk
W www.britemb.cl
Ambassador Extraordinary and Plenipotentiary, HE Howard Drake, *apptd* 2005

BRITISH COUNCIL
Eliodoro Yáñez 832, 750-0651 Providencia, Santiago
T (+56) (2) 410 6900 W www.britishcouncil.cl
Director, Sarah Barton

DEFENCE

The army has 375 main battle tanks, 139 armoured infantry fighting vehicles and 648 armoured personnel carriers. The navy has 4 submarines, 8 frigates, 38 patrol and coastal vessels and 18 combat aircraft. There are bases at Valparaíso, Talcahuano, Puerto Montt, Puerto Williams, Iquique and Punta Arenas. The marines have 8 light tanks and 25 armoured personnel carriers. The air force has 74 combat aircraft.
Military expenditure – US$4,670m (2006)
Military personnel – 64,966: army 36,016, navy 20,450, air force 8,500; paramilitary 38,000

ECONOMY AND TRADE

Economic reforms in the late 1970s and the 1980s and sound management of government finances and financial institutions have made Chile one of the most successful economies in Latin America. GDP growth is based on high copper prices, a strong export base and growing domestic demand, but wealth distribution is uneven and tackling poverty is a priority of President Bachelet.

Chile is the world's largest producer of copper, and the world's only commercial producer of nitrate of soda (Chile saltpetre) from natural resources. The chief industries are mining, forestry, fishing, food and fish processing, and wine-making. Agriculture, which contributes 4.9 per cent of GDP, produces fruit, vegetables, cereals, meat and wool.

The main trading partners are the USA, China, Brazil, Argentina, Japan, South Korea and the EU. Principal exports are copper, fruit, fish products, paper and pulp, chemicals and wine. The main imports are petrol and petroleum products, chemicals, electrical and telecommunications equipment, industrial machinery, vehicles and natural gas.
GNI – US$111,900m; US$6,810 per capita (2006)
Annual average growth of GDP – 5.2 per cent (2007 est)
Inflation rate – 6.5 per cent (2007 est)
Unemployment – 7 per cent (2007 est)
Total external debt – US$49,180m (2007)
Imports – US$38,400m (2006)
Exports – US$58,100m (2006)

BALANCE OF PAYMENTS
Trade – US$19,707m surplus (2006)
Current Account – US$5,256m surplus (2006)

Trade with UK	*2006*	*2007*
Imports from UK	£186,624,000	£182,397,199
Exports to UK	£530,386,000	£496,122,179

COMMUNICATIONS

The main ports are Valparaíso, Antofagasta, Arica, Iquique and Punta Arenas. There is a 6,585km railway system, but lines in some areas are not in use as rail travel is increasingly superseded by road and air travel. Services are run by a state-owned company. The road network is about 80,000km in length, of which 16,000km is surfaced. There are over 300 airports and airfields; the principal airport is at Santiago. The national air carrier is LAN Airlines, with Sky Airline and Aerolíneas del Sur also providing domestic flights. Mobile phone distribution is growing rapidly, reaching 75 per 100 people in 2006, and fixed-line connections are decreasing as a result.

EDUCATION AND HEALTH

Education is free and compulsory for 12 years, although the education system has suffered from years of under-investment and mismanagement. Following student demonstrations and strikes in 2006, the government announced plans to reorganise and make further investments in education infrastructure.
Literacy rate – 95.7 per cent (2004 est)
Gross enrolment ratio (percentage of relevant age group) – primary 104 per cent; secondary 91 per cent; tertiary 48 per cent (2006 est)
Health expenditure (per capita) – US$397 (2005)
Hospital beds (per 1,000 people) – 2.4 (2000–6)

MEDIA AND CULTURE

Television is a combination of national and local, private and state-run, cable and terrestrial channels. Radio is the country's most important news medium, with 800 stations country-wide. Chile has a good record for press freedom and 2001 legislation abolished several media restrictions remaining from the Pinochet era.

Chile has a vibrant arts culture and is considered the most European of the Latin American countries. Chilean Nobel Prize winners for literature include the writers Gabriela Mistral (1889–1957) in 1945, and poet Pablo Neruda (1904–73) in 1971.

Chile's island possessions include the Juan Fernández group about 576km from Valparaíso; one of these islands is the reputed scene of Alexander Selkirk's shipwreck (the inspiration for Daniel Defoe's novel *Robinson Crusoe*). Easter Island, about 3,200km away in the South Pacific Ocean, contains stone platforms and hundreds of mysterious stone figures, *moai,* thought to be carved from volcanic ash by Polynesian colonisers between 1100 and 1600.

CHILEAN ANTARCTIC TERRITORY

The Chilean Antarctic Territory covers the Antarctic peninsula and an area of the landmass that extends from 53°W to 90°W along a latitude of 60°S. This area is also claimed by the UK and Argentina, although the Antarctic treaty has frozen all disputes over territory. (*See also* The North and South Poles.)

CHINA

Zhonghua Renmin Gongheguo – People's Republic of China

Area – 9,596,960 sq. km
Capital – Beijing; population, 11,106,000 (2007 est)
Major cities – Changchun, Chengdu, Chongqing, Guangzhou, Harbin, Nanjing, Shanghai, Shenyang, Tianjin, Wuhan, Xi'an
Currency – Renminbi yuan of 10 jiao or 100 fen
Population – 1,321,851,888 rising at 0.61 per cent per year (2007 est); Han Chinese (91.9 per cent) (est). The remainder of the population belongs to around 55 ethnic minorities
Religion – Buddhism (8 per cent), Christianity (3 per cent), Islam (1 per cent) (est). Most of the country's population does not subscribe to any religious faith
Language – Mandarin (official), Cantonese, Fuzhou, Xiang, Gan, Taiwanese
Population density – 141 per sq. km (2006)
Urban population – 40.5 per cent (2005 est)
Median age (years) – 33.2 (2007 est)
National anthem – 'Yiyongjun Jinxingqu' ['The March of the Volunteers']
National day – 1 October (Founding of People's Republic)
Life expectancy (years) – 72.88 (2007 est)
Mortality rate – 7 (2007 est)
Birth rate – 13.45 (2007 est)
Infant mortality rate – 22.12 (2007 est)
Death penalty – Retained
CPI score – 3.5 (2007)
Population below poverty line – 10 per cent (2004 est)

CLIMATE AND TERRAIN

China is twice the size of western Europe and contains a vast range of landscapes and climates. Two-thirds of the country is hilly or mountainous. The highest mountains are on the Tibetan plateau, in the west of the country, where the highest elevation is 8,850m (Mt Everest). To the north of the Tibetan plateau, the land drops to the arid, semi-desert steppes bisected by the Tian Shan mountains; the country's lowest elevation is −154m at Turpan Pendi. The southern plains and east coast have the most fertile land, irrigated by the Huang He (Yellow), Chang Jiang (Yangtze) and Xi Jiang (West) rivers, and therefore are the most heavily populated areas.

There are seven climate zones. The north-east has cold winters, fierce winds, hot and humid summers and erratic rainfall. The south-west has mild winters and warm summers. Inner Mongolia has cold winters and hot summers. Central China has hot and humid summers with the occasional tropical cyclone. South China is partly tropical with heavy rainfall. Xizang is a high plateau surrounded by mountains that is subject to harsh winters. Xinjiang and the west have a desert climate, cold winters and year-round rain.

HISTORY AND POLITICS

China was ruled by imperial dynasties from the second millennium BC. The last emperor of the Qing dynasty abdicated in 1912 after a revolution broke out in 1911. Central authority collapsed, leading to a period of chaos and regional warlord domination as neither the Guomindang, led by Sun Yat-sen, nor the Chinese Communist Party (CCP), founded in 1921, were able to unify China. The conflict between them also hindered their individual and joint efforts to resist Japanese encroachment; Japan occupied Manchuria in 1932, and most northern and coastal areas of China by 1939. Japan's occupation was ended by its defeat by the Allies in 1945. Despite Allied support after 1941 for the Guomindang, now led by Chiang Kai-shek, the Communists established control over large areas of China in the early 1940s, seizing the territory abandoned by Japan in 1945. Following a civil war (1946–9) the successful CCP inaugurated the People's Republic of China (PRC), and the Guomindang went into exile in Taiwan. The USA continued to recognise the Chiang Kai-shek regime as the rightful government of China until 1971, when the PRC took over China's membership of the UN from Taiwan.

Under Mao Zedong, China was ruled on the basis of four 'cardinal principles': Marxist-Leninist-Maoist thought, the Socialist Road, the dictatorship of the proletariat, and the leadership of the CCP. Mao's 'Great Leap Forward' (1958–61) was an attempt to industrialise rural areas that resulted in a famine in which 30–40 million people died. China was plunged into chaos during the Cultural Revolution (1966–70) when the Red Guards were used to rid the country of 'rightist elements'.

Following Mao Zedong's death in 1976, the disgraced Deng Xiaoping was recalled and he became the dominant force within the party, eliminating leftist influence, rehabilitating fallen leaders and promoting an 'open door' policy of economic liberalisation. The party congresses of 1982 and 1987 reaffirmed Deng's policies, and in 1987 most of the revolutionary generation was replaced in the most senior posts by younger, more liberal supporters of reform.

Liberalisation suffered a setback in 1989, when student-led pro-democracy demonstrations in April and May, centred on Tiananmen Square in Beijing, were brutally repressed by the army. Over 2,000 protesters died. The events strengthened the position of hardliners within the leadership, who readopted policies of centralisation based on Marxist ideology.

Although Deng retired from his last official post in 1989, he retained effective control until late 1994, and at his instigation, the emphasis switched back to economic reform in 1992 and the power of the hardliners waned. The 1992 party congress endorsed Deng's calls for faster, bolder economic reforms and a socialist market economy. Following Deng's death in 1997, Jiang Zemin became leader and continued the economic reforms whilst also seeking to improve China's standing in the international community. In 2003 Hu Jintao was elected by the National People's Congress as the new state president and Wen Jaibao was elected as premier; both were re-elected to their posts at the 2008 party congress.

China's violent suppression of anti-China riots in Tibet in spring 2008 was condemned internationally, and overshadowed the run-up to the Beijing Olympic Games in August. A severe earthquake in May 2008 devastated the western province of Sichuan and killed an estimated 70,000 people.

INSURGENCIES

Economic liberalisation has not been matched by political liberalisation or an improvement in respect for human rights, and the regime firmly suppresses dissent by ethnic minorities or any other group that it perceives as a threat to its authority. This has led to moves against separatists from the Uighur Muslim minority group in Xinjiang Autonomous Region since the 1990s, violent suppression of demonstrations in Tibet in 2008, and the 1999 banning of the Falun Gong spiritual sect, which had claimed to have 70 million followers, after it was revealed that a large number of party officials and senior army officers had joined the cult.

POLITICAL SYSTEM

Under the 1982 constitution, the National People's Congress is the highest organ of state power. It has 2,979 members indirectly elected for a five-year term and it is supposed to hold one session a year. It is empowered to amend the constitution, make laws, select the president and vice-president and other leading state officials, approve the national economic plan, the state budget and the final state accounts, and to decide on questions of war and peace. The head of state is the president, elected by the National Party Congress for a five-year term, renewable only once. The State Council is the highest organ of the state administration and is elected by the National People's Congress on the nomination of the premier. It is composed of the premier, the vice-premiers, the state councillors, heads of ministries and commissions, the auditor-general and the secretary-general. Command over the armed forces is vested in the Central Military Commission.

Deputies to congresses at the primary level are directly elected by the voters through a secret ballot after democratic consultation. This is now extended to county level. These congresses elect the deputies to the congress at the next higher level. Deputies to the National People's Congress are elected by the people's congresses of the provinces, autonomous regions and municipalities directly under the central government, and by the armed forces.

Local government is conducted through people's governments at provincial, municipal and county levels. Autonomous regions, prefectures and counties exist for national minorities and are described as self-governing.

HEAD OF STATE

President of the Republic, Hu Jintao, *elected* 15 March 2003, *re-elected* March 2008

Vice-President, Xi Jinping

STATE COUNCIL *as at May 2008*

Premier, Wen Jiabao

Vice-Premiers, Li Keqiang; Wang Qishan; Zhang Dejiang; Hui Liangyu

State Councillors, Meng Jianzhu *(Public Security);* Liang Guanglie *(National Defence);* Dai Bingguo; Ma Kai *(Secretary-General of the State Council);* Liu Yandong

SELECTED GOVERNMENT MEMBERS *as at May 2008*

Civil Affairs, Li Xueju

Finance, Xie Xuren

Foreign Affairs, Yang Jiechi

State Security, Geng Huichang

EMBASSY OF THE PEOPLE'S REPUBLIC OF CHINA

49–51 Portland Place, London W1B 1JL

T 020-7299 4049 **W** www.chinese-embassy.org.uk

Ambassador Extraordinary and Plenipotentiary, HE Fu Ying, *apptd* 2007

BRITISH EMBASSY

11 Guang Hua Lu, Jian Guo Men Wai, Beijing 100600

T (+86) (10) 5192 4000 **E** commercialmail.beijing@fco.gov.uk

W www.britishembassy.org.cn

Ambassador, HE Sir William Ehrman, *apptd* 2006

BRITISH COUNCIL

Cultural and Education Section, British Embassy, 4th Floor Landmark Building Tower 1, 8 North Dongsanhuan Road, Chaoyang District, Beijing 100004

T (+86) (10) 6590 6903 **W** www.britishcouncil.org/china

Director, Robin Rickard

DEFENCE

All three military arms are parts of the People's Liberation Army (PLA). China has at least 46 intercontinental, 725 short range and 35 intermediate ballistic missiles, and 3 submarine-launched nuclear ballistic missiles. The army has over 7,660 main battle tanks, 1,000 light tanks, 1,000 armoured infantry fighting vehicles, over 3,500 armoured personnel carriers and 31 armed helicopters.

The navy has 62 submarines (3 strategic), 29 destroyers, 46 frigates, 233 patrol and coastal vessels and 792 combat aircraft. The marines have 150 light tanks and 60 armoured personnel carriers. The air force has 1,762 combat aircraft.

Military expenditure – US$122,000m (2006 est)

Military personnel – 2,105,000: army 1,600,000, navy 255,000, air force 250,000; paramilitary 1,500,000

Conscription duration – 24 months (selective)

ECONOMY AND TRADE

Liberalisation since the 1980s has transformed the economy from centrally planned to a more market-orientated one with a rapidly growing private sector and a significant presence in global trade and finance. A massive industrial base and transport infrastructure have been constructed, especially in the coastal regions, and the economy has become a free market in all but name, with several stock markets and Shanghai's emergence as a financial centre. China attracts considerable foreign investment and is becoming a major investor overseas, usually in joint ventures and particularly in production of raw materials for industry and fuel supplies such as oil and gas. The economy has grown more than five-fold since 1980.

However, the effects of the rapid transformation have been unevenly distributed, with rural incomes rising only 6.2 per cent in 2005 compared to a 9.6 per cent increase in urban areas. This has caused social unrest and, in 2005, officials recorded 87,000 protests by those who have so far missed out on the benefits or been adversely affected by the effects of economic growth. Another serious downside of industrialisation is environmental degradation of land, water and air. Officials estimate that pollution costs China between 8 per cent and 15 per cent of GDP, and the latest five-year plan, approved in 2006, makes environmental protection a priority.

Tensions are also arising from China's effects on world trade; the cheapness of its exports, especially garments, has provoked protective measures by the EU and USA. Its need for greater supplies of oil have put it in competition with countries such as Japan for supplies. The urgency of this need may decline as the increasing availability of domestic coal and oil help to reduce energy imports and the Three Gorges Dam reaches its full capacity to generate hydroelectric power (18.2 million kilowatts per hour by 2011). The government has also contracted to purchase five nuclear power generators.

Although rural areas have seen few benefits from the economic transformation and are suffering the effects of rural depopulation and pollution, agriculture remains of great importance; it contributes 11.7 per cent of GDP but employs 43 per cent of the workforce. The size of the country, and the variations in terrain and climate, allow a wide variety of produce to be grown. The main crops are rice, cereals, vegetables, peanuts, tea, fruit, cotton and oilseed crops. Livestock is raised in large numbers. Sericulture is one of the oldest industries. Cotton, woollen and silk textiles are manufactured in large quantities.

The highly diversified industrial sector, encompassing heavy industry, manufacturing and construction, contributes 49.2 per cent of GDP and employs 25 per cent of the workforce. The services sector accounts for 39.1 per cent of GDP and 32 per cent of employment. Tourism has become a major industry, and experienced a boom in 2008 with Beijing hosting the Olympic Games. Exports include machinery, electrical equipment, data processing equipment, garments, textiles, steel and mobile phones. The principal imports are machinery and equipment, oil and mineral fuels, plastics, LED screens, data processing equipment, optical and medical equipment, organic chemicals, steel and copper. The main trading partners are the USA, Japan, Hong Kong, South Korea, Germany and Taiwan, although trade with Latin America and Africa is growing rapidly.

GNI – US$2,621,000m; US$2,000 per capita (2006)
Annual average growth of GDP – 11.4 per cent (2007 est)
Inflation rate – 4.7 per cent (2007 est)
Unemployment – 9 per cent (2004 est)
Total external debt – US$363,000m (2007 est)
Imports – US$792,000m (2006)
Exports – US$969,000m (2006)

BALANCE OF PAYMENTS
Trade – US$177,775m surplus (2006)
Current Account – US$249,866m surplus (2006)

Trade with UK	*2006*	*2007*
Imports from UK	£3,278,879,000	£3,780,531,195
Exports to UK	£15,559,074,000	£18,794,464,822

COMMUNICATIONS

The infrastructure was created after the civil war and has been expanded and modernised considerably since liberalisation began. In the past the principal means of internal communication was by river, the most important of which are the Huang He (Yellow), Chang Jiang (Yangtze) and Xi Jiang (West). These, together with the network of canals connecting them, are still much used, but their overall importance has declined. Coastal port facilities are being improved and the merchant fleet expanded. The main seaports are Shanghai and Dalian in the north, and Guangzhou in the south; Nanjing is the largest river port.

Long-distance internal travel is mostly by air and rail. The length of civil air routes has more than tripled in the past two decades. There are 467 airports and airfields and several national air carriers. The rail system has 75,438km of track, although only 20,151km is electrified; the Qinghai–Tibet railway opened in 2006, opening up the remote western provinces. The road network has been expanded to over 1.8 million km, making all towns and villages accessible, and the major cities are linked by 34,000km of modern highways. Motor vehicle ownership is growing rapidly, leading to rising problems of congestion, road safety and pollution.

The telecommunications infrastructure is also expanding, although facilities for personal subscribers are unevenly distributed, concentrated in the cities, industrial centres and major towns. Mobile phone distribution is growing rapidly and, at 461 million in 2006, has overtaken land-line subscriptions. There were 162 million internet users in 2007.

EDUCATION AND HEALTH

Primary education lasts six years and secondary education six years (three years in junior middle school and three years in senior middle school).

Literacy rate – 90.9 per cent (2004 est)
Gross enrolment ratio (percentage of relevant age group) – primary 111 per cent; secondary 76 per cent; tertiary 22 per cent (2006 est)
Health expenditure (per capita) – US$81 (2005)
Hospital beds (per 1,000 people) – 2.5 (2000–6)

MEDIA

China's media industry is huge, with 25,000 newspapers and magazines, 750,000 journalists and 12,000 radio and television stations. In 2002 officials put the domestic television audience at 1.1 billion. Subscription services are expected to have a market of 128 million by the year 2010. The Communist Party has always maintained a firm grip on the nation's news reporting but when Hu Jintao became president, a more liberal approach was adopted, and since December 2006 foreign journalists have been allowed to travel freely and interview people without official permission. Market reforms have also been introduced into the media industry with the closure in 2004 of hundreds of state-funded publications that relied on government departments for their readership. Despite these reforms, journalists still exercise a significant degree of self-censorship and the Communist Party still attempts to restrict access to foreign news media by blocking websites and radio broadcasts and limiting the distribution of overseas newspapers. Several bloggers have also found themselves the target of Beijing officials.

CULTURE

The Chinese language has many dialects, notably Cantonese, Hakka, Amoy, Foochow, Changsha, Nanchang, Wu (Shanghai) and the northern dialect. The common speech or *putonghua* (often referred to as Mandarin) is based on the northern dialect. The Communists have promoted it as the national language and it is taught throughout the country. As *putonghua* encourages the use of the spoken language in writing, the old literary style and ideographic form of writing has fallen into disuse. Since 1956 simplified characters have been introduced to make reading and writing easier. In 1958 the National People's Congress adopted a system of romanisation known as *pinyin*.

Chinese literature is one of the oldest in the world. Paper has been employed for writing and printing for nearly 2,000 years. The Confucian classics, which formed the basis of traditional Chinese culture, date from the Warring States period (fourth to third centuries BC), as do the earliest texts of Taoism. Histories, philosophical and scientific works, poetry, literary and art criticism, novels and romances survive from most periods.

TIBET

Area – 1,199,164 sq. km
Population – 2,610,000 (2001 est)
Capital – Lhasa

Tibet is a plateau, seldom lower than 3,000m, in south-west China which forms the frontier with India (boundary imperfectly demarcated), from Kashmir to Myanmar, from which it is separated by the Himalayas. The Indus, Brahmaputra, Mekong and Yangtze rivers all rise on the Tibet plateau.

Tibet was under Mongol rule almost continuously from the 13th to the 17th century. Chinese control grew from the 18th century and direct rule began in 1910, but with the collapse of the Chinese Empire in 1911, Tibet declared its independence and the Dalai Lama ruled undisturbed until Communist rule was established in China. In 1950 Chinese Communist forces invaded Tibet, and in 1951 the Tibetan authorities signed a treaty agreeing joint Chinese-Tibetan rule. A series of revolts against Chinese rule culminated in a 1959 uprising in the capital, which was crushed after several days of fighting and military rule was imposed. The Dalai Lama fled to India where he and his followers were granted political asylum and established a government in exile. Tibet became an Autonomous Region of China in 1965. Martial law was declared in Tibet in 1989.

The Panchen Lama remained in Lhasa after 1959; when he died in 1989, China rejected the Dalai Lama's choice of successor and enthroned its own candidate. Subsequent appointments have been handled in a similar manner, increasing tension between the Chinese authorities and the Tibetan government-in-exile. The Chinese government has held occasional talks with representatives of the Dalai Lama since 2002 in an attempt to improve the situation but relations remain poor.

Another source of tension is the large number of Chinese migrants who have settled in Tibet since the 1970s, a development that the Tibetan government-in-exile regards as an attempt to eradicate the culture of the Tibetan people. Chinese now considerably outnumber Tibetans and have benefited disproportionately from the economic development of recent years.

Anti-Chinese demonstrations in Tibet increased in early 2008 as the imminence of the Beijing Olympics put China's human rights record under greater international scrutiny. In March the authorities' violent attempt to suppress a peaceful demonstration marking the anniversary of the 1959 uprising erupted into rioting in Lhasa which then spread across Tibet and into neighbouring Chinese provinces with large Tibetan populations. The violence of the Chinese crackdown was condemned worldwide, and pro-Tibet activists abroad disrupted the Olympic torch relay in several countries.

SPECIAL ADMINISTRATIVE REGIONS

HONG KONG

Xianggang Tebie Xingzhengqu – Hong Kong Special Administrative Region
Area – 1,092 sq. km
Currency – Hong Kong dollar (HK$) of 100 cents
Population – 6,980,412, rising at 0.56 per cent per year (2007 est)
Population density – 6,581 per sq. km (2006)
Urban population – 93.1 per cent (2000 est)
Flag – Red, with a white bauhinia flower of five petals each containing a red star
National day – 1 July (Establishment Day)
Life expectancy (years) – 81.59 (2006 est)
Birth rate – 7.34 (2007 est)
Mortality rate – 6.45 (2007 est)
Infant mortality rate – 2.94 (2007 est)
Death penalty – Abolitionist for all crimes (since 2003)
CPI score – 8.3 (2007)

CLIMATE AND TERRAIN

Hong Kong consists of more than 230 islands and a portion of the mainland (Kowloon and the New Territories, a peninsula in the southern part of Guangdong province and adjacent islands) on the south-east coast of China, situated on the eastern side of the mouth of the Pearl river. Hong Kong Island is about 18km long and 3–8km wide. It is separated from the mainland by a narrow strait. The highest point is Tai Mo Shan (958m). The climate is subtropical, tending towards the temperate for nearly half the year. Mean monthly temperatures range from 16°C to 29°C. Tropical cyclones occur between May and November, and nearly 80 per cent of the average annual rainfall of 2,214mm falls between May and September.

HISTORY AND POLITICS

Hong Kong Island was first occupied by Britain in 1841 and formally ceded to Britain in 1842. Kowloon was acquired in 1860 and the New Territories by a 99-year lease signed in 1898.

In 1984, the UK and China agreed that China would resume sovereignty over Hong Kong in 1997, and on 1 July 1997, Hong Kong became a Special Administrative Region (SAR) of the People's Republic of China. The 1984 joint declaration and the Basic Law (1990) guarantee that the SAR's social and economic systems will remain unchanged for 50 years and grant it a high degree of autonomy.

The Basic Law provides for the development of democratic processes, but political reform has been slow, prompting frequent demonstrations to demand full democracy or to oppose to measures perceived to be repressive. In December 2007 the Chinese government said that the chief executive would be directly elected from 2017 and the legislature members from 2020.

After the 2004 legislative elections, pro-China parties held 34 of the 60 elected seats and pro-democracy parties 25. Tung Chee-hwa resigned in March 2005 and in June, Donald Tsang was elected as chief executive to serve out the rest of the term of office. Tsang was re-elected in March 2007. The next legislative elections are due in September 2008.

POLITICAL SYSTEM

The Basic Law, approved in 1990, has served as Hong Kong's constitution since 1997. Its government is headed by the chief executive, who is elected by a 800-member election committee and serves a five-year term. The chief executive is aided by an executive council consisting of 14 official members, who are the heads of administrative departments, and 15 non-official members. The legislative council consists of 60 members, 30 directly elected by geographic constituencies, and 30 elected by functional constituencies composed of professional and business groups. They serve a four-year term.

Chief Executive, Donald Tsang, *elected* 16 June 2005, *sworn in* 24 June 2005, *re-elected* 2007

SELECTED GOVERNMENT MEMBERS *as at May 2008*
Chief Secretary for Administration, Rafael Hui
Economy and Finance, Francis Tam Pak Yuen

CONSULATE-GENERAL
PO Box 528, 1 Supreme Court Road, Central Hong Kong
T (+852) 2901 3000 E consular@bcg.org.hk
Consul-General, Andrew Seaton, *apptd* 2008

BRITISH COUNCIL
3 Supreme Court Road, Admiralty, Hong Kong
T (+852) 2913 5100 W www.britishcouncil.org/hongkong
Deputy Director, Georgina Pearce

ECONOMY AND TRADE

The economy has moved away from manufacturing (which has mostly relocated to mainland China) and is now service-based, with a high reliance on international trade. It has developed into a regional corporate and banking centre, and has benefited in recent years from closer integration with China through increased trade, tourism and financial links. The growth in GDP has averaged 5 per cent a year since 1989.

The economy is dominated by the service sector, which accounted for 91.8 per cent of GDP in 2007. The main contributors to this were tourism, financial services and shipping. Industry contributed 8.1 per cent of GDP, and manufacturing occupied 6.5 per cent of the workforce. Principal products are textiles, clothing, electronics, plastics, toys, and clocks and watches.

The principal export markets are China, the USA and Japan. China is Hong Kong's principal supplier of imported goods.

GNI – US$199,100m; US$29,040 per capita (2006)
Annual average growth of GDP – 5.8 per cent (2007 est)
Inflation rate – 2 per cent (2007 est)
Unemployment – 5.5 per cent (2005 est)
Imports – US$335,000m (2006)
Exports – US$317,000m (2006)

BALANCE OF PAYMENTS
Trade – US$17,865m deficit (2006)
Current Account – US$22,936m surplus (2006)

Trade with UK	*2006*	*2007*
Imports from UK	£2,869,960,000	£2,651,154,220
Exports to UK	£7,494,492,000	£6,988,436,513

EDUCATION

Education is free of charge and compulsory for children up to the age of 15.

Gross enrolment ratio (percentage of age group) – secondary 85 per cent; tertiary 33 per cent (2005 est)

COMMUNICATIONS

Hong Kong has one of the world's finest natural harbours, and is the busiest container port in the world. Dockyard facilities include eight floating drydocks, the largest being capable of docking vessels up to 150,000 tonnes deadweight. There are two airports, one accommodating international flights. Modern telecommunications systems supported 3.8 million main lines, 9.9 million mobile phone subscribers and 3.7 million internet users in 2007.

MACAO (AOMEN)

Aomen Tebie Xingzhengqu – Macau Special Administrative Region
Area – 28.2 sq. km
Currency – Pataca of 100 avos
Population – 456,989, rising at 0.84 per cent per year (2007 est)
Flag – Green, with a white lotus flower above a white stylised bridge and water, under a large gold five-point star and four gold stars in crescent
National day – 20 December (Establishment Day)
CPI score – 5.7 (2007)

CLIMATE AND TERRAIN

Macao consists of a peninsula and the islands of Coloane and Taipa, situated at the mouth of the Pearl river. It is 64km from Hong Kong. The highest point is Coloane Alto (172.4m). The climate is subtropical.

HISTORY AND POLITICS

The first Portuguese ship arrived at Macao in 1513 and trade with China commenced in 1553. Macao became a Portuguese colony in 1557; China recognised Portugal's sovereignty over Macao by treaty in 1887. An agreement to transfer the administration of Macao to the Chinese authorities was signed in 1987, and Macao became the Macao Special Administrative Region (MSAR) of China on 19 December 1999. Edmund Ho Hao Wah, elected as the first chief executive in 1999, was re-elected in 2004. The last legislative election was in 2005. Pro-democracy supporters are campaigning for the introduction of universal suffrage for the next elections, due in 2009.

The Basic Law, approved in 1993, has served as Macao's constitution since 1999. The chief executive is elected by a 300-member election committee and serves a five-year term of office, which may be renewed once. The chief executive is assisted in policy-making by the 10-member executive council. The legislative council has 29 members, who serve for four years; 12 are directly elected, 10 are indirectly elected by corporate constituencies and seven are appointed by the chief executive.

Chief Executive, Edmund Ho Hao Wah

SELECTED GOVERNMENT MEMBERS *as at May 2008*
Economy and Finance, Francis Tam Pak Yuen
Secretary for Administration and Justice, Florida Rosa Silver Chan

CONSUL-GENERAL
Andrew Seaton, resident at Hong Kong

ECONOMY AND TRADE

The economy is based on tourism and gambling, which have grown rapidly since 2001–2, and garment manufacturing, which is in decline. The service sector contributes about 96 per cent of GDP and industry 3.9 per cent. Gambling is the largest employer, occupying 19.8 per cent of the workforce in 2006; restaurants and hotels employed 11.3 per cent, wholesale and retail trade 13.7 per cent and manufacturing 11.1 per cent. The principal products and exports are clothing, textiles, electronics, footwear and toys. The main trading partners are China, the USA, Hong Kong and Japan.

Annual average growth of GDP – 6.7 per cent (2005)
Inflation rate – 4.4 per cent (2005)
Imports – US$4,560m (2006)
Exports – US$2,560m (2006)

BALANCE OF PAYMENTS
Trade – US$2,008m deficit (2006)
Current Account – US$4,163m surplus (2004)

Trade with UK	*2006*	*2007*
Imports from UK	£20,993,000	£17,621,567
Exports to UK	£23,644,000	£28,761,122

COLOMBIA

República de Colombia – Republic of Colombia

Area – 1,138,910 sq. km
Capital – Bogotá; population, 7,772,000 (2007 est)
Major cities – Barranquilla, Cali, Medellín
Currency – Colombian peso of 100 centavos
Population – 44,379,598 rising at 1.43 per cent per year (2007 est)
Religion – Roman Catholicism (80 per cent), other Christian denominations (13 per cent) (est)
Language – Spanish (official)
Population density – 41 per sq. km (2006)
Urban population – 77.4 per cent (2005 est)
Median age (years) – 26.6 (2007 est)
National anthem – 'Himno Nacional de la República de Columbia' ['National Anthem of the Republic of Columbia']
National day – 20 July (Independence Day)
Life expectancy (years) – 72.27 (2007 est)
Mortality rate – 5.54 (2007 est)
Birth rate – 20.16 (2007 est)
Infant mortality rate – 20.13 (2007 est)
Death penalty – Abolished for all crimes (since 1910)
CPI score – 3.8 (2007)
Population below poverty line – 49.2 per cent (2005)

CLIMATE AND TERRAIN

Colombia lies in the extreme north-west of South America, having a coastline on both the Caribbean Sea and the Pacific Ocean. Elevation extremes range from 5,775m (Pico Cristobal Colon) at the highest point to 0m (Pacific Ocean) at the lowest. The country is divided by the Andes into a coastal region in the north and west and extensive plains in the east. The eastern range of the Colombian Andes is a series of vast tablelands. This temperate region is the most densely populated portion of the country. The principal rivers are the Magdalena, Guaviare, Cauca, Caquetá, Putumayo and Patia. The climate is predominantly tropical but the Caribbean coastline is typically drier than the rest of the country.

HISTORY AND POLITICS

The Colombian coast was visited in 1502 by Columbus, and in 1536 a Spanish expedition penetrated the interior and established a government. The country remained under Spanish rule until 1819 when Simón Bolivar established the Republic of Gran Colombia, consisting of the territories now known as Colombia, Panama, Venezuela and Ecuador. In 1829–30 Venezuela and Ecuador withdrew, and in 1831 the remaining territories formed a separate state. The name of Colombia was adopted in 1866. Panama seceded in 1903.

In 1949, a civil war broke out which lasted until 1957, when the Conservative and Liberal parties formed a coalition government known as the National Front. This arrangement continued until 1974 and was revived in 1978 in an attempt to maintain the rule of law in the face of violence by drugs cartels, a left-wing insurgency and counter-attacks by right-wing paramilitaries. Despite foreign assistance and increased military spending, drugs trafficking continues to be widespread, although less of a threat to civil order than hitherto, but the government has been unable to suppress or reach a negotiated settlement with insurgents' leaders despite peace talks.

In the 2006 legislative elections, the Liberal Party (PL) remained the largest party in the lower chamber of the legislature, but was only the third largest in the upper chamber. President Uribe, seen by many as closely aligned with the USA, was re-elected in 2006 with 62.2 per cent of the vote.

INSURGENCIES
Since the 1960s Colombia has been dogged by insurgency by several guerrilla groups, mainly the Revolutionary Armed Forces of Colombia (FARC), the National Liberation Army (ELN) and the right-wing United Self-Defence Forces of Colombia (AUC), which is suspected of having links with the security forces. All the groups are known to be involved in drugs trafficking and other crime, and now act to protect these sources of funding as much as to further their political aims. Talks between the government and the FARC began in 1998 but were broken off by the government in 2002 after further violence. The AUC declared an indefinite ceasefire in 2002 and peace talks from 2004 led to the start of demobilisation, which continued despite some AUC leaders pulling out of further talks in 2006. Talks with the ELN began in December 2005.

Action against the insurgents was a key election pledge of President Uribe in 2002 and the government's increased efforts since then have extended state control so that it now has a presence in every municipality. The level of violence has dropped but drug-eradication programmes are aggressively resisted.

Mediation between the government and left-wing rebels by President Chavez of Venezuela ended in late 2007 because of a row over his powers. After Colombian forces crossed the Ecuadorean border in pursuit of FARC rebels in March 2008, both Ecuador and Venezuela broke off diplomatic relations with Colombia and moved troops to their borders.

POLITICAL SYSTEM
Under the 1991 constitution, the executive president is directly elected for a four-year term; a 2005 amendment allows an incumbent president to stand for a second term. The bicameral Congress comprises a lower house, the House of Representatives, with 166 members directly elected for a four-year term. The senate has 102 members, directly elected for a four-year term; two seats are reserved for representatives of indigenous people.

HEAD OF STATE
President, Álvaro Uribe Vélez, *elected* 26 May 2002, *re-elected* 28 May 2006
Vice-President, Francisco Santos Calderon

SELECTED GOVERNMENT MEMBERS *as at May 2008*
Defence, Juan Manuel Santos
Finance, Oscar Ivan Zuluaga
Foreign Affairs, Fernando Araujo
Interior, Justice, Carlos Holguin Sardi

EMBASSY OF COLOMBIA
3 Hans Crescent, London SW1X 0LN
T 020-7589 9177 E mail@colombianembassy.co.uk
Ambassador Extraordinary and Plenipotentiary, HE Dr Carlos Eduardo Medellin Becerra, *apptd* 2006

BRITISH EMBASSY
Edificio Ing Barings, Carrera 9, No 96–49, Piso 5, Santafe de Bogotá
T (+57) (1) 317 6690 E britain@cable.net.co
W www.britain.gov.co
Ambassador Extraordinary and Plenipotentiary, HE Haydon Warren-Gash, *apptd* 2005

BRITISH COUNCIL
c/o British Embassy
T (+57) (1) 325 9090 W www.britishcouncil.org/colombia
Director, Charles Nuttall

DEFENCE

The army has over 228 armoured personnel carriers. The navy has 4 submarines, 4 corvettes, and 93 patrol and coastal vessels at 9 bases. The air force has 115 combat aircraft and 31 armed helicopters.
Military expenditure – US$7,140m (2007)
Military personnel – 254,259: army 216,921, navy 27,605, air force 9,733; paramilitary 144,097

ECONOMY AND TRADE

The improving security situation, government austerity budgets and international funding have aided economic growth. Public sector debt has been reduced and inflation and unemployment levels are declining, although nearly half the population is still below the poverty line. The government has encouraged diversification to reduce dependence on coffee as the major export and this has led to the growth of new export-orientated industries, particularly textiles, clothing and footwear.

Services accounted for around 52.4 per cent of GDP, industry 36 per cent and agriculture 11.5 per cent in 2007. Coal, oil, natural gas and hydroelectricity resources are being exploited, and Colombia is a net exporter of electricity and oil. Hydrocarbons account for half of mining output, with iron ore, nickel, gold, emeralds, copper and other minerals accounting for the remainder. Major cash crops are coffee, bananas and cut flowers. Cattle are raised in large numbers, and forestry is also important.

The principal trading partners are the USA, other Latin American countries and China. Principal exports are oil, coffee, coal, nickel, emeralds, garments, bananas and cut flowers. The main imports are industrial and transport equipment, consumer goods, chemicals, paper products and fuels.
GNI – US$142,000m; US$3,120 per capita (2006)
Annual average growth of GDP – 6.5 per cent (2007 est)
Inflation rate – 5.5 per cent (2007 est)
Unemployment – 10.6 per cent (2007 est)
Total external debt – US$43,300m (2007)
Imports – US$26,000m (2006)
Exports – US$24,400m (2006)

BALANCE OF PAYMENTS
Trade – US$1,658m deficit (2006)
Current Account – US$2,909m deficit (2006)

Trade with UK	*2006*	*2007*
Imports from UK	£133,040,000	£139,647,539
Exports to UK	£305,628,000	£370,226,072

COMMUNICATIONS

The terrain has always hampered internal transport, and historically travel was largely along the rivers, especially the Magdalena. This is still used for some bulk cargo but most long-distance internal travel is now by air, although the growing road network (113,000km) is the main means of freight transport, superseding the 3,304km rail system as well as the waterways. There are 934 airports and airstrips, although only 103 have surfaced runways. The principal airports are at Bogotá, Barranquilla and Cali. The main seaports are Barranquilla, Cartagena and Santa Marta on the Caribbean Sea and Buenaventura on the Pacific coast. A modern telephone system covers the whole of the country but with only 18 main lines per 100 people in 2006; mobile phone density is 70 per 100 people.

EDUCATION AND HEALTH

Elementary education is free of charge and compulsory for nine years. Most primary schools are run by the Roman Catholic church and courses in Roman Catholicism are compulsory. There are some Protestant church schools (mainly in the capital). The government finances secondary and university level education.
Literacy rate – 94.2 per cent (2004 est)
Gross enrolment ratio (percentage of relevant age group) – primary 116 per cent; secondary 82 per cent; tertiary 31 per cent (2006 est)
Health expenditure (per capita) – US$201 (2005)
Hospital beds (per 1,000 people) – 1.2 (2000–6)

MEDIA

There are state-owned television (Inravision) and radio stations (Radiodifusora Nacional de Colombia) as well as private commercial networks. There are five main daily newspapers, but television remains the most popular medium. Colombia is one of the most dangerous countries in the world for journalists, who are often targeted by drug-traffickers, guerrillas and paramilitary groups. More than 120 Colombian journalists were killed during the 1990s.

THE COMOROS

L'Union des Comores – Union of the Comoros

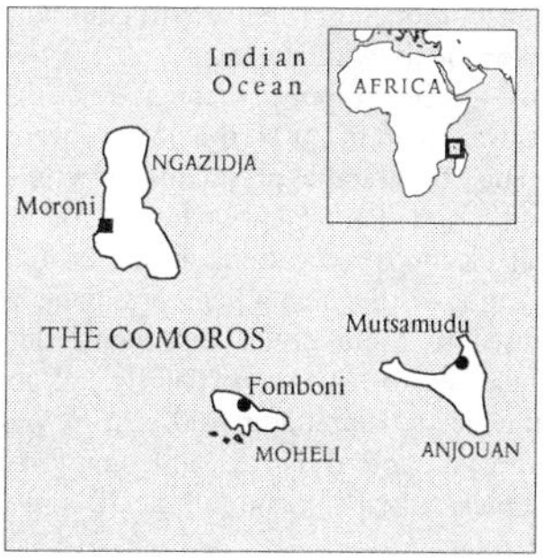

Area – 2,170 sq. km. The Comoros includes the islands of Ngazidja (formerly Grande Comore), Anjouan (also known as Nzwani), Moheli (also known as Mwali) and certain islets in the Indian Ocean. The easternmost island of the archipelago, Mayotte, is a French dependency.
Capital – Moroni; population, 46,000 (2007 est), on Ngazidja
Major towns – Domoni, Fomboni, Mutsamudu
Currency – Comorian franc (KMF) of 100 centimes. The Franc CFA of 100 centimes is also used
Population – 711,417 rising at 2.84 per cent per year (2007 est)
Religion – Islam (99 per cent) (est)
Language – Arabic, French (both official), Shikomoro
Population density – 330 per sq. km (2006)
Urban population – 36.3 per cent (2005 est)
Median age (years) – 18.7 (2007 est)
National anthem – 'Udzima wa ya Masiwa' ['The Union of the Great Islands']
National day – 6 July (Independence Day)
Life expectancy (years) – 62.73 (2007 est)
Mortality rate – 7.95 (2007 est)
Birth rate – 36.35 (2007 est)
Infant mortality rate – 70.66 (2007 est)
Death penalty – Retained
Population below poverty line – 60 per cent (2002 est)
CPI score – 2.6 (2007)
Literacy rate – 56.2 per cent (2004 est)

CLIMATE AND TERRAIN

Located in the Mozambique Channel between Africa and Madagascar, Njazidja, Anjouan and Moheli are volcanic islands in the Comoros archipelago. The highest point is Karthala (2,360m) on Njazidja, an active volcano that last erupted in 2005, and the lowest is 0m (Indian Ocean). There is a tropical climate with a dry season from May to October and a hot season from November to April. The average temperature ranges from 20°C to 28°C. Cyclones afflict the islands between January and April.

HISTORY AND POLITICS

The islands became a French protectorate in the late 19th century, and achieved internal self-government in 1961. In 1974, the islanders voted on independence from France and three main islands became independent on 6 July 1975; Mayotte voted to remain part of France. The republic experienced a number of coups between 1976 and 1999, some supported by European mercenaries. Anjouan and Moheli seceded in 1997 but after another coup in 1999, the military took control of the other islands' governments and reunited them with the Comoros. Talks on the secessionist crisis produced a new constitution, introducing a federal structure with greater autonomy for the individual islands.

Elections to the union parliament and the islands' legislatures were held in 2004; the union government is a coalition. The 2006 federal presidential election was won by Ahmed Abdallah Sambi from Anjouan. The presidential elections were held in the islands in June 2007; in Anjouan, the incumbent president, Mohamed Bacar, refused to stand down and then held elections which he claimed to have won. The federal government declared the elections null and void, and in March 2008 federal troops, supported by African Union forces, ousted Bacar. The presidential election in June 2008 was won by Moussa Toybou.

POLITICAL SYSTEM

The 2002 constitution created a federal structure. Under this, the union president is elected from each of the three islands in turn and serves a four-year term. The executive president appoints the union ministers. The unicameral Assembly of the Union has 33 members; five are appointed by each of the three island parliaments and 18 are directly elected for a five-year term. Each island has its own president and legislative assembly, and each island president appoints the island's eight ministers. The islands' governments deal with local issues; foreign affairs, finance, defence, judicial and religious matters remain the responsibility of the union government. There are still areas of dispute, principally over security, budget control and customs revenue.

HEAD OF STATE

President of the Union, Ahmed Abdallah Sambi, *elected* 14 May 2006, *sworn in* 25 May 2006

SELECTED GOVERNMENT MEMBERS *as at May 2008*
Vice-President, Transport, Tourism, Post and Communications, Idi Nadhoim
Vice-President, Health, Solidarity and Gender Equality, Ikililou Dhoinine
Foreign Relations and Cooperation, Francophone and Arab Affairs, Ahmed ben Said Jaffar
Finance, Budget and Planning, Mohamed Ali Soilihi

HONORARY CONSULATE
Flat 6, 24–26 Avenue Road, London, NW8 6BU
T 020 7722-1146 E comorosuk@gmail.com
Honorary Consul, Khaleb Chehabi

BRITISH AMBASSADOR
HE Anthony Godson, *apptd* 2005, resident at Port Louis, Mauritius

ECONOMY AND TRADE

The Comoros is very poor and heavily dependent on foreign aid and technical assistance. It has few natural resources, an uneducated workforce and a poor transport infrastructure. Continuing political tensions hinder government attempts to reform and develop the economy and social welfare provision. Unemployment is high and over 20 per cent of the workforce is employed abroad; remittances are a valuable contribution to the economy. Agriculture, fishing and forestry account for about 40 per cent of GDP and employ 80 per cent of the population; service industries account for 56 per cent and the manufacturing industry 4 per cent. The principal exports are vanilla, perfume essence, copra and cloves; coconuts, bananas and cassava are also cultivated. The main industries are fishing, tourism and perfume distillation.
GNI – US$406m; US$660 per capita (2006)
Annual average growth of GDP – −1 per cent (2007 est)
Inflation rate – 3 per cent (2005 est)
Total external debt – US$177m (2001)

BALANCE OF PAYMENTS
Trade – US$97m deficit (2006)
Current Account – US$21m deficit (2006)

Trade with UK	*2006*	*2007*
Imports from UK	£87,000	£318,180
Exports to UK	£65,000	£71,881

MEDIA

Radio is the country's primary source of information and there is healthy competition between state and privately-owned radio broadcasters. Television Nationale Comorienne is the state-run television channel, which exists alongside programmes broadcast from Mayotte, which can be received on several of the islands. Most newspapers are published weekly and have small circulations owing to a weak advertising market and poor distribution. Much of their content is restricted by self-censorship, practised because of the government's willingness to close down media who broadcast material deemed offensive.

DEMOCRATIC REPUBLIC OF CONGO

République Démocratique du Congo – Democratic Republic of the Congo

Area – 2,345,410 sq. km
Capital – Kinshasa; population, 7,843,000 (2007 est)
Major cities – Boma, Kananga, Kisangani, Kolwezi, Lubumbashi, Mbuji-Mayi
Currency – Congolese franc of 100 centimes
Population – 65,751,512 rising at 3.39 per cent per year (2007 est). The population is composed of Bantu, Hamitic, Nilotic, Sudanese and Pygmoid groups, divided into more than 200 tribes
Religion – Roman Catholicism (55 per cent), Protestantism (30 per cent), Kimbanguism (5 per cent), Islam (5 per cent) (est). The remainder mostly practise indigenous religious beliefs
Language – French (official), Lingala, Kingwana, Kikongo, Tshiluba
Population density – 27 per sq. km (2006)
Urban population – 32.7 per cent (2005 est)
Median age (years) – 16.1 (2007 est)
National anthem – 'Debout Congolais' ['Stand Up, Congolese']
National day – 30 June (Independence Day)
Life expectancy (years) – 57.2 (2007 est)
Mortality rate – 10.34 (2007 est)
Birth rate – 42.96 (2007 est)
Infant mortality rate – 65.52 (2007 est)
HIV/AIDS adult prevalence – 2.9 per cent (2005 est)
Death penalty – Retained
CPI score – 1.9 (2007)
Literacy rate – 65.3 per cent (2004 est)
Gross enrolment ratio (percentage of relevant age group) – primary 62 per cent; secondary 22 per cent (2005 est)
Health expenditure (per capita) – US$5 (2005)

CLIMATE AND TERRAIN

The Democratic Republic of the Congo is Africa's third largest country. Most of the state lies in the basin of the river Congo and its principal tributaries, the Lualaba and the Kasai. A chain of mountains and lakes (Albert, Edward, Kivu and Tanganyika) run along the eastern border. Elevation extremes range from 5,110m (Mt Ngaliema, also known as Mt Stanley) at the highest point to 0m (Atlantic Ocean) at the lowest. The central region has an equatorial climate with high humidity and an average temperature of 26°C. The equator passes through the north of the country and there are different climatic cycles either side of it, with a dry season in the north from December to February and in the south from May to September.

HISTORY AND POLITICS

The state of the Congo, founded in 1885 by King Leopold II of Belgium, became a Belgian colony in 1908 and gained its independence in 1960. Mobutu Sésé Seko came to power in a coup in 1965 and was elected president in 1970. The *Mouvement Populaire de la Révolution* (MPR) was the sole legal political party until the late 1980s, when the regime began moves towards a multiparty system, but progress was hindered by army revolts and political disagreements.

In 1996 ethnic conflict, largely resulting from the influx of refugees from the Rwandan genocide, sparked a civil war in which the army found itself outgunned by anti-Mobutu rebels, backed by the Rwandan and Ugandan governments. Under the leadership of Laurent Kabila, the Alliance of Democratic Forces for the Liberation of Congo-Zaire (AFDL) captured Kinshasa in May 1997 and President Mobutu fled. Zaire was then renamed the Democratic Republic of the Congo.

In 1998 a rebellion against Kabila's government began in the east, initiating years of fighting between government forces and a shifting alliance of rebel groups, with neighbouring countries lending support to either the government (Angola, Chad, Kenya, Namibia, Zimbabwe) or the rebels (Rwanda, Uganda). All parties to the conflict plundered the country's rich natural resources and left an estimated 3.5 million dead from violence, famine and disease. A number of ceasefires were negotiated and broken, but by December 2000 the government and rebel groups had signed a disengagement agreement, and withdrew their troops 15km from their frontline positions by the end of March 2001. UN-sponsored peace talks in 2002 concluded in a power-sharing agreement between the government and the main rebel groups.

In 2003 a transitional government was established under the incumbent president, Maj.-Gen. Joseph Kabila (who had succeeded his father Laurent, assassinated in 2001) and an interim legislature was inaugurated. Despite a number of coup attempts and occasional clashes with renegade rebels, a fragile peace has held in much of the country, apart from the eastern provinces. Rebel militia in the east signed a peace agreement with the government in January 2008 but violence against the civilian population continues, much of it perpetrated by renegade Rwandan militia. There are still 18,000 UN peacekeeping troops in the country.

A new constitution came into effect with presidential and legislative elections on 30 July 2006. The presidential election was won in the second round in October 2006 by the incumbent, Joseph Kabila. His People's Party for Reconstruction and Development (PPRD) won the largest number of seats in the lower legislative chamber but not an overall majority; supporters of the president won an overall majority in the senate in elections in January 2007. The PPRD became the major partner in the coalition government formed in February 2007.

POLITICAL SYSTEM

Under the 2006 constitution, the executive president is directly elected for a five-year term, renewable only once. The bicameral *Parlement* consists of the National Assembly, which has 500 members directly elected for a five-year term, and the senate, which has 108 members indirectly elected by provincial assemblies to serve a five-year term, plus former elected presidents, who are senators for life.

HEAD OF STATE

President, Maj.-Gen. Joseph Kabila, *sworn in* 26 January 2001, *sworn in as president of the transitional government* 7 April 2003, *elected* 29 October 2006

Vice-President, Abdoulaye Yerodia Ndombasi

SELECTED GOVERNMENT MEMBERS *as at May 2008*

Prime Minister, Antonie Gizenga

Defence, Chikez Diemu

Finance, Athanase Matenda Kyelu

Foreign Affairs and International Co-operation, Antipas Mbusa Nyamwisi

Interior, Gen. Denis Kalume Numbi

EMBASSY OF THE DEMOCRATIC REPUBLIC OF THE CONGO

281 Gray's Inn Road, London WC1X 8QF

T 020-7278 9825

Ambassador Extraordinary and Plenipotentiary, HE Eugénie Tshiela Compton, *apptd* 2005

BRITISH EMBASSY

83 Avenue du Roi Baudouin, Kinshasa

T (+243) 98 169 100 E ambrit@ic.cd

Ambassador Extraordinary and Plenipotentiary, HE Nicholas Kay, *apptd* 2007

DEFENCE

The army has 49 main battle tanks, 20 armoured infantry fighting vehicles and 138 armoured personnel carriers. The navy has 3 patrol and coastal combatant vessels. The air force has 5 combat capable aircraft and 4 armed helicopters.

Military budget – US$181m (2007 est)

Military personnel – 134,484: army 125,233, navy 6,703, air force 2,548

ECONOMY AND TRADE

The country has immense natural resources, including copper, diamonds, gold, silver, uranium, other minerals, coal, oil, timber and hydroelectric power, and so great potential wealth. But the years of civil war devastated the economy and the country now has a huge external debt, little infrastructure, widespread corruption and an environment that discourages foreign investment. Improved stability since 2003 has allowed some economic growth. The government has obtained financing from international organisations and donors and begun reforms. It was also granted US$10bn (£5bn) of debt relief by the IMF in 2003.

Over half of GDP was contributed by agriculture, about 35 per cent by the services sector and 11 per cent by industry. Apart from mining and mineral processing, the main industrial activities are the production of textiles, footwear, cigarettes, processed food, beverages and cement, and ship repair. Oil deposits are exploited off the Congo estuary, and hydroelectric schemes on the river Congo supply power to the major cities.

The main trading partners are Belgium, which takes 29 per cent of exports, China, South Africa and Brazil. Principal exports are diamonds, copper, crude oil, coffee and cobalt. The main imports are foodstuffs, mining and other machinery, transport equipment and fuels.

GNI – US$7,700m; US$130 per capita (2006)

Annual average growth of GDP – 7 per cent (2007 est)

Inflation rate – 18.2 per cent (2006 est)

Total external debt – US$10,000m (2006 est)

BALANCE OF PAYMENTS

Trade – US$500m deficit (2006)

Current Account – US$212m deficit (2006)

Trade with UK	*2005*	*2006*
Imports from UK	£11,592,000	£16,912,000
Exports to UK	£6,083,000	£786,000

COMMUNICATIONS

The transport infrastructure is undeveloped owing to the terrain, poverty and warfare. The river Congo and its main tributaries provide 15,000km of waterways, and the 5,138km rail system links the interior to the rivers and to the great lakes in the east. The system also connects with neighbouring states, through which east and south African ports can be accessed. There are approximately 153,000km of roads, of which 3,000km are surfaced. The country has over 230 airports and airfields, the principal airports being at Kinshasa, Kananga, Goma, Gemena and Mbandaka. The principal seaports are at Matadi and Boma.

The telecommunications infrastructure is also poor, with limited coverage in and between urban areas; fixed-line connections have decreased to fewer than 10,000. Mobile phone distribution is growing rapidly, doubling between 2005 and 2006 to about 7 per 100 people.

MEDIA

The state-controlled Radio-Télévision Nationale Congolaise (RTNC) and La Voix du Congo have the greatest influence and broadcast reach. There are about eight other private and commercial television stations and ten radio stations (some run by the Roman Catholic Church, some by the UN). Around 15 newspapers are published regularly in Kinshasa.

REPUBLIC OF CONGO

République du Congo – Republic of the Congo

Area – 342,000 sq. km
Capital – Brazzaville; population, 1,355,000 (2007 est)
Major cities – Loubomo, Pointe Noire
Currency – Franc CFA of 100 centimes
Population – 3,800,610 rising at 2.64 per cent per year (2007 est); Kongo (48 per cent), Sangha (20 per cent), Teke (17 per cent), M'Bochi (12 per cent) (est)
Religion – Roman Catholicism (45 per cent), Islam (2 per cent) (est). Others practise indigenous religious beliefs, belong to messianic groups or have no religious affiliation
Language – French (official), Lingala, Monokutuba, Kikongo
Population density – 11 per sq. km (2006)
Urban population – 54.4 per cent (2005 est)
Median age (years) – 16.7 (2007 est)
National anthem – 'La Congolaise' ['The Congolese']
National day – 15 August (Independence Day)
Life expectancy (years) – 53.29 (2007 est)
Mortality rate – 12.59 (2007 est)
Birth rate – 42.16 (2007 est)
Infant mortality rate – 83.26 (2007 est)
HIV/AIDS adult prevalence – 4.7 per cent (2005 est)
Death penalty – Retained, but not used
CPI score – 2.1 (2007)

CLIMATE AND TERRAIN

The republic is covered by grassland, mangrove and dense rainforest. The land rises from sea-level on the narrow Atlantic coastal plain to a central plateau, and then falls to the northern part of the basin of the river Congo, which forms part of the border with the Democratic Republic of the Congo. In the north, the main rivers are the Sangha and Alima. Elevation extremes range from 903m (Mt Berongou) at the highest point to 0m at the lowest (Atlantic Ocean). The climate is equatorial. The annual daily temperature in Brazzaville is between 28°C and 33°C. The dry season is June to September but the country is prone to flooding during the wet season (March to June).

HISTORY AND POLITICS

The first European visitors to the area were the Portuguese, who established slave trading in the 16th century. The French established a colonial presence in the area in the 1880s and, as Middle Congo, it was part of French Equatorial Africa from 1908. It became independent as the Republic of Congo on 17 August 1960.

In 1968, a military coup created the first Marxist state in Africa, under the Congolese Labour Party (PCT). Marxism was renounced and, after popular pressure, the PCT abandoned its monopoly of power in 1990. The following decade was a period of ethnically derived political instability, with factional fighting after the 1993 election and a civil war between 1997 and 2003, incited by Denis Sassou-Nguesso's deposition of the elected president. A peace accord ended the civil war in 2003 but the peace is fragile and remnants of the rebel militias are still active in the south of the country, where many have turned to banditry.

In the 2002 presidential election, Sassou-Nguesso was elected legitimately with nearly 90 per cent of the vote, although his victory was criticised after his candidature was unopposed owing to the barring of his main rivals. A prime minister was appointed in 2005, the first time the post had been filled since 1997. In the 2007 legislative election, which was boycotted by about 40 opposition parties, the PCT and its allies retained their large majority. Senate elections were due in July 2008.

POLITICAL SYSTEM

Under the 2002 constitution, the executive president is directly elected for a seven-year term, and appoints the cabinet. The bicameral *Parlement* comprises the National Assembly, of 137 members directly elected for a five-year term, and the senate, which has 66 members indirectly elected for a six-term term, half of the members retiring every three years.

HEAD OF STATE

President, Denis Sassou-Nguesso, *took power* October 1997, *elected* 10 March 2002

SELECTED GOVERNMENT MEMBERS *as at May 2008*

Prime Minister, Isidore Mvouba
Economy, Finance and Budget, Pacifique Issoibeka
Foreign and Francophone Affairs, Rodolphe Adada
Defence, Brig.-Gen. Jacques Yvon Ndolou

EMBASSY OF THE REPUBLIC OF CONGO

37 bis rue Paul Valéry, 75116 Paris, France
T (+33) (1) 4500 6057
Ambassador Extraordinary and Plenipotentiary, HE Henri Lopes, *apptd* 1999

BRITISH AMBASSADOR

HE Nicholas Kay, *apptd* 2007, resident at Kinshasa, DR of Congo

DEFENCE

The army has 40 main battle tanks and 68 armoured personnel carriers. The navy has 3 patrol and coastal combatant vessels at a base at Pointe Noire. The air force has 2 armed helicopters.
Military budget – US$97m (2007 est)
Military personnel – 10,000: army 8,000, navy 800, air force 1,200; paramilitary 2,000

ECONOMY AND TRADE

Oil revenues enabled the government to embark on development schemes in the 1980s but the slump in oil prices in the late 1990s and a decade of civil conflict have left the country with a high external debt, a budget deficit and widespread poverty. Since 2003 the government has made efforts to address these problems and in 2006 qualified for debt relief under the IMF–World Bank heavily indebted poor countries initiative; most of Congo's debt was cancelled in 2007.

Oil production is the backbone of the economy and the recovery in oil prices has boosted GDP. Mining, especially diamonds, forestry, brewing, agricultural processing and cement production are the other main industries. Agriculture, which is mostly at subsistence level, accounts for 5.6 per cent of GDP, industry for 57.1 per cent and services for 37.3 per cent.

The main markets are China, the USA, France and Taiwan. Principal exports are oil, timber, plywood, sugar, cocoa, coffee and diamonds. Imports are mainly capital equipment, construction materials and foodstuffs.
GNI – US$3,800m; US$1,050 per capita (2006)
Annual average growth of GDP – 2.8 per cent (2007 est)
Inflation rate – 7 per cent (2007 est)
Total external debt – US$5,000m (2000)
Imports – US$1,850m (2006)
Exports – US$6,780m (2006)

BALANCE OF PAYMENTS
Trade – US$4,926m surplus (2006)
Current Account – US$125m surplus (2006)

Trade with UK	*2005*	*2006*
Imports from UK	£20,494,000	£26,892,000
Exports to UK	£7,980,000	£9,747,000

COMMUNICATIONS

Pointe Noire is the main seaport and is the centre of the offshore oil industry. It is linked to Brazzaville by rail and road. Brazzaville is the main river port, lying on the river Congo, which, with the Ubango river, provides 1,125km of commercially navigable waterways. There are 894km of railways and 17,289km of roads, 864km of which are surfaced. Five of the 31 airports and airfields have surfaced runways. Telecommunications are poor and frequently out of order. Mobile phone distribution was 490,000 in 2005.

EDUCATION AND HEALTH

Literacy rate – 82.8 per cent (2004 est)
Gross enrolment ratio (percentage of relevant age group) – primary 108 per cent; secondary 43 per cent (2006 est)
Health expenditure (per capita) – US$31 (2005)
HIV/AIDS adult prevalence – 4.9 per cent (2003 est)

MEDIA

Brazzaville is the centre of the country's print media industry with five privately owned newspapers regularly published there. TV Congo is the only television station and it is state-owned and controlled by Radiodiffusion Télévision Congolaise. Radio Congo is also state-controlled. Prison sentences for libel and insult were abolished under a 2001 reform law, but punishments for incitement to violence and racism are still enforceable.

COSTA RICA

República de Costa Rica – Republic of Costa Rica

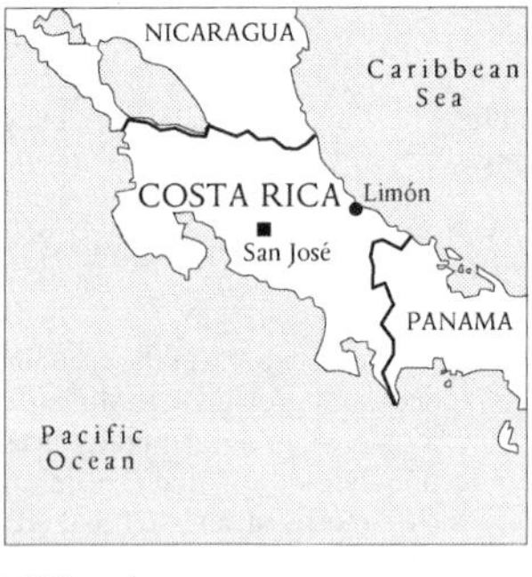

Area – 51,100 sq. km
Capital – San José; population, 1,284,000 (2007 est)
Major towns – Alajuela, Liberia, Limón, Paraíso, San Francisco
Currency – Costa Rican colón of 100 céntimos
Population – 4,133,884 rising at 1.41 per cent per year (2007 est)
Religion – Roman Catholicism (74 per cent), Protestantism (13 per cent) (est). Around 9 per cent of the population has no religious affiliation
Language – Spanish (official), English
Population density – 86 per sq. km (2006)
Urban population – 61.7 per cent (2005 est)
Median age (years) – 26.8 (2007 est)
National anthem – 'Noble Patria, Tu Hermosa Bandera' ['Noble Fatherland, Your Beautiful Flag']
National day – 15 September (Independence Day)
Life expectancy (years) – 77.21 (2007 est)
Mortality rate – 4.39 (2007 est)
Birth rate – 18.02 (2007 est)
Infant mortality rate – 9.45 (2007 est)
Death penalty – Abolished for all crimes (since 1877)
CPI score – 5.0 (2007)
Population below poverty line – 18 per cent (2004 est)
Literacy rate – 95.8 per cent (2004 est)
Gross enrolment ratio (percentage of relevant age group) – primary 111 per cent; secondary 86 per cent; tertiary 25 per cent (2006 est)
Health expenditure (per capita) – US$327 (2005)
Hospital beds (per 1,000 people) – 1.4 (2000–6)

CLIMATE AND TERRAIN

The Cordillera de Guanacaste (north-west), Cordillera Central and Cordillera de Talamanca (south-east) form a chain of volcanic mountain ranges that traverse the country from north to south. Elevation extremes range from 3,810m (Chirripó Grande) to 0m (Pacific Ocean) at the lowest. The climate is tropical, with an average annual temperature of 26°C. The wet season runs from May to November. The area is subject to occasional earthquakes, hurricanes, flooding and landslides.

HISTORY AND POLITICS

Visited by Columbus in 1502, Costa Rica was under Spanish rule for nearly three centuries (1530–1821). In 1821 the country gained independence and from 1824 became a member of the United Provinces (Federation) of Central America until its secession in 1839. Political unrest in the mid-20th century led to a brief civil war in 1948, after which the army was abolished and replaced with a national guard. Since then power has alternated between the two main political parties, the Social Christian Unity Party (PUSC) and the National Liberation Party (PLN).

In the 2006 legislative elections, the PLN became the largest party, with 25 seats, but without an outright majority. The simultaneous presidential election was won narrowly by the PLN candidate Oscar Arias Sanchez, president in 1986–90 and the winner of the Nobel Peace prize in 1987 for devising the strategy that ended the civil wars in Nicaragua and El Salvador; he received 40.92 per cent of the vote.

POLITICAL SYSTEM
Under the 1949 constitution, the executive president is directly elected for a four-year term. Legislative power is vested in the unicameral legislative assembly), which has 57 members directly elected for a four-year term.

HEAD OF STATE
President, Oscar Arias, *elected* 5 February 2006, *sworn-in* 9 May 2006
First Vice-President, Justice, Laura Chinchilla
Second Vice-President, Kevin Casas

SELECTED GOVERNMENT MEMBERS *as at May 2008*
Finance, Guillermo Zuniga
Foreign Affairs, Bruno Stagno

EMBASSY OF COSTA RICA
14 Lancaster Gate, London W2 3LH
T 020-7706 8844 E costarica@btconnect.com
Ambassador Extraordinary and Plenipotentiary, HE Pilar Saborio de Rocafort, *apptd* 2007

BRITISH EMBASSY
Apartado 815, Edificio Centro Colón (11th Floor), San José 1007
T (+506) 258 2025 E britemb@racsa.co.cr
W www.britishembassycr.com
Ambassador Extraordinary and Plenipotentiary, HE Tom Kennedy, LVO, *apptd* 2006

DEFENCE
The armed forces consist of 9,800 paramilitaries. The coast guard has 20 patrol and coastal vessels at 6 bases.
Security budget – US$132m (2007 est)
Military personnel – 9,800: Civil Guard 4,500, Border Police 2,500, Coast Guard Unit 400, Air Surveillance Unit 400, Rural Guard 2,000

ECONOMY AND TRADE
Sixty years of political stability has allowed economic growth, the creation of a social welfare system and a reduction in poverty; less than 20 per cent of the population is below the poverty line. The economic problems of the 1990s were overcome by diversification, but budget and trade imbalances have created large internal and external debt and inflation is high. Economic reforms are difficult because of inflexibility in the labour market and the last administration's reform attempts provoked widespread public protests, as did the country's ratification of the Central America Free Trade Agreement with the USA in 2007.

Tourism is the largest single industry, and with one-third of the country now national parkland or nature reserve, eco-tourism is on the increase. The manufacturing industry accounts for around 29.4 per cent of GDP, the principal products being microprocessors, foodstuffs, medical equipment, textiles, clothing, construction materials and plastic goods. The agricultural sector contributes 8.6 per cent of GDP; the principal products are tropical fruit, coffee, ornamental plants, sugar, rice, vegetables, beef and timber.

The main trading partners are the USA, China, the Netherlands and other Central American states. The chief exports are agricultural products, seafood, electrical components and medical equipment. The chief imports are raw materials, consumer goods, capital equipment, petroleum and construction materials.
GNI – US$21,900m; US$4,980 per capita (2006)
Annual average growth of GDP – 6.1 per cent (2007 est)
Inflation rate – 9.3 per cent (2007 est)
Unemployment – 5.5 per cent (2007 est)
Total external debt – US$7,163m (2007)
Imports – US$11,500m (2006)
Exports – US$8,200m (2006)

BALANCE OF PAYMENTS
Trade – US$3,305m deficit (2006)
Current Account – US$1,108m deficit (2006)

Trade with UK	*2006*	*2007*
Imports from UK	£33,643,000	£46,101,961
Exports to UK	£501,352,000	£495,317,929

COMMUNICATIONS
The chief seaports are Limón on the Atlantic coast, through which passes most of the coffee exported, and Puntarenas on the Pacific coast. There are 151 airports and airfields, 36 of which have surfaced runways; the principal ones are at San José and Limón. The national air carrier is LACSA. There are 278km of railways, none of which is in use, and 35,330km of roads, 8,621km of which are surfaced. The telephone system is modern and efficient, although mobile phone coverage is restricted.

CÔTE D'IVOIRE

République de la Côte d'Ivoire – Republic of Côte d'Ivoire

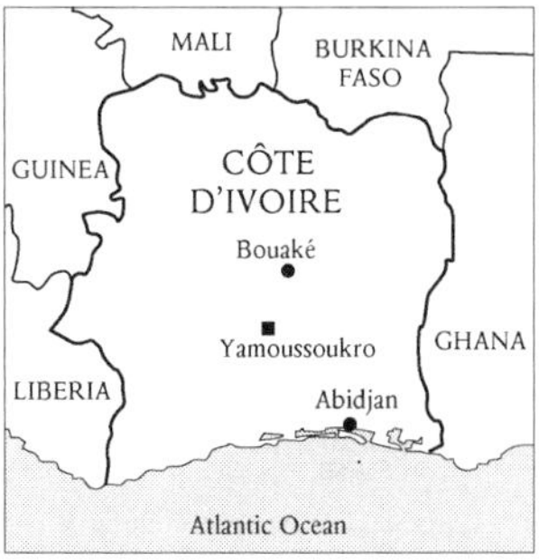

Area – 322,460 sq. km
Capital – Yamoussoukro; population, 668,000 (2007 est), the political and administrative capital since 1983
Major cities – Abidjan, Bouaké, Daloa, Korhogo
Currency – Franc CFA of 100 centimes
Population – 18,013,409 rising at 2 per cent per year (2007 est); Akan (42.1 per cent), Voltaiques or Gur (17.6 per cent), Northern Mandes (16.5 per cent), Krous (11 per cent), Southern Mandes (10 per cent) (est)
Religion – Christianity (35 per cent), Islam (35 per cent), indigenous religions (25 per cent) (est). Many Christians and Muslims incorporate some indigenous belief into their worship
Language – French (official), Dioula
Population density – 59 per sq. km (2006)
Urban population – 45.8 per cent (2005 est)
Median age (years) – 19.3 (2007 est)
National anthem – 'L'Abidjanaise' ['Song of Abidjan']
National day – 7 August (Independence Day)
Life expectancy (years) – 49 (2007 est)
Mortality rate – 14.74 (2007 est)
Birth rate – 34.69 (2007 est)
Infant mortality rate – 87.41 (2007 est)
HIV/AIDS adult prevalence – 6.4 per cent (2005 est)
Death penalty – Abolished for all crimes (since 2000)
CPI score – 2.1 (2007)
Literacy rate – 48.1 per cent (2004 est)
Gross enrolment ratio (percentage of relevant age group) – primary 71 per cent (2006 est)
Health expenditure (per capita) – US$34 (2005)

CLIMATE AND TERRAIN
The land rises from a coastal plain through tropical rainforest to savannah and low mountains in the north. Elevation extremes range from 1,752m (Mt Nimba) at the highest point to 0m (Gulf of Guinea) at the lowest. The climate is tropical in the south and semi-arid in the north.

The south has two rainy seasons (May–July, October–November) and the north one (June–September). Average temperatures range from 24°C in August to 27°C in March.

HISTORY AND POLITICS

The first European visitors were Portuguese navigators in the 1460s, and Europeans established the ivory trade and some slave trading in the 16th century. The area came under French influence from 1842, and Côte d'Ivoire became a protectorate in 1889 and a colony in 1893, although it was not pacified until 1912. It achieved self-government in 1958, and became independent on 7 August 1960 as a one-party state with Felix Houphouët-Boigny as president. A multiparty system was introduced in 1990.

The post-independence period of stability ended after President Houphouët-Boigny's death in 1993. The adoption of xenophobia as a political tool in the late 1990s opened up religious and ethnic divisions, particularly between the Muslim north and the Christian south and west of the country. These emerged in violence between supporters of different candidates in the 2000 presidential election, won by Laurent Gbagbo of the Ivorian Popular Front. Reconciliation moves were progressing when a mutiny in 2002 developed into a rebellion that plunged the country into civil war.

The civil war ended in 2003 with a ceasefire that left the country divided between the government-controlled south and the rebel-held north, with international peacekeeping troops deployed in 2003 to maintain a buffer zone between the two. Despite the ceasefire, clashes continued, drawing in UN peacekeepers in late 2004. Further talks between the government and rebels in 2006–7 resulted in a power-sharing peace agreement in March 2007 and the rebel leader Guillaume Soro became prime minister of the transitional government. Presidential and legislative elections are expected in November 2008.

POLITICAL SYSTEM

Under the 2000 constitution, the executive president is directly elected for a five-year term, renewable only once. The president appoints the prime minister. The unicameral National Assembly has 225 members, directly elected for a five-year term.

HEAD OF STATE

President, Laurent Gbagbo, *elected* 22 October 2000, *sworn in* 26 October 2000

SELECTED GOVERNMENT MEMBERS *as at May 2008*

Prime Minister, Guillaume Soro
Defence, Michel Amani N'guessan
Interior, Desire Tagro Assegnini
Foreign Affairs, Youssouf Bakayoko
Finance and Economy, Charles Dibi Koffi

EMBASSY OF THE REPUBLIC OF CÔTE D'IVOIRE

2 Upper Belgrave Street, London SW1X 8BJ
T 020-7235 6991
Ambassador Extraordinary and Plenipotentiary, HE Philippe Djangoné-Bi, *apptd* 2007

BRITISH HIGH COMMISSIONER

HE Dr Nicholas Westcott, CMG, *apptd* 2007, resident at Accra, Ghana

DEFENCE

The army has 10 main battle tanks, 10 armoured infantry fighting vehicles and 41 armoured personnel carriers. The navy has 3 patrol and coastal combatant vessels. The air force has 6 combat capable aircraft.

Military budget – US$300m (2007 est)
Military personnel – 17,050: army 6,500, navy 900, air force 700, Presidential Guard 1,350, Gendarmerie 7,600; paramilitary 1,500

ECONOMY AND TRADE

Political instability has damaged an economy that was performing well. It is heavily dependent on agriculture, leaving it vulnerable to fluctuations in world prices of its key exports. Although diversification has been hampered by the civil war and its aftermath, discouraging foreign investment, revenue from oil and refined products is now outstripping earnings from cocoa.

Agriculture accounts for 22.7 per cent of GDP, industry for 26.3 per cent and services for 51 per cent. Agriculture employs around 68 per cent of the workforce, producing cocoa (of which Côte d'Ivoire is the world's largest producer and exporter), coffee, cotton, bananas, pineapples and palm oil for export. The principal industries are food processing, forestry, oil refining, vehicle assembly, textiles, fishing and the production of oil, natural gas and hydroelectric power; the country is a net exporter of electricity. The main trading partners are France and Nigeria.

GNI – US$16,600m; US$880 per capita (2006)
Annual average growth of GDP – 1.4 per cent (2007 est)
Inflation rate – 1.8 per cent (2007 est)
Total external debt – US$10,910m (2007 est)
Imports – US$5,300m (2006)
Exports – US$8,700m (2006)

BALANCE OF PAYMENTS

Trade – US$3,415m surplus (2006)
Current Account – US$529m surplus (2006)

Trade	*2005*	*2006*
Imports from UK	£54,022,000	£39,841,000
Exports to UK	£74,919,000	£83,252,000

COMMUNICATIONS

Côte d'Ivoire has 660km of railways and 80,000km of roads, 6,500km of which are surfaced. There are 980km of navigable rivers, canals and lagoons. The main seaports are Abidjan and San Pedro. There are 34 airports and airfields, the principal international airport being at Abidjan. Although the telephone system is well developed, fixed-line density is only 2 per 100 people. Mobile phone distribution was 4 million in 2006 (23 per 100 people), and internet users numbered 300,000.

MEDIA

The state broadcaster is Radiodiffusion Télévision Ivoirienne (RTI). RTI operates two national radio stations and two television channels, all of which have frequently been used as propaganda tools by the government. There are no private terrestrial television stations although subscription services are available.

Radio is the most popular medium for news, with around 30 non-commercial community radio stations located throughout the country. In August 2004, UN peacekeepers launched their own radio station, ONUCI FM. Initially available only in Abidjan, the station now covers rebel-held towns in the north.

The print media is represented by two government-owned and around 20 privately owned daily newspapers. Several opposition newspapers have been raided by government officials and ceased publication.

CROATIA

Republika Hrvatska – Republic of Croatia

Area – 56,542 sq. km
Capital – Zagreb; population, 690,000 (2007 est)
Major cities – Osijek, Rijeka, Split
Currency – Kuna of 100 lipa
Population – 4,493,312 falling at 0.04 per cent per year (2007 est); Croat (89.6 per cent), Serb (4.5 per cent)
Religion – Roman Catholicism (85 per cent), Orthodox Christianity (6 per cent), Islam (1 per cent) (est); 2 per cent of the population is thought to be atheist
Language – Croatian (official), Serbian, Italian, Hungarian, Czech, Slovak, German
Population density – 79 per sq. km (2006)
Urban population – 59.9 per cent (2005 est)
Median age (years) – 40.6 (2007 est)
National anthem – 'Lijepa Nasa Domovina' ['Our Beautiful Homeland']
National day – 8 October (Independence Day)
Life expectancy (years) – 74.9 (2007 est)
Mortality rate – 11.57 (2007 est)
Birth rate – 9.63 (2006 est)
Infant mortality rate – 6.6 (2007 est)
Death penalty – Abolished for all crimes (since 1990)
CPI score – 4.1 (2007)
Population below poverty line – 11 per cent (2003)

CLIMATE AND TERRAIN

There are three major geographic areas: the Pannonian region in the north, the central mountain belt, and the Adriatic coast region of Istria and Dalmatia, which has 1,185 islands and islets and 1,778km of coastline. Elevation extremes range from 1,830m (Dinara) at the highest point to 0m (Adriatic Sea) at the lowest. The climate varies significantly between the Dalmatian coast, where the winters are mild and the summers hot, and inland areas, which are more typical of eastern Europe with colder temperatures and rain in the summer. Average temperatures in Zagreb, away from the coast, range from 2°C in January to 26°C in July.

HISTORY AND POLITICS

Croatia was ruled by the Habsburgs from 1526 to 1918. With the collapse of the Austro-Hungarian Empire at the end of the First World War, Croatia declared its independence on 29 October 1918 and soon after joined with Slovenia, Bosnia-Hercegovina, Serbia and Montenegro to form the Kingdom of Serbs, Croats and Slovenes (renamed Yugoslavia in 1929). From 1941 to 1945, Yugoslavia was occupied by the Axis powers; Italy and Hungary annexed parts of Croatia and a pro-Nazi Croat puppet state was established in the remainder of Croatia and Bosnia-Hercegovina. The armed extremists of this state (the Ustae) engaged in fierce fighting with Serbian royalists, communist partisans and pro-allied Croat partisans. At the end of the Second World War, Croatia became a republic within the Socialist Federal Republic of Yugoslavia, which gradually disintegrated following the death of President Tito in 1980.

In 1991 Croatia declared its independence from the Yugoslav federation. The efforts of the Federal Yugoslav Army (JNA) and ethnic Serbs in Croatia to prevent Croatia's secession led to civil war until January 1992, when a ceasefire was declared. Fighting restarted the following year as Croatian forces set out to retake the ethnic Serb areas of the country that had seceded; Krajina and Western Slavonia were recaptured in 1995, and Eastern Slavonia agreed in 1995 to re-integration by 1998. From 1992 to 1995 Croatian forces were also involved in the war in Bosnia-Hercegovina. Croatia signed the Dayton accord in 1995.

Post-independence politics was dominated by the authoritarian President Franjo Tudjman, a former partisan who was first elected president in 1990. Since his death in 1999, Croatia has become more outward-looking, and applied to join the EU in 2003; its expected accession date is 2010.

President Stipe Mesic, first elected in 2000, was re-elected in 2005 in the second round of voting. In the 2007 legislative election, the Croatian Democratic Union (HDZ) retained its position as the largest party in the legislature but without an overall majority, and formed a coalition government with the Croatian Social Liberal Party, the Independent Democratic Serb Party and the Croatian Peasant Party.

POLITICAL SYSTEM

The 1990 constitution was amended in 2000 to increase the powers of the legislature, making the presidency a largely ceremonial role, and in 2001 to abolish the upper house of the legislature. The head of state is a president, who is directly elected for a five-year term. Executive power is vested in the prime minister, who is appointed by the legislature, and government. Legislative power is vested in the unicameral House of Representatives, which has 153 members directly elected for a four-year term.

HEAD OF STATE

President, Stipe Mesic, *elected* 7 February 2000, *re-elected* 17 January 2005

SELECTED GOVERNMENT MEMBERS *as at May 2008*

Prime Minister, Ivo Sanader
Deputy Prime Ministers, Jadranka Kosor; Damir Polancec; Djurdja Adlesic; Slobodan Uzelac
Defence, Branko Vukelic
Finance, Ivan Suker
Foreign Affairs, Gordan Jandrokovic
Interior, Berislav Roncevic

EMBASSY OF THE REPUBLIC OF CROATIA

21 Conway Street, London W1T 6BN
T 020-7387 2022 **E** croemb.london@mvp.hr **W** http://uk.mvp.hr

Ambassador Extraordinary and Plenipotentiary, HE Josip Paro, *apptd* 2002

BRITISH EMBASSY
ul Ivana Lucica 4, 10000 Zagreb
T (+385) 600 9100 E british.embassyzagreb@fco.gov.uk
W www.britishembassy.gov.uk/croatia
Ambassador Extraordinary and Plenipotentiary, HE Sir John Ramsden, Bt., *apptd* 2000

BRITISH COUNCIL
Illica 12, PP 55, 10001 Zagreb
T (+385) 1489 9500 W www.britishcouncil.org/croatia
Director, Adrian Chadwick

DEFENCE

The armed forces are subject to an arms limitation regime established under the Dayton accord. The army has 297 main battle tanks, 104 armoured infantry fighting vehicles and 33 armoured personnel carriers. The navy has 2 submarines and 5 patrol and coastal combatant vessels at five major bases. The air force has 12 combat aircraft.

Military budget – US$875m (2007)
Military personnel – 17,660: army 12,300, navy 1,700, air force 1,800, joint staff 1,860; paramilitaries 3,000
Conscription duration – 6 months

ECONOMY AND TRADE

As part of Yugoslavia, Croatia was a prosperous and industrialised area but the conflict in 1991–5 damaged the infrastructure, large areas of farmland, industrial production and the tourist industry. Since 2000 there has been steady economic growth, led by a recovery in tourism, banking and public investment. However, there are budget and trade deficits, high unemployment, a large public sector and a lack of political will to address these problems, although structural reform will be necessary to meet the criteria for EU membership.

The service sector accounts for 60.7 per cent of GDP, industry for 32 per cent, and agriculture for 7.2 per cent. Industry produces chemicals and plastics, machine tools, metal and metals, electronics, wood products and textiles, and includes food processing, shipbuilding and oil refining. Agricultural production includes grains, fruit and vegetables, livestock and dairy products. Most trade is with neighbouring countries.

GNI – US$41,400m; US$9,310 per capita (2006)
Annual average growth of GDP – 5.6 per cent (2007 est)
Inflation rate – 2.2 per cent (2007 est)
Unemployment – 11.8 per cent (2007 est)
Total external debt – US$41,560m (2007)
Imports – US$21,500m (2006)
Exports – US$10,400m (2006)

BALANCE OF PAYMENTS
Trade – US$11,112m deficit (2006)
Current Account – US$3,377m deficit (2006)

Trade with UK	*2006*	*2007*
Imports from UK	£146,557,000	£159,110,908
Exports to UK	£68,769,000	£74,281,020

COMMUNICATIONS

Those parts of the transport infrastructure destroyed in fighting in the 1990s have mostly been reconstructed, and parts of the rail and road networks have been modernised and expanded. There are 2,726km of railways and 28,436km of roads, including 792km of motorway. The principal airports are at Zagreb and Split. The national carrier is Croatia Airlines. There are 785km of inland waterways, including a stretch of the river Danube, and frequent ferry services to the many Adriatic islands. The main seaports are Rijeka (Fiume), Zadar, Split, Sibenik and Dubrovnik. The telephone system is being modernised and extended. There were 4.5 million mobile phone subscribers in 2006, compared to 1.8 million main line users.

EDUCATION AND HEALTH

Literacy rate – 98.1 per cent (2004 est)
Gross enrolment ratio (percentage of relevant age group) – primary 93 per cent; secondary 89 per cent; tertiary 46 per cent (2006 est)
Health expenditure (per capita) – US$812 (2005)
Hospital beds (per 1,000 people) – 5.5 (2000–6)

MEDIA

The constitution guarantees freedom of the press. Croatian Radio-Television (HRT) is the national state-owned broadcaster and is the main source of news. Nove TV is the country's first national private network. There are three main news publications: *Vecernji List* (daily), *Feral Tribune* (weekly), *Nacional* (weekly).

CUBA

República de Cuba – Republic of Cuba

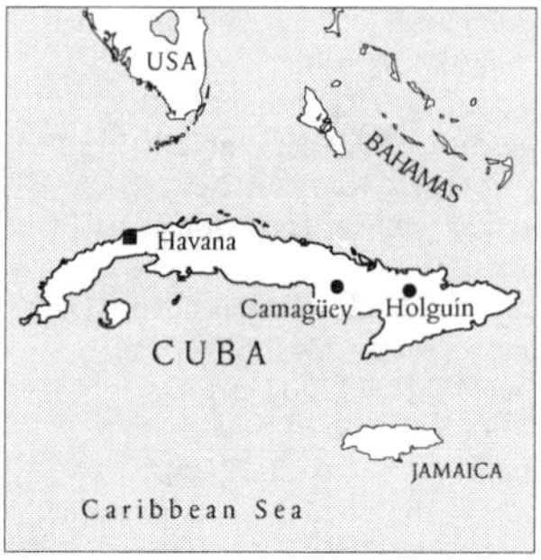

Area – 110,860 sq. km
Capital – Havana; population, 2,174,000 (2007 est)
Major cities – Camagüey, Guantánamo, Holguín, Santa Clara, Santiago de Cuba
Currency – Cuban peso of 100 centavos
Population – 11,394,043 rising at 0.27 per cent per year (2007 est)
Religion – Roman Catholicism (40 per cent), Protestantism (4 per cent) (est)
Language – Spanish (official)
Population density – 103 per sq. km (2006)
Urban population – 76 per cent (2005 est)
Median age (years) – 36.3 (2007 est)
National anthem – 'La Bayamesa' ['The Bayamo Song']
National day – 1 January (Triumph of the Revolution)
Life expectancy (years) – 77.08 (2007 est)
Mortality rate – 7.14 (2007 est)
Birth rate – 11.44 (2007 est)
Infant mortality rate – 6.04 (2007 est)
Death penalty – Retained
CPI score – 4.2 (2007)

CLIMATE AND TERRAIN

Cuba, the largest island in the Caribbean, is part of an archipelago that also includes Isla de la Juventud and 1,600 other islets and cays. The island of Cuba has three mountainous ranges running from east to west. Elevation extremes range from 2,005m (Pico Turquino) at the highest point to 0m (Caribbean Sea) at the lowest. The climate is subtropical, with an average annual temperature of 25°C.

HISTORY AND POLITICS

The island was visited by Columbus in 1492. In the early 16th century the island was settled by the Spanish and remained under rule until 1898, when power was transferred to the USA as part of the spoils of the Spanish-American War. Cuba became independent in 1902, albeit with a condition allowing the USA to retain naval bases on the island. The dictatorship of Gen. Batista (1933–44, 1952–9) was overthrown in 1959 in a revolution led by Fidel Castro. A communist state was established in 1961 which quickly became allied with the USSR. This alliance and the regime's policies on the one hand, and the USA's support of exiled Cuban opponents on the other, created great friction in US-Cuban relations, to the extent that the USA has maintained an economic and trade embargo since 1961.

When the USSR collapsed in 1991, Cuba lost the economic, commercial and military support it had enjoyed since 1960. Faced with severe economic deterioration, the government introduced rationing and relaxed state controls on economic activity. The latter resulted in increased overseas investment and a growing tourist sector, although state control has been reasserted in recent years. Since 2003 the EU has restricted its political and cultural contacts with Cuba over its poor human rights record.

Fidel Castro, who had been elected president for successive terms from the revolution until 2003, underwent surgery in July 2006 and his brother Raúl became acting president for the rest of his term of office. Fidel Castro announced in February 2008 that he would not accept another term of office and Raúl Castro was elected president later that month by the national assembly.

POLITICAL SYSTEM

The Communist Party of Cuba (PCC), formed in 1965, is the only authorised political party. The 1976 constitution was amended in 1991 to allow direct election of the National Assembly by secret ballot, and in 2002 to enshrine socialism in the constitution. The president is indirectly elected by the legislature for a five-year term. The unicameral National Assembly of the People's Power has 614 members directly elected for a five-year term; all candidates are approved by the PCC and stand unopposed. Between its sessions, the assembly is represented by the Council of State, whose members are elected by the assembly.

HEAD OF STATE

President of Council of State and Council of Ministers, Gen. Raúl Castro Ruz, *elected* 24 February 2008

Vice Presidents, Jose Ramon Machado Ventura; Jose Ramon Fernandez Alvarez; Osmany Cienfuegos Gorriaran; Jose Luis Rodriguez Garcia; Otto Rivero Torres

SELECTED GOVERNMENT MEMBERS *as at May 2008*

Armed Forces, Maj.-Gen. Julio Casas Requeiro
Finance and Prices, Georgina Barreiro Fajardo
Foreign Relations, Felipe Ramon Pérez Roque
Interior, Gen. Abelardo Colomé Ibarra

EMBASSY OF THE REPUBLIC OF CUBA
167 High Holborn, London WC1 6PA
T 020-7240 2488 E embacuba@cubaldn.com
W www.cubaldn.com
Ambassador Extraordinary and Plenipotentiary, HE René Juan Mujica Cantelar, *apptd* 2005

BRITISH EMBASSY
Calle 34, No 702, Miramar, Havana
T (+53) (0) 7204 1771 E embrit@ceniai.inf.cu
W www.britishembassy.gov.uk/cuba
Ambassador Extraordinary and Plenipotentiary, HE John Dew, *apptd* 2001

BRITISH COUNCIL
c/o British Embassy
T (+53) (0) 7204 1771/2 W www.britishcouncil.org/cuba
Director, Jenny White

DEFENCE

The army has about 900 main battle tanks, 50 armoured infantry fighting vehicles and 500 armoured personnel carriers. The navy has 7 patrol and coastal vessels and bases. The air force has 179 combat aircraft (of which only some 31 are operational) and 4 armed helicopters.

The USA has 592 joint task force personnel at Guantánamo Bay Naval Base, which has been leased since before the 1959 revolution.

Military expenditure – US$1,660m (2006)
Military personnel – 49,000: army 38,000, navy 3,000, air force 8,000; paramilitary 26,500
Conscription duration – 24 months

ECONOMY AND TRADE

After the revolution virtually all land and industrial and commercial enterprises were nationalised. With the collapse of communism in Europe in 1989–91, the economy deteriorated sharply, necessitating rationing of energy, food and consumer goods, and obliging the government to introduce reforms. Since 1993, the government has permitted private enterprise, cut subsidies to loss-making state industries, allowed prices for some goods and services to rise, and introduced income tax. Once ownership of property and business enterprises was opened to foreign investors in 1995, foreign companies have started to operate, especially in the oil and mining industries. The reforms, some now reversed, resulted in steady growth but the standard of living for most Cubans is still below the pre-1991 level. Energy shortages, which caused frequent power cuts from 1991, were overcome in 2006 with the import of electricity generators, run on fuel supplied by Venezuela.

State farms have been transformed into privately run cooperatives and are permitted to sell 20 per cent of their produce on the open market. Agriculture contributes 4.6 per cent of GDP but employs about 20 per cent of the workforce. The main crop is sugar, one of the mainstays of the economy although it is subject to fluctuating world prices. Industrial activities include sugar refining, oil production, tobacco processing, construction, nickel mining and production of steel, cement, agricultural machinery and pharmaceuticals. Industry contributes 26.1 per cent of GDP, and the service sector 69.3 per cent. About 78 per cent of the workforce is employed in the state sector.

The main trading partners are China, Canada, Venezuela, the Netherlands and Spain; Venezuela provides oil at preferential terms. Principal exports are sugar, nickel, tobacco, fish, medical products, citrus fruits and coffee. The main imports are oil, food, machinery and equipment and chemicals.

Annual average growth of GDP – 7 per cent (2007 est)
Inflation rate – 3.6 per cent (2007 est)
Unemployment – 1.9 per cent (2007 est)
Total external debt – US$16,790m (2007 est)

Trade with UK	*2006*	*2007*
Imports from UK	£20,533,000	£16,537,301
Exports to UK	£8,050,000	£6,170,013

COMMUNICATIONS

The transport system has suffered as a result of recent economic difficulties, although the growth in tourism has stimulated and paid for some remedies. Even so, road and rail services are subject to cancellation owing to breakdowns or fuel shortages. There are 4,226km of railways, with an additional 7,742km of track used exclusively by the sugar plantations. There are 60,858km of roads, 29,820km of which are surfaced, including 638km of motorway. Air services link the major cities and offshore islands; the islands are also served by ferries. There are 165 airports and airfields, of which 70 are surfaced; the main international airport is at Havana. The main ports are Havana, Cienfuegos and Matanzas.

The telephone system has been improved since 2000 but land-line density is low, with fewer than 10 lines per 100 residents. Mobile phone ownership has been permitted since March 2008 but the cost is prohibitive. Ownership of computers and other electrical consumer goods has been permitted since March 2008, but internet access is still largely restricted to foreigners and the government elite.

EDUCATION AND HEALTH

Education is free of charge and compulsory at all levels. In some rural areas children attend boarding schools where agricultural tasks are compulsory in addition to schoolwork. After basic education students can choose to go to a pre-collegiate school or a technical school. The pre-collegiate school is free to graduates.

Literacy rate – 99.8 per cent (2004 est)
Gross enrolment ratio (percentage of relevant age group) – primary 101 per cent; secondary 94 per cent; tertiary 88 per cent (2006 est)
Health expenditure (per capita) – US$310 (2005)
Hospital beds (per 1,000 people) – 4.9 (2000–6)

MEDIA

The media is tightly controlled by the government so journalists practise self-censorship. Conviction for libel or insulting officials can result in a three-year prison term. Private ownership of electronic media is prohibited and foreign news agencies are permitted only to hire local journalists through government offices. The official Communist Party newspaper is *Granma*. The main television stations are Cubavision, Tele-Rebelde and CHTV. The main radio stations are Radio Rebelde and Radio Reloj. Radio-TV Marti is a US government-backed station that transmits from Florida.

CULTURE

Cubans are perhaps most famous for their music, a vibrant mix of Spanish traditional guitar melodies and African rhythms. Rumba, mambo, bolero, salsa and cha-cha-cha all evolved from *son,* a type of Cuban music that originated in the hills of Oriente at the turn of the 20th century. Cuban music returned to the world stage with the success of the Buena Vista Social Club (publicised by the Wim Wenders film of the same name) in the late 1990s. Writers of international standing include Cirilo Villaverde y de la Paz (1812–94), José Martí (1853–95), Alejo Carpentier (1904–80), Nicolás Guillén (1902–89) and Guillermo Cabrera Infante (1929–2005).

CYPRUS

Kypriaki Dimokratía/Kibris Cumhuriyeti – Republic of Cyprus

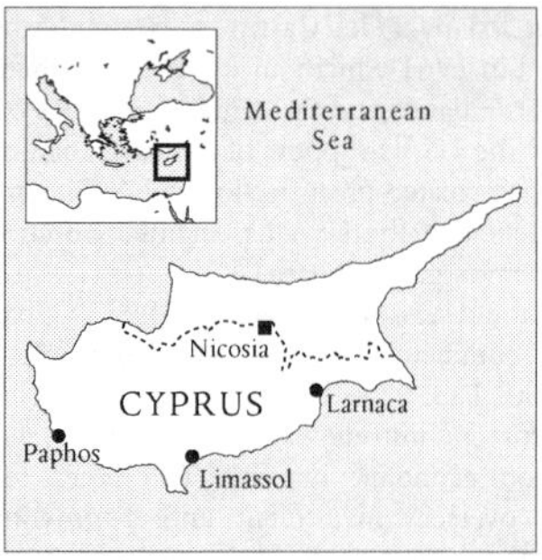

Area – 9,250 sq. km, of which 3,355 sq. km are in the Turkish Cypriot-administered area
Capital – Nicosia; population 233,000 (2007 est)
Major cities – Larnaca; Limassol; Paphos
Currency – Cyprus pound (C£) of 100 cents
Population – 788,457 rising at 0.53 per cent per year (2007 est); Greek (77 per cent), Turkish (18 per cent)
Religion – 95 per cent Greek Orthodox south of the partition; 99 per cent Muslim north of the partition
Language – Greek, Turkish (both official), English
Population density – 83 per sq. km (2006)
Urban population – 69.5 per cent (2005 est)
Median age (years) – 35.1 (2007 est)
National anthem – 'Ymnos eis tin Eleftherian' ['Hymn to Freedom']
National day – 1 October (Independence Day)
Life expectancy (years) – 77.98 (2007 est)
Mortality rate – 7.72 (2007 est)
Birth rate – 12.56 (2007 est)
Infant mortality rate – 6.89 (2007 est)
Death penalty – Abolished for all crimes (since 2002)
CPI score – 5.3 (2007)
Literacy rate – 96.8 per cent (2004 est)

CLIMATE AND TERRAIN

Cyprus is the third largest island in the Mediterranean. It has two mountain ranges, the Pentadaktylos range along the north coast, and the Troodos range (which includes Mt Olympus) in the centre and west. Elevation extremes range from 1,951m (Mt Olympus) at the highest point to 0m (Mediterranean Sea) at the lowest. The climate is Mediterranean with very warm summers.

HISTORY AND POLITICS

Cyprus has a recorded history of over 4,000 years, and its rulers have included the Greeks, Phoenicians, Ptolemaic

Egyptians, Romans, Byzantines, Arabs, Franks, Venetians, Turks and the British. Cyprus was ceded to Britain by Turkey in 1878, then formally annexed by Britain in 1914, and became a crown colony in 1925. Greek Cypriot demands for union with Greece *(enosis)* led to guerrilla warfare against the British administration in the 1950s and a four-year state of emergency (1955–9). An agreement was signed in 1959 between Britain, Greece, Turkey and the Greek and Turkish Cypriots which stipulated that Cyprus would become an independent republic; the island became independent on 16 August 1960, with Britain retaining sovereignty over the military bases at Akrotiri and Dhekelia.

The constitution provided for power-sharing between the Greek and Turkish Cypriots but this proved unworkable and led to intercommunal trouble throughout the 1960s and in 1971. The UN Peacekeeping Force in Cyprus was deployed in 1964. In 1974, a coup against the government backed by the mainland Greek government led Turkey, which feared *enosis,* to invade. It occupied the northern third of the island, partitioning the island and displacing over 160,000 Greek Cypriots. Talks on reunification in the 1980s and 1990s were unsuccessful, and there were further sporadic outbreaks of intercommunal violence. The approach of Cyprus' admission to the EU gave added impetus to the search for a settlement from 1999, but a UN-sponsored reunification plan was rejected by Greek Cypriots in a referendum in April 2004, and only the southern part of the island joined the EU in May 2004. Relations have eased since, and the Greek and Turkish Cypriot leaders agreed in March 2008 to resume reunification talks.

In the 2006 legislative election, the Progressive Party of the Working People (AKEL) and the Democratic Rally (DISY) each won 18 seats. AKEL formed a coalition government with DIKO and another smaller party. Demetris Christofias, the AKEL candidate, was elected president in February 2008.

HEAD OF STATE

President, Demetris Christofias, *elected* 24 February 2008, *sworn in* 28 February 2008

SELECTED GOVERNMENT MEMBERS *as at May 2008*

Defence, Costas Papacostas
Finance, Charilaos Stavrakis
Foreign Affairs, Marcos Kyprianou
Interior, Neoclis Sylikiotis

HIGH COMMISSION FOR THE REPUBLIC OF CYPRUS

93 Park Street, London W1K 7ET
T 020-7499 8272 E cyphclondon@dial.pipex.com
High Commissioner, HE George Iacovou, *apptd* 2006

BRITISH HIGH COMMISSION

PO Box 21978, Alexander Pallis Street, 1587 Nicosia
T (+357) 2286 1100 E infobhc@cylink.cy
W www.britain.org.cy
High Commissioner, HE Peter Millett, *apptd* 2005

BRITISH COUNCIL

1–3 Aristotelous Street, 1011 Nicosia
T (+357) 2258 5000 W www.britishcouncil.org/cyprus
Director, Richard Law

BRITISH SOVEREIGN BASE AREAS

The Sovereign Base Areas (SBAs) of Akrotiri and Dhekelia are those parts of the island which remained under British sovereignty and jurisdiction when Cyprus became independent in 1960. They have the status of a British overseas territory and are around 253 sq. km in size. There are approximately 15,700 residents: 7,700 Cypriots, 3,900 service and UKBC personnel, of whom 3,600 live in the SBAs, and nearly 5,000 dependants, of whom over 4,400 live in the SBAs. There are also nearly 2,700 locally employed civilians.

Administrator of the British Sovereign Base Areas, Air Vice-Marshal Richard Lacey, CBE, *apptd* 2006

DEFENCE

The National Guard has 154 main battle tanks, 43 armoured infantry fighting vehicles and 310 armoured personnel carriers. Turkey has around 36,000 troops in northern Cyprus.

A military airfield in Paphos provides a base for Greek military aircraft, as Cyprus does not possess its own air force.

Military budget – US$346m (2007)
Military personnel – National Guard 10,000, paramilitaries 750; Northern Cyprus Army 5,000, paramilitaries 150
Conscription duration – 25 months

ECONOMY AND TRADE

The Greek Cypriot economy is dominated by the service sector, which accounted for 77.8 per cent of GDP in 2007; this was derived mainly from tourism and financial services. With about 2.5 million visitors each year, tourism represents around 20 per cent of GDP. Shipping services are also important; about 20 per cent of the world's shipping is Cypriot-registered. Industry contributes 19.1 per cent of GDP and agriculture 3.1 per cent. The main products for export are citrus fruits, potatoes, pharmaceuticals, cement, clothing and cigarettes. Imports are primarily consumer goods, fuel and lubricants, intermediate goods and machinery. Over 50 per cent of trade is with other EU countries. Cyprus adopted the euro in January 2008.

The Turkish Cypriot economy suffers from a small domestic market, international isolation and a large public sector. It is heavily dependent on financial support from the Turkish government. Services accounted for about 69 per cent of GDP in 2003, industry for 20 per cent and agriculture for 11 per cent. The main products for export are citrus fruits, dairy products, potatoes and textiles. The main imports are vehicles, fuel, cigarettes, food, minerals, chemicals and machinery. The tourist industry is small because the only international transport links are via Turkey.

GNI – US$17,948m; US$23,270 per capita (2006)
Annual average growth of GDP – 3.9 per cent (2007 est)
Inflation rate – 2.3 per cent (2005 est)
Unemployment – 3.8 per cent (2005 est)
Total external debt – US$26,120m (2007 est)
Imports – US$6,950m (2006)
Exports – US$1,150m (2006)

BALANCE OF PAYMENTS

Trade – US$5,798m deficit (2006)
Current Account – US$1,081m deficit (2006)

Trade with UK	*2006*	*2007*
Imports from UK	£995,300,000	£410,955,898
Exports to UK	£1,246,800,000	£180,100,058

COMMUNICATIONS

There are no railways. The road network (12,280km in the Greek part of the island and 2,350km in the Turkish part) serves the main population centres, although crossings between the Greek and Turkish areas are closed or controlled. In the Greek area, the main airports are at Larnaca and Paphos, and the principal ports are Limassol, Larnaca and Paphos. In the Turkish area, the main ports are Famagusta and Kyrenia; there is an airport but flight connections are with Turkey only.

MEDIA

The division of the country is mirrored in the media, with the Turkish north operating its own services and broadcasts. There is competition between state and privately owned television and radio stations. Newspapers on both sides of the divide are free to criticise the authorities.

TURKISH REPUBLIC OF NORTHERN CYPRUS

In 1974, a coup against the Cypriot government backed by the mainland Greek government led Turkey, fearing the coup was a precursor to the union of Cyprus with Greece, to invade northern Cyprus and occupy over a third of the island. The next year, a Turkish Federated State of Cyprus under Rauf Denktash was declared and in 1983 a declaration of statehood was issued which purported to establish the Turkish Republic of Northern Cyprus. The declaration was condemned by the UN security council and only Turkey has recognised the new state. In 1985 Denktash was elected president and a general election was held. Denktash was re-elected in 1990, 1995 and 2000, retiring at the 2005 election. A UN plan for the reunification of the island was approved by the Turkish Cypriot population in a 2004 referendum, but the plan's rejection by the Greek Cypriots has left the status of northern Cyprus unchanged. Confidence-building measures instituted by both governments have improved relations between the two communities, and reunification talks were scheduled to resume in June 2008.

The legislative election in February 2005 was won by the party of the incumbent prime minister, Mehmet Ali Talat, and his allies. Talat subsequently won the presidential election in April 2005.

DE FACTO HEAD OF STATE
President, Mehmet Ali Talat, *elected* 17 April 2005, *sworn in* 24 April 2005
Prime Minister, Ferdi Sabit Soyer

CZECH REPUBLIC

Ceska Republika – Czech Republic

Area – 78,866 sq. km
Capital – Prague (Praha); population, 1,162,000 (2007 est)
Major cities – Brno (Brünn), Ostrava, Plzen (Pilsen)
Currency – Koruna (Kcs) of 100 haleru
Population – 10,228,744 falling at 0.07 per cent per year (2007 est); Czech (90.4 per cent), Moravian (3.7 per cent), Slovak (1.9 per cent) (est)
Language – Czech (official), Slovak
Population density – 133 per sq. km (2006)
Urban population – 74.5 per cent (2005 est)
Median age (years) – 39.5 (2007 est)
National anthem – 'Kde Domov Muj?' ['Where is My Motherland?']
National day – 28 October (Founding Day)
Life expectancy (years) – 76.42 (2007 est)
Mortality rate – 10.64 (2007 est)
Birth rate – 8.96 (2007 est)
Infant mortality rate – 3.86 (2007 est)
Death penalty – Abolished for all crimes (since 1990)
CPI score – 5.2 (2007)

CLIMATE AND TERRAIN

The landlocked republic is composed of Bohemia (the west and centre) and Moravia (the east). Bohemia contains the fertile plain of the river Elbe surrounded by hills and low mountains, while the hilly region of Moravia extends towards the basin of the river Danube. Roughly a third of the country is covered by forest. Elevation extremes range from 1,602m (Snezka) at the highest point to 115m (Elbe) at the lowest. The climate is continental, with warm, humid summers and cold, dry winters. The average temperature in Prague ranges from 2°C in January to 19°C in July.

HISTORY AND POLITICS

The area came under the rule of the Habsburg dynasty in 1526 and remained part of the Austro-Hungarian Empire until 1918. The rise of Czech nationalism in the late 19th century led to Czechoslovakia's independence on 28 October 1918 following an amalgamation of Bohemia, Moravia, Slovakia and Ruthenia. It was officially confirmed at the Versailles Peace Conference of 1919.

Czechoslovakia was forced to cede the ethnic German Sudetenland to Nazi Germany in 1938 after the Munich agreement. German forces invaded the Czech lands in 1939 and incorporated them into Germany while Slovakia became a puppet state. The republic was liberated by Soviet and US forces in 1945. The pre-war democratic Czechoslovak state was re-established in 1945, having ceded Ruthenia to the Soviet Union. Communists took power in a coup in 1948 and remained in power until 1989.

In 1968, the Communist Party under Alexander Dubcek embarked on a political and economic reform programme (known as the Prague Spring). The reforms were suppressed following an invasion by Warsaw Pact troops on 20 August 1968, and were abandoned when Gustav Husak became leader of the Communist Party in 1969.

After mass protests in November 1989, the Communist Party central committee resigned, and the party was forced to concede its monopoly on power. On 10 December a new government was appointed in which only half the ministers were Communists. Husak resigned as president and was replaced by the dissident writer Vaclav Havel. Free elections were held in 1990 in which the Communist Party was defeated.

In late 1992, the leaders of the Czech and Slovak republics agreed to dissolve the federation and form two sovereign states; this took effect on 1 January 1993. The Czech Republic joined the EU in 2004.

President Havel left office in February 2003 but parliament was unable to agree on a successor until, at the third attempt, Vaclav Klaus of the Civic Democrat Party (ODS) was elected on 28 February; he was narrowly re-elected in 2008. The 2006 legislative elections were inconclusive and after a minority ODS government lost a vote of confidence in October 2006, the ODS formed a three-party centre-right coalition government with the Christian Democrats and the Green Party in January 2007.

POLITICAL SYSTEM

The 1992 constitution provided for the separation of the Czech Republic and Slovakia; federal laws remain in place unless superseded by Czech ones. The president is elected by both chambers of the legislature for a five-year term, with a maximum of two consecutive terms. The bicameral parliament comprises a 200-member Chamber of Deputies directly elected for a four-year term, and an 81-member senate directly elected for a six-year term, one-third being elected every two years. Executive power is held by the council of ministers, appointed by the president on the recommendation of the prime minister.

HEAD OF STATE

President, Vaclav Klaus, *elected by parliament* 28 February 2003, *sworn in* 7 March 2003, *re-elected* February 2008

SELECTED GOVERNMENT MEMBERS *as at May 2008*

Prime Minister, Mirek Topolanek
Minister of Vice-Premiers, Finance, Bohuslav Sabotka
Deputy Prime Ministers, Martin Bursik; Petr Necas; Alexandr Vondra; Jiri Cunek
Defence, Vlasta Parkanova
Interior, Ivan Langer
Foreign Affairs, Karel Schwarzenberg
Finance, Miroslav Kalousek

EMBASSY OF THE CZECH REPUBLIC

26 Kensington Palace Gardens, London W8 4QY
T 020-7243 1115 E london@embassy.mzv.cz
W www.czechembassy.org.uk
Ambassador Extraordinary and Plenipotentiary, HE Jan Winkler, *apptd* 2005

BRITISH EMBASSY

Thunovska 14, 11800 Prague 1
T (+420) (2) 5740 2111 E info@britain.cz W www.britain.cz
Ambassador Extraordinary and Plenipotentiary, HE Linda Duffield, *apptd* 2004

BRITISH COUNCIL

Bredovsky dvur, Politickych veznu 13, 11000 Prague 1
T (+420) 221 991 111 W www.britishcouncil.org/czechrepublic
Director (acting), Matt Burney

DEFENCE

The army has 181 main battle tanks, 508 armoured infantry fighting vehicles and 72 armoured personnel carriers. The air force has 50 combat aircraft and 38 armed helicopters.
Military expenditure – US$2,460m (2006)
Military personnel – 23,092: joint staff 23,092; paramilitary 3,100

ECONOMY AND TRADE

Economic reforms since 1990 have produced a stable and prosperous market economy. Accession to the EU has encouraged further reform and restructuring, as well as contributing to the continuing steady growth by expanding export markets and encouraging investment. A customs union between the Czech and Slovak republics is in place but separate currencies were introduced in 1993 following speculation.

Services account for 57.9 per cent of GDP, industry for 39.7 per cent and agriculture for 2.4 per cent. The principal agricultural products are sugar beet, potatoes and cereal crops; the timber industry is also very important. Having been the major industrial area of the Austro-Hungarian Empire, the country has long been industrialised, and metals, machinery, vehicles, glass and armaments are major products. The principal trading partners are EU countries, especially Germany, and Russia.
GNI – US$131,400m; US$12,790 per capita (2006)
Annual average growth of GDP – 5.7 per cent (2007 est)
Inflation rate – 2.6 per cent (2007 est)
Unemployment – 6.6 per cent (2007 est)
Total external debt – US$61,740m (2007)
Imports – US$93,000m (2006)
Exports – US$95,000m (2006)

BALANCE OF PAYMENTS

Trade – US$1,707m surplus (2006)
Current Account – US$4,462m deficit (2006)

Trade with UK	*2006*	*2007*
Imports from UK	£1,503,100,000	£1,384,132,908
Exports to UK	£2,151,400,000	£2,962,904,172

COMMUNICATIONS

There are extensive road (127,865km) and rail (9,597km) networks linking the main population centres. Navigable inland waterways include 664km on the Elbe, Vltava, Oder and other rivers, lakes and canals. The principal airport is at Prague and the national carrier is Czech Airlines, which operates international and domestic services. The telecommunications system was privatised recently and is being modernised. Mobile phone distribution has grown rapidly, to 120 phones per 100 people.

EDUCATION AND HEALTH

Education is free of charge and compulsory for all children from the age of six to 15. Primary education lasts for nine years, divided into two stages of five and four years respectively. Secondary education comprises three main types of school: general schools, technical schools and vocational schools.
Gross enrolment ratio (percentage of relevant age group) – primary 102 per cent; secondary 96 per cent; tertiary 48 per cent (2006 est)
Health expenditure (per capita) – US$868 (2005)
Hospital beds (per 1,000 people) – 8.4 (2000–6)

MEDIA AND CULTURE

The public broadcaster is Ceska Televize (CT) and it runs two networks and a 24-hour news channel. There are several private television stations. Czech public radio, Cesky Rozhlas (CRo), operates three national networks and local services alongside over 70 private radio stations throughout the country.

Prague is famous for its Art Nouveau architecture, cobbled streets and squares and thriving cultural life (particularly its contemporary jazz scene). The best-known Czech composers include Antonin Dvorak (1841–1904), Bedrich Smetana (1824–84) and Leos Janacek (1854–1928). Among its important writers are Franz Kafka (1883–1924), Milan Kundera (*b.* 1929), Ivan Klima (*b.* 1931) and Vaclav Havel (*b.* 1936).

DENMARK

Kongeriget Danmark – Kingdom of Denmark

Area – 43,094 sq. km (excluding the Faeroe Islands and Greenland)
Capital – Copenhagen; population, 1,085,000 (2007 est)
Major cities – Alborg, Arhus, Odense
Currency – Danish krone of 100 ore
Population – 5,468,120 rising at 0.31 per cent per year (2007 est)
Religion – Protestant (Lutheran) (83 per cent), Islam (4 per cent) (est). Around 1 per cent of the population is atheist
Language – Danish (official), English, German, Faroese, Greenlandic
Population density – 128 per sq. km (2006)
Urban population – 85.5 per cent (2005 est)
Median age (years) – 40.1 (2007 est)
National anthem – 'Det er et Yndigt Land' ['There is a Lovely Land']
National day – 5 June (Constitution Day)
Life expectancy (years) – 77.96 (2007 est)
Mortality rate – 10.3 (2007 est)
Birth rate – 10.91 (2007 est)
Infant mortality rate – 4.45 (2007 est)
Death penalty – Abolished for all crimes (since 1978)
CPI score – 9.4 (2007)

CLIMATE AND TERRAIN

Denmark consists of most of the Jutland peninsula and 406 islands, mainly in the Baltic Sea or among the northern Frisian Islands in the North Sea. The largest islands are Sjaelland (Zealand), Fyn, Lolland, Faister and Bornholm. It is a low-lying country, indented by fjords on its east coast and with lagoons and sand dunes along the west coast. Elevation extremes range from 173m (Yding Skovhoej) at the highest point to −7m (Lammefjord) at the lowest. There are cold winters and warm summers. Average temperatures range from 0°C in January to 17°C in July.

HISTORY AND POLITICS

The Danes were at the forefront of Viking expansionism from the eighth century. Denmark was unified in the 10th century and was the centre of the short-lived empire, also including Norway and England, created by Cnut (Canute) in the 11th century. The Union of Kalmar (1397) brought Norway and Sweden (including Finland) under Danish rule. Danish power waned during the 16th century, enabling Sweden to re-establish its independence in 1523. In 1814 Norway was ceded to Sweden under the Treaty of Kiel, and in 1864 Schleswig and Holstein, which had been subsumed in 1460, were lost to Germany. Northern Schleswig was returned in 1919 after a plebiscite. Denmark was neutral during the First World War, but in the Second World War it was invaded and occupied by Germany.

Iceland declared its independence from Denmark in 1944 and the Faeroe Islands were granted home rule in 1948. Greenland, which previously had the status of a colony, was integrated into Denmark in 1953 and granted home rule in 1979.

Denmark joined the European Community in 1973. In a referendum in 2000, it rejected membership of the European single currency.

Social Democrat-led coalitions dominated the post-war era, creating a welfare state. They lost the 1982 election but were in power again from 1993 to 2001. In the 2001 legislative election, the Liberal Party became the largest party in parliament, and formed a coalition government with the Conservative People's Party. This coalition government retained power in the 2005 and 2007 general elections, winning 89 of the 179 seats in 2007.

POLITICAL SYSTEM

The country is a constitutional monarchy, with the hereditary monarch as head of state. The head of government is the prime minister, who appoints the cabinet. The unicameral legislature, the *Folketing*, has 179 members, including two for the Faeroes and two for Greenland; members are elected for a four-year term by proportional representation.

HEAD OF STATE

HM The Queen of Denmark, Queen Margrethe II, KG, *born* 16 April 1940, *acceded* 14 January 1972
Heir, HRH Crown Prince Frederik, *born* 26 May 1968

SELECTED GOVERNMENT MEMBERS *as at May 2008*

Prime Minister, Anders Fogh Rasmussen
Defence, Soeren Gade Jensen
Finance, Lars Loekke Rasmussen
Foreign Affairs, Per Stig Moeller
Interior, Karen Jespersen

ROYAL DANISH EMBASSY

55 Sloane Street, London SW1X 9SR
T 020-7333 0200 E lonamb@um.dk W www.denmark.org.uk
Ambassador Extraordinary and Plenipotentiary, HE Birger Riis-Jorgensen, *apptd* 2006

BRITISH EMBASSY

Kastelsvej 36–40, 2100 Copenhagen
T (+45) 3544 5200 E brit-emb@post6.tele.dk
W www.britishembassy.dk
Ambassador Extraordinary and Plenipotentiary, HE Nicholas Archer, MVO, *apptd* 2008

BRITISH COUNCIL

Gammel Mont 12.3, 1117 Copenhagen K
T (+45) (33) 369 400 W www.britishcouncil.org/denmark
Director, Dr Michael Sorensen-Jones

DEFENCE

The army has 231 main battle tanks, 395 armoured personnel carriers and 12 armed helicopters. The navy has 49 patrol and coastal vessels at 2 bases. The air force has 48 combat aircraft.

Military expenditure – US$3,870m (2006)
Military personnel – 29,960: army 14,240, navy 3,650, air force 3,830, joint staff 8,240
Conscription duration – 4–10 months

ECONOMY AND TRADE

Denmark has a diversified and industrialised market economy. Sound management of public finances means the budget and balance of trade are in surplus. It is a net exporter of food and energy (oil, natural gas and electricity). The service sector contributes 72.1 per cent of GDP, industry 26.3 per cent and the highly efficient agricultural sector 1.6 per cent.

The main trading partners are other EU countries, especially Germany and Sweden. Principal exports are machinery and instruments, meat and meat products, dairy products, fish, pharmaceuticals, furniture and windmills. The main imports are machinery and equipment, industrial raw materials and semi-manufactures, chemicals, grain and foodstuffs, and consumer goods.

GNI – US$283,300m; US$52,110 per capita (2006)
Annual average growth of GDP – 1.7 per cent (2007 est)
Inflation rate – 1.5 per cent (2007 est)
Unemployment – 3.5 per cent (2007 est)
Total external debt – US$492,600m (2007)
Imports – US$85,100m (2006)
Exports – US$91,700m (2006)

BALANCE OF PAYMENTS
Trade – US$6,613m surplus (2006)
Current Account – US$7,415m surplus (2006)

Trade with UK	*2006*	*2007*
Imports from UK	£3,711,700,000	£2,150,318,040
Exports to UK	£4,258,800,000	£3,376,169,772

COMMUNICATIONS

The main ports are Arhus, Odense, Copenhagen, Alborg and Esbjerg. The principal airports are at Copenhagen, Arhus, Alborg and near Vejle. There are 2,644km of railway, of which 636km is electrified. A rail tunnel and a bridge link the islands of Sjaelland (Zealand) and Fyn, and a road and rail tunnel and a bridge across the Oresund link Copenhagen with Malmo (Sweden). There are 72,257km of roads, including 1,032km of motorways. The telecommunications network is modern and extensive; mobile phone distribution is, at 5.8 million in 2006, over 100 per cent.

EDUCATION AND HEALTH

Education is free of charge and compulsory for nine years. Specialist schools are numerous, with commercial, technical and agricultural predominating.

Gross enrolment ratio (percentage of relevant age group) – primary 99 per cent; secondary 124 per cent; tertiary 81 per cent (2006 est)
Health expenditure (per capita) – US$4,350 (2005)
Hospital beds (per 1,000 people) – 3.8 (2000–6)

MEDIA

The public broadcaster is Danmarks Radio, which operates two television networks and national and regional radio stations. Private television stations can be obtained via satellite and cable. There are around 250 local commercial and community radio stations in operation. The country's commitment to a free press was reiterated in 2006 following the publication of satirical cartoons of the Prophet Muhammad in the *Jyllands-Posten* daily newspaper, which led to violent protests.

CULTURE

Denmark has made significant contributions to science and its Nobel laureates include atomic physicist Niels Bohr (1885–1962), who collaborated on the Manhattan project to develop nuclear power during the Second World War, and medical researcher Niels Finsen (1860–1904). Notable contributions have been made in music by Carl Nielsen (1865–1931), in design by Arne Jacobsen (1902–71) and Georg Jensen (1866–1935), in philosophy by Soren Kierkegaard (1813–55), and in literature by Hans Christian Andersen (1805–75) and Karen Blixen (1885–1962). Perhaps the most famous Dane of all, however, remains William Shakespeare's Prince Hamlet.

THE FAEROE ISLANDS

Area – 1,399 sq. km
Population – 47,511, rising at 2.44 per cent per year (2007 est)
Capital – Torshavn; population, 20,000 (2007 est)
National day – 29 July (Olaifest)

The Faeroe (Sheep) Islands are a group of 18 islands (17 inhabited) and a few islets in the North Atlantic Ocean, between the Shetland Islands and Iceland. First settled in the ninth century, the islands were a Norwegian province and, with Norway, came under Danish rule in the 14th century. Since 1948 the Faeroes have been self-governing. The islands are not part of the EU.

The sovereign is represented in the islands by a high commissioner. The government *(Landsstryri)* of three to six members deals with internal affairs. The parliament *(Logting)* has 33 members, elected for a four-year term. The islands send two representatives to the *Folketing* at Copenhagen. In the 2008 election to the *Logting*, the Republican Party won most seats but the coalition government of the Social Democrats, Union Party and People's Party formed in 2004 retained its majority and continued in office.

Prime Minister, Joannes Eidesgaard

ECONOMY AND TRADE
The economy has grown steadily in recent years, but remains highly dependent on fishing and fish processing; fish and fish products account for 94 per cent of exports. Offshore oil discoveries raise the possibility of future diversification.

BALANCE OF PAYMENTS
Trade – US$90m deficit (2003)
Current Account – US$7m deficit (2003)

Trade with UK	*2006*	*2007*
Imports from UK	£11,558,000	£20,748,269
Exports to UK	£103,851,000	£91,777,522

BRITISH CONSULATE
P/F Damfar, PO Box 1154, Niels Finsengota 5, FR-110 Torshavn
T (+298) 35 00 77
Honorary Consul, Tummas H. Dam

GREENLAND (KALAALLIT NUNAAT)

Area – 2,166,086 sq. km
Population – 56,344, falling at 0.03 per cent per year (2007 est)
Capital – Godthab (Nuuk); population 15,000 (2007 est)
National day – 21 June

Greenland, the world's largest island, lies between the Atlantic and Arctic oceans, to the east of Canada and to the west of Iceland. Most of Greenland is within the Arctic Circle, with permafrost covering about 80 per cent of the island. Elevation extremes range from 3,700m (Gunnbjorn) at the highest point to 0m (Atlantic Ocean) at the lowest.

Greenland was first discovered by small groups of hunters and nomadic groups who travelled from Canada *c.*500 BC. In the late 10th century, Viking invaders began establishing settlements along the south-eastern coast and started subsistence farming and trading with northern Europe. These colonies came under Norwegian rule in 1261 and had died out by the 16th century, though some Inuit settlements continued. Greenland became a Danish colony in the 18th century, and was granted internal autonomy in 1979. Greenland negotiated its withdrawal from the EU, without discontinuing relations with Denmark, and left in 1985. The USA has acquired the right to maintain air bases in Greenland.

The sovereign is represented by a high commissioner. The government *(Landsstyre)* is elected by the parliament *(Landsting)*, which has 31 members, elected for a four-year term. Greenland sends two representatives to the *Folketing* at Copenhagen. In the 2005 election to the *Landsting*, the Siumut ('Forward') party retained its ten seats and formed a coalition government with the Inuit Brotherhood and Atassut parties.
Prime Minister, Hans Enoksen (Siumut)

ECONOMY AND TRADE

Natural resources include zinc, lead, iron ore, coal, molybdenum, gold, platinum and uranium, some of which are mined, but the economy is dependent on fishing; fish and fish products comprise 94 per cent of exports. Hydrocarbon and mineral exploration is in progress, and tourism is being encouraged.

Trade with UK	*2005*	*2006*
Imports from UK	£464,000	£856,000
Exports to UK	£65,000	£578,000

DJIBOUTI

Jumhuriyat Jibuti/République du Djibouti – Republic of Djibouti

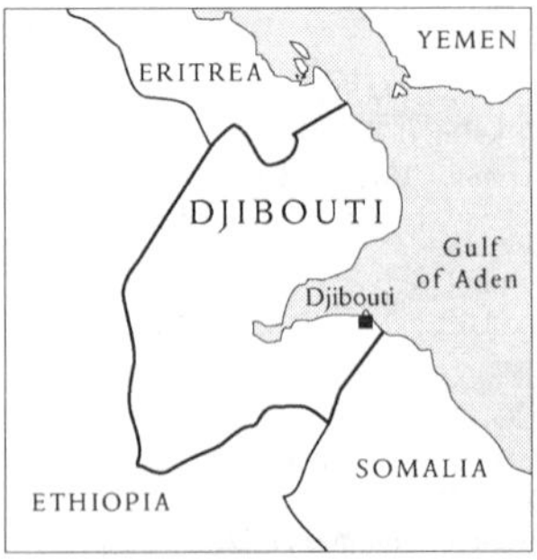

Area – 23,000 sq. km
Capital – Djibouti
Currency – Djibouti franc of 100 centimes
Population – 496,374 rising at 1.98 per cent per year (2007 est); Somali (60 per cent), Afar (35 per cent) (est)
Religion – Islam (99 per cent) (est). This number may be inflated as citizens are officially considered Muslims if they do not specifically identify with a faith
Language – French, Arabic (official), Somali, Afar
Population density – 35 per sq. km (2006)
Urban population – 84.6 per cent (2005 est)
Median age (years) – 18.2 (2007 est)
National anthem – 'Djibouti'
National day – 27 June (Independence Day)
Life expectancy – 43.25 (2007 est)
Mortality rate – 19.23 (2007 est)
Birth rate – 39.07 (2007 est)
Infant mortality rate – 100.77 (2007 est)
HIV/AIDS adult prevalence – 3 per cent (2005 est)
Death penalty – Abolished for all crimes (since 1995)
CPI score – 2.9 (2007)
Population below poverty line – 50 per cent (2001 est)

CLIMATE AND TERRAIN

Djibouti is situated on the east coast of Africa, at the point where the Gulf of Aden and the Red Sea meet. Elevation extremes range from 2,028m (Moussa Ali) at the highest point to −155m (Lake Assal) at the lowest. The country is prone to flash floods as well as cyclones, droughts and earthquakes. The climate is semi-arid with a hot season between May and September.

HISTORY AND POLITICS

Settled by the Afars (Ethiopian) and Issas (Somali) about 2,000 years ago, the area was annexed by the French in 1888 and became French Somaliland; in 1967 it was renamed the French Territory of the Afars and the Issas. The territory became independent as Djibouti on 27 June 1977, under President Hassan Gouled Aptidon (an Issa), the leader of the *Rassemblement Populaire pour le Progrès* (RPP) party, which became the only legal political party in 1981.

In 1991, Afar discontent with Issa domination of government under one-party rule led to civil war between the government and the *Front pour la Restauration de L'Unité et de la Democratie* (FRUD), an alliance of rebel groups. A multiparty constitution was introduced and multiparty elections were held in 1992, but fighting continued until a power-sharing agreement was reached in 1994. The civil war ended with the signing of a peace accord in 1996, although a breakaway faction of the FRUD continued its armed opposition to the government until 2001.

In the 2005 presidential election, President Guelleh was re-elected unopposed. In the 2008 legislative elections, which were boycotted by the opposition, the Union for a Presidential Majority (UMP), an alliance of the RPP, FRUD and two other parties supporting President Guelleh, retained all 65 seats in the legislature.

POLITICAL SYSTEM

Under the 1992 constitution, the president is directly elected for a six-year term, renewable only once. The unicameral National Assembly has 65 members, directly elected for a five-year term. The president appoints the council of ministers.

HEAD OF STATE
President, C.-in-C. of the Armed Forces, Ismail Omar Guelleh, *elected* 9 April 1999, *re-elected* 8 April 2005

SELECTED GOVERNMENT MEMBERS *as at May 2008*
Prime Minister, Dileita Muhammad Dileita
Defence, Ougoureh Kifleh Ahmed
Interior, Yacin Elmi Bouh
Economy, Finance, Ali Farah Assoweh
Foreign Affairs, Mahamoud Ali Youssouf

EMBASSY OF THE REPUBLIC OF DJIBOUTI
26 rue Emile Ménier, 75116 Paris, France
T (+33) (1) 4727 4922 E webmaster@ambdjibouti.org
W www.ambdjibouti.org
Ambassador Extraordinary and Plenipotentiary, HE Rachad Farah, *apptd* 2005

BRITISH AMBASSADOR
HE Norman Ling, *apptd* 2008, resident at Addis Ababa, Ethiopia

DEFENCE
The army has 12 armoured personnel carriers. The navy has 7 patrol and coastal combatant vessels. The Gendarmerie has 1 patrol and coastal combatant vessel.
Military budget – US$16.9m (2007 est)
Military personnel – 10,950: army 8,000, navy 200, air force 250, National Security Force 2,500; paramilitary 1,400

ECONOMY AND TRADE
A barren country with few natural resources and little industry, Djibouti's chief asset is its location. It is a transit port for neighbouring landlocked countries, a transshipment and refuelling centre, and a military base for US and EU forces because of its strategic position. The service sector accounts for 81.9 per cent of GDP, agriculture for 3.2 per cent, and industry for 14.9 per cent. The country is highly dependent on foreign aid and has fallen behind with external debt servicing in recent years. The main trading partners are Somalia, Ethiopia, Saudi Arabia, India, China and Yemen. Principal exports are re-exports, hides and skins, and coffee (in transit). The main imports are foodstuffs, transport equipment, chemicals and petroleum products.
GNI – US$864m; US$1,060 per capita (2006)
Annual average growth of GDP – 3.2 per cent (2005 est)
Inflation rate – 3 per cent (2005 est)
Unemployment – 50 per cent (2004 est)
Total external debt – US$394m (2004 est)
Imports – US$300m (2006)

BALANCE OF PAYMENTS
Trade – US$250m deficit (2006)
Current Account – US$109m deficit (2006)

Trade with UK	*2005*	*2006*
Imports from UK	£5,617,000	£5,183,000
Exports to UK	£1,311,000	£2,172,000

COMMUNICATIONS
There is 100km of railway, the Djibouti section of the Addis Ababa–Djibouti railway, controlled by both Djibouti and Ethiopia. The government is keen to expand the rail network into neighbouring countries to improve trade. Of the 2,890km of roads, 364km are surfaced. Djibouti is the main port, and the location of the principal airport. Three of the country's 13 airports and airfields have surfaced runways. The telephone system in Djibouti city, home to much of the population, is adequate but mobile phone distribution is now over three times greater than fixed-line density.

MEDIA
The government owns *La Nation,* the main newspaper, as well as Radiodiffusion-Télévision de Djibouti (RTD), the company which operates the national radio and television stations. There are a number of privately owned newspapers including *Al Qarn, La République,* and *Le Renouveau.* Independent newspapers are generally allowed to circulate freely, but journalists exercise self-censorship.

DOMINICA

Commonwealth of Dominica

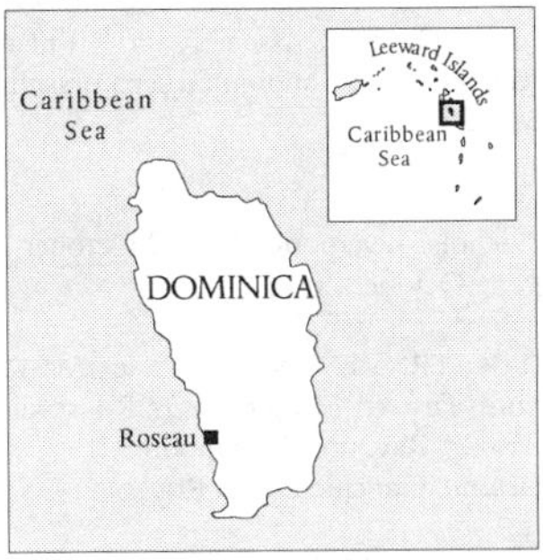

Area – 754 sq. km
Capital – Roseau; population, 14,000 (2007 est)
Currency – East Caribbean dollar (EC$) of 100 cents
Population – 72,386 rising at 0.18 per cent per year (2007 est)
Religion – Roman Catholicism (61 per cent), Protestantism (28 per cent) (est). Around 6 per cent of the population has no religious affiliation
Language – English (official), French patois
Population density – 97 per sq. km (2006)
Urban population – 72.7 per cent (2005 est)
Median age (years) – 29.1 (2007 est)
National anthem – 'Isle of Beauty, Isle of Splendour'
National day – 3 November (Independence Day)
Life expectancy – 75.1 (2007 est)
Mortality rate – 8.44 (2007 est)
Birth rate – 15.75 (2007 est)
Infant mortality rate – 14.61 (2007 est)
Death penalty – Retained
CPI score – 5.6 (2007)
Population below poverty line – 30 per cent (2002 est)

CLIMATE AND TERRAIN
Dominica, in the Lesser Antilles, lies in the Windward Islands group 95 miles south of Antigua. It is about 46km long and 25km wide, with a mountainous central ridge. Elevation extremes range from 1,447m (Morne Diablatins) at the highest point to 0m (Caribbean Sea) at the lowest. The climate is tropical with average daily temperatures ranging from 25°C to 32°C. The island is located within a hurricane zone.

HISTORY AND POLITICS

Dominica was discovered by Columbus in 1493, when it was a stronghold of the Caribs, the sole inhabitants of the island until the French founded settlements in the 18th century. It was captured by the British in 1759 but passed back and forth between France and Britain until 1805, after which British possession was unchallenged. From 1871 to 1939 Dominica was part of the Leeward Islands federation, then from 1940 part of the Windward Islands federation, and from 1958 part of the West Indies federation. Internal self-government from 1967 was followed on 3 November 1978 by independence as a republic.

The United Workers' Party (UWP) lost the 2000 election to the Dominica Labour Party (DLP), which formed a coalition government with the Dominica Freedom Party (DFP). The DLP remained the largest party after the 2005 election and continued in government in coalition with the DFP.

POLITICAL SYSTEM
Under the 1978 constitution, the president is elected by the legislature for a five-year term, renewable only once. The unicameral House of Assembly has 30 members, 21 directly elected, and nine appointed senators; all members sit for a five-year term.

HEAD OF STATE
President, Nicholas Liverpool, *elected* 2 October 2003, *took office* 6 October 2003

SELECTED GOVERNMENT MEMBERS *as at May 2008*
Prime Minister, Finance, Foreign Affairs, Roosevelt Skerrit
National Security, Rayburn Blackmoore
Attorney-General, Francine Baron-Royer

OFFICE OF THE HIGH COMMISSIONER FOR THE COMMONWEALTH OF DOMINICA
1 Collingham Gardens, London SW5 0HW
T 020-7370 5194 **E** dominicahighcom@btconnect.com
High Commissioner, Agnes Adonis

BRITISH HIGH COMMISSIONER
High Commissioner, HE Duncan Taylor, *apptd* 2005, resident at Bridgetown, Barbados

ECONOMY AND TRADE

Traditionally dependent on banana exports, the economy suffered a negative growth rate in 2003 after EU preferential treatment for this trade ended and was further damaged in 2007 by Hurricane Dean, which wiped out 99 per cent of the banana crop. Tourism is growing but is limited by poor facilities, including the lack of an international airport. The government is encouraging diversification into offshore financial services, fishing, forestry and light industry. An IMF-funded economic restructuring programme began in 2003 and the economy is growing again but at the expense of jobs.

Agriculture is the principal occupation, employing 40 per cent of the workforce but producing only 17.7 per cent of GDP. Services now contribute 49.5 per cent of GDP and industry 32.8 per cent. The main trading partners are China, the USA, the UK, South Korea and other Caribbean countries. Principal exports are bananas, soap, bay oil, vegetables and citrus fruits. The main imports are manufactured goods, machinery and equipment, food and chemicals.

GNI – US$300m; US$4,160 per capita (2006)
Annual average growth of GDP – 3.2 per cent (2007 est)
Inflation rate – –0.1 per cent (2005 est)
Unemployment – 23 per cent (2000 est)
Total external debt – US$213m (2004)
Imports – US$200m (2006)
Exports – US$100m (2000)

BALANCE OF PAYMENTS
Trade – US$127m deficit (2006)
Current Account – US$58m deficit (2006)

Trade with UK	*2006*	*2007*
Imports from UK	£5,698,000	£5,295,746
Exports to UK	£13,866,000	£5,890,940

MEDIA

Although there is no national television service, a private cable network covers part of the island. There are no daily newspapers but there are weekly publications. Private and public radio stations are in operation throughout the country. All media are free of government interference.

DOMINICAN REPUBLIC

República Dominicana – Dominican Republic

Area – 48,730 sq. km
Capital – Santo Domingo; population, 2,154,000 (2007 est)
Major cities – La Romana, San Pedro de Macorís, Santiago de los Caballeros
Currency – Dominican Republic peso (RD$) of 100 centavos
Population – 9,365,818 rising at 1.5 per cent per year (2007 est)
Religion – Roman Catholicism (69 per cent), Protestantism (18 per cent) (est). Many Catholics also practise a combination of Christianity and Afro-Caribbean beliefs (Santería) or witchcraft (brujería), but because these practices are rarely admitted, the number of adherents is impossible to estimate. Around 10 per cent of the population is atheist
Language – Spanish (official)
Population density – 199 per sq. km (2006)
Urban population – 60.1 per cent (2005 est)
Median age (years) – 24.5 (2007 est)
National anthem – 'Quisqueyanos Valientes' ['Valiant Sons of Quisqueya']
National day – 27 February (Independence Day)
Life expectancy (years) – 73.07 (2007 est)
Mortality rate – 5.32 (2007 est)
Birth rate – 22.91 (2007 est)

Infant mortality rate – 27.94 (2007 est)
HIV/AIDS adult prevalence – 1 per cent (2005 est)
Death penalty – Abolished for all crimes (since 1966)
CPI score – 3.0 (2007)
Population below poverty line – 42.2 per cent (2004)
Literacy rate – 87.7 per cent (2004 est)
Gross enrolment ratio (percentage of relevant age group) – primary 98 per cent; secondary 69 per cent; tertiary 35 per cent (2006 est)
Health expenditure (per capita) – US$197 (2005)
Hospital beds (per 1,000 people) – 2.2 (2000–6)

CLIMATE AND TERRAIN

The republic forms the eastern two-thirds of the island of Hispaniola (the remainder is Haiti) and is crossed from the north-west to the south-east by the Cordillera Central mountain range. Many of the mountains are over 3,000m. Elevation extremes range from 3,175m (Pico Duarte) at the highest point to −46m (Lake Enriquillo) at the lowest. The climate is maritime tropical with average temperatures of between 23°C and 27°C.

HISTORY AND POLITICS

The island was discovered by Columbus in 1492, and became a Spanish colony. The eastern province of Santo Domingo remained Spanish after the partition of Hispaniola in 1697, but was ceded to France in 1795. It was restored to Spanish rule in 1809. Independence was declared in 1821, but in 1822 it was subjugated by the neighbouring Haitians who remained in control until 1844, when the Dominican Republic was proclaimed. Under Spanish occupation for a third time in 1861–5, a long dictatorship at the end of the 19th century was followed by revolution and bankruptcy, which led to occupation by US forces from 1916 until 1924. A military coup in 1930 established the dictatorship of Gen. Rafael Trujillo, who ruled until his assassination in 1961. After a period of political instability, a new constitution was adopted in 1966 and democracy was restored.

The 2008 presidential election was won by Leonel Fernandez (president 1996–2000, 2004–) of the Dominican Liberation Party (PLD). The 2006 legislative elections were won in both houses by the PLD, which defeated the ruling Dominican Revolutionary Party.

POLITICAL SYSTEM

Under the 1966 constitution (amended in 2002), the executive president is directly elected for a four-year term, renewable only once. The bicameral National Congress comprises a lower chamber, the Chamber of Deputies, which has 178 members directly elected for a four-year term, and the senate, with 30 members, one for each province and one for Santo Domingo, directly elected for a four-year term.

HEAD OF STATE

President, Leonel Fernández Reyna, *elected* May 2004, *sworn in* August 2004, *re-elected* 17 May 2008
Vice-President, Rafael Alburquerque

SELECTED GOVERNMENT MEMBERS *as at May 2008*

Foreign Affairs, Carlos Morales Troncoso
Armed Forces, Gen. Ramon Aquino Garcia
Finance, Vincente Bengoa
Interior, Franklin Almeyda

EMBASSY OF THE DOMINICAN REPUBLIC

139 Inverness Terrace, London W2 6JF
T 020-7727 7091 E embassy@dominicanembassy.org.uk
W www.dominicanembassy.org.uk
Ambassador Extraordinary and Plenipotentiary, HE Anibal de Castro, *apptd* 2005

BRITISH EMBASSY

Edificio Corominas Pepín, Ave 27 de Febrero No 233, Santo Domingo
T (+1) (829) 472 7111 E brit.emb.sadom@codetel.net.do
Ambassador Extraordinary and Plenipotentiary, HE Ian Worthington, *apptd* 2006

DEFENCE

The army has 9 light tanks and 8 armoured personnel carriers. The navy has 16 patrol and coastal combatant vessels at two bases.
Military budget – US$268m (2007 est)
Military personnel – 49,910: army 40,410, navy 4,000, air force 5,500; paramilitary 15,000

ECONOMY AND TRADE

In recent years, tourism and the free trade zones have overtaken agriculture as the mainstay of the economy, and services now account for 60.2 per cent of GDP. Agriculture accounts for 11.5 per cent of GDP, and industry for 28.3 per cent. The main crops are sugar, coffee, cotton, cocoa, tobacco, rice, vegetables and bananas, and the main industrial activities are tourism, sugar processing, mining of ferro-nickel, gold and silver, and the production of textiles, cement and tobacco products. Remittances from expatriate workers represent nearly 10 per cent of GDP. A free-trade agreement with Central American states in 2007 is expected to boost trade, but unemployment and fluctuations in nickel prices remain problems.

The main trading partner is the USA, which takes 73 per cent of exports and provides nearly half of imports. Principal exports are ferro-nickel, sugar, gold, silver, coffee, cocoa, tobacco, meats and consumer goods. The chief imports are foodstuffs, fuel, cotton and fabrics, chemicals and pharmaceuticals.
GNI – US$28,000m; US$2,910 per capita (2006)
Annual average growth of GDP – 7.2 per cent (2007 est)
Inflation rate – 5.8 per cent (2007 est)
Unemployment – 15.5 per cent (2007 est)
Total external debt – US$8,842m (2007 est)
Imports – US$10,100m (2006)
Exports – US$1,930m (2006)

BALANCE OF PAYMENTS

Trade – US$9,900m deficit (2006)
Current Account – US$1,122m deficit (2006)

Trade with UK	*2006*	*2007*
Imports from UK	£51,449,000	£54,753,640
Exports to UK	£113,994,000	£83,959,987

COMMUNICATIONS

Santo Domingo and Rio Haina are the main seaports. There are 34 airports and airfields, seven of which handle international flights; the principal airport is at Santo Domingo. There are over 12,600km of roads, 6,224km of which are surfaced. There is 57km of railway, plus a further 1,226km operated by sugar companies. A metro system is under construction in Santo Domingo. Mobile phone distribution, at 50 per 100 people in 2006, is five times greater than main line density, which was 10 per 100 people. There are 1.2 million internet users.

MEDIA

There are several terrestrial commercial broadcasting stations and 30 multi-channel cable TV operators. The government-owned channel is Radio Television Dominicana (Canal 4). There are more than 200 commercial radio stations as well as two government stations. Press freedom is guaranteed by law.

EAST TIMOR

Republika Demokratika Timor Lorosa'e' – Democratic Republic of Timor-Leste

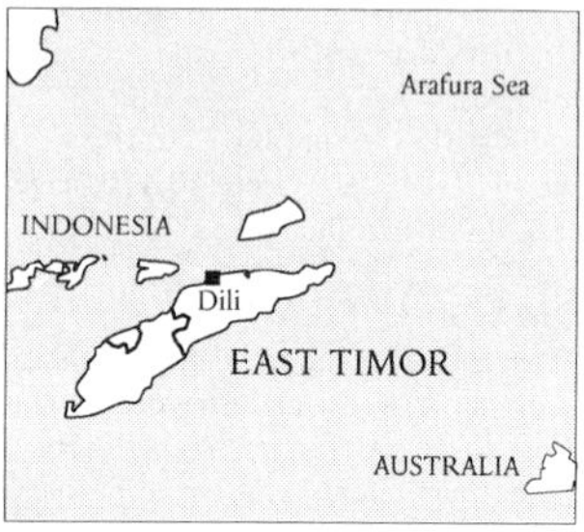

Area – 15,007 sq. km. The enclave of Oekussi is separated from the rest of East Timor by the Indonesian province of West Timor
Capital – Dili; population, 159,000 (2007 est)
Currency – Currency is that of the USA
Population – 1,084,971 rising at 2.06 per cent per year (2007 est)
Religion – Roman Catholicism (98 per cent), Protestantism (1 per cent), Islam (1 per cent) (est)
Language – Tetum, Portuguese (both official), Indonesian, English
Population density – 69 per sq. km (2006)
Urban population – 7.8 per cent (2005 est)
Median age (years) – 21.1 (2007 est)
National anthem – 'Patria' ['Fatherland']
National day – 28 November (Independence Day)
Life expectancy – 66.6 (2007 est)
Mortality rate – 6.19 (2007 est)
Birth rate – 26.77 (2007 est)
Infant mortality rate – 44.46 (2007 est)
Death penalty – Abolished for all crimes (since 1999)
CPI score – 2.6 (2007)
Population below poverty line – 42 per cent (2003 est)
Military personnel – 1,286: army 1,250, Naval Element 36
Gross enrolment ratio (percentage of relevant age group) – primary 99 per cent; secondary 53 per cent (2006 est)
Health expenditure (per capita) – US$45 (2005)

CLIMATE AND TERRAIN

The republic comprises the eastern half of the island of Timor, plus the enclave of Oekussi on the northern coast. The island, about 296km long and 72km wide, lies at the eastern end of the Indonesian archipelago. The interior is covered in forests and mountains. Elevation extremes range from 2,963m (Mt Tatamailau) at the highest point to 0m (Timor Sea) at the lowest. The climate is tropical.

HISTORY AND POLITICS

East Timor was a Portuguese colony from 1702 until 1975, when Portuguese rule was withdrawn following the 1974 coup in Portugal, but without a formal handover of power. The Revolutionary Front for an Independent East Timor (Fretilin), which supported independence, emerged as the strongest party in the 1975 election, but opposition by supporters of the integration of the territory into Indonesia led to civil war. Despite Fretilin's success in suppressing opposition, Indonesia used the civil war as an excuse to invade in December 1975 and declared East Timor Indonesia's 27th province in July 1976. By 1979, most of East Timor was under Indonesia's control, although Fretlin continued to engage in guerrilla warfare until the 1990s. The UN never recognised the annexation.

Following the fall of the Suharto regime in Indonesia, a plebiscite was held in August 1999 offering East Timor autonomy within Indonesia or independence; in a turnout of 98.5 per cent, 78.5 per cent voted for independence; the Indonesian consultative assembly unanimously ratified the result in October. This result provoked violence by pro-Indonesian militias and Indonesian troops, who murdered hundreds of people and devastated towns. Indonesia agreed to the deployment in September 1999 of UN peacekeeping troops, and the UN security council set up a transitional administration. East Timor became independent on 20 May 2002.

The UN mission left in 2005 when its peacekeeping duties ended. Troops returned in May 2006 to re-establish law and order; almost half the army had been dismissed in March for going on strike, and subsequent clashes between protesting ex-soldiers and the authorities had escalated into wider factional violence. A non-military UN peacekeeping mission was set up in August 2006. Instability continues, with violent protests in August 2007 over the appointment of the prime minister, and attacks on the president and prime minister by renegade soldiers in February 2008 which left the president seriously injured.

The 2007 presidential election was won in the second round by Jose Ramos-Horta, the former prime minister. In the 2007 legislative election, Fretilin won the largest number of seats, but without an overall majority. Negotiations with the National Congress for Timorese Reconstruction (CNRT) over forming a coalition failed, and the CNRT formed a coalition government with smaller parties under its leader, Xanana Gusmao, the former president; his appointment provoked violent protests by Fretilin supporters.

POLITICAL SYSTEM

The 2002 constitution established a parliamentary democracy. The president is directly elected for a five-year term, renewable only once. The unicameral national parliament has 65 members, directly elected for a five-year term. The council of ministers is nominated by the prime minister, who is appointed by the president.

HEAD OF STATE

President, Jose Ramos-Horta, *elected* 9 May 2007, *took office* 20 May 2007

SELECTED GOVERNMENT MEMBERS *as at May 2008*

Prime Minister, Defence, Xanana Gusmao
Deputy Prime Minister, Jose Louis Guterres
Foreign Affairs, Zacarias da Costa
Finance, Emilia Pires

BRITISH EMBASSY

Ambassador Extraordinary and Plenipotentiary, HE Charles Humfrey, *apptd* 2006, resident at Jakarta, Indonesia

ECONOMY AND TRADE

An internationally funded programme in 2002–5 achieved substantial reconstruction of the infrastructure destroyed in the 1999 post-referendum violence, but the 2006 outbreak of civil unrest and looting caused further damage and disrupted economic activity. It also displaced about 10 per cent of the population, many of whom remain in camps in Dili. Although the economy has grown since independence, this is largely owing to revenue from the exploitation of offshore oil and gas deposits, with other areas of the economy contracting. The new government has to address the high levels of poverty and unemployment (both over 40 per cent) and weak civil administration as well as the continuing security problems.

Services contribute 55 per cent of GDP, industry 12.8 per cent and agriculture 32.2 per cent. The main commercial crops are coffee, timber, rice, maize, vegetables, tropical fruits and vanilla. There are some light manufacturing industries and quarrying. Crude oil is piped to Australia for processing as there are no production facilities in East Timor. Principal exports are coffee, sandalwood and marble. The main imports are food, fuels and machinery. The main trading partners are EU countries, Australia and Indonesia.

GNI – US$900m; US$840 per capita (2006)
Annual average growth of GDP – 1.8 per cent (2005 est)
Inflation rate – 1.4 per cent (2005)
Unemployment – 50 per cent (2001 est)

BALANCE OF PAYMENTS
Current Account – US$679m surplus (2006)

Trade with UK	*2006*	*2007*
Imports from UK	£503,000	£963,631
Exports to UK	£18,000	£24,530

COMMUNICATIONS

There are no railways or waterways, and Dili is the only port. There is one major road, which links the main townships along the northern coast to the east of Dili. There are 6,000km of roads in total, 2,600km of which are surfaced. There are eight airports and airfields; the only international airport is at Dili.

MEDIA

East Timor's national public radio and television services began broadcasting in 2002. Radio coverage extends to around 90 per cent of the country, but access to television broadcasts is largely limited to the capital. Two newspapers are published daily.

ECUADOR

República del Ecuador – Republic of Ecuador

Area – 283,560 sq. km
Capital – Quito; population, 1,701,000 (2007 est)
Major cities – Cuenca, Guayaquil, Machala, Santo Domingo
Currency – Currency is that of the USA
Population – 13,755,680 rising at 1.55 per cent per year (2007 est)
Language – Spanish (official), Quechua
Population density – 48 per sq. km (2006)
Urban population – 62.8 per cent (2005 est)
Median age (years) – 23.9 (2007 est)
National anthem – 'Salve, Oh Patria' ['We Salute You Our Homeland']
National day – 10 August (Independence Day)
Life expectancy (years) – 76.62 (2007 est)
Mortality rate – 4.21 (2007 est)
Birth rate – 21.91 (2007 est)
Infant mortality rate – 22.1 (2007 est)
Death penalty – Abolished for all crimes (since 1906)
CPI score – 2.1 (2007)
Population below poverty line – 38.3 per cent (2006)

CLIMATE AND TERRAIN

Ecuador is an equatorial state lying on the north-west coast of South America. Its territory includes the Galápagos Islands in the Pacific Ocean. It has five different climatic zones and is one of the most bio-diverse countries on earth. The Andes run north to south through the centre of the country, dividing the coastal plain in the west from the low-lying rainforest in the east. Elevation extremes range from 0m (Pacific Ocean) at the lowest point to 6,267m (Chimborazo) at the highest. Other Andean peaks include Cotopaxi (5,896m) and Cayambe (5,790m) in the Eastern Cordillera. Ecuador is located in an earthquake zone and has two active volcanoes (Pichincha, only 12km away from the capital, and Tungurahua). The average annual temperature in Quito is 15°C.

HISTORY AND POLITICS

The former kingdom of Quito was conquered by the Incas of Peru in the 15th century. In 1534, Francisco Pizarro's (1475–1541) acquisitions led to the inclusion of the present territory of Ecuador in the Spanish viceroyalty of Quito. Independence from Spain was achieved in a revolutionary war that culminated in the battle of Mount Pichincha (1822). Ecuador then formed part of Gran Colombia with Colombia, Panama and Venezuela but left this union to become a fully independent state in 1830. Since then, the country has experienced periods of political instability interspersed with dictatorships and military rule. The country has been a democracy since 1979.

The oil-generated economic and social transformation from the 1970s onwards also caused rapid inflation and increased foreign debt, and the austerity measures introduced by various governments in the 1980s and 1990s caused widespread civil unrest. In recent years, these problems have worsened due to economic recession, provoking strikes and demonstrations. The most notable of these were by indigenous people, who have benefited least from the oil boom but been hardest hit by the economic downturn. Civil unrest has forced three presidents from office in eight years.

In the 2006 legislative election, the Institutional Renewal Party of Democratic Action (PRIAN) was the largest party with 28 seats, but without an overall majority. The 2006 presidential election was won in the second round by the Country Alliance (AP) candidate, Rafael Correa. The AP won a majority of seats in the national assembly elected in September 2007 to draft a new constitution, and President Correa indicated that he would dissolve the current legislature and hold early elections, but none have been scheduled at present.

POLITICAL SYSTEM

The 1998 constitution provides for an executive president who is directly elected for a four-year term, which is not renewable. The unicameral National Congress has 121 members, 101 elected on a provincial basis and 20 elected on a national basis, all for a four-year term. The republic is divided into 22 provinces.

A 130-member National Constituent Assembly was elected in September 2007 to draft a new constitution.

HEAD OF STATE

President, Rafael Correa *took office* 15 January 2007
Vice-President, Lenin Moreno

SELECTED GOVERNMENT MEMBERS *as at May 2008*
Finance and Economy, Fausto Ortiz
Foreign Relations, Maria Isabel Salvador
National Defence, Javier Ponce Cevallos

EMBASSY OF ECUADOR
Flat 3B, 3 Hans Crescent, London SW1X 0LS
T 020-7584 1367 E eecugranbretania@mmrree.gov.ec
Ambassador Extraordinary and Plenipotentiary, vacant

BRITISH EMBASSY
Citiplaza Building, Av. Naciones Unidas y Republica de El Salvador, Piso 14, Quito
T (+593) (2) 2970 800 E britembq@interactive.net.ec
W www.britembquito.org.ec
Ambassador Extraordinary and Plenipotentiary, HE Bernard Whiteside, *apptd* 2006

DEFENCE

The army has 24 light tanks, 123 armoured personnel carriers and 18 armed helicopters. The navy has 2 submarines, 2 frigates, 6 corvettes, and 13 patrol and coastal combatant vessels at two bases. The air force has over 57 combat aircraft.

Military budget – US$918m (2007)
Military personnel – 57,100: army 47,000, navy 6,100, air force 4,000; paramilitary 400
Conscription duration – 12 months (selective)

ECONOMY AND TRADE

Oil is Ecuador's principal export, accounting for half of export earnings and a quarter of government revenue in recent years. The economy has recovered from the severe economic crisis in 1999 owing to structural reforms in 2000, including the adoption of the US dollar in place of the sucre. Growth was strong from 2002 to 2006 and the poverty rate declined, although it is still high at 38 per cent. However, underinvestment in the state oil company caused production to drop in 2007, and higher taxation of foreign oil companies since 2006 has created uncertainty, causing investment to drop and economic growth to slow.

After oil, agriculture, fishing and forestry are the most important activities, providing products both for export and for the food and timber processing industries. The main products for export are oil, bananas, cut flowers, shrimps, cacoa, coffee, hemp and timber. The main imports are industrial materials, fuels and lubricants and consumer goods. Principal trading partners are the USA and other Latin American countries.

GNI – US$38,500m; US$2,910 per capita (2006)
Annual average growth of GDP – 1.8 per cent (2007 est)
Inflation rate – 2.2 per cent (2007 est)
Unemployment – 9.8 per cent (2007 est)
Total external debt – US$17,560m (2007)
Imports – US$12,100m (2006)
Exports – US$12,700m (2006)

BALANCE OF PAYMENTS
Trade – US$615m surplus (2006)
Current Account – US$1,503m surplus (2006)

Trade with UK	*2006*	*2007*
Imports from UK	£41,052,000	£35,257,205
Exports to UK	£43,705,000	£61,613,374

COMMUNICATIONS

There are 43,197km of roads, 6,467km of which are surfaced, and there are 966km of railways. The road and rail networks are largely to the west of the Andes. Travel to the east is mostly by air, with internal services between all major towns. There are 406 airports and airfields, of which 84 have surfaced runways, and international flights operate to Quito and Guayaquil. The main ports are Guayaquil and Esmeraldas. The land-line telephone system is being expanded but the service is limited. Mobile phone distribution has grown quickly and there were about 65 per 100 people in 2006.

EDUCATION AND HEALTH

Elementary education is free of charge and compulsory until age 14.

Literacy rate – 91 per cent (2004 est)
Gross enrolment ratio (percentage of relevant age group) – primary 117 per cent; secondary 65 per cent (2006 est)
Health expenditure (per capita) – US$147 (2005)
Hospital beds (per 1,000 people) – 1.4 (2000–6)

MEDIA AND CULTURE

Newspapers include *El Mercurio, El Universo* and *Diario Hoy*. There are six commercial television stations, including Ecuavision, Teleamazon, ETV Telerama and TC Television. Radio Nacional del Ecuador is the government-owned radio station. By law, the media is required to accede to government demands for free space or air time so programmes by the state are occasionally broadcast.

The capital Quito has been a UNESCO World Heritage Site since 1978, while South America's oldest market, which predates the Inca period, can be found in the small town of Otavalo. The most popular sport is football, while tennis also attracts a lot of support, since the success of former world number one Pancho Segura (*b.* 1921).

GALÁPAGOS ISLANDS

The Galápagos (Giant Tortoise) Islands, forming the province of the Archipelago de Colón, were annexed by Ecuador in 1832. The archipelago lies in the Pacific, about 800km from the mainland. There are 12 large and several hundred smaller islands with a total area of about 7,769 sq. km and an estimated population of 18,640. The capital is Puerto Barquerizo Moreno, on San Cristóbal Island. Although the archipelago lies on the equator, the temperature of the surrounding water is well below quatorial average owing to the Humboldt current. The province consists mostly of a national park, where unique narine birds, iguanas and the giant tortoises are conserved. The islands' wildlife provided naturalist Charles Darwin (1809–82) with inspiration and research material for his theory of natural selection, explained in *The Origin of the Species* (1859). There is some local ubsistence farming; the main industry, apart from tourism, is tuna and lobster fishing.

EGYPT

umhuriyat Misr al-Arabiyah – Arab Republic of Egypt

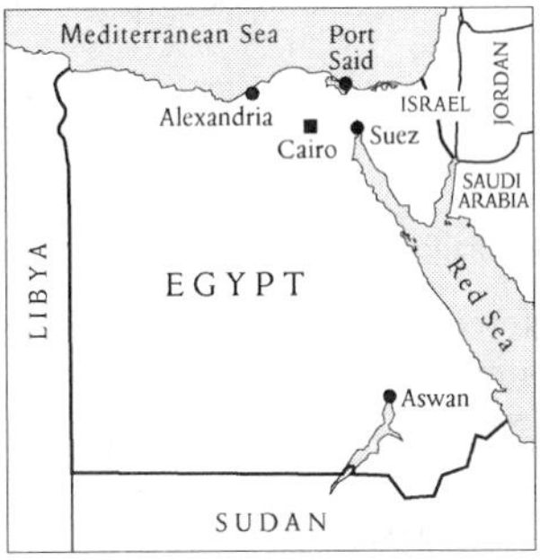

Area – 1,001,450 sq. km
Capital – Cairo; population, 11,893,000 (2007 est), stands on the Nile about 14 miles from the head of the delta
Major cities – Alexandria (founded 332 BC by Alexander the Great, was the capital for over 1,000 years), Giza, Port Said, Shubra el Khayma, Suez
Currency – Egyptian pound (£E) of 100 piastres or 1,000 millièmes
Population – 80,335,036 rising at 1.72 per cent per year (2007 est); Egyptian (98 per cent) (est). The remainder includes the Bedouin, or nomadic Arabs of the Western and Eastern deserts, who are now mainly semi-sedentary tent-dwellers. Another element is the Nubian of the Nile Valley, of mixed Arab and African blood
Religion – Islam (91 per cent), Coptic Christianity (8 per cent) (est)
Language – Arabic (official), English, French
Population density – 75 per sq. km (2006)
Urban population – 42.3 per cent (2005 est)
Median age (years) – 24.2 (2007 est)
National anthem – 'Biladi' ['My Homeland']
National day – 23 July (Revolution Day)
Life expectancy (years) – 71.57 (2007 est)
Mortality rate – 5.11 (2007 est)
Birth rate – 22.53 (2007 est)
Infant mortality rate – 29.5 (2007 est)
Death penalty – Retained
CPI score – 2.9 (2007)
Population below poverty line – 20 per cent (2005 est)

CLIMATE AND TERRAIN

The country is mainly flat but there are mountainous areas in the south-west, along the Red Sea coast and in the south of the Sinai peninsula. Elevation extremes range from 2,629m (Mt Catherine, Sinai) at the highest point to –133m (Qattara Depression) at the lowest. Most of the land is desert and the Nile Valley and delta were the only fertile areas until the construction of the Aswan dam allowed areas of desert to be irrigated. West of the Nile Valley is the Western desert, containing some depressions whose springs irrigate oases. The Eastern desert between the Nile and the mountains along the Red Sea coast is mostly plateaux dissected by wadis (dry watercourses). The average daily temperature ranges from 18°C to 30°C.

HISTORY AND POLITICS

The unification of the kingdoms of Lower Egypt and Upper Egypt *c.*3100 BC marked the establishment of the Egyptian state, with Memphis as its capital. Egypt was ruled for nearly 2,800 years by a succession of 31 pharaonic dynasties, which built the pyramids at Giza. Egypt's independence was lost to the Assyrians in 666 BC, and it was conquered by the Persians in 525 BC and then by Alexander the Great in 332 BC. Subsequently ruled by Alexander's general Ptolemy and his descendants, it was conquered and ruled by Rome (30 BC to AD 324) and then by the Byzantine Empire. In AD 640 Egypt was subjugated by Arab Muslim invaders. In 1517 the country was incorporated into the Ottoman Empire, under which it remained until the early 19th century. Britain occupied Egypt in 1882, and a British protectorate over Egypt lasted from 1914 to 1922, when Sultan Ahmed Fuad was proclaimed King of Egypt. Full independence was achieved in 1936. In 1953 the monarchy was deposed and Egypt became a republic.

Egypt was involved in the Arab-Israeli wars in 1948, 1967 and 1973. In the 1967 war (the Six Day War), the Sinai peninsula was lost to Israel. Sinai was returned to Egypt in 1982 under the 1979 treaty that resulted from the Camp David talks (1978–9) and formally terminated the 31-year-old state of war between the two countries. The treaty led to strained relations with other Arab nations until the mid-1980s.

President Hosni Mubarak, who took office after the assassination of President Sadat in 1981, played an active part in the Middle East peace process in the 1990s but was unable to suppress internal terrorism by Islamic fundamentalists. Frustration and resentment at the lack of political freedom has found expression in public demonstrations in recent years. President Mubarak was re-elected in 2005 for a fifth term. In the 2005 elections to the People's Assembly, the ruling National Democratic Party (NDP) won an overall majority; 88 seats (20 per cent of the total) were won by members of the Muslim Brotherhood standing as independents because of the ban on religious political parties. The NDP also held the majority of seats on the Consultative Council after the 2007 elections. In spring 2008, rising food prices led to demonstrations, strikes and riots.

INSURGENCIES

Militant Islamic fundamentalists emerged in the 1980s. Their campaign against the government became increasingly violent from the early 1990s, and was eventually directed against foreign tourists as well as domestic targets. Although the largest fundamentalist organisation, Gamaat-i-Islamiya, renounced violence in 1999, attacks continue, often aimed at foreign tourists.

POLITICAL SYSTEM

The 1971 constitution was amended in 2005 to allow for direct elections to the presidency and in 2007 to introduce changes increasing the president's powers. It provides for an executive president who appoints the council of ministers and determines government policy. The president is directly elected from multiple candidates (who must meet strict criteria) and serves a six-year term. The unicameral People's Assembly has 454 members, 444 directly elected and ten appointed by the president to increase the ethnic or religious diversity of the representatives; all serve a five-year term. The Consultative Council has an advisory role; its 264 members include 176 who are directly elected and 88 presidential appointees, all serving a six-year term. Religious political parties are banned.

HEAD OF STATE
President, Mohammed Hosni Mubarak, *elected* 1981, *re-elected* 1987, 1993, 1999, 2005

SELECTED GOVERNMENT MEMBERS *as at May 2008*
Prime Minister, Economy, Ahmed Nazif
Defence, Field Marshal Mohammad Hussein Tantawi
Finance, Youssef Boutros Ghali
Foreign Affairs, Ahmed Aboul Gheit
Interior, Maj.-Gen. Habib al-Adli

EMBASSY OF THE ARAB REPUBLIC OF EGYPT
26 South Street, London W1K 1DW
T 020-7499 2401 E etembuk@hotmail.com
Ambassador Extraordinary and Plenipotentiary, HE Gehad Madi, *apptd* 2004

BRITISH EMBASSY
7 Ahmed Ragheb Street, Garden City, Cairo
T (+20) (2) 794 0852 E info@britishembassy.org.eg
W www.britishembassy.org.eg
Ambassador Extraordinary and Plenipotentiary, HE Dominic Asquith, CMG, *apptd* 2007

BRITISH COUNCIL
192 El Nil Street, Agouza, Cairo
T (+20) (2) 219 789 W www.britishcouncil.org/egypt
Director, Paul Smith

DEFENCE

The army has 3,505 main battle tanks, 610 armoured infantry fighting vehicles and 4,160 armoured personnel carriers. The navy has 4 submarines, 1 destroyer, 10 frigates 41 patrol and coastal vessels and 5 armed helicopters at 8 bases. The air force has 489 combat aircraft and 115 armed helicopters.
Military expenditure – US$4,330m (2006)
Military personnel – 468,500: army 340,000, navy 18,500, air force 30,000, Air Defence Command 80,000; paramilitary 397,000
Conscription duration – 12–36 months

ECONOMY AND TRADE

Economic liberalisation in recent years has promoted strong growth in GDP but living standards for most of the population remain low, with nearly a quarter below the poverty line. There is a growing budget deficit, partly owing to price subsidies for basic necessities, and public debt was more than 100 per cent of GDP in 2007. Although the dams on the Nile have expanded the area of land under cultivation, other factors, such as population growth, are putting resources under pressure.

The services sector contributes 45.1 per cent to GDP and employs 51 per cent of the workforce; tourism is the largest component of this sector, visitor numbers having increased by over 50 per cent since the late 1990s. Industry accounts for 41.1 per cent of GDP and 17 per cent of employment, but despite increasing industrialisation, agriculture still employs 32 per cent of the workforce, contributing 13.8 per cent of GDP. Egypt is a net importer of foodstuffs, especially grain, and a food security programme has been set up with the aim of achieving self-sufficiency. The main cash crop is cotton, of which Egypt is one of the world's main producers. Other important crops are rice, maize, wheat, vegetables, fruit and livestock. Industry is centred on processing oil, cotton and other agricultural products, producing textiles, chemicals and pharmaceuticals. Oil is the backbone of the economy and, alongside considerable reserves of natural gas and the hydroelectric power produced by the Aswan and High dams, helps to make Egypt self-sufficient in energy.

The main trading partners are the USA, EU countries, Saudi Arabia, China and Syria. Principal exports are crude oil and petroleum products, cotton, textiles, metal products and chemicals. The main imports are machinery and equipment, foodstuffs, chemicals, wood products and fuels.
GNI – US$100,900m; US$1,360 per capita (2006)
Annual average growth of GDP – 7.2 per cent (2007 est)
Inflation rate – 8.8 per cent (2007 est)
Unemployment – 10.1 per cent (2007 est)
Total external debt – US$29,900m (2007)
Imports – US$17,600m (2006)
Exports – US$13,700m (2006)

BALANCE OF PAYMENTS
Trade – US$3,909mm deficit (2006)
Current Account – US$868m surplus (2006)

Trade with UK	*2006*	*2007*
Imports from UK	£579,169,000	£707,824,913
Exports to UK	£676,744,000	£555,235,287

COMMUNICATIONS

Egypt has 5,063km of railways and 92,000km of roads, 75,000km of which are surfaced. Road and rail networks link the Nile Valley and delta with the main development areas east and west of the river, but there are few routes in the interior. There are 88 airports and airfields; the principal airports are at Cairo, Luxor, Alexandria, Aswan and Hurgadah. Egypt has 3,500km of waterways, including the river Nile, the Alexandria–Cairo waterway, numerous small canals in the Nile delta, and the Suez Canal, which was re-opened in 1975. The main seaports are Alexandria, Damietta and Port Said on the Mediterranean Sea and Suez on the Red Sea. The telephone system was modernised in the 1990s; there were 10.8 million main-line, 18 million mobile phone and 6 million internet subscribers in 2006.

EDUCATION AND HEALTH

Education is free between the ages of six and 15.
Literacy rate – 55.6 per cent (2004 est)
Gross enrolment ratio (percentage of relevant age group) – primary 102 per cent; secondary 86 per cent; tertiary 35 per cent (2006 est)
Health expenditure (per capita) – US$78 (2005)
Hospital beds (per 1,000 people) – 2.2 (2000–6)

MEDIA

The Egyptian media plays a central role in the Arab world and its newspapers are some of the most influential in the region. There are two state-run national television channels and six regional channels. Egypt has an important satellite television industry (Egypt was the first Arab country to have its own satellite, Nilesat 101) that is watched all over the Arab-speaking world. In 2001, the country's first three private television stations went on air. The state has a monopoly on all radio broadcasting. The government has actively encouraged foreign media to base themselves in Egypt by setting up a free media zone in 2000 that offers economic incentives and access to its media infrastructure.

CULTURE

Egyptian culture dates back five thousand years to one of the earliest-known civilisations on Earth; ancient Egyptian hieroglyphic scripts provide some of the world's oldest records of written communication. The country has experienced ages of Hellenism, Christianity, Arab and Islamic culture and remains most famous for the Pyramids of Giza, the Library of Alexandria and the art and architecture of its ancient periods (beginning in the fourth millennium BC and waning around 31 BC). Modern Egypt retains cultural significance. The country has the highest number of Nobel laureates in Africa, including author Naguib Mahfouz (1911–2006) and politician Boutros Boutros-Ghali (*b.* 1922); actor Omar Sharif (*b.* 1932) is an Academy Award winner, while Cairo is home to Al-Ahly, the most widely supported football club in Africa.

EL SALVADOR

República de El Salvador – Republic of El Salvador

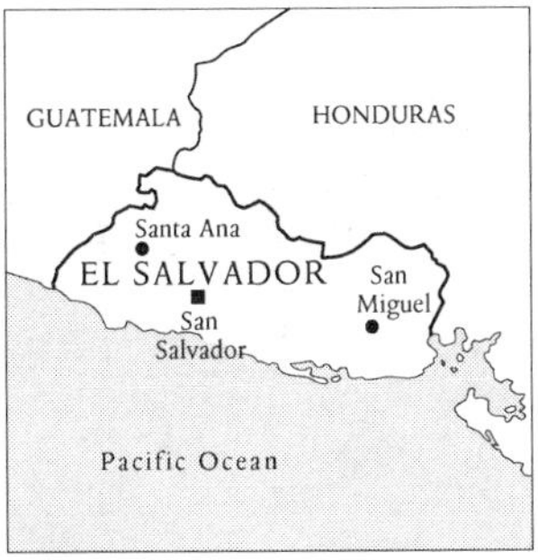

Area – 21,040 sq. km
Capital – San Salvador; population, 1,433,000 (2007 est)
Major cities – Mejicanos, San Miguel, Santa Ana, Soyapango
Currency – US dollar (US$) of 100 cents
Population – 6,948,073 rising at 1.7 per cent per year (2007 est)
Religion – Roman Catholicism (48 per cent), Protestantism (28 per cent) (est). Around 14 per cent of the population has no religious affiliation
Language – Spanish (official), Nahua
Population density – 326 per sq. km (2006)
Urban population – 60.1 per cent (2005 est)
Median age (years) – 22 (2007 est)
National anthem – 'Himno Nacional de El Salvador' ['National Anthem of El Salvador']
National day – 15 September (Independence Day)
Life expectancy (years) – 71.78 (2007 est)
Mortality rate – 5.6 (2007 est)
Birth rate – 26.13 (2007 est)
Infant mortality rate – 22.88 (2007 est)
Death penalty – Retained for certain crimes
CPI score – 4.0 (2007)
Population below poverty line – 35.2 per cent (2005 est)
Military personnel – 15,500: army 13,850, navy 700, air force 950; paramilitaries 12,000
Conscription duration – 12 months (selective)

CLIMATE AND TERRAIN

El Salvador extends along the Pacific coast of Central America for 307km. The country is very mountainous (much of the interior has an average altitude of 600m) and many of its peaks are volcanoes; most are extinct, but Ilamatepec (or Santa Ana) erupted in 2005. There are also numerous volcanic lakes. Elevation extremes range from 2,730m (Cerro El Pital) at the highest point to 0m (Pacific Ocean) at the lowest. Average temperatures vary with altitude, with coastal areas tending to be hotter. The average annual temperature in San Salvador is 23°C. Earthquakes and volcanic activity are common, and the country is susceptible to hurricanes and tropical storms.

HISTORY AND POLITICS

El Salvador was part of the Aztec kingdom conquered in 1524 by Pedro de Alvarado, and formed part of the Spanish viceroyalty of Guatemala until 1821. It became part of the United Provinces of Central America in 1823 until the federation's dissolution, and became fully independent in 1841.

There was political unrest in the 1970s, and guerrilla activity by the left-wing Farabundo Martí National Liberation Front (FMLN), which intensified from 1977 amid reports of human rights abuses by government-backed militias. Decades of military rule ended in 1979, but elections in 1982 were boycotted by left-wing parties and the right-wing National Republican Alliance (ARENA) took office. The civil war between the FMLN and the US-backed government lasted throughout the 1980s, until a UN-sponsored peace agreement was signed in 1991. The FMLN was recognised as a political party, and it won a few seats in the 1994 election, which returned ARENA to power. Since then, the FMLN has increased its vote, often being the largest party in parliament, but it has never held office, as ARENA has always formed coalition governments with smaller right-wing parties.

In 2004, Antonio Saca of ARENA won the presidential election with 57 per cent of the vote. Following the 2006 legislative elections, ARENA was the largest party in the legislature and continued its coalition with the National Conciliation Party.

POLITICAL SYSTEM

Under the 1983 constitution, the executive president is directly elected for a five-year term. The unicameral legislative assembly has 84 members, who are directly elected for a three-year term. The country is divided into 14 departments.

HEAD OF STATE

President, Elias Antonio Saca Gonzalez, *elected* 21 March 2004, *took office* 1 June 2004
Vice-President, Ana Vilma Albanez de Escobar

SELECTED GOVERNMENT MEMBERS *as at May 2008*

Defence, Maj.-Gen. Jorge Alberto Molina Contreras
Economy, Yolanda Mayora de Gavidia

Foreign Affairs, Marisol Argueta de Barillas
Interior, Juan Miguel Bolanos

EMBASSY OF EL SALVADOR
8 Dorset Square, London NW1 6PU
T 020-7224 9800 E embajadalondres@rree.gob.sv
Ambassador Extraordinary and Plenipotentiary, HE Dr Vladimiro P. Villalta, *apptd* 2005

BRITISH AMBASSADOR
HE Ian Hughes, *apptd* 2006, resident at Guatemala City, Guatemala

DEFENCE

The army has 43 armoured personnel carriers. The navy has 39 patrol and coastal combatant vessels. The air force has 14–15 combat aircraft.
Military budget – US$111m (2007)
Military personnel – 15,660: army 13,850, navy 860, air force 950; paramilitary 12,000
Conscription duration – 18 months voluntary

ECONOMY AND TRADE

The country is one of the most industrialised in Central America and has the third largest economy despite being the smallest country and having few natural resources. Recovery after the civil war has been set back by a series of natural disasters since the late 1990s, resulting in a sluggish economy and 30 per cent of the population living below the poverty line. Remittances from El Salvadoreans working abroad and foreign aid help to offset the large trade deficit. The free trade agreement with the USA and other Central American states that came into effect in 2006 is strengthening exports, and government diversification efforts have promoted textile production, international port services and tourism. Telecommunications, electricity distribution, banking and pension funds are being privatised.

Agriculture contributes 10.2 per cent to GDP and employs 19 per cent of the workforce. The principal agricultural products are coffee, sugar, maize, rice, beans, oilseed, cotton, sorghum, beef, dairy products and shrimps. Industry contributes 29.3 per cent of GDP, mostly through food processing, beverages, petroleum, chemicals, fertilizer, textiles, furniture and light metals. Services contribute 60.5 per cent of GDP.

The main trading partners are the USA, Guatemala, Honduras and Mexico. Principal exports are offshore assembly products, coffee, sugar, shrimps, textiles, chemicals and electricity. The chief imports are raw materials, consumer goods, capital goods, fuels, foodstuffs, petroleum and electricity.
GNI – US$18,100m; US$2,680 per capita (2006)
Annual average growth of GDP – 3.4 per cent (2007 est)
Inflation rate – 4.3 per cent (2007 est)
Unemployment – 6.2 per cent (2007 est)
Total external debt – US$9,991m (2007)
Imports – US$7,600m (2006)
Exports – US$3,500m (2006)

BALANCE OF PAYMENTS
Trade – US$4,115m deficit (2006)
Current Account – US$700m deficit (2006)

Trade with UK	*2006*	*2007*
Imports from UK	£25,813,000	£9,851,054
Exports to UK	£4,331,000	£7,851,434

COMMUNICATIONS

The principal ports are Cutuco and Acajutla, and ports in Honduras and Guatemala are also used. There are 10,886km of roads, of which 2,827km are surfaced. The Pan-American Highway from the Guatemalan frontier passes through Santa Ana and San Salvador, continuing to the Honduran frontier. The rail network has not been in operation since 2005 because of lack of maintenance. There are 65 airports and airfields, although only four have surfaced runways. There is an international airport at San Salvador.

EDUCATION AND HEALTH

Primary education is state-run and is compulsory and free of charge.
Literacy rate – 79.7 per cent (2004 est)
Gross enrolment ratio (percentage of relevant age group) – primary 114 per cent; secondary 64 per cent; tertiary 21 per cent (2006 est)
Health expenditure (per capita) – US$220 (2005)
Hospital beds (per 1,000 people) – 0.9 (2000–6)

MEDIA

Television is dominated by a small number of large private broadcasters, but there are hundreds of private radio stations (70 operate in San Salvador alone). Press freedom is guaranteed by the country's constitution.

EQUATORIAL GUINEA

República de Guinea Ecuatorial/Republique de Guinee equatoriale – Republic of Equatorial Guinea

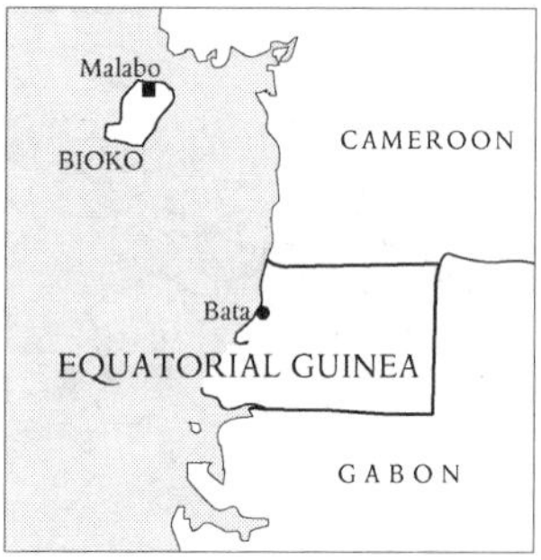

Area – 28,051 sq. km
Capital – Malabo; population, 96,000 (2007 est) on Bioko Island
Major towns – Bata is the principal town and port of Río Muni; Ebebiyín
Currency – Franc CFA of 100 centimes
Population – 551,201 rising at 2.02 per cent per year (2007 est)
Religion – Roman Catholicism (87 per cent), other Christian denominations (6 per cent), indigenous religions (5 per cent) (est)
Language – Spanish, French (both official), Fang, Bubi
Population density – 18 per sq. km (2006)
Urban population – 50 per cent (2005 est)
Median age (years) – 18.8 (2007 est)
National anthem – 'Caminemos Pisando la Senda' ['Let's Walk Down the Path']
National day – 12 October (Independence Day)
Life expectancy – 49.51 (2007 est)
Mortality rate – 15.01 (2007 est)

Birth rate – 35.16 (2007 est)
Infant mortality rate – 87.15 (2007 est)
HIV/AIDS adult prevalence – 2.9 per cent (2005 est)
Death penalty – Retained
CPI score – 1.9 (2007)
Literacy rate – 84.2 per cent (2004 est)

CLIMATE AND TERRAIN

There are two provinces: Bioko Island and the mainland, Río Muni, where 80 per cent of the population lives. Bioko is of volcanic origin. The mainland rises from a narrow coastal plain to a mountainous interior plateau, and is covered in dense vegetation. Elevation extremes range from 3,008m (Pico Basile) at the highest point to 0m (Atlantic Ocean) at the lowest. The climate is tropical, with a rainy season from July to January on Bioko and from April to May and October to December on the mainland.

HISTORY AND POLITICS

The island of Fernando Po (Bioko) was claimed by the Portuguese in 1494 and held until 1778, when it was ceded to Spain. The mainland territory of Río Muni came under Spanish rule in 1885, and the whole colony became known as Spanish Guinea. Constituted as two provinces of metropolitan Spain in 1959, the colony became autonomous in 1963, and fully independent in 1968 under its present name.

The first president, Francisco Macias Nguema, established a one-party state in 1970. His regime was brutal and he was overthrown in 1979 in a military coup led by his nephew, Col. Obiang Nguema. A military regime was established after the coup and only presidential nominees could stand in the 1983 and 1988 elections. Constitutional amendments were introduced in 1991 to allow multiparty elections, and ten opposition parties were legalised, operating alongside the ruling Equatorial Guinea Democratic Party (PDGE). However, President Nguema and the PDGE have retained power since 1992; most elections have been boycotted by the opposition parties because of election irregularities and intimidation. The regime has been accused of human rights abuses and the suppression of political opposition, and in 2003 opposition leaders set up a government-in-exile in Spain.

President Nguema won the 2002 presidential election unopposed, opposition candidates having withdrawn after voting began, alleging irregularities. In the 2008 legislative election, the PDGE and its allies retained their overwhelming majority in parliament.

POLITICAL SYSTEM

The 1991 constitution introduced a multiparty system. The president is directly elected for a seven-year term. The unicameral House of Representatives of the People has 100 members, who are directly elected for a five-year term.

HEAD OF STATE

President, Brig.-Gen. Teodoro Obiang Nguema Mbasogo, *took office* August 1979, *re-elected* 1989, 1996, 2002

SELECTED GOVERNMENT MEMBERS *as at May 2008*

Prime Minister, Ricardo Mangue Obama Nfubea
Economy, Jaime Ela Ndong
Foreign Affairs, Pastor Micha Ondo Bile
Interior, Clemente Engonga Nguema Onguene
Defence, Gen. Antonio Mba Nguema Mikwe

EMBASSY OF THE REPUBLIC OF EQUATORIAL GUINEA

13 Park Place, London SW1A 1LP
T 020-7499 6867 E embarege-londres@embarege-londres.org
W www.embarege-londres.org
Ambassador Extraordinary and Plenipotentiary, Agustin Nze Nfumu, *apptd* 2005

BRITISH AMBASSADOR

HE Syd Maddicott, *apptd* 2006, resident at Yaoundé, Cameroon

DEFENCE

The army has 10 armoured personnel carriers. The navy has 5 patrol and coastal combatant vessels at 2 bases. The coast guard has 1 patrol and coastal combatant vessel.
Military personnel – 1,320: army 1,100, navy 120, air force 100

ECONOMY AND TRADE

Large oil and natural gas deposits discovered off Bioko in the 1990s have transformed the economy, which has grown dramatically since production began in 1996. The country has the reputation of being one of the most corrupt in the world; oil exploitation has not benefited much of the population as most businesses are owned by government officials or their families and, despite the oil revenues, the country has external debt.

Industry contributes 92.5 per cent of GDP, agriculture 2.8 per cent and services 4.6 per cent. The oil-driven growth in the GDP masks stagnation in other sectors; agriculture, once the mainstay of the economy, has declined to subsistence level owing to neglect and lack of investment. The main crops are coffee, cocoa, rice, fruit, nuts, livestock and timber. Industrial activities include oil and natural gas production, fishing and timber processing. The main trading partners are the USA, China, Spain and Taiwan. Principal exports are petroleum, methanol, timber and cocoa. The main imports are oil industry equipment and other industrial equipment.
GNI – US$4,216m (2006); US$8,510 per capita (2006)
Annual average growth of GDP – 12.7 per cent (2007 est)
Inflation rate – 5.5 per cent (2007 est)
Total external debt – US$288m (2007 est)
Imports – US$2,500m (2006)
Exports – US$8,900m (2006)

BALANCE OF PAYMENTS

Trade – US$6,400m surplus (2006)
Current Account – US$385m surplus (2006)

Trade with UK	*2005*	*2006*
Imports from UK	£38,878,000	£45,434,000
Exports to UK	£16,691,000	£17,183,000

MEDIA

Television and radio broadcasts are state-controlled and the government owns the only television and radio stations, Television Nacional and Radio Nacional de Guinea Ecuatorial. The main newspaper, *Ebano,* is state-owned. A few privately owned publications appear sporadically. Criticism of the authorities is extremely rare.

ERITREA

Hagere Ertra – State of Eritrea

Area – 121,320 sq. km
Capital – Asmara; population, 601,000 (2007 est)
Major towns – Assab, Keren, Mitsiwa
Currency – Nakfa of 100 cents
Population – 4,906,585 rising at 2.46 per cent per year (2007 est); Tigrinya (50 per cent), Tigre and Kunama (40 per cent), Afar (4 per cent), Saho (3 per cent) (est)
Religion – Islam (50 per cent), Coptic Christianity (30 per cent), Roman Catholicism (13 per cent), indigenous religions (2 per cent) (est)
Language – Arabic, Tigrinya, Afar, Kunama
Population density – 46 per sq. km (2006)
Urban population – 20.8 per cent (2005 est)
Median age (years) – 17.9 (2007 est)
National anthem – 'Ertra, Ertra, Ertra' ['Eritrea, Eritrea, Eritrea']
National day – 24 May (Independence Day)
Life expectancy – 59.55 (2007 est)
Mortality rate – 9.36 (2007 est)
Birth rate – 33.97 (2007 est)
Infant mortality rate – 45.24 (2007 est)
HIV/AIDS adult prevalence – 2.2 per cent (2005 est)
Death penalty – Retained, but not used
CPI score – 2.8 (2007)
Population below poverty line – 50 per cent (2004 est)
Gross enrolment ratio (percentage of relevant age group) – primary 62 per cent; secondary 31 per cent; tertiary 1 per cent (2006 est)
Health expenditure (per capita) – US$8 (2005)

CLIMATE AND TERRAIN

The northern end of the Ethiopian Highlands extends into central Eritrea, where the average altitude is over 2,000m. The mountains fall in the west to a plateau, then rise to the hills on the Sudan border. To the east of the mountains, the land falls to the narrow coastal plain. The coastal strip extending to the Djibouti border is low-lying, the border with Ethiopia running along the edge of the Denakil desert. Elevation extremes range from 3,018m (Soira) at the highest point to −75m (Denakil depression) at the lowest. The climate changes with the country's varying altitudes, from temperatures averaging 16°C in the mountains and 30°C on the arid coastal plain.

HISTORY AND POLITICS

From the mid-16th century, the area was under the control of the Ottoman Empire. It was occupied by Italy in the late 19th century and was the base for Italy's 1936 invasion of Abyssinia (now Ethiopia). After the Italian defeat in North Africa in 1941, Eritrea became a British protectorate until 15 September 1952, when a federation with Ethiopia was created by the UN. In 1962, Ethiopia annexed Eritrea.

The Eritrean Liberation Front (ELF) fought a guerrilla war for independence from 1961 and the Eritrean People's Liberation Front (a breakaway faction of the ELF) emerged as the dominant rebel group in the 1980s and joined with Ethiopian resistance groups, including the People's Front for Democracy and Justice (PFDJ), to help overthrow the Mengistu regime in 1991. The EPLF secured the whole of Eritrea and formed a provisional government. The new PFDJ-led government in Ethiopia agreed to an Eritrean referendum on independence, which was held in April 1993 and recorded a 99.89 per cent vote in favour. Independence was declared on 24 May 1993.

Following independence, a transitional government for a four-year period was formed under Issaias Afwerki, and the EPLF became the ruling political party, renaming itself the People's Front for Democracy and Justice (PFDJ) in 1994. The post-independence regime has become increasingly authoritarian; although a new constitution was introduced in 1997, no presidential election has taken place since independence, and legislative elections scheduled for 2001 did not take place and have not been rescheduled.

FOREIGN RELATIONS

Since independence, Eritrea has been involved in disputes with Yemen over the Hanish and Mohabaka islands in the Red Sea (possession divided between Yemen and Eritrea by international arbitration), and with Djibouti over their common border. Sudan has accused Eritrea of supporting rebels in eastern Sudan.

There has been fighting with Ethiopia in disputes over border territory, especially in Tigray, since 1998. Though usually sporadic, fighting escalated in 1999–2000 into a war that left thousands of people dead. The independent Eritrea–Ethiopia Boundary Commission (EEBC) defined the international border between the two countries in 2002 but both countries have failed to abide by the original demarcation or a revised ruling in 2006. The UN, which deployed peacekeeping troops in 2000, continues to monitor the disputed area despite obstructiveness by the Eritrean government, which has also violated the ceasefire agreement.

POLITICAL SYSTEM

Under the 1997 constitution, the head of state is the president, elected for a five-year term by the legislature, and the 150-member unicameral National Assembly is directly elected for a four-year term; however, presidential and legislative elections have yet to be held and the transitional president, state council (cabinet) and legislature remain in place. The People's Front for Democracy and Justice (PFDJ) is the only legal political party.

HEAD OF STATE

President, Chairman of the National Assembly, C.-in-C. of the Armed Forces, Issaias Afewerki, *elected by the national assembly* 22 May 1993

SELECTED GOVERNMENT MEMBERS *as at May 2008*

Defence, Gen. Sebhat Ephrem
Foreign Affairs, Osman Saleh
Finance, Berhane Abrehe

EMBASSY OF THE STATE OF ERITREA
96 White Lion Street, London N1 9PF
T 020-7713 0096 E eriemba@eriembauk.com
W www.eritrean-embassy.org.uk
Ambassador Extraordinary and Plenipotentiary, HE Tesfamicael Gerahtu Ogbaghiorghis, *apptd* 2007

BRITISH EMBASSY
PO Box 5584, 66–68 Mariam Ghimbi Street, Asmara
T (+291) (1) 120 145 E asmara.enquiries@fco.gov.uk
Ambassador Extraordinary and Plenipotentiary, HE Nick Astbury, *apptd* 2006

BRITISH COUNCIL
PO Box 997, 175 – 11 Street No 23, Asmara
T (+291) (1) 123 415/120 529
W www.britishcouncil.org/eritrea
Director, Dr Negusse Araya

DEFENCE

The army has 150 main battle tanks and 40 armoured infantry fighting vehicles and armoured personnel carriers. The navy has 13 patrol and coastal combatant vessels at 3 bases. The air force has 18 combat aircraft and 1 armed helicopter.
Military budget – US$65m (2005 est)
Military personnel – 201,750: army 200,000, navy 1,400, air force 350
Conscription duration – 16 months

ECONOMY AND TRADE

Over 30 years of conflict left the country's economy devastated, and it has struggled to recover since independence. The command economy has concentrated business ownership in military and party hands, while agricultural output is restricted by the failure to demobilise agricultural workers from the large army, the conflict with Ethiopia, which has affected the most productive regions, and the frequent droughts and ensuing famines. Currently agriculture is the means of subsistence of around 80 per cent of the population, but food production is insufficient and emergency food aid is needed for two-thirds of the people.

Mineral reserves include zinc, potash, gold, copper and possibly oil; these are not fully exploited at present, although mining production should begin in 2010. Industries include food processing, beverages, clothing and textiles, salt, cement and light manufacturing. The opening of a free trade zone at Massawa, planned for 2008, may boost revenues, currently heavily dependent on remittances from expatriates.

The main trade partners are Italy, China, Saudi Arabia and France. Principal exports are livestock, sorghum, textiles, food and light manufactures. The main imports are machinery, petroleum products, food and manufactured goods.
GNI – US$900m; US$190 per capita (2006)
Annual average growth of GDP – 2 per cent (2007 est)
Inflation rate – 15.5 per cent (2007 est)
Total external debt – US$311m (2000 est)

BALANCE OF PAYMENTS
Current Account – US$41m deficit (2006)

Trade with UK	*2005*	*2006*
Imports from UK	£5,678,000	£2,011,000
Exports to UK	£274,000	£189,000

COMMUNICATIONS

Infrastructure reconstruction has focused on the ports of Massawa and Assab, the roads from these ports to Ethiopia, and the railway from Massawa to Sudan via Asmara. There are 306km of railways and 4,010km of roads, of which 874km are surfaced. There are 18 airports and airfields, of which four have surfaced runways; the international airport is at Asmara. The fixed-line telephone system is poor and largely confined to Asmara; mobile phone subscriptions are nearly double the number of main-line subscribers, at 62,000 in 2006.

MEDIA

Eritrea is the only country in Africa to have no privately owned news media. Existing organisations were closed down by the government in 2001, helping Eritrea supplant North Korea as the worst country in the world for press freedom in 2007 according to Reporters Without Borders. Eri TV is the state-run television station. There are no private networks or radio stations.

ESTONIA

Eesti Vabariik – Republic of Estonia

Area – 45,226 sq. km
Capital – Tallinn; population, 397,000 (2007 est)
Major towns – Kohtla-Jarve, Narva, Parnu, Tartu
Currency – Kroon of 100 senti
Population – 1,315,912 falling at 0.64 per cent per year (2007 est); Estonian (67.9 per cent), Russian (25.6 per cent), Ukrainian (2.1 per cent), Belarusian (1.3 per cent), Finn (0.9 per cent)
Religion – Protestantism (Lutheranism) (13 per cent), Orthodox Christianity (13 per cent) (est). Fifty years of Soviet occupation has diminished the role of religion in society
Language – Estonian (official), Russian
Population density – 32 per sq. km (2006)
Urban population – 69.6 per cent (2005 est)
Median age (years) – 39.4 (2007 est)
National anthem – 'Mu Isamaa, Mu Onn Ja Room' ['My Native Land, My Joy, Delight']
National day – 24 February (Independence Day)
Life expectancy (years) – 72.3 (2007 est)
Mortality rate – 13.3 (2007 est)
Birth rate – 10.17 (2007 est)
Infant mortality rate – 7.59 (2007 est)
Death penalty – Abolished for all crimes (since 1998)
CPI score – 6.5 (2007)
Population below poverty line – 5 per cent (2003)

CLIMATE AND TERRAIN

The country is mostly a plain of lakes, marshes and forests, with a low range of hills in the south-east. Elevation extremes range from 318m (Munamagi) at the highest point to 0m (Baltic Sea) at the lowest. Part of the border with Russia runs through the large Lake Peipus. The climate is mild, with average temperatures ranging from −6°C in January to 17°C in July.

HISTORY AND POLITICS

Estonia came under Swedish control between 1561 and 1629, and was ceded in 1721 to the Russian Empire. An Estonian nationalist movement developed in the late 19th century and fought against occupying German forces during the First World War. Estonia declared its independence in February 1918 and defended it against Soviet forces until 1920, when independence was recognised by the USSR. However, the USSR annexed Estonia in 1940, and the country was subsequently occupied by German forces when they invaded the USSR in 1941. In 1944 the USSR expelled the Germans and reannexed the country, beginning a process of 'Sovietisation'.

There was a resurgence of nationalist feeling in the 1980s, and in 1989 the Estonian Supreme Soviet declared the republic to be sovereign and its 1940 annexation by the USSR to be illegal. In 1990, the Communist Party's monopoly of power was abolished and, following multiparty elections in which pro-independence candidates won the majority of seats, a period of transition to independence was inaugurated, culminating in its declaration on 20 August 1991. The last Russian troops withdrew in 1994. Since independence, Estonia has pursued pro-Western policies. It joined NATO and the EU in 2004 and its parliament ratified the EU constitution in 2006.

In 2006 Toomas Hendrik Ilves was elected president by an electoral assembly. In the March 2007 legislative election, the Reform Party (ER), the main partner in the coalition government since 2005, became the largest party and formed a new coalition with the Union of Pro Patria and Res Publica (IRL) and the Estonian Social Democratic Party (SDE).

POLITICAL SYSTEM

Under the 1992 constitution, the president is elected for a five-year term by the legislature by a two-thirds majority or, if no candidate receives this majority after three rounds of voting, by an electoral assembly composed of the legislature members and local government representatives. The unicameral legislature, the *Riigikogu,* has 101 members, directly elected for a four-year term. The prime minister is appointed by the president and nominates the government. Members of the government need not be members of the *Riigikogu.*

HEAD OF STATE

President, Toomas Hendrik Ilves, *elected by electoral assembly* 23 September 2006, *sworn in* 9 October 2006

SELECTED GOVERNMENT MEMBERS *as at May 2008*

Prime Minister, Andrus Ansip
Defence, Jaak Aaviksoo
Finance, Ivari Padar
Foreign Affairs, Urmas Paet
Internal Affairs, Juri Pihl

EMBASSY OF THE REPUBLIC OF ESTONIA

16 Hyde Park Gate, London SW7 5DG
T 020-7589 3428 E embassy.london@estonia.gov.uk
W www.estonia.gov.uk
Ambassador Extraordinary and Plenipotentiary, HE Dr Margus Laidre, *apptd* 2006

BRITISH EMBASSY

Wismari 6, Tallinn 10136
T (+372) 677 4700 E information@britishembassy.ee
W www.britishembassy.ee
Ambassador Extraordinary and Plenipotentiary, HE Peter Carter, *apptd* 2007

BRITISH COUNCIL

Vana-Posti 7, Tallinn 10146
T (+372) 625 7788 W www.britishcouncil.org/estonia
Director, Kyllike Tohver

DEFENCE

The army has 57 armoured personnel carriers. The navy has 1 principal surface combatant vessel. The paramilitary Border Guard has 31 patrol and coastal combatant vessels.
Military budget – US$386m (2007 est)
Military personnel – 4,100: army 3,600, navy 300, air force 200; paramilitary 2,600
Conscription duration – 8–11 months

ECONOMY AND TRADE

Economic reforms and restructuring since 1992 have resulted in a market economy. Accession to the EU has boosted economic growth, but its aim of joining the eurozone has had to be delayed owing to persistently high inflation. There is a high trade deficit, but the government budget is in balance and public debt is low.

Agriculture engages 11 per cent of the workforce and accounts for 2.9 per cent of GDP, the main products being potatoes, vegetables, livestock and dairy products, and fish. Industry accounts for 20 per cent of employment and 28.9 per cent of GDP, concentrating on engineering, electronics, wood and wood products, textiles, information technology and telecommunications; electronics and telecommunications are particularly strong. The services sector accounts for 69 per cent of both employment and 68.2 per cent of GDP.

The main trading partners are Finland, Sweden and Russia. Principal exports are machinery and equipment, wood and paper, textiles and clothing, foodstuffs, furniture, metals and chemicals. The main imports are machinery and equipment, chemicals, textiles, foodstuffs and vehicles. Estonia is still dependent on Russian natural gas supplies, although it is a net exporter of electricity.
GNI – US$15,300m; US$11,400 per capita (2006)
Annual average growth of GDP – 7.9 per cent (2007 est)
Inflation rate – 6 per cent (2007 est)
Unemployment – 4.7 per cent (2007 est)
Total external debt – US$20,240m (2007)
Imports – US$11,900m (2006)
Exports – US$8,800m (2006)

BALANCE OF PAYMENTS

Trade – US$3,129m deficit (2006)
Current Account – US$2,575m deficit (2006)

Trade with UK	*2006*	*2007*
Imports from UK	£456,700,000	£227,336,495
Exports to UK	£467,400,000	£225,836,373

EDUCATION AND HEALTH

Estonia has a three-tier education system, consisting of primary level (four years), secondary level (six years) and university level (four to six years). Primary and secondary level education is compulsory between the ages of seven and 17. The country's best known university is Tartu, founded in 1632.

Literacy rate – 99.8 per cent (2004 est)
Gross enrolment ratio (percentage of relevant age group) – primary 100 per cent; secondary 100 per cent; tertiary 66 per cent (2006 est)
Health expenditure (per capita) – US$516 (2005)
Hospital beds (per 1,000 people) – 5.8 (2000–6)

MEDIA AND CULTURE

Freedom of the press is guaranteed in the constitution, and the state monopoly on television and radio ended soon after independence. All newspapers have been privatised and public broadcasting channels compete with private-sector companies. Russian-language news and programmes are provided on Estonian television.

The old town area of Tallinn is a UNESCO World Heritage Site. The city has suffered many occupations but apart from a Soviet bombing raid in 1944, its medieval and 18th-century architecture has never been harmed. Estonia's heritage is rich in traditional folk songs and poetry, which influences much of its contemporary culture, and the country has produced many well-known names in modern classical music, including conductors Neeme Jarvi (*b.* 1937) and Tonu Kaljuste (*b.* 1953), and composers Arvo Part (*b.* 1935) and Veljo Tormis (*b.* 1930).

ETHIOPIA

Ityop'iya Federalawi Demokrasiyawi Ripeblik – Federal Democratic Republic of Ethiopia

Area – 1,127,127 sq. km
Capital – Addis Ababa; population, 3,100,000 (2007 est)
Major cities – Bahir Dar, Dese, Dire Dawa, Gonder, Mek'ele, Nazret
Currency – Ethiopian birr (EB) of 100 cents
Population – 76,511,887, rising at 2.27 per cent per year (2007 est); Oromo (40 per cent), Amhara and Tigre (32 per cent), Sidamo (9 per cent), Shankella (6 per cent), Somali (6 per cent), Afar (4 per cent), Gurage (2 per cent) (est)
Religion – Coptic Christianity (45 per cent), Islam (45 per cent) (est)
Language – Amharic (official), Tigrinya, Oromigna, Somali, Arabic, English, Guaragigna, Hadiyigna
Population density – 77 per sq. km (2006)
Urban population – 16.2 per cent (2005 est)
Median age (years) – 18 (2007 est)
National anthem – 'Wodefit Gesgeshi Widd Innat Ityopp'ya' ['March Forward, Dear Mother Ethiopia']
National day – 28 May
Life expectancy (years) – 49.23 (2007 est)
Mortality rate – 14.67 (2007 est)
Birth rate – 37.39 (2007 est)
Infant mortality rate – 91.92 (2007 est)
HIV/AIDS adult prevalence – 4.4 per cent (2003 est)
Death penalty – Retained
CPI score – 2.4 (2007)
Population below poverty line – 38.7 per cent (2005/6 est)

CLIMATE AND TERRAIN

Ethiopia is a landlocked country dominated by a central plateau, rising to the mountains of the Ethiopian Highlands, which are divided by the Great Rift Valley. The western mountains are the source of the Blue Nile. The land drops to desert plains in the east (Ogaden) and north-east (Denakil desert). Elevation extremes range from 4,533m (Ras Dejen) at the highest point to −125m (Denakil depression) at the lowest. There is a tropical monsoon climate that varies according to altitude. The wet season is April to September.

HISTORY AND POLITICS

The Hamitic culture was heavily influenced by Semitic immigration from Arabia around the time of Christ, and Coptic Christianity was introduced in the fourth century. The empire attained its zenith in the sixth century under the Axum rulers but was checked by Islamic expansion from the east. The independent kingdom of Abyssinia emerged in the 11th century. Modern Ethiopia dates from 1855 when Theodros established supremacy over the various tribes. Menelik II repulsed an Italian invasion in 1896, but Italy conquered Abyssinia in 1936 and occupied the country until its liberation and the return of the emperor, Haile Selassie, in 1941. Ethiopia was federated with Eritrea in 1952 and annexed the area in 1962.

Following a severe famine in 1973–4, Emperor Haile Selassie was deposed in a military coup in 1974 and a military government was installed. By 1977 Lt.-Col. Mengistu Haile Mariam had become head of state and his single-party Marxist regime initiated reforms based on the Soviet model, brutally suppressing opposition. War with Somalia over the Ogaden (1977–8), internal conflict with Ethiopian resistence and Eritrean separatist forces, drought and severe famine (1984–5), and government mismanagement and corruption undermined the regime until its collapse in 1991. A transitional administration comprising the Ethiopian People's Revolutionary Democratic Front (EPRDF) and other opposition groups governed until a new federal constitution was adopted in 1994. The Federal Democratic Republic of Ethiopia was proclaimed on 22 August 1995.

The 2001 presidential election was won by Lt. Girma Wolde Giorgis, the EPRDF candidate, and he was elected for a second term in October 2007. In the 2005 legislative election, the EPRDF retained an overall but reduced majority in parliament; opposition parties accused the EPRDF of electoral fraud and there were reruns of polls in over 30 seats. Popular protests against the irregularities were violently suppressed amid a crackdown on the opposition and the media, leading foreign donors to cut direct aid.

FOREIGN RELATIONS

There has been fighting with Eritrea in disputes over border territory, especially in Tigray, since 1998. Though usually sporadic, fighting escalated in 1999–2000 into a war in which thousands of people died. The independent Eritrea–Ethiopia Boundary Commission (EEBC) defined the international border between the two countries in 2002 but both countries have failed to abide by the original demarcation or a revised ruling in 2006. Relations remain strained. The UN, which deployed peacekeeping troops in 2000, continues to monitor the disputed area.

Ethiopia intervened in Somalia from July 2006 in support of the Somali transitional government, based in Baidoa. Ethiopian forces joined with those loyal to the transitional government to push back an Islamist offensive towards Baidoa and then went on to capture Mogadishu in December and Kismaayo in January 2007. Its troops remain in Somalia.

POLITICAL SYSTEM

The 1994 constitution provides for a federal government responsible for foreign affairs, defence and economic policy, and nine ethnically based states. The president is elected by both houses of the legislature for a six-year term, renewable only once. The prime minister is appointed by the lower chamber of the legislature and appoints the government. The Federal Parliamentary Assembly is bicameral. The lower chamber, the House of People's Representatives), has 547 members, directly elected for a five-year term. The House of the Federation has 110 members, indirectly elected for a five-year term by the government councils of the nine states in the federation. These regional administrations have considerable autonomy and the right to secede.

HEAD OF STATE

President, Lt. Girma Wolde Giorgis, *elected by parliament* 8 October 2001

SELECTED GOVERNMENT MEMBERS *as at May 2008*

Prime Minister, C.-in-C. of the National Armed Forces, Meles Zenawi

Deputy Prime Minister, Addisu Legesse

Finance and Economic Development, Sufian Ahmed

Foreign Affairs, Seyoum Mesfin

National Defence, Kuma Demekesa

EMBASSY OF THE FEDERAL DEMOCRATIC REPUBLIC OF ETHIOPIA

17 Princes Gate, London SW7 1PZ

T 020-7589 7212 E info@ethioembassy.org.uk

W www.ethioembassy.org.uk

Ambassador Extraordinary and Plenipotentiary, HE Berhanu Kebede, *apptd* 2006

BRITISH EMBASSY

PO Box 858, Fikre Mariam Abatechan Street, Addis Ababa

T (+251) (11) 661 2354

E britishembassy.addisababa@fco.gov.uk

W www.britishembassy.gov.uk/ethiopia

Ambassador Extraordinary and Plenipotentiary, HE Norman Ling, *apptd* 2008

BRITISH COUNCIL

PO Box 1043, Artistic Building, Adwa Avenue, Addis Ababa

T (+251) (11) 155 0022 W www.britishcouncil.org/ethiopia

Director, Barbara Wickham

DEFENCE

The army has over 246 main battle tanks and around 450 armoured infantry fighting vehicles and armoured personnel carriers. The air force has 48 combat aircraft and 25 armed helicopters.

Military budget – US$330m (2007)

Military personnel – 138,000: army 135,000, air force 3,000

ECONOMY AND TRADE

Since 1993 the government has implemented a programme of economic reforms. The economy is highly dependent on agriculture, and therefore on the rains; recurring droughts led to famine conditions in 1984–5, 1992, 1997, 2000 and 2002, and much of the population is dependent on food aid. In 2004, a government resettlement programme began to move more than two million people away from the drought-stricken and overworked highlands in the east of the country; the government claimed this would be a long-term solution to food shortages. There is a high level of foreign debt, but in 2001 Ethiopia met the criteria of the IMF-World Bank heavily indebted poor countries initiative, and in 2005 its debt to the IMF was cancelled.

Agriculture and herding account for approximately 48.8 per cent of GDP, and around 80 per cent of the population is dependent upon the land for a living. The main crops are cereals, pulses, coffee, oilseed, cotton, sugar, potatoes, qat, cut flowers, livestock products and fish. Natural resources, including gold, platinum, copper, potash, oil and natural gas, are largely unexploited; most industrial activity involves the processing of agricultural products, gold mining and metalworking, and textiles. The main trade partners are Saudi Arabia, China, Germany and Italy. Principal exports are coffee (which normally provides over 20 per cent of foreign exchange earnings), qat, gold, leather products, livestock and oilseeds. The main imports are food, livestock, petroleum and petroleum products, chemicals, machinery, vehicles, cereals and textiles.

GNI – US$12,900m; US$170 per capita (2006)

Annual average growth of GDP – 9.8 per cent (2007 est)

Inflation rate – 15.9 per cent (2007 est)

Total external debt – US$3,793m (2007 est)

Imports – US$4,710m (2006)

Exports – US$1,050m (2006)

BALANCE OF PAYMENTS

Trade – US$3,660m deficit (2006)

Current Account – US$1,386m deficit (2006)

Trade with UK	*2005*	*2006*
Imports from UK	£31,497,000	£38,273,000
Exports to UK	£20,723,000	£21,615,000

COMMUNICATIONS

A network of roads links the major cities with each other, with the Sudanese and Kenyan borders and through Eritrea to the Red Sea coast. There are 36,469km of roads, 6,980km of which are surfaced. The only railway line, 699km in length, links Addis Ababa to the capital, Djibouti. There are over 80 airports and airfields, including the international airport at Addis Ababa. Ethiopian Airlines maintains regular services throughout Africa and to Europe. There is a limited telephone service, with only 725,000 main lines in use in 2006. Mobile phone distribution overtook fixed-line connections in 2006 to reach 867,000, but only about two per 100 people have access to either type of telephone.

EDUCATION AND HEALTH

Non-compulsory elementary and secondary education are provided by government schools in the main centres of population; there are also mission schools. The National University (founded 1961) coordinates the institutions of higher education.

Literacy rate – 41.5 per cent (2004 est)

Gross enrolment ratio (percentage of relevant age group) – primary 83 per cent; secondary 27 per cent; tertiary 2 per cent (2006 est)

Health expenditure (per capita) – US$6 (2005)

Hospital beds (per 1,000 people) – 0.2 (2000–6)

MEDIA

There are over 50 privately owned newspapers in addition to the state-owned daily *Addis Zemen*. There is only one television station, the state-owned Ethiopian Television (ETV). Radio Ethiopia is state-owned but several private stations were given licences in 2006.

FIJI

Matanitu ko Viti – Republic of the Fiji Islands

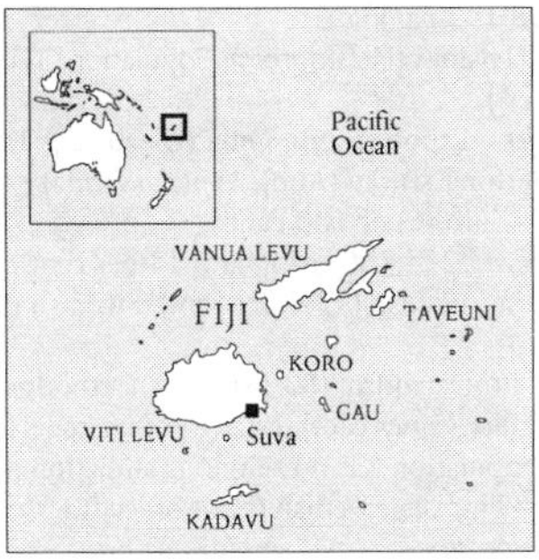

Area – 18,270 sq. km

Capital – Suva; population, 224,000 (2007 est), on Viti Levu Island

Major towns – Lautoka, Nasinu, Nausori

Currency – Fiji dollar (F$) of 100 cents

Population – 918,675 rising at 1.39 per cent per year (2007 est); Fijian (54.8 per cent), Indian (37.4 per cent) (est). After the 1987 coup many Indians left, and by 1994 Melanesian Fijians formed the largest population group

Religion – Christianity (52 per cent), Hinduism (30 per cent), Islam (7 per cent) (est)

Language – English, Fijian (both official), Hindustani

Population density – 46 per sq. km (2006)

Urban population – 53.2 per cent (2005 est)

Median age (years) – 24.9 (2007 est)

National anthem – 'God Bless Fiji'

National day – second Monday of October (Independence Day)

Life expectancy (years) – 70.12 (2007 est)

Mortality rate – 5.66 (2007 est)

Birth rate – 22.37 (2007 est)

Infant mortality rate – 11.99 (2007 est)

Death penalty – Retained for certain crimes

Literacy rate – 92.9 per cent (2004 est)

CLIMATE AND TERRAIN

Fiji is a Melanesian island group of roughly 332 islands (around 100 are permanently inhabited) and over 500 islets in the South Pacific, about 1,760km north of New Zealand. The group extends 480km from east to west and 480km north to south. The International Date Line has been diverted to the east of the island group. The largest islands are Viti Levu and Vanua Levu. The terrain is mountainous and volcanic, with tropical rainforest and grassland, and most islands are surrounded by coral reefs. Elevation extremes range from 1,324m (Tomaniivi, on Viti Levu) at the highest point to 0m (Pacific Ocean) at the lowest. Fiji has a tropical oceanic climate with high humidity and an average annual temperature of 27°C.

HISTORY AND POLITICS

The islands were visited by Dutch explorer Abel Tasman in 1643, and by Captain Cook in 1774. They became a British colony in 1874, and sugar plantations, employing more than 60,000 indentured Indian labourers, were established. Fiji became independent as a constitutional monarchy within the Commonwealth on 10 October 1970, and became a republic after the 1987 coups.

Racial and political tension between the native Melanesians and the growing ethnic Indian population has caused political instability since the 1980s. There have been four coups in 20 years: two in 1987 and one in 2000 as ethnic Fijians attempted to reassert their political dominance; and one in 2006 over the government's proposed amnesty for those involved in the 2000 coup.

In December 2006 Commodore Frank Bainimarama overthrew the coalition government led by Laisenia Qarase and assumed executive authority. President Iloilo was reinstated in January 2007, when Commodore Bainimarama became interim prime minister and appointed an interim coalition government. Bainimarama announced in 2007 that elections would be held in 2010. In 2008 he appointed himself chairman of the Great Council of Chiefs.

POLITICAL SYSTEM

Under the 1997 constitution, the head of state is the president, appointed for a five-year term by the Great Council of Chiefs. The lower house of the bicameral parliament is the House of Representatives, which has 71 members directly elected for a five-year term. Of the 71 seats, 25 are open to all races and elected in single-member constituencies, while the other 46 are allocated for election by the country's various ethnic communities. The upper house, the senate, has 32 members, who are appointed for a five-year term by the president on the recommendation of the political parties (in proportion to their representation in the lower house) and the Great Council of Chiefs.

HEAD OF STATE

President, Ratu Josefa Iloilo, *appointed* 13 July 2000, *reappointed* 13 March 2001, 8 March 2006

SELECTED GOVERNMENT MEMBERS *as at May 2008*

Prime Minister, Commodore Frank Voreqe Bainimarama
Finance, Mahendra Chaudhry
Foreign Affairs, Ratu Epeli Nailatikau
Attorney-General, Aiyaz Sayed-Khaiyum
Defence, Ratu Epeli Ganilau

HIGH COMMISSION OF THE REPUBLIC OF THE FIJI ISLANDS

34 Hyde Park Gate, London SW7 5DN
T 020-7584 3661 E mail@fijihighcommission.org.uk
W www.fijihighcommission.org.uk
High Commissioner, vacant

BRITISH HIGH COMMISSION
PO Box 1355, Victoria House, 47 Gladstone Road, Suva
T (+679) 322 9100 E publicdiplomacysuva@fco.gov.uk
W www.britishhighcommission.gov.uk/fiji
High Commissioner, HE Roger Sykes, *apptd* 2006

DEFENCE

The navy has 7 patrol and coastal combatant vessels at 2 bases.
Military budget – US$51m (2007 est)
Military personnel – 3,500: army 3,200, navy 300

ECONOMY AND TRADE

Fiji has abundant natural resources and a developed and diverse economy. However, economic problems arose after the 1987 coup because of the large-scale emigration of Indian Fijians and the impact of continuing political instability on the tourist industry; a drop in tourist numbers after the 2006 coup caused the economy to contract in 2007. Tourism has overtaken the sugar industry as the mainstay of the economy. Budget and trade deficits are long-term problems, and remittances from Fijians working abroad are important but have decreased significantly.

Agriculture accounts for 8.9 per cent of GDP and employs 70 per cent of the workforce. The principal cash crop is sugar cane; in 2002 the government announced the privatisation of the industry, threatened with collapse by the withdrawal of EU subsidies. The other main crops are coconuts, cassava, rice, sweet potatoes, bananas, livestock and fish. Light industry is being encouraged in order to diversify the economy. The main industries are tourism, sugar processing, manufacturing of clothing, copra, gold and silver mining, forestry and small cottage industries. The main trade partners are Australia, Singapore, the USA, New Zealand and the UK. Principal exports are sugar, garments, gold, timber, fish, molasses and coconut oil. The chief imports are manufactured goods, machinery and transport equipment, petroleum products, food and chemicals.
GNI – US$3,098m; US$3,720 per capita (2006)
Annual average growth of GDP – –3.1 per cent (2007 est)
Inflation rate – 3 per cent (2005)
Total external debt – US$127m (2004 est)
Imports – US$1,800m (2006)
Exports – US$680m (2006)

BALANCE OF PAYMENTS
Trade – US$1,123m deficit (2006)
Current Account – US$552m deficit (2006)

Trade with UK	*2006*	*2007*
Imports from UK	£5,143,000	£4,864,172
Exports to UK	£74,616,000	£62,458,647

COMMUNICATIONS

Fiji is one of the main aerial crossroads in the Pacific, providing services to New Zealand, Australia and other Pacific states; the 28 airports and airfields include international airports at Suva and Nadi. The main seaports are Suva and Lautoka. There are 3,440km of roads, 1,692km of which are surfaced. There are 597km of railway track, principally used by the sugar industry. The telephone system is modern and covers all the islands.

MEDIA

Fiji's privately owned newspapers are published in English, Fijian and Hindi. Government-owned newspapers are also multilingual. Radio (both public and private) is the main source of news, particularly on the more remote outer islands. There are two main television networks, operated by Fiji Television Ltd: Fiji 1, a national channel, and Sky Fiji, accessed via subscription.

FINLAND

Suomen tasavalta / Republiken Finland – Republic of Finland

Area – 338,145 sq. km
Capital – Helsinki (Helsingfors); population, 1,115,000 (2007 est)
Major cities – Espoo (Esbo), Oulu (Uleaborg), Tampere (Tammerfors), Turku (Abo), Vantaa (Vanda)
Currency – Euro (€) of 100 cents
Population – 5,238,460 rising at 0.13 per cent per year (2007 est); Finnish (93.4 per cent), Swedish (5.7 per cent) (est)
Religion – Protestantism (83 per cent), Orthodox Christianity (1 per cent) (est). An estimated 10 per cent of the population has no religious affiliation
Language – Finnish, Swedish (both official)
Population density – 17 per sq. km (2006)
Urban population – 60.9 per cent (2005 est)
Median age (years) – 41.6 (2007 est)
National anthem – 'Maamme'/'Vart Land' ['Our Land']
National day – 6 December (Independence Day)
Life expectancy (years) – 78.66 (2007 est)
Mortality rate – 9.93 (2007 est)
Birth rate – 10.42 (2007 est)
Infant mortality rate – 3.52 (2007 est)
Death penalty – Abolished for all crimes (since 1972)
CPI score – 9.4 (2007)

CLIMATE AND TERRAIN

Most of the country is a glaciated plain of forests (over 65 per cent of the land area) and over 60,000 lakes, with low hills along the eastern border with Russia and in the far north. Elevation extremes range from 1,328m (Haltaitunturi) at the highest point to 0m (Baltic Sea) at the lowest. A third of the country is north of the Arctic Circle and temperatures there can range from −20°C in January to 10°C in July. Temperatures in Helsinki range from −6°C in January to 17°C in July.

Owing to isostatic uplift (the vertical movement of post-glaciated land masses), the surface area of Finland is growing by an estimated 7 sq. km a year.

HISTORY AND POLITICS

Finland was part of the Swedish Empire from the Middle Ages until it was ceded to Russia in 1809 and became an autonomous grand duchy of the Russian Empire. After the

Russian Revolution in 1917, Finland declared its independence. An attempted coup by Finnish Bolsheviks led to a short civil war that ended in their defeat in 1918, and in 1919 a republic was set up. It resisted the 1939 invasion by the USSR but was defeated in 1940 and forced to cede territory; in the hope of recovering this territory it joined Germany's attack on the USSR in 1941. After agreeing an armistice with the USSR in 1944, Finland concluded a peace treaty in 1947 that conceded further territory to the USSR and obliged it to pay reparations. A Soviet-Finnish cooperation treaty in 1948 forced Finland to demilitarise its Soviet border and to adopt a stance of neutrality; these terms lasted until the demise of the USSR in 1991.

Since the mid-1960s the majority of Finnish governments have been coalitions of centre and moderate left-wing parties, with the Social Democratic Party (SDP) or the Centre Party (KESK) leading coalitions. Finland joined the EU in 1995 and the European Monetary Union in 1998; its parliament voted in favour of ratifying the EU constitution in 2006.

In the 2006 presidential election, Tarja Halonen of the SDP was re-elected with 51.8 per cent of the vote. Following the 2007 legislative election, KESK remained the largest party and formed a new coalition government with the National Coalition Party, the Greens and the Swedish People's Party.

POLITICAL SYSTEM

Under the 2000 constitution, the president is directly elected for a six-year term. There is a unicameral legislature, the *Eduskunta,* with 200 members directly elected for a four-year term. The prime minister is elected by the *Eduskunta* and appointed by the president.

HEAD OF STATE

President, Tarja Halonen, *elected* 6 February 2000, *inaugurated* 1 March 2000, *re-elected* January 2006

SELECTED GOVERNMENT MEMBERS *as at May 2008*

Prime Minister, Matti Vanhanen
Deputy Prime Minister, Finance, Jyrki Katainen
Defence, Jyri Hakamies
Foreign Affairs, Alexander Stubb
Interior, Anne Holmlund

EMBASSY OF FINLAND

38 Chesham Place, London SW1X 8HW
T 020-7838 6200 E sanomat.lon@formin.fi
W www.finemb.org.uk
Ambassador Extraordinary and Plenipotentiary, HE Jaakko Laajava, *apptd* 2005

BRITISH EMBASSY

Itainen Puistotie 17, 00140 Helsinki
T (+358) (9) 2286 5100 E info@ukembassy.fi
W www.ukembassy.fi
Ambassador Extraordinary and Plenipotentiary, HE Valerie Caton, *apptd* 2006

BRITISH COUNCIL

Urho Kekkosen Katu 2 C, 00100 Helsinki
T (+358) (9) 774 3330 W www.britishcouncil.fi
Director, Tuija Talvitie

DEFENCE

The army has 163 main battle tanks, 182 armoured infantry fighting vehicles and 538 armoured personnel carriers. The navy has 12 patrol and coastal vessels. The air force has 61 combat aircraft.

Military expenditure – US$2,750m (2006)
Military personnel – 29,300: army 20,500, navy 4,100, air force 4,700; paramilitary 3,100
Conscription duration – 6–12 months

ECONOMY AND TRADE

The country has a highly industrialised market economy which is thriving as a result of its telecommunications and electronics industries, particularly the manufacture of mobile phones, as well as its traditional timber and metals industries. High unemployment persists, however, and the pulp and paper industry will be adversely affected if Russia implements plans to impose high tariffs on timber exports to Finland.

Most trade is with other EU countries and Russia. Principal exports are machinery and equipment (especially electronic and electrical goods), chemicals, metals, timber, paper and wood pulp. The main imports are foodstuffs (especially grain), petroleum and petroleum products, chemicals, transport equipment, iron and steel, machinery, textile yarn and fabrics, and components for manufactured goods. Finland is also a net importer of energy.

GNI – US$217,800m; US$41,360 per capita (2006)
Annual average growth of GDP – 3.9 per cent (2007 est)
Inflation rate – 2.7 per cent (2007 est)
Unemployment – 6.6 per cent (2007 est)
Total external debt – US$271,200m (2007)
Imports – US$69,400m (2006)
Exports – US$77,300m (2006)

BALANCE OF PAYMENTS

Trade – US$7,839m surplus (2006)
Current Account – US$9,550m surplus (2006)

Trade with UK	*2006*	*2007*
Imports from UK	£1,772,700,000	£1,937,396,407
Exports to UK	£2,713,400,000	£2,585,369,249

COMMUNICATIONS

The road and rail networks are concentrated in the southern half of the country, where most of the population and industry are located. There are 78,189km of roads, 50,760km of which are surfaced. There are 5,741km of railways. The main seaports are Helsinki, Kotka, Rauma and Turku, and there are passenger services with Sweden, Estonia and Germany as well as countries outside the Baltic. The principal airports are at Helsinki, Turku and Vaasa. Mobile phone distribution, at 5.6 million subscribers in 2006, is over 100 per cent.

EDUCATION AND HEALTH

Primary education is free of charge and compulsory for children from seven to 16 years.

Gross enrolment ratio (percentage of relevant age group) – primary 100 per cent; secondary 111 per cent; tertiary 92 per cent (2006 est)
Health expenditure (per capita) – US$2,824 (2005)
Hospital beds (per 1,000 people) – 7.0 (2000–6)

MEDIA

Finland is highly rated for press freedom by Reporters Without Borders; every citizen has the right to publish and is guaranteed a right of reply. Newspapers are privately owned and offer a wide spectrum of political views. There are both commercial and state-owned broadcasters; the state broadcaster is Yleisradio Oy (YLE). The analogue television signal was switched off during 2007. Newspapers, books, plays and films appear in both Finnish and Swedish.

FRANCE

République française – French Republic

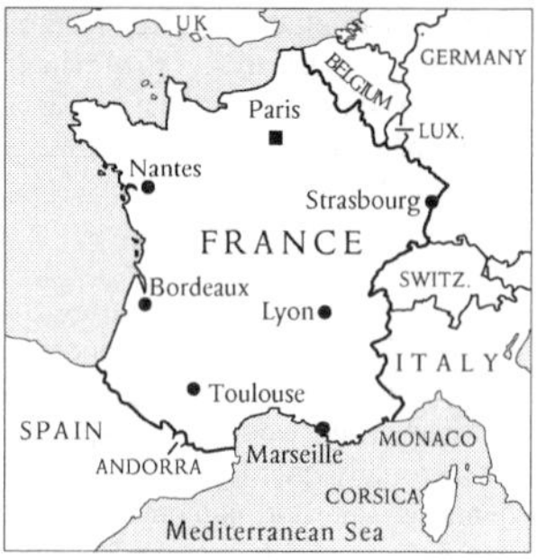

Area – 547,030 sq. km
Capital – Paris; population, 9,904,000 (2007 est)
Major cities – Bordeaux, Lille, Lyon, Marseilles, Montpellier, Nantes, Nice, Reims, Rennes, Strasbourg, Toulouse. The chief towns of Corsica are Ajaccio and Bastia
Currency – Euro (€) of 100 cents
Population – 63,713,926 rising at 0.59 per cent per year (2007 est)
Religion – Roman Catholicism (51 per cent), Islam (8 per cent), Protestantism (3 per cent), Judaism (1 per cent), Buddhism (1 per cent) (est). Although the majority of the population is nominally Roman Catholic, only about 8 per cent of Catholics practice their religion
Language – French (official)
Population density – 111 per sq. km (2006)
Urban population – 76.7 per cent (2005 est)
Median age (years) – 39 (2007 est)
National anthem – 'La Marseillaise' ['Song of Marseille']
National day – 14 July (Fete de la Federation)
Life expectancy (years) – 80.59 (2007 est)
Mortality rate – 8.55 (2007 est)
Birth rate – 12.91 (2007 est)
Infant mortality rate – 3.41 (2007 est)
Death penalty – Abolished for all crimes (since 1981)
CPI score – 7.3 (2007)
Population below poverty line – 6.2 per cent (2004)

CLIMATE AND TERRAIN

The north and west are flat plains, especially in the basins of the Somme, Seine, Loire and Garonne rivers, with some low hills. The centre of the south is occupied by the Massif Central plateau, which is divided by the valley of the Rhone and Soane rivers from the French Alps and the Jura mountains on the eastern border with Switzerland. The Pyrenees range lies along the southern border with Spain. Elevation extremes range from 4,807m (Mt Blanc, Alps) at the highest point to −2m (Rhone delta) at the lowest. The south has a Mediterranean climate with warm winters and hot, arid summers. The east has a continental climate.

HISTORY AND POLITICS

The area that is now France was conquered by the Romans in the first century BC and, as the province of Gaul, remained part of the Roman Empire until the Frankish invasions of the fifth and sixth centuries. The Treaty of Verdun (AD 843) divided the Frankish Empire created by Charlemagne into three parts, of which the western part, *Francia Occidentalis,* became the basis for modern France. Weak central government allowed the great nobles to form virtually independent duchies, and the assertion of royal power over these nobles was not completed until the 16th century. France's attempts to establish itself as the supreme European power from the 16th century were hindered by civil and religious wars (1562–98), but by the early 18th century this ambition was achieved, along with a large overseas empire.

The *ancien régime* was overthrown in the French Revolution (1789), a republic was declared in 1792 and the king, Louis XVI, was executed. The republic was overthrown by Napoléon Bonaparte, who established the first French Empire (1804–14). After Bonaparte's defeat, the congress of Vienna restored the monarchy, but in 1848 the Second Republic was declared, which lasted only until 1852, when the Second Empire was proclaimed under Napoléon III. He was forced to abdicate following the defeat of France in the Franco-Prussian war (1870–71), after which the Third Republic (1870–1940) was established.

France was one of the victors in the First World War (1914–18), when German offensives in the north and east of the country were held and eventually defeated. However, the country was invaded in the Second World War and the north was occupied by Germany from 1940 until 1944, with a pro-German government in the south. The Fourth Republic was declared in 1946, but collapsed in 1958, when a new constitution was adopted and the Fifth Republic was proclaimed. France granted most of its colonies independence between 1954 and 1962.

France was a founder member of the EEC in 1958, and joined the European Monetary Union in 1999. In a 2005 referendum, the population rejected the EU constitution.

The 2007 presidential election was won in the second round by Nicolas Sarkozy, the Rally for the Republic (RPR) candidate. In the 2007 national assembly elections, the RPR-led Union for a Popular Movement (UMP) won 313 seats, and the UMP-dominated coalition government continued in office after a reshuffle. The next elections to the senate, currently dominated by the Socialist Party, are due in September 2008.

INSURGENCIES

Corsican separatists began a campaign of bombings and shootings in the mid-1970s. The French government's proposals to combine the island's two departments and to give the Corsican regional parliament a degree of autonomy by 2004 were accepted by the regional parliament in 2000 and narrowly passed by the national assembly in 2001. But the constitutional council rejected the legislation as unconstitutional in 2002, and a referendum in 2003 voted narrowly against the proposals. In spring 2005 the main separatist faction announced an end of its 2003 ceasefire and the resumption of its campaign.

POLITICAL SYSTEM

Under the 1958 constitution, the head of state is a president directly elected for a five-year term. The legislature, the *Parlement,* consists of the National Assembly and the senate. The National Assembly has 577 deputies, 555 for metropolitan France and 22 for the overseas departments and territories; members are directly elected for a five-year term. The senate currently has 331 senators, elected by an electoral college to serve a nine-year term, with one-third being elected every three years. By 2011, 15 new seats will be added to make a total of 348 senators (326 for metropolitan France and the overseas departments, two each for New Caledonia and Mayotte, one each for St Pierre and Miquelon, St Barthelemy and St Martin, three for overseas territories and 12 for French nationals living abroad), and from 2008 members will serve for a six-year term, with one half of the seats being elected every three years.

The prime minister is nominated by the national assembly and appointed by the president, as is the council of ministers. They are responsible to the legislature, but as the executive is constitutionally separate from the legislature, ministers may not sit in the legislature and must hand over their seats to a substitute.

A government plan for decentralisation of power from Paris was initiated in 2002, and constitutional amendments in 2003 paved the way for the devolution to the 22 regions and 96 departments of powers over economic development, transport, tourism, culture and further education.

HEAD OF STATE

President of the French Republic, Nicolas Sarkozy, *elected* 6 May 2007

SELECTED GOVERNMENT MEMBERS *as at May 2008*

Prime Minister, Francois Fillon
Defence, Hervé Morin
Economy, Christine Lagarde
Foreign, Bernard Kouchner
Interior, Michèle Alliot-Marie

EMBASSY OF FRANCE

58 Knightsbridge, London SW1X 7JT
T 020-7073 1000 W www.ambafrance-uk.org
Ambassador Extraordinary and Plenipotentiary, HE Maurice Gourdault-Montagne, *apptd* 2007

BRITISH EMBASSY

35 rue du Faubourg St Honoré, 75383 Paris Cédex 08
T (+33) (1) 4451 3100 W www.britishembassy.gov.uk/france
Ambassador Extraordinary and Plenipotentiary, HE Sir Peter Westmacott, KCMG, LVO, *apptd* 2007

BRITISH COUNCIL

9 rue de Constantine, 75340 Paris Cédex 07
T (+33) (1) 4955 7300 W www.britishcouncil.org/france
Director, Paul de Quincey

DEFENCE

The army has 968 main battle tanks, 601 armoured infantry fighting vehicles, 4,413 armoured personnel carriers and 2 armed helicopters.

The navy has 10 submarines including 4 strategic submarines, 2 aircraft carriers, 13 destroyers, 20 frigates and 20 patrol and coastal vessels, 60 combat aircraft and 77 armed helicopters. The navy has 4 domestic and 5 overseas bases. The air force has 256 combat aircraft. There are currently 2 military satellites in service.

Military expenditure – US$54,000m (2006)
Military personnel – 254,895: army 133,500, navy 43,995, air force 63,600, central staff 5,200, Service de Santé 8,600; paramilitary 199,148

ECONOMY AND TRADE

The economy is in transition from a state of extensive government ownership and intervention to one of greater market orientation. Reform was begun because of poor economic growth and high unemployment. Implementation has been difficult because of the constraints of eurozone membership and the strong resistance to the government's privatisation and labour, pension and welfare reform plans, particularly by the trade unions and the large public sector, provoking demonstrations and strikes.

Nearly 40 per cent of the land area of metropolitan France is utilised for agricultural production and a further quarter is accounted for by forests. Viniculture is extensive, though France has lost market share to other countries in recent years. Cognac, liqueurs and cider are also produced. Other important agricultural products include cereals, sugar beet, potatoes, beef, dairy products and fish. Agriculture employs 4.1 per cent of the workforce but contributes only 2.0 per cent of GDP.

Oil is produced from fields in the Landes area, but France is a net importer of crude oil, for processing by its oil-refining industry. Natural gas is produced in the foothills of the Pyrenees.

Industry contributes 20.7 per cent of GDP, employing 24.4 per cent of the workforce. The sector is highly diversified and includes the production of machinery, iron, steel, aluminium, chemicals, vehicles, aircraft, electronic goods, textiles and food processing. The services sector contributes 77.3 per cent of GDP and employs 71.5 per cent of the workforce. Tourism is an important contributor to GDP.

The main trading partners are other EU countries. Principal exports are machinery, vehicles, aircraft, plastics, chemicals, pharmaceutical products, iron and steel, and beverages. The main imports are raw materials for industry (eg crude oil, chemicals, plastics), machinery and equipment, vehicles and aircraft.

GNI – US$2,306,700m; US$36,560 per capita (2006)
Annual average growth of GDP – 1.8 per cent (2007 est)
Inflation rate – 1.5 per cent (2007 est)
Unemployment – 8 per cent (2007 est)
Total external debt – US$4,396,000m (2007)
Imports – US$538,000m (2006)
Exports – US$487,000m (2006)

BALANCE OF PAYMENTS

Trade – US$48,486m deficit (2006)
Current Account – US$28,192m deficit (2006)

Trade with UK	*2006*	*2007*
Imports from UK	£28,314,000,000	£17,895,395,303
Exports to UK	£20,746,100,000	£21,599,133,113

COMMUNICATIONS

There are extensive road and rail networks covering the whole country, with approximately 956,300km of roads, including 10,490km of motorways, and around 29,370km of railways. The world's tallest road bridge was opened at Millau in 2004.

The principal seaports are Marseille on the Mediterranean Sea, Bordeaux and Nantes on the Atlantic coast, and Le Havre, Calais and Dunkirk on the Channel coast. There are 8,500km of navigable inland waterways, 1,686km navigable by large vessels, and Paris, Rouen and Strasbourg are significant river ports. The French mercantile marine consisted in 2007 of 141 ships of 1,000 gross tonnage or over, 56 of which are registered overseas. There are two international airports serving Paris, and many regional airports capable of accepting international flights.

In 2006, there were 33.9 million main telephone lines in use and 51.6 million mobile phone users. There were 30.8 million internet users in 2007.

EDUCATION AND HEALTH

Education is compulsory, free of charge and secular from the ages of six to 16. Schools may be single-sex or co-educational. Primary education is given in nursery schools, primary schools and *collèges d'enseignement général* (four-year secondary modern course), and secondary education in *collèges d'enseignement technique, collèges d'enseignement secondaire* and *lycées* (a seven-year course leading to one of the five *baccalauréats*). Specialist schools are numerous.

There are many *grandes écoles* in France which award diplomas in subjects not taught at university, especially applied science and engineering. Most of these are state institutions but have a competitive system of entry, unlike the universities.

Gross enrolment ratio (percentage of relevant age group) – primary 110 per cent; secondary 114 per cent; tertiary 56 per cent (2006 est)
Health expenditure (per capita) – US$3,807 (2005)
Hospital beds (per 1,000 people) – 7.5 (2000–6)

MEDIA

There are over 100 daily newspapers in France including *Le Monde, Le Figaro* and *Libération*. The press is mostly privately owned and not linked to political parties. State radio broadcasting caters for both domestic (Radio France) and overseas (Radio France Internationale) audiences. TV5 is an international French-language television channel co-financed by Belgium, Canada, France and Switzerland. The main domestic channel, TF1, was privatised in 1987. A global news channel, France 24, was launched in 2006 and broadcasts in both French and English.

CULTURE

French literature contains two of the masterpieces of the Middle Ages, the anonymous *Song of Roland* and *The Romance of the Rose* by Guillaume de Lorris, later lengthened by Jean de Meun. Philosophers Voltaire (1694–1778) and Rousseau (1712–78) also used fiction to illustrate their thought, creating *Candide* (1759) and *Julie* (1761), respectively. The 19th century saw a flowering of French literature in novels of Victor Hugo (1802–85), Alexandre Dumas (1802–70), Jules Verne (1828–1905), Gustave Flaubert (1821–80) and Émile Zola (1840–1902). Marcel Proust's (1871–1922) *Remembrance of Things Past* remains the weightiest of the French literary landmarks.

France's many artistic movements have inspired generations of artists all over the world. The first significant French painter is commonly believed to be classicist Nicholas Poussin (1594–1665). The works of Édouard Manet (1832–83) represent the change from the Romanticism characterised by Eugène Delacroix (1798–1863) to Impressionism, one of France's most productive artistic periods as demonstrated by Edgar Degas (1834–1917), Pierre-Auguste Renoir (1841–1919), Paul Cézanne (1839–1906), along with sculptors Auguste Rodin (1840–1917) and Marcel Duchamp (1887–1968).

French cinema is characterised by experimental auteurs such as Jean-Luc Godard (*b.* 1930) and François Truffaut (1932–1984). Actresses to succeed in Hollywood include Brigitte Bardot (*b.* 1934), Catherine Deneuve (*b.* 1943) and Juliette Binoche (*b.* 1964). In music, Edith Piaf (1915–63) and Serge Gainsbourg (1928–91) are the best-known proponents of the uniquely French musical form *chansons*. In classical music, Hector Berlioz (1803–69), Georges Bizet (1838–75) and Claude Debussy (1862–1918) are among the country's best-known composers.

OVERSEAS DEPARTMENTS/REGIONS

French Guiana, Guadeloupe, Martinique and Réunion have had departmental status since 1946. They were given regional status with greater powers of self-government and elected assemblies in 1982, and under recent constitutional changes they were redesignated as Overseas Regions. Their regional and departmental status is identical to that of regions and departments of metropolitan France, and they can choose to replace these with a single structure by merging their regional and departmental assemblies. The French government is represented by a *prefect* in each.

FRENCH GUIANA

Area – 83,534 sq. km
Capital – Cayenne; population, 63,000 (2007 est)
Population – 199,000 (2006 est)

Situated on the north-eastern coast of South America, French Guiana is flanked by Suriname on the west and by Brazil on the south and east. Under the administration of French Guiana is the Îles du Salut group of islands (St Joseph, Île Royal and Île du Diable). The European Space Agency rocket launch site is situated at Kourou, and accounts for 25 per cent of GDP. Fishing and forestry are the main activities, and the main exports are timber, shrimp and gold. Tourism is restricted by the lack of infrastructure, as much of the interior is accessible only by river.

Prefect, Ange Mancini

GUADELOUPE

Area – 1,705 sq. km
Capital – Basse-Terre; population 12,000 (2007 est), on Guadeloupe
Population – 405,000 (2006 est, adjusted for separation of St Bartelemy and St Martin)

Consists of a number of islands in the Leeward Islands group of the West Indies, including Guadeloupe (or Basse-Terre), Grande-Terre, Marie-Galante, La Désirade and the Îles des Saintes. The main towns are Les Abymes; Pointe-à-Pitre (Grande-Terre) and Grand Bourg (Marie-Galante). The main industries are tourism, agriculture, sugar refining and rum distilling. Bananas, sugar, rum and vanilla are the main exports.

Prefect, Paul Girot de Langlade

MARTINIQUE

Area – 1,128 sq. km
Capital – Fort-de-France; population, 93,000 (2007 est)
Population – 436,000 (2006 est)

An island in the Windward Islands group of the West Indies, between Dominica in the north and St Lucia in the south. Mount Pelée (1,397m) is an active volcano that last erupted in 1902. Tourism is a major industry. The main

exports are bananas, rum and petroleum products.
Prefect, Yves Dassonville

RÉUNION

Area – 2,547 sq. km
Capital – St-Denis; 143,000 (2007 est)
Population – 787,000 (2006 est)

A French possession since 1638, Réunion lies in the Indian Ocean, about 650km east of Madagascar and 180km south-west of Mauritius. The main industries are tourism, and sugar and rum production.
Prefect, Gonthier Friederici

TERRITORIAL COLLECTIVITIES

Overseas collectivities are administrative divisions with a degree of autonomy but without the status of a similar administrative division in metropolitan France; each has its own laws and elected assembly. The French government is represented by a *prefect* in each. Constitutional changes in 2003 redesignated most of the former overseas territories as collectivities; New Caledonia is treated in this category because this is its de facto status at present but its official designation depends upon the outcome of independence referendums to be held between 2014 and 2019.

FRENCH POLYNESIA

Pays d'outre-mer de la Polynésie français – Overseas Lands of French Polynesia
Area – 4,167 sq. km
Capital – Papeete; population, 131,000 (2007 est), in Tahiti
Population – 278,963; rising at 1.46 per cent per year (2007 est)

French Polynesia consists of over 118 volcanic and coral islands and atolls in the South Pacific. There are five archipelagos: the Society Islands (Windward Islands group includes Tahiti, Moorea, Makatea, Mehetia, Tetiaroa, Tubuai Manu; Leeward Islands group includes Huahine, Raiatea, Tahaa, Bora-Bora, Maupiti), the Tuamotu Islands (Rangiroa, Hao, Turéia, etc), the Gambier Islands (Mangareva, etc), the Tubuai Islands (Rimatara, Rurutu, Tubuai, Raivavae, Rapa, etc) and the Marquesas Islands (Nuku-Hiva, Hiva-Oa, Fatu-Hiva, Tahuata, Ua Huka, etc). Some of the atolls were used by France for testing nuclear weapons between 1966 and 1996. The main industries are tourism, pearl-farming, fishing, coconut products and vanilla production.
High Commissioner, Anne Boquet

MAYOTTE

Area – 374 sq. km
Population – 208,783 rising at 3.62 per cent per year (2007 est)
Capital – Mamoudzou; population, 45,458 (2004 est)

Part of the Comoros archipelago, Mayotte remained a French dependency when the other three islands became independent as the Comoros Republic in 1975, and became a *collectivité territoriale* in 1976; there will be a vote in 2010 on whether to become an overseas department/region. The main products are vanilla, ylang-ylang (perfume essence), coffee and copra. Lobster and shrimp fishing is being established.
Prefect, Jean-Paul Kihl

NEW CALEDONIA

Territoire des Nouvelle-Caledonie et Dependances – Territory of New Caledonia and Dependencies
Area – 19,060 sq. km
Capital – Nouméa; population, 156,000 (2007 est)
Population – 221,943 rising at 1.2 per cent per year (2007 est)

New Caledonia is a large island in the western Pacific, 1,120km off the eastern coast of Australia. Dependencies are the Isles of Pines, the Loyalty Islands (Mahé, Lifou, Urea, etc), the Bélep Archipelago, the Chesterfield Islands, the Huon Islands and Walpole. New Caledonia was discovered in 1774 and annexed by France in 1853. Agitation for independence from the 1980s ended with the Nouméa accord in 1998, under which an increasing degree of autonomy will be transferred to the territory up to 2018, with referendums on independence to be held between 2014 and 2018. The territory is divided into three provinces, each with a provincial assembly; these combine to form the territorial assembly.

A quarter of the world's nickel deposits are found in the territory, and nickel mining and smelting are the main industries, as well as tourism. Ferronickel, nickel ore and fish are the main exports.
High Commissioner, Michel Mathieu

ST BARTHÉLEMY

Area – 21 sq. km
Population – 7,492 (2008 est)
Capital – Gustavia

The island lies in the Caribbean Sea about 240km north-west of Guadeloupe. It was settled by the French from 1648. France sold the island to Sweden in 1784 but bought it back again in 1878 and placed it under the administration of Guadeloupe. In 2003 the population voted to secede from Guadeloupe and in February 2007 the island became a *collectivité territoriale.* The economy is based on luxury tourism and duty-free commerce in luxury goods. Freshwater resources are limited, so all food and energy and most manufactured goods are imported.
Prefect, Dominique Lacroix

ST MARTIN

Area – 54.4 sq. km
Population – 29,376
Capital – Marigot

The territory occupies the northern part of the island of St Martin over 240km to the north-west of Guadeloupe; the southern part is a territory of the Netherlands. The island was claimed for Spain by Columbus in 1493 but the Dutch occupied it from 1631 until ousted by Spain in 1633. In 1648 Spain relinquished the island to the Dutch and French, who divided it between them. The French part was administered from Guadeloupe until, after its population voted to secede in 2003, it was made a *collectivité territoriale* in February 2007. The economy is dependent on tourism, which employs 85 per cent of the workforce. Nearly all food, energy and manufactured goods are imported.
Prefect, Dominique Lacroix

ST PIERRE AND MIQUELON

Département de Saint-Pierre et Miquelon – Territorial Collectivity of Saint Pierre and Miquelon
Area – 242 sq. km

Population – 7,036 rising at 0.13 per cent per year (2007 est)
Capital – St-Pierre; population, 6,000 (2007)

These two small groups of eight islands off the south coast of Newfoundland became a *collectivité territoriale* in 1985. The main industry of fishing and servicing fishing fleets has declined in step with the decline in cod stocks, and fish farming, crab fishing and agriculture are being developed. Tourism is of growing importance.
Prefect, Albert Dupuy

WALLIS AND FUTUNA ISLANDS

Area – 274 sq. km
Capital – Mata-Utu; population, 1,000 (2007 est), on Uvea, the main island of the Wallis group
Population – 16,309 (2007 est)

The two groups of islands (the Wallis Archipelago and the Îles de Horne) lie in the South Pacific, north-east of Fiji. The main products are copra, vegetables, bananas, livestock products, fish and timber.
Administrator, Xavier de Furst

OVERSEAS TERRITORIES

FRENCH SOUTHERN AND ANTARCTIC TERRITORIES

Territoire des Terres australes et antarctiques françaises – Territory of the French Southern and Antarctic Lands

Created in 1955 from former Réunion dependencies, the territory comprises the islands of Amsterdam (64 sq. km) and St Paul (7 sq. km), the Kerguelen Islands (6,992 sq. km) and Crozet Islands (300 sq. km) archipelagos, Adélie Land (302,500 sq. km) in the Antarctic continent and, since 2007, the islands of Bassas da India (80 sq. km), Europa (28 sq. km), les Glorieuses (5 sq. km), Juan de Nova (4.4 sq. km) and Tromelin (1 sq. km). The population consists only of members of staff of the scientific stations.
Administrator, Michel Champon

THE FRENCH COMMUNITY OF STATES

The 1958 constitution envisaged the establishment of a French Community of States. A number of the former French states in Africa have seceded from the community but for all practical purposes continue to enjoy the same close links with France as those that remain formal members. Most former French African colonies are closely linked to France by financial, technical and economic agreements.

GABON

République gabonaise – Gabonese Republic

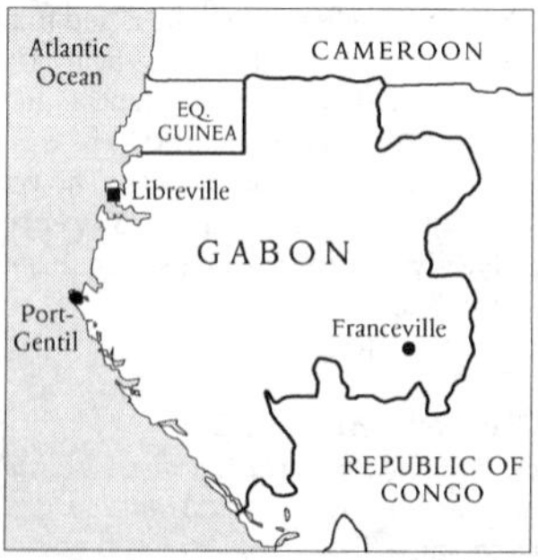

Area – 267,667 sq. km
Capital – Libreville; population, 576,000 (2007 est)
Major towns – Franceville, Moanda, Oyem, Port-Gentil
Currency – Franc CFA of 100 centimes
Population – 1,454,867 rising at 2.04 per cent per year (2007 est)
Religion – Christianity (73 per cent), Islam (12 per cent), indigenous religions (10 per cent) (est). It is estimated that 5 per cent of the population practises no religion
Language – French (official), Fang, Myene, Nzebi, Bapounou, Bandjabi
Population density – 5 per sq. km (2006)
Urban population – 85.2 per cent (2005 est)
Median age (years) – 18.6 (2007 est)
National anthem – 'La Concorde' ['The Concord']
National day – 17 August (Independence Day)
Life expectancy (years) – 53.99 (2007 est)
Mortality rate – 12.45 (2007 est)
Birth rate – 35.96 (2007 est)
Infant mortality rate – 53.65 (2007 est)
HIV/AIDS adult prevalence – 6.8 per cent (2005 est)
Death penalty – Retained, but not used
CPI score – 3.3 (2007)
Gross enrolment ratio (percentage of relevant age group) – primary 152 per cent (2006 est)
Health expenditure (per capita) – US$276 (2005)

CLIMATE AND TERRAIN

The terrain rises from a narrow coastal plain to a hilly interior; approximately 85 per cent of the land is rainforest, with savannah in the east and south. Elevation extremes range from 1,575m (Mt Iboundji) at the highest point to 0m (Atlantic Ocean) at the lowest. The climate is hot and humid with an average temperature of 27°C. There are two wet seasons each year, from February to May, and from October to December.

HISTORY AND POLITICS

The first Europeans to visit the region were the Portuguese in the 15th century; Dutch, French and English traders arrived soon after. Sovereignty was signed over to the French in 1839 by a local Mpongwe ruler. In 1849, a slave ship was captured by the French and the freed slaves formed a settlement which they called Libreville, the current capital. The country was occupied by the French in 1885 and became part of French Equatorial Africa in 1910. Gabon became autonomous within the French Community in 1958 and gained full independence on 17 August 1960.

President Bongo came to power in 1967, and in 1968 a one-party state was established with the *Parti Démocratique Gabonais* (PDG) as the only party. By the late 1980s, the deteriorating economy was provoking unrest, and in 1991 a multiparty system was reintroduced.

Under the multiparty system, the PDG has remained in power (amid allegations of electoral fraud) although it has included opposition party members in coalition governments since 1994. President Bongo was re-elected for a sixth term of office in 2005 with nearly 80 per cent of the vote. The 2006 legislative elections were again won by the PDG, which formed a coalition government with two smaller parties.

POLITICAL SYSTEM

The 1991 constitution, amended in 1995, 1997 and 2003, provides for a president who is directly elected for a seven-year term; since 2003, there has been no limit on the number of terms a president may serve. The prime minister is appointed by the president, and then appoints the council of ministers. There is a bicameral *Parlement*, comprising the 120-member National Assembly (111 directly elected and nine appointed by the president for a five-year term), and the senate, which has 91 members elected for a six-year term by municipal and regional councillors.

HEAD OF STATE
President, Omar Bongo, *assumed office* December 1967, *re-elected* 1973, 1979, 1986, 1993, 1998, 2005
Vice-President, Didjob Divungi di Ndinge

SELECTED GOVERNMENT MEMBERS *as at May 2008*
Prime Minister, Jean Eyeghe Ndong
Deputy Prime Ministers, Georgette Koko; Paul Mba Abessole; Honorine Dossou Naki
Defence, Ali Bongo Ondimba
Finance, Economy, Paul Toungui
Interior, André Mba Obame
Foreign Affairs, Laure Olga Gondjout

EMBASSY OF THE GABONESE REPUBLIC
27 Elvaston Place, London SW7 5NL
T 020-7823 9986 W www.gaboneseembassy.org
Ambassador Extraordinary and Plenipotentiary, HE Alain Mensah-Zoguelet, *apptd* 2003

BRITISH AMBASSADOR
HE Syd Maddicott, *apptd* 2005, resident at Yaoundé, Cameroon

DEFENCE
The army has 12 armoured infantry fighting vehicles and 23 armoured personnel carriers. The navy has 9 patrol and coastal combatant vessels at a base at Port Gentil. The air force has 16 combat capable aircraft and 5 armed helicopters.
Military personnel – 4,700: army 3,200, navy 500, air force 1,000; paramilitary 2,000

ECONOMY AND TRADE
Gabon is one of the most stable and prosperous countries in Africa, largely owing to its small population and abundance of oil and mineral resources. The economy is heavily dependent on oil (which contributes 50 per cent of GDP) and on other mineral resources, including manganese and uranium, and timber, all of which can be subject to fluctuating prices. Despite the country's wealth, a large proportion of the population remains poor, and weak fiscal management has resulted in a high foreign debt which has had to be rescheduled several times.

Agriculture is largely at subsistence level, employing 60 per cent of the workforce but contributing only 5.8 per cent of GDP. The main products include cocoa, coffee, sugar, palm oil, rubber, cattle, timber and fish. Industry contributes 58.8 per cent of GDP and employs 15 per cent of the workforce, mainly in oil and mineral extraction, oil refining, chemicals, ship repair, textiles, and processing agricultural and forestry products. The service sector contributes 35.5 per cent of GDP and employs 25 per cent of the workforce. The main trading partners are the USA, France and China. Principal exports are crude oil (77 per cent), timber, manganese and uranium. The main imports are machinery and equipment, food, chemicals and construction materials.
GNI – US$7,000m; US$5,630 per capita (2006)
Annual average growth of GDP – 4.5 per cent (2007 est)
Inflation rate – 5 per cent (2007 est)
Unemployment – 21 per cent (2006 est)
Total external debt – US$3,579m (2007 est)
Imports – US$1,500m (2006)
Exports – US$5,600m (2006)

BALANCE OF PAYMENTS
Trade – US$4,100m surplus (2006)
Current Account – US$1,717m surplus (2006)

Trade with UK	*2005*	*2006*
Imports from UK	£29,335,000	£28,415,000
Exports to UK	£10,091,000	£6,350,000

MEDIA
The biggest broadcaster, Radiodiffusion-Télévision Gabonaise, is state controlled and operates two stations. There are two other main channels: TéléAfrica, which is privately owned, and TV Sat, a subscription operator. There are several privately owned newspapers that usually publish on a weekly basis. The only daily newspaper, *L'Union,* is government-run. Radio is an important news medium because of rural illiteracy. Africa No1, a pan-African broadcaster based in Gabon, is partly French-owned.

THE GAMBIA

Republic of the Gambia

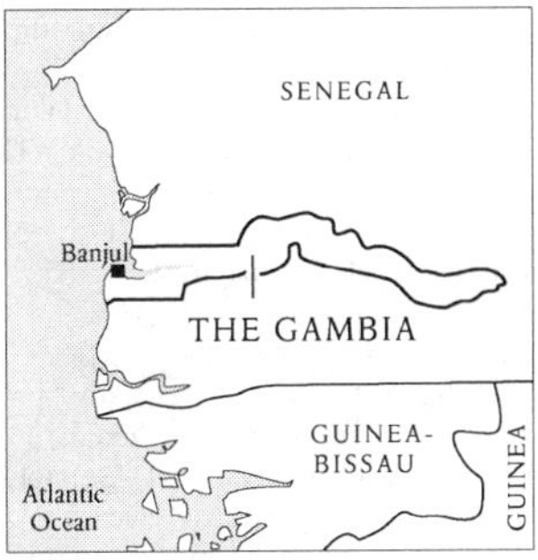

Area – 11,300 sq. km
Capital – Banjul; population, 406,000 (2007 est)
Major towns – Bakau, Brikama, Kanifeng
Currency – Dalasi (D) of 100 butut
Population – 1,688,359 rising at 2.78 per cent per year (2007 est); Mandinka (42 per cent), Fula (18 per cent), Wolof (16 per cent), Jola (10 per cent), Soninke (9 per cent) (est)
Religion – Islam (90 per cent), Christianity (9 per cent), indigenous religions (1 per cent) (est)
Language – English (official), Mandinka, Wolof, Fula
Population density – 166 per sq. km (2006)
Urban population – 26.1 per cent (2005 est)
Median age (years) – 17.8 (2007 est)
National anthem – 'For The Gambia Our Homeland'
National day – 18 February (Independence Day)
Life expectancy (years) – 54.54 (2007 est)
Mortality rate – 11.99 (2007 est)
Birth rate – 38.86 (2007 est)
Infant mortality rate – 70.14 (2007 est)
HIV/AIDS adult prevalence – 2.1 per cent (2005 est)
Death penalty – Retained, but not used
CPI score – 2.3 (2007)

CLIMATE AND TERRAIN

The Gambia consists of a narrow strip of land along the Gambia river; the low-lying land is mostly a flood plain flanked by hills. Elevation extremes range from 53m at the highest point to 0m (Atlantic Ocean) at the lowest. The climate is tropical, with an average temperature of between 23°C and 40°C. The wet season lasts from June to September.

HISTORY AND POLITICS

The Gambia river basin was part of a region dominated from the 10th to 16th centuries by the Mali and Songhai kingdoms. The Portuguese reached the Gambia river in 1447; English merchants began to trade along the river from 1588. Merchants from France, Courland (now Latvia) and the Netherlands also established trading posts there. In 1816, the British stationed a garrison on an island at the river mouth that became the capital of a small British-administered colony; this became a crown colony in 1843. In 1889, France agreed that the British rights along the upper river should extend to 10km from the river on either bank. The Gambia became independent within the Commonwealth on 18 February 1965 and a republic on 24 April 1970.

The post-independence prime minister, Sir Dawda Jawara, was president from 1970 until he was overthrown in 1994, in a military coup. The coup leader, Lt. (later Capt.) Jammeh, assumed the presidency, the constitution was suspended and a civilian-military government was formed to govern in conjunction with the ruling military council. A referendum approved a new constitution in 1996, Jammeh was elected president and the military council was dissolved.

In the 2006 presidential election, Jammeh was re-elected with 67 per cent of the vote. The 2007 legislative election was won by the Alliance for Patriotic Reorientation and Construction (APRC), the president's party, with an overwhelming majority.

POLITICAL SYSTEM

Under the 1996 constitution, the executive president is directly elected for a five-year term; there is no limit on re-election. The unicameral National Assembly has 53 members, of whom 48 are directly elected and five are appointed by the president, for a five-year term.

HEAD OF STATE

President, Defence, Agriculture, Col. Yahya Jammeh, *took power* July 1994, *elected* September 1996, *re-elected* 2001, 2006

Vice-President, Women and Social Affairs, Ajaratou Isatou Njie-Saidy

SELECTED GOVERNMENT MEMBERS *as at May 2008*

External Affairs, Omar Touray
Finance and Economic Affairs, Musa Gibril Bala Gaye
Interior, Col. Ousman Sonko
Justice, Attorney-General, Marie Sainte Firdaus

GAMBIA HIGH COMMISSION

57 Kensington Court, London W8 5DG
T 020-7937 6316 E gambia@gamhighcom.wanadoo.co.uk
High Commissioner, vacant

BRITISH HIGH COMMISSION

PO Box 507, 48 Atlantic Road, Fajara, Banjul
T (+220) 449 5133 E bhcbanjul@gamtel.gm
High Commissioner, HE Philip Sinkinson, *apptd* 2006

DEFENCE

The Marine Unit has 4 patrol and coastal combatant vessels at a base at Banjul.
Military budget – US$1.6m (2006 est)
Military personnel – army 800

ECONOMY AND TRADE

The country has limited natural resources and agricultural land and, historically, the mainstay of the economy was re-export trade with neighbouring countries. This has declined owing to the government's imposition of pre-shipment inspection plans in 1999 and the instability of the currency. Although the discovery of offshore oil deposits was announced in 2004, none are currently exploited. There are high levels of public and foreign debt and the country is dependent on financial and technical aid from foreign donors. An important revenue source is remittances from Gambians working abroad.

Most of the population is dependent on subsistence agriculture, which employs 75 per cent of the workforce and contributes 32.8 per cent of GDP. The chief product, peanuts, is the basis of the main industrial activity and the main export, leaving the economy vulnerable to market fluctuations. Industry contributes 8.7 per cent to GDP and employs 19 per cent of the workforce, chiefly in light manufacturing: processing peanuts, fish and hides, assembling agricultural machinery, metalworking, woodworking and production of beverages and clothing. The services sector employs only 6 per cent of the workforce but contributes 58.5 per cent of GDP, largely owing to the growing tourism industry.

The main trade partners are India, China, the UK and Senegal. Principal exports are peanut products, fish, cotton lint, palm kernels and re-exports. The main imports are foodstuffs, manufactures, fuel and machinery and transport equipment.
GNI – US$500m; US$290 per capita (2006)
Annual average growth of GDP – 7 per cent (2007 est)
Inflation rate – 3.5 per cent (2007 est)
Total external debt – US$628.8m (2003 est)
Imports – US$250m (2006)
Exports – US$10m (2006)

BALANCE OF PAYMENTS

Trade – US$235m deficit (2006)
Current Account – US$58m deficit (2006)

Trade with UK	*2005*	*2006*
Imports from UK	£16,468,000	£14,042,000
Exports to UK	£3,055,000	£3,513,000

EDUCATION AND HEALTH

Education is compulsory until the age of eight.
Gross enrolment ratio (percentage of relevant age group) – primary 74 per cent; secondary 45 per cent; tertiary 1 per cent (2006 est)
Health expenditure (per capita) – US$15 (2005)
Hospital beds (per 1,000 people) – 0.8 (2000–6)

MEDIA

Since 2002 private newspapers and radio stations have been regulated by a government-run commission that has the power to suspend publication or transmission licences and imprison journalists. The state operates the only national television station, Gambia Television. There is one private satellite channel, Premium TV Network. State-run Radio Gambia produces carefully controlled news broadcasts, which are relayed by private radio stations.

GEORGIA

Sak'art'velo – Georgia

Area – 69,700 sq. km
Capital – Tbilisi; population, 1,100,000 (2007 est)
Major cities – Batumi, Kutaisi, Rustavi
Currency – Lari of 100 tetri
Population – 4,646,003, falling at 0.33 per cent per year (2007 est); Georgian (83.8 per cent), Azeri (6.5 per cent), Armenian (5.7 per cent); Russian (1.5 per cent)
Religion – Orthodox Christianity (80 per cent), Islam (10 per cent) (est)
Language – Georgian (official), Russian, Armenian, Azeri, Abkhaz
Population density – 64 per sq. km (2006)
Urban population – 51.5 per cent (2005 est)
Median age (years) – 38 (2007 est)
National anthem – 'Tavisupleba' ['Freedom']
National day – 26 May (Independence Day)
Life expectancy (years) – 76.3 (2007 est)
Mortality rate – 9.37 (2007 est)
Birth rate – 10.54 (2007 est)
Infant mortality rate – 17.36 (2007 est)
Death penalty – Abolished for all crimes (since 1997)
CPI score – 3.4 (2007)
Population below poverty line – 54.5 per cent (2003)
Gross enrolment ratio (percentage of relevant age group) – primary 96 per cent; secondary 85 per cent; tertiary 38 per cent (2006 est)
Health expenditure (per capita) – US$123 (2005)
Hospital beds (per 1,000 people) – 3.8 (2000–6)

CLIMATE AND TERRAIN

Georgia lies in the western part of the Caucasus region, on the eastern shore of the Black Sea. It is mountainous, with the Great Caucasus mountain range in the north and the Lesser Caucasus in the south, divided by the valleys of the Kura and Rioni rivers. Elevation extremes range from 5,201m (Mt Shkhara) at the highest point to 0m (Black Sea) at the lowest. The climate is almost tropical in the summer, while cold winters affect both the mountains and valleys. Average temperatures in Tbilisi range from 3°C in January to 28°C in July.

HISTORY AND POLITICS

The Georgians formed two states, Colchis and Iberia, on the edge of the Black Sea around 1000 BC. After several centuries of Arab rule, Georgia was liberated and entered a period of prosperity in the 12th century AD, when trade, irrigation and communications were developed. Invasions by the Khazars and Mongols led to the division of Georgia into several states. These precarious states struggled against the Turkish and Persian empires from the 16th to the 18th centuries, gradually turning to the Russian Empire for protection and support. Eastern Georgia signed a treaty of alliance with Russia which recognised Russian supremacy in 1783 and joined the Russian Empire in 1801, followed soon after by western Georgia.

In the late 19th century, nationalist and Marxist movements competed for limited political influence under autocratic Russian rule. One of the most prominent Marxist activists was Iosif Dzhugashvili (Joseph Stalin). After the Russian Revolution of 1917, an independent nationalist government came to power in Georgia supported by Allied intervention forces. In 1921 Soviet forces occupied Tbilisi, and in 1922 Georgia joined the USSR as part of the Transcaucasian Soviet Socialist Republic, becoming a separate republic in 1936.

In the 1980s there were growing demands for autonomy, and in 1990 the Communist Party's monopoly on power was abolished. In multiparty elections held in autumn 1990, the nationalist leader Zviad Gamsakhurdia was elected president. Georgia declared its independence from the USSR in May 1991.

Demonstrations against Gamsakhurdia's increasingly dictatorial government in 1991 developed into civil war that resulted in Gamsakhurdia's overthrow and replacement by Eduard Shevardnadze in 1992. The war continued until 1993, when, with most government forces engaged in Abkhazia, Georgia was forced to accept Russian armaments and troops to defeat the rebels and in return agreed to join the Commonwealth of Independent States.

President Shevardnadze was re-elected in 2000, but resigned in 2003 after mass demonstrations against alleged electoral fraud in parliamentary elections. Mikhail Saakashvili, leader of the National Movement, was elected president in a landslide victory in January 2004. Following rerun elections in the 150 disputed parliamentary seats in March 2004, the National Movement-Democratic Front held 135 of the 235 parliamentary seats. President Saakashvili won a second term with 53 per cent of then vote in the first round of a presidential election brought forward to January 2008 after demonstrations in late 2007 caused a state of emergency to be declared; the opposition disputed the results but international monitors considered the election democratic.

Relations between Georgia and Russia remained fraught owing to Russia's support for the secessionists in South Ossetia and Abkhazia, Georgia's increasingly pro-Western stance and ties with the US government (including joint military exercises), and Russia's use of trade embargos and disruption of energy supplies.

A series of clashes between Georgian and South Ossetian forces in the summer of 2008 prompted Georgia to launch an aerial and ground attack on secessionist South Ossetia. In response, Russia launched bombing raids both over the province and on targets in the rest of Georgia and the Georgian troops were ejected from South Ossetia and Abkhazia. An EU-brokered ceasefire brought a formal end to the conflict, although both sides have accused each other of breaking the agreement.

SECESSION

The growth of Georgian nationalism and demands for autonomy from the USSR in the 1980s led to unilateral declarations of independence by the central region of South Ossetia (1991) and the north-western region of Abkhazia (1992). The Georgian government resisted these moves and there was conflict with both regions, which received support from Russia. Fighting flared up in 2008 into a four-day armed conflict triggered by clashes between Georgian troops and South Ossetian and Abkhazian separatist forces. An EU-brokered ceasefire was signed by both sides but Russia was slow to withdraw, insisting on a 'buffer zone' on the Georgian side of the border. With Russian support, both South Ossetia and Abkhazia declared their independence of Georgia, but this has not been internationally recognised. Russian peacekeeping forces remain in both areas, but are regularly accused by Tbilisi of siding with the separatists. The UN operates a military observer mission alongside.

Relations between Georgia and Ajaria, a semi-autonomous region in the south-west and a key trade hub, deteriorated in 2004 when Aslan Abashidze, Ajaria's leader from 1991, refused to recognise the authority of the newly elected President Saakashvili, and accused Georgia of planning to invade Ajaria, ordering the destruction of connecting bridges. Public demonstrations against Abashidze followed and he was forced to resign. In the subsequent elections to the Ajarian legislature, the pro-Georgian Saakashvili-Victorious Ajaria (SUA) party won 28 of the 30 seats. The Georgian parliament granted the Ajarian assembly powers over local affairs but the Georgian president retains the power to nominate the region's head of government and to dissolve its government and assembly.

POLITICAL SYSTEM

The 1995 constitution provides for a federal republic with a unicameral legislature, to become bicameral 'following the creation of appropriate conditions'. The president is directly elected for a five-year term, renewable only once. The unicameral parliament has 235 members, 85 elected in single-member constitutencies and the rest from party lists by proportional representation, who serve for a four-year term.

HEAD OF STATE

President, Mikhail Saakashvili, *elected* 4 January 2004, *sworn in* 25 January 2004, *re-elected* 5 January 2008

SELECTED GOVERNMENT MEMBERS *as at July 2008*

Prime Minister, Lado Gurgenidze
Deputy Prime Minister, Giorgi Baramidze
Defence, Davit Kezerashvili
Finance, Nika Gilauri
Foreign Affairs, Eka Tkeshelashvili

EMBASSY OF GEORGIA

4 Russell Gardens, London W14 8EZ
T 020-7603 7799 E embassy@geoemb.plus.com
W www.geoemb.org.uk
Ambassador Extraordinary and Plenipotentiary, HE Gela Charkviani, *apptd* 2006

BRITISH EMBASSY

GMT Plaza, 4 Freedom Square, 0105 Tbilisi
T (+995) (32) 274 747 E british.embassy.tbilisi@fco.gov.uk
Ambassador Extraordinary and Plenipotentiary, HE Denis Keefe, *apptd* 2007

BRITISH COUNCIL

34 Rustaveli Avenue, 0108 Tbilisi
T (+995) (32) 250 407/ 988 014 W www.britishcouncil.org.ge
Director, Lena Milosevic

DEFENCE

The army has 128 main battle tanks, 91 armoured infantry fighting vehicles and 44 armoured personnel carriers. The navy has 6 patrol and coastal combatant vessels, based at Tbilisi and Poti, while the coastguard has 14 patrol and coastal combatant vessels. The air force has 9 combat aircraft and 9 armed helicopters.

Military budget – US$583m (2007)
Military personnel – 21,150: army 17,767, navy 495, air force 1,310, National Guard 1,578; paramilitaries 11,700
Conscription duration – 18 months

ECONOMY AND TRADE

The economy has made good progress towards recovery from the near-collapse of the 1990s, although a trade deficit and rising inflation are potential problems. The post-Shevardnadze government has reformed the tax system, nearly quadrupling government revenue, and given added impetus to the privatisation and anti-corruption programmes, hoping to attract greater foreign investment. Dependence on Russian oil and gas led to fuel crises in 2005–6, prompting the renovation of the hydroelectric power plants and the repair of a pipeline from Azerbaijan which now brings in gas supplies. The government hopes Georgia's position as a transit state for oil and gas pipelines and for trade between central Asia and Europe will provide economic growth.

The most productive sector of the economy is agriculture, which employs 55.6 per cent of the workforce and generates 12.3 per cent of GDP, with a concentration on grapes for viniculture, tea, citrus fruits and hazelnuts. Industry, which contributes 29.7 per cent of GDP, produces steel, aircraft, machine tools, electrical appliances, manganese, copper, chemicals, wood products and wine. The main trading partners are Turkey, Russia, Azerbaijan and other former Soviet states. Principal exports are scrap metal, wine, mineral water, mineral ores, vehicles, fruit and nuts. The main imports are fuels, vehicles, machinery and parts, food (especially grain) and pharmaceuticals.

GNI – US$7,000m; US$1,580 per capita (2006)
Annual average growth of GDP – 10 per cent (2007 est)
Inflation rate – 8 per cent (2007 est)
Unemployment – 13.8 per cent (2005 est)
Total external debt – US$2,040m (2004)
Imports – US$4,000m (2006)
Exports – US$1,000m (2006)
BALANCE OF PAYMENTS
Trade – US$2,688m deficit (2006)
Current Account – US$1,235m deficit (2006)

Trade with UK	*2006*	*2007*
Imports from UK	£37,771,000	£34,335,483
Exports to UK	£230,961,000	£144,177,562

MEDIA

A government-funded public broadcaster, Georgian State TV, has replaced former state television and radio networks. The state has also handed over control of newspapers and news agencies; there are now over 200 privately owned newspapers, although readership is generally low. A 2004 law decriminalised slander and libel, but the suspension of several private publications and a private television station during a state of emergency in 2007 cast doubt on the freedom of the media.

GERMANY

Bundesrepublik Deutschland – Federal Republic of Germany

Area – 357,021 sq. km
Capital – Berlin; population, 3,406,000 (2007 est)
Major cities – Bremen, Cologne, Dortmund, Dresden, Düsseldorf, Essen, Frankfurt, Hamburg, Hannover, Leipzig, Munich, Nuremberg, Stuttgart
Currency – Euro (€) of 100 cents
Population – 82,400,996 falling at 0.03 per cent per year (2007 est); German (91.5 per cent), Turkish (2.4 per cent) (est)
Religion – Protestantism (32 per cent), Roman Catholicism (31 per cent), Islam (4 per cent), Orthodox Christianity (2 per cent) (est)
Language – German (official)
Population density – 236 per sq. km (2006)
Urban population – 88.5 per cent (2005 est)
Median age (years) – 43 (2007 est)
National anthem – 'Einigkeit und Recht und Freiheit' ['Unity and Right and Freedom']
National day – 3 October (Unity Day)
Life expectancy (years) – 78.95 (2007 est)
Mortality rate – 10.71 (2007 est)
Birth rate – 7.8 (2007 est)
Infant mortality rate – 4.08 (2007 est)
Death penalty – Abolished for all crimes (since 1949 in FRG and 1987 in GDR)
CPI score – 7.8 (2007)

CLIMATE AND TERRAIN

The north of the country is low-lying, rising in the central region to uplands, Alpine foothills and then to the Bavarian Alps in the south. Elevation extremes range from 2,963m (Zugspitze, Bavaria) at the highest point to −3.5m (Neuendorf bei Wilster) at the lowest. The Rhine, Weser and Elbe rivers flow from the south to the North Sea, the Oder and Neisse rivers flow north to the Baltic Sea, and the river Danube flows east from its source in the south of the country to the Austrian border. More than a third of the land is covered by forest. The climate is temperate, with average temperatures ranging from −5°C in January to 19°C in July.

HISTORY AND POLITICS

Charlemagne extended Frankish authority over the Germanic tribes in the eighth century, and took the title of Holy Roman Emperor. The treaty of Verdun (843) divided this empire into three, the eastern part (corresponding to modern Germany) comprising hundreds of small dukedoms and principalities that enjoyed virtual independence under the hegemony of a nominally elective Holy Roman Emperor. Although a succession of dynasties succeeded at times in centralising power between 962 and 1806, shifting allegiances and alliances enabled the states to challenge the authority of the emperor, which was never sufficient to overcome the fragmentation and achieve unification into a nation state.

The empire was replaced in 1806 by a loose association of sovereign states known as the German Confederation, which was dissolved in 1866 and replaced by the Prussian-dominated North German Federation. The south German principalities united with the northern federation to form a second German Empire in 1871 and the King of Prussia was proclaimed emperor.

Defeat in the First World War led to the abdication of the emperor, and the country became a republic. The treaty of Versailles (1919) ceded Alsace-Lorraine to France, and large areas in the east were lost to Poland. The world economic crisis of 1929 contributed to the collapse of the Weimar Republic and the subsequent rise to power of the National Socialist movement of Adolf Hitler, who became chancellor in 1933.

After concluding a treaty of non-aggression with the Soviet Union in August 1939, Germany invaded Poland (1 September 1939), precipitating the Second World War, which lasted until 1945. Hitler committed suicide on 30 April 1945. On 8 May 1945, Germany unconditionally surrendered.

Germany was divided into American, French, British and Soviet zones of occupation. The Federal Republic of Germany (FRG) was created out of the three Western zones in 1949. A Communist government was established in the Soviet zone (henceforth the German Democratic Republic (GDR)). In 1961 the Soviet zone of Berlin was sealed off, and the Berlin Wall was built along the zonal boundary, partitioning the western sectors of the city from the eastern.

Soviet-initiated reform in eastern Europe during the late 1980s led to unrest in the GDR, culminating in the opening of the Berlin Wall in November 1989 and the collapse of the Communist government. The 'treaty on the final settlement with respect to Germany' concluded between the FRG, GDR and the four former occupying powers in September 1990, unified Germany with effect from 3 October 1990 as a fully sovereign state. Economic and monetary union preceded formal union on 1 July 1990. Constitutionally, unification was the accession of Berlin and the five reformed *Länder* (states) of the GDR to the FRG, which remains in being. Berlin was declared the capital of the unified Germany and the legislature and government departments were transferred from Bonn.

Germany was a founder member of the EEC in 1958 and joined the eurozone in 1999. Its parliament ratified the EU constitution in 2005.

Horst Köhler was elected federal president in 2004. An early legislative election was held in 2005 after Chancellor Gerhard Schröder's Social Democratic Party (SPD) lost control of several *Länder* governments in the 2005 regional elections and Schröder lost a subsequent parliamentary vote of no confidence. In the general election, the opposition Christian Democratic Union/Christian Social Union (CDU/CSU) coalition won four more seats than the SDP, but Chancellor Schröder refused to concede defeat. To break the political deadlock, a grand coalition of the SDP and CDU/CSU was formed under the CDU/CSU leader Angela Merkel, who became Germany's first female chancellor in November 2005.

POLITICAL SYSTEM
The Basic Law (constitution) provides for a president, elected for a five-year term by the *Bundesversammlung* (an electoral college comprising the members of the Bundestag and an equal number of representatives elected by the state legislatures), and a bicameral legislature. The lower house, *Bundestag*, has 614 members directly elected by proportional representation for a four-year term. The upper house, *Bundesrat*, has 69 members appointed by the governments of the states *(Länder)* in proportion to *Länder* populations, without a fixed term of office. The head of government is the chancellor, who is proposed by the president and elected by the *Bundestag*.

HEAD OF STATE
Federal President, Horst Köhler, *elected* 23 May, *sworn in* 1 July 2004

SELECTED GOVERNMENT MEMBERS *as at May 2008*
Federal Chancellor, Angela Merkel
Federal Vice-Chancellor, Foreign Affairs, Frank-Walter Steinmeier
Defence, Franz Josef Jung
Interior, Wolfgang Schäuble
Finance, Peer Steinbrück

EMBASSY OF THE FEDERAL REPUBLIC OF GERMANY
23 Belgrave Square/Chesham Place, London SW1X 8PZ
T 020-7824 1300 E info@london.diplo.de
W www.london.diplo.de
Ambassador Extraordinary and Plenipotentiary, HE Wolfgang Ischinger, *apptd* 2006

BRITISH EMBASSY
Wilhelmstrasse 70, 10117 Berlin
T (+49) (30) 204 570 W www.britischebotschaft.de
Ambassador Extraordinary and Plenipotentiary, HE Sir Michael Arthur, KCMG, *apptd* 2007

BRITISH COUNCIL
Alexanderplatz 1, 10178 Berlin
T (+49) (30) 311 0990 W www.britishcouncil.de/e
Director, Michael Bird, OBE

FEDERAL STRUCTURE
Germany is a federal republic composed of 16 states *(Länder)* (ten from the former FRG, five from the former GDR, and Berlin). Each *Land* has its own directly elected legislature and government led by Minister-Presidents (prime ministers) or equivalents. The 1949 Basic Law vests executive power in the *Länder* governments except in those areas reserved for the federal government.

State	*Capital*	*Population (millions) (2005 est)*
Baden-Württemberg	Stuttgart	10.7
Bavaria	Munich	12.5
Berlin	—	3.4
Brandenburg	Potsdam	2.6
Bremen	—	0.7
Hamburg	—	1.7
Hesse	Wiesbaden	6.1
Lower Saxony	Hannover	8.0
Mecklenburg-West Pomerania	Schwerin	1.7
North Rhine-Westphalia	Düsseldorf	18.1
Rhineland-Palatinate	Mainz	4.1
Saarland	Saarbrücken	1.1
Saxony	Dresden	4.3
Saxony-Anhalt	Magdeburg	2.5
Schleswig-Holstein	Kiel	2.8
Thuringia	Erfurt	2.3

DEFENCE
The army has 2,035 main battle tanks, 2,300 armoured personnel carriers, 2,218 armoured infantry fighting vehicles and 192 armed helicopters. The navy has 12 submarines, 15 frigates, 2 corvettes, 10 patrol and coastal vessels and 22 armed helicopters at 6 bases. The air force has 298 combat aircraft.
Military expenditure – US$37,770m (2006)
Military personnel – 245,702: army 160,794, navy 24,328, air force 60,580.
Conscription duration – 9 months

ECONOMY AND TRADE
Germany has one of the world's largest economies but decades of strong economic performance gave way in the 1990s to Germany's most severe post-war recession, largely an aftermath of reunification and of macroeconomic stagnation. The economy in the east remains weak despite costly modernisation and integration measures. However, an overall revival began in 2006, with growth in GDP exceeding 2 per cent for the first time since 2001, a drop in unemployment and the budget deficit being reduced to less than 3 per cent. Government reforms of the labour and welfare systems contributed to the improvement.

The country has a modern, diverse, highly industrialised and technologically advanced market economy. The services sector contributes 69.5 per cent of GDP, industry 9.6 per cent and agriculture 0.9 per cent. The industrial sector is among the world's largest producers of iron, steel, coal, cement, chemicals, machinery, vehicles, machine tools, electronics, food and beverages, ships and textiles. Germany depends on imports to meet its oil and natural gas needs but is a net exporter of electricity; this may change, though, as all 19 of its nuclear power stations, which supply over 30 per cent of its energy, are to be closed down by 2032.

The main trading partners are other EU countries, the USA and China. Machinery, vehicles, chemicals, metals and manufactures, footstuff and textiles are the principal imports and exports.
GNI – US$3,032,600m; US$36,810 per capita (2006)
Annual average growth of GDP – 2.6 per cent (2007 est)
Inflation rate – 2 per cent (2007 est)
Unemployment – 9.1 per cent (2007 est)
Total external debt – US$4,489,000m (2007)
Imports – US$919,000m (2006)
Exports – US$1,126,000m (2006)

BALANCE OF PAYMENTS
Trade – US$199,732m surplus (2006)
Current Account – US$147,134m surplus (2006)

Trade with UK	*2006*	*2007*
Imports from UK	£26,366,500,000	£24,391,695,250
Exports to UK	£38,882,800,000	£44,040,584,686

COMMUNICATIONS
There is an extensive road network of around 232,000km, including 12,000km of motorways *(autobahn)*. There are 48,000km of railways. Around 20 per cent of domestic freight is carried on the 7,500km of inland waterways. The Rhine and the Danube are linked

by the Rhine-Maine-Danube canal, creating a through route from the North Sea to the Black Sea. The Kiel canal links the North Sea and the Baltic Sea. The main river ports are Duisburg, Frankfurt, Karlsruhe and Mainz; the main seaports are Hamburg, Kiel, Bremen, Bremerhaven, Rostock and Wilhemshaven. The busiest airport is at Frankfurt, other principal airports include Berlin, Munich and Bonn. The telephone system in the east has been modernised and integrated with the rest of the country. Mobile phone distribution is widespread, with 84 million subscribers in 2006. There were 38.6 million internet users in 2006.

EDUCATION AND HEALTH

Education is free of charge and compulsory between the ages of six and 18 and comprises nine years of full-time education at primary and main schools and three years of vocational education on a part-time basis. The secondary school leaving examination *(Abitur)* entitles the holder to a place at a university or another institution of higher education.

Children below the age of 18 who are not attending a general secondary or a full-time vocational school have compulsory day-release at a vocational school.

The largest universities are in Munich, Berlin, Hamburg, Bonn, Frankfurt and Cologne. Germany's oldest university is Heidelberg, founded in 1386.

Gross enrolment ratio (percentage of relevant age group) – primary 101 per cent; secondary 100 per cent (2006 est)
Health expenditure (per capita) – US$3,628 (2005)
Hospital beds (per 1,000 people) – 8.4 (2000–6)

MEDIA

Each of the country's 16 states operates its own television stations, both private and public. Germany is implementing digital radio and television and will cease analogue services in 2010. Over 90 per cent of households receive cable or satellite television. Germany also has a considerable press industry and is home to many international media companies.

CULTURE

Germany has produced a wealth of composers, among them Bach (1685–1750), Beethoven (1770–1827), Schubert (1797–1828), Wagner (1813–83) and Brahms (1833–97). Philosophers include Immanuel Kant (1724–1804), Karl Marx (1818–83), Friedrich Engels (1820–95) and Friedrich Nietzsche (1844–1900). The work of playwrights Goethe (1749–1832) and Friedrich Schiller (1759–1805) had a European-wide influence. Novelists Thomas Mann (1875–1955), Hermann Hesse (1877–1962) and Günter Grass (*b.* 1927) have all received the Nobel prize for literature.

Key figures in the visual arts are Hans Holbein the Younger (1497–1543), who achieved success in England as a court painter in the Renaissance, surrealist Max Ernst (1891–1976) and Joseph Beuys (1921–86), and in film-making, directors Friedrich Murnau (1888–1931), Leni Riefenstahl (1902–2003), Werner Herzog (*b.* 1942) and Wim Wenders (*b.* 1945), and actor Klaus Kinski (1926–91) all gained Hollywood recognition.

Physicist Albert Einstein (1879–1955) is perhaps the world's best-known modern scientist, having introduced his theory of relativity to the wider world in 1905. Other notable German scientists include Max Planck (1858–1947), Hans Geiger (1882–1945) and Wilhelm Röntgen (1845–1923).

GHANA

Republic of Ghana

Area – 239,460 sq. km
Capital – Accra; population, 2,121,000 (2007 est)
Major cities – Ashiman, Kumasi, Sekondi-Takoradi, Tamale
Currency – Cedi of 100 pesewas
Population – 22,931,299 rising at 1.97 per cent per year (2007 est); Akan (45.3 per cent), Moshi-Dagomba (15.2 per cent), Ewe (11.7 per cent), Ga-Dangme (7.3 per cent), Guan (4 per cent), Gurma (3.6 per cent), Grusi (2.6 per cent)
Religion – Christianity (69 per cent), Islam (16 per cent), indigenous religions (15 per cent) (est). Around 6 per cent of the population has no religious affiliation
Language – English (official), Asante, Fante, Akan, Moshi-Dagomba, Ewe, Ga, Dangme, Akyem
Population density – 101 per sq. km (2006)
Urban population – 46.3 per cent (2005 est)
Median age (years) – 20.2 (2007 est)
National anthem – 'God Bless Our Homeland Ghana'
National day – 6 March (Independence Day)
Life expectancy (years) – 59.12 (2007 est)
Mortality rate – 9.55 (2007 est)
Birth rate – 29.85 (2007 est)
Infant mortality rate – 53.56 (2007 est)
HIV/AIDS adult prevalence – 2.2 per cent (2005 est)
Death penalty – Retained, but not used
CPI score – 3.7 (2007)

CLIMATE AND TERRAIN

Ghana consists mostly of tropical interior plains bisected by the Volta river basin and the great central Lake Volta, and rising to the Ashanti plateau in the west. Elevation extremes range from 880m (Mt Afadjato) at the highest point to 0m (Atlantic Ocean) at the lowest. The climate is tropical but there is also a warm and dry coastal area in the south-east. The average temperature in Accra is 30°C.

HISTORY AND POLITICS

First reached by Europeans in the 15th century, after which it became a centre for gold and slave trading, the constituent parts of Ghana came under British administration at various times. The original Gold Coast colony was constituted in 1874 and Ashanti and the Northern Territories Protectorate in 1901. Trans-Volta-Togoland, part of the former German colony of Togo, was mandated to Britain by the League of Nations after the First World War and was integrated with the Gold Coast colony in 1956 following a plebiscite.

The colony became independent on 6 March 1957 and was proclaimed a republic in 1960 under Kwame Nkrumah.

Since 1966, Ghana has experienced long periods of military rule interspersed with short-lived civilian governments. A coup in 1978 led to the formation of an Armed Forces Revolutionary Council chaired by Flt. Lt. Jerry Rawlings. Civilian rule was restored in 1979 but another coup in 1981 brought Rawlings back to power. Civilian rule was restored again in 1992 after a referendum approved a new multiparty constitution and the legalisation of political parties. A reconciliation commission was set up in 2002 to investigate human rights violations during military rule.

Since the mid-1990s there have been intermittent clashes over land ownership between different ethnic groups in the Northern Region. A state of emergency was in place for two years after the latest ethnic violence in 2002.

In the 2004 elections, President John Kufuor was re-elected with 52.75 per cent of the vote, and the New Patriotic Party retained its parliamentary majority.

POLITICAL SYSTEM

Under the 1993 constitution, the executive president is directly elected for a four-year term, renewable only once. The president nominates members of the council of ministers subject to approval by the legislature. The unicameral parliament has 230 members, who are directly elected for a four-year term.

HEAD OF STATE
President, National Security, John Kufuor, *elected* 28 December 2000, *sworn in* 7 January 2001, *re-elected* 7 December 2004
Vice-President, Aliu Mahama

SELECTED GOVERNMENT MEMBERS *as at May 2008*
Defence, Albert Kan-Dapaah
Finance and Economic Planning, Kwadwo Baah Wiredu
Foreign Affairs, Akwasi Osei Adjei
Interior, Kwamena Bartels

OFFICE OF THE HIGH COMMISSION FOR GHANA
13 Belgrave Square, London SW1X 8PS
T 020-7201 5900 E ghmfa31@yahoo.com
W www.ghanahighcommissionuk.com
High Commissioner, HE Annan Arkyin Cato, *apptd* 2006

BRITISH HIGH COMMISSION
PO Box 296, Osu Link, off Gamel Abdul Nasser Avenue, Accra
T (+233) (21) 221 665 E high.commission.accra@fco.gov.uk
W www.britishhighcommission.gov.uk/ghana
High Commissioner, HE Dr Nicholas Westcott, CMG, *apptd* 2007

BRITISH COUNCIL
PO Box GP 771, Liberia Road, Accra
T (+233) (21) 683 068/663 979
W www.britishcouncil.org/ghana
Director, Moses Anibaba

DEFENCE

The army has 19 armoured infantry fighting vehicles and 50 armoured personnel carriers. The navy has 6 patrol and coastal combatant vessels at 2 bases. The air force has 9 combat capable aircraft.

Military budget – US$104m (2007 est)
Military personnel – 13,500: army 10,000, navy 2,000, air force 1,500

ECONOMY AND TRADE

Ghana has abundant natural resources, but high foreign debt and budget and trade deficits make it dependent on international financial and technical aid. It qualified for the IMF/World Bank heavily indebted poor countries intitiative in 2002 and benefited from debt relief in 2006. Economic priorities include tighter management of government finances, further privatisation and reduction of inflation.

Subsistence agriculture forms the basis of the economy, along with forestry and fishing. The sector employs 56 per cent of the workforce and generates 37.3 per cent of GDP. The main cash crops are cocoa, timber and tuna. Industry employs 15 per cent of the workforce and contributes 25.3 per cent of GDP, mainly from mining (manganese, gold, bauxite, diamonds), forestry, light manufacturing, aluminium smelting, food processing and shipbuilding. Services employ 29 per cent and account for 37.5 per cent of GDP. Hydroelectric power is generated at dams on the Volta and is fed into a power transmission network for most of Ghana, Togo and Benin. Oil was discovered offshore in 2007 but is not yet exploited.

The main export markets are EU countries and the USA. Principal exports are gold, cocoa, timber, tuna, metals, minerals and diamonds. Imports are provided mainly by Nigeria, China, EU countries and the USA. The main imports are capital equipment, fuel and foodstuffs.

GNI – US$11,800m; US$510 per capita (2006)
Annual average growth of GDP – 5.8 per cent (2007 est)
Inflation rate – 10 per cent (2007 est)
Total external debt – US$4,668m (2007 est)
Imports – US$5,500m (2006)
Exports – US$3,700m (2006)

BALANCE OF PAYMENTS
Trade – US$1,795m deficit (2006)
Current Account – US$1,381m deficit (2006)

Trade with UK	*2005*	*2006*
Imports from UK	£155,043,000	£189,834,000
Exports to UK	£117,690,000	£148,788,000

EDUCATION AND HEALTH

The government provides nine years of compulsory basic education for all children free of charge. Ghana has one of Africa's oldest universities, at Legon in Accra (established in 1948).

Literacy rate – 54.1 per cent (2004 est)
Gross enrolment ratio (percentage of relevant age group) – primary 98 per cent; secondary 47 per cent; tertiary 5 per cent (2006 est)
Health expenditure (per capita) – US$30 (2005)
Hospital beds (per 1,000 people) – 0.9 (2000–6)

MEDIA

The Ghana Broadcasting Corporation (GBC) is the state-owned broadcaster. GBC operates a television network and various radio stations that transmit in English and Ghanaian dialects. TV3 is a private television channel, Multichoice is a cable television operator and Metro TV is jointly owned by the government and private backers. Radio is the country's most popular medium and there are hundreds of private stations. Ghana's private press and broadcasters operate without significant restrictions.

GREECE

Elliniki Dhimokratia – Hellenic Republic

Area – 131,940 sq. km
Capital – Athens; population, 3,242,000 (2007 est)
Major cities – Iraklion (Heraklion), Larissa, Patrai (Patras), Peristerion, Piraieus, Thessaloniki (Salonika)
Currency – Euro (€) of 100 cents
Population – 10,706,290 rising at 0.16 per cent per year (2007 est)
Religion – Greek Orthodox Christianity (97 per cent) (est)
Language – Greek (official), English, French
Population density – 86 per sq. km (2006)
Urban population – 61.4 per cent (2005 est)
Median age (years) – 41.2 (2007 est)
National anthem – 'Imnos eis tin Eleftherian' ['Hymn to Freedom']
National day – 25 March (Independence Day)
Life expectancy (years) – 79.38 (2007 est)
Mortality rate – 10.33 (2007 est)
Birth rate – 9.62 (2007 est)
Infant mortality rate – 5.34 (2007 est)
Death penalty – Abolished for all crimes (since 2004)
CPI score – 4.6 (2007)

CLIMATE AND TERRAIN

The main areas of Greece are: Macedonia, Thrace, Epirus, Thessaly, Continental Greece, the Peloponnese and the island of Crete. The main island groups are the Sporades, the Dodecanese or Southern Sporades, the Cyclades, the Aegean and Ionian islands and Corfu. Low-lying coastal areas rise to a hilly or mountainous interior on the mainland and the islands. The Pindos mountains form a spine down the centre of the mainland, continuing down the Peloponnese, which is divided from the mainland by the Gulf of Corinth, the largest of the gulfs and bays indenting the coast. Elevation extremes range from 2,917m (Mt Olympus) at the highest point to 0m (Mediterranean Sea) at the lowest. The coastline and islands have a Mediterranean climate with hot, dry summers and mild, wet winters. The average temperature in Athens ranges from 9°C in January to 28°C in July.

HISTORY AND POLITICS

Successive civilisations flourished in ancient Greece from the second millennium BC until it was conquered by Philip II of Macedon in the fourth century BC and the Romans in 146 BC. When the western Roman Empire fell, the eastern part continued as the Byzantine Empire until it was conquered by the Turks in the mid-15th century. Turkish rule began to be overthrown in a war of independence (1821–7) that led to the establishment of a Greek kingdom in the Peloponnese in 1829. Other islands and territories were added gradually over the next century, culminating in the return of the Dodecanese by Italy in 1947.

After the German Nazi occupation of 1941–4, a civil war broke out between monarchist and communist groups that lasted from 1946 to 1949, and although it resulted in the restoration of democracy, tension between right-wing and radical groups continued. In 1967, right-wing elements in the army seized power and established a military regime (the Greek Colonels). The king went into voluntary exile in 1967. Unrest in Athens intensified after the government was involved in a coup against President Makarios of Cyprus in July 1974 and led the Colonels to surrender power. Konstantinos Karamanlis (prime minister 1955–63) returned from exile to form a provisional government, and the first elections for ten years were held. The restoration of the monarchy was rejected by referendum in December 1974 and Greece became a republic. The restored democracy has proved stable, with political life dominated for the next two decades by Karamanlis, founder of the conservative New Democracy (ND) party, and Andreas Papandreou, who founded the left-wing Panhellenic Socialist Party (PASOK). Greece joined the European Community in 1981 and the eurozone in 2000. The parliament ratified the EU constitution in 2005.

The 2005 presidential election was won by Karolos Papoulias. In a legislative election in September 2007, the ND party was returned to power, albeit with a much-reduced majority, despite public criticism of the government's handling of the summer's spate of forest fires on the mainland and some islands.

POLITICAL SYSTEM

Under the 1975 constitution, the head of state is the president, elected by the legislature for a five-year term, renewable only once. The unicameral legislature, *Vouli*, has 300 members directly elected for a four-year term.

HEAD OF STATE

President of the Hellenic Republic, Karolos Papoulias, *elected by parliament* 8 February 2005, *sworn in* 12 March 2005

SELECTED GOVERNMENT MEMBERS *as at May 2008*

Prime Minister, Costas Karamanlis
Foreign Affairs, Theodora Bakoyiannis
Internal Affairs, Prokopis Pavlopoulos
Defence, Evangelos Meimarakis
Economy and Finance, Georgios Alogoskoufis

EMBASSY OF GREECE

1A Holland Park, London W11 3TP
T 020-7229 3850 E political@greekembassy.org.uk
W www.greekembassy.org.uk
Ambassador Extraordinary and Plenipotentiary, Vassilis Achilleas Pispinis, *apptd* 2007

BRITISH EMBASSY

1 Ploutarchou Street, 106 75 Athens
T (+30) (210) 727 2600 E information.athens@fco.gov.uk
W www.british-embassy.gr
Ambassador Extraordinary and Plenipotentiary, HE Simon Gass, CMG, CVO, *apptd* 2004

BRITISH COUNCIL

17 Kolonaki Square (Plateia Philikis Etairias), 106 73, Athens
T (+30) (210) 369 2333 W www.britishcouncil.org/greece
Director, Richard Walker

DEFENCE

The army has 1,514 main battle tanks, 2,105 armoured personnel carriers, 377 armoured infantry fighting vehicles and 32 armed helicopters. The navy has 9 submarines, 14 frigates, 3 corvettes, 40 patrol and coastal vessels and 11 armed helicopters, with bases at Salamis, Patras and Soudha Bay. The air force has a total of 357 combat aircraft.

Greece maintains 950 army personnel in Cyprus.

Military expenditure – US$7,280m (2006)
Military personnel – 156,600: army 93,500, navy 20,000, air force 31,500, joint staff 11,600; paramilitary 4,000
Conscription duration – Up to 12 months

ECONOMY AND TRADE

Greece experienced rapid economic growth in the final quarter of the 20th century, partly through revenues from tourism and partly through accession to the EC. It has a capitalist economy, though with a large public sector which accounts for 40 per cent of GDP. Economic growth has slowed recently, but the high levels of public debt, unemployment and inflation are being reduced, and the budget deficit has been brought below 3 per cent of GDP. Government measures to reduce its spending and the size of the public sector, and reform pension and labour systems have provoked strikes and demonstrations.

Though there has been substantial industrialisation, agriculture still employs 12 per cent of the workforce and contributes 3.2 per cent of GDP. The most important agricultural products are cereals, vegetables, fruit, tobacco, beef and dairy products. Industrial activities, which contribute 20.6 per cent of GDP, include food and tobacco processing, textiles, chemicals, metal products, mining and petroleum production. The service sector employs 68 per cent of the workforce and generates 76.3 per cent of GDP; much of this is derived from tourism, which accounts for about 15 per cent of GDP, and shipping. Greece is a net importer of energy, including oil for refining and re-export.

The main trading partners are other EU countries (especially Germany and Italy), the USA, Bulgaria, Russia and Turkey. Principal exports are food and wine, manufactured goods, petroleum products, chemicals and textiles. The main imports are machinery, transport equipment, fuels and chemicals.

GNI – US$305,300m; US$27,390 per capita (2006)
Annual average growth of GDP – 3.7 per cent (2007 est)
Inflation rate – 2.6 per cent (2007 est)
Unemployment – 8.4 per cent (2007 est)
Total external debt – US$371,500m (2007)
Imports – US$59,100m (2006)
Exports – US$20,200m (2006)

BALANCE OF PAYMENTS
Trade – US$38,940m deficit (2006)
Current Account – US$29,684m deficit (2006)

Trade with UK	*2006*	*2007*
Imports from UK	£1,403,300,000	£1,333,820,366
Exports to UK	£640,400,000	£626,775,503

COMMUNICATIONS

There are extensive rail and road networks. The 2,500km of railways are state-owned, with the exception of the Athens–Piraeus Electric Railway. There are 115,000km of roads, including 880km of motorways. The main seaports are Piraeus, Thessaloniki and Patrai on the mainland and Iraklion on Crete. An extensive ferry system connects the islands to one another and to the mainland. The 6km Corinth canal across the Corinth isthmus shortens the sea journey by 325km. There are 81 airports and airfields, of which 66 have surfaced runways; the main airports are at Athens, Thessaloniki, Iraklion (Crete) and Corfu town (Corfu), although several other islands, especially tourist destinations, have airports. In 2006 there were 6.1 million main-line and 11 million mobile telephone subscribers, and 2 million internet users.

EDUCATION AND HEALTH

Education is free of charge and compulsory between the ages of six and 15, and is maintained by state grants.

Literacy rate – 91 per cent (2004 est)
Gross enrolment ratio (percentage of relevant age group) – primary 102 per cent; secondary 102 per cent; tertiary 90 per cent (2006 est)
Health expenditure (per capita) – US$2,580 (2005)
Hospital beds (per 1,000 people) – 4.7 (2000–6)

MEDIA

Although the Greek media is largely free from regulation, editors and publishers risk prosecution should their material be deemed offensive to religious beliefs or the president. A sizeable proportion of the country's 1,700 private radio and television stations are unlicensed. State-run broadcasters have lost a large segment of the market to commercial services in recent years.

CULTURE

Greek civilisation emerged *c.*1300 BC and underpins the philosophy, politics, literature, art and mathematics of the Western world. The epic poems of Homer, the *Iliad* and the *Odyssey*, are thought to date from *c.*800 BC, making them the earliest recorded works in Western literature. Aeschylus (*c.*525–*c.*456 BC) is credited with inventing modern drama through the use of dialogue; prior to this, actors could only communicate through the chorus. Other dramatists whose work has survived include Euripedes (480–406 BC) and Aristophanes (446–388 BC), author of the earliest known comedies. Socrates (470–399 BC), Plato (*c.*428–*c.*348 BC) and Aristotle (384–322 BC), whose *Poetics* is the earliest work of literary criticism, are considered the founders of philosophy. Hippocrates (*c.*460–370 BC) was the first to separate medicine from philosophy and religion; his theory of the body being ruled by four humours persisted until late medieval times.

The spoken language of modern Greece is descended from the common Greek of Alexander the Great's empire. *Katharevousa,* a conservative literary dialect evolved by Adamantios Korais (1748–1833), which was used for official and technical matters, has been phased out. Novels and poetry are mostly written in *dimotiki,* a progressive literary dialect which owes much to Yannis Psycharis (1854–1929). Giorgos Seferis (1900–71) and Odysseus Elytis (1911–96) won the Nobel prize for literature, in 1963 and 1979 respectively.

GRENADA

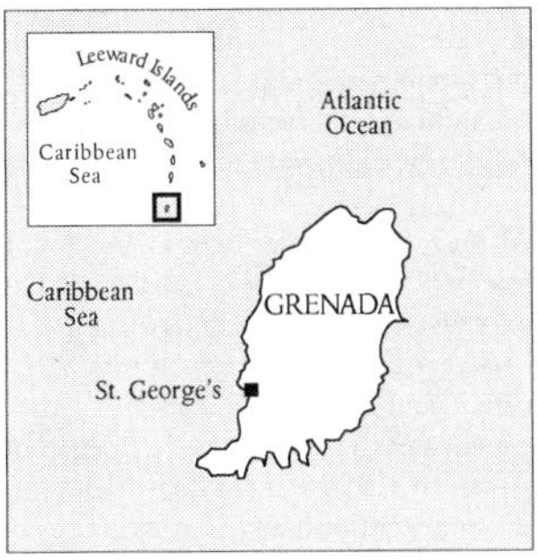

Area – 344 sq. km
Capital – St George's; population, 32,000 (2007 est)
Currency – East Caribbean dollar (EC$) of 100 cents
Population – 89,971 rising at 0.34 per cent per year (2007 est)
Religion – Roman Catholicism (44 per cent), Protestantism (34 per cent) (est)
Language – English (official), French patois
Population density – 318 per sq. km (2006)
Urban population – 42.4 per cent (2005 est)
Median age (years) – 22.1 (2007 est)
National anthem – 'Hail Grenada'
National day – 7 February (Independence Day)
Life expectancy (years) – 65.21 (2007 est)
Mortality rate – 6.61 (2007 est)
Birth rate – 21.87 (2007 est)
Infant mortality rate – 13.92 (2007 est)
Death penalty – Retained, but not used
CPI score – 3.4 (2007)
Population below poverty line – 32 per cent (2000)

CLIMATE AND TERRAIN

The most southerly of the Windward Islands, Grenada comprises three islands: Grenada (the largest at 18km in length and 34km in width), Carriacou and Petite Martinique. Elevation extremes range from 840m (Mt St Catherine) at the highest point to 0m (Caribbean Sea) at the lowest. The climate is subtropical, with a wet season running from June to December. Grenada is in a hurricane zone.

HISTORY AND POLITICS

Discovered by Columbus in 1498 and named Concepción, Grenada was originally colonised by France and was ceded to Great Britain in 1763. It became a crown colony in 1877, an associated state in 1967 and an independent nation within the Commonwealth on 7 February 1974.

The government was overthrown in 1979 by the New Jewel Movement led by Maurice Bishop, and a People's Revolutionary Government (PRG) was set up with Bishop as prime minister. In 1983, disagreements within the PRG led to the deposition and execution of Bishop, whose government was replaced by a revolutionary military council. These events prompted the intervention of Caribbean and US forces. After a period of interim government, democracy was restored with a general election in 1984. Since the restoration of democracy, power has alternated between the New National Party (NNP) and the National Democratic Congress (NDC).

In the 2008 general election, the NDC, led by Tillman Thomas, won a small overall majority to defeat the NNP who had been in power since 1995.

POLITICAL SYSTEM

Under the 1974 constitution, reinstated in 1984, the British monarch is head of state and is represented locally by a governor-general. The bicameral parliament consists of a lower house, the house of representatives, with 15 members directly elected for a five-year term, and a senate with 13 members appointed by the governor-general on the advice of the prime minister and the leader of the opposition.

Governor-General, HE Sir Daniel Williams, GCMG, QC, *apptd* 1996

SELECTED GOVERNMENT MEMBERS *as at July 2008*

Prime Minister, National Security, Tillman Thomas
Finance, Nazim Burke
Foreign Affairs, Peter David

HIGH COMMISSION FOR GRENADA

The Chapel, Archel Road, London W14 9QH
T 020-7385 4415 E grenada@high-commission.demon.co.uk
High Commissioner, HE Joseph Charter, *apptd* 2005

BRITISH HIGH COMMISSION

High Commissioner, Duncan Taylor, *apptd* 2005, resident at Bridgetown, Barbados

ECONOMY AND TRADE

Grenada's economy has grown considerably in recent decades owing to the development of tourism and offshore financial services. Tourism and agriculture have recovered from the severe damage caused by hurricanes Ivan (2004) and Emily (2005) but reconstruction has left the country with considerable debt.

Agriculture now employs only 24 per cent of the workforce and produces 5.4 per cent of GDP. Industry consists of processing agricultural products, textiles manufacturing, light assembly operations and construction, and contributes 18 per cent of GDP. The service sector, including tourism and financial services, accounts for 62 per cent of employment and 76.6 per cent of GDP.

The main trading partners are Trinidad and Tobago, the USA, other Caribbean countries and the UK. Principal exports are bananas, cocoa, nutmeg, fruit, vegetables, clothing and mace. Imports include foodstuffs, manufactured goods, machinery, chemicals and fuels.

GNI – US$495m; US$4,650 per capita (2006)
Annual average growth of GDP – 0.9 per cent (2005 est)
Inflation rate – 3 per cent (2005 est)
Unemployment – 12.5 per cent (2004 est)
Total external debt – US$347m (2004)
Imports – US$280m (2006)
Exports – US$20m (2006)

BALANCE OF PAYMENTS

Trade – US$136m deficit (2000)
Current Account – US$129m deficit (2006)

Trade with UK	*2006*	*2007*
Imports from UK	£7,250,000	£6,093,702
Exports to UK	£165,000	£260,399

MEDIA

There are no daily newspapers but several private weekly publications which enjoy a considerable amount of independence. There are two television stations: GBN TV, which is operated by the public broadcaster Grenada Broadcasting Network, and MTV, which is US-owned. There are several radio stations jointly owned by the public and private sector.

GUATEMALA

República de Guatemala – Republic of Guatemala

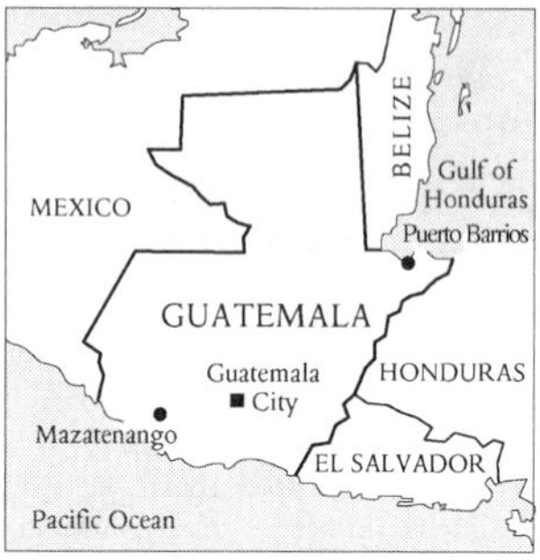

Area – 108,890 sq. km
Capital – Guatemala City; population, 1,024,000 (2007 est)
Major cities – Mixco, San Juan Sacatepéquez, Villa Nueva
Currency – Quetzal (Q) of 100 centavos
Population – 12,728,111 rising at 2.15 per cent per year (2007 est); *mestizo* and European (59.4 per cent), K'iche (9.1 per cent), Kaqchikel (8.4 per cent), Mam (7.9 per cent), Q'eqchi (6.3 per cent)
Religion – Roman Catholicism (50 per cent), Protestantism (40 per cent) (est)
Language – Spanish (official)
Population density – 120 per sq. km (2006)
Urban population – 47.2 per cent (2005 est)
Median age (years) – 18.9 (2007 est)
National anthem – 'Himno Nacional de Guatemala' ['Guatemala National Anthem']
National day – 15 September (Independence Day)
Life expectancy (years) – 69.69 (2007 est)
Mortality rate – 5.27 (2007 est)
Birth rate – 29.09 (2007 est)
Infant mortality rate – 29.77 (2007 est)
Death penalty – Retained
CPI score – 2.8 (2007)
Population below poverty line – 56.2 per cent (2004 est)

CLIMATE AND TERRAIN

Narrow plains on both the north (Caribbean) and south (Pacific) coasts rise to a mountainous interior in the centre and south. The mountains fall in the north to a plateau, which drops further to low-lying marshland. Elevation extremes range from 4,211m (Tajumulco volcano) at the highest point to 0m (Pacific Ocean) at the lowest. There are 33 volcanoes. The climate is tropical but is cooler in the highlands. The wet season runs from May to October, when mudslides and hurricanes can occur. There are also frequent minor earth tremors and some earthquakes.

HISTORY AND POLITICS

Mayan civilisation flourished in the area until the Spanish conquest in 1523, when the area became a Spanish colony. It gained its independence in 1821, and formed part of the United Provinces of Central America from 1823 to 1835. After independence, the country was ruled by a series of dictatorships and military regimes, interspersed with periods of democratic government. The latest restoration of civilian rule in 1984 has survived an attempted coup in 1989 and the mass protests and military intervention that ousted President Serrano in 1993 when he attempted to introduce rule by decree.

Alvaro Alvarez, elected president in 1996, concluded a peace agreement with the left-wing Guatemalan Revolutionary National Unity guerrillas in 1996 that ended the 36-year civil war, in which over 200,000 died or disappeared, and began a reduction in the size and political influence of the army that has been continued by his successors. In 1999, an independent commission found that 93 per cent of human rights abuses during the war had been instigated by the security forces, and in 2000 and 2004 the state formally admitted guilt in several human rights crimes, paying damages to the victims. Only a small number of the military personnel found to be responsible for the atrocities have been prosecuted so far.

The National Unity of Hope party (UNE) won the 2007 legislative election with 48 seats. The 2007 presidential election was won in the second round by the UNE candidate Alvaro Colom, with 52.8 per cent of the vote.

POLITICAL SYSTEM

Under the 1986 constitution, the executive president is directly elected for a four-year term, which is not renewable. He is responsible to the Congress and appoints the cabinet. Legislative authority is vested in the unicameral Congress of the Republic, whose 158 members are directly elected for a four-year term.

HEAD OF STATE

President, Alvaro Colom Caballeros, *elected* 4 November 2007, *sworn in* 14 January 2008
Vice-President, Rafael Espada

SELECTED GOVERNMENT MEMBERS *as at May 2008*

Defence, Marco Tulio Garcia Franco
Economy, José Carlos García
Foreign Affairs, Haroldo Rodas
Interior, Vinicio Gomez

EMBASSY OF GUATEMALA

13A Fawcett Street, London SW10 9HN
T 020-7351 3042 E embassy.gtm@btconnect.com
Ambassador Extraordinary and Plenipotentiary, Edmundo Urrutia Garcia, *apptd* 2006

BRITISH EMBASSY

Edificio Torre Internacional, Nivel 11, 16 Calle 00-55, Zona 10, Guatemala City
T (+502) 2367 5425 E embassy@intelnett.com
Ambassador Extraordinary and Plenipotentiary, Ian Hughes, *apptd* 2006

DEFENCE

The army has 52 armoured personnel carriers. The navy has 36 patrol and coastal combatant vessels at 2 bases. The air force has 10 combat capable aircraft.
Military budget – US$164m (2007 est)
Military personnel – 15,500: army 13,444, navy 986, air force 1,070; paramilitary 19,000

ECONOMY AND TRADE

The country suffers from a huge imbalance in wealth, and a civic structure and infrastructure still recovering from the civil war. IMF funding and foreign aid have underpinned the government's economic reforms and stabilisation programmes, but the trade deficit and high levels of corruption and violence remain a problem. Remittances from expatriates, equivalent to about two-thirds of export revenue, are vital to the economy. Around 56 per cent of the population is below the poverty line and nearly half depends on agriculture, which contributes 13.8 per cent of GDP. Industry accounts for 27.9 per cent of GDP, and the services sector, which includes tourism, for 58.3 per cent of GDP.

The main trading partners are the USA, El Salvador, Mexico and Honduras. The principal exports are coffee, sugar, oil, clothing, bananas, fruit, vegetables and cardamom. The chief imports are fuels, machinery and transport equipment, construction materials, grain, fertilisers and electricity.

GNI – US$33,700m; US$2,590 per capita (2006)
Annual average growth of GDP – 5.6 per cent (2007 est)
Inflation rate – 6.6 per cent (2007 est)
Unemployment – 3.2 per cent (2005 est)
Total external debt – US$5,561m (2007 est)
Imports – US$10,200m (2006)
Exports – US$3,700m (2006)

BALANCE OF PAYMENTS
Trade – US$6,492m deficit (2006)
Current Account – US$1,510m deficit (2006)

Trade with UK	*2006*	*2007*
Imports from UK	£28,852,000	£24,520,486
Exports to UK	£18,923,000	£15,623,133

EDUCATION AND HEALTH

There are six years of compulsory education.
Literacy rate – 69.1 per cent (2004 est)
Gross enrolment ratio (percentage of relevant age group) – primary 114 per cent; secondary 53 per cent; tertiary 9 per cent (2006 est)
Health expenditure (per capita) – US$132 (2005)
Hospital beds (per 1,000 people) – 0.7 (2000–6)

MEDIA AND CULTURE

Freedom of the press is enshrined in the constitution, but journalists who pursue controversial stories are often subjected to threats. There are four major daily newspapers, including *Prensa Libre* and *El Periodico*. Four privately run television channels are under the same ownership and monopolise Guatemalan television.

Guatemala enjoys a rich and varied cultural history. The ruins of the Mayan civilisation (AD *c*.300–900) dot the country, while the influences of African culture are evident along the Caribbean coast. Distinguished Guatemalans include the writers Miguel Angel Asturias (1899–1974), who won the Nobel prize for literature in 1967; Luis Cardoza y Aragon (1901–92), who edited the influential periodical *Revista de Guatemala* after the 1944 revolution; and Rigoberta Menchu (*b.* 1959), who won the Nobel peace prize in 1992.

GUINEA

République de Guinée – Republic of Guinea

Area – 245,857 sq. km
Capital – Conakry; population, 1,494,000 (2007 est)
Major cities – Guéckédou, Kankan, Nzérékoré
Currency – Guinea franc of 100 centimes
Population – 9,947,814 rising at 2.62 per cent per year (2007 est); Fula (40 per cent), Malinke (30 per cent), Susu (20 per cent) (est)
Religion – Islam (85 per cent), Christianity (10 per cent), indigenous religions (5 per cent) (est)
Language – French (official)
Population density – 37 per sq. km (2006)
Urban population – 36.5 per cent (2005 est)
Median age (years) – 17.7 (2007 est)
National anthem – 'Liberté' ['Liberty']
National day – 2 October (Independence Day)
Life expectancy – 49.65 (2007 est)
Mortality rate – 15.33 (2007 est)
Birth rate – 41.53 (2007 est)
Infant mortality rate – 88.58 (2007 est)
HIV/AIDS adult prevalence – 1.5 per cent (2005 est)
Death penalty – Retained
CPI score – 1.9 (2007)
Population below poverty line – 47 per cent (2006 est)
Gross enrolment ratio (percentage of relevant age group) – primary 88 per cent; secondary 35 per cent; tertiary 3 per cent (2006 est)
Health expenditure (per capita) – US$21 (2005)

CLIMATE AND TERRAIN

Guinea has a flat coastal plain that rises to a mountainous interior, where the Senegal and Niger rivers rise. The river Gambia rises on the Fouta Djallon plateau in the north-west of the country. Elevation extremes range from 1,752m (Mt Nimba) at the highest point to 0m at the lowest (Atlantic Ocean). The south-east is forested. There is a wet season from June to November and the average daily temperature is 27°C.

HISTORY AND POLITICS

Susi kingdoms were established in the area by the 13th century, and in the 16th century the north-east of the country was part of the Mali Empire. The Portuguese established ivory and slave trading from the mid-15th century. In 1849 the French established a protectorate over the coastal areas, and the country was governed with Senegal until the 1890s, when it was renamed French Guinea, becoming part of French West Africa in 1904.

Guinea became independent on 2 October 1958 under President Ahmed Sekou Touré, who established a one-party state pursuing Marxist policies in the 1960s and 1970s. After decades of economic stagnation Touré introduced limited economic liberalisation in response to strong opposition to his policies in 1984. His death shortly afterwards was followed by a military coup that brought Lansana Conté to power. Conté introduced greater economic liberalisation and, following strikes and mass protests in 1991, reintroduced a multiparty system. President Conté narrowly won the presidential election in 1993, was re-elected in 1998 with 54 per cent of the vote, and again in 2003 with 95 per cent of the vote after several opposition parties boycotted the election.

The civil wars in neighbouring Sierra Leone and Liberia caused an influx of nearly half a million refugees in 2000 that has severely strained the economy, exacerbating the poor conditions which have contributed to the growing unpopularity of the government and creating ethnic tension.

The 2002 legislative election was won by President Conté's Party of Unity and Progress (PUP), which gained 85 of the 114 seats. President Conté has repeatedly clashed with and dismissed prime ministers, presiding over the cabinet himself for nine months in 2004 and from April 2006 until February 2007, when Lansana Kouyaté was appointed to the post. His appointment was part of a deal to end a two-week general strike and violent demonstrations against the government. Kouyaté nominated a new government that included only one member of the outgoing administration, but he himself resigned in May 2008 and was replaced by Ahmed Souare. The legislative election due in June 2007 was postponed and is now expected to take place in late 2008.

POLITICAL SYSTEM

Under the 1991 constitution, the executive president is directly elected for a five-year term, renewable only once; a 2001 amendment allowed the president to stand for a third term, lasting seven years, in 2003. The unicameral National Assembly has 114 members, who are directly elected for a five-year term. The president appoints the council of ministers.

HEAD OF STATE

President, Maj.-Gen. Lansana Conté, *took power* 3 April 1984, *elected* 19 December 1993, *re-elected* 1998, 2003

SELECTED GOVERNMENT MEMBERS *as at May 2008*

Prime Minister, Ahmed Tidiane Souaré
Economy, Finance, Ousmane Dorè
Foreign Affairs, Abdoul Kabèlè Camara
Defence, Gen. Bailo Diallo
Interior, M'Boh Keita

EMBASSY OF THE REPUBLIC OF GUINEA

48 Onslow Gardens, London SW7 3PY
T 020-7594 4809 E ambaguineeuk@yahoo.co.uk
Ambassador Extraordinary and Plenipotentiary, Lansana Keita, *apptd* 2005

BRITISH AMBASSADOR

Ambassador Extraordinary and Plenipotentiary, HE John McManus, *apptd* 2004, resident at Freetown, Sierra Leone

DEFENCE

The army has 38 main battle tanks and 40 armoured personnel carriers. The navy has 2 patrol and coastal combatant vessels at 2 bases. The air force has 7 combat capable aircraft and 1 attack helicopter.

Military budget – US$52m (2007 est)
Military personnel – 12,300: army 8,500, navy 400, air force 800, Gendarmerie 1,000, Republican Guard 1,600; paramilitary 7,000
Conscription duration – 24 months

ECONOMY AND TRADE

Despite an abundance of natural resources, including over 40 per cent of the world's bauxite reserves, decades of mismanagement have left Guinea's economy undeveloped, and 47 per cent of the population is below the poverty line. There is a large foreign debt, budget and trade deficits and inflation at 20 per cent in 2007, but little foreign aid as most IMF and World Bank aid was suspended in 2003. Agriculture, much of it at subsistence level, employs 76 per cent of the population but contributes only 22 per cent of GDP. Industry accounts for 40.5 per cent of GDP, mostly through mining and the processing of minerals and agricultural produce.

The main trading partners are France, Russia, China, Ukraine, South Korea and EU countries. Principal exports are bauxite, alumina, gold, diamonds, coffee, fish and other agricultural products. The main imports are petroleum products, metals, machinery, transport equipment, textiles, grain and other foodstuffs.

GNI – US$3,700m; US$400 per capita (2006)
Annual average growth of GDP – 1.5 per cent (2007 est)
Inflation rate – 20 per cent (2007 est)
Total external debt – US$3,298m (2007 est)
Exports – US$900m (2006)

BALANCE OF PAYMENTS

Trade – US$0m (2006)
Current Account – US$185m deficit (2006)

Trade with UK	*2005*	*2006*
Imports from UK	£22,186,000	£33,252,000
Exports to UK	£4,426,000	£1,728,000

COMMUNICATIONS

Guinea has over 837km of railways, 44,348km of roads (only 10 per cent of which are surfaced) and 1,300km of inland waterways navigable by shallow-draught craft. The major seaports are Conakry and Kamsar. Guinea has 16 airports, including five with surfaced runways; the principal airport is at Conakry. The fixed-line telephone system is small in scope, with 26,300 main line subscribers, but mobile phone distribution is more extensive, with 189,000 subscribers in 2005. There were 50,000 internet users in 2006.

MEDIA

Government control over the media has tightened considerably in 2007 after the president declared a state of emergency and many private radio stations and cybercafes have been closed. Criticism of the government is rare in the five national newspapers. There is a single state-run television broadcaster, Radiodiffusion-Television Guineenne (RTG).

GUINEA-BISSAU

Republica da Guine-Bissau – Republic of Guinea-Bissau

Area – 36,120 sq. km
Capital – Bissau; population, 330,000 (2007 est)
Currency – Franc CFA of 100 centimes
Population – 1,472,780 rising at 2.05 per cent per year (2007 est); Balanta (30 per cent), Fula (20 per cent), Manjaca (14 per cent), Mandinga (13 per cent), Papel (7 per cent) (est)
Religion – Islam (38 per cent), Christianity (5 per cent) (est), the remainder follow indigenous religions
Language – Portuguese (official), Creole
Population density – 59 per sq. km (2006)
Urban population – 35.6 per cent (2005 est)
Median age (years) – 19.1 (2007 est)
National anthem – 'Esta e a Nossa Patria Ben Amada' ['This is Our Beloved Country']
National day – 24 September (Independence Day)
Life expectancy (years) – 47.18 (2007 est)
Mortality rate – 16.29 (2007 est)
Birth rate – 36.81 (2007 est)
Infant mortality rate – 103.5 (2007 est)
HIV/AIDS adult prevalence – 3.5 per cent (2005 est)
Death penalty – Abolished for all crimes (since 1993)
CPI score – 2.2 (2007)
Gross enrolment ratio (percentage of relevant age group) – primary 70 per cent; secondary 18 per cent (2002)
Health expenditure (per capita) – US$10 (2005)

CLIMATE AND TERRAIN

Guinea-Bissau has a low coastal plain that rises to savannah in the east. Elevation extremes range from 300m (in the north-east) at the highest point to 0m (Atlantic Ocean) at the lowest. Average temperatures range from 24°C in January to 27°C in October, with a wet season from June to November.

HISTORY AND POLITICS

A part of the ancient African empire of Mali, Guinea-Bissau was once the kingdom of Gabu, which became independent of the empire in 1546 and survived until 1867. In 1446, Portuguese traders discovered the coast and established slave trading there, subsequently administering Guinea-Bissau with the Cape Verde islands. After becoming a separate colony in 1879, Guinea-Bissau achieved independence in 1974 after a guerrilla war led by the left-wing African Party for the Independence of Guinea and Cape Verde (PAIGC).

Since independence, Guinea-Bissau has suffered periods of political instability interspersed with military rule. From 1981 until 1994, the country was under military and one-party rule by the PAIGC. A multiparty system was introduced in 1991 after popular agitation. The first multiparty elections in 1994 were won by the PAIGC, and General Joao Vieira was confirmed as president. An army mutiny against him in 1998 developed into a civil war that ended in 1999 with Vieira's deposition, and a military junta appointed an interim president. In 2000 Kumba Yala was elected president, but his increasingly erratic behaviour and the worsening economic situation led to his overthrow in a military coup in 2003. Under ECOWAS influence, the military accepted the formation of a civilian-led transitional government.

In the 2004 legislative election, the PAIGC won the most seats but without an overall majority. The 2005 presidential election was won in the second round by Joao Vieira (president 1980–99) with 52 per cent of the vote. The PAIGC did not accept Vieira's election initially, and objected to his choice of prime minister; it refused to participate in the coalition government and expelled party members who remained in their ministerial posts. The government was defeated in a vote of no confidence in March 2007 and a new coalition government was formed under PAIGC leadership. The next legislative election is due in late 2008.

POLITICAL SYSTEM

Under the 1999 constitution, the executive president is directly elected for a five-year term, which is renewable only once. The president appoints the council of ministers. The unicameral National People's Assembly has 102 members, who are directly elected for a four-year term.

HEAD OF STATE

President, Brig.-Gen. Joao Vieira, *elected* June 2005, *took office* October 2005

SELECTED GOVERNMENT MEMBERS *as at May 2008*

Prime Minister, Martinho N'Dafa Cabi
Economy, Abubcar Demba Dahahba
Foreign Affairs, Maria de Concicao Nobre Cabral
Defence, Marciano Silva Barbeiro
Interior, Certorio Biote

EMBASSY OF THE REPUBLIC OF GUINEA-BISSAU

94 rue St Lazare, Paris 75009, France
T (+33) (1) 4526 1851
Ambassador Extraordinary and Plenipotentiary, vacant

BRITISH CONSULATE

Ambassador Extraordinary and Plenipotentiary, HE Christopher Trott, *apptd* 2007, resident in Dakar, Senegal

DEFENCE

The army has 10 main battle tanks and 55 armoured personnel carriers. The navy has 2 patrol and coastal combatant vessels at a base at Bissau. The air force has 3 combat capable aircraft.
Military budget – US$16m (2007 est)
Military personnel – 9,250: army 6,800, navy 350, air force 100, Gendarmerie 2,000

ECONOMY AND TRADE

The economy is in a poor state, with one of the world's greatest extremes of wealth distribution, after decades of mismanagement and corruption and the devastating effects of the 1998–9 civil war. There is a massive foreign debt and the country is heavily dependent on foreign aid;

emergency aid provided over 80 per cent of the national budget in 2004.

Although Guinea-Bissau has mineral resources, including oil, the high cost of exploiting these has prevented development and the economy is based almost exclusively on agriculture and fishing. This sector employs 82 per cent of the population and contributes 62 per cent of GDP. The small industrial sector generates 12 per cent of GDP through the processing of agricultural products and beer and soft drink production.

The main trading partners are India, Portugal, Nigeria, Senegal and Italy. Principal exports include cashew nuts, fish, peanuts, palm kernels and timber. The main imports are foodstuffs, machinery and transport equipment, and fuels.

GNI – US$300m; US$190 per capita (2006)
Annual average growth of GDP – 3.7 per cent (2007 est)
Inflation rate – 4 per cent (2002 est)
Total external debt – US$941.5m (2000 est)
Imports – US$110m (2006)
Exports – US$75m (2006)

BALANCE OF PAYMENTS
Trade – US$35m deficit (2006)
Current Account – US$35m deficit (2006)

Trade with UK	*2005*	*2006*
Imports from UK	£389,000	£672,000
Exports to UK	£1,000	£91,000

COMMUNICATIONS
Guinea-Bissau has 3,455km of roads, of which only 965km are surfaced, but no railways. There are 27 airports and airfields, three of which have surfaced runways; the principal airport is at Bissau. The main rivers are navigable for part of their lengths, and shallow-draught craft can access much of the interior through creeks, etc. Bissau is the main seaport. The fixed-line telephone system is small, with fewer than one per 100 people in 2005, while mobile phone density was 7 per 100 people. There were 37,000 internet users in 2006.

MEDIA
Since the 2003 military coup, media organisations have been able to operate with greater freedom. Government interference is often less of an concern than reliable power supplies. Of the four national newspapers, three are privately owned. Guinea-Bissau's principal television station, Radio Televisao de Guinea-Bissau (RTGB), is state-run. Radio consists of the national broadcaster, Radio Nacional, and three commercial stations.

GUYANA

Cooperative Republic of Guyana

Area – 214,970 sq. km
Capital – Georgetown; population, 133,000 (2007 est)
Major towns – Linden, New Amsterdam
Currency – Guyana dollar (G$) of 100 cents
Population – 769,095 rising at 0.23 per cent per year (2007 est)
Religion – Protestantism (29 per cent), Hinduism (28 per cent), other Christian denominations (20 per cent), Roman Catholicism (8 per cent, Islam (7 per cent) (est)
Language – English (official), Creole, Hindi, Urdu
Population density – 4 per sq. km (2006)
Urban population – 38.5 per cent (2005 est)
Median age (years) – 27.8 (2007 est)
National anthem – 'Dear Land of Guyana'
National day – 23 February (Republic Day)
Life expectancy (years) – 66.17 (2007 est)
Mortality rate – 8.28 (2007 est)
Birth rate – 18.09 (2007 est)
Infant mortality rate – 31.35 (2007 est)
HIV/AIDS adult prevalence – 2.1 per cent (2005 est)
Death penalty – Retained
CPI score – 2.6 (2007)

CLIMATE AND TERRAIN
The land rises from a coastal plain to highlands in the west and savannah in the south. Much of the interior is covered in rainforest, with elevation extremes ranging from 2,835m (Mt Roraima) at the highest point to 0m (Atlantic Ocean) at the lowest. The average daily temperature is 28°C.

HISTORY AND POLITICS
Carib and Arawak Indians inhabited the coastal region of Guyana and began trading with the Dutch merchants who founded the first European settlement in 1615. Guyana became an important producer of sugar, grown on plantations worked first by African slaves and then, after the abolition of slavery, by indentured Indian labourers. Several areas were ceded to Britain in 1815, and were consolidated as British Guiana before coming formally under British rule in 1831. The country became independent, as Guyana, on 26 May 1966, and became a republic in 1970.

Guyana's first political party, the People's Progressive Party (PPP), divided along ethnic lines in 1957; the PPP continued as a predominantly Indian party under Cheddi Jagan while those of African descent formed the People's National Congress (PNC), led by Forbes Burnham. Burnham dominated political life after independence, as prime minister from 1966 until 1980 and then as executive president until his death in 1985. Under his autocratic rule, politics became characterised by suspect elections and the disregard of civil liberties and human rights. The PPP's electoral victory in 1992 ended the PNC's monopoly of power but the persistent ethnic tension continues to destabilise politics.

Bharrat Jagdeo of the PPP was elected president in 2001. His presidency has seen attempts to encourage joint action between the government and the private sector, and soon after the 2001 elections he called for reconciliation between the PPP and Guyana's other political parties in order to prevent further political violence.

The 2006 legislative election was won by the PPP, with 54.6 per cent of the vote, securing its fourth consecutive term of office. President Jagdeo was confirmed in office for a further five-year term.

POLITICAL SYSTEM
The 1980 constitution provides for an executive president who is nominated by the majority party in the legislature after legislative elections and serves a five-year term. The unicameral National Assembly has 65 members, of whom 53 are elected by proportional representation and 12 are regional representatives; they serve a five-year term.

HEAD OF STATE
President, Bharrat Jagdeo, *succeeded* 11 August 1999, *elected* 2001, *re-elected* 28 August 2006

SELECTED GOVERNMENT MEMBERS *as at May 2008*
Prime Minister, Samuel Hinds
Finance, Ashni Kumar Singh
Foreign Affairs, Carolyn Rodrigues
Home Affairs, Clement Rohee

HIGH COMMISSION FOR GUYANA
3 Palace Court, Bayswater Road, London W2 4LP
T 020-7229 7684 E guyanahc1@btconnect.com
W www.guyanahc.com
High Commissioner, HE Laleshwar Singh, *apptd* 1993

BRITISH HIGH COMMISSION
PO Box 10849, 44 Main Street, Georgetown
T (+592) 226 5881 E consular@georgetown.mail.fsc.gov.uk
High Commissioner, HE Fraser Wheeler, *apptd* 2006

DEFENCE
The navy has 5 patrol and coastal combatant vessels at 2 bases. The air force has 2 utility helicopters.
Military personnel – 1,100: army 900, navy 100, air force 100; paramilitary 1,500

ECONOMY AND TRADE
Serious economic problems arose in the late 1980s because of mismanagement of the largely state-owned industries and falling commodity prices. In the 1990s the government privatised many industries but recovery was slow and fitful until 2001. Since then, growth has improved owing to expansion in agriculture and mining, the cancellation of over one-third of Guyana's external debt in 2006–7, and increases in remittances from expatriate workers and foreign direct investment. The poor infrastructure and a skills shortage inhibit growth, especially attempts to develop tourism.

Agriculture is the principal economic activity, accounting for 35.2 per cent of GDP and providing the raw materials for the major industries of sugar processing and rice milling. Industry accounts for 19 per cent of GDP, non-agricultural activities including bauxite and gold mining, forestry and textile manufacturing. Oil deposits have been found; these are mainly in offshore areas which were disputed with neighbouring Suriname until a 2007 UN ruling shared the territory between the two countries.

The main trading partners are the USA, Trinidad and Tobago, Canada, the UK and China. Principal exports include sugar, gold, bauxite, alumnia, rice, shrimps, molasses, rum and timber. The main imports are manufactured goods, machinery, fuel and food.
GNI – US$849m; US$1,150 per capita (2006)
Annual average growth of GDP – 4.5 per cent (2007 est)
Inflation rate – 10.4 per cent (2007 est)
Total external debt – US$1,200m (2002)
Imports – US$880m (2006)
Exports – US$570m (2006)

BALANCE OF PAYMENTS
Trade – US$274m deficit (2006)
Current Account – US$172m deficit (2006)

Trade with UK	*2006*	*2007*
Imports from UK	£20,329,000	£24,571,593
Exports to UK	£35,379,000	£40,077,040

COMMUNICATIONS
Roads and navigable waterways (the Berbice, Demerara and Essequibo rivers) form the main arteries of communication in the country, though only 590km of roads, out of a total of 7,970km, are surfaced. The railway system is only 187km in length and is used only for transporting minerals. Georgetown is the main seaport and the location of the principal airport. There are 95 airports and airfields in total, though only nine have surfaced runways. Many areas lack fixed-line services; density is about 15 per 100 people in 2005. Mobile phone distribution has grown quickly and density was 37 per 100 people in 2005.

MEDIA
Guyana has six radio and three television stations. One television station is state-run and the remaining two are privately owned. Journalists operate freely but practise self-censorship.

HAITI

République d'Haïti/Repiblik d'Ayiti – Republic of Haiti

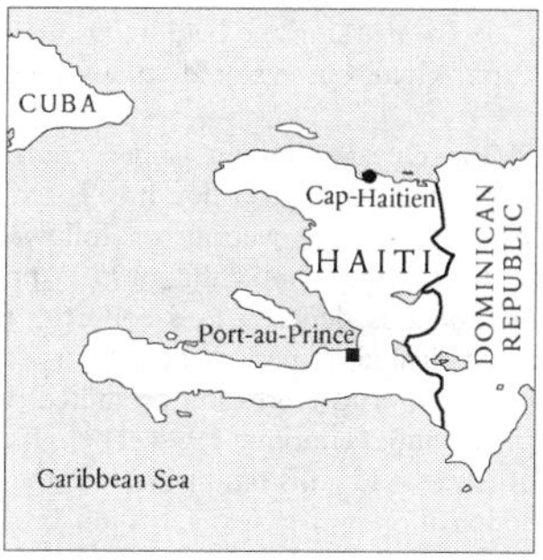

Area – 27,750 sq. km
Capital – Port-au-Prince; population, 1,998,000 (2007 est)
Major cities – Carrefour, Delmas
Currency – Gourde of 100 centimes
Population – 8,706,497 rising at 2.45 per cent per year (2007 est)
Religion – Roman Catholicism (55 per cent), Protestantism (29 per cent) (est). At least half of the country is believed to also practise voodoo, which was recognised as an official religion in 2003. Around 10 per cent of the population has no religious affiliation
Language – French, Creole (both official)
Population density – 343 per sq. km (2006)
Urban population – 38.8 per cent (2005 est)
Median age (years) – 18.4 (2007 est)
National anthem – 'La Dessalinienne' ['Song of Dessalines']
National day – 1 January (Independence Day)
Life expectancy (years) – 57.03 (2007 est)
Mortality rate – 10.4 (2007 est)

Birth rate – 35.87 (2007 est)
Infant mortality rate – 63.83 (2007 est)
HIV/AIDS adult prevalence – 3.4 per cent (2005 est)
Death penalty – Abolished for all crimes (since 1987)
CPI score – 1.6 (2007)
Population below poverty line – 80 per cent (2003 est)
Literacy rate – 51.9 per cent (2004 est)
Health expenditure (per capita) – US$28 (2005)
Hospital beds (per 1,000 people) – 0.8 (2000–6)

CLIMATE AND TERRAIN

The country occupies the western third of the island of Hispaniola (the remainder is the Dominican Republic). The terrain is mountainous, with lower-lying coastal areas in the north. Elevation extremes range from 2,680m (Châine de la Selle) at the highest point to 0m (Caribbean Sea) at the lowest. The climate is tropical.

HISTORY AND POLITICS

Haiti was ceded to France by Spain in 1697. It was named Saint Domingue and was popularly known as the pearl of the Antilles, as it became the richest colony in the French Empire. This wealth was generated by African slaves working in the sugar and coffee plantations. In 1791, a slave rebellion expelled the French from the northern part of the colony and instigated a long war between freed slaves and colonists. By 1804 the Republic of Haiti was founded, marking the inception of the world's first black republic and, after the USA, the oldest republic in the western hemisphere.

Haiti has experienced very little stability since. The country endured 22 changes of government between 1843 and 1915. The resulting upheaval led the USA to intervene in 1915, marking the beginning of 19 years of US occupation. Haiti was restored to sovereign rule in 1934.

In 1957, the Duvalier family gained control of the country and began a dictatorial rule which lasted 29 years. A series of transitional governments followed before Jean-Bertrand Aristide won the 1990 presidential election. Aristide was deposed in a coup the following year which instigated a period of military rule. The severity of the military's repression prompted the UN to authorise US-led intervention in 1994. Though re-elected in 2000, Aristide's administration became the focus of mounting opposition. An armed rebellion broke out in January 2004 and by late February the rebels controlled most of the country. Under pressure from the USA and France, Aristide resigned and went into exile. An interim government was sworn in and a UN-led multinational stabilisation force was deployed, although its presence has done little to counteract the widespread violence, lawlessness and corruption. The presidential election in February 2006 was won by René Préval (president 1996–2000) of the Front for Hope (Lespwa) party, with 51.2 per cent of the vote. In the legislative election, held in two rounds in February and April 2006, the Lespwa party won most seats but not an overall majority. A six-party coalition government was formed under Jacques-Édouard Alexis. Parliament dismissed Alexis in April 2008 and the government announced emergency action on prices after food riots over the spiralling cost of rice.

POLITICAL SYSTEM

Under the 1987 constitution, the head of state is the president, directly elected for a five-year term that may not be renewed immediately. The bicameral National Assembly comprises a lower house, the Chamber of Deputies, with 99 members directly elected for a four-year term, and the senate, with 30 members directly elected for a six-year term; one-third of the senators is elected every two years. The president appoints the prime minister, who must be approved by the legislature.

HEAD OF STATE

President, René Préval, *elected* February 2006, *sworn in* 14 May 2006

SELECTED GOVERNMENT MEMBERS *as at May 2008*

Prime Minister, vacant
Foreign Affairs, Jean Renald Clerisme
Finance and Economy, Daniel Dorsainvil
Interior, Paul Antoine Bien-Aime

BRITISH AMBASSADOR

HE Ian Worthington, *apptd* 2006, resident at Santo Domingo, Dominican Republic

ECONOMY AND TRADE

The country is the poorest in the western hemisphere, with a huge imbalance in wealth, a devastated infrastructure, and high levels of violence and corruption; around 80 per cent of the population lives below the poverty line. Remittances from the estimated one in six Haitians living abroad, principally in the USA, are the main source of foreign revenue, worth nearly a quarter of GDP. The government is completely dependent on international economic aid; an IMF-assisted programme has stimulated moderate economic growth since 2005, and Haiti should benefit from recent foreign aid pledges, but the insecurity and limited infrastructure deter foreign investment. Two-thirds of the population depends on agriculture – predominantly small-scale subsistence farming – but this is vulnerable to natural disasters. Industrial activities include sugar refining, flour milling, textiles and garments, and assembly of goods, especially vehicle parts, for re-export.

The main trading partners are the USA, Netherlands Antilles, Dominican Republic, Canada and Brazil. Principal exports are garments, manufactured goods, oils, cocoa, mangoes and coffee. The main imports are foodstuffs, manufactured goods, machinery and transport equipment, fuels and raw materials.
GNI – US$4,000m; US$430 per capita (2006)
Annual average growth of GDP – 3.5 per cent (2007 est)
Inflation rate – 8.9 per cent (2007 est)
Total external debt – US$1,248m (2007 est)
Imports – US$1,875m (2006)
Exports – US$476m (2006)

BALANCE OF PAYMENTS

Trade – US$1,400m deficit (2006)
Current Account – US$19m deficit (2006)

Trade with UK	*2006*	*2007*
Imports from UK	£7,102,000	£5,042,346
Exports to UK	£401,000	£1,301,728

COMMUNICATIONS

Less than a quarter of the country's 4,160km of highways are surfaced. There are 14 airports, four of which have surfaced runways; the international airports are at Port-au-Prince and Cap-Haitien. Cap-Haitien is the main port. The telephone system is poor, with only 145,000 main lines in use; mobile phone distribution is greater, with 500,000 subscribers in 2005, but the combined density of the two is only about 8 per 100 people. There were 650,000 internet users in 2006.

MEDIA

Radio is the most important medium owing to low literacy levels, and there are more than 250 radio stations, broadcasting in French and Creole. A single state broadcaster, Télévision Nationale d'Haiti, provides four television channels and these have been joined by two privately owned French-language stations. Press freedom is reported to have improved significantly since the fall of Jean-Bertrand Aristide.

HONDURAS

República de Honduras – Republic of Honduras

Area – 112,090 sq. km
Capital – Tegucigalpa; population, 946,000 (2007 est)
Major cities – Choloma, La Ceiba, San Pedro Sula
Currency – Lempira of 100 centavos
Population – 7,483,763 rising at 2.09 per cent per year (2007 est) of mixed Spanish and Indian descent. The Garinagu in the north are of West Indian origin.
Religion – Roman Catholicism (63 per cent), Protestantism (23 per cent) (est)
Language – Spanish (official)
Population density – 62 per sq. km (2006)
Urban population – 46.4 per cent (2005 est)
Median age (years) – 19.7 (2007 est)
National anthem – 'Tu Bandera es un Lampo de Cielo ['Your Flag is a Heavenly Light']
National day – 15 September (Independence Day)
Life expectancy – 69.35 (2007 est)
Mortality rate – 5.32 (2007 est)
Birth rate – 27.59 (2007 est)
Infant mortality rate – 25.21 (2007 est)
HIV/AIDS adult prevalence – 1.4 per cent (2005 est)
Death penalty – Abolished for all crimes (since 1956)
CPI score – 2.5 (2007)
Population below poverty line – 50.7 per cent (2004)

CLIMATE AND TERRAIN

Honduras has a mountainous interior, falling to narrow coastal plains. Elevation extremes range from 2,870m (Cerro Las Minas) at the highest point to 0m (Caribbean Sea) at the lowest. The climate is subtropical in the lowlands and temperate in the mountains. Average temperatures range from 19°C in January to 23°C in June.

HISTORY AND POLITICS

Honduras was home to part of the Mayan civilisation between the fourth and ninth centuries AD. Christopher Columbus first set foot on the American mainland at Trujillo in Honduras in 1502, but it was 1525 before Spanish colonisation began. In 1821, the country became independent and was part of the United Provinces of Central America from 1823 until it became fully independent in 1838. Thereafter the country underwent periods of political instability interspersed with military rule until 1981, when a civilian government was elected. It became embroiled in the civil wars of Nicaragua and El Salvador as a base for US forces and anti-Sandinista Contras. The ending of the civil wars meant a decline in the power of the army, which was brought under civilian control in 1999.

The presidential election in November 2005 was won by Manuel Zelaya of the Liberal Party (PLH). In the simultaneous legislative election, the PLH won the most seats, though not an overall majority, and formed a government after the inauguration of President Zelaya.

POLITICAL SYSTEM

Under the 1982 constitution, the executive president is directly elected for a four-year term, which is not renewable, and appoints the government. The unicameral National Congress has 128 members, elected for a four-year term.

HEAD OF STATE

President, C.-in-C. of the Armed Forces, Manuel Zelaya Rosales, *elected* 27 November 2005, *took office* 27 January 2006
Vice-President, Elvin Santos Ordonez

SELECTED GOVERNMENT MEMBERS *as at May 2008*

Defence, Aristides Mejia
Finance, Rebeca Santos
Foreign Relations, Angel Edmundo Orellana
Interior, Justice, Victor Meza

EMBASSY OF HONDURAS

115 Gloucester Place, London W1U 6JT
T 020-7486 4880 E hondurasuk@lineone.net
Ambassador Extraordinary and Plenipotentiary, HE Ivan Romero-Martinez, *apptd* 2008

BRITISH AMBASSADOR

HE Ian Hughes, *apptd* 2006, resident at Guatemala City, Guatemala

DEFENCE

The army has 12 light tanks. The navy has 31 patrol and coastal combatant vessels at 3 bases. The air force has 16 combat capable aircraft.
Military budget – US$76m (2007 est)
Military personnel – 12,000: army 8,300, navy 1,400, air force 2,300; paramilitary 8,000

ECONOMY AND TRADE

The country has a huge imbalance in wealth and high levels of corruption and violent crime, often connected with drug-trafficking. Qualification for debt relief under the IMF/World Bank heavily indebted poor countries initiative and expanded trade since the US-Central American Free Trade Agreement came into force have reduced public debt from 67 per cent of GDP to 29.3 per cent in 2007. However, nearly half the population lives below the poverty line and over a quarter of the workforce is unemployed. Remittances from expatriate workers, equivalent to nearly three-quarters of export revenue, are vital to the economy.

The economy is dependent on agriculture, fishing and forestry, whose products form the basis of industrial activity and are the main exports. Agriculture employs 34 per cent of the workforce and contributes 13.5 per cent of GDP. Industry accounts for 31 per cent of GDP and 23 per cent of employment, and the services sector for 55.6 per cent of GDP and 43 per cent of employment.

The main trading partners are the USA, Guatemala and El Salvador. Principal exports are coffee, shrimps, bananas, gold, palm oil, fruit, lobster and timber. The main imports are machinery and transport equipment, industrial raw materials, chemical products, fuels and foodstuffs.

GNI – US$8,800m; US$1,270 per capita (2006)
Annual average growth of GDP – 6 per cent (2007 est)
Inflation rate – 6.4 per cent (2007 est)
Unemployment – 27.8 per cent (2007 est)
Total external debt – US$3,871m (2007 est)
Imports – US$5,400m (2006)
Exports – US$1,900m (2006)

BALANCE OF PAYMENTS
Trade – US$3,488m deficit (2006)
Current Account – US$508m deficit (2006)

Trade with UK	*2006*	*2007*
Imports from UK	£7,750,000	£9,695,210
Exports to UK	£17,897,000	£19,723,620

COMMUNICATIONS

Honduras has ports on its Caribbean (Puerto Castilla, Puerto Cortes, Tela) and Pacific (San Lorenzo) coasts. There are 699km of railway and 13,603km of roads, 2,775km of which are surfaced. The mountainous interior has led to the development of a large number of airports, though only 12 of the 112 have surfaced runways; the principal airports are at Tegucigalpa, La Ceiba and San Pedro Sula. The land-line telephone system is poor and mobile phone distribution has grown rapidly, to 2.2 million in 2006. Internet usage is low, at 337,000 users in 2006.

EDUCATION AND HEALTH

Primary and secondary education is free of charge and primary education is compulsory between the ages of seven and 12. The government has launched a campaign to eradicate illiteracy.

Literacy rate – 80 per cent (2004 est)
Gross enrolment ratio (percentage of relevant age group) – primary 118 per cent; secondary 76 per cent; tertiary 17 per cent (2006 est)
Health expenditure (per capita) – US$91 (2005)
Hospital beds (per 1,000 people) – 1.0 (2000–6)

MEDIA

Honduras has a state-owned radio station as well as several privately run broadcasters and newspapers. Televicentro operates several television channels. Journalists are known to restrict their coverage of controversial events.

HUNGARY

Magyar Koztarsasag – Republic of Hungary

Area – 92,030 sq. km
Capital – Budapest; population, 1,679,000 (2007 est)
Major cities – Debrecen, Gyor, Miskolc, Pecs, Szeged
Currency – Forint of 100 filler
Population – 9,956,108 falling at 0.25 per cent per year (2007 est); Hungarian (92.3 per cent). There are minorities of Romanies, ethnic Germans, Serbs, Romanians and Slovaks
Religion – Roman Catholicism (55 per cent), other Christian denominations (18 per cent), Judaism (1 per cent) (est). An estimated 15 per cent of the population has no religious affiliation
Language – Hungarian (official)
Population density – 112 per sq. km (2006)
Urban population – 65.9 per cent (2005 est)
Median age (years) – 38.9 (2007 est)
National anthem – 'Himnusz' ['Hymn']
National day – 20 August (Saint Stephen's Day)
Life expectancy (years) – 72.92 (2007 est)
Mortality rate – 13.05 (2007 est)
Birth rate – 9.66 (2007 est)
Infant mortality rate – 8.21 (2007 est)
Death penalty – Abolished for all crimes (since 1990)
CPI score – 5.3 (2007)

CLIMATE AND TERRAIN

A landlocked state in central Europe, Hungary is mostly low-lying with a mountainous region in the north. Elevation extremes range from 1,014m (Kekes) at the highest point to 78m (Tisza river) at the lowest. The main rivers are the Danube and the Tisza. Lake Balaton lies in the west. Average temperatures range from −1°C in January to 21°C in July.

HISTORY AND POLITICS

Hungary became a Christian kingdom in 1000 but had been settled by Magyar tribes (the ancestors of modern Hungarians) since 896. Between 1699 and 1867, Hungary was ruled as a province of the Austrian Habsburg Empire. Following years of Hungarian agitation, a dual monarchy was created in 1867, giving Hungary control of its internal affairs in return for the continued union of the Austrian and Hungarian crowns. The Austro-Hungarian Empire is remembered as a time of great cultural achievement and economic success. Nevertheless, the union took the country into the First World War on the side of Germany, resulting in defeat for the Hungarians and the fall of the Habsburg dynasty.

Initially a communist republic after the war, in 1920 the country became a kingdom, with Admiral Horthy as regent. Hungary signed the Anti-Comintern Pact with Germany, Italy and Japan in 1939 but remained neutral when the Second World War began, joining the conflict in 1941 on the side of the Axis powers. Horthy was deposed in 1944 after seeking an armistice with advancing Soviet troops, who drove out German forces in 1945.

The Communists came to power in the 1947 elections, and in 1949 Hungary became a communist state aligned with the Soviet Union. A national uprising broke out in 1956, with protesters demanding the withdrawal of Soviet forces from the country, but this was brutally suppressed. In the 1960s Janos Kadar introduced limited liberalisation, which encouraged the development of the most prosperous and permissive regime in the Soviet bloc.

The opening of Hungary's border with Austria in 1989 triggered the developments that led to the fall of communism throughout eastern Europe. Communist rule ended in Hungary, which began the transition to a free-market democracy. The country became a member of NATO in 1999 and joined the EU in 2004. Its parliament ratified the EU constitution in the same year.

Laszlo Solyom was elected president in 2005. In the 2006 legislative election, the Hungarian Socialist Party (MSzP) remained the largest party in the legislature and continued its coalition with the Free Democrats.

POLITICAL SYSTEM

The 1949 constitution has been amended several times, most radically in 1989 to allow a return to a multiparty democracy. The president is elected by the legislature for a five-year term, renewable only once; the post is largely ceremonial but powers include the appointment of the prime minister. The unicameral National Assembly has 386 members directly elected for a four-year term.

HEAD OF STATE

President, Laszlo Solyom, *elected* June 2005, *sworn in* 5 August 2005

SELECTED GOVERNMENT MEMBERS *as at May 2008*

Prime Minister, Ferenc Gyurcsany
Deputy Prime Minister, Peter Kiss
Defence, Imre Szekeres
Finance, Janos Veres
Foreign Affairs, Kinga Goencz

EMBASSY OF THE REPUBLIC OF HUNGARY

35 Eaton Place, London SW1X 8BY
T 020-7201 3440 E office.lon@kum.hu
W www.mfa.gov.hu/emb/london
Ambassador Extraordinary and Plenipotentiary, HE Borbala Czako, *apptd* 2007

BRITISH EMBASSY

Harmincad Utca 6, 1051 Budapest
T (+36) (1) 266 2888 E info@britemb.hu
W www.britishembassy.hu
Ambassador Extraordinary and Plenipotentiary, HE Gregory Dorey, *apptd* 2007

BRITISH COUNCIL

Benczur Utca 26, 1068 Budapest
T (+36) (1) 478 4700 W www.britishcouncil.org/hungary
Director, David Martin

DEFENCE

The army has 238 main battle tanks, 178 armoured infantry fighting vehicles and 458 armoured personnel carriers. The air force has 28 combat aircraft and 12 armed helicopters.

Military expenditure – US$1,320m (2006)
Military personnel – 32,300: army 23,950, air force 7,500, joint staff 850; paramilitary 12,000
Conscription duration – 6 months

ECONOMY AND TRADE

Hungary has made a successful transition to a market economy since 1989, with 80 per cent of GDP now generated by the private sector, and it has attracted high levels of foreign direct investment. The strong, sustained economic growth of the post-Communist years started to slow in 2006–7, partly as a result of the government's austerity programme, intended to reduce the budget deficit and public debt so Hungary can qualify for eurozone membership. The trade deficit has been eliminated, but inflation is rising and unemployment remains high.

Nearly half the land is under cultivation, but agriculture accounts for only 3.3 per cent of GDP; the main crops are cereals, sunflower seeds, vegetables, livestock, dairy products and grapes for wine. Industry contributes 32.4 per cent of GDP; the main activities include mining, metallurgy, construction materials, food processing, textiles, chemicals (especially pharmaceuticals) and motor vehicles. The main trading partners are other EU countries, Russia and China. Machinery and manufactured goods account for 90 per cent of exports and 87 per cent of imports. The country is a net importer of fuels and electricity.

GNI – US$109,500m; US$10,870 per capita (2006)
Annual average growth of GDP – 2.1 per cent (2007 est)
Inflation rate – 7.8 per cent (2007 est)
Unemployment – 7.1 per cent (2007 est)
Total external debt – US$142,900m (2007)
Imports – US$76,000m (2006)
Exports – US$73,500m (2006)

BALANCE OF PAYMENTS

Trade – US$2,990m deficit (2006)
Current Account – US$7,352m deficit (2006)

Trade with UK	*2006*	*2007*
Imports from UK	£807,000,000	£856,956,778
Exports to UK	£2,028,400,000	£2,353,358,749

COMMUNICATIONS

Hungary has 159,600km of roads, about 40 per cent of which is surfaced, and 8,000km of railways (including a cross-border line to Austria, jointly managed by the two countries). There are 1,622km of permanently navigable waterways, mainly on the river Danube, and several major river ports and harbours on the Danube, including Budapest. There are 46 airports and airfields, 20 of which have surfaced runways; the principal airport is at Budapest. The land-line telephone system has been modernised since 2003. Mobile phone distribution is very widespread, at 9.9 million subscribers in 2006. There were 3.5 million internet users in 2006.

EDUCATION AND HEALTH

Hungarians have ten years of compulsory education until age 16, though a further two years at secondary level is optional.

Literacy rate – 99.3 per cent (2004 est)
Gross enrolment ratio (percentage of relevant age group) – primary 98 per cent; secondary 96 per cent; tertiary 65 per cent (2006 est)

Health expenditure (per capita) – US$855 (2005)
Hospital beds (per 1,000 people) – 7.9 (2000–6)

MEDIA AND CULTURE

The state-run broadcaster, Magyar Televizio, has recently lost ground in competition with privately owned television and radio stations. Hungary has a wide range of weekly and daily newspapers, many of which are owned by foreign investors.

The strong folk music culture has influenced the classical music tradition, including the composers Franz Liszt (1811–86), Bela Bartok (1881–1945), Zoltan Kodaly (1882–1967) and Gyorgy Ligeti (1923–2006). Hungary's best known author is Imre Kertesz (*b.* 1929), who won the Nobel prize for literature in 2002.

ICELAND

Lydveldid Island – Republic of Iceland

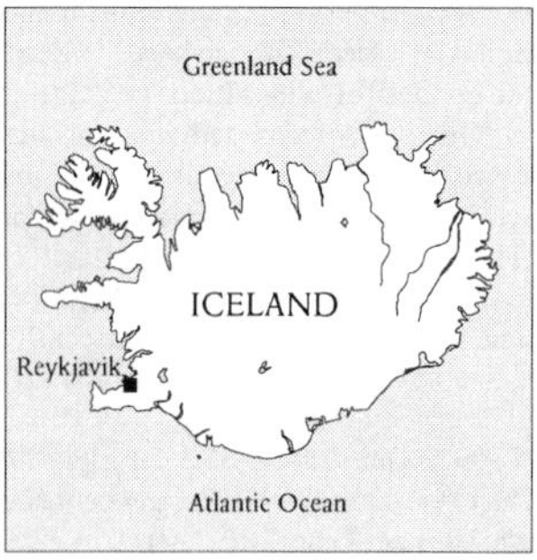

Area – 103,000 sq. km
Capital – Reykjavik; population, 192,000 (2007 est)
Major towns – Hafnarfjordur, Kopavogur
Currency – Icelandic krona (Kr) of 100 aurar
Population – 301,931 rising at 0.82 per cent per year (2007 est)
Religion – Protestantism (Lutheranism) (82 per cent), Roman Catholicism (3 per cent) (est)
Language – Icelandic (official), English, German
Population density – 3 per sq. km (2006)
Urban population – 93 per cent (2005 est)
Median age (years) – 34.5 (2007 est)
National anthem – 'Lofsongur' ['Hymn']
National day – 17 June (Independence Day)
Life expectancy (years) – 80.43 (2007 est)
Mortality rate – 6.77 (2007 est)
Birth rate – 13.57 (2007 est)
Infant mortality rate – 3.27 (2007 est)
Death penalty – Abolished for all crimes (since 1928)
CPI score – 9.2 (2007)
Military budget – US$59.5m (2007) (spent mostly on coast guard)
Military personnel – paramilitary 130
Gross enrolment ratio (percentage of relevant age group) – primary 101 per cent (2002)

CLIMATE AND TERRAIN

Iceland is located in the North Atlantic Ocean, to the east of Greenland and to the west of Norway, and its northernmost coasts reach the Arctic Circle. Some parts of the coastline have narrow strips of low-lying land, others sheer cliffs. An inland plateau of glaciers, lakes and lava fields covers 79 per cent of the interior, with mountainous areas in the north and at the four glaciers in the centre and south. Elevation extremes range from 2,110m (Hvannadalshnukur) at the highest point to 0m (North Atlantic Ocean) at the lowest. There are geysers and hot springs owing to the numerous active volcanoes, which can create new islands, such as Surtsey in 1963. It is estimated that over the past 500 years, Iceland has emitted a third of the earth's total lava flow. The climate is influenced by the Gulf Stream and is therefore temperate, in spite of the country's location. Average temperature ranges from −3°C in January to 11°C in July.

HISTORY AND POLITICS

The first major settlements occurred from around AD 870 onwards, as turmoil in Scandinavia drove migrants to seek new homelands. Iceland hosted a flourishing Viking culture in the ninth and tenth centuries, becoming a fully Christian country in 999. Iceland recognised Norwegian sovereignty in 1263, and along with Norway, came under Danish rule in 1397. When Norway was ceded to Sweden in 1814, Iceland remained Danish territory, achieving autonomy in domestic affairs in 1874. Though it became an independent state with the same sovereign as Denmark in 1918, Copenhagen continued to control its foreign policy and defence. The treaty of union with Denmark expired in 1943, while Denmark was under German occupation, and in a referendum Icelanders voted to become a fully independent republic, proclaimed on 17 June 1944.

The country's dependence on the fishing industry has led occasionally to fraught foreign relations. The introduction and extensions of an exclusive fishing limit around Iceland in 1958, 1972 and 1975 caused the so-called 'Cod War' disputes with the UK with clashes between Icelandic patrol boats and British trawlers and navy vessels. Subsequent restrictions on fishing in Icelandic waters in the 1990s were less controversial.

Post-independence politics has been dominated by the Conservative Independence Party (SSF), which governed in coalition with the Progressive Party (FSF) from 1995 to 2007. The coalition retained its legislative majority by one seat in the 2007 election but the FSF had performed badly and the SSF formed a new coalition with the Social Democratic Alliance. The 2008 presidential election – due in May – was cancelled due to a lack of opposition to incumbent Olafur Grimsson.

POLITICAL SYSTEM

Under the 1944 constitution, the head of state is the president, who is directly elected for a four-year term, which is renewable. The unicameral legislature, the *Althing*, has 63 members, who are directly elected for a four-year term. Founded in AD 930, the *Althing* is the world's oldest parliament.

HEAD OF STATE

President, Olafur Ragnar Grimsson, *elected* 29 June 1996, *re-elected* 2000, 2004, 2008

SELECTED GOVERNMENT MEMBERS *as at June 2008*

Prime Minister, Geir Hilmar Haarde
Finance, Arni M. Mathiesen
Foreign Affairs, Ingibjorg Solrun Gisladottir
Social Affairs, Johanna Sigurdardottir

EMBASSY OF ICELAND

2A Hans Street, London SW1X 0JE
T 020-7259 3999 E icemb.london@utn.stjr.is
W www.iceland.org/uk

Ambassador Extraordinary and Plenipotentiary, HE Sverrir Haukur Gunnlaugsson, *apptd* 2003

BRITISH EMBASSY
PO Box 460, Laufasvegur 31, 101 Reykjavik
T (+354) 550 5100 E britemb@centrum.is
Ambassador Extraordinary and Plenipotentiary and Consul-General, HE Alp Mehmet, MVO, *apptd* 2004

ECONOMY AND TRADE

Iceland has a market economy with an extensive welfare system. The economy is heavily dependent on the fishing industry; although fishing contributes only about 10 per cent of GDP, it accounts for 70 per cent of exports. However, economic diversification has been encouraged in recent years, and aluminium smelting, ferrosilicon production, geothermal power, financial services and tourism now account for industry's 26.3 per cent contribution to GDP and the service sector's 68.4 per cent. Owing to the plentiful supply of geothermal power, which runs industrial complexes and provides most of the island's heating, the island is self-sufficient in energy apart from vehicle fuels.

The main trading partners are EU countries and the USA. Principal exports are fish and fish products, aluminium, animal products, ferrosilicon and diatomite. The main imports are machinery, petroleum products, foodstuffs and textiles.

GNI – US$15,078m; US$49,960 per capita (2006)
Annual average growth of GDP – 1.8 per cent (2007 est)
Inflation rate – 4.9 per cent (2007 est)
Unemployment – 1 per cent (2007 est)
Total external debt – US$3,073m (2002)
Imports – US$5,080m (2006)
Exports – US$3,240m (2006)

BALANCE OF PAYMENTS
Trade – US$1,844m deficit (2006)
Current Account – US$4,232m deficit (2006)

Trade with UK	*2006*	*2007*
Imports from UK	£190,067,000	£201,531,965
Exports to UK	£411,776,000	£421,810,771

COMMUNICATIONS

Iceland has no railways and no navigable waterways. Although the country has about 13,000km of roads, about two-thirds are unsurfaced and in winter these are often blocked by snow. Consequently much internal travel is by air or sea. Iceland has 99 airports and airfields, the principal ones being at Keflavik, near Reykjavik, in the south and Akureyri in the north. The national carrier, Icelandair, is a major employer. There are nine major ports and the capital, Reykjavik, operates shipping services to the USA and Europe. The land-line telephone system has 194,000 main lines in use; mobile phone subscribers numbered 328,500 and there were 194,000 internet users in 2006.

MEDIA AND CULTURE

The state provides public service broadcasting on television and radio via the Icelandic National Broadcasting Service (RUV), which is mandated to promote Icelandic culture and history. There are several commercial stations and a wide variety of newspapers. Reporters Without Borders ranked the country the joint highest for press freedom in 2007.

Iceland enjoys a rich literary tradition. The anonymous Icelandic prose sagas, dating from the 12th to the 14th centuries, are among the most important works of medieval European literature. One of Iceland's best known modern writers is Halldor Laxness (1902–98), winner of the Nobel prize for literature in 1955. The country has also become a successful exporter of popular music through groups including the Sugarcubes (whose singer Bjork has enjoyed worldwide recognition) and Sigur Ros.

INDIA

Bharatiya Ganarajya – Republic of India

Area – 3,287,590 sq. km
Capital – New Delhi; population, 15,926,000 (2007 est)
Major cities – Ahmadabad, Bengaluru/Bangalore, Hyderabad, Jaipur, Kanpur, Kolkata/Calcutta, Madras, Mumbai/Bombay, Pune, Surat
Currency – Indian rupee (Rs) of 100 paise
Population – 1,129,866,154 rising at 1.61 per cent per year (2007 est); Indo-Aryan (72 per cent), Dravidian (25 per cent) (est)
Religion – Hinduism (81 per cent), Islam (13 per cent), Christianity (2 per cent), Sikhism (1 per cent) (est)
Language – English, Hindi, Bengali, Bodo, Dogri, Kannada, Konkani, Maithili, Manipuri, Nepali, Telugu, Marathi, Tamil, Urdu, Gujurati, Malayalam, Santhali, Oriya, Punjabi, Assamese, Kashmiri, Sindhi, Sanskrit (all official), Hindustani
Population density – 373 per sq. km (2006)
Urban population – 28.7 per cent (2005 est)
Median age (years) – 24.8 (2007 est)
National anthem – 'Jana Gana Mana' ['Thou Art the Ruler of the Minds of all People']
National day – 26 January (Republic Day)
Life expectancy (years) – 68.59 (2007 est)
Mortality rate – 6.58 (2007 est)
Birth rate – 22.69 (2007 est)
Infant mortality rate – 34.61 (2007 est)
Death penalty – Retained
CPI score – 3.5 (2007)

CLIMATE AND TERRAIN

India has three well-defined regions: the mountain range of the Himalayas, the Indo-Gangetic plain, and the southern peninsula. The Himalayas along the northern border reach 8,598m (Kanchenjunga) at the highest point of elevation, then drop to the northern plains formed by the basins of the Indus, Ganges and Brahmaputra rivers before rising to low hills running east to west that mark the division with the southern, Deccan peninsula. The peninsula has narrow coastal plains rising to a central plateau, with the Western Ghats and Eastern Ghats ranges of hills lying along the west and east coasts respectively. The Thar Desert lies in the north-west. The average temperature in New Delhi ranges from 14°C in January to 34°C in June. The climate is influenced by the south-west monsoon; the main rainy season is between June and October. During the drier season from December to May, the weather is cooler until February and then becomes increasingly hot until the monsoon breaks.

HISTORY AND POLITICS

The Indus civilisation emerged in the Indus river valley region *c.*2500 BC, and the beginnings of Hinduism date from this period. This civilisation was destroyed by Aryan tribes from central Asia between 1500 and 200 BC. Buddhism emerged in India from *c.*500 BC and was embraced by the Emperor Ashoka; it spread to the rest of eastern Asia via trade routes, but a Hindu revival from AD 40 onwards pushed Buddhism into decline in the subcontinent.

The first Muslim advances into India occurred in the 10th and 11th centuries. Incursions swept across the north of the country, where large Muslim communities were established. India thus became a country with two great religious traditions: a Muslim-dominated north and a largely Hindu south. Europeans arrived in India in the 15th century and had established territorial holdings by the 18th century, though it was not until 1803, when the British East India Company consolidated its influence, that a single power came to dominate the entire subcontinent. In 1857 rule passed to the British government. From the late 19th century, opposition to British rule, led by the Indian National Congress (INC), latterly under the leadership of Mahatma Gandhi, became a concerted nationwide movement, and India achieved its independence in 1947. Against a backdrop of violence, its predominantly Muslim regions were partitioned off to became the separate state of Pakistan. India then became a republic in 1950.

The INC has been the dominant party in Indian politics in the decades since independence, holding power almost continuously for four decades, with periods in opposition in 1977–80, 1989–91 and 1996–2004. Jawaharlal Nehru's appointment as prime minister at independence began the rise of the Gandhi family, which has dominated the INC. Nehru was succeeded by his daughter, Indira Gandhi, who was succeeded after her assassination in 1984 by her son Rajiv until he too was assassinated in 1991; Rajiv's widow Sonia became president of the party in 1998. The INC's dominance appeared to be over in the early 1990s when the Hindu nationalist Bharatiya Janata Party (BJP) began to beat the INC at the polls and formed a series of coalition governments. The INC returned to power with a surprise victory in the 2004 parliamentary election, winning 217 seats in the *Lok Sabha.* Sonia Gandhi was nominated as prime minister but declined the office, and Manmohan Singh became India's first Sikh prime minister at the head of an INC-dominated coalition government called the United Progressive Alliance. A presidential election in July 2007 was won by Pratibha Patil, who became the country's first female head of state.

COMMUNALISM

Tensions between India's Hindu majority and large Muslim minority have never been fully resolved. Violence between the two at the time of partition in 1947 is thought to have cost up to one million lives. The rise of Hindu nationalism in the 1990s accompanied a rise in communal clashes. In 1992, a mosque in the town of Ayodhya was destroyed by Hindus who claimed it was built on the birthplace of the Hindu god Rama. Anti-Muslim mobs rampaged through many parts of India and the army was called upon to restore order. Intercommunal violence flared up again in 2002 when the massacre of pilgrims returning from Ayodhya prompted revenge killings.

Sikh separatist agitation for an independent state in the Punjab became increasingly violent in the 1980s. The suppression of militant Sikh separatism, and particularly the Indian army offensive at the Golden Temple at Amritsar, led to the assassination of Indira Gandhi by her Sikh bodyguards in 1984.

FOREIGN RELATIONS

Since partition, sovereignty over the predominantly Muslim state of Jammu and Kashmir has been disputed by India and Pakistan. A short war in 1947–8 resulted in the state being partitioned between the two countries; its status remains unresolved, despite further outbreaks of war in 1965 and 1971, low-level conflict for control of the Siachen glacier since 1985 and occasional increases in military exchanges, most recently in 1999–2002 and 2003. Tension was exacerbated by Pakistan's support of the Muslim insurgency in the Indian part of the state, which began in the 1980s and has included terrorist attacks in Indian cities, and by both countries' acquisition of nuclear weapons. Moves towards a peaceful settlement began in 2003, when diplomatic missions were reopened and the resumption of transport links was initiated (a bus service across the line of control began in 2005). Formal diplomatic talks began in 2004 and have achieved several accords intended to reduce tension between the two countries, but the status of Kashmir has yet to be addressed.

In the Sino-Indian war in 1962, India lost territory to China. In addition, China claims Arunachal Pradesh and does not recognise Indian sovereignty over Sikkim. Talks between India and China in 2003 resulted in India's formal recognition of the Tibetan Autonomous Region as a part of China and a cross-border trade agreement on Sikkim.

POLITICAL SYSTEM

Under the 1950 constitution, executive power is vested in the president, who is elected for a five-year term by an electoral college consisting of members of the upper and lower chambers of the legislature. The president appoints the prime minister, who is responsible to the legislature. The vice-president, who is elected by both chambers for a five-year term, is *ex-officio* chair of the upper chamber. The legislature, the *Sansad,* consists of two chambers. The upper chamber, the *Rajya Sabha* (Council of States), has up to 250 members serving a six-year term; up to 238 members are elected by the state legislative assemblies as individual terms expire, and the rest are nominated by the president. The *Lok Sabha* (House of the People) has 545 members; 543 are directly elected for a five-year term, and two representatives of the Anglo-Indian community are nominated by the president.

HEAD OF STATE

President of the Republic of India, Pratibha Patil, *elected* 19 July 2007, *took office* 25 July 2007

Vice-President, Hamid Ansari

SELECTED GOVERNMENT MEMBERS *as at June 2008*
Prime Minister, Manmohan Singh
Defence, A. K. Antony
Finance, Palaniappan Chidambaram
Home Affairs, Shivraj V. Patil
External Affairs, Pranab Mukherjee

OFFICE OF THE HIGH COMMISSIONER FOR INDIA
India House, Aldwych, London WC2B 4NA
T 020-7836 8484 E communicationwing@hcilondon.net
W www.hcilondon.net
High Commissioner, HE Kamalesh Sharma, *apptd* 2004

BRITISH HIGH COMMISSION
Chanakyapuri, New Delhi 21 1100-21
T (+91) (11) 2687 2161 E postmaster.newdelhi@fco.gov.uk
W www.ukinindia.org
High Commissioner, Richard Stagg, CMG, *apptd* 2007

BRITISH COUNCIL
17 Kasturba Gandhi Marg, New Delhi 110001
T (+91) (11) 2371 1401/2371 0111
W www.britishcouncil.org/india
Regional Director, Rod Pryde

FEDERAL STRUCTURE
There are 28 states, six union territories and the national capital territory. Each state is headed by a governor, who is appointed by the president and holds office for five years, and by a council of ministers. All states have a legislative assembly, and some also have a legislative council, elected directly for a maximum period of five years. The union territories are administered, except where otherwise provided by parliament, by the president acting through an administrator or lieutenant-governor, or other authority appointed by him. The states have considerable autonomy, although the union government controls such matters as foreign policy, defence and external trade.

DEFENCE
The army has 4,059 main battle tanks, over 1,700 armoured infantry fighting vehicles, 12 combat helicopters and more than 817 armoured personnel carriers. The navy has 16 submarines, 1 aircraft carrier, 8 destroyers, 15 frigates, 24 corvettes, 18 patrol and coastal vessels, 34 combat aircraft and 25 armed helicopters. The air force has 565 combat aircraft and 20 armed helicopters.

India has had nuclear weapon technology since the mid-1970s, and by the mid-1990s had also successfully developed intermediate-range ballistic missiles.
Military expenditure – US$22,400m (2006)
Military personnel – 1,288,000: army 1,100,000, navy 55,000, air force 125,000, coast guard 8,000; paramilitary 1,300,586

ECONOMY AND TRADE
The economy was closed for three decades after independence, with high import tariffs and limits on foreign investment to stimulate domestic growth. Since the late 1980s, economic liberalisation and more foreign investment have generated rapid expansion, with GDP growing by an average 7 per cent a year. India's large skilled workforce, especially its pool of English-speaking graduates, has enabled it to develop knowledge-based industries, such as IT and telecommunications, becoming a global centre for manufacturing and services. Pharmaceuticals is another area of growth, as are tourism and the provision of services to the burgeoning urban middle class. The service sector now accounts for 55 per cent of GDP and industry for 28.4 per cent, employing 28 per cent and 12 per cent of the workforce respectively. The government's plans to set up over 600 special economic zones to stimulate the growth of manufacturing industries has met with opposition in the mainly agricultural areas earmarked for development.

Although about 1 per cent of the population has been lifted out of poverty each year since 1997, rural areas have benefited disproportionately little from the economic growth. Since 2004 the government has initiated schemes intended to reduce rural poverty, which has been exacerbated by prolonged drought in some areas and the effects of the Indian Ocean tsunami of 2004. Agriculture, forestry and fishing support 60 per cent of the population and contribute 16.6 per cent of GDP. The main food crops are rice, cereals (principally wheat) and pulses. The major cash crops include sugar cane, jute, cotton and tea. Agriculture and forestry are threatened by deforestation, soil erosion, over-grazing and desertification.

Despite the economic growth, there is a high trade deficit and growing inflation. Problems that threaten to constrain continued growth include the halting of the privatisation of state enterprises, under-investment in the infrastructure (especially transport and power supply), excessive regulation and corruption. Shortfalls in energy generation cause frequent power cuts, and output is not expected to meet demand until at least 2010.

The main trading partners are the USA, China, the UAE, EU and ASEAN countries. Principal exports include petroleum products, textiles and garments, gemstones and jewellery, engineering goods, chemicals and leather manufactures. Its main imports are crude oil, machinery, gemstones, fertiliser and chemicals.
GNI – US$909,100m; US$820 per capita (2006)
Annual average growth of GDP – 8.5 per cent (2007 est)
Inflation rate – 5.9 per cent (2007 est)
Unemployment – 7.2 per cent (2007 est)
Total external debt – US$165,400m (2007)
Imports – US$174,800m (2006)
Exports – US$120,300m (2006)

BALANCE OF PAYMENTS
Trade – US$54,381m deficit (2006)
Current Account – US$9,800m deficit (2006)

Trade with UK	*2006*	*2007*
Imports from UK	£2,703,856,000	£2,964,285,676
Exports to UK	£3,187,831,000	£3,772,901,088

COMMUNICATIONS
India has over 63,000km of railways and 3.38 million km of roads, although fewer than half are surfaced. There are 346 airports and airfields, the principal ones being at Delhi, Mumbai/Bombay, Chennai/Madras and Kolkata/Calcutta. The chief seaports are Mumbai, Kolkata, Haldia, Chennai, Cochin, Visakhapatnam, Mangalore and Tuticorin. The merchant fleet includes 477 ships of over 1,000 tonnes. There are 485km of canals and the great rivers provide over 5,200km of navigable waterways.

Deregulation and liberalisation has prompted rapid expansion of the telephone system, although services are still concentrated in urban areas. Mobile phone distribution is expanding even more quickly; there were 166 million subscribers (2006) compared to 50 million main-line subscribers (2005). There were 60 million internet users in 2005, and 2.3 million internet hosts in 2007.

EDUCATION AND HEALTH

Education is free of charge, but not compulsory.
Literacy rate – 61 per cent (2004 est)
Gross enrolment ratio (percentage of relevant age group) – primary 115 per cent; secondary 54 per cent; tertiary 11 per cent (2006 est)
Health expenditure (per capita) – US$36 (2005)
Hospital beds (per 1,000 people) – 0.9 (2000–6)

MEDIA

The state's monopoly of television broadcasting ended in 1992, since when the number of channels available has increased rapidly; Doordarshan and Zee TV are major broadcasters, while satellite and cable channels are also popular. The private press is a thriving and diverse industry, often outspoken and critical of the government; in 2004 some 142 million newspapers were sold throughout the country.

CULTURE

Contemporary writers of international standing include Vikram Seth (*b.* 1952), Salman Rushdie (*b.* 1947) and Arundhati Roy (*b.* 1961). Bollywood is the common name for the Mumbai-based Indian film industry which produces over 800 films a year. The influence of Bollywood in the West is growing, as shown by the success of collaborative efforts such as *Bride and Prejudice* (2004) and Andrew Lloyd Webber's 2004 musical *Bombay Dreams*.

Cricket, the most popular sport in India, was introduced by the British and matches have been played in the country since 1721. Notable players include spin bowlers Bishan Singh Bedi (*b.* 1946) and Anil Kumble (*b.* 1970), batsman Sachin Tendulkar (*b.* 1973) and *Wisden*'s Indian Cricketer of the Century Kapil Dev (*b.* 1959).

INDONESIA

Republik Indonesia – Republic of Indonesia

Area – 1,919,440 sq. km
Capital – Jakarta; population, 9,125,000 (2007 est)
Major cities – Bandung, Bekasi, Depok, Makasar, Medan, Palembang, Semarang, Surabaya, Tangerang
Currency – Rupiah (Rp) of 100 sen
Population – 234,693,997 rising at 1.21 per cent per year (2007 est); Javanese (40.6 per cent), Sundanese (15 per cent), Madurese (3.3 per cent), Minangkabau (2.7 per cent), Betawi (2.4 per cent), Bugis (2.4 per cent), Banten (2 per cent), Banjar (1.7 per cent) (est)
Religion – Islam (88 per cent), Protestantism (6 per cent), Roman Catholicism (3 per cent), Hinduism (2 per cent), Buddhism (1 per cent) (est)
Language – Bahasa Indonesian (official), English, Dutch, Javanese
Population density – 123 per sq. km (2006)
Urban population – 47.9 per cent (2005 est)
Median age (years) – 26.9 (2007 est)
National anthem – 'Indonesia Raya' ['Great Indonesia']
National day – 17 August (Independence Day)
Life expectancy (years) – 70.16 (2007 est)
Mortality rate – 6.25 (2007 est)
Birth rate – 19.65 (2007 est)
Infant mortality rate – 32.14 (2007 est)
Death penalty – Retained
CPI score – 2.3 (2007)
Population below poverty line – 17.8 per cent (2006)
Literacy rate – 87.9 per cent (2004 est)
Gross enrolment ratio (percentage of relevant age group) – primary 115 per cent; secondary 62 per cent; tertiary 17 per cent (2006 est)
Health expenditure (per capita) – US$26 (2005)

CLIMATE AND TERRAIN

Indonesia comprises over 13,000 islands, of which over 6,000 are inhabited. They include the islands of Java, Madura, Sumatra, the Riouw-Lingga archipelago, Bangka and Billiton, part of the island of Borneo (Kalimantan), Sulawesi (formerly Celebes), the Maluku (formerly Moluccas) archipelago, Bali, Lombok, Sumbawa, Sumba, Flores and others comprising the provinces of East and West Nusa Tenggara, and the western half of the islands of New Guinea (Papua; formerly Irian Jaya) and Timor. Elevation extremes range from 5,030m (Puncak Jaya, in Papua) at the highest point to 0m (Indian Ocean) at the lowest. Many of the islands have narrow coastal plains with hilly or mountainous interiors, and over half of the country is covered by tropical rainforest.

Average temperatures in Jakarta range from 23°C in January to 32°C in August. The country is located at the junction of tectonic plates, making it susceptible to natural disasters such as earthquakes and tsunamis, and its weather patterns are being affected by climate change.

HISTORY AND POLITICS

Hindu and Buddhist kingdoms existed in some parts of the Indonesian islands until the 14th century. Islam was introduced in the 13th century and spread over the next three centuries. Trading by the Portuguese began in the 16th century, but the Portuguese were displaced by the Dutch who, lured by the rich spice trade, came to

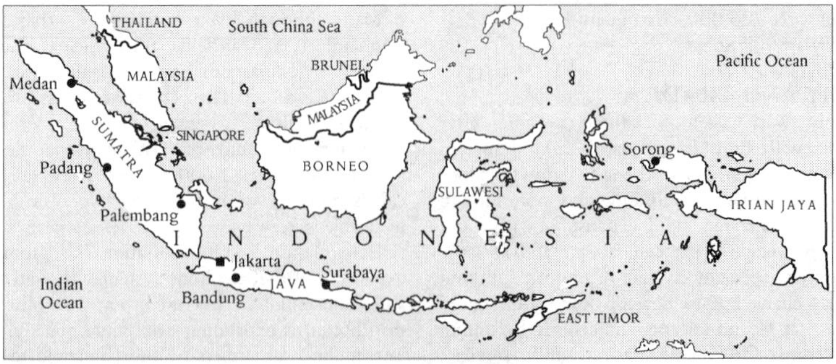

dominate Indonesia by the early 20th century. Opposition to Dutch rule grew in the 1920s and the Japanese occupation of Indonesia during the Second World War strengthened nationalism, leading to a declaration of independence after liberation in 1945. This was not recognised by the Dutch, who attempted to reassert control, but after four years of guerrilla warfare they granted independence to the Netherlands Indies in 1949 and Irian Jaya in 1963. East Timor was invaded and annexed in 1975 but gained independence in 2002.

Achmed Soekarno, the foremost proponent of self-rule since the 1920s, became president in 1949 but was deposed in 1966 in a military coup that brought General Suharto to power. Suharto remained in power until 1998 when, amidst economic and social upheaval, he was succeeded by his deputy B. J. Habibie. Habibie's cautious introduction of social and economic reforms led to him being defeated in 1999 by Abdurrahman Wahid, in the first democratically held elections for 44 years. President Wahid was impeached for alleged financial corruption and in 2001 the legislature appointed Megawati Soekarnoputri (daughter of Achmed Soekarno) to replace him.

In the 2004 legislative elections, the greatest number of seats was won by Golkar, the former ruling party. The 2004 presidential election was won by Susilo Bambang Yudhoyono of the Democratic Party, who defeated Megawati Soekarnoputri in the second round; Yudhoyono appointed a coalition government that included two Golkar ministers.

INSURGENCIES

Separatist movements developed in several parts of Indonesia after independence, including Maluku, which fought an unsuccessful separatist war in the 1950s; Irian Jaya (now Papua), which was granted greater autonomy in 2001, although separatist agitation continues; East Timor, from its annexation in 1975 until independence in 2002; and Aceh province in Sumatra, granted a degree of autonomy after a peace accord between the separatist movement and the government in 2005.

Since the fall of Suharto in 1998, tensions between different racial or religious groups have surfaced, and there has been intercommunal violence in Kalimantan (1996–7, 1999 and 2001), Sulawesi (1998–2000 and 2001) and Maluku (1999–2002).

At least two Muslim extremist groups are based in Indonesia and claim links with al-Qaida. They have been held responsible for bombings in Bali in 2002, 2003 and 2005.

POLITICAL SYSTEM

The 1959 constitution was amended in 2001 to provide for the establishment of the upper chamber of the legislature, and in 2002 to provide for the direct election of the president and the abolition of parliamentary seats reserved for the armed forces. The executive president, who is directly elected for a five-year term of office, appoints the cabinet. The bicameral People's Consultative Assembly, is the state's highest authority, with powers to alter the constitution. It comprises the House of Representatives, which has 550 members directly elected for a five-year term, and the House of Representatives of the Regions; this upper house was created in 2001 to deal with regional matters, and has 128 members, four for each province, directly elected on a non-partisan basis for a five-year term.

HEAD OF STATE

President, Susilo Bambang Yudhoyono, *sworn in* 20 October 2004

Vice-President, Muhammad Jusuf Kalla

SELECTED GOVERNMENT MEMBERS *as at June 2008*

Defence, Juwono Sudarsono

Finance, Mulyani Indrawati

Foreign Affairs, Hasan Wirayuda

Home Affairs, Mardiyanto

EMBASSY OF THE REPUBLIC OF INDONESIA

38 Grosvenor Square, London W1K 2HW

T 020-7499 7661 W www.indonesianembassy.org.uk

Ambassador Extraordinary and Plenipotentiary, vacant

BRITISH EMBASSY

Jalan M. H. Thamrin 75, Jakarta 10310

T (+62) (21) 315 6264 E consulate.jakarta@fco.gov.uk

W www.british-emb-jakarta.or.id

Ambassador Extraordinary and Plenipotentiary, HE Martin Hatfull, *apptd* 2008

BRITISH COUNCIL

Jakarta Stock Exchange, Tower II, 16th Floor, Jalan Jenderal Sudirman Kav. 52–53, Jakarta 12190

T (+62) (021) 515 5561 W www.britishcouncil.org/indonesia

Director, Prof. Mike Hardy, OBE

DEFENCE

The army has 356 armoured personnel carriers, 11 armoured infantry fighting vehicles and 2 armed helicopters. The navy has 2 submarines, 11 frigates, 18 corvettes, 41 patrol and coastal vessels and 9 armed helicopters. There are 5 principal naval bases. The air force has 94 combat aircraft.

Military expenditure – US$10,300m (2006 est)

Military personnel – 302,000: army 233,000, navy 45,000, air force 24,000; paramilitaries 280,000

Conscription duration – 24 months (selective)

ECONOMY AND TRADE

The economy has struggled since the late 1990s, when the Asian financial crisis coincided with the fall of Suharto and the ensuing period of political upheaval. Owing to the caution, corruption and indecision of subsequent governments, the economy drifted, its recovery hit by a downturn in tourism following the Bali bombings and the devastation caused by a succession of natural disasters since 2004. President Yudhoyono's government has introduced significant economic reforms which have reduced debt and boosted investment, and unemployment and inflation levels are falling. However, poverty, poor infrastructure, corruption, a complex regulatory regime and inequitable resource distribution among its regions continue to present problems.

Natural resources include oil, tin, natural gas, nickel, timber, bauxite, copper, coal, gold and silver. However, a lack of investment in finding new sources of oil has led to a decline in oil production that has made Indonesia a net importer since 2004. The exploitation and processing of mineral assets, production of textiles, clothing, timber, chemicals and rubber, and tourism are the main industrial activities; industry accounts for 47.7 per cent of GDP and services 39.9 per cent, employing 18 per cent and 39 per cent of the workforce respectively. Agriculture contributes only 12.4 per cent of GDP but employs 43 per cent of the workforce. The main crops are rice, cassava, peanuts, rubber, cocoa, coffee, palm oil, copra and livestock products.

The main trading partners are Singapore, Japan, China, the USA, South Korea and other Pacific Rim nations. Principal exports are oil and natural gas, electrical appliances, plywood, textiles and rubber. The main imports are machinery and equipment, chemicals, fuel and foodstuffs.

GNI – US$315,900m; US$1,420 per capita (2006)
Annual average growth of GDP – 6.1 per cent (2007 est)
Inflation rate – 6.3 per cent (2007 est)
Unemployment – 9.7 per cent (2007 est)
Total external debt – US$137,200m (2007)
Imports – US$80,300m (2006)
Exports – US$103,500m (2006)

BALANCE OF PAYMENTS
Trade – US$23,153m surplus (2006)
Current Account – US$10,836m surplus (2006)

Trade with UK	*2006*	*2007*
Imports from UK	£318,173,000	£288,585,650
Exports to UK	£1,021,567,000	£992,288,962

COMMUNICATIONS

Indonesia has 368,400km of highways, 6,458km of railways and 21,579km of navigable waterways. An extensive network of ferry services links the islands. There are 652 airports and airfields, of which 158 have surfaced runways; each of the main islands has a major airport, most capable of accepting international flights. There are nine major ports, usually the chief towns of the major islands, and the merchant fleet contains 965 ships of over 1,000 tonnes. The telephone system covers the whole country, and access has improved with the installation of over 200,000 kiosks, many in remote areas. Mobile phone distribution is growing quickly and, at 64m subscribers in 2006, exceeds fixed-line use at 15m lines.

MEDIA

A state-run television broadcaster, Televisi Republik Indonesia (TVRI), competes with several commercial stations. There are several newspapers and many radio stations with national coverage. In 2003 more than 2,000 unlicensed radio and television stations were given the chance to apply for licences.

IRAN

Jomhuri-ye-Eslami-ye-Iran – Islamic Republic of Iran

Area – 1,648,000 sq. km
Capital – Tehran; population 7,873,000 (2007 est)
Major cities – Ahvaz, Esfahan, Karaj, Mashhad, Qom, Shiraz, Tabriz
Currency – Iranian rial of 100 dinar
Population – 65,397,521 rising at 0.66 per cent per year (2007 est); Persian (51 per cent), Azeri (24 per cent), Mazandarani (8 per cent), Kurdish (7 per cent), Arab (3 per cent), Lurs (2 per cent), Baloch (2 per cent), Turkmen (2 per cent) (est)
Religion – Islam (98 per cent) (est), the majority practise Shia Islam
Language – Persian (official), Turkic, Kurdish, Arabic, Luri, Balochi
Population density – 43 per sq. km (2006)
Urban population – 68.1 per cent (2005 est)
Median age (years) – 25.8 (2007 est)
National anthem – 'Sorud-e Melli-e Iran' ['Anthem of the Islamic Republic of Iran']
National day – 1 April (Republic Day)
Life expectancy (years) – 70.56 (2007 est)
Mortality rate – 5.65 (2007 est)
Birth rate – 16.57 (2007 est)
Infant mortality rate – 38.12 (2007 est)
Death penalty – Retained
CPI score – 2.5 (2007)
Population below poverty line – 18 per cent (2007 est)

CLIMATE AND TERRAIN

Apart from narrow coastal strips at sea-level on the Gulf coasts and the shores of the Caspian Sea, the interior is a plateau rising to mountains in the north, west and east. The western and eastern ranges are divided by the Dasht-e Kavir desert. Elevation extremes range from 5,671m (Qolleh-ye Damavand) at the highest point to −28m (Caspian Sea) at the lowest. Earthquakes are frequent. Average temperatures in Tehran are 3°C in January and 30°C in July.

HISTORY AND POLITICS

Iran is part of the Middle East's so-called fertile crescent, an area associated with the development of sophisticated agriculture. In the sixth century BC, the Achaemenian king Cyrus the Great developed control over the area. His dynasty founded the Persian Empire under the Zoroastrian religion. Two hundred years later, Persia was conquered by Alexander the Great. Alexander's death led to a period of economic turbulence, civil conflict and foreign invasion until the Sassanian Persian Empire was founded in the second century AD. This was destroyed in AD 637 by Arab conquerors who introduced Islam, converting the majority of the population and initiating a cultural revolution. The area was ruled by the Arabs, Turks and Mongols until the accession of the Safavid dynasty, which ruled between the 16th and 18th centuries, a time recognised as one of great cultural production; it was followed by the Qajar dynasty in the 19th and 20th centuries.

The Qajar dynasty was overthrown in 1921 by Reza Khan, who became prime minister in 1923 and was crowned Shah in 1925. He was succeeded in 1941 by his son, Mohammad Reza Shah Pahlavi, who began a programme of economic modernisation, Westernisation and secularisation in the 1960s. Opposition to reform and popular protests against the Shah's regime in the 1970s led to a revolution in 1978. The Shah went into exile and in 1979 a non-party theocratic Islamic republic was proclaimed under Ayatollah Khomeini.

Since Ayatollah Khomeini's death in 1989, there has been a struggle for political dominance between conservatives and more liberal reformers. Although the reformists were generally in the ascendancy until 2004, liberalisation has been blocked by the religious authorities and the conservative judiciary, which also constitutes the membership of the Council of Guardians and so is able to influence the selection of parliamentary candidates. There is a vocal popular pro-democracy movement.

The 2005 presidential election was won in the second round by a conservative, Mahmoud Ahmadinejad, with 61.6 per cent of the vote. The Assembly of Experts was last elected in December 2006. At the 2008 legislative election, most pro-reform candidates were disqualified from standing by the Council of Guardians; conservatives won 170 seats, independents 71 seats, reformers 46 seats and religious minorities 3 seats.

FOREIGN RELATIONS

Between 1980 and 1988, Iran was engaged in a bitter war with Iraq; ostensibly a boundary dispute over the Shatt-al-Arab waterway, it was fuelled by Iran's fear that Iraq was encouraging demands for autonomy by Arabs in its westernmost province. Fighting ended in 1988 and a peace settlement was agreed in 1990. Iran remained neutral in the Gulf War (1991) and the Iraq War (2003).

Since the 1978 revolution, Iran's relations with the West, and especially the USA, have been strained. It has not cooperated with international efforts to achieve peace in the Middle East, and has long been suspected of sponsoring terrorism by Islamic fundamentalists, especially in Lebanon; since 2003 it has been accused of subverting Western efforts at reconstruction in Iraq by arming insurgents. Since 2002 relations with the West have deteriorated further because of concerns over Iran's nuclear power programme (for which Russia provides technical support and equipment), especially its acquisition of the ability to enrich uranium. Iran denies that this is a precursor to developing nuclear weapons, but refuses to halt its enrichment of uranium, although following talks with the IAEA it allowed inspectors to visit its nuclear plant in summer 2007. UN sanctions on trade in nuclear materials and technology were imposed following votes in December 2006 and March 2007.

POLITICAL SYSTEM

Under the 1979 constitution, overall authority rests with the spiritual leader of the republic, who is elected by the Assembly of Experts; this consists of 83 clerics who are directly elected every eight years and decide on religious and spiritual matters. The executive president is directly elected for a four-year term, renewable only once. Ministers are nominated by the president but must be approved by the legislature. The unicameral *Majlis al-Shoura* (Consultative Council) has 290 members who are directly elected for a four-year term on a non-party basis; five seats are reserved for religious minorities. Laws passed by the legislature must be approved by the Council of Guardians of the Constitution, a 12-member judicial body elected by the legislature for an eight-year term, which also has a supervisory role in elections. In 1997, the Constitutional Surveillance Council, a five-member body, was established to supervise the proper application of constitutional laws.

Spiritual Leader of the Islamic Republic and C.-in-C. of Armed Forces, Ayatollah Seyed Ali Khamenei, *appointed* June 1989
President, Mahmoud Ahmadinejad, *elected* 24 June 2005
First Vice-President, Parviz Dawoodi

SELECTED GOVERNMENT MEMBERS *as at June 2008*
Defence and Logistics, Brig.-Gen. Mohammad Mostafa Najjar
Economic Affairs and Finance, Hoseyn Samsami
Foreign Affairs, Manouchehr Mottaki
Interior, Seyyed Mehdi Hashemi

EMBASSY OF THE ISLAMIC REPUBLIC OF IRAN
16 Prince's Gate, London SW7 1PT
T 020-7225 3000 W www.iran-embassy.org.uk
Ambassador Extraordinary and Plenipotentiary, HE Rasoul Movahedian Attar, *apptd* 2006

BRITISH EMBASSY
PO Box 11365–4474, 198 Ferdowsi Avenue, Tehran 11344
T (+98) (21) 6670 5018 E britishembassytehran@fco.gov.uk
W www.britishembassy.gov.uk/iran
Ambassador Extraordinary and Plenipotentiary, HE Geoffrey Adams, KCMG, *apptd* 2006

BRITISH COUNCIL
North Entrance, British Embassy Compound, Shariati Street, Qolhak, Tehran 19396 13661
T (+98) (21) 2200 1222 W www.britishcouncil.org/iran
Director, Neville McBain

DEFENCE

The army has over 1,613 main battle tanks, 640 armoured personnel carriers, 610 armoured infantry fighting vehicles and 50 armed helicopters. The navy has 3 submarines, 3 frigates, 2 corvettes, 140 patrol and coastal vessels, 3 combat aircraft and 10 armed helicopters. There are 7 naval bases. The air force has some 319 combat aircraft, of which about 60–80 per cent are serviceable.
Military budget – US$7,160m (2007)
Military personnel – 545,000: army 350,000, Islamic Revolutionary Guard Corps 125,000, navy 18,000, air force 52,000; paramilitary 40,000

ECONOMY AND TRADE

Iran has one of the best-performing economies in the Middle East owing to its vast reserves of oil and natural gas and the buoyancy of oil prices in recent years. But the predominantly state-controlled economy is inefficient and despite high revenues, unemployment and inflation are serious problems. Economic liberalisation and diversification have made little progress with privatisation, deregulation and the abolition of subsidies, and there is a flourishing unofficial economy.

Oil and gas extraction and processing dominate the economy, but Iran also produces textiles, construction materials, metals and armaments. Agricultural production includes wheat, rice, other grains, sugar cane, fruit, nuts, cotton, dairy products, wool and caviar. The main trading partners are China, Japan, Germany, Italy, South Korea and the UAE. Principal exports are petroleum (80 per cent), chemical and petrochemical products, fruit and nuts, and carpets. The main imports are industrial raw materials and intermediate goods, capital goods, foodstuffs, consumer goods and technical services.
GNI – US$205,000m; US$2,930 per capita (2006)
Annual average growth of GDP – 4.3 per cent (2007 est)
Inflation rate – 17 per cent (2007 est)
Unemployment – 11 per cent (2007)
Total external debt – US$13,800m (2007 est)
Imports – US$42,000m (2005)
Exports – US$58,000m (2005)

BALANCE OF PAYMENTS
Trade – US$13,138m surplus (2000)
Current Account – US$20,650m surplus (2006)

Trade with UK	*2005*	*2006*
Imports from UK	£463,944,000	£431,404,000
Exports to UK	£38,789,000	£71,689,000

COMMUNICATIONS

Iran's seaports include Asaluyeh, Bushehr and Abadan (largely destroyed in the 1980–8 war with Iraq) on the Persian Gulf and Bandar Abbas on the Strait of Hormuz. Its merchant fleet includes 131 ships of over 1,000 tonnes. The 850km of navigable waterways are mainly on the river Karun and Lake Urmia. There are a total of 179,388km of roads, of which 120,782km are surfaced, and 8,367km of railways. There are over 300 airports and airfields; the principal airports are at Tehran and Shiraz.

The state-owned telephone system is being modernised and expanded to include rural as well as urban areas. The land-line network has more than doubled in capacity, to 21.9 million, between 2000 and 2006. Mobile phone distribution has grown dramatically and there were 13.7 million subscribers in 2006. Internet users numbered 18 million in 2006.

EDUCATION AND HEALTH

Since 1943 primary education has been compulsory and free of charge.
Literacy rate – 77 per cent (2004 est)
Gross enrolment ratio (percentage of relevant age group) – primary 118 per cent; secondary 81 per cent; tertiary 27 per cent (2006 est)
Health expenditure (per capita) – US$212 (2005)
Hospital beds (per 1,000 people) – 1.7 (2000–6)

MEDIA

The relative freedom of the press under previous reformist governments is now being challenged by the conservatives and a number of more liberal publications have been closed down. The Islamic Republic of Iran Broadcasting (IRIB) is a state-run national television broadcaster which is supplemented by regional channels. Viewing of satellite television channels is widespread and tolerated by the authorities despite the ban on receivers. Internet usage is the most common method of circumventing censorship, although several bloggers have attracted the attention of the authorities by publishing controversial views.

CULTURE

Iran is rich in Islamic and pre-Islamic architecture. Persepolis, constructed by Darius in the sixth century BC and the capital of the Achaemenian Empire, lies 644km south of Tehran. It was declared a UNESCO World Heritage Site in 1979.

The flourishing film industry was boosted in 1998 by the government's decision to subsidise productions. Director Abbas Kiarostami (*b.* 1940), whose films include Palme d'Or winner *Taste of Cherry* and *Ten*, has received much critical acclaim, while author and filmmaker Marjane Satrapi (*b.* 1969) received widespread critical acclaim for her graphic novel and film *Persepolis*.

IRAQ

Al-Jumhuriyah al-Iraqiyah – Republic of Iraq

Area – 437,072 sq. km
Capital – Baghdad; population, 5,054,000 (2007 est)
Major cities – Arbil, Basra, Hillah, Karbala, Kirkuk, Mosul, Najaf, Sulaymaniyah
Currency – New Iraqi dinar (NID) of 1,000 fils
Population – 27,499,638 rising at 2.62 per cent per year (2007 est); Arab (75 per cent), Kurdish (15 per cent) (est)
Religion – Islam (97 per cent) (est); the majority of Muslims practise Shia Islam
Language – Arabic (official), Kurdish (official in Kurdish Autonomous Region), Assiryan, Armenian
Population density – 55 per sq. km (2001 est)
Urban population – 66.8 per cent (2005 est)
Median age (years) – 20 (2007 est)
National anthem – 'Mawtini' ['My Homeland']
National day – 17 July (Revolution Day)
Life expectancy (years) – 69.31 (2007 est)
Mortality rate – 5.26 (2007 est)
Birth rate – 31.44 (2007 est)
Infant mortality rate – 47.04 (2007 est)
Death penalty – Retained
CPI score – 1.5 (2007)

CLIMATE AND TERRAIN

Most of Iraq is a desert plain, with mountainous areas in the north. The Euphrates and Tigris rivers run across the country from north-west to south-east, discharging into the Persian Gulf. Elevation extremes range from 3,611m at the highest point to 0m (Persian Gulf) at the lowest. Average temperatures in Baghdad range from 9°C in January to 35°C in July.

HISTORY AND POLITICS

The Sumerians, the world's oldest civilisation, were the first people to populate the areas around the Tigris and Euphrates rivers. They began to build city-states from around 3000 BC of which Ur, Lagash and Eridu are the earliest examples; the city-states were unified into an empire *c.*2350 BC. In the seventh century BC, the area became part of the Assyrian Empire until this was destroyed by the Babylonians and the Medes. Apart from 150 years of Roman rule (AD 114–266), Iraq was under Persian rule from the mid-sixth century BC until the Persian defeat and conquest by Arab Muslims in AD 637.

The Battle of Karbala in AD 680 marked a decisive moment in Islamic history: the split between Sunnis and Shias was created when the Shi'ite leader Hussein was killed attempting to claim the Caliphate. Iraq came under the control of the Ottoman Empire from 1533 until 1916, when the Ottomans, weakened by the First World War, ceded control to the British. A provisional government was set up in 1920, and in 1921 the Emir Faisal was elected king of Iraq. King Faisal II was assassinated in 1958 in a military-led revolution, following which a left-wing military regime assumed power. Iraq came under the control of the socialist Ba'ath Party temporarily after a coup in 1963 and then from 1968. In 1979, Saddam Hussein deposed President Bakr and became president.

Iraq fought a bitter war with Iran from 1980–8. Ostensibly a border dispute over the Shatt-al-Arab waterway, it arose from Iraq's fear that Iran was encouraging a Shi'ite majority uprising against its predominantly Sunni regime. Fighting ended with a ceasefire in 1988 and a peace settlement in 1990. In August 1990, Iraq invaded and annexed Kuwait, ignoring international and UN demands for it to withdraw. In January 1991, a US-led alliance of NATO and Middle East countries launched a military offensive against Iraq that liberated Kuwait the following month. UN sanctions remained in place owing to Iraq's obstruction of attempts to verify the decommissioning of its weapons of mass destruction; further refusal to comply led to an invasion by US-led military forces in March 2003. Saddam Hussein was captured in December 2003, and was executed in December 2006, after being convicted of crimes against humanity.

Following the invasion and occupation between March and May 2003, a coalition provisional authority became the occupying authority in Iraq before handing over sovereignty in June 2004 to the Iraqi interim governing council, despite deteriorating internal security.

Elections to the transitional national assembly took place in January 2005; the turnout was high generally, but low among Sunni Muslims, who won only 17 seats. Elections for a permanent legislature took place in December 2005, but as no party or bloc commanded an outright majority, there were four months of political deadlock before Jalal Talabani, the Kurdish president of the transitional government, was re-elected president in April 2006 and asked Nouri Jawad al-Maliki (leader of a Shia party) to form a government. Maliki's coalition government, including the four main parliamentary blocs and one minor party, was sworn in on 20 May. The Sunni blocs began boycotts of the government in summer 2007 over the arrest of a Sunni minister; in April 2008 they agreed in principle to rejoin the government.

INSURGENCIES

There are about four million Kurds in north-east Iraq, in areas adjoining the predominantly Kurdish areas in Iran and Turkey. Iraq's Kurdish nationalists have demanded an autonomous homeland, Kurdistan, since the 1960s, and turned to militant tactics in the 1970s. Their demands were opposed by Saddam Hussein's regime with great brutality. An uprising after the Gulf War (1991) was suppressed by Iraqi troops, prompting the creation of UN safe havens which enabled the Kurds to set up a semi-autonomous region in the north. An air exclusion zone was also established, but there was further conflict with Iraqi forces and between the two main Kurdish parties in the 1990s. During the war in 2003, Kurdish fighters fought alongside US troops in the north, taking control of the northern cities and establishing a relatively stable administration in the area, which is now autonomous. The Kurdish Alliance, made up of the two main Kurdish parties, is the second largest party in the Iraqi legislature, holds the presidency and participates in the government.

The Shi'ites in southern Iraq also rebelled after the Gulf War and were brutally suppressed. The UN established an air exclusion zone over southern Iraq in 1992 to protect the population, but persecution continued until the Iraq War.

Since the end of the Iraq War in May 2003, there has been insurgent activity throughout the country, particularly in the Baghdad area and the predominantly Sunni-populated towns in the centre and west of the country. Initially the targets were foreign troops, Iraqi military and police, and foreign aid and reconstruction workers, but from early 2005 the attacks became increasingly sectarian in nature. The level of violence dropped after one of the main militias, the Mahdi Army, declared a ceasefire in August 2007, but rose again after government forces began an offensive in March 2008 against militias in Basra and parts of Baghdad. The approximate number of deaths as at March 2008 was estimated at: Iraqi civilians 75,000–81,000, US troops *c.*4,000, other coalition troops *c.*300.

POLITICAL SYSTEM

Under the 2005 constitution, the president serves a four-year term, renewable only once. The legislature elects the president and two vice-presidents (by a two-thirds majority) to form the presidency council, which nominates a prime minister to form a government; this must be approved by the legislature. The unicameral *Majlis al-Nuwab* (Council of Representatives) has 275 members, of whom 69 must be women, directly elected for a four-year term.

HEAD OF STATE

President, Jalal Talabani, *elected* 6 April 2005, *re-elected* 22 April 2006
Vice-Presidents, Tariq al-Hashimi; Adil Abd al-Mahdi

SELECTED GOVERNMENT MEMBERS *as at June 2008*

Prime Minister, Nouri Jawad al-Maliki
Deputy Prime Ministers, Barham Salih *(Economic Affairs);* Salam Zaubai
Foreign Affairs, Hoshyar al-Zebari
Defence, Gen. Abdel Qader Jassim
Interior, Jawad Kadem al-Bolani

EMBASSY OF THE REPUBLIC OF IRAQ

3 Elvaston Place, London SW7 5QH
T 020-7590 9220 E lonemb@iraqmofamail.net
W www.iraqembassy.org.uk
Ambassador Extraordinary and Plenipotentiary, vacant

BRITISH EMBASSY

International Zone, Baghdad
T (+964) 790 192 6280 E britishconsulbaghdad@gtnet.gov.uk
Ambassador Extraordinary and Plenipotentiary, HE Christopher Prentice, *apptd* 2007

BRITISH COUNCIL

c/o British Embassy, International Zone, Baghdad *(no postal service available)*
T (+962) 790 191 1971 W www.britishcouncil.org/iraq
Director, Karen Giblin

DEFENCE

Iraq's armed forces were officially disbanded by the coalition provisional authority in May 2003. Since then, new Iraqi security forces have been recruited and trained by coalition troops. As at April 2008 the Iraqi security forces numbered 494,800: army 163,500, navy 1,100, air 1,200, police 135,000 and other Ministry of Interior forces 194,000. The army has 77 main battle tanks and 352 armoured personnel carriers. The navy has 12 patrol and coastal combatant vessels at a base at Umm Qasr.

ECONOMY AND TRADE

The economy declined dramatically after the 1991 Gulf War because of damage sustained in the conflict and subsequent UN sanctions. Although the UN oil-for-food programme improved conditions from the mid-1990s, productivity and standards of living in 2003 were still well below pre-1991 standards. The Allied invasion in May 2003 damaged relatively little of the infrastructure but subsequent looting, insurgency and sabotage have undermined reconstruction and restricted productivity and foreign exchange earnings. However, government revenue has been higher than expected owing to high oil prices, the institutions needed to implement economic policy are now in place and a debt reduction programme has been arranged. Economic activity has improved with the recent reduction in the level of violence and although unemployment remains high (18–30 per cent), inflation has been reduced considerably.

Oil is Iraq's main resource and export, and production returned to pre-war levels in 2005. Other industries include textiles, chemicals and construction materials. The main market for exports is the USA (46.7 per cent in 2006) and the main sources of imports were Syria (26.5 per cent) and Turkey (20.5 per cent). Principal exports are crude oil (84 per cent), other crude materials, food and livestock. The main imports are food, medicine and manufactured goods.

Annual average growth of GDP – 1 per cent (2007 est)
Inflation rate – 20 per cent (2007 est)
Total external debt – US$56,310m (2007 est)

Trade with UK	*2006*	*2007*
Imports from UK	£77,449,000	£133,208,256
Exports to UK	£1,768,000	£3,717,154

COMMUNICATIONS

The transport infrastructure was severely damaged during the wars in 1991 and 2003 and reconstruction is slow. There are 2,272km of railways and 45,550km of roads, the majority surfaced. Railway services between Baghdad and Basra resumed in 2008. There are 5,279km of waterways, primarily on the Tigris and Euphrates rivers. The main seaport is Basra, and the principal airport is at Baghdad.

The telephone system was badly disrupted in 2003 but has been repaired and now has a greater capacity than previously. Mobile phone services are expanding rapidly. There were 1.5 million main lines in use and 36,000 internet users in 2005, and 10.9 million mobile phone subscribers in 2007.

EDUCATION AND HEALTH

Since May 2003 the country's education system has been reviewed, and over 2,500 schools have been refurbished. Primary education is compulsory.

Gross enrolment ratio (percentage of relevant age group) – primary 98 per cent; secondary 45 per cent; tertiary 15 per cent (2005 est)
Health expenditure (per capita) – US$58 (2004)
Hospital beds (per 1,000 people) – 1.3 (2000–5)

MEDIA

Once strictly controlled, the media has begun to flourish since 2003, although media workers have fallen victim to the insurgency. There are more than 200 newspapers and periodicals, many with an ethnic or religious affiliation, and private radio and television stations have also begun to thrive. The television and radio stations set up by the coalition provisional authority now form part of the publicly-funded Iraqi Public Broadcasting Service. The Iraqi Media Network operates the *Al-Iraqiya* television station and publishes the *Al-Sabah* newspaper. The *Al-Zaman* daily newspaper is based in London but printed in Baghdad and Basra. In the autonomous Kurdish areas, rival factions operate their own media.

IRELAND

Eire – Ireland

Area – 70,280 sq. km
Capital – Dublin *(Baile Átha Cliath)*; population, 1,059,000 (2007 est)
Major towns – Cork *(Corcaigh)*, Galway *(Gaillimh)*, Limerick *(Liumneach)*, Waterford *(Port Láirge)*
Currency – Euro (€) of 100 cents
Population – 4,109,086 rising at 1.14 per cent per year (2007 est)
Religion – Roman Catholicism (87 per cent), Protestantism (4 per cent) (est)
Language – English, Irish (both official), Gaelic
Population density – 62 per sq. km (2006)
Urban population – 60.4 per cent (2005 est)
Median age (years) – 34.3 (2007 est)
National anthem – 'Amhran na bhFiann' ['The Soldier's Song']
National day – 17 March (St Patrick's Day)
Life expectancy (years) – 77.9 (2007 est)
Mortality rate – 7.79 (2007 est)
Birth rate – 14.4 (2007 est)
Infant mortality rate – 5.22 (2007 est)
Death penalty – Abolished for all crimes (since 1990)
CPI score – 7.5 (2007)
Population below poverty line – 7 per cent (2005 est)

CLIMATE AND TERRAIN

The greatest length of the island is 486km, from Torr Head in the north-east to Mizen Head in the south-west, and the greatest breadth is 280km, from Dundrum Bay in the east to Annagh Head in the west. The republic has a central plain surrounded by hills and low mountains, including the Wicklow, Knockmealdown, Galty and Boggeragh mountains, and drained by the principal river, the Shannon (386km), which flows into the Atlantic Ocean. On the north coast of Achill Island (Co. Mayo) are the highest cliffs in the British Isles, 609m above sea level. Elevation extremes range from 1,041m (Carrauntoohil, Co. Kerry) at the highest point to 0m (Irish Sea) at the lowest.

HISTORY AND POLITICS

Settled by the Celts around 300 BC, Ireland developed a flourishing and distinct culture that remained largely intact until Christianity was introduced in the fifth century AD, after which Christian Ireland established itself as a centre of learning and high culture, a place of intellectual thought and spiritual refuge. Viking raiders began sustained attacks *c.*800 and established settlements from the mid-ninth century. In the 12th century, Anglo-Norman barons, invited to Ireland by a Gaelic king seeking allies, brought much of the south of the island under their own control, and Henry II of England declared himself Lord of Ireland in 1171. The island was unified under English control in Elizabeth I's reign. From the early 17th century, England began to promote the settlement of Protestant Scots in the north-eastern kingdom of Ulster, the final stronghold of Celtic power. This policy produced a long-standing antagonism between the north's Protestant and Catholic populations.

In the mid-17th century, widespread support in Ireland for the royalist side in the English Civil War prompted bloody reprisals from Oliver Cromwell, who invaded Ireland and reasserted English control in 1649–50. Catholic Irish support for the deposed Catholic king James II was defeated by William III at the Battle of the Boyne (1690) and penal laws passed in 1695 suppressed Catholic wealth and power. Popular discontent in the late 18th century and a rebellion in 1798 led to the abolition of the Irish parliament by the Act of Union (1800), which united Britain and Ireland. Simultaneously, Catholic opposition to English rule became increasingly organised with the formation of the Catholic Association, but agitation for home rule failed until 1912, when legislation was passed but did not come into effect because of the First World War.

By 1916, demands in some quarters had shifted from home rule to independence from Britain, and a rebellion broke out in Dublin. Known as the Easter Uprising, it was eventually repressed by the British but served to inspire Irish nationalists to contest the 1918 elections and, on gaining a majority of the Irish seats, to declare Irish independence under the leadership of Eamon de Valera. The British response was an attempt at violent suppression of the nationalists. The ensuing Anglo-Irish War lasted from 1919 to 1921 when the two sides negotiated the Anglo-Irish treaty, giving Ireland internal self-government as the Irish Free State, with dominion status within the Commonwealth, but leaving the six predominantly Protestant counties in the north part of the UK. This partition was not accepted by all nationalists and opposition developed into civil war in 1922–3. In 1937, the Irish Free State declared itself independent and sovereign, and in 1948 it left the Commonwealth and became a republic.

The status of Northern Ireland remained divisive, with the partition unacknowledged by the Irish constitution of 1937. The Anglo-Irish agreement in 1985 gave the Irish government a consultative role in the government of Northern Ireland, and in 1993 the Downing Street declaration set out a joint Anglo-Irish peace proposal to end the conflict in the north. The Irish government was involved in the negotiation of the 1998 Good Friday agreement; its proposals, including Irish recognition of the partition and the right of the north to self-determination, were approved in a referendum by 94 per cent of voters in the Irish Republic.

Ireland joined the EEC in 1973 and the eurozone in 1999. In a referendum in June 2008, the majority voted against ratification of the Lisbon treaty reforming EU institutions.

The 1997 presidential election was won by Mary McAleese, and she was confirmed in office unopposed in 2004. In the 2007 elections to the house of representatives, Fianna Fail (FF), led by Bertie Ahern (prime minister since 1997), remained the largest party but without an overall majority. The coalition government of the FF and the Progressive Democrats (PD) was expanded to include the Green Party. Bertie Ahern stood down as prime minister in May 2008 and was replaced as party leader and prime minister by Brian Cowen, previously the deputy prime minister, who appointed a reshuffled cabinet.

POLITICAL SYSTEM

Under the 1937 constitution, the president, *Uachtaran na Eireann,* is directly elected for a term of seven years, renewable only once. The bicameral parliament, *Oireachtas,* consists of the *Dail Eireann* (House of Representatives) and the *Seanad Eireann* (senate). *Dail Eireann* has 166 members, elected for a five-year term on a basis of proportional representation. *Seanad Eireann* has 60 members, who serve a five-year term; of these, 11 are nominated by the *Taoiseach* (prime minister) and 49 are elected, six by institutions of higher education and 43 from panels of candidates representing various sectoral interests.

Executive power is vested in the government, which is responsible to the *Dail Eireann.* The *Taoiseach* is appointed by the president on the nomination of the *Dail Eireann,* while other members of the government are appointed by the president on the nomination of the *Taoiseach* with the previous approval of the *Dail Eireann.* The *Taoiseach* appoints a member of the government to be the *Tanaiste* (deputy prime minister).

HEAD OF STATE

President, Mary McAleese, *elected* 30 October 1997, *confirmed in office* 1 October 2004, *sworn in* 11 November 2004

SELECTED GOVERNMENT MEMBERS *as at June 2008*

Taoiseach (Prime Minister), Brian Cowen
Tánaiste (Deputy PM), Mary Coughlan
Defence, Willie O'Dea
Finance, Brian Lenihan
Foreign Affairs, Michael Martin

EMBASSY OF IRELAND

17 Grosvenor Place, London SW1X 7HR
T 020-7235 2171
Ambassador Extraordinary and Plenipotentiary, HE David Cooney, *apptd* 2007

BRITISH EMBASSY
29 Merrion Road, Ballsbridge, Dublin 4
T (+353) (1) 205 3700 E dubembassy@internet-ireland.ie
W www.britishembassy.ie
Ambassador Extraordinary and Plenipotentiary, HE David Reddaway, *apptd* 2006

BRITISH COUNCIL
Newmount House, 22/24 Lower Mount Street, Dublin 2
T (+353) (1) 676 4088 W www.britishcouncil.org/ireland
Director, Tony Reilly, MBE

DEFENCE

The army has 82 armoured personnel carriers. The navy has 8 patrol and coastal combatant vessels at 2 bases. The air force has 11 utility helicopters.

Military budget – US$1,380m (2007 est)
Military personnel – 10,460: army 8,500, navy 1,100, air force 850

ECONOMY AND TRADE

In the past few decades Ireland's economy has been transformed from a mainly agricultural to a modern, export-led economy which has experienced strong growth since the mid-1990s; GDP per head is now the second highest in the EU. Government action to keep inflation low, improve labour skills and attract foreign investment means that light industry and services have overtaken agriculture, which now accounts for only 5 per cent of GDP and 6 per cent of employment; services contributes 49 per cent and industry 46 per cent of GDP, and the sectors account for 67 per cent and 27 per cent of employment respectively. Major industries include computer software, information technology, food and drink production, chemicals, pharmaceuticals and tourism. Although the Kinsale gas field off the south coast provides for some of its gas needs, and hydroelectric power is generated from the Shannon barrage and other schemes, Ireland still imports nearly half the fuel needed for power generation.

The main trading partners are other EU countries and the USA. Principal exports are machinery, computers, chemicals, pharmaceuticals, livestock and livestock products. The main imports are data processing equipment, other machinery, chemicals, petroleum and petroleum products, textiles and clothing.

GNI – US$191,300m; US$44,830 per capita (2006)
Annual average growth of GDP – 5.3 per cent (2007 est)
Inflation rate – 4.7 per cent (2007 est)
Unemployment – 5 per cent (2007 est)
Total external debt – US$1,841,000m (2007)
Imports – US$83,700m (2006)
Exports – US$104,900m (2006)

BALANCE OF PAYMENTS
Trade – US$37,649m surplus (2005)
Current Account – US$9,136m deficit (2006)

Trade with UK	*2006*	*2007*
Imports from UK	£15,941,700,000	£17,573,666,895
Exports to UK	£10,001,100,000	£11,216,180,536

COMMUNICATIONS

Ireland has 96,600km of roads and 3,237km of railways. There are over 950km of waterways, although these are used only by leisure craft. The main ports are Cork, Dun Laoghaire, Galway, Limerick and Waterford. The principal airport is at Dublin, with others at Shannon, Waterford, Cork, Killarney, Galway and Knock. There were 2 million main telephone lines in use, 4.7 million mobile subscribers and 1.4 million internet users in 2006.

EDUCATION AND HEALTH

Primary education is directed by the state, with the exception of several private primary schools. Education is compulsory until age 16.

Gross enrolment ratio (percentage of relevant age group) – primary 104 per cent; secondary 112 per cent; tertiary 58 per cent (2006 est)
Health expenditure (per capita) – US$3,993 (2005)
Hospital beds (per 1,000 people) – 5.7 (2000–6)

MEDIA

Irish broadcasting is regulated by a commission appointed by the Department of Communications. The main broadcaster is the state-run Radio Telefis Eireann (RTE), and the British satellite service BSkyB is widely available. There are three national newspapers: the *Irish Times, Irish Independent* and *Irish Examiner.*

CULTURE

Ireland has a disproportionately rich literary history given the size of the country. Irish poetry is among the oldest in Europe, with extracts dating back to the sixth century. Jonathan Swift (1667–1745) created one of the English language's finest satires in *Gulliver's Travels,* and Bram Stoker (1847–1912) one of the most enduring horror stories in *Dracula.* Ireland has produced four Nobel prize-winning writers: poets W. B. Yeats (1865–1939) and Seamus Heaney (*b.* 1939) and dramatists George Bernard Shaw (1856–1950) and Samuel Beckett (1906–89). The country's greatest literary icons remain Oscar Wilde (1854–1900) and James Joyce (1882–1941), one of the 20th century's most influential, if often inscrutable, novelists.

In the fields of sport and music, Ireland has maintained a strong interest in traditional forms. Hurling and Gaelic football attract passionate support, as do the more recently introduced rugby and football. Similarly, musicians adopting and adapting musical folklore, such as Van Morrison (*b.* 1945), Clannad and Enya (*b.* 1961), have achieved international success, alongside rock groups U2 and Thin Lizzy and boybands Westlife and Boyzone.

ISRAEL AND PALESTINIAN TERRITORIES

Medinat Yisra'el/Dawlat Isra'il – State of Israel

Area – 20,770 sq. km
Capital – Most of the government departments are in Jerusalem; population 736,000 (2007 est). A resolution proclaiming Jerusalem as the capital of Israel was adopted by the *Knesset* in 1950. It is not, however, recognised as the capital by the UN because East Jerusalem is part of the Occupied Territories captured in 1967. The UN and international law continues to reject the Israeli annexation of East Jerusalem and considers the pre-1950 capital Tel Aviv (population, 382,500) to be the capital.
Major cities – Haifa; Rishon Le'Zion
Currency – Shekel of 100 agora
Population – 6,426,679 rising at 1.15 per cent per year (2007 est). Since independence Israel has had a policy of granting an immigration visa to every Jew who expresses a desire to settle in the country. Between 1948 and 1992, 2.3 million immigrants entered Israel from over 100 different countries.
Religion – Judaism (79 per cent), Islam (16 per cent), Christianity (2 per cent) (est)
Language – Hebrew (official), Arabic, English
Population density – 326 per sq. km (2006)
Urban population – 91.7 per cent (2005 est)
Median age (years) – 29.9 (2007 est)
National anthem – 'Hatikvah' ['The Hope']
National day – 14 May (Independence Day)
Life expectancy (years) – 79.59 (2007 est)
Mortality rate – 6.17 (2007 est)
Birth rate – 17.71 (2007 est)
Infant mortality rate – 6.75 (2007 est)
Death penalty – Retained for certain crimes
CPI score – 6.1 (2007)
Population below poverty line – 21.6 per cent (2005)

CLIMATE AND TERRAIN

Israel comprises the hill country of Galilee and parts of Judea and Samaria, the coastal plain from the Gaza Strip to north of Acre (including the plain of Esdraelon running from Haifa Bay to the south-east); the Negev, a semi-desert triangular-shaped region, and parts of the Jordan valley, including the Hula region, Tiberias and the south-western extremity of the Dead Sea. Elevation extremes range from 1,208m (Har Meron) at the highest point to –408m (Dead Sea) at the lowest, which is the Earth's deepest depression. Average temperatures in Tel Aviv range from 14°C in January to 27°C in August.

HISTORY AND POLITICS

Regarded by Jews as their homeland since the Israelite settlement in Old Testament times, Palestine was conquered by the Babylonians, the Greeks and the Romans between the sixth and first centuries BC, beginning the diaspora. Conquered by Muslim Arabs in the seventh century AD, the area was contested between Muslims and Christians during the Crusades before becoming part of the Turkish Ottoman Empire in the 16th century. Zionist settlement in Palestine began in the 1880s and the British declared support for a Jewish homeland there in 1917 after capturing much of the Middle East from the Ottoman Empire during the First World War. Britain administered the area under a League of Nations mandate from 1918 to 1947, during which period Jewish immigration from Europe was encouraged, but this resulted in tension with the Arab population of Palestine, who had also been promised recognition for an Arab state by the British.

After the Second World War, the British mandate became increasingly untenable and they withdrew in 1947. The UN voted to partition Palestine, creating a Jewish and an Arab state, but the proposal was rejected by the Arabs, prompting the Jews to announce the creation of the independent State of Israel on 14 May 1948. This led to the first of a series of conflicts between Israel and neighbouring Arab states, creating a large number of Palestinian refugees. Further conflict occurred in 1956, when Israel attacked the Suez Canal zone; in 1967 (the Six-Day War) when Israel gained control of the Gaza Strip, the Sinai peninsula, the West Bank and east Jerusalem, and the Golan Heights in Syria (the 'Occupied Territories'); in 1973, when Egypt and Syria attempted to regain their lost territory; and in 1982, when Israel invaded Lebanon to drive Palestinian guerrillas out of Beirut, occupying a buffer zone in the south until 2000. Southern Lebanon was the scene of further conflict in summer 2006, when Israeli forces attempted to dislodge Hezbollah guerrillas. A peace agreement with Egypt was reached in 1979, as a result of which Israel withdrew from Sinai, and a similar agreement with Jordan in 1994.

From the 1960s, the Palestine Liberation Organisation (PLO), under Yasser Arafat, fought a guerrilla war against Israeli occupation of the territories taken in 1967, and in 1974 the PLO was recognised by the Arab League as the official representative of the Palestinian people. Talks between Israel and the PLO resulted in the Oslo accords (1993–5), which led to the establishment of the Palestinian Autonomous Areas in 1994. This appeared to end the popular Palestinian uprising *(intifada)* in the Gaza Strip and West Bank but the situation deteriorated from the mid-1990s, with further violence in the West Bank and suicide bombings in Israeli cities. These attacks evoked an increasingly hard line from a new Israeli government already critical of the peace accords. Implementation of the Oslo accords stalled and negotiations on outstanding issues reached deadlock. Palestinian frustration was inflamed by the visit of Israeli opposition leader Ariel Sharon to the Temple Mount in Jerusalem in 2000, triggering a second *intifada*. In 2002, Israel began building a security wall between Jewish and Palestinian areas to prevent suicide bombings despite international diplomatic and legal opposition to a *de facto* partitioning of the country. Plans to impose a permanent border unilaterally were announced in March 2006 but shelved a few months later.

In 2003, the USA, Russia, the EU and the UN proposed a 'road map' for peace which envisioned a two-state solution to the conflict. Progress stalled until the death of Yasser Arafat in 2004. Despite the Israeli goverment's action on a key issue – the evacuation and dismantling of Jewish settlements in, and military disengagement from, the Gaza Strip (achieved by September 2005) – no further progress has been made owing to the Israeli refusal to deal with the militant Palestinian government elected in January 2006, and the Palestinian power struggle in 2007 that led to the creation of rival administrations in Gaza and the West Bank. Israel resumed talks in 2007 with the Palestinian administration headed by President Abbas, but its tight blockade of Gaza has continued, worsening conditions for Gaza's residents.

In the March 2006 legislative election, the largest number of seats was won by Kadima, a centrist party set up in autumn 2005 by Ariel Sharon, the prime minister and former leader of the Likud party; after his incapacitation by a series of strokes in early 2006, Ehud Olmert became prime minister. As it lacked an overall majority, Kadima formed a coalition government with

Labour, Shas and the Gil; the Yisrael Beitenu party joined the coalition in October 2006 but left in January 2008. The 2007 presidential election was won by Shimon Peres. In July 2008, Ehud Olmert announced he would resign as prime minister and head of Kadima after September's leadership election.

POLITICAL SYSTEM
There is no written constitution; most constitutional provision is set out in the basic law on government; this was amended in 2001 to end the system of separate prime ministerial elections. The head of state is the president, elected by the legislature for a seven-year term, which is not renewable. The unicameral *Knesset* has 120 members elected by proportional representation for a four-year term. The prime minister is responsible to the *Knesset,* and appoints the cabinet, subject to the approval of the *Knesset.*

HEAD OF STATE
President of Israel, Shimon Peres, *elected* 13 June 2007, *sworn in* 15 July 2007

SELECTED GOVERNMENT MEMBERS *as at June 2008*
Prime Minister, Ehud Olmert
Vice Prime Ministers, Haim Ramon; Tzipi Livni *(Foreign Affairs)*
Deputy Prime Ministers, Elijahi Yishai; Gen. Shaul Mofaz; Ehud Barak *(Defence)*
Finance, Ronnie Bar-On
Interior, Meir Sheetrit

EMBASSY OF ISRAEL
2 Palace Green, London W8 4QB
T 020-7957 9500 W www.israel-embassy.org.uk
Ambassador Extraordinary and Plenipotentiary, HE Ron Prosor, *apptd* 2007

BRITISH EMBASSY
192 Hayarkon Street, Tel Aviv 63405
T (+972) (3) 725 1222 E webmaster.telaviv@fco.gov.uk
W www.britemb.org.il
Ambassador Extraordinary and Plenipotentiary, HE Tom Phillips CMG, *apptd* 2006

BRITISH COUNCIL
PO Box 3302, Crystal House, 12 Hahilazon Street, Ramat Gan 52136 T (+972) (3) 611 3600 W www.britishcouncil.org/israel
Director, Jim Buttery

DEFENCE
Israel is believed to have a nuclear capacity of around 200 warheads which could be delivered by aircraft or Jericho I and II missiles. The army has 3,501 main battle tanks and around 10,419 armoured personnel carriers. The navy has 3 submarines, 3 corvettes and 52 patrol and coastal vessels at 4 bases. The air force has 393 combat aircraft and 94 armed helicopters.
Military expenditure – US$11,030m (2006)
Military personnel – 176,500: army 133,000, navy 9,500, air force 34,000; paramilitary 8,050
Conscription duration – 24–48 months (Jews and Druze only; Christians, Circassians and Muslims may volunteer)

ECONOMY AND TRADE
Israel has a technically advanced market economy, having developed its agriculture and industry intensively since the 1970s despite limited natural resources. After a short recession in the early 2000s, structural reforms and tighter fiscal control were implemented, resulting in steady growth since 2003, increased foreign investment and a rising demand for exports. However, there is a high level of external debt and budget and trade deficits. These are covered by foreign aid and loans; the USA is the main source of economic and military aid and is Israel's main creditor, owed about half of its external debt.

Israel has developed a strong technology sector, central to which are the aviation, electronics, biotechnology and software industries. Other important industries include timber and paper, mineral and metal products, cement, chemicals, plastics, diamond cutting and tourism, which is reviving. The country is also an important producer of citrus fruits, vegetables, cotton, beef, poultry and dairy products. In 2007, service industries accounted for 67.6 per cent of GDP, industry for 30 per cent and agriculture for 2.4 per cent.

The main trading partners are the USA, accounting for 38.4 per cent of exports, Belgium and other EU states. Principal exports are high-technology machinery and equipment, software, cut diamonds, agricultural products, chemicals, textiles and clothing. The main imports are raw materials, military equipment, investment goods, rough diamonds, fuels, grain and consumer goods.
GNI – US$142,200m; US$20,170 per capita (2006)
Annual average growth of GDP – 5.1 per cent (2007 est)
Inflation rate – 0.4 per cent (2007 est)
Unemployment – 7.6 per cent (2007 est)
Total external debt – US$87,430m (2007)
Imports – US$50,300m (2006)
Exports – US$47,000m (2006)

BALANCE OF PAYMENTS
Trade – US$3,544m deficit (2006)
Current Account – US$8,546m surplus (2006)

Trade with UK	*2006*	*2007*
Imports from UK	£1,293,047,000	£1,242,728,509
Exports to UK	£985,634,000	£1,057,974,558

COMMUNICATIONS
Israel State Railways operates a network of 853km, serving Haifa, Tel Aviv, Jerusalem, Lod, Nahariya, Beersheba, Dimona, Ashdod and intermediate stations. There are 17,446km of roads, including 144km of motorway. A major road-building programme has been under way in the West Bank since 1992. The chief seaports are Haifa and Ashdod on the Mediterranean, and Eilat on the Red Sea; Acre has an anchorage for small vessels. There are 53 airports and airfields; the chief international airport is Ben Gurion between Tel Aviv and Jerusalem. The highly developed telephone system provides services for 3 million main-line users, 8.4 million mobile phone subscribers and 1.9 million internet users.

EDUCATION AND HEALTH
Education is compulsory between the ages of five and 16 and is free of charge. Youths aged 16–18 who are in work but have not completed their education can be given time off to finish their studies.
Literacy rate – 96.9 per cent (2004 est)
Gross enrolment ratio (percentage of relevant age group) – primary 110 per cent; secondary 93 per cent; tertiary 58 per cent (2006 est)
Health expenditure (per capita) – US$1,533 (2005)
Hospital beds (per 1,000 people) – 6.3 (2000–6)

MEDIA AND CULTURE

The Israeli Broadcasting Authority (IBA) is a public broadcaster operating television and radio services funded largely by a licence fee. It competes with two main terrestrial commercial channels and a number of satellite and cable stations. The radio sector features a number of commercial stations, but there are also a large number of unlicensed radio stations. There are five national daily newspapers.

The Israel Museum in Jerusalem houses the Dead Sea Scrolls along with an extensive collection of Jewish religious and folk art. Jerusalem has a vast number of historic sites, including the Church of the Holy Sepulchre, sacred to Christians, and the al-Aqsa Mosque, which stands on the Temple Mount.

PALESTINIAN AUTONOMOUS AREAS

Area – The total area is 6,231 sq. km. The area which is fully autonomous is 412 sq. km, of which the Gaza Strip is 352 sq. km and the Jericho enclave 60 sq. km
Capital – Although Palestinians claim East Jerusalem as their capital, the administrative capital has been established in Gaza City; population 479,400 (2005 est)
Major cities – Khan Yunis, Rafah in the Gaza Strip, Hebron and Nablus on the West Bank
Population – 3,634,585 (2003 est)
Religion – Islam (98 per cent (est)); the vast majority practise Sunni Islam
Flag – Three horizontal stripes of black, white, green with a red triangle based on the hoist (the PLO flag)
National anthem – 'Fidai, Fidai' ['Freedom Fighter, Freedom Fighter']
Death penalty – Retentionist

HISTORY AND POLITICS

Since 1967 the West Bank and Gaza Strip have been under Israeli occupation and until 1994 were administered by the Israeli ministry of defence. Frustration at continued Israeli occupation led to the start of a popular Palestinian uprising, the *intifada,* in 1987. Negotiations between Israel and the Palestinian Liberation Organisation (PLO) led to the signing of the Oslo accords in 1993. The accords established self-government in the Palestinian areas and set a timetable for progress towards a final settlement; the 1993 provisions were intended to be for a five-year interim period during which the final status of the West Bank, Gaza and Jerusalem was to be resolved.

The Oslo B or Taba accord, signed in 1995, provided for Israeli withdrawal from six West Bank towns and 85 per cent of Hebron; the extension of self-rule to most of the West Bank by 1998; the release of 5,300 Palestinian prisoners and the striking out of the demand for Israel's destruction from the PLO's charter. On 29 December 1995 an agreement was reached on the transfer of 17 areas of civilian power to the Palestinian National Authority (PNA) in Hebron.

The first areas, the Gaza Strip and the town of Jericho on the West Bank, were handed over to the PNA in 1994, and the six West Bank towns in 1995. The final status talks opened in 1996, but stalled in the late 1990s and broke down in 2001. Efforts to restart negotiations were hindered by the election of Israeli governments critical of the peace accords and the outbreak of the second *intifada.*

In 2003, the USA, Russia, the EU and the UN proposed the road map peace plan, a staged process leading to the establishment of an autonomous Palestinian state by 2005, which also sought political reforms in the PNA. Although endorsed by most parties, implementation of the peace plan made little progress because of the continuing *intifada,* internal power struggles within the Palestinian administration and the refusal of Israel and the USA to negotiate with the Palestinian president Yasser Arafat. This stalemate was broken only by the death of Arafat in November 2004 and the election of a moderate as his successor. Talks with Israel resumed but the peace process continued to be jeopardised by the Palestinian authorities' inability to rein in the violence of extremists, and it stalled in early 2006 with the victory of the extremist group Hamas in the Palestinian legislative election; Hamas refused to renounce violence, to recognise Israel's right to exist or to abide by existing peace agreements with Israel, which led international donors to cut off funding, causing increasingly severe hardship, especially in Gaza.

The 2005 presidential election was won by the Fatah candidate Mahmoud Abbas, who secured 67.4 per cent of the vote. In the 2006 legislative election, the Hamas movement, regarded internationally as a terrorist organisation, received 44.45 per cent of the vote and won 76 seats, forming the new government. Relations between Hamas and the more moderate Fatah, always tense, were often violent in 2006–7 and the power struggle between the two descended into a near civil war in June 2007 that left Hamas in control of the Gaza Strip and Fatah in control of the West Bank areas. On 14 June, President Abbas declared a state of emergency and dissolved the unity government appointed in March 2007, subsequently appointing a new, transitional government. Hamas politicians rejected the dissolution of the unity government and called for further talks; President Abbas has ruled out negotiations until Hamas restores Gaza to the control of the Palestinian Authority and recognises the transitional government. Talks between President Abbas and the Israeli government resumed in 2007 and a new target of late 2008 was set for the achievement of a final peace settlement.

POLITICAL SYSTEM

The president is directly elected for a five-year term. Legislative authority is vested in the unicameral Palestinian Legislative Council, which has one seat reserved for the president and 132 seats for members who are directly elected from party lists for a five-year term. The president appoints the prime minister, who appoints the council of ministers, which must be approved by the legislature.

SELECTED GOVERNMENT MEMBERS *as at June 2008*
President, Mahmoud Abbas
Prime Minister, Finance, Salam Khaled Abdallah Fayyad
Interior, Brig.-Gen. Abd-al-Razzaq Aqqab Mahmud al-Yahya
Foreign Affairs, Riyad Najib Abd-al-Rahman al-Maliki

PALESTINIAN GENERAL DELEGATION
5 Galena Road, London W6 0LT
T 020-8563 0008
General Delegate, Afif Safieh

BRITISH CONSULATE-GENERAL
PO Box 19690, 19 Nashashibi Street, East Jerusalem 97200
T (+972) (2) 541 4100 E british.jerusalem@fco.gov.uk
W www.britishconsulate.org
Consul-General, Richard Makepeace, *apptd* 2006

BRITISH COUNCIL
PO Box 19136, 31 Nablus Road, East Jerusalem 97200
T (+972) (2) 626 7111 W www.britishcouncil.org/ps
Director, Dr Ken Churchill, OBE

ECONOMY AND TRADE

The economy of the Palestinian areas has been severely affected in recent years by the *intifada* and Israeli security restrictions. The authority's main sources of revenue are the customs dues collected on its behalf by Israel and funding from the EU, the USA, Russia and the UN. These funds have been withheld since Hamas came to power in 2006, causing severe hardship and prompting fears of a humanitarian crisis; emergency aid, provided through channels that bypass the government, was resumed in late 2006, while the Hamas government sought alternative funding from other, predominantly Muslim, countries. The effects are more severe in Gaza than in the West Bank, where salary payments and provision of services have resumed since June 2007.

Most economic activity consists of small family businesses producing construction materials, textiles, metal goods and agricultural produce. The main exports are fruit and olives, and the main trading partners are Israel, Jordan and Egypt.

Annual average growth of GDP – 19.1 per cent (2002 est)
Inflation rate – 23.6 per cent (2002 est)
Population below poverty line – 59 per cent (2002 est)

Trade with UK	*2006*	*2007*
Imports from UK	£1,096,000	£876,220
Exports to UK	£882,000	£958,172

ITALY

Repubblica Italiana – Italian Republic

Area – 301,230 sq. km
Capital – Rome; population, 3,339,000 (2007 est). The Eternal City was founded, according to legend, by Romulus in 753 BC. It was the centre of Latin civilisation and capital of the Roman Republic and Roman Empire
Major cities – Bari, Bologna, Catania, Florence, Genoa, Milan, Naples, Palermo, Turin, Venice, Verona
Currency – Euro (€) of 100 cents
Population – 58,147,733 rising at 0.01 per cent per year (2007 est)
Religion – Roman Catholicism (87 per cent) (est). An estimated 14 per cent of the population is agnostic or atheist
Language – Italian (official), German, French, Slovene
Population density – 200 per sq. km (2006)
Urban population – 67.5 per cent (2005 est)
Median age (years) – 42.5 (2007 est)
National anthem – 'L'Inno di Mameli' ['The Song of the Italians']
National day – 2 June (Republic Day)
Life expectancy (years) – 79.94 (2007 est)
Mortality rate – 10.5 (2007 est)
Birth rate – 8.54 (2007 est)
Infant mortality rate – 5.72 (2007 est)
Death penalty – Abolished for all crimes (since 1994)
CPI score – 5.2 (2007)

CLIMATE AND TERRAIN

Italy consists of a peninsula, the islands of Sicily, Sardinia, Elba and about 70 smaller islands. The smaller islands include Pantelleria, the Pelagian islands, the Aeolian islands, Capri, the Flegrean islands, the Pontine archipelago, the Tremiti islands and the Tuscan archipelago. Most of the islands are mountainous.

The peninsula is also largely mountainous, but between the spine of the Apennines and the eastern coastline are two large fertile plains: Emilia-Romagna in the north and Apulia in the south. Italy is divided from France and Switzerland by the Alps, and from Austria and Slovenia by both the Alps and the Dolomites. Three volcanoes, Vesuvius, Etna and Stromboli, are still active. Elevation extremes range from 4,748m (Mt Bianco di Courmayeur) at the highest point to 0m (Mediterranean Sea) at the lowest. At the foot of the Alps lie the great lakes of Como, Maggiore and Garda. The chief rivers are the Po (651km) and the Adige, flowing through the northern plain to the Adriatic Sea, and the Arno (Florentine plain) and the Tiber (flowing through Rome to Ostia), which flow to the west coast. The climate is Mediterranean, with warm dry summers and mild winters.

HISTORY AND POLITICS

The Etruscans were the first people to control the Italian peninsula. Their empire flourished between the 12th and eighth centuries BC, but was eventually overtaken by the Romans. At the height of its power, the Roman Empire spread from Italy across Europe, Asia Minor and North Africa. Conquered and settled by a variety of invaders throughout the Dark Ages, Italy began to develop into a number of competing city states. These, with their powerful and wealthy merchant classes, became the locations (and provided the capital) for the Renaissance. Italian nationalists began to agitate for a unified Italy in the 19th century, culminating in the declaration of the Kingdom of Italy in 1861; unification was achieved by 1870. The major figures in Italian unification were Mazzini (1805–72), Garibaldi (1807–82) and Cavour (1810–61).

In 1923, the Fascist leader Benito Mussolini seized power and promised a firm rule to end political instability. He tied Italy into an alliance with Nazi Germany and thus led Italy into the Second World War on the Axis side. The Allied invasion of Sicily in 1943 led to a coup to depose Mussolini, who was eventually captured and killed by partisans in April 1945. Italy became a republic after the war; the king abdicated when the country's new constitution came into force and the monarchy was abolished.

A post-war economic boom lasted until the late 1970s, when high inflation and unemployment ensued. This was a time of serious civil unrest, with unions opposed to often corrupt governments, and extreme right- and left-wing groups conducting violent campaigns. In the early 1990s, there was a drive to reform the political establishment after links were exposed between the government and organised crime; many politicians were arrested. In 1993, the electoral system was changed from proportional representation to majority voting in 75 per cent of the seats, helping to remedy the political instability that had resulted in 45 governments in 47 years. Although governments have continued to be coalitions, those of the past ten years have generally lasted longer. Corruption in public administration and business remains a problem.

Italy was a founding member of the EEC in 1957 and of the eurozone in 1999. Its parliament ratified the EU constitution in April 2005.

The 2006 presidential election was won, after four rounds of voting, by Giorgio Napolitano. Romano Prodi's centre-left coalition government, in power since the 2006 election, resigned in January 2008 after losing a vote of confidence. In the ensuing legislative election in April, the People of Freedom party (PdL) won the most seats in both chambers, achieving a majority through the support of the Northern League and the Movement for Autonomy. The PdL and Northern League formed a coalition government under PdL leader Silvio Berlusconi (prime minister 1994, 2001–6).

POLITICAL SYSTEM

The 1948 constitution has been amended several times, notably in 2001 to provide for greater autonomy for the 20 regions in tax, education and environment matters. The president, who must be over 50 years of age, is elected for a seven-year term by an electoral college which consists of both chambers of the legislature and 58 regional representatives. The bicameral *Parlamento* comprises a chamber of deputies and a senate. The Chamber of Deputies has 630 members directly elected for a five-year term. The senate has 315 members directly elected by proportional representation on a regional basis for a five-year term, and a variable number of life senators, who are past presidents and senators appointed by incumbent presidents.

HEAD OF STATE

President, Giorgio Napolitano, *elected* 11 May 2006, *took office* 15 May 2006

SELECTED GOVERNMENT MEMBERS *as at June 2008*

Prime Minister, Silvio Berlusconi
Foreign Affairs, Franco Frattini
Defence, Ignazio La Russa
Economy and Finance, Giulio Tremonti
Interior, Roberto Maroni

ITALIAN EMBASSY

14 Three Kings Yard, Davies Street, London W1K 4EH
T 020-7312 2200 E ambasciata.london@esteri.it
Ambassador Extraordinary and Plenipotentiary, HE Sir Giancarlo Aragona, KCVO, *apptd* 2004

BRITISH EMBASSY

Via XX Settembre 80A, 00187 Rome
T (+39) (6) 4220 0001 E info@rome.mail.foc.gov.uk
W www.britain.it
Ambassador Extraordinary and Plenipotentiary, HE Edward Chaplin, *apptd* 2006

BRITISH COUNCIL

Palazzo del Drago, Via Quattro Fontane 20, 00184 Rome
T (+39) (6) 478 141 W www.britishcouncil.org/italy
Director, Paul Docherty

DEFENCE

The army has 320 main battle tanks, 200 armoured infantry fighting vehicles and 1,692 armoured personnel carriers. The navy has 7 submarines, 2 aircraft carriers, 3 destroyers, 12 frigates, 8 corvettes, 14 patrol and coastal vessels, 17 combat aircraft and 41 armed helicopters. The air force has 250 combat aircraft.
Military expenditure – US$30,630m (2006)
Military personnel – 186,049: army 108,000, navy 34,000, air force 44,049; paramilitary 254,300
Conscription duration – 10 months

ECONOMY AND TRADE

Italy has a diversified industrial economy, divided between a prosperous and industrially developed north and a largely agricultural and welfare-dependent south that has high unemployment levels. The growth rate has been low in recent years, with a budget deficit that has now breached the 3 per cent limit set by eurozone rules. Although inflation and unemployment rates have fallen, public debt remains over 100 per cent of GDP. The Prodi government, elected on a platform of improving the economy, has introduced short-term measures to promote growth and competitiveness but more extensive economic restructuring has progressed little because of the economic slowdown and opposition.

Tourism is the main industry. Other industries centre around manufactured goods, including motor vehicles, chemicals, electrical goods, textiles, clothing, footwear and ceramics. The services sector contributes 69.3 per cent of GDP, industry 28.8 per cent and agriculture 1.9 per cent. The main trading partners are other EU states, especially Germany. Principal exports are the products of the main industries, plus foodstuffs, beverages, minerals and non-ferrous metals. The main imports are industrial raw materials and energy and fuel.
GNI – US$1,882,500m; US$31,990 per capita (2006)
Annual average growth of GDP – 1.9 per cent (2007 est)
Inflation rate – 1.7 per cent (2007 est)
Unemployment – 6.7 per cent (2007 est)
Total external debt – US$2,345,000m (2007)
Imports – US$441,000m (2006)
Exports – US$416,000m (2006)

BALANCE OF PAYMENTS

Trade – US$24,624m deficit (2006)
Current Account – US$47,566m deficit (2006)

Trade with UK	*2006*	*2007*
Imports from UK	£9,194,100,000	£9,070,532,645
Exports to UK	£11,801,500,000	£13,118,231,551

COMMUNICATIONS

A 6,620km network of motorways *(autostrade)* covers the country but there are 484,688km of roads in total. There are 19,460km of railways; the main railway system is run by the state-owned *Ferrovia dello Stato.* In 2001, Italy and France agreed plans to build a 52km rail tunnel through the Alps as part of a high-speed rail link between Turin and Lyons; commissioning of the project is scheduled for 2012. Alitalia is the principal international and domestic airline. There are 132 airports and airfields, the major ones being at Rome, Milan, Naples and Venice, Palermo and Catania (Sicily) and Cagliari (Sardinia). The main seaports are Naples, Genoa, Livorno, Trieste, Venice, Palermo and Catania. In 2005, there were 25 million main telephone lines in use, 72 million mobile phone subscribers and 29 million internet users.

EDUCATION AND HEALTH

Education is free of charge and compulsory between the ages of six and 16. Pupils who obtain a middle school certificate may seek admission to any senior secondary school, which may be a lyceum with a classical or scientific or artistic bias, or an institute directed at technology, trade or industry, or teacher training. Courses at the lyceums and technical institutes usually last five years and success in the final examination qualifies students for admission to university. The universities at Bologna, Modena, Parma and Padua were established in the 12th century.

Gross enrolment ratio (percentage of relevant age group) – primary 102 per cent; secondary 99 per cent; tertiary 65 per cent (2006 est)
Health expenditure (per capita) – US$2,692 (2005)
Hospital beds (per 1,000 people) – 4.0 (2000–6)

MEDIA

Rai is Italy's public broadcaster and competes with a number of private broadcasters, including Mediaset, part of the media empire of prime minister Silvio Berlusconi. Rupert Murdoch's Sky Italia, launched in 2003, has control of the cable subscriptions market. The press includes many regional publications, as well as five national dailies, including *La Stampa* and *La Repubblica*, but readership is generally low, with television the primary source of news.

CULTURE

Florence, the capital of Tuscany, was one of the greatest cities in Europe from the 11th to the 16th centuries, and the 'cradle' of the Renaissance. Under the Medici family in the 15th century flourished many of the greatest names in Italian art, including Donatello (1386–1466) and Botticelli (1445–1510) and, in the 16th century, Michelangelo (1475–1564) and Leonardo da Vinci (1452–1519). Significant non-Florentine artists include Titian (*c.*1490–1576), Caravaggio (1571–1610) and Modigliani (1884–1920).

In music, Italy has produced a wealth of composers, including Monteverdi (1567–1643), whose *Orfeo* (1607) is the oldest opera still regularly performed, Vivaldi (1678–1741), Verdi (1813–1901) and Puccini (1858–1924).

Dante Alighieri (1265–1321) and Boccaccio (1313–75) were two of the earliest writers to compose works in vernacular languages. The works of the poet Petrarch (1304–74) and diplomat Baldassare Castiglione (1478–1529) had a strong influence on the writers of the English Renaissance. Notable contemporary writers include Dario Fo (*b.* 1926), winner of the Nobel prize for literature in 1997, and Umberto Eco (*b.* 1932).

Italian cinema has produced world-renowned auteurs such as Luchino Visconti (1906–76), Federico Fellini (1920–93) and Michelangelo Antonioni (1912–2007). Director Sergio Leone (1929–89) and composer Ennio Morricone (*b.* 1928) are famed for their work on spaghetti westerns.

Sport has been an integral part of Italian life since the days of the Roman Empire. Football is now the most popular sport and the country's national team have won the World Cup four times, most recently in 2006. Formula 1 motor racing also attracts significant interest and Ferrari has won more World Championships than any other constructor.

JAMAICA

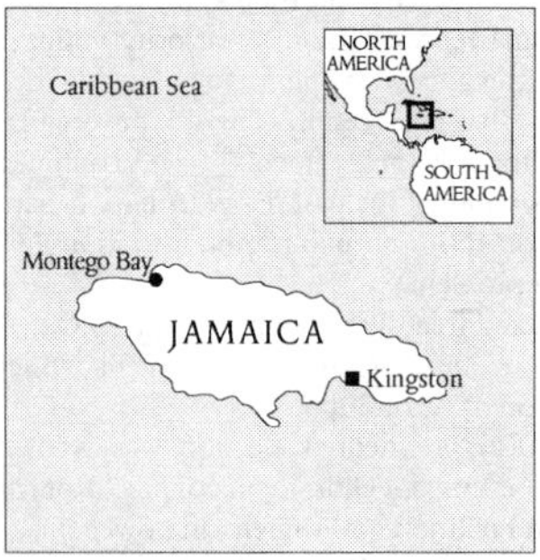

Area – 10,991 sq. km
Capital – Kingston; population, 580,000 (2007 est)
Major towns – Montego Bay, Portmore, Spanish Town
Currency – Jamaican dollar (J$) of 100 cents
Population – 2,780,132 rising at 0.78 per cent per year (2007 est)
Religion – Protestantism (64 per cent), Roman Catholicism (2 per cent) (est); 21 per cent has no religious affiliation
Language – English (official)
Population density – 246 per sq. km (2006)
Urban population – 52.2 per cent (2005 est)
Median age (years) – 23.2 (2007 est)
National anthem – 'Jamaica, Land We Love'
National day – 6 August (Independence Day)
Life expectancy (years) – 73.12 (2007 est)
Mortality rate – 6.59 (2007 est)
Birth rate – 20.44 (2007 est)
Infant mortality rate – 15.73 (2007 est)
HIV/AIDS adult prevalence – 1.4 per cent (2005 est)
Death penalty – Retained
CPI score – 3.3 (2007)
Population below poverty line – 14.8 per cent (2003 est)

CLIMATE AND TERRAIN

An island in the Caribbean Sea, south of Cuba and west of Hispaniola, Jamaica is mountainous, with tropical vegetation. Elevation extremes range from 2,256m (Blue Mountain Peak) at the highest point to 0m (Caribbean Sea) at the lowest. The climate is hot and humid, with average temperatures ranging from 25°C in January to 29°C in July.

HISTORY AND POLITICS

Jamaica was visited by Columbus in 1494 and settled by the Spanish from 1509. Captured by the British in 1655, it became a crown colony in 1865. Autonomy was achieved in 1947 and independence in 1962.

Post-independence politics has been dominated by the conservative Jamaican Labour Party (JLP) and social-democratic People's National Party (PNP). Relations between the two parties, often fraught, degenerated in the 1970s into violence that marred elections and political life for some years. Despite the current political stability, there is widespread poverty and lawlessness that is often connected to drug-trafficking.

In the 2007 legislative election, the PNP, which had been in power since 1989, was narrowly defeated by the JLP, which won 33 of the 60 seats. The JLP formed a government under Bruce Golding.

POLITICAL SYSTEM

Under the 1962 constitution, the head of state is the British monarch, represented locally by a governor-general. The bicameral parliament consists of the House of Representatives, with 60 members directly elected for a five-year term, and the senate of 21 appointed members, 13 nominated by the prime minister and eight by the leader of the opposition. The prime minister is the leader of the majority party in the elected chamber.

Governor-General, HE Sir Kenneth Hall, GCMG, *apptd* 2006

SELECTED GOVERNMENT MEMBERS *as at June 2008*

Prime Minister, Defence, Bruce Golding
Finance and Planning, Audley Shaw
Foreign Affairs, Kenneth Baugh
National Security, Col. Trevor MacMillan

JAMAICAN HIGH COMMISSION

1–2 Prince Consort Road, London SW7 2BZ
T 020-7823 9911 E jamhigh@jhcuk.com W www.jhcuk.com
High Commissioner, HE the Hon. Burchell Whiteman, *apptd* 2007

BRITISH HIGH COMMISSION

PO Box 575, 28 Trafalgar Road, Kingston 10
T (+1) (876) 926 9050 E bhckingston@cw.com
W www.britishhighcommission.gov.uk/jamaica
High Commissioner, HE Jeremy Cresswell, CVO, *apptd* 2005

BRITISH COUNCIL

c/o British High Commission
T (+1) (876) 929 6915 W www.britishcouncil.org/jamaica
Manager, Pauline Samuels

DEFENCE

The army has 4 armoured personnel carriers. The coast guard has 14 patrol and coastal combatant vessels at 3 bases.

Military budget – US$105m (2007 est)
Military personnel – 2,830: army 2,500, coast guard 190, air force 140

ECONOMY AND TRADE

The economy is weak owing to high interest rates, increased foreign competition, unemployment, growing internal and external debt, and hurricane damage in 2004 and 2007. Economic growth is hindered by the high level of violent crime. Tourism, the main foreign exchange earner, is particularly vulnerable. The economy depends on foreign aid and remittances from expatriates; remittances are worth nearly 20 per cent of GDP.

The economy is dominated by the service sector, which makes up 61 per cent of GDP; industry accounts for 34 per cent, and agriculture for 5 per cent. Natural resources include alumina and bauxite (extraction of which is the main industry after tourism), processing of agricultural produce and light manufacturing.

The main trading partners are the USA, Canada, China, Trinidad and Tobago and the UK. Principal exports are alumina, bauxite, sugar, bananas, rum, coffee, yams, beverages, chemicals and clothing. The main imports are food, consumer goods, industrial supplies, fuel, and parts and accessories for capital goods.

GNI – US$9,500m; US$3,560 per capita (2006)
Annual average growth of GDP – 1.5 per cent (2007 est)
Inflation rate – 7.1 per cent (2007 est)
Unemployment – 10.2 per cent (2007 est)
Total external debt – US$7,138m (2007 est)
Imports – US$5,310m (2006)
Exports – US$1,870m (2006)

BALANCE OF PAYMENTS

Trade – US$3,439m deficit (2006)
Current Account – US$1,197m deficit (2006)

Trade with UK	*2006*	*2007*
Imports from UK	£71,727,000	£62,727,564
Exports to UK	£131,481,000	£125,408,393

COMMUNICATIONS

There are several harbours, Kingston being the main seaport. The principal airports are at Kingston and Montego Bay. The island has 20,996km of roads, of which 15,386km are surfaced. The rail network is no longer in use. The number of fixed telephone lines has declined as mobile phone usage has grown; mobile phone density was over 100 per cent by 2006.

EDUCATION AND HEALTH

Education is compulsory to age 14.

Literacy rate – 87.6 per cent (2004 est)
Gross enrolment ratio (percentage of relevant age group) – primary 95 per cent; secondary 87 per cent (2006 est)
Health expenditure (per capita) – US$170 (2005)
Hospital beds (per 1,000 people) – 1.7 (2000–6)

MEDIA

The state broadcaster was privatised in 1997 and now operates as Television Jamaica Ltd (TVJ). It competes with a commercial and a religious broadcaster. The press operates independently and freely criticises the establishment.

CULTURE

Jamaica's cultural heritage includes a vibrant music scene. Kingston is widely regarded as the birthplace of reggae, and Jamaica is also the home of ska, dub and dancehall. The most significant Jamaican musician is reggae pioneer Bob Marley (1945–81); others include Jimmy Cliff (*b.* 1948) and Desmond Dekker (1941–2006). Closely connected to reggae is the Rastafari religious movement, which originated in the 1930s among descendants of slaves brought from Africa.

The most widely recognised literary figures are the Nobel prize winning poet Derek Walcott (*b.* 1930) and the novelist Jean Rhys (1890–1979).

JAPAN

Nihon-koku/Nippon-koku – Japan

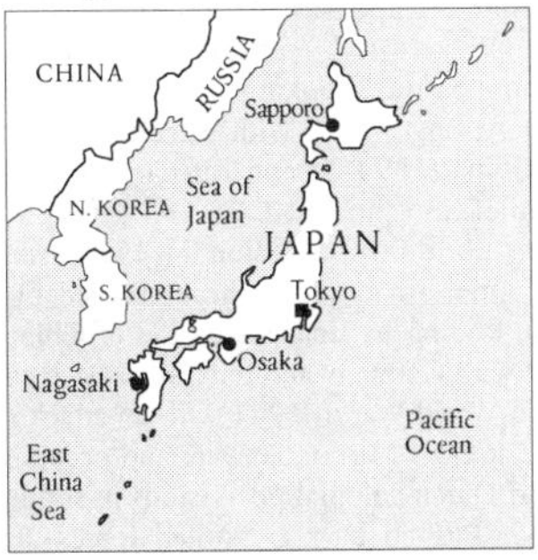

Area – 377,835 sq. km
Capital – Tokyo; population, 35,676,000 (2007 est)
Major cities – Fukuoka, Hiroshima, Kawasaki, Kitakyushu, Kobe, Kyoto, Nagoya, Osaka, Saitama, Sapporo, Sendai, Yokohama
Currency – Yen of 100 sen
Population – 127,433,494 falling at 0.09 per cent per year (2007 est)
Religion – Shintoism (78 per cent), Buddhism (71 per cent), Christianity (2 per cent) (est). Much of the population combines Shinto and Buddhist beliefs
Language – Japanese (official)
Population density – 350 per sq. km (2006)
Urban population – 65.7 per cent (2005 est)
Median age (years) – 43.5 (2007 est)
National anthem – 'Kimi ga Yo' ['Imperial Reign']
National day – 23 December (Birthday of Emperor Akihito)
Life expectancy (years) – 82.02 (2007 est)
Mortality rate – 8.98 (2007 est)
Birth rate – 8.1 (2007 est)
Infant mortality rate – 2.8 (2007 est)
Death penalty – Retained
CPI score – 7.5 (2007)

CLIMATE AND TERRAIN

Japan consists of four large islands: Honshu (or Mainland), 230,448 sq. km; Shikoku, 18,757 sq. km; Kyushu, 42,079 sq. km; Hokkaido, 78,508 sq. km and many smaller islands. Typically, the islands have coastal plains and wooded, mountainous interiors. The mountains running across the mainland from the Sea of Japan to the Pacific Ocean include a number of volcanoes, mainly extinct or dormant. Elevation extremes range from 3,776m (Mt Fuji) at the highest point to –4m (Hachiro-gata) at the lowest. Average temperatures in Tokyo range from 3°C in January to 27°C in August.

The islands are located on the boundaries of three tectonic plates and are prone to earthquakes; 20 per cent of the world's earthquakes occur in this area.

HISTORY AND POLITICS

A single empire had been established in what is now Japan by the ninth century AD. In the 12th century, the country was plunged into centuries of rivalry and conflict between different *samurai* (feudal warrior class) families, who were subdued and ruled by successive dynasties of *shoguns* (military overlords) nominally appointed by the emperor. Imperial control was re-established in 1868 after long periods of civil warfare.

Contact with the West was severely restricted until the 19th century, when the visit of a US naval officer, Commodore Perry, led to the Japanese opening their ports to foreign trade. Industrialisation followed and Japan adopted a Western-style constitution in 1889. Policies became more outward-looking and, in the case of foreign policy, more aggressive, with successful wars against imperial China (1894–5) and Russia (1904–5), and the annexation of Korea in 1910.

Emperor Hirohito's accession in 1926 ushered in a period of intense nationalism accompanied by a rise in militarism, leading to Japan's invasion of China in 1931 and a pact with Germany and Italy in 1940. Japan entered the Second World War in 1941 with an attack on the US naval base at Pearl Harbor, Hawaii, and occupied British, French and Dutch colonial possessions in south-east Asia in 1941–2. Pushed back by Allied forces in 1943–5, Japan surrendered after atomic bombs were dropped on Hiroshima and Nagasaki in 1945.

The Liberal Democrat Party (LDP) has dominated post-war politics, holding power continuously from 1955 until 1993. It returned to power in 1995, although usually as the main party in coalition governments. Following a year dominated by political scandals, the LDP and its coalition partners lost their majority in the upper house of the legislature in the July 2007 elections. This prompted the resignation of Shinzo Abe in September; he was replaced as prime minister by Yasuo Fukuda.

POLITICAL SYSTEM

The 1947 constitution established Japan as a constitutional monarchy with the emperor as head of state. Legislative authority rests with the bicameral Diet, which comprises the House of Representatives) and the House of Councillors. The House of Representatives has 480 members directly elected for a four-year term, 180 by proportional representation in 11 regional blocks, and 300 in single-member, first-past-the-post constituencies. It elects the prime minister from among its ranks. The House of Councillors has 242 members who serve for six years, with half elected every three years; unlike the lower house, it cannot be dissolved by the prime minister. Executive authority is vested in the cabinet, which is responsible to the legislature.

HEAD OF STATE

His Imperial Majesty the Emperor of Japan, Emperor Akihito, *born* 23 December 1933, *succeeded* 8 January 1989, *enthroned* 12 November 1990
Heir, HRH Crown Prince Naruhito Hironomiya, *born* 23 February 1960

SELECTED GOVERNMENT MEMBERS *as at June 2008*

Prime Minister, Yasuo Fukuda
Finance, Fukushiro Nukaga
Foreign Affairs, Masahiko Koumura
Defence, Gen. Shigeru Ishiba
Internal Affairs, Hiroya Masuda

EMBASSY OF JAPAN

101–104 Piccadilly, London W1J 7JT
T 020-7465 6500 W www.uk.emb-japan.go.jp
Ambassador Extraordinary and Plenipotentiary, HE Yoshiji Nogami, *apptd* 2004

BRITISH EMBASSY

No. 1 Ichiban-cho, Chiyoda-ku, Tokyo 102–8381
T (+81) (3) 5211 1100 E embassy.tokyo@fco.gov.uk
W www.uknow.or.jp
Ambassador Extraordinary and Plenipotentiary, HE Sir Graham Fry, KCMG, *apptd* 2004

BRITISH COUNCIL

1–2 Kagurazaka, Shinjuku-ku, Tokyo 162–0825
T (+81) (3) 3235 8031 W www.britishcouncil.org/japan
Director, Jason James

DEFENCE

The constitution prohibits the maintenance of armed forces, although internal security forces were created in the 1950s and their mission was extended in 1954 to include the defence of Japan against aggression. In the 1990s, legislation was passed permitting limited participation by the armed forces in UN peacekeeping missions and allowing them to enter foreign conflicts in order to rescue Japanese nationals. A revision to the USA–Japan defence cooperation guidelines agreed in 1997 permits Japan to play a supporting role in US military operations in areas surrounding Japan. In 2003, the Japanese parliament passed legislation approving the deployment of Japanese troops in Iraq to assist with post-war reconstruction; it withdrew its troops in 2006.

The Ground Self-Defence Force (GSDF) has some 900 main battle tanks, 790 armoured personnel carriers, 70 armoured infantry fighting vehicles, 20 aircraft and 85 armed helicopters. The Maritime Self-Defence Force (MSDF) has 16 submarines, 44 destroyers, 9 frigates, 9 patrol and coastal vessels, 80 combat aircraft and 99 armed helicopters at five bases. The Air Self-Defence Force (ASDF) has 280 combat aircraft.

Military budget – US$43,650m (2007)
Military personnel – 240,400: GSDF 148,300, MSDF 44,500, ASDF 45,900, central staff 1,700; paramilitary 12,250

ECONOMY AND TRADE

Japan has the third-largest economy in the world after the USA and China. Its rapid post-war economic growth, based largely on car and consumer electronics manufacturing, experienced a marked contraction in the early 1990s. Exacerbated by the 1997 Asian economic crisis, the recession lasted 14 years, causing unprecedented levels of bankruptcy, unemployment and homelessness and leaving the government with a huge public debt (194 per cent of GDP in 2007). Reforms introduced since 2001, particularly to the financial sector, public spending and private sector have improved economic growth since 2002. This has been boosted by the buoyancy of export markets and domestic business, and improved consumer confidence.

High-technology industries remain the mainstay of the economy, producing vehicles, electronic equipment, machine tools, steel and other metals, ships, chemicals, textiles and processed food. Financial services is also a major sector, supplying a global market. Agriculture is constrained by the mountainous terrain but intensive cultivation produces high yields, and there is a large fishing industry. The service sector contributes 73.3 per cent of GDP, industry 25.2 per cent and agriculture 1.5 per cent.

The main trading partners are China, the USA, South Korea, other Pacific Rim countries and the Gulf states. Principal exports include transport equipment, motor vehicles, semiconductors, electrical machinery and chemicals. The main imports are machinery and equipment, fuels, foodstuffs, chemicals, textiles and raw materials.

GNI – US$4,934,700m; US$38,630 per capita (2006)
Annual average growth of GDP – 2 per cent (2007 est)
Inflation rate – 0 per cent (2007 est)
Unemployment – 3.8 per cent (2007 est)
Total external debt – US$1,492,000m (2007)
Imports – US$580,000m (2006)
Exports – US$650,000m (2006)

BALANCE OF PAYMENTS
Trade – US$70,357m surplus (2006)
Current Account – US$170,437m surplus (2006)

Trade with UK	*2006*	*2007*
Imports from UK	£4,014,803,000	£3,761,703,115
Exports to UK	£7,983,607,000	£7,980,720,014

COMMUNICATIONS

Japan has a large merchant fleet, with 676 ships of over 1,000 tonnes in 2007. The main seaports are Tokyo, Osaka, Nagoya, Yokohama, Kobe and Kawasaki. There are 176 airports and airfields; the principal airports are at Tokyo, Hiroshima, Nagoya, Osaka and Sendai. There are 23,474km of railway track and 1,183,000km of roads. *Shinkansen* (bullet train) tracks are currently being expanded. The Seikan rail tunnel and the Seto Ohashi rail bridge link the four major islands. In 2005, there were 55.1 million fixed telephone lines in use, 101.7 million mobile phone subscribers and 87.5 million internet users.

EDUCATION AND HEALTH

Elementary education is free of charge, and compulsory at elementary level (six-year course) and lower secondary (three-year course).

Gross enrolment ratio (percentage of relevant age group) – primary 100 per cent; secondary 102 per cent; tertiary 55 per cent (2006 est)
Health expenditure (per capita) – US$2,936 (2005)
Hospital beds (per 1,000 people) – 14.3 (2000–6)

MEDIA

A public broadcaster, NHK, competes with four national terrestrial television companies and a growing number of satellite and cable providers. NHK also runs national radio networks. Satellite and cable television is widespread and digital broadcasting is increasingly significant. Around 80 per cent of the population reads a newspaper, creating huge markets for dailies such as *Asahi Shimbun, Nikkei Net* and the English language title *The Japan Times*.

CULTURE

The popularity of technology in Japan has not obliterated traditional culture, instead creating a mixture of the old and new. Traditional woodblock printing and imported Western cartoons have been combined into Manga, a form of comic book illustration. Animated Manga, known as 'anime', are broadcast on television, included in computer games and have spawned a number of internationally successful films, most notably *Spirited Away* (2002), the first anime film to win an Academy Award. Akira Kurosawa (1910–98), awarded an Oscar for Lifetime Achievement, directed *Rashomon* (1950) and *Seven Samurai* (1954).

Japan has responded with enthusiasm to imported sports such as football and baseball. The country co-hosted the 2002 football World Cup with South Korea, while the national baseball league has existed since 1936. However, sumo remains the perennial Japanese sport. Its roots are lost, but references to its earlier name, Sumai, exist in texts from the eighth century. The sport is immersed in ceremony, which has largely survived despite its huge commercial success.

JORDAN

Al-Mamlakah al-Urduniyah al-Hashimiyah – Hashemite Kingdom of Jordan

Area – 92,300 sq. km
Capital – Amman; population, 1,060,000 (2007 est)
Major cities – Ar Rusayfah, Az Zarqa, Irbid
Currency – Jordanian dinar (JD) of 10 dirhams
Population – 6,053,193 rising at 2.41 per cent per year (2007 est); Arab (98 per cent), Circassian (1 per cent), Armenian (1 per cent) (est)
Religion – Islam (92 per cent), Christianity (6 per cent) (est). The vast majority of Muslims practise Sunni Islam
Language – Arabic (official), English
Population density – 63 per sq. km (2006)
Urban population – 79.3 per cent (2005 est)
Median age (years) – 23.5 (2007 est)
National anthem – 'As-Salam a-Malaki al-Urdoni' ['Long Live the King']
National day – 25 May (Independence Day)
Life expectancy (years) – 78.55 (2007 est)
Mortality rate – 2.68 (2007 est)
Birth rate – 20.69 (2007 est)
Infant mortality rate – 16.16 (2007 est)
Death penalty – Retained
CPI score – 4.7 (2007)
Population below poverty line – 14.2 per cent (2002)

CLIMATE AND TERRAIN

Most of the country is a desert plateau, with a range of hills in the south along the edge of the Great Rift Valley and a hilly outcrop in the centre of the desert. The Great Rift Valley is an important topographical feature that separates the east and west banks of the river Jordan. Elevation extremes range from 1,734m (Jabal Ram) at the highest point to –408m (Dead Sea) at the lowest. Average temperatures in Amman range from 7°C in January to 26°C in August, although temperatures in the Jordan Valley have been known to reach an oppressive 49°C.

HISTORY AND POLITICS

The area was part of the Roman Empire and subsequently of the Byzantine Empire. It came under Arab control in the seventh century, and in the 16th century became part of the Turkish Ottoman Empire. With the collapse of the latter in 1918, the state of Transjordan was created and administered by the British under a League of Nations mandate. Transjordan became independent in 1946 and changed its name to Jordan.

During the first Arab–Israeli War of 1948, Jordan seized the West Bank and part of Jerusalem, but these areas were recaptured by Israel in the Six Day War of 1967, resulting in an influx of Palestinian refugees into Jordan; the descendants of these refugees now constitute the majority of the Jordanian population. Jordan attempted to expel Palestinian guerrillas from the West Bank in 1970–1, causing a brief civil war. Jordan recognised the Palestinian Liberation Organisation (PLO) as the sole representative of the Palestinian people in the Occupied Territories in 1974, but severed links with the PLO and expelled its personnel in 1986. Jordan formally renounced sovereignty over the West Bank and East Jerusalem in 1999, having signed a peace agreement with Israel in 1994.

The economy declined in the 1980s and internal stability became increasingly precarious. Riots in 1989 forced the government to initiate a process of political, social and economic reform. The country's first free elections under universal suffrage took place in 1989, and a ban on political parties was lifted in 1992. Real power, however, effectively rests with the king, with parliament amending or approving legislation originating with the monarch. Although support for Islamist parties has grown, the system favours people's tribal loyalties over their religious affiliation; consequently there has been little constitutionally expressed opposition to the peace treaty with Israel or the close ties with the USA, both generally unpopular.

The first local elections since 1999 were held in July 2007, followed by legislative elections in November. Over 90 per cent of the legislative seats were won by tribal leaders and other pro-government candidates; the Islamist share of the vote dropped to 5.5 per cent.

POLITICAL SYSTEM

The 1952 constitution provides for a constitutional monarchy with the king as head of state. The bicameral national assembly comprises a House of Deputies and a senate. The House of Deputies has 110 members, directly elected for a four-year term; six seats are reserved for women. The senate has 55 members, who are appointed by the king for a four-year term. The king appoints the prime minister, who chooses the council of ministers.

HEAD OF STATE

His Majesty The King of Jordan, Abdullah II, *born* 30 January 1962, *succeeded* 7 February 1999
Crown Prince, Hamzeh ibn al-Hussein, *born* 29 March 1982

SELECTED GOVERNMENT MEMBERS *as at June 2008*

Prime Minister, Defence, Nader Dahabi
Finance, Hamad Kasasbeh
Foreign Affairs, Salah Bashir
Interior, Eid Fayez

EMBASSY OF THE HASHEMITE KINGDOM OF JORDAN

6 Upper Phillimore Gardens, London W8 7HB
T 020-7937 3685 E info@jordanembassyuk.org
W www.jordanembassyuk.org
Ambassador Extraordinary and Plenipotentiary, HE Dr Alia Bouran, *apptd* 2006

BRITISH EMBASSY

PO Box 87, Abdoun, Amman 11118
T (+962) (6) 592 3100 E becommercial@nets.com.jo
W www.britain.org.jo
Ambassador Extraordinary and Plenipotentiary, HE James Watt, *apptd* 2006

BRITISH COUNCIL
PO Box 634, Rainbow Street, First Circle, Jebel Amman, Amman 11118
T (+962) (6) 463 6147 W www.britishcouncil.org/jordan
Director, Charlie Walker

DEFENCE

The army has 1,100 main battle tanks, 1,345 armoured personnel carriers and 235 armoured infantry fighting vehicles. The navy has 13 patrol and coastal vessels at its base at Aqaba. The air force has 100 combat aircraft and over 20 armed helicopters.

Military budget – US$1,590m (2007)
Military personnel – 100,500: army 88,000, navy 500, air force 12,000; paramilitary 10,000

ECONOMY AND TRADE

High levels of poverty, unemployment and government and foreign debt are long-term problems. In recent years these have been exacerbated by the conflict between Israel and Palestine and the impact of the 2003 war and post-war insurgency in Iraq, which is normally a significant export market. Since 1999, King Abdullah has implemented economic reforms, including a reduction of the public sector, privatisation and trade liberalisation. These measures have increased productivity and exports, started to attract foreign direct investment and won agreement to debt rescheduling from international donors. Even so, the economy is still dependent on foreign aid, of which the USA is the largest provider.

Jordan has no oil reserves of its own and few natural resources. Since 2003, several Gulf states have temporarily extended aid to Jordan in order to compensate for the loss of its usual oil supplies from Iraq. The country imports natural gas as well as oil but aims to become a net exporter of electricity via its national grid's links with those of Syria and Egypt. Jordan has also begun joint ventures with Israel and Syria to guarantee water supplies.

The service sector, including tourism, accounts for 85.8 per cent of GDP. Industry generates 10.5 per cent, from activities that include clothing, phosphate mining, fertilisers, pharmaceuticals, oil refining, cement, potash and light manufacturing. Agriculture, which accounts for 3.7 per cent of GDP, produces citrus and other fruit, tomatoes, cucumbers, olives, sheep, poultry and dairy products.

The main export markets are the USA and Iraq, and the main sources of imports are Saudi Arabia, Germany, China and the USA. Principal exports are clothing, pharmaceuticals, potash, phosphates, fertilisers, vegetables and manufactured goods. The main imports are crude oil, fabrics, machinery, transport equipment and manufactured goods.

GNI – US$14,700m; US$2,650 per capita (2006)
Annual average growth of GDP – 5.7 per cent (2007 est)
Inflation rate – 4.9 per cent (2007 est)
Unemployment – 13.5 per cent (2007 est)
Total external debt – US$7,483m (2007 est)
Imports – US$11,400m (2006)
Exports – US$5,170m (2006)

BALANCE OF PAYMENTS
Trade – US$6,272m deficit (2006)
Current Account – US$1,598m deficit (2006)

Trade with UK	*2005*	*2006*
Imports from UK	£186,270,000	£159,536,000
Exports to UK	£21,801,000	£19,796,000

COMMUNICATIONS

Jordan has 7,500km of roads; Amman is linked to Jordan's seaport at Aqaba, the Saudi Arabian port of Jeddah and the Syrian and Iraqi capitals by roads which are of considerable importance in the overland trade of the Middle East. The 505km of rail track includes the former Hejaz Railway, used mainly for freight between Amman and Damascus, and the railway carrying phosphate rock from the mines of al-Hasa and al-Abiad to Aqaba. There are 17 airports and airfields; the principal airports are at Amman and Aqaba. The telephone system is modern and growing, but fixed-line services are declining as mobile phone use grows. Mobile phone subscribers numbered 4.3 million in 2006, and there were 614,000 main lines in use and 796,900 internet users.

EDUCATION AND HEALTH

Literacy rate – 89.9 per cent (2004 est)
Gross enrolment ratio (percentage of relevant age group) – primary 97 per cent; secondary 89 per cent; tertiary 40 per cent (2006 est)
Health expenditure (per capita) – US$241 (2005)
Hospital beds (per 1,000 people) – 1.7 (2000–6)

MEDIA

There is strict media censorship, but legislation permitting imprisonment for anyone criticising the king or harming the country's reputation was repealed in 2003. Jordan Radio and Television, the state-run broadcaster, operates three terrestrial channels and a satellite channel. There are radio services in Arabic, English and French. Radio Fann is an entertainment station run by the armed forces.

KAZAKHSTAN

Qazaqstan Respublikasy – Republic of Kazakhstan

Area – 2,717,300 sq. km
Capital – Astana; population, 585,000 (2007 est); previously known as Akmola and Tselinograd. The capital was moved from Almaty in 1997
Major cities – Almaty, Oskemen, Pavlodar, Qaraghandy, Semey, Shymkent, Taraz
Currency – Tenge of 100 tiyn
Population – 15,284,929 rising at 0.35 per cent per year (2007 est); Kazakh (53.4 per cent), Russian (30 per cent), Ukrainian (3.7 per cent), Uzbek (2.5 per cent), German (2.4 per cent), Tatar (1.7 per cent), Uygur (1.4 per cent). The Russian population is concentrated in the north of the country, where it forms a significant majority, and in Almaty
Language – Kazakh, Russian (both official)
Population density – 6 per sq. km (2006)

Urban population – 55.9 per cent (2005 est)
Median age (years) – 29.1 (2007 est)
National anthem – 'Menin Qazaqstanym' ['My Kazakhstan']
National day – 16 December (Independence Day)
Life expectancy (years) – 67.22 (2007 est)
Mortality rate – 9.4 (2007 est)
Birth rate – 16.23 (2007 est)
Infant mortality rate – 27.41 (2007 est)
Death penalty – Retained
CPI score – 2.1 (2007)
Population below poverty line – 14 per cent (2007 est)
Gross enrolment ratio (percentage of relevant age group) – primary 105 per cent; secondary 93 per cent; tertiary 51 per cent (2006 est)
Literacy rate – 99.5 per cent (2004 est)
Health expenditure (per capita) – US$204 (2005)
Hospital beds (per 1,000 people) – 7.7 (2000–6)

CLIMATE AND TERRAIN

Kazakhstan stretches from the basin of the river Volga and the Caspian Sea in the west to the Altai and Tien Shan mountains in the east. The terrain consists of arid steppes and semi-deserts, flat in the west, hilly in the east and mountainous in the south-east (southern Altai and Tien Shan mountains). Elevation extremes range from 6,995m (Khan Tangiri Shyngy) at the highest point to −132m (Vpadina Kaundy) at the lowest. It includes the northern part of the Aral Sea in the west, and Lake Balkhash and Lake Zaysan in the east. The climate is warm and dry in much of the country, but can be Siberian in the north. Average yearly temperatures in the capital Astana range from −16°C in January to 24°C in July.

HISTORY AND POLITICS

Kazakhstan was inhabited by nomadic tribes before being invaded by Ghenghis Khan and incorporated into his empire in 1218. After this empire disintegrated, feudal towns emerged based on large oases and the nomadic tribes formed federations led by khans. The towns affiliated and established a Kazakh state in the late 15th century which engaged in almost continuous warfare with the marauding khanates on its southern border. After turning to Russia for protection in the 1730s, the Kazakh khanates formally acceded to the Russian Empire in the early 19th century.

The 1917 Bolshevik revolution in Russia was followed by civil war in Kazakhstan, which became an autonomous republic in the USSR in 1920 and a full union republic in 1936. Kazakhstan suffered severely under Stalin's policies of agricultural collectivisation and 'sedentarisation', which forced nomadic tribes to become farmers; around 1.5 million people died of famine or disease. Later Soviet rule saw the country used as a testing ground for nuclear weapons.

Growing nationalism in the 1980s and a reformist leader led to economic and cultural reforms in 1989 and a declaration of sovereignty in 1990. Kazakhstan declared its independence in December 1991, and became a founding member of the Commonwealth of Independent States. It entered an economic, social and military union with Kyrgyzstan and Uzbekistan in 1994, and an economic and military pact with Russia in 1995, when it achieved nuclear-free status. Privatisation and other economic reforms began in 1993, but despite these and considerable foreign investment, the country has serious economic, social and environmental problems, while its international standing is tarnished by political illiberalism and corruption.

Nursultan Nazarbayev, the reformist communist leader of 1989, became head of state in 1990 and was re-elected in 1991, 1999 and 2005; the 2005 election, in which he received over 90 per cent of the vote, was considered seriously flawed by the Organisation for Security and Cooperation in Europe (OSCE). A 2007 constitutional reform allows him to serve for an unlimited number of terms. He has been criticised for concentrating power in the presidency and suppressing political and media freedom.

In 2005, opposition parties joined together to form the For a Just Kazakhstan movement, led by Zharmakhan Tuyakbai, the former parliamentary speaker. In 2006, three pro-government parties merged with Nazarbayev's Fatherland Republican Party (Otan), which subsequently changed its name to Nur-Otan. Nur-Otan won every seat in the lower legislative chamber in the 2007 legislative elections, which observers said were better conducted than the 2004 elections but still did not meet international standards of fairness.

POLITICAL SYSTEM

The 1995 constitution was amended in 1998 to extend the presidential term from five to seven years, in 2000 to give President Nazarbayev special powers for life, and in 2007 to reduce the presidential term to five years, renewable only once, but exempting Nazarbayev from this restriction. The president is directly elected. The bicameral *Parlament* is composed of a lower house, the *Majlis,* and the senate. The *Majlis* has 107 members, 98 directly elected on a single constituency basis and nine seats reserved for ethnic groups; all serve a five year term. The senate has 39 members, of whom 32 are indirectly elected and seven are appointed for a six-year term, with half elected every three years. At the next renewal, the senate is to be expanded to 47 members. The president appoints the prime minister and other senior ministers.

HEAD OF STATE

President, Commander-in-Chief of the Armed Forces, Nursultan Nazarbayev, *elected* 1 December 1991, *confirmed in office by referendum* 1995, *re-elected* 1999, 2005

SELECTED GOVERNMENT MEMBERS *as at June 2008*

Prime Minister, Karim Masimov
Deputy Prime Ministers, Umirzak Shukeyev; Yerbol Orynbayev
Defence, Daniyal Akhmetov
Foreign Affairs, Marat Tazhin
Interior, Baurzhan Mukhamedzhanov
Economy, Bakhyt Sultanov

EMBASSY OF THE REPUBLIC OF KAZAKHSTAN

33 Thurloe Square, London SW7 2SD
T 020-7581 4646 E london@kazakhstan-embassy.org.uk
W www.kazakhstanembassy.org.uk
Ambassador Extraordinary and Plenipotentiary, vacant

BRITISH EMBASSY

6th Floor, Renco Building, 62 Kosmonavtov Street, Astana 010000
T (+7) (317) 255 6200 E britishembassy@mail.online.kz
Ambassador Extraordinary and Plenipotentiary, HE Paul Brummell, *apptd* 2005

RITISH COUNCIL
3 Republic Square, Almaty 050013
(+7) (327) 272 0111 W www.britishcouncil.org/kazakhstan
irector, Christopher Baxter

DEFENCE

'he CIS mutual defence treaty of 1993, to which Kazakhstan is a signatory, retains a common air defence orce, and Kazakh forces also take part in the CIS eacekeeping force on the Tajikistan–Afghanistan border. An agreement signed with Russia in 1995 provides for ventual reunification of the two states' armed forces. By 996, all nuclear warheads had been returned to Russia, lthough Kazakhstan retained 48 SS-18 intercontinental allistic missiles. Kazakhstan participates in the NATO artnership for peace programme. The army has 980 main attle tanks, 370 armoured personnel carriers and 1,430 rmoured infantry fighting vehicles. The navy has 12 atrol and coastal combatant vessels. The Caspian Sea 'lotilla, which Kazakhstan shares with Russia and Turkmenistan, operates under Russian command. The air orce has 163 combat aircraft and over 40 armed helicopters.

Military expenditure – US$1,183m (2007)
Military personnel – 49,000: army 30,000, navy 3,000, air force 12,000, MoD 4,000; paramilitary 31,500
Conscription duration – 24 months

ECONOMY AND TRADE

Economic reforms and privatisation in the 1990s have nabled GDP to grow by at least 8 per cent a year since 2002. This has largely been achieved through xploitation of the vast oil and natural gas reserves, articularly since the opening of export pipelines to Black Sea ports in 2001 and to China in 2006. As a result of the oom, the government has eliminated the budget deficit, ut it is also trying to stimulate growth in other industries o reduce dependency on oil. A fund was set up in 2001 o manage state finances and protect the economy from volatile oil prices. Despite these revenues, poverty is widespread, with 14 per cent living below the poverty ine in 2007.

Other economic sectors also perform well. Mineral esources are considerable and there is a significant ndustry mining coal, iron ore, manganese, chrome, lead, zinc, copper, titanium, bauxite, silver, gold and phosphates. A large and well-developed agricultural ndustry produces grain, wool, cotton and livestock as cash crops. The main industries are mineral extraction and processing and machine-building, especially construction equipment, tractors, agricultural machinery and electric motors. Services contribute 54.8 per cent of GDP, industry 39.4 per cent and agriculture 5.8 per cent, although agriculture employs over 30 per cent of the workforce.

The main trading partners are Russia, China, Germany and other EU states. Principal exports are oil and oil products (59 per cent), ferrous metals, chemicals, machinery, grain, wool, meat and coal. The main imports are machinery and equipment, metal products and foodstuffs.

GNI – US$59,200m; US$3,870 per capita (2006)
Annual average growth of GDP – 9.5 per cent (2007 est)
Inflation rate – 9.5 per cent (2007 est)
Unemployment – 7.1 per cent (2007 est)
Total external debt – US$92,080m (2007)
Imports – US$25,000m (2006)
Exports – US$40,500m (2006)

BALANCE OF PAYMENTS
Trade – US$15,515m surplus (2006)
Current Account – US$1,795m deficit (2006)

Trade with UK	*2006*	*2007*
Imports from UK	£208,754,000	£296,886,105
Exports to UK	£81,726,000	£199,878,123

COMMUNICATIONS

Because of Kazakhstan's size, long-distance internal travel is usually by air, and the country has 97 airports and airfields; the principal airports are at Astana, Almaty and Atyrau. There are extensive rail and road networks (13,700km of railways and 90,018km of roads), although the roads are concentrated in the more populous east. There are important ports on the Caspian and Aral seas which permit international trade while the Syr Darya and Irtysh rivers provide 3,900km of navigable waterways.

The telephone system is antiquated. Fixed-line services are being extended and there were 2.9 million lines in use in 2006. Mobile phone services cover most of the country and subscribers numbered 7.8 million in 2006. In the same year, there were 1.2 million internet users.

MEDIA

There are several public television broadcasters, including Kazakh Television and Khabar TV (which is broadcast in Russian). Popular newspapers include the government-backed *Kazakhstanskaya Pravda, Yegemen Qazaqstan* and the private *Karavan* and *Vremya.* There is also the English language *Almaty Herald.* Although freedom of the press is protected by the constitution, opposition and privately owned media are subject to censorship.

KENYA

Jamhuri y Kenya – Republic of Kenya

Area – 582,650 sq. km
Capital – Nairobi; population, 3,010,000 (2007 est)
Major cities – Eldoret, Kisumu, Mombasa, Nakuru
Currency – Kenyan shilling (Ksh) of 100 cents
Population – 36,913,721, rising at 2.8 per cent per year (2007 est); Kikuyu (22 per cent), Luhya (14 per cent), Luo (13 per cent), Kalenjin (12 per cent), Mukamba (11 per cent), Kisii (6 per cent), Ameru (6 per cent) (est)
Religion – Protestantism (46 per cent), Roman Catholicism (33 per cent), Islam (10 per cent) (est)
Language – English, Swahili (both official)
Population density – 64 per sq. km (2006)
Urban population – 41.6 per cent (2005 est)

Median age (years) – 18.6 (2007 est)
National anthem – 'Ee Mungu Nguvu Yetu' ['Oh God of All Creation']
National day – 12 December (Independence Day)
Life expectancy (years) – 55.31 (2007 est)
Mortality rate – 10.95 (2007 est)
Birth rate – 38.94 (2007 est)
Infant mortality rate – 57.44 (2007 est)
HIV/AIDS adult prevalence – 6.1 per cent (2005 est)
Death penalty – Retained, but not used
CPI score – 2.1 (2007)

CLIMATE AND TERRAIN

The coastal plain in the south-east and semi-desert terrain in the east rise to an arid interior of highlands and mountains in the centre and west. Elevation extremes range from 5,199m (Mt Kenya) at the highest point to 0m (Indian Ocean) at the lowest. The country includes part of Lake Victoria in the south-west and most of Lake Turkana (Rudolph) in the north. As an equatorial country, the climate is tropical, with average temperatures reaching 27°C in February and 22°C in June.

HISTORY AND POLITICS

Fossils of early hominids found in the Lake Turkana region suggest that the area was inhabited some 2.6 million years ago. Arabs and Persians settled on the Kenyan coast from the eighth century AD. The Portuguese gained control of coastal areas in the 16th century but Arab overlordship was reasserted in the 18th century.

European exploration of the interior began in the 19th century and in 1895, Kenya became part of Britain's East African Protectorate, becoming a colony in 1920. Demands for internal self-government by white settlers were rejected in 1923, but from 1944 a nationalist group, the Kenya African Union (KAU), was founded to campaign for African rights. The Mau Mau rebellion of 1952–6, intended to drive white settlers from African tribal lands, resulted in a state of emergency that lasted until 1960, when preparations for majority African rule began. Kenya became independent in 1963, and a republic in 1964. Kenyatta's death in 1978 brought Daniel arap Moi to power, where he remained until 2002, when he was barred from standing for re-election.

Kenya was a one-party state ruled by the Kenya African National Union (KANU) from 1964 (in effect, although not formally declared until 1982) until 1991. A multiparty system was reintroduced after violent agitation and international pressure in the early 1990s but KANU maintained its grip on power until the 2002 elections, which were won by the National Rainbow Coalition (NARC). After decades of stability, intercommunal violence and conflict over land and water rights have become more frequent since the 1990s, exacerbated by a rural food crisis since 2004 following persistent drought.

Despite the NARC coalition's anti-corruption electoral platform, once in government it made little headway against the endemic official corruption and in 2005 and 2006 several serving government ministers were implicated in corruption scandals. It is estimated that up to US$1,000m (£500m) of official funds were misappropriated in 2002–7, and some aid donors suspended funding to pressurise the government into addressing the problem.

The December 2007 legislative elections were won by the Orange Democratic Movement, led by Raila Odinga. The announcement that President Kibaki had won the simultaneous presidential election was greeted with accusations of electoral fraud by the opposition and triggered weeks of serious rioting that resulted in over 800 deaths. A political stalemate ensued until, after international mediation, a power-sharing agreement was signed in February 2008; under this, Kibaki remained president, the post of prime minister was created for Raila Odinga and, after several weeks of further negotiation, a coalition government was formed and took office in April.

POLITICAL SYSTEM

The 1963 constitution is still in effect, after a proposed new constitution was rejected in a national referendum in 2005.

The head of state is the president, directly elected for a five-year term; under the constitution, the president is also head of government, but the power-sharing agreement of February 2008 created the post of prime minister and assigned some of the president's powers to this post. The unicameral national assembly, the *Bunge,* has 224 members, of whom 210 are directly elected for a five-year term, 12 are nominated by the president, and two, the attorney-general and the speaker, are *ex-officio* members.

HEAD OF STATE

President and C.-in-C. Armed Forces, Mwai Kibaki, *elected* 27 December 2002, *took office* 30 December 2002, *re-elected* 27 December 2007
Vice-President, Home Affairs, Stephen Musyoka

SELECTED GOVERNMENT MEMBERS *as at June 2008*

Prime Minister, Raila Odinga
Finance, Amos Kimunya
Foreign Affairs, Moses Wetangula
Defence, Yussuf Haji

KENYA HIGH COMMISSION

45 Portland Place, London W1B 1AS
T 020-7636 2371 E kcomm45@aol.com
W www.kenyahighcommission.net
High Commissioner, HE Joseph Muchemi, *apptd* 2003

BRITISH HIGH COMMISSION

PO Box 30465, Upper Hill Road, Nairobi
T (+254) (20) 284 4000 E nairobi-chancery@fco.gov.uk
W www.britishhighcommission.gov.uk/kenya
High Commissioner, HE Robert Macaire, *apptd* 2008

BRITISH COUNCIL

Upper Hill Road, Nairobi
T (+254) (20) 283 6000 W www.britishcouncil.org.uk/kenya
Director, David Higgs

DEFENCE

The army has 78 main battle tanks and 62 armoured personnel carriers. The navy has 10 patrol and coastal combatant vessels based at Mombasa. The air force has 29 combat aircraft and 11 armed helicopters.
Military budget – US$355m (2006)
Military personnel – 24,120: army 20,000, navy 1,620, air force 2,500; paramilitary 5,000

ECONOMY AND TRADE

Kenya acts as a regional trade and finance hub for its landlocked neighbours. However, its own economy is weak owing to endemic corruption, low commodity prices, low investor confidence and the frequent suspension of international aid because of successive governments' failure to tackle corruption. These problems are exacerbated by occasional severe droughts. There are high budget and trade deficits, a huge foreign debt, widespread unemployment and extreme poverty, with 50 per cent of the population living below the poverty line.

The country is overwhelmingly agricultural, with 75 per cent of the population engaged in agricultural and horticultural production; this sector contributes 23.8 per cent of GDP. The world's fourth largest producer of tea, it also grows coffee, maize, wheat, sugar cane, fruit and vegetables. Natural resources include gold, limestone, soda ash, salt, rubies, garnets and hydroelectric power, which makes it self-sufficient in energy.

The industrial sector has grown over the past two decades, developing a manufacturing base in consumer goods (such as textiles) and agricultural products (such as dehydrated vegetables), as well as oil refining, commercial ship repair and the production of steel, aluminium, lead and cement. Tourism generates some US$400m (£200m) a year and has now recovered from the slump following terrorist bombings in 1998 and 2002. Industry contributes 19 per cent to GDP and the service sector 65 per cent.

The main export markets are Uganda, the UK, the USA, the Netherlands, Tanzania and Pakistan, while imports come mainly from the UAE, the USA, India, Saudi Arabia, South Africa, the UK, China and Japan. Principal exports are tea, horticultural products, coffee, petroleum products, fish and cement. The main imports are machinery and transport equipment, petroleum products, vehicles, iron and steel, resins and plastics.

GNI – US$21,300m; US$580 per capita (2006)
Annual average growth of GDP – 6.3 per cent (2007 est)
Inflation rate – 9.3 per cent (2007 est)
Unemployment – 40 per cent (2001 est)
Total external debt – US$7,715m (2007 est)
Imports – US$7,300m (2006)
Exports – US$3,400m (2006)

BALANCE OF PAYMENTS
Trade – US$3,875m deficit (2006)
Current Account – US$561m deficit (2006)

Trade with UK	*2005*	*2006*
Imports from UK	£192,299,000	£214,977,000
Exports to UK	£223,411,000	£255,875,000

COMMUNICATIONS

The Kenya Railways Corporation operates 2,778km of railways. There are 177,765km of roads, of which 63,265km connect the urban areas. The principal seaport is Mombasa, operated by the Kenya Ports Authority, and Lake Victoria also provides transport and trade routes. There are 225 airports and airfields; the international airports are at Nairobi, Mombasa and Eldoret.

The telephone system is antiquated and domestic services are unreliable, although business fares better. Mobile phone distribution has grown rapidly and subscribers numbered 6.5 million in 2006. There were 2.7 million internet users in 2006.

EDUCATION AND HEALTH

The state provides eight years of free primary education. A free secondary education programme was initiated in 2008.
Literacy rate – 73.6 per cent (2004 est)
Gross enrolment ratio (percentage of relevant age group) – primary 108 per cent; secondary 48 per cent; tertiary 3 per cent (2006 est)
HIV/AIDS adult prevalence – 6.7 per cent (2003 est)
Health expenditure – US$24 per capita (2005)
Hospital beds (per 1,000 people) – 1.9 (2000–6)

MEDIA

There are a number of television channels, including the state-run Kenya Broadcasting Corporation (KBC). Radio is a popular medium outside urban areas. There are six national newspapers that report a range of political views, including *The Daily Nation, The Standard* and *The East African*. Kenya has a more relaxed attitude towards press freedom than many of its neighbours. However, several recent incidents, such as the storming of the Standard Press offices by police, have caused concern.

KIRIBATI

Republic of Kiribati

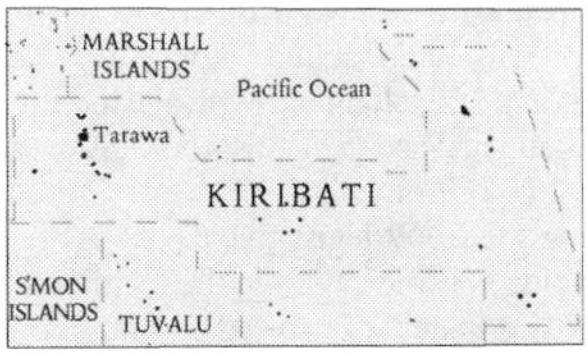

Area – 811 sq. km
Capital – Tarawa (Bairiki); population, 42,000 (2007 est)
Currency – Australian dollar ($A) of 100 cents
Population – 107,817 rising at 2.24 per cent per year (2007 est)
Religion – Roman Catholicism (55 per cent), Protestantism (36 per cent), Mormonism (3 per cent), Baha'i (2 per cent) (est). An estimated 5 per cent of the population is atheist
Language – English, I-Kiribati (both official)
Population density – 124 per sq. km (2006)
Urban population – 50.2 per cent (2005 est)
Median age (years) – 20.4 (2007 est)
National anthem – 'Teirake kaini Kiribati' ['Stand Kiribati']
National day – 12 July (Independence Day)
Life expectancy (years) – 62.45 (2007 est)
Mortality rate – 8.12 (2007 est)
Birth rate – 30.48 (2007 est)
Infant mortality rate – 46.02 (2007 est)
Death penalty – Abolished for all crimes (since 1979)
CPI Score – 3.3 (2007)

CLIMATE AND TERRAIN

Kiribati (pronounced Kiri-bas) comprises 36 islands, of which about 20 are inhabited: the Kiribati (Gilbert) group (17), including Banaba; the Rawaki (Phoenix) Islands (8); and some of the Line Islands (11), including Kiritimati (Christmas Island). They are situated in the southern central Pacific Ocean, crossed by the Equator; the area was also crossed by the international date line until 1995, when the government unilaterally moved the date line eastwards so that the whole country shared the same day. The atolls are coral, and few are more than 800m wide or more than 3m high, making the the country particularly vulnerable to rising sea levels. The highest elevation is 81m (on Banaba) and the lowest is 0m (Pacific Ocean). The climate is tropical.

HISTORY AND POLITICS

The islands were settled by Austronesian-speaking peoples in the first millennium BC and Samoans, Fijians and Tongans migrated there in the 11th to 14th centuries. British seafarers visited the islands in the 18th century. In 1892, the Gilbert (Kiribati) and Ellice (Tuvalu) Islands were proclaimed a British protectorate and in 1916 became a British colony, which subsequently incorporated the Line Islands and Phoenix Islands. During the Second World War, the islands were occupied by the Japanese and were the scene of fierce fighting between Japanese and US troops. Kiritimati (Christmas) Island became the site of British nuclear weapons tests in the 1950s and 1960s. In 1975, the territories separated and the Gilbert, Phoenix and Line Islands became independent as the Republic of Kiribati in 1979.

The republic faces a number of environmental problems. Open-cast phosphate mining left Banaba unfit for human habitation and the population was evacuated in 1945, now living on Rabi Island, Fiji; they have since been compensated for the environmental damage. The rise in the sea level owing to global warming threatens low-lying countries such as Kiribati, which reported in 1999 that two uninhabited atolls were completely submerged. In 2002, along with Tuvalu and the Maldives, Kiribati began legal action against the USA over its refusal to sign the Kyoto Protocol.

Following the 2007 legislative elections, the Pillars of Truth grouping was the largest in the legislature, although still fewer in number than the other independent members. The incumbent president, Anote Tong, was re-elected in the 2007 presidential election.

POLITICAL SYSTEM

Under the 1979 constitution, the president is head of state and head of government, and is directly elected for a four-year term, with a maximum of three terms; presidential candidates are selected by and from members of the legislature. The unicameral legislature, the House of Assembly, has 46 members: 44 members directly elected for a four-year term, an appointed representative of the Banaban community on Rabi Island, and the attorney-general. There are no formal political parties but some associations of politicians formed for elections have proved durable enough to be given names.

HEAD OF STATE

President, Foreign Affairs, Anote Tong, *elected* 4 July 2003, *sworn in* 6 July 2003, *re-elected* 17 October 2007
Vice-President, Teima Onorio

SELECTED GOVERNMENT MEMBERS *as at June 2008*

Internal Affairs, Amberoti Nikora
Finance, Naatan Teewe

KIRIBATI HIGH COMMISSION

c/o Office of the President, PO Box 68, Bairiki, Tarawa, Kiribati
High Commissioner (acting), Makurita Baaro

BRITISH HIGH COMMISSIONER

HE Roger Sykes, *apptd* 2006, resident at Suva, Fiji

ECONOMY AND TRADE

Since the phosphate deposits on Banaba ran out in 1979, the economy has been weak, dependent on coconuts, fish and tourism (over 20 per cent of GDP) as the main economic activities; tourism is hampered by remoteness, poor transport connections and the lack of funding, infrastructure and skills. Additional revenue comes from international aid (over 10 per cent of GDP), the sale of fishing licences, remittances from expatriates and monies from the trust fund established with phosphate mining revenues. A financial sector is being developed. The main trading partners are Pacific Rim countries and EU states. The principal exports are copra (62 per cent), coconuts, seaweed and fish. The principal imports are foodstuffs, machinery and transport equipment, manufactured goods and fuel.

GNI – US$124m; US$1,240 per capita (2006)
Annual average growth of GDP – 0.3 per cent (2005)
Inflation rate – 0.5 per cent (2005 est)

BALANCE OF PAYMENTS

Current Account – US$17m deficit (2006)

Trade with UK	*2006*	*2007*
Imports from UK	£177,000	£62,357
Exports to UK	£8,000	£11,039

COMMUNICATIONS

Air communication exists between most of the islands and is operated by the state-owned Air Kiribati. Flights to other Pacific states are provided by Air Marshall Islands and Air Nauru. There are 19 airports and airfields on the islands; the international airport is on Tarawa. Inter-island shipping is operated by the state-owned Shipping Corporation of Kiribati. The main seaport is Betio, on Tarawa. There are no railways, and only *c.*670km of roads.

The telephone system provides good national and international services. Mobile phones are not widespread.

MEDIA

Kiribati has no domestic television, so radio forms the islands' main source of communication. There is one state-run and one private weekly newspaper.

KOREA

Independent kingdoms in the Korean peninsula were united by the Buddhist Silla dynasty in AD 668, and a distinct culture developed. The Silla were succeeded by the Koryo dynasty in 935 and the Yi dynasty from 1395 to 1910, during which period Korea became a vassal of China and Confucianism replaced Buddhism. Contact with outside cultures was discouraged by successive Korean rulers until 1876, when Japan forced the country to open up to foreign trade. Subsequently, Japan, China and Russia competed for influence, with Japan emerging as the dominant state, formally annexing Korea in 1910.

Japanese rule ended with its Second World War defeat in 1945, when Korea was divided along the 38th parallel by the occupying armies of liberation: US troops in the south and Soviet troops in the north. The Republic of Korea was founded in the south on 15 August 1948, following a general election and the adoption of a constitution. The Democratic People's Republic of Korea was established in the north on 9 September 1948; a Supreme People's Soviet was elected and a Soviet-style constitution was adopted.

UN plans to reunify the country after nationwide elections in 1950 were defied by North Korea. After elections in the south, South Korea declared its independence, which prompted its invasion by North Korea. A multinational UN force, with a large US contingent, intervened and pushed the North Korean troops back to the Chinese frontier. This brought China into the war in support of North Korea and their combined forces pushed back the UN troops, occupying Seoul. A UN counter-attack retook all territory south of the 28th parallel by the time an armistice was signed in 1953; a demilitarised border zone was established. The war devastated the entire peninsula, particularly North Korea, and left over two million people dead.

Reunification talks between North and South Korea have taken place intermittently; they were broken off by North Korea in 1980 but further talks took place in 1990, 1997–9 and 2000. A non-aggression pact was signed in 1991 and an agreement on mutual inspection of nuclear facilities in 1992. The 2000 talks ended with a joint declaration under which both sides agreed to work independently for reunification and to recognise the common elements in each side's proposals for federation-confederation. Since the declaration, meetings have become more frequent, although tensions remain, primarily over North Korea's nuclear programme; high-level talks were suspended in 2006–7 over North Korea's testing of a nuclear missile. South Korea is concerned about the prospect of a reduction in US troop numbers in the demilitarised zone.

DEMOCRATIC PEOPLE'S REPUBLIC OF KOREA

Choson-minjujuui-inmin-konghwaguk – Democratic People's Republic of Korea

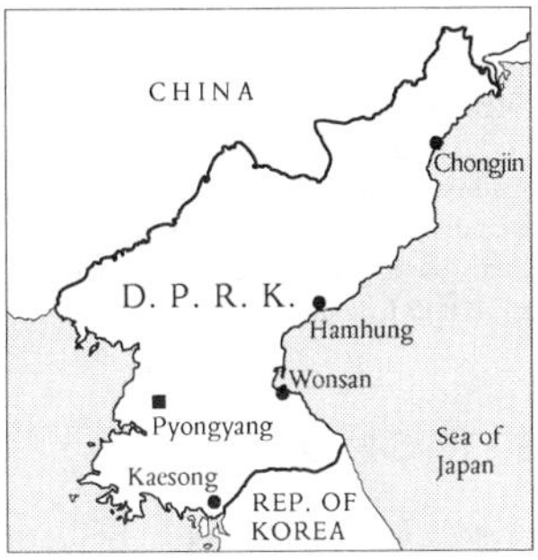

Area – 120,540 sq. km
Capital – Pyongyang; population, 3,300,000 (2007 est)
Major cities – Chongjin, Hamhung, Hungnam, Kaesong, Nampo, Wonsan
Currency – Won of 100 chon
Population – 23,301,725 rising at 0.79 per cent per year (2007 est)
Religion – Religious activity is almost non-existent outside government-sponsored religious groups. Historically, the main religions were Buddhism and Confucianism
Language – Korean (official)
Population density – 197 per sq. km (2006)
Urban population – 61.7 per cent (2005 est)
Median age (years) – 32.4 (2007 est)
National anthem – 'Aegukka' ['The Patriotic Song']
National day – 9 September (Founding of the Democratic People's Republic of Korea)
Life expectancy (years) – 71.92 (2007 est)
Mortality rate – 7.21 (2007 est)
Birth rate – 15.06 (2007 est)
Infant mortality rate – 22.56 (2007 est)
Death penalty – Retained
Hospital beds (per 1,000 people) – 13.2 (2000–6)

CLIMATE AND TERRAIN

The republic occupies the northern half of the Korean peninsula. A wide coastal plain in the west rises to mountains divided by deep valleys in the interior. Elevation extremes range from 2,744m (Paektu-san) at the highest point to 0m (Sea of Japan) at the lowest. The climate is more extreme than in South Korea. Temperatures in January can fall as far as −10°C in Pyongyang. The average July temperature is 25°C.

HISTORY AND POLITICS

After the Korean war ended in 1953, Kim Il-sung continued the process of Soviet-style reform that began with land reform and nationalisation in 1946. He also developed *Juche* (self-reliance), an ideology demanding total economic independence. North Korea pursued an isolationist foreign policy for several decades, only signing a mutual assistance treaty with China in 1961 and improving relations with the USSR in 1985. It established diplomatic contacts with South Korea and Japan in 1990, raising hopes that it was abandoning its isolationism, but it remains a secretive, closed country under tight Communist Party control.

This situation has had serious consequences domestically and internationally. The economy has suffered a long decline, and a series of natural disasters in the 1990s caused severe famine, obliging the government to request international aid. It is estimated that two million people have died since the 1990s as a result of the acute food shortages, which continue despite international food and fuel aid.

There has been international concern over North Korea's attempts to develop a nuclear capability. In 1994, North Korea agreed to freeze its nuclear development programme in return for US oil shipments and assistance in building two nuclear power stations. However, in 2002 it became clear that it had reactivated the programme, and it subsequently expelled international nuclear inspectors. The following year the government withdrew from the nuclear non-proliferation treaty and in 2006 it test-fired several ballistic missiles (July) and claimed to have tested a nuclear weapon (October), prompting the UN security council to impose weapons and financial sanctions. Six-nation talks to resolve the nuclear issue began in 2003; two denuclearisation agreements were concluded in 2007 with which North Korea had partially complied by spring 2008.

Kim Il-sung died in 1994. His son, Kim Jong-il, became chairman of the National Defence Commission, designated as the highest post of the state, and general secretary of the Korean Workers' Party in 1997. The next legislative elections are due in August 2008.

POLITICAL SYSTEM

The (communist) Korean Workers' Party, which was founded in 1946 by Kim Il-sung, is the only permitted political party. However, political control and leadership is maintained by the cult of personality created by Kim Il-sung and continued by his son and successor Kim Jong-il.

The 1972 constitution was amended in 1998 to designate leading state posts; it made Kim Il-sung the Eternal President and the chairmanship of the National Defence Commission, held by Kim Jong-il, the highest post in the state, while providing that the chairman of the

Presidium of the Supreme People's Assembly would represent the state on formal occasions. There is a unicameral legislature, the Supreme People's Assembly, which has 687 members directly elected from a single list of candidates for a five-year term. The assembly elects a presidium and the premier, appointing the government on the recommendation of the premier. The Central People's Committee, which is also elected by the assembly, directs the administrative council (government), which implements the policy formulated by the committee.

HEAD OF STATE
Eternal President, Kim Il-sung (deceased)
Chair of the National Defence Commission, Kim Jong-il
Chair of the Presidium of the Supreme People's Assembly, Kim Yong-nam

SELECTED GOVERNMENT MEMBERS *as at June 2008*
Premier, Kim Yong-il
Deputy Premiers, Kwak Pon-ki, Ro Tu-chol, Chon Sung-hun; Thae Jong-su
Finance, Mun Il-bong
Foreign Affairs, Pak Ui-chun

EMBASSY OF THE DEMOCRATIC PEOPLE'S REPUBLIC OF KOREA
73 Gunnersbury Avenue, London W5 4LP
T 020-8992 4965
Ambassador Extraordinary and Plenipotentiary, HE Ja Song-nam, *apptd* 2007

BRITISH EMBASSY
Munsu Dong, Pyongyang
T (+850) (2) 381 7980
Ambassador Extraordinary and Plenipotentiary, HE John Everard, *apptd* 2006

DEFENCE

The army has about 3,500 main battle tanks and over 2,500 armoured personnel carriers. The navy has 63 submarines, 3 frigates, 5 corvettes and over 335 patrol and coastal vessels at 15 bases. The air force has 590 combat aircraft and 24 armed helicopters.
Military budget – US$2,300m (2006 est)
Military personnel – 1,106,000: army 950,000, navy 46,000, air force 110,000; paramilitary 189,000
Conscription duration – 3–12 years

ECONOMY AND TRADE

Although North Korea is rich in natural resources and Japan developed heavy industry during its years of occupation in the first half of the 20th century, the economy is in a critical state. Internal mismanagement and underinvestment, low export levels and increasing debt sent the economy into a long decline that was compounded by the collapse of Soviet communism in the 1990s.

Severe floods and a series of disastrous harvests in the 1990s brought famine, and the centrally planned economy has not been able to pull North Korea out of its desperate condition. Lack of arable land, collective farming and chronic shortages of fuel and fertilisers hamper food production even with better weather conditions. Massive amounts of food aid since the mid-1990s from bilateral donors and international agencies have averted famine but malnutrition is widespread. A relaxation of restrictions on farmers' markets and private farming in 2003 reduced shortages but these measures were partially rescinded in 2005 and a centralised rationing system was reinstated. Industrial output is centred on coal, steel, chemicals and machine tools, but antiquated machinery and fuel shortages have limited capacity to a fraction of pre-1989 levels.

The main trading partners are China, South Korea, Thailand and Russia. Principal exports are minerals, metallurgical products, armaments, textiles, and agricultural and fish products. The main imports are petroleum, coal, machinery and equipment, textiles and grain.
Annual average growth of GDP – 1.6 per cent (2006 est)
Imports – US$431m (2002)
Exports – US$298m (2002)

BALANCE OF PAYMENTS
Trade – US$1,280m deficit (2006)
Current Account – US$82m deficit (2002)

Trade with UK	*2006*	*2007*
Imports from UK	£343,000	£288,083
Exports to UK	£9,278,000	£7,531,688

COMMUNICATIONS

North Korea has 5,235km of railways and 25,554km of roads, although few are surfaced. There are some 2,250km of waterways but these are navigable only by small craft. The main seaports are Chongjin, Nampo and Wonsan. There are 77 airports and airfields; the principal airport is at Pyongyang.

MEDIA

There are no independent media in North Korea. All televisions and radios are pre-tuned to government stations which broadcast state propaganda. Anyone found listening to foreign broadcasts is harshly punished. In 2007 Reporters Without Borders rated the country as the second worst in the world for press freedom. There are four national papers in circulation, including *Rodong Sinmun* and *Minju Choson.*

REPUBLIC OF KOREA

Taehan-min'guk – Republic of Korea

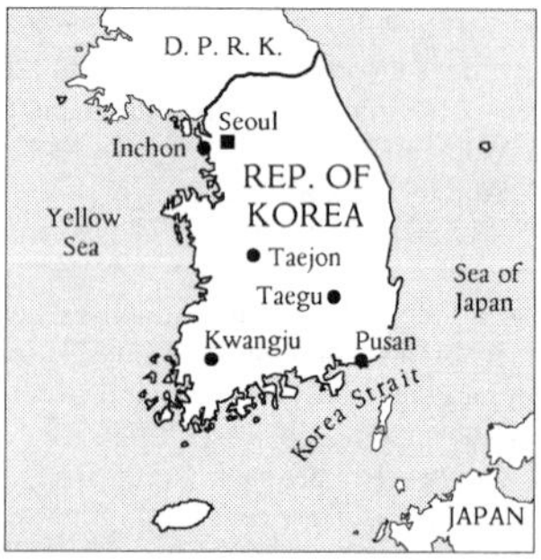

Area – 98,480 sq. km
Capital – Seoul; population, 9,796,000 (2007)
Major cities – Inchon, Kwangju, Pusan, Songnam, Suwon, Taegu, Taejon
Currency – Won of 100 jeon
Population – 49,044,790 rising at 0.39 per cent per year (2007 est)

Religion – Buddhism (22 per cent), Protestantism (18 per cent), Roman Catholicism (11 per cent) (est). An estimated 45 per cent of the population is atheist
Language – Korean (official), English
Population density – 490 per sq. km (2006)
Urban population – 80.8 per cent (2005 est)
Median age (years) – 35.8 (2007 est)
National anthem – 'Aegukka' ['The Patriotic Song']
National day – 15 August (Liberation Day)
Life expectancy (years) – 77.23 (2007 est)
Mortality rate – 5.99 (2007 est)
Birth rate – 9.93 (2007 est)
Infant mortality rate – 6.05 (2007 est)
Death penalty – Retained, but not used
CPI score – 5.1 (2007)

CLIMATE AND TERRAIN

The country occupies the southern part of the mountainous Korean peninsula, with highlands and mountains accounting for around 70 per cent of the land area. Elevation extremes range from 1,950m (Halla-san) at the highest point to 0m (Sea of Japan) at the lowest. The climate is temperate, although winters are very cold for the country's latitude. Temperatures in Seoul range from from −5°C in January to 29°C in July. The rainy season runs from June to September.

HISTORY AND POLITICS

Since 1948, South Korea has experienced mostly authoritarian, often military, rule and great industrial development. Syngman Rhee, president from 1948, resigned in 1960 in the face of popular protests at corruption and electoral fraud. A military coup in 1961 brought General Park Chung-hee to power and he instigated a programme of industrial development; by 1979 Korea was a leading shipbuilding nation and producer of electronic goods. Park's repressive regime introduced military law in 1972, and he was assassinated in 1979.

Following riots against the interim government, General Chun Do-hwan assumed power. Pro-democracy agitation in the mid-1980s led to constitutional changes in 1987 and the first multiparty elections in 1988, but despite the anti-corruption campaign of the new democratically elected president Roh Tae-woo, politics continued to be plagued by allegations of corruption and fraud, and was subject to military influence. The first civilian president and the first wholly civilian government since 1961 were appointed as recently as 1993. Kim Dae-jung's inauguration as president in 1998 saw the adoption of the 'sunshine policy' of engagement with North Korea.

The presidential election in December 2007 was won by Lee Myung-bak, the Grand National Party (GNP) candidate. In the 2008 legislative election, the GNP won a majority of seats in the legislature.

POLITICAL SYSTEM

A new constitution was adopted when the Sixth Republic was inaugurated in 1988. Under this, the president is directly elected for a five-year term, which is not renewable. He appoints the prime minister with the approval of the legislature and members of the state council (cabinet) on the recommendation of the prime minister. The president is also empowered to take wide-ranging measures in an emergency, including the declaration of martial law, but must obtain the agreement of the legislature. The unicameral national assembly has 299 members who are directly elected for a four-year term.

HEAD OF STATE

President, Lee Myung-bak, *elected* 19 December 2007, *sworn in* 25 February 2008

SELECTED GOVERNMENT MEMBERS *as at June 2008*

Prime Minister, Han Seung-soo
Finance, Kang Man-soo
Defence, Gen. Lee Sang-hee
Foreign Affairs, Yu Myung-hwan
Justice, Kim Kyung-han

EMBASSY OF THE REPUBLIC OF KOREA

60 Buckingham Gate, London SW1E 6AJ
T 020-7227 5500
Ambassador Extraordinary and Plenipotentiary, HE Dr Yoon-Je Cho, *apptd* 2005

BRITISH EMBASSY

Taepyeongno 40, 4 Jeong-dong, Jung-gu, Seoul 100-120
T (+82) (2) 3210 5500 E postmaster.seoul@fco.gov.uk
W www.uk.or.kr
Ambassador Extraordinary and Plenipotentiary, HE Martin Uden, *apptd* 2008

BRITISH COUNCIL

4F Hungkuk Life Insurance Building, 226 Shinmunro 1-ga, Jongro-gu, Seoul 110-786
T (+82) (2) 3702 0600 W www.britishcouncil.org/korea
Director, Dr Ian Simm

DEFENCE

The army has 2,330 main battle tanks, 2,480 armoured personnel carriers, 2,040 armoured infantry fighting vehicles and 60 armed helicopters. The navy has 12 submarines, 7 destroyers, 9 frigates, 28 corvettes, around 75 patrol and coastal vessels, 8 combat aircraft, 24 armed helicopters and 60 main battle tanks. There are 8 naval bases. The air force has 555 combat aircraft.
Military budget – US$26,900m (2007)
Military personnel – 687,000: army 560,000, navy 63,000, air force 64,000; paramilitary 4,500
Conscription duration – 26–30 months

ECONOMY AND TRADE

Industrialisation from the 1960s transformed South Korea from a predominantly agrarian country into one of the Asian 'miracle' economies by the 1980s. Initially based on shipbuilding and electrical goods, production shifted towards electronics and IT goods in the 1980s. By 1997 South Korea was the world's eleventh largest economy, with an annual GDP growth rate of 8 per cent. However, the Asian financial crisis in 1997 caused severe financial difficulties for the dominating conglomerates *(chaebols)* and a number collapsed in the late 1990s, causing a 6.9 per cent drop in GDP in 1998. Despite a speedy recovery in 1999, it was clear that corporate and financial reforms were needed and these have since been introduced. Growth in GDP has been more modest since the early 2000s, but the economy is stable owing to sound fiscal management, budget and trade surpluses, and low rates of unemployment and inflation.

Services contribute 57.2 per cent to GDP, industry 39.6 per cent and agriculture 3.2 per cent. Major manufacturing industries include electronics, telecommunications, motor vehicles, chemicals, shipbuilding and steel. Tourism is of growing importance.

The main trading partners are China, Japan, the USA, Hong Kong and Saudi Arabia. Principal exports are semiconductors, telecommunications equipment, motor vehicles, computers, steel, ships and petrochemicals. The main imports are machinery, electronics and electronic equipment, oil, steel, transport equipment, organic chemicals and plastics.

GNI – US$856,600m; US$17,690 per capita (2006)
Annual average growth of GDP – 4.8 per cent (2007 est)
Inflation rate – 2.5 per cent (2007 est)
Unemployment – 2.9 per cent (2007 est)
Total external debt – US$311,100m (2007)
Imports – US$309,000m (2006)
Exports – US$325,000m (2006)

BALANCE OF PAYMENTS
Trade – US$16,082m surplus (2006)
Current Account – US$5,385m surplus (2006)

Trade with UK	*2006*	*2007*
Imports from UK	£1,702,036,000	£1,812,521,752
Exports to UK	£3,116,358,000	£3,027,040,715

COMMUNICATIONS

There are 3,472km of railway in commercial operation, of which 1,361km are electrified. A high-speed railway line is being constructed between Seoul and Pusan and there are plans to build high-speed rail links from Seoul to Mokp'o and to Kangnung. There are 100,279km of roads, of which 3,060km are motorways. There are 105 airports and airfields and there are international airports at Seoul (Kimpo), Kimhae (near Pusan), Taegu, Cheju city and Inchon. Pusan, Inchon and P'ohang are the major ports, although development and operations at Inchon are hampered by tidal variations of 9–10m.

A modern telephone system provides 26.8 million main lines. In 2006, there were 40 million mobile phone subscribers and 34 million internet users.

EDUCATION AND HEALTH

Primary education is free of charge and compulsory for nine years from the age of six. Secondary and higher education is extensive, with the option of middle school to age 15 and high school to age 18.

Gross enrolment ratio (percentage of relevant age group) – primary 105 per cent; secondary 96 per cent; tertiary 91 per cent (2006 est)
Health expenditure (per capita) – US$973 (2005)
Hospital beds (per 1,000 people) – 7.1 (2000–6)

MEDIA

Korea has a number of public broadcasters, such as Korea Broadcasting System (KBS), Munhwa Broadcasting Corporation (MBC) and Education Broadcasting System (EBS). RTV, South Korea's first public-access television channel, is run by the Citizen's Broadcast Foundation. Newspaper readership is very high. Popular publications include *Hangyore Sinmun,* and the English language title *Korea Daily News.*

KUWAIT

Dawlat al-Kuwayt – State of Kuwait

Area – 17,820 sq. km
Capital – Kuwait City (Al Kuwayt); population, 2,063,000 (2007 est)
Major towns – Al Qurain, Jaleeb, Salmiya, Sabah Al Salem
Currency – Kuwaiti dinar (KD) of 1,000 fils
Population – 2,505,559 rising at 3.56 per cent per year (2007 est); 45 per cent are Kuwaiti citizens, the remainder being other Arabs, Iranians, Indians, Pakistanis and Westerners
Religion – Islam (70 per cent), Christianity (12 per cent), Hinduism (9 per cent) (est)
Language – Arabic (official), English
Population density – 146 per sq. km (2006)
Urban population – 96.4 per cent (2005 est)
Median age (years) – 26 (2007 est)
National anthem – 'Al-Nasheed al-Watani' ['National Anthem']
National day – 25 February
Life expectancy (years) – 77.36 (2007 est)
Mortality rate – 2.39 (2007 est)
Birth rate – 21.95 (2007 est)
Infant mortality rate – 9.47 (2007 est)
Death penalty – Retained
CPI score – 4.3 (2007)

CLIMATE AND TERRAIN

Kuwait is an almost entirely flat and arid country with elevation extremes ranging from 306m at the highest point to 0m (Persian Gulf) at the lowest. Its territory includes the island of Bubiyan and others at the head of the Persian Gulf. Average temperatures range from 10°C in January to 37°C in July. High levels of humidity often compound the summer temperatures.

HISTORY AND POLITICS

The area was under the nominal control of the Ottoman Empire from the late 16th century, but in 1756 an autonomous sheikdom was founded that has been ruled by the al-Sabah family ever since. Kuwait entered into a treaty of friendship with Britain in 1899, in order to protect itself from Ottoman and Saudi domination, and it became a British protectorate in 1914. The borders with Saudi Arabia and Iraq were agreed between 1922 and 1933. Full independence was achieved in 1961, although Britain retained a military presence in the country until 1971.

An attempted Iraqi invasion shortly after independence in 1961 was discouraged by British troops in the Gulf. However, in August 1990 Iraq invaded and occupied Kuwait, proclaiming it a province of Iraq. In 1991, a short military campaign by a US-led coalition force expelled the Iraqi forces, although there were further Iraqi incursions in 1993 before Iraq renounced its claim and recognised the new UN-demarcated border in 1994. Extensive damage was caused to the country's infrastructure and environment during the Iraqi occupation and the liberation campaign, and reconstruction was a priority throughout the 1990s. In 2003, Kuwait was a base for the build-up of forces for the Iraq War, and it remains an important transit route for military and civilian traffic into and out of Iraq.

In recent years, there have been clashes between security forces and militant Islamists, some of whom are alleged to have links to al-Qaida.

Although Kuwait was the first Arab country in the Gulf to have an elected legislature, it was suspended from 1977 to 1981 and again from 1986 to 1992. Apart from a brief suspension in 1999 because of a dispute between members and the government, it has since sat regularly, with frequent democratic elections. The government resigned in March 2008 after disagreements with the legislature and the emir called a legislative election for May, following which Islamists were again the largest bloc.

POLITICAL SYSTEM

The 1962 constitution was amended in 2005 to extend the franchise to women, who are now allowed to vote and to stand for election. The head of state is the emir, chosen from among the ruling family. He exercises executive power through the council of ministers. In 2003, the post of prime minister was separated from the role of heir to the throne for the first time. The unicameral National Assembly has 50 members directly elected for a four-year term. There are no political parties. There are six governorates: Capital, Hawalli, Ahmadi, Al-Jahrah, Al-Farwaniya and Al-Asimah.

HEAD OF STATE

HH The Emir of Kuwait, Shaikh Sabah al-Ahmad al-Jaber al-Sabah, *born* 1929, *acceded* 29 January 2006
Crown Prince, HH Shaikh Nawaf al-Ahmad al-Jaber al-Sabah

SELECTED GOVERNMENT MEMBERS *as at June 2008*

Prime Minister, Shaikh Nasser al-Muhammad al-Ahmad al-Sabah
First Deputy Prime Minister, Defence, Shaikh Jaber al-Mubarak al-Hamad al-Sabah
Deputy Prime Ministers, Shaikh Mohammad al-Salem al-Sabah *(Foreign Affairs);* Faisal Mohammed al-Hajji
Interior, Shaikh Jabir Khalid al-Jabir al-Sabah
Finance, Mustafa Jasim Al-Shimali

EMBASSY OF THE STATE OF KUWAIT

2 Albert Gate, London SW1X 7JU
T 020-7590 3400
Ambassador Extraordinary and Plenipotentiary, HE Khaled Al-Duwaisan, GCVO, *apptd* 1993

BRITISH EMBASSY

PO Box 13001, Arabian Gulf Street, Safat 13001
T (+965) 240 3334 E britemb@qualitynet.net
Ambassador Extraordinary and Plenipotentiary, HE Stuart Laing, *apptd* 2005

BRITISH COUNCIL

PO Box 345, 2 Al Arabi Street, Block 2, Mansouriya, Safat 13004
T (+965) 251 5512 W www.britishcouncil.org/kuwait
Director, Graham McCulloch

DEFENCE

The army has 368 main battle tanks, 321 armoured personnel carriers and up to 450 armoured infantry fighting vehicles. The navy has 10 patrol and coastal vessels, based at Ras al-Qalaya. The air force has 50 combat aircraft and 32 armed helicopters.
Military budget – US$3,920m (2007 est)
Military personnel – 15,500: army 11,000, navy 2,000, air force 2,500; paramilitary 7,100

ECONOMY AND TRADE

Oil was discovered in 1938 and the development of the oil industry after 1945 transformed the country from one of the poorest in the world to one of the richest. Petroleum accounts for 95 per cent of export revenues and 80 per cent of government income. Income from foreign reserves and investment is also high.

The climate and terrain limit agriculture and, with the exception of fish, all food is imported; the primary sector contributes only 0.4 per cent of GDP. Services account for 44.9 per cent of GDP and industry for 54.7 per cent. Apart from the oil and petrochemical industries, other activities include production of cement and construction materials, shipbuilding and repair, water desalination and food processing. Immigrant labour, mainly from Pakistan, India and Iran makes up about 80 per cent of the 1.17 million-strong workforce.

The main export markets are Japan, South Korea, Taiwan, Singapore and the USA, and the main sources of imports are the USA, Germany, Japan, Saudi Arabia and China. Principal exports are oil and refined products, and fertilisers. The main imports are food, construction materials, vehicles and vehicle parts, and clothing.
GNI – US$77,700m; US$30,630 per capita (2006)
Annual average growth of GDP – 5.6 per cent (2007 est)
Inflation rate – 3.9 per cent (2007 est)
Unemployment – 2.2 per cent (2004 est)
Total external debt – US$33,610m (2007 est)
Imports – US$16,000m (2006)
Exports – US$57,300m (2006)

BALANCE OF PAYMENTS

Trade – US$41,306m surplus (2006)
Current Account – US$51,050m surplus (2005)

Trade with UK	*2005*	*2006*
Imports from UK	£436,649,000	£446,530,000
Exports to UK	£395,705,000	£789,549,000

COMMUNICATIONS

Kuwait has 5,749km of roads, most of which are surfaced, but no railway or internal waterways. There are seven airports and airstrips; the international airport is at Kuwait City. The main seaports are Ash Shu'aybah, Ash Shuwaykh, Kuwait City, Mina' 'Abd Allah, Mina' al Ahmadi and Mina' Su'ud. A modern telephone system provides 510,300 main lines; there were 2.5 million mobile phone subscribers in 2006 and 816,700 internet users.

EDUCATION AND HEALTH

Education is free of charge and compulsory from six to 14 years.

Literacy rate – 82.9 per cent (2004 est)
Gross enrolment ratio (percentage of relevant age group) – primary 96 per cent; secondary 89 per cent; tertiary 18 per cent (2006 est)

Health expenditure (per capita) – US$687 (2005)
Hospital beds (per 1,000 people) – 1.9 (2000–6)

MEDIA

Kuwaiti newspapers are far more outspoken in their coverage of politics than newspapers in neighbouring Arab nations, although coverage of the emir and the royal family is often restrained and insulting references to God are banned. KUNA (Kuwaiti News Agency) is the official media agency; *Kuwait Times* is the English language daily newspaper and Radio Kuwait is the state radio broadcaster.

KYRGYZSTAN

Kyrgyz Respublikasy – Kyrgyz Republic

Area – 198,500 sq. km
Capital – Bishkek; population, 837,000 (2007 est)
Major city – Osh
Currency – Som of 100 tyiyn
Population – 5,284,149 rising at 1.35 per cent per year (2007 est); Kyrgyz (64.9 per cent), Uzbek (13.8 per cent), Russian (12.5 per cent), Dungan (1.1 per cent), Ukrainian (1 per cent), Uygur (1 per cent)
Religion – Islam (80 per cent) (est). The majority of the population practises Sunni Islam
Language – Kyrgyz, Russian (both official), Uzbek, Dungun
Population density – 27 per sq. km (2006)
Urban population – 33.7 per cent (2005 est)
Median age (years) – 23.9 (2007 est)
National anthem – 'Mamlekettik Gimni' ['National Anthem of the Kyrgyz Republic']
National day – 31 August (Independence Day)
Life expectancy (years) – 68.81 (2007 est)
Mortality rate – 7.02 (2007 est)
Birth rate – 23.08 (2007 est)
Infant mortality rate – 33.38 (2007 est)
Death penalty – Retained for certain crimes
CPI score – 2.1 (2007)
Population below poverty line – 40 per cent (2004 est)
Gross enrolment ratio (percentage of relevant age group) – primary 97 per cent; secondary 86 per cent; tertiary 43 per cent (2006 est)
Literacy rate – 98.7 per cent (2004 est)
Health expenditure (per capita) – US$29 (2005)
Hospital beds (per 1,000 people) – 5.1 (2000–6)

CLIMATE AND TERRAIN

Kyrgyzstan is a landlocked and mountainous country lying in the Tien Shan mountain range, with the Pamirs in the extreme south. Elevation extremes range from 7,439m (Jengish Chokusu/Pik Pobedy) at the highest point to 132m (Kara-Darya) at the lowest, though most of the country lies at over 1,000m. The principal rivers are the Naryn and the Chu, and the vast Issyk-Kul lake lies in the north-east. The climate is continental but with temperatures and humidity moderated by the altitude; typical temperatures in the valleys range from 0°C in January to 25°C in July. Rainfall is low for the altitude, owing to Kyrgyzstan's distance from the sea and the rain-shadow effect of the Himalayan and Pamir mountain ranges.

HISTORY AND POLITICS

After a long period under Turkic, Mongol and Chinese rule, the Kyrgyz became part of the Russian Empire in the 1860s and 1870s. After the October 1917 revolution in Russia, the area became part of the Turkestan autonomous republic within the USSR until 1924, when the Kirgiz Autonomous Region was formed; it became an autonomous republic in 1926 and a constituent republic of the USSR in 1936. Soviet rule brought land reforms in the 1920s that resulted in the settlement of many of the nomadic Kyrgyz.

Reform in the USSR in the 1980s provoked an upsurge in nationalism in Kyrgyzstan and agitation for independence. Following the attempted coup in Moscow in 1991, Kyrgyzstan became an independent republic and joined the Commonwealth of Independent States. Kyrgyzstan formed the Central Asian Union with Kazakhstan and Uzbekistan in 1994, agreeing to create a single economic market in 1996.

Since independence, there has been tension between the Kyrgyz and ethnic Uzbeks, concentrated around Osh, and this has flared into intercommunal violence on occasions. There have also been clashes between security forces and militant Islamists, active near the border with Tajikistan.

Askar Akayev, a pro-reform communist, was elected president in 1990 and re-elected 1991, 1995 and 2000, although the 2000 election was considered flawed. After growing unrest from 2002 over political and media suppression, persistent economic problems and corruption, Akayev was deposed in March 2005 in a popular uprising over alleged government interference in the 2005 legislative election. The opposition leader Kurmanbek Bakiyev was elected president in July but throughout the following year he faced mass protests demanding action against corruption and crime after several politicians were murdered.

President Bakiyev signed a new constitution limiting his powers in November 2006 but soon pushed through legislation restoring some of these powers. Renewed protests and calls for his resignation and early elections continued in 2007. After a new constitution was approved in a referendum in October 2007, legislative elections were held in December; these resulted in the president's Ak Zhol party winning 71 of the 90 seats in polls that observers considered to be marred by fraud.

POLITICAL SYSTEM

The 2007 constitution restored some of the presidential powers reduced in the 2006 constitution. The president is directly elected for a five-year term, renewable only once. The unicameral Supreme Council has 90 members directly elected for a five-year term. The largest party in the legislature nominates the prime minister, and the president appoints the cabinet; the appointments are subject to the approval of the Supreme Council.

HEAD OF STATE
President, Kurmanbek Bakiyev, *elected* 10 July 2005

SELECTED GOVERNMENT MEMBERS *as at June 2008*
Prime Minister, Igor Chudinov
Deputy Prime Minister, Nur uluu Dosbol
Finance, Tazhikan Kalimbetova
Foreign Affairs, Ednan Karabayev
Interior, Moldomusa Kongantiyev
Defence, Bakytbek Kalyev

EMBASSY OF THE KYRGYZ REPUBLIC
Ascot House, 119 Crawford Street, London W1U 6BJ
T 020-7935 1462 E embassy@kyrgyz-embassy.org.uk
W www.kyrgyz-embassy.org.uk
Ambassador Extraordinary and Plenipotentiary, HE Kuban Mambetaliev, *apptd* 2006

BRITISH AMBASSADOR
HE Paul Brummell, *apptd* 2005, resident at Almaty, Kazakhstan

BRITISH COUNCIL
Director, Christopher Baxter, resident at Almaty, Kazakhstan

DEFENCE

The army has 150 main battle tanks, 35 armoured personnel carriers and 320 armoured infantry fighting vehicles. The air force has 52 combat aircraft and 9 armed helicopters.

The USA and Russia have troops stationed in the country as part of the international fight against terrorism.
Military budget – US$41m (2007)
Military personnel – 10,900: army 8,500, air force 2,400; paramilitary 9,500
Conscription duration – 18 months

ECONOMY AND TRADE

Economic reforms in the early 1990s caused severe hardship; since the late 1990s productivity and exports have grown, but the economy remains heavily dependent on gold and vulnerable to fluctuations in global prices. The government has reduced its fiscal deficit and, with international support, is pursuing poverty reduction and economic growth programmes. These will require further economic restructuring and greater foreign direct investment, though the latter may be deterred by the recent political instability.

The economy is predominantly agrarian, with agriculture accounting for 31.7 per cent of GDP and employing over 50 per cent of the workforce. There are deposits of gold, uranium, mercury and natural gas, and hydroelectric potential. Apart from mining and energy, industry consists of light manufacturing and contributes 19.8 per cent of GDP; services contribute 48.4 per cent.

The main trading partners are Russia, Kazakhstan, Switzerland, China, Afghanistan and the USA. Principal exports are cotton, wool, meat, tobacco, gold, mercury, uranium, natural gas and electricity. The main imports are oil, gas, machinery and equipment, chemicals and foodstuffs.
GNI – US$2,600m; US$500 per capita (2006)
Annual average growth of GDP – 6.5 per cent (2007 est)
Inflation rate – 6.4 per cent (2007 est)
Unemployment – 18 per cent (2005 est)
Total external debt – US$2,966m (2007)
Imports – US$1,800m (2006)
Exports – US$800m (2006)

BALANCE OF PAYMENTS
Trade – US$1,052m deficit (2006)
Current Account – US$186m deficit (2006)

Trade with UK	*2006*	*2007*
Imports from UK	£3,160,000	£3,400,607
Exports to UK	£5,473,000	£1,245,691

COMMUNICATIONS

Kyrgyzstan has 18,500km of roads, 470km of railways and 600km of waterways. There are 30 airports and airfields; the international airport is at Bishkek.

Both fixed-line and mobile telephone systems are expanding, though density is currently low and, for fixed lines, concentrated in urban areas. In 2006, there were 458,900 main lines in use, 1.3 million mobile phone subscribers and 298,000 internet users.

MEDIA

There are a large number of newspapers in circulation, several of which have affiliations to particular political parties. There are also a number of private and independent television and radio broadcasters, mostly concentrated in Bishkek. While still enjoying greater freedom than in neighbouring countries, the media has come under increasing pressure in recent years, with heavy fines for slander acting as a deterrent to opposition outlets.

LAOS

Sathalanalat Paxathipatai Paxaxon Lao – Lao People's Democratic Republic

Area – 236,800 sq. km
Capital – Vientiane; population, 745,000 (2007 est)
Major towns – Pakse, Savannakhet
Currency – Kip (K) of 100 att
Population – 6,521,998 rising at 2.37 per cent per year (2007 est); Lao Loum (68 per cent), Lao Theung (22 per cent), Lao Soung (9 per cent) (est)
Religion – Buddhism (40 per cent), Christianity (2 per cent) (est). The remainder of the population is animist
Language – Lao (official), French, English
Population density – 25 per sq. km (2006)
Urban population – 21.6 per cent (2005 est)
Median age (years) – 19 (2007 est)
National anthem – 'Pheng Xat Lao' ['Hymn of the Lao People']
National day – 2 December (Republic Day)
Life expectancy – 55.89 (2007 est)
Mortality rate – 11.28 (2007 est)
Birth rate – 34.98 (2007 est)
Infant mortality rate – 81.44 (2007 est)

Death penalty – Retained, but not used
CPI score – 1.9 (2007)
Population below poverty line – 30.7 per cent (2005 est)
Literacy rate – 68.7 per cent (2004 est)
Gross enrolment ratio (percentage of age group) – primary 116 per cent; secondary 43 per cent; tertiary 9 per cent (2006 est)
Health expenditure (per capita) – US$18 (2005)
Hospital beds (per 1,000 people) – 0.9 (2000–6)

CLIMATE AND TERRAIN

Laos is landlocked, the land rising from the Mekong river basin in the west to a range of hills in the east of the country and mountains in the north. Elevation extremes range from 2,817m (Phon Bia) at the highest point to 70m (Mekong) at the lowest. Much of the land is covered by rainforest. The climate is tropical, with a wet season from May to November, during which humidity levels are very high. Average temperatures in Vientiane range from 14°C in January to 34°C in July.

HISTORY AND POLITICS

From the ninth to the 13th centuries, Laos was part of the Khmer Empire centred on Angkor in Cambodia. Small principalities developed from the 12th century and were united in the 14th century into the kingdom of Lan Xang ('the land of a million elephants'), which dominated until 1713, when it split into the separate kingdoms of Luang Prabang, Vientiane and Champassac, which became tributaries of Siam (Thailand) in the late 18th century and then a protectorate of France from 1893.

Japanese occupation during World War II inspired a Lao nationalist movement, which proclaimed independence in 1945, but the French regained control of the country in 1946. Independence as a constitutional monarchy was granted in 1953, but much of the following 20 years was spent in civil war between the communist Pathet Lao, backed first by China and then by North Vietnam, and royalists, who attracted US support from the early 1960s. A ceasefire in 1973 partitioned the country between the two sides, but in 1975 the Pathet Lao seized power in the rest of the country and proclaimed a republic, introducing a one-party state and initiating socialist policies. Greater economic liberalisation was introduced from the mid-1980s, and the first legislative elections since 1975 were held in 1989.

Ethnic Hmong minority groups have maintained a low-level insurgency against the communist regime since 1975. In 2000 and 2003, Laos suffered some serious civil disturbances, including bombings and armed attacks on buses. These were variously attributed to Hmong insurgents and anti-government groups based abroad.

In the April 2006 legislative election, Lao People's Revolutionary Party (LPRP) candidates won all but one of the seats, the remaining seat being taken by an approved non-partisan candidate. In June 2006, the legislature elected Choummaly Sayasone as president and approved a reshuffled council of ministers.

POLITICAL SYSTEM

Under the 1991 constitution, the head of state is a president elected by the legislature for a five-year term. The unicameral National Assembly has 115 members, who are party-approved candidates directly elected for a five-year term. The LPRP is the only legal political party, although non-partisan candidates for legislative seats have been approved by it. Party congresses are held every five years.

HEAD OF STATE

President, Lt.-Gen. Choummaly Sayasone, *elected* 8 June 2006
Vice-President, Bounnhang Vorachit

SELECTED GOVERNMENT MEMBERS *as at June 2008*

Prime Minister, Bouasone Bouphavanh
Deputy Prime Ministers, Maj.-Gen. Asang Laoly; Somsavat Lengsavad; Maj.-Gen. Douangchay Phichit *(Defence);* Thongloun Sisoulit *(Foreign Affairs)*
Finance, Somdy Douangdy

EMBASSY OF THE LAO PEOPLE'S DEMOCRATIC REPUBLIC

74 avenue Raymond-Poincaré, 75116 Paris, France
T (+33) (1) 4553 0298 E ambalaoparis@wanadoo.fr
W www.laoparis.com
Ambassador Extraordinary and Plenipotentiary, HE Soutsakhone Pathammavong, *apptd* 2003

BRITISH AMBASSADOR

HE Quinton Quayle, *apptd* 2007, resident at Bangkok, Thailand

DEFENCE

The army has 25 main battle tanks and 50 armoured personnel carriers. The navy has 52 patrol and coastal combatant vessels. The air force has 22 combat capable aircraft.

Military budget – US$13.3m (2006 est)
Military personnel – 29,100: army 25,600, air force 3,500; paramilitary 100,000
Conscription duration – 18 months

ECONOMY AND TRADE

Economic liberalisation and a measure of private enterprise were introduced from the mid-1980s, producing growth averaging 6 per cent a year since 1988, except during the 1997 Asian financial crisis. Economic growth is currently being driven by dam and road construction projects and foreign investment in hydroelectric power and mining. Despite this, the country remains very poor, with only a rudimentary transport, communications and energy infrastructure, and is dependent on international aid.

Subsistence agriculture, principally rice, accounts for 41 per cent of GDP and about 80 per cent of employment. Deposits of copper, tin, gold and gypsum are exploited, as is the abundance of timber in the rainforests. Other activities include food processing, manufacture of garments and cement, and tourism. A hydro-electric dam under construction on the Mekong will export electricity to Thailand, earning valuable additional revenue.

Main trading partners are Thailand, China and Vietnam. Principal exports are garments, timber products, coffee, electricity, tin, copper and gold. The main imports are machinery and equipment, vehicles, fuel and consumer goods.

GNI – US$2,900m; US$500 per capita (2006)
Annual average growth of GDP – 7 per cent (2007 est)
Inflation rate – 5 per cent (2007 est)
Unemployment – 2.4 per cent (2005 est)
Total external debt – US$3,179m (2006)
Imports – US$1,100m (2006)
Exports – US$900m (2006)

BALANCE OF PAYMENTS

Trade – US$178m deficit (2006)
Current Account – US$435m deficit (2006)

Trade with UK	*2006*	*2007*
Imports from UK	£911,000	£3,355,271
Exports to UK	£816,000	£1,118,602

COMMUNICATIONS

There are no railways and only a limited road network (31,210km), although expansion of the road system is under way. The Friendship Bridge over the river Mekong connects Laos with Thailand, and links up the road routes from Singapore to China. There are around 4,600km of navigable waterways, principally on the Mekong and its tributaries. There are 42 airports and airfields; the principal airports are at Vientiane and Luang Prabang.

The telephone system is poor and limited in extent but services are improving. Mobile phone distribution is growing rapidly and subscribers numbered 638,200 in 2006, compared to 90,067 main lines. There were 25,000 internet users in 2005.

MEDIA

All media is strictly controlled by the government. Slandering the state, distorting party policies and spreading false rumours are all criminal offences, which discourages objectivity. There are three state-run newspapers, although circulation is very low, and also state-run television and radio broadcasters.

LATVIA

Latvijas Republika – Republic of Latvia

Area – 64,589 sq. km
Capital – Riga; population, 722,000 (2007 est)
Major cities – Daugavpils, Jelgava, Liepaja
Currency – Lats of 100 santims
Population – 2,259,810 falling at 0.65 per cent per year (2007 est); Latvian (57.7 per cent), Russian (29.6 per cent), Belarusian (4.1 per cent), Ukrainian (2.7 per cent), Polish (2.5 per cent), Lithuanian (1.4 per cent)
Religion – Roman Catholicism (22 per cent), Protestantism (20 per cent), Orthodox Christianity (15 per cent) (est)
Language – Latvian (official), Russian, Lithuanian
Population density – 37 per sq. km (2006)
Urban population – 65.9 per cent (2005 est)
Median age (years) – 39.6 (2007 est)
National anthem – 'Dievs, Sveti Latviju' ['God Bless Latvia']
National day – 18 November (Independence Day)
Life expectancy (years) – 71.6 (2007 est)
Mortality rate – 13.64 (2007 est)
Birth rate – 9.43 (2007 est)
Infant mortality rate – 9.16 (2007 est)
Death penalty – Retained for certain crimes
CPI score – 4.8 (2007)

CLIMATE AND TERRAIN

Latvia is a flat, low-lying country on the eastern shore of the Baltic Sea. Elevation extremes range from 312m (Gaizinkalns) at the highest point to 0m (Baltic Sea) at the lowest. Average temperatures in Riga range from −4°C in January to 18°C in July.

HISTORY AND POLITICS

Conquered and Christianised in the 13th century by the Teutonic Knights, Latvia was successively under Polish, Lithuanian and Swedish rule in the 16th and 17th centuries, until it was incorporated into the Russian Empire in 1721. Under partial German occupation during the First World War, it declared its independence in 1918 and successfully defended this against the Bolsheviks in 1918–20. A dictatorship was established in 1934 following political instability and economic depression. The USSR invaded and annexed Latvia in 1940, and regained control in 1944 after ousting the German forces that had invaded in 1941. Latvia suffered huge civilian losses during the Second World War, including the destruction of its large Jewish community. Many more Latvians died after the war in purges and deportations ordered by Stalin.

Agitation by nationalist groups grew from the mid-1980s and in 1990 talks on independence began with the USSR. Following the failed coup in Moscow in 1991, the Latvian parliament declared the country's independence and this was internationally recognised. The last Russian troops left in 1994 but a large Russian minority remains and there are intercommunal tensions. Since the first post-Soviet elections in 1993, there has been a succession of centre-right coalition governments.

Latvia joined the EU in 2004. Its parliament ratified the EU constitution in June 2005.

In the 2006 legislative election, the People's Party won the most seats and continued in coalition with its previous government partners, Latvia's First Party–Latvia's Way and the Union of Latvian Greens and Farmers Party, plus the For Fatherland and Freedom party, under Aigars Kalvitis. The presidential election in May 2007 was won by Valdis Zatlers. In December 2007, the government resigned and Ivars Godmanis became prime minister at the head of a reshuffled coalition government.

POLITICAL SYSTEM

The 1922 constitution was restored in 1993. The head of state is a president, who is elected by the legislature for a four-year term which may be renewed only once. The president appoints the prime minister, who appoints the cabinet subject to approval by the legislature. The unicameral *Saeima* has 100 deputies who are elected for a four-year term by proportional representation.

HEAD OF STATE

President, Valdis Zatlers, *elected* 31 May 2007, *sworn in* 7 July 2007

SELECTED GOVERNMENT MEMBERS *as at June 2008*

Prime Minister, Ivars Godmanis
Defence, Vinets Veldre
Finance, Atis Slakteris
Foreign Affairs, Maris Riekstins
Interior, Mareks Seglins

EMBASSY OF THE REPUBLIC OF LATVIA
45 Nottingham Place, London W1U 5LY
T 020-7312 0040 E embassy.uk@mfa.gov.lv
W www.london.mfa.gov.lv
Ambassador Extraordinary and Plenipotentiary, HE Indulis Berzins, *apptd* 2005

BRITISH EMBASSY
5 J. Alunana Street, Riga 1010
T (+371) 777 4700 E british.embassy@apollo.lv
Ambassador Extraordinary and Plenipotentiary, HE Richard Moon, *apptd* 2007

BRITISH COUNCIL
5A Blaumana Street, Riga 1011
T (+371) 728 1730 W www.britishcouncil.org/latvia
Director, Agita Kalvina

DEFENCE

The army has 3 main battle tanks, the navy has 4 patrol and coastal vessels and the air force has 3 aircraft and 6 helicopters. Latvia, Lithuania and Estonia operate a joint naval unit, BALTRON, which is located at 5 naval bases: Liepaja, Riga, Ventspils, Tallinn and Klaipeda.
Military expenditure – US$279m (2006)
Military personnel – 5,696: army 1,526, navy 603, air force 480, administration, central support and other forces 3,087; paramilitary 11,034

ECONOMY AND TRADE

The country has made the transition from a planned to a market economy, although a few large enterprises remain in state ownership. The economy is growing rapidly, causing inflation to rise, which is delaying Latvia's adoption of the euro, now expected no earlier than 2012.

The economy has shifted towards service industries since independence. Transit, services and banking are large sectors, with services contributing 75.2 per cent of GDP. Industry contributes 21.3 per cent of GDP and includes the manufacture of commercial and public transport vehicles, synthetic fibres, agricultural machinery, fertilisers, washing machines, radios, electronics and pharmaceuticals. The agricultural sector accounts for 3.5 per cent of GDP, employs 13 per cent of the workforce and specialises in rearing livestock, dairy farming and cultivation of crops including grain, sugar beet, vegetables and potatoes.

The main trading partners are other EU states and Russia. Principal exports are timber and wood products, machinery and equipment, metals, textiles and foodstuffs. The main imports are machinery and equipment, chemicals, fuel and vehicles.
GNI – US$18,500m; US$8,100 per capita (2006)
Annual average growth of GDP – 10.3 per cent (2007 est)
Inflation rate – 9.6 per cent (2007 est)
Unemployment – 5.9 per cent (2007 est)
Total external debt – US$29,850m (2007)
Imports – US$11,000m (2006)
Exports – US$6,000m (2006)

BALANCE OF PAYMENTS
Trade – US$5,535m deficit (2006)
Current Account – US$4,479m deficit (2006)

Trade with UK	*2006*	*2007*
Imports from UK	£339,300,000	£144,582,407
Exports to UK	£861,400,000	£577,893,101

COMMUNICATIONS

Latvia has 2,303km of railway track and some 69,600km of roads. There are two major ports, Riga and Ventspils, which are warm-water ports. The main airports are at Riga, Ventspils and Liepaja. The telecommunications sector has become increasingly competitive since 2003. Fixed-line use is declining as mobile services expand. In 2006, there were 657,000 main lines in use, 2.1 million mobile phone subscribers and 1 million internet users.

EDUCATION AND HEALTH

Education is compulsory from the age of seven until 16 years, after which there is the option for a further three years of either secondary or vocational study.
Literacy rate – 99.7 per cent (2004 est)
Gross enrolment ratio (percentage of relevant age group) – primary 95 per cent; secondary 99 per cent; tertiary 75 per cent (2006 est)
Health expenditure (per capita) – US$443 (2005)
Hospital beds (per 1,000 people) – 7.7 (2000–6)

MEDIA

There are around 140 newspapers in circulation, including 24 national dailies. The most popular include *Diena Panorama, Latvii* and *Neatkariga RA*. Latvian Television is a public service broadcaster that has two channels, and Latvijas Neatkariga Televizija is the biggest private broadcaster. Latvian versions of the main Russian networks are also available.

LEBANON

Al-Jumhuriyah al-Lubnaniyah – Lebanese Republic

Area – 10,400 sq. km
Capital – Beirut (Bayrut); population, 1,846,000 (2007 est)
Major city – Tripoli
Currency – Lebanese pound (L£) of 100 piastres
Population – 3,925,502 rising at 1.2 per cent per year (2007 est); Arab (95 per cent), Armenian (4 per cent) (est)
Religion – Islam (62 per cent), including Druze (6 per cent), Christianity (34 per cent), including Orthodox Christianity (8 per cent) (est)
Language – Arabic (official), French, English, Armenian
Population density – 396 per sq. km (2006)
Urban population – 88 per cent (2005 est)
Median age (years) – 28.3 (2007 est)
National anthem – 'Koullouna Liloutaan Lil Oula Lil Alam' ['All of Us! For Our Country, For Our Flag and Glory']
National day – 22 November (Independence Day)

Life expectancy (years) – 73.15 (2007 est)
Mortality rate – 6.1 (2007 est)
Birth rate – 18.08 (2007 est)
Infant mortality rate – 23.39 (2007 est)
Death penalty – Retained
CPI score – 3.0 (2007)

CLIMATE AND TERRAIN

There is a narrow plain on the Mediterranean Sea coast, and the fertile Bekaa valley runs from north to south between the Lebanon and Anti-Lebanon mountain ranges. Elevation extremes range from 3,088m (Qurnat as Sawda') at the highest point to 0m (Mediterranean Sea) at the lowest. The climate is Mediterranean, with average temperatures of 13°C in January and 29°C in August.

HISTORY AND POLITICS

Lebanon was part of the Phoenician Empire from the fifth century BC until the first century AD, when it came under Roman rule and Christianity was introduced. Islam was introduced by Arabs in the seventh century AD, and the Druze faith was developed by local Muslims in the 11th century. The area was contested between Muslims and Christians during the Crusades before becoming part of the Turkish Ottoman Empire in the 16th century. Following the Ottoman collapse at the end of the First World War, Lebanon became a French-administered mandated territory, achieving independence in 1943 with a constitution that enshrined power-sharing by all the country's religions.

The complicated system of government established by the constitution created tensions between Christians and Muslims that in 1975 erupted into a civil war that pitted a coalition of Christian groups against Druze and Muslim militias. Conflict continued for 15 years, drawing in the Palestine Liberation Organisation (PLO), then based in Beirut, and Syrian forces in support of the Muslim factions, and Israel, which invaded in 1978 and 1982 in response to PLO guerrilla raids on Israel; Israel forced the PLO to withdraw from Lebanon in 1982. By 1985, the country was close to partition as rival political and religious factions sought to gain control.

An Arab League-sponsored ceasefire came into effect in 1989 and a peace plan, the Ta'if accord, proposed revisions to the constitution that would reduce Christian Maronite dominance. This was rejected by some Christian factions and fighting continued until this opposition was crushed by Syrian forces. A fragile peace was achieved in 1991, and elections in 1992 were peaceful, although they were boycotted by some Christian parties. In the security zones established by Israel in south Lebanon in 1985, clashes continued between occupying Israeli troops, or the Israeli-backed South Lebanon Army (SLA), and Hezbollah guerrillas throughout the 1990s. The SLA collapsed after Israel withdrew its forces in 2000.

Regional tensions continue to exert a strong influence on Lebanese politics. Conflict broke out in the south in July 2006 after Hezbollah guerrillas kidnapped Israeli soldiers and launched rocket attacks on northern Israel; Israel retaliated with air, sea and land attacks that killed or displaced thousands and severely damaged infrastructure. A UN peacekeeping force and Lebanese troops deployed on the border from August; it was the first deployment of government forces on the southern border in decades. The government also extended its control in the north of the country in 2007, taking over a militia-controlled refugee camp after a four-month siege.

Syria's influence is most pervasive, even though it was obliged to withdraw its troops in 2005 after huge protest rallies brought down the pro-Syrian government following the assassination of former prime minister Rafik Hariri, for which Syria was blamed. Since 2005, Lebanese politics has been dominated by a power struggle between pro- and anti-Syrian factions and militias. Although an alliance of anti-Syria parties won an overall majority of seats in the 2005 legislative elections, the subsequent coalition government included pro-Syrian ministers until their resignation in November 2006 over the number of seats offered to them in a proposed national unity government. The pro-Syria factions then pursued a greater role in the government through popular protests and a legislative boycott that left the state moribund for months. The failure to agree on a successor to President Emile Lahoud after his term of office ended in November 2007 created a political vacuum that led to a rise in factional violence, raising fears of renewed civil conflict. After six months, a neutral candidate, General Michel Suleiman, the head of the armed forces, was elected president in May 2008. He reappointed Fouad Siniora as prime minister, to head a national unity government.

POLITICAL SYSTEM

The constitution dates from 1926 but has been heavily amended, most significantly in 1943, when the National Covenant set out the division of power between the religious communities, and in 1989 to incorporate the provisions of the Ta'if accord. By convention, the presidency is held by a Maronite Christian, the prime minister is a Sunni Muslim and the speaker is a Shia Muslim. The president is elected by the legislature for a six-year term, which is not renewable. The unicameral National Assembly has 128 members, directly elected for a four-year term; seats are divided equally between Christians and Muslims. The prime minister is appointed by the president following consultation with the legislature.

HEAD OF STATE

President of the Republic of Lebanon, Gen. Michel Suleiman, *elected* 25 May 2008, *sworn in* 26 May 2008

SELECTED GOVERNMENT MEMBERS *as at June 2008*

Prime Minister, Fouad Siniora
Deputy Prime Minister, Defence, Elias Murr
Finance, Jihad Azour
Foreign Affairs, Fawzi Salloukh
Interior, Hasan al-Sabaa

EMBASSY OF LEBANON

21 Palace Gardens Mews, London W8 4RB
T 020-7727 6696 E emb.leb@btinternet.com
Ambassador Extraordinary and Plenipotentiary, vacant

BRITISH EMBASSY

PO Box 11-471 Serail Hill, Beirut Centre-Ville, Beirut
T (+961) (1) 990 400 E britemb@cyberia.net.lb
W www.britishembassy.org.lb
Ambassador Extraordinary and Plenipotentiary, HE Frances Guy, *apptd* 2006

BRITISH COUNCIL

Berytech Technology and Health, Sodeco Street, Damascus Road, 2064 1509 Beirut
T (+961) (1) 428 900 W www.britishcouncil.org/lebanon
Director, Amanda Burrell

DEFENCE

The army has 310 main battle tanks and 1,257 armoured personnel carriers. The navy has 21 patrol and coastal vessels at 2 bases. The air force has 14 aircraft and 13 armed helicopters.

Military budget – US$631m (2007)
Military personnel – 56,000: army 53,900, navy 1,100, air force 1,000; paramilitary 20,000

ECONOMY AND TRADE

The civil war devastated Lebanon's economy and infrastructure, and its role as an entrepôt and financial services centre for the region. A government reconstruction programme launched in 1993 succeeded in stimulating economic growth and reducing inflation as well as rebuilding the infrastructure and financial systems. This was financed by heavy borrowing, creating a high level of debt. Austerity measures, foreign debt rescheduling and international aid had begun to stabilise government finances until economic and financial reforms stalled from the mid-2000s, and the Israeli attacks in 2006 caused an estimated US$3.6bn (£1.8bn) of damage to the country's infrastructure. Internal political tensions continue to hinder economic activity and recovery.

In 2007, the service sector contributed 76.4 per cent of GDP, largely through banking and tourism, which are the two main economic activities. Industry accounted for 18.4 per cent, through food processing, wine production and the manufacture of jewellery, cement, textiles, mineral and chemical products, timber and furniture, oil refining and metal fabrication. Agriculture contributed 5.2 per cent of GDP, producing fruit, vegetables, tobacco and livestock.

The main export markets are Syria, the UAE, Switzerland, Saudi Arabia and Turkey, while imports come mainly from Syria, EU countries, the USA and China. Principal exports include jewellery, chemicals, consumer goods, fruit, vegetables, tobacco and construction materials. The main imports are petroleum products, cars, medicines, clothing, foodstuffs and consumer goods.

GNI – US$22,600m; US$5,580 per capita (2006)
Annual average growth of GDP – 0.3 per cent (2007 est)
Inflation rate – 5.6 per cent (2007 est)
Unemployment – 20 per cent (2006 est)
Total external debt – US$34,670m (2007 est)
Imports – US$9,600m (2006)
Exports – US$2,800m (2006)

BALANCE OF PAYMENTS
Trade – US$6,833m deficit (2006)
Current Account – US$1,372m deficit (2006)

Trade with UK	*2005*	*2006*
Imports from UK	£212,065,000	£207,737,000
Exports to UK	£20,169,000	£20,414,000

COMMUNICATIONS

The Israeli attacks in 2006 destroyed much of the country's infrastructure, including about 80 per cent of the major roads. The 401km railway system, some still not usable following the civil war, was rendered completely inoperable. There are seven airports and airfields, although the international airport at Beirut was also damaged by airstrikes in 2006. The principal seaports are Tripoli, Tyre, Sidon and Jounieh.

The telephone system was repaired after the civil war but privatisation and modernisation have been hampered by political tensions. In 2006, there were 681,400 main lines in use, 1.1 million mobile phone subscribers and 950,000 internet users.

EDUCATION AND HEALTH

There are eight years of compulsory education.
Gross enrolment ratio (percentage of relevant age group) – primary 94 per cent; secondary 81 per cent; tertiary 48 per cent (2006 est)
Health expenditure (per capita) – US$460 (2005)
Hospital beds (per 1,000 people) – 3.6 (2000–6)

MEDIA

Lebanon was the first Arab country to permit private radio and television stations. There are a number of daily newspapers in circulation, including French and English language publications. Tele-Liban is the state-run broadcaster and competes with several commercial stations, including the pro-Hezbollah al-Manar TV, targeted by Israeli air raids during the conflict in 2006.

LESOTHO

Kingdom of Lesotho

Area – 30,355 sq. km
Capital – Maseru; population, 210,000 (2007 est)
Currency – Loti (M) of 100 lisente. The South African rand is also legal tender
Population – 2,125,262 rising at 0.14 per cent per year (2007 est); Sotho (99.7 per cent) (est)
Religion – Christianity (90 per cent) (est). Incorporating indigenous beliefs alongside Christianity is very common
Language – English (official), Sesotho, Zulu, Xhosa
Population density – 66 per sq. km (2006)
Urban population – 18.2 per cent (2005 est)
Median age (years) – 21.1 (2007 est)
National anthem – 'Lesotho, Fatse la Bontata Rona' ['Lesotho, Land of Our Fathers']
National day – 4 October (Independence Day)
Life expectancy – 39.97 (2007 est)
Mortality rate – 22.49 (2007 est)
Birth rate – 24.72 (2007 est)
Infant mortality rate – 79.85 (2007 est)
HIV/AIDS adult prevalence – 22.7 per cent (2005 est)
Death penalty – Retained
CPI score – 3.3 (2007)
Military budget – US$34m (2007 est)
Military personnel – army 2,000
Health expenditure (per capita) – US$69 (2005)

CLIMATE AND TERRAIN

Lesotho is a landlocked country consisting of a highland plateau with hilly and mountainous areas. Elevation extremes range from 3,482m (Thabana Ntlenyana) at the highest point to 1,400m (the junction of the Orange and Makhaleng rivers) at the lowest. Due to the country's elevation, the climate is temperate. Average temperatures range from 25°C in January to 8°C in July.

HISTORY AND POLITICS

The area was organised into a single territory by Moshoeshoe the Great around 1820. Later in the 19th century, the Sotho people came under pressure from both the expanding Zulu nation and Europeans (the Boers) to give up land. In 1868, after fighting two wars with the Europeans, pressure from the Boers forced the Sotho to seek protection from the British government, and Basutoland became first a British territory in 1868, and then a crown colony in 1884.

The country gained independence in 1966 as the kingdom of Lesotho, under Moshoeshoe II and with Chief Lebua Jonathan as prime minister. The post-independence period has been one of political instability, with a number of coups and mutinies as rival political parties, army factions and the royal family competed for power. Chief Jonathan declared a state of emergency in 1970, fearing defeat in the elections. Although the constitution was restored in 1973, Jonathan was overthrown in a military coup in 1986, and another military coup in 1990 forced King Moshoeshoe II into exile, his son then ruling as Letsie III. Military rule ended with multiparty elections in 1993, although serious civil unrest followed the ousting of the military rulers; democratic rule was restored in 1994 and King Moshoeshoe II was reinstated in 1995. He died in a car accident in 1996 and King Letsie III returned to the throne.

Lesotho continued to be troubled by civil violence, and the 1998 elections were followed by particularly severe disturbances, which were quelled by an intervention force from neighbouring countries at the government's request. An interim political authority set up to review the constitution introduced a more representative electoral system in time for the 2002 election. In the 2007 legislative election, the Lesotho Congress for Democracy retained its majority, with 61 seats, and formed a new government. A state of emergency was declared in July 2007 as the country experienced its most severe drought in 30 years.

POLITICAL SYSTEM

Under the 1993 constitution, subsequently amended, the head of state is a hereditary monarch, with ceremonial duties but no executive or legislative powers. The bicameral parliament comprises the National Assembly, with 120 members elected for a five-year term, one-third by proportional representation, and the senate, whose 33 members comprise 22 principal chiefs and 11 members nominated by the king. The prime minister is the leader of the majority party in the legislature and appoints the council of ministers.

HEAD OF STATE

HM The King of Lesotho, King Letsie III, *acceded* February 1996, *crowned* 31 October 1997

SELECTED GOVERNMENT MEMBERS *as at June 2008*

Prime Minister, Defence, Bethuel Pakalitha Mosisili
Deputy Prime Minister, Home Affairs, Archibald Lesao Lehohla
Finance, Timothy Thahane
Foreign Affairs, Mohlabi Tsekoa

HIGH COMMISSION OF THE KINGDOM OF LESOTHO

7 Chesham Place, London SW1X 8HN
T 020-7235 5686 E lhc@lesotholondon.org.uk
W www.lesotholondon.org.uk
High Commissioner, HE HRH Prince Seeiso Bereng Seeiso, *apptd* 2005

BRITISH HIGH COMMISSION

High Commissioner, HE Paul Boateng, *apptd* 2005, resident at Pretoria (Tshwane), South Africa

ECONOMY AND TRADE

The country is one of the poorest in the world, with 49 per cent of the population living below the poverty line, and the situation has worsened with the severe droughts since 2001. With few natural resources apart from water, the main sources of government revenue are customs dues from the South African customs union and, since 1998, the export of water and electricity to South Africa from the hydroelectric facilities created by the Lesotho Highlands Water Project. One traditional source of revenue, remittances from miners employed in South Africa (35 per cent of the male workforce), is declining as the mines become exhausted. This decline is partially compensated for by the development of a small manufacturing base processing agricultural products, producing textiles and assembling garments, and the development of tourism, especially in the highlands. Even so, nearly half of the population is unemployed.

The economy has always been dependent on subsistence agriculture, which engages 86 per cent of the population, although productivity has declined in recent years because of drought, erosion and the loss of labour as farmers succumb to AIDS; nearly a quarter of the adult population is infected with HIV or AIDS. The main market for exports is the USA (82 per cent); imports come mainly from Hong Kong and China. Principal exports are clothing, footwear, road vehicles, wool and mohair, food and livestock. The main imports are food, construction materials, vehicles, machinery, medicines and petroleum products.

GNI – US$2,000m; US$980 per capita (2006)
Annual average growth of GDP – 4.8 per cent (2007 est)
Inflation rate – 12 per cent (2007 est)
Unemployment – 45 per cent (2002)
Total external debt – US$693m (2007 est)
Imports – US$1,360m (2006)
Exports – US$690m (2006)

BALANCE OF PAYMENTS

Trade – US$668m deficit (2006)
Current Account – US$66m surplus (2006)

Trade with UK	*2006*	*2007*
Imports from UK	£1,303,000	£472,337
Exports to UK	£363,000	£182,373

COMMUNICATIONS

Most travel is by foot or by air, as there is little transport infrastructure other than to link the main towns to each other and to South Africa, and to access the highland hydroelectric facilities. Of the 5,940km of roads,

1,087km are surfaced. There are 28 airports and airfields; the international airport is at Maseru.

The telephone system is rudimentary but expanding. Mobile phone distribution is growing rapidly; density is about 15 per 100 people.

EDUCATION AND HEALTH

Literacy rate – 81.4 per cent (2004 est)
Gross enrolment ratio (percentage of relevant age group) – primary 114 per cent; secondary 37 per cent; tertiary 4 per cent (2006 est)
Health expenditure (per capita) – US$69 (2005)

MEDIA

Lesotho has a mixture of state-run and private media. Radio is the most important medium and reforms in 1998 prompted the growth of a number of commercial stations. State-run Radio Lesotho is the only national station. South African broadcasts can also be received. The press publishes a range of weekly papers in both Sesotho and English.

LIBERIA

Republic of Liberia

Area – 111,370 sq. km
Capital – Monrovia; population, 1,041,000 (2007 est)
Currency – Liberian dollar (L$) of 100 cents
Population – 3,195,931 rising at 4.84 per cent per year (2007 est); indigenous African (95 per cent), Americo-Liberians (descendants of free immigrants from the USA) (2.5 per cent), Congo People (descendants of free immigrants from the Caribbean) (2.5 per cent) (est)
Religion – Indigenous religions (40 per cent), Christianity (40 per cent), Islam (20 per cent) (est)
Language – English (official)
Population density – 37 per sq. km (2006)
Urban population – 47.9 per cent (2005 est)
Median age (years) – 18.1 (2007 est)
National anthem – 'All Hail, Liberia, Hail!'
National day – 26 July (Independence Day)
Life expectancy (years) – 40.39 (2007 est)
Mortality rate – 22.24 (2007 est)
Birth rate – 43.75 (2007 est)
Infant mortality rate – 149.73 (2007 est)
HIV/AIDS adult prevalence – 5.9 per cent (2003 est)
Death penalty – Abolished for all crimes (since 2005)
CPI score – 2.1 (2007)
Population below poverty line – 80 per cent (2000 est)
Military personnel – 2,400
Literacy rate – 55.9 per cent (2004 est)
Gross enrolment ratio (percentage of relevant age group) – primary 91 per cent (2006 est)
Health expenditure (per capita) – US$10 (2005)

CLIMATE AND TERRAIN

Liberia lies on the west African coast, just north of the equator. There are forested highlands in the interior and swampy plains on the coast, where several rivers enter the ocean. Elevation extremes range from 1,380m (Mt Wuteve) at the highest point to 0m (Atlantic Ocean) at the lowest. The climate is tropical and average annual temperature is consistently around 28°C.

HISTORY AND POLITICS

The land was purchased by the American Colonisation Society in 1821 and turned into a settlement for liberated black slaves from the USA, gaining recognition as an independent state in 1847; it is the only west African country never to have been colonised.

Much of the first century of statehood was dominated by the True Whig Party, but political stability ended in 1980 when a coup installed a military government under Samuel Doe. When civilian rule was restored in 1985, Doe became president, but his regime's arbitrary, corrupt rule combined with an economic collapse led to a revolt in 1990 by Charles Taylor's National Patriotic Forces of Liberia (NPFL) and the Armed Forces of Liberia (AFL). The country descended into a civil war that, despite various peace initiatives and ceasefires, lasted until 2003. Around 250,000 people were killed and thousands were displaced. Following mediation by a number of African and European countries, all factions in the conflict signed a peace agreement in 2003 and a UN peacekeeping force was deployed. The disarming of militias was completed in late 2004 but the situation remains volatile. After the international criminal court issued a warrant for his arrest, Charles Taylor was captured in March 2006 and a trial began at the Hague in June 2007, where Taylor is charged with war crimes and crimes against humanity.

After a period of transitional government, presidential and legislative elections were held at the end of 2005. In the legislative election, the Congress for Democratic Change (CDC) won the most seats but without an overall majority. The Unity Party leader Ellen Johnson-Sirleaf was elected president in the second round of voting and took office in January 2006, nominating a new government that included members of two smaller parties and some independents. In the same year, a commission was set up to investigate human rights abuses between 1979 and 2003.

POLITICAL SYSTEM

Under the 1986 constitution, the head of state is an executive president who is directly elected for a six-year term, renewable only once. There is a bicameral National Assembly, consisting of a lower chamber, the House of Representatives, with 64 members directly elected for a six-year term, and a senate, with 30 members (two from each of the 15 counties) normally elected for a nine-year term, although half of this reconvened senate will serve for only six years. The president appoints the cabinet, which must be approved by the legislature.

HEAD OF STATE

President, Ellen Johnson-Sirleaf, *elected* 8 November 2005, *sworn in* 16 January 2006
Vice-President, Joseph N. Boakai

SELECTED GOVERNMENT MEMBERS, *as at June 2008*
Defence, Brownie Samukai
Finance, Antoinette Sayeh
Foreign Affairs, Olubanke King-Akerele
Internal Affairs, Ambulai Johnson

EMBASSY OF THE REPUBLIC OF LIBERIA
23 Fitzroy Square, London W1T 6EW
T 020-7388 5489 E info@embassyofliberia.org.uk
W www.embassyofliberia.org.uk
Ambassador Extraordinary and Plenipotentiary, Wesley M. Johnson, *apptd* 2007

BRITISH AMBASSADOR
HE John Mitchiner, *apptd* 2003, resident at Freetown, Sierra Leone

ECONOMY AND TRADE

The civil war devastated an economy already weakened by government mismanagement and corruption, and drove those with expertise and capital into exile. Since the war ended, over US$500m (£250m) of foreign aid has been pledged to finance reconstruction, conditional on the adoption of anti-corruption measures, and economic activity has revived. UN sanctions on timber and diamond exports, used by civil war factions as a source of finance, were lifted in 2006 and 2007 respectively, opening up new sources of revenue.

Natural resources include iron ore, timber, gold, diamonds and hydroelectric power potential, and Liberia benefits from reliable water resources and a climate suited to agriculture. Agriculture is the main economic activity, engaging 70 per cent of the workforce and generating 77 per cent of GDP. Industry centres on the processing of rubber and palm oil, forestry and diamond mining.

The main export markets are EU countries, South Africa and the USA, while imports come mainly from South Korea, Singapore, Japan and China. Principal exports are rubber, timber, iron, diamonds, cocoa and coffee. The main imports are fuels, chemicals, machinery, transport equipment, manufactured goods and foodstuffs.

GNI – US$500m; US$130 per capita (2006)
Annual average growth of GDP – 8.5 per cent (2007 est)
Inflation rate – 15 per cent (2003 est)
Unemployment – 85 per cent (2003 est)
Total external debt – US$3,200m (2005 est)

BALANCE OF PAYMENTS
Current Account – US$189m deficit (2006)

Trade with UK	*2006*	*2007*
Imports from UK	£11,920,000	£14,208,653
Exports to UK	£9,882,000	£8,005,201

COMMUNICATIONS

The main seaports are Monrovia and Buchanan, and there is a merchant fleet of 1,948 ships of over 1,000 tonnes, as well as 1,904 foreign-owned ships registered in Liberia. There are 10,600km of roads, of which only 657km are surfaced, and 490km of railway track, although little of this is operational due to war damage. There are 53 airports and airfields; the international airports, Robertsfield and Spriggs Payne, are at Monrovia.

Telephone services are limited and confined mostly to Monrovia. Mobile phone coverage extends services to other towns and rural areas, but combined fixed-line and mobile phone density is low, at about five per 100 people.

MEDIA

Liberia has no television service so radio is the main medium for news. The state-run broadcaster runs one station but does not provide national coverage. Many private radio stations were shut down under President Taylor's regime, but there is now a growing number of community radio stations, often supported by international agencies.

LIBYA

Al-Jumahiriyah al-Arabiya al-Libiyah ash Shabiyah al-Ishtirakiyah al-Uzma – Great Socialist People's Libyan Arab Jamahiriya

Area – 1,759,540 sq. km
Capital – Tripoli (Tarabulus); population, 2,189,000 (2007 est)
Major cities – Al Hums, Az Zawiyah, Benghazi, Misratah, Tarhunah, Zuwarah
Currency – Libyan dinar (LD) of 1,000 dirhams
Population – 6,036,914 rising at 2.26 per cent per year (2007 est); the people are principally Arab, with some Berbers in the west and some Tuareg tribesmen in the Fezzan
Religion – Islam (97 per cent), Christianity (2 per cent) (est). The vast majority of the Muslim population practises Sunni Islam
Language – Arabic (official), Italian, English
Population density – 3 per sq. km (2006)
Urban population – 86.9 per cent (2005 est)
Median age (years) – 23.3 (2007 est)
National anthem – 'Allahu Akbar' ['God is Greatest']
National day – 1 September (Revolution Day)
Life expectancy (years) – 76.88 (2007 est)
Mortality rate – 3.47 (2007 est)
Birth rate – 26.09 (2007 est)
Infant mortality rate – 22.82 (2007 est)
Death penalty – Retained
CPI score – 2.5 (2007)
Population below poverty line – 7.4 per cent (2005 est)

CLIMATE AND TERRAIN

Plains in the north rise to plateaus and depressions in the centre and south, with some hills on the north-west and north-east coasts and in the far south. The terrain is arid, and much of it is desert. Elevation extremes range from 2,267m (Bikku Bitti) at the highest point to −47m (Sabkhat Guzayyil) at the lowest. The climate is Mediterranean on the coast and hot and dry in the interior. Average temperatures in Tripoli range from 13°C in January to 31°C in August.

HISTORY AND POLITICS

Libya comprises the three ancient regions of Tripolitania, Cyrenaica and Phazzania (Fezzan). Tripolitania was settled by the Phoenicians in the seventh century BC and then became the eastern part of the kingdom of Carthage. Cyrenaica was colonised by the Greeks in the fourth century BC. All three regions became provinces of the Roman Empire in the first century BC, and subsequently were under the control of the Byzantine Empire until conquered by the Arabs in the seventh century AD, when Islam was introduced.

Libya was part of the Turkish Ottoman Empire from the mid-16th century until 1911, when the country was conquered and colonised by Italy. Libya suffered heavy fighting in the Second World War, and then came under British and French control until 24 December 1951, when it achieved independence as the Kingdom of Libya through a UN resolution.

The discovery of oil in 1959 made the country wealthy but created social disharmony. In 1969 the king was deposed in a military coup led by Col. Muammar al-Gaddafi and a Revolutionary Command Council was installed that proclaimed the country a republic. Economic activity, including the oil industry, was nationalised in the 1970s, but a degree of liberalisation was introduced in the late 1980s.

Col. Gaddafi developed a brand of Islamic socialism and sought to promote pan-Arab unity and Islam abroad. This led Libya to support militant and revolutionary groups and to become involved in international terrorism. Relationships with Western governments became increasingly strained, bringing US military reprisals for terrorist activities in the 1980s and UN sanctions from 1992 after Libya refused to extradite the two men suspected of the 1988 bombing of a Pan Am aircraft over Lockerbie, Scotland. Sanctions were suspended in 1999 after the suspects were handed over for trial, and were lifted in 2003 after Libya admitted responsibility for the bombing and paid compensation.

Since 2003 Col. Gaddafi has made further moves to end Libya's isolation and normalise relations with the West, such as abandoning its development of weapons of mass destruction and a promise in 2004 to allow UN nuclear weapons inspections.

POLITICAL SYSTEM

Under the 1977 constitution, the head of state is the 'Leader of the Revolution', Col. Muammar al-Gaddafi, who is in effect an absolute ruler. The legislature is the General People's Congress, which has 750 members appointed by local people's congresses for a three-year term. The General People's Congress is the highest policy-making body in the country. It appoints the General People's Committee, which exercises executive power; the secretary-general of the General People's Committee is in effect the prime minister. The General People's Congress also has its own administrative secretariat. The Arab Socialist Union is the only legal political party.

HEAD OF STATE

Leader of the Revolution, Col. Muammar al-Gaddafi

SELECTED GOVERNMENT MEMBERS *as at June 2008*

Secretary-General of the People's Congress, Miftah Muhammad Keba
Secretary-General of the General People's Committee, Prime Minister, Al-Baghdadi Ali al-Mahmudi
Secretary, Economy, Ali Abd-al-Aziz al-Isawi
Secretary, Finance, Muhammad al-Huwayj
Secretary, Foreign Affairs, Abdel Rahman Muhammad Shalqam

LIBYAN PEOPLE'S BUREAU

15 Knightsbridge, London SW1X 7LY
T 020-7201 8280
Ambassador Extraordinary and Plenipotentiary, vacant

BRITISH EMBASSY

PO Box 4206, Sharia Uahran 1, Tripoli
T (+218) (21) 340 3644
Ambassador Extraordinary and Plenipotentiary, HE Sir Vincent Fean, *apptd* 2006

BRITISH COUNCIL

PO Box 6797, Casablanca Street, Siyahia, Tripoli
T (+218) (21) 483 2541 W www.britishcouncil.org/libya
Director, Anna Searle

DEFENCE

The army has 2,025 main battle tanks, over 1,000 armoured infantry fighting vehicles and 945 armoured personnel carriers. The navy has 2 submarines, 2 frigates, 1 corvette, 18 patrol and coastal vessels, and 7 helicopters at 4 major bases. The air force has 374 combat aircraft and 35 armed helicopters.

Military expenditure – US$650m (2007)
Military personnel – 76,000: army 50,000, navy 8,000, air force 18,000
Conscription duration – 12 to 24 months (selective)

ECONOMY AND TRADE

Normalisation of relations with the West has stimulated economic liberalisation and a slow transition towards a more market-orientated economy; some subsidies have been reduced and some privatisation is planned. Libya has also attracted more foreign direct investment, mainly in the energy sector, since UN sanctions ended.

The oil industry, which is state-controlled, dominates the economy, accounting for 95 per cent of total exports and about 25 per cent of GDP; as the population is small, this gives the country a relatively high per capita GDP. Oil and natural gas reserves are considerable and relatively undeveloped, and Libya has licensed further exploration in recent years in auctions open to foreign companies. Attempts to diversify the economy have led to expansion of the manufacturing and construction sectors, which account for more than 20 per cent of GDP, to include the production of petrochemicals, iron, steel and aluminium in addition to food processing. Owing to the terrain and climate, agriculture is a small sector, contributing only 2.1 per cent of GDP, and Libya imports about 75 per cent of its food.

The main trading partners are Italy, Germany and other EU countries, Turkey and China. Principal exports are crude oil, refined petroleum products, natural gas and chemicals. The main imports are machinery, semi-finished goods, food, transport equipment and consumer products.

GNI – US$44,000m; US$7,290 per capita (2006)
Annual average growth of GDP – 5.4 per cent (2007 est)
Inflation rate – 3.3 per cent (2007 est)
Unemployment – 30 per cent (2004 est)
Total external debt – US$4,837m (2007 est)
Imports – US$8,200m (2006)
Exports – US$38,000m (2006)

BALANCE OF PAYMENTS
Trade – US$30,150m surplus (2006)
Current Account – US$25,646m surplus (2006)

Trade with UK	*2006*	*2007*
Imports from UK	£203,493,000	£231,990,898
Exports to UK	£592,042,000	£577,010,804

COMMUNICATIONS

There are about 83,200km of roads; the coastal road running from the Tunisian frontier through Tripoli, Benghazi and Tubruq to the Egyptian border, serves the main population centres. Main roads also link the provincial centres, and the oil-producing areas of the south with the coastal towns. Libya has had no railway services since 1965, but seven lines with a total of 2,757km of track are undergoing work with a view to resuming services from 2008. There are 141 airports and airfields; the principal airports are at Tripoli, Benghazi and Sebha. The main seaports are Benghazi, Tripoli and Tobruq.

The telephone system is being modernised and expanded. Combined fixed-line and mobile phone density was 75 per 100 people in 2006, with 483,000 main lines and 3.9 million mobile phone subscribers. There were 205,000 internet users in 2005.

EDUCATION AND HEALTH

There are nine years of compulsory education. The education system allows for six years each at primary and secondary level.
Literacy rate – 81.7 per cent (2004 est)
Gross enrolment ratio (percentage of relevant age group) – primary 110 per cent; secondary 111 per cent (2006 est)
Health expenditure (per capita) – US$223 (2005)
Hospital beds (per 1,000 people) – 3.4 (2000–6)

MEDIA

The state maintains strict control over the media, although the first private television channel was permitted to broadcast in 2007. Great Jamahiriya TV is the state-run television broadcaster. Pan-Arab satellite television stations are available and internet access is generally free from disruption, but still closely monitored. Some international publications are available, but are routinely censored by the authorities.

LIECHTENSTEIN

Fürstentum Liechtenstein – Principality of Liechtenstein

Area – 160 sq. km
Capital – Vaduz; population, 5,000 (2007 est)
Currency – Swiss franc of 100 rappen (or centimes)
Population – 34,247 rising at 0.75 per cent per year (2007 est)
Religion – Roman Catholicism (78 per cent), Protestantism (8 per cent), Islam (5 per cent), Orthodox Christianity (1 per cent) (est)
Language – German (official)
Population density – 21·8 per sq. km (2006)
Median age (years) – 40.1 (2007 est)
National anthem – 'Oben am Jungen Rhein' ['High Above the Young Rhine']
National day – 15 August (Assumption Day)
Life expectancy (years) – 79.81 (2007 est)
Mortality rate – 7.3 (2007 est)
Birth rate – 10.02 (2007 est)
Infant mortality rate – 4.58 (2007 est)
Death penalty – Abolished for all crimes (since 1987)

CLIMATE AND TERRAIN

Liechtenstein is a small landlocked principality in the Alps, with part of the Rhine river valley running through the west of the country. Elevation extremes range from 2,599m (Grauspitz) at the highest point to 430m (Ruggeller Riet) at the lowest. There is heavy snowfall in winter and average temperatures range from 0°C in January to 21°C in July.

HISTORY AND POLITICS

Although there was a sovereign state within the present boundaries from the 14th century, the present state of Liechtenstein was formed from the lordships of Schellenberg and Vaduz in 1719. Part of the Holy Roman Empire, the principality became a member of the Confederation of the Rhine that succeeded the Empire in 1806, and then of the German Confederation from 1815 until 1866. It was the only German principality to remain outside the German Empire when it was formed in 1871. The country abolished its armed forces and declared permanent neutrality in 1868. The country's neutrality was not violated in either of the world wars.

Economic decline in the years following the First World War led Liechtenstein to adopt the Swiss currency in 1921 and to enter into a Swiss customs union in 1923. The country became extremely prosperous as an international finance centre after the Second World War. After criticism of the laxness of its financial regulation it tightened its laws in 2000 to prevent money laundering. Nevertheless, it was threatened with sanctions by the OECD in 2002 for failing to meet international financial transparency and information exchange standards and remains on the OECD blacklist.

Governments in the 20th century have been formed by the two main parties, each dominating at different periods: the northern-based Progressive Citizens' Party (FBP) from 1938 to 1970, and the southern-based Patriotic Union (VU) from 1970 to 2001, except for 1974–8. In the 2001 legislative election, the FBP returned to power for the first time since 1978, but although it remained the largest party after the 2005 election, it did not have an overall majority and formed a coalition government with the VU. However, the government's power is limited by the role and power of the monarchy, which has resisted attempts at reform. Prince Hans Adam II threatened to step down as head of state when the government suggested a reduction in his powers in 1995, and a referendum in 2003 approved constitutional changes that give the monarchy greater powers over the government and judiciary. Prince Hans

Adam remains head of state but in 2004 he handed over day-to-day responsibility for running the principality to his son and heir, Prince Alois.

POLITICAL SYSTEM
Under the 1921 constitution, Liechtenstein is a constitutional monarchy, with the hereditary prince as head of state. The unicameral legislature, the *Landtag*, has 25 members directly elected for a four-year term. There is a threshold of 8 per cent for parties to gain representation. The cabinet is appointed by the prince on the advice of the *Landtag* and consists of the head of government and four ministers.

HEAD OF STATE
HSH The Prince of Liechtenstein, Hans Adam II, *born* 14 February 1945; *succeeded* 13 November 1989
Heir, HSH Prince Alois, *born* 11 June 1968

SELECTED GOVERNMENT MEMBERS *as at June 2008*
Head of Government, Finance, Otmar Hasler
Deputy Head of Government, Justice, Economy, Klaus Tschütscher
Foreign Affairs, Rita Kieber-Beck
Home Affairs, Martin Meyer

BRITISH AMBASSADOR
HE Simon Featherstone, resident at Bern, Switzerland

ECONOMY AND TRADE

Liechtenstein has a prosperous, highly industrialised and diversified economy. Its mainstay is the financial services sector, which, with other service industries such as tourism, employs over half of the workforce. A light industrial base produces electronics, metal manufactures, dental products, ceramics, pharmaceuticals, food products, precision instruments and optical instruments, and employs 44 per cent of the workforce. Almost half the workforce commutes daily from Austria, Switzerland and Germany.

Liechtenstein became a member of the European Free Trade Association in 1991, and joined the European Economic Area in 1995. Most of its trade is with EU countries and Switzerland. The principal exports are its industrial products. The main imports are agricultural products, industrial raw materials, energy, machinery, metal goods, textiles, foodstuffs and vehicles.
Inflation rate – 1 per cent (2001)
Unemployment – 1.3 per cent (2002)

Trade with UK	*2006*	*2007*
Imports from UK	£23,322,000	£5,743,390
Exports to UK	£39,076,000	£37,389,395

COMMUNICATIONS

Liechtenstein has no airports and only 380km of roads, 28km of waterways, and 9km of rail track which is part of the Austrian system and connects Austria and Switzerland. In 2005, there were 20,000 main telephone lines in use and 27,500 mobile phone subscribers; there were 22,000 internet users in 2006. Liechtenstein relies on foreign broadcasters for television. Circulation for its two newspapers, *Liechtenstein News* and *Liechtensteiner Vaterland,* is under 10,000.

LITHUANIA

Lietuvos Respublika – Republic of Lithuania

Area – 65,200 sq. km
Capital – Vilnius; population, 543,000 (2007 est)
Major cities – Kaunas, Klaipeda
Currency – Litas of 100 centas, pegged to the euro
Population – 3,575,439 falling at 0.29 per cent per year (2007 est); Lithuanian (83.4 per cent), Polish (6.7 per cent), Russian (6.3 per cent)
Religion – Roman Catholicism (79 per cent), Orthodox Christianity (4 per cent) (est). Around 9 per cent of the population does not identify itself with any religious group
Language – Lithuanian (official), Russian, Polish
Population density – 54 per sq. km (2006)
Urban population – 66.6 per cent (2005 est)
Median age (years) – 38.6 (2007 est)
National anthem – 'Tautiska Giesme' ['The National Song']
National day – 16 February (Independence Day)
Life expectancy (years) – 74.44 (2007 est)
Mortality rate – 11.05 (2007 est)
Birth rate – 8.87 (2007 est)
Infant mortality rate – 6.68 (2007 est)
Death penalty – Abolished for all crimes (since 1998)
CPI score – 4.8 (2007)
Population below poverty line – 4 per cent (2003)

CLIMATE AND TERRAIN

Lithuania is a low-lying country with low hills in the west and south-east. It contains over 2,800 lakes, many of which lie in the east of the country. Elevation extremes range from 293.8m (Aukstojas Hill) at the highest point to 0m (Baltic Sea) at the lowest. The climate is mainly continental and average temperatures range from −3°C in January to 17°C in July.

HISTORY AND POLITICS

Lithuania became a nation in the late 12th century. It remained pagan for far longer than any other European country and only became fully Christian in the 15th century, when the Samogitians and the Aukstaitiai, the two main ethnic groups in the region, were converted. In the 14th century, a strong grand duchy was formed that stretched from the Baltic to the Black Sea and eastwards almost to Moscow. It confederated with Poland in the 16th century, before coming under Russian rule in 1795. The country joined Poland in rebelling against Russian domination twice in the 19th century.

Occupied by Germany during the First World War, Lithuania declared its independence in 1918 and successfully defended its autonomy against the Bolsheviks in 1918–19. However, the province and city of Vilnius were occupied by the newly independent Poland from 1920 until 1939. The USSR invaded and annexed Lithuania in 1940, but the country revolted in 1941 and briefly established its own government before being invaded and occupied by the Germans in their 1941 offensive against the USSR. Around 210,000 Lithuanians, mainly Jews, were killed during the German occupation. Soviet troops ousted the Germans in 1944 and re-established Soviet control, against which Lithuanians carried on a guerrilla war until 1952.

Growing nationalist sentiment led to the formation of the pro-democracy *Sajudis* ('The Movement') in 1988 to campaign for greater autonomy. A unilateral declaration of independence in 1990 was blocked by the USSR but following the failed August coup in Moscow in 1991, Lithuania declared its independence a second time, and this was internationally recognised. The last Russian troops left the country in 1993. Lithuania joined the EU and ratified its constitution in 2004.

Rolandas Paksas was elected president in 2003 but was impeached and dismissed the following year. He was succeeded by Valdus Adamkus (president 1998–2003), who was elected in June 2004. In the October 2004 legislative elections, the Labour Party became the largest party but without a majority, and in November joined the ruling coalition. This coalition collapsed in May 2006 and the government resigned. Gediminas Kirkilas of the Social Democratic party formed a four-party coalition government that was approved by the *Seimas* in July. A legislative election is scheduled for 12 October 2008.

POLITICAL SYSTEM

Under the 1992 constitution, the head of state is a president, who is directly elected for a five-year term, renewable only once. The unicameral *Seimas* has 141 members who are directly elected for a four-year term; 71 members are elected in first past the post constituencies and 70 by proportional representation. The prime minister is appointed by the president with the approval of the *Seimas*, and ministers are appointed upon the recommendation of the prime minister.

HEAD OF STATE

President, Valdas Adamkus, *sworn in* 12 July 2004

SELECTED GOVERNMENT MEMBERS *as at June 2008*

Prime Minister, Gediminas Kirkilas
Defence, Juozas Olekas
Foreign Affairs, Petras Vaitiekunas
Interior, Regimantas Ciupaila
Economy, Vytas Navickas
Finance, Rimantas Sadzius

EMBASSY OF THE REPUBLIC OF LITHUANIA

84 Gloucester Place, London W1U 6AU
T 020-7486 6401 E chancery@lithuanianembassy.co.uk
W http://uk.mfa.lt
Ambassador Extraordinary and Plenipotentiary, HE Vygaudas Usackas, *apptd* 2006

BRITISH EMBASSY

2 Antakalnio, Vilnius 10308
T (+370) (5) 246 2900 W www.britain.lt
Ambassador Extraordinary and Plenipotentiary, HE Simon Butt, *apptd* 2008

BRITISH COUNCIL

4 Jogailos, Vilnius 01116
T (+370) (5) 264 4890 W www.britishcouncil.org/lithuania
Director, Lina Balenaite

DEFENCE

The army has over 190 armoured personnel carriers; the navy has 2 frigates and 3 patrol and coastal vessels based at Klaipeda; the air force has 10 aircraft and 9 helicopters.

Military expenditure – US$349m (2006)
Military personnel – 13,850: army 12,500, navy 450, air force 900; paramilitary 14,600
Conscription duration – 12 months

ECONOMY AND TRADE

Lithuania's transition to a market economy is nearly complete, with most enterprises now privatised. Initially it caused a deep recession, but the economy has recovered and growth has been steady and sustained in the period up to and since Lithuania's accession to the EU. However, the inflation rate is rising, causing its adoption of the euro to be postponed until at least 2010.

The economy is diverse, industries including amber extraction and jewellery-making, metal-cutting machine tools, electric motors, domestic appliances, oil refining, shipbuilding, furniture-making and textiles. Industry contributes 34.2 per cent to GDP, services 60.6 per cent and agriculture 5.2 per cent.

The main trading partners are other EU countries and Russia. Principal exports are mineral products, textiles and clothing, machinery and equipment, chemicals, timber and wood products, and foodstuffs. The main imports are mineral products, machinery, transport equipment, chemicals, textiles, clothing, and metals.
GNI – US$26,900m; US$7,930 per capita (2006)
Annual average growth of GDP – 8 per cent (2007 est)
Inflation rate – 5.4 per cent (2007 est)
Unemployment – 3.2 per cent (2007 est)
Total external debt – US$22,700m (2007)
Imports – US$19,000m (2006)
Exports – US$14,000m (2006)

BALANCE OF PAYMENTS

Trade – US$5,259m deficit (2006)
Current Account – US$3,218m deficit (2006)

Trade with UK	*2006*	*2007*
Imports from UK	£219,000,000	£307,026,268
Exports to UK	£282,500,000	£294,555,011

COMMUNICATIONS

There are 79,497km of roads, and a railway system of 1,771km linking the major towns with Vilnius and Klaipeda, the main seaport. The 87 airports and airfields include major airports at Vilnius, Kaunas and Palanga.

The telephone system is being modernised, although fixed-line use is declining as mobile phone coverage expands. In 2006 there were 792,400 main lines in use, 4.7 million mobile phone subscribers and 1.1 million internet users.

EDUCATION AND HEALTH

Education is free of charge and compulsory from seven to 16 years, with the system comprising elementary schools (four years), nine-year schools (five years), and secondary schools (three years). The language of instruction is

predominantly Lithuanian, but there are also Russian and Polish schools. Vilnius University, founded in 1579, is one of the oldest in eastern Europe.
Literacy rate – 99.6 per cent (2004 est)
Gross enrolment ratio (percentage of relevant age group) – primary 94 per cent; secondary 100 per cent; tertiary 76 per cent (2006 est)
Health expenditure (per capita) – US$448 (2005)
Hospital beds (per 1,000 people) – 8.1 (2000–6)

MEDIA

The daily newspapers operate independently of the state and are free to criticise the government. A mix of public and private television broadcasters operate; BTV is the largest commercial company while LRT is the publicly run station.

LUXEMBOURG

Groussherzogtom Lëtzebuerg/Grand-Duché de Luxembourg/Großherzogtum Luxembourg – Grand Duchy of Luxembourg

Area – 2,586 sq. km
Capital – Luxembourg; population, 84,000 (2007 est)
Currency – Euro (€) of 100 cents
Population – 480,222 rising at 1.21 per cent per year (2007 est)
Religion – Roman Catholicism (91 per cent), Islam (1 per cent) (est)
Language – German, French (both official), Luxembourgish
Population density – 178 per sq. km (2006)
Urban population – 92.4 per cent (2005 est)
Median age (years) – 38.9 (2007 est)
National anthem – 'Ons Hemecht' ['Our Homeland']
National day – 23 June
Life expectancy (years) – 79.03 (2007 est)
Mortality rate – 8.42 (2007 est)
Birth rate – 11.84 (2007 est)
Infant mortality rate – 4.68 (2007 est)
Death penalty – Abolished for all crimes (since 1979)
CPI score – 8.4 (2007)
Military expenditure – US$253m (2006)
Military personnel – army 900; paramilitary 612

CLIMATE AND TERRAIN

A landlocked principality, Luxembourg has the forested plateau of the Ardennes in the north, forming part of the Natural Germano-Luxembourg Park which extends east into Germany. The south of the country is mainly fertile farmland and in the east is the wine-growing region of the Moselle valley. Elevation extremes range from 559m (Buurgplaatz) at the highest point to 133m (Moselle river) at the lowest. The climate is mild and average temperatures range from 1°C in January to 22°C in July.

HISTORY AND POLITICS

The area was part of the Roman Empire and then became part of the Frankish Empire in the fifth century AD. It became autonomous within the Holy Roman Empire under Siegfried, Count of Ardennes and was given the status of a duchy in 1354. Controlled by a succession of European powers after 1437, when the House of Luxembourg died out, it was made a grand duchy after the Napoleonic wars and passed to the Netherlands. Much of Luxembourg joined the Belgians in their revolt against the Netherlands in 1830; in 1838 the western, French-speaking region was assigned to Belgium, and the remainder was granted autonomy. The treaty of London in 1867 confirmed its independence and neutrality. Occupation by Germany in both world wars prompted Luxembourg to give up its neutrality and it was a founding member of NATO in 1949.

Luxembourg entered into economic union with Belgium in 1921 and joined the Benelux economic union in 1948. It was a founder member of the European Economic Community in 1958 and joined the eurozone in 1999. A referendum in 2005 approved ratification of the EU constitution.

In the 2004 legislative election, the Christian Social Party (CSV) remained the largest party in the legislature, but without an overall majority. It formed a new coalition government with the Luxembourg Socialist Workers' Party, under the leadership of Jean-Claude Juncker of the CSV, who has been prime minister since 1995.

POLITICAL SYSTEM

Under the 1868 constitution, the head of state is a hereditary grand duke. There is a unicameral legislature, the Chamber of Deputies, which has 60 members directly elected for a five-year term. There is also a Council of State, which has 21 members nominated by the grand duke; this acts as the supreme administrative tribunal and has some legislative functions. The prime minister is appointed by the grand duke on the basis of the election results and appoints the cabinet.

HEAD OF STATE

HRH The Grand Duke of Luxembourg, HRH Grand Duke Henri, *born* 16 April 1955; *succeeded* 7 October 2000
Heir, HRH Prince Guillaume, *born* 11 November 1981

SELECTED GOVERNMENT MEMBERS *as at June 2008*

Prime Minister, Finance, Jean-Claude Juncker
Deputy Prime Minister, Foreign Affairs, Jean Asselborn
Home Affairs, Jean-Marie Halsdorf

EMBASSY OF LUXEMBOURG

27 Wilton Crescent, London SW1X 8SD
T 020-7235 6961 E londres.amb@mae.etet.lu
Ambassador Extraordinary and Plenipotentiary, HE Hubert Wurth, *apptd* 2007

BRITISH EMBASSY

14 Boulevard Roosevelt, 2450 Luxembourg
T (+352) 229 864 E britemb@pt.lu
W www.webplaza.pt.lu/public/britemb
Ambassador Extraordinary and Plenipotentiary, HE Peter Bateman, *apptd* 2007

ECONOMY AND TRADE

The economy is stable, with steady growth, low unemployment and low inflation providing an exceptionally high standard of living. Banking and financial services are the dominant sector, contributing 28 per cent of GDP. Steel production used to dominate the industrial sector, but this has diversified to include IT, telecommunications, freight transport, food processing, chemicals, metal products and engineering. Tourism is also important. The small agricultural sector consists mainly of family-owned farms. Services account for 86 per cent of GDP, industry for 13 per cent and agriculture for 1 per cent. Over 50 per cent of the workforce are foreign residents or commute daily from France, Belgium and Germany.

The main trading partners are other EU countries and China. Principal exports are the products of industrial activities. The main imports are minerals, metals, foodstuffs and quality consumer goods.

GNI – US$32,904m; US$71,240 per capita (2006)
Annual average growth of GDP – 5 per cent (2007 est)
Inflation rate – 2.1 per cent (2007 est)
Unemployment – 4.4 per cent (2007 est)
Imports – US$19,000m (2006)
Exports – US$14,000m (2006)

BALANCE OF PAYMENTS
Trade – US$5,259m deficit (2006)
Current Account – US$4,389m surplus (2006)

Trade with UK	*2006*	*2007*
Imports from UK	£1,621,900,000	£267,255,793
Exports to UK	£1,512,400,000	£675,090,046

COMMUNICATIONS

Luxembourg has one airport. There are 5,227km of roads (including 147km of motorways), and 275km of railways. The river Moselle provides 37km of navigable waterway. In 2006, there were 246,700 main telephone lines in use, 714,000 mobile phone subscribers and 339,000 internet users.

MEDIA

Despite its size, Luxembourg has significant international media influence. The media group RTL broadcasts to audiences in France, Germany and the UK as well as serving the domestic market. Luxembourg also hosts the Société Européenne des Satellites (SES), which operates the Astra satellite fleet, Europe's largest satellite operation. The two best-selling daily newspapers are *Luxemburger Wort* and *Tageblatt*.

MACEDONIA

Republika Makedonija – Republic of Macedonia

Area – 25,333 sq. km
Capital – Skopje; population, 480,000 (2007 est)
Major city – Kumanovo
Currency – Denar of 100 deni
Population – 2,055,915 rising at 0.26 per cent per year (2007 est); Macedonian (64.2 per cent), Albanian (25.2 per cent), Turkish (3.9 per cent), Romani (2.7 per cent), Serb (1.8 per cent)
Religion – Macedonian Orthodox Christianity (65 per cent), Islam (32 per cent), Protestantism (2 per cent), Roman Catholicism (1 per cent) (est)
Language – Macedonian (official), Albanian, Turkish, Romani, Serbian (each official in different regions)
Population density – 80 per sq. km (2006)
Urban population – 59.7 per cent (2005 est)
Median age (years) – 34.4 (2007 est)
National anthem – 'Denes Nad Makedonija' ['Today Over Macedonia']
National day – 2 August (Ilinden Uprising Day)
Life expectancy (years) – 74.21 (2007 est)
Mortality rate – 8.78 (2007 est)
Birth rate – 12.02 (2007 est)
Infant mortality rate – 9.53 (2007 est)
Death penalty – Abolished for all crimes (since 1991)
CPI score – 3.3 (2007)
Population below poverty line – 30 per cent (2005)
Military budget – US$161m (2007)
Military personnel – 10,890: army 9,760, air force 1,130; paramilitaries 7,600
Conscription duration – Six months
Gross enrolment ratio (percentage of relevant age group) – primary 98 per cent; secondary 84 per cent; tertiary 30 per cent (2006 est)
Literacy rate – 96.1 per cent (2004 est)
Health expenditure (per capita) – US$224 (2005)
Hospital beds (per 1,000 people) – 4.7 (2000–6)

CLIMATE AND TERRAIN

The landlocked country is a mountainous plateau divided by the valleys of the rivers Struma and Vardar. Elevation extremes range from 2,764m (Golem Korab) at the highest point to 50m (Vardar river) at the lowest. Lakes Ohrid and Prespa lie on the south-west border with Albania. The climate is Mediterranean, with average temperatures ranging from 1°C in January to 23°C in July.

HISTORY AND POLITICS

The area of the former Yugoslav republic was part of the ancient kingdom of Macedonia, which also included northern Greece and south-west Bulgaria, in the fourth century BC. Macedonia became a province of the Roman Empire in the second century BC, coming under the control of the Byzantine Empire from the fourth century AD. Slav peoples settled the area in the seventh century and mixed with the Greek, Illyrian, Thracian, Scythian and Turkish peoples.

From the ninth to the 14th centuries it was under the rule successively of the Bulgars, Byzantium and the Serbs, and became part of the Turkish Ottoman Empire in the late 14th century. Following the Balkan wars of 1912 and 1913 the country was partitioned between Bulgaria, Serbia and Greece. The Serbian part was awarded to the newly created state that became Yugoslavia after the First World War. During the Second World War, this area was occupied by Bulgaria from 1941 to 1944, and after liberation became a republic within the communist Federal Republic of Yugoslavia.

Nationalist sentiment grew after the death of the

Yugoslav leader Josip Tito in 1980, and Macedonia formally seceded from Yugoslavia in 1992. International recognition was initially delayed by Greece's objections to the republic's name (Greece claims that its region of Macedonia is the only one entitled to the name), but the country joined the UN in 1993 as the Former Yugoslav Republic of Macedonia; Greece recognised it under this name and lifted its trade blockade in 1995, but blocked NATO's invitation to the republic to join the alliance in 2008 because of its name.

Throughout the 1990s there was tension and sporadic violence between the ethnic Albanians and Macedonians. Instability in neighbouring Kosovo spilled over into Macedonia in 2001, sparking off a two-month uprising by ethnic Albanian separatists aggrieved at their lack of civil rights. Peace talks facilitated by international bodies resulted in the Ohrid framework agreement, giving Albanians greater recognition within Macedonia and making Albanian an official language.

The prime minister Branko Crvenkovski was elected president in 2004 after President Trajkovski died in an air crash. After Macedonia's admission to NATO was blocked in April 2008, an early election was called for June, as the government sought a mandate for its policies. The election was won by the government but was marred by violence and electoral irregularities, causing voting to be suspended in five areas.

POLITICAL SYSTEM

The 1991 constitution was amended in 2001 in accordance with the Ohrid agreement to incorporate provisions relating to ethnic Albanian rights, and in 2004 to give ethnic Albanians greater local autonomy in areas where they predominate. The head of state is a president, who is directly elected for a five-year term. The unicameral assembly, the *Sobranie,* has 120 members directly elected for a four-year term. The prime minister is appointed by the president. Government ministers are elected by the assembly but are not members of it.

HEAD OF STATE

President, Branko Crvenkovski, *elected* 28 April 2004, *sworn in* 12 May 2004

SELECTED GOVERNMENT MEMBERS *as at June 2008*

Prime Minister, Nikola Gruevski
Deputy Prime Ministers, Zivko Jankulovski; Gabriela Konevska-Trajkovska; Zoran Stavrevski *(Economy)*
Foreign Affairs, Antonio Milososki
Interior, Gordana Jankulovska
Finance, Trajko Slavevski
Defence, Lazar Elenovski

EMBASSY OF THE REPUBLIC OF MACEDONIA

Suites 2.1/2.2, Buckingham Court, 75–83 Buckingham Gate, London SW1E 6PE
T 020-7976 0535 E info@macedonianembassy.org.uk
W www.macedonianembassy.org.uk
Ambassador Extraordinary and Plenipotentiary, vacant

BRITISH EMBASSY

Dimitrija Chupovski 4/26, 1000 Skopje
T (+389) (2) 329 9299 E britishembassyskopje@fco.gov.uk
W www.britishembassy.org.mk
Ambassador Extraordinary and Plenipotentiary, HE Andrew Key, *apptd* 2007

BRITISH COUNCIL

PO Box 562, Bulevar Goce Delcev 6, 1000 Skopje
T (+389) (2) 313 5035 W www.britishcouncil.org/macedonia
Director, Frank Fitzpatrick

DEFENCE

The army has 61 main battle tanks, 11 armoured infantry fighting vehicles and 207 armoured personnel carriers. The Marine Wing has 4 patrol and coastal combatant vessels. The air force has 4 combat aircraft and 10 armed helicopters.

MILITARY BUDGET – US$161m (2007 est)
MILITARY PERSONNEL – 10,890: army 9,760, air force 1,130; paramilitary 7,600
CONSCRIPTION DURATION – 6 months

ECONOMY AND TRADE

Macedonia was the least developed republic in the former Yugoslavia before 1991 and economic growth was hindered by the trade embargo by Greece (1993–5), suffering a further setback with the 2001 ethnic Albanian uprising. Although economic growth has recovered and is steady, the number of jobs has not risen and officially 35 per cent of the workforce is unemployed, although the grey economy is estimated to be worth more than 20 per cent of GDP. The country remains poor, with 29 per cent of the population living below the poverty line. Crime and corruption are other factors deterring foreign investment.

In 2007, 61.6 per cent of GDP was produced by the service industries, 28.1 per cent by industry and 10.3 per cent by agriculture. The main crops are grapes, tobacco, vegetables, fruit and dairy products. Food processing and wine-making are major industries, along with textiles, chemicals, iron, steel, cement, energy and pharmaceuticals. The main trading partners are Montenegro, Germany, Greece, Italy, Russia, Serbia and other Balkan states. Principal exports are food, wine, tobacco, textiles, manufactured goods, iron and steel. The main imports are machinery and equipment, cars, chemicals, fuels and foodstuffs.

GNI – US$6,300m; US$3,070 per capita (2006)
Annual average growth of GDP – 4.6 per cent (2007 est)
Inflation rate – 2 per cent (2007 est)
561m (2007 est)
Unemployment – 35 per cent (2007 est)
Total external debt – US$2,561m (2007 est)
Imports – US$3,800m (2006)
Exports – US$2,400m (2006)

BALANCE OF PAYMENTS

Trade – US$1,355m deficit (2006)
Current Account – US$24m deficit (2006)

Trade with UK	*2006*	*2007*
Imports from UK	£17,610,000	£18,151,728
Exports to UK	£25,538,000	£32,450,032

COMMUNICATIONS

Macedonia has 8,684km of roads, of which 5,500km are surfaced. There are 699km of railways, of which 223km are electrified. A 53km railway line from Beljakovci to the Bulgarian border was scheduled for completion in 2005 but is still under construction. The principal airports are at Skopje and Ohrid, and there are a further 15 airports and airfields around the country.

In 2006, there were 490,900 main telephone lines in use, 1.4 million mobile phone subscribers and 268,000 internet users.

MEDIA

Three channels of state-run television service compete with a growing number of commercial stations. Broadcasters are loosely regulated and many are unlicensed. There are 12 major daily and weekly press publications, reflecting a range of views. The partially government-owned *Nova Makedonija* is the leading newspaper.

MADAGASCAR

Repoblikan'i Madagasikara/République de Madagascar – Republic of Madagascar

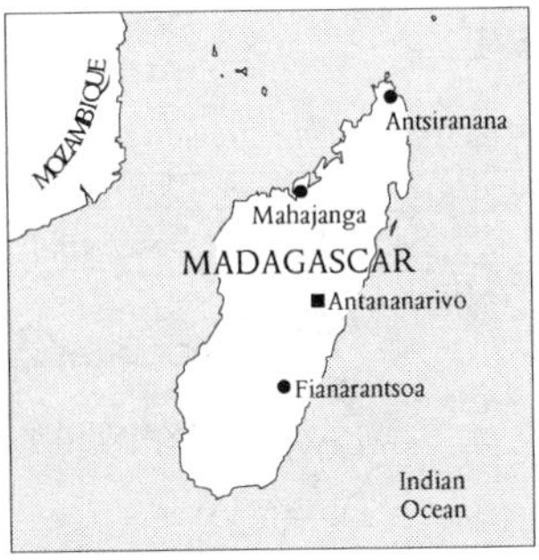

Area – 587,040 sq. km
Capital – Antananarivo; population, 1,697,000 (2007 est)
Major cities – Antsirabe, Fianarantsoa, Mahajanga, Toamasina
Currency – Ariary (MGA) of five iraimbilanja
Population – 19,448,815 rising at 3.01 per cent per year (2007 est); the people are of mixed Malayo-Indonesian, Arab and African origin. There are sizeable French, Chinese and Indian communities
Religion – Christianity (50 per cent), Islam (9 per cent) (est)
Language – English, French, Malagasy (all official)
Population density – 33 per sq. km (2006)
Urban population – 27 per cent (2005 est)
Median age (years) – 17.8 (2007 est)
National anthem – 'Ry Tanindrazanay malala ô' ['Oh, Our Beloved Fatherland']
National day – 26 June (Independence Day)
Life expectancy (years) – 62.14 (2007 est)
Mortality rate – 8.51 (2007 est)
Birth rate – 38.6 (2007 est)
Infant mortality rate – 57.02 (2007 est)
Death penalty – Retained, but not used
CPI score – 3.2 (2007)
Population below poverty line – 50 per cent (2004 est)

CLIMATE AND TERRAIN

Madagascar, the fourth-largest island in the world, lies 386km off the south-east coast of Africa, from which it is separated by the Mozambique Channel. Coastal plains rise to central highlands indented with river valleys. The terrain is arid in the south. Elevation extremes range from 2,876m (Maromokotro) at the highest point to 0m (Indian Ocean) at the lowest. Because of its isolation, most mammals and plants and half of its bird species are unique to the island. The climate is tropical along the coastline and temperate in the highlands. Average temperatures range from 9°C in July to 29°C in January. Madagascar is subject to tropical cyclones, which cause torrential rain and flooding.

HISTORY AND POLITICS

The island was settled by Indonesians from the first century AD and by African traders from the eighth century. Although first visited by Europeans *c.*1500, local kingdoms ruled until 1885, when the island became a French protectorate; it became a colony in 1895 after the last indigenous resistance was defeated. During the Second World War, the British invaded to replace the pro-Vichy government with a Free French government. At the end of the war Madagascar was returned to France, which suppressed a nationalist uprising in 1947–8. Nationalist agitation continued throughout the 1950s and resulted in independence in 1960.

The military took control in 1972 following civil disturbances, and in 1975 martial law was imposed after a coup. A Marxist one-party state was created with Lt-Com. Didier Ratsiraka as president. Marxism was abandoned in 1980 and – following pro-democracy agitation throughout the 1980s and early 1990s – other political parties were legalised in 1990 and a new constitution, adopted in 1992, made Madagascar a parliamentary democracy.

Didier Ratsiraka was defeated in the 1993 presidential elections but returned to office in 1997 after winning the 1996 election. He refused to accept his defeat in the 2001 presidential election and the six-month struggle between his supporters and those of Marc Ravalomanana, the successful candidate, brought the country close to civil war until, in July 2002, Ratsiraka went into exile and his supporters surrendered.

President Ravalomanana was elected for a second term in December 2006. The I Love Madagascar party (TIM), which supports President Ravalomanana, retained its large majority in the 2007 legislative election, winning 106 of the 127 seats; it also has a majority in the Senate.

POLITICAL SYSTEM

The 1992 constitution was amended in 1998 to create an upper chamber in the legislature, increase the powers of the presidency and increase the autonomy of the six provinces; amendments approved in a 2007 referendum further increased the powers of the president. The president is directly elected and serves a five-year term. The legislature is bicameral, comprising the National Assembly, which has 127 members (reduced from 160 in July 2007) directly elected for a five-year term, and the senate, which has 90 members, of whom two-thirds are elected by an electoral college and one-third are nominated by the president; they serve a five-year term. The prime minister is appointed by the president, and appoints the ministers.

HEAD OF STATE
President, Marc Ravalomanana, *declared elected* 29 April 2002, *sworn in* 6 May 2002, *accepted* 5 July 2002, *re-elected* 3 December 2006

SELECTED GOVERNMENT MEMBERS *as at June 2008*
Prime Minister, Interior, Gen. Charles Rabemananjara
Defence, Cecile Manorohanta
Foreign Affairs, Gen. Marcel Ranjeva
Finance, Haja Nirina Razafinjatoro

EMBASSY OF THE REPUBLIC OF MADAGASCAR
8–10 Hallam Street, London W1W 6JE
T 020-3008 4550 E embamadlon@yahoo.co.uk
W www.embassy-madagascar-uk.com
Ambassador Plenipotentiary and Extraordinary, vacant

BRITISH AMBASSADOR
HE Anthony Godson, resident in Port Louis, Mauritius

DEFENCE

The army has 12 light tanks and 30 armoured personnel carriers. The navy has 6 patrol and coastal combatant vessels at 5 bases. The Gendarmerie has 5 patrol and coastal combatant vessels.

Military budget – US$385m (2007 est)
Military personnel – 13,500: army 12,500, navy 500, air force 500; paramilitary 8,100
Conscription duration – 18 months

ECONOMY AND TRADE

Economic liberalisation and privatisation since the mid-1990s have resulted in slow but steady growth, although the political disturbances in 2002 and cyclone devastation in 2000 and 2004 were serious setbacks. President Ravalomanana's reforms and anti-corruption measures attracted increased international aid and in 2004 half of the country's foreign debt was written off. Even so, poverty remains endemic, with half the population living below the poverty line, and unemployment is widespread. For his second term the president has set out an action plan that aims to cut poverty levels by 50 per cent over five years.

Agriculture is the mainstay of the economy, accounting for 27 per cent of GDP and employing 80 per cent of the workforce. The main cash crops include coffee, vanilla, fish, sugar cane, cocoa and spices. The industrial sector contributes 16 per cent of GDP, producing processed meat, soap, beer, leather, sugar, textiles, glassware, cement and paper, assembling cars and extracting oil. Tourism is of growing importance. The main trading partners are the USA and France. Principal exports are agricultural products, cotton cloth, chromite and petroleum products. The main imports are capital goods, petroleum, consumer goods and food.

GNI – US$5,300m; US$280 per capita (2006)
Annual average growth of GDP – 6.3 per cent (2007 est)
Inflation rate – 10 per cent (2007 est)
Total external debt – US$4,600m (2002)
Imports – US$1,380m (2006)
Exports – US$830m (2006)

BALANCE OF PAYMENTS
Trade – US$550m deficit (2006)
Current Account – US$476m deficit (2006)

Trade with UK	*2006*	*2007*
Imports from UK	£4,223,000	£7,175,657
Exports to UK	£25,771,000	£32,238,638

COMMUNICATIONS

The main seaports are Toamasina, Antsiranana, Mahajanga and Toliara. There are over 100 airports and airfields, of which the major airports are at Antananarivo and Mahajanga. Surface transport is by the 49,827km of roads and 854km of railways.

In 2006, there were 129,800 main telephone lines in use, 1.04 million mobile phone subscribers and 110,000 internet users.

EDUCATION AND HEALTH

Education is free of charge and compulsory for five years, but attendance is variable; primary education is followed by a possible seven years of secondary education.

Literacy rate – 70.6 per cent (2004 est)
Gross enrolment ratio (percentage of relevant age group) – primary 139 per cent; secondary 24 per cent; tertiary 3 per cent (2006 est)
Health expenditure (per capita) – US$9 (2005)
Hospital beds (per 1,000 people) – 0.4 (2000–6)

MEDIA

An increasing number of private local radio stations are challenging the monopoly of state-run national broadcasting. A wide range of press publications print a diverse range of opinions. The independence of the press has been protected by law since 1990.

MALAWI

Dziko la Malawi – Republic of Malawi

Area – 118,480 sq. km
Capital – Lilongwe; population, 732,000 (2007 est)
Major cities – Blantyre, incorporating Blantyre and Limbe, the major commercial and industrial centre, Mzuzu, Zomba (the former capital)
Currency – Kwacha (K) of 100 tambala
Population – 13,603,181 rising at 2.38 per cent per year (2007 est)
Religion – Christianity (80 per cent), Islam (13 per cent) (est). Around 4 per cent of the population is atheist
Language – Chichewa, English (both official), Chinyanja, Chiyao, Chitumbuka
Population density – 144 per sq. km (2006)
Urban population – 17.2 per cent (2005 est)
Median age (years) – 16.7 (2007 est)
National anthem – 'Mlungu dalitsani Malawi' ['Oh God Bless Our Land of Malawi']
National day – 6 July (Independence Day)
Life expectancy (years) – 42.98 (2007 est)
Mortality rate – 18.25 (2007 est)
Birth rate – 42.09 (2007 est)
Infant mortality rate – 92.1 (2007 est)
HIV/AIDS adult prevalence – 12.5 per cent (2005 est)
Death penalty – Retained, but not used
CPI score – 2.7 (2007)
Population below poverty line – 53 per cent (2004)

CLIMATE AND TERRAIN

Malawi is a landlocked state lying along the western and southern shores of Lake Nyasa (Malawi). The northern and central regions are plateaux with rolling terrain, the south is mainly highlands. Elevation extremes range from 3,002m (Sapitwa) at the highest point to 37m (junction of Shire river and Mozambique border) at the lowest. There is a wet season from November to May and average temperatures range from 9°C in June to 30°C in January.

HISTORY AND POLITICS

Until contact was made with European missionaries in the mid-19th century, Malawi was dominated by a succession of powerful tribes that included the Maravi, the Yao and the Nogni. In 1891, the area was claimed as the Nyasaland and District Protectorate, renamed the British Central Africa Protectorate in 1893, before becoming the British colony of Nyasaland in 1907. The country was joined with Northern and Southern Rhodesia (now Zambia and Zimbabwe) between 1953 and 1963. It became independent, as Malawi, in 1964, with Dr Hastings Banda as prime minister.

In 1966, the country became a one-party state ruled by the Malawi Congress Party (MCP) and Dr Banda became president, declaring himself president for life in 1971. In the early 1990s, there was increasing pro-democracy agitation at home, and the civil disturbances and pressure from abroad forced Banda to introduce multiparty democracy in 1994.

In the 2004 legislative election, the MCP became the largest party with 60 seats, but without an overall majority. The simultaneous presidential election was won by the United Democratic Front (UDF) candidate Bingu wa Mutharika, who appointed a coalition government made up of the UDF and smaller parties.

In 2005, President Mutharika resigned from the UDF over the apparent hostility of the party and his predecessor, Bakili Muluzi, to his anti-corruption campaign and founded a new party, the Democratic Progressive Party. A power struggle ensued between President Mutharika and his predecessor, Bakili Muluzi, and the vice-president, Cassim Chilumpha; both were arrested in 2006, the former on corruption charges and the latter on charges of treason.

POLITICAL SYSTEM

Under the 1995 constitution, the head of state and government is the president, who is directly elected for a five-year term, renewable only once. The unicameral national assembly consists of 193 members, who are directly elected for a five-year term.

HEAD OF STATE
President, C-in-Cf of the Armed Forces, Bingu wa Mutharika, *elected* 20 May 2004

SELECTED GOVERNMENT MEMBERS *as at June 2008*
Finance, Goodall Gondwe
Foreign Affairs, Joyce Banda
Home Affairs, Ernest Malenga
Defence, Aaron Sangala

HIGH COMMISSION OF THE REPUBLIC OF MALAWI
70 Winnington Road, Hampstead, London N2 0TX
T 020-8455 5624 E malawihighcom@btconnect.com
W www.malawihighcom.org.uk
High Commissioner, HE Dr Francis Moto, *apptd* 2006

BRITISH HIGH COMMISSION
PO Box 30042, Lingadzi House, Lilongwe 3
T (+265) (1) 772 400 E bhclilongwe@fco.gov.uk
High Commissioner, Richard Wildash, LVO, *apptd* 2006

BRITISH COUNCIL
PO Box 30222, Plot No. 13/20 City Centre, Lilongwe 3
T (+265) (1) 773 244 W www.britishcouncil.org/malawi
Director, Marc Jessel

DEFENCE

The maritime wing has 14 patrol and coastal combatant vessels at a base on Lake Nyasa.
Military budget – US$21m (2007 est)
Military personnel – 5,300: army 5,300; paramilitary 1,500

ECONOMY AND TRADE

The economy has suffered from years of mismanagement and corruption and Malawi is one of the poorest countries in Africa. These problems and the vulnerability of agricultural production to both drought and severe flooding make the country heavily dependent on food and economic aid from international agencies and donor nations. Debt relief under the IMF's heavily indebted poor countries programme and tighter fiscal control have reduced public debt from over 200 per cent of GDP to 42 per cent by 2007.

The economy is primarily agricultural, with 90 per cent of the workforce engaged in agriculture, which accounts for 36.3 per cent of GDP and 90 per cent of export revenue. Tobacco is the most important cash crop, providing over half of export earnings, along with tea, sugar, cotton, coffee and peanuts. A number of light manufacturing industries have been established, mainly in agricultural processing, sawmill products, cement, clothing and consumer goods. The main export markets are South Africa, Germany, Egypt and the USA. The main sources of imports are South Africa, India and neighbouring countries. Apart from tobacco and other agricultural products, wood products and clothing are principal exports. The main imports are food, fuels, semi-manufactures, consumer goods and transport equipment.
GNI – US$3,100m; US$230 per capita (2006)
Annual average growth of GDP – 5.7 per cent (2007 est)
Inflation rate – 8 per cent (2007 est)
Total external debt – US$622m (2007 est)
Imports – US$1,020m (2006)
Exports – US$620m (2006)

BALANCE OF PAYMENTS
Trade – US$400m deficit (2006)
Current Account – US$195m deficit (2006)

Trade with UK	*2006*	*2007*
Imports from UK	£10,485,000	£13,563,290
Exports to UK	£11,461,000	£11,092,859

COMMUNICATIONS

Much internal transport is by water; there are 700km of navigable waterways on Lake Nyasa (Malawi) and the river Shire. Communication with the Indian Ocean coast is by rail through Mozambique; the route to the port of Beira was severed during Mozambique's civil war but the route to Nacala reopened in 2002. There are 797km of railways, including a single-track line linking Blantyre with the Zambian border, via Lilongwe and Salima. There are 15,451km of roads, of which 6,956km are surfaced. The main airports are at Blantyre and Lilongwe, with 37 smaller airports and airstrips around the country.

Privatisation of telecommunications services was completed in 2006. Fixed-line density is less than one per 100 people. Mobile phone services are expanding but coverage is limited to urban areas at present.

EDUCATION AND HEALTH

The government is responsible for primary and secondary schools, technical education and primary teacher training.

Literacy rate – 64.1 per cent (2004 est)
Gross enrolment ratio (percentage of relevant age group) – primary 119 per cent; secondary 29 per cent (2006 est)
Health expenditure (per capita) – US$19 (2005)
Hospital beds (per 1,000 people) – 1.3 (2002)

MEDIA

There are four national newspapers, two of which are dailies. Television Malawi is state-run, and the Malawi Broadcasting Corporation, which is the chief provider of information for the country, is a state-run radio network that competes with a number of private channels.

MALAYSIA

Area – 329,750 sq. km. Peninsular Malaysia is bordered by Thailand to the north. On Borneo, the Malaysian states of Sarawak and Sabah are bordered by Indonesia to the south, and enclose Brunei to the north
Capital – Kuala Lumpur; population, 1,448,000 (2007 est); Putrajaya is the administrative capital
Major cities – Ampang Jaya, Ipoh, Johor Bahru, Klang, Kota Kinabalu, Kuching, Petaling Jaya, Shah Alam, Subang Jaya
Currency – Malaysian dollar (M$) (ringgit) of 100 sen
Population – 24,821,286 rising at 1.76 per cent per year (2007 est); Malay (50.4 per cent), Chinese (23.7 per cent), Indian (7.1 per cent) (est)
Religion – Islam (60 per cent), Buddhism (19 per cent), Christianity (9 per cent), Hinduism (6 per cent), Chinese traditional religions (3 per cent) (est)
Language – Bahasa Melayu (official), English, Cantonese, Mandarin, Tamil, Telugu, Malayalam, Punjabi, Thai
Population density – 79 per sq. km (2006)
Urban population – 65.1 per cent (2005 est)
Median age (years) – 24.4 (2007 est)
National anthem – 'Negaraku' ['My Country']
National day – 31 August (Malaysia Day)
Life expectancy (years) – 72.76 (2007 est)
Mortality rate – 5.05 (2007 est)
Birth rate – 22.65 (2007 est)
Infant mortality rate – 16.62 (2007 est)
Death penalty – Retained
CPI score – 5.1 (2007)
Population below poverty line – 5.1 per cent (2002 est)

CLIMATE AND TERRAIN

Malaysia comprises the 11 states of peninsular Malaya plus Sabah and Sarawak on the island of Borneo. Each is separated from the other by 1,029km of the South China Sea. The Malay peninsula, which extends from the isthmus of Kra to the Singapore Strait, is a plain with two highland areas in the north. The Malaysian part of Borneo is mostly high plateau, rising to mountains in western Sabah and eastern Sarawak, while Sarawak also has lower-lying land along the coast and in the Rajang river valley. Elevation extremes range from 4,100m (Gunung Kinabalu, Sabah) at the highest point to 0m (Indian Ocean) at the lowest. There are monsoon seasons from April to October in the south-west of the country and from October to February in the north-east. Average temperatures in Kuala Lumpur range from 22°C in January to 31°C in September.

HISTORY AND POLITICS

Malaysia formed part of the Srivijaya Empire from the ninth to the 14th century. From the 16th century, the Portuguese, Dutch and British vied for control in the region. The British possessions of Singapore, Penang and Malacca were formed in 1826 into the Straits Settlement, which became a crown colony in 1867. British protection was extended over four Malay states, which federated in 1896, and protection treaties were agreed with several other states between 1885 and 1930. Following occupation by the Japanese from 1941 to 1945, the United Malay National Organisation (UMNO) was founded in 1946 to oppose plans for centralisation. The nine peninsular states were federated as the Federation of Malaya in 1948. The Federation of Malaya became independent in 1957, and in 1963 it combined with Singapore, Sarawak and Sabah to form the Federation of Malaysia; Singapore withdrew from the federation in 1965.

UMNO has dominated post-independence politics, initially as the governing party and since 1971 as the dominant partner in the Barisan Nasional (National Front) coalition governments. Mahathir bin Muhammad became prime minister in 1981 and his 22-year tenure of office saw increasingly authoritarian rule, particularly as opposition to Malay dominance of political life grew in the 1980s and 1990s. There is considerable tension between the ethnic groups in Malaysia; Malay resentment of the large Chinese minority's economic dominance led to the adoption in 1971 of policies that favour ethnic Malays in education and employment, although the Chinese remain the wealthiest section of society. In recent

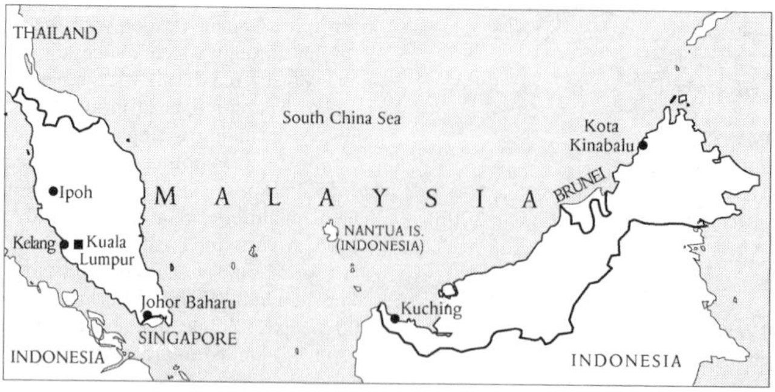

years there has been intercommunal violence between ethnic Indians, the poorest group, and Malays.

The Barisan Nasional coalition won the legislative election in March 2008, but with a majority reduced from 198 to 140 seats after a significant swing to the opposition parties.

POLITICAL SYSTEM

The 1957 constitution provides for a federal government and a degree of autonomy for the state governments. The supreme head of state *(Yang di-Pertuan Agong)* is elected by the state rulers from among their number and serves a five-year term.

The federal legislature has two houses, the House of Representatives and the senate. The latter, *Dewan Rakyat,* is the lower house and has 222 members, directly elected for a five-year term. The senate, *Dewan Negara,* has 70 members who serve a six-year term; the legislative assembly of each state elects two members, and 44 are nominated by the head of state.

HEAD OF STATE

Supreme Head of State, HM Sultan Mizan Zainal Abidin ibni al-Marhum Sultan Mahmud, *sworn in* 13 December 2006
Deputy Head of State, Abdul Halim Mu'adzam Shah

SELECTED GOVERNMENT MEMBERS *as at June 2008*

Prime Minister, Finance, Abdullah Ahmed Badawi
Deputy Prime Minister, Defence, Najib Tun Abdul Razak
Foreign Affairs, Rais Yatim
Home Affairs, Hamid Albar

MALAYSIAN HIGH COMMISSION

45 Belgrave Square, London SW1X 8QT
T 020-7235 8033 E mwlon@btconnect.com
High Commissioner, HE Abd Aziz bin Mohammed, *apptd* 2003

BRITISH HIGH COMMISSION

PO Box 11030, 185 Jalan Ampang, 50450 Kuala Lumpur
T (+60) (3) 2148 2122 E consular.kualalumpur@fco.gov.uk
W www.britain.org.my
High Commissioner, HE Boyd McCleary, CVO, *apptd* 2006

BRITISH COUNCIL

Ground Floor, West Block, Wisma Selangor Dredging, 142 C Jalan Ampang, 50450 Kuala Lumpur
T (+60) (3) 2723 7900 W www.britishcouncil.org/malaysia
Director, Gerry Liston, CMG

FEDERAL STRUCTURE

Each state has its own constitution, which must not be inconsistent with the federal constitution. The Malay rulers are either chosen or succeed to their position in accordance with the custom of their particular state; in other states of Malaysia, choice of the head of state is at the discretion of the *Yang di-Pertuan Agong* after consultation with the chief minister of the state. The ruler or governor acts on the advice of an executive council appointed on the advice of the chief minister and a single-chamber legislative assembly. The legislative assemblies are elected on the same basis as the lower chamber of the federal legislature.

DEFENCE

The army has 6 main battle tanks, 111 armoured infantry fighting vehicles, 1,020 armoured personnel carriers. The navy has 3 frigates, 8 corvettes, 14 patrol and coastal vessels and 12 armed helicopters at 6 bases. The air force has 68 combat aircraft and 20 armed helicopters.
Military budget – US$3,960m (2007)
Military personnel – 109,000: army 80,000, navy 14,000, air force 15,000; paramilitary 24,600

ECONOMY AND TRADE

The economy has grown vigorously since the 1970s, transforming the country into a diversified emerging economy; the government's goal is to achieve developed nation status by 2020. To this end, it has encouraged investment in high technology industries, medical technology and pharmaceuticals. Growth has been largely export-driven and the economy depends on continued buoyancy in its key export markets. The agricultural sector produces the raw materials for its highly developed industries. Industrial production includes rubber manufacturing, palm oil processing, electronics, tin mining and smelting, and logging and timber processing; oil and timber are produced in Sabah and Sarawak, and oil is refined in Sarawak, which also processes agricultural and forestry products. Tourism is a major industry. The services sector contributed 44 per cent of GDP, industry 48 per cent and agriculture 8 per cent in 2007.

The main trading partners are the USA, Japan, Singapore, China and other south-east Asian countries. Principal exports are electronic equipment, petroleum and liquefied natural gas, timber and wood products, palm oil, rubber, textiles and chemicals. The main imports are electronics, machinery, petroleum products, plastics, vehicles, iron and steel products, and chemicals.
GNI – US$146,800m; US$5,620 per capita (2006)
Annual average growth of GDP – 5.7 per cent (2007 est)
Inflation rate – 2.1 per cent (2007 est)
Unemployment – 3.1 per cent (2007 est)
Total external debt – US$57,830m (2007)
Imports – US$131,100m (2006)
Exports – US$160,600m (2006)

BALANCE OF PAYMENTS

Trade – US$29,493m surplus (2006)
Current Account – US$25,313m surplus (2006)

Trade with UK	*2006*	*2007*
Imports from UK	£881,626,000	£953,947,949
Exports to UK	£1,935,419,000	£1,716,064,403

COMMUNICATIONS

There are six main seaports in peninsular Malaysia, plus Kita Kinabalu (Sabah) and Kuching (Sarawak), and a merchant fleet of 304 ships of over 1,000 tonnes, as well as 7,200km of navigable waterways. There are 98,721km of roads, and in peninsular Malaysia 1,890km of railways. The main airports are at Kuala Lumpur, Kuala Terengganu and Penang, with over 110 smaller airports and airfields around the country.

A modern telephone system provides services nationwide. In 2006, there were 4.3 million fixed telephone lines in use, 19.5 million mobile phone subscribers and 11 million internet users.

EDUCATION AND HEALTH

There are six years of compulsory education.
Literacy rate – 88.7 per cent (2004 est)
Gross enrolment ratio (percentage of relevant age group) – primary 100 per cent; secondary 72 per cent; tertiary 31 per cent (2006 est)
Health expenditure (per capita) – US$222 (2005)
Hospital beds (per 1,000 people) – 1.8 (2000–6)

MEDIA

The government operates extremely strict censorship of all media outlets and newspapers must renew their licences annually; a renewal is granted subject to the opinion of the home minister. Scenes including kissing or swearing are routinely censored. Controversial political websites and blogs have begun to attract the attention of the government.

The four main national daily newspapers are English-language and include *The Star*, *Business Times* and *The Malay Mail*. Radio Television Malaysia is the state-run broadcaster and competes with three main commercial broadcasters.

MALDIVES

Dhivehi Raajjeyge ge Jumhooriyyaa – Republic of Maldives

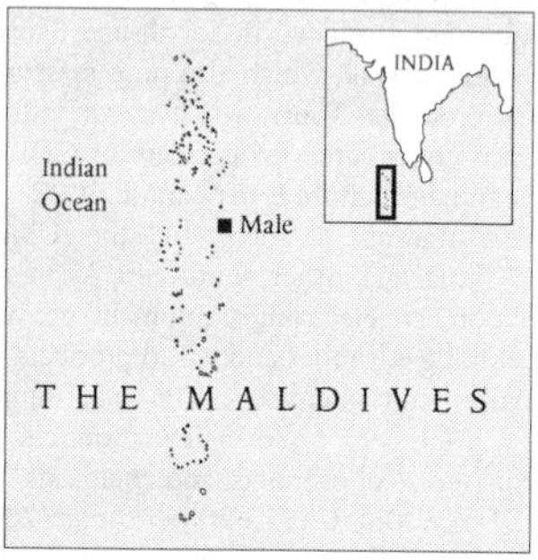

Area – 300 sq. km
Capital – Male; population, 111,000 (2007 est)
Currency – Rufiyaa of 100 laaris
Population – 369,031 rising at 2.73 per cent per year (2007 est)
Language – Dhivehi (official), English
Population density – 1,001 per sq. km (2006)
Urban population – 29.7 per cent (2005 est)
Median age (years) – 18.1 (2007 est)
National anthem – 'Gavmii mi ekuverikan matii tibegen kuriime salaam' ['In National Unity Do We Salute Our Nation']
National day – 26 July (Independence Day)
Life expectancy (years) – 64.76 (2007 est)
Mortality rate – 6.88 (2007 est)
Birth rate – 34.2 (2007 est)
Infant mortality rate – 53.25 (2007 est)
Death penalty – Retained, but not used
CPI Score – 3.3 (2007)
Population below poverty line – 21 per cent (2004)
Literacy rate – 96.3 per cent (2004 est)

CLIMATE AND TERRAIN

The republic is a chain of coral atolls in the Indian Ocean, 643km to the south-west of Sri Lanka. There are about 1,196 coral islands grouped into 12 clusters of atolls, about 198 of which are inhabited. The islands are all flat and low-lying; none is more than 2.4m above sea level. There is a tropical climate and daytime temperatures rarely drop below 28°C.

HISTORY AND POLITICS

The Maldives converted to Islam in the 12th century and came under Portuguese rule in the 16th century. After becoming a dependency of Ceylon in 1645, the islands were under Dutch and then British rule until 1887, when they became an internally self-governing British protectorate. Full independence was achieved in 1968, when the Maldives became a republic under President Ibrahim Nasir. The autocratic Nasir retired in 1978 and was succeeded by Maumoon Abdul Gayoom. Despite attempted coups in the 1980s, his tenure has ensured political stability and allowed economic development, although he has been accused of authoritarianism and human rights abuses. Unprecedented violence during anti-government demonstrations in 2003 and 2004 led to the introduction of constitutional reforms in 2005; a 2007 referendum approved the continuation of the current presidential system, although the opposition disputed the results. The 2004 Indian Ocean tsunami devastated the islands, destroying many homes and tourist resorts, but the number of dead and missing was low compared to other countries in the region.

In the 2003 presidential election, President Gayoom was re-elected for a sixth term. In the 2005 legislative election, all candidates for the elected seats ran as independents, although some were backed by the Maldivian Democratic Party, based in Sri Lanka. Following the legalisation of political parties, President Gayoom became leader of the Dhivehi Raiyyithunge Party. The first multiparty elections are due to be held before April 2009.

POLITICAL SYSTEM

The 1998 constitution was amended in 2005 to legalise political parties. The executive president, who serves a five-year term, is elected by the legislature and confirmed by national referendum. The unicameral People's Assembly has 50 members, two elected from each of the 21 provinces and eight appointed by the president, to serve a five-year term.

HEAD OF STATE
President, Commander-in-Chief of the Armed Forces, Maumoon Abdul Gayoom, *elected* 1978, *re-elected* 1983, 1989, 1993, 1998, 2003

SELECTED GOVERNMENT MEMBERS *as at June 2008*
Defence, Ismail Shafeeu
Foreign Affairs, Abdullah Shahid
Finance, Qasim Ibrahim
Home Affairs, Abdullah Kamaaludheen

HIGH COMMISSION OF THE REPUBLIC OF MALDIVES
22 Nottingham Place, London W1U 5NJ
T 020-7224 2135 E info@maldives.high.commission.org
W www.maldiveshighcommission.org
High Commissioner (acting), Adam Hassan

BRITISH HIGH COMMISSIONER
HE Dr Peter Hayes, *apptd* 2008, resident at Colombo, Sri Lanka

ECONOMY AND TRADE

Political stability and economic liberalisation have produced steady economic growth since the 1980s; although the economy contracted sharply in 2005 owing to the devastation caused by the 2004 tsunami, growth has resumed, driven by post-tsunami construction and a recovery and subsequent expansion in tourism. The economy is heavily dependent on tourism, which accounts for 28 per cent of GDP and 60 per cent of foreign exchange receipts. Import duties and tourism-related taxes provide over 90 per cent of government tax revenue. Fishing is the second largest activity. Agriculture and manufacturing are constrained by a shortage of cultivatable land and domestic labour, and so most food must be imported. Industry concentrates on clothing manufacture, boat-building and handicrafts, contributing 7 per cent to GDP.

The main trading partners are Thailand, Singapore and Sri Lanka. The only significant export is fish. Imports include fuel, ships, food and clothing.

GNI – US$903m; US$3,010 per capita (2006)
Annual average growth of GDP – 18 per cent (2006 est)
Inflation rate – 6 per cent (2005 est)
Total external debt – US$482m (2006 est)
Imports – US$900m (2006)
Exports – US$100m (2006)

BALANCE OF PAYMENTS
Trade – US$791m deficit (2006)
Current Account – US$369m deficit (2006)

Trade with UK	*2005*	*2006*
Imports from UK	£8,858,000	£6,187,000
Exports to UK	£11,667,000	£14,342,000

COMMUNICATIONS

None of the islands is more than 13 sq. km in area. The larger islands have some roads. Transport between islands is by water or air, and the country's five airports handle 6,000 departures a year. The main port is Male. Telephone services are available on the inhabited islands and mobile phone distribution is expanding rapidly.

MEDIA

The government controls the only television station. Minivan Radio, the country's only independent radio station, broadcasts from overseas as the government has failed to honour its promise to give licences to proposed private stations. The three daily newspapers are *Haveeru Daily*, *Aafathis News* and *Miadhu News*.

MALI

République de Mali – Republic of Mali

Area – 1,240,000 sq. km
Capital – Bamako; population, 1,494,000 (2007 est)
Major cities – Kayes, Mopti, Ségou, Sikasso
Currency – Franc CFA of 100 centimes
Population – 11,995,402 rising at 2.68 per cent per year (2007 est); Mandé (50 per cent), Fula (17 per cent), Voltaic (12 per cent), Songhai (6 per cent), Tuareg and Moor (10 per cent) (est)
Religion – Islam (90 per cent), Christianity (5 per cent) (est). The remainder either practise indigenous beliefs or have no religious affiliation
Language – French (official), Bambara
Population density – 10 per sq. km (2006)
Urban population – 33.7 per cent (2005 est)
Median age (years) – 15.9 (2007 est)
National anthem – 'Pour l'Afrique et Pour Toi, Mali' ['For Africa and For You, Mali']
National day – 22 September (Independence Day)
Life expectancy – 49.51 (2007 est)
Mortality rate – 16.51 (2007 est)
Birth rate – 49.61 (2007 est)
Infant mortality rate – 105.65 (2007 est)
HIV/AIDS adult prevalence – 1.6 per cent (2005 est)
Death penalty – Retained, but not used
CPI score – 2.7 (2007)
Population below poverty line – 36 per cent (2001 est)

CLIMATE AND TERRAIN

A landlocked state in west Africa, Mali is mainly savannah in the south and arid desert in the north, with some hills in the north-east. The centre is drained by the river Niger and the south-west by the river Senegal. Elevation extremes range from 1,155m (Hombori Tondo) at the highest point to 23m (Senegal river) at the lowest. Average temperatures range from 17°C in January to 31°C in September.

HISTORY AND POLITICS

Mali was successively part of the empire of the Malinke people from the 13th to 15th centuries, and the Songhai Empire in the 15th to 16th centuries. With the fall of the Songhai Empire, it was divided between the Tuareg and the Fulani and Bambara kingdoms, and then the Tukolor and Samori kingdoms. It was conquered by the French in 1880–95 and became a French colony. In 1959, it formed the Federation of Mali with Senegal before becoming a separate independent state in 1960 under a socialist regime. A military coup in 1968 resulted in Lt Moussa Traoré becoming president, and in 1974 Mali became a one-party state. Traoré was ousted in 1991 in a military coup led by Gen. Amadou Toumani Touré. Multiparty elections were held in 1992, returning the country to civilian government.

In the early 1990s there was a revolt by the Tuareg, who were seeking greater land, linguistic and cultural rights. A peace agreement in the mid 1990s brought calm but further unrest began in 2006 as the Tuareg sought greater autonomy for their region. Incidents increased in 2007 as activity by Tuareg rebels in Niger spilled over the border. The government talks with Tuareg groups are being mediated by Algeria.

Amadou Toumani Touré, standing as an independent candidate, won the 2002 presidential elections, and was re-elected in April 2007 in the first round of voting. In the 2007 legislative elections, the Alliance for Democracy in Mali (ADEMA), which had dominated government coalitions since 1992, won the largest number of seats, and the three-party Alliance for Democracy and Progress coalition of which ADEMA is a part retained its overall majority.

POLITICAL SYSTEM

Under the 1992 constitution, the president is directly elected for a five-year term. The unicameral National Assembly has 160 members, 147 directly elected for a five-year term and 13 to represent Malians abroad. The president appoints the prime minister and other ministers.

HEAD OF STATE

President, Amadou Toumani Touré, *elected* 12 May 2002, *took office* 8 June 2002, *re-elected* 2007

SELECTED GOVERNMENT MEMBERS *as at June 2008*

Prime Minister, Modibo Sidibe
Defence, Natie Pleah
Economy, Ba Fatoumata Nene Sy
Foreign Affairs, Moctar Ouane

EMBASSY OF THE REPUBLIC OF MALI

Avenue Molière 487, 1050 Brussels, Belgium
T (+32) (2) 345 7432
Ambassador Extraordinary and Plenipotentiary, HE Ibrahim Bocar Ba, *apptd* 2003

BRITISH AMBASSADOR

HE Christopher Trott, *apptd* 2007, resident at Dakar, Senegal

DEFENCE

The army has 33 main battle tanks and 50 armoured personnel carriers. The navy has 3 patrol and coastal combatant vessels at 4 bases. The air force has 16 combat capable aircraft.
Military budget – US$162m (2007 est)
Military personnel – 7,350: army 7,350; paramilitary 7,000; militia 3,000

ECONOMY AND TRADE

Mali is one of the world's poorest countries, with over 30 per cent of the population living below the poverty line. Economic reform since the mid-1990s has produced steady growth, but Mali is heavily dependent on foreign aid and remittances from expatriates. There are severe budget and foreign trade deficits, but the huge foreign debt has been reduced to a manageable size by debt cancellation and rescheduling. The economy is based primarily on subsistence farming and animal husbandry, which contribute 45 per cent of GDP and occupy 80 per cent of the population.

Gold and phosphate mining, and cotton and food processing are also important; industry accounts for 17 per cent of GDP. Export of electricity from hydroelectric plants is expected to contribute to future earnings. The main export markets are China, other Asian countries and Germany; imports come mainly from France, Senegal and Côte d'Ivoire. Principal exports are cotton, gold and livestock. The main imports are fuel, machinery and equipment, construction materials, foodstuffs and textiles.
GNI – US$5,600m; US$460 per capita (2006)
Annual average growth of GDP – 4.3 per cent (2007 est)
Inflation rate – 4.5 per cent (2002 est)
Unemployment – 14.6 per cent (2001 est)
Total external debt – US$2,800m (2002)
Imports – US$1,600m (2006)
Exports – US$1,350m (2006)

BALANCE OF PAYMENTS

Trade – US$250m deficit (2006)
Current Account – US$302m deficit (2006)

Trade with UK	*2006*	*2007*
Imports from UK	£4,304,000	£4,202,996
Exports to UK	£279,000	£593,573

COMMUNICATIONS

Mali has 18,700km of roads, 729km of railway line and 1,815km of waterways. Bamako is the centre of the transport network and the main shipping point for freight, with links to ports in Côte d'Ivoire, where civil war has disrupted trade routes, Guinea and Senegal. The main port is Koulikoro on the river Niger, and the principal airport is at Bamako.

The telephone system is limited in extent and services are unreliable, though improving. Mobile phone distribution is growing rapidly. In 2006, fixed-line density was less than one per 100 people, while mobile phone density was 13 per 100 people.

EDUCATION AND HEALTH

Literacy rate – 19 per cent (2004 est)
Gross enrolment ratio (percentage of relevant age group) – primary 80 per cent; secondary 28 per cent; tertiary 3 per cent (2006 est)
Health expenditure (per capita) – US$28 (2005)
Hospital beds (per 1,000 people) – 0.2 (2002)

MEDIA AND CULTURE

The media is among the most free-spoken in Africa. Laws exist to punish the slandering of public officials but these are rarely invoked. The print media consists of 40 privately owned newspapers, and there are a further 50 private television and radio stations. The state operates its own daily newspaper, *L'Essor.*

The music of Mali has become increasingly popular internationally in the last decade, and has absorbed some Western influences. Important names include blues guitarist Ali Farka Toure (1939–2006), kora player Toumani Diabaté (1965–), duo Amadou et Mariam and Tuareg nomads Tinariwen.

MALTA

Repubblika ta' Malta – Republic of Malta

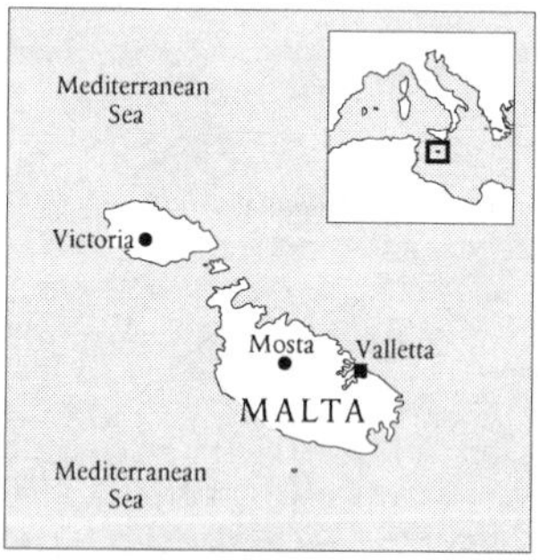

Area – 316 sq. km
Capital – Valletta; population, 199,000 (2007)
Major towns – Birkirkara, Mosta, Qormi, Saint Paul's Bay
Currency – Euro (€) of 100 cents
Population – 401,880 rising at 0.41 per cent per year (2007 est)
Religion – Roman Catholicism (95 per cent), Islam (1 per cent). Around 2 per cent of the population is atheist
Language – Maltese, English (both official)
Population density – 1,269 per sq. km (2006)
Urban population – 92.1 per cent (2005 est)
Median age (years) – 39 (2007 est)
National anthem – 'L-Innu Malti' ['Hymn of Malta']
National day – 21 September (Independence Day)

Life expectancy (years) – 79.15 (2007 est)
Mortality rate – 8.19 (2007 est)
Birth rate – 10.28 (2007 est)
Infant mortality rate – 3.82 (2007 est)
Death penalty – Abolished for all crimes (since 2000)
CPI score – 5.8 (2007)

CLIMATE AND TERRAIN

Malta is an archipelago of six islands in the Mediterranean Sea; Malta, Gozo and Comino are the largest. The island of Malta has a coastal plain in the north-east, rising to low hills on the south-west. Elevation extremes range from 253m (Ta'Dmejrek) at the highest point to 0m (Mediterranean Sea) at the lowest. The climate is warm and temperate with average summer temperatures reaching 30°C.

HISTORY AND POLITICS

The islands were controlled at various times by the Phoenicians, Greeks, Carthaginians, Romans, Arabs and the Spanish. Spain gave them to the Sovereign Military Order of Malta (known as the Knights of St John), which held them from 1530 until 1798. Recaptured from the French by Britain during the Napoleonic wars, the island became a British colony in 1814, and was developed into a substantial naval base and dockyard. Malta was strategically important in both world wars – particularly the second – when it was blockaded and subjected to aerial bombardment for five months. Its resistance led to the people of Malta being awarded the George Cross, the UK's highest award for civilian bravery, in 1942.

Malta gained independence in 1964 and became a republic in 1974. In the 1970s it developed close links with communist and Arab states, but more pro-European and pro-US policies were adopted after the election of the Nationalist Party in 1987. Malta became a member of the EU in 2004, and its legislature ratified the EU constitution in 2005.

Edward Fenech Adami, prime minister in 1987–96 and 1998–2004, stood down to contest the 2004 presidential election, which he won. The Nationalist Party was returned to power in the 2008 legislative election with a small majority.

POLITICAL SYSTEM

Under the 1974 constitution, the president is elected by the legislature for a five-year term, renewable only once. The unicameral legislature, the House of Representatives, has 69 members directly elected for a five-year term; if a party wins the majority of votes in a general election without winning a majority of seats, new seats are created until that party holds a majority of one seat. The prime minister is appointed by the president and nominates the other ministers.

HEAD OF STATE

President, Edward Fenech Adami, *took office* 15 April 2004

SELECTED GOVERNMENT MEMBERS *as at June 2008*

Prime Minister, Defence, Lawrence Gonzi
Deputy Prime Minister, Foreign Affairs, Tonio Borg
Home Affairs, Carmelo Mifsud Bonnici
Finance, Tonio Fenech

MALTA HIGH COMMISSION

Malta House, 36–38 Piccadilly, London W1J 0LE
T 020-7292 4800 E maltahighcommission.london@gov.mt
W www.foreign.gov.mt
High Commissioner, HE Dr Michael Refalo, *apptd* 2005

BRITISH HIGH COMMISSION

Whitehall Mansions, Ta'Xbiex Seafront, Msida MSD 11
T (+356) 2323 0000 E bhccomm@vol.net.mt
W www.britishhighcommission.gov.uk/malta
High Commissioner, vacant

BRITISH COUNCIL

Exchange Buildings, Republic Street, Valletta VLT 05
T (+356) 2122 6377 W www.britishcouncil.org/malta
Director, Ronnie Micallef

DEFENCE

The Maritime Squadron has 9 patrol and coastal combatant vessels. The air force has 4 combat capable aircraft.
Military budget – US$45m (2007 est)
Military personnel – 1,609: armed forces 1,609

ECONOMY AND TRADE

The mainstay of the economy for over a century was the dockyard, and ship-building and ship repairs remain significant industries, but since the 1980s Malta has developed into a tourist destination, financial services centre and freight trans-shipment point. Tourism is now the main source of income, followed by foreign trade and manufacturing, especially of electronics and pharmaceuticals. The service sector accounts for 74.9 per cent of GDP, industry for 22.3 per cent and agriculture for 2.7 per cent; Malta produces only about 20 per cent of its own food. The main trading partners are other EU states, the USA and Singapore. Principal exports are machinery and transport equipment. The main imports are machinery and transport equipment, manufactured and semi-manufactured goods, foodstuffs, beverages and tobacco.
GNI – US$6,216m; US$15,310 per capita (2006)
Annual average growth of GDP – 3.4 per cent (2007 est)
Inflation rate – 0.9 per cent (2007 est)
Unemployment – 6.8 per cent (2005 est)
Total external debt – US$188.8m (2005)
Imports – US$4,080m (2006)
Exports – US$2,710m (2006)

BALANCE OF PAYMENTS

Trade – US$1,371m deficit (2006)
Current Account – US$426m deficit (2006)

Trade with UK	*2006*	*2007*
Imports from UK	£293,300,000	£356,362,882
Exports to UK	£150,600,000	£174,465,209

EDUCATION

Education is free at all levels and compulsory between the ages of five and 16.
Literacy rate – 87.9 per cent (2004 est)

COMMUNICATIONS

The main ports are Marsaxlokk and Valletta, and there is a large merchant fleet of 1,281 ships of over 1,000 tonnes. There are 2,227km of roads, but no railways. The only airport is at Valletta.

The telephone system extends to all the islands. In 2006, fixed-line density was 50 per 100 people and mobile phone density was about 90 per 100 people.

MEDIA

Radio broadcasting began in the 1930s, partly to counter Fascist broadcasts from Italy. Malta Television, the public broadcaster, was set up in 1963. There are seven major daily and weekly news publications, which include *Malta Independent* and *It-Torca*. The newspapers usually have strong political affiliations.

MARSHALL ISLANDS

Republic of the Marshall Islands

Area – 11,854 sq. km
Capital – Majuro; population, 28,000 (2007 est)
Major towns – Ebeye, Rita
Currency – US dollar (US$) of 100 cents
Population – 61,815 rising at 2.21 per cent per year (2007 est). About 60 per cent of the population is concentrated on the two atolls of Majuro and Kawjalein
Religion – Protestantism (81 per cent), Roman Catholicism (8 per cent), Mormonism (2 per cent) (est). Around 1 per cent of the population is atheist
Language – Marshallese, English (both official)
Population density – 363 per sq. km (2006)
Urban population – 66.7 per cent (2005 est)
Median age (years) – 20.7 (2007 est)
National anthem – 'Forever Marshall Islands'
National day – 1 May (Constitution Day)
Life expectancy (years) – 70.61 (2007 est)
Mortality rate – 4.66 (2007 est)
Birth rate – 32.37 (2007 est)
Infant mortality rate – 27.3 (2007 est)
Death penalty – Abolished for all crimes (since 1986)

CLIMATE AND TERRAIN

The republic consists of an archipelago of 29 coral atolls, five islands and over 1,000 islets in the western Pacific Ocean. All of the islands are low-lying (the highest point is 10m) and a 1989 UN report warned that a rise in sea level could submerge them all by 2030. There is a wet season from May to November and average temperatures range from 25°C in January to 31°C in August.

HISTORY AND POLITICS

The Marshall Islands were first claimed by Spain in 1592 but were left largely undisturbed. Subsequently they were seized by Germany and formally became a protectorate in 1886. Japan took control of the islands in 1914 on behalf of the Allied powers and administered them from 1920 until 1944, when they were seized by US forces. In 1947 the islands became part of the UN Trust Territory of the Pacific Islands, administered by the USA. Between 1946 and 1962, US nuclear weapon tests were held on Bikini and Enewetak atolls. Enewetak has been partially decontaminated but Bikini is uninhabitable; the USA paid compensation to the test victims in the 1980s but the government is seeking US$2.7bn (£1.4bn) in further compensation to cover the medical care of radiation victims and rectify environmental damage.

The islands became internally self-governing in 1979, and the US–UN trusteeship administration came to an end in 1986, when a free association agreement between the USA and the Republic of the Marshall Islands came into effect. Under this agreement, the USA recognised the republic as a fully sovereign and independent state but retained control of external security and defence as well as giving financial help; the USA controls the Kwajalein Atoll, where it has a military base and missile test site. UN trust territory status was terminated in 1990 and full independence was granted in December 1990. A renegotiated compact with the USA was signed in 2003.

In the legislative election in November 2007, the Our Islands (AKA) grouping won the largest number of seats. Litokwa Tomeing, the former speaker, was elected president in January 2008.

POLITICAL SYSTEM
Under the 1979 constitution, the executive president is elected by the legislature from among its members to serve a four-year term. The unicameral legislature, the *Nitijela*, has 33 members, directly elected for a four-year term. There are no formal political parties, although groupings of like-minded independents have emerged in recent years. There is also a 12-member *Iroij* (Council of Chiefs) who are traditional leaders with a consultative and advisory role.

HEAD OF STATE
President, Litokwa Tomeing, *elected* 5 January 2008

SELECTED GOVERNMENT MEMBERS *as at June 2008*
Finance, Jack Ading
Foreign Affairs, Tony deBrum
Internal Affairs, Norman Matthew

BRITISH AMBASSADOR
HE Peter Beckingham, *apptd* 2005, resident at Manila, the Philippines

ECONOMY AND TRADE

The Marshall Islands has few natural resources, apart from possible seabed mineral deposits, and the economy is dependent on aid from the USA, supplemented by ship registration fees and the sale of fishing licences. Most islanders live by subsistence farming and fishing, with coconuts, breadfruit and fish the main commercial crops. A small-scale industrial sector produces copra and handicrafts and processes tuna. Tourism is being encouraged, but as yet employs less than 10 per cent of the workforce. The government is the largest employer. The main trading partners are the USA, Japan, Australia and China. Principal exports are copra and coconut products, handicrafts and fish. The main imports include foodstuffs and fuel.
GNI – US$195m; US$2,980 per capita (2006)
Annual average growth of GDP – 3.5 per cent (2005 est)
Inflation rate – 3 per cent (2005 est)
Unemployment – 30.9 per cent (2000 est)

Trade with UK	*2006*	*2007*
Imports from UK	£2,733,000	£4,476,851
Exports to UK	£560,000	£2,586,611

COMMUNICATIONS

Air transport provides the main means of internal travel, and there are 15 airports and airfields throughout the islands, with internal and international flights operated by Air Marshall Islands and Continental Air Micronesia. Majuro is the main airport as well as the main port, with a merchant fleet of 902 ships of over 1,000 tonnes; a further 857 foreign-owned ships are registered in the republic. There are 65km of surfaced roads on the two main islands. The modern telephone system extends to most of the islands. Mobile phone distribution in 2004 was less than 15 per cent of main-line density.

MEDIA

The media operates freely, although occasionally it practises self-censorship over controversial issues. US forces' radio and television broadcasts can be received. The print media consists of the *Marshall Islands Journal*, a private weekly newspaper, and the *Marshall Islands Gazette*, a government-owned monthly publication.

MAURITANIA

Al-Jumhuriyah al-Islamiyah al-Muritaniyah – Islamic Republic of Mauritania

Area – 1,030,700 sq. km
Capital – Nouakchott; population, 673,000 (2007 est)
Major towns – Kayhaydi, Kifah, Nouadhibou, Rosso
Currency – Ouguiya (UM) of 5 khoums
Population – 3,270,065 rising at 2.87 per cent per year (2007 est)
Religion – Islam (99 per cent) (est). Almost all Muslims practise Sunni Islam
Language – Arabic (official), Pulaar, Soninke, French, Hassaniya, Wolof
Population density – 3 per sq. km (2006)
Urban population – 64.3 per cent (2005 est)
Median age (years) – 17.1 (2007 est)
National anthem – 'National Anthem of Mauritania'
National day – 28 November (Independence Day)
Life expectancy (years) – 53.51 (2007 est)
Mortality rate – 11.89 (2007 est)
Birth rate – 40.56 (2007 est)
Infant mortality rate – 68.07 (2007 est)
Death penalty – Retained, but not used
CPI score – 2.6 (2007)
Population below poverty line – 40 per cent (2004 est)
Literacy rate – 51.2 per cent (2004 est)
Gross enrolment ratio (percentage of relevant age group) – primary 102 per cent; secondary 22 per cent; tertiary 4 per cent (2006 est)
Health expenditure (per capita) – US$17 (2005)
Hospital beds (per 1,000 people) – 0.6 (2000–6)

CLIMATE AND TERRAIN

The terrain is arid, apart from in the Senegal river valley, and flat, with some hilly regions in the centre of the country. Elevation extremes range from Kediet Ijill (915m) at the highest point to −5m (Sebkhet Te-n-Dghamcha) at the lowest. The climate is hot and dry; the north of the country is virtually rainless, while the south receives some unreliable rainfall between June and October. Humidity during the summer period is very high. Average temperatures range from 16°C in January to 34°C in July.

HISTORY AND POLITICS

Eastern Mauritania was part of the Ghana Empire and then the Mali and Songhai empires from the seventh to the 16th century. The area came under French influence in the 19th century, becoming a protectorate in 1903 and then a colony in 1920. The country became independent as the Islamic Republic of Mauritania on 28 November 1960. There were military coups in 1978 and 1984, the latter bringing to power Col. Maaouya ould Sid Ahmed Taya. Civilian rule was restored after multiparty elections in 1992; the presidential election was won by Col. Taya.

In the 1990s and early 2000s, ethnic tension between the Arab north and African south and internal unrest caused by opposition groups was exacerbated by several years of drought. These led to serious civil disturbances and several attempted coups. President Taya was deposed in a military coup in 2005 and a transitional government was installed.

Constitutional changes were approved by referendum in June 2006 and legislative elections were held in late 2006 and early 2007. The national assembly election was won by the Coalition of the Forces for Democratic Change, led by the Rally of Democratic Forces, with 41 seats; the senate election was won by independents grouped into the Al-Mithaq coalition, with 36 seats. The presidential election in March 2007 was won by Sidi ould Cheikh Abdallahi, who became the country's first democratically elected president since independence. President Abdallahi established the National Pact for Democracy and Development (PNDD-ADIL) in 2007, and the government appointed after a reshuffle in May 2008 was a five-party coalition dominated by the PNDD-ADIL but including opposition groups.

A bloodless military coup removed Abdallahi in August 2008, following his attempt to sack a number of military leaders. The junta appointed former EU ambassador Moulaye ould Mohamed as the new prime minister.

POLITICAL SYSTEM

The 1991 constitution was amended in 2006 to reduce the term of office of the president from six to five years and to limit the number of terms to two. The bicameral parliament comprises the National Assembly, the lower house, and the senate. The National Assembly has 95 members who are directly elected for a five-year term. The senate has 56 members (including three representing Mauritanians abroad), who are indirectly elected for a six-year term; one-third is elected every two years.

HEAD OF STATE

President, Sidi ould Cheikh Abdallahi, *elected* 25 March 2007, *sworn in* 19 April 2007

SELECTED GOVERNMENT MEMBERS *as at June 2008*

Prime Minister, Yahya ould Ahmed el Wagh
Finance, Abderrahmane ould Hamma Vezzaz
Foreign Affairs, Cheikh el Avia ould Mohamed Khouna
Interior, Mohamed Yehdih ould Moctar el Hacen
Defence, Mohamed Mahmoud ould Mohamed Lemine

EMBASSY OF THE ISLAMIC REPUBLIC OF MAURITANIA

5 rue de Montevideo, Paris 75016, France
T (+33) 4504 8354
Ambassador Extraordinary and Plenipotentiary, vacant

BRITISH AMBASSADOR
HE Charles Gray, *apptd* 2005, resident at Rabat, Morocco

DEFENCE

The army has 35 main battle tanks and 25 armoured personnel carriers. The navy has 10 patrol and coastal combatant vessels at 2 bases.

Military budget – US$18.6m (2007 est)
Military personnel – 15,870: army 15,000, navy 620, air force 250; paramilitary 7,000
Conscription duration – 24 months

ECONOMY AND TRADE

Mauritania is one of the poorer countries in the region, with 40 per cent of the population living below the poverty line and unemployment at 20 per cent. Past economic mismanagement and droughts created a huge foreign debt, although the country qualified for debt relief under the IMF heavily indebted poor country initiative in 2002, and in 2005 it was promised 100 per cent debt relief by the G8 countries.

Natural resources include iron ore, gypsum, gold, oil (off-shore production began in 2006) and rich fishing waters, although the latter are threatened by over-exploitation. Agriculture and animal husbandry, mainly at subsistence level, are the mainstay of the economy, accounting for 25 per cent of GDP and engaging 50 per cent of the population. The main industries are fish processing and mining.

The main trading partners are China and EU countries. Principal exports are iron ore (nearly 40 per cent), fish and fish products, and gold. The main imports are machinery, petroleum products, capital goods, food and consumer goods.
GNI – US$2,300m; US$760 per capita (2006)
Annual average growth of GDP – 1.5 per cent (2007 est)
Inflation rate – 7 per cent (2003 est)
Unemployment – 20 per cent (2004 est)
Total external debt – US$2,500m (2000)

BALANCE OF PAYMENTS
Trade – US$360m deficit (2006)
Current Account – US$36m deficit (2006)

Trade with UK	*2006*	*2007*
Imports from UK	£22,699,000	£9,738,189
Exports to UK	£13,952,000	£11,789,709

COMMUNICATIONS

The main seaports are Nouakchott and Nouadhibou. There are 717km of railways and 7,660km of roads. Mauritania operates ferry services on the Senegal river. There are 25 airports and airfields. The telephone system is limited but improvements are being made. Mobile phone distribution is growing rapidly, with 1 million subscribers in 2006, compared to 34,900 main lines in use.

MEDIA

The media is forbidden by law to publish opinions or information that undermine Islam or threaten national security. Television and radio services are state-owned. There are seven main national press publications, including the state-run dailies *Chaab* and *Horizon*.

MAURITIUS

Republic of Mauritius

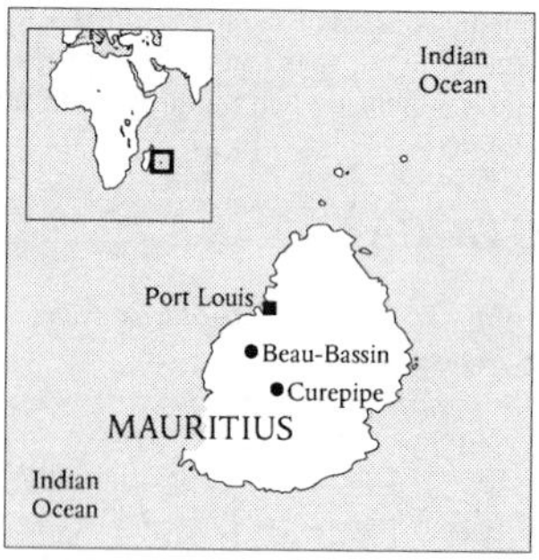

Area – 2,040 sq. km
Capital – Port Louis; population, 150,000 (2007 est)
Major towns – Beau-Bassin, Curepipe, Quatre Bornes, Vacoas-Phoenix
Currency – Mauritius rupee of 100 cents
Population – 1,250,882 rising at 0.8 per cent per year (2007 est); Indo-Mauritian (68 per cent), Creole (27 per cent), Sino-Mauritian (3 per cent), Franco-Mauritian (2 per cent) (est)
Religion – Hinduism (50 per cent), Roman Catholicism (23 per cent), Islam (17 per cent), other Christian denominations (9 per cent) (est). Less than 1 per cent of the population is atheist
Language – English, French (both official), Creole, Bhojpuri
Population density – 617 per sq. km (2006)
Urban population – 43.8 per cent (2005 est)
Median age (years) – 31.2 (2007 est)
National anthem – 'Motherland'
National day – 12 March (Independence Day)
Life expectancy (years) – 72.88 (2007 est)
Mortality rate – 6.88 (2007 est)
Birth rate – 15.26 (2007 est)
Infant mortality rate – 14.14 (2007 est)
Death penalty – Abolished for all crimes (since 1995)
CPI score – 4.7 (2007)
Population below poverty line – 10 per cent (2001 est)

CLIMATE AND TERRAIN

The republic is an island group in the Indian Ocean, approximately 885km east of Madagascar. The volcanic island of Mauritius rises from a narrow coastal plain to a central plateau ringed by mountains. Elevation extremes range from 828m (Mt Piton) at the highest point to 0m (Indian Ocean) at the lowest. The island of Rodrigues, formerly a dependency but now part of Mauritius, is about 563km east of Mauritius, with an area of 64km; the population is 36,907 (2005 est). The islands of Agalega and St Brandon are dependencies of Mauritius; the total population is 289 (2002).

There is a tropical climate, modified by south-east trade winds, and average temperatures range from 25°C in July to 31°C in January.

HISTORY AND POLITICS

The island was discovered by the Dutch in 1598; the colonists withdrew in 1710. A decade later they were replaced by the French, who established plantations that were worked by African slaves. In 1814 Mauritius was ceded to the British, who had occupied it in 1810. The

British abolished slavery in 1834 and imported indentured Indian and Chinese labourers to work on the plantations. Independence was achieved on 12 March 1968 and the state became a republic in 1992.

The Mauritian Socialist Party (MSM) under Sir Anerood Jugnauth held power from 1982 until 1995, and then returned to power in the 2000 election in coalition with the Mouvement Militant Mauricien (MMM). Jugnauth stood down as party leader and prime minister in 2003 and was elected president later in the same year. The MSM-MMM coalition lost the 2005 election to the opposition Socialist Alliance led by Navinchandra Ramgoolam, who became prime minister. The next presidential election is due in 2008.

POLITICAL SYSTEM

The 1968 constitution was amended in 1992 to introduce a republican form of government, and in 2001 to give the island of Rodrigues a degree of autonomy. The head of state is a president elected by the legislature for a five-year term. The unicameral legislature, the National Assembly has 62 elected members (Mauritius has 20 three-member constituencies and Rodrigues returns two members) and eight appointed members, who serve a five-year term; the electoral commission allocates the appointed seats on a 'best loser' basis to give more equitable representation to ethnic minorities. The prime minister is the leader of the majority party in the legislature.

Rodrigues has an 18-member regional assembly, inaugurated in 2002, when a chief commissioner and chief executive were appointed.

HEAD OF STATE

President, Sir Anerood Jugnauth, *took office* 7 October 2003

Vice-President, Angidi Chettiar

SELECTED GOVERNMENT MEMBERS *as at June 2008*

Prime Minister, Defence, Foreign Affairs, Home Affairs, Navinchandra Ramgoolam

Deputy Prime Ministers, Ahmed Rashid Beebeejaun; Charles Gaeten Xavier Luc Duval; Rama Krishna Sithanen

MAURITIUS HIGH COMMISSION

32–33 Elvaston Place, London SW7 5NW

T 020-7581 0294

High Commissioner, HE Abhimanu Kundasamy, *apptd* 2005

BRITISH HIGH COMMISSION

PO Box 1063, Les Cascades Building, Edith Cavell Street, Port Louis

T (+230) 202 9400 E bhc@intnet.mu

High Commissioner, HE Anthony Godson, *apptd* 2004

BRITISH COUNCIL

PO Box 111, Royal Road, Rose Hill

T (+230) 403 0200 W www.britishcouncil.org/mauritius

Director, Simon Ingram-Hill

DEFENCE

The army has 2 armoured infantry fighting vehicles and 16 armoured personnel carriers. The navy has 21 patrol and coastal combatant vessels.

Military budget – US$20m (2007 est)

Military personnel – none active; paramilitary 2,000

ECONOMY AND TRADE

Since independence Mauritius has diversified its economy from a predominantly agricultural base into one concentrating on the industrial, financial and tourism sectors. Agriculture continues to play a part; sugar cane is grown on 90 per cent of cultivated land and produces 15 per cent of export earnings. Industrial activity is centred on food processing, mining, offshore financial services and manufacturing textiles, clothing, chemicals, metal products, transport equipment and non-electrical machinery. Information and communications technology, hospitality and property are priorities for development. The services sector accounts for 70 per cent of GDP, industry for 25 per cent and agriculture for 5 per cent.

The main trading partners are the UK, France, India, the UAE, China and the USA. Principal exports are clothing, textiles, sugar, cut flowers, molasses and fish. The main imports are manufactured goods, capital equipment, food, fuels and chemicals.

GNI – US$6,800m; US$5,430 per capita (2006)

Annual average growth of GDP – 5.5 per cent (2007 est)

Inflation rate – 9.1 per cent (2007 est)

Unemployment – 9.2 per cent (2007 est)

Total external debt – US$2,583m (2007 est)

Imports – US$3,630m (2006)

Exports – US$2,330m (2006)

BALANCE OF PAYMENTS

Trade – US$1,297m deficit (2006)

Current Account – US$336m deficit (2006)

Trade with UK	*2006*	*2007*
Imports from UK	£45,144,000	£52,105,714
Exports to UK	£368,768,000	£349,908,462

COMMUNICATIONS

Port Louis handles the bulk of the island's external trade. The international airport is located at Plaisance. The 2,020km of roads are all surfaced. There are no railways. The telephone system offers a good service; mobile phone distribution, at 772,400 subscribers, was more than double the density of main telephone lines, recorded at 357,300 in 2006.

EDUCATION AND HEALTH

Eleven years of primary education are free of charge and compulsory. There are a number of facilities offering vocational training. The Institute of Education is responsible for training primary and secondary school teachers and for curriculum development.

Literacy rate – 84.3 per cent (2004 est)

Gross enrolment ratio (percentage of relevant age group) – primary 102 per cent; secondary 86 per cent; tertiary 17 per cent (2006 est)

Health expenditure (per capita) – US$218 (2005)

Hospital beds (per 1,000 people) – 3.0 (2000–6)

MEDIA

Freedom of expression is guaranteed by the constitution and four daily newspapers and eight weekly publications offer a range of political viewpoints. Mauritius was the highest-rated African country for press freedom in 2007, according to Reporters Without Borders. The Mauritius Broadcasting Corporation is state-owned and runs television and radio services funded through advertising and a licence fee. Satellite television is available and private radio stations began broadcasting in 2002.

MEXICO

Estados Unidos Mexicanos – United Mexican States

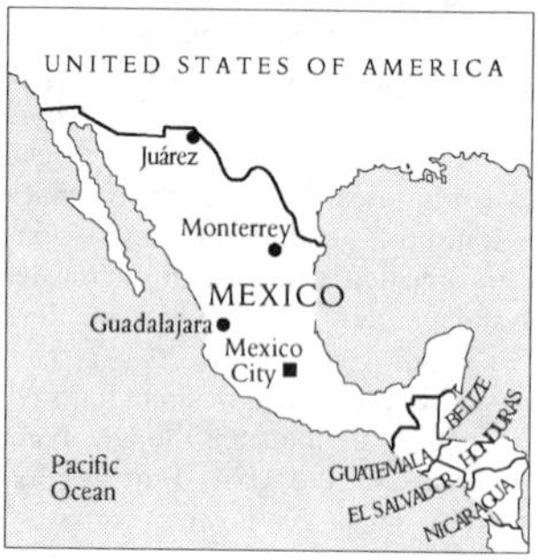

Area – 1,972,550 sq. km
Capital – Mexico City; population, 19,028,000 (2007)
Major cities – Ecatpec, Guadalajara, Juárez, León, Monterrey, Nezuhualcoyotl, Puebla, Tijuana, Zapopan
Currency – Peso of 100 centavos
Population – 108,700,891 rising at 1.15 per cent per year (2007 est)
Religion – Roman Catholicism (88 per cent), Protestantism (6 per cent) (est). An estimated 3 per cent of the population has no affiliation
Language – Spanish, Nahuatl
Population density – 54 per sq. km (2006)
Urban population – 76 per cent (2005 est)
Median age (years) – 25.6 (2007 est)
National anthem – 'Himno Nacional Mexicano' ['Mexican National Anthem']
National day – 16 September (Independence Day)
Life expectancy (years) – 75.63 (2007 est)
Mortality rate – 4.76 (2007 est)
Birth rate – 20.36 (2007 est)
Infant mortality rate – 19.63 (2007 est)
Death penalty – Abolished for all crimes (since 2005)
CPI score – 3.5 (2007)
Population below poverty line – 17.6 per cent (2004)

CLIMATE AND TERRAIN

Coastal plains rise to a central plateau and then to a spine of high mountains, the Sierra Madre, running from the north-west to south-east. The Yucatán peninsula in the south-east is low-lying, and marshy on the coast. The narrow Lower California peninsula, separated from the rest of the country by the Gulf of California, has a range of hills running along it. The mountains include volcanoes such as Popocatepetl. Elevation extremes range from 5,700m (Volcan Pico de Orizaba) at the highest point to −10m (Laguna Salada) at the lowest. The Rio Grande forms the eastern part of the northern border with the USA. Average temperatures in Mexico City range from 10°C in January to 23°C in July.

HISTORY AND POLITICS

Mexico was the centre of Mesoamerican civilisations for over 2,500 years: the Olmecs (*c.*1200–600 BC), based on the Mexican Gulf Coast; the Zapotecs (*c.*300 BC to 300 AD) in the Oaxaca valley; the Mayas (*c.*300–900 AD) in southern Mexico and the Yucatán peninsula; the Mixtecs (*c.*800–1300) in the Oaxaca valley; and the Toltecs (*c.*900–1170) in central Mexico and the Yucatán peninsula. The Aztecs, who came to the region in the 13th century, ruled until their civilisation fell to the Spanish under Hernán Cortés in 1519–21. As the viceroyalty of New Spain, Mexico remained under Spanish rule until the 19th century. In the first century of Spanish occupation, the indigenous population fell from around 21 million to one million, largely through lack of resistance to European diseases, such as bubonic plague, smallpox and influenza.

After an unsuccessful revolt in 1810, independence was declared in 1821 and a federal republic was instituted in 1824. Mexico suffered extreme instability, civil war and invasion throughout much of the 19th century. War with the USA in 1836 and 1846–8 led to the loss of about one-third of its territory. There was civil war in 1858–61 and in 1862–7 war with Britain, France and Spain after Mexico defaulted on its foreign debt. Porfirio Díaz ruled as a dictator between 1876 and 1911, until his repressive regime was overthrown in a revolution that introduced radical land and labour reforms, but instability continued.

The National Revolutionary Party, founded in 1929, came to dominate political life. Renamed the Institutional Revolutionary Party (PRI) in 1946, it formed a succession of authoritarian governments. Although unrest was not eliminated under its regime, the 1960s saw rapid industrialisation and the 1970s an oil-fuelled economic boom. Falling oil prices led to a serious financial crisis in 1982 and Mexico defaulted on its debt. Economic difficulties were eased in the 1990s with the introduction of market reforms and privatisation, and free trade agreements.

These reforms led to a degree of social upheaval. Fearing for the status of the already marginalised indigenous peoples, the Zapatista National Liberation Front (EZLN) led revolts in the south of the country in 1994 and 1995. Although violence tailed off in the late 1990s, civil campaigning continued, culminating in a mass march from Chiapas to Mexico City in 2001 in support of a bill of indigenous rights. The bill was enacted later that year but the Zapatistas claimed its provisions had been watered down and vowed to continue their campaign. The government also faces problems with corruption and violent crime, often drug-related; former president Vincente Fox said in 2005 that drugs cartels were trying to infiltrate state institutions. Violent crime rates have risen in recent years, and a new federal force was created in 2006 to combat drugs-related crime.

The PRI's political dominance ended at the 1997 election, when it lost its absolute majority in the lower house of the legislature, although it continued in government until 2000 and was again in power from 2003 until 2006. However, in the July 2006 legislative election the Partido de Accion Nacional (PAN) became the largest party in the lower house. The simultaneous presidential election was won by Felipe Calderón of the PAN, with 35.88 per cent of the vote; his closest rival, Lopez Obrador, received 35.31 per cent of the vote and challenged the result, his supporters staging mass protests for several months. Calderón's victory was confirmed in September after recounts in 9 per cent of polling districts, although Obrador and his supporters refused to accept the result, alleging voting irregularities.

POLITICAL SYSTEM

Under the 1917 constitution, the federal republic consists of 31 states and the federal capital. The head of state is an executive president, directly elected for a six-year term that may not be renewed. The bicameral legislature is the Congress of the Union. The lower house, the Chamber of Deputies, has 500 members, directly elected for a three-year term. The senate has 128 members, directly elected for a six-year term. The president appoints the cabinet. Each of the states has its own constitution and is administered by a governor, elected for a six-year term, and a state chamber of deputies, elected for a three-year term.

HEAD OF STATE
President, Felipe Calderón, *elected* 2 July 2006, *sworn in* 1 December 2006

SELECTED GOVERNMENT MEMBERS *as at June 2008*
Defence, Gen. Guillermo Galván Galván
Economy, Eduardo Sojo Garza-Aldape
Foreign Affairs, Patricia Espinosa Cantellano
Interior, Juan Camilo Mourino Terrazo

EMBASSY OF MEXICO
16 St George Street, London W1S 1FD
T 020-7499 8586 E mexuk@easynet.co.uk
W www.sre.gov.mx/reinounidoeng
Ambassador Extraordinary and Plenipotentiary, HE Juan José Bremer de Martino, CVO, *apptd* 2004

BRITISH EMBASSY
PO Box 96, Río Lerma 71, Col. Cuauhtémoc, 06500 Mexico City
T (+52) (55) 5242 8500 E ukinmex@att.net.mx
W www.embajadabritanica.com.mx
Ambassador Extraordinary and Plenipotentiary, HE Giles Paxman, *apptd* 2005

BRITISH COUNCIL
Lope de Vega 316, Col. Chapultepec Morales, 11570 Mexico City
T (+52) (55) 5263 1900 W www.britishcouncil.org/mexico
Director, Chris Rawlings

DEFENCE

The army has 746 armoured personnel carriers. The navy has 1 destroyer, 6 frigates, 168 patrol and coastal vessels, and 8 combat aircraft. There are 18 naval bases. The air force has 78 combat aircraft and 167 helicopters.
Military budget – US$3,980m (2007)
Military personnel – 248,700: army 178,000, navy 46,400, air force 11,700, marines 12,600; paramilitary 30,700

ECONOMY AND TRADE

Economic liberalisation and privatisation in the 1990s and membership of NAFTA (since 1994) have stimulated economic growth and development. This is especially true in the industrial sector, as Mexico's cheap labour has led US companies to establish factories in the north to assemble goods for the US market. But despite this and its oil, natural gas and mineral resources, Mexico remains a poor country with 40 per cent of the population living below the poverty line. A large proportion of the male population works overseas, predominantly in the USA, and much of the remaining population, especially in poor and rural areas, is dependent on their remittances. Further economic growth and poverty reduction measures are needed; so far, President Calderón's economic programme, which prioritises job creation and infrastructure development, has had opposition support.

Agriculture is diverse and productive; major crops include maize, wheat, soya beans, rice, beans, cotton, coffee, fruit, tomatoes, beef, poultry and dairy products. Agriculture accounts for 4 per cent of GDP and 18 per cent of employment. The main industries include production of food, beverages, tobacco, chemicals, iron and steel, oil production, mining, textiles, clothing, motor vehicles, consumer durables and tourism. The services sector accounts for 70 per cent of GDP and industry for 26 per cent.

Mexico has free trade agreements with over 40 countries, covering 90 per cent of its trade. The main trading partner is the USA (85 per cent of exports; 51 per cent of imports). Canada is the other main export market, and China and Japan the other main sources of imports. Principal exports include manufactured goods, oil and oil products, silver, fruit, vegetables, coffee and cotton. The main imports include metal-working machines, steel mill products, agricultural machinery, electrical equipment, car parts for assembly, vehicle repair parts, aircraft and aircraft parts.
GNI – US$815,700m; US$7,830 per capita (2006)
Annual average growth of GDP – 3 per cent (2007 est)
Inflation rate – 4 per cent (2007 est)
Unemployment – 3.7 per cent (2007 est)
Total external debt – US$182,000m (2007)
Imports – US$268,000m (2006)
Exports – US$250,000m (2006)

BALANCE OF PAYMENTS
Trade – US$17,728m deficit (2006)
Current Account – US$2,220m deficit (2006)

Trade with UK	*2006*	*2007*
Imports from UK	£743,227,000	£764,709,225
Exports to UK	£454,803,000	£573,831,430

COMMUNICATIONS

Veracruz, Tampico and Coatzacoalcos are the chief seaports on the Atlantic coast, and Guaymas, Mazatlán, Lázaro Cárdenas and Salina Cruz on the Pacific. There are 17,665km of railways; the rail network is currently undergoing reorganisation. There are 235,670km of roads, of which 116,751km are surfaced, and 2,900km of navigable rivers and coastal canals. The main international airport is at Mexico City, with 20 others across the country.

The telephone system is limited in scope, with a low density of provision for domestic users, and mobile phone distribution has grown rapidly. In 2006 there were 19.8 million main telephone lines in use, 57 million mobile phone subscribers and 22 million internet users.

EDUCATION AND HEALTH

Although Mexico allows for eleven years of free and compulsory education, on average adults have only completed 7.2 years. The country's largest university is the National Autonomous University of Mexico, situated in Mexico City.
Literacy rate – 90.3 per cent (2004 est)
Gross enrolment ratio (percentage of relevant age group) – primary 112 per cent; secondary 85 per cent; tertiary 25 per cent (2006 est)
Health expenditure (per capita) – US$474 (2005)
Hospital beds (per 1,000 people) – 1.0 (2000–6)

MEDIA

The Televisa group used to control all Mexican broadcasting but now competes with other channels and a huge number of independent radio stations operating in a competitive sector, some of which broadcast to Mexicans working in the USA. There are six national newspapers, which represent a variety of political opinions.

CULTURE

The dominant figures in Mexican art are husband and wife Diego Rivera (1886–1957) and Frida Kahlo (1907–1954). In literature, essayist and poet Octavio Paz (1914–98) won the Nobel prize in 1990, while Carlos Fuentes (*b.* 1928) is a respected political commentator and novelist.

As in other Latin American countries, football has a huge following, and the country has hosted the World Cup twice, in 1970 and 1986. Bullfighting is also very popular and Mexico City is home to the largest ring in the world, seating 55,000.

FEDERATED STATES OF MICRONESIA

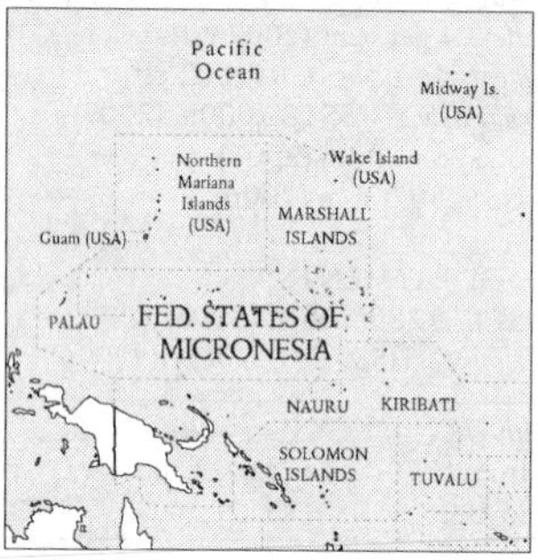

Area – 702 sq. km
Federal capital – Palikir; population, 7,000 (2007), on Pohnpei
Major city – Weno
Currency – US dollar
Population – 107,862 falling at 0.15 per cent per year (2007 est); Chuukese (48.8 per cent), Pohnpeian (24.2 per cent), Kosraean (6.2 per cent), Yapese (5.2 per cent), Yap outer islands (4.5 per cent), Asian (1.8 per cent), Polynesian (1.5 per cent)
Religion – Protestantism (40 per cent), Roman Catholicism (40 per cent) (est)
Language – English (official), Trukese, Pohnpeian, Yapese, Kosrean, Ulithian
Population density – 158 per sq. km (2006)
Urban population – 30 per cent (2005 est)
Median age (years) – 21.2 (2007 est)
National anthem – 'Patriots of Micronesia'
National day – 10 May (Constitution Day)
Life expectancy (years) – 70.35 (2007 est)
Mortality rate – 4.66 (2007 est)
Birth rate – 24.14 (2007 est)
Infant mortality rate – 28.15 (2007 est)
Death penalty – Abolished for all crimes (since 1986)
Population below poverty line – 26.7 per cent (2001 est)

CLIMATE AND TERRAIN

The republic consists of more than 600 volcanic islands extending 2,900km across the archipelago of the Caroline Islands in the western Pacific Ocean. Elevation extremes range from 791m (Totolom) at the highest point to 0m (Pacific Ocean) at the lowest. The islands lie to the north of the Equator; the climate is tropical, with only slight variations in temperatures, which are usually between 20°C and 30°C.

HISTORY AND POLITICS

Inhabited since around 4,000 BC by migrants from the Philippines and Indonesia, Micronesia experienced contact with Europeans from the 1520s and the islands were colonised by Spain from the 16th century. German encroachment in the 1870s and 1880s was resisted until 1899, when Germany purchased the islands from Spain. The islands were occupied by Japan on behalf of the Allies during the First World War, and administered as a League of Nations mandated territory by Japan from 1920 until the Japanese defeat in the Second World War. In 1947 the islands became part of the UN Trust Territory of the Pacific, administered by the USA.

A constitution was adopted in 1979 and the islands became independent in 1986 under a free association agreement with the USA by which the USA retains responsibility for defence and provides substantial financial aid; a renegotiated agreement was signed in 2003. The UN trusteeship was formally terminated in 1990. The most recent presidential and legislative elections were in spring 2007. Emmanuel ('Manny') Mori was elected president in May.

The republic is threatened by the effects of global warming, particularly an increase in the frequency and intensity of storms in the region. A typhoon in 2004 devastated the island of Yap, badly damaging nearly all its infrastructure.

POLITICAL SYSTEM

The 1979 constitution established a federal republic of four states: Chuuk, Kosrae, Pohnpei and Yap. The federal head of state is an executive president, who is elected by the federal legislature for a four-year term. The unicameral congress has 14 members, ten senators directly elected for a two-year term and four senators 'at large' (one from each state) elected for a four-year term; the president and vice-president must be selected from among the 'at large' senators. The federal cabinet is appointed by the president and approved by the congress. There are no formal political parties. Each state has its own government and legislative system.

HEAD OF STATE
President, Emmanuel Mori, *elected* 11 May 2007
Vice-President, Alik L. Alik

SELECTED GOVERNMENT MEMBERS *as at June 2008*
Finance, Finley S. Perman
Foreign Affairs, Lorin S. Robert
Health, Vita Akapito Skilling

BRITISH AMBASSADOR
HE Peter Beckingham, *apptd* 2005, resident at Manila, the Philippines

ECONOMY AND TRADE

Micronesia has few natural resources apart from phosphate, which is not exploited, and is highly dependent on aid from the USA, which constitutes over a quarter of GDP. The main economic activities are subsistence farming and fishing, which account for nearly 30 per cent of GDP, but both are threatened by climate change and over-fishing. The islands' remoteness and lack of facilities and air links has constrained the development of tourism, the main industry; other industries include construction, fish processing, specialised aquaculture and handicrafts. Two-thirds of the workforce is employed by the government. The main trading partners are the USA

World Physical

Europe
0 100 200 300 400 Miles
0 100 200 300 400 500 600 Kms
Conical Orthomorphic Projection
© Oxford Cartographers, 96706
+44 (0)1865 882 884
E & OE
40°W
30°W
20°W
10°W
0°
10°E
70°N
60°N
50°N
40°N
Arctic Circle
ICELAND
Reykjavík
Norwegian Sea
Faeroe Is. (Denmark)
Shetland Is.
Orkney Is.
Hebrides
ATLANTIC OCEAN
North Sea
Skagerrak
NORWAY
SWEDEN
Trondheim
Bergen
Oslo
Stavanger
Kristiansand
Gothenburg
Helsingborg
Copenhagen
Malmo
DENMARK
Alborg
Arhus
Odense
UNITED KINGDOM
Inverness
Aberdeen
Dundee
Glasgow
Edinburgh
Londonderry
Belfast
Newcastle upon Tyne
Leeds
Liverpool
Manchester
Sheffield
Stoke-on-Trent
Birmingham
Norwich
Swansea
Cardiff
Bristol
London
Southampton
Plymouth
REP. OF IRELAND
Galway
Dublin
Cork
English Channel
NETHERLANDS
Amsterdam
Rotterdam
Antwerp
Brussels
BELGIUM
Lille
LUX.
Luxembourg
GERMANY
Kiel
Rostock
Hamburg
Bremen
Elbe
Osnabrück
Hanover
Berlin
Munster
Essen
Dortmund
Düsseldorf
Cologne
Leipzig
Dresden
Chemnitz
Frankfurt
Nuremberg
Regensburg
Mannheim
Stuttgart
Munich
Rhine
Danube
Plzeň
CZECH
Salzburg
Innsbruck
AUSTRIA
LIECH.
SWITZERLAND
Zurich
Bern
Geneva
Mt. Blanc 4808
ALPS
SLOVENIA
Ljubljana
Trieste
FRANCE
Cherbourg
Le Havre
Amiens
Rouen
Caen
Seine
Paris
Reims
Metz
Strasbourg
Nancy
Brest
Rennes
Nantes
Loire
Orléans
Tours
Dijon
Limoges
Clermont-Ferrand
Lyon
Grenoble
Rhône
Bordeaux
Toulouse
Montpellier
Nîmes
Marseille
Nice
MONACO
Bay of Biscay
ANDORRA
Pyrenees
SPAIN
La Coruña
Gijón
Vigo
León
Bilbao
San Sebastian
Pamplona
Burgos
Valladolid
Zaragoza
Salamanca
Madrid
Lerida
Barcelona
Tagus
Badajoz
Valencia
Balearic Is. (Sp.)
Palma
Mallorca
Córdoba
Seville
Huelva
Granada
Murcia
Cartagena
Cadiz
Málaga
Almeria
Gibraltar(U.K.)
Ceuta(Sp.)
PORTUGAL
Oporto
Douro
Coimbra
Amadora
Lisbon
Setubal
Faro
ITALY
Trento
Milan
Verona
Venice
Turin
Genoa
Parma
Bologne
SAN MARINO
La Spezia
Livorno
Florence
Ancona
Apennines
Pescara
Rome
Naples
Corsica (Fr.)
Ajaccio
Sardinia (It.)
Sassari
Cagliari
Palermo
Sicily
Valletta
MALTA
Mediterranean Sea
Adriatic
MOROCCO
Tangier
Tétouan
Rabat
Casablanca
Fès
Meknès
Oujda
Atlas Mountains
ALGERIA
Melilla(Sp.)
Oran
Sidi Bel Abbès
Algiers
Blida
Bejaia
Skikda
'Annaba
Constantine
TUNISIA
Aryanah
Tunis
Sousse
Sfax

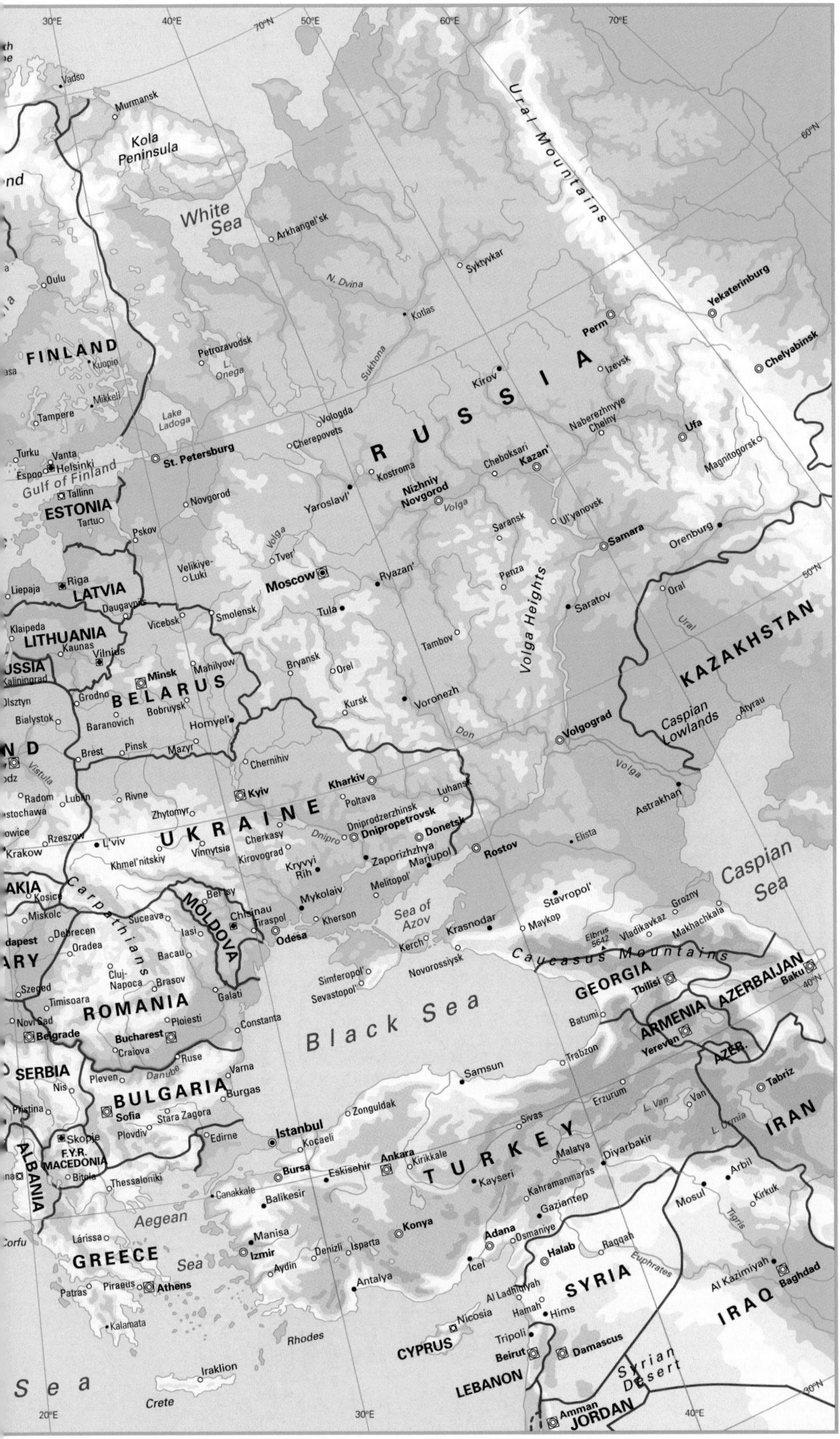

30°E
40°E
70°N
50°E
60°E
70°E
Vadso
Murmansk
Kola Peninsula
White Sea
Arkhangel'sk
Ural Mountains
60°N
Syktyvkar
N. Dvina
Oulu
Kotlas
Yekaterinburg
Perm
FINLAND
Kuopio
Petrozavodsk
L. Onega
Sukhona
Chelyabinsk
Izevsk
Kirov
Mikkeli
Tampere
Lake Ladoga
Vologda
RUSSIA
Naberezhnyye Chelny
Ufa
Turku
Vanta
Helsinki
Espoo
St. Petersburg
Cherepovets
Gulf of Finland
Kostroma
Cheboksari
Kazan'
Magnitogorsk
Tallinn
ESTONIA
Tartu
Novgorod
Yaroslavl'
Nizhniy Novgorod
Volga
Saransk
Ul'yanovsk
Orenburg
Pskov
Volga
Tver'
Samara
Velikiye-Luki
Moscow
Ryazan'
Penza
Volga Heights
50°N
Liepaja
Riga
LATVIA
Daugavpils
Smolensk
Tula
Oral
Saratov
Klaipeda
LITHUANIA
Kaunas
Vilnius
Vicebsk
Ural
KAZAKHSTAN
Kaliningrad
Minsk
Mahilyow
Bryansk
Orel
Tambov
BELARUS
Olsztyn
Grodno
Bobruysk
Bialystok
Baranovich
Homyel'
Kursk
Voronezh
Caspian Lowlands
Atyrau
Brest
Pinsk
Mazyr
Don
Volgograd
Vistula
Chernihiv
Volga
Radom
Lublin
Rivne
Kyiv
Kharkiv
Poltava
Luhansk
Astrakhan
Zhytomyr
UKRAINE
Dniprodzerzhinsk
Dnipropetrovsk
Rzeszow
L'viv
Cherkasy
Dnipro
Donetsk
Elista
Krakow
Khmel'nitskiy
Vinnytsia
Kirovograd
Kryvyi Rih
Zaporizhzhya
Mariupol
Rostov
Caspian Sea
Kosice
Carpathians
MOLDOVA
Beltsy
Melitopol'
Stavropol'
Mykolaiv
Miskolc
Suceava
Chisinau
Tiraspol
Kherson
Sea of Azov
Grozny
Debrecen
Iasi
Odesa
Krasnodar
Maykop
Makhachkala
Oradea
Bacau
Kerch
Elbrus 5642
Vladikavkaz
Caucasus Mountains
Cluj-Napoca
Brasov
Simferopol'
Novorossiysk
GEORGIA
Tbilisi
AZERBAIJAN
Baku
40°N
Szeged
Timisoara
ROMANIA
Galati
Sevastopol'
Black Sea
Batumi
ARMENIA
Novi Sad
Ploiesti
Constanta
Yerevan
Belgrade
Bucharest
Craiova
AZER.
SERBIA
Ruse
Trabzon
Pleven
Danube
Varna
Samsun
Tabriz
Nis
BULGARIA
Burgas
Erzurum
Pristina
Sofia
Stara Zagora
Zonguldak
L. Van
Van
L. Urmia
IRAN
Skopje
Plovdiv
Edirne
Istanbul
Kocaeli
Sivas
F.Y.R. MACEDONIA
ALBANIA
Bitola
Thessaloniki
Bursa
Eskisehir
Ankara
Kirikkale
TURKEY
Malatya
Diyarbakir
Arbil
Kayseri
Kahramanmaras
Mosul
Canakkale
Balikesir
Kirkuk
Gaziantep
Aegean Sea
Tigris
Lárissa
Manisa
Konya
Adana
Osmaniye
Corfu
Izmir
Denizli
Isparta
Halab
Raqqah
GREECE
Aydin
Icel
Euphrates
SYRIA
Al Kazimiyah
Baghdad
Patras
Piraeus
Athens
Antalya
Al Ladhiqiyah
IRAQ
Hamah
Hims
Nicosia
Kalamata
Rhodes
CYPRUS
Tripoli
Beirut
Damascus
Iraklion
LEBANON
Syrian Desert
Sea
Crete
30°N
20°E
30°E
Amman
JORDAN
40°E

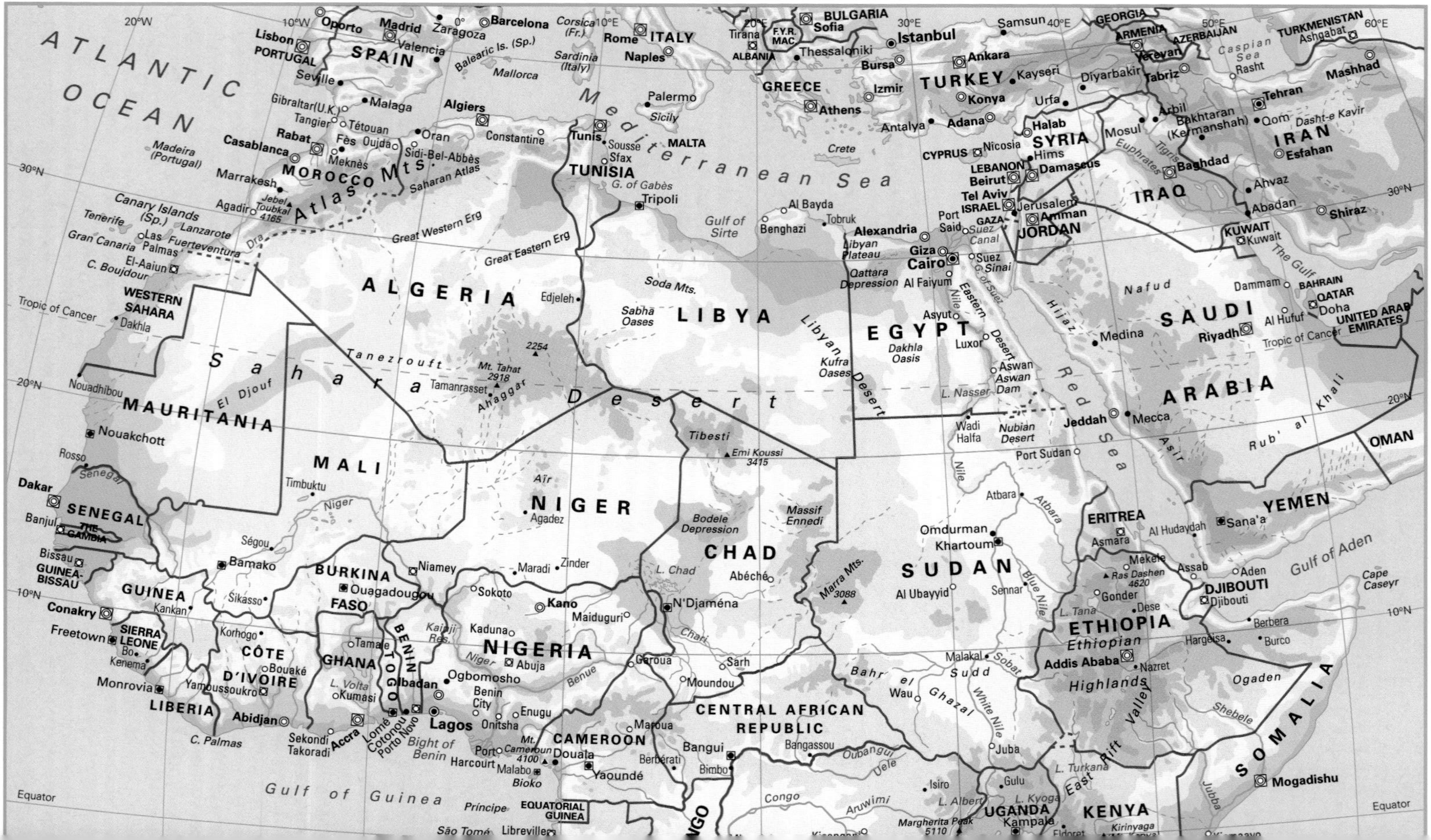

ATLANTIC OCEAN
Madeira (Portugal)
Canary Islands (Sp.)
Tenerife
Gran Canaria
Las Palmas
Lanzarote
Fuerteventura
El-Aaiun
C. Boujdour
WESTERN SAHARA
Dakhla
Tropic of Cancer
Nouadhibou
MAURITANIA
Nouakchott
Rosso
Senegal
Dakar
SENEGAL
Banjul
THE GAMBIA
Bissau
GUINEA-BISSAU
GUINEA
Conakry
Kankan
SIERRA LEONE
Freetown
Bo
Kenema
Monrovia
LIBERIA
C. Palmas
CÔTE D'IVOIRE
Korhogo
Bouaké
Yamoussoukro
Abidjan
Sekondi Takoradi
GHANA
Tamale
L. Volta
Kumasi
Accra
TOGO
Lomé
BENIN
Cotonou
Porto Novo
Ibadan
Lagos
Bight of Benin
Gulf of Guinea
Equator
Lisbon
PORTUGAL
Oporto
Madrid
SPAIN
Zaragoza
Barcelona
Valencia
Seville
Malaga
Gibraltar(U.K.)
Tangier
Tétouan
Balearic Is. (Sp.)
Mallorca
Rabat
Casablanca
Fès
Oujda
Meknès
MOROCCO
Marrakesh
Agadir
Jebel Toubkal 4165
Atlas Mts
Saharan Atlas
Dra
Oran
Sidi-Bel-Abbès
Algiers
Constantine
ALGERIA
Great Western Erg
Great Eastern Erg
Edjeleh
Tanezrouft
Tamanrasset
Mt. Tahat 2918
Ahaggar
2254
Sahara Desert
El Djouf
MALI
Timbuktu
Niger
Ségou
Bamako
Sikasso
BURKINA FASO
Ouagadougou
Niamey
NIGER
Aïr
Agadez
Maradi
Zinder
Sokoto
Kano
Kaduna
Kainji Res.
NIGERIA
Abuja
Ogbomosho
Benin City
Enugu
Onitsha
Port Harcourt
Maiduguri
Benue
Mt. Cameroun 4100
CAMEROON
Douala
Malabo
Bioko
Yaoundé
Garoua
Maroua
Berbérati
EQUATORIAL GUINEA
Príncipe
São Tomé
Libreville
Corsica (Fr.)
Sardinia (Italy)
Rome
ITALY
Naples
Palermo
Sicily
MALTA
Tunis
Sousse
Sfax
TUNISIA
G. of Gabès
Tripoli
Mediterranean Sea
Gulf of Sirte
Benghazi
Al Bayda
Tobruk
LIBYA
Soda Mts.
Sabha Oases
Libyan Desert
Kufra Oases
Tibesti
Emi Koussi 3415
CHAD
Bodele Depression
Massif Ennedi
L. Chad
N'Djaména
Abéché
Chari
Sarh
Moundou
CENTRAL AFRICAN REPUBLIC
Bangui
Bimbo
Bangassou
Oubangui
Uele
Congo
Aruwimi
Tirana
ALBANIA
F.Y.R. MAC
Sofia
BULGARIA
Thessaloniki
GREECE
Athens
Crete
Istanbul
Bursa
Izmir
TURKEY
Ankara
Konya
Antalya
Adana
Kayseri
Samsun
CYPRUS
Nicosia
Alexandria
Libyan Plateau
Qattara Depression
Giza
Cairo
Al Faiyum
EGYPT
Dakhla Oasis
Asyut
Luxor
Eastern Desert
Aswan
Aswan Dam
L. Nasser
Wadi Halfa
Nubian Desert
Nile
Port Said
Suez Canal
Suez
Sinai
G. of Suez
GAZA
ISRAEL
Tel Aviv
Jerusalem
Amman
JORDAN
LEBANON
Beirut
Damascus
Hims
SYRIA
Halab
Urfa
Diyarbakir
Mosul
Euphrates
Tigris
Arbil
Bakhtaran (Kermanshah)
Baghdad
IRAQ
GEORGIA
ARMENIA
Yerevan
AZERBAIJAN
Tabriz
Caspian Sea
Rasht
TURKMENISTAN
Ashgabat
Mashhad
Tehran
Qom
Dasht-e Kavir
IRAN
Esfahan
Ahvaz
Abadan
Shiraz
KUWAIT
Kuwait
The Gulf
BAHRAIN
QATAR
Doha
UNITED ARAB EMIRATES
Dammam
Al Hufuf
Riyadh
SAUDI ARABIA
Nafud
Hijaz
Medina
Jeddah
Mecca
Asir
Rub' al Khali
Red Sea
OMAN
YEMEN
Sana'a
Al Hudaydah
Aden
Gulf of Aden
Cape Caseyr
Port Sudan
Atbara
SUDAN
Omdurman
Khartoum
Sennar
Blue Nile
Al Ubayyid
Marra Mts. 3088
Bahr el Ghazal
Wau
Sudd
Malakal
Sobat
White Nile
Juba
ERITREA
Asmara
Mekele
Ras Dashen 4620
Gonder
Dese
L. Tana
Assab
DJIBOUTI
Djibouti
ETHIOPIA
Ethiopian Highlands
Addis Ababa
Nazret
Hargeisa
Berbera
Burco
Ogaden
Shebele
SOMALIA
Mogadishu
Jubba
East Rift Valley
L. Turkana
KENYA
Kirinyaga
Eldoret
UGANDA
Gulu
L. Kyoga
Kampala
L. Albert
Isiro
Margherita Peak 5110
Tropic of Cancer
Equator
10°W
20°W
0°
10°E
20°E
30°E
40°E
50°E
60°E
30°N
20°N
10°N

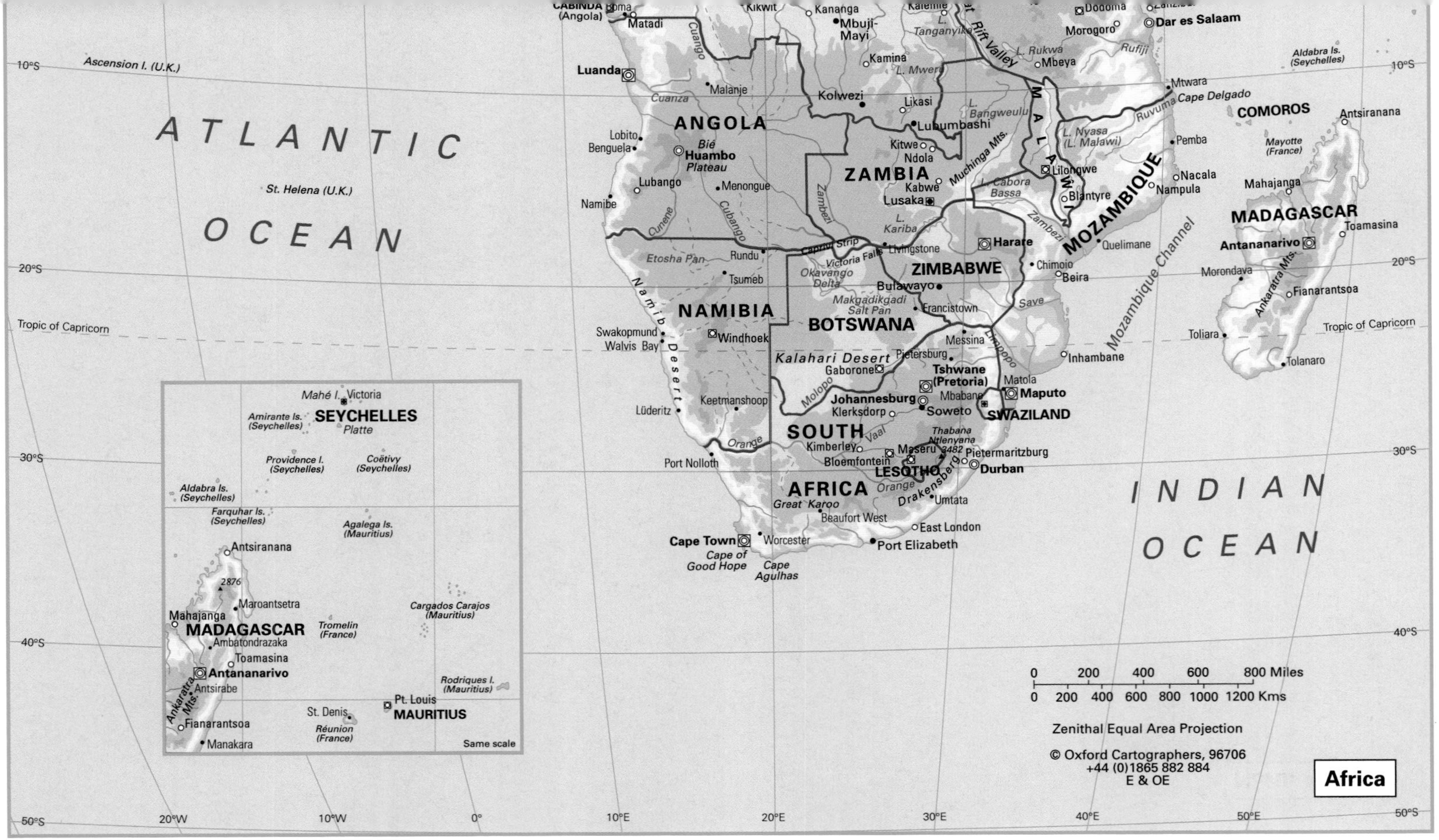
Africa
ATLANTIC OCEAN
INDIAN OCEAN
Ascension I. (U.K.)
St. Helena (U.K.)
Tropic of Capricorn
CABINDA (Angola)
Boma
Matadi
Kikwit
Kananga
Mbuji-Mayi
Kamina
Kolwezi
Likasi
Lubumbashi
L. Tanganyika
L. Mweru
L. Bangweulu
Rift Valley
L. Rukwa
Mbeya
Dodoma
Morogoro
Dar es Salaam
Rufiji
Luanda
Malanje
Cuanza
Cuango
ANGOLA
Lobito
Benguela
Bié
Huambo
Plateau
Lubango
Menongue
Namibe
Cunene
Cubango
Etosha Pan
Rundu
Tsumeb
NAMIBIA
Namib Desert
Swakopmund
Walvis Bay
Windhoek
Keetmanshoop
Lüderitz
Orange
Port Nolloth
ZAMBIA
Kitwe
Ndola
Kabwe
Lusaka
Zambezi
Muchinga Mts.
L. Kariba
Caprivi Strip
Victoria Falls
Livingstone
Okavango Delta
Makgadikgadi Salt Pan
ZIMBABWE
Harare
Bulawayo
Francistown
Cabora Bassa
BOTSWANA
Kalahari Desert
Gaborone
Molopo
Pietersburg
Messina
Limpopo
Tshwane (Pretoria)
Johannesburg
Soweto
Klerksdorp
Mbabane
SWAZILAND
Matola
Maputo
SOUTH AFRICA
Vaal
Kimberley
Bloemfontein
Maseru
LESOTHO
Thabana Ntlenyana
3482
Pietermaritzburg
Durban
Drakensberg
Umtata
East London
Port Elizabeth
Great Karoo
Beaufort West
Worcester
Cape Town
Cape of Good Hope
Cape Agulhas
MALAWI
L. Nyasa (L. Malawi)
Lilongwe
Blantyre
MOZAMBIQUE
Ruvuma
Mtwara
Cape Delgado
Pemba
Nacala
Nampula
Quelimane
Chimoio
Beira
Save
Inhambane
Mozambique Channel
COMOROS
Mayotte (France)
Aldabra Is. (Seychelles)
Antsiranana
Mahajanga
MADAGASCAR
Toamasina
Antananarivo
Ankaratra Mts.
Morondava
Fianarantsoa
Toliara
Tolanaro
10°S
20°S
30°S
40°S
50°S
20°W
10°W
0°
10°E
20°E
30°E
40°E
50°E
Mahé I.
Victoria
SEYCHELLES
Platte
Amirante Is. (Seychelles)
Providence I. (Seychelles)
Coëtivy (Seychelles)
Aldabra Is. (Seychelles)
Farquhar Is. (Seychelles)
Agalega Is. (Mauritius)
Antsiranana
2876
Maroantsetra
Mahajanga
MADAGASCAR
Ambatondrazaka
Toamasina
Antananarivo
Antsirabe
Ankaratra Mts.
Fianarantsoa
Manakara
Cargados Carajos (Mauritius)
Tromelin (France)
Rodriques I. (Mauritius)
Pt. Louis
MAURITIUS
St. Denis
Réunion (France)
Same scale
0 200 400 600 800 Miles
0 200 400 600 800 1000 1200 Kms
Zenithal Equal Area Projection
© Oxford Cartographers, 96706
+44 (0)1865 882 884
E & OE

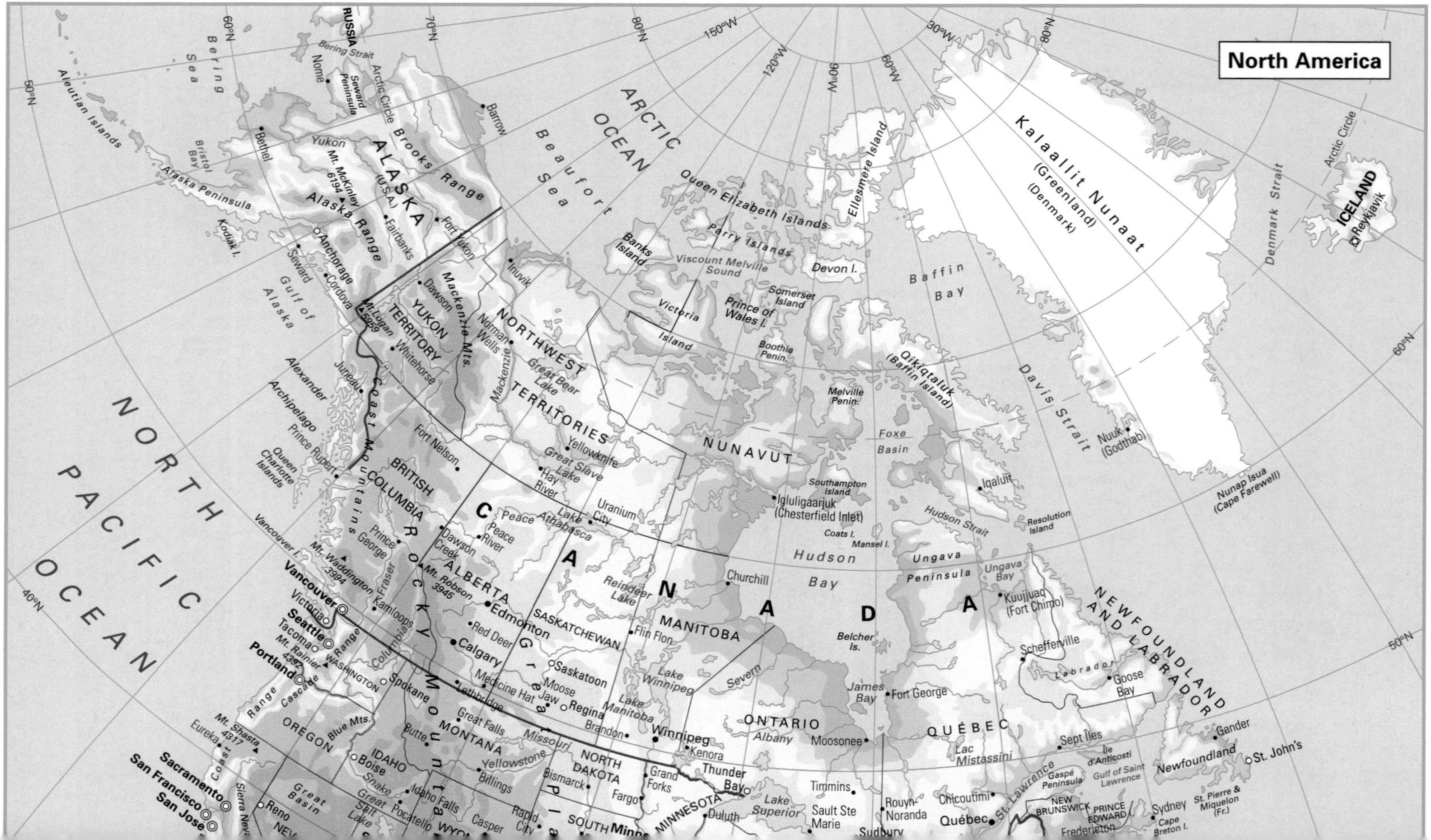
North America
ARCTIC OCEAN
Beaufort Sea
NORTH PACIFIC OCEAN
Bering Sea
Bering Strait
Gulf of Alaska
Alexander Archipelago
Queen Charlotte Islands
Vancouver I.
Aleutian Islands
Alaska Peninsula
Kodiak I.
Bristol Bay
RUSSIA
Nome
Seward Peninsula
Arctic Circle
Bethel
Yukon
ALASKA (U.S.A.)
Brooks Range
Barrow
Mt. McKinley 6194
Alaska Range
Fairbanks
Fort Yukon
Anchorage
Seward
Cordova
Mt. Logan 5959
Juneau
Whitehorse
YUKON TERRITORY
Dawson
Mackenzie Mts.
Inuvik
Norman Wells
Mackenzie
NORTHWEST TERRITORIES
Great Bear Lake
Great Slave Lake
Yellowknife
Hay River
Fort Nelson
BRITISH COLUMBIA
Coast Mountains
Prince Rupert
Prince George
Mt. Waddington 3994
Fraser
Kamloops
Columbia
Vancouver
Victoria
Seattle
Tacoma
Mt. Rainier 4392
Portland
Cascade Range
WASHINGTON
OREGON
Blue Mts.
Mt. Shasta 4317
Eureka
Coast
Sacramento
San Francisco
San Jose
Sierra Nevada
Reno
Great Basin
Great Salt Lake
IDAHO
Boise
Snake
Idaho Falls
Pocatello
Spokane
Butte
MONTANA
Great Falls
Yellowstone
Billings
Casper
Rapid City
Rocky Mountains
Great Plains
Missouri
NORTH DAKOTA
SOUTH
Bismarck
Fargo
Grand Forks
MINNESOTA
Duluth
Lethbridge
Medicine Hat
Calgary
Red Deer
Edmonton
ALBERTA
Mt. Robson 3945
Dawson Creek
Peace River
Peace
Lake Athabasca
Uranium City
CANADA
SASKATCHEWAN
Saskatoon
Moose Jaw
Regina
Brandon
Reindeer Lake
Flin Flon
MANITOBA
Lake Winnipeg
Lake Manitoba
Winnipeg
Kenora
Thunder Bay
Lake Superior
Sault Ste Marie
Sudbury
Timmins
Albany
ONTARIO
Severn
Moosonee
James Bay
Fort George
Rouyn-Noranda
Belcher Is.
Churchill
Hudson Bay
Coats I.
Mansel I.
Igluligaarjuk (Chesterfield Inlet)
Southampton Island
NUNAVUT
Melville Penin.
Foxe Basin
Boothia Penin.
Prince of Wales I.
Somerset Island
Victoria Island
Banks Island
Viscount Melville Sound
Parry Islands
Queen Elizabeth Islands
Devon I.
Ellesmere Island
Qikiqtaluk (Baffin Island)
Baffin Bay
Iqaluit
Hudson Strait
Resolution Island
Ungava Peninsula
Ungava Bay
Kuujjuaq (Fort Chimo)
Schefferville
Labrador
Goose Bay
NEWFOUNDLAND AND LABRADOR
QUÉBEC
Lac Mistassini
Chicoutimi
Québec
St. Lawrence
Sept Îles
Île d'Anticosti
Gaspé Peninsula
Gulf of Saint Lawrence
NEW BRUNSWICK
PRINCE EDWARD I.
Fredericton
Sydney
Cape Breton I.
St. Pierre & Miquelon (Fr.)
Newfoundland
Gander
St. John's
Kalaallit Nunaat (Greenland) (Denmark)
Davis Strait
Nuuk (Godthab)
Nunap Isua (Cape Farewell)
Denmark Strait
ICELAND
Reykjavik
150°W
120°W
90°W
60°W
30°W
80°N
70°N
60°N
50°N
40°N

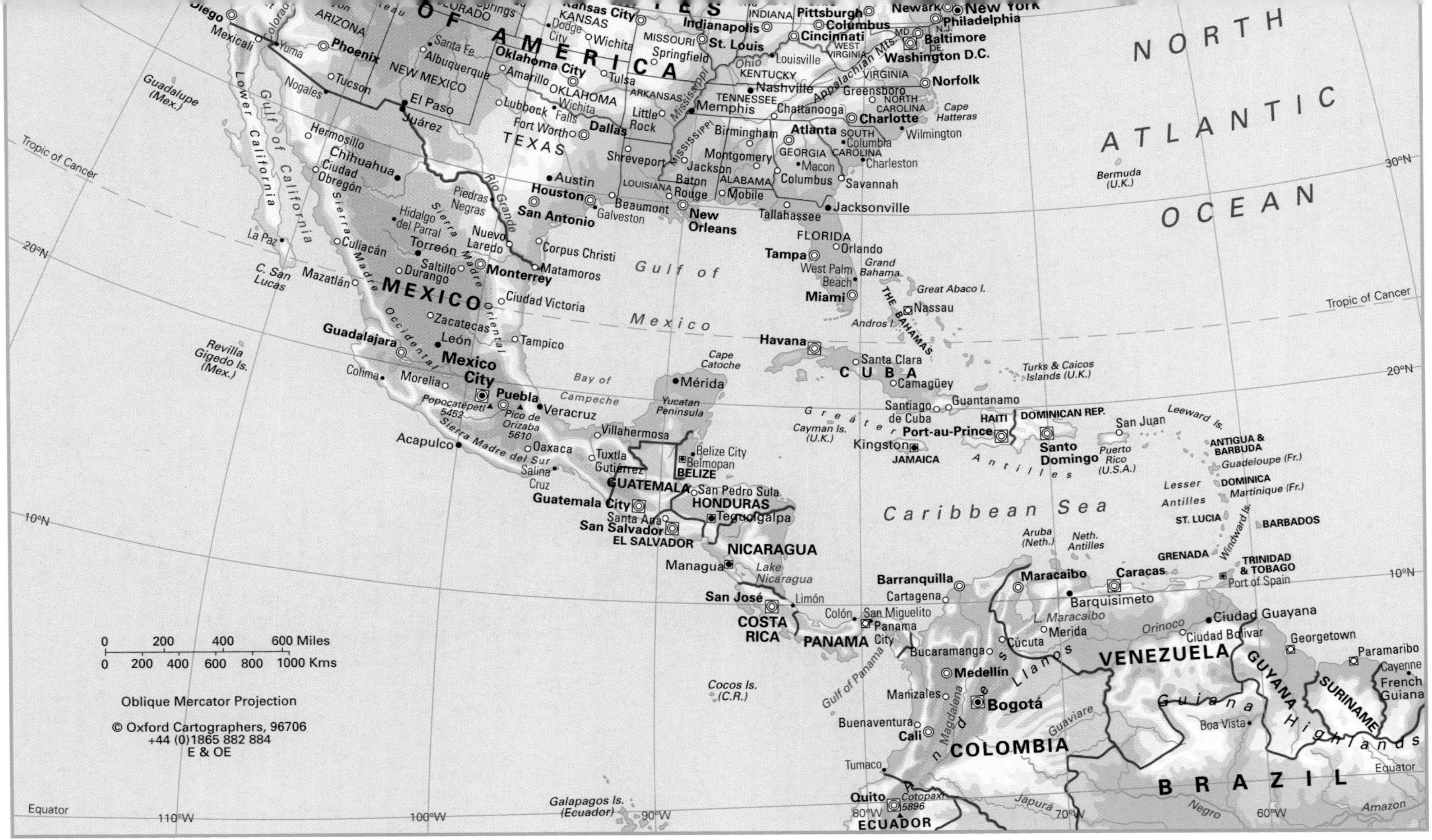
NORTH ATLANTIC OCEAN
Gulf of Mexico
Caribbean Sea
Greater Antilles
Lesser Antilles
MEXICO
CUBA
THE BAHAMAS
JAMAICA
HAITI
DOMINICAN REP.
BELIZE
GUATEMALA
HONDURAS
EL SALVADOR
NICARAGUA
COSTA RICA
PANAMA
COLOMBIA
VENEZUELA
GUYANA
SURINAME
French Guiana
ECUADOR
BRAZIL
TEXAS
Tropic of Cancer
Equator
30°N
20°N
10°N
110°W
100°W
90°W
80°W
70°W
60°W
Bermuda (U.K.)
Mexico City
Guadalajara
Monterrey
Havana
Miami
Houston
Dallas
New Orleans
Caracas
Bogotá
Panama City
Kingston
Port-au-Prince
Santo Domingo
Quito
0 200 400 600 Miles
0 200 400 600 800 1000 Kms
Oblique Mercator Projection
© Oxford Cartographers, 96706
+44 (0)1865 882 884
E & OE

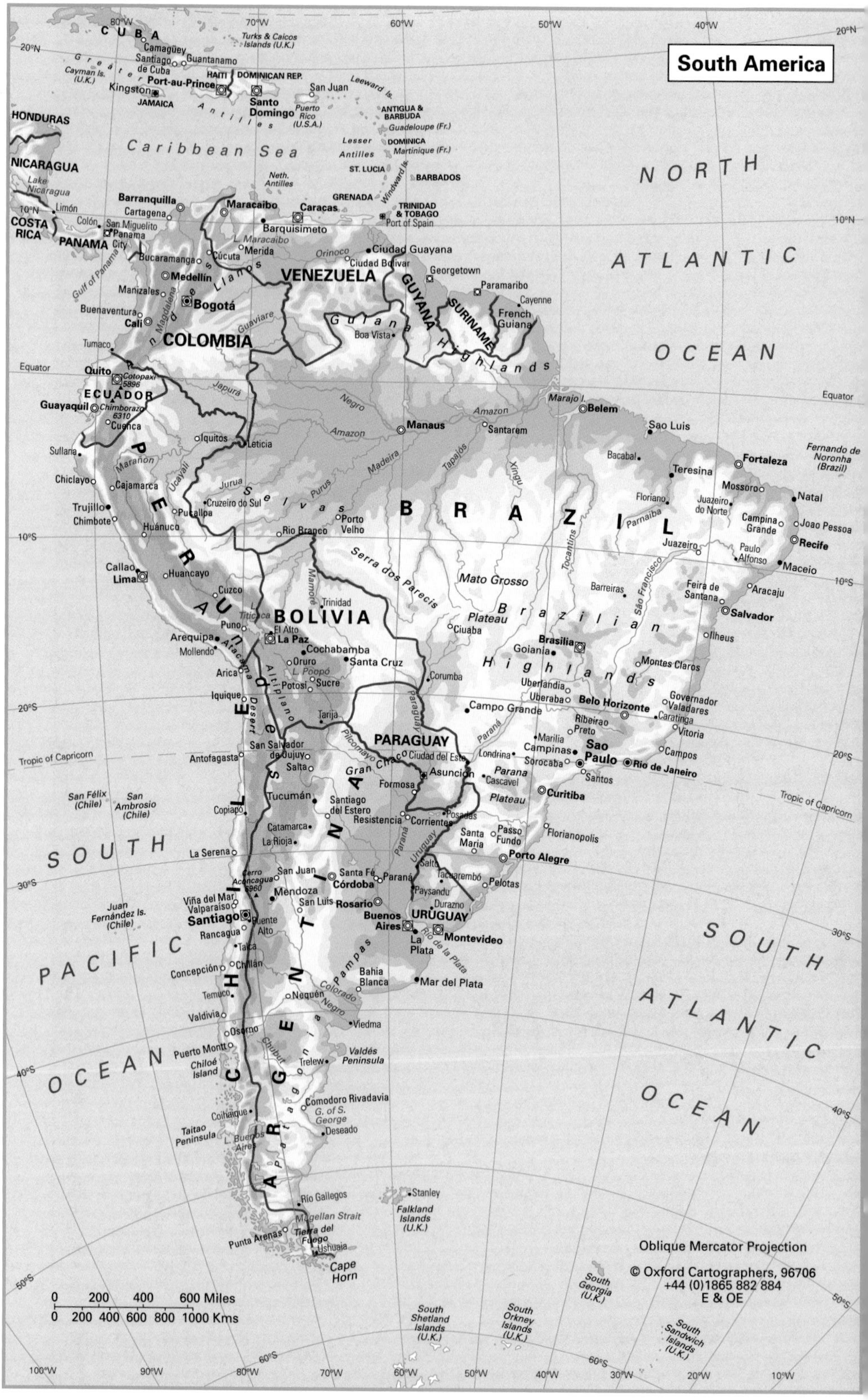
South America
CUBA
Camagüey
Santiago de Cuba
Guantanamo
Cayman Is. (U.K.)
Greater Antilles
HAITI
DOMINICAN REP.
Port-au-Prince
Santo Domingo
Kingston
JAMAICA
Turks & Caicos Islands (U.K.)
San Juan
Puerto Rico (U.S.A.)
Leeward Is.
ANTIGUA & BARBUDA
Guadeloupe (Fr.)
DOMINICA
Martinique (Fr.)
Lesser Antilles
ST. LUCIA
BARBADOS
Windward Is.
GRENADA
TRINIDAD & TOBAGO
Port of Spain
HONDURAS
NICARAGUA
Lake Nicaragua
Caribbean Sea
Neth. Antilles
COSTA RICA
Limón
Colón
PANAMA
San Miguelito
Panama City
Gulf of Panama
Barranquilla
Cartagena
Maracaibo
L. Maracaibo
Barquisimeto
Caracas
Cúcuta
Merida
Bucaramanga
Medellín
Manizales
Bogotá
Buenaventura
Cali
Tumaco
COLOMBIA
Llanos
Magdalena
Guaviare
Orinoco
Ciudad Guayana
Ciudad Bolívar
VENEZUELA
GUYANA
Georgetown
Paramaribo
SURINAME
Cayenne
French Guiana
Guiana Highlands
Boa Vista
Equator
Quito
Cotopaxi 5896
ECUADOR
Guayaquil
Chimborazo 6310
Cuenca
Japurá
Negro
Amazon
Manaus
Santarem
Marajo I.
Belem
Sao Luis
Iquitos
Leticia
Sullana
Chiclayo
Cajamarca
Marañon
Ucayali
Trujillo
Chimbote
Huánuco
Pucallpa
Cruzeiro do Sul
Juruá
Selvas
Purus
Madeira
Tapajós
Xingu
Porto Velho
Rio Branco
PERU
Callao
Lima
Huancayo
Cuzco
L. Titicaca
Puno
Arequipa
Mollendo
Arica
Iquique
Serra dos Parecis
Mamoré
Trinidad
BOLIVIA
El Alto
La Paz
Cochabamba
Oruro
L. Poopó
Santa Cruz
Potosí
Sucre
Altiplano
Tarija
Atacama Desert
ANDES
BRAZIL
Bacabal
Teresina
Fortaleza
Fernando de Noronha (Brazil)
Mossoro
Natal
Floriano
Juazeiro do Norte
Parnaiba
Campina Grande
Joao Pessoa
Recife
Juazeiro
Paulo Alfonso
Maceio
Tocantins
São Francisco
Mato Grosso Plateau
Barreiras
Feira de Santana
Aracaju
Salvador
Brazilian Highlands
Ciuaba
Brasilia
Goiania
Ilheus
Montes Claros
Uberlandia
Uberaba
Belo Horizonte
Governador Valadares
Caratinga
Corumba
Paraguay
Campo Grande
Ribeirao Preto
Vitoria
Marilia
Campinas
Sao Paulo
Campos
Rio de Janeiro
Londrina
Sorocaba
Santos
Paraná
Parana Plateau
Cascavel
Curitiba
Tropic of Capricorn
Antofagasta
San Salvador de Jujuy
Salta
Pilcomayo
Gran Chaco
PARAGUAY
Ciudad del Este
Asunción
Formosa
Tucumán
Santiago del Estero
Resistencia
Corrientes
Posadas
San Félix (Chile)
San Ambrosio (Chile)
Copiapó
Catamarca
La Rioja
Santa Maria
Passo Fundo
Florianopolis
Uruguay
Porto Alegre
La Serena
Cerro Aconcagua 6960
San Juan
Santa Fé
Córdoba
Paraná
Salto
Tacuarembó
Pelotas
Paysandu
Durazno
Viña del Mar
Valparaíso
Mendoza
San Luis
Rosario
Santiago
Puente Alto
Buenos Aires
URUGUAY
Montevideo
La Plata
Rio de la Plata
Juan Fernández Is. (Chile)
Rancagua
Talca
Chillán
Concepción
Pampas
Bahia Blanca
Mar del Plata
Temuco
Neuquén
Colorado
Negro
Viedma
Valdivia
Osorno
Puerto Montt
Chiloé Island
Chubut
Trelew
Valdés Peninsula
CHILE
ARGENTINA
Patagonia
Comodoro Rivadavia
G. of S. George
Coihaique
Deseado
Taitao Peninsula
L. Buenos Aires
Río Gallegos
Stanley
Falkland Islands (U.K.)
Magellan Strait
Punta Arenas
Tierra del Fuego
Ushuaia
Cape Horn
NORTH ATLANTIC OCEAN
SOUTH ATLANTIC OCEAN
SOUTH PACIFIC OCEAN
South Georgia (U.K.)
South Shetland Islands (U.K.)
South Orkney Islands (U.K.)
South Sandwich Islands (U.K.)
Oblique Mercator Projection
© Oxford Cartographers, 96706
+44 (0)1865 882 884
E & OE
0 200 400 600 Miles
0 200 400 600 800 1000 Kms
100°W
90°W
80°W
70°W
60°W
50°W
40°W
30°W
20°W
10°W
20°N
10°N
10°S
20°S
30°S
40°S
50°S
60°S

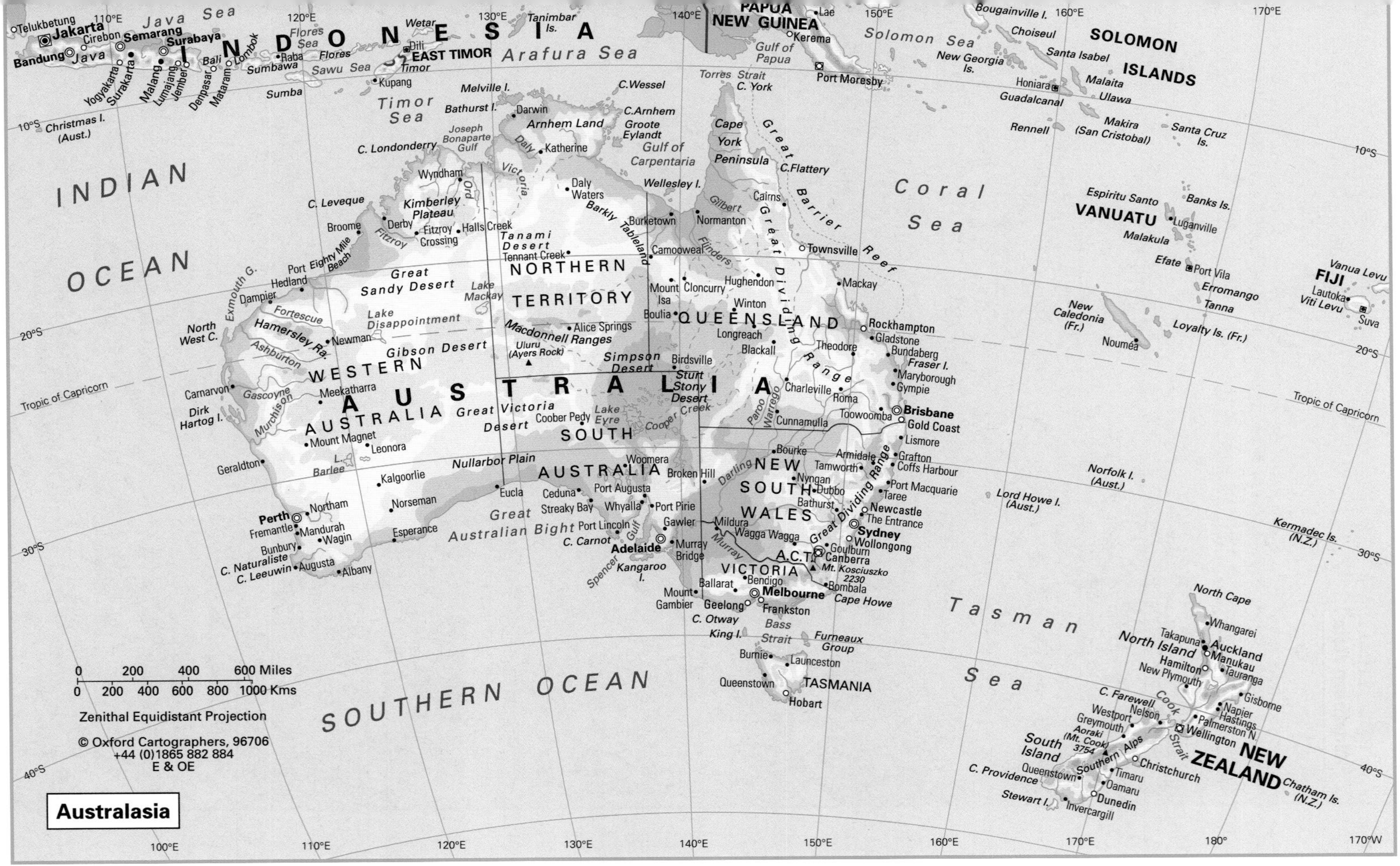
Australasia
INDONESIA
PAPUA NEW GUINEA
EAST TIMOR
SOLOMON ISLANDS
VANUATU
FIJI
NEW ZEALAND
AUSTRALIA
WESTERN AUSTRALIA
NORTHERN TERRITORY
QUEENSLAND
SOUTH AUSTRALIA
NEW SOUTH WALES
VICTORIA
A.C.T.
TASMANIA
INDIAN OCEAN
SOUTHERN OCEAN
Java Sea
Flores Sea
Sawu Sea
Timor Sea
Arafura Sea
Solomon Sea
Coral Sea
Tasman Sea
Gulf of Carpentaria
Gulf of Papua
Torres Strait
Bass Strait
Cook Strait
Great Australian Bight
Spencer Gulf
Joseph Bonaparte Gulf
Exmouth G.
Great Barrier Reef
Great Dividing Range
Great Sandy Desert
Gibson Desert
Great Victoria Desert
Tanami Desert
Simpson Desert
Sturt Stony Desert
Nullarbor Plain
Kimberley Plateau
Barkly Tableland
Hamersley Ra.
Macdonnell Ranges
Arnhem Land
Cape York Peninsula
Lake Eyre
Lake Mackay
Lake Disappointment
L. Barlee
Uluru (Ayers Rock)
Mt. Kosciuszko 2230
Aoraki (Mt. Cook) 3754
Southern Alps
Jakarta
Bandung
Surabaya
Semarang
Dili
Port Moresby
Honiara
Port Vila
Nouméa
Suva
Perth
Darwin
Adelaide
Melbourne
Sydney
Canberra
Brisbane
Hobart
Alice Springs
Townsville
Cairns
Rockhampton
Wellington
Auckland
Christchurch
Dunedin
Christmas I. (Aust.)
Norfolk I. (Aust.)
Lord Howe I. (Aust.)
Kermadec Is. (N.Z.)
Chatham Is. (N.Z.)
New Caledonia (Fr.)
Loyalty Is. (Fr.)
North Island
South Island
Stewart I.
King I.
Kangaroo I.
Tropic of Capricorn
10°S
20°S
30°S
40°S
100°E
110°E
120°E
130°E
140°E
150°E
160°E
170°E
180°
170°W
0 200 400 600 Miles
0 200 400 600 800 1000 Kms
Zenithal Equidistant Projection
© Oxford Cartographers, 96706
+44 (0)1865 882 884
E & OE

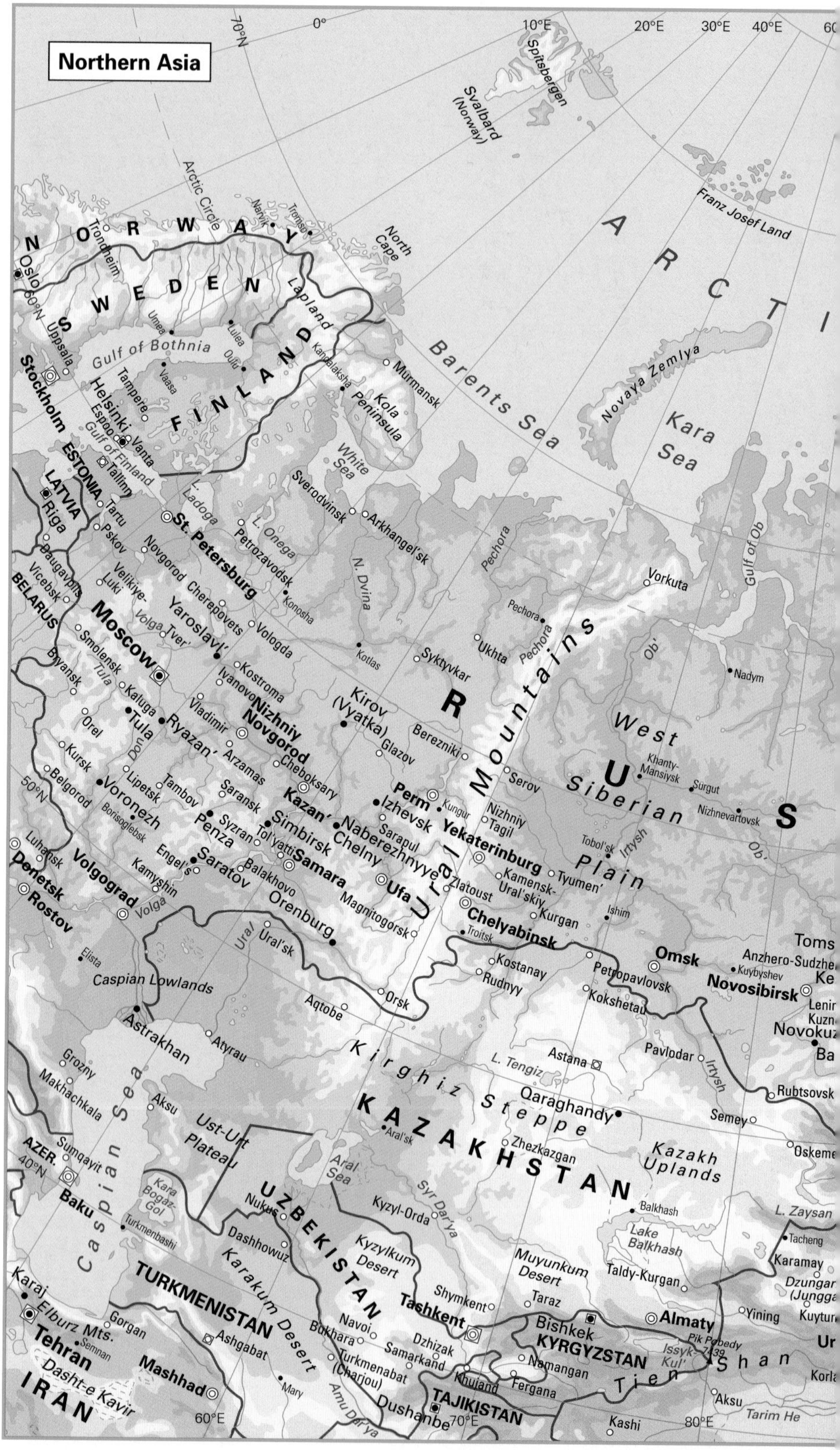
Northern Asia
70°N
0°
10°E
20°E
30°E
40°E
Spitsbergen
Svalbard (Norway)
Franz Josef Land
ARCTI
Arctic Circle
Narvik
Tromsø
North Cape
NORWAY
Trondheim
Oslo
60°N
SWEDEN
Umeå
Luleå
Lapland
Oulu
Gulf of Bothnia
Uppsala
Stockholm
Vaasa
Tampere
FINLAND
Kandalaksha
Murmansk
Kola Peninsula
Barents Sea
Novaya Zemlya
Kara Sea
Helsinki
Espoo
Vantaa
Gulf of Finland
Tallinn
ESTONIA
LATVIA
Riga
Tartu
Pskov
L. Ladoga
St. Petersburg
L. Onega
Petrozavodsk
White Sea
Sverodvinsk
Arkhangel'sk
Pechora
Gulf of Ob
Vorkuta
Daugavpils
Vicebsk
BELARUS
Velikiye-Luki
Novgorod
Cherepovets
Konosha
N. Dvina
Pechora
Ukhta
Ob'
Nadym
Moscow
Volga
Tver'
Yaroslavl'
Vologda
Kotlas
Syktyvkar
Ural Mountains
Smolensk
Bryansk
Tula
Kaluga
Kostroma
Ivanovo
Kirov (Vyatka)
R
West
Orel
Tula
Vladimir
Nizhniy Novgorod
Glazov
Berezniki
Kursk
Don
Ryazan'
Arzamas
Cheboksary
Serov
U
Khanty-Mansiysk
Surgut
Siberian
Belgorod
Lipetsk
Tambov
Saransk
Perm
Kungur
Nizhniy Tagil
Nizhnevartovsk
S
50°N
Voronezh
Borisoglebsk
Kazan'
Izhevsk
Yekaterinburg
Tobol'sk
Irtysh
Ob'
Luhansk
Penza
Syzran
Simbirsk
Tol'yatti
Naberezhnyye Chelny
Sarapul
Plain
Donetsk
Volgograd
Engel's
Kamyshin
Saratov
Samara
Balakhovo
Ufa
Zlatoust
Kamensk-Ural'skiy
Tyumen'
Rostov
Volga
Orenburg
Magnitogorsk
Chelyabinsk
Kurgan
Ishim
Ural
Ural'sk
Troitsk
Omsk
Toms
Elista
Kostanay
Petropavlovsk
Anzhero-Sudzhe
Kuybyshev
Caspian Lowlands
Rudnyy
Novosibirsk
Orsk
Aqtobe
Kokshetau
Astrakhan
Atyrau
Kirghiz Steppe
Astana
Pavlodar
Irtysh
Grozny
L. Tengiz
Makhachkala
Aksu
Qaraghandy
Rubtsovsk
Ust-Urt Plateau
KAZAKHSTAN
Aral'sk
Semey
AZER.
40°N
Sumqayit
Baku
Caspian Sea
Kara Bogaz-Gol
Turkmenbashi
Aral Sea
Zhezkazgan
Kazakh Uplands
Oskeme
UZBEKISTAN
Nukus
Kyzyl-Orda
Syr Dar'ya
Balkhash
L. Zaysan
Dashhowuz
Kyzylkum Desert
Lake Balkhash
Tacheng
Karaj
Elburz Mts.
TURKMENISTAN
Karakum Desert
Muyunkum Desert
Taldy-Kurgan
Karamay
Dzungar (Jungga
Tehran
Semnan
Gorgan
Ashgabat
Navoi
Bukhara
Shymkent
Tashkent
Taraz
Bishkek
KYRGYZSTAN
Almaty
Yining
Kuytun
Dasht-e Kavir
Mashhad
Mary
Turkmenabat (Charjou)
Samarkand
Dzhizak
Khujand
Namangan
Fergana
Issyk-Kul'
Pik Pobedy 7439
Tien Shan
Ur
Korla
IRAN
60°E
Amu Dar'ya
Dushanbe
TAJIKISTAN
70°E
Kashi
80°E
Aksu
Tarim He

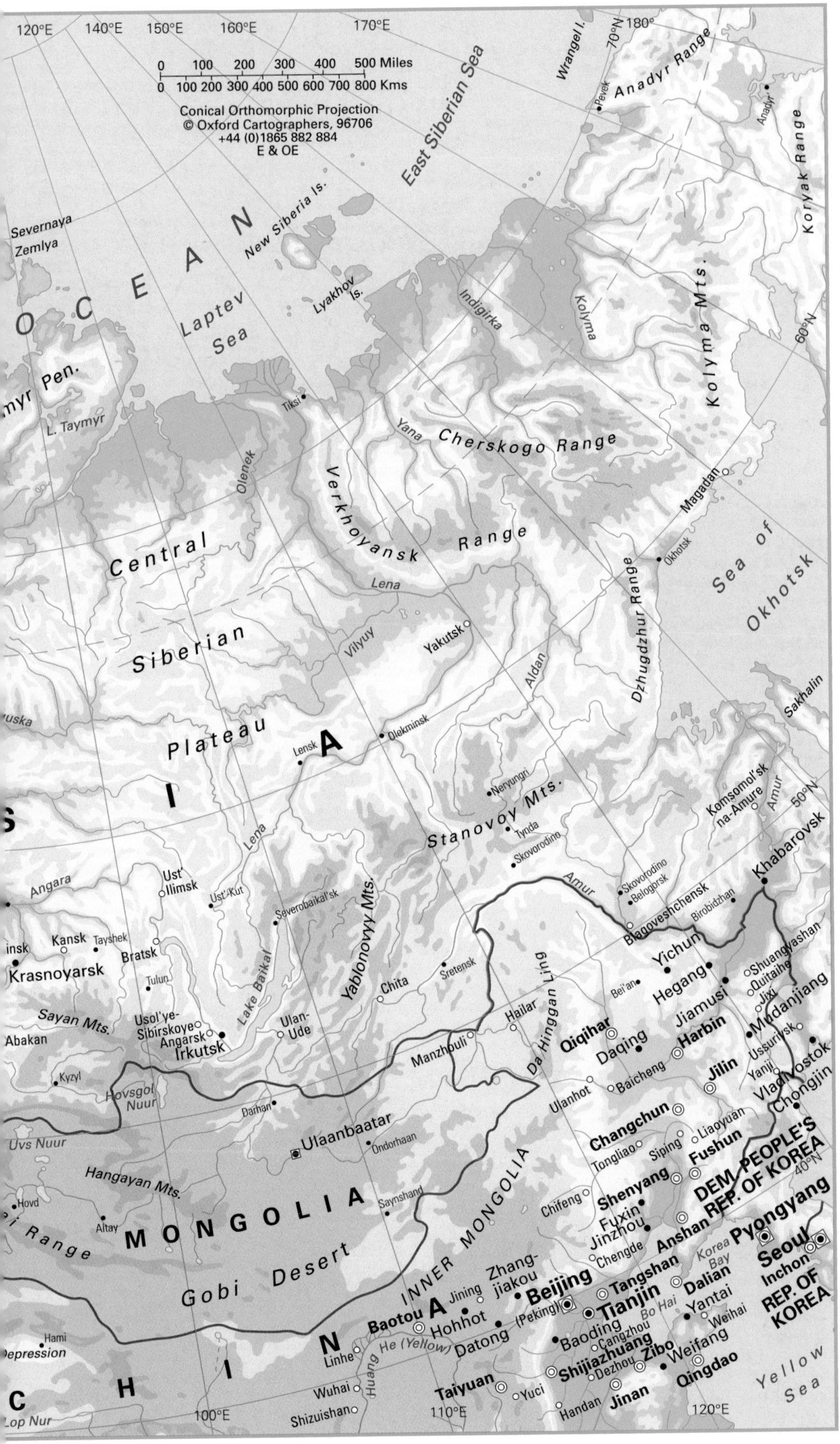
120°E
140°E
150°E
160°E
170°E
180°
70°N
60°N
50°N
40°N
100°E
110°E
120°E
0 100 200 300 400 500 Miles
0 100 200 300 400 500 600 700 800 Kms
Conical Orthomorphic Projection
© Oxford Cartographers, 96706
+44 (0)1865 882 884
E & OE
East Siberian Sea
Wrangel I.
Pevek
Anadyr Range
Anadyr
Koryak Range
OCEAN
New Siberia Is.
Severnaya Zemlya
Laptev Sea
Lyakhov Is.
Indigirka
Kolyma
Kolyma Mts.
Taymyr Pen.
L. Taymyr
Tiksi
Yana
Cherskogo Range
Olenek
Verkhoyansk Range
Magadan
Okhotsk
Central Siberian Plateau
Lena
Dzhugdzhur Range
Sea of Okhotsk
Vilyuy
Yakutsk
Aldan
Sakhalin
Olekminsk
Lensk
A
I
S
Neryungri
Stanovoy Mts.
Tynda
Skovorodino
Komsomol'sk na-Amure
Amur
Khabarovsk
Angara
Ust' Ilimsk
Ust'-Kut
Severobaikal'sk
Yablonovyy Mts.
Belogorsk
Blagoveshchensk
Birobidzhan
Kansk
Tayshek
Bratsk
Krasnoyarsk
Tulun
Lake Baikal
Chita
Sretensk
Yichun
Shuangyashan
Qitaihe
Hegang
Jiamusi
Jixi
Bei'an
Da Hinggan Ling
Sayan Mts.
Abakan
Usol'ye-Sibirskoye
Angarsk
Irkutsk
Ulan-Ude
Hailar
Qiqihar
Daqing
Harbin
Mudanjiang
Ussuriysk
Manzhouli
Kyzyl
Hovsgol Nuur
Baicheng
Jilin
Yanji
Vladivostok
Chongjin
Ulanhot
Darhan
Uvs Nuur
Ulaanbaatar
Ondorhaan
Changchun
Liaoyuan
Tongliao
Siping
Fushun
Hangayan Mts.
Hovd
Altay
Range
MONGOLIA
Saynshand
INNER MONGOLIA
Shenyang
DEM. PEOPLE'S REP. OF KOREA
Chifeng
Fuxin
Jinzhou
Anshan
Pyongyang
Chengde
Korea Bay
Seoul
Inchon
Gobi Desert
Zhangjiakou
Jining
Beijing
(Peking)
Tangshan
Tianjin
Dalian
REP. OF KOREA
Baotou
Hohhot
Bo Hai
Yantai
Weihai
Hami
Depression
Linhe
Huang He (Yellow)
Datong
Baoding
Cangzhou
Shijiazhuang
Dezhou
Zibo
Weifang
Qingdao
Yellow Sea
CHINA
Wuhai
Taiyuan
Yuci
Handan
Jinan
Shizuishan
Lop Nur

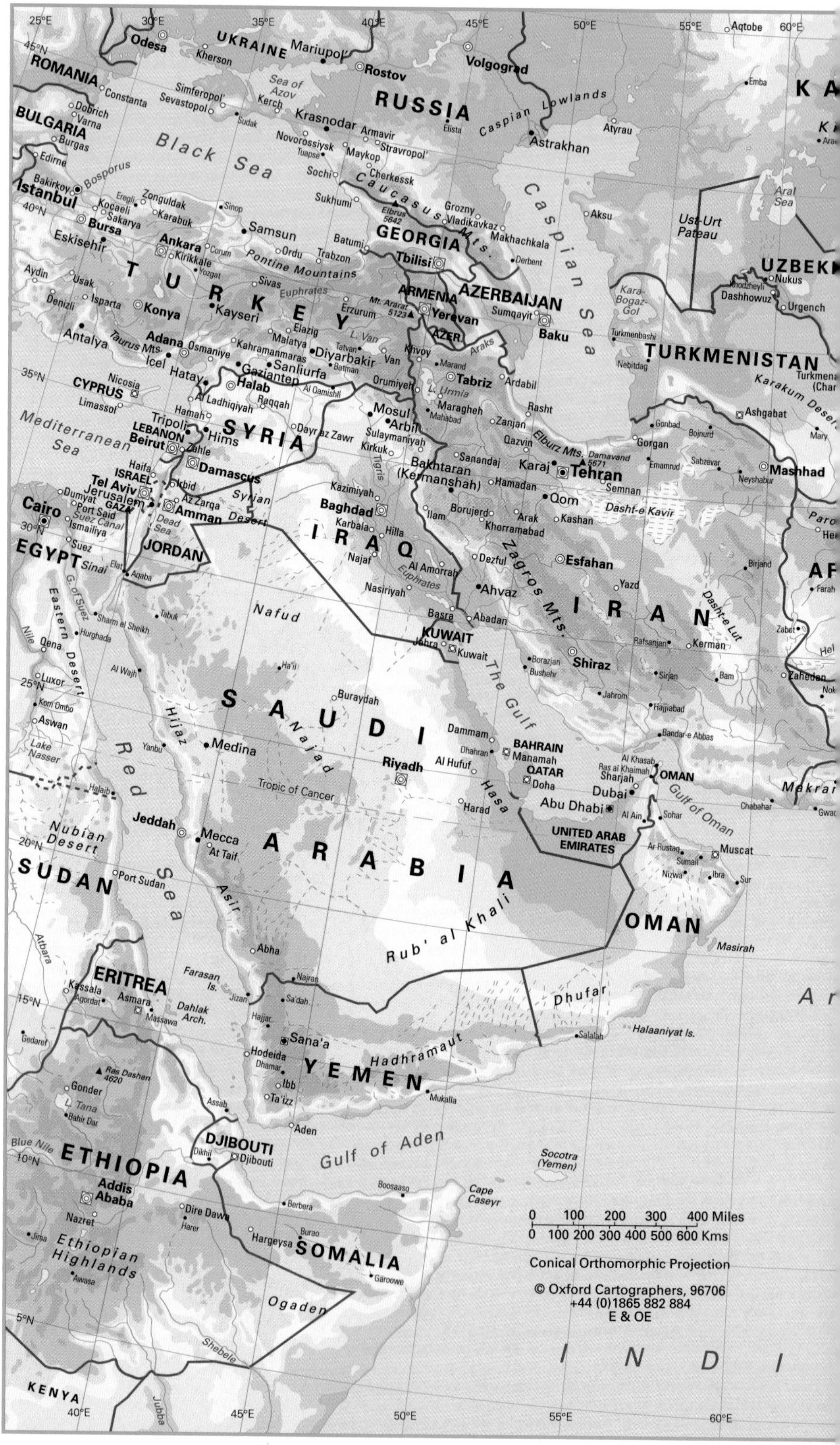

25°E
30°E
35°E
40°E
45°E
50°E
55°E
60°E
45°N
40°N
35°N
30°N
25°N
20°N
15°N
10°N
5°N
Odesa
UKRAINE
Kherson
Mariupol'
Rostov
Volgograd
Aqtobe
Emba
ROMANIA
Constanta
Simferopol'
Sevastopol
Sea of Azov
Kerch
Sudak
RUSSIA
Elista
Caspian Lowlands
Atyrau
Dobrich
Varna
BULGARIA
Burgas
Edirne
Black Sea
Krasnodar
Armavir
Novorossiysk
Tuapse
Maykop
Stavropol'
Astrakhan
Sochi
Cherkessk
Caucasus Mts.
Bakirkoy
Bosporus
Istanbul
Eregli
Zonguldak
Kocaeli
Sakarya
Karabuk
Sinop
Sukhumi
Elbrus 5642
Grozny
Vladikavkaz
Makhachkala
Derbent
Caspian Sea
Aksu
Aral Sea
Ust-Urt Pateau
Bursa
Eskisehir
Ankara
Corum
Kirikkale
Yozgat
Samsun
Ordu
Trabzon
Batumi
GEORGIA
Tbilisi
Pontine Mountains
Aydin
Usak
TURKEY
Sivas
Euphrates
Erzurum
ARMENIA
AZERBAIJAN
Sumqayit
Baku
Kara-Bogaz-Gol
UZBEK
Nukus
Dashhowuz
Urgench
Denizli
Isparta
Konya
Kayseri
Mt. Ararat 5123
Yerevan
AZER.
Turkmenbashi
Nebitdag
TURKMENISTAN
Antalya
Taurus Mts.
Adana
Osmaniye
Elazig
Malatya
L. Van
Tatvan
Kahramanmaras
Diyarbakir
Batman
Van
Khvoy
Araks
Marand
Tabriz
Ardabil
Icel
Hatay
Sanliurfa
Gaziantep
Halab
Al Qamishli
Orumiyeh
L. Urmia
Karakum Desert
Nicosia
CYPRUS
Limassol
Al Ladhiqiyah
Raqqah
Hamah
Mosul
Arbil
Maragheh
Mahabad
Rasht
Zanjan
Ashgabat
Gonbad
Bojnurd
Mary
Mediterranean Sea
Tripoli
LEBANON
Beirut
Hims
SYRIA
Zahle
Dayr az Zawr
Sulaymaniyah
Kirkuk
Tigris
Qazvin
Elburz Mts.
Damavand 5671
Gorgan
Haifa
ISRAEL
Damascus
Sanandaj
Bakhtaran (Kermanshah)
Karaj
Tehran
Semnan
Emamrud
Sabzevar
Neyshabur
Mashhad
Tel Aviv
Jerusalem
GAZA
Dumyat
Port Said
Suez Canal
Ismailiya
Irbid
Az Zarqa
Amman
Dead Sea
Syrian Desert
Kazimiyah
Baghdad
Hamadan
Qom
Dasht-e Kavir
Cairo
Suez
JORDAN
Karbala
Hilla
IRAQ
Ilam
Borujerd
Khorramabad
Arak
Kashan
EGYPT
Sinai
Elat
Aqaba
Najaf
Al Amorrah
Euphrates
Dezful
Zagros Mts.
Esfahan
Yazd
Birjand
Farah
G. of Suez
Eastern Desert
Nasiriyah
Ahvaz
IRAN
Dasht-e Lut
Tabuk
Sharm el Sheikh
Nafud
Basra
Abadan
Zabol
Nile
Qena
Hurghada
KUWAIT
Jahra
Kuwait
Rafsanjan
Kerman
Luxor
Al Wajh
Ha'il
The Gulf
Borazjan
Bushehr
Shiraz
Sirjan
Bam
Zahedan
Kom Ombo
Aswan
Buraydah
Jahrom
Hajjiabad
SAUDI ARABIA
Najd
Hijaz
Dammam
Dhahran
BAHRAIN
Manamah
Bandar-e Abbas
Lake Nasser
Yanbu
Medina
Riyadh
Al Hufuf
QATAR
Doha
Al Khasab
Ras al Khaimah
Sharjah
OMAN
Dubai
Red Sea
Halaib
Tropic of Cancer
Hasa
Harad
Abu Dhabi
Al Ain
Sohar
Gulf of Oman
Chabahar
Makran
Jeddah
Mecca
At Taif
UNITED ARAB EMIRATES
Ar Rustaq
Sumail
Muscat
Nizwa
Ibra
Sur
Nubian Desert
SUDAN
Port Sudan
Asir
Rub' al Khali
OMAN
Masirah
Atbara
Abha
ERITREA
Kassala
Agordat
Asmara
Massawa
Farasan Is.
Dahlak Arch.
Jizan
Najran
Sa'dah
Dhufar
Salalah
Halaaniyat Is.
Gedaref
Hajjar
Sana'a
Hadhramaut
Hodeida
Dhamar
YEMEN
Ras Dashen 4620
Gonder
L. Tana
Bahir Dar
Ibb
Ta'izz
Mukalla
Assab
Aden
Blue Nile
ETHIOPIA
DJIBOUTI
Dikhil
Djibouti
Gulf of Aden
Socotra (Yemen)
Addis Ababa
Boosaaso
Cape Caseyr
Berbera
Nazret
Dire Dawa
Harer
Burao
Jima
Ethiopian Highlands
Hargeysa
SOMALIA
Awasa
Garoowe
Ogaden
Shebele
KENYA
Juba
INDI
0 100 200 300 400 Miles
0 100 200 300 400 500 600 Kms
Conical Orthomorphic Projection
© Oxford Cartographers, 96706
+44 (0)1865 882 884
E & OE

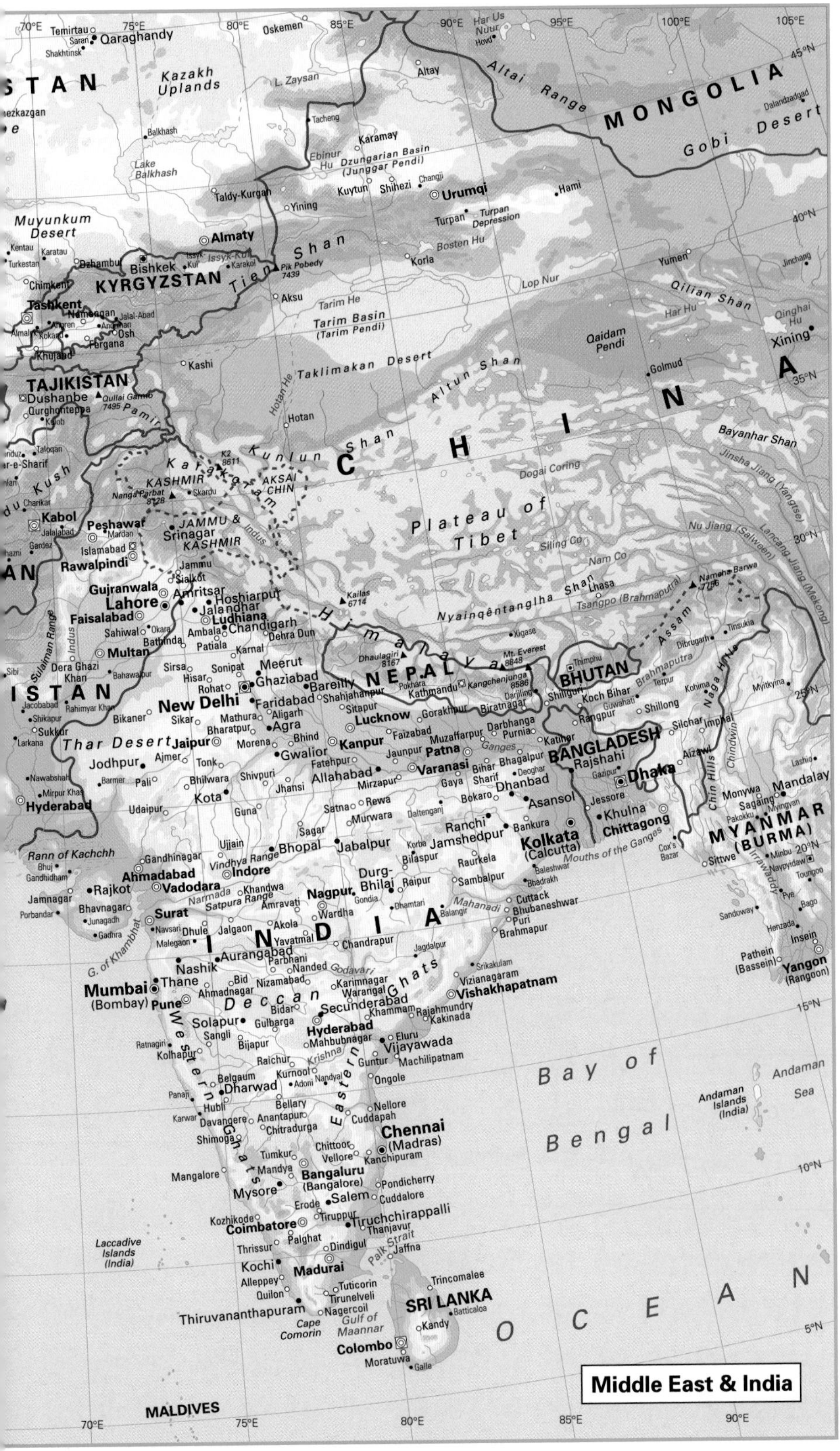
Middle East & India
70°E
75°E
80°E
85°E
90°E
95°E
100°E
105°E
45°N
40°N
35°N
30°N
25°N
20°N
15°N
10°N
5°N
Temirtau
Saran
Qaraghandy
Shakhtinsk
Oskemen
Har Us Nuur
Hovd
STAN
Kazakh Uplands
L. Zaysan
Altay
Altai Range
MONGOLIA
Dalandzadgad
Gobi Desert
Tacheng
Balkhash
Lake Balkhash
Karamay
Ebinur Hu
Dzungarian Basin (Junggar Pendi)
Changji
Kuytun
Shihezi
Urumqi
Hami
Taldy-Kurgan
Yining
Muyunkum Desert
Turpan
Turpan Depression
Almaty
Bosten Hu
Kentau
Karatau
Turkestan
Dzhambul
Bishkek
Issyk-Kul
Karakol
Tien Shan
Pik Pobedy 7439
Korla
Yumen
Jinchang
Chimkent
KYRGYZSTAN
Lop Nur
Qilian Shan
Tashkent
Namangan
Jalal-Abad
Aksu
Tarim He
Andijan
Osh
Tarim Basin (Tarim Pendi)
Har Hu
Qinghai Hu
Kokand
Fergana
Xining
Khujand
Qaidam Pendi
Kashi
Taklimakan Desert
Altun Shan
Golmud
TAJIKISTAN
Dushanbe
Qullai Garmo 7495
Qurghonteppa
Pamir
Hotan He
Hotan
C H I N A
Bayanhar Shan
Kunlun Shan
K2 8611
Karakoram
Taloqan
Jinsha Jiang (Yangtse)
Dogai Coring
KASHMIR
AKSAI CHIN
Nanga Parbat 8128
Skardu
Hindu Kush
Charikar
Kabol
Peshawar
Mardan
Jalalabad
JAMMU & KASHMIR
Srinagar
Plateau of Tibet
Nu Jiang (Salween)
Lancang Jiang (Mekong)
Gardez
Islamabad
Rawalpindi
Indus
Siling Co
Jammu
Nam Co
Sialkot
Gujranwala
Amritsar
Hoshiarpur
Kailas 6714
Lhasa
Namcha Barwa 7756
Lahore
Jalandhar
Ludhiana
Nyainqêntanglha Shan
Tsangpo (Brahmaputra)
Faisalabad
Okara
Sahiwal
Ambala
Chandigarh
Dehra Dun
Himalaya
Assam
Sulaiman Range
Bathinda
Patiala
Xigase
Tinsukia
Multan
Karnal
Dibrugarh
Dhaulagiri 8167
Mt. Everest 8848
Thimphu
Sibi
Dera Ghazi Khan
Sirsa
Sonipat
Meerut
BHUTAN
Brahmaputra
Bahawalpur
Hisar
Ghaziabad
NEPAL
Kangchenjunga 8586
Tezpur
Kohima
Myitkyina
Rohtak
Bareilly
Pokhara
Kathmandu
Darjiling
Koch Bihar
Naga Hills
ISTAN
Jacobabad
Rahimyar Khan
New Delhi
Faridabad
Shahjahanpur
Biratnagar
Shiliguri
Guwahati
Shikapur
Bikaner
Sikar
Mathura
Aligarh
Sitapur
Gorakhpur
Rangpur
Shillong
Sukkur
Bharatpur
Agra
Lucknow
Darbhanga
Silchar
Imphal
Larkana
Thar Desert
Jaipur
Morena
Bhind
Kanpur
Faizabad
Muzaffarpur
Purnia
Katihar
BANGLADESH
Chindwin
Jodhpur
Ajmer
Tonk
Gwalior
Fatehpur
Jaunpur
Patna
Ganges
Rajshahi
Aizawl
Lashio
Nawabshah
Barmer
Pali
Bhilwara
Shivpuri
Allahabad
Varanasi
Bihar Sharif
Bhagalpur
Gazipur
Dhaka
Chin Hills
Mandalay
Mirpur Khas
Jhansi
Mirzapur
Gaya
Dhanbad
Monywa
Sagaing
Hyderabad
Udaipur
Kota
Guna
Satna
Rewa
Bokaro
Asansol
Jessore
Myingyan
Murwara
Daltenganj
Ranchi
Khulna
Pakokku
MYANMAR (BURMA)
Bankura
Sagar
Jamshedpur
Chittagong
Rann of Kachchh
Gandhinagar
Ujjain
Bhopal
Jabalpur
Korba
Kolkata (Calcutta)
Mouths of the Ganges
Cox's Bazar
Sittwe
Minbu
Naypyidaw
Bhuj
Vindhya Range
Bilaspur
Raurkela
Ahmadabad
Indore
Baleshwar
Irrawaddy
Toungoo
Gandhidham
Rajkot
Vadodara
Khandwa
Durg-Bhilai
Raipur
Sambalpur
Bhadrakh
Jamnagar
Narmada
Satpura Range
Nagpur
Pye
Bhavnagar
Amravati
Gondia
Cuttack
Bago
Porbandar
Surat
Wardha
Dhamtari
Mahanadi
Bhubaneshwar
Junagadh
Balangir
Sandoway
Navsari
Dhule
Akola
Puri
Gadhra
Malegaon
Jalgaon
Yavatmal
Chandrapur
Brahmapur
Henzada
I N D I A
Insein
Aurangabad
Jagdalpur
G. of Khambhat
Parbhani
Srikakulam
Pathein (Bassein)
Yangon (Rangoon)
Nashik
Nanded
Godavari
Bid
Vizianagaram
Thane
Nizamabad
Karimnagar
Mumbai (Bombay)
Ahmadnagar
Warangal
Ghats
Vishakhapatnam
Pune
Deccan
Bidar
Secunderabad
Khammam
Rajahmundry
Solapur
Gulbarga
Kakinada
Hyderabad
Sangli
Mahbubnagar
Eluru
Ratnagiri
Bijapur
Vijayawada
Kolhapur
Western Ghats
Krishna
Raichur
Guntur
Machilipatnam
Bay of Bengal
Andaman Sea
Belgaum
Kurnool
Nandyal
Ongole
Adoni
Eastern Ghats
Panaji
Dharwad
Andaman Islands (India)
Bellary
Nellore
Hubli
Karwar
Davangere
Anantapur
Cuddapah
Chitradurga
Chennai (Madras)
Shimoga
Chittoor
Tumkur
Vellore
Kanchipuram
Mandya
Bangaluru (Bangalore)
Mangalore
Pondicherry
Mysore
Erode
Salem
Cuddalore
Kozhikode
Coimbatore
Tiruppur
Tiruchchirappalli
Thanjavur
Laccadive Islands (India)
Thrissur
Palghat
Dindigul
Palk Strait
Jaffna
Kochi
Madurai
Alleppey
Tuticorin
Trincomalee
Quilon
Tirunelveli
SRI LANKA
Batticaloa
Thiruvananthapuram
Nagercoil
Cape Comorin
Gulf of Maannar
Kandy
Colombo
Moratuwa
Galle
OCEAN
MALDIVES

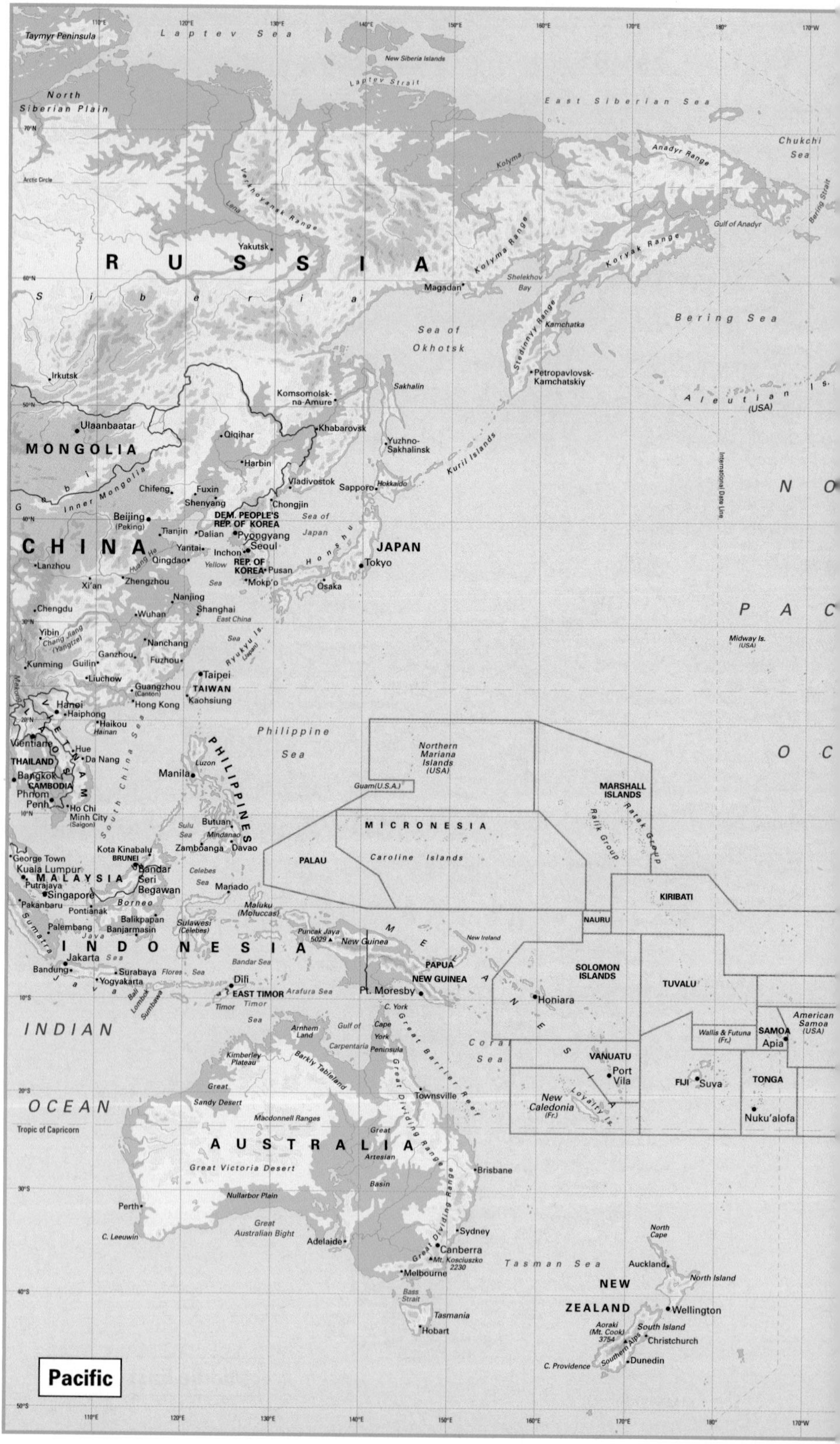
Pacific
Taymyr Peninsula
Laptev Sea
New Siberia Islands
Laptev Strait
North Siberian Plain
East Siberian Sea
Chukchi Sea
Anadyr Range
Kolyma
Verkhoyansk Range
Lena
Arctic Circle
Gulf of Anadyr
Bering Strait
Yakutsk
RUSSIA
Kolyma Range
Koryak Range
Shelekhov Bay
Magadan
Siberia
Bering Sea
Sea of Okhotsk
Kamchatka
Stedinnyy Range
Petropavlovsk-Kamchatskiy
Irkutsk
Sakhalin
Komsomolsk-na-Amure
Aleutian Is. (USA)
Khabarovsk
Ulaanbaatar
Qiqihar
Yuzhno-Sakhalinsk
MONGOLIA
Harbin
Kuril Islands
International Date Line
Gobi
Inner Mongolia
Chifeng
Fuxin
Vladivostok
Sapporo
Hokkaido
Shenyang
Chongjin
Beijing (Peking)
DEM. PEOPLE'S REP. OF KOREA
Sea of Japan
Tianjin
Dalian
Pyongyang
Honshu
CHINA
Yantai
Seoul
Inchon
JAPAN
Lanzhou
Huang He
Qingdao
Yellow Sea
REP. OF KOREA
Pusan
Tokyo
Xi'an
Zhengzhou
Mokp'o
Osaka
Nanjing
Shanghai
Chengdu
Wuhan
East China Sea
PACIFIC OCEAN
Yibin
Chang Jiang (Yangtze)
Nanchang
Ryukyu Is. (Japan)
Midway Is. (USA)
Ganzhou
Fuzhou
Kunming
Guilin
Taipei
Liuchow
Guangzhou (Canton)
TAIWAN
Mekong
Hanoi
Hong Kong
Kaohsiung
Haiphong
Haikou
Hainan
Philippine Sea
Vientiane
LAOS
VIETNAM
Hue
Da Nang
Northern Mariana Islands (USA)
THAILAND
Luzon
PHILIPPINES
Bangkok
Manila
Guam(U.S.A.)
CAMBODIA
MARSHALL ISLANDS
Phnom Penh
Ho Chi Minh City (Saigon)
South China Sea
MICRONESIA
Ralik Group
Ratak Group
Sulu Sea
Butuan
Mindanao
Kota Kinabalu
Zamboanga
Davao
PALAU
Caroline Islands
BRUNEI
George Town
Bandar Seri Begawan
Kuala Lumpur
Celebes Sea
MALAYSIA
Putrajaya
Manado
KIRIBATI
Singapore
Borneo
Pakanbaru
Pontianak
Maluku (Moluccas)
NAURU
Balikpapan
Sulawesi (Celebes)
Palembang
Banjarmasin
Puncak Jaya 5029
New Guinea
MELANESIA
New Ireland
Sumatra
Java Sea
INDONESIA
SOLOMON ISLANDS
Jakarta
Bandar Sea
PAPUA NEW GUINEA
TUVALU
Bandung
Surabaya
Flores Sea
Java
Yogyakarta
Dili
Bali
Lombok
Sumbawa
EAST TIMOR
Arafura Sea
Pt. Moresby
Honiara
Timor
Timor Sea
C. York
American Samoa (USA)
INDIAN OCEAN
Arnhem Land
Gulf of Carpentaria
Cape York Peninsula
Coral Sea
Wallis & Futuna (Fr.)
SAMOA
Apia
Kimberley Plateau
Barkly Tableland
VANUATU
Port Vila
FIJI
Suva
TONGA
Great Sandy Desert
Great Barrier Reef
Townsville
New Caledonia (Fr.)
Loyalty Is.
Nuku'alofa
Tropic of Capricorn
Macdonnell Ranges
Great Artesian Basin
AUSTRALIA
Great Dividing Range
Great Victoria Desert
Brisbane
Nullarbor Plain
Perth
Great Australian Bight
Sydney
C. Leeuwin
Adelaide
Canberra
North Cape
Mt. Kosciuszko 2230
Tasman Sea
Auckland
Melbourne
NEW ZEALAND
North Island
Bass Strait
Wellington
Tasmania
Aoraki (Mt. Cook) 3754
South Island
Hobart
Southern Alps
Christchurch
C. Providence
Dunedin

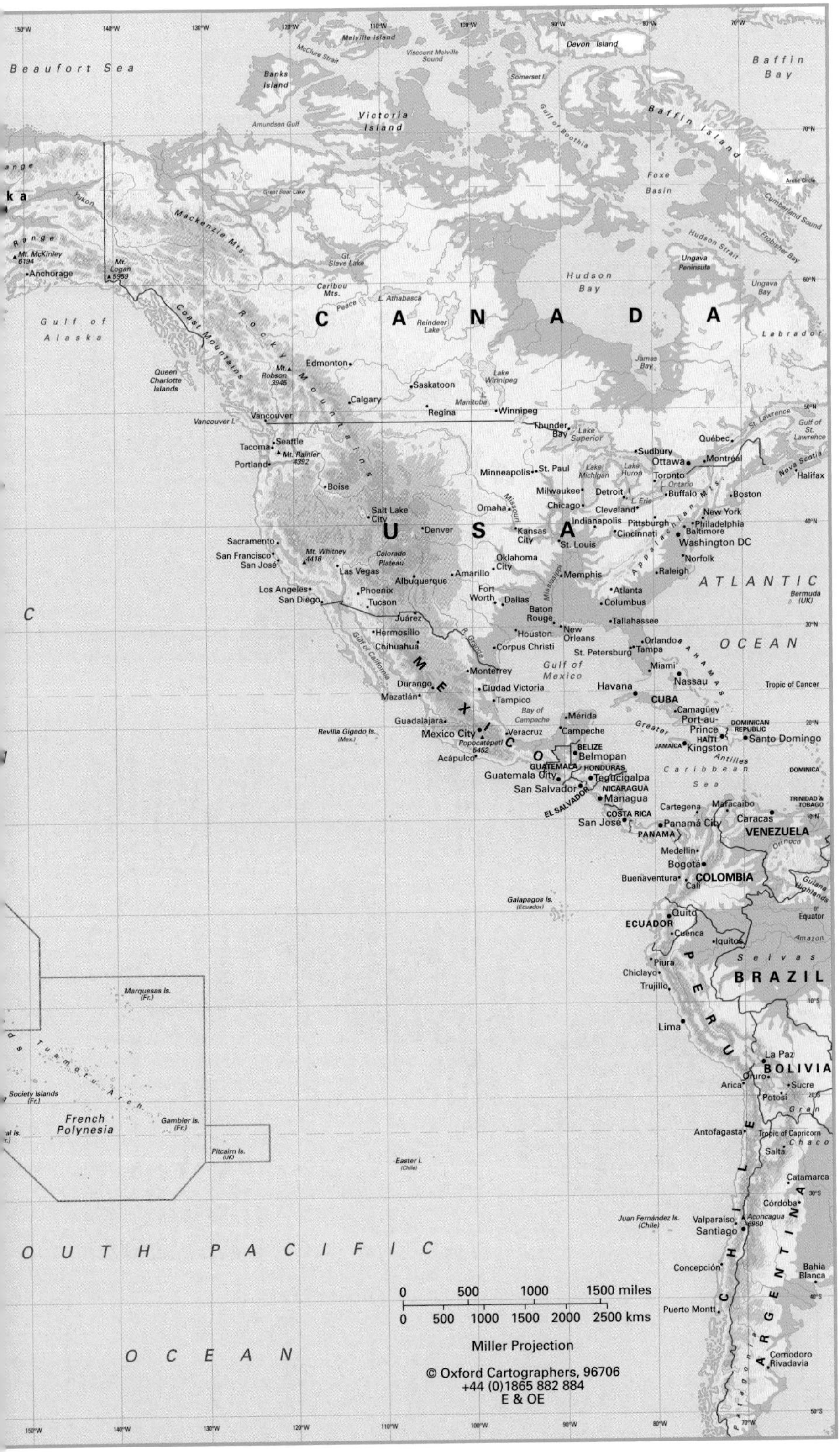

Beaufort Sea
Melville Island
McClure Strait
Viscount Melville Sound
Banks Island
Devon Island
Baffin Bay
Somerset I.
Victoria Island
Amundsen Gulf
Gulf of Boothia
Baffin Island
Foxe Basin
Great Bear Lake
Yukon
Mackenzie Mts.
Arctic Circle
Cumberland Sound
Frobisher Bay
Hudson Strait
Ungava Peninsula
Range
Mt. McKinley 6194
Anchorage
Mt. Logan 5959
Gt. Slave Lake
Caribou Mts.
Hudson Bay
Ungava Bay
Peace
L. Athabasca
Reindeer Lake
CANADA
Gulf of Alaska
Coast Mountains
Rocky Mountains
Labrador
James Bay
Edmonton
Queen Charlotte Islands
Mt. Robson 3945
Saskatoon
Lake Winnipeg
Calgary
Manitoba
Regina
Winnipeg
Vancouver
Vancouver I.
Thunder Bay
Lake Superior
St. Lawrence
Gulf of St. Lawrence
Seattle
Tacoma
Mt. Rainier 4392
Portland
Québec
Sudbury
Ottawa
Montréal
Nova Scotia
Halifax
Minneapolis
St. Paul
Lake Michigan
Lake Huron
Toronto
Ontario
Boise
Milwaukee
Detroit
L. Erie
Buffalo
Boston
Missouri
Omaha
Chicago
Cleveland
New York
Salt Lake City
Indianapolis
Pittsburgh
Philadelphia
USA
Denver
Kansas City
Cincinnati
Baltimore
Washington DC
St. Louis
Sacramento
San Francisco
San José
Mt. Whitney 4418
Colorado Plateau
Las Vegas
Oklahoma City
Amarillo
Memphis
Norfolk
Raleigh
Appalachian Mts.
Mississippi
Albuquerque
Los Angeles
San Diego
Phoenix
Tucson
Fort Worth
Dallas
Atlanta
Columbus
ATLANTIC
Bermuda (UK)
Juárez
Baton Rouge
Tallahassee
Hermosillo
Houston
New Orleans
Orlando
Tampa
OCEAN
Chihuahua
Gulf of California
R. Grande
Corpus Christi
St. Petersburg
BAHAMAS
Miami
Nassau
Gulf of Mexico
Monterrey
Durango
Ciudad Victoria
Havana
Tropic of Cancer
Mazatlán
MEXICO
Tampico
CUBA
Camagüey
Bay of Campeche
Mérida
Guadalajara
Campeche
Revilla Gigedo Is. (Mex.)
Mexico City
Veracruz
Greater
Port-au-Prince
DOMINICAN REPUBLIC
Santo Domingo
HAITI
Popocatépetl 5452
JAMAICA
Kingston
BELIZE
Belmopan
Antilles
Acápulco
GUATEMALA
HONDURAS
DOMINICA
Caribbean Sea
Guatemala City
Tegucigalpa
San Salvador
NICARAGUA
Managua
TRINIDAD & TOBAGO
EL SALVADOR
Cartegena
Maracaibo
COSTA RICA
Caracas
San José
Panamá City
PANAMA
VENEZUELA
Orinoco
Medellín
Bogotá
Buenaventura
Cali
COLOMBIA
Guiana Highlands
Galapagos Is. (Ecuador)
Quito
Equator
ECUADOR
Cuenca
Iquitos
Amazon
Piura
Selvas
Chiclayo
BRAZIL
Trujillo
PERU
Lima
Marquesas Is. (Fr.)
Tuamotu Arch.
La Paz
BOLIVIA
Oruro
Arica
Sucre
Potosí
Society Islands (Fr.)
French Polynesia
Gambier Is. (Fr.)
Gran Chaco
Antofagasta
Tropic of Capricorn
Salta
Pitcairn Is. (UK)
Easter I. (Chile)
Catamarca
Córdoba
Juan Fernández Is. (Chile)
Aconcagua 6960
Valparaíso
Santiago
SOUTH PACIFIC OCEAN
CHILE
ARGENTINA
Concepción
Bahia Blanca
Puerto Montt
Comodoro Rivadavia
Patagonia
0 500 1000 1500 miles
0 500 1000 1500 2000 2500 kms
Miller Projection
© Oxford Cartographers, 96706
+44 (0)1865 882 884
E & OE

World Political
180° 160°W 140°W 120°W 100°W 60°W 20°W 0° 20°E 40°E 60°E 80°E 100°E 120°E 140°E 160°E 180°
60°N
40°N
Tropic of Cancer
20°N
0° Equator
International Date Line
20°S
Tropic of Capricorn
40°S
60°S
Antarctic Circle
Arctic Circle
INTERNATIONAL DATE LINE
Kalaallit Nunaat
(Greenland)
(Denmark)
Alaska
(USA)
Canada
United States of America
Mexico
Bahamas
Cuba
Haiti
Dom. Rep.
Belize
Jamaica
Guatemala
Honduras
El Salvador
Nicaragua
Costa Rica
Panama
Trinidad and Tobago
Venezuela
Guyana
Sur.
French Guiana
Colombia
Ecuador
Brazil
Peru
Bolivia
Paraguay
Chile
Uruguay
Argentina
Iceland
Norway
Sweden
Finland
Denmark
UK
Rep. of Ireland
Neth.
Belg.
Lux.
Ger.
Poland
Rus.
Es.
La.
Li.
Belarus
Ukraine
Mol.
Cz. Rep.
Slov.
Aust.
Hungary
Sw.
Slo.
Cro.
Serb.
B&H
Mo.
Ma.
Romania
Bulgaria
Alb.
Greece
France
Portugal
Spain
Italy
Gibraltar
Malta
Morocco
Tunisia
Algeria
Libya
Egypt
Western Sahara
Mauritania
Cape Verde
Senegal
Gambia
Guinea Bissau
Gui.
SL
Liberia
Mali
Burkina Faso
Côte d'Ivoire
Ghana
T.
Benin
Niger
Nigeria
Chad
Sudan
Eritrea
Ethiopia
Djibouti
Somalia
Cam.
Cen. Af. Rep.
Eq. Gui.
Gabon
Rep. of Congo
Cabinda (Angola)
Dem. Rep. of Congo
Uganda
Kenya
Rwanda
Burundi
Tanzania
Angola
Zambia
Mal.
Mozambique
Zim.
Namibia
Botswana
Swaziland
South Africa
Lesotho
Madagascar
Mauritius
Seychelles
Maldives
Turkey
Georgia
Ar.
Azer.
Cyp.
Syria
Leb.
Isr.
Jor.
Iraq
Kuwait
Q.
UAE
Saudi Arabia
Yemen
Oman
Iran
Turk.
Uzbekistan
Kazakhstan
Kyrg.
Taj.
Afghanistan
Pakistan
India
Nepal
Bh.
Bangladesh
Sri Lanka
Russia
Mongolia
China
Myanmar
Laos
Thai.
Vietnam
Cam.
Malaysia
Singapore
Brn.
Indonesia
East Timor
Philippines
Taiwan
Dem. People's Rep. of Korea
Rep. of Korea
Japan
Micronesia
Papua New Guinea
Australia
Vanuatu
Fiji
New Zealand
Antarctica
Alb. Albania
Ar. Armenia
Aust. Austria
Azer. Azerbaijan
Belg. Belgium
Bh. Bhutan
B&H Bosnia-Hercegovina
Brn. Brunei
Cam. Cambodia
Cam. Cameroon
Cen. Af. Rep. Central African Republic
Cro. Croatia
Cyp. Cyprus
Cz. Rep. Czech Republic
Dom. Rep. Dominican Republic
Eq. Gui. Equatorial Guinea
Es. Estonia
Ger. Germany
Gui. Guinea
Isr. Israel
Jor. Jordan
Kyrg. Kyrgyzstan
La. Latvia
Leb. Lebanon
Li. Lithuania
Lux. Luxembourg
Ma. F.Y.R.Macedonia
Mal. Malawi
Mo. Montenegro
Mol. Moldova
Neth. Netherlands
Q. Qatar
Rus. Russia
SL Sierra Leone
Slov. Slovakia
Slo. Slovenia
Serb. Serbia
Sur. Suriname
Sw. Switzerland
Taj. Tajikistan
Thai. Thailand
T. Togo
Turk. Turkmenistan
UAE United Arab Emirates
UK United Kingdom
Zim. Zimbabwe
Modified Gall Projection
Equatorial Scale 1:166,000,000
© Oxford Cartographers, 96706
+44 (0)1865 882 884
E & OE

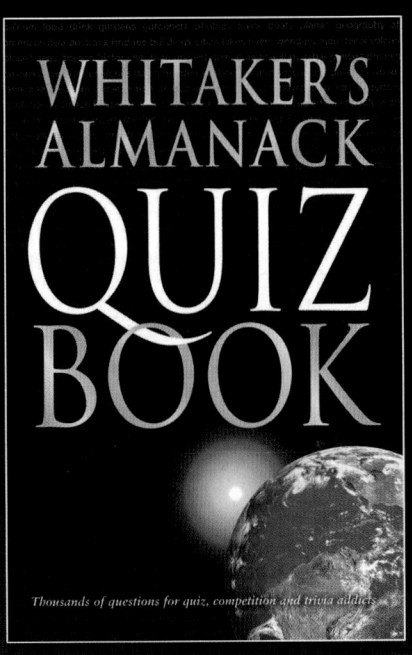

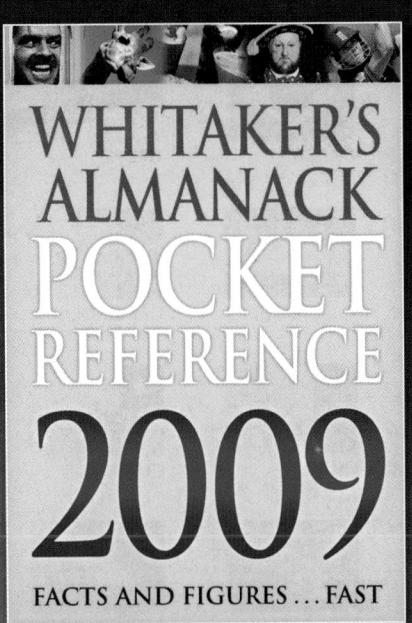

FLAGS OF THE WORLD

The following four pages show the national flag of each country, as it is used for international purposes. In some cases this means that the state flag is shown. Where this is the case the country name is marked (†).

AFGHANISTAN | ALBANIA | ALGERIA | ANDORRA | ANGOLA

ANTIGUA AND BARBUDA | ARGENTINA | ARMENIA | AUSTRALIA | AUSTRIA

AZERBAIJAN | THE BAHAMAS | BAHRAIN | BANGLADESH | BARBADOS

BELARUS | BELGIUM | BELIZE | BENIN | BHUTAN

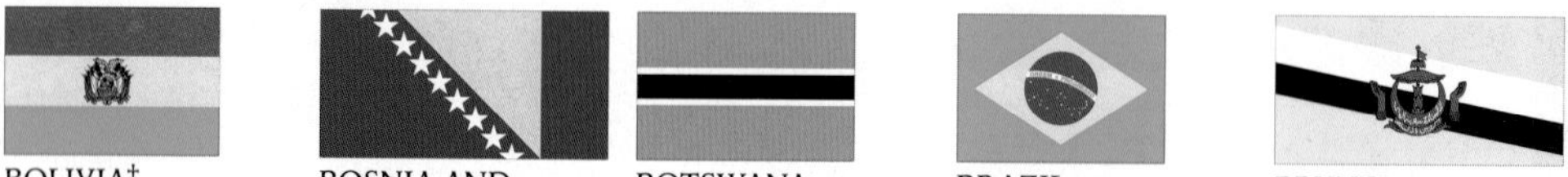

BOLIVIA† | BOSNIA AND HERCEGOVINA | BOTSWANA | BRAZIL | BRUNEI

BULGARIA | BURKINA FASO | BURUNDI | CAMBODIA | CAMEROON

CANADA | CAPE VERDE | CENTRAL AFRICAN REPUBLIC | CHAD | CHILE

CHINA | COLOMBIA | THE COMOROS | DEM. REPUBLIC OF THE CONGO | REPUBLIC OF THE CONGO

COSTA RICA | CÔTE D'IVOIRE | CROATIA | CUBA | CYPRUS

CZECH REPUBLIC — DENMARK — DJIBOUTI — DOMINICA — DOMINICAN REPUBLIC

EAST TIMOR — ECUADOR — EGYPT — EL SALVADOR — EQUATORIAL GUINEA

ERITREA — ESTONIA — ETHIOPIA — FIJI — FINLAND

FRANCE — GABON — THE GAMBIA — GEORGIA — GERMANY

GHANA — GREECE — GRENADA — GUATEMALA — GUINEA

GUINEA-BISSAU — GUYANA — HAITI† — HONDURAS — HUNGARY

ICELAND — INDIA — INDONESIA — IRAN — IRAQ

IRELAND — ISRAEL — ITALY — JAMAICA — JAPAN

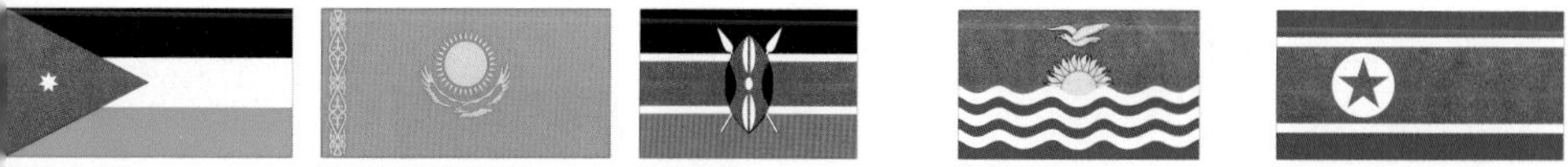

JORDAN — KAZAKHSTAN — KENYA — KIRIBATI — DEM. PEOPLE'S REPUBLIC OF KOREA

REPUBLIC OF KOREA — KUWAIT — KYRGYZSTAN — LAOS — LATVIA

LEBANON | LESOTHO | LIBERIA | LIBYA | LIECHTENSTEIN

LITHUANIA | LUXEMBOURG | MACEDONIA | MADAGASCAR | MALAWI

MALAYSIA | MALDIVES | MALI | MALTA | MARSHALL ISLANDS

MAURITANIA | MAURITIUS | MEXICO | FEDERATED STATES OF MICRONESIA | MOLDOVA

MONACO | MONGOLIA | MONTENEGRO | MOROCCO | MOZAMBIQUE

MYANMAR | NAMIBIA | NAURU | NEPAL | THE NETHERLANDS

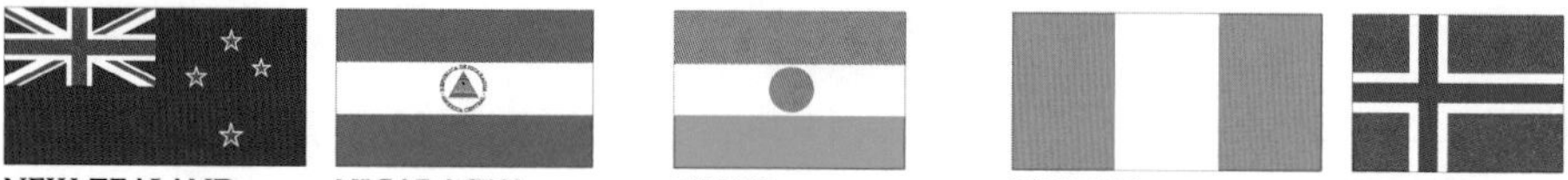

NEW ZEALAND | NICARAGUA | NIGER | NIGERIA | NORWAY

OMAN | PAKISTAN | PALAU | PANAMA | PAPUA NEW GUINEA

PARAGUAY | PERU | THE PHILIPPINES | POLAND | PORTUGAL

QATAR | ROMANIA | RUSSIAN FEDERATION | RWANDA

ST CHRISTOPHER AND NEVIS | ST LUCIA | ST VINCENT AND THE GRENADINES | SAMOA | SAN MARINO†

SAO TOME AND PRINCIPE | SAUDI ARABIA | SENEGAL | SERBIA† | SEYCHELLES

SIERRA LEONE | SINGAPORE | SLOVAKIA | SLOVENIA | SOLOMON ISLANDS

SOMALIA | SOUTH AFRICA | SPAIN | SRI LANKA | SUDAN

SURINAME | SWAZILAND | SWEDEN | SWITZERLAND | SYRIA

TAIWAN | TAJIKISTAN | TANZANIA | THAILAND | TOGO

TONGA | TRINIDAD AND TOBAGO | TUNISIA | TURKEY | TURKMENISTAN

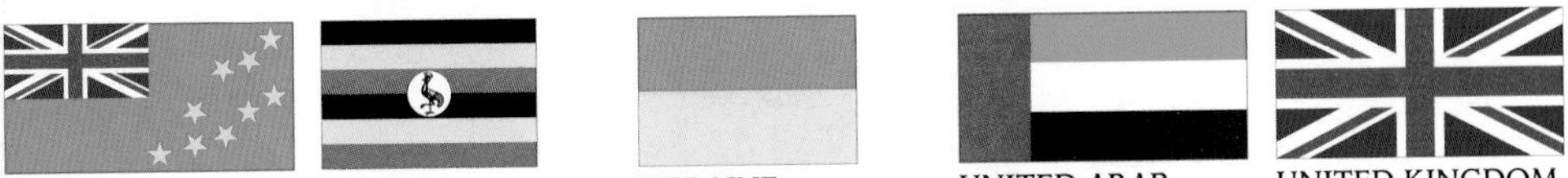

TUVALU | UGANDA | UKRAINE | UNITED ARAB EMIRATES | UNITED KINGDOM

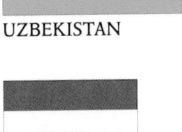

UNITED STATES OF AMERICA | URUGUAY | UZBEKISTAN | VANUATU | VATICAN CITY STATE

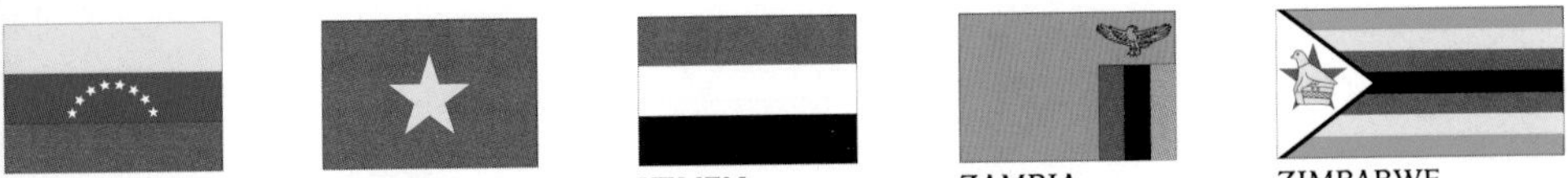

VENEZUELA | VIETNAM | YEMEN | ZAMBIA | ZIMBABWE

GLOBAL FOOD CRISIS

Prices of basic international food commodities, such as wheat, rice, milk and maize, have risen in 2006–8 due to a combination of economic and social factors. Buoyant oil prices have pushed up the cost of producing food, making fertilisers and food transport more expensive. Meanwhile, droughts in exporting countries, such as Australia, have reduced the size of harvests. The enthusiasm for growing biofuels as a green alternative to fossil fuels has also cut the amount of land available for crop production. As prices have risen, many governments have imposed export tariffs on grain, further reducing the amount available to trade globally.

These problems of supply have been matched by a rise in demand for meat and dairy from emerging economies such as China and India. The price rises have affected parts of Africa and Asia most severely leading to many protests and riots in late 2007 and 2008.

PETROL PRICES WORLDWIDE

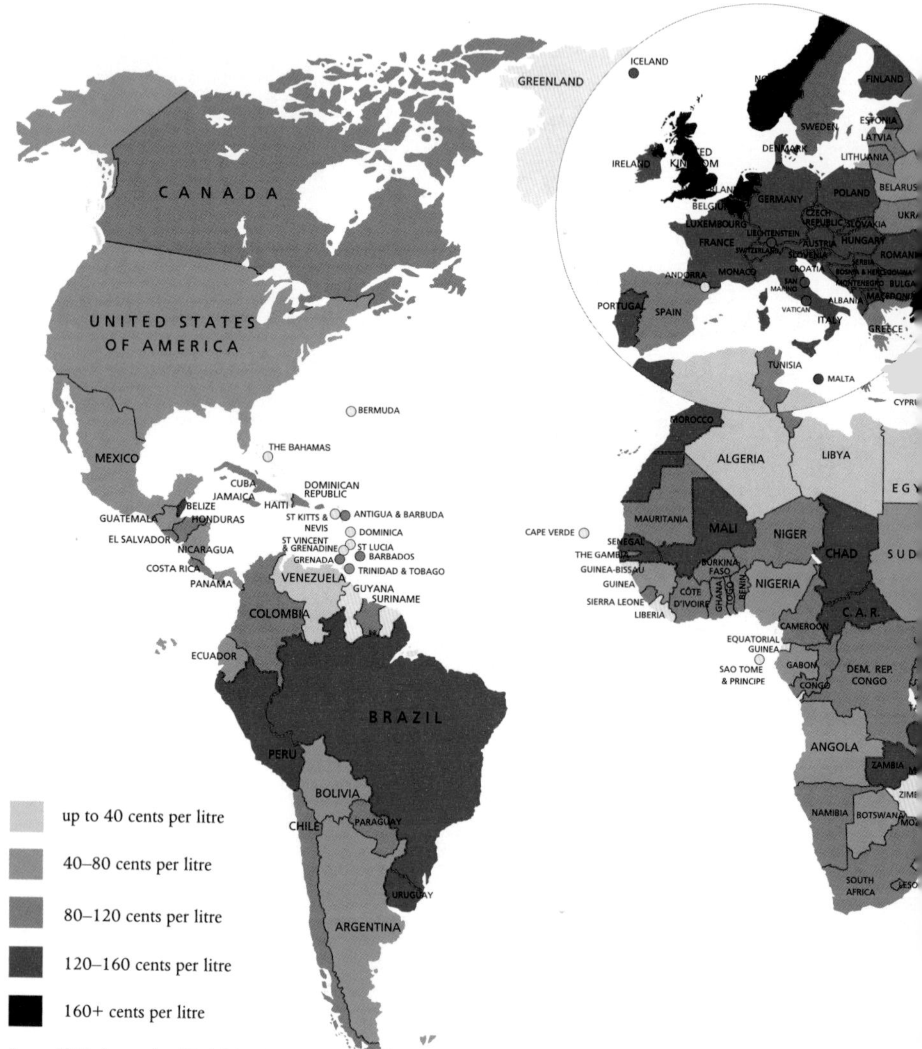

Source: GTZ, *International Fuel Prices 2007*

The price at which oil retails is set on world markets, however the price which consumers pay for fuel at the pump varies enormously. This difference reflects the variety of national fiscal policies. Prices above a rough benchmark figure (for 2007 this is 53 cents a litre) suggest that governments are taxing fuel, while prices below imply a policy of subsidising. In addition, high demand, political instability, the rising price of crude oil and OPEC's protectionist policy have driven up the cost of fuel in recent years.

The most expensive fuel prices are typically found in Western Europe, where governments have historically imposed significant taxes. In the UK, fuel duty is set at 52.35p for every litre of unleaded petrol and diesel, while VAT is a further 17.5 per cent. Low prices are centred around the Gulf and other net oil exporters such as Venezuela and Turkmenistan.

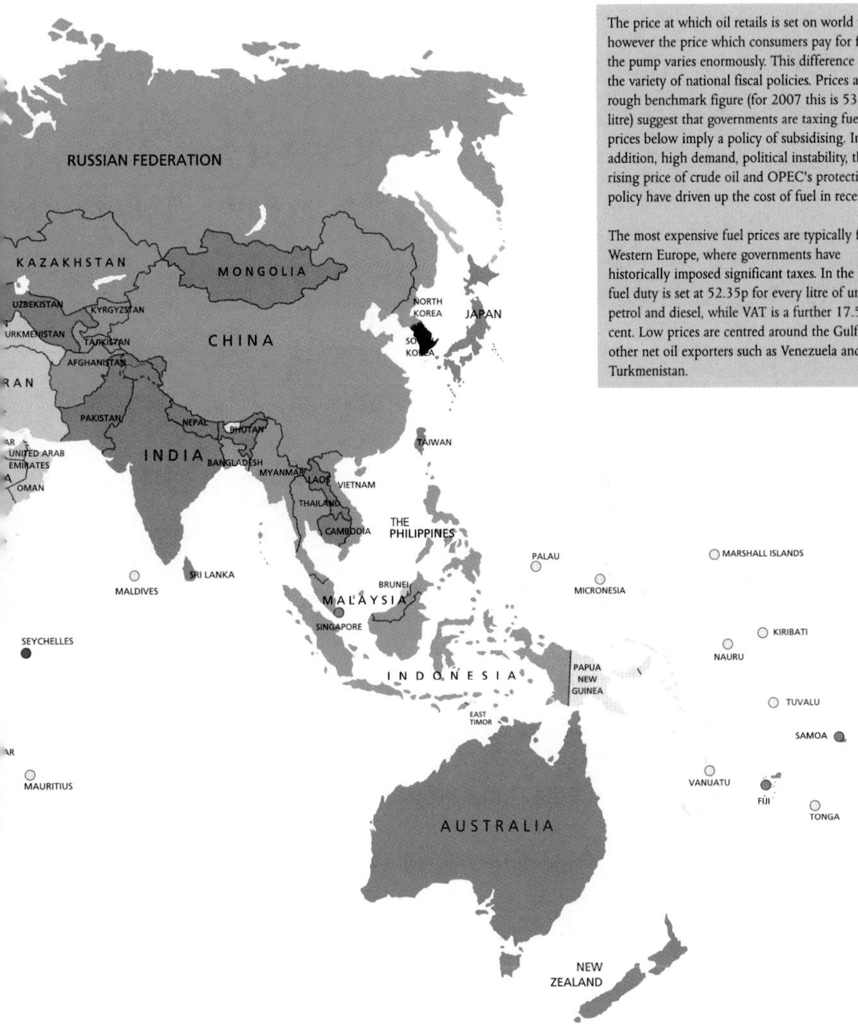

INFLATION RATES WORLDWIDE

2008 estimates

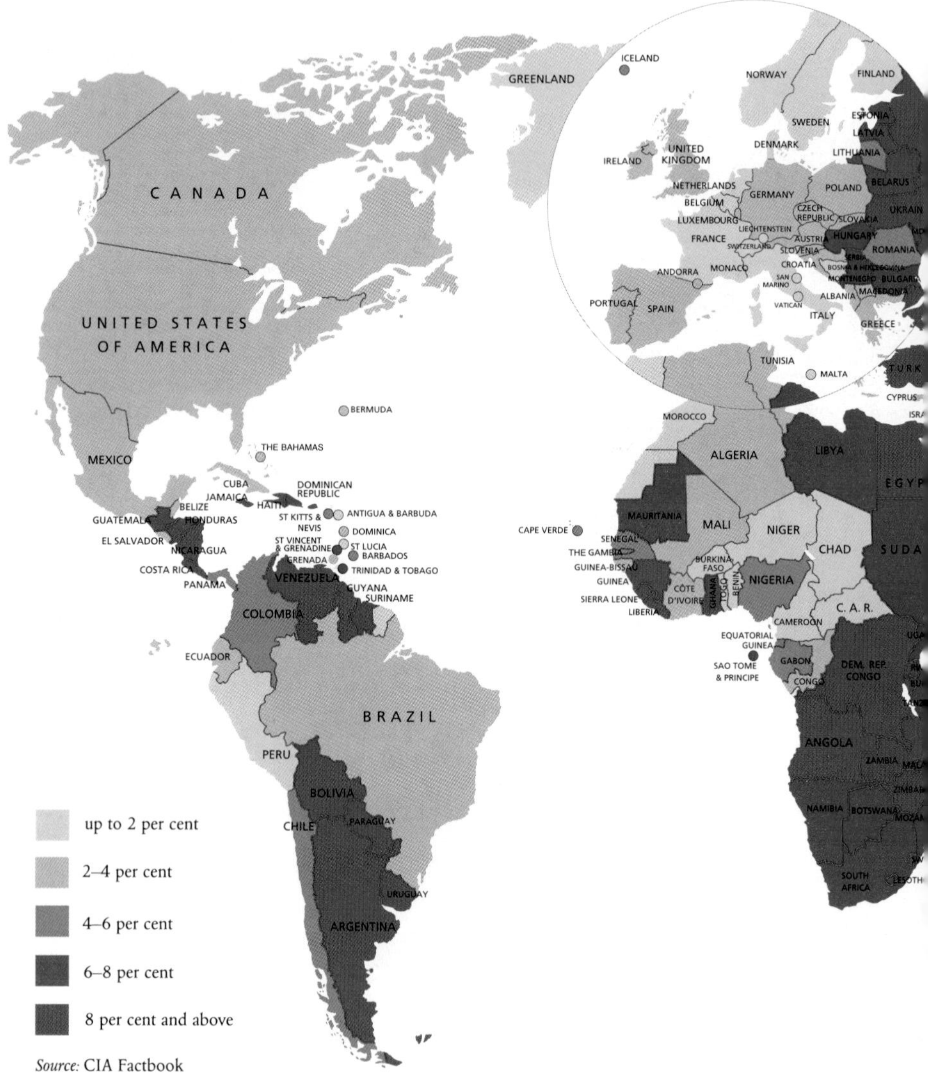

Source: CIA Factbook

Price stability is generally the goal of many central banks' monetary policies. The Bank of England is expected to achieve an inflation rate of 2.5 per cent, while the European Central Bank's target is between 0 and 2 per cent.

Zimbabwe has the world's highest rate of inflation – considered to be hyperinflation at 2,200,000 per cent in July 2008. Even this figure has to be estimated as the country's statistical office suspended monthly updates during 2007 because shops were short of supplies used to calculate a regular basket of goods.

The most prominent example of deflation is Japan, where the consumer price index has been falling since the 1990s and remains at 0. Since their peak in 1989, assets such as equity and property have been reducing in value, while many banks and businesses became bankrupt. The decreasing prices of imported goods, particularly from China, have also contributed to the deflationary pressure.

The recent global rise in food prices is partly to blame for the substantial increases in inflation in developing countries, where food has a bigger weight in household spending – over 30 per cent for Argentina compared to 15 per cent in G7 countries.

POPULATION GROWTH RATES

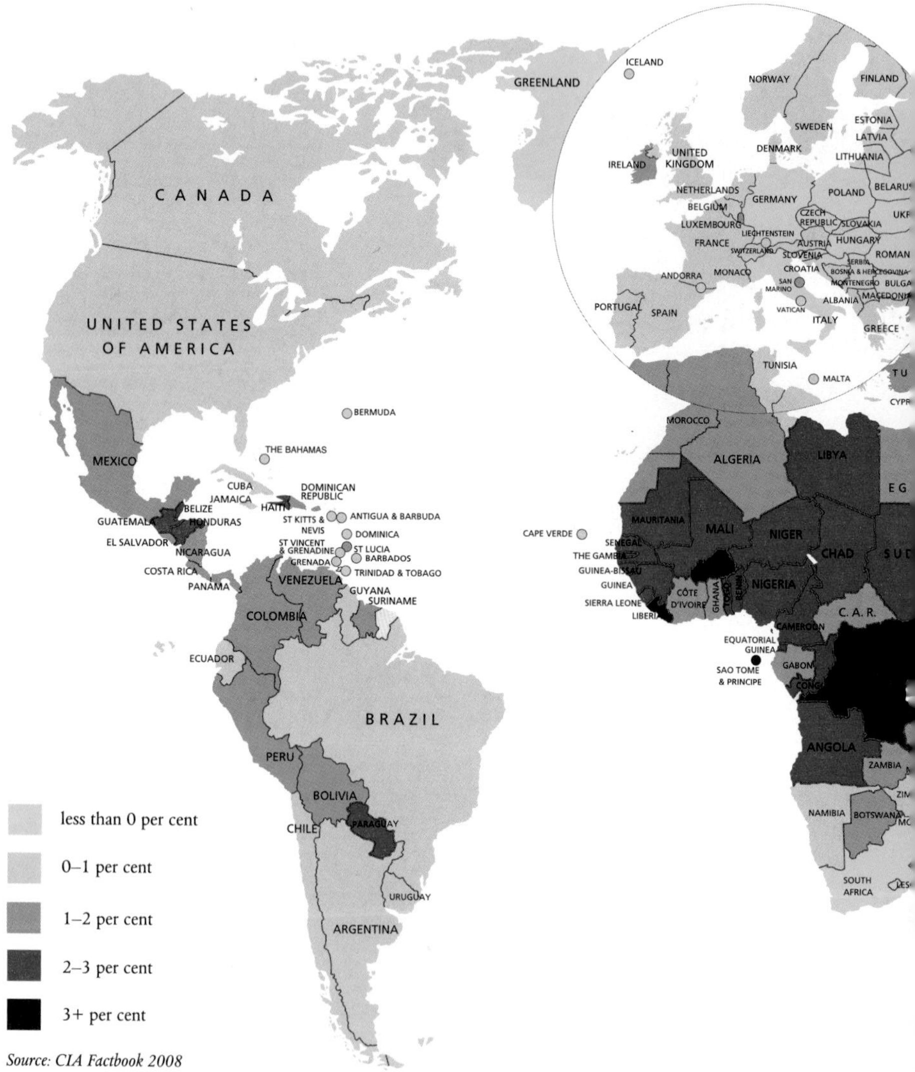

Source: CIA Factbook 2008

A review of population growth rates in this year's Countries of the World section shows that 169 of 194 countries have populations larger than last year. The global population is continuing to grow, albeit more slowly than in the 1970s and 80s. However, declining fertility means that half of the world's population now lives in countries where the number of births each year is smaller than the number of deaths, a phenomenon known as sub-replacement fertility.

In the Mediterranean, Eastern Europe and the Far East, declining populations are thought to be due to a combination of fertility rates falling and standards of living improving. For developed countries with industrialised economies, the effects of a fall in population growth can be far-reaching – leading to labour shortages, a decline in economic growth and a greater burden on social security systems.

GAY AND LESBIAN RIGHTS
legislation worldwide

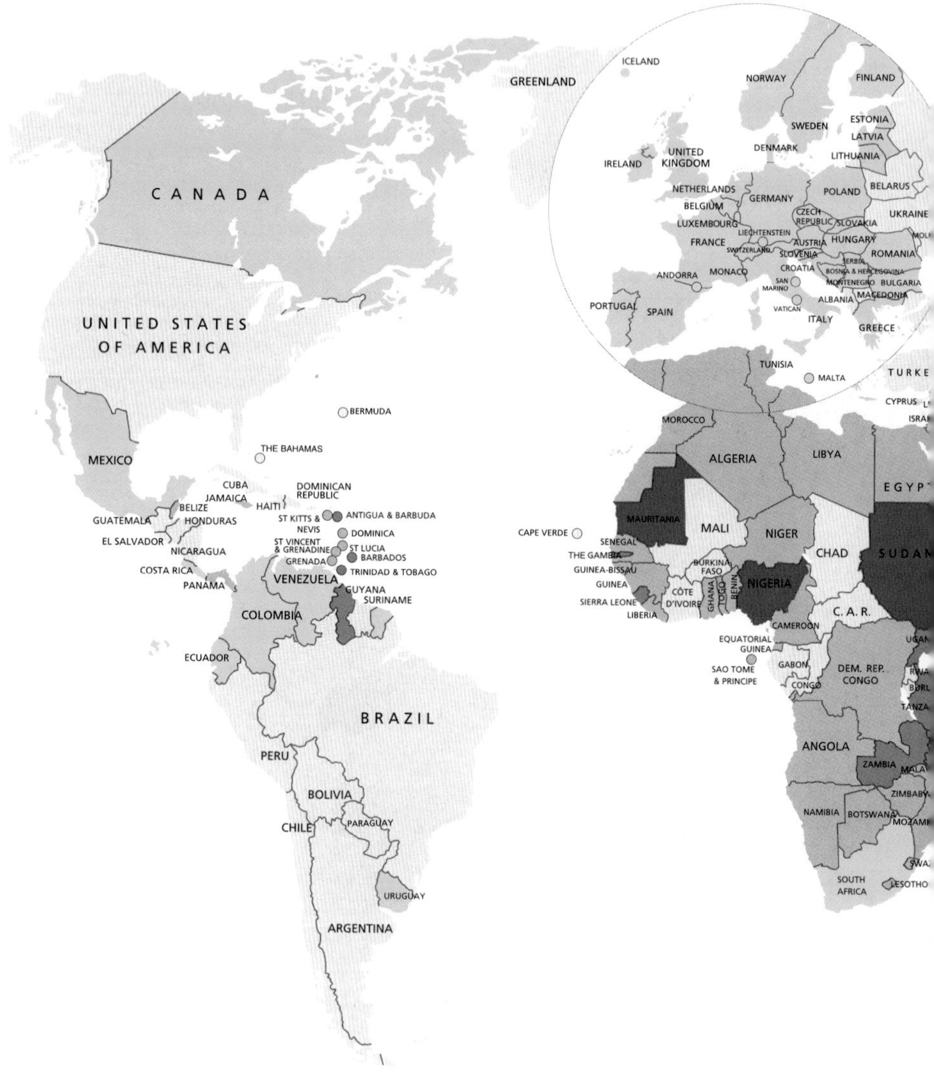

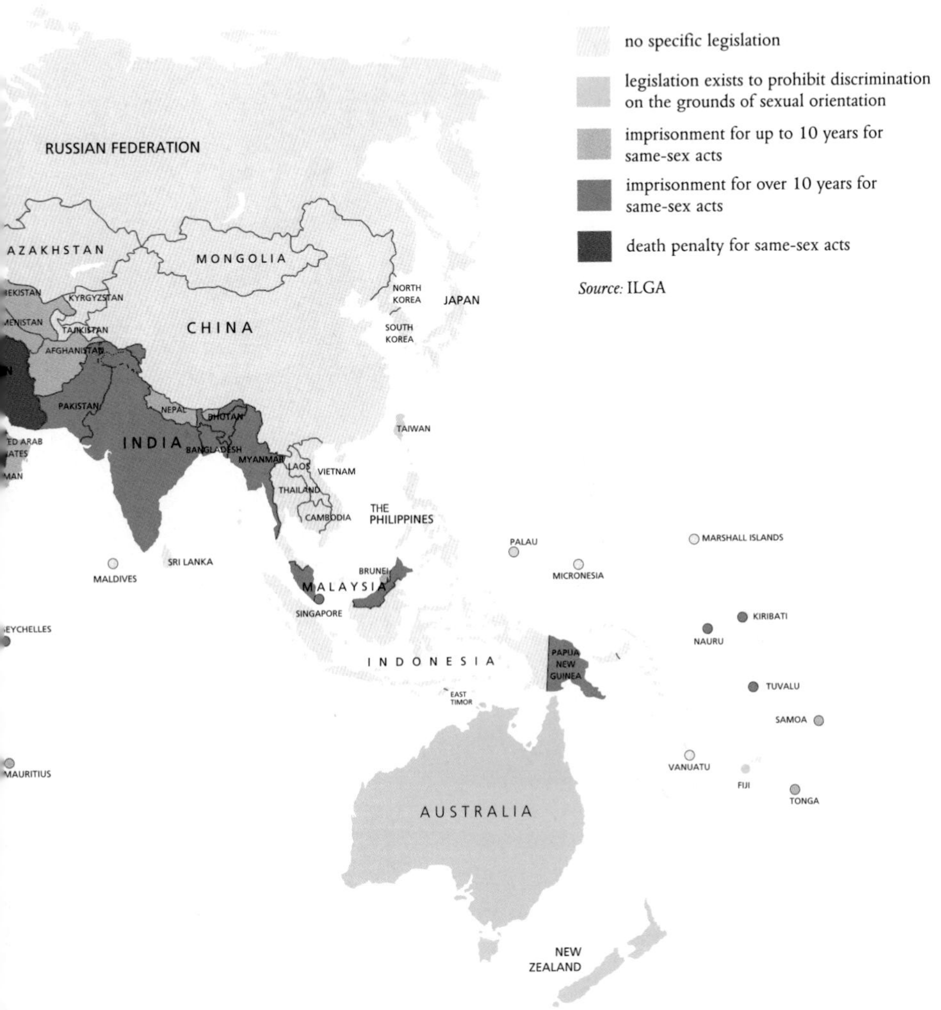
no specific legislation
legislation exists to prohibit discrimination on the grounds of sexual orientation
imprisonment for up to 10 years for same-sex acts
imprisonment for over 10 years for same-sex acts
death penalty for same-sex acts
RUSSIAN FEDERATION
AZAKHSTAN
MONGOLIA
EKISTAN
KYRGYZSTAN
MENISTAN
TAJIKISTAN
CHINA
NORTH KOREA
JAPAN
SOUTH KOREA
AFGHANISTAN
PAKISTAN
NEPAL
BHUTAN
INDIA
BANGLADESH
MYANMAR
ED ARAB
ATES
MAN
TAIWAN
LAOS
VIETNAM
THAILAND
CAMBODIA
THE PHILIPPINES
PALAU
MARSHALL ISLANDS
MICRONESIA
MALDIVES
SRI LANKA
BRUNEI
MALAYSIA
SINGAPORE
KIRIBATI
NAURU
EYCHELLES
INDONESIA
PAPUA NEW GUINEA
EAST TIMOR
TUVALU
SAMOA
VANUATU
FIJI
TONGA
MAURITIUS
AUSTRALIA
NEW ZEALAND

Source: ILGA

and Japan. Principal exports are fish, garments, bananas and black pepper.
GNI – US$264m; US$2,390 per capita (2006)
Annual average growth of GDP – 0.3 per cent (2005 est)
Inflation rate – 2.2 per cent (2005)
Unemployment – 22 per cent (2000 est)
Total external debt – US$60.8m (2005 est)

Trade with UK	*2006*	*2007*
Imports from UK	£17,000	£24,179
Exports to UK	£15,000	£18,444

COMMUNICATIONS
Most transport is by air or sea. There are six airports and airfields, with major airports on the four main islands, and the main seaports are Colonia (Yap), Kolonia (Pohnpei), Lele and Moen. There are 240km of roads. The islands are all connected to the telephone system. In 2005 there were 12,400 main telephone lines in use and 14,100 mobile phone subscribers.

MEDIA
There are no daily newspapers; the federal government produces a fortnightly information bulletin and state governments produce weekly news publications. One government television channel competes with two commercial channels, and there are several radio stations.

MOLDOVA

Republica Moldova – Republic of Moldova

Area – 33,843 sq. km
Capital – Chisinau; population, 592,000 (2007 est)
Major towns – Balti, Tighina, Tiraspol
Currency – Moldovan leu (plural lei) of 100 bani
Population – 4,320,490 falling at 0.11 per cent per year (2007 est): Moldovan (78.2 per cent), Ukrainian (8.4 per cent), Russian (5.8 per cent), Gagauz (4.4 per cent); Bulgarian (1.9 per cent)
Religion – Orthodox Christianity (90 per cent) (est)
Language – Moldovan (official), Russian, Gagauz
Population density – 117 per sq. km (2006)
Urban population – 46.3 per cent (2005 est)
Median age (years) – 34 (2007 est)
National anthem – 'Limba Noastra' ['Our Language']
National day – 27 August (Independence Day)
Life expectancy (years) – 70.2 (2007 est)
Mortality rate – 10.85 (2007 est)
Birth rate – 10.88 (2007 est)
Infant mortality rate – 13.88 (2007 est)
Death penalty – Abolished for all crimes (since 1995)
CPI score – 2.8 (2007)
Population below poverty line – 29.5 per cent (2005)

CLIMATE AND TERRAIN
A landlocked country to the north-west of the Black Sea, Moldova is a hilly plain lying mostly between the Prut and Dniester rivers. Elevation extremes range from 430m (Dealul Bulanesti) at the highest point to 2m (Dniester river) at the lowest. The climate is continental and average temperatures range from –4°C in January to 20°C in August.

HISTORY AND POLITICS
Part of the Roman province of Dacia from AD 106, Moldova saw centuries of invasion and occupation after the fall of the Roman Empire but formed part of an independent Moldovan state from the mid-14th century. The principality was absorbed into the Ottoman Empire in the 16th century, then came under Russian protection in the 18th century. Partition saw the west (Bukovina) lost to Austria in the 18th century and the east (Bessarabia) to Russia in 1812. The remainder became independent of Turkish overlordship in 1856 and in 1859 joined with Wallachia to form the principality of Romania.

After the Russian revolution in 1917, Bessarabia was seized and incorporated into Romania in 1918, and the area east of the Dniester formed the Moldovan autonomous republic in the USSR from 1924. Romania was forced to return Bessarabia to the USSR in 1940 but, with the help of its German allies, invaded and occupied the Soviet republic of Moldova in 1941 until its reconquest by Soviet forces in 1944.

Moldovan nationalism grew in the late 1980s and the parliament declared political and economic sovereignty in 1990, achieving independence and joining the Commonwealth of Independent States in 1991 after the collapse of the USSR. Nationalist advocacy of unification with Romania was defeated in a plebiscite in 1994.

The rise in Moldovan nationalism was matched by growing demands for autonomy by the republic's Russian and Ukrainian ethnic minorities in the Transdniestria region (east of the Dniester) and the Gagauz in the south-west. Both areas declared their independence in 1990, though this was not recognised. Both regions were granted special autonomy status by the 1994 constitution, and the Gagauz exercise a degree of autonomy over political, economic and cultural affairs.

A stalemate has developed over the status of Transdniestria. Fighting between separatists and government forces in 1991 was followed by a fragile peace settlement in 1992, maintained by Russian peacekeeping troops. Despite talks sponsored by the OSCE, EU, Russia and Ukraine since the late 1990s, the situation has not been resolved. Although the Moldovan parliament backed a 2005 Ukrainian settlement proposal that would give the region autonomy within Moldova, Transdniestria's population voted for independence and eventual union with Russia in a 2006 referendum.

The governments in the first decade after independence were made up of moderate reformists, but their ineffectiveness led to a resurgence in support for the Communist Party of Moldova (PCM), which won the majority of seats in the 1998, 2001 and 2005 legislative elections. After the 2005 election, the PCM leader Vladimir Voronin was re-elected president and Vasile Tarlev, an independent member of parliament and prime minister since 2001, was reappointed prime minister. Vasile Tarlev resigned in March 2008 and was replaced by the first deputy prime minister Zinaida Greceanii, who reshuffled the cabinet.

POLITICAL SYSTEM
The 1997 constitution was amended in 2000 to increase the powers of the legislature and the executive. The head of state is a president who (since 2000) is elected by the legislature for a four-year term. The unicameral legislature, the *Parlamentul*, has 101 members, who are directly elected for a four-year term. The prime minister and government are nominated by the president.

HEAD OF STATE
President, Vladimir Voronin, *elected* 4 April 2001, *re-elected* 4 April 2005

SELECTED GOVERNMENT MEMBERS *as at June 2008*
Prime Minister, Zinaida Greceanii
First Deputy Prime Minister, Economy, Igor Dodon
Deputy Prime Ministers, Victor Stepaniuc; Andrei Stratan
Defence, Vitalie Vrabie
Finance, Mariana Durlesteanu
Interior, Gen. Valentin Mejinschi

EMBASSY OF THE REPUBLIC OF MOLDOVA
5 Dolphin Square, Edensor Road, London W4 2ST
T 020-8995 6818 E mail@moldovanembassy.org.uk
W www.moldovanembassy.org.uk
Ambassador Extraordinary and Plenipotentiary, HE Mariana Durlesteanu, *apptd* 2005

BRITISH EMBASSY
18 Nicolae Iorga str., Chisinau MD2012
T (+373) 222 225902 E enquiries.chisinau@fco.gov.uk
W www.britishembassy.gov.uk/moldova
Ambassador Extraordinary and Plenipotentiary, HE John Beyer, *apptd* 2006

DEFENCE
The army has 44 armoured infantry fighting vehicles and 315 armoured personnel carriers.
Military budget – US$17.2m (2007 est)
Military personnel – 6,750: army 5,150, air force 850; paramilitary 3,279
Conscription duration – 12 months

ECONOMY AND TRADE
Moves towards a market economy after independence were slow but have been given impetus by and from 2000 to 2005 experienced sustained growth. But with the most industrialised areas lying in the breakaway Transdniestria region, it has struggled to reduce poverty or its large foreign debt. About 30 per cent of the population lives below the poverty line, and although unemployment is low, an estimated 25 per cent of the workforce is employed abroad. Its dependence on Russia, as an export market and main energy supplier, caused an economic downturn in 2006 owing to Russia's trade embargo.

The agricultural sector is the mainstay of the economy, accounting for 21.5 per cent of GDP. Principal crops include vegetables, fruit, wine, grain, sugar beet, sunflower seed, tobacco, beef and milk. Major industrial activities include food processing and production of sugar, vegetable oil, agricultural machinery, foundry equipment, domestic appliances and textiles. Industry accounts for 22 per cent of GDP and services for 56.5 per cent.

The main trading partners are Russia, Ukraine, Romania, Italy and Germany. Principal exports are foodstuffs, textiles and machinery. The main imports are fuel and energy, machinery and equipment, chemicals and textiles.

GNI – US$3,700m; US$1,080 per capita (20056)
Annual average growth of GDP – 6 per cent (2007 est)
Inflation rate – 12.5 per cent (2007 est)
Unemployment – 2.1 per cent (2007 est)
Total external debt – US$2,774m (2007)
Imports – US$3,000m (2006)
Exports – US$1,000m (2006)

BALANCE OF PAYMENTS
Trade – US$1,650m deficit (2006)
Current Account – US$404m deficit (2006)

Trade with UK	*2006*	*2007*
Imports from UK	£18,205,000	£12,886,423
Exports to UK	£12,358,000	£15,221,154

COMMUNICATIONS
Moldova has 12,730km of roads and 1,130km of railways. There are 10 airports and airstrips; the principal airport is at Chisinau. There are 424km of navigable waterways on the Prut and Dniester rivers.

The telephone system is antiquated and service is poor outside the capital, although some modernisation is under way. In 2006 there were 1.01 million main telephone lines in use, 1.4 million mobile phone subscribers and 727,700 internet users.

EDUCATION AND HEALTH
Literacy rate – 96.2 per cent (2004 est)
Gross enrolment ratio (percentage of relevant age group) – primary 91 per cent; secondary 82 per cent; tertiary 36 per cent (2006 est)
Health expenditure (per capita) – US$58 (2005)
Hospital beds (per 1,000 people) – 6.4 (2000–6)

MEDIA
Freedom of media expression is guaranteed by the constitution, but laws existing to prevent insulting the state. There are five main newspapers. State-run television and radio stations compete with a single commercial channel. The breakaway Transdniestria region operates its own television and radio stations.

MONACO

Principaute de Monaco – Principality of Monaco

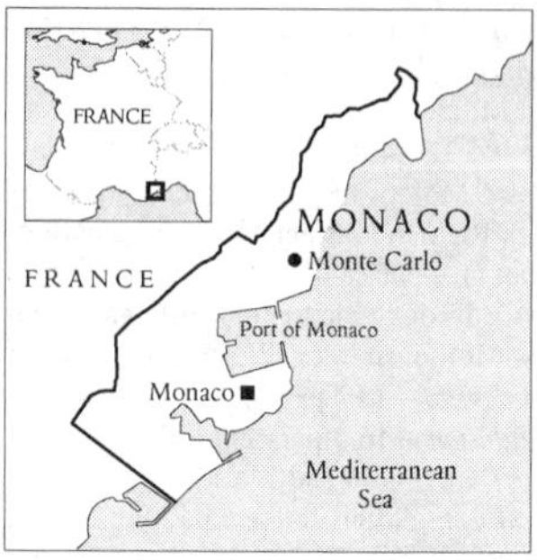

Area – 1.95 sq. km
Capital – Monaco
Major town – Monte Carlo
Currency – Euro (€) of 100 cents
Population – 32,671 rising at 0.39 per cent per year (2007 est); French (47 per cent), Monegasque (16 per cent), Italian (16 per cent) (est)

Religion – Roman Catholicism (90 per cent) (est)
Language – French (official), English, Italian, Monegasque
Population density – 16,718 per sq. km (2006)
Urban population – 100 per cent (2005 est)
Median age (years) – 45.5 (2007 est)
National anthem – 'Hymne Monégasque' ['Hymn of Monaco']
National day – 19 November
Life expectancy (years) – 79.82 (2007 est)
Mortality rate – 12.92 (2007 est)
Birth rate – 9.12 (2007 est)
Infant mortality rate – 5.27 (2007 est)
Death penalty – Abolished for all crimes (since 1962)

CLIMATE AND TERRAIN

Monaco has a steep, rugged terrain on the Mediterranean coast; Fontvieille, a district in the south of the country, has been expanded into the sea by infilling. Elevation extremes range from 140m (Mt Agel) at the highest point to 0m (Mediterranean Sea) at the lowest. The climate is Mediterranean, with average temperatures that range from 10°C in January to 23°C in July.

HISTORY AND POLITICS

Monaco has been ruled by the Grimaldi family since the 13th century. Monarchical France recognised Monaco's independence in the 15th century, but Revolutionary France annexed it in the 18th century. Monaco did not regain its independence until 1861 and the principality remains under French protection. It was occupied by the Italians and subsequently by the Germans in the Second World War.

The 1962 constitution was amended in 2002 to allow the throne to pass in the female line in the absence of male heirs. Legislative power is held jointly by the prince and a 24-member national council, which is directly elected for a five-year term. Executive power is exercised by the prince and a six-member Council of Government, headed by a minister of state who is nominated by the prince from a list of three French diplomats submitted by the French government. The judicial code is based on that of France.

In the 2008 legislative election, the Union for Monaco (UPM) retained its 21 seats, an overwhelming majority, in the legislature.

HEAD OF STATE
HSH The Prince of Monaco, Prince Albert II Alexandre Louis Pierre, *born* 14 March 1958, *succeeded* 6 April 2005
Heir, HSH Princess Caroline von Hannover, *born* 23 January 1957

SELECTED GOVERNMENT MEMBERS *as at June 2008*
Minister of State, Jean-Paul Proust
Finance and Economy, Gilles Tonelli
Interior, Paul Masseron
Foreign Affairs, Jean Pastorelli

CONSULATE-GENERAL OF MONACO
7 Upper Grosvenor Street, London W1K 2LX
T 020-7318 1081 W www.monaco-consulate-uk.gouv.mc
Consul-General, Evelyne Genta, *apptd* 2006

BRITISH CONSULATE-GENERAL
PO Box 265, 33 Boulevard Princesse Charlotte, 98005 Monaco
T (+377) 9350 9966
Hon. Consul-General, Simon Lever, resident in Marseille, France

ECONOMY AND TRADE

The economy has diversified away from its historic dependence on tourism and gambling to benefit from financial services, real estate revenue and some light industry. A large floating jetty, installed in 2002, has extended the harbour facilities, doubling the port's capacity to handle cruise ships. Since the state collects no taxes from individuals and little from businesses, it has become a tax haven for the wealthy, and non-Monegasques make up 84 per cent of the population. The state retains monopolies in a number of sectors, including tobacco, the telephone network and the postal service. It is in a customs union with France, which collects and rebates its trade duties.
Unemployment – 0 (2005)
Total external debt – US$18,000m (2000 est)

MEDIA

Radio Monte-Carlo started broadcasting to France in the 1960s and Italy in the 1970s. Monaco does not have an indigenous daily press (French newspapers are widely available) but does publish two weekly journals.

MONGOLIA

Mongol Uls – Mongolia

Area – 1,564,116 sq. km
Capital – Ulaanbaatar; population, 885,000 (2007 est)
Major towns – Darhan, Erdenet
Currency – Tugrik of 100 mongo
Population – 2,951,786 rising at 1.49 per cent per year (2007 est); Mongol (94.9 per cent), Turkic (5 per cent) (est)
Religion – Buddhism (93 per cent), Islam 4 per cent (est)
Language – Mongolian (official), Turkic, Russian
Population density – 2 per sq. km (2006)
Urban population – 57 per cent (2005 est)
Median age (years) – 24.6 (2007 est)
National anthem – 'National Anthem of Mongolia'
National day – 11 July (Revolution Day)
Life expectancy (years) – 66.99 (2007 est)
Mortality rate – 6.21 (2007 est)
Birth rate – 21.07 (2007 est)
Infant mortality rate – 42.65 (2007 est)
Death penalty – Retained
CPI score – 3.0 (2007)
Population below poverty line – 36.1 per cent (2004)
Literacy rate – 97.8 per cent (2004 est)
Gross enrolment ratio (percentage of relevant age group) – primary 101 per cent; secondary 89 per cent; tertiary 47 per cent (2006 est)
Health expenditure (per capita) – US$35 (2005)
Hospital beds (per 1,000 people) – 7.5 (2000–6)

CLIMATE AND TERRAIN

The eastern part of landlocked Mongolia lies on a semi-desert plateau, with steppes rising to the Mongolian Altai and Hangai mountain ranges in the west. The Gobi desert covers part of the south of the country. Elevation extremes range from 4,374m (Nayramadlin Orgil) at the highest point to 518m (Hoh Nuur) at the lowest. The country has long, very cold Siberian winters, which quickly turn into short and warm summers. The wet season runs from June to September. Average temperatures in Ulaanbaatar range from −27°C in January to 19°C in July.

HISTORY AND POLITICS

The nomadic tribes of Mongolia, mostly Turks and Uighurs, were united in the early 13th century by Genghis Khan, forming the nucleus of a Mongol Empire that reached its zenith under Kublai Khan, Genghis' grandson, when it stretched from Hungary to China and as far south as Vietnam. After Kublai's death in 1294, the empire declined. Many of the khanates formed under Genghis survived as increasingly independent petty kingdoms, but Mongolia itself was conquered by China in the late 17th century and became the provinces of Inner and Outer Mongolia.

When imperial rule in China collapsed in 1911, Outer Mongolia declared itself an independent monarchy under a Buddhist lama king. Chinese rule was reasserted in 1915, but in 1921 Mongolian revolutionaries, supported by the Soviets, overthrew Chinese rule and the Mongolian People's Revolutionary Party (MPRP) formed a government. When the king died in 1924, the monarchy was abolished and the ensuing republic introduced communist-inspired defeudalisation and collectivisation programmes and suppressed Buddhism. With the assistance of Soviet troops, Mongolia resisted Japanese attacks in the late 1930s and after the Second World War, Mongolia seemed likely to remain under Soviet control, but in a 1946 UN plebiscite the people voted for independence.

Mongolia became more open to external contacts from the mid-1980s and, influenced by events in eastern Europe, a democratisation campaign led to the first multiparty elections in 1990 and a massive privatisation programme, which began in 1991. The MPRP, which had eschewed communism, continued to dominate political life until 1996, when an alliance of nationalists and social democrats displaced it. The alliance quickly became the subject of corruption scandals and its transition to a market economy caused widespread social disruption and poverty. The MPRP returned to power in the 2001 election, having already regained the presidency in 1997, but lost nearly half of its seats in the legislature in the 2004 election.

The 2005 presidential election was won by the MPRP candidate, Nambariyn Enkhbayar. The coalition government formed by the MPRP and the Motherland Democratic Coalition (MDC) after the 2004 legislative election collapsed in 2006 after the MPRP members withdrew. The MPRP leader Miyeegombo Enkhbold was appointed prime minister and he formed a predominantly MPRP coalition. In November 2007, Enkhbold was replaced as party leader by Sanj Bayar; Enkhbold resigned as prime minister and Bayar was appointed as his replacement. In the July 2008 legislative election the MPRP won 47 of the 76 parliamentary seats, but the vote was marred by outbreaks of violence and accusations of electoral fraud.

POLITICAL SYSTEM

The 1992 constitution established a parliamentary democracy. It was amended in 2000 to give the president the right to dissolve the legislature if it is unable to reach agreement on appointing a prime minister. The president is directly elected for a four-year term, which is renewable. The unicameral State Great Hural has 76 members who are directly elected for a four-year term. The prime minister is elected by the legislature and appoints the cabinet.

HEAD OF STATE

President, Nambariyn Enkhbayar, *elected* 22 May 2005, *sworn in* 24 June 2005

SELECTED GOVERNMENT MEMBERS *as at June 2008*

Prime Minister, Sanj Bayar
Deputy Prime Minister, Miyegombo Enkhbold
Defence, Jamiyandorj Batkhuyag
Finance, Chultem Ulaan
Foreign Affairs, Sanjaasuren Oyun
Justice and Internal Affairs, Tsendiyn Munkh-Orgil

EMBASSY OF MONGOLIA

7 Kensington Court, London W8 5DL
T 020-7937 0150 E office@embassyofmongolia.co.uk
W www.embassyofmongolia.co.uk
Ambassador Extraordinary and Plenipotentiary, HE Dalrain Davaasambuu, *apptd* 2001

BRITISH EMBASSY

PO Box 703, 30 Enkh Taivny Gudamzh, Ulaanbaatar 13
T (+976) (11) 458 133 E britemb@mongol.net
Ambassador Extraordinary and Plenipotentiary, HE Christopher Osborne, *apptd* 2006

DEFENCE

The army has 370 main battle tanks, 150 armoured personnel carriers and 310 armoured infantry fighting vehicles. The air force has 9 aircraft and 11 armed helicopters.

Military budget – US$20m (2007)
Military personnel – 8,600: army 7,500, air force 800, construction troops 300; paramilitaries 7,200
Conscription duration – 12 months

ECONOMY AND TRADE

The economy suffered after the withdrawal of Soviet support and during the transition to a market economy, though in recent years it has experienced growth. Mongolia has been successful in attracting foreign investment, particularly in mining, agricultural processing and infrastructure. However, economic growth is hindered by administrative corruption, the country's dependency on imported energy supplies (mostly from Russia) and the vulnerability of the agrarian sector to climate extremes, which decimated herds in 2000–2. Around 36 per cent of the population lives below the poverty line.

Deposits of copper, coal, molybdenum, fluorspar, tin, tungsten, gold and oil are being exploited; copper and gold sales are major drivers of recent economic growth. The agrarian sector, which makes up 18.8 per cent of GDP, engages 40 per cent of the workforce in agriculture and herding. The main products are grains, vegetables, forage crops, sheep, goats and other livestock. The main industries are construction, mining, processing animal products and the production of oil, food and beverages, cashmere and natural yarns.

The main export markets are China, the USA and Canada; the main import providers are Russia and China. Principal exports are copper, clothing, livestock, animal products, cashmere, wool, hides and metals. The main imports are machinery and equipment, fuels, cars, foodstuffs, industrial consumer goods, chemicals and construction materials.

GNI – US$2,600m; US$1,000 per capita (2006)
Annual average growth of GDP – 8.4 per cent (2006)
Inflation rate – 9.5 per cent (2005 est)
Unemployment – 3.2 per cent (2006)
Total external debt – US$1,380m (2005)
Imports – US$1,500m (2006)
Exports – US$1,500m (2006)

BALANCE OF PAYMENTS
Trade – US$57m surplus (2006)
Current Account – US$222m surplus (2006)

Trade with UK	*2006*	*2007*
Imports from UK	£3,593,000	£3,553,730
Exports to UK	£4,621,000	£3,820,930

COMMUNICATIONS

Mongolia has 1,810km of railways and 49,250km of roads, though only about 4 per cent of the roads are surfaced. The main airport is at Ulaanbaatar, although there are over 40 other airports and airfields around the country. The lakes and main rivers are navigable in the summer months but ice-bound in winter. International trade is via Russia and China.

The telephone system is improving but fixed-line density is very low. Mobile phone distribution has risen rapidly. In 2006 there were 159,000 main telephone lines in use and 775,300 mobile phone subscribers.

MEDIA

There are five daily newspapers, including *Onoodor,* which has the biggest circulation, and *Unen,* the organ of the Mongolian People's Revolutionary Party and the country's oldest newspaper. In 2005, the state-run radio and television was transformed into a public-service broadcaster. Violations of press freedom are rare.

MONTENEGRO

Republika Crna Gora – Republic of Montenegro

Area – 14,026 sq. km
Capital – Podgorica; population, 142,000 (2007 est)
Major city – Niksic
Currency – Euro (€) of 100 cents
Population – 684,736, falling at 1 per cent per year (2007 est); Montenegrin (43 per cent), Serbian (32 per cent), Bosniak (8 per cent), Albanian (5 per cent) (est)
Religion – Orthodox Christianity (74 per cent), Islam (18 per cent), Roman Catholicism (4 per cent) (est)
Language – Serbian (official), Bosnian, Albanian, Croatian
Population density – 44 per sq. km (2006)
National anthem – 'Oj, Svijetla Majska Zoro' ['O, Bright Dawn of May']
National day – 13 July
Life expectancy (years) – 74.73 (2005 est)
Mortality rate – 8.39 (2007 est)
Birth rate – 11.18 (2007 est)
Infant mortality rate – 12.89 (2005 est)
Death penalty – Abolished for all crimes (since 2002)
CPI score – 3.3 (2007)
Population below poverty line – 7 per cent (2007 est)
Gross enrolment ratio (percentage of relevant age group) – primary 99 per cent; secondary 89 per cent; tertiary 36 per cent (2002)

CLIMATE AND TERRAIN

The terrain is mountainous in the north and centre of the country, intersected by the deep canyon of the Tara river valley, and falls to a narrow plain on the highly indented Adriatic coast. About half of the country is forested. Elevation extremes range from 2,522m (Bobotov Kuk) at the highest point to 0m (Adriatic Sea) at the lowest. The main rivers are the Piva (Drina), the Tara and the Lim. Lake Skadarsko straddles the border with Albania. The climate inland is moderate and continental, while along the coast a Mediterranean-Adriatic climate prevails. Average temperatures in Podgorica range from 5°C in January to 31°C in July.

HISTORY AND POLITICS

The area was part of the Roman province of Illyria, and then was settled by Slavs in the seventh century. In the late 12th century it was incorporated into the medieval kingdom of Serbia and so became part of the Ottoman Empire after Serbia's defeat by the Turks in 1389. When Serbia became independent in 1878, Montenegro followed and remained an independent monarchy until the end of the First World War. In 1918, Montenegro joined with Serbia and the former Austro-Hungarian provinces of Slovenia, Croatia and Bosnia-Hercegovina to form the Kingdom of Serbs, Croats and Slovenes, which was renamed Yugoslavia in 1929. Yugoslavia was occupied by Axis forces in 1941 and after liberation it reformed as a communist federal republic under the presidency of partisan leader Josip Tito in 1945. When the federation disintegrated in 1991, Serbia and Montenegro formed the Federal Republic of Yugoslavia, which was declared on 27 April 1992.

Montenegro's desire for independence led in 2002 to an EU-brokered agreement between the leaders of Serbia, Montenegro and the Federal Republic of Yugoslavia to restructure the republic into a union of two semi-independent states; the union was renamed Serbia and Montenegro. The constitutional charter for the new union, which came into effect in March 2003, provided for the two republics to hold referendums on whether to retain or end the union after a minimum of three years. A referendum was held in Montenegro on 21 May 2006 and 55.5 per cent voted in favour of independence, which was declared on 3 June and acknowledged by the Serbian legislature on 5 June. Montenegro was admitted as a member of the UN on 26 June. Negotiations on separating the two states' assets continue.

The 2006 legislative election was won by the For a European Montenegro coalition. A coalition government was formed by the Democratic Party of Socialists, Social Democratic Party and Democratic Union of Albanians. Zeljko Sturanovic resigned as prime minister in January 2008 because of ill-health and was replaced by his immediate predecessor, Milo Djukanovic. In the April 2008 presidential election, Filip Vujanovic was returned for a second term.

POLITICAL SYSTEM

Under the 2007 constitution, the head of state is a president who is directly elected for a five-year term. The unicameral legislature, the Assembly of the Republic of Montenegro, has 81 members directly elected for a four-year term; five members are elected from the ethnic Albanian community. The prime minister appoints the cabinet, subject to the approval of the assembly.

HEAD OF STATE

President, Filip Vujanovic, *elected* 11 May 2003

SELECTED GOVERNMENT MEMBERS *as at June 2008*

Prime Minister, Milo Djukanovic

Deputy Prime Ministers, Gordana Djurovic; Vujica Lazovic

Finance, Igor Luksic

Foreign Affairs, Milan Rocen

Defence, Boro Vucinic

EMBASSY OF MONTENEGRO

5th Floor, Trafalgar House 11–12 Waterloo Place, London SW1Y 4AU

T 020-7863 8806 E dragisa_burzan@yahoo.co.uk

Ambassador Extraordinary and Plenipotentiary, HE Dragisa Burzan, *apptd* 2007

BRITISH EMBASSY

First Floor, No. 3, Bulevar Svetog Petra Cetinjskog nn, 81000 Podgorica

T (+381) (81) 205 460 E britishoffice@cg.yu

Ambassador Extraordinary and Plenipotentiary, John Dyson, MVO, *apptd* 2006

DEFENCE

The navy has 6 submarines, 2 frigates and 6 patrol and coastal combatant vessels at 4 bases.

Military budget – US$321m (2006 est)

Military personnel – 5,800: army 2,500, navy 3,300; paramilitary 10,100

ECONOMY AND TRADE

Montenegro achieved fiscal autonomy from the Yugoslav federation in the 1990s, managing its own budget, collecting customs tariffs on its own account, maintaining its own central bank and adopting the euro in place of the dinar. However, it faced the same problems as Serbia – slow growth, foreign debt, lack of foreign investment, high unemployment, corruption and organised crime – as well as having more limited health and educational facilities and a poor administrative capacity. It has privatised its aluminium industry and financial sector, and is beginning to attract foreign direct investment in tourism.

Since independence, it has pursued international integration, and especially its bid for EU membership, which is a priority of the post-independence government. The main agricultural products are grain, tobacco, fruit and vegetables. Major industrial activities include production of steel, aluminium and consumer goods, processing of agricultural products and tourism. The main trading partners are Switzerland, Italy, Bosnia and Hercegovina, Greece and Germany.

GNI – US$2,481m; US$4,130 per capita (2006)

Annual average growth of GDP – 6 per cent (2007 est)

**Inflation rate* – 3.4 per cent (2004)

Unemployment – 14.7 per cent (2007 est)

Total external debt – US$650m (2006 est)

* Figure is for Serbia and Montenegro

BALANCE OF PAYMENTS

Trade – US$171m deficit (2004)

Current Account – US$755m deficit (2006)

Trade with UK	*2006*	*2007*
Imports from UK	£1,583,000	£8,976,455
Exports to UK	£1,154,000	£1,633,745

COMMUNICATIONS

Montenegro's independence leaves Serbia landlocked, although access to the Adriatic ports of Bar and Kotor is expected to be negotiated. There is 250km of rail track, part of the European system linking Bar with Belgrade, via Podgorica. The 7,300km of roads include major roads linking Podgorica and the coastal ports with the hinterland and neighbouring countries. There are five airports, including international airports at Podgorica and Tivat. Modernised telecommunications systems provide services to 353,300 main-line subscribers, 821,800 mobile phone subscribers and 266,000 internet users.

MEDIA

Freedom of the press is guaranteed and media laws passed in 2002 provide for the transformation of the state-funded RCTG into a public broadcaster. Overseas donors and organisations have contributed funds to stimulate private media growth, but this has been limited by low advertising revenue.

MOROCCO

Al-Mamlakah al-Maghribiyah – Kingdom of Morocco

Area – 446,550 sq. km

Capital – Rabat; population, 1,705,000 (2007 est)

Major cities – Agadir, Casablanca, Fez, Marrakesh, Meknès, Tangier

Currency – Dirham (DH) of 100 centimes

Population – 33,757,175 rising at 1.53 per cent per year (2007 est)

Religion – Islam (99 per cent); almost all Muslims practise Sunni Islam

Language – Arabic (official), French, Berber dialects
Population density – 68 per sq. km (2006)
Urban population – 58.8 per cent (2005 est)
Median age (years) – 24.3 (2007 est)
National anthem – 'Hymne Cherifien' ['Moroccan Anthem']
National day – 30 July (Throne Day)
Life expectancy (years) – 71.22 (2007 est)
Mortality rate – 5.54 (2007 est)
Birth rate – 21.64 (2007 est)
Infant mortality rate – 38.85 (2007 est)
Death penalty – Retained, but not used
CPI score – 3.5 (2007)
Population below poverty line – 15 per cent (2007 est)

CLIMATE AND TERRAIN

Fertile coastal plains in the west rise to a mountainous centre, with ranges, including the Atlas range, running north-east to south-west. The Rif mountains lie along the northern, Mediterranean coast. Elevation extremes range from 4,165m (Jbel Toubkal) at the highest point to −55m (Sebkha Tah) at the lowest. Average temperatures in Rabat range from 7°C in January to 29°C in July, although summer temperatures in the desert interior can reach as high as 41°C.

HISTORY AND POLITICS

From the tenth century BC, the northern coast was settled by the Phoenicians. Morocco was part of the Roman Empire from the first century AD until it was invaded by first the Vandals and then the Visigoths in the fifth and sixth centuries. Arab conquest of the area began in the seventh century and Morocco was part of a succession of Arab empires, but successfully resisted inclusion in the Turkish Ottoman Empire in the 16th century. The current Alawite dynasty was founded in the mid-17th century and under its rule Morocco remained independent but isolated until the mid-19th century, when the country opened up to European trade. The subsequent growth in Spanish and French influence resulted in its partition into two protectorates. In the Second World War, Morocco was a base for the Allied offensives that drove German forces out of North Africa.

Nationalist campaigning for independence began in the 1940s. French and Spanish forces withdrew in 1956, leaving Morocco independent under Sultan Mohammed V, who adopted the title of king in 1957; the coastal towns of Ceuta and Melilla remain under Spanish control. King Hassan II, who ruled from 1961 to 1999, annexed the mineral-rich Western Sahara region in 1975.

Since the accession of King Mohammed VI in 1999, Morocco has been moving away from absolute monarchy, increasing civil liberties and addressing human rights issues. In the 2007 legislative election the Independence Party (Istiqlal), one of the parties in the coalition government, became the largest party by a small majority. Its leader, Abbas el Fassi, was appointed prime minister and formed a coalition government that includes five parties and a number of independents.

POLITICAL SYSTEM

The 1992 constitution was amended in 1996 to introduce a bicameral legislature. The head of state is a hereditary constitutional monarch. The king appoints the prime minister and, on the latter's recommendation, appoints the members of the council of ministers. There is a bicameral legislature; the lower house, the House of Representatives *(Majlis al-Nuwab)* has 325 members who are directly elected for a five-year term. The House of Councillors *(Majlis al-Mustashareen)* has 270 members, indirectly elected by local councils, professional organisations and the 'salaried classes'. One-third of its members is elected every three years, to serve a nine-year term.

HEAD OF STATE

HM The King of Morocco, King Mohammed VI (Sidi Mohammed Ben Hassan), *born* 21 August 1963, *acceded* 23 July 1999
Heir, HRH Crown Prince Moulay Hassan, *born* 2003

SELECTED GOVERNMENT MEMBERS *as at June 2008*

Prime Minister, Abbas el-Fassi
Economy and Finance, Salaheddine Mezouar
Foreign Affairs, Taieb Fassi Fihri
Interior Affairs, Chakib Benmoussa

EMBASSY OF THE KINGDOM OF MOROCCO

49 Queen's Gate Gardens, London SW7 5NE
T 020-7581 5001 E ihilan@yahoo.co.uk
Ambassador Extraordinary and Plenipotentiary, HE Mohammed Belmahi, *apptd* 1999

BRITISH EMBASSY

PO Box 45, 17 Boulevard de la Tour Hassan, Rabat
T (+212) (37) 238 600 E consular.rabat@fco.gov.uk
W www.britain.org.ma
Ambassador Extraordinary and Plenipotentiary, HE Charles Gray, *apptd* 2005

BRITISH COUNCIL

36 rue de Tanger, BP 427, Rabat
T (+212) (37) 760 836 W www.britishcouncil.org/morocco
Director, Adam Ladbury

DEFENCE

The army has 580 main battle tanks, 70 armoured infantry fighting vehicles, and 765 armoured personnel carriers. The navy has 3 frigates and 27 patrol and coastal combatant vessels at five bases. The air force has 89 combat aircraft and 19 armed helicopters.
Military budget – US$2,470m (2007)
Military personnel – 195,800: army 175,000, navy 7,800, air force 13,000; paramilitary 50,000
Conscription duration – 18 months

ECONOMY AND TRADE

Economic liberalisation since 1999 has attracted foreign direct investment, but private-sector enterprises are few, the financial system is rudimentary and the country is dependent on foreign energy imports, factors which inhibit growth. Morocco remains a poor country, with 15 per cent of the population living below the poverty line and unemployment averaging 15 per cent, though it is often nearly 20 per cent in urban areas; the remittances of expatriate workers are crucial to the domestic economy.

The large agrarian sector generates 15 per cent of GDP and engages 40 per cent of the workforce, producing cereals, citrus fruits, vegetables, wine, olives and livestock; production levels were lower in 2007 because of drought and wheat had to be imported. It faces environmental problems such as desertification and soil erosion. Another major sector is the exploitation of mineral reserves, especially phosphate. Other industries include food processing, textiles, leather goods, construction and tourism, which the government wishes to expand. Industry accounts for 38.2 per cent of GDP and services for 46.8 per cent.

The main trading partners are EU countries, especially France and Spain. Principal exports are clothing, textiles, electrical components, inorganic chemicals, transistors, crude minerals, fertilisers, petroleum products and foodstuffs. The main imports are crude petroleum, fabrics, telecommunications equipment, wheat, gas and electricity.
GNI – US$65,800m; US$2,160 per capita (2006)
Annual average growth of GDP – 2.1 per cent (2007 est)
Inflation rate – 2.1 per cent (2007 est)
Unemployment – 15 per cent (2007 est)
Total external debt – US$16,860m (2007 est)
Imports – US$22,500m (2006)
Exports – US$11,500m (2006)

BALANCE OF PAYMENTS
Trade – US$10,987m deficit (2006)
Current Account – US$1,856m surplus (2006)

Trade with UK	*2006*	*2007*
Imports from UK	£290,102,000	£313,392,818
Exports to UK	£380,820,000	£440,134,384

COMMUNICATIONS

There are 1,907km of railways linking the major towns and there are 57,500km of roads; a 32,700km network of surfaced roads connects the main towns. The main ports are Tangier, Casablanca and Agadir, on the Atlantic coast. The principal airports are at Rabat, Agadir, Casablanca and Marrakesh; Royal Air Maroc is the national airline. There is a modern telephone system, although main-line density is low. In 2006 there were 1.3 million main-line subscribers, 16 million mobile phone subscribers and 6.1 million internet users; internet access is expensive.

EDUCATION AND HEALTH

Education is compulsory between the ages of seven and 16. There are government primary, secondary and technical schools. At Fez there is a theological university. Schools for special denominations, Jewish and Catholic, are permitted and may receive government grants.
Literacy rate – 50.7 per cent (2004 est)
Gross enrolment ratio (percentage of relevant age group) – primary 106 per cent; secondary 52 per cent; tertiary 12 per cent (2006 est)
Health expenditure (per capita) – US$89 (2005)
Hospital beds (per 1,000 people) – 0.9 (2000–6)

MEDIA

State control of the media has eased since the accession of King Mohammad VI, although its freedom to cover some topics is limited. There are three daily newspapers, one of which is state-owned. State-owned television and radio compete with a private broadcaster.

WESTERN SAHARA

Al-Jumhuriyya al-'Arabiyya as-Sahrawiyya ad-Dimuqratiyya – *Sahrawi Arab Democratic Republic*
Area – 266,000 sq. km. Neighbours: Morocco (north), Algeria (north-east), Mauritania (east and south)
Population – 382,617 (2007 est)
Administrative centre – El-Aaiun (Laayoune); population, 200,000 (2007 est)
Religion – Islam (99 per cent) (est)
Language – Arabic, Hassaniya, Spanish
Flag – Three horizontal stripes of black, white and green with a red crescent and a five-pointed star in the centre and a red triangle based on the hoist

Western Sahara came under Spanish rule in 1884, and became a province in 1934. Following Spain's withdrawal in 1975, Morocco and Mauritania annexed the territory and divided it between them. The Polisario Front began a guerrilla war to secure the Western Sahara's independence as the Sahrawi Arab Democratic Republic, which they declared in 1976, setting up a government in exile. In 1979, Mauritania withdrew from its part of the territory, which was annexed by Morocco. Fighting between Polisario and Moroccan forces continued at varying levels of intensity until 1991, when a UN-brokered ceasefire came into effect. Around 180,000 Sahrawis were driven into exile, some to Algeria and some to Mauritania.

The 1991 ceasefire was established following both sides' agreement in 1988 to UN proposals for a peace settlement, which included the holding of a referendum on the future status of Western Sahara. But the precise terms of the referendum have proved a sticking point and an impasse was reached that has still not been overcome despite further proposals in the period 2001–4; Polisario agreed to a referendum offering the options of independence, semi-autonomy or integration for Western Sahara, but Morocco is only prepared to accept semi-autonomy or integration. The UN suspended the process of preparing for the referendum in 1996 because of disagreements over voter registration; the ceasefire remains in place.

MOZAMBIQUE

República de Moçambique – Republic of Mozambique

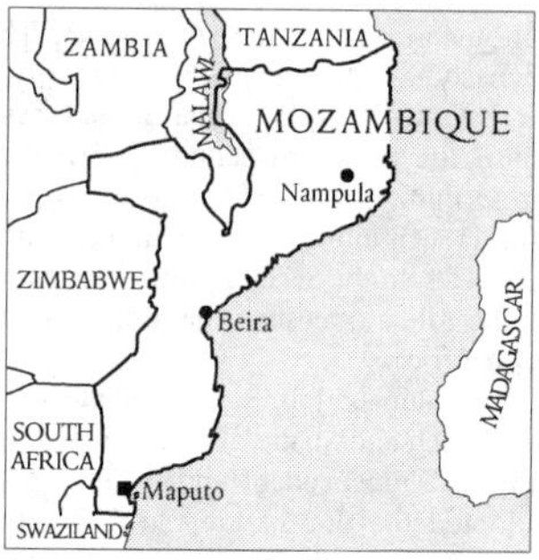

Area – 801,590 sq. km
Capital – Maputo; population, 1,446,000 (2007 est)
Major cities – Beira, Chimoio, Matola, Nampula
Currency – New metical (MT) of 100 centavos
Population – 20,905,585 rising at 1.8 per cent per year (2007 est)
Religion – Roman Catholicism (24 per cent), Protestantism (22 per cent), Islam (20 per cent) (est). Indigenous practices are present in most Christian and Muslim worship. Much of the population does not practice an organised religion
Language – Portuguese (official), Emakhuwa, Xichangana, Elomwe, Cisena
Population density – 27 per sq. km (2006)
Urban population – 38 per cent (2005 est)
Median age (years) – 17.4 (2007 est)
National anthem – 'Patria Amada' ['Beloved Fatherland']
National day – 25 June (Independence Day)
Life expectancy (years) – 40.9 (2007 est)
Mortality rate – 20.51 (2007 est)

Birth rate – 38.54 (2007 est)
Infant mortality rate – 109.93 (2007 est)
HIV/AIDS adult prevalence – 14.4 per cent (2005 est)
Death penalty – Abolished for all crimes (since 1990)
CPI score – 2.8 (2007)
Population below poverty line – 70 per cent (2001 est)
Gross enrolment ratio (percentage of relevant age group) – primary 105 per cent; secondary 16 per cent; tertiary 1 per cent (2006 est)
Health expenditure (per capita) – US$14 (2005)

CLIMATE AND TERRAIN

Coastal plains rise to plateaux in the centre and west, with mountains on the western borders. Elevation extremes range from 2,436m (Mt Binga) at the highest point to 0m (Indian Ocean) at the lowest. A number of rivers run from the western highlands to the Indian Ocean coast, including the Zambezi, Limpopo, Sava and Ruvuma. The climate is tropical, with average temperatures in the capital an almost constant 28°C.

HISTORY AND POLITICS

Between the first and fourth centuries Mozambique was settled by Bantu peoples. Trade with India and the Arabian peninsula grew and migrants from both these regions settled in the coastal areas. The first European contact was with the Portuguese explorer Vasco de Gama, who landed in 1498. Over the next three centuries the Portuguese exploited Mozambique for gold, ivory, spices and slaves. Proximity to the South African gold mines led to Mozambique's development as an important trading post from the late 19th century, and also as a source of cheap labour. It was administered as part of Portuguese India from 1751, becoming a separate colony in the late 19th century and an overseas province of Portugal in 1951. Concessions to private companies that had operated as *de facto* rulers over much of the country were ended in 1930.

The *Frente de Libertacao de Mocambique* (Frelimo) was founded in 1962 to fight for independence and a ten-year guerrilla war against Portuguese forces began in 1964. Independence was achieved in 1975, when a one-party socialist republic was set up. Opposition to this was led from 1977 by the *Resistencia Nacional de Mocambique* (Renamo) and a brutal civil war broke out that lasted until 1992. It was ended by a peace settlement that gave Renamo political party status. Mozambique joined the Commonwealth in 1996, becoming the only member country never to have been under British rule. Reconstruction of the economy and infrastructure progressed quickly after the civil war, although a series of natural catastrophes since 2000 have been major setbacks. An additional problem is the large number of remaining landmines, and the resulting amputees. The level of HIV/AIDS infection is also high.

In 1990 Frelimo abandoned Marxist-Leninism and ended one-party rule, introducing a multiparty system. The first elections under the new constitution were held in 1994 and won by Frelimo. Frelimo retained power in the 1999 and 2004 legislative and presidential elections, prompting allegations of vote-rigging by Renamo, though monitors believe that any irregularities were minor. In the December 2004 elections, the Frelimo candidate, Armando Guebuza, was elected president with 63.7 per cent of the vote, and Frelimo won 160 seats in the legislature, retaining its overall majority.

POLITICAL SYSTEM

Under the 2004 constitution, the executive president is directly elected and serves for a five-year term, which is renewable only once. The unicameral Assembly of the Republic *(Assembleia da Republica)* has 250 members, who are directly elected for a five-year term. The president appoints the prime minister and the council of ministers.

HEAD OF STATE

President, Armando Emilio Guebuza, *elected* 22 December 2004, *sworn in* 2 February 2005

SELECTED GOVERNMENT MEMBERS *as at June 2008*

Prime Minister, Luisa Dias Diogo
Foreign Affairs, Oldemiro Baloi
Interior, Jose Pacheco
Finance, Manuel Chang
Defence, Filipe Nhussi

HIGH COMMISSION FOR THE REPUBLIC OF MOZAMBIQUE

21 Fitzroy Square, London W1T 6EL
T 020-7383 3800 W www.mozambiquehc.org.uk
High Commissioner, HE Antonio Gumende, *apptd* 2002

BRITISH HIGH COMMISSION

PO Box 55, Av. Vladimir I Lenine 310, Maputo
T (+258) (21) 420 111 E info.maputo@fco.gov.uk
High Commissioner, HE Andrew Soper, *apptd* 2007

BRITISH COUNCIL

PO Box 4178, Rua John Issa 226, Maputo
T (+258) (1) 355 000 W www.britishcouncil.org/mozambique
Director, Peter Brown

DEFENCE

The army has 60 main battle tanks, 40 armoured infantry fighting vehicles and 260 armoured personnel carriers. The navy has 5 patrol and coastal combatant vessels. The air force has 4 armed helicopters.
Military budget – US$57m (2007 est)
Military personnel – 11,200: army 10,000, navy 200, air force 1,000
Conscription duration – 24 months

ECONOMY AND TRADE

Political stability and economic liberalisation have attracted foreign direct investment and donor support, and achieved economic growth despite setbacks from devastating flooding (2000, 2001, 2007, 2008), droughts (2002, 2003) and an earthquake (2006). The country remains poor, with 70 per cent of the population living below the poverty line, and is dependent on foreign aid. The huge foreign debt has been reduced to a more manageable size by debt cancellation and rescheduling, but there is a substantial ongoing trade imbalance.

Agriculture and forestry are the mainstay of the economy, accounting for 23.1 per cent of GDP and engaging 81 per cent of the workforce; shellfish, cashew nuts, cotton, sugar, citrus fruits and timber are important exports. There are considerable oil, gas, mineral and hydroelectric power resources, which are increasingly being exploited. Industries include aluminium extraction and smelting, food processing, production of beverages, fertiliser and petroleum products. There are plans to expand titanium extraction and processing, and garment-manufacturing. Industry generates 30.2 per cent of GDP and services 46.7 per cent.

The main trading partners are the Netherlands and South Africa. Principal exports are aluminium, agricultural products, timber and electricity. The main imports are machinery, vehicles, fuel, chemicals, metal products, foodstuffs and textiles.
GNI – US$6,500m; US$310 per capita (2006)
Annual average growth of GDP – 7.5 per cent (2007 est)
Inflation rate – 8 per cent (2007 est)
Total external debt – US$4,284m (2007 est)
Imports – US$3,000m (2005)

BALANCE OF PAYMENTS
Trade – US$550m deficit (2006)
Current Account – US$1,335m surplus (2006)

Trade with UK	*2006*	*2007*
Imports from UK	£11,364,000	£8,917,220
Exports to UK	£5,754,000	£45,990,361

COMMUNICATIONS

The main seaports are Maputo, Beira and Nacala; these handle trade also for landlocked countries such as Malawi and Zimbabwe, to which they are linked by rail. A new rail link to South Africa has been commissioned, and there are plans to develop new rail and road links to Malawi and Zambia. There is currently a total of 3,123km of railways. Of the 30,400km of roads, only about one sixth is surfaced. The 460km of navigable waterways are on Cahora Bassa Lake and the lower reaches of the Zambezi river. The principal airports are at Maputo and Beira, with over 140 smaller airports and airstrips around the country.

The telephone system is efficient but fixed-line availability is limited and mobile phone distribution has grown rapidly. There were 67,000 main lines in use and 2.3 million mobile phone subscribers in 2006, and 138,000 internet users in 2005.

MEDIA

Freedom of speech is guaranteed in the constitution. There are two daily newspapers and three weekly publications, which have little influence outside urban areas because of low literacy levels, plus three television stations. Radio is the main medium for most people, with UNESCO and the government funding around 40 stations.

MYANMAR

Pyidaungzu Myanma Naingngandaw – Union of Myanmar

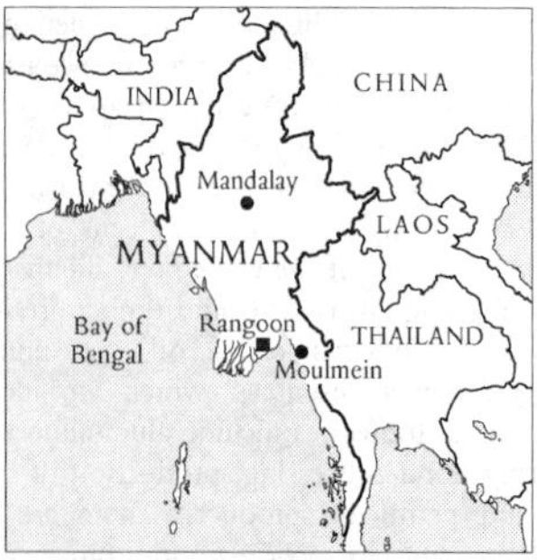

Area – 678,500 sq. km
Capital – Naypyidaw; population, 930,000 (2007 est)
Major cities – Bago, Mandalay, Mawlamyine (Moulmein), Pathein (Bassein), Yangon (Rangoon)
Currency – Kyat (K) of 100 pyas
Population – 47,373,958 rising at 0.82 per cent per year (2007 est); Burman (68 per cent), Shan (9 per cent), Karen (7 per cent), Rakhine (4 per cent), Chinese (3 per cent), Indian (2 per cent), Mon (2 per cent) (est)
Religion – Buddhism (90 per cent), Christianity (6 per cent), Islam (4 per cent) (est)
Language – Burmese (official)
Population density – 74 per sq. km (2006)
Urban population – 30.6 per cent (2005 est)
Median age (years) – 27.4 (2007 est)
National anthem – 'Kaba Ma Kyei' ['Till the End of the World, Myanmar']
National day – 4 January (Independence Day)
Life expectancy (years) – 62.49 (2007 est)
Mortality rate – 9.33 (2007 est)
Birth rate – 17.48 (2007 est)
Infant mortality rate – 50.68 (2007 est)
Death penalty – Retained, but not used
CPI score – 1.4 (2007)
Population below poverty line – 25 per cent (2000 est)

CLIMATE AND TERRAIN

Central lowlands are ringed by mountains in the west, north (part of the foothills of the Himalayas) and east, and running down the Kra isthmus that Myanmar shares with Thailand. Elevation extremes range from 5,881m (Hkakabo Razi) at the highest point to 0m (Andaman Sea) at the lowest. The lowlands are drained by the Irrawaddy river and its chief tributary, the Chindwin, and the eastern mountains by the Salween. The climate is tropical, with a wet season from May to October. Average temperatures range from 16°C in January to 36°C in July, although summer temperatures in the interior can reach 43°C.

HISTORY AND POLITICS

Myanmar (also known as Burma) was first unified in the 11th century by King Anawrahta, who adopted Theravada Buddhism. The Mongols under Kublai Khan invaded in 1287. The country was reunified in the 15th century but was weakened by internal dissension and wars with Siam (Thailand). King Alaunghpaya reunited the nation in the 18th century. In the first half of the 19th century, border disputes with British India spiralled into a series of wars. Following the third Anglo-Burmese war, Burma was annexed as part of British India in 1885. It became a separate crown colony in 1937, and was occupied by the Japanese during the Second World War. Following liberation by British troops and Burmese nationalists, the country gained its independence as the quasi-federal Union of Burma in 1948.

Following a left-wing military coup led by Gen. Ne Win in 1962, the federal system was abolished and the economy nationalised. In 1974, a one-party socialist republic was formally established. Another coup in 1988 brought to power Gen. Saw Maung, who replaced all existing state institutions with the State Law and Order Council (SLORC), imposed martial law and changed the country's name to Myanmar; the SLORC was replaced by the State Peace and Development Council in 1997.

Pro-democracy forces, notably the National League for Democracy (NLD) under Aung San Suu Kyi, oppose military rule. In 1990 the NLD won a landslide victory in the first multiparty elections for 30 years. The military ignored the election results, prevented the constituent assembly from convening, and have continued to rule by diktat, suppressing and persecuting pro-democracy campaigners. Aung San Suu Kyi was under house arrest from 1989 to 1995 and almost continuously from 2000 to date. The NLD took part in UN-brokered talks with the government in 2000 but these stalled in 2003.

A constitutional convention set up in 1993 was reconvened in 2004, but without the participation of the NLD and other opposition and ethnic groups. Shortly after it closed in September 2007 there were widespread anti-government demonstrations, which were brutally suppressed, attracting international condemnation. A new constitution was put to a referendum on 10 May 2008 in two-thirds of the country; the government claimed that 92 per cent of the 99 per cent turnout voted in favour.

The referendum was postponed until 24 May in the areas worst affected by Cyclone Nargis, which devastated the Irrawaddy basin on 3 May, leaving an estimated 134,000 dead or missing. The government appealed for international aid but restricted aid workers' access to the country to distribute supplies, raising fears of further deaths from starvation and disease. *See also* Events of the Year, Asia.

INSURGENCIES

Since independence in 1948 the government has fought various insurgencies, mostly by ethnic groups. These have included the Kachin, Kayin (Karen), Karenni, Wa, Shan, Mon, Arakan and Chin ethnic minorities. Since 1992, 15 ethnic groups have signed ceasefire agreements following government offensives against them; the most significant group, the Kayin National Union (KNU), began talks about a ceasefire in 2004. Many governments and non-governmental organisations believe that abuse of the country's ethnic minorities continues.

POLITICAL SYSTEM

The constitution was effectively abrogated in 1988 when the executive and legislature were abolished and replaced by the State Law and Order Restoration Council (SLORC); the SLORC was replaced by the State Peace and Development Council (SPDC) in 1997. The *de facto* head of state is the chair of the SPDC. A unicameral 485-member constituent assembly was elected in 1990 but has not been allowed to convene. There are no permitted political parties. The draft constitution put to a referendum in May 2008 proposes that 25 per cent of seats in both legislative chambers would be reserved for the military and excludes Aung San Suu Kyi from holding office.

HEAD OF STATE

Chair of State Peace and Development Council, Defence, Senior Gen. Than Shwe

SELECTED GOVERNMENT MEMBERS *as at June 2008*

Prime Minister, Lt.-Gen. Thein Sein
Finance and Revenue, Maj.-Gen. Hla Tun
Foreign Affairs, Maj.-Gen. U Nyan Win
Home Affairs, Maj.-Gen. Maung Oo

EMBASSY OF THE UNION OF MYANMAR

19A Charles Street, London W1J 5DX
T 020-7499 4340 E melondon@btconnect.com
Ambassador Extraordinary and Plenipotentiary, HE Nay Win, *apptd* 2005

BRITISH EMBASSY

PO Box 638, 80 Strand Road, Rangoon
T (+95) (1) 256 918 E consular.rangoon@fco.gov.uk
Ambassador Extraordinary and Plenipotentiary, HE Mark Canning, *apptd* 2006

BRITISH COUNCIL

PO Box 638, 78 Kanna Road, Rangoon
T (+95) (1) 254 658/256 290 W www.britishcouncil.org/burma
Director, Alan Smart

DEFENCE

The army has 150 main battle tanks and 325 armoured personnel carriers. The navy has 3 corvettes and 67 patrol and coastal vessels at 6 bases. The air force has 125 combat aircraft.

Military budget – US$6,900m (2006 est)
Military personnel – 406,000: army 375,000, navy 16,000, air force 15,000; paramilitary 107,250

ECONOMY AND TRADE

Myanmar has fertile soil and an abundance of natural resources such as timber (it is the world's largest exporter of teak), precious gems (jade, pearls, rubies and sapphires), oil and natural gas, but the economy is characterised by corruption and mismanagement. The country has become increasingly poverty-stricken under military rule and around a third of the population lives below the poverty line. The economy suffers from fiscal and currency instability, and inflation and foreign debt are very high. The regime's suppression of the pro-democracy movement has lost it development aid and attracted economic and trade sanctions since the 1990s. There is a large grey economy and considerable unofficial cross-border trade.

Agriculture is the dominant economic activity, accounting for 54 per cent of GDP and engaging 70 per cent of the workforce; the most important export crops are pulses, beans, fish and rice. The 2008 cyclone flooded large tracts of arable land in the Irrawaddy delta, killed livestock and destroyed fishing boats; with foreign aid prevented from reaching survivors, the pace of recovery is uncertain. The main industries are forestry and the extraction of minerals, gemstones, oil and gas; manufacturing and services are struggling, and the growing tourist industry was adversely affected by the demonstrations of September 2007. Industry contributes 11 per cent of GDP and services 35 per cent.

The main trading partners are Thailand, China, Singapore and India. Principal exports are natural gas, wood products, agricultural produce, clothing and gems. The main imports are fabric, petroleum products, fertiliser, plastics, machinery, transport equipment, construction materials, crude oil and food.

Annual average growth of GDP – 3.5 per cent (2007 est)
Inflation rate – 40.2 per cent (2007 est)
Unemployment – 5.2 per cent (2007 est)
Total external debt – US$6,914m (2007 est)
Imports – US$2,100m (2006)
Exports – US$4,500m (2006)

BALANCE OF PAYMENTS

Trade – US$2,398m surplus (2006)
Current Account – US$958m surplus (2006)

Trade with UK	*2006*	*2007*
Imports from UK	£3,653,000	£3,641,251
Exports to UK	£26,676,000	£27,521,864

COMMUNICATIONS

The 12,800km of navigable waterways includes the Irrawaddy and Chindwin rivers; the main stream of the Irrawaddy is navigable for 1,440km and carries most of the country's traffic. The chief seaports are Yangon (Rangoon), Mawlamyine (Moulmein) and Akyab (Sittwe). The railway network of 3,955km covers most of the country. There are 27,000km of roads. The main airports are at Rangoon, Mandalay and Tavoy.

The telephone system is rudimentary and domestic services are poor. Mobile phone services are more efficient than fixed-line and are growing more quickly, with 214,200 mobile phones in 2006, compared to 503,900 fixed lines.

EDUCATION AND HEALTH

Most children attend primary school; attendance at secondary level is much more variable.

Gross enrolment ratio (percentage of relevant age group) – primary 114 per cent; secondary 49 per cent (2006 est)
Health expenditure (per capita) – US$4 (2005)
Hospital beds (per 1,000 people) – 0.6 (2000–6)

MEDIA

The government controls and censors nearly all the media outlets, including the four national newspapers and four television stations. Editors and journalists are answerable to the military authorities, ensuring that self-censorship is widespread. The English-language daily newspaper *New Light of Myanmar* publishes heavily edited versions of foreign news reports from international agencies, but its domestic news strictly adheres to the government line. An opposition radio station, Democratic Voice of Myanmar, broadcasts on short-wave from Norway.

NAMIBIA

Republic of Namibia

Area – 825,418 sq. km
Capital – Windhoek; population, 313,000 (2007 etc)
Major towns – Rundu, Walvis Bay
Currency – Namibian dollar of 100 cents, at parity to South African rand
Population – 2,055,080 rising at 0.48 per cent per year (2007 est); Ovambo (50 per cent), Kavangos (9 per cent), Herero (7 per cent), Damara (7 per cent), Nama (5 per cent) (est)
Religion – Christianity (90 per cent), indigenous religions (4 per cent) (est)
Language – English (official), Afrikaans, German
Population density – 2 per sq. km (2006)
Urban population – 33.5 per cent (2005 est)
Median age (years) – 20.2 (2007 est)
National anthem – 'Namibia, Land of the Brave'
National day – 21 March (Independence Day)
Life expectancy (years) – 43.11 (2007 est)
Mortality rate – 19.15 (2007 est)
Birth rate – 23.52 (2007 est)
Infant mortality rate – 47.23 (2007 est)
HIV/AIDS adult prevalence – 17.7 per cent (2005 est)
Death penalty – Abolished for all crimes (since 1990)
CPI score – 4.5 (2007)
Population below poverty line – 50 per cent (2002 est)
Literacy rate – 85 per cent (2004 est)
Gross enrolment ratio (percentage of relevant age group) – primary 107 per cent; secondary 57 per cent; tertiary 6 per cent (2006 est)
Health expenditure (per capita) – US$165 (2005)

CLIMATE AND TERRAIN

The Namib desert runs along the Atlantic coast and the Kalahari desert covers south-eastern Namibia, with veld in the north-east. The interior and coastal desert areas are divided by a line of hills and higher land. The terrain is almost completely arid and dry. Elevation extremes range from 2,606m (Konigstein) at the highest point to 0m (Atlantic Ocean) at the lowest. The only rivers not dependent on rains are the Orange, which forms the southern border with South Africa, and the Zambezi, which runs through the Caprivi Strip in the extreme north-east of the country. Average temperatures range from 21°C in July to 36°C in January.

HISTORY AND POLITICS

Pre-colonial Namibia was inhabited by Bantu tribes and San (Bushmen). It was annexed by Germany in 1884 and named South West Africa. From 1904, the Germans brutally suppressed indigenous uprisings, killing over half of some tribes and an estimated 80 per cent of the Herero. The territory was occupied by South Africa on behalf of the Allies in 1914 and after the First World War it became a League of Nations mandated territory, administered by South Africa.

The arrangement continued under the UN after the Second World War, but South Africa exceeded its mandate by effectively annexing the country, extending representation in the South Africa parliament to the white population in 1949, and applying apartheid in 1966. These actions were taken despite the UN's refusal to permit the country's incorporation into South Africa in 1946 and its vote to end the mandate in 1964. In 1968, the UN changed the country's name to Namibia, and the South West Africa People's Organisation (SWAPO), which had campaigned for racial equality and independence since the late 1950s, began a guerrilla war against South Africa.

In 1978, South Africa accepted and then rescinded its acceptance of UN security council Resolution 435 for the granting of full independence to Namibia. South Africa's peace talks with Angola in 1988 led to agreement on independence for Namibia, and this was achieved on 21 March 1990; South Africa's Walvis Bay enclave was returned to Namibia in 1994.

The country has enjoyed stability since independence, apart from a brief period of secessionist violence in the Caprivi Strip in the late 1990s. In recent years there has been agitation for an acceleration of land reform, and the government programme moved from voluntary sales to expropriation of white-owned farms in 2005. The country's main problems arise from the demographic, economic and social impact of the high level of HIV/AIDS infection amongst the population.

SWAPO has been the dominant party since independence, holding the presidency and commanding a parliamentary majority without interruption. The 2004 presidential election was won by Hifikepunye Pohamba, who replaced Sam Nujoma, the president since independence. In the 2004 legislative elections, SWAPO retained its majority in both legislative chambers.

POLITICAL SYSTEM
Under the 1990 constitution, the executive president is directly elected for a five-year term, renewable only once. There is a bicameral parliament consisting of a National Assembly, with 72 members directly elected for a five-year term and up to six additional non-voting members appointed by the president, and a National Council, whose 26 members are indirectly elected by the regional councils from among their own members for a six-year term; the latter's main function is to review and consider legislation from the lower chamber. The president appoints the prime minister and the other ministers.

HEAD OF STATE
President, Hifikepunye Pohamba, *elected* 16 November 2004, *sworn in* 21 March 2005

SELECTED GOVERNMENT MEMBERS *as at June 2008*
Prime Minister, Nahas Angula
Deputy Prime Minister, Libertina Amathila
Defence, Maj-Gen.Charles Namoloh
Finance, Saarah Kuugongelwa-Amathila
Foreign Affairs, Marco Hausiku
Home Affairs, Rosalia Nghidinwa

HIGH COMMISSION FOR THE REPUBLIC OF NAMIBIA
6 Chandos Street, London W1G 9LU
T 020-7636 6244 E namibia-highcomm@btconnect.com
High Commissioner, HE George Mbanga Liswaniso, *apptd* 2006

BRITISH HIGH COMMISSION
PO Box 22202, 116 Robert Mugabe Avenue, Windhoek
T (+264) (61) 274 800 E bhc@mweb.com.na
W www.britishhighcommission.gov.uk/namibia
High Commissioner, HE Mark Bensberg, *apptd* 2007

BRITISH COUNCIL
1–5 Fidel Castro Street, Windhoek
T (+264) (61) 226 776 W www.britishcouncil.org/namibia
Director, Julian Baker

DEFENCE
The army has 60 armoured personnel carriers. The navy has 6 patrol and coastal combatant vessels at a base at Walvis Bay. The air force has 2 combat capable aircraft and 2 armed helicopters.
Military budget – US$248m (2007 est)
Military personnel – 9,200: army 9,000, navy 200; paramilitary 6,000

ECONOMY AND TRADE
Namibia is a poor country, with much of the population living below the poverty line. Its arid terrain limits agriculture, but the emphasis on environmental protection (enshrined in the constitution) is helping the development of tourism. The country has rich mineral deposits; extraction of these is the main industrial activity and minerals account for over 50 per cent of foreign exchange earnings. Other industries process the meat, fish and dairy products of the agricultural and fisheries sector. This operates mostly at subsistence level, accounting for 10.6 per cent of GDP but engaging nearly half the workforce.

The main trading partners are South Africa (33 per cent of exports; 85 per cent of imports) and the USA. Principal exports are diamonds, copper, gold, zinc, lead, uranium, cattle, processed fish and skins. The main imports are foodstuffs (particularly grain), petroleum products and fuel, machinery and equipment, and chemicals.
GNI – US$6,600m; US$3,210 per capita (2006)
Annual average growth of GDP – 4.5 per cent (2007 est)
Inflation rate – 6.7 per cent (2007 est)
Unemployment – 5.3 per cent (2006 est)
Total external debt – US$1,429m (2007 est)
Imports – US$2,730m (2006)
Exports – US$2,720m (2006)

BALANCE OF PAYMENTS
Trade – US$10m deficit (2006)
Current Account – US$1,106m surplus (2006)

Trade with UK	*2006*	*2007*
Imports from UK	£13,191,000	£11,897,438
Exports to UK	£346,552,000	£249,697,541

COMMUNICATIONS
Namibia has 2,382km of railways and 42,237km of roads. In 2002, a road bridge across the Zambezi opened, linking Namibia with Zambia and raising hopes of an increase in regional trade. The main airports are at Windhoek and Odangwa, with over 130 smaller airports and airfields around the country. The two main seaports are Luderitz and Walvis Bay.

Telephone services are good in both urban and rural areas. There were 138,900 main telephone lines in use and 495,000 mobile phone subscribers in 2005.

MEDIA
Freedom of the press is guaranteed by the constitution and government interference in reportage is rare. There are six national newspapers, including *The Namibian* and the Afrikaans language title *Die Republikein*. The state-administered Namibian Broadcasting Corporation runs alongside Desert TV, a private network based at Windhoek.

NAURU

Republic of Nauru

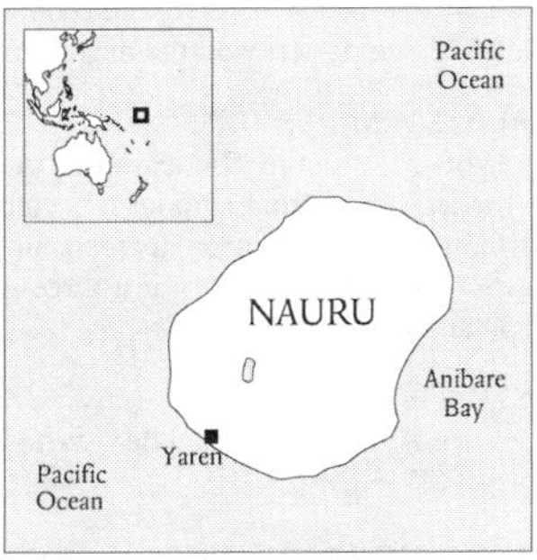

Area – 21 sq. km
Capital – Yaren District (unofficial); population, 10,000 (2007 est)

Currency – Australian dollar ($A) of 100 cents
Population – 13,528 rising at 1.78 per cent per year (2007 est); Nauruan (58 per cent), other Pacific Islander (26 per cent), Chinese (8 per cent) (est)
Religion – The majority of the population is predominantly Christian, with around twice as many Protestants as Roman Catholics; around 3 per cent practise traditional Chinese religions, including Confucianism
Language – Nauruan, English (both official)
Population density – 609.9 per sq. km (2004 est)
Urban population – 100 per cent (2005 est)
Median age (years) – 21 (2007 est)
National anthem – 'Nauru Bwiema' ('Nauru, Our Homeland')
National day – 31 January (Independence Day)
Life expectancy (years) – 63.44 (2007 est)
Mortality rate – 6.65 (2007 est)
Birth rate – 24.47 (2007 est)
Infant mortality rate – 9.6 (2007 est)
Death penalty – Retained, but not used

CLIMATE AND TERRAIN

Nauru is a low-lying coral island in the southern Pacific Ocean, 42km south of the Equator and 4,000km north-east of Sydney, Australia. The land rises from 0m at sea level to a central plateau; the plateau rim is the highest point, at 61m. The climate is tropical, with daily temperatures an almost constant 29°C.

HISTORY AND POLITICS

Nauru was first settled by Polynesian and Melanesian groups. The first Europeans to visit the island were British whalers in 1798 and by 1888 Nauru was annexed by Germany. At the outbreak of the First World War, Nauru was occupied by Australia, which continued to administer the island under a League of Nations mandate from 1920. During the Second World War, the island was occupied by the Japanese in 1942–3. UN trusteeship status superseded the mandate in 1947 and Nauru continued to be administered by Australia until it became independent on 31 January 1968.

The financial crisis since 2003 has caused some political instability, with five changes of president between January and August 2003 and two different presidents in 2004. In the October 2004 general election, Ludwig Scotty's supporters won a majority of seats and Scotty (president May–August 2003 and from June 2004) was re-elected president unopposed. He was returned to office in August 2007 but lost a vote of confidence in December and was replaced by Marcus Stephen. President Stephen called a legislative election in April 2008 in which his supporters won the majority of seats.

POLITICAL SYSTEM

Under the 1968 constitution, the executive president is elected by the legislature from among its members for a three-year term. The unicameral parliament has 18 members, who are directly elected for a three-year term. The president appoints the cabinet.

HEAD OF STATE

President, Internal Affairs Marcus Stephen, *elected* 19 December 2007

SELECTED GOVERNMENT MEMBERS *as at June 2008*

Foreign Affairs, Kieren Keke
Justice, Roland Kun
Finance, Frederic Pitcher

HONORARY CONSULATE

Romshed Courtyard, Underriver, Sevenoaks, Kent TN15 0SD
T 01732-746061 E nauru@weald.co.uk
Honorary Consul, Martin W. L. Weston

BRITISH HIGH COMMISSIONER

HE Roger Sykes, *apptd* 2006, resident at Suva, Fiji

ECONOMY AND TRADE

The economy is almost entirely dependent on phosphate extraction, but reserves are nearing exhaustion. Using profits derived from the mining industry, the government had invested in trust funds to provide for the post-mining future. Heavy spending from the funds has left the country virtually bankrupt, causing it to default on loans and have assets seized in 2004. In response, Australian officials took charge of the state's finances, and Nauru is now dependent on international aid. The future is very uncertain as phosphate is the island's only resource and all other goods, including food and water, have to be imported. Diversification efforts include offshore banking and small-scale tourism.

Most of the phosphate is exported to South Africa (64 per cent), South Korea and Canada. Imports come mainly from South Korea, Australia, the USA and Germany.
Unemployment – 90 per cent (2004 est)
Total external debt – US$33.3m (2002)

Trade with UK	*2006*	*2007*
Imports from UK	£186,000	£68,232
Exports to UK	£48,000	£17,423

EDUCATION AND MEDIA

Education is free of charge and compulsory between the ages of six and 17.

Nauru has no daily press but there are three weekly or fortnightly publications. A domestic radio service broadcasts material from the BBC and Radio Australia, and is supplemented by the government-owned Nauru Television (NTV), which broadcasts programmes from New Zealand.

NEPAL

Area – 147,181 sq. km
Capital – Kathmandu; population, 895,000 (2007 est)
Major cities – Biratnagar, Lalitpur, Pokhara
Currency – Nepalese rupee of 100 paisa
Population – 28,901,790 rising at 2.13 per cent per year (2007 est); Chhettri (15.5 per cent), Brahman-Hill (12.5 per cent), Magar (7 per cent), Tharu (6.6 per

cent), Tamang (5.5 per cent), Newar (5.4 per cent), Kami (3.9 per cent), Yadav (3.9 per cent)
Religion – Hinduism (81 per cent), Buddhism (11 per cent), Islam (4 per cent), indigenous religions (4 per cent) (est)
Language – Nepali (official), Maithali, Bhojpuri, Tamang, English, Tharu, Newar, Magar, Awadhi
Population density – 193 per sq. km (2006)
Urban population – 15.8 per cent (2005 est)
Median age (years) – 20.5 (2007 est)
National anthem – 'Sayaun Thunga Phool Ka' ['Hundreds of Flowers']
Life expectancy (years) – 60.56 (2007 est)
Mortality rate – 9.14 (2007 est)
Birth rate – 30.46 (2007 est)
Infant mortality rate – 63.66 (2007 est)
Death penalty – Abolished for all crimes (since 1997)
CPI score – 2.5 (2007)
Population below poverty line – 30.9 per cent (2004)

CLIMATE AND TERRAIN

The north of landlocked Nepal lies in the Himalayas, with the snowline at about 4,880m. The terrain descends from the mountains through a hilly central belt with fertile valleys to a southern region, the Terai, that lies in the valley of the Ganges. Elevation extremes range from 8,850m (Mt Everest) at the highest point, to 70m (Kanchan Kalan) at the lowest. Average temperatures in Kathmandu range from 2°C in January to 29°C in July. The rainy season lasts from June to September.

HISTORY AND POLITICS

Modern Nepal was formed from a number of hill states that were unified in the 18th century by the Gurkha ruler Prithvi Naryan Shah. After war with the British in 1815–16, Nepal became a British-dependent buffer state; its independence was formally recognised in 1923.

Power was seized by Jung Bahdur in 1846. He assumed the title Rana and his family became hereditary chief ministers, reducing the monarchy to a purely ceremonial role and keeping the country isolated. In 1950–1, the Ranas were overthrown in the so-called 'palace revolution' and the monarchy was restored to power. Apart from the period 1959–60, when a parliamentary system of government was in place, the kings ruled as absolute monarchs until 1990, when major constitutional reforms were introduced after violent pro-democracy demonstrations.

Under the reforms, the monarchy's powers were restricted and a multiparty parliamentary system was reintroduced. However, factionalism led to frequent changes of government, causing political and social instability, which was exacerbated from 1996 by a Maoist insurgency led by the Nepal Communist Party. The insurgency began in the west and quickly spread, despite the government's often brutal attempts at suppression. King Gyanendra, who succeeded to the throne in 2001 after Crown Prince Dipendra killed King Birendra and eight other members of the royal family before fatally injuring himself, assumed direct control of the government in 2005–6 in an attempt to defeat the insurgents.

The king found himself increasingly isolated from November 2005 as politicians from seven opposition parties allied themselves with the Maoists to achieve the restoration of democracy, and in April 2006 the king agreed to reinstate the legislature after three months of violent pro-democracy protests. The legislature voted to curtail the king's powers, to hold elections to a constituent assembly to draft a new constitution and to open peace talks with the Maoists, who controlled 80 per cent of the country; a peace accord was signed in November.

An interim constitution was approved and an interim legislature was set up in January 2007, with Maoists participating in both the legislature and the multiparty government that took office in April. They withdrew from the government in September 2007 over the timetable for abolition of the monarchy but returned after the rest of the government agreed to the immediate declaration of a republic by the legislature, in December 2007, and that the constituent assembly's first meeting would endorse the declaration. Elections to the assembly were postponed twice in 2007 but went ahead in April 2008, when candidates of the Communist Party of Nepal–Maoists (CPN-M) won the most seats. The assembly met on 28 May 2008, when it declared the country a republic and abolished the monarchy; the interim legislature was dissolved. The assembly elected Ram Baran Yadav at the country's first president, rejecting the candidate proposed by the CPN-M, which, at the time of going to press, threatened to withdraw from the assembly.

POLITICAL SYSTEM

The 1990 constitution will be superceded by a new constitution, to be drafted by the constituent assembly; the 2007 interim constitution transfers all the king's powers to the prime minister. The monarchy was abolished in May 2008 and the country declared a republic. The head of state is the president. The interim legislature was replaced in May 2008 by a constituent assembly with 601 members, 575 directly elected and 26 appointed by the council of ministers. Executive power is now vested in the council of ministers.

HEAD OF STATE

President, Ram Baran Yadav, *sworn in* 23 July 2008
Vice-President, Paramananda Jha

SELECTED GOVERNMENT MEMBERS *as at June 2008*

Chair of the Council of Ministers, Defence, Prachanda
Vice-Chair, Khadga Prasad Sharma Oli
Finance, Ram Sharan Mahat
Home Affairs, Krishna Sitaula
Foreign Affairs, Sahana Pradhan

EMBASSY OF NEPAL

12A Kensington Palace Gardens, London W8 4QU
T 020-7229 1594 E eon@nepembassy.org.uk
W www.nepembassy.org.uk
Ambassador Extraordinary and Plenipotentiary, HE Murari Raj Sharma

BRITISH EMBASSY

PO Box 106, Lainchaur, Kathmandu
T (+977) (1) 441 0583 E britemb@wlink.com.np
W www.britishembassy.gov.uk/nepal
Ambassador Extraordinary and Plenipotentiary, HE Andrew Hall, *apptd* 2006

BRITISH COUNCIL

PO Box 640, Lainchaur, Kathmandu
T (+977) (1) 4410 798 W www.britishcouncil.org/nepal
Country Manager, John Fry

DEFENCE

The army has 40 armoured personnel carriers.
Military budget – US$173m (2007 est)
Military personnel – 69,000: army 69,000; paramilitary 62,000

ECONOMY AND TRADE

The country is very poor, with nearly one-third of the population living below the poverty line, and is dependent on foreign aid and trade with India. Agriculture is the main economic sector, generating 38 per cent of GDP and engaging about 76 per cent of the workforce; principal crops are rice, maize, wheat, sugar cane, jute, root crops and milk. The main industry is tourism; other industries manufacture carpets, textiles, cigarettes, cement and bricks, and process rice, jute, sugar and oilseed. Industry accounts for 20 per cent of GDP and services for 42 per cent. Tourism's contribution has decreased recently because of the Maoist insurgency but has potential for development, although this might compound growing environmental problems.

The main export markets are India (70 per cent) and the USA; the main import providers are India (62 per cent), China and Indonesia. Principal exports are carpets, clothing, leather goods, jute goods and grain. The main imports are gold, machinery and equipment, petroleum products and fertilisers.

GNI – US$8,800m; US$320 per capita (2006)
Annual average growth of GDP – 2.5 per cent (2007 est)
Inflation rate – 8.6 per cent (2006 est)
Unemployment – 42 per cent (2004 est)
Total external debt – US$3,070m (2006)
Imports – US$2,100m (2006)
Exports – US$760m (2006)

BALANCE OF PAYMENTS
Trade – US$1,340m deficit (2006)
Current Account – US$192m surplus (2006)

Trade with UK	*2006*	*2007*
Imports from UK	£4,597,000	£5,512,780
Exports to UK	£10,354,000	£9,695,083

COMMUNICATIONS

There is a total of 17,380km of roads, of which 9,886km are surfaced. A major highway runs the length of the country through the Terai, linking the main lowland centres and extending into the hills to Kathmandu and Pokhara. Other highways connect Kathmandu with India and Tibet. There are 59km of railways. The principal airport is at Kathmandu, and there are over 40 smaller airports and airfields around the country.

The telephone system is extensive but services are poor and mobile phone distribution is expanding rapidly. In 2006 there were 595,800 main telephone lines in use, 1.04 million mobile phone subscribers and 249,400 internet users.

EDUCATION AND HEALTH

Literacy rate – 48.6 per cent (2004 est)
Gross enrolment ratio (percentage of relevant age group) – primary 126 per cent; secondary 43 per cent; tertiary 6 per cent (2006 est)
Health expenditure (per capita) – US$16 (2005)
Hospital beds (per 1,000 people) – 0.2 (2000–6)

MEDIA

Nepal has had notoriously strict media laws for many years and is responsible for a large proportion of world censorship cases. These laws have been eased since the appointment of a multiparty government in 2006 but remain comparatively draconian. The two most widely circulated newspapers are the *Kathmandu Post* and *Rising Nepal*. The government-run Radio Nepal is the most influential media outlet.

THE NETHERLANDS

Koninkrijk der Nederlanden – Kingdom of the Netherlands

Area – 41,526 sq. km
Capital – Amsterdam; population, 1,031,000 (2007 est)
Seat of government – The Hague (Den Haag or, in full, 's-Gravenhage), population 624,000 (2007 est)
Major cities – Eindhoven, Rotterdam, Tilburg, Utrecht
Currency – Euro (€) of 100 cents
Population – 16,570,613 rising at 0.46 per cent per year (2007 est)
Religion – Christianity (55 per cent), Islam (6 per cent) (est). An estimated 36 per cent of the population is agnostic or atheist
Language – Dutch, Frisian (both official), English
Population density – 482 per sq. km (2006)
Urban population – 66.8 per cent (2005 est)
Median age (years) – 39.7 (2007 est)
National anthem – 'Het Wilhelmus' ['The William']
National day – 30 April (Queen's Day)
Life expectancy (years) – 79.11 (2007 est)
Mortality rate – 8.69 (2007 est)
Birth rate – 10.7 (2007 est)
Infant mortality rate – 4.88 (2007 est)
Death penalty – Abolished for all crimes (since 1982)
CPI score – 9.0 (2007)
Population below poverty line – 10.5 per cent (2005)

CLIMATE AND TERRAIN

The Netherlands is a low-lying country, below sea level in many places, making it susceptible to flooding despite the coastal defences and a network of dykes and canals. Its land area has been extended over the centuries by land reclamation (polders), found especially in the west around the huge freshwater lake of Yssel, created in the 1930s by damming the Zuider Zee. The country is crossed by three major European rivers, the Rhine, Mass and Scheldt, whose estuaries are in the south-west. Elevation extremes range from 322m (Vaalserberg) at the highest point to –7m (Zuidplaspolder) at the lowest point. The climate is temperate with average temperatures ranging from 0°C in January to 23°C in July.

HISTORY AND POLITICS

The area was part of the Frankish Empire by the eighth century and was subsequently part of the Holy Roman Empire. From the 12th century the mercantile towns of the Low Countries became virtually independent principalities. In the 15th century these came under the influence of the dukes of Burgundy and then of the Habsburgs from 1477, passing to the Spanish branch of the Habsburgs in 1555. The northern provinces, led by William, Prince of Orange, rebelled against Spanish rule in 1568. The war of independence ended with the seven northern provinces forming the Union of Utrecht in 1579, and in 1581 independence was declared; the United Provinces were formally recognised as an independent republic in 1648.

The 17th century was a golden age in which the Dutch led the world in trade, art and science, founding colonies in the East and West Indies. Commercial and colonial rivalries led to three wars with Britain in the late 17th century, and resisting French attempts at domination exhausted the country in the 18th century. In 1795, French revolutionary armies overran the country and it remained under French rule until 1814. In 1815, the northern and southern provinces were reunited into one kingdom, with the hereditary stadtholder of the northern provinces becoming King William I of the Netherlands and grand duke of Luxembourg; the southern provinces seceded to form Belgium in 1830 and the Duchy of Luxembourg was made an independent state in 1867. The Netherlands was neutral during the First World War, but during the Second World War the country was invaded and occupied by Germany from 1940 until 1945.

The post-war period was marked by economic expansion and the construction of a liberal welfare state. The Netherlands formed the Benelux economic union with Belgium and Luxembourg in 1948, was a founder member of the EEC in 1958 and joined the eurozone in 1999. In a referendum in June 2005, its population rejected ratification of the EU constitution.

Although it is a stable democracy, one party has rarely commanded a sufficient parliamentary majority to govern alone and post-war governments have usually been coalitions of two or more parties. Following the 2006 legislative election, the Christian Democratic Appeal (CDA) remained the largest party, but without an overall majority. After three months of negotiation, a new coalition comprising members of the CDA, the Labour Party (PvdA) and the Christian Union (CU) was sworn into office in February 2007, led by Jan Peter Balkenende, prime minister since 2002.

POLITICAL SYSTEM

Under the 1983 constitution, the kingdom consists of three autonomous elements: the Netherlands, the Netherlands Antilles and Aruba. The head of state is a hereditary constitutional monarch. The legislature, the *Staten-Generaal* (States-General), consists of the *Eerste Kamer* (First Chamber) of 75 members, elected for a four-year term by provincial councillors; and the *Tweede Kamer* (Second Chamber) of 150 members, directly elected for a four-year term. The head of government is the prime minister, who is responsible to parliament.

HEAD OF STATE

HM The Queen of the Netherlands, Queen Beatrix Wilhelmina Armgard, KG, GCVO, *born* 31 January 1938; *succeeded* 30 April 1980
Heir, HRH Prince Willem Alexander, *born* 27 April 1967

SELECTED GOVERNMENT MEMBERS *as at June 2008*

Prime Minister, Jan Peter Balkenende
Deputy Prime Ministers, Wouter Bos *(Finance)*; André Rouvoet
Defence, Eimert van Middelkoop
Economic Affairs, Maria van der Hoeven
Foreign Affairs, Maxime Verhagen
Interior, Guusje ter Horst

ROYAL NETHERLANDS EMBASSY

38 Hyde Park Gate, London SW7 5DP
T 020-7590 3200 E london@netherlands-embassy.org.uk
W www.netherlands-embassy.org.uk
Ambassador Extraordinary and Plenipotentiary, HE Pieter Willem Waldeck, *apptd* 2007

BRITISH EMBASSY

Lange Voorhout 10, The Hague, 2514 ED
T (+31) (70) 427 0427 W www.britain.nl
Ambassador Extraordinary and Plenipotentiary, HE Lyn Parker, *apptd* 2005

BRITISH COUNCIL

Weteringschans 85A, Amsterdam, 1017 RZ
T (+31) (20) 550 6060 W www.britishcouncil.org/netherlands
Director, Ben Harris

DEFENCE

The army has 170 main battle tanks, 569 armoured infantry fighting vehicles and 93 armoured personnel carriers. The navy has 4 submarines, 4 destroyers, 4 frigates and 34 helicopters. The air force has 105 combat aircraft and 24 armed helicopters.
Military expenditure – US$9,900m (2006)
Military personnel – 45,608: army 18,266, navy 10,401, air force 10,141, paramilitary 6,800

ECONOMY AND TRADE

The Netherlands has a highly industrialised and diversified market economy, and is a European transport hub. The economy depends heavily on foreign trade. Economic growth slowed in 2001–5, but has recovered strongly since 2006 owing to increased exports and investment.

The highly mechanised agricultural sector employs only 3 per cent of the workforce but output supplies the food processing industries and the export as well as the domestic market. Flower bulbs and cut flowers are a major contributor to this sector, as is the fishing industry. The industrial sector contributes 24 per cent of GDP; major industries include food processing, and the manufacture of metal and engineering products, electrical machinery and equipment, chemicals, oil refining, construction and micro-electronics. The service industries represent 74 per cent of the economy. Other EU countries account for most overseas trade. Principal exports are machinery and equipment, chemicals, fuels and foodstuffs. The main imports are machinery and transport equipment, chemicals, fuels, foodstuffs and clothing.
GNI – US$703,500m; US$43,050 per capita (2006)
Annual average growth of GDP – 2.8 per cent (2007 est)
Inflation rate – 1.8 per cent (2007 est)
Unemployment – 4.5 per cent (2007 est)
Total external debt – US$2,277,000m (2007)
Imports – US$358,000m (2006)
Exports – US$400,000m (2006)

BALANCE OF PAYMENTS
Trade – US$41,074m surplus (2006)
Current Account – US$55,874m surplus (2006)

Trade with UK	*2006*	*2007*
Imports from UK	£16,063,200,000	£14,943,482,443
Exports to UK	£20,024,700,000	£22,744,217,357

COMMUNICATIONS

The main seaport is Rotterdam, although there are a number of other ports on the river estuaries or linked to the coast by the canals; 6,183km of inland waterways, including canals, are navigable by ships of up to 50 tonnes. The large merchant fleet includes 566 ships of over 1,000 tonnes. There are 134,000km of roads and 2,811km of railways, of which 2,064km are electrified. The principal airports are at Amsterdam, Rotterdam, Eindhoven and Maastricht, with a further 23 smaller airports and airfields around the country.

There is a modern telephone system and a very high density of mobile phone ownership. In 2005 there were 7.6 million main telephone lines in use and 15.8 million mobile phone subscribers; in 2006, there were 14.5 million internet users.

EDUCATION AND HEALTH

Ten years of primary and secondary education are available at both denominational and state schools and are compulsory. The principal universities are at Leiden, Utrecht, Groningen, Amsterdam, Nijmegen, Maastricht and Rotterdam.
Gross enrolment ratio (percentage of relevant age group) – primary 107 per cent; secondary 118 per cent; tertiary 59 per cent (2006 est)
Health expenditure (per capita) – US$3,560 (2005)
Hospital beds (per 1,000 people) – 5.0 (2000–6)

MEDIA

Ownership of the five national newspapers is highly concentrated. A competitive television sector includes Nederlandse Omroep Stichting (NOS), which oversees the country's three public networks and a large number of commercial stations. Freedom of the press is guaranteed by the constitution and, as such, violations are very rare.

CULTURE

The Netherlands has produced many of the world's major artists, particularly in the period 1580–1700, known as the Dutch Golden Age. Rembrandt (1606–69) and Johannes Vermeer (1632–75) have become the most enduring artists from the period, while mathematician and physicist Christiaan Huygens (1629–95) created the first pendulum clock, rendering time-keeping accurate for the first time, and Baruch Spinoza (1632–77) wrote *Ethics*, a ground-breaking work in rationalist philosophy.

After the Golden Age, the works of Vincent van Gogh (1853–90), Piet Mondrian (1872–1944) and M. C. Escher (1898–1972) ensured that Dutch art remained inventive. Less celebrated is the life of Han van Meegeren (1889–1947), an expert forger of Golden Age painters until his confession in 1945.

OVERSEAS TERRITORIES

ARUBA

Area – 193 sq. km
Capital – Oranjestad; population, 32,000 (2007 est)
Major town – Sint Nicolaas
Currency – Aruban florin of 100 cents
Population – 100,018, rising at 1.52 per cent per year (2007 est)
Language – Dutch (official), Papiamento
National Day – 18 March (Flag Day)

The Caribbean island became part of the Dutch West Indies from 1828 and part of the Netherlands Antilles from 1845. On 1 January 1986 it became a separate territory with full internal autonomy. The governor is responsible for external affairs; internal government is in the hands of the prime minister and council of ministers, who are responsible to the 21-member unicameral legislature. The principal economic activities are tourism, oil refining and offshore financial services.
Governor, Fredis Refunjol
Prime Minister, Nelson O. Oduber, *elected* 30 October 2001

CURACAO

Area – 444 sq. km
Capital – Willemstad; population, 120,000 (2007 est)
Currency – Netherlands Antilles guilder of 100 cents
Population – 137,094 (2007 est)
Language – Dutch (official), Papiamento

Curacao was colonised by the Dutch in the 17th century and became part of the self-governing Netherlands Antilles federation in 1954. The federation will be dissolved in December 2008, when Curacao will become autonomous. The governor is responsible for external affairs; internal affairs are in the hands of the executive council, chaired by the lieutenant-governor, and the 21-member island council. The principal economic activities are tourism, oil refining and light manufacturing.
Lieutenant-Governor, Lizanne Richards-Dindial

NETHERLANDS ANTILLES

Nederlandse Antillen
Area – 960 sq. km
Capital – Willemstad; population, 120,000 (2007 est), on Curaçao
Currency – Netherlands Antilles guilder of 100 cents
Population – 223,652, rising at 0.78 per cent per year (2006 est)
Language – Dutch (official), Papiamentu

The Netherlands Antilles currently comprise the Caribbean islands of Curacao, Bonaire, part of St Maarten, St Eustatius and Saba. The islands were colonised by the Dutch in the 17th century and became a self-governing federation in 1954. The federation will be dissolved in December 2008, when Curacao and St Maarten will become autonomous and the other three islands will be given city status within the Netherlands. At present, the governor is responsible for external affairs; internal affairs are in the hands of a prime minister and council of ministers, who are elected by the 21-member unicameral legislature. The principal economic activities are tourism, oil refining and offshore financial services.
Governor, Gen. Frits Goedgedrag
Prime Minister, Emily de Jongh-Elhage

ST MAARTEN

Area – 34 sq. km
Capital – Philipsburg; population, 1,578 (2008 est)
Currency – Netherlands Antilles guilder of 100 cents; the US dollar is also in circulation
Population – 38,959 (2007 est)
Language – Dutch (official), Papiamentu

St Maarten consists of the southern third of the island of St Martin in the Leeward group of the Lesser Antilles; the rest of the island is the French overseas territory of St Martin. The island was colonised by the Dutch and the French, who agreed to divide it in 1648, although the boundary was not settled until 1817. The Dutch territory became part of the self-governing Netherlands Antilles federation in 1954. The federation will be dissolved in December 2008, when St Maarten will become autonomous. The Netherlands Antilles governor is responsible for external affairs; internal affairs are in the hands of a five-member executive council chaired by the lieutenant-governor, and there is an 11-member island council. The principal economic activities are tourism and offshore financial services.
Lieutenant-Governor, Franklyn Richards

NEW ZEALAND

Aotearoa – New Zealand

Area – 268,680 sq. km
Capital – Wellington; population, 366,000 (2007 est)
Major cities – Auckland, Christchurch, Hamilton, Manakau, North Shore, Waitakere
Currency – New Zealand dollar (NZ$) of 100 cents
Population – 4,115,771 rising at 0.95 per cent per year (2007 est); 7.9 per cent are Maori (2001)
Religion – Protestantism (26 per cent), Roman Catholicism (14 per cent), other Christian denominations (17 per cent), Buddhism (2 per cent), Hinduism (2 per cent), Islam (1 per cent) (est). A large proportion of the population has no religious affiliation
Language – English, Maori, sign language (all official)
Population density – 16 per sq. km (2006)
Urban population – 86 per cent (2005 est)
Median age (years) – 34.2 (2007 est)
National anthem – 'God Save the Queen'/'God Defend New Zealand'
National day – 6 February (Waitangi Day)
Life expectancy (years) – 78.96 (2007 est)
Mortality rate – 7.54 (2007 est)
Birth rate – 13.61 (2007 est)
Infant mortality rate – 5.67 (2007 est)
Death penalty – Abolished for all crimes (since 1989)
CPI score – 9.4 (2007)

CLIMATE AND TERRAIN

New Zealand consists of a number of islands in the South Pacific Ocean, and also administers a number of territories and associated states in the region. The two larger islands, North Island and South Island, are separated by the relatively narrow Cook Strait. The remaining islands are much smaller and more widely dispersed.

Much of the North and South Islands is mountainous. The North Island mountains include several volcanoes, three of which are active. The principal range is the Southern Alps, extending the entire length of the South Island to the west of the Canterbury Plains. There are geysers and hot springs in the Rotorua district and glaciers in the Southern Alps. Elevation extremes range from 3,754m (Aoraki/Mt Cook) at the highest point to 0m (Pacific Ocean) at the lowest. The climate is temperate and average temperatures in Christchurch (South Island) range from 1°C in July to 24°C in January.

HISTORY AND POLITICS

Settled by Polynesian tribes since the ninth century, New Zealand was sighted by the Dutch navigator Abel Tasman in 1642 but he did not land. The British explorer James Cook surveyed the coastline in 1769, the year in which the islands were claimed by the British. In 1840, under the treaty of Waitangi, the Maoris accepted British sovereignty, with Maoris retaining some territorial rights. The Maoris attempted to resist the loss of their land in the 1840s and 1860s; their resistance was defeated but concessions such as parliamentary representation were won. New Zealand was administered as part of the New South Wales colony until 1841, when it became a separate colony. In 1907 it was granted dominion status; in 1931 the Statute of Westminster tacitly acknowledged its independence, which was formally confirmed in 1947.

New Zealand forces took part in the First and Second World Wars, the Korean War and the Vietnam War (1965–72). The UK's entry into the EEC in 1973 forced New Zealand to form closer trade links with Australia; the two countries entered into a free-trade agreement in 1988. In the 1990s, Maori demands for compensation for land lost to European settlers were settled either by compensation payments or grants of land.

Post-war politics has been dominated by the National Party and the Labour Party, either forming governments on their own or in coalition with smaller parties. In the 2005 legislative election, the Labour Party won the most seats (50 to the National Party's 48) and formed a government with the Progressive Coalition, with additional support from the United Future, New Zealand First and Green parties. A legislative election is due in November 2008.

POLITICAL SYSTEM

There is no written constitution. The head of state is the British sovereign, represented by the governor-general, who is appointed on the advice of the New Zealand government. The unicameral House of Representatives has 121 members, elected for a three-year term; there are 69 members from single-member constituencies, which include seven Maori constituencies, and 52 allocated from party lists. A non-binding referendum in 1999 approved a reduction in the number of members to 100 in future parliaments. The prime minister and the cabinet are appointed by the governor-general on the advice of the legislature.

GOVERNOR-GENERAL
Governor-General and Commander-in-Chief, HE Anand Satyanand, *sworn in* August 2006

SELECTED GOVERNMENT MEMBERS *as at June 2008*
Prime Minister, Helen Clark
Deputy Prime Minister, Finance, Attorney-General, Michael Cullen
Defence, Phil Goff
Internal Affairs, Rick Barker
Foreign Affairs, Winston Peters

NEW ZEALAND HIGH COMMISSION
2nd Floor, New Zealand House, 80 Haymarket, London SW1Y 4TQ
T 020-7930 8422 W www.nzembassy.com/uk
High Commissioner, HE Rt. Hon. Jonathan Hunt, ONZ, *apptd* 2005

BRITISH HIGH COMMISSION
PO Box 1812, 44 Hill Street, Wellington 1
T (+64) (4) 924 2888 E bhc.wel@xtra.co.nz
W www.britain.org.nz
High Commissioner, HE George Fergusson *apptd* 2006

BRITISH COUNCIL
PO Box 1812, 44 Hill Street, Wellington 1
T (+64) (4) 924 2880 W www.britishcouncil.org/nz
Director, Paula Middleton

DEFENCE

With Australia and the USA, New Zealand formed the ANZUS Pacific security treaty in 1951, but its non-nuclear military policy led to disagreements with the USA and France in 1985, and in 1986 the USA suspended its ANZUS obligations towards New Zealand.

The army has 105 armoured personnel carriers. The navy has 2 frigates and 6 patrol and coastal vessels based at Auckland. The air force has 6 combat aircraft.
Military budget – US$1,680m (2007)
Military personnel – 9,051: army 4,580, navy 2,034, air force 2,437

ECONOMY AND TRADE

The economy is based largely on agriculture, although since the 1980s it has become more industrialised. Growth is driven by trade, particularly in agricultural products. The agricultural sector contributes 4.3 per cent of GDP, employs 7 per cent of the workforce and provides 70–80 per cent of exports. The main products are dairy products, meat, cereals, pulses, fruits, vegetables, wool and fish. The major industries are food processing, wood and paper products, textiles, machinery, transport equipment, financial services and tourism, which is growing steadily. Non-metallic minerals such as coal, limestone and dolomite are heavily exploited, while gold and iron production is economically important. Natural gas deposits in offshore and onshore fields are used for electricity generation, though a significant amount of the country's energy is derived from sustainable sources such as hydroelectric power. Industry contributes 26.2 per cent of GDP and services 69.6 per cent.

The main trading partners are Australia, the USA, Japan and China. Principal exports are dairy products, meat, wood, fish and machinery. The main imports are machinery and equipment, vehicles and aircraft, petroleum, electronics, textiles and plastics.
GNI – US$112,000m; US$26,750 per capita (2006)
Annual average growth of GDP – 3 per cent (2007 est)
Inflation rate – 2.5 per cent (2007 est)
Unemployment – 3.5 per cent (2007 est)
Total external debt – US$50,020m (2007 est)
Imports – US$26,400m (2006)
Exports – US$22,400m (2006)

BALANCE OF PAYMENTS
Trade – US$3,996m deficit (2006)
Current Account – US$9,082m deficit (2006)

*Trade with UK**	*2006*	*2007*
Imports from UK	£364,334,000	£346,286,995
Exports to UK	£610,229,000	£667,150,326

* Includes Niue, Tokelau and Cook Islands

COMMUNICATIONS

The national railway system is owned and operated by Tranz Rail Ltd; there are 4,128km of railway track. There are 92,931km of roads, of which about 64 per cent are surfaced. The principal airports are at Auckland, Wellington (North Island), Christchurch and Dunedin (South Island) and there are over 110 smaller airports and airfields around the country; the government holds an 83 per cent stake in Air New Zealand. Tauranga, Auckland, Christchurch, Dunedin and Napier are the main seaports.

The telephone system provided 1.7 million main lines in 2005, and there were 3.5 million mobile phone subscribers. In 2006 there were 3.2 million internet users.

EDUCATION AND HEALTH

Education is free of charge and compulsory between the ages of six and 16.
Gross enrolment ratio (percentage of relevant age group) – primary 102 per cent; secondary 121 per cent; tertiary 82 per cent (2006 est)
Health expenditure (per capita) – US$2,403 (2005)
Hospital beds (per 1,000 people) – 6.0 (2000–6)

MEDIA AND CULTURE

The broadcasting sector was deregulated in 1988. Two public networks, Television New Zealand and Maori TV, compete with four major private networks. There are four main national daily papers, including *The Press* and the *New Zealand Herald,* and a large number of radio stations, including Ruai Mai, a Maori-owned and operated broadcaster.

New Zealand's cultural history stretches back to the first Maori settlers, who brought the artform *Whakapapa,* a type of oral genealogy, to the islands. Notable cultural figures include the writer Katherine Mansfield (1888–1923), poet Sam Hunt (*b.* 1946), filmmakers Jane Campion (*b.* 1954) and Peter Jackson (*b.* 1961), opera singer Kiri Te Kanawa (*b.* 1944), and pop musicians Tim and Neil Finn (*b.* 1952 and 1958) who achieved international success under the names Split Enz and Crowded House.

TERRITORIES

TOKELAU

Tokelau is a group of three atolls: Fakaofo, Nukunonu and Atafu. Formerly part of Britain's Gilbert and Ellis Islands colony, they were transferred to New Zealand administration in 1926 and proclaimed part of New Zealand in 1949.

The Council of Ongoing Government (cabinet) omprises three *Faipule* (village leaders) and three *ulenuku* (village mayors), one from each atoll; the osition of *Ulu-o-Tokelau* (leader) is rotated among the ıree *Faipule* members annually. The *General Fono*, which as 20 members elected for a three-year term, has ·gislative powers. Each atoll has a *Taupulega* (council of lders). Referendums on self-government in 2006 and 007 failed to achieve the two-thirds majority required to hange Tokelau's status. The principal economic activities re subsistence farming, copra, handicrafts and the sale of ostage stamps and coins.

dministrator, David Payton, *apptd* 2006

'HE ROSS DEPENDENCY

Jew Zealand has administrative responsibility for the Ross Dependency. This is defined as all the Antarctic slands and territories between 160° E. and 150° W. ongitude which are situated south of the 60° S. parallel, ncluding Edward VII Land and portions of Victoria Land *ee also* The North and South Poles).

ASSOCIATED STATES

COOK ISLANDS

'he Cook Islands consist of the 15 volcanic islands and oral atolls of Rarotonga, Aitutaki, Mangaia, Atiu, Mauke, Aitiaro, Manuae, Takutea, Palmerston, Penrhyn or 'ongareva, Manihiki, Rakahanga, Suwarrow, Pukapuka or)anger, and Nassau in the southern Pacific Ocean. A ormer British protectorate, since 1965 the islands have een self-governing in free association with New Zealand. Queen Elizabeth II has a representative on the islands, and here is a New Zealand high commissioner. There is a 24-member legislative assembly, and a house of Ariki nade up of traditional leaders which advises on raditional matters; executive power is exercised by a rime minister and a cabinet responsible to the legislature. 'he main economic activities are tourism, agriculture especially tropical fruits), fruit processing, fishing, nanufacture of clothing and handicrafts, and earl-fishing.

HM Representative, Sir Frederick Goodwin, KBE

Prime Minister, Jim Marurai

NIUE

Niue was part of the Cook Islands group but was dministered separately after 1903. Since 1974 the island has been self-governing in free association with New Zealand. A New Zealand high commissioner represents both the Queen and the New Zealand government. There s a 20-member legislative assembly, and executive power s exercised by a prime minister and a three-member abinet drawn from the assembly's members. The principal economic activities are agriculture and fishing, ourism, handicrafts, food processing and the sale of postage stamps.

New Zealand High Commissioner, Anton Ojala, *apptd* 2005

NICARAGUA

República de Nicaragua – Republic of Nicaragua

Area – 129,494 sq. km
Capital – Managua; population, 920,000 (2007 est)
Major cities – Chinandega, Esteli, León, Masaya
Currency – Córdoba (C$) of 100 centavos
Population – 5,675,356 rising at 1.86 per cent per year (2007 est). Three quarters are of mixed race, around 15 per cent are white and the remaining 10 per cent are West Indian or Indian
Religion – Roman Catholicism (59 per cent), Protestantism (22 per cent) (est). An estimated 16 per cent of the population has no religious affiliation
Language – Spanish (official), English, Miskito
Population density – 46 per sq. km (2006)
Urban population – 58.1 per cent (2005 est)
Median age (years) – 21.3 (2007 est)
National anthem – 'Salve a ti, Nicaragua' ['Hail to You, Nicaragua']
National day – 15 September (Independence Day)
Life expectancy (years) – 70.92 (2007 est)
Mortality rate – 4.42 (2007 est)
Birth rate – 24.12 (2007 est)
Infant mortality rate – 27.14 (2007 est)
Death penalty – Abolished for all crimes (since 1979)
CPI score – 2.6 (2007)
Population below poverty line – 48 per cent (2005)

CLIMATE AND TERRAIN

The narrow Pacific coastal plain is separated from the broad Atlantic coastal plain by volcanic mountains and lakes Managua and Nicaragua. Elevation extremes range from 2,438m (Mogoton) at the highest point to 0m (Pacific Ocean) at the lowest. The climate is generally tropical near the coast, with average temperatures in Managua ranging from 20°C in January to 34°C in August. The country is subject to frequent earthquakes.

HISTORY AND POLITICS

The area was settled by Indians from Mexico and Mesoamerica from the tenth century AD. Spanish colonisation began in 1523 but in the 17th and 18th centuries the British were the dominant presence on the Caribbean coast, with the Spanish controlling the Pacific plain. Independence from Spain was achieved in 1821 and the area was initially part of Mexico. In 1823 it became part of the United Provinces of Central America but seceded from the federation and became fully independent in 1838. British control of the Caribbean coast was ceded to Nicaragua in 1860.

In 1893, José Santos Zelaya established a dictatorship that lasted until 1909, when he was overthrown by US marines. Anastasio Somoza established a dictatorship in 1938 and ruled until his assassination in 1956, when he was succeeded by his sons Luis and Anastasio. The family amassed a huge fortune in its 44 years in power, until it was overthrown in 1979 by a popular revolt led by the *Frente Sandinista de Liberacíon Nacional* (FSLN), popularly known as the Sandinistas.

The Sandinistas' socialist government redistributed land and promoted education and health services, but was opposed by US-backed right-wing guerrillas (the Contras). The civil war lasted until the Sandinistas were unexpectedly defeated in the 1990 elections by a coalition of opposition parties. Ceasefires and disarmament were agreed with different Contra factions in 1990 and 1994. The country has struggled to recover from the effects of the civil war. Although some foreign debt has been cancelled, poverty is widespread and rises in fuel prices and the cost of living provoked protests, some violent, in 2005.

After the civil war, governments were liberal or liberal-dominated coalitions, keeping the FSLN from power even though it was often the largest party in the legislature. However, in the 2006 presidential and legislative elections, the FSLN candidate, Daniel Ortega (president 1984–90) was elected president and the FSLN became the largest party in the assembly, with 38 seats.

POLITICAL SYSTEM

The 1987 constitution was amended in 1995 to reduce the presidential term; further changes reducing the power of the presidency came into effect in 2007. The executive president is directly elected for a five-year term; a second term may be served, but terms may not be consecutive. There is a unicameral legislature, the National Assembly, with 90 members directly elected for a five-year term; unsuccessful presidential and vice-presidential candidates may be awarded a seat if they receive more than the average percentage of the vote in each electoral district. The cabinet is appointed by the president.

HEAD OF STATE

President, Daniel Ortega, *elected* 5 November 2006, *sworn in* 11 January 2007
Vice-President, Jaime Morales

SELECTED GOVERNMENT MEMBERS *as at June 2008*

Defence, Ruth Tapia Roa
Finance, Alberto Guevara
Foreign Affairs, Samuel Santos
Interior, Ana Isabel Morales Mazún

EMBASSY OF NICARAGUA

Suite 31, Vicarage House, 58–60 Kensington Church Street, London W8 4DP
T 020-7938 2373 E embaniclondon@btconnect.com
Ambassador Extraordinary and Plenipotentiary, HE Piero P. Coen, *apptd* 2005

BRITISH AMBASSADOR

Ambassador Extraordinary and Plenipotentiary, HE Tom Kennedy, resident at San José, Costa Rica

DEFENCE

The army has 127 main battle tanks and 166 armoured personnel carriers. The navy has 24 patrol and coastal vessels at 3 bases. The air force has 7 aircraft and 16 helicopters.
Military budget – US$36m (2007)
Military personnel – 14,000: army 12,000, navy 800, air force 1,200
Conscription duration – 18–36 months

ECONOMY AND TRADE

Progress towards economic recovery and reconstruction after the civil war was reversed in 1998 by Hurricane Mitch, which caused widespread devastation and left 20 per cent of the population homeless. Economic growth since has been slow and the country is dependent on foreign aid, creating a large foreign debt. Some debt relief was provided in 2004 and 2006, but the country remains very poor. Nearly half the population lives below the poverty line, and unemployment and underemployment are widespread. Ratification of the US-Central America Free Trade Agreement in 2005 has helped to expand exports and attract investment.

Agriculture is the mainstay of the economy, accounting for 17 per cent of GDP and 29 per cent of employment. The main commercial crops are coffee, beef, prawns, lobsters, tobacco, sugar and peanuts. Industry includes food and timber processing, the manufacture of chemicals, machinery, metal products, textiles and clothing, oil refining and tourism. Industry contributes 26 per cent of GDP and services 57 per cent. The main trading partners are the USA, Mexico, Venezuela and other Central and South American countries. Principal exports are the main commercial crops and gold. The main imports are consumer goods, machinery and equipment, raw materials and petroleum products.
GNI – US$5,200m; US$930 per capita (2006)
Annual average growth of GDP – 2.9 per cent (2007 est)
Inflation rate – 9.8 per cent (2005 est)
Unemployment – 5.6 per cent (2007 est)
Total external debt – US$3,702m (2007 est)
Imports – US$3,000m (2006)
Exports – US$1,000m (2006)

BALANCE OF PAYMENTS

Trade – US$1,949m deficit (2006)
Current Account – US$700m deficit (2006)

Trade with UK	*2005*	*2006*
Imports from UK	£2,291,000	£3,124,000
Exports to UK	£6,694,000	£11,584,000

COMMUNICATIONS

The Inter-American Highway runs between Nicaraguan's Honduran and Costa Rican borders while the Inter-Oceanic Highway runs from Corinto on the Pacific coast via Managua to Rama, where there is a natural waterway to Bluefields on the Atlantic. There are 19,036km of roads and 6km of operable railway. The main airport is at Managua, and there are a further 160 airports and airfields around the country. The chief ports are Corinto (Pacific) and Bluefields and El Bluff (Caribbean Sea). There are 2,220km of inland waterways, mostly on lakes Managua and Nicaragua, and Lake Nicaragua is the chief element in a 2006 proposal to construct a canal linking the Pacific and Caribbean coasts.

The telephone system is being expanded and upgraded with the help of foreign investment. In 2006 there were 248,000 main telephone lines in use, 1.8 million mobile phone subscribers, and 155,000 internet users.

EDUCATION AND HEALTH

Literacy rate – 76.7 per cent (2004 est)
Gross enrolment ratio (percentage of relevant age group) –

primary 116 per cent; secondary 66 per cent (2006 est)
Health expenditure (per capita) – US$75 (2005)
Hospital beds (per 1,000 people) – 0.9 (2000–6)

MEDIA

There are three daily newspapers, including the pro-Sandinista *El Nuevo Diario.* Three commercial networks provide television services, while there are a large number of radio stations, mostly concentrated in Managua.

NIGER

République du Niger – Republic of Niger

Area – 1,267,000 sq. km
Capital – Niamey; population, 915,000 (2007 est)
Major cities – Maradi, Zinder
Currency – Franc CFA of 100 centimes
Population – 12,894,865 rising at 2.9 per cent per year (2007 est); Hausa (56 per cent), Djerma (22 per cent), Tuareg (9.3 per cent), Fula (8.5 per cent), Kanouri Manga (4.7 per cent)
Religion – Islam (90 per cent), Christianity (5 per cent) (est)
Language – French (official), Hausa, Djerma
Population density – 11 per sq. km (2006)
Urban population – 23.3 per cent (2005 est)
Median age (years) – 16.5 (2007 est)
National anthem – 'La Nigérienne'
National day – 18 December (Republic Day)
Life expectancy (years) – 44.03 (2007 est)
Mortality rate – 20.59 (2007 est)
Birth rate – 50.16 (2007 est)
Infant mortality rate – 116.83 (2007 est)
Death penalty – Retained, but not used
CPI score – 2.6 (2007)
Health expenditure (per capita) – US$9 (2005)
Literacy rate – 14.4 per cent (2004 est)
Gross enrolment ratio (percentage of relevant age group) – primary 51 per cent; secondary 11 per cent; tertiary 1 per cent (2006 est)

CLIMATE AND TERRAIN

A landlocked state, the country is mostly desert, with low hills in the north and savannah in the south. Elevation extremes range from 2,022m (Mt Bagzane) at the highest point to 200m (Niger river) at the lowest. The Niger valley in the south-west and the seasonal part of Lake Chad in the south-east are the only well-watered areas. Average temperatures range from 24°C in January to 34°C in May.

HISTORY AND POLITICS

The area was divided between several kingdoms formed by different tribes (Tuareg, Songhai, Hausa, Fulani) from the 10th to 19th centuries. French colonial expansion from the 1880s brought the whole area under its control in 1898 and in 1904 it became part of French West Africa. The country became autonomous in 1958 and achieved full independence in 1960.

After a coup in 1974 the country was under military rule until popular agitation led to the reintroduction of civilian government in 1989, albeit under a one-party system. Other parties were legalised in 1990 and a multi-party constitution was introduced in 1992. This political liberalisation was reversed following a military coup in 1996 led by Brig. Ibrahim Barre Mainassara. He was assassinated in 1999 by the military, and political pluralism was restored.

In presidential and legislative elections in November 1999, Mamadou Tandja of the National Movement for Society in Development (MNSD) was elected president and the MNSD won an overall majority in the national assembly. In the 2004 elections, President Tandja was re-elected president, and the MNSD remained the largest party in the legislature but lost its overall majority.

In the early 1990s there was a revolt in the north by the Tuareg, who were seeking greater social equality and political representation. A 1995 peace agreement brought calm until 2007, when another armed revolt began, the rebels claiming that the 1995 agreement had not been fully implemented.

POLITICAL SYSTEM

Under the 1999 constitution, the head of state is a president directly elected for a five-year term, renewable only once. The unicameral legislature, the National Assembly, has 83 members, who are directly elected for a five-year term. The prime minister is appointed from the party with the parliamentary majority.

HEAD OF STATE

President, Mamadou Tandja, *elected* 24 November 1999, *sworn in* 22 December 1999, *re-elected* 4 December 2004

SELECTED GOVERNMENT MEMBERS *as at June 2008*

Prime Minister, Seyni Oumarou
Finance and Economy, Ali Mahamane Lamine Zène
Foreign Affairs, Aissatou Mindaoudou
Interior, Albade Abouba
Defence, Djida Hamadou

EMBASSY OF THE REPUBLIC OF NIGER

154 rue de Longchamp, 75116 Paris, France
T (+33) (1) 4504 8060
Ambassador Extraordinary and Plenipotentiary, HE Adamou Seydou, *apptd* 2003

BRITISH AMBASSADOR

HE Dr Nicholas Westcott, CMG, *apptd* 2007, resident at Accra, Ghana

DEFENCE

The army has 22 armoured personnel carriers.
Military budget – US$47m (2007 est)
Military personnel – 5,300: army 5,200, air force 100; paramilitary 5,400
Conscription duration – 24 months (selective)

ECONOMY AND TRADE

Niger is one of the poorest countries in the world, with the majority of the population living below the poverty line. Economic progress has been constrained by political instability, recurrent droughts, desertification, over-grazing and rapid population growth, leaving the country dependent on foreign aid. Its huge foreign debt burden was much reduced by debt relief and cancellation in 2000 and 2005.

The mainstay of the economy is subsistence agriculture and herding, which account for 39 per cent of GDP and engage 90 per cent of the population; the main crops are cowpeas, cotton, peanuts, millet, sorghum, cassava, rice and livestock. The main industry and most lucrative export is uranium, but this makes the economy vulnerable to fluctuations in global prices. Efforts are being made to diversify into exploitation of other mineral resources. The other industries are food processing and manufacturing of cement, bricks, soap, textiles and chemicals. Industry contributes 17 per cent of GDP and services 44 per cent.

The main trading partners are France, the USA and Nigeria. Principal exports are uranium ore, livestock and cowpeas. The main imports are foodstuffs, machinery, vehicles and parts, petroleum and cereals.

GNI – US$3,700m; US$270 per capita (2006)
Annual average growth of GDP – 4.5 per cent (2007 est)
Inflation rate – 0.2 per cent (2004 est)
Total external debt – US$2,100m (2003 est)
Imports – US$800m (2006)
Exports – US$540m (2006)

BALANCE OF PAYMENTS
Trade – US$260m deficit (2006)
Current Account – US$307m deficit (2006)

Trade with UK	*2006*	*2007*
Imports from UK	£4,649,000	£3,913,716
Exports to UK	£261,000	£231,950

COMMUNICATIONS

Niger has no railways. Of the 14,500km of roads, less than 4,000km is surfaced. The Niger is navigable between September and March for 300km from Niamey to the Benin frontier. The principal airport is at Niamey; there are a further 27 airports and airfields around the country.

The telephone system is limited in extent, concentrated mainly in the south-west, and mobile phone distribution has grown rapidly. In 2005 there were 24,000 main lines in use, 300,000 mobile phone subscribers and 24,000 internet users.

MEDIA

Radio is the most important form of communication, and a growing sector; the state-owned broadcaster *Tele Sahel* faces competition from a number of private stations. Similarly, the single state-owned daily newspaper, *Le Sahel,* competes with a proliferating number of private publications.

NIGERIA

Federal Republic of Nigeria

Area – 923,768 sq. km
Capital – Abuja (declared the federal capital in 1991) population, 1,576,000 (2007 est)
Major cities – Abu, Benin City, Ibadan, Kaduna, Kano, Lagos, Maiduguri, Port Harcourt
Currency – Naira (N) of 100 kobo
Population – 135,031,164 rising at 2.38 per cent per year (2007 est); Hausa and Fula (29 per cent), Yoruba (21 per cent), Igbo (18 per cent), Ijaw (10 per cent), Kanuri (4 per cent), Ibibio (3.5 per cent), Tiv (2.5 per cent) (est)
Religion – Islam (50 per cent), Christianity (50 per cent) (est); indigenous beliefs are practised alongside Christianity or Islam
Language – English (official), Hausa, Yoruba, Igbo, Fulani
Population density – 159 per sq. km (2006)
Urban population – 48.3 per cent (2005 est)
Median age (years) – 18.7 (2007 est)
National anthem – 'Arise O Compatriots, Nigeria's Call Obey'
National day – 1 October (Independence Day)
Life expectancy (years) – 47.44 (2007 est)
Mortality rate – 16.68 (2007 est)
Birth rate – 40.2 (2007 est)
Infant mortality rate – 95.52 (2007 est)
HIV/AIDS adult prevalence – 3.5 per cent (2005 est)
Death penalty – Retained
CPI score – 2.2 (2007)
Population below poverty line – 60 per cent (2000 est)
Literacy rate – 66.8 per cent (2004 est)
Gross enrolment ratio (percentage of relevant age group) – primary 96 per cent; secondary 32 per cent; tertiary 10 per cent (2006 est)
Health expenditure (per capita) – US$27 (2005)
Hospital beds (per 1,000 people) – 1.2 (2000–6)

CLIMATE AND TERRAIN

The north is arid savannah and semi-desert. The south is tropical rainforest, with mangrove swamps along the coast. The Niger river forms a broad delta in the south, and there are mountains in the south-east. Elevation extremes range from 2,419m (Chappal Waddis) at the highest point to 0m (Atlantic Ocean) at the lowest. The climate varies across the country, with the north experiencing a single rainy season and colder winter temperatures; by contrast the south has two rainy seasons (in the spring and autumn) and an average temperature between 20°C and 30°C all year round.

HISTORY AND POLITICS

Nigeria was at the centre of the Nok culture from 500 BC to AD 200. Various kingdoms flourished in the area in the Middle Ages, and Islam was introduced to the north in the 13th century. The Oyo Empire was dominant in the south in the 17th century and the Muslim Sokoto Empire in the north in the 19th century. European traders had arrived on the coast in the 15th century and participated in the gold and slave trades. After Britain abolished slavery, several other powers attempted to exploit the slave trade in Nigeria, which led Britain to annex Lagos in 1861. Britain occupied the rest of Nigeria in stages during the late 19th century, uniting the whole of modern Nigeria into a single political and administrative unit by 1914. The country became a federation in 1954, and increasing degrees of internal self-government were introduced until the country became fully independent in 1960.

Independence unleashed ethnic and regional tensions, and there were two military coups in 1966; the first coup was Igbo-led and provoked an anti-Igbo counter-coup from the north. The following year, three eastern states seceded and set up the Igbo state of Biafra, sparking off a civil war. The conflict lasted until 1970, when Biafra surrendered and was reunited with Nigeria; despite an international relief effort, bombing and famine killed around one million people.

In the 30 years after 1967 there were several military coups and the governments during most of the period were military or military-dominated. Some of the regimes made efforts to reintroduce civilian government, legalise political parties and restore democracy but invariably suspended these when the results were unfavourable to them. Nigeria was suspended from the Commonwealth in 1995 because of human rights abuses against pro-democracy campaigners (most notably the hanging of activist Ken Saro-Wiwa) but was readmitted in 1999 after moves towards civilian rule began. Following presidential and legislative elections in 1999, a civilian president and government took office and military rule ended. The first civilian-run elections in 20 years were held in 2003.

Ethnic and regional tensions have been more openly and violently expressed since 1999, including calls for secession by various groups. The main source of tension is the religious divide between the predominantly Muslim north, where Shariah law has been introduced, and the predominantly Christian south. There have been sporadic violent clashes in which thousands have died, leading to internal migration of Christians from the north. The latest trouble spot is the Niger delta, where militants have attacked oil facilities and kidnapped foreign oil workers, demanding greater local control over oil revenues.

The 2007 presidential and legislative elections were condemned as undemocratic by international observers amid reports of violence, intimidation and ballot-rigging. The presidential election was won by Umaru Musa Yar'Adua of the People's Democratic Party (PDP), which also retained its majority in both houses of parliament.

POLITICAL SYSTEM

The country is a federal democratic republic. Under the 1999 constitution, the executive president is directly elected for a four-year term, renewable only once. As head of the government, the president appoints the federal executive council, which must be approved by the senate. The National Assembly is bicameral; the House of Representatives has 360 members and the senate has 109 members, both elected for a four-year term.

HEAD OF STATE

President, Umaru Musa Yar'Adua, *elected* 21 April 2007, *re-elected* 29 May 2007
Vice-President, Goodluck Jonathan

SELECTED GOVERNMENT MEMBERS *as at June 2008*

Defence, Mahmud Yayale Ahmed
Finance, Shamsudeen Usman
Foreign Affairs, Ojo Maduekwe
Internal Affairs, Maj.-Gen. (retd) Godwin Abbe

HIGH COMMISSION FOR THE FEDERAL REPUBLIC OF NIGERIA

Nigeria House, 9 Northumberland Avenue, London WC2N 5BX
T 020-7839 1244 **E** information@nigeriahc.org.uk
W www.nigeria.org.uk
High Commissioner, vacant

BRITISH HIGH COMMISSION

Shehu Shagari Way (North), Maitama, Abuja
T (+234) (1) 523 2010 **E** chancery@abuja.mail.fco.gov.uk
High Commissioner, HE Robert Dewar, CMG, *apptd* 2007

BRITISH COUNCIL

Plot 3645, IBB Way, Maitama, PMB 550, Garki, Abuja
T (+234) (9) 4137 8707 **W** www.britishcouncil.org/nigeria
Director, Peter Upton

FEDERAL STRUCTURE

The federal republic is divided into 36 states and the Federal Capital Territory: Abia, Adamawa, Akwa Ibom, Anambra, Bauchi, Bayelsa, Benue, Borno, Cross River, Delta, Ebonyi, Edo, Ekiti, Enugu, Gombe, Imo, Jigawa, Kaduna, Kano, Katsina, Kebbi, Kogi, Kwara, Lagos, Nassarawa, Niger, Ogun, Ondo, Osun, Oyo, Plateau, Rivers, Sokoto, Taraba, Yobe and Zamfara.

DEFENCE

The army has 276 main battle tanks, 157 light tanks and over 437 armoured personnel carriers. The navy has 1 frigate, 1 corvette and 21 patrol and coastal vessels at 3 bases. The air force has 75 combat aircraft and 5 armed helicopters.
Military budget – US$988m (2007)
Military personnel – 80,000: army 62,000, navy 8,000, air force 10,000; paramilitaries 82,000

ECONOMY AND TRADE

Nigeria is the leading sub-Saharan oil producer, enjoying an oil boom in the 1970s and currently benefiting again from high oil prices. The profits from the 1970s boom were dissipated by mismanagement and corruption. The majority of the population received little benefit, and 70 per cent live below the poverty line. Past governments also failed to diversify the economy away from its dependence on the oil industry, which accounts for 20 per cent of GDP, 80 per cent of budgetary revenues and 95 per cent of foreign exchange earnings. However, the current government is showing the political will to introduce market-oriented reforms that will improve fiscal and monetary management, curb inflation and address regional agitation for wider distribution of oil revenues. Factors such as security and the inadequate infrastructure remain obstacles to foreign investment, but infrastructure improvements are a 2008 budget priority. The recent high oil revenues have, however, freed Nigeria from much of its foreign debt, enabling it to pay off US$30bn (£15bn) in 2006.

Apart from crude oil, Nigeria exploits its reserves of coal, tin and columbite. The mainstay of the economy is agriculture, mostly at subsistence level, which generates 17.6 per cent of GDP and engages 70 per cent of the population. The main crops include cocoa, peanuts, palm oil, maize, rice, sorghum and millet. In addition to its main activities of oil production, mining and processing agricultural products, the industrial sector produces textiles, cement and other construction materials and footwear. Industry contributes 53.1 per cent of GDP and services 29.3 per cent.

The main trading partners are the USA (49 per cent of exports), Brazil, China and EU countries. Principal exports are oil and oil products, cocoa and rubber. The main imports are machinery, chemicals, transport equipment, manufactured goods, food and live animals. Agricultural output has failed to keep pace with rapid population growth, changing Nigeria from a net food exporter to a food importer.

GNI – US$90,000m; US$620 per capita (2006)
Annual average growth of GDP – 6.1 per cent (2007 est)
Inflation rate – 6.5 per cent (2007 est)
Unemployment – 5.8 per cent (2006 est)
Total external debt – US$5,815m (2007 est)
Imports – US$21,800m (2006)
Exports – US$31,000m (2004)

BALANCE OF PAYMENTS
Trade – US$23,307m surplus (2006)
Current Account – US$13,891m surplus (2006)

Trade with UK	*2006*	*2007*
Imports from UK	£836,230,000	£1,012,798,363
Exports to UK	£217,960,000	£337,655,042

COMMUNICATIONS

Internal long-distance travel is mostly by air; there are 70 airports and airfields, including the principal airports at Lagos, Kano and Port Harcourt. The Nigerian railway network, which is controlled by the Nigerian Railway Corporation, has 3,505km of track. There are 194,394km of roads, and 8,600km of waterways, mostly on the Niger and Benue rivers. The main seaports are Lagos, Port Harcourt, Warri and Calabar.

Both the fixed-line and mobile phone telephone networks are expanding quickly. In 2006 there were 1.7 million main lines in use, 32.3 million mobile phone subscribers and 8 million internet users.

MEDIA

There are ten main daily newspapers, supplemented by weekly publications, and popular titles include *The Guardian* and *Punch*. The Nigerian Television Authority (NTA) is a government-run broadcaster operating alongside a large number of private and commercial networks and in addition to local services. Radio provides Nigerians with their main access to the media, and international broadcasters such as the BBC are popular.

CULTURE

Nigerians are responsible for several key post-colonial works of literature, most notably *Things Fall Apart* (1958) by Chinua Achebe (*b.* 1930), a historical novel examining the effects of British colonialism on the Igbo tribe. It has been translated into 50 languages, making Achebe the most translated author in Africa. Other significant writers include Nobel prize winner Wole Soyinka (*b.* 1934) and Ken Saro-Wiwa (1941–1995), whose political activism resulted in his death at the hands of the military government.

'Nollywood' is the colloquial name for the Nigerian film industry, reported by *Time* magazine to be the third biggest in the world, behind the USA and India, and worth around US$250m (£125m) a year. It is estimated that up to 2,000 films a year are produced, many of which outsell even the biggest Hollywood blockbusters in Africa. Most films go straight to DVD or VCD (video CD) and are sold at low prices, helping to spread popularity and increase demand.

Fela Kuti (1938–97) is Nigeria's most famous musician. He pioneered Afrobeat, a style combining traditional Yoruba rhythms with jazz and funk. The movement became inextricably linked with Kuti's personal politics, which saw him embrace black power, campaign against suppression of human rights in Africa and later twice run (unsuccessfully) for the Nigerian presidency.

NORWAY

Kongeriket Norge – Kingdom of Norway

Area – 323,802 sq. km, of which Svalbard and Jan Mayen have a combined area of 63,080 sq. km
Capital – Oslo; population, 835,000 (2007 est)
Major cities – Bergen, Stavanger, Trondheim
Currency – Krone of 100 ore
Population – 4,627,926 rising at 0.36 per cent per year (2007 est)
Religion – Protestantism (88 per cent), Islam (2 per cent), Roman Catholicism (1 per cent) (est)
Language – Bokmal and Nynorsk Norwegian (both official), Sami (official in six municipalities)
Population density – 15 per sq. km (2006)
Urban population – 80.5 per cent (2005 est)
Median age (years) – 38.7 (2007 est)
National anthem – 'Ja, Vi Elsker Dette Landet' ['Yes, We Love This Country']
National day – 17 May (Constitution Day)
Life expectancy (years) – 79.67 (2007 est)
Mortality rate – 9.37 (2007 est)
Birth rate – 11.27 (2007 est)
Infant mortality rate – 3.64 (2007 est)
Death penalty – Abolished for all crimes (since 1979)
CPI score – 8.7 (2007)

CLIMATE AND TERRAIN

The terrain is mountainous, with elevated, barren tablelands separated by deep, narrow valleys. The coastline is deeply indented with numerous fjords and fringed with rocky islands; in 2005 Geirangerfjord and

Naeroyfjord in the west were awarded UNESCO World Heritage status. Elevation extremes range from 2,469m (Galdhopiggen) at the highest point to 0m (Norwegian Sea) at the lowest.

Part of the country lies north of the Arctic Circle, and at the North Cape the sun does not appear to set between about 14 May and 29 July, causing the phenomenon known as the midnight sun; conversely, there is no apparent sunrise from about 18 November to 24 January. Average temperatures in Oslo range between −7°C in February to 22°C in August, though winter temperatures in the north can drop to −15°C.

HISTORY AND POLITICS

Norway became a unified country under rule of King Harald Fairhair in *c.*900 but dissolved after his death and was reunified by Olav II in *c.*1016–28. Canute brought Norway under Danish rule in 1028 but the throne reverted on his death to Magnus I. When the royal house died out in the 14th century, the Danish monarch was the nearest heir and in 1397 Norway, Denmark and Sweden were united under a single monarch in the Kalmar Union. Sweden seceded from the union in 1523, but Norway continued to be ruled by the Danish monarch until the end of the Napoleonic wars.

In 1814 Norway was ceded to Sweden; it continued to have its own parliament although the cabinet was appointed by the king of Sweden. Internal self-government was achieved in 1884, but growing tension over the government's lack of control led to the union being dissolved and Norway became independent in 1905. The first king of the newly independent country was a Danish prince who took the throne as King Haakon VII.

The country was neutral in the First World War, but in the Second World War Norway was invaded and occupied by Germany from 1940 until 1945. Norway joined NATO in 1949 and was a founder member of the European Free Trade Association in 1960. Despite this integration with Europe, the Norwegians rejected opportunities to join the EU in referendums in 1972 and 1994.

Since 1945 the Labour Party has held office for long periods, either on its own or in coalition with smaller parties, and pursued policies of economic planning and an extensive welfare state. After a period in opposition, the Labour Party returned to power in 2005 after winning a majority of seats in the legislative election, forming a coalition government with the Socialist Left and Centre parties.

POLITICAL SYSTEM

Norway is a constitutional monarchy with a hereditary monarch as head of state. Under the 1814 constitution, the unicameral *Storting* has 169 members who are directly elected for a four-year term. When legislative matters are under discussion, the *Storting* divides into two chambers, the *Lagting* (upper chamber) and the *Odelsting* (lower chamber); a 2007 constitutional amendment abolished this bicameral division with effect from the next election (due 2009). The prime minister, who is responsible to parliament, appoints the other ministers.

HEAD OF STATE

HM The King of Norway, King Harald V, KG, GCVO, *born* 21 February 1937; *succeeded* 17 January 1991
Heir, HRH Crown Prince Haakon Magnus, *born* 20 July 1973

SELECTED GOVERNMENT MEMBERS *as at June 2008*

Prime Minister, Jens Stoltenberg
Defence, Anne-Grete Strom-Erichsen
Finance, Kristin Halvorsen
Foreign Affairs, Jonas Gahr Store

ROYAL NORWEGIAN EMBASSY

25 Belgrave Square, London SW1X 8QD
T 020-7591 5500 E emb.london@mfa.no
W www.norway.org.uk
Ambassador Extraordinary and Plenipotentiary, HE Bjarne Lindstrom, *apptd* 2005

BRITISH EMBASSY

Thomas Heftyesgate 8, 0244 Oslo
T (+47) 2313 2700 W www.britishembassy.gov.uk/norway
Ambassador Extraordinary and Plenipotentiary, HE David Powell, *apptd* 2006

BRITISH COUNCIL

Storgaten 10 B, 0155 Oslo
T (+47) (22) 396 190 W www.britishcouncil.org/norway
Director, Simon Giverin

DEFENCE

The army has 165 main battle tanks, 157 armoured infantry fighting vehicles and 189 armoured personnel carriers. The navy has 6 submarines, 5 frigates and 7 patrol and coastal vessels at two bases. The air force has 52 combat aircraft.

Military expenditure – US$5,010m (2006)
Military personnel – 15,800: army 6,700, navy 4,100, air force 5,000
Conscription duration – 12 months plus refresher training

ECONOMY AND TRADE

Norway's prosperity depends primarily upon its oil and gas sectors and fisheries. The third largest oil exporter after Saudi Arabia and Russia, oil and gas account for one-third of net exports. Reserves in currently operating fields will be exhausted in the next 20 years but there are plans, opposed by environmentalists, to explore for oil and gas in the Barents Sea and other areas that are becoming more accessible as the Arctic ice cap retreats. Norway has planned for the time when current oil and gas reserves are exhausted by investing its budget surpluses in a government petroleum fund, now valued at US$250bn (£125bn).

The nature of the terrain restricts agriculture, which generates 2.4 per cent of GDP. The main industries apart from oil and gas are fishing, forestry, food processing, shipbuilding, pulp and paper products, metals, chemicals, mining and textiles. Shipping freight services are also significant, with Norwegian companies controlling 10 per cent of the world's shipping fleet. Industry contributes 42.9 per cent of GDP and services 54.7 per cent.

The main trading partners are EU countries, the USA and China. Principal exports are crude oil and petroleum products, machinery and equipment, metals, chemicals, ships and fish. The main imports are machinery and equipment, chemicals, metals and foodstuffs.

GNI – US$318,900m; US$68,440 per capita (2006)

Annual average growth of GDP – 4.9 per cent (2007 est)
Inflation rate – 0.4 per cent (2007 est)
Unemployment – 2.4 per cent (2007 est)
Total external debt – US$469,100m (2007)
Imports – US$63,400m (2006)
Exports – US$120,500m (2006)

BALANCE OF PAYMENTS
Trade – US$57,098m surplus (2006)
Current Account – US$58,278m surplus (2006)

Trade with UK	*2006*	*2007*
Imports from UK	£2,123,700,000	£2,749,742,456
Exports to UK	£14,755,152,000	£14,595,002,100

COMMUNICATIONS

There are 4,043km of railways and 92,513km of roads. The rail network stops at Bodo, a little way north of the Arctic Circle, and there are few roads in the far north, to which the main means of transport is by sea; the state ferries operating between Bergen and Kirkenes carry freight, vehicles and passengers. There are 98 airports and airfields, including the principal airports at Oslo, Bergen, Kristiansand and Stavanger. The main ports are Oslo, Bergen, Kristiansand, Tonsberg, Stavanger and Narvik, and there is a large merchant fleet, with 715 ships of over 1,000 tonnes registered in Norway and 872 registered abroad.

The fixed-line telephone system serves all parts of the country and mobile phone distribution has grown rapidly. In 2006 there were 2.05 millon main lines in use, 5.04 million mobile phone subscribers and 4.07 million internet users.

EDUCATION AND HEALTH

Education from six to 16 is free of charge and compulsory in the basic schools, and free from 16 to 19 years. The majority of pupils receive post-compulsory schooling at upper secondary schools, regional colleges, and universities and specialist colleges.
Gross enrolment ratio (percentage of relevant age group) – primary 98 per cent; secondary 113 per cent; tertiary 78 per cent (2006 est)
Health expenditure (per capita) – US$5,910 (2005)
Hospital beds (per 1,000 people) – 4.2 (2000–6)

MEDIA AND CULTURE

Broadcasting is deregulated and there are a number of commercial channels, with satellite networks becoming increasingly popular. There are five widely read national daily newspapers and a single national weekly newspaper, *Morgenbladet*.

Celebrated cultural figures include the artist Edvard Munch (1863–1944), responsible for one of the world's most recognisable paintings, *The Scream* (1893); writer Knut Hamsun (1859–1952), winner of the Nobel prize in 1920; dramatist Henrik Ibsen (1828–1906); the composer Edvard Grieg (1843–1907) and the 1980s pop group A-ha, which has sold over 30 million albums worldwide.

TERRITORIES

SVALBARD, area 61,020 sq. km; population 2,214 (2007 est)
The Svalbard archipelago consists of Spitsbergen, the main island, North East Land, the Wiche Islands, Barents Island, Edge Island, Prince Charles Foreland, Hope Island and Bear Island. Around 60 per cent of the islands in the archipelago are covered by ice. Over half of the Svalbard archipelago has been designated as a national park, such is the diversity of its wildlife, and a global seed repository has been established there. Norway's sovereignty was recognised by treaty in 1920 but the other signatories were granted equal rights to exploit mineral deposits, although this right is now only exercised by Russia. The main economic activity is coal mining, with some hunting of seal, reindeer and arctic fox.

JAN MAYEN ISLAND, area 377 sq. km; the only residents are the staff of the radio and meteorological stations. The island is barren, volcanic and partially covered by glaciers, with no exploitable natural resources. It became Norwegian territory in 1929.

NORWEGIAN ANTARCTIC TERRITORY

The Norwegian Antarctic Territory consists of Queen Maud Land, Bouvet Island and Peter the First Island. Claimed in 1938, Queen Maud Land is a sector of the Antarctic content which extends from 45° E. to 20° E. Peter the First Island was formally claimed in 1931 and is the only claimed area covered under the Antarctic treaty that is not part of the main land mass. Bouvet Island was claimed in 1930 (*see also* The North and South Poles).

OMAN

Saltanat Uman – Sultanate of Oman

Area – 212,460 sq. km
Capital – Muscat (Masqat); population, 620,000 (2007 est)
Major cities – Bawsar, Matrah, Salalah, As Sib
Currency – Rial Omani (OR) of 1,000 baisas
Population – 3,204,897 rising at 3.23 per cent per year (2007 est)
Religion – The majority of the population practises Islam, while there are also Hindu and Christian minorities
Language – Arabic (official), English, Baluchi, Urdu
Population density – 8 per sq. km (2006)
Urban population – 78.6 per cent (2005 est)
Median age (years) – 18.9 (2007 est)
National anthem – 'Nashid as-Salaam as-Sultani' ['The Sultan's Anthem']
National day – 18 November (Birthday of Sultan Qaboos)
Life expectancy (years) – 73.62 (2007 est)
Mortality rate – 3.78 (2007 est)
Birth rate – 35.76 (2007 est)
Infant mortality rate – 18.28 (2007 est)
Death penalty – Retained
CPI score – 4.7 (2007)

CLIMATE AND TERRAIN

Oman lies at the south-eastern corner of the Arabian peninsula and includes territory at the tip of the Musandam peninsula which is separated from the rest of the country by the UAE. There are mountains in the north and the south-west of the country, divided by nearly 643km of high desert plateau. This descends to a fertile plain on the Arabian Sea coast. Elevation extremes range from 2,980m (Jabal Shams) at the highest point to 0m (Arabian Sea) at the lowest. Temperatures and humidity are high throughout the year; the highest temperatures are recorded inland, but the high humidity often makes coastal areas the most inhospitable. Rainfall is low and falls mostly in December and January. Average temperatures in Muscat range from 20°C in January to 40°C in July.

HISTORY AND POLITICS

Oman began to build an empire in the Middle East from the eighth century AD and remained largely unchallenged until the arrival in 1507 of the Portuguese, who were ousted in 1650. Following a civil war in the early 18th century, an independent sultanate was established in 1749 by the founder of the dynasty that still rules the country. By the early 19th century, Omani rule extended to the east African coast and parts of Persia and Baluchistan (in modern Pakistan). The kingdom came under British influence from the late 19th century until 1951.

The country was divided from 1913, with religious leaders in control of the interior and the sultan of the coastal regions; the sultan recognised the autonomy of the interior in 1920. The interior's attempts to assert its independence led to further clashes between the sultan and religious leaders in the 1950s, but by 1959 the sultan had established control over the whole country. An insurrection in the south by left-wing rebels supported by South Yemen began in 1965 and was defeated with British military assistance in 1975. The discovery and subsequent exploitation of oil in the mid-1960s led to the steady economic transformation of Oman, and in 1970 the sultan was overthrown in a bloodless coup by his son, Sultan Qaboos bin Said al-Said, who initiated a modernisation programme.

A degree of political liberalisation has occurred in the past 20 years but the country is still essentially an absolute monarchy. In 1996 a succession mechanism was established and the system of government codified. Universal adult suffrage was introduced in 2002; the franchise was previously restricted to an electoral college of tribal leaders, intellectuals and businessmen (including some women) from 1997. The first direct election to the consultative council was held in 2000 and the first by universal adult suffrage in 2003. In the 2007 election, 38 members were returned and 46 new members were elected.

POLITICAL SYSTEM

In 1996 the sultan issued the basic statute of the state, which decreed Oman to be a hereditary absolute monarchy. There is no legislature; legislation is by decree of the sultan, and is implemented by the cabinet of ministers, which the sultan appoints. The sultan is advised by the Consultative Council *(Majlis al-Shura)*, which has 84 members directly elected for a four-year term. The council has the right to review legislation, question ministers and make policy proposals. In 1997 the sultan set up the Council of State *(Majlis al-Dawlah)*, which has 59 members appointed by him; it is intended to facilitate 'constructive cooperation between the government and the citizens'. There are no political parties.

HEAD OF STATE

HM The Sultan of Oman, Prime Minister, C-in-C of the Armed Forces, Sultan Qaboos bin Said al-Said, *succeeded following a coup,* 23 July 1970

SELECTED GOVERNMENT MEMBERS *as at June 2008*

Deputy Prime Minister, Fahd bin Mamud al-Said
Defence, Badr bin Saud bin Hareb al-Busaidi
Foreign Affairs, Yusuf bin Alawi bin Abdullah
Interior, Saud bin Ibrahim al-Busaidi
Economy, Ahmed bin Abdul Nabi Makki

EMBASSY OF THE SULTANATE OF OMAN
167 Queen's Gate, London SW7 5HE
T 020-7225 0001
Ambassador Extraordinary and Plenipotentiary, HE Hussain Ali Abdullatif, *apptd* 1995

BRITISH EMBASSY
PO Box 185, Mina al Fahal, 113 Muscat
T (+968) (24) 609 000 E enquiries.muscat@fco.gov.uk
W www.britishembassy.gov.uk/oman
Ambassador Extraordinary and Plenipotentiary, HE Noel Guckian, *apptd* 2005

BRITISH COUNCIL
PO Box 73, Road One, Madinat al Sultan, Qaboos West, 115 Muscat
T (+968) (24) 681 000 W www.britishcouncil.org/oman
Director, Steve McNulty

DEFENCE

The army has 117 main battle tanks and 216 armoured personnel carriers. The navy has 2 corvettes and 11 patrol and coastal vessels at 6 bases. The air force has 64 combat aircraft.

Military budget – US$3,230m (2007)
Military personnel – 42,600: army 25,000, navy 4,200, air force 5,000, Royal Household 6,400, foreign forces 2,000; paramilitary 4,400

ECONOMY AND TRADE

Although its production is more modest than other Gulf states, oil is the mainstay of Oman's economy and accounts for 80 per cent of government revenue. Oil reserves are dwindling and development plans centre on diversification, industrialisation and privatisation, with the aim of reducing the oil sector's contribution to GDP to 9 per cent by 2020. Industrial development is focused on natural gas production, metal manufacturing, petrochemicals and trans-shipment ports, with plans also to develop tourism and communication technology industries. Improved training, especially in IT and business skills, is intended to enable the local population to replace expatriate workers.

Agriculture and fishing account for 22.2 per cent of GDP, producing dates, limes, bananas, alfalfa and vegetables as well as fish. The main industries apart from oil and natural gas extraction are oil refining, liquefied natural gas production, construction and production of cement, copper, steel, chemicals and optic fibre. Industry accounts for 38.3 per cent of GDP and services for 59.5 per cent.

The main trading partners are the UAE, Japan, China, South Korea and Thailand. Principal exports are petroleum, re-exports, fish, metals and textiles. The main imports are machinery and transport equipment, manufactured goods, food and livestock.

GNI – US$27,900m; US$11,120 per capita (2006)
Annual average growth of GDP – 5.3 per cent (2007 est)
Inflation rate – 4 per cent (2007 est)
Unemployment – 15 per cent (2004 est)
Total external debt – US$3,483m (2007 est)
Imports – US$10,920m (2006)
Exports – US$21,600m (2006)

BALANCE OF PAYMENTS
Trade – US$10,670m surplus (2006)
Current Account – US$4,328m surplus (2006)

Trade with UK	*2006*	*2007*
Imports from UK	£211,023,000	£268,417,691
Exports to UK	£83,778,000	£83,120,736

COMMUNICATIONS

There are some 34,900km of roads, of which 9,700km are surfaced, but there are no railways. The main airports are at Muscat and Salalah, with over 130 other airports and airfields around the country. The main ports are Salalah and Port Qaboos at Mutrah, which has eight deep-water berths.

The modern telephone system served 278,300 main-line subscribers, 1.8 million mobile phone subscribers and 319,200 internet users in 2006.

EDUCATION AND HEALTH

Literacy rate – 74.4 per cent (2004 est)
Gross enrolment ratio (percentage of relevant age group) – primary 82 per cent; secondary 89 per cent; tertiary 25 per cent (2006 est)
Health expenditure (per capita) – US$312 (2005)
Hospital beds (per 1,000 people) – 2.1 (2000–6)

MEDIA

The first private television station launched in May 2007, breaking a government monopoly on television and radio broadcasters. Satellite dishes are permitted and so stations from neighbouring Saudi Arabia, the UAE and Yemen can be received. There are a large number of newspapers, including four national dailies. The press can be subject to political and cultural censorship by the government.

PAKISTAN

Jamhuryat Islami Pakistan – Islamic Republic of Pakistan

Area – 803,940 sq. km
Capital – Islamabad; population, 780,000 (2007 est)
Major cities – Faisalabad, Gujranwala, Hyderabad, Karachi, Lahore, Multan, Peshawar, Quetta, Rawalpindi
Currency – Pakistan rupee of 100 paisa
Population – 164,741,924, rising at 1.83 per cent per year (2007 est)
Religion – Islam (96 per cent) (est). The majority of the population practises Sunni Islam
Language – Urdu, English (both official), Punjabi, Sindhi, Siraiki, Pashto, Balochi
Population density – 206 per sq. km (2006)
Urban population – 34.8 per cent (2005 est)
Median age (years) – 20.9 (2007 est)
National anthem – 'Qaumi Tarana' ['National Anthem']
National day – 23 March (Republic Day)
Life expectancy (years) – 63.75 (2007 est)
Mortality rate – 8 (2007 est)
Birth rate – 27.52 (2007 est)
Infant mortality rate – 68.84 (2007 est)
Death penalty – Retained
CPI score – 2.4 (2007)
Population below poverty line – 24 per cent (2006 est)

CLIMATE AND TERRAIN

The arid Thar desert in the east gives way to the fertile Indus valley in the centre of the country. The terrain then rises to the Makran, Kirthar and Sulaiman mountain ranges in the west and the Karakoram and Himalayan ranges in the north. Elevation extremes range from 8,611m (K2) at the highest point to 0m (Indian Ocean) at the lowest. The climate varies greatly across the country. For the majority, the rainy season runs from June to October and is accompanied by very high humidity. Average temperatures in Islamabad range from 5°C in January to 38°C in June.

HISTORY AND POLITICS

Islam was introduced to the area from the eighth century onwards. From the 12th century, the territory formed part of successive empires covering northern India, including the Delhi sultanate and the Mughal Empire, and came under British control by the mid-19th century, when it formed part of the territory of British India.

In 1940, Muslim leaders in British India campaigned for a separate state for Muslims, and the predominantly Muslim areas were partitioned at independence in 1947, forming the state of Pakistan. This state comprised West Pakistan (now Pakistan) and East Pakistan, the Muslim areas of Bengal, which became the independent state of Bangladesh in 1971 following a short civil war.

Pakistan became an Islamic republic in 1956. A coup in 1958 led to military rule until 1971, when Zulfiqar Ali Bhutto became head of a civilian government following Bangladesh's secession. He was overthrown and eventually executed after another military coup in 1977 which brought General Zia ul-Haq to power. Zia's government abandoned secularism and initiated an Islamisation programme. Following Zia's death in 1988, civilian government was again restored but proved unstable, with several rapid changes of government in the 1990s amid allegations of corruption.

In 1999 the government was overthrown in a military coup led by General Pervez Musharraf, who became head of government (until 2002) and, in 2001, also head of state. His presidency has been dogged by controversy over his failure to resign his army post and become a civilian president at the end of 2004, reneging on a 2002 agreement.

Since September 2001 President Musharraf has aligned Pakistan with the West in its war on terror, providing support to the Allies in the Afghan War. This policy has angered militant factions, who are believed to be responsible for terrorist attacks in the major cities.

President Musharraf's suspension of the chief justice in March 2007 acted as a focus for dissatisfaction with his rule, triggering months of violent demonstrations and strikes. He was re-elected president by the national and provincial assemblies in October 2007 but formal confirmation of his success was delayed until the supreme court had considered his eligibility to stand while still head of the military; President Musharraf declared a state of emergency in November, dismissed the supreme court and appointed new judges who ruled his election valid. He resigned his military commission and his position as head of the army in November. The state of emergency was lifted in December.

The exiled opposition leaders Benazir Bhutto and Nawaz Sharif were allowed to return to Pakistan in advance of elections to the lower chamber of the legislature; originally scheduled for January 2008, the elections were postponed to February after the assassination of Benazir Bhutto in December 2007. The two main opposition parties, Bhutto's Pakistan People's Party (PPP) and Sharif's Pakistan Muslim League–Nawaz Sharif (PML-N), won the most seats and formed a coalition government that also included two smaller parties. The PML-N withdrew from the coalition in May 2008 after the legislature failed to reinstate the supreme court judges dismissed in November 2007. President Musharraf resigned in August 2008 and presidential elections were scheduled for 6 September.

INSURGENCIES

Factional violence between Shia and Sunni fundamentalists has been a problem in Balochistan, Punjab and Sindh provinces since the 1980s, and has led to thousands of deaths. The government has banned several extremist groups. Government troops are also fighting in Balochistan against guerrilla forces seeking greater autonomy and financial resources for the province.

Since the early 1990s there has been civil disorder in Sindh province, especially in Karachi, where armed militants of the Mohajir Qaumi Movement (MQM), which represents Urdu-speaking Indian Muslims who fled India at partition and their descendants, are fighting for an autonomous Karachi province.

FOREIGN RELATIONS

Since partition, sovereignty over the predominantly Muslim state of Jammu and Kashmir has been disputed between Pakistan and India. A short war in 1947–8 resulted in the state being partitioned between the two countries; its status remains unresolved, despite further outbreaks of war in 1965 and 1971, low-level conflict at altitude for control of the Siachen glacier since 1985 and occasional increases in military exchanges, most recently in 1999–2002 and 2003. Tension was exacerbated by Pakistan's support of the Muslim insurgency in the Indian part of the state, which began in the 1980s, and by both countries' acquisition of nuclear weapons. Moves towards a peaceful settlement began in 2003, when diplomatic missions were reopened and the resumption of transport links was initiated (a bus service across the line of control began in 2005). Formal diplomatic talks began in 2004 and have achieved several accords intended to reduce tension between the two countries, but the status of Kashmir has yet to be addressed

International concern was raised in 2004 by disclosures that Pakistan has sold its nuclear technology to other countries, but President Musharraf continues to receive Western support.

POLITICAL SYSTEM

Pakistan is a federal republic. The 1973 constitution has been suspended and restored several times, and was amended in 2002 by a legal framework order that increased the size of the legislature and extended the powers of the presidency. Under the constitution, the head of state is a president elected by parliament for a five-year term; Musharraf's term as president was extended for a further five years by a national referendum in 2002 and confirmed by the parliament and provincial assemblies in 2004.

The parliament *(Majlis as-Shura)* comprises a lower house, the National Assembly, and the senate. Under the 1973 constitution, the former has 237 members; this total was increased in 2002 to 342 members, of whom 60 are women and ten are elected by non-Muslim minorities; members serve for a five-year term. The senate has 100 members, 88 elected by provincial assemblies, eight chosen by tribal agencies and four elected by the national assembly; they serve a six-year term. General Musharraf was 'chief executive' from 1999 until 2002, when a new prime minister was appointed to lead the cabinet. The prime minister is nominated by and is responsible to the legislature.

There are four provinces: Balochistan, North-West Frontier Province, Punjab and Sindh. Each has a provincial assembly and government. In addition, there is the Federal Capital Territory and the Federally Administered Tribal Areas.

HEAD OF STATE

President, Gen. (retd) Pervez Musharraf, *assumed office* 20 June 2001, *confirmed in office by referendum* 30 April 2002, *re-elected* 6 October 2007

SELECTED GOVERNMENT MEMBERS *as at June 2008*

Prime Minister, Yusuf Raza Gilani
Defence, Chaudhry Ahmed Mukhtar
Foreign Affairs, Shah Mehmood Qureshi

HIGH COMMISSION FOR THE ISLAMIC REPUBLIC OF PAKISTAN

35–36 Lowndes Square, London SW1X 9JN
T 020-7664 9200 W www.pakmissionuk.gov.pk
High Commissioner, HE Dr Maleeha Lodhi, *apptd* 2003

BRITISH HIGH COMMISSION

PO Box 1122, Diplomatic Enclave, Ramna 5, Islamabad
T (+92) (51) 282 2131 E bhcmedia@isb.comsats.net.pk
High Commissioner, HE Robert Brinkley, *apptd* 2006

BRITISH COUNCIL

PO Box 1135, Islamabad
T (+92) (51) 111 424 424 W www.britishcouncil.org/pakistan
Director, Sue Beaumont

DEFENCE

The army has over 2,461 main battle tanks, 1,266 armoured personnel carriers and 26 armed helicopters. The navy has 8 submarines, 6 frigates, 8 patrol and coastal vessels, 16 combat aircraft and 12 armed helicopters at three bases. The air force has 360 combat aircraft and 19 helicopters.

Military expenditure – US$4,140m (2006)
Military personnel – 619,000: army 550,000, navy 24,000, air force 45,000; paramilitary 304,000

ECONOMY AND TRADE

Political instability, confrontations between political institutions, inefficiency, corruption and high military expenditure have inhibited the development of the economy. About one-quarter of the population lives below the poverty line and a high proportion of its labour force works abroad, especially in the Middle East, providing valuable remittances, but also causing a growth in the use of child labour within Pakistan. Since 2000, however, economic reforms, international aid and greater foreign investment have produced steady growth of 6–8 per cent a year, notably in the industrial and service sectors, and reduced poverty levels, although inflation remains a concern.

Agriculture employs 42 per cent of the labour force, producing cotton, wheat, rice, sugar cane, fruit, vegetables, milk, beef, mutton and eggs, and contributing 19.6 per cent to GDP. Significant manufacturing industries include textiles and clothing, food processing, pharmaceuticals, construction materials, paper products, fertiliser and seafood. Industry accounts for 26.8 per cent of GDP and services for 53.7 per cent. The main trading partners are the USA, the UAE, China, Saudi Arabia and Afghanistan. Principal exports are textiles (clothing, bed linen, cotton cloth and yarn), rice, leather goods, sports goods, chemicals, manufactures and carpets. The main imports are petroleum, petroleum products, machinery, plastics, transport equipment, edible oils, paper, iron, steel and tea.
GNI – US$126,700m; US$800 per capita (2006)
Annual average growth of GDP – 6.3 per cent (2007 est)
Inflation rate – 6.9 per cent (2007 est)
Unemployment – 7.5 per cent (2007 est)
Total external debt – US$40,320m (2007 est)
Imports – US$29,800m (2006)
Exports – US$16,900m (2006)

BALANCE OF PAYMENTS
Trade – US$12,895m deficit (2006)
Current Account – US$5,015m deficit (2006)

Trade with UK	*2006*	*2007*
Imports from UK	£489,948,000	£426,267,161
Exports to UK	£523,353,000	£514,826,682

COMMUNICATIONS

There are some 258,000km of roads and 8,163km of railways. The principal airports are at Karachi, Islamabad, Lahore, Peshawar and Sialkot. Pakistan International Airlines operates domestic air services between the principal cities as well as international services. The main seaports are Karachi and Port Qasim. The government is planning to build a deepwater port at Gwadar in Balochistan, and a road link from there to Afghanistan and central Asia.

Recent investment has resulted in dramatic improvements in the fixed-line and mobile telephone infrastructure. Since 2000, main-line availability has risen gradually but mobile phone distribution has rocketed; in 2006 there were 5.2 million main lines in use, while mobile phone subscribers numbered 63.1 million in 2007. In 2006 there were 12 million internet users.

EDUCATION AND HEALTH

Education is free of charge to upper secondary level. The system consists of five years of primary education (five to nine years), three years of middle or lower secondary (general or vocational), two years of upper secondary, two years of higher secondary (intermediate) and two to five years of higher education in colleges and universities.
Literacy rate – 48.7 per cent (2004 est)
Gross enrolment ratio (percentage of relevant age group) – primary 84 per cent; secondary 30 per cent; tertiary 5 per cent (2006 est)
Health expenditure (per capita) – US$15 (2005)
Hospital beds (per 1,000 people) – 0.7 (2000–6)

MEDIA

There are eight national newspapers, and the state-owned broadcaster, Pakistan Television Corporation Ltd, competes with several private networks. In keeping with the liberalisation of the media under President Musharraf, the government has granted licences for a number of satellite television and radio stations since 2004. A number of unlicensed broadcasters are believed to exist in the north of the country.

PALAU

Beluu er a Belau – Republic of Palau

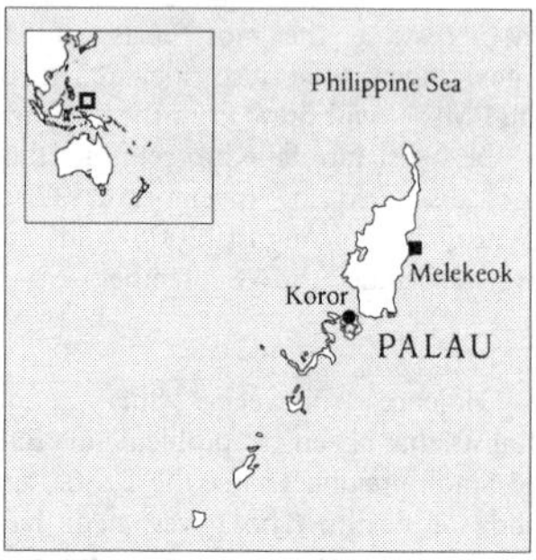

Area – 458 sq. km
Capital – Melekeok; population, 581 (2005)
Major town – Koror
Currency – Currency is that of the USA
Population – 20,842 rising at 1.23 per cent per year (2007 est); Palauan (69.9 per cent), Filipino (15.3 per cent), Chinese (4.9 per cent)
Religion – Roman Catholicism (65 per cent), other Christian denominations (16 per cent), Modekngei (9 per cent) (est). Modekngei is unique to Palau and combines elements of animism and Christian beliefs
Language – Palauan, English, Tobi, Sonsoralese, Japanese, Angaur (all official), Filipino
Population density – 44 per sq. km (2006)
Urban population – 68.2 per cent (2005 est)
Median age (years) – 32 (2007 est)
National anthem – 'Belau rekid' ['Our Palau']
National day – 9 July (Constitution Day)
Life expectancy (years) – 70.71 (2007 est)
Mortality rate – 6.77 (2007 est)
Birth rate – 17.7 (2007 est)
Infant mortality rate – 14.07 (2007 est)
Death penalty – Abolished for all crimes (since 1994)

CLIMATE AND TERRAIN

The republic consists of 340 volcanic and coral islands and islets in the western Pacific Ocean, of which only eight are inhabited. The islands are mainly low-lying, with elevation extremes ranging from 242m (Mt Ngerchelchauus) at the highest point to 0m (Pacific Ocean) at the lowest. The climate is tropical, with a wet season from May to November. Average daily temperatures are an almost constant 27°C.

HISTORY AND POLITICS

Britain became Palau's main trading partner in the 18th century, but did not colonise the islands. In 1889 Spain sold the islands to Germany, which exploited the phosphate deposits and developed coconut plantations.

apan occupied the islands on behalf of the Allies in 1914 nd administered them after the First World War under a eague of Nations mandate. Japanese forces were ousted y the USA during the Second World War.

In 1947 the islands became part of the UN Trust Territory of the Pacific, administered by the USA. In 1982 a compact of free association was signed with the USA under which the USA retained responsibility for defence and foreign policy in return for providing economic aid; the compact was implemented in 1993. Palau became independent on 1 October 1994.

In the 2004 presidential and legislative elections, President Remengesau was re-elected president and Elias Camsek Chin was elected vice-president. Presidential and legislative elections were scheduled for 4 November 2008.

POLITICAL SYSTEM

Under the 1981 constitution, the executive president is directly elected for a four-year term, renewable only once. The president appoints the cabinet. The bicameral National Congress comprises the House of Delegates, which is the lower house, and the senate. The House of Delegates has 16 members (one member from each of the 16 constituent states), directly elected for a four-year term. The senate has 14 members elected for a four-year term. Members of both houses stand for election as independents. A council of indigenous chiefs, composed of the paramount chief from each of the 16 constituent states, acts as an advisory body to the president on matters concerning traditional law and customs. Each of the 16 component states has its own elected governor and legislature.

HEAD OF STATE

President, Tommy Remengesau, *elected* 7 November 2000, *took office* 19 January 2001, *re-elected* 2 November 2004

Vice-President; Justice, Elias Camsek Chin

SELECTED GOVERNMENT MEMBERS *as at June 2008*

Commerce and Trade, Otoichi Besebes

Finance, Elbuchel Sadang

BRITISH AMBASSADOR

HE Peter Beckingham, *apptd* 2005, resident at Manila, the Philippines

ECONOMY AND TRADE

The economy is reliant on economic aid from the USA and so the government is keen to diversify. Tourism is growing and now caters for around 60,000 people a year, but the government is limiting development to protect the environment. The other main industries are handicrafts, construction and clothing manufacturing. Subsistence agriculture and fishing remain important, engaging 20 per cent of the workforce and producing crops such as coconuts, copra, cassava and sweet potatoes as well as fish. Revenue is also derived from the sale of licences to fishing fleets.

The main trading partners are the USA, Japan, Singapore and South Korea. Principal exports are shellfish, tuna, copra and clothing. The main imports are machinery and equipment, fuels, metals and foodstuffs.

GNI – US$161m; US$7,990 per capita (2006)

Annual average growth of GDP – 5.5 per cent (2005 est)

Inflation rate – 2.7 per cent (2005 est)

Unemployment – 4.2 per cent (2005 est)

Trade with UK	*2006*	*2007*
Imports from UK	£59,000	£208,216
Exports to UK	–	–

COMMUNICATIONS

There are 61km of roads, but no railways. There are three airports, on Koror, Peleliu and Angaur, which have daily flights from Guam operated by Continental Micronesia. Koror is also the main seaport.

MEDIA

Most Palauans rely on satellite and cable services from the USA. T8AA Eco Paradise is the government-run radio station. There are a further two commercial stations. Palau has three weekly news publications, including *Tia Belau* and *Palau Horizon.*

PANAMA

República de Panamá – Republic of Panama

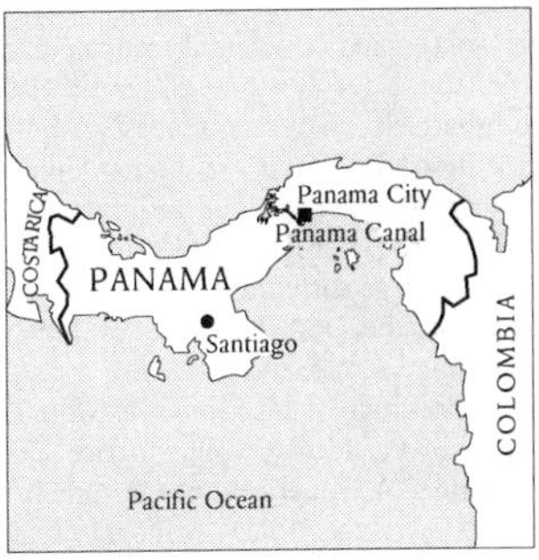

Area – 78,200 sq. km

Capital – Panama City; population, 1,281,000 (2007 est)

Major city – San Miguelito

Currency – Balboa of 100 centésimos (the US dollar is also in circulation)

Population – 3,242,173 rising at 1.56 per cent per year (2007 est)

Religion – Roman Catholicism (75 per cent), Protestantism (15 per cent) (est)

Language – Spanish (official), English

Population density – 44 per sq. km (2006 est)

Urban population – 57.8 per cent (2005 est)

Median age (years) – 26.4 (2007 est)

National anthem – 'Himno Istmeño' ['Isthmus Hymn']

National day – 3 November (Independence Day)

Life expectancy (years) – 75.19 (2007 est)

Mortality rate – 5.44 (2007 est)

Birth rate – 21.45 (2007 est)

Infant mortality rate – 15.96 (2007 est)

Death penalty – Abolished for all crimes (since 1903)

CPI score – 3.2 (2007)

CLIMATE AND TERRAIN

Coastal plains on the Pacific and Atlantic coasts rise to a mountainous interior. There is rainforest in the north-west and the east. Elevation extremes range from 3,475m (Volcan Baru) at the highest point to 0m (Pacific Ocean) at the lowest. The climate is tropical, with a prolonged wet season from May to January. Average temperatures range from 20°C in January to 31°C in June.

HISTORY AND POLITICS

Panama was visited by Spanish explorers in 1502 and subsequently became part of the Viceroyalty of New Andalucia, later New Grenada. It became a strategically important centre of trade. When it gained its independence from Spain in 1821, Panama joined the confederacy of Gran Colombia (comprising Colombia, Venezuela, Ecuador, Peru and Bolivia). The confederacy split up in 1830 and Panama became part of Colombia until 1903, when it achieved its independence.

In the 1880s, France attempted to construct a canal across Panama to link the Atlantic and Pacific oceans, and so avoid the longer and more dangerous journey between the oceans via Cape Horn. The French attempt failed, but the lucrative trade possibilities persuaded the USA to buy the rights to build the canal, which it completed in 1914. The USA was also given control of the canal and land to either side of it, known as the Canal Zone, in perpetuity. In 1979, Panama and the USA agreed that sovereignty over the Canal Zone would transfer to Panama from 2000, with the USA guaranteeing the zone's protection and providing an annual payment.

Panama was under the military rule of General Omar Torrijos from 1968 until his death in 1981. In 1983, General Noriega seized power and instigated a period of military rule, supported by the USA until 1987, when, following an attack on a US embassy, the American authorities ordered his arrest for money laundering and drug trafficking. An internal coup to unseat Noriega was unsuccessful in 1988, but in 1989 US forces invaded and deposed him. Noriega surrendered in 1990 and was tried and sentenced in the USA in 1992. In 1991, Panama abolished its armed forces.

The 2004 presidential election was won by Martín Torrijos of the Partido Revolucionario Democrática (PRD), who gained 47.4 per cent of the vote. In the 2004 legislative election, the PRD won 41 seats in the legislative assembly.

POLITICAL SYSTEM

Under the 1972 constitution, as amended, the executive president is directly elected for a five-year term, which is not renewable. The unicameral legislative assembly has 78 members, who are directly elected for a five-year term. The president, who is responsible to the assembly, appoints the cabinet.

HEAD OF STATE

President, Martín Torrijos, *elected* 2 May 2004, *sworn in* 14 September 2004
First Vice-President, Foreign Affairs, Samuel Lewis Navarro
Second Vice-President, Rubén Arosemena

SELECTED GOVERNMENT MEMBERS *as at June 2008*

Interior, Daniel Delgado Diamante
Economy and Finance, Hector Alexander

EMBASSY OF PANAMA

40 Hertford Street, London W1J 7SH
T 020-7493 4646 E panama1@btconnect.com
Ambassador Extraordinary and Plenipotentiary, HE Liliana Fernandez, *apptd* 2005

BRITISH EMBASSY

Swiss Tower, Calle 53 (Apartado 889) Zona 1, Panama City
T (+507) 269 0866 E britemb@cwpanama.net
Ambassador Extraordinary and Plenipotentiary, HE Richard Austen, MBE, *apptd* 2006

DEFENCE

The National Maritime Service has 41 patrol and coastal combatant vessels at 3 bases.
Military budget – US$200m (2007 est)
Military personnel – none active; paramilitary 12,000

ECONOMY AND TRADE

The economy is based on a large service sector and has experienced steady growth in recent years. However, the distribution of wealth is very uneven and about one-third of the population lives below the poverty line. Reform of the social welfare system, which was close to bankruptcy, and the tax system have been implemented despite widespread protests.

The service sector accounts for 77 per cent of GDP, derived from the operation of the Panama Canal and the Colón free trade zone, financial services, ports, ship registry and tourism. Plans to enlarge the canal to take more and larger vessels were approved in a 2006 referendum; work began in 2007 and is scheduled for completion in 2014. Industry, which contributes 16.2 per cent of GDP, includes construction, brewing, the manufacture of cement and other construction materials and sugar refining. Agriculture, which accounts for 6.8 per cent of GDP, is centred on bananas, rice, maize, coffee, sugar cane, vegetables, livestock and prawns.

The main trading partners are the USA, Netherlands Antilles, Costa Rica, EU countries, Japan and other Central and South American countries. Principal exports are bananas, prawns, sugar, coffee and clothing. The main imports are capital goods, foodstuffs, consumer goods and chemicals.
GNI – US$16,400m; US$5,000 per capita (2006)
Annual average growth of GDP – 7.8 per cent (2007 est)
Inflation rate – 5.1 per cent (2007 est)
Unemployment – 7.2 per cent (2007 est)
Total external debt – US$10,560m (2007 est)
Imports – US$4,830m (2006)
Exports – US$1,040m (2006)

BALANCE OF PAYMENTS

Trade – US$3,794m deficit (2006)
Current Account – US$552m deficit (2006)

Trade with UK	*2006*	*2007*
Imports from UK	£108,297,000	£169,785,600
Exports to UK	£17,638,000	£17,947,981

COMMUNICATIONS

The Panama Canal was built between 1903 and 1914 to connect the Pacific and Atlantic oceans, shortening sea journeys significantly. Each year the canal handles over 14,000 transits, containing 200 million tonnes of cargo; this represents about 5 per cent of world trade and over 40 per cent of trade between Asia and the east coast of the USA. The chief ports are Colón, Cristóbal and Balboa, at either end of the canal. Because of its role as a ship registry, there were 5,764 Panamanian-owned and 4,949 foreign-owned ships over 1,000 tonnes registered under its flag in 2007.

Apart from the 82km of the canal, there are over 700km of navigable waterways. These are supplemented by 355km of railways and 11,600km of roads. There are 116 airports and airfields; the principal airport is at Panama City. Modern telephone systems serve 433,000 main-line subscribers, 1.7 million mobile phone subscribers and 220,000 internet users.

EDUCATION AND HEALTH

There are six years of compulsory education.

Literacy rate – 91.9 per cent (2004 est)

Gross enrolment ratio (percentage of relevant age group) – primary 112 per cent; secondary 70 per cent; tertiary 45 per cent (2006 est)

Health expenditure (per capita) – US$351 (2005)

Hospital beds (per 1,000 people) – 2.4 (2000–6)

MEDIA

The freedom of the media has improved markedly in recent years owing to the repeal of restrictive legislation. Four television and five radio networks, all commercial, and six daily newspapers constitute the news media. *La Prensa*, *Panama News* and *El Siglo* are popular newspapers.

PAPUA NEW GUINEA

Gau Hedinarai ai Papua-Matamata Guinea – Independent State of Papua New Guinea

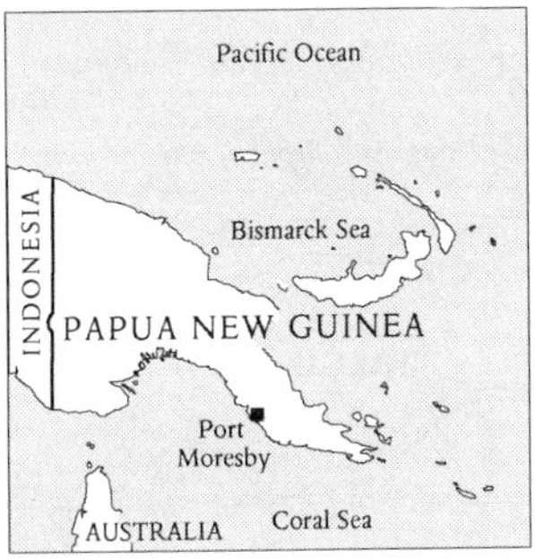

Area – 462,840 sq. km

Capital – Port Moresby; population, 299,000 (2007 est)

Major town – Lae

Currency – Kina (K) of 100 toea

Population – 5,795,887 rising at 2.16 per cent per year (2007 est)

Religion – Christianity (96 per cent) (est)

Language – English, Motu (both official); 820 indigenous languages are spoken, representing over 10 per cent of the world total

Population density – 14 per sq. km (2006)

Urban population – 13.2 per cent (2005 est)

Median age (years) – 21.4 (2007 est)

National anthem – 'O Arise, All You Sons'

National day – 16 September (Independence Day)

Life expectancy (years) – 65.62 (2007 est)

Mortality rate – 7.14 (2007 est)

Birth rate – 28.76 (2007 est)

Infant mortality rate – 48.46 (2007 est)

HIV/AIDS adult prevalence rate – 1.6 per cent (2005 est)

Death penalty – Retained, but not used

CPI score – 2.0 (2007)

Population below poverty line – 37 per cent (2002 est)

Literacy rate – 57.3 per cent (2004 est)

Gross enrolment ratio (percentage of relevant age group) – primary 55 per cent (2006 est)

Health expenditure (per capita) – US$34 (2005)

CLIMATE AND TERRAIN

Papua New Guinea lies in the south-western Pacific Ocean and consists of the eastern half of the island of New Guinea, the islands of Bougainville, New Britain and New Ireland, the Admiralty Islands, the D'Entrecasteaux Islands and the Louisiade archipelago. A range of densely forested mountains runs across the centre of the Papuan part of New Guinea, descending to coastal plains. Elevation extremes range from 4,509m (Mt Wilhelm) at the highest point to 0m (Pacific Ocean) at the lowest. The climate is tropical and temperatures in Port Moresby are around 26°C throughout the year.

HISTORY AND POLITICS

New Guinea was visited by the Portuguese and Spanish in the 16th century before being colonised by the British and Dutch in the late 19th century. The western part of the island (now Papua province, Indonesia) was incorporated into the Netherlands East Indies in 1828. In 1884 a British protectorate, British New Guinea, was proclaimed over south-eastern New Guinea and the adjacent islands, which were annexed outright in 1888. The territory was placed under Australian administration in 1906. The north-east of the island was claimed by Germany in 1884 and became a colony in 1899. It was occupied by Australia in the First World War and both the British territory and the German-mandated territory were administered by Australia from 1920 until 1942. The territories were occupied by Japan between 1942 and 1945. After the Second World War the territories were combined and administered by Australia before becoming independent on 16 September 1975.

In 1989 fighting began on Bougainville island between separatists led by the Bougainville Revolutionary Army and government forces. A ceasefire came into effect in 1998 and further talks led to a peace agreement in 2001 which provided for autonomy for the island and guaranteed a referendum on independence in 2009. The first elections for an autonomous government were held in 2005.

Border areas are sometimes affected by the overspill from fighting between separatists and Indonesian forces in the Indonesian province of Papua. Thousands of refugees from this conflict live in camps along the border.

Following the 2007 legislative election, the National Alliance Party (NAP) remained the largest party in parliament, and the NAP leader Sir Michael Somare was elected prime minister for the fourth time, forming a new coalition government.

POLITICAL SYSTEM

The 1975 constitution was amended in 1998 to permit greater autonomy for Bougainville. The head of state is the British sovereign, represented by a governor-general who is elected by the legislature for a six-year term. The unicameral National Parliament has 109 members, 20 from provincial electorates and the remainder from open electorates, who are directly elected for a five-year term. The prime minister is nominated by the legislature and appointed by the governor-general.

Governor-General, Sir Paulias Matane, *sworn in* 29 June 2004

SELECTED GOVERNMENT MEMBERS *as at June 2008*

Prime Minister, Sir Michael Somare

Deputy Prime Minister, Puka Temu

Finance and Treasury, Patrick Pruaitch

Foreign Affairs, Sam Abal

PAPUA NEW GUINEA HIGH COMMISSION

14 Waterloo Place, London SW1Y 4AR

T 020-7930 0922 E kunduldnhc.@btconnect.com
W www.pnghighcomm.org.uk
High Commissioner, HE Jean L. Kekedo, OBE, *apptd* 2002

BRITISH HIGH COMMISSION
PO Box 212, Waigani NCD 131, Port Moresby
T (+675) 325 1643 E bhcpng@datec.com.pg
High Commissioner, HE David Dunn, *apptd* 2007

DEFENCE

The Maritime Element has 4 patrol and coastal combatant vessels at four bases.
Military budget – US$33m (2007 est)
Military personnel – 3,100: army 2,500, air 200, Maritime Element 400

ECONOMY AND TRADE

Political instability, corruption, a weak economy and high unemployment and crime levels have brought the economy to a parlous state, with an Australian report in 2004 warning that the country was in imminent danger of economic and social collapse. The economy has grown slightly since, owing to higher commodity prices and tight control of the national budget, but the country remains poor and underdeveloped, with about one-third of the population living below the poverty line and unemployment in some urban areas as high as 80 per cent. It continues to struggle to attract foreign investment and is dependent on foreign aid, mostly from Australia, which accounts for nearly 20 per cent of the budget.

Only about 1 per cent of the land area is suitable for commercial crops. Over 80 per cent of the population practises subsistence farming, including some tribes in the interior so isolated that they live within an unmonetised economy. Mineral deposits, including copper, gold, silver, oil and natural gas, are abundant and constitute the main sources of revenue, although exploitation is hampered by the terrain and poor infrastructure. The main industries are mining, oil extraction and refining, forestry, processing of agricultural products, construction and tourism. Industry contributes 37 per cent of GDP and services 27 per cent.

The main trading partners are Australia, Singapore, Japan and China. Principal exports are oil, gold, copper ore, logs, palm oil, coffee, cocoa and shellfish. The main imports are machinery and transport equipment, manufactured goods, food, fuels and chemicals.
GNI – US$4,600m; US$740 per capita (2006)
Annual average growth of GDP – 4 per cent (2007 est)
Inflation rate – 1.8 per cent (2007 est)
Unemployment – 2.8 per cent (2004)
Total external debt – US$1,814m (2007 est)
Imports – US$1,730m (2005)
Exports – US$4,100m (2006)

BALANCE OF PAYMENTS
Trade – US$881m surplus (2001)
Current Account – US$163m surplus (2006)

Trade with UK	*2006*	*2007*
Imports from UK	£4,881,000	£7,793,493
Exports to UK	£40,275,000	£36,449,048

COMMUNICATIONS

There are 19,600km of roads, of which less than 700km are surfaced; the most important road links Lae with the populous highlands. There are 578 airports and airstrips, the principal airports being at Port Moresby, Lae and Rabaui. Air Niugini operates regular flights internally and to other countries in the region. The main seaports are Port Moresby, Lae and Madang on New Guinea and Rabaul on New Britain. Several shipping companies operate cargo services around the world, but cargo and passenger services between the main ports and outports are very limited.

The telephone system provides a minimal service and access is not widespread; combined density of fixed lines and mobile phones was less than 3 per 100 people in 2005, although mobile phone ownership is growing quickly.

MEDIA

Radio is the most important medium owing to the widely scattered population and low levels of literacy. The state-run National Broadcasting Corporation operates a radio network that competes with the commercial NAU FM. EMTV is the sole television broadcaster; coverage is limited to Port Moresby and regional capitals. There are two foreign-owned daily newspapers, *The National* and *The Post-Courier,* and a number of weekly publications.

PARAGUAY

República del Paraguay – Republic of Paraguay

Area – 406,750 sq. km
Capital – Asunción; population, 1,870,000 (2007 est)
Major cities – Capiatá, Ciudad del Este, Luque, San Lorenzo
Currency – Guaraní (Gs) of 100 céntimos
Population – 6,669,086 rising at 2.42 per cent per year (2007 est)
Religion – Roman Catholicism (89 per cent), other Christian denominations (6 per cent) (est)
Language – Spanish, Guarani (both official)
Population density – 15 per sq. km (2006)
Urban population – 58.5 per cent (2005 est)
Median age (years) – 21.6 (2007 est)
National anthem – 'Paraguayos, República o Muerte' ['Paraguayans, the Republic or Death']
National day – 15 May (Independence Day)
Life expectancy (years) – 75.34 (2007 est)
Mortality rate – 4.54 (2007 est)
Birth rate – 28.77 (2007 est)
Infant mortality rate – 26.45 (2007 est)
Death penalty – Abolished for all crimes (since 1992)
CPI score – 2.4 (2007)
Population below poverty line – 32 per cent (2005 est)

CLIMATE AND TERRAIN

The country is landlocked and lies in the grassy and occasionally marshy plains of the river Paraguay, which divides the country, and the rivers Parana and Pilcomayo. Elevation extremes range from 842m (Cerro Pero) at the highest point to 46m (the junction of the Paraguay and Parana rivers) at the lowest. Average temperatures in Asunción range from 23°C in June to 34°C in January.

HISTORY AND POLITICS

Spanish colonisation of Paraguay began in the early 16th century and Asunción was founded in 1537. Paraguay became independent from Spain in 1811 under the dictator José Gaspar Rodriguez de Francia, who ruled until his death in 1840. His successors instigated a period of reform and modernisation which ended in 1865–70 with the catastrophic War of the Triple Alliance against Brazil, Uruguay and Argentina over access to the sea. The war resulted in the loss of over half the population as well as 150,000 sq. km of territory, and initiated a period of political instability that lasted until 1912. In the Chaco War of 1932–5, Paraguay gained territory in the west from Bolivia.

Political instability and conflict after the Second World War ended with a coup in 1954 in which General Alfredo Stroessner seized power. His rule was autocratic and increasingly repressive, marked by corruption and human rights abuses. He was ousted in a coup in 1989 that paved the way for free multiparty elections to the presidency and legislature in 1993. These were won by the National Republican Association-Colorado Party (ANR-PC) and its presidential candidate. The ANR-PC has won the subsequent elections but splits in the party have contributed to the instability that has prevailed since the 1990s, with the assassination of a vice-president, an attempted coup, widespread corruption and the growth of organised crime.

In the 2008 presidential and legislative elections, the ANR-PC remained the largest party in both chambers of the legislature, but for the first time in 61 years lost the presidency. This was won by Fernando Lugo of the Patriotic Alliance for Change coalition, with 42.3 per cent of the vote, and he took office in August 2008 at the head of a coalition government.

POLITICAL SYSTEM

Under the 1992 constitution, the executive president is directly elected for a five-year term, which is not renewable. The bicameral Congress consists of a 45-member senate and an 80-member Chamber of Deputies, both directly elected for a five-year term. Deputies are elected on a regional basis, the number of seats allocated to each regional department being directly proportional to the department's population. Voting is compulsory for all citizens over 18. The president, who is responsible to congress, appoints the council of ministers.

HEAD OF STATE

President, Fernando Lugo, *elected* 20 April 2008, *sworn in* 15 August 2008
Vice-President, Francisco Oviedo

SELECTED GOVERNMENT MEMBERS *as at June 2008*

Defence, Nelson Mora
Foreign Affairs, Ruben Ramirez Lezcano
Interior, Rogelio Raimundo Benítez Vargas

EMBASSY OF THE REPUBLIC OF PARAGUAY

3rd Floor, 344 High Street Kensington, London W14 8NS
T 020-7610 4180 E embapar@btconnect.com
W www.paraguayembassy.co.uk

BRITISH AMBASSADOR

HE Dr John Hughes, *apptd* 2004, resident in Buenos Aires, Argentina

DEFENCE

The army has 5 main battle tanks and 10 armoured personnel carriers. The navy has 28 patrol and coastal combatant vessels at 3 bases. The air force has 10 combat aircraft.

Military budget – US$101m (2007)
Military personnel – 10,650: army 7,600, navy 1,950, air force 1,100; paramilitary 14,800
Conscription duration – 12–24 months

ECONOMY AND TRADE

The economy contracted in 2002, partly owing to the financial crisis in Argentina, but has shown modest growth since 2003. Economic reforms, a condition of IMF loans in 2002, have not progressed owing to popular and parliamentary resistance. Political instability, corruption, national and foreign debt, an inadequate infrastructure and high crime levels have resulted in poor economic performance and the existence of a large unofficial economy. About one-third of the population lives below the poverty line, although this is higher in the cities because of migration from the countryside by families made landless by the increasing commercialisation of agriculture and forest clearances.

The country has few mineral resources and the economy is largely agricultural, much of it at subsistence level. Agricultural production, which accounts for 21.9 per cent of GDP and engages 31 per cent of the workforce, is centred on cotton, sugar cane, soya beans, maize, wheat, tobacco, cassava, timber and other foodstuffs. The main industries are sugar refining and manufacture of cement, textiles, beverages, wood products, steel and electric power. Industry accounts for 18.7 per cent of GDP and services for 59.4 per cent. The main trading partners are Brazil, China, Argentina, Uruguay and Russia. Principal exports are soya beans, feed, cotton, meat, edible oils, electricity and wood. The main imports are vehicles, consumer goods, tobacco and petroleum products.

GNI – US$8,500m; US$1,410 per capita (2006)
Annual average growth of GDP – 4 per cent (2007 est)
Inflation rate – 8.6 per cent (2007 est)
Unemployment – 15.9 per cent (2007 est)
Total external debt – US$3,632m (2007 est)
Imports – US$6,100m (2006)
Exports – US$1,900m (2006)

BALANCE OF PAYMENTS

Trade – US$4,184m deficit (2006)
Current Account – US$118m deficit (2006)

Trade with UK	*2006*	*2007*
Imports from UK	£13,649,000	£10,708,959
Exports to UK	£1,371,000	£2,112,349

COMMUNICATIONS

Although landlocked, Paraguay has 3,100km of navigable waterways on its rivers. Direct shipping services operate between Asunción and Europe and the USA, and river steamer services provide internal transport. There are 29,500km of roads, including connections with Sao Paulo and Buenos Aires, but many are impassable in severe weather. Paraguay has 36km of railways. There are about 12 airports, including the principal airport at

Asunción, and around 820 airfields and airstrips around the country.

The fixed-line telephone system is not extensive so mobile phone distribution has risen rapidly. In 2006 there were 331,100 main lines in use, 3.2 million mobile phone subscribers and 260,000 internet users.

EDUCATION AND HEALTH

Basic education is free of charge and compulsory for nine years.

Literacy rate – 91.6 per cent (2004 est)
Gross enrolment ratio (percentage of relevant age group) – primary 112 per cent; secondary 67 per cent; tertiary 25 per cent (2006 est)
Health expenditure (per capita) – US$92 (2005)
Hospital beds (per 1,000 people) – 1.2 (2000–6)

MEDIA

Paraguay has three private-owned daily newspapers, *ABC Color, La Nacion* and *Ultima Hora,* as well as five commercial television channels and a range of radio broadcasters. Intimidation of journalists covering politically sensitive issues is common.

PERU

Republica del Peru – Republic of Peru

Area – 1,285,220 sq. km
Capital – Lima; including Callao, population, 8,012,000 (2007 est)
Major cities – Arequipa, Chiclayo, Iquitos, Piura, Trujillo
Currency – New sol of 100 centimos
Population – 28,674,757 rising at 1.29 per cent per year (2007 est)
Religion – Roman Catholicism (85 per cent), Protestantism (11 per cent) (est). Around 1 per cent of the population is agnostic or atheist
Language – Spanish, Quechua (official), Aymara
Population density – 22 per sq. km (2006)
Urban population – 74.6 per cent (2005 est)
Median age (years) – 25.5 (2007 est)
National anthem – 'Somos libres, seámoslo siempre' ['We Are Free, Let Us Remain So Forever']
National day – 28 July (Independence Day)
Life expectancy (years) – 70.14 (2007 est)
Mortality rate – 6.21 (2007 est)
Birth rate – 20.09 (2007 est)
Infant mortality rate – 29.96 (2007 est)
Death penalty – Retained for certain crimes
CPI score – 3.5 (2007)
Population below poverty line – 44.5 per cent (2006)

CLIMATE AND TERRAIN

Peru has three main regions: the Costa, the coastal plain west of the Andes; the Sierra or mountain range of the Andes, which runs parallel to the Pacific coast; and the Montaña (or Selva), a vast area of jungle stretching from the eastern foothills of the Andes to the country's eastern and north-eastern borders. Elevation extremes range from 6,768m (Nevado Huascaran) at the highest point to 0m (Pacific Ocean) at the lowest. The country typically receives very little rain, but occasionally, due to the El Niño weather system, the northern districts receive several days of higher temperatures accompanied by torrential rain. Average temperatures in Lima range from 16°C in July to 26°C in January.

HISTORY AND POLITICS

The Inca Empire centred on Cuzco had superseded earlier civilisations in Peru by the 15th century, when the Empire reached its zenith before falling to Spanish conquistadores led by Francisco Pizarro in 1532–3. The territory formed the Viceroyalty of Peru and its gold and silver mines made Peru the principal source of wealth in Spain's American empire. After 1810, Peru became the centre for the Spanish government as its other colonies rebelled. Although it declared its independence in 1821, this was achieved only with the final defeat of Spanish forces in 1824.

Peru entered into several border disputes with its neighbours in the 19th and 20th centuries, including the Pacific War (1879–83) in which it lost three southern coastal provinces to Chile. A border dispute with Ecuador was renewed in 1981, leading to a short, inconclusive war in 1995, but was resolved in 1998 following adjudication. A border dispute with Chile ended in 1999 with the implementation of accords first agreed in 1929.

Following independence, Peru alternated between military dictatorships and periods of democratic rule. The last military dictator was General Francisco Morales Bermundez, who guided the country to democracy in 1980. Civilian rule has not brought greater political stability or improved economic and social equality. Two left-wing insurgencies, by the Maoist *Sendero Luminoso* (Shining Path) and the *Movimento Revolucionario Tupac Amaru* (MRTA), began in the 1980s. The activities of the *Sendero Luminoso* in particular destabilised the government and the economy; the conflict caused about 69,000 deaths and provoked human rights abuses by both the security forces and the guerrillas. By the late 1990s both insurgencies had been overcome, although a few Maoists remain active. The conflict has left a legacy of criminal violence, much of it related to drug trafficking.

The economy deteriorated badly in the late 1980s and by 1990 inflation had reached 400 per cent. Alberto Fujimori was elected president in 1990 on a platform of economic reform. Within two years he had dismantled the existing order in Peru by dismissing the legislature, sacking senior judges, imposing order through a so-called Emergency National Reconstruction Government and changing the constitution. He fled to Japan in 2000 to escape corruption charges and was succeeded by Alejandro Toledo, who won the 2001 presidential election, becoming the country's first president of Quechan descent.

In the 2006 legislative election, the Union for Peru (UPP) party won the most seats, but although the UPP candidate was leading in the first round of the presidential election, the second round was won by the Peruvian Aprista Party (APRA) candidate Alan Garcia (president

1985–90). In 2007 President Garcia was granted emergency powers allowing him to rule by decree on issues related to organised crime and drug trafficking.

POLITICAL SYSTEM
Under the 1993 constitution, the executive president is directly elected for a five-year term, renewable only once. The unicameral legislature, the Congress of the Republic, has 120 members, directly elected for a five-year term. The president, who is responsible to the congress, appoints the council of ministers.

HEAD OF STATE
President of the Republic, Alan Garcia, *elected* 4 June 2006, *sworn in* 28 July 2006
Vice-Presidents, Jose Vega; Fabiola Morales; Luisa Cuculiza

SELECTED GOVERNMENT MEMBERS *as at June 2008*
Defence, Antero Flores-Araoz
Economy and Finance, Luis Carranza
Foreign Affairs, José Antonio García Belaunde
Interior, Luis Alva Castro

EMBASSY OF PERU
52 Sloane Street, London SW1X 9SP
T 020-7235 1917 E postmaster@peruembassy-uk.com
W www.peruembassy-uk.com
Ambassador Extraordinary and Plenipotentiary, HE Ricardo Luna, *apptd* 2006

BRITISH EMBASSY
PO Box 854, Torre Parque Mar (Piso 22), Avenida José Larco 1301, Lima
T (+51) (1) 617 3000 E britemb@terra.com.pe
W www.britemb.org.pe
Ambassador Extraordinary and Plenipotentiary, HE Catherine Nettleton, *apptd* 2006

DEFENCE
The army has 240 main battle tanks and 299 armoured personnel carriers. The navy has 6 submarines, 1 cruiser, 8 frigates, 14 patrol and coastal combatant vessels and 3 armed helicopters at 7 bases. The air force has 70 combat aircraft and 16 armed helicopters.
Military budget – US$1,270m (2007)
Military personnel – 114,000: army 74,000, navy 23,000, air force 17,000; paramilitary 84,000

ECONOMY AND TRADE
The economy has grown steadily since 2002 but poverty remains widespread, with over half the population living below the poverty line and over a third of the wealth in the hands of 10 per cent of society. The inadequate infrastructure hinders development and also deterred trade and investment.

Mineral resources, including copper, silver, gold, oil and natural gas, are abundant, and extracting and refining these is the mainstay of the economy, although this makes it vulnerable to global price fluctuations. Other industries include steel and metal fabrication, fishing and fish processing, textiles and clothes manufacture and food processing. Agriculture is centred on asparagus, coffee, cotton, sugar cane, rice, maize, vegetables, fruit, coca, meat and dairy products. Services contribute 66 per cent to GDP, industry 25.6 per cent and agriculture 8.4 per cent.

The main trading partners are the USA, China, Chile, other South American countries, Canada and Switzerland. Principal exports are copper, gold, zinc, crude oil and petroleum products, coffee, vegetables, textiles and guinea pigs. The main imports are oil and petroleum products, plastics, machinery, vehicles, iron and steel, wheat and paper.
GNI – US$82,200m; US$2,980 per capita (2006)
Annual average growth of GDP – 7.5 per cent (2007 est)
Inflation rate – 3.5 per cent (2007 est)
Unemployment – 7.4 per cent (2000 est)
Total external debt – US$27,810m (2007 est)
Imports – US$17,900m (2006)
Exports – US$23,700m (2006)

BALANCE OF PAYMENTS
Trade – US$5,873m surplus (2006)
Current Account – US$2,589m surplus (2006)

Trade with UK	*2006*	*2007*
Imports from UK	£52,831,000	£67,542,448
Exports to UK	£199,564,000	£134,213,334

COMMUNICATIONS
There are 78,829km of roads, of which 11,351km are surfaced. These include sections of two transnational highways: the east-west Andean Highway, linking the Pacific and Atlantic coasts, and the north-south Pan-American Highway running along the Pacific coast. The state-run railways have 1,989km of track, and 8,600km of inland waterways are navigable, on tributaries of the Amazon and Lake Titicaca. The main seaports are Callao and Matarani. There are over 230 airports and airstrips, including the international airport at Lima.

In 2006 there were 2.3 million main telephone lines in use, 8.5 million mobile phone subscribers and 6.1 million internet users.

EDUCATION AND HEALTH
Education is free of charge and compulsory for 11 years.
Literacy rate – 87.7 per cent (2004 est)
Gross enrolment ratio (percentage of relevant age group) – primary 116 per cent; secondary 92 per cent; tertiary 34 per cent (2006 est)
Health expenditure (per capita) – US$125 (2005)
Hospital beds (per 1,000 people) – 1.1 (2000–6)

MEDIA
Media freedom has greatly improved since the end of the Fujimori administration in 2000. There are six national daily newspapers and a host of commercial radio broadcasters. The state-owned Television Nacional de Peru competes with four commercial broadcasters, including America TV and Panamericana.

THE PHILIPPINES

Repúblika ng Pilipinas – Republic of the Philippines

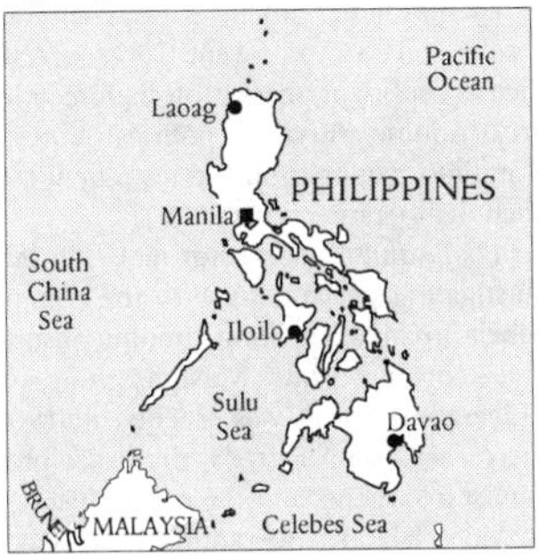

Area – 300,000 sq. km
Capital – Manila (including Quezon City); population, 11,100,000 (2007 est)
Major cities – Antipolo, Cagayan, Calamba, Cebu, Dadiangas, Dasmariñas, Davao, Zamboanga
Currency – Philippine peso (P) of 100 centavos
Population – 91,077,287 rising at 1.76 per cent per year (2007 est); Tagalog (28.1 per cent), Cebuano (13.1 per cent), Ilocano (9 per cent), Bisaya (7.6 per cent); Hiligaynon Ilonggo (7.5 per cent), Bikol (6 per cent), Waray (3.4 per cent)
Religion – Roman Catholicism (80 per cent), other Christian denominations (5 per cent), Islam (5 per cent) (est)
Language – Filipino, English (both official)
Population density – 289 per sq. km (2006)
Urban population – 62.6 per cent (2005 est)
Median age (years) – 22.7 (2007 est)
National anthem – 'Lupang Hinirang' ['Beloved Land']
National day – 12 June (Independence Day)
Life expectancy (years) – 70.51 (2007 est)
Mortality rate – 5.36 (2007 est)
Birth rate – 24.48 (2007 est)
Infant mortality rate – 22.12 (2007 est)
Death penalty – Abolished for all crimes (since 2006)
CPI score – 2.5 (2007)
Population below poverty line – 40 per cent (2001 est)

CLIMATE AND TERRAIN

The Philippines comprises over 7,000 islands in the western Pacific Ocean. The principal islands are Luzon, Mindanao, Samar, Negros, Palawan, Panay and Leyte. Other groups include the Sulu islands (capital, Jolo), Babuyanes and Batanes, Calamian and Kalayaan islands. The larger islands are traversed by volcanic mountain ranges; some volcanoes are still active. Elevation extremes range from 2,954m (Mt Apo) at the highest point to 0m (Philippine Sea) at the lowest. The climate is tropical with temperatures fairly constant between 23°C in January and 31°C in June. The country is particular susceptible to typhoons during the rainy season from August to October, which cause widespread damage and frequent loss of life. Humidity is often oppressive, particularly in June and July.

HISTORY AND POLITICS

The Philippine islands were conquered by Spain in 1565 and colonial rule lasted until 1898, when Spain ceded the colony to the USA following the Spanish-American War. The country became internally self-governing in 1935, was occupied by Japan from 1942 to 1944, and achieved independence from the USA in 1946.

Ferdinand Marcos seized power in 1965, imposing martial law in 1972. His regime became increasingly repressive, corrupt and violent, and when he falsified election results in 1986 to prevent Corazon Aquino from taking office as president, mass protests forced him to flee the country. Aquino survived political unrest and six attempted military coups to introduce a new constitution and entrench democratic politics.

Fidel Ramos, Aquino's successor in 1992, built on her work by instigating peace talks with the communist and Muslim rebels involved in long-running insurgencies; a peace agreement with one Muslim group, the Moro National Liberation Front, was reached in 1996. Under Ramos' successor, Joseph Estrada, the peace process with the communist insurgents and the main Muslim insurgent group, the Moro Islamic Liberation Front (MILF), began to stall. Popular dissatisfaction with Estrada grew and he was forced out of office in 2001; his term was completed by Vice-President Gloria Arroyo. She re-established peace talks with the MILF and the National Democratic Front (NDF), a front organisation for the communist insurgents. The talks with the MILF, though often interrupted by violence, achieved a ceasefire in 2003 and a breakthrough on key issues in 2005. Progress with the NDF has proved more problematic and clashes have continued despite six months of peace talks in 2004. Since the 11 September 2001 attacks, Abu Sayyaf, a Muslim group suspected of links with al-Qaida, has emerged on the island of Jolo, undertaking a spate of violent kidnappings.

Gloria Arroyo was elected president in 2004. Since the election, her popularity has plummeted. Her anti-corruption measures and economic reforms have been undermined by a series of corruption scandals and she came under intense pressure to resign in 2005 over accusations that she tried to influence the 2004 presidential election result. Despite these setbacks, pro-government parties remained in the majority in the lower legislative chamber in the 2007 legislative elections, although they were defeated by opposition groups in the upper house.

POLITICAL SYSTEM

Under the 1987 constitution, the executive president is directly elected for a six-year term, which is not renewable. There is a bicameral Congress. The lower house, the House of Representatives, and a senate. The House of Representatives has 236 members, of whom 218 are directly elected and the rest are appointed from party and minority group lists by the president; all serve a three-year term. The senate has 24 members directly elected for a six-year term, with half re-elected every three years.

The autonomous region of Muslim Mindanao consists of four provinces: Lanao del Sur, Maguindanao, Sulu, Tawi-Tawi and Basilan. There is a 24-member regional assembly and a governor.

HEAD OF STATE

President, Gloria Macapagal Arroyo, *assumed office* 20 January 2001
Vice-President, Manuel Noli de Castro

SELECTED GOVERNMENT MEMBERS *as at June 2008*

Finance, Margarito Teves
Interior, Ronaldo Puno
Foreign, Alberto Romulo
Defence, Hermogenes Ebdane

EMBASSY OF THE REPUBLIC OF THE PHILIPPINES

8 Suffolk Street, London SW1Y 4HH
T 020-7937 1600 E embassy@philemb.co.uk
W http://philembassy-uk.org
Ambassador Extraordinary and Plenipotentiary, HE Edgardo Espiritu, *apptd* 2003

BRITISH EMBASSY

PO Box 2927 MCPO, Floors 15–17, LV Locsin Building, 6752 Ayala Avenue, 1226 Makati, Manila
T (+63) (2) 816 7116 E uk@info.com.ph
W www.britishembassy.gov.uk/philippines
Ambassador Extraordinary and Plenipotentiary, HE Peter Beckingham, *apptd* 2005

BRITISH COUNCIL
10th Floor, Taipan Place, Emerald Avenue, Ortigas Centre, Pasig City 1605
T (+63) (2) 914 1011 E britishcouncil@britishcouncil.org.ph
Director, Andrew Picken

DEFENCE

The army has 85 armoured infantry fighting vehicles and 370 armoured personnel carriers. The navy has 1 frigate and 62 patrol and coastal vessels at 3 bases. The air force has 30 combat aircraft and 25 armed helicopters.
Military budget – US$1,121m (2006)
Military personnel – 106,000: army 66,000, navy 24,000, air force 16,000; paramilitary 40,500

ECONOMY AND TRADE

The economy was one of the best-performing in the region until the Asian economic crisis of 1997, but it has steadily recovered since 2002 owing to growth in exports, agricultural output and the service industries. Greater and more rapid economic expansion is needed to offset the high rate of population growth. Privatisation of state-owned industries has yielded revenue that, along with tighter budget management, has reduced public debt. However, about 30 per cent of the population lives below the poverty line, and remittances from the millions of Filipinos working abroad are vital to the economy.

Major industries include electronics assembly, manufacture of clothing, footwear, pharmaceuticals, chemicals and wood products, food processing, oil refining and fishing. The large agricultural sector employs 35 per cent of the workforce, producing sugar cane, coconuts, rice, maize, tropical fruits and livestock products. Agriculture accounts for 14 per cent of GDP, industry for 31 per cent and services for 55 per cent.

The main trading partners are the USA, Japan, China, Singapore, Taiwan and Hong Kong. Principal exports are semiconductors and electronic products, transport equipment, clothing, copper products, petroleum products, coconut oil and fruit. The main imports are electronic products, fuels, machinery and transport equipment, iron and steel, fabrics, grains, chemicals and plastics.
GNI – US$120,200m; US$1,390 per capita (2006)
Annual average growth of GDP – 6.3 per cent (2007 est)
Inflation rate – 2.8 per cent (2007 est)
Unemployment – 7.9 per cent (2007 est)
Total external debt – US$62,840m (2007 est)
Imports – US$53,600m (2006)
Exports – US$47,000m (2006)

BALANCE OF PAYMENTS
Trade – US$6,665m deficit (2006)
Current Account – US$5,347m surplus (2006)

Trade with UK	*2006*	*2007*
Imports from UK	£243,583,000	£247,929,984
Exports to UK	£755,698,000	£723,849,857

COMMUNICATIONS

There are about 200,000km of roads, and Philippine National Railway operates 897km of railways. The main ports are Manila (Luzon), Cebu, Davao, Iloilo and Zamboanga (Mindanao), and there are over 400 smaller ports. There are 255 airports and airfields, including international airports at Manila, Cebu and Davao City.

There is a good telephone system, and mobile phone distribution has grown rapidly. There were 3.6 million fixed line in use in 2006, and 42.8 million mobile phone subscribers.

EDUCATION AND HEALTH

There are six years of free and compulsory primary education, followed by four years of free but non-compulsory secondary education.
Literacy rate – 92.6 per cent (2004 est)
Gross enrolment ratio (percentage of relevant age group) – primary 111 per cent; secondary 85 per cent; tertiary 28 per cent (2006 est)
Health expenditure (per capita) – US$37 (2005)
Hospital beds (per 1,000 people) – 1.2 (2000–6)

MEDIA

The government-owned IBC television network competes with two commercial broadcasters. There is a large number of radio stations and four main national publications that include *The Daily Tribune* and *Malaya*.

POLAND

Rzeczpospolita Polska – Republic of Poland

Area – 312,685 sq. km
Capital – Warsaw; population, 1,707,000 (2007 est)
Major cities – Bydgoszcz, Gdansk, Katowice, Krakow, Lodz, Lublin, Poznan, Szczecin, Wroclaw
Currency – Zloty of 100 groszy
Population – 38,518,241 falling at 0.05 per cent per year (2007 est)
Religion – Roman Catholicism (96 per cent), Orthodox Christianity (2 per cent) (est). Around 3 per cent of the population is atheist
Language – Polish (official)
Population density – 124 per sq. km (2006)
Urban population – 62 per cent (2005 est)
Median age (years) – 37.3 (2007 est)
National anthem – 'Mazurek Dabrowskiego' ['Poland Is Not Yet Lost']
National day – 3 May (Constitution Day)
Life expectancy (years) – 75.19 (2007 est)
Mortality rate – 9.94 (2007 est)
Birth rate – 9.94 (2007 est)
Infant mortality rate – 7.07 (2007 est)
Death penalty – Abolished for all crimes (since 1997)
CPI score – 4.2 (2007)
Population below poverty line – 17 per cent (2003 est)

CLIMATE AND TERRAIN

Poland lies mostly in a great plain crossed by the Oder, Neisse and Vistula rivers. The land rises to the Carpathian, Tatra and Sudeten mountains along the southern border.

Elevation extremes range from 2,499m (Rysy) at the highest point to −2m (Raczki Elblaskie) at the lowest. The climate is continental and average temperatures in Warsaw range from −5°C in January to 24°C in July.

HISTORY AND POLITICS

Poland emerged as an independent kingdom in the ninth century. It formed a union with Lithuania in 1569 that stretched from the Baltic to the Black Sea. This commonwealth was weakened by attacks by its neighbours and in 1772, 1793 and 1795 its territory was partitioned between Russia, Prussia and Austria. Following the congress of Vienna in 1815, eastern Poland became a semi-independent kingdom within the Russian Empire.

After the First World War, Poland became independent for a second time with the signing of the treaty of Versailles. The Second World War began with the German invasion of western Poland on 1 September 1939; on 17 September, Soviet forces invaded eastern Poland, and on 21 September Germany and the USSR declared that Poland had ceased to exist. In 1941 the rest of Poland was occupied by Germany. The USSR aligned with the Allies, and the country was liberated by Soviet forces in 1944–5. After the war, its boundaries were redrawn. Eastern Poland was ceded to the USSR but the country gained German territory in Silesia along the Oder and Neisse rivers, effectively shifting the state 240km westwards.

The post-war coalition government was Soviet-influenced and in 1947 a communist republic was proclaimed. Nationalisation and agricultural collectivisation programmes were introduced and the Roman Catholic Church was persecuted. By the 1970s attempts to boost the economy had failed and the country had a large foreign debt. In 1980, following a strike at the Gdansk shipyard prompted by economic crisis and popular discontent, a mass movement for civil and national rights coalesced around the newly formed independent Solidarity trade union, led by Lech Walesa. The following year, the demoralised Communist government declared martial law and interned Walesa and other leaders, driving Solidarity underground. Economic decline and continuing unrest in the 1980s eventually resulted in talks between Solidarity, the government and the Roman Catholic Church in 1989. In multiparty parliamentary elections later that year, the Communists lost power and Solidarity helped to form a coalition government. In 1990 Walesa was elected president. The Communist Party subsequently dissolved and reformed as the Democratic Left Alliance (SLD).

The post-communist governments introduced economic reforms from 1990 but the transition to a market economy caused unemployment and a sharp drop in living standards. Popular discontent and a fragmented parliament led to a succession of short-lived governments. In 1997 a new constitution was adopted that eradicated all signs of the former communist system. Poland joined NATO in 1999 and the EU in 2004.

The Law and Justice Party (PiS) candidate, Lech Kaczynski, won the presidential election in October 2005. The PiS had won the legislative election a month earlier, forming first a minority and then a coalition government. The coalition government collapsed in August 2007, leading to an early election in which the liberal Civic Platform (PO) won most of the seats in both chambers, although without an outright majority in the lower house. The PO formed a coalition government with the Polish Popular Party and independents, under the PO leader Donald Tusk.

POLITICAL SYSTEM

Under the 1997 constitution, the head of state is the president, who is directly elected for a five-year term, renewable only once. The president nominates the prime minister and has the right to be consulted over the appointment of the foreign, defence and interior ministers. The National Assembly is bicameral; the lower house, the *Sejm* (Diet), has 460 members elected by proportional representation for a four-year term. The senate has 100 members elected on a provincial basis for a four-year term.

HEAD OF STATE
President, Lech Kaczynski, *elected* 23 October 2005, *sworn in* 23 December 2005

SELECTED GOVERNMENT MEMBERS *as at June 2008*
Prime Minister, Donald Tusk
Deputy Prime Ministers, Waldemar Pawlak *(Economy);* Grzegorz Schetyna *(Interior)*
Defence, Radoslaw Sikorski
Foreign Affairs, Bogdan Klich
Finance, Jan Vincent Rostowski

EMBASSY OF THE REPUBLIC OF POLAND
47 Portland Place, London W1B 1JHST
T 0870-774 2700 E polishembassy@polishembassy.org.uk
W www.polishembassy.org.uk
Ambassador Extraordinary and Plenipotentiary, HE Barbara Tuge-Erecinska, *apptd* 2006

BRITISH EMBASSY
Aleje Roz No. 1, 00-556 Warsaw
T (+48) (22) 628 1001 E britemb@it.com.pl
W www.britishembassy.pl
Ambassador Extraordinary and Plenipotentiary, HE Ric Todd, *apptd* 2007

BRITISH COUNCIL
Al. Jerozolimskie 59, 00-697 Warsaw
T (+48) (22) 695 5900 W www.britishcouncil.org/poland
Director, Tony O'Brien

DEFENCE

The army has 946 main battle tanks, 1,402 armoured infantry fighting vehicles, 693 armoured personnel carriers and 54 armed helicopters. The navy has 5 submarines, 3 frigates, 5 corvettes, and 14 armed helicopters at 5 bases. The air force has 103 combat aircraft.

The government has agreed in principle to host a US missile defence system.
Military expenditure – US$6,230m (2006)
Military personnel – 127,266: army 79,000, navy 11,600, air force 28,466, joint staff 8,200; paramilitary 21,400
Conscription duration – 9 months

ECONOMY AND TRADE

Poland's successful transition to a market economy in the 1990s was at the cost of high levels of public debt, unemployment and inflation. Recent governments have reduced these, and the economy has expanded since accession to the EU, owing to growing exports and access to EU funding. Further economic development is hindered by inefficiency, rigidity and low-level corruption, although the new government is committed to further privatisation and structural reforms.

Poland has vast mineral resources, especially of coal. The main industries are machine-building, iron and steel production, coal-mining, chemicals, shipbuilding, food processing, glass, beverages and textiles. Industry accounts for 31.9 per cent of GDP. The large agricultural sector has been modernised but remains inefficient; it employs 16 per cent of the workforce but contributes only 4.1 per cent of GDP. The main crops are vegetables, fruit, wheat, meat, eggs and dairy products.

The main trading partners are other EU countries (especially Germany) and Russia. Principal exports include machinery and vehicles, manufactured goods, foodstuffs and livestock. The main imports are machinery and vehicles, semi-manufactured goods, chemicals, minerals, fuels and lubricants.

GNI – US$313,000m; US$8,210 per capita (2006)
Annual average growth of GDP – 6.5 per cent (2007 est)
Inflation rate – 2.1 per cent (2007 est)
Unemployment – 12.8 per cent (2007 est)
Total external debt – US$187,800m (2007)
Imports – US$125,000m (2006)
Exports – US$110,000m (2006)

BALANCE OF PAYMENTS
Trade – US$15,063m deficit (2006)
Current Account – US$11,084m deficit (2006)

Trade with UK	*2006*	*2007*
Imports from UK	£2,677,500,000	£2,364,778,709
Exports to UK	£3,083,400,000	£3,595,494,740

COMMUNICATIONS

The country has a total of 23,072km of railways, 423,997km of roads, and 3,997km of navigable rivers and canals. Around 123 airports and airfields are in use; the principal airports are at Warsaw, Gdansk, Krakow and Szczecin. The principal seaports are Gdansk, Gdynia, Szczecin and Swinoujscie.

The fixed-line telephone system is being modernised but progress has been slow, especially in rural areas. Mobile phone distribution has, by contrast, grown very rapidly. In 2006 there were 11.5 million main lines in use, 36.7 million mobile phone subscribers and 11 million internet users.

EDUCATION AND HEALTH

Elementary education (ages seven to 15) is free of charge and compulsory. Secondary education is also free, but optional.

Gross enrolment ratio (percentage of relevant age group) – primary 98 per cent; secondary 100 per cent; tertiary 64 per cent (2006 est)
Health expenditure (per capita) – US$495 (2005)
Hospital beds (per 1,000 people) – 5.3 (2000–6)

MEDIA

Poland's broadcasting network is the largest in eastern and central Europe, and while freedom of speech is generally respected, laws against criticism of the political system are still in force. State-owned television (TVP) still has the largest audience share for its two national channels. State-owned radio reaches just over half the population and there are more than 200 other commercial local and regional stations on air. Poland has over 300 newspapers, most of them local or regional, and popular titles include *Fakt, Polityka* and *Rzeczpospolita*.

CULTURE

Polish literature dates from before the 14th century. Major writers include Nobel Prize winners Henryk Sienkiewicz (1846–1916), Wladyslaw Stanislaw Reymont (1867–1925), Czeslaw Milosz (1911–2004) and Wislawa Szymborska (*b.* 1923).

Other notable cultural figures include the pianist and composer Frédéric Chopin (1810–49); film directors Krzysztof Kieslowski (1941–1996) and Academy Award winner Roman Polanski (*b.* 1933); astronomer Nicolaus Copernicus (1473–1543), who formulated the first heliocentric theory of the solar system, and physicist Marie Curie (1867–1934), the first woman to win a Nobel prize.

PORTUGAL

República Portuguesa – Portuguese Republic

Area – 92,391 sq. km
Capital – Lisbon; population, 2,812,000 (2007 est)
Major cities – Amadora, Oporto
Currency – Euro (€) of 100 cents
Population – 10,642,836 rising at 0.33 per cent per year (2007 est)
Language – Portuguese, Mirandese (both official)
Population density – 116 per sq. km (2006)
Urban population – 55.6 per cent (2005 est)
Median age (years) – 38.8 (2007 est)
National anthem – 'A Portuguesa' ['The Portuguese']
National day – 10 June (Portugal Day)
Life expectancy (years) – 77.87 (2007 est)
Mortality rate – 10.56 (2007 est)
Birth rate – 10.59 (2006 est)
Infant mortality rate – 4.92 (2007 est)
Death penalty – Abolished for all crimes (since 1976)
CPI score – 6.5 (2007)

CLIMATE AND TERRAIN

The terrain is mountainous north of the river Tagus, with rolling hills and plains in the south. Elevation extremes range from 2,351m (Ponta do Pico, Azores) at the highest point to 0m (Atlantic Ocean) at the lowest. Forests of pine, cork and eucalyptus cover about 38 per cent of the country. The climate is mild, with average temperatures in Lisbon ranging from 8°C in January to 28°C in July.

HISTORY AND POLITICS

Part of the Roman Empire from the second century BC, the country was overrun by Vandals and Visigoths in the fifth century AD. The Visigoths were ousted by Muslims from north Africa in the eighth century but Christian reconquest began in the tenth century and an independent Christian kingdom was established in the 12th century.

Portuguese navigators led the 15th-century European age of exploration and the country soon became a major commercial and colonial power; its empire expanding to include Brazil, parts of China and vast areas of Africa. In 1807 Portugal was invaded by Napoleonic France and then became the base from which Allied forces liberated Portugal and Spain in the Peninsular War. The 19th century was politically turbulent, with power struggles between conservative and liberal politicians and between different factions of the royal family. In 1910 an armed uprising in Lisbon drove King Manuel II into exile and a republic was declared.

A period of political instability ensued until the military intervened in 1926. The constitution of 1933 gave formal expression to the authoritarian *Estado Novo* (New State) introduced by Dr Antonio Salazar, prime minister from 1932 until 1968. Marcello Caetano succeeded Salazar in 1968 but the regime's failure to liberalise at home or to conclude wars in the African colonies resulted in the government's overthrow by a military coup in 1974. Great political turmoil followed in 1974–5, a period in which most of the colonies gained their independence. Elections in 1976 stabilised the situation and full civilian government was restored in 1982. Portugal joined the EEC in 1986 and the eurozone in 1999.

The Socialist Party won the 2005 legislative election with 120 seats, giving it its first absolute majority in the assembly since Portugal returned to democracy in 1974. The 2006 presidential election was won by the Social Democrat candidate Anibal Cavaco Silva (prime minister 1985–95), with 50.6 per cent of the vote.

POLITICAL SYSTEM

Under the 1976 constitution, amended in 1982 and 1989, the head of state is a president who is elected for a five-year term, renewable only once. The unicameral Assembly of the Republic has 230 members, directly elected by proportional representation for a four-year term. The prime minister, appointed by the president, is usually the leader of the largest party in the assembly.

HEAD OF STATE

President of the Republic, Anibal Cavaco Silva, *elected* 22 January 2006, *sworn in* 9 March 2006

SELECTED GOVERNMENT MEMBERS *as at June 2008*

Prime Minister, Jose Socrates
Foreign Affairs, Luis Amado
Interior, Rui Pereira
Finance, Fernando Teixeira dos Santos
Defence, Nuno Severiano Teixeira

EMBASSY OF PORTUGAL

11 Belgrave Square, London SW1X 8PP
T 020-7235 5331 E london@portembassy.co.uk
Ambassador Extraordinary and Plenipotentiary, HE Antonio Santana Carlos, *apptd* 2006

BRITISH EMBASSY

Rua de Sao Bernardo 33, 1249-082 Lisbon
T (+351) (21) 392 4000 E britembassy@mail.telepac.pt
W www.uk-embassy.pt
Ambassador Extraordinary and Plenipotentiary, HE Alexander Ellis, *apptd* 2007

BRITISH COUNCIL

1–3 Rua Luís Fernandes, 1249-062 Lisbon
T (+351) (21) 321 4500 W www.britishcouncil.org/portugal
Director, Rosemary Hilhorst, OBE

DEFENCE

The army has 224 main battle tanks and 353 armoured personnel carriers. The navy has 1 submarine, 5 frigates, 7 corvettes and 17 patrol and coastal vessels at 6 bases. The air force has 25 combat aircraft.
Military expenditure – US$3,080m (2006)
Military personnel – 42,910: army 26,700, navy 9,110, air force 7,100; paramilitary 47,700

ECONOMY AND TRADE

Portugal has experienced rapid economic growth since joining the EU in 1986, developing a diversified and increasingly service-based economy. Since the mid-1990s, much of the economy has been liberalised and many state enterprises privatised. Economic growth slowed in 2001–6, leading to a large budget deficit, although this has now been brought below the eurozone's 3 per cent limit. Scope to boost growth is limited by a shortage of foreign direct investment and a poor education system.

Around 10 per cent of the workforce is engaged in agriculture, contributing 3.5 per cent of GDP. The chief products are grain, fruit and vegetables, livestock, fish, dairy products and timber and cork from the forests. The main industries are tourism, manufacturing (textiles, footwear, cork, paper, chemicals, rail and aerospace equipment, porcelain, ceramics, glassware), metalworking, shipbuilding and repair and wine-making. Natural resources are being exploited to generate electricity from hydroelectric and solar sources, to reduce Portugal's dependence on imported fuel and energy. Industry accounts for 25.3 per cent of GDP and services for 71.2 per cent.

The main trading partners are other EU countries, especially Spain, and the USA. Principal exports are textiles, clothing, wood products, agricultural products and electrical equipment. The main imports include machinery, vehicles, chemicals, oil, textiles and agricultural products.
GNI – US$189,000m; US$17,850 per capita (2006)
Annual average growth of GDP – 1.7 per cent (2007 est)
Inflation rate – 2.4 per cent (2007 est)
Unemployment – 8 per cent (2007 est)
Total external debt – US$415,500m (2007)
Imports – US$65,600m (2006)
Exports – US$42,900m (2006)

BALANCE OF PAYMENTS

Trade – US$22,712m deficit (2006)
Current Account – US$18,283m deficit (2006)

Trade with UK	*2006*	*2007*
Imports from UK	£2,271,500,000	£1,464,719,378
Exports to UK	£2,742,300,000	£1,451,949,559

COMMUNICATIONS

There are 2,786km of railways, of which 1,351km are electrified, and 78,470km of roads. There are 66 airports and airfields, including international airports at Lisbon, Oporto, Faro and Santa Maria (Azores) and Funchal (Madeira). The main ports are Lisbon, Oporto and Setubal.

Modern telephone systems serve 4.2 million main-line

subscribers, 12.2 million mobile phone subscribers and 3.2 million internet users.

EDUCATION AND HEALTH

Education is free of charge and compulsory for nine years from the age of six. Secondary education is mainly conducted in state general unified schools, lyceums, technical and professional schools and private schools. There are also military, naval, polytechnic and other specialist schools. The university at Coimbra was founded in 1290.

Gross enrolment ratio (percentage of relevant age group) – primary 116 per cent; secondary 97 per cent; tertiary 55 per cent (2006 est)
Health expenditure (per capita) – US$1,800 (2005)
Hospital beds (per 1,000 people) – 3.7 (2000–6)

MEDIA

The monopoly of the public broadcaster RTP ended in 1992 with the launch of commercial television. Public radio networks are operated by RTP, while the Roman Catholic Church owns Radio Renascenca. There are some 300 other local and regional commercial radio stations. Principal national newspapers include the daily titles *Diario de Noticias, Publico, Correio da Manha* and *Jornal de Noticias.*

AUTONOMOUS REGIONS

Madeira and the Azores are both autonomous regions, each with its own locally elected assembly and government.
MADEIRA is a group of islands in the Atlantic Ocean about 990km south-west of Lisbon, and consists of Madeira, Porto, Santo and three uninhabited islands. Total area is 779 sq. km; population, 243,007 (2003 est). Funchal in Madeira, the largest island, is the capital.
THE AZORES is an archipelago of nine islands in the Atlantic Ocean 1,400–1,800 km west of Lisbon, and consists of Flores, Corvo, Terceira, Sao Jorge, Pico, Faial, Graciosa, Sao Miguel and Santa Maria. Total area is 2,330 sq. km; population, 240,042 (2003 est). Ponta Delgada, on Sao Miguel, is the capital.

QATAR

Dawlat Qatar – State of Qatar

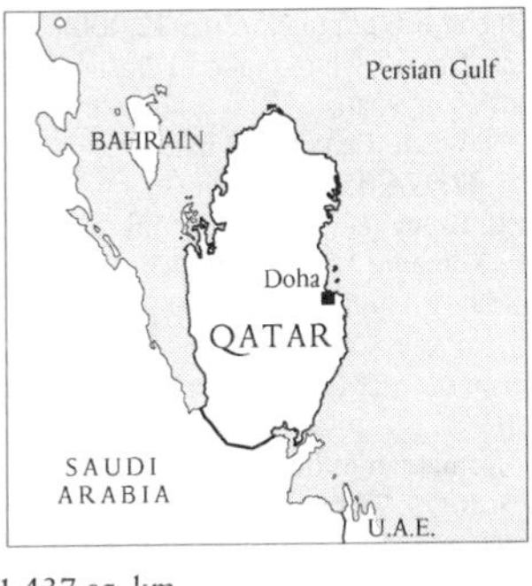

Area – 11,437 sq. km
Capital – Doha; population, 384,000 (2007 est)
Major city – Ar Rayyan
Currency – Qatar riyal of 100 dirhams
Population – 907,229 rising at 2.39 per cent per year (2007 est); Arab (40 per cent), Indian (18 per cent), Pakistani (18 per cent), Iranian (10 per cent) (est)
Religion – Islam (75 per cent), Christianity (10 per cent) (est)
Language – Arabic (official), English
Population density – 75 per sq. km (2006)
Urban population – 92.3 per cent (2005 est)
Median age (years) – 31.9 (2007 est)
National anthem – 'As-Salam al-Amiri' ['The Peace of the Amir']
National day – 3 September (Independence Day)
Life expectancy (years) – 74.14 (2007 est)
Mortality rate – 4.82 (2007 est)
Birth rate – 15.56 (2007 est)
Infant mortality rate – 17.46 (2007 est)
Death penalty – Retained
CPI score – 6.0 (2007)
Literacy rate – 89.2 per cent (2004 est)

CLIMATE AND TERRAIN

The terrain is mostly desert, with salt flats in the south. Elevation extremes range from 103m (Qurayn Abu al-Bawl) at the highest point to 0m (Persian Gulf) at the lowest. The country has a desert climate and average temperatures range from 23°C in January to 35°C in July. Humidity along the coast often reaches 90 per cent during the summer. Average annual rainfall is below 75mm.

HISTORY AND POLITICS

Qatar developed into an important trading centre from the eighth century. It came under the rule of the al-Khalifa family, which in the 18th century moved its base to Bahrain island. A revolt against al-Khalifa rule in the 1860s was suppressed, but Britain intervened in 1867. The al-Khalifas were removed and replaced by the al-Thani family. Nominally under the rule of the Ottoman Empire from 1871 until the outbreak of the First World War, Qatar became a British protectorate in 1916. It became independent in 1971.

In 1972 Shaikh Ahmad was overthrown by the crown prince and prime minister, Shaikh Khalifa. Another coup followed in 1995 when Khalifa was overthrown by his son and heir, Shaikh Hamad, who has since introduced liberal reforms. Municipal elections, the first democratic polls since independence, were held in 1999. A referendum in 2003 approved a new constitution, which was endorsed by the amir in 2004. Elections to the partially elected consultative council established by the constitution were expected in 2007 but have yet to take place.

POLITICAL SYSTEM

A new constitution was promulgated in 2004. The head of state is a hereditary absolute monarch, the amir. There is no legislature at present, although the 2004 constitution provides for a *Shura* council with 45 members, 30 directly elected and 15 appointed by the amir, and this will have legislative powers. At present there is an advisory council with 35 members appointed by the amir. There are no political parties. Women have been permitted to vote and stand for election since 1999; the first female cabinet member was appointed in 2003.

HEAD OF STATE

HH Amir of Qatar, Defence, C-in-C of Armed Forces, Shaikh Hamad bin Khalifa al-Thani, KCMG, *assumed power* 27 June 1995
Crown Prince, HH Shaikh Tamim bin Hamad al-Thani

SELECTED GOVERNMENT MEMBERS *as at July 2008*
Prime Minister, Foreign Affairs, HH Shaikh Hamad bin Jassem bin Jabr al-Thani
Deputy Prime Minister, Abdullah bin Hamad al-Attiyah
Internal Affairs, Shaikh Abdulla bin Khalid al-Thani
Economy and Finance, Yousef bin Hussain Kamal

EMBASSY OF THE STATE OF QATAR
1 South Audley Street, London W1K 1NB
T 020-7493 2200
Ambassador Extraordinary and Plenipotentiary, HE Khalid Rashid al-Hamoudi al-Mansouri, *apptd* 2005

BRITISH EMBASSY
PO Box 3, Doha
T (+974) 442 1991 E bembcomm@qatar.net.qa
Ambassador Extraordinary and Plenipotentiary, vacant

BRITISH COUNCIL
PO Box 2992, 93 Al Sadd Street, Doha
T (+974) 425 1888 W www.britishcouncil.org/qatar
Director, Simon Winetroube

DEFENCE

The army has 30 main battle tanks, 226 armoured personnel carriers and 40 armoured infantry fighting vehicles. The navy has 21 patrol and coastal combatant vessels at 2 bases. The air force has 18 combat aircraft and 19 armed helicopters.
Military budget – US$2,330m (2006 est)
Military personnel – 11,800: army 8,500, navy 1,800, air force 1,500

ECONOMY AND TRADE

The economy is based largely on the production of oil and gas, which account for more than 60 per cent of GDP, about 85 per cent of export earnings and 70 per cent of government revenues. The state-owned Qatar General Petroleum Corporation controls the industry, and is responsible for oil production onshore and offshore. There has been substantial foreign investment in exploitation of the large gasfields, and Qatar became the world's leading exporter of liquefied natural gas in 2007.

Other industries include oil refining, production of ammonia, fertilisers, petrochemicals, steel and cement, and ship repairing. Industry contributes 71.2 per cent of GDP, services 28.7 per cent and agriculture, which is constrained by the terrain and climate, just 0.1 per cent. The economy depends on foreign workers, who outnumber the indigenous population.

The main export markets are Japan, South Korea and Singapore. Principal exports are liquefied natural gas, petroleum products, fertilisers and steel. The chief sources of imports are EU states, especially France, Japan, the USA, Saudi Arabia and South Korea. The main imports are machinery and transport equipment, foodstuffs and chemicals.
Annual average growth of GDP – 7.8 per cent (2007 est)
Inflation rate – 12 per cent (2007 est)
Unemployment – 0.7 per cent (2007 est)
Total external debt – US$31,070m (2007 est)
Imports – US$15,860m (2006)
Exports – US$31,300m (2006)

BALANCE OF PAYMENTS
Trade – US$14,837m surplus (2006)
Current Account – US$16,113m surplus (2006)

Trade with UK	*2006*	*2007*
Imports from UK	£488,809,000	£624,144,571
Exports to UK	£199,329,000	£187,938,516

COMMUNICATIONS

There are 1,230km of roads, of which 1,107km are surfaced, but no railways. There are five airports, of which Doha is the principal one, as well as being the main seaport. Gulf Air and Qatar Airways provide regular international air services. Halul is the terminal for offshore oilfields. There is a modern telephone system, which served 228,300 main lines and 289,900 internet users in 2006; mobile phone subscriptions numbered 919,800 in 2006.

MEDIA

Qatar officially lifted media censorship in 1995 and since then the press has essentially been free from government interference, although some self-censorship is practised. The Qatari satellite station Al Jazeera, launched in 1996, has become one of the most important broadcasters in the Middle East. It launched an English-language network, Al-Jazeera International, in 2006. Radio is state-run by the Qatar Broadcasting Service (QBS), and the BBC World Service is available in Doha. The most popular newspapers are *Al-Watan* and the English-language *Gulf Times.*

ROMANIA

Area – 237,500 sq. km
Capital – Bucharest; population, 1,942,000 (2007 est)
Major cities – Brasov, Cluj-Napoca, Constanta, Craiova, Galati, Iasi, Timisoara
Currency – New leu (Lei) of 100 bani
Population – 22,276,056 falling at 0.13 per cent per year (2007 est); Romanian (89.5 per cent), Hungarian (6.6 per cent), Romani (2.5 per cent). There are German, Russian, Turkish and Ukrainian minorities
Religion – Orthodox Christianity (87 per cent), Roman Catholicism (54 per cent), Greek Catholicism (4 per cent) (est)
Language – Romanian (official), Hungarian, Romani
Population density – 94 per sq. km (2006)
Urban population – 54.7 per cent (2005 est)
Median age (years) – 36.9 (2007 est)
National anthem – 'Desteapta-te, Romane' ['Awake Thee, Romanian']
National day – 1 December (Unification Day)
Life expectancy (years) – 71.91 (2007 est)
Mortality rate – 11.81 (2007 est)
Birth rate – 10.67 (2007 est)

Infant mortality rate – 24.6 (2007 est)
Death penalty – Abolished for all crimes (since 1989)
CPI score – 3.7 (2007)
Population below poverty line – 25 per cent (2005 est)

CLIMATE AND TERRAIN

The Carpathian mountains, running south into the centre of the country and then turning west, and the Transylvanian Alps, enclose a central plateau, which falls towards the basin of the river Tisa. To the south lies the plain of the river Danube, which forms part of the southern border, and to the east the plain of the river Siret and the Black Sea coast. The mountains are thickly forested. Elevation extremes range from 2,544m (Moldoveanu) at the highest point to 0m (Black Sea) at the lowest. The climate is continental, with average temperatures in Bucharest ranging from −2°C in January to 22°C in July.

HISTORY AND POLITICS

Romania was incorporated into the Roman Empire in the early part of the second century AD but was abandoned 200 years later when the power of Rome started to decline. After centuries of rule by invading and often disparate tribal forces, Romania was incorporated into the Ottoman Empire during the 15th century. The principalities of Moldavia and Wallachia were unified under a single native ruler in 1859, and independence was recognised by the Congress of Berlin in 1878. Romania joined the Allies in the First World War, and in the post-war peace settlement acquired Transylvania, Bukovina and Bessarabia.

In 1940 Romania was forced to cede territory to the USSR and Hungary, and power was seized by the Romanian fascists, who took the country into the Second World War on the Axis side. When its leaders were overthrown in 1944, Romania changed sides. It was occupied in 1945 by Soviet forces and a communist-dominated government was installed. In 1947 King Michael abdicated, the monarchy was abolished and Romania became a communist republic. In 1965 Nicolae Ceausescu became leader of the Romanian Communist Party and pursued a foreign policy increasingly independent of the USSR, forming relationships with China and several Western countries. Ceausescu's regime was brutal and corrupt, and when the rest of eastern Europe threw off communist rule in 1989, violent suppression of reformers provoked an uprising in December 1989 that deposed and executed the dictator and his wife. A provisional government led by Ion Iliescu abolished the leading role of the Communist Party and held elections in 1990.

Although Romania became a multiparty democracy in 1991, governments continued to be dominated by former communists until 1996. Popular unrest and demonstrations have persisted throughout the post-communist period, as most of the population has yet to benefit much from the transition to a market economy. Further economic (and constitutional) changes were introduced to prepare for EU membership and Romania joined the EU in 2007.

Presidential and legislative elections were held in November and December 2004. Traian Basescu, the candidate of a coalition of the Democratic and National Liberal parties, won the presidential election with 51.2 per cent of the vote. In the legislative election, the Social Democratic Party (PSD) remained the largest party, with 189 seats, but without an overall majority. It formed a coalition government with three other centre parties under Calin Tariceanu. The Democratic Party left the government in April 2007, prompting a cabinet reshuffle. Tension between the government and the president over the pace of anti-corruption reforms led to a government attempt to impeach President Basescu; a referendum in May 2007 endorsed the president and he resumed his powers. The next legislative elections are due in late 2008.

POLITICAL SYSTEM

The 1991 constitution was amended in 2003 to bring it into line with EU requirements. The head of state is a president who is directly elected for a five-year term, renewable only once. The bicameral parliament comprises the Chamber of Deputies with 345 seats, of which 18 are reserved for ethnic minorities, and the senate with 140 seats. Both houses are directly elected for a four-year term. The prime minister is appointed by the president.

HEAD OF STATE

President of the Republic, Traian Basescu, *elected* 12 December 2004

SELECTED GOVERNMENT MEMBERS *as at July 2008*

Prime Minister, Calin Tariceanu
Defence, Radu Stroe
Economy and Finance, Varujan Vosganian
Foreign Affairs, Lazar Comanescu
Interior, Cristian David

EMBASSY OF ROMANIA

Arundel House, 4 Palace Green, London W8 4QD
T 020-7937 9666 E roemb@roemb.co.uk
W www.londra.mae.ro
Ambassador Extraordinary and Plenipotentiary, vacant

BRITISH EMBASSY

24 Strada Jules Michelet, 70154 Bucharest
T (+40) (21) 201 7200
Ambassador Extraordinary and Plenipotentiary, HE Robin Barnett, *apptd* 2006

BRITISH COUNCIL

Calea Dorobantilor 14, 010572 Bucharest
T (+40) (21) 307 9600 W www.britishcouncil.org/romania
Director (acting), Liliana Biglou

DEFENCE

The army has 366 main battle tanks, 1,081 armoured personnel carriers and 95 armoured infantry fighting vehicles. The navy has 3 frigates, 4 corvettes and 23 patrol and coastal vessels at 4 bases. The air force has 74 combat aircraft.

Under an agreement signed in 2005, the USA is allowed to use military bases in Romania.

Military expenditure – US$2,320m (2006)
Military personnel – 74,267: army 42,200, navy 8,067, air force 10,500, joint staff 13,500; paramilitary 79,900

ECONOMY AND TRADE

Transition to a market economy was slow to begin and made sluggish progress. The president and government elected in 2004 accelerated reform and the campaign against corruption to meet the requirements for accession to the EU. Although the economy has grown steadily since 2000, it was from a low base and the effects have only recently started to have an impact on the country's widespread poverty; about 25 per cent of the population lives below the poverty line. Corruption and red tape continue to deter foreign investment. The high inflation of past years has been reduced, and the currency was revalued in 2005.

Agriculture employs 29.7 per cent of the workforce and contributes 7.9 per cent of GDP. The principal crops are cereals, sugar beet, vegetables, sunflower seeds and livestock products. Vines and fruit are grown, and extensive forests in the mountains support an important timber industry. There are reserves of natural gas and oil, but Romania is a net importer of fossil fuels, although it exports electricity. Mineral deposits including coal, iron ore, bauxite, chromium and uranium support a mining industry. Other industries include manufacturing, machinery and car assembly, food processing and oil refining.

The main trading partners are EU states (especially Italy and Germany), Turkey and Russia. Principal exports include textiles, footwear, metallurgical products, machinery components, minerals and fuels, chemicals and agricultural products. The main imports are machines and equipment, fuels, minerals, chemicals, textiles, base metals and agricultural products.

GNI – US$104,400m; US$4,830 per capita (2006)
Annual average growth of GDP – 5.9 per cent (2007 est)
Inflation rate – 4.6 per cent (2007 est)
Unemployment – 4.5 per cent (2007 est)
Total external debt – US$85,860m (2007 est)
Imports – US$51,100m (2006)
Exports – US$32,300m (2006)

BALANCE OF PAYMENTS
Trade – US$18,770m deficit (2006)
Current Account – US$12,748m deficit (2006)

Trade with UK	*2006*	*2007*
Imports from UK	£606,466,000	£657,011,981
Exports to UK	£827,115,000	£921,708,684

COMMUNICATIONS

There are 11,385km of railways, over one-third of which are electrified. There are 198,817km of roads, of which 60,043km are surfaced and 228km are motorway. Navigable waterways include 1,599km on the river Danube and its tributaries and 132km of canals, principally the canal linking the Danube to the Black Sea. The principal ports are Braila, Constanta, Galati and Tulcea. The main airports are at Bucharest and Timisoara.

Liberalisation of telecommunications in 2003 has led to rapid growth, and fixed-line density is now about 20 per 100 people. In 2006 there were 4.2 million main lines in use, 17 million mobile phone subscribers and 5 million internet users.

EDUCATION AND HEALTH

Primary and secondary education is free of charge and compulsory for ten years.
Literacy rate – 97.3 per cent (2004 est)
Gross enrolment ratio (percentage of relevant age group) – primary 105 per cent; secondary 86 per cent; tertiary 45 per cent (2006 est)
Health expenditure (per capita) – US$250 (2005)
Hospital beds (per 1,000 people) – 6.6 (2000–6)

MEDIA

Most households in Bucharest have cable TV. There are more than 100 private radio stations. State-run Radio Romania operates four national networks and regional and local stations. There are four main daily newspapers. Law reforms in 2007 mean that journalists can no longer be imprisoned for defamation.

RUSSIA

Rossiyskaya Federatsiya – Russian Federation

Area – 17,075,200 sq. km. Neighbours: Norway (west), Georgia, Azerbaijan, Kazakhstan, China, Mongolia and North Korea (south). The Kaliningrad enclave borders Lithuania and Poland
Capital – Moscow; population, 10,452,000 (2007 est). Founded about 1147, it became the centre of the rising Moscow principality and in the 15th century the capital of the whole of Russia (Muscovy). In 1703 Peter the Great transferred the capital to St Petersburg, but on 14 March 1918 Moscow was again designated the capital
Major Cities – Chelyabinsk, Kazan, Nizhniy Novgorod (Gorky 1932–90), Novosibirsk (Novonikolayevsk until 1926), Omsk, Perm, Rostov, St Petersburg (Petrograd 1914–24; Leningrad 1924–91), Samara (Kuibyshev 1935–90), Ufa, Volgograd (Stalingrad 1925–61), Yekaterinburg (Sverdlovsk 1924–91)
Currency – Rouble of 100 kopeks
Population – 141,377,752 falling at 0.48 per cent per year (2007 est); Russian (79.8 per cent), Tatar (3.8 per cent), Ukrainian (2 per cent). There are a further 150 nationalities living in the country
Religion – Orthodox Christianity (70 per cent), Islam (10 per cent), other Christian denominations (2 per cent), Buddhism (1 per cent) (est)
Language – Russian (official)
Population density – 9 per sq. km (2006)
Urban population – 73.3 per cent (2005 est)

Median age (years) – 38.2 (2007 est)
National anthem – 'National Anthem of Russia'
National day – 12 June (Russia Day)
Life expectancy (years) – 65.87 (2007 est)
Mortality rate – 16.04 (2007 est)
Birth rate – 10.92 (2007 est)
Infant mortality rate – 11.06 (2006 est)
Death penalty – Retained, but not used
CPI score – 2.3 (2007)
Population below poverty line – 17.6 per cent (2004)

CLIMATE AND TERRAIN

Russia includes the easternmost areas of Europe and the whole of northern Asia. There are three principal geographic areas: a low-lying flat western area stretching eastwards up to the Yenisei river and divided in two by the Ural mountain range; the eastern area between the Yenisei and the Pacific, consisting of plateaux and mountain ranges; and a southern mountainous area. The Kuril Islands form an archipelago in the north Pacific Ocean and are under Russian administration as part of the Sakhalin *oblast*. Elevation extremes range from 5,633m (Mt El'brus, Caucasus) at the highest point to −28m (Caspian Sea) at the lowest. Russia has the longest Arctic coastline in the world (over 27,000km).

The most important rivers are the Volga, the Northern Dvina, the Neva, the Don and the Kuban in the European part, and in the Asiatic part, the Ob, the Irtysh, the Yenisei, the Lena, the Amur and, further north, the Khatanga, Olenek, Yana, Indigirka and Kolyma. Lake Baikal in eastern Siberia is the deepest lake in the world.

The climate varies dramatically, from the frozen tundra of the north Siberian plain to the temperate regions of the far east. Throughout the country, winters are cold, while summers are hot in the south and relatively warm elsewhere. Rainfall is highest in the westerly mountain regions, which have an average annual precipitation of up to 2,000mm. Average temperatures in Moscow range from −16°C in January to 23°C in July.

HISTORY AND POLITICS

Russia was settled by many ethnic groups, including Slavs, Turks and Bulgars in the third to seventh centuries AD, and in the 13th century came under the overlordship of the Mongols. In the 15th century the grand duke of Muscovy threw off Mongol overlordship and began a process of unification and territorial expansion continued by his successors. Internal disorder and war with neighbouring countries held back Russian development until the reign of Peter I (The Great) (1682–1725), who introduced Western ideas of government, modernised the army and founded the navy. Under Catherine II (The Great) (1762–96) Russia extended its territory further. Russian expansion in Asia led to a war with Japan in 1904–5 that ended in an unexpected defeat. This provoked a revolution in 1905 which, though suppressed, forced the emperor to establish Russia's first parliament *(Duma)*.

The *Duma's* powers were limited and it was unable to ameliorate the Tsarist regime's endemic misgovernment or the conditions of the increasingly militant urban working class. During the First World War discontent caused by autocratic rule, the poor military conduct of the war and wartime privation led to a revolution which broke out in March 1917. The emperor abdicated and a power struggle ensued between the provisional government and the Bolshevik Party. This led to a second revolution in November 1917 in which the Bolsheviks, led by Vladimir Lenin (1870–1924), seized power.

Civil war between 'red' Bolshevik forces and 'white' monarchist and anti-communist forces, the latter supported by foreign powers, lasted until the end of 1922. During the civil war, Russia was declared a Soviet republic and other Soviet republics were formed in Ukraine, Belorussia and Transcaucasia. These four republics merged to form the Union of Soviet Socialist Republics (USSR) on 30 December 1922.

During the 1930s Joseph Stalin introduced a policy of rapid industrialisation under a series of five-year plans, brought all sectors of industry under government control, abolished private ownership and enforced the collectivisation of agriculture, causing severe famine. Many ethnic minority groups suffered under Stalin's regime and it is estimated that up to 1.5 million people were deported to the Gulags of Siberia and the central Asian republics. After being attacked by Nazi Germany in 1941, the USSR joined the Second World War on the side of the Allies. In 1944–5 Soviet forces liberated much of eastern Europe and the post-war communist regimes in these countries were closely tied to the Soviet government.

The post-war period was dominated for 40 years by the Cold War with the West, especially the USA, prompting massive expenditure on the military-industrial sector and the provision of aid to developing countries as a means of extending Soviet influence. Tight political and economic control was maintained over the countries in the Soviet bloc, including military intervention in support of communist regimes in Europe and Afghanistan.

Mikhail Gorbachev became Soviet leader in 1985 and introduced the policies of *perestroika* (complete restructuring) and *glasnost* (openness) in order to revamp the economy, which had stagnated since the 1970s, to root out corruption and inefficiency, and to end the Cold War. The retreat from total control by the Communist Party unleashed ethnic and nationalist tensions.

Following the defeat of an attempted coup by hardline Communists in August 1991, effective political power was in the hands of the republican leaders, especially Russian President Yeltsin, and the USSR began to break up as the constituent republics declared their independence. Gorbachev resigned as Soviet president on 25 December 1991 and the following day the USSR formally ceased to exist. The Russian Federation took over the USSR's seat at the UN in December 1991, was recognised as an independent state by the EC and USA in January 1992, and joined the G7 group of industrialised countries in 1996.

Vladimir Putin was elected president in 2000, and re-elected in 2004. His presidency saw an increasing degree of centralisation, the partial renationalisation of industry (especially oil and gas), the re-assertion of state control over the media, an increasingly authoritarian stance on democracy and an aggressive approach to relations with former Soviet states. In the 2007 legislative elections, the pro-Putin United Russia party retained its majority in the *Duma*, and President Putin won a parliamentary seat. This enabled him to be appointed chair of the council of ministers in May 2008 after his successor as president, Dmitry Medvedev, took office. President Medvedev was elected outright in the first round of the presidential election in March, but he is widely regarded as a figurehead, with Putin continuing to wield the most political power and to determine government policy.

INSURGENCIES

Chechnya occupies an area that is strategically important to Russia because routes from central Russia to the Black and Caspian seas, and oil and gas pipelines from neighbouring countries pass through it. The republic declared itself independent in November 1991 but its attempts to assert its independence have led to two wars with the federal government.

The first of these, from 1994–6, occurred after a civil war in 1994 between the Chechen government and armed opposition forces tacitly supported by the federal government was followed by a Russian military invasion in December 1994. Peace negotiations in 1996 resulted in the signing of the Khasavyurt accords and Russian troops withdrew in January 1997. The uneasy peace broke down in September 1999 when Russian forces invaded Chechnya again. Refusing to negotiate with the Chechen government, President Putin imposed direct rule from Moscow in May 2000. Violent unrest has continued in Chechnya, and there have been reports of human rights violations, particularly by Russian troops. Chechen separatists have carried out suicide bombings and other attacks in Russia, such as the Moscow theatre siege in 2002 and the Beslan school siege in 2004.

In a 2003 referendum in Chechnya, the majority voted in favour of a new constitution promising autonomy for the republic but also stating that Chechnya was an integral part of the Russian Federation. The election of a Russian-backed candidate, Alu Alkhanov, as president of Chechnya in August 2004 (following the assassination of his predecessor, Akhmad Kadyrov, in May) has helped reduce the level of violence; Alkhanov was succeeded in 2007 by Ramzan Kadyrov, son of Akhmad Kadyrov. Violence has spilled over into other parts of the northern Caucasus as Russian forces attempt to capture Chechen separatists based in the republics neighbouring Chechnya.

POLITICAL SYSTEM

The 1993 constitution introduced multiparty democracy and enshrines various human rights and civil liberties. The head of state is a president, who is directly elected for a four-year term, renewable only once consecutively. Legislative power is vested in the Federal Assembly, comprising the State *Duma* (lower house) of 450 members, all elected by proportional representation for a four-year term, and the Council of the Federation, which has 166 members (two from each member of the federation), appointed for terms of varying lengths. The president appoints the chairman of the council of ministers (prime minister) but is also entitled to chair sessions of the council.

HEAD OF STATE

President, Dmitry Medvedev, *elected* 2 March 2008, *inaugurated* 7 May 2008

SELECTED GOVERNMENT MEMBERS *as at July 2008*

Prime Minister, Vladimir Putin
First Deputy Chairs, Igor Shuvalov; Viktor Zubkov
Deputy Chairs, Sergei Ivanov; Igor Sechin; Sergei Sobyanin; Aleksandr Zhukov
Foreign Affairs, Sergey Lavrov
Interior, Rashid Nurgaliyev
Finance, Alexei Kudrin
Defence, Anatoliy Serdyukov

EMBASSY OF THE RUSSIAN FEDERATION

13 Kensington Palace Gardens, London W8 4QX
T 020-7229 2666
Ambassador Extraordinary and Plenipotentiary, HE Yury Fedotov, *apptd* 2005

BRITISH EMBASSY

Smolenskaya Naberezhnaya 10, 121099 Moscow
T (+7) (495) 956 7200 E moscow@britishembassy.ru
W www.britemb.msk.ru
Ambassador Extraordinary and Plenipotentiary, HE Anthony Brenton, *apptd* 2005

BRITISH COUNCIL

Ulitsa Nikoloyamskaya 1, 109189 Moscow
T (+7) (495) 782 0200 W www.britishcouncil.ru
Director, James Kennedy

FEDERAL STRUCTURE

Following the break-up of the USSR in 1991, a new federal treaty was signed in 1992 between the central government and the autonomous republics of the Russian Federation. Tatarstan and Bashkortostan signed the treaty in 1994 after securing considerable legislative and economic autonomy.

The Russian Federation comprises 46 *oblasti* (regions), 9 *krai* (autonomous territories), 21 *respubliki* (autonomous republics), 4 *okrugi* (autonomous areas), two cities of federal status (Moscow and St Petersburg) and one autonomous Jewish *oblast,* Yevrey. The *oblasti* are Amur, Arkhangelsk, Astrakhan, Belgorod, Bryansk, Chelyabinsk, Irkutsk, Ivanovo, Kaliningrad, Kaluga, Kemerovo, Kirov, Kostroma, Kurgan, Kursk, Leningrad, Lipetsk, Magadan, Moscow, Murmansk, Nizhny-Novgorod, Novgorod, Novosibirsk, Omsk, Orenburg, Oryol, Penza, Pskov, Rostov, Ryazan, Sakhalin, Samara, Saratov, Smolensk, Sverdlovsk, Tambov, Tomsk, Tula, Tver, Tyumen, Ulyanovsk, Vladimir, Volgograd, Vologda, Voronezh and Yaroslavl. The *krai* are Altai, Kamchatka, Khabarovsk, Krasnodar, Krasnoyarsk, Perm, Primorsky, Stavropol and Zabaykalsky. The *respubliki* are Adygeia, Altai, Bashkortostan, Buryatia, Chechnya, Chuvashia, Dagestan, Ingushetia, Kabardino-Balkaria, Kalmykiya, Karachai-Cherkessia, Karelia, Khakassia, Komi, Mari-El, Mordovia, North Ossetia-Alania, Sakha, Tatarstan, Tuva and Udmurtia. The *okrugi* are Chukotka, Khanty-Mansi, Nenets and Yamal-Nenets.

DEFENCE

Since the demise of the USSR, Russia's armed forces have been considerably reduced. Major army reform is planned for the period 2004–10, including transition from conscription to voluntary service.

A joint CIS air defence system covers Russia, Armenia, Belarus, Georgia, Kazakhstan, Kyrgyzstan, Tajikistan, Turkmenistan, Ukraine and Uzbekistan. The Black Sea fleet was divided between Russian and Ukraine under an agreement signed in 1997.

The Strategic Deterrent Forces have 15 nuclear-powered ballistic missile submarines and 508 intercontinental ballistic missiles equipped with some 1,600 nuclear warheads. Russia also has 89 long-range strike aircraft capable of carrying strategic missiles.

The army has about 23,000 main battle tanks, 9,900 armoured personnel carriers and over 15,140 armoured infantry fighting vehicles. The navy has 67 submarines, 1 aircraft carrier, 9 cruisers, 16 destroyers, 14 frigates, 26 corvettes, 74 patrol and coastal vessels, 245 combat aircraft and 166 armed helicopters. The air force has 1,860 combat aircraft.

Russia deploys forces in Armenia (3,170), Georgia (1,000), Moldova (1,199) and Tajikistan (5,500).

Military expenditure – US$70,000m (2006)

Military personnel – 1,027,000: Strategic Deterrent Forces 80,000, army 360,000, airborne 35,000, navy 142,000, air force 160,000, command and support 250,000; paramilitary 418,000

ECONOMY AND TRADE

Under the Soviet regime, an essentially agrarian economy in 1917 was transformed by the early 1960s into the second-greatest industrial power in the world. However, by the early 1970s the concentration of resources on the military-industrial complex had caused the civilian economy to deteriorate. Economic reforms were introduced by President Gorbachev, including the legalisation of small private businesses, the reduction of state control over the economy, and denationalisation and privatisation. The first stage of mass privatisation of state industries began in 1992 and by 1996, 80 per cent of the economy had been privatised. The largest and most economically significant industries, oil and gas, were partially renationalised after President Putin took office.

The transition to a market economy caused a severe economic crisis in 1993 and again in 1998, when the rouble collapsed. But since 1999, the economy has sustained growth averaging 7 per cent a year, and average incomes have grown by more than 12 per cent a year since 2002; the middle class is expanding and poverty is declining, with only 15.8 per cent still living below the poverty line. Investment and consumer demand have both increased significantly since 2000. Foreign debt now stands at around one-third of GDP, inflation has been reduced, the budget has been in surplus every year since 2001 and there is a healthy trade surplus.

Recent banking and fiscal reforms have stimulated foreign investment, although political uncertainties, corruption and a lack of trust in institutions continue to be inhibiting factors. Other problems include the economy's vulnerability to fluctuations in global commodity prices for its main exports, a dilapidated manufacturing base and the small size of its banking sector.

Russia has some of the world's richest natural resources, especially mineral deposits, and oil, natural gas, timber and minerals account for 80 per cent of its exports and 30 per cent of government revenue. The recent growth in the economy is founded on the exploitation and export of its oil and natural gas reserves, and Russia is becoming the leading supplier to European countries and China, a position that has led the country into disputes with its neighbours; Ukraine, Georgia and Belarus have all had gas supplies cut for short periods during negotiations over cutting price subsidies.

Oil is produced in the northern Caucasus, between the Volga and the Urals, and in western Siberia, which also has large deposits of natural gas. Coal is mined in the Kuznetsk area, in the Urals, south of Moscow, in the Donets basin and in the Pechora area in the north. Coal and gas deposits in Siberia and the far east (especially Yakutia) are being developed, and Russia is keen to exploit the shrinking of the Arctic ice-cap to prospect for previously inaccessible deposits under the Arctic Sea. The Ural mountains contain many valuable natural resources, including high-quality iron ore, coal and oil. Iron ore is also mined near Kursk, Tula, Lipetsk, in several areas in Siberia and in the Kola Peninsula. Non-ferrous metals are found in the Altai, eastern Siberia, the northern Caucasus, the Kuznetsk basin, and the far east and north.

The vast area and the great variety in climatic conditions are reflected in the structure of agriculture. In the far north reindeer breeding, hunting and fishing predominate. Further south, the timber industry is combined with grain growing. In the southern half of the forest zone and in the adjacent forest–steppe zone, the acreage under grain crops is larger and agriculture more complex. The southern part of the western Siberian plain is an important grain-growing and stock-breeding area. In the extreme south, cotton is cultivated. Vine, tobacco and other southern crops are grown on the Black Sea shore of the Caucasus.

The service sector is the largest, accounting for 56.2 per cent of GDP and employing 60.5 per cent of the workforce; industry contributes 39.1 per cent of GDP and employs 28.8 per cent; and agriculture accounts for 4.7 per cent of GDP and 10.8 per cent of employment. Moscow and St Petersburg are still the two largest industrial centres, but new industrial areas have been developed in the Urals, the Kuznetsk basin, Siberia and the far east.

Russia's main trading partners are EU countries (especially Germany), China, Ukraine, Japan, South Korea, Turkey and the USA. Principal exports are oil and petroleum products, natural gas, timber and timber products, metals, chemicals, manufactured goods, military vehicles and defence equipment. The main imports are machinery and equipment, consumer goods, medicines, meat, sugar and semi-finished metal products.

GNI – US$822,300m (2006); US$5,770 per capita (2006)

Annual average growth of GDP – 7.4 per cent (2007 est)

Inflation rate – 9 per cent (2007 est)

Unemployment – 5.9 per cent (2007 est)

Total external debt – US$384,800m (2007)

Imports – US$180,000m (2006)

Exports – US$305,000m (2006)

BALANCE OF PAYMENTS

Trade – US$122,765m surplus (2006)

Current Account – US$94,257m surplus (2006)

Trade with UK	*2006*	*2007*
Imports from UK	£2,057,506,000	£2,832,399,450
Exports to UK	£5,819,732,000	£5,460,522,604

COMMUNICATIONS

The European area of Russia is well served by railways, which are state-run, but there are still large areas, notably in the far north and Siberia, with few or no railways. There are 117,000km of railways, of which 87,000km were used for passenger transport and the rest by industry. The road system is similarly concentrated in the more densely populated European part of the country, and in the southernmost parts of Asian Russia. There are 871,000km of roads, 738,000km of which are surfaced.

The most important ports include Taganrog, Rostov and Novorossiysk around the Black Sea and the Sea of Azov. Two of the three northern ports, St Petersburg and Arkhangelsk, are icebound during winter; only Murmansk is accessible. Several ports have been built along the Arctic Sea route between Murmansk and Vladivostok and are in regular use in summer. The far eastern port of Vladivostok, Russia's Pacific naval base, is kept open by icebreakers all the year round.

There are 102,000km of waterways. The great rivers of European Russia flow outwards from the centre, linking all parts of the plain with the chief ports. They are supplemented by a 72,000km system of canals which provides a through route between the White Sea and Baltic Sea in the north and the Black Sea, Caspian Sea and the Sea of Azov in the south; the most notable are the White Sea–Baltic Canal, the Moscow–Volga Canal and the Volga–Don Canal.

Because of the vast distances, the terrain and the harsh winter climate, air transport is the quickest form of long-distance internal travel. There are over 1,260 airports and airfields, although only about 600 have surfaced runways. The principal international airports are at Moscow, St Petersburg and Novosibirsk. The main national carriers are Aeroflot and Sibir Airlines.

The telecommunications infrastructure is expanding and modernising, although less quickly for fixed lines than for mobile phones, and rural services are still inadequate. There were 40 million main lines in use in 2005, and 150 million mobile phone subscribers and 25.6 million internet users in 2006.

EDUCATION AND HEALTH

There are 11 years of compulsory education: nine at basic school level and a further two at senior secondary level. Higher education is provided by public and private accredited higher education institutions.

Literacy rate – 99.4 per cent (2004 est)
Gross enrolment ratio (percentage of relevant age group) – primary 129 per cent; secondary 91 per cent; tertiary 70 per cent (2006 est)
Health expenditure (per capita) – US$277 (2005)
Hospital beds (per 1,000 people) – 9.7 (2000–6)

MEDIA

The main national television networks, Channel One, Radio Broadcasting Company (RTR) and NTV, are state-run, ensuring the government controls media content. Many of the country's 400 newspapers are privately owned and popular titles include *Kommersant, Komsomolskaya Pravda, Izvestia* and the English-language *Moscow Times*. The principal radio network is run by Russian State Television and RTR, alongside numerous regional and external services.

CULTURE

Russian is a branch of the Slavonic family of languages and is written in the Cyrillic script.

Before the westernisation of Russia under Peter the Great, Russian literature consisted mainly of *byliny* (folk songs), epic songs, chronicles and works of moral theology. The 19th century proved to be the most fertile period for Russian writing: poetry reached its zenith with Alexander Pushkin (1799–1837) and Mikhail Lermontov (1814–41), while novelists Nikolai Gogol (1809–52), Ivan Turgenev (1818–83), Fyodor Dostoyevsky (1821–81) and Leo Tolstoy (1828–1910) created masterpieces such as *Dead Souls, Fathers and Sons, Crime and Punishment* and *War and Peace* respectively. In the 20th century, Mikhail Bulgakov (1891–1940), Vladimir Nabokov (1899–1977) and Nobel laureate Alexander Solzhenitsyn (1918–2008) have been especially acclaimed. Anton Chekhov (1860–1904) is best-known as a playwright but also produced short stories.

Russia has made an equally impressive contribution to classical music. Mikhail Glinka (1804–57) was an innovator to match Pushkin, while those that followed him include Mussorgsky (1839–81), Rimsky-Korsakov (1844–1908), Tchaikovsky (1840–93) – arguably the most internationally successful Russian composer, whose ballets include *Swan Lake* and *The Nutcracker* – Rachmaninov (1873–1943), Prokofiev (1891–1953), Stravinsky (1882–1971) and Shostakovich (1906–75).

Directors Sergey Eisenstein (1898–1948), Andrei Tarkovsky (1932–86) and Nikita Mikhalkov (*b.* 1945) are celebrated figures in Russian cinema.

RWANDA

Republika y'u Rwanda/République rwandaise – Republic of Rwanda

Area – 26,338 sq. km
Capital – Kigali; population, 860,000 (2007 est)
Major towns – Butare; Gisenyi; Gitarama; Ruhengeri
Currency – Rwanda franc of 100 centimes
Population – 9,907,509 rising at 2.77 per cent per year (2007 est); Hutu (84 per cent), Tutsi (15 per cent), Twa (1 per cent) (est)
Religion – Roman Catholicism (57 per cent), Protestantism (37 per cent), Islam (4 per cent) (est). A very small minority practises indigenous religions; an estimated 2 per cent of the population is atheist
Language – Kinyarwanda, French, English (all official), Swahili
Population density – 384 per sq. km (2006)
Urban population – 21.8 per cent (2005 est)
Median age (years) – 18.6 (2007 est)
National anthem – 'Rwanda nziza' ['Rwanda, Our Beautiful Country']
National day – 1 July (Independence Day)
Life expectancy (years) – 48.99 (2007 est)
Mortality rate – 14.91 (2007 est)
Birth rate – 40.16 (2007 est)
Infant mortality rate – 85.27 (2007 est)
HIV/AIDS adult prevalence – 3.1 per cent (2005 est)
Death penalty – Abolished for all crimes (since 2007)
CPI score – 2.8 (2007)
Population below poverty line – 60 per cent (2001 est)
Literacy rate – 64 per cent (2004 est)
Gross enrolment ratio (percentage of relevant age group) – primary 140 per cent; secondary 13 per cent; tertiary 3 per cent (2006 est)
Health expenditure (per capita) – US$19 (2005)
Hospital beds (per 1,000 people) – 1.7 (2000–6)

CLIMATE AND TERRAIN

Landlocked Rwanda's terrain is mostly savannah uplands and mountains, including the volcanic Virunga range in the north-west. Elevation extremes range from 4,519m (Volcan Karisimbi) at the highest point to 950m (river Rusizi) at the lowest. Rwanda's western border runs through Lake Kivu. The climate is tropical, with two wet seasons, from February to April and November to January. Average daily temperatures range from 15°C in January to 35°C in July.

HISTORY AND POLITICS

Rwanda was settled by Hutu peoples from the tenth century. From the 14th century, they came under the dominance of Tutsi migrants, who established a monarchy in the 15th century and a unified state in the late 19th century. The historic dominance of the majority Hutus by the minority Tutsis is the source of the conflict between the two ethnic groups that has overshadowed the country's history.

Rwanda became a German protectorate in the 1890s and was occupied by Belgium when the First World War broke out. After the war, it became a mandated territory administered by Belgium. In 1959, the Hutu population rebelled against Tutsi domination, causing the king and some 150,000 Tutsis to flee the country. Rwanda became a republic in 1961 and independence was achieved in July 1962 under a Hutu president. He was overthrown in 1973 in a military coup led by Maj.-Gen. Juvenal Habyarimana, whose National Revolutionary Development Movement (MRND) was the only legal party until 1991.

Armed Tutsi exiles in Uganda repeatedly attempted to invade Rwanda in the 1960s and 1970s but were defeated by the predominantly Hutu army. Continued conflict left thousands dead over a period of 30 years. The exiles and opponents of the MRND regime eventually formed the Tutsi-led Rwandan Patriotic Front (FPR), and in 1990 they again invaded the country, winning control of parts of the north. After the government reneged on a 1992 peace agreement, the FPR advanced on Kigali and forced the government to restart negotiations, which led to the Arusha peace accord in 1993.

In April 1994, President Habyarimana, who had retained the interim presidency, died in a plane crash blamed variously on extremist sections of the Hutu army and the FPR. His death was the trigger for the army and militia *(interahamwe)* to massacre the Tutsi minority and moderate Hutus; 800,000 people were killed in three months and millions escaped to neighbouring countries. The FPR's forces mobilised to counter the bloodshed and took control of the country, causing the defeated government forces and millions more Hutus to flee.

In July 1994 the FPR established a broad-based government of national unity in which moderate Hutus were given the presidency and premiership and the FPR took eight of the 22 seats. An International Criminal Tribunal for Rwanda was established in 1995 to bring to trial those directly responsible for the 1994 genocide; so far, 27 people have been convicted. A government report in 2002 stated that 1,074,017 people, more than 93 per cent of them Tutsis, were killed between 1990 and 1994.

Attacks by extremist Hutu insurgents continued in the west, drawing Rwanda into the civil war in the neighbouring Democratic Republic of the Congo from 1996 until 2002, and the Congolese border areas remain volatile. Internally, reconciliation efforts and political reforms since 1994 have been more successful in stabilising the country. Local elections were held in 1999, and presidential and legislative elections took place in 2003 following the approval of a new constitution.

In the 2003 presidential election, the FPR leader Paul Kagame was elected with 95.1 per cent of the vote. The FPR won the 2003 legislative elections and formed a coalition government with four other parties and a number of independent members; a legislative election is scheduled for 15 September 2008. The FPR is regarded as authoritarian, suppressing dissent, but the country has achieved relative stability under its rule.

POLITICAL SYSTEM

Under the 2003 constitution, the head of state is a president directly elected for a seven-year term, renewable only once. The bicameral parliament consists of the Chamber of Deputies, the lower house, and the senate. The Chamber of Deputies has 80 members, of whom 53 are directly elected, 24 are women members elected by the provinces, two represent youth organisations and one represents organisations of disabled people; all serve a five-year term. The senate has 26 members indirectly elected for an eight-year term.

In 2006 the 12 provinces were replaced by five provinces, North, East, South, West and Kigali, with the aim of creating more ethnically diverse administrative areas.

HEAD OF STATE

President, Maj-Gen. Paul Kagame, *appointed* 17 April 2000, *sworn in* 22 April 2000, *elected* 25 August 2003

SELECTED GOVERNMENT MEMBERS *as at July 2008*

Prime Minister, Bernard Makuza
Defence and National Security, Maj.-Gen. Marcel Gatsinzi
Finance and Economic Planning, James Musoni
Foreign Affairs, Rosemary Museminari

EMBASSY OF THE REPUBLIC OF RWANDA

120–122 Seymour Place, London W1H 1NR
T 020-7224 9832 E uk@ambarwanda.org.uk
W www.ambarwanda.org.uk
Ambassador Extraordinary and Plenipotentiary, HE Claver Gatete, *apptd* 2005

BRITISH EMBASSY

Parcelle No. 1131, Blvd de l'Umuganda, Kacyira-Sud, BP 576 Kigali T (+250) 584 098 E ppao@rwanda1.com
W www.britishembassykigali.org.rw
Ambassador Extraordinary and Plenipotentiary, HE Nicholas Cannon, OBE, *apptd* 2008

DEFENCE

The army has 24 main battle tanks and 16 armoured personnel carriers. The air force has at least 5 armed helicopters.
Military budget – US$62m (2007)
Military personnel – 33,000: army 32,000, air force 1,000; paramilitary 2,000

ECONOMY AND TRADE

Rwanda is the most densely populated country in Africa, with few natural resources and minimal industry. Reconstruction efforts have restored the economy to pre-1994 levels, but 60 per cent of the population lives below the poverty line and Rwanda struggles to attract direct investment. IMF/World Bank heavily indebted poor country status has afforded some debt relief, and it was promised 100 per cent debt relief and additional development aid from the G8 countries in 2005. Around

90 per cent of the population is engaged in agriculture, mainly at subsistence level, but population growth is outpacing production, which contributes 36.9 per cent of GDP. There is a small industrial sector, processing agricultural products and producing small-scale manufactured goods. Primary foreign exchange earners are coffee, tea, tin ore and hides; the lack of adequate transport infrastructure handicaps export growth. The main trading partners are Kenya, Germany, China, Uganda, Belgium and the USA. The principal imports are foodstuffs, machinery and equipment, steel and petroleum products.
GNI – US$2,300m (2006); US$250 per capita (2006)
Annual average growth of GDP – 6 per cent (2007 est)
Inflation rate – 8 per cent (2007 est)
Total external debt – US$1,400m (2004 est)
Imports – US$490m (2006)
Exports – US$140m (2006)

BALANCE OF PAYMENTS
Trade – US$350m deficit (2006)
Current Account – US$186m deficit (2006)

Trade with UK	*2006*	*2007*
Imports from UK	£3,632,000	£6,516,875
Exports to UK	£279,000	£283,994

COMMUNICATIONS
Rwanda has received considerable foreign aid to upgrade its transport infrastructure since the 1994 genocide. The main internal transport system is the 14,000km road network, which links with those of neighbouring countries to provide access to Kenyan and Tanzanian ports for international trade. There are no railways, but in late 2006 a feasibility study was planned into the possibility of including Rwanda in a project to expand the rail network in central Africa. Lake Kivu is navigable by shallow boats, and provides access, but no regular services, to the Democratic Republic of the Congo. The principal airport is at Kigali.

The limited fixed-line telephone system mostly serves government and business, and mobile phone distribution has grown rapidly. There were 22,000 main lines in use and 290,000 mobile phone subscribers in 2005, and 65,000 internet users in 2006.

MEDIA
The broadcast media is mainly government-controlled, and the state-run Radio Rwanda has the largest audience. The first private radio station to open since the genocide began broadcasting in 2004. The BBC World Service, Voice of America and Deutsche Welle all broadcast in Kigali. Television is mostly confined to urban areas. There is a growing number of newspapers but they face government restrictions and generally exercise self-censorship.

ST CHRISTOPHER AND NEVIS

Federation of St Christopher and Nevis (Federation of St Kitts and Nevis)

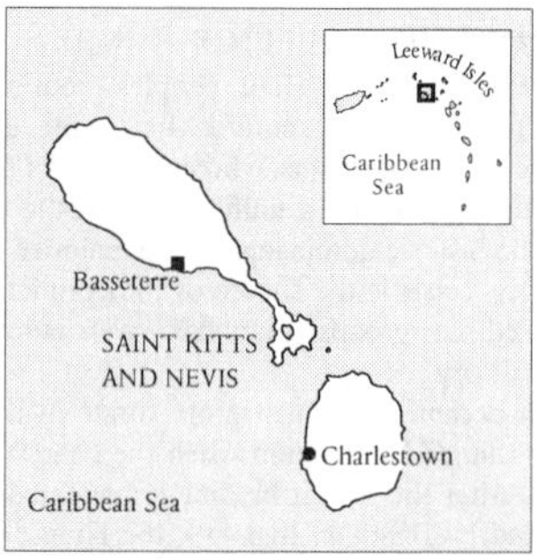

Area – 261 sq. km
Capital – Basseterre; population, 13,000 (2007 est)
Major town – Charlestown, the chief town of Nevis
Currency – East Caribbean dollar (EC$) of 100 cents
Population – 39,349 rising at 0.62 per cent per year (2007 est)
Religion – Protestantism (50 per cent), Roman Catholicism (25 per cent) (est)
Language – English (official)
Population density – 186 per sq. km (2006)
Urban population – 31.9 per cent (2005 est)
Median age (years) – 28.1 (2007 est)
National anthem – 'Oh Land of Beauty!'
National day – 19 September (Independence Day)
Life expectancy (years) – 72.66 (2007 est)
Mortality rate – 8.16 (2007 est)
Birth rate – 17.89 (2007 est)
Infant mortality rate – 13.74 (2007 est)
Death penalty – Retained

CLIMATE AND TERRAIN
The volcanic islands of St Christopher (St Kitts) (109.5 sq. km) and Nevis (58 sq. km) are part of the Leeward group in the eastern Caribbean Sea. The central area of St Christopher is forest-clad and mountainous, with elevation extremes that range from 1,156m (Mount Liamuiga) at the highest point to 0m (Caribbean Sea) at the lowest. Nevis, separated from the southern tip of St Christopher by a strait 3km wide, is dominated by Nevis Peak (985m). The climate is tropical and influenced by north-east trade winds. The average annual rainfall, principally during May to September, is 1,375mm, with average daily temperatures of 24°C.

HISTORY AND POLITICS
The islands were visited in 1493 by Christopher Columbus, who named St Christopher. It was settled by the British, becoming the first British colony in the West Indies in 1623; Nevis was settled from 1628. Control was disputed between the British and French in the 17th and 18th centuries, until France dropped its claims in 1783. The islands of St Christopher and Nevis were united in the late 19th century, and in 1967 became a state in association with Britain with internal self-government. Independence was achieved in September 1983.

A separatist movement was formed on Nevis in 1970, and in 1997 the Nevis government voted to secede. A referendum on the issue in 1998 resulted in a 61.8 per cent vote in favour of secession, which fell short of the two-thirds majority required.

In the 2004 legislative election the Labour Party retained its overall majority and began its third consecutive term of office.

POLITICAL SYSTEM
Under the 1983 constitution, the head of state is the British monarch, represented by a governor-general appointed on the advice of the prime minister. The unicameral National Assembly has 15 members: 11 directly elected for a five-year term, a speaker, and three appointed by the governor-general on the advice of the prime minister and the leader of the opposition. The prime minister, who is responsible to the legislature, and the cabinet are appointed by the governor-general. Nevis is responsible for its own internal affairs, has an eight-member Nevis Island assembly and is governed by the Nevis Island administration, headed by the premier.
Governor-General, HE Sir Cuthbert Montraville Sebastian, GCMG, OBE, *apptd* 1996

SELECTED GOVERNMENT MEMBERS *as at July 2008*
Prime Minister, Finance, Denzil Douglas
Deputy Prime Minister, Sam Condor
Foreign Affairs, Timothy Harris
National Security, Gerald Astaphan

HIGH COMMISSION FOR ST CHRISTOPHER AND NEVIS
10 Kensington Court, London W8 5DL
T 020-7937 9718 E sknhighcomm@btconnect.com
High Commissioner, HE James Ernest Williams, *apptd* 2001

BRITISH HIGH COMMISSIONER
HE Duncan Taylor, *apptd* 2005, resident at Bridgetown, Barbados

ECONOMY AND TRADE
The sugar industry was the mainstay of the economy for over 300 years but was closed down in 2005 after decades of losses at the state-run sugar company. Tourism (the chief source of foreign exchange), offshore financial services and light manufacturing – concentrating on distilling, food processing, clothing and electronics – are being developed; services now account for 71 per cent of GDP, industry for 26 per cent and agriculture for 3 per cent. The economy of Nevis relies on farming, but a sea-island cotton industry is being developed for export. The main trading partners are the USA, Trinidad and Tobago and Canada. Principal exports are machinery, foodstuffs, electronic equipment, beverages and tobacco. The main imports are machinery, manufactured goods, foodstuffs and fuels.
GNI – US$406m; US$8,460 per capita (2006)
Annual average growth of GDP – 6 per cent (2007 est)
Inflation rate – 8.7 per cent (2005 est)
Total external debt – US$314m (2004)

BALANCE OF PAYMENTS
Trade – US$255m deficit (2006)
Current Account – US$144m deficit (2006)

Trade with UK	*2006*	*2007*
Imports from UK	£7,217,000	£9,917,351
Exports to UK	£383,000	£373,829

COMMUNICATIONS
The islands have a total of 320km of roads, of which 138km are surfaced, and 50km of narrow-gauge railways on St Christopher. Basseterre is a port of registry and has deep-water harbour facilities. There are two airports; that on St Christopher can take most large jet aircraft, and Nevis' airport can take small aircraft and has night-time landing facilities. The sea ferry route from Basseterre to Charlestown is 18km. There are modern telecommunications systems.

MEDIA
ZIZ is the government-owned national broadcaster and operates both television and radio stations. Cable television services carry both local and international channels. *The Sun* is the sole daily newspaper and is privately owned.

ST LUCIA

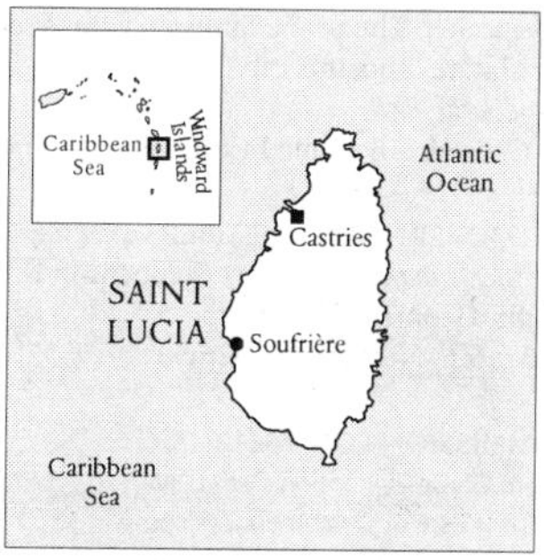

Area – 616 sq. km
Capital – Castries; population, 14,000 (2007 est)
Currency – East Caribbean dollar (EC$) of 100 cents
Population – 170,649 rising at 1.3 per cent per year (2007 est)
Religion – Roman Catholicism (67 per cent) (est)
Language – English (official), French patois
Population density – 272 per sq. km (2006)
Urban population – 31.3 per cent (2005 est)
Median age (years) – 25.6 (2007 est)
National anthem – 'Sons and Daughters of Saint Lucia'
National day – 22 February (Independence Day)
Life expectancy (years) – 74.08 (2007 est)
Mortality rate – 5.03 (2007 est)
Birth rate – 19.28 (2007 est)
Infant mortality rate – 12.81 (2007 est)
Death penalty – Retained
CPI score – 6.8 (2007)
Literacy rate – 90.1 per cent (2004 est)

CLIMATE AND TERRAIN
St Lucia, the second largest of the Windward group, is 43.5km in length, with an extreme breadth of 22.5km. The terrain is mountainous, with elevation extremes that range from 950m (Mt Gimie) at the highest point to 0m (Caribbean Sea) at the lowest. The volcanic peaks of Gros Piton and Petit Piton were declared a UNESCO World Heritage Site in 2004. The climate is tropical and there is a wet season from June to September. The average daily temperature is 25°C.

HISTORY AND POLITICS
Originally inhabited by Arawak Indians and then settled by Carib Indians from AD 800, the island was sighted by Columbus in 1502. French settlement began in 1635 but control was disputed with Britain from 1659 until 1814, when the island was ceded to Britain. It achieved internal

self-government in 1967 and became independent on 22 February 1979.

The St Lucia Labour Party, in power since 1997, lost the 2006 general election to the United Workers Party, which formed a government under Sir John Compton; he became died in September 2007 and Stephenson King became prime minister.

POLITICAL SYSTEM

Under the 1979 constitution, the head of state is the British monarch, represented by a governor-general appointed on the advice of the prime minister. The bicameral parliament consists of the House of Assembly and the senate. The senate has 11 members, six appointed by the government, three by the opposition and two by the governor-general. The House of Assembly, which serves for a five-year term, has 17 elected members and an appointed speaker. The prime minister, who is responsible to the legislature, and the cabinet are appointed by the governor-general.

Governor-General, HE Dame Pearlette Louisy, *apptd* 1997

SELECTED GOVERNMENT MEMBERS *as at July 2008*
Prime Minister, Finance, Economy, Stephenson King
Home Affairs, George Guy Mayers
Attorney-General, Nicholas Frederick

HIGH COMMISSION FOR ST LUCIA
1 Collingham Gardens, London SW5 0HW
T 020-7370 7123 E hcslu@btconnect.com
High Commissioner, vacant

BRITISH HIGH COMMISSIONER
HE Duncan Taylor, *apptd* 2005, resident at Bridgetown, Barbados

ECONOMY AND TRADE

The economy was dependent on bananas (which still account for about 40 per cent of export earnings), but has been diversified since preferential access to EU markets ended in 1999. Offshore financial services and tourism have developed, and the manufacturing sector is the most diverse in the Caribbean, processing agricultural products, assembling electronic components and producing clothing, beverages and corrugated cardboard boxes. Services now account for 80 per cent of GDP, industry for 15 per cent and agriculture for 5 per cent.

The main trading partners are France, the USA, the UK and Trinidad and Tobago. Principal exports are bananas, clothing, cocoa, vegetables, fruit and coconut oil. The main imports are foodstuffs, manufactured goods, machinery, transport equipment, chemicals and fuels.

GNI – US$833m; US$5,060 per capita (2006)
Annual average growth of GDP – 5.1 per cent (2005 est)
Inflation rate – 2.9 per cent (2005 est)
Unemployment – 20 per cent (2003 est)
Total external debt – US$257m (2004)
Imports – US$600m (2006)
Exports – US$100m (2006)

BALANCE OF PAYMENTS
Trade – US$535m deficit (2006)
Current Account – US$298m deficit (2006)

Trade with UK	*2006*	*2007*
Imports from UK	£27,166,000	£14,695,275
Exports to UK	£16,678,000	£13,536,254

COMMUNICATIONS

St Lucia contains around 910km of roads, of which 48km are surfaced. The island has two airports, at Castries and Vieux Fort. Castries also has a deep-water harbour. There are modern telecommunications systems.

MEDIA

The television and radio outlets are mainly privately owned. The government operates a radio network, which broadcasts in English and Creole. The island has two main newspapers, *The Star* and *The Voice,* both published three times a week.

ST VINCENT AND THE GRENADINES

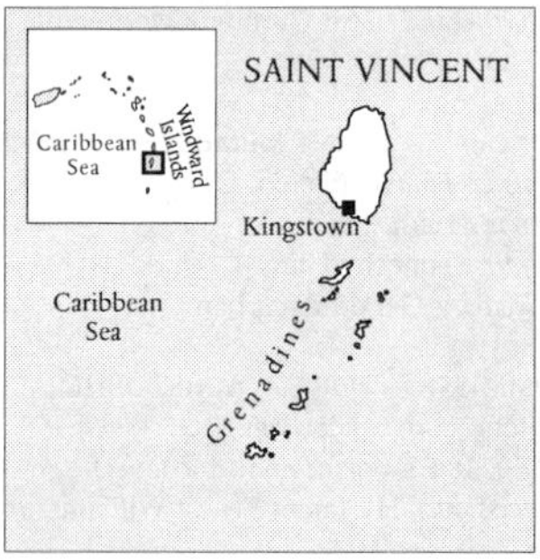

Area – 389 sq. km
Capital – Kingstown; population, 26,000 (2007 est)
Currency – East Caribbean dollar (EC $) of 100 cents
Population – 118,149 rising at 0.25 per cent per year (2007 est)
Religion – Protestantism (59 per cent), Roman Catholicism (6 per cent) (est)
Language – English (official), French patois
Population density – 307 per sq. km (2006)
Urban population – 60.5 per cent (2005 est)
Median age (years) – 27.4 (2007 est)
National anthem – 'St Vincent, Land So Beautiful'
National day – 27 October (Independence Day)
Life expectancy (years) – 74.09 (2007 est)
Mortality rate – 5.97 (2007 est)
Birth rate – 16.02 (2007 est)
Infant mortality rate – 14.01 (2007 est)
Death penalty – Retained
CPI score – 6.1 (2007)

CLIMATE AND TERRAIN

The state, which lies in the Windward group, includes some of the northern Grenadines, a chain of small islands stretching 64km across the eastern Caribbean Sea between Grenada and St Vincent; the larger of these include Bequia, Canouan, Mayreau, Mustique, Union Island, Petit St Vincent and Prune Island. St Vincent itself has volcanic mountains, which are densely forested. Elevation extremes range from 1,234m (La Soufriére volcano) at the highest point to 0m (Caribbean Sea) at the lowest. The climate is tropical with an average daily temperature of 28°C.

HISTORY AND POLITICS

St Vincent was discovered by Christopher Columbus in 1498. It was granted by Charles I to the Earl of Carlisle in 1627 but British settlement did not begin until 1762, and was resisted by the French and the native Caribs. It was recognised as a British colony by the French in 1783. A Carib uprising in 1795–7 resulted in thousands of Caribs being deported. It became internally self-governing in 1969 and achieved full independence as St Vincent and the Grenadines on 27 October 1979.

An early election was called in 2001 after anti-government protests and strikes in 2000 over proposals to increase the pensions of parliamentarians. It was won decisively by the opposition Unity Labour Party (ULP); the ULP was returned for a second term in the 2005 general election.

POLITICAL SYSTEM
Under the 1979 constitution, the head of state is the British monarch, represented by a governor-general appointed on the advice of the prime minister. The unicameral House of Assembly has 21 members: 15 directly elected for a five-year term and six senators appointed by the governor-general (four on the advice of the government and two on the advice of the opposition). The prime minister, who is responsible to the legislature, and the cabinet are appointed by the governor-general.
Governor-General, Sir Frederic Ballantyne, GCMG, *apptd* 2002

SELECTED GOVERNMENT MEMBERS *as at July 2008*
Prime Minister, Finance, Economy, National Security, Ralph Gonsalves
Deputy Prime Minister, Foreign Affairs, Louis Straker

HIGH COMMISSION FOR ST VINCENT AND THE GRENADINES
10 Kensington Court, London W8 5DL
T 020-7565 2874 E info@svghighcom.co.uk
High Commissioner, HE Cenio E. Lewis, *apptd* 2001

BRITISH HIGH COMMISSIONER
HE Duncan Taylor, *apptd* 2005, resident at Bridgetown, Barbados

ECONOMY AND TRADE

The economy was based on bananas (which still account for 39 per cent of exports) but since preferential access to EU markets ended in 1999, efforts have been made to diversify. Tourism, the development of which has been hampered by drug-related crime, manufacturing and offshore banking services have all expanded. Services now account for 64 per cent of GDP, industry for 26 per cent and agriculture for 10 per cent.

The main export markets are France, Greece and Italy. Imports come mostly from Singapore, Trinidad and Tobago, the USA and Italy. Principal exports are bananas, vegetables, starch and tennis racquets. The main imports are foodstuffs, machinery and equipment, chemicals, fertilisers, minerals and fuel.
GNI – US$395m; US$3,320 per capita (2006)
Annual average growth of GDP – 4.4 per cent (2007 est)
Inflation rate – 1 per cent (2005 est)
Unemployment – 15 per cent (2001 est)
Total external debt – US$223m (2004)
Imports – US$250m (2006)
Exports – US$20m (2006)

BALANCE OF PAYMENTS
Trade – US$222m deficit (2006)
Current Account – US$120m deficit (2006)

Trade with UK	*2006*	*2007*
Imports from UK	£8,863,000	£8,170,274
Exports to UK	£7,902,000	£5,887,881

COMMUNICATIONS

The islands have around 829km of roads, of which 580km are surfaced. The main harbour is at Kingstown, which is a port of registry for shipping. There is a large merchant marine of 582 ships of over 1,000 tonnes; 536 ships are foreign-owned. There are six airports, although none can accommodate international flights.

MEDIA

The press is privately owned, and its freedom to criticise the government is guaranteed by the constitution. Most newspapers are published weekly. There are several private radio stations and a national radio service which is partly government-funded. Television broadcasting is operated by the St Vincent and the Grenadines Broadcasting Corporation.

SAMOA

Malo Sa'oloto Tuto'atasi o Samoa – Independent State of Samoa

Area – 2,944 sq. km
Capital – Apia; population, 43,000 (2007), on Upolu
Currency – Tala (S$) of 100 sene
Population – 214,265 rising at 1.29 per cent per year (2007 est). Samoans are a Polynesian people, though the population also includes other Pacific Islanders, Euronesians, Chinese and Europeans
Religion – Protestantism (68 per cent), Roman Catholicism (20 per cent), Mormonism (13 per cent) (est)
Language – English (official), Samoan
Population density – 66 per sq. km (2006)
Urban population – 22.5 per cent (2005 est)
Median age (years) – 20.4 (2007 est)
National anthem – 'The Banner of Freedom'
National day – 1 June (Independence Day)
Life expectancy (years) – 71.3 (2007 est)
Mortality rate – 5.88 (2007 est)
Birth rate – 28.28 (2007 est)
Infant mortality rate – 25.89 (2007 est)
Death penalty – Abolished for all crimes (since 2004)
Literacy rate – 98.7 per cent (2004 est)
CPI score – 4.5 (2007)

CLIMATE AND TERRAIN

Samoa consists of the islands of Savai'i, Upolu, Apolima, Manono, Fanuatapu, Namua, Nuutele, Nuulua and

Nuusafee in the south Pacific Ocean. All the islands are mountainous and volcanic, with elevation extremes ranging from 1,857m (Mauga Silisili, Savai'i) at the highest point to 0m (Pacific Ocean) at the lowest. The climate is tropical with a wet season from November to April. Average temperatures range between 22 and 30°C all year round.

HISTORY AND POLITICS

Inhabited since *c.*1000 BC, Samoa was visited by Dutch traders and French explorers in the 18th century. In 1889, Germany took control of the nine western islands (Western Samoa) and the USA of the other Samoan islands (American Samoa). Western Samoa was occupied by New Zealand on the outbreak of the First World War and became a mandated territory administered by New Zealand from 1920. Internal self-government was established in 1959, and Western Samoa became fully independent on 1 June 1962. The state was treated as a member country of the Commonwealth until its formal admission in 1970. In 1997 the state changed its name to the Independent State of Samoa.

The Human Rights Protection Party, which has been in power since 1981, remained the largest party in the legislature after the 2006 election; it won 35 seats, the Samoan National Development Party won 10 seats and independents won four. The head of state for life, Malietoa Tanumafili, died in May 2007; his successor, the former prime minister Tuiatua Tupua Tamasese Efi, was elected the following month.

POLITICAL SYSTEM

Under the 1962 constitution, the head of state is an elected monarch whose functions are analogous to those of a constitutional monarch. Initially an office held for life, the monarch is now elected by the legislature for a five-year term. The unicameral legislative assembly, *Fono*, has 49 members elected for a five-year term; only members of the Matai (elected clan leaders) are eligible to stand for election. The prime minister is appointed by the monarch on the recommendation of the legislature and appoints the cabinet.

HEAD OF STATE

Head of State, Tuiatua Tupua Tamasese Efi, *elected* 16 June 2007, *sworn in* 20 June 2007

SELECTED GOVERNMENT MEMBERS *as at July 2008*

Prime Minister, Foreign Affairs, Tuilaepa Sailele Malielegaoi
Deputy Prime Minister, Misa Telefoni Retzlaff
Finance, Niko Lee Hang

HIGH COMMISSION OF THE INDEPENDENT STATE OF SAMOA

20 avenue de l'Oree, Brussels 1000, Belgium
T (+32) (2) 660 8454 E samoanembassy@skynet.be
High Commissioner, HE Tuala Falani Chan Tung, *apptd* 2006

BRITISH HIGH COMMISSIONER

HE George Fergusson, CVO, *apptd* 2006, resident at Wellington, New Zealand

ECONOMY AND TRADE

The economy is underdeveloped and dependent on fishing, agriculture (which is vulnerable to cyclones), remittances from migrant workers and international aid. Agriculture generates 11 per cent of GDP, employing about two-thirds of the labour force and supplying about 90 per cent of exports. Attempts at diversification are proving successful; manufacturing is branching out from small-scale processing of agricultural products into light manufacturing, and offshore financial services are being developed. Tourism has grown rapidly and now accounts for about 25 per cent of GDP.

The main trading partners are Australia, New Zealand, American Samoa, Fiji and Singapore. Principal exports are fish, coconut oil and cream, copra, taro, vehicle parts, garments and beer. The main imports are machinery and equipment, industrial supplies and foodstuffs.

GNI – US$421m (2006); US$2,270 per capita (2006)
Annual average growth of GDP – 5.5 per cent (2005 est)
Inflation rate – 3.3 per cent (2005)
Total external debt – US$177m (2004)
Imports – US$219m (2006)
Exports – US$11m (2006)

BALANCE OF PAYMENTS

Trade – US$175m deficit (2005)
Current Account – US$23m deficit (2006)

Trade with UK	*2006*	*2007*
Imports from UK	£64,000	£647,040
Exports to UK	£453,000	£1,055,771

COMMUNICATIONS

There are 2,300km of roads, of which 332km are surfaced. Upolu contains the harbours of Apia and Mulifanua, and Savai'i the harbour of Salelologa. There are four airports, including an international airport 35km west of Apia on Upolu.

Telecommunications systems are adequate, with mobile phones distribution now more widespread than fixed-line telephones; in 2005 there were 19,500 main lines in use and 24,000 mobile phones, with 8,000 internet users in 2006.

MEDIA

There are two daily papers, one weekly and one fortnightly. The press is generally free to report as it chooses, although the *Samoa Observer* has been sued by the government for reporting about alleged corruption. The government operates Televise Samoa, which competes with three private networks and there are three FM radio stations and one state-run commercial radio service.

SAN MARINO

Repubblica di San Marino – Republic of San Marino

Area – 61.2 sq. km
Capital – San Marino; population, 4,000 (2007 est)
Currency – Euro (€) of 100 cents
Population – 29,615 rising at 1.22 per cent per year (2007 est)
Religion – Roman Catholicism (95 per cent) (est)
Language – Italian (official)
Population density – 477 per sq. km (2006)
Urban population – 88.7 per cent (2005 est)
Median age (years) – 40.9 (2007 est)
National anthem – 'Inno Nazionale della Repubblica' ['National Anthem']
National day – 3 September (Republic Day)
Life expectancy (years) – 81.8 (2007 est)
Mortality rate – 8.27 (2007 est)
Birth rate – 9.89 (2007 est)
Infant mortality rate – 5.53 (2007 est)
Death penalty – Abolished for all crimes (since 1865)

CLIMATE AND TERRAIN

A landlocked enclave in central Italy, the republic lies in the foothills of the Apennines, 20km from the Adriatic Sea. Elevation extremes range from 755m (Mt Titano) at the highest point to 55m (Torrente Ausa) at the lowest. The climate is Mediterranean, characterised by cool winters and warm summers. Average annual rainfall is 762mm, while average temperatures range from –6°C in January to 25°C in June.

HISTORY AND POLITICS

The republic is said to have been founded in the fourth century by a Christian stonecutter seeking refuge from religious persecution. By the 12th century a self-governing commune was established, and a parliamentary constitution was adopted in 1600. The republic resisted papal claims and those of neighbouring dukedoms from the 15th to 18th centuries, and the papacy recognised its independence in 1631. In 1862 it signed a treaty with the newly united kingdom of Italy which recognised its integrity and sovereignty and accorded it the protection of Italy. San Marino became a member of the UN in 1992.

The Socialist Party (PSS) and the Party of Democrats (PdD), partners at various times in a number of coalition governments that have held office since 2001, merged to form the Party of Socialists and Democrats (PSD) in 2005. Following the 2006 election to the Grand and General Council, the Christian Democratic Party (PDCS) remained the largest party in the legislature, but a coalition government was formed by the PSD, United Left and Popular Alliance parties.

POLITICAL SYSTEM

The 1600 constitution has been amended several times. The joint heads of state are two captains-regent who are elected at six-monthly intervals (March and September) by the Great and General Council, taking office the month after the election. Executive power is vested in the captains-regent and the Congress of State (cabinet), which is also elected by the Great and General Council. The latter, a unicameral legislature, has 60 members, directly elected for a five-year term. The Council of Twelve forms in certain cases a supreme court of justice.

HEADS OF STATE *as at July 2008*

Captains-Regent, Federico Pedini Amati; Rosa Zafferani

SELECTED GOVERNMENT MEMBERS *as at July 2008*

Finance, Stefano Macina
Foreign Affairs, Fiorenzo Stolfi
Internal Affairs, Valeria Ciavatta

EMBASSY OF THE REPUBLIC OF SAN MARINO

c/o Consulate of the Republic of San Marino, Flat 51, 162 Sloane Street, London SW1X 9BS
T 020-7823 4762
Ambassador Extraordinary and Plenipotentiary, HE Countess Marina Meneghetti de Camillo, *apptd* 2002, resident in Rome, Italy

BRITISH AMBASSADOR

HE Sir Ivor Roberts, KCMG, *apptd* 2003, resident at Rome, Italy

ECONOMY AND TRADE

Tourism is the basis of the economy, contributing over 50 per cent of GDP. Sales of postage stamps and coins also generate significant revenue. The principal agricultural products are wine, cheeses, cereals and fruits, and the other main industries are banking and the manufacture of clothing, electronics and ceramics. The enclave is in a customs union with the EU.
GNI – US$1,291m; US$45,130m per capita (2006)
Annual average growth of GDP – 4.6 per cent (2004 est)
Inflation rate – –1.5 per cent (2006)
Unemployment – 3.8 per cent (2004)

Trade with UK	*2006*	*2007*
Imports from UK	£6,818,000	£7,196,835
Exports to UK	£5,085,000	£6,751,980

MEDIA

San Marino has one state-run broadcasting station, providing radio and television services. The two daily newspapers are *La Tribuna Sammarinese* and *San Marino Oggi.*

SAO TOME AND PRINCIPE

Republica Democratica de Sao Tome e Principe – Democratic Republic of Sao Tome and Principe

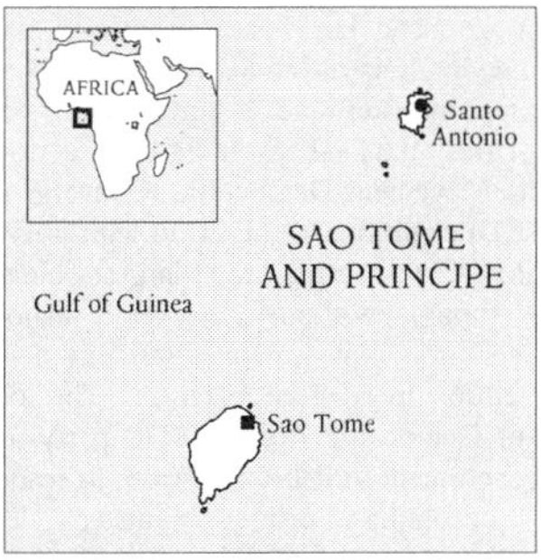

Area – 1,001 sq. km
Capital – Sao Tome; population, 58,000 (2007 est)
Currency – Dobra of 100 centavos
Population – 199,579 rising at 3.13 per cent per year (2007 est)
Religion – Roman Catholicism (72 per cent), Protestantism (23 per cent), Islam (3 per cent) (est). An estimated 2 per cent of the population is atheist

Language – Portuguese (official)
Population density – 162 per sq. km (2006)
Urban population – 37.9 per cent (2005 est)
Median age (years) – 16.2 (2007 est)
National anthem – 'Independencia total' ['Total Independence']
National day – 12 July (Independence Day)
Life expectancy (years) – 67.64 (2007 est)
Mortality rate – 6.28 (2007 est)
Birth rate – 39.72 (2007 est)
Infant mortality rate – 40.54 (2007 est)
Death penalty – Abolished for all crimes (since 1990)
CPI score – 2.7 (2007)
Population below poverty line – 54 per cent (2004 est)

CLIMATE AND TERRAIN

The republic consists of the islands of Sao Tome, Principe and several smaller islands in the Gulf of Guinea, off the west coast of Africa. All the islands are volcanic, thickly forested and fertile. Elevation extremes range from 2,024m (Pico de Sao Tome) at the highest point to 0m (Atlantic Ocean) at the lowest. The climate is tropical with a wet season from October to May. Average daily temperatures are an almost constant 30°C.

HISTORY AND POLITICS

The uninhabited islands were discovered by the Portuguese between 1469 and 1472, and settlement began in 1493. Plantations were established that became important producers of sugar cane, cocoa and coffee in the 18th and 19th centuries. Resistance to Portuguese rule began in the 1950s. The islands gained independence from Portugal in July 1975 and became a one-party state under the rule of the Movement for the Liberation of Sao Tome and Príncipe (MLSTP). The government nationalised the plantations and formed close links with the communist bloc. These were scaled down in the 1980s as the economy deteriorated and in 1990 the MLSTP abandoned Marxism and introduced a democratic constitution. The first multiparty elections were held in 1991. Democracy has brought a degree of political instability, and tensions have been heightened recently by disagreements over how to use the expected revenue from exploitation of offshore oil reserves.

President Fradique de Menezes was deposed briefly in July 2003 in a military coup that occurred while he was out of the country. He was reinstated a week later following negotiations and in September 2003 appointed a new prime minister and a government comprising members of the MLSTP-PSD and the Force for Change Democratic Movement-Democratic Convergence Party (MDFM-PCD) coalition. In the 2006 legislative election, the MDFM-PCD became the largest bloc in the legislature, though without an overall majority, and formed a coalition government. President de Menezes won the 2006 presidential election. The opposition Independent Democratic Action (ADI) party joined the coalition government in February 2008, its leader Patrice Trovoada becoming prime minister. Trovoada's government lost a vote of confidence in May and he was dismissed. In June the MLSTP leader Joaquim Rafael Branco was invited to form a government.

POLITICAL SYSTEM

Under the 1990 constitution, the head of state is the president, who is directly elected for a five-year term, renewable only once. The unicameral National Assembly has 55 members, directly elected for a four-year term. The prime minister is appointed by the president and appoints the cabinet. Since 1995 Principe has been internally self-governing, with an eight-member regional council.

HEAD OF STATE

President, C-in-C of the Armed Forces, Fradique de Menezes, *elected* 29 July 2001, *sworn in* 3 September 2001, *re-elected* July 2006

SELECTED GOVERNMENT MEMBERS *as at July 2008*

Prime Minister, Joaquim Rafael Branco
Defence, Elsa Teixeira Pinto
Economy, Angela Viegas Santiago
Foreign Affairs, Carlos Alberto Pires Tiny

EMBASSY OF SAO TOME AND PRINCIPE

175 avenue de Tervuren, 1150 Brussels, Belgium
T (+32) (2) 734 8966 E ambassade.sao.tome@skynet.be
Ambassador Extraordinary and Plenipotentiary, vacant

BRITISH AMBASSADOR

HE Patricia Phillips, *apptd* 2007, resident at Luanda, Angola

ECONOMY AND TRADE

Economic mismanagement and over-dependency on cocoa contributed to a large foreign debt that stood at about US$318m (£159m) in 2002. A debt-reduction package worth about US$200m (£100m) was agreed with the IMF and World Bank in 2000, and about 90 per cent of the debt was cancelled in 2007. The government is encouraging diversification away from cocoa; tourism is being promoted, and the exploitation of recently discovered offshore oil reserves in the Gulf of Guinea is expected to generate considerable revenue in the future. Most of the population is engaged in subsistence farming and fishing, and 54 per cent live below the poverty line. The principal trading partners are Portugal, the Netherlands, Belgium and France. Principal exports are cocoa (80 per cent), copra, coffee and palm oil. The main imports are machinery and electrical equipment, foodstuffs and petroleum products.
GNI – US$124m; US$800 per capita (2006)
Annual average growth of GDP – 6.5 per cent (2007 est)
Inflation rate – 17 per cent (2007 est)
Total external debt – US$318m (2002)

BALANCE OF PAYMENTS

Trade – US$171m deficit (2004)
Current Account – US$56m deficit (2006)

Trade with UK	*2006*	*2007*
Imports from UK	£319,000	£159,278
Exports to UK	£133,000	£35,858

COMMUNICATIONS

There are 320km of roads, 218km of which are surfaced but in poor condition. There are two airports, and the ports are Santo Antonio and Sao Tome. The telephone system is minimal in extent; in 2005 there were 7,100 main lines in use, 12,000 mobile phone subscribers and 23,000 internet users.

MEDIA

Freedom of expression is guaranteed by the constitution. The islands' only radio and television stations are state-run, but opposition parties are given free airtime. There are three privately owned newspapers and one published by the government.

SAUDI ARABIA

Al-Mamlakah al-Arabiyah as Suudiyah – Kingdom of Saudi Arabia

Area – 2,149,690 sq. km
Capital – Riyadh (Ar-Riyad); population, 4,465,000 (2007 est)
Major cities – Ad Dammam, Jeddah, Mecca, Medina, Tabuk, At Taif
Currency – Saudi riyal (SR) of 100 halala
Population – 27,601,038 rising at 2.06 per cent per year (2007 est); includes some 5,576,076 non-nationals (2006 est)
Religion – Islam is the state religion
Language – Arabic (official)
Population density – 12 per sq. km (2006)
Urban population – 88.5 per cent (2005 est)
Median age (years) – 21.4 (2007 est)
National anthem – 'Aash al Maleek' ['The Royal Saudi Salute']
National day – 23 September (Unification Day)
Life expectancy (years) – 75.88 (2007 est)
Mortality rate – 2.55 (2007 est)
Birth rate – 29.1 (2007 est)
Infant mortality rate – 12.41 (2007 est)
Death penalty – Retained
CPI score – 3.4 (2007)

CLIMATE AND TERRAIN

Saudi Arabia comprises most of the Arabian peninsula. The Nejd ('plateau') extends over the centre, including the Nafud and Dahna deserts. The Hejaz ('boundary') province runs along the Red Sea coast to Asir and contains the holy towns of Mecca and Medina. The Asir ('inaccessible') area is so named for its mountainous terrain, and, with the coastal plain of the Tihama, lies along the southern Red Sea coast from the Hejaz to the border with Yemen. The east and south-east of the country are low-lying and largely desert. Elevation extremes range from 3,133m (Jabal Sawda) at the highest point to 0m (Persian Gulf) at the lowest. The climate is hot and dry, particularly in the interior, and extremely humid in coastal areas between May and October. Average temperatures in Riyadh range from 21°C in January to 42°C in July.

HISTORY AND POLITICS

The Arabian peninsula was the birthplace of the Muslim faith in the seventh century and the base from which the religion and a Muslim empire expanded, eventually stretching from India to Spain. When this empire declined in the 12th century, Arabia became isolated and internally divided. The rise of the al-Saud family began in the 18th century, when it united the Nejd in support of the Wahhabi religious movement. The modern state was formed in 1932 when the head of the dynasty, Abd-al Aziz al-Saud (often known as Ibn Saud), united the four tribal provinces of the Hejaz, Asir, Najd and Al Hasa; the Kingdom of Saudi Arabia was proclaimed on 23 September 1932.

The ruling family preserved stability for many years by suppressing dissent and resisting calls for greater democracy, with some of its actions raising international concerns over human rights abuses. Internal tension grew in the 1990s because of the continuing presence of foreign, particularly US, troops in the country after the 1991 Gulf War, and troops and foreign nationals became terrorist targets. Despite the troops' redeployment to Qatar in early 2003, the frequency of attacks increased following the start of the Iraq War in 2003 and included Saudi as well as foreign victims. Some dissident groups are believed to have links with al-Qaida. Since 2003 demand for political reform has grown and become more militant. In 2005, the country's first nationwide elections were held for half the seats on municipal councils, with voting by universal male suffrage.

King Abdullah acceded to the throne after the death of his half-brother King Fahd in August 2005; he had carried out many of the king's official functions after King Fahd suffered a debilitating stroke in 1996.

POLITICAL SYSTEM

There is no written constitution; constitutional practice is provided for by articles of government based on the Koran *(Qur'an)* and the teachings and sayings of the Prophet Muhammad *(Sunnah)* and issued by royal decree.

Saudi Arabia is a hereditary monarchy. The king is head of government and appoints the council of ministers (established in 1953), whose term of office was fixed in 1993 at four years.

There is no legislature; the *Majlis-al-Shura* (Consulative Council) debates policy and proposes legislation in the areas of the budget, defence, foreign and social affairs, and makes recommendations to the king. The council's 150 members are appointed by the king and serve a four-year term. Its decisions are taken by majority vote. There are no political parties.

There are 13 provinces: Al-Jawf, Asir, Al-Madinah, Al-Qassim, Baha, Eastern, Ha'il, Al-Hudud ash Shamaliyah, Jizan, Makkah, Najran, Riyadh and Tabuk. Each province has a governor appointed by the king and a council of prominent local citizens to advise the governor on local government, budgetary and planning issues.

HEAD OF STATE

HM The King of Saudi Arabia, Custodian of the Two Holy Mosques, Prime Minister, Commander of the National Guard, King Abdullah ibn Abdul Aziz al-Saud, *born* 1923, *succeeded* 2 August 2005
HRH Crown Prince, Deputy Prime Minister, Defence, Prince Sultan ibn Abdul Aziz al-Saud

SELECTED GOVERNMENT MEMBERS *as at July 2008*
Interior, HRH Prince Nayef ibn Abdul Aziz al-Saud
Finance, Ibrahim ibn Abdel Aziz al-Assaf
Foreign Affairs, HRH Prince Saud al-Faisal ibn Abdul Aziz al-Saud
Economy, Khaled ibn Mohammad al-Qussaibi

ROYAL EMBASSY OF SAUDI ARABIA
30 Charles Street, London W1J 5DZ
T 020-7917 3000

Ambassador Extraordinary and Plenipotentiary, HE HRH Prince Mohamed bin Nawaf bin Abdulaziz al-Saud, *apptd* 2005

BRITISH EMBASSY
PO Box 94351, Diplomatic Quarter, Riyadh 11693
T (+966) (1) 488 0077
Ambassador Extraordinary and Plenipotentiary, HE William Patey, CMG, *apptd* 2007

BRITISH COUNCIL
PO Box 58012, C-14, 3rd Floor, Al-Fazari Square, Diplomatic Quarter, Riyadh 11594
T (+966) (1) 483 1818 W www.britishcouncil.org/saudiarabia
Director, Jim Scarth

DEFENCE

The army has 910 main battle tanks, 2,240 armoured personnel carriers, 780 armoured infantry fighting vehicles and 12 armed helicopters. The navy has 7 frigates, 4 corvettes, 65 patrol and coastal vessels and 15 armed helicopters at 8 bases. The air force has 278 combat aircraft.
Military budget – US$33,330m (2007 est)
Military personnel – 223,500: army 75,000, navy 15,500, air force 20,000, Air Defence Force 4,000, Industrial Security Force 9,000, National Guard 100,000; paramilitary 15,500

ECONOMY AND TRADE

The economy is based on oil extraction and processing, but since 1970 the government has used a series of five-year development plans to encourage diversification, and the non-oil sector now accounts for around 60 per cent of GDP. The 2000–5 development plan encouraged the growth of the private sector (now responsible for about 40 per cent of GDP) and an increase in the proportion of Saudi Arabian citizens in the workforce (over 35 per cent of workers are foreign nationals). The 2005–9 plan extends privatisation further, covering a wide range of infrastructure and services, including the development of mineral industries, housing and transport schemes, petrochemical plants, electricity generation, water supplies and desalination, telecommunications and ports. To promote diversification and foreign investment, Saudi Arabia joined the World Trade Organisation in 2005.

Oil extraction since the 1940s has brought great wealth. Proven oil reserves of 264 billion barrels account for over 20 per cent of the world total, and recoverable gas reserves are estimated at over 6.5 trillion cubic metres. Depending on world prices, the oil and gas industry contributes around 45 per cent of GDP and about 75 per cent of government revenue. The main industries apart from oil extraction and refining include production of ammonia, industrial gases, caustic soda, cement, fertiliser, plastics and metals, commercial ship and aircraft repair and construction. Industry accounts for 65.9 per cent of GDP and the service sector for 31.1 per cent. Agriculture contributes 3 per cent but is limited by the terrain, although productivity has been increased by extensive irrigation, desalination and the use of aquifers. The main products are cereals, fruit, meat and dairy products.

The main export markets are the USA, Japan, South Korea and China; the leading suppliers of imports are the USA, Japan, China, South Korea and Germany. Oil and petroleum products constitute 90 per cent of exports. The main imports are machinery and equipment, foodstuffs, chemicals, motor vehicles and textiles.
GNI – US$331,000m (2006); US$13,980 per capita (2006)
Annual average growth of GDP – 4.7 per cent (2007 est)
Inflation rate – 3.4 per cent (2007 est)
Total external debt – US$52,890m (2007 est)
Imports – US$66,000m (2006)
Exports – US$181,000m (2005)

BALANCE OF PAYMENTS
Trade – US$141,506m surplus (2006)
Current Account – US$95,514mm surplus (2006)

Trade with UK	*2006*	*2007*
Imports from UK	£1,676,209,000	£1,873,205,430
Exports to UK	£1,309,707,000	£922,347,876

COMMUNICATIONS

Jeddah is the main cargo port on the Red Sea coast and Dammam on the Gulf coast. The main oil port (the world's largest) is Ras Tanura. There are 1,392km of railways, operated by the Saudi Government Railway Organisation, which link Riyadh with the Gulf ports; there are plans to build a railway from Jeddah to Dammam. In 2000 the road network totalled 152,044km (of which 45,461km were surfaced), including a motorway system connecting all the cities and main towns. The 25km-long King Fahd Causeway connects the Eastern Province to Bahrain. There are over 200 airports and airfields; the three international airports are at Riyadh, Jeddah (serving Mecca) and Dammam. There is a modern telecommunications system; there were 4.5 million main telephone lines in use, 19.6 million mobile phone subscribers and 4.7 million internet users in 2006.

EDUCATION AND HEALTH

With the exception of a few schools for expatriate children, all schools are supervised by the government and are segregated. There are universities in Jeddah, Mecca, Riyadh (branches in Abha and Qassim), Dammam (branch at Al-Hufuf) and Az-Zahran, and Islamic universities in Medina and Riyadh. There is great emphasis on vocational training, provided at literacy and artisan skill training centres and more advanced industrial, commercial and agricultural education institutes.
Literacy rate – 79.4 per cent (2004 est)
Gross enrolment ratio (percentage of relevant age group) – primary 108 per cent; secondary 96 per cent; tertiary 27 per cent (2006 est)
Health expenditure (per capita) – US$448 (2005)
Hospital beds (per 1,000 people) – 2.3 (2000–6)

MEDIA AND CULTURE

Saudi Arabia's media is one of the most tightly controlled in the Middle East. Criticism of the government and royal family and the questioning of religious doctrine are not tolerated.

The state-run Broadcasting Service of the Kingdom of Saudi Arabia (BSKSA) is responsible for all broadcasting, operating four TV networks. Private radio and TV stations cannot operate from Saudi soil, but the country is a key market for pan-Arab satellite and subscription-based broadcasters. Saudi newspapers are created by royal decree. There are 10 dailies and many magazines. Pan-Arab newspapers, subject to censorship, are also available. The government has invested heavily in creating security systems to block websites with material deemed unsuitable.

Saudi culture revolves around Islam – it was the birthplace of the religion and two of Islam's holiest sites are situated in the country. Mecca was the site of the Prophet Muhammad's birth, and contains the Great Mosque, within which is the *Ka'abah* or sacred shrine of the Muslim religion. This is the focus of the annual *Hajj* ('pilgrimage'). Medina ('city of light'), some 300km north of Mecca, is celebrated as the first city to embrace Islam and as the burial place of the Prophet.

SENEGAL

République du Sénégal – Republic of Senegal

Area – 196,190 sq. km
Capital – Dakar; population, 2,604,000 (2007 est)
Major cities – Kaolack, Mbour, Saint-Louis, Thiès, Ziguinchor
Currency – Franc CFA of 100 centimes
Population – 12,521,851 rising at 2.65 per cent per year (2007 est); Wolof (43.3 per cent), Fula (23.8 per cent), Serer (14.7 per cent), Jola (3.7 per cent), Mandinka (3 per cent) (est)
Religion – Islam (94 per cent), Christianity (4 per cent) (est). The remaining 2 per cent practise indigenous beliefs or no religion
Language – French (official), Wolof, Pulaar, Jola, Mandinka
Population density – 63 per sq. km (2006)
Urban population – 51 per cent (2005 est)
Median age (years) – 18.7 (2007 est)
National anthem – 'Pincez Tous vos Koras, Frappez les Balafons' ['All Pluck Your Koras, Strike the Balafons']
National day – 4 April (Independence Day)
Life expectancy (years) – 56.69 (2007 est)
Mortality rate – 10.96 (2007 est)
Birth rate – 37.4 (2007 est)
Infant mortality rate – 60.15 (2007 est)
Death penalty – Abolished for all crimes (since 2004)
CPI score – 3.6 (2007)
Population below poverty line – 54 per cent (2001 est)

CLIMATE AND TERRAIN

The terrain is generally low and rolling, with plains rising to foothills in the south-east. There is desert in the north and tropical forest in the south. Elevation extremes range from 581m (Nepen Diakha) at the highest point to 0m (Atlantic Ocean) at the lowest. The river Senegal runs close to the northern border and the river Gambia flows through the south-east of the county. The climate is tropical, with a wet season from June to September. Average temperatures in Dakar range from 18°C in January to 32°C in July.

HISTORY AND POLITICS

Senegal was part of the Mali Empire in the 14th to 15th centuries. The first European visitors were the Portuguese in 1445. The French established a fort at Saint-Louis in 1659 and European traders exported slaves, ivory, gold and other commodities from there in the 17th and 18th centuries. The interior was occupied by the French in the mid-19th century and the territory became part of French West Africa in 1902. It became an autonomous state in 1958 and achieved independence as part of the Federation of Mali in June 1960, seceding to form the Republic of Senegal in September 1960. In 1966 the country became a one-party state under the rule of the Senegalese Progressive Union (UPS), which changed its name to the Socialist Party (PS) in 1976. Although a three-party system was introduced in 1978, the PS dominated political life until 2000. Senegal joined with the Gambia to form the Confederation of Senegambia from 1982 to 1989.

In the early 1980s a violent separatist insurgency led by the Movement of Democratic Forces of Casamance (MFDC) began in the Casamance region south of the river Gambia. A 2001 peace agreement was not implemented because of splits and leadership changes among the separatists. Violence in the region increased during the 2001 election campaign, but subsequently declined. In 2003 the MFDC leader said that the secessionist war was over, and a peace agreement with the government was signed in 2004 after two years of relative calm.

The Socialist Party's 40 years of political domination ended in 2000 with the election of Abdoulaye Wade, leader of the Senegalese Democratic Party (PDS), as president. The 2001 legislative election was won by an alliance of 40 parties, the *Sopi* (Change) coalition, led by the PDS; the PS retained only ten seats. President Wade was re-elected in the first round of the presidential election in February 2007. The Sopi coalition retained its majority in June 2007 in legislative elections boycotted by opposition parties.

POLITICAL SYSTEM

The 2001 constitution was amended in 2007 to re-establish the senate as the upper chamber of a bicameral legislature. The executive president is directly elected for a five-year term (reduced from seven years in 2001), renewable only once. The bicameral parliament comprises the National Assembly, the lower chamber, which has 150 members directly elected for a five-year term; and the senate, which has 100 members, 35 indirectly elected and 65 appointed by the president, for a five-year term. The president appoints the prime minister, who nominates the other ministers.

HEAD OF STATE

President, Commander of the Armed Forces, Abdoulaye Wade, *elected* 19 March 2000, *sworn in* 1 April 2000, *re-elected* 25 February 2007

SELECTED GOVERNMENT MEMBERS *as at July 2008*

Prime Minister, Cheikh Hadjibou Soumare
Finance and Economy, Abdoulaye Diop
Interior, Cheikh Tidiane Sy
Foreign Affairs, Cheikh Tidiane Gadio

EMBASSY OF THE REPUBLIC OF SENEGAL

39 Marloes Road, London W8 6LA
T 020-7938 4048 E mail@senegalembassy.co.uk
W www.senegalembassy.com

Ambassador Extraordinary and Plenipotentiary, HE Abdou Sourang, *apptd* 2007

BRITISH EMBASSY
PO Box 6025, 20 rue du Docteur Guillet, Dakar
T (+221) 823 7392 E britemb@sentoo.sn
Ambassador Extraordinary and Plenipotentiary, HE Christopher Trott, *apptd* 2005

BRITISH COUNCIL
Rue AAB-68, Amitie Zone A&B, BP 6232, Dakar
T (+221) 869 27008 W www.britishcouncil.org/senegal
Director, Adrian Odell

DEFENCE

The army has over 28 armoured personnel carriers. The navy has 9 patrol and coastal combatant vessels at 2 bases. The air force has 8 combat capable aircraft.
Military budget – US$173m (2007 est)
Military personnel – 13,620: army 11,900, navy 950, air force 770; paramilitary 5,000
Conscription duration – 24 months (selective)

ECONOMY AND TRADE

An economic reform programme in the 1990s has resulted in GDP growth averaging over 5 per cent a year since 1995 and the reduction of inflation. Even so, the country is poor, with over half the population living below the poverty line and unemployment at over 40 per cent. The country is heavily dependent on foreign aid and had high foreign debt, although two-thirds of this has been cancelled under the IMF/World Bank heavily indebted poor countries programme.

Agriculture is the mainstay of the economy, engaging 77.5 per cent of the workforce and contributing 16.7 per cent of GDP. The main industries are food and fish processing, mining (phosphate, iron, zircon, gold), oil refining, production of fertiliser and construction materials, ship construction and repair, and tourism. Industry accounts for 18.9 per cent of GDP and services for 64.4 per cent. The trading partners are France, Mali, Spain and other EU countries, India, the Gambia, Thailand and China. The principal exports are fish, groundnuts (raw and processed), petroleum products, phosphates and cotton. Principal imports are foodstuffs, beverages, capital goods and fuels.
GNI – US$9,100m (2006); US$760 per capita (2006)
Annual average growth of GDP – 4.6 per cent (2007 est)
Inflation rate – 5.4 per cent (2007 est)
Unemployment – 48 per cent (2001 est)
Total external debt – US$1,604m (2007 est)
Imports – US$3,510m (2006)
Exports – US$1,510m (2006)

BALANCE OF PAYMENTS
Trade – US$1,995m deficit (2006)
Current Account – US$895m deficit (2006)

Trade with UK	*2006*	*2007*
Imports from UK	£190,924,000	£138,633,895
Exports to UK	£7,446,000	£14,810,410

COMMUNICATIONS

Senegal has a road network of some 13,576km, of which 3,972km are surfaced. There are also 906km of railways and 1,000km of navigable waterways, mainly on the Senegal, Saloum and Casamance rivers. Dakar is the main port and the location of the principal airport; there are around 20 other airports and airfields. The telephone system is good although not extensive; in 2006 there were 282,600 main lines in use, 2.9 million mobile phone subscribers and 650,000 internet users.

EDUCATION AND HEALTH

Literacy rate – 39.3 per cent (2004 est)
Gross enrolment ratio (percentage of relevant age group) – primary 80 per cent; secondary 22 per cent; tertiary 6 per cent (2006 est)
Health expenditure (per capita) – US$38 (2005)
Hospital beds (per 1,000 people) – 0.4 (2002)

MEDIA

The constitution guarantees media freedom. RTS is the state-run broadcaster and produces two channels. There are many private radio stations, and subscription-based television is readily available. Publications must be registered as a formality, but foreign media circulate freely. There are at least five daily newspapers, of which one is state-owned.

SERBIA

Republika Srbija – Republic of Serbia

Area – 88,361 sq. km
Capital – Belgrade; population, 1,099,000 (2007 est)
Major cities – Kragujevac, Nis, Novi Sad
Currency – Dinar of 100 paras
Population – 10,150,265 (2007 est); Serb (82.9 per cent), Hungarian (3.9 per cent), Bosniak (1.8 per cent), Romani (1.4 per cent), Yugoslav (1.1 per cent), Montenegrin (0.9 per cent)
Religion – Orthodox Christianity (78 per cent), Islam (5 per cent), Roman Catholicism (4 per cent), Protestantism (1 per cent) (est)
Language – Serbian (official), Romanian, Hungarian, Slovak, Ukrainian, Croatian, Albanian (official in different regions), Bosnian, Romani
Population density – 96 per sq. km (2006)
Median age (years) – 37.3 (2007 est)
National anthem – 'Boze Pravde' ['God the Righteous']
National day – 15 February
Life expectancy (years) – 75.06 (2006 est)
Mortality rate – 10.49 (2005 est)
Birth rate – 12.12 (2005 est)
Infant mortality rate – 12.89 (2005 est)
Death penalty – Abolished for all crimes (since 2002)
CPI score – 3.4 (2007)
Gross enrolment ratio (percentage of relevant age group) – primary 99 per cent; secondary 89 per cent; tertiary 36 per cent (2002 est)

Health expenditure (per capita) – US$212 (2005)
Hospital beds (per 1,000 people) – 5.9 (2000–6)
Note: All statistics include Kosovo

CLIMATE AND TERRAIN

The landlocked country has an extremely mountainous south, while the north is dominated by the low-lying plains of the Danube. The highest point 2,656m (Daravica, Kosovo) or 2,169m (Midzor). The major rivers are the Danube, the Sava, the Tisa and the Morava. The climate is moderate and continental. Average temperatures in Belgrade range from 2°C in January to 18°C in July.

HISTORY AND POLITICS

The medieval kingdom of Serbia emerged from the rule of the Byzantine Empire in the 12th century to form a large and prosperous state in the Balkans. Defeat by the Turks in 1389 led to almost 500 years of Turkish rule. After gaining autonomy within the Ottoman Empire in 1815, Serbia became fully independent in 1878 and a kingdom in 1881. At the end of the First World War Serbia joined with the former Austro-Hungarian provinces of Slovenia, Croatia and Bosnia-Hercegovina and the kingdom of Montenegro to form the Kingdom of Serbs, Croats and Slovenes, which was renamed Yugoslavia in 1929. Yugoslavia was occupied by Axis forces in 1941 and reformed after liberation as a communist federal republic under the presidency of partisan leader Josip Tito in 1945. When the federation disintegrated in 1991–2, Serbia and Montenegro were left to form the rump Federal Republic of Yugoslavia (FRY), which was declared on 27 April 1992.

Slobodan Milosevic, president of Serbia from 1989 until 1996, supported various military and militia efforts to unite ethnic Serbs in neighbouring republics into a 'Greater Serbia'. All of these efforts were ultimately unsuccessful. Milosevic dominated Serbian and federal politics in the 1990s, becoming president of the Federal Republic in 1997. His corrupt and repressive regime was ended by the 2000 federal elections, in which the Democratic Opposition of Serbia became the largest party in both chambers of the legislature and the Democratic Party of Serbia presidential candidate, Vojislav Kostunica, won the most votes. Milosevic's attempts to pervert the outcome of the presidential election and remain in power were met with mass demonstrations and strikes, forcing him to stand down. He was arrested in 2001 and extradited to the UN International Criminal Tribunal for the Former Yugoslavia, where his trial began in 2002; he died unexpectedly in 2006 while still on trial.

In 2003 the Federal Republic of Yugoslavia was restructured into a union of Serbia and Montenegro, each with semi-independent status. Montenegro voted to become independent in May 2006 and the union was dissolved in June, with Serbia succeeding to the union's membership of international bodies. The Serbian province of Kosovo unilaterally declared its independence in February 2008 after nine years under UN administration (*see* below).

After the 2004 presidential election was invalidated owing to a low turnout, the legislature abolished the minimum turnout requirement, and in June 2004 Boris Tadic, leader of the Democratic Party (DS), was elected president; he was re-elected in early 2008. In the 2007 legislative election, the nationalist Serbian Radical Party remained the largest party but without an overall majority. A new coalition government was formed by the DS, the Democratic Party of Serbia (DSS) and two smaller parties, under the incumbent prime minister, Vojislav Kostunica of the DSS.

The government resigned in March 2008 because of disagreements between the coalition partners over policy towards the EU following Kosovo's declaration of independence, and elections were held in May. The For a European Serbia coalition led by the DS won the most seats but without an overall majority, and formed a coalition government with the Socialist Party.

POLITICAL SYSTEM

Under the 2006 constitution, the president is directly elected for a five-year term, renewable only once. The unicameral National Assembly has 250 members, directly elected for a four-year term. The prime minister is appointed by the president.

HEAD OF STATE
President, Boris Tadic, *elected* 27 June 2004, *took office* 11 July 2004, *re-elected* 3 February 2008

SELECTED GOVERNMENT MEMBERS *as at July 2008*
Prime Minister, Vojislav Kostunica
Deputy Prime Minister, Bozidar Djelic
Finance, Mirko Cvetkovic
Interior, Dragan Jocic
Foreign Affairs, Vuk Jeremic
Defence, Dragan Sutanovac

EMBASSY OF THE REPUBLIC OF SERBIA
28 Belgrave Square, London SW1X 8QB
T 020-7235 9049 E londre@jugisek.demon.co.uk
W www.serbianembassy.org.uk
Ambassador Extraordinary and Plenipotentiary, vacant

BRITISH EMBASSY
Resavska 46, 11000 Belgrade
T (+381) (11) 264 5055
Ambassador Extraordinary and Plenipotentiary, HE Stephen Wordsworth, *apptd* 2006

BRITISH COUNCIL
Terazije 8/1, 11000 Belgrade
T (+381) (11) 302 3800 W www.britishcouncil.org/serbia
Director, Andrew Glass

DEFENCE

The army has 224 main battle tanks and 332 armoured infantry fighting vehicles. The air force has 57 combat aircraft.
Military budget – US$1,040m (2007)
Military personnel – 24,257: army 11,180, air force and air defence 4,155, training command 3,108, MoD 5,814
Conscription duration – 6 months

ECONOMY AND TRADE

Economic mismanagement, UN sanctions in the 1990s and damage to infrastructure and industry from NATO bombing in 1999 had reduced the economy to about 40 per cent of its 1990 size by 2000. Since 2000 governments have pursued economic reforms and international reintegration, obtained international support for economic restructuring and rescheduled payments or received debt relief on much of its foreign debt. Progress remains slow, and only the country's agricultural self-sufficiency has kept it afloat. Industrial production remains extremely low and there is high unemployment, although this has fallen from the 2005 peak of 32 per cent. Foreign aid and EU negotiations on accession, suspended in 2005 because of Serbia's failure to surrender alleged war criminals for trial, have resumed.

Agriculture accounts for 12.3 per cent of GDP and employs 30 per cent of the workforce. The main agricultural products are cereals, sugar beet, sunflowers, fruit, meat and milk. Industry includes production of sugar, paper and pulp, lead and agricultural, transport and electrical and communications equipment. Industry contributes 24.2 per cent of GDP and services 63.5 per cent. Principal exports are manufactured goods, food and livestock, machinery and transport equipment.

GNI – US$30,000m (2006); US$4,030 per capita (2006)
Annual average growth of GDP – 5.9 per cent (2005 est)
Inflation rate – 8.9 per cent (2007 est)
Unemployment – 18.8 per cent (2007 est)
**Total external debt* – US$28,240m (2007 est)
*Figure includes Montenegro and Kosovo

BALANCE OF PAYMENTS
Trade – US$171m deficit (2004)
Current Account – US$3,966m deficit (2006)

Trade with UK	*2006*	*2007*
Imports from UK	£85,285,000	£95,562,847
Exports to UK	£63,629,000	£72,108,992

COMMUNICATIONS

Serbia has some 37,800km of roads, around 32,000km of which are surfaced. There are also 3,300km of railways, linking Belgrade directly to Athens, Bucharest, Budapest, Istanbul, Ljubljana, Munich, Skopje, Sofia, Thessaloniki, Vienna and Zagreb. There are 587km of navigable waterways on the Danube and Sava rivers; the principal ports include Belgrade and Novi Sad on the Danube. The main international airport is at Belgrade.

Modernisation of the telephone system has been slow and rural services are not as good as those in urban areas. There were 2.7 million main lines in use, 6.6 million mobile phone subscribers and 1.4 million internet users in 2006.

MEDIA

The ousting of Milosevic allowed the media much greater freedom and outlets proliferated. A media regulatory system is in operation and issues licences to the hundreds of private-sector radio and television broadcasters. The state-funded national broadcaster RTS aims to develop into a public service, and state-funded local and regional media outlets are to be privatised. Newspapers include the daily *Danas*, the weekly *Vreme* and *NIN*.

KOSOVO

Area – 10,887 sq. km
Capital – Pristina
Major towns – Kosovska Mitrovica; Pec; Prizren
Currency – Euro (€) of 100 cents; the Serbian dinar is also in circulation
Population – 2,126,708 (2007 est); Albanian (88 per cent), Serb (7 per cent)
Religion – Islam, Orthodox Christianity, Roman Catholicism
Language – Albanian, Serbian (official)

HISTORY AND POLITICS

Kosovo was at the centre of the medieval kingdom of Serbia and was the location of the Serbian defeat by the Turks in 1389 that led to the kingdom becoming part of the Ottoman Empire; the historic and cultural resonances of these events underlie Serbia's refusal to countenance the independence of what it views as the heartland of its nation. Kosovo was under Turkish rule from 1389 until 1913, when Serbia regained control following the First Balkan War. As a province of Serbia, Kosovo became part of the Kingdom of Serbs, Croats and Slovenes (subsequently Yugoslavia) in 1918.

During the period of Ottoman rule, migration gradually altered the population's ethnicity, and Albanians had become the dominant ethnic group by the end of the 19th century. After the Second World War, the Yugoslav federal government made Kosovo an autonomous republic within Serbia, granting greater autonomy (almost equivalent to that of one of the constituent republics) in 1974. Even so, Albanian nationalism grew during the 1980s, leading to calls for independence. Complaints of mistreatment by Serbs in Kosovo led to a crackdown by the Serbian republican government, which stripped the province of its autonomy in 1989 and introduced repressive measures that progressively excluded the Albanian majority from public life and suppressed the culture. The Kosovans' decisive vote in a 1991 referendum for independence from both Serbia and Yugoslavia was declared illegal by the Serbian government, which tightened its control further.

Passive resistance in the 1990s failed to secure any concessions from the Serbian government, and militants formed the Kosovan Liberation Army (KLA) in 1995. The subsequent KLA insurgency provoked Serbian military reprisals that from 1998 developed into a brutal and systematic process of ethnic cleansing. Over 800,000 people sought refuge in Albania, Macedonia or Montenegro, and over 500,000 were internally displaced. Despite international condemnation, the attacks continued until NATO intervened in March 1999, bombing military targets in Kosovo and Serbia. Serbia accepted a peace plan proposed by NATO and Russia in June 1999 and withdrew its forces. The UN then placed Kosovo under the transitional administration of the UN Interim Administration Mission in Kosovo (UNMIK), pending determination of the province's future status. UNMIK established autonomous democratic institutions, to which it gradually devolved administrative responsibilities, and held legislative elections.

UN-sponsored talks on Kosovo's future began in 2005 but failed to make any progress. In February 2007 the UN's special envoy, Martti Ahtisaari, published a 12-point plan setting out the steps towards Kosovo's eventual independence. After further talks in 2007 proved fruitless, the Kosovan government unilaterally declared independence from Serbia on 17 February 2008 and began to implement the Ahtisaari plan. The declaration of independence has been recognised by 43 countries, including the USA, the UK and other EU countries, but condemned by Serbia, supported by Russia and China among others, and is not recognised by the UN. The UN completed its hand-over of administrative powers in June 2008, when the constitution came into force, but UNMIK remains in Kosovo to maintain stability and protect the Serb minority.

Fatmir Sejdiu was elected president in February 2006, in place of Ibrahim Rugova, who died in office, and was re-elected in January 2008. In the November 2007 legislative election, the Democratic Party of Kosovo, led by Hashim Thaci, became the largest party in the legislature and formed a coalition government with the

Democratic League of Kosovo, under the leadership of Mr Thaci. The Serbs in Kosovo set up their own assembly in June 2008.

POLITICAL SYSTEM

A draft constitution was approved in April 2008 and came into effect in June when the UN completed its hand-over of powers. The head of state is a president elected by the legislature for a five-year term. The unicameral legislature, the Assembly of the Republic of Kosovo, has 120 members, elected for a four-year term; ten of the seats are reserved for Serbs and ten for other minorities. The majority party or coalition nominates the prime minister, who is appointed by the president. Both the prime minister and the government must be approved by the legislature.

SELECTED GOVERNMENT MEMBERS *as at July 2008*

President, Fatmir Sejdiu, *elected* 10 February 2006, *re-elected* January 2008
Prime Minister, Hashim Thaci
Deputy Prime Ministers, Hajredin Kuci; Rame Manaj
Economy, Ahmet Shala
Interior, Zenun Pajaziti
Foreign Affairs, Skender Hyseni

BRITISH EMBASSY

Ismail Qemali 6, Arberi, Dragodan, Pristina
T (+381) 3825 4700 E britishoffice.pristina@fco.gov.uk
Ambassador Extraordinary and Plenipotentiary, HE Andrew Sparkes, *apptd* 2008

BRITISH COUNCIL

Perandori Justinian 6, Qyteza Pejton, 10000 Pristina
T (+381) 3824 3292 E info@ks.britishcouncil.org
Director, Arjeta Emra

ECONOMY AND TRADE

Under UN administration Kosovo began the transition to a market economy and over half of state-owned businesses have been privatised. However, income levels are the lowest in Europe, and the economy is dependent on international and foreign aid and the remittances of expatriates; Kosovo received US$324m (£160m) of economic aid in 2007 and remittances contributed nearly one-third of GDP. Agriculture is close to subsistence level and inefficient, industrial output has declined because of insufficient investment and an unemployment level of over 40 per cent encourages emigration. International agencies and foreign governments are working with the Kosovan government to stimulate economic growth, attract investment and reduce unemployment.

Natural resources include lignite, lead, zinc, nickel, chrome, magnesium and aluminium, and the mainstay of the economy is mining and the production of construction materials. Production is held back by ageing equipment and inadequacies in the power sector, although these are being addressed.

UNMIK signed Kosovo's accession to the Central Europe Free Trade Area (CEFTA) in 2006 and its members are the main markets for exports of minerals and processed metal products, scrap metals, leather goods, machinery and appliances. Imports of foodstuffs, wood, fuels, chemicals, machinery and electrical equipment come mainly from EU countries and Kosovo's neighbours.

SEYCHELLES

République des Seychelles/Repiblik Sesel – Republic of Seychelles

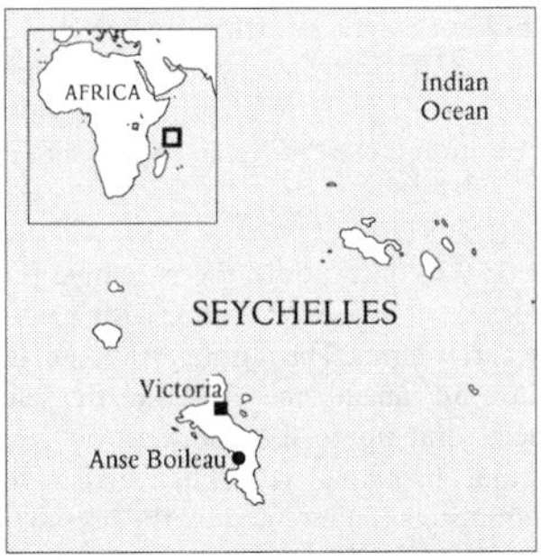

Area – 455 sq. km
Capital – Victoria; population, 26,000 (2007 est), on Mahé
Currency – Seychelles rupee of 100 cents
Population – 81,895 rising at 0.43 per cent per year (2007 est)
Religion – Roman Catholicism (82 per cent), Protestantism (6 per cent) (est)
Language – English (official), Creole
Population density – 184 per sq. km (2006)
Urban population – 50.2 per cent (2005 est)
Median age (years) – 28.4 (2007 est)
National anthem – 'Koste Seselwa' ['Seychelles Unite']
National day – 18 June (Constitution Day)
Life expectancy (years) – 72.34 (2007 est)
Mortality rate – 6.25 (2007 est)
Birth rate – 15.83 (2007 est)
Infant mortality rate – 14.75 (2007 est)
Death penalty – Abolished for all crimes (since 1993)
CPI score – 4.5 (2007)
Literacy rate – 91.9 per cent (2004 est)

CLIMATE AND TERRAIN

Seychelles consists of 115 islands spread over 643,737 sq. km of the south-west Indian Ocean, north of Madagascar. There is a relatively compact granitic group of 32 islands, with high hills and mountains, of which Mahé is the largest and most populated (90 per cent of the population lives on Mahé), and an outlying coralline group, for the most part only a little above sea-level. Elevation extremes range from 905m (Morne Seychellois) at the highest point to 0m (Indian Ocean) at the lowest. The climate is tropical, with an average temperature of 26°C.

HISTORY AND POLITICS

The islands were first sighted by European navigators in the early 15th century and were proclaimed French territory in 1756. The Mahé group was settled as a dependency of Mauritius from 1770, but was captured by the British in 1794 and ceded to Britain in 1814. In 1903 these islands, together with the coralline group, were formed into a colony separate from Mauritius. On 29 June 1976, the islands became an independent republic. Following a coup d'état in 1977, when France-Albert René became president, Seychelles became a one-party state ruled by the Seychelles People's Progressive Front (SPPF) in 1979. Opposition parties were permitted from 1991 and in 1993 President René reintroduced a multiparty democratic system. Power has remained with the SPPF under the pluralist system as it dominates the legislature and holds the presidency, although opposition parties are beginning to achieve a greater share of the vote.

President René stepped down in mid-term in 2004 and the rest of his term was served by the vice-president James Michel, who was elected president in 2006. In the 2007 legislative election, the SPPF retained its overall majority.

POLITICAL SYSTEM

Under the 1993 constitution, the executive president is directly elected for a five-year term, with a maximum of three consecutive terms. The unicameral national assembly has up to 34 members: 23 directly elected by constituencies and up to 11 allocated by proportional representation; members serve a five-year term. The council of ministers is appointed by the president.

HEAD OF STATE

President, Head of Government, Defence, James Michel, *assumed office* 14 April 2004
Vice-President, Internal Affairs, Joseph Belmont

SELECTED GOVERNMENT MEMBERS *as at July 2008*
Foreign Affairs, Patrick Pillay
Finance, Danny Faure

SEYCHELLES HIGH COMMISSION
51 avenue Mozart, 75016 Paris, France
T (+33) (1) 4230 5747
High Commissioner, HE Claude Morel, *apptd* 2007

BRITISH HIGH COMMISSION
PO Box 161, Oliaji Trade Centre, Victoria, Mahé
T (+248) 283 666 E bhcvictoria@fco.gov.uk
High Commissioner, HE Fergus Cochrane-Dyet, *apptd* 2007

DEFENCE

The navy has 9 patrol and coastal combatant vessels at a base at Port Victoria.
Military budget – US$10m (2007 est)
Military personnel – 200: army 200; paramilitary 250

ECONOMY AND TRADE

Seychelles has prospered since independence owing to the development of the tuna fishing and tourism industries. Tourism now provides 70 per cent of foreign exchange earnings and employs about 30 per cent of the workforce. Agriculture, fishing and small-scale manufacturing industries are being developed to diversify the economy, and the government is promoting offshore financial services. Apart from tourism and fishing, the main industries involve processing fish, coconuts and vanilla, producing coir rope, furniture and beverages, boat-building and printing. The main trading partners are EU countries, Saudi Arabia and South Africa. The principal exports are canned tuna, frozen fish, copra and re-exports of petroleum products. The principal imports are machinery and transport equipment, foodstuffs, petroleum products and chemicals.
GNI – US$751m; US$8,870 per capita (2006)
Annual average growth of GDP – 5.8 per cent (2007 est)
Inflation rate – 2.9 per cent (2007 est)
Total external debt – US$957m (2007 est)
Imports – US$760m (2006)
Exports – US$430m (2006)

BALANCE OF PAYMENTS
Trade – US$325m deficit (2006)
Current Account – US$133mm deficit (2006)

Trade with UK	*2006*	*2007*
Imports from UK	£16,522,000	£16,119,736
Exports to UK	£52,837,000	£43,383,241

COMMUNICATIONS

There are around 458km of roads, most of which are surfaced. The main port is Victoria, and ferries run regularly between Mahé, Praslin and la Digue. Some 15 airports, nine with surfaced runways, serve the islands; the principal airport is at Mahé.

The telephone system serves all the islands. In 2006 there were 20,700 main lines in use, 70,300 mobile phone subscribers and 29,000 internet users.

MEDIA

Freedom of speech has improved since one-party rule was abolished in 1993, but the government continues to control most of the media and operates the only radio and television stations and the sole daily newspaper. Expensive licensing fees have discouraged the development of privately owned broadcast media, and the opposition weekly newspaper, *Regar,* has been sued regularly by the government. The BBC World Service and Radio France Internationale broadcast in the area.

SIERRA LEONE

Republic of Sierra Leone

Area – 71,740 sq. km
Capital – Freetown; population, 827,000 (2007 est)
Major towns – Bo, Kenema
Currency – Leone (Le) of 100 cents
Population – 6,144,562 rising at 2.29 per cent per year (2007 est); Temne (30 per cent), Mende (30 per cent) (est)
Religion – Islam (60 per cent), Christianity (20 per cent), indigenous religions (5 per cent) (est)
Language – English (official), Mende, Temne, Krio
Population density – 80 per sq. km (2006)
Urban population – 40.2 per cent (2005 est)
Median age (years) – 17.5 (2007 est)
National anthem – 'High We Exalt Thee, Realm of the Free'
National day – 27 April (Independence Day)
Life expectancy (years) – 40.58 (2007 est)
Mortality rate – 22.64 (2007 est)
Birth rate – 45.41 (2007 est)
Infant mortality rate – 158.27 (2007 est)

HIV/AIDS adult prevalence – 1.4 per cent (2005 est)
Death penalty – Retained
CPI score – 2.1 (2007)
Population below poverty line – 70.2 per cent (2004)

CLIMATE AND TERRAIN

The terrain rises from coastal mangrove swamps to wooded hill country, upland plateau and mountains in the east. Elevation extremes range from 1,948m (Loma Mansa) at the highest point to 0m (Atlantic Ocean) at the lowest. The climate is tropical, with a wet season from May to October. Average daily temperatures in Freetown are 30°C all year round.

HISTORY AND POLITICS

Coastal trading posts were established by the Portuguese in the 15th century and the British in the 17th century. In the late 18th century British philanthropists bought land to establish a settlement for liberated and escaped African slaves on the Freetown peninsula. In 1808 the settlement was declared a crown colony and became the main base in West Africa for enforcing the 1807 Act outlawing the slave trade. Africans from North America and the West Indies and Africans rescued from slave ships also settled there. In 1896 a protectorate was declared over the hinterland. In 1951 the colony of Freetown and the protectorate were united and on 27 April 1961 Sierra Leone became a fully independent state.

The country became a republic in 1971 and a one-party state in 1978. Transition to a multiparty democracy began in 1991 but was aborted by a military coup in 1992. Civilian rule was restored for the 1996 elections, but another short-lived coup in May 1997 required military intervention by the ECOWAS Monitoring Group, which eventually ousted the military regime. A peace agreement in October enabled President Ahmad Tejan Kabbah, elected in 1996, to return to the country in March 1998.

The transition to multiparty and civilian rule was complicated by the civil war with the Revolutionary United Front (RUF), which began in 1991. Fighting lasted until 2001, when a ceasefire was agreed that was not broken, and the war was declared over in 2002. An estimated 50,000 people were killed and thousands mutilated between 1991 and 2002. In 2004 a UN-supported war crimes tribunal began to try senior militia leaders from both sides of the civil war.

The 2007 presidential election was won by Ernest Bai Koroma, the All People's Congress (APC) candidate, in the second round. The APC won an outright majority of seats in the simultaneous legislative election, defeating the Sierra Leone People's Party, which has been in power since 2002.

POLITICAL SYSTEM

Under the 1991 constitution, the head of state is an executive president who is directly elected for a five-year term, renewable only once. The unicameral parliament has 124 members: 112 directly elected for a five-year term and 12 indirectly elected to represent the 12 provincial districts. The president appoints and chairs the cabinet.

HEAD OF STATE

President, Ernest Bai Koroma, *elected* 18 September 2007
Vice-President, Samuel Sam-Sumana

SELECTED GOVERNMENT MEMBERS *as at July 2008*

Finance, David Carew
Foreign Affairs, Zainab Bangura
Internal Affairs, Dauda Kamara
Defence, Paolo Conteh

SIERRA LEONE HIGH COMMISSION

41 Eagle Street, London WC1R 4TL
T 020-7404 0140 E info@slhc-uk.org.uk
High Commissioner, HE Melvin H. Chalobah, *apptd* 2006

BRITISH HIGH COMMISSION

Spur Road, Freetown
T (+232) (22) 232 961 E bhc@sierratel.sl
High Commissioner, HE Sarah MacIntosh, *apptd* 2006

BRITISH COUNCIL

PO Box 124, Tower Hill, Freetown
T (+232) (22) 222 223 W www.britishcouncil.org/sierraleone
Director, Tom Walsh

DEFENCE

The process of disarming the country's various factions after the civil war was completed in 2004. The army took over full responsibility for internal security in December 2005 when the UN peacekeeping forces left. The navy has 4 patrol and coastal combatant vessels at a base in Freetown.
Military budget – US$25m (2007 est)
Military personnel – 10,500: Joint Staff 10,500

ECONOMY AND TRADE

The country has been devastated by a decade of civil war, and unemployment has increased with the demobilisation of former combatants. Economic activity has grown since the end of the war but the country depends on substantial foreign aid to offset its trade imbalance and support reconstruction. It benefited from having around 90 per cent of foreign debt written off in 2006.

There are significant mineral deposits, mainly diamonds, bauxite, rutile, iron and gold, and agricultural and fishery resources, although the lack of infrastructure hampers development. Diamonds account for about half of export earnings, but nearly 50 per cent of GDP is generated by agriculture, much of which is at subsistence level. Industry consists mainly of diamond mining, processing agricultural products, light manufacturing for the domestic market, oil refining and ship repair. The main export market is Belgium (over 50 per cent); the chief import suppliers are Côte d'Ivoire, the USA, China, Brazil and EU countries. Principal exports are diamonds, rutile, cocoa, coffee and fish. The main imports are foodstuffs, machinery and equipment, fuels and lubricants and chemicals.
GNI – US$1,400m (2006); US$240 per capita (2006)
Annual average growth of GDP – 6.8 per cent (2007 est)
Inflation rate – 1 per cent (2002 est)
Total external debt – US$1,610m (2003 est)
Imports – US$390m (2006)
Exports – US$220m (2006)

BALANCE OF PAYMENTS

Trade – US$173m deficit (2006)
Current Account – US$51m deficit (2006)

Trade with UK	*2006*	*2007*
Imports from UK	£18,553,000	£18,021,824
Exports to UK	£4,374,000	£2,832,019

COMMUNICATIONS

The railway system was phased out in 1974, but an extensive road network has been developed since; there are now 11,300km of roads in the country, although only 904km is surfaced. A bridge over the Mano river links Sierra Leone with Liberia. There is an international airport at Freetown and nine airfields around the country. Freetown, which has one of the world's largest natural harbours, is the main port and there are smaller ports at Pepel, Bonthe and Niti.

The fixed-line telephone system is poor and mobile phone distribution has grown rapidly. In 2002–5 there were about 24,000 main lines in use, 113,000 mobile phone subscriptions and 10,000 internet users.

EDUCATION AND HEALTH

Technical education is provided in two government technical institutes, situated in Freetown and Kenema, in two trade centres and in the technical training establishments of the mining companies.

Literacy rate – 29.6 per cent (2004 est)
Gross enrolment ratio (percentage of relevant age group) – primary 145 per cent; secondary 32 per cent (2006 est)
Health expenditure (per capita) – US$8 (2005)
Hospital beds (per 1,000 people) – 0.4 (2000–6)

MEDIA

Media freedom is limited by the government's use of the libel laws to restrict coverage of politically sensitive issues. Broadcasters also have to contend with unreliable electricity supplies and a lack of advertising revenue. The UN Mission in Sierra Leone operates a number of radio services, and the BBC World Service and Radio France Internationale are broadcast from Freetown. Dozens of privately run newspapers are published in Freetown, despite low literacy levels.

SINGAPORE

Repablik Singapura/Xinjiapo Gongheguo – Republic of Singapore

Area – 692.7 sq. km
Capital – Singapore; population, 4,436,000 (2007 est)
Currency – Singapore dollar (S$) of 100 cents
Population – 4,553,009 rising at 1.28 per cent per year (2007 est); Chinese (76.8 per cent), Malay (13.9 per cent), Indian (7.9 per cent)
Religion – Buddhism and other Chinese religions (51 per cent), Islam (15 per cent), Christianity (15 per cent), Hinduism (4 per cent) (est)
Language – English, Mandarian, Tamil (all official), Malay, Hokkien, Teochew, Cantonese
Population density – 6,508 per sq. km (2006)
Urban population – 100 per cent (2005 est)
Median age (years) – 37.8 (2007 est)
National anthem – 'Majulah Singapura' ['May Singapore Progress']
National day – 9 August
Life expectancy (years) – 81.8 (2007 est)
Mortality rate – 4.4 (2007 est)
Birth rate – 9.17 (2007 est)
Infant mortality rate – 2.3 (2007 est)
Death penalty – Retained
CPI score – 9.3 (2007)
Literacy rate – 92.5 per cent (2004 est)
Gross enrolment ratio (percentage of relevant age group) – primary 78 per cent; secondary 63 per cent (2006 est)
Health expenditure (per capita) – US$944 (2005)
Hospital beds (per 1,000 people) – 2.8 (2000–6)

CLIMATE AND TERRAIN

Singapore consists of the island of Singapore and 63 islets. Singapore island is 42km long and 22.5km wide and is situated just north of the Equator off the southern extremity of the Malay peninsula, from which it is separated by the Straits of Johore. A causeway crosses the 1.21km to the mainland. Elevation extremes range from 166m (Bukit Timah) at the highest point to 0m (Singapore Strait) at the lowest. The average temperature is 29°C all year round. Average annual rainfall is high at 2,410mm and flooding is common during the monsoon months of December and June.

HISTORY AND POLITICS

Singapore, a trading site since the 12th century, was leased from the Sultan of Johore by the British East India Company in 1819. In 1826 it was incorporated with Penang and Malacca to form the Straits Settlements and they became a crown colony in 1867. Singapore became the principal British military base in the Far East in the 1920s and in 1942, during the Second World War, fell to Japanese forces. Liberated in 1945, it became a separate colony in 1946. Internal self-government was introduced in 1959 and it became part of the Federation of Malaysia in 1963, before withdrawing to become an independent sovereign state on 9 August 1965.

Although Singapore is a multiparty state, the People's Action Party (PAP) has dominated politics since 1959; opposition candidates were elected to parliament for the first time in 1984. The PAP leader, Lee Kuan Yew, was prime minister from 1959 until he retired in 1990.

Sellapan Rama Nathan became president in September 1999 and was declared re-elected in August 2005, although no election was held on either occasion as he was the sole eligible candidate. In the 2006 general election, the PAP won 82 seats in parliament and opposition parties two. Lee Hsien Loong, the son of Lee Kuan Yew, continued in office as prime minister, a post he has held since 2004.

POLITICAL SYSTEM

The 1959 constitution was amended in 1965 to enable Singapore to become a republic, and in 1991 to make the presidency directly elective with increased responsibilities. The head of state is the president, directly elected for a six-year term, who has the power to veto government decisions relating to internal security, the budget, financial reserves and the appointment of senior civil servants. The president appoints the prime minister and, on his advice, the members of the cabinet. There is a unicameral parliament with 84 directly elected members and up to three extra members from opposition parties (NCMPs), depending on their share of the vote; they serve a five-year term. Up to nine members can also be nominated by the government for a two-year term (NMPs).

HEAD OF STATE
President, Sellapan Rama Nathan, *took office* 1 September 1999, *re-elected* 17 August 2005

SELECTED GOVERNMENT MEMBERS *as at July 2008*
Prime Minister, Lee Hsien Loong
Deputy Prime Ministers, Shanmugam Jayakumar; Wong Kan Seng
Foreign Affairs, George Yong Boon Yeo
Defence, Rear-Adm. Teo Chee Hean
Finance, Tharman Shanmugaratnam

HIGH COMMISSION FOR THE REPUBLIC OF SINGAPORE
9 Wilton Crescent, London SW1X 8SP
T 020-7235 8315 E singhc_lon@sgmfa.gov.sg
W http://mfa.gov.sg/london
High Commissioner, HE Michael Eng Cheng Teo, *apptd* 2002

BRITISH HIGH COMMISSION
Tanglin Road, Singapore 247919
T (+65) 6424 4200 E commercial.singapore@fco.gov.uk
W www.britain.org/sg
High Commissioner, HE Paul Madden, *apptd* 2007

BRITISH COUNCIL
30 Napier Road, Singapore 258509
T (+65) 6473 1111 W www.britishcouncil.org/sg
Director, Eunice Crook

DEFENCE

The army has 196 main battle tanks, over 1,280 armoured personnel carriers and over 272 armoured infantry fighting vehicles. The navy has 4 submarines, 3 frigates, 6 corvettes and 29 patrol and coastal combatant vessels at 2 bases. The air force has 102 combat aircraft and 12 armed helicopters.
Military budget – US$7,240m (2007)
Military personnel – 72,500: army 50,000, navy 9,000, air force 13,500; paramilitary 93,800
Conscription duration – 24 months

ECONOMY AND TRADE

Historically based on the sale and distribution of raw materials from surrounding countries and on entrepot trade in finished products, the economy has been diversified and industrialised since independence. Singapore has also developed as a financial centre for the region, with significant insurance and foreign exchange markets, a stock exchange, and a large commercial and merchant banking sector. Agriculture is limited and contributes little to GDP. Industries include the manufacture of electronic, electrical, telecommunications and oil-drilling equipment, and chemicals, oil refining, rubber processing, food processing, ship repair, offshore oil platform construction and life sciences; industry contributes 31.2 per cent of GDP. The service sector, which includes tourism as well as financial and business services and the entrepot trade, accounts for 68.8 per cent of GDP and employs 42 per cent of the workforce.

The main trading partners are Malaysia, the USA, China, Japan, Indonesia, Hong Kong and Taiwan. Principal exports are machinery and equipment (especially electronic), consumer goods, chemicals and mineral fuels. The main imports are machinery and equipment, mineral fuels, chemicals and foodstuffs.
GNI – US$128,800m (2006); US$28,730 per capita (2006)
Annual average growth of GDP – 7.4 per cent (2007 est)
Inflation rate – 1.8 per cent (2007 est)
Unemployment – 2.6 per cent (2007 est)
Total external debt – US$25,530m (2007 est)
Imports – US$239,000m (2006)
Exports – US$271,800m (2006)

BALANCE OF PAYMENTS
Trade – US$33,097m surplus (2006)
Current Account – US$29,765m surplus (2006)

Trade with UK	*2006*	*2007*
Imports from UK	£2,325,114,000	£2,465,111,959
Exports to UK	£3,834,344,000	£4,111,468,139

COMMUNICATIONS

There are 30km of railway, connected to the Malaysian rail system by a causeway across the Straits of Johore, and an extensive light rail system on the island. There are 3,234km of roads, all surfaced. Singapore is one of the largest and busiest seaports in the world, with deep-water wharves and six terminals. It has a large merchant fleet of 1,131 ships of over 1,000 tonnes registered in Singapore and a further 293 ships registered in other countries, while 652 foreign-owned ships are registered in Singapore. There is one international airport, at Changi.

There is a modern telecommunications system. In 2006 there were 1.8 million main telephone lines in use, 4.7 million mobile phone subscribers and 1.7 million internet users.

MEDIA

Singapore's media is highly regulated by the government. Private satellite dishes are outlawed and internet access is controlled, although the government sees the country as a digital media pioneer and plans to create thousands of new jobs in this sector. The television sector is dominated by MediaCorp, owned by a state investment agency. Singapore Press Holdings, which has close links to the ruling party, has a virtual monopoly of the newspaper industry, and publishes 15 newspapers and six periodicals.

SLOVAKIA

Slovenska Republika – Slovak Republic

Area – 48,845 sq. km
Capital – Bratislava; population, 424,000 (2007 est), on the Danube
Major city – Kosice
Currency – Koruna (Sk) of 100 halierov
Population – 5,447,502 rising at 0.15 per cent per year (2007 est); Slovak (85.8 per cent), Hungarian (9.7 per cent), Romani (1.7 per cent)
Religion – Roman Catholicism (69 per cent), other Christian denominations (18 per cent) (est)
Language – Slovak (official), Hungarian, Romani, Ukrainian
Population density – 112 per sq. km (2006)
Urban population – 58 per cent (2005 est)
Median age (years) – 36.1 (2007 est)
National anthem – 'Nad Tatrou sa blyska' ['Storm Over the Tatras']
National day – 1 September (Constitution Day)
Life expectancy (years) – 74.95 (2007 est)
Mortality rate – 9.48 (2007 est)
Birth rate – 10.65 (2007 est)
Infant mortality rate – 7.12 (2007 est)
Death penalty – Abolished for all crimes (since 1990)
CPI score – 4.9 (2007)
Population below poverty line – 21 per cent (2002)
Literacy rate – 99.6 per cent (2004 est)
Gross enrolment ratio (percentage of relevant age group) – primary 99 per cent; secondary 96 per cent; tertiary 41 per cent (2006 est)
Health expenditure (per capita) – US$626 (2005)
Hospital beds (per 1,000 people) – 6.9 (2000–6)

CLIMATE AND TERRAIN

Slovakia is landlocked and mostly mountainous, lying in the western Carpathian range and including the Tatra and Beskid mountains to the north. The lower-lying plain of the river Danube is in the south-west. Elevation extremes range from 2,655m (Gerlachorsky Stit) at the highest point to 94m (Bodrok river) at the lowest. The climate is continental, with warm humid summers and cold dry winters. Average temperatures range from 1°C in January to 21°C in July.

HISTORY AND POLITICS

The area was part of the kingdom of Greater Moravia in the ninth century, became part of the Hungarian Magyar Empire in the tenth century and came under Austrian Habsburg rule from the 16th century. After the dissolution of the Austro-Hungarian Empire in 1918, Slovakia became part of Czechoslovakia.

Following the German annexation of Czechoslovakia in 1939, Slovakia became a nominally independent state but was exploited as part of the German war effort. After an abortive uprising in 1944, Slovakia was liberated by Soviet forces in 1945 and returned to Czechoslovakia, where a communist regime assumed power in 1948. The formation of a federal republic between the Czech lands and Slovakia was the only Prague Spring reform to survive the Soviet invasion of 1968. Following the collapse of communist rule in 1989, the Slovak separatist movement gained ground and the Czech and Slovak republics negotiated the dissolution of the federation into two sovereign states in 1992. Dissolution took effect on 1 January 1993.

The Movement for a Democratic Slovakia (HZDS), led by the authoritarian Vladimir Meciar, dominated the coalition governments that held office in the 1990s, pursuing populist nationalist policies. It was ousted at the 1998 election by an alliance of liberals, centrists, left-wingers and ethnic Hungarians, which formed a coalition government under Mikulas Dzurinda of the Slovak Democratic and Christian Union (SDKU). This government, which was re-elected in 2002, introduced the constitutional and economic reforms necessary to meet the requirements for membership of the EU. Slovakia joined NATO and the EU in 2004. Its parliament ratified the EU constitution in 2005.

The 2004 presidential election was won by Ivan Gasparovic, with 59.9 per cent of the vote; he was chair of the Movement for Democracy (HZD) but resigned from this position after his election. After the 2006 legislative election, the Smer-SD (Direction–Social Democracy) party became the largest party in the legislature, with 50 seats. It formed a coalition government with the HZD and the Slovak National Party, led by Smer leader Robert Fico.

POLITICAL SYSTEM

The 1993 constitution has been amended several times, most recently in 1999 to allow direct elections to the presidency. The head of state is the president, directly elected for a five-year term, renewable only once. The unicameral National Council of the Slovak Republic has 150 members, who are directly elected for a four-year term by proportional representation. The prime minister, who is appointed by the president, nominates the cabinet.

HEAD OF STATE

President, Ivan Gasparovic, *elected* 17 April 2004, *sworn in* 15 June 2004

SELECTED GOVERNMENT MEMBERS *as at July 2008*

Prime Minister, Robert Fico
Deputy Prime Ministers, Dusan Caplovic; Stefan Harabin; Robert Kalinak *(Interior)*
Defence, Jaroslav Baska
Foreign Affairs, Jan Kubis
Finance, Jan Pociatek

EMBASSY OF THE SLOVAK REPUBLIC

25 Kensington Palace Gardens, London W8 4QY
T 020-7243 0803 E emb.london@mzv.sk
W www.slovakembassy.co.uk
Ambassador Extraordinary and Plenipotentiary, Juraj Zervan, *apptd* 2007

BRITISH EMBASSY

Panska 16, Bratislava 811 01
T (+421) (2) 5998 2000 E bebra@internet.sk
W www.britemb.sk
Ambassador Extraordinary and Plenipotentiary, HE Michael Roberts, *apptd* 2007

BRITISH COUNCIL

PO Box 68, Panska 17, 814 99 Bratislava
T (+421) (2) 5443 1074 W www.britishcouncil.org/slovakia
Director, Huw Jones

DEFENCE

The army has 245 main battle tanks, 134 armoured personnel carriers and 387 armoured infantry fighting vehicles. The air force has 46 combat aircraft and 16 armed helicopters.
Military expenditure – US$957m (2006)
Military personnel – 17,129: army 7,324, air force 4,280, central staff 2,621, support and training 2,904
Conscription duration – 6 months

ECONOMY AND TRADE

Slovakia has nearly completed the transition from a centrally planned to a free-market economy, following structural reforms and privatisation begun after 1998. As a result, foreign investment has risen, especially in the vehicle industry, and since 2000 the GDP has grown steadily. Unemployment has fallen from the 2003 peak of 20 per cent but remains high. Slovakia aims to adopt the euro in 2009.

Natural resources include brown coal and lignite, natural gas, oil, iron ore, copper and manganese. Major industries include production of metal and metal products, food and beverages, fuel and energy (electricity, gas, coke, oil and nuclear), chemicals and synthetic fibres, machinery, paper and printing, ceramics, transport vehicles, textiles and electrical and optical equipment. Industry accounts for 33.5 per cent of GDP, services 63.9 per cent and agriculture 2.6 per cent.

The main trading partners are other EU countries (especially Germany and the Czech Republic) and Russia. Principal exports are vehicles, machinery and electrical equipment, base metals, chemicals, minerals and plastics. The main imports are machinery and transport equipment, intermediate manufactured goods and fuels.

GNI – US$51,800m (2006); US$9,610 per capita (2006)
Annual average growth of GDP – 8.8 per cent (2007 est)
Inflation rate – 2.7 per cent (2007 est)
Unemployment – 8.6 per cent (2007 est)
Total external debt – US$36,660m (2007)
Imports – US$47,000m (2006)
Exports – US$42,000m (2006)

BALANCE OF PAYMENTS
Trade – US$5,120m deficit (2006)
Current Account – US$3,963m deficit (2006)

Trade with UK	*2006*	*2007*
Imports from UK	£260,300,000	£375,494,822
Exports to UK	£636,300,000	£1,267,971,788

COMMUNICATIONS

Slovakia has a total of 42,993km of roads, including 316km of motorways. There are 3,662km of railways, and 172km of navigable waterways on the river Danube. The main Danube ports are Bratislava and Komarno, and the principal airport is at Bratislava.

The modern telecommunications system has expanded rapidly in recent years, especially for mobile phones. In 2006 there were 1.2 million main telephone lines in use, 4.9 million mobile phone subscribers and 2.3 million internet users.

MEDIA

Since the collapse of communism the public broadcaster Slovak TV has lost much of its audience share to the private sector TV Markiza. Cable and satellite television channels are also popular. All three major daily newspapers are privately owned and there are more than 20 private radio stations in addition to the public broadcaster Slovak Radio, which operates five national networks and an external service.

SLOVENIA

Republika Slovenija – Republic of Slovenia

Area – 20,273 sq. km
Capital – Ljubljana; population, 244,000 (2007 est)
Major city – Maribor
Currency – Euro (€) of 100 cents
Population – 2,009,245 falling at 0.07 per cent per year (2007 est); Slovene (83.1 per cent), Serb (2 per cent), Croat (1.8 per cent), Bosnian (1.1 per cent)
Religion – Roman Catholicism (58 per cent), Islam (2 per cent), Orthodox Christianity (2 per cent) (est). An estimated 10 per cent of the population is atheist
Language – Slovene (official), Serbian, Croatian
Population density – 100 per sq. km (2006)
Urban population – 50.8 per cent (2005 est)
Median age (years) – 41 (2007 est)
National anthem – 'Zdravljica' ['A Toast']
National day – 25 June (Statehood Day)
Life expectancy (years) – 76.53 (2007 est)
Mortality rate – 10.41 (2007 est)
Birth rate – 9 (2007 est)
Infant mortality rate – 4.35 (2007 est)
Death penalty – Abolished for all crimes (since 1989)
CPI score – 6.6 (2007)
Population below the poverty line – 12.9 per cent (2004)

CLIMATE AND TERRAIN

The terrain is mountainous, the only low-lying areas being the valleys of the rivers Sava and Drava and the short Adriatic coastline. Elevation extremes range from 2,864m (Triglav) at the highest point to 0m (Adriatic Sea) at the lowest. The majority of the country has an Eastern European climate; the exception is the stretch of Adriatic coastline, which has milder winters and more hours of sunshine. Average temperatures in Ljubljana range from 0°C in January to 25°C in July.

HISTORY AND POLITICS

Settled by Slovenes in the sixth century, the area was later ruled by Slavs, Franks and Hungarians before coming under the control of the Austrian Habsburg Empire in the 14th century. Following the collapse of the Austro-Hungarian Empire in 1918, Slovenia became part of the Kingdom of the Serbs, Croats and Slovenes (later Yugoslavia). German forces invaded Yugoslavia in 1941 and Slovenia was divided between Germany, Italy and Hungary. In 1945 it was reformed as a constituent republic of Yugoslavia, which became a communist state in 1946. After a dispute with Italy and nine years of international administration, the Adriatic coast and hinterland were returned to Slovenia in 1954, while Italy retained Trieste.

Slovenia's fears of Serbian dominance led the Slovene Assembly in 1989 to amend the republican constitution to allow secession. The first multiparty elections, held in April 1990, were won by the pro-independence 'Demos' coalition. In a referendum in December 1990, 88 per cent of the electorate voted for independence, which was declared on 25 June 1991. A ten-day war with the Yugoslav National Army followed before the army withdrew under the terms of an EU-brokered ceasefire. Slovenia became a member of NATO and the EU in 2004, and joined the eurozone in January 2007. The legislature ratified the EU constitution in 2005.

The Liberal Democracy of Slovenia party (LDS) was the major party in every government from 1991 to 2004, when the Slovenian Democratic Party became the largest party in the legislature following the legislative election; its leader, Janez Jansa, formed a four-party coalition government. The 2007 presidential election was won by an independent candidate, Danilo Turk, in the second round of voting. A legislative election is scheduled for September 2008.

POLITICAL SYSTEM

Under the 1991 constitution, the head of state is the president, directly elected for a five-year term. The unicameral legislature, the National Assembly, has 90 members directly elected for a four-year term. The National Council, which has 40 members indirectly elected for a five-year term, has an advisory role. The prime minister, who is nominated by the president and elected by the national assembly, appoints the cabinet.

HEAD OF STATE

President, Danilo Turk, *elected* 11 November 2007; *sworn in* 22 December 2007

SELECTED GOVERNMENT MEMBERS *as at July 2008*

Prime Minister, Janez Jansa
Defence, Karl Erjavec
Finance, Andrej Bajuk
Foreign Affairs, Dimitrij Rupel
Internal Affairs, Dragutin Mate

EMBASSY OF THE REPUBLIC OF SLOVENIA

10 Little College Street, London SW1P 3SH
T 020-7222 5700 E vlo@gov.si
Ambassador Extraordinary and Plenipotentiary, HE Iztok Mirosic, *apptd* 2004

BRITISH EMBASSY

4th Floor, Trg Republike 3, 1000 Ljubljana
T (+386) (1) 200 3910 E info@british-embassy.si
W www.british-embassy.si
Ambassador Extraordinary and Plenipotentiary, HE Timothy Simmons, *apptd* 2004

BRITISH COUNCIL

Tivoli Center, Tivolska 30, 1000 Ljubljana
T (+386) (1) 300 2030 W www.britishcouncil.org/slovenia
Director, Robert Munro

DEFENCE

The army has 70 main battle tanks, 64 armoured personnel carriers and 26 armoured infantry fighting vehicles. The army Maritime Element has 1 patrol and coastal combatant vessel.
Military expenditure – US$629m (2006)
Military personnel – army 5,973; paramilitary 4,500

ECONOMY AND TRADE

Always the most prosperous republic of the former Yugoslavia, Slovenia's transition to a market economy has been relatively smooth. It has a good infrastructure and a well-educated workforce, and it has successfully re-orientated its exports towards Western markets. Much of the economy remains in state ownership and taxes are high, deterring foreign investment and inhibiting its competitiveness in international markets.

Agriculture contributes 2 per cent of GDP, industry 34.4 per cent and the service sector 63.5 per cent. The main agricultural products are potatoes, hops, wheat, sugar beet, maize and grapes. Industries include metal extraction and processing, electronics, vehicles, electric power equipment, wood products, textiles, chemicals and machine tools.

The main trading partners are other EU countries, Croatia and Russia. Principal exports are manufactured goods, machinery and transport equipment, chemicals and food. These items, along with fuels and lubricants, are also the main imports.
GNI – US$37,400m (2005); US$18,660 per capita (2006)
Annual average growth of GDP – 5.6 per cent (2007 est)
Inflation rate – 3.2 per cent (2007 est)
Unemployment – 7.8 per cent (2007 est)
Total external debt – US$40,420m (2007)
Imports – US$23,000m (2006)
Exports – US$21,000m (2006)

BALANCE OF PAYMENTS

Trade – US$2,029m deficit (2006)
Current Account – US$1,076m deficit (2006)

Trade with UK	*2006*	*2007*
Imports from UK	£187,600,000	£201,392,433
Exports to UK	£267,300,000	£316,308,611

COMMUNICATIONS

There are 38,400km of roads and 1,229km of railways, of which 504km are electrified. Major international road and rail routes cross the country. There are 14 airports and airfields, with international airports at Ljubljana, Maribor and Portoroz. Koper is the main port, receiving shipments from landlocked central European countries.

In 2006 there were 837,500 main telephone lines in use, 1.8 millon mobile phone subscribers and 1.2 million internet users.

EDUCATION AND HEALTH

Education is free of charge and compulsory between the ages of six and 14.
Literacy rate – 99.7 per cent (2004 est)
Gross enrolment ratio (percentage of relevant age group) – primary 98 per cent; secondary 96 per cent; tertiary 79 per cent (2006 est)
Health expenditure (per capita) – US$1,495 (2005)
Hospital beds (per 1,000 people) – 4.8 (2000–6)

MEDIA

Slovenia saw a rapid development of its media market after the fall of communism. The main newspapers are privately owned, and the broadcasting sector is a mix of public and private ownership. The television market is mainly shared between the public service, RTV Slovenia, and the private stations Pop TV and Kanal A. About two-thirds of households are connected to cable or satellite.

SOLOMON ISLANDS

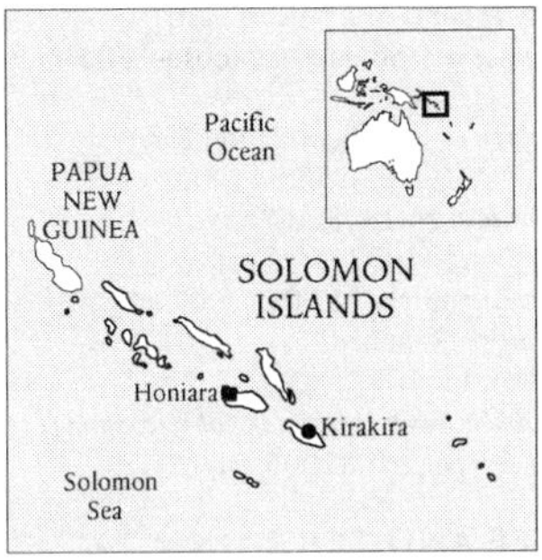

Area – 28,450 sq. km
Capital – Honiara, on Guadalcanal; population, 66,000 (2007 est)
Currency – Solomon Islands dollar (SI$) of 100 cents
Population – 66,842 rising at 2.54 per cent per year (2007 est); Melanesian (94.5 per cent), Polynesian (3 per cent), Micronesian (1.2 per cent)
Religion – Protestantism (63 per cent), Roman Catholicism (19 per cent), other Christian denominations (13 per cent), animist (5 per cent) (est)
Language – English (official), Melanesian pidgin
Population density – 17 per sq. km (2006)
Urban population – 17.1 per cent (2005 est)
Median age (years) – 19.1 (2007 est)
National anthem – 'God Save Our Solomon Islands'
National day – 7 July (Independence Day)
Life expectancy (years) – 73.16 (2007 est)
Mortality rate – 3.87 (2007 est)
Birth rate – 29.27 (2007 est)
Infant mortality rate – 19.97 (2007 est)
Death penalty – Abolished for all crimes (since 1966)
CPI score – 2.8 (2007)

CLIMATE AND TERRAIN

Forming a scattered archipelago of mountainous islands and low-lying coral atolls in the south-west Pacific Ocean, the Solomon Islands stretch about 1,448km in a south-easterly direction from the Shortland Islands to the Santa Cruz islands. The six biggest islands are Choiseul, New Georgia, Santa Isabel, Guadalcanal, Malaita and Makira (San Cristobal). They are characterised by thickly forested mountain ranges intersected by deep, narrow valleys. Elevation extremes range from 2,447m (Mt Makarakomburu) at the highest point to 0m (Pacific Ocean) at the lowest. The climate is tropical and the average temperature in Honiara is 27°C. The islands are occasionally prone to earthquakes, tsunamis and volcanic activity.

HISTORY AND POLITICS

The islands were discovered by the Spanish in 1568 and visited by Europeans intermittently for about 300 years. Following the inauguration of sugar plantations in Queensland and Fiji (which created a need for labour) and the arrival of missionaries and traders, Britain declared a protectorate in 1893 over the southern Solomons, adding the Santa Cruz group in 1898. The Shortland Islands were transferred from Germany to Britain by treaty in 1900. The islands were occupied by the Japanese in 1942, and recaptured by US forces in 1943 after fierce fighting, especially on Guadalcanal. After the Second World War, campaigns began for self-government, which was achieved in 1976; independence followed in July 1978.

Ethnic tension on Guadalcanal between the native population and migrants from the island of Malaita began in 1998 and descended into conflict between rival militias. A fragile peace began with an agreement signed in October 2000, allowing elections to be held in 2001. Escalating economic and social problems in early 2002 led to growing lawlessness throughout the country. In June 2003 the government requested assistance from neighbouring countries and an Australian-led peacekeeping force was deployed, restoring public order and economic stability, and disarming the militias.

In the April 2006 legislative election, the governing People's Alliance Party (PAP) and the opposition won an equal number of seats. Snyder Ridi of the PAP was elected prime minister on 20 April but resigned six days later after rioting in protest at his appointment. Manasseh Sogavare (prime minister 2000–1) of the Social Credit Party was elected to replace him and formed a coalition government. Sogavare was defeated in a vote of no confidence in December 2007 and Derek Sikua was elected prime minister.

POLITICAL SYSTEM

Under the 1978 constitution, the Solomon Islands is a constitutional monarchy. The head of state is the British monarch, represented by a governor-general, who is chosen by the legislature. The unicameral national parliament has 50 members who are directly elected for a four-year term. The prime minister is elected by the legislature from among its members, and nominates the cabinet, which is formally appointed by the governor-general.
Governor-General, Sir Nathaniel Waena, *apptd* 2004

SELECTED GOVERNMENT MEMBERS *as at July 2008*
Prime Minister, Derek Sikua
Deputy Prime Minister, Fred Fono
Foreign Affairs, William Haomae
Home Affairs, James Tora
Finance, Snyder Rini

HIGH COMMISSION FOR THE SOLOMON ISLANDS
17B Avenue Edouard Lacombe, 1040 Brussels, Belgium
T (+32) (2) 732 7085
High Commissioner, HE Joseph Ma'ahanua, *apptd* 2006

BRITISH HIGH COMMISSION
PO Box 676, Telekom House, Mendana Avenue, Honiara
T (+677) 21705 E bhc@solomon.com.sb
High Commissioner, HE Richard Lyne, *apptd* 2005

ECONOMY AND TRADE

The civil conflict of 1998–2003 left the country virtually bankrupt but the restoration of law and order has enabled the economy to recover and it has grown slightly, although rioting and looting in April 2006 were a temporary setback. Owing to recent events, the country's dependency on foreign aid, principally from Australia, has increased.

Abundant mineral resources are largely undeveloped, although there is some mining. Agriculture, much at subsistence level, is the largest economic sector, accounting for over 40 per cent of GDP and engaging 75 per cent of the population. The main industries are fishing, mining, forestry and processing agricultural products; industry contributes 11 per cent of GDP.

The main export markets are China, South Korea and Japan; most imports come from Australia and Singapore. Principal exports are timber, fish, copra, palm oil and cocoa. The main imports are foodstuffs, machinery and equipment, manufactured goods, fuels and chemicals.
GNI – US$333m (2006); US$690 per capita (2006)
Annual average growth of GDP – 4.4 per cent (2005 est)
Inflation rate – 6.6 per cent (2005 est)
Total external debt – US$166m (2004)
Imports – US$210m (2006)
Exports – US$120m (2006)

BALANCE OF PAYMENTS
Trade – US$90m deficit (2006)
Current Account – US$87m deficit (2006)

Trade with UK	*2005*	*2006*
Imports from UK	£982,000	£1,440,000
Exports to UK	£419,000	£442,000

COMMUNICATIONS

There are 1,360km of roads, of which only 34km are surfaced. The main ports are Honiara and Yandina. There are 35 airports and airfields, the main one being at Honiara. Solomon Airlines operates international services to other Pacific states and Australia. Air Niugini flies from Papua New Guinea to Honiara.

Telephone services are limited; in 2005 there were 7,400 main telephone lines in use, 6,000 mobile phone subscribers and 8,000 internet users.

MEDIA

The Solomon Islands Broadcasting Corporation (SIBC) operates a public radio service; there are no television services on the islands, although external satellite services can be received. Low literacy levels mean that SIBC has greater influence than the press, which consists of one daily, two weekly and two monthly newspapers. Australia and Taiwan have donated funds and equipment to develop the domestic media.

SOMALIA

Jamhuuriyada Demuqraadiga Soomaaliyeed – Somalia

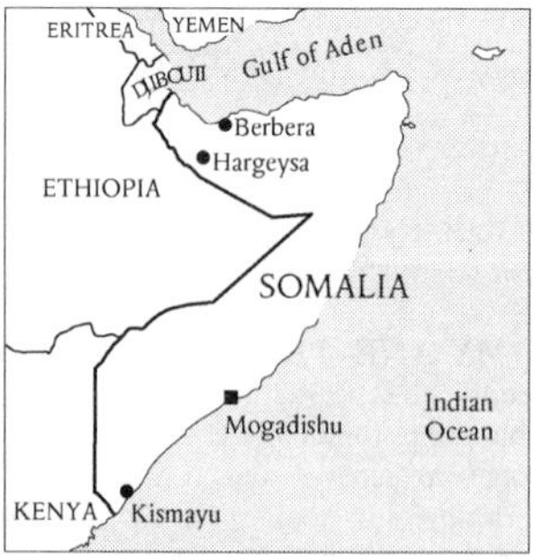

Area – 637,657 sq. km
Capital – Mogadishu; population, 1,100,000 (2007 est)
Major cities – Burco, Hargeisa
Currency – Somali shilling of 100 cents
Population – 9,118,773 rising at 2.83 per cent per year (2007 est)
Religion – The vast majority of the population follow Sunni Islam. There is a small Christian community
Language – Somali (official), Arabic, Italian, English
Population density – 13 per sq. km (2006)
Urban population – 35.9 per cent (2005 est)
Median age (years) – 17.6 (2007 est)
National anthem – 'Somaliyaay toosoo' ['Somalia Wake Up']
National day – 1 July (Foundation Day)
Life expectancy (years) – 48.84 (2007 est)
Mortality rate – 16.28 (2007 est)
Birth rate – 44.6 (2007 est)
Infant mortality rate – 113.08 (2007 est)
Death penalty – Retained
CPI score – 1.4 (2007)
Gross enrolment ratio (percentage of relevant age group) – primary 17 per cent (2005 est)

CLIMATE AND TERRAIN

The terrain is mostly arid, flat or undulating plateau, rising to hills in the north. Elevation extremes range from 2,416m (Shimbiris) at the highest point to 0m (Indian Ocean) at the lowest. The climate is tropical, influenced by the north-east and south-west monsoons. Rainfall is greater in the south than the north, but is low and irregular throughout the country, leading to frequent droughts. Temperatures in Mogadishu are an almost constant 30°C.

HISTORY AND POLITICS

Arab settlement from the eighth century onwards introduced Islam and established coastal trading towns that developed into sultanates. European contact began in the early 16th century, with Italian, French and British interest intensifying after the Suez Canal opened in 1869. Protectorates were established in the north by the British and in the centre (subsequently taking in the south) by the Italians in the 1880s. Italian Somalia was returned to Italian administration as a UN Trust Territory in 1950. The two protectorates became independent and merged to form the United Republic of Somalia in July 1960.

In 1969 the armed forces seized power in a coup led by Maj.-Gen. Muhammad Siad Barre, and established a socialist Islamic regime which became a one-party state in 1979. Insurrection in the north began in 1978 and by the late 1980s opposition to the government had developed into a civil war. In January 1991 the rebels captured Mogadishu, forcing Siad Barre to flee. Attempts to establish a new central government failed as political and clan rivalries split the former rebels. The situation degenerated into civil war between rival 'warlords' and the state effectively disintegrated. The conflict has prevented effective response to disasters such as the recurrent famines and the 2004 Indian Ocean tsunami; conflict, disasters and disease have resulted in an estimated one million deaths.

Internationally sponsored peace talks between 2002 and 2004 led to the establishment of a federal government and a transitional federal legislature, which elected Col. Abdullahi Yusuf Ahmed as president in 2004 and a transitional federal government in January 2005. Members of the federal institutions returned to Somalia in 2005–6, basing themselves in the central town of Baidoa because of the security situation in Mogadishu.

In early 2006 Muslim militias loyal to the Union of Islamic Courts (UIC) defeated the warlords in the south, taking control of Mogadishu in June. A UIC advance in the direction of Baidoa in December 2006 was repulsed by government troops, supported by Ethiopian armed forces, and in January 2007 they forced the UIC to abandon the capital to the transitional government.

African Union peacekeeping forces were deployed in March 2007 but fighting between government and Ethiopian forces and the UIC-led insurgents continues. The government agreed a ceasefire with one insurgent group in June 2008, but the UIC rejected any settlement while foreign troops remain in the country.

Ali Muhammed Ghedi, who was appointed prime minister in 2004, resigned in October 2007 and was replaced by Nur Hassan Hussein.

SECESSION

The northern-based Somali National Movement (SNM) took control of the north-west (the former British Somaliland protectorate) after Siad Barre's deposition and in May 1991 declared unilateral independence as the 'Somaliland Republic'. A 2001 referendum on a new constitution, which confirmed the independence of Somaliland, was approved by 97.09 per cent of the voters. The leaders of the regime have refused to take part in the peace process since 1999 and have not signed the 2004 peace agreement; they are seeking international recognition of Somaliland's independence.

The north-east of the country proclaimed its autonomy as the region of Puntland in 1998. Puntland does not seek independence but participation in a federal Somalia. Its leaders have taken part in the peace process, signing the 2004 peace agreement; its former leader, Col. Abdullahi Yusuf Ahmed, was elected national president in October 2004.

There has been sporadic fighting between Somaliland and Puntland over Somaliland's Sool and Sanaag regions, which Puntland claims on the grounds of ethnicity.

POLITICAL SYSTEM

Somalia has been without an effective central government since 1991. The 2004 peace agreement produced a charter which outlines the powers of the transitional federal institutions (TFI) and their five-year mandate to draw up a constitution and hold elections. The TFI include the Transitional Federal Parliament, which has 275 seats; 244 members are appointed by each of the country's four major clans (61 per clan) and 31 seats are allocated to smaller clans. The parliament elects the president, who serves a four-year term, and approves the appointment of ministers to the transitional federal government.

HEAD OF STATE

President, Col. Abdullahi Yusuf Ahmed, *sworn in* 10 October 2004

SELECTED GOVERNMENT MEMBERS *as at July 2008*

Prime Minister, Col. Nur Hassan Hussein
Deputy Prime Ministers, Muhammad Abdisalan Adan; Aydid Abdullahi Ilka Hanaf; Salim Aliyow Ibrow
Defence, Col. Muhyadin Muhammad Ibrahim
Foreign Affairs, Ali Ahmed Jama Jangali
Finance, Muhammad Ali Hamud
Interior, Muse Nur Amin

DEFENCE

There has been no national armed forces since 1991, despite attempts at re-establishment by the transitional government. Somaliland and Puntland have their own militias with limited amounts of equipment.

ECONOMY AND TRADE

Political instability, damaged infrastructure and a lack of education and health services have prevented broad-based economic development and assistance from international aid. Many people are dependent on remittances from relatives abroad. Natural resources are not exploited and industry is virtually non-existent but the lack of regulation has led to a thriving entrepreneurial economy in some sectors, especially agriculture, remittance/money transfer services and telecommunications; the three main telecommunications companies are cooperating to fund the internet infrastructure. Businesses have also built small airfields and use natural harbours to trade with overseas countries. The main factor inhibiting trade is the lack of a central bank.

Agriculture, primarily livestock-raising by nomads or semi-nomads, is the most important economic sector. It normally accounts for about 40 per cent of GDP and 65 per cent of export earnings, but has been hit by drought in 2008. The main export markets are the Gulf states, especially the UAE; imports come mainly from Djibouti, Brazil, India and Kenya. Principal exports are livestock, bananas, hides, fish, charcoal and scrap metal. The main imports are manufactures, petroleum products, foodstuffs and construction materials.

Annual average growth of GDP – 2.6 per cent (2007 est)
Total external debt – US$3,000m (2001 est)

Trade with UK	*2006*	*2007*
Imports from UK	£772,000	£872,356
Exports to UK	£71,000	£177,007

COMMUNICATIONS

The main ports are Mogadishu, Kismayu and Merca in the south, and Berber (in Somaliland) in the north, although these have all been damaged by war. The international airports are at Mogadishu and Hargeisa (in Somaliland).

Little of the public telephone system has survived the civil wars, but mobile phone services are available in most major population centres; there were 100,000 main lines in use and 500,000 mobile phone subscribers in 2005, and 94,000 internet users in 2006.

MEDIA

Many new print and broadcast outlets emerged after Siad Barre was ousted in 1991, but most were tied to one of the country's warring factions. Recent years have seen the emergence of stronger regional media, but broadcasters and journalists operate in a dangerous environment, limiting their ability to report freely and objectively. Many Somalis rely on foreign broadcasts for news and information.

SOUTH AFRICA

Republic of South Africa

Area – 1,219,912 sq. km
Capital – The seat of the government is Pretoria (Tshwane): population 1,338,000 (2007 est): the seat of the legislature is Cape Town; population, 3,215,000 (2007 est) and the seat of the judiciary is Bloemfontein (417,000) (2007 est)
Major cities – Durban, Johannesburg, Port Elizabeth, Pietermaritzburg
Currency – Rand (R) of 100 cents
Population – 43,997,828 falling at 0.46 per cent per year (2007 est)
Religion – Christianity (80 per cent) and small numbers of Muslims, Hindus, Jews and adherents of indigenous religions (est). An estimated 15 per cent of the population is atheist or agnostic
Language – Sotho, Northern Sotho, Tswana, Swati, Venda, Tsonga, Afrikaans, English, Ndebele, Xhosa, Zulu (all official)
Population density – 39 per sq. km (2006)
Urban population – 57.9 per cent (2005 est)
Median age (years) – 24.3 (2007 est)
National anthems – 'Nkosi Sikelel' iAfrika' ['God Bless Africa'], incorporating 'Die Stem van Suid Afrika' ['The Call of South Africa']
National day – 27 April (Freedom Day)
Life expectancy (years) – 42.45 (2007 est)
Mortality rate – 22.45 (2007 est)
Birth rate – 17.94 (2007 est)
Infant mortality rate – 59.44 (2007 est)
HIV/AIDS adult prevalence – 16.6 per cent (2005 est)
Death penalty – Abolished for all crimes (since 1997)
CPI score – 5.1 (2007)
Population below poverty line – 50 per cent (2000 est)

CLIMATE AND TERRAIN

South Africa occupies the southernmost part of the African continent from the courses of the Limpopo, Marico, Molopo, Nosop and Orange rivers to the Cape of Good Hope, with the exception of Lesotho, Swaziland and the extreme south of Mozambique. To the west, south and east lie the south Atlantic and southern Indian oceans. Some 1,920km to the south-east of Cape Town lie Prince Edward and Marion Islands, part of South Africa since 1947. The country lies mostly on a high plateau fringed by hills and mountains, including the Drakensberg range, with lower-lying strips along the coast. Elevation extremes range from 3,408m (Njesuthi) at the highest point to 0m (Atlantic Ocean) at the lowest. The climate is temperate and is influenced by the warm Agulhas current from Mozambique. Average temperatures in Pretoria (Tshwane) range from 3°C in June to 29°C in January.

HISTORY AND POLITICS

Hunter-gatherers, the San (Bushmen) and Khoikhoi (Hottentots), inhabited southern Africa from *c.*8000 BC. By the eighth century AD, Bantu-speaking peoples had arrived from the north and settled. The Portuguese navigator Bartolomeu Días charted the coast in 1488 and the Dutch founded the colony of the Cape of Good Hope in 1652. The British occupied the Cape in 1795 after Revolutionary France had conquered the Netherlands, and the colony was ceded to Britain in 1806. From 1836 the Boers (descendants of Dutch settlers) migrated north-east in the Great Trek to escape British rule, and founded the republic of Natal in 1839; the British annexed Natal in 1844, made it a colony in 1856 and added Zululand to it in 1897 after victory in the Zulu wars. The Boer republics of Transvaal (founded 1852) and Orange Free State (founded 1854) were recognised by Britain in 1853–4.

The discovery in the Boer republics of diamonds and gold, and the Boers' need for British assistance in defeating the Zulus in the 1870s, led to disputes and political tension that eventually resulted in the Boer Wars of 1880–1 and 1899–1902. After the British victory in the Second Boer War, Transvaal and the Orange Free State became British colonies. The four self-governing colonies were united in 1910 to form the Union of South Africa, with dominion status. It became a sovereign state within the Commonwealth in 1931. South Africa left the Commonwealth and became a republic on 31 May 1961, largely as a result of international condemnation of the Sharpeville massacre, in which 67 protesters were killed by police.

The Afrikaner National Party came to power in 1948 and adopted a policy of apartheid ('separateness'), which it pursued until 1991. As a result, South Africa's social and political structure came to be based on racial segregation, with separate institutions and facilities for different racial groups. The African National Congress (ANC) and other opposition groups mounted a civil disobedience campaign, following which most opposition groups were banned. Internal opposition continued, with strikes and violence in the 1980s leading to the declaration of a state of emergency in 1985. Internationally, the country became isolated as economic and cultural sanctions were imposed.

In 1984, a new constitution extended the franchise to mixed race and Asian people, but the progressive dismantling of apartheid began with the desegregation of public facilities in 1989. This was followed by the lifting of the bans on the ANC and other anti-apartheid groups, the release from prison of ANC leader Nelson Mandela (1990) and the effective abolition of the laws implementing apartheid in 1991. Negotiations between the government of F. W. de Klerk, the ANC and other political and civic groups reached agreement in 1991 on the establishment of an interracial administration and the formation of a five-year coalition government following multiracial elections. In 1993 the franchise was extended to all adults, and elections took place in April 1994. The ANC won a majority in both legislative chambers, and Nelson Mandela was elected president. South Africa rejoined the Commonwealth and took its UN seat again in 1994.

The legislature passed two significant pieces of legislation to settle the legacy of the apartheid era. The first, in 1994, restored the rights of those dispossessed of their land, and the second, in 1995, established the Truth and Reconciliation Commission to assess confessions, grant amnesties for political crimes and set compensation for victims.

The high levels of HIV/AIDS infection, a very high crime rate, social disruption and lack of education resulting from apartheid and opposition are serious problems. Despite these, South Africa is widely regarded as the dominant political, economic and diplomatic force in the region.

The ANC has won both the legislative elections held since 1994, increasing its majority each time. In the 2004 election, it won 279 seats in the national assembly and majorities in all the provincial assemblies. As a result, the ANC's candidate holds the presidency; Thabo Mbeki was elected to succeed Nelson Mandela in 1999 and was re-elected in 2004.

POLITICAL SYSTEM
Under the 1997 constitution, the executive president is elected by the National Assembly for a five-year term, renewable only once. The president, who is responsible to parliament, appoints the cabinet. The bicameral parliament consists of the National Assembly, the lower house, and the National Council of Provinces. The national assembly has 400 members directly elected by proportional representation for a five-year term. The National Council of Provinces has 90 members, ten for each province, elected by the provincial legislatures for a five-year term.

South Africa is divided into nine provinces (Eastern Cape, Free State, Gauteng, KwaZulu-Natal, Limpopo, Mpumalanga, Northern Cape, North-West, Western Cape). Each province has its own premier, legislature and constitution.

HEAD OF STATE
President, C-in-C of the Armed Forces, Thabo Mbeki, *elected by parliament* 14 June 1999, *sworn in* 16 June 1999, *re-elected* 24 April 2004
Executive Deputy President, Phumzile Mlambo-Ngcuka

SELECTED GOVERNMENT MEMBERS *as at July 2008*
Defence, Mosiuoa Lekota
Finance, Trevor Manuel
Foreign Affairs, Nkosazana Dlamini-Zuma
Home Affairs, Nosiviwe Mapisa-Nqakula

SOUTH AFRICAN HIGH COMMISSION
South Africa House, Trafalgar Square, London WC2N 5DP
T 020-7451 7299 W www.southafricahouse.com
High Commissioner, HE Dr Lindiwe Mabuza, *apptd* 2001

BRITISH HIGH COMMISSION
255 Hill Street, Arcadia 0002, Pretoria (Tshwane)
T (+27) (12) 405 2400 E media.pretoria@fco.gov.uk
W www.britain.org.za
High Commissioner, HE Rt. Hon. Paul Boateng, *apptd* 2005

BRITISH COUNCIL
Ground Floor, Forum 1, Braampark, 33 Hoofd Street, Braamfontein, Johannesburg 2001
T (+27) (11) 718 4300 W www.britishcouncil.org/southafrica
Director, Shoba Ponnappa, OBE

DEFENCE
The South African National Defence Force (SANDF) was created from the merger of the South African Defence Forces (SADF), the Umkhonto we Sizwe (MK) armed wing of the ANC, the Azanian People's Liberation Army (APLA) of the Pan Africanist Congress of Azania, and the defence forces of the four former independent homelands.

The army has 167 main battle tanks, 810 armoured personnel carriers and 1,200 armoured infantry fighting vehicles. The navy has 3 submarines, 4 corvettes and 22 patrol and coastal vessels at 3 bases. The air force has 29 combat aircraft and 11 armed helicopters.
Military expenditure – US$3,520m (2006)
Military personnel – 62,334: army 41,350, navy 5,801, air force 9,183, military health service 6,000

ECONOMY AND TRADE
South Africa is rich in natural resources and has well-developed financial, legal, energy and transport sectors. Its infrastructure is modern, though outdated in some sectors; electricity supply has been increasingly unreliable since 2007, causing power cuts that are affecting production in a number of industries, especially mining. GDP growth is strong and state-owned enterprises are being used to create jobs and raise incomes. However, poverty remains widespread (50 per cent of the population lives below the poverty line) and unemployment is high.

Agriculture, forestry and fishing account for 3.2 per cent of GDP and employ 9 per cent of the workforce. Principal crops are maize, wheat, sugar cane, fruit and vegetables. Livestock farming and cotton and viticulture are also widespread.

The largest industry is mining; South Africa is the world's largest producer of gold, platinum and chromium, as well as producing diamonds, manganese, coal, copper, iron ore, tin, uranium and titanium. Other industries include car assembly, metalworking, food processing, ship repair and production of machinery, textiles, iron and steel, chemicals and fertiliser; manufacturing is concentrated most heavily around Johannesburg, Pretoria (Tshwane) and the major ports. Tourism is a significant industry, attracting nearly six million visitors in 2000. Industry contributes 31.3 per cent of GDP.

Energy production is based upon coal and natural gas and the production of synthetic liquid fuel from coal. One nuclear power station is in operation and others are planned. South Africa exports electricity through its electricity grid connections to all states in southern Africa. Water resources are inadequate to meet demand and so water is imported from the highlands of Lesotho.

The main trading partners are Germany, the USA, Japan, the UK and China. Principal exports are gold, diamonds, platinum, other metals and minerals, and machinery and equipment. Principal imports are machinery and equipment, chemicals, petroleum products, scientific instruments and foodstuffs.
GNI – US$255,400m (2006); US$5,390 per capita (2006)
Annual average growth of GDP – 5 per cent (2007 est)
Inflation rate – 6 per cent (2007 est)
Unemployment – 24.2 per cent (2007 est)
Total external debt – US$66,200m (2007 est)
Imports – US$62,000m (2005)
Exports – US$58,200m (2006)

BALANCE OF PAYMENTS
Trade – US$13,612m deficit (2006)
Current Account – US$16,602m deficit (2006)

Trade with UK	*2006*	*2007*
Imports from UK	£2,187,910,000	£2,159,860,515
Exports to UK	£3,988,533,000	£3,157,840,361

COMMUNICATIONS
The country has 20,872km of railways and 362,099km of roads, of which 73,506km are surfaced. There are over 700 airports and airfields, with international airports at Johannesburg, Durban and Cape Town. South African Airways operates international services worldwide and it is the principal operator of domestic flights. Durban is the largest seaport. Other major ports are Cape Town, Port Elizabeth, East London, Saldanha, Mossel Bay and Richards Bay.

The telephone system is the best developed in Africa, and there is a high level of mobile phone ownership, with 39.6 million subscribers in 2006. In 2005 there were 4.7 million main lines in use and 5.1 million internet users.

EDUCATION AND HEALTH

Education is compulsory between the ages of seven and 15. It is provided by the state and organised into three levels: general education and training, further education and training, and higher education. The nine provincial legislatures manage education facilities, subject to a national policy framework.

Literacy rate – 82.4 per cent (2004 est)
Gross enrolment ratio (percentage of relevant age group) – primary 106 per cent; secondary 95 per cent; tertiary 15 per cent (2006 est)
Health expenditure (per capita) – US$437 (2005)

MEDIA AND CULTURE

South Africa's media industry is the largest and most influential in Africa. The South African Broadcasting Corporation (SABC) is a major state-owned television and radio broadcaster, while Channel Africa (owned by SABC) is an external radio service that reaches the entire continent. Deregulation in 1996 saw a large number of new radio stations. *The Star* is Johannesburg's oldest daily newspaper, while the *Sunday Times* is the longest running weekly title. *Beeld* is a popular Afrikaans daily title. Press freedom is generally respected, with little evidence of repressive measures against journalists.

South Africa is home to a diversity of cultures, and black cultures – such as Zulu, Xhosa and Ndebele – are reviving after suppression during the apartheid years. Celebrated figures include the writers Nadine Gordimer (*b.* 1923), winner of the Nobel prize for literature in 1991 and J. M. Coetzee (*b.* 1940), who won the same award in 2003. The Nobel peace prize was won by Archbishop Desmond Tutu (*b.* 1931) in 1984, and shared by Nelson Mandela (*b.* 1918) and F. W. de Klerk (*b.* 1936) in 1993.

SPAIN

Reino de España – Kingdom of Spain

Area – 504,782 sq. km
Capital – Madrid; population, 5,567,000 (2007 est)
Major cities – Barcelona, Bilbao, Las Palmas (Gran Canaria), Málaga, Murcia, Palma (Majorca), Seville, Valencia, Zaragoza
Currency – Euro (€) of 100 cents
Population – 40,448,191 rising at 0.12 per cent per year (2007 est)
Religion – Roman Catholicism (79 per cent) (est). An estimated 6 per cent of the population is atheist
Language – Spanish (official), Catalan, Galician, Basque (all are official in certain regions)
Population density – 88 per sq. km (2006)
Urban population – 76.7 per cent (2005 est)
Median age (years) – 40.3 (2007 est)
National anthem – 'La Marcha Real' ['The Royal March']
National day – 12 October
Life expectancy (years) – 79.78 (2007 est)
Mortality rate – 9.81 (2007 est)
Birth rate – 9.98 (2007 est)
Infant mortality rate – 4.31 (2007 est)
Death penalty – Abolished for all crimes (since 1995)
CPI score – 6.7 (2007)
Population below the poverty line – 19.8 per cent (2005)

CLIMATE AND TERRAIN

The interior consists of an elevated tableland surrounded and traversed by mountain ranges: the Pyrenees on the border with France, the Cantabrian Mountains (north-west), the Sierra de Guadarrama, Sierra Morena, Montes de Toledo (centre) and the Sierra Nevada (south). The principal rivers are the Duero, the Tajo (Tagus), the Guadiana, the Guadalquivir, the Ebro and the Miño. Elevation extremes range from 3,718m (Pico de Teide, Tenerife, Canary Islands) at the highest point to 0m (Mediterranean Sea) at the lowest. The climate is Mediterranean in the southern and eastern coastal areas, and temperate further inland and at altitude. Average temperatures in Madrid range from 1°C in January to 31°C in July.

HISTORY AND POLITICS

The Romans conquered the Iberian peninsula in the second century BC. It was overrun by Vandals and Visigoths in the fifth century AD, and invaded and occupied by Muslims from Africa in the eighth century. Christians in the north formed small kingdoms which reconquered the peninsula by 1492. Spain's modern form derives from the dynastic union of the kingdoms of Castile and Aragón in 1479. In the 16th century, Spain's exploration and colonisation of the New World made it one of the richest and most powerful nations in Europe, with an empire that covered most of central and southern America. However, a succession of costly wars and revolts in the 17th and 18th centuries saw this empire go into steady decline. Its central and southern American possessions declared independence in the early 19th century and most other overseas possessions had been lost by 1900.

The restoration of the Bourbon monarchy after the Napoleonic occupation of 1808–14 initiated over a century of political instability, with power struggles between conservative and liberal factions in royal, political and military circles. The dictatorship of Gen. Primo de Rivera (1923–30) ended with the exiling of King Alfonso XIII and the declaration of the Second Republic in 1931. The success of moderate and religious candidates in the 1933 elections provoked a socialist and Catalan insurrection in 1934. A narrow victory by the left-wing Popular Front (PF) in fresh elections in 1936 led to an army revolt in military garrisons in Spanish Morocco and this spread throughout Spain, led by Gen. Francisco Franco. Civil war ensued until March 1939, when the PF governments in Madrid and Barcelona surrendered to the Nationalists (as Gen. Franco's followers were then called). Gen. Franco became president and ruled the country until his death in 1975. His death was followed, according to his wishes, by the restoration of the monarchy, and Prince Juan Carlos of Bourbon (grandson of Alfonso XIII) became head of state as King Juan Carlos I. The first free election was held in 1977, and a referendum in 1978 endorsed a democratic constitution.

Spain joined NATO in 1982 and the EEC in 1986, becoming a member of the eurozone in 1999. A referendum in 2005 approved the ratification of the EU constitution.

The Spanish Socialist Workers' Party (PSOE) won an unexpected victory in the 2004 election, held three days after the bombing of commuter trains in Madrid by a group linked to al-Qaida. In the March 2008 legislative elections the PSOE increased its seats, remaining the largest party in the congress of deputies but without a majority; the main opposition party, the Popular Party, won the most seats in the senate. José Luis Rodríguez Zapatero continued as prime minister at the head of a minority PSOE government, which has the support of five small parties.

INSURGENCIES

The Basque separatist organisation ETA (*Euzkadi ta Azkatasuna* – Basque Nation and Liberty), formed in 1959, has carried out a terrorist campaign of bombings, shootings and kidnappings since 1961 in an attempt to gain independence for the Basque country. ETA rejected regional autonomy for the Basque country in 1979 as insufficient and continued its campaign, but has been greatly weakened since the early 1990s by increased cooperation between Spanish security forces and their European counterparts. The Basque political party *Herri Batasuna,* regarded as ETA's political wing, was banned in 2003. ETA has announced a number of ceasefires since 1998, during some of which it has held talks with the government or political parties, but no progress has been made towards a political settlement that it considers acceptable; its latest ceasefire was called off in June 2007.

POLITICAL SYSTEM

The 1978 constitution has been amended at various times to devolve powers to the 19 autonomous regions. The head of state is a hereditary constitutional monarch. There is a bicameral legislature, the *Cortes Generales,* comprising a 350-member Congress of Deputies *(Congreso de los Diputados)* directly elected for a four-year term, and a senate with 264 members, 208 directly elected and 56 appointed by the assemblies of the autonomous regions, for a four-year term.

There are 19 autonomous regions: Andalucía, Aragón, Asturias, Balearic Islands, the Basque Country, Canary Islands, Cantabria, Castilla-La Mancha, Castilla y León, Catalonia, Ceuta, Extremadura, Galicia, Madrid, Melilla, Murcia, Navarra, La Rioja and Valencia. Each has its own elected legislature and government. In 2006 a referendum endorsed the *Cortes'* approval of greater autonomy for Catalonia.

HEAD OF STATE

HM The King of Spain, King Juan Carlos I de Borbón, KG, GCVO, *born* 5 January 1938, *acceded to the throne* 22 November 1975

Heir, HRH The Prince of the Asturias (Prince Felipe Juan Pablo Alfonso y Todos los Santos), *born* 30 January 1968

SELECTED GOVERNMENT MEMBERS *as at July 2008*

Prime Minister, José Luis Rodríguez Zapatero

First Deputy Prime Minister, Maria Teresa Fernandez de la Vega

Second Deputy Prime Minister, Economy, Pedro Solbes

Foreign Affairs, Miguel Ángel Moratinos

Interior, Alfredo Pérez Rubalcaba

Defence, Carmen Chacon Piqueras

EMBASSY OF SPAIN

39 Chesham Place, London SW1X 8SB

T 020-7235 5555 E embespuk@mail.mae.es

W www.mae.es/embajadas/londres/es/home

Ambassador Extraordinary and Plenipotentiary, Count Carlos Miranda, *apptd* 2004

BRITISH EMBASSY

Calle de Fernando el Santo 16, 28010 Madrid

T (+34) (91) 700 8200 E madridconsulate@ukinspain.com

W www.ukinspain.com

Ambassador Extraordinary and Plenipotentiary, HE Denise Holt, CMG, *apptd* 2007

BRITISH COUNCIL

Paseo del General Martínez, Campos 31, E-28010 Madrid

T (+34) (91) 337 3500 W www.britishcouncil.org/spain

Director, Chris Hickey

DEFENCE

The army has 323 main battle tanks, 144 armoured infantry fighting vehicles and 2,022 armoured personnel carriers. The navy has 4 submarines, 1 aircraft carrier, 11 frigates, 31 patrol and coastal vessels, 16 combat aircraft and 24 armed helicopters at 6 bases. The air force has 181 combat aircraft.

Military expenditure – US$14,410m (2006)

Military personnel – 149,150: army 95,600, navy 23,200, air force 20,900, joint staff 9,450; paramilitary 73,360

ECONOMY AND TRADE

The conservatism and isolation of Franco's regime initially held back economic development in the mid-20th century, but the economy improved from the 1950s with industrialisation and the development of tourism. Since the mid-1990s the mixed capitalist economy has shown steady moderate growth, stimulated by liberalisation, privatisation and deregulation, although unemployment remains high.

The generally fertile country produces cereals, vegetables, olives, sugar beets, citrus and other fruits, meat and dairy products. Viticulture is widespread. Spain also has one of Europe's largest fishing industries. The agricultural sector contributes 3.5 per cent of GDP and employs 5.3 per cent of the workforce. Abundant mineral resources include coal, iron ore, copper, zinc, lead, uranium and tungsten. Metal extraction and the manufacture of metal products, including steel, are major industries. A diverse industrial sector includes manufacturing (principally textiles, clothing, footwear, beverages, chemicals, cars, machine tools, clay products, pharmaceuticals and medical equipment), food processing, shipbuilding and tourism; the tourist industry caters for over 52 million visitors a year. Industry accounts for 29.8 per cent of GDP and the service sector for 66.6 per cent.

The main trading partners are other EU countries, especially Germany and France. Principal exports include machinery, vehicles, foodstuffs, pharmaceuticals, medicines and other consumer goods. The main imports are machinery and equipment, fuels, chemicals, semi-finished goods, foodstuffs, consumer goods, and measuring and medical control instruments.

GNI – US$1,206,200m (2006); US$27,340 per capita (2006)

Annual average growth of GDP – 3.8 per cent (2007 est)

Inflation rate – 2.4 per cent (2007 est)

Unemployment – 7.6 per cent (2007 est)

Total external debt – US$2,047,000m (2007 est)

Imports – US$326,000m (2006)
Exports – US$213,300m (2006)

BALANCE OF PAYMENTS
Trade – US$112,692m deficit (2006)
Current Account – US$106,399m deficit (2006)

Trade with UK	*2006*	*2007*
Imports from UK	£12,156,000,000	£9,867,692,941
Exports to UK	£10,194,100,000	£10,106,914,655

COMMUNICATIONS

Spain has a total of 666,292km of roads, nearly all of which are surfaced (including 12,009km of motorways). Railways total 14,873km. The main ports are Algeciras, Alicante, Barcelona, Bilbao, Cádiz, Santander and Valencia, and Las Palmas in the Canary Islands, and there are 1,000km of navigable inland waterways. The principal airports are at Madrid, Barcelona, Alicante, Málaga, Valencia and Bilbao, and there are over 100 other airports and airfields around the country.

The modern telephone system has a density of 45 per cent but mobile phone distribution is very high. There were 18.3 million main telephone lines in use, 46.1 million mobile phone subscribers and 18.5 million internet users in 2006.

EDUCATION AND HEALTH

Education is free from age six to 18, and compulsory to the age of 16. Private schools (30 per cent of primary and 60 per cent of secondary schools) have to fulfil certain criteria to receive government maintenance grants. There are 73 universities, the oldest of which, Salamanca, was founded in 1218. Other historic foundations are Valladolid (1346), Barcelona (1430), Zaragoza (1474), Santiago (1495), Valencia (1500), Seville (1505) and Madrid (1508).

Literacy rate – 97.1 per cent (2004 est)
Gross enrolment ratio (percentage of relevant age group) – primary 105 per cent; secondary 118 per cent; tertiary 66 per cent (2006 est)
Health expenditure (per capita) – US$2,152 (2005)
Hospital beds (per 1,000 people) – 3.5 (2000–6)

MEDIA

Broadcasting has expanded in recent years and digital services are increasingly popular. Public radio and TV services are run by RadioTelevision Espanola (RTVE), which is funded by advertising and state subsidies. Many private radio and TV stations operate alongside, on both a national and regional level. There are plans to switch off the analogue signal in 2010. There are four Madrid-based daily newspapers and another two based in Barcelona. Popular titles include *El Mundo, ABC, La Razon* and *El Periodico de Catalunya.*

CULTURE

Spain's literature is one of the oldest in the world. The *Poem of the Cid,* the earliest of Spain's heroic songs, was written *c.*1140. The outstanding writers of Spain's Golden Age are Miguel de Cervantes (1547–1616), Lope Felix de Vega Carpio (1562–1635) and Pedro Calderón de la Barca (1600–81). The Nobel prize for literature has been awarded to five Spanish authors: J. Echegaray (1832–1916), J. Benavente (1866–1954), Juan Ramón Jiménez (1881–1958), Vicente Aleixandre (1898–1984) and Camilo José Cela (1916–2002). Federico Garciá Lorca (1898–1936) is the most significant modern dramatist.

Spain's long tradition in fine art includes the work of El Greco (1541–1614), Velázquez (1599–1660), Goya (1746–1828), Picasso (1881–1973), Miró (1893–1983) and Dali (1904–89).

ISLANDS AND ENCLAVES

THE BALEARIC ISLES form an archipelago off the east coast of Spain. There are four large islands (Majorca, Minorca, Ibiza and Formentera) and seven smaller ones (Aire, Aucanada, Botafoch, Cabrera, Dragonera, Pinto and El Rey). Area 5,014 sq. km; population 1,001,062. The archipelago forms a province of Spain. The capital is Palma on Majorca.

THE CANARY ISLANDS are an archipelago in the Atlantic off the African coast, consisting of seven islands and six islets. Area 7,270 sq. km; population 1,995,833 (2006 est). The Canary Islands form two provinces of Spain: Las Palmas, comprising Gran Canaria, Lanzarote, Fuerteventura and the islets of Alegranza, Roque del Este, Roque del Oeste, Graciosa, Montaña Clara and Lobos, with the seat of administration at Las Palmas in Gran Canaria; and Santa Cruz de Tenerife, comprising Tenerife, La Palma, Gomera, and Hierro, with the seat of administration at Santa Cruz in Tenerife

ISLA DE FAISANES is an uninhabited Franco-Spanish condominium, at the mouth of the Bidassoa in La Higuera bay

CEUTA is a fortified post on the Moroccan coast, opposite Gibraltar. Area 13 sq. km; population 75,861 (2006 est)

MELILLA is a town on a rocky promontory of the Moroccan coast, connected with the mainland by a narrow isthmus. Population 66,871 (2006 est). Ceuta and Melilla are autonomous regions of Spain

OVERSEAS TERRITORIES

The following territories, which are Spanish settlements on the Moroccan seaboard, come under direct Spanish administration.

PENON DE ALHUCEMAS is a bay including six islands; population 366

PENON DE LA GOMERA (or Peñón de Velez) is a fortified rocky islet; population 450

THE CHAFFARINAS (or Zaffarines) is a group of three islands near the Algerian frontier; population 610

SRI LANKA

Shri Lamka Prajatantrika Samajaya di Janarajaya/Ilankai Jananayaka Choshalichak Kutiyarachu – Democratic Socialist Republic of Sri Lanka

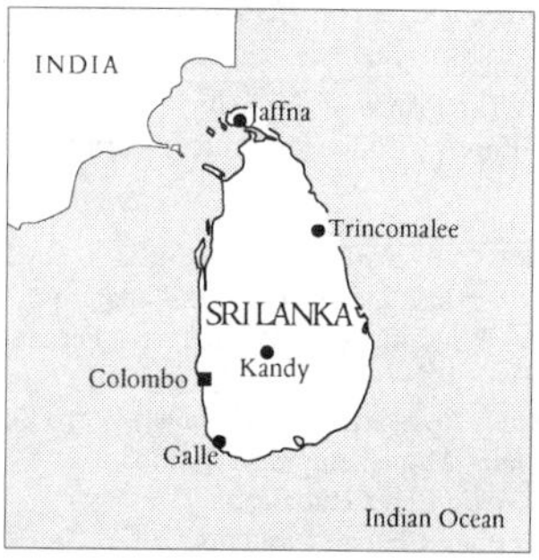

Area – 65,610 sq. km
Capital – Colombo; population, 656,000 (2007 est), Sri Jayewardenepura Kotte is the administrative capital
Major cities – Dehiwala-Mount Lavinia, Jaffna, Kandy, Kotte, Moratuwa, Negombo, Trincomalee
Currency – Sri Lankan rupee of 100 cents
Population – 20,926,315 rising at 0.98 per cent per year (2007 est); Sinhalese (73.8 per cent), Sri Lankan Moor (7.2 per cent), Indian Tamil (4.6 per cent), Sri Lankan Tamil (3.9 per cent)
Religion – Buddhism (70 per cent), Hinduism (15 per cent), Christianity (8 per cent), Islam (7 per cent) (est)
Language – Sinhala (official), Tamil, English
Population density – 308 per sq. km (2006)
Urban population – 21 per cent (2005 est)
Median age (years) – 30 (2007 est)
National anthem – 'Sri Lanka Matha' ['Sri Lanka, Motherland']
National day – 4 February (Independence Day)
Life expectancy (years) – 74.8 (2007 est)
Mortality rate – 6.01 (2007 est)
Birth rate – 17 (2007 est)
Infant mortality rate – 19.45 (2007 est)
Death penalty – Retained, but not used
CPI score – 3.2 (2007)
Population below poverty line – 22 per cent (2002 est)
Literacy rate – 90.4 per cent (2004 est)
Gross enrolment ratio (percentage of relevant age group) – primary 108 per cent; secondary 87 per cent (2006 est)
Health expenditure (per capita) – US$51 (2005)
Hospital beds (per 1,000 people) – 3.1 (2000–6)

CLIMATE AND TERRAIN

Sri Lanka (formerly Ceylon) is an island in the Indian Ocean, off the southern tip of India and separated from it by the narrow Palk Strait. The land is low-lying in the north and along the coasts, with hills and mountains in the south and centre of the interior. Forests, jungle and scrub cover the greater part of the island. In areas over 600m above sea level, grasslands *(patanas* or *talawas)* are found. Elevation extremes range from 2,524m (Pidurutalagala) at the highest point to 0m (Indian Ocean) at the lowest. The climate is tropical with little seasonal variation in conditions and humidity, which often reaches around 90 per cent. The island experiences the south-west monsoon in May and the north-east monsoon in November. Average temperature in Colombo is approximately 29°C all year round.

HISTORY AND POLITICS

Modern Sri Lanka is a product of its long history of occupation, which began with the arrival of the Sinhalese late in the sixth century BC. They settled in the north, but gradually moved southwards under pressure from Tamil invasions from southern India, which began in the third century BC. These Tamils settled in the northern and eastern coastal areas. The Portuguese landed in the early 16th century and established control over most of the island by 1618. These territories were conquered by the Dutch in 1658 and held until 1798, when they were ceded to the British, becoming a British crown colony in 1802. With the annexation of the kingdom of Kandy in 1815, all Ceylon came under British rule, and was subsequently used as a front-line base for British forces fighting the Japanese in the Second World War. Ceylon achieved independence on 4 February 1948. A republican constitution was adopted in 1972 and the country was renamed Sri Lanka (meaning 'Resplendent Island').

Tension between the Buddhist Sinhalese majority and the Hindu Tamil minority dates from the early 20th century, and policies discriminating against Tamils were introduced after independence. Separatist movements developed in the 1970s to campaign for an independent Tamil state in the north and east of the island, and in the early 1980s the Liberation Tigers of Tamil Eelam (LTTE) began a guerrilla war against government forces for control of these areas. Although fighting has tended to be confined to the north, especially the Jaffna peninsula, bombings have occurred throughout the island. The LTTE succeeded in capturing large areas of the north and along the east coast. Various attempts at peace talks in the 1980s and 1990s were unsuccessful. The latest began in May 2002, following the establishment of a ceasefire in January, stalled in 2003 and resumed only briefly in 2006. Although the 2002 ceasefire remained formally in place, conflict between Tamil and government forces has escalated from early 2006, and in 2007 the government regained control of the Eastern province. The government withdrew from the 2002 ceasefire in January 2008 and began an offensive against the LTTE in the north.

After the 2004 legislative election, the United People's Freedom Alliance, dominated by the Sri Lanka Freedom Party (SLFP) and the People's Liberation Front (JVP), controlled 105 seats. The SLFP leader Mahinda Rajapakse became prime minister and formed a coalition government. Two coalition partners withdrew in 2005, and membership of the coalition has fluctuated since, with the government often struggling to achieve a parliamentary majority. The 2005 presidential election was won by Mahinda Rajapakse, who was replaced as prime minister by Ratnasiri Wickremanayake (prime minister 2000–1).

POLITICAL SYSTEM

The 1978 constitution was amended in 1983 to ban parties advocating separatism and in 1987 to create provincial councils. The executive president is directly elected for a six-year term, which may be renewed. The unicameral parliament has 225 members directly elected by proportional representation for a six-year term. The president appoints the cabinet.

Under the Indo-Sri Lankan peace accord in 1987, elected councils were set up in the eight provinces in an attempt to defuse ethnic tensions. Since 1988 all provinces, except for the temporarily merged North-East province, have elected provincial councils.

HEAD OF STATE
President; Defence; Finance, Mahinda Rajapakse, *elected* 17 November 2005 *took office* 19 November 2005

SELECTED GOVERNMENT MEMBERS *as at July 2008*
Prime Minister, Ratnasiri Wickremanayake
Home Affairs, Karu Jayasuriya
Foreign Affairs, Rohitha Bogollagama

HIGH COMMISSION OF THE DEMOCRATIC SOCIALIST REPUBLIC OF SRI LANKA
13 Hyde Park Gardens, London W2 2LU
T 020-7262 1841 E mail@slhc-london.co.uk
W www.slhclondon.org
High Commissioner, HE Kshenuka Senewiratne, *apptd* 2005

BRITISH HIGH COMMISSION
PO Box 1433, 190 Galle Road, Kollupitiya, Colombo 3
T (+94) (11) 243 7336 E bhc@eureka.lk
High Commissioner, HE Peter Hayes, *apptd* 2008

BRITISH COUNCIL
PO Box 753, 49 Alfred House Gardens, Colombo 3
T (+94) (1) 1258 1171 W www.britishcouncil.org/srilanka
Director, Gill Westaway

DEFENCE

The army has 62 main battle tanks, 217 armoured personnel carriers and 62 armoured infantry fighting vehicles. The navy has 131 patrol and coastal vessels at 5 bases. The air force has 22 combat aircraft and 13 armed helicopters.
Military budget – US$1,230m (2007)
Military personnel – 150,900: army 117,900, navy 15,000, air force 18,000; paramilitary 62,200

ECONOMY AND TRADE

The economy, already damaged by decades of violence, was devastated by the Indian Ocean tsunami in December 2004. The central highlands, the centre of most cash crop production, were unscathed but the damage to the coastal areas wiped out cultivation there, destroyed the fishing industry and tourist resorts. Reconstruction boosted the economic growth rate in 2005 and 2006, but renewed conflict between the government and the LTTE since early 2006 has caused a slump in tourism, an important source of revenue which usually attracts over 400,000 visitors a year.

In recent decades the importance of agriculture has declined as manufacturing and service industries have grown, but it still accounts for 16.5 per cent of GDP and about one-third of employment. The main crops are rice, sugar cane, grains, pulses, oilseed, spices, tea, rubber, coconuts, livestock products and fish. Manufacturing is based on processing the main cash crops of rubber, tea, coconuts, tobacco and other commodities, and production of clothing, textiles and cement; other industries include mining and oil refining. Service industries such as telecommunications, banking and insurance and tourism are also important; the sector accounts for 56.5 per cent of GDP and industry for 26.9 per cent. Remittances from expatriate workers are economically significant.

The main trading partners are India, the USA, the UK, China and Singapore. Principal exports are textiles and clothing, tea, spices, diamonds, emeralds, rubies, coconut products, rubber manufactures and fish. The main imports are textile fabrics, mineral products, oil, foodstuffs, machinery and transport equipment.
GNI – US$26,000m (2006); US$1,310 per capita (2006)
Annual average growth of GDP – 6 per cent (2007 est)
Inflation rate – 15.6 per cent (2007 est)
Unemployment – 6.3 per cent (2007 est)
Total external debt – US$13,520m (2007 est)
Imports – US$10,260m (2006)
Exports – US$6,890m (2006)

BALANCE OF PAYMENTS
Trade – US$3,373m deficit (2006)
Current Account – US$1,339m deficit (2006)

Trade with UK	*2006*	*2007*
Imports from UK	£104,675,000	£95,140,501
Exports to UK	£508,230,000	£544,828,169

COMMUNICATIONS

There are 97,287km of roads, of which 78,802km are surfaced. The rail network is government-run and there are 1,449km of railway. Colombo is the main port, and the principal airport is Bandaranaike International, to the north of the capital.

Fixed-line telephone services now extend to most of the country, and mobile phone distribution is expanding rapidly. There were 2.7 million main lines in use and 7.9 million mobile phone users in 2007, and 428,000 internet users in 2006.

MEDIA

Many of the main media outlets are government-controlled, including two major TV stations and radio networks operated by the Sri Lanka Broadcasting Corporation (SLBC). There are also privately owned broadcast media and newspapers. As part of the peace process, in 2002 the government permitted the Tamil Tigers to broadcast their Voice of Tigers radio station in the north of the island. The escalation in violence during 2006–7 increased the dangers faced by journalists, with threats and arrests occurring frequently.

SUDAN

Jumhuriyat as-Sudan – Republic of the Sudan

Area – 2,505,810 sq. km
Capital – Khartoum; population, 4,754,000 (2007 est)
Major cities – Khartoum Bahri, Kassala, Kusti, Omdurman, Nyala, Port Sudan, Al Ubayyid
Currency – Sudanese pound (SDP) of 100 piastres
Population – 39,379,358 rising at 2.08 per cent per year (2007 est); Arab and Nubian peoples populate the north and centre with Nilotic and black African peoples in the south
Religion – Precise figures showing the proportion of religious adherents are unavailable, but the population is predominantly Islamic in the north and Christian in the south, although Christianity is often combined with syncretic indigenous beliefs
Language – Arabic (official), Nubian, Ta Bedawie, English
Population density – 16 per sq. km (2006)
Urban population – 40.8 per cent (2005 est)
Median age (years) – 18.7 (2007 est)
National anthem – 'Nahnu Djundulla Djundulwatan' ['We Are the Army of God and of Our Land']
National day – 1 January (Independence Day)
Life expectancy (years) – 49.11 (2007 est)
Mortality rate – 14.39 (2007 est)
Birth rate – 34.86 (2007 est)
Infant mortality rate – 91.78 (2007 est)

HIV/AIDS adult prevalence – 1.5 per cent (2005 est)
Death penalty – Retained
CPI score – 1.8 (2007)
Population below poverty line – 40 per cent (2004 est)

CLIMATE AND TERRAIN

Sudan is the largest country in Africa and is predominately desert. The Libyan Desert in the west is separated from the high rocky Nubian Desert in the east by the fertile valley of the Nile and its tributaries. There are mountains in the west and along the Red Sea coast in the east. Elevation extremes range from 3,187m (Kinyeti) at the highest point to 0m (Red Sea) at the lowest. The climate is as varied as the terrain, with arid conditions in the desert, tropical conditions on the plains and cooler conditions in the highlands. There is a wet season from April to October. Average temperatures in Khartoum, in the north of the country, range from 15°C in January to 38°C in July.

HISTORY AND POLITICS

Parts of northern Sudan formed part of the Egyptian Empire from 1900 BC and of the Nubian Empire from the sixth century BC. The country was converted to Coptic Christianity in the sixth century AD, and Islam was introduced in the seventh century by Arab invaders, but did not become widespread until the 15th century. From the eighth century onwards, northern Sudan was conquered and occupied by several Arab and Arab-African powers. The south remained independent. Egypt established its control over the north in the early 19th century. The Mahdi revolt in the 1880s led to a joint Anglo-Egyptian campaign to subdue the country, and it was administered as an Anglo-Egyptian condominium from 1899. On 19 December 1955 the Sudanese legislature declared Sudan an independent sovereign state, and on 1 January 1956 a republic was proclaimed and was recognised by Britain and Egypt.

Tensions between the dominant Arab Muslim north and the black African Christian and animist south have dominated the entire post-independence period. The first civil war in the south began in 1955 and lasted until 1972, when the south was given greater autonomy. A second civil war broke out in 1983, largely because of attempts to impose Shari'ah law on the whole country. A peace process began in 2000 and the parties to it – Omar al-Bashir's government, the Sudan People's Liberation Army (SPLA) and the southern National Democratic Alliance – finalised a peace agreement in 2004. Under this, a largely autonomous administration (installed in October 2005) governs in the south, and a referendum on independence for the south will be held after six years. The war caused an estimated 1.5 million deaths, including over 300,000 in the 1988 and 1994 war-induced famines. Some three million people were displaced or became refugees. Large areas of the south are now desolate and uninhabitable.

The civil wars caused years of political instability in the country as a whole, resulting in several coups, and Sudan spent much of the period between 1958 and 1996 under military or one-party rule. Elections were held in 1996 and 2000 but the 2004 legislative election was postponed owing to the peace process.

Following the conclusion of the 2004 peace agreement, a new constitution was approved in July 2005. The president was sworn into office under this constitution and John Garang, the leader of the SPLM (the renamed SPLA), was sworn in as vice-president; Garang died a few weeks later and was succeeded as SPLM leader, president of the government of southern Sudan and national vice-president by Salva Kiir Mayardit. A power-sharing government took office in September 2005. A census was held in 2008 as part of the preparations for the next elections, which under the 2005 peace agreement must be held by July 2009.

INSURGENCIES

The western region of Darfur has two main ethnic groupings, both predominantly Muslim: Arabs, who tend to be nomadic livestock herders, and black African peoples, who tend to be farmers. There has long been competition over resources, but prolonged drought and increasing desertification exacerbated tensions from the late 1990s, leading to increased intercommunal violence.

In 2003, black African rebels began to attack government targets, demanding more state resources for the region and an end to discrimination. The government responded with severe reprisals, operating through Arab militia *(Janjaweed)* which carried out mass executions and forcible depopulation, leading to accusations of ethnic cleansing. Since 2003 an estimated 300,000 have died, and over two million people have been displaced or become refugees in Chad and the Central African Republic. Aid agencies have struggled to prevent starvation in the refugee camps inside Darfur, and in some cases even to gain access to certain areas, because of continuing violence and government obstructiveness.

Although the government acceded to settlements brokered by the African Union (AU) and the UN in 2004, it has not acted upon them and continues to resist international pressure to disarm the militias. It opposed and then obstructed the deployment of AU peacekeeping troops, and resisted their replacement by UN peacekeepers until 2007. In 2006 the government and the largest of the three main rebel groups signed a peace agreement, but the government has not met the implementation deadlines and fighting between rebel forces supporting the agreement and those opposing it has increased the levels of violence and displacement in the region.

POLITICAL SYSTEM

Under the 2005 constitution, the executive president will be directly elected for a five-year term. The unicameral legislature was replaced in August 2005 by a bicameral Transitional National Legislature that comprises a 450-member Transitional National Assembly and a Transitional Council of States with two members from each of the 26 states. The president appoints the cabinet.

The south has a largely autonomous government. The president of the south is also the national vice-president.

HEAD OF STATE

President, Prime Minister, Field Marshal Omar Hassan Ahmad al-Bashir, *seized power* 1989, *elected* 1996, *re-elected* 2000, *sworn in under new constitution* 9 July 2005
First Vice-President, Salva Kiir Mayardit
Second Vice-President, Ali Osman Mohammed Taha

SELECTED GOVERNMENT MEMBERS *as at July 2008*

Defence, Lt.-Gen. Abdel-Rahim Hussein
Finance, Awad Ahmad al-Jaz
Foreign Affairs, Deng Alor Kol
Interior, Ibrahim Mahmud Hama

EMBASSY OF THE REPUBLIC OF THE SUDAN
3 Cleveland Row, London SW1A 1DD
T 020-7839 8080 E admin@sudanembassy.co.uk
W www.sudanembassy.co.uk
Ambassador Extraordinary and Plenipotentiary, Omer Mohammed Ahmed Siddig, *apptd* 2006

BRITISH EMBASSY
PO Box 801, Off Sharia Al Baladiya, Khartoum East
T (+249) (1) 8377 7105 E british@sudanmail.net
W www.britishembassy.gov.uk/sudan
Ambassador Extraordinary and Plenipotentiary, HE Rosalind Marsden, CMG, *apptd* 2007

BRITISH COUNCIL
PO Box 1253, 14 Abu Sinn Street, Khartoum Central
T (+249) 183 780817 W www.britishcouncil.org/sudan
Director, David Codling

DEFENCE

The army has 350 tanks, 409 armoured personnel carriers and 75 armoured infantry fighting vehicles. The navy has 16 patrol and coastal combatant vessels at 3 bases. The air force has 51 combat aircraft and 23 armed helicopters.
Military budget – US$579m (2007)
Military personnel – 109,300: army 105,000, navy 1,300, air force 3,000; paramilitary 17,500
Conscription duration – 24 months

ECONOMY AND TRADE

Since 1997 Sudan has been implementing IMF economic reforms which, despite the country's political instability and vulnerability to drought, have stabilised the economy and enabled infrastructure improvements. In 1999 Sudan began exporting crude oil, and increases in oil production, light industry and exports have resulted in growth in GDP in recent years. However, development started from a low base and about 40 per cent of the population lives below the poverty line.

Agriculture, much as subsistence level, provides employment for around 80 per cent of the workforce and contributes 31.8 per cent of GDP. The industry is based on large and medium-sized public sector irrigation projects; mechanised and traditional agriculture is practised in areas with sufficient rainfall. The principal crops include cotton, groundnuts, sorghum, millet, wheat, gum arabic and sugar cane. Industry consists of oil extraction and refining, cotton ginning, manufacture of textiles, cement, edible oils, sugar, soap, shoes, pharmaceuticals and armaments, and vehicle assembly. Industry contributes 34.2 per cent of GDP and services 33.9 per cent.

The main trading partners are Japan and China. Principal exports are oil and petroleum products, cotton, sesame, livestock, groundnuts, gum arabic and sugar. The main imports are foodstuffs, manufactured goods, refinery and transport equipment, medicines, chemicals, textiles and wheat.
GNI – US$30,100m (2006); US$800 per capita (2006)
Annual average growth of GDP – 12.8 per cent (2007 est)
Inflation rate – 5.3 per cent (2007 est)
Unemployment – 18.7 per cent (2002 est)
Total external debt – US$29,600m (2007 est)
Imports – US$8,100m (2006)
Exports – US$5,700m (2006)

BALANCE OF PAYMENTS
Trade – US$2,417m deficit (2006)
Current Account – US$5,489m deficit (2006)

Trade with UK	*2006*	*2007*
Imports from UK	£155,148,000	£114,990,429
Exports to UK	£10,021,000	£20,512,462

COMMUNICATIONS

Large areas of the country lack basic infrastructure, which has been a focus of development since the late 1990s. The railway network is about 5,970km in length. There are 11,900km of roads, of which 4,320km are surfaced, and there are over 4,000km of navigable waterways, including 1,700km on the White and Blue Nile rivers. Port Sudan, on the Red Sea, is the main seaport. The principal airports are at Khartoum and Juba, and there are over 90 other airports and airfields. Sudan Airways provides domestic and international flights.

The fixed-line telephone system is being upgraded; mobile phone services are growing rapidly. In 2006 there were 637,000 main lines in use, 4.6 million mobile phone subscribers and 3.5 million internet users.

EDUCATION AND HEALTH

Education is free of charge for most children but not compulsory. Six years of primary education is followed by three years of secondary education; there are three types of secondary school: general, academic and vocational. The language of instruction is Arabic.
Literacy rate – 59 per cent (2004)
Gross enrolment ratio (percentage of relevant age group) – primary 66 per cent; secondary 34 per cent (2006 est)
Health expenditure (per capita) – US$29 (2005)
Hospital beds (per 1,000 people) – 0.7 (2000–6)

MEDIA

Radio and television are controlled by the government, and a permanent military censor ensures that the news reflects official views. There are no wholly privately owned television or radio stations. Satellite dishes are becoming common in affluent areas and pan-Arab TV stations are popular, as are foreign radio stations such as the BBC World Service and Paris-based Radio Monte Carlo, which broadcast in Khartoum. There are several privately owned newspapers.

SURINAME

Republiek Suriname – Republic of Suriname

Area – 163,270 sq. km
Capital – Paramaribo; population, 252,000 (2007 est)
Currency – Suriname dollar of 100 cents
Population – 470,784 rising at 1.1 per cent per year (2007 est); Hindustani (37 per cent), Creole (31 per cent), Javanese (15 per cent) (est)

Religion – Christianity (40 per cent), Hinduism (20 per cent), Islam (13 per cent), indigenous religions (3 per cent) (est). Around 4 per cent of the population is atheist
Language – Dutch (official), English, Surinamese, Hindustani, Javanese
Population density – 3 per sq. km (2006)
Urban population – 77.2 per cent (2005 est)
Median age (years) – 27.1 (2007 est)
National anthem – 'God zij met ons Suriname' ['God Be With Our Suriname']
National day – 25 November (Independence Day)
Life expectancy (years) – 73.23 (2007 est)
Mortality rate – 5.5 (2007 est)
Birth rate – 17.31 (2007 est)
Infant mortality rate – 20.11 (2007 est)
HIV/AIDS adult prevalence – 1.6 per cent (2005 est)
Death penalty – Retained, but not used
CPI score – 3.5 (2007)
Population below poverty line – 70 per cent (2002 est)
Literacy rate – 88 per cent (2004 est)

CLIMATE AND TERRAIN

Suriname is situated in the north-east of South America, with a coastline on the Atlantic Ocean. A narrow coastal plain rises to a hilly, forested interior. Elevation extremes range from 1,230m (Juliana Top) at the highest point to −2m (coastal plain) at the lowest. The climate is tropical, with high rainfall, high humidity and high temperatures which are tempered by the north-east trade winds. There are two wet seasons, from April to August and November to February. Average annual precipitation in Paramaribo is 2,200mm and average temperatures are an almost constant 27°C.

HISTORY AND POLITICS

Although visited and claimed by Spanish explorers in 1593, the first European settlement was by the Dutch in 1602. A British colony was founded in 1651 but this was ceded to the Dutch in 1667. Dutch rule was interrupted by British occupation during the French Revolutionary and Napoleonic wars, but was restored in 1816. The colony, known as Dutch Guiana, remained part of the Netherlands West Indies until 25 November 1975, when it achieved independence as Suriname. At independence, about 40 per cent of the population emigrated to the Netherlands.

The early years of independence were politically unstable, with coups in 1980, 1982 and 1990. A guerrilla campaign for the restoration of democracy began in 1986. A peace accord with the guerrillas in 1989, following the return to civilian rule in 1988, was opposed by the military leader and former dictator Desi Bouterse, who engineered a coup in 1990 that deposed the president. Elections in 1991 were won by the New Front for Democracy and Development alliance, led by Ronald Venetiaan, who became president. President Venetiaan introduced an unpopular austerity programme, which improved the economy but lost him the 1996 election.

Suriname has a long-running dispute with its neighbour, Guyana, over the ownership of a potentially oil-rich offshore area. In 2007, a UN tribunal ruled that the two countries should both have a share in the area.

After the 2005 legislative election the New Front for Democracy, a four-party alliance, remained the largest bloc in the legislature, but lost its overall majority. Two rounds of voting in the July 2005 presidential election failed to produce the necessary majority, requiring a third round of voting by a United People's Conference (UPC); this re-elected President Venetiaan to another term in office.

POLITICAL SYSTEM

Under the 1987 constitution, the executive president is elected for a five-year term by a two-thirds majority in the legislature or, if the required majority cannot be achieved, by a specially convened United Peoples' Assembly including district and local council representatives. The vice-president is elected in the same way. The unicameral National Assembly has 51 members directly elected for a five-year term.

HEAD OF STATE

President, Ronald Venetiaan, *sworn in* 12 August 2000, *re-elected* 2005
Vice-President, Ram Sardjoe

SELECTED GOVERNMENT MEMBERS *as at July 2008*

Defence, Ivan Fernald
Finance, Humphrey Hildenberg
Foreign Affairs, Lygia Kraag-Keteldijk
Internal Affairs, Maurits Hassankhan

EMBASSY OF THE REPUBLIC OF SURINAME

Alexander Gogelweg 2, 2517 JH The Hague, The Netherlands
T (+31) (70) 365 0844 E ambassade.suriname@wxs.nl
Ambassador Extraordinary and Plenipotentiary, HE Urmila Joella-Sewnundun

BRITISH AMBASSADOR

HE Fraser Wheeler, *apptd* 2006, resident at Georgetown, Guyana

DEFENCE

The army has 15 armoured personnel carriers. The navy has 8 patrol and coastal combatant vessels at a base in Paramaribo. The air force has 4 combat capable aircraft.
Military budget – US$22m (2007)
Military personnel – 1,840: army 1,400, navy 240; air force 200

ECONOMY AND TRADE

The mainstays of the economy are mining, especially of bauxite and gold, and oil and alumina production, although these make the economy vulnerable to global price fluctuations. Bauxite reserves are declining, but oil production is increasing from existing offshore fields and onshore exploration has begun. Agriculture employs only 8 per cent of the population but produces 10.8 per cent of GDP. Industries other than mining and oil production are forestry, food processing and fishing. Industry accounts for 24.4 per cent of GDP and services for 64.8 per cent.

The main trading partners are the the USA, Norway, the Netherlands, Canada and Trinidad and Tobago. Principal exports are alumina, gold, crude oil, timber, fish and prawns, rice and bananas. The main imports are capital equipment, oil, foodstuffs, cotton and consumer goods.
GNI – US$1,918m; US$4,210 per capita (2006)
Annual average growth of GDP – 5.1 per cent (2007 est)
Inflation rate – 9.5 per cent (2005 est)
Unemployment – 9.5 per cent (2004)
Total external debt – US$504.3m (2005 est)
Imports – US$280m (2005)
Exports – US$270m (2005)

BALANCE OF PAYMENTS
Trade – US$37m deficit (2006)
Current Account – US$3m surplus (2006)

Trade with UK	*2006*	*2007*
Imports from UK	£9,666,000	£7,996,432
Exports to UK	£540,000	£314,657

COMMUNICATIONS

There are 4,300km of roads in total, of which approximately one-quarter is surfaced. There are no railways. The 1,200km of inland waterways provide the most effective means of transport. The main seaport is Paramaribo. There are over 40 airports and airfields, the principal airport being at Paramaribo.

The telephone system is good and mobile phone services have expanded rapidly. There were 81,500 main lines and 320,000 mobile phone subscribers in 2006, and 32,000 internet users in 2005.

MEDIA

State-owned broadcast media offer a range of views, and operate alongside commercial radio and TV stations. The two daily newspapers, *De West* and *De Ware Tijd,* are privately owned. The government is tolerant of freedom of expression.

SWAZILAND

Umbuso we Swatini – Kingdom of Swaziland

Area – 17,363 sq. km
Capital – Mbabane; population, 78,000 (2007 est)
Major town – Manzini
Currency – Lilangeni (E; plural *Emalangeni*) of 100 cents; South African currency is also in circulation. Swaziland is a member of the Common Monetary Area and the Lilangeni has a par value with the South African rand
Population – 1,133,066 falling at 0.34 per cent per year (2007 est)
Religion – Protestantism (35 per cent), Zionism (30 per cent), Roman Catholicism (25 per cent), Islam (1 per cent) (est).
Language – English, siSwati (both official)
Population density – 66 per sq. km (2006)
Urban population – 23.9 per cent (2005 est)
Median age (years) – 18.6 (2007 est)
National anthem – 'Nkulunkulu Mnikati wetibuiso temaSwati' ['Oh God, Bestower of Blessings on the Swazi']
National day – 6 September (Independence Day)
Life expectancy (years) – 32.23 (2007 est)
Mortality rate – 30.35 (2007 est)
Birth rate – 26.98 (2007 est)
Infant mortality rate – 70.66 (2007 est)
HIV/AIDS adult prevalence – 34.5 per cent (2005 est)
Death penalty – Retained, but not used
CPI score – 3.3 (2007)
Population below poverty line – 69 per cent (2006)
Literacy rate – 79.2 per cent (2004 est)
Gross enrolment ratio (percentage of relevant age group) – primary 106 per cent; secondary 47 per cent; tertiary 4 per cent (2006 est)
Health expenditure (per capita) – US$146 (2005)

CLIMATE AND TERRAIN

The three regions of the landlocked country are the densely forested and mountainous Highveld along the western border, with an average altitude of 1,219m; the Middleveld, averaging about 609m, which is a mixed farming area; and the Lowveld in the east, which was mainly scrubland until the introduction of sugar cane plantations. Four rivers, the Komati, Usutu, Mbuluzi and Ngwavuma, flow from west to east. Elevation extremes range from 1,862m (Emlembe) at the highest point to 21m (Great Usutu river) at the lowest.

The climate varies from region to region. The Highveld is humid and temperate, the Middleveld and Lebombo range are subtropical and the Lowveld is tropical and semi-arid. Average temperatures in Mbabane, in the Highveld, range from 6°C in June to 25°C in January.

HISTORY AND POLITICS

The Swazi people are believed to have arrived in the area in the 16th century. They developed a strong kingdom which by the mid-19th century was three times the size of the present country. It became a protectorate of the Transvaal in 1884, of the Transvaal and Britain jointly in 1894 and of Britain solely in 1903. The Kingdom of Swaziland became independent on 6 September 1968. In 1973 King Sobhuza II suspended the constitution, banned political parties and assumed absolute power. The parliamentary system was replaced by traditional tribal communities *(tinkhundla)*. Sobhuza II died in 1982, but as his son was a minor he did not succeed until 1986 as King Mswati III. The regency between 1982 and 1986 led to power struggles within the royal family, but the real power passed to the Dlamini family, which dominates the government.

Demands for democratisation of the constitution have grown over the past 20 years, with the campaigning of trade unions and political movements supported by popular demonstrations, general strikes and blockades of the border with South Africa.

Swaziland has one of the highest levels of HIV/AIDS infection in the world and faces severe demographic, economic and social problems as a consequence. Erratic rainfall, droughts and food shortages have left over a quarter of the population in need of food aid in recent years.

POLITICAL SYSTEM

The 2005 constitution retains the wide extent of the king's powers and the ban on political parties. The head of state is a hereditary king who is effectively an absolute monarch. There is a bicameral parliament comprising a 30-member senate and a 65-member House of Assembly; members of both serve a five-year term. Each of the country's 55 administrative districts *(tinkhundla)* directly elects one member to the house of assembly and the king appoints ten members. The members of the House of Assembly elect ten of their own number to the senate and a further 20 senators are appointed by the king.

HEAD OF STATE
King of Swaziland, HM King Mswati III, *inaugurated* 25 April 1986

SELECTED GOVERNMENT MEMBERS *as at July 2008*
Prime Minister, Absalom Themba Dlamini
Deputy Prime Minister, Constance Simelane
Finance, Majozi Sithole
Foreign Affairs, Mathendele Moses Dlamini
Home Affairs, Prince Gabheni Dlamini

KINGDOM OF SWAZILAND HIGH COMMISSION
20 Buckingham Gate, London SW1E 6LB
T 020-7630 6611 E swaziland@swaziland.btinternet.com
High Commissioner, Mary M. Kanya, *apptd* 2005

BRITISH HIGH COMMISSIONER
HE Paul Boateng, *apptd 2005,* resident at Pretoria (Tshwane), South Africa

ECONOMY AND TRADE

The country is very poor, with 69 per cent of the population living below the poverty line. Customs dues from the South African Customs Union and remittances from expatriates working in South Africa are a vital supplement to the domestic economy. Subsistence agriculture occupies about 70 per cent of the population and contributes 11.8 per cent of GDP. Sugar cane, cotton, citrus fruits and pineapples are the main cash crops and the basis of industries producing sugar, canned fruit and soft drink concentrates. The mining industry has scaled back in recent years but still produces some coal and asbestos. Other industries produce wood pulp, textiles, clothing and refrigerators, although a shift in global trading concessions has devastated sugar and clothing exports, making thousands unemployed. Industry contributes 45.7 per cent of GDP and services 42.5 per cent.

South Africa accounts for about 60 per cent of exports and provides about 95 per cent of imports. Principal exports are the products of agriculture and manufacturing. The main imports are vehicles, machinery, transport equipment, foodstuffs, petroleum products and chemicals.
GNI – US$2,700m; US$2,400 per capita (2006)
Annual average growth of GDP – 1.6 per cent (2007 est)
Inflation rate – 6 per cent (2007 est)
Unemployment – 40 per cent (2006 est)
Total external debt – US$538.6m (2007 est)
Imports – US$2,200m (2006)
Exports – US$2,100m (2006)

BALANCE OF PAYMENTS
Trade – US$101m deficit (2006)
Current Account – US$103m deficit (2006)

Trade with UK	*2006*	*2007*
Imports from UK	£5,925,000	£5,005,789
Exports to UK	£35,113,000	£28,798,384

COMMUNICATIONS

The railway network is 301km long and connects with the Mozambique port of Maputo and the South African railway to Richards Bay and Durban. There are 3,600km of roads, of which 1,078km are surfaced. There is an international airport at Manzini. Royal Swazi National Airways provides scheduled air services to southern and eastern Africa.

Although modern, the fixed-line telephone system is not extensive and mobile phone services have grown rapidly. There were 44,000 main lines in use and 250,000 mobile phone subscribers in 2006, and 41,600 internet users in 2005.

MEDIA

The state controls the media; all radio and TV stations, with the exception of a Christian radio station, are under government control, and the country's only private daily newspaper, *The Times of Swaziland,* is strictly monitored. Criticism of the monarchy is banned.

SWEDEN

Konungariket Sverige – Kingdom of Sweden

Area – 449,964 sq. km
Capital – Stockholm; population, 1,264,000 (2007 est)
Major cities – Gothenburg, Malmo, Uppsala
Currency – Swedish krona of 100 ore
Population – 9,031,088 rising at 0.16 per cent per year (2007 est)
Religion – Protestantism (77 per cent), Roman Catholicism (2 per cent), Orthodox Christianity (1 per cent), Islam (1 per cent) (est). An estimated 10 per cent of the population is atheist
Language – Swedish (official)
Population density – 22 per sq. km (2006)
Urban population – 83.4 per cent (2005 est)
Median age (years) – 41.1 (2007 est)
National anthem – 'Du Gamla, Du Fria' ['Thou Ancient, Thou Freeborn']
National day – 6 June (Flag Day)
Life expectancy (years) – 80.63 (2007 est)
Mortality rate – 10.27 (2007 est)
Birth rate – 10.2 (2007 est)
Infant mortality rate – 2.76 (2007 est)
Death penalty – Abolished for all crimes (since 1972)
CPI score – 9.3 (2007)

CLIMATE AND TERRAIN

The terrain is mostly flat or rolling lowlands in the south and along the east coast, with mountains in the west. Elevation extremes range from 2,111m (Kebnekaise) at the highest point to –2.4m (reclaimed bay of Lake Hammarsjon) at the lowest. There are many lakes, including Vanern, Vattern, Malaren and Hjalmaren in the south, and over 20,000 islands off the coast near Stockholm. The climate is continental, with average temperatures in Stockholm ranging from –5°C in January to 22°C in July.

HISTORY AND POLITICS

Sweden takes its name from the Svear people who inhabited the region during the seventh century AD. The country was united *c.*1000, apart from the south and west, which remained under Danish rule until conquered in the 17th century. The Swedes participated in the Viking expansion from the ninth to 11th centuries and established sovereignty over Finland in the 13th century. The Union of Kalmar (1397) brought Sweden and Norway under Danish rule. Sweden regained its independence following a rebellion by noblemen in 1521 which resulted in the election of Gustav I to the Swedish throne.

Sweden's power reached its zenith in the 17th century under Gustavus II. The Danes were driven out of southern Sweden, the Baltic coast of Russia was seized and the Swedish army pushed into Germany after vanquishing the Catholic League. Swedish power waned in the late 17th and 18th centuries. Finland was lost to Russia in 1809; Norway was ceded to Sweden by the congress of Vienna (1814–15) but gained independence in 1905.

Sweden remained neutral during both world wars. Post-war governments have been dominated by Social Democrat-led coalitions which established a mixed economy and a generous welfare state between 1946 and 1969. Right-wing and centrist parties held power in 1976–82 and 1991–4. Sweden joined the EU in 1995, but decided against membership of the eurozone in 1997, a decision confirmed in a 2003 national referendum.

After the 2006 general election, the Swedish Social Democratic Labour Party (SAP) remained the largest party in the legislature but a larger number of seats were won by a coalition led by the Moderate Party. A four-party Alliance for Sweden coalition government comprising the Moderate Party, Centre Party, Liberal Party and Christian Democrat Party took office in October 2006.

POLITICAL SYSTEM

Sweden is a constitutional hereditary monarchy. The 1975 constitution was amended in 1979 to vest the succession in the monarch's eldest child irrespective of sex.

The *Riksdag* is the unicameral legislature of 349 members directly elected by proportional representation for a four-year term. The prime minister appoints the council of ministers; the cabinet is responsible to the *Riksdag*. Sweden is divided into 21 counties *(lan)* and 290 municipalities *(kommun)*.

HEAD OF STATE

HM The King of Sweden, Carl XVI Gustaf, KG, *born* 30 April 1946, *succeeded* 15 September 1973
Heir, HRH Crown Princess Victoria Ingrid Alice Desiree, Duchess of Vastergotland, *born* 14 July 1977

SELECTED GOVERNMENT MEMBERS *as at July 2008*

Prime Minister, Fredrik Reinfeldt
Deputy Prime Minister, Maud Olofsson
Defence, Sten Tolgfors
Finance, Anders Borg
Foreign Affairs, Carl Bildt

EMBASSY OF SWEDEN

11 Montagu Place, London W1H 2AL
T 020-7917 6400 W www.swedenabroad.com/london
Ambassador Extraordinary and Plenipotentiary, HE Staffan Carlsson, *apptd* 2004

BRITISH EMBASSY

PO Box 27819, Skarpogatan 6–8, 115 93 Stockholm
T (+46) (8) 671 3000 E info@britishembassy.se
W www.britishembassy.se
Ambassador Extraordinary and Plenipotentiary, HE Andrew Mitchell, *apptd* 2006

BRITISH COUNCIL

c/o British Embassy
T (+46) (8) 671 3110 W www.britishcouncil.org/sweden
Country Manager, Roger Budd

DEFENCE

The army has 280 main battle tanks, 799 armoured personnel carriers and 485 armoured infantry fighting vehicles. The navy has 5 submarines, 5 corvettes and 18 patrol and coastal vessels at 3 bases. The air force has 130 combat aircraft.

Sweden has a policy of non-alignment in peace and neutrality in war and has declined to become a member of NATO.

Military budget – US$7,300m (2007)
Military personnel – 24,000: army 10,200, navy 7,900, air force 5,900; paramilitary 600; voluntary auxiliary organisations 42,000
Conscription duration – 7–15 months

ECONOMY AND TRADE

Sweden developed from an agricultural to an industrial economy in the early 20th century. The prosperity that had funded the generous welfare state after 1946 ended in the early 1990s, when Sweden experienced a deep recession. Austerity measures and free-market reforms enabled an economic recovery. The government plans to privatise more state assets in coming years to stimulate economic growth further.

Industrial prosperity is based on natural resources including forests, mineral deposits and water power. The forests cover about half the total land surface and sustain the timber, finished wood products, pulp and paper milling industries. Mineral resources include iron ore, lead, zinc, sulphur, granite, marble, precious and heavy metals (the latter not exploited) and extensive deposits of low-grade uranium ore. Industries based on mining are important but it is the general engineering industry that provides 50 per cent of output and exports, particularly specialised machinery and systems, motor vehicles, aircraft, electrical and electronic equipment, armaments, pharmaceuticals, plastics and chemical industries.

Hydroelectricity supplies about 15 per cent of energy needs. Sweden has no significant indigenous resources of conventional hydrocarbon fuels and relies upon imported gas and coal for 50 per cent of its energy needs. Less than 10 per cent of the land area is farmland and only 2 per cent of the labour force is employed in farming. Agriculture contributes 1.4 per cent of GDP, industry 28.9 per cent and services 69.8 per cent.

The main trading partners are other EU states, Norway and the USA. Principal exports include machinery, cars, trucks, paper products, pulp and wood, iron and steel products, and chemicals. The main imports are machinery, oil and petroleum products, chemicals, vehicles, iron and steel, foodstuffs and clothing.

GNI – US$395,400m (2006); US$43,530 per capita (2006)
Annual average growth of GDP – 3.4 per cent (2007 est)
Inflation rate – 2 per cent (2007 est)
Unemployment – 4.5 per cent (2007 est)
Total external debt – US$598,200m (2006)
Imports – US$126,600m (2006)
Exports – US$147,200m (2006)

BALANCE OF PAYMENTS
Trade – US$20,601m surplus (2006)
Current Account – US$33,303m surplus (2006)

Trade with UK	*2006*	*2007*
Imports from UK	£4,972,300,000	£4,851,216,782
Exports to UK	£5,547,500,000	£5,210,005,189

COMMUNICATIONS

The railway network is 11,528km in length. There are 424,900km of roads, of which 130,000km are surfaced (including 1,600km of motorways). There are also 2,052km of waterways, navigable for small steamers and barges. The main ports are Gothenburg, Helsingborg, Malmo and Stockholm. The principal airports are at Stockholm, Gothenburg, Kalmar, Linkoping, Malmo, Norrkoping and Orebro. Scandinavian Airlines System provides international and domestic flights, and domestic flights are also provided by Malmo Aviation. The Oresund Bridge connects Sweden to Denmark.

The modern telecommunications systems provided services to 6.4 million main-line subscribers and 9 million mobile phone subscribers in 2005, and 6.9 million internet users in 2006.

EDUCATION AND HEALTH

The state education system provides nine years of free and compulsory schooling from the age of seven to 16 in the comprehensive elementary schools. Around 95 per cent continue into further education of two to four years' duration in the upper secondary schools and a unified higher education system administered in six regional areas containing one of the universities: Uppsala (founded 1477); Lund (1668); Stockholm (1878); Gothenburg (1887); Umea (1963) and Linkoping (1967).

Gross enrolment ratio (percentage of relevant age group) – primary 98 per cent; secondary 103 per cent; tertiary 82 per cent (2006 est)
Health expenditure (per capita) – US$3,598 (2005)
Hospital beds (per 1,000 people) – 3.6 (2000–6)

MEDIA

Public television is run by Sveriges Television (SVT). There are a number of commercial stations and around two-thirds of households have cable or satellite television. The switch from analogue to digital services is expected to be completed in 2008. Commercial radio began in 1993, and some of the main stations now have near-national networks, in competition with public broadcaster Sveriges Radio. The country is among the world's top consumers of newspapers and the government provides subsidies to newspapers regardless of their political affiliation. There are four Stockholm-based daily newspapers and one based in Gothenburg.

CULTURE

Several Swedish writers have become globally successful, among them crime-fiction writer Henning Mankel (*b.* 1948) and Astrid Lindgren (1907–2002), the creator of *Pippi Longstocking*. A number of Swedes have received Academy awards, including directors Ingmar Bergman (1918–2007), and Lasse Hallstrom (*b.* 1946) and actors Greta Garbo (1905–90) and Ingrid Bergman (1915–82). ABBA is the country's most recognisable musical export and has sold over 370 million albums; founders Bjorn Ulvaeus and Benny Andersson have repeated their success in musical theatre, writing the international hits *Mamma Mia!* and *Chess*. In science, astronomer Anders Celsius (1701–44) devised the eponymous temperature scale and the polymath Alfred Nobel (1833–96) invented dynamite and founded the Nobel prizes for physics, chemistry, medicine, literature and world peace.

SWITZERLAND

Schweizerische Eidgenossenschaft/Confédération Suisse/Confederazione Svizzera/Confederaziun Svizra – *Swiss Confederation*

Area – 41,290 sq. km
Capital – Bern; population, 337,000 (2007 est)
Major cities – Basel, Geneva, Lausanne, Zurich
Currency – Swiss franc of 100 rappen (or centimes)
Population – 7,554,661 rising at 0.38 per cent per year (2007 est); German (65 per cent), French (18 per cent), Italian (10 per cent), Romansch (1 per cent) (est)
Religion – Roman Catholicism (42 per cent), Protestantism (35 per cent), Islam (4 per cent) (est); 11 per cent have no religious affiliation
Language – German, French, Italian, Romansch (all official), Serbian, Croatian, English, Albanian, Portuguese, Spanish
Population density – 187 per sq. km (2006)
Urban population – 67.5 per cent (2005 est)
Median age (years) – 40.4 (2007 est)
National anthem – 'Schweizerpsalm' ['Swiss Psalm']
National day – 1 August (Confederation Day)
Life expectancy (years) – 80.62 (2007 est)
Mortality rate – 8.51 (2007 est)
Birth rate – 9.66 (2007 est)
Infant mortality rate – 4.28 (2007 est)
Death penalty – Abolished for all crimes (since 1992)
CPI score – 9.0 (2007)

CLIMATE AND TERRAIN

Landlocked Switzerland is the most mountainous country in Europe. The Alps, at no point lower than 1,700m, occupy the south and east, and include peaks such as Dufourspitze (4,634m), Matterhorn (4,478m), Finsteraarhorn (4,274m), Aletschhorn (4,195m) and Jungfrau (4,158m). The Jura mountains lie in the north-west, and the area between these and the Alps is a plateau of hills, flatland and lakes. Elevation extremes range from 4,634m (Dufourspitze) at the highest to 195m (Lake Maggiore) at the lowest. The climate is temperate, with conditions that vary with altitude. Average temperatures in Zurich range from −3°C in January to 24°C in July.

HISTORY AND POLITICS

The area was conquered by the Romans in 58 BC and then overrun by Germanic tribes in the fourth century AD.

It was a province of the medieval Holy Roman Empire from 1033. The Swiss confederation began in 1291 as an alliance of three cantons to resist Habsburg control, and expanded during the 14th century when it became independent of the Habsburgs. Its independence was recognised under the Treaty of Westphalia in 1648. French revolutionary forces seized Switzerland in 1789 and named it the Helvetic Republic. Independence was restored in 1814, and the congress of Vienna (1815) joined Geneva, Neuchatel and Valais to the confederation and recognised the country's perpetual neutrality in international affairs. In 1847 a brief civil war between the federal government and seven Roman Catholic cantons over centralisation ended in the latter's defeat. A new constitution was adopted in 1848 which enhanced the powers of the central government.

Many policy decisions are submitted to national referendums. Although the federal government has pursued a policy of gradual integration with the EU and applied for membership in 1992, referendums have rejected membership of the European Economic Area (1992), approved bilateral trade agreements with the EU (2000), and rejected EU membership (2001).

Proportional representation, introduced in 1919, resulted in coalition governments throughout the 20th and into the 21st century. From 1959 until December 2007, the federal government was an unchanged coalition of four parties: the Swiss People's Party, the Social Democratic Party, the Christian Democratic People's Party and the Radical Democratic Party. Following the October 2007 legislative election, the Swiss People's Party remained the largest party in the legislature, increasing its number of seats to 62, but in December 2007 it left the coalition government in protest after one of its ministers was voted out of office; two party members who continued in their cabinet posts were excluded from the party.

POLITICAL SYSTEM

Under the 1998 constitution, the head of state is a president elected annually (along with the vice-president) for a one-year term by the Federal Assembly from the members of the Federal Council. The federal legislature, the Federal Assembly, has two chambers: the National Council has 200 members, directly elected for a four-year term; the Council of States has 46 members (two from each canton and one from each half-canton) directly elected within each canton for a four-year term.

Executive power is in the hands of a Federal Council of seven members, elected for a four-year term by the Federal Assembly after every legislative election. The Federal Council is chaired by the president. Not more than one person from the same canton may be elected a member of the Council; however, there is a tradition that Italian- and French-speaking areas should between them be represented on the council by at least two members.

Any citizen able to obtain 100,000 voters' signatures in support of holding a referendum on a given issue can initiate a national referendum.

SELECTED GOVERNMENT MEMBERS *as at July 2008*
President of the Swiss Confederation, Interior, Pascal Couchepin
Vice-President, Finance, Hans-Rudolf Merz
Defence, Samuel Schmid
Foreign Affairs, Micheline Calmy-Rey

EMBASSY OF SWITZERLAND
16–18 Montagu Place, London W1H 2BQ
T 020-7616 6000 E swissembassy@lon.rep.adminh.ch
W www.swissembassy.org.uk
Ambassador Extraordinary and Plenipotentiary, HE Alexis Lautenberg, *apptd* 2004

BRITISH EMBASSY
Thunstrasse 50, 3005 Bern
T (+41) (31) 359 7700 W www.britain-in-switzerland.ch
Ambassador Extraordinary and Plenipotentiary, HE Simon Featherstone, *apptd* 2003

BRITISH COUNCIL
PO Box 532, Sennweg 2, 3000 Bern 9
T (+41) (31) 301 1473 W www.britishcouncil.org/switzerland
Director, Caroline Morrissey

CONFEDERAL STRUCTURE

There are 23 cantons, three of which are subdivided making 20 cantons and six half-cantons, or 26 in all. Each canton and half-canton has its own government and a substantial degree of autonomy. The main language in 19 of the cantons is German; in the others it is French (*) or Italian (†).

The confederation consists of: Aargau, Appenzell-Ausserrhoden, Appenzell-Innerrhoden, Basel-Country, Basel-Town, Bern, *Fribourg, *Geneva, Glarus, Graubünden/Grischun, *Jura, Lucerne, *Neuchatel, Nidwalden, Obwalden, St Gallen, Schaffhausen, Schwyz, Solothurn, Thurgau, †Ticino, Uri, *Valais, *Vaud, Zug and Zurich.

DEFENCE

The army has 224 main battle tanks, 1,123 armoured personnel carriers and 186 armoured infantry fighting vehicles. The air force has 90 combat aircraft.
Military budget – US$3,780m (2007)
Military personnel – 22,600: joint 3,900; 18,700 conscript
Conscription duration – 18 weeks, then 3-week refresher courses

ECONOMY AND TRADE

Switzerland has a prosperous and stable market economy with low unemployment and a highly skilled labour force. Although it has rejected EU membership, it has brought many of its practices into line with EU members to maintain its competitiveness. GDP per capita is higher than in the EU and unemployment is much lower.

Agriculture is practised chiefly in the valleys and the central plateau, where cereals, fruits and vegetables are grown. Dairy farming and stock-raising are also important. The chief manufacturing industries comprise engineering and electrical engineering, metalworking, chemicals and pharmaceuticals, watchmaking, textiles, precision instruments, woodworking, foodstuffs and footwear. Banking, insurance and tourism are also major industries. Agriculture contributes 1.5 per cent of GDP, industry 34 per cent and services 64.5 per cent.

The main trading partners are the EU countries (especially Germany) and the USA. Principal exports are machinery, chemicals, metals, watches and agricultural products. The main imports are machinery, chemicals, vehicles, metals, agricultural products and textiles.
GNI – US$434,800m; US$58,050 per capita (2006)
Annual average growth of GDP – 2.6 per cent (2007 est)

nflation rate – 0.6 per cent (2007 est)
Jnemployment – 3.1 per cent (2007 est)
Total external debt – US$1,340,000m (2007)
mports – US$132,000m (2006)
xports – US$142,000m (2006)

BALANCE OF PAYMENTS
Trade – US$9,648m surplus (2006)
Current Account – US$58,7080m surplus (2006)

Trade with UK	*2006*	*2007*
Imports from UK	£4,204,719,000	£3,843,276,005
Exports to UK	£4,475,953,000	£4,878,440,710

COMMUNICATIONS

There are 71,300km of roads, including 1,728km of motorways. Railway track totals 4,800km, almost all of which is electrified. Transnational Alpine routes are served by all-weather road and rail tunnels. The Rhine carries heavy shipping traffic on the 65km of the Basel-Rheinfelden and Schaffhausen-Bodensee stretches, and there are 12 navigable lakes. The principal airports are at Zurich, Basel, Bern and Geneva.

Modern telecommunications systems provided services to 5.1 million main-line subscribers, 7.4 million mobile phone subscribers and 4.6 million internet users in 2006.

EDUCATION AND HEALTH

Education is controlled by cantonal and communal authorities and is free and compulsory from age seven to 16. Special schools make a feature of commercial and technical instruction. The universities are Basel (founded 1460), Bern (1834), Fribourg (1889), Geneva (1873), Lausanne (1890), Zurich (1832), and Neuchatel (1909), the technical universities of Lausanne and Zurich and the economics university of St Gall.

Gross enrolment ratio (percentage of relevant age group) – primary 98 per cent; secondary 93 per cent; tertiary 45 per cent (2006 est)
Health expenditure (per capita) – US$5,694 (2005)
Hospital beds (per 1,000 people) – 5.7 (2000–6)

MEDIA AND CULTURE

Broadcasting is dominated by the public service Swiss Broadcasting Corporation (SRG/SSR), which operates seven TV networks and 18 radio stations, mainly funded through licence fees. Private radio and TV stations operate at regional level, and television stations from France, Germany and Italy are widely available through multi-channel cable and satellite television. The press has full editorial freedom and operates mainly along regional lines, reflecting linguistic divisions: there are two German-language dailies based in Zurich, two French-language dailies in Geneva and an Italian-language daily in Lugano.

Important cultural figures include the writer and philosopher Jean-Jacques Rousseau (1712–78), the psychoanalyst Carl Gustav Jung (1875–1961), the poet Carl Spitteler (1845–1924), who won the Nobel prize for literature in 1919, and the writer and founder of modern structural linguistics Ferdinand de Saussure (1857–1913).

SYRIA

Al-Jumhuriyah al-Arabiyah as Suriyah – *Syrian Arab Republic*

Area – 185,180 sq. km
Capital – Damascus; population, 2,466,000 (2007 est)
Major cities – Halab, Hamah, Hims, Al Ladhiqiyah
Currency – Syrian pound (S£) of 100 piastres
Population – 19,314,747 rising at 2.24 per cent per year (2007 est)
Religion – Islam (90 per cent), Christianity (10 per cent) (est)
Language – Arabic (official), Kurdish, Armenian, Aramaic, Circassian, French
Population density – 106 per sq. km (2006)
Urban population – 50.3 per cent (2005 est)
Median age (years) – 21.1 (2007 est)
National anthem – 'Homat el Diyar' ['Guardians of the Homeland']
National day – 17 April (Independence Day)
Life expectancy (years) – 70.61 (2007 est)
Mortality rate – 4.74 (2007 est)
Birth rate – 27.19 (2007 est)
Infant mortality rate – 27.7 (2007 est)
Death penalty – Retained
CPI score – 2.4 (2007)
Population below poverty line – 11.9 per cent (2006 est)

CLIMATE AND TERRAIN

The terrain is primarily semi-arid and desert plateaux in the interior, with a narrow coastal plain and mountains in the west, and the fertile basin of the river Euphrates in the east. Elevation extremes range from 2,814m (Mt Hermon) at the highest point to −200m (Lake Tiberias) at the lowest. The climate varies; the coast has a Mediterranean climate, the mountains have moderate summers, the interior plateaux have very hot summers and cold winters, and the Hamad region has a desert climate. Average temperatures in Damascus range from 0°C in January to 37°C in August.

HISTORY AND POLITICS

The country was successively part of the Phoenician, Persian, Roman and Byzantine empires. It was conquered by Muslim Arabs in the seventh century, and was subsequently ruled by foreign dynasties before being conquered by the Turks in the 11th century. The location of many battles during the medieval Crusades, Syria became part of the Ottoman Empire in 1516. Following the empire's collapse after the First World War, Syria became a mandated territory in 1920, administered by France with the mandated territory of Lebanon as 'Greater Lebanon'. Syria's declaration of independence in

1944 was resisted by the French, but was effectively achieved in 1946 when French forces withdrew. Syria formed part of the United Arab Republic with Egypt from 1958 to 1961, when it seceded. It was involved in the Arab-Israeli wars in 1948, 1967 and 1973, losing the Golan Heights to Israel in 1967.

Syrian intervention in Lebanon began in 1976, its military presence influencing politics there after the civil war ended. Forces remained until 2005, when they were withdrawn in response to massive popular protests in Lebanon and intense international pressure following the assassination of a Lebanese politician. However, following the withdrawal, many Western states continued to accuse Syria of supporting and arming Lebanese militants. Relations with the USA, already strained by Syria's attempts to develop weapons of mass destruction, deteriorated in 2006 following the conflict between Israel and Lebanon, but have since improved.

The Arab Socialist Renaissance (Ba'ath) Party has been the ruling party since 1963. Hafez al-Assad seized power in a coup in 1970 and was elected president in 1971. He remained president until his death in 2000, when he was succeeded by his son, Bashar al-Assad, who was re-elected unopposed in 2007. Following the 2007 legislative election, the Ba'ath Party and its allies retained a large majority in the legislature.

POLITICAL SYSTEM

The 1973 constitution declares that the Arab Socialist Renaissance (Ba'ath) Party is the leading party in the state and society. The president is head of state and head of government. He is elected for a seven-year term by the legislature and confirmed in office by a national referendum. The president appoints the council of ministers. The unicameral People's Council *(Majlis al-Sha'ab)* has 250 members directly elected for a four-year term. The only candidates permitted to stand in elections are those from the Ba'ath Party, parties allied with it or independents.

HEAD OF STATE

President, Lt-Gen. Bashar al-Assad, *elected by parliament* 27 June 2000, *approved by referendum* 10 July 2000, *re-elected* May 2007
Vice-Presidents, Farouk al-Shara; Najah al-Attar

SELECTED GOVERNMENT MEMBERS *as at July 2008*

Prime Minister, Mohammed Naji al-Otari
Foreign Affairs, Waleed al-Muallem
Defence, Lt.-Gen. Hassan al-Turkmani
Interior, Gen. Bassam Abdel Majeed
Finance, Mohammad al-Husayn

EMBASSY OF THE SYRIAN ARAB REPUBLIC

8 Belgrave Square, London SW1X 8PH
T 020-7245 9012 W www.syrianembassy.co.uk
Ambassador Extraordinary and Plenipotentiary, Sami Khiyami, *apptd* 2004

BRITISH EMBASSY

PO Box 37, 11 Mohammad Kurd Ali Street, Malki, Damascus
T (+963) (11) 373 9241
Ambassador Extraordinary and Plenipotentiary, HE Simon Collis *apptd* 2007

BRITISH COUNCIL

PO Box 33105, Maysaloun Street, Shalaan, Damascus
T (+963) (11) 331 0631 W www.britishcouncil.org/syria
Director, Paul Doubleday

DEFENCE

The army has 4,950 main battle tanks, 1,500 armoured personnel carriers and up to 2,450 armoured infantry fighting vehicles. The navy has 2 frigates, 18 patrol and coastal vessels and 13 armed helicopters at 3 bases. The air force has 583 combat aircraft and 71 armed helicopters.
Military budget – US$1,460m (2007)
Military personnel – 292,600: army 215,000, navy 7,600, air force 70,000; paramilitary 108,000
Conscription duration – 30 months

ECONOMY AND TRADE

The economy is state-controlled and predominantly state-owned, although recent modest economic reforms included some privatisation. Oil and agriculture account for nearly half of GDP; recent high oil prices have cushioned the impact of declining production and exports on government revenue. Gas is also produced, for domestic use, and phosphate is mined. An industrialisation programme is developing steadily; the main activities are the manufacture of textiles, processed food, beverages, tobacco and cement, and car assembly. Agriculture contributes 23.6 per cent of GDP, industry 27.5 per cent and services 48.9 per cent.

The main export markets are Iraq, Germany, Lebanon and Italy; imports come chiefly from Saudi Arabia, China, Egypt, the UAE and Italy. Principal exports are crude oil, minerals, petroleum products, fruit and vegetables, cotton fibre, textiles, clothing, meat, livestock and wheat. The main imports are machinery and transport equipment, electrical power machinery, food and livestock, metals and metal products, chemicals, plastics, yarn and paper.
GNI – US$30,300m (2006); US$1,560 per capita (2006)
Annual average growth of GDP – 3.5 per cent (2007 est)
Inflation rate – 7 per cent (2007 est)
Unemployment – 10 per cent (2007 est)
Total external debt – US$6,610m (2007 est)
Imports – US$44,800m (2005)
Exports – US$37,800m (2005)

BALANCE OF PAYMENTS

Trade – US$374m deficit (2004)
Current Account – US$2,133m deficit (2006)

Trade with UK	*2006*	*2007*
Imports from UK	£81,594,000	£72,392,007
Exports to UK	£272,693,000	£56,810,460

COMMUNICATIONS

There are 2,711km of railways, which link with the networks of neighbouring countries. The country has 94,890km of roads, 19,000km of which are surfaced. The principal airports are at Aleppo and Damascus; internal air services operate between all major cities. The main port is Latakia.

Telecommunications systems are being improved. In 2006 there were 3.2 million main telephone lines in use, 4.6 million mobile phone subscribers and 1.5 million internet users.

EDUCATION AND HEALTH

Education is under state control. Elementary education is free at state schools and is compulsory from the age of seven. Secondary education is not compulsory and is free only at state schools. There are universities at Damascus, Halab, Tishrin, Latakia and a Ba'ath University at Hims.
Literacy rate – 82.9 per cent (2004 est)

Gross enrolment ratio (percentage of relevant age group) – primary 126 per cent; secondary 70 per cent (2006 est)
Health expenditure (per capita) – US$61 (2005)
Hospital beds (per 1,000 people) – 1.3 (2000–6)

MEDIA

There was a brief period of press freedom when Bashar al-Assad became president in 2000 and instigated the first licensing of private publications in almost 40 years, but restrictions have since been imposed. It is now illegal to criticise the president or his family, and reportage of both foreign and domestic events is heavily censored. Most of the print and broadcast media are owned by the government and the Ba'ath Party. There are three state-run television networks, but satellite receivers are permitted so many viewers have access to foreign television broadcasts.

TAIWAN

T'ai-wan – Taiwan

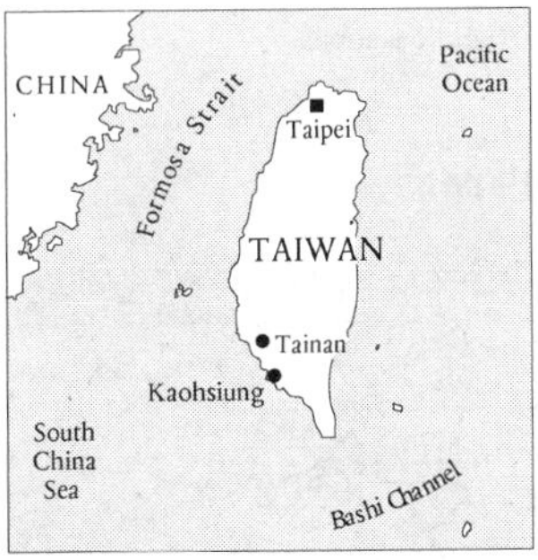

Area – 35,980 sq. km
Capital – Taipei; population, 2,646,474 (2001 est)
Major cities – Kaohsiung, Taichung, Tainan
Currency – New Taiwan dollar (NT$) of 100 cents
Population – 22,858,872 rising at 0.3 per cent per year (2007 est); Hoklo (70 per cent), Hakka (14 per cent), mainland Chinese (14 per cent), aborigine (2 per cent) (est)
Religion – Taoism (33 per cent), Buddhism (24 per cent), I Kuan Taoism (3 per cent), Christianity (2 per cent) (est). Many also practise Chinese folk beliefs, among which are shamanism, ancestor worship, magic and aspects of animism
Language – Mandarin (official), Taiwanese
Population density – 618 per sq. km (2001)
Median age – 35.5 (2007 est)
National anthem – 'National Anthem of the Republic of China'
National day – 10 October (Republic Day)
Life expectancy (years) – 77.56 (2007 est)
Mortality rate – 6.54 (2007 est)
Birth rate – 8.97 (2007 est)
Infant mortality rate – 5.54 (2007 est)
Death penalty – Retained
CPI score – 5.7 (2007)
Population below poverty line – 0.95 per cent (2007 est)

CLIMATE AND TERRAIN

An island in the China Sea, Taiwan (formerly Formosa) lies 145km east of the Chinese mainland. The island is mountainous and forested in the east, with lowlands in the west. Elevation extremes range from 3,952m (Yu Shan) at the highest point to 0m (South China Sea) at the lowest. The climate is tropical and influenced by the monsoons. Typhoons bring heavy rains between July and September. Average temperatures in Taipei range from 12°C in January to 34°C in July.

Territories include the Penghu (Pescadores) islands (80.47 sq. km), some 56km west of Taiwan, as well as Kinmen (Quemoy) (109 sq. km) and Matsu (7 sq. km), which are only a few kilometres from mainland China.

HISTORY AND POLITICS

Settled for centuries by Chinese, the island was annexed by China in the 17th century, and ceded to Japan in 1895 at the end of the Sino-Japanese War. It was returned to China after Japan's defeat in the Second World War. The Kuomintang (KMT) government, led by Gen. Chiang Kai-shek, withdrew to Taiwan in 1949 after being defeated by the communists in mainland China. The territory remained under Chiang Kai-shek's presidency until his death in 1975. He was succeeded as president by his son, Gen. Chiang Ching-kuo, who ruled until his death in 1988. Martial law was lifted in 1987 after 38 years. In 1991 the Taiwanese government declared an end to the state of war with China, officially recognising the People's Republic of China for the first time, and ended emergency measures that had frozen political life in Taiwan since 1949.

Demands for democratisation of the authoritarian one-party state in the late 1980s led to the first multiparty elections in 1992. The 'Senior Parliamentarians' who had retained their seats since being elected on the mainland in 1948 were forcibly retired in 1991–2. From this point, power has shifted away from the mainlanders to the native Taiwanese, and 50 years of KMT rule ended when the Democratic Progressive Party (DPP), which favours self-determination, won the presidency in 2000 and the 2001 legislative election.

The DPP retained the presidency and continued in government after the 2004 elections. However, in the 2008 elections the KMT returned to power, winning a majority of seats in the legislature, and the KMT candidate, Ma Ying-jeou, was elected president.

FOREIGN RELATIONS

Legally, most nations acknowledge the position of the Chinese government that Taiwan is a province of the People's Republic of China, and as a result Taiwan has formal diplomatic relations with only 25 countries and no seat at the UN. China has sanctioned the use of force to prevent Taiwan declaring itself independent.

Direct tourism, trade and communications links between mainland China and the Taiwanese islands of Kinmen and Matsu were inaugurated in 2001, the first direct links between Taiwan and China since 1949.

POLITICAL SYSTEM

The 1947 constitution (which originally applied to the whole of China) has been amended a number of times since 1991; in 2004 an amendment provided for future proposed constitutional changes to be put to a referendum instead of the National Assembly (formerly the upper house of the legislature), which was disbanded under 2005 provisions that also reduced the number of legislative seats with effect from the 2008 election. The head of state is a president directly elected for a four-year term, renewable only once. The unicameral Legislative Yuan has 113 members: 73 directly elected, 34 elected proportionately by party and six elected by aboriginal voters in two constituencies; all serve a four-year term.

HEAD OF STATE
President, Ma Ying-jeou, *elected* 22 March 2008
Vice-President, Vincent Siew

SELECTED GOVERNMENT MEMBERS *as at July 2008*
Premier, Liu Chao-shiuan
Economy, Yiin Chii-ming
Foreign Affairs, Francisco Ou
Interior, Liao Liou-yi
Defence, Chen Chao-min

BRITISH COUNCIL
2F-1, 106 XinYi Rd, Sec. 5, Taipei 110
T (+886) (2) 8722 1000 W www.britishcouncil.org/taiwan
Director, Christine Skinner

DEFENCE

The army has over 926 main battle tanks, 950 armoured personnel carriers, 225 armoured infantry fighting vehicles and 101 armed helicopters. The navy has 4 submarines, 4 destroyers, 22 frigates, 70 patrol and coastal vessels, 32 combat aircraft and 20 armed helicopters at 5 bases. The air force has 478 combat aircraft.
Military budget – US$9,580m (2007)
Military personnel – 290,000: army 200,000, navy 45,000, air force 45,000; paramilitary 17,000
Conscription duration – 20 months

ECONOMY AND TRADE

Since the 1950s Taiwan has transformed itself from a mainly agricultural country into a highly developed industrial economy. This transition was driven by exports, and the trade surplus and foreign reserves are very high. There has been a gradual shift away from state domination of the economy, with a reduction in government influence on investment and foreign trade, and privatisation in the financial and industrial sectors.

The soil is very fertile and a quarter of the land area is used for agriculture, producing rice, corn, vegetables, fruit, tea, meat, dairy products and fish. The industrial base includes electronics, oil refining, armaments, chemicals, textiles, iron and steel, machinery, cement, food processing and vehicles. Agriculture contributes 1.4 per cent of GDP, industry 27.5 per cent and services 71.1 per cent.

The main trading partners are China, Japan, the USA, Hong Kong and South Korea. Principal exports are computer products and electrical equipment, metals, textiles, plastics, chemicals and vehicle parts. The main imports are electronic and electrical equipment, machinery and oil.
Average annual growth of GDP – 4.6 per cent (2007 est)
Inflation rate – 1.1 per cent (2007 est)
Unemployment – 3.9 per cent (2007 est)
Total external debt – US$96,720m (2007 est)
Imports – US$202,700m (2006)
Exports – US$224,000m (2006)

BALANCE OF PAYMENTS
Trade – US$21,282m surplus (2006)
Current Account – US$24,661m surplus (2006)

Trade with UK	*2006*	*2007*
Imports from UK	£912,853,000	£938,618,747
Exports to UK	£2,390,453,000	£2,421,774,928

COMMUNICATIONS

Taiwan has 1,588km of railways and a total road network of 40,000km, most of which is surfaced (including 976km of motorways). The main ports are Keelung, Kaohsiung and Taichung, and there are international airports at Taoyuan (near Taipei) and Kaohsiung. There are internal flights between all the major cities.

Modern, digital telecommunications systems provided services to 14.4 million main-line telephone subscribers and 23.2 million mobile phone subscribers in 2006, and 13.2 million internet users in 2005.

MEDIA

The media is among the most liberal and competitive in Asia. There are some 350 newspapers, all privately owned and reflecting a wide range of views. There are four main Chinese-language dailies, and three published in English. The broadcast media, especially television, has a high level of ownership by the government, the military and political parties; the government is taking steps to end this. Both terrestrial and cable television services operate, and cable subscription is the highest in the region. There are over 170 radio stations.

TAJIKISTAN

Jumhurii Tojikiston – Republic of Tajikistan

Area – 143,100 sq. km
Capital – Dushanbe; population, 553,000 (2007 est)
Major town – Khujand
Currency – Somoni of 100 dirams
Population – 7,076,598 rising at 1.9 per cent per year (2007 est); Tajik (79.9 per cent), Uzbek (15.3 per cent). There are also Russian, Tatar, Kyrgyz, German and Ukrainian minorities
Religion – Islam (97 per cent), Christianity (2 per cent) (est). The majority of the population practises Sunni Islam
Language – Tajik (official), Russian
Population density – 47 per sq. km (2006)
Urban population – 24.2 per cent (2005 est)
Median age (years) – 21.3 (2007 est)
National anthem – 'Surudi Milli' ['Tajik National Anthem']
National day – 9 September (Independence Day)
Life expectancy (years) – 64.61 (2007 est)
Mortality rate – 7.05 (2007 est)
Birth rate – 27.33 (2007 est)
Infant mortality rate – 43.64 (2007 est)
Death penalty – Retained
CPI score – 2.1 (2007)
Population below poverty line – 64 per cent (2004 est)

iteracy rate – 99.5 per cent (2004 est)
'ross enrolment ratio (percentage of relevant age group) – primary 100 per cent; secondary 83 per cent; tertiary 19 per cent (2006 est)
'ealth expenditure (per capita) – US$18 (2005)
'ospital beds (per 1,000 people) – 6.2 (2000–6)

:LIMATE AND TERRAIN

he landlocked country is mountainous, with the Pamir ighlands in the east and the high ridges of the amir-Altai ranges in the centre. Plains are formed by 'ide stretches of the Syr-Darya valley in the north and of e Amu-Darya and its tributaries in the south. Elevation xtremes range from 7,495m (Qullai Ismoili Somoni) at e highest point to 300m (Syr Darya) at the lowest. The imate is continental, with average temperatures ranging 'om –4°C in January to 18°C in July.

IISTORY AND POLITICS

he area that is now Tajikistan was conquered by lexander the Great in the fourth century BC and emained under Greek and Greco-Persian rule for 200 ears, until the kingdom of Kusha was established, based n Bacharia (Bukhara).

Tajikistan was invaded by both the Arabs and the amanid Persians between the seventh and ninth centuries .D. The cities of Bukhara and Samarkand (now in Jzbekistan) were two of the most important cultural and ducational centres in the Islamic world. The area became art of the Mongol Empire in the 13th century, and emained under the control of various feudal emirates ntil the 19th century. In 1868, the northern part was ubsumed within the Russian Empire, while the south was nnexed by the Emirate of Bukhara. At the time of the ussian revolution in 1917 the Central Asian emirates ttempted to establish their independence. Bolshevik ower was established in northern Tajikistan by 1 April 1918, when the Turkestan Soviet Socialist Republic was ormed, and the Bukhara emirate was overthrown by oviet forces in 1920. In 1924 the Tajikistan Autonomous Soviet Socialist Republic was formed as part of the Uzbek Republic, before Tajikistan was given full epublican status within the USSR in 1929.

Tajikistan declared its independence on 9 September 1991, and Rahmon Nabiyev, communist leader in 1982–5, was elected president. In 1992, anti-government demonstrations escalated into a five-year civil war between pro-government forces and Islamic and pro-democracy groups. A four-part peace accord signed in 1997 was implemented by a National Reconciliation Commission by 2000. There have been several assassinations and bombings, targeted at government ministers and buildings, since the end of the civil war.

Former communists have dominated the presidency and the governments since 1991. Some elections have been boycotted by opposition parties, and most have been deemed by international observers not to meet international standards of fairness. A number of opposition leaders have been arrested on criminal charges, moves that their supporters claim are politically motivated.

President Rakhmonov has served as head of state since 1992, and was re-elected for a third term in 2006. The 2005 legislative elections were won by the incumbent (former communist) People's Democratic Party of Tajikistan (HDKT), which continued in office. The government was reshuffled after the 2006 presidential election.

POLITICAL SYSTEM

The 1994 constitution was amended in 1999 and 2003, following referendums, to introduce changes to the presidential term of office and the legislative structure. The executive president is directly elected for a single seven-year term, although the 2003 amendment permits the current incumbent to stand for two further terms. The bicameral legislature consists of the Assembly of Representatives *(Majlisi Namoyandogan)*, which has 63 members directly elected for a five-year term, and a national assembly *(Majlisi Milli)*, which has 33 members, 25 elected by five regional assemblies and eight appointed by the president, to serve a five-year term. Administratively Tajikistan is divided into two regions and the Gorno-Badakhstan autonomous region.

HEAD OF STATE

President, Emomali Rakhmonov, *elected by Supreme Soviet* 19 November 1992, *elected* 6 November 1994, *re-elected* 1999, 2006

SELECTED GOVERNMENT MEMBERS *as at July 2008*

Prime Minister, Akil Akilov
First Deputy Prime Minister, Asadullo Ghulomov
Deputy Prime Ministers, Murodali Alimardonov; Ruqiya Qurbonova
Defence, Col.-Gen. Sherali Khayrulloyev
Finance, Safarali Najmiddinov
Foreign Affairs, Hamrokhon Zaripov
Internal Affairs, Mahmadnazar Solehov

HONORARY CONSULATE

33 Ovington Square, London SW3 1LJ
T 020-7584 5111
Honorary Consul, Benjamin Brahms

BRITISH EMBASSY

65 Tursunzade Street, Dushanbe 734002
T (+992) 372 42221 E dushanbe.reception@fco.gov.uk
W www.britishembassy.gov.uk/tajikistan
Ambassador Extraordinary and Plenipotentiary, HE Graeme Loten, *apptd* 2004

DEFENCE

The army has 37 main battle tanks, 23 armoured infantry fighting vehicles and 23 armoured personnel carriers. The air force has 4 armed helicopters.
Military budget – US$87m (2007)
Military personnel – 8,800: army 7,300, air force 1,500; paramilitary 7,500
Conscription duration – 24 months

ECONOMY AND TRADE

Since the civil war, there has been steady economic growth but the economy remains fragile owing to inconsistent implementation of structural reforms, corruption, weak industrial infrastructure, widespread unemployment and high foreign debt. A debt restructuring and write-off agreement was reached with Russia in 2002, and the country has received US$67m (£34m) in aid from the USA. However, around 60 per cent of the population lives below the poverty line.

Agriculture is the major sector of the economy, accounting for 23 per cent of GDP but 67 per cent of employment. Cotton-growing and cattle-raising predominate; other crops are cereals, fruit, grapes and vegetables. Abundant mineral deposits are not fully exploited. Industry consists of aluminium and hydro-electric power production, zinc and lead extraction, food processing and light industries making chemicals and fertilisers, cement, metal-cutting machine tools, refrigerators and freezers. The sector contributes 30 per cent of GDP and employs 7.5 per cent of the workforce.

The main export markets are the Netherlands and Turkey; imports come chiefly from Russia, Uzbekistan and Kazakhstan. Principal exports are aluminium, electricity, cotton, fruit, vegetable oil and textiles. The main imports are electricity, petroleum products, aluminium oxide, machinery and equipment, and foodstuffs.

GNI – US$2,600m (2006); US$390 per capita (2006)
Annual average growth of GDP – 7.2 per cent (2007 est)
Inflation rate – 9.8 per cent (2007 est)
Unemployment – 12 per cent (2004 est)
Total external debt – US$1,308m (2007 est)

BALANCE OF PAYMENTS
Trade – US$200m deficit (2006)
Current Account – US$84m deficit (2006)

Trade with UK	*2006*	*2007*
Imports from UK	£5,016,000	£1,291,418
Exports to UK	£511,000	£11,407,992

COMMUNICATIONS

There are 482km of railway and 27,767km of roads; many roads, including the main highways, are only open in the summer months. About 200km of the river Vakhsh is navigable. The main airport is at Dushanbe, and there are over 20 other airports and airfields around the country.

Telecommunications systems are poor, with many towns not linked to the national network and limited mobile phone coverage. There were 280,200 main telephone lines in use, 265,000 mobile phone subscribers and 19,500 internet users in 2005.

MEDIA

Broadcasting is dominated by state-run radio and television, alongside more than 30 local and regional private television stations and a few private radio stations. There are more than 200 registered newspapers, some government-owned and others linked to political parties and movements. Journalists regularly come under pressure from the authorities, who control printing presses.

TANZANIA

Jamhuri ya Muungano wa Tanzania – *United Republic of Tanzania*

Area – 945,087 sq. km
Capital – Dodoma; population, 183,000 (2007 est)
Major cities – Arusha, Dar es Salaam, Mbeya, Mwanza, Zanzibar
Currency – Tanzanian shilling of 100 cents
Population – 39,384,223 rising at 2.09 per cent per year (2007 est); Africans form a large majority, with European, Asian and other non-African minorities
Religion – Christianity (30 per cent), Islam (30 per cent) (est)
Language – Swahili, English (both official), Arabic
Population density – 45 per sq. km (2006)
Urban population – 37.5 per cent (2005 est)
Median age (years) – 17.7 (2007 est)
National anthem – 'Mungu ibariki Afrika' ['God Bless Africa']
National day – 26 April (Union Day)
Life expectancy (years) – 50.71 (2007 est)
Mortality rate – 13.36 (2007 est)
Birth rate – 35.95 (2007 est)
Infant mortality rate – 71.69 (2007 est)
HIV/AIDS adult prevalence – 5.9 per cent (2005 est)
Death penalty – Retained, but not used
CPI score – 3.2 (2007)
Population below poverty line – 36 per cent (2002 est)

CLIMATE AND TERRAIN

Tanzania comprises the former Tanganyika, on the mainland of east Africa, and the islands of Zanzibar, Pemba and Mafia. Most of the country lies on the central African plateau, from which rise mountains that run across the centre of the country from north-east to south-west. Peaks include Mt Kilimanjaro (5,895m), the highest point on the continent of Africa, and Mt Meru (4,564m). The lowest point is 0m (Indian Ocean). The land falls to plains in the south-east and along the coast, and to swamps in the west. Large areas of lakes Victoria, Tanganyika and Nyasa lie on the northern and western borders, and there are smaller lakes in the north-east and south-west. The Serengeti National Park covers an area of 9,656 sq. km in the north of the country. The climate is tropical equatorial, modified by altitude. The north has two wet seasons, from March to May and from November to December, while the rest of the country has one wet season from November to May. The average temperature in Dar es Salaam is 29°C all year round.

HISTORY AND POLITICS

The area was settled by Bantu people from the fifth century AD, and city states developed along the coast from the eighth century, trading with Arab, Indian and Persian merchants. Portuguese explorers arrived in the 15th century, and in the 16th century the Portuguese conquered Zanzibar, periodically controlling the coastal states on the mainland. They were ousted from Zanzibar in 1699 by Arabs from Oman, and Oman exercised overlordship over the east African coast from Zanzibar until 1861, when the sultanates of Oman and Zanzibar were separated. The sultanate of Zanzibar became a British protectorate in 1890 and Germany established the colony of German East Africa on the mainland in the 1890s. After the First World War, Tanganyika became a mandated territory under British administration, and achieved independence on 9 December 1961. It became a republic in 1962. Zanzibar became independent as a constitutional monarchy on 10 December 1963. The sultan was overthrown in a revolution in 1964 and anzibar united with Tanganyika on 26 April 1964 to rm the United Republic of Tanzania.

The sole legal political party from 1977 to 1992 was e Revolutionary Party of Tanzania (CCM). The onstitution was amended in 1992 to allow multiparty olitics, with the stipulation that all parties must be active both the mainland and Zanzibar and that parties must ot be formed on regional, religious, tribal or racial rounds. The first multiparty presidential and arliamentary elections were held in 1995 and were won y the CCM, which has continued to dominate politics.

In the 2005 elections, the CCM candidate Jakaya Irisho Kikwete was elected president with 80.3 per cent f the vote, and the CCM retained its overwhelming ajority in the legislature. Three ministers resigned in ebruary 2008 because of corruption allegations and the resident reshuffled the cabinet.

In Zanzibar's 2005 presidential and legislative elections, resident Amani Abeid Karume was re-elected with 53 per ent of the vote, and the CCM retained its majority in the egislature. The elections were characterised by violence nd accusations of electoral fraud.

OLITICAL SYSTEM

The 1977 constitution was amended in 1992 to introduce ultiparty elections and in 2000 to allow the president to ominate some members of parliament. The executive resident is directly elected for a five-year term, renewable nly once. The president is always from Tanganyika and he vice-president is always from Zanzibar. The nicameral National Assembly *(Bunge)* has 323 members: 32 directly elected, 75 seats reserved for women, five hosen by Zanzibar's legislature, and the speaker; up to en further members may be appointed by the president. All serve a five-year term. The Bunge enacts laws that pply to the whole of the United Republic of Tanzania nd those that apply only to the mainland; laws that apply pecifically to Zanzibar are enacted by the island's own egislature, the 50-member House of Representatives. Zanzibar also has its own directly elected president, who s a member of the Bunge, and government.

HEAD OF STATE

President of the United Republic, Jakaya Mrisho Kikwete, *elected* 14 December 2005, *took office* 21 December 2005

Vice-President, Ali Mohamed Shein

President of Zanzibar, Amani Abeid Karume

SELECTED GOVERNMENT MEMBERS *as at July 2008*

Prime Minister, Mizengo Kayanza Peter Pinda

Defence, Hussein Mwinyi

Finance, Mustapha Mkullo

Foreign Affairs, Bernard Membe

Home Affairs, Lawrence Masha

HIGH COMMISSION FOR THE UNITED REPUBLIC OF TANZANIA

3 Stratford Place, London W1C 1AS

T 020-7569 1470 E tanzarep@tanzania-online.gov.uk

W www.tanzania-online.gov.uk

High Commissioner, HE Mwanaidi Sinare Maajar, *apptd* 2006

BRITISH HIGH COMMISSION

PO Box 9200, Umoja House, Garden Avenue, Dar es Salaam

T (+255) (22) 211 0101 E bhc.dar@dar.mail.fco.gov.uk

W www.britishhighcommission.gov.uk/tanzania

High Commissioner, HE Philip Parham, *apptd* 2006

BRITISH COUNCIL

PO Box 9100, Samora Avenue/Ohio Street, Dar es Salaam

T (+255) (22) 211 6574 W www.britishcouncil.org/tanzania

Director, Kate Ewart-Biggs

DEFENCE

The army has 45 main battle tanks and around 10 armoured personnel carriers. The navy has 7 patrol and coastal combatant vessels at 3 bases. The air force has 19 combat capable aircraft.

Military budget – US$173m (2007 est)

Military personnel – 27,000: army 23,000, navy 1,000, air force 3,000; paramilitary 1,400

Conscription duration – 24 months

ECONOMY AND TRADE

State control has been dismantled gradually since the mid-1980s. Liberalisation and modernisation policies have been supported by the World Bank, IMF and aid donors, increasing private-sector growth and investment and producing steady growth in GDP in recent years, but around one-third of the population still lives below the poverty line.

Agriculture is the mainstay of the economy, accounting for 42.8 per cent of GDP, about 80 per cent of employment and 85 per cent of exports. It provides coffee, sisal, tea, cotton, pyrethrum, cashew nuts, cereals, fruit and vegetables as well as the raw materials for industries producing sugar, beer, and cigarettes. Zanzibar and Pemba produce cloves and clove oil, and coconuts and their derivatives. Output of minerals (chiefly diamonds, gold and iron) has increased substantially, and soda ash, cement, petroleum products, footwear, clothing, wood products and fertiliser are also produced. Tourism is a major source of revenue. Industry accounts for 18.4 per cent of GDP and services for 38.7 per cent.

The main trading partners are China, India, UAE, South Africa, Kenya, Japan and EU countries. Principal exports are gold, coffee, cashew nuts, manufactures and cotton. The main imports are consumer goods, machinery and transport equipment, industrial raw materials and crude oil.

GNI – US$13,400m (2006); US$350 per capita (2006)

Annual average growth of GDP – 6.9 per cent (2007 est)

Inflation rate – 7 per cent (2007 est)

Total external debt – US$4,984m (2007 est)

Imports – US$4,300m (2006)

Exports – US$1,660m (2006)

BALANCE OF PAYMENTS

Trade – US$2,599m deficit (2006)

Current Account – US$1,110m deficit (2006)

Trade with UK	*2006*	*2007*
Imports from UK	£85,748,000	£85,656,774
Exports to UK	£29,490,000	£30,852,662

COMMUNICATIONS

There are 78,900km of roads, only 6,808km of which are surfaced. The 3,690km of railways connect Dar es Salaam with Zambia, northern Tanzania and Kenya, and lakes Tanganyika and Victoria. The three major lakes in the east are the main trade routes with neighbouring countries, via ports at Mwanza, Musoma, Bukoba (Lake Victoria) and Kigoma (Lake Tanganyika). The main seaports are Dar es Salaam, Tanga, Mtwara, Zanzibar, Mkoani and Wete (Pemba). Coastal shipping services connect the mainland to Zanzibar, and lake services operate on Lake Tanganyika and Lake Nyasa. The principal international airports are Dar es Salaam, Kilimanjaro and Zanzibar.

The fixed-line telephone system is being modernised; mobile phone distribution has grown rapidly. There were 169,100 main lines and 6.7 million mobile phone subscribers in 2007, and 384,000 internet users in 2005.

EDUCATION AND HEALTH

The school system is administered in Swahili but the government is making efforts to improve English standards in secondary and higher education.

Literacy rate – 69.4 per cent (2004 est)
Gross enrolment ratio (percentage of relevant age group) – primary 112 per cent; tertiary 1 per cent (2006 est)
Health expenditure (per capita) – US$17 (2005)

MEDIA

There are many state-owned and private newspapers available and popular titles include *Daily News, The Express* and *Uhuru.* Radio is prevalent in urban areas and channels include Radio Free Africa and Radio Tanzania Dar es Salaam. Television was not officially launched until 1994 and does not yet provide national coverage. Zanzibar has a less liberal media policy and there are no private broadcasters or newspapers on the island, although locals can access mainland media.

THAILAND

Ratcha Anachak Thai – Kingdom of Thailand

Area – 514,000 sq. km
Capital – Bangkok; population, 6,704,000 (2007 est)
Major cities – Nonthaburi, Samut Prakan, Udon Thani
Currency – Baht of 100 satang
Population – 65,068,149 rising at 0.66 per cent per year (2007 est); Thai, including Lao (75 per cent), Chinese (14 per cent) (est)
Religion – Buddhism (94 per cent), Islam (5 per cent) (est)
Language – Thai (official), English
Population density – 124 per sq. km (2006)
Urban population – 32.5 per cent (2005 est)
Median age (years) – 32.4 (2007 est)
National anthem – 'Phleng Chat' ['National Song']
National day – 5 December (The King's Birthday)
Life expectancy (years) – 72.55 (2007 est)
Mortality rate – 7.1 (2007 est)
Birth rate – 13.73 (2007 est)
Infant mortality rate – 18.85 (2007 est)
HIV/AIDS adult prevalence – 1.1 per cent (2005 est)
Death penalty – Retained
CPI score – 3.3 (2007)
Population below poverty line – 10 per cent (2004 est)

CLIMATE AND TERRAIN

Thailand is divided geographically into four regions: the centre is a fertile plain; to the north-east there is a semi-arid plateau; to the north-west, mountains; and the south is a narrow tropical isthmus with a spine of mountains. Extremes of elevation range from 2,576m (Doi Inthanon) at the highest point to 0m (Gulf of Thailand) at the lowest. The principal rivers are the Chao Phraya and its tributories in the central plains and the Mekong on the northern and north-eastern borders. The climate is tropical, with high humidity all year round and average temperatures in Bangkok range from 20°C in January to 35°C in July.

HISTORY AND POLITICS

The Thai nation was founded in the 13th century and expanded in the following centuries at the expense of the declining Khmer Empire. Although trade with China, Japan and Europe developed in the 17th century, in 1699 an isolationist policy was adopted. Burma invaded in the 18th century, leaving the country in a state of anarchy until reunification in 1782 under the first king of the present Chakri dynasty. From the late 19th century Thailand opened up to European contact and trade under a series of modernising kings who reformed the country's administration and commerce. It was the only country in the region to escape colonisation by a European power.

Following a revolution in 1932, Thailand became a constitutional monarchy with parliamentary government. It was occupied by Japan from 1941 until 1945, after which it was under military or military-controlled governments for most of the following 50 years. In 1992, mass demonstrations in Bangkok supported by the king, forced from power the military-aligned government that had won the 1992 election. Military power was curbed, the 1978 constitution was restored and the interim government sacked military chiefs. Another election in September 1992 resulted in a majority for parties not allied with the military. A new constitution was introduced in 1997.

The military again intervened in politics in September 2006, staging a coup against the prime minister, Thaksin Shinawatra, while he was out of the country. Shinawatra's Thai Rak Thai (TRT) party, in government from 2001 until the coup, was dissolved in 2007 after being found guilty of electoral irregularities by the constitutional court, but he is believed to be one of the main sponsors of the People Power Party (PPP). The PPP won nearly half the seats in the lower legislative chamber in the December 2007 election and is the dominant party in the six-party coalition government led by the PPP leader Samak Sundaravej which took office in February 2008 when civil rule was restored.

INSURGENCY

The Muslim minority is concentrated in the southern provinces of Narathiwat, Pattani, Songhkla and Yala. A separatist campaign in the region began in the 1970s but died down in the 1990s following promises of increased government resources and political representation. Renewed violence since early 2004 has claimed over 1,500 lives. The military government offered to negotiate with the rebels, but this has had little impact on the level of violence.

POLITICAL SYSTEM

Thailand is a constitutional monarchy with a hereditary monarch as head of state. A new constitution was troduced in 2007; the new civil government wishes to nange this and its proposals are before a parliamentary ommittee. The 2007 constitution provides for a icameral National Assembly comprising a 480-member ouse of representatives, elected for a four-year term, and senate with 150 members: 76 elected members (one om each province) and 74 members appointed by a election committee; senators serve a six-year term. The rime minister is appointed by the king and approved by nd responsible to the House of Representatives.

EAD OF STATE

IM The King of Thailand, King Bhumibol Adulyadej (Rama IX), *born* 5 December 1927, *succeeded* 9 June 1946

Ieir, HRH Crown Prince Maha Vajiralongkorn, *born* 28 July 1952

ELECTED GOVERNMENT MEMBERS *as at July 2008*

rime Minister, Defence, Samak Sundaravej

irst Deputy Prime Minister, Somchai Wongsawat

Deputy Prime Ministers, Sahas Bunditkul; Sanan Kajornprasart; Suwit Khunkitti; Mingkwan Saengsuwan; Surapong Suebwonglee *(Finance)*

nterior, Chalerm Yoobamrung

ROYAL THAI EMBASSY

9–30 Queen's Gate, London SW7 5JB

020-7225 5500 E csinfo@thaiembassy.org.uk

V www.thaiembassyuk.org.uk

Ambassador Extraordinary and Plenipotentiary, HE Kitti Wasinondh, *apptd* 2007

BRITISH EMBASSY

4 Wireless Road, Bangkok 10330

(+662) 305 8333

Ambassador Extraordinary and Plenipotentiary, HE Quinton Quayle, *apptd* 2007

BRITISH COUNCIL

254 Chulalongkorn Soi 64, Siam Square, Phayathai Road,

Pathumwan, Bangkok 10330

T (+662) 652 5480 W www.britishcouncil.or.th/en

Director, John Whitehead

DEFENCE

The army has 333 main battle tanks, 950 armoured personnel carriers and 5 armed helicopters. The navy has 1 aircraft carrier, 10 frigates, 9 corvettes, 87 patrol and coastal vessels, 17 combat aircraft and 8 armed helicopters at 5 bases. The air force has 165 combat aircraft.

Military budget – US$3,370m (2007)

Military personnel – 306,600: army 190,000, navy 70,600, air force 46,000; paramilitary 113,700

Conscription duration – 24 months

ECONOMY AND TRADE

Thailand made a quick recovery from the 1997 economic crisis in south-east Asia and in 2002–4 was one of its best performing economies. Growth slowed in 2005 owing to higher oil prices, weaker export performance, a tsunami-related decline in tourism and drought in rural areas, but revived in 2007. This was owing to strong export growth, especially in manufacturing and agricultural products, and a recovery in tourism.

The agricultural sector generates 11.4 per cent of GDP and employs nearly half the workforce. The main crops are rice, cassava, rubber, maize, sugar cane, coconuts and soya beans. In recent years fishing and livestock production have gained importance. There are reserves of natural gas, lignite, tin, tungsten and lead; Thailand is a leading producer of both tin and tungsten.

The main industry is tourism, which has been the chief foreign exchange earner since the 1980s. Other industries include textiles and clothing, agricultural processing, beverages, tobacco, cement, mining and light manufacturing, which produces jewellery, electrical appliances, computers and parts, and cars. Industry contributes 43.9 per cent of GDP and services 44.7 per cent.

The main trading partners are Japan, the USA, China, Malaysia and Singapore. Principal exports are textiles and footwear, fish products, rice, rubber, jewellery, cars, computers and electrical appliances. The main imports are capital goods, intermediate goods and raw materials, consumer goods and fuels.

GNI – US$193,700m (2006); US$3,050 per capita (2006)

Annual average growth of GDP – 4.3 per cent (2007 est)

Inflation rate – 2 per cent (2007 est)

Unemployment – 1.7 per cent (2007 est)

Total external debt – US$58,600m (2007)

Imports – US$129,000m (2006)

Exports – US$131,000m (2006)

BALANCE OF PAYMENTS

Trade – US$2,080m surplus (2006)

Current Account – US$2,174m surplus (2006)

Trade with UK	*2006*	*2007*
Imports from UK	£567,654,000	£598,479,920
Exports to UK	£1,963,844,000	£2,017,285,286

COMMUNICATIONS

There are 57,403km of roads, almost all of which are surfaced, and 4,071km of railways. Bangkok is the international airport, though airports at Chiang Mai, Phuket and Hat Yai also receive international flights. The main ports are Bangkok and Sattahip, and there are 3,701km of inland waterways navigable by small boats.

A competitive telecommunications sector has seen a rapid growth in mobile phone take-up. In 2006 there were 7 million main lines in use, 40.8 million mobile phone subscribers and 8.4 million internet users.

EDUCATION AND HEALTH

Primary education is compulsory and free, and secondary education in government schools is free. Private universities and colleges are playing an increasing role in higher education.

Literacy rate – 92.6 per cent (2004 est)

Gross enrolment ratio (percentage of relevant age group) – primary 108 per cent; secondary 78 per cent; tertiary 46 per cent (2006 est)

Health expenditure (per capita) – US$98 (2005)

Hospital beds (per 1,000 people) – 2.2 (2000–6)

MEDIA

Nearly all the national terrestrial television networks and many of the country's radio networks are controlled by the government and the military. Media reforms are currently in progress, aimed at reducing military interest and opening up more opportunities to the private sector. Although free to criticise policy and uncover abuses, the media tends towards self-censorship regarding the monarchy and judiciary. Newspapers are largely privately run, with popular titles including *Bangkok Post* and *Thairath*.

TOGO

République togolaise – Togolese Republic

Area – 56,785 sq. km
Capital – Lomé; population, 1,452,000 (2007 est)
Major cities – Atakpamé, Kara, Kpalimé, Sodoké
Currency – Franc CFA of 100 centimes
Population – 5,701,579 rising at 2.72 per cent per year (2007 est)
Religion – Animism (33 per cent), Roman Catholicism (28 per cent), Islam (14 per cent), Protestantism (10 per cent), other Christian denominations (10 per cent) (est). An estimated 5 per cent of the population is atheist
Language – French (official), Ewe, Mina, Kabye, Dagomba
Population density – 118 per sq. km (2006)
Urban population – 36.3 per cent (2005 est)
Median age (years) – 18.4 (2007 est)
National anthem – 'Salut à toi, pays de nos aïeux' ['Hail to Thee, Land of Our Forefathers']
National day – 27 April (Independence Day)
Life expectancy (years) – 57.86 (2007 est)
Mortality rate – 9.65 (2007 est)
Birth rate – 36.83 (2007 est)
Infant mortality rate – 59.12 (2007 est)
HIV/AIDS adult prevalence – 2.9 per cent (2005 est)
Death penalty – Retained, but not used
CPI score – 2.3 (2007)
Literacy rate – 53 per cent (2004 est)
Gross enrolment ratio (percentage of relevant age group) – primary 102 per cent; secondary 40 per cent (2006 est)
Health expenditure (per capita) – US$18 (2005)
Hospital beds (per 1,000 people) – 0.9 (2000–6)

CLIMATE AND TERRAIN

From hills in the centre of the country, the terrain flattens out to savannah in the north and a plateau leading to a marshy coastal plain in the south. Elevation extremes range from 986m (Mt Agou) at the highest point to 0m (Atlantic Ocean) at the lowest. The climate is tropical, with two wet seasons (March to July and September to November). The average temperature in Lomé is 27°C all year round.

HISTORY AND POLITICS

Formerly part of the kingdom of Togoland, the territory became a German protectorate in 1884 but was occupied on the outbreak of the First World War by Britain and France. The country was divided between Britain and France as a League of Nations mandate after the war and the mandate was renewed by the UN in 1946. In 1957 following a plebiscite, British Togoland integrated with Ghana when it became independent. French Togoland achieved independence as the Republic of Togo in 1960.

There were military coups in 1963 and 1967, the latter bringing to power the army commander Lt.-Col. (later Gen.) Gnassingbé Eyadéma, who proclaimed himself president. Political parties were banned, and in 1969 the president's *Rassemblement du peuple togolais* (RPT) became the sole legal political party. Violent anti-government demonstrations in 1990 forced the government to legalise other political parties and introduce a multiparty constitution in 1992. Eyadéma and the RPT were returned to power in the first multiparty elections in 1993 and in two subsequent elections. The regime continued its brutal suppression of opposition, particularly before and after the 1998 elections, when an international inquiry concluded there was systematic abuse of human rights.

Following President Eyadéma's death in February 2005, the military attempted to install his son, Faure Gnassingbé, as president but this attracted domestic and international condemnation. Gnassingbé resigned as acting president, only to be elected to the presidency in April 2005. Following reconciliation talks in 2006, the government and opposition leaders signed an accord providing for the participation of opposition parties in a transitional government, and a national unity government was appointed until a legislative election was held in October 2007. The election, the first without an opposition boycott for two decades, was nevertheless won by the RPT, which retained its majority; the polls were declared free and fair by observers.

POLITICAL SYSTEM

Under the 1993 constitution, the head of state is a president directly elected for a five-year term. The unicameral National Assembly has 81 members, who are directly elected for a five-year term. The prime minister, who is appointed by the president, is head of government and appoints the cabinet in consultation with the president.

HEAD OF STATE

President, Defence, Faure Gnassingbé, *elected* 24 April 2005, *sworn in* 4 May 2005

SELECTED GOVERNMENT MEMBERS *as at July 2008*

Prime Minister, Komlan Mally
Economic Affairs, Adji Otheth Ayassor
Foreign Affairs, Leopold Messan Gnininvi

EMBASSY OF THE REPUBLIC OF TOGO

8 rue Alfred Roll, 75017 Paris, France
T (+33) (1) 4380 1213
Ambassador Extraordinary and Plenipotentiary, HE Tchao Sotou Bere, *apptd* 2003

BRITISH AMBASSADOR

HE Dr Nicholas Westcott, CMG, *apptd* 2007, resident at Accra, Ghana

DEFENCE

The army has 2 main battle tanks, 20 armoured infantry fighting vehicles and 30 armoured personnel carriers. The navy has 2 patrol and coastal combatant vessels at a base at Lomé. The air force has 16 combat capable aircraft.
Military budget – US$43m (2007 est)

Military personnel – 8,550: army 8,100, navy 200, air force 250; paramilitary 750
Conscription duration – 24 months (selective)

ECONOMY AND TRADE

Progress on economic reform, intended to attract foreign investment and balance the budget, is slow; greater impetus is needed on privatisation and financial transparency. Resumption of aid to Togo, mostly suspended in the 1990s because of its human rights record, has increased since the 2007 election, and the country is working with donors on a debt reduction scheme.

The economy is predominantly based on agriculture, accounting for 40 per cent of GDP, engaging 65 per cent of the workforce and providing most of the country's exports as well as the raw materials for industry. Industrial activity centres on phosphate mining, agricultural processing and manufacture of cement, handicrafts, textiles and beverages. Industry accounts for 25 per cent of GDP and 5 per cent of employment. The main export markets are Ghana, Burkina Faso and Benin; imports come mainly from China, the UK and France. Principal exports are re-exports, cotton, phosphates, coffee and cocoa. The main imports are machinery and equipment, foodstuffs and petroleum products.

GNI – US$2,300m; US$350 per capita (2006)
Annual average growth of GDP – 2.5 per cent (2007 est)
Inflation rate – 3 per cent (2007 est)
Total external debt – US$2,000m (2005)
Imports – US$1,200m (2006)
Exports – US$630m (2006)

BALANCE OF PAYMENTS
Trade – US$570m deficit (2006)
Current Account – US$133m deficit (2006)

Trade with UK	*2006*	*2007*
Imports from UK	£140,196,000	£34,102,038
Exports to UK	£489,000	£7,578,595

COMMUNICATIONS

Togo has about 7,500km of roads, of which approximately one-third is surfaced. There are about 500km of railways. The chief waterway is the Mono river, depending on rainfall, and the main ports are Lomé and Kpeme. The principal airport is at Lomé.

The adequate telephone system served 82,100 main telephone lines, 708,000 mobile phone subscribers and 320,000 internet users in 2006.

MEDIA

The government owns Television Togolaise, the sole national television station, and the national radio station, Radiodiffusion Togolaise, and, in association with the ruling party RPT, some of the private radio stations. Togo's only daily newspaper, the *Togo-Presse,* is also government-owned. The constitution promises freedom of expression but this right is regularly abused, with journalists subject to harassment and law suits.

TONGA

Pule'anga Tonga – Kingdom of Tonga

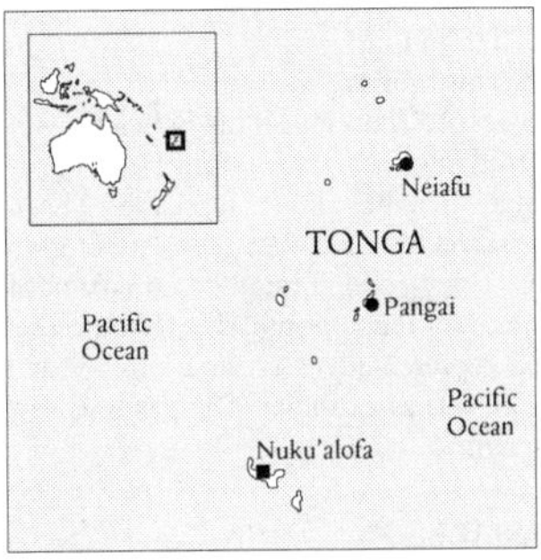

Area – 748 sq. km
Capital – Nuku'alofa on Tongatapu; population, 25,000 (2007 est)
Currency – Pa'anga (T$) of 100 seniti
Population – 116,921 rising at 1.85 per cent per year (2007 est)
Religion – Protestantism (53 per cent), Roman Catholicism (16 per cent), other Christian denominations (17 per cent), Mormonism (14 per cent) (est)
Language – English (official), Tongan
Population density – 139 per sq. km (2006)
Urban population – 34 per cent (2005 est)
Median age (years) – 21.3 (2007 est)
National anthem – 'Fasi Fakafonua' ['National Song']
National day – 4 June (Emancipation Day)
Life expectancy (years) – 70.12 (2007 est)
Mortality rate – 5.2 (2007 est)
Birth rate – 23.67 (2007 est)
Infant mortality rate – 11.99 (2007 est)
Death penalty – Retained, but not used
CPI score – 1.7 (2007)
Literacy rate – 98.9 per cent (2004 est)

CLIMATE AND TERRAIN

Tonga comprises over 170 islands in three groups, situated in the south Pacific Ocean some 724km east-south-east of Fiji. Most of the islands are of coral formation, but some are volcanic (Tofua, Kao and Niuafo'ou or 'Tin Can' Island). Elevation extremes range from 1,033m (unnamed location on Kao Island) at the highest point to 0m (Pacific Ocean) at the lowest. The climate is subtropical, influenced by prevailing south-west trade winds with average temperatures of 26°C all year round.

HISTORY AND POLITICS

The islands were settled by Polynesians from *c.*1000 AD. They were visited by Dutch explorers in 1643 and by Captain Cook in 1773. The country was reunited in 1845 after a civil war and a modern constitution adopted in 1875. Tonga became a British protectorate in 1900, and gained its independence on 4 June 1970.

A pro-democracy movement began in 1992 and gathered momentum throughout the 1990s, with the first political party being established in 1994. Following pro-democracy rioting in 2006, the government has agreed to hold elections in 2010 in which at least 21 of the 33 legislative seats will be directly elected by popular vote. In the 2008 legislative election, the Human Rights and Democracy Movement won seven of the popularly elected seats and other pro-democracy candidates the remaining two.

POLITICAL SYSTEM

The 1875 constitution was amended in 2003 to give greater powers to the king, limit judicial review of royal decisions and increase state control of the media. The head of state is a hereditary monarch. The unicameral legislative assembly, *Fale Alea,* consists of the king, the 16-member privy council, nine hereditary nobles elected by their peers, and nine popularly elected representatives; the elected representatives serve a three-year term. The privy council acts as a cabinet. The prime minister is head of government.

HEAD OF STATE

King of Tonga, HM King Siaosi (George) Tupou V, *born* 4 May 1948, *acceded* 11 September 2006, *crowned* 1 August 2008

Heir, HRH Crown Prince Tupouto'a Lavaka, *born* 12 July 1959

SELECTED GOVERNMENT MEMBERS *as at July 2008*

Prime Minister, Feleti (Fred) Sevele

Deputy Prime Minister, Villiami Tau Tangi

Finance, Afu'alo Matoto

Foreign Affairs; Defence (acting), Sonatane Tu'a Taumoepeau Tupou

TONGA HIGH COMMISSION

36 Molyneux Street, London W1H 5BQ

T 020-7724 5828 E snkioa@tongahighcom.co.uk

High Commissioner, HE Dr Sione Ngongo Kioa, *apptd* 2006

BRITISH HIGH COMMISSIONER

HE Roger Sykes, resident at Suva, Fiji, *apptd* 2006

ECONOMY AND TRADE

There are few natural resources and the country is dependent on foreign aid and remittances from Tongans working abroad. Tourism is the second-largest source of foreign exchange revenue after remittances. The government is encouraging the development of a private sector. Unemployment is high and inflation is rising.

Agriculture, fishing and tourism are the main economic activities. The main crops are squashes, coconuts, bananas, vanilla beans, cocoa, coffee, ginger and black pepper. Fish is an important staple food. A small light industry sector processes agricultural produce.

The main export markets are the USA and Japan; imports come chiefly from Fiji and New Zealand. Principal exports are squashes, fish, vanilla beans and root crops. The main imports are foodstuffs, machinery and transport equipment, fuels and chemicals.

GNI – US$225m (2006); US$2,250 per capita (2006)

Annual average growth of GDP – 2.4 per cent (2005 est)

Inflation rate – 11.1 per cent (2005 est)

Unemployment – 13 per cent (2004 est)

Total external debt – US$80.7m (2004)

Imports – US$130m (2006)

Exports – US$11m (2006)

BALANCE OF PAYMENTS

Trade – US$119m deficit (2006)

Current Account – US$18m deficit (2006)

Trade with UK	*2006*	*2007*
Imports from UK	£3,228,000	£860,765
Exports to UK	£3,000	£48,192

COMMUNICATIONS

There are 680km of roads in Tonga, 184km of which are surfaced. Its principal port is Nuku'alofa. There are six airfields on the islands; one has a surfaced runway.

Competition between providers has stimulated rapid expansion of telecommunications services. There were 13,700 main telephone lines in use and 29,900 mobile phone subscribers in 2005, and 3,100 internet users in 2006.

MEDIA

An amendment to the constitution in 2003 increased state control of the media. The primary television and radio broadcasters, Television Tonga and A3Z Radio Tonga, and the weekly newspaper, *Tonga Chronicle,* are all government-run. The private television station OBN TV7 ceased broadcasting in 2006 after a march originating at its headquarters ended in riots in the capital.

TRINIDAD AND TOBAGO

Republic of Trinidad and Tobago

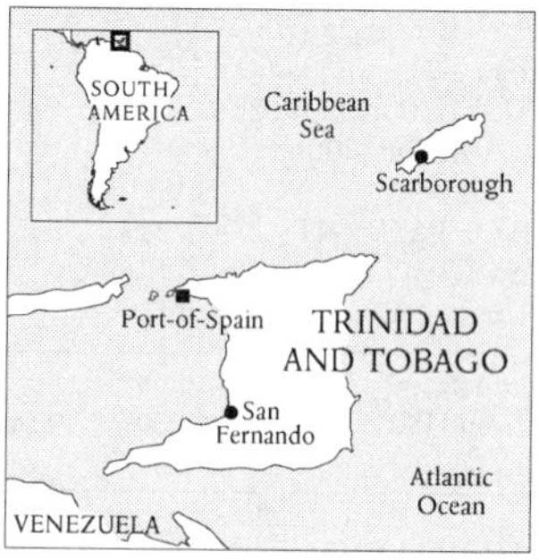

Area – 5,128 sq. km

Capital – Port of Spain; population, 54,000 (2007 est)

Major towns – Chaguanas, San Fernando, San Juan, Scarborough

Currency – Trinidad and Tobago dollar (T$) of 100 cents

Population – 1,056,608 falling at 0.88 per cent per year (2007 est)

Religion – Roman Catholicism (26 per cent), Protestantism (24 per cent), Hinduism (22 per cent), Islam (6 per cent), indigenous religions (5 per cent) (est). An estimated 2 per cent of the population is atheist

Language – English (official), Hindustani, French, Spanish, Chinese

Population density – 259 per sq. km (2006)

Urban population – 76.2 per cent (2005 est)

Median age (years) – 31.8 (2007 est)

National anthem – 'Forged From the Love of Liberty'

National day – 31 August (Independence Day)

Life expectancy (years) – 66.85 (2007 est)

Mortality rate – 10.76 (2007 est)

Birth rate – 13.07 (2007 est)

Infant mortality rate – 24.33 (2007 est)

HIV/AIDS adult prevalence – 2.5 per cent (2005 est)

Death penalty – Retained

CPI score – 3.4 (2007)

CLIMATE AND TERRAIN

Trinidad, the most southerly of the West Indian islands, lies 11km off the north coast of Venezuela. The island is mostly flat, with low mountains, the Northern Range, across almost its entire northern width and some low hills in the centre. Elevation extremes range from 940m (Mt Aripo) at the highest point to 0m (Caribbean Sea) at the lowest. Pitch Lake on the south-west coast is one of the world's largest natural sources of asphalt.

Tobago lies 30km north-east of Trinidad. The island has a range of hills, Main Ridge, running along its length; the highest point is 565m. Several islands, of which Chacachacare, Huevos, Monos and Gaspar Grande are the most important, lie west of Corozal Point, the north-west extremity of Trinidad.

There is a wet season from June to December. The average temperature in coastal regions is 27°C all year round.

HISTORY AND POLITICS

Trinidad is believed to be the oldest site of human habitation in the Caribbean archipelago, with excavated human remains dating back 7,200 years. For much of its history, the islands were home to a number of indigenous peoples, including the Nepuyo, Yaio and Carib peoples.

Trinidad and Tobago were discovered by Columbus in 1498. Trinidad was colonised in 1532 by Spain, capitulated to the British in 1797, and was ceded to Britain in 1802. Tobago was colonised by the Dutch from 1632 but subsequently changed hands numerous times until it was ceded to Britain by France in 1814. The two islands were amalgamated as a British colony in 1889. The Territory of Trinidad and Tobago became independent on 31 August 1962, and became a republic in 1976.

The republic has been politically stable since independence, with power passing between the People's National Movement (PNM), principally supported by those of African descent, and the United National Congress (UNC), most of whose supporters are of Asian descent. In the 2007 legislative election the PNM was returned to power with an increased majority, and its leader Patrick Manning remained prime minister. The PNM had also won the 2005 election for the Tobago legislature. President Richards, first elected in 2003, was declared re-elected in February 2008, when he was the only candidate for the presidency.

POLITICAL SYSTEM

Under the 1976 constitution, the head of state is a president elected for a five-year term by an electoral college consisting of both houses of the legislature. The bicameral parliament comprises the House of Representatives, the lower house, and the senate. The former has 41 members directly elected for a five-year term. The senate has 31 members, of whom 16 are appointed on the advice of the prime minister, six on the advice of the leader of the opposition and nine at the discretion of the president, to serve a five-year term.

Since 1980 Tobago has had internal self-government through its House of Assembly, which has 15 members, 12 directly elected and three chosen by the house for a four-year term.

HEAD OF STATE

President, George Maxwell Richards, *elected* 14 February 2003, *took office* 17 March 2003, *re-elected* 2008

SELECTED GOVERNMENT MEMBERS *as at July 2008*

Prime Minister, Patrick Manning
Attorney-General, Bridgid Annisette-George
Foreign Affairs, Paula Gopee-Scoon
National Security, Donna Cox
Finance, Karen Nynez-Tesheira

HIGH COMMISSIONER OF THE REPUBLIC OF TRINIDAD AND TOBAGO

42 Belgrave Square, London SW1X 8NT
T 020-7245 9351 E tthc@btconnect.com
High Commissioner, HE Glenda P. Morean-Phillip, *apptd* 2003

BRITISH HIGH COMMISSION

PO Box 778, 19 St Clair Avenue, St Clair, Port of Spain
T (+868) 622 2748 W http://britain-in-trinidad.org
High Commissioner, HE Eric Jenkinson OBE, *apptd* 2007

BRITISH COUNCIL

c/o British High Commission
T (+868) 628 0565 W www.britishcouncil.org/tt.htm
Manager, Peredur Evans

DEFENCE

The navy has 25 patrol and coastal combatant vessels at 5 bases.
Military budget – US$56m (2007)
Military personnel – 2,700: army 2,000, coast guard 700

ECONOMY AND TRADE

The country is the most prosperous in the Caribbean owing largely to its oil and natural gas reserves. This dependence makes the economy vulnerable to fluctuations in global prices; low prices in the 1980s and 1990s led to the build-up of a large foreign debt, but the high prices of recent years have produced a growing trade surplus. The agricultural sector is small, accounting for 0.6 per cent of GDP and 4 per cent of employment; the main products are cocoa, rice, citrus fruits, coffee, vegetables and poultry. Sugar production decreased in 2003 when the state-owned sugar company was closed. Apart from oil and gas extraction, the main industries are tourism, food processing, production of chemicals, cement, beverages, cotton textiles, and car and appliance assembly.

The main trading partners are the USA (60 per cent of exports; 31 per cent of imports), Brazil, Venezuela, Spain and Jamaica. Principal exports are oil and petroleum products, liquified natural gas, chemicals, steel products, beverages, cereals and cereal products, sugar, cocoa, coffee, citrus fruits, vegetables and flowers. The main imports are fuels and lubricants, machinery, transport equipment, manufactured goods, food, livestock and grain.
GNI – US$16,600m; US$12,500 per capita (2006)
Annual average growth of GDP – 5.8 per cent (2007 est)
Inflation rate – 8 per cent (2007 est)
Unemployment – 6.5 per cent (2007 est)
Total external debt – US$3,025m (2007 est)
Imports – US$6,500m (2006)
Exports – US$14,200m (2006)

BALANCE OF PAYMENTS

Trade – US$7,666m surplus (2006)
Current Account – US$4,654m surplus (2006)

Trade with UK	*2006*	*2007*
Imports from UK	£102,138,000	£118,360,062
Exports to UK	£184,339,000	£124,742,649

COMMUNICATIONS

The two islands have about 8,300km of roads, of which about half are surfaced. The three main ports are Scarborough (Tobago), Port of Spain and Point Lisas, where new industries powered by local natural gas are located. The international airport is at Port of Spain on Trinidad, and Tobago is served by Crown Point airport.

Modern telecommunications systems provided services to 323,500 main-line subscribers and 1.6 million mobile phone subscribers in 2006, and 163,000 internet users in 2005.

EDUCATION AND HEALTH

Education is free at all state-owned and government-assisted denominational schools, and at certain faculties at the University of the West Indies. Attendance is compulsory for children aged six to 12 years, after which attendance at free secondary schools is determined by success in the secondary school entrance examination at 11 years.

Literacy rate – 98.5 per cent (2004 est)
Gross enrolment ratio (percentage of relevant age group) – primary 95 per cent; secondary 76 per cent; tertiary 11 per cent (2006 est)
Health expenditure (per capita) – US$513 (2005)
Hospital beds (per 1,000 people) – 3.3 (2000–6)

MEDIA

There are both private and state-run media organisations. Private television and radio stations predominate and the freedom of the press is constitutionally protected. *Newsday* and *Trinidad Guardian* are popular newspapers.

TUNISIA

Al-Jumhuriyah at Tunisiyah – *Tunisian Republic*

Area – 163,610 sq. km
Capital – Tunis; population, 745,000 (2007 est)
Major cities – Aryanah, Ettadhamen Douar Hicher, Sfax, Sousse
Currency – Tunisian dinar of 1,000 millimes
Population – 10,276,158 rising at 0.99 per cent per year (2007 est)
Religion – Islam (99 per cent) (est)
Language – Arabic (official), French
Population density – 65 per sq. km (2006)
Urban population – 64.4 per cent (2005 est)
Median age (years) – 28.3 (2007 est)
National anthem – 'Himat al-Hima' ['Defenders of the Homeland']
National day – 20 March (Independence Day)
Life expectancy (years) – 75.34 (2007 est)
Mortality rate – 5.17 (2007 est)
Birth rate – 15.54 (2007 est)
Infant mortality rate – 22.94 (2007 est)
Death penalty – Retained, but not used
CPI score – 4.2 (2007)
Population below poverty line – 7.4 per cent (2005 est)

CLIMATE AND TERRAIN

The north is mountainous with a central plateau that gives way to the semi-arid desert plains of the south. There are salt lakes in the west. Elevation extremes range from 1,544m (Jebel ech Chambi) at the highest point to −17m (Shatt al Gharsah) at the lowest. The climate varies considerably from north to south; the northern coastal regions have a Mediterranean climate, while the south is both drier and hotter. Average temperatures in Tunis, on the northern tip of the country, range from 11°C in January to 34°C in June.

HISTORY AND POLITICS

The area was ruled successively by the Phoenicians, Carthaginians, Romans, Byzantines, Arabs, Turks and French before formally becoming a French protectorate in 1883. It was briefly occupied by Germany during the Second World War (1942–3), and became independent as a monarchy under the bey in 1956. In 1957 the bey was deposed and the country became a republic under one-party rule with Habib Bourguiba as president.

There was a growing demand throughout the 1970s for the legalisation of other political parties and the government's resistance to these led to serious unrest. Multiparty legislative elections were held in 1981, but the ruling party (now known as the Constitutional Democratic Rally (RCD)) has retained its grip on power over the past two decades. Although proclaimed president for life in 1975, President Bourguiba was deposed in 1987 on the grounds of senility by the prime minister Zine el-Abidine Ben Ali. Ben Ali was subsequently elected president in unopposed elections in 1989 and 1994, and in multiparty elections in 1999 and 2004.

The main opposition party pulled out of the 2004 presidential election beforehand, claiming that its participation would only legitimise a show of democracy. The simultaneous legislative election was won by the ruling RCD, again with an overwhelming majority of seats after capturing 87.7 per cent of the vote. The new upper house of the legislature, the Chamber of Councillors, was elected for the first time in July 2005; membership is dominated by the RCD.

POLITICAL SYSTEM

The 1959 constitution has been amended a number of times, most recently in 2002 to remove the restriction on the number of presidential terms and to establish a second parliamentary chamber. The executive president is directly elected for a five-year term. The parliament *(Barlaman)* comprises the Chamber of Deputies *(Majlis al-Nuwaab)*, with 189 members directly elected for a five-year term, and the Chamber of Councillors *(Majlis al-Mustasharin)*, which has 126 members, (85 indirectly elected by regions and professional organisations and 41 appointed by the president) who serve a six-year term with half elected every three years.

HEAD OF STATE

President, Gen. Zine el-Abidine Ben Ali, *took office* 7 November 1987, *elected* 2 April 1989, *re-elected* 1994, 1999, 2004

SELECTED GOVERNMENT MEMBERS *as at July 2008*
Prime Minister, Mohammed Ghannouchi
Finance, Mohamed Rachid Kechiche
Foreign Affairs, Abdelwahab Abdallah
Interior, Rafik Belhaj Kacem
Defence, Kamel Morjane

EMBASSY OF TUNISIA
29 Prince's Gate, London SW7 1QG
T 020-7584 8117
Ambassador Extraordinary and Plenipotentiary, HE Hamida M'Rabet Labidi, *apptd* 2007

BRITISH EMBASSY
Rue du Lac Windemere, Les Berges du Lac, 1053 Tunis
T (+216) (71) 108 703 E british.emb@planet.tn
W www.britishembassy.gov.uk/tunisia
Ambassador Extraordinary and Plenipotentiary, HE Alan Goulty, CMG, *apptd* 2004

BRITISH COUNCIL
87 Avenue Mohamed V, 1002 Tunis Belvédère
T (+216) 7184 8588 W www.britishcouncil.org/tunisia
Director, Peter Skelton

DEFENCE

The army has 84 main battle tanks and 268 armoured personnel carriers. The navy has 25 patrol and coastal combatant vessels at 3 bases. The air force has 27 combat aircraft.
Military budget – US$500m (2007)
Military personnel – 35,800: army 27,000, navy 4,800, air force 4,000; paramilitary 12,000
Conscription duration – 12 months (selective)

ECONOMY AND TRADE

The economy is diverse and an increasing proportion is in private ownership. Further liberalisation is planned to attract foreign investment and barriers to trade with the EU are being removed with the aim of creating a free trade zone. Agriculture and fisheries account for 11.6 per cent of GDP; the main products are olives, grain, tomatoes, citrus fruits, sugar beets, dates, almonds, meat and dairy products. The main industries are oil production, mining (principally phosphate and iron ore), tourism, processing agricultural products and manufacture of textiles, footwear and beverages. Tourism is the chief foreign exchange earner.

The main trading partners are EU countries, especially France and Italy. Principal exports are clothing, semi-finished goods and textiles, agricultural products, mechanical goods, phosphates and chemicals and hydrocarbons. The main imports are textiles, machinery and equipment, hydrocarbons, chemicals and food.
GNI – US$30,100m (2006); US$2,970 per capita (2006)
Annual average growth of GDP – 6.3 per cent (2007 est)
Inflation rate – 2.9 per cent (2007 est)
Unemployment – 13.9 per cent (2007 est)
Total external debt – US$18,560m (2007)
Imports – US$14,900m (2006)
Exports – US$11,500m (2006)

BALANCE OF PAYMENTS
Trade – US$3,352m deficit (2006)
Current Account – US$630m deficit (2006)

Trade with UK	*2006*	*2007*
Imports from UK	£128,883,000	£107,245,119
Exports to UK	£160,857,000	£192,130,708

COMMUNICATIONS

Tunisia has 19,000km of roads, over 12,000km of which are surfaced. There are 2,100km of railways. The main ports include Bizerte, Sfax, Sousse and Tunis-La Goulette. The principal airports are at Tunis, Monastir and Djerba.

The telephone system is being upgraded. In 2006 there were 1.3 million main lines in use, 7.3 million mobile phone subscribers and 1.2 million internet users.

EDUCATION AND HEALTH

There are nine years of compulsory primary education.
Literacy rate – 74.3 per cent (2004 est)
Gross enrolment ratio (percentage of relevant age group) – primary 110 per cent; secondary 83 per cent; tertiary 30 per cent (2006 est)
Health expenditure (per capita) – US$158 (2005)
Hospital beds (per 1,000 people) – 1.8 (2000–6)

MEDIA

In addition to the state-run radio and television stations, many satellite television channels are available and a private radio station has recently ended the state monopoly on radio broadcasting. An independent press exists but its coverage of local political issues is monitored by the government. Self-censorship is common as breaches of the press code are punishable with a prison sentence. Editions of foreign publications are frequently seized and internet access is monitored.

TURKEY

Turkiye Cumhuriyeti – Republic of Turkey

Area – 780,580 sq. km
Capital – Ankara (Angora), in Asia; population, 3,716,000 (2007 est)
Major cities – Adana, Antalya, Bursa, Gaziantep, Istanbul, Izmir, Konya
Currency – New Turkish lira (TL) of 100 kurus
Population – 71,158,647 rising at 1.04 per cent per year (2007 est): Turkish (80 per cent), Kurdish (20 per cent) (est)
Religion – Islam (99 per cent) (est)
Language – Turkish (official), Kurdish, Dimli, Azeri, Kabardian
Population density – 95 per sq. km (2006)
Urban population – 67.3 per cent (2005 est)
Median age (years) – 28.6 (2007 est)
National anthem – 'Istiklal Marsi' ['The Independence March']
National day – 29 October (Republic Day)
Life expectancy (years) – 72.88 (2007 est)
Mortality rate – 6 (2007 est)

Birth rate – 16.4 (2007 est)
Infant mortality rate – 38.33 (2007 est)
Death penalty – Abolished for all crimes (since 2004)
CPI score – 4.1 (2007)
Population below poverty line – 20 per cent (2002)

CLIMATE AND TERRAIN

Turkey in Europe consists of the relatively low-lying area of Eastern Thrace, including the cities of Istanbul and Edirne, and is separated from Asia by the Bosporus at Istanbul and by the Sea of Marmara and the Dardanelles (about 64km in length, with a width varying from 1.6km to 6.4km).

Turkey in Asia comprises the whole of Asia Minor or Anatolia. The western part of Anatolia is a central plateau with narrow coastal plains fringed by mountains in the north and south. The eastern part is mountainous, the land falling to a plateau lying between the mountains and the Syrian border. Elevation extremes range from 5,166m (Mt Ararat) at the highest point to 0m (Mediterranean Sea) at the lowest. There are many lakes in the eastern mountains, where the Euphrates and Tigris rivers rise.

Climate varies greatly from region to region. The coastal areas and the mountains (except in the east) have fairly hot summers and wet, mild winters. Average temperatures in Ankara range from −4°C in January to 31°C in June.

HISTORY AND POLITICS

Part of the empire of Alexander the Great and then of the Roman and Byzantine empires, Anatolia came under Turkish rule in the 11th century. The Ottoman Turkish Empire was founded in the 13th century and reached its zenith in the 16th century, its rule encompassing much of western Asia, northern Africa and south-eastern Europe. In the 17th century it began a steady decline, and after defeat in the First World War the Empire's remaining territory was partitioned. Following a revolution and the expulsion of foreign forces, the sultanate was abolished and Turkey was proclaimed a republic on 29 October 1923, under Gazi Mustafa Kemal (later known as Kemal Atatürk), who was elected president. Policies of secularism, rapid modernisation, economic development and neutrality were introduced. Turkey was neutral for much of the Second World War, but joined the Allies in 1945. It joined NATO in 1952.

In 1945 a multiparty system was introduced but in 1960 the government was overthrown by the armed forces. A new constitution was adopted in 1961 and a civilian government took office. Civilian governments remained in power until 1980 when mounting problems with the economy and terrorism resulted in another military coup. After the 1983 general election the military leadership handed power to a civilian government.

Since becoming a candidate for EU membership in 1999, Turkey has introduced a number of human and civil rights reforms to meet the preconditions for membership negotiations. These include abolition of the death penalty and reform of the penal code, easing restrictions on freedom of speech, improving rights for women and Kurds, and reducing the political role of the military. Formal EU membership talks began in 2005.

Tension between secularists and Islamists has grown in recent years, particularly since the Islamic-based Justice and Development Party (AKP), led by Recep Tayyip Erdogan, came to power in 2002. Seculists' concerns about the AKP's agenda caused a four-month political crisis in 2007, preventing the election of a new president and leading outgoing President Sezer to refuse approval of constitutional amendments. The impasse was ended by early legislative elections in July 2007, in which the AKP won a greatly increased majority. In August the AKP candidate, Abdullah Gul, was elected president in the third round of voting. Since October 2007 referendums have approved constitutional changes replacing indirect with direct presidential elections and lifting the ban on women wearing the Islamic headscarf in universities.

INSURGENCIES

From 1984 until 1999, government forces fought armed guerrillas of the secessionist Kurdistan Workers' Party (PKK) in the south and east of the country, where Turkey's 12 million Kurds are the majority population. The PKK seeks greater political and cultural rights for the Kurds. In 2004 it suspended its 1999 ceasefire because of what it called 'annihilation' attacks against its forces by the government. There were subsequently several armed clashes in south-east Turkey, and tensions mounted there again in summer 2007; in spring 2008, Turkish troops crossed into Iraq to destroy PKK bases. The government has blamed bombings in 2004 and 2005 on the PKK, which has mostly denied responsibility for the attacks and which unilaterally reinstated its ceasefire in September 2006.

Pro-Islamic parties have become increasingly popular since the 1990s, and a number have been banned since 1998 for acting as a focus for anti-secular activities. A number of bombings, attributed to Muslim extremists, occurred in Istanbul in 2003 and 2004.

POLITICAL SYSTEM

The 1982 constitution has been amended several times; in May 2007 amendments were passed by the legislature but the president refused to approve them, although the introduction of direct elections to the presidency was approved by referendum in October 2007. The head of state is a president elected by the legislature for a single seven-year term. The unicameral Turkish Grand National Assembly has 550 members who are directly elected for a five-year term. The prime minister, who is appointed by the president, is head of government and appoints the cabinet.

HEAD OF STATE

President, Abdullah Gul, *elected* 27 August 2007

SELECTED GOVERNMENT MEMBERS *as at August 2008*

Prime Minister, Recep Tayyip Erdogan
Deputy Prime Ministers, Cemil Cicek; Nazim Ekren Hayati Yazici
Finance, Kemal Unakitan
Interior, Besir Atalay
Foreign Affairs, Ali Babacan

EMBASSY OF THE REPUBLIC OF TURKEY

43 Belgrave Square, London SW1X 8PA
T 020-7393 0202 E turkish.emb@btclick.com
W www.turkishembassylondon.org
Ambassador Extraordinary and Plenipotentiary, HE Mehmet Yigit Alpogan, *apptd* 2007

BRITISH EMBASSY

Sehit Ersan Caddesi 46/A, Cankaya, Ankara
T (+90) (312) 455 3344 E britembinf@turk.net
W www.britishembassy.org.tr
Ambassador Extraordinary and Plenipotentiary, HE Nicholas Baird *apptd* 2006

BRITISH COUNCIL
Karum Is Merkezi, D Blok 437 Kat 5, Kavalklidere, Ankara
T (+90) (312) 455 3600 W www.britishcouncil.org.tr
Director, Chris Brown, OBE

DEFENCE

The army has 4,205 main battle tanks, 3,643 armoured personnel carriers, 650 armoured infantry fighting vehicles and 37 armed helicopters. The navy has 13 submarines, 24 frigates, 42 patrol and coastal vessels and 10 armed helicopters at 12 bases. The air force has 435 combat aircraft. Since its invasion of Cyprus in 1974, Turkey has maintained forces in the north of the island and at present has about 36,000 personnel stationed there.

As a member of NATO, Turkey is host to the Headquarters Joint Command South East and the Sixth Allied Tactical Air Force Headquarters. US air force detachments (1,650 personnel) are based at Incirlik in southern Turkey.

Military expenditure – US$11,630m (2006)
Military personnel – 510,600: army 402,000, navy 48,600, air force 60,000; paramilitary 102,200
Conscription duration – 15 months

ECONOMY AND TRADE

After years of economic difficulty, a stringent recovery programme agreed with the IMF in 2002 has begun to turn round the economy. Growth has averaged over 5 per cent a year since 2005 and inflation has fallen considerably, although there are still large foreign and public debts. The government's main priorities are to make progress with tax reforms and privatisation and to reduce employment in the public sector.

The agricultural sector accounts for 8.9 per cent of GDP and employs 35.9 per cent of the workforce. The principal crops are tobacco, cotton, cereals, olives, sugar beets, pulses, citrus and other fruits, and livestock products. A diverse modern industrial sector is dominated by textiles and clothing (which employ one-third of the industrial workforce), food processing, vehicle assembly, electronics, mining, iron and steel, oil, construction, timber and paper. Turkey is also a destination and a transit route for oil and gas from central Asian countries. Tourism is a major industry and source of foreign revenue. Industry contributes 28.3 per cent of GDP and services 62.8 per cent.

The main trading partners are EU countries (especially Germany), Russia, the USA and China. Principal exports are clothing, foodstuffs, textiles, metal manufactures and transport equipment. The main imports are machinery, chemicals, semi-finished manufactures, fuels and transport equipment.

GNI – US$393,900m (2006); US$5,400 per capita (2006)
Annual average growth of GDP – 5.1 per cent (2007 est)
Inflation rate – 8.5 per cent (2007 est)
Unemployment – 9.7 per cent (2007 est)
Total external debt – US$226,400m (2007)
Imports – US$134,000m (2006)
Exports – US$82,000m (2006)

BALANCE OF PAYMENTS
Trade – US$51,672m deficit (2006)
Current Account – US$32,193m deficit (2006)

Trade with UK	*2006*	*2007*
Imports from UK	£2,480,948,000	£2,337,551,857
Exports to UK	£4,038,493,000	£4,728,559,416

COMMUNICATIONS

Turkey has nearly 430,000km of roads, of which about a third are surfaced. There are over 8,600km of railways, and 1,200km of navigable waterways. The principal ports are Istanbul (Europe) and Izmir (Asia). There is a large merchant fleet, with 565 ships of 1,000 tonnes or over registered in Turkey and 470 Turkish-owned ships registered overseas. The principal airports are at Istanbul and Ankara.

Telecommunications systems are being modernised and expanded, especially the mobile phone network. There were 18.9 million main lines in use in 2005, and 52.6 million mobile phone subscribers and 12.2 million internet users in 2006.

EDUCATION AND HEALTH

Education is free, secular and compulsory from the ages of six to 14. There are elementary, secondary and vocational schools.

Literacy rate – 88.3 per cent (2004 est)
Gross enrolment ratio (percentage of relevant age group) – primary 94 per cent; secondary 74 per cent; tertiary 31 per cent (2006 est)
Health expenditure (per capita) – US$383 (2005)
Hospital beds (per 1,000 people) – 2.6 (2000–6)

MEDIA

The authorities monitor and censor broadcasts that cover sensitive political subjects, and the press is also subject to some censorship, although many of the restrictions have been lifted to comply with EU requirements. Turkey has one state television and radio station, TRT, over 300 private television channels and more than 1,000 private radio stations. TRT has begun to broadcast Kurdish-language programmes, to conform with the EU criteria on minority rights. There are several daily newspapers, including *Hurriyet, Milliyet* and *Cumhuriyet,* and the English-language *Turkish Daily News.*

CULTURE

Turkey is rich in archaeological remains, including Ephesus, a religious and cultural centre in Greek and Roman times, and an important centre of early Christianity; Troy, the Homeric city of Ilium; and a wealth of sites from Roman, Byzantine, early Christian and Ottoman periods. Ankara (or Ancyra as it was known in Roman times) was the capital of the Roman province of *Galatia Prima,* and a marble temple (now in ruins), dedicated to Augustus, contains the *Monumentum (Marmor) Ancyranum,* inscribed with a record of the reign of Augustus Caesar.

The Roman city of Byzantium was selected by Constantine the Great as the capital of the eastern Roman Empire in AD 328 and was renamed Constantinople after the emperor's death. Now Istanbul, it contains the celebrated church of St Sophia, which, after becoming a mosque, was made a museum in 1934, and Topkapi, the former palace of the Ottoman sultans. In 2006 author Orhan Pamuk (*b.* 1952) became the first Turkish Nobel laureate.

TURKMENISTAN

Area – 488,100 sq. km
Capital – Ashgabat; population, 744,000 (2007 est)
Major cities – Dashhowuz, Turkmenabat
Currency – Manat of 100 tennesi
Population – 5,097,028 rising at 1.62 per cent per year (2007 est): Turkmen (85 per cent), Uzbek (5 per cent), Russian (4 per cent) (est)
Religion – Islam (89 per cent) (est)
Language – Turkmen (official), Russian, Uzbek
Population density – 10 per sq. km (2006)
Urban population – 45.8 per cent (2005 est)
Median age (years) – 22.3 (2007 est)
National anthem – 'Garashciiz Bitarap Turkmenistaniin Devlet Gimni' ['Independent Neutral Turkmenistan State Anthem']
National day – 27 October (Independence Day)
Life expectancy (years) – 68.3 (2007 est)
Mortality rate – 6.17 (2007 est)
Birth rate – 25.36 (2007 est)
Infant mortality rate – 53.40 (2007 est)
Death penalty – Abolished for all crimes (since 1999)
CPI score – 2.0 (2007)
Population below poverty line – 27 per cent (2002)
Literacy rate – 98.8 per cent (2004 est)
Health expenditure (per capita) – US$156 (2005)
Hospital beds (per 1,000 people) – 4.9 (2000–6)

CLIMATE AND TERRAIN

Over 80 per cent of the country is taken up by the Kara Kum (Black Sands) desert. There are mountains in the south, and areas below sea level along the edges of the Caspian Sea. Elevation extremes range from 3,139m (Gora Ayribaba) at the highest point to −81m (Lake Akchanaya; because of fluctuations in its water level, Lake Sarykamysh sometimes has a lower elevation) at the lowest. Average temperatures in Ashgabat range from 0°C in January to 34°C in July. The heat of the summers is tempered by low humidity.

HISTORY AND POLITICS

Turkmenistan has been invaded and occupied by many empires, including the Persian, Greek (under Alexander the Great), Parthian and Mongol. From the early 19th century until 1886 Turkmenistan was gradually incorporated into the Russian Empire. A Turkmen revolt against Russian rule in 1916 brought a period of autonomy until 1921, when Soviet control over Turkmenistan was established and it became an Autonomous Soviet Socialist Republic. Turkmenistan became a full republic of the USSR in 1925. It declared its independence from the USSR on 27 October 1991.

Saparmurat Niyazov became leader of the Turkmen Communist Party in 1985, and was elected president in 1990 and re-elected in 1992. After extending his term of office to 2002 the legislature removed it altogether and elected him president for life in 2004. His autocratic regime, through harassment and authoritarianism, prevented the development of any effective political opposition or press freedom, rejecting political pluralism in favour of a cult of personality.

The Democratic Party of Turkmenistan (DP), the renamed Communist Party, is the only legal political party, and held all the seats in the parliament after the elections of 1998 and 2004–5. President Niyazov died in December 2006 and Kurbanguly Berdymukhamedov became interim president before being elected to the post in February 2007. Although the regime remains authoritarian, President Berdymukhamedov has introduced some economic and social welfare reforms.

POLITICAL SYSTEM

The 1992 constitution was amended in 1999 to remove restrictions on the number of terms a president can serve, and in 2003 to alter the status, powers and composition of the People's Council. The president is head of state and head of government, directly elected for a five-year term. The parliament *(Majlis)* has 50 members directly elected for a five-year term. The People's Council *(Khalk Maslakhaty)* is the supreme representative, legislative and supervisory body. It has 2,507 members: the president, the council of ministers, the 50 members of the parliament, regional governors, 50 elected and 10 appointed members from each region, and ethnic and regional representatives.

The country is divided into five regions: Ahal, Balkan, Dashowuz, Lebap and Mary, plus the city of Ashgabat.

HEAD OF STATE

President, Chair of the Council of Ministers, Kurbanguly Berdymukhamedov, *elected* 14 February 2007

SELECTED GOVERNMENT MEMBERS *as at July 2008*

First Deputy Chair, Foreign Affairs, Rashid Meredov
Defence, Col.-Gen. Agageldy Mamedgeldiyev
Economy and Finance, Hojamyrat Geldimyradov
Interior, Orazgeldi Amanmyradov

EMBASSY OF TURKMENISTAN

2nd Floor, St George's House, 14–17 Wells Street, London W1T 3PD
T 020-7255 1071
Ambassador Extraordinary and Plenipotentiary, HE Yazmurad N. Seryayev, *apptd* 2003

BRITISH EMBASSY

3rd Floor, Office Building, Four Points Ak Altin Hotel, Ashgabat
T (+993) (12) 363 462 E beasb@online.tm
W www.britishembassy.gov.uk/turkmenistan
Ambassador Extraordinary and Plenipotentiary, HE Peter Butcher, *apptd* 2005

DEFENCE

The army has 670 main battle tanks, 829 armoured personnel carriers and 942 armoured infantry fighting vehicles. The navy has 6 patrol and coastal combatant vessels. The air force has 94 combat aircraft and 10 armed helicopters.

Military expenditure – US$450m (2005)

Military personnel – 22,000: army 18,500, navy 500, air force 3,000
Conscription duration – 24 months

ECONOMY AND TRADE

The post-independence regime has been reluctant to adopt market reforms; most economic activity remains in state control and is inefficient. Although Turkmenistan has large reserves of natural gas and oil, exports have hitherto been restricted by the lack of export routes. However, new gas pipelines are being built westwards to Turkey, eastwards to China and northwards through Kazakhstan to Russia. However, government misuse of the revenues from these commodities means that little has been done to alleviate the widespread poverty or high level of unemployment.

Agriculture is intensive around the irrigated oases, with half the irrigated land used to grow cotton, although exports of this commodity have halved in recent years owing to poor harvests. Agriculture accounts for 11.5 per cent of GDP and 48 per cent of employment; grain and livestock are the other main products. The principal industries are gas and oil production, petroleum products, the silk industry and food processing.

The main export markets are Ukraine and Iran; imports come chiefly from the UAE, Turkey, Ukraine and Russia. Principal exports are gas, crude oil, petrochemicals, textiles and cotton fibre. The main imports are machinery and equipment, chemicals and foodstuffs.

GNI – US$5,400m (2003); US$1,120 per capita (2003)
Annual average growth of GDP – 7 per cent (2007 est)
Inflation rate – 11.3 per cent (2007 est)
Unemployment – 60 per cent (2004 est)
Total external debt – US$2,259m (2000)

BALANCE OF PAYMENTS
Trade – US$554m surplus (2006)
Current Account – US$3,351m surplus (2006)

Trade with UK	*2006*	*2007*
Imports from UK	£15,591,000	£16,714,492
Exports to UK	£26,613,000	£5,612,940

COMMUNICATIONS

Turkmenistan has 24,000km of roads, nearly 20,000km of which are surfaced. There are 2,440km of railways. There are two important waterways, the Amu Darya river in the north-east and the Niyazov (formerly Kara Kum) canal running across the Kara Kum desert from the Amu Darya to the Caspian Sea, providing 1,300km of transport routes. The main port is Turkmenbashi, on the Caspian Sea, and the main airport is at Ashgabat.

Telecommunications networks are underdeveloped but are to be upgraded. There were 495,000 main lines in use, 216,900 mobile phone subscribers and 64,800 internet users in 2006.

MEDIA

The government has total control of broadcast and print media. Newspapers are produced on government-owned presses, programmes from broadcasters other than the state channels are censored before airing in Turkmenistan, and internet access is controlled by the country's communication authorities. According to Reporters Without Borders, only Eritrea has lower press freedom.

TUVALU

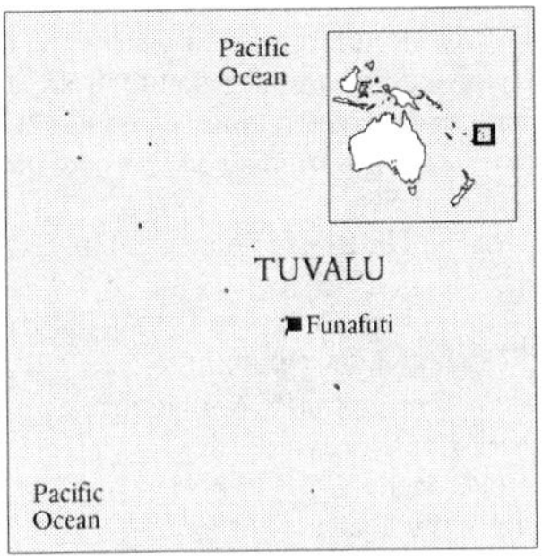

Area – 26 sq. km
Capital – Funafuti; population, 5,000 (2007 est)
Currency – The Australian dollar (A$) of 100 cents is legal tender. In addition there are Tuvalu dollar and cent coins in circulation
Population – 11,992 rising at 1.54 per cent per year (2007 est): Polynesian (96 per cent), Micronesian (4 per cent) (est)
Religion – Protestantism (96 per cent), Baha'i (3 per cent), Roman Catholicism (1 per cent) (est)
Language – English (official), Tuvaluan, Samoan, I-Kiribati
Population density – 423 per sq. km (1999)
Urban population – 57 per cent (2005 est)
Median age (years) – 24.9 (2007 est)
National anthem – 'Tuvalu mo te Atua' ['Tuvalu for the Almighty']
National day – 1 October (Independence Day)
Life expectancy (years) – 68.63 (2007 est)
Mortality rate – 7 (2007 est)
Birth rate – 22.43 (2007 est)
Infant mortality rate – 18.9 (2007 est)
Death penalty – Abolished for all crimes (since 1978)

CLIMATE AND TERRAIN

Tuvalu comprises nine low-lying islands, five of them coral atolls, in the south-west Pacific Ocean. The highest elevation is 5m and the lowest 0m (Pacific Ocean). The climate is tropical, with average temperatures of 26°C all year round.

HISTORY AND POLITICS

The islands were discovered by Europeans in the 18th century and, as the Ellice Islands, came under the control of the British in 1877. They formed part of the Gilbert and Ellice Islands protectorate (later a colony) from 1892, but were granted separate status from the Gilbert Islands in 1975. Tuvalu became a fully independent state on 1 October 1978. The country is seriously affected by rising sea levels, which are threatening its economic viability.

There are no political parties; allegiances are influenced by geography and personalities. Although politically stable as a democracy, there are frequent changes in government as support in parliament shifts. Most of the government lost their seats in the 2006 legislative election and a new cabinet was appointed following the election of Apisai Ielemia as prime minister.

POLITICAL SYSTEM
Under the 1978 constitution, Tuvalu is a constitutional monarchy with the British monarch as head of state,

represented by a governor-general who is appointed on the advice of the prime minister. The unicameral legislature, the Parliament of Tuvalu, has 15 members who are directly elected for a four-year term. The prime minister is elected by the legislature from among its members, and appoints the cabinet, who must be members of parliament. Local government services are provided by elected island councils.

Governor-General, HE Revd Filoimea Telito, GCMG, MBE

SELECTED GOVERNMENT MEMBERS *as at July 2008*
Prime Minister, Foreign Affairs, Apisai Ielemia
Deputy Prime Minister, Taavau Teii
Finance, Lotoala Metia
Home Affairs, Willy Telavi

HONORARY CONSULATE OF TUVALU
Tuvalu House, 230 Worple Road, London SW20 8RH
T 020-8879 0985
Honorary Consul, Dr Iftikhar A. Ayaz

BRITISH HIGH COMMISSIONER
HE Roger Sykes, *apptd* 2006, resident at Suva, Fiji

ECONOMY AND TRADE

The main economic activities are subsistence agriculture and fishing, although agricultural productivity is threatened by the increasing salinity of the soil as the sea level rises; the only cash crop is coconuts. Tourism is small-scale. Most employment is in the public sector or abroad, often as merchant seamen; many families rely on remittances from expatriate workers. The government receives substantial annual income from a trust fund set up in 1987, and raises revenue through the sale of fishing licences, postage stamps and coins, and the leasing of its 900 telephone code and .tv internet suffix. The main trading partners are Fiji and Germany. The only exports are copra and fish. The main imports are foodstuffs, livestock, fuels, machinery and manufactured goods.
Annual average growth of GDP – 1.2 per cent (2002 est)
Inflation rate – 3.9 per cent (2005 est)

Trade with UK	*2006*	*2007*
Imports from UK	£174,000	£5,161
Exports to UK	—	—

COMMUNICATIONS

Funafuti has an airfield, from which a service operates regularly to Fiji and Kiribati, and it is also the main port. There are 8km of roads on the islands. The telephone system provides an adequate service, with 900 main lines in use in 2005 and 1,300 internet users in 2002.

MEDIA

The government runs Radio Tuvalu, the primary source of information. There is no domestic television, although many islanders watch foreign programming via satellite. The state-owned Tuvalu Media Corporation publishes a newspaper in both Tuvaluan and English. The state respects the freedom of the press.

UGANDA

Republic of Uganda

Area – 236,040 sq. km
Capital – Kampala; population, 1,420,000 (2007 est)
Major towns – Gulu, Lira
Currency – Uganda shilling of 100 cents
Population – 30,262,610 rising at 3.57 per cent per year (2007 est); Banganda (16.9 per cent), Banyakole (9.5 per cent), Basoga (8.4 per cent), Bakiga (6.9 per cent), Iteso (6.4 per cent), Langi (6.1 per cent), Acholi (4.7 per cent), Bagisu (4.6 per cent), Lugbara (4.2 per cent), Bunyoro (2.7 per cent)
Religion – Roman Catholicism (36 per cent), Protestantism (31 per cent), Islam (12 per cent) (est). Indigenous beliefs are often blended into or are observed alongside recognised religions
Language – English (official), Ganda, Swahili, Arabic
Population density – 152 per sq. km (2006)
Urban population – 12.4 per cent (2005 est)
Median age (years) – 14.9 (2007 est)
National anthem – 'O Uganda, Land of Beauty'
National day – 9 October (Independence Day)
Life expectancy (years) – 51.75 (2007 est)
Mortality rate – 12.64 (2007 est)
Birth rate – 48.12 (2007 est)
Infant mortality rate – 67.22 (2007 est)
HIV/AIDS adult prevalence – 6.3 per cent (2005 est)
Death penalty – Retained
CPI score – 2.8 (2007)
Population below poverty line – 35 per cent (2001 est)

CLIMATE AND TERRAIN

The landlocked country lies on a high plateau with mountain ranges in the south and along the north-eastern border. Elevation extremes range from 5,110m (Mt Stanley) at the highest point to 621m (Lake Albert) at the lowest. Nearly 20 per cent of the country is covered by lakes, rivers and wetlands, and it contains about half of lakes Victoria, Edward and Albert (Mobuto), as well as lakes Kyoga, Kwania, George and Bisina (formerly Salisbury) and the course of the Nile from its outlet from Lake Victoria to the Sudan border at Nimule. There is a wet season from December to February. The average temperature in Kampala is an almost constant 24°C.

HISTORY AND POLITICS

Indigenous people had formed several kingdoms in the area by the 14th century. External contact began in the early 19th century with Arab traders and then European explorers. A British protectorate was established over the kingdom of Buganda in 1893 and gradually extended to other territory by 1903. Uganda became an independent state on 9 October 1962, as a federation of the kingdoms of Ankole, Buganda, Bunyoro, Busoga and Toro.

In 1963 it was proclaimed a federal republic but in 1966 prime minister Milton Obote overthrew the president, ended the federal status and became executive president. In 1971 President Obote was deposed in an army coup led by Maj.-Gen. Idi Amin, who proclaimed himself head of state. His repressive dictatorship was overthrown in 1979 after a failed attempt to invade northern Tanzania.

Milton Obote was re-elected president in 1980 but political instability and human rights abuses continued. He was ousted by a military coup in 1985 amid a civil war with the rebel National Resistance Army (NRA) led by Yoweri Museveni. A military council was installed but the NRA captured Kampala in January 1986, securing control of the rest of the country in the following few months. Museveni began a process of reconstruction which has resulted in Uganda becoming relatively peaceful and stable, and restored a degree of prosperity.

Museveni was sworn in as president in January 1986, and won the first direct presidential election in May 1996. In the subsequent legislative election, the majority of seats were won by supporters of his 'Movement' system of government, under which political parties are allowed to exist but not to contest elections. President Museveni was re-elected in 2001, and in the 2001 legislative election most of the seats were won by his supporters. A 2005 referendum resulted in an overwhelming vote in favour of a return to multiparty politics, suspended since 1986, and also abolished the restriction on the number of terms a president may serve. In multiparty elections held in 2006, President Museveni was re-elected in the second round of the presidential election with 59 per cent of the vote, and the National Resistance Movement retained its majority in parliament.

INSURGENCIES

The Lord's Resistance Army (LRA) is an insurgent group whose aims have never been specified. In its low-level insurgency from the late 1980s, thousands were massacred or mutilated, an estimated 20,000 children abducted to serve in its forces, and over 1.6 million displaced into camps. Originally confined to the north of the country, in 2003 LRA attacks also started to occur in the east. Peace talks between the government and the LRA began in 2006 and a permanent ceasefire was signed in February 2008.

POLITICAL SYSTEM

The 1995 constitution was amended in 2005 to allow multiparty elections and to remove the restriction on the number of terms a president can serve. The president is directly elected for a five-year term. The unicameral parliament has 215 directly elected members and 94 (including 69 women) elected indirectly to represent particular groups; all serve a five-year term. The prime minister is appointed by the president, subject to the approval of parliament.

HEAD OF STATE

President, Commander-in-Chief of the Armed Forces, Yoweri Museveni, *sworn in* 29 January 1986, *elected* 9 May 1996, *re-elected* 2001, 2006

Vice-President, Gilbert Balibaseka Bukenya

SELECTED GOVERNMENT MEMBERS *as at July 2008*

Prime Minister, Apolo Nsibambi

Deputy Prime Ministers, Henry Muganwa Kajura; Eriya Kategaya; Ali Kirunda Kivejinja

Defence, Crispus W. C. B. Kiyonga

Finance, Ezra Sumura

Internal Affairs, Ruhakana Rugunda

Foreign Affairs, Sam Kutesa

UGANDA HIGH COMMISSION

Uganda House, 58–59 Trafalgar Square, London WC2N 5DX

T 020-7839 5783 E info@ugandahighcommission.co.uk

W www.ugandahighcommission.co.uk

High Commissioner, HE Joan Kakima Rwabyomere, *apptd* 2006

BRITISH HIGH COMMISSION

PO Box 7070, 10–12 Parliament Avenue, Kampala

T (+256) (31) 312 000 E bhcinfo@starcom.co.ug

W www.britain.or.ug

High Commissioner, HE Francois Gordon, CMG, *apptd* 2005

BRITISH COUNCIL

PO Box 7070, Rwenzori Courts, Plot 2 and 4A, Nakasero Road, Kampala

T (+256) (41) 456 800 W www.britishcouncil.org/uganda

Director, Richard Weyers

DEFENCE

The army has 152 main battle tanks and 79 armoured personnel carriers. The air force has 14 combat capable aircraft and 6 armed helicopters.

Military budget – US$226m (2007)

Military personnel – 45,000: Ugandan People's Defence Force 45,000; paramilitary 1,800

ECONOMY AND TRADE

Economic reforms introduced after 1986 have produced steady economic growth and the reduction of inflation since 1990, but there has been little industrialisation and the economy is vulnerable to fluctuations in the global price of coffee, its main export. Uganda's debt burden has been reduced by the US$2bn (£1bn) debt relief received since 2000 but it is still dependent on foreign aid; some of this has been withheld recently because of donors' concerns about the regime's increasing autocracy.

Agriculture is the most important economic sector, contributing 30.2 per cent of GDP and engaging about 80 per cent of the workforce. The principal crops are coffee, tea, cotton, tobacco, cassava, potatoes, maize, millet, pulses, cut flowers and livestock products. Industrial activity centres on production of sugar, tobacco, cotton textiles, cement and steel, brewing and fishing. The main export markets are EU countries; imports come chiefly from Kenya and the UAE. Principal exports are coffee, fish and fish products, tea, cotton, cut flowers, horticultural products and gold. Electricity is exported to Kenya, Tanzania and Rwanda. The main imports are capital equipment, vehicles, petroleum, medical supplies and cereals.

GNI – US$9,000m (2006); US$300 per capita (2006)

Annual average growth of GDP – 6 per cent (2007 est)

Inflation rate – 5.8 per cent (2007 est)

Total external debt – US$1,390m (2007 est)

Imports – US$2,500m (2006)

Exports – US$970m (2006)

BALANCE OF PAYMENTS

Trade – US$1,535m deficit (2006)

Current Account – US$379m deficit (2006)

Trade with UK	*2006*	*2007*
Imports from UK	£38,978,000	£46,654,544
Exports to UK	£12,946,000	£16,423,974

COMMUNICATIONS

There is over 1,200km of rail track, and 70,700km of roads, of which 16,300km are surfaced. Having no coast, Uganda is dependent upon rail and road links to Mombasa in Kenya and Dar es Salaam in Tanzania for much of its trade, although the lakes and the river Nile provide navigable routes internally and to neighbouring countries. There is an international airport at Entebbe, and 30 other airports and airfields around the country.

The fixed-line telephone system is inadequate and mobile phone distribution is growing rapidly. In 2006 there were 108,000 main lines in use, 2 million mobile phone subscribers and 750,000 internet users.

EDUCATION AND HEALTH

Education is a joint undertaking by the government, local authorities and voluntary agencies. In 1996 the Universal Primary Programme was launched, under which four children per family are entitled to receive free primary education.

Literacy rate – 68.9 per cent (2004 est)
Gross enrolment ratio (percentage of relevant age group) – primary 117 per cent; secondary 18 per cent; tertiary 3 per cent (2006 est)
Health expenditure (per capita) – US$22 (2005)
Hospital beds (per 1,000 people) – 0.7 (2000–6)

MEDIA

In addition to one television station and one radio station in state ownership, there are more than 100 private radio and television stations, most of which have appeared after the loosening of media laws in 1993. There are two main newspapers, *New Vision* and *The Monitor*. The state has been known to interfere when reporting is perceived to raise racial tension.

UKRAINE

Ukrayina – Ukraine

Area – 603,700 sq. km
Capital – Kyiv (Kiev); population, 2,709,000 (2007 est)
Major cities – Dnipropetrovsk, Donetsk, Kharkiv, L'viv, Odesa, Zaporizhzhya
Currency – Hryvna of 100 kopiykas
Population – 46,299,862 falling at 0.68 per cent per year (2007 est); Ukrainian (77.8 per cent), Russian (17.3 per cent). There are smaller Belarusian, Molodovan, Tatar, Polish, Hungarian and Greek communities
Religion – Orthodox Christianity (23 per cent), other Christian denominations (10 per cent) (est)
Language – Ukrainian (official), Russian
Population density – 81 per sq. km (2006)
Urban population – 67.3 per cent (2005 est)
Median age (years) – 39.2 (2007 est)
National anthem – 'Shche ne vmerla, Ukrainy' ['Thou Hast Not Perished, Ukraine']
National day – 24 August (Independence Day)
Life expectancy (years) – 67.88 (2007 est)
Mortality rate – 16.07 (2007 est)
Birth rate – 9.45 (2007 est)
Infant mortality rate – 9.5 (2007 est)
HIV/AIDS adult prevalence – 1 per cent (2005 est)
Death penalty – Abolished for all crimes (since 1999)
CPI score – 2.7 (2007)
Population below poverty line – 37.7 per cent (2003)

CLIMATE AND TERRAIN

Much of the country lies in a plain, rising to steppes and then to the Carpathian mountains in the west, and the mountains in the south of the Crimean peninsula. Elevation extremes range from 2,061m (Hora Hoverla) at the highest point to 0m (Black Sea) at the lowest. The main rivers are the Dnieper, which runs through the centre of the country, the Dniester in the west, the Southern Buh and the Northern Donets (a tributary of the Don). Despite cold winters, the climate is more temperate than in neighbouring Russia. Average temperatures in Kyiv, in the colder north of the country, range from −8°C in January to 28°C in June.

HISTORY AND POLITICS

The earliest Slavic state was formed in the middle reaches of the river Dnieper with its capital at Kyiv in the ninth century AD. The area was invaded successively by the Goths, Huns and Khazars, and then by the Tatar-Mongols in the 13th century. It came under Lithuanian rule in the 14th to 15th centuries, Polish rule in the 16th century, and gradually became part of Russia in the 17th to 18th centuries.

Ukraine declared its independence in 1918, and a civil war ensued between Ukrainian nationalists, Bolsheviks, anarchists, Russian monarchists and the Poles, which ended in 1921 with the partitioning of Ukraine between the USSR and Poland. In 1922 Ukraine became a constituent republic of the USSR. Germany invaded and occupied Ukraine from 1941 until forced to withdraw by the Red Army in 1944. Ukraine gained territory in the west in the aftermath of the Second World War, and in 1954 the Crimea was transferred from Russia to Ukraine.

In 1986 Ukraine was the scene of the world's worst nuclear disaster, when a reactor at the Chernobyl nuclear plant exploded. At least 10,000 people have died from radiation poisoning, the long-term health of millions more has been affected and a large area of the country is permanently contaminated.

Ukraine declared itself independent of the USSR on 24 August 1991. Independence was confirmed by a referendum in December 1991 and Leonid Kravchuk was elected to the presidency. In the 1994 presidential election Leonid Kuchma defeated President Kravchuk and won a further term of office in 1999. His resignation was demanded in mass protests after the 2002 legislative election resulted in a hung parliament amid allegations of electoral fraud. The Our Ukraine bloc, an alliance of parties opposed to President Kuchma, was the largest party but a coalition government was formed by supporters of the president and a number of independents.

The 2004 presidential election illustrated Ukraine's divide between the Russian-influenced and industrial east and the pro-European west. The announcement of a victory for the pro-Russian Viktor Yanukovych, despite observers' reports of widespread vote-rigging, triggered mass demonstrations and civil disobedience by supporters of the rival candidate, pro-western Viktor Yushchenko, with counter-demonstrations by Yanukovych's followers. The supreme court annulled the result and ordered a rerun, which was held in December 2004 and won by Viktor Yushchenko, with 52 per cent of the vote.

The tensions between the pro-Russian and pro-western political blocs, and divisions within the pro-western parties, has caused political instability since 2004, with three changes of government and two legislative elections. The latest election, in September 2007, was called after a power struggle between President Yushchenko and Viktor Yanukovych, prime minister from July 2006, produced a political impasse. Yanukovych's Party of Regions remained the largest party in the legislature but without an outright majority, and President Yushchenko's Our Ukraine–People's Self Defence Bloc and the Yuliya Tymoshenko Bloc formed a coalition government headed by Yuliya Tymoshenko (prime minister January–September 2005).

SECESSION

The predominantly Russian Crimea was transferred to Ukrainian rule in 1954. In September 1991 the Crimean parliament voted to make Crimea an autonomous republic, a vote that was accepted by the newly independent Ukraine. However, when the Crimean parliament voted in favour of independence in 1992, Ukraine did not accept the decision and the parliament was suspended. In 1994 the parliament attempted to restore the declaration of sovereignty, leading eventually to Ukraine imposing direct presidential rule over Crimea that ended only after parliamentary elections in 1995 saw a dramatic drop in support for pro-Russian parties. Since 1999 Crimea has had considerable autonomy.

FOREIGN RELATIONS

In the aftermath of the USSR's disintegration in 1991, relations between Ukraine and Russia were strained by disputes over the Black Sea fleet and the status of Crimea. Agreement over the division of the fleet was reached in 1997, but Russia's lease for the use of Sevastapol as a naval base until 2017 is a continuing focus of tension. Disputes over Crimea have flared up intermittently, most recently in 2003 over a border in the region. The main causes of tension are the pro-Western policies pursued by recent governments, particularly the possibility of Ukraine joining NATO, and the economic interdependence of the two countries; Ukraine is heavily dependent on Russia for gas supplies, and the pipelines carrying Russia's gas exports to Europe pass through Ukraine. In January 2006 Russia briefly cut Ukraine's supplies in a price dispute; in Ukraine the move was perceived to be politically motivated.

Ukraine signed a partnership and cooperation agreement with the EU in 1994, and EU membership is a declared long-term objective of the current president. Ukraine was involved in NATO's Partnership for Peace programme in the 1990s, and its application for NATO membership is under consideration.

POLITICAL SYSTEM

The 1996 constitution was amended in 2006 to transfer some powers from the president to the legislature. The head of state is a president, directly elected for a five-year term. The unicameral legislature, the Supreme Council, has 450 members, who are directly elected for a five-year term.

The country is divided into 24 provinces, the autonomous republic of Crimea and two municipalities (Kyiv and Sevastapol) with provincial status.

HEAD OF STATE

President, Viktor Yushchenko, *elected* 26 December 2004, *sworn in* 23 January 2005

SELECTED GOVERNMENT MEMBERS *as at July 2008*

Prime Minister, Yuliya Tymoshenko
First Deputy Prime Minister, Oleksandr Turchynov
Deputy Prime Ministers, Vitaliy Hayduk; Hryhoriy Nemyrya; Ivan Vasyunyk
Finance, Viktor Pynzenyk
Interior, Yuriy Lutsenko
Defence, Yuriy Yekhanurov
Foreign Affairs, Volodymyr Ohryzko
Economy, Anatoliy Kinakh

EMBASSY OF UKRAINE

60 Holland Park, London W11 3SJ
T 020-7727 6312 E emb_gb@mfa.gov.ua
W www.ukremb.org.uk
Ambassador Extraordinary and Plenipotentiary, Dr Ihor Y. Kharchenko, *apptd* 2005

BRITISH EMBASSY

Desyatinna 9, 01025 Kyiv
T (+380) (44) 462 0011 E ukembinf@sovamua.com
W www.britemb-ukraine.net
Ambassador Extraordinary and Plenipotentiary, HE Timothy Barrow, CMG, *apptd* 2006

BRITISH COUNCIL

4/12 Vul. Hryhoriya Skovorody, Kyiv 04070
T (+380) (44) 490 5600 W www.britishcouncil.org/ukraine
Director, Terry Sandell, OBE, FRSA

DEFENCE

The army has 2,984 main battle tanks, 1,432 armoured personnel carriers, 2,818 armoured infantry fighting vehicles and 139 armed helicopters. The navy has 1 submarine, 1 frigate, 4 corvettes 5 patrol and coastal vessels, 10 combat aircraft and 72 armed helicopters at 6 bases. The air force has 211 combat aircraft.

Military budget – US$1,810m (2007)
Military personnel – 129,925: army 70,753, navy 13,932, air force 45,240; paramilitaries 84,900
Conscription duration – 18–24 months

ECONOMY AND TRADE

The first decade of independence was characterised by economic mismanagement and opposition to economic restructuring. Reform began in the late 1990s and brought economic growth, with rises in output and exports and a reduction in inflation. However, the slow progress of reform is proving a drag on the economy, leaving it vulnerable to external factors, and corruption remains a major problem, discouraging overseas investors.

Ukraine's agricultural sector is large and productive, with over half the land under cultivation. The main crops are cereals, sugar beet, sunflowers and vegetables; stock-raising and dairy-farming are also important. Agriculture accounts for 9.1 per cent of GDP and nearly a quarter of employment. There are large deposits of coal, iron ore and other minerals. Mining and metal processing, along with the manufacture of machinery and transport equipment and chemical and petrochemical industries are major contributors to Ukraine's GDP. Industrial activities also include electricity generation and food processing, especially of sugar.

The main trading partners are Russia (21 per cent of exports; 28 per cent of imports), Germany, Poland, Turkey, China and Italy. Principal exports are ferrous and non-ferrous metals, fuel and petroleum products, chemicals, machinery and transport equipment, and foodstuffs. The main imports are energy (primarily gas), machinery and equipment, and chemicals.

GNI – US$90,700m (2006); US$1,940 per capita (2006)
Annual average growth of GDP – 6.9 per cent (2007 est)
Inflation rate – 11.3 per cent (2007 est)
Unemployment – 2.5 per cent (2007 est)
Total external debt – US$65,380m (2007)
Imports – US$45,000m (2006)
Exports – US$38,000m (2006)

BALANCE OF PAYMENTS
Trade – US$6,671m deficit (2006)
Current Account – US$1,617m deficit (2006)

Trade with UK	*2006*	*2007*
Imports from UK	£337,863,000	£439,574,718
Exports to UK	£128,552,000	£129,545,797

COMMUNICATIONS

Ukraine has a total of 170,000km of roads, 165,000km of which are surfaced. it has 22,500km of railways, and 2,200km of waterways, mostly on the River Dnieper. its main seaports are Mariupol on the Sea of Azov, and Kherson, Mykolayiv, Odesa and Sevastopol on the Black Sea. there is a large merchant fleet of 193 ships of 1,000 tonnes and over, with a further 194 Ukrainian-owned ships registered in other countries. the principal airports are at Kyiv and Odesa.

The fixed-line telephone system was antiquated and is being improved, although density remains low, and mobile phone distribution is rising rapidly. There were 12.3 million main lines in use, over 30 million mobile phone subscribers and 5.5 million internet users in 2006.

EDUCATION AND HEALTH

Literacy rate – 99.4 per cent (2004 est)
Gross enrolment ratio (percentage of relevant age group) – primary 102 per cent; secondary 93 per cent; tertiary 73 per cent (2006 est)
Health expenditure (per capita) – US$128 (2005)
Hospital beds (per 1,000 people) – 8.7 (2000–6)

MEDIA

There are several private and state-owned television and radio networks. Ukraine has seven daily newspapers, many of which are mass-circulation publications; titles include *Silski Visti* and *Segodnya*. The independence of the press has become much more apparent since the disputed presidential election of 2004, and has been encouraged by President Yushchenko.

UNITED ARAB EMIRATES

Al-Imarat al-Arabiyah al-Muttahidah – United Arab Emirates

Area – 83,600 sq. km approximately.
Capital – Abu Dhabi; population, 603,000 (2007 est)
Major cities – Ajman, Al-Ain, Ash Shariqah, Dubai
Currency – UAE dirham (Dh) of 100 fils
Population – 4,444,011 rising at 4 per cent per year (2007 est)
Religion – Islam (76 per cent), Christianity (9 per cent) (est)
Language – Arabic (official), Persian, English, Hindi, Urdu
Population density – 51 per sq. km (2006)
Urban population – 85.5 per cent (2005 est)
Median age (years) – 30.1 (2007 est)
National anthem – 'Ishy Bilady' ['Long Live My Homeland']
National day – 2 December (Independence Day)
Life expectancy (years) – 75.69 (2007 est)
Mortality rate – 2.16 (2007 est)
Birth rate – 16.09 (2007 est)
Infant mortality rate – 13.52 (2007 est)
Death penalty – Retained
CPI score – 5.7 (2007)
Population below poverty line – 19.5 per cent (2003)

CLIMATE AND TERRAIN

The United Arab Emirates (UAE) is situated in the south-east of the Arabian peninsula. Six of the emirates lie on the shore of the Gulf, between the Musandam peninsula in the east and the Qatar peninsula in the west, while the seventh, Fujairah, lies on the Gulf of Oman. Much of the inland terrain is desert, leading to a flat coastal plain, and there are mountains in the east. Elevation extremes range from 1,527m (Jabal Yibir) at the highest point to 0m (Persian Gulf) at the lowest. Average temperatures in Sharjah range between 12°C in January to 38°C in August. Humidity is very high between May and September.

HISTORY AND POLITICS

The United Arab Emirates (formerly the Trucial States) is composed of seven emirates. Six of these came together as an independent state on 2 December 1971 when they ended their individual special treaty relationships with the British government, and they were joined by Ras al-Khaimah on 10 February 1972. On independence, the union government assumed full responsibility for all internal and external affairs apart from some internal matters that remained the prerogative of the individual emirates.

Sheikh Zayed of Abu Dhabi was president from

independence until his death in 2004. He was succeeded as Sultan of Abu Dhabi by his son, Sheikh Khalifa, who was also elected president of the UAE. The first national elections were held in 2006, when half the members of the Federal National Council were elected by a small electoral college.

POLITICAL SYSTEM
The provisional constitution in use since 1971 was finally approved in 1996. Overall authority lies with the Supreme Council of Rulers, comprising the hereditary rulers of the seven emirates, each of whom also governs in his own territory. The president and vice-president are elected every five years by the Supreme Council from among its members. The president appoints the prime minister and the council of ministers. The unicameral Federal National Council is a consultative body which considers draft legislation proposed by the council of ministers. It has 40 members, eight members each from Abu Dhabi and Dubai, six each from Sharjah and Ras al-Khaimah and four each for Fujairah, Umm al-Qaiwain and Ajman, who serve a two-year term; half are elected by an electoral college and half are appointed by the rulers of each emirate.

HEAD OF STATE
President, HH Sheikh Khalifa bin Zayed al-Nahyan *(Abu Dhabi), elected* 3 November 2004
Vice-President, Prime Minister, Defence, HH Sheikh Mohammed bin Rashid al-Maktoum *(Dubai)*

SELECTED GOVERNMENT MEMBERS *as at July 2008*
Deputy Prime Ministers, Sheikh Sultan bin Zayed al-Nahyan; Sheikh Hamdan bin Zayed al-Nahyan
Finance, HH Sheikh Hamdan bin Rashid al-Maktoum
Foreign Affairs, Sheikh Abdullah bin Zayed al-Nahyan
Interior, Lt.-Gen. Sheikh Saif bin Zayed al-Nahyan

EMBASSY OF THE UNITED ARAB EMIRATES
30 Prince's Gate, London SW7 1PT
T 020-7581 1281 E information@uaeembassyuk.net
Ambassador Extraordinary and Plenipotentiary, HE Easa Saleh al-Gurg, CBE, *apptd* 1991

BRITISH EMBASSY
PO Box 248, Abu Dhabi
T (+971) (2) 610 1100 E chancery.abudhabi@fco.gov.uk
W www.britain-uae.org
Ambassador Extraordinary and Plenipotentiary, HE Edward Oakden, CMG, *apptd* 2006

BRITISH COUNCIL
PO Box 46523, Villa No. 7, Al-Nasr Street, Khalidiya, Abu Dhabi
T (+971) (2) 691 0600 W www.britishcouncil.org/uae
Director, Paul Sellers

FEDERAL STRUCTURE
The emirates are: Abu Dhabi, Ajman, Dubai, Fujairah, Ras al-Khaimah, Sharjah and Umm al-Qaiwain. Each emirate has its own government, court system and penal code. Abu Dhabi has an executive council chaired by the crown prince.

DEFENCE
The army has 471 main battle tanks, 880 armoured personnel carriers and 430 armoured infantry fighting vehicles. The navy has 2 frigates, 2 corvettes and 14 patrol and coastal vessels at 8 bases. The air force has 184 combat aircraft and over 40 armed helicopters.
Military budget – US$10,080m (2007 est)
Military personnel – 51,000: army 44,000, navy 2,500, air force 4,500

ECONOMY AND TRADE
Exploitation of the territories' oil reserves began in the 1960s and has transformed the UAE from poor rural principalities into modern states. Oil revenues have been invested in the infrastructure and agriculture as well as education, health and social systems. The government is expanding infrastructure and job creation, and encouraging foreign investment. Oil and gas production dominate the economy, although diversification means that the hydrocarbon sector now accounts for less than 40 per cent of GDP. Other industries include fishing, manufacturing (aluminium, cement, petrochemicals, fertilisers, construction materials, handicrafts, textiles), commercial ship repair, boat-building, financial services and tourism.

There is no personal or corporate taxation, apart from on oil companies and foreign banks. There are several zones where overseas companies can trade tax-free. Agriculture is limited by the terrain but the area under cultivation has been extended by irrigation and water desalination projects. The main products are dates, vegetables, watermelons, poultry, eggs and dairy products.

The main export markets are Japan, South Korea, Thailand and India; imports come chiefly from the USA, China, India, Japan, EU countries and Japan. Principal exports are crude oil (45 per cent), natural gas, re-exports, dried fish and dates. The main imports are machinery and transport equipment, chemicals and food.
GNI – US$103,500m; US$26,210 per capita (2006)
Annual average growth of GDP – 8.5 per cent (2007 est)
Inflation rate – 12 per cent (2007 est)
Unemployment – 2.4 per cent (2001)
Total external debt – US$41,510m (2007 est)
Imports – US$95,000m (2006)
Exports – US$139,000m (2006)

BALANCE OF PAYMENTS
Trade – US$44,683m surplus (2006)
Current Account – US$35,942m surplus (2006)

Trade with UK	*2006*	*2007*
Imports from UK	£3,637,426,000	£2,755,525,064
Exports to UK	£1,101,024,000	£1,061,002,496

COMMUNICATIONS
Roads total 1,088km, all of which are surfaced, but there is no railway system. There are 15 ports, of which Abu Dhabi, Dubai and Sharjah are the most significant, and an international airport in every emirate except Ajman.

Modern telecommunications systems provide services to 1.3 million main-line subscribers, 5.5 million mobile phone subscribers and 1.7 million internet users.

EDUCATION AND HEALTH
Education is free in state schools and compulsory for ages six to 12
Literacy rate – 77.3 per cent (2004 est)
Gross enrolment ratio (percentage of relevant age group) – primary 104 per cent; secondary 90 per cent (2006 est)
Health expenditure (per capita) – US$833 (2005)
Hospital beds (per 1,000 people) – 2.2 (2000–6)

MEDIA

Dubai is an important media hub and is home to pan-Arab satellite television channels and other international media organisations, including Reuters and Sony. Residents can receive several local and pan-Arab television and radio stations. There are three national newspapers, *Al-Bayan, Gulf News* and *Khaleej Times.* A 1988 law requires the licensing of publications and outlines acceptable subjects for coverage. Self-censorship is common, despite the guarantee of freedom of speech in the constitution.

UNITED KINGDOM

United Kingdom of Great Britain and Northern Ireland

Area – 244,820 sq. km
Capital – London; population, 8,567,000 (2007 est)
Major cities – Birmingham, Bristol, Edinburgh, Glasgow, Leeds, Liverpool, Manchester, Sheffield
Currency – Pound sterling (£) of 100 pence
Population – 60,776,238 rising at 0.28 per cent per year (2007 est)
Religion – Protestantism (43 per cent), Roman Catholicism (10 per cent) Islam (3 per cent) (est)
Language – English, Welsh, Scottish Gaelic (none official)
Population density – 250 per sq. km (2006)
Urban population – 90 per cent (2005 est)
Median age (years) – 39.6 (2007 est)
National anthem – 'God Save the Queen'
Life expectancy (years) – 78.7 (2007 est)
Mortality rate – 10.09 (2007 est)
Birth rate – 10.67 (2007 est)
Infant mortality rate – 5.01 (2007 est)
Death penalty – Abolished for all crimes (since 1998)
CPI score – 8.4 (2007)
Population below poverty line – 14 per cent (2006 est)

CLIMATE AND TERRAIN

The terrain of Great Britain is higher in the north and east, with low mountains and rugged hills in Scotland, northern England and Wales; the land declines towards the south and west, with its lowest points in the south-east. Northern Ireland is more low-lying, with low mountains in the east and north. The heavily indented coastline varies in height between high cliffs and sea level. Elevation extremes range from 1,343m (Ben Nevis, Scotland) at the highest point to −4m (the Fens, eastern England) at the lowest. Although Scotland contains numerous large lochs and northern England includes a region known as the Lake District, the largest freshwater lake is Lough Neagh in Northern Ireland. The main rivers are the Thames, the Severn and the Trent in England and Wales, and the Tay in Scotland. The climate is temperate and extremes are rare, but the convergence of Atlantic, Arctic and European weather systems produces unusually changeable weather conditions. Average temperatures in London range from 2°C in January to 22°C in July.

HISTORY AND POLITICS

England, the largest of the United Kingdom's four constituent countries, was unified by the early tenth century. It experienced a period of Danish rule in the early 11th century, and then in 1066 was conquered by Duke William of Normandy. The Norman kings and their successors sought to expand their rule over the whole of Britain. Wales was conquered in the 13th century and politically united with England in 1535. English involvement in Ireland began in the 12th century and control of the whole island was finally established in Elizabeth I's reign. The succession of Elizabeth I by James VI of Scotland in 1603 united the two countries under one crown, followed by the transfer of Scottish government to Westminister by the Act of Union in 1707, creating Great Britain. Government of Ireland was transferred to Westminster in 1801, when the state became known as the United Kingdom. When the rest of Ireland became independent in 1921, the six counties of Northern Ireland chose to remain under British rule. Sectarian violence broke out in 1968 between the Protestant majority and the Roman Catholic minority over civil rights, and was continued by paramilitary forces seeking union with the Republic of Ireland until a peace process began in the 1990s. Self-government was granted to Scotland, Wales and Northern Ireland in 1999.

In 1215, facing a revolt by the barons, King John signed Magna Carta, which attempted to define good kingship and began the country's constitutional development. The attempts of the Stuart kings to extend royal powers at the expense of Parliament in the mid 17th century led to the English Civil Wars, which established the relationship of the executive to the legislature. From the late 17th century Britain embarked on a period of massive trade expansion, emerging as a major colonial power in the 18th century with control over large territories, particularly in North America and India; 13 of the North American colonies seceded in 1776 and formed the United States of America.

Industrialisation began in Britain in the second half of the 18th century, and entered a second phase after 1830 that stimulated great economic growth and further colonial expansion throughout the 19th century. But Britain's economic and political dominance declined in the 20th century, undermined by the two world wars, the second war leaving the country close to economic collapse. Most of its colonies were granted independence between 1947 and the mid 1980s, many joining the Commonwealth. After the UK joined the European Community in 1973, its economic and diplomatic focus shifted from the Commonwealth to Europe.

The Labour government elected in 1945 pursued socialist economic and welfare policies, nationalising key industries, setting up the National Health Service and expanding the social security system. Economic decline continued until the 1980s, when it was reversed by the Conservative government led by Margaret Thatcher, the country's first woman prime minister. Her administration privatised nationalised industries, opened up welfare services to market forces and reduced the role of local government, polarising politics and public opinion. She also established a close relationship with the USA that was supportive of its foreign policy. This has been continued by her successors, most recently in the support for the US 'war on terror' and the deployment of British forces in Afghanistan since 2001 and Iraq since 2003.

The 1997 legislative election was won by the Labour Party, led by Tony Blair, and it was returned to power in 2001 and 2005, although with a smaller majority in the 2005 election. Tony Blair stood down as prime minister in June 2007 and was replaced by Gordon Brown (Chancellor of the Exchequer 1997–2007).

POLITICAL SYSTEM

There is no written constitution. The head of state is a hereditary constitutional monarch. The bicameral parliament consists of the House of Commons, the lower house, and the House of Lords. The House of Commons has 659 members, directly elected for a five-year term. The House of Lords is appointed and numbers vary; in July 2007 it had 747 members, comprising 26 archbishops and bishops of the Church of England, 26 appeal judges, 603 life peers and 92 hereditary peers. The prime minister is the leader of the majority party or coalition in the lower chamber of the legislature.

Powers over certain internal matters were devolved in 1999 to Scotland, Wales and Northern Ireland, which each has its own legislature and government; devolution was suspended in Northern Ireland several times between 2000 and 2007 owing to the breakdown of power-sharing arrangements.

HEAD OF STATE

HM The Queen of the United Kingdom of Great Britain and Northern Ireland, Head of the Commonwealth, Queen Elizabeth II, *born* 21 April 1926; *succeeded* 6 February 1952; *crowned* 2 June 1953

Heir, HRH The Prince of Wales (Prince Charles Philip Arthur George), *born* 14 November 1948

SELECTED GOVERNMENT MEMBERS *as at July 2007*

Prime Minister, First Lord of the Treasury, Civil Service, Gordon Brown

Chancellor of the Exchequer, Alistair Darling

Foreign and Commonwealth Affairs, David Miliband

Justice, Lord Chancellor, Jack Straw

Home Affairs, Jacqui Smith

Defence, Des Browne

DEFENCE

The army has 386 main battle tanks, 2,718 armoured personnel carriers, 575 armoured infantry fighting vehicles and 67 armed helicopters. The navy has 13 submarines, 3 aircraft carriers, 9 destroyers, 17 frigates, 24 patrol and coastal combatant vessels, 13 combat aircraft and 109 armed helicopters at 7 bases. The air force has 341 combat aircraft.

Military expenditure – US$55,440m (2006)

Military personnel – 180,527: army 99,707, navy 38,900, air force 41,920

ECONOMY AND TRADE

The UK has a highly developed and technologically advanced economy that is now dominated by services and trade. It was the first industrialised nation, developing an economy in the 19th century based on heavy industry, mass manufacturing and global trade. It became less predominant as industrialisation spread to other countries, and the demands of the Second World War caused a postwar industrial decline that left the economy less efficient than many of its competitors and increasingly undercut by cheaper production in the developing world. In the 1980s, privatisation of state industries and constraints on public spending improved government finances, and primary industrial activities were increasingly replaced by service industries. Since emerging from recession in the early 1990s, the economy has experienced the longest-recorded period of expansion, outperforming the rest of the EU states, although uncertainties in the financial sector, high levels of debt and rising inflation are growing problems.

The service sector, especially banking, insurance and business services, electronics, telecommunications and tourism, now contributes 75.7 per cent of GDP and employs 80 per cent of the workforce. Agriculture is intensive, highly mechanised and efficient, meeting about 60 per cent of the UK's food needs with 1.4 per cent of the workforce, although contributing only 0.9 per cent of GDP. The UK has large reserves of oil, gas and coal, and production of these accounts for 10 per cent of GDP. Other industrial output is mostly of manufactured goods, including machine tools, electrical power equipment, automation and transport equipment, aircraft, ships, motor vehicles and parts, electronics and communications equipment, metals, chemicals, paper and paper products, food processing, textiles, clothing and other consumer goods.

The main trading partners are other EU countries and the USA. The principal exports are manufactured goods, fuels, chemicals, foodstuffs, beverages and tobacco. The main imports are manufactured goods, machinery and transport equipment, fuels and foodstuffs.

GNI – US$2,455,700m; US$40,560 per capita (2006)

Annual average growth of GDP – 2.9 per cent (2007 est)

Inflation rate – 2.4 per cent (2007 est)

Unemployment – 5.4 per cent (2007 est)

Total external debt – US$10,450,000m (2007)

Imports – US$547,000m (2006)

Exports – US$428,000m (2006)

BALANCE OF PAYMENTS

Trade – US$119,117m deficit (2006)

Current Account – US$92,566m deficit (2006)

COMMUNICATIONS

Traditionally a seafaring nation, the UK has a large merchant navy, with 474 ships of over 1,000 tonnes registered in the UK and a further 412 ships registered overseas. The main ports are at Grimsby and Immingham, Tees and Hartlepool, London, Southampton, Milford Haven, Liverpool, Forth, Felixstowe, Dover, Sullom Voe and Belfast. There is an extensive road network of 388,351km, including 3,555km of motorways. Railway passenger services are operated by 27 private companies. The network is being upgraded, and nearly a third of the 16,567km of track is now electrified. The Channel tunnel links the UK railway network to those of mainland Europe. About 3,200 km of waterways are navigable, although most are used for leisure and only about 600km for commerce. There are about 140 licensed civil airports, of which Heathrow (the world's busiest international airport), Gatwick, Stansted and Manchester handle the highest volume of passengers.

Technologically advanced telecommunications systems provide services to 33.6 main telephone lines, 69.6 million mobile phone subscribers and 33.5 internet users in 2006.

Technologically advanced telecommunications systems provide services to 33.6 main telephone lines, 69.6

million mobile phone subscribers and 33.5 internet users in 2006.

EDUCATION AND HEALTH

Full-time education is compulsory between the ages of five and 16 in Great Britain and four and 16 in Northern Ireland. Education between the ages of 16 and 18 is currently voluntary, but under recent government legislation, will become compulsory from 2013. There are 106 universities, including the Open University, which offers distance-learning access to further and higher education.

Gross enrolment ratio (percentage of relevant age group) – primary 107 per cent; secondary 105 per cent; tertiary 59 per cent (2006 est)
Health expenditure (per capita) – US$3,064 (2005)
Hospital beds (per 1,000 people) – 3.9 (2000–6)

MEDIA

The media is free, rarely censored and exerts considerable influence, particularly over political life. The press is mostly owned by large communications companies and therefore financially independent of any political party, although most newspapers adopt a political stance. The British Broadcasting Corporation is a public service broadcaster with a worldwide reputation. It provides radio and television programmes, in competition with several commercial radio and television stations, including cable and satellite services. There are plans for the analogue television signal to be switched off by 2012.

OVERSEAS TERRITORIES

See pp 1069–1076

UNITED STATES OF AMERICA

Area – 9,826,630 sq. km
Capital – Washington DC; population, 4,338,000 (2007 est). The area of the District of Columbia (with which the City of Washington is considered co-extensive) is 98.2 sq. km
Major cities – Chicago, Dallas, Houston, Los Angeles, New York, Philadelphia, Phoenix, San Antonio, San Diego
Currency – US dollar (US$) of 100 cents
Population – 301,139,947 rising at 0.89 per cent per year (2007 est)
Religion – Protestantism (52 per cent), Roman Catholicism (24 per cent), Mormonism (2 per cent), Judaism (2 per cent), Islam (1 per cent) (est). An estimated 10 per cent of the population is atheist
Language – English, Spanish, Hawaiian (official in Hawaii)
Population density – 33 per sq. km (2006)
Urban population – 80.8 per cent (2005 est)
Median age (years) – 36.6 (2007 est)
National anthem – 'The Star-Spangled Banner'
National day – 4 July (Independence Day)
Life expectancy (years) – 78 (2007 est)
Mortality rate – 8.26 (2007 est)
Birth rate – 14.16 (2007 est)
Infant mortality rate – 6.37 (2007 est)
Death penalty – Retained in 37 states
CPI score – 7.2 (2007)
Population below poverty line – 12 per cent (2004 est)

CLIMATE AND TERRAIN

The coastline has a length of about 3,329km on the Atlantic Ocean, 12,268km on the Pacific, 1,705km on the Arctic, and 2,624km on the Gulf of Mexico. The principal river is the Mississippi-Missouri-Red (5,970km long), traversing the whole country to its mouth in the Gulf of Mexico. The chain of the Rocky Mountains separates the western portion of the country from the remainder. West of these, bordering the Pacific coast, the Cascade Mountains and Sierra Nevada form the outer edge of a high tableland, consisting partly of stony and sandy desert and partly of grazing land and forested mountains, and including the Great Salt Lake, which extends to the Rocky Mountains. In the eastern states large forests still exist, the remnants of the forests which formerly extended over the entire Atlantic slope. Elevation extremes range from 6,198m (Mt McKinley, Alaska) to −86m (Death Valley, Inyo, California). Temperatures vary dramatically throughout the country; average temperatures in Washington DC range from 6°C in January to 27°C in June.

Two states are detached: Alaska and Hawaii. Alaska occupies the north-western extremity of North America, separated from the rest of the USA by the Canadian province of British Columbia. The terrain is arctic tundra with mountain ranges, and the climate is arctic. The state of Hawaii is a chain of about 20 volcanic islands in the north Pacific Ocean, of which the chief islands are Hawaii, Maui, Oahu, Kauai and Molokai. The climate there is tropical.

HISTORY AND POLITICS

The area which is now the USA was first inhabited by nomadic hunters who probably arrived from Asia *c.*30,000 BC. The continent was explored by the Norse in the ninth century and by the Spanish after their first landfall in North America in 1513. European colonisation began in the 16th century, with Spanish settlements in the south, and British, Dutch, French, German and Swedish settlements in the east. In the first century of European settlement, much of the native population was killed by diseases brought by the colonists. Many black Africans were introduced as slaves to work on the plantations in the Caribbean and southern US states.

By 1733 there were 13 British colonies, composed mostly of religious non-conformists who had left Britain to escape persecution. A rebellion broke out in these colonies in 1775, largely because of the colonists' objection to being taxed by, but having no representation in, the British parliament. The British government's forces were defeated with French, Spanish and Dutch assistance. The Declaration of Independence which inaugurated the United States of America was signed on 4 July 1776; Britain recognised American sovereignty in 1783. The first federal constitution was drawn up in 1787; ten amendments, termed the Bill of Rights, were added in

1791. The 13 original states of the Union ratified the constitution between 1787 and 1790. Vermont, Kentucky and Tennessee were admitted in the 1790s, but most of the states acceded in the 19th century, as the opening up of the centre and west led to the creation of new states, and European or neighbouring countries ceded or sold their territories to the USA.

The Civil War (1861–5) was fought over the issue of slavery, which was integral to the economy of the southern states but was opposed by the northern states. The northern states defeated the Confederacy of 11 southern states (Virginia, North Carolina, South Carolina, Georgia, Alabama, Florida, Tennessee, Mississippi, Louisiana, Texas, Arkansas) after they seceded in 1860–1.

The USA industrialised rapidly in the late 19th century. It emerged as a world economic and military superpower in the 20th century and played a decisive role in the two world wars. Its economic and military (including nuclear) supremacy has given the USA a key role in shaping the post-war world. The Cold War with the USSR after the Second World War ended in 1990. Following terrorist attacks in New York and Washington DC on 11 September 2001, President George W. Bush declared a 'war on terror'. As part of this, the USA led multi-national forces into conflicts in Afghanistan in 2001 (*see* Afghanistan) and Iraq in 2003 (*see* Iraq); US troops remain in both countries to help stabilise internal security. In response to the threat of terrorist attacks on US territory, the Department of Homeland Security was created in 2002.

The 2000 presidential election was won by the Republican candidate George W. Bush, and he was re-elected in 2004. In the 2004 legislative election, the Republican Party retained its majorities in both houses of Congress. Control of both houses was lost to the Democratic Party in the mid-term elections in 2006. The next presidential and legislative elections are scheduled for 4 November 2008.

POLITICAL SYSTEM

By the constitution of 17 September 1787 (which has been amended 15 times, most recently in 1992), the government of the USA is entrusted to three separate authorities: the federal executive (the president and cabinet), the legislature (congress, which consists of a senate and a house of representatives) and the judicature. The president is indirectly elected by an electoral college to serve a four-year term, and may serve a maximum of two consecutive terms. If a president dies in office, the vice-president serves the remainder of his term. The president appoints the cabinet officers and all the chief officials, subject to confirmation by the senate. He makes recommendations of a general nature to Congress, and when laws are passed, he may return them to Congress with a veto. But, if a measure so vetoed is again passed by both houses of Congress by a two-thirds majority in each house, it becomes law, notwithstanding the objection of the president.

Each of the 50 states has its own executive, legislature and judiciary. In theory, they are sovereign, but in practice their autonomy is increasingly circumscribed.

PRESIDENTIAL ELECTIONS

Candidates for the presidency must be at least 35 years of age and a native citizen of the USA. The electoral college for each state is directly elected by universal adult suffrage in the November preceding the January in which the presidential term expires. The number of members of the electoral college is equal to the whole number of senators and representatives to which the state is entitled in Congress. The electoral college for each state meets in its state in December and each member votes for a presidential candidate by ballot. The ballots are sent to Washington, and opened on 6 January by the president of the senate in the presence of congress. The candidate who has received a majority of the whole number of electoral votes cast is declared president for the ensuing term. If no one has a majority, then from the highest on the list (not exceeding three) the house of representatives elects a president, the votes being taken by states, the representation from each state having one vote. A presidential term begins at noon on 20 January.

HEAD OF STATE

President of the United States, George Walker Bush, *elected* 2000, *sworn in* 20 January 2001, *re-elected* 2004
Vice-President, Dick Cheney

SELECTED GOVERNMENT MEMBERS *as at August 2008*

Secretary of State, Condoleezza Rice
Defence, Robert Gates
Interior, Dirk Kempthorne
Treasury, Henry M. Paulson
Secretary for Homeland Security, Michael Chertoff

THE CONGRESS

Legislative power is vested in the bicameral Congress, comprising the senate and the House of Representatives. The senate has 100 members, two from each state, elected for a six-year term, with one-third elected every two years. The House of Representatives has 435 members directly elected in each state for a two-year term; a resident commissioner from Puerto Rico and a delegate each from American Samoa, the District of Columbia, Guam and the Virgin Islands serve as non-voting members of the house. Members of the 110th congress were elected on 7 November 2006. As at July 2008, the 110th congress is constituted as follows:

Senate: Democrats 49; Republicans 49; Independent 2; total 100
House of Representatives: Democrats 236; Republicans 199; vacancies 0; total 435
President of the Senate, The Vice-President
Senate Majority Leader, Harry Reid *(D), Nevada*
Speaker of the House of Representatives, Nancy Pelosi *(D), California*

THE JUDICATURE

The federal judiciary consists of three sets of federal courts: the supreme court at Washington DC, consisting of a Chief Justice and eight Associate Justices, the United States courts of appeals, consisting of 168 circuit judges within 13 regional circuits, and the 94 United States district courts served by 575 district court judges.

THE SUPREME COURT

US Supreme Court Building, Washington DC 20543
Chief Justice, John Roberts, *apptd* 2005

UNITED STATES EMBASSY

24 Grosvenor Square, London W1A 1AE
T 020-7499 9000 **W** www.usembassy.org.uk
Ambassador Extraordinary and Plenipotentiary, HE Robert Tuttle, *apptd* 2005

THE STATES OF THE UNION

The USA is a federal republic consisting of 50 states and the federal District of Columbia, and also of organised territories. Of the present 50 states, 13 are original states, seven were admitted without previous organisation as territories, and 30 were admitted after such organisation.

§ The 13 original states
(D) Democratic Party; (I) Independent; (R) Republican Party; (PDP) Popular Democratic Party; (C) Covenant

State (with date and order of admission)	*Area sq. km*	*Population (2006 est)*	*Capital*	*Governor (end of term in office)*
Alabama (AL) (1819, 22)	133,915	4,599,030	Montgomery	Bob Riley (R), Jan. 2011
Alaska (AK) (1959, 49)	1,530,694	670,053	Juneau	Sarah Palin (R), Dec. 2010
Arizona (AZ) (1912, 48)	295,259	6,166,318	Phoenix	Janet Napolitano (D), Jan. 2011
Arkansas (AR) (1836, 25)	137,754	2,810,872	Little Rock	Mike Beebe (D), Jan. 2011
California (CA) (1850, 31)	411,047	36,457,549	Sacramento	Arnold Schwarzenegger (R), Jan. 2011
Colorado (CO) (1876, 38)	269,595	4,753,377	Denver	Bill Ritter (D), Jan. 2011
Connecticut (CT) § (1788, 5)	12,997	3,504,809	Hartford	M. Jodi Rell (R), Jan. 2011
Delaware (DE) § (1787, 1)	5,297	853,476	Dover	Ruth Ann Minner (D), Jan. 2009
Florida (FL) (1845, 27)	151,939	18,089,888	Tallahassee	Charlie Crist (R), Jan. 2011
Georgia (GA) § (1788, 4)	152,576	9,363,941	Atlanta	Sonny Perdue (R), Jan. 2011
Hawaii (HI) (1959, 50)	16,760	1,285,498	Honolulu	Linda Lingle (R), Dec. 2010
Idaho (ID) (1890, 43)	216,430	1,466,465	Boise	C. L. Otter (R), Jan. 2011
Illinois (IL) (1818, 21)	145,933	12,831,970	Springfield	Rod R. Blagojevich (D), Jan. 2011
Indiana (IN) (1816, 19)	93,719	6,313,520	Indianapolis	Mitchell E. Daniels (R), Jan. 2009
Iowa (IA) (1846, 29)	145,752	2,982,085	Des Moines	Chet Culver (D), Jan. 2011
Kansas (KS) (1861, 34)	213,097	2,764,075	Topeka	Kathleen Sebelius (D), Jan. 2011
Kentucky (KY) (1792, 15)	104,661	4,206,074	Frankfort	Steve Beshear (D), Dec. 2011
Louisiana (LA) (1812, 18)	123,677	4,287,768	Baton Rouge	Bobby Jindal (R), Jan. 2012
Maine (ME) (1820, 23)	86,156	1,321,574	Augusta	John Baldacci (D), Jan. 2011
Maryland (MD) § (1788, 7)	27,091	5,615,727	Annapolis	Martin O'Malley (D), Jan. 2011
Massachusetts (MA) § (1788, 6)	21,455	6,437,193	Boston	Deval Patrick (D), Jan. 2011
Michigan (MI) (1837, 26)	151,584	10,095,643	Lansing	Jennifer Granholm (D), Jan. 2011
Minnesota (MN) (1858, 32)	218,600	5,167,101	St Paul	Tim Pawlenty (R), Jan. 2011
Mississippi (MS) (1817, 20)	123,514	2,910,540	Jackson	Haley Barbour (R), Jan. 2008
Missouri (MO) (1821, 24)	180,514	5,842,713	Jefferson City	Matt Blunt (R), Jan. 2009
Montana (MT) (1889, 41)	380,848	944,632	Helena	Brian Schweitzer (D), Jan. 2009
Nebraska (NE) (1867, 37)	200,349	1,768,331	Lincoln	Dave Heineman (R), Jan. 2011
Nevada (NV) (1864, 36)	286,352	2,495,529	Carson City	Jim Gibbons (R), Jan. 2011
New Hampshire (NH) § (1788, 9)	24,033	1,314,895	Concord	John Lynch (D), Jan. 2009
New Jersey (NJ) § (1787, 3)	20,168	8,724,560	Trenton	Jon Corzine (D), Jan. 2010
New Mexico (NM) (1912, 47)	314,925	1,954,599	Santa Fé	Bill Richardson (D), Jan. 2011
New York (NY) § (1788, 11)	127,189	19,306,183	Albany	David Paterson (D), Jan. 2011
North Carolina (NC) § (1789, 12)	136,412	8,856,505	Raleigh	Mike Easley (D), Jan. 2009
North Dakota (ND) (1889, 39)	183,117	635,867	Bismarck	John Hoeven (R), Dec. 2008
Ohio (OH) (1803, 17)	107,044	11,478,006	Columbus	Ted Strickland (D), Jan. 2011
Oklahoma (OK) (1907, 46)	181,185	3,579,212	Oklahoma City	Brad Henry (D), Jan. 2011
Oregon (OR) (1859, 33)	251,418	3,700,758	Salem	Ted R. Kulongoski (D), Jan. 2011
Pennsylvania (PA) § (1787, 2)	117,347	12,440,621	Harrisburg	Edward G. Rendell (D), Jan. 2011
Rhode Island (RI) § (1790, 13)	3,139	1,067,610	Providence	Don Carcieri (R), Jan. 2011
South Carolina (SC) § (1788, 8)	80,582	4,321,249	Columbia	Mark Sanford (R), Jan. 2011
South Dakota (SD) (1889, 40)	199,730	781,919	Pierre	Mike Rounds (R), Jan. 2011
Tennessee (TN) (1796, 16)	109,153	6,038,803	Nashville	Phil Bredesen (D), Jan. 2011
Texas (TX) (1845, 28)	691,027	23,507,783	Austin	Rick Perry (R), Jan. 2011
Utah (UT) (1896, 45)	219,888	2,550,063	Salt Lake City	Jon Huntsman Jr (R), Jan. 2009
Vermont (VT) (1791, 14)	24,900	623,908	Montpelier	James Douglas (R), Jan. 2009
Virginia (VA) § (1788, 10)	105,586	7,642,884	Richmond	Tim Kaine (D), Jan. 2010
Washington (WA) (1889, 42)	176,479	6,395,798	Olympia	Christine Gregoire (D), Jan. 2009
West Virginia (WV) (1863, 35)	62,761	1,818,470	Charleston	Joe Manchin III (D), Jan. 2009
Wisconsin (WI) (1848, 30)	145,436	5,556,506	Madison	Jim Doyle (D), Jan. 2011
Wyoming (WY) (1890, 44)	253,324	515,004	Cheyenne	Dave Freudenthal (D), Jan. 2011
Dist. of Columbia (DC) (1791)	179	581,530	–	Adrian M. Fenty (D), *(Mayor)*

OUTLYING TERRITORIES AND POSSESSIONS

	Area sq. km	*Population (2008 est)*	*Capital*	*Governor (end of term in office)*
American Samoa	199	57,496	Pago Pago	Togiola Tulafono (D), Jan. 2009
Guam	541	175,877	Hagatna	Felix Perez Camacho (R), Jan. 2011
Northern Mariana Islands	477	86,816	Saipan	Benigno Fitial (C), Jan. 2010
Puerto Rico	13,790	3,958,128	San Juan	Anibal Acevedo Vila (PDP), Jan. 2009
US Virgin Islands	363	108,2108	Charlotte Amalie	John Percy De Jongh Jr (D), Jan. 2011

BRITISH EMBASSY
3100 Massachusetts Avenue NW, Washington DC 20008
T (+1) (202) 588 6500 E washi@fco.gov.uk
W www.britainusa.com
Ambassador Extraordinary and Plenipotentiary, Sir Nigel Sheinwald, KCMG, *apptd* 2006

BRITISH COUNCIL
c/o The British Embassy
T (+1) (202) 588 6500 W www.britishcouncil.org/usa
Director, Sharon Memis

RESIDENT POPULATION BY RACE (2005 EST)

White	237,854,954
Black	37,909,341
Asian	12,687,472
American Indian and Alaska Native	2,863,001
Native Hawaiian and other Pacific Islanders	516,612
† Hispanic origin	42,687,224
Two or more races	4,579,024

† Persons of Hispanic origin may be of any race

DEFENCE

Each military department is separately organised and functions under the direction, authority and control of the Secretary of Defence. The air force has primary responsibility for the Department of Defence space development programmes and projects. Under US strategic command the USA has 730 submarine-launched ballistic missiles, 500 laser-guided nuclear missiles *(Minuteman III)* and 110 heavy nuclear-capable bombers. There are currently 4 space-based early warning satellites in orbit and the USA operates land-based early warning systems throughout the world. The army has over 7,620 main battle tanks, 6,719 armoured infantry fighting vehicles, 19,931 armoured personnel carriers and 1,009 armed helicopters.

The navy has 14 strategic submarines, 57 tactical submarines, 11 aircraft carriers, 22 cruisers, 52 destroyers, 21 frigates, 16 patrol and coastal vessels, 32 amphibious and support ships, 1,171 combat aircraft and 224 armed helicopters. The Marine Corps has 403 main battle tanks, 362 combat aircraft and 140 armed helicopters. The air force has 2,658 combat aircraft.

Military expenditure – US$571,000m (2007)
Military personnel – 1,498,157: army 593,327, navy 341,588, Marine Corps 186,661, air force 336,081, coast guard 40,500

ECONOMY AND TRADE

The USA is one of the world's leading industrial nations, with a sophisticated market economy that saw huge growth during the 20th century. This economic development was due in part to an industrial revolution that mechanised the agrarian economy, the expansion of the country's transport infrastructure and large amounts of relatively cheap migrant labour. More recently, the economy has shifted reliance from industry to services, and government involvement in the economy has steadily reduced. In recent years, the economy has experienced steady growth, low unemployment and inflation, and rapid advances in technology, but there are large budget and trade deficits and an increasingly uneven distribution of wealth; an estimated 12 per cent of the population lives below the poverty line.

Most economic activity is in the private sector, so the main feature of government economic policy is the annual budget proposal, which is put forward by the president, and drafted into a budget resolution by the house and senate committees before being debated in congress. The 2008 budget estimate totalled US$2,931.2bn. The largest areas of expenditure by government department were health and human services (US$709.4bn), social security administration (US$656.6bn), defence (US$583.1), agriculture (US$94.8bn) and veterans' affairs (US$86.6bn).

Agriculture is a major industry in the USA, with about 18 per cent of the land under cultivation. Principal crops are wheat, maize, other grains, fruit, vegetables, cotton, soya beans, meat and dairy products. Agriculture, fishing and forestry contribute 0.9 per cent of GDP and employ 0.6 per cent of the workforce.

Mining and extraction are also important to the economy. Large quantities of iron ore, phosphate rock, copper, zinc and lead are mined. About one-third of its oil requirements are supplied by domestic production, principally from fields in the Gulf of Mexico; production in 2005 was 7.61 million barrels per day. Most oil refining capacity is located on the Gulf coast; production is returning to normal levels after the damage caused by Hurricane Katrina in 2005. Natural gas is also produced. Despite its domestic oil and natural gas resources and its electricity generating capacity, the USA is a net importer of energy; the largest exporters of oil to the USA are Canada (782.5 million barrels in 2005) and Mexico (609 million barrels in 2005).

The industrial sector is highly diversified and technologically advanced. The main manufacturing industries produce steel, vehicles, aircraft and aerospace equipment, telecommunications equipment, chemicals, electronic equipment and consumer goods, and process food. Industry contributes 20.5 per cent of GDP and employs about 22.6 per cent of the workforce; services account for 78.5 per cent of GDP and 76.8 per cent of employment.

The main trading partners are Canada, Mexico, China, Japan, Germany and the UK. Principal exports are capital goods (chiefly transistors, aircraft, vehicle parts, computers, telecommunications equipment), industrial supplies, consumer goods (cars, medicines) and agricultural produce (soya beans, fruit, maize). The main imports are consumer goods (cars, clothing, medicines, furniture, toys), capital goods (computers,

telecommunications equipment, vehicle parts, office machines, electric power machinery), industrial goods (especially crude oil) and agricultural products.
GNI – US$13,386,900m (2006); US$44,710 per capita (2006)
Annual average growth of GDP – 2 per cent (2007 est)
Inflation rate – 2.7 per cent (2007 est)
Unemployment – 4.6 per cent (2007 est)
Total external debt – US$12,250,000m (2007)
Imports – US$1,919,000m (2006)
Exports – US$1,038,000m (2006)

BALANCE OF PAYMENTS
Trade – US$881,160m deficit (2006)
Current Account – US$811,483m deficit (2006)

Trade with UK	*2006*	*2007*
Imports from UK	£31,800,605,000	£32,072,312,637
Exports to UK	£26,088,161,000	£26,068,455,759

GDP BY INDUSTRY (2007)

	US$bn
Private industries	13,841.3
Agriculture, forestry, fisheries	319.3
Mining	439.2
Construction	431.2
Manufacturing	4,932.3
Transportation and warehousing	756.9
Wholesale trade	1,158.7
Retail trade	1,352.6
Finance, insurance and real estate	4,405,2
Information	1,274.8

Source: Bureau of Economic Analysis

COMMUNICATIONS

There are approximately 6.4 million km of roads, with surfaced roads accounting for 64.7 per cent of the total. There are 226,600km of railways, and more than 41,000km of navigable waterways, of which 19,300km are used for commerce. The main seaports are at Anchorage, Baltimore, Boston, Charleston, Chicago, Corpus Christi, Duluth, Hampton Roads, Honolulu (Hawaii), Houston, Jacksonville, Long Beach, Los Angeles, New Orleans, New York, Philadelphia, Port Canaveral, Portland (Oregon), Prudhoe Bay, San Francisco, Savannah, Seattle, Tampa and Toledo. There are over 14,900 airports and airfields; nearly 200 are capable of handling international flights, but the rest cater for the high domestic demand as air travel is the main form of transport for long-distance internal journeys.

Technologically advanced systems provide multi-purpose telecommunications facilities, and the mobile phone network is growing rapidly. There were 176 million main-line subscribers, 233 million mobile phone subscribers and 208 million internet users in 2006.

EDUCATION AND HEALTH

All the states have compulsory school attendance laws. In general, children are obliged to attend school from seven to 16 years of age. Most of the revenue for public elementary and secondary school purposes comes from federal, state and local governments. Less than 3 per cent comes from gifts and from tuition and transportation fees. Among the better-known universities are Harvard (founded in 1636), Yale (1701) and Princeton (1746).
Gross enrolment ratio (percentage of relevant age group) – primary 98 per cent; secondary 94 per cent; tertiary 82 per cent (2006 est)
Health expenditure (per capita) – US$6,657 (2005)
Hospital beds (per 1,000 people) – 3.3 (2000–6)

MEDIA

The media industry is the largest and most influential in the world. Both television and radio are regulated by the Federal Communications Commission and programming is exported around the world (via the major networks of ABC, CBS, NBC, CNN, Fox, MTV, HBO and PBS). There are around 10,000 commercial radio stations and more than 1,500 daily newspapers, including *The Wall Street Journal*, *USA Today*, *The Washington Post* and *The New York Times*. *Time*, *Newsweek* and *US News and World Report* are influential current affairs magazines, while *Rolling Stone* and *Vanity Fair* are popular entertainment titles.

CULTURE

The culture of the USA is indebted to the diverse origins of its immigrants; European, African and Latin American influences are particularly strong. Often at the forefront of modern philosophical, literary or artistic movements (such as feminism, postmodernism and postcolonialism), the USA boasts many important writers, film-makers and artists.

The best-known early novelists include Nathaniel Hawthorne (1804–64) and Mark Twain (1835–1910), and poets Walt Whitman (1819–92) and Emily Dickinson (1830–86). The 20th century saw the emergence of writers such as William Faulkner (1897–1962), Ernest Hemingway (1899–1961) and John Steinbeck (1902–68); postwar US literature was personified by the 'beat poet' generation of writers that included Jack Kerouac (1922–69), William Burroughs (1914–97) and Allen Ginsberg (1926–1997). African American literature has been assimiliated into the literary canon in the last 50 years through the works of Ralph Ellison (1913–94), Toni Morrison (*b.* 1931) and Alice Walker (*b.* 1944).

The Hollywood film industry is the most wide-reaching in the world; celebrated directors include Orson Welles (1915–85), Frank Capra (1897–1991), Stanley Kubrick (1928–99), Francis Ford Coppola (*b.* 1939) and Martin Scorsese (*b.* 1942).

Modern art found a spiritual home on the east coast and the Guggenheim and Metropolitan museums in New York house vast collections. Renowned artists include Edward Hopper (1882–1967), Jackson Pollock (1912–56), Roy Lichtenstein (1923–97) and Andy Warhol (1928–87).

The music of the USA reflects the country's ethnic diversity, with superior recording and distribution methods ensuring that rock and roll, country, blues, jazz and hip-hop became known worldwide. Musical icons include Elvis Presley (1935–77) and Bob Dylan (*b.* 1941) in rock, Hank Williams (1923–53) and Johnny Cash (1932–2003) in country music, Leadbelly (1888–1949) and Muddy Waters (1915–83) in blues, and Louis Armstrong (1901–71), Miles Davis (1926–91) and John Coltrane (1926–67) in jazz.

US TERRITORIES, ETC

Responsibility within the federal government for the US insular areas other than Puerto Rico and Kingman Reef lies with the US Department of the Interior; the Office of Insular Affairs deals with American Samoa, Guam, the Northern Mariana Islands, the US Virgin Islands, Navassa Island (7.8 sq. km), Palmyra Atoll (4 sq. km) and Wake

Atoll (6.4 sq. km), shared with the US army Space and Missile Defence Command; and the US Fish and Wildlife Service deals with Baker Island (1.5 sq. km), Howland Island (2.5 sq. km) and Jarvis Island (4.2 sq. km), Midway Atoll (5.2 sq. km) and Johnston Atoll (2.5 sq. km), shared with the Defence Special Weapons Agency. The Aleutian Islands (17,666 sq. km) form part of the Alaskan archipelago.

Four of the eight populated insular areas are represented in the house of representatives: Puerto Rico by a resident commissioner, and American Samoa, Guam and the US Virgin Islands by one non-voting delegate each. Although represented in the house of representatives by a delegate, the District of Columbia was an incorporated territory for only three years (1871–4).

THE COMMONWEALTH OF PUERTO RICO

Area – 13,790 sq. km
Population – 3,958,128 rising at 0.39 per cent per year (2007 est). The majority of the inhabitants are of Spanish descent; Spanish and English are the official languages
Capital – San Juan; population, 2,690 (2007 est est). Other major towns are: Bayamón, Carolina, Ponce
National day – 25 July (Constitution Day)

Puerto Rico (Rich Port) is an island of the Greater Antilles group in the West Indies and was discovered in 1493 by Columbus. It was a Spanish possession until 1898, when it was ceded to the USA after the Spanish–American War. Residents are US citizens and Puerto Rico is represented in congress by a resident commissioner, elected for a four-year term, who is a non-voting member of the house of representatives. Under its 1952 constitution, Puerto Rico has full powers of internal self-government. The governor is directly elected for a four-year term. The bicameral legislative assembly consists of a 29-member senate and a 51-member house of representatives, whose members serve a four-year term; proposals to replace these bodies with a one-chamber legislature were approved by referendum in 2005. Tourism, pharmaceuticals, electronics, clothing and food processing are the main economic activities.
Governor, Anibal Acevedo Vila (PDP)

Trade with UK	*2005*	*2006*
Imports from UK	£179,136,000	£187,164,000
Exports to UK	£349,402,000	£283,688,000

GUAM

Guahan – Territory of Guam
Area – 541.3 sq. km
Population – 175,877; rising at 1.4 per cent per year (2008 est); Chamorro (37 per cent), Filipino (26 per cent), other Pacific islander (11 per cent). Chamorro (a language of the Malayo-Polynesian family with admixtures of Spanish) and English are the official languages; most Chamorro residents are bilingual
Capital – Hagatna (also known as Agana); population, 149,000 (2007 est)
National day – first Monday in March (Discovery Day)

Guam is the largest of the Mariana Islands, in the north Pacific Ocean. A Spanish colony for centuries, it was ceded to the USA in 1898 after the Spanish–American War. Guam was occupied by the Japanese in 1941 but was recaptured by US forces in 1944. Any person born in Guam is a US citizen. Guam is represented in congress by a delegate directly elected for a two-year term who is a non-voting member of the house of representatives. Under the Organic Act of Guam 1950, Guam has statutory powers of self-government. The governor and lieutenant-governor are directly elected for a four-year term. The 15-member unicameral legislature is directly elected every two years. The main sources of revenue are tourism (particularly from Japan) and US military spending.
Governor, Felix Perez Camacho (R)

Trade with UK	*2005*	*2006*
Imports from UK	£3,922	£6,912,000
Exports to UK	£1,247	£351,000

AMERICAN SAMOA

Area – 199 sq. km
Population – 57,496, falling at 0.26 per cent per year (2008 est)
Capital – Pago Pago; population, 3,519 (2007)
National day – 17 April (Flag Day)

American Samoa consists of the islands of Tutuila, Aunu'u, Ofu, Olesega, Ta'u, Rose and Swains Islands. The islands were discovered by Europeans in the 18th century and the USA took possession in 1900. Those born in American Samoa are US non-citizen nationals, although some have acquired citizenship through service in the US armed forces or other naturalisation procedures. American Samoa is represented in congress by a delegate directly elected for a two-year term who is a non-voting member of the House of Representatives. Under the 1966 constitution, American Samoa has a measure of self-government, with certain powers reserved to the US Secretary of the Interior. The governor and deputy governor are directly elected for a four-year term. The bicameral legislative Assembly comprises a 21-member house of representatives (one appointed member and 20 members directly elected for a two-year term) and an 18-seat senate with members elected from among the traditional chiefs for a four-year term. Tuna fishing and canning are the principal economic activities.
Governor, Togiola Tulafono (D)

THE UNITED STATES VIRGIN ISLANDS

Area – 1,910 sq. km
Population – 108,210 falling at 0.2 per cent per year (2008 est)
Capital – Charlotte Amalie; population, 53,000 (2007 est), on St Thomas
National day – 27 March (Transfer Day)

There are three main islands, St Thomas, St Croix and St John, and about 50 small islets or cays. These constituted the Danish part of the Virgin Islands from the 17th century until purchased by the USA in 1917. Those born in the US Virgin Islands are US nationals. The Virgin Islands are represented in congress by a representative directly elected for a two-year term who is a non-voting member of the house of representatives. Under the provisions of the Revised Organic Act of 1954, the islands have powers of self-government. The governor and lieutenant-governor are directly elected for a four-year term. The unicameral senate has 15 senators

directly elected for a two-year term. Tourism, oil refining and manufacturing are the main industries.
Governor, John DeJongh Jr (D)

NORTHERN MARIANA ISLANDS

Area – 477 sq. km
Population – 86,616 rising at 2.46 per cent per year (2008 est)
Seat of government – Saipan; population, 76,000 (2007 est)
National day – 8 January (Commonwealth Day)

The USA administered the Northern Mariana Islands, in the north-west Pacific Ocean, as part of a UN Trusteeship until the trusteeship agreement was terminated in 1986, when the islands became a commonwealth under US sovereignty. Those resident in 1976 or subsequently born in the islands are US citizens. The islands are not represented in congress but have a resident representative in Washington DC. Under the 1978 constitution, the islands are self-governing. The governor and lieutenant-governor are directly elected for a four-year term. The bicameral legislature comprises a 20-member house of representatives and a nine-member senate; members are directly elected, representatives for two years and senators for four years. Tourism and manufacturing, especially of clothing, are the main industries.
Governor, Benigno Fitial (C)

URUGUAY

República Oriental del Uruguay – Oriential Republic of Uruguay

Area – 176,220 sq. km
Capital – Montevideo; population, 1,513,000 (2007 est)
Major town – Salto
Currency – Uruguayan peso of 100 centésimos
Population – 3,460,607 rising at 0.5 per cent per year (2007 est)
Religion – Roman Catholicism (54 per cent), Protestantism (11 per cent) (est). An estimated 35 per cent of the population is atheist or agnostic
Language – Spanish (official), Portunol
Population density – 19 per sq. km (2006)
Urban population – 93 per cent (2005 est)
Median age (years) – 32.9 (2007 est)
National anthem – 'Orientales, la Patria o la Tumba' ['Uruguayans, the Fatherland or Death']
National day – 25 August (Independence Day)
Life expectancy (years) – 75.93 (2007 est)
Mortality rate – 9.16 (2007 est)
Birth rate – 14.41 (2007 est)
Infant mortality rate – 12.02 (2007 est)
Death penalty – Abolished for all crimes (since 1907)
CPI score – 6.7 (2007)

CLIMATE AND TERRAIN

The country consists mainly of undulating grassy plains, with low hills. Elevation extremes range from 514m (Cerro Catedral) at the highest point to 0m (Atlantic Ocean) at the lowest. The principal river is the Rio Negro (with its tributary, the Yi), flowing from north-east to south-west into the Rio Uruguay. Average temperatures in Montevideo range from 6°C in July to 28°C in January.

HISTORY AND POLITICS

Originally populated by the Charras Amerindians, the Rio de la Plata was first visited by the Spanish in 1515. Although initially colonised by the Portuguese, the *Banda Oriental,* as the territory lying on the eastern bank of the river Uruguay was then called, formed part of Spanish South America from 1726 to 1814. Briefly independent and then a a province of Brazil, its independence was recognised in 1828 and a republic was inaugurated in 1830. In the mid-19th century there was a power struggle, descending into civil war, between the conservatives *(Blancos)* and liberals *(Colorados)* which ended when the latter took office in the 1860s and governed until 1958.

The period from 1962 until 1973 saw unrest caused by the Marxist Tupamaros guerrillas. They were crushed by a military dictatorship that held power from 1973 until 1985, when a return to civilian rule was agreed after violent anti-government protests at the regime's repressive rule and the deteriorating economy. The presidential and general elections returned the Colorado Party to power and Julio Sanguinetti became president. The first fully free presidential and legislative elections since 1971 were held in 1989, and were won by the National *(Blanco)* Party.

The Colorado and National parties now both occupy the centre ground, but their dominance of politics has been eroded by left-wing parties such as New Space and coalitions such as the Progressive Encounter-Broad Front (EP-FA). In the 2004 legislative election, the EP-FA won outright majorities in both houses. The 2004 presidential election was won by Tabaré Vázquez of the EP-FA, the first left-wing president to hold office, and he appointed an EP-FA coalition government including other left-wing parties.

POLITICAL SYSTEM

Under the 1997 constitution, the executive president is directly elected for a five-year term; a president cannot serve two consecutive terms. The president, who appoints the council of ministers, is responsible to the legislature. The bicameral legislature, the General Assembly, consists of a Chamber of Representatives, the lower house, and a Chamber of Senators. The Chamber of Representatives has 99 members directly elected for a five-year term. The Chamber of Senators has 31 members, 30 directly elected for a five-year term and the vice-president as an *ex officio* member.

The republic is divided into 19 departments, each with an elected governor and legislature.

HEAD OF STATE

President, Tabaré Vázquez, *elected* October 2004, *took office* 1 March 2005
Vice-President, Rodolfo Nin Novoa

SELECTED GOVERNMENT MEMBERS *as at July 2008*
Economy and Finance, Danilo Astori
Foreign Relations, Gonzalo Fernandez
Interior, Daisy Tourne
Defence, Jose Bayardi

EMBASSY OF URUGUAY
140 Brompton Road, London SW3 1HY
T 020-7589 8835 E emburuguay@emburuguay.org.uk
Ambassador Extraordinary and Plenipotentiary, HE Dr Ricardo Varela, *apptd* 2004

BRITISH EMBASSY
PO Box 16024, Calle Marco Bruto 1073, 11300 Montevideo
T (+598) (2) 622 3630 E ukinuruguay@gmail.com
Ambassador Extraordinary and Plenipotentiary, HE Patrick Mullee, *apptd* 2008

DEFENCE

The army has 15 main battle tanks, 104 armoured personnel carriers and 18 armoured infantry fighting vehicles. The navy has 2 frigates, 10 patrol and coastal combatant vessels and 1 aircraft at 4 bases. The air force has 19 combat aircraft.
Military budget – US$262m (2007)
Military personnel – 25,400: army 16,800, navy 5,600, air force 3,000; paramilitary 920

ECONOMY AND TRADE

After years of steady growth, Uruguay suffered a recession in 1999–2002 largely owing to the economic problems of Brazil and Argentina, its main export markets and sources of tourists. The recession culminated in a banking crisis in 2002; IMF loans, the rescheduling of foreign debt repayments and the government's emergency measures achieved a recovery and the economy has grown strongly since 2004. However, the recession reduced many to poverty in what had previously been a moderately prosperous society; 27 per cent of households still lived below the poverty line in 2006.

Ranching and livestock products (beef, mutton, wool) have been the mainstay of the economy since the mid-19th century, generating the prosperity that enabled Uruguay to develop an extensive welfare system in the early 20th century. Dependence on these products leaves the economy vulnerable to price fluctuations, a factor contributing to the recent recession. Other crops include rice, grains, soya beans, citrus fruits, wine grapes, linseed and sunflower seed. Agricultural produce is the basis of the food processing and beverages industries. Other industries include fishing, forestry and the manufacture of electrical machinery, transport equipment, petroleum products, textiles and chemicals. Exploited minerals include clinker, dolomite, marble and granite. Tourism and offshore financial services also contribute substantially to revenue. Agriculture contributes 10.1 per cent of GDP, industry 32 per cent and services 57.9 per cent.

The main trading partners are Brazil, Argentina, the USA and China. Principal exports are meat, rice, leather products, wool, fish and dairy products. The main imports are crude oil and petroleum products, machinery, chemicals, vehicles and paper.
GNI – US$17,600m; US$5,310 per capita (2006)
Annual average growth of GDP – 5.7 per cent (2007 est)
Inflation rate – 8.3 per cent (2007 est)
Unemployment – 10.3 per cent (2007 est)
Total external debt – US$10,800m (2007)
Imports – US$4,800m (2006)
Exports – US$4,000m (2006)

BALANCE OF PAYMENTS
Trade – US$804m deficit (2006)
Current Account – US$457m deficit (2006)

Trade with UK	*2006*	*2007*
Imports from UK	£40,112,000	£35,137,443
Exports to UK	£65,239,000	£70,233,103

COMMUNICATIONS

There are nearly 78,000km of roads, 8,000km of which are surfaced, and over 2,000km of railway, of which 1,200km is in full or partial use. There are 1,600km of navigable waterways, mainly on the Uruguay and Negro rivers. A bridge across the Rio de la Plata links Uruguay and Argentina. The main ports are Montevideo and Colonia on the coast, and Fray Bentos and Paysandú on the river Uruguay. There is an international airport near Montevideo, and about 60 smaller airports and airfields around the country.

Modernised telephone systems provided services to 1 million main-line subscribers, 2.3 million mobile phone subscribers, and 756,000 internet users in 2006.

EDUCATION AND HEALTH

Primary and secondary education is compulsory and free, and technical and trade schools and evening courses for adult education are state-controlled. The university at Montevideo was founded in 1849.
Literacy rate – 97.7 per cent (2004 est)
Gross enrolment ratio (percentage of relevant age group) – primary 113 per cent; secondary 107 per cent; tertiary 42 per cent (2006 est)
Health expenditure (per capita) – US$404 (2005)
Hospital beds (per 1,000 people) – 2.4 (2000–6)

MEDIA

The constitution enshrines freedom of expression. There are more than 100 daily and weekly newspapers, all privately owned, and more than 100 radio stations, as well as 20 television channels. The government runs one television and one radio station.

UZBEKISTAN

Osbekiston Respublikasi – Republic of Uzbekistan

Area – 447,400 sq. km
Capital – Tashkent; population, 2,184,000 (2007 est)
Major cities – Andijan, Bukhara, Karsi, Namangan, Nukus, Samarkand

Currency – Sum of 100 tiyin
Population – 27,780,059 rising at 1.73 per cent per year (2007 est); Uzbek (80 per cent), Russian (5.5 per cent), Tajik (5 per cent), Kazakh (3 per cent), Karakalpak (2.5 per cent), Tatar (1.5 per cent) (est)
Religion – Islam (91 per cent), Orthodox Christianity (5 per cent) (est). The majority of the population practises Sunni Islam
Language – Uzbek (official), Russian, Tajik
Population density – 62 per sq. km (2006)
Urban population – 36.4 per cent (2005 est)
Median age (years) – 22.9 (2007 est)
National anthem – 'Osbekistan Respublikasining Davlat Madhiyasi' ['National Anthem of the Republic of Uzbekistan']
National day – 1 September (Independence Day)
Life expectancy (years) – 64.98 (2007 est)
Mortality rate – 7.73 (2006 est)
Birth rate – 26.46 (2007 est)
Infant mortality rate – 68.89 (2007 est)
Death penalty – Abolished for all crimes (since 2008)
CPI score – 1.7 (2007)
Population below poverty line – 33 per cent (2004 est)

CLIMATE AND TERRAIN

The terrain of landlocked Uzbekistan falls from the Tien Shan mountains and the Pamir highlands in the east and south-east to the desert lowlands in the west and north-west, in the basin of the Amu Darya river and the southern part of the Aral Sea. Elevation extremes range from 4,301m (Adelunga Toghi) at the highest point to −12m (Sariqarnish Kuli) at the lowest. Average temperatures in Tashkent range from −2°C in January to 33°C in June.

HISTORY AND POLITICS

Part of the Persian Empire and then the empire of Alexander the Great, Samarkand developed as an important transit point on the ancient 'Silk Road' in the first century BC. In the 13th century the area became part of the Mongol Empire, with Samarkand as its capital during the reign of Amir Timur (Tamerlane). With the decline of the Mongol Empire, independent emirates and khanates emerged. The three khanates in what is now Uzbekistan, Khiva, Kokand and Bukhara, were annexed by the Russian Empire in the second half of the 19th century. In 1917 a Bolshevik revolution broke out in Tashkent and by 1921 all of Uzbekistan had been absorbed into the USSR. Under Soviet rule a massive land irrigation programme was implemented to allow the cultivation of cotton, but this also led to the drying up of the Aral Sea.

Uzbekistan declared its independence from the USSR on 1 September 1991 but post-independence political life has been dominated by the former communists. The main opposition parties, *Erk* (Freedom) and *Birlik* (Unity), have been banned since 1992, other forms of opposition are suppressed and the government has been accused of human rights abuses, including the systematic use of torture. The former communist leader Islam Karimov, who came to power in 1990, was elected president in 1991 and has retained the presidency since, in unopposed elections or through the extension of his term of office in referendums. He was re-elected in 2007 for a third term, despite the constitutional restriction to two terms.

All legislative elections since independence have been won by the People's Democratic Party (the former Communist Party) or its allies. After the latest legislative election in December 2004 and January 2005, the largest party in the legislative chamber was the pro-Karimov Liberal Democratic Party; opposition parties were barred from contesting the election. Most elections have been reported by observers to be neither free nor fair and have attracted international criticism.

INSURGENCIES

The Islamic Movement of Uzbekistan (IMU), which seeks to establish an Islamic state, was founded in 1996. Whilst it has carried out car bombings in Tashkent, its activities have centred on the Fergana valley, where it has clashed with Kyrgyz armed forces. The government has used the insurgency as an excuse to curtail human rights and suppress political opposition and protests, such as those in Andijan in May 2005.

POLITICAL SYSTEM

The 1992 constitution was amended in 2002 to create a bicameral legislature and extend the president's term of office. The president is directly elected; his term of office was five years, renewable only once, but was extended in 2002 to seven years. The legislature, the Supreme Assembly, became bicameral after the 2004–5 elections. The lower house, the Legislative Assembly, has 120 members directly elected for a five-year term. The senate has 100 members, 16 appointed by the president and the rest elected by regional deputies to represent the regions and the capital; they serve a five-year term. The president appoints the cabinet, which is chaired by the prime minister.

The country is divided into the autonomous republic of Karakalpakstan, 12 provinces (Andijan, Bukhara, Fergana, Jizak, Kashka-Darya, Khorezm, Namanghan, Navoi, Samarkand, Surhan-Darya, Syr-Darya, Tashkent) and the city of Tashkent.

HEAD OF STATE

President, Islam Karimov, *elected* 29 December 1991, *elected by referendum for a five-year term* 26 March 1995, *re-elected* 2000, 2007

SELECTED GOVERNMENT MEMBERS *as at July 2008*

Prime Minister, Shavkat Mirziyaev
First Deputy Prime Minister, Finance, Rustam Azimov
Deputy Prime Ministers, Farida Akbarova; Abdulla Aripov; Nordirkhon Khanov; Azimzhon Parpiev; Ergash Shoismatov
Defence, Ruslan Mirzayev
Foreign Affairs, Vladimir Norov
Interior, Bahodir Matlubov

EMBASSY OF THE REPUBLIC OF UZBEKISTAN

41 Holland Park, London W11 3RP
T 020-7229 7679 E info@uzbekembassy.org
W www.uzbekembassy.org
Ambassador Extraordinary and Plenipotentiary, HE Otabek Akbarov, *apptd* 2007

BRITISH EMBASSY

Ul. Gulyamova 67, UZ-700000 Tashkent
T (+998) (71) 120 6451 E brit@emb.uz
Ambassador Extraordinary and Plenipotentiary, HE Iain Kelly, *apptd* 2007

BRITISH COUNCIL

University of World Languages Building, 11 Mirobod St, Tashkent 700031

T (+998) (71) 140 0660/61/62/63
W www.britishcouncil.org.uk/uzbekistan
Director, Jeremy Jacobson

DEFENCE

The army has 340 main battle tanks, 399 armoured infantry fighting vehicles and 309 armoured personnel carriers. The air force has 135 combat capable aircraft and 29 armed helicopters.

Military budget – US$84m (2006 est)
Military personnel – 67,000: army 50,000, air force 17,000; paramilitary 20,000
Conscription duration – 12 months

ECONOMY AND TRADE

The economy remains centrally planned and control has increased in some areas, stifling economic activity. Economic growth and living standards are among the worst in the former Soviet republics, with 33 per cent of the population living below the poverty level. Much foreign aid has been cut or withdrawn in protest at the country's poor human rights record.

The economy is based on intensive agricultural production, particularly of cotton, made possible by extensive irrigation schemes. Vegetables, fruit, grains and livestock are also produced. The main industries are textile manufacture, food processing, mineral mining (especially for gold), oil and natural gas production, machine building, metallurgy and chemicals. Oil and gas exports offer potential for economic growth and may attract foreign investment, possibly from Russia and China, but this is unlikely in the immediate future owing to a basic lack of modern oil pipelines and infrastructure. Agriculture contributes 29.4 per cent of GDP, industry 33.1 per cent and services 37.4 per cent.

The main trading partners are Russia, China, South Korea, Kazakhstan and Turkey. Principal exports are cotton (41 per cent), gold, oil and natural gas, mineral fertilisers, metals, textiles, food products, machinery and motor vehicles. The main imports are machinery and equipment, foodstuffs, chemicals and metals.

GNI – US$16,200m (2006); US$610 per capita (2006)
Annual average growth of GDP – 8.1 per cent (2007 est)
Inflation rate – 16 per cent (2007 est)
Unemployment – 0.8 per cent (2007 est)
Total external debt – US$5,398m (2007 est)

BALANCE OF PAYMENTS
Trade – US$372m surplus (2006)
Current Account – US$3,198m surplus (2006)

Trade with UK	*2006*	*2007*
Imports from UK	£28,419,000	£36,556,937
Exports to UK	£18,520,000	£42,198,688

COMMUNICATIONS

Uzbekistan has 81,600km of roads, 71,000km of which are paved. It has nearly 4,000km of railway, and 1,100km of waterways. The principal airport is at Tashkent.

The fixed-line telephone system is antiquated and mobile phone distribution is growing rapidly, doubling in 2005. There were 1.7 million main lines in use in 2005, 5.8 million mobile phone subscribers in 2007 and 1.7 million internet users in 2006.

EDUCATION AND HEALTH

Literacy rate – 99.3 per cent (2004 est)
Gross enrolment ratio (percentage of relevant age group) – primary 95 per cent; secondary 102 per cent; tertiary 10 per cent (2006 est)
Health expenditure (per capita) – US$26 (2005)
Hospital beds (per 1,000 people) – 5.2 (2000–6)

MEDIA

Despite constitutional protection of free speech, the government strictly controls the political content of the media and much of the population relies on foreign broadcasts. Self-censorship is a way of life because of the frequent harassment of journalists. There is a mixture of government-run and private television and radio stations. Almost all newspapers are produced by the state or by pro-government organisations.

VANUATU

Ripablik blong Vanuatu/République de Vanuatu – Republic of Vanuatu

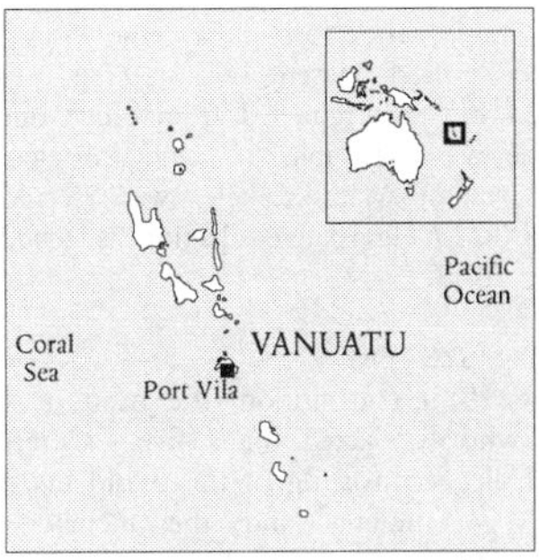

Area – 12,200 sq. km
Capital – Port Vila; population, 40,000 (2007 est), on Efaté
Major town – Luganville, on Espiritu Santo
Currency – Vatu
Population – 211,971 rising at 1.46 per cent per year (2007 est). About 95 per cent are Melanesian, the rest being mostly Micronesian, Polynesian and European
Religion – Protestantism (56 per cent), Roman Catholicism (13 per cent), other Christian denominations (14 per cent) (est)
Language – English, French (official), Bislama; over 100 local languages exist
Population density – 18 per sq. km (2006)
Urban population – 23.7 per cent (2005 est)
Median age (years) – 23.4 (2007 est)
National anthem – 'Yumi, Yumi, Yumi' ['We, We, We']
National day – 30 July (Independence Day)
Life expectancy (years) – 63.22 (2007 est)
Mortality rate – 7.75 (2007 est)
Birth rate – 22.35 (2007 est)
Infant mortality rate – 52.45 (2007 est)
Death penalty – Abolished for all crimes (since 1980)
CPI score – 3.1 (2005)
Literacy rate – 74 per cent (2004 est)

CLIMATE AND TERRAIN

Situated in the south Pacific Ocean, Vanuatu includes 13 large and some 70 small islands, of coral and volcanic origin, including the Banks and Torres Islands in the north. The principal islands are Vanua Lava, Espiritu Santo, Maewo, Pentecost, Ambae, Malekula, Ambrym, Epi, Efaté, Erromango, Tanna and Aneityum. Most islands are mountainous and there are active volcanoes on several. Elevation extremes range from 1,877m (Tabwemasana) at the highest point to 0m (Pacific Ocean) at the lowest. The climate is tropical, and the average temperature in Tana is around 29°C all year round.

HISTORY AND POLITICS

Some of the islands of Vanuatu have been inhabited for over 4,000 years. Europeans first visited in the early 17th century, and Captain Cook named the islands the New Hebrides in 1774. The islands were settled in the 19th century by the British and the French, who established plantations, and from 1906 were jointly administered as the Condominium of the New Hebrides. This became independent as the Republic of Vanuatu in 1980.

In the July 2004 legislative elections, the National United Party (NUP) won 10 seats, becoming the largest party in parliament. Serge Vohor of the Union of Moderate Parties (UMP) was elected prime minister and formed a six-party coalition government. Vohor lost a vote of confidence in December 2004 and was replaced by Ham Lini, who formed a nine-party coalition government. Alfred Maseng was elected president in April 2004 but was removed from office on 10 May because he was ineligible to stand for election. His successor, Kalkot Mataskelekele, was elected on 17 August 2004. A legislative election is scheduled for September 2008.

POLITICAL SYSTEM

Under the 1980 constitution, the head of state is a president who is elected for a five-year term by an electoral college consisting of the presidents of the six provincial governments and the members of the legislature. The unicameral parliament has 52 members, directly elected for a four-year term. The executive is the prime minister, who is elected by parliament from among its members, and the council of ministers. A Council of Chiefs advises on matters of custom.

HEAD OF STATE

President, Kalkot Mataskelekele, *elected* 17 August 2004

SELECTED GOVERNMENT MEMBERS *at July 2008*

Prime Minister, Ham Lini
Deputy Prime Minister, Edward Natapei
Finance and Economic Development, Willie Jimmy Tapangararua
Foreign Affairs, George Andre Wells
Internal Affairs, Joe Natuman

BRITISH HIGH COMMISSIONER

HE Roger Sykes, *apptd* 2006, resident at Suva, Fiji

ECONOMY AND TRADE

The economy is based on small-scale agriculture and fishing; 65 per cent of the population is employed on plantations or in subsistence agriculture. Subsistence crops include yams, taro, fruit and vegetables; the principal cash crops are coconuts, cocoa and coffee. Cattle are kept on the plantations. There is a small light industrial sector producing frozen food and fish, canned meat and processing wood. Eco-tourism and offshore financial services are of growing importance.

The main export markets are Thailand (59.6 per cent), India and Japan; imports come chiefly from Australia, Japan and Singapore. Principal exports are copra, beef, cocoa, timber, kava and coffee. The main imports are machinery and equipment, foodstuffs and fuels.

GNI – US$373m); US$1,690 per capita (2006)
Annual average growth of GDP – 6.8 per cent (2005 est)
Inflation rate – –1.6 per cent (2005 est)
Total external debt – US$81.2m (2004)
Imports – US$155m (2006)
Exports – US$40m (2006)

BALANCE OF PAYMENTS

Trade – US$116m deficit (2006)
Current Account – US$33m deficit (2006)

Trade with UK	*2006*	*2007*
Imports from UK	£802,000	£773,870
Exports to UK	£894,000	£576,673

COMMUNICATIONS

Vanuatu has just over 1,000km of roads, of which about one quarter is surfaced. The islands have no waterways or railways. The main ports are Forari, Port Vila and Santo. There are about 30 airports and airfields on the islands; the international airport is at Port Vila.

There were 7,000 main telephone lines in use and 12,700 mobile phone subscribers in 2005, and 7,500 internet users in 2004.

VATICAN CITY STATE

Status Civitatis Vaticanae/Stato della Città del Vaticano or Santa Sede – State of the Vatican City or The Holy See

Area – 0.44 sq. km
Capital – Vatican City; population, 1,000 (2007 est)
Currency – Euro (€) of 100 cents
Population – 821 (2007 est)
Religion – Roman Catholicism
Language – Italian, Latin, French
Population density – 2,273 per sq. km (1997)
National anthem – 'Inno e Marcia Pontificale' ('Hymn and Pontifical March')
National day – 24 April (Inauguration of present Pontiff)
Death penalty – Abolished for all crimes (since 1969)

HISTORY

The Vatican City is surrounded on all sides by Rome. The head of the Roman Catholic Church became a temporal ruler in the eighth century, holding territory in central Italy. The Papal States were annexed in 1860 by the newly unified kingdom of Italy and Rome was captured by Italian troops in 1870–1, when the pope withdrew into the Vatican Palace. In the Lateran treaties (1929), Italy recognised the pope's sovereignty over the city of the Vatican, and declared the state to be neutral and inviolable territory. The Vatican City State has special observer status at the United Nations.

The head of state is the the Pope, the Sovereign Pontiff. He is elected for life by a conclave consisting of members of the Sacred College of Cardinals. Administration of the Vatican City State is carried out by the Pontifical Commission and the Secretariat of State, which are appointed by the pope. All Vatican officials vacate their offices on the death of a pope. Pope Benedict XVI confirmed in office the president of the Pontifical Commission and the members of the Secretariat of State after his election.

Sovereign Pontiff, His Holiness Pope Benedict XVI (Joseph Ratzinger), *born* 16 April 1927, *elected* 19 April 2005, *inaugurated* 24 April 2005

SECRETARIAT OF STATE *as at July 2008*
Secretary of State, Cardinal Tarcisio Bertone
Substitute for General Affairs, Archbishop Leonardo Sandri
Secretary for Relations with States, Archbishop Dominique Mamberti

PONTIFICAL COMMISSION
President, Archbishop Giovanni Lajolo

APOSTOLIC NUNCIATURE
54 Parkside, London SW19 5NE
T 020-8944 7189
Apostolic Nuncio, HE Archbishop Faustino Sainz Munoz, *apptd* 2005

BRITISH EMBASSY TO THE HOLY SEE
Via XX Settembre 80/A, 00187 Rome
T (+39) (6) 4220 4000 **E** holysee@fco.gov.uk
W www.britishembassy.gov.uk/holysee
Ambassador Extraordinary and Plenipotentiary, HE Francis Campbell, *apptd* 2005

ECONOMY

The Vatican City is unique in having a non-commercial economy. It is supported by financial contributions by Roman Catholic dioceses worldwide. Revenue is also generated by the sale of postage stamps, coins, medals and tourist mementoes, and from income from investments and property.

MEDIA AND CULTURE

There is one official television channel in the Vatican City, and one official radio station (Vatican Radio), broadcasting seven channels. The Vatican Information Service is the state's official news service. The city is a World Heritage Site. Its architectural masterpiece, St Peter's Basilica, is famed for its domed roof and the Sistine Chapel ceiling, respectively designed and painted by Michelangelo. Much of the state's wealth is in a vast art collection.

VENEZUELA

República Bolivariana de Venezuela – Bolivarian Republic of Venezuela

Area – 912,050 sq. km
Capital – Caracas; population, 2,985,000 (2007 est)
Major cities – Barquisimeto, Ciudad Guayana, Maracaibo, Valencia
Currency – Bolívar fuerte (Bs. F) of 100 céntimos
Population – 26,023,528 rising at 1.49 per cent per year (2007 est)
Religion – Roman Catholicism (92 per cent), Protestantism (8 per cent) (est)
Language – Spanish (official)
Population density – 31 per sq. km (2006)
Urban population – 88.1 per cent (2005 est)
Median age (years) – 24.9 (2007 est)
National anthem – 'Gloria al Bravo Pueblo' ['Glory to the Brave People']
National day – 5 July (Independence Day)
Life expectancy (years) – 73.28 (2007 est)
Mortality rate – 5.08 (2007 est)
Birth rate – 21.22 (2006 est)
Infant mortality rate – 22.52 (2007 est)
Death penalty – Abolished for all crimes (since 1863)
CPI score – 2.0 (2007)
Population below poverty line – 37.9 per cent (2005 est)

CLIMATE AND TERRAIN

The Andean mountains, of which the main range is the Sierra Nevada de Mérida, run across the north-west of the country, separating the northern coast from the central plains. The Guiana Highlands occupy the south-east of the country. Elevation extremes range from 5,007m (Pico Bolivar) at the highest point to 0m (Caribbean Sea) at the lowest. The Orinoco flows across the centre of the country to its delta on the Atlantic coast. Its upper waters are united with those of the Rio Negro (a Brazilian tributary of the Amazon) by a natural river or canal, known as the Brazo Casiquiare. The coastal regions contain many lagoons and lakes, including Maracaibo (area 13,351 sq. km), the largest lake in South America. The wet season lasts from May to November. Average temperatures in Caracas range from 16°C in January to 29°C in June.

HISTORY AND POLITICS

The first Spanish settlement was established at Cumaná in 1520 and Venezuela became part of the Viceroyalty of New Granada in the early 18th century. There were several revolts against Spanish colonial rule, and a declaration of independence in 1811 was followed by several years of struggle until troops led by Simón Bolivar defeated the Spanish at the battle of Carabobo in 1821.

Venezuela became part of Gran Colombia (with Colombia, Ecuador and Panama), and then an independent republic in 1830 under the first of a series of *caudillos* (military leaders). The first truly democratic elections were held in 1947 but the government was overthrown by the military within months. An enduring civilian democracy was established in 1958 and introduced a period of relative political stability.

Oil revenues supported a buoyant economy in the 1970s but a price collapse in the mid-1980s led to economic difficulties and widespread poverty, causing social unrest and a number of attempted coups. President Hugo Chávez's economic reforms and his authoritarian style have polarised domestic opinion, provoking strikes and demonstrations, an attempted military coup in 2002 and a recall referendum in 2004, which he won.

President Chávez was originally elected in 1998 under the 1961 constitution but in 2000 successfully sought re-election under the 1999 constitution; he was elected for a third term in December 2006. In the 2005 legislative election, the president's Fifth Republic Movement won an overall majority in the legislature and parties allied to it took the remaining seats because of an opposition boycott of the election; international observers declared the polls fair. President Chávez's proposed constitutional reforms, increasing his powers and accelerating his 'socialist revolution' were approved by the legislature in November 2007 but rejected in a referendum in December 2007.

POLITICAL SYSTEM

Under the 1999 constitution, the executive president is directly elected for a six-year term, renewable only once. The unicameral National Assembly *(Asamblea Nacional)* has 165 members, directly elected for a five-year term. The president appoints the vice-president and the council of ministers.

The country is divided into 22 states, two federal territories, one federal district (around the capital) and 72 federal dependencies. The states have considerable autonomy and each has its own legislature and elected governor.

HEAD OF STATE

President, Col. Hugo Chávez Frías (retd), *elected* 6 December 1998, *sworn in* 2 February 1999, *re-elected* 2000, 2006

Vice-President, Col. Ramon Carrizalez (retd)

SELECTED GOVERNMENT MEMBERS *as at July 2008*

Interior and Justice, Ramon Rodriguez Chacin

Defence, Gen. Gustavo Rangel Briceno

Economy, Pedro Morejon

Foreign Relations, Nicolas Maduro

EMBASSY OF THE BOLIVARIAN REPUBLIC OF VENEZUELA

1 Cromwell Road, London SW7 2HW

T 020-7584 4206 E info@venezlon.co.uk

Ambassador Extraordinary and Plenipotentiary, HE Samuel Moncada, *apptd* 2007

BRITISH EMBASSY

Edificio Torre la Castellana, Piso 11, Avenida la Principal de la Castellana, Caracas 1601

T (+58) (212) 263 8411 E britishembassy@internet.ve

W www.britain.org.ve

Ambassador Extraordinary and Plenipotentiary, HE Catherine Royle, *apptd* 2007

BRITISH COUNCIL

Torre Credicard, Piso 3, Avenida Principal El Bosque, Chacaito, Caracas

T (+58) (212) 952 9965 W www.britishcouncil.org/venezuela

Director, Cherry Gough

DEFENCE

The army has 81 main battle tanks, 71 armoured personnel carriers and 13 armed helicopters. The navy has 2 submarines, 6 frigates, 6 patrol and coastal vessels and 10 combat aircraft at 10 bases. The air force has 94 combat aircraft.

Military expenditure – US$2,580m (2006)

Military personnel – 115,000: army 63,000, navy 17,500, air force 11,500, National Guard 23,000

Conscription duration – 30 months (selective)

ECONOMY AND TRADE

Much of industry is state-owned, and since President Chávez came to power a number of private assets, some foreign-owned, have been nationalised; these include major oil, electricity and telecommunications companies. The oil and gas industries are the mainstays of the economy, providing 90 per cent of exports and over 50 per cent of government revenue, but the heavy dependence on them makes the economy vulnerable to global price fluctuations. Recent high prices have funded an expansion in government spending but this has combined with a consumption boom to produce inflation of over 20 per cent.

Agriculture comprises large-scale commercial farms and subsistence farming. Land distribution is uneven, but redistribution of land to the rural poor, breaking up the larger estates, has begun. Agricultural products include maize, sorghum, sugar cane, rice, bananas, vegetables and coffee. There is an extensive beef and dairy farming industry. Agriculture provides 3.8 per cent of GDP and engages over 10 per cent of the workforce.

There are very large deposits of minerals, especially coal, iron ore, bauxite and gold, which are being mined. Apart from oil and gas extraction and mining, the main industries are production of construction materials, textiles, steel and aluminium, food processing and vehicle assembly. Industry contributes 41 per cent of GDP and services 55 per cent.

The main trading partners are the USA (46 per cent of exports; 31 per cent of imports) and neighbouring countries. Principal exports are oil, bauxite and aluminium, steel, chemicals, agricultural products and basic manufactures. The main imports are raw materials, machinery, transport equipment and construction materials.

GNI – US$164,000m; US$6,070 per capita (2006)

Annual average growth of GDP – 8.3 per cent (2007 est)

Inflation rate – 20.7 per cent (2007 est)

Unemployment – 9.1 per cent (2007 est)

Total external debt – US$45,440m (2007 est)

Imports – US$33,600m (2006)

Exports – US$59,000m (2006)

BALANCE OF PAYMENTS

Trade – US$25,592m surplus (2006)

Current Account – US$27,167m surplus (2006)

Trade with UK	*2006*	*2007*
Imports from UK	£235,951,000	£250,313,520
Exports to UK	£604,960,000	£488,614,650

COMMUNICATIONS

There are 96,155km of roads, some 32,308km of them surfaced. Road and river communications have made railways of negligible importance, except for carrying iron ore in the south-east, although the government is expanding the network and there are now some 682km of lines. The 7,100km of inland waterways include 400km on the river Orinoco which, with Lake Maracaibo, is navigable for ocean-going ships. The main ports are Maracaibo, Puerto Cabello and Caracas-La Guaira. There are over 300 airports and airfields, the principal airports being at Caracas and Maracaibo.

Telecommunications are being modernised and expanded. In 2006 there were 4.2 million main lines in use, 18.7 million mobile phone subscribers and 4.1 million internet users.

EDUCATION AND HEALTH

There are nine years of compulsory education.

Literacy rate – 93 per cent (2004 est)

Gross enrolment ratio (percentage of relevant age group) – primary 104 per cent; secondary 78 per cent; tertiary 52 per cent (2006 est)

Health expenditure (per capita) – US$247 (2005)

Hospital beds (per 1,000 people) – 0.9 (2000–6)

MEDIA

Media watchdogs have accused President Chávez of creating a climate of fear amongst journalists; in May 2007 Radio Caracas Television, the country's most influential private network and an outspoken critic of the president, was closed after the government refused to renew its licence. Chávez has his own television and radio shows on the government-run networks There are six daily newspapers, including *El Mundo* and *El Nacional*.

VIETNAM

Cong Hoa Xa Hoi Chu Nghia Viet Nam – Socialist Republic of Vietnam

Area – 329,560 sq. km

Capital – Hanoi; population, 4,378,000 (2007 est)

Major cities – Da Nang, Haiphong, Ho Chi Minh City

Currency – Dong of 10 ho or 100 xu

Population – 85,262,356 rising at 1 per cent per year (2007 est)

Religion – Buddhism (50 per cent), Roman Catholicism (8 per cent), Cao Dai (2 per cent), Hoa Hao (2 per cent) (est). Cao Dai is a syncretistic religion that combines elements of several faiths. Hoa Hao is a branch of Buddhism that focuses on private acts of worship and devotion

Language – Vietnamese (official), English, French, Khmer

Population density – 271 per sq. km (2006)

Urban population – 26.7 per cent (2005 est)

Median age (years) – 26.4 (2007 est)

National anthem – 'Tien Quan Ca' ['The March to the Front']

National day – 2 September (Independence Day)

Life expectancy (years) – 71.07 (2007 est)

Mortality rate – 6.19 (2007 est)

Birth rate – 16.63 (2007 est)

Infant mortality rate – 24.37 (2007 est)

Death penalty – Retained

CPI score – 2.6 (2007)

Population below poverty line – 19.5 per cent (2004 est)

CLIMATE AND TERRAIN

The terrain consists of flat river deltas, of the Hong (Red) in the north and of the Mekong in the south, divided by central highlands. The country is mountainous in the far north and north-west. Elevation extremes range from 3,144m (Fan Si Pan) at the highest point to 0m (South China Sea) at the lowest. The climate is tropical, with a monsoon season that lasts from May to September in the north of the country, and from September to January in the south. Average temperatures in Hanoi range from 17°C in January to 29°C in June.

HISTORY AND POLITICS

Independent kingdoms in Vietnam were unified in the 15th century but power became decentralised until the early 19th century, when central power was reasserted with the assistance of France. From 1858 to 1884 France conquered Vietnam, establishing three protectorates which in 1887 became part of France's Indo-Chinese Union with Cambodia and Laos. Vietnam was under Japanese occupation from 1940 to 1945; Vietnamese communists fought a guerrilla war of resistance against the occupiers and, controlling most of the country when the Second World War ended, declared independence.

France's attempts to reassert its control led to the Indo-China War (1946–54) that ended with France's withdrawal and an armistice dividing the country into communist North Vietnam and non-communist South Vietnam. In 1957 a communist insurgency that began in South Vietnam escalated into war between the communist north and the US-backed south. A ceasefire and peace talks led to the withdrawal of US troops in 1973. North Vietnam violated the peace agreements to capture Saigon and took control of the south in 1975. North and South Vietnam were reunified in 1976 as the Socialist Republic of Vietnam.

A degree of economic liberalisation was introduced from 1986 and was enshrined in a new constitution in 1992 which approved many economic and political reforms, but power remains with the ruling Communist Party. The party leadership's request in early 2006 for comments on its political platform prompted a public debate about the party's role, criticism of government and some calls for political pluralism.

At its five-yearly meeting in 2006, the Communist Party Congress elected a new politburo and secretariat. A few months later the president and prime minister resigned to allow a younger leadership to be appointed; Nguyen Minh Triet was elected president to complete his predecessor's term of office, and he appointed Nguyen Tan Dung as prime minister. In the 2007 legislative election, the Communist Party won 450 of the 500 seats; subsequently Nguyen Minh Triet was re-elected president and Nguyen Tan Dung was reappointed prime minister.

POLITICAL SYSTEM
The 1992 constitution was amended in 2001 to allow small-scale capitalism greater freedom. The head of state is a president elected by the legislature to serve a five-year term. The unicameral National Assembly *(Quoc-Hoi)* has 500 members, who are directly elected for a five-year term. The head of government is the prime minister, who is responsible to the National Assembly, which appoints the council of ministers. However, effective power lies with the Communist Party of Vietnam. Its highest executive body is the Central Committee, elected by the national party congress held every five years. The politburo and the secretariat of the central committee, which exercise the real power, are elected at the party congress.

HEAD OF STATE
President, Nguyen Minh Triet, *elected* 27 June 2006
re-elected 24 June 2007
Vice-President, Truong My Hoa

SELECTED GOVERNMENT MEMBERS *as at July 2008*
Prime Minister, Nguyen Tan Dung
Deputy Prime Ministers, Pham Gia Khiem (Foreign Affairs); Troung Vinh Trong; Nguyen Sinh Hung; Nguyen Thien Nhan; Hoang Trung Hai
Finance, Vu Van Ninh
Internal Affairs, Tran Van Tuan
National Defence, Gen. Phung Quang Thanh

EMBASSY OF THE SOCIALIST REPUBLIC OF VIETNAM
12–14 Victoria Road, London W8 5RD
T 020-7937 1912 E embassy@vietnamembassy.org.uk
Ambassador Extraordinary and Plenipotentiary, HE Tran Quang Hoan, *apptd* 2007

BRITISH EMBASSY
Central Building, 31 Hai Ba Trung, Hanoi
T (+84) (4) 936 0500 E bcghcmc@hcm.vnn.vn
W www.uk-vietnam.org
Ambassador Extraordinary and Plenipotentiary, HE Mark Kent, *apptd* 2008

BRITISH COUNCIL
40 Cat Linh Street, Dong Da, Hanoi
T (+84) (4) 843 6780 W www.britishcouncil.org/vietnam
Director, Keith Davies

DEFENCE
The army has 1,315 main battle tanks, 1,380 armoured personnel carriers and 300 armoured infantry fighting vehicles. The navy has 2 submarines, 5 frigates, 6 corvettes and 38 patrol and coastal vessels at 7 principal bases. The air force has 219 combat aircraft and 26 armed helicopters.
Military budget – US$3,730m (2007)
Military personnel – 455,000: army 412,000, navy 13,000, air force 30,000; paramilitary 40,000
Conscription duration – 24–36 months

ECONOMY AND TRADE
The economy struggled for a decade after 1975 owing to the devastation of war and the imposition of a centrally planned economy. Since economic liberalisation and international integration were adopted in 1986, the economy has grown substantially, albeit from a low base, and competitive, export-driven industries are being developed, attracting foreign investment and international aid. Poverty has been reduced, although rural areas have benefited less, so there is a disparity in wealth distribution between the urban and rural populations. The government aims to turn Vietnam into an industrialised country by 2020.

Although its contribution is gradually shrinking, agriculture is still a mainstay of the economy, accounting for 19.5 per cent of GDP and employing 55.6 per cent of the workforce. The main industries are food processing, machine building, coal mining, manufacture of clothing, footwear, steel, cement, chemical fertiliser, glass, tyres and paper, and oil and gas production from large offshore reserves. Industry now contributes 42.3 per cent of GDP and services 38.2 per cent.

The main trading partners are China, Japan, the USA, Singapore and Taiwan. Principal exports are crude oil, fish and seafood, rice, coffee, rubber, tea, clothing and footwear. The main imports are machinery and equipment, petroleum products, fertiliser, steel products, raw cotton, grain, cement and motorcycles.
GNI – US$58,500m (2006); US$700 per capita (2006)
Annual average growth of GDP – 8.2 per cent (2007 est)
Inflation rate – 8.1 per cent (2007 est)
Unemployment – 4.2 per cent (2007 est)
Total external debt – US$24,410m (2007 est)
Imports – US$44,000m (2006)
Exports – US$40,000m (2006)

BALANCE OF PAYMENTS
Trade – US$4,805m deficit (2006)
Current Account – US$244m deficit (2006)

Trade with UK	*2006*	*2007*
Imports from UK	£95,701,000	£133,727,245
Exports to UK	£809,500,000	£860,473,562

COMMUNICATIONS
Vietnam has 222,000km of roads, 180,000km of which are unsurfaced. It has 2,600km of railways and 17,700km of navigable waterways. The main ports are Haiphong and Ho Chi Minh City. The principal airports are at Ho Chi Minh City, Hanoi and Da Nang.

Telecommunications systems are being modernised and expanded, and mobile phone distribution is growing rapidly. There were 10.8 million main lines in use, 33.2 million mobile phone subscribers and 17.8 million internet users in 2007.

EDUCATION AND HEALTH
Literacy rate – 90.3 per cent (2004 est)
Gross enrolment ratio (percentage of relevant age group) – primary 90 per cent; secondary 76 per cent; tertiary 16 per cent (2006 est)
Health expenditure (per capita) – US$37 (2005)
Hospital beds (per 1,000 people) – 1.4 (2000–6)

MEDIA
The Communist Party has a firm grip on the media and has closed down television and radio stations that have expressed dissent from the party line. There is one national television station and many local stations; some satellite channels are also available. The state-run radio network operates several national stations. The Communist Party and the People's Army both publish a daily newspaper and there are also newspapers published in English and French.

YEMEN

Al-Jumhuriyah al-Yamaniyah – Republic of Yemen

Area – 527,970 sq. km
Capital – Sana'a; population, 2,008,000 (2007 est)
Major cities – Aden (the former capital of South Yemen), Al Hudaydah, Ibb, Al Mukulla, Ta'izz
Currency – Riyal of 100 fils
Population – 22,230,531 rising at 3.46 per cent per year (2007 est)
Religion – Islam is practised by the majority of the population
Language – Arabic (official)
Population density – 41 per sq. km (2006)
Urban population – 26.3 per cent (2005 est)
Median age (years) – 16.7 (2007 est)
National anthem – 'United Republic'
National day – 22 May (Unification Day)
Life expectancy (years) – 62.52 (2007 est)
Mortality rate – 8.05 (2007 est)
Birth rate – 42.67 (2007 est)
Infant mortality rate – 57.88 (2007 est)
Death penalty – Retained
CPI score – 2.5 (2007)
Population below poverty line – 45.2 per cent (2003)

CLIMATE AND TERRAIN

A mountainous region in the west and south divides the desert interior from the coastal regions. Elevation extremes range from 3,760m (Jabal an Nabi Shu'ayb) at the highest point to 0m (Arabian Sea) at the lowest. The coastal area has high humidity, but rainfall throughout the country is unpredictable, resulting in droughts and severe floods. Average temperatures in Aden range from 22°C in January to 37°C in June.

Included in the state of Yemen are the offshore islands of Perim and Kamaran in the Red Sea, and Suqutra in the Gulf of Aden. The border with Saudi Arabia, except for the north-west corner, is unclear and is being delineated following an agreement between the two countries in 2000.

HISTORY AND POLITICS

Northern Yemen became part of the Ottoman Empire in the early 16th century and although it achieved some independence in the 17th century, Ottoman control was re-established in the 1870s and the area remained part of the empire until it collapsed at the end of the First World War. In 1918 north Yemen became an independent kingdom under the rule of the Hamid al-Din dynasty. A revolution in 1962 overthrew the monarchy and the Yemen Arab Republic was declared. Fighting between royalists and republicans continued until 1967, when the republican regime was recognised internationally.

Aden, on the south coast, came under British rule in 1839, and a protectorate was gradually established over the sultanates of the southern hinterland in the second half of the 19th century. An armed rebellion against British rule began in 1963. After British troops withdrew in 1967, power was seized by the National Liberation Front, which established a repressive communist regime in the People's Republic of South Yemen (later renamed the People's Democratic Republic of Yemen).

There were border clashes between the two Yemeni states in 1971–2 and again in 1978, when a ceasefire agreement included a commitment to merge the two states. Negotiations began in 1979 and the two countries united as the Republic of Yemen on 22 May 1990. A power struggle between the former northern and southern elites led to a three-month civil war in 1994 in which a southern attempt to secede was crushed by northern government forces. Tensions remain between the north and south; southerners perceived the south to be marginalised and their resentment has led to public protests. Tourists have been kidnapped on several occasions by groups seeking concessions from the government.

Fighting occurred in the north-west in 2004–5 as government forces suppressed an uprising by some members of the Zaidi sect, a Shia sect in the predominantly Sunni country. There were brief resurgences in the fighting in early 2007 and early 2008.

Lt.-Gen. Ali Abdullah Saleh, president of North Yemen from 1978, became president of the united country in 1990. He was elected president for a five-year term by the house of representatives in 1994 and, following constitutional changes, re-elected for a seven-year term in the first direct presidential election in 1999; he was re-elected again in 2006. In the 2003 legislative election, the ruling General People's Congress (GPC) won 228 seats and formed a coalition government with the Yemeni Alliance for Reform (YAR or al-Islah) led by Abd al-Qadir Abd al-Rahman Bajammal. Bajammal was replaced as prime minister by Ali Mohammad Mujawar in March 2007.

POLITICAL SYSTEM

The 1991 constitution was amended following a referendum in 2001. The head of state is a president who is directly elected for a seven-year term, renewable once only. The unicameral House of Representatives *(Majlis al-Nowab)* has 301 members directly elected for a six-year term. In addition, there is an advisory Shura council, whose 111 members are appointed by the president. The prime minister is appointed by the president.

HEAD OF STATE
President, Field Marshal Ali Abdullah Saleh, *took office* 22 May 1990, *elected* 1 October 1994, *re-elected* 1999, 2006
Vice-President, Gen. Abdrabo Mansour Hadi

SELECTED GOVERNMENT MEMBERS *as at July 2008*
Prime Minister, Ali Mohammad Mujawar
Deputy Prime Ministers, Gen. Rashad Mohammad al-Alimi *(Defence);* Abdul-Karim Ismail al-Arhabi; Sadiq Abu Ras
Foreign Affairs, Abu-Bakr Abdallah al-Qirbi
Finance, Numan Saleh al-Suhaibi

EMBASSY OF THE REPUBLIC OF YEMEN
57 Cromwell Road, London SW7 2ED
T 020-7584 6607 E yemen.embassy@btconnect.com
Ambassador Extraordinary and Plenipotentiary, HE Mohamed Taha Mustafa, *apptd* 2005

BRITISH EMBASSY
PO Box 1287, 129 Haddah Road, Sana
T (+967) (1) 264 081 W www.britishembassy.gov.uk/yemen
Ambassador Extraordinary and Plenipotentiary, HE Tim Torlot, *apptd* 2007

BRITISH COUNCIL
PO Box 2157, 3rd Floor, Administrative Tower, Sana'a Trade Centre, Algiers Street, Sana'a
T (+967) (1) 448 356/7 W www.britishcouncil.org/yemen
Director, Elizabeth White

DEFENCE

The army has 790 main battle tanks, 710 armoured personnel carriers and 200 armoured infantry fighting vehicles. The navy has 20 patrol and coastal vessels at 2 bases. The air force has 79 combat aircraft and 8 armed helicopters.
Military budget – US$908m (2007)
Military personnel – 66,700: army 60,000, navy 1,700, air force 3,000; paramilitary 71,200
Conscription duration – 24 months

ECONOMY AND TRADE

Despite its oil industry, the mainstay of the economy, Yemen is one of the poorest countries in the Arab world. It has received IMF support for restructuring and modernising the economy, though the political will to implement the programme has flagged in recent years and the government is also struggling to rein in high spending and corruption. Agriculture is largely of a subsistence nature, and, with herding and fishing, engages about 75 per cent of the population, contributing 12.3 per cent of GDP. Apart from oil producing and refining, industry consists of small-scale manufacturing of cotton textiles, leather goods, handicrafts, aluminium products and cement, food processing and ship repair. The main trading partners are China, the UAE, India, Thailand and the USA. Principal exports are crude oil, coffee, and dried and salted fish. The main imports are food and livestock, machinery and equipment, and chemicals.
GNI – US$16,400m (2006); US$760 per capita (2006)
Annual average growth of GDP – 3.2 per cent (2007 est)
Inflation rate – 10.7 per cent (2007 est)
Unemployment – 35 per cent (2003 est)
Total external debt – US$6,122m (2007 est)
Imports – US$6,000m (2006)
Exports – US$8,000m (2006)

BALANCE OF PAYMENTS
Trade – US$2,260m surplus (2006)
Current Account – US$206m surplus (2006)

Trade with UK	*2006*	*2007*
Imports from UK	£61,876,000	£67,728,633
Exports to UK	£16,206,000	£15,093,255

COMMUNICATIONS

Yemen has 71,000km of roads, of which 6,000km are surfaced. Its main ports are at Aden, Al Hudaydah and Al-Mukalla. The principal airports are at Sana'a and Aden.
Since unification a national telephone network has been created. Mobile phone distribution is expanding rapidly. There were 968,000 main lines in use, 2 million mobile phone users and 270,000 internet users in 2006.

EDUCATION AND HEALTH

Literacy rate – 49 per cent (2004 est)
Gross enrolment ratio (percentage of relevant age group) – primary 87 per cent; secondary 46 per cent; tertiary 9 per cent (2006 est)
Health expenditure (per capita) – US$39 (2005)
Hospital beds (per 1,000 people) – 0.6 (2000–6)

MEDIA

All broadcasting is state-run and administered through the Ministry of Information. Television and radio are the main means of communication owing to low levels of literacy. The government also funds some newspapers and controls most of the printing. There are four main newspapers: *Al-Thawrah, Yemen Times, Yemen Observer* and *Al-Ayyam*.

ZAMBIA

Republic of Zambia

Area – 752,614 sq. km
Capital – Lusaka; population, 1,328,000 (2007 est)
Major cities – Kitwe, Ndola
Currency – Kwacha (K) of 100 ngwee
Population – 11,477,447 rising at 1.66 per cent per year (2007 est)
Religion – Christianity (87 per cent), indigenous religions (7 per cent), Hinduism and Islam (1 per cent) (est)
Language – English (official); over 70 indigenous languages are spoken
Population density – 16 per sq. km (2006)
Urban population – 36.5 per cent (2005 est)
Median age (years) – 16.8 (2007 est)
National anthem – 'Stand and Sing of Zambia, Proud and Free'
National day – 24 October (Independence Day)
Life expectancy (years) – 38.44 (2007 est)
Mortality rate – 21.46 (2007 est)
Birth rate – 40.78 (2007 est)
Infant mortality rate – 100.71 (2007 est)
HIV/AIDS adult prevalence – 15.8 per cent (2005 est)
Death penalty – Retained, but not used
CPI score – 2.6 (2007)
Literacy rate – 67.9 per cent (2004 est)
Gross enrolment ratio (percentage of relevant age group) – primary 117 per cent; secondary 36 per cent (2006 est)
Health expenditure (per capita) – US$36 (2005)
Hospital beds (per 1,000 people) – 2.0 (2000–6)

CLIMATE AND TERRAIN

Landlocked Zambia lies in central Africa on a forested plateau cut through by river valleys and with higher land in the north and north-east. Elevation extremes range from 2,301m (Mafinga Hills) at the highest point to 329m (Zambezi river) at the lowest. Lake Bangweulu and parts of Lakes Tanganyika, Mweru and Kariba lie within its boundaries. The climate is tropical, with an average temperature of 28°C all year.

HISTORY AND POLITICS

Most of the ethnic groups in Zambia migrated there between the 16th and the 18th centuries. Portuguese explorers arrived in the late 18th century and, with Arab traders, began slave-trading in the 19th century. The area came under British administration as Barotseland in 1889, was named Northern Rhodesia in 1911 and became a British protectorate in 1924. It was part of the Central African Federation with South Rhodesia (Zimbabwe) and Nyasaland (Malawi) from 1953 to 1963, when the federation was dissolved and Northern Rhodesia achieved internal self-government. It became an independent republic on 24 October 1964 under the name of Zambia. Kenneth Kaunda of the United National Independence Party (UNIP) became president at independence and remained in power until 1991.

Zambia was a one-party state ruled by the UNIP from 1972 until 1990, when pressure from opposition groups led to a new constitution, under which multiparty legislative and presidential elections were held in 1991. The Movement for Multiparty Democracy (MMD) won a majority of seats in the parliament, and the MMD candidate Frederick Chiluba defeated Kenneth Kaunda in the presidential election. President Chiluba was re-elected in 1996, surviving coup attempts in 1993 and 1997.

Serious food shortages have occurred in recent years owing to floods and drought, leading to appeals for international food aid in 2001 and 2005. The country also faces serious demographic, economic and social problems because of the high levels of HIV/AIDS infection.

The 2001 presidential election was won by MMD candidate Levy Mwanawasa. In the simultaneous legislative election, the MMD won 69 seats, the United Party for National Development (UPND) won 49 seats, other parties and independents won 32 seats. In the 2006 presidential and legislative elections, President Mwanawasa was re-elected and the MMD remained the largest party in the legislature, although it commands a majority only because of the appointed members.

President Mwanawasa died in August 2008; under the country's constitution, presidential elections must be held within 90 days.

POLITICAL SYSTEM

Under the 1991 constitution, the executive president is directly elected for a five-year term, renewable only once. The unicameral National Assembly has 158 members: 150 directly elected, up to eight nominated by the president and a speaker; all serve a five-year term. The president appoints the cabinet.

HEAD OF STATE

President, Levy Mwanawasa, *elected* 27 December 2001, *sworn in* 2 January 2002, *re-elected* 2 October 2006
Vice-President, Rupiah Banda

SELECTED GOVERNMENT MEMBERS *as at July 2008*

Home Affairs, Lt.-Gen. Ronnie Shikapwasha
Foreign Affairs, Kabinga Pande
Finance, Peter Ng'andu Magande

HIGH COMMISSION FOR THE REPUBLIC OF ZAMBIA

Zambia House, 2 Palace Gate, London W8 5NG
T 020-7589 6655 E zhal@btconnect.com W www.zhcl.org.uk
High Commissioner, HE Anderson K. Chibwa, *apptd* 2003

BRITISH HIGH COMMISSION

PO Box 50050, 5210 Independence Avenue, 15101 Ridgeway, Lusaka
T (+260) (21) 1251 133 E bhc-lusaka@fco.gov.uk
High Commissioners, HE Thomas Carter and HE Carolyn Davidson, *apptd* 2008

BRITISH COUNCIL

PO Box 34571, Heroes Place, Cairo Road, Lusaka
T (+260) (21) 122 8332 W www.britishcouncil.org/zambia
Director, Paul Clementson

DEFENCE

The army has 30 main battle tanks and 13 armoured personnel carriers. The air force has 29 combat capable aircraft.
Military budget – US$243m (2007 est)
Military personnel – 15,100: army 13,500, air 1,600; paramilitary 1,400

ECONOMY AND TRADE

Although prosperous at independence, the economy was devastated by the drop in world copper prices in the 1970s and Zambia remains one of the world's poorest countries, with about three-quarters of the population living below the poverty line. The transition in the 1990s from a state-controlled to a free-market system improved productivity, especially in the now privatised copper industry, which is the mainstay of the economy. Despite budgetary reform, foreign debt is high, although more than 50 per cent has been written off in recent years.

Copper is the main source of foreign earnings and increased demand in recent years for electronics has spurred investment and greater output, increasing revenue and making the industry a driver of recent economic growth. However, 85 per cent of the workforce remains engaged in agriculture, mostly at subsistence level, which accounts for 17.3 per cent of GDP. The main industries are copper mining and processing, construction, food processing, manufacture of beverages, chemicals, textiles and fertiliser, and horticulture. The main trading partners are South Africa, Switzerland, the UAE and China. Principal exports are copper, cobalt, electricity, tobacco, cut flowers and cotton. The main imports are machinery, transport equipment, petroleum products, electricity, fertiliser, foodstuffs and clothing.
GNI – US$7,400m (2006); US$630 per capita (2006)
Annual average growth of GDP – 5.3 per cent (2007 est)
Inflation rate – 10.5 per cent (2007 est)
Unemployment – 50 per cent (2000 est)
Total external debt – US$2,798m (2007 est)
Imports – US$2,920m (2006)
Exports – US$3,690m (2006)

BALANCE OF PAYMENTS

Trade – US$769m surplus (2006)
Current Account – US$120m surplus (2006)

Trade with UK	*2006*	*2007*
Imports from UK	£35,323,000	£35,787,011
Exports to UK	£17,772,000	£20,993,422

MEDIA

The broadcast media is dominated by the government-run television and radio networks. The only television service is provided by the state-run Zambia National Broadcasting Association. There are private radio stations but they do not provide much political content. Three of the four newspapers are state-owned.

ZIMBABWE

Republic of Zimbabwe

Area – 390,580 sq. km
Capital – Harare; population, 1,572,000 (2007 est)
Major cities – Bulawayo, Chitungwiza, Gweru, Mutare
Currency – Zimbabwe dollar (Z$) of 100 cents
Population – 12,311,143 rising at 0.6 per cent per year (2007 est); Shona (82 per cent), Ndebele (14 per cent) (est)
Religion – Christianity (70 per cent), Islam (1 per cent) (est). Indigenous beliefs are widely followed, often combined with Christian faiths
Language – English (official), Shona, Ndebele
Population density – 34 per sq. km (2006)
Urban population – 35.9 per cent (2005 est)
Median age (years) – 20.1 (2007 est)
National anthem – 'Simudzai Mureza wedu WeZimbabwe' ['Blessed Be the Land of Zimbabwe']
National day – 18 April (Independence Day)
Life expectancy (years) – 39.5 (2007 est)
Mortality rate – 21.76 (2007 est)
Birth rate – 27.72 (2007 est)
Infant mortality rate – 51.12 (2007 est)
HIV/AIDS adult prevalence – 19.2 per cent (2005 est)
Death penalty – Retained
CPI score – 2.1 (2007)
Population below poverty line – 68 per cent (2004)

CLIMATE AND TERRAIN

A landlocked country, Zimbabwe's terrain is mainly high plateau with a central high veld and mountains in the east. Elevation extremes range from 2,592m (Inyangani) at the highest point to 162m (confluence of the Runde and Save rivers) at the lowest. The wet season coincides with the summer, which runs from November to March. Average temperatures in Harare range from 7°C in June to 29°C in November.

HISTORY AND POLITICS

Organised settlement of the region began at least 20,000 years ago and culminated in the establishment of a powerful settlement at Great Zimbabwe in the 12th century AD. In the 19th century this was taken over by the Ndebele people and became the kingdom of Matabeleland, which was often in dispute with the people of Mashonaland to the north. The area came under British influence from the 1880s, when the British started to exploit the mineral resources. Britain invaded Mashonaland in 1890 and seized Matabeleland in 1893. The two areas became a British protectorate as Southern Rhodesia in 1898, which became a self-governing colony in 1923.

It was part of the Central African Federation from 1953 until 1963, when Northern Rhodesia (Zambia) and Nyasaland (Malawi) became independent. Opposition to independence under black majority rule in Southern Rhodesia prompted a unilateral declaration of independence (UDI) by the white-dominated colonial government in 1965. Economic sanctions and guerrilla warfare by African nationalist groups forced the government to negotiate, and UDI was terminated in 1979. Power was transferred to the majority population and the country became independent as the Republic of Zimbabwe on 18 April 1980.

Robert Mugabe became prime minister at independence and executive president in 1987. His regime has become increasingly autocratic, brutally suppressing opposition and dissent, and rejecting international criticism of human rights and other abuses; Zimbabwe left the Commonwealth in 2003 because its membership had been suspended indefinitely over the political situation. The appropriation of white-owned farms, which began in 2000, was accompanied by intimidation and violence. The seizures caused an agricultural collapse that, combined with a long drought, led to widespread food shortages in 2001, and a state of disaster was declared in 2002; international food aid is still required but distribution is inequitable, used by the government to garner and reward supporters.

Mass anti-government protests, including a general strike in 2003, provoked a brutal crackdown by the authorities; opposition leaders were arrested and allegedly tortured for holding demonstrations in 2006 and 2007. Talks in South Africa between government and opposition representatives began in June 2007 but made little progress towards solving the country's political and economic crises.

In the legislative elections held in March 2008, the main opposition party, the Movement for Democratic Change (MDC) won 99 seats in the lower chamber, defeating President Mugabe's party, the Zimbabwe African National Union–Patriotic Front (ZANU-PF), which won 97. In the senate, ZANU-PF won 30 of the elected seats and the MDC 24.

The results of the simultaneous presidential election were delayed for several weeks. When eventually announced, they showed that the MDC leader Morgan Tsvangirai had received more of the vote (47.9 per cent, compared with 43.2 per cent for President Mugabe) but his majority was insufficient for a first-round victory and a second round of voting was scheduled for 27 June. ZANU-PF began a savage campaign of violence and intimidation, specifically targeting MDC supporters, and this became so severe that Morgan Tsvangirai withdrew from the run-off election on 22 June.

The victor by default, President Mugabe, defiant in the

face of international condemnation and the threat of sanctions, persisted with polling. He won 85 per cent of the vote, the turnout for which was 42 per cent; Morgan Tsvangirai, whose name remained on the ballot papers, won about 9 per cent of the vote and about 5 per cent of ballots were spoilt. Talks to create a national unity government are currently ongoing.

POLITICAL SYSTEM
The 1980 constitution was amended in 1987, 1990, 2005 and 2007. The executive president is directly elected for a six-year term. The bicameral parliament comprises the House of Assembly and a senate. The former has 210 members, directly elected for a five-year term. The senate (re-introduced in 2005) has 93 members, 60 elected (six from each province), five appointed by the president, ten provincial governors and 18 traditional chiefs, who serve a five-year term. The president appoints the cabinet.

The country is divided into eight provinces and two cities (Bulawayo and Harare) with provincial status. The provinces are: Manicaland, Mashonaland Central, Mashonaland East, Mashonaland West, Masvingo, Matabeleland North, Matabeleland South and Midlands.

HEAD OF STATE
President, C.-in-C. of the Defence Forces, Robert Gabriel Mugabe, *elected* 30 December 1987, *re-elected* 1990, 1996, 2002, 2008
Vice-Presidents, Joseph Msika; Joyce Mujuru

SELECTED GOVERNMENT MEMBERS *as at July 2008*
Defence, Sidney Sekeramayi
Finance, Samuel Mumbengegwi
Foreign Affairs, Simbarashe Mumbengegwi
Home Affairs, Kembo Mohadi

EMBASSY OF THE REPUBLIC OF ZIMBABWE
Zimbabwe House, 429 Strand, London WC2R 0JR
T 020-7836 7755 **E** zimlondon@yahoo.co.uk
Ambassador Extraordinary and Plenipotentiary, HE Gabriel Mharadze Machinga, *apptd* 2005

BRITISH EMBASSY
PO Box 4490, Corner House, Samora Machel Avenue/Leopold Takawira Street, Harare
T (+263) (4) 772 990 **E** british.info@fco.gov.uk
W www.ukinzimbabwe.fco.gov.uk
Ambassador Extraordinary and Plenipotentiary, HE Dr Andrew Pocock CMG, *apptd* 2006

BRITISH COUNCIL
PO Box 664, Corner House, Samora Machel Avenue, Harare
T (+263) (4) 775 313-4/756 668
W www.britishcouncil.org/zimbabwe
Director, Rajiv Bendre

DEFENCE
The army has 40 main battle tanks, 80 armoured infantry fighting vehicles and 85 armoured personnel carriers. The air force has 45 combat capable aircraft and 6 armed helicopters.
Military budget – US$155m (2006)
Military personnel – 29,000: army 25,000, air force 4,000; paramilitary 21,800

ECONOMY AND TRADE
The seizure of almost all the white-owned commercial farms caused a devastating drop in production and the agriculture-based economy has collapsed. Unemployment was 80 per cent in 2005 and hyperinflation, officially 26,000 per cent in 2007 but unofficially estimated at over 2,200,000 per cent, has caused huge rises in the prices of basic commodities and fuel; about 80 per cent of the population is living below the poverty line and many are dependent on food aid. Other forms of international aid have been suspended because repayment of past loans has fallen into arrears, and the government has failed to introduce economic stabilisation measures. The economy and social services have been badly hit by the migration of professional and skilled labour.

Agriculture accounted for 28 per cent of GDP in 1998 and engaged two-thirds of the workforce, but in 2007 accounted for only 18.1 per cent of GDP. The most important crops are cotton and tobacco for export and maize for domestic consumption. Other crops include wheat, coffee, sugar cane, peanuts and livestock.

The mining sector, although contributing a relatively small portion to GDP, is important to the economy as a foreign exchange earner. Almost all mineral production is exported. Gold is the most important product; others are coal, platinum, copper, nickel, tin, iron ore and other metal and non-metal ores. Mining is now the largest industrial activity and supports a ferro-alloy industry and a steel works. Manufacturing, traditionally highly dependent on the agricultural sector for raw materials, produces wood products, cement, chemicals, fertiliser, clothing, footwear, foodstuffs and beverages; output has dropped in some industries because of transport difficulties and power rationing. Industry generates 22.6 per cent of GDP and services 59.3 per cent.

The main trading partners are South Africa, Zambia, Democratic Republic of Congo, Botswana and the USA. Principal exports are platinum, cotton, tobacco, gold, ferro-alloys, textiles and clothing. The main imports are machinery and transport equipment, other manufactures, chemicals and fuels.
GNI – US$4,500m; US$340 per capita (2006)
Annual average growth of GDP – −5.7 per cent (2007 est)
Inflation rate – 6,072 per cent (2007 est)
Unemployment – 80 per cent (2005 est)
Total external debt – US$4,876m (2007 est)
Imports – US$2,100m (2006)
Exports – US$1,920m (2006)

BALANCE OF PAYMENTS
Trade – US$180m deficit (2006)
Current Account – US$333m deficit (2006)

Trade with UK	*2006*	*2007*
Imports from UK	£19,609,000	£22,893,365
Exports to UK	£26,661,000	£19,617,552

COMMUNICATIONS
Zimbabwe has 97,400km of roads, over 18,500km of which are surfaced. There are 3,000km of railways but services have become increasingly restricted by lack of diesel and spare parts, leading to the reintroduction into service of steam locomotives. It relies on rail connections through Mozambique and South Africa for access to seaports. The main airports are at Harare and Bulawayo.

The telephone system, once one of the best in Africa, is now badly maintained. Mobile phone distribution is growing quickly, but internet access is limited to Harare and some of the major towns. In 2006 there were 332,000 main lines in use, 833,000 mobile phone subscribers and 1.2 million internet users.

EDUCATION AND HEALTH

Education is compulsory at primary level, and the language of instruction is English. Over 80 per cent of schools are government-aided.

Literacy rate – 90 per cent (2004 est)

Gross enrolment ratio (percentage of relevant age group) – primary 96 per cent; secondary 36 per cent; tertiary 4 per cent (2005 est)

Health expenditure (per capita) – US$21 (2005)

MEDIA

The government exercises strict control over the print and broadcast media, and some foreign correspondents are prevented from reporting from within the country. The only television and radio stations are state-run, but overseas radio stations can be received. Two of the main daily newspapers, *The Herald* and *The Chronicle,* are run by the government. Readership of newspapers has been badly hit by rising inflation as their price often exceeds daily wages. Journalists who write anti-government reports face imprisonment.

UK OVERSEAS TERRITORIES

ANGUILLA

Area – 102 sq. km
Capital – The Valley; population, 1,000 (2007 est)
Currency – East Caribbean dollar (EC$) of 100 cents
Population – 13,677 rising at 1.38 per cent per year (2007 est)
Religion – Protestantism (83 per cent), Roman Catholicism (5 per cent), other Christian denominations (1 per cent) (est)
Language – English (official)
Population density – 134 per sq. km (1999)
Flag – British blue ensign with the coat of arms and three dolphins in the fly
National day – 30 May (Anguilla Day)
Life expectancy (years) – 77.28 (2006 est)
Mortality rate – 5.34 (2007 est)
Birth rate – 13.97 (2007 est)
Infant mortality rate – 19.61 (2007 est)
Population below poverty line – 23 per cent (2002)

CLIMATE AND TERRAIN

Anguilla is a flat coralline island in the Caribbean, and is the most northerly of the Leeward Islands. Elevation extremes range from 65m (Crocus Hill) at the highest point to 0m (Caribbean Sea) at the lowest. The climate is tropical, modified by north-east trade winds, with temperatures ranging from 24°C to 30°C throughout the year.

HISTORY AND POLITICS

Anguilla has been a British colony since 1650. For much of its history it was linked administratively with St Kitts, but three months after the Associated State of Saint Christopher (St Kitts)-Nevis-Anguilla came into being in 1967, the Anguillans repudiated government from St Kitts. A commissioner was installed in 1969 and in 1976 Anguilla was given a new status and separate constitution. Final separation from St Kitts and Nevis was effected in December 1980 and Anguilla reverted to a British dependency.

The 1982 constitution (amended in 1990) provides for a governor, an executive council comprising four elected ministers and two *ex-officio* members (the attorney-general and deputy governor), and a 12-member legislative House of Assembly, consisting of a speaker, seven elected members, two nominated members and two *ex-officio* members (the attorney-general and deputy governor). The 2005 general election was won by the Anguilla United Front with four seats.

Governor, HE Andrew George, *apptd* 2006
Chief Minister, Hon. Osbourne Fleming

ECONOMY

Tourism is the main economic activity, stimulating construction, and the offshore financial services sector is of growing importance. Export earnings are mainly from sales of fish, lobsters, livestock, concrete blocks and rum.

Imports – US$143m (2006)
Exports – US$13m (2006)

BALANCE OF PAYMENTS
Trade – US$57m deficit (2002)
Current Account – US$35m deficit (2002)

Trade with UK	*2006*	*2007*
Imports from UK	£1,236,000	£1,974,094
Exports to UK	£33,000	£14,288,300

COMMUNICATIONS

The road network is gradually expanding but less than half is paved. The main ports are Blowing Point ferry port and Wallblake airport, near The Valley.

BERMUDA

Area – 53.3 sq. km
Capital – Hamilton; population, 11,000 (2007 est)
Currency – Bermuda dollar of 100 cents
Population – 66,163 rising at 0.58 per cent per year (2007 est)
Religion – Protestantism (52 per cent), Roman Catholicism (15 per cent) (est)
Language – English (official), Portuguese
Population density – 1,231 per sq. km (2001)
Flag – British red ensign with the shield of the arms in the fly
National day – 24 May (Bermuda Day)
Life expectancy (years) – 77.96 (2006 est)
Mortality rate – 7.84 (2007 est)
Birth rate – 11.26 (2007 est)
Infant mortality rate – 8.08 (2007 est)
Population below poverty line – 19 per cent (2000)

CLIMATE AND TERRAIN

Bermuda is a group of over 130 small islands, of which about 20 are inhabited, in the North Atlantic Ocean. All the islands are volcanic in origin, with hilly interiors, surrounded by coral reefs. Elevation extremes range from 76m (Town Hill) at the highest point to 0m (Atlantic Ocean) at the lowest. The climate is subtropical, regulated by the Gulf Stream, with an average temperature of 23°C.

HISTORY AND POLITICS

Bermuda was discovered by the Spanish *c.*1503 but colonised by the British in the 17th century, becoming a colony in 1684. Independence from the UK was rejected in a 1995 referendum.

Internal self-government was introduced in 1968. The governor retains responsibility for external affairs, defence, internal security and the police, although administrative matters for the police service have been delegated to the minister of labour, home affairs and public safety. The cabinet comprises the premier and six elected members. The parliament consists of the senate of 11 appointed members and the house of assembly with 36 elected members. At the December 2007 election, the ruling Progressive Labour Party retained its 22 seats and continued in office.

Governor and Commander-in-Chief, HE Sir Richard Gozney, KCMG, *apptd* 2007
Premier, Hon. Ewart Brown

ECONOMY

The economy is based on offshore financial services for international business, especially re-insurance and tourism. Other activities include light manufacturing (re-exports of pharmaceuticals are the main export) and construction.

Trade with UK	*2006*	*2007*
Imports from UK	£19,580,000	£18,293,214
Exports to UK	£73,687,000	£25,342,286

COMMUNICATIONS

There are 447km of roads, all of which are paved, and one airport, near Ferry Reach on St David's Island. The main ports are at Hamilton and St George. The telephone system is extensive, and mobile telephone distribution is widespread.

BRITISH ANTARCTIC TERRITORY

Area – 1,709,340 sq. km
Population – There is no indigenous population; the British Antarctic Survey maintains two permanently staffed research stations at Halley and Rothera, and two part-time (summer only) stations at Fossil Bluff (Alexander Island) and Signy (South Orkney Islands)
Flag – British white ensign, without the cross of St George, with the coat of arms of the territory in the fly

CLIMATE AND TERRAIN

The British Antarctic Territory (BAT) consists of the areas south of 60°S. latitude between longitudes 20°W. and 80°W. The territory includes the South Orkney Islands, the South Shetland Islands, the mountainous Antarctic Peninsula and all adjacent islands, and the land mass extending to the South Pole.

Only around 0.7 per cent of the BAT remains ice-free and the ice sheet that permanently covers the remainder is, in places, 5km thick. The climate is polar desert with very little precipitation, and the annual average temperature at the South Pole is −49°C. The highest point of elevation is 3,184m (Mt Jackson).

HISTORY AND POLITICS

Britain made its first territorial claim to part of the Antarctic in 1908. Since 1943, a permanent presence has been maintained which became the British Antarctic Survey (BAS) in 1962. In the same year, the territory, originally administered as a dependency of the Falkland Islands, became a UK overseas territory in its own right.

The BAT is administered by the Foreign and Commonwealth Office, and has a full suite of laws, and legal and postal administrations. All activities are governed by the Antarctic Treaty of 1961, which has the objectives of keeping Antarctica demilitarised and promoting international scientific cooperation. The territory is self-financing from income tax revenue and the sale of postage stamps and coins.

GOVERNMENT OF THE BRITISH ANTARCTIC TERRITORY
Polar Regions Unit, Overseas Territory Department, Foreign and Commonwealth Office, London SW1A 2AH
T 020-7008 2617
Commissioner (non-resident), Leigh Turner, *apptd* 2006
Administrator, Dr Michael Richardson

BRITISH INDIAN OCEAN TERRITORY

Area – 54,400 sq. km, of which 60 sq. km is land
Population – No indigenous population now lives in the archipelago; in 2004, around 4,000 military personnel and civilian contract employees were based at the joint UK–US naval support facility on Diego Garcia
Flag – Divided horizontally into blue and white wavy stripes, with the Union Flag in the canton and a crowned palm-tree over all in the fly

CLIMATE AND TERRAIN

The British Indian Ocean Territory (BIOT) comprises the Chagos Archipelago of 55 islands in six main groups, situated on the Great Chagos Bank in the Indian Ocean, about 1,900km north-east of Mauritius. The largest and most southerly of the islands is Diego Garcia, a sand cay with an area of about 44 sq. km. The main island groups are Peros Banhos (29 islands with a total land area of 6.5 sq. km) and Salamon (11 islands with a total land area of 3.2 sq. km).

The flat and low terrain rarely rises more than 2m above sea level, while the climate is hot and humid.

HISTORY AND POLITICS

The Chagos Archipelago was ceded to Britain after the Napoleonic Wars and was administered from Mauritius until 1965, when the British Indian Ocean Territory was established. The islands of Farquhar, Desroches and Aldabra became part of the Seychelles when it became independent in 1976; since then the territory has consisted of the Chagos Archipelago only. Since the 1980s successive Mauritian governments have asserted a sovereignty claim to the islands, arguing that they were annexed illegally.

Diego Garcia is used as a joint naval support facility by Britain and the USA. The islands' former inhabitants (the Ilois) were expelled between 1967 and 1973 to allow for the construction of the naval base, most being resettled in Mauritius and the Seychelles. Since the 1990s the Ilois have taken legal action to obtain the right to return to and settle in the islands; the first visit by former residents took place in spring 2006, on a day trip funded by the Foreign Office and the government of Mauritius. In May 2006, the Ilois won a case before the High Court allowing them to return home to the archipelago, but not to Diego Garcia. The British government's appeal against the ruling was defeated in 2007 but a further appeal to the House of Lords is expected to be heard in 2008.

Commissioner (non-resident), Leigh Turner, *apptd* 2006
Administrator, Tony Humphries, *apptd* 2005

BRITISH VIRGIN ISLANDS

Area – 153 sq. km
Capital – Road Town; population, 9,000 (2007 est)
Currency – US dollar (US$)
Population – 23,552 rising at 1.92 per cent per year (2007 est)
Religion – Protestantism (86 per cent), Roman Catholicism (10 per cent) (est)
Language – English (official)
Population density – 134 per sq. km (2001)
Flag – British blue ensign with the shield of arms in the fly
National day – 1 July (Territory Day)

Life expectancy (years) – 76.68 (2006 est)
Mortality rate – 4.42 (2007 est)
Birth rate – 14.82 (2007 est)
Infant mortality rate – 16.13 (2007 est)

CLIMATE AND TERRAIN

Part of the Virgin Islands archipelago, the northernmost of the Leeward Islands in the Caribbean Sea, the British Virgin Islands comprise Tortola, Virgin Gorda, Anegada, Jost Van Dyke and about 40 islets; 16 of the islands are inhabited. Apart from Anegada, which is a flat coral island, the British Virgin Islands are hilly. The highest point of elevation is 521m (Sage Mountain). The climate is sub-tropical and there is little variation in temperature; typically 25°C in January and 29°C in July. The hurricane season runs from June to October.

HISTORY AND POLITICS

Initially settled by Arawak Indians from South America, the islands were named by Christopher Columbus in 1493 and annexed by the British in 1672. The islands were administered as part of the Leeward Islands colony from 1872 until 1960, when direct administration was introduced. A measure of self-government was introduced by the 1977 constitution and extended in 2000.

Under a new constitution introduced in 2007, the governor, appointed by the crown, continues to be responsible for defence, security, external affairs and the civil service and chairs the executive council. This comprises one *ex-officio* member (the attorney-general), the premier (the post replaced that of chief minister in 2007) and four other ministers. The legislative council consists of a speaker chosen from outside the council, one *ex-officio* member (the attorney-general) and 13 elected members.

The 2007 election was won by the opposition Virgin Islands Party with ten seats, and Ralph O'Neal became the territory's first premier.

Governor, HE David Pearey, *apptd* 2006
Premier, Ralph O'Neal

ECONOMY

The main industries are tourism, which generates about 45 per cent of GDP, and offshore financial services. Other industries include a rum distillery, three stone-crushing plants and factories manufacturing concrete blocks and paint. The major export items are rum, fish, fruit, livestock, gravel and sand. Chief imports are building materials, machinery, cars and foodstuffs.

Trade with UK	*2006*	*2007*
Imports from UK	£15,011,000	£13,446,517
Exports to UK	£23,656,000	£29,766,949

COMMUNICATIONS

The principal airport is on Beef Island, linked by bridge to Tortola, and there are also airfields on Anegada and Virgin Gorda. Road Harbour, at Road Town, is the main port, and ferry services connect the main islands. Many of the 177km of roads are steep and narrow.

CAYMAN ISLANDS

Area – 262 sq. km
Capital – George Town; population, 28,000 (2007 est)
Currency – Cayman Islands dollar (CI$) of 100 cents
Population – 46,600 rising at 2.5 per cent per year (2007 est)
Language – English (official)
Population density – 163 per sq. km (2002)
Flag – British blue ensign with the arms on a white disc in the fly
National day – first Monday in July (Constitution Day)
Life expectancy (years) – 80.07 (2006 est)
Mortality rate – 4.98 (2007 est)
Birth rate – 12.6 (2007 est)
Infant mortality rate – 7.8 (2007 est)
GNI – US$43,703 per capita (2002)
Annual average growth of GDP – 1.7 per cent (2002)

CLIMATE AND TERRAIN

The Cayman Islands comprise Grand Cayman, Cayman Brac and Little Cayman. Situated about 241km south of Cuba, the low-lying islands are divided from Jamaica, 289km to the south-east, by the Cayman Trench, the deepest part of the Caribbean Sea. Typical temperatures are 20°C in January and 30°C in July. The hurricane season is from June to November.

HISTORY AND POLITICS

The territory derives its name from the Carib word *caymanas* (crocodile). Permanent settlement followed the first land grant by Britain in 1734 and the islands were placed under direct control of Jamaica in 1863. When Jamaica became independent in 1962, the islands opted to remain under the British crown.

The constitution provides for a governor, a legislative assembly and a cabinet, and allows a large measure of self-government, the governor acting on the advice of the cabinet. This comprises three appointed official members and five ministers elected by the legislative assembly from among its elected members. The assembly has 18 members, 15 elected by popular vote and the three appointed official members of the cabinet. The governor has responsibility for the police, civil service, defence and external affairs. The normal life of the assembly is four years; a general election took place in May 2005 and was won by the People's Progressive Movement, which won nine seats in the assembly.

Following a modernisation review in 2002, a new constitution was drafted but was not implemented owing to disagreements. A new constitutional review began in 2007.

Governor, HE Stuart Jack, *apptd* 2005
Leader of Government Business, Hon. Kurt Tibbetts

CAYMAN ISLANDS GOVERNMENT OFFICE
6 Arlington Street, London SW1A 1RE **T** 020-7491 7772
W www.gov.ky

ECONOMY

The mainstays of the economy are offshore financial services, largely owing to the absence of direct taxation; tourism, with an emphasis on scuba diving; and real estate. Government revenue is derived from fees and duties. Reconstruction, especially of housing, is still in progress after the devastation of Hurricane Ivan in 2004.

Trade with UK	*2006*	*2007*
Imports from UK	£14,662,000	£31,326,687
Exports to UK	£31,226,000	£14,978,753

COMMUNICATIONS

The islands are served by airports at George Town and on Cayman Brac and by an airfield on Little Cayman. George

Town is the main port and there are 785km of surfaced roads.

FALKLAND ISLANDS

Area – 12,173 sq. km
Capital – Stanley; population, 2,000 (2007 est)
Currency – Falkland Island pound of 100 pence
Population – 3,105 rising at 2.44 per cent per year (2007 est)
Urban population – 84 per cent (2001)
Flag – British blue ensign with the arms on a white disc in the fly
National day – 14 June (Liberation Day)

CLIMATE AND TERRAIN

The Falkland Islands consist of East Falkland (6,759 sq. km), West Falkland (5,413 sq. km) and around 700 small islands in the South Atlantic Ocean, about 480km from the South American mainland. Elevation extremes range from 705m (Mount Usbourne) at the highest point to 0m (Atlantic Ocean) at the lowest. Temperatures in Stanley range from –5°C in winter to 24°C in summer, and annual rainfall is low (around 626mm per year).

HISTORY AND POLITICS

The Falkland Islands have a long history of occupation by European countries, including France, Spain and the UK, which claimed sovereignty in 1765 and established its first settlement in 1766.

After Argentina declared independence from Spain, the Argentine government in 1820 proclaimed its sovereignty over the Falklands and a settlement was founded in 1826 but was subsequently destroyed by the USA in 1831. In 1833 occupation was resumed by the British for the protection of the seal-fisheries, and the islands were permanently colonised. Argentina continued to claim sovereignty over the islands (known to them as *las Islas Malvinas*), and invaded the islands on 2 April 1982. A British naval and military task force recaptured the islands on 14 June 1982. A naval and military garrison of 1,265 personnel remains in the area.

Under the 1985 constitution, the governor is advised by an executive council consisting of three elected members of the legislative council and two *ex-officio* members, the chief executive and the financial secretary. The legislative council consists of eight elected members and the same two *ex-officio* members. The last election was held in November 2005; there are no political parties and all members sit as independents.

Governor and Chair of the Executive Council, HE Alan Huckle, *apptd* 2006
Chief Executive, Dr Tim Thorogood

FALKLAND ISLANDS GOVERNMENT OFFICE
Falkland House, 14 Broadway, London SW1H 0BH
T 020-7222 2542 W www.falklands.gov.fk

ECONOMY

Since the establishment of a conservation and managed fishing zone around the islands in 1987, the economy has been transformed, with revenue from fishing and related activities replacing sheep-farming as the main industry. Fishing licence fees now provide about half of government revenue, making the islands self-supporting in all but defence costs and funding the provision of health, education and welfare facilities. Tourism, especially wildlife tourism, is growing. Fish, meat, wool and hides are the principal exports. Chief imports are fuel, food and drink, construction materials and clothing.

There are believed to be substantial reserves of oil offshore and the Falkland Islands government is encouraging exploration for exploitable sites. Onshore, exploration is under way for gold.

Trade with UK	*2006*	*2007*
Imports from UK	£26,560,000	£25,448,591
Exports to UK	£8,335,000	£4,269,454

COMMUNICATIONS

There is an international airport at Mount Pleasant, served by military flights to the UK (also carrying civilian passengers) and commercial flights to Chile. The main port is Stanley Harbour and a regular shipping service operates to the UK. The road network is gradually expanding but only roads in and around Stanley are paved, and most longer internal journeys are by light aircraft. Telecommunications are possible through a satellite link and about half of the households have internet access.

GIBRALTAR

Area – 6.5 sq. km
Capital – Gibraltar
Currency – Gibraltar pound of 100 pence
Population – 27,967 rising at 0.13 per cent per year (2007 est)
Religion – Roman Catholicism (78 per cent), other Christian denominations (10 per cent), Islam (4 per cent), Judaism (2 per cent), Hinduism (1 per cent) (est)
Language – English (official), Spanish, Italian, Portuguese
Population density – 4,338 per sq. km (2001)
Flag – White with a red stripe along the lower edge; over all a red castle with a key hanging from its gateway
National day – 10 September
Life expectancy (years) – 79.8 (2006 est)
Mortality rate – 9.4 (2007 est)
Birth rate – 10.69 (2007 est)
Infant mortality rate – 4.98 (2007 est)

CLIMATE AND TERRAIN

Gibraltar is a rocky promontory, 426m at its highest point, that juts southwards from the south-east coast of Spain, with which it is connected by a low isthmus. It is about 32km from the opposite coast of Africa.

HISTORY AND POLITICS

Gibraltar was captured in 1704, during the War of the Spanish Succession, by a combined Dutch and English force, and was ceded to Great Britain by the treaty of Utrecht (1713). This treaty stipulates that if Britain ever relinquishes colonial rights over Gibraltar, the colony would return to Spain.

Spanish claims to the territory have been a source of tension for many years but after the overwhelming rejection of a joint sovereignty arrangement in a referendum in 2002, Spain moderated its attitude and the previously bilateral Anglo-Spanish talks about the territory became tripartite with the inclusion of Gibraltar from 2006.

Gibraltar is part of the EU (with the UK government

responsible for enforcing EU directives affecting Gibraltar), but is not a full member and is exempt from the common policies on customs, commerce, agriculture, fisheries and VAT. Gibraltarians have voted in EU elections since 2004.

The 1969 constitution made provision for self-government in respect of certain domestic matters, but full internal autonomy came into effect with the constitution introduced in January 2007. This limited the governor's responsibilities to external affairs, defence, internal security and public service. The house of assembly was restyled the parliament, and may determine its own size; at present, it consists of an independent speaker, 15 elected members, the attorney-general and the financial and development secretary. The government is formed by ministers appointed by the elected members of the assembly.

The 2003 elections were won by the Gibraltar Social Democrats with eight seats, and it formed a government under Peter Caruana. The next elections are due to be held in 2008.

Governor and Commander-in-Chief, HE Sir Robert Fulton, KBE, *apptd* 2006
Chief Minister, Hon. Peter Caruana

GOVERNMENT OF GIBRALTAR
178–179 The Strand, London WC2R 1EL T 020-7836 0777
W www.gibraltar.gov.uk

ECONOMY

The economy is dominated by offshore financial services, shipping and tourism (especially retail for day visitors), and these three sectors account for nearly 70 per cent of GDP. Diversification efforts have encouraged telecommunications in particular and Gibraltar has become a centre for internet businesses, especially internet gaming. A shift from a predominantly public-sector to a private-sector economy has occurred in recent years, although government spending still has a significant impact on the local economy. The chief sources of government revenue are port dues, the rent of the crown estate in the town, and duties on consumer items (although value added tax is not applied in the territory).

GNI – US$5,000 per capita (2001)

Trade with UK	*2006*	*2007*
Imports from UK	£254,586,000	£212,176,992
Exports to UK	£30,045,000	£41,745,807

COMMUNICATIONS

Gibraltar has one international airport; in December 2006 air links to Spain and through Spanish air space reopened. The 29km road network is all paved; road links to Spain reopened in the 1980s. The port services the large shipping industry, cruise liners and a regular ferry service to Tangiers (Morocco).

MONTSERRAT

Area – 102 sq. km
Capital – Plymouth (abandoned 1997); the government's administrative headquarters is now at Brades, in the north-west of the island; population, 1,000 (2007 est)
Currency – East Caribbean dollar (EC$) of 100 cents
Population – 9,538 rising at 1.05 per cent per year (2007 est)
Language – English (official)
Population DENSITY – 108 per sq. km (1999)
Flag – British blue ensign with the shield of arms in the fly
National day – second Saturday in June (Queen's Birthday)
Life expectancy (years) – 78.85 (2006 est)
Mortality rate – 7.02 (2007 est)
Birth rate – 17.51 (2007 est)
Infant mortality rate – 7.03 (2007 est)

CLIMATE AND TERRAIN

Montserrat is a mountainous volcanic island in the Leeward group in the Caribbean Sea, with elevation extremes ranging from 914m (Chances Peak) at the highest point to 0m (Caribbean Sea) at the lowest. Volcanic activity since 1995 has left over half of the island devastated by lava flows and ash. The climate is tropical and the average temperature is 29°C.

HISTORY AND POLITICS

Discovered by Columbus in 1493, Montserrat became a British colony in 1632. The first settlers were predominantly Irish indentured servants from St Kitts. France and Britain fought over the island during the 17th and 18th centuries but Montserrat was finally assigned to Great Britain in 1783.

Volcanic activity by the Soufrière Hills volcano since 1995, particularly the severe 1996 and 1997 eruptions, has left over half of the island uninhabitable, and prompted the migration of two-thirds of the population in the late 1990s. Reconstruction and the return of migrants is hampered by continuing volcanic activity. An 'unsafe zone', to which access is prohibited, covers two-thirds of the island and there are maritime exclusion zones off the west, south and east coasts.

The present constitution came into force in 1990; talks are in progress about modernisation measures proposed by the Montserrat government in 2005, but some modifications were made in 1999 as over half of the constituencies were unoccupied owing to volcanic activity. The executive council is presided over by the governor and is composed of four elected members and two *ex-officio* members (the attorney-general and the financial secretary). The legislative council consists of the speaker, two *ex-officio* members (the attorney-general and the financial secretary) and nine elected members. Following the 2006 general election a coalition of the New People's Liberation Movement and the Montserrat Democratic Party, headed by the MDP leader, Lowell Lewis.

Governor, HE Peter A. Waterworth, *apptd* 2007
Chief Minister, Hon. Lowell Lewis

GOVERNMENT OF MONTSERRAT
180–186 Kings Cross Road, London WC1X 9DE
T 020-7520 2622

ECONOMY

Continuing volcanic activity has restricted reconstruction, agriculture and industry; the limited economic activity includes mining and quarrying, construction (mostly public sector), financial and professional services, and tourism. Communications improved with the opening of Gerald's airport in the north in 2005, allowing regular commercial air services to resume. There are port facilities at Little Bay.

Trade with UK	*2006*	*2007*
Imports from UK	£664,000	£1,247,459
Exports to UK	£121,000	£563,687

PITCAIRN ISLANDS

Pitcairn, Henderson, Ducie and Oeno Islands
Area – 47 sq. km
Capital – Adamstown
Currency – Currency is that of New Zealand
Population – 48 (2007 est)
Language – English (official), Pitcairnese (official)
Flag – British blue ensign with the arms in the fly
National day – second Saturday in June (Queen's Birthday)

CLIMATE AND TERRAIN

Pitcairn is the chief of a group of islands situated about midway between New Zealand and Panama in the South Pacific Ocean. The other three islands of the group are Henderson, lying 168km east-north-east of Pitcairn; Oeno, lying 120km north-west; and Ducie, lying 470km east; all are uninhabited. Henderson Island is a UNESCO World Heritage site. The climate is tropical, and the average temperature is 29°C.

HISTORY AND POLITICS

Pitcairn was settled in 1790 by the *Bounty* mutineers and their Tahitian companions. It became a British settlement under the British Settlement Act 1887 and was administered by the governor of Fiji from 1952 until 1970. In 1970 the office of governor, usually held by the British high commissioner to New Zealand, was established and administration was transferred to the British High Commission in New Zealand. Most administration is carried out by the Pitcairn Islands Office, under a commissioner appointed by the governor. The Local Government Ordinance of 1964 provides for an island council, which manages internal affairs. It has ten members, of whom six are elected; elections are held yearly in December.

Governor (non-resident), HE George Fergusson, *apptd* 2006 *(British High Commissioner to New Zealand)*
Commissioner, Leslie Jaques

ECONOMY

The islanders live by subsistence fishing and gardening and the sale of handicrafts. Apart from small fees charged for licences there are no taxes and government revenue is derived almost solely from the sale of postage stamps and .pn internet domain names, and income from investments. Since financial reserves became exhausted a few years ago the islands have received budgetary aid from the UK.

Trade with UK	*2005*	*2006*
Imports from UK	£58,000	£203,000
Exports to UK	£5,000	£11,000

COMMUNICATIONS

There is no airfield and the only means of access is by sea; cruise and container ships stop irregularly but a regular shipping supply route to French Polynesia was established in 2006. There are 6.4km of dirt roads on the islands. A telephone system, a limited television service and internet access have been introduced in recent years.

SOUTH GEORGIA AND THE SOUTH SANDWICH ISLANDS

Area – 3,903 sq. km
Capital – King Edward Point (administrative centre)
Currency – Pound sterling
Population – There is no indigenous population. The British Antarctic Survey maintains two permanently staffed research stations, at King Edward Point and on Bird Island, to the north-west of South Georgia; in addition, there is the Government Officer at King Edward Point, and the curators of the museum at Grytviken, South Georgia
Flag – British blue ensign, with the shield of arms in the fly

CLIMATE AND TERRAIN

South Georgia is an island 1,390km east-south-east of the Falkland Islands. More than half of the island is covered by permanent ice with many large glaciers reaching the sea at the head of fjords. The main mountain range is the Allardyce and elevation extremes range from 2,934m (Mount Paget) at the highest point to 0m (Atlantic Ocean) at the lowest. The South Sandwich Islands, lying some 750km miles south-east of South Georgia, consist of a chain of 11 uninhabited volcanic islands some 350km long. Some of these volcanoes are still active.

HISTORY AND POLITICS

South Georgia was used by whalers and sealers of many nationalities following its discovery by Captain Cook in the 18th century. Britain annexed South Georgia and the South Sandwich Islands in 1908 and since then they have been under continuous British occupation apart from a brief period during the Falklands war in 1982. Following the conflict, a small British army garrison was maintained at King Edward Point on South Georgia, but this was withdrawn in 2001.

The present constitution came into effect in 1985. It provides for a commissioner who, for the time being, is the officer administering the government of the Falkland Islands.

Commissioner (non-resident), HE Alan Huckle *apptd* 2006

ECONOMY

A conservation and management fishing zone was established around the islands in 1993 and a licensing regime introduced for fishing vessels. Sale of fishing licences, postage stamps and commemorative coins, customs and harbour dues, and harbour and landing fees are the main sources of revenue. Tourism, especially wildlife tourism, is growing, but prior permission to land on the islands must be sought and is subject to environmental impact assessments and landing fees.

Access is possible only by sea; there are no scheduled services but cruise ships and other vessels call at South Georgia.

ST HELENA AND DEPENDENCIES

ST HELENA

Area – 122 sq. km
Capital – Jamestown; population, 1,000 (2007 est)
Currency – St Helena pound (£) of 100 pence
Population – 7,543 rising at 0.53 per cent per year (2007 est)

Language – English (official
Flag – British blue ensign with the shield of arms in the fly
National day – second Saturday in June (Queen's Birthday)
Life expectancy (years) – 77.93 (2006 est)
Mortality rate – 6.63 (2007 est)
Birth rate – 11.93 (2007 est)
Infant mortality rate – 17.67 (2007 est)

CLIMATE AND TERRAIN

St Helena is situated in the South Atlantic Ocean, 1,500km south of the Equator and about 1,900km west of Africa. The island is rugged and volcanic, with sheer cliffs rising to a central plateau. The climate is tropical but mild, tempered by trade winds, and the annual average temperature is 27°C.

HISTORY AND POLITICS

St Helena is believed to have been discovered by the Portuguese navigator João da Nova in 1502. It was used as a port of call for vessels of all nations trading to the East until it was annexed by the Dutch in 1633. It was never occupied by them, however, and the English East India Company seized it in 1659. From 1815 to 1821 the island was lent to the British government as a place of exile for the Emperor Napoleon Bonaparte, who died in St Helena on 5 May 1821, and in 1834 it was annexed to the British crown. The Zulu chief Dinizulu was exiled to the island in 1890, and up to 6,000 Boer prisoners were held there between 1900 and 1903.

Under the 1989 constitution, government is administered by a governor, with the aid of an executive council comprising three *ex-officio* members (the chief secretary, financial secretary and attorney-general) and five elected members of the legislative council. The legislative council consists of a speaker, the three *ex-officio* members of the executive council, and 12 elected members.
Governor, HE Andrew Gurr, *apptd* 2007

GOVERNMENT OF ST HELENA
7 Portland Place, London W1B 1PP **T** 020-7031 0314

ECONOMY AND TRADE

St Helena was intended as a maritime base, with an economy dedicated to the provision of supplies for shipping and the local garrison, rather than as a self-sufficient colony. Its importance as a port of call declined after the opening of the Suez Canal reduced the amount of shipping on passing routes. Consequently, its economy is dependent on an annual grant from the UK. The main economic activities are agriculture, the sale of fishing licences and tourism, and the only significant exports are frozen, canned and dried fish and coffee.

Trade with UK	*2005*	*2006*
Imports from UK	£16,744,000	£8,946,000
Exports to UK	£874,000	£972,000

COMMUNICATIONS

Regular access is by sea at present, but plans are progressing for the establishment of an airport by 2010, when the regular supply ship is due to be withdrawn from scheduled service. Jamestown is the only port. St Helena has 138km of roads, most of which are single track. Telecommunication services are provided via satellite links, which also enable television programmes to be received for distribution by cable. There is a local radio station and two weekly newspapers.

ASCENSION ISLAND

Area – 90 sq. km
Capital – Georgetown; population, 560 (2003 est)
Currency – Currency is that of the UK
Population – 1,100 (2003 est)

CLIMATE AND TERRAIN

The island lies in the South Atlantic Ocean some 1,200km north-west of St Helena. It is a rocky peak of purely volcanic origin. The highest point (Green Mountain), some 860m, is covered with lush vegetation. It is an important breeding place for the green turtle and a number of seabird species.

HISTORY AND POLITICS

Ascension is said to have been discovered by João da Nova in 1501 and two years later was visited on Ascension Day by Alphonse d'Albuquerque, who gave the island its present name. It was uninhabited until the arrival of Napoleon in St Helena in 1815 when a small British naval garrison was stationed on the island. As HMS *Ascension* it remained under the supervision of the Board of Admiralty until 1922, when it was made a dependency of St Helena.

In 2002 new constitutional arrangements introduced a measure of democratic self-government. The governor, resident in St Helena, retains responsibility for defence, external affairs, internal security and public service. The governor, represented locally by the island administrator, chairs the island council, which consists of seven elected members and two *ex-officio* members (the director of financial services and the attorney-general). An election was called for May 2007 after most of the elected council members resigned, but there were so few candidates that the governor suspended the council for 12 months and began a consultation about constitutional changes.
Administrator, Michael Hill, *apptd* 2005

ECONOMY

Before 2002 the island was governed and financed by the main commercial users (the BBC and Cable and Wireless) and the military. With the change in governance in 2002, a fiscal regime was introduced to finance public services through taxation. This funds public services, a school, a hospital, police and judicial services. A private sector is developing following the sale of previously government-owned concerns to commercial operators and the establishment of a sports fishing industry.

COMMUNICATIONS

Communications with the outside world are by sea and air. Georgetown is the only port and there are regular scheduled shipping services, as well as regular air links to the UK and the USA by military aircraft and occasional charter flights. Ascension has 40km of roads. Telecommunication services are provided via satellite links.

TRISTAN DA CUNHA

Area – 201 sq. km
Capital – Edinburgh of the Seven Seas
Currency – Currency is that of the UK
Population – 277 (2003 est)
Flag – British blue ensign with the shield of arms in the fly

CLIMATE AND TERRAIN

Tristan da Cunha is the chief of a group of islands in the South Atlantic Ocean which lie some 2,333km south-south-west of St Helena. All of the islands are volcanic and steep-sided with cliffs or narrow beaches. The highest point of elevation is 2,060m (Queen Mary's Peak) while the lowest is 0m (Atlantic Ocean). Gough and Inaccessible islands are UNESCO World Heritage sites.

HISTORY AND POLITICS

Tristan da Cunha was discovered in 1506 by the Portuguese navigator Tristão da Cunha. In 1760 a British naval officer visited the islands and gave his name to Nightingale Island. In 1816 the group was annexed to the British crown and a garrison was placed on Tristan da Cunha. When this force was withdrawn in 1817, four adults and two children remained at their own request and formed a settlement, which was joined in 1827 by five women from St Helena and afterwards by others from Cape Colony. Due to its position on a main sailing route the colony thrived, with an economy based on trading with passing ships, until the late 19th century, when the opening of the Suez Canal led to decline.

In 1961 a volcano, believed to have been extinct for thousands of years, erupted and the danger of further volcanic activity led to the evacuation of inhabitants to the UK until 1963.

In 1938 Tristan da Cunha and Inaccessible, Nightingale and Gough islands were made dependencies of St Helena. They are administered by the governor of St Helena through a resident administrator. Under the 1985 constitution, the administrator is advised by an island council of eight elected members, of whom one must be a woman, and three appointed members. Elections are held every three years.

Administrator, David Morley, *apptd* 2007

ECONOMY

The island is almost financially self-sufficient; UK government aid finances training scholarships and a resident medical officer at the hospital. The main activities are crayfish fishing, fish processing, agriculture and the sale of postage stamps and coins.

COMMUNICATIONS

Communications with the outside world are by sea as there is no airport. Scheduled visits to the island are restricted to about nine calls a year by fishing vessels from Cape Town and annual calls by the St Helena supply ship and a South African research vessel. Tristan da Cunha has 20km of roads.

TURKS AND CAICOS ISLANDS

Area – 430 sq. km
Capital – Cockburn Town, on Grand Turk; population, 6,000 (2007 est)
Currency – US dollar (US$)
Population – 21,746 rising at 2.72 per cent per year (2007 est)
Religion – Protestantism (86 per cent) (est)
Language – English (official)
Population density – 37 per sq. km (2001)
Flag – British blue ensign with the shield of arms in the fly
National day – 30 August (Constitution Day)
Life expectancy (years) – 74.73 (2006 est)
Mortality rate – 4.23 (2007 est)
Birth rate – 21.48 (2007 est)
Infant mortality rate – 14.7 (2007 est)

CLIMATE AND TERRAIN

The Turks and Caicos Islands are about 80km south-east of the Bahamas, of which they are geographically an extension. There are around 40 islands and cays, of which six are permanently inhabited. The climate is marine tropical, moderated by trade winds; the average annual temperature is 27°C.

HISTORY AND POLITICS

The islands were settled by Bermudans in the 17th century. They were part of the Bahamas from 1799 until 1848, had separate colonial status from 1848, were administered from Jamaica between 1872 and 1962, and from the Bahamas between 1965 and 1973. Since the Bahamas' independence in 1973, the territory has had its own governor.

Internal self-government was introduced in the 1970s, and a new constitution was introduced in 2006. The governor is responsible for defence, external affairs, internal security and the regulation of financial services. The cabinet is presided over by the governor and comprises the premier and six elected ministers, together with an *ex-officio* member (the attorney-general). The house of assembly comprises the speaker, 15 elected members, four appointed members and the attorney-general.

The general election of 9 February 2007 was won by the Progressive National party, with 13 seats.

Governor, HE Richard Tauwhare, *apptd* 2005
Premier, Michael Eugene Misick

GOVERNMENT OF TURKS AND CAICOS ISLANDS
42 Westminster Palace Gardens, 1–7 Artillery Row, London SW1P 1RR **T** 020-7222 9024

ECONOMY

The main industries are tourism, property development, offshore financial services and fishing. The main trade partner is the USA.

Trade with UK	*2006*	*2007*
Imports from UK	£2,241,000	£2,542,135
Exports to UK	£100,000	£19,896

COMMUNICATIONS

The principal airports are on the islands of Grand Turk and Providenciales and provide international air links. There are smaller airports on the other main islands, and regular internal air services between them. The main seaports are on Grand Turk and Providenciales. The islands also have a total of 121km of roads, 24km of which are surfaced.

THE YEAR 2007–8

EVENTS OF THE YEAR

OBITUARIES

ARCHAEOLOGY

ARCHITECTURE

ART

BROADCASTING

BUSINESS AND FINANCE

CONSERVATION

DANCE

FILM

LITERATURE

MUSIC

OPERA

PARLIAMENT

ACTS OF PARLIAMENT

WHITE PAPERS

SCIENCE AND DISCOVERY

THEATRE

WEATHER

SPORTS

EVENTS OF THE YEAR 2007–8

UK AFFAIRS

AUGUST 2007
4. Sixty cattle were found to be infected with foot and mouth disease at a farm in Surrey leading to a nationwide ban on the movement of all livestock. **5.** A second farm in Surrey confirmed its cattle were also infected with foot and mouth disease; Merial, an American-owned research company, and the government-funded Institute of Animal Health, whose laboratories share a site at Pirbright, were identified as possible sources of the outbreak. **9.** A calving glacier bombarded an arctic cruise ship with ice in northern Norway, injuring nine British tourists on board. **12.** Climate change campaigners set up a campsite together with local residents near Heathrow to protest against proposals to build a third runway at the airport; the protests lasted for over a week and led to 11 arrests on 20 August. **29.** Members of the Prison Officers' Association called off an unannounced 24-hour strike over pay after the Ministry of Justice obtained a court injunction to end the strike with immediate effect. **30.** The Health Protection Agency announced that the number of confirmed cases of childhood measles in 2007 had risen from 136 in June to 480 in 11 weeks and advised that all children were fully immunised.

SEPTEMBER 2007
2. Around 2,000 members of the Rail, Maritime and Transport Workers Union began a three-day London Underground (LU) strike; the workers were seeking assurances on job and pension security following the collapse of the LU maintenance contractor Metronet; the strike was called off during the second day after Transport for London confirmed no jobs or pensions would be lost. **4.** A Eurostar train completed the 306-mile journey from Paris to London, via the new high-speed rail link from Southfleet Junction to London's St Pancras station, in a record 2hr 3min and 39sec. **6.** The RAF scrambled four Tornado F3 fighter jets after eight Russian Tupolev-95 Bear bombers approached UK airspace; Russian authorities insisted that the mission was non-confrontational. **7.** A report by the Health and Safety Executive concluded that a leaking underground drainage pipe at the Pirbright research site was likely to have been the source of the August outbreak of foot and mouth disease in Surrey (*see* 4 August). **12.** Urgent investigations into another suspected foot and mouth outbreak at a farm in Surrey began; the virus was later identified as the same strain found which caused the August cases. **23.** The first incidence of bluetongue disease in the UK was identified in a cow at a farm in Suffolk; tests confirmed that the strain was the same as that affecting farms in mainland Europe. **24.** Tornadoes of around 70–80mph swept across central and southern England causing damage to property in Farnborough, Luton and Nuneaton. **25.** An investigation, chaired by Baroness Finlay of Llandaff, into the treatment of allergies in the UK recommended that a network of allergy centres staffed by specialists in chest medicine, immunologists, dermatologists and gastroenterologists should be established throughout the country. A second incidence of bluetongue disease was confirmed in Suffolk, 80km (50 miles) from the first infected farm; all transportation of sheep and cattle in Norfolk, Suffolk and Essex was banned.

OCTOBER 2007
4. Postal workers began the first of two 48-hour strikes as part of an ongoing dispute between the Communications Workers Union and Royal Mail over pay and pensions. **8.** The prime minister, Gordon Brown, announced that the number of troops in Iraq would be halved to 2,500 by spring 2008; in addition Mr Brown said that all Iraqis that had been employed by the British armed forces in Iraq for more than one year would be entitled to apply for a financial package to help with resettlement, either within Iraq or, in some circumstances, for admission to the UK. **10.** An investigation by the Healthcare Commission concluded that two serious outbreaks of *clostridium difficile* between April 2004 and September 2006 at three hospitals run by Maidstone and Tunbridge Wells NHS trust were the result of poor hygiene, inadequate staffing levels and unsatisfactory isolation procedures; 21 patients died as a direct result of the infection. **15.** Sir Menzies Campbell resigned as leader of the Liberal Democrats. **23.** The Food Standards Agency ordered an urgent audit of lamb for sale in the UK after discovering that breeding animals recently treated with organophosphate sheep dips and anti-parasitic drugs had been slaughtered for human consumption. **26.** Health secretary Alan Johnson announced that from September 2008 girls aged 12–13 will be routinely vaccinated against the sexually transmitted human papilloma virus, which is responsible for an estimated 70 per cent of cervical cancer cases. **30.** King Abdullah of Saudi Arabia was received formally by the Queen on his first state visit to Britain since 1987.

NOVEMBER 2007
3. Four firefighters died when the roof of a blazing warehouse collapsed at Atherstone on Stour in Warwickshire. **6.** The Queen officially opened the 110km (68 mile) high-speed rail link from London to the Channel tunnel at the newly restored St Pancras station. **8.** The Environment Agency issued flood warnings for the Norfolk, Suffolk and Kent coasts after the Met Office predicted that high tides could reach up to 3m above normal levels due to a combination of spring tides and gales; sea defences withstood the high tides and the evacuees returned to their homes the following day. **12.** The chief executive of the National Policing Improvement Agency, Peter Neyroud, said that, despite exceeding the government's target of bringing 1.25 million offences a year to justice by 2007–8, the police had failed to significantly improve the detection rate for serious sexual and violent crimes. **13.** A cull of around 6,500 poultry began at a Suffolk farm near Diss after vets identified the H5N1 strain of avian flu in birds on the premises. It emerged that a non-departmental public body reporting to the Home Office issued thousands of licences to illegal immigrants, allowing them to work in the security industry; home secretary Jacqui Smith denied claims that she had tried to cover up the problem. **20.** The Queen and the Duke of Edinburgh celebrated their 60th wedding

anniversary. The chancellor, Alistair Darling, announced that the personal details, including bank account information, of every child benefit claimant in the country had gone missing after two CDs containing the confidential data were posted to the National Audit Office. **23.** One hundred and thirty people, including 24 Britons, aboard the MV *Explorer* had to be rescued after their Antarctic cruise ship hit an iceberg near the South Shetland Islands. **25.** The Labour Party began an inquiry into an estimated £600,000 of its donations to establish whether they breached the regulations governing party funding; two days later the prime minister announced that the party would be returning the donation to David Abrahams as the contribution had not been lawfully declared. Gillian Gibbons, a British woman teaching in Sudan, was arrested after being accused of insulting Islam when she named a teddy bear Mohamed as part of a school project; she was later convicted of inciting religious hatred and sentenced to 15 days in prison. **26.** Two European elk were introduced to a wildlife reserve on a private estate in the Highlands of Scotland; the first time in 3,000 years that the species inhabited the wild in Britain. **29.** The leader of the Scottish Labour party, Wendy Alexander, asked the Electoral Commission to investigate the legitimacy of a £950 donation made to her leadership campaign by Paul Green, a property developer residing in Jersey.

DECEMBER 2007

3. Gillian Gibbons (*see* 25 November) was released and flown back to the UK after a diplomatic effort involving two British Muslim peers secured her a pardon from the Sudanese president Omar al-Bashir. **12.** An inquiry confirmed that the second wave of the foot and mouth outbreak discovered on a farm at Virginia Water in September was likely to have been caused by contaminated top soil, spread on land adjacent to the farm; the soil was accidentally transported by building contractors working at the Pirbright research laboratory. **16.** British forces formally handed back control of Iraq's Basra province to the Iraqi security forces. **18.** Nick Clegg was elected leader of the Liberal Democrats. **19.** Jamil el-Banna, Omar Deghayes and Abdennour Sameur arrived back in the UK after being released by US authorities from the internment camp at Guantanamo Bay, on arrival all three were detained for questioning; Mr el-Banna and Mr Deghayes were later released on bail and Mr Sameur was released without charge.

JANUARY 2008

2. Thousands of commuters endured delays and cancellations as Network Rail failed to complete major engineering work on the West Coast main line. A fire destroyed much of the roof and badly damaged a number of wards and operating theatres at the Royal Marsden Hospital in London; patients and staff were evacuated. **4.** Around 100 hospital wards across the UK were closed to new admissions due to a national outbreak of the highly infectious norovirus. **10.** Business secretary John Hutton announced plans to build a new generation of nuclear power stations; funding for building new facilities, disposing of waste and decommissioning old stations would be met by the private sector. Three dead swans discovered at the Abbotsbury swannery in Dorset were found to be infected by the H5N1 strain of avian flu after being sent for routine testing. **11.** The Electoral Commission began an investigation into the failure by Peter Hain, the Secretary of State for Work and Pensions and Secretary of State for Wales, to declare £103,000 donated to his campaign for the deputy leadership of the Labour Party. **17.** A British Airways flight from Beijing crash-landed short of the runway at Heathrow after experiencing a twin engine failure; 13 people suffered minor injuries. **23.** The business secretary, John Hutton, announced a two-year feasibility study to establish whether the environmental benefits of building a hydroelectric barrage across the Severn Estuary to provide almost 5 per cent of Britain's electricity, would outweigh the costs of destroying large areas of wetland. **24.** The Electoral Commission referred its investigation into Peter Hain's deputy leadership campaign to the Metropolitan Police; Mr Hain immediately announced his resignation from the cabinet, stepping down both as work and pensions secretary and as secretary of state for Wales. **29.** A report by the Standards and Privileges Committee concluded that payments made by Derek Conway, MP for Old Bexley and Sidcup, to his family members constituted misuse of parliamentary allowances; Mr Conway was suspended from the Commons for 10 days and had his Conservative Party whip withdrawn. **31.** Gale force winds caused numerous power cuts and road closures in the North; 23 people had to be rescued after a passenger ferry ran aground off the coast at Blackpool and 14 people had to be winched to safety from a stricken trawler off St Kilda, in the Outer Hebrides.

FEBRUARY 2008

7. Comments on the adoption of Shariah law in the UK made by the Archbishop of Canterbury, Dr Rowan Williams, caused widespread controversy amongst politicians, the Church of England and other faith bodies; the Archbishop later apologised for his 'misleading choice of words' during his lecture at the Royal Courts of Justice, but stood by his right to express an opinion on such issues. **15.** Concern grew over the number of suicides amongst young people in Bridgend, Wales, after the deaths of a 15 and a 20-year-old brought the total number to 16 since January 2007. **19.** The Welsh assembly government announced a suicide prevention strategy for Wales following another suicide in Bridgend. **20.** A 13-week public consultation began on new flight path plans for Stansted, Luton and Heathrow airports, proposed by National Air Traffic Services. **21.** Despite assurances that UK territory had not been used since 1998 to facilitate the transfer of any individual to a place where they could face the risk of torture, foreign secretary David Miliband confirmed that the British Indian Ocean Territory Diego Garcia had been used twice in 2002 by US planes carrying two detainees to offshore internment facilities. **24.** The Parliamentary Commissioner for Standards was officially asked to investigate whether £4,000 claimed on expenses by the Speaker of the House of Commons, Michael Martin, for taxi journeys made by his wife amounted to a misuse of public funds. **26.** Peter Moore, one of five Britons kidnapped from the Iraqi finance ministry in Baghdad in May 2007, was seen for the first time since his abduction in a television broadcast; the group holding him identified themselves as the Shia Islamic Resistance in Iraq. **27.** A 10-second earthquake measuring 5.3 on the Richter scale was felt across the UK; no-one was injured although some buildings near the epicentre in Market Rasen, Lincolnshire, suffered minor structural damage. **28.** Emergency plans to extract Prince Harry from Afghanistan were implemented after his covert 10-week mission in the Helmand province was revealed on a US website. **29.** The prime minister found himself embroiled in controversy after Downing Street and the Labour Party gave permission for Mr Brown's face to be used in an advertising campaign to promote Fiji as a holiday destination; the Fiji Visitors Bureau later confirmed that the advertisements would be withdrawn.

MARCH 2008

4. Revd Ian Paisley announced his intention to step down as First Minister of Northern Ireland and leader of the Democratic Unionist Party in May. **7.** Flight Lieutenant Michelle Goodman became the first woman to be awarded the Distinguished Flying Cross for rescuing a wounded comrade under heavy fire while on duty in Basra, Iraq. **10.** Hurricanes reaching 82mph caused widespread flooding, disruption to transport services and cut the power to around 10,000 homes. **11.** The Chief Constable of Greater Manchester Police, Michael Todd, was found dead at a foot of a cliff in Snowdonia, North Wales. A committee on parliamentary expenses chaired by the speaker announced that the amount of petty cash MPs can draw would be reduced from £250 to £50 per month and that receipts should be presented for all items over £25, excluding food. A review of the government's reaction to the 2007 outbreak of foot and mouth disease led by Dr Iain Anderson concluded that the condition of the government's Pirbright animal disease research laboratory in Surrey, the source of the outbreak, was 'shabby and dilapidated'. **16.** In response to a 50 per cent increase in the number of ethical concerns referred by doctors to the General Medical Council (GMC) since 2007, the GMC published guidelines to assist hospital doctors and GPs in dealing with cases that conflict with their personal beliefs. **21.** Greater Glasgow and Clyde health board reported Britain's first case of a rare strain of extremely drug-resistant tuberculosis (XDR-TB). **23.** Royal Mail announced that it was selling off 40 vacant post-office properties after agreeing a deal with WHSmith to relocate around 76 crown post offices into branches of the newsagent by the end of 2008. **26.** The Office for National Statistics reported that the proportion of single adults getting married was at its lowest (2.2 per cent) since records began in 1862. **27.** BAA's Heathrow Terminal 5 was reduced to chaos on its opening day due to the failure of its baggage system. **30.** A private jet suffered major engine failure minutes after taking off from Biggin Hill airport in Kent and crashed into a house in Farnborough; all five people on board the aircraft were killed.

APRIL 2008

2. The schools minister, Ed Balls, published a report which found that one in six schools of the sample tested (Manchester, Northamptonshire and Barnet, north London) was breaching the admissions code; the most common concern was failing to give priority to children in local authority care or to those with special needs. **6.** Gatwick and Heathrow airports cancelled flights as Arctic winds brought a blanket of heavy snow to much of the UK. The London-leg of the Beijing Olympic torch relay was disrupted by pro-Tibet demonstrators. **8.** The chief veterinary officer for Wales announced that a badger-culling zone would be established in Wales in order to stop the spread of bovine TB; the culling initiative to remove diseased animals was expected to last for four years. **9.** The Reform (Sark) Law 2007 and the Real Property (Transfer Tax, Charging and Related Provisions) (Sark) Law 2007 were given royal assent, allowing universal suffrage to replace the feudal system of governance on the Channel Island of Sark. **23.** Following a backbench rebellion by Labour MPs against the abolition of the 10p tax rate for low-earners, the prime minister and the chancellor announced a package of measures to compensate low-paid workers. **24.** Lessons at almost a third of schools in England and Wales were disrupted due to a strike called by the National Union of Teachers in protest at a pay settlement below the rate of inflation. **30.** The House of Lords ruled that government guidance which recommended that doctors from outside Europe should only be offered training posts if there were no suitable candidates from Britain or the EU was an illegal limitation of the employment rights of overseas doctors.

MAY 2008

1. The Conservative mayoral candidate Boris Johnson defeated Labour's incumbent Ken Livingstone in the London mayoral election. In the English and Welsh local elections the Labour Party lost nine councils and the Conservative Party gained 12 of the 159 councils up for election. **7.** In his first policy announcement, London mayor Boris Johnson, declared that alcohol consumption would be banned from all public transport in the capital from 1 June 2008. **19.** A cross-party attempt to ban hybrid human animal embryos for use in stem cell research was defeated in the House of Commons on a free vote, by 336 to 176; in addition, an attempt to ban 'saviour siblings' (whose cells can be used to treat an older sibling's genetic condition), was voted down by 342 votes to 163. **20.** MPs voted in favour of keeping the 24-week abortion upper limit after rejecting options ranging from 12 to 22 weeks in a series of votes; earlier in the day MPs also voted in favour of abolishing the legal requirement that fertility clinics consider a child's need for a father when offering treatment. **22.** The Princesshay shopping centre in Exeter was evacuated after an explosive device was detonated at a restaurant in the complex; only one man, who was arrested at the scene, was injured. A report by the NHS showed that the number of alcohol-related hospital admissions in the year to April 2007 reached 200,000, a 7 per cent increase on the previous year. **27.** Around 300 lorry drivers converged in London to protest at rising fuel costs, a further 100 drivers joined a similar protest in Wales. **29.** The British ambassador to Iraq made a public appeal for the safe release of five British men taken hostage there in May 2007; the men were working as civilian contractors at the Iraqi finance ministry in Baghdad. **31.** In Northern Ireland, Revd Ian Paisley formerly handed over the leadership of the Democratic Unionist Party to his long-term deputy Peter Robinson.

JUNE 2008

5. Giles Chichester resigned as the Conservative party leader in Europe after admitting that he had broken European parliament rules on staff expenses. In Northern Ireland, the DUP leader, Peter Robinson, was appointed first minister and Martin McGuinness was reappointed as deputy first minister. **10.** The House of Commons voted by a majority of just nine votes in favour of the government's proposal to extend the pre-charge detention for terrorist suspects from 28 to 42 days. **12.** The shadow home secretary and MP for Haltemprice and Howden, David Davis, announced that he was resigning from the House of Commons in opposition to the 42-day pre-charge detention period and that he would contest his seat in a single-issue by-election. **23.** A study by the Department of Health, which measured the BMI of children in England in their first year of school, reported that 9.9 per cent of them were obese; the borough of Hackney in London had the highest rate at 16 per cent, while Teesdale in County Durham had the lowest at 5 per cent. **30.** Ahead of the General Synod's vote on whether legislation should be introduced to consecrate women, the archbishops of Canterbury and York received a letter signed by 1,300 clergy, including 11 serving bishops, which stated their intention to defect from the Church of England if such legislation was introduced. The findings of a review of NHS services, conducted by health minister Lord Darzi was published alongside a draft NHS constitution.

JULY 2008

1. A report by the Commons Health Select Committee concluded that reforms to NHS dentists' contracts introduced in 2006 – under which dentists were paid an annual income rather than a fee for each treatment provided – had decreased, rather than increased, the number of preventative treatments carried out. **3.** The MoD signed a contract for the production of two 65,000-tonne aircraft carriers for the Royal Navy to be built in a joint venture between BAE Systems and VT Group; the contract was expected to sustain 1,200 jobs at VT Group's shipbuilding operation in Portsmouth until at least 2014. **6.** A government inquiry into food policy found that British households dispose of a total of four million tonnes of food each year. **7.** The General Synod of the Church of England voted in favour of introducing legislation to consecrate women bishops. **9.** A review by the Healthcare Commission which surveyed more than 26,000 women and 5,000 staff, examining all aspects of maternity care, concluded that significant weaknesses persisted in maternity and neonatal services across England. **16.** Thousands of local authority employees took part in a two-day strike over pay and working conditions. **22.** A report by the chief medical officer, Sir Liam Donaldson, outlined plans for all practising doctors to undergo mandatory annual performance reviews in order to identify those that repeatedly made poor clinical decisions; trials for the scheme were expected to start in 2009. **28.** A fire broke out on the 104-year-old pier at Weston-super-Mare; the pier was destroyed in 90 minutes, no-one was injured in the blaze.

ARTS AND MEDIA

AUGUST 2007

1. Michael Grade, the executive chairman of ITV, ordered an independent inquiry into a documentary that falsely claimed to show the death of an Alzheimer's sufferer. Channel 4 stopped all phone-in competitions on its programmes after a company that operated a phone-in quiz for the channel was fined in July 2007 for overcharging viewers. **7.** Mark Paton caused over £10,000 of damage to an 18th-century portrait of Samuel Johnson by smuggling a hammer into the National Portrait Gallery and attacking the painting. **16.** Radio audience figures released by RAJAR revealed that the number of people listening to digital-only stations had increased by a third in the past 12 months, and that 26 per cent of adults used digital services to listen to the radio. **26.** US writer Cormac McCarthy won the James Tait Black memorial prize for fiction. **28.** The Heritage Lottery Fund announced that it would cut the amount of money for large projects by £60m to fund the 2012 London Olympics. **30.** Damien Hirst's work, *For the Love of God,* was bought by a group of investors; the diamond-encrusted skull sold for its asking price of £50m, setting a record for a work by a living artist.

SEPTEMBER 2007

2. The Museum of Rural Life in Devon received a surprise gift of £1.5m in the will of an elderly woman living in a local village. **4.** A painting by Francis Bacon given to the Royal College of Art in lieu of rent on a studio sold for over £8m at auction. **5.** The BBC cancelled Planet Relief, an event similar to Live Earth and Comic Relief, as it breached guidelines on impartiality. **7.** A previously unseen portrait of Isabel Rawsthorne by Francis Bacon was put up for auction and was expected to raise at least £2m; the painting was a gift to Bacon's doctor and had been passed down to his children. **17.** At the Emmy Awards in Los Angeles Dame Helen Mirren won the award for best actress in a mini series, and Ricky Gervais won best comedy actor. **19.** The Best Jazz accolade was reinstated at the MOBO Awards following protests at its removal from the ceremony in 2006. The makers of the television programme *Blue Peter* were accused of deceiving children by ignoring the results of a viewer poll to name the programme's new cat. **20.** The Tate announced record number of visitors in 2006, with a total of 7.7 million people visiting its four galleries. **21.** ITV dropped the British Comedy Awards from its broadcasting schedule and announced an investigation into voting irregularities on the programme. **23.** A premium-rate phone services company responsible for falsely charging over 18 million GMTV viewers over a period of four years was given a record £20m fine from the regulator ICSTIS. **27.** The National Portrait Gallery bought David Hockney's *Self-Portrait with Charlie,* the first artwork to be purchased by the gallery using gift aid receipts from visitors.

OCTOBER 2007

3. Sean O'Brien won the main Forward poetry award for the third time with his collection, *The Drowned Book.* **4.** Police recovered Leonardo Da Vinci's *Madonna of the Yarnwinder* in south-west Scotland, arresting four men; the painting was stolen from Drumlanrig Castle in Dumfriesshire in 2003 and was valued at over £30m. **5.** The controller of BBC1, Peter Fincham, resigned after a report highlighted errors of judgment made by him and his colleagues regarding a television programme that showed misleading footage of the Queen. **11.** The British writer Doris Lessing, 87, was awarded the Nobel prize for literature. **12.** The government announced an extra £50m of funding for Arts Council England by 2011 and further subsidies to guarantee free admission to England's national museums and galleries for a further three years. **16.** Anne Enright won the Booker prize for *The Gathering*, beating the two favourites for the award, Ian McEwan and Lloyd Jones. **18.** The director-general of the BBC, Mark Thompson, announced 2,500 redundancies from the corporation's workforce. **23.** British and Dutch police closed down OiNK, one of the largest filesharing websites used to download music illegally. The State Hermitage museum in St Petersburg confirmed that its centre at Somerset House in London, the Hermitage Rooms, would be closing due to financial problems. **25.** Figures released by RAJAR showed that the number of adults listening to radio each week fell by 760,000 compared to the previous quarter. **26.** A painting listed as in the style of Rembrandt and valued at £1,500, sold for £2.2m at auction to a collector on speculation that it was genuine; it was confirmed as authentic in July and its value was estimated at £30m. **29.** The Tate and the National Gallery unveiled a donation of 18 paintings valued at up to £100m from collector Simon Sainsbury.

NOVEMBER 2007

5. The charity Art Fund awarded five museums and galleries £1m each to spend on contemporary artworks; the Gallery of Modern Art in Glasgow and the Towner Art Gallery in Eastbourne were among these. **7.** Thomas Schutte's *Model for a Hotel* was installed as the latest artwork on the empty fourth plinth in Trafalgar Square. **16.** Three members of the Greenhalgh family from Bolton were found guilty of fraud after attempting to sell 120 fake artworks to museums; the family had made at least £850,000 from the forgeries. **20.** At the International Emmy Awards, British television programmes won seven prizes, including best documentary for Stephen Fry's *The Secret Life of a Manic Depressive* and best comedy for *Little Britain Abroad*. **27.** The missing section of a 17th-century cabinet commissioned by Pope Clement IX was found in a pizza restaurant in York. **28.** At the British Independent Film Awards, Anton Corbijn's *Control* won five awards, including best film and best director; the award for best actor was won by Viggo Mortensen and the award for best actress by Dame Judy Dench.

DECEMBER 2007

3. Mark Wallinger won the Turner prize for *State Britain*, a recreation of an anti-war protest originally staged in Parliament Square. **5.** The culture secretary, James Purnell, announced a £50m grant towards the expansion of Tate Modern. **6.** The Public Catalogue Foundation launched a catalogue containing the 2,500 oil paintings held by the Government Art Collection. **13.** The Tate announced that Damien Hirst had agreed to donate four of his works, worth an estimated £10m, to its collection. **15.** The Arts Council announced that it would end funding for nearly 200 arts organisations from April 2008, including the Bristol Old Vic and the National Student Drama Festival. **20.** Channel 4 was fined £1.5m by OFCOM for charging viewers to enter phone-in competitions that they had no chance of winning. **26.** Manchester city council announced its intention to sue the artist Thomas Heatherwick after spikes from his sculpture, *B of the Bang*, fell off in high winds. *The Stage* named Cameron Mackintosh as the most influential figure in British theatre; Andrew Lloyd Webber took second place.

JANUARY 2008

4. The poet Philip Larkin came top in a survey of the 50 greatest British writers since 1945 commissioned by *The Times*. **9.** Russian authorities gave official approval for the exhibition From Russia at the Royal Academy to go ahead after the culture secretary, James Purnell, implemented anti-seizure legislation early; previously it was feared that there was insufficient legal protection to prevent descendants of the original artists claiming the work. **11.** A launch party officially marked the beginning of Liverpool's year as European Capital of Culture. Over 100 British artists signed a letter condemning changes made by the British Council to its arts programme abroad, including the closure of visual arts, theatre, film and dance departments. **12.** The Golden Globes ceremony was replaced with a news conference due to an ongoing writers' strike affecting the film and television industry in the USA; British awards included best drama for *Atonement*, best actor for Daniel Day-Lewis and best actress for Julie Christie. **15.** BBC Radio 3 presenter Andy Kershaw was jailed for three months for breaking a restraining order banning him from approaching his former partner. **17.** Figures from the Society of London Theatre showed an annual increase of 1.25 million people attending shows in Central London in 2007; the figures were boosted by musicals featuring winners of TV talent shows **22.** A. L. Kennedy won the overall Costa Book award for her novel, *Day*.

FEBRUARY 2008

1. The Arts Council confirmed that it would end funding for 185 arts organisations and reduce it for a further 27; only 17 of the originally proposed organisations, including the Bush theatre and the National Student Drama Festival managed to get the decision reversed (*see* 15 December 2007). **7.** Figures published by British libraries showed that in the year to June 2007, Patricia Cornwell's *At Risk* was the most borrowed book, and James Patterson the most borrowed author. **10.** At the Bafta Film Awards *La Vie en Rose* won four awards including best actress, *No Country for Old Men* won three awards including best director, and *Atonement* won two awards including best film. **11.** Amy Winehouse won five Grammy awards, including song of the year, best new artist and best pop vocal album. GCap announced the closure of digital-only radio stations *The Jazz* and *Planet Rock* in an attempt to save £8.8m a year. **20.** At the Brit Awards, Arctic Monkeys won best British group, Kate Nash won best female solo artist and Mark Ronson won best male solo artist. **21.** *The Lion, the Witch and the Wardrobe* by C. S. Lewis was voted the best children's book of all time in a poll conducted by the charity Booktrust. **22.** A museum devoted to cinematic history opened in County Hall, London. **24.** At the Academy Awards, best picture was won by *No Country for Old Men*, best actor by Daniel Day-Lewis, and best actress by Marion Cotillard. **26.** Anthony d'Offay, a London art dealer, gave 725 works worth over £125m to the Tate and the national galleries of Scotland for £26.5m, the price he originally paid for them. **28.** Peter Fincham became the director of ITV after resigning from his post as controller of BBC1 (*see* 5 October 2007). The Arctic Monkeys won three prizes at the NME Awards, including best British band.

MARCH 2008
9. At the Olivier Awards, Chiwetel Ejiofor won best actor for *Othello*, Kristin Scott Thomas won best actress for *The Seagull* and Rupert Goold won best director for *Macbeth*. **16.** Figures released by the Film Distributor's Association showed a 7.7 per cent rise in box office takings and a 3.7 per cent rise in admissions for UK cinemas in 2007. **20.** Christie's in London withdrew Pieter de Grebber's *Study of a Reading Man* from auction after the Polish embassy revealed that it had been looted by the Nazis; the painting was later returned to its Polish owner. **26.** The Pushkin Museum of Fine Arts in Moscow announced that it would host an exhibition of 112 paintings by J. M. W. Turner in a joint project with Tate Britain. **27.** Sammy Ofer, an Israeli billionaire who once served in the Royal Navy, donated £20m to the National Maritime Museum to pay for the construction of a new wing. Leona Lewis became the first British woman to reach number one in the USA for over 20 years with her single, 'Bleeding Love'.

APRIL 2008
7. David Hockney donated his largest landscape painting, *Bigger Trees Near Water*, to the Tate. **8.** An anonymous donor gave over 4,000 classical LPs valued at a total of £25,000 to an Oxfam shop in Tavistock. **9.** At the Galaxy British Book Awards, book of the year was won by Ian McEwan's *On Chesil Beach*, and the outstanding achievement award was won by J. K. Rowling. **16.** Figures obtained by the Council for the Advancement of Arts, Recreation and Education showed that Arts Council England had not allocated £152m received from lottery ticket sales. **17.** Leona Lewis became the first UK female solo artist to go straight to number one in the USA's album chart with her debut, *Spirit*. **19.** The widow of T. S. Eliot donated £2.5m to help to build a new wing in the London Library. **20.** At the BAFTA Television Awards, the sitcom *Gavin and Stacey* won best comedy performance and the audience award for programme of the year; Bruce Forsyth won the BAFTA Fellowship award. **25.** *Casablanca* was named as the best film in history in a list compiled by film critics for *The Times*. **29.** The Advertising Standards Authority reported a 9.6 per cent rise in complaints about adverts in 2007 compared with the previous year; objections to violent images in advertising doubled.

MAY 2008
1. RAJAR figures showed an increase in listeners across all analogue BBC radio stations except for Radio 3, which had 155,000 fewer listeners than in the previous quarter. **2.** Banksy and 29 other artists turned a disused road tunnel near Waterloo station in London into an exhibition space, covering it in murals and graffiti. **5.** The first international literary festival to be held in the occupied Palestinian territories was launched; it was supported by the British Council and UNESCO. **6.** ITV and the BBC announced the commencement of Freesat, a digital satellite television service offering up to 200 channels for a one-off payment. **8.** The results of an investigation by the legal firm Olswang into the 2005 British Comedy Awards shown on ITV1 revealed that the People's Choice Award had been fixed in favour of *Ant and Dec's Saturday Night Takeaway*, when in fact *The Catherine Tate Show* received more telephone votes (*see* 21 September 2007). ITV was fined £5.7m by OFCOM for misleading its audience on 86 separate occasions over four years. **13.** Lucian Freud's *Benefits Supervisor Sleeping* became the most expensive painting by a living artist after it sold for $33.6m (£17.2m) at Christie's in New York. **18.** A retired GP's collection of over 200 British surrealist works went on display at Middlesbrough Institute of Modern Art; the collection included works by Henry Moore and Damien Hirst. **22.** At the Ivor Novello Awards, the best song musically and lyrically was named as 'Love is a Losing Game' by Amy Winehouse and the best album was *In Rainbows* by Radiohead. **24.** Russia won the Eurovision song contest, the UK came last with 'Even If' by Andy Abraham. **26.** Three drawings by Goya that had been missing since 1877 were discovered in Switzerland; they were expected to sell for over £2m at Christie's in London. **27.** A gold cup given by a scrap metal dealer to his grandson was identified as a 2,500-year-old Persian artefact, worth up to £500,000.

JUNE 2008
4. Rose Tremain won the Orange Broadband prize for women's fiction with her novel, *The Road Home*. **5.** The Tate made a public appeal for help to raise £6m to save a sketch by Paul Rubens from being sold overseas; the sketch was a design for the ceiling of the Banqueting House in Whitehall, London. Over 80 authors, illustrators and booksellers joined a campaign led by Philip Pullman against the proposed introduction of age guidelines on children's books. **11.** Michael Rosen was chosen as the new Children's Laureate, replacing Jacqueline Wilson. **16.** At the Mojo Awards, best song was won by Duffy for 'Mercy', best breakthrough act by The Last Shadow Puppets, and best live act by Led Zeppelin. Craig Wylie won the BP portrait prize with a painting of his girlfriend, Katherine Raw; the prize included a £25,000 cheque and a commission from the National Portrait Gallery. **23.** Antony Gormley was selected as the next artist to produce a work for the Fourth Plinth in Trafalgar Square; his proposal, *One and Other*, was for volunteers chosen by a lottery to take turns to occupy the plinth for an hour. **24.** Monet's *Le Bassin aux Nymphéas*, one of a series of waterlily paintings, sold for a record price for the artist of £40.1m at Christie's in London.

JULY 2008
1. The British Museum reported a record six million visitors during 2007–8; the museum beat Tate Modern to become the most visited cultural attraction in the UK. **10.** Salman Rushdie's novel *Midnight's Children* was named as the winner of the Best of the Booker, an award created to celebrate the 40th birthday of the literary prize. **11.** A First Folio of Shakespeare's plays, stolen from Durham University in 1998, was recovered; an international businessman claimed to have bought the manuscript in Cuba. **15.** The Samuel Johnson prize for non-fiction was won by Kate Summerscale, for her book *The Suspicions of Mr Whicher*. **17.** A watercolour by Beatrix Potter sold for £289,500 at auction at Sotheby's in London, a record amount for a book illustration. **21.** The Film Council reported worldwide takings of over £1.65bn for British films in 2007, an increase of more than 50 per cent on the previous year. OFCOM ruled that Channel 4's documentary, *The Great Global Warming Swindle*, broke guidelines on impartiality, but the channel was cleared of misleading viewers; the programme claimed man-made global warming was a conspiracy and a fraud. **28.** Sotheby's announced that an auction of 233 new Damien Hirst pieces would take place in September; it was expected to raise £65–90m. **30.** OFCOM fined the BBC £400,000 for breaches of the Broadcasting Code, including deliberately conducting competitions unfairly.

BUSINESS AND ECONOMIC AFFAIRS

AUGUST 2007

1. Figures published by financial markets analyst Dealogic revealed that leading investment banks in the USA and Europe had nearly $500bn (£246bn) in agreed leveraged loans that they were unable to sell to other investors. **9.** The European Central Bank (ECB) made €95bn (£65bn) available to banks in order to stabilise European credit markets after the interest rate on the overnight markets lending rose to 4.62 per cent, exceeding the ECB's target level of 4 per cent. **14.** The Office of National Statistics (ONS) published the consumer price index (CPI): inflation decreased to 1.9 per cent in July 2007 from 2.4 per cent in June; supermarket-led price reductions in food and non-alcoholic drink were the biggest factor behind the decrease. The Council of Mortgage Lenders revealed that, in the first half of 2007 buy-to-let mortgages accounted for 10 per cent of all outstanding home loans – a 7 per cent rise over five years. **21.** The Bank of England disclosed that it had provided £314m of emergency funding to an unnamed financial institution. **24.** The Northern Rock bank announced increases in its fixed-rate mortgages for sub-prime home loans and stopped offering tracker mortgages to such borrowers altogether.

SEPTEMBER 2007

4. Premier Foods, owner of the Hovis and Mothers Pride brands, announced that wheat prices had doubled in the past year due to a series of poor harvests and the company would therefore be increasing bread and flour prices due to rises in production costs. **5.** The three-month London inter-bank offered rate (LIBOR) reached 6.8 per cent, its highest level for nine years, prompting the Bank of England to announce that it would provide £4.4bn of additional reserves to banking institutions to enable them to continue to borrow at the rate of 5.75 per cent. **10.** Citizens Advice reported that the number of households seeking debt advice increased by 20 per cent in 2007, credit and store card debt arrears accounted for almost half of the enquiries it received; over the same time period, problems with utility arrears had increased by a third and council tax debt by a quarter. **14.** Northern Rock revealed it had asked the Bank of England for financial help in order to cope with the lack of liquidity in the short-term debt markets; shares in the bank plummeted by 31 per cent and hundreds of its customers queued at branches throughout Britain to withdraw their savings. **17.** Despite reassurances from the chief executive of Northern Rock, Adam Applegarth, and the chancellor Alistair Darling, queues at the bank's branches continued and an estimated £2bn was withdrawn over three days. **19.** The Bank of England announced that it would make £10bn of funds available to banking institutions and that it would accept mortgages and mortgage-backed securities as collateral for these loans in order to alleviate pressure on the inter-bank lending market.

OCTOBER 2007

1. The chancellor, Alistair Darling, announced that the first £35,000 of all deposits in bank and building society accounts would be guaranteed by the Bank of England with immediate effect. **16.** The Office of National Statistics (ONS) reported that the CPI measure of inflation for September remained below the Bank of England's 2 per cent target at 1.8 per cent, despite steep increases in food and petrol prices. **17.** The International Monetary Fund published a report on world economic prospects warning that house prices in Britain were overvalued by up to 40 per cent. **19.** The price of diesel in the UK increased to above £1 per litre for the first time. **22.** British Energy announced the indefinite closure of both its Hartlepool and Heysham-1 nuclear power stations after a corroded steel wire was discovered in the concrete casing of one of the reactors at Hartlepool; this lead to a drop of nearly £500m in the company's value on the London Stock Exchange. **24.** The Bank of England's half-yearly *Financial Stability Review* concluded that global problems in the credit markets had constituted the most severe challenge to the UK financial system for several decades and banks needed to adapt their business models to ensure that funds were available when problems arose. **25.** BP America was ordered to pay fines totalling approximately $370m (£185m) to the US Department of Justice: $50m (£25m) for the Texas City refinery explosion in 2005, $20m (£10m) for pipeline leaks at the Prudhoe Bay oil fields in Alaska and $300m (£150m) for price fixing US propane contracts in 2004.

NOVEMBER 2007

1. The Markets in Financial Instruments directive came into force across the European Union; designed to facilitate a single EU-wide market for cross-border trading in securities and to allow smaller trading platforms to compete with established national stock exchanges, the regulations were met with resistance by some EU countries. **5.** Moneyexpert.com reported that the number of credit card applications refused by card providers had increased by 17 per cent to an estimated 3.27 million in the six-month period from March 2007. **7.** The London Stock Exchange experienced its first serious technical problem since 2000 when the system failed at 3.50pm forcing the exchange to extend trading by over an hour. **29.** The Bank of England released figures showing that mortgage approvals had dropped by 31 per cent over the year to the end of October, reaching their lowest levels since the beginning of 2005.

DECEMBER 2007

4. The Council of Mortgage Lenders warned that as much as a third of the £90bn required to finance new mortgage loans in 2008 would need to come from wholesale credit markets that had effectively been closed since August 2007; the Financial Services Authority (FSA) warned that market conditions would remain difficult for a sustained period and urged banks to protect themselves from a collapse in liquidity. **5.** The Halifax building society published data showing that the average house price in the UK decreased for the third consecutive month. **6.** The Bank of England reduced its base rate of interest to 5.5 per cent, the first decrease since August 2005. **7.** The Office of Fair Trading announced that the retailers Asda, Sainsbury's and Safeway had been in a cartel with the dairy companies Wiseman, Dairy Crest and the Cheese Company in order to fix prices of milk, butter and cheese; the companies were fined a total of £116m. **12.** A consortium consisting of the Bank of England, the Swiss Central Bank, the Bank of Canada, the European Central Bank (ECB) and the US Federal Reserve announced that they would release a total of £53.7bn into the global money markets via a series of auctions in order to ease the worldwide credit crisis. **18.** Inter-bank lending rates dropped in the UK and Europe after the Bank of England's auction of funds, worth £10bn, was fully taken up and the ECB distributed £250bn in two-week loans to any banking institution offering at least 4.21 per cent.

JANUARY 2008
2. The price of crude oil reached $100 per barrel for the first time on New York's Nymex exchange; Brent crude oil, the British benchmark price, rose to just over $98 a barrel. **3.** LSL Property Services, owner of Your Move estate agents, announced that it had closed 12 of its branches and cut 315 jobs across its surveying and estate agency businesses due to a weakening property market in the UK. **4.** The Bank of England published figures showing that mortgage approvals fell for the fifth consecutive month in November with only 83,000 loans, worth a total of £11.4bn, approved. **7.** The British Bankers' Association announced changes to the Banking Code, followed by most banks, due to take effect from March 2008; the new code moves the onus of debt responsibility from borrower to lender, with British banks expected to warn borrowers if they are in danger of getting into financial difficulties. **21.** The FTSE-100 index of leading shares fell by 323 points, reducing the value of Britain's stock market by more than £77bn. **22.** The US Federal Reserve cut interest rates from 4.25 to 3.5 per cent, the biggest one-day rate reduction by the American central bank for 25 years. **24.** It emerged that the previous day's fall in the world stock markets may have been precipitated by the actions of Jérôme Kerviel, a junior trader at the French investment bank Société Générale, who had lost his employer £3.7bn by fraudulently gambling the bank's money on stock market futures. **30.** The US Federal Reserve cut interest rates for the second time in eight days to 3 per cent.

FEBRUARY 2008
1. The 317-store bargain bookseller, The Works, went into administration with debts of around £20m. **7.** The Bank of England reduced interest rates by a quarter point to 5.25 per cent. **10.** The Royal Institution of Chartered Surveyors reported that the price of agricultural land in England and Wales was at a record high of £10,439 per hectare, a 28 per cent increase since the beginning of 2007. **19.** Credit Suisse suspended a small group of London traders after the investment bank discovered a £1.5bn asset writedown during an audit of its structured credit division; the bank said the writedown was due to mispriced trades and was not the result of any fraudulent activity. **20.** The high street bank Alliance and Leicester issued a profit warning and said that it would restrict its new mortgage and savings business in 2008. **21.** OFGEM, the energy industry regulator, launched a formal inquiry into the UK's energy supply market after 70 MPs signed an early day motion stating that the UK market was not competitive enough and was unhealthily dominated by six suppliers. **22.** Three British bankers, David Bermingham, Giles Darby and Gary Mulgrew, who were extradited to the USA in 2006 to stand trial for fraud, were jailed for 37 months each by a Houston district judge, for their part in a plot to deceive the National Westminster Bank about the true value of its stake in Enron, the energy trader which collapsed with debts of £18bn in December 2001. **28.** As part of a general tightening of mortgage lending criteria amongst banks and building societies, Lloyds TSB became the biggest lender to refuse mortgages to buyers that do not have a 10 per cent deposit, the move followed Nationwide building society's announcement that it would now offer higher rates to borrowers without a 25 per cent deposit. **29.** The Bank of England announced that mortgage approvals for new buyers had dropped by 40 per cent in January 2008 compared with January 2007, with just 74,000 new-buyer loans approved.

MARCH 2008
12. The Chancellor, Alistair Darling, announced in his 2008 budget statement that he would be writing to the governor of the Bank of England to instruct him to keep a 2 per cent target on inflation and predicted that the British economy will experience growth of between 1.75 and 2.25 per cent in 2008–9. **13.** The price of gold reached $1,000 (£500) per ounce for the first time as fears of a global credit crisis escalated. Carlyle Capital Corporation, a £10.8bn US-owned investment fund collapsed with debts of around £8bn, despite investing in high-quality mortgages rather than the sub-prime market. **14.** Bear Stearns, America's fifth largest investment bank, announced a significant deterioration in its liquidity and secured an emergency loan from New York's Federal Reserve Bank under legislation that had not been invoked for 50 years. **19.** The Bank of England was forced to issue a statement that no British bank had requested emergency funding after false rumours that HBOS (Halifax, Bank of Scotland) had requested a multi-billion-pound emergency loan, which resulted in HBOS's shares falling by more than 17 per cent. **20.** The Bank of England announced a £5bn weekly increase in the amount of money it would make available via auction to the credit markets; despite the additional liquidity, the cost of inter-bank borrowing for three months increased for the tenth day in a row to 5.99 per cent.

APRIL 2008
1. The chair of Swiss bank UBS, Marcel Ospel, resigned after the bank revealed losses of £18.73bn. **7.** *The Times* reported that personal financial and mortgage advisers were facing a sharp downturn in revenues due to the withdrawal of mortgage products by major lenders and the decision by some building societies that they would no longer lend money through intermediaries. **10** The Bank of England reduced the base rate of interest by a quarter point to 5 per cent; despite the reduction, most high street banks and building societies increased rates on a range of loan products, including mortgages. **15.** Fashion retailer Ethel Austin went into administration, later announcing the loss of 420 jobs. **17.** Investment bank Merrill Lynch revealed that it would be making 4,000 employees redundant worldwide as a consequence of the sub-prime mortgage crisis. **20.** The Bank of England announced the issue of around £50bn of Treasury bills to allow banks to swap mortgage-backed securities for government bonds; the chancellor confirmed that the move was intended to help stabilise the UK financial market and ease lending criteria. **22.** The Royal Bank of Scotland announced its intention to seek £12bn from its shareholders in a rights issue in order to raise its equity capital. **28.** A review of the collapse of the Northern Rock building society by the FSA showed that it knew in April 2007 that Northern Rock had breached its capital requirements, months before the bank run which occurred in September.

MAY 2008
6. The Channel Island of Jersey introduced a goods and services tax (GST); similar to VAT in the UK, the rate was set at 3 per cent for three years by the States of Jersey government. **9.** *The Times* reported that the number of house repossessions in the first three months of 2008 increased to 27,530, up by 17 per cent in one year and by

) per cent on the previous quarter. **13.** The chancellor, Alistair Darling, increased the basic personal tax allowance from £5,435 to £6,035 and decreased the higher rate tax threshold from £41,435 to £40,835 in order offset the losses of lower earners after the abolishment of the 10p starting income tax rate in the March budget. **14.** The Governor of the Bank of England, Mervyn King, forecast that inflation could reach 3.7 per cent during 2008 and remain high for a further two years, he also warned that households could face a protracted period of financial strain as food and utility bills continued to rise. **20.** The executive chair of Northern Rock, Ron Sandler, reported to the Treasury Select Committee that the bank planned to repay at least 25 per cent of the £27bn loaned by the Treasury by the end of 2008, a further 50 per cent by the end of 2009 and the total amount by the end of 2010. **22.** The chief executive of the London Stock Exchange, Clara Furse, confirmed that there had been a slowdown in client business at the exchange; the admission came after the exchange's own share price dropped to £10.38 following year-on-year monthly increases since May 2005. **29.** Figures published by Nationwide Building Society showed that the cost of an average British home had fallen by 2.5 per cent during May. **30.** The business class airline Silverjet went into administration, grounding all flights after it failed to secure a £2.5m loan from a Gulf investor; the Civil Aviation Authority estimated that around 7,000 UK and 2,500 non-UK customers had been affected by the collapse and would not be covered by the air travel industry's insurance scheme.

JUNE 2008

4. The European Commission initiated an in-depth investigation into Northern Rock's restructuring operation after its report concluded that a more aggressive downsizing of the bank's market share should be implemented to ensure a quicker redemption of the government's loan and prevent the bank from having an unfair advantage due to its nationalised status. **10.** In an address at the British Bankers' Association conference, the Governor of the Bank of England, Mervyn King, proposed that banks should make upfront payments into a new scheme in order to compensate savers who might lose money in a bank collapse. **19** The deputy governor of the Bank of England, Sir John Gieve, announced his intention to stand down from the post in January 2009, with two years of his five-year term left to run. **26.** Tesco declared it was cutting the cost of around 3,000 in-store items by 50 per cent; in response ASDA announced it was to sell ten staple products such as bread, butter and eggs from just 50p in order to win back customers caught in the credit crunch. ALDI, the German-owned discount grocery retailer, reported a 20 per cent rise in sales.

JULY 2008

3. A survey by the online financial comparison website Moneysupermarket.com reported that more than four million households had resorted to personal loans or credit cards in order to cover mortgage or rent payments in the past year. **9.** Figures from the British Retail Consortium showed that the cost of groceries in June 2008 was 7 per cent higher than in June 2007, equalling a £360 increase in the average yearly food bill for a family of four. **10.** The Housebuilding firm Barratt Developments announced 1,200 job cuts, amounting to a fifth of its workforce. **12.** The Office of Fair Trading issued £173.3m in fines and costs after a number of retailers (including ASDA, Somerfield and Threshers) admitted that they had colluded with the tobacco company Gallagher in fixing the price of a number of cigarette brands. **14.** Alliance and Leicester building society was bought by Spanish bank Santander, which also owns Abbey, in a deal worth £1.3bn. The ONS reported that the CPI rate of inflation for June was 3.8 per cent, nearly double the Bank of England's 2 per cent target. **30.** British Gas confirmed price rises of 35 per cent for gas customers and 9 per cent for electricity customers; utility company EDF, which supplies energy to around five million people in London and the South East, also confirmed that it was increasing the price of electricity by 17 per cent and gas by 22 per cent.

CRIMES AND LEGAL AFFAIRS

AUGUST 2007

1. The Youth Justice Board, created in 2000 to cut youth crime, released its annual report; it failed to meet any of its targets for the previous 12 months. **2.** An Independent Police Complaints Commission report into the shooting of Jean Charles de Menezes by police in 2005 recommended that Assistant Commissioner Andy Hayman should be disciplined for the mistakes that led to Mr de Menezes' death. **16.** The Sentencing Advisory Panel told courts that teenagers who breached antisocial behaviour orders (ASBOs) should not be jailed except in the most serious cases; 45 per cent of those prosecuted for the breach of an ASBO in 2005 were given prison terms. **18.** The number of robberies in England and Wales involving knives doubled in 2005–7, according to a study by King's College London. **20.** Learco Chindamo, who was sentenced to a minimum of 12 years in prison for the murder of headteacher Philip Lawrence in 1995, won his appeal with immigration judges to be allowed to remain in Britain at the end of his prison term in 2008. A high court judge warned of the possibility of hundreds of prisoners being released after their minimum term due to lack of facilities. **23.** A high court judge overruled the home secretary Jacqui Smith and ordered that 70 asylum seekers due to be deported to the Democratic Republic of the Congo should not be sent back until the risk of torture or persecution on their return had been assessed. **25.** Figures released by the Home Office showed that the number of gun-related injuries and deaths was four times higher in 2006 than in 1998. **30.** Raymond Gilmour, 45, was freed after 21 years in prison; appeal judges ruled that his confession to the rape and murder of a 16-year-old girl in 1982 was based on police intimidation. **31.** Five boys, aged between 12 and 14, were found guilty of the manslaughter of 67-year-old Ernest Norton, who died from a heart attack caused by the children throwing stones at him and his son; the boys were sentenced to two years in youth custody on 19 October.

SEPTEMBER 2007

2. Data released under the Freedom of Information Act revealed that children under ten were named as the prime suspects in just under 3,000 crimes in 2006. **5.** Five gang members were jailed for the murder of Somalian student Mahir Osman in north London; Faisal Wangita, the son of Ugandan dictator Idi Amin, was jailed for five years in May 2007 for his part in the attack. **8.** The parents of Madeleine McCann were named as official suspects by Portuguese police in the case of their daughter's disappearance; the four-year-old went missing from a holiday resort in Portugal in May 2007. **11.** The grandmother of Ellie Lawrenson, a five-year-old girl killed by a pitbull terrier in 2007, was cleared of manslaughter and gross negligence for allowing the dog to enter the house. **14.** The actor Chris Langham was sentenced to ten months in prison for downloading video clips showing children being sexually abused. The second inquest into the death of 21-year-old Rachel Whitear in 2000 confirmed that she died of a heroin overdose; the inquest could not establish whether anyone else was with her at the time of her death. **20.** Figures released by the Home Office showed that only one in eight crimes recorded in England and Wales resulted in a suspect being charged or appearing in court in 2006–7. **21.** A Labour councillor was found guilty of making false accusations about a rival Liberal Democrat candidate in an election campaign; Miranda Gell was ordered to pay a fine of £1,000, prosecution costs of £3,000 and was disqualified from holding office as a councillor for three years. **27.** Miles Cooper, a primary school caretaker, was found guilty of sending seven letter bombs in 2007 which injured eight people; he was given an indeterminate jail sentence with a minimum term of five years on 28 September.

OCTOBER 2007

1. Legislation for the enduring power of attorney was replaced by the lasting power of attorney (*see* Legal Notes). The minimum legal age for buying cigarettes or tobacco was raised from 16 to 18. **2.** The Portuguese detective in charge of the investigation into the disappearance of Madeleine McCann was dismissed from the case and demoted; he accused the British police of covering up the role the girl's parents played in her disappearance. **4.** The Serious Organised Crime Agency seized £8.5m in fraudulent cheques and documents in overnight raids across the UK; parallel operations were carried out in the USA, Canada and Nigeria. **9.** A survey conducted by the Howard League found that 95 per cent of 10 to 15-year-olds in Britain had experienced some form of crime at least once. **12.** Two men jailed for the rape of underage girls had their sentences doubled from two to four years at the court of appeal; the four-year sentence became the minimum term for cases of this kind as a result of the ruling. **15.** The Association of Muslim Lawyers and the Society of Black Lawyers released figures demonstrating that the Law Society was twice as likely to investigate allegations of misconduct against ethnic minority solicitors than against white solicitors. **22.** A report from the Ministry of Justice revealed that the number of high-risk offenders that committed a serious crime while on probation rose by a third in the year 2006–7. **30.** Government figures for 2005–6 showed that only one in 400 people stopped and searched under the Terrorism Act 2000 was subsequently arrested. **31.** The House of Lords ruled that control orders placed on terrorist suspects could include a curfew of a maximum of 12 hours; previously 18 hours was the maximum curfew.

NOVEMBER 2007

1. The Metropolitan Police was fined £175,000 and ordered to pay £385,000 in costs for breaking health and safety regulations in the case of the shooting of Jean Charles de Menezes in July 2005. A British student was found dead in her apartment in Perugia, Italy; an Italian judge ordered three suspects to be held on remand for Meredith Kerchner's murder on 9 November. **5.** Adel Yahya, 25, was jailed for six years and nine months for passing on terrorist information; counts of conspiracy to murder and conspiracy to cause explosions were withdrawn. **8.** Samina Malik, 22, from west London, became the first woman in Britain to be convicted under the Terrorism Act 2000; she was found guilty of possessing material that could be used for terrorism and was given a suspended prison sentence on 10 December. **12.** Ronald Castree was given a life sentence for the murder of 11-year-old Lesley Molseed in 1975; Castree was charged after he gave a DNA sample in an unrelated case. **14.** A body found at a house in Margate was identified as 15-year-old Vicky Hamilton who went missing in 2001; Peter Tobin, already serving a life sentence for the murder of Angelika Kluk in 2006, was charged with her murder. **15.** The court of appeal quashed Barry George's conviction for the murder of television presenter Jill Dando in 1999; the court ruled that the original verdict was unsafe and that he should face a retrial. **16.** The body of Dinah McNicol, who went missing in 1991, was found at the house in Margate where Vicky Hamilton's remains were found on 14 November. **28.** Robert Napper was charged with the murder of Rachel Nickell, who was stabbed to death on Wimbledon Common in 1992. **29.** Seventy-year-old Anthony Hall was convicted of the murder of 15-year-old Jacqueline Thomas in Birmingham in 1961; the case was reopened following advances in DNA profiling.

DECEMBER 2007

1. John Darwin, who disappeared on a canoeing trip in 2002 and was believed to be dead, walked into a police station alleging memory loss; both he and his wife Anne were later arrested on suspicion of fraud after a newspaper published a photo of the couple taken in Panama in 2006. **5.** The chairman of the Association of Chief Police Officers' road safety committee was banned from driving for six weeks and fined £300 for driving at 90mph in a 60mph zone. **10.** Conrad Black, the former owner of the Telegraph Group, was sentenced to six years in prison by Chicago's federal court for fraud totalling £3m. **13.** The National Audit Office revealed that over 84,000 victims of violent crime would have to wait 17 months for compensation; the average time for responding to a claim had risen from 364 days in 1998 to 515 days in 2006–7. The court of appeal quashed the convictions of five boys that were found guilty of the manslaughter of Ernest Norton (*see* 31 August 2007); they received 12-month supervision orders for violent disorder on 11 January. **16.** A British terrorist suspect, Rashid Rauf, escaped from outside an Islamabad court after attending an extradition hearing. **20**. Sean Hoey, the only person to be prosecuted for the Omagh bombing carried out by the Real IRA in 1998, was cleared of all charges, including 29 counts of murder. **26.** The Home Office announced that it had met its target to deport over 4,000 foreign prisoners in 2007.

JANUARY 2008

7. A British man, Kenny Richey, was freed after a successful fourth appeal against his sentence; he had spent 21 years on death row in Ohio for the alleged murder of a two-year-old girl in 1986. **8.** A dentist from London was jailed for four-and-a-half years for terrorist offences; Sohail Qureshi tried to board a flight to Pakistan carrying military equipment. **12.** Garry Weddell, a senior police officer due to stand trial for the murder of his wife in May 2008, was found dead after apparently killing his mother-in-law; Mr Weddell had been released on bail and his mother-in-law was due to give evidence in the case. **15.** Mr Justice Ousley ruled that the murder trial of Wang am, accused of killing the writer Allan Chappelow in 006, would mostly be held in camera for reasons of ational security; the home secretary, Jacqui Smith applied or the unprecedented Public Interest Immunity certificate n December. **23.** John Hogan, who jumped from a hotel alcony with his two children, killing his son, while on oliday in August 2006, was found to be mentally nstable by a Greek jury, and therefore not guilty of nurder. **24.** Home Office figures showed a 9 per cent lrop in crime overall in the year to September 2007, espite a 21 per cent increase in drug offences and a 4 er cent rise in gun crime. Police carried out dawn raids gainst suspected child-traffickers in Slough, Berkshire, nd 11 Romanian children were taken into care; ten hildren were returned on 1 February and no charges vere brought due to lack of evidence. **25.** Wayne Cook nd Steven Robinson were each jailed for six years for ending vodka containing lethal doses of caustic soda to wo randomly chosen people; they were campaigning n behalf of the Scottish National Liberation Army to orce Scottish independence. **28.** Five men who stole 53m from the Securitas depot in Kent in 2006 were onvicted of kidnap, robbery and firearms offences; they vere sentenced to between 20 and 30 years' mprisonment.

EBRUARY 2008

4. Five men were jailed for assisting the terrorists that ttempted attacks on the London Underground on 21 July 2005; their sentences ranged from seven to 17 years in prison. **5.** At the inquest of Mayra Cabrera, a jury ruled a verdict of unlawful killing by the Swindon and Marlborough NHS Trust; Mrs Cabrera died immediately after giving birth when she was given a powerful naesthetic instead of a saline drip. **11.** Three teenagers were jailed for life for the murder of Garry Newlove, who died from being repeatedly punched and kicked after confronting the group. **18.** Parviz Khan was jailed for life for planning to kidnap and behead a British soldier. The body of 15-year-old Scarlett Keeling was found on a beach in Goa, India; two men were later arrested on suspicion of rape and murder. **21.** An official report by the chief surveillance commissioner into a recorded conversation between a terrorist suspect and Sadiq Khan, MP, found that Scotland Yard had not broken the law by surveiling Mr Khan's communications. **22.** Steve Wright, 49, was given a life sentence for the murders of five women who worked as prostitutes in Ipswich in December 2006. Mark Dixie was sentenced to life in prison for the murder of 18-year-old Sally Anne Bowman in September 2005. **23.** Detectives investigating suspected child abuse at the Haut de la Garenne children's home in Jersey found a number of human bone fragments. **24.** A survey by the Courts Service revealed that nearly one in seven people awaiting trial for murder in January had been released on bail. **26.** Levi Bellfield was given a life sentence for killing two women and attacking a third; he had also been named as the prime suspect in the murder investigation of 13-year-old Milly Dowler, killed in 2002. **29.** Gil Magira was found guilty of using an instrument to procure a miscarriage and sentenced to three years and nine months in prison; in the first case of its kind in 40 years, Mr Magira crushed abortion pills into his pregnant wife's food.

MARCH 2008

3. A 19-year-old woman was awarded more than £16,000 compensation under the Employment Equality (Age) Regulations 2006; Leanne Wilkinson was dismissed from her job because her employers claimed she was too young for the role. **4.** Colin Norris, a nurse at Leeds General Infirmary, was given four life sentences and a concurrent 20-year sentence for murdering four elderly patients and attempting to murder a fifth by injecting them with overdoses of insulin. **7.** Mohammed Hamid was jailed indefinitely for recruiting and training potential terrorists; Hamid's accomplice Attilla Ahmet was jailed for six years and 11 months. **10.** The inspectors of the Crown Prosecution Service reported that over 2,000 planned cases did not go to court in 2006–7 because prosecutors were not fully prepared. **13.** Marianna Telles won compensation from the NHS in a landmark ruling; she suffered brain damage as a baby as a result of high-risk heart surgery carried out at Bristol hospital. **14.** Shannon Matthews, a nine-year-old who went missing on 19 February, was found alive in a house a mile from her home; police later charged the uncle of Shannon's stepfather, Michael Donovan, with kidnapping and unlawful imprisonment and her mother, Karen Matthews, with perverting the course of justice and child neglect. **18.** A 15-year-old girl became the first person in England and Wales to be successfully prosecuted for filming a fatal attack on her mobile phone; she was sentenced to two years' detention and training for aiding and abetting manslaughter. **28.** The justice secretary, Jack Straw, banned the early release of convicted terrorists after it was revealed that they had been freed before the end of their sentences under a programme designed to reduce prison overcrowding.

APRIL 2008

7. At the inquest into the deaths of Princess Diana and Dodi al-Fayed the jury delivered a verdict of unlawful killing; it found that chauffeur Henri Paul and paparazzi photographers pursuing the Princess' vehicle were responsible for the crash. **8.** The high court ruled that the government acted unlawfully by changing the immigration regulations that allowed skilled workers to remain in the UK; the new regulations affected up to 44,000 people. **9.** The court of appeal blocked the deportation of the radical Islamist preacher Abu Qatada on the basis that he would be at risk of torture if he returned to Jordan. **10.** The high court ruled that the Serious Fraud Office acted improperly by halting an enquiry in December 2006 into an arms deal between the defence firm BAE and Saudi officials; the ruling was overturned by the House of Lords on 30 July. The forensic science regulator declared that it was safe to use very small samples of DNA in criminal prosecutions; the investigation followed allegations that the technique used to analyse the low-template DNA was scientifically unsound. **11.** The high court judged that the Human Rights Act applies to British troops even when they are in combat and therefore sending troops on military operations without adequate equipment constitutes a breach of law. **15.** The court of appeal ruled that the justice secretary, Jack Straw, would no longer be able to overrule the parole board to block the release of dangerous prisoners. **18.** Abu Izzadeen, a radical Muslim cleric, was sentenced to four-and-a-half years in prison for inciting and funding terrorism. **24.** The Prison Service agreed to pay over £120,000 to 15 former inmates of Leeds prison who sued the service, claiming they had suffered beatings and racial discrimination by prison officers. Ruling on an appeal brought by five terrorist suspects, a high court judge found that the Treasury's entitlement to freeze suspects' bank accounts was unlawful.

MAY 2008
1. The court of appeal found Suzanne Holdsworth's murder conviction unsafe due to new medical evidence; Ms Holdsworth was sentenced to life in prison for the murder of a two-year-old while babysitting in March 2005. **2.** Ian Strachan and Sean McGuigan were jailed for five years for attempting to blackmail a member of the Royal family. **7.** Barrister Mark Saunders was shot dead by police after a five-hour siege at his flat in Chelsea, London. **8.** The high court ruled that Abu Qatada should be released from prison under strict bail conditions; Qatada appealed against being kept in prison indefinitely following the ruling against his deportation to Jordan (*see* 9 April). Home Office figures showed that 37 per cent fewer ASBOs were issued in 2006 than in 2005, but the number of ASBOs breached rose from 47 to 61 per cent. **9.** Statistics published by the Ministry of Justice showed that 41 per cent of adults released from jail or community punishment in the first three months of 2005 reoffended within a year. **12.** The judiciary announced new robes for court of appeal and high court judges in civil cases; judges would also not be required to wear wigs, wing collars and bands from 1 October. **15.** The Youth Justice Board released figures showing that violent acts committed by girls aged 10–17 rose by 25 per cent in the past three years. **23.** Habib Khan was was cleared of murder and convicted of the manslaughter of his neighbour, Keith Brown, in July 2007; evidence presented showed that Mr Brown, a BNP activist, had conducted a campaign of racist threats and violence towards Mr Khan and his family.

JUNE 2008
17. The court of appeal quashed Samina Malik's terrorism conviction (*see* 8 November); judges decided that the jury could have been confused by some of the trial documents. **18.** Law lords ruled that a government plan to guarantee anonymity to witnesses giving evidence against gang members could make a trial unfair, and quashed a double-murder conviction originally secured by two anonymous witnesses. **20.** Abu Hamza, a radical Muslim cleric, lost his appeal against a decision to extradite him to the USA where he was due to face up to 11 terror-related charges. **23.** Seventeen-year-old Armel Gnango was sentenced to life in prison for starting a gunfight that accidentally killed Magda Pniewska, a Polish care worker, in October 2007, in the first criminal case where a defendant was convicted of murder despite not firing the fatal shot. **26.** A US court issued Neil Entwistle, of Nottinghamshire, with two life sentences for killing his wife and daughter in 2006. **28.** Anandakumar Ratnasabapathy committed suicide in court by taking an overdose of sleeping pills after being found guilty of assaulting his three-month-old daughter. **29.** Two French students, Laurent Bonomo and Gabriel Ferez, were found stabbed to death and subsequently set alight in their flat in south-east London.

JULY 2008
7. A court in Equatorial Guinea sentenced Simon Mann, former British soldier, to 34 years in prison for his role i an attempted coup to overthrow president Teodor Nguema in 2004. It was confirmed that Sir Igor Judg would be appointed as Lord Chief Justice on Lord Phillip of Worth Matravers' retirement in October 2008. **8.** Th high court ruled that a 78-year-old woman who wa sexually assaulted over 20 years previously had the righ to sue her attacker for a share of his subsequent £7n lottery winnings; similar claims previously had to b brought to court within six years. **11.** The case brough against firms allegedly fixing the price of prescribed NH drugs, the biggest ever brought by the Serious Frau Office, was thrown out of court; it lasted for six years an cost an estimated £40m. **17.** The European court o justice upheld a landmark ruling that allowed Sharo Coleman, a legal secretary and unpaid carer for he disabled son, to take time off work to care for her child **21.** Kate and Gerry McCann were officially cleared o their status as suspects in the case of the disappearance o their daughter in Portugal in May 2007; Portugues police closed the investigation due to lack of evidence **23.** Anne and John Darwin were each sentenced to ove six years in prison for money laundering and fraud; Joh Darwin faked his own death so that the couple coul claim £250,000 in life insurance (*see* 1 December 2007) **29.** The high court ruled that Sarika Singh, a Sik teenager who was excluded from her school for wearing a steel bracelet to school should be readmitted, as the bracelet, the *kara,* was central to her faith. **31.** Police found the remains of up to five children buried on the site of Haut de la Garenne home in Jersey (*see* 23 February); the names of the children and when they were killed could not be identified. Barry George was cleared of the murder of Jill Dando at his retrial after serving eight years in prison (*see* 15 November 2007).

NVIRONMENT AND SCIENCE

UGUST 2007

. Scientists at the Cleveland Clinic, USA, revealed that ey had successfully used a deep brain stimulation chnique, where electrodes are inserted through the kull to stimulate the thalamus, to revive a patient in a inimally conscious state. **2.** The Heritage Lottery Fund warded an £8.9m grant to the Great Fen Project, which ntends to turn over 3,000ha (7,400 acres) of ambridgeshire farmland into fenland. **7.** In China, cientists announced that the Yangtze river dolphin, the aiji, had become the first extinct large vertebrate for over 0 years. **8.** The journal *Nature* published a research paper hallenging the widely accepted view of human evolution the detailed analysis of two hominid fossils discovered Kenya showed that rather than *Homo habilis* evolving nto the more advanced *Homo Sapiens* as previously ought, the two may have been sister species that verlapped in time. **14.** The *British Journal of Nutrition* ublished a study suggesting that babies' future eating abits can be influenced while in the womb by the diet of eir mothers. **19.** Scientists presented research in Boston, SA, suggesting that natural pigments that give certain uit and vegetables a red, blue or purple colour can act as nti-cancer agents. **27.** The government published its UK iodiversity Action Plan, which cited twice as many pecies of plants and animals in need of special protection s ten years ago, including hedgehogs, harvest mice, almon and sparrows. **30.** The journal *Science* published esearch showing that the world's most successful acterial parasite – *Wolbachia* – has effectively become a art of 11 different animals, by enveloping its entire enetic code into theirs.

EPTEMBER 2007

. The journal *Nature Genetics* published research on the iscovery of the first common gene shown to have a direct nk to a person's height (HMGA2). **5.** The Human ertilisation and Embryology Authority agreed in rinciple to the creation of human-animal embryos for use n research emphasising that scientists must make ndividual applications and ensure that the embryos are lestroyed after 14 days. **9.** The Campaign to Protect ural England released maps that were commissioned to hart the pace of construction over the past 40 years; the naps show that almost 50 per cent of the country is now ffected by urbanisation, compared to 26 per cent in the arly 1960s. **11.** The *British Medical Journal* reported the esults of a large study, which concluded that taking the ontraceptive pill reduced the overall risk of developing ancer; however, if the pill was taken for over eight years, he risk was shown to increase. **15.** The European Space Agency announced that the Northwest Passage, the sea oute that connects Europe and Asia, opened for the first ime since records began 30 years due to the shrinking ummer ice in the Arctic. **21.** The journal *Atmospheric Chemistry and Physics* published research showing that ertain biofuels derived from rapeseed and maize produce nore greenhouse gas emissions than they save in omparison to fossil fuels. **23.** Scientists in Italy revealed hat they had identified a gene, Trop-2, that plays an mportant role in tumour growth in almost 75 per cent of ancers. **27.** The environment secretary, Hilary Benn, nnounced that supermarkets and energy suppliers have greed to gradually phase out incandescent light bulbs in avour of low-energy versions by 2012; the scheme is expected to save 5 million tonnes of carbon dioxide a year.

OCTOBER 2007

7. The Royal Society for the Protection of Birds outlined its plans for a £12m wetland wildlife reserve near Southend, Essex; it is to be created by allowing the sea to flood 728ha (1,800 acres) of reclaimed coastline. **8.** Sir Martin Evans of Cardiff University shared his Nobel prize for medicine with two US scientists for their research on embryonic stem cells. **10.** The *New England Journal of Medicine* published the results of a study of 6,500 men taking statins (cholesterol-lowering drugs); it found that they were 25 per cent less likely to suffer a fatal heart attack in the ten years after finishing the medication. **19.** The International Council for the Exploration of the Seas issued advice to the government that stocks of cod around Britain were showing signs of reversing a severe decline. **25.** The UN published an environmental audit concluding that the speed at which mankind has consumed the Earth's resources over the past 20 years has put 'humanity's very survival at risk'; it urged immediate action with the most pressing concerns being climate change and the condition of fresh water supplies, agricultural land and biodiversity. **27.** Honda announced that the first mass-produced hydrogen fuel cell car, which has zero carbon emissions and emits only water from its exhaust, would be on sale in the USA and Japan within a year. British scientists discovered that a clam dredged off the coast of Iceland was the oldest living animal ever known, with an age of 405 years.

NOVEMBER 2007

1. The journal *Science* published genetic research claiming to show that the colugo, a mammal from South-East Asia that glides between trees, is the closest animal relative to humans after primates. **4.** The power company E.ON in partnership with Lunar Energy announced that they would begin the construction of the world's first deep-sea tidal-energy farm in the summer of 2008; the farm will be based off St David's peninsula in Pembrokeshire, South Wales. **5.** The British Trust for Ornithology stated that the summer of 2007 was the worst breeding season on record for a number of species, including the blue tit, great tit and treecreeper. **7.** A team of scientists from King's College London reported the results of a study showing that women with low levels of vitamin D showed the greatest signs of biological ageing. **12.** Five ships, including an oil tanker, sank during a storm in the Black Sea; 2,000 tonnes of fuel oil were spilt, killing more than 30,000 birds. A study published in the *Journal of Neurology* found that a diet rich in omega-3 oils such as rapeseed, flaxseed and walnut oil could reduce the risk of dementia by 60 per cent. **14.** Scientists in the USA created cloned embryos from a primate for the first time. **19.** Prime Minister Gordon Brown stated that UK carbon emissions should be cut by up to 80 per cent by 2050. **28.** Paleontologists in Spain revealed the discovery of a collection of dinosaur fossils, thought to be the largest in Europe.

DECEMBER 2007

2. The journal *Nature Geoscience* published a paper claiming that due to global warming the tropics have expanded at least 500 miles north and south over the past 30 years. **6.** *Science* reported that researchers had cured sickle cell anaemia in mice using stem cells produced without embryos – it was the first instance that the new technique for obtaining stem cells by genetically reprogramming skin tissue was successfully used to cure a disease. Researchers at the University of Bristol revealed the results of a study that concluded that regular exercise can cut the risk of developing Alzheimer's disease by 30–40 per cent. **7.** A supertanker collided with a barge off of the coast of South Korea, releasing 10.5 million litres of crude oil into the sea. **10.** A team of scientists from the University of Wisconsin, USA, presented research claiming that in the past 5,000 years, humans have evolved up to 100 times more quickly than at any time since their split with the ancestors of modern chimpanzees 6 million years ago. **15.** At a UN summit in Bali representatives of 186 countries agreed a deal aimed at curbing climate change, though environmental campaigners criticised the lack of firm targets for the reduction of greenhouse gas emissions. **19.** *Nature* published details of the discovery of a fossil, found in India and dating from 48 million years ago, believed to be the earliest ancestor of the cetaceans (the group that includes whales, dolphins and porpoises); the *Indohyus*, a small deer-like herbivore, is the first cetacean ancestor known to have lived on land. **24.** The journal *Headache* published research linking activity in the hypothalamus gland to migraine attacks.

JANUARY 2008

1. Researchers in Germany reported finding an 'infant' planet, named TW Hya b; the planet is thought to be under ten million years old, the youngest yet discovered. **3.** Scientists announced the discovery of 11 previously unknown animal and plant species, including frogs and salamanaders, in La Amistad national park in Costa Rica. **8.** A 20-year study of over 11,000 people found that moderate drinkers have 30 per cent less risk of developing heart disease than teetotallers. **9.** The Chinese government banned shops from handing out free plastic bags from 1 June; at the time of writing China was thought to use 3 billion bags per day. **13.** An international team of scientists mapping the ice cover around Antarctica's coast concluded that the rate of annual ice loss had almost doubled in a decade, increasing by around 80 billion tonnes. **17.** *Science* reported the discovery of cells that are thought to be the source of the most common form of childhood leukaemia. A government watchdog granted one-year licences to two research teams planning to create human-animal hybrid embryos; the experiments are intended to provide insight into diseases caused by genetic defects. **22.** An international consortium of scientists announced the launch of the 1,000 Genomes Project, which in two years aims to identify every genetic variant carried by at least 1 per cent of mankind. **30.** A report in *Nature* concluded that a 0.5°C rise in sea temperatures in the North Atlantic since 1965 has led to a 40 per cent increase in the frequency, strength and duration of hurricanes in the region.

FEBRUARY 2008

5. The journal *Archives of Disease in Childhood* published a study dismissing any link between the measles, mumps and rubella (MMR) vaccine and autism. **7.** *New Scientist* reported the results of successful experiments on rats to bypass paralysis through reattaching nerves to the spine. **10.** *Nature Genetics* published the findings of three research teams who had between them discovered 12 genes linked to prostate cancer tumours, doubling the known tally of genes that influence the disease. **14.** *Science* presented a paper showing that 41 per cent of the world's oceans have been damaged significantly by human activity. **18.** In a statement to the American Advancement of Science annual meeting in Boston researchers asserted that 'the global cardiovascular health burden from air pollution is likely to escalate dramatically over the coming decades'. **20.** *Nature* detailed the invention of supramolecular rubber, which exhibits unique self-healing properties; when a sample is broken or cut into pieces and the pieces are then brought into contact at room temperature, they self-repair without the application of heat or pressure. **26.** The journal *PLoS (Public Library of Science) Medicine* published a study casting serious doubt over the effectiveness of a range of antidepressant drugs, including Prozac and Seroxat. The Svalbard Global Seed Bank was officially opened; the vault, built inside a mountain 800km (500 miles) from the North Pole, will act as a failsafe against disaster for up to 2 billion seeds.

MARCH 2008

5. Scientists from the University of California announced the development of a computerised mind-reading technique which lets the user, in nine out of ten cases accurately predict the images a person is looking at by using scanners to study brain activity. **6.** The government's chief scientific adviser, Professor John Beddington, warned that the rush to produce biofuels threatened world food production and could lead to billions suffering acute food shortages. **12.** Plans were outlined for the world's largest butterfly sanctuary near St Albans at the launch of Butterfly World in London; the sanctuary, founded by property developer and entomologist Clive Farrell, is expected to be completed by 2001 at a cost of £25m. **15.** The World Glacier Monitoring Service released a report stating that 2006 showed the biggest 'net loss' of ice since records began. **23.** Scientists in New York published the results of successful experiments using stem cells to treat Parkinson's disease in mice. **26.** *Nature* reported the discovery of a hominin jawbone fossil in Spain, dating between 1.1 million and 1.2 million years ago; it was previously thought that early humans did not reach Europe until 800,000 years ago. **31.** The *British Journal of Psychiatry* published a study indicating that paranoia among people with no mental health problems was more common than previously thought; around a third of the general population often experience an exaggerated sense of persecution or threat.

APRIL 2008

1. Scientists at Newcastle University announced that they had created Britain's first human-animal hybrid embryos, known as cytoplasmic hybrids. **5.** The Zoological Society of London revealed that it has observed the presence of short-snouted seahorses in the Thames Estuary over the past 18 months. **9.** Scientists in Germany warned that households storing organic waste are at risk of health problems, stating that exposure to the moulds that develop as the material decays can cause skin problems and breathing difficulties. **15.** A report on the development of agricultural science and technology, written by 400 international scientists over four years, was published; it concluded that radical changes were needed in world farming to avert increasing regional food shortages, escalating prices and growing environmental concerns. **17.** Britain's first hydrogen fuel station opened in Birmingham. **21.** Surgeons fitted the first 'bionic eyes' in Britain to two men at Moorfields Eye hospital in London; the artificial retinas enable viewing of basic images through the use of a video camera mounted on a pair of glasses. **23.** The Gloucester Wildlife Trust announced plans for the country's first wildlife highway; the scheme will establish a corridor in the Severn Vale to allow animals to move north in the event of climate change altering their original habitat irrevocably.

MAY 2008
4. *Nature Genetics* published a study detailing a genetic variation that raises the risk of obesity; people who inherit two copies of the variant gene were shown to weigh on average 2kg more than those with no copies. **6.** Researchers at Harvard medical school in the USA presented a study demonstrating that within five years of stopping, a former smoker's risk of death from all causes fell by 13 per cent, and after 20 years there was no risk connected to their past smoking history at all. **8.** The Office for National Statistics published a report showing that Britain's carbon footprint was growing; the report stated that any improvements gained from recycling were far outweighed by the increased number of car journeys and commercial flights taken. **14.** *Nature* published a study which examined reports of environmental damage to over 28,000 animal and plant species dating back to 1970; the study concluded that at least 90 per cent of such disruption could be explained by climate change caused by human activity. **18.** Surgeons in Canada used a remotely controlled robot to remove a woman's brain tumour, in the first operation of its kind. **19.** The House of Commons voted to reject an amendment to the Human Fertilisation and Embryology Bill, which would have outlawed the creation of human-animal embryos for use in scientific research. **26.** NASA's *Phoenix* Mars lander touched down safely in the first mission to the planet in four years.

JUNE 2008
3. A seven-year-old boy from Wales became the second person in the world to be declared cured of a genetic defect known as 'Nemo' which destroyed his immune system; Rhys Harris underwent a complete bone marrow transplant, chemotherapy and months in isolation. **4.** At the British Wind Energy conference in London the Crown Estate named 11 zones around Britain's coastline as locations for new offshore wind farms. **9.** Over 20 dolphins died after being trapped in a creek as the tide fell near St Mawes in Cornwall. **10.** Raloxifene, a drug prescribed to treat osteoporosis in post-menopausal women, was found to reduce the risk of developing invasive oestrogen-positive breast cancer by 55 per cent; the findings were reported in the *Journal of the National Cancer Institute.* **11.** An audit by the NHS and the Association of Breast Surgery concluded that women whose breast cancers are detected early have the same life expectancy as those who have never developed the disease. **13.** A series of images of the exact moment of a star's death were published in the journal *Science*; combining data from ground-based and orbiting telescopes, astronomers were able to chart the final explosion of an individual red supergiant for the first time. **17.** The World Land Trust, a British conservation charity, announced it was to jointly manage a million hectares of forest in the Chaco, northern Paraguay, with a local conservation organisation; the forest is home to a number of rare species including the giant peccary and the fairy armadillo.

JULY 2008
3. The journal *Science* published research offering new insight into the origins of Sudden Infant Death Syndrome; the European Molecular Biology Laboratory in Monterotondo, Italy, demonstrated that an imbalance of serotonin in the brain stem can kill infant animals. **15.** The government of the Netherlands informed the press that 12 British-reared calves exported to the Netherlands in March had tested positive for bovine TB. **22.** Initial results from a small trial of a new drug for prostate cancer, abiraterone acetate, were published; the Institute of Cancer Research and the Royal Marsden Hospital, London, found the drug benefited 21 men with advanced prostate cancer. **24.** Scientists at the NASA Themis observatory announced that they had been able to identify the cause of magnetic substorms in space; details of their observations were published in *Science.* **29.** Scientists from the University of Aberdeen presented their research at the International Conference on Alzheimer's Disease in Chicago, showing the efficacy of the drug Rember in reducing the mental decline of Alzheimer's patients.

SPORT

AUGUST 2007

2. The internet betting exchange company Betfair declared void £3.5m of bets placed on a low-profile tennis match between Nikolay Davydenko and Martin Vassallo Arguello at the Orange Prokom Open in Poland, because of concerns over unusual betting patterns. **4.** The England rugby union team beat Wales by 62–5 in the Investec Challenge at Twickenham, its greatest-ever winning margin against Wales. **8.** In the USA, Barry Bonds hit his 756th home run in major league baseball, breaking Hank Aaron's 33-year-old record; on 16 November, a federal grand jury indicted Bonds on perjury and obstruction of justice charges relating to his alleged use of steroids. **13.** Bristol rugby union club was fined £20,000 by the Rugby Football Union after being found guilty of making illegal approaches to players at another club. **17.** The British showjumping team won a bronze medal at the European championships, its best result for nine years, and qualified for the 2008 Olympic Games. **19.** Cyclist Nicole Cooke won the British road race championship for a record eighth time in nine years. **28.** The 22-year-old Seville and Spain footballer Antonio Puerta died in hospital three days after suffering a heart attack during the first game of the season. **29.** At the world athletics championships in Osaka, Japan, the British runners Christine Ohuruogu and Nicola Sanders took first and second place respectively in the 400m; the Great Britain team finished the competition in tenth position with five medals in total.

SEPTEMBER 2007

2. At the world rowing championships in Munich, Great Britain finished top of the medals table for the first time, winning three gold, two silver and six bronze medals. **9.** Asafa Powell of Jamaica set a new world record for the 100m of 9.74 seconds. **13.** The governing body of Formula One motor racing, the FIA, ejected the McLaren Mercedes team from the constructors' championship and fined it £50m, the biggest financial penalty in sporting history, for using technical information stolen from Ferrari. **15.** Colin McRae, the former world motor rally champion, was killed after his helicopter crashed near his home in Lanark; his five-year-old son and two others also died. **16.** The Great Britain baseball team qualified for the world cup for the first time since 1938. **19.** England was knocked out of the ICC world Twenty20 competition at the group stage after losing to the eventual winners, India; in the match, the Indian batsman Yuvraj Singh scored the fastest 50 runs in international cricket, off just 12 balls. **20.** Arbitrators upheld a guilty verdict against the US cyclist Floyd Landis after concluding that he had used synthetic testosterone to win the 2006 Tour de France; he became the first winner of the event to be stripped of his title and was also given a two-year ban. **22.** The tennis player Tim Henman, former British number one and four-time Wimbledon semi-finalist, retired from the game after contributing to the British team's victory over Croatia in the Davis Cup. **25.** Giles Clarke was appointed chairman of the England and Wales Cricket Board. **29.** Gareth Jenkins was sacked as head coach of the Welsh rugby union team after Wales was eliminated from the world cup at the group stage. In football, Portsmouth beat Reading 7–4 in the highest scoring match in premier league history. **30.** Haile Gebreselassie of Ethiopia broke the marathon world record by 29 seconds, setting a time of 2hr 4min 26sec in Berlin, Germany.

OCTOBER 2007

2. In speedway, Coventry Bees won the Sky Sports Elite League title. **5.** The US sprinter Marion Jones admitted to the use of performance-enhancing drugs before winning five medals at the 2000 Olympics; subsequently, Jones was stripped of her medals, ordered to repay £340,000 in prize money and banned from competition for two years. **6.** Jonny Wilkinson became the leading points scorer in the history of the rugby union world cup, with 234 points, after scoring all England's points during the team's 12–10 quarter-final victory over Australia. **7.** Eighteen-year-old Rory McIlroy became the youngest golfer to secure a European Tour card, after finishing third in the Alfred Dunhill Links Championship. **8.** James Roby, the 21-year-old St Helens and Great Britain hooker won rugby league's Man of Steel award. **10.** The Olympic Delivery Authority confirmed that the final cost of the main stadium for the 2012 Games would be £496m, a 77 per cent increase on the initial forecast of £280m. **17.** The World Anti-Doping Agency appointed John Fahey, an Australian former politician, as its new president. **21.** Twenty-two-year-old Lewis Hamilton finished second in the Formula One drivers' championship, the highest ranking ever achieved by a driver in his debut season. **28.** The New York Giants won the first competitive NFL game to be held outside the Americas, beating the Miami Dolphins 13–10 at Wembley. **29.** The IOC granted the British Olympic Association permission to field Great Britain football teams in the 2012 Games, although the Irish, Welsh and Scottish teams refused to be involved. **30.** The governing body of world football, FIFA, appointed Brazil host of the 2014 World Cup finals; the following day, the English FA announced that it would bid to host the 2018 tournament.

NOVEMBER 2007

4. The British boxer Joe Calzaghe successfully defended his WBO title for the 21st time and also became the undisputed world super-middleweight champion after beating Mikkel Kessler to take the WBA and WBC titles. Paula Radcliffe won the New York City marathon. **6.** The Football League announced that it had agreed a broadcasting rights deal worth £264m with the BBC and Sky, running for three years from the start of the 2009–10 season. **9.** Glasgow won the contest to host the 2014 Commonwealth Games. **10.** The Jockeys' Championship was shared for the first time since 1923 after Seb Sanders and Jamie Spencer both finished the flat season with 190 winners. The Great Britain rugby league team beat New Zealand 28–22, completing a 3–0 series victory. The British boxer David Haye won the WBA and WBC cruiserweight titles after beating Jean-Marc Mormeck of France. **15.** The RFU and Premier Rugby (the organisation that represents the 12 premiership clubs in England) agreed an eight-year deal intended to end conflicts between players' club and country commitments; the RFU agreed to pay the clubs a total of £110m in return for more time with elite players. **18.** Andy Priaulx won his third successive FIA World Touring Car title. **19.** In golf, the European Tour announced a £97m sponsorship deal with Dubai that includes the opening of an international headquarters in the emirate, renaming the Order of Merit the Race to Dubai, and inaugurating an end-of-season tournament with £10m in prize money. **20.** Gerald Davies was appointed coach of the British Lions rugby union team. **21.** In football, England lost 3–2 to Croatia and so, like the other home nations, failed to qualify for the 2008 European Championship; Steve

McClaren was sacked as England manager the following day. **22.** The organising committee of the America's Cup announced that the sailing event would not take place in 2009 because of ongoing legal proceedings. **27.** The Sports Disputes Resolution Panel lifted Christine Ohuruogu's lifetime Olympic ban, which was imposed after she missed three out-of-competition drugs tests. **28.** The Portsmouth FC manager Harry Redknapp was among five people arrested on suspicion of conspiracy to defraud and false accounting; on 23 May 2008, Redknapp was awarded £1,000 damages after a judge deemed the police raid on his house unlawful.

DECEMBER 2007

3. The Sri Lankan cricket player Muttiah Muralitharan took his 709th test wicket in a match against England, setting a new record for the greatest number of test wickets taken. **5.** The British Olympic Association named Nicola Sanders, the 400m runner, as its athlete of the year. **6.** The FIA found Renault guilty of possessing confidential technical information belonging to McLaren; no charges were brought. **7.** The champion jockey Kieren Fallon and five other men were cleared of all charges of race-fixing after a two-month trial. **9.** The American boxer Floyd Mayweather Jr beat Ricky Hatton in a WBC welterweight title contest in Las Vegas; Hatton's unsuccessful challenge ended his record of 43 undefeated bouts. The boxer Joe Calzaghe won the BBC Sports Personality of the Year award. **11.** Padraig Harrington was named European Tour golfer of the year. **12.** England won the squash world men's team title, beating Australia 2–1. **14.** The FA appointed Fabio Capello as the new manager of the England football team. **20.** The FA approved in principle the development of a National Football Centre; the FA also announced the appointment of the Labour life peer Lord Triesman as its first independent chairman, with effect from February 2008. The British Horseracing Authority banned the jockey Eddie Ahern for three months for bringing racing into disrepute through excessive use of the whip. **29.** The Motherwell and Scotland footballer Phil O'Donnell died of heart failure as he was being substituted in a match against Dundee United.

JANUARY 2008

1. The US Anti-Doping Agency banned the 100m sprinter and Olympic champion Justin Gatlin from competition for four years, backdated to May 2006; Gatlin had appealed against an eight-year ban he received for a second doping offence. **4.** The Dakar Motor Rally across the Sahara desert was cancelled for the first time in its 30-year history owing to the threat of terrorist attack; it was announced that the 2009 rally would be held in Argentina and Chile. **11.** The French footballer Nicolas Anelka was signed by Chelsea, becoming the most expensive player in the history of the sport, with combined transfer fees of £85m over his career. The discredited US sprinter Marion Jones was sentenced to six months in prison for lying to federal investigators about doping and cheque fraud (*see* 5 October). **15.** The 34-year-old cyclist Jason MacIntyre, three times the British champion, was hit by a vehicle and killed while training near Fort William. **20.** A 51-year-old French sailor, Francis Joyon, set a new record of 57 days for solo circumnavigation of the globe, beating Ellen MacArthur's record by two weeks. **24.** The Scottish FA appointed George Burley as manager of the national team. **25.** The French horse racing authority France Galop imposed a worldwide 18-month ban on the champion jockey Kieren Fallon after he provided a positive drugs test. **29.** In sailing, Ben Ainslie won the Finn Gold Cup, the class's world championship, for a record fifth time.

FEBRUARY 2008

2. The British boxer Amir Khan retained his Commonwealth lightweight title after beating Gairy St Clair of Australia. **6.** A service was held at Old Trafford to mark the 50th anniversary of the Munich air crash, which killed 23 people, including eight Manchester United players. **12.** UK Athletics included the sprinter Dwain Chambers in the Great Britain team for the World Indoor Championships (*see* 7 March); Chambers had previously served a two-year doping ban. **15.** In sailing, Sarah Ayton, Sarah Webb and Pippa Wilson retained the Yngling World Championship title. **18.** The England women's cricket team beat Australia in a one-off test match, retaining the Ashes. **20.** The Indian Premier League, an ICC-sanctioned Twenty20 cricket tournament, held its inaugural auction of players; Mahendra Dhoni was the highest-priced player after attracting a bid of £770,000 from Chennai. **22.** Kristan Bromley became the first Briton to win the bob skeleton world championship; he also became the first person to be European champion, World Cup champion and world champion in the same season.

MARCH 2008

7. The sprinter Dwain Chambers won a silver medal and set a personal best time of 6.54sec in the 60m at the World Indoor Championships. **8.** Jonny Wilkinson became the highest-ever points scorer in rugby union during England's international against Scotland in the Six Nations tournament. **9.** Portsmouth became the only club from the top division to reach the semi-finals of the FA Cup. Great Britain finished fourth in the medals table at the athletics World Indoor Championships; Phillips Idowu won the triple jump with a new British indoor record of 17.75m. David Haye beat Enzo Maccarinelli in a cruiserweight title bout that added the WBO title to his WBA and WBC titles (*see* 10 November); Haye subsequently declared his intention to relinquish these titles and fight in the heavyweight division. **15.** In rugby union, Wales beat France 29–12 to win the Six Nations tournament with a grand slam; the England ladies side became the first to win three consecutive grand slams after beating Ireland 17–7. **20.** The BBC signed a five-year deal worth £200m for the broadcasting rights for Formula One motor racing. **24.** The Olympic torch was lit at Olympia in Greece and began its 20-country tour to the 2008 Beijing Games; its progress was marred, especially in European countries and the USA, by protests at human rights abuses in China, in particular the recent crack-down on demonstrations in Tibet. Britain's Tom Daley won the 10m diving competition at the European Championships, becoming the youngest-ever winner, at 13 years and 308 days. **26.** The footballer David Beckham made his 100th appearance for England in a friendly match that England lost 1–0 to France; he is the fifth player to win 100 caps. **28.** The Indian batsman Virender Sehwag scored the fastest triple hundred in test match history, making 300 runs off 278 balls, on his way to a 319 score against South Africa. **29.** Oxford won the University Boat Race. **30.** The Great Britain team won nine gold medals at the cycling world track championships, its best-ever performance.

APRIL 2008

6. The Olympic torch relay through London was disrupted by protests at China's human rights record, in particular its suppression of recent demonstrations in Tibet. The Whitaker family made history by taking the top three places in an international showjumping competition; Robert Whitaker won the British Open Show Jumping Championship, with his uncle Michael finishing second and his cousin William in third place. **9.** Police arrested David Sullivan, co-owner of Birmingham City football club, and Karren Brady, the club's managing director, on suspicion of conspiracy to defraud and false accounting. **13.** Martin Lel of Kenya won the London Marathon for the third time in four years and set a new course record of 2hr 5min 15sec. **16.** The RFU dismissed Brian Ashton as England's head coach and appointed Martin Johnson, the former World Cup-winning captain, as team manager. **18.** The first Indian Premier League cricket match was played (*see* 20 February); New Zealander Brendon McCullum achieved the highest-ever individual score in Twenty20 cricket, with 158 runs off 73 balls. **20.** The British boxer Joe Calzaghe beat Bernard Hopkins in Las Vegas, USA, to win a world light-heavyweight title and extend his unbeaten career record to 45 bouts. **28.** In the snooker world championship, Ronnie O'Sullivan made a maximum break (147), the ninth of his professional career and more than any other player.

MAY 2008

1. The International Rugby Board, the rugby union governing body, approved a one-year trial of 13 'experimental law variations' from 1 August. **3.** The South African swimmer Natalie du Toit, an amputee, qualified for the 2008 able-bodied Olympic Games by finishing fourth in the 10km open water world championships; du Toit will also compete in the Paralympic Games. **4.** West Bromwich Albion and Stoke City were promoted to the football premier league; Hull City was promoted on 24 May after winning a play-off match. **5.** Arsenal beat Leeds United 4–1 to win the women's FA Cup for the third time in succession and a record ninth time in total. **11.** Manchester United won its 17th football league title, its tenth under Sir Alex Ferguson's management. The Great Britain rowing team finished top of the world cup medals table with five golds and three silvers. **14.** The Belgian tennis player Justine Henin, ranked number one in the world, retired at the age of 25. **16.** The Court of Arbitration for Sport overturned an IAAF ban on the South African 400m runner Oscar Pistorius competing at the 2008 Olympic Games; Pistorius' lower legs were amputated as a child and he races with prosthetic limbs that the IAAF considered gave him an unfair advantage over able-bodied athletes; in July, Pistorius failed to meet the qualifying time and was not selected for the South African team. **17.** Portsmouth won the FA Cup for the first time since 1939. **20.** The Newcastle United footballer Joey Barton was jailed for six months after being found guilty of assault and affray over an incident in December 2007. **21.** Manchester United won the European Cup for the third time, after beating Chelsea in the first-ever all-England final. **22.** Celtic won the Scottish football premier league title for the third successive season. **31.** The Jamaican athlete Usain Bolt, hitherto a 200m runner, broke the world 100m record with a new time of 9.72 seconds.

JUNE 2008

1. The unfancied Rajasthan Royals, led by Shane Warne of Australia, won the inaugural Indian Premier League Twenty20 tournament with a last-ball victory over the Chennai Super Kings. In golf, the USA won the Curtis Cup for the sixth consecutive time with a 13–7 victory over Great Britain and Ireland. **3.** Max Mosley, president of the FIA, won a vote of confidence to retain his position following tabloid allegations about his sex life. **7.** The 2008 European football championships began with a victory for Croatia over joint host nation Switzerland. Ana Ivanovic of Serbia won the women's singles at the French Open, and became the tennis world number one. **8.** Rafael Nadal won the French Open for the fourth consecutive time, equalling Bjorn Borg's record. **9.** Manchester United reported Real Madrid to FIFA, the governing body of international football, over an alleged illegal approach to Cristiano Ronaldo. **11.** The England and Wales Cricket Board announced an agreement with the US billionaire Sir Allen Stanford under which an England team will take part in an annual winner-takes-all Twenty20 cricket match against a Caribbean team for five years beginning in November 2008; the prize money of £10m is believed to be the highest prize for a single match in any sport. Zara Phillips was forced to withdraw from the British Olympic equestrian team following an injury to her horse, Toytown. The former coach of the Brazilian national team, Luiz Felipe Scolari, was appointed manager of Chelsea, following the sacking of Avram Grant. **16.** Tiger Woods won his third US Open following an 18-hole play-off and a single sudden-death hole. **19.** Yeats won the Ascot Gold Cup for the third time, the first horse to achieve three successes in the event since 1977. **22.** The former Manchester United player Paul Ince became manager of Blackburn Rovers. Scott Redding's victory in the motorcycling grand prix at Donington Park made him, at 15 years and 170 days, the youngest-ever grand prix winner. **29.** Spain defeated Germany in the final to win the 2008 European football championships; it was the country's first major trophy for 44 years.

JULY 2008

1. The Newcastle United footballer Joey Barton (*see* 20 May) was given a four-month suspended sentence for assaulting Ousmane Dabo, a former Manchester United teammate, in May 2007. **3.** The British driver David Coulthard announced his retirement at the end of the 2008 Formula One season. **4.** A mystery investor pledged £100m for the rights to stage the British Grand Prix at Donington Park from 2010. **5.** The British teenager Laura Robson won the girls' singles championship at Wimbledon; in the women's singles, Venus Williams defeated her sister Serena to win her fifth title. **6.** Lewis Hamilton won the British grand prix at Silverstone in very wet conditions. In tennis, Rafael Nadal defeated Roger Federer to win the men's singles title at Wimbledon in a match that lasted nearly five hours, the longest-ever men's final. **18.** The cyclist Mark Cavendish won a fourth stage in the Tour de France, the first British man to win so many stages. The sprinter Dwain Chambers lost a legal battle to overturn the British Olympic Association's lifelong ban on him competing at the Olympics. **20.** In golf, Padraig Harrington won the British Open for the second successive year. Lewis Hamilton won the German grand prix, moving to the top of the Formula One drivers' championship. **26.** Middlesex won the Twenty20 cup with a last-ball victory over the 2007 champions Kent; Owais Shah scored 75 off just 35 balls. **27.** Carlos Sastre of Spain won the Tour de France. **31.** Yeats, ridden by Johnny Murtagh, won the Goodwood Cup for the second time in three years.

INTERNATIONAL EVENTS

AFRICA

AUGUST 2007

2. Libya signed a £200m arms deal with France, its first since a European Union embargo was lifted in 2004. **4.** President Mugabe of Zimbabwe passed legislation enabling the security services to intercept postal, telephone and internet communications. **8.** In Namibia, ten men were found guilty of treason for leading a secessionist rebellion in the northern Caprivi region; they were given prison sentences of between 30 and 32 years. **13.** A report on the state of Somalia by the lobby group Human Rights Watch stated that war crimes had been committed by both Islamic insurgents and Ethiopian soldiers during the current phase of the conflict. **16.** At a meeting of the Southern African Development Community, the Zimbabwean government denied the need for reform to counter the adverse effects of the country's economic collapse on its neighbours. **17.** Adriaan Vlok, a law and order minister in South Africa during the apartheid era, received a suspended ten-year prison sentence for ordering the murder of a black cleric in 1989. **20.** Flooding in central Sudan killed at least 90 people. **23.** The legislative election in Sierra Leone was won by the opposition All People's Congress party; Ernest Bai Koroma, an opposition candidate, won the presidential election after a second round run-off against vice-president Solomon Berewa on 17 September. **31.** President Mugabe banned businesses from awarding pay rises to employees because of Zimbabwe's rampant inflation.

SEPTEMBER 2007

2. The UN began to airlift thousands of peacekeeping troops into eastern DR Congo after General Laurent Nkunda, a Congolese Tutsi, withdrew his soldiers from the national army and instigated attacks on government troops who he believed to be collaborating with Hutu extremists responsible for the 1994 genocide in Rwanda. **4.** Thousands of Congolese sought refuge in Uganda from the fighting in eastern DR Congo. Fighting in Bujumbura between rival factions of Burundi's last remaining rebel group, the Hutu National Liberation Force, left 26 people dead. **7.** A bomber attempting to assassinate President Bouteflika of Algeria killed 22 people in the town of Batna; the following day, a car bomb in Dellys killed 30 people; al-Qaida's north African wing claimed responsibility for both incidents. Morocco's parliamentary elections resulted in a surprise victory for the conservative Istiqlal party, which won 52 seats, six more than the moderate Islamic PJD party. **11.** The World Health Organisation confirmed an outbreak of the Ebola virus in the Kasai region of DR Congo, where an estimated 166 people are thought to have died. **12.** Ethiopia, which uses the Coptic calendar, celebrated the start of the third millennium. **19.** Burkina Faso, Togo and Ghana each declared a state of disaster following weeks of heavy rain; an estimated 1.5 million people were affected. **30.** Hundreds of rebels attacked a camp of African Union (AU) peacekeeping troops in Darfur, Sudan, killing at least ten peacekeepers.

OCTOBER 2007

4. In South Africa, 3,200 miners were rescued after an electrical fault left them trapped more than a mile underground. **9.** After losing a key stronghold, renegade General Nkunda (*see* 2 September) called for a ceasefire in eastern DR Congo, and announced that he wished to reintegrate his forces into the national army. Girma Wolde Giorgis was re-elected president of Ethiopia. **11.** The Sudan People's Liberation Movement (SPLM), a former southern rebel group, pulled out of the country's national unity government amid complaints that its northern counterparts had failed to honour the terms of the 2005 peace agreement. **14.** Togo's ruling party, the RPT, won the majority of seats in the legislative election; it was the first election for 20 years in which all the opposition parties participated. **22.** Joaquim Chissano, president of Mozambique 1986–2005, won the inaugural Mo Ibrahim prize, a £2.5m bursary awarded to a former African state leader in recognition of good governance. **26.** A peace agreement was signed between the government of Chad and the country's four main rebel groups. **29.** The Chadian government charged 18 people, including Europeans, with attempting to abduct 103 local children; the suspects, associated with a French charity arranging adoptions in Europe, believed that the children were Darfuri orphans. Ali Mohamed Ghedi resigned as prime minister of Somalia after his government's mandate expired; Nur Hassan Hussein was appointed to the post on 22 November.

NOVEMBER 2007

5. A state-backed human rights group in Kenya accused the police of 500 execution-style murders in Nairobi since June; the targets are believed to have been members of the outlawed Mungiki sect. **6.** At least 50 Africans died sailing from Senegal to the Canary Islands; their boat was discovered drifting off the coast of Mauritania. **8.** Renewed fighting in Mogadishu, Somalia, caused around 50 deaths, and the bodies of two Ethiopian soldiers were dragged through the streets; UN secretary-general Ban Ki-moon said the security situation was so poor that a peacekeeping mission was 'neither realistic nor viable'. **12.** Twenty-one Cameroonian soldiers were killed by unknown gunmen in the oil-rich Bakassi peninsula, handed over to Cameroon by Nigeria in 2006. **20.** President Mugabe announced a new law giving the state a controlling stake in Zimbabwe's lucrative mines. **23.** After two days of violent clashes between protesters and police in Dakar, the Senegalese government reversed its decision to ban street vendors from the capital.

DECEMBER 2007

1. Thirty-seven people died in an outbreak of the Ebola virus in western Uganda. **5.** Pre-election violence in the Rift Valley region of Kenya left 16 people dead. **11.** Two car bombs in the capital of Algeria killed 76 people; al-Qaida in the Islamic Maghreb claimed responsibility. **12.** Following talks between the president and vice-president of Sudan, the SPLM announced its return to the power-sharing government (*see* 11 October); one of the measures adopted to further the peace process was the rotation of the seat of government between Khartoum and the southern town of Juba every three months. **12.** At least 17 people were killed by a mortar attack on a market in Mogadishu. **18.** In South Africa, Jacob Zuma defeated Thabo Mbeki to win the presidency of the ruling African National Congress party. **20.** A suspected gas leak caused three explosions in the capital of Sierra Leone and killed 17 people. **26.** Six French charity workers charged with kidnapping Chadian children (*see* 29 October) were found guilty by a court in N'Djaména and sentenced to eight years' hard labour; they were returned to France under the terms of a repatriation treaty two days later. An explosion at a ruptured oil pipeline in southern Nigeria killed over 40 looters. **27.** Presidential and legislative elections were held in Kenya; the opposition Orange Democratic Movement (ODM) made significant gains, winning 99 seats to the ruling Party of National Unity's 43. Despite early indications of a large lead for the ODM candidate, Raila Odinga, in the presidential election, on 30 December President Kibaki was declared the winner, leading to widespread accusations of electoral fraud.

JANUARY 2008

1. Post-election violence in Kenya resulted in over 300 deaths, including 30 people who died in a church in Eldoret that was set on fire by a mob; the violence reflected ethnic divisions, with members of the Kikuyu, President Kibaki's tribe, comprising the majority of victims. **10.** Flooding on the Zambezi river displaced around 60,000 people in Mozambique. **12.** Jackie Selebi, South Africa's chief of police and the head of Interpol, resigned from both positions after he was charged with corruption. **19.** The government of the Central African Republic resigned following widespread strikes; Faustin-Archange Touadera was appointed prime minister by President Bozize. **21.** Musa Hilal, a tribal leader accused of perpetrating Janjaweed atrocities in Darfur, was appointed as a special adviser to the Sudanese government. **23.** The Congolese government and over 20 rebel groups concluded a peace agreement to end conflict in eastern DR Congo; the forces of renegade General Nkunda (*see* 9 October) received an amnesty and re-integration into the Congolese national army. **25.** The South African government announced the introduction of electricity rationing after years of economic growth and the expansion of the power network to black townships left the state provider Eskom struggling to cope with demand. **27.** Post-electoral unrest continued in Kenya's Rift Valley region, where police clashed with members of the Kikuyu, Luo and Kalenjin tribes; 69 people died, raising the death toll since December to 900. **28.** EU foreign ministers approved the deployment of a multinational EU peacekeeping force in Chad and the Central African Republic to improve security and humanitarian relief. **29.** At least 100 people died in Lake Tanganyika after a boat carrying passengers from DR Congo sank. **31.** A post-election mediation meeting between President Kibaki of Kenya, presidential contender Raila Odinga and former UN secretary-general Kofi Annan was postponed following the murder of an opposition MP.

FEBRUARY 2008

2. In Chad, thousands of people fled N'Djaména after rebels entered the capital city and surrounded President Déby's residence before being repulsed by government troops; at least 160 people were killed. **3.** Two earthquakes – in Bukavu, DR Congo, and the Rusizi district of Rwanda – killed over 40 people. **24.** Cyclone Ivan left 44 people dead and 145,000 homeless in Madagascar. **26.** A specially convened tribunal in Nigeria rejected two challenges to the legality of the 2007 presidential election, won by Umaru Yar'Adua amid accusations of vote-rigging and fraud. **28.** Two days after post-election peace talks brokered by Kofi Annan were abandoned, President Kibaki of Kenya and opposition leader Raila Odinga agreed a power-sharing arrangement under which Kibaki retained the presidency, Odinga became the country's first prime minister and a coalition government was appointed that reflected the parliamentary strength of the parties; the new cabinet was sworn in on 17 April. Four days of protests over rising fuel prices in Yaoundé, Cameroon, resulted in the deaths of 20 people following clashes between protesters and the police.

MARCH 2008

3. The USA launched an air strike on the Somali town of Dhoble while in pursuit of al-Qaida associate Hassan Turki; four people died in the attack but Turki's fate was undisclosed. **7.** Zimbabwe banned Western observers from monitoring its forthcoming elections. **11.** President Museveni of Uganda refused a International Criminal Court request to hand over the rebel leader Joseph Kony and two of his commanders, who had been indicted for war crimes; Museveni claimed that victims would prefer Kony to be tried before Ugandan courts, which prefer compensation to punishment. **13.** The Chadian and Sudanese governments signed a peace agreement, their sixth in five years; none of the rebel groups in either country was party to the agreement. **15.** Around 70 people were killed in fighting in DR Congo between members of Bundu Dia Kongo, a political and religious organisation, and police. **25.** In the Comoros, federal troops, supported by AU forces, seized control of the island of Anjouan from Mohamed Bacar, the island's president since 2001; Bacar had refused to stand down when federal and island presidential elections were held in 2006 and had effected the island's secession from the federation in 2007. **29.** Presidential and legislative elections were held in Zimbabwe; the Zanu-PF party lost its parliamentary majority, for the first time since independence, to the opposition Movement for Democratic Change (MDC); delays in announcing the result of the presidential election led to a growing suspicion that the MDC candidate, Morgan Tsvangirai, had defeated President Mugabe. Heavy rains in north-east Tanzania flooded a tanzanite mine, killing 66 workers.

APRIL 2008

1. President Festus Mogae of Botswana retired and was replaced by the vice-president, Seretse Ian Khama. After two days of strikes in Côte d'Ivoire over rising food prices, President Gbagbo cut customs duties and forcibly lowered the price of household goods to pacify protesters. **6.** Post-election harassment of known opposition supporters in Zimbabwe started to escalate into violence by the police, armed forces and government-sponsored militia against those believed to be opposition sympathisers as speculation grew about a run-off presidential election. **14.** In Zimbabwe, the MDC called for a general strike in an attempt to force the authorities to release the results of the March presidential election. **17.** The World Food Programme announced a reduction in food aid deliveries in Darfur because of the frequent hijacking of its vehicles on supply routes. **25.** Zimbabwean police raided the offices of the MDC and the Zimbabwe Election Support Network, which helped to monitor the presidential election, and arrested over 100 people.

MAY 2008

1. A US air strike on the Somali town of Dusamareb killed Aden Hashi Ayro (believed to be al-Qaida's leader in the country) and up to 30 others. **2.** The Zimbabwean electoral commission confirmed that the opposition leader Morgan Tsvangirai had defeated President Mugabe in the March presidential election but with less than 50 per cent of the vote, necessitating a second round of polling. **5.** Tens of thousands of people demonstrated in Mogadishu in protest at rises in food prices. **6.** Over 50 people were killed in Burundi as fighting continued between government forces and Hutu FNL rebels near Bujumbura; the government signed a peace agreement with the FNL on 26 May. **10.** There was heavy fighting in the Sudanese city of Omdurman as Darfuri rebels, with support from neighbouring Chad, attacked government forces. **11.** Morgan Tsvangirai announced that he would stand against President Mugabe in the second round of the Zimbabwean presidential election. **15.** An oil pipeline explosion in the Nigerian city of Lagos killed at least 100 people. **17.** Islamist fighters in Somalia captured the town of Jilib from government forces. **18.** Armed gangs in the suburbs of Johannesburg, South Africa, attacked immigrants, mostly from neighbouring countries, who they accused of taking local jobs and housing; at least 50 people were killed. **24.** Jean-Pierre Bemba, the former vice-president of DR Congo, was arrested in Belgium and charged with war crimes relating to assistance he gave in 2002 to the then-president of the Central African Republic in putting down an attempted coup. **26.** The Ethiopian supreme court sentenced former president Mengistu Haile Mariam to death in absentia; the sentence was a revision of the original sentence of life imprisonment that he received in January 2007 for genocide and crimes against humanity.

JUNE 2008

2. President Mugabe of Zimbabwe made a surprise appearance at a UN summit on global rises in food prices, provoking an angry response from members of the international community. **4.** The Zimbabwean opposition leader Morgan Tsvangirai was detained by police for several hours before being released without charge; his arrest was part of an escalating campaign of violent intimidation by the authorities before the presidential election. **5.** British and US diplomats travelling to meet opposition activists in Zimbabwe were attacked and detained by government-sponsored militia; meanwhile the government indefinitely suspended the activities of all aid workers and NGOs operating in the country, a move described by the UN as 'scandalous'. **6.** Morgan Tsvangirai was banned from holding rallies. **10.** The government of Somalia signed a three-month ceasefire agreement with a major opposition bloc in the hope of ending the country's civil war. **16.** At least 40 illegal immigrants died when their boat capsized on a journey from Libya to Italy. **18.** The Chadian army announced that it had killed 161 rebels during a battle in the eastern town of Am Zoer. **22.** Morgan Tsvangirai withdrew from the Zimbabwean presidential election because of pre-election violence; this had been systematically directed at MDC politicians, activists and supporters, leading to over 120 deaths, 5,000 abductions and the displacement of 200,000 people. **27.** The presidential election in Zimbabwe went ahead even though Robert Mugabe was the only candidate; he polled 85 per cent of the votes in a turnout of 42 per cent, Morgan Tsvangirai (whose name was still on ballot papers because of his late withdrawal) received 9 per cent, and 5 per cent of ballot papers were spoiled; Mr Mugabe was sworn in for a sixth term as president on 29 June.

JULY 2008

2. Seventy-two people died when police opened fire on the supporters of an Islamic preacher in south-eastern Chad. **10.** Talks began in South Africa between Zimbabwe's ruling ZANU-PF party and the two main opposition parties to establish the conditions for negotiations to resolve the country's political crisis. **12.** An attempt by the UN security council to impose sanctions on Zimbabwe was vetoed by Russia and China. **14.** The International Criminal Court called for the arrest of President Bashir of Sudan on ten counts of genocide, crimes against humanity and war crimes relating to the conflict in Darfur. **21.** President Mugabe and Morgan Tsvangirai signed an agreement outlining the framework for talks on forming a power-sharing government; talks began on 24 July. **31.** In an attempt to facilitate business dealings, Zimbabwe's central bank revalued the currency, striking ten zeros off old dollar notes to make ten billion dollars now equal one dollar; it issued new banknotes in the new denominations and reintroduced coins.

THE AMERICAS

AUGUST 2007

1. A motorway bridge collapsed into the Mississippi river in Minnesota, USA, killing at least 13 people. **5.** Nicaragua signed agreements with Iran to provide agricultural produce in exchange for assistance with infrastructure projects. **10.** During a visit to Canada's Arctic region, the Canadian prime minister Stephen Harper reasserted Canada's sovereignty in the region, a response to Russia's territorial claim the week before (*see* Europe, 2 August); Canada had already announced plans to expand naval patrols and build two new military bases in the area. **13.** Karl Rove, the deputy chief of staff and senior adviser to US president George W. Bush, resigned. **15.** Over 500 people were killed in Peru in an earthquake that measured 8.0 on the Richter scale. **20.** President da Silva of Brazil unveiled a $3.3bn (£1.7bn) five-year national security plan to tackle the country's high crime rate. **21.** A declassified CIA report on the 9/11 terrorist attacks criticised the performance of its former chief George Tenet for failing to create a strategic plan to counter al-Qaida. President Chavez proposed changes to the Venezuelan constitution, including removing the limit on presidential terms, extending the term from six years to seven and removing the autonomy of the central bank. **23.** Fighting between inmates at a prison in Sao Paulo, Brazil, resulted in the deaths of 25 prisoners. Hurricane Dean hit the Caribbean and Central America, leaving about 40 people dead. **27.** The US attorney-general Alberto Gonzales resigned after months of criticism and allegations of perjury; he was replaced by a former federal judge, Michael Mukasey. **28.** Hugo Salas Wenzel, a former Chilean military leader, became the first member of General Pinochet's former regime to be convicted of human rights violations; he received a sentence of life imprisonment. **29.** Over 650 people were arrested in Santiago, Chile, following demonstrations against the government's economic policies.

SEPTEMBER 2007

3. In the Jamaican general election, the opposition Jamaica Labour Party won a narrow overall majority, ending the People's National Party's 18 years in office; JLP leader Bruce Golding succeeded Portia Simpson Miller as prime minister on 12 September. Hurricane Felix triggered mudslides and flooding in Honduras and Nicaragua that killed over 100 people. **9.** Presidential and legislative elections were held in Guatemala; the legislative election was won by the National Union for Hope (UNE), while the UNE candidate Alvaro Colom was elected president in a run-off election on 4 November. **10.** In a report to the US Congress, General David Petraeus announced uneven but substantial progress in Iraq and said that 30,000 troops could be withdrawn by summer 2008. **12.** The government of Paraguay declared a state of emergency after fires destroyed 100,000 hectares of land. **21.** President da Silva announced a $270m (£134m) fund to protect indigenous tribes in the Amazon region of Brazil. **30.** A 130-member Constituent National Assembly was elected in Ecuador to draft a new constitution.

OCTOBER 2007

3. President Bush vetoed a bill imposing higher taxes on tobacco to subsidise child health insurance. **7.** A 20-year-old sheriff's deputy killed five people in Wisconsin, USA, before committing suicide. **8.** Seven South American countries announced the creation of a new development bank, to be based in Venezuela, that will reduce the region's dependence on the World Bank and the International Monetary Fund. A service in Santa Clara, Cuba, to mark the 40th anniversary of the death of the revolutionary Che Guevara was attended by over 10,000 people. **12.** The Nobel peace prize was awarded jointly to the former US vice-president Al Gore and the UN climate change panel for raising awareness of global warming. **13.** In Colombia, a makeshift gold mine collapsed, triggering an avalanche of mud and rock that killed 22 workers. **22.** Wildfires in California, USA, forced the evacuation of a million people. **28.** Presidential and legislative elections were held in Argentina; Peronist parties retained their majority in the Congress, and the presidential election was won by Cristina Fernandez de Kirchner, the wife of the outgoing president and the country's first female leader. **29.** Tropical storm Noel caused flooding in the Dominican Republic and Haiti that left 56 dead. **31.** The US supreme court halted the implementation of death sentences while it considered whether execution by lethal injection constituted 'cruel and unusual punishment'; the case was rejected and executions were permitted to resume in April.

NOVEMBER 2007

2. The Venezuelan parliament approved constitutional changes proposed by President Chavez (*see* 21 August). Flooding in the Mexican state of Tabasco made 450,000 people homeless. **5.** In Trinidad and Tobago, the ruling People's National Movement party was returned to power in the legislative election. A fire started by inmates in a prison in northern Argentina killed 31 people. **8.** The US Congress overturned a presidential veto for the first time in the Bush administration, to rescue a water resources bill that included authorisation for flood protection measures on the Gulf coast. The Brazilian state oil company Petrobas discovered an enormous oilfield off the coast of Rio de Janeiro. **27.** President Chavez of Venezuela froze bilateral ties with Colombia after his role as a negotiator with the Colombian FARC rebel group was terminated by the Colombian president. **29.** Hundreds of thousands of Venezuelans demonstrated in Caracas against proposed reforms to the constitution (*see* 2 November); the reforms were rejected in a national referendum on 2 December.

DECEMBER 2007

5. Robert Hawkins, a 19-year-old American, shot dead eight people in a shopping mall in Omaha, Nebraska, before shooting himself. **6.** The CIA and the US Justice Department announced a joint investigation into claims that the agency destroyed tapes showing 'enhanced' interrogation of terror suspects in 2005. **9.** Robert Pickton, a Canadian pig farmer, received a life sentence after being convicted of the murders of six women; he faces a second trial for another 20 murders he is suspected of committing. Bolivia's constituent assembly approved a draft constitution that would increase the political rights of the majority indigenous population, who would also benefit from the proposed redistribution of land and resources from the richer to the poorer provinces. **11.** Ice storms in the mid-western states of the USA killed over 20 people. A former president of Peru, Alberto Fujimori, was sentenced to six years in prison and fined $92,000 (£45,000) for abuse of power; the conviction related to an incident in 2000 in which he illegally removed surveillance equipment monitoring the wife of his former intelligence chief. **16.** Thousands of people in Bolivia's richest provinces protested against President Evo Morales' constitutional reforms and wealth redistribution plans; sustained opposition to the new constitution in the richer eastern provinces led to a political crisis in 2008 as several provinces demanded greater autonomy. **17.** The US state of New Jersey abolished capital punishment.

JANUARY 2008

3. The contests for the Democrat and Republican nominations in the 2008 US presidential election began with the caucus in Iowa, USA; Barack Obama won the Democrat caucus, with Hillary Clinton in third place; Mike Huckabee won the Republican caucus. **8.** Hillary Clinton won the Democrat primary in New Hampshire; John McCain won the Republican contest. **10.** Two women held captive by the FARC rebel group in Colombia for over five years were freed after talks brokered by President Chavez of Venezuela. **15.** Mitt Romney won the Republican primary in Michigan. **19.** The Democratic caucus in Nevada was won by Hillary Clinton; John McCain won the Republican primary in South Carolina. **23.** The Brazilian government announced a significant increase in the rate of Amazon deforestation since 2004. **26.** Barack Obama won the South Carolina Democratic primary with over 50 per cent of the vote, the first candidate from either party to achieve a majority of the vote. **28.** In his final state of the union address, President Bush hailed improving security in Iraq, warned the USA about its dependence on oil and urged Congress to pass a $150bn (£75bn) package of economic reforms to ward off the threat of recession. **29.** John McCain became the favourite for the Republican presidential nomination after defeating Mitt Romney to win the Florida primary; Rudy Giuliani and John Edwards withdrew from the contest after poor results in the polls.

FEBRUARY 2008

2. Heavy rains and flooding in northern Bolivia killed over 45 people. **3.** A million people demonstrated in Bogota, Colombia, against the FARC rebel group. **5.** In the US presidential nomination campaign, 24 states voted on so-called 'Super Tuesday'; a strong showing from Mike Huckabee in several southern states prevented John McCain from securing the Republican nomination, while the Democrat contenders Hillary Clinton and Barack Obama won similar numbers of delegates. Tornadoes in eight southern US states caused over 50 deaths. **7.** Mitt Romney withdrew from the contest for the Republican presidential nomination after disappointing results on Super Tuesday, effectively ceding the nomination to John McCain. **9.** The Democrat contender Barack Obama won the primaries in all five of the states contested; in the Republican contest, John McCain won in Louisiana and Washington and Mike Huckabee in Kansas. **11.** US military prosecutors charged six men held at the Guantanamo Bay base with 169 offences relating to the 9/11 terrorist attacks; the men included the alleged ringleader Khalid Sheikh Mohammed, who, the CIA admitted, had been subjected to torture. **12.** Barack Obama won the primaries in Virginia, Maryland and the District of Columbia, taking the lead in the Democrat nomination contest for the first time; John McCain won the Republican contest in the states. Torrential rain in northern Bolivia caused floods that killed 60 people. **19.** Fidel Castro, president of Cuba since 1959, announced that he would not accept another term after his present term expired in March; his brother Raul was elected as his successor on 24 February. **19.** Barack Obama won the primaries in Wisconsin and Hawaii, extending his lead over Hillary Clinton.

MARCH 2008

1. Colombian troops attacked a camp used by the Colombian rebel group FARC that was located two kilometres inside Ecuador; Raul Reyes, a prominent FARC member, was among 21 people killed. **2.** Following Colombia's military incursion into Ecuador, President Chavez of Venezuela cut diplomatic ties with Colombia and sent 9,000 soldiers to their joint border. **4.** John McCain won four more primaries, securing the Republican presidential nomination; the Democrat contenders continued neck-and-neck as Hillary Clinton won the primaries in Ohio and Texas to close the gap on Barack Obama. Diplomatic relations between Venezuela and Colombia worsened as the Colombian government accused President Chavez of providing the FARC with funding. **7.** Bolivia's National Electoral Court postponed the national referendum on the draft constitution (*see* 9 December) scheduled for May; the court also postponed the provinces' referendums on declarations of greater autonomy, although several provinces went ahead with referendums between March and June. **9.** Diplomatic relations in South America were restored to normal after Colombia apologised to Ecuador for its cross-border incursion. Barack Obama won the Wyoming caucus. President Bush vetoed a Democrat-sponsored bill that proposed to outlaw the use of force (including waterboarding) by the CIA when interrogating terror suspects. **11.** Barack Obama won the Democrat primary in Mississippi. **12.** Eliot Spitzer resigned as governor of New York after he was revealed to have used prostitutes belonging to a ring under criminal investigation. **13.** The Cuban government eased restrictions on the sale of computers, DVD players and other electronic goods, although they can still only be bought using hard currency. Farmers in Argentina staged a nationwide strike against a sharp rise in export taxes on agricultural products.

APRIL 2008

1. Juana Barraza was convicted of the murders of 16 elderly women in Mexico City; she was sentenced to 759 years in prison. **8.** In his latest report to the US Congress, General Petraeus labelled progress in Iraq 'fragile and reversible'. **9.** The capital of Haiti was paralysed by two days of violent protests against rising food prices; UN peacekeepers fired rubber bullets at rioters who attempted to storm the presidential palace. Fears of violent clashes between pro-Chinese and pro-Tibet demonstrators during the Olympic torch relay through San Francisco led to last-minute changes to the relay's route. **13.** The prime minister of Haiti, Jacques Edouard Alexis, was dismissed after losing a parliamentary vote of confidence over the government's response to the food price riots. **20.** Presidential and legislative elections were held in Paraguay; the Colorado Party retained its majority in the Congress, and Fernando Lugo was elected president. **22.** Hillary Clinton won the Democratic primary in Pennsylvania, keeping herself in contention for the Democrat presidential nomination. **27.** In Tijuana, Mexico, at least 13 people were killed during car chases and gun battles between rival drug gangs.

MAY 2008

2. Two weeks after being convicted of running a prostitution ring for the Washington political elite, Deborah Jeane Palfrey, dubbed the 'DC Madam', hanged herself. **4.** In an unofficial referendum in Santa Cruz, Bolivia's richest province, 85 per cent of voters approved a proposal of greater autonomy for the region; President Morales called the vote unconstitutional. **6.** Barack Obama won the Democratic primary in North Carolina, extending his lead over Hillary Clinton, who won the Indiana primary. **11.** Tornadoes in the southern US states of Georgia, Missouri and Oklahoma left 22 people dead. **12.** President Morales of Bolivia approved legislation setting 10 August as the date for recall referendums on the continuation in office of himself, the vice-president and the regional governors. **13.** Hillary Clinton won the Democratic primary in West Virginia and vowed to continue her campaign for the Democratic nomination. **15.** The supreme court in the US state of California recognised the validity of same-sex marriages, in defiance of federal legislation. **20.** Barack Obama won the Democratic primary in Oregon and Hillary Clinton won in Kentucky, taking Obama to the brink of the Democratic nomination. **25.** The founder of Colombia's FARC rebel group, Manuel Marulanda, died aged 78 from a heart attack.

JUNE 2008

2. Barack Obama became the Democratic presidential nominee after victory in the Montana primary gave him the greater share of the delegates. Two more provinces of Bolivia (*see* 4 May) voted for greater autonomy in unofficial referendums. **11.** The Canadian government apologised for the government policy of forcing aboriginal children to attend state-funded residential schools throughout the 20th century in an attempt at enforced assimilation. **12.** The US supreme court ruled that the 270 prisoners held at Guantanamo Bay had a constitutional right to have their cases heard by the US civil courts instead of facing trial by the military commissions created by the Bush administration. **19.** Flooding in the USA's mid-western farm belt left 24 people dead and devastated crops, threatening to drive record food prices even higher.

JULY 2008

2. A Colombian army raid on a FARC camp freed 15 hostages, including a former presidential candidate, Ingrid Betancourt, who had been held captive since 2002. **20.** An estimated one million Colombians demonstrated in Bogotá against the FARC rebel group, calling for the release of its 27 remaining hostages. **21.** The first military trial at Guantanamo Bay began; Osama bin Laden's former driver, Salim Ahmed Hamdan, faced charges of conspiracy and providing material support for terrorism.

ASIA

AUGUST 2007

1. Monsoon rains devastated parts of India, Bangladesh, Pakistan and Nepal; by 13 August, 2,500 people had been killed and 20 million displaced. **7.** Satsuki Eda of the Democratic Party of Japan was elected head of the upper chamber of the Diet; Eda is the first leader in over 50 years from a party other than the Liberal Democrat Party (LDP). **8.** Over 10,000 Tibetan exiles living in India demonstrated in New Delhi against China's human rights abuses in Tibet. **11.** Flooding caused by a tropical storm killed at least 56 people in central Vietnam. **14.** The collapse of a bridge under construction in the town of Fenghuang, China, killed 41 people. Pakistan celebrated 60 years of independence; India marked the same anniversary the following day. **16.** Temperatures in Japan reached 40.9°C, the highest ever recorded; the heat caused at least 13 deaths. North Korea's state media reported 600 deaths caused by widespread flooding. **17.** In China's Shandong province, 181 workers died when a mine was flooded. **18.** A referendum in the Maldives endorsed the continuation of a presidential system of government and supported President Gayoom's proposed reforms. In a legislative election in Kazakhstan the pro-presidential Otan party won all 98 seats; observers said the poll fell short of international standards. **19.** Protesters in Rangoon, Myanmar, demonstrated against steep rises in fuel prices. In Thailand, a draft constitution was approved by referendum; the constitution was enacted by the king on 24 August. **22.** The supreme court of Pakistan released from prison dozens of Islamic militants who had been held without charge for up to three years; the following day the court ruled that the former prime minister Nawaz Sharif could return from exile. After three days of rioting by students in Dhaka, the military-backed government of Bangladesh imposed curfews in the country's largest cities. **25.** Bomb attacks killed 43 people in the Indian city of Hyderabad.

SEPTEMBER 2007

3. Khaleda Zia, the former president of Bangladesh, was arrested and charged with extortion and corruption. **4.** Two suicide bombers in Rawalpindi, Pakistan, killed 25 people. **6.** Protests against price increases in Myanmar (*see* 19 August) escalated as 300 Buddhist monks confronted the police and ten were arrested; the following day monks held government officials hostage for five hours in the town of Pakokku until those arrested were released. **8.** A truck carrying Hindu pilgrims fell into a gorge in north-west India, killing 85 people. **9.** Twenty people died in Hyderabad when a motorway flyover collapsed. **10.** President Musharraf of Pakistan ordered the deportation of Nawaz Sharif within hours of his return, in defiance of a supreme court ruling (*see* 22 August). **12.** Shinzo Abe resigned as prime minister of Japan after less than a year in office, during which his administration suffered from a series of scandals and poor poll ratings; he was replaced by Yasuo Fukuda on 25 September. Joseph Estrada, a former president of the Philippines, was jailed for life for embezzling $87m (£42m) from state funds. **16.** A Taiwanese plane travelling from Bangkok to Phuket crashed in bad weather, killing 90 people. **18.** The four Maoist ministers in Nepal's coalition government resigned after the government failed to agree a timetable for the abolition of the monarchy; this caused planned elections to a constituent assembly to be postponed. **19.** Nuon Chea, Pol Pot's deputy in Cambodia's Khmer Rouge, was charged with war crimes by a UN-backed tribunal. **22.** Forty people died in Karachi, Pakistan, after drinking toxic liquor. **24.** Demonstrations continued in Rangoon, where about 100,000 people protested against Myanmar's military junta, which responded by imposing a 60-day curfew. **26.** The Myanmar junta began a crackdown on demonstrators in which nine people were killed and up to 200 were arrested.

OCTOBER 2007

1. The border between India and Pakistan was opened to freight traffic for the first time since the partitioning of the subcontinent in 1947. **2.** The presidents of North and South Korea met for only the second time in 54 years. **5.** Pakistan passed legislation giving immunity to politicians, public officials and bankers suspected of corruption between 1986 and 1999; this permitted the return of former prime minister Benazir Bhutto to contest parliamentary elections. **6.** President Musharraf of Pakistan won the most votes in an indirect presidential election, but the supreme court said that his inauguration could not take place until it had ruled on his eligibility to stand for election while still head of the army. **7.** Typhoon Lekima killed 55 people in Vietnam. **15.** The 17th Chinese Communist Party Congress opened. **18.** Benazir Bhutto returned to Pakistan from exile; her arrival was marred by a suicide bombing that killed 140 people surrounding her convoy in Karachi. **31.** Monks staged street protests in Myanmar for the first time since the September crackdown; the demonstrations in Pakkoku were ignored by the military junta.

NOVEMBER 2007

3. President Musharraf declared a state of emergency in Pakistan and suspended the constitution; the chief justice and eight other supreme court judges were dismissed for refusing to endorse the move. **13.** In the Philippines, four people were killed by a bomb outside the House of Representatives in Quezon City; among the dead was Wahab Akbar, an MP and former Islamist who was believed to be the target of the attack. **15.** Cyclone Sidr destroyed three villages in southern Bangladesh, killing over 3,500 people. **22.** Pakistan's newly appointed supreme court dismissed the last of the legal challenges to the validity of President Musharraf's re-election. Pakistan was suspended from the Commonwealth because of the imposition of emergency rule. **24.** Two suicide bombers killed at least 30 members of Pakistan's military intelligence service in Rawalpindi. **25.** Nawaz Sharif returned to Pakistan from exile for the second time in three months. **28.** President Musharraf stepped down from his army post, handing over command of the Pakistani army to General Ashfaq Kiyani; Musharraf was sworn in for another term as president the following day. Two suicide bombers killed 18 people in Colombo, Sri Lanka. **29.** A group of Filipino army rebels seized a hotel in Manila and demanded the resignation of President Arroyo; the attempted coup was ended after six hours by state military intervention.

DECEMBER 2007

5. A gas explosion in a coal mine at Linfeng in eastern China killed 105 workers. **13.** Military scientists in India announced plans to install a missile defence system by 2010. **15.** President Musharraf lifted the state of emergency in Pakistan. **17.** In Kyrgyzstan, the president's Ak Zhol party won the majority of seats and the rest were taken by parties sympathetic to the government in a legislative election that was criticised as falling short of international standards. **19.** The presidential election in South Korea was won by Lee Myung-bak of the conservative Grand National Party. **21.** A suicide bomb attack on a mosque in Pakistan's North-West Frontier Province killed over 50 worshippers. **23.** Islam Karimov, the autocratic leader of Uzbekistan, was re-elected for a third term as president. In the first elections to the new lower chamber of Thailand's National Assembly, the majority of seats were won by the People Power Party, formed by supporters of the exiled former prime minister Thaksin Shinawatra. **27.** Benazir Bhutto, the leader of the Pakistan People's Party (PPP), was assassinated at an election rally in Rawalpindi; she was among 20 people killed in a gun and bomb attack; rioting and other civil disturbances in the days after her assassination led to the deaths of 31 people. **31.** Elections were held to the new upper chamber of Bhutan's parliament, the first stage in its transition from an absolute monarchy to a parliamentary democracy.

JANUARY 2008

2. The chief election commissioner in Pakistan announced that the election scheduled for 8 January would be postponed to 18 February as violence following Benazir Bhutto's asssassination had disrupted election preparations. Following an escalation in violence, the government of Sri Lanka formally withdrew from the six-year ceasefire with the Tamil Tiger rebels. **7.** Islamic militants shot dead eight tribal leaders in the South Waziristan region of Pakistan, hours before a discussion on a ceasefire between Pakistan's security forces and al-Qaida and Taliban operatives in the region. **10.** A suicide bomber blew himself up outside the high court in Lahore, Pakistan, killing 24 people. **12.** In Taiwan's legislative election, the opposition Nationalist Party (Kuomintang) won an overall majority. **15.** A bus bombing blamed on Tamil Tiger rebels killed 31 people in south-eastern Sri Lanka. **20.** In central India, a bus carrying Hindu pilgrims fell into a gorge, killing 38 people. **22.** A court in Mumbai sentenced 11 Hindu men to life imprisonment for the gang-rape of Bilkis Bano, a pregnant Muslim, and the murder of 13 of her relatives during anti-Muslim riots in Gujarat six years previously. **23.** The Pakistani army claimed to have killed several hundred militants in South Waziristan following an air and ground attack on the base of a Taliban commander suspected of orchestrating the assassination of Benazir Bhutto. **30.** At least 55 people died in China following the country's heaviest snowfall in 50 years.

FEBRUARY 2008

6. The swearing-in of a six-party coalition government in Thailand restored civilian rule after the 2006 military coup. **11.** The 600-year-old Namdaemun Gate, South Korea's greatest cultural treasure, was largely destroyed in an arson attack; a 69-year-old man admitted starting the fire as a protest against low levels of compensation from land developers. **12.** Steven Spielberg withdrew from his role as artistic adviser to the Beijing Olympics because of the Chinese government's failure to use its influence with the Sudanese government over the conflict in Darfur. **16.** A suicide bomber killed 47 people in Pakistan. **18.** In the Pakistani legislative election, the Pakistan People's Party (PPP), now led by Benazir Bhutto's widower, won 121 of the 335 seats, the Pakistan Muslim League (PML-N) led by Nawaz Sharif won 91 and the pro-Musharraf PML party won 54; 26 people were killed in election-related violence. **26.** The New York Philharmonic Orchestra played a concert in Pyongyang, North Korea; the act of cultural diplomacy introduced the largest number of Americans into the country since the Korean war. **28.** A collision between a ferry and a cargo ship in Bangladesh left at least 39 people dead.

MARCH 2008

1. A bomb killed 38 people attending a funeral in Pakistan. **2.** A suicide bomber killed 40 people in Pakistan's North-West Frontier Province. **3.** The Indian government announced a cash incentive scheme for poor families to discourage female foeticide; the sex ratio in parts of India is as low as 900 girls for every 1,000 boys. **6.** Viktor Bout, an international arms dealer known as the 'Merchant of Death' for his role in supplying weapons in a number of conflicts in Asia and Africa, was arrested in a 'sting' operation in Thailand. **8.** In the Malaysian legislative election, a coalition of opposition parties united under Anwar Ibrahim made unprecedented gains, reducing the majority of the ruling Barisan Nasional party. **9.** In Pakistan, the PPP and the PML-N agreed to form a coalition government. **10.** Hundreds of Tibetan monks demonstrated in Lhasa in the biggest anti-communist protest in 20 years. **11.** Two suicide bombs in Lahore, Pakistan, killed 24 people. **15.** Clashes between Tibetans, local Chinese and riot police in Tibet spread from Lhasa to surrounding districts, leaving dozens dead. **22.** The Taiwan presidential election was won by the Kuomintang candidate Ma Ying-jeou. **24.** In the first elections to the lower chamber of Bhutan's parliament, the Bhutan Harmony Party won 45 of the 47 seats. Yousuf Raza Gilani, a former speaker of the National Assembly nominated by the PPP, was sworn in as prime minister of Pakistan; his five-party coalition government was sworn into office on 31 March.

APRIL 2008

1. The Sri Lankan army killed at least 54 Tamil Tiger rebels during fighting in the rebel-held Mannar district. **6.** A suicide bomber, suspected to be a Tamil Tiger rebel, killed 14 people at an athletics event in Sri Lanka, including a government minister and several leading athletes; the following day renewed fighting between government troops and the rebels led to the deaths of 28 people. **9.** Fifty-four illegal immigrants were discovered suffocated in the back of a lorry in Thailand. South Korea's legislative election was won by the conservative Grand National Party with 153 of the 299 seats. **10.** In Nepal, elections were held to a constituent assembly that replaced the interim legislature and will draft a new constitution; the Communist Party of Nepal-Maoists won 220 of the 575 elected seats. **14.** Clashes between police and striking garment industry workers over rising food prices in Dhaka, Bangladesh, left 50 people injured. **22.** Fighting between Sri Lankan troops and Tamil Tiger rebels in the Jaffna peninsula left over 90 people dead, the majority of them Tamil Tiger rebels. **26.** A bomb exploded on a bus in Colombo, Sri Lanka, killing 24 people.

MAY 2008

2. A series of 24-hour power blackouts provoked rioting by thousands of people in the Indian state of Uttar Pradesh. **3.** Cyclone Nargis devastated much of southern Myanmar, killing an estimated 78,000 people and displacing 150,000; an estimated 2.4 million people were affected, of whom 1.4 million were in severely affected areas. The military junta's internal response to the catastrophe was inadequate, and its unwillingness to allow foreign aid and aid workers to enter the country delayed the relief effort for several weeks, raising fears of further deaths from starvation and disease, and attracted international condemnation. **10.** A referendum on a draft constitution went ahead in Myanmar, except in the areas worst affected by the cyclone, where voting took place two weeks later; a reported 92 per cent of voters approved the constitution. **12.** An earthquake measuring 8.3 on the Richter scale shook Sichuan province in central China, killing an estimated 69,000 people, injuring 400,000 and leaving 20,000 missing and 5 million homeless. Pakistan Muslim League ministers in the Pakistani government resigned because of the parliament's failure to reinstate all the judges dismissed by President Musharraf in November; the party continued to support the government in parliament. **13.** A number of bombs killed 63 people in the Indian city of Jaipur; an obscure Islamist group, Indian Mujahideen, claimed responsibility. **14.** The military junta in Myanmar sealed off the cyclone disaster zone from the outside world and began to expel foreign aid workers; the areas were reopened on 23 May following talks with the UN secretary-general Ban Ki-moon. **20.** Poisonous home-made alcohol killed over 150 people in southern India. **21.** In Pakistan's North-West Frontier Province, the provincial government agreed a peace deal with local Taliban fighters under which Shariah law would be introduced and Islamist prisoners released in exchange for an end to suicide bombings and attacks on government buildings. **23.** Thousands of members of India's Gujjar caste blocked roads and railways to demand the lowering of their social status to give them greater access to education and employment benefits; at least 15 people died in the disturbances. **28.** The Constituent Assembly of Nepal abolished the monarchy and declared the country a republic; Ram Baran Yadav was elected as the country's first president on 21 July.

JUNE 2008

2. A bomb blast outside the Danish embassy in Islamabad, Pakistan, killed six people; the attack was thought to be a reprisal for the republication of an anti-Islam cartoon in Danish newspapers (*see* Europe, 12 February). **6.** A bomb in Colombo, Sri Lanka, killed over 20 people. **8.** Seven people were killed in Tokyo after 25-year-old Tomohiro Kato crashed his truck into a group of pedestrians and embarked on a stabbing spree; he was eventually subdued by police. **9.** Thousands of South Koreans attended a rally in Seoul to protest at the government's decision in April to lift a ban on US beef imports imposed following a 2003 outbreak of BSE; the entire government offered their resignations the following day, but the president accepted only three, on 7 July. **10.** Lawyers in Pakistan began a march across the country in protest at the failure of the president and government to reinstate judges sacked when Pakistan was under emergency rule (*see* 12 May). **11.** Pakistan reacted angrily to a US air strike on the border with Afghanistan which killed 11 of its soldiers. **15.** Flooding caused by ten days of torrential rain in southern China killed 57 people. **17.** Amnesty International announced that it was unable to account for 1,000 Tibetans detained during anti-Chinese demonstrations in March. **29.** The legislative election in Mongolia was won by the ruling Mongolian People's Revolutionary Party (MPRP); when the results were released on 1 July, the opposition accused the MPRP of vote-rigging, although international observers considered the elections free and fair.

JULY 2008

1. The president of Mongolia declared a four-day state of emergency in the capital Ulaanbaatar after violence by opposition supporters reacting to the election results (*see* 29 June) left five people dead and caused widespread damage. **7.** UNESCO accorded world heritage site status to the Preah Vihear temple, which stands on the Cambodian–Thai border on territory claimed by both countries; the listing led to tension between the two countries, which both moved troops to the border. **16.** The Malaysian opposition leader Anwar Ibrahim was arrested over allegations of sodomy that he insisted were politically motivated. **20.** In Beijing measures were introduced to improve air quality for the Olympic Games in August; these included relocation or temporary closures of industrial plants and restrictions on motor access to the city. **23.** The Indian government narrowly survived a parliamentary vote of confidence over a controversial nuclear cooperation agreement with the USA under which India would keep its nuclear weapons and access to nuclear technology in return for separating its military and industrial reactors. **26.** Sixteen bombs exploded in the Indian city of Ahmadabad, killing 49 people; the Indian Mujahideen (*see* 13 May) was believed to be responsible. **29.** Pakistani and Indian forces exchanged gunfire across the demarcation line in Kashmir, following the death of an Indian soldier.

AUSTRALASIA AND THE PACIFIC

AUGUST 2007

6. President Jose Ramos-Horta of East Timor appointed his predecessor, Xanana Gusmao, prime minister. **13.** Following legislative elections in Papua New Guinea in July, Michael Somare, prime minister since 2002, was re-elected to the post by parliament. **28.** Ludwig Scotty was re-elected president of Nauru by the parliament.

SEPTEMBER 2007

5. Indonesia and Russia announced an arms deal under which the Pacific nation will purchase £500m of Russian helicopters, submarines and tanks. **12.** Following party criticism, the Australian prime minister John Howard announced that he would step down midway through his next term if elected in the country's forthcoming general election. An earthquake registering 8.2 in magnitude killed at least 23 people on the Indonesian island of Sumatra. **25.** The Australian government promised A$714m (£308m) of aid to farmers, affected by several years of severe drought.

OCTOBER 2007

2. The Australian government announced a freeze on immigration from Africa.

NOVEMBER 2007

19. A legislative election took place in the Marshall Islands. **21.** At least 170 people were killed by flooding on the north-east coast of Papua New Guinea. **24.** In the Australian general election, the Labor party defeated the Liberal party, which had been in government since 1996; the Labor leader Kevin Rudd became prime minister.

DECEMBER 2007

3. Australia's new government ratified the Kyoto protocol on climate change, reversing the previous government's stance. **13.** The prime minister of the Solomon Islands, Manessah Sogavare, was defeated in a parliamentary vote of confidence; parliament elected Derek Sikua to replace him on 20 December. **15.** Leaders from more than 180 countries meeting in Indonesia agreed the 'Bali roadmap', which initiates two years of negotiations to agree new emissions targets to replace those in the expiring Kyoto protocol. **18.** President Scotty of Nauru lost a parliamentary vote of confidence; parliament elected Marcus Stephen as president on 19 December. **30.** Heavy rain in the centre and east of Java triggered mudslides and flooding that killed over 150 people.

JANUARY 2008
5. The inaugural session of the Marshall Islands' new parliament elected Litokwa Tomeing president of the republic. **7.** A week of heavy rain in eastern Australia resulted in the worst floods in 20 years, with thousands of people cut off by floodwater and damage to infrastructure. **22.** The Australian state of Tasmania announced a compensation scheme for more than 100 Aborigines who were forcibly removed from their parents, a practice that ended in 1970.

FEBRUARY 2008
8. The last asylum seekers held on the island of Nauru under the immigration policy of the former Australian government were transferred to Australia; the Liberal government had created camps on Nauru and Papua New Guinea where would-be immigrants were held while their applications were processed. **11.** President Ramos-Horta of East Timor was shot and severely injured by armed rebels believed to be plotting a coup; the prime minister, Xanana Gusmao, escaped unhurt from a second assassination attempt later the same day. **13.** The Australian prime minister Kevin Rudd issued a formal apology to the country's Aborigines for wrongs perpetrated by past governments. **20.** An earthquake with a magnitude of 7.5 shook the Aceh province of Indonesia; three people were killed.

APRIL 2008
29. Gastao Salshina, the leader of the East Timorese rebels who attempted to assassinate the country's president and prime minister (*see* 11 February), surrendered to police.

JUNE 2008
1. Kevin Rudd announced the withdrawal of Australian troops from Iraq, condemning his predecessor's decision to join the war in Iraq. **22.** Up to 800 people died when a ferry capsized off the Philippine island of Sibuyan during a typhoon.

EUROPE

AUGUST 2007
1. Russian explorers planted the country's flag on the Arctic seabed two and a half miles beneath the North Pole, in support of Russia's claim to the waters off its northern coast; this claim is based on its assertion that an underwater feature known as the Lomonosov Ridge is an extension of the Russian continental shelf. **15.** Six Italian men were shot dead outside a restaurant in the German town of Duisberg; police arrested 32 suspected mafia members in the southern Italian town of San Luca on 30 August. **27.** Forest fires in Greece, believed to have been started deliberately, killed over 60 people and destroyed 300,000 hectares of land. **28.** After months of opposition to his nomination by secularists, especially in the military, Abdullah Gul, the candidate of the ruling AK party, was elected president of Turkey by the legislature.

SEPTEMBER 2007
1. French and Spanish police raided a house in France where they found 350 kg of explosives, and claimed to have foiled a terrorist attack by the Basque separatist group Eta. **5.** Police in Germany arrested three men on suspicion of planning terrorist attacks on US facilities in the country. **12.** Mikhail Fradkov resigned as prime minister of Russia and was replaced by Viktor Zubkov, a political unknown. **14.** The Russian military announced the creation of the 'father of all bombs', reputedly the world's most powerful non-nuclear weapon. **16.** In Greece's legislative election, the ruling New Democracy party was re-elected, but with a smaller majority, despite widespread criticism of its handling of forest fires in August. **29.** Thirteen people were shot dead by Kurdish separatists in south-east Turkey. **30.** In the Ukrainian legislative election, the pro-Russian Party of the Regions remained the largest single party, with 175 seats, but the pro-Western parties of President Yushchenko and Yuliya Tymoshenko won a combined total of 228 seats; on 17 October the two parties announced that they had agreed to form a coalition government. Milan Jelic, the president of the Serb republic within Bosnia and Hercegovina since 2006, died of a heart attack, aged 51.

OCTOBER 2007
6. Left-wing radicals rioted in Bern, Switzerland, during an election rally by the right-wing Swiss People's Party, whose election campaign was condemned as racist by the UN. **7.** Thirteen Turkish soldiers were killed in an attack by members of the separatist Kurdish Workers Party (PKK) in south-eastern Turkey. **9.** The Turkish prime minister said that the army had been authorised to cross the border into Iraq if necessary to counter PKK insurgents; parliamentary approval for cross-border military incursions was given on 17 October. **11.** Turkey withdrew its ambassador to the USA after a congressional committee passed a resolution labelling as genocide the mass killings of Armenians in 1915–17. **21.** Poland's legislative election was won by the opposition Civic Platform party, whose leader, Donald Tusk, replaced Jaroslaw Kaczynski as prime minister. In Switzerland's legislative election, the far-right Swiss People's Party (*see* 6 October) received 29 per cent of the vote, the highest recorded by a single party since 1919. A referendum in Turkey approved a constitutional change making future presidents directly rather than indirectly elected. At least 12 Turkish soldiers and 23 PKK guerrillas died during clashes on the border between Turkey and Iraq. **24.** Alexander Pichushkin was convicted of 48 murders and three attempted murders in Moscow; he was sentenced to life imprisonment. **28.** Twenty Kurdish rebels were killed in raids by the Turkish army. **31.** After a four-month trial, a Spanish court convicted three men of mass murder for their roles in the 2004 Madrid train bombings which killed 191 people; another 18 of the 28 defendants were convicted on other charges, but Rabei Osman, the alleged ringleader of the gang, was acquitted.

NOVEMBER 2007
1. The prime minister of Bosnia and Hercegovina, Nikola Spiric, offered his resignation after disagreements with the UN High Representative; the presidency accepted his resignation on 12 November and consultations began on

his successor. Following the alleged rape and murder of an Italian woman by a Romanian immigrant, the Italian government passed emergency legislation granting local authorities the power to expel EU citizens believed to pose a threat to public security. **5.** A fire in a retirement home near the Russian city of Tula killed 32 people. **7.** An 18-year-old gunman killed eight students and staff at a school in southern Finland; Pekka-Eric Auvinen declared his intentions a few hours beforehand in a video posted on YouTube. President Saakashvili of Georgia declared a 15-day state of emergency after six days of anti-government protests; on 8 November the president announced that a presidential election would be held in January 2008. **11.** The presidential election in Slovenia was won in the second round by Danilo Tuerk, an independent supported by centre-left parties. **14.** The centre-right coalition government in Denmark won a snap general election to secure a third term in office but with a majority of only six seats. **17.** A legislative election in the UN-administered Serbian province of Kosovo was won by the pro-independence Democratic Party of Kosovo. **18.** An underground methane explosion killed 90 miners in the Donetsk region of Ukraine. Around 35,000 people marched through Brussels in protest at the political stalemate that had left Belgium without a government for six months. **25.** In Croatia's legislative election, the ruling Croatian Democratic Union won the most seats, but gains by the Social Democrats obliged the ruling party to form a four-party coalition government, which was sworn in on 12 January 2008. **29.** The exiled Russian billionaire Boris Berezovsky was convicted in absentia by a Moscow court and sentenced to six years in prison for defrauding the national airline Aeroflot; Berezovsky was granted asylum in the UK in 2003.

DECEMBER 2007

2. In the legislative election in Russia, which observers considered neither free nor fair, the United Russia party retained its commanding parliamentary majority and President Putin won a parliamentary seat. **10.** UN-sponsored talks between Serbia and Kosovo over the future status of the province ended without a resolution being reached. **11.** The Ukrainian parliament rejected Yulia Tymoshenko's nomination as prime minister; it approved her appointment in a second vote on 18 December. **12.** Nikola Spiric was nominated as prime minister of Bosnia and Hercegovina after six parliamentary parties supported his reappointment to the post (*see* 1 November); the parliament approved his appointment on 28 December. A former Bosnian Serb general, Dragomir Milosevic, was jailed for 33 years by the international war crimes tribunal at The Hague for his role in the siege of Sarajevo. A general strike in Greece brought Athens to a standstill as 100,000 people protested at government plans to reform the pension system. The right-wing Swiss People's Party (*see* 21 October) withdrew from Switzerland's coalition government after the parliament failed to confirm the appointment to the cabinet of one of its ministers. **13.** In Lisbon, EU leaders signed a new treaty incorporating many of the provisions of the proposed constitution rejected in referendums in the Netherlands and France in 2005. **17.** The United Russia party conference confirmed Dmitry Medvedev, President Putin's preferred successor, as its presidential candidate in the March 2008 election; the following day President Putin said he would become prime minister if Mr Medvedev was elected president. **20.** The borders of the EU's Schengen agreement, allowing passport-free travel, were extended to include nine new countries. **22.** The Belgian parliament approved a new interim coalition government for a three-month term to break the country's political deadlock; Yves Leterme, the leader of the Christian Democrats, took control of a permanent five-party coalition on 20 March.

JANUARY 2008

1. Cyprus and Malta adopted the euro. **5.** Mikhail Saakashvili was re-elected president of Georgia (*see* 7 November), winning outright in the first round of voting. **22.** The French government announced a €1bn (£750m) scheme to tackle social deprivation in the country's *banlieues,* in response to the rioting in 2005 and 2007. **23.** The Greek prime minister Costas Karamanlis began a three-day visit to Turkey, the first by a Greek leader for almost 50 years. **24.** Romano Prodi resigned as prime minister of Italy after his government lost a vote of confidence in the Senate; after the speaker proved unable to form a new government, elections were called and parliament was dissolved. **31.** An explosion at an illegal fireworks factory in Turkey killed at least 20 people.

FEBRUARY 2008

3. President Tadic was re-elected for a second term in the second round of voting in Serbia's presidential election. **9.** The Turkish parliament voted to ease the ban on women wearing Islamic headscarves at the country's universities. **12.** Danish police arrested three men of North African origin suspected of plotting to attack Kurt Westergaard, the creator of a cartoon satirising the Prophet Muhammad that caused riots on its initial publication in 2005; the following day, several Danish newspapers reprinted the cartoon, provoking renewed protests by Muslims worldwide. **15.** President Klaus of the Czech Republic was elected by parliament for a second term of office. **17.** Kosovo unilaterally declared its independence; this was recognised by several countries, including the USA and most EU states, but rejected by Serbia, Russia, China and a number of other countries. **19.** The Armenian prime minister Serzh Sarkisian won the country's presidential election, which observers considered to be generally democratic. **21.** In Belgrade, thousands of Serbs protested at western support for Kosovan independence and set fire to the US embassy. **22.** The EU suspended talks with Serbia following attacks on embassies of its member states in Belgrade. **24.** Demetrius Christofias, a communist, was elected president of Cyprus in the second round of voting.

MARCH 2008

1. The Armenian government declared a 20-day state of emergency after days of violent protests by opposition supporters over alleged vote-rigging in the presidential election (*see* 19 February) left eight people dead. **2.** Dmitry Medvedev won a landslide victory in the Russian presidential election, with over 70 per cent of the vote. **8.** The Serbian prime minister Vojislav Kostunica resigned and requested early elections, after his government collapsed because of differences between the coalition partners over policy towards Kosovo. **9.** In Spain's general election, the governing Socialist Party won an increased number of seats but fell short of an overall majority. **11.** At The Hague, the trial began of Ante Gotovina, a Croatian general charged with nine counts of war crimes and crimes against humanity relating to the expulsion of Serbs from Croatia in 1995. **17.** Germany held its weekly cabinet session in Jerusalem to mark the 60th anniversary of the establishment of Israel. Serbs clashed with UN troops and riot police in the ethnically divided city of Mitrovica in northern Kosovo, in the worst disturbances since Kosovo declared independence. **24.** Serbia proposed to the UN that Kosovo should be partitioned along ethnic lines to allow Belgrade control over areas with a predominantly Serb population. **27.** A US agent exposed Alexander Kramar, a UN official who was instrumental in the Oil for Food programme, as a Russian spy who diverted almost $500m (£250m) to Russian officials and helped Saddam Hussein circumvent UN sanctions on Iraq imposed after the invasion of Kuwait. **28.** The prime minister of Poland, the president of the Czech Republic and the chancellor of Germany announced that they would not attend the Olympic Games in Beijing because of recent events in Tibet (*see* Asia, March).

APRIL 2008

2. Bertie Ahern announced his resignation as prime minister of Ireland with effect from 6 May amid reports of financial irregularities; Brian Cowan was elected unopposed as his successor on 9 April. **3.** Greece vetoed Macedonia's accession to NATO because of its continuing objection to the country's name. The barricades dividing Ledra Street in Nicosia, Cyprus, between the Greek- and Turkish-controlled zones were officially dismantled as relations between the two communities began to improve. The Turkish parliament approved the reform of an article of the Turkish constitution that made 'insulting Turkishness' illegal; the article, which was deemed to prevent freedom of speech and had been a stumbling block to Turkey's EU accession negotiations, had been used to prosecute writers such as the Nobel prize winner Orhan Pamuk and murdered journalist Hrant Dink. **15.** In the Italian general election, the People of Freedom (PdL) party won the majority of seats in both legislative chambers; on 8 May the PdL leader Silvio Berlusconi began a third term as prime minister at the head of a two-party coalition government. **26.** Police in Amstetten, Austria, discovered that 73-year-old Josef Fritzl had imprisoned his daughter for 23 years in a purpose-built cellar in his house and fathered her seven children, three of whom were also held captive. **28.** A Ukrainian helicopter crashed into the Black Sea after striking an offshore gas platform, killing all 20 people on board.

MAY 2008

11. In Serbia's legislative election, the pro-western Democratic Party won the largest number of seats, but not an overall majority. **13.** Barcelona received delivery of 23 million litres of drinking water to cope with its worst drought in 60 years. **21.** In the legislative election in Georgia, the president's United National Movement won a landslide victory. **22.** Thousands of French workers held a one-day strike in protest at President Sarkozy's planned pension reforms. Italy, the world's largest net importer of electricity, announced plans to restart its nuclear energy programme, closed down 20 years ago in the wake of the Chernobyl disaster. **28.** In France, Michel Fourniret, nicknamed 'the ogre of Ardennes', was sentenced to life imprisonment for the rape and murder of seven young women and girls; his wife Monique was given a life sentence for assisting him. **30.** Thousands of fishermen in central and southern Europe protested against the rising price of oil.

JUNE 2008

1. Legislative elections in Macedonia were marred by violence and disruptions which caused results to be cancelled in nearly 200 constituencies, where elections were re-run on 15 June; the elections were won by the ruling VMRO-DPMNE, which in July formed a coalition government with parties representing the Albanian, Turk and Roma ethnic minorities. **2.** Six children were killed in the French Alps when a school bus was hit by a passenger train on a level crossing. **5.** Turkey's constitutional court ruled that the parliament's easing of the ban on women wearing Islamic headscarves at universities (*see* 9 February) violated the constitution. At a summit in Rome, UN members vowed to combat hunger caused by rising food prices, but failed to reach consensus on the use of crops for biofuels. **13.** In a referendum in Ireland, 53.6 per cent of voters rejected ratification of the EU Lisbon treaty. **15.** Kosovo's constitution came into force with the completion of the UN handover of powers. Bosnia and Hercegovina signed a stabilisation and association agreement with the EU, a preliminary step towards membership. **18.** In Moscow, Russian police announced that three men had been charged with the murder of journalist Anna Politovskaya in 2006. **23.** A Macedonian journalist, Vlado Taneski, committed suicide in police custody after being charged with the rape and murder of two women whose deaths he had reported on for his newspaper.

JULY 2008

8. The USA signed an agreement with the Czech Republic to build a radar station south of Prague; it was the first agreement to be concluded as part of the USA's controversial plan to build a missile defence system in eastern Europe. **13.** President Sarkozy of France opened the inaugural meeting of the Union of the Mediterranean, a new international body with 43 members from countries bordering the Mediterranean Sea. **14.** After only four months in power, the Belgian government offered its resignation after failing to push through reforms giving greater autonomy to the regions, but its resignation was rejected on 17 July. **21.** The French parliament narrowly passed constitutional reforms proposed by President Sarkozy; the reforms restricted the president's tenure of office to two five-year terms and expanded parliament's scope for exercising its veto. **22.** After more than a decade on the run, the Serbian war crimes suspect Radovan Karadzic was arrested in Belgrade; he had been living under an assumed name and practising alternative medicine. **23.** The EU froze £400m of aid to Bulgaria because of the country's failure to combat corruption and organised crime. **24.** French MPs passed employment reforms which would end the 35-hour restriction on the working week. **27.** Two bombs exploded in Istanbul, killing at least 17 people; no group claimed responsibility. **30.** Turkey's constitutional court ruled by a narrow margin against a case that sought to have the country's governing party, the AKP, banned and its leaders barred from office for being anti-secular; however, the court did impose financial penalties on the party. **31.** Ukraine's worst flooding in 200 years killed 30 people.

MIDDLE EAST

AUGUST 2007

2. The US secretary of state, Condoleezza Rice, signed an agreement with the Fatah-led Palestinian Authority to give it $80m (£39m) to rebuild its security services. **6.** Israeli and Palestinian officials met in the Palestinian territories for the first time in seven years to discuss the outline of a future Palestinian state. In Iraq, a truck bomb killed 28 people in a Shia district of Tall' Afar. An official report by the US Government Accountability Office stated that the Pentagon had lost track of 190,000 firearms given to Iraqi security forces. **8.** US raids on the Sadr City suburb of Baghdad, a Shia stronghold, killed 32 militants suspected of smuggling arms from Iran. **10.** The UN security council voted unanimously to expand the UN's role in Iraq, raising the possibility that the organisation might act as a moderator in discussions on political reform. **14.** In the deadliest attack since the 2003 coalition invasion, four coordinated bombs exploded in a Yazidi area in northern Iraq, killing at least 500 people. **22.** A helicopter crash in northern Iraq killed 14 US soldiers. **27.** The UN announced that despite the presence of foreign troops, opium production in Afghanistan had grown by 34 per cent in 2007. **29.** The Iraqi Shia cleric Muqtada al-Sadr announced a six-month freeze on military activity by his Mahdi Army following criticism of their conduct during street battles with government troops in Karbala, which killed 50 people, the previous day. US forces in Afghanistan announced the deaths of 100 militants following a major battle in Kandahar province. **29.** Twelve South Koreans taken hostage by Taliban militants in Afghanistan in July were freed; seven others were released the following day.

SEPTEMBER 2007

2. The Lebanese army regained control of the Nahr el-Bared Palestinian refugee camp that had been occupied by Fatah militants since May; over 50 people died in the final days of fighting. **11.** Sixty-nine Israeli soldiers were wounded by a rocket fired by Palestinian militants from inside the Gaza Strip; the attack caused the Israeli government to debate a military assault on the area. **17.** The Iraqi government banned employees of Blackwater, a US private security firm, from the country after some of them were involved in a shoot-out that killed 11 civilians the previous day. **19.** An explosion at a secret weapons facility near the Syrian city of Aleppo killed over 15 workers. **26.** US-led coalition forces in Afghanistan claimed to have killed 165 Taliban fighters following air and artillery strikes in the Helmand and Uruzgan provinces. **29.** Taliban militants claimed responsibility for the suicide bombing of a bus in Kabul, Afghanistan, that killed 30 soldiers.

OCTOBER 2007

2. Israel admitted that it had carried out an air attack on a Syrian military base on 6 September; satellite photographs taken of the site later in the month showed that the base had been dismantled, suggesting the site may have contained a partially completed nuclear facility. **8.** Two car bombs killed 19 people in the Iraqi town of Baiji. **9.** The Palestinian group Hamas announced its desire for reconciliation talks with rival group Fatah and hinted that it might relinquish control of Gaza. **10.** The Palestinian president, Mahmoud Abbas, announced for the first time the amount of territory (6,205 sq. km in the West Bank and Gaza Strip) that he was seeking from Israel to form a Palestinian state. **11.** The US military in Iraq announced that 15 civilians were among 32 people killed by air strikes in the Lake Thartha region. **18.** Thousands of people protested in northern Iraq at the Turkish parliament's approval of cross-border incursions by the Turkish army (*see* Europe, 9 October) in pursuit of militants belonging to the Kurdistan Workers Party (PKK), which has bases in northern Iraq. **25.** The USA imposed its most severe sanctions on Iran since the 1979 revolution and classified the Quds (the elite group of the state military) as a terrorist organisation. **29.** A suicide bomb attack on a police headquarters in the Iraqi town of Baquba left 28 people dead. **30.** The Iraqi government approved a draft law to make foreign private security firms such as Blackwater (*see* 17 September) subject to Iraqi law.

NOVEMBER 2007

6. Sixty-eight people, including 59 children and six MPs, were killed in a suicide bombing in the Afghan town of Pul-i-Khumri during a visit from a parliamentary committee. **12.** At a rally in Gaza to mark the third anniversary of the death of Yasser Arafat, clashes between Hamas's paramilitary police and Fatah supporters left six people dead. **15.** A report by the International Atomic Energy Agency revealed that Iran had installed 3,000 centrifuges for uranium enrichment, enough to produce a nuclear warhead within a year. **18.** A fire in a coal mine killed 28 people in eastern Saudi Arabia. **22.** Over 30 people died in gun battles between soldiers and suspected al-Qaida militants in three locations in Iraq. **23.** President Lahoud of Lebanon stood down on the expiry of his term of office, leaving the country in a political vacuum as the parliament had failed to elect his successor. **25.** Local media reported the deaths of 80 Taliban members in air strikes in eastern Afghanistan. **27.** The first official convoy of Iraqi refugees returned from Syria to Baghdad, reflecting the improving security situation in the Iraqi capital. Israeli and Palestinian leaders met at a peace summit in Annapolis, USA, and made a commitment to create a Palestinian state, but could not agree on its borders, the status of Jerusalem or the future of Jewish settlements on the West Bank. **28.** The Saudi Arabian government announced the arrests of 208 people suspected of plotting terrorist attacks on state infrastructure.

DECEMBER 2007

2. A report by the US National Intelligence Council concluded that Iran's nuclear weapons programme had been inactive since 2003 and its current uranium enrichment programme was civilian in nature. Israel freed 429 Palestinian detainees. **3.** A consensus emerged in Lebanon as all political factions expressed support for the army chief General Michel Suleiman becoming the next president (*see* 23 November); his election required a constitutional amendment, which was delayed for several months because of disputes over the make-up of a power-sharing government. **5.** Car bombs in Baghdad, Mosul, Kirkuk and Baquba killed over 20 people. **7.** Suicide bombers in Iraq's Diyala province killed over 25 people. **10.** After four days of heavy fighting with Taliban militants, NATO forces recaptured the town of Musa Qala in southern Afghanistan; the town was overrun by the Taliban in February, four months after British troops withdrew. **12.** Three car bombs in the southern Iraqi town of Amara killed 40 people. A car bomb in Beirut killed five people, including General Francois Hajj, the army commander expected to take over as army chief from General Suleiman. **16.** British forces handed over control of Basra, the last of the four Iraqi provinces it had controlled since 2003, to the Iraqi authorities. Fifty Turkish warplanes attacked Kurdish PKK rebels in northern Iraq; the Turkish military claimed that hundreds of rebels were killed. **17.** The king of Saudi Arabia pardoned a female gang-rape victim who was sentenced to 200 lashes and a six-month jail term for being alone with an unrelated man, after the widely publicised case attracted international criticism. At a summit in Paris, world leaders pledged $7.4bn (£3.6bn) to support Palestinians because of their economic difficulties, although none of the aid was to Gaza because it was under Hamas control. **18.** Israeli military strikes killed 12 people in Gaza, all of whom were believed to have belonged to an Islamic jihadist group. **25.** More than 30 people were killed by a suicide bomber in northern Iraq. **28.** An illegally extended tenement block collapsed in Alexandria, Egypt, killing 28 people. **29.** At least 16 Afghan policemen were killed by a Taliban raid on their checkpoint in Kandahar province.

JANUARY 2008

2. A suicide bomber killed 30 people attending a funeral in eastern Baghdad. **8.** A joint survey by the World Health Organisation and the Iraqi government estimated the total number of deaths since the coalition invasion in 2003 at 151,000. **12.** The Iraqi parliament passed legislation that reversed the 2003 ban on Ba'ath party members holding public office, making thousands eligible for reinstatement in the civil service, education and armed forces. **14.** Taliban militants attacked a Kabul hotel, killing eight people. **15.** Israel launched an incursion into Gaza, killing 19 Palestinians. **18.** An Israeli air strike on Gaza in retaliation for rocket attacks on southern Israel destroyed the interior ministry building. **19.** Over 70 people were killed in the Iraqi cities of Basra and Nasiriya by members of a messianic cult known as Soldiers of Heaven, who opened fire on pilgrims marking the Ashura festival. **20.** Gaza's only electricity plant closed down after Israel cut off fuel supplies. **21.** After intense diplomatic pressure, Israel agreed to a one-off delivery of fuel and emergency provisions to Gaza. **23.** After militants blew holes in the wall along Gaza's border with Egypt, thousands of Palestinians crossed into Egypt to obtain food and other supplies. In Mosul, northern Iraq, militants exploded a huge bomb after their building was surrounded by security forces who suspected it was being used as a weapons cache; 36 people were killed in the blast. **28.** Hamas militants and Egyptian security forces began to close the Gaza border. **30.** The report of an Israeli inquiry into the 2006 war against Lebanon found serious failures and shortcomings in the country's military and political leadership, but criticism of the government and especially the prime minister Ehud Olmert was less severe than expected.

FEBRUARY 2008

1. Two female suicide bombers with Down's syndrome killed 99 people in Baghdad. **4.** Two people died in the first suicide bombing in Israel for over a year, while a second bomber was shot dead after his explosives failed to detonate; Hamas claimed responsibility for the attacks. **7.** Israeli military raids in Gaza killed eight members of Hamas; the electricity supply was also cut off as part of a new economic campaign against the group. **12.** A senior Hezbollah commander, Imad Mughnieh, was killed by a car bomb in Damascus, Syria. **17.** Over 80 people were killed by a suicide bomber in Kandahar, the deadliest attack in Afghanistan since 2001. **18.** A suicide bomber in Kandahar killed 37 people in an attack on a Canadian military convoy. **22.** Thousands of Turkish troops moved into northern Iraq to pursue Kurdish PKK rebels; 170 people were killed in the first three days of fighting. **24.** A suicide bomber killed over 50 people in Iskandariya, Iraq, after targeting a group of Shia pilgrims. **28.** Attacks by Israel and Hamas across the Gaza border killed over 20 people. **29.** Turkey announced the withdrawal of its troops from northern Iraq, prompting the PKK to claim a victory.

MARCH 2008

1. Israel launched raids on Gaza, targeting those believed to be responsible for firing rockets at Israeli towns; at least 109 people died in the raids. **2.** The Palestinian president Mahmoud Abbas suspended peace negotiations with Israel because of the increasing violence in Gaza. President Ahmedinejad of Iran began a visit to Iraq, the first by an Iranian president. **4.** Hundreds of members of Egypt's Muslim Brotherhood, the country's main opposition party, were detained by state authorities to prevent them from registering as political candidates in the local elections in April. **6.** Eight people were killed in Jerusalem by a Palestinian gunman; it was the deadliest attack in the city in four years. Two bomb blasts in Baghdad killed 54 people. **12.** Ismail Haniyeh, the leader of Hamas in Gaza, called for an immediate truce with Israel. **14.** In northern Syria, a mechanical failure caused a school bus to crash into a house, killing 24 people. In Iran's legislative elections, conservative candidates won the majority of seats; many reformist candidates were refused permission to stand by the state body that supervises elections. **17.** A female suicide bomber killed 39 people near a Shia mosque in Karbala, Iraq. The Kuwaiti government resigned over the alleged lack of cooperation of the opposition-dominated national assembly; the emir dissolved the assembly and called elections for May. **25.** Fighting broke out in Basra, Iraq, between government forces and Moqtada al-Sadr's Mahdi Army. **27.** After 210 deaths in the violence in Basra, the Iraqi prime minister, Nouri al-Maliki, offered militias a ten-day amnesty to hand in their weapons. **30.** Moqtada al-Sadr withdrew his forces from Basra and, in response, the government lifted a curfew imposed during the violence.

APRIL 2008

6. Coalition forces in Iraq raided the Baghdad stronghold of the Mahdi Army; at least 73 people died in the clashes. **8.** Seventeen people, mostly civilians, were killed in a Taleban attack in the Afghan province of Zabul. President Ahmedinejad announced that Iran had started to install 6,000 uranium enrichment centrifuges, in defiance of UN security council sanctions. **13.** The Iraqi government sacked 1,300 soldiers and policemen following widespread desertions from government forces during the previous month's fighting in Basra. **15.** More than 70 people were killed in three car bombings in Iraq. The former US president Jimmy Carter held informal talks with Hamas in the West Bank; he was accused by President Bush of legitimising the organisation. **17.** A suicide bomber in Diyala, northern Iraq, killed 50 people attending the funeral of two Sunni militia members. **24.** The UN was forced to halt food aid deliveries to 800,000 Palestinians owing to a severe fuel shortage caused by Israeli sanctions. **25.** Israel rejected an offer of a six-month ceasefire from Hamas, claiming it was a smokescreen to allow to the organisation to rearm. **27.** President Karzai of Afghanistan narrowly escaped assassination when Taliban gunmen attacked an independence day parade; three people were killed. **28.** A suicide bomb in eastern Afghanistan killed 15 people.

MAY 2008

2. A bomb exploded outside a mosque in Yemen, killing 18 people; Shia rebels were believed to be responsible. **5.**

The Lebanese government declared Hezbollah's telecommunications network illegal and moved to close it down the following day; on 7 May a strike over pay developed into protests against the closure, and then degenerated into fighting between pro-government and pro-opposition supporters; by 9 May Hezbollah fighters had captured most of western Beirut and closed down pro-government media offices. **10.** Hezbollah forces withdrew from Beirut, handing over control to the army. **11.** Lebanese troops deployed in Tripoli and areas east of Beirut to end sectarian violence. **12.** Moqtada al-Sadr ordered his supporters to observe an indefinite ceasefire. **15.** Two days of talks brokered by the Arab League in Beirut achieved an agreement to end the fighting in Lebanon that had left at least 65 dead. **16.** The leaders of Lebanon's political factions began negotiations in Doha, Qatar, to end the country's political deadlock. **17.** In the Kuwaiti legislative election, Islamicists again won the majority of seats. **21.** Lebanese leaders in Doha reached an agreement that provided for a government of national unity, gave the opposition the power of the veto in cabinet and banned the use of weapons in internal conflicts. The opposition sit-in outside the government headquarters in central Beirut since 2006 was ended. **25.** General Michel Suleiman, commander of the army, was elected president of Lebanon, ending a six-month political vacuum. An explosion and fire at a chemical plant near Arak, Iran, killed at least 30 people.

JUNE 2008

12. At a conference in Paris, world leaders pledged over $20bn (£10.3bn) in aid to Afghanistan to shore up its fragile government. **16.** Taliban militants stormed a prison in Kandahar and freed 400 Taliban prisoners. **17.** Israel and Hamas signed an Egyptian-brokered six-month ceasefire; Hamas agreed to stop all attacks from Gaza by its militants in return for an end to Israel's military strikes and economic blockade. A bomb in northern Baghdad killed at least 63 people; the USA blamed a Shia militant group it believes to be armed by Iran. **19.** Coalition troops in Iraq recaptured the south-eastern city of Al Amarah, which had been occupied by the Mahdi Army for two years; there were no casualties. **26.** Thirty-eight people were killed by a bomb in Iraq's Anbar province. **30.** Iraq opened its main oilfields to exploitation by international companies.

JULY 2008

1. The UAE announced an agreement to cultivate 30,000 hectares of land in Sudan to protect itself from food shortages. **2.** A Palestinian construction worker went on the rampage in a bulldozer in Jerusalem, killing three people. **6.** A US air strike killed 47 civilians attending a wedding in eastern Afghanistan. **7.** A suicide bomber exploded a car bomb at the Indian embassy in Kabul, killing 41 people. **9.** Iran conducted long-range missile tests, including a missile capable of reaching Israel. **13.** Nine US soldiers were killed in Afghanistan in an attack on their base by Taliban militants. **14.** Two suicide bombings at an army training centre in Iraq killed at least 35 people. **16.** Israel released five Lebanese prisoners in exchange for the bodies of two Israeli soldiers captured by Hezbollah in 2006. In northern Egypt, a lorry that failed to stop at a level crossing pushed waiting vehicles in front of a train; the crash killed at least 37 people. **19.** The UN security council gave Iran two weeks to agree to freeze its uranium enrichment programme or face international sanctions. **27.** Iran hanged 29 convicted people in a mass execution. **28.** In Iraq, 57 people were killed in bomb attacks in Baghdad and Kirkuk. **30.** Ehud Olmert, the prime minister of Israel, whose tenure had been dogged by allegations of corruption, announced his intention to stand down in September 2008.

OBITUARIES

Allen, Marit, fashion editor and film costume designer, aged 66 – *d.* 26 November 2007, *b.* 17 September 1941
Allen of Abbeydale, Lord, GCB, civil servant, aged 95 – *d.* 27 November 2007, *b.* 8 July 1912
Antonioni, Michelangelo, Italian film director, aged 94 – *d.* 30 July 2007, *b.* 29 September 1912
Asquith, Brian, silversmith and designer, aged 78 – *d.* 16 March 2008, *b.* 23 February 1930
Astor, Brooke, American philanthropist, aged 105 – *d.* 13 August 2007, *b.* 31 March 1902
Badham, Molly, MBE, co-founder of Twycross Zoo, aged 93 – *d.* 19 October 2007, *b.* 18 May 1914
Barnes, Carol, television journalist and newsreader, aged 63 – *d.* 8 March 2008, *b.* 13 September 1944
Barraclough, Air Chief Marshal Sir John, KCB, CBE, DFC, AFC, aged 90 – *d.* 10 May 2008 *b.* 2 May 1918
Bartlett, Elizabeth, poet, aged 84 – *d.* 18 June 2008, *b.* 24 April 1924
Beadle, Jeremy, TV and radio presenter, aged 59 – *d.* 30 January 2008, *b.* 12 April 1948
Beaumont of Whitley, Lord, politician and Anglican priest, aged 79 – *d.* 8 April 2008, *b.* 22 November 1928
Bethell (4th), Lord, Conservative MEP (1999–2003), aged 69 – *d.* 8 September 2007, *b.* 19 July 1938
Bevan, Natalie, artist, aged 98 – *d.* 15 August 2007, *b.* 22 May 1909
Bhan Bhagta Gurung, Havildar, VC, awarded the Victoria Cross for actions in Burma (1945) while a member of the 2nd Gurkha Rifles, aged 86 – *d.* 1 March 2008, *b.* September 1921
Bhutto, Benazir, prime minister of Pakistan (1988–90 and 1993–6), aged 54 – *d.* 27 December 2007, *b.* 21 June 1953
Bide, Sir Austin, chair of Glaxo Holdings (1973–85), aged 92 – *d.* 11 May 2008, *b.* 11 September 1915
Biffen, Lord, PC, Conservative cabinet minister and leader of the House of Commons (1982–7), aged 76 – *d.* 14 August 2007, *b.* 3 November 1930
Blease, Lord, trade unionist, aged 93 – *d.* 16 May 2008, *b.* 28 May 1914
Blond, Anthony, publisher and writer, aged 79 – *d.* 27 February 2008, *b.* 20 March 1928
Bradshaw, Sir Kenneth, KCB, clerk of the House of Commons (1983–7), aged 85 – *d.* 31 October 2007, *b.* 1 September 1922
Bramall, Margaret, OBE, social worker and director of the National Council for One-Parent Families (1962–79), aged 90 – *d.* 11 August 2007, *b.* 1 October 1916
Brandram, HRH Lady Katherine (Princess Katherine of Greece and Denmark), last surviving great-granddaughter of Queen Victoria, aged 94 – *d.* 2 October 2007 *b.* 4 May 1913
Bridge of Harwich, Lord, PC, Lord of Appeal in Ordinary (1980–92), aged 90 – *d.* 20 November 2007, *b.* 26 February 1917
Brown, Ron, Labour MP for Edinburgh Leith (1979–92), aged 67 – *d.* 3 August 2007, *b.* 29 June 1940
Buccleuch (9th) and Queensberry (11th), Duke of, KT, VRD, MP for Edinburgh North (1960–73), aged 83 – *d.* 4 September 2007, *b.* 28 September 1923
Burlison, Lord, footballer and trade unionist, aged 71 – *d.* 20 May 2008, *b.* 23 May 1936
Butler, Rt. Hon. Sir Adam, Conservative MP for Bosworth (1970–87), aged 76 – *d.* 9 January 2008, *b.* 11 October 1931
Campbell, Sir Alan, GCMG, diplomat, ambassador to Ethiopia (1969–72) and Italy (1976–9), aged 88 – *d.* 7 October 2007, *b.* 1 July 1919
Chadwick, Rt. Revd Graham, British-born Bishop of Kimberley and Kuruman, South Africa (1976–82, when he was expelled by the authorities for anti-apartheid activities), aged 84 – *d.* 28 October 2007, *b.* 3 January 1923
Clare, Prof. Anthony, psychiatrist and broadcaster, aged 64 – *d.* 28 October 2007, *b.* 24 December 1942
Clarke, Sir Arthur C., CBE, science fiction writer, aged 90 – *d.* 19 March 2008, *b.* 16 December 1917
Colledge, Cecilia, ice skating champion, aged 87 – *d.* 12 April 2008, *b.* 28 November 1920
Compton, Rt. Hon. Sir John, KCMG, prime minister of St Lucia (1979, 1982–96 and 2006-7), aged 82 – *d.* 7 September 2007, *b.* 29 April 1925
Cook, Beryl, OBE, artist, aged 81 – *d.* 28 May 2008, *b.* 10 September 1926
Coren, Alan, writer and broadcaster, aged 69 – *d.* 18 October 2007, *b.* 27 June 1938
Cosgrove, Prof. Denis, cultural geographer, aged 59 – *d.* 21 March 2008, *b.* 3 May 1948
Cotton, Sir William, broadcasting executive, aged 80 – *d.* 11 August 2008, *b.* 23 April 1928
Court, Hazel, actress known for her roles in horror films of the fifties and sixties, aged 82 – *d.* 15 April 2008, *b.* 10 February 1926
Cox, Sir Geoffrey, CBE, editor and chief executive of ITN (1956–68), aged 97 – *d.* 2 April 2008, *b.* 7 April 1910
Crocket, Rt. Revd Anthony, 80th Bishop of Bangor (2004–8), aged 62 – *d.* 30 June 2008, *b.* 23 August 1945
Croll, Prof. Elisabeth, CMG, sinologist, vice-principal of SOAS and elected chair of the UN council in Tokyo (2002–4), aged 63 – *d.* 3 October 2007, *b.* 21 September 1944
Darcy De Knayth, Baroness, one of the 92 hereditary peers elected to remain in the House of Lords in 1999, campaigner for disabled rights, aged 69 – *d.* 24 February 2008, *b.* 19 July 1938
DeBakey, Michael, American cardiovascular surgeon, aged 99 – *d.* 11 July 2008, *b.* 7 September 1908
Devi, Kinkri, environmental campaigner against illegal quarrying in her home region of Himachal Pradesh in Northern India, aged 82 – *d.* 30 December 2007, *b.* 1925
Diddley, Bo, rock'n'roll singer, songwriter and guitarist, aged 79 – *d.* 2 June 2008, *b.* 30 December 1928
Drabble, Phil, OBE, TV presenter of *One Man and His Dog* (1976–93), aged 93 – *d.* 29 July 2007, *b.* 14 May 1914
Drnovsek, Janez, prime minister of Slovenia (1992–

2002), president of Slovenia (2002–7), aged 57 – *d.* 23 February 2008, *b.* 17 May 1950

Dunwoody, Gwyneth, Labour MP for Exeter (1966–70), Crewe (1974–83) and Crewe and Nantwich (1983–2008); at the time of her death the longest serving female member of the House of Commons, aged 77 – *d.* 17 April 2008, *b.* 12 December 1930

Elwell, Charles, OBE, MI5 officer, aged 88 – *d.* 11 January 2008, *b.* 16 May 1919

Fairhurst, Angus, artist, member of the Young British Artists group, aged 41 – *found dead* 29 March 2008, *b.* 4 October 1966

Fields, Terry, MP for Liverpool Broadgreen (Labour 1983–91, Independent 1991–2), aged 71 – *d.* 28 June 2008, *b.* 8 March 1937

Fischer, Bobby, American world chess grandmaster (1972), aged 64 – *d.* 17 January 2008, *b.* 9 March 1943

Fossett, Steve, American businessman and adventurer, aged 63 – *declared dead* 15 February 2008, *b.* 22 April 1944

Fraser, George MacDonald, OBE, screenwriter and author of the *Flashman* novels, aged 82 – *d.* 2 January 2008, *b.* 2 April 1925

Garden, Air Marshal Lord, KCB, aged 63 – *d.* 9 August 2007, *b.* 23 April 1944

Gilmour of Craigmillar, Lord, PC, editor of *The Spectator* (1954–9), Conservative MP for Norfolk Central (1962–74) and Chesham and Amersham (1974–92), secretary of state for defence (1974), aged 81 – *d.* 21 September 2007, *b.* 8 July 1926

Goldberg, Prof. Sir Abraham, MD, DSC, FRCP, regius professor of the practice of medicine, University of Glasgow (1978–89), aged 83 – *d.* 1 September 2007, *b.* 7 December 1923

Goldman, Sir Samuel, KCB, second permanent secretary to the Treasury (1968–72), aged 95 – *d.* 28 July 2007, *b.* 10 March 1912

Grima, Andrew, jewellery designer, aged 86 – *d.* 26 December 2007, *b.* 31 May 1921

Guines, Tata, Cuban percussionist, aged 77 – *d.* 4 February 2008, *b.* 30 June 1930

Hacker, Rose, political activist, social worker, counsellor, author and journalist, aged 101 – *d.* 4 February 2008, *b.* 3 March 1906

Hardwick, Elizabeth, American writer, literary critic and co-founder of *The New York Review of Books*, aged 91 – *d.* 2 December 2007, *b.* 27 July 1916

Harris, John, TD, architect who designed the Dubai World Trade Centre (completed in 1979), aged 88 – *d.* 15 February 2008, *b.* 5 June 1919

Harvey, John, CBE, Conservative MP for Walthamstow East (1955–66), aged 87 – *d.* 13 January 2008, *b.* 24 April 1920

Harvey-Jones, Sir John, business executive, chair of ICI (1982–7), aged 83 – *d.* 9 January 2008, *b.* 16 April 1924

Hassett, Gen. Sir Francis, KBE, CB, DSO, LVO, Chief of Defence Force Staff Australia (1975–7), aged 90 – *d.* 11 June 2008, *b.* 11 April 1918

Hawley, Sir Donald, KCMG, MBE, high commissioner in Malaysia (1977–81), aged 86 – *d.* 31 January 2008, *b.* 22 May 1921

Hay, Bruce, Scottish rugby player and coach, aged 57 – *d.* 1 October 2007, *b.* 23 May 1950

Hazlehurst, Ronnie, composer of TV theme tunes, including *Last of the Summer Wine* and *Are You Being Served?*, aged 79 – *d.* 1 October 2007, *b.* 13 March 1928

Healey, Jeff, Canadian guitarist, aged 41 – *d.* 2 March 2008, *b.* 25 March 1966

Heston, Charlton, American actor, aged 83 – *d.* 5 April 2008, *b.* 4 October 1924

Hezlet, Vice-Admiral Sir Arthur, KBE, CB, DSO and Bar, submariner, aged 93 – *d.* 7 November 2007, *b.* 7 April 1914

Hill, Sir John, PHD, FRS, FRENG, nuclear physicist, chair of the UKAEA (1967–81), aged 86 – *d.* 14 January 2008, *b.* 21 February 1921

Hillary, Sir Edmund, KG, KBE, mountaineer and author, aged 88 – *d.* 11 January 2008, *b.* 20 July 1919

Hobbs, Peter, business partner of William Russell, who in 1956 invented the automatic kettle, aged 91 – *d.* 11 April 2008, *b.* 3 May 1916

Hofmann, Albert, Swiss chemist, aged 102 – *d.* 29 April 2008, *b.* 11 January 1906

Holme of Cheltenham, Lord, CBE, PC, Liberal politician and businessman, aged 71 – *d.* 4 May 2008, *b.* 27 May 1936

Howell, Sir Ralph, Conservative MP for North Norfolk (1970–97), aged 84 – *d.* 14 February 2008, *b.* 25 May 1923

Hurwicz, Leonid, winner of the Nobel prize for economic sciences (2007) and the US national medal of science (1990), aged 90 – *d.* 24 June 2008, *b.* 21 August 1917

Illy, Ernesto, Italian coffee merchant, aged 82 – *d.* 3 February 2008, *b.* 18 July 1925

Johnston, Ollie, one of the nine original Disney animators, aged 95 – *d.* 14 April 2008, *b.* 31 October 1912

Jones, Rt. Revd Alwyn Rice, Archbishop of Wales (1991–9), aged 73 – *d.* 12 August 2007, *b.* 25 March 1934

Kerr, Deborah, CBE, screen and stage actor, aged 86 – *d.* 16 October 2007, *b.* 30 September 1921

Knerr, Richard, co-founder of the Wham-O toy company that produced the hula hoop and the frisbee, aged 82 – *d.* 14 January 2008, *b.* 30 June 1925

Knievel, Robert Craig 'Evel', American motorcycle stuntman, aged 69 – *d.* 30 November 2007, *b.* 17 October 1938

Kornberg, Prof. Arthur, biochemist and joint winner of the Nobel prize in physiology or medicine (1959), aged 89 – *d.* 26 October 2007, *b.* 3 March 1918

Lambert, Verity, OBE, television drama producer, aged 71 – *d.* 22 November 2007, *b.* 27 November 1935

Langley, Maj.-Gen. Sir Desmond, KCVO, MBE, governor and commander-in-chief, Bermuda (1988–92), aged 77 – *d.* 14 February 2008, *b.* 16 May 1930

Laurance, Patrick, co-founder of the Family Holiday Association charity, aged 88 – *d.* 11 January 2008, *b.* 24 December 1919

Laurus, Metropolitan, head of the Russian Orthodox Church outside Russia who re-united the church with the Moscow patriarchate in 2007, aged 80 – *d.* 16 March 2008, *b.* 1 January 1928

Leblanc, Raymond, comic-strip publisher who established Éditions du Lombard, publisher of *Tintin*, aged 92 – *d.* 21 March 2008, *b.* 22 May 1915

Lederberg, Prof. Joshua, American geneticist and microbiologist who was a joint winner of the Nobel prize for physiology or medicine (1958), aged 82 – *d.* 2 February 2008, *b.* 23 May 1925

Ledger, Heath, Australian-born actor, aged 28 – *d.* 22 January 2008, *b.* 4 April 1979

Leigh, Dorian, model, aged 91 – *d.* 7 July 2008, *b.* 23 April 1917
Lorenz, Prof. Edward, American meteorologist and mathematician who coined the term 'butterfly effect' in a 1972 paper on chaos theory, aged 90 – *d.* 16 April 2008, *b.* 23 May 1917
Loveridge, Sir John, Conservative MP for Hornchurch (1970–4) and Upminster (1974–83), aged 82 – *d.* 13 November 2007, *b.* 25 September 1925
Lowry, Sunny, swimmer who swam the Channel in 1933, aged 97 – *d.* 21 February 2008, *b.* 2 January 1911
Lyttelton, Humphrey, jazz trumpeter and bandleader, broadcaster and writer, aged 86 – *d.* 25 April 2008, *b.* 23 May 1921
MacArthur, Ian, OBE, Conservative MP for Perth and East Perthshire (1959–74), aged 82 – *d.* 30 November 2007, *b.* 17 May 1925
MacCready, Paul, American aeronautical engineer who invented the first human-powered and the first solar-powered aircraft, aged 81 – *d.* 28 August 2007, *b.* 29 September 1925
McGeoch, Vice-Adm. Sir Ian, KCB, DSO, DSC, wartime submarine commander and Flag Officer Submarines (1966–7), aged 93 – *d.* 12 August 2007, *b.* 26 March 1914
McRae, Colin, rally driver, aged 39 – *d.* 15 September 2007, *b.* 5 August 1968
Mabon, Rt. Hon. Dr Dickson Mabon, MP (Labour and Co-op 1955–81, SDP 1981–3) for Greenock (1955–74), Greenock and Port Glasgow (1974–83); minister of state, Scottish Office (1967–70) and Department of Energy (1976–9), aged 83 – *d.* 10 April 2008, *b.* 1 November 1925
Mailer, Norman, American writer, aged 84 – *d.* 10 November 2007, *b.* 31 January 1923
Marceau, Marcel, French mime artist, aged 84 – *d.* 22 September 2007, *b.* 22 March 1923
Mason, Sir Frederick, KCVO, CMG, ambassador to Chile (1966–70) and the UN (1971–3), aged 94 – *d.* 18 January 2008, *b.* 15 May 1913
Mason, Sir John, KCMG, British high commissioner in Australia (1980–4), aged 80 – *d.* 16 March 2008, *b.* 13 May 1927
Michie of Gallanach, Liberal Democrat MP for Argyll and Bute (1987–2001), aged 74 – *d.* 6 May 2008, *b.* 4 February 1934
Mills, Richard, press photographer, aged 41 – *found dead* 14 July 2008, *b.* 25 August 1966
Minghella, Anthony, CBE, scriptwriter and film director, chair of the British Film Institute (2003–8), aged 54 – *d.* 18 March 2008, *b.* 6 January 1954
Mitty, Joe, Oxfam's first paid employee and head of retail who was instrumental in setting-up the first Oxfam shop (1949–82), aged 88 – *d.* 30 September 2007, *b.* 7 May 1919
Moberg, Gunnie, Swedish-born photographer of the Orkney Islands, aged 66 – *d.* 31 October 2007, *b.* 8 May 1941
Moore, Maj.-Gen. Sir Jeremy, KCB, OBE, MC and Bar, Royal Marines Falklands campaign Land Force Commander (1982) and Major-General Commando Forces RM (1979–82), aged 79 – *d.* 15 September 2007, *b.* 5 July 1928
Musson, Gen. Sir Geoffrey, GCB, CBE, DSO, Adjutant-General of the Army (1967–70), aged 97 – *d.* 10 January 2008, *b.* 9 June 1910
Nabb, Magdalen, author, aged 60 – *d.* 18 August 2007, *b.* 16 January 1947
Newton, Peter, entrepreneur and winemaker, aged 81 – *d.* 4 February 2008, *b.* 27 August 1926
Noakes, Rt. Revd George, Archbishop of Wales (1987–91), aged 83 – *d.* 14 July 2008, *b.* 13 September 1924
O'Donnell, Phil, footballer, aged 35 – *d.* 29 December 2007, *b.* 25 March 1972
Oerter, Alfred, American four-time Olympic discus gold medallist, aged 71 – *d.* 1 October 2007, *b.* 19 September 1936
Oliver of Aylmerton, Lord, Lord of Appeal in Ordinary (1986–92), PC, aged 86 – *d.* 17 October 2007, *b.* 7 March 1921
Orr, Sir David, MC and Bar, chair of Unilever (1974–82), aged 85, *d.* 2 February 2008, *b.* 10 May 1922
Pavarotti, Luciano, Italian opera singer, aged 71 – *d.* 6 September 2007, *b.* 12 October 1935
Piasecki, Frank, American aeronautical engineer who designed the twin-rotor helicopter, aged 88 – *d.* 11 February 2008, *b.* 24 October 1919
Pirro, Ugo, Italian Oscar-winning screenwriter and author, aged 87 – *d.* 18 January 2008, *b.* 24 April 1920
Pollack, Sydney, film director, producer and actor, aged 73 – *d.* 26 May 2008, *b.* 1 July 1934
Pym, Lord, MC, PC, Conservative MP for Cambridgeshire (1961–83) and Cambridgeshire South East (1983–7), secretary of state for defence (1979–81) and foreign and commonwealth affairs (1982–3), aged 86 – *d.* 7 March 2008, *b.* 13 February 1922
Quinn, James, director of the British Film Institute (1955–64), aged 88 – *d.* 11 February 2008, *b.* 23 August 1919
Rathbone, Julian, writer, aged 73 – *d.* 28 February 2008, *b.* 10 February 1935
Rauschenberg, Robert, American pop artist, aged 82 – *d.* 12 May 2008, *b.* 22 October 1925
Reid, Sir Norman, director of the Tate Gallery (1964–79), aged 91 – *d.* 17 December 2007, *b.* 27 December 1915
Robbe-Grillet, French writer and film-maker, aged 85 – *d.* 18 February 2008, *b.* 18 August 1922
Roberts, Eirlys, CBE, editor of *Which?* (1958–73), aged 97 – *d.* 18 March 2008, *b.* 3 January 1911
Roddick, Dame Anita, DBE, entrepreneur and environmentalist, aged 64 – *d.* 10 September 2007, *b.* 23 October 1942
Routh, Jonathan, painter, writer and broadcaster, aged 80 – *d.* 4 June 2008, *b.* 24 November 1927
Russell-Johnston, Lord, Scottish Liberal Party leader (1974–88) and president of the Council of Europe Parliamentary Assembly (1999–2002), aged 75 – *d.* 25 July 2008, *b.* 28 July 1932
Rutherford, Paul, jazz trombonist, aged 67 – *d.* 6 August 2007, *b.* 29 February 1940
Saint Laurent, Yves, couturier, aged 71 – *d.* 1 June 2008, *b.* 1 August 1936
Scofield, Paul, CH, CBE, actor, aged 86 – *d.* 19 March 2008, *b.* 21 January 1922
Shakhlin, Boris, Siberian-born gymnast who won 13 Olympic medals, aged 76 – *d.* 30 May 2008, *b.* 27 January 1932
Shepperd, Sir Alfred, chair and chief executive of the Wellcome Trust (1977–90), aged 82 – *d.* 15 October 2007, *b.* 19 June 1925
Sheridan, Roger, physician who was one of 15 medical students from UCL, London, sent to treat survivors at the Bergen Belsen concentration camp, aged 83 – *d.* 28 October 2007, *b.* 11 November 1923

Siegbahn, Kai, Swedish physicist and joint winner of the Nobel prize in physics (1981), aged 89 – *d.* 20 July 2007, *b.* 20 April 1918

Sinnott, Steve, general secretary of the National Union of Teachers (2004–8), aged 56 – *d.* 5 April 2008, *b.* 2 June 1951

Smith, Ian, prime minister of Rhodesia (1964–79), aged 88 – *d.* 20 November 2007, *b.* 8 April 1919

Speight, Mark, children's television presenter, aged 42 – *found dead* 13 April 2008, *b.* 6 August 1965

Stallard, Lord, Labour MP for St Pancras North (1970–83), aged 86 – *d.* 30 March 2008, *b.* 5 November 1921

Stanier, Field Marshal Sir John, GCB, MBE, Chief of the General Staff (1982–5), aged 82 – *d.* 10 November 2007, *b.* 6 October 1925

Stockhausen, Karlheinz, German composer, aged 79 – *d.* 5 December 2007, *b.* 22 August 1928

Stokes, Lord, industrialist, chair and managing director of the British Leyland Motor Corporation (1968–75), aged 94 – *d.* 21 July 2008, *b.* 22 March 1914

Suharto, General, president of Indonesia (1968–98), aged 86 – *d.* 27 January 2008, *b.* 8 June 1921

Svensson, Esbjorn, Swedish jazz pianist, aged 44 – *d.* 14 June 2008, *b.* 16 April 1964

Telford, Sir Robert, CBE, life president of Marconi, aged 92 – *d.* 10 March 2008, *b.* 1 October 1915

Thomas of Gwydir, Lord, Conservative MP for Conway (1951–66) and Hendon South (1970–87), chair of the Conservative Party (1970–2) and secretary of state for Wales (1970–4), aged 87 – *d.* 4 February 2008, *b.* 31 July 1920

Thompson, Dr Colin, CBE, director of the National Galleries of Scotland (1977–84), aged 87 – *d.* 5 October 2007, *b.* 2 November 1919

Thurnham, Peter, Conservative MP for Bolton North East (1983–97), aged 69 – *d.* 10 May 2008, *b.* 21 August 1938

Todd, Michael, QPM, chief constable of Greater Manchester Police (2002–8), aged 50 – *found dead* 10 March 2008, *b.* 10 August 1957

Tomlinson, Jane, CBE, charity fundraiser who raised millions of pounds through feats of athletic endurance while suffering from terminal cancer, aged 43 – *d.* 3 September 2007, *b.* 21 February 1964

Trant, Gen. Sir Richard, KCB, Quartermaster-General of the Army (1983–6), aged 79 – *d.* 3 October 2007, *b.* 30 March 1928

Troup, Vice-Adm. Sir Anthony Troup, KCB, DSC and Bar, Flag Officer Scotland and Northern Ireland (1974-7), aged 86 – *d.* 8 June 2008, *b.* 18 July 1921

Turner, Ike, American musician, aged 76 – *d.* 12 December 2007, *b.* 5 November 1931

Tweedsmuir (3rd), Lord, publisher and writer, aged 92 – *d.* 29 June 2008, *b.* 10 January 1916

Uemera, Shu, Japanese make-up artist and cosmetics designer, aged 79 – *d.* 29 December 2007, *b.* 19 June 1928

Vallat, Sir Francis, GBE, KCMG, QC, international jurist, aged 95 – *d.* 6 April 2008, *b.* 25 May 1912

Vallings, Vice-Adm. Sir George, KCB, Flag Officer Scotland and Northern Ireland, aged 75 – *d.* 25 December 2007, *b.* 31 May 1932

Varley, Lord, Labour MP for Chesterfield (1964–84), secretary of state for energy (1974–5) and industry (1975–9), aged 75 – *d.* 29 July 2008, *b.* 11 August 1932

Walker, Diana Barnato, MBE, wartime Air Transport Auxiliary (ATA) pilot, aged 90 – *d.* 28 April 2008, *b.* 15 January 1918

Watkins, Rt. Hon. Sir Tasker, VC, GBE, Lord Justice of Appeal (1980–93) and Deputy Chief Justice of England (1988–93), aged 88 – *d.* 9 September 2007, *b.* 18 November 1918

Weatherstone, Sir Dennis, KBE, chair and chief executive of JPMorgan (1990–4), aged 77 – *d.* 13 June 2008, *b.* 29 November 1930

Webster, Very Revd Alan, KCVO, dean of Norwich Cathedral (1970–8) and St Paul's Cathedral (1978–87), aged 89 – *d.* 2 September 2007, *b.* 1 July 1918

Wheeler, Sir Charles, CMG, journalist and broadcaster, aged 85 – *d.* 4 July 2008, *b.* 26 March 1923

Wilde, Brian, actor, aged 80 – *d.* 19 March 2008, *b.* 13 June 1927

Wilkinson, Sir Philip, chief executive of National Westminster bank (1983–7), aged 80 – *d.* 23 August 2007, *b.* 8 May 1927

Willis, Air Chief Marshal Sir John, GBE, KCB, Vice-Chief of the Defence Staff (1995–7), aged 70 – *d.* 9 January 2008, *b.* 27 October 1937

Wilson, Tony, music industry entrepreneur who founded Factory Records and the Haçienda nightclub in Manchester, aged 57 – *d.* 10 August 2007, *b.* 20 February 1950

Yates, Rt. Revd John, Bishop of Gloucester (1975–91), aged 82 – *d.* 26 February 2008, *b.* 17 April 1925

ARCHAEOLOGY

Dr Nadia Durrani and Dr Neil Faulkner

DEBATING PREHISTORIC RITUAL AT STONEHENGE AND SEAHENGE

Stonehenge, Britain's most famous prehistoric site, was the location of a new and privileged dig. Professors Tim Darvill of Bournemouth University, and Geoffrey Wainwright, president of the Society of Antiquaries, were granted the opportunity to dig inside the stone circle at Stonehenge – the first time this has been allowed since 1964. Their aim was to discover more about the so-called Double Bluestone Circle. This was the first stone structure erected on the site, and built from bluestones. But when exactly was it built? How long it was in use for? And at what point was it dismantled and the stones reused in later phases of the monument? Limited dating evidence and poor recording in earlier excavations has left the answers uncertain. The team's new trench, measuring just 3.5m by 2.5m, was located in the south-east quadrant of the Double Bluestone Circle. The excavators' attention was focused on the 'Stonehenge Layer'; a varied stratum of debris and stone chippings that extends across the whole stone circle and contains a large proportion of bluestone chippings. A critical question was whether this layer dates to the construction or the demolition of the Double Bluestone Circle, and whether it could be closely dated. The results were not quite what was expected. Roman pottery and coins were recovered from two pits – clearly implying ritual use of the site in the Romano-British period – and, incidentally, providing circumstantial support for antiquarian speculations that Stonehenge was used by the Druids of that era! The better news is that some carbonised grain was also recovered, with the possibility of a radiocarbon date for the actual erection of the bluestones. But at the time of writing, the results are unknown. The dig was funded by BBC2's *Timewatch*, so the excavators cannot spill the beans until the programme, scheduled for autumn 2008, has gone out. A similar constraint has afflicted Mike Parker Pearson's new *National Geographic*-funded work at the nearby prehistoric site of Durrington Walls: the price one has to pay for media support is having to keep one's professional colleagues on tenterhooks.

What can be revealed, however, is that Parker Pearson, the excavator of Durrington Walls, sees the Stonehenge complex of monuments as a landscape rich with ancient religious meaning. To him, it is one in which rituals associated with the transition from life to death were enacted – where the passage of the seasons, and the rising and setting of the sun, offered rich symbolic references to this major rite of passage. In this scenario, wooden uprights represent the recently deceased, the gradual rotting of the timber signifying the decay of the flesh. The stones, at sites such as Stonehenge, would have represented the completion of the journey into the afterlife. They were the embodiment of the realm of the ancestors, where the dead, having completed the passage to the other side, would have become ancestors themselves. But is this interpretation of ancient ritual and landscape correct? The beauty of prehistoric archaeology is that it can be open to multiple interpretation. And Mike Parker Pearson's academic rival, Tim Darvill, is indeed offering a radically different interpretation of Stonehenge.

For the past six years, Prof. Darvill has been working at Carn Meini in the Preseli Hills, Pembrokeshire, Wales. This is some 250 miles from Stonehenge, and the source of the bluestones. Darvill has been trying to understand why the builders of Stonehenge should have gone to all the trouble of moving these massive chunks of stone over such huge distances. The bluestones, he argues, must have some special significance: Carn Meini was not just a stone quarry – it was hardly conveniently located – rather, it was a place of high ritual significance in itself. The stones here, he thinks, were associated with springs thought to have healing properties, and the stones therefore had magical significance when they were transported to the Stonehenge site in Wiltshire. In this scenario, they would have carried with them the sanctity of their place of origin, and perhaps formed the basis for some sort of healing cult centre at their new location.

In contrast to Parker Pearson's view, this would make Stonehenge a place for the living, not the dead, albeit the living who were ill, perhaps even facing imminent death – a kind of Stone Age Lourdes. This would certainly explain certain folk traditions, such as that recounted by Geoffrey of Monmouth in the 12th century, who associates the Arthurian magician Merlin – a man from the West – with the site.

However, as a final prosaic aside, Open University geologists have been suggesting that the stones were in fact moved to Salisbury Plain by glaciers. This is a long-running argument, but for them, the idea that prehistoric humans brought the stones such long distances is simply not credible. Whatever the case, the debate among the Stonehenge specialists is likely to continue for a long while yet.

Meanwhile, another famous henge – the preserved timber circle found on a Norfolk beach in 1998 and dubbed 'Seahenge' – has also been in the news this year. It was originally excavated amid great controversy by an archaeological team determined to save the monument from destruction by the elements, but against much opposition from druids and local people. The timbers have spent the last several years being conserved. This is an arduous process that involves slowly replacing all the salt-water in the timbers with preservatives. Waterlogged timbers from archaeological sites are formed overwhelmingly of water: they retain their form as timber, but have lost most of their wood content. The danger is that they dry out and crumble to dust when excavated. The only way to avoid this is to slowly remove the water and substitute a bulky, waxy preservative. The process is now complete and the timbers have finally gone on display at the King's Lynn Museum where they have pride of place in a newly opened Seahenge Gallery.

The timber circle is about 4,000 years old, dating to the Early Bronze Age (like the main phase of stone building at Stonehenge). It comprises a ring of split tree trunks, set close together, ranged around an upturned, centrally placed trunk. Speculation about the meaning of the Seahenge monument continues. Was the upturned central stump used as a platform for excarnation – the laying out of dead bodies so that they could be picked clean by carrion birds, so releasing the soul for an ascent to the heavens? Or was the central stump itself a ritual object, one precious enough to be enclosed by a palisade that obscured it from view or restricted access, its upturned condition perhaps symbolising some return to the earth from which it was sprung? Or is it a gigantic phallus, placed there to guarantee the fertility of the soil, the fecundity of flocks and herds, and the procreation of the community that placed it? As with the debate around Stonehenge, this one is likely to run and run.

CELTIC, ROMAN, AND VIKING HOARDS

A metal-detectorist in a Wiltshire field near Chiseldon made one of the archaeological scoops of the year: the discovery of an Iron Age hoard comprising 12 bronze cauldrons. It was then investigated by a local archaeologist, and carefully excavated by a Wessex archaeology team.

The Chiseldon Cauldrons – a 'gobsmackingly unique' find according to one expert – varied from around 400mm to 700mm in diameter, and had been placed in a round pit, roughly 2m in diameter and up to 1m deep. Beneath two of them were ox-skulls. The latter possibly represent the remains of a feast held to celebrate a major event. The find-spot is close to *The Ridgeway* prehistoric track, which seems to have marked the boundary between different tribes in the Iron Age. So was the major event – marked by the feast and cauldrons – the sealing of some ancient political alliance?

This is not mere fanciful speculation for agreements were often sealed by feasting, and then, in a symbolic sharing of the feast with the gods, were completed with some form of ritual deposition. The Irish epics also make clear the role of cauldrons in such events: in the story *Mac Datho's Pig*, revellers ate from seven cauldrons on seven hearths in the great hall of Mac Datho, and each man would thrust a flesh-fork into the cauldron to spear a portion of meat. When the feast marked an especially important occasion, one that the gods were required to sanctify and guarantee, it may have been thought appropriate to bury the cauldrons themselves as a high-value offering. Analysis is planned to establish whether or not the insides of the cauldrons contain tell-tale food residues. An early to mid-Iron Age date seems likely for the Chiseldon Cauldrons, but half a millennium later, Roman soldiers and Romano-British natives were still throwing offerings into the River Tees at Piercebridge – as located by a pair of amateur divers. Their discoveries, known as the Piercebridge finds, have been catalogued and identified by Finds Liaison Officer, Philippa Walton. Some 2,000 objects have since been recovered. Most of them date to the middle of the Roman period and include 415 identifiable coins, 72 brooches, 24 finger-rings, and numerous other items of jewellery, military equipment, and votive objects. Among the most telling objects are the high proportion of coins depicting females – perhaps implying worship of a female deity in the waters. In addition, a horse-and-rider brooch suggests worship of the Celtic deity Epona. But the archaeologists also discovered a small silver plaque depicting the god Jupiter, and a pipe-clay figurine probably of the god Mercury. Worship of deities, presumed to reside in rivers, marshes, and springs, was widespread in both the Celtic and Roman worlds. The evidence suggests that this particular sacred place attracted the attentions of the worshippers of many different gods. Offerings were sometimes made along with a prayer for some favour, or, if the favour was done, to honour a previous vow to the deity to make an appropriate offering in return.

Also of Roman date was the discovery of a hoard of well-preserved, mainly bronze vessels at the bottom of a well excavated at Drapers Gardens in the heart of the City of London. The cache included a mix of 'ritual' vessels, such as buckets for mixing water and wine, 'dippers' (shallow-handled bowls), a flagon, and part of a hanging-bowl, along with everyday items, such as a cauldron, a set of three nested bowls and a ladle. The potential religious use of all these items suggests that the deposit was ritual. However, the probable date – the end of the fourth century AD – may imply otherwise. Paganism was on the retreat at this period, London was largely ruined and abandoned, and Roman power was collapsing. Thus, this find should perhaps be interpreted as a security hoard – a cache of valuables that the owners were hiding and expected to return to reclaim at some future date.

Another equally spectacular find-of-the-year was the Harrowgate Hoard, which dates to some 1,000 years after the Drapers Gardens discovery. The hoard, so experts assert, is the most important Viking find made in Britain for 150 years, and is the second largest Viking hoard ever found. It was uncovered by two metal-detectorists, a father and son team, in a field near Harrowgate in Yorkshire. They discovered almost the entire hoard, which comprises hundreds of glorious objects. The hoard centres on a decorated silver-gilt cup, packed with 617 coins. Buried with the cup were 11 ingots of silver, and 67 pieces of silver including arm-rings and hack-silver, a gold arm-ring, and lead fragments. The origin of the objects is also of great interest for they come from as far afield as Afghanistan, Russia, Scandinavia, and Ireland. The coins, dating from the late 9th and early 10th centuries, include Anglo-Saxon, Anglo-Viking, Carolingian and Islamic types – typical of Viking hoards of this period. The latest coins are those of King Aethelstan (*c.*AD 924–939). Close analysis of these latest coins strongly implies that the hoard was deposited around AD 930.

BARBARIANS AND ROMANS ON THE NORTHERN FRONTIER

Both Hadrian's Wall, and its less well-known, more northerly cousin, the Antonine Wall, have been in the news this year. Following the spectacular success of the British Museum's blockbuster Terracotta Army *First Emperor* exhibition in 2007, the Roman emperor Hadrian is the focus of their main 2008 exhibition. Hadrian, of course, has a special relationship with the UK, because the British wall that bears his name is the single best surviving example of Roman frontier defences of the early second century AD anywhere in the world. Yet far less well-known than the wall itself is the global political context in which it was built: that of defeat in Mesopotamia (modern Iraq) and turmoil in the wider Middle East. It was Hadrian's decision to end his predecessor's disastrous invasion of the East, to recognise that the empire was overextended, and to adopt a policy of retrenchment and consolidation that gave rise to his great campaigns of building-work on the frontiers. The exhibition had provided a superb context for understanding the archaeological remains unearthed along the wall.

As for recent work at the wall itself, of note is the reconstruction of an entire barrack-block at South Shields. The reconstruction is complete with centurion's quarters at one end, and is directly overlying the excavated remains of the actual barrack-block on which it is based. The barrack-block now stands beside an earlier reconstructed commandant's house, plus the long-standing reconstruction of a fort gateway. Together they make South Shields one of the premier visitor attractions on Hadrian's Wall.

Meanwhile, David Breeze of Historic Scotland had been lobbying for the Antonine Wall to be granted World Heritage Site status, and his efforts were crowned with success shortly before this was written. The Antonine Wall ran from the Firth of Forth to the Firth of Clyde – that is through the Central Lowlands – but, except for its stone forts, it was constructed entirely of earth and timber. It therefore survives along its length mainly as a huge earthwork of ditch and rampart. It was occupied for a far shorter period than Hadrian's Wall – a couple of decades in the middle of the second century AD – and therefore represents the failure of Roman imperialism to subjugate the Picts from what is now Scotland. On the other hand, this relatively brief period of occupation means that the archaeology of the Antonine Wall offers a rich microcosm of mid-second century AD Roman military occupation. World Heritage status is likely to lead to a ramping up of visitor facilities, and perhaps additional funding for further research.

The Romans' problems in the far north have been exemplified by evidence from a site recently excavated at Culduthel Farm on the outskirts of Inverness. The site, excavated by a professional team from Headland Archaeology, comprised a substantial settlement of 17 native roundhouses dating from the Middle Iron Age to the mid-Roman period. It included two exceptionally large roundhouses of up to 20m in diameter – the residences of local chieftains. But the most telling aspect of the site was the abundant evidence for large-scale ironworking, bronzeworking, enamelling, and glassworking – on a scale without parallel in the archaeology of mainland Scotland at this time. It seems likely that the chieftains residence here were true iron-masters, providing metalwork for the Caledonian tribes nearby – and quite possibly some of the armaments with which local men fought the Roman army at the Battle of Mons Graupius in AD 84, as recorded in the pages of Tacitus.

THE FIRST GREAT PLAGUE?

Recent work analysing human remains and finds from a Roman cemetery excavation in Gloucester has reached startling conclusions. Excavators have discovered a large square pit during otherwise fairly routine work on a known Roman cemetery site in the Wotton area of the city. The pit measured a little over 3.5m in extent, and was less than a metre deep. However, this small space was crammed with a huge tangle of human remains, which presented major challenges, and major results, for the excavators. Lab-based work has since established that there were at least 91 bodies in the pit, that the skeletons represent a fairly typical cross-section of population, and that they all seem to have been tipped into the pit in a single event. Why had these people been thrown together like this? It is unlikely that they were the victims of battle or massacre since none of the bodies revealed any evidence of violent trauma. The burial has been dated to late second century AD. So what happened at this time that suddenly struck down 91 citizens of Roman Gloucester?

The grave is contemporary with the great plague of the second century AD. Historical sources report that it began in the East in AD 165 and spread rapidly westwards, to infect the heartlands of the Roman Empire by AD 167. Thereafter, for the next three decades, there were recurrent outbreaks of deadly disease in the Roman world – possibly small-pox, according to the pernicious symptoms recorded in the ancient accounts. An outbreak in AD 189 is said to have killed 2,000 per day at its height. No-one can prove that the mass-grave in Gloucester is a plague pit, but the circumstantial evidence seems compelling, in which case it is the first example of such from anywhere in the empire, and the only evidence so far that the plague reached the empire's westernmost province.

THE END OF ROMAN BRITAIN

Excavations beside St Martin-in-the-Fields, Trafalgar Square, London, by Museum of London archaeologists have unearthed the remains of a man in his forties who has been dubbed 'London's last Roman'. He was placed in a stone sarcophagus, and his remains have been radiocarbon-dated to AD 390–430, ie to the very end of the Roman period. Thus he dates from a time when most of Roman London is known to have been a wasteland of ruined buildings, blocked streets, and heaps of rubble and refuse. His stone sarcophagus shows him to have been a man of high rank, and he may have belonged to the small class of top officials and officers still maintaining some sort of Roman authority in the twilight of Roman rule. His burial lay some distance from the westernmost gates leading into the Roman town (which corresponded roughly to the modern City of London), and it is even possible that it can be regarded for evidence for an extramural Roman church – a possible very early precursor to the present-day St Martin's. Other finds from the dig included an Anglo-Saxon pot of *c.*AD 500, a discovery that perhaps creates some sort of chronological bridge between *Londinium* – the Roman town underlying the City – and *Lundenwic* – the Middle Saxon town underlying the West End.

The end of Roman Britain continues to be a controversial subject. Two new contributions are represented in two new overviews published in the last year, Roger White's *Britannia Prima: Britain's last Roman province*, and Stuart Laycock's *Britannia: a failed state?* Roger White argues that Britannia Prima, the westernmost of the four (later five) provinces forming the diocese of late Roman Britain continued to evolve as a coherent political entity after the end of Roman rule. It was, he suggests, the territorial base of a distinct, early medieval British and Christian culture, which contrasted with the Germanic and Pagan culture of the eastern parts of the island that succumbed to Anglo-Saxon domination during the fifth and sixth centuries AD. White draws on a wide range of evidence, including later historical accounts, metalwork finds, and place-name evidence.

Somewhat similar in approach is Stuart Laycock's focus on metalwork finds to assess what was going on at the end of Roman Britain. Laycock has plotted the distribution of distinct types of late Roman military belt-fittings – presumably worn by Roman soldiers who belonged to local tribal militia units – found in different tribal areas. Fascinatingly, the distributions correspond closely to the pre-Roman Celtic tribal territories, which are in turn essentially the same as the Roman-period local government units. This indicates that the late Romans (like all 'good' colonials) maintained the old tribal divisions and were simply raising local militias on a tribal basis. Consequently, when the central Roman authority collapsed in the years around AD 400, Britain fragmented into a series of tribal territories. To Laycock, Rome's legacy to Britain was thus a 'failed state' because of the tribal divisions and animosities that had been fostered by the imperial state on the principle of divide-and-rule. Laycock's argument is based partly on personal experience in the recent Balkan wars following the break-up of Yugoslavia – he sees the same scenario played out in Yugoslavia's fragmentation into national territories in the 1990s.

A further ingredient for the pot is Sam Moorhead's research on late Roman coinage, a study facilitated by the huge increase in data arising from the development of the Portable Antiquities Scheme (PAS). Moorhead is the British Museum-based Roman coins expert for the PAS. Some 68,000 Roman coins have been recorded on the PAS database since the scheme was established in 1997. This work has revealed evidence for significant coin use in the very late and immediate post-Roman periods. Moreover, relatively large numbers of clipped *siliquae* – a distinctive late Roman type of silver coin – have now been found. This clipping is thought by experts to have taken place only after the supply of Roman coins ended – the purpose being to maintain a precious metal currency into the fifth century on the part of native rulers.

THE ARCHAEOLOGY OF URBAN POVERTY

Building redevelopment ensures a steady flow of new discoveries from our historic cities, of which the Drapers Garden hoard of Roman vessels described above is a good example. However, an unusual variant on the typical range of Roman, Anglo-Saxon, medieval, and early modern discoveries comes from current excavations on the Hungate site at York – the largest single dig in the city for 25 years. Traditionally, archaeologists tend to focus on one period of an excavation, but the approach this time has been to excavate and record all phases in equal detail – including the most recent. This has allowed archaeologists to explore an area of slum housing dating from the 19th and the first half of the 20th century. What makes the dig especially significant is the fact that working-class York was the subject of the first great survey of urban poverty in Britain by Seebohm Rowntree, the York chocolate manufacturer and social reformer.

Rowntree organised a landmark investigation of poverty across the entire city – a study that supported the great Liberal reforms in the years after 1906, and which effectively founded the welfare state. Archaeologists have been able to flesh out the statistics of Rowntree's survey with countless human details and many socio-economic nuances. Thus, for example, their work has revealed how some 50 people had to share a communal toilet located just outside the front-doors of a row of tiny back-to-back houses. Equally, they have been able to assess the degree to which standards of housing might vary, sometimes significantly, from one street to another. Later phases of the project will carry the excavations down to the natural on one part of the site over a five-year period, and this will provide a complete sequence from Roman to modern through 2,000 years of the city's history.

LOOTERS, BUREAUCRATS AND CRANKS

Looting has been a feature of archaeology ever since people first started burying rich objects in the ground. The issue that has hit the headlines this year, however, is marine salvage, with attention focussed on the *Odyssey Explorer*, a huge, state-of-the-art, specialised salvage vessel. The commercial value of bullion, other precious objects, and antiquities lost with ships at sea over centuries and millennia of time, is vast. There are thousands of underwater wrecks, a very high proportion of them lying in relatively shallow water, easily accessible to modern, high-tech salvage operations. Big capitalist interest is therefore involved, providing a steady supply of objects for the global art and antiquities market.

While the *Odyssey Explorer* operates behind a veil of academic respectability and seriousness, its true purpose is plunder for profit. It has been involved in salvaging from ships once considered to be the property of distinct nation-states, sparking political outrage. The issue was highlighted by a very public clash between the Spanish government and Odyssey Marine Exploration, the owners of *Odyssey Explorer*, over what the Spanish authorities claim is the naked plundering of a Spanish wreck, the *Black Swan*, at an undisclosed location in the Atlantic. The company had announced that it was recovering a hoard of 500,000 gold and silver coins, weighing some 17 tons, from the shipwreck. The Spanish government argued strongly against the actions of Odyssey, who had disregarded the assumed national ownership of the wreck, as well as its heritage value to Spain. Meanwhile, from earlier similar ventures a company called New World Treasures is selling a range of coins for up to £268 each, while the Canadian version of eBay is selling Mexican silver 'pieces of eight' for £193. The potential profits from the looting of wrecks are clearly considerable and the threat to the global heritage represented by shipwrecks very real. Pressure is mounting for world governments to sign up to the 2001 UNESCO convention on the protection of the underwater cultural heritage, which aims to preserve all wrecks over 100 years old, and thus to make the looting of them illegal.

By contrast, one of the greatest success stories of recent years in terms of reining back the removal of archaeological objects from sites without record is threatened by major government cutbacks. The Portable Antiquities Scheme (PAS) has recorded more than 300,000 objects in its ten-year life, most of them metal-detected. But the Department of Culture, Media and Sport is cutting 25 per cent from the Museum, Libraries and Archives Council's budget, and in consequence PAS funding has been frozen at £1.3m, which, allowing for inflation, represents a substantial cut, at the possible cost of five main office jobs. The cuts are wrapped in the usual apparatchik gobbledygook: 'the best value for government money'. this will 'have the potential to strengthen the PAS overall'. Yet the reality is that the huge gains that have been made since the scheme's introduction in bringing metal-detectorists – previously the great pariahs of British archaeology – into the fold will be undermined. Leading Cambridge archaeologist Martin Millett has headed up an open letter signed by 17 top academic archaeologists opposing the cuts, and an Early Day Motion has attracted 68 MP signatures at the time of writing.

Too much government – in the form of unwelcome interference and regulation – is, however, the problem for community archaeology. Gabriel Moshenka, writing polemically in the pages of *Current Archaeology* magazine, argues against key features of what might be called 'public archaeology from above'. He and his colleagues critique a 'bureaucratic pantomime' in which local government based professional archaeologists attempt to impose the apparatus of 'project designs, impact assessments, and regional research agendas' used in commercial rescue archaeology on small-scale community projects with local volunteers. Pat Reid takes the argument a stage further in a follow-up opinion piece published in a subsequent edition of the same magazine. She rejects Moshenka's proposal for official guidelines for community archaeology: 'The idea fills me with dread. What starts out as helpful support so easily becomes a regulatory stranglehold.' Instead, she argues, 'true community archaeology should be a living process, embedded in a local community.'

Coincidentally, there are growing concerns about the ineffectiveness of what might be called 'official' community archaeology – that which is staffed by professional archaeologists appointed and funded by external bodies. Steve Watson and Emma Waterton have issued a call for papers for a prospective volume of the *International Journal of Heritage Studies* which will address this head on: 'Our rationale behind this proposal is that while there is a lot of noise in policy and practice and a profusion of case studies about 'community' involvement, participation and consultation, we do not believe that, on the whole, it has been quite as successful, even in its own terms, and all-encompassing as the rhetoric suggests'. The current vogue for 'public archaeology' has generated a minor industry of professional staff, outreach departments and community initiatives, but it is afflicted with a bureaucratic mindset of regulation and control, instead of attempting to create *real* community projects, in which it is local amateurs who control and shape the work.

Finally, on archaeological politics, another old perennial that has surfaced this year is the question of human remains. Or, more specifically, who is entitled to claim their ownership and make decisions about what happens to them – in particular, whether or not they should be left in the ground, returned to the ground, perhaps even repatriated to their former place of origin. The Tasmanian Aboriginal Centre (TAC) has succeeded in persuading the British Museum to repatriate two human 'ash bundles' and, more controversially, the Natural History Museum 17 skeletons. The lobbying of this group has been challenged by academic archaeologists of the British Association for Biological Anthropology and Osteoarchaeology (BABAO). They argue that since the indigenous population of Tasmania was effectively wiped out in the 19th century, the membership of the modern TAC has no biological relationship with the remains in question, and therefore no right to 'speak for' these deceased. Even more questionable has been the intervention of an organisation called Honouring the Ancient Dead (HAD), a lobby group of pagans and druids allegedly speaking for the British dead of pre-Christian times – a claim which threatens the integrity of numerous archaeological collections of prehistoric human remains. HAD's arguments have surfaced in apparently reputable organs like the *Museums Journal*, and BABAO archaeologists have found themselves having to argue their case with some members of their own profession. BABAO's Martin Smith is deeply concerned that the small and valuable existing collection of prehistoric human remains in various collections might be under threat from charlatans setting themselves up as 'spokespersons' for people who died thousands of years ago and about whose culture and beliefs virtually nothing is known. Fortunately, as the letters pages of the *Museums Journal* have revealed, HAD's antics have evoked criticism even from fellow pagans, and it seems unlikely that their arguments will be widely endorsed.

ARCHITECTURE

John Hitchman

TERMINAL 5, HEATHROW AIRPORT, LONDON

Architect: Rogers, Stirk, Harbour & Partners

As high profile projects go, few have been burdened with a higher profile than the newly completed fifth terminal at Heathrow, the UK's premier international airport and allegedly the busiest in the world. The £4.5bn development has taken 20 years to come to fruition, following the initial proposals and the design competition (won by Richard Rogers) in 1988–9. For so long the subject of a heated national debate about whether Heathrow should continue to expand or relocate to a more efficient location elsewhere, the project was subjected to the longest public inquiry on record, lasting 46 months, before it received approval in 2001. By that time design work was already well advanced, as BAA took the decision to proceed with the work in anticipation of a positive outcome.

Due to the evolving nature of air travel, the scheme itself has progressed through many iterations in its development from the original concept. This envisaged a much larger site than ultimately proved to be available and accommodated its functions in a low single-storey structure rather than the multi-level building eventually realised, which is in direct contrast to the horizontality of most recently completed airport buildings. The need to fit the building in between the airport's two existing main runways without encroaching on green belt land to the west necessitated squeezing the 300,000 sq. m of accommodation into a more compact and taller structure.

If it ultimately lacks the spatial freedom and visual ease of, for example, the 2006 Stirling prize-winning scheme by the same architect at Madrid's Barajas Airport, it is nevertheless an impressive achievement considering the enormous constraints on design. Given the continually changing requirements of the client and numerous stakeholders over the long gestation period of the design, one of the early and most significant decisions taken was to separate the enclosing envelope and its structural support from the internal accommodation, creating the scenario of a building within a building. By this means it was possible to continue to play around with the three dimensional organisation of the airport functions and adapt the internal structure where necessary, without impinging on the development of the major structural elements.

All passenger arrivals and departures at Terminal 5 are contained within an independent structure rising to four storeys above ground level under a soaring single span roof, with three levels dedicated to support functions, servicing, baggage handling and the rail transport interchange located below ground level. In the future the isolation of the main building from the envelope may offer future flexibility if it becomes necessary to reconfigure parts of the building to keep up with the operational and commercial needs of 21st century air travel as the entire internal structure could be demolished and rebuilt without affecting the external envelope.

The 'no touching' concept is expressed visually by the narrow canyons of space around the perimeter, occupied by the muscular and dramatic roof support 'trees' on the long elevations and angled support struts on the end elevations. The main roof is a single span modular steel framed construction comprising a central 110m curved arch, supported on each side by an arrangement of struts carrying a continuation of the curved profile of the central arch member. Each module of the roof is formed from two arch members 18m apart, supported by the framework of the 'trees' and with a clear bay between, so that the trees occupy alternate bays.

The end result is a clear span of 156.6m across the building's width, and an array of arches extending 390m in length. A method of assembly on site had to be developed avoiding the use of tower cranes, which would have interfered with aircraft movements. A system of jacking towers was devised whereby three modules of the roof were assembled at ground level into a single unit of 54 × 110m and then raised into place between the opposing bracing tree structures.

Along its western side, the terminal building is confronted by a five-storey car park structure, almost as long as the terminal itself, set back across a long narrow pedestrianised street, landscaped like a plaza, with paved areas, water features and tree planting. The street is spanned at intervals by pedestrian bridges connecting the top deck of the car park to the highest floor of the main terminal, devoted to the check-in and departures hall. The full drama of the roof structure is thus only fully visible upon the first arrival of departing passengers at the check-in hall, and then after check-in while waiting for the familiar experience of the security check. From here departing passengers progress down one floor to the main departures lounge, with its extensive array of shops, bars and restaurants. Two cut-backs in the top floor provide a welcome spatial release and a view of the roof for the main seating areas.

To cater for the anticipated number of passengers, the terminal has aircraft stands with connecting piers on the north, east and south sides and the complete complex includes space for two further satellite buildings, of which only the first has been completed to date, the second being due to open in 2010. Departing passengers, called to their gate, will proceed either by lift to the lower level in the main terminal, where arriving and departing passengers are separated and channelled by glazed screens and armoured glass doors, or via escalators to the subterranean un-manned shuttle rail link that will speed them to the base of the satellite buildings.

The satellite buildings are in many ways mini-versions of the main terminal, long and narrow on plan, with a similar but smaller scaled version of the structural system, incorporating the curved roof arches and multi-strut 'trees'. The first to be built, T5B, is 442m long and 52m wide, and provides linked stands for 15 aircraft.

Arriving passengers are processed through the two lower levels of the main terminal, proceeding via the links from the stands or from the shuttle link from the satellites to the passport control area at first floor level and thence down to the ground floor baggage hall. The baggage reclaim area is a generous double height space running almost the entire length of the building, characterised by hard and shiny surfaces, with stainless steel column casings, green tinted opaque glass cladding and a ceiling of suspended white metal discs that veil the structure and services paraphernalia above. From here it is but a short step to the arrivals hall, at a level with the landscaped street outside, from where banks of lifts are available to transfer people to the upper car park levels for their onward journey. As arriving passengers approach the exit doors to the arrivals hall, the ceiling of discs terminates and the structure is cut away above to reveal the 'canyon' of free space between the external envelope and the internal structure, with the 'trees' visible to their full height and the ends of the great vault of the roof just visible overhead.

Terminal 5 was officially opened by the Queen on 14th March 2008. BA's initial operational teething problems attracted a disastrous reception from the media but as time passes, all the baggage handling problems will hopefully be resolved and the terminal can get on with the business of handling BA's worldwide services. The building is hugely impressive in its mastery of the complex requirements of a modern international airport within an unusually constrained site, and the achievement has been recognised by a RIBA national award in 2008. If it lacks anything, it is that spark of imagination and flair in the spaces at the heart of the building and a sense of either uniqueness or specifically British identity. It is an international air terminal that could be almost anywhere. For now the debate will no doubt return to the longer-term scenario as to whether Heathrow will be allowed to continue with its planned expansion with further terminal buildings and the highly contentious third runway.

ST PANCRAS INTERNATIONAL STATION, LONDON

Architect: Foster & Partners

The Queen formally opened the Eurostar Terminal on 6 November 2007 at the newly refurbished and extended St Pancras Station in London, heralding the completion of the final part of the long anticipated high-speed rail link via the Channel tunnel to mainland Europe.

Parliamentary approval was gained for the initial proposals in 1996, since when this enormously complex £800m project has required the attention and sustained hard work of a legion of consultants, contractors and suppliers, each bringing their particular expertise to this multi-faceted, £800m undertaking.

The redevelopment can be broadly said to fall into three distinct major elements: the refurbishment and restoration of the great train shed designed by Thomas Barlow; a new extension to the existing train shed to accommodate the platforms serving local and regional trains; and the conversion of the undercroft of the old station into the new retail arcade with links to the London Underground and car and taxi drop-off points.

The key strategic decisions underpinning the redevelopment derive from the fact that at a quarter of a mile in length the Eurostar trains are twice as long as those used for domestic services. Early on, the decision was made that all arriving trains would terminate with an alignment at a common point at the outgoing 'country' end, rather than the arrivals end. Of the 13 platforms provided overall, only six, for the Eurostar trains, penetrate into the original train shed, leaving the remaining domestic services housed under the new extension to the north. As a consequence, one side of the vaulted space has been left free of tracks, enabling a wide pedestrian concourse to be inserted at the original undercroft level, running parallel to the tracks, with generous views opened up at platform level enabling daylight to flood down to the lower level while simultaneously affording the opportunity of dramatic views back up into the vaulted roof.

When it was first built Barlow's magnificent 1868 train shed was the world's widest span building, a single vault over 30m high, 210m long and spanning 75m, constructed from steel and wrought iron, a record that it held for the next 50 years. Along with George Gilbert Scott's extraordinary gothic concoction fronting the station, it was accorded Grade 1 status, and as such attracted the unremitting attention of English Heritage when it came to restoring and adapting it for use in the 21st century.

Over the years leading up to its transformation, St Pancras had been allowed to degenerate into a dirty, run down and gloomy structure, badly in need of attention. The restoration project, overseen by Pascall & Watson Architects, has removed all the old boarding that formerly concealed the centre of the vault, the substitute Georgian wired glass and panels that were introduced as a result of wartime bomb damage, restored the original cast iron arches and secondary structural members, and provided a

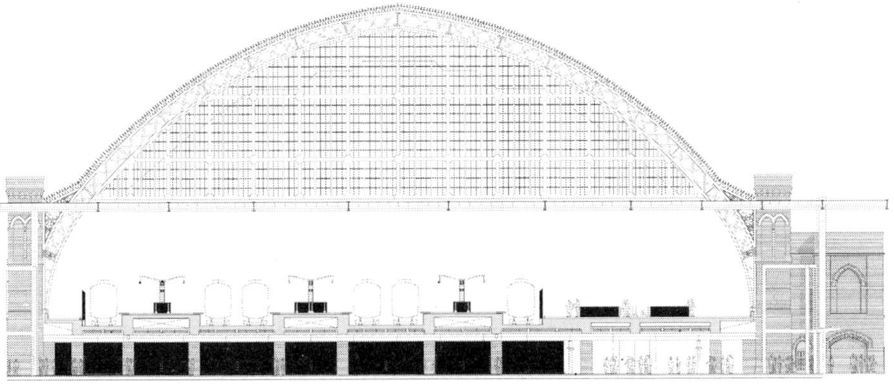

Fig. 1 St Pancras

new part-solid, part-glazed roof system designed to follow Barlow's original intentions as closely as possible.

Layers of paint were stripped off the metalwork, and after repairing the rusted metal and a careful microscopic paint analysis it was all repainted in a pale sky blue colour closely matching that found overlaying the original red lead finish, and honouring Barlow's intention that in sunny conditions the roof vault would merge into the sky. Along each side of the train shed the orange-red brickwork and stone-trimmed arcades of the enclosing walls have been cleaned up and restored and provide a stimulating counterpoint to the sky blue filigree framework of the roof.

The main platform level of the Barlow shed was located over an enormous undercroft that was originally constructed as a bonded warehouse for storing beer delivered by train from the breweries in Burton-on-Trent. The loads of the platforms and train tracks were borne on a forest of cast iron columns laid out at roughly 4.5m centres (the dimensions derived incidentally directly from the size of a beer cask). This area has now been opened up to the public to accommodate both a shopping arcade comprising some 62 shop units and an adjoining market and the substantial Eurostar concourse areas. Integrating the requirements of modern retailers with English Heritage's concern to retain the integrity and fabric of the original construction imposed considerable demands on the designers of the fit-out of the undercroft areas, led by the architects Chapman Taylor.

The western flank wall of the train shed is supported on a series of massive brick arches, which English Heritage was adamant had to be respected. The original proposal placed the shop-fronts within the arches (and generated unrealistically small units), but in attempting to maximise the retail area a compromise was reached in which a line of full-height glazed shop-fronts was established forward of the brick arches but still set back behind the row of cast iron columns supporting the edge of the concourse void above. This was sufficient to create a colonnade that helps to separate a browsing area for shoppers from people dashing to and from the trains.

The detailing of the retail units had to be rigorously pursued, with a clear policy established of 'don't touch' details separating new from old. Glass separating screens are carefully scribed around the over-sailing brickwork courses at the springing of the arches, structural fixings are kept to an absolute minimum, and the glazed shop-fronts are even cantilevered from the floor to avoid interference with the original fabric above. Tenants are subject to a rigorous level of control over signage, merchandising and finishes that is untypical of most shopping environments but which here allows a subtle and restrained ambience to play second fiddle to the historic setting.

Banks of escalators placed centrally in the concourse provide intermittent vertical connection to the main platform level, where there is to be found, running alongside the adjacent Eurostar track, the much anticipated 'longest champagne bar in Europe', at 92m in length it is an ad-man's dream and proving to be, so far, a highly popular and successful meeting point. From the north end of the concourse, further stairs and escalators connect to the platforms serving the local train services, where the third major component, in the form of a new 200m long flat-roofed extension to the train shed has been added, on the basis of a design originally proposed by Foster & Partners.

The new train shed extension is linked to the old with a band of glazed roof-lights illuminating the mall below, but rather than pursue any kind of a vaulted solution, which might have suffered in comparison with the Barlow shed, the new extension adopts an essentially flat format of narrow saw-tooth roof-lights, arranged transversely to the platforms, with north-facing glazing. The main plane of the roof is aligned with the lowest member of the vertical glazed screen defining the end of the original vaulted roof. While to this end it avoids a direct confrontation with the powerful volume of the original, its lack of height and limited glazing unfortunately creates an oppressive and at times gloomy space, offering compression just at the point where disembarking passengers would expect to enjoy a sense of arrival. Had the roof-lights faced south, east or west, or a combination of these, the opportunity for shafts of sunlight to illuminate the space could have been exploited.

However, the restored Barlow shed is a triumph, a colourful, bright, airy and dramatic space that comes across as a fitting environment for the sleek high-speed Eurostar trains. With links to King's Cross mainline station and its several underground lines, as well as a coach station and road transport links, St Pancras now lies at the heart of the capital's largest transport interchange. The project has been awarded a RIBA regional award for 2008 and it is a tribute to the vision of both the original designer, the engineer Thomas Barlow, as well as the many who have worked on its transformation that one of London's finest historic buildings has taken on a significant 21st century role with such panache.

CIVIL JUSTICE CENTRE, SPINNINGFIELDS, MANCHESTER

Architect: Denton Corker Marshall

Manchester's new Civil Justice Centre is the largest courtroom complex to be built in the UK since the Royal Courts of Justice were completed in 1870. This striking new building functions as the north-west regional headquarters of the Ministry of Justice, and is an impressive addition to the city's central business district, extending from Deansgate to the river Irwell. Its unconventional articulated form is the outcome of an international design competition held in 2002 which was set out in two parts, one a competition to select the design architect, the other a developer competition to locate an appropriate site.

The original competition brief called for an additional 20,000 sq. m of office space, but the architects chose instead to isolate this into a separate building, squeezing the court onto an awkward triangular area of the site. By increasing its height beyond that of the surrounding developments, and stacking the accommodation within a narrow footprint, the architects have managed to create a public piazza that brings daylight, greenery and fresh air into a very densely developed area. Its 15-storey height gives the building a very strong visual presence and enables it to act as a gateway marker to one of the main crossings over the river into Salford.

The highly articulated form of the building is the result of separating out its various functions into a series of parallel zones, which are treated as though they could each slip past each other to suit particular internal requirements. The most obvious manifestation of this feature is the treatment of the major zone containing the courtrooms and judges' offices. At each floor level the larger courtroom spaces are grouped at each end of the long narrow fingers of space; their varying sizes are

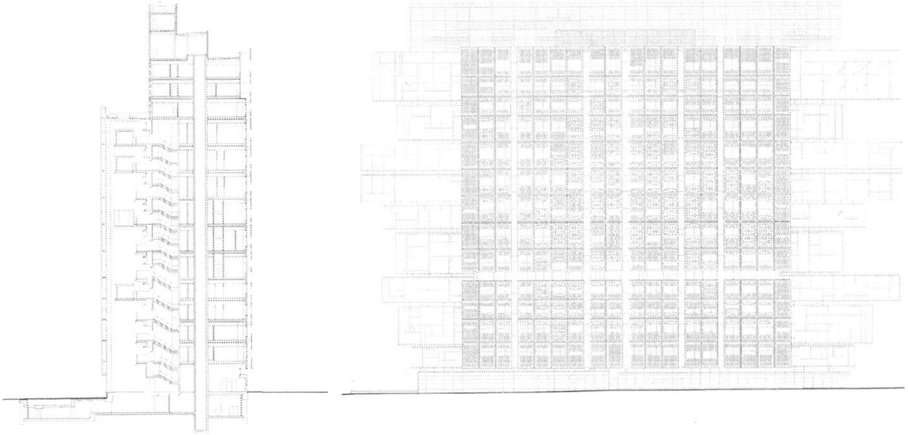

Fig. 2 Civil Justice Centre, Manchester

expressed by the differing lengths by which they cantilever out beyond the sheer vertical ends of the narrow central core, which contains the lifts and staircases. With the ends of the courtrooms projecting out a variety of distances from each end of the building the appearance is reminiscent of a ransacked double-sided filing cabinet, its drawers left in general disorder in a quite random manner.

Viewed from the street, four distinct elements become apparent. On the west side facing the new landscaped square is a huge 11-storey glazed atrium, providing daylight to the public concourses that run along its length at each storey, its soaring space populated at a number of the upper levels by waiting or consultation rooms suspended like boxes in the space between the concourses and the outer window wall.

The atrium backs onto a narrow central spine, which is predominantly solid and, rising to the full 15-storey height, acts visually as the anchor to the whole building. It is clad in a sleek aluminium panel system that provides an effective backdrop to the complexities of the atrium glazing and the courtroom area. This central zone contains the main lifts and stairs and provides access to the various meeting rooms and court spaces at each end of the building.

Covering the east face of the building is a thin veil of perforated painted aluminium panels, projected a metre forward from the main building façade. These display a variety of geometric arrangements of large openings, horizontal projecting 'light shelves' and areas of slatted screening, within a consistent overall modular panel arrangement. The effect calls to mind the traditional window shutters seen in Arabic architecture, and it performs a similar multi-functional role.

The placing of the openings responds to the needs of the spaces behind for daylight and privacy and provides a unifying visual screening of a disparate array of openings, ventilation grilles, panels and windows in the main building façade behind. Its somewhat forbidding and geometric discipline allies it to the silver panelled central core, and the two elements provide an appropriate enclosure to the slip-sliding forms of the courtrooms projecting beyond each end.

As courtrooms are essentially private and inward-looking, the need for windows is limited, and the placing of individual window elements in the courtroom walls has been disguised by incorporating them within a random pattern of panels, utilising different colours, materials and finishes. The window, wherever it occurs, is thus seen as part of an overall artistic geometric composition that is different on each face of each projecting courtroom space. The concept has been aptly described by the architect as a 'Mondrian wall'.

The construction incorporates a number of sustainable environmental features and has been awarded a BREEAM environmental rating of 'excellent'. For most of the time the building can operate on a naturally ventilated basis, utilising a complex array of horizontal and vertical plenum spaces linking one side of the building to the other. A key feature is the glazed clerestory created over the line of meeting rooms placed between the concourse and courtrooms at each level, which have an internal height lower than the general storey height on each side.

The void thus created is glazed on both sides, providing a source of borrowed daylight from the atrium into the courtrooms. It also acts as a natural ventilation plenum connecting the courtrooms on the floor above, via rising shafts venting at low level, to fresh air from louvres placed at each end of the central spine's west elevation. The predominantly north-south alignment of the building minimises the extent of south facing façade, while the 'veil' and the atrium to the east and west provide passive solar control and allow selective use of daylight in order to reduce demand for artificial lighting.

The main public entrance to the building addresses the busy public thoroughfare of Bridge Street. Judges are provided with their own separate access on the east elevation and the zoning of the floor plans provides an effective means of separating the public from the judiciary and administrative staff. This is always a key aspect for court buildings, with their need for strict separation of the public, criminal defendants and judges. At Manchester, the court is a civil rather than criminal court, so there is less complexity involved in separating the circulation, one factor which has made the multi-storey solution adopted a more viable one. From a central suite of offices the judges have their own discrete circulation and a private corridor extends along the outside face of each courtroom zone to provide direct access to each individual judge's bench.

The structure has cost in the region of £110m and the quality of the building, as evidenced by the detailing and materials, is high, with the end result worthy of its role as a highly visible and important civic institution. With this building, which has received an RIBA national award for 2008, Manchester has acquired a stunning new addition to its skyline and architectural heritage, which clearly raises the bar for others charged with creating significant new public buildings.

ARENA AND CONVENTION CENTRE, KING'S WATERFRONT, LIVERPOOL
Architect: Wilkinson Eyre

With the onset of its year as European Capital of Culture in 2008, Liverpool has acquired a major new events arena and convention centre, occupying one of the prime sites on the city's famed waterfront immediately adjacent to the historic warehouse buildings of Albert Dock and a short distance from the city's iconic Liver Building. The winning design by Wilkinson Eyre combines three very substantial conference and entertainment facilities within a long, low, quayside-hugging building. The accommodation is enclosed within a double-sided envelope whose spreading form might suggest that of an opened clamshell, placed on the quayside with its outer surfaces uppermost, sloping gently upwards and away from a central concourse inserted along the hinge-line.

The site was created by filling a disused dock and shares its location with a substantial multi-storey car park, two hotels and a small café pavilion, all placed to the rear of the site to allow the centre to dominate the waterfront vistas.

The largest of the centre's three major elements is the arena, a U-shaped space with seating for 10,000 on the three sides of the 'U', and this occupies on its own the larger of the two shell-like segments. On the opposite side of the central concourse there is a large multi-purpose hall at the lower ground floor level, tucked under the raking floor of a 1,350 seat auditorium and its foyer, which opens directly off the balcony level within the concourse. At this upper level a number of flexible meeting rooms and breakout spaces are arranged around the perimeter of the auditorium.

The potentially intrusive bulk of all these spaces has been reduced by sinking the floors of the arena and exhibition hall 1.5m below the original site level. The resulting spoil has been used to raise the level of the newly landscaped piazza around the buildings by approximately 3m, so that the main entrance to the central concourse opening directly off the piazza is at this higher level, a full storey height above the arena floor level.

The placing of the main piazza at this higher level has enabled the considerable delivery and servicing requirements of the centre to be met by placing the lorry loading and unloading bays below the piazza level, providing direct level access to both the arena and multi-purpose halls. The absence of any delivery bays at the main pedestrian level is a great help in allowing the building to be read as a stand-alone sculptural form, with no suggestion of 'front' and 'back' elevations.

Flexibility is a key requirement of such centres, to ensure that no potential event is excluded by virtue of the constraints of the layout, maximising potential revenues. The lowest level of the central concourse can be adapted and opened up to form a direct link between the main floor of the arena on one side and the multi-purpose hall on the other. By this means can be created one enormous space extending to some 200m in length and 7,000 sq. m in area that can function as a major convention space or with the multi-purpose hall section acting as a back-up space for a major event in the arena. Other combinations can be achieved through the use of bleacher seating and moveable partitions.

The raking auditorium has its own special flexibility feature in the form of two rotating drum-like spaces placed on each side at the rear of the auditorium that allow it to be reconfigured in minutes into three separate performance spaces. The revolving drums can function either as independent 250 seat mini-theatres closed off from the main hall, or be rotated to open up and work in combination with the main auditorium space.

Seen from the river the building presents a long, low horizontal profile characterised by gently sweeping bands of metal and glass cladding. These break up the ground hugging form of the two shell-like wings into three overlapping and outward leaning layers that help to break down the bulk and emphasise the horizontality of the building in its riverfront setting. Its low profile succeeds in avoiding any visual competition with the city's famous Anglican and Metropolitan cathedrals, which dominate the skyline.

The arena is circumscribed at piazza level by a public concourse for access and circulation, and the lowest of the three bands of cladding enclosing this is arranged as clear glazing, which provides exciting glimpses of the raking underside of the arena seating tiers from the piazza outside. The intermediate band utilises a delicately framed glazing system filled with semi-translucent panels featuring a sub-grid of jazzy green lines, both set at a jaunty angle that adds to the dynamism and sense of flow of the façade. At one point the gridded pattern modulates into a line of diamond-shaped window elements that add a welcome highlight to the elevations.

The uppermost layer is formed from narrow metallic cladding panels set vertically but again on the angle, acting as a kind of peaked cap and terminating the progression logically from clear to semi-clear to solid. The gently moulded plane of the roof folds into the upper layer and is covered with a grey single ply membrane. The continually changing angles and orientation of the various cladding systems generate an ever changing sequence of lighting effects and reflections as the daylight and weather conditions modulate throughout the day.

By contrast with the inward looking 'black box' approach of the major spaces, the concourse galleria, at the centre of the building, is flooded with daylight that streams in through a steel-framed vaulted roof. At the waterfront end a semicircular external balcony is provided beneath an elliptical projecting glazed canopy and from this vantage point can be gained superb views out over the Mersey. To the rear the grey granite paving of the piazza steps gently down towards the landward side, with one section arranged in a raked fan shape that might provide an interesting location for impromptu external events.

Given the huge amount of accommodation that has been placed on the site the architect has engineered a solution that does not present an intrusive barrier at the water's edge, at the same time providing an elegant and assured response to an exposed site. A number of significant events had been lined up by the time the arena element was opened and it is interesting to note that as well as receiving a RIBA regional award for 2008 it was chosen as the venue for the 2008 RIBA Stirling prize dinner. Hopefully the centre will go on to provide the citizens of Liverpool with a vibrantly successful commercial and cultural programme for the future, far beyond 2008.

DESIGN CENTRE, BERKHAMSTED COLLEGIATE SCHOOL, HERTFORDSHIRE
Architect: Short & Associates

Berkhamsted Collegiate School was founded as a grammar school in the 16th century. Housed originally in a range of Tudor buildings, right in the centre of the town, the school has grown incrementally over the years, with late Victorian Gothic and neo-Georgian insertions, and now boasts this rather quirky new addition, providing a dining hall and art and design facilities. Short & Associates won a limited competition held in 2003 with a design that follows a strong environmental agenda and responds cleverly to its site and the immediate context of the town with a highly articulated composition using small-scale elements and traditional materials.

The site is a tapering plot of land at the north end of the grammar school campus, defined by Castle Street to the east and Mill Street to the west. The accommodation has been divided into two wings, each one aligned with one of the two street frontages, creating a tapering courtyard space between, widening towards the south end where a footpath approaching from the campus to the south passes over the landscaped banks of the river Bulbourne. The two wings are joined together in the centre of the courtyard by a circular rotunda that acts like a hinge and cleverly resolves the question of how to align the access and circulation requirements across a tapering space. Two further circular drums have been inserted in the west wing either side of the rotunda, one containing a staircase, the other accommodating lavatories at the ground and first floors and an office at the second floor.

The rotunda is open at the ground floor, a ring of slender tubular steel columns supporting a circular ambulatory and display space at the first floor, the doughnut shape leaving an octagonal central void and a clear view of the sky above. The display spaces have been created around the inner face of the ring by the insertion of small projecting walls at each point of the octagon, thus creating a series of shallow alcoves with sufficient room left for students to circulate around the outside.

The west wing is divided into two large rooms at each floor level separated by a service core of a lift and escape stair, and these function as meeting room and teaching spaces for art and design technology. The east, the wider of the two wings, contains the substantial dining hall at ground level. At first floor level a range of teaching rooms is provided for sculpture and ceramics, art history and photographic studies, each with a generous display of east-facing windows set into a tile-hung gable, reflecting the 'room-in-the-roof' volumes of the studio spaces behind.

The external appearance of the building is driven by the decision to give each component part of the building its own individual roof form, coupled with the expression of the underlying natural ventilation system as a number of independent stacks rising above the general roof levels. The end result is a very complicated three-dimensional array of gables, pitched roofs, dormer windows and vent stacks that breaks down the apparent bulk of the building and enables it to bed down well in its immediate context. While the ground floor is expressed in facing brick walls, the remainder of the cladding is carried out in plain clay tile-hanging and roofing, resulting in a tour-de-force of this particular craft. Even the quirky ventilation chimneys, with their tiny pitched roofs and banks of louvres along each long side, are tile-hung.

The east elevation is broken down into three central gabled sections, with the roof to the bay at each end set traditionally to present a gable to the flanking elevations. The tile-hung upper parts project forward in a series of shallow steps, providing the opportunity for fresh air inlet through a perforated soffit panel into a plenum at first floor level as well as a degree of shading to the upper level windows.

Recent changes to the acoustic regulations for schools have attempted to address the problem of excess noise, from outside or from other classrooms, but these have had an unfortunate knock-on effect on ventilation, to the extent that in many instances it is not possible to provide opening windows. If air conditioning is to be avoided then passive ventilation systems such as those deployed here need to be developed, with attention to acoustic attenuation at the air entry and exit points.

Here, each of the main spaces effectively has its own passive ventilation system, with fresh air inlets at low level driven by the stack effect of the tall air chimneys rising above the roof level. At ground level the fresh air inlets are organised as banks of square fire-clay sections set into the brick walls, providing an air supply to a plenum unit fitted with damper, acoustic baffle and a heater battery. First floor rooms have a similar arrangement with air intake through a perforated soffit panel into a plenum unit sited underneath the lowest bank of windows. Exhaust plenums are created at high level either in the pitched internal ceiling spaces or directly into the vertical air chimneys, which are made high enough to create the desired pressure drop and consequent flow of air. While the system is complicated and requires careful co-ordination with the building envelope, and the rising ducts from the ground floor take up valuable space at first floor, the end result is a commendably energy efficient ventilation system capable of close environmental control.

The brick and tile-hung elevations, broken down into recognisable and domestically scaled components, are reminiscent of much vernacular building in the south of England. This is leavened with a nod towards some of the typical stylistic features of the Arts and Crafts movement and topped off with the rather more exotic forms of the ventilation stacks, which for some might suggest the appearance of a series of dovecotes but which actually have more in common functionally with the wind towers of middle eastern houses. The architects have worked hard to turn the prevailing environmental constraints to good advantage and the school has, as a result, gained a charming, if idiosyncratic, addition to its very mixed architectural heritage. This will no doubt serve it well in the future as the cost of energy soars and buildings are required to achieve an ever smaller carbon footprint.

AWARDS

RIBA AWARDS 2007

The Stirling Prize – Museum of Modern Literature, Marbach am Neckar, Germany; David Chipperfield Architects

THE STIRLING SHORTLIST

The Savill Building Visitor Centre, Windsor Great Park; Glenn Howells Architects

Casa Da Musica Concert Hall, Porto, Portugal; Office for Metropolitan Architecture

America's Cup Building, Valencia, Spain; David Chipperfield Architects

Young Vic Theatre, London; Haworth Tompkins

Dresden Station Redevelopment, Dresden, Germany; Foster & Partners

SPECIAL AWARDS

The Manser Medal – The Salt House, Essex; Alison Brooks Architects

The Stephen Lawrence Prize – Wooda (drama space), Cornwall; David Sheppard Architects

The RIBA Sustainability Award – Upper Twyford Barn, Hereford; Architype

The RIBA Inclusive Design Award – Portland College New Learning Centre, Mansfield; Patel Taylor

Crown Estate Conservation Award – SS Great Britain and Historic Dockyard, Bristol; Alec French Architects

RIBA Client of the Year Award – Derwent London

RIBA Sorrell Schools Award – The Marlowe Academy, Ramsgate

BRITISH CONSTRUCTION INDUSTRY AWARDS 2007

Prime Minister's Better Public Building Award – Dalby Forest Visitor Centre, North Yorkshire; White Design

The Lubetkin Prize – Casa Kike, Costa Rica; Gianni Botsford Architects

RIBA Client of the Year Award – Coin Street Community Builders

ART

Ossian Ward

WHAT CREDIT CRUNCH?

As world stock markets and confidence in financial and banking institutions went into freefall, the art world appeared to be heading resolutely the other way. Hungry for a doom story, commentators and journalists were almost willing on an art market recession, spurred on by a 50 per cent fall in Sotheby's share price over the second half of the year. However, despite much feverish hand-wringing in the press, a rise in auction house debt was put down to the increase in the value of works for sale and the greater risk of guaranteeing high returns for clients. Against all trends, the hammer prices for sales of Impressionism, modern and contemporary art kept going through the roof: the February sales were up 50 per cent with Francis Bacon pictures going for £26m and £30m a piece. Even Old Masters held their own at around £100m, but couldn't keep up with the rampant contemporary art sales that clocked up £250m between Christie's, Sothebys and Phillips de Pury & Co.

With no sign of a bursting bubble in the £8.5bn UK art economy, attention shifted onto sustainability of demand for such stratospherically expensive works of art. One sign of London's strength over New York was the sudden influx of sellers from the USA, many of whom came to avoid the weakening dollar. Another was the change in nationalities of the buyers, with new mega-collectors emerging from cash-rich nations such as India, China and Russia. Although the auction houses had long been courting big Arab spenders, especially Sheikh Saud Al-Thani, it was the Russian energy oligarch Roman Abramovich who made the headlines by purchasing Lucian Freud's portrait of Sue Tilley – *Benefits Supervisor Sleeping* – for £17.2m, achieving the highest price ever for a work by a living artist. Abramovich, the billionaire owner of Chelsea Football Club, subsequently went on a £60m art spree, his sudden interest perhaps precipitated by the influence of his girlfriend, Daria 'Dasha' Zhukova who opened her own gallery in Moscow with a lavish party featuring pop singer Amy Winehouse.

In addition to a successful Russian sale at Christie's London, which notched up a record for the category in Konstantin Somov's *The Rainbow* of 1927, the admiration between countries clearly went both ways as London-based collector Charles Saatchi made a deal to show some of his works on rotating display in a dedicated room at the prestigious Hermitage Museum in St Petersburg. Saatchi had a relatively quiet year as he waited for his new gallery in Chelsea to be completed for an October 2008 unveiling, but other collectors began opening up their own spaces in London, most notably Anita Zabludowicz's 176 Project Space in Camden. The Mancunian collector Frank Cohen, dubbed 'the Saatchi of the North', also began exhibiting his contemporary art holdings in a warehouse space near Wolverhampton.

HIRSTS MAKE THE WORLD GO ROUND

Having shaken off accusations of plagiarism for his diamond-studded skull *For the Love of God,* Damien Hirst took his career and growing brand name to new heights – designing a collection for Levi's and opening up his first art shop in Marylebone which sells the wares of his print and book publishing arm, Other Criteria. The announcement that he was to hold an auction of his own work at Sotheby's in September 2008, without any gallery involvement whatsoever, showed how Hirst's once controversial art was fast becoming a nakedly commercial and corporate enterprise.

Christie's purchase of an entire London gallery, the Haunch of Venison, made waves in the gallery community. The acquisition will enable Christie's to compete for primary market business and increase its non-auction sales. Haunch of Venison was subsequently denied entry to the major art fairs including the Frieze Art Fair in Regent's Park due to a perceived conflict of interest, but was in discussion with the Royal Academy to take over the former Museum of Mankind for its new headquarters. The opposite fortune befell one of London's oldest fine art dealerships, Agnew's, as it sold up its Old Bond Street space to the Italian fashion house Etro, after occupying the same space since 1877.

DIRECTOR COMINGS AND GOINGS

Strangely, one of the biggest surprises of the year came when it was announced that one of the UK's leading cultural institutions would *not* lose its director. The British Museum's Neil MacGregor committed himself to another five years at the helm, at least until after the 2012 Olympic Games, after deflecting rumours that he was in line for the recently vacated post at the Metropolitan Museum of Art in New York. He was also named Chairman of World Collections by the then-culture secretary James Purnell and put in charge of a new global scheme to widen exposure of London's wonderful collections (including the Tate, the V&A, the British Library, the Natural History Museum and the Royal Botanic Gardens in Kew) to the rest of the world.

John Tusa, who gave up his position as managing director of the Barbican, was named chairman of the V&A, while the beleaguered Baltic Centre for Contemporary Art in Gateshead lost yet another director when Peter Doroshenko stepped down after being accused of promoting a 'climate of fear' among employees. The Baltic was also in the news when police seized a photograph by American artist Nan Goldin (from the collection of Elton John) on the eve of its exhibition, under suspicion that it could be violating child pornography laws.

After a long period of uncertainty without a director, the National Gallery hired back a former curator of Renaissance art, Nicholas Penny, to take over the reins. He left his post at the National Gallery in Washington and immediately set out his stall by rubbishing the importance of so-called blockbuster exhibitions and by denying that the National Gallery would ever break its dateline cut-off of 1900 in order to show modern and contemporary art, despite their commercial allure.

Penny's predecessor, Charles Saumarez Smith, began his new tenure at the Royal Academy of Arts just as the long-standing Exhibitions Secretary, Sir Norman

Rosenthal, was about to bow out, after 31 years of exemplary service. His final exhibition, From Russia: French and Russian Art Masterpieces of 1870–1925 was to be one of the most spectacular (and most fraught) of his distinguished time at the RA. At the eleventh hour, Russian officials withdrew the 120 or so works borrowed from the State Hermitage Museum, the Tretyakov Gallery and the Russian Museum for From Russia, citing their dissatisfaction with the UK's anti-seizure laws that might allow disgruntled heirs of the previous owners of many paintings to begin legal claims for their return. There was also a background of worsening Anglo-Russian political relations; first came the scandal of the poisoned spy Alexander Litvinenko, followed by the Kremlin's decision to close the British Council's two regional offices in St Petersburg and Yekaterinburg. Early in January, the necessary legislation was rushed through British parliament, allowing 'immunity from seizure' for the masterpieces by Matisse, Renoir, Cézanne, Gauguin and others to be shown from 26 January to 18 April. A group of descendants of the collectors Sergei Shchukin and Ivan Morosov whose works made up the RA's show, did attempt to lay claim to the proceeds of ticket sales, but Sir Norman's last major show was nevertheless regarded as a fitting end to his tenure.

POLICY MATTERS

A further reduction in lottery grants for the arts to a total of £20m (down from £80m and then £40m in 2007) was announced and the maximum amount for any one project was reduced to £5m. The freeze on dozens of Arts Council grants to UK art organisations was also due in large part to the impending 2012 Olympics, although the Department for Culture, Media, and Sport then promised that 20 new country-wide initiatives would be introduced to turn the UK into the 'the world's creative hub'. The government's plans were woolly to say the least, but a new film centre, a creative festivals season and a proposal to turn the Olympic Park into a national attraction after the games, were all mooted.

All endeavours moved instead towards encouraging private donation and how the level of charitable funding could be raised above its woeful fraction of the annual £9.5bn given by individuals, which was hovering at pre-1992 levels for the arts sector. A Campaign for Private Giving was launched and attractive breaks in inheritance tax rules were bandied about in order to encourage donors to posthumously bequeath their collections to the nation, with the added carrot of concessions during their lifetimes. One step in the right direction was a significant climb-down over a proposed raise in taxes for all non-domiciled residents in Britain – the so-called non-doms. Foreign-born individuals were threatened with an annual, non-negotiable tax of £30,000 for undisclosed international earnings, but the danger of alienating rich collectors and philanthropists from settling was largely averted when it was revealed that art works coming into Britain for public display would not be taxed at all.

Artists began campaigning for legislative reform to the already controversial 2006 Droit de Suite bill, asking to receive royalties on their works bought and sold, for a further 70 years after their death, a deal already enforced for writers and musicians. The sum would be capped at 4 per cent of the sale to a maximum of €12,500 (£9,580), but would obviously impact most on future auction sales, hence the industry's initial displeasure at the idea.

MUSEUMS MATTER

Despite the guarantee of free admissions until 2011 and the threat of an economic dip, some museums bucked the belt-tightening trend by extending ever higher and wider. The Whitechapel Gallery advanced in its reconstruction, with a schedule to reopen in early 2009 and the National Museum of Scotland in Edinburgh partially closed for a £46.4m renovation. Tate Modern managed to raise £70m (about a third) of its total for the new TM2 building, which is to be designed by the architects of the original scheme Jacques Herzog and Pierre de Meuron. With a permeable deadline of 2012 in place, the design also shifted slightly halfway through the year, from a ziggurat of tumbling glass boxes to a sturdier-looking and ecologically sound perforated brick structure, with the existing power plant's oil tanks forming the base from which the new 11-storey tower would rise.

Architecture fans were not so fortunate when Pritzker Prize-winning British-Iraqi architect Zaha Hadid's first permanent building in London was scrapped due to a lack of funds. The Architecture Foundation's new triangular headquarters were due to be built on Southwark Street just behind the TM2's new East Wing development, but despite the setback, Hadid was still on course to have her increasingly expensive Aquatic Centre ready in time for the Olympics. While Hadid's failed project stirred echoes of the V&A's 2004 failure to get money and permission to realise Daniel Libeskind's ambitious Spiral Project, London does get to see a construction by a world-famous 'starchitect' every summer, with Olafur Eliasson and Frank Gehry designing the Serpentine Pavilion in Kensington Gardens in 2007 and 2008. Gwyn Miles, who headed the ill-fated Spiral at the V&A, had much more success transforming the defunct Hermitage Rooms and Gilbert Collection into contemporary art, design and photography galleries. The south side of Somerset House was freed up, thanks also to the departure of the remaining Inland Revenue officers, for the inauguration of the Embankment Galleries with a slick exhibition of fashion and architecture crossovers called Skin + Bones (24 April–10 August 2008).

The collections of the National Galleries of Scotland and Tate were significantly swelled after a agreement to secure 725 works owned by former art dealer Anthony d'Offay was finalised. The works by Jeff Koons, Diane Arbus, Gerhard Richter, Joseph Beuys and many others will be displayed in 50 Artist Rooms that will be jointly owned and managed for the nation, but most importantly should tour across the UK to smaller galleries and regional museums. Although valued at over £125m, d'Offay reduced the cost, roughly to the historic amount he would have paid for the entire collection, at £26.5m.

CRIMES AND DISCOVERIES

Although one homeless man took a few swipes at a picture of Samuel Johnson in the National Portrait Gallery, it was the staff who were to blame next door, where National Gallery handlers dropped a portion of Domenico Beccafumi's *Marcia* while removing it from an exhibition in January.

Much more embarrassing was the revelation that a family in Bolton had duped numerous galleries over many years by forging at least 120 works – including Anglo Saxon rings and Assyrian reliefs – which had been bought and valued at millions of pounds. Although members of the family were apprehended in 2003 and in 2005, they were only sentenced after a court hearing in 2007, when Shaun Greenhalgh received four years in prison, while his mother and father, both in their 80s, were given suspended sentences. The case was similar to that of John Myatt, jailed for forgery in 1999, who was for the first time given an exhibition of his copies, called The Masters Collection in a Birmingham Gallery. A former public school teacher, Jeremy Broadway, was also convicted of fakery, passing off his ceramics as the work of Bernard Leach and Lucie Rie.

The art world loves a discovery as much as a scandal, so it was good news that Edvard Munch's *The Scream* was finally returned to an Oslo museum after being stolen in 2004, while in this country, the British Library stumbled across a John Constable sketch that was tucked into the pages of one of the catalogues of his work. Similarly, a watercolour by Dante Gabriel Rossetti and an oil painting by Sir Edward Coley Burne-Jones were fortuitously discovered in manuscript curator Jean Preston's Oxford home after she died. An even more unlikely setting for a masterpiece was a small auction house in Leicestershire, where it was rumoured that a picture sold for £205,000 was actually a Titian, painted in Venice *c.*1510 (with a market value nearer £5m). Not a discovery, but a close shave: the Tate secured the acquisition of JMW Turner's watercolour *The Blue Rigi,* shortly before the export deferral deadline of 20 March. The price was £4.95m making it the most expensive painting ever bought by the gallery.

PEOPLE AND PRIZES

While American celebrity photographer Annie Leibovitz photographed the Queen, a British performance artist caused no little consternation by eating one of Her Majesty's favourite creatures, a Corgi. Mark McGowan, who had previously eaten a swan, did his stunt live on air to raise awareness of the RSPCA, or so he claimed. David Hockney too was in campaigning mood, helping not only to retain Turner's *Blue Rigi,* but also coming out in defence of fellow smokers who were being banned from lighting up in public places. Hockney's friend and Pop Art contemporary R. B. Kitaj died on 21 October in California, while the suicide of one of Damien Hirst's YBA colleagues, Angus Fairhurst, on the last day of his London show aged just 41, was a shock to the art world.

The demise of one of the UK's countless art prizes, the Beck's Futures award, was not much lamented, while Mark Wallinger was generally accepted as the rightful winner of this year's Turner prize (staged in Liverpool to coincide with their Capital of Culture celebrations), mainly in recognition of his ingenious *State Britain* installation that recreated Brian Haw's Parliament Square peace protest.

The first Northern art prize of £15,000 was awarded to artist duo Karen Guthrie and Nina Pope while the Finnish photographer Esko Mannikko took home the 2008 Deutsche Börse photography prize. Steve McQueen was given the honour of representing the UK at the forthcoming Venice Biennale in 2009, although his controversial set of stamps depicting more than 100 troops who had died in Iraq, *Queen and Country* was officially declined by Royal Mail.

PUBLIC ART

Mega-scale public art came to the fore this year and not just because Antony Gormley's *Angel of the North* was voted the most recognisable landmark in Britain, beating competition from the likes of St Paul's Cathedral. A new scheme to create a similar monument for the south got underway with shortlisted artists Mark Wallinger, Rachel Whiteread, Richard Deacon, Christopher le Brun, and Daniel Buren producing proposals for the Ebbsfleet Valley that ranged from a giant horse to a blinking signal tower.

The temporary sculptures on the fourth plinth in Trafalgar Square briefly came under threat from new London mayor Boris Johnson whose pre-election promise to install a permanent statue to honour British war hero Keith Park was thankfully dropped after he won. Instead the two designs by Yinka Shonibare and Antony Gormley – respectively a ship in a bottle and a platform for members of the public – will go up on the empty pedestal in 2009.

Not all public sculpture was welcomed, indeed a hideously huge embracing couple at the new St Pancras Eurostar station was just one recent commission that came under fire from curators and officials in a list of 'horrors and Frankenstein monster memorials', according to Tim Knox, director of the Sir John Soane's Museum. The venerable artist Anthony Caro couldn't find a home for his 100-ton *Millbank Steps,* despite offering it as gift to Westminster council, who said they had reached saturation point with around 300 public works of art. In Scotland, a row over what kind of sculpture should sit outside Holyrood caused the director of the Henry Moore Foundation, Richard Calvocoressi, and artist Alison Watt to resign from the presiding body. *The Lion of Scotland* by Edinburgh-based Ronald Rae was deemed of insufficient quality by the outspoken panel members, but received popular support from the Scottish MPs.

EXHIBITIONS

Antony Gormley raised his profile by placing dozens of cast clones of himself all along the London skyline for his exhibition at the Hayward Gallery (17 May–19 August 2007). The centrepiece of the show was a new work, *Blind Light,* which created an impenetrable fog or cloud of mist, around which viewers happily stumbled and meandered. American curator Ralph Rugoff had a good first year in charge of the Hayward, overseeing the 40th-birthday celebrations and putting on stunning shows of painting (The Painting of Modern Life, 4 October–3 December 2007) and of architectural interventions by artists (Psycho Buildings, 28 May–25 August 2008). Not exactly coming under the rubrik of public art, but an unprecedented outdoor show of 28 large-scale works by Henry Moore drew visitors to the Royal Botanic Gardens at Kew throughout the winter and spring months (15 September 2007–30 March 2008).

The most highly anticipated exhibition was certainly the British Museum's First Emperor: China's Terracotta Army (13 September 2007–6 April 2008), which attracted such large numbers (over 800,000) that the museum extended its opening hours until midnight, even going all-night before the show's end. The 20 life-size terracotta warriors were the highlight, borrowed from the 2,200-year-old burial site of Emperor Qin Shihuan at Xi'an. This blockbuster went head-to-head with a travelling Tutankhamun show in London at the former Millennium Dome site, now rebranded as the O_2 Arena (22 November 2007–30 August 2008). Presided over by antiquities chief, Zahi Hawass, the Egyptian extravaganza was also a success, but deemed too commercial and tacky by many commentators.

The Barbican also divided opinion with its lurid autumn offering, Seduced: Sex from Antiquity to Now (12 October 2007–27 January 2008) but clearly pushed the thematic envelope too far in its contemporary art grouping titled The Martian Museum of Terrestrial Art

(16 March–18 May 2008). Weirder still is the work of American filmmaker Matthew Barney, who not only had his first major London solo show at the Serpentine Gallery (20 September–11 November 2007), but resolutely stole the show at the first ever Manchester International Festival (28 June–15 July 2007). *Il Tempo del Postino* was a performance art stage show including contributions from other well-known artists such as Douglas Gordon and Carsten Höller, but all eyes were on Barney's 45-minute procession of female contortionists, on-stage urination, a live bull and the artist himself wearing a dog on his head.

Liverpool also made a splash with its year as Capital of Culture, the artistic highlight being an expensive loan exhibition of works by Viennese maestro, Gustav Klimt (30 May–31 August 2008).

Tate Modern's packed autumn programme included a show of nonagenarian female artist Louise Bourgeois (10 October 2007–20 January 2008) as well as a new Turbine Hall commission by Colombian artist Doris Salcedo, who dug an enormous crack out of the concrete floor, leaving a rupture the length of the gallery's transept. The media focused more on members of the public who got their foot stuck in the split than on the dark meaning behind the work 'shibboleth', which was a comment on the underclasses of society who are not generally noticed or involved in cultural life.

The best Old Master show of the year was the RA's show of Lucas Cranach the Elder (8 March—8 June 2008) although the medievalist managed to court debate after the London Underground banished his 1532 painting of a nude Venus (only to later relent). It was also revealed that Cranach was one of Hitler's favourite artists.

If the Old Masters are on the wane, then it seems that the superstardom of one graffiti artist in particular could only grow stronger. The shadowy *plein-air* dauber known as Banksy, whose identity was supposedly revealed in a Sunday paper, saw his work fetch a total of £455,000 at a Bonham's auction but also kept his street credentials by organising an impromptu exhibition in a tunnel near Waterloo station, called the Cans Festival.

BROADCASTING

Steve Clarke

TELEVISION

As fears of the British economy sliding into recession alarmed the public and policy-makers alike, broadcasting organisations were forced to tighten their belts during the year under review. In the autumn the BBC announced an economy drive that would lead to the loss of 1,800 jobs. Programme budgets were cut and the new, somewhat optimistic mantra from Television Centre was 'fewer, bigger, better' programmes. In April Channel 4 posted its first loss since 1992. As for ITV, a sceptical City wondered if the broadcaster's so-called 'turnaround plan' would deliver the desired results. By the summer, ITV's share price sank to an all-time low amidst predictions of a tough advertising market igniting speculation regarding a possible takeover. Even pay-TV giant Sky was not immune to the harsh economic climate; its controversial 17.9 per cent stake in ITV, under scrutiny from regulators, led to a £112m loss when in February the company announced results for the first half of its financial year.

Against this background the official countdown to digital switchover, due to be completed by 2012, commenced on 17 October when the analogue signal for BBC Two was turned off in Whitehaven, Cumbria. The significance of this was more symbolic than real because around 85 per cent of homes in the UK already received digital services on their main TV sets. Moreover, the long-delayed launch of Freesat in May, backed by the BBC and ITV, was designed partly to ensure that those parts of the UK unable to receive digital terrestrial signals were covered by this new service. More important in terms of the impact on viewing habits was the relaunch of the BBC on-demand catch-up service, the iPlayer, on Christmas Day. This enables audiences to watch the past week's BBC TV programmes online. By March viewers had made 17.2 million requests for BBC shows. 'Audiences of all ages embraced it quickly', claimed the BBC director-general Mark Thompson. However, he insisted there was no evidence to suggest the iPlayer was taking audiences away from the BBC's traditional broadcasting outlets, but it was too early to draw any meaningful conclusions.

During 2007–8 there were indications that despite the onward march of digital media, traditional network television was staging a comeback. Britain's most popular channel, BBC One, recorded its highest Christmas Day figures for four years. Dominating the list of most watched programmes were such warhorses as *EastEnders*, *Doctor Who* and the one-off return of 1970s sitcom *To the Manor Born*. The figures provided further evidence for the growing popularity of shows that appealed to family audiences and suggested that the long-predicted decline of mainstream channels was premature. 'The simple fact is that television remains the dominant medium, despite all the communication wonders that technology offers', observed veteran media writer Raymond Snoddy in *The Independent* in July. It was the case, however, that an increasing number of TV dramas were failing to win big ratings; in the spring ITV's much-hyped *Rock Rivals* only managed an audience of around three million, but flagship entertainment like *Doctor Who, The X Factor, Strictly Come Dancing, Britain's Got Talent* and *The Apprentice* continued to generate very healthy audiences. And premium sport, be it the Rugby World Cup final (13.1 million viewers), the Champions League final between Chelsea and Manchester United (in excess of 14.5 million), or the longest Wimbledon men's final in history (over 12.5 million), reaffirmed television's unique status as a mass medium.

BBC AND ITV FOUND WANTING

Following the phone-in scandals of the previous year, the main terrestrial broadcasters sought to avoid any repetition of these transgressions; BBC staff, including senior management, were sent on so-called 'safeguarding trust' seminars, designed to instil a greater sense of ethical awareness. In May media regulator OFCOM fined ITV £5.7m for abusing premium rate phone services in shows such as *Ant and Dec's Saturday Night Takeaway*. It was the biggest fine in ITV's 53-year history but some commentators felt the network had got off too easily. 'For a company that's delivering to its shareholders £150–200m a year of free cash flow . . . this is on the pathetic end of not very much', broadcasting analyst Steve Hewlett told the BBC. Two months later the BBC was fined £400,000 – another record financial penalty – by OFCOM for breaches of the broadcasting code in a range of programmes that had featured phone-in quizzes across TV and radio. Among these were *Children In Need, Comic Relief* and BBC 6 Music's *Liz Kershaw Show;* the latter received the biggest fine, £115,000, because OFCOM said it was 'extremely concerned by the repeated instances of premeditated, deliberate deception . . . spanning nearly 17 months'.

DOCTOR WHO DEFIES GRAVITY – AGAIN

During the period under review few TV dramas, with the notable exception of big-ticket soaps like *Coronation Street* and *EastEnders*, could rival the perennial popularity of *Doctor Who*. The fourth series of the revived classic bowed out with almost 9.5 million viewers in July as fans were kept guessing over actor David Tennant's future – or lack of it – as the intrepid time traveller starred in a specially extended 65-minute episode. Overall weekend drama on the main channels was more successful than the weekday equivalent. Encouraged by BBC One hits such as *Doctor Who* and *Robin Hood*, ITV1's special-effects laden Saturday evening family drama *Primeval* proved popular; on Sundays Morse spin-off *Lewis* continued to be a good draw. In recent years ITV1 has avoided showing American drama series because home-made shows perform much better, but in the winter *Pushing Daisies*, a quirky show about a man who can bring the dead back to life simply by touching their bodies, starring Anna Friel, was given a peak-time Saturday night slot on ITV1. The show performed adequately and is due to return next year.

If some critics despaired at the BBC for not screening more edgy, contemporary drama, fans of period adaptations had plenty to choose from. An undoubted highlight was BBC One's autumn treat *Cranford*, based on Elizabeth Gaskell's stories and starring Judi Dench and Eileen Atkins; the latter's performance was good enough to win the septuagenarian actress her first BAFTA in a lengthy career. As Nancy Banks-Smith wrote in *The Guardian*: 'The power of her performance is all the more remarkable considering the company she keeps. The gang's all here. Judi Dench with that heartbreaking catch in her voice, Jim Carter, Imelda Staunton, Francesca Annis looking deliciously delicious, Julia McKenzie and Julia Sawalha.' Adaptations of *Lark Rise To Candleford* and *Sense and Sensibility* also won approval, but a Christmas serialisation of the already over-adapted *Oliver Twist* left critics underwhelmed.

Not every reviewer approved of another literary adaptation, albeit a contemporary crime story, *The No. 1 Ladies' Detective Agency*, directed by the greatly admired Anthony Minghella, who unexpectedly died days before the film's transmission on Easter Monday. Writing in *The Guardian* Sam Wollaston derided this interpretation of Alexander McCall Smith's novel, co-written by the ubiquitous Richard Curtis, as 'twee, quaint, shallow, possibly patronising'. Others, however, welcomed the opportunity to see an uplifting version of Africa that attempted to rise above media stereotypes – and *The No. 1 Ladies' Detective Agency* achieved a more than decent audience as 6.3 million people tuned in.

Throughout the period under review the main channels' attempts to find a new hit 9pm weekday returning drama series were largely fruitless. There were exceptions such as BBC One's *Mistresses*, a contemporary story about the intertwined lives of four women. This built a loyal following. Another hit was *Ashes to Ashes*, the follow-up to *Life on Mars*. The BBC One show was set in the 1980s and starred Philip Glenister and Keeley Hawes, but success on this scale was unusual. 'The networks' season launches have been peppered with hopeful new dramas that have come and gone almost without trace', opined Neil Midgley writing in the *Daily Telegraph*.

Critics were divided over the merits of Stephen Poliakoff's latest BBC offerings *Joe's Palace*, *Capturing Mary* and *A Real Summer*, but visually and in terms of the very high standard of acting they contained, their inclusion in prime slots on BBC One and Two offered some useful ammunition against those convinced that the BBC was too populist for its own good. In common with many a screenwriter, Poliakoff was scathing about the organisation's priorities. He told *The Independent* in November: 'There's not enough creative energy at the BBC. There are far too many people on quite big salaries who have no power to get anything on screen. Until that is unlocked in some way, the place is going to be in perpetual crisis. It's in the very difficult area of civil service meets showbiz.'

ITV'S RELAUNCH RUNS AGROUND

ITV1's attempts to revamp its schedule in January, bolstered by the return of *News At Ten*, was hyped as a turning point in the troubled broadcaster's fortunes, but the performance of the new line-up failed to live up to expectations. As a result the former BBC1 controller Peter Fincham, forced to resign from the corporation the previous autumn following the publication of a report into his handling of a documentary about the Queen, was hired as ITV's new director of television. There were, however, some signs that ITV1 was trying to be more inventive. Critics praised the ambition of the network's two new linked dramas *Moving Wallpaper* and *Echo Beach*, but expressed doubts about their execution. *Echo Beach* was a soap opera set in a Cornish holiday resort, while *Moving Wallpaper* was a comedy drama based on the machinations involved in the making of the former. Both shows failed to win broad appeal; *Echo Beach* was axed but *Moving Wallpaper* was re-commissioned for a second series.

For a grittier take on the world, viewers could turn to Channel 4. Following two high-profile series disasters – *Goldplated* and *Cape Wrath* – the broadcaster received plaudits for its edgy one-off dramas, *Boy A*, about a child murderer, and Peter Kosminsky's *Britz*. The two-parter examined the radicalisation of a young British Muslim from two different and contrasting viewpoints. The second series of Channel 4's teen drama *Skins* confirmed that the station had succeeded in making a series that was a genuine hit with the demanding and far from loyal teenage audience who were apparently abandoning TV for social networking sites and video games. Meanwhile transmission of Channel 4's American dramas, including *Desperate Housewives* and *Ugly Betty*, were disrupted by the three-month strike by Hollywood writers over payments for new media rights. This was settled in February, too late to film fresh episodes of these shows in time for their inclusion in the winter Channel 4 schedule. While a lot of British TV series drama found it difficult to win viewers, let alone critical admirers, the cult success of the year was *The Wire*, an amoral account of crime in Baltimore shown by FX in Britain. *Sunday Times* commentator Bryan Appleyard praised the programme's 'harsh and dirty realism'. Linking it with two other American TV series, *Dexter* and *The Shield*, he claimed that these shows demonstrated why the USA is 'uniquely capable of making and sustaining the best television in the world'.

GAVIN AND STACEY REINVENT THE SITCOM

If American programme makers consistently raised the bar in long-running drama series, the year under review proved once again that in comedy the British were in a class of their own. The outstanding success was the second series of *Gavin and Stacey*, the multi award-winning BBC Three sitcom co-written by Ruth Jones and James Corden, who also star in the show. '*Gavin and Stacey* is both a welcome throwback to the pre-Gervais days of accessible comedies with wide appeal and a knowing no-laughter-track critique of modern sexual manners', opined Bruce Dessau in *The Times*. Politically the show was of enormous importance to the BBC since its success helped deflect the views of high-profile in-house critics like John Humphrys and Jeremy Paxman. They argued that youth-focused BBC Three should be axed in order to claw back budgets for news and current affairs because there were already enough rival stations providing similar material, but Mark Thompson said that distinctive comedy was as much a key ingredient of the organisation's public service purposes as news and current affairs.

During the autumn BBC One gave the British-Iranian comic Omid Djalili his own Saturday night show, but not everyone was impressed. 'Going for a Dave Allen mix of sketches and gags, it ended up misfiring on both counts', observed the *Daily Telegraph*. Perhaps the TV sketch show looked increasingly tired, a criticism levelled at *That Mitchell and Webb Look*. Screened by BBC Two in the winter, the consensus was that David Mitchell and Robert Webb were far funnier in Channel 4's *Peep Show*, in which they left the writing duties to others. ITV's new investment in comedy was unlikely to pay instant dividends, but the network's attempt to reinvent *Spitting Image* for the 21st century in the form of *Headcases*, a topical satirical show using computer generated images, was a brave move to widen the scope of its entertainment shows.

It was a bleak year for children's television. ITV stopped commissioning children's programmes because they were no longer considered profitable while annual budget cuts to the tune of 5 per cent at the BBC increased fears for the future of British produced children's programmes. As the BBC annual report noted in the summer: 'The CBBC channel is now almost the only source of new UK originated content for 6–12 year olds in news, factual, drama and entertainment.' Earlier in the year OFCOM published an analysis demonstrating that while children had never experienced so much choice – some 25 channels – there was very little new British programming available. Moreover, spending by the main broadcasters on children's shows had halved in real terms over a decade. Nevertheless policy makers seemed reluctant to intervene.

In the ongoing debate about television's future in the digital era OFCOM announced a second review of public service broadcasting in the autumn. Arguably in this context provision of news and current affairs programmes was seen as the real litmus test of a network's credentials. Media commentators welcomed *News at Ten's* return to ITV1's schedules in January. But the move wasn't quite all it was cracked up to be. The programme was broadcast on four instead of five evenings a week and within months of the launch speculation began to emerge over Sir Trevor McDonald's long-term commitment to the programme. More worryingly still, while most reviewers praised the programme, the better-resourced BBC was virtually guaranteed to win any ratings battle. On the first night the two news bulletins went head-to-head, *News at Ten* secured a very healthy 3.8 million viewers compared to the BBC's 4.9 million for the *Ten O'Clock News*. By the summer, the gap had widened considerably; on some evenings more than twice as many people chose the *Ten O'Clock News* in preference to *News at Ten*.

THE 'NATASHA EFFECT' IS GOOD NEWS FOR FIVE

Throughout the year under review Five struggled to compete against its more generously funded rivals, but the re-launch of its nightly news show, *Five News*, in February hosted by the former BBC presenter Natasha Kaplinsky, impressed observers by virtue of its viewer-friendly style which included reports from members of the audience. The so-called 'Natasha effect' led to a 43 per cent increase in viewing figures. Unfortunately for Five, Kaplinsky, reputed to be paid £1m a year, subsequently announced she was pregnant – less than two months after arriving at the station. On the plus side, acquiring *Neighbours* gave Five a much-needed ratings boost and the network continued to broadcast some of the best US imports, not least *House*, starring Hugh Laurie.

In July the death was announced of the veteran reporter Sir Charles Wheeler, the BBC's longest serving foreign correspondent. For more than four decades Wheeler, who was 85, had reported for radio and television from most of the world's trouble spots. 'The doyen of BBC foreign correspondents, Charles Wheeler earned a permanent niche in television history through his coverage of the Watergate scandal during his years as the corporation's chief correspondent in the United States', said *The Times*. 'Often ahead of the American press corps, he exploited the contacts he had built up during seven years in Washington to provide the fullest and most comprehensive reporting available in the British media — and more than matching in quality, though not in quantity, that of the American networks.'

Meanwhile another great BBC octogenarian Sir David Attenborough showed little signs of slowing down. His flagship BBC One documentary *Life in Cold Blood*, looking at reptiles and amphibians did, however, mark the end of a cycle of programmes that had begun in 1979 with *Life on Earth*. Inevitably the programme was one of the highlights of the channel's winter schedule.

Other documentaries that made a big impact included *Ross Kemp in Afghanistan* on Sky One, the BBC's *Sacred Music* and *The Art of Spain* – both screened by the increasingly successful BBC Four – and *Malcolm and Barbara: Love's Farewell* on ITV. Over at Channel 4 there was praise for a winter food season in which celebrity chef Hugh Fearnley-Whittingstall campaigned against intensively farmed chickens.

The controversy over presenters' salaries was often in the headlines, but a report published by the BBC Trust concluded that there was 'no evidence' that the Corporation was distorting the market by paying stars such as Jonathan Ross huge fees. In July *Countdown* presenter Carol Vorderman caused a stir when it was reported she was leaving the long-running programme because hard-up Channel 4 intended to cut her fee by 90 per cent. However, several days later it was announced that comic Alan Carr was being paid £3m over two years by the broadcaster following attempts by rivals to poach the *Friday Night Project* star.

RADIO

In common with television, in the period under review radio was also tested by the growth of internet-based technologies and a challenging economic climate. As wireless internet radio receivers become more widely available and the spread of high-speed broadband connections allowed more listeners to tune in via the web, digital audio broadcasting was beginning to feel the strain. It was too early too tell how the BBC iPlayer would affect radio listening, but in this uncertain environment BBC Radio continued to dominate. In the summer the BBC announced a new head of Audio and Music (running the organisation's radio networks) in the guise of the relatively untested Tim Davie. Three years earlier Davie had joined the BBC from Pepsi to run the corporation's marketing and communications team. Following in the footsteps of the BBC veteran Jenny Abramsky, whose career at the broadcaster began in 1969, represented a huge challenge. Media commentator Maggie Brown, writing in *The Guardian*, observed that the departure of the hugely respected Abramsky marked 'the end of an era'. Her impressive legacy was a portfolio of stations in remarkably good health, notwithstanding the continued decline in audiences for Radio 3 and the failure of 1Xtra to make an impact.

RADIOS 1, 2, 3 AND 4 HIT MIDDLE AGE

In September, BBC Radios 1, 2, 3, and 4 all celebrated their 40th birthdays. Remarkably, each had survived more or less in tact. The *Daily Telegraph*'s seasoned radio critic Gillian Reynolds struck a sour note and warned her readers not to take Radio 4 for granted. 'Is it safe now?' she asked rhetorically, 'Current controller Mark Damazer thinks it is. I wouldn't be so sure. A decade hence, when digital switchover is complete and the BBC's charter expires, the licence fee will probably go, leaving Radio 4's future to subscription and market forces. Enjoy it while you can.'

Throughout 2007–8, there was much to enjoy across BBC Radio. Radio 1 in the BBC's annual statement of programme policy, published in June, promised, not for the first time, to focus on 'emerging' rock and pop artists through coverage of music festivals such as Glastonbury and the Big Weekend. It remains to be seen, however, if the BBC will respond to criticism from both the Church of England and the Roman Catholic Church. In April both organisations wrote to the BBC Trust demanding that religion be included Radio 1's remit, arguing that the present distinction between the stations was 'illogical and inconsistent' and failed to reflect young people's 'thirst for spiritual input'. They added: 'Religion figures strongly in the output of Radio 2, 3, and 4 under the proposed licences . . . but it does not appear under Radio 1. Unless religion is appropriately included in the Radio 1 licence, audience needs may not be met.' The network's most popular DJ, Chris Moyles, recorded his biggest ever audience when RAJAR figures released in May showed 7.72 million people tuning in every week. Meanwhile Radio 1's audience of 11.07 million was the first time in seven years it had broken the 11 million barrier.

It was, however, a different situation at spin-off digital station, the relatively well-resourced 1Xtra, which failed to attract more than 500,000 listeners. The station was criticised as an example of the BBC over-reaching itself. Sceptics asked why licence fee funds were deployed to fund services of marginal appeal.

CALLS TO SELL OFF RADIO 1 AND 2

Radio 2's position as the nation's most popular radio listening choice remained undiminished throughout the year. There were calls for its privatisation – and that of Radio 1 – including a proposal put forward by Peter Bazalgette, the TV executive who'd helped bring *Big Brother* to Britain, who also suggested selling off Channel 4. But policy makers dismissed these suggestions, while in her final interview as head of BBC Radio Jenny Abramsky said such a move would be a 'cultural travesty'. Politicians did complain about BBC Radio driving up talent costs at a time when commercial rivals could least afford it. Radio 2's biggest star, 70-year-old Terry Wogan, was more popular than ever, according to RAJAR figures for the first quarter of 2008. Some 8.1 million listeners made a regular date with *Wake Up To Wogan*. As *The Guardian* pointed out, with popularity on this scale, there was no reason to suspect that the garrulous Irishman would be retiring at any time in the near future. One Radio 2 stalwart who did exit during the year was Michael Parkinson, who announced in the autumn that he would be leaving his Sunday morning Radio 2 show to concentrate on other projects including writing his autobiography. His successor was the singer and actor Michael Ball. Radio 2's music documentaries again proved popular with critics. Among the programmes praised were *Jerseybeat – The Four Seasons Story* and *Let Freedom Ring*, an examination of how the legacy of Martin Luther King was taken up by musicians such as James Brown and Stevie Wonder. Radio 2 was less sure-footed in comedy. The *Telegraph*'s Gillian Reynolds identified Vic Reeves' *House Arrest* as a new low in radio comedy. The waspish reviewer dismissed the show as 'aural sewage'.

Radio 3 attempted to shrug off more bad listening figures by insisting that greater numbers of people were listening on demand via the internet, which is not covered by RAJAR's surveys. When for the first time ever Radio 3's listening share dropped below 1 per cent, the BBC commented that the network was a 'great bastion of arts and culture'. In any case, listening figures were not the only measure of success. According to Sarah Spilsbury, the co-ordinator of Friends of Radio 3, the new schedule introduced in February 2007 was still putting people off tuning in. But critics were impressed by Radio 3's Sunday plays and the Sunday night sequence *Words & Music* although world music devotees missed Andy Kershaw, whose troubled private life kept him off the air.

FORGET THE BODY PIERCINGS, IT'S THE INTERVIEWS THAT MATTER

Not every commentator was impressed by Radio 4's attempts to broaden its appeal beyond its loyal middle-aged and elderly listeners. But clearly the network was doing something right; in May it was once again voted station of the year at the Sony awards. In the same month RAJAR's quarterly listening report showed Radio 4's audience share had increased from 11.8 per cent to 12.2 per cent. During the year under review Radio 4's flagship current affairs programme *Today* celebrated its 50th anniversary – the programme had started life on the Home Service – and in April the BBC's economics editor Evan Davis joined the regular presenting team. Despite some initial misgivings from critics, he was generally regarded as an asset to *Today*. Gillian Reynolds advised in the *Daily Telegraph*: 'Forget all the prior excitements in the press about his haircut, his sex life, his possible body piercings. If it took him only a couple of days to get to grips with *Today's* backstairs rivalries and on-air rigidities, he'll do.'

Radio 4's news and current affairs coverage is rarely far from the headlines. So it was in February when *The World at One* interviewed the Archbishop of Canterbury, Dr Rowan Williams. In the interview he said that introducing parts of Shariah law in the UK seemed unavoidable and would be good for social cohesion. His comments, taken out of context by certain newspapers, sparked a media feeding frenzy and led to calls for his resignation.

The network was in the spotlight again two months later when one of its most familiar voices was silenced. The death of Humphrey Lyttleton, who was 86, was considered important enough to be the lead news item on the *Today* programme. For 36 years he had hosted *I'm Sorry I Haven't a Clue*. His demise was the subject of considerable comment. 'As the deadpan chairman of the long-running radio show . . . Lyttelton's droll stage persona allowed him to negotiate the most outrageous doubles entendres – many of them directed at the imaginary hostess, Samantha – while he also demonstrated his mastery of the show's impossibly arcane parlour game Mornington Crescent', said *The Times*. During the year 2007–8 two other eminent Radio 4 broadcasters died – Ned Sherrin and Miles Kington.

DAB – A DIGITAL DISASTER IN THE MAKING?

With the UK experiencing an economic slowdown and more advertising migrating to the internet, commercial radio once again experienced difficulties. The single biggest change affecting the sector was a far-reaching shake-up in ownership leaving most of British commercial radio in private hands. The German media group H Bauer gained Magic and Kiss in December when they acquired the British media company EMAP. Three months later Global Radio, owners of Heart, Galaxy and LBC, finally bought GCap Media, operators of Classic FM, Xfm and London's Capital 95.8, for a reported £375m following a hostile takeover bid. The move made Global, led by ex-ITV boss Charles Allen, Britain's biggest radio company. Fears were expressed that Allen, known for his cost-cutting regime at ITV, would pursue a similar strategy at the ambitious radio company. In June GCap's CEO and chairman Fru Hazlitt and Richard Eyre departed as Allen assumed the chairmanship on an interim basis while Ashley Tabor stepped in as CEO. During the same month the £1.1m fine for GCap over a phone-in competition scandal by media watchdog, OFCOM, the biggest ever financial penalty imposed on a British commercial radio company, was regarded by commentators as a wake-up call for the industry. The regulator accused the company's management of 'inexcusable' behaviour that showed a 'fundamental disregard' for its broadcasting obligations. Thirty stations had run the competition in which GCap was alleged to have deliberately selected people who gave the wrong answers to go on air. As a result the competition was artificially prolonged as more contestants paid to enter.

In the summer the sale of Virgin Radio, part of the troubled SMG Group, to the Times of India Group was completed, another sign of the sub-continent's growing economic power. The new owner's plans involve dropping the Virgin name and rebranding the station. The economic climate was harsh but at least one commentator was optimistic that the lack of pressure from the City, now that much of British commercial radio was in private hands, might encourage greater investment in programmes. In June *Sunday Times* columnist Paul Donovan wrote: 'It can at last afford to take risks and, if it has access to cash, to splash out on programmes without complaints from shareholders.' As evidence, Donovan praised new shows broadcast by Smooth, *Rolling River of Rock*, a musical history of the Mississippi, and *Grease at 30*, an analysis of the stage show and film presented by Sue Perkins. 'We are trying to attract new audiences and to present a serious challenge to Radio 2', said John Simons, programme director at GMG, Smooth's owner. 'We want to add depth and substance to our output.'

Listening figures announced in May suggested that BBC Radio was experiencing an even bigger lead over rival broadcasters than ever. In the first three months of 2008 the corporation achieved a record share of 56.8 per cent of radio listening, up from 55.4 per cent the previous quarter. Commercial radio's share fell to 41.1 per cent, down from 42.4 per cent.

As even greater numbers of listeners tuned into their favourite radio stations on their digital TVs or listened via personal computers, the prospects for the digital audio broadcasting (DAB) platform looked increasingly bleak. The high cost of transmission and slow growth in advertising revenue was undermining confidence in DAB and forcing commercial radio companies to rethink their strategy. GCap's decision to all but abandon DAB only heightened concern. A string of national digital stations closed during the year. Among those hit were GCap Media's Core and The Jazz, UBC's Oneword and Virgin Radio's Groove. Rock star Brian May from Queen led a rescue bid for Planet Rock, nominated for three Sony awards, claiming the station was 'a symbol of free radio – radio which is not run by large corporate organisations for the purpose of making tons of money'. Against the odds a consortium involving rock musicians Ian Anderson and Gary Moore stepped in and Planet Rock survived.

It was a less optimistic picture elsewhere. GCap's Chill and Fun Radio were scaled back, while Virgin jettisoned plans to launch new national station Virgin Radio Viva. *The Guardian*'s radio writer Elisabeth Mahoney predicted more casualties: 'The culling of radio stations will continue. . . driven by poor audience figures and falling advertising revenue as digital radio matures.'

GCap Media's chief executive Fru Hazlitt had pinpointed part of the problem when she told *The Guardian* in February: 'The majority of people who are listening through DAB receivers are listening to stations that are 'simulcasting' [simultaneously broadcasting] on FM. . . If you put that against a background of the cost structure of DAB, it cannot be commercially viable.' She predicted that radio's growth opportunities were on FM and broadband. But with around 6.5 million DAB receivers sold and the BBC committed to the technology, there was pressure to ensure that DAB survived. Said BBC audio and music director Jenny Abramsky: 'Recent RAJAR listening figures show that nearly 5.6 million people tune into BBC Radio via DAB each week and the BBC's digital-only networks continue to grow, with two networks – 6 Music and BBC7 – recently posting record listening figures.' Subsequently Abramsky urged commercial radio to work with the BBC collaborating on a joint marketing push and the introduction of a higher quality DAB signal. She warned that the emergence of new technologies was presenting radio with bigger threats than at any time in the past five decades. Long-term growth in average radio listening per head had declined by about 6 per cent since 2004. New media was changing consumption patterns, but programme quality remained paramount, she told the Radio Reborn conference in London in April: 'Without content there will be no future. Content is everything. Content is what matters to audiences. Everything else, all the digital technology in the world, comes down to convenience.'

ANGER AT CHANNEL 4'S RADIO SIGNALS

Despite the setbacks Channel 4 was due to launch ten national digital stations by the autumn of 2008 although the broadcaster's much-trailed rival to BBC Radio 4, Channel 4 Radio, was not expected to start broadcasting until the beginning of 2009. However, there was criticism of Channel 4's treatment of digital speech station Oneword, axed in January after the TV organisation had initially rescued the station only to then sell it for £1. Oneword was replaced by a continuous loop of birdsong. Classic FM, which during the year saw its share of the radio market fall from 4.2 per cent to 3.7 per cent, announced an overhaul of its schedules in February. The new initiative featured what was apparently the station's biggest ever commission, a 100-part series fronted by the former Blur bass player, the ubiquitous Alex James. Other new signings were Laurence Llewelyn-Bowen and ex-Capital DJ Margherita Taylor, hired to present *Smooth Classics at Six*. The musician Howard Goodall was appointed Classic's latest composer in residence and joined the regular team of Saturday presenters.

BUSINESS AND FINANCE

Timothy Hindle

FROM NORTHERN ROCK TO SOUTHERN CRUMBLE

For British businessmen, there was only one question during the year: would the collapse of Northern Rock turn into a southern crumble? Would the financial crisis at an ambitious Newcastle building society extend so far that the engine of the economy, the services industries of the south would stall? By the end of the year the question was still unanswered, but by then pessimists comfortably outnumbered optimists.

Encouraging those remaining optimists were figures showing that the percentage of working age Britons in jobs in March 2008 was the highest for three years (at 74.9 per cent), and that GDP, though slowing, was nowhere near the two consecutive quarters of negative growth that technically defines a recession. The pessimists' case was backed by the frightening sight of queues outside Northern Rock branches and inflation rates not experienced for more than two decades. Manufacturers' output prices rose at an annual rate of more than 10 per cent in June 2008, the highest level since records began in 1986.

The economy became a subject of high street chit-chat, not least because its problems focused first and foremost on house prices. By Easter 2008 they had started to fall – a phenomenon unprecedented this century – as banks froze in fear after the Northern Rock collapse and virtually stopped lending. At times the gloom seemed overdone. One reliable measure – the Land Registry's record of all completed sales – was still showing positive growth in prices as late as May 2008, albeit for a much lower number of transactions. In any case, falls were uneven across the country and nowhere near as bad as in the USA. By the summer of 2008, house prices in Los Angeles and Phoenix were dropping at an annual rate of over 30 per cent.

Falling house prices were in stark contrast to rising prices elsewhere. The price of oil rose from \$70 (£35) a barrel in July 2007 to \$145 (£72) a year later, before starting to drop. Chancellor of the Exchequer Alistair Darling said we must end our oil dependency, and alternative energy sources suddenly seemed more economically viable. Britain's Wellcome Trust was among a number of investors backing a California company called Sapphire Energy which claimed to be able to turn algae into crude oil. The bad news? It will be five years before Sapphire's alternative fuel is on the market.

The price of many other commodities hit new highs, pushed up partially by increasing demand from China and India. The gold price exceeded \$1,000 (£502) an ounce for the first time ever in March. Its previous nominal high (\$850 (£426) an ounce) was reached as long ago as 1980, and in real terms that still stands as the record. Nevertheless the price was high enough in 2008 for a proposal to open a new gold mine in Ireland to be floated, and the UK's only working mine, near Tyndrum in Scotland, to be reopened.

Food prices also shot up in the year causing riots around the world, from Egypt to Haiti. The increasing use of 'green' biofuels was one of a number of factors blamed for the rise. A leaked report from the World Bank in mid-2008 said that biofuels for use in cars had pushed food prices up by 75 per cent. From April 2008 2.5 per cent of all petrol and diesel in the UK must be produced from biofuels. An independent British study found that plant fuels – produced mostly from maize – which is now the exclusive occupant of large swathes of America's mid-western farmland – played a 'significant' part in pushing up food prices.

The Bank of England was left with a classic dilemma. What to do about interest rates? Should it cut them further to reduce the possibility of recession (in the five months to April 2008 it cut rates three times, down to 5 per cent)? Or should it raise them to help fend off the threat of inflation?

THE RETURN OF NATIONALISATION

Northern Rock, Britain's fifth biggest mortgage lender, had been a pillar of the north-eastern business community (and a major sponsor of Newcastle United Football Club) until it changed its business model to work like a commercial bank. Limited by its small number of branches and its regional deposit base, it went into the wholesale money markets to increase its size by borrowing short-term funds to lend as long-term mortgages. This mix has long been a potential recipe for disaster. When economies turn down, short-term money runs away and long-term obligations do not. In the summer of 2007, in the wake of problems in America's sub-prime mortgage market, short-term money stopped running the way of Northern Rock.

A report from America's Securities and Exchange Commission (SEC) laid some blame for the mortgage market's troubles at the door of the ratings agencies – dominated by Fitch, Moody's and Standard & Poor's. They, it claimed, rated securities (in the mortgage market and elsewhere) indiscriminately. A security 'could be structured by cows', said one analyst, 'and we would rate it'. The agencies sacked a few senior people and vowed to do better in future. But who will now rate the raters?

On 13 September Northern Rock was forced to seek help from the Bank of England, which it received in the form of loans backed ultimately by £55bn of taxpayers' money. For a while it searched for a white knight to solve its problems, but in February the government felt compelled to nationalise the bank when the last potential private-sector bidder, Sir Richard Branson's Virgin Group, dropped out.

Prime Minister Gordon Brown had previously described this – the first nationalisation of a British company since the 1970s – as 'the least favourable option', but it was the option that the government finally had to accept. It appointed Ron Sandler as executive chairman to oversee the slimming of the business to 'a more sustainable size' and, it hoped, to a sale at some future date.

In March Northern Rock announced that it had made a loss of £167.6m in 2007, a figure that included £127.7m of professional fees paid to lawyers and PR firms in the wake of its collapse. It also included £760,000 for its former CEO Adam Applegarth, one of the main architects of the company's disastrous growth strategy.

Other banks' reluctance to lend continued and ısinesses found their credit lines cut drastically. In April, ıe Bank of England introduced a special liquidity :heme designed to persuade constipated financial ıstitutions to release funds onto the market. The scheme 'lowed commercial banks to swap their illiquid ıortgage-backed securities with the central bank in :turn for government bills, but at a discount.

'LACK BY NAME

ıesperate times lead to desperate actions. But the actions ınd their consequences take time to unravel. Most of the nancial scandals in the headlines this year related to ettling previous misdemeanours. In July 2008, Phillip ßennett, a British citizen who was formerly chief xecutive of Refco, a global commodity broker that went pectacularly bust in 2005, was jailed for 16 years by a ourt in Manhattan for conspiracy and securities fraud. In 'ebruary, three British bankers, known as 'The NatWest 'hree', were sentenced by a court in Texas to 37 months ı jail after being found guilty of embezzling $7.3m €3.6m) in an Enron-related fraud that dated back to 2000.

In March Conrad Black began a six-and-a-half year entence in a Florida prison. The former owner of the *Daily Telegraph* (and of over 200 other publications round the world), was jailed for embezzling more than 36m (£3m) from a public company which he controlled. With typical arrogance he said, ahead of an appeal, that 'a noron who seriously looks at this case will see that it is a 'rock and I expect that it will ultimately be determined to ıe so'. Time will tell.

The biggest scandal of the year centred on Paris and nirrored the demise of Britain's Barings Bank more than ı decade earlier. In January Jérôme Kerviel, a 31-year-old employee of Société Générale nicknamed 'the mad trader', was charged with breach of trust and falsifying documents during a month of wildly spiralling deals that cost the bank $7bn (£3.5bn). As when Britain's own 'rogue trader' Nick Leeson brought down the venerable Barings Bank in 1995, questions subsequently focused on how and why one man, who had worked for only two years for Société Générale, could be in a position to single-handedly expose one of the biggest banks in the world to such risk. Kerviel said all he wanted was respect and a big bonus. He got neither.

A TOUCH OF QATAR

Northern Rock was not the only British financial institution to reel from the mortgage market's weakness. Many went into the same uncharted territory, heavy with assets and liabilities that few understood. The Financial Services Authority (FSA), the regulator of Britain's financial institutions, said in its annual report at the beginning of the year that new mortgage loans had been 'concentrated in groups which historically have not been homeowners'. Their behaviour under pressure was unpredictable.

Several institutions had to find new capital to improve their balance sheets. The Royal Bank of Scotland raised a record £12bn from its shareholders in May. But not all found it so easy. Only 8 per cent of a rights issue from HBOS was taken up by its existing shareholders, while a big capital-raising exercise by Barclays in July left 8 per cent of the big British bank in the hands of investors from Qatar. Vacillations in the stock market at the time were such that the Qataris made a profit of more than £200m on their investment in less than a week.

The Qatari Investment Authority and Temasek, a Singapore state investment fund, are now both major shareholders in Barclays Bank. These two sovereign wealth funds are typical of a new breed of investor on the world scene. State-owned funds belonging to wealthy nations such as Norway, Singapore, Abu Dhabi and Kuwait – many of them oil-based economies – are buying ever more significant stakes in corporations around the world. Temasek, for example, also owns 17 per cent of Standard Chartered bank.

Britain could have had its own sovereign wealth fund had it chosen to invest the proceeds of North Sea oil rather than using them to cut taxes and boost government expenditure. A report by PricewaterhouseCoopers in early 2008 reckoned that such a fund would now be worth over £450bn, more than those of Russia, Kuwait and Qatar put together.

Regrets at the missed opportunity increased in line with the price of oil. The AA said that British drivers spent an extra £110m on fuel in the late May bank holiday of 2008 than they spent at the same time in 2007. Speculators were among those blamed for the oil-price hike, and financial regulators launched an investigation into trading in the oil-futures market.

As motorists groaned, the oil giant Royal Dutch Shell announced profits of £13.9bn, an all-time record for a UK quoted company. 'Obscene,' cried the trade unions and called for a windfall tax. Behind the headlines, though, the picture was less rosy. The company's total oil and gas output fell for the fifth year running and civil unrest in Nigeria's Niger Delta region caused it particular problems.

The world's oil and gas resources are increasingly being nationalised, as demonstrated by Russia and Venezuela. According to one estimate, some 85 per cent of oil and gas supplies are now in governments' hands. That leaves little for the once mighty oil 'majors', such as Shell.

The oil price rise had a marked effect on the world's airlines. British Airways said its traffic fell by 3.7 per cent in June 2008 while Willie Walsh, its chief executive, declared that the era of cheap flights was over. Low-cost carriers like easyJet and Ryanair tried to recoup some of their increased costs by charging more for extras, such as baggage and car-hire. However, both airlines reported that their passenger-load factor, the percentage of occupied seats per plane, remained static.

High fuel costs had a broad impact on the way people travelled. There were significant increases in the use of public transport, for instance, and train services in particular benefited. Eurostar, the cross-Channel train operator, which for years had struggled to compete with low-cost airlines, saw its passenger traffic increase by over 10 per cent, boosted by the new high-speed line from London's St Pancras station. Opened in November 2007, the dedicated line helped cut journey times to Paris and Brussels by 20 minutes and for the first time in its 20-year history, the Eurostar operation made a profit.

TERMINAL ILLNESS

The oil price was not the only cause for concern for British airlines in 2008. The ill-fated opening of Heathrow's Terminal 5 at the end of March, a 'state-of-the-art' building designed by Richard Rodgers, was a fiasco that raised questions about the capability of British management. Over 300 British Airways flights had to be cancelled immediately after its opening and the transfer of BA's long-distance routes had to be postponed until September. The airline (for whose exclusive use the terminal was designed) had originally said the opening had presented it with 'a few minor problems'.

The government criticised BA for subjecting passengers to an 'unacceptably poor travelling experience'. Heathrow had the worst record in Europe for lost bags in the first half of 2008, managing to misplace as many as 30,000 following the opening of the new terminal. Stephen Nielson, the CEO of BAA, the company that runs Heathrow and most of Britain's airports, was removed from his job in February. Willie Walsh clung on to his by his fingernails.

Holidaymakers began to think again about taking trips abroad. Blacks Leisure, a camping and outdoor pursuits supplier, reported a sharp increase in sales in summer 2008. British campsites were said to be having a bumper season despite indifferent weather in July. But few of these campers were in the mood to buy a new camera for their holiday snaps. Leading retailer Jessops saw its sales plunge.

Shoppers tried to cut their bills by moving downmarket. Among the food retailers, Asda and the European discount chains Aldi and Lidl benefited greatly, while relatively expensive Waitrose and Marks & Spencer suffered.

In May 700 jobs were lost at Northern Foods. The company said it could no longer fulfil its contract with Marks & Spencer to supply pre-prepared foods while turning a profit. Despite seemingly driving at least one of its suppliers to the limit, Marks & Spencer's sales in the three months to the end of June 2008 were 5.3 per cent down on the previous year, forcing the company to issue a profit warning. The head of its food division, Steve Epsom, resigned unexpectedly in early July, after only a year on the job. He had been poached from Waitrose. Upmarket grocers were not flavour of the year.

The big supermarket grocers were shown a yellow card by the Competition Commission in February when it produced its third report on the sector in eight years. The main focus of the report was the massive 'banks' of development land controlled by the big four – Asda, Morrisons, Sainsbury's and Tesco – which have 75 per cent of the UK groceries market between them. Does their land bank prevent new competitors from (literally) getting anywhere near them? The commission (more or less) said yes.

Some indication of the limitations to further growth at home for Tesco, the largest of these stores, came three months later when it paid £464 million for a chain of discount shops in faraway South Korea.

Consumers also cut back on both eating and drinking out. By April, four pubs a day were said to be closing, hit not only by consumer parsimony but also by the smoking ban, and by deeply discounted alcohol prices in supermarkets. These prices encouraged more drinking at home and, less felicitously, on the streets. One of the first acts of the new Mayor of London, Boris Johnson, was to ban drinking alcohol on London's public transport system.

Premium coffee shops also felt the pinch. Starbucks' profits fell by 28 per cent in the first quarter of 2008 and the store said it would close 600 of its outlets in the USA. Starbucks' UK trade was hit as much by strong competition from Costa and Café Nero as by any hint of recession. During the year the company chose the city of Cardiff for its first European drive-through outlet.

Not all food outlets had a bad year. Domino's, the UK franchise of a US operation, reported a 32.7 per cent rise in pre-tax profits in the first half of 2008. Such was its confidence in the future that it announced that it intend to open 50 new stores in the second half of the year. The *Financial Times* described this as a demonstration of the 'Aldi effect', the movement downmarket of traditional ABC shoppers on tighter budgets.

Women seemed to be more resolute in their shopping than men. While sales of electronic goods and cameras fell, Burberry, an upmarket fashion retailer, saw its sales rise by 25 per cent in the first quarter of the year, while more downmarket H&M reported an 8 per cent increase in sales in June.

BOYS' TOYS

One company that could benefit if Britons were to stay at home more would be Hornby. In May, the famous maker of model railways added Corgi to its portfolio of hobby businesses, buying the once-British manufacturer of die-cast metal model vehicles from its American owners. Corgi's products have become collectible over the years, with some items changing hands for hundreds of pounds on eBay. Hornby also owns Scalextric, a car-racing game, and Airfix, the firm which makes the famous model kits.

Another famous British name crossed the Atlantic in the opposite direction. The Guinness World Records brand was sold to the Florida-based company behind Ripley's 'Believe it or Not' museums; tourist attractions that are stuffed with oddities from around the world. A London branch is due to open in 2008 and is rumoured to contain a four-metre long matchstick model of Tower Bridge and a 69cm hairball found inside a cow's stomach. Could it become a bigger attraction even than the London Eye?

Two brands that many people still think of as British – Land Rover and Jaguar – moved from one foreign owner (Ford) to another (Tata, an Indian conglomerate) for around $2.3bn (£1.1bn). This was Tata's second big foray into Britain in recent years. In 2007 it paid $13bn (£6.3bn) for the Corus Group, a company in which rest the remains of the once mighty British Steel Corporation.

There were signs that the UK was becoming a less attractive destination for international companies. One study placed it 12th out of 22 European nations, with Cyprus, Ireland and Switzerland at the top. As if to confirm that ranking, Yahoo!, an American internet company that spent much of the year fending off an unwelcome $45bn (£22bn) takeover bid from Microsoft, moved its European headquarters from the UK to Switzerland, while Shire, a quoted pharmaceuticals company based in Basingstoke, Hampshire, decided to move its head office to Ireland.

WPP, the huge advertising conglomerate run by Sir Martin Sorrell, threatened to move its headquarters too, influenced particularly by government proposals to spread the net of corporation tax to include hitherto excluded items like overseas royalties. The Confederation of British Industry criticised the proposals, at the same time calling for a simplification of the country's corporate tax system and a headline tax rate of 18 per cent. In July the government backed away from its proposal, confirming that it would retain the exemption for foreign profits while looking at new ways to prevent avoidance of corporation tax on UK earnings.

BONUS ISSUES

However bad the economy in 2008, British companies had rarely if ever been in a better position to endure some eavy weather: 2007 was a bumper year for profits. The rvices sector (which now accounts for two-thirds of the K economy) recorded record profitability of 21 per cent r the year.

Another group in a good position to take the strain ere the perennially over-rewarded City of London ankers whose bonuses in 2007 amounted to some £7bn, ot a penny of which they will have to repay should the vestors, whose earnings paid for the bonuses, lose their nirts in 2008.

In May came belated recognition that bankers' reward structures have some bearing on the risks they are prepared to take. Hector Sants, the FSA's chief executive, said that the regulator would henceforth take account of an organisation's remuneration packages when assessing how much risk it is taking. 'We will,' he said, 'do this with increasing intensity.' Rewarding employees without regard for losses that may emerge later, he said, is 'a risk for shareholders'. Indeed it is. This is not the first year that this has been made evidently clear.

CONSERVATION

THE NATURAL ENVIRONMENT

Peter Marren

BADGERS AND TB

The government's attempts to control TB in cattle are not working. The number of infected cattle in England has doubled in the past four years, and 28,000 were slaughtered as a result during 2007. The disease has put an intolerable strain on the farming industry as well as being an unsustainable cost to the taxpayer, concluded the report of the Environment, Food and Rural Affairs Select Committee in February 2008.

TB is also increasing in badgers. Last year 8,000 badgers tested positive for TB, compared with only 700 in 1997. The committee's advice was that government should adopt a multi-faceted approach to tackling the disease, including improved testing, better biosecurity, the fast-tracking of vaccines both for cattle and for badgers, and continued work on the epidemiology of the disease. Another option is to cull badgers in TB hotspots. The committee did not rule out this out, but pointed out that 'patchy, disorganised or short-term culling could make matters worse'. Snaring and gassing have been ruled out as inhumane, leaving trapping and shooting as the only acceptable ways of control.

In June 2008 the Rural Affairs Minister, Hilary Benn, decided against a cull of badgers in England partly on the grounds that there is insufficient public support for it. While he was criticised by angry farmers for ducking the issue, the government seems to have accepted scientific arguments that culling badgers would be costly without any certainty that it would ease the situation. Experience in Ireland supports this. In the Irish Republic a scorched earth policy aimed at exterminating badgers failed to control the disease. But in Northern Ireland, bovine TB is in decline despite the absence of an organised cull. Better surveillance and biosecurity measures, such as erecting electric fences around farm buildings to keep the badgers out, seem to be the key.

Benn's decision means that policies regarding the control of TB in cattle are different in England, Scotland and Wales. In May 2008 the Welsh Assembly opted for culling in identified intensive-treatment areas (such as Pembrokeshire) along with improvements in husbandry. The Badger Trust intends to mount a legal challenge to this ruling, while the National Trust said it would not cooperate over culling on its land unless the cull has legal backing.

MORE AGRICULTURE, LESS WILDLIFE?

The EU has abolished set-aside, the rule that required all farmers to keep 10 per cent of their land fallow, introduced in the 1990s. Some 644,000 hectares of agricultural land was in set-aside, a vastly greater area than most natural habitats. The abolition is driven both by the current high price of grain and the desire to free up more land for biofuels. Currently 6,140 square kilometers of farmland produce biofuels in the UK, but this is set to increase dramatically.

The abandonment of set-aside will impact wildlife, which, according to conservationists, was not properl considered. The EU expects biofuels to supply 10 per cen of our energy needs by the year 2020. Its renewabl transport fuel obligation requires that 5 per cent of fue sold on garage forecourts comes from renewables b 2010; from April 2009 it will no longer be possible t buy petrol that does not contain biofuel. To fulfil thes targets, much, perhaps most, land formerly in set-asid will have to be ploughed. This will worsen an alread serious situation for farm birds and other wildlife Set-aside and other marginal land offered a haven fo wildlife in intensively farmed areas as a source o weed-seeds and insects, and as nesting space Environmentalists are not the only ones to hav reservations about the threat of oil-seed rape monoculture which will colour whole landscapes bright yellow anc create a pungent unspring-like smell.

According to researchers at the University o Strathclyde, even if all set-aside land was planted with biofuels, it would scarcely dent the nation's dependence on fossil fuels. The 850 million litres of oil it would produce is a drop in the ocean beside the 20 billion litres of diesel consumed by the UK each year. Campaigners point out that large-scale biofuel production will generate large amounts of nitrous oxide, itself a greenhouse gas, as well as a pollutant. In the meantime, BP is building an industrial plant near Hull to produce bioethanol from wheat. It should begin production in 2009, and will encourage farmers in the East Midlands to turn over yet more land to the production of cereals, this time as a fuel for our cars.

STATE OF THE NATION'S BIRDS

The ups and downs of Britain's breeding and migratory birds are the responsibility of the British Trust for Ornithology, which celebrated its 75th birthday in 2008. The latest of a long series of reports on the state of the nation's birds suggests a chaotic situation as birds struggle to come to terms with changes in the countryside and climate. Very broadly speaking, water birds and some birds of prey are doing well, while woodland birds and long-distance migrants, as well as farm birds, are doing badly. The list of priority species of conservation concern has increased from 26 to 59.

Many remarked on the scarcity of cuckoos in 2007. The breeding season began with unusually dry weather followed by an exceptionally cool, wet summer, in which insect-eating birds, such as the spotted and pied flycatchers, struggled to find enough food for their broods. Farm birds, meanwhile, continued to decline. We have only half the number of bullfinches that were present in 1970. Other decreasing birds reliant on farming include yellowhammer, grey partridge, turtle dove, linnet and yellow wagtail, although in some cases there are signs that this decline may be easing as more environmentally friendly farming methods kick in.

Sea birds such as guillemot and kittiwake have suffered a succession of poor seasons, especially on the east coast. Climate change and overfishing are responsible; sand-eels, on which many birds depend, have become scarce and therefore harder to find. A survey of puffins at their largest nglish colony on the Farne Islands found that their ımbers had fallen from 55,674 pairs in 2003 to 36,500 2008. They have declined by a similar ratio on the Isle f May in the Firth of Forth. Conservationists believe that inter storms are an additional hazard, and that fewer ıffins are surviving the winter.

On the other hand, some birds did well. Woodlark and artford warbler continue to expand their range, helped the latter case by milder British winters, while little gret and Mediterranean gull consolidated their hold as reeding residents. Cattle egrets visited the south coast in nprecedented numbers and may be on the threshold of ecoming established. A modest increase in tree sparrows nd corncrakes following a long period of decline can be ttributed to conservation efforts. The ring-tailed parakeet also increasing and has become a familiar garden bird in ne London area.

Perhaps the best news has been the increase of uzzards across England, and the continued rise of red ites, mostly the progeny of releases in the 1990s. Kites ircling overhead are now a familiar sight in many parts f Britain, and they can appear in spectacular numbers at oosts, especially in mid-winter. In Scotland, however, the SPB reported the deliberate killing of 11 red kites by amekeepers, part of a worrying degree of persecution of irds of prey.

NEW APPROACH TO CONSERVATION?

n its first report into the state of the natural environment, Natural England called for a new, more inclusive approach o nature conservation. Our current system of nature eserves and protected sites (sites of special scientific nterest or SSSIs), devised in the 1940s, is not enough for he challenges of the 21st century, said the organisation's hief executive Helen Phillips. 'We need to find ways to nanage our landscape to create a mosaic of uses so that ve can help wildlife survive', she concluded. These hould include a national park around the coast of ngland, better use of the green belt and improved unding to farmers to deliver a better natural environment.

Natural England found that environment in Britain is nuch less rich in natural habitats and wildlife than fifty years ago. Although the character of the landscape has been broadly maintained, there are many problems. Woods are growing too shady (or deer-nibbled) to naintain butterflies; only 3 per cent of grassland remains rich in wild flowers; the rising sea has bitten away at coastal habitat, especially salt-marsh. Lowland heaths are, overall, in a poor and deteriorating condition despite much money and attention being poured into them in recent years. Other habitats in poor repair include chalk rivers, lowland lakes, fens, limestone pavement and blanket bog.

Some habitats are improving. These include arable field margins, coastal grazing marsh, reedbeds, and some kinds of woodlands. The condition of the country's most important wildlife sites, the SSSIs, has improved dramatically over the past ten years, claims Phillips. In its *Manifesto for the Natural Environment,* Natural England pledges to set the nation on a greener path by helping to store carbon in peat, soaking up rainwater to prevent flooding, and connecting existing wildlife sites by creating 'wildlife super highways'. And it will transform some National Nature Reserves into first-class visitor destinations to reconnect the public with nature. Watch this space.

BEAVERS REVISITED

The release of beavers is back on the agenda. A public consultation in Scotland found that most members of the public now support the introduction of European beavers. No doubt this influenced the Scottish environment minister, Mike Russell, when he announced that he would look kindly on the project, and in June 2008 approved a licence for the Scottish Wildlife Trust and the Royal Zoological Society of Scotland to release beavers at a location in Knapdale, Argyll. (After years of dithering, the previous application was rejected in 2005 on the grounds that beavers might cause damage and that it would be illegal, as a protected species, to control them.) The licence is for four beaver families collected from Norway, which, after six months in quarantine, will be released in spring 2009. If successful, the project is likely to pave the way for other releases elsewhere in Britain. Beaver enthusiasts Derek Gow and Roy Dennis have been asked to scour the country for potential sites.

Conservationists claim that beavers benefit the natural environment in a number of ways. Their activities create healthy ponds and streams that can be beneficial for other wildlife. For example by felling young trees beavers maintain a form of open woodland. They also raise the water level in periods of drought and boost the local economy by attracting tourists. An unknown number of European beavers already live in Britain within fenced enclosures on private estates, and one nature reserve in Kent. A few of these have escaped. A beaver living wild on the Thames near Oxford has not been seen recently, while, of two beavers living close to the River Earn in Perthshire, one has been recaptured. At Lower Mill Estate in the Cotswold Water Park, where a family of beavers was released within a 20-hectare enclosure in 2005, twelve baby beavers (kits) were seen in 2008, the first outdoor British-born beavers since the animal died out four hundred years ago.

A CONFUSION OF TARGETS

Recovery schemes have been prepared for a large number of declining British wild animals, insects and plants. But what happens when they affect other species? The capercaillie is the UK's largest and rarest species of grouse. Two thousand of the turkey-like birds live in the ancient pine forests of the Scottish Highlands. Some of their nests are monitored by video cameras, and a wildlife volunteer going through 500 hours of footage noticed that they had suffered an intruder in the form of another protected species. It seems that about one third of the capercaillie's egg production is eaten by pine martens.

Capercaillies and pine martens are both the subject of conservation action plans. Some capercaillie specialists are now calling for a different kind of action involving the trapping and relocation of marauding martens. Marten experts are understandably less keen to interfere.

A similar clash of priorities has caused the abandonment of ambitious plans to introduce the white-tailed eagle to East Anglia. The eagle, which has a 3m wingspan, was reintroduced to western Scotland during the 1980s and 1990s, and is doing well. There are 42 breeding pairs, which in 2007 had one of their best-ever seasons, rearing 34 young. More white-tailed eagles from Norway are being released on the east coast of Scotland. However plans to release the bird in Suffolk were abandoned when the RSPB objected that the eagle might take another, even rarer bird, the bittern (the Country Landowner's Association, meanwhile, complained that it might take piglets). The wildlife writer

Richard Mabey commented that all this smacks more of gamekeeping than conservation.

PRICKLY PROBLEMS

Where have all the hedgehogs gone? An analysis of road-kill statistics suggested that hedgehog numbers had fallen by 20 per cent between 2001 and 2005. Traffic-flattened hedgehogs are less common than they used to be. The reason is not that they have become better at dodging speeding cars but that there are fewer hedgehogs.

The causes of the hedgehog's downfall are various. One of them is removing hedges. A study in the Netherlands found that the animals do not like big open fields and stay close to hedges for safety, most of the places where they lie up during the day were located in hedgerows or along the edges of woods. Some experts believe that predation by badgers is another cause. Badgers certainly do kill and eat hedgehogs, and the former have increased as the latter have declined. The British Hedgehog Preservation Society has even received letters from farmers trying to muster its support for more badger culling.

As for urban hedgehogs, every large garden or allotment that is built on removes hedgehog habitat, as does the replacement of traditional garden lawns and shrubberies with modern, low-maintenance decking and patios. Urban hedgehogs find themselves faced with fewer places to forage, and face still greater danger from difficult-to-climb fences, more busy roads and denser housing.

One place where hedgehogs are doing well was the Outer Hebrides, especially on the islands of North and South Uist where the animals had been introduced by gardeners in the 1970s to keep down their slugs. In the absence of their natural predators, foxes and badgers, and with a plentiful supply of food in the form of birds' eggs, the hedgehogs thrived and multiplied. Unfortunately this brought them into conflict with nature conservation interests since some of those eggs belonged to vulnerable and declining birds such as dunlin, corncrake, lapwing, redshank and snipe.

Scottish Natural Heritage (SNH) decided to trap and remove the hedgehogs. Between 2001 and 2005, around 200 hedgehogs were caught annually and dispatched by lethal injection. This brought down the wrath of animal lovers and the hedgehogs were subsequently released on the Scottish mainland. After a round-up of more than a thousand animals, the Uists have been declared virtually hedgehog-free. SNH is now looking for volunteers to tackle the neighbouring island of Benbecula.

THE IMPACT OF WINDFARMS

Plans to build Europe's largest onshore windfarm on the Hebridean island of Lewis, which had the enthusiastic approval of the local Western Islands Council, were rejected by the Scottish government. The development of 181 giant turbines, each the height of the London Eye, was expected to provide around 10 per cent of Scotland's electricity. Thousands of objections were received from islanders and conservation bodies. Many of the turbines would have been uncomfortably close to a large special protection area for birds (SPA), designated under EU law because of its concentration of rare nesting birds. Some of these, notably golden eagles and divers, are known to be vulnerable to wind turbines. Campaigners were also concerned that transmitting energy from the remote Lewis to Scotland's cities would require the construction of pylons across the western Highlands. Stuart Housden, the RSPB's Scotland director, said the reprieve 'sent a strong message that in meeting our ambitious and welcome renewables targets, we do not have to sacrifice our most important environmental resources'.

Scotland is, however, still committed to generating half of its electricity from renewables by 2020. The Klondike rush of applications for windfarms, big and small, has all but overwhelmed Scottish Natural Heritage's capacity to deal with any but the most significant ones. In the far north of Scotland, especially, many windfarms will be sited on deep peat. The danger, say conservationists, is that disturbance to peat will result in the release of more carbon than the turbines will ever save.

An example is a windfarm at Gordonbush in Sutherland, at the edge of another large SPA set up to preserve moorland birds such as golden plovers, as well as the only pair of golden eagles in that part of Scotland. After being reassured that the development would contain mitigation measures, SNH withdrew its objection. In an attempt to guide local planning authorities, SNH and RSPB have circulated a map showing all the most sensitive areas for birds.

TRUMP GOLF COURSE

The American billionaire Donald Trump has been reported to be planning to build a golf course on the Aberdeenshire coast. The billion-pound development would include two championship golf courses, a luxury hotel, almost a thousand holiday homes and 500 private houses within a gated community. It would transform that part of the coast. But Trump's plan brought him into conflict with conservation bodies since the development will destroy part of Foveran Links SSSI, part of Scotland's largest sand dune system. The controversial development has divided Scottish public opinion. Some saw it as of vital importance to Scotland's economy and tourist industry, and so overriding planning policies and protective legislation. By a narrow margin, Aberdeen's local authority turned down the application, which was subsequently called in by the Scottish government.

At a public inquiry held in Aberdeen in June 2008, Donald Trump insisted that his golf resort would be very special for Scotland, with 'the potential to be the greatest golf course in the world'. The current state of the site, he said, was desolate and 'kind of disgusting' with dead bird carcasses lying around. Scottish public opinion, he insisted, was on his side, despite objections from a minority. The inquiry closed on 4 July and a decision was expected by the end of the year.

MIXED FORTUNES FOR BUTTERFLIES

The charity Butterfly Conservation celebrated its 40th birthday in 2008. As expected, the cold wet summer of 2007 has had a knock-on effect on butterflies the following year, and, with a few exceptions, numbers are unusually low. Climate change has already made a marked impact on British butterflies, favouring some while disadvantaging others. The red admiral is a beneficiary and now appears early in the year after hibernating successfully in gardens. The small tortoiseshell, by contrast, has declined by 80 per cent since 1990. A possible cause is a parasitic fly, which has reached Britain from Europe and attacks the butterfly's caterpillars. The red light is on for some woodland butterflies, such as the pearl-bordered and high brown fritillaries whose populations have plummeted during the past 20 years probably through changes in woodland management.

At the launch of a Save Our Butterflies Week in July 08, Sir David Attenborough outlined a new strategy to lp butterflies by designating 20 'butterfly survival nes' in key landscapes across Britain. The plan involves king colonies of butterflies by butterfly-friendly bitats, thus avoiding the isolation which is believed to the main cause of local extinction. This approach has eady helped to save the marsh fritillary on Dartmoor, d Butterfly Conservation claims to have the expertise to ake the idea work.

HE ADVANCE OF THE HARLEQUIN LADYBIRD

ntil 2004 everyone loved a ladybird. Unfortunately itish ladybirds are threatened as never before by one of eir own kind, an invader called the harlequin. A native Asia, it has been spread around the globe to control hids and scale-insects. The harlequin arrived in Britain summer 2004 and has since appeared throughout ngland, though it is commonest in the south-east. It is an tractive beetle, larger than Britain's native ladybirds, and curs as two forms: either orange-with-black spots or ack-with-red spots. It is most conspicuous in autumn hen it often hibernates in buildings in large numbers.

Its rapid increase suggests that the harlequin is not eing controlled, as native insects are, by predators and arasites. It therefore has the competitive edge over fellow dybirds. Worse, the harlequin will on occasion attack nd kill native ladybirds, and experts believe it is a threat their survival, perhaps the worst they have ever faced. he harlequin also has the potential to become an gricultural pest, particularly in vineyards, and a nuisance homes. There are no easy ways to control it other than secticides, which will also kill many non-target insects. has proven resistant to a fungal pathogen which infects native ladybirds, and also to one of their main parasites. The solution? There isn't one as yet.

THE RAGWORT MYTH

In 2003 in response to pressure from the owners of horses and ponies, the government passed a Ragwort Control Act. It was claimed that up to 6,500 animals had died of liver damage after eating ragwort. The new law introduces a code of conduct for controlling the weed which relies on good neighbourliness rather than compulsion.

Ragwort has generated many headlines, but public fear of it as a super weed is unwarranted. There is no evidence that the plant, which is native to Britain, has increased. Nor is it as poisonous as is supposed. There is no significant risk to humans, while horses normally avoid it. Cattle and sheep do not live long enough to show symptoms of ragwort poisoning, and there is no evidence that consuming ragwort harms the meat. The few fatalities (around 13 horses in 2005) were probably due to the animals eating dried ragwort in hay or being forced by hunger to eat it after the grass had been grazed bare. On the other hand, ragwort is important for wildlife because, along with another injurious weed, the creeping thistle, it is often the main source of pollen and nectar for bees and other insects at the warmest time of the year.

Long-term research by Imperial College London at Silwood Park in Berkshire suggests that pulling ragwort may actually worsen the situation. Ragwort is a short-lived plant that naturally burns itself out in the process of seeding. Pulling ragwort ensures that the plant lives longer as it fragments the root and so produces several new plants. Ragwort seed cannot establish in closed turf; it is only when bare soil is exposed, for example by over-grazing, that it can gain a hold.

DANCE

Bridie Macmahon

As in politics, so in dance: the east rises to challenge the west. London hosted the first visit for 25 years of the entire New York City Ballet company in a major season at the London Coliseum in the spring of 2008. This followed the hugely successful mounting of Balanchine's 1967 work *Jewels* by the Royal Ballet in November 2007 and the long-awaited revival of Jerome Robbins's *Dances at a Gathering* by the company in May 2008. Meanwhile venues around the country hosted 'China Now', designed as a showcase for various forms of contemporary art from China, Beijing Modern Dance Company performed at the Linbury Studio Theatre in February 2008, and the National Ballet of China made its debut at the Royal Opera House, Covent Garden in July–August 2008, in the run-up to the opening of the Olympic Games in Beijing. The company performed a western production of *Swan Lake* and a Chinese ballet, *Raise the Red Lantern,* based on the successful film of the same name. The Olympic Games were in fact the springboard throughout the year for promoting all aspects of China to the west; but in dance terms, the response of China to the strength, depth and history of classical ballet in the west is still in its very early stages.

CROWNING GLORY

Jewels glittered appropriately and magnificently at the heart of the Royal Ballet's 2007–8 season. The company had staged the central section of the three-part work, *Rubies,* in 1989, but this was the first time it had danced it in its entirety. Set to Fauré, Stravinsky and Tchaikovsky, the work pays tribute (in *Emeralds* and *Diamonds*) to the French and Russian schools that so powerfully shaped Balanchine's development, and (in *Rubies*) to the American school that emerged from the fusion of the two in his choreography. The Royal Ballet danced the work with glamour and conviction, in Karinska's original costume designs but with new sets provided by Jean-Marc Puissant, and the great ballerina roles were seized with relish by Tamara Rojo, Sarah Lamb and Alina Cojocaru.

Balanchine's seminal one-act work, *Serenade,* was also presented by the Royal Ballet, and provided an interesting opportunity to compare and contrast with the 'parent' company who danced the work at the London Coliseum a few weeks earlier. In spite of the plethora of non-British trained dancers at the Royal Ballet, the British version was still markedly more precise than its American counterpart, which was presented instead with an exhilarating boldness and energy. The US input into the Royal's repertoire culminated with the revival of Jerome Robbins' *Dances at a Gathering,* last presented by the company in the 1970s. Created by Robbins in 1969, the work is a series of dances for soloists and couples set to Chopin piano music, with, at the choreographer's clear insistence, no story and no roles to be played: 'the dancers are themselves dancing with each other to that music in that space'. Nevertheless the result is a work full of tenderness, humour and affection, and the impression of spontaneity in the choreography is belied by its structural and dramatic discipline. *Dances at a Gathering* had enjoyed enormous success in the last Royal Ballet production, with the starriest possible of casts including Rudolf Nureyev, Anthony Dowell, Antoinette Sibley, Lynn Seymour and the company's current director, Monica Mason (who was awarded a DBE in the Queen's Birthday Honours in 2008). The new cast as a whole could not perhaps immediately banish the ghosts of its predecessors, but there were individual performances of great quality, especially from Tamara Rojo, Johan Kobborg, Alina Cojocaru and Lauren Cuthbertson.

The company staged two wholly new works during the season. In February 2008 Christopher Wheeldon (recently departed from new York City Ballet) mounted his fourth work for them, entitled *Electric Counterpoint* and set to Bach and Steve Reich. The work focussed on the thoughts and fears of four of the company's dancers about their art and craft; it is therefore dancer-specific and therefore possibly of limited life. It did however highlight the talents of Edward Watson, Sarah Lamb, Zenaida Yanowsky and Eric Underwood, using taped interviews with the dancers, their digital images projected onto screens and their actual bodies to interesting if slightly self-absorbed effect. The other new work, *Rushes – Fragments of a Lost Story,* was the first for the full company by the Danish choreographer Kim Brandstrup. Its inspiration was Dostoevsky's novel *The Idiot,* although the resulting work was difficult to relate in any meaningful way to its literary source. An elaborate set by Richard Hudson with video input from Dick Straker combined with urgent but stubbornly inexpressive steps to produce a tired reworking of the 'love triangle' theme with valiant but ultimately ineffective performances by Carlos Acosta, Alina Cojocaru and Laura Morera.

NORMAN MORRICE

Norman Morrice, director of the Royal Ballet from 1977 until 1986, died in January 2008 at the age of 76. He also played a major role as associate artistic director in the reshaping of Ballet Rambert in the 1960s, from a classical company to one comprising a smaller number of dancers performing contemporary works to a high standard, and as a dancer, teacher and choreographer he was at the heart of the British dance world for much of his career. His appointment to the directorship of the Royal Ballet was controversial, partly because he was the first 'outsider' to run the company; during his tenure he did much to encourage young dancers and choreographers from within the company, and this aspect of his talent was put to good use in his subsequent appointment as director of choreographic studies at the Royal Ballet School. Maryon Lane, a talented and popular ballerina with Sadler's Wells Theatre Ballet and then the Royal Ballet from 1947 until 1968, died in June 2008 at the age of 77.

One of Norman Morrice's protegés, Michael Corder, produced a new full-length classical work – in itself a rarity – for English National Ballet during the year. *The Snow Queen,* adapted from the Hans Christian Andersen fairy tale, was premiered in Liverpool in October 2007, to an arrangement of Prokofiev's score *The Stone Flower* and with designs by Mark Bailey. Corder's choreography is always elegant, fluent and expressive, and the work is carefully structured and well danced. It fails however to convey the urgency and chill of the fairy tale's plot in a way that engages real attention. It nevertheless gives great opportunities to Daria Klimentova in the title role and Yosvani Ramos as her victim Kay, and the company as a whole will benefit hugely from having this ambitious work in the repertoire.

ENB's director, Wayne Eagling, mounted a new work of his own at the Royal Festival Hall in July 2008, his first as director and marking the company's first return to it's 'home' venue since 1997. Set to Mahler's Rückert-Lieder, *Resolution* was a frequently beautiful but uneven work inspired in part by Eagling's work with sufferers of muscular dystrophy. ENB continues to make technical progress under Eagling, while maintaining the audience appeal nurtured over the preceding decades. One of the company's former directors, Derek Deane, returned to the company to stage another of his in-the-round productions at the Royal Albert Hall in June 2008. This 'extravaganza', *Strictly Gershwin,* celebrated George Gershwin and the age of the Hollywood musical and provided a glossy and highly entertaining blend of ballet, tap and ballroom dancing performed with relish by ENB members and guest stars including Tamara Rojo, Guillaume Côté and Friedemann Vogel, with four of the numbers sung by the 80-year-old Hollywood legend Barbara Cook.

Rather less escapist in nature was the return of Birmingham Royal Ballet's *Edward II.* David Bintley's 1995 work, based on Christopher Marlowe's play, was marketed with the tag 'Ever seen a ballet with a health warning?'; though perhaps not actually injurious to its audience's well-being, it does tell a black story with no hint of light relief, a mood enhanced by the rich, heavy costuming designed by Jasper Conran and graced by Robert Tewsley's impressive portrayal of Edward. BRB did intersperse this work with lighter fare in the shape of Ashton's *Daphnis and Chloë,* several jazz ballets showing a different side of Bintley's talent, and performances of its excellent productions of *Swan Lake, The Nutcracker* and *Giselle.* In July 2008 Michael Corder turned from one chilling Hans Christian Andersen fairy tale to another: he staged a new version of *Le Baiser de la fée* set to Stravinsky's score and designed by John Macfarlane. This work displayed similar strengths and weaknesses to *The Snow Queen,* with choreographic fluency and imagination failing to be matched by innate dramatic sensibility.

MOVING ON

BRB's assistant director Desmond Kelly, a teacher and former dancer of distinction, retired from the company at the end of the season. He had held the post of assistant director since 1990, having previously been a principal dancer with both Royal Ballet companies after coming to Britain from his native Zimbabwe in the 1960s. Kelly was subsequently appointed artistic director of Elmhurst School for Dance from September 2008. His retirement from the company was marked by a gala at the Birmingham Hippodrome on 28 June 2008 in honour of a great career culminating in his work on *Ballet Hoo! Ballet Changed My Life,* for which he and Marion Tait were awarded a National Dance Awards Special Award for 2007. The company also announced at the end of the season that David Bintley would combine his role as director of BRB with the post of artistic director of the New National Theatre Ballet in Tokyo from 2010.

Another Royal Ballet alumnus, Ashley Page, is marking his stamp on Scottish Ballet with ever-growing confidence; certainly he cannot be accused of under-ambition. His new production of *The Sleeping Beauty,* staged in December 2007, drastically reworked the traditional scenario and substituted a knowing modern perspective for the innocence and grandeur of the original. Page's choreographic style and sensibilities are not suited to the combination of formality and yearning romance of ballet's classic works, and, as is sometimes the case with Matthew Bourne's reworkings, Page too often ignores or mistreats the magnificent music at the heart of these works. This *Beauty* is more concerned with its plot ideas and its lavish and sometimes outrageous costume conceptions than it is with the ideas of love, evil and the triumph of good that are central not just to the plot of *The Sleeping Beauty* but also to its score. A new version of *Romeo and Juliet* by Krzyzstof Pastor mounted in May 2008 displayed much of the same insensitivity to the central drama of Shakespeare's plot and Prokofiev's score by attempting to encompass great swathes of 20th-century history and a whole range of 'messages' in place of choreographic or dramatic coherence.

Tchaikovsky fared somewhat better at the hands of Northern Ballet Theatre's director, David Nixon, this time in a visually imaginative new production of *The Nutcracker.* Nixon also turned his hand to *Hamlet,* in a frequently tasteless production with a completely re-written scenario set in Nazi-occupied Paris and designed by Christopher Giles to a score by Philip Feeney.

Tastelessness is not often a charge that can be levelled at Rambert Dance Company. *Infinity,* a new work mounted in the autumn of 2007 by Garry Stewart, director of Australian Dance Theatre, did however create other problems. It sought to deal with birth, growth, metamorphosis, symbiosis, conflict, death and the hope of eternal life; and while the choreography was athletic and strongly danced the work was unfocussed and unable to shed real light on these great themes. Melanie Teall's *L'éveil* was by contrast an overly-restrained exploration of 'aspects of femininity' set to songs by Kurt Weill and Leslie Bricusse. Rambert also revived Christopher Bruce's powerful *Swansong,* created in 1987 for English National Ballet and exploring the themes of torture and interrogation.

FIRST UMBRELLA

Dance Umbrella 2007 was the first under new director Betsy Gregory. It presented a range of established and new companies, including the London premiere of Siobhain Davies's *Two Quartets* and the Michael Clark Company in the final instalment of his Stravinsky Project works – *I do,* set to *Les Noces. I do* evoked Nijinska's influential 1923 staging but found a fresh and personal way of expressing the power of the music as a Russian peasant bride is led with a ritual inevitability to her wedding. This Dance Umbrella's main innovation was to stage two free outdoor events, one on the South Bank (the Compagnie Beau Geste in *Transports Exceptionnels*) and one adjacent to Liverpool Street Station (Paul-André Fortier in *Solo 30 × 30*).

Possibly the most keenly anticipated season of the year was the inaugural season of Christopher Wheeldon's new company, Morphoses, at Sadler's Wells Theatre in September 2007. The full company is not in fact due to be assembled until 2009, and so these performances formed more of a statement of intent than a final product. And although Wheeldon brought together a fine group of dancers from both sides of the Atlantic, including Wendy Whelan, Craig Hall, Angel Corella, Alina Cojocaru and Johan Kobborg, the programmes on offer were strangely low-key and performed (as seems inevitable at Sadler's

Wells) in near-darkness, thereby eliminating any sense of excitement that may have been generated in advance. Mainly small-scale works by Wheeldon himself, Balanchine, William Forsythe and Edwaard Liang gave no real indication of how Wheeldon hopes to invigorate contemporary ballet, and if anything, they served to reinforce doubts about the creative future of this art form that has such an illustrious past.

Wayne McGregor, resident choreographer at the Royal Ballet but still running his own company, Random Dance, is a key figure in dance's creative present. He presented a new work, *Entity*, for Random Dance in April 2008, again at Sadler's Wells. As with earlier works, McGregor uses a range of media including dance, film, art, music and technology to explore the relationship between the brain and the body. To music by Coldplay, Jon Hopkins and Jody Talbot, *Entity* is work of intensity and visceral beauty that literally stretches its dancers to their physical utmost. Less dramatic were the new works mounted by Richard Alston's company – a sparkling piece by Alston himself set to Hoagy Carmichael songs, and two rather less inspiring offerings from Darren Ellis *(No More Ghosts)* and Martin Lawrance *(Body and Soul)*. A collaboration between Akram Khan and dancers from the National Ballet of China in February 2008 produced one of the more new interesting works of the year: *Bahok*, choreographed by Khan and set to a score by Nitin Sawhney, explored the meaning of home in a constantly changing world, and was a powerful and absorbing piece superbly danced and with a real sense of authority and purpose.

Maurice Béjart, a controversial but influential choreographer and director, died in November 2007 at the age of 80. Born in Marseilles, he trained there and in Paris and formed his own company, Les Ballets de l'Etoile, in Paris in 1954. International success came with his move to Brussels, where his version of *Le Sacre du printemps* in 1959 led to his appointment the following year as director of ballet at the Théâtre Royale de la Monnaie where he renamed the company Le Ballet du XXme Siècle. His work, little seen in Britain, has been variously interpreted as profound and groundbreaking or vulgar and clichéd. His spectacular early productions, often with explicit political messages, were hugely popular, and his work had a notable influence on the development of dance in continental Europe.

'BABY BALLERINA'

The last surviving of the three 'baby ballerinas' of the Ballets Russes in the 1930s, Irina Baronova, died in June 2008 at the age of 89. Born in Petrograd, she studied under the former Imperial ballerina Olga Preobajenska in Paris, and was chosen by Balanchine at the age of 13 to join the new Ballets Russes de Monte Carlo. When Balanchine left the company, Baronova stayed and worked under Léonide Massine, creating roles in works by him including *Les Présages, Le Beau Danube* and *Jeux d'enfants*. She later joined Ballet Theatre (now American Ballet Theatre) at the invitation of its founder, Lucia Chase. She retired from dancing in 1946, but retained links with the dance world until her death.

Following New York City Ballet's major London season in the spring of 2008 came a short but equally interesting visit by the Stuttgart Ballet, who performed John Cranko's 1962 version of *Romeo and Juliet* set to Prokofiev's familiar score and originally created for Stuttgart Ballet. Parts of the choreography and staging also proved to be unnervingly familiar to London ballet-goers steeped in Kenneth MacMillan's 1965 production, and showed the direct influence Cranko's work clearly had on MacMillan. The performances by Pina Bausch's company at Sadler's Wells in February 2008 also allowed for the comparison of different versions of the same work, this time Stravinsky's *The Rite of Spring*. Bausch's grimly physical 1975 work contrasted with MacMillan's lighter but still powerful 1962 work performed by the Royal Ballet during the season and with Michael Clark's idiosyncratic contemporary version *Mmm*, given as part of his Dance Umbrella performances.

A highlight of this dance year came in the shape not of a staged work but a book. Julie Kavanagh's new biography of Rudolf Nureyev was a beautifully written and researched account of the life of a complex, difficult and driven man who changed the face of ballet after his defection in 1961. His intensity and passion both enriched and blighted his personal life, but they combined with his talent and determination to transform the role of the male dancer, to inspire other dancers both male and female, and to give audiences a glimpse of the transcendent reality behind all great art.

NEW PRODUCTIONS

ROYAL BALLET
Founded 1931 as the Vic-Wells Ballet
Royal Opera House, Covent Garden, London WC2E 9DD

Electric Counterpoint (Christopher Wheeldon), 28 February 2008. A one-act work. *Music,* Bach and Steve Reich; *design,* Jean-Marc Puissant; *video artists,* Michael Nunn and William Trevitt; *sound design,* Mukul Patel. *Cast,* Edward Watson, Sarah Lamb, Zenaida Yanowsky and Eric Underwood

Rushes - Fragments of a Lost Story (Kim Brandstrup), 23 April 2008. A one-act work. *Music,* Prokofiev, arranged by Michael Berkeley; *design,* Richard Hudson; *video design,* Dick Straker. Cast led by Carlos Acosta, Alina Cojocaru and Laura Morera

BIRMINGHAM ROYAL BALLET
Founded 1946 as the Sadler's Wells Opera Ballet
Birmingham Hippodrome, Thorp Street, Birmingham B5 4AU

Le Baiser de la fée (Michael Corder), 3 July 2008. A one-act work. *Music,* Stravinsky; *design,* John Macfarlane and Paule Constable. Cast led by Alexander Campbell, Jenna Roberts and Natasha Oughtred

ENGLISH NATIONAL BALLET
Founded 1950 as London Festival Ballet
Markova House, 39 Jay Mews, London SW7 2ES

The Snow Queen (Michael Corder), 11 October 2007. A full-length work. *Music,* Prokofiev, arranged by Julian Phillips; *design,* Mark Bailey. Cast led by Daria Klimentova, Yosvani Ramos and Fernanda Oliveira

Strictly Gershwin (Derek Deane), 13 June 2008. An in-the-round production at the Royal Albert Hall, London. *Music,* George Gershwin, adapted by Gareth Valentine; *costumes,* Roberta Guidi di Bagno

Resolution (Wayne Eagling), 2 July 2008. A one-act work. *Music,* Mahler; *design,* Wayne Eagling and Wizzy Shawyer

RAMBERT DANCE COMPANY
Founded 1926 as the Marie Rambert Dancers
94 Chiswick High Road, London W4 1SH

Infinity (Garry Stewart), 26 September 2007. *Score,* Luke Smiles; *design,* Georg Mayer-Wiel

L'éveil (Melanie Teall), 26 September 2007 following workshop performances in July 2007. *Music,* Kurt Weill and Leslie Bricusse; *design,* Melanie Teall, with costumes inspired by Roland Mouret

Scribblings (Doug Varone), 20 February 2008. *Music,* John Adams; *design,* Jon Bausor

RICHARD ALSTON DANCE COMPANY
Founded 1994
The Place, 17 Duke's Road, London WC1H 9AB

Shuffle It Right (Richard Alston), 12 February 2008. *Music,* Hoagy Carmichael

No More Ghosts (Darren Ellis), 13 June 2008. *Music,* Wayne Walker-Allen

Body and Soul (Martin Lawrance), 13 June 2008. *Music,* Schubert

SCOTTISH BALLET
Founded 1956 as the Western Theatre Ballet
261 West Princes Street, Glasgow G4 9EE

Ride the Beast (Stephen Petronio), 18 August 2007. A one-act work. *Music,* Radiohead; *design,* Benjamin Cho

The Sleeping Beauty (Ashley Page), 13 December 2007. A full-length work. *Music,* Tchaikovsky; *design,* Antony McDonald. Cast led by Claire Robertson, Erik Cavallari, Soon Ja Lee and Limor Ziv

Romeo and Juliet (Krzyzstof Pastor), 13 May 2008. A full-length work. *Music,* Prokofiev; *design,* Tatyana van Walsum. Cast led by Sophie Martin and Erik Cavallari

Lull (Diana Loosmore), 26 June 2008. A one-act work. *Music,* Basquiat Strings; *design,* Diana Loosmore

Träume (Gregory Dean), 26 June 2008. A one-act work. *Music,* Colleen; *design,* Gregory Dean

AWARDS

CRITICS' CIRCLE NATIONAL DANCE AWARDS 2007

De Valois Award for Outstanding Achievement in Dance – Celeste Dandeker (co-founder of Candoco)

Dancing Times Award for Best Male Dancer – Jonathan Goddard (Richard Alston Dance Company)

Richard Sherrington Award for Best Female Dancer – Natalia Osipova (Bolshoi Ballet, for performances with the company in London in summer 2007)

Patron's Award – Darcey Bussell

National Dance Awards Special Award – Desmond Kelly and Marion Tait (Birmingham Royal Ballet) for their work on *Ballet Hoo! Ballet Changed My Life*

Best Choreography (Modern) – Michael Keegan-Dolan (*The Bull,* Fabulous Beast Dance Theatre)

SPOTLIGHT AWARDS 2008

Female Modern Dancer – Kialea-Nadine Williams (Phoenix Dance Company)

Male Modern Dancer – Dane Hurst (Rambert Dance Company)

Female Classical Dancer – Carol-Anne Miller (Birmingham Royal Ballet)

Male Classical Dancer – Ivan Vasiliev (Bolshoi Ballet)

Dance UK Industry Award – Celeste Dandeker

Company Prize for Outstanding Repertoire (Classical) – Scottish Ballet

Company Prize for Outstanding Repertoire (Modern) – Henri Oguike Dance Company

Working Title Billy Elliot Award – Brandon Lawrence

LAURENCE OLIVIER AWARDS 2008 (DANCE)

Best New Dance Production – *Jewels* (The Royal Ballet)

Outstanding Achievement in Dance – The Royal Ballet for its revival of George Balanchine's *Jewels* at the Royal Opera House

Best Theatre Choreographer – Toby Sedgewick *(War Horse)*

ROYAL ACADEMY OF DANCE QUEEN ELIZABETH II CORONATION AWARD 2007
Alexander Grant

YOUNG BRITISH DANCER OF THE YEAR COMPETITION

2001	Lauren Cuthbertson	2005	Ruth Bailey
2002	Anniek Soobroy	2006	James Hay
2003	Joseph Caley	2007	Sergiy Polunin
2004	Aaron Robison	2008	William Bracewell

FILM

Jonathan Theodore

HOLLYWOOD IN TURMOIL

The past year has been an unusual one for cinema, as for much of it Hollywood, and indeed the entire entertainment industry, has been in disarray. The writers' strike of November 2007 to February 2008, a struggle over the spoils of the digital media revolution, brought the US film industry to a grinding halt and threatened to turn the entire studio system upside down. It provoked 'End of Hollywood' headlines in the *New York Times* and derailed not just cinema but the TV industry as a whole. A hasty settlement by the big studios has contained the damage to $2bn (£1bn) – not exactly pocket money – but the consequences of the strike are far from over, and with an actors' strike now on the cards its long-term significance for the industry is yet to be seen.

The film industry may have stuttered through the preceding year but this has not stopped it from being a superb time for quality drama. The first example of this was the stellar *No Country for Old Men*, written and directed by the Coen brothers of *O Brother, Where Art Thou?* and *Fargo* fame. Goofy and excessive comedy has made the Coens famous but *No Country* is a triumphant return to their starker, ragged roots. Based on the 2005 novel by Cormac McCarthy, *No Country* is a cat-and-mouse drama set along the bleak and unforgiving borderlands of Texas by the Rio Grande. This is Western country, and the Coens have crafted a bleak and brutal vision – reminiscent of Sam Peckinpah's *The Wild Bunch*, a bloody and notorious film about the decline of the old West.

The story opens with the aftermath of a drug deal gone wrong. Llewelyn Moss (Josh Brolin, in what is probably his breakthrough role), a quiet and taciturn Vietnam veteran, stumbles upon the money while out hunting deer and heads with it to the Mexican border. Hot on his trail is the sociopathic hitman Anton Chigurh (Javier Bardem, in another Oscar-winning performance) hired by shadowy corporate interests to recover the money. Chigurh is less hitman than Hannibal Lecter, an existential disciple of slaughter who is as happy to dispatch his employers as his target. Also following him is Tommy Lee Jones in a pitch-perfect performance as Sheriff Ed Tom Bell, a gruff, upright lawman disillusioned by the excesses of criminality he has borne witness to. Bell is convinced that Moss is a good man gone astray and is determined, against the evidence, that he can save and redeem him.

No Country is a dark and pessimistic film. It portrays a borderland American in a state of rot, with all norms and codes of conduct in permanent decline. The soul of the story can be found after all the action is over, in a conversation between the now-retired Ed Tom and his uncle, another former police officer, in which the latter states that America as a nation is inherently cruel and savage, with little possibility of redemption. The tone of the film is that of the 11th hour before the Apocalypse, and it hints, subtly but darkly, at a future devoid of all remaining norms and restraints.

The only real rival for the cinematic top spot this year was Paul Thomas Anderson's mad and brilliant *There Will Be Blood*. Loosely based on the Upton Sinclair novel *Oil* (1927), it tells the story of self-proclaimed 'oil-man' Daniel Plainview (played by Daniel Day-Lewis) on a ruthless quest for power during southern California's oil boom of the late 19th and early 20th centuries.

The film speaks of the industry's savage and reckless history, but its greatness lies not in the extravagance one might expect of such a film, but rather its subtlety of mood and tone. Where many a lesser film would have settled for a montage of boom-town scenes of the oil rush, *There Will Be Blood* is only ever coloured with a moody alienated texture. For all his wealth and success, Plainview leads a lonely and miserable existence, the expanse of the desert mirroring his isolation from humanity in a way reminiscent of the Wim Wenders classic *Paris, Texas*. The blood in the title suggests something gratuitous but any real violence only occurs in the final scene, spewing out of an arterial vein in the way that oil, the then-new blood of the nation, has been pumped out of holes for the course of the film.

The film focuses overwhelmingly on Daniel Day-Lewis, who, on usual flamboyant form, dominates the screen. Shrewd and manipulative, he is driven by ego, a disguised atheism and a misanthropic contempt for humanity (though, curiously, not children). In an era where naturalism has permeated screen acting, the intense theatricality of his performances often draws criticism – most notably in Scorsese flop *Gangs of New York* – but here he kills any possible objection stone dead. The only cloud on this film's horizon is the promise of a gratuitous cash-in sequel in the wake of its success.

Viewers in need of an adrenaline rush at the big screen were left disappointed. Where 2007 saw *Casino Royale*, a magnificent dark and gritty rejuvenation of the Bond genre, and the critically lauded *Bourne Ultimatum*, last year's most hyped action film was *Rambo*, complete with the tagline 'A Hero Never Dies, He Just Reloads'. Written and directed by Sylvester Stallone, the film is a running bloodbath, a collection of all the worst liberal nightmares presented without apology or irony.

No better was *Wanted*, macho erotica for the under-15 demographic starring James McAvoy, a serious actor selling out to the A-league action scene, and Angelina Jolie. For those looking for more fun there was *Iron Man*, a gleeful poke-in-the-eye at the Neo-Conservative world view. Its titular *Marvel Comics* hero was played by Robert Downey Jr, whose recent rise to stardom is justified by his electrifying charisma on screen. A darker comic turn could be found in *Sweeney Todd*, the latest slice of Tim Burton gothica starring his favourite muse Johnny Depp. A horror-panto musical about the fictitious psycho-barber, it ironically suffers from being too tasteful and restrained for the subject matter, and none of the tunes leave any lasting imprint in the mind.

The most notable example of the 'true crime' genre this year was *American Gangster*, directed by Ridley Scott, about a black kingpin (Frank Lucas, played by Denzel Washington) from Harlem who smuggles heroin into the USA on American planes returning from the Vietnam War, hiding it in the coffins of dead US servicemen. Lucas is memorable for breaking the Italian mafia's monopoly on heroin by smuggling it directly from a source in the Golden Triangle. His trial and testimony revealed drug-dealing and bribery among the US military, which provided Frank Lucas with his supply chain, and endemic corruption in the NYPD. It is unfortunate, then, that the film distorted so much of this fascinating true story. Sterling Johnson, a federal judge who served as a narcotics prosecutor in the trial of Lucas, depressingly described the film as '1 per cent reality and 99 per cent Hollywood'.

Releases over the last few years have been increasingly demonstrating a creeping creative exhaustion in Hollywood, and this year was no different, with the two biggest summer blockbusters being *Indiana Jones and the Kingdom of the Crystal Skull* and the *Sex and the City* movie. Both of these films, while fantastic money-spinners, feel late in the day and gratuitous. The relatively long gestation of *Sex and the City* (the series ended in 2004), allegedly due to a falling out between Sarah Jessica Parker and Kim Cattrall over pay and prominence, means the characters are now all in their forties and fifties, making this difficult ground for a show that defined itself as the bible of the 30-something single woman. At two-and-a-half hours, the feature-film showcase for New York's famous foursome is long enough to be a full mini-series of the show. Unfortunately that is where the similarity to its ancestor ends: *Sex and the City* has been transformed from a hip, niche programme into a cartoonish remake of itself. Exploiting the trendsetting reputation of the series to the hilt by stuffing the opening half hour full of product placement, it feels like seeing a fashion catalogue in 3D, and though things improve as the film takes a more sombre and reflective turn, *Sex and the City* lacks any of the originality, sass or relevance that gave the TV show its edge.

Coming twenty years after its predecessor *The Last Crusade, Indiana Jones and the Kingdom of the Crystal Skull* was one of the most eagerly anticipated films for years. It is a shame then that, though not a complete disaster, it largely disappointed. Spielberg was the king of family entertainment in the VHS age, and the new *Indiana* retains some of its old charm. In fact there is one scene of pure old-school genius, where Dr Jones blunders into a quiet suburban town that turns out to be a nuclear test site in the desert, ten seconds from detonation. But that is where the Indy magic ends. In order to keep aesthetic continuity with the previous films, the crew relied on traditional stunt work, but this much-lauded fact is redundant because many of the stunts are so overflowing with CGI that they look ropey and inauthentic. In fact the whole film, from Indy's continual lucky escapes to an ending complete with *Close Encounters*-style UFO, strains credulity, and bar the one scene mentioned above, there are no original flourishes. Shia LaBeouf, a rising star in Hollywood, plays Jones's son, successor and verbal sparring partner, but there is none of the golden cross-generational wisecracking of Harrison Ford and Sean Connery in *The Last Crusade*, and Cate Blanchett's icy Soviet nemesis is not convincing.

If last year was the year of superheroes – *Spiderman 3, X-Men 3,* and the metal behemoths in *Transformers* – this year's biggest releases were mostly fantasy films. *The Golden Compass* marks the latest attempt by Hollywood to spin a famous fantasy series into box-office gold. Based on Philip Pullman's trilogy *His Dark Materials* – a much more contemporary and controversial than the old favourites like Tolkien and C. S. Lewis – the story concerns Lyra, an orphan living in a fantastical parallel universe in which a dogmatic theocracy, called the Magisterium, threatens to dominate the world. This retro-futurist fairy-tale is visually impressive, and Nicole Kidman steals the show as the embodiment of icy blonde evil. But otherwise this adaptation feels cold. The books attained notoriety in the use of the Magisterium as a thinly veiled attack on organised faith and especially the Catholic Church, but this message has been surgically removed for the onscreen version. While understandable from a commercial point of view – an anti-Christian message would have spelled box office suicide in the USA – it strips the story of its whole point. In its desperation to ape the success of the big fantasy franchises, *The Golden Compass* looks like a hurried amalgamation of everything Hogwarts, Tolkien and *Narnia*, leaving little in the way of characters or ideas to root for.

The other running fantasy franchise, C. S. Lewis' *Narnia* tales, saw its second outing with *The Chronicles of Narnia: Prince Caspian*, directed by Andrew Adamson, who also directed *Shrek*. The film was shot in New Zealand for the Tolkienesque scenery (and convenient tax breaks). Set in a brutally occupied Narnia, *Prince Caspian* ramps up the pace of the original, throwing the viewer straight into the action and multiplying the number of battle scenes while somehow keeping the violence as bloodless and PG-friendly as possible. The plucky children share their screen time with newcomer to the series Ben Barnes, who plays the brooding and impassioned Prince Caspian. For a supposedly more adult film, the characters have been streamlined and lost much of their richness. Former black sheep Edmund loses his flirtations with the dark side, depriving the film of a moral dimension and undermining C. S. Lewis's Christian message of redemption. Tilda Swinton reprises her role as the White Witch, a superfluous but energising interlude that reminds us of just what this film is lacking in antagonists. Save that single scene, there is no dark temptation, no sense of mystery or dread. In fact the whole film seems streamlined to make as much space as possible for the staple fantasy medieval battle scenes, an ill omen for future *Narnia* adaptations to come.

Less sombre, but far more entertaining fantasy fare was found this year in the whimsical and irreverent *Stardust.* A cobbling together of fairytale stereotypes – dark lords, witches and damsels in distress – the film lacks the grandeur or self-conviction of the *Lord of the Rings* or *Narnia* franchises, but is thankfully devoid of any pretensions as a result. *Stardust* is less weighty Tolkien than panto with special effects. Trading a serious tone for satirical swipes works wonderfully with the star-studded cast – Michelle Pfeiffer revels in her over-the-top witch, and Robert De Niro camps up his role as a cross-dressing, effeminate pirate captain with gusto. Entertaining cameos by Peter O'Toole as a gleefully nasty monarch and Ricky Gervais in a reprisal of his David Brent persona are also enjoyable. With many big pictures such as *The Golden Compass* failing to ignite the box office, some smaller indie films achieved considerable success. Notable among these was *Juno*, which drew considerable media attention by inserting itself right in the middle of the US culture war and taking fire at both sides. *Juno* confronted the issue of abortion – a subject sensitive in American culture that most pregnancy-themed films don't even mention – and in aiming squarely at everyone's pieties drew equal amounts of praise and criticism from both sides of the debate. Initially on only limited release, *Juno* benefited from its controversy coupled with overwhelmingly positive reviews to recoup its modest investment of $6.5m 40 times over.

Since the days of the now-laughable *Jason* and *Friday the 13th* slasher-fests of the 1980s, Hollywood horror has been suffering from a form of inflation – the more it ramps up the gore and shock, the more apathetic its audiences become to the gratuity of violence on screen. Western directors struggling to re-engage with their audiences have been remaking the remarkable horror films coming out of Japan. Very little violence or otherworldly horror is actually witnessed in these films, which instead generate atmosphere through mystery and artful suspense. *The Ring*, *The Grudge* and *Dark Water* are all eastern films rewired for the English-speaking market, and the latest offering in this mould comes in the form of *The Eye*, an adaptation of a 2002 Hong Kong ghost film about a blind girl who, when her sight is restored in a cataract transplant, realises she can see ghosts as well as the living, and travels to Mexico to uncover the identity of her donor. The biggest looming spectre in this film is therefore *The Sixth Sense*-style concept of 'seeing the dead', so thoroughly engrained in popular lore, it strips *The Eye* of much of its thunder. The fact that *The Eye* is a star vehicle for screen beauty Jessica Alba is another issue, though in the end she fulfils her quota of glum stares and grimacing reasonably well. *The Eye* retains several of the most unnerving sequences from the original, though their impact is undermined by the upping of the thrills and shocks elsewhere – most Hollywood directors are still failing to learn the lessons that forced them to turn East in the first place.

The prime example of a horror director repeating the same mistakes is seen in *The Happening*, the latest attempt by writer-director M. Night Shyamalan to resurrect his career. Burnt at the box office by his laughable fairy tale *Lady in the Water* – in which he notoriously cast himself as a visionary writer who would save mankind – Shyamalan returns in *The Happening* to the more familiar horror-with-a-twist formula that made him famous, showing an America struck by a new mystery plague. The film drips with new-age spirituality and mysticism and an earnest belief in its power to engage and provoke. But, as always, the stylised wrapping conceals a lack of hard substance. *The Sixth Sense* was original, creepy, and brilliantly plotted, and is also now a decade old, and Shyamalan cannot continue to base his entire reputation on the fading memories of that one hit.

BRITISH CINEMA

One of the best examples of British cinema this year was Anton Corbijn's *Control*, a biopic about Ian Curtis, the troubled front-man of post-punk Mancunian band *Joy Division*. His story is the great northern rock-and-roll tragedy of recent decades, as the epileptic Curtis hanged himself, instantly enshrining his bittersweet posthumous release 'Love Will Tear us Apart' with legendary doomed romantic status. The film is shot in monochrome, highlighting the grimness of 70s working class Macclesfield.

The big British period piece of the year was the drama *Atonement*. Directed by Joe Wright and starring Keira Knightley and James McAvoy, it is the film adaptation of Ian McEwan's critically acclaimed 2001 novel of the same name, which became an international hit. Wright (who directed *Pride and Prejudice* in 2005) pitches this tale of lies and redemption as a heady mix of comedy melodrama and tragedy, and it largely works. The book is a difficult-to-adapt, dense concoction of secrets and lies but *Atonement* pulls it off. In particular, the chemistry between its leads, Knightley and McAvoy, is white-hot. Somewhat less impressive was *The Edge of Love*. The film may nominally be about a notorious scandal involving Welsh poet Dylan Thomas but the director, John Maybury, seems far more interested in Keira Knightley, with his camera continually lingering lovingly over her face. Knightley plays a singer, and unfortunately we are forced to endure a series of ill-fated attempts to prove that the pouting star can croon seductively with the best of them. The fact that the script was written by her mother probably didn't help with the attention, but why one could be as drawn to her cold and conceited manner as is Dylan Thomas remains a mystery. Unfocused and underpowered, *The Edge of Love* is full of stock images of louche artists and bohemians as a substitute for real depth, with Knightley and co-star Sienna Miller sharing many scenes but little chemistry.

AWARD CEREMONIES

Saved from cancellation by a last-minute settlement of the screenwriters strike, the 80th Academy Awards were a hasty and rushed ceremony. With this year's catalogue of films far from ideal, the main contenders were critically acclaimed character dramas rather than billion-dollar earning blockbusters. Daniel Day-Lewis was voted best actor for his punishing *tour de force* as brutal oilman Daniel Plainview, but *No Country For Old Men* was the evening's big winner. Despite that, it gained only four Oscars, far fewer than most best-picture winners. That left more Oscars to be handed out as consolation prizes to many of the year's other top films. *Atonement* won best original score; *Sweeney Todd* won best art direction; *The Bourne Ultimatum* won best editing and sound mixing; even *The Golden Compass*, a commercial flop in the US, was given best visual effects.

The scatter-shot spread of the Oscars reflected the Academy's feeling that this was a strong roster of films, perhaps the strongest since the 1970s. Both *No Country* and *There Will Be Blood* seem to have reflected the dark mood of a country mired in war and sliding into recession. Yet neither film hit a chord with Middle America, and ratings were amongst the lowest recorded yet. *Juno*, the year's crowd-pleaser, which some had feared might win best picture, took just one Oscar – best original screenplay for Hollywood's newest writing sensation, ex-stripper Diablo Cody.

Cannes followed a more predictable pattern, with European films taking the top prizes while Hollywood stars worked the red carpet. Despite Sean Penn's appearance on the jury panel, American cinema received its requisite snubbing; the only film receiving any attention was Steven Soderbergh's *Che*, a Spanish-language film starring Benicio Del Toro as the titular revolutionary icon. The top prize, the Palme d'Or, went unanimously to Laurent Cantet's *Entre les Murs*, which traces a year in a Paris high school class. Cannes is as vulnerable to Hollywood glitz and glamour as any other award ceremony, and that *Indiana Jones and the Kingdom of the Crystal Skull* premiered to such excitement there shows the continuing importance of Hollywood to a festival otherwise preoccupied with its snobbishly high ideals of cinema.

AWARDS

ACADEMY AWARDS 2008

Best Picture – *No Country for Old Men* (Joel and Ethan Coen)
Best Director – Joel and Ethan Coen *(No Country For Old Men)*
Best Actor – Daniel Day-Lewis *(There Will Be Blood)*
Best Actress – Marion Cotillard *(La Vie En Rose)*
Best Supporting Actor – Javier Bardem *(No Country For Old Men)*
Best Supporting Actress – Tilda Swindon *(Michael Clayton)*
Best Animated Feature – *Ratatouille* (Brad Bird)
Best Documentary – *An Inconvenient Truth* (Alex Gibney and Eva Orner)
Best Foreign Language Film – *The Counterfeiters* (Stefan Ruzowitzky)
Best Adapted Screenplay – Joel and Ethan Coen *(No Country For Old Men)*
Best Original Screenplay – Diablo Cody *(Juno)*

CANNES FILM FESTIVAL 2008

Palme d'Or – *Entre les Murs* (Laurent Cantet)
Grand Prix – *Gomorra* (Matteo Garrone)
Best Director – *Three Monkeys* (Nuri Bilge Ceylan)
Best Screenplay – *The Silence of Lorna* (Luc and Jean Pierre Dardenne)
Best Actor – Benicio del Toro *(Che)*
Best Actress – Sandra Corveloni *(Linha de Passe)*
Jury Prize – *Il Divo* (Paolo Sorrentino)
61st Anniversary Prize – Clint Eastwood *(Changeling)* and Catherine Deneuve *(A Christmas Tale)*
Camera d'Or – *Hunger* (Steve McQueen)

BERLIN FILM FESTIVAL 2008

Golden Bear – *The Elite Squad* (Jose Padilha)
Grand Jury Prize – *Standard Operating Procedure* (Errol Morris)
Silver Bear for Best Director – *There Will Be Blood* (Paul Thomas Anderson)

VENICE FILM FESTIVAL 2007

Golden Lion – *Lust, Caution* (Ang Lee)
Special Jury Prize – *I'm Not There* (Todd Haynes)

LITERATURE

Nick Rennison

FICTION

Who are the two most powerful people in the British book trade? A good case could be made for two women. Until the Queen decides to publish her memoirs, J. K. Rowling is certainly the wealthiest person in the book world and wealth typically translates into power. In 2007 Rowling dominated the bestseller lists once again. *Harry Potter and the Deathly Hallows* (Bloomsbury), the final book in the series, sold more than four million copies in the UK alone between July and December. Look down that list, however, and evidence of another power in the land could be easily detected. Rather fewer people have heard of Amanda Ross but, as the *éminence grise* of the Richard and Judy Book Club, her ability to turn a book into a bestseller is clear enough. Third in the 2007 bestseller list, behind two Harry Potter editions, was Jed Rubenfeld's *The Interpretation of Murder* (Headline), a clever and compelling crime novel which imagines Freud and Jung involved in a murder mystery during their 1909 trip to America; fourth in the list was Kim Edwards' *The Memory-Keeper's Daughter* (Penguin), the moving story of the consequences that follow from a doctor's unwillingness to accept a daughter with Down's syndrome. Both would have doubtless sold well enough had they not been included among Richard and Judy's recommendations but selection by Ross propelled them even further up the chart. Kate Morton's *The House at Riverton* (Pan), another Richard and Judy choice, finished in sixth place.

It thus becomes not too demanding a task to predict some of the books that will feature in this year's bestseller charts when they are announced in December. Put money on Margaret Cezair-Thompson's *The Pirate's Daughter* (Headline), a tale that mixes together real and fictional characters in 1940s Jamaica; Julia Gregson's historical romance set in 1920s India, *East of the Sun* (Orion); and James Bradley's story of Regency body-snatching, *The Resurrectionist* (Faber), taking their places in the higher reaches of lists. They all sold well from the moment of publication and selection for the Richard and Judy Summer Reads 2008 will guarantee that they do even better in the second half of the year.

What else can be deduced from the bestseller charts? Probably not much more than we know already – that being on the TV and in celebrity magazines is a big help if you are selling a book that you have either written or paid somebody else to write. The ubiquitous Jeremy Clarkson called his latest *Don't Stop Me Now* (Michael Joseph). For better or for worse, it was impossible to do so. Two other titles by Clarkson featured in the top 50, although all three were beaten by *On the Edge* (Weidenfeld & Nicolson), the autobiography of his fellow *Top Gear* petrolhead Richard Hammond, which told the story of how Hammond's obsession with fast cars nearly cost him his life. Comedian Russell Brand's obsession with fast women (in fact, with women of all kinds) is well-known and his gratingly titled memoir *My Booky Wook* (Hodder) recorded both his sexual antics and his struggles with substance addiction in some detail. It was no sooner published in the autumn of 2007 than it headed rapidly towards the top of the non-fiction charts. Meanwhile Katie Price, the cultural phenomenon still occasionally known as Jordan, was pursuing her campaign to have more books in the bestseller lists than J. K. Rowling. Not to be outdone by Literary Spice, Geri Halliwell – who published three children's stories in the year – she even turned her hand to a series of Perfect Ponies books.

One work that didn't feature in the top 100 titles of 2007, sadly, was the winner of the Man Booker prize. This was Irish novelist Anne Enright's book *The Gathering* (Jonathan Cape), the story of a troubled Dublin family coming together to mourn the death of one of its members. It was praised by one reviewer for its 'exhilarating bleakness', a description which may go some way to explaining its absence from the list. Bleakness and bestseller status rarely go together in a novel. *The Gathering* won out over five other shortlisted titles – Nicola Barker's *Darkmans* (Fourth Estate), Mohsin Hamid's *The Reluctant Fundamentalist* (Hamish Hamilton), Lloyd Jones's *Mister Pip* (John Murray), Ian McEwan's *On Chesil Beach* (Jonathan Cape) and *Animal's People* (Simon & Schuster) by Indra Sinha.

The 2008 prize will be awarded after this piece goes to print but the year has already seen some newsworthy Booker-related activity. As the prize approached its 40th birthday, the search was on for the Best of the Booker, the finest novel from four decades of winners. When a similar exercise was undertaken on the prize's 25th anniversary, the winner was Salman Rushdie for *Midnight's Children*. On that occasion the decision was made by three wise men meeting in secret. For the 40th anniversary, the decision was more democratic. A panel chose a shortlist of six and the vote was then thrown open to the public via the Booker prize's website. And the winner this time was . . . Salman Rushdie for *Midnight's Children*.

Other prizes jostled with the Booker for media attention. Now in its 13th year, the Orange prize for fiction has attracted controversy from the start but has also established itself as one of the most prestigious in Britain. The 'women-only' status of the prize was again at the centre of debate earlier this year with some male writers claiming positive discrimination was increasingly unnecessary in the modern literary world. A distinguished *grande dame* of fiction, A. S. Byatt, argued that it was sexist and that her publishers had been instructed never to submit her books for it. Whatever the arguments, the shortlist drawn up by a team of judges led by the broadcaster and journalist Kirsty Lang was an intriguing one. Three of the six titles – *The Outcast* (Chatto & Windus) by Sadie Jones, Heather O'Neill's *Lullabies for Little Criminals* (Quercus) and Patricia Wood's *Lottery* (Heinemann) – were first novels. Charlotte Mendelson's *When We Were Bad* (Picador) was a third novel by the admired young British novelist. The list was completed by *Fault Lines* (Atlantic) by Nancy Huston, a Canadian novelist who writes first in French and then translates her own work into English, and *The Road Home* (Chatto & Windus) by Rose Tremain. Any of the six would have been a deserving winner but the prize was won by Tremain. The 2008 Orange award for new writers was won by Joanna Kavenna for *Inglorious* (Faber), her darkly comic story of a successful metropolitan woman who chooses to turn her back on the comforts of her life in search of deeper meanings.

At the Costa Book Awards the first novel award for 2007 went to Catherine O'Flynn for *What Was Lost* (Tindal Street Press); the novel award went to A. L. Kennedy and *Day* (Jonathan Cape), a brilliantly convincing recreation of the experiences of a young aircraftman during and after the Second World War. In the biography category the winner was Simon Sebag Montefiore's *Young Stalin* (Weidenfeld & Nicolson), a memorable portrait of the formative years of one of the twentieth century's greatest monsters. The poetry prize was won by Jean Sprackland for *Tilt* (Jonathan Cape), her third collection of what the judges called 'crafted and delicate poems that tell us what it is to be alive now'; the children's book winner was Ann Kelley for *The Bower Bird* (Luath Press). The judges of the awards carry out one final duty when they choose the Costa book of the year from the victors in the five categories. The overall winner and recipient of an extra £25,000 was A. L. Kennedy.

The biggest prize of all – the Nobel prize for literature – has gone to writers in English three times already in the 21st century. As winner of the 2007 prize, the name of Doris Lessing was added to those of V. S. Naipaul, Harold Pinter and J. M. Coetzee. Announcing the award, the Swedish Academy spoke of her 'scepticism, fire and visionary power' which have 'subjected a divided civilisation to scrutiny'. Her scepticism at least seemed to be on display in her distinctly underwhelmed first response to word that she had been awarded the prize. 'Oh, Christ', she said to reporters who waylaid her outside her north London home with the news, 'I couldn't care less.' Lessing's name has been mentioned in connection with the prize for the last thirty years at least and, it seemed, the thrill of possible victory had long since faded.

The first half of 2008 saw a varied array of interesting novels published. The latest writer to inherit the mantle of Ian Fleming was Sebastian Faulks, whose new James Bond novel, *Devil May Care*, was published to mostly complimentary reviews. Its success must have both shaken *and* stirred executives at Penguin as the book went on to become one of the company's fastest-selling hardbacks ever. Salman Rushdie mixed Mughals with Medicis in his historical romance *The Enchantress of Florence* (Jonathan Cape), the story of a young Florentine traveller turning up at the court of Akbar the Great with claims that he is the son of a lost Indian princess. In *The Northern Clemency* (Fourth Estate) Philip Hensher looked outside the metropolis for clues to the zeitgeist and found them in 1970s Sheffield. Another bold and ambitious narrative, this one by a debut novelist, also sought to define the state of the nation, in this instance in Newcastle. Richard T. Kelly's *Crusaders* (Faber) turned the tale of a naive Church of England vicar despatched northwards in the early years of New Labour to establish a mission church in a deprived area of the city into an absorbing analysis of what's gone wrong with the country.

Some much-lauded and highly respected writers published new novels in the early months of the year. Helen Dunmore's *Counting the Stars* (Fig Tree) was her version of the passionate but destructive affair between the Roman poet Catullus and his muse. Louis de Bernières recorded the progress of this unlikely love story in *A Partisan's Daughter* (Harvill Secker) and Melvyn Bragg revisited the most painful episode in his own past – the suicide of his first wife – in the heavily autobiographical *Remember Me* (Sceptre). In *His Illegal Self* (Faber) Peter Carey followed the complicated relationship of a woman and a child as they made their way through the radical counterculture of the 1960s and 1970s; Hanif Kureishi's *Something to Tell You* (Faber) also looked back to the 1970s in its story of a middle-aged psychoanalyst still haunted by his youthful misdeeds. Since his debut stories were published nearly 30 years ago, Adam Mars-Jones has not been the most prolific of fiction writers but he has often won the admiring attention of the critics and was officially hailed as one of the best of young British novelists as long ago as 1983. None the less *Pilcrow* (Faber) was only his second published novel, a funny and poignant story of the childhood and adolescence of a precocious outsider.

Debut novelist Nick Harkaway is the son of John Le Carré, as every reviewer of the book was keen to tell us, but it was hard to find any echoes of George Smiley in *The Gone Away World* (Heinemann), a sprawling and ambitious work of post-apocalyptic fantasy in which survivors of a future war struggle with the new world that a devastating superweapon has created. Madly inventive and often very funny, Harkaway's novel was probably the only one published this year to be compared to both the work of Salman Rushdie and a *Mad Max* film. Equally impressive in its own very different way was Ross Raisin's *God's Own Country* (Viking), in which a gangling young misfit from an isolated Yorkshire hill-farm told his own tale of obsession and delusion in a powerfully original narrative voice. Victoria Hislop was a debut novelist herself as recently as 2005 with *The Island.* Few novels were as keenly anticipated this year as her second book, *The Return* (Headline), which moves between present-day Spain and the terrible years of the country's civil war to tell its story of romance, heroism and the revelation of family secrets.

In the crime genre, perhaps the most eagerly awaited novel was *Revelation* (Pan Macmillan), C. J. Sansom's fourth tale of the Tudor lawyer Matthew Shardlake, but other well-known writers had new books to their names. Reginald Hill published *A Cure for All Diseases* (HarperCollins), a further instalment in his long-running Dalziel and Pascoe series, Elizabeth George provided her aristocratic Inspector Lynley with another adventure in *Careless in Red* (Hodder), Susan Hill's series character Simon Serailler made a fourth appearance in *The Vows of Silence* (Chatto & Windus) and Donna Leon's humane Venetian policeman Commissario Brunetti was on hand again in *The Girl of his Dreams* (Heinemann). As the popularity of Shardlake shows, the public's taste for historical crime fiction seems as strong as ever and other writers were there to satisfy it. The Russian novelist Boris Akunin's suave 19th-century investigator Erast Fandorin was given his sixth outing in *The State Counsellor* (Weidenfeld & Nicolson). Fandorin fans need have no concerns that the supply of their favourite fiction will dry up. Another half-dozen titles await translation and, since Akunin claims to have identified sixteen sub-genres of crime fiction, we can probably expect even more.

Two British novelists, in very different ways, made clever use of real-life writers from the past in their books. Gyles Brandreth gave Oscar Wilde the leading role in another murder mystery in *Oscar Wilde and the Ring of Death* (John Murray) and did a creditable job of recreating his hero's legendary wit and wisdom; Nicola Upson's debut novel *An Expert in Murder* (Faber) revolves around the crime writer Josephine Tey and murder in London's theatreland of the 1930s. Some of the big hitters in American crime fiction also had novels published in the UK during the year. Sue Grafton reached the 20th letter of the alphabet in her Kinsey Milhone series with *T is for Trespass* (Macmillan), Harlan Coben produced another tautly-plotted thriller in *Hold Tight* (Orion) and Tess Gerritsen moved between past and present crime in *The Bone Garden* (Bantam).

The Oscars of the crime and mystery fiction world are the CWA Dagger Awards. Eight prizes are handed out on the night of the awards dinner in July including the Duncan Lawrie International Dagger for the best crime novel translated into English which went to Dominique Manotti's *Lorraine Connection* (Eurocrime), the Ian Fleming Steel Dagger for best contemporary thriller, awarded to Tom Rob Smith for *Child 44* (Simon & Schuster), and the John Creasey New Blood Dagger, for best debut novel, won by Matt Rees for *The Bethlehem Murders* (Atlantic Books). The most prestigious prize of all, however, is the Duncan Lawrie Dagger, which was given this year to Frances Fyfield for *Blood from Stone* (Little, Brown), the story of the investigation into the apparent suicide of a successful female barrister and the murky secrets it revealed. Ms Fyfield accepted the award with the memorable words, 'Thank you from the bottom of my little black heart'.

In science fiction (SF), the glittering prizes for which British authors yearn are the British Science Fiction Association award for Best Novel and Arthur C. Clarke award. The first of these went to Ian McDonald's *Brasyl* (Gollancz), a kaleidoscopic thriller which moved between past, present and future states of the South American country. The BSFA celebrated its own 50th anniversary by handing out a special prize to the best novel of 1958. Winner was *Non-Stop* by Brian Aldiss who was unable to collect the award but is still publishing new and mind-stretching fiction in his eighties. *Harm* (Duckworth), a story of the real world and a fictional world colliding, appeared in the autumn of 2007. The Arthur C. Clarke award was won by Richard Morgan for his novel *Black Man* (Gollancz), a gripping, often violent story of a manhunt 100 years in the future. Other SF highlights in the first half of 2008 included *Matter* (Orbit), Iain M. Banks's return to the multiple civilisations of the Culture, Stephen Baxter's *Weaver* (Gollancz), a startling work of alternative history set in Second World War England, and *House of Suns* (Gollancz), a space opera set against a vast backdrop of time and space by Alastair Reynolds.

Fantasy fiction has a tendency to come in multi-volume form and there was, as usual, no shortage of entrants in already popular and highly-acclaimed series. *Toll the Hounds* (Bantam) was the eighth book in Steven Erikson's 'Malazan Book of the Fallen' sequence; Raymond E. Feist published *Wrath of a Mad God* (Harper Voyager) the third and final book in his 'Darkwar Saga'; and Katharine Kerr's *The Shadow Isle* (Harper Voyager) was the latest in her cycle of novels set in the fictional land of Deverry. Meanwhile Darren Shan, who has already written enough horror and fantasy fiction for teenagers to terrify and traumatise one generation, aimed at another and began a series for adults with *Procession of the Dead* (Harper Voyager).

NON-FICTION

In its tenth year, the Samuel Johnson Prize is firmly established as the most prestigious of non-fiction awards and the books chosen for its shortlist are now given extra publicity in a number of TV programmes produced by its sponsor, BBC4. The shortlist this year was as eclectic as always and showed just what a vast range of writing comes under the broad label of non-fiction. Titles included *Blood River* (Vintage), Tim Butcher's hair-raising account of his travels along the Congo, Mark Cocker's *Crow Country* (Jonathan Cape), a celebration of a seemingly commonplace British bird and the countryside it inhabits, *The Whisperers* (Allen Lane) by Orlando Figes which vividly reconstructed the hidden histories of ordinary people living under Stalin's tyranny, Patrick French's *The World Is What It Is* (Picador), an authorised biography of V. S. Naipaul which was frank where other authorised biographies tend to be coy, and *The Rest Is Noise* (Fourth Estate), the American critic Alex Ross's idiosyncratic and stimulating overview of 20th century music. The prize was won by the sixth book on the list – Kate Summerscale's remarkable *The Suspicions of Mr Whicher* (Bloomsbury), a reconstruction of the circumstances surrounding a Victorian murder and its aftermath.

The year saw no slowing down in the torrent of celebrity autobiography that the book trade directs at the reading public. Katie Price, who has only just passed her 30th birthday, is already on her third memoir, the latest is entitled *Pushed to the Limit* (Century). And every politician who retires from the front bench expects to be given the opportunity to settle scores on the printed page. However, John Prescott's account of his life as deputy Prime Minister, *Prezza* (Headline Review), was chiefly remarkable for its startling revelation that the generously proportioned Labour stalwart had suffered for years from bulimia.

The first half of 2008 also saw the publication of several memoirs by individuals better known for their literary skills than for their appearances in the pages of Hansard or *Heat*. *Nothing to be Frightened Of* (Jonathan Cape) by Julian Barnes was a characteristically elegant and intelligent meditation on death (and life) by one of the best of contemporary novelists; *Miracles of Life* (Fourth Estate) subtitled 'From Shanghai to Shepperton', was the autobiography of J. G. Ballard. Ferdinand Mount, novelist, journalist and sometime head of Mrs Thatcher's policy unit, produced a witty and self-deprecating account of his life in *Cold Cream* (Bloomsbury). Julia Blackburn's *The Three of Us* (Jonathan Cape), the candid story of the unusual relationship between the author and her parents, was hailed by many critics as a small masterpiece.

In the year of the Olympics it was perhaps unsurprising that a fascination with all things Chinese was in evidence in publishers' lists. Readers looking for a panorama of 2,000 years and more of China's past could pick up John Keay's *China: A History* (HarperPress); those searching for insights into the country's fall and subsequent rise in the last century-and-a-half could turn to Jonathan Fenby's *The Penguin History of Modern China* (Allen Lane). Both were weighty volumes by respected historians. *What Does China Think?* (Fourth Estate) was the question posed by another book and publishers were queuing up to provide answers.

The Olympics themselves were the focus of much attention. Dozens of books appeared, although they were nearly all, by their very nature, as ephemeral as mayflies. Arguably the only essential book on the subject is *The Complete Book of the Olympics* (Aurum), given a new edition this year, in which David Wallechinsky is given ample scope to demonstrate his lifetime obsession with Olympic facts and figures. Thoughts of the Beijing Olympics in 2008 sent writers and publishers back to the previous times London was host to the games. *The Austerity Olympics* (Aurum) by Janie Hampton looked back to 1948 and at least two books – *The First London Olympics* (Piatkus) by Rebecca Jenkins and *Olympic Follies* (JR Books) by Graeme Kent – returned even further in time to the 1908 games.

Connoisseurs of curious book titles usually have to content themselves with the Bookseller/Diagram prize for oddest title of the year (the most recent winner was *If You Want Closure in Your Relationship, Start With Your Legs)* but, in 2008, they could look to the popular science shelves of their local bookshop. *Your Inner Fish* (Allen Lane) by Neil Shubin could have been a contender for the Diagram prize but was, in fact, a look at the history of the human body and the ways in which it still carries reminders of its evolutionary past. Other science titles of note in the year included *The Kingdom of Infinite Space* (Atlantic) by Raymond Tallis, an introduction to the brain and consciousness, Steven Pinker's *The Stuff of Thought* (Allen Lane) and *Physics of the Impossible* (Allen Lane) in which the well-known American physicist Michio Kaku journeyed in search of what future technology will hold for us. *Darwin's Garden* (Constable) by Michael Boulter was a reminder that what the future of science publishing holds for us is lots of books about Darwin. 2009 is the 200th anniversary of Darwin's birth and the 150th anniversary of the publication of *On the Origin of Species*, probably the most influential science book of all time. Expect a swathe of new titles on the great man next year.

POETRY

Ten poets were shortlisted for the T. S. Eliot prize, from the veteran Scottish writer Edwin Morgan, born in 1920, to Frances Leviston, born in 1982. The eventual winner was Sean O'Brien for his latest collection, *The Drowned Book* (Picador). *The Drowned Book* also took the other major poetry prize in the UK, the Forward prize for best collection. It was the third time that O'Brien had left the ceremony with this particular award tucked under his arm. Daljit Nagra's *Look We Have Coming to Dover!* (Faber), a brilliant and witty take on multicultural Britain, won the Forward award for best first collection.

Simon Armitage, one of the country's most high-profile poets, published his own version of the medieval tale of chivalry and the supernatural, *Sir Gawain and the Green Knight* (Faber). Other poets with significant collections appearing in the year included Selima Hill, whose new volume entitled *The Dress* was jointly published with *Gloria* (both Bloodaxe), a selection from more than twenty years of writing, John Fuller who published *Song and Dance* (Chatto & Windus), Matthew Francis whose book *Mandeville* (Faber) gave a new voice to a legendary medieval traveller and Sujata Bhatt, author of *Pure Lizard* (Carcanet). Wendy Cope collected the best of earlier volumes of verse, including a number from the idiosyncratically titled *Making Cocoa for Kingsley Amis* and combined them with a selection of more recent poems in *Two Cures for Love* (Faber). *All Things Tire of Themselves* (Flambard) was a first collection of poetry by the veteran playwright Arnold Wesker.

CHILDREN'S

Should children's books be officially labelled with age ranges? This was the most contentious question which divided publishers and authors in 2008. Age-banding was proposed by publishers eager to see their books targeted at the appropriate audience. Most publishers seemed to want a book to state quite clearly the age it was aimed at. Most authors, it seemed, didn't. The authors' revolt against age-banding was led by Philip Pullman, writer of the bestselling *His Dark Materials* trilogy, who objected to prescriptive statements about the audience for his books. 'I write books for whoever is interested', he told one newspaper, 'When I write a book I don't have an age group in mind.' Many writers seemed to agree with him. Signatories to an online petition condemning the proposals as 'damaging to the interests of young readers' included J. K. Rowling, the current children's laureate Michael Rosen, and all four of his predecessors.

As yet, the dispute is unresolved although children's books remain unbanded for the time-being. Among those published unsullied by age ranges was an array of actual and potential bestsellers and prize-winners. For some reason children's writers are given medals rather than prizes or awards for their achievements. The two biggest accolades to win in British children's literature are the Carnegie medal, given in 2008 to Philip Reeve for *Here Lies Arthur* (Scholastic), a vividly imaginative re-telling of Arthurian legend, and the Kate Greenaway medal, awarded this year to Emily Gravett for her highly original picture book, *Little Mouse's Big Book of Fears* (Macmillan).

Among the best children's and young adult fiction to appear in the period under review were Philip Pullman's addition to the imaginative universe of the *His Dark Materials* trilogy entitled *Once Upon a Time in the North* (David Fickling); *Airman* (Puffin), in which Eoin Colfer left behind the world of Artemis Fowl for a tale of swashbuckling fantasy; *Just Henry* (Egmont), a long and rewarding mystery story set in 1940s London and written by Michelle Magorian, the author of the contemporary classic *Goodnight Mister Tom*; Eva Ibbotson's *The Dragonfly Pool* (Macmillan); *Sovay* (Bloomsbury), another historical blockbuster by Celia Rees and the latest novel by the much-loved Jacqueline Wilson entitled *My Sister Jodie* (Doubleday). *Bog Child* (David Fickling), a story set amidst the Troubles in 1980s Ireland, was by Siobhan Dowd and was published posthumously after her untimely death in the late summer of 2007.

Although the Harry Potter series came to a triumphant conclusion in July last year, there was no way that J. K. Rowling would be able to keep out of the news in 2008. The attention and imagination of the media at least were grabbed by *The Tales of Beedle the Bard*, supposedly the book which has a role to play in the plot of *Harry Potter and the Deathly Hallows*. This was given the most limited of editions when seven copies, each handwritten and illustrated by Rowling herself, were produced. One went to auction and was eventually sold to Amazon for an eye-watering £1.95m, thus making it the highest price ever achieved at auction by a modern literary manuscript. For those unable to fork out millions to own the stories, several less expensive editions will be released simultaneously in December 2008.

NEWS AND FAREWELLS

What happens to the book in a world of increasing technological sophistication? Book sales remain buoyant in the UK, despite all the talk of recession and the undoubted difficulties faced by high street shops, particularly in the independent sector. Two possible futures beckoned in the year under review. Amazon Kindle, launched in November 2007 by the online bookselling giant, is an e-book reader which allows readers to download up to 200 titles. 'This is the future of book reading', proclaimed bestselling author Michael Lewis with conviction, 'It will be everywhere.' No sign of such ubiquity yet but there's still time for Lewis to be proved right. Many retailers were busy linking themselves with other e-book readers. Borders began to push the rival iLiad in May and Waterstone's was soon offering the Sony reader to UK customers. Meanwhile chain booksellers Blackwell's announced that the 'Espresso Book Machine', a print-on-demand device invented in the USA, will be given a trial run in some of their shops in the autumn. The EBM can brew up a book – potentially any book, in print or out of print – and produce an edition of it for you within minutes. Perhaps the bookshop of the future will be no bigger than a telephone kiosk.

Other news stories in the book world varied, as always, from the sublime to the ridiculous. There was joy at Durham University library when a Shakespeare First Folio stolen a decade ago reappeared. A man took the book, worth several million pounds at the very least, to an American library to be authenticated, claiming he had acquired it in Cuba and it turned out to be the missing Durham volume. Piracy of a subtler kind was reported to be growing as academic publishers claimed that students were increasingly downloading textbooks online, using the same methods employed by those intent on stealing music and films.

And Salman Rushdie had no sooner been acclaimed winner of the best of Booker than he was claiming another, less exalted accolade. On a tour to promote his new novel *The Enchantress of Florence*, he signed 1,000 copies of the book with his full name in less than an hour, thus allegedly breaking a signing record held by the wine writer Malcolm Gluck for ten years. There has, as yet, been no word of confirmation from the Guinness Book of Records.

The most melancholy task for anyone reviewing a year in books is scanning the obituary pages and recording losses in the literary world. Two very different writers, both of world renown, passed away. Norman Mailer, whose work stretched from his Second World War epic *The Naked and the Dead*, first published in 1948, to a controversial novel about the childhood of Hitler which appeared in the last few months of his life, died in November 2007 at the age of 84. Four months later, Sir Arthur C. Clarke died in his adopted home of Sri Lanka at the age of 90. The man who once said, 'I sometimes think that the universe is a machine designed for the perpetual astonishment of astronomers', had been astonishing and delighting readers of science fiction for more than 60 years with works such as *2001: A Space Odyssey*, *Childhood's End* and *Rendezvous with Rama*.

Other writers who deserted their desks for good included Grace Paley, the American poet, short-story writer and political activist; Magdalen Nabb, the crime writer and creator of the Florentine detective Marshal Guarnaccia; John Gardner, the thriller writer who took on Ian Fleming's mantle in the 1980s and published a series of James Bond novels; the novelist Angela Lambert; Robert Jordan, author of the 'Wheel of Time' fantasy novels; the humourist and former editor of *Punch* Alan Coren; Richard Leigh, one of the authors of *The Holy Blood and the Holy Grail*; the poet Vernon Scannell; Ira Levin, author of two classic horror novels in *Rosemary's Baby* and *The Stepford Wives*; the humourist Miles Kington, inventor of Franglais; George MacDonald Fraser who, in the late 1960s, had the brilliant idea of resurrecting Flashman, the bully from *Tom Brown's Schooldays* and making him the anti-hero of a series of novels; the novelist Julian Rathbone; Robin Moore, the author of *The French Connection*; the poet E. A. Markham; Jeff Torrington, the Scottish novelist who won the Whitbread Book of the Year in 1992 for *Swing, Hammer, Swing!*; the Irish writer Nuala O'Faolain; Elaine Dundy, author of the 1950s bestseller *The Dud Avocado*; and the historian Angus Calder, writer of the groundbreaking work on the Second World War, *The Myth of the Blitz*.

One other name from the obituary columns is worth noting. In April 2008 an elderly Hampshire lady named Joan Jackson died. Her death would have meant little to anyone outside friends and family had she not known the poet John Betjeman during the Second World War. Her maiden name was Hunter Dunn and she was the Joan Hunter Dunn of Betjeman's famous poem, 'A Subaltern's Love-Song'.

MUSIC

MUSIC (CLASSICAL)

Lewis Morgan-Klein

ANNIVERSARIES

Composers' anniversaries have become perennial, and as the 2007–8 season proved, they are, once again, the concert-programmer's best friend. Only the querulous few had grounds for complaint – classical music is becoming increasingly popular, judging by ticket sales. Celebrations generally eschewed shallow, 'greatest hits' style of programming: a few offered performances of lesser-known works alongside old favourites, challenging audiences to reconsider the less popular composers. British orchestras must be commended too, for the considerable effort and resources poured into educational and outreach work, in which anniversaries and festivals help introduce audiences to unfamiliar works.

In the year in review Elgar continued to be well-served, although less was heard from his contemporary Grieg, who also enjoyed his 150th birthday. Scarlatti celebrations were dauntingly telescoped – the 250th year since his death was most memorably marked by a complete cycle of 555 of his keyboard sonatas in Manchester, played simultaneously, in different locations and on a variety of keyboards, involving over 230 different musicians – and all in 12 hours. Philip Glass aficionados were surely delighted with a surfeit of performances and premieres celebrating his 70th birthday. He remains the darling of most critics, despite his collaboration on his latest commission with pop icon Leonard Cohen. The provocative *Book of Longing*, based on Cohen's poetry and images, was performed repeatedly, most notably as part of the Barbican's Glassworks concerts.

Sibelius fared best in the second half of 2007, with a series of events commemorating 50 years since his death. The coincidence of the 90th anniversary of Finnish independence probably helped: London's Finnish Institute and the English Chamber Orchestra promoted the composer through the Sibelius and Beyond series, involving 54 of his works in 23 concerts, including a symphony cycle. This was given a fiery rendering by the composer's compatriot Esa-Pekka Salonen and the Los Angeles Philharmonic. The opening recital included songs by Sibelius, arrangements of Finnish folk songs by Ralf Gothoni, and songs by Oskar and Aarre Merikanto. Wigmore Hall saw a performance of Sibelius's D minor String Quartet from Finnish quartet Meta4, followed by some of the composer's finest vocal writing, his Runeberg setting *Seven Songs*, performed commendably by baritone Jorma Hynninen. More fine singing came from Ben Heppner and Finnish soprano Karita Mattila. The Hallé's retrospective, The Origin of Fire, comprised four concerts, offering his seven symphonies and lesser-known works. Not to be outdone, the City of Birmingham Symphony Orchestra (CBSO) not only offered a sensational cycle of the symphonies but also the British premiere of the long-lost *Three Symphonic Pieces for Cello and Orchestra*, played beautifully by Martti Rousi.

Ralph Vaughan Williams died half a century ago in 1958 and the anniversary of his death was enthusiastically observed. Plenty of his work could be heard in the Royal Philharmonic's Green and Pleasant Land series eulogising quintessentially English composers. Paul Daniel's concert at the Cadogan Hall achieved extremely high standards. Finzi's moving, underappreciated Cello Concerto was accompanied by an introspective rendering of Vaughan Williams's Fifth Symphony and the *Fantasia on a Theme by Thomas Tallis*. Vernon Handley, a virtually peerless exponent of British composers, conducted Symphonies 3 and 4 and Sir Andrew Davis led a performance of the *'London' Symphony*, paired with Elgar's *'Enigma' Variations*. The Philharmonia, however, has offered the most: its year-long series, under the aegis of brilliant artistic advisor Michael Kennedy and conductor Richard Hickox involves performances of choral works, opera, a complete symphony cycle and a special event at the British Library. The rarely given *Song for All Seas, All Ships*, named after Walt Whitman's poem, and the *Sea Symphony* were given in an immaculate Royal Festival Hall performance in May 2008 as part of this series, with sought-after soloists Gerald Finley and Susan Gritton. More Whitman via Vaughan Williams was on offer in a BBC Symphony Orchestra concert in May, under Andrew Davis, compensating for Dominic Muldowney's unimpressive *Tsunami* premiere, with the beautifully sung *Toward the Unknown Region* and the Sixth Symphony amidst works by Ives and Holst.

Charges of musical parochialism, however, were unfair; hitherto far more has been done in Britain to celebrate Olivier Messiaen's centenary than in his homeland across the channel. His former student, pianist Pierre-Laurent Aimard, deserves much of the credit for a series of events, which inspired the rediscovery of his teacher. As the artistic director and star performer, Aimard has been central to the Southbank Centre's year-long series of concerts, From the Canyons to the Stars, with an impressive array of artists performing virtually all of Messiaen's major works. Punctuated by performances of the *Quatuor pour la fin du temps*, the festival opened with *Des canyons aux étoile* conducted by Susanna Malkki – a transcendent performance, with Aimard in the solo piano role and Jean-Christophe Vervoitte playing the solo horn section. Messiaen's epic *Turangalêla-symphonie* was performed in February by the Philharmonia, Salonen and Aimard. After this colourful orchestral tour de force came the vocal and choral components of Messiaen's recherché triology, the *Cinq rechants* and *Harawi* – both pieces poorer relations, but nonetheless remarkable. Yet more Messiaen the following night: the birdsong transcription *Oiseaux exotiques*, played by pianist Tamara Stefanovich, followed by Prokofiev's Piano Concerto No. 5 and Stravinsky's *Rite of Spring*. In March Joanna MacGregor tackled the pianistic endurance test that is Messiaen's two-hour-long *Vingt regards sur l'enfant Jésus* at the Cadogan Hall.

MUSICAL HIGHLIGHTS OF SEASON 2007–8

Daniel Barenboim's survey of the 32 Beethoven piano sonatas at the Royal Festival Hall left critics stuck for superlatives in the lengthy and virtually unanimously positive reviews. It was not so much the technical aspects of Barenboim's pianism that attracted attention as much as his intelligent interpretations and the articulacy of his playing. Barenboim aside, the last year offered a veritable feast of highlights: Itzhak Perlman's Barbican appearance in November; visits of the Bavarian Radio Symphony Orchestra under Mariss Jansons; Chailly's Leipzig Gewandhaus Orchestra's Barbican concert in June; the South Bank's Early Music Weekend in September; Riccardo Muti's 35th anniversary concert with the Philharmonia; Rozhdestvensky's Mahler Symphony No. 3 and Jaap van Zweden's account of Mahler's Fifth with the London Philharmonic. Thomas Zehetmair and his quartet offered a rare performance of Hindemith's String Quartet No. 4, later giving the composer's Horn Concerto with the Northern Sinfonia. Sakari Oramo's mammoth four-year 'Igorfest', a celebration of Stravinsky's entire oeuvre has carried on apace, and Sir Colin Davis' 80th birthday in 2007 occasioned London Symphony Orchestra concerts devoted to favourite composers such as Berlioz and Mozart. Best of all was Davis' wonderful September *Eroica*, with Evgeny Kissin playing Beethoven's Piano Concerto No. 3.

The London Philharmonic celebrated its 75th anniversary with a programme recalling its inaugural concert with founder Sir Thomas Beecham in 1932. A specially composed fanfare commenced celebrations, followed by Mozart's *'Prague' Symphony*, Beethoven's Piano Concerto No. 4 with Maurizio Pollini and Rachmaninoff's *Symphonic Dances*. Vladimir Jurowski, who opened the 2007–8 season as the orchestra's impressive new principal conductor with Wagner's *Parsifal* prelude, Berg's *Three Pieces for Orchestra* and Mahler's *Das klagende Lied* in its original version has thus far garnered the orchestra deservedly good reviews, broadening the repertory significantly. Jurowski's concert in March, in which he conducted Shostakovich's *'Leningrad' Symphony*, laid bare some of that score's many secrets. Jurowski's interpretations are often revelatory: nothing drags under his baton and he brings out colours and textures like few other conductors.

Mark Elder's Hallé celebrated its 150th anniversary this year, giving a gala performance featuring Sir John Tomlinson. Elder's Verdi Requiem, performed in December with the Hallé, was lively and dramatic, with the Hallé Chorus augmented by the London Symphony Chorus. In June Elder's concert in St Paul's Cathedral of Brahms *Vier ernste Gesänge* showcased the terrific baritone of Johan Reuter, including the Prelude and 'Good Friday Spell' from *Parsifal* – a cathedral in sound in its own right, whose vaulted arches Elder articulated splendidly. St Paul's is not the Bayreuth Festspielhaus but its resounding acoustic made for an unusual experience, particularly in Orla Boylan's gorgeous performance of Strauss' much-adored *Four Last Songs*. The 82-year-old Sir Charles Mackerras' series of three concerts in the spring brought out the very best of the rich Philharmonia sound, each pairing a Richard Strauss tone poem *(Don Juan, Also Sprach Zarathustra* and *Till Eulenspiegel)* along with a third symphony (Beethoven, Brahms and Schumann), piano concerti by Mozart and Beethoven and the *Four Last Songs*. Mackerras' Mozart-only concert in the intimate Edinburgh Queen's Hall in March was a delight, confirming his status as the foremost living Mozart interpreter.

Meanwhile, the LSO's dynamic Valery Gergiev – purportedly engaged in unacknowledged competition with his LPO counterpart Jurowski – continued to attract attention, in particular for his Mahler cycle. For the latter, supposedly rather uneven and episodic, Gergiev was criticised, sometimes unfairly, thanks to his often unconventional interpretations, iconoclastic tempi and an inability to communicate musical architecture. Regardless, the quality of Gergiev's work with the orchestra is indisputable and his intrepid offerings continue to be popular with concert-goers. His love affair with the Vienna Philharmonic and its unique *klang* was in evidence at the Barbican in February. The first concert took in Berlioz's *Scenes from Roméo et Juliette*, the Prelude and the eponymous heroine's transfiguration from *Tristan und Isolde* – a clever juxtaposition, which emphasised the composer's not inconsiderable Saxon influence – and Debussy's luminous *La Mer*. The performance was made more potent with an encore of Strauss waltzes. On the following night, Gergiev gave Verdi's *La forza del destino overture*, Tchaikovsky's Sixth *('Pathétique')* and Prokofiev's Piano Concerto No. 2, with virtuoso Yefim Bronfman earning well-deserved plaudits, before the audience were sent home with a small dose of Tchaikovsky's *Sleeping Beauty*. Also at the LSO, Pierre Boulez made an outstanding guest appearance as part of the orchestra's Great Conductors series, giving two concerts, the first included his still-in-progress *Notations*. In the second, another intelligently chosen combination: works by Arnold Schoenberg, a Matthias Pintscher premiere and Bela Bartok's haunting *Duke Bluebeard's Castle*.

The piano fared well: even excluding Barenboim's achievement, some extremely fine playing was to be heard. Konstantin Lifschitz's performance of Bach's *Well-Tempered Klavier*'s second book was marvellous, and Angela Hewitt's Festival Hall performances of both books in January and May rank especially high. Maurizio Pollini's June concert at the Royal Festival Hall (Schumann, Chopin and Debussy) was a reminder of his considerable gifts as a pianist, and the good fortune of those lucky enough to hear his compelling, authoritative delivery. In November 2007, a recital in the capital's Queen Elizabeth Hall with works by Schoenberg, Alban Berg and Luigi Nono, was dazzling. Among many fine performances, Richard Goode's recital at the same venue in February, his Homage to Chopin, exhibited his detailed, sensitive and masterly playing. The concert also paid homage to Bach, Mozart and Debussy. Goode richly deserves the honour of the 2007–8 residency, offered to him as part of the Southbank Centre's new Artists in Residence series.

Amidst the 80th-birthday celebrations was Sir Colin Davis' December concert with the LSO and its chorus, presenting Michael Tippett's oratorio *A Child of Our Time* and his Piano Concerto, which was notable for the trouble it occasionally caused pianist Lang Lang. The 25-year-old's appearances – customarily in sparkling, glittery suits – utterly divided critics. Some feared that Lang Lang is all bravura and no technique, conforming to the worst caricature of the virtuoso concert pianist. Yet he is obviously prodigiously talented, as a November Royal Festival Hall recital revealed. Such attention should not cause us to ignore other, quieter talents. Piotr Anderszewski, in some way's Lang Lang's opposite, gave several outstanding piano recitals. He is a fastidious, intense performer characterised as a perfectionist by critics – one who often meets his own high standards. Stephen Hough is still supreme at the keyboard, having given many concerts in the UK and abroad. His Brahms'

Piano Concerto No. 1 in November at the Queen Elizabeth Hall was popular, and a Wigmore Hall recital in January offered an impressively varied programme – from Mendelssohn and Webern to Chopin and Saint-Saëns. His playing was as superbly showy and versatile as Lang Lang's but also sensitive and imbued with understanding and insight.

The 2007–8 season saw some memorable vocal performances. Lieder festivals in Oxford, Leeds and elsewhere continued to attract singers of the highest calibre. Thomas Quasthoff's *Winterreise* at the Wigmore in October was enjoyable, but the chance to hear Schubert's song cycle by female voice, via Alice Coote's stunning mezzo was even better. Her performance in March displayed a rich, colourful vocal palette and total mastery of the piece's bleak moods and shifting emotions. Just days before, Coote had appeared in an iridescent performance in Mark Elder's massive, unapologetically 'inauthentic' full symphony orchestra *St Matthew Passion*, with the huge Hallé Choir. It was a pleasing change from virtually ubiquitous period instruments and small ensembles. Andreas Scholl's countertenor was lavishly praised by critics after his June concert of Handel, Vivaldi, Bach and Purcell in Gateshead with the Orchestra of the Age of Enlightenment. And it would be difficult for a lieder concert with such gifted performers as Martineau, soprano Lisa Milne (who gets better and better) and tenor John Mark Ainsley not to have satisfied. Their April recital at the Wigmore featured settings by Poulenc in the first half and in the second works by Jake Heggie, Honegger's *Saluste du Bartas* and Rosenthal's *Chansons de Monsieur Bleu*.

Christopher Maltman's recital with Martineau formed part of the Wigmore Hall's survey of the songs of Poulenc (much in vogue) and in the same month a magnificent all-Schubert lieder programme combined soprano Dorothea Röschmann, baritone Thomas Quasthoff and Ian Bostridge in the latter's Homeward Bound series at the Barbican. January was also graced by noted baritone Simon Keenlyside, accompanied by Martineau, in Schumann's *Dichterliebe*, Butterworth's cycle from *A Shropshire Lad* and Poulenc's Éluard settings *Tel jour, telle nuit*. Paul Plummer's Strauss Song Series, a weekend in January focusing on Strauss lieder at the Wigmore Hall, was inspired, although the vocal talent simply could not compete with last year's Straussian high noons, featuring Brewer, Isokoski and Kaufmann.

CONTEMPORARY MUSIC

It was an inordinately successful year for contemporary music. There were so many premieres and performances that it is difficult to do more than list some of the most significant. Last October's Southbank Centre Luigi Nono festival demonstrated real commitment to modern music and included some first performances. The Royal Liverpool Philharmonic announced in September that it would premiere 30 new works over the subsequent 15 months, commissioned to mark the 800th anniversary of the city and to celebrate its year as European Capital of Culture. Conducted by Vasily Petrenko, the opening concert of the new season kicked off with two new works, both by prominent Liverpudlian composers Kenneth Hesketh and John McCabe. James MacMillan's important May premiere of his gigantic, demanding *St John Passion*, commissioned as an 80th-birthday present for Sir Colin Davis was given by the LSO and its chorus was central to Davis' celebrations. For many contemporary works, the first often turns out to be its only performance, but MacMillan's piece was generally well-received and has already been performed several times since. The same is true of John Taverner's much-mooted *Requiem*, given in Liverpool's Metropolitan Cathedral by Petrenko, conducting the Royal Liverpool Philharmonic Orchestra and its choir. The religioso theme is a Taverner hallmark, but the *Requiem*, has received a mixed reception. Premiers of a string quartet by Harrison Birtwistle and a violin concerto by John Woolrich were both given at the 2008 Aldeburgh Festival by the Arditti Quartet and violinist Carolin Widmann with the Northern Sinfonia.

At the Festival Hall, Thomas Adès conducted the London Sinfonietta and Nicholas Hodges in the first performance of his own *Seven Days*, a minimalist yet rather complicated audio and visual experience, described as 'a piano concerto with moving image'. Notably, Simon Holt's percussion concerto, *A Table of Noises*, was premiered by Colin Currie with Martyn Brabbins conducting the CBSO at the Symphony Hall in May. The jazzy *Riffs and Refrains* with its ostentatious clarinet writing, specially composed by Mark-Anthony Turnage for Michael Collins, received its London premiere with the LPO under Alsop.

Best of all was, perhaps, the Britten Sinfonia's outstanding premiere of Robin Holloway's *Five Temperaments*, for a wind quintet, bookended by Beethoven's Quintet for Piano and Wind Quartet, with Imogen Cooper, and Ravel's *Mother Goose Suite*. Fears that contemporary music exists in a ghetto sealed off from mainstream classical music were belied by programmes which featured a mixture of both, like the Zehetmair Quartet's performance of Schumann's final quartet combined with the UK premiere of Heinz Holliger's String Quartet No. 2. Judith Weir had an excellent year of premieres and performances, too, but what was the BBC thinking of letting her January composer weekend, Telling the Tale, clash with the premiere of Ronald Stevenson's landmark *Praise of Ben Doran* at Glasgow's Celtic Connections festival, particularly in Stevenson's 80th year? Stevenson's work will not feature in either the Proms or this year's Edinburgh International Festival, and has hitherto been neglected even on BBC Radio 3. Why has so little of Stevenson's amazing output been heard?

MOVES AND NEW APPOINTMENTS

2007–8 was a year of many losses. No-one could have escaped the extensive coverage following the death of tenor Luciano Pavarotti in September, which brought forth tributes to the artistry and vocal majesty of the great Italian and provoked much worthwhile debate about the popularisation of classical music and opera. Music lovers mourned the loss of other great singers too, including tenor, Giuseppe di Stefano; baritone John Noble; Danish soprano Inga Nielsen; sopranos Teresa Stich-Randall, Beverly Sills and Régine Crespin; American tenor Jerry Hadley; the Czech Republic's most celebrated composer, Petr Eben; and Canadian Henry Bran.

Among composers, the most prominent departure came in December with the death of Karlheinz Stockhausen, the central figure in the Darmstadt School and one of the most controversial figures of the last century. His vocal work, *Stimmung*, was given at this year's Aldeburgh Festival by the London Voices under Ben Parry and as part of the Stockhausen day at the 2008 Proms, in what would have been Stockhausen's 80th year. Lastly, March saw the death of the versatile English National Opera stalwart, conductor Noel Davies, who enjoyed a successful career spanning three decades with the company.

At 77, Alfred Brendel announced that he would give his final recital in 2008, although he plans to continue writing and lecturing. He will probably be most fondly remembered for the intelligent, powerful and the sophisticated yet understated simplicity of his playing – excelling particular in Mozart. The rest of the year affords us with a definitive survey of some of the works which have made his name. Connoisseurs of the Alban Berg Quartet have already bid its musicians a fond farewell after three valedictory Queen Elizabeth Hall recitals in February, May and June. Performances featured composers important to the quartet, in particular Berg, whose *Lyric Suite* was performed with the group's trademark technical accomplishment and insight in February and a typically understated all-Schubert recital in June. That these farewells have saddened music-lovers is something of a truism – much more important is the opportunity they have afforded to celebrate great musicianship. The musicianship of Thomas Adès, Julian Anderson, Edwin Roxburgh, Oliver Knussen and Harrison Birtwistle – among others – was recognised in the 2007 British Composer Awards. Luke Bedford, who has enjoyed several premieres this year, was named by the Wigmore Hall in January as its first ever composer-in-residence. And Mark Elder, mentioned above, received a knighthood for services to music.

New appointments generally rewarded the meritorious. The Scottish conductor Donald Runnicles, it was announced in October 2007, takes over from Ilan Volkov in September 2009 as conductor of the BBC Scottish Symphony Orchestra (BBCSSO). Already, in April, he conducted the BBCSSO at Glasgow's City Halls: a Scottish premiere of MacMillan's Third Symphony and Mahler's *Das Lied von der Erde*. Runnicles has not been entirely reclaimed for the UK; his appointment at the BBCSSO coincides with a new job as music director at the Deutsche Oper Berlin. In October the LPO announced that 32-year-old Canadian Yannick Nézet-Séguin, a name to watch out for in future, would assume the position of principal guest conductor in the 2008–9 season. Nézet-Séguin's Glasgow concert in April with the Scottish Chamber Orchestra revealed panache and an outstanding, articulate sense of style, especially in Mendelssohn's *Italian Symphony*, and the evidence of his guest appearance with the CBSO to conduct Bruckner's Ninth and Beethoven's Third Piano Concerto has whetted many appetites.

Nézet-Séguin is just one among a new generation of young and relatively unknown conductors rising to prominence and great success. The promising 21-year-old Lionel Bringuier made his debut conducting the BBCSO with a performance of Maurice Ravel, Giya Kancheli and Modest Mussorgsky. The Bournemouth Symphony Orchestra parted with its principal conductor Marin Alsop, under whose baton the orchestra has flourished over the last six years; she was replaced by 30-year-old Kirill Karabits, of Ukraine. Alsop, having devoted her final appearances with the orchestra in May to performances of Mahler's Ninth and the reconstructed Tenth Symphony, will certainly be missed. She is now conductor of the Baltimore Symphony Orchestra – and the first woman to lead a major American orchestra. Karabits' concerts thus far have been most successful.

In a similar move, the CBSO (selling more tickets than ever before) announced that 28-year-old Andris Nelsons, of Latvia, will become the orchestra's music director from the beginning of the 2008–9 season. The post's previous occupant, Sakari Oramo, becomes chief conductor of the Royal Stockholm Philharmonic and the Finnish Radio Symphony, although he will return as guest conductor.

Birmingham's fine orchestra came back to the refurbished neoclassical Town Hall, a musical seat of great historical significance in October. After the completion of a £35m restoration programme, a two-week festival featured Richard Hickox and the OAE in a programme recalling the hall's concerts of old. It was a remarkably varied selection for the OAE – Mendelssohn, Mozart, Gounod, Grieg, Sullivan, Elgar and Bach played by organist Thomas Trotter. As part of the re-opening festival Simon Halsey conducted the CBSO and its chorus in an all-English programme of Hubert Parry's *I Was Glad* and Samuel Coleridge-Taylor's Violin Concerto.

THE FESTIVAL SEASON

The 113th Proms season marked Roger Wright's seamless takeover from Sir Nicholas Kenyon. Elgar and Sibelius received plenty of attention, but much of the best music-making came from visiting companies, notably Claudio Abbado and his Lucerne Festival Orchestra, or Mariss Jansons' two Proms with the Bavarian Radio Symphony Orchestra and Bernhard Haitink's two evenings with the Royal Concertgebouw. Haitink's Bruckner is a force to be reckoned with, and his marvellous reading of the Eighth Symphony complimented the accompanying Wagner pieces. The best Bruckner came from 80-year-old Kurt Masur, with his Seventh and Tchaikovsky's *Serenade for Strings*, also with some Wagner thrown in for good measure – in this case the festive prelude to *Die Meistersinger*. The Bayreuth Master featured again in Donald Runnicles' fantastic concert *Götterdämmerung* with the BBC Symphony Orchestra, with Christine Brewer as a Brünnhilde that Wagnerites must be desperate to see on stage. Contrastingly, the debut appearance of Michael Ball at Prom 58 appalled some – popular hits from musicals were deemed too lowbrow for the Proms. Culture minister Margaret Hodge provoked much sound and fury, accusing the Proms of being insufficiently diverse and inclusive.

Venezuela's Simón Bolívar National Youth Orchestra produced a sensation with its energetic, *con brio* performance of works by Bernstein and Shostakovich along with various Latin American confections. Ilan Volkov's Proms with the BBCSSO and Jac van Steen's with the BBC National Orchestra of Wales (BBCNOW) reminded how well-served the British musical landscape is by the BBC's many orchestras. Volkov is a great advocate of Sibelius and Mahler, while the BBCNOW gave a very fine premiere of Michael Tippett's Sixth Symphony. Modern music, then, was by no means under-represented. Prom 25 brought an important Boulez premiere, the elaborate, endlessly self-generating *Dérive* 2, and John Adams conducted the BBCSO in his *Dr Atomic Symphony*. Aimard's Haydn, Ligeti and, in particular, his delicate Beethoven's Piano Concerto No. 2 could not fail to impress. Where else could three days' worth of concerts take in names like Daniel Barenboim, Riccardo Chailly and James Levine, or have Anna Netrebko delivering gorgeous top E-flats with the same astonishing equanimity as when tossing red roses to her admirers on Jiri Behlolavek's first opening night?

The 2007 Edinburgh Festival was director Jonathan Mills' first, ending not so much with a bang than with a threat of resignation, should the EIF not receive a level of funding commensurate with its artistic significance. Mills is clearly fond of Early music, a major component of the festival: the Tallis Scholars made an appearance and a performance of fourteenth century composer Carlo Gesualdo's *Tenebrae* was given by Italian group La Venexiana. Vivaldi's *Orlando Furioso*, Purcell's *Dido and Aeneas* in concert performance, Monteverdi's *L'Orfeo* and a diet of his madrigals performed by the Concerto Italiano all featured. Other highlights included Brendel's concert, featuring works by Mozart, Schubert, Beethoven and Haydn and a performance of Haydn's *Creation,* in which bass Matthew Rose and, in particular, Ian Bostridge distinguished themselves. Other vocal treats included mezzo Jane Irwin's *Kindertotenlieder*, tenor Mark Padmore's Bach and Silvana Dussmann's gleaming soprano singing Wagner's *Wesendonck Lieder* and Schumann's *Frauenliebe und-leben.* Best of all was soprano Christine Brewer's two appearances, the first a lieder recital which, after an unannounced change of programme, featured five Strauss songs and Wolf's *Vier Mignon Lieder.* Brewer's is a mighty voice with a beautiful, burnished golden timbre. The mood of the second half was much less intense: a humorous performance of Benjamin Britten's Auden settings, the *Cabaret Songs*, featuring mighty whistles that still ring in the ears, before ending the recital with John Carter's virtually unknown *Cantata.* Brewer's second performance was at a splendid all-Poulenc concert, featuring his *Stabat Mater*, Organ Concerto and excerpts from *Les dialogues des Carmélites.*

It is not just the Proms and the EIF that thrived. This year the Aldeburgh Festival celebrated its 60th anniversary in which Thomas Adès' final season, after ten years as artistic director, saw a wide-ranging programme featuring Robert Holl, Ian Bostridge, and Steven Isserlis. The 2008 City of London Festival was also a great success, featuring Peter Maxwell Davies' *A Sad Pavan for these Distracted Tymes* and the premiere of Alexander Goehr's *Since Brass, nor Stone.* The Cambridge and Chester summer festivals and the Cheltenham, Buxton and Bath festivals all go from strength to strength, while the East Neuk Festival in Fife has flourished in just a few years. These vibrant signs bode well for the future.

AWARDS

GRAMOPHONE AWARDS 2007

Orchestral – Prokofiev, Complete Symphonies. London Symphony Orchestra/Valery Gergiev

Chamber – Haas and Janácek, String Quartets. Pavel Haas Quartet

Solo vocal – R. Strauss, Lieder. Jonas Kaufmann; Helmut Deutsch

Instrumental – Bach, Cello Suites. Steven Isserlis

Choral – Brahms, *Ein Deutsches Requiem.* Dorothea Röschmann; Thomas Quasthoff; Berlin Radio Choir; Berlin Philharmonic Orchestra/Sir Simon Rattle

Early music – Byrd, *Laudibus in sanctis.* The Cardinall's Music

Baroque instrumental – Handel, *Concerto Grossi.* Academy of Ancient Music/Richard Egarr

Baroque vocal – Handel, *Messiah* (Dublin version, 1742). Dunedin Consort & Players/John Butt

Contemporary – Julian Anderson, *Alhambra Fantasy.* BBC Symphony Orchestra/Oliver Knussen

Historic archive – Wagner, *Götterdämmerung.* Bayreuth Festival/Joseph Keilberth

Record of the year – Brahms, Piano Concertos. Nelson Freire; Leipzig Gewandaus Orchestra/Riccardo Chailly

Editor's choice – Mahler, Symphony No. 2. Budapest Festival Orchestra/Ivan Fisher

Artist of the year – Julia Fischer

Lifetime achievement award – Montserrat Caballè

Young artist of the year – Vasily Petrenko

MUSIC (POPULAR)

Piers Martin

DIGITAL DEMAND

There have been signs this year that the beleaguered British record industry is adapting to the changing business environment in its ongoing bid to offset dwindling record sales and combat piracy. Try as it might, however, and in keeping with the trend of recent years, the industry endured a rotten 12 months. Figures released by the British Phonographic Industry (BPI), the body that represents the British music business, show total industry revenue fell by 13.4 per cent in 2007, dipping below £1bn for the first time since 1994. Much of this revenue loss can be attributed to sales of CD albums, which tumbled by £145m in 2007, a drop of 15.1 per cent, the BPI reported. On a brighter note, digital sales reached £71.5m during the same period, an increase of more than 50 per cent on 2006, but still not enough to offset losses from physical sales. Nevertheless, as digital music continues to evolve at a dramatic pace, it is conceivable that this balance might be redressed in the next few years.

As expected, the digital market in the UK grew substantially. The BPI estimates there are now more than six million tracks available to download from legitimate services such as iTunes and Napster. Some 200 million tracks have been legally downloaded in the UK since 2004. In 2007, sales of single track downloads topped 77 million, up 48 per cent on the previous year, according to the BPI, which also noted that in the run up to Christmas average weekly sales approached two million. Sales of the year's biggest selling single, 'Bleeding Love' by former *X Factor* winner Leona Lewis, reached 800,000, although only half of these were digital downloads. Meanwhile, 2007's *X Factor* champion, Leon Jackson, sold 400,000 copies of 'When You Believe' in the last two weeks of December, making it the year's fourth best-seller. The year's other notable big sellers included chart-toppers from R&B star Rihanna ('Umbrella'), flamboyant newcomer Mika ('Grace Kelly') and the reunited Take That ('Rule The World'), each of which sold most on the digital format.

In spite of efforts by music companies to tackle digital music piracy, illegal file-sharing remained a thorn in the industry's side. For the majority of young people, downloading MP3s for free and swapping them among friends has become second-nature and as a consequence most are unwilling to pay for music. Acquiring tracks via torrent sites, blogs, instant messaging, email and other channels is now so prevalent that, according to Jupiter Research, 15 per cent of internet users in the UK are file-sharers. The International Federation of the Phonographic Industry (IFPI), the trade body that represents the music companies, estimates that for every track legally bought, 20 tracks are downloaded illegally. An IFPI survey conducted by Ipsos suggested that one in ten office workers download while at their desk, and two-thirds of those do so from illegal sites.

Recent measures aimed at clamping down on illegal file-sharing barely scratch the surface of the problem. In October, for example, the BPI helped shut down OiNK, an illegal download site with an estimated membership of 180,000 users, while in July, the UK's main internet service providers (ISPs), such as BT, BSkyB and Orange, signed up to a Memorandum of Understanding. Backed by the BPI, these ISPs will deliver warning letters to serial file-sharers, who may have their account cancelled if law-breaking persists.

RADIOHEAD'S MEDIA STUNT

Rather than resist illegal downloading, many major labels now turn the public's thirst for free music to their advantage. This year, comeback singles by stadium rockers Coldplay ('Violet Hill') and Keane ('Spiralling') were made available as a free download weeks before the albums were released. Two million people downloaded the Coldplay track in its first week. One particular giveaway that grabbed headlines and took the industry by surprise was the decision by eco-friendly Oxford outfit Radiohead to self-release their seventh album, *In Rainbows*, exclusively online as a digital download in October, two months ahead of the conventional physical CD release. Not only that, but once online, fans were invited to choose their own price for the album in what was dubbed an 'honesty box'. Customers could even opt to pay nothing, bar the 49 pence administration fee, though a survey by industry newsletter *Record of the Day* estimated that an average of £3.88 was paid for the album. At the same time, fans could also pre-order a deluxe package of *In Rainbows* for £40. 'It's fun to make people stop for a few seconds and think about what music is worth', said Radiohead's guitarist Jonny Greenwood. One industry commentator labelled the experiment 'a stunt by the most credible band on the planet'. Regardless of the nature of the release, the album was unanimously praised by critics, many of whom posted their reviews online within minutes of downloading and listening to the record.

Nevertheless, once the dust had settled, a study by music rights holders MCPS-PRS Alliance and media company Big Champagne discovered that not only had more fans illegally downloaded *In Rainbows* than had bought it in shops, but they'd downloaded it from illegal sites rather than the official Radiohead site where it was available at no cost. With this release, Radiohead also ended their deal with troubled major label EMI Records and signed to leading independent XL Recordings, which has since sold 180,000 copies of *In Rainbows*. If anything, Radiohead's initiative proved that platinum artists no longer need a major label to promote and market their music. Sure enough, soon after *In Rainbows*, new albums by industrial rockers Nine Inch Nails, rapper Saul Williams and British indie stalwarts The Charlatans were each made available as free or pay-what-you-like downloads in a bid to target fans directly and fill column inches. The various versions of the Nine Inch Nails album, *Ghosts I–V*, made the band $1.6m (£800,000) during its first week of release.

EMI AND TERRA FIRMA

Radiohead enjoyed a walk-on – or rather, walk-out – role in the other high-profile music news story of the year: the takeover of struggling major record company EMI by the private equity group Terra Firma. EMI, the world's fourth largest label, is the original home of The Beatles, Queen and Pink Floyd, but it had become a shadow of its former self. The company had only six entries in a list of 2007's 100 top-selling albums, and three of those were compilations of old material by Phil Collins, Spice Girls and Cliff Richard. Terra Firma, run by ex-bond trader Guy Hands, acquired EMI for £3.2bn in August 2007. To the horror of many of the label's high-profile artists, Hands quickly set about streamlining the business, putting in place measures to curtail excesses traditionally associated with the record industry. To help revitalise the company, he recruited business executives with no previous music experience, including former BBC director-general Lord Birt and Post Office chairman Allan Leighton. During an internal investigation, Hands uncovered costs ranging from multi-million-pound 'hand out and hope' advances to a £20,000-a-month bill for candles, and was said to be surprised by the £200,000 EMI splashed out annually on fruit and flowers for its Hammersmith headquarters. 'Fruit and flowers' transpired to be a euphemism for artists' party supplements.

Relations between the new EMI board and some of the label's key artists appeared strained. Radiohead left EMI, comparing the new regime to 'a confused bull in a china shop', while representatives of Robbie Williams, Coldplay and the Verve made disapproving noises. Williams effectively went on strike, refusing to deliver another album until the management's plans were made clearer. He was last spotted heavily bearded in the Nevada desert, discussing his preoccupation with UFOs and aliens in an interview with *The Guardian*. Arguably the biggest blow to EMI came in July when The Rolling Stones, the world's highest-earning band, defected to Universal, the world's largest music company. Hands claimed a shallow victory that same month when, following company restructuring at the expense of 1,500 jobs, EMI reported a £100m rise in quarterly profits.

This year, two of pop's biggest names, Madonna and Jay-Z, exchanged their deals with major labels for lucrative contracts with Live Nation, the concert promoter. In October, Madonna left Warner, her label for 24 years, and signed a $120m (£60m) deal. This was a landmark contract for the music industry as it combined touring and recording rights, giving Live Nation exclusive rights to promote the 50-year-old star's hugely profitable tours; her 2006 *Confessions* world tour grossed £130m. Live Nation manages a number of venues around the world, including Wembley Arena, and also handles merchandise and online ticket sales. In April, the company secured a similar deal with New York rap mogul and former Def Jam Records president Jay-Z for $150m (£75m). Live Nation hopes to capitalise on the star's entrepreneurial skills. Analysts questioned the company's logic, pointing out that Jay-Z's album sales figures have halved in recent years. However, the worldwide live music market is undergoing a boom and the company aims to recoup most of its investment through the rapper's tours and exclusive shows.

Jay-Z proved his popularity when he headlined a number of festivals in Europe in the summer, including the coveted Saturday night slot at the Glastonbury Festival. In the run-up to the event, Oasis guitarist Noel Gallagher sparked fierce debate among fans when he told the BBC he believed organisers were wrong to book a hip-hop act to headline a festival which has a tradition of focusing on guitar bands. On the night, Jay-Z took to the stage performing an ironic cover of the Oasis hit 'Wonderwall' before blasting into his own track, '99 Problems'. With all eyes on this one show, Jay-Z triumphed.

STATESIDE SUCCESS

British acts flourished in the US this year. In February, troubled soul singer Amy Winehouse won five Grammy Awards, picking up gongs for record of the year and best new artist, despite being absent from the ceremony in Los Angeles. The 24-year-old's 2006 album, *Back To Black*, was 2007's best-seller in the UK, with 1.6 million copies sold. With predictable alacrity, Winehouse's drug addiction and erratic performances continued to make tabloid headlines. In April, Leona Lewis entered the record books when she scored US number ones with her debut single, 'Bleeding Love', and album, *Spirit*, in the same week. She became the first British female artist in history to debut at number one in the Billboard Top 200 album chart, and was the first British female to top the Billboard Hot 100 singles chart since Kim Wilde's 1987 Supremes cover, 'You Keep Me Hanging On'. In January, Radiohead entered the US album chart at number one with *In Rainbows*, selling a modest 122,000 in its first week. Indie giants Coldplay released their fourth album, the curiously titled *Viva La Vida Or Death And All His Friends*, which raced to the top spot around the world in June, selling a million copies in the US in its first three weeks. By August, the album had sold 750,000 copies in the UK, a respectable tally for a band seemingly going through the motions.

NEW FACES

The Arctic Monkeys are one British success story yet to fully translate across the Atlantic. In the UK, the Sheffield quartet sold 680,000 copies of their second album, *Favourite Worst Nightmare*, and scooped Brit Awards in February for best band and best album, which they picked up dressed as country squires. Two months later, the band's chief songwriter Alex Turner scored another number one album as the Last Shadow Puppets, his collaboration with Miles Kane of The Rascals. Evoking the rich 1960s orchestral pop of The Walker Brothers, *The Age Of The Understatement* sold 179,000 copies, underscoring the 22-year-old Turner's songwriting prowess.

It was a good year for Salford boy-girl duo The Ting Tings, whose debut album *We Started Nothing* rapidly sold half-a-million copies around the world largely because their infectious single, 'Shut Up And Let Me Go', appeared in an iTunes TV commercial. Adele Adkins, best known as soulful 19-year-old singer Adele, won the inaugural critics' choice award at the Brits in February, a few weeks after her debut album, *19*, had reached number one. The Londoner's LP sold steadily during 2008, selling 372,000 copies. *Rockferry*, the debut album by pint-sized diva Duffy, easily seduced the record-buying public with its tuneful pastiche of Motown pop and feel-good soul. Aimee Duffy, a 24-year-old newcomer from north Wales, is blessed with an authentically soulful voice that helped root February's debut single, 'Mercy', to the number one spot. Released in March, *Rockferry* has sold well over two million copies worldwide. A pop veteran by Duffy's standards, Kylie Minogue turned 40 this year and made a glittering comeback after a well-publicised battle with breast cancer. The Australian singer's album, *X*, a fruity electro-pop confection, sold 440,000 copies in the UK but contained few memorable moments.

REFORMED ROCKERS

Two other notable comebacks also took place this year. After much fanfare, the five original Spice Girls reformed for a string of arena shows in December that received, at best, mixed reports. Their uninspired single for Children In Need, 'Headlines (Friendship Never Ends)', limped into the UK top ten in October. By contrast, 1970s rock legends Led Zeppelin performed their first show in 19 years at a concert at London's O2 Arena in December. More than one million people took part in a ballot for the

9,000 pairs of tickets to witness original members Robert Plant, Jimmy Page and John Paul Jones play with Jason Bonham, son of their late drummer John Bonham. After more than two hours of exceptional entertainment, no one left disappointed. Future Led Zeppelin activity was thrown into doubt when Plant announced that he was to tour in 2008 with US country star Alison Krauss. The pair's joyful album, *Raising Sand*, was one of 2007's critical and commercial successes.

Elsewhere, US rock dinosaurs The Eagles underwhelmed with new album *Long Road Out Of Eden* in October. The band's decision to strike an exclusive distribution deal with US supermarket chain Wal-Mart rankled fans, who found it hard to square Eagles singer Don Henley's longstanding green credentials with this bastion of American consumerism.

A host of promising new bands from the States made waves in Britain this year. Heartwarming debuts from newcomers Bon Iver and Fleet Foxes bowled over critics and fans alike. With their rousing single 'Blind', colourful New York ensemble Hercules & Love Affair could claim responsibility for reviving an interest in disco in the UK. Fellow New Yorkers Vampire Weekend, MGMT and Yeasayer, meanwhile, mixed psychedelic rock, pop and ethnic elements to mesmeric effect, captivating festival-goers all summer long.

AWARDS

BRIT AWARDS 2008
British Male – Mark Ronson
British Female – Kate Nash
British album – Arctic Monkeys, *Favourite Worst Nightmare*
British group – Arctic Monkeys
British Breakthrough Act – Mika
British Live Act – Take That
British Single – Take That, 'Shine'
International Male Solo Artist – Kanye West
International Female Solo Artist – Kylie Minogue
International Group – Foo Fighters
International album – Foo Fighters, *Echoes, Silence, Patience & Grace*
Critics' Choice – Adele

MERCURY MUSIC PRIZE 2007
Klaxons – *Myths Of The Near Future*

NME AWARDS 2008
British Band – Arctic Monkeys
Album – Klaxons, *Myths Of The Near Future*
Track – Arctic Monkeys, 'Fluorescent Adolescent'
Solo Artist – Kate Nash
Live Band – Muse
New Band – The Enemy
International Band – The Killers
Radio Show – Zane Lowe, Radio 1
Website – Facebook
Music Blog – The Modern Age

OPERA

Elizabeth Forbes

Opera companies are particularly susceptible to cancellations by singers and during the first months of the season. The Royal Opera suffered a double loss: first Welsh baritone Bryn Terfel withdrew from Wagner's *Der Ring des Nibelungen* in October for personal reasons; then Mexican tenor Rolando Villazón cancelled his appearances as Nemorino in Donizetti's *L'elisir d'amore* during November for reasons of health. Terfel was scheduled to sing Wotan in two of the three *Ring* cycles, while John Tomlinson sang one. In the event Tomlinson sang the role in all three cycles, giving up the role of Hagen he was due to sing in *Götterdämmerung*. Tomlinson, in magnificent voice and commanding dramatic presence, dominated the first three parts of the cycle, and received the 2007 Royal Philharmonic Society Singer Award for his efforts.

This complete *Ring* was in any case more dramatic than were the original, separate performances. Keith Warner had tightened his production and music director Antonio Pappano obtained even more compelling playing from the Royal Opera Orchestra. The new production of *L'elisir d'amore*, directed by Laurent Pelly, was very enjoyable. Villazón, though obviously missed, was adequately replaced by Stefano Secco and the young Russian tenor Dmitriy Korchak offered a delightfully gentle portrait of Nemorino. The performances were dedicated to the memory of Luciano Pavarotti, the great Italian tenor who died on 6 September 2007, aged 70, and who had sung Nemorino, among many other roles, at Covent Garden.

Pavarotti made his debut with the Royal Opera in 1963 as Rodolfo in Puccini's *La Bohème*. During the 1960s he also sang Alfredo in Verdi's *La traviata*, Elvino in Bellini's *La sonnambula* and Tonio in Donizetti's *La Fille du régiment*, the last two with Joan Sutherland. In the 1970s he sang the Duke of Mantua in Verdi's *Rigoletto*, Edgardo in Donizetti's *Lucia di Lammermoor*, Gustavo in Verdi's *Un ballo in maschera*, Cavaradossi in Puccini's *Tosca* and Rodolfo in Verdi's *Luisa Miller*. Later performances included Nemorino in 1990. Though in the latter part of his career the dramatic aspect of his performances was not always very credible, vocally he remained peerless, his singing superbly stylish, his diction perfect.

Harrison Birtwistle's new opera, *The Minotaur*, was given its world premiere at Covent Garden on 15 April 2008. The libretto by David Harsent, who provided the text for *Gawain*, Birtwistle's previous commission by the Royal Opera, is based on the familiar Greek myth in which Theseus goes to Crete to kill the Minotaur, half bull, half man, assisted by Ariadne, the daughter of King Minos. Pappano conducted the broadly lyrical score with great sympathy, while Stephen Langridge's production made the events crystal clear. The role of the Minotaur, who can only bellow when awake, but who dreams in human speech, was specially written for John Tomlinson, who consequently gave an amazing account of the often very beautiful music in his dreams.

Ian Judge's staging of Verdi's *Simon Boccanegra*, though dating from 1997, contained important new material. Originally the 1857 version, the production was now that of 1881, the music revised by Verdi and the text largely rewritten by Arrigo Boito (librettist of *Otello* and *Falstaff*). The most important addition is the great Council Chamber scene, which ends the first act. The cast was dominated by Italian bass Ferruccio Furlanetto, who sang Jacopo Fiesco, father-in-law to Boccanegra, as a last minute replacement for a sick colleague. Furlanetto was in London rehearsing for Verdi's *Don Carlo* at Covent Garden. His complete dramatic involvement in *Simon Boccanegra* was the more impressive as he had had almost no rehearsal.

The new production of *Don Carlo* was staged by Nicholas Hytner, at present director of the National Theatre, and designed by Bob Crowley. Conducted by Pappano and with a splendid cast, this was the most eagerly-awaited event in the Royal Opera's whole season. Nor were the audiences disappointed. Musically the orchestra and chorus under Pappano were in superb form, while all the singers filled their roles more than adequately. Dramatically there were few cavils; Hytner's staging was powerful, though older operagoers can never quite forget Luchino Visconti's 1958 production. Furlanetto as Philip II and his fellow bass Eric Halfvarson as the Grand Inquisitor were magnificent; their scene together made the hairs rise on the back of one's neck. Elsewhere the tension seldom dropped.

In the Linley Studio Theatre below the opera house, a new staging of *Powder Her Face*, the first opera by Thomas Adès, written when he was 24 years old, displayed the composer's precocious talents to their best effect. Conducted by Timothy Redmond, directed by Carlos Wagner and designed by Conor Murphy, the production framed a superb performance by soprano Joan Rodgers as Margaret, Duchess of Argyll who, while admitting all the sordid details of her divorce, never entirely lost the audience's sympathy. Soprano Rebecca Bottone, tenor Iain Paton and bass Alan Ewing were excellent in multiple roles. Adès also conducted a very controversial new production in the main auditorium of Stravinsky's *Rake's Progress*. Instead of 18th-century England, director Robert Lepage placed the opera in 1950s USA. Carl Fillion's sets brilliantly evoked scenes in Texas, Las Vegas and Hollywood. Most of the critics hated the staging, but a younger than usual audience loved it, applauding soprano Sally Matthews' delightful Anne, tenor Charles Castronovo's lyrical Tom and bass John Relyea's saturnine Nick.

Among the revivals, Christof Loy's revival of *Ariadne auf Naxos* was perhaps the most noteworthy. Strauss's gorgeous score was superbly conducted by Mark Elder, recently knighted in the Queen's Birthday Honours. A very strong cast included American mezzo Kristine Jepson's poignant young composer and Thomas Allen's kindly Music Master. Canadian soprano Gillian Keith's Zerbinetta was as comfortable in the stratospheric fireworks of her aria as in the lyric duet with the Composer in the Prologue. As Ariadne and Bacchus, soprano Deborah Voigt and tenor Robert Dean Smith, both from the USA, sang their hearts out in the final scene. Herbert Murauer's monumental set for the

Prologue still takes 40 minutes to change, but the wait is well worth it.

Edward Gardner, English National Opera's music director, was awarded the 2007 Royal Philharmonic Society Music Award for Conductor. The jury cited 'his consistently high musical standards across a wide repertoire.' Gardner conducted two large-scale new productions in the early part of the season, Bizet's *Carmen* and Verdi's *Aida*, both of which illustated the high musical standard quoted above, but dramatically the staging of *Carmen* was less successful. Sally Potter, a film director making her operatic debut, chose to update the action, making Don José a security guard instead of a soldier, thus removing the threat of the death penalty for desertion. In *Aida* director Jo Davies kept the tension firmly taut, helped by a fine performance of Aida by Claire Rutter and some extremely colourful designs by Zandra Rhodes.

Other successful new ENO productions included Monteverdi's *Coronation of Poppea*, in which Kate Royal, winner of both the Kathleen Ferrier and John Christie awards, sang splendidly as Poppea, and Britten's *The Turn of the Screw*, originally directed by David McVicar for the Maryinsky Theatre, St Petersburg. Better still were Donizetti's *Lucia di Lammermoor*, conducted by ENO's former music director, Paul Daniel and staged by David Alden with an excellent cast headed by American soprano Anna Christy as Lucia; and McVicar's production of Strauss's *Der Rosenkavalier* (first seen at Scottish Opera), conducted by Gardner, with two outstanding performances from mezzo Sarah Connolly as Octavian, and bass John Tomlinson as Baron Ochs.

In somewhat lighter mood, Lehár's ever-popular *Merry Widow* was newly and opulently staged by John Copley. Soprano Amanda Roocroft sang beautifully as Hanna Glawari, though she was dramatically miscast, but tenor John Graham Hall made a perfect match for Danilo, being especially good in the dialogue. The evergreen score was idiomatically conducted by Oliver von Dohnányi. Robert Carsen's new production of Leonard Bernstein's *Candide*, conducted by Rumon Gamba, divided public and critical opinion. Carsen brought the satire of American politics right up to date, while Michael Levine's spectacular designs evoked Hollywood's golden age, with Anna Christy's Cunégonde as Marilyn Monro. Tenor Toby Spence made an attractive if gullible Candide and Alex Jennings dominated proceedings as the ever- optimistic Voltaire/Pangloss.

In April 2008 ENO collaborated with the Young Vic in mounting, at the latter venue, two contemporary music theatre pieces. The British premiere of *Lost Highway*, by Austrian composer Olga Neuwirth, first performed in 2004, was the adaptation by Nobel prize-winner Elfriede Jellinek and Neuwirth of the cult film made by David Lynch and Barry Gifford. *Lost Highway* was staged by American director Diane Paulus; soprano Lisa Saffer, renowned for her performance of Lulu in Berg's opera at ENO, sang the dual role of Renee/Alice. The second work given at the Young Vic was Birtwistle's *Punch and Judy*; conducted by Gardner and directed by Daniel Kramer, this work, though now 40 years old, still has the power to shock; another production, by Music Theatre Wales, was given at the Linbury Studio Theatre as an introduction to *The Minotaur*.

Opera North gave the British premiere of an opera first staged at Hamburg in 1730, *The Fortunes of King Croesus* by Reinhold Keiser, the first major composer of German Baroque. This turned out to be a real find, a work full of delightful music and telling dramatic situations, a Shakespearean medley of the serious and comic. Opera North also staged a genuine Shakespeare season, beginning with a revival of Verdi's *Falstaff* in autumn 2007 and continuing with new productions of Verdi's *Macbeth*, Britten's *A Midsummer Night's Dream* and Gounod's *Roméo et Juliette* in spring 2008. Of these *Macbeth* was particularly successful, strongly conducted by music director Richard Farnes, tautly staged by Tim Albery, with an exciting Lady Macbeth in Italian soprano Antonia Cifrone. The same basic set, designed by Johan Engels, was used for all three operas. Opera North also gave the world premiere of Jonathan Dove's *The Adventures of Pinocchio*, based on the well-known children's book with libretto by Alasdair Middleton.

Scottish Opera managed four new full-scale productions, all with points of interest: Rossini's *Il barbiere di Siviglia* was directed by Thomas Allen, better known as a singer; Mozart's *Die Entführung aus dem Serail* was staged by Tobias Hoheisel, better known as a designer; Judith Weir's *A Night at the Chinese Opera* was sensitively conducted by Sian Edwards; while Verdi's *Falsttaff* was particularly well and evenly cast. Scottish Opera also put on *Five:15*, five newly commissioned 15 minute operas by different composers and librettists. These proved extremely – and perhaps unexpectedly – successful, with four of the five mini-operas achieving real dramatic tension and musical interest.

Welsh National Opera opened the season with the world premiere of James MacMillan's *The Sacrifice*, with libretto by Michael Symmons Roberts, conducted by the composer and directed by Katie Mitchell. In a country torn by civil war Sian, daughter of the General, marries Mal, head of the opposing faction, in a vain attempt to broker peace. As Sian, soprano Lisa Milne was outstanding. A revival of Peter Stein's nearly 20-year-old production of Verdi's *Falstaff* featured Bryn Terfel in the title role (he sang Ford in a 1993 revival) and a very strong cast conducted by music director Carlo Rizzi. Terfel, in superb voice, made every note, every little gesture tell in his outsize portrait of the fat Knight; a truly magnificent performance. Also conducted by Rizzi, a new staging of Verdi's *Aida* was musically satisfying.

Glyndebourne could be said to have 'discovered' Monteverdi in 1962, when Raymond Leppard's version of *L'incoronazione di Poppea* was first given there. Opening the 2008 festival, a new production, with the Orchestra of the Age of Enlightenment conducted by Emmanuelle Haïm, was more authentic musically. Dramatically Robert Carsen's production was very different from Günther Rennert's staging in the sixties. Carsen set the action in the present: the Emperor Nero and the Gentlemen of his Court wore dark suits; Poppea, in a mini-nightdress most of the time, wore a ball-gown for her coronation. None of this distracted from the beauty and overpowering sensuality of the scenes between Nero and Poppea. American soprano Danielle de Niese (Glyndebourne's much-praised Cleopatra in Handel's *Giulio Cesare*) portrayed not only the overwhelming attraction of Poppea, but also her boundless ambition. She was strongly partnered by mezzo Alice Coote as Nero.

Revivals at Glyndebourne included Peter Hall's classic 1985 staging of Britten's *Albert Herring*, with a splendid performance by young tenor Allan Clayton as Albert. The original Albert of this production, John Graham-Hall, now sang Mr Upfold the Mayor. David McVicar's popular staging of Bizet's *Carmen* was also revived, with a new, exciting protagonist in mezzo Tania Kross. After a new production of Humperdinck's *Hänsel und Gretel*, with tenor Wolfgang Ablinger-Sperrhacke (Poppea's nurse Arnalta, earlier in the season) as a really frightening Witch, the season ended with the world premiere of *Love and other Demons* by Peter Eötvös. The text, by Kornél Márquez, adapted from a novel by Gabriel García Márquez, is set in 18th-century Columbia and deals with the love of a priest for a young girl. American baritone Nathan Gunn sang Father Delaura, while soprano Allison Bell made a touching Sierva Maria.

Among other summer festivals, Garsington Opera exhumed an interesting rarity in Vivaldi's *L'incoronazione di Dario*, first performed at Venice in 1717 but not heard before in the UK. David Freeman's production drew attention to the similarities between the Persia of the Emperor Darius and the Iran of Shah Reza Pahlevi in the 1950s. Stravinsky's *The Rake's Progress*, staged by Olivia Fuchs with tremendous energy, also found a parallel in the punk culture of the 1950s. Baritone Christopher Purves made a really devilish Nick Shadow, totally in command of tenor Robert Murray's gullible Tom Rakewell. Garsington Opera will have to leave the Manor from which it derives its name in 2010, but hopes to finds a suitable new venue before then.

Grange Park Opera offered an impressive staging by Stephen Medcalf of Puccini's *La fanciulla del West*, with a compelling Minnie in soprano Cynthia Makris, who was well supported by an excellent Dick Johnson in John Hudson and a notable cast of assorted miners. Rory Macdonald conducted the English Chamber Orchestra. Dvorák's *Rusalka*, directed and designed by Antony McDonald, was also very enjoyable, with French soprano Anne-Sophie Duprels as a bewitching Rusalka, tenor Jeffery Lloyd-Roberts a strong-voiced Prince and soprano Janis Kelly a cruel but attractive Foreign Princess. The ECO played particularly well for conductor Stephen Barlow, who brought out all the beauties of Dvorák's score.

Scottish Opera made a welcome return to the Edinburgh International Festival with a new production of Smetana's *The Two Widows*, conducted by the company's new music director Francesco Corti and directed and designed by Tobias Hoheisel. The Maryinsky Opera from St Petersburg staged *King Roger* by Polish composer Karol Szymanowski. This was conducted by Valery Gergiev, who also conducted concert performances of Rachmaninov's *Aleko* with Act 3 of Prokofiev's *Semyon Kotko* and the British premiere of contemporary Russian composer Rodion Shchedrin's *The Enchanted Warrior*. The Kurt Weill/Bertold Brecht *Aufstieg und Fall der Stadt Mahagonny* was conducted by Austrian composer H. K. Gruber in yet another concert performance.

The Aldeburgh Festival staged a world premiere, *Ocean of Rain* by Anglo-Cypriot composer Yannis Kyriakides and Canadian writer Daniel Davis, directed by Cathie Boyd. The four principal characters are all female. On May 31 2008 Music Theatre Wales gave the world premiere of Michael Berkeley's new opera, *For You*, with text by novelist Ian McEwan, a study of jealousy. This will tour to the Linbury Studio Theatre next season. Meanwhile, the Pacific Road Arts Centre, Birkenhead, put on the first UK performance of George Benjamin's *Into the Little Hill*, with libretto by Martin Crimp. This short work, for two singers and 15 instrumentalists, was premiered in Paris in 2006; it is based on the legend of the Pied Piper of Hamelin. It too will be presented at the Linbury next season.

Buxton Festival celebrated its 30th anniversary with a varied programme that included Lortzing's *Der Wildschütz*, sung in English as *The Poacher*. The 50th anniversary of the death of Ralph Vaughan Williams in 1958 was marked by a staging of his one-act opera *Riders to the Sea*, based on the play by J. M. Synge; this was preceded by two short operas by Gustav Holst (a great friend of Vaughan Williams), *The Wandering Scholar* and *Savitri*. There were also performances of Handel's *Samson* which, though technically an oratorio, can very well be staged as an opera, with tenor Thomas Randle in the title role; Kurt Weill's *Street Scene* and the English premiere of Welsh composer John Metcalf's *A Chair in Love*, a comedy for young people.

Operas given at the BBC Promenade Concerts at the Royal Albert Hall included the Glyndebourne production (semi-staged) of *L'incoronazione di Poppea* and, in honour of the centenary of the composer's birth, Olivier Messiaen's *Saint François d'Assise*, performed by Netherlands Opera with baritone Rod Gilfrey in the title role. Other operatic Proms were Puccini's one-acter *Il tabarro*, with the BBC Philharmonic Orchestra conducted by Gianandrea Noseda, Janácek's *Osud* (*Fate*), with the BBC Symphony orchestra conducted by Jiri Belohlavek and Rimsky-Korsakov's *Kashchei the Immortal*, with the London Philharmonic conducted by Glyndebourne's music director Vladimir Jurowski.

DEATHS

Sicilian tenor Guiseppe di Stefano died on 3 March 2008 aged 86. Gifted by nature with a voice of great beauty, as well as dark good looks, Di Stefano had a meteoric international career. But lack of good vocal technique and his insistence on singing roles too heavy for him resulted in the loss of that wonderful velvety bloom at a far too early age. He made his British debut with the Piccola Scala at the 1957 Edinburgh Festival, singing Nemorino in Donizetti's *L'elisir d'amore*. His Covent Garden debut was as Cavaradossi in *Tosca* in 1961, and he returned there two years later as Rodolfo in *La Bohème* (at one performance he was replaced by Luciano Pavarotti, making his Covent garden debut). However, his voice was known to a much greater number of British opera lovers through the ten commercial recordings he made with Maria Callas, including *Tosca*, Verdi's *Un ballo in maschera* and *Rigoletto*, Donizetti's *Lucia di Lammermoor* and Puccini's *Manon Lescaut*, as well as a number of unofficial recordings of the many live performances they gave together during the years 1951 to 1957.

British tenor Edmund Barham died on 7 May 2008, aged 56. He started his professional career in Germany at Wuppertal, later moving to Munich. In 1985 he was engaged by English National Opera, making his debut as Jenik in Smetana's *The Bartered Bride* and later singing Turiddu in Mascagni's *Cavalleria rusticana*, Pinkerton in *Madam Butterfly* and Cavaradossi in *Tosca*. After Boris in Janácek's *Katya Kabanova* and Don José in *Carmen* for Opera North in 1988, Barham returned to ENO for his first Verdi role with the company, Gabriele Adorno in *Simon Boccanegra*. This was followed by Alfredo in *La traviata* and Macduff in *Macbeth* in 1990 and two years later the title role of *Don Carlos* and Don Alvaro in *The Force of Destiny*. Alvaro, in particular, was magnificently sung. He also sang Calaf in Puccini's *Turandot* for both Welsh National Opera and ENO. In Australia he sang two more Verdi roles, Radames in *Aida*, as well as the title role of *Otello*, which unfortunately he never sang in the UK.

PRODUCTIONS

In the summaries of company activities shown below, the dates in brackets indicate the year that the current productions entered the company's repertory.

ROYAL OPERA

Founded 1946

Royal Opera House, Covent Garden, London WC2E 9DD

REPERTORY: *Das Rheingold* (2004), *Die Walküre* (2005), *Siegfried* (2005), *Götterdämmerung* (2006), *Parsifal* (2001), *La Cenerentola* (2000), *La traviata* (1994), *Die Zauberflöte* (2003), *Eugene Onegin* (2006), *Carmen* (2006), *Simon Boccanegra* (1997), *Tosca* (2006), *Ariadne auf Naxos* (2002), *Le nozze di Figaro* (2006), *La Bohème* (1974)

NEW PRODUCTIONS: *Iphigénie en Tauride* (Gluck), 10 September 2007. Conductor, Ivor Bolton; director, Robert Carsen; designer, Tobias Hoheisel. Susan Graham (Iphigénie), Simon Keenlyside (Oreste), Paul Groves (Pylade)

L'elisir d'amore (Donizetti) 13 November 2007. Conductor, Mikko Franck; director, Laurent Pelly; designer, Chantal Thomas. Aleksandra Kurzak (Adina), Stefano Secco (Nemorino), Ludovic Tézier (Belcore), Paolo Gavanelli (Dulcamara)

Salome (Strauss), 21 February 2008. Conductor Philippe Jordan; director, David McVicar; designer, Es Devlin. Nadja Michael (Salome), Michael Volle (Jochanaan), Michaela Schuster (Herodias), Robin Leggate (Herod)

The Minotaur (Birtwistle), 15 April 2008 (world premiere). Conductor, Antonio Pappano; director, Stephen Langridge; designer, Alison Chitty. John Tomlinson (Minotaur), Christine Rice (Ariadne), Johan Reuter (Theseus)

Don Carlo (Verdi), 6 June 2008. Conductor, Antonio Pappano; director, Nicholas Hytner; designer, Bob Crowley. Ferruccio Furlanetto (Philip II), Rolando Villazón (Don Carlo), Marina Polavskaya (Elisabeth), Sonia Ganassi (Eboli), Simon Keenlyside (Posa)

The Rake's Progress (Stravinsky), 7 July 2008. Conductor, Thomas Adès; director, Robert Lepage; designers, Carl Fillion (sets), François Barbeau (costumes). Charles Castronovo (Tom Rakewell), John Relyea (Nick Shadow), Sally Matthews (Anne Trulove)

ENGLISH NATIONAL OPERA

Founded 1931

London Coliseum, St Martin's Lane, London WC2N 4BS

REPERTORY: *The Magic Flute* (1988), *Madam Butterfly* (2005), *The Mikado* (1986)

NEW PRODUCTIONS: *Carmen* (Bizet), 29 September 2007. Conductor, Edward Gardner; director, Sally Potter; designers, Es Devlin (sets), Catherine Zuber (costumes). Alice Coote (Carmen), Julian Gavin (Don José), Katie van Kooten (Micaela), David Kampster (Escamillo)

The Coronation of Poppea (Monteverdi), 18 October 2007. Conductor, Laurence Cummings; director, Chen Shi-Zheng; designers, Walt Spangler (sets), Elizabeth Caitlin Ward (costumes). Kate Royal (Popea), Anna Grevelius (Nero), Robert Lloyd (Seneca), Tim Mead (Ottone), Doreen Curran (Ottavia), Lucy Crowe (Drusilla)

Aida (Verdi), 8 November 2007. Conductor, Edward Gardner; director, Jo Davies; designer, Zandra Rhodes. Claire Rutter (Aida), John Hudson (Radames), Jane Dutton (Amneris), Iain Patterson (Amonasro)

The Turn of the Screw (Britten), 26 November 2006. Conductor, Garry Walker; director, David McVicar; designer, Tanya McCallin. Rebecca Evans (Governess), Ann Murray (Mrs Grose), Timothy Robinson (Peter Quint)

Lucia di Lammermoor (Donizetti), 16 February 2008. Conductor, Paul Daniel; director, David Alden; designers, Charles Edwards (sets), Brigitte Reiffenstuel (costumes). Anna Christy (Lucia), Barry Banks (Edgardo), Mark Stone (Enrico), Clive Bailey/Paul Whelan (Raimondo)

The Merry Widow (Lehár), 24 April 2008. Conductor, Oliver von Dohnányi; director, Peter Copley; designers, Tim Reed (sets), Deirdre Clancy (costumes). Amanda Roocroft (Hanna), John Graham-Hall (Danilo), Fiona Murphy (Valencienne), Alfie Boe (Camille)

Der Rosenkavalier (Strauss), 22 May 2008. Conductor, Edward Gardner; director/set designer, David McVicar; costume designer, Tania McCallin. Sarah Connolly (Octavian), Janice Watson (Marschallin), Sarah Tynan (Sophie). John Tomlinson (Baron Ochs), Andrew Shore (Faninal)

Candide (Bernstein), 25 June 2008. Conductor, Rumon Gamba; director, Robert Carsen; designers, Michael Levine (sets), Buki Schiff (costumes). Toby Spence (Candide), Anna Christy (Cunégonde), Alex Jennings (Pangloss/Voltaire)

OPERA NORTH

Founded 1978

Grand Theatre, 40 New Briggate, Leeds LS1 6NU

REPERTORY: *Falstaff* (1996), *Peter Grimes* (2006)

NEW PRODUCTIONS: *Madama Butterfly* (Puccini), 15 September 2007. Conductor, Wyn Davies; director, Tim Albery; designers, Hildegard Bechtler (sets), Ana Jebens (costumes). Anne Sophie Duprels (Butterfly), Rafael Rojas (Pinkerton), Ann Taylor (Suzuki), Peter Savidge (Sharpless)

The Fortunes of King Croesus (Keiser), 17 October 2007. Conductor, Harry Bicket; director, Tim Albery; designer, Leslie Travers. Paul Nilon (Croesus), Gillian Keith (Elmira), Michael Maniaci (Atis), John Graham-Hall (Ellcius)

The Adventures of Pinocchio (Dove), 21 December 2007 (world premiere). Conductor, David Parry; director, Martin Duncan; designer, Francis O'Connor. Victoria Simmonds (Pinocchio), Mary Plazas (Blue Fairy), Jonathan Summers (Gepetto)

Macbeth (Verdi), 23 April 2008. Conductor, Richard Farnes; director, Tim Albery; designer, Johan Engels (sets), Brigitte Reiffenstuel (costumes). Robert Hayward (Macbeth), Antonia Cifrone (Lady Macbeth), Ernesto Morillo Hoyt (Banquo), Peter Auty (Macduff)

A Midsummer Night's Dream (Britten), 3 May 2008. Conductor, Stuart Stratford; director, Martin Duncan; designers, Johan Engels (sets), Ashley Martin Davies, costumes). James Laing (Oberon). Jeni Bern (Tytania), Henry Waddington (Bottom)

Roméo et Juliette (Gounod), 17 May 2008. Conductor, Martin André; director, John Fulljames; designers, Johan Engels (sets), Adam Wiltshire (costumes). Leonardo Capalbo (Roméo), Bernarda Bobro (Juliette), Grant Doyle (Mercutio)

SCOTTISH OPERA
Founded 1962
39 Elmbank Crescent, Glasgow G2 4PT

NEW PRODUCTIONS: *Il barbiere di Siviglia* (Rossini), 3 October 2007. Conductor, Sergio La Stella; director, Thomas Allen; designer, Simon Higlett. Karen Cargill (Rosina), Adrian Dwyer (Almaviva), Thomas Oliemans (Figaro), Nicholas Folwell (Bartolo)

Die Entführung aus dem Serail (Mozart), 19 October 2007. Conductor, Jeremy Carnall; director, Tobias Hoheisel; designer, Andreas Grüter. Julia Borchert (Constanze), Rebecca Bottone (Blonde), Eric Laporte (Belmonte), Dmitry Ivashchenko (Osmin)

A Night at the Chinese Opera (Weir), 11 April 2008. Conductor, Sian Edwards; director, Lee Blakeley; designer, Jean-Marc Puissant. Damien Thantrey (Chao Lin), Toby Stafford-Allen (Chao Sun), Fiona Kimm (Mrs Chin)

Falstaff (Verdi), 13 May 2008. Conductor, Peter Robinson; director, Dominic Hill; designer, Tom Piper. Peter Sidhom (Falstaff), Maria Costanza Nocentini (Alice), William Dazeley (Ford), Lucy Crowe (Nannetta), Sally Burgess (Mistress Quickly)

WELSH NATIONAL OPERA
Founded 1946
Wales Millenium Centre, Bute Place, Cardiff Bay CG10 5AL

REPERTORY: *Il trovatore* (2003), *Eugene Onegin* (2004), *Falstaff* (1988), *The Magic Flute* (2005), *Hansel and Gretel* (1998)

NEW PRODUCTIONS: *The Sacrifice* (James MacMillan), 22 September 2008 (world premiere). Conductor, MacMillan; director, Katie Mitchell; designer, Vicki Mortimer. Christopher Purves (General), Lisa Milne (Sian), Sarah Tynan (Megan)

La Cenerentola (Rossini), 27 September 2007. Conductor, Carlo Rizzi; director, Joan Font; designer, Joan Guillén. Marianna Pizzolato (Angiolina), Colin Lee (Ramiro), Roberto de Candia (Dandini), Robert Poulton (Don Magnifico)

Aida (Verdi), 27 May 2008. Conductor, Carlo Rizzi; director, John Caird; designers, Yannis Thavoris (sets), Emma Ryott (costumes). Svetelina Vassilieva (Aida), Dennis O'Neill (Radames), Margaret Jane Wray (Amneris), Philip Joll (Amonasro)

GLYNDEBOURNE FESTIVAL OPERA
Founded 1934
Glyndebourne, Lewes, East Sussex BN8 5UU

The Festival ran from 18 May to 31 August 2008.

REPERTORY: *Eugene Onegin* (1994), *Albert Herring* (1985), *Carmen* (2002)

NEW PRODUCTIONS: *L'incoronazione di Poppea* (Monteverdi), 18 May 2008. Conductor, Emmanuelle Haïm; director, Robert Carsen; designers, Michael Levine (sets), Constance Hoffman (costumes). Danielle de Niese (Poppea), Alice Coote (Nerone), Tamara Mumford (Ottavia), Paolo Battaglia (Seneca), Marie Arnet (Drusilla)

Hänsel und Gretel (Humperdinck), 20 July 2008. Conductor, Kazushi Ono; director/costume designer, Laurent Pelly; set designer, Barbara de Limburg Stirum. Jennifer Holloway (Hänsel), Adriana Kucerova (Gretel), Wolfgang Ablinger-Sperrhacke (Witch)

Love and other Demons (Peter Eötvös) 10 August 2008 (world premiere). Conductor, Vladimir Jurowski; director, Silviu Pucarete; designer, Helmut Stürmer. Allison Bell (Sierva Maria), Nathan Gunn (Father Delaura), Robert Brubaker (Don Ignacio), Mats Almgren (the Bishop)

PARLIAMENT

Patrick Robathan

The first full year of Gordon Brown's tenure as prime minister began with his popularity running high and the opposition parties unsure as to how to handle the new incumbent, who wrong-footed them from an early stage. As parliament rose for the summer recess, however, things were entirely different: the government had seen significant backbench rebellions against core policies (a total of 90 so far up to August 2008 in addition to 10 from the end of the 2006–7 session), they suffered the loss of Labour's third safest seat in Scotland when the Scottish Nationalist Party overturned Labour's majority of 13,507 to win the by-election in Glasgow East by 365 votes and the leader of the Conservative Party David Cameron challenged the prime minister to call a general election. The opinion polls consistently showed a 22-point lead for the Conservatives over Labour, with one poll showing that 67 per cent of those questioned regarded Mr Brown as 'weak, a loser and not up for the job as prime minister'.

The parliamentary year began with much promise for the prime minister, although his decision not to call an early general election in the autumn soon reflected in the opinion polls with the Conservatives breaking through the 40 per cent barrier for the first time since 1992 to establish a three point lead over the Labour party and with Mr Brown's approval ratings as prime minister plummeting from 44 to 34 per cent. During the year he experienced a series of parliamentary setbacks that undermined his position – a selection of these issues are examined below.

SPILL-OVER PERIOD: FOOT AND MOUTH

The government's handling of the foot and mouth outbreak over the summer of 2007 did little to improve their standing. Environment secretary Hilary Benn reported back on the situation to the House on 8 October, when Conservative environment spokesman Peter Ainsworth was scathing, 'The government have been caught red-handed and are damned by their negligence. We know that the source of the outbreak was a government-regulated and licensed laboratory'. Liberal Democrat environment spokesperson Chris Huhne wondered, 'Do the government now accept that they have a legal obligation, and certainly a moral one, to compensate those whose businesses have been damaged by the outbreak?'

PRE-BUDGET REPORT

Chancellor Alistair Darling delivered his first pre-budget report on 9 October, under pressure from the opposition over policies relating to non-domiciles and inheritance tax, areas where the Conservatives were widely believed to have stolen a march on the government. The main points were:

- growth forecast cut by 0.5 per cent
- tax receipts down by £1.8bn, public sector net borrowing up by £4.3bn
- inheritance tax threshold raised to £600,000 for married people or those in civil partnerships
- crackdown pledged on non-domicile tax payers
- 10 per cent tax rate on private equity capital gains abolished so private equity bosses would pay more in tax
- green taxes on flights not passengers from 2009

He said, 'The theme of this year's pre-budget report is that, provided we maintain the course for economic stability that we have set, we can respond to the uncertain global environment. We will do so by taking no risks with stability and no risks with unaffordable promises that put the public finances at risk . . . We propose not unaffordable tax cuts that deprive public services of the money they need, but an affordable tax cut and improved investment in health and education, founded on economic stability.'

Shadow chancellor George Osborne said Mr Brown had ten years to address issues like inheritance tax but 'now, a week after we put forward our plans, the prime minister and the chancellor are scrabbling around in a panic trying to think of something to say . . . He talks about setting out his vision of the country, but he has to wait for us to tell him what it is . . . we have had a pre-election budget without the election.'

LIBERAL DEMOCRATS LEADERSHIP CONTEST

A good showing at his party conference could not silence mutterings about his style of leadership and his age, and so Liberal Democrat leader Sir Menzies Campbell resigned after only 19 months as leader on 15 October saying, 'It has become clear that following the prime minister's decision not to hold an election, questions about leadership are getting in the way of further progress by the party.' Deputy leader Vince Cable declined to stand but was acting leader until the conclusion of the leadership election on 18 December. He provided some memorable performances whilst deputising, notably at prime minister's question time (PMQs) on 28 November, 'the House has noticed the Prime Minister's remarkable transformation in the past few weeks from Stalin to Mr. Bean, creating chaos out of order, rather than order out of chaos.'

The two candidates in the contest were home affairs spokesperson Nick Clegg and environment spokesperson Chris Huhne. The former was the victor, winning under the alternative vote system by a narrow margin of 1.2 per cent. He was welcomed to the post by Mr Brown at PMQs on 9 January: 'I look forward to working with him on many of the issues facing the country. I have said to him in our private conversations that there is an open door for him, and we are ready to discuss the major issues that affect the country where there is common ground.' Mr Cameron was more light-hearted, 'He is the fourth Liberal Democrat leader that I have faced, and I wish him well, although not that well. I am simply relieved that it is no longer my party that has this habit of replacing its leader on quite such a regular basis.'

NEW SESSION: QUEEN'S SPEECH

The Queen's Speech on 6 November contained proposals for 31 bills for the coming session (including two carried over from the previous session and six bills that would be introduced in draft) and hinted at possible further legislation on other matters such as party political funding. The prime minister felt this was 'a legislative programme that takes the next step forward for a stronger, fairer Britain . . . with the first law in the world to curb carbon emissions; the biggest educational reform for 60 years; the first universal right for adults to study free of charge; the first new towns for 40 years; building three million more homes by 2020; youth centres for every area of the country; progress on health, social care, transport and energy'. This enthusiasm was not shared by the opposition leaders. Mr Cameron said: 'There are bills that we support, not least because we proposed them in the first place . . . but the real problem with the Queen's Speech is simple. It is the same as the problem with this prime minister. Whether it is on housing, immigration or youth unemployment, it is all short-term tricks instead of long-term problem solving. We now see a prime minister bereft of vision, bending with the wind, buffeted by events. There is day after day of dithering.' Stand-in Liberal Democrat leader Vince Cable thought: 'The Queen's Speech has been long in anticipation. The prime minister has been waiting for it for ten years. He has had a 35-year political career distilling many of the ideas that have come forward today. He postponed the election in order to inject more vision, but the sense of anticlimax is deafening. We have heard little new, no ideas and little vision.' Support from Mr Brown's own backbenches was more solid, 'The last couple of months have been a bit bumpy . . . He said himself when he called off the election that he hadn't done enough in terms of stating his vision. He can't do that overnight; it's not an on-off switch you hit and I think he has done a lot of good work today to begin to build that', argued Labour MP Jon Cruddas.

COUNTER-TERRORISM BILL – 28 vs 42 DAYS DETENTION

One of the most contentious of the bills announced was the Counter-Terrorism Bill, under which the 28-day limit for police to hold terror suspects without charge would be increased. Speaking in the debate on the Queen's speech on 7 November Home Secretary Jacqui Smith argued that the time was right for an extension. Conservative home affairs spokesman David Davis said, 'We do not accept the need to extend detention without charge, based either on the evidence of operations to date or the most horrendous hypothetical scenarios dreamt up by ministers.' Liberal Democrat home affairs spokesperson Nick Clegg said extending the period was 'divisive, wrong in practice and wrong in principle'. From the government backbenches veteran Labour MP David Winnick warned, 'If we are to go beyond 28 days, the House should have compelling evidence that it's absolutely essential.'

When the bill was debated at second reading in the Commons on 1 April the government proposal was for a 'reserve power' for an extension from 28 to 42 days. Whilst the bill was not opposed at second reading, both main opposition parties and several government backbenchers said that they expected to vote against this part of the bill during the later stages of its passage through parliament. By the time the bill came to the Commons for remaining stages on 11 June there had been weeks of behind-the-scenes negotiation to try to gain sufficient support. During the debate Ms Smith said, 'It is the job of government, police and prosecutors to protect the public from terrorist attack, and thereby to defend everybody's right to life, but today it is the job of parliament to give them the tools to do that. We need the support of the House for the proposals in the bill. We need the support of the House to do the right thing for this country's security.' Liberal Democrat Chris Huhne felt: 'The fight against terrorism is far too important to be reduced to populist symbols that would substantially curb our hard-won freedoms.' Rebel Labour backbench MP Diane Abbott said: 'Because the government do not have the votes, they have spent the past ten days putting good, conscientious colleagues – who naturally enough want to support the leader of their party, our prime minister – under incredible pressure. People whom the prime minister has never spoken to in his life have been ushered into his presence twice in 48 hours.'

In the event the clause extending the maximum time police can hold terror suspects to 42 days was passed by 315 MPs to 306, with 36 Labour MPs voting with Conservatives and Liberal Democrats against the proposals. The 'yes' votes of the nine Democratic Unionist Party MPs proved crucial leading to claims that they had been bought off with a string of inducements – including extra financial help for Northern Ireland and guarantees that the government would block efforts to use the Human Embryology and Fertility Bill, currently going through parliament, to loosen abortion rules in Northern Ireland.

As a result of this vote, Mr Davis resigned his front bench position and his seat (Haltemprice and Howden) to stand again on a platform of defending 'British liberties'. When neither the Liberal Democrats nor Labour put up a candidate against him, he won the by-election on 10 July with a majority of 15,355 votes. The government still faces a battle in the House of Lords where the bill will be debated in the October spill-over period.

CREDIT CRUNCH – NORTHERN ROCK

The credit crunch began in late July 2007 when banks became reluctant to lend to each other due to market fears over exposure to potential losses on high-risk US 'sub-prime' mortgages. During the 2007 summer recess, Northern Rock was caught up in the crisis and a potential run on the bank caused the chancellor to pledge on 17 September that the government would guarantee all deposits with Northern Rock. On 1 October Mr Darling announced that the government would guarantee 100 per cent of each individual's bank and building society savings up to £35,000. On 11 October he came to the House to update MPs on these developments: 'When problems occur, we need to have a system in place that is clear and which reassures depositors. We will introduce legislation in the next session to establish a new regime.'

On 21 January Mr Darling announced plans to back a private-sector rescue of Northern Rock through the sale of government-guaranteed bonds to pay off the lender's £24bn debts. When this strategy failed and the two actual bids were rejected because they would require a 'very significant implicit subsidy', on 17 February Mr Darling announced legislation to take Northern Rock into a period of temporary public ownership, 'Having made the decision to save the bank, maintain financial stability and protect savers, we are now taking this decision to protect the taxpayer.' George Osborne was scathing: 'Never before in the long history of his office has a chancellor had to come to parliament to announce the nationalisation of a high street bank. For months, the prime minister dithered and delayed, doing everything he could to avoid the very course of action that he now recommends.' Mr Osborne confirmed his party would oppose the bill. On behalf of the Liberal Democrats Vince

Cable was more welcoming: 'They were right to decide that temporary nationalisation is a better option than a bad private sale whereby the taxpayer would have underwritten the risks and the private buyer would have acquired the profits.' The Banking (Special Provisions) Bill was introduced the next day, receiving second reading in the Commons by 367 votes to 164 and completed its legislative passage in 2 days, gaining royal assent on 21 February.

On 21 April Mr Darling made a statement on moves by the Bank of England to improve conditions in the financial markets, making some £50bn available to banks and reporting on the measures that he was taking to strengthen the stability of the banking system, as well as to help home owners with their mortgages. Mr Osborne thought: 'It is time for the government to stop fighting themselves and start fighting for the country. It is time for a government who are on the people's side, not on people's backs.' Vince Cable felt: 'the chancellor is in the process of being slowly devoured by the British banking system.'

During the 2008 summer recess Northern Rock announced bigger-than-expected losses for the first six months of the year, prompting the government to give the bank a maximum of £3bn more in funds, this time turned into equity in the state-owned bank. Conservative Treasury spokesman Philip Hammond said the taxpayer 'was being forced to hand over yet more money in order to keep this bank afloat' and Vince Cable added: 'Alistair Darling assured parliament that taxpayer loans to Northern Rock would be fully secured on mortgage assets. This is clearly not true.'

BUDGET – 10P TAX RATE/VEHICLE EXCISE DUTY

In his first Budget speech on 12 March, Chancellor of the Exchequer Alistair Darling outlined the following proposals:

- delay 2p rise in fuel duty for six months
- 6 per cent increase in alcohol tax – with 2 per cent above inflation rise for each of next four years
- 4p on pint of beer, 3p on cider, 14p on wine, 55p on spirits
- 11p on packet of 20 cigarettes, 4p on five cigars
- £950 higher first year rate of road tax for most polluting cars
- new top band for the most polluting vehicles that emit more than 255g of carbon dioxide per kilometre
- air passenger duty scrapped in favour of flight tax
- winter fuel payment up to £250 for over-60s and to £400 for over-80s
- require supermarkets to charge for plastic bags if they do not scrap them
- more cash to tackle child poverty
- help with rising energy costs for poorer families
- forecasts for economic growth for this year cut by 0.25 per cent – to between 1.75 per cent and 2.25 per cent – with big increase in government borrowing, which is set to go up by £14bn over the next two years

He called it 'a responsible Budget to secure Britain's stability in the face of global uncertainty. I have made my choice: responsible decisions, not irresponsible, unfunded promises; fairness and opportunity for everyone in Britain to secure a strong and sustainable future.' Mr Cameron dismissed the statement as 'a dire list of reviews and re-announcements'. Liberal Democrat leader Nick Clegg said the chancellor had delivered a 'meagre tinkering budget which gives precious little help to the poor but maintains special treatment to the rich'. As the year unfolded various parts of the government's budgetary announcements came back to haunt them.

The abolition of the 10p tax rate, announced by Mr Brown in his final budget in 2007 prompted Labour MP Greg Pope to table an early-day motion calling on the government to compensate losers from the tax change, which gained the signatures of 26 Labour MPs. When the Treasury select committee report on the 2008 budget concluded: 'it seems strange that the abolition of the 10p starting rate of income tax disadvantages mainly low income households', pressure grew on the chancellor to back down. On 21 April Chief Secretary to the Treasury Yvette Cooper announced a review of the impact of tax changes on the childless poor and Mr Brown made an unscheduled address to the parliamentary Labour Party, assuring MPs he was listening to their concerns. Labour MP Frank Field however, still tabled an amendment to the Finance Bill at committee stage on the issue, supported by 45 Labour MPs. The following day Mr Darling promised compensation would be delivered within this financial year and later announced that assistance would be given to low-paid workers without children and pensioners aged 60–64, backdated to the start of the financial year. As a result Mr Field withdrew his amendment. On 13 May the chancellor announced that this help would amount to £600 on top of this year's personal tax allowance. George Osborne was damning: 'the chancellor serves up a compensation con after a tax con and expects people to believe it. What utter cynicism, what total incompetence – and what a complete humiliation for this chancellor.' But Labour rebel Mr Field congratulated the chancellor on putting an end to the issue and apologised for having allowed his campaign to become personal. A new clause was added to the Finance Bill which received royal assent on 21 July.

On the issue of Vehicle Excise Duty (VED) the chancellor revealed a major reform, which he hoped would 'encourage manufacturers to produce cleaner cars' but he had not said explicitly that higher charges would apply to anyone who had bought a car since 1 March 2001. As this became clear, another backbench revolt began to emerge, led by Labour MP Ronnie Campbell who tabled a motion calling for the government to reconsider its plans which was signed by nearly 50 Labour MPs. The issue dominated PMQs on 4 June where Mr Cameron said: 'the next tax hike planned by the government is to hit family cars, including those bought seven years ago, with massive increases in vehicle excise duty. Is the prime minister really going to go ahead with this deeply unpopular tax when families are struggling with the cost of living, or can he give us another of his trademark u-turns?' In a reply that was to come back to haunt him, Mr Brown replied: 'the majority of drivers will benefit from it'. Mr Cameron countered: 'the Treasury has said that under this regime, 81 per cent of cars will be worse off. Once again, dodgy statistics from the prime minister'.

During the third reading debate on the Finance Bill on 2 July, the Exchequer Secretary Angela Eagle announced that the government would re-examine the plans at the pre-budget report in the autumn, with the expectation that the measures would be phased in rather than brought in straight away. As a result the measure was passed by 303 votes to 240 with only six Labour rebels voting against the government. Mr Campbell, who ended up voting with the government said: 'We are considering a heavy tax on working people who need the car to get to work because our transport system is not that good. It is a retrospective tax . . . on working people . . . I will vote with the government, with a heavy heart, in the hope that they come up with something in the autumn statement that will give the working-class people of this country a bit of a break.'

DRAFT LEGISLATIVE PROGRAMME

As in the previous year, the government published their draft legislative programme for the following year on 14 May. The consultation proposed 18 bills and other non-legislative actions, organised into four themes: economic stability; making the most of your potential; personalisation and improvement of public services; and handing power back to the people. Hoping to regain the initiative in light of the global economic problems, with food and fuel prices rising and mortgages more difficult to obtain, Mr Brown said the purpose of the proposals was 'building a more prosperous Britain and a fairer Britain'. Mr Cameron was less than impressed, 'The draft Queen's Speech reveals the prime minister's deeper problem . . . his ideas have run out of steam. He no longer has the solutions.' Mr Clegg was similarly dismissive, 'it is now clear that the prime minister will try anything to cling to power. He has scraped the legislative barrel to save himself.'

EUROPE

Usually seen as a problem for the Conservative Party, the need to ratify the Lisbon treaty and the passage of the European Union (Amendment) Bill also caused much embarrassment to the government. The bill had its second reading in the Commons on 21 January with the foreign secretary David Miliband declaring that the treaty was 'good for Britain and good for Europe' and arguing that no referendum was needed as the treaty merely amended the EU's existing constitution, rather than overwriting it – as the failed constitution would have done. The second reading was passed by 362 votes to 224.

Controversially an amendment supported by 18 Labour and four nationalist MPs calling for a referendum was not selected for debate by Commons Speaker Michael Martin. One of those Labour MPs, Austin Mitchell, said: 'If it looks like a constitution, if it smells like a constitution, if it reads like a constitution, so far as I'm concerned it's a constitution.' On 28 January MPs agreed by 299 votes to 243 a timetable motion to limit clause by clause committee debate on the bill to 12 days on the floor of the Commons. Conservative foreign affairs spokesman William Hague felt: 'There could not be a more cynical approach to the conduct of government policy, deeply lacking in openness, transparency or honesty' while Liberal Democrat Simon Hughes added: 'The modernising tendencies of the government wanting to do something good in terms of procedure have been overridden by the old tendency . . . of the Stalin in Number 10 and his friends wanting to be very authoritarian about the timetable of this bill.'

On the seventh day of committee debate, on 26 February, the Liberal Democrats staged an orchestrated Commons walkout after the speaker blocked debate on their bid to force a referendum on UK membership of the EU and on the tenth day a vote was forced on their call for referendum, but it was defeated by 471 votes to 68. On the eleventh day of committee debate on 5 March MPs rejected the Conservative call for a referendum on whether the Lisbon treaty should be ratified by 311 votes to 248, a majority of 63. Twenty-nine Labour MPs supported the Conservative motion and three Conservative MPs voted against it. Thirteen Liberal Democrat MPs rebelled against party leader Nick Clegg's orders to abstain on the vote, with three frontbench spokesmen resigning their posts as a result (Scottish affairs spokesperson Alistair Carmichael, countryside spokesman Tim Farron and justice spokesman David Heath).

At third reading on 11 March Mr Miliband told MPs: 'every mainstream political party in Europe believes the treaty is good for the UK and good for Europe, because it reforms the EU's "foundations" and allows us to move on to the agenda of prosperity and development and climate change.' To which Mr Hague replied, 'the truth is the foreign secretary and prime minister now believe the former prime minister made a serious error when he promised a referendum and it was that error which has reduced them to arguing that something, which is 90 per cent the same, is fundamentally different'. The refusal to give one was nothing to do with constitutional practice, but 'everything to do with the sharp practice of ministers focused solely on what they could or could not get away with'. In the end MPs voted by 346 votes to 206, a majority of 140, to approve the bill.

When the bill moved to the House of Lords for second reading on 1 April (with a marathon 12-hour debate) Conservative hopes of forcing a referendum on the treaty were given a blow after Liberal Democrat leader in the Lords, Lord McNally, said peers would not be asked to abstain like their MP colleagues, 'Let there be no doubt that we on these benches want to see this bill passed and this treaty ratified. Our general election commitment to a referendum was on a constitutional treaty. That commitment died with the constitution, which was rejected by the French and the Dutch. We have taken the view that the present treaty is an amending treaty which should be carried through by the parliamentary process.' The bill had seven days in committee in the Lords and on the final day (20 May) peers rejected an amendment moved by Conservative peer Lord Blackwell to put into law a requirement that a referendum be held before Britain joins the euro by 195 votes to 135, a majority of 60. On the third and final day of report stage (11 June – one day before the referendum in the Irish Republic) the Lords voted against holding a referendum by 280 to 218, (only two Labour peers voted for the referendum but eight Conservative peers voted against). Conservative foreign affairs spokesman in the Lords, Lord Howell said: 'What has happened is that the treaty drafters and this government have achieved an illusion by using a methodological device which is used to say the constitution position is abandoned . . . the public is being hoodwinked and the public knows that as well.' As the Lords debated the third reading on 18 June and following the 'No' vote in Ireland, David Cameron asked Gordon Brown at PMQs to show 'backbone' and declare the EU treaty 'dead . . . this is not a treaty Britain wanted or needed . . . It would be ridiculous to ask the Irish to vote twice, when we haven't even been allowed to vote once.' Mr Brown replied: 'Just as we have respect for the Irish, we should have respect for the other countries that are processing the treaty and ratifying the treaty as well. And perhaps we should also have respect for this House, which has also voted for ratification of the treaty.' The last-ditch Conservative bid in the Lords to delay the process for four months was defeated by 277 votes to 184, and peers then gave the bill an unopposed third reading. The bill received royal assent on 19 June and the United Kingdom became the 19th EU country to ratify the Lisbon treaty when the 'instruments of ratification' were deposited in Rome on 16 July.

IRAQ/AFGHANISTAN

The involvement of British troops in both Iraq and Afghanistan continued to undermine the government, with Mr Brown beginning most PMQs with an expression of regret and sending condolences to relatives of British troops who had been killed. On 8 October he made a statement on the situation in Iraq: 'Our strategy in Iraq as a government has been first, political reconciliation, to work to bring together the political groupings in Basra and across Iraq; secondly, security, to ensure that the security of the Iraqi people and the new Iraqi democracy is properly safeguarded, as well as the security of our own armed forces; and thirdly, economic reconstruction, to work for an economy in Iraq where people have a stake in the future.' He also outlined plans to reduce force numbers in southern Iraq to a figure of 2,500 from next spring. This announcement was generally welcomed on all sides of the House, even by those opposed to the presence of British troops.

On 12 December Mr Brown updated MPs on the situation in Afghanistan: 'Britain will continue to fulfil our obligations to the Afghan people and the international community. We will support the Afghan army, police and government as they progressively take over greater responsibility for their own security. We will work with our international partners and help the Afghans themselves to strengthen stability, foster democracy and build prosperity. At all times we will support the hard work, dedication, professionalism and courage of our armed forces, who are doing everything in their power to defeat terrorism and to lay the foundations of a stable and secure future for Afghanistan.' Whilst this statement was also generally welcomed, there was some dissent. Senior Conservative backbencher Sir Peter Tapsell pointed out: that 'the basic stumbling block to all the admirable aims that he has announced is the fact that the one thing that unites all Afghans is their hatred of foreign troops in their country'.

Just before the summer recess Mr Brown made a further statement on Iraq to MPs on 22 July, 'We have . . . sought to foster democratic and accountable government and support national reconciliation, giving all of Iraq's communities a genuine say in the future of their country. And we have worked to help the Iraqis build their economy and give their people an economic stake in the future . . . It is now right to complete the tasks we have set ourselves . . . we expect a further fundamental change of mission in the first months of 2009, as we make the transition to a long-term bilateral relationship with Iraq, similar to the normal relationships that our military forces have with other important countries in the region.' Mr Cameron wanted to know more about the troop withdrawals: 'we need the government to be as clear and transparent as possible on troop numbers. Is it not the case that over the past few days we have been in danger of hearing two quite contradictory things? Does the prime minister agree that we are discussing not abstract numbers and . . . announcements, but people with families and responsibilities who are already coping with the consequence of overstretch and who deserve the very best treatment?'

On 25 March the Conservatives instigated a debate on the need for an inquiry into the war in Iraq and Labour backbenchers lined up to criticise the government. Bob Marshall-Andrews said: 'this is a war without an apparent or defined end. It was said we had a victory four years ago, and it is a gloomy symbiosis that the fourth anniversary of that victory marked the death of the 4,000th US serviceman in Iraq. He will not be the last; and nor will our next casualty be our last.' Alan Simpson added: 'We should not be afraid to say that in a catastrophic experience for the British government we have led ourselves into a disastrous, dishonest, destabilising and downright illegal war. We owe it to our credibility with our own people and our own armed forces to address the questions of why and at what point people signed up to a war that was a betrayal of the interest of the UK rather than an honouring of it.'

Whilst the Conservatives were generally supportive of the government, they were more critical on the issues of equipment and support – covered by two defence committee reports. On equipment, James Arbuthnot MP said: 'for too long the MoD has had an unaffordable equipment programme and needs to confront the problem rather than giving the usual response of salami-slicing and moving programmes to the right. A realistic equipment programme will give confidence to our armed forces that the programmes that remain will be delivered in the numbers and to the timescale required, and will also allow industry to make informed investment decisions.' On medical care he said: 'there is no doubt that armed forces medical personnel do a brilliant job in treating and rehabilitating wounded servicemen and women . . . but the MoD needs to do more to look after families and veterans . . . and there also has to be better long-term mental healthcare for veterans.'

ENERGY REVIEW

The government's decision to press ahead with a new generation of nuclear power stations also upset many backbenchers. On 10 January Business Secretary John Hutton told MPs they would give a 'safe and affordable' way of securing the UK's future energy supplies while fighting climate change, that any plants would be built at or near existing reactors by private firms and he hoped the first one would be completed 'well before 2020'. Bearing in mind the costs, former Labour minister Michael Meacher thought: 'is not the whole nuclear project the mother of all white elephants?' These sentiments were echoed by Labour MP Colin Challen, 'we have to be honest and recognise that the statement is as full of holes as the Sellafield reprocessing plant.'

DATA LOSS

The government's competence was further questioned, with several high profile losses of personal data by government departments, the most serious of which was the loss of unregistered and unencrypted discs containing 25 million child benefit records in October. When this came to light Mr Darling told the Commons on 20 November, 'This is an extremely serious matter. HMRC has a responsibility towards the general public, who entrust it with highly sensitive personal information. It has failed to meet the high standards that should be expected of it. I recognise that millions of people across the country will be very concerned about what has happened. I deeply regret that and apologise for the anxiety that will undoubtedly be caused.' Mr Osborne felt 'half the country will be very anxious about the safety of their family and the security of their bank accounts, and the whole country will be wondering how on earth the government allowed this to happen . . . This autumn, the prime minister said he had shown that the government could be competent, and now needed to set out his vision . . . Never mind the lack of vision; just get a grip, and deliver a basic level of competence.'

On 21 January Defence Secretary Des Browne had to report to MPs the loss of laptop computers from the MoD containing personal information on some 600,000 people. Conservative defence spokesman Liam Fox said, 'lately, it has been shown that the government take a cavalier approach to the confidential details of UK citizens, but in the case that we are considering, the security aspects make things worse,' and Liberal Democrat defence spokesperson Nick Harvey called for a 'change of culture across Whitehall'.

On 12 June Minister for the Cabinet Office Ed Miliband had to report to MPs on the loss of two Joint Intelligence Committee documents, left on a train, while two weeks later Mr Darling published the final Poynter report into the lost HMRC discs, which made it clear that the incident was 'entirely avoidable'.

SLEAZE

Whilst it was the Conservative Party who suffered the most embarrassing incident over alleged sleaze when Old Bexley and Sidcup MP Derek Conway was suspended from the House of Commons for 10 days in January after a Standards and Privileges Committee report said he overpaid his son from parliamentary allowances (he also had the party whip withdrawn and subsequently announced he would not stand at the next election) and Conservative party chairman Caroline Spelman referring her use of expenses to pay her nanny for investigation by the parliament's Standards Commissioner, John Lyon, on 17 June. But the issue also damaged the government. Welsh Secretary Peter Hain resigned from the cabinet on 24 January in order to clear his name after his Labour deputy leadership campaign donations had been referred to the police. In Scotland, Labour lost its party leader when Wendy Alexander, MSP, resigned 'with deep regret' on 28 June after breaking rules on declaring donations when she faced a one-day ban from Holyrood after failing to register donations to her leadership campaign.

As a result of the Conway affair, the Commons Members Estimate Committee instigated a review into the wider system of MPs' expenses, but when this was debated on 3 July MPs rejected the tougher auditing and alternative expenses regime proposed by the review and voted to keep their £24,000 additional costs allowance. Liberal Democrat MP Nick Harvey, a member of the committee, said: 'it was a total own-goal on the part of the House of Commons. An opportunity to put our house in order and be seen to put our house in order has been passed up. They took all the nice bits of the package but not the ones they didn't like. They took the spoonful of sugar but refused the medicine.' As a result the Leader of the House of Commons, Harriet Harman, announced a further consultation on steps to improve financial control and audit on 16 July.

OTHER NOTABLE BACKBENCH REBELLIONS

The scale of Mr Brown's difficulties can be illustrated by the fact that he has faced 100 backbench revolts (involving no less than 79 MPs) since becoming prime minister, admittedly some of them very small. This compares to just 96 in Tony Blair's first full four-year term as prime minister. Among the largest (not alluded to above) in this year were:

- 19 March: 19 Labour MPs voted for a Conservative motion condemning Post Office closures, reducing the government's majority to 20, albeit on a relatively low turnout.
- 25 March: 12 Labour MPs supported a Conservative motion calling for an inquiry into the war in Iraq, more than halving the government's majority to just 28.
- 31 March: 30 Labour MPs supported Labour MP Austin Mitchell's new clause 8 at the report stage of the Housing and Regeneration Bill, which would have required the secretary of state to take certain matters into account when determining what subsidy to give to local authorities to support their housing revenue accounts, in particular, ensuring they had the necessary resources needed to meet the decent homes standard and the need for affordable housing.
- 22 April: 21 Labour MPs supported Labour MP Jim Cousins' amendment to the Pensions Bill that would have implemented the restoration of the earnings link with pensions in 2010 at the latest.
- 30 April: 38 Labour MPs voted for Labour MP Alan Simpson's new clause 4 at the report stage of the Energy Bill, requiring designated energy suppliers to introduce a renewable energy tariff for specified producers of renewable energy.
- 2 June: 24 Labour MPs voted against the government during the report stage of the Planning Bill, reducing their majority to 15.
- 25 June: Having postponed the second day of the remaining stages of the Planning Bill in order to try and head off a rebellion from 60 Labour MPs, the government saw some seven separate rebellions, but by accepting two amendments from Labour MP Clive Betts – requiring the Infrastructure Planning Commission to take account of local communities' views and to hold public hearings if compulsory purchases were involved – only six Labour MPs actually opposed the third reading of the bill.

The House rose for an 11-week summer recess on 22 July, due to return on 6 October amid a row over the fact that thousands of children were still waiting for the results of SATs in English, maths and science. Schools Secretary Ed Balls said the delays were 'unacceptable . . . and we need to learn lessons from that'. He declined to apologise – claiming it was the job of the exams watchdog to manage the process – and as a result was forced to make a statement to the Commons when his Conservative counterpart Michael Gove wondered, 'Does not this just underline the incompetence at the heart of this government when it comes to education?'

A very mixed year for the government ended with Labour MP Gordon Prentice urging Gordon Brown to resign. He felt that the role of prime minister required 'a different set of skills from being a chancellor'. Up to ten junior ministers were rumoured willing to resign to force Mr Brown to do so.

PUBLIC ACTS OF PARLIAMENT

This list of public acts commenced with five public acts which received the royal assent before 1 August 2007 and which were mentioned briefly in the last edition. Those public acts which follow received the royal assent after 31 July 2007. The date stated after each act is the date on which it came into operation.

Statistics and Registration Service Act 2007 c.18 (various dates, some to be appointed) establishes and makes provision about the Statistics Board; about offices and office-holders under the Registration Service Act 1953; and for connected purposes.

Corporate Manslaughter and Corporate Homicide Act 2007 c. 19 (various dates, some to be appointed) creates a new offence, in England and Wales or Northern Ireland 'corporate manslaughter' and, in Scotland, 'corporate homicide'; and makes provision therefor.

Forced Marriage (Civil Protection) Act 2007 c. 20 (day or days to be appointed) makes provision for protecting individuals against being forced to enter into marriage without their free and full consent and for protecting individuals who have been forced to enter into marriage without such consent; and for connected purposes.

Offender Management Act 2007 c. 21 (various dates, some to be appointed) makes provision about providing probation services, prisons and other matters relating to the management of offenders; and for connected purposes.

Pensions Act 2007 c. 22 (various dates, some to be appointed) makes provision about pensions and other benefits payable to persons in connection with bereavement or by reference to pensionable age; about the establishment and functions of the Personal Accounts Delivery Authority; and for connected purposes.

Sustainable Communities Act 2007 c. 23 (23 October 2007) makes provision about promoting the sustainability of local communities; and for connected purposes.

Greater London Authority Act 2007 c. 24 (various dates, some to be appointed) makes further provision with respect to the Greater London Authority; amends the 1999 act; and provides with respect to the functional bodies, within the meaning of that act, and the Museum of London; and for connected purposes.

Further Education and Training Act 2007 c. 25 (various dates, some to be appointed) makes provision about the Learning and Skills Council for England; about institutions within the further education sector; with respect to industrial training levies; about the formation of, and investment in, companies and charitable incorporated organisations by higher education corporations; and enables the making of Assembly Measures in relation to the field of education and training; and for connected purposes.

Building Societies (Funding) and Mutual Societies (Transfers) Act 2007 c. 26 (day or days to be appointed) makes provision in relation to funding limits in respect of building societies; provides consequential rights to building society members; and in connection with the transfer of the business of certain mutual societies.

Serious Crime Act 2007 c. 27 (various dates, some to be appointed) makes provision about serious crime prevention orders; creates offences in respect of the encouragement or assistance of crime; enables information to be shared or processed to prevent fraud or for purposes relating to proceeds of crime, and data matching to be conducted both in relation to fraud and for other purposes; amends the Proceeds of Crime Act 2002 in relation to certain investigations and in relation to accredited financial investigators, management receivers and enforcement receivers, cash recovery proceedings and search warrants; extends stop and search powers in connection with incidents involving serious violence; and for various other purposes connected with serious crime.

Local Government and Public Involvement in Health Act 2007 c. 28 (various dates, some to be appointed) provides with respect to local government and the functions and procedures of local authorities and certain other authorities; with respect to persons with functions of inspection and audit in relation to local government; establishes the Valuation Tribunal for England; provides for the abolishing of Patients' Forums and the Commission for Patient and Public Involvement in Health; and with respect to local consultation in connection with health services; and for connected purposes.

Legal Services Act 2007 c. 29 (various dates, some to be appointed) provides for the establishment of the Legal Services Board and in respect of its functions; for, and in connection with, the regulation of persons who carry on certain legal activities; for the establishment of the Office for Legal Complaints and for a scheme to consider and determine legal complaints; makes provision about claims management services and about immigration advice and immigration services, and about the application of the Legal Profession and Legal Aid (Scotland) Act 2007, and about the Scottish legal services ombudsman; and for connected purposes.

UK Borders Act 2007 c. 30 (various dates, some to be appointed) makes provisions about immigration and asylum; and for connected purposes.

Consolidated Fund Act 2007 c. 31 (13 December 2007) authorises the use of resources for the service of the years ending 31 March 2008 and 31 March 2009 and applies certain sums out of the Consolidated Fund to the service of the years ending 31 March 2008 and 31 March 2009.

European Communities (Finance) Act 2008 c. 1 (19 February 2008) amends the definition of 'the treaties' and 'the community treaties' in section 1(2) of the European Communities Act 1972 so as to include the decision of 7 June 2007 of the Council on the Communities' system of own resources.

Banking (Special Provisions) Act 2008 c. 2 (21 February 2008) enables the Treasury in certain circumstances to make an order relating to the transfer of securities issued by, or of property, rights or liabilities belonging to, an authorised deposit-taker; makes further provision in relation to building societies; and for connected purposes.

Appropriation Act 2008 c. 3 (20 March 2008) authorises the use of resources for the service of the years ending 31 March 2007 and 31 March 2008 and applies certain sums out of the Consolidated Fund to the service of the year ending with 31 March 2008; and appropriates the supply authorised in this session of parliament for the service of the years ending 31 March 2007 and 31 March 2008.

Criminal Justice and Immigration Act 2008 c. 4 (various dates, some to be appointed) provides further for criminal justice (including provision about the police) and dealing with offenders and defaulters; about the management of offenders; for combating crime and disorder; about the mutual recognition of financial penalties; amends the criminal law, and the Repatriation of Prisoners Act 1984; provides for a new immigration status in certain cases involving criminality; about the automatic deportation of criminals under the UK Borders Act 2007; and for connected purposes.

Channel Tunnel Rail Link (Supplementary Provisions) Act 2008 c. 5 (22 July 2008) makes provision amending, and supplementary to, the 1996 act.

Child Maintenance and Other Payments Act 2008 c. 6 (various dates, some to be appointed) establishes the Child Maintenance and Enforcement Commission; amends the law relating to child support; makes provision about lump sum payments to or in respect of persons with diffuse mesothelioma; and for connected purposes.

European Union (Amendment) Act 2008 c. 7 (day or days to be appointed) makes provision in connection with the treaty of Lisbon amending the treaty on European Union and the treaty establishing the European Community, signed at Lisbon on 13 December 2007.

Appropriation (No 2) Act 2008 c. 8 (21 July 2008) authorises the use of resources for the service of the year ending 31 March 2009 and applies certain sums out of the Consolidated Fund to the service of the year ending 31 March 2009; appropriates the supply authorised in this session of parliament for the service of the year ending with 31 March 2009; and repeals certain Consolidated Fund and appropriation acts.

Finance Act 2008 c. 9 (21 July 2008) grants certain duties, alters others and amends the law relating to the national debt and the public revenue, makes further provision in connection with finance.

Sale of Student Loans Act 2008 c. 10 (21 July 2008) enables the sale of rights to repayments of student loans; and for connected purposes.

Special Educational Needs (Information) Act 2008 c. 11 (various dates, some to be appointed) amends the Education Act 1996 in relation to the provision and publication of information about children who have special educational needs; and for connected purposes.

Statute Law (Repeals) Act 2008 c. 12 (21 July 2008) promotes the reform of the statute law by the repeal, in accordance with recommendations of the Law Commission and the Scottish Law Commission, of certain enactments which (except in so far as their effect is preserved) are no longer of practical utility, and makes other provision in connection with the repeal of those enactments.

Regulatory Enforcement and Sanctions Act 2008 c. 13 (various dates, some to be appointed) makes provision for the establishment of the Local Better Regulation Office; for the co-ordination of regulatory enforcement by local authorities; for the creation of civil sanctions in relation to regulatory offences; for the reduction and removal of regulatory burdens; and for connected purposes.

Health and Social Care Act 2008 c. 14 (various dates, some to be appointed) establishes and makes provision in connection with a Care Quality Commission; makes provision about health care (including provision about the National Health Service) and about social care; makes provision about reviews and investigations under the Mental Health Act 1983; establishes and makes provision in connection with an Office of the Health Professions Adjudicator, and makes other provision about the regulation of the health care professions; and for various other matters connected with health and social care.

Criminal Evidence (Witness Anonymity) Act 2008 c.15 (21 July 2008) makes provision for the making of orders for securing the anonymity of witnesses in criminal proceedings.

National Insurance Contributions Act 2008 c. 16 (various dates, one to be appointed) makes provision as to the upper earnings limit for NIC.

Housing and Regeneration Act 2008 c. 17 (various dates, some to be appointed) establishes and provides for the Homes and Communities Agency; abolishes the Urban Regeneration Agency and the Commission for New Towns; makes provision about landlord and tenant matters, building regulations and mobile homes; and for other matters connected with housing and regeneration.

Crossrail Act 2008 c. 18 (22 July 2008) makes provision for a railway system to run from Maidenhead and Heathrow Airport, through central London to Shenfield and Abbey Wood; and for connected purposes.

Statistics and Registration Service Act 2007 c.19 (day or days to be appointed) establishes and makes provision about the Statistics Board; and about offices and office-holders under the Registration Service Act 1953; and for connected purposes.

WHITE PAPERS

This section provides an outline of a selection of white papers that have been published in the last year. For further information see W www.official-documents.co.uk or www.parliament.uk. Alternatively, visit the websites of individual government departments – *see* Government Departments section.

The Children's Plan: Building Brighter Futures was presented to parliament by the Secretary of State for Children, Schools and Families in December 2007. The paper outlines the plans for improving the lives of children and young people over the next decade. It introduces a package of measures including £225m to upgrade 3,500 playgrounds, the possible end of SATs tests by 2009, and £200m extra childcare provision for two-year-olds in families in deprived areas. The paper also recommends a review of the primary curriculum, and the option for children born in August to begin school a year later.

Meeting the Energy Challenge: A White Paper on Nuclear Power was presented to parliament by the Secretary of State for Business, Enterprise and Regulatory Reform in January 2008. The paper constitutes a formal response to a 2007 consultation on the future of nuclear power. It concludes that it is in the public interest that new nuclear power stations should have a role to play alongside other low-carbon sources, and that energy companies should be given the option of investing in new nuclear power stations. The paper describes the steps that the government will take to facilitate this, including meeting European law requirements, and enhancing the transparency of the regulatory regime to give greater confidence to the public and investors.

Innovation Nation was presented to parliament by the Secretary of State for Innovation, Universities and Skills, the Chancellor of the Exchequer and the Secretary of State for Business, Enterprise and Regulatory Reform in March 2008. The paper argues that innovation is essential to the UK's future economic prosperity and quality of life, and sets out the government's aim to form closer links between industry and higher education. Key commitments proposed include innovation vouchers to support and fund businesses to work with universities and colleges; doubling the number of knowledge transfer partnerships between businesses, universities and colleges; and expanding the network of national skills academies.

Pharmacy in England: Building on Strengths – Delivering the Future was presented to parliament by the Secretary of State for Health in April 2008. The paper reflects the views and ideas of pharmacists in the UK and builds on the existing strengths of pharmacies to give them a wider role in the community. The paper introduces new roles for pharmacies: to become healthy-living centres; to offer some NHS treatments for minor ailments; to provide support for people beginning courses of treatment for long-term conditions; to offer screening for those at risk of vascular disease; and to be commissioned based on the range and quality of their services.

Joint Birth Registration – Recording Responsibility was presented to parliament by the Secretary of State for Work and Pensions in June 2008. The paper proposes changes to the law in England and Wales to make joint birth registration a legal requirement for all unmarried parents unless it is decided by the registrar to be impossible, impractical or unreasonable. The paper also proposes to give mothers the right to insist that the father acknowledges his responsibilities to his child by registering on the birth certificate, and equally outlines the right of the father to insist that he is registered. It will offer sole-registering mothers the opportunity to re-register the birth with the father within six months of the first registration.

Framework for a Fairer Future – The Equality Bill was published by the Lord Privy Seal, Leader of the House of Commons and Minister for Women and Equality in June 2008. The paper argues for the simplification of existing legislation into a single equality bill. The bill outlined in the paper has powers to outlaw age discrimination; to require public bodies to report inequalities in gender pay, ethnic minority employment and disability employment; to allow employers to take into account the under-representation of disadvantaged groups when choosing between two equally qualified candidates; and to allow tribunals to make wider recommendations in discrimination cases that could benefit the whole workforce.

Communities in Control: Real People, Real Power was presented to parliament by the Secretary of State for Communities and Local Government in July 2008. The paper focuses on passing more power to local communities and giving control over local decisions and services to a wider selection of people. Policies outlined include introducing a duty to promote democracy; a new duty to involve local people in key decisions; a task force to support frontline staff; and an empowerment fund of at least £7.5m to support organisations to turn key proposals into action. The paper also introduced a new duty for local councils to respond to petitions, and measures to allow a wider range of people to stand for office.

An Elected Second Chamber: Further Reform of the House of Lords was presented to parliament by the Lord Chancellor and Secretary of State for Justice in July 2008. The paper sets out the government's proposals for a reformed second chamber of the UK parliament based on House of Commons votes for an 80 or 100 per cent elected second chamber. The reforms create a second chamber with directly elected members, and remove the rights of the remaining hereditary peers to sit and vote in the chamber. The changes are intended to strengthen the role of the House of Lords in holding the government to account and revising legislation, and to make the second chamber more accountable.

SCIENCE AND DISCOVERY

Neil Bone

ASTEROID MISSION ON ITS WAY

Following several delays, NASA's *Dawn* spacecraft was launched on a Delta 2 rocket from Cape Canaveral on 27 September 2007. *Dawn* will rendezvous with and orbit asteroid Vesta from September 2011 until April 2012, and then be targetted to the dwarf planet/asteroid Ceres between February 2015 and the nominal mission end in July of that year. A Discovery mission, *Dawn* will map and study the composition of these contrasting bodies: Vesta is irregular, dense and iron-rich, while Ceres is spherical and has significant amounts of carbonaceous material. With respective diameters of 525 and 930 km, Vesta and Ceres are by far the largest asteroidal bodies targetted for spacecraft study.

Meanwhile, another spacecraft on a long interplanetary journey briefly caused some excitement on its return to Earth's vicinity in November 2007. Launched in 2004, ESA's *Rosetta* probe is scheduled to rendezvous with Comet 67P/Churyumov-Gerasimenko in 2014. The mission calls for several gravity-assisted flybys of Earth and Mars. The spacecraft was detected as a moving object – initially thought to be a 20-metre asteroid making a potentially hazardous close approach – by the 0.68-metre Catalina Sky Survey Telescope in Arizona on 7 November 2007, and briefly given the minor planet designation 2007VN84 before its true nature was realised. During its close (5,300km) flyby on 13 November, *Rosetta*'s systems were tested by taking images of the Earth and Moon. Rosetta's next target is asteroid (2867) Steins, which it will encounter on 5 September 2008.

MERCURY FLYBY REVEALS HIDDEN SIDE

NASA's *Messenger* (MErcury Surface Space ENvironment GEochemistry and Ranging) spacecraft made its first close passage, 200km above the surface of Mercury on 14 January 2008. The probe, launched in 2004, is the first to examine Mercury in detail since the Mariner 10 mission of 1974–5. *Messenger*'s cameras imaged parts of Mercury's surface which were inaccessible to Mariner 10. Scientists have now had a first view of the giant Caloris Basin impact feature in its entirety: this has proved larger than initially thought (1,720km diameter as opposed to earlier estimates of 1,280km). Crater counts show that the western half of the basin has been resurfaced by lava flows, perhaps similar to those that produced the Moon's dark maria. *Messenger* also imaged a complex crater, nicknamed 'The Spider', near the centre of the Caloris Basin and from which an unusual system of about 100 narrow, flat-floored troughs radiate. Lobate scarp features, resulting from wrinkling of the planet's crust as Mercury cooled and shrank in the past were also recorded in detail among the 1,300 or so images returned.

Messenger will make a further close pass over Mercury on 6 October 2008, as part of a series of manoeuvres designed to place it in orbit around the planet in 2011.

FOSSIL TEETH ADD NEW LINK TO APE EVOLUTIONARY CHAIN

The Afar rift region of Ethiopia has been a rich source of fossil evidence documenting early human and ape evolution. Excavations by a Japanese–Ethiopian team in the Chorora formation in southern Afar between 2005 and 2007 have found remains of a new gorilla-like ape, which suggest that divergence between human and gorilla lineages may have occurred earlier than previously thought.

The remains are in the form of teeth – one canine and eight molars – from at least three individuals. In terms of size, these are indistinguishable from those of modern gorillas. The molars show adaptation for a fibrous diet including plant leaves and stems. Named *Chororapithecus abyssinicus*, the newly discovered fossil species is the first large-bodied Miocene ape to be found on the African continent north of Kenya. The region's fossil assemblage suggests that at the time *C.abysssinicus* lived, the area was a forest environment on a lake margin. The teeth were found in sediments which date back to between 10 and 10.5 million years ago, at least two million years earlier than previous (genome-based) estimates for the split between human and gorilla lineages.

EARLY HUMAN HABITATION IN SOUTH AFRICA

Archaeological and genetic evidence indicates that *Homo sapiens* originated in Africa around 200,000 years ago, later spreading out to colonise Europe and Asia. Excavations in a cave at Pinnacle Point, overlooking the Indian Ocean in South Africa, offer new evidence for early development of recognisably human traits – tool-making and the use of ochre for symbolic purposes – 165,000 years ago. A team, led by Prof. Curtis Marean of Arizona State University, published their findings in *Nature* in October 2007.

Between 196,000 and 130,000 years ago, conditions in Africa were harsh – cool and arid – as a result of glaciation. Responding to these, early humans expanded their range to coastal regions and adopted a diet supplemented by shellfish. Charred remains of mussels and other species were found at Pinnacle Point. Haematite rock fragments at the site were used as a source of ochre pigment. The strong red colouration of these points to the use of the pigment in symbolic or ritualistic practices. Bladelet tools, flaked from quartz and suitable for attachment to wooden shafts, were also found at the site. The findings suggest that modern human cognitive and symbolic behaviour had developed some 40,000 years earlier than previously suspected.

THE EARLIEST EUROPEAN HUMAN

Spanish researchers have found evidence for the earliest recognisably modern human habitation in western Europe during excavations at the Sima del Elefante cave in the Sierra de Atapuerca in northern Spain. A lower mandible fragment, including some teeth preserved *in situ*, was recovered from a stratigraphic layer dating back to the early Pleistocene, 1.1 to 1.2 million years ago. The jawbone shows both primitive and modern anatomical features and appears – like many other fossils from the Atapuerca site – to come from *Homo antecessor* ('Pioneer Man'). Stone tools were also found, alongside animal remains showing traces of processing (butchery) by hominins. This find, reported in March 2008, suggests that early humans rapidly colonised western Europe following their initial spread out of Africa. It would also appear that a major speciation event, leading to new hominin lineages, occurred in the Atapuerca region during the early Pleistocene.

GRAPEVINE GENOME SEQUENCE PUBLISHED

The grapevine *Vitis vinifera* is a crop of enormous commercial importance, and has become the fourth flowering plant to have its complete genome sequence determined. Results of the project were published by the French-Italian Public Consortium for Grapevine Genome Characterisation in August 2007. To obviate the problem of variation between strains, the sequence was determined from PN40024, a highly inbred derivative of the Pinot Noir Burgundy grapevine. The genome was found to consist of 475 million basepairs of DNA, in which 30,434 protein-coding genes were identified.

Relative to other available plant genomes, *V.vinifera* shows increased representation (perhaps three-fold) of genes for terpene synthases, enzymes involved in synthesis of resins and essential oils which are important components of the aroma and flavour of wine. A modest amplification of stilbane synthase genes was also found. These are associated with synthesis of resveratol, an antioxidant which has been suggested to offer health benefits to moderate drinkers of wine.

While it is unlikely that availability of the complete grapevine genome sequence will lead to changes in wine-making – growth conditions and traditional production methods are far more significant – it is possible that selective transfer between strains of factors offering resistance to various pathogens may be more effectively carried out in the future.

PRIMATE CLONING BREAKTHROUGH

The procedure of somatic cell nuclear transfer (SCNT) has been used to produce clones from several mammalian species: sheep (the celebrated Dolly in 1996), cow, cat, horse, dog and mouse. In SCNT, the nucleus of an unfertilised ooctyte (egg cell) is removed and replaced by that of a mature cell. The first successful cloning of a primate – using nuclei from skin cells taken from a nine-year-old rhesus macaque monkey named Semos – was reported in *Nature* in November 2007.

The research team, led by Shoukhrat Mitalipov at the Oregon National Primate Research Centre, overcame a number of technical obstacles to achieve their success. Critically, when preparing oocytes for SCNT, they avoided the use of fluorescent DNA-binding dyes and ultraviolet light, instead using polarised-light microscopy to effect identification and removal of recipient cell nuclei. Nuclear transfer was carried out with a brief electrical pulse, followed by a recovery period, then cells were stimulated to grow and divide, producing blastocysts in culture.

While attempts to implant cloned embryos to surrogate mothers have so far failed, two lines of embryonic stem (ES) cells have been successfully derived from blastocysts cultured *in vitro*. The stem cell lines showed the ability to develop into neuronal and muscular tissues. Use of SCNT to produce ES cell lines, described by some as therapeutic cloning, offers the hope of future treatments for degenerative diseases, allowing replacement of defective host cells with compatible, differentiated ES cells. Technical and ethical barriers, however, are such that this procedure is a long way from human application. Perhaps more significant is the potential for developing patient-specific ES lines for drug testing and analysis of cellular processes.

'DESIGNER GENOMES' A STEP CLOSER

Molecular biologists have for some time been able to construct reasonably long stretches of DNA *in vitro* from the bases A, G, C and T. Short oligonucleotides are routinely synthesised by the polymerase chain reaction (PCR), for example. Synthetic 'designer genomes' have been brought a step closer by the work of a team led by J. Craig Venter in Rockville, Maryland. Venter and co-workers had previously (in 2003) succeeded in synthesising from scratch the entire 5,386 base genome of the bacteriophage fX174.

In a much more ambitious project, reported in *Science* in January 2008, they describe their work in recreating a synthetic genome for the bacterium *Mycoplasma genitalium*. The aim is to eventually introduce the synthetic genome – containing all the essential *M.genitalium* genes, but with a gene for pathogenicity deliberately removed – into a receptive, DNA-free bacterial cell. Ethical issues remain, and it is technically more difficult to remove the relatively structureless resident bacterial DNA than it is to extract the discrete, packaged nucleus of an animal cell in SCNT procedures. In the much longer term, this approach may lead to development of bacteria tailored to particular tasks such as removal of pollutants or synthesis of biofuels.

METHANE DETECTED IN EXOPLANET ATMOSPHERE

By mid-2008, the number of planets detected orbiting other stars was rapidly approaching 300. Many of the known exoplanets are 'hot Jupiters' – massive gaseous bodies in orbits close to their parent star. Observations often reveal little more than the (considerable) mass of the exoplanets, and it is difficult to determine much more about their nature. Spectroscopic analysis of HD 189733b, a hot Jupiter orbiting a faint star 63 light years away in the constellation Vulpecula, as for the first time revealed the presence of an organic molecule – methane (CH_4) – in an exoplanet's atmosphere.

The planet's 2.2-day orbit is aligned so that, from out terrestrial perspective, it periodically crosses in front of the star, causing a slight dip in brightness. Comparison of infrared spectra obtained during such transits with those obtained when the planet is clear of the star, allows identification of absorption features specific to the planet's atmosphere. The observations, made with the NICMOS instrument aboard the Hubble Space Telescope, also confirmed earlier detection (by the Spitzer infrared space telescope) of water vapour. As usual, the media were quick to seize on the presence of water and organic molecules as key indicators for the possibility of life. The high temperatures (in excess of 1,000°C) on HD 189733b of course preclude this, the planet's orbit being only 0.03 astronomical units (AU; 1 AU is equivalent to Earth's mean orbital distance from the Sun, approximately 150,000,000km) from the star. Perhaps more importantly, the observations of heavy elements such as carbon in the atmospheres of such hot Jupiters afford some insight to the nature of the protostellar clouds from which other planetary systems condensed: relative to that which gave rise to our own Solar System, HD 189733's protostellar cloud may have been less rich in carbonaceous material.

PLATYPUS GENOME REVEALS KEY DIFFERENCES FROM OTHER MAMMALS

Long seen as an oddity of the animal world, the duck-billed platypus *Ornithorynchus anatinus* has had its genome sequence determined by an international team of researchers. The results, reported in May 2008, offer some interesting insights to mammalian evolution. Mammals are thought to have first evolved from a common reptilian ancestor around 315 million years ago. The platypus is part of a separate lineage – the monotremes, so named because they have a single external opening for their urogenital and digestive systems – which diverged from other mammals 166 million years ago. Marsupial and eutherian (placental) mammals in turn diverged from each other slightly later, around 148 million years ago.

In most respects, the platypus has a lifestyle very much in common with other mammals. A significant difference is that, rather than giving birth to live young, the platypus lays eggs. The female does, however, lactate and the hatched young are fed on milk secreted from her abdominal skin (the platypus lacks nipples). In common with that of marsupials, the milk alters in composition as the young develop. Male platypus have the particularly reptilian trait of producing venom, released from their hind claws and used in defence of territory.

Analysis of the genomic data explains some of these characteristics. The platypus genome is arranged in 52 chromosomes, and contains 18,527 protein-encoding genes – a total similar to the 18,600–20,800 for human or opossum (as a representative marsupial). Most platypus genes show reasonable homology to their equivalents in other mammals. The genes for venom production, however, are clearly reptilian in nature. An interesting difference is found in the sex-determining X and Y chromosomes. Whereas other mammals have a single pair (XX for females, XY for males), the platypus has five pairs – females have five XX pairs, males five XY pairs. This is more typical of the situation in birds and, at DNA sequence level, the platypus X chromosome far more closely resembles that of chicken than other mammals.

As the research team who produced the genome sequence put it, the platypus represents a remarkable amalgam of mammalian and reptilian characteristics.

MOST LUMINOUS GAMMA RAY BURST

Among the most energetic events in the Universe, gamma ray bursts come in two types: short bursts (lasting less than two seconds) resulting from the merger of neutron stars in close binary systems, and long bursts associated with supernova explosions in which a massive star abruptly collapses to become a black hole. Jets of high-energy photons ejected during these violent events can be detected by satellites, and afterglows produced as the jets plough through the interstellar medium can be observed with ground-based telescopes.

A long burst at 0612 GMT on 19 March 2008, detected by NASA's Swift satellite, was the most intrinsically-luminous event in the Universe thus far observed. Designated GRB 080319B – the second gamma ray burst to be detected that day – the event produced an afterglow that reached magnitude +5.8 for an interval of about 30 seconds: had anyone chanced to be looking in the right direction, towards the constellation Bootes, at the time, they would have just been able to glimpse the most distant object ever visible to the naked eye. Observations of the afterglow with the Very Large Telescope in Chile and the Hobby-Eberly Telescope in Texas established a distance of 7.5 billion light years or the event – far beyond the accepted naked eye limit of 2.9 million light years for the relatively nearby galaxy M33 in Triangulum. Indeed, GRB 080819B represented the demise of a star perhaps 40 times as massive as the Sun, in a galaxy halfway towards the edge of the visible Universe. The burst's intrinsic luminosity was 2.5 million times greater than that of the most luminous supernova observed (2005ap). Astronomers are unsure why GRB 080319B was so bright: one suggestion is that the jet was, by chance, directed straight towards Earth.

The burst was one of four detected on 19 March by the Swift satellite, the largest number in a single day since its launch in 2004.

BEE IN AMBER REVEALS ORCHID ORIGINS

While they constitute the most diverse plant family on Earth, the orchids have a poorly understood evolutionary history and little representation in the fossil record. The situation has been clarified following analysis of pollen-containing structures attached to an extinct stingless bee (*Proplebeia dominicanum*), found preserved in amber from the Miocene 15–20 million years ago and recovered in 2000 at a mine in the Dominican Republic.

Analysis, published in August 2007, shows that the two pollinaria – structures consisting of stalks and supporting structures along with a mass of pollen grains – attached to the bee's thorax could only have come from the flower of an orchid, similar to the still-extant Goodyerinae. While flowers of the extinct orchid (*Meliorchis caribea*) have not been fossilised, their structure can be inferred from the location of the pollen-containing structures on the bee: in order to feed from the flower, the bee had to insert its front half. One implication is that, as with modern orchids, plant and pollinator had a close relationship.

Phylogenetic analysis used to fit *M.caribea* into an evolutionary tree suggests that orchids arose from a common ancestor between 76 and 84 million years ago, with a rapid expansion in the range of forms following the Cretaceous-Tertiary mass extinction which accounted for the dinosaurs 65 million years ago.

AMPHIOXUS GENOME OFFERS CLUES TO VERTEBRATE EVOLUTION

Also known as lancelets, amphioxus are small sand-dwelling primitive animals which feed on detritus filtered from seawater. Around 25 species are recognised, and the amphioxus is a surviving example of the type of animal believed to be the ancestor of all chordates – animals which possess at some stage in their embryonic development a supporting rod of tissue between the nerve cord and gut – including the vertebrates. Fossil amphioxus from the Cambrian 550 million years ago are morphologically very similar to those still extant. The genome sequence determined from the Florida lancelet *Branchiostoma floridae*, published in June 2008, has shed light on vertebrate evolution.

The *B.floridae* genome comprises about 520 million basepairs of DNA, in 19 chromosome pairs. A total of 21,900 protein-coding genes are present, similar to the number in vertebrates including humans. Interestingly, there is a remarkable level of conservation of macro-synteny all the way from amphioxus to human: blocks of genes found together in amphioxus are also found together – though not necessarily in the same order (micro-synteny) – in the human genome.

Much of the interesting information to come from this

project results from comparison with other genomes. Tunicates (sea squirts), for example, are seen to be a sister-group, divergent from the evolutionary line leading to vertebrates: *Ciona intestinalis*, whose genome was published in 2002, shows far less synteny in common with vertebrates, suggesting that amphioxus is indeed a much better model basal chordate.

Examining rearrangements of connected genes (Chordate Linkage Groups or CLGs, as observed in amphioxus) in the vertebrate lineage indicates that, early in evolutionary history, two genome-duplication (diploidisation) events occurred. These came after the tunicates had split from the line, but before the divergence of teleosts (cartilaginous fish) and bony vertebrates around 385 million years ago. It has been speculated that gene-doubling events may have been the stimulus for the development of limbs and other more sophisticated vertebrate anatomical structures.

COMET OUTBURST SURPRISES ASTRONOMERS

A normally very faint comet, 17P/Holmes, surprised astronomers by undergoing a dramatic increase in brightness on 23–24 October 2007. The comet flared by a factor of about 400,000 in the course of 24 hours to become a second-magnitude object, easily visible to the naked eye against the stars of Perseus, high in the midnight sky for observers in the northern hemisphere. Over the following weeks both professional and amateur astronomers made thousands of observations, following the expansion of the comet's diffuse coma (atmosphere), which reached an apparent diameter nearly twice as large as that of the Moon against the sky. Moulded by the outflowing solar wind, the coma had a teardrop shape, and during the early part of the outburst was estimated to be expanding at 600km/sec.

Most comets become bright only when close to the Sun. 17P/Holmes has a rather distant orbit, lying outside that of Mars, and reaching its closest to the Sun (perihelion at a distance of 2.05 AU, as last occurred) on 4 May 2007, some months before the outburst. One of the large family of comets whose orbits are governed by Jupiter's gravitational influence, 17P/Holmes has an orbital period of 6.88 years. Its ice-dust nucleus is relatively small, 3.3 km in diameter. Despite several spacecraft flybys of comet nuclei (including 1P/Halley, 81P/Wild2 and 9P/Tempel), uncertainties remain as to the precise nature of these bodies. Many are clearly very fragile, and have been seen to disintegrate on passage close to the Sun. The mechanism by which 17P/Holmes underwent its outburst is unclear, but many astronomers believe that explosive sublimation of water just below the surface led to detachment of a large slab of nucleus which underwent rapid disintegration as it escaped, filling the coma with reflective dust and fluorescing gas.

The comet was discovered in November 1892 by London amateur astronomer Edwin Holmes during a previous outburst. At its discovery apparition, 17P/Holmes underwent a secondary brightening the following January. Observers watched with interest to see if this behaviour would recur in early 2008, but any re-brightening would appear to have been very minor, and the comet has faded slowly from view.

PHOENIX EXPLORES MARTIAN ARCTIC

Launched aboard a Delta 2 rocket from Cape Canaveral on 4 August 2007, NASA's ambitious Phoenix lander successfully touched down in the northwest of Mars' Vastitas Borealis Arctic plain on May 25 2008. Previous attempts to land at high Martian latitudes had ended in failure, but Phoenix safely survived initial atmospheric entry at 22,300km/hr, decelerating to 1,770km/hr before deploying a parachute, then completing its descent on thrusters at 8km/hr. During its parachute descent, Phoenix was imaged by the HiRISE camera on the Mars Reconnaissance Orbiter – the first time a landing on another planet has been so captured.

Once on the surface, Phoenix deployed its camera-equipped 2.4m robotic arm for sample recovery, and began taking images of its surroundings using the Surface Stereo Imager. Confirming results from orbiting spacecraft, Phoenix's camera showed flat terrain with relatively few rocks, and polygonal structures consistent with thawing and re-freezing of sub-surface ice: similar features are found in Earth's Arctic regions. A primary goal of the Phoenix mission is to investigate Martian ice, whose presence had been revealed by the Mars Odyssey orbiter in 2002.

The robotic arm has been used initially to dig shallow trenches in the soil. White material exposed in a 5cm trench dug on 15 June and still present on 16 June had disappeared by 19 June – indicating this to be water ice (rather than salt) sublimating in the cold, tenuous Martian atmosphere. In due course, ice samples will be collected for chemical studies in the lander's thermal and evolved gas analyser. This instrument can heat samples to 1,000°C, providing material for mass spectrometry.

Early analyses of soil samples show these to be slightly alkaline (pH 8–9), and quite similar in composition to soil from the Upper Dry Valleys of Antarctica on Earth. Salts of magnesium, sodium and potassium, and chloride ions, are present, indicative of past interaction of the Martian soil with water. Soil samples will also be subjected to microscopic examination to a resolution of four microns.

Further sampling of the soil should continue for about 80 sols (Martian days of 24h 37min), and may go as deep as two metres below the surface. The mission will end as the northern Martian winter sets in, and the lander is likely to be covered in condensing carbon dioxide dry ice, reducing the efficiency of its power-providing solar panels.

MARS ROVERS STILL ROLL ON AND ORBITER MISSIONS CONTINUE

Meanwhile, elsewhere on the Martian surface, the remarkable success of the Mars exploration rovers *Spirit* and *Opportunity* continues. Operating since January 2004, these have far exceeded their nominal 90-sol missions, having respectively travelled 7.6 and 11.6km from their landing sites. In July 2008 *Spirit* was riding out local winter conditions at Gusev Crater, where it has recently been exploring a silica-rich feature called Home Plate, possibly evidence of past hot spring or volcanic fumarole activity. On the opposite side of the planet at Meridiani Planum, *Opportunity* has begun a cautious descent into the 800m wide, 70m deep Victoria Crater, where it will explore exposed rock layers. Sulphur deposits here are indicative of a past wet epoch on Mars prior to conditions becoming more arid. Mechanically, both Rovers continue to function well, though *Opportunity* has experienced some problems with its robotic arm since April 2008. The Rovers survived planet-encircling dust storms, which limited the amount of sunlight available to their solar panels between June and September 2007.

Three orbiters continue their missions mapping Mars. Mars Odyssey, in orbit around the red planet since October 2001, has found evidence of salt deposits (again indicative of past surface water) and acts as a communications relay for the rovers on the ground. ESA's Mars Express continues its high-resolution surface imaging and has been in orbit since December 2003. NASA's Mars Reconnaissance Orbiter (MRO), which reached the planet in March 2006, is following up the Odyssey observations of sub-surface ice, and is also acting as a valuable telecommunications link for the other missions in orbit and on the surface. Its HiRISE camera can resolve surface features as small as 0.3 metres across. In June 2008 MRO observations revealed what may be the largest impact crater in the Solar System. The 'Borealis basin', covering 40 per cent of the Martian surface, is 8,500km across – four times the size of the Hellas basin in Mars' southern hemisphere – and is believed to be the result of a colossal impact early in the planet's history, 3.9 billion years ago. This could account for the marked contrast between the rugged, cratered (more ancient) terrain of the Martian southern hemisphere, and the smoother northern hemisphere.

ICE CORE REVEALS 800,000 YEARS OF CLIMATE HISTORY

Deep ice cores drilled in Greenland and the Antarctic offer valuable insights to past atmospheric and climatic conditions. Measurements allow reconstruction of temperature changes, and the concentrations of the important greenhouse gases carbon dioxide (CO_2) and methane (CH_4) trapped in the ice can be determined. Present-day levels of CO_2 and CH_4 far exceed those in the distant past, and ice core samples allow assessment of how these were influenced by non-anthropogenic effects, including those associated with long-term changes in Earth's orbital eccentricity and precession of its axis.

The European Project for Ice Coring in Antarctica (EPICA) has obtained a sample reaching to just above the bedrock at a depth of 3,270m at Dome C in Dronning Maud land in East Antarctica. Results published in 2005 presented a record of climate variations back to 650,000 years ago. Further analysis, presented in May 2008, covers the deepest 200m of the core and extends the record to 800,000 years before present, adding data from a further two 100,000-year glacial cycles.

CO_2 and CH_4 concentrations in the core correlate reasonably well with temperature reconstructions. CO_2 variations show that there was a change in the amplitude of the glacial-interglacial cycle around 450,000 years ago, with the interglacial periods becoming warmer. Oceanic circulation and biological productivity appear to have strongly influenced CO_2 concentrations, whilst CH_4 levels were affected by patterns of rainfall and temperature in the tropics and boreal regions. A long-term aim of the EPICA project is to extend the record back still farther, to 1.5 million years ago: other sites in East Antarctica are likely to be the best locations for drilling.

Climate scientists continue to keep a close eye on the current apparent rapid melting of the Greenland ice sheet. Containing one-twentieth of the world's ice, were this to melt in its entirety it would raise sea levels by seven metres. Several key glaciers are in retreat. Others have, in recent years, accelerated the rate at which they deposit ice into the sea, leading to a thinning of the sheet's interior. The summer of 2007 saw a loss of 500 billion tonnes of ice, a 30 per cent increase on the previous year. Ice is being lost more rapidly than it is replaced by winter snowfall.

The US-German GRACE satellites and a network of GPS stations on the ground are being used to monitor developments. The current ice sheet is a relic from the previous ice age, and core samples taken from Greenland show that below this is ice from an earlier glacial period, the Eemian 120,000 years ago. On this basis, complete loss of the ice – even on millennial timescales – can probably be considered unlikely. The behaviour of the Greenland ice sheet does, however, appear to be a very sensitive indicator of subtle changes in global temperature: the effects of small changes at lower latitudes are amplified in the polar regions.

LARGE HADRON COLLIDER READY TO GO ON LINE

Described as the biggest machine in the world, the Large Hadron Collider (LHC) at CERN – the European Organisation for Nuclear Research – is finally ready to begin investigations into some of the fundamental particles and forces that govern our physical Universe. The giant particle accelerator occupies a 27-km circumference, 3.8-metre diameter tunnel 50–175 metres underground on the border between Switzerland and France on the outskirts of Geneva. The tunnel is maintained at a high vacuum, and within it beams of protons will be accelerated by an array of 9,300 superconducting magnets, cryogenically cooled to 2K (−271°C), to 99.999999 per cent of the speed of light.

Protons – positively charged components of atomic nuclei – are classified as hadrons, strongly interacting subatomic particles comprised of still smaller units known as quarks. By colliding opposed beams of protons, each carrying 7 TeV of energy, and observing the resulting decay products, particle physicists expect to gain an improved understanding of the forces that hold matter together, and recreate on a microscopic scale conditions that prevailed immediately after the Big Bang moment of the Universe's creation.

Collision products will be analysed by four principal instruments – ALICE, ATLAS, CMS and LHCb. It is hoped that data from ATLAS (A Large Toroidal LHC apparatus) and CMS (Compact Muon Solenoid) will provide evidence for the elusive Higgs boson, an elementary particle postulated to confer the property of mass on other particles, and critical to explaining how they stay together. LHC was expected to produce its first particle beams in August 2008, with a gradual build-up to full experimental operation in the following couple of months.

VOYAGER 2 REACHES THE HELIOSHEATH

Launched in August 1977, the *Voyager 2* spacecraft made important discoveries at Jupiter, Saturn, Uranus and Neptune during its epic journey outwards from the Sun. Now, thirty years later, it has joined *Voyager 1* in having passed beyond the termination shock in the outer reaches of the Solar System and, like its sister craft, is expected to continue to reveal new information about the fringes of the Sun's zone of influence – the heliosphere – for at least another decade. The heliosphere is dominated by the outflowing solar wind emerging from the Sun, forming a local 'bubble' in interstellar space: interstellar winds and magnetic fields are thought to mould this into a teardrop shape. The termination shock marks the boundary where the solar wind is rapidly decelerated by the interstellar wind. *Voyager 1* crossed this to enter a region known as the heliosheath, underlying the very edge of the heliosphere (the heliopause), in December 2004 at a distance of 94 AU. *Voyager 2* crossed the termination shock at a distance of 84 AU, suggesting that the heliosphere is, as expected, asymmetrical. Voyagers 1 and 2 are departing the Solar System on trajectories separated by an angle of 45 degrees as seen from the Sun, and have therefore encountered somewhat different parts of the termination shock. It may take them a further ten years to reach the heliopause, but it is hoped that they will still be functioning and able to provide direct measurements of the interstellar medium.

Another well-travelled spacecraft, the ESA/NASA *Ulysses,* is coming to the end of its mission of heliospheric exploration. Launched in 1990, *Ulysses* was placed in a high-inclination 6-year orbit – out of the ecliptic plane where the planets' orbits lie – allowing investigation of the Sun's polar regions and the solar wind at high heliocentric latitudes. Ulysses also made measurements of the ion tails of comets Hyakutake in 1996 and McNaught in 2007 as it passed through them. Now, however, its radioactive power source is failing, and the hydrazine fuel used to maintain *Ulysses'* orientation is likely to freeze, leading to loss of control and contact. The mission reached a nominal end of July 1 2008, but some operations have been able to continue beyond this date.

SATURN MISSION EXTENDED

In orbit around the planet since July 2004, the NASA/ESA *Cassini* spacecraft continues its detailed exploration of Saturn, its rings, magnetosphere and satellites. Observations of the dimming of starlight by the rings have revealed the presence of transient clumps of material up to 10km in diameter. 'Recycling' of these clumps suggests that the rings may be ancient – dating back to Saturn's formation 4.5 billion years ago – rather than a cosmologically short-lived feature perhaps produced by disruption of a satellite in more recent times (hundreds of millions of years ago).

Cassini made a close (1,640km) flyby of the 1,440-km diameter satellite Iapetus on 10 September, during which detailed images were taken. *Cassini's* plasma spectrometer has detected charged particles ejected from the satellites Tethys and Dione (1,060 and 1,120km diameter respectively), suggesting that these are geologically active.

Much interest has centred on the 500-km diameter satellite Enceladus, whose south polar 'tiger stripe' terrain is a source of water vapour plumes. On 12 March 2008 *Cassini* skimmed just 48km above Enceladus, and directly sampled plume material, which was found to contain water, carbon dioxide, carbon monoxide and organic molecules in proportions similar to those observed in comets. Some scientists believe Enceladus to have a reservoir of liquid water about 40m below the surface in its south polar region. Another close pass by *Cassini* was planned for 11 August 2008.

The Cassini mission was originally scheduled to end in July 2008, but with the spacecraft continuing to perform superbly and producing huge amounts of new data, this has been extended by two years. The extension will allow a further 26 flybys at the satellite Titan, and seven more visits to Enceladus during 60 orbits around the planet.

THEATRE

Josh Spero

From the Royal Shakespeare Company's epic histories cycle – eight three-hour plays over four days – to Mark Ravenhill's sixteen bite-size dramas; from the orgies of ancient Greece to the grief of Spanish mothers; and from countless opening nights to the lights going dark in several important theatres, the year on stage (and off) has covered all the terrains of geography and mind. Theatrical companies grappled with funding cuts from the Arts Council and some critics turned their eyes from the stage to their own typewriters, but a year of enduring triumphs and monumental failures rolled on regardless.

This year proved that the 'straight' play is stronger than ever, despite the perpetual presentiments of its death under the churning wheel of the musical whose star has been chosen by Saturday night television viewers. There were three stand-out new dramas: *Black Watch*, about an army regiment in Iraq and from the National Theatre of Scotland; Complicite's *A Disappearing Number*, about maths, love and time; and *That Face*, an Oedipal drama by 19-year-old Polly Stenham. The first two of these seized on all the possibilities not just of theatre but of dance and film and technology, to expand the boundaries of what a stage can contain.

The National Theatre of Scotland, without a permanent home but with a stunning reputation, continued its run of acclaimed productions with *Black Watch* at the Barbican, the story of the historic Scottish regiment's deployment to Iraq. Spun from three threads – real interviews with Black Watch soldiers back from their tour of duty, scenes from their Iraqi base imagined by Gregory Burke and transitional scenes of dance and song inspired by military life and history – *Black Watch* was a tremendously moving piece of theatre. The word 'play' is inadequate for something which burst off the stage with such a multiplicity of ideas and forms and passions. There was graveyard levity on the field of combat, barely concealed anger at home. The most moving scene was when the soldiers, to a rending soundtrack, gently, ritually enacted the contents of the letters from their loved ones, each alone yet caught in the same trance of distant tenderness. One scene of particular virtuosity was where a constantly moving soldier – running, walking, being spun, being turned around the stage – was clothed by his comrades in all the previous costumes of the Black Watch, to emphasise the 'golden thread' of unbroken history that runs through the regiment and its members. It was split-second perfect, balletic in its simple elegance of steps.

Another company whose reputation precedes it is Complicite. Now in its twenty-fifth year, Complicite has thrived by producing startling, original, thoughtful, visually stunning pieces of theatre, both devised and revived, under artistic director Simon McBurney. *A Disappearing Number* was an archetypal yet unique project, devised by the company and integrating text, music and image to tell of how maths and love and India and travel and beauty intersect through the stories of several lives. Rather than being theoretical and pretentious, critical reaction lauded it to the skies as deeply moving and intellectually profound. It won all three Best Play awards of the year and after touring returned to the Barbican in September.

That Face proves that the spirit of Tennessee Williams is alive and well, at least in its new instantiation of Polly Stenham, who wrote her Oedipal drama aged 19. After a sell-out initial run at the Royal Court, it transferred to the Duke of York's, where its limited season continued to have theatregoers clasping their mouths in horror. Stenham, still only 21 when *That Face* hit the West End, created a work of terrifying emotional entanglements and abandonments and of the most acute perceptiveness about the eternal ways families can hurt one another. Lindsay Duncan plays the Blanche du Bois-like mother (called Martha, presumably in homage to that other notable theatrical monster, from *Who's Afraid of Virginia Woolf?*) who shuts out the real world with a haze of booze and an inappropriate attachment to her son (Matt Smith), while her daughter (Hannah Murray) tortures a classmate and her ex-husband makes a new life with a new family in Hong Kong. Duncan takes her cue from Vivien Leigh and Elizabeth Taylor as Blanche and Martha, mixing the sharpest bitching with desperate pleading and a seductive, fatal manner. Instead of just being over-blown Gothic nonsense, Stenham's acute eye and fine feel for dialogue were used to create an emotional genocide, waged from all sides. The ties that bind have bound too close or snapped.

There was a welcome return to the West End for Yasmina Reza, whose play *Art* ran for six years in London, with *God of Carnage*, starring Ralph Fiennes and Tamsin Greig. A vicious comedy satirising the bourgeoisie even as the bourgeoisie laughed at it, *God of Carnage* subtly said a lot about the revenge of art over life while showing two middle class couples descend into violence.

Violence was the only thing that the Lyric Hammersmith's *Contains Violence* had going for it. A site-specific piece, where the audience sat on the theatre's terrace and spied into an office building opposite (binoculars and headphones were provided) as a man was repeatedly battered to death, it surely counts as one of the emptiest things on (or at least near) stage this year. The play is largely speechless, as was the critic at the play's vacuity: a thin plot, no discernible acting, and a gimmick – the voyeurism – which added nothing but novelty. This was in sharp contrast to the Lyric's epic staging of Tony Kushner's seven-hour *Angels in America*, which used its set astonishingly: by the final scene, the whole stage was covered like a hurricane had passed through, evoking the chaos of the characters and their universe.

Mark Ravenhill made a brave effort to get his audience moving – not by including songs so toe-tapping it just had to get up and dance but by staging his sixteen shorts plays (no more than twenty minutes a piece) in several locations over several days. *Shoot/Get Treasure/Repeat* (which takes its unfortunate name from the description of a video game) tackled war in all its forms. Their reception was mixed, but the diversity of the subjects and approaches and the achievement of the successes shone out. The problem with such a piece of theatre is that it can seem gimmicky, as opposed to innovative; perhaps the plays would stand up better in two three-hour slots.

British theatrical royalty met Spanish cinematic majesty as Dame Diana Rigg starred in Pedro Almodóvar's *All About My Mother* at the Old Vic. The story of how several women's lives are connected by the tragic death of a son was adapted from the Oscar-winning movie, certainly one of the most moving films ever made. With its references to and deep connections with *A Streetcar Named Desire* and *All About Eve*, the play was a celebration of the varying forms of femininity and the love they can engender. Lesley Manville received raves as the grieving mother who goes in search of her dead son's father, on her journey crossing the paths of an old transsexual friend and a theatrical legend. This was a triumph of the movie-as-play, but other movies did not survive the translation.

Two of the year's greatest disasters were musicals based on non-musical movies, which was perhaps a sign. *Desperately Seeking Susan*, adapted from the Madonna movie but with songs added from Blondie's back catalogue, lost £3.5m and closed after only a month. The critical reaction tended to the view that shoehorning great songs into a fine adaptation of a great movie made it less than the sum of its parts. The popular reaction tended to avoidance.

The other white elephant was one with much grander claims for itself than just the assembly of a seventies band's songs with an eighties film: *Gone with the Wind*, the £4m musical, with music, lyrics and book by first time composer Margaret Martin, discovering the meaning of hubris. If making the four-hour film in 1939 nearly killed its directors, actors and screenwriters, sitting through the four-hour musical nearly killed the critics, audiences and the actors' careers. Even by chopping out chunks of it, critical reaction derided poor acting, poor song-writing and shocking direction (under the usually reliable Trevor Nunn, on whose uninteresting *Lear* more below). It closed after 79 performances, going down in flames almost as quickly as Atlanta did in the film.

Three of the year's most successful musicals were just as diverse beasts. *Hairspray*, against the prevailing trend, was a well-received movie-cum-musical with original songs. The strong performances of newcomer Leanne Jones as sixties schoolgirl Tracy Turnblad, stuck in the backwater of Baltimore and just wanting to dance, and her mother (the effervescent Michael Ball, padded out and dragged up in a housecoat) helped it stand out, as well as its witty songs and uplifting message of tolerance.

Jersey Boys, based on the story of the rise of Frankie Valli and the Four Seasons, was impressively popular, if depressingly predictable, trite and dull. Packing out the house every night, the only difference between this and a tribute album was the £60 it now costs to sit in the stalls of a West End theatre. The acting was poor, the actors presumably feeling the need to swing their arms (when not dancing) and shout (when not singing) to reach the back of the house. They need not have bothered. The story was the traditional drama of small-town kids making it big, except to say 'drama' is to overstate the interest the show provoked. Perhaps the worst crime is the tactless use of the songs: by identifying songs with particular 'relevant' moments in the story, rather than with the context of their composition, we lose any real meaning they might have had (if indeed they ever had any); instead, songs are applied for humour or pathos, in which case they might as well have been from any group.

The final 'musical' was a far less traditional beast. The National Theatre of Scotland brought its *Bacchae* all over the country. A version of Euripides' violent tragedy of impiety and wine-filled orgiastic rites, it starred Alan Cumming as the sensual, cruel god Dionysus, who comes back to Thebes to punish his family for refusing to acknowledge his divinity. From the moment Cumming was lowered, head-first, bottom-out, onto the stage, until the scenery ran with blood, this was a transfixing production. The best aspect was the use of original gospel and rock songs for the choral scenes, which normally feature interminable mumbling about nature while actors bump into one another. The true meaning of the play is about the ecstatic transportation that Dionysos, the god of wine and theatre, brings out in his followers, and by intoxicating the audience with the music, we too felt the full Bacchic force. Cumming was magnetically seductive and repulsive, dominating the play by talent and force of personality.

Shakespeare must be wishing his earliest critics could read his current reviews: the Bard has drawn a stream of plaudits throughout the year, climaxing in the rapturous reception of the RSC's 'Glorious Moment'. One of the most intensive theatrical undertakings of recent years, the RSC rehearsed all eight Wars of the Roses plays *(Richard II, Henry IV 1 and 2, Henry V, Henry VI 1, 2 and 3, and Richard III)* for two years, with the company of 34 actors sharing 264 roles. Running for three months in Stratford-upon-Avon and two at the Camden Roundhouse, nearly 200,000 tickets were sold, with many lucky souls seeing the full 24 hours – 210,000 of Shakespeare's words.

Sheer statistics, although they express the mind-boggling size of the enterprise and popularity of the series, cannot do a full measure of justice to Michael Boyd's astounding direction and his cast's brilliance. Setting it with period costume and sets which evolved over the hundred years of the drama into modern dress and sets (helicopters, PR advisers), Boyd – with Richard Twyman directing *Henry IV part 2* – made at once a cycle historically specific but eternally applicable, noting that the nature of power never changes and is never neutral. Richard II, with his ruff, painted face and ginger curls, resembled the reigning monarch, Elizabeth I, while Henry VII assumes power at the end of Richard III as his heavies train machine guns on the audience.

The performances of Jonathan Slinger, bookending the Glorious Moment as vacillating, capricious Richard II and cruel, violent Richard III, will certainly guarantee his place among the great Shakespearean actors. With an instinct for just how to pitch his character at any one moment, a transfixing way with his hands and a fine voice, Slinger created two kings of depth and complexity, bringing out Shakespeare's genius and adding one all his own. Katy Stephens as Joan of Arc and Margaret of Anjou in *Henry VI 1, 2* and *3* (plays rarely seen either individually or as a trilogy but thoroughly engrossing studies of what happens when power is neglected) staked her own claim to inspiration, with a triumphant, calculating, vicious but ultimately broken performance. These highlights should not shut out the rest of the ensemble, whose continually strong acting unified the cycle and helped to lift it into the realm of theatrical legend.

The triumph of Shakespeare did not stop there. Patrick Stewart's *Macbeth*, in a clinical, bloody production, shared the Critics' Circle Award for best Shakespearean performance with Chiwetel Ejiofor's *Othello*. Although Ejiofor was not the main draw for the Donmar Warehouse production – Ewan McGregor as Iago probably sold most of the tickets – he emerged as the star. The Olivier auditorium at the National Theatre saw probably Britain's greatest living actor, Simon Russell Beale, as a saucy, sad Benedick in *Much Ado About Nothing*, alongside Zoe Wanamaker as a feisty Beatrice.

King Lear starring Sir Ian McKellen and directed by Trevor Nunn was perhaps the biggest theatrical disappointment of the year. Instead of a powerful, revelatory performance from McKellen, he seemed to overact when a sparer portrayal would have been more effective. It was a paint-by-numbers, colour-within-the-lines production, distinguished only by its failure to be original. If anything, it was heavy-handed, providing banal interpretations of things best left to the imagination, such as the Fool's death and Kent's last sighs. Critics were initially put out by the production when Frances Barber, playing Goneril, fell off a bicycle and the press preview was put back several weeks. Its great success, then, was disgruntling the critics. Many of the audience were shocked, too, when McKellen entirely disrobed during the heath scene; gasps of astonishment at his proportions competed with howling winds.

The National Theatre enjoyed a largely controversy-free year, in contrast with the previous one where its artistic director, Nicholas Hytner, took on the perceived chauvinism of male theatre critics and exchanged barbs with them until a score-draw was called. His missions this year included the rehabilitation of George Bernard Shaw and an evangelism for new drama. This meant the repertoire of the National was lighter on the classics than usual, which gave the whole company a forward-looking face, even if there were fewer 'safe' plays an audience would immediately be attracted by. New plays included Tony Harrison's *Fram*, about a Norwegian Arctic explorer; Howard Brenton's *Never So Good*, about the rise and fall of Harold Macmillan, as portrayed by Jeremy Irons; and *Afterlife*, by Michael Frayn, telling of a theatrical impresario under the iron boot as Hitler invaded Austria in 1938. Less established playwrights than this venerable triumvirate received plenty of stage-time too: Lucinda Coxon's *Happy Now?*, a middle-class crisis; Matt Charman's *Five Wives of Maurice Pinder*, a polygamous crisis; and Lee Hall's *Pitmen Painters*, which received its London premiere, about miners and their cultural crisis after they take up painting.

The Shaw revival was the biggest surprise of the National's year. Previously a dramatist whom most theatres wouldn't touch (*Pygmalion* aside) with a Shakespearean bargepole, Hytner has been showing the relevance of Shaw's themes as well as the eloquence of his language. He has been very successful in his effort, drawing Simon Russell Beale to play Andrew Undershaft, the arms manufacturer, in *Major Barbara* and winning a clutch of awards for *Saint Joan*, including Best Revival at the Oliviers. Anne-Marie Duff, the titular martyr, won Best Actress at the Critics' Circle awards and Evening Standard Theatre awards.

Among the canon at the National, Katie Mitchell's *Women of Troy* was a traumatic triumph, transferring the action from defeated Troy to an anonymous refugee deportation centre, where death came to all, young and old, and the horror continued right until the last seconds as the set fell victim to off-stage explosions. Mitchell continues to refine her technique and aesthetic to great success, and the National is giving her more avant-garde productions *(The Waves, . . . some trace of her)* the space to flourish. There was also *Much Ado*, Noel Coward's *Present Laughter*, and Harold Pinter's *Hothouse*.

Offstage, the theatre world was battered and bloodied by the Arts Council's settlement of grants. Eight days before Christmas, 990 arts bodies were promised substantial increases to their funding, but almost 200 were told that theirs would be reduced or even entirely cut. The Exeter Northcott Theatre's Christmas card from the Arts Council told them they would lose their £547,000 grant, while season's greetings came to the National Student Drama Festival in the form of the removal of its £52,000 grant. The logic behind the grants was faultless – cut some perceived dead branches, encourage strong ones, let younger ones flourish – but the feeling was lacking, and if the Arts Council expected a quiet submission from the arts world, it was wrong, indeed was dealt its own bloody nose.

Actors may worry about facing hostile audiences, but spare a thought for the chief executive of the Arts Council, who had to face an audience of hostile actors in January. Peter Hewitt endured a two-hour inquisition from the stalls, where the star-studded crowd included Sir Ian McKellen, Kevin Spacey and Joanna Lumley. There were complaints about the process of and criteria for deciding on changes to grants, the lack of notice given and the brief time allowed for an appeal. Although Hewitt promised that some of the Council's decisions might be reversible on appeal (indeed, the Northcott's grant has now been restored), the bad press the meeting gathered, as well as letters pages full of eloquent protests and a vitriolic internet response, ensured that the Arts Council's reputation suffered nearly mortal damage, largely serving to alienate it from the very people it was supposed to help. With a new chief executive, Alan Davey, in April came the chance for the Arts Council to put the fiasco behind itself and begin to regain the trust of its constituency, as well as restore the parlous state of regional theatre. Time will tell.

The theatre had disasters and surprises inflicted on it from within as well. The Bristol Old Vic, a regional theatre of two centuries' standing, announced in May 2007 that it would close for development as of August, shocking everyone with the sharpness of the close, with the refurbishment plans not even thought to be complete. An autumn production, *Rough Crossings*, had to be cancelled since there was no indication the theatre would be closed by then, and the Arts Council was taken by surprise too. There were 45 redundancies, and the artistic director, Simon Reade, left too. The Bristol Old Vic was certainly in need of its £7m refurbishment – structural work, electrical work, air conditioning, lifts for the disabled, lifting of the stalls – but the sudden closure perturbed many. It is due to reopen in December 2008.

An even sharper lights-out came to the Derby Playhouse in December, when it failed to agree a financial plan with the city council to save itself and closed within a week, going into administration. Slings and arrows assaulted both sides, with the council alleging mismanagement and the theatre saying council works had made it hard to reach. 20,000 people were given refunds on tickets for *Treasure Island*, and all 60 staff were made redundant. It did not help that two weeks after the closure, the Playhouse lost its funding in the Arts Council's purge. At the time of writing, the curtain was still down in Derby, but it had been saved from going into liquidation and hoped to reopen in time for its 60th anniversary in November 2008.

Two theatre critics made notable turns away from daily poison penmanship. The *Evening Standard's* Nicholas de Jongh saw his play *Plague Over England* produced to general acclaim; his colleagues came to praise him, not to bury him, despite the temptation of the target. Telling of the humiliation of John Gielgud in the fifties after his arrest for homosexual acts, it took in the establishment's view of the subject with all its fear and hatred. Out of sight of the stage, but not out of mind, *The Guardian*'s Michael Billington wrote *State of the Nation*, an analysis of British theatre since the war; it won the Theatre Book Prize.

The next year in theatre is already promising much: the Donmar is putting on *Hamlet* with Jude Law, *Twelfth Night* with Derek Jacobi, *Madame de Sade* with Judi Dench and Tom Stoppard's new version of *Ivanov* with Kenneth Branagh; the National is bringing over *August: Osage County*, which won the Best Play award at the Tony awards; and there will no doubt be a host of non-West End shows which completely trump theatreland's behemoths for invention and excellence. Surpassing this year, however, will not come easily.

AWARDS

2008 LAURENCE OLIVIER AWARDS

Best New Play – *A Disappearing Number* by Simon McBurney and Complicite at the Barbican
Best New Comedy – *Rafta, Rafta* by Ayub Khan-Din at the National Theatre
Best Revival – *Saint Joan* by George Bernard Shaw at the National Theatre
Best Actor – Chiwetel Ejiofor for *Othello* at the Donmar Warehouse
Best Actress – Kristin Scott Thomas for *The Seagull* at the Royal Court
Best Performance in a Supporting Role – Rory Kinnear for *The Man of Mode* at the National Theatre
Best Newcomer in a Play – Tom Hiddleston for *Cymbeline* at the Barbican
Best Director – Rupert Goold for *Macbeth* at the Gielgud
Outstanding Achievement or Performance in an Affiliate Theatre – *Gone Too Far!* at the Jerwood Theatre Upstairs at the Royal Court
Best New Musical – *Hairspray* by Marc Shaiman and Scott Wittman at the Shaftesbury
Best Musical Revival – *The Magic Flute* by Impempe Yomlingo at the Young Vic
Best Actor in a Musical – Michael Ball for *Hairspray* at the Shaftesbury
Best Actress in a Musical – Leanne Jones for *Hairspray* at the Shaftesbury
Best Performance in a Supporting Role in a Musical – Tracie Bennett in *Hairspray* at the Shaftesbury
Best New Dance Production – The Royal Ballet for the revival of George Balanchine's ballet *Jewels* at the Royal Opera House
Outstanding Achievement in Dance – The Royal Ballet for the revival of George Balanchine's ballet *Jewels* at the Royal Opera House
Best New Opera Production – *Pelléas et Mélisande* at the Royal Opera House
Outstanding Achievement in Opera – Natalie Dessay for *La Fille du régiment* at the Royal Opera House
Best Lighting Design – Howard Harrison for *Macbeth* at the Chichester Festival Theatre
Best Sound Design – Paul Arditti and Jocelyn Pook for *Saint Joan* at the National Theatre
Best Costume Design – Vicki Mortimer for *The Man Of Mode* at the National Theatre
Best Set Design – Rae Smith and Handspring Puppet Company for *War Horse* at the National Theatre
Best Theatre Choreographer – Toby Sedgewick for *War Horse* at the National Theatre
Special Award – Andrew Lloyd Webber

CRITICS' CIRCLE AWARDS FOR 2007

Best New Play – *A Disappearing Number* by Simon McBurney and Complicite
Best Actor – Charles Dance for *Shadowlands*
Best Actress – Anne-Marie Duff for *Saint Joan*
The John and Wendy Trewin Award for Best Shakespearean Performance – Patrick Stewart for *Macbeth* and Chiwetel Ejiofor for *Othello.*
Best Director – Rupert Goold for *Macbeth*
The Peter Hepple Award for Best Musical – *Hairspray* by Marc Shaiman and Scott Wittman
Most Promising Playwright – Polly Stenham for *That Face*
Best Designer – Rae Smith and the Handspring Puppet Company for *War Horse*
The Jack Tinker Award for Most Promising Newcomer – Leanne Jones for *Hairspray*

EVENING STANDARD THEATRE AWARDS FOR 2007

Best Play – *A Disappearing Number* by Simon McBurney and Complicite
Best Actor – Patrick Stewart for *Macbeth*
Best Actress – Anne-Marie Duff for *Saint Joan*
The Sydney Edwards Award for Best Director – Rupert Goold for *Macbeth*
The Ned Sherrin Award for Best Musical – *Hairspray*
Best Design – Rae Smith and The Handspring Puppet Company for *War Horse*
The Charles Wintour Award for Most Promising Playwright – Polly Stenham for *That Face*
The Milton Shulman Award for Outstanding Newcomer – Stephen Wight for *Dealer's Choice* and *Don Juan In Soho*
Special Award – Stephen Tompkins for innovative theatre architecture

WEATHER

The year 2007 will long be remembered for the summer flooding which affected much of the country, but it was by no means wet throughout. Indeed the early spring and most of the autumn were notably dry. Although much was made of the fact that the three-month period between May and July 2007 was wetter than any other May–July period in almost three centuries, it was not the wettest three month period on record at any time of the year – in fact in ranked 43rd, which means that it has a probability of recurring once every five to six years on average. Furthermore, the major flooding events were caused by individual downpours which were far from unprecedented. There was something of a mismatch between these severe but not unprecedented rainfall events on the one hand, and the extreme and destructive floods on the other. Rainfall does, of course, make a very important contribution to flooding, but it is not the only factor. The wide-ranging human influences on river catchments in general, and flood-plains in particular, also play a major part.

The autumn in 2007 was, in general, the quietest for decades, but a severe north-westerly gale in the North Sea on 8–9 November triggered a major storm surge – the worst since 1996 – which threatened to engulf low-lying coastal districts of eastern England, although mercifully the surge did not coincide with the high tide and serious flooding was therefore averted. The first half of 2008 was characterised by dramatic contrasts: January was exceptionally wet, February unusually sunny, March and April often wintry, while May was the warmest and driest on record in the northern half of the UK. Flooding returned to many parts of Scotland, north Wales and northern England during the middle of January, and low-lying parts of Leeds were particularly badly hit when the River Aire overtopped its banks. The heaviest snowfalls of the winter half-year in southern districts did not occur until late-March and early-April: heavy snow disrupted traffic on Easter Sunday (23 March), and again a fortnight later on 6 April when as much as 11cm was registered in the Home Counties. Thundery downpours during the fourth week of May led to severe though short-lived local flooding in the Torbay district and also in south Somerset.

THE YEAR 2007

The Central England temperature for the entire year stands at 10.6°C which is 0.8°C above the average for the standard reference period of 1971–2000. The only warmer years in 350 years of records were 1949, 1990, 1999, 2002 and 2006. Rainfall, averaged over England and Wales, totalled 992mm over the year, just 6 per cent above the long-term normal, making it wetter than 2006 and 2005, but not as wet as 2004. The sun shone for 1,664 hours, again averaged over England and Wales, some seven per cent above normal – rather less than in 2006 but a little more than in 2005.

TEMPERATURE

The long succession of warmer-than-average months ended in June 2007, and between July 2007 and June 2008 eight of the 12 months reported a mean temperature close to or below the average for the standard reference period 1971–2000. As measured by the Central England Temperature, the mean temperature for the 12 months ending June 2008 was 10.2°C, just 0.1°C above the long-term average, and it was the coldest such period since 2000–1. Notable months were July and August, which were both the coolest since 1993; May, which was the equal warmest (alongside 1992) since 1848; and June, which was the coolest since 1999. There was no single heat wave of note during the summer of 2007, and the highest individual temperature during that season was 30.1°C at Terrington St Clement, near King's Lynn in Norfolk, on August 5; this is the lowest absolute maximum in the UK for any year since 1993. No daily maximum above 28°C was recorded during the first six months of 2008. The lowest temperature of winter 2007–8 was –13.0°C at Aboyne, Aberdeenshire, on the night of 21 December.

MEAN MONTHLY TEMPERATURE (°C)

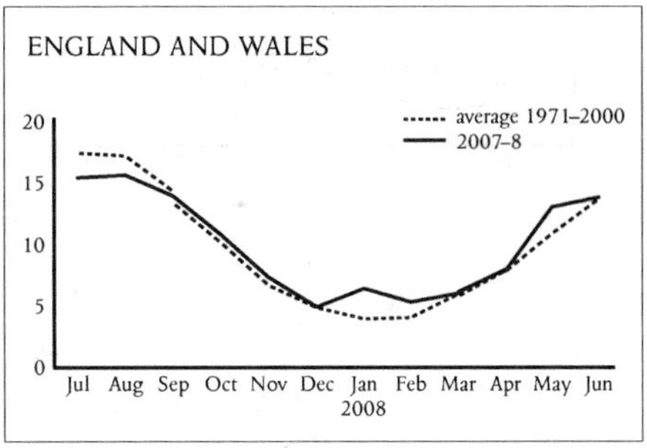

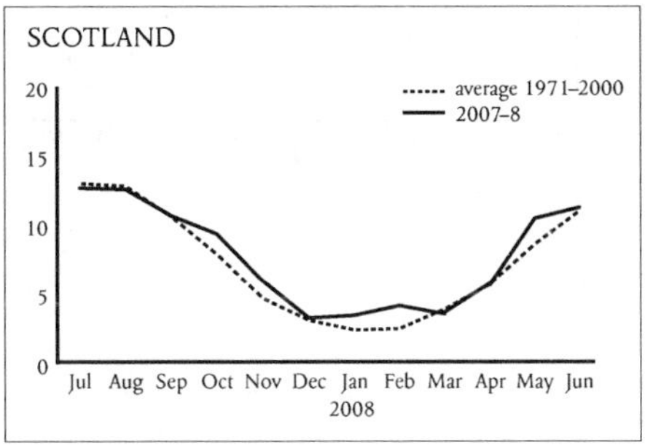

	Mean temp. °C	*Diff. from normal °C*	*Rainfall mm*	*Proportion of ave. %*	*Sunshine hours*	*Proportion of ave. %*
England	10.1	+0.7	966	106	1,662	108
Wales	9.7	+0.7	1,159	105	1,652	109
Scotland	9.2	+0.7	1,042	109	1,363	106
Northern Ireland	10.4	+0.7	827	92	1,518	113
United Kingdom	9.8	+0.7	1,000	106	1,559	108

RAINFALL

July 2007 was the wettest since 1936 with more than twice the normal rainfall over the UK as a whole, three times the normal over the Midlands region, and five times the normal over parts of the southwest Midlands. During the downpour which triggered the disastrous floods along the River Severn, 163mm of rain fell in less than 36 hours on 19–20 July at Sudeley Lodge, near Cheltenham. Persistently dry weather followed from the last week of July onwards, and the last five months of the year, from August to December, constituted the driest such period since 1947 over a large part of the country. The rains returned during the last few days of December, and January was excessively wet especially in Scotland; averaged nationally it was the wettest January since 1995, but at several sites in eastern Scotland, including Edinburgh, new records were established. After a respite in February, March was also very wet – the wettest since 1981, taking the UK as a whole – and heavy rains continued throughout April in eastern Scotland and northeast England. May was an odd month: the driest on record at several locations in the north and west of Scotland and in Northern Ireland, but the wettest on record in east Kent and in east Devon.

MONTHLY RAINFALL 2007–8 (mm)

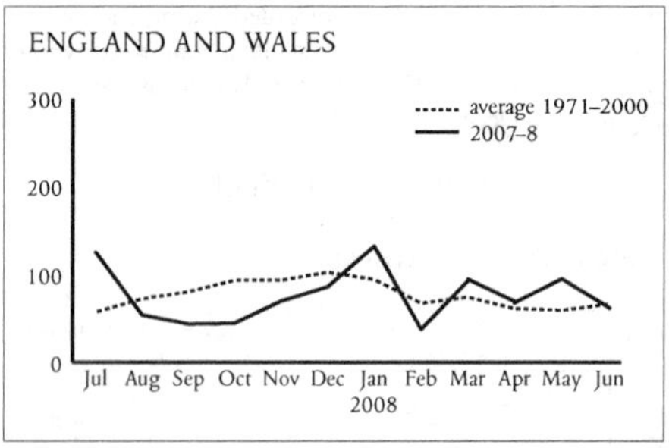

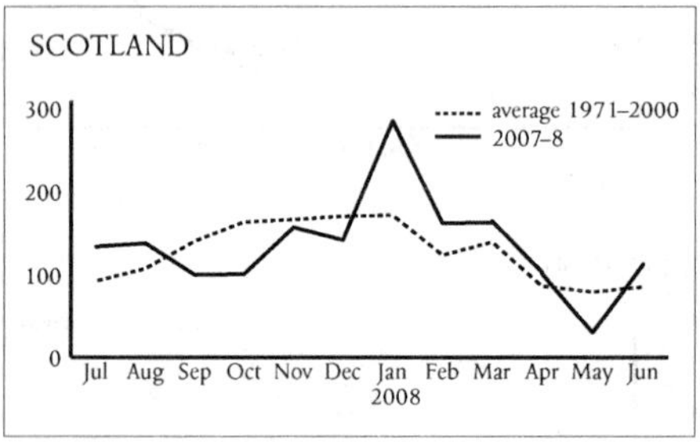

SUNSHINE

Sunshine was plentiful during the last five months of 2007 in most parts of the country with some excellent totals in Scotland, Northern Ireland and northern England during October, in the eastern half of England during November, and in Scotland, Northern Ireland, and southeast England during December. However, there was a general shortage of sunshine during January 2008, especially in Scotland where the monthly total at Eskdalemuir (Dumfriesshire) was just 11 hours. February, by contrast was a brilliant month with previous records smashed out of sight over England and Wales, and at Norwich the monthly total of 157 hours was more than twice the normal amount. March and April were unremarkable months for sunshine, but new records were established for May in the far north of Scotland, and at Fair Isle, between Orkney and Shetland, an aggregate of 304 hours was achieved. June was a fairly sunny month, especially along English Channel and Bristol Channel coasts.

MONTHLY SUNSHINE (hours)

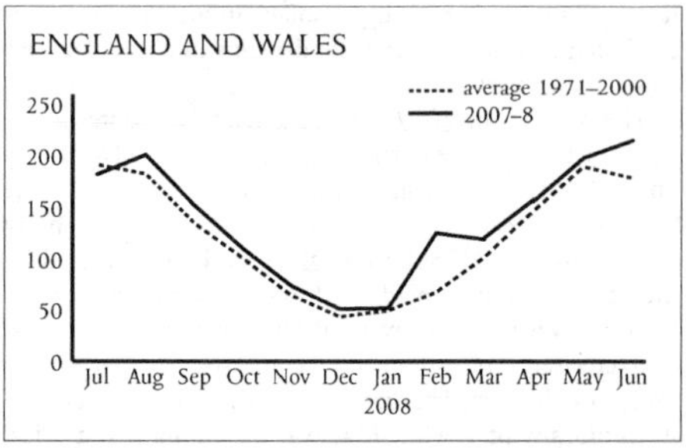

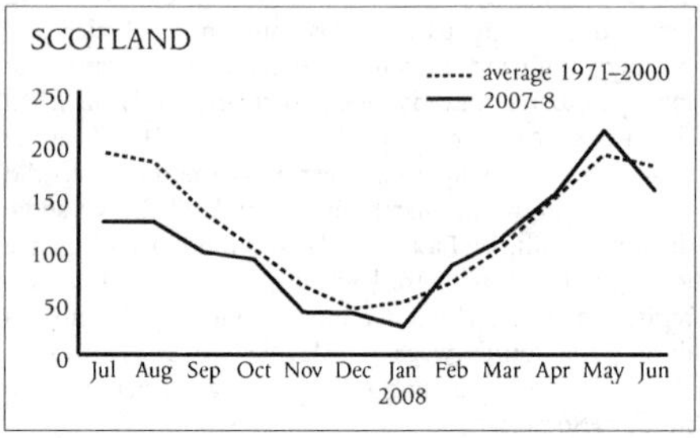

UK WEATHER STATIONS

Given below are temperature, rainfall and sunshine at selected climatological stations for July 2007 to June 2008

Ht height of station above mean sea-level
Temp mean monthly air temperature
Rain total monthly rainfall
Sun total monthly sunshine duration

		July 2007			*August 2007*			*September 2007*			*October 2007*		
	Ht m	*Temp °C*	*Rain mm*	*Sun hrs*	*Temp °C*	*Rain mm*	*Sun hrs*	*Temp °C*	*Rain mm*	*Sun hrs*	*Temp °C*	*Rain mm*	*Sun hrs*
Stornoway	15	13.5	86	112	13.1	134	69	11.5	107	99	11.1	81	59
Aberdeen	65	14.1	116	103	13.9	85	120	12.3	68	89	10.3	23	119
Glasgow	59	14.5	90	137	14.5	129	118	12.3	65	103	10.7	81	99
Belfast	68	14.5	104	135	14.7	82	98	13.2	25	94	11.7	31	92
Durham	102	14.9	75	127	14.9	23	154	13.3	19	106	10.3	15	91
York	8	15.7	96	161	15.9	28	190	14.3	27	143	10.9	25	114
Manchester	69	14.7	132	109	15.0	35	144	13.3	73	103	10.8	50	92
Holyhead	10	15.1	99	184	15.3	59	159	14.3	85	117	12.3	35	124
Nottingham	117	15.3	132	154	16.0	34	185	13.9	28	129	11.1	23	102
Norwich	32	16.3	111	161	15.9	85	180	14.5	53	169	10.7	61	103
Birmingham	140	15.3	153	165	15.9	53	193	13.9	36	133	11.1	49	90
Cardiff	46	15.3	160	179	16.0	73	194	14.5	41	153	11.9	49	109
Bristol	42	15.7	156	171	16.5	37	206	14.3	25	146	11.8	50	103
London	137	16.5	89	155	16.4	55	162	14.9	18	131	11.5	41	87
Bournemouth	10	15.7	119	172	15.8	44	217	14.4	28	150	11.0	33	106
Newquay	103	15.0	94	201	15.9	57	243	14.7	29	177	12.7	55	133

		November 2007			*December 2007*			*January 2008*			*February 2008*		
	Ht	*Temp*	*Rain*	*Sun*	*Temp*	*Rain*	*Sun*	*Temp*	*Rain*	*Sun*	*Temp*	*Rain*	*Sun*
Stornoway	15	7.5	110	20	6.1	133	33	5.3	146	22	5.7	112	64
Aberdeen	65	6.9	119	61	4.0	42	62	4.3	119	47	5.8	20	107
Glasgow	59	7.5	113	51	4.4	87	27	4.9	255	22	5.5	141	68
Belfast	68	8.3	51	33	6.0	54	43	5.5	151	38	5.9	34	91
Durham	102	7.3	32	68	4.1	23	48	5.3	49	58	5.1	13	112
York	8	7.7	41	70	5.0	37	33	6.5	125	46	5.1	25	106
Manchester	69	7.2	68	51	4.9	90	59	6.3	150	29	5.4	38	115
Holyhead	10	9.9	90	53	7.0	90	61	7.8	123	43	6.9	32	121
Nottingham	117	7.3	63	66	4.8	63	33	6.3	113	51	5.3	32	122
Norwich	32	7.1	67	61	5.0	53	63	7.9	83	62	5.7	30	145
Birmingham	140	6.9	60	57	4.8	54	40	6.3	117	37	5.1	40	108
Cardiff	46	8.7	69	65	6.2	131	42	7.6	100	30	6.3	21	124
Bristol	42	8.3	58	85	5.8	89	42	7.5	116	43	6.1	39	123
London	137	7.7	77	91	5.6	62	80	6.8	85	71	6.6	15	135
Bournemouth	10	7.5	108	84	5.7	55	58	7.3	115	47	5.5	40	130
Newquay	103	9.7	83	66	8.0	94	68	8.3	118	45	7.7	42	117

		March 2008			*April 2008*			*May 2008*			*June 2008*		
	Ht	*Temp*	*Rain*	*Sun*	*Temp*	*Rain*	*Sun*	*Temp*	*Rain*	*Sun*	*Temp*	*Rain*	*Sun*
Stornoway	15	4.9	119	96	6.9	69	178	11.3	13	286	11.5	88	136
Aberdeen	65	4.6	58	128	6.5	86	146	10.4	14	169	12.5	89	142
Glasgow	59	5.3	165	105	7.7	61	129	12.5	22	170	12.1	87	143
Belfast	68	5.8	87	120	8.1	21	173	12.9	8	234	13.4	41	151
Durham	102	5.5	45	118	7.3	67	98	11.6	12	155	13.3	41	125
York	8	6.1	63	128	7.7	55	112	12.5	27	191	14.1	65	157
Manchester	69	5.4	74	87	7.6	69	104	13.4	34	167	13.5	55	139
Holyhead	10	7.1	66	128	8.3	83	168	13.9	28	232	13.3	83	222
Nottingham	117	6.1	62	122	7.7	70	107	12.9	63	151	14.4	42	146
Norwich	32	6.5	114	115	8.1	47	163	12.5	35	243	14.5	43	167
Birmingham	140	6.2	90	119	7.9	60	117	12.1	88	159	14.3	49	182
Cardiff	46	7.2	74	130	8.3	42	186	14.0	73	171	14.5	36	219
Bristol	42	7.1	76	113	8.7	43	179	14.1	91	158	15.1	24	212
London	137	6.5	76	97	8.8	56	136	14.3	91	176	15.5	35	188
Bournemouth	10	7.0	96	109	8.6	76	197	14.3	72	188	14.7	40	236
Newquay	103	7.5	102	140	8.5	52	223	13.7	124	209	13.9	28	262

METEOROLOGICAL OBSERVATIONS LONDON *(Hampstead Observatory)*

Maximum temperature is for the period 9am to 9pm; minimum temperature is for the period 9pm to 9am; the 'rainfall day' is the 24 hours starting at 9am on the day of entry; the 'wet hours' column counts all clock-hours during the rainfall day during which 0.2mm or more has fallen; sunshine is for the calendar day. All times are GMT.

July 2007

	Temperature Min (°C)	Max (°C)	*Rain* mm	*Wet* hours	*Sun* hours
1	14.4	18.9	0.7	2	5.2
2	13.4	20.1	13.9	9	3.3
3	11.2	20.3	2.9	5	5.1
4	11.6	18.4	0.4	2	5.0
5	13.0	18.9	1.3	4	3.0
6	12.9	18.9	0.0	0	2.8
7	10.7	21.7	0.0	0	8.9
8	9.6	21.2	0.0	0	6.3
9	10.5	20.9	5.5	3	7.7
10	10.7	18.6	0.0	0	3.0
11	12.2	19.2	0.2	1	2.7
12	12.6	22.8	0.0	0	1.9
13	15.6	22.1	0.7	3	3.0
14	15.8	21.8	0.0	0	6.0
15	14.8	22.2	3.1	1	4.3
16	16.8	21.9	2.0	4	3.8
17	13.0	20.9	0.2	1	6.8
18	13.0	23.2	0.0	0	7.7
19	11.9	23.3	4.4	4	4.3
20	14.7	19.1	22.4	3	3.6
21	11.3	20.3	4.0	4	4.8
22	11.1	20.8	0.0	0	7.6
23	13.7	18.3	4.2	6	0.1
24	11.8	21.9	0.0	0	8.9
25	12.4	20.9	0.9	3	2.2
26	13.7	18.1	7.7	3	1.3
27	12.5	21.3	0.0	0	4.6
28	11.9	21.7	14.3	9	7.7
29	10.7	19.5	0.0	0	5.2
30	9.1	20.2	0.0	0	8.1
31	9.1	21.8	0.0	0	9.8

August 2007

	Temperature Min (°C)	Max (°C)	*Rain* mm	*Wet* hours	*Sun* hours
1	11.2	23.9	0.0	0	7.1
2	12.5	20.0	0.7	3	3.9
3	11.1	24.2	0.0	1	9.7
4	13.8	25.6	0.0	0	11.5
5	15.2	28.9	0.0	0	11.2
6	15.4	23.2	0.0	0	6.0
7	10.6	21.5	1.5	2	6.1
8	10.6	21.5	0.2	1	9.3
9	11.1	21.5	0.0	0	9.0
10	10.1	23.7	0.0	0	10.9
11	12.9	25.2	0.0	0	9.7
12	12.8	21.0	0.0	0	3.8
13	10.8	20.8	4.8	4	4.6
14	13.9	18.4	7.0	7	0.0
15	15.4	21.2	7.9	6	2.7
16	10.2	19.0	1.5	2	6.1
17	9.2	18.7	0.7	1	5.4
18	13.6	18.8	12.8	11	1.0
19	14.5	16.8	2.6	7	0.2
20	11.2	15.8	0.4	1	0.4
21	11.8	15.5	3.1	4	0.0
22	13.2	14.8	4.4	8	0.0
23	13.0	15.6	7.5	5	0.0
24	13.8	18.1	0.2	1	0.7
25	11.9	25.5	0.0	0	9.9
26	14.9	22.4	0.0	0	8.6
27	10.5	19.6	0.0	0	7.5
28	11.4	19.9	0.0	0	6.8
29	11.7	20.5	0.0	0	7.4
30	9.6	18.3	0.0	0	0.2
31	11.0	19.5	0.0	0	2.5

September 2007

1	14.2	21.7	0.0	0	3.0
2	12.0	20.8	0.2	1	3.9
3	12.0	18.6	0.0	1	5.4
4	9.5	18.6	0.0	0	7.3
5	11.9	24.0	0.0	0	2.3
6	13.4	23.9	0.0	0	6.2
7	15.6	22.9	0.0	0	4.2
8	11.0	18.7	0.0	0	0.6
9	12.2	21.0	0.0	0	4.6
10	12.9	20.7	0.0	0	4.6
11	9.1	19.8	0.0	0	9.2
12	9.8	20.9	0.0	0	5.3
13	11.5	22.0	0.0	0	7.2
14	11.3	20.5	0.0	0	3.9
15	8.4	20.3	0.0	0	8.6
16	9.7	20.0	0.0	0	6.8
17	11.7	16.5	0.0	0	1.0
18	5.4	15.3	0.0	0	8.7
19	7.9	17.7	0.4	2	1.1
20	13.3	18.4	1.1	2	1.2
21	14.1	19.0	0.0	0	1.4
22	12.7	21.5	0.0	0	3.8
23	12.3	20.2	7.5	4	5.0
24	11.3	17.1	0.0	0	5.0
25	8.4	16.9	0.9	1	4.0
26	7.0	12.9	0.7	2	5.3
27	5.9	13.5	0.0	0	3.2
28	9.0	13.1	5.3	8	0.2
29	11.9	17.6	0.0	0	1.8
30	6.2	16.0	2.0	4	6.0

October 2007

1	11.6	13.5	5.5	5	0.2
2	11.1	13.9	0.7	3	0.0
3	12.2	16.8	0.0	0	2.3
4	11.3	18.3	0.0	0	6.0
5	7.7	17.4	0.0	0	6.1
6	10.1	15.8	0.0	0	2.1
7	8.3	15.5	0.0	0	1.6
8	10.8	15.5	2.2	3	0.5
9	9.6	13.9	16.7	13	0.1
10	10.3	16.4	0.0	0	2.2
11	7.8	16.5	0.2	1	7.8
12	11.3	16.5	0.0	0	0.0
13	13.4	17.6	0.0	0	0.8
14	10.3	18.4	0.0	0	4.9
15	9.8	17.0	1.8	2	2.0
16	12.1	15.8	5.7	11	0.2
17	8.6	14.3	0.0	0	4.7
18	4.1	13.8	0.0	0	6.7
19	4.0	13.6	0.0	0	5.6
20	5.0	14.0	0.0	0	5.1
21	3.8	14.2	0.0	0	7.3
22	4.3	12.7	0.0	0	1.2
23	3.4	12.0	0.0	0	7.3
24	5.0	9.7	0.0	0	0.0
25	8.3	9.0	1.5	6	0.0
26	8.1	10.2	0.0	0	0.0
27	8.5	13.2	0.2	1	0.3
28	11.3	13.9	6.6	9	0.0
29	8.0	13.3	0.0	0	4.3
30	5.6	13.9	0.0	0	6.9
31	5.3	14.2	0.0	0	1.2

November 2007

	Temperature Min (°C)	Max (°C)	Rain mm	Wet hours	Sun hours
1	8.9	17.7	0.0	0	3.4
2	8.8	17.3	0.0	0	4.2
3	7.5	15.8	0.0	0	4.3
4	6.1	13.7	0.0	0	6.3
5	3.3	10.6	0.0	0	1.4
6	4.7	11.9	0.0	0	7.0
7	5.6	14.0	0.0	0	3.4
8	8.6	13.6	4.6	3	1.1
9	3.9	9.4	0.2	1	6.8
10	6.6	13.6	0.0	0	1.0
11	9.3	13.3	0.2	1	1.4
12	–0.2	8.4	1.3	4	7.1
13	0.7	9.0	0.2	1	0.3
14	5.0	9.4	0.2	1	3.1
15	1.1	9.4	0.0	0	6.7
16	–1.3	8.9	0.0	0	7.0
17	1.4	7.6	0.7	2	0.0
18	5.1	5.7	7.5	13	0.0
19	1.8	9.2	27.7	15	0.7
20	5.7	8.9	5.3	11	0.0
21	8.1	11.4	13.4	11	4.5
22	6.9	11.2	0.7	3	4.3
23	2.1	5.5	0.0	0	6.2
24	–2.2	6.8	0.0	0	0.7
25	4.9	9.4	0.0	0	3.2
26	3.5	9.3	0.2	1	2.8
27	6.9	9.2	0.9	3	0.0
28	7.5	10.2	1.3	4	0.2
29	6.8	11.5	0.2	1	3.2
30	3.8	13.2	12.8	7	0.7

December 2007

	Temperature Min (°C)	Max (°C)	Rain mm	Wet hours	Sun hours
1	5.1	10.1	0.7	2	5.3
2	6.6	12.4	3.1	5	0.9
3	5.2	10.0	0.0	0	4.7
4	5.4	12.7	2.9	5	0.0
5	11.3	13.5	10.6	7	2.2
6	8.3	13.6	6.8	9	0.0
7	6.8	10.2	0.2	1	5.3
8	2.4	10.6	6.8	7	0.0
9	4.4	8.2	4.8	10	1.1
10	4.4	6.0	0.2	1	1.1
11	–0.8	7.9	0.0	0	5.4
12	0.0	7.6	0.2	1	6.3
13	–0.6	6.8	0.2	1	3.6
14	1.9	4.2	0.0	0	0.0
15	2.4	3.0	0.0	0	1.9
16	0.7	3.9	0.2	1	6.0
17	0.2	4.2	0.0	0	2.0
18	1.7	3.9	0.0	0	4.1
19	1.2	4.5	0.0	0	4.7
20	–1.6	3.5	0.2	1	3.7
21	0.7	3.9	0.0	0	3.5
22	–1.5	7.8	0.2	1	2.6
23	–0.7	3.8	0.2	1	4.0
24	1.7	9.0	5.5	4	1.2
25	7.6	8.3	8.6	8	0.0
26	2.6	8.4	0.0	0	4.5
27	7.0	11.6	0.2	1	0.0
28	8.5	10.3	9.9	6	0.0
29	4.2	8.3	0.0	0	5.0
30	4.4	8.9	0.0	0	0.8
31	5.0	7.7	0.9	2	0.0

January 2008

1	6.5	8.5	2.0	6	0.0
2	2.8	3.4	0.2	1	2.6
3	–0.3	2.2	0.0	0	0.0
4	2.2	7.8	6.2	6	0.0
5	5.0	7.9	0.0	0	1.7
6	0.6	8.2	0.7	3	5.6
7	6.1	8.9	0.4	2	3.8
8	3.8	9.7	6.8	6	0.6
9	4.0	8.0	0.0	0	4.2
10	6.2	10.3	10.6	10	0.0
11	6.7	9.2	11.4	11	0.9
12	0.7	7.8	1.5	5	6.3
13	6.5	10.3	3.7	6	0.6
14	6.5	10.2	7.5	11	1.7
15	7.0	10.9	6.8	7	0.0
16	4.0	9.7	0.2	1	6.2
17	2.1	11.1	3.5	4	1.0
18	6.6	12.4	0.9	3	0.0
19	11.7	12.9	3.3	4	0.0
20	11.7	13.3	0.4	2	0.0
21	10.0	10.3	8.6	7	0.4
22	1.3	7.6	0.2	1	5.9
23	6.4	11.5	0.2	1	0.1
24	9.6	10.0	0.0	0	3.2
25	2.3	9.5	0.0	0	3.0
26	4.7	10.2	0.0	0	5.2
27	3.9	11.1	0.0	0	7.1
28	1.2	6.6	0.2	1	2.7
29	3.7	9.3	4.0	6	1.0
30	2.7	8.0	0.0	0	5.6
31	2.8	8.0	3.3	1	0.9

February 2008

1	2.1	8.3	0.0	0	6.9
2	–1.9	6.5	0.0	0	5.9
3	3.7	7.1	1.1	2	4.8
4	1.8	8.9	3.3	6	5.3
5	5.5	12.3	2.2	3	1.8
6	6.5	10.3	0.0	0	4.9
7	3.4	12.3	0.0	0	4.2
8	5.1	13.4	0.0	0	7.5
9	5.5	15.9	0.0	0	7.6
10	4.1	14.1	0.0	0	7.4
11	2.3	11.6	0.2	1	7.5
12	3.1	12.2	0.2	1	7.5
13	4.1	12.5	0.0	0	7.7
14	2.5	4.2	0.0	0	0.0
15	2.3	5.8	0.0	0	2.1
16	–1.1	5.6	0.0	0	7.0
17	–1.5	9.3	0.2	1	7.5
18	0.0	8.8	0.0	0	7.6
19	0.5	6.4	0.2	1	6.5
20	0.9	3.9	0.0	0	0.8
21	3.2	9.9	0.2	1	1.4
22	9.2	11.6	0.0	0	0.0
23	5.8	10.3	0.0	0	0.0
24	7.9	13.0	2.0	4	4.1
25	1.1	9.5	4.6	6	5.6
26	8.6	12.5	0.0	0	5.3
27	2.8	11.2	0.0	0	5.7
28	3.5	11.0	0.0	0	1.6
29	1.9	10.2	1.5	4	0.5

March 2008

	Temperature Min (°C)	Max (°C)	*Rain* mm	*Wet* hours	*Sun* hours
1	6.8	12.6	0.0	0	6.7
2	9.2	12.6	0.0	0	4.4
3	2.1	9.0	0.2	1	4.9
4	–0.4	8.8	0.0	0	5.0
5	–2.2	9.4	0.2	1	6.4
6	5.3	11.7	1.3	1	0.9
7	5.2	11.5	0.0	0	7.0
8	3.4	9.8	3.5	7	0.6
9	4.5	9.4	11.2	8	2.4
10	3.3	8.3	9.5	8	1.7
11	4.4	13.9	2.0	4	2.5
12	4.7	10.6	0.0	0	3.7
13	4.4	10.0	2.2	5	1.3
14	6.1	12.4	0.7	2	3.3
15	8.8	13.6	17.8	15	1.0
16	7.0	7.0	2.0	4	0.0
17	3.7	8.1	0.0	0	1.6
18	0.6	6.4	0.0	0	0.7
19	0.7	7.4	0.0	0	3.1
20	0.3	9.2	4.4	10	0.6
21	3.1	9.7	4.4	10	5.8
22	0.5	5.1	2.8	3	4.6
23	–2.6	2.4	0.2	1	0.3
24	–1.4	5.2	0.0	0	2.7
25	–0.4	6.1	3.4	0	5.4
26	4.0	11.0	1.0	0	1.5
27	2.7	11.4	5.7	0	6.8
28	4.3	11.9	3.2	0	2.0
29	4.0	11.4	0.0	0	3.5
30	7.3	13.7	0.4	0	5.6
31	5.3	11.9	0.0	0	0.7

April 2008

	Temperature Min (°C)	Max (°C)	*Rain* mm	*Wet* hours	*Sun* hours
1	6.2	15.5	0.0	0	3.9
2	7.1	13.2	0.2	0	0.3
3	7.6	15.2	0.0	0	4.0
4	7.2	17.4	0.4	2	7.4
5	5.5	10.6	5.6	5	3.7
6	–1.0	4.4	2.2	3	3.8
7	–1.7	8.9	0.0	0	4.0
8	–0.6	10.5	0.0	0	6.8
9	–0.4	12.4	0.0	0	8.3
10	1.3	12.8	0.0	0	6.4
11	4.0	11.2	2.0	2	5.9
12	4.4	12.7	0.2	1	4.6
13	3.7	11.6	4.0	4	4.8
14	2.0	12.2	1.8	4	6.9
15	–0.3	12.3	2.6	3	7.4
16	3.6	10.2	0.0	0	2.2
17	2.7	9.1	0.0	0	5.6
18	3.1	8.0	0.0	0	0.0
19	6.1	8.0	0.0	0	0.0
20	6.8	14.5	0.2	1	3.3
21	8.0	14.7	0.0	0	3.1
22	5.3	17.6	1.5	2	9.1
23	7.1	17.1	1.1	2	4.5
24	6.2	15.7	3.7	3	6.2
25	7.2	16.1	0.0	0	4.3
26	9.0	21.1	0.0	0	8.9
27	13.4	16.8	1.1	3	1.7
28	7.3	14.3	5.1	7	5.3
29	5.9	12.6	14.7	12	2.1
30	5.5	9.5	9.7	12	1.3

May 2008

1	5.9	14.4	3.1	4	4.9
2	5.8	15.1	0.4	2	4.7
3	6.7	20.0	0.0	0	7.8
4	11.7	21.3	0.0	0	1.5
5	13.3	21.2	0.0	0	9.7
6	9.6	21.3	0.0	0	11.7
7	11.6	24.0	0.0	0	11.4
8	11.9	23.6	0.0	0	11.5
9	12.5	24.6	0.0	0	5.5
10	14.3	25.5	0.0	0	5.6
11	14.0	25.5	0.0	0	11.5
12	11.3	23.9	0.0	0	11.4
13	9.2	20.7	0.0	0	11.6
14	8.9	19.0	0.0	0	7.0
15	8.8	13.4	0.2	1	0.0
16	8.5	11.8	0.0	0	0.0
17	8.4	11.6	2.0	6	0.0
18	5.9	15.2	1.5	0	5.8
19	3.5	13.7	0.0	0	5.7
20	3.4	15.5	0.0	0	6.0
21	5.6	18.4	0.0	0	10.2
22	8.1	20.8	0.0	0	5.9
23	10.9	21.0	0.0	0	3.2
24	10.8	20.0	21.8	8	8.1
25	10.8	15.7	21.8	9	0.1
26	10.6	11.2	23.5	16	0.0
27	9.1	18.2	11.2	6	3.3
28	13.3	16.2	0.4	1	0.0
29	10.3	20.7	0.0	0	4.7
30	10.9	18.0	0.0	0	0.9
31	12.7	21.2	1.3	3	5.3

June 2008

1	11.8	17.7	0.0	0	2.0
2	11.2	18.0	8.6	12	1.3
3	13.0	14.7	10.3	19	0.0
4	9.9	19.8	0.0	0	7.1
5	9.9	21.2	0.0	0	11.3
6	10.0	18.1	0.0	0	1.4
7	9.9	18.4	0.2	1	7.0
8	12.7	24.7	0.0	0	10.7
9	12.4	26.2	0.0	0	11.3
10	15.0	22.4	0.0	0	8.6
11	10.5	20.0	10.3	6	4.4
12	9.8	15.1	0.0	0	3.4
13	8.4	16.6	0.0	0	4.5
14	8.7	18.9	0.0	0	7.0
15	9.3	18.2	0.0	0	8.6
16	7.6	18.8	0.0	0	6.2
17	10.3	20.1	0.0	0	9.0
18	10.7	17.5	0.7	2	0.7
19	12.6	19.6	0.0	0	7.2
20	10.7	18.5	2.0	4	5.2
21	12.0	18.4	0.4	2	0.2
22	16.3	20.9	0.0	0	9.6
23	9.8	21.0	0.0	0	9.6
24	10.9	21.4	0.0	0	8.3
25	14.0	21.5	0.0	0	6.5
26	10.2	21.1	2.2	3	8.7
27	12.4	19.9	0.7	3	3.8
28	15.5	21.8	0.0	0	8.9
29	11.7	20.9	0.0	0	5.1
30	9.9	21.6	0.0	0	10.4

SPORTS RESULTS

ALPINE SKIING

WORLD CUP 2007–8

MEN
Downhill: Didier Cuche (Switzerland), 584pts
Slalom: Manfred Moelgg (Italy), 531pts
Giant Slalom: Ted Ligety (USA), 485pts
Super Giant Slalom: Hannes Reichelt (Austria), 341pts
Overall: Bode Miller (USA), 1,409pts

WOMEN
Downhill: Lindsey Vonn (USA), 755pts
Slalom: Marlies Schild (Austria), 640pts
Giant Slalom: Denise Karbon (Italy), 592pts
Super Giant Slalom: Maria Riesch (Germany), 374pts
Overall: Lindsey Vonn (USA), 1,403 pts

AMERICAN FOOTBALL

AFC Championship 2007–8: New England Patriots beat San Diego Chargers 21–12
NFC Championship 2007–8: New York Giants beat Green Bay Packers 23–20
XLII Superbowl 2008: New York Giants beat New England Patriots 17–14

ANGLING

BRITISH CHAMPIONSHIPS 2007
Individual: Scott Rispin

TEAMS
First Division: Garbolino Osets
Second Division: Team Daiwa Dorking
Third Division: Littleport AC
Ladies: Barnsley and District

ASSOCIATION FOOTBALL

LEAGUE COMPETITIONS 2007–8

ENGLAND AND WALES
Premiership
1. Manchester United, 87pts
2. Chelsea, 85pts
3. Arsenal, 83pts
Relegated: Reading, Birmingham City, Derby County

Championship
1. West Bromwich Albion, 81pts
2. Stoke City, 79pts
Play-off winner and third promotion place: Hull City
Relegated: Leicester City, Scunthorpe United, Colchester United

League 1
1. Swansea City, 92pts
2. Nottingham Forest, 82pts
Play-off winner and third promotion place: Doncaster Rovers
Relegated: Bournemouth, Gillingham, Port Vale, Luton Town

League 2
1. Milton Keynes Dons, 97pts
2. Peterborough United, 92pts
3. Hereford United, 88pts
Play-off winner and fourth promotion place: Stockport County
Relegated: Mansfield Town and Wrexham

Football Conference
1. Aldershot, 101pts
Play-off winner and second promotion place: Exeter City

Welsh Premier League
1. Llanelli, 85pts
2. The New Saints, 78pts
3. Rhyl, 69pts

Women's Premier League National Division
1. Arsenal, 62pts
2. Everton, 57pts
3. Leeds United, 40pts

SCOTLAND
Premier Division
1. Celtic, 89pts
2. Rangers, 86pts
Relegated: Gretna *(to Division 3 owing to financial problems)*

Division 1
1. Hamilton Academicals, 76pts
Relegated: Stirling Albion

Division 2
1. Ross County, 73pts
Also promoted: Airdrie United
Relegated: Berwick and Cowdenbeath

Division 3
1. East Fife, 88pts
Play-off winner and second promotion place: Arbroath
Also promoted: Stranraer
Bottom: Forfar Athletic

NORTHERN IRELAND
Premier League
1. Linfield, 74pts
2. Glentoran, 71pts
3. Cliftonville, 60pts

REPUBLIC OF IRELAND
Premier Division 2007: 1. Drogheda United, 68pts; 2. St Patrick's Athletic, 61pts; 3. Bohemians, 58pts

FRANCE
Ligue 1: 1. Lyon, 79pts; 2. Bordeaux, 75pts; 3. Marseille, 62pts

GERMANY
Bundesliga: 1. Bayern Munich, 76pts; 2. Werder Bremen, 66pts; 3. Schalke 04, 64pts

ITALY
Serie A: 1. Internazionale, 85pts; 2. Roma, 82pts; 3. Juventus, 72pts

NETHERLANDS
Eredivisie: 1. PSV, 72pts; 2. Ajax, 69pts; 3. NAC, 63pts

SPAIN
Primera Liga: 1. Real Madrid, 85pts; 2. Villarreal, 77pts; 3. Barcelona, 67pts

CUP COMPETITIONS 2007–8
ENGLAND
FA Cup final 2008: Portsmouth beat Cardiff City 1–0
League Cup final 2008: Tottenham beat Chelsea 2–1
Football League Trophy final 2008: Milton Keynes Dons beat Grimsby Town 2–0
FA Vase final 2008: Kirkham and Wesham beat Lowestoft Town 2–1
FA Trophy final 2008: Ebbsfleet United beat Torquay United 1–0
Community Shield 2008: Manchester United beat Portsmouth 3–1 on penalties (0–0 aet)

WOMEN
FA Cup final 2008: Arsenal beat Leeds United 4–1
Premier League Cup final 2008: Everton beat Arsenal 1–0
Community Shield 2008: Arsenal beat Everton 1–0

WALES
FA Wales Cup final 2008: Bangor City beat Llanelli 4–2
FA Wales Premier Cup final 2008: Newport County beat Llanelli 1–0

SCOTLAND
Scottish Cup final 2008: Rangers beat Queen of the South 3–2
League Cup final 2008: Rangers beat Dundee United 3–2 on penalties (2–2 aet)

NORTHERN IRELAND
Irish Cup final 2008: Linfield beat Coleraine 2–1

EUROPE
Champions League final 2008: Manchester United beat Chelsea 6–5 on penalties (1–1 aet)
UEFA Cup final 2008: Zenit St Petersburg beat Rangers 2–0

EUROPEAN CHAMPIONSHIP
Austria and Switzerland, June 2008

Group A

	Played	*Won*	*Drawn*	*Lost*	*F*	*A*	*Pts*
Portugal	3	2	0	1	5	3	6
Turkey	3	2	0	1	5	5	6
Czech Rep.	3	1	0	2	4	6	3
Switzerland	3	1	0	2	3	3	3

Czech Republic beat Switzerland 1–0
Portugal beat Turkey 2–0
Portugal beat Czech Republic 3–1
Turkey beat Switzerland 2–1
Switzerland beat Portugal 2–0
Turkey beat Czech Republic 3–2

Group B

	Played	*Won*	*Drawn*	*Lost*	*F*	*A*	*Pts*
Croatia	3	3	0	0	4	1	9
Germany	3	2	0	1	4	2	6
Austria	3	0	1	2	1	3	1
Poland	3	0	1	2	1	4	1

Croatia beat Austria 1–0
Germany beat Poland 2–0
Croatia beat Germany 2–1
Austria and Poland drew 1–1
Germany beat Austria 1–0
Croatia beat Poland 1–0

Group C

	Played	*Won*	*Drawn*	*Lost*	*F*	*A*	*Pts*
Netherlands	3	3	0	0	9	1	9
Italy	3	1	1	1	3	4	4
Romania	3	0	2	1	1	3	2
France	3	0	1	2	1	6	1

Romania and France drew 0–0
Netherlands beat Italy 3–0
Italy and Romania drew 1–1
Netherlands beat France 4–1
Netherlands beat Romania 2–0
Italy beat France 2–0

Group D

	Played	*Won*	*Drawn*	*Lost*	*F*	*A*	*Pts*
Spain	3	3	0	0	8	3	9
Russia	3	2	0	1	4	4	6
Sweden	3	1	0	2	3	4	3
Greece	3	0	0	3	1	5	0

Spain beat Russia 4–1
Sweden beat Greece 2–0
Spain beat Sweden 2–1
Russia beat Greece 1–0
Spain beat Greece 2–1
Russia beat Sweden 2–0

Quarter-finals
Germany beat Portugal 3–2
Turkey beat Croatia 3–1 on penalties (1–1 aet)
Russia beat Netherlands 3–1
Spain beat Italy 4–2 on penalties (0–0 aet)

Semi-finals
Germany beat Turkey 3–2
Spain beat Russia 3–0

Final
Spain beat Germany 1–0

WORLD PLAYER OF THE YEAR
2007 – Kaka (Brazil)
2006 – Fabio Cannavaro (Italy)
2005 – Ronaldinho (Brazil)
2004 – Ronaldinho (Brazil)
2003 – Zinedine Zidane (France)
2002 – Ronaldo (Brazil)
2001 – Luis Figo (Portugal)
2000 – Zinedine Zidane (France)
1999 – Rivaldo (Brazil)
1998 – Zinedine Zidane (France)
1997 – Ronaldo (Brazil)
1996 – Ronaldo (Brazil)
1995 – George Weah (Liberia)
1994 – Romario (Brazil)
1993 – Roberto Baggio (Italy)

ATHLETICS

EUROPEAN CROSS COUNTRY CHAMPIONSHIPS
Toro, Spain, 9 December 2007

SENIOR MEN (10.7km)
Individual: Sergiy Lebid (Ukraine), 31min 47sec
Team: Spain, 33pts

U23 MEN (8.2km)
Individual: Kemal Koyuncu (Turkey), 24min 31sec
Team: Great Britain, 52pts

JUNIOR MEN (6.7km)
Individual: Mourad Amdouni (France), 20min 08sec
Team: France, 29pts

SENIOR WOMEN (8.2km)
Individual: Marta Dominguez (Spain), 26min 58sec
Team: Spain, 33pts

U23 WOMEN (6.7km)
Individual: Ancuta Bobocel (Romania), 22min 35sec
Team: Great Britain, 47pts

JUNIOR WOMEN (4.2km)
Individual: Stephanie Twell (Great Britain), 14min 12sec
Team: Great Britain, 14pts

UK INDOOR CHAMPIONSHIPS
Sheffield, 9–10 February 2008

MEN
60m: Dwain Chambers (Belgrave), 6.56sec
200m: Chris Clarke (Milton Keynes), 20.98sec
400m: Richard Buck (York), 46.53sec
800m: Richard Hill (Notts), 1min 48.26sec
1,500m: James McIlroy (Windsor, Slough, Eton and Hounslow), 3min 44.90sec
3,000m: Nick McCormick (Morpeth), 8min 16.73sec
60mH: Allan Scott (Shaftesbury Barnet), 7.61sec
High jump: Samson Oni (Belgrave), 2.30m
Pole vault: Steve Lewis (Newham and Essex Beagles), 5.61m
Long jump: Chris Tomlinson (Newham and Essex Beagles), 7.80m
Triple jump: Phillips Idowu (Belgrave), 17.24m
Shot: Gareth Johnson (Shaftesbury Barnet/USA), 20.66m

WOMEN
60m: Laura Turner (Harrow), 7.32sec
200m: Joice Maduaka (Woodford Green and Essex Ladies), 23.43sec
400m: Meghan Beesley (Tamworth), 54.88sec
800m: Jenny Meadows (Wigan), 2min 01.97sec
1,500m: Jemma Simpson (Newquay and Par), 4min 13.99sec
3,000m: Helen Clitheroe (Preston), 8min 56.13sec
60mH: Sarah Paxton (Woodford Green and Essex Ladies), 8.09sec
High jump: Jessica Ennis (City of Sheffield), 1.92m
Pole vault: Kate Dennison (Sale), 4.25m
Long jump: Kelly Sotherton (Birchfield), 6.41m
Triple jump: Nadia Williams (Shaftesbury Barnet), 13.39m
Shot: Eden Francis (Birchfield), 16.11m

ENGLISH NATIONAL CROSS COUNTRY CHAMPIONSHIPS
Alton Towers, Staffordshire, 23 February 2008

SENIOR MEN (12km)
Individual: Tom Humphries (Cannock and Stafford), 32min 03sec
Team: Leeds City, 183pts

JUNIOR MEN (9.6km)
Individual: Lee Carey (Nuneaton), 27min 19sec
Team: Aldershot, Farnham and District, 86pts

SENIOR WOMEN (8km)
Individual: Liz Yelling (Bedford), 23min 44sec
Team: Winchester and District, 96pts

JUNIOR WOMEN (5km)
Individual: Stephanie Twell (Aldershot, Farnham), 13min 53sec
Team: Aldershot, Farnham and District, 55pts

WORLD INDOOR CHAMPIONSHIPS
Valencia, Spain, 7–9 March 2008

MEN
60m: Olusoji Fasuba (Nigeria), 6.51sec
400m: Tyler Christopher (Canada), 45.67sec
800m: Abubaker Kaki (Sudan), 1min 44.81sec
1,500m: Deresse Mekonnen (Ethiopia), 3min 38.23sec
3,000m: Tariku Bekele (Ethiopia), 7min 48.23sec
60mH: Liu Xiang (China) 7.46sec
4 × 400m: USA, 3min 06.79sec
High jump: Stefan Holm (Sweden), 2.36m
Pole vault: Yevgeni Lukyanenko (Russia) 5.90m
Long jump: Khotso Mokoena (South Africa), 8.08m
Triple jump: Phillips Idowu (Great Britain), 17.75m
Shot: Christian Cantwell (USA), 21.77m
Heptathlon: Bryan Clay (USA), 6,371pts

WOMEN
60m: Angela Williams (USA), 7.06sec
400m: Olesya Zykina (Russia), 51.09sec
800m: Tamsyn Lewis (Australia), 2min 02.57sec
1,500m: Yelena Soboleva (Russia), 3min 57.71sec
3,000m: Meseret Defar (Ethiopia), 8min 38.79sec
60mH: Lolo Jones (USA), 7.80sec
4 × 400m: Russia, 3min 28.17sec
High jump: Blanka Vlasic (Croatia), 2.03m
Pole vault: Yelena Isinibayeva (Russia), 4.75m
Long jump: Naide Gomes (Portugal), 7.00m
Triple jump: Yargelis Savigne (Cuba), 15.05m
Shot: Valerie Vili (New Zealand), 20.19m
Pentathlon: Tia Hellebaut (Belgium), 4,867pts

IAAF WORLD CROSS COUNTRY CHAMPIONSHIPS
Edinburgh, 30 March 2008

SENIOR MEN (12km)
Individual: Kenenisa Bekele (Ethiopia), 34min 38sec
Team: Kenya, 39pts

JUNIOR MEN (8km)
Individual: Ibrahim Jeilan (Ethiopia), 22min 38sec
Team: Kenya, 21pts

SENIOR WOMEN (8km)
Individual: Tirunesh Dibaba (Ethiopia), 25min 10sec
Team: Ethiopia, 18pts

JUNIOR WOMEN (6km)
Individual: Genzebe Dibaba (Ethiopia), 19min 59sec
Team: Ethiopia, 16pts

LONDON MARATHON
London, 13 April 2008
Men: Martin Lel (Kenya), 2hr 05min 15sec
Women: Irina Mikitenko (Germany), 2hr 24min 14sec

EUROPEAN CUP SUPER LEAGUE
Annecy, France, 21–22 June 2008

MEN
100m: Tyrone Edgar (Great Britain), 10.20sec
200m: Marlon Devonish (Great Britain), 20.52sec
400m: Martyn Rooney (Great Britain), 45.33sec
800m: Manuel Olmedo (Spain), 1min 49.98sec
1,500m: Mehdi Baala (France), 3min 40.55sec
3,000m: Andy Baddeley (Great Britain), 8min 01.28sec
5,000m: Mo Farah (Great Britain), 13min 44.07sec
3,000mSt: Mahiedine Mehkhissi Benabbad (France), 8min 33.10sec
110mH: Jackson Quinonez (Spain), 13.40sec
400mH: Periklis Iakovakis (Greece), 49.15sec
4 × 100m: Great Britain, 38.48sec
4 × 400m: France, 3min 02.33sec
High jump: Andrei Silnov (Russia), 2.32m
Pole vault: Danny Edcker (Germany), 5.55m
Long jump: Louis Tsatoumas (Greece), 8.17m
Triple jump: Phillips Idowu (Great Britain), 17.46m
Shot: Peter Sack (Germany), 20.41m
Discus: Mario Pestano (Spain), 68.34m
Hammer: Szymon Ziolkowski (Poland), 79.26m
Javelin: Peter Esenwein (Germany), 79.23m
Points: Great Britain 112; Poland 98; France 96; Germany 95; Russia 84; Italy 82; Spain 81; Greece 68

WOMEN
100m: Yulia Nestsiarenka (Belarus), 11.17sec
200m: Muriel Hurtis-Houairi (France), 22.75sec
400m: Nicola Sanders (Great Britain), 51.17sec
800m: Jenny Meadows (Great Britain), 2min 01.20sec
1,500m: Sylwia Ejdys (Poland), 4min 19.17sec
3,000m: Lidia Chojecka (Poland), 9 min 03.49sec
5,000m: Nataliya Berkut (Ukraine), 15min 23.97sec
3,000mSt: Gulnara Galkina (Russia), 9min 35.32sec
100mH: Yevheniya Snihur (Ukraine), 12.81sec
400mH: Anastasiya Rabchenyuk (Ukraine), 54.64sec
4 × 100m: Russia, 42.80sec
4 × 400m: Russia, 3min 23.77sec
High jump: Ariane Friedrich (Germany), 2.03m
Pole vault: Yuliya Golubchikova (Russia), 4.73m
Long jump: Ludmila Kolchanova (Russia), 7.04m
Triple jump: Olha Saladuha (Ukraine), 14.73m
Shot: Yulia Leantsiuk (Belarus), 19.43m
Discus: Svetlana Saykina (Russia), 62.56m
Hammer: Aksana Menkova (Belarus), 75.97m
Javelin: Natalia Shymchuk (Belarus), 63.24m
Points: Russia 122; Ukraine 108.5; Great Britain 89; Poland 86; France 81; Italy 79.5; Belarus 78; Germany 74

UK TRIALS AND CHAMPIONSHIPS
Birmingham, 12–13 July 2008

MEN
100m: Dwain Chambers (Belgrave), 10.00sec
200m: Christian Malcolm (Cardiff), 20.52sec
400m: Martyn Rooney (Croydon), 45.31sec
800m: Michael Rimmer (Liverpool Pembroke), 1min 49.13sec
1,500m: Tom Lancashire (Bolton), 3min 38.92sec
5,000m: Andy Vernon (Aldershot, Farnham and District), 13min 54.26sec
*10,000m:** Surendra Singh (India), 28min 22.79sec
3,000mSt: Adam Bowden (Harrow), 8min 36.17sec
110mH: Andy Turner (Sale), 13.58sec
400mH: Richard Yates (Trafford), 49.50sec
5,000m Walk: Daniel King (Colchester), 21min 06.37sec
High jump: Tom Parsons (Birchfield), 2.30m
Pole vault: Steve Lewis (Newham and Essex Beagles), 5.60m
Long jump: Greg Rutherford (Milton Keynes), 8.20m
Triple jump: Phillips Idowu (Belgrave), 17.58m
Shot: Carl Myerscough (Blackpool and Fylde), 20.15m
Discus: Emeka Udechuku (Woodford Green), 59.35m
Hammer: Mike Floyd (Sale), 69.68m
Javelin: Michael Allen (Trafford), 75.07m
†*Decathlon:* Daniel Awde (Woodford Green), 7,704pts

WOMEN
100m: Jeanette Kwakye (Woodford Green and Essex Ladies), 11.26sec
200m: Emily Freeman (Wakefield), 22.92sec
400m: Lee McConnell (Shaftesbury Barnet), 52.31sec
800m: Marilyn Okoro (Shaftesbury Barnet), 1min 59.81sec
1,500m: Lisa Dobriskey (Ashford), 4min 15.84sec
5,000m: Jo Pavey (Exeter), 15min 12.55sec
**10,000m:* Jo Pavey (Exeter), 31min 56.90sec
3,000mSt: Helen Clitheroe (Preston), 9min 36.98sec
100mH: Sarah Claxton (Woodford Green and Essex Ladies), 13.12sec
400mH: Perri Shakes Drayton (Victoria Park), 56.00sec
5,000m walk: Johanna Jackson (Redcar), 21min 30.75sec
High jump: Stephanie Pywell (Sale), 1.88m
Pole vault: Emma Lyons (Sale), 4.12m
Long jump: Jade Johnson (Herne Hill), 6.30m
Triple jump: Nadia Williams (Shaftesbury Barnet), 13.35m
Shot: Jo Duncan (Woodford Green and Essex Ladies), 15.99m
Discus: Emma Carpenter (Windsor, Slough, Eton and Hounslow), 57.26m
Hammer: Zoe Derham (Birchfield), 67.27m
Javelin: Goldie Sayers (Belgrave), 62.62m
†*Heptathlon:* Julie Hollman (Birchfield), 5,941pts
* Held at Watford, 14 June 2008
† Held at Birmingham, 31 May–1 June 2008

BADMINTON

WORLD CHAMPIONSHIPS 2007
Kuala Lumpur, Malaysia, August

Men's Singles: Dan Lin (China) beat Sony Dwi Kuncoro (Indonesia) 2–0
Women's Singles: Lin Zhu (China) beat Chen Wang (Hong Kong) 2–0

Men's Doubles: Markis Kido and Hendra Setiawan (Indonesia) beat Jae Sung Jung and Yong Dae Lee (Rep. of Korea) 2–0
Women's Doubles: Wei Yang and Jiewen Zhang (China) beat Ling Gao and Sui Huang (China) 2–0
Mixed Doubles: Liliyana Natsir and Nova Widianto (Indonesia) beat Ling Gao and Bo Zheng (China) 2–0

ALL-ENGLAND CHAMPIONSHIPS 2008
Birmingham, March

Men's Singles: Jin Chen (China) beat Dan Lin (China) 2–0
Women's Singles: Tine Rasmussen (Denmark) beat Lan Lu (China) 2–1
Men's Doubles: Jae Sung Jung and Yong Dae Lee (Rep. of Korea) beat Ji Man Hwang and Jae Jin Lee (Rep. of Korea) 2–1
Women's Doubles: Hyo Jung Lee and Kyung Won Lee (Rep. of Korea) beat Jing Du and Yang Yu (China) 2–1
Mixed Doubles: Ling Gao and Bo Zheng (China) beat Liliyana Natsir and Nova Widianto (Indonesia) 2–1

ENGLISH NATIONAL CHAMPIONSHIPS 2008
Manchester, February

Men's Singles: Rajiv Ouseph beat Aamir Ghaffar 2–1
Women's Singles: Elizabeth Cann beat Tracey Hallam 2–0
Men's Doubles: Anthony Clark and Nathan Robertson beat Richard Eidestedt and Chris Langridge 2–0
Women's Doubles: Tracey Hallam and Donna Kellogg beat Natalie Munt and Joanne Nicholas 2–1
Mixed Doubles: Donna Kellogg and Anthony Clark beat Liza Smith and Robin Middleton 2–0

SCOTTISH NATIONAL CHAMPIONSHIPS 2008
Perth, February

Men's Singles: Craig Goddard beat Gordon Thomson 2–0
Women's Singles: Susan Hughes beat Rita Yuan Gao 2–0
Men's Doubles: Andrew Bowman and David Gilmour beat Watson Briggs and Thomas Bethell 2–0
Women's Doubles: Imogen Bankier and Emma Mason beat Susan Hughes and Rita Yuan Gao 2–0
Mixed Doubles: Imogen Bankier and Watson Briggs beat Rita Yuan Gao and Andrew Bowman 2–1

WELSH NATIONAL CHAMPIONSHIPS 2008
Cwmbran, February

Men's Singles: Martyn Lewis beat Daniel Van Hooijdonk 2–0
Women's Singles: Caroline Harvey beat Bethan Higginson 2–0
Men's Doubles: Martyn Lewis and Matthew Hughes beat James Phillips and Jo Morgan 2–0
Women's Doubles: Vikki Jones and Nicole Walkley beat Bethan Higginson and Kelly Blake 2–0
Mixed Doubles: Katy Howell and James Phillips beat Bethan Higginson and Michael Lewis 2–0

BASEBALL

American League Championship Series 2007: Boston Red Sox beat Cleveland Indians 4–3
National League Championship Series 2007: Colorado Rockies beat Arizona Diamondbacks 4–0
World Series 2007: Boston Red Sox beat Colorado Rockies 4–0

BASKETBALL

BRITISH

MEN
BBL Play-off final 2008: Guildford Heat beat Milton Keynes Lions 100–88
BBL Trophy final 2008: Guildford Heat beat Newcastle Eagles 86–79
BBL Cup final 2008: Milton Keynes Lions beat Newcastle Eagles 69–66
BBL Champions 2007–8: Newcastle Eagles

WOMEN
EBL Division 1 2007–8: Sheffield Hatters
EBL Division 1 Play-off final 2007–8: Rhondda Rebels beat Sheffield Hatters 72–70
National Cup final 2008: Rhondda Rebels beat Sheffield Hatters 71–59

USA – NATIONAL BASKETBALL LEAGUE (NBA)
Eastern Conference final 2008: Boston Celtics beat Detroit Pistons 4–2
Western Conference final 2008: LA Lakers beat San Antonio Spurs 4–1
NBA final 2008: Boston Celtics beat LA Lakers 4–2

BOWLS — INDOOR

WORLD CHAMPIONSHIPS 2008
Norfolk, January

Men's Singles: Alex Marshall (Scotland) beat Ian Bond (England) 2–0
Women's Singles: Ceri Ann Davies (Australia) beat Debbie Stavrou (England) 2–0
Men's Pairs: Andy Thomson and Ian Bond (England) beat Greg Harlow and Mark McMahon (England) 2–1
Mixed Pairs: Ceri Ann Davies and David Gourlay (Australia) beat Caroline Brown and Alex Marshall (Scotland) 2–1

BRITISH ISLES INDOOR BOWLS CHAMPIONSHIPS 2008
Perth, March

Singles: Craig Docherty (England) beat Ian Merrien (Channel Islands) 21–12
Pairs: England beat Scotland 25–11
Triples: Wales beat Scotland 23–8
Fours: Ireland beat England 18–15

ENGLISH NATIONAL CHAMPIONSHIPS 2008
Nottingham, April

Singles: Gary R. Smith beat Glenn Skipp 21–12
Pairs: Gallow beat Nottingham 19–7
Triples: Cumbria beat Clarrie Dunbar 17–3
Fours: Cyphers beat Egham 21–17
Liberty Trophy (Inter-County Championship) final: Durham beat Hampshire 133–98
Champion of Champions (Lowestoft, February): Jayson Parkinson beat Mathew Orrey 21–14

SCOTTISH NATIONAL CHAMPIONSHIPS 2008
Cumbernauld, March

Pairs: Ardrossan beat Coatbridge 20–18
Triples: West of Scotland beat Midlothian 21–12
Fours: Midlothian beat Prestwick 27–18

BOWLS — OUTDOOR

BRITISH ISLES CHAMPIONSHIPS 2008
Llandrindod Wells, June

Singles: Scotland beat Ireland 21–18
Pairs: England beat Wales 20–16
Triples: Jersey beat Wales 20–13
Fours: England beat Scotland 26–15

ENGLISH NATIONAL CHAMPIONSHIPS 2008
Worthing, August

Singles: King's Devon beat Stute 21–8
Pairs: Felixstowe beat Carlisle Subscription 20–10
Triples: Kingsthorpe beat Elm Park 14–12
Fours: Clevedon beat Trent Vale 18–17
Inter-county Championship: Devon beat Norfolk 120–109

SCOTTISH NATIONAL CHAMPIONSHIPS 2008
Ayr, August

MEN
Singles: Markinch beat Port Glasgow 21–8
Pairs: Carrick Knowe beat Maidens 18–10
Triples: Clackmannan beat Polmaise 24–20
Fours: Gourock Park beat Haddington 18–7

WELSH NATIONAL CHAMPIONSHIPS 2008
Llandrindod Wells, August

Singles: Panteg Park beat Caerphilly Town 21–18
Pairs: Caerphilly Town beat Crosskeys 20–15
Triples: Caerau Welfare beat Pontrhydyfen 18–17
Fours: Machynlleth beat Aberavon 21–12

BOXING

WORLD CHAMPIONS
as at 1 August 2008

WORLD BOXING COUNCIL (WBC)
Heavy: Samuel Peter (Nigeria)
Cruiser: Vacant
Light-heavy: Adrian Diaconu (Romania)
Super-middle: Vacant
Middle: Kelly Pavlik (USA)
Super-welter: Sergio Mora (USA)
Welter: Andre Berto (USA)
Super-light: Timothy Bradley (USA)
Light: Manny Pacquiao (Philippines)
Super-feather: Manny Pacquiao (Philippines)
Feather: Jorge Linares (Venezuela)
Super-bantam: Israel Vazquez (Mexico)
Bantam: Hozumi Hasegawa (Japan)
Super-fly: Cristian Mijares (Mexico)
Fly: Daisuke Naito (Japan)
Light-fly: Edgar Sosa (Mexico)
Straw: Oleydong Sithsamerchai (Thailand)

WORLD BOXING ASSOCIATION (WBA)
Heavy: Ruslan Chagaev (Uzbekistan)
Cruiser: Firat Arslan (Germany)
Light-heavy: Hugo Hernan Garay (Argentina)
Super-middle: Mikkel Kessler (Denmark)
Middle: Felix Sturm (Germany)
Super-welter: Danial Santos (Puerto Rico)
Welter: Antonio Margarito (Mexico)
Super-light: Andreas Kotelnik (Ukraine)
Light: Yusuke Kobori (Japan)
Super-feather: Edwin Valero (Venezeula)
Feather: Chris John (Indonesia)
Super-bantam: Celestino Caballero (Panama)
Bantam: Anselmo Moreno (Panama)
Super-fly: Cristian Mijares (Mexico)
Fly: Takefumi Sakata (Japan)
Light-fly: Brahmin Asloum (France)
Straw: Yukata Niida (Japan)

WORLD BOXING ORGANISATION (WBO)
Heavy: Wladimir Klitschko (Ukraine)
Cruiser: Vacant
Light-heavy: Zsolt Erdei (Hungary)
Super-middle: Joe Calzaghe (Great Britain)
Middle: Kelly Pavlik (USA)
Super-welter: Sergei Dzindziruk (Ukraine)
Welter: Paul Williams (USA)
Super-light: Kendall Holt (USA)
Light: Nate Campbell (USA)
Super-feather: Alex Arthur (Great Britain)
Feather: Steve Luevano (USA)
Super-bantam: Juan Manuel Lopez (Puerto Rico)
Bantam: Gerry Penalosa (Philippines)
Super-fly: Fernando Montiel (Mexico)
Fly: Omar Narvaez (Argentina)
Light-fly: Ivan Calderon (Puerto Rico)
Straw: Donnie Nietes (Philippines)

INTERNATIONAL BOXING FEDERATION (IBF)
Heavy: Wladimir Klitschko (Ukraine)
Cruiser: Steve Cunningham (USA)
Light-heavy: Antonio Tarver (USA)
Super-middle: Lucian Bute (Romania)
Middle: Arthur Abraham (Germany)
Super-welter: Verno Phillips (USA)
Welter: Joshua Clottey (Ghana)
Super-light: Paulie Malignaggi (USA)
Light: Nate Campbell (USA)
Super-feather: Cassius Baloyi (South Africa)
Feather: vacant
Super-bantam: Steve Molitor (Canada)
Bantam: Joseph Agbeko (Ghana)
Super-fly: Vic Darchinyan (Armenia)
Fly: Nonito Donaire (Philippines)
Light-fly: Ulises Solis (Mexico)
Straw: Raul Garcia (Mexico)

BRITISH CHAMPIONS
Heavy: Danny Williams
Cruiser: Vacant
Light-heavy: Dean Francis
Super-middle: Carl Froch
Middle: Wayne Elcock
Light-middle: Ryan Rhodes
Welter: Kell Brook
Light-welter: David Barnes
Light: John Murray
Super-feather: Kevin Mitchell
Feather: Paul Appleby
Super-bantam: Matthew Marsh
Bantam: Ian Napa
Super-fly: Andy Bell
Fly: Vacant

CHESS

FIDE World Champion 2007: Viswanathan Anand (Sri Lanka)
British Champion 2008: Stuart Conquest

CRICKET

TEST SERIES

SRI LANKA V ENGLAND
Kandy (1–5 December 2007): Sri Lanka beat England by 88 runs. Sri Lanka 188 and 442–8; England 281 and 261
Colombo (SSC) (9–13 December 2007): Sri Lanka drew with England. England 351 and 250–3. Sri Lanka 548–9
Galle (18–22 December 2007): Sri Lanka drew with England. Sri Lanka 499–8; England 81 and 251–6

NEW ZEALAND V ENGLAND
Hamilton (5–9 March 2008): New Zealand beat England by 189 runs. New Zealand 470 and 177–9; England 348 and 110
Wellington (13–17 March 2008): England beat New Zealand by 126 runs. England 342 and 293; New Zealand 198 and 311
Napier (22–26 March 2008): England beat New Zealand by 121 runs. England 253 and 467–7; New Zealand 168 and 431

ENGLAND V NEW ZEALAND
Lord's (15–19 May 2008): England drew with New Zealand. New Zealand 277 and 269–6; England 319
Old Trafford (23–26 May 2008): England beat New Zealand by 6 wickets. New Zealand 381 and 114; England 202 and 294–4
Trent Bridge (5–8 June 2008): England beat New Zealand by an innings and 9 runs. England 364; New Zealand 123 and 232

ENGLAND V SOUTH AFRICA
Lord's (10–14 July 2008): England drew with South Africa. England 593–8; South Africa 247 and 393–3
Headingley (18–21 July 2008): South Africa beat England by 10 wickets. England 203 and 327; South Africa 522 and 9–0
Edgbaston (30 July–2 August 2008): South Africa beat England by 5 wickets. England 231 and 363; South Africa 314 and 283–5
The Oval (7–11 August 2008): England beat South Africa by 6 wickets. South Africa 194 and 318; England 316 and 198–4

[D] ONE-DAY INTERNATIONALS

ENGLAND V INDIA
Rose Bowl (21 August 2007): England beat India by 104 runs. England 288–2; India 184
Nevil Road (24 August 2007): India beat England by 9 runs. India 329–7; England 320–8
Edgbaston (27 August 2007): England beat India by 42 runs. England 281–8; India 239
Old Trafford (30 August 2007): England beat India by 3 wickets. India 212; England 213–7
Headingley (2 September 2007): India beat England by 38 runs (Duckworth-Lewis method). India 324–6; England 242–8
The Oval (5 September 2007): India beat England by 2 wickets. England 316–6; India 317–8
Lord's (8 September 2007): England beat India by 7 wickets. India 187; England 188–3

SRI LANKA V ENGLAND
Dambulla (1 October 2007): Sri Lanka beat England by 119 runs. Sri Lanka 269–7; England 150
Dambulla (4 October 2007): England beat Sri Lanka by 65 runs. England 234–8; Sri Lanka 169
Dambulla (7 October 2007): England beat Sri Lanka by 2 wickets (Duckworth-Lewis method). Sri Lanka 164; England 164–8
Colombo (RPS) (10 October 2007): England beat Sri Lanka by 5 wickets. Sri Lanka 211–9; England 212–5
Colombo (RPS) (13 October 2007): Sri Lanka beat England by 107 runs. Sri Lanka 211; England 104

NEW ZEALAND V ENGLAND
Wellington (9 February 2008): New Zealand beat England by 6 wickets. England 130; New Zealand 131–4
Hamilton (12 February 2008): New Zealand beat England by 10 wickets (Duckworth-Lewis method). England 158; New Zealand 165–0
Auckland (15 February 2008): England beat New Zealand by 6 wickets (Duckworth-Lewis method). New Zealand 234–9; England 229–4
Napier (20 February 2008): New Zealand tied with England. England 340–6; New Zealand 340–7
Christchurch (23 February 2008): New Zealand beat England by 34 runs (Duckworth-Lewis method). England 242–7; New Zealand 213–6

ENGLAND V NEW ZEALAND
Chester-le-Street (15 June 2008): England beat New Zealand by 114 runs. England 307–5; New Zealand 193
Edgbaston (18 June 2008): No result. England 162; New Zealand 127–2
Nevil Road (21 Jun 2008): New Zealand beat England by 22 runs. New Zealand 182; England 160
The Oval (25 June 2008): New Zealand beat England by 1 wicket. England 245; New Zealand 246–9
Lord's (28 June 2008): New Zealand beat England by 51 runs. New Zealand 266–5; England 215

TWENTY20 INTERNATIONALS
Auckland (5 February 2008): England beat New Zealand by 32 runs. England 184–8; New Zealand 152
Christchurch (7 February 2007): England beat New Zealand by 50 runs. England 193–8; New Zealand 143–8
Old Trafford (13 June 2008): England beat New Zealand by nine wickets. New Zealand 123–9; England 127–1

WORLD TWENTY20

West Indies, March–April 2007

Group A

	Matches	*Won*	*Lost*	*Tied*	*N/R*	*Pts*	*Net RR*
South Africa	2	2	0	0	0	4	+0.974
Bangladesh	2	1	1	0	0	2	+0.149
West Indies	2	0	2	0	0	0	–1.233

Group B

	Matches	*Won*	*Lost*	*Tied*	*N/R*	*Pts*	*Net RR*
Australia	2	1	1	0	0	2	+0.987
England	2	1	1	0	0	2	+0.209
Zimbabwe	2	1	1	0	0	2	–1.196

Group C

	Matches	Won	Lost	Tied	N/R	Pts	Net RR
Sri Lanka	2	2	0	0	0	4	+4.721
N. Zealand	2	1	1	0	0	2	+2.396
Kenya	2	0	2	0	0	0	–8.047

Group D

	Matches	Won	Lost	Tied	N/R	Pts	Net RR
India	2	0	0	1	1	3	0.000
Pakistan	2	1	0	1	0	2	+1.275
Scotland	2	0	1	0	1	1	–2.550

Group E

	Matches	Won	Lost	Tied	N/R	Pts	Net RR
India	3	2	1	0	0	4	+0.750
N. Zealand	3	2	1	0	0	4	+0.050
South Africa	3	2	1	0	0	4	–0.116
England	3	0	3	0	0	0	–0.700

Group F

	Matches	Won	Lost	Tied	N/R	Pts	Net RR
Pakistan	3	3	0	0	0	6	+0.843
Australia	3	2	1	0	0	4	+2.256
Sri Lanka	3	1	2	0	0	2	–0.697
Bangladesh	3	0	3	0	0	0	–2.031

Semi-finals

Cape Town (22 September 2007): Pakistan beat New Zealand by 6 wickets. New Zealand 143–8; Pakistan 147–4

Durban (22 September 2007): India beat Australia by 15 runs. India 188–5; Australia 173–7

Final

Johannesburg (24 September 2007): India beat Pakistan by 5 runs. India 157–5; Pakistan 152

ENGLAND AND WALES DOMESTIC COMPETITIONS

County Championship 2007, Division 1: Sussex, 202pts; *Relegated* Warwickshire, 139pts; Worcestershire, 95pts – *Division 2:* Somerset, 266pts; *Promoted* Nottinghamshire, 214.5pts

Pro40 2007, Division 1: Worcestershire, 13pts; *Relegated* Northamptonshire, 6pts; Warwickshire, 5pts; Essex, 5pts – *Division 2:* Durham, 12pts; *Promoted* Somerset, 11pts; Middlesex, 10pts

FP Trophy final 2008: Essex beat Kent by 5 wickets. Kent 214; Essex 218–5

Twenty20 Cup final 2008: Middlesex beat Kent by 3 runs. Middlesex 187–6; Kent 184–5

OTHER INTERNATIONAL DOMESTIC CHAMPIONSHIPS

Australia: Pura Cup final 2007–8: New South Wales beat Victoria by 258 runs. New South Wales 281 and 563–8; Victoria 216 and 370. *Ford Cup final 2007–8:* Tasmania beat Victoria by 1 wicket (Duckworth-Lewis method). Victoria 158; Tasmania 131–9. *KFC Twenty20 Cup final 2007–8:* Victoria beat Western Australia by 32 runs. Victoria 203–8; Western Australia 171

Bangladesh: National League 2007–8: Khulna Division, 108pts. *National One-Day League 2007–8:* Rajshahi Division, 14pts

India: Irani Trophy final 2007–8: Rest of India beat Mumbai by 9 wickets. Mumbai 453 and 106; Rest of India 472 and 91–1. *Ranji Trophy Super League final 2007–8:* Delhi beat Uttar Pradesh by 9 wickets. Uttar Pradesh 342 and 177; Delhi 290 and 230–1. *Vijay Hazare Trophy final 2007–8:* Saurashtra beat Bengal by 6 wickets. Bengal 86; Saurashtra 89–4. *Deodhar Trophy 2007–8:* Central Zone, 17pts. *Duleep Trophy final 2007–8:* North Zone beat West Zone by 6 wickets. West Zone 274 and 231; North Zone 340 and 166–4. *Indian Premier League Twenty20 final 2008:* Rajasthan Royals beat Chennai Super Kings by 3 wickets. Chennai Super Kings 163–5; Rajasthan Royals 164–7

New Zealand: State Championship final 2007–8: Canterbury beat Wellington by 49 runs. Canterbury 215 and 221–8; Wellington 188 and 199. *State Shield final 2007–8:* Otago beat Auckland by 7 wickets. Auckland 310–7; Otago 311–3. *Twenty20 final 2007–8:* Central Districts beat Northern Districts by 5 wickets. Central Districts 150–5; Northern Districts 148–8

Pakistan: Quaid-e-Azam Trophy final 2007–8: Sui Northern Gas Pipelines Limited drew with Habib Bank Limited. Sui Northern Gas Pipelines Limited won the trophy. Sui Northern Gas Pipelines Limited 351 and 304–9; Habib Bank Limited 192 and 166–1. *ABN Amro Pentangular Cup 2007–8:* Sind, 21pts. *ABN Amro Cup final 2007–8:* Sui Northern Gas Pipelines Limited beat Habib Bank Limited by 7 wickets. Habib Bank Limited 127; Sui Northern Gas Pipelines Limited 128–3.

South Africa: SuperSport Series 2007–8: Eagles, 117.52pts. *Provincial One-Day Challenge final 2007–8:* Gauteng beat Northerns by 6 wickets (Duckworth-Lewis method). Gauteng 130–4; Northerns 132. *Pro20 Series final 2007–8:* Titans beat Dolphins by 18 runs. Titans 153–6; Dolphins 135. *Provincial Challenge final 2007–8:* Griqualand West beat Western Province by 42 runs. Griqualand West 144 and 277; Western Province 155 and 174. *Domestic Championship final 2007–8:* Titans beat Warriors by 38 runs. Titans 269–6; Warriors 231

Sri Lanka: Premier League Tournament 2007–8: Sinhalese, 129.995pts. *Premier Limited Overs Tournament final 2007–8:* Sinhalese beat Moors by 6 runs (Duckworth-Lewis method). Sinhalese 243–7; Moors 205–7. *Twenty20 Cup final 2008:* Wayamba beat Ruhuna by 31 runs. Wayamba 174–9; Ruhuna 143. *Inter-Provincial Limited-Overs tournament final 2008:* Kandurata 131–5; Wayamba 37–0. No result, trophy shared.

West Indies: Carib Challenge final 2007–8: Jamaica beat Trinidad and Tobago by 9 wickets. Trinidad and Tobago 121 and 241; Jamaica 293 and 71–1. *KFC Cup final 2007-8:* Jamaica beat Trinidad and Tobago by 28 runs. Jamaica 230; Trinidad and Tobago 202

Zimbabwe: Logan Cup 2007–8: Northerns. *Faithwear Cup 2007–8:* Easterns. *Provincial A Twenty20 final 2007-08:* Easterns beat Westerns by 7 runs. Easterns 142–9; Westerns 135

CURLING

MEN'S WORLD CHAMPIONSHIP 2008
Grand Forks, USA, April

Final: Canada beat Scotland 6–3

WOMEN'S WORLD CHAMPIONSHIP 2008
Vernon, Canada, March

Final: Canada beat China 7–4

EUROPEAN CHAMPIONSHIPS 2007
Fussen, Germany, December

Men's final: Scotland beat Norway 5–3
Women's final: Sweden beat Scotland 9–4

CYCLING

Vuelta D'Espana 2007: Denis Menchov (Russia)
Giro d'Italia 2008: Alberto Contador (Spain)
Tour de France 2008: Carlos Sastre (Spain)

WORLD ROAD RACE CHAMPIONSHIPS 2007
Stuttgart, Germany, September

MEN
Elite Time Trial: Fabian Cancellara (Switzerland)
Road Race: Paolo Bettini (Italy)

WOMEN
Elite Time Trial: Hanka Kupfernagel (Germany)
Road Race: Marta Bastianelli (Italy)

BRITISH NATIONAL ROAD RACE CHAMPIONSHIPS 2008
North Yorkshire, June

MEN
Road Race: Rob Hayles

WOMEN
Road Race: Nicole Cooke

WORLD TRACK CHAMPIONSHIPS 2008
Manchester, Great Britain, March–April

MEN
Points Race: Vasili Kiryienka (Belarus)
Olympic Sprint: Chris Hoy (Great Britain)
1km Time Trial: Teun Mulder (Netherlands)
Individual Pursuit: Bradley Wiggins (Great Britain)
Scratch Race: Aliaksandr Lisouski (Belarus)
Keirin: Chris Hoy (Great Britain)
Team Pursuit: Great Britain
Madison: Mark Cavendish and Bradley Wiggins (Great Britain)
Team Sprint: France
Omnium: Hayden Godfrey (New Zealand)

WOMEN
Points Race: Marrianne Vos (Netherlands)
500m Time Trial: Lisandra Guerra Rodriguez (Cuba)
Individual Pursuit: Rebecca Romero (Great Britain)
Scratch Race: Eleonora van Dijk (Netherlands)
Keirin: Jennie Reed (USA)
Sprint: Victoria Pendleton (Great Britain)
Team Sprint: Great Britain
Team Pursuit: Great Britain

DARTS

BDO World Championship 2008: Mark Webster (Wales) beat Simon Whitlock (Australia) 7–5
PDC World Championship 2007–8: John Part (Canada) beat Kirk Shepherd (England) 7–2

EQUESTRIANISM

Burghley Horse Trials 2007: William Fox-Pitt (Great Britain) on Parkmore Ed
Badminton Horse Trials 2008: Nicolas Touzaint (France) on Hildago de L'Ile
British Open Horse Trials 2008 (Gatcombe Park): Ruth Edge (Great Britain) on Mayhem III

ETON FIVES

Amateur Championship (Kinnaird Cup) final 2008: James Toop and Howard Wiseman beat Tom Dunbar and Peter Dunbar 3–2
Alan Barber Cup final 2008: Old Olavians beat Old Harrovians 2–1
County Championship final 2008: Hertfordshire beat Middlesex 3–0
Schools' Championship 2008: Highgate 1 beat Shrewsbury 1 3–0
Preparatory Schools' Tournament 2008: Highgate 1 beat Highgate 2 2–0

FENCING

WORLD CHAMPIONSHIPS 2007
St Petersburg, Russia, September–October

MEN
Individual Foil: Peter Joppich (Germany)
Individual Epée: Krisztian Kulcsar (Hungary)
Individual Sabre: Stanislav Pozdniakov (Russia)
Team Foil: France
Team Epée: France
Team Sabre: Hungary

WOMEN
Individual Foil: Valentina Vezzali (Italy)
Individual Epée: Britta Heidemann (Germany)
Individual Sabre: Elena Netchaeva (Russia)
Team Foil: Poland
Team Epée: France
Team Sabre: France

EUROPEAN CHAMPIONSHIPS 2008
Kiev, Ukraine, July

MEN
Individual Foil: Andrea Cassara (Italy)
Individual Epée: Geza Imre (Hungary)
Individual Sabre: Aliaksandr Buikevich (Belarus)
Team Foil: Poland
Team Epée: France
Team Sabre: Russia

WOMEN
Individual Foil: Adeline Wuilleme (France)
Individual Epée: Adrienn Hormay (Hungary)
Individual Sabre: Sophia Velikaia (Russia)
Team Foil: Russia
Team Epée: Romania
Team Sabre: Poland

BRITISH CHAMPIONSHIPS 2008
Sheffield, July

MEN
Individual Foil: David Riseley
Individual Epée: Jon Willis

Individual Sabre: Chris Buxton
Team Foil: Sussex House A
Team Epée: Stockport
Team Sabre: Laszlo's Fencing

WOMEN
Individual Foil: Anna Bentley
Individual Epée: Hannah Lawrence
Individual Sabre: Chrystall Nicoll
Team Foil: Salle Stretton
Team Epée: LTFC Students
Team Sabre: Scimitar A

GOLF (MEN)

THE MAJOR CHAMPIONSHIPS 2008
US Masters (Augusta, 10–13 April): Trevor Immelman (South Africa), 280
US Open (Torrey Pines, 12–15 June): Tiger Woods (USA), 283
The Open (Royal Birkdale, 17–20 July): Padraig Harrington (Ireland), 283
US PGA Championship (Oakland Hills, 7–10 August): Padraig Harrington (Ireland), 277

WORLD RANKINGS
as at 1 August 2008

1. Tiger Woods (USA); 2. Phil Mickelson (USA); 3. Padraig Harrington (Ireland); 4. Vijay Singh (Fiji); 5. Ernie Els (South Africa)

PGA EUROPEAN TOUR 2007
Scandinavian Masters (Arlandastad, Sweden): Mikko Ilolen (Finland), 274
KLM Open (Kennemer, Netherlands): Ross Fisher (England), 268
Johnnie Walker Championship (Gleneagles, Scotland): Marc Warren (Scotland), 280
Omega European Masters (Crans-sur-Sierre, Switzerland): Brett Rumford (Australia), 268
Mercedes Benz Championship (Gut Laerchenhof, Germany): Soren Hansen (Denmark), 271
British Masters (The Belfry, England): Lee Westwood (England), 273
Alfred Dunhill Links Championship (St Andrews, Carnoustie and Kingsbarns, Scotland): Nick Dougherty (England), 270
HSBC World Match-Play Championship (Wentworth, England): Ernie Els (South Africa)
Open De Madrid Valle Romano (Real Sociedad Hipica Espanola, Spain): Mads Vibe-Hastrup (Denmark), 272
Portugal Masters (Vilamoura): Steve Webster (England), 263
Mallorca Classic (Pula): Gregory Bourdy (France), 268
Volvo Masters (Valderrama, Spain): Justin Rose (England), 283

TEAM CHAMPIONSHIPS
Seve Trophy (Heritage, Ireland): Great Britain & Ireland beat Europe, $16\frac{1}{2}$–$11\frac{1}{2}$
Omega Mission Hills World Cup (Mission Hills, China): Scotland

EUROPEAN TOUR ORDER OF MERIT 2007
1. Justin Rose *(England)*; 2. Ernie Els *(South Africa)*; 3. Padraig Harrington *(Ireland)*; 4. Henrik Stenson *(Sweden)*; 5. Niclas Fasth *(Sweden)*

PGA EUROPEAN TOUR 2008
Champions' Tournament (Sheshan, China): Phil Mickelson (USA), 278
Hong Kong Open (Hong Kong): Miguel Angel Jimenez (Spain), 265
Mastercard Masters (Huntingdale, Australia): Aaron Baddeley (Australia), 275
New Zealand Open (The Hills): Richard Finch (England), 274
Afred Dunhill Championship (Leopard Creek, South Africa): John Bickerton (England), 275
South African Airways Open (Pearl Valley): James Kingston (South Africa), 284
Joburg Open (Royal Johannesburg and Kensington): Richard Sterne (South Africa), 271
Abu Dhabi Golf Championship (Abu Dhabi): Martin Kaymer (Germany), 273
Qatar Masters (Doha): Adam Scott (Australia), 268
Dubai Desert Classic (Emirates): Tiger Woods (USA), 274
Indian Masters (Delhi): SSP Chowrasia (India), 279
Indonesia Open (Cengkareng): Felipe Aguilar (Chile), 262
WGC – Accenture Match Play (Gallery, Arizona): Tiger Woods (USA)
Johnnie Walker Classic (DLF, India): Mark Brown (New Zealand), 270
Malaysian Open (Kota Permai): Arjun Atwal (India), 270
Ballantine's Championship (Jeju Island, Rep. of Korea): Graeme McDowell (Northern Ireland), 264
WGC – CA Championship (Doral Resort, Florida): Geoff Ogilvy (Australia), 271
Madeira Island Open (Santo da Serra): Alastair Forsyth (Scotland), 273
Open de Andalucia (Aloha, Spain): Thomas Levet (France), 272
Estoril Open de Portugal (Oitavos Dunes): Gregory Bourdy (France), 266
China Open (Beijing CBD International): Damien McGrane (Ireland), 278
Asian Open (Shanghai Pudong): Darren Clarke (Northern Ireland), 280
Open de Espana (Real Club Sevilla): Peter Lawrie (Ireland), 273
Italian Open (Castello di Tolcinasco): Hennie Otto (South Africa), 263
Irish Open (Adare Manor): Richard Finch (England), 278
BMW PGA Championship (Wentworth, England): Miguel Angel Jimenez (Spain), 277
Wales Open (Celtic Manor): Scott Strange (Australia), 262
Bank Austria Open (Fontana, Austria): Jeev Milkha Singh (India), 198
Open de St Omer (Aa St Omer, France): David Dixon (England), 279
BMW International Open (Munchen Eichenried, Germany): Martin Kaymer (Germany), 273
Open de France (Le Golf National): Pablo Larrazabal (Spain), 269
European Open (London Club): Ross Fisher (England), 268
Scottish Open (Loch Lomond): Graeme McDowell (Northern Ireland), 271
WGC – Bridgestone Invitational (Firestone, USA): Vijay Singh (Fiji), 270
SAS Masters (Arlandastad, Sweden): Peter Hanson (Sweden), 271
KLM Open (Kennemer, Netherlands): Darren Clarke (Great Britain), 264
Johnnie Walker Championship (Gleneagles, Scotland): Gregory Harret (France), 278

AMATEUR CHAMPIONSHIPS 2008
British Amateur Championship (Turnberry): Reinier Saxton (Netherlands)
English Amateur Championship (Woodhall Spa): Todd Adcock (England)
Brabazon Trophy (English Open Strokeplay) (Trevose): Steven Uzzell (England), 197
Scottish Amateur Championship (Carnoustie): Callum Macaulay (Scotland)
Scottish Open Strokeplay (The Duke's St Andrews): Wallace Booth (Scotland), 210
Welsh Amateur Championship (Royal Porthcawl): Ben Westgate (Wales)
Welsh Open Strokeplay (Conwy): Chris Wood (England), 289
Irish Amateur Open Championship (Royal Dublin): Pedro Figueiredo (Portugal), 278
Irish Amateur Close Championship (Belvoir Park): Paul O'Hanlon (Ireland)
Lytham Trophy (Royal Lytham Golf Club): Matthew Haines (England), 284
Berkshire Trophy (The Berkshire): Farren Keenan (England), 279

TEAM CHAMPIONSHIPS 2007
Walker Cup: USA beat Great Britain and Ireland $12\frac{1}{2}$–$11\frac{1}{2}$

GOLF (WOMEN)

THE MAJOR CHAMPIONSHIPS 2008
Kraft Nabisco Championship (Mission Hills Country Club, USA, 3–6 April): Lorena Ochoa (Mexico), 277
US Women's Open (Interlachen, 26–29 June): Inbee Park (Rep. of Korea), 283
LPGA Championship (Bulle Rock, USA, 5–8 June): Yani Tseng (Taiwan), 276
Women's British Open (Sunningdale, 31 July–3 August): Ji-Yai Shin (Rep. of Korea), 270

EUROPEAN LPGA TOUR 2007
Scandinavian TPC (Barseback, Sweden): Catriona Matthew (Scotland), 279
Wales Ladies' Championship of Europe (Machynys Peninsular): Joanne Mills (Australia), 282
SAS Masters (Losby, Norway): Suzann Pettersen (Norway), 204
Finnair Masters (Helsinki): Bettina Hauert, 207
Nykredit Masters (Helsingor, Denmark): Lisa Hall (England), 275
Scottish Open (Carrick Cameron House): Sophie Gustafson (Sweden), 210
UNIQA Open (Fohrenwald-Wiener Neustadt, Austria): Laura Davies (England), 200
Madrid Masters (Casino Club, Spain): Martina Eberl (Germany), 206
EMAAR-MGF Masters (Eagleton, India): Gwladys Nocera (France), 281
Dubai Masters (Emirates): Annika Sorenstam (Sweden), 278

EUROPEAN LPGA TOUR ORDER OF MERIT 2007
1. Sophie Gustafson *(Sweden)*; 2. Bettina Hauert *(Germany)*; 3 Gwladys Nocera *(France)*; 4. Trish Johnson *(England)*; 5. Maria Hjorth (Sweden*)*

TEAM CHAMPIONSHIP 2007
Solheim Cup: USA beat Europe 16–12

EUROPEAN LPGA TOUR 2008
Australian Open (Kingston Heath): Karrie Webb (Australia), 284
ANZ Ladies' Masters (Royal Pines, Australia): Lisa Hall (England), 203
Catalonia 2008 (Emporda, Spain): Lotta Wahlin (Sweden), 133
Open de Espana (Panoramica): Emma Zackrisson (Sweden), 281
Scottish Open (Carrick Cameron House): Gwladys Nocera (France), 208
Turkish Open (National): Lotta Wahlin (Sweden), 285
Swiss Open (Gerre Losone): Suzann Pettersen (Norway), 194
German Open (Gut Hausern): Amy Yang (Rep. of Korea), 267
ABN AMRO Open (Eindhovensche, Netherlands): Gwladys Nocera (France), 203
Open de Portugal (Quinta de Cima): Anne-Lise Caudal (France), 203
Tenerife Open (Costa Adeje): Rebecca Hudson (England), 278
English Open (The Oxfordshire): Rebecca Hudson (England), 206
Irish Open (Portmarnock): Suzann Pettersen (Norway), 205
Italian Open (Argentario): Martina Eberl (Germany), 275
Evian Masters (Evian Les Bains, France): Helen Alfredsson (Sweden), 273
Scandinavian TPC (Frosaker, Sweden): Amy Yang (Rep. of Korea), 202
Wales Championship of Europe (Machynys Peninsula): Lotta Wahlin (Sweden), 209
SAS Masters (Haga Golf Course, Norway): Gwladys Nocera (France), 203
Finnair Masters (Helsinki, Finland): Minea Blomqvist (Finland), 202

TEAM CHAMPIONSHIPS
World Cup (Gary Player, South Africa): Philippines, 198
European Cup (La Sella, Spain): England

AMATEUR CHAMPIONSHIPS 2008
British Open Championship (North Berwick): Anna Nordqvist (Sweden)
Ladies' British Open Amateur Strokeplay Championship (Malone): Roseanne Niven (Scotland), 288
English Close Amateur Championship (Ganton): Hannah Barwood (England)
English Strokeplay Championship: Jodi Ewart (England), 285
Helen Holm (Scottish Open Strokeplay Championship) (Troon): Barbara Genuini (France), 214
Scottish Ladies Close Amateur Championship (Moray): Michele Thomson (Scotland)
Welsh Open Strokeplay (Pyle and Kenfig): Rhian Wyn Thomas (Wales), 228
Welsh Close Championship (Monmouthshire): Kirsty O'Connor (Wales)
Irish Open Strokeplay Championship (Elm Park): Breanne Loucks (Wales), 214
Irish Close Championship (Westport): Leona Maguire (Ireland)

GREYHOUND RACING

2007
St Leger (Wimbledon): Spiridon Louis

2008
The Regency (Hove): Flying Winner
Pall Mall (Oxford): Spears Tarquynn
Golden Jacket (Crayford): Shelbourne Merc
Grand National (Wimbledon): Kildare Lark
The Derby (Wimbledon): Loyal Honcho

GYMNASTICS

WORLD CHAMPIONSHIPS 2007
Stuttgart, Germany, September

MEN
Team: China
Overall: Wei Yang (China)
Individual Apparatus Champions
Floor: Diego Hypolito (Brazil)
Pommel Horse: Qin Xiao (China)
Still Rings: Yibing Chen (China)
Vault: Leszek Blanik (Poland)
Parallel Bars: Mitja Petkovsek (Slovenia)
High Bar: Fabian Hambuechen (Germany)

WOMEN
Team: USA
Overall: Shawn Johnson (United States)
Individual Apparatus Champions
Floor: Shawn Johnson (United States)
Beam: Anastasia Liukin (United States)
Vault: Fei Cheng (China)
Uneven Bars: Ksenia Semenova (Russia)

MEN'S EUROPEAN CHAMPIONSHIPS 2008
Lausanne, Switzerland, May

Team: Russia
Individual Apparatus Champions
Floor: Anton Golotsutskov (Russia)
Pommel Horse: Krisztian Berki (Hungary)
Still Rings: Yuri van Gelder (Netherlands)
Vault: Leszek Blanik (Poland)
Parallel Bars: Mitja Petkovsek (Slovenia)
High Bar: Fabian Hambuechen (Germany)

WOMEN'S EUROPEAN CHAMPIONSHIPS 2008
Clermont-Ferrand, France, April

Team: Romania
Individual Apparatus Champions
Floor: Sandra R Izbasa (Romania)
Beam: Ksenia Semenova (Russia)
Vault: Oksana Chusovitina (Germany)
Uneven Bars: Ksenia Semenova (Russia)

BRITISH MEN'S CHAMPIONSHIPS 2007
Wigan, November

Overall Champion: Daniel Keatings
Individual Apparatus Champions
Floor: Daniel Keatings
Pommel Horse: Louis Smith
Still Rings: Luke Folwell
Vault: Luke Folwell
Parallel Bars: Daniel Keatings
High Bar: Daniel Keatings

BRITISH WOMEN'S CHAMPIONSHIPS 2008
Guildford, June

Overall Champion: Beckie Downie
Individual Apparatus Champions
Floor: Beckie Downie
Beam: Beckie Downie
Vault: Beckie Downie
Assymetric Bars: Elizabeth Tweddle

HOCKEY

MEN
English Hockey League 2007–8: Premier Division: Reading, 46pts; *Division One:* Southgate, 42pts; *National North Division:* University of Birmingham, 51pts; *National South Division:* University of Exeter, 53pts
English Hockey League Indoor Championship final 2008: Loughborough Students beat East Grinstead 5–4
English Hockey League Cup final 2007–8: Beeston beat Bowdon 4–3
County Championship final 2008: Cheshire beat Yorkshire 2–1

WOMEN
English Hockey League 2007–8: Premier Division: Slough, 42pts; *Division One:* Trojans, 43pts; *National North Division:* Cannock, 58pts; *National South Division:* Staines, 51pts
English Hockey League Indoor Championship final 2008: Slough beat Bowden Hightown 5–2
English Hockey League Cup final 2007–8: Leicester beat Slough 1–0
County Champions 2008: Cumbria

HORSE RACING

NATIONAL HUNT

HENNESSY GOLD CUP
(1957) Newbury, 3 miles and about 2½ f

2004 Celestial Gold (6y), T. Murphy
2005 Trabolgan (7y), M. Fitzgerald
2006 State of Play (6y), P. Moloney
2007 Denman (7y), S. Thomas

TINGLE CREEK CHASE
(1957) Sandown, 2 miles

2004 Moscow Flyer (10y), B. Geraghty
2005 Kauto Star (5y), M. Fitzgerald
2006 Kauto Star (6y), R. Walsh
2007 Twist Magic (5y), S. Thomas

KING GEORGE VI CHASE
(1937) Kempton, about 3 miles

2004 Kicking King (6y), B. Geraghty
2005 Kicking King (7y), B. Geraghty
2006 Kauto Star (6y), R. Walsh
2007 Kauto Star (7y), R. Walsh

CHAMPION HURDLE
(1927) Cheltenham, 2 miles and about ½ f

2005 Hardy Eustace (8y), C. O'Dwyer
2006 Brave Inca (8y), T. McCoy
2007 Sublimity (7y), P. Carberry
2008 Katchit (5y), R. Thornton

QUEEN MOTHER CHAMPION CHASE
(1959) Cheltenham, about 2 miles

2005 Moscow Flyer (11y), B. Geraghty
2006 Newmill (8y), A. McNamara
2007 Voy Por Ustedes (6y), R. Thornton
2008 Master Minded (5y), R. Walsh

CHELTENHAM GOLD CUP
(1924) 3 miles and about 2½ f

2005 Kicking King (7y), B. Geraghty
2006 War Of Attrition (7y), C. O'Dwyer
2007 Kauto Star (7y), R. Walsh
2008 Denman (8y), S. Thomas

GRAND NATIONAL
(1837) Liverpool, 4 miles and about 4 f

2005 Hedgehunter (9y), R. Walsh
2006 Numbersixvalverde (10y), N. Madden
2007 Silver Birch (10y), R. Power
2008 Comply or Die (9y), T. Murphy

BET365 GOLD CUP
(1957) Sandown, 3 miles and about 5 f

2005 Jack High (10y), G. Cotter
2006 Lacdoudal (7y), R. Johnson
2007 Hot Weld (8y), G. Lee
2008 Monkerhostin (11y), R. Johnson

STATISTICS
WINNING NATIONAL HUNT TRAINERS 2007–8

P. F. Nicholls	£3,507,643
D. E. Pipe	2,349,040
A. King	1,977,315
P. J. Hobbs	1,234,117
N. A. Twiston-Davies	1,213,350
N. J. Henderson	989,048
J. O'Neill	968,321
J. Howard Johnson	798,236
Miss V. Williams	696,738
G. L. Moore	539,257

WINNING NATIONAL HUNT JOCKEYS 2007–8

	1st	*2nd*	*3rd*	*Unpl.*	*Total mts*
A. P. McCoy	140	99	80	329	648
R. Johnson	122	109	101	448	780
R. Thornton	105	91	63	339	598
P. J. Brennan	104	98	72	353	627
G. Lee	89	81	71	358	599
S. Thomas	88	64	61	350	563
J. Moore	75	56	57	260	448
M. Fitzgerald	71	43	35	182	331
T. J. O'Brien	70	70	64	350	554
T. J. Murphy	70	56	50	326	502

The above statistics have been provided by *Timeform*, publishers of the *Racehorses* and *Chasers and Hurdlers* annuals

THE FLAT

THE CLASSICS

ONE THOUSAND GUINEAS
(1814) Rowley Mile, Newmarket, for three-year-old fillies

Year	*Winner*	*Betting*	*Owner*	*Jockey*	*Trainer*	*Runners*
2004	Attraction	11–2	Duke of Roxburghe	K. Darley	M. Johnston	16
2005	Virginia Waters	12–1	Mrs J. Magnier and M. Tabor	K. Fallon	A. O'Brien	20
2006	Speciosa	10–1	M. H. Sly	M. Fenton	Mrs P. Sly	13
2007	Finsceal Beo	5–4	M. A. Ryan	K. Manning	J. Bolger	21
2008	Natagora	11–4	Stefan Friborg	C-P Lemaire	P. Bary	15

TWO THOUSAND GUINEAS
(1809) Rowley Mile, Newmarket, for three-year-olds

Year	*Winner*	*Betting*	*Owner*	*Jockey*	*Trainer*	*Runners*
2004	Haafhd	11–2	Sheikh Hamdan Al Maktoum	R. Hills	B. Hills	14
2005	Footstepsinthesand	13–2	Mrs J. Magnier and M. Tabor	K. Fallon	A. O'Brien	19
2006	George Washington	6–4	Mrs J. Magnier and M. Tabor	K. Fallon	A. O'Brien	14
2007	Cockney Rebel	25–1	P. Cunningham	O. Peslier	G. Huffer	24
2008	Henrythenavigator	11–1	Mrs J. Magnier	J. Murtagh	A. O'Brien	15

THE DERBY
(1780) Epsom, 1 mile and about 4 f, for three-year-olds
The first winner was Sir Charles Bunbury's Diomed in 1780. The owners with the record number of winners are Lord Egremont, who won in 1782, 1804, 1805, 1807, 1826 (also won five Oaks); and the late Aga Khan, who won in 1930, 1935, 1936, 1948, 1952. Other winning owners are: Duke of Grafton (1802, 1809, 1810, 1815); Mr J. Bowes (1835, 1843, 1852, 1853); Sir J. Hawley (1851, 1858, 1859, 1868); the 1st Duke of Westminster (1880, 1882, 1886, 1899); and Sir Victor Sassoon (1953, 1957, 1958, 1960).
The Derby was run at Newmarket in 1915–18 and 1940–5.

Year	*Winner*	*Betting*	*Owner*	*Jockey*	*Trainer*	*Runners*
2004	North Light	7–2	Exors of the late Lord Weinstock	K. Fallon	Sir Michael Stoute	14
2005	Motivator	3–1	Royal Ascot Racing Club	J. Murtagh	M. Bell	13
2006	Sir Percy	6–1	A. E. Pakenham	M. Dwyer	M. Tregoning	18
2007	Authorized	5–4	Saleh Al Homeizi and Imad Al Sagar	L. Dettori	P. Chapple-Hyam	17
2008	New Approach	5–1	H. R. H. Princess Haya of Jordan	K. Manning	J. Bolger	16

THE OAKS
(1779) Epsom, 1 mile and about 4 f, for three-year-old fillies

Year	*Winner*	*Betting*	*Owner*	*Jockey*	*Trainer*	*Runners*
2004	Ouija Board	7–2	Lord Derby	K. Fallon	E. Dunlop	7
2005	Eswarah	11–4	Sheikh Hamdan Al Maktoum	R. Hills	M. Jarvis	12
2006	Alexandrova	9–4	Mrs J. Magnier and M. Tabor	K. Fallon	A. O'Brien	10
2007	Light Shift	13–2	Niarchos family	T. Durcan	H. Cecil	14
2008	Look Here	33–1	J. H. Richmond-Watson	S. Sanders	R. M. Beckett	16

ST LEGER
(1776) Doncaster, 1 mile and about 6 f, for three-year-olds (2006 run at York)

Year	*Winner*	*Betting*	*Owner*	*Jockey*	*Trainer*	*Runners*
2003	Brian Boru	5–4	Mrs J. Magnier	J. Spencer	A. O'Brien	12
2004	Rule Of Law	3–1	Godolphin	K. McEvoy	Saeed bin Suroor	9
2005	Scorpion	10–11	Mrs J. Magnier and M. Tabor	L. Dettori	A. O'Brien	6
2006	Sixties Icon	11–8	Mrs S. Roy	L. Dettori	J. Noseda	11
2007	Lucarno	7–2	Mr G. Strawbridge	J. Fortune	J. H. M. Gosden	10

RESULTS

CAMBRIDGESHIRE HANDICAP
(1839) Newmarket, 1 mile and 1 f

2004 Spanish Don (6y), L. Keniry
2005 Blue Monday (4y), S. Drowne
2006 Formal Decree (3y), J. Spencer
2007 Pipedreamer (3y), J. Fortune

PRIX DE L'ARC DE TRIOMPHE
(1920) Longchamp, 1½ miles

2004 Bago (3y), T. Gillet
2005 Hurricane Run (3y), K. Fallon
2006 Rail Link (3y), S. Pasquier
2007 Dylan Thomas (4y), K. Fallon

CESAREWITCH
(1839) Newmarket, 2 miles and about 2 f

2004 Contact Dancer (5y), R. Ffrench
2005 Sergeant Cecil (6y), A. Munro
2006 Detroit City (4y), J. Spencer
2007 Leg Spinner (6y), J. Murtagh

CHAMPION STAKES
(1877) Newmarket, 1 mile and 2 f

2004 Haafhd (3y), R. Hills
2005 David Junior (3y), J. Spencer
2006 Pride (6y), C-P. Lemaire
2007 Literato (3y), C-P Lemaire

DUBAI WORLD CUP
(1996) Dubai, 1 mile and 2 f

2005 Roses In May (5y), J. Velazquez
2006 Electrocutionist (5y), L. Dettori
2007 Invasor (5y), F. Jara
2008 Curlin (4y), R. Albarado

LINCOLN HANDICAP
(1965) Doncaster, 1 mile

2005 Stream Of Gold (5y), R. Winston
2006 Blythe Knight (6y), G. Gibbons
2007 Very Wise (5y), J. Fanning
2008 Smokey Oakey (4y), J. Quinn

JOCKEY CLUB STAKES
(1894) Newmarket, 1½ miles

2005 Alkaased (5y), J. Fortune
2006 Shirocco (5y), C. Soumillon
2007 Sixties Icon (4y), L. Dettori
2008 Getaway (5y), S. Pasquier

PRIX DU JOCKEY CLUB
(1836) Chantilly, 1 mile and about 2½ f, for three-year-olds

2005 Shamardal, L. Dettori
2006 Darsi, C. Soumillon
2007 Lawman, L. Dettori
2008 Vision D'Etat, I. Mendizabal

ASCOT GOLD CUP
(1807) Ascot, 2 miles and about 4 f

2005 Westerner (6y), O. Peslier
2006 Yeats (5y), K. Fallon
2007 Yeats (6y), M. J. Kinane
2008 Yeats (7y), J. Murtagh

IRISH DERBY
(1866) Curragh, 1½ miles, for three-year-olds

2005 Hurricane Run, K. Fallon
2006 Dylan Thomas, K. Fallon
2007 Soldier of Fortune, J. A. Heffernan
2008 Frozen Fire, J. A. Heffernan

ECLIPSE STAKES
(1886) Sandown, 1 mile and about 2 f

2005 Oratorio (3y), K. Fallon
2006 David Junior (4y), J. Spencer
2007 Notnowcato, (5y), R. Moore
2008 Mount Nelson (4y), J. Murtagh

KING GEORGE VI AND QUEEN ELIZABETH DIAMOND STAKES
(1952) Ascot, 1 mile and about 4 f

2005 Azamour (4y), M. J. Kinane
2006 Hurricane Run (4y), C. Soumillon
2007 Dylan Thomas (4y), J. P. Murtagh
2008 Duke of Marmalade (4y), J. Murtagh

GOODWOOD CUP
(1812) Goodwood, about 2 miles

2005 Distinction (6y), M. J. Kinane
2006 Yeats (5y), M. J. Kinane
2007 Alegretto (4y), R. Moore
2008 Yeats (7y), J. Murtagh

STATISTICS
WINNING FLAT OWNERS 2007

Godolphin	£1,561,810
Hamdan Al Maktoum	1,548,259
Saleh Al Homeizi & Imad Al Sagar	1,368,997
Cheveley Park Stud	1,185,880
Mrs J. Magnier & M. Tabor	907,088
Mr D. Smith, Mrs J. Magnier & M. Tabor	845,873
Sheikh Mohammed	697,730
K. Abdulla	689,171
Jaber Abdullah	604,957
Mr G. Strawbridge	507,972

WINNING FLAT TRAINERS 2007

A. P. O'Brien	£3,267,317
Sir Michael Stoute	2,400,234
R. Hannon	1,867,496
P. W. Chapple-Hyam	1,830,729
B. W. Hills	1,641,157
Saeed bin Suroor	1,561,810
M. Johnston	1,552,001
M. R. Channon	1,525,332
J. H. M. Gosden	1,486,640
R. A. Fahey	1,041,983

WINNING FLAT SIRES 2007

	Races won	*Stakes*
Montjeu by Sadler's Wells	47	£2,011,030
Danehill by Danzig	44	1,889,748
Pivotal by Polar Falcon	89	1,145,898
Galileo by Sadler's Wells	57	1,144,090
Sadler's Wells by Northern Dancer	55	1,134,212
Danehill Dancer by Danehill	75	1,128,703
Royal Applause by Waajib	86	869,726
Rock of Gibraltar by Danehill	35	835,329
Dansili by Danehill	78	811,993
Acclamation by Royal Applause	35	766,558

WINNING FLAT JOCKEYS 2007

	1st	*2nd*	*3rd*	*Unpl.*	*Total mts*
S. Sanders	213	167	147	717	1,244
J. P. Spencer	207	151	119	563	1,040
N. Callan	170	155	132	679	1,136
R. Hughes	139	115	108	506	868
R. L. Moore	128	100	72	375	675
C. Catlin	112	119	114	947	1,292
J. Fortune	109	83	92	435	719
S. Drowne	106	104	91	669	970
T. Durcan	96	96	74	527	793
D. O'Neill	92	92	107	648	939

ICE HOCKEY

MEN'S WORLD CHAMPIONSHIP 2008

Quebec City, Canada, May
Final: Russia beat Canada 5–4

WOMEN'S WORLD CHAMPIONSHIP 2008
Harbin, China, April

Final: USA beat Canada 4–3

DOMESTIC COMPETITIONS
Elite League Champions 2007–8: Coventry Blaze
Play-off Champions 2008: Sheffield Steelers
Challenge Cup final 2008: Nottingham Panthers beat Sheffield Steelers 9–7

NATIONAL HOCKEY LEAGUE
Stanley Cup final 2007–8: Detroit Red Wings beat Pittsburgh Penguins 4–2

ICE SKATING

WORLD CHAMPIONSHIPS 2008
Gothenburg, Sweden, March

Men: Jeffrey Buttle (Canada)
Women: Mao Asada (Japan)
Pairs: Aliona Savchenko and Robin Szolkowy (Germany)
Ice Dance: Isabelle Delobel and Olivier Schoenfelder (France)

EUROPEAN CHAMPIONSHIPS 2008
Zagreb, Croatia, January

Men: Tomas Verner (Czech Republic)
Women: Carolina Kostner (Italy)
Pairs: Aliona Savchenko and Robin Szolkowy (Germany)
Ice Dance: Oksana Domnina and Maxim Shabalin (Russia)

BRITISH CHAMPIONSHIPS 2008
Sheffield, January

Men: Elliot Hilton
Women: Jenna McCorkell
Pairs: Stacey Kemp and David King
Ice Dance: Sinead Kerr and John Kerr

JUDO

EUROPEAN CHAMPIONSHIPS 2008
Sarajevo, Bosnia-Hercegovina, May

MEN
Heavyweight (over 100kg): Aleksandar Petkovic (Serbia)
Light-heavyweight (100kg): Novica Milovic (Serbia)
Middleweight (90kg): Nikola Nikolic (Serbia)
Welterweight (81kg): Uros Nenkovic (Serbia)
Lightweight (73kg): Pedro Guedes Ferreira Lucio (Brazil)
Junior Lightweight (66kg): Michael Popiel (Canada)
Bantamweight (60kg): Matjaz Trbovc (Slovenia)

WOMEN
Heavyweight (over 78kg): Ekaterina Sheremetova (Russia)
Light-heavyweight (78kg): Lea Murko (Slovenia)
Middleweight (70kg): Margarita Gurtsieva (Russia)
Welterweight (63kg): Tina Razinger (Slovenia)
Lightweight (57kg): Dijana Moric (Serbia)
Junior Lightweight (52kg): Tatjana Trivic (Serbia)
Bantamweight (48kg): Kelmendli Majlinda (Albania)

BRITISH OPEN CHAMPIONSHIPS 2008
Crawley, May

MEN
Heavyweight (over 100kg): Matthias Schmunk (Germany)
Light-heavyweight (100kg): Ricky Turner (Great Britain)
Middleweight (90kg): Victor Semenov (Russia)
Welter (81kg): Matthew Purssey (Great Britain)
Lightweight (73kg): Colin Oates (Great Britain)
Junior Lightweight (66kg): Sugoi Uriarte (Spain)
Bantamweight (60kg): Ashley McKenzie (Great Britain)

WOMEN
Heavyweight (over 78kg): Sarah Adlington (Great Britain)
Light-heavyweight (78kg): Sian Wilson (Great Britain)
Middleweight (70kg): Elisabeth Greve (Germany)
Welter (63kg): Hilde Drexler (Austria)
Lightweight (57kg): Yahaira Aguirre (Spain)
Junior Lightweight (52kg): Samantha Clark (Great Britain)
Bantamweight (48kg): Bianca Ockedahl (Canada)

MOTORCYCLING

MOTOGP 2007
San Marino (Misano): Casey Stoner (Australia), Ducati
Portuguese (Estoril): Valentino Rossi (Italy), Yamaha
Japanese (Motegi): Loris Capirossi (Italy), Ducati
Australian (Phillip Island): Casey Stoner (Australia), Ducati
Malaysian (Sepang): Casey Stoner (Australia), Ducati
Spanish (Valencia): Dani Pedrosa (Spain), Honda
Riders' Championship 2007: 1. Casey Stoner (Australia), Ducati, 367pts; 2. Dani Pedrosa (Spain), Honda, 242pts; 3. Valentino Rossi (Italy), Yamaha, 241pts

MOTOGP 2008
Qatari (Losail): Casey Stoner (Australia), Ducati
Spanish (Jerez): Dani Pedrosa (Spain), Honda
Portuguese (Estoril): Jorge Lorenzo (Spain), Yamaha
Chinese (Shanghai): Valentino Rossi (Italy), Yamaha
French (Le Mans): Valentino Rossi (Italy), Yamaha
Italian (Mugello): Valentino Rossi (Italy), Yamaha
Catalunyan (Montmelo): Dani Pedrosa (Spain), Honda
British (Donington Park): Casey Stoner (Australia), Ducati
Dutch (Assen): Casey Stoner (Australia), Ducati
German (Sachsenring): Casey Stoner (Australia), Ducati
United States (Laguna Seca): Valentino Rossi (Italy), Yamaha
Czech Republic (Brno): Valentino Rossi (Italy), Yamaha
San Marino (Misano): Valentino Rossi (Italy), Yamaha

250CC GRAND PRIX 2007
San Marino (Misano): Jorge Lorenzo (Spain), Aprilia
Portuguese (Estoril): Alvaro Bautista (Spain), Aprilia
Japanese (Motegi): Mika Kallio (Finland), KTM
Australian (Phillip Island): Jorge Lorenzo (Spain), Aprilia
Malaysian (Sepang): Hiroshi Aoyama (Japan), KTM
Spanish (Valencia): Mika Kallio (Finland), KTM
Riders' Championship 2007: 1. Jorge Lorenzo (Spain), Aprilia, 312pts; 2. Andrea Dovizioso (Italy), Honda, 260pts; 3. Alex De Angelis (San Marino), Aprilia, 235pts

250CC GRAND PRIX 2008
Qatari (Losail): Mattia Pasini (Italy), Aprilia
Spanish (Jerez): Mika Kallio (Finland), KTM
Portuguese (Estoril): Alvaro Bautista (Spain), Aprilia
Chinese (Shanghai): Mika Kallio (Finland), KTM
French (Le Mans): Alex Debon (Spain), Aprilia
Italian (Mugello): Marco Simoncelli (Italy), Gilera
Catalunyan (Montmelo): Marco Simoncelli (Italy), Gilera
British (Donington Park): Mika Kallio (Finland), KTM
Dutch (Assen): Alvaro Bautista (Spain), Aprilia
German (Sachsenring): Marco Simoncelli (Italy), Gilera
Czech Republic (Brno): Alex Debon (Spain), Aprilia
San Marino (Misano): Alvaro Bautista (Spain), Aprilia

125CC GRAND PRIX 2007
San Marino (Misano): Mattia Pasini (Italy), Aprilia
Portuguese (Estoril): Hector Faubel (Spain), Aprilia
Japanese (Motegi): Mattia Pasini (Italy), Aprilia
Australian (Phillip Island): Lukas Pesek (Czech Republic), Derbi
Malaysian (Sepang): Gabor Talmacsi (Hungary), Aprilia
Spanish (Valencia): Hector Faubel (Spain), Aprilia
Riders' Championship 2007: 1. Gabor Talmacsi (Hungary), Aprilia, 282pts; 2. Hector Faubel (Spain), Aprilia, 277pts; 3. Tomoyoshi Koyama (Japan), KTM, 193pts

125CC GRAND PRIX 2008
Qatari (Losail): Sergio Gadea (Spain), Aprilia
Spanish (Jerez): Simone Corsi (Italy), Aprilia
Portuguese (Estoril): Simone Corsi (Italy), Aprilia
Chinese (Shanghai): Andrea Iannone (Italy), Aprilia
French (Le Mans): Mike Di Meglio (France), Derbi
Italian (Mugello): Simone Corsi (Italy), Aprilia
Catalunyan (Montmelo): Mike Di Meglio (France), Derbi
British (Donington Park): Scott Redding (Great Britain), Aprilia
Dutch (Assen): Gabor Talmacsi (Hungary), Aprilia
German (Sachsenring): Mike Di Meglio (France), Derbi
Czech Republic (Brno): Stefan Bradl (Germany), Aprilia
San Marino (Misano): Gabor Talmacsi (Hungary), Aprilia

ISLE OF MAN TOURIST TROPHY 2008
Senior: John McGuinness (England), Honda
Supersport: Race 1 – Steve Plater (England), Yamaha; Race 2 – Bruce Anstey (New Zealand), Suzuki

WORLD SUPERBIKES 2007
Germany (Lausitzring): Race 1 – Noriyuki Haga (Japan), Yamaha; Race 2 – Troy Bayliss (Australia), Ducati
Spain (Vallelunga): Race 1 – Max Biaggi (Italy), Suzuki; Race 2 – Troy Bayliss (Australia), Ducati
France (Magny Cours): Race 1 – Noriyuki Haga (Japan), Yamaha; Race 2 – Noriyuki Haga (Japan), Yamaha
Riders' World Championship 2007: 1. James Toseland (Great Britain), Honda, 415pts; 2. Noriyuki Haga (Japan), Yamaha, 413pts; 3. Max Biaggi (Italy), Suzuki, 397pts

WORLD SUPERBIKES 2008
Qatar (Losail): Race 1 – Troy Bayliss (Australia), Ducati: Race 2 – Fonsi Nieto (Spain), Suzuki
Australia (Philip Island): Race 1 – Troy Bayliss (Australia), Ducati; Race 2 – Troy Bayliss (Australia), Ducati
Spain (Valencia): Race 1 – Lorenzo Lanzi (Italy), Ducati; Race 2 – Noriyuki Haga (Japan), Yamaha
Netherlands (Assen): Race 1 – Troy Bayliss (Australia), Ducati; Race 2 – Troy Bayliss (Australia), Ducati
Italy (Monza): Race 1 – Max Neukirchner (Germany), Suzuki; Race 2 – Noriyuki Haga (Japan), Yamaha
US (Miller Motorsports Park): Race 1 – Carlos Checa (Spain), Honda; Race 2 – Carlos Checa (Spain), Honda
Germany (Nurburgring): Race 1 – Noriyuki Haga (Japan), Yamaha; Race 2 – Noriyuki Haga (Japan), Yamaha
San Marino (Mizano): Race 1 – Max Neukirchner (Germany), Suzuki; Race 2 – Ruben Xaus (Spain), Ducati

Czech (Brno): Race 1 – Troy Bayliss (Australia), Ducati; Race 2 – Troy Bayliss (Australia), Ducati
British (Brands Hatch): Race 1 – Ryuichi Kiyonari (Japan), Honda; Race 2 – Ryuichi Kiyonari (Japan), Honda

MOTOR RACING

FORMULA ONE GRAND PRIX 2007
Italian (Monza): Fernando Alonso (Spain), McLaren
Chinese (Shanghai): Kimi Raikkonen (Finland), Ferrari
Japanese (Suzuka): Lewis Hamilton (Great Britain), McLaren
Brazilian (Interlagos): Kimi Raikkonen (Finland), Ferrari
Drivers' World Championship 2007: 1. Kimi Raikkonen (Finland), Ferrari, 110pts; 2. Lewis Hamilton (Great Britain), McLaren, 109pts; 3. Fernando Alonso (Spain), McLaren 109pts
Constructors' World Championship 2007: 1. Ferrari, 204pts; 2. BMW, 101pts; 3. Renault, 51pts

FORMULA ONE GRAND PRIX 2008
Australian (Melbourne): Lewis Hamilton (Great Britain), McLaren
Malaysian (Sepang): Kimi Raikkonen (Finland), Ferrari
Bahraini (Sakhir): Felipe Massa (Brazil), Ferrari
Spanish (Barcelona): Kimi Raikkonen (Finland), Ferrari
Turkish (Istanbul): Felipe Massa (Brazil), Ferrari
Monaco (Monte Carlo): Lewis Hamilton (Great Britain), McLaren
Canada (Montreal): Robert Kubica (Poland), BMW
French (Magny Cours): Felipe Massa (Brazil), Ferrari
British (Silverstone): Lewis Hamilton (Great Britain), McLaren
German (Hochenheim): Lewis Hamilton (Great Britain), McLaren
Hungarian (Budapest): Heikki Kovalainen (Finland), McLaren
European (Valencia): Felipe Massa (Brazil), Ferrari

INDIANAPOLIS 500 2008
Indianapolis, USA, May
Scott Dixon (New Zealand), Ganassi

LE MANS 24-HOUR RACE 2008
Le Mans, France, June
Allan McNish (Great Britain), Rinaldo Capello (Italy) and Tom Kristensen (Denmark), Audi

MOTOR RALLYING

WORLD RALLY CHAMPIONSHIP 2007
Germany: Sebastien Loeb (France), Citroen
New Zealand: Marcus Gronholm (Finland), Ford
Spain: Sebastien Loeb (France), Citroen
France: Sebastien Loeb (France), Citroen
Japan: Mikko Hirvonen (Finland), Ford
Ireland: Sebastien Loeb (France), Citroen
Great Britain: Mikko Hirvonen (Finland), Ford
Drivers' World Championship 2007: 1. Sebastien Loeb, (France), 116pts; 2. Marcus Gronholm, (Finland), 112pts; 3. Mikko Hirvonen (Finland), Ford, 99pts
Manufacturers' World Championship 2007: 1. Ford, 212pts; 2. Citroen, 183pts; 3. Subaru, 87pts

WORLD RALLY CHAMPIONSHIP 2008
Monte Carlo: Sebastien Loeb (France), Citroen
Sweden: Jari-Matti Latvala (Finland), Ford
Mexico: Sebastien Loeb (France), Citroen
Argentina: Sebastien Loeb (France), Citroen
Jordan: Mikko Hirvonen (Finland), Ford
Italy: Sebastien Loeb (France), Citroen
Greece: Sebastien Loeb (France), Citroen
Turkey: Mikko Hirvonen (Finland), Ford
Finland: Sebastien Loeb (France), Citroen
Germany: Sebastien Loeb (France), Citroen
New Zealand: Sebastien Loeb (France), Citroen

BRITISH RALLY CHAMPIONSHIP 2007
Ulster: Kris Meeke (Great Britain), Subaru
Yorkshire: Mark Higgins (Great Britain), Mitsubishi
Wales: Guy Wilks (Great Britain), Mitsubishi

BRITISH RALLY CHAMPIONSHIP 2008
Cumbria: Guy Wilks (Great Britain), Mitsubishi
Scottish Borders: Eamonn Boland (Ireland), Subaru
Isle of Man: Mark Higgins (Great Britain), Subaru

DAKAR RALLY 2008
Cancelled

NETBALL

Superleague 2007–8: Loughborough
Superleague play-off 2008: Mavericks
Challenge Cup final 2007–8: Academy beat Linden 43–36

NORDIC EVENTS

BIATHLON WORLD CUP 2007–8

MEN
Overall: Ole Einar Bjoerndalen (Norway), 869pts

WOMEN
Overall: Magdalena Neuner (Germany), 818pts

BIATHLON WORLD CHAMPIONSHIPS 2008
Oestersund, Sweden, February

MEN
10km sprint: Maxim Tchoudov (Russia)
12.5km pursuit: Ole Einar Bjoerndalen (Norway)
15km mass start: Emil Hegle Svendsen (Norway)
20km individual: Emil Hegle Svendsen (Norway)
4 × 7.5km relay: Russia

WOMEN
7.5km sprint: Andrea Henkel (Germany)
10km pursuit: Andrea Henkel (Germany)
12.5km mass start: Magdalena Neuner (Germany)
15km individual: Ekaterina Iourieva (Russia)
4 × 6km relay: Germany

MIXED
2 × 6km + 2 × 7.5km relay: Germany

NORDIC WORLD CUP 2007–8

CROSS COUNTRY
Men: Lukas Bauer (Czech Republic), 1,462pts
Women: Virpi Kuitunen (Finland), 1,552pts

SKI-JUMPING
Thomas Morgenstern (Austria), 1,794pts

NORDIC COMBINED
Ronny Ackermann (Germany), 1,174pts

POLO

Prince of Wales Trophy 2008: Broncos beat Zacara 8–7
Queen's Cup final 2008: Ellerston beat Sumaya 10–9
Warwickshire Cup 2008: Les Lions II beat Lovelocks 8–7
Gold Cup (British Open) final 2008: Loro Piana beat Ellerston 11–10
Coronation Cup 2008: England beat Australia 10–9

RACKETS

Noel Bruce Cup 2007: Harry Foster and Charlie Danby (Harrow) beat Mark Hubbard and Ben Bomford (Malvern) 4–2
Amateur Singles Championship final 2007: Harry Foster beat Jonathan Larken 3–1
The Foster Cup final 2007 (public schools' singles championship): Sam Northeast (Harrow) beat Dan Shiner (Cheltenham) 3–1
British Professional Singles Championship final 2008: Mark Hubbard beat Neil Smith 3–1
British Open Singles Championship final 2008: Jamie Stout beat Alex Titchener-Barrett 4–1
British Open Doubles Championship final 2008: Harry Foster and Mark Hue Williams beat Alex Titchener-Barrett and Will Hopton 4–0
Amateur Doubles Championship 2008: Tim Cockroft & Alex Titchener-Barrett beat Jonathan Larken and Toby Sawrey-Cookson 4–3
Public Schools Doubles 2008: Christian Portz and Sean Knight (Winchester) beat Sam Northeast and Will Jones (Harrow) 4–1

REAL TENNIS

MEN
IRTPA Championship final 2007 (British Professional Singles Championship): Robert Fahey (Australia) beat Ruaraidh Gunn (Australia) 3–0
British Open Singles final 2007: Robert Fahey (Australia) beat Steve Virgona (Australia) 3–1
British Open Doubles final 2007: Robert Fahey and Ruaraidh Gunn (Australia) beat Steve Virgona (Australia) and James Willcocks (Great Britain) 3–1
World Singles Championship 2008: Robert Fahey (Australia) beat Camden Riviere (USA) 7–5
Field Trophy final 2007: Petworth House beat The Queen's Club 3–2
Henry Leaf Cup final 2008 (public schools' old boys' doubles championship): Gilberd beat Newhall 2–0
National League final 2008: Cambridge beat Prested Hall 2–0

WOMEN
British Open Singles Championship final 2008: Charlotte Cornwallis (Great Britain) beat Claire Vigrass (Great Britain) 2–0
British Open Doubles Championship final 2008: Charlotte Cornwallis and Penny Lumley (Great Britain) beat Sally Grant and Jo Iddles (Great Britain) 2–1

ROWING

BRITISH CHAMPIONSHIPS 2008
Nottingham, July

MEN
Single sculls: Ian Lawson (Leander), 7min 29.61sec
Double sculls: Leander, 7min 03.08sec
Quadruple sculls: Leander, 6min 37.05sec
Coxless pairs: Leander 7min, 04.43sec
Coxless fours: Leander, 7min 00.83sec
Coxed fours: Leander, 6min 56.56sec
Eights: Leander Club, 6min 08.37sec

WOMEN
Single sculls: Fran Jacob (Glasgow), 8min 27.95sec
Double sculls: Rhwyfo Cymru/Worcester, 8min 09.11sec
Quadruple sculls: Imperial College, 7min 20.17sec
Coxless pairs: Worcester, 8min 28.07sec
Coxless fours: Leander, 7min 25.85sec
Coxed fours: Furnivall Sculling Club, 7min 40.20sec
Eights: Thames, 7min 19.08sec

HENLEY ROYAL REGATTA 2008
Grand Challenge Cup: Victoria City R. C. and Kingston R. C. (Canada) beat University of Southern California (USA) by 2 lengths
Stewards' Challenge Cup: Cambridge University beat O. E. A. and N. A. V. Volos and N. C. Thessaloniki (Greece) by 3½ lengths
Queen Mother Challenge Cup: R. C. Viljandi and R. C. Narva Energia (Estonia) beat California R. C. (USA) by 2¼ lengths
Silver Goblets and Nickalls' Challenge Cup: S. B. Keeling and R. P. Di Clemente (South Africa) beat O. L. E. Rueckbrodt and F. Otto (Germany) by 4¾ lengths
Double Sculls Challenge Cup: W. D. Piermarini and E. M. Hovey (USA) beat P. F. Graves and T. H. Graves (USA) by 1¼ lengths
Diamond Challenge Sculls: I. J. Lawson (Great Britain) beat S. M. Jacob (Ireland) easily
Remenham Challenge Cup: Leander Club and Wallingford R. C. beat Furnivall Scullers and Leander Club by 3 lengths
Princess Grace Challenge Cup: Wallingford R. C. and Reading University beat Upper Thames R. C. easily
Princess Royal Challenge Cup: C. Ryan (Ireland) beat M. H. Pauls (Great Britain) by 3½ lengths
Ladies' Challenge Plate: Leander Club beat R. S. V. U. Okeanos and D. S. R. Laga (Netherlands) by ⅔ of a length
Visitors' Challenge Cup: Imperial College London and Kingston R. C. beat Martyrs B. C. and Christ Church Oxford by 1¼ lengths
Prince of Wales Challenge Cup: California R. C. (USA) beat Leander Club and London R. C. by 1¼ lengths
Thames Challenge Cup: Leander Club beat Tideway Scullers by a canvas
Wyfold Challenge Cup: Tyne R. C. beat London R. C. 'B' by 1 length
Britannia Challenge Cup: Molesey R. C. beat Ortner B. C. 'A' by 2½ lengths
Temple Challenge Cup: University of Western Ontario (Canada) beat Trinity College, Hartford (USA) by 2¾ lengths
Prince Albert Challenge Cup: Newcastle University beat University of the West of England by 2 lengths
Princess Elizabeth Challenge Cup: Shawnigan Lake School (Canada) beat Eton College by ¾ length
Fawley Challenge Cup: Peterborough City R. C. and Nottingham R. C. beat Marlow R. C. 'A' by 1 length

THE 154TH UNIVERSITY BOAT RACE
Putney–Mortlake, 4 miles, 1 f, 180 yd, 29 March 2008

Oxford beat Cambridge by 6 lengths; 20min 52sec
Cambridge have won 79 times, Oxford 74 and there has

been one dead heat. The record time is 16min 19sec, rowed by Cambridge in 1998.

OTHER ROWING EVENTS
Wingfield Sculls 2007: Men, Mahe Drysdale (Tideway Scullers); *Women,* Elise Laverick (Thames)
Oxford Torpids 2008: Men, Magdalen; *Women,* St Catherine's
Oxford Summer Eights 2008: Men, Balliol; *Women,* St Edmund Hall
Head of the River 2008: Men, Leander I; *Women,* Osiris A

RUGBY FIVES

National Open Singles Championship final 2007: H. Buchanan beat J. Toop 2–0
National Ladies' Singles Championship final 2007: C. Knowles beat E. Seton 2–0
National Ladies' Doubles Championship final 2007: C. Knowles and M. Whitehead beat E. Seton and I. Bravo 2–0
National Open Doubles Championship final 2008: H. Buchanan and R. Perry beat M. Cavanagh and E. Fuller 2–0
National Club Championship final 2008: Manchester Y Club beat Alleyn Old Boys 107–76
National Schools' Singles Championship final 2008: I. Ackland (Alleyn's) beat J. Faber (St Paul's) 2–0
National Schools' Doubles Championship final 2008: I. Ackland and J. Brubert (Alleyn's) beat J. Faber and T. Hoolahan (St Paul's) 2–1
Varsity Match 2008: Oxford beat Cambridge 260–193

RUGBY LEAGUE

Challenge Cup final 2008: St Helens beat Hull FC 28–16
Super League Grand Final 2007: Leeds beat St Helens 33–6
World Club Challenge 2008: Leeds beat Melbourne 11–4

AMATEUR COMPETITIONS 2007–8
National Conference League Premier Division Grand Final: Leigh Miners Rangers beat Skirlaugh 38–4
Division One: Wigan St Judes
Division Two: Normanton Knights
BARLA National Cup final: East Hull beat Wath Brow Hornets 32–10
Varsity Match 2008: Oxford beat Cambridge 38–12

RUGBY UNION

WORLD CUP 2008
France and Wales, September–October
Pool A

	P	*W*	*D*	*L*	*BP*	*Pts*
South Africa	4	4	0	0	3	19
England	4	3	0	1	2	14
Tonga	4	2	0	2	1	9
Samoa	4	1	0	3	1	5
USA	4	0	0	4	1	1

England beat USA 28–10
South Africa beat Samoa 59–7
Tonga beat USA 25–15
South Africa beat England 36–0
Tonga beat Samoa 19–15
South Africa beat Tonga 30–25
England beat Samoa 44–22
Samoa beat USA 25–21
England beat Tonga 36–20
South Africa beat USA 64–15

Pool B

	P	*W*	*D*	*L*	*BP*	*Pts*
Australia	4	4	0	0	4	20
Fiji	4	3	0	1	3	15
Wales	4	2	0	2	4	12
Japan	4	0	1	3	1	3
Canada	4	0	1	3	0	2

Australia beat Japan 91–3
Wales beat Canada 42–17
Fiji beat Japan 35–31
Australia beat Wales 32–20
Fiji beat Canada 29–16
Wales beat Japan 72–18
Australia beat Fiji 55–12
Canada drew with Japan 12–12
Australia beat Canada 37–6
Fiji beat Wales 38–34

Pool C

	P	*W*	*D*	*L*	*BP*	*Pts*
New Zealand	4	4	0	0	4	20
Scotland	4	3	0	1	2	14
Italy	4	2	0	2	1	9
Romania	4	1	0	3	1	5
Portugal	4	0	0	4	1	1

New Zealand beat Italy 76–14
Scotland beat Portugal 56–10
Italy beat Romania 24–18
New Zealand beat Portugal 108–13
Scotland Romania 42–0
Italy beat Portugal 31–5
New Zealand beat Scotland 40–0
Romania beat Portugal 14–10
Scotland beat Italy 18–16
New Zealand beat Romania 85–8

Pool D

	P	*W*	*D*	*L*	*BP*	*Pts*
Argentina	4	4	0	0	2	18
France	4	3	0	1	3	15
Ireland	4	2	0	2	1	9
Georgia	4	1	0	3	1	5
Namibia	4	0	0	4	0	0

Argentina beat France 17–12
Ireland beat Namibia 32–17
Argentina beat Georgia 33–3
Ireland beat Georgia 14–10
France beat Namibia 87–10
France beat Ireland 25–3
Argentina beat Namibia 63–3
Georgia beat Namibia 30–0
France beat Georgia 64–7
Argentina beat Ireland 30–15

Quarter-finals
England beat Australia 12–10
France beat New Zealand 20–18
South Africa beat Fiji 37–20
Argentina beat Scotland 19–13

Semi-finals
England beat France 14–9
South Africa beat Argentina 37–13

Third-place play-off
Argentina beat France 34–10

Final
South Africa beat England 15–6

SIX NATIONS' CHAMPIONSHIP 2008

2 February	Dublin	Ireland beat Italy 16–11
	London	Wales beat England 26–19
3 February	Edinburgh	France beat Scotland 27–6
9 February	Cardiff	Wales beat Scotland 30–15
	Paris	France beat Ireland 26–21
10 February	Rome	England beat Italy 23–19
23 February	Cardiff	Wales beat Italy 47–8
	Dublin	Ireland beat Scotland 34–13
	Paris	England beat France 24–13
8 March	Dublin	Wales beat Ireland 16–12
	Edinburgh	Scotland beat England 15–9
9 March	Paris	France beat Italy 25–13
15 March	Rome	Italy beat Scotland 23–20
	London	England beat Ireland 33–10
	Cardiff	Wales beat France 29–12

Final standings: 1. Wales, 10pts; 2. England, 6pts; 3. France, 6pts; 4. Ireland, 4pts; 5. Scotland, 2pts; 6. Italy, 2pts

EUROPEAN COMPETITIONS 2007–8
Heineken European Cup final: Munster beat Toulouse 16–13
European Challenge Cup: Bath beat Worcester 24–16

DOMESTIC COMPETITIONS 2007–8

ENGLAND
Premiership: Gloucester, 74pts
Championship final: Wasps beat Leicester 26–16
National League: Division 1, Northampton, 143pts; *Division 2,* Otley, 105pts; *Division 3* (North), Tynedale, 112pts; (South) Mounts Bay, 107pts
National Trophy final: Northampton beat Exeter 24–13
County Championship final: Yorkshire beat Devon 33–13
County Shield: Northumberland beat Cornwall 25–11
County Plate: Hampshire beat Leicestershire 22–12
125th Varsity Match: Cambridge beat Oxford 22–16

ANGLO-WELSH
EDF Cup final: Ospreys beat Leicester 23–6

CELTIC
Magners League: Lenster, 61pts

SCOTLAND
Premier League: Division 1, Boroughmuir, 96pts; *Division 2,* West of Scotland, 94pts; *Division 3,* Gala, 84pts
Cup final: Melrose beat Heriots 31–24

WALES
Premiership: Neath, 93pts; *National League:* Division 1 (East), Pontypool, 89pts; (West), Tonmawr, 85pts
Cup final: Neath beat Pontypridd 28–22

IRELAND
All Ireland League: Division 1, Cork Constitution, 58pts; *Division 2,* Buccaneers, 53pts; *Division 3,* Bruff, 65pts

SHOOTING

139TH NATIONAL RIFLE ASSOCIATION IMPERIAL MEETING
Bisley, July 2008

Queen's Prize: Zainal Abidin Md Zain, 294.36 v-bulls
Grand Aggregate: N. J. Ball, 690.91 v-bulls
Prince of Wales Prize: A. N. R. Walker, 75.11 v-bulls
St George's Vase: Dr G. C. D. Barnett, 150.19 v-bulls
All Comers' Aggregate: Miss J. H. Messer, 369.36 v-bulls
Kolapore Cup: Great Britain, 1,179.155 v-bulls
Chancellor's Trophy: Cambridge University, 1,141.99 v-bulls
National Trophy: England, 2,046.204 v-bulls
Musketeers Cup: Exeter University, 585.49 v-bulls
County Championship Long Range: London, 590.75 v-bulls
Mackinnon Challenge Cup: England, 1,153.106 v-bulls
The Albert: J. M. B. Baillie-Hamilton, 220.26 v-bulls
Hopton Challenge Cup: C. N. Tremlett, 997.108 v-bulls

SNOOKER

2007–8
Pot Black Cup (Sheffield): Ken Doherty (Ireland) beat Shaun Murphy (England) 1–0
Grand Prix (Aberdeen): Marco Fu (Hong Kong) beat Ronnie O'Sullivan (England) 9–6
Northern Ireland Trophy (Belfast): Stephen Maguire (Scotland) beat Fergal O'Brien 9–5
UK Championship (York): Ronnie O'Sullivan (England) beat Stephen Maguire (Scotland) 10–2
Masters (Wembley): Mark Selby (England) beat Stephen Lee (England) 10–3
Malta Cup (Portomaso): Shaun Murphy (England) beat Ken Doherty (Ireland) 9–3
Welsh Open (Newport): Mark Selby (England) beat Ronnie O'Sullivan (England) 9–8
China Open (Beijing): Stephen Maguire (Scotland) beat Shaun Murphy (England) 10–9
World Championship (Sheffield): Ronnie O'Sullivan (England) beat Ali Carter (England) 18–8

SPEED SKATING

WORLD ALL-ROUND CHAMPIONSHIPS 2008
Berlin, Germany, February

MEN
500m: Denny Morrison (Canada), 35.81sec
1,500m: Shani Davis (USA), 1min 45.93sec
5,000m: Sven Kramer (Netherlands), 6min 13.35sec
10,000m: Sven Kramer (Netherlands), 13min 09.06sec

WOMEN
500m: Christine Nesbitt (Canada), 39.03sec
1,500m: Ireen Wust (Netherlands), 1min 57.59sec
3,000m: Paulien van Deutekom (Netherlands), 4min 03.33sec
5,000m: Martina Sablikova (Czech Rep.), 6min 59.26sec

WORLD SINGLE-DISTANCE CHAMPIONSHIPS 2008
Nagano, Japan, March

MEN
500m: Jeremy Wotherspoon (Canada), 69.46sec *(over two legs)*
1,000m: Shani Davis (USA), 1min 08.99sec
1,500m: Denny Morrison (Canada), 1min 45.22sec
5,000m: Sven Kramer (Netherlands), 6min 17.24sec
10,000m: Sven Kramer (Netherlands), 12min 57.71sec
Team pursuit: Netherlands, 3min 41.69sec

WOMEN
500m: Jenny Wolf (Germany), 37.74sec
1,000m: Anni Friesinger (Germany), 1min 15.37sec
1,500m: Anni Friesinger (Germany), 1min 56.06sec
3,000m: Kristina Groves (Canada), 4min 05.03sec
5,000m: Martina Sablikova (Czech Rep.), 6min 58.22sec
Team pursuit: Netherlands, 3min 02.19sec

EUROPEAN CHAMPIONSHIPS 2008
Kolomna, Russia, January

MEN
500m: Sven Kramer (Netherlands), 36.20sec
1,500m: Yevgeny Lalenkov (Russia), 1min 45.24sec
5,000m: Sven Kramer (Netherlands), 6min 11.78sec
10,000m: Sven Kramer (Netherlands), 13min 03.30sec

WOMEN
500m: Yekaterina Lobysheva (Russia), 39.24sec
1,500m: Ireen Wust (Netherlands), 1min 56.88sec
3,000m: Martina Sablikova (Czech Rep.), 4min 01.67sec
5,000m: Martina Sablikova (Czech Rep.), 6min 53.42sec

WORLD SHORT TRACK CHAMPIONSHIPS 2008
Gangneung City, Rep. of Korea, March

MEN
500m: Apolo Anton Ohno (USA), 41.935sec
1,000m: Ho-Suk Lee (Rep. of Korea), 1min 26.462sec
1,500m: Kyung-Taek Song (Rep. of Korea), 2min 16.770sec
3,000m: Seung-Hoon Lee (Rep. of Korea), 4min 53.620sec
5,000m relay: Rep. of Korea, 6min 51.148sec
Overall: Apolo Anton Ohno (USA), 68pts

WOMEN
500m: Meng Wang (China), 43.888sec
1,000m: Meng Wang (China), 1min 32.527sec
1,500m: Meng Wang (China), 2min 22.819sec
3,000m: Yang Zhou (China), 5min 46.063sec
3,000m relay: Rep. of Korea, 4min 16.261sec
Overall: Meng Wang (China), 107pts

EUROPEAN SHORT TRACK CHAMPIONSHIPS 2008
Ventspils, Latvia, January

MEN
500m: Jon Eley (Great Britain), 42.945sec
1,000m: Niels Kerstholt (Netherlands), 1min 26.625sec
1,500m: Haralds Silovs (Latvia), 2min 16.032sec
3,000m: Haralds Silovs (Latvia), 5min 03.706sec
5,000m relay: Italy, 6min 57.853sec
Overall: Haralds Silovs (Latvia), 89pts

WOMEN
500m: Annita van Doorn (Netherlands), 45.754sec
1,000m: Evgenia Radanova (Bulgaria), 1min 32.849sec
1,500m: Arianna Fontana (Italy), 2min 28.559sec
3,000m: Arianna Fontana (Italy), 5min 43.030sec
3,000m relay: Great Britain, 4min 23.172sec
Overall: Arianna Fontana (Italy), 89pts

SQUASH

MEN
World Team Championship 2007: England beat Australia 2–1
World Open 2007: Amr Shabana (Egypt) beat Gregory Gaultier (France) 3–0
British Open 2007: Gregory Gaultier (France) beat Thierry Lincou (France), 3–1
European Championship 2008: Gregory Gaultier (France) beat Thierry Lincou (France), 3–2
European Team Championship 2008: England beat France 3–0
British Open 2008: David Palmer (Australia) beat James Willstrop (England) 3–2
British National Championship 2008: James Willstrop beat Lee Beachill 3–0

WOMEN
World Open 2007: Rachael Grinham (Australia) beat Natalie Grinham (Australia) 3–0
British Open 2007: Rachael Grinham (Australia) beat Nicol David (Malaysia), 3–2
European Championship 2008: Isabelle Stoehr (France) beat Sarah Kippax (England) 3–1
European Team Championship 2008: England beat Netherlands 3–0
British Open 2008: Nicol David (Malaysia) beat Jenny Duncalf (England) 3–0
British National Championship 2008: Alison Waters beat Laura Lengthorn-Massaro 3–1

SWIMMING

EUROPEAN CHAMPIONSHIPS 2008
Eindhoven, Netherlands, March

MEN
50m freestyle: Alain Bernard (France), 21.66sec
100m freestyle: Alain Bernard (France), 47.50sec
200m freestyle: Paul Biedermann (Germany), 1min 46.59sec
400m freestyle: Yury Prilukov (Russia), 3min 45.10sec
800m freestyle: Gergo Kis (Hungary), 7min 51.94sec
1500m freestyle: Yury Prilukov (Russia), 14min 50.40sec
4 × 100m freestyle relay: Sweden 3min 15.41sec
4 × 200m freestyle relay: Italy, 7min 09.94sec
50m backstroke: Aristeidis Grigoriadis (Greece), 25.13sec
100m backstroke: Marcus Rogan (Austria), 54.03sec
200m backstroke: Marcus Rogan (Austria), 1min 55.85sec
50m breaststroke: Oleg Lisogor (Ukraine), 27.43sec
100m breaststroke: Alexander Dale Oen (Norway), 59.76sec
200m breaststroke: Grigory Falko (Russia), 2min 09.64sec
50m butterfly: Milorad Cavic (Serbia), 23.11sec
100m butterfly: Evgeny Korotyshkin (Russia), 51.89sec
200m butterfly: Ioannis Drymonakos (Greece), 1min 54.16sec
200m individual medley: Laszlo Cseh (Hungary), 1min 58.02sec

400m individual medley: Laszlo Cseh (Hungary), 4min 09.59sec
4 × 100m medley relay: Russia, 3min 34.25sec

WOMEN
50m freestyle: Marleen Veldhuis (Netherlands), 24.09sec
100m freestyle: Marleen Veldhuis (Netherlands), 53.77sec
200m freestyle: Sara Isakovic (Slovenia), 1min 57.45sec
400m freestyle: Federica Pellegrini (Italy), 4min 01.53sec
800m freestyle: Alessia Filippi (Italy), 8min 23.50sec
1500m freestyle: Flavia Rigamonti (Switzerland), 15min 58.54sec
4 × 100m freestyle relay: Netherlands, 3min 33.62sec
4 × 200m freestyle relay: France, 7min 52.09sec
50m backstroke: Anastasia Zueva (Russia), 28.05sec
100m backstroke: Anastasia Zueva (Russia), 59.41sec
200m backstroke: Laure Manaudou (France), 2min 07.99sec
50m breaststroke: Janne Schaefer (Germany), 31.08sec
100m breaststroke: Mirna Jukic (Austria), 1min 08.18sec
200m breaststroke: Yuliya Efimova (Russia), 2min 24.09sec
50m butterfly: Chantal Groot (Netherlands), 26.03sec
100m butterfly: Sarah Sjoestroem (Sweden), 58.44 sec
200m butterfly: Aurore Mongel (France), 2min 06.59sec
200m individual medley: Mireia Belmonte Garcia (Spain), 2min 11.16sec
400m individual medley: Alessia Filippi (Italy), 4min 36.68sec
4 × 100m medley relay: Great Britain, 3min 59.33sec

BRITISH CHAMPIONSHIPS 2008
Sheffield, March–April

MEN
50m freestyle: Mark Foster (Bath University), 22.30sec
100m freestyle: Benjamin Hockin (Swansea), 49.63sec
200m freestyle: Ross Davenport (Loughborough University), 1min 47.66sec
400m freestyle: David Carry (Aberdeen), 3min 49.78sec
1,500m freestyle: Richard Charlesworth (Hatfield), 15min 10.99sec
100m backstroke: Gregor Tait (]Edinburgh), 54.22sec
200m backstroke: Gregor Tait (Edinburgh), 1min 56.67sec
100m breaststroke: Christopher Cook (Newcastle), 59.88sec
200m breaststroke: Kristopher Gilchrist (Edinburgh), 2min 10.44sec
100m butterfly: Michael Rock (Stockport), 52.30sec
200m butterfly: Michael Rock (Stockport), 1min 56.92sec
200m medley: James Goddard (Loughborough University), 1min 57.72sec
400m medley: Thomas Hatfield (Cardiff), 4min 14.01sec

WOMEN
50m freestyle: Francesca Halsall (Liverpool), 24.79sec
100m freestyle: Caitlin Mcclatchey (Loughborough University), 54.58sec
200m freestyle: Rebecca Adlington (Nova), 1min 57.94sec
400m freestyle: Rebecca Adlington (Nova), 4min 04.50sec
800m freestyle: Rebecca Adlington (Nova), 8min 20.29sec
100m backstroke: Gemma Spofforth (Portsmouth), 59.90sec
200m backstroke: Elizabeth Simmonds (Lincoln), 2min 08.99sec
100m breaststroke: Kate Haywood (Loughborough University), 1min 07.84sec
200m breaststroke: Georgia Holderness (Millfield), 2min 29.99sec
100m butterfly: Francesca Halsall (Liverpool), 58.16sec
200m butterfly: Jemma Lowe (Stockton), 2min 07.61sec
200m medley: Hannah Miley (Garioch), 2min 12.17sec
400m medley: Hannah Miley (Garioch), 4min 37.34sec

TABLE TENNIS

WORLD TEAM CHAMPIONSHIPS 2008
Guangzhou, China, February–March

Men's final: China beat Rep. of Korea 3–0
Women's final: China beat Singapore 3–1

ENGLISH NATIONAL CHAMPIONSHIPS 2008
Sheffield, March

Men's Singles: Andrew Baggaley (Buckinghamshire) beat Paul Drinkhall (Cleveland) 4–1
Women's Singles: Kelly Sibley (Warwickshire) beat Joanna Parker (Surrey) 3–1
Men's Doubles: Paul Drinkhall (Cleveland) and Darius Knight (Surrrey) beat Tim Yarnall (Northamptonshire) and Andrew Rushton (Lancashire) 3–0
Women's Doubles: Kelly Sibley (Warwickshire) and Joanna Parker (Surrey) beat Lindsey Reynolds (Lancashire) and Abigail Embling (Essex), 3–0
Mixed Doubles: Joanna Parker (Surrey) and Paul Drinkhall (Cleveland) beat Kelly Sibley (Warwickshire) and Darius Knight (Surrrey) 3–1

TENNIS

US OPEN CHAMPIONSHIPS 2007
New York, August–September

Men's Singles: Roger Federer (Switzerland) beat Novak Djokovic (Serbia) 7–6, 7–6, 6–4
Women's Singles: Justine Henin (Belgium) beat Svetlana Kuznetsova (Russia) 6–1, 6–3
Men's Doubles: Simon Aspelin (Sweden) and Julian Knowle (Austria) beat Lukas Dlouhy and Pavel Vizner (Czech Republic) 7–5, 6–4
Women's Doubles: Nathalie Dechy (France) and Dinara Safina (Russia) beat Chan Yung-Jan and Chuang Chia-Jung (Taipei) 6–4, 6–2
Mixed Doubles: Victoria Azarenka and Max Mirnyi (Belarus) beat Meghann Shaughnessy (USA) and Leander Paes (India) 6–4, 7–6

AUSTRALIAN OPEN CHAMPIONSHIPS 2008
Melbourne, January

Men's Singles: Novak Djokovic (Serbia) beat Jo-Wilfried Tsonga (France) 4–6, 6–4, 6–3, 7–6
Women's Singles: Maria Sharapova (Russia) beat Ana Ivanovic (Serbia) 7–5, 6–3
Men's Doubles: Jonathan Erlich and Andy Ram (Israel) beat Arnaud Clement and Michael Llodra (France) 7–5, 7–6
Women's Doubles: Alona Bondarenko and Kateryna Bondarenko (Ukraine) beat Victoria Azerenka (Belarus) and Shahar Peer (Israel) 2–6, 6–1, 6–4
Mixed Doubles: Tiantian Sun (China) and Nenad Zimoniic (Serbia) beat Sania Mirza and Mahesh Bhupathi (India) 7–6, 6–4

FRENCH OPEN CHAMPIONSHIPS 2008
Paris, May–June

Men's Singles: Rafael Nadal (Spain) beat Roger Federer (Switzerland) 6–1, 6–3, 6–0
Women's Singles: Ana Ivanovic (Serbia) beat Dinara Safina (Russia) 6–4, 6–3
Men's Doubles: Pablo Cuevas (Uruguay) and Luis Horna (Peru) beat Daniel Nestor (Canada) and Nenad Zimonjic (Serbia) 6–2, 6–3
Women's Doubles: Anabel Medina Garrigues and Virginia Ruano Pascual (Spain) beat Casey Delacqua (Australia) and Francesca Schiavone (Italy) 2–6, 7–5, 6–4
Mixed Doubles: Victoria Azarenka (Belarus) and Bob Bryan (USA) beat Katarina Srebotnik (Slovenia) and Nenad Zimonjic (Serbia) 6–2, 7–6

ALL-ENGLAND CHAMPIONSHIPS 2008
Wimbledon, June–July

Men's Singles: Rafael Nadal (Spain) beat Roger Federer (Switzerland) 6–4, 6–4, 6–7, 6–7, 9–7
Ladies' Singles: Venus Williams (USA) beat Serena Williams (USA) 7–5, 6–4
Men's Doubles: Daniel Nestor (Canada) and Nenad Zimonjic (Serbia) beat Jonas Bjorkman (Sweden) and Kevin Ullyett (Zimbabwe) 7–6, 6–7, 6–3, 6–3
Ladies' Doubles: Venus Williams and Serena Williams (USA) beat Samantha Stosur (Australia) and Lisa Raymond (USA) 6–2, 6–2
Mixed Doubles: Samantha Stosur (Australia) and Bob Bryan (USA) beat Katarina Srebotnik (Slovenia) and Mike Bryan (USA) 7–5, 6–4

TEAM CHAMPIONSHIPS
Davis Cup final 2007: USA beat Russia 4–1
Federation Cup final 2007: Russia beat Italy 4–0

OLYMPIC GAMES

Beijing, China, 2008

GOLD MEDALLISTS

ARCHERY
MEN
Individual: Viktor Ruban (Ukraine)
Team: Korea

WOMEN
Individual: Juan Juan Zhang (China)
Team: Korea

ATHLETICS
MEN
100m: Usain Bolt (Jamaica)
200m: Usain Bolt (Jamaica)
400m: LaShawn Merritt (USA)
800m: Wilfred Bungei (Kenya)
1500m: Rashid Ramzi (Bahrain)
5000m: Kenenisa Bekele (Ethiopia)
10,000m: Kenenisa Bekele (Ethiopia)
Marathon: Sammy Wanjiru (Kenya)
3000m Steeplechase: St Brimin Kipruto (Kenya)
110m Hurdles: Dayton Robles (Cuba)
400m Hurdles: Angelo Taylor (USA)
4 × 100m Relay: Jamaica
4 × 400m Relay: USA
High Jump: Andrei Silnov (Russia)
Pole Vault: Steve Hooker (Australia)
Long Jump: Irving Saladino (Panama)
Triple Jump: Nelson Evora (Portugal)
Shot: Tomasz Majewski (Poland)
Discus: Gerd Kanter (Latvia)
Hammer: Primoz Kosmus (Slovenia)
Javelin: Andreas Thorkkildsen (Norway)
Decathlon: Bryan Clay (USA)
20km Walk: Valeri Borchin (Russia)
50km Walk: Alex Schwazer (Italy)

WOMEN
100m: Shelly-Ann Fraser (Jamaica)
200m: Veronica Campbell-Brown (Jamaica)
400m: Christine Ohuruogu (Great Britain)
800m: Pamela Jelimo (Kenya)
1500m: Nancy Lagat (Kenya)
5000m: Tirunesh Dibaba (Ethiopia)
10,000m: Tirunesh Dibaba (Ethiopia)
Marathon: Constantina Dita-Tomescu (Romania)
3000m Steeplechase: Gulnara Galkina (Russia)
100m Hurdles: Dawn Harper (USA)
400m Hurdles: Melaine Walker (Jamaica)
4 × 100m Relay: Russia
4 × 400m Relay: USA
High Jump: Tia Hellebaut (Belgium)
Pole Vault: Yelena Isinbayeva (Russia)
Long Jump: Maurren Maggi (Brazil)
Triple Jump: Francoise Mbango (Cameroon)
Shot: Valerie Vili (New Zealand)
Discus: Stephanie Brown Trafton (USA)
Hammer: Aksena Miankova (Belarus)
Javelin: Barbora Spotáková (Czech Republic)
Heptathlon: Natalia Dobrynska (Ukraine)
20km Walk: Olga Kaniskina (Russia)

BADMINTON
MEN
Singles: Dan Lin (China)
Doubles: Indonesia

WOMEN
Singles: Ning Zhang (China)
Doubles: China

MIXED
Doubles: Korea

BASEBALL
MEN: Korea

BASKETBALL
MEN: USA

WOMEN: USA

BOXING
Light Fly: Shiming Zou (China)
Fly: Somjit Jongjohor (Thailand)
Bantam: Badar-Uygan Enkhbat (Mongolia)
Feather: Vasyl Lomachenko (Ukraine)
Light: Alexei Tishchenko (Russia)
Light Welter: Felix Diaz (Dominican Republic)
Welter: Bakhyt Sarsekbayev (Kazakhstan)
Middle: James DeGale (Great Britain)
Light Heavy: Xiaoping Zhang (China)
Heavy: Rakhim Chakhkiev (Russia)
Super Heavy: Roberto Cammarelle (Italy)

CANOEING

MEN

K-1 500m: Ken Wallace (Australia)
K-1 1000m: Tim Brabants (Great Britain)
K-2 500m: Spain
K-2 1000m: Germany
K-4 1000m: Belarus
C-1 500m: Maxim Opalev (Russia)
C-1 1000m: Attila Sandor Vajda (Hungary)
C-2 500m: China
C-2 1000m: Belarus
K-1 Slalom: Alexander Grimm (Germany)
C-1 Slalom: Michal Martikan (Slovakia)
C-2 Slalom: Slovakia

WOMEN

K-1 500m: Inna Osypenko-Radomska (Ukraine)
K-2 500m: Hungary
K-4 500m: Germany
K-1 Slalom: Elena Kaliska (Slovakia)

CYCLING

MEN

Individual Sprint: Chris Hoy (Great Britain)
4000m Individual Pursuit: Bradley Wiggins (Great Britain)
4000m Team Pursuit: Great Britain
Points Race: Joan Llanaris (Spain)
Team Sprint: Great Britain
Madison: Argentina
Keirin: Chris Hoy (Great Britain)
BMX: Maris Strombergs (Latvia)
Individual Road Race: Samuel Sanchez (Spain)
Individual Road Time Trial: Fabian Cancellara (Italy)
Mountain Bike: Julien Absalon (France)

WOMEN

Individual Sprint: Victoria Pendleton (Great Britain)
3000m Individual Pursuit: Rebecca Romero (Great Britain)
Points Race: Marianne Vos (Netherlands)
BMX: Anne-Caroline Chausson (France)
Individual Road Race: Nicole Cooke (Great Britain)
Individual Road Time Trial: Kristin Armstrong (USA)
Mountain Bike: Sabine Spitz (Germany)

DIVING

MEN

3m Springboard: Chong He (China)
10m Platform Diving: Matthew Mitcham (Australia)
3m Synchronised: China
10m Synchronised: China

WOMEN

3m Springboard: Jingjing Guo (China)
10m Platform Diving: Ruolin Chen (China)
3m Synchronised: China
10m Synchronised: China

EQUESTRIAN

Individual Jumping: Eric Lamaze (Canada) on *Hickstead*
Team Jumping: USA
Individual Dressage: Anky van Grunsven (Netherlands) on *Salinero*
Team Dressage: Germany
Individual 3-Day Event: Hinrich Romeike (Germany) on *Marius*
Team 3-Day Event: Germany

FENCING

MEN

Individual Foil: Benjamin Kleibrink (Germany)
Individual Sabre: Man Zhong (China)
Individual Epee: Matteo Tagliarol (Italy)
Team Sabre: France
Team Epee: France

WOMEN

Individual Foil: Maria Vezzali (Italy)
Individual Sabre: Mariel Zagunis (USA)
Individual Epee: Britta Heidemann (Germany)
Team Foil: Russia
Team Sabre: Ukraine

FOOTBALL

MEN: Argentina
WOMEN: USA

HANDBALL

MEN: France
WOMEN: Norway

GYMNASTICS

MEN

Team: China
Individual All-Around: Wei Yang (China)
Floor: Kai Zou (China)
Pommel Horse: Qin Xiao (China)
Rings: Yibing Chen (China)
Vault: Leszek Blanik (Poland)
Parallel Bars: Xiaopeng Li (China)
Horizontal Bar: Kai Zou (China)
Trampolining: Chunlong Lu (China)

WOMEN

Team: China
Individual All-Around: Nastia Liukin (USA)
Floor: Sandra Izbasa (Romania)
Vault: Un Jong Hong (North Korea)
Uneven Bars: Kexin He (China)
Balance Beam: Shawn Johnson (USA)
Rhythmic Individual: Evgeniya Kanaeva (Russia)
Rhythmic Team: Russia
Trampolining: Wenna He (China)

HOCKEY

MEN: Germany
WOMEN: Netherlands

JUDO

MEN

60kg: Minho Choi (Korea)
66kg: Masato Uchishiba (Japan)
73kg: Elnur Mammadli (Azerbaijan)
81kg: Ole Bischof (Germany)
90kg: Irakli Tsirekidze (Georgia)
100kg: Tuvshinbayar Naidan (Mongolia)
+100kg: Satoshi Ishii (Japan)

WOMEN

48kg: Alina Dumitru (Romania)
52kg: Dongmei Xian (China)
57kg: Giulia Quintavalle (Italy)
63kg: Ayumi Tanimoto (Japan)
70kg: Masae Ueno (Japan)
78kg: Xiuli Yang (China)
+78kg: Wen Tong (China)

MODERN PENTATHLON
MEN: Andrey Moiseev (Russia)
WOMEN: Lena Schöneborn (Germany)

ROWING
MEN
Single Scull: Olaf Tufte (Norway)
Coxless Pairs: Australia
Coxless Double Sculls: Australia
Coxless Fours: Great Britain
Coxless Quad Sculls: Poland
Coxed Eight: Canada
L/w Coxless Double Sculls: Great Britain
L/w Coxless Fours: Denmark

WOMEN
Single Sculls: Rumyana Neykova (Bulgaria)
Coxless Pairs: Romania
Coxless Double Sculls: New Zealand
Coxless Quad Sculls: China
Coxed Eight: USA
Lightweight Coxless Double Sculls: Netherlands

SAILING
MEN
Windsurfer (RS:X): Tom Ashley
Laser: Paul Goodison (Great Britain)
Finn Dinghy: Ben Ainslie (Great Britain)
470 Dinghy: Australia
Star: Great Britain

WOMEN
Windsurfer (RS:X): Jian Yin (China)
Laser: Anna Tunnicliffe (USA)
470 Dinghy: Australia
Yngling: Great Britain

MIXED
Tornado: Spain
49er: Denmark

SOFTBALL
WOMEN: Japan

SWIMMING
MEN
50m Freestyle: Cesar Cielo Filho (Brazil)
100m Freestyle: Alain Bernard (France)
200m Freestyle: Michael Phelps (USA)
400m Freestyle: Taehwan Park (Korea)
1500m Freestyle: Oussama Mellouli (Tunisia)
4 × 100m Freestyle: USA
4 × 200m Freestyle: USA
100m Back: Aaron Peirsol (USA)
200m Back: Ryan Lochte (USA)
100m Breast: Kosuke Kitajima (Japan)
200m Breast: Kosuke Kitajima (Japan)
100m Butterfly: Michael Phelps (USA)
200m Butterfly: Michael Phelps (USA)
200m Medley: Michael Phelps (USA)
400m Medley: Michael Phelps (USA)
4 × 100m Medley: USA
10,000m Open Water: Maarten van der Weijden (Netherlands)

WOMEN
50m Freestyle: Britta Steffen (Germany)
100m Freestyle: Britta Steffen (Germany)
200m Freestyle: Federica Pellegrini (Italy)
400m Freestyle: Rebecca Adlington (Great Britain)
800m Freestyle: Rebecca Adlington (Great Britain)
4 × 100m Freestyle: Netherlands
4 × 200m Freestyle: Australia
100m Back: Natalie Coughlin (USA)
200m Back: Kirsty Coventry (Zimbabwe)
100m Breast: Leisel Jones (Australia)
200m Breast: Rebecca Soni (USA)
100m Butterfly: Lisbeth Trickett (Australia)
200m Butterfly: Zige Liu (China)
200m Medley: Stephanie Rice (Australia)
400m Medley: Stephanie Rice (Australia)
4 × 100m Medley: Australia
10,000m Open Water: Larisa Ilchenko (Russia)

SYNCHRONIZED SWIMMING
Duet: Russia
Team: Russia

SHOOTING
MEN
25m Rapid-Fire Pistol: Oleksandr Petriv (Ukraine)
50m Pistol: Jong-Oh Jin (Korea)
10m Air Pistol: Wei Pang (China)
50m Rifle Prone: Artur Ayvazian (Ukraine)
50m Rifle 3-pos: Jian Qiu (China)
10m Air Rifle: Abhinav Bindra (India)
Trap: David Kostelecky (Czech Republic)
Double Trap: Walton Eller (USA)
Skeet: Vincent Hancock (USA)

WOMEN
25m Pistol: Ying Chen (China)
10m Air Pistol: Wenjun Guo(China)
50m Rifle 3-pos: Li Du (China)
10m Air Rifle: Katerina Emmons (Czech Republic)
Trap: Satu Makela-Nummela (Finland)
Skeet: Chiara Cainero (Italy)

TAEKWONDO
MEN
58kg: Guillermo Perez (Mexico)
8kg: Taejin Son (Korea)
80kg: Hadi Saei (Iran)
+80kg: Dongmin Cha (Korea)

WOMEN
49kg: Jingju Wu (China)
57kg: Sujeong Lim (Korea)
67kg: Kyungseon Hwang (Korea)
+67kg: Maria del Rosario Espinoza (Mexico)

TABLE TENNIS
MEN
Singles: Lin Ma (China)
Team: China

WOMEN
Singles: Yining Zhang (China)
Team: China

TENNIS
MEN
Singles: Rafael Nadal (Spain)
Doubles: Switzerland

WOMEN
Singles: Elena Dementieva (Russia)
Doubles: USA

TRIATHLON
MEN: Jan Frodeno (Germany)
WOMEN: Emma Snowsill (Australia)

VOLLEYBALL
MEN
Indoor: USA
Beach: USA

WOMEN
Indoor: Brazil
Beach: USA

WATER POLO
MEN: Netherlands
WOMEN: Hungary

WEIGHTLIFTING
MEN
56kg: Qingquan Long(China)
62kg: Xiangxiang Zhang (China)
69kg: Hui Liao (China)
77kg: Jaehyouk Sa (Korea)
85kg: Yong Lu (China)
94kg: Ilya Ilin (Kazakhstan)
105kg: Andrei Aramnau (Belarus)
+105kg: Matthias Steiner (Germany)

WOMEN
48kg: Xiexia Chen (China)
53kg: Prapawadee Jaroenrattanatarakoon (Thailand)
58kg: Yanging Chen (China)
63kg: Hyon Suk Pak (North Korea)
69kg: Chunhong Liu (China)
75kg: Lei Cao (China)
+75kg: Miran Jang (Korea)

WRESTLING
MEN
Freestyle
55kg: Henry Cejudo (USA)
60kg: Mavlet Batirov (Russia)
66kg: Ramazan Sahin (Turkey)
74kg: Buvaysa Saytiev (Russia)
84kg: Revazi Mindorashvili (Georgia)
96kg: Shirvani Muradov (Russia)
120kg: Artur Taymanov (Uzbekistan)
Greco-Roman
55kg: Nazyr Mankiev (Russia)
60kg: Islam-Beka Albiev (Russia)
66kg: Steeve Guénot (France)
74kg: Manuchar Kvirkelia (Georgia)
84kg: Andrea Minguzzi (Italy)
96kg: Aslanbek Khushtov (Russia)
120kg: Mijain Lopez (Cuba)

WOMEN
Freestyle
48kg: Carol Huynh (Canada)
55kg: Saori Yoshida (Japan)
63kg: Kaori Icho (Japan)
72kg: Jiao Wang (China)

OLYMPICS MEDAL TABLE

Country	*Gold*	*Silver*	*Bronze*	*Total*
China	51	21	28	100
USA	36	38	36	110
Russia	23	21	28	72
Great Britain	19	13	15	47
Germany	16	10	15	41
Australia	14	15	17	46
Korea	13	10	8	31
Japan	9	6	10	25
Italy	8	10	10	28
France	7	16	17	40
Ukraine	7	5	15	27
Netherlands	7	5	4	16
Jamaica	6	3	2	11
Spain	5	10	3	18
Kenya	5	5	4	14
Belarus	4	5	10	19
Romania	4	1	3	8
Ethiopia	4	1	2	7
Canada	3	9	6	18
Poland	3	6	1	10
Hungary	3	5	2	10
Norway	3	5	2	10
Brazil	3	4	8	15
Czech Republic	3	3	0	6
Slovakia	3	2	1	6
New Zealand	3	1	5	9
Georgia	3	0	3	6
Cuba	2	11	11	24
Kazakhstan	2	4	7	13
Denmark	2	2	3	7
Mongolia	2	2	0	4
Thailand	2	2	0	4
DPR Korea	2	1	3	6
Argentina	2	0	4	6
Switzerland	2	0	4	6
Mexico	2	0	1	3
Turkey	1	4	3	8
Zimbabwe	1	3	0	4
Azerbaijan	1	2	4	7
Uzbekistan	1	2	3	6
Slovenia	1	2	2	5
Bulgaria	1	1	3	5
Indonesia	1	1	3	5
Finland	1	1	2	4
Latvia	1	1	1	3
Belgium	1	1	0	2
Dominican Republic	1	1	0	2
Estonia	1	1	0	2
Portugal	1	1	0	2
India	1	0	2	3
Iran	1	0	1	2
Bahrain	1	0	0	1
Cameroon	1	0	0	1
Panama	1	0	0	1
Tunisia	1	0	0	1
Sweden	0	4	1	5
Croatia	0	2	3	5
Lithuania	0	2	3	5
Greece	0	2	2	4
Trinidad and Tobago	0	2	0	2
Nigeria	0	1	3	4
Austria	0	1	2	3
Ireland	0	1	2	3
Serbia	0	1	2	3
Algeria	0	1	1	2

Country	*Gold*	*Silver*	*Bronze*	*Total*
Bahamas	0	1	1	2
Colombia	0	1	1	2
Kyrgyzstan	0	1	1	2
Morocco	0	1	1	2
Tajikistan	0	1	1	2
Chile	0	1	0	1
Ecuador	0	1	0	1
Iceland	0	1	0	1
Malaysia	0	1	0	1
South Africa	0	1	0	1
Singapore	0	1	0	1
Sudan	0	1	0	1
Vietnam	0	1	0	1
Armenia	0	0	6	6
Taiwan	0	0	4	4
Afghanistan	0	0	1	1
Egypt	0	0	1	1
Israel	0	0	1	1
Moldova	0	0	1	1
Mauritius	0	0	1	1
Togo	0	0	1	1
Venezuela	0	0	1	1

SPORTS RECORDS

ATHLETICS WORLD RECORDS

as at 30 August 2008

All the world records given below have been accepted by the International Amateur Athletic Federation except those marked with an asterisk* which are awaiting homologation or ratification. Fully automatic timing to 1/100th second is mandatory up to and including 400 metres. For distances up to and including 10,000 metres, records will be accepted to 1/100th second if timed automatically, and to 1/10th if hand timing is used.

MEN

TRACK EVENTS	*hr*	*min*	*sec*
100m Usain Bolt (Jamaica) 2008			9.72*
200m Usain Bolt (Jamaica) 2008			19.30
400m Michael Johnson (USA) 1999			43.18
800m Wilson Kipketer (Denmark) 1997		1	41.11
1,000m Noah Ngeny (Kenya) 1999		2	11.96
1,500m Hicham El Guerrouj (Morocco) 1998		3	26.00
1 mile Hicham El Guerrouj (Morocco) 1999		3	43.13
2,000m Hicham El Guerrouj (Morocco) 1999		4	44.79
3,000m Daniel Komen (Kenya) 1996		7	20.67
5,000m Kenenisa Bekele (Ethiopia) 2004		12	37.35
10,000m Kenenisa Bekele (Ethiopia) 2005		26	17.53
20,000m Haile Gebrselassie (Ethiopia) 2007		56	26.0
21,285m Haile Gebrselassie (Ethiopia) 2007	1	00	00.0
25,000m Toshihiko Seko (Japan) 1981	1	13	55.8
30,000m Toshihiko Seko (Japan) 1981	1	29	18.8
Marathon Paul Tergat (Kenya) 2003	2	04	55
110m hurdles (1.07m) Dayron Robles (Cuba) 2008			12.87*
400m hurdles (0.97m) Kevin Young (USA) 1992			46.78
3,000m steeplechase Saif Saaeed Shaheen (Qatar) 2004		7	53.63

RELAYS	*min*	*sec*
4 × 100m Jamaica, 2008		37.10
4 × 200m USA, 1994	1	18.68
4 × 400m USA, 1993	2	54.29
4 × 800m Kenya, 2006	7	02.43*
4 × 1,500m Federal Republic of Germany, 1977	14	38.8

FIELD EVENTS	*m*	*ft*	*in*
High jump Javier Sotomayor (Cuba) 1993	2.45	8	0½
Pole vault Sergei Bubka (Ukraine) 1994	6.14	20	1¾
Long jump Mike Powell (USA) 1991	8.95	29	4½
Triple jump Jonathan Edwards (GB) 1995	18.29	60	0¼
Shot Randy Barnes (USA) 1990	23.12	75	10¼
Discus Jürgen Schult (GDR) 1986	74.08	243	0
Hammer Yuriy Sedykh (USSR) 1986	86.74	284	7
Javelin Jan Zelezny (Czech Rep.) 1996	98.48	323	1
Decathlon † Roman Sebrle (Czech Rep.) 2001	9,026pts		

† Ten events comprising 100m, long jump, shot, high jump, 400m, 110m hurdles, discus, pole vault, javelin, 1500m

WALKING (TRACK)	*hr*	*min*	*sec*
20,000m Bernard Segura (Mexico) 1994	1	17	25.6
29,572m Maurizio Damilano (Italy) 1992	2	00	00.0
30,000m Maurizio Damilano (Italy) 1992	2	01	44.1
50,000m Thierry Toutain (France) 1996	3	40	57.9

WOMEN

TRACK EVENTS	*hr*	*min*	*sec*
100m Florence Griffith-Joyner (USA) 1988			10.49
200m Florence Griffith-Joyner (USA) 1988			21.34
400m Marita Koch (GDR) 1985			47.60
800m Jarmila Kratochvilova (Czechoslovakia) 1983		1	53.28
1,500m Qu Yunxia (China) 1993		3	50.46
1 mile Svetlana Masterkova (Russia) 1996		4	12.56
3,000m Wang Junxia (China) 1993		8	06.11
5,000m Tirunesh Dibaba (Ethiopia) 2008		14	11.15
10,000m Wang Junxia (China) 1993		29	31.78
Marathon Paula Radcliffe (GB) 2003	2	15	25
100m hurdles (0.84m) Yordanka Donkova (Bulgaria) 1988			12.21

	min	sec
400m hurdles (0.76m)		52.34
Yuliya Pechonkina (Russia) 2003		
3,000m steeplechase	8	58.81
Gulnara Galkina (Russia) 2008		

RELAYS	*min*	*sec*
4 × 100m		41.37
GDR, 1985		
4 × 200m	1	27.46
USA, 2000		
4 × 400m	3	15.17
USSR, 1988		
4 × 800m	7	50.17
USSR, 1984		

FIELD EVENTS	*m*	*ft*	*in*
High jump	2.09	6	10¼
Stefka Kostadinova (Bulgaria) 1987			
Pole vault	5.05	16	6¾
Yelena Isinbayeva (Russia) 2008			
Long jump	7.52	24	8¼
Galina Chistyakova (USSR) 1988			
Triple jump	15.50	50	10¼
Inessa Kravets (Ukraine) 1995			
Shot	22.63	74	3
Natalya Lisovskaya (USSR) 1987			
Discus	76.80	252	0
Gabriele Reinsch (GDR) 1988			
Hammer	77.80	255	3
Tatyana Lysenko (Russia) 2006			
Javelin (new implement in 1999)	71.70	235	3
Osleidys Menendez (Cuba) 2005			
Heptathlon†		7,291pts	
Jackie Joyner-Kersee (USA) 1986			

† Seven events comprising 100m hurdles, shot, high jump, 200m, long jump, javelin, 800m

ATHLETICS NATIONAL (UK) RECORDS

as at 30 August 2008

Records set anywhere by athletes eligible to represent Great Britain and Northern Ireland

MEN

TRACK EVENTS	*hr*	*min*	*sec*
100m			9.87
Linford Christie, 1993			
Dwain Chambers, 2002			
200m			19.87
John Regis, 1994			
400m			44.36
Iwan Thomas, 1997			
800m		1	41.73
Sebastian Coe, 1981			
1,000m		2	12.18
Sebastian Coe, 1981			
1,500m		3	29.67
Sebastian Coe, 1985			
1 mile		3	46.32
Steve Cram, 1985			
2,000m		4	51.39
Steve Cram, 1985			
3,000m		7	32.79
David Moorcroft, 1982			
5,000m		13	00.41
David Moorcroft, 1982			
10,000m		27	18.14
Jon Brown, 1998			
20,000m		57	28.7
Carl Thackery, 1990			
20,855m	1	00	00.0
Carl Thackery, 1990			
25,000m	1	15	22.6
Ron Hill, 1965			
30,000m	1	31	30.4
Jim Alder, 1970			
Marathon	2	07	13
Steve Jones, 1985			
3,000m steeplechase		8	07.96
Mark Rowland, 1988			
110m hurdles			12.91
Colin Jackson, 1993			
400m hurdles			47.82
Kriss Akabusi, 1992			

RELAYS	*min*	*sec*
4 × 100m		37.73
GB team, 1999		
4 × 200m	1	21.29
GB team, 1989		
4 × 400m	2	56.60
GB team, 1996		
4 × 800m	7	03.89
GB team, 1982		

FIELD EVENTS	*m*	*ft*	*in*
High jump	2.37	7	9¼
Steve Smith, 1993			
Pole vault	5.80	19	0¼
Nick Buckfield, 1998			
Long jump	8.29*	27	2½
Chris Tomlinson, 2007			
Triple jump	18.29	60	0¼
Jonathan Edwards, 1995			
Shot	21.92	71	11
Carl Myerscough, 2003			
Discus	66.64	218	8
Perris Wilkins, 1998			
Hammer	77.54	254	5
Martin Girvan, 1984			
Javelin	91.46	300	1
Steve Backley, 1992			
Decathlon		8,847pts	
Daley Thompson, 1984			

WALKING (TRACK)	*hr*	*min*	*sec*
20,000m	1	23	26.5
Ian McCombie, 1990			
30,000m	2	19	18
Christopher Maddocks, 1984			
50,000m	4	05	44.6
Paul Blagg, 1990			
26,037m	2	00	00.0
Ron Wallwork, 1971			

WOMEN

TRACK EVENTS	*hr*	*min*	*sec*
100m			11.05
Montell Douglas, 2008			
200m			22.10
Kathy Cook, 1984			
400m			49.43
Kathy Cook, 1984			
800m		1	56.21
Kelly Holmes, 1995			

	min	sec
1,500m Kelly Holmes, 2004	3	57.90
1 mile Zola Budd, 1985	4	17.57
3,000m Paula Radcliffe, 2002	8	22.20
5,000m Paula Radcliffe, 2004	14	29.11
10,000m Paula Radcliffe, 2002	30	01.09
Marathon Paula Radcliffe, 2003	2 15	25
100m hurdles Angela Thorp, 1996		12.80
400m hurdles Sally Gunnell, 1993		52.74
3,000m steeplechase Helen Clitheroe, 2008	9	29.14*

RELAYS	*min*	*sec*
4 × 100m GB team, 1980		42.43
4 × 200m GB team, 1977	1	31.57
4 × 400m GB team, 1991	3	22.01
4 × 800m GB team, 1971	8	23.8

FIELD EVENTS	*m*	*ft*	*in*
High jump Diana Elliott, 1982 Susan Jones, 2001 Jessica Ennis, 2007	1.95	6	4¾
Pole vault Janine Whitlock, 2002	4.47	14	8
Long jump Beverley Kinch, 1983	6.90	22	7¾
Triple jump Ashia Hansen, 1997	15.15	49	8½
Shot Judy Oakes, 1988	19.36	63	6¼
Discus Margaret Ritchie, 1981	67.48	221	5
Hammer Lorraine Shaw, 2001	68.93	226	1
Javelin (new implement) Goldie Sayers, 2008	65.75*	215	8
Heptathlon Denise Lewis, 2000		6,831pts	

* Awaiting ratification

SWIMMING WORLD RECORDS

as at 30 August 2008

MEN

	min	*sec*
50m freestyle Eamon Sullivan, Australia		21.28
100m freestyle Eamon Sullivan, Australia		47.05
200m freestyle Michael Phelps, USA	1	42.96
400m freestyle Ian Thorpe, Australia	3	40.08
800m freestyle Grant Hackett, Australia	7	38.65
1,500m freestyle Grant Hackett, Australia	14	34.56
50m breaststroke Oleg Lisogor, Ukraine		27.18
100m breaststroke Kosuke Kitajima, Japan		58.91
200m breaststroke Brendan Hansen, USA	2	07.51
50m butterfly Roland Schoeman, South Africa		22.96
100m butterfly Ian Crocker, USA		50.40
200m butterfly Michael Phelps, USA	1	52.03
50m backstroke Liam Tancock, Great Britain		24.47
100m backstroke Aaron Peirsol, USA		52.54
200m backstroke Ryan Lochte, USA	1	53.94
200m medley Michael Phelps, USA	1	54.23
400m medley Michael Phelps, USA	4	03.84
4 × 100m freestyle relay USA	3	08.24
4 × 200m freestyle relay USA	6	58.56
4 × 100m medley relay USA	3	29.34

WOMEN

	min	*sec*
50m freestyle Libby Trickett, Australia		23.97
100m freestyle Britta Steffen, Germany		52.88
200m freestyle Federica Pellegrini, Italy	1	54.82
400m freestyle Federica Pellegrini, Italy	4	01.53
800m freestyle Rebecca Adlington, Great Britain	8	14.10
1,500m freestyle Kate Ziegler, USA	15	42.54
50m breaststroke Jade Edmistone, Australia		30.31
100m breaststroke Leisel Jones, Australia	1	05.09
200m breaststroke Rebecca Soni, USA	2	20.22
50m butterfly Therese Alshammar, Sweden		25.46
100m butterfly Inge de Bruijn, the Netherlands		56.61
200m butterfly Liu Zige, China	2	04.18
50m backstroke Sophie Edington, Australia		27.67
100m backstroke Kirsty Coventry, Zimbabwe		58.77
200m backstroke Kirsty Coventry, Zimbabwe	2	05.24
200m medley Stephanie Rice, Australia	2	08.45
400m medley Stephanie Rice, Australia	4	29.45
4 × 100m freestyle relay The Netherlands	3	33.62
4 × 200m freestyle relay Australia	7	44.31
4 × 100m medley relay Australia	3	52.69

TIME AND SPACE

ASTRONOMY

TIME MEASUREMENT AND CALENDARS

TIDAL PREDICTIONS

ASTRONOMY

The following pages give astronomical data for each month of the year 2009. There are four pages of data for each month. All data are given for 0h Greenwich Mean Time (GMT), ie at the midnight at the beginning of the day named. This applies also to data for the months when British Summer Time is in operation (for dates, *see* below).

The astronomical data are given in a form suitable for observation with the naked eye or with a small telescope. These data do not attempt to replace the *Astronomical Almanac* for professional astronomers.

A fuller explanation of how to use the astronomical data is given on pages 1277–82.

CALENDAR FOR EACH MONTH

The calendar for each month comprises dates of general interest plus the dates of birth or death of well-known people. For key religious, civil and legal dates *see* page 9. For details of flag-flying days *see* page 23. For royal birthdays *see* pages 23 and 24–5. Public holidays are given in italics. *See also* pages 10 and 11.

Fuller explanations of the various calendars can be found under Time Measurement and Calendars.

The zodiacal signs through which the Sun is passing during each month are illustrated. The date of transition from one sign to the next, to the nearest hour, is given under Astronomical Phenomena.

JULIAN DATE

The Julian date on 2009 January 0.0 is 2454831.5. To find the Julian date for any other date in 2008 (at 0h GMT), add the day-of-the-year number on the extreme right of the calendar for each month to the Julian date for January 0.0.

SEASONS

The seasons are defined astronomically as follows:

Spring from the vernal equinox to the summer solstice
Summer from the summer solstice to the autumnal equinox
Autumn from the autumnal equinox to the winter solstice
Winter from the winter solstice to the vernal equinox

The time when seasons start in 2009 (to the nearest hour) are:

Northern Hemisphere

Vernal equinox	March 20d 12h GMT
Summer solstice	June 21d 06h GMT
Autumnal equinox	September 22d 21h GMT
Winter solstice	December 21d 18h GMT

Southern Hemisphere

Autumnal equinox	March 20d 12h GMT
Winter solstice	June 21d 06h GMT
Vernal equinox	September 22d 21h GMT
Summer solstice	December 21d 18h GMT

The longest day of the year, measured from sunrise to sunset, is at the summer solstice. The longest day in the United Kingdom will fall on 21 June in 2009.

The shortest day of the year is at the winter solstice. The shortest day in the United Kingdom will fall on 21 December in 2008.

The equinox is the point at which day and night are of equal length all over the world.

In popular parlance, the seasons in the northern hemisphere comprise the following months:

Spring	March, April, May
Summer	June, July, August
Autumn	September, October, November
Winter	December, January, February

BRITISH SUMMER TIME

British Summer Time is the legal time for general purposes during the period in which it is in operation (*see also* pages 1273–4). During this period, clocks are kept one hour ahead of Greenwich Mean Time. The hour of changeover is 01h Greenwich Mean Time. The duration of Summer Time in 2009 is from March 29 01h GMT to October 25 01h GMT.

JANUARY 2009

FIRST MONTH, 31 DAYS. *Janus*, god of the portal, facing two ways, past and future

1	*Thursday*	Euro notes and coins entered circulation in twelve European Union countries 2002	day 1
2	*Friday*	The Jameson raid ended in failure 1896	2
3	*Saturday*	General Washington's revolutionary forces defeated the British at the battle of Princeton 1777	3
4	*Sunday*	Burma regained its independence from the United Kingdom 1948	4
5	*Monday*	Pol Pot renamed Cambodia as Kampuchea and legalised its communist government 1976	week 2 day 5
6	*Tuesday*	Henry VIII married Anne of Cleves 1540	6
7	*Wednesday*	Calais was regained by the French 1558	7
8	*Thursday*	American forces under General Jackson defeated the British army at the battle of New Orleans 1815	8
9	*Friday*	280,000 coal miners began a seven-week strike against the government 1972	9
10	*Saturday*	The Metropolitan line, the first underground railway in the world, opened 1863	10
11	*Sunday*	Insulin was first administered to a diabetic patient in Canada 1922	11
12	*Monday*	The Royal Aeronautical Society of Great Britain was founded 1866	week 3 day 12
13	*Tuesday*	Pope Honorius II granted papal sanction to the military order the Knights Templar 1128	13
14	*Wednesday*	The American War of Independence ended 1784	14
15	*Thursday*	The British Museum opened to the public in Montagu House, Bloomsbury, London 1759	15
16	*Friday*	Prohibition, the attempt to ban alcohol sale and consumption, began in the USA 1920	16
17	*Saturday*	Operation Desert Storm began with bombing raids in Iraq 1991	17
18	*Sunday*	Captain Scott reached the South Pole 1912	18
19	*Monday*	The first air raid on Britain took place in Great Yarmouth 1915	week 4 day 19
20	*Tuesday*	The House of Commons assembled for the first time 1265	20
21	*Wednesday*	Concorde entered service 1976	21
22	*Thursday*	The first British Labour government came to power 1924	22
23	*Friday*	Vietnam peace treaty was agreed by the USA 1973	23
24	*Saturday*	German cruiser *Blücher* was sunk at the battle of Dogger Bank 1915	24
25	*Sunday*	Edward III acceded to the throne 1327	25
26	*Monday*	India proclaimed itself a republic 1950	week 5 day 26
27	*Tuesday*	John Logie Baird first demonstrated television 1926	27
28	*Wednesday*	The space shuttle *Challenger* exploded killing all seven astronauts on board 1986	28
29	*Thursday*	The Victoria Cross was instituted for outstanding bravery on the field of battle 1856	29
30	*Friday*	Adolf Hitler became Chancellor of Germany 1930	30
31	*Saturday*	Nauru declared independence from Australia 1968	31

ASTRONOMICAL PHENOMENA

d	*h*	
4	14	Mercury at greatest elongation E.19°
4	16	Earth at perihelion (147 million km)
11	17	Mercury at stationary point
14	21	Venus at greatest elongation E.47°
15	08	Saturn in conjunction with Moon. Saturn 6°N.
18	19	Jupiter in conjunction with Mercury. Jupiter 3°S.
19	23	Sun's longitude 300° ♒
20	16	Mercury in inferior conjunction
24	06	Jupiter in conjunction
25	03	Mars in conjunction with Moon. Mars 0°.7N.
25	09	Mercury in conjunction with Moon. Mercury 5°N.
26	05	Jupiter in conjunction with Moon. Jupiter 0°.02S.
26	08	Annular eclipse of Sun
27	06	Mars in conjunction with Mercury. Mars 4°S.
30	09	Venus in conjunction with Moon. Venus 3°S.

MINIMA OF ALGOL

d	*h*	*d*	*h*	*d*	*h*
2	16.2	14	16.2	25	16.2
5	13.0	17	13.0	28	13.0
8	09.9	19	09.9	31	09.9
11	06.7	22	06.7		

CONSTELLATIONS

The following constellations are near the meridian at

	d	*h*		*d*	*h*
December	1	24	January	16	21
December	16	23	February	1	20
January	1	22	February	15	19

Draco (below the Pole), Ursa Minor (below the Pole), Camelopardalis, Perseus, Auriga, Taurus, Orion, Eridanus and Lepus

THE MOON

Phases, Apsides and Node	*d*	*h*	*m*
☽ First Quarter	4	11	56
○ Full Moon	11	03	27
☾ Last Quarter	18	02	46
● New Moon	26	07	55
Perigee (357,503km)	10	10	57
Apogee (406,094km)	23	00	21

Mean longitude of ascending node on January 1, 311°

THE SUN

s.d. 16′.3

Day	Right Ascension	Dec. –	Equation of time	Rise 52°	Rise 56°	Transit	Set 52°	Set 56°	Sidereal time	Transit of first point of Aries
	h m s	° ′	*m s*	*h m*	*h m*	*h m*	*h m*	*h m*	*h m s*	*h m s*
1	18 46 33	23 01	−3 26	8 08	8 31	12 04	15 59	15 36	6 43 07	17 14 03
2	18 50 58	22 55	−3 54	8 08	8 31	12 04	16 00	15 38	6 47 04	17 10 07
3	18 55 22	22 50	−4 22	8 08	8 31	12 05	16 02	15 39	6 51 00	17 06 11
4	18 59 46	22 44	−4 50	8 08	8 30	12 05	16 03	15 40	6 54 57	17 02 15
5	19 04 10	22 37	−5 17	8 07	8 30	12 06	16 04	15 42	6 58 53	16 58 19
6	19 08 33	22 30	−5 43	8 07	8 29	12 06	16 05	15 43	7 02 50	16 54 24
7	19 12 56	22 23	−6 09	8 06	8 28	12 06	16 07	15 45	7 06 46	16 50 28
8	19 17 18	22 15	−6 35	8 06	8 28	12 07	16 08	15 46	7 10 43	16 46 32
9	19 21 40	22 07	−7 00	8 05	8 27	12 07	16 09	15 48	7 14 39	16 42 36
10	19 26 01	21 58	−7 25	8 05	8 26	12 08	16 11	15 50	7 18 36	16 38 40
11	19 30 21	21 49	−7 49	8 04	8 25	12 08	16 12	15 51	7 22 33	16 34 44
12	19 34 41	21 39	−8 12	8 03	8 24	12 08	16 14	15 53	7 26 29	16 30 48
13	19 39 01	21 29	−8 35	8 03	8 23	12 09	16 15	15 55	7 30 26	16 26 52
14	19 43 19	21 19	−8 57	8 02	8 22	12 09	16 17	15 57	7 34 22	16 22 56
15	19 47 37	21 08	−9 18	8 01	8 21	12 09	16 18	15 58	7 38 19	16 19 00
16	19 51 55	20 57	−9 39	8 00	8 20	12 10	16 20	16 00	7 42 15	16 15 04
17	19 56 11	20 45	−10 00	7 59	8 19	12 10	16 22	16 02	7 46 12	16 11 09
18	20 00 28	20 33	−10 19	7 58	8 17	12 10	16 23	16 04	7 50 09	16 07 13
19	20 04 43	20 21	−10 38	7 57	8 16	12 11	16 25	16 06	7 54 05	16 03 17
20	20 08 58	20 08	−10 56	7 56	8 15	12 11	16 27	16 08	7 58 02	15 59 21
21	20 13 12	19 55	−11 13	7 55	8 13	12 11	16 28	16 10	8 01 58	15 55 25
22	20 17 25	19 42	−11 30	7 54	8 12	12 12	16 30	16 12	8 05 55	15 51 29
23	20 21 37	19 28	−11 46	7 53	8 10	12 12	16 32	16 14	8 09 51	15 47 33
24	20 25 49	19 14	−12 01	7 51	8 09	12 12	16 34	16 16	8 13 48	15 43 37
25	20 30 00	18 59	−12 15	7 50	8 07	12 12	16 35	16 18	8 17 44	15 39 41
26	20 34 10	18 44	−12 29	7 49	8 05	12 13	16 37	16 20	8 21 41	15 35 45
27	20 38 19	18 29	−12 42	7 47	8 04	12 13	16 39	16 23	8 25 38	15 31 49
28	20 42 28	18 13	−12 54	7 46	8 02	12 13	16 41	16 25	8 29 34	15 27 53
29	20 46 35	17 57	−13 05	7 44	8 00	12 13	16 43	16 27	8 33 31	15 23 58
30	20 50 42	17 41	−13 15	7 43	7 58	12 13	16 44	16 29	8 37 27	15 20 02
31	20 54 48	17 24	−13 24	7 41	7 57	12 13	16 46	16 31	8 41 24	15 16 06

DURATION OF TWILIGHT (in minutes)

Latitude	*52°*	*56°*	*52°*	*56°*	*52°*	*56°*	*52°*	*56°*
	1 January		*11 January*		*21 January*		*31 January*	
Civil	41	47	40	45	38	43	37	41
Nautical	84	96	82	93	80	90	78	87
Astronomical	125	141	123	138	120	134	117	130

THE NIGHT SKY

Mercury reaches its greatest eastern elongation (19 degrees) on the 4th and is visible in the early evenings for the first two weeks of the month, low above the south-western horizon at the end of evening civil twilight. Mercury's magnitude fades from −0.7 to +1.2 during this period.

Venus reaches greatest eastern elongation (47 degrees) on the 14th and therefore is visible as a brilliant evening object, magnitude −4.4, completely dominating the western evening sky for several hours after sunset. The Moon, 4 days old, will be seen near the planet on the 30th

Mars is unsuitably placed for observation throughout the month.

Jupiter passes through conjunction on the 24th and therefore remains too close to the Sun for observation throughout the month.

Saturn, magnitude +0.8, is a morning object, moving retrograde in the constellation of Leo, and is actually visible from the mid-evening onwards when it rises above the eastern horizon, right through until dawn. The rings are becoming more difficult to observe even with moderately sized telescopes, as the angular width is only about one arcsecond; later in the year the Earth actually passes through the ring-plane.

THE MOON

Day	R.A.		Dec.	Hor. Par.	Semi-diam.	Sun's Co-Long.	PA of Br. Limb	Ph.	Age	Rise				Transit		Set			
										52°		56°				52°		56°	
	h	*m*	°	′	′	°	°	%	*d*	*h*	*m*	*h*	*m*	*h*	*m*	*h*	*m*	*h*	*m*
1	22	05	−9.8	55.1	15.0	325	248	17	4.5	10	19	10	25	15	49	21	32	21	28
2	22	50	−4.4	55.7	15.2	337	246	25	5.5	10	31	10	33	16	31	22	46	22	47
3	23	35	+1.3	56.3	15.3	349	245	35	6.5	10	43	10	40	17	14	—		—	
4	0	21	+7.1	57.1	15.5	2	246	45	7.5	10	56	10	48	18	00	0	02	0	09
5	1	10	+12.8	57.9	15.8	14	248	56	8.5	11	12	10	58	18	49	1	22	1	34
6	2	03	+18.0	58.8	16.0	26	252	66	9.5	11	33	11	13	19	43	2	47	3	05
7	3	00	+22.4	59.6	16.3	38	257	77	10.5	12	03	11	36	20	43	4	14	4	40
8	4	02	+25.6	60.4	16.5	50	264	86	11.5	12	47	12	14	21	48	5	40	6	12
9	5	08	+27.0	61.0	16.6	62	272	93	12.5	13	50	13	16	22	55	6	54	7	29
10	6	16	+26.5	61.3	16.7	74	282	98	13.5	15	12	14	42	—		7	50	8	21
11	7	23	+23.9	61.3	16.7	87	320	100	14.5	16	44	16	22	0	00	8	29	8	53
12	8	26	+19.7	60.9	16.6	99	101	99	15.5	18	18	18	03	1	02	8	56	9	13
13	9	24	+14.4	60.3	16.4	111	110	95	16.5	19	47	19	38	1	58	9	15	9	26
14	10	18	+8.3	59.5	16.2	123	114	89	17.5	21	11	21	09	2	49	9	31	9	36
15	11	08	+2.0	58.5	15.9	135	115	81	18.5	22	32	22	35	3	37	9	44	9	44
16	11	56	−4.1	57.5	15.7	147	115	71	19.5	23	50	23	58	4	22	9	57	9	52
17	12	44	−9.9	56.6	15.4	159	114	61	20.5	—		—		5	07	10	11	10	00
18	13	31	−15.1	55.8	15.2	172	112	51	21.5	1	06	1	21	5	52	10	27	10	11
19	14	20	−19.5	55.1	15.0	184	108	41	22.5	2	21	2	42	6	38	10	46	10	24
20	15	09	−23.1	54.6	14.9	196	104	32	23.5	3	34	4	01	7	26	11	11	10	43
21	16	01	−25.5	54.3	14.8	208	98	24	24.5	4	43	5	15	8	15	11	44	11	12
22	16	53	−26.9	54.1	14.7	220	93	16	25.5	5	43	6	18	9	06	12	28	11	53
23	17	46	−27.0	54.0	14.7	232	87	10	26.5	6	31	7	05	9	57	13	24	12	51
24	18	39	−25.8	54.0	14.7	245	81	5	27.5	7	09	7	38	10	46	14	30	14	01
25	19	30	−23.5	54.2	14.8	257	75	2	28.5	7	37	8	01	11	35	15	41	15	18
26	20	20	−20.2	54.4	14.8	269	67	0	29.5	7	58	8	16	12	21	16	54	16	37
27	21	08	−16.0	54.7	14.9	281	249	0	0.7	8	14	8	27	13	05	18	08	17	57
28	21	54	−11.1	55.1	15.0	293	245	3	1.7	8	28	8	35	13	48	19	22	19	16
29	22	39	−5.7	55.5	15.1	306	243	7	2.7	8	40	8	43	14	30	20	36	20	35
30	23	24	−0.0	56.0	15.3	318	243	13	3.7	8	52	8	50	15	13	21	51	21	56
31	0	10	+5.8	56.5	15.4	330	243	20	4.7	9	04	8	58	15	57	23	09	23	19

MERCURY

Day	R.A.		Dec.	Diam.	Phase	Transit		5° high			
								52°		56°	
	h	*m*	°	″	%	*h*	*m*	*h*	*m*	*h*	*m*
1	20	08	−21.8	6	71	13	26	16	41	16	11
3	20	18	−21.0	7	65	13	27	16	50	16	21
5	20	27	−20.1	7	58	13	28	16	57	16	30
7	20	33	−19.3	7	49	13	26	17	01	16	36
9	20	38	−18.5	8	40	13	22	17	02	16	39
11	20	40	−17.8	8	30	13	15	17	00	16	37
13	20	39	−17.2	9	21	13	05	16	53	16	32
15	20	34	−16.8	9	12	12	52	16	42	16	21
17	20	27	−16.7	10	6	12	37	16	27	16	06
19	20	18	−16.7	10	2	12	19	16	09	15	48
21	20	07	−16.9	10	1	12	00	15	49	15	27
23	19	56	−17.2	10	3	11	42	7	56	8	18
25	19	47	−17.6	10	7	11	26	7	42	8	04
27	19	40	−18.0	10	13	11	11	7	30	7	53
29	19	35	−18.4	9	19	10	59	7	20	7	44
31	19	32	−18.8	9	26	10	49	7	13	7	38

VENUS

Day	R.A.		Dec.	Diam.	Phase	Transit		5° high			
								52°		56°	
	h	*m*	°	″	%	*h*	*m*	*h*	*m*	*h*	*m*
1	22	00	−13.8	21	58	15	17	19	29	19	13
6	22	20	−11.6	22	56	15	17	19	44	19	30
11	22	40	−9.3	23	53	15	17	19	57	19	45
16	22	58	−6.9	25	51	15	16	20	09	20	00
21	23	16	−4.5	26	48	15	13	20	19	20	13
26	23	32	−2.1	28	45	15	10	20	29	20	24
31	23	48	+0.3	29	42	15	06	20	37	20	34

MARS

Day	R.A.		Dec.	Diam.	Phase	Transit		5° high			
								52°		56°	
	h	*m*	°	″	%	*h*	*m*	*h*	*m*	*h*	*m*
1	18	15	−24.1	4	100	11	32	8	39	9	18
6	18	32	−24.0	4	100	11	29	8	34	9	13
11	18	48	−23.8	4	100	11	26	8	29	9	07
16	19	05	−23.4	4	100	11	22	8	23	8	59
21	19	22	−23.0	4	100	11	19	8	16	8	51
26	19	38	−22.4	4	99	11	16	8	08	8	41
31	19	54	−21.8	4	99	11	13	7	59	8	30

SUNRISE AND SUNSET

	London		*Bristol*		*Birmingham*		*Manchester*		*Newcastle*		*Glasgow*		*Belfast*	
	0° 05′	*51° 30′*	*2° 35′*	*51° 28′*	*1° 55′*	*52° 28′*	*2° 15′*	*53° 28′*	*1° 37′*	*54° 59′*	*4° 14′*	*55° 52′*	*5° 56′*	*54° 35′*
d	*h m*	*h m*	*h m*	*h m*	*h m*	*h m*	*h m*	*h m*	*h m*	*h m*	*h m*	*h m*	*h m*	*h m*
1	8 06	16 02	8 16	16 12	8 18	16 05	8 25	16 01	8 31	15 49	8 47	15 54	8 46	16 09
2	8 06	16 03	8 16	16 13	8 18	16 06	8 25	16 02	8 31	15 50	8 47	15 55	8 46	16 10
3	8 06	16 04	8 15	16 15	8 18	16 07	8 24	16 03	8 31	15 52	8 47	15 57	8 46	16 11
4	8 05	16 06	8 15	16 16	8 18	16 08	8 24	16 04	8 30	15 53	8 46	15 58	8 45	16 13
5	8 05	16 07	8 15	16 17	8 17	16 09	8 24	16 06	8 30	15 54	8 46	15 59	8 45	16 14
6	8 05	16 08	8 15	16 18	8 17	16 11	8 23	16 07	8 29	15 56	8 45	16 01	8 44	16 15
7	8 04	16 09	8 14	16 20	8 16	16 12	8 23	16 08	8 29	15 57	8 44	16 02	8 44	16 17
8	8 04	16 11	8 14	16 21	8 16	16 13	8 22	16 10	8 28	15 59	8 44	16 04	8 43	16 18
9	8 03	16 12	8 13	16 22	8 15	16 15	8 22	16 11	8 27	16 00	8 43	16 06	8 42	16 20
10	8 03	16 13	8 13	16 24	8 15	16 16	8 21	16 13	8 27	16 02	8 42	16 07	8 42	16 21
11	8 02	16 15	8 12	16 25	8 14	16 18	8 20	16 14	8 26	16 04	8 41	16 09	8 41	16 23
12	8 01	16 16	8 11	16 26	8 13	16 19	8 19	16 16	8 25	16 05	8 40	16 11	8 40	16 25
13	8 01	16 18	8 11	16 28	8 13	16 21	8 19	16 17	8 24	16 07	8 39	16 12	8 39	16 26
14	8 00	16 19	8 10	16 29	8 12	16 22	8 18	16 19	8 23	16 09	8 38	16 14	8 38	16 28
15	7 59	16 21	8 09	16 31	8 11	16 24	8 17	16 21	8 22	16 10	8 37	16 16	8 37	16 30
16	7 58	16 22	8 08	16 33	8 10	16 26	8 16	16 22	8 21	16 12	8 36	16 18	8 36	16 32
17	7 57	16 24	8 07	16 34	8 09	16 27	8 15	16 24	8 20	16 14	8 35	16 20	8 35	16 33
18	7 56	16 26	8 06	16 36	8 08	16 29	8 14	16 26	8 19	16 16	8 34	16 22	8 34	16 35
19	7 55	16 27	8 05	16 37	8 07	16 31	8 13	16 28	8 17	16 18	8 32	16 24	8 33	16 37
20	7 54	16 29	8 04	16 39	8 06	16 32	8 11	16 29	8 16	16 20	8 31	16 26	8 31	16 39
21	7 53	16 31	8 03	16 41	8 05	16 34	8 10	16 31	8 15	16 22	8 29	16 28	8 30	16 41
22	7 52	16 32	8 02	16 42	8 03	16 36	8 09	16 33	8 13	16 24	8 28	16 30	8 29	16 43
23	7 51	16 34	8 01	16 44	8 02	16 38	8 08	16 35	8 12	16 25	8 27	16 32	8 27	16 45
24	7 50	16 36	8 00	16 46	8 01	16 39	8 06	16 37	8 10	16 27	8 25	16 34	8 26	16 47
25	7 48	16 38	7 58	16 48	7 59	16 41	8 05	16 39	8 09	16 29	8 23	16 36	8 24	16 49
26	7 47	16 39	7 57	16 49	7 58	16 43	8 03	16 40	8 07	16 31	8 22	16 38	8 23	16 51
27	7 46	16 41	7 56	16 51	7 57	16 45	8 02	16 42	8 06	16 34	8 20	16 40	8 21	16 53
28	7 44	16 43	7 54	16 53	7 55	16 47	8 00	16 44	8 04	16 36	8 18	16 42	8 20	16 55
29	7 43	16 45	7 53	16 55	7 54	16 49	7 59	16 46	8 02	16 38	8 17	16 44	8 18	16 57
30	7 42	16 46	7 51	16 57	7 52	16 50	7 57	16 48	8 01	16 40	8 15	16 46	8 16	16 59
31	7 40	16 48	7 50	16 58	7 51	16 52	7 56	16 50	7 59	16 42	8 13	16 49	8 14	17 01

JUPITER

Day	*R.A.*		*Dec.*		*Transit*		*5° high*			
							52°		*56°*	
	h	*m*	°	′	*h*	*m*	*h*	*m*	*h*	*m*
1	20	04.6	−20	47	13	20	16	41	16	13
11	20	14.3	−20	18	12	50	16	16	15	48
21	20	24.1	−19	46	12	21	15	50	15	23
31	20	33.9	−19	13	11	51	15	24	14	59

Diameters – equatorial 32″ polar 30″

SATURN

Day	*R.A.*		*Dec.*		*Transit*		*5° high*			
							52°		*56°*	
	h	*m*	°	′	*h*	*m*	*h*	*m*	*h*	*m*
1	11	33.0	+5	09	4	49	22	52	22	51
11	11	32.7	+5	14	4	09	22	12	22	11
21	11	31.8	+5	23	3	29	21	31	21	30
31	11	30.2	+5	35	2	48	20	49	20	48

Diameters – equatorial 19″ polar 17″

Rings – major axis 43″ minor axis 1″

URANUS

Day	*R.A.*		*Dec.*		*Transit*		*10° high*			
							52°		*56°*	
	h	*m*	°	′	*h*	*m*	*h*	*m*	*h*	*m*
1	23	21.6	−4	57	16	36	21	02	20	51
11	23	22.8	−4	49	15	58	20	25	20	14
21	23	24.2	−4	40	15	20	19	48	19	37
31	23	25.9	−4	29	14	42	19	11	19	00

Diameter 4″

NEPTUNE

Day	*R.A.*		*Dec.*		*Transit*		*10° high*			
							52°		*56°*	
	h	*m*	°	′	*h*	*m*	*h*	*m*	*h*	*m*
1	21	39.6	−14	22	14	54	18	21	17	56
11	21	40.9	−14	16	14	16	17	43	17	19
21	21	42.2	−14	09	13	38	17	06	16	42
31	21	43.7	−14	02	13	00	16	29	16	05

Diameter 2″

FEBRUARY 2009

SECOND MONTH, 28 or 29 DAYS. *Februa*, Roman festival of Purification

1	*Sunday*	Ayatollah Khomeini returned to Iran after 14 years in exile 1979	day 32
2	*Monday*	The British embassy in Dublin was burnt down 1972	week 6 day 33
3	*Tuesday*	Harold Macmillan made the 'winds of change' speech in the parliament in Cape Town 1960	34
4	*Wednesday*	George Washington was elected as the first president of the USA 1789	35
5	*Thursday*	Sweet rationing ended in Great Britain 1953	36
6	*Friday*	Tony Blair became the longest-serving Labour prime minister 2005	37
7	*Saturday*	The EU became official with the signing of the Maastricht Treaty 1991	38
8	*Sunday*	Mary Queen of Scots was beheaded 1587	39
9	*Monday*	Conscription began in Great Britain with the Military Service Act 1916	week 7 day 40
10	*Tuesday*	France ceded Canada to Great Britain in the Treaty of Paris 1763	41
11	*Wednesday*	The Lateran Treaty between Italy and the Holy See was signed 1929	42
12	*Thursday*	Lady Jane Grey was beheaded 1554	43
13	*Friday*	Allied forces bombed Dresden, Germany 1945	44
14	*Saturday*	The Spanish fleet was defeated by the British at the battle of Cape St Vincent 1797	45
15	*Sunday*	Decimal currency was introduced in the UK 1971	46
16	*Monday*	Fidel Castro became prime minister of Cuba 1959	week 8 day 47
17	*Tuesday*	China invaded Vietnam 1979	48
18	*Wednesday*	A ban on hunting came into force in the UK 2005	49
19	*Thursday*	The phonograph was patented by Thomas Edison 1878	50
20	*Friday*	John Glenn became the first American astronaut orbiting three times around the Earth 1962	51
21	*Saturday*	Battle of Verdun began and continued into the summer 1916	52
22	*Sunday*	1,700 Frenchmen landed at Fishguard in the 'last invasion of Britain' 1797	53
23	*Monday*	Benito Mussolini formed the Fascist party in Italy 1919	week 9 day 54
24	*Tuesday*	Vladimir Putin dismissed the entire Russian government 2004	55
25	*Wednesday*	Pope Pius V excommunicated Elizabeth I 1570	56
26	*Thursday*	£1 and £2 notes were first issued 1797	57
27	*Friday*	The Reichstag building burnt down in Berlin 1933	58
28	*Saturday*	Olof Palme, the Swedish prime minister, was assassinated 1986	59

ASTRONOMICAL PHENOMENA

d	*h*	
1	07	Mercury at stationary point
11	16	Saturn in conjunction with Moon. Saturn 6°N.
12	13	Neptune in conjunction
13	21	Mercury at greatest elongation W.26°
17	16	Jupiter in conjunction with Mars. Jupiter 0°.6N.
18	13	Sun's longitude 330° ♓
19	16	Venus at greatest brilliancy
22	22	Mercury in conjunction with Moon. Mercury 1°S.
23	01	Jupiter in conjunction with Moon. Jupiter 0°.7S.
23	07	Mars in conjunction with Moon. Mars 2°S.
24	07	Jupiter in conjunction with Mercury. Jupiter 0°.6N.
28	00	Venus in conjunction with Moon. Venus 1°N.

MINIMA OF ALGOL

d	*h*	*d*	*h*	*d*	*h*
3	16.2	14	16.2	26	16.2
6	13.0	17	13.0		
8	09.9	20	09.9		
11	06.7	23	06.7		

CONSTELLATIONS

The following constellations are near the meridian at

	d	*h*		*d*	*h*
January	1	24	February	15	21
January	16	23	March	1	20
February	1	22	March	16	19

Draco (below the Pole), Camelopardalis, Auriga, Taurus, Gemini, Orion, Canis Minor, Monoceros, Lepus, Canis Major and Puppis

THE MOON

Phases, Apsides and Node	*d*	*h*	*m*
☽ First Quarter	2	23	13
○ Full Moon	9	14	49
☾ Last Quarter	16	21	37
● New Moon	25	01	35
Perigee (361,504km)	7	20	15
Apogee (405,094km)	19	17	04

Mean longitude of ascending node on February 1, 309°

THE SUN

s.d. 16′.2

Day	Right Ascension			Dec. –		Equation of time		Rise 52°		Rise 56°		Transit		Set 52°		Set 56°		Sidereal time			Transit of first point of Aries		
	h	*m*	*s*	°	′	*m*	*s*	*h*	*m*	*h*	*m*	*h*	*m*	*h*	*m*	*h*	*m*	*h*	*m*	*s*	*h*	*m*	*s*
1	20	58	53	17	07	−13	33	7	40	7	55	12	14	16	48	16	33	8	45	20	15	12	10
2	21	02	58	16	50	−13	41	7	38	7	53	12	14	16	50	16	35	8	49	17	15	08	14
3	21	07	01	16	33	−13	48	7	37	7	51	12	14	16	52	16	38	8	53	13	15	04	18
4	21	11	04	16	15	−13	54	7	35	7	49	12	14	16	54	16	40	8	57	10	15	00	22
5	21	15	06	15	57	−13	59	7	33	7	47	12	14	16	56	16	42	9	01	07	14	56	26
6	21	19	07	15	38	−14	04	7	32	7	45	12	14	16	57	16	44	9	05	03	14	52	30
7	21	23	07	15	20	−14	07	7	30	7	43	12	14	16	59	16	46	9	09	00	14	48	34
8	21	27	06	15	01	−14	10	7	28	7	41	12	14	17	01	16	49	9	12	56	14	44	38
9	21	31	05	14	42	−14	12	7	26	7	38	12	14	17	03	16	51	9	16	53	14	40	43
10	21	35	03	14	23	−14	13	7	24	7	36	12	14	17	05	16	53	9	20	49	14	36	47
11	21	39	00	14	03	−14	14	7	23	7	34	12	14	17	07	16	55	9	24	46	14	32	51
12	21	42	56	13	43	−14	14	7	21	7	32	12	14	17	09	16	57	9	28	42	14	28	55
13	21	46	52	13	23	−14	13	7	19	7	30	12	14	17	10	17	00	9	32	39	14	24	59
14	21	50	46	13	03	−14	11	7	17	7	27	12	14	17	12	17	02	9	36	36	14	21	03
15	21	54	40	12	42	−14	08	7	15	7	25	12	14	17	14	17	04	9	40	32	14	17	07
16	21	58	34	12	22	−14	05	7	13	7	23	12	14	17	16	17	06	9	44	29	14	13	11
17	22	02	26	12	01	−14	01	7	11	7	20	12	14	17	18	17	08	9	48	25	14	09	15
18	22	06	18	11	40	−13	57	7	09	7	18	12	14	17	20	17	11	9	52	22	14	05	19
19	22	10	10	11	18	−13	51	7	07	7	16	12	14	17	22	17	13	9	56	18	14	01	23
20	22	14	00	10	57	−13	45	7	05	7	13	12	14	17	23	17	15	10	00	15	13	57	28
21	22	17	50	10	35	−13	39	7	03	7	11	12	14	17	25	17	17	10	04	11	13	53	32
22	22	21	40	10	14	−13	32	7	01	7	09	12	13	17	27	17	19	10	08	08	13	49	36
23	22	25	28	9	52	−13	24	6	59	7	06	12	13	17	29	17	21	10	12	05	13	45	40
24	22	29	17	9	29	−13	16	6	56	7	04	12	13	17	31	17	24	10	16	01	13	41	44
25	22	33	04	9	07	−13	07	6	54	7	01	12	13	17	33	17	26	10	19	58	13	37	48
26	22	36	51	8	45	−12	57	6	52	6	59	12	13	17	34	17	28	10	23	54	13	33	52
27	22	40	38	8	22	−12	47	6	50	6	56	12	13	17	36	17	30	10	27	51	13	29	56
28	22	44	23	8	00	−12	36	6	48	6	54	12	13	17	38	17	32	10	31	47	13	26	00

DURATION OF TWILIGHT (in minutes)

Latitude	*52°*	*56°*	*52°*	*56°*	*52°*	*56°*	*52°*	*56°*
	1 February		*11 February*		*21 February*		*31 February*	
Civil	37	41	35	39	34	38	34	37
Nautical	77	86	75	83	74	81	73	80
Astronomical	117	130	114	126	113	124	112	124

THE NIGHT SKY

Mercury is unsuitably placed for observation throughout the month, despite attaining a greatest western elongation of 26 degrees on the 13th.

Venus continues to be visible as a magnificent object in the south-western sky in the evenings after sunset. It attains its greatest brilliancy on the 19th with a magnitude of −4.6. On the evening of the 27th the thin crescent Moon, only about 3 days old, will be seen 4 degrees below.

Mars continues to be unsuitably placed for observation. The planet will not be available for observation until the second half of June, when it reappears as a morning object.

Jupiter is still too close to the Sun for observation.

Saturn, in the constellation of Leo, is rising in the eastern sky in the evenings and remains visible until the morning twilight inhibits observation. Its magnitude is +0.6.

Zodiacal Light. The evening cone may be observed stretching up from the western horizon, along the ecliptic, after the end of twilight, from the 11th to the 25th. This faint phenomenon is only visible under good conditions and in the absence of both moonlight and artificial lighting.

THE MOON

Day	R.A.		Dec.	Hor. par.	Semi-diam.	Sun's Co-Long.	PA of Br. Limb	Ph.	Age	Rise 52°		Rise 56°		Transit		Set 52°		Set 56°	
	h	*m*	°	′	′	°	°	%	*d*	*h*	*m*	*h*	*m*	*h*	*m*	*h*	*m*	*h*	*m*
1	0	58	+11.5	57.1	15.6	342	245	29	5.7	9	19	9	07	16	44	—		—	
2	1	48	+16.7	57.8	15.7	354	248	40	6.7	9	37	9	19	17	35	0	30	0	46
3	2	42	+21.3	58.4	15.9	6	252	50	7.7	10	02	9	38	18	31	1	54	2	17
4	3	41	+24.7	59.1	16.1	19	258	62	8.7	10	38	10	07	19	31	3	18	3	48
5	4	44	+26.7	59.7	16.3	31	265	72	9.7	11	30	10	55	20	35	4	35	5	09
6	5	49	+26.9	60.2	16.4	43	272	82	10.7	12	41	12	08	21	39	5	37	6	11
7	6	54	+25.3	60.6	16.5	55	279	90	11.7	14	07	13	40	22	41	6	23	6	50
8	7	57	+21.8	60.7	16.5	67	284	96	12.7	15	39	15	20	23	40	6	55	7	15
9	8	57	+17.0	60.5	16.5	79	285	99	13.7	17	11	16	59	—		7	17	7	31
10	9	53	+11.2	60.0	16.4	91	127	100	14.7	18	39	18	33	0	33	7	35	7	42
11	10	46	+4.9	59.4	16.2	104	120	97	15.7	20	03	20	04	1	24	7	49	7	52
12	11	36	−1.5	58.6	16.0	116	119	92	16.7	21	25	21	31	2	11	8	03	8	00
13	12	25	−7.6	57.7	15.7	128	118	86	17.7	22	44	22	56	2	58	8	17	8	08
14	13	14	−13.2	56.8	15.5	140	116	78	18.7	—		—		3	44	8	32	8	18
15	14	03	−18.1	56.0	15.2	152	112	68	19.7	0	02	0	20	4	31	8	50	8	30
16	14	53	−22.0	55.3	15.1	164	108	59	20.7	1	18	1	42	5	19	9	13	8	47
17	15	45	−24.9	54.7	14.9	176	103	49	21.7	2	30	3	00	6	09	9	43	9	12
18	16	37	−26.6	54.4	14.8	189	97	40	22.7	3	34	4	08	6	59	10	23	9	49
19	17	30	−27.0	54.2	14.8	201	91	31	23.7	4	27	5	02	7	50	11	15	10	40
20	18	23	−26.3	54.1	14.7	213	86	22	24.7	5	08	5	40	8	40	12	17	11	46
21	19	15	−24.3	54.2	14.8	225	81	15	25.7	5	39	6	06	9	29	13	26	13	01
22	20	05	−21.3	54.5	14.8	237	77	9	26.7	6	03	6	23	10	16	14	39	14	20
23	20	54	−17.3	54.8	14.9	250	75	4	27.7	6	21	6	36	11	02	15	54	15	40
24	21	41	−12.6	55.3	15.1	262	77	1	28.7	6	35	6	45	11	45	17	08	17	01
25	22	27	−7.2	55.7	15.2	274	140	0	29.7	6	48	6	53	12	28	18	23	18	21
26	23	12	−1.5	56.2	15.3	286	230	1	0.9	7	00	7	00	13	12	19	39	19	42
27	23	59	+4.4	56.7	15.4	298	237	4	1.9	7	13	7	08	13	56	20	57	21	05
28	0	46	+10.1	57.2	15.6	311	240	9	2.9	7	27	7	17	14	42	22	18	22	32

MERCURY

Day	R.A.		Dec.	Diam.	Phase	Transit		5° high 52°		5° high 56°	
	h	*m*	°	″	%	*h*	*m*	*h*	*m*	*h*	*m*
1	19	32	−19.0	9	29	10	45	7	10	7	36
3	19	33	−19.3	8	35	10	39	7	06	7	32
5	19	36	−19.6	8	41	10	34	7	03	7	30
7	19	40	−19.8	8	46	10	31	7	02	7	29
9	19	46	−19.9	7	51	10	29	7	01	7	28
11	19	53	−20.0	7	55	10	29	7	01	7	28
13	20	01	−20.0	7	59	10	29	7	01	7	28
15	20	10	−19.9	7	62	10	30	7	01	7	28
17	20	19	−19.7	7	66	10	31	7	01	7	28
19	20	29	−19.4	6	68	10	34	7	01	7	27
21	20	40	−19.1	6	71	10	36	7	01	7	26
23	20	51	−18.7	6	73	10	39	7	01	7	25
25	21	02	−18.2	6	75	10	42	7	00	7	24
27	21	13	−17.6	6	77	10	46	7	00	7	22
29	21	25	−16.9	6	79	10	50	6	59	7	20
31	21	36	−16.1	6	81	10	54	6	57	7	17

VENUS

Day	R.A.		Dec.	Diam.	Phase	Transit		5° high 52°		5° high 56°	
	h	*m*	°	″	%	*h*	*m*	*h*	*m*	*h*	*m*
1	23	51	+ 0.8	30	41	15	05	20	38	20	36
6	0	05	+ 3.0	32	38	14	59	20	44	20	43
11	0	17	+ 5.2	34	34	14	52	20	47	20	48
16	0	28	+ 7.2	37	30	14	42	20	48	20	51
21	0	37	+ 9.1	40	26	14	31	20	46	20	50
26	0	43	+10.6	43	22	14	17	20	40	20	45
31	0	46	+11.9	47	17	14	00	20	29	20	35

MARS

Day	R.A.		Dec.	Diam.	Phase	Transit		5° high 52°		5° high 56°	
	h	*m*	°	″	%	*h*	*m*	*h*	*m*	*h*	*m*
1	19	58	−21.6	4	99	11	12	7	57	8	28
6	20	14	−20.9	4	99	11	09	7	47	8	16
11	20	30	−20.0	4	99	11	05	7	37	8	04
16	20	46	−19.1	4	99	11	01	7	26	7	51
21	21	02	−18.0	4	99	10	57	7	15	7	38
26	21	18	−16.9	4	98	10	53	7	03	7	24
31	21	33	−15.7	4	98	10	49	6	51	7	10

SUNRISE AND SUNSET

	London		*Bristol*		*Birmingham*		*Manchester*		*Newcastle*		*Glasgow*		*Belfast*	
	0° 05′	*51° 30′*	*2° 35′*	*51° 28′*	*1° 55′*	*52° 28′*	*2° 15′*	*53° 28′*	*1° 37′*	*54° 59′*	*4° 14′*	*55° 52′*	*5° 56′*	*54° 35′*
d	*h m*	*h m*	*h m*	*h m*	*h m*	*h m*	*h m*	*h m*	*h m*	*h m*	*h m*	*h m*	*h m*	*h m*
1	7 38	16 50	7 48	17 00	7 49	16 54	7 54	16 52	7 57	16 44	8 11	16 51	8 13	17 03
2	7 37	16 52	7 47	17 02	7 47	16 56	7 52	16 54	7 55	16 46	8 09	16 53	8 11	17 05
3	7 35	16 54	7 45	17 04	7 46	16 58	7 50	16 56	7 53	16 48	8 07	16 55	8 09	17 07
4	7 34	16 56	7 44	17 06	7 44	17 00	7 49	16 58	7 51	16 50	8 05	16 57	8 07	17 09
5	7 32	16 57	7 42	17 07	7 42	17 02	7 47	17 00	7 50	16 52	8 03	17 00	8 05	17 11
6	7 30	16 59	7 40	17 09	7 41	17 04	7 45	17 02	7 48	16 54	8 01	17 02	8 03	17 13
7	7 29	17 01	7 39	17 11	7 39	17 06	7 43	17 04	7 46	16 56	7 59	17 04	8 01	17 15
8	7 27	17 03	7 37	17 13	7 37	17 07	7 41	17 06	7 44	16 59	7 57	17 06	7 59	17 17
9	7 25	17 05	7 35	17 15	7 35	17 09	7 39	17 08	7 42	17 01	7 55	17 08	7 57	17 19
10	7 23	17 06	7 33	17 17	7 33	17 11	7 37	17 10	7 39	17 03	7 53	17 10	7 55	17 21
11	7 22	17 08	7 31	17 18	7 31	17 13	7 35	17 12	7 37	17 05	7 51	17 13	7 53	17 23
12	7 20	17 10	7 30	17 20	7 29	17 15	7 33	17 14	7 35	17 07	7 48	17 15	7 51	17 25
13	7 18	17 12	7 28	17 22	7 28	17 17	7 31	17 16	7 33	17 09	7 46	17 17	7 49	17 27
14	7 16	17 14	7 26	17 24	7 26	17 19	7 29	17 18	7 31	17 11	7 44	17 19	7 47	17 30
15	7 14	17 16	7 24	17 26	7 24	17 21	7 27	17 20	7 29	17 13	7 42	17 21	7 45	17 32
16	7 12	17 17	7 22	17 28	7 22	17 23	7 25	17 22	7 27	17 15	7 39	17 24	7 43	17 34
17	7 10	17 19	7 20	17 29	7 20	17 25	7 23	17 24	7 24	17 17	7 37	17 26	7 41	17 36
18	7 08	17 21	7 18	17 31	7 18	17 26	7 21	17 26	7 22	17 20	7 35	17 28	7 38	17 38
19	7 06	17 23	7 16	17 33	7 15	17 28	7 19	17 28	7 20	17 22	7 32	17 30	7 36	17 40
20	7 04	17 25	7 14	17 35	7 13	17 30	7 17	17 30	7 18	17 24	7 30	17 32	7 34	17 42
21	7 02	17 27	7 12	17 37	7 11	17 32	7 15	17 31	7 15	17 26	7 28	17 34	7 32	17 44
22	7 00	17 28	7 10	17 38	7 09	17 34	7 12	17 33	7 13	17 28	7 25	17 37	7 29	17 46
23	6 58	17 30	7 08	17 40	7 07	17 36	7 10	17 35	7 11	17 30	7 23	17 39	7 27	17 48
24	6 56	17 32	7 06	17 42	7 05	17 38	7 08	17 37	7 08	17 32	7 20	17 41	7 25	17 50
25	6 54	17 34	7 04	17 44	7 03	17 40	7 06	17 39	7 06	17 34	7 18	17 43	7 22	17 52
26	6 52	17 35	7 02	17 46	7 01	17 41	7 03	17 41	7 03	17 36	7 15	17 45	7 20	17 54
27	6 50	17 37	7 00	17 47	6 58	17 43	7 01	17 43	7 01	17 38	7 13	17 47	7 18	17 56
28	6 48	17 39	6 57	17 49	6 56	17 45	6 59	17 45	6 59	17 40	7 11	17 49	7 15	17 58

JUPITER

Day	*R.A.*		*Dec.*		*Transit*		*5° high*			
							52°		*56°*	
	h	*m*	°	′	*h*	*m*	*h*	*m*	*h*	*m*
1	20	34.8	−19	10	11	48	8	14	8	40
11	20	44.4	−18	35	11	18	7	40	8	05
21	20	53.9	−17	59	10	48	7	06	7	29
31	21	03.0	−17	22	10	18	6	31	6	54

Diameters – equatorial 33″ polar 31″

SATURN

Day	*R.A.*		*Dec.*		*Transit*		*5° high*			
							52°		*56°*	
	h	*m*	°	′	*h*	*m*	*h*	*m*	*h*	*m*
1	11	30.0	+ 5	37	2	44	20	45	20	44
11	11	27.9	+ 5	52	2	03	20	02	20	00
21	11	25.4	+ 6	10	1	21	19	19	19	17
31	11	22.5	+ 6	30	0	39	18	35	18	33

Diameters – equatorial 20″ polar 17″
Rings – major axis 44″ minor axis 1″

URANUS

Day	*R.A.*		*Dec.*		*Transit*		*10° high*			
							52°		*56°*	
	h	*m*	°	′	*h*	*m*	*h*	*m*	*h*	*m*
1	23	26.0	−4	28	14	38	19	08	18	57
11	23	27.9	−4	16	14	01	18	31	18	21
21	23	29.8	−4	03	13	24	17	55	17	45
31	23	31.9	−3	50	12	46	17	19	17	09

Diameter 4″

NEPTUNE

Day	*R.A.*		*Dec.*		*Transit*		*10° high*			
							52°		*56°*	
	h	*m*	°	′	*h*	*m*	*h*	*m*	*h*	*m*
1	21	43.8	−14	01	12	56	9	27	9	51
11	21	45.3	−13	54	12	19	8	49	9	13
21	21	46.7	−13	47	11	41	8	10	8	34
31	21	48.2	−13	39	11	03	7	31	7	55

Diameter 2″

MARCH 2009

THIRD MONTH, 31 DAYS. *Mars*, Roman god of battle

1	*Sunday*	A new Official Secrets Act came into force 1990	day 60
2	*Monday*	Concorde made its maiden flight 1969	week 10 day 61
3	*Tuesday*	Serfdom was abolished in Russia 1861	62
4	*Wednesday*	The Royal National Lifeboat Institution was founded 1824	63
5	*Thursday*	Churchill stated that an 'iron curtain has descended across the continent' 1946	64
6	*Friday*	The Siege of El Alamo, known as Thermopylae of America, ended 1836	65
7	*Saturday*	Alexander Graham Bell patented the telephone 1876	66
8	*Sunday*	The New York Stock exchange was founded 1817	67
9	*Monday*	Joseph Stalin's daughter Svetlana Alliluyeva defected to the USA 1967	week 11 day 68
10	*Tuesday*	Charles I dissolved parliament, starting 11 years known as the 'Personal Rule' 1629	69
11	*Wednesday*	The Madrid train bombings killed 192 people 2004	70
12	*Thursday*	Germany annexed Austria in the *Anshluss* 1938	71
13	*Friday*	German-born astronomer William Herschell discovered Uranus 1781	72
14	*Saturday*	The first patient was successfully treated with penicillin 1942	73
15	*Sunday*	In Russia, Tsar Nicholas II abdicated 1917	74
16	*Monday*	Harold Wilson resigned 1976	week 12 day 75
17	*Tuesday*	The Kingdom of Italy was proclaimed 1861	76
18	*Wednesday*	The Commune Rising began in Paris 1871	77
19	*Thursday*	Argentines hoisted a flag on South Georgia Island precipitating the Falklands War 1982	78
20	*Friday*	A sarin gas attack killed 12 people on the underground in Tokyo 1995	79
21	*Saturday*	The Sharpeville Massacre took place, in which South African police shot 69 black demonstrators 1960	80
22	*Sunday*	The Football League was formed 1888	81
23	*Monday*	Pakistan became a republic 1956	week 13 day 82
24	*Tuesday*	The union of English and Scottish crowns 1603	83
25	*Wednesday*	The EEC was established by the treaty of Rome 1957	84
26	*Thursday*	Women were admitted to the London Stock Exchange 1973	85
27	*Friday*	The first international radio transmission was achieved by Guglielmo Marconi 1899	86
28	*Saturday*	Britain declared war on Russia and the Crimean War began 1854	87
29	*Sunday*	Queen Victoria opened the Royal Albert Hall 1871	88
30	*Monday*	Russia sold Alaska to the USA for US$7.2bn 1867	week 14 day 89
31	*Tuesday*	200,000 marched in the Poll Tax riots 1990	90

ASTRONOMICAL PHENOMENA

d	*h*	
2	03	Mars in conjunction with Mercury. Mars 0°.6N.
6	17	Venus at stationary point
8	20	Saturn at opposition
10	22	Saturn in conjunction with Moon. Saturn 6°N.
13	01	Uranus in conjunction
20	12	Sun's longitude 0° ♈
22	21	Jupiter in conjunction with Moon. Jupiter 1°S.
24	11	Mars in conjunction with Moon. Mars 4°S.
26	07	Mercury in conjunction with Moon. Mercury 6°S.
26	19	Venus in conjunction with Moon. Venus 4°N.
27	19	Venus in inferior conjunction
29	03	Venus in conjunction with Mercury. Venus 9°N.
31	03	Mercury in superior conjunction

MINIMA OF ALGOL

d	*h*	*d*	*h*	*d*	*h*
1	16.2	12	16.2	23	16.2
3	13.0	15	13.0	26	13.0
6	09.9	18	09.9	29	09.9
9	06.7	21	06.7		

CONSTELLATIONS

The following constellations are near the meridian at

	d	*h*		*d*	*h*
February	1	24	March	16	21
February	15	23	April	1	20
March	1	22	April	15	19

Cepheus (below the Pole), Camelopardalis, Lynx, Gemini, Cancer, Leo, Canis Minor, Hydra, Monoceros, Canis Major and Puppis

THE MOON

Phases, Apsides and Node	*d*	*h*	*m*
☽ First Quarter	4	07	46
○ Full Moon	11	02	38
☾ Last Quarter	18	17	47
● New Moon	26	16	06
Perigee (367,043km)	7	15	15
Apogee (404,259km)	19	13	17

Mean longitude of ascending node on March 1, 308°

THE SUN

s.d. 16′.1

Day	Right Ascension h m s	Dec. ° ′	Equation of time m s	Rise 52° h m	Rise 56° h m	Transit h m	Set 52° h m	Set 56° h m	Sidereal time h m s	Transit of first point of Aries h m s
1	22 48 09	−7 37	−12 25	6 46	6 51	12 12	17 40	17 34	10 35 44	13 22 04
2	22 51 54	−7 14	−12 13	6 43	6 49	12 12	17 42	17 36	10 39 40	13 18 08
3	22 55 38	−6 51	−12 01	6 41	6 46	12 12	17 43	17 39	10 43 37	13 14 13
4	22 59 22	−6 28	−11 48	6 39	6 44	12 12	17 45	17 41	10 47 34	13 10 17
5	23 03 05	−6 05	−11 35	6 37	6 41	12 11	17 47	17 43	10 51 30	13 06 21
6	23 06 48	−5 42	−11 21	6 35	6 39	12 11	17 49	17 45	10 55 27	13 02 25
7	23 10 30	−5 18	−11 07	6 32	6 36	12 11	17 51	17 47	10 59 23	12 58 29
8	23 14 12	−4 55	−10 53	6 30	6 33	12 11	17 52	17 49	11 03 20	12 54 33
9	23 17 54	−4 32	−10 38	6 28	6 31	12 11	17 54	17 51	11 07 16	12 50 37
10	23 21 35	−4 08	−10 22	6 26	6 28	12 10	17 56	17 53	11 11 13	12 46 41
11	23 25 16	−3 45	−10 07	6 23	6 26	12 10	17 58	17 55	11 15 09	12 42 45
12	23 28 57	−3 21	−9 51	6 21	6 23	12 10	17 59	17 57	11 19 06	12 38 49
13	23 32 37	−2 58	−9 35	6 19	6 20	12 09	18 01	18 00	11 23 02	12 34 53
14	23 36 17	−2 34	−9 18	6 16	6 18	12 09	18 03	18 02	11 26 59	12 30 58
15	23 39 57	−2 10	−9 01	6 14	6 15	12 09	18 05	18 04	11 30 56	12 27 02
16	23 43 37	−1 46	−8 44	6 12	6 13	12 09	18 06	18 06	11 34 52	12 23 06
17	23 47 16	−1 23	−8 27	6 10	6 10	12 08	18 08	18 08	11 38 49	12 19 10
18	23 50 55	−0 59	−8 10	6 07	6 07	12 08	18 10	18 10	11 42 45	12 15 14
19	23 54 34	−0 35	−7 52	6 05	6 05	12 08	18 12	18 12	11 46 42	12 11 18
20	23 58 13	−0 12	−7 35	6 03	6 02	12 07	18 13	18 14	11 50 38	12 07 22
21	0 01 52	+0 12	−7 17	6 00	5 59	12 07	18 15	18 16	11 54 35	12 03 26
22	0 05 31	+0 36	−6 59	5 58	5 57	12 07	18 17	18 18	11 58 31	11 59 30
23	0 09 09	+1 00	−6 41	5 56	5 54	12 07	18 18	18 20	12 02 28	11 55 34
24	0 12 48	+1 23	−6 23	5 53	5 52	12 06	18 20	18 22	12 06 25	11 51 39
25	0 16 26	+1 47	−6 05	5 51	5 49	12 06	18 22	18 24	12 10 21	11 47 43
26	0 20 05	+2 10	−5 47	5 49	5 46	12 06	18 24	18 26	12 14 18	11 43 47
27	0 23 43	+2 34	−5 29	5 46	5 44	12 05	18 25	18 28	12 18 14	11 39 51
28	0 27 22	+2 57	−5 11	5 44	5 41	12 05	18 27	18 30	12 22 11	11 35 55
29	0 31 00	+3 21	−4 53	5 42	5 38	12 05	18 29	18 32	12 26 07	11 31 59
30	0 34 39	+3 44	−4 35	5 39	5 36	12 04	18 31	18 34	12 30 04	11 28 03
31	0 38 17	+4 07	−4 17	5 37	5 33	12 04	18 32	18 36	12 34 00	11 24 07

DURATION OF TWILIGHT (in minutes)

Latitude	*52°*	*56°*	*52°*	*56°*	*52°*	*56°*	*52°*	*56°*
	1 March		*11 March*		*21 March*		*31 March*	
Civil	34	37	34	37	34	37	34	38
Nautical	73	80	73	80	74	81	75	84
Astronomical	112	124	113	125	115	128	120	135

THE NIGHT SKY

Mercury remains too close to the Sun for observation throughout the month, passing through superior conjunction on the 31st.

Venus is a brilliant object in the western sky in the early evenings after sunset. Its magnitude fades slightly during the month from −4.6 to −4.1 because the illuminated crescent gets thinner as Venus approaches inferior conjunction on the 27th. However Venus attains its greatest northern ecliptic latitude in the middle of the month. As a result it may be possible to see it as a morning object from the 20th onwards low above the eastern horizon shortly before sunrise. Thus there are several days, between the 20th (the 17th from Scotland) and the 25th, approximately, when it can be seen both as an evening and a morning object. Rarely are observers in Scotland more favoured than those further south! After the 25th it is only visible in the mornings.

Mars is still unsuitably placed for observation.

Jupiter, magnitude −2.1, is gradually emerging from the morning twilight and for the last ten days of the month should be visible low above the south-eastern horizon about half-an-hour before sunrise.

Saturn, magnitude +0.5, reaches opposition on the 8th and thus remains visible throughout the hours of darkness. Saturn is in Leo. The rings of Saturn are difficult to observe, as the angular width is only three arcseconds. The Moon, almost Full, passes about six degrees south of the planet on the night of the 10th.

Zodiacal Light. The evening cone may be observed stretching up from the western horizon, along the ecliptic, after the end of twilight, from the 12th to the 27th. This faint phenomenon is only visible under good conditions and in the absence of both moonlight and artificial lighting.

THE MOON

Day	R.A.		Dec.	Hor. par.	Semi-diam.	Sun's Co-Long.	PA of Br. Limb	Ph.	Age	Rise				Transit		Set			
										52°		56°				52°		56°	
	h	m	°	′	′	°	°	%	d	h	m	h	m	h	m	h	m	h	m
1	1	36	+15.5	57.7	15.7	323	244	16	3.9	7	44	7	28	15	32	23	41	—	—
2	2	30	+20.2	58.1	15.8	335	249	25	4.9	8	07	7	45	16	26	—	—	0	02
3	3	27	+23.9	58.5	15.9	347	254	35	5.9	8	38	8	10	17	24	1	04	1	32
4	4	28	+26.3	58.9	16.1	359	261	46	6.9	9	24	8	50	18	25	2	23	2	56
5	5	31	+27.0	59.3	16.1	11	268	58	7.9	10	26	9	52	19	27	3	29	4	03
6	6	34	+25.9	59.5	16.2	24	274	69	8.9	11	44	11	15	20	28	4	19	4	49
7	7	36	+23.1	59.7	16.3	36	280	79	9.9	13	11	12	49	21	26	4	54	5	17
8	8	35	+18.9	59.7	16.3	48	285	88	10.9	14	40	14	25	22	20	5	20	5	36
9	9	31	+13.6	59.6	16.2	60	286	94	11.9	16	08	16	00	23	11	5	39	5	49
10	10	24	+7.5	59.3	16.1	72	283	98	12.9	17	33	17	31	—	—	5	54	5	59
11	11	15	+1.2	58.8	16.0	84	226	100	13.9	18	56	18	59	0	00	6	08	6	08
12	12	04	−5.0	58.1	15.8	97	133	99	14.9	20	17	20	26	0	47	6	22	6	16
13	12	54	−10.9	57.4	15.6	109	123	96	15.9	21	37	21	52	1	34	6	37	6	26
14	13	43	−16.2	56.7	15.4	121	118	90	16.9	22	55	23	17	2	21	6	54	6	37
15	14	34	−20.5	55.9	15.2	133	113	83	17.9	—	—	—	—	3	10	7	15	6	52
16	15	26	−23.8	55.3	15.1	145	107	75	18.9	0	11	0	38	3	59	7	42	7	14
17	16	19	−26.0	54.8	14.9	157	101	66	19.9	1	19	1	52	4	50	8	19	7	46
18	17	13	−26.9	54.4	14.8	169	95	57	20.9	2	18	2	52	5	42	9	06	8	32
19	18	06	−26.5	54.3	14.8	182	89	48	21.9	3	04	3	37	6	32	10	04	9	32
20	18	58	−24.9	54.3	14.8	194	84	38	22.9	3	39	4	07	7	22	11	11	10	43
21	19	49	−22.3	54.4	14.8	206	79	29	23.9	4	05	4	28	8	09	12	22	12	01
22	20	37	−18.6	54.7	14.9	218	75	21	24.9	4	25	4	42	8	55	13	36	13	20
23	21	25	−14.2	55.2	15.0	230	73	14	25.9	4	41	4	53	9	39	14	50	14	40
24	22	11	−9.0	55.7	15.2	243	73	8	26.9	4	55	5	02	10	23	16	05	16	00
25	22	57	−3.4	56.3	15.3	255	76	3	27.9	5	08	5	10	11	06	17	21	17	21
26	23	44	+2.4	56.9	15.5	267	92	1	28.9	5	20	5	17	11	51	18	39	18	45
27	0	32	+8.3	57.5	15.7	279	199	0	0.3	5	34	5	26	12	37	20	00	20	12
28	1	22	+14.0	58.1	15.8	291	232	2	1.3	5	51	5	37	13	27	21	24	21	43
29	2	16	+19.0	58.5	15.9	304	242	7	2.3	6	12	5	52	14	21	22	49	23	15
30	3	13	+23.0	58.8	16.0	316	249	13	3.3	6	41	6	15	15	19	—	—	—	—
31	4	14	+25.7	59.1	16.1	328	257	22	4.3	7	23	6	51	16	20	0	11	0	42

MERCURY

Day	R.A.		Dec.	Diam.	Phase	Transit		5° high			
								52°		56°	
	h	m	°	″	%	h	m	h	m	h	m
1	21	25	−16.9	6	79	10	50	6	59	7	20
3	21	36	−16.1	6	81	10	54	6	57	7	17
5	21	48	−15.3	5	83	10	58	6	56	7	14
7	22	00	−14.4	5	85	11	02	6	54	7	11
9	22	13	−13.3	5	86	11	07	6	52	7	08
11	22	25	−12.2	5	88	11	11	6	50	7	04
13	22	38	−11.1	5	89	11	16	6	47	7	01
15	22	51	− 9.8	5	91	11	21	6	45	6	57
17	23	03	− 8.4	5	92	11	26	6	42	6	53
19	23	17	− 7.0	5	94	11	31	6	39	6	49
21	23	30	− 5.5	5	95	11	37	6	36	6	44
23	23	43	− 3.9	5	97	11	42	6	34	6	40
25	23	57	− 2.3	5	98	11	48	6	31	6	36
27	0	11	− 0.6	5	99	11	54	6	28	6	31
29	0	25	+1.2	5	100	12	01	17	38	17	37
31	0	39	+3.0	5	100	12	07	17	55	17	54

VENUS

Day	R.A.		Dec.	Diam.	Phase	Transit		5° high			
								52°		56°	
	h	m	°	″	%	h	m	h	m	h	m
1	0	45	+11.4	45	19	14	07	20	34	20	40
6	0	46	+12.4	49	14	13	48	20	19	20	26
11	0	43	+13.0	52	10	13	26	19	59	20	06
16	0	37	+12.9	56	6	13	00	19	32	19	39
21	0	28	+12.2	58	3	12	31	18	58	19	05
26	0	18	+10.9	59	1	12	00	18	21	18	27
31	0	07	+ 9.3	59	1	11	30	17	42	17	46

MARS

Day	R.A.		Dec.	Diam.	Phase	Transit		5° high			
								52°		56°	
	h	m	°	″	%	h	m	h	m	h	m
1	21	27	−16.2	4	98	10	51	6	56	7	16
6	21	42	−15.0	4	98	10	46	6	43	7	01
11	21	58	−13.7	4	98	10	42	6	30	6	47
16	22	13	−12.3	4	98	10	37	6	17	6	32
21	22	28	−10.9	4	98	10	33	6	04	6	18
26	22	42	−9.5	4	97	10	28	5	51	6	03
31	22	57	−8.0	4	97	10	23	5	38	5	48

SUNRISE AND SUNSET

	London		*Bristol*		*Birmingham*		*Manchester*		*Newcastle*		*Glasgow*		*Belfast*	
	0° 05′	*51° 30′*	*2° 35′*	*51° 28′*	*1° 55′*	*52° 28′*	*2° 15′*	*53° 28′*	*1° 37′*	*54° 59′*	*4° 14′*	*55° 52′*	*5° 56′*	*54° 35′*
d	*h m*	*h m*	*h m*	*h m*	*h m*	*h m*	*h m*	*h m*	*h m*	*h m*	*h m*	*h m*	*h m*	*h m*
1	6 45	17 41	6 55	17 51	6 54	17 47	6 57	17 47	6 56	17 42	7 08	17 52	7 13	18 00
2	6 43	17 43	6 53	17 53	6 52	17 49	6 54	17 49	6 54	17 44	7 06	17 54	7 10	18 02
3	6 41	17 44	6 51	17 54	6 49	17 51	6 52	17 51	6 51	17 46	7 03	17 56	7 08	18 04
4	6 39	17 46	6 49	17 56	6 47	17 52	6 50	17 53	6 49	17 48	7 00	17 58	7 06	18 06
5	6 37	17 48	6 47	17 58	6 45	17 54	6 47	17 55	6 46	17 50	6 58	18 00	7 03	18 08
6	6 34	17 50	6 44	18 00	6 43	17 56	6 45	17 56	6 44	17 52	6 55	18 02	7 01	18 10
7	6 32	17 51	6 42	18 01	6 40	17 58	6 43	17 58	6 41	17 54	6 53	18 04	6 58	18 12
8	6 30	17 53	6 40	18 03	6 38	18 00	6 40	18 00	6 39	17 56	6 50	18 06	6 56	18 14
9	6 28	17 55	6 38	18 05	6 36	18 01	6 38	18 02	6 37	17 58	6 48	18 08	6 53	18 16
10	6 26	17 57	6 36	18 07	6 34	18 03	6 35	18 04	6 34	18 00	6 45	18 10	6 51	18 18
11	6 23	17 58	6 33	18 08	6 31	18 05	6 33	18 06	6 31	18 02	6 43	18 12	6 48	18 20
12	6 21	18 00	6 31	18 10	6 29	18 07	6 31	18 08	6 29	18 04	6 40	18 14	6 46	18 22
13	6 19	18 02	6 29	18 12	6 27	18 09	6 28	18 10	6 26	18 06	6 37	18 17	6 44	18 24
14	6 17	18 03	6 27	18 13	6 24	18 10	6 26	18 11	6 24	18 08	6 35	18 19	6 41	18 26
15	6 14	18 05	6 24	18 15	6 22	18 12	6 23	18 13	6 21	18 10	6 32	18 21	6 39	18 28
16	6 12	18 07	6 22	18 17	6 20	18 14	6 21	18 15	6 19	18 12	6 29	18 23	6 36	18 30
17	6 10	18 08	6 20	18 19	6 17	18 16	6 19	18 17	6 16	18 14	6 27	18 25	6 34	18 32
18	6 08	18 10	6 17	18 20	6 15	18 18	6 16	18 19	6 14	18 16	6 24	18 27	6 31	18 34
19	6 05	18 12	6 15	18 22	6 13	18 19	6 14	18 21	6 11	18 18	6 22	18 29	6 28	18 36
20	6 03	18 14	6 13	18 24	6 10	18 21	6 11	18 23	6 09	18 20	6 19	18 31	6 26	18 37
21	6 01	18 15	6 11	18 25	6 08	18 23	6 09	18 24	6 06	18 22	6 16	18 33	6 23	18 39
22	5 58	18 17	6 08	18 27	6 05	18 25	6 07	18 26	6 04	18 24	6 14	18 35	6 21	18 41
23	5 56	18 19	6 06	18 29	6 03	18 26	6 04	18 28	6 01	18 26	6 11	18 37	6 18	18 43
24	5 54	18 20	6 04	18 30	6 01	18 28	6 02	18 30	5 58	18 28	6 09	18 39	6 16	18 45
25	5 52	18 22	6 02	18 32	5 58	18 30	5 59	18 32	5 56	18 30	6 06	18 41	6 13	18 47
26	5 49	18 24	5 59	18 34	5 56	18 32	5 57	18 34	5 53	18 32	6 03	18 43	6 11	18 49
27	5 47	18 25	5 57	18 35	5 54	18 33	5 54	18 35	5 51	18 34	6 01	18 45	6 08	18 51
28	5 45	18 27	5 55	18 37	5 51	18 35	5 52	18 37	5 48	18 36	5 58	18 47	6 06	18 53
29	5 42	18 29	5 52	18 39	5 49	18 37	5 50	18 39	5 46	18 38	5 55	18 49	6 03	18 55
30	5 40	18 30	5 50	18 40	5 47	18 39	5 47	18 41	5 43	18 40	5 53	18 51	6 01	18 57
31	5 38	18 32	5 48	18 42	5 44	18 40	5 45	18 43	5 41	18 42	5 50	18 53	5 58	18 59

JUPITER

Day	*R.A.*		*Dec.*		*Transit*		*5° high*			
							52°		*56°*	
	h	*m*	°	′	*h*	*m*	*h*	*m*	*h*	*m*
1	21	01.2	−17	29	10	24	6	38	7	01
11	21	10.0	−16	53	9	54	6	04	6	25
21	21	18.3	−16	17	9	23	5	29	5	49
31	21	26.1	−15	42	8	51	4	53	5	13

Diameters – equatorial 34″ polar 32″

SATURN

Day	*R.A.*		*Dec.*		*Transit*		*5° high*			
							52°		*56°*	
	h	*m*	°	′	*h*	*m*	*h*	*m*	*h*	*m*
1	11	23.1	+6	26	0	47	6	47	6	49
11	11	20.2	+6	45	0	05	6	06	6	08
21	11	17.3	+7	04	23	19	5	25	5	28
31	11	14.6	+7	21	22	37	4	45	4	48

Diameters – equatorial 20″ polar 18″
Rings – major axis 45″ minor axis 2″

URANUS

Day	*R.A.*		*Dec.*		*Transit*		*10° high*			
							52°		*56°*	
	h	*m*	°	′	*h*	*m*	*h*	*m*	*h*	*m*
1	23	31.5	−3	53	12	54	8	21	8	32
11	23	33.6	−3	39	12	17	7	43	7	53
21	23	35.7	−3	25	11	39	7	04	7	14
31	23	37.7	−3	12	11	02	6	26	6	35

Diameter 4″

NEPTUNE

Day	*R.A.*		*Dec.*		*Transit*		*10° high*			
							52°		*56°*	
	h	*m*	°	′	*h*	*m*	*h*	*m*	*h*	*m*
1	21	47.9	−13	41	11	10	7	39	8	02
11	21	49.3	−13	34	10	33	7	00	7	23
21	21	50.6	−13	27	9	54	6	21	6	44
31	21	51.8	−13	21	9	16	5	43	6	05

Diameter 2″

APRIL 2009

FOURTH MONTH, 30 DAYS. *Aperire*, to open; Earth opens to receive seed.

1	*Wednesday*	VAT was introduced in the UK 1973	day 91
2	*Thursday*	Argentina invaded the Falklands Islands 1982	92
3	*Friday*	The Pony Express ran for the first time 1860	93
4	*Saturday*	The North Atlantic Treaty was signed bringing NATO into existence 1949	94
5	*Sunday*	Winston Churchill resigned as prime minister 1955	95
6	*Monday*	The modern Olympic Games were revived at Athens 1896	week 15 day 96
7	*Tuesday*	The Entente Cordiale was signed between Britain and France 1904	97
8	*Wednesday*	Clint Eastwood was elected mayor of Carmel, California 1986	98
9	*Thursday*	Captain Cook discovered Australia 1770	99
10	*Friday*	The *Titanic* embarked on her maiden voyage 1912	100
11	*Saturday*	William III and Mary II were crowned joint sovereigns 1689	101
12	*Sunday*	Yuri Gagarin became the first person to orbit the Earth 1961	102
13	*Monday*	The Catholic Emancipation Act was passed 1829	week 16 day 103
14	*Tuesday*	Abraham Lincoln was shot 1865	104
15	*Wednesday*	The *Titanic* sank with estimates of 1,520 people perishing 1912	105
16	*Thursday*	Bonnie Prince Charlie was defeated at the Battle of Culloden 1746	106
17	*Friday*	Martin Luther appeared before the Diet of Worms 1521	107
18	*Saturday*	The Irish Free State became the Republic of Ireland 1949	108
19	*Sunday*	An office complex was bombed in Oklahoma claiming 168 lives 1995	109
20	*Monday*	Apollo 16 landed on the Moon 1972	week 17 day 110
21	*Tuesday*	Women in France received the right to vote 1944	111
22	*Wednesday*	Germany first used poison gas against British troops 1915	112
23	*Thursday*	The first decimal coins, 5p and 10p pieces, were issued 1968	113
24	*Friday*	The Easter Rising in Dublin began 1916	114
25	*Saturday*	Scientists announced the discovery of the structure of DNA 1953	115
26	*Sunday*	A reactor at the Chernobyl Nuclear Power Plant exploded 1986	116
27	*Monday*	Britain formally recognised the state of Israel 1950	week 18 day 117
28	*Tuesday*	The League of Nations was founded 1919	118
29	*Wednesday*	Women were admitted to Oxford University examinations 1885	119
30	*Thursday*	George Washington was inaugurated as the first president of the USA 1789	120

ASTRONOMICAL PHENOMENA

d	*h*	
4	18	Pluto at stationary point
7	03	Saturn in conjunction with Moon. Saturn 5°N.
17	19	Venus at stationary point
19	15	Jupiter in conjunction with Moon. Jupiter 2°S.
19	23	Sun's longitude 30° ♉
21	23	Mars in conjunction with venus. Mars 4°S.
22	13	Venus in conjunction with Moon. Venus 1°S
22	14	Mars in conjunction with Moon. Mars 5°S.
26	08	Mercury at greatest elongation E.20°
26	16	Mercury in conjunction with Moon. Mercury 2°S.

MINIMA OF ALGOL

d	*h*	*d*	*h*	*d*	*h*
1	16.2	13	16.2	24	16.2
4	13.0	15	13.0	27	13.0
7	09.9	18	09.9	30	09.9
10	06.7	21	06.7		

CONSTELLATIONS

The following constellations are near the meridian at

	d	*h*		*d*	*h*
March	1	24	April	15	21
March	16	23	May	1	20
April	1	22	May	16	19

Cepheus (below the Pole), Cassiopeia (below the Pole), Ursa Major, Leo Minor, Leo., Sextans, Hydra and Crater

THE MOON

Phases, Apsides and Node	*d*	*h*	*m*
☽ First Quarter	2	14	34
○ Full Moon	9	14	56
☾ Last Quarter	17	13	36
● New Moon	25	03	23
Perigee (370,050 km)	2	02	15
Apogee (404,192 km)	16	09	14
Perigee (366,062 km)	28	06	17

Mean longitude of ascending node on April 1, 306°

THE SUN

s.d. 16′.0

Day	Right Ascension			Dec. +		Equation of time		Rise 52°		Rise 56°		Transit		Set 52°		Set 56°		Sidereal time			Transit of first point of Aries		
	h	*m*	*s*	°	′	*m*	*s*	*h*	*m*	*h*	*m*	*h*	*m*	*h*	*m*	*h*	*m*	*h*	*m*	*s*	*h*	*m*	*s*
1	0	41	56	4	31	−3	59	5	35	5	30	12	04	18	34	18	38	12	37	57	11	20	11
2	0	45	35	4	54	−3	41	5	33	5	28	12	04	18	36	18	40	12	41	54	11	16	15
3	0	49	14	5	17	−3	24	5	30	5	25	12	03	18	37	18	43	12	45	50	11	12	19
4	0	52	53	5	40	−3	06	5	28	5	23	12	03	18	39	18	45	12	49	47	11	08	24
5	0	56	32	6	03	−2	49	5	26	5	20	12	03	18	41	18	47	12	53	43	11	04	28
6	1	00	11	6	25	−2	31	5	23	5	17	12	02	18	42	18	49	12	57	40	11	00	32
7	1	03	51	6	48	−2	14	5	21	5	15	12	02	18	44	18	51	13	01	36	10	56	36
8	1	07	30	7	10	−1	57	5	19	5	12	12	02	18	46	18	53	13	05	33	10	52	40
9	1	11	10	7	33	−1	41	5	17	5	10	12	02	18	48	18	55	13	09	29	10	48	44
10	1	14	50	7	55	−1	24	5	14	5	07	12	01	18	49	18	57	13	13	26	10	44	48
11	1	18	31	8	17	−1	08	5	12	5	05	12	01	18	51	18	59	13	17	23	10	40	52
12	1	22	12	8	39	−0	53	5	10	5	02	12	01	18	53	19	01	13	21	19	10	36	56
13	1	25	53	9	01	−0	37	5	08	4	59	12	00	18	54	19	03	13	25	16	10	33	00
14	1	29	34	9	23	−0	22	5	05	4	57	12	00	18	56	19	05	13	29	12	10	29	04
15	1	33	16	9	44	−0	07	5	03	4	54	12	00	18	58	19	07	13	33	09	10	25	09
16	1	36	58	10	06	+0	07	5	01	4	52	12	00	19	00	19	09	13	37	05	10	21	13
17	1	40	40	10	27	+0	21	4	59	4	49	12	00	19	01	19	11	13	41	02	10	17	17
18	1	44	23	10	48	+0	35	4	57	4	47	11	59	19	03	19	13	13	44	58	10	13	21
19	1	48	07	11	09	+0	48	4	55	4	44	11	59	19	05	19	15	13	48	55	10	09	25
20	1	51	50	11	29	+1	01	4	52	4	42	11	59	19	06	19	17	13	52	52	10	05	29
21	1	55	34	11	50	+1	14	4	50	4	39	11	59	19	08	19	19	13	56	48	10	01	33
22	1	59	19	12	10	+1	26	4	48	4	37	11	58	19	10	19	21	14	00	45	9	57	37
23	2	03	04	12	30	+1	37	4	46	4	35	11	58	19	12	19	23	14	04	41	9	53	41
24	2	06	50	12	50	+1	48	4	44	4	32	11	58	19	13	19	25	14	08	38	9	49	45
25	2	10	36	13	10	+1	59	4	42	4	30	11	58	19	15	19	27	14	12	34	9	45	49
26	2	14	22	13	29	+2	09	4	40	4	27	11	58	19	17	19	29	14	16	31	9	41	54
27	2	18	09	13	49	+2	18	4	38	4	25	11	58	19	18	19	31	14	20	27	9	37	58
28	2	21	57	14	08	+2	27	4	36	4	23	11	57	19	20	19	33	14	24	24	9	34	02
29	2	25	45	14	26	+2	36	4	34	4	21	11	57	19	22	19	36	14	28	21	9	30	06
30	2	29	33	14	45	+2	44	4	32	4	18	11	57	19	23	19	38	14	32	17	9	26	10

DURATION OF TWILIGHT (in minutes)

Latitude	*52°*	*56°*	*52°*	*56°*	*52°*	*56°*	*52°*	*56°*
	1 April		*11 April*		*21 April*		*31 April*	
Civil	34	38	35	39	37	42	39	44
Nautical	76	84	79	89	83	96	89	106
Astronomical	120	136	127	147	137	165	152	204

THE NIGHT SKY

Mercury reaches greatest eastern elongation (20 degrees) on the 26th. It becomes visible low in the western sky in the evenings, at around the end of civil twilight, after the first ten days of the month. The magnitude of Mercury fades from −1.3 to +1.0 during its period of visibility. On the evening of the 26th the thin crescent Moon, a mere 1.5 days old, will be seen above the planet, given good conditions. This evening apparition is the most suitable one of the year for observers in the British Isles.

Venus is a magnificent morning object, its magnitude brightening during the month from −4.1 to −4.5. It can be seen low above the east-north-east horizon for a short while before sunrise. On the morning of the 22nd the old crescent Moon, three days before New, will be seen about five degrees to the right of Venus and about one degree higher in altitude.

Mars continues to be unsuitably placed for observation throughout the month.

Jupiter, magnitude −2.1, is becoming easier to observe as the month progresses, low above the south-eastern horizon in early mornings. By the end of April it becomes visible to observers in England by about 1.5 hours before sunrise, and to observers in Scotland by about an hour before sunrise, given a good clear horizon. The waning crescent Moon, just past Last Quarter, passes one degree north of the planet on the 19th.

Saturn, magnitude +0.5, continues to be visible as an evening object and remains visible for most of the night in the south-western quadrant of the sky. The waxing gibbous Moon is in the vicinity of the planet on the morning of the 7th.

THE MOON

Day	R.A.		Dec.	Hor. Par.	Semi-diam.	Sun's Co-Long.	PA of Br. Limb	Ph.	Age	Rise				Transit		Set			
										52°		56°				52°		56°	
	h	m	°	′	′	°	°	%	d	h	m	h	m	h	m	h	m	h	m
1	5	16	+26.8	59.2	16.1	340	264	32	5.3	8	20	7	46	17	21	1	22	1	55
2	6	20	+26.1	59.3	16.1	353	272	43	6.3	9	33	9	03	18	22	2	16	2	47
3	7	21	+23.7	59.2	16.1	5	278	55	7.3	10	56	10	32	19	20	2	55	3	20
4	8	20	+19.9	59.1	16.1	17	283	66	8.3	12	23	12	06	20	14	3	23	3	42
5	9	15	+15.0	58.9	16.1	29	287	76	9.3	13	48	13	38	21	04	3	44	3	56
6	10	08	+9.4	58.7	16.0	41	289	85	10.3	15	12	15	07	21	52	4	00	4	07
7	10	58	+3.3	58.3	15.9	53	288	92	11.3	16	33	16	34	22	39	4	15	4	16
8	11	47	−2.9	57.9	15.8	66	283	97	12.3	17	53	18	00	23	25	4	28	4	25
9	12	35	−8.8	57.3	15.6	78	263	99	13.3	19	13	19	25	—		4	42	4	34
10	13	25	−14.2	56.8	15.5	90	159	100	14.3	20	32	20	50	0	12	4	58	4	44
11	14	15	−18.9	56.2	15.3	102	126	98	15.3	21	49	22	14	1	00	5	18	4	58
12	15	07	−22.6	55.6	15.2	114	115	94	16.3	23	01	23	31	1	50	5	43	5	17
13	16	00	−25.2	55.1	15.0	126	107	88	17.3	—		—		2	41	6	16	5	45
14	16	54	−26.5	54.7	14.9	139	100	81	18.3	0	05	0	38	3	32	6	59	6	25
15	17	48	−26.5	54.4	14.8	151	93	73	19.3	0	56	1	30	4	24	7	53	7	20
16	18	41	−25.4	54.3	14.8	163	87	65	20.3	1	36	2	06	5	14	8	57	8	28
17	19	32	−23.1	54.3	14.8	175	81	55	21.3	2	06	2	30	6	02	10	06	9	42
18	20	21	−19.8	54.5	14.8	187	77	46	22.3	2	28	2	47	6	48	11	18	11	00
19	21	08	−15.6	54.8	14.9	200	73	37	23.3	2	45	2	59	7	32	12	31	12	18
20	21	54	−10.8	55.3	15.1	212	71	27	24.3	3	00	3	09	8	16	13	44	13	37
21	22	40	−5.4	56.0	15.3	224	70	19	25.3	3	13	3	17	8	59	14	59	14	57
22	23	26	+0.3	56.7	15.5	236	71	12	26.3	3	26	3	25	9	42	16	15	16	19
23	0	13	+6.2	57.5	15.7	248	75	6	27.3	3	40	3	34	10	28	17	35	17	45
24	1	03	+11.9	58.2	15.9	261	85	2	28.3	3	55	3	44	11	17	18	59	19	15
25	1	56	+17.2	58.9	16.0	273	139	0	29.3	4	15	3	58	12	10	20	26	20	48
26	2	54	+21.7	59.4	16.2	285	230	1	0.9	4	42	4	18	13	08	21	52	22	21
27	3	55	+24.9	59.7	16.3	297	249	5	1.9	5	20	4	50	14	10	23	09	23	42
28	4	59	+26.4	59.9	16.3	310	259	11	2.9	6	13	5	40	15	13	—		—	
29	6	04	+26.2	59.9	16.3	322	268	19	3.9	7	23	6	51	16	16	0	11	0	42
30	7	07	+24.2	59.7	16.3	334	276	29	4.9	8	45	8	19	17	15	0	55	1	22

MERCURY

Day	R.A.		Dec.	Diam.	Phase	Transit		5° high			
								52°		56°	
	h	m	°	″	%	h	m	h	m	h	m
1	0	47	+4.0	5	100	12	11	18	03	18	03
3	1	02	+5.8	5	99	12	18	18	19	18	21
5	1	16	+7.7	5	98	12	25	18	36	18	40
7	1	31	+ 9.6	5	96	12	32	18	53	18	58
9	1	46	+11.4	5	92	12	39	19	10	19	16
11	2	01	+13.2	6	88	12	46	19	26	19	34
13	2	16	+14.8	6	82	12	52	19	41	19	51
15	2	30	+16.4	6	76	12	59	19	55	20	07
17	2	44	+17.7	6	70	13	04	20	08	20	21
19	2	56	+19.0	7	63	13	08	20	19	20	33
21	3	08	+20.0	7	56	13	12	20	29	20	43
23	3	19	+20.9	7	49	13	15	20	36	20	52
25	3	28	+21.6	8	42	13	16	20	41	20	57
27	3	37	+22.2	8	36	13	16	20	44	21	01
29	3	43	+22.6	8	30	13	15	20	44	21	01
31	3	49	+22.8	9	25	13	12	20	42	20	59

VENUS

Day	R.A.		Dec.	Diam.	Phase	Transit		5° high			
								52°		56°	
	h	m	°	″	%	h	m	h	m	h	m
1	0	05	+8.9	59	2	11	24	5	13	5	09
6	23	57	+7.0	57	4	10	56	4	55	4	52
11	23	51	+5.3	54	7	10	32	4	39	4	38
16	23	50	+3.9	50	11	10	11	4	25	4	25
21	23	52	+2.9	46	16	9	54	4	12	4	13
26	23	58	+2.4	43	21	9	40	4	01	4	03
31	0	06	+2.3	39	25	9	29	3	51	3	52

MARS

Day	R.A.		Dec.	Diam.	Phase	Transit		5° high			
								52°		56°	
	h	m	°	″	%	h	m	h	m	h	m
1	23	00	−7.7	4	97	10	22	5	35	5	45
6	23	14	−6.2	4	97	10	16	5	21	5	30
11	23	29	−4.6	4	97	10	11	5	08	5	15
16	23	43	−3.1	4	96	10	06	4	54	5	00
21	23	57	−1.5	4	96	10	00	4	41	4	45
26	0	12	0.0	4	96	9	55	4	27	4	30
31	0	26	+1.6	4	96	9	49	4	14	4	16

SUNRISE AND SUNSET

	London		*Bristol*		*Birmingham*		*Manchester*		*Newcastle*		*Glasgow*		*Belfast*	
	0° 05′	*51° 30′*	*2° 35′*	*51° 28′*	*1° 55′*	*52° 28′*	*2° 15′*	*53° 28′*	*1° 37′*	*54° 59′*	*4° 14′*	*55° 52′*	*5° 56′*	*54° 35′*
d	*h m*	*h m*	*h m*	*h m*	*h m*	*h m*	*h m*	*h m*	*h m*	*h m*	*h m*	*h m*	*h m*	*h m*
1	5 36	18 34	5 46	18 44	5 42	18 42	5 42	18 45	5 38	18 44	5 48	18 55	5 56	19 01
2	5 33	18 35	5 43	18 45	5 40	18 44	5 40	18 46	5 36	18 46	5 45	18 57	5 53	19 02
3	5 31	18 37	5 41	18 47	5 37	18 46	5 37	18 48	5 33	18 48	5 42	18 59	5 51	19 04
4	5 29	18 39	5 39	18 49	5 35	18 47	5 35	18 50	5 31	18 50	5 40	19 01	5 48	19 06
5	5 27	18 40	5 37	18 50	5 33	18 49	5 33	18 52	5 28	18 51	5 37	19 03	5 46	19 08
6	5 24	18 42	5 34	18 52	5 30	18 51	5 30	18 54	5 26	18 53	5 35	19 05	5 43	19 10
7	5 22	18 44	5 32	18 54	5 28	18 53	5 28	18 55	5 23	18 55	5 32	19 07	5 41	19 12
8	5 20	18 45	5 30	18 55	5 26	18 54	5 26	18 57	5 20	18 57	5 29	19 09	5 38	19 14
9	5 18	18 47	5 28	18 57	5 23	18 56	5 23	18 59	5 18	18 59	5 27	19 11	5 36	19 16
10	5 15	18 49	5 26	18 59	5 21	18 58	5 21	19 01	5 16	19 01	5 24	19 13	5 34	19 18
11	5 13	18 50	5 23	19 00	5 19	19 00	5 18	19 03	5 13	19 03	5 22	19 15	5 31	19 20
12	5 11	18 52	5 21	19 02	5 17	19 01	5 16	19 05	5 11	19 05	5 19	19 18	5 29	19 22
13	5 09	18 54	5 19	19 04	5 14	19 03	5 14	19 06	5 08	19 07	5 17	19 20	5 26	19 23
14	5 07	18 56	5 17	19 05	5 12	19 05	5 11	19 08	5 06	19 09	5 14	19 22	5 24	19 25
15	5 05	18 57	5 15	19 07	5 10	19 07	5 09	19 10	5 03	19 11	5 12	19 24	5 21	19 27
16	5 02	18 59	5 12	19 09	5 08	19 08	5 07	19 12	5 01	19 13	5 09	19 26	5 19	19 29
17	5 00	19 01	5 10	19 10	5 06	19 10	5 05	19 14	4 58	19 15	5 07	19 28	5 17	19 31
18	4 58	19 02	5 08	19 12	5 03	19 12	5 02	19 15	4 56	19 17	5 04	19 30	5 14	19 33
19	4 56	19 04	5 06	19 14	5 01	19 13	5 00	19 17	4 54	19 19	5 02	19 32	5 12	19 35
20	4 54	19 06	5 04	19 15	4 59	19 15	4 58	19 19	4 51	19 21	4 59	19 34	5 10	19 37
21	4 52	19 07	5 02	19 17	4 57	19 17	4 56	19 21	4 49	19 23	4 57	19 36	5 07	19 39
22	4 50	19 09	5 00	19 19	4 55	19 19	4 53	19 23	4 47	19 25	4 54	19 38	5 05	19 41
23	4 48	19 11	4 58	19 20	4 53	19 20	4 51	19 25	4 44	19 27	4 52	19 40	5 03	19 43
24	4 46	19 12	4 56	19 22	4 51	19 22	4 49	19 26	4 42	19 28	4 50	19 42	5 00	19 45
25	4 44	19 14	4 54	19 24	4 48	19 24	4 47	19 28	4 40	19 30	4 47	19 44	4 58	19 46
26	4 42	19 16	4 52	19 25	4 46	19 26	4 45	19 30	4 37	19 32	4 45	19 46	4 56	19 48
27	4 40	19 17	4 50	19 27	4 44	19 27	4 43	19 32	4 35	19 34	4 43	19 48	4 54	19 50
28	4 38	19 19	4 48	19 29	4 42	19 29	4 41	19 34	4 33	19 36	4 40	19 50	4 52	19 52
29	4 36	19 20	4 46	19 30	4 40	19 31	4 38	19 35	4 31	19 38	4 38	19 52	4 49	19 54
30	4 34	19 22	4 44	19 32	4 38	19 33	4 36	19 37	4 29	19 40	4 36	19 54	4 47	19 56

JUPITER

Day	*R.A.*		*Dec.*		*Transit*		*5° high*			
							52°		*56°*	
	h	*m*	°	′	*h*	*m*	*h*	*m*	*h*	*m*
1	21	26.9	−15	39	8	48	4	50	5	09
11	21	34.0	−15	07	8	15	4	14	4	33
21	21	40.3	−14	37	7	42	3	38	3	56
31	21	45.9	−14	11	7	09	3	01	3	19

Diameters – equatorial 36″ polar 34″

SATURN

Day	*R.A.*		*Dec.*		*Transit*		*5° high*			
							52°		*56°*	
	h	*m*	°	′	*h*	*m*	*h*	*m*	*h*	*m*
1	11	14.3	+7	22	22	32	4	41	4	44
11	11	12.0	+7	36	21	51	4	00	4	03
21	11	10.1	+7	47	21	10	3	20	3	23
31	11	08.7	+7	54	20	29	2	40	2	43

Diameters – equatorial 19″ polar 17″
Rings – major axis 44″ minor axis 3″

URANUS

Day	*R.A.*		*Dec.*		*Transit*		*10° high*			
							52°		*56°*	
	h	*m*	°	′	*h*	*m*	*h*	*m*	*h*	*m*
1	23	37.9	− 3	11	10	58	6	22	6	32
11	23	39.9	− 2	58	10	21	5	43	5	53
21	23	41.8	− 2	46	9	43	5	05	5	14
31	23	43.5	− 2	35	9	06	4	26	4	35

Diameter 4″

NEPTUNE

Day	*R.A.*		*Dec.*		*Transit*		*10° high*			
							52°		*56°*	
	h	*m*	°	′	*h*	*m*	*h*	*m*	*h*	*m*
1	21	51.9	−13	20	9	13	5	39	6	01
11	21	53.0	−13	15	8	34	5	00	5	22
21	21	53.8	−13	11	7	56	4	21	4	43
31	21	54.5	−13	07	7	17	3	42	4	04

Diameter 2″

MAY 2009

FIFTH MONTH, 31 DAYS. *Maia*, goddess of growth and increase

1 *Friday*	The union of Scotland and England was proclaimed 1707		day 121
2 *Saturday*	The King James version of the Bible was published 1611		122
3 *Sunday*	Christopher Columbus first sighted present-day Jamaica 1494		123
4 *Monday*	The Yorkists defeated the Lancastrians in the battle of Tewksbury 1471	week 19	day 124
5 *Tuesday*	Bobby Sands died in prison after 66 days on hunger strike 1981		125
6 *Wednesday*	Postage stamps were introduced 1840		126
7 *Thursday*	Germany signed unconditional surrender 1945		127
8 *Friday*	The monarchy was restored under King Charles II after the interregnum 1660		128
9 *Saturday*	Australia opened its first parliament in Melbourne 1901		129
10 *Sunday*	The Indian Mutiny began with a rising at Meerut 1857		130
11 *Monday*	Spencer Perceval was assassinated in the House of Commons 1812	week 20	day 131
12 *Tuesday*	George VI was crowned 1937		132
13 *Wednesday*	Pope John Paul II survived an assassination attempt in Rome with four bullet wounds 1981		133
14 *Thursday*	The Home Guard was formed 1940		134
15 *Friday*	The Royal Opera House in Covent Garden opened 1858		135
16 *Saturday*	James Boswell first met Dr Samuel Johnson 1763		136
17 *Sunday*	Compact discs were introduced by Phillips 1978		137
18 *Monday*	Napoleon Bonaparte was proclaimed emperor of France 1804	week 21	day 138
19 *Tuesday*	Anne Boleyn was beheaded on Tower Green for adultery 1536		139
20 *Wednesday*	The USA's military rule of Cuba ended 1902		140
21 *Thursday*	Daylight saving time was first used in Britain 1916		141
22 *Friday*	The Blackwall tunnel was opened 1897		142
23 *Saturday*	Bonnie Parker and Clyde Barrow were shot by the Texas and Louisiana state police 1934		142
24 *Sunday*	Samuel Morse transmitted the world's first telegraph message 1844		144
25 *Monday*	Oscar Wilde was convicted of gross indecency 1895	week 22	day 145
26 *Tuesday*	The last public hanging in Britain took place 1868		146
27 *Wednesday*	British and French troops began to evacuate from Dunkirk in operation Dynamo 1940		147
28 *Thursday*	The Spanish Armada set sail from Lisbon 1588		148
29 *Friday*	Edmund Hillary and Tenzing Norgay conquered Mount Everest 1953		149
30 *Saturday*	Joan of Arc was burnt at the stake 1431		150
31 *Sunday*	South Africa left the British Commonwealth 1961		151

ASTRONOMICAL PHENOMENA

d	*h*	
2	08	Venus at greatest brilliancy
4	07	Saturn in conjunction with Moon. Saturn 6°N.
7	05	Mercury at stationary point
17	02	Saturn at stationary point
17	06	Jupiter in conjunction with Moon. Jupiter 3°S.
18	10	Mercury in inferior conjunction
20	22	Sun's longitude 60° ♊
21	03	Venus in conjunction with Moon. Venus 6°S.
21	15	Mars in conjunction with Moon. Mars 6°S.
23	22	Mercury in conjunction with Moon. Mercury 7°S.
29	05	Neptune at stationary point
31	01	Mercury at stationary point
31	13	Saturn in conjunction with Moon. Saturn 6°N.

MINIMA OF ALGOL

Algol is inconveniently situated for observation during May

CONSTELLATIONS

The following constellations are near the meridian at

	d	*h*		*d*	*h*
April	1	24	May	16	21
April	15	23	June	1	20
May	1	22	June	15	19

Cepheus (below the Pole), Cassiopeia (below the Pole), Ursa Minor, Ursa Major, Canes Venatici, Coma Berenices, Bootes, Leo, Virgo, Crater, Corvus and Hydra

THE MOON

Phases, Apsides and Node	*d*	*h*	*m*
☽ First Quarter	01	20	44
○ Full Moon	09	04	01
☾ Last Quarter	17	07	26
● New Moon	24	12	11
☽ First Quarter	31	03	22
Apogee (404,882 km)	14	02	52
Perigee (361,168 km)	26	03	38

Mean longitude of ascending node on May 1, 305°

THE SUN

s.d. 15′.8

Day	Right Ascension			Dec. +		Equation of time		Rise				Transit		Set				Sidereal time			Transit of first point of Aries		
								52°		56°				52°		56°							
	h	*m*	*s*	°	′	*m*	*s*	*h*	*m*	*h*	*m*	*h*	*m*	*h*	*m*	*h*	*m*	*h*	*m*	*s*	*h*	*m*	*s*
1	2	33	22	15	03	+2	52	4	30	4	16	11	57	19	25	19	40	14	36	14	9	22	14
2	2	37	12	15	21	+2	59	4	28	4	14	11	57	19	27	19	42	14	40	10	9	18	18
3	2	41	02	15	39	+3	05	4	26	4	12	11	57	19	28	19	44	14	44	07	9	14	22
4	2	44	52	15	57	+3	11	4	25	4	09	11	57	19	30	19	46	14	48	03	9	10	26
5	2	48	43	16	14	+3	17	4	23	4	07	11	57	19	32	19	48	14	52	00	9	06	30
6	2	52	35	16	31	+3	21	4	21	4	05	11	57	19	33	19	50	14	55	56	9	02	34
7	2	56	27	16	48	+3	26	4	19	4	03	11	57	19	35	19	52	14	59	53	8	58	39
8	3	00	20	17	04	+3	30	4	17	4	01	11	56	19	37	19	53	15	03	50	8	54	43
9	3	04	13	17	20	+3	33	4	16	3	59	11	56	19	38	19	55	15	07	46	8	50	47
10	3	08	07	17	36	+3	36	4	14	3	57	11	56	19	40	19	57	15	11	43	8	46	51
11	3	12	02	17	52	+3	38	4	12	3	55	11	56	19	41	19	59	15	15	39	8	42	55
12	3	15	57	18	07	+3	39	4	11	3	53	11	56	19	43	20	01	15	19	36	8	38	59
13	3	19	52	18	22	+3	40	4	09	3	51	11	56	19	45	20	03	15	23	32	8	35	03
14	3	23	48	18	37	+3	40	4	08	3	49	11	56	19	46	20	05	15	27	29	8	31	07
15	3	27	45	18	51	+3	40	4	06	3	47	11	56	19	48	20	07	15	31	25	8	27	11
16	3	31	43	19	05	+3	39	4	05	3	45	11	56	19	49	20	09	15	35	22	8	23	15
17	3	35	41	19	19	+3	38	4	03	3	43	11	56	19	51	20	11	15	39	19	8	19	19
18	3	39	39	19	32	+3	36	4	02	3	42	11	56	19	52	20	12	15	43	15	8	15	24
19	3	43	38	19	45	+3	34	4	00	3	40	11	56	19	54	20	14	15	47	12	8	11	28
20	3	47	38	19	58	+3	30	3	59	3	38	11	57	19	55	20	16	15	51	08	8	07	32
21	3	51	38	20	10	+3	27	3	58	3	37	11	57	19	56	20	18	15	55	05	8	03	36
22	3	55	39	20	22	+3	23	3	56	3	35	11	57	19	58	20	19	15	59	01	7	59	40
23	3	59	40	20	34	+3	18	3	55	3	34	11	57	19	59	20	21	16	02	58	7	55	44
24	4	03	42	20	45	+3	12	3	54	3	32	11	57	20	01	20	23	16	06	54	7	51	48
25	4	07	44	20	56	+3	07	3	53	3	31	11	57	20	02	20	24	16	10	51	7	47	52
26	4	11	47	21	07	+3	00	3	52	3	29	11	57	20	03	20	26	16	14	48	7	43	56
27	4	15	50	21	17	+2	54	3	51	3	28	11	57	20	05	20	27	16	18	44	7	40	00
28	4	19	54	21	27	+2	46	3	50	3	27	11	57	20	06	20	29	16	22	41	7	36	04
29	4	23	59	21	36	+2	39	3	49	3	25	11	57	20	07	20	30	16	26	37	7	32	09
30	4	28	03	21	45	+2	31	3	48	3	24	11	58	20	08	20	32	16	30	34	7	28	13
31	4	32	08	21	54	+2	22	3	47	3	23	11	58	20	09	20	33	16	34	30	7	24	17

DURATION OF TWILIGHT (in minutes)

Latitude	52°	56°	52°	56°	52°	56°	52°	56°
	1 May		*11 May*		*21 May*		*31 May*	
Civil	39	44	41	48	44	53	46	57
Nautical	89	106	97	120	106	141	115	187
Astronomical	152	204	176	TAN	TAN	TAN	TAN	TAN

THE NIGHT SKY

Mercury passes through inferior conjunction on the 18th and is therefore unsuitably placed for observation throughout the month.

Venus continues to be visible as a magnificent morning object, attaining its greatest brilliancy with a magnitude of −4.5 on the 2nd. However, it is never visible for more than an hour before sunrise, low in the eastern sky before dawn. On the morning of the 21st the thin waning crescent Moon passes five degrees north of the planet. As seen through a telescope, the apparent diameter of Venus shrinks from 39 to 26 arcseconds during May as its distance from the Earth increases. At the same time its phase increases from 47 to 62 per cent illuminated.

Mars remains unsuitably placed for observation throughout May.

Jupiter continues to be visible as a brilliant object, magnitude −2.3, low in the south-eastern sky for several hours before dawn. The Moon, at Last Quarter, passes two degrees north of Jupiter on the morning of the 17th. Jupiter is in the constellation of Capricornus.

Saturn, magnitude +0.9, is still visible in the south-western sky in the evenings, though by the end of the month it will not be visible for long after midnight. The waxing gibbous Moon is in the vicinity of the planet on the 3rd and 4th, and again, when at First Quarter, on the last day of the month. Saturn reaches its second stationary point on the 17th, resuming its direct motion.

THE MOON

Day	R.A.		Dec.	Hor. Par.	Semi-diam.	Sun's Co-Long.	PA of Bright Limb	Ph.	Age	Rise				Transit		Set			
										52°		56°				52°		56°	
	h	m	°	′	′	°	°	%	d	h	m	h	m	h	m	h	m	h	m
1	8	07	+20.7	59.3	16.2	346	282	40	5.9	10	11	9	52	18	10	1	26	1	47
2	9	03	+16.0	58.9	16.1	358	287	52	6.9	11	37	11	24	19	02	1	49	2	03
3	9	55	+10.5	58.5	15.9	11	289	63	7.9	12	59	12	53	19	49	2	07	2	15
4	10	45	+4.6	58.0	15.8	23	291	73	8.9	14	19	14	19	20	35	2	21	2	25
5	11	34	−1.4	57.5	15.7	35	290	82	9.9	15	38	15	43	21	21	2	35	2	33
6	12	22	−7.3	57.0	15.5	47	288	89	10.9	16	56	17	06	22	06	2	49	2	42
7	13	10	−12.7	56.5	15.4	59	282	95	11.9	18	14	18	30	22	53	3	04	2	52
8	13	59	−17.5	56.1	15.3	72	271	98	12.9	19	31	19	53	23	42	3	22	3	05
9	14	50	−21.5	55.6	15.1	84	219	100	13.9	20	45	21	13	—	—	3	45	3	22
10	15	43	−24.4	55.1	15.0	96	128	99	14.9	21	52	22	24	0	32	4	15	3	46
11	16	37	−26.0	54.8	14.9	108	108	97	15.9	22	48	23	21	1	24	4	54	4	22
12	17	31	−26,5	54.5	14.8	120	98	92	16.9	23	32	—	—	2	16	5	44	5	11
13	18	24	−25.6	54.2	14.8	133	90	87	17.9	—	—	0	03	3	07	6	45	6	15
14	19	15	−23.7	54.2	14.8	145	84	80	18.9	0	05	0	31	3	55	7	52	7	27
15	20	05	−20.7	54.2	14.8	157	78	71	19.9	0	30	0	51	4	42	9	03	8	43
16	20	52	−16.8	54.4	14.8	169	74	63	20.9	0	49	1	05	5	27	10	14	10	00
17	21	38	−12.2	54.8	14.9	181	71	53	21.9	1	05	1	15	6	09	11	26	11	17
18	22	23	−7.1	55.4	15.1	194	69	43	22.9	1	18	1	24	6	52	12	39	12	35
19	23	08	−1.7	56.0	15.3	206	68	34	23.9	1	31	1	32	7	34	13	53	13	54
20	23	54	+4.1	56.9	15.5	218	69	24	24.9	1	44	1	40	8	18	15	09	15	16
21	0	42	+9.8	57.7	15.7	230	71	16	25.9	1	58	1	50	9	05	16	30	16	43
22	1	34	+15.2	58.6	16.0	242	76	9	26.9	2	16	2	02	9	56	17	56	18	15
23	2	29	+20.0	59.4	16.2	255	85	3	27.9	2	39	2	19	10	51	19	23	19	49
24	3	30	+23.8	60.1	16.4	267	109	1	28.9	3	12	2	45	11	52	20	46	21	18
25	4	34	+26.0	60.5	16.5	279	232	0	0.5	3	59	3	28	12	57	21	57	22	30
26	5	41	+26.4	60.7	16.5	291	260	3	1.5	5	05	4	32	14	02	22	50	23	19
27	6	47	+24.9	60.6	16.5	304	272	9	2.5	6	25	5	58	15	05	23	27	23	49
28	7	49	+21.6	60.3	16.4	316	280	17	3.5	7	54	7	33	16	04	23	53	—	—
29	8	48	+17.1	59.8	16.3	328	286	27	4.5	9	22	9	08	16	58	—	—	0	09
30	9	43	+11.7	59.1	16.1	340	290	37	5.5	10	47	10	39	17	47	0	12	0	22
31	10	34	+5.8	58.4	15.9	353	292	49	6.5	12	09	12	07	18	34	0	28	0	33

MERCURY

Day	R.A.		Dec.	Diam.	Phase	Transit		5° high			
								52°		56°	
	h	m	°	″	%	h	m	h	m	h	m
1	3	49	+22.8	9	25	13	12	20	42	20	59
3	3	53	+22.8	9	20	13	08	20	37	20	55
5	3	56	+22.7	10	15	13	02	20	30	20	48
7	3	57	+22.4	10	11	12	55	20	21	20	38
9	3	57	+22.0	11	8	12	46	20	09	20	26
11	3	55	+21.5	11	5	12	37	19	56	20	12
13	3	53	+20.9	12	3	12	26	19	41	19	56
15	3	49	+20.1	12	1	12	15	19	25	19	39
17	3	45	+19.3	12	0	12	03	19	09	19	22
19	3	41	+18.5	12	0	11	51	4	48	4	36
21	3	37	+17.7	12	1	11	39	4	41	4	29
23	3	33	+16.9	12	2	11	27	4	34	4	23
25	3	30	+16.2	12	4	11	17	4	26	4	16
27	3	27	+15.7	12	6	11	07	4	19	4	09
29	3	26	+15.2	11	9	10	57	4	12	4	03
31	3	26	+14.9	11	12	10	50	4	06	3	56

VENUS

Day	R.A.		Dec.	Diam.	Phase	Transit		5° high			
								52°		56°	
	h	m	°	″	%	h	m	h	m	h	m
1	0	06	+2.3	39	25	9	29	3	51	3	52
6	0	17	+2.5	36	29	9	20	3	40	3	41
11	0	29	+3.0	34	33	9	13	3	30	3	31
16	0	43	+3.8	31	37	9	07	3	20	3	21
21	0	58	+4.9	29	40	9	03	3	11	3	10
26	1	15	+6.1	27	43	9	00	3	01	3	00
31	1	32	+7.4	26	46	8	57	2	52	2	49

MARS

Day	R.A.		Dec.	Diam.	Phase	Transit		5° high			
								52°		56°	
	h	m	°	″	%	h	m	h	m	h	m
1	0	26	+1.6	4	96	9	49	4	14	4	16
6	0	40	+3.1	5	95	9	43	4	00	4	01
11	0	54	+4.6	5	95	9	38	3	47	3	46
16	1	08	+6.1	5	95	9	32	3	34	3	32
21	1	22	+7.5	5	95	9	27	3	21	3	18
26	1	36	+9.0	5	94	9	21	3	08	3	04
31	1	50	+10.3	5	94	9	16	2	55	2	50

SUNRISE AND SUNSET

	London		*Bristol*		*Birmingham*		*Manchester*		*Newcastle*		*Glasgow*		*Belfast*	
	0° 05′	*51° 30′*	*2° 35′*	*51° 28′*	*1° 55′*	*52° 28′*	*2° 15′*	*53° 28′*	*1° 37′*	*54° 59′*	*4° 14′*	*55° 52′*	*5° 56′*	*54° 35′*
d	*h m*	*h m*	*h m*	*h m*	*h m*	*h m*	*h m*	*h m*	*h m*	*h m*	*h m*	*h m*	*h m*	*h m*
1	4 32	19 24	4 42	19 34	4 36	19 34	4 34	19 39	4 26	19 42	4 33	19 56	4 45	19 58
2	4 30	19 25	4 40	19 35	4 34	19 36	4 32	19 41	4 24	19 44	4 31	19 58	4 43	20 00
3	4 28	19 27	4 39	19 37	4 33	19 38	4 30	19 43	4 22	19 46	4 29	20 00	4 41	20 02
4	4 27	19 29	4 37	19 39	4 31	19 39	4 28	19 44	4 20	19 48	4 27	20 02	4 39	20 03
5	4 25	19 30	4 35	19 40	4 29	19 41	4 26	19 46	4 18	19 50	4 25	20 04	4 37	20 05
6	4 23	19 32	4 33	19 42	4 27	19 43	4 25	19 48	4 16	19 52	4 23	20 06	4 35	20 07
7	4 21	19 33	4 31	19 43	4 25	19 44	4 23	19 50	4 14	19 53	4 20	20 08	4 33	20 09
8	4 20	19 35	4 30	19 45	4 23	19 46	4 21	19 51	4 12	19 55	4 18	20 10	4 31	20 11
9	4 18	19 37	4 28	19 47	4 22	19 48	4 19	19 53	4 10	19 57	4 16	20 12	4 29	20 13
10	4 16	19 38	4 26	19 48	4 20	19 49	4 17	19 55	4 08	19 59	4 14	20 14	4 27	20 14
11	4 15	19 40	4 25	19 50	4 18	19 51	4 15	19 56	4 06	20 01	4 12	20 16	4 25	20 16
12	4 13	19 41	4 23	19 51	4 16	19 53	4 14	19 58	4 04	20 03	4 10	20 17	4 23	20 18
13	4 11	19 43	4 22	19 53	4 15	19 54	4 12	20 00	4 02	20 04	4 08	20 19	4 22	20 20
14	4 10	19 44	4 20	19 54	4 13	19 56	4 10	20 02	4 01	20 06	4 07	20 21	4 20	20 22
15	4 08	19 46	4 19	19 56	4 12	19 57	4 09	20 03	3 59	20 08	4 05	20 23	4 18	20 23
16	4 07	19 47	4 17	19 57	4 10	19 59	4 07	20 05	3 57	20 10	4 03	20 25	4 16	20 25
17	4 06	19 49	4 16	19 59	4 09	20 00	4 05	20 06	3 55	20 11	4 01	20 27	4 15	20 27
18	4 04	19 50	4 14	20 00	4 07	20 02	4 04	20 08	3 54	20 13	3 59	20 29	4 13	20 28
19	4 03	19 52	4 13	20 02	4 06	20 03	4 02	20 10	3 52	20 15	3 58	20 30	4 11	20 30
20	4 01	19 53	4 12	20 03	4 04	20 05	4 01	20 11	3 51	20 17	3 56	20 32	4 10	20 32
21	4 00	19 55	4 10	20 04	4 03	20 06	4 00	20 13	3 49	20 18	3 54	20 34	4 08	20 33
22	3 59	19 56	4 09	20 06	4 02	20 08	3 58	20 14	3 47	20 20	3 53	20 36	4 07	20 35
23	3 58	19 57	4 08	20 07	4 00	20 09	3 57	20 16	3 46	20 21	3 51	20 37	4 06	20 36
24	3 57	19 59	4 07	20 08	3 59	20 11	3 55	20 17	3 45	20 23	3 50	20 39	4 04	20 38
25	3 55	20 00	4 06	20 10	3 58	20 12	3 54	20 19	3 43	20 25	3 48	20 40	4 03	20 39
26	3 54	20 01	4 05	20 11	3 57	20 13	3 53	20 20	3 42	20 26	3 47	20 42	4 02	20 41
27	3 53	20 02	4 03	20 12	3 56	20 15	3 52	20 21	3 41	20 28	3 46	20 44	4 00	20 42
28	3 52	20 04	4 03	20 13	3 55	20 16	3 51	20 23	3 39	20 29	3 44	20 45	3 59	20 44
29	3 51	20 05	4 02	20 15	3 54	20 17	3 50	20 24	3 38	20 30	3 43	20 47	3 58	20 45
30	3 50	20 06	4 01	20 16	3 53	20 18	3 49	20 25	3 37	20 32	3 42	20 48	3 57	20 47
31	3 50	20 07	4 00	20 17	3 52	20 20	3 48	20 26	3 36	20 33	3 41	20 49	3 56	20 48

JUPITER

Day	*R.A.*		*Dec.*		*Transit*		*5° high*			
							52°		*56°*	
	h	*m*	°	′	*h*	*m*	*h*	*m*	*h*	*m*
1	21	45.9	−14	11	7	09	3	01	3	19
11	21	50.5	−13	50	6	34	2	24	2	41
21	21	54.1	−13	33	5	58	1	47	2	03
31	21	56.6	−13	23	5	21	1	09	1	25

Diameters – equatorial 40″ polar 37″

SATURN

Day	*R.A.*		*Dec.*		*Transit*		*5° high*			
							52°		*56°*	
	h	*m*	°	′	*h*	*m*	*h*	*m*	*h*	*m*
1	11	08.7	+7	54	20	29	2	40	2	43
11	11	08.0	+7	57	19	49	2	00	2	03
21	11	07.8	+7	56	19	10	1	21	1	24
31	11	08.4	+7	51	18	31	0	41	0	45

Diameters – equatorial 18″ polar 16″
Rings – major axis 42″ minor axis 3″

URANUS

Day	*R.A.*		*Dec.*		*Transit*		*10° high*			
							52°		*56°*	
	h	*m*	°	′	*h*	*m*	*h*	*m*	*h*	*m*
1	23	43.5	−2	35	9	06	4	26	4	35
11	23	45.0	−2	26	8	28	3	47	3	57
21	23	46.3	−2	18	7	50	3	09	3	18
31	23	47.4	−2	11	7	12	2	30	2	39

Diameter 4″

NEPTUNE

Day	*R.A.*		*Dec.*		*Transit*		*10° high*			
							52°		*56°*	
	h	*m*	°	′	*h*	*m*	*h*	*m*	*h*	*m*
1	21	54.5	−13	07	7	17	3	42	4	04
11	21	55.0	−13	05	6	38	3	03	3	25
21	21	55.3	−13	04	5	59	2	23	2	46
31	21	55.4	−13	04	5	20	1	44	2	07

Diameter 2″

♊ JUNE 2009 ♋

SIXTH MONTH, 30 DAYS. *Junius*, Roman *gens* (family)

1	*Monday*	The British fleet defeated the French at the battle of the Glorious First of June 1794	week 23 day 152
2	*Tuesday*	The coronation of HM Queen Elizabeth II took place 1953	153
3	*Wednesday*	The Duke of Windsor, who had abdicated as Edward VIII, married Wallis Simpson 1937	154
4	*Thursday*	The first hot air balloon was flown by the Montgolfier brothers 1783	155
5	*Friday*	US senator Robert Kennedy was shot in Los Angeles 1968	156
6	*Saturday*	D-day: the Allied forces landed in Normandy 1944	157
7	*Sunday*	The US navy defeated a Japanese attack at the battle of Midway 1942	158
8	*Monday*	Margaret Bondfield became Britain's first woman cabinet minister 1929	week 24 day 159
9	*Tuesday*	The first live broadcast from the House of Commons was transmitted 1975	160
10	*Wednesday*	The first Oxford and Cambridge boat race took place 1829	161
11	*Thursday*	James III of Scotland was murdered after the battle of Sauchieburn 1488	162
12	*Friday*	Nelson Mandela was sentenced to life in prison for plotting to sabotage the South African state 1964	163
13	*Saturday*	The Peasants' Revolt: Wat Tyler marched into London leading a mob of peasants 1381	164
14	*Sunday*	German troops entered Paris 1940	165
15	*Monday*	The Magna Carta was signed by King John 1215	week 25 day 166
16	*Tuesday*	Russian astronaut Valentina Tereshkova became the first woman in space 1963	167
17	*Wednesday*	The Statue of Liberty, a gift from France, arrived in New York 1885	168
18	*Thursday*	Napoleon was defeated by Wellington at the battle of Waterloo 1815	169
19	*Friday*	The Metropolitan Police Service was founded 1829	170
20	*Saturday*	Queen Victoria became Queen of England at the age of 18 1837	171
21	*Sunday*	Britain annexed Zululand in southern Africa 1887	172
22	*Monday*	Germany invaded the Soviet Union 1941	week 26 day 173
23	*Tuesday*	A terrorist bomb on an Air India jet killed all 330 passengers 1985	174
24	*Wednesday*	Robert Bruce defeated Edward II's army at the battle of Bannockburn 1314	175
25	*Thursday*	The Korean War began as North Korean troops crossed the 38th parallel 1950	176
26	*Friday*	Francisco Pizzaro, the Spanish conqueror of Peru, was murdered by his followers 1541	177
27	*Saturday*	Tony Blair resigned as prime minister 2007	178
28	*Sunday*	Archduke Franz Ferdinand, heir to the Austrian throne, was assassinated in Sarajevo 1914	179
29	*Monday*	The *Daily Telegraph* was first published 1855	week 27 day 180
30	*Tuesday*	Hundreds of leading Nazis were murdered in the Night of the Long Knives 1934	181

ASTRONOMICAL PHENOMENA

d	*h*	
5	20	Venus at greatest elongation W.46°
13	12	Mercury at greatest elongation W.23°
13	16	Jupiter in conjunction with Moon. Jupiter 3°S.
15	08	Jupiter at stationary point
19	13	Venus in conjunction with Moon. Venus 8°S.
19	14	Mars in conjunction with Moon. Mars 6°S.
21	06	Sun's longitude 90°. ♋
21	07	Mercury in conjunction with Moon. Mercury 7°S.
21	13	Mars in conjunction with Venus. Mars 2°N.
23	08	Pluto at opposition
27	22	Saturn in conjunction with Moon. Saturn 6°N.

MINIMA OF ALGOL

Algol is inconveniently situated for observation during June

CONSTELLATIONS

The following constellations are near the meridian at

	d	*h*		*d*	*h*
May	1	24	June	15	21
May	16	23	July	1	20
June	1	22	July	16	19

Cassiopeia (below the Pole), Ursa Minor, Draco, Ursa Major, Canes Venatici, Bootes, Corona, Serpens, Virgo and Libra

THE MOON

Phases, Apsides and Node	*d*	*h*	*m*
○ Full Moon	7	18	12
☾ Last Quarter	15	22	15
● New Moon	22	19	35
☽ First Quarter	29	11	28
Apogee (405,766 km)	10	15	53
Perigee (358,020 km)	23	10	33

Mean longitude of ascending node on June 1, 303°

THE SUN

s.d. 15′.8

Day	Right Ascension			Dec. +		Equation of time		Rise 52°		Rise 56°		Transit		Set 52°		Set 56°		Sidereal time			Transit of first point of Aries		
	h	*m*	*s*	°	′	*m*	*s*	*h*	*m*	*h*	*m*	*h*	*m*	*h*	*m*	*h*	*m*	*h*	*m*	*s*	*h*	*m*	*s*
1	4	36	14	22	03	+2	13	3	46	3	22	11	58	20	10	20	35	16	38	27	7	20	21
2	4	40	19	22	11	+2	04	3	45	3	21	11	58	20	12	20	36	16	42	23	7	16	25
3	4	44	26	22	18	+1	54	3	44	3	20	11	58	20	13	20	37	16	46	20	7	12	29
4	4	48	32	22	25	+1	44	3	44	3	19	11	58	20	14	20	38	16	50	17	7	08	33
5	4	52	39	22	32	+1	34	3	43	3	18	11	59	20	15	20	40	16	54	13	7	04	37
6	4	56	46	22	39	+1	23	3	42	3	17	11	59	20	15	20	41	16	58	10	7	00	41
7	5	00	54	22	45	+1	13	3	42	3	17	11	59	20	16	20	42	17	02	06	6	56	45
8	5	05	01	22	50	+1	01	3	41	3	16	11	59	20	17	20	43	17	06	03	6	52	49
9	5	09	10	22	55	+0	50	3	41	3	15	11	59	20	18	20	44	17	09	59	6	48	53
10	5	13	18	23	00	+0	38	3	41	3	15	11	59	20	19	20	45	17	13	56	6	44	58
11	5	17	26	23	05	+0	26	3	40	3	14	12	00	20	19	20	45	17	17	52	6	41	02
12	5	21	35	23	09	+0	14	3	40	3	14	12	00	20	20	20	46	17	21	49	6	37	06
13	5	25	44	23	12	+0	02	3	40	3	14	12	00	20	21	20	47	17	25	46	6	33	10
14	5	29	53	23	16	−0	11	3	40	3	13	12	00	20	21	20	48	17	29	42	6	29	14
15	5	34	02	23	18	−0	24	3	39	3	13	12	01	20	22	20	48	17	33	39	6	25	18
16	5	38	12	23	21	−0	37	3	39	3	13	12	01	20	22	20	49	17	37	35	6	21	22
17	5	42	21	23	23	−0	50	3	39	3	13	12	01	20	23	20	49	17	41	32	6	17	26
18	5	46	31	23	24	−1	03	3	39	3	13	12	01	20	23	20	50	17	45	28	6	13	30
19	5	50	41	23	25	−1	16	3	39	3	13	12	01	20	23	20	50	17	49	25	6	09	34
20	5	54	50	23	26	−1	29	3	40	3	13	12	02	20	24	20	50	17	53	21	6	05	38
21	5	59	00	23	26	−1	42	3	40	3	13	12	02	20	24	20	50	17	57	18	6	01	43
22	6	03	10	23	26	−1	55	3	40	3	13	12	02	20	24	20	51	18	01	15	5	57	47
23	6	07	19	23	26	−2	08	3	40	3	14	12	02	20	24	20	51	18	05	11	5	53	51
24	6	11	29	23	25	−2	21	3	41	3	14	12	02	20	24	20	51	18	09	08	5	49	55
25	6	15	39	23	23	−2	34	3	41	3	14	12	03	20	24	20	51	18	13	04	5	45	59
26	6	19	48	23	22	−2	47	3	41	3	15	12	03	20	24	20	51	18	17	01	5	42	03
27	6	23	57	23	19	−3	00	3	42	3	16	12	03	20	24	20	50	18	20	57	5	38	07
28	6	28	06	23	17	−3	12	3	42	3	16	12	03	20	24	20	50	18	24	54	5	34	11
29	6	32	15	23	14	−3	24	3	43	3	17	12	04	20	24	20	50	18	28	51	5	30	15
30	6	36	23	23	11	−3	36	3	44	3	18	12	04	20	23	20	49	18	32	47	5	26	19

DURATION OF TWILIGHT (in minutes)

Latitude	52°	56°	52°	56°	52°	56°	52°	56°
	1 June		*11 June*		*21 June*		*31 June*	
Civil	46	58	48	61	49	63	48	61
Nautical	116	TAN	124	TAN	127	TAN	124	TAN
Astronomical	TAN	TAN	TAN	TAN	TAN	TAN	TAN	TAN

THE NIGHT SKY

Mercury reaches greatest western elongation (23 degrees) on the 13th but the long duration of twilight means that it remains unsuitably placed for observation throughout the month.

Venus is a brilliant morning object in the eastern sky, magnitude −4.2. It reaches greatest western elongation (46 degrees) on the 5th and by the end of June it is visible for nearly two hours before sunrise. The waning crescent Moon passes seven degrees north of Venus on the 19th, while two days later Venus passes two degrees south of Mars.

Mars, by almost the end of the month, becomes visible to observers for the first time this year, though it will be a difficult object to detect. Then it may be seen very low above the eastern horizon for a short while about two hours before sunrise. Its magnitude is +1.1.

Jupiter, magnitude −2.6, continues to be visible as a conspicuous object in the night sky, becoming visible above the south-eastern horizon by about 01h at the beginning of the month, and two hours earlier by the end of the month. The waning gibbous Moon will be seen in the vicinity of Jupiter around the 13th. Jupiter reaches its first stationary point on the 15th, on the borders of the constellations of Capricornus and Aquarius, and commences its retrograde motion in Capricornus.

Saturn, magnitude +1.1, continues to be visible low in the western sky in the evenings. Saturn is in the constellation of Leo. The waxing crescent Moon is near the planet on the evening of the 27th.

THE MOON

Day	R.A.		Dec.	Hor. Par.	Semi-diam.	Sun's Co-Long.	PA. of Br. Limb	Ph.	Age	Rise				Transit		Set			
										52°		56°				52°		56°	
	h	m	°	′	′	°	°	%	d	h	m	h	m	h	m	h	m	h	m
1	11	23	−0.2	57.7	15.7	5	292	60	7.5	13	28	13	31	19	19	0	42	0	42
2	12	10	−6.1	57.1	15.6	17	292	70	8.5	14	45	14	54	20	05	0	56	0	51
3	12	58	−11.6	56.5	15.4	29	289	79	9.5	16	02	16	17	20	51	1	11	1	00
4	13	47	−16.5	55.9	15.2	41	285	87	10.5	17	19	17	39	21	38	1	28	1	12
5	14	37	−20.6	55.4	15.1	54	280	93	11.5	18	33	18	59	22	27	1	49	1	27
6	15	29	−23.7	55.0	15.0	66	271	97	12.5	19	42	20	12	23	18	2	16	1	49
7	16	22	−25.7	54.7	14.9	78	254	99	13.5	20	41	21	14	—		2	51	2	20
8	17	15	−26.4	54.4	14.8	90	146	100	14.5	21	29	22	01	0	10	3	38	3	05
9	18	09	−25.9	54.2	14.8	102	99	99	15.5	22	06	22	34	1	01	4	35	4	04
10	19	01	−24.2	54.1	14.7	115	87	95	16.5	22	33	22	56	1	51	5	41	5	14
11	19	51	−21.5	54.0	14.7	127	80	91	17.5	22	54	23	11	2	38	6	51	6	29
12	20	39	−17.8	54.1	14.8	139	75	85	18.5	23	10	23	22	3	23	8	02	7	46
13	21	25	−13.5	54.4	14.8	151	71	77	19.5	23	24	23	32	4	06	9	13	9	02
14	22	09	−8.6	54.8	14.9	163	68	69	20.5	23	37	23	40	4	48	10	24	10	18
15	22	53	−3.3	55.3	15.1	176	67	59	21.5	23	49	23	48	5	29	11	35	11	35
16	23	38	+2.3	56.0	15.2	188	67	49	22.5	—		23	56	6	11	12	49	12	53
17	0	24	+7.9	56.8	15.5	200	68	39	23.5	0	03	—		6	55	14	06	14	16
18	1	13	+13.3	57.7	15.7	212	70	29	24.5	0	18	0	07	7	43	15	27	15	43
19	2	06	+18.3	58.6	16.0	225	74	20	25.5	0	38	0	21	8	35	16	52	17	15
20	3	03	+22.4	59.5	16.2	237	80	11	26.5	1	05	0	42	9	33	18	17	18	46
21	4	06	+25.3	60.3	16.4	249	88	5	27.5	1	45	1	15	10	35	19	35	20	08
22	5	12	+26.4	60.9	16.6	261	102	1	28.5	2	41	2	08	11	41	20	37	21	08
23	6	19	+25.7	61.2	16.7	274	230	0	0.2	3	56	3	26	12	47	21	22	21	47
24	7	25	+23.0	61.2	16.7	286	275	2	1.2	5	25	5	00	13	50	21	53	22	12
25	8	27	+18.8	60.9	16.6	298	284	7	2.2	6	57	6	40	14	47	22	16	22	28
26	9	25	+13.4	60.3	16.4	310	290	15	3.2	8	27	8	17	15	40	22	34	22	40
27	10	18	+7.5	59.5	16.2	323	293	24	4.2	9	53	9	48	16	30	22	49	22	50
28	11	09	+1.3	58.7	16.0	335	294	34	5.2	11	14	11	16	17	17	23	03	22	59
29	11	58	−4.8	57.8	15.7	347	294	45	6.2	12	34	12	41	18	03	23	18	23	09
30	12	46	−10.5	57.0	15.5	359	292	56	7.2	13	52	14	04	18	49	23	34	23	20

MERCURY

Day	R.A.		Dec.	Diam.	Phase	Transit		5° high			
								52°		56°	
	h	m	°	″	%	h	m	h	m	h	m
1	3	26	+14.9	11	14	10	46	4	02	3	53
3	3	27	+14.8	10	17	10	40	3	56	3	47
5	3	30	+14.9	10	21	10	34	3	50	3	41
7	3	33	+15.1	9	24	10	30	3	45	3	36
9	3	38	+15.4	9	28	10	27	3	40	3	30
11	3	43	+15.9	9	32	10	25	3	35	3	25
13	3	50	+16.4	8	36	10	24	3	31	3	20
15	3	58	+17.0	8	40	10	24	3	28	3	16
17	4	07	+17.7	8	45	10	25	3	25	3	13
19	4	16	+18.4	7	49	10	28	3	22	3	10
21	4	27	+19.2	7	54	10	31	3	21	3	07
23	4	39	+20.0	7	59	10	35	3	20	3	06
25	4	52	+20.7	6	64	10	40	3	21	3	06
27	5	06	+21.5	6	69	10	46	3	23	3	06
29	5	20	+22.2	6	75	10	53	3	25	3	09
31	5	36	+22.8	6	80	11	02	3	30	3	12

VENUS

Day	R.A.		Dec.	Diam.	Phase	Transit		5° high			
								52°		56°	
	h	m	°	″	%	h	m	h	m	h	m
1	1	36	+7.7	25	47	8	57	2	50	2	47
6	1	54	+9.1	24	50	8	55	2	41	2	37
11	2	13	+10.6	22	52	8	55	2	33	2	27
16	2	32	+12.1	21	55	8	54	2	24	2	18
21	2	52	+13.6	20	57	8	55	2	17	2	09
26	3	13	+15.1	19	60	8	56	2	10	2	01
31	3	34	+16.4	19	62	8	58	2	04	1	54

MARS

Day	R.A.		Dec.	Diam.	Phase	Transit		5° high			
								52°		56°	
	h	m	°	″	%	h	m	h	m	h	m
1	1	53	+10.6	5	94	9	14	2	53	2	47
6	2	08	+11.9	5	94	9	09	2	40	2	34
11	2	22	+13.2	5	94	9	04	2	28	2	21
16	2	36	+14.4	5	93	8	58	2	16	2	08
21	2	51	+15.5	5	93	8	53	2	05	1	55
26	3	05	+16.6	5	93	8	48	1	54	1	43
31	3	19	+17.6	5	93	8	42	1	43	1	31

SUNRISE AND SUNSET

d	London 0° 05′	51° 30′	Bristol 2° 35′	51° 28′	Birmingham 1° 55′	52° 28′	Manchester 2° 15′	53° 28′	Newcastle 1° 37′	54° 59′	Glasgow 4° 14′	55° 52′	Belfast 5° 56′	54° 35′
	h m	h m	h m	h m	h m	h m	h m	h m	h m	h m	h m	h m	h m	h m
1	3 49	20 08	3 59	20 18	3 51	20 21	3 47	20 28	3 35	20 34	3 40	20 51	3 55	20 49
2	3 48	20 09	3 58	20 19	3 50	20 22	3 46	20 29	3 34	20 36	3 39	20 52	3 54	20 50
3	3 47	20 10	3 57	20 20	3 49	20 23	3 45	20 30	3 33	20 37	3 38	20 53	3 53	20 51
4	3 47	20 11	3 57	20 21	3 49	20 24	3 44	20 31	3 32	20 38	3 37	20 54	3 52	20 53
5	3 46	20 12	3 56	20 22	3 48	20 25	3 44	20 32	3 32	20 39	3 36	20 56	3 51	20 54
6	3 45	20 13	3 56	20 23	3 48	20 26	3 43	20 33	3 31	20 40	3 35	20 57	3 51	20 55
7	3 45	20 14	3 55	20 24	3 47	20 27	3 42	20 34	3 30	20 41	3 34	20 58	3 50	20 56
8	3 44	20 15	3 55	20 25	3 46	20 28	3 42	20 35	3 30	20 42	3 34	20 59	3 50	20 57
9	3 44	20 16	3 54	20 25	3 46	20 28	3 41	20 36	3 29	20 43	3 33	21 00	3 49	20 58
10	3 44	20 16	3 54	20 26	3 46	20 29	3 41	20 36	3 29	20 44	3 33	21 01	3 48	20 58
11	3 43	20 17	3 54	20 27	3 45	20 30	3 41	20 37	3 28	20 45	3 32	21 01	3 48	20 59
12	3 43	20 18	3 53	20 27	3 45	20 30	3 40	20 38	3 28	20 45	3 32	21 02	3 48	21 00
13	3 43	20 18	3 53	20 28	3 45	20 31	3 40	20 39	3 27	20 46	3 31	21 03	3 47	21 01
14	3 43	20 19	3 53	20 29	3 44	20 32	3 40	20 39	3 27	20 47	3 31	21 04	3 47	21 01
15	3 43	20 19	3 53	20 29	3 44	20 32	3 40	20 40	3 27	20 47	3 31	21 04	3 47	21 02
16	3 42	20 20	3 53	20 30	3 44	20 33	3 39	20 40	3 27	20 48	3 31	21 05	3 47	21 02
17	3 42	20 20	3 53	20 30	3 44	20 33	3 39	20 41	3 27	20 48	3 31	21 05	3 47	21 03
18	3 42	20 21	3 53	20 30	3 44	20 33	3 39	20 41	3 27	20 49	3 31	21 06	3 47	21 03
19	3 43	20 21	3 53	20 31	3 44	20 34	3 40	20 41	3 27	20 49	3 31	21 06	3 47	21 03
20	3 43	20 21	3 53	20 31	3 44	20 34	3 40	20 42	3 27	20 49	3 31	21 06	3 47	21 04
21	3 43	20 21	3 53	20 31	3 45	20 34	3 40	20 42	3 27	20 49	3 31	21 06	3 47	21 04
22	3 43	20 22	3 53	20 31	3 45	20 34	3 40	20 42	3 27	20 50	3 31	21 07	3 47	21 04
23	3 43	20 22	3 54	20 31	3 45	20 35	3 40	20 42	3 28	20 50	3 32	21 07	3 48	21 04
24	3 44	20 22	3 54	20 31	3 46	20 35	3 41	20 42	3 28	20 50	3 32	21 07	3 48	21 04
25	3 44	20 22	3 54	20 32	3 46	20 35	3 41	20 42	3 28	20 50	3 32	21 07	3 49	21 04
26	3 45	20 22	3 55	20 31	3 46	20 35	3 42	20 42	3 29	20 50	3 33	21 06	3 49	21 04
27	3 45	20 22	3 55	20 31	3 47	20 34	3 42	20 42	3 29	20 49	3 34	21 06	3 50	21 04
28	3 46	20 21	3 56	20 31	3 47	20 34	3 43	20 42	3 30	20 49	3 34	21 06	3 50	21 04
29	3 46	20 21	3 56	20 31	3 48	20 34	3 43	20 41	3 31	20 49	3 35	21 06	3 51	21 03
30	3 47	20 21	3 57	20 31	3 49	20 34	3 44	20 41	3 31	20 49	3 36	21 05	3 51	21 03

JUPITER

Day	R.A.	Dec.	Transit	5° high 52°	5° high 56°
	h m	° ′	h m	h m	h m
1	21 56.8	−13 22	5 18	1 05	1 21
11	21 58.0	−13 19	4 39	0 27	0 43
21	21 58.0	−13 21	4 00	23 44	0 04
31	21 56.7	−13 31	3 19	23 04	23 21

Diameters – equatorial 44″ polar 41″

SATURN

Day	R.A.	Dec.	Transit	5° high 52°	5° high 56°
	h m	° ′	h m	h m	h m
1	11 08.5	+7 50	18 27	0 38	0 41
11	11 09.7	+7 40	17 49	23 55	0 02
21	11 11.5	+7 27	17 12	23 16	23 19
31	11 13.8	+7 11	16 35	22 38	22 40

Diameters – equatorial 17″ polar 16″
Rings – major axis 39″ minor axis 3″

URANUS

Day	R.A.	Dec.	Transit	10° high 52°	10° high 56°
	h m	° ′	h m	h m	h m
1	23 47.4	−2 11	7 08	2 26	2 35
11	23 48.2	−2 06	6 29	1 47	1 56
21	23 48.7	−2 04	5 50	1 08	1 17
31	23 48.8	−2 03	5 11	0 29	0 37

Diameter 4″

NEPTUNE

Day	R.A.	Dec.	Transit	10° high 52°	10° high 56°
	h m	° ′	h m	h m	h m
1	21 55.4	−13 04	5 16	1 40	2 03
11	21 55.2	−13 05	4 37	1 01	1 23
21	21 54.9	−13 07	3 57	0 22	0 44
31	21 54.3	−13 10	3 17	23 38	0 05

Diameter 2″

JULY 2009

SEVENTH MONTH, 31 DAYS. *Julius* Caesar, formerly *Quintilis*, fifth month of Roman pre-Julian calendar

1	*Wednesday*	James II was defeated by William III at the battle of the Boyne 1690	day 182
2	*Thursday*	Live 8 concerts were held around the globe to persuade political leaders to tackle poverty in Africa 2005	183
3	*Friday*	The first RAF air display took place 1920	184
4	*Saturday*	Israeli commandoes freed hostages at Entebbe Airport, Uganda 1976	185
5	*Sunday*	The National Health Service Act came into effect 1948	186
6	*Monday*	The Piper Alpha oil rig caught fire 1988	week 28 day 187
7	*Tuesday*	Four suicide bomb attacks on London's transport system killed 66 2005	188
8	*Wednesday*	The National Society for the Prevention of Cruelty to Children (NSPCC) was founded 1884	189
9	*Thursday*	The International Olympic Committee reinstated South Africa as a member after a 21–year boycott 1991	190
10	*Friday*	Lady Jane Grey was proclaimed queen of England, her reign only lasted 13 days 1553	191
11	*Saturday*	The Srebrenica Massacre began: an estimated 8,000 Bosnian boys and men were killed 1995	192
12	*Sunday*	The city of Acre was captured by Crusaders 1191	193
13	*Monday*	Ruth Ellis, the last woman to be executed in Britain, was hanged 1955	week 29 day 194
14	*Tuesday*	The Bastille, the state prison in Paris, was stormed beginning the French Revolution 1789	195
15	*Wednesday*	Jerusalem was captured by the Crusaders 1099	196
16	*Thursday*	The first atomic bomb was tested in New Mexico 1945	197
17	*Friday*	The first issue of *Punch* was published 1841	198
18	*Saturday*	The Spanish Civil War began 1936	199
19	*Sunday*	A French soldier found the Rosetta Stone during Napoleon's Egyptian campaign 1799	200
20	*Monday*	Sirimavo Bandaranaike became the world's first female prime minister in Ceylon 1960	week 30 day 201
21	*Tuesday*	Neil Armstrong became the first man to walk on the Moon 1969	202
22	*Wednesday*	The Tate Gallery opened 1897	203
23	*Thursday*	Military rule collapsed in Greece 1974	204
24	*Friday*	Treaty of Lausanne partitioning the Otttoman Empire was signed 1923	205
25	*Saturday*	Louis Blériot made the first flight across the English Channel 1909	206
26	*Sunday*	Liberia became the first African colony to become an independent state 1847	207
27	*Monday*	The Bank of England was established by royal charter 1694	week 31 day 208
28	*Tuesday*	The First World War began when Austria-Hungary declared war on Serbia 1914	209
29	*Wednesday*	Prince Charles and Lady Diana Spencer married 1982	210
30	*Thursday*	England won the football World Cup, defeating Germany 4–2 1966	211
31	*Friday*	Cigarette adverts were banned on television in the UK 1965	212

ASTRONOMICAL PHENOMENA

d	*h*	
1	08	Uranus at stationary point
4	02	Earth at aphelion (152 million km)
10	20	Jupiter in conjunction with Moon. Jupiter 3°S.
14	02	Mercury in superior conjunction
18	10	Mars in conjunction with Moon. Mars 5°S.
19	04	Venus in conjunction with Moon. Venus 6°S.
22	03	Total eclipse of Sun
22	17	Sun's longitude 120° ♌
22	19	Mercury in conjunction with Moon. Mercury 3°N.
25	10	Saturn in conjunction with Moon. Saturn 6°N.

MINIMA OF ALGOL

d	*h*	*d*	*h*	*d*	*h*
2	16.2	13	16.2	25	16.2
5	13.0	16	13.0	28	13.0
8	09.9	19	09.9	31	09.9
10	06.7	22	06.7		

CONSTELLATIONS

The following constellations are near their meridian at

	d	*h*		*d*	*h*
June	1	24	July	16	21
June	15	23	August	1	20
July	1	22	August	16	19

Ursa Minor, Draco, Corona, Hercules, Lyra, Serpens, Ophiuchus, Libra, Scorpius and Sagittarius

THE MOON

Phases, Apsides and Node	*d*	*h*	*m*
○ Full Moon	7	09	21
☾ Last Quarter	15	09	53
● New Moon	22	02	35
☽ First Quarter	28	22	00
Apogee (406,228 km)	7	21	23
Perigee (357,460 km)	21	20	08

Mean longitude of ascending node on July 1, 301°

THE SUN

s.d. 15′.8

Day	Right Ascension			Dec. +		Equation of time		Rise 52°		Rise 56°		Transit		Set 52°		Set 56°		Sidereal time			Transit of first point of Aries		
	h	*m*	*s*	°	′	*m*	*s*	*h*	*m*	*h*	*m*	*h*	*m*	*h*	*m*	*h*	*m*	*h*	*m*	*s*	*h*	*m*	*s*
1	6	40	32	23	07	–3	48	3	44	3	18	12	04	20	23	20	49	18	36	44	5	22	23
2	6	44	40	23	03	–4	00	3	45	3	19	12	04	20	23	20	48	18	40	40	5	18	27
3	6	48	48	22	58	–4	11	3	46	3	20	12	04	20	22	20	48	18	44	37	5	14	32
4	6	52	55	22	53	–4	22	3	47	3	21	12	04	20	22	20	47	18	48	33	5	10	36
5	6	57	02	22	48	–4	32	3	47	3	22	12	05	20	21	20	46	18	52	30	5	06	40
6	7	01	09	22	42	–4	42	3	48	3	23	12	05	20	21	20	46	18	56	26	5	02	44
7	7	05	15	22	36	–4	52	3	49	3	24	12	05	20	20	20	45	19	00	23	4	58	48
8	7	09	21	22	29	–5	02	3	50	3	26	12	05	20	19	20	44	19	04	20	4	54	52
9	7	13	27	22	22	–5	11	3	51	3	27	12	05	20	19	20	43	19	08	16	4	50	56
10	7	17	32	22	15	–5	19	3	52	3	28	12	05	20	18	20	42	19	12	13	4	47	00
11	7	21	37	22	07	–5	28	3	53	3	29	12	06	20	17	20	41	19	16	09	4	43	04
12	7	25	41	21	59	–5	35	3	54	3	31	12	06	20	16	20	40	19	20	06	4	39	08
13	7	29	45	21	50	–5	43	3	56	3	32	12	06	20	15	20	39	19	24	02	4	35	12
14	7	33	49	21	41	–5	50	3	57	3	33	12	06	20	14	20	37	19	27	59	4	31	17
15	7	37	52	21	32	–5	56	3	58	3	35	12	06	20	13	20	36	19	31	55	4	27	21
16	7	41	54	21	23	–6	02	3	59	3	36	12	06	20	12	20	35	19	35	52	4	23	25
17	7	45	56	21	13	–6	08	4	00	3	38	12	06	20	11	20	33	19	39	49	4	19	29
18	7	49	58	21	02	–6	12	4	02	3	40	12	06	20	10	20	32	19	43	45	4	15	33
19	7	53	59	20	52	–6	17	4	03	3	41	12	06	20	09	20	30	19	47	42	4	11	37
20	7	57	59	20	40	–6	21	4	04	3	43	12	06	20	07	20	29	19	51	38	4	07	41
21	8	01	59	20	29	–6	24	4	06	3	44	12	06	20	06	20	27	19	55	35	4	03	45
22	8	05	58	20	17	–6	27	4	07	3	46	12	06	20	05	20	26	19	59	31	3	59	49
23	8	09	57	20	05	–6	29	4	09	3	48	12	07	20	04	20	24	20	03	28	3	55	53
24	8	13	55	19	53	–6	31	4	10	3	50	12	07	20	02	20	22	20	07	24	3	51	57
25	8	17	53	19	40	–6	32	4	11	3	51	12	07	20	01	20	21	20	11	21	3	48	02
26	8	21	50	19	27	–6	32	4	13	3	53	12	07	19	59	20	19	20	15	18	3	44	06
27	8	25	46	19	14	–6	32	4	14	3	55	12	07	19	58	20	17	20	19	14	3	40	10
28	8	29	42	19	00	–6	31	4	16	3	57	12	07	19	56	20	15	20	23	11	3	36	14
29	8	33	37	18	46	–6	30	4	17	3	58	12	06	19	55	20	13	20	27	07	3	32	18
30	8	37	32	18	32	–6	28	4	19	4	00	12	06	19	53	20	11	20	31	04	3	28	22
31	8	41	25	18	17	–6	25	4	20	4	02	12	06	19	51	20	09	20	35	00	3	24	26

DURATION OF TWILIGHT (in minutes)

Latitude	52°	56°	52°	56°	52°	56°	52°	56°
	1 July		*11 July*		*21 July*		*31 July*	
Civil	48	61	47	58	44	53	42	49
Nautical	124	TAN	117	TAN	107	146	98	123
Astronomical	TAN	TAN	TAN	TAN	TAN	TAN	182	TAN

THE NIGHT SKY

Mercury passes through superior conjunction on the 14th and therefore remains too close to the Sun for observation throughout the month.

Venus, magnitude –4.1, continues to be visible as a magnificent morning object in the eastern sky before dawn. The old crescent Moon is in the vicinity of Venus on the morning of the 19th. Venus is moving eastwards amongst the stars, passing three degrees north of Aldebaran on the 14th.

Mars, magnitude +1.1, is slowly emerging from the morning twilight and may be detected low above the eastern horizon some three hours before sunrise, but the sky will soon become too bright to continue observation. The waning crescent Moon passes five degrees north of Mars on the morning of the 18th. Mars passes about five degrees north of Aldebaran, in Taurus, on the 27th.

Jupiter, magnitude −2.8, becomes visible low in the south-eastern sky well before midnight, in the eastern part of Capricornus. On the 10th and 11th the waning crescent Moon is in the vicinity of the planet. A good opportunity of locating Neptune (with only small optical aid) occurs within a few days either side of July 13 when Neptune will be found only 0.6 degrees north of Jupiter. Do not confuse Neptune (magnitude 7.8) with the star Mu Capricorni (magnitude 5.1), which is roughly halfway between the two planets.

Saturn, magnitude +1.2, is becoming increasingly difficult to observe low above the western horizon in the long evening twilight and will be lost to view before the end of the month.

Twilight. Reference to the section above shows that astronomical twilight lasts all night for a period around the summer solstice (ie in June and July), even in southern England. Under these conditions the sky never gets completely dark as the Sun is always less than 18 degrees below the horizon.

THE MOON

Day	*R.A.*		*Dec.*	*Hor. Par.*	*Semi-diam.*	*Sun's Co-Long.*	*PA of Br. Limb*	*Ph.*	*Age*	*Rise*				*Transit*		*Set*			
										52°		*56°*				*52°*		*56°*	
	h	*m*	°	′	′	°	°	%	*d*	*h*	*m*	*h*	*m*	*h*	*m*	*h*	*m*	*h*	*m*
1	13	35	–15.6	56.2	15.3	11	290	66	8.2	15	09	15	27	19	36	23	53	23	34
2	14	25	–19.8	55.6	15.1	24	286	75	9.2	16	23	16	48	20	24	—	—	23	53
3	15	16	–23.2	55.1	15.0	36	281	83	10.2	17	34	18	03	21	14	0	18	—	—
4	16	09	–25.4	54.7	14.9	48	275	90	11.2	18	36	19	09	22	06	0	51	0	21
5	17	02	–26.4	54.3	14.8	60	268	95	12.2	19	27	20	00	22	57	1	34	1	01
6	17	55	–26.2	54.1	14.7	73	260	98	13.2	20	07	20	37	23	47	2	28	1	55
7	18	48	–24.7	54.0	14.7	85	243	100	14.2	20	37	21	01	—	—	3	31	3	02
8	19	38	–22.2	54.0	14.7	97	86	100	15.2	21	00	21	19	0	35	4	40	4	17
9	20	27	–18.8	54.0	14.7	109	75	98	16.2	21	17	21	31	1	21	5	51	5	33
10	21	13	–14.6	54.2	14.8	121	70	94	17.2	21	32	21	41	2	04	7	02	6	50
11	21	58	–9.8	54.4	14.8	133	67	89	18.2	21	45	21	49	2	46	8	13	8	06
12	22	42	–4.6	54.8	14.9	146	65	82	19.2	21	57	21	57	3	27	9	24	9	21
13	23	26	+0.8	55.3	15.1	158	65	74	20.2	22	09	22	05	4	08	10	35	10	38
14	0	10	+6.3	55.9	15.2	170	65	65	21.2	22	23	22	14	4	51	11	49	11	57
15	0	57	+11.7	56.7	15.4	182	67	54	22.2	22	41	22	26	5	36	13	06	13	20
16	1	47	+16.7	57.5	15.7	195	70	44	23.2	23	03	22	42	6	24	14	27	14	47
17	2	41	+21.1	58.4	15.9	207	74	33	24.2	23	35	23	08	7	18	15	50	16	17
18	3	40	+24.4	59.3	16.2	219	80	23	25.2	—	—	23	50	8	16	17	10	17	42
19	4	43	+26.2	60.1	16.4	231	87	14	26.2	0	22	—	—	9	20	18	20	18	52
20	5	49	+26.3	60.8	16.6	244	94	7	27.2	1	27	0	54	10	25	19	12	19	41
21	6	56	+24.4	61.2	16.7	256	101	2	28.2	2	49	2	21	11	29	19	50	20	12
22	8	00	+20.8	61.3	16.7	268	110	0	29.2	4	21	4	00	12	30	20	17	20	32
23	9	00	+15.8	61.1	16.7	280	292	1	0.9	5	55	5	41	13	27	20	37	20	46
24	9	57	+9.9	60.6	16.5	293	295	5	1.9	7	25	7	18	14	19	20	54	20	57
25	10	50	+3.5	59.8	16.3	305	297	12	2.9	8	51	8	51	15	09	21	09	21	07
26	11	41	–2.8	59.0	16.1	317	297	21	3.9	10	15	10	19	15	57	21	24	21	17
27	12	31	–8.8	58.0	15.8	329	295	30	4.9	11	35	11	46	16	44	21	40	21	27
28	13	21	–14.2	57.1	15.6	341	293	41	5.9	12	55	13	11	17	32	21	58	21	40
29	14	11	–18.8	56.2	15.3	354	290	51	6.9	14	11	14	34	18	21	22	22	21	58
30	15	03	–22.4	55.5	15.1	6	285	61	7.9	15	24	15	52	19	11	22	52	22	23
31	15	55	–25.0	55.0	15.0	18	280	70	8.9	16	30	17	02	20	02	23	31	22	59

MERCURY

Day	*R.A.*		*Dec.*	*Diam.*	*Phase*	*Transit*		*5° high*			
								52°		*56°*	
	h	*m*	°	″	%	*h*	*m*	*h*	*m*	*h*	*m*
1	5	36	+22.8	6	80	11	02	3	30	3	12
3	5	53	+23.3	6	85	11	11	3	36	3	17
5	6	11	+23.6	5	90	11	20	3	43	3	24
7	6	29	+23.8	5	94	11	31	3	52	3	33
9	6	47	+23.9	5	97	11	42	4	03	3	44
11	7	06	+23.7	5	99	11	53	4	15	3	56
13	7	25	+23.4	5	100	12	04	19	38	19	57
15	7	44	+22.9	5	100	12	14	19	45	20	03
17	8	02	+22.2	5	99	12	25	19	51	20	07
19	8	19	+21.4	5	98	12	34	19	55	20	11
21	8	36	+20.5	5	96	12	43	19	58	20	12
23	8	53	+19.4	5	94	12	51	20	00	20	13
25	9	08	+18.3	5	91	12	59	20	01	20	12
27	9	23	+17.0	5	89	13	06	20	00	20	11
29	9	37	+15.8	5	86	13	12	19	59	20	09
31	9	51	+14.5	5	84	13	17	19	58	20	06

VENUS

Day	*R.A.*		*Dec.*	*Diam.*	*Phase*	*Transit*		*5° high*			
								52°		*56°*	
	h	*m*	°	″	%	*h*	*m*	*h*	*m*	*h*	*m*
1	3	34	+16.4	19	62	8	58	2	04	1	54
6	3	57	+17.7	18	64	9	00	2	00	1	48
11	4	19	+18.9	17	66	9	03	1	56	1	43
16	4	42	+19.9	16	68	9	07	1	54	1	40
21	5	06	+20.7	16	70	9	11	1	53	1	38
26	5	30	+21.3	15	72	9	15	1	54	1	38
31	5	55	+21.7	15	73	9	20	1	56	1	40

MARS

Day	*R.A.*		*Dec.*	*Diam.*	*Phase*	*Transit*		*5° high*			
								52°		*56°*	
	h	*m*	°	″	%	*h*	*m*	*h*	*m*	*h*	*m*
1	3	19	+17.6	5	93	8	42	1	43	1	31
6	3	34	+18.6	5	92	8	37	1	32	1	19
11	3	49	+19.4	5	92	8	32	1	22	1	08
16	4	03	+20.2	5	92	8	27	1	12	0	58
21	4	18	+20.9	5	92	8	22	1	03	0	48
26	4	32	+21.5	5	91	8	17	0	54	0	38
31	4	47	+22.1	5	91	8	11	0	46	0	29

SUNRISE AND SUNSET

	London		*Bristol*		*Birmingham*		*Manchester*		*Newcastle*		*Glasgow*		*Belfast*	
	0° 05′	*51° 30′*	*2° 35′*	*51° 28′*	*1° 55′*	*52° 28′*	*2° 15′*	*53° 28′*	*1° 37′*	*54° 59′*	*4° 14′*	*55° 52′*	*5° 56′*	*54° 35′*
d	*h m*	*h m*	*h m*	*h m*	*h m*	*h m*	*h m*	*h m*	*h m*	*h m*	*h m*	*h m*	*h m*	*h m*
1	3 47	20 21	3 58	20 30	3 49	20 33	3 45	20 41	3 32	20 48	3 36	21 05	3 52	21 03
2	3 48	20 20	3 58	20 30	3 50	20 33	3 45	20 40	3 33	20 48	3 37	21 04	3 53	21 02
3	3 49	20 20	3 59	20 30	3 51	20 33	3 46	20 40	3 34	20 47	3 38	21 04	3 54	21 02
4	3 50	20 19	4 00	20 29	3 52	20 32	3 47	20 39	3 35	20 46	3 39	21 03	3 55	21 01
5	3 51	20 19	4 01	20 29	3 53	20 32	3 48	20 39	3 36	20 46	3 40	21 02	3 56	21 00
6	3 51	20 18	4 02	20 28	3 53	20 31	3 49	20 38	3 37	20 45	3 41	21 02	3 57	21 00
7	3 52	20 18	4 02	20 28	3 54	20 30	3 50	20 37	3 38	20 44	3 42	21 01	3 58	20 59
8	3 53	20 17	4 03	20 27	3 55	20 30	3 51	20 37	3 39	20 43	3 43	21 00	3 59	20 58
9	3 54	20 16	4 04	20 26	3 56	20 29	3 52	20 36	3 40	20 43	3 45	20 59	4 00	20 57
10	3 55	20 16	4 05	20 25	3 57	20 28	3 53	20 35	3 41	20 42	3 46	20 58	4 01	20 56
11	3 56	20 15	4 06	20 25	3 59	20 27	3 54	20 34	3 43	20 41	3 47	20 57	4 02	20 55
12	3 57	20 14	4 08	20 24	4 00	20 26	3 55	20 33	3 44	20 40	3 48	20 56	4 04	20 54
13	3 59	20 13	4 09	20 23	4 01	20 25	3 57	20 32	3 45	20 38	3 50	20 55	4 05	20 53
14	4 00	20 12	4 10	20 22	4 02	20 24	3 58	20 31	3 46	20 37	3 51	20 53	4 06	20 52
15	4 01	20 11	4 11	20 21	4 03	20 23	3 59	20 30	3 48	20 36	3 53	20 52	4 08	20 51
16	4 02	20 10	4 12	20 20	4 05	20 22	4 01	20 29	3 49	20 35	3 54	20 51	4 09	20 50
17	4 03	20 09	4 13	20 19	4 06	20 21	4 02	20 28	3 51	20 34	3 56	20 49	4 10	20 48
18	4 04	20 08	4 15	20 18	4 07	20 20	4 03	20 26	3 52	20 32	3 57	20 48	4 12	20 47
19	4 06	20 07	4 16	20 17	4 08	20 19	4 05	20 25	3 54	20 31	3 59	20 46	4 13	20 46
20	4 07	20 06	4 17	20 15	4 10	20 17	4 06	20 24	3 55	20 29	4 01	20 45	4 15	20 44
21	4 08	20 04	4 19	20 14	4 11	20 16	4 08	20 22	3 57	20 28	4 02	20 43	4 16	20 43
22	4 10	20 03	4 20	20 13	4 13	20 15	4 09	20 21	3 58	20 26	4 04	20 42	4 18	20 41
23	4 11	20 02	4 21	20 12	4 14	20 13	4 11	20 19	4 00	20 25	4 06	20 40	4 20	20 40
24	4 13	20 00	4 23	20 10	4 15	20 12	4 12	20 18	4 02	20 23	4 07	20 38	4 21	20 38
25	4 14	19 59	4 24	20 09	4 17	20 10	4 14	20 16	4 03	20 22	4 09	20 37	4 23	20 37
26	4 15	19 57	4 25	20 07	4 18	20 09	4 15	20 15	4 05	20 20	4 11	20 35	4 24	20 35
27	4 17	19 56	4 27	20 06	4 20	20 07	4 17	20 13	4 07	20 18	4 13	20 33	4 26	20 33
28	4 18	19 55	4 28	20 04	4 21	20 06	4 18	20 12	4 08	20 16	4 14	20 31	4 28	20 32
29	4 20	19 53	4 30	20 03	4 23	20 04	4 20	20 10	4 10	20 15	4 16	20 29	4 29	20 30
30	4 21	19 51	4 31	20 01	4 25	20 03	4 22	20 08	4 12	20 13	4 18	20 28	4 31	20 28
31	4 23	19 50	4 33	20 00	4 26	20 01	4 23	20 07	4 14	20 11	4 20	20 26	4 33	20 26

JUPITER

Day	*R.A.*		*Dec.*		*Transit*		*5° high*			
							52°		*56°*	
	h	*m*	°	′	*h*	*m*	*h*	*m*	*h*	*m*
1	21	56.7	−13	31	3	19	23	04	23	21
11	21	54.3	−13	46	2	38	22	24	22	41
21	21	50.8	−14	07	1	55	21	43	22	01
31	21	46.5	−14	31	1	11	21	02	21	20

Diameters – equatorial 47″ polar 44″

SATURN

Day	*R.A.*		*Dec.*		*Transit*		*5° high*			
							52°		*56°*	
	h	*m*	°	′	*h*	*m*	*h*	*m*	*h*	*m*
1	11	13.8	+7	11	16	35	22	38	22	40
11	11	16.7	+6	51	15	58	22	00	22	02
21	11	20.0	+6	29	15	22	21	22	21	24
31	11	23.6	+6	05	14	46	20	44	20	46

Diameters – equatorial 17″ polar 15″

Rings – major axis 38″ minor axis 2″

URANUS

Day	*R.A.*		*Dec.*		*Transit*		*10° high*			
							52°		*56°*	
	h	*m*	°	′	*h*	*m*	*h*	*m*	*h*	*m*
1	23	48.8	−2	03	5	11	0	29	0	37
11	23	48.7	−2	04	4	32	23	45	23	54
21	23	48.3	−2	07	3	52	23	06	23	15
31	23	47.6	−2	12	3	12	22	26	22	35

Diameter 4″

NEPTUNE

Day	*R.A.*		*Dec.*		*Transit*		*10° high*			
							52°		*56°*	
	h	*m*	°	′	*h*	*m*	*h*	*m*	*h*	*m*
1	21	54.3	−13	10	3	17	23	38	0	05
11	21	53.6	−13	14	2	37	22	59	23	21
21	21	52.8	−13	18	1	57	22	19	22	42
31	21	51.8	−13	24	1	17	21	39	22	02

Diameter 2″

AUGUST 2009

EIGHTH MONTH, 31 DAYS. *Augustus*, formerly *Sextilis*, sixth month of Roman pre-Julian calendar

1	*Saturday*	Christopher Columbus landed in South America in present-day Venezuela 1498	day 213
2	*Sunday*	Paul von Hindenburg died and Adolf Hitler assumed the title *Der Fuhrer* 1934	214
3	*Monday*	John Speke discovered and named Lake Victoria 1858	week 32 day 215
4	*Tuesday*	Germany invaded Belgium and Britain declared war on Germany 1914	216
5	*Wednesday*	22 members of the IRA were sentenced to a total of over 4,000 years 1983	217
6	*Thursday*	The first atomic bomb was dropped by the USA on Hiroshima 1945	218
7	*Friday*	Côte d'Ivoire became independent 1960	219
8	*Saturday*	President Nixon announced his resignation 1974	220
9	*Sunday*	Singapore became an independent sovereign state 1965	221
10	*Monday*	The foundation stone was laid for the Royal Observatory at Greenwich 1675	week 33 day 222
11	*Tuesday*	The first Royal Ascot horse race took place 1711	223
12	*Wednesday*	The Royal Ulster Constabulary used tear gas for the first time during riots in Londonderry 1969	224
13	*Thursday*	Barbed wire fences were put up overnight dividing East and West Berlin 1961	225
14	*Friday*	Japan surrendered unconditionally to the Allied forces 1945	226
15	*Saturday*	The Panama Canal was officially opened 1914	227
16	*Sunday*	Gold was found in the Yukon Territory sparking the last gold rush in the American West 1896	228
17	*Monday*	Charles Blondin crossed the Niagara Falls on a tightrope 1859	week 34 day 229
18	*Tuesday*	The National Fire Service was formed 1941	230
19	*Wednesday*	Mary Queen of Scots returned to Scotland aged 18 after spending 13 years in France 1561	231
20	*Thursday*	The *Marchioness* collided with a dredger on the river Thames, killing 51 1989	232
21	*Friday*	Hawaii was admitted as the 50th state of the USA 1959	233
22	*Saturday*	Twelve nations signed the first Geneva Convention, forming the Red Cross 1864	234
23	*Sunday*	Scottish leader William Wallace was hung, drawn and quartered for treason by the English 1305	235
24	*Monday*	Mount Vesuvius erupted destroying Pompeii and Herculaneum in Italy AD 79	week 35 day 236
25	*Tuesday*	The *Voyager 2* spacecraft reached Neptune after travelling for 12 years 1989	237
26	*Wednesday*	The battle of Crécy of the Hundred Years' War was won by Edward III's army 1346	238
27	*Thursday*	Julius Caesar and 10,000 Romans landed in Britain 55 BC	239
28	*Friday*	Martin Luther King delivered his famous speech against racial discrimination 1963	240
29	*Saturday*	Hurricane Katrina devastated New Orleans, 80 per cent of the city was flooded 2005	241
30	*Sunday*	Melbourne, Australia, was founded 1835	242
31	*Monday*	Princess Diana died in a car crash in Paris 1997	week 36 day 243

ASTRONOMICAL PHENOMENA

d	*h*	
6	20	Jupiter in conjunction with Moon. Jupiter 3°S.
14	18	Jupiter at opposition
16	03	Mars in conjunction with Moon. Mars 3°S.
17	15	Saturn in conjunction with Mercury. Saturn 3°N.
17	21	Neptune at opposition
17	21	Venus in conjunction with Moon. Venus 2°S.
22	01	Saturn in conjunction with Moon. Saturn 6°N.
22	10	Mercury in conjunction with Moon. Mercury 3°N.
23	00	Sun's longitude 150° ♍
24	16	Mercury at greatest elongation E.27°

MINIMA OF ALGOL

d	*h*	*d*	*h*	*d*	*h*
2	16.2	14	16.2	25	16.2
5	13.0	17	13.0	28	13.0
8	09.9	20	09.9	31	09.9
11	06.7	22	06.7		

CONSTELLATIONS

The following constellations are near their meridian at

	d	*h*		*d*	*h*
July	1	24	August	16	21
July	16	23	September	1	20
August	1	22	September	15	19

Draco, Hercules, Lyra, Cygnus, Sagitta, Ophiuchus, Serpens, Aquila and Sagittarius

THE MOON

Phases, Apsides and Node	*d*	*h*	*m*
○ Full Moon	6	00	55
☾ Last Quarter	13	18	55
● New Moon	20	10	02
☽ First Quarter	27	11	42
Apogee (406,043 km)	4	00	29
Perigee (359,628 km)	19	04	51
Apogee (405,299 km)	31	10	55

Mean longitude of ascending node on August 1, 300°

THE SUN

s.d. 15′.8

Day	Right Ascension h	m	s	Dec. + °	′	Equation of time m	s	Rise 52° h	m	Rise 56° h	m	Transit h	m	Set 52° h	m	Set 56° h	m	Sidereal time h	m	s	Transit of first point of Aries h	m	s
1	8	45	19	18	02	−6	22	4	22	4	04	12	06	19	50	20	07	20	38	57	3	20	30
2	8	49	11	17	47	−6	18	4	23	4	06	12	06	19	48	20	05	20	42	53	3	16	34
3	8	53	03	17	31	−6	13	4	25	4	08	12	06	19	46	20	03	20	46	50	3	12	38
4	8	56	55	17	16	−6	08	4	26	4	10	12	06	19	45	20	01	20	50	47	3	08	42
5	9	00	46	16	59	−6	02	4	28	4	12	12	06	19	43	19	59	20	54	43	3	04	46
6	9	04	36	16	43	−5	56	4	30	4	13	12	06	19	41	19	57	20	58	40	3	00	51
7	9	08	25	16	26	−5	49	4	31	4	15	12	06	19	39	19	55	21	02	36	2	56	55
8	9	12	14	16	10	−5	41	4	33	4	17	12	06	19	37	19	53	21	06	33	2	52	59
9	9	16	03	15	52	−5	33	4	34	4	19	12	05	19	35	19	50	21	10	29	2	49	03
10	9	19	51	15	35	−5	25	4	36	4	21	12	05	19	34	19	48	21	14	26	2	45	07
11	9	23	38	15	17	−5	15	4	38	4	23	12	05	19	32	19	46	21	18	22	2	41	11
12	9	27	25	15	00	−5	05	4	39	4	25	12	05	19	30	19	44	21	22	19	2	37	15
13	9	31	11	14	41	−4	55	4	41	4	27	12	05	19	28	19	41	21	26	16	2	33	19
14	9	34	56	14	23	−4	44	4	42	4	29	12	05	19	26	19	39	21	30	12	2	29	23
15	9	38	42	14	04	−4	33	4	44	4	31	12	04	19	24	19	37	21	34	09	2	25	27
16	9	42	26	13	46	−4	21	4	46	4	33	12	04	19	22	19	34	21	38	05	2	21	31
17	9	46	10	13	27	−4	08	4	47	4	35	12	04	19	20	19	32	21	42	02	2	17	36
18	9	49	54	13	07	−3	56	4	49	4	37	12	04	19	18	19	29	21	45	58	2	13	40
19	9	53	37	12	48	−3	42	4	51	4	39	12	04	19	15	19	27	21	49	55	2	09	44
20	9	57	20	12	28	−3	28	4	52	4	41	12	03	19	13	19	25	21	53	51	2	05	48
21	10	01	02	12	08	−3	14	4	54	4	43	12	03	19	11	19	22	21	57	48	2	01	52
22	10	04	44	11	48	−2	59	4	56	4	45	12	03	19	09	19	20	22	01	45	1	57	56
23	10	08	25	11	28	−2	44	4	57	4	47	12	03	19	07	19	17	22	05	41	1	54	00
24	10	12	06	11	08	−2	28	4	59	4	49	12	02	19	05	19	15	22	09	38	1	50	04
25	10	15	46	10	47	−2	12	5	00	4	51	12	02	19	03	19	12	22	13	34	1	46	08
26	10	19	26	10	26	−1	55	5	02	4	53	12	02	19	00	19	10	22	17	31	1	42	12
27	10	23	05	10	05	−1	38	5	04	4	55	12	01	18	58	19	07	22	21	27	1	38	16
28	10	26	44	9	44	−1	21	5	05	4	57	12	01	18	56	19	05	22	25	24	1	34	21
29	10	30	23	9	23	−1	03	5	07	4	58	12	01	18	54	19	02	22	29	20	1	30	25
30	10	34	02	9	02	−0	45	5	09	5	00	12	01	18	52	18	59	22	33	17	1	26	29
31	10	37	40	8	40	−0	26	5	10	5	02	12	00	18	49	18	57	22	37	14	1	22	33

DURATION OF TWILIGHT (in minutes)

Latitude	52°	56°	52°	56°	52°	56°	52°	56°
	1 August		*11 August*		*21 August*		*31 August*	
Civil	41	49	39	45	37	42	35	40
Nautical	97	121	90	107	84	97	79	90
Astronomical	179	TAN	154	210	139	168	128	148

THE NIGHT SKY

Mercury, despite reaching greatest eastern elongation (27 degrees) on the 24th, remains unsuitably placed for observation throughout the month.

Venus, magnitude −4.0, is a magnificent morning object, visible in the eastern sky for several hours before dawn. The waning crescent Moon is near the planet on the 17th–18th. Around the 22nd, Venus, continuing its easterly motion, passes south of the twins Castor and Pollux, in the constellation of Gemini.

Mars continues to be visible as a morning object and by the end of the month it is rising above the east-north-eastern horizon around five hours before sunrise. Its magnitude is +1.0. At the beginning of the month Mars is in Taurus, north-east of Aldebaran, but its eastward motion carries it into Gemini before the end of the month. The waning crescent Moon, four days before New, passes two degrees north of Mars on the 16th.

Jupiter, magnitude −2.9, reaches opposition on the 14th and therefore remains visible throughout the hours of darkness. Jupiter is in the constellation of Capricornus. The Full Moon passes north of the planet on the 6th–7th.

Saturn is too close to the Sun for observation during August. In any case, as the Sun passes through the ring plane from south to north on the 10th, while the Earth remains south of this plane until next month, the rings would not be visible from the Earth anyway.

Neptune is at opposition on the 17th, in the constellation of Capricornus. It is not visible to the naked eye since its magnitude is +7.9.

Meteors. The maximum of the famous Perseid meteor shower occurs on the 12th and will be best seen from the late evening of that day, though there will be interference from the waning gibbous Moon.

THE MOON

Day	R.A.		Dec.	Hor. Par.	Semi-diam.	Sun's Co-Long.	PA of Br. Limb	Ph.	Age	Rise				Transit		Set			
										52°		56°				52°		56°	
	h	m	°	′	′	°	°	%	d	h	m	h	m	h	m	h	m	h	m
1	16	49	−26.3	54.5	14.9	30	274	79	9.9	17	25	17	58	20	53	—		23	49
2	17	42	−26.4	54.2	14.8	43	269	86	10.9	18	08	18	39	21	43	0	22	—	
3	18	35	−25.2	54.1	14.7	55	263	92	11.9	18	41	19	07	22	32	1	22	0	52
4	19	26	−23.0	54.0	14.7	67	259	96	12.9	19	06	19	26	23	18	2	29	2	04
5	20	14	−19.7	54.0	14.7	79	258	99	13.9	19	25	19	40	—		3	40	3	21
6	21	02	−15.7	54.2	14.8	91	324	100	14.9	19	40	19	50	0	03	4	52	4	38
7	21	47	−11.0	54.4	14.8	104	59	99	15.9	19	53	19	59	0	46	6	03	5	54
8	22	31	−5.9	54.7	14.9	116	60	96	16.9	20	06	20	07	1	27	7	14	7	10
9	23	15	−0.5	55.1	15.0	128	61	92	17.9	20	18	20	15	2	08	8	25	8	26
10	0	00	+5.0	55.5	15.1	140	62	86	18.9	20	31	20	23	2	50	9	38	9	44
11	0	45	+10.4	56.1	15.3	152	64	78	19.9	20	47	20	34	3	33	10	53	11	05
12	1	34	+15.4	56.7	15.5	164	66	69	20.9	21	07	20	48	4	20	12	11	12	29
13	2	26	+19.9	57.4	15.6	177	70	59	21.9	21	34	21	10	5	10	13	32	13	56
14	3	21	+23.4	58.2	15.8	189	75	48	22.9	22	13	21	43	6	05	14	51	15	21
15	4	21	+25.7	58.9	16.1	201	82	37	23.9	23	08	22	35	7	04	16	03	16	36
16	5	25	+26.4	59.7	16.3	213	88	26	24.9	—		23	50	8	07	17	01	17	33
17	6	29	+25.4	60.3	16.4	226	95	16	25.9	0	20	—		9	10	17	45	18	10
18	7	33	+22.5	60.8	16.6	238	100	9	26.9	1	46	1	22	10	11	18	16	18	35
19	8	34	+18.2	61.0	16.6	250	103	3	27.9	3	18	3	01	11	10	18	39	18	51
20	9	32	+12.6	60.9	16.6	262	91	0	28.9	4	50	4	40	12	04	18	58	19	04
21	10	27	+6.4	60.5	16.5	275	312	1	0.6	6	20	6	16	12	56	19	14	19	15
22	11	20	−0.1	59.9	16.3	287	303	4	1.6	7	46	7	48	13	46	19	29	19	24
23	12	12	−6.4	59.0	16.1	299	300	9	2.6	9	10	9	18	14	35	19	45	19	35
24	13	03	−12.2	58.1	15.8	311	297	17	3.6	10	32	10	46	15	23	20	03	19	47
25	13	54	−17.3	57.2	15.6	324	293	26	4.6	11	53	12	13	16	13	20	25	20	03
26	14	47	−21.3	56.4	15.4	336	289	35	5.6	13	09	13	35	17	04	20	52	20	26
27	15	40	−24.2	55.6	15.1	348	284	45	6.6	14	19	14	50	17	56	21	29	20	58
28	16	34	−25.9	55.0	15.0	0	278	55	7.6	15	18	15	52	18	47	22	16	21	43
29	17	27	−26.4	54.5	14.9	12	272	65	8.6	16	06	16	38	19	38	23	13	22	42
30	18	20	−25.6	54.2	14.8	25	267	73	9.6	16	43	17	10	20	28	—		23	51
31	19	12	−23.6	54.1	14.7	37	262	81	10.6	17	10	17	32	21	15	0	18	—	

MERCURY

Day	R.A.	Dec.	Diam.	Phase	Transit	5° high	
						52°	56°
	h m	°	″	%	h m	h m	h m
1	9 57	+13.8	5	83	13 20	19 56	20 04
3	10 10	+12.4	6	80	13 25	19 54	20 00
5	10 22	+11.1	6	78	13 29	19 50	19 56
7	10 34	+9.7	6	76	13 32	19 47	19 51
9	10 45	+8.3	6	73	13 35	19 42	19 45
11	10 55	+6.9	6	71	13 37	19 38	19 40
13	11 05	+5.6	6	68	13 39	19 33	19 34
15	11 14	+4.3	6	66	13 41	19 27	19 27
17	11 23	+3.0	7	63	13 42	19 22	19 20
19	11 32	+1.7	7	61	13 42	19 16	19 13
21	11 40	+0.5	7	58	13 42	19 09	19 06
23	11 47	−0.6	7	55	13 41	19 03	18 59
25	11 54	−1.7	7	52	13 40	18 56	18 51
27	12 00	−2.7	8	49	13 38	18 49	18 43
29	12 05	−3.6	8	45	13 35	18 41	18 34
31	12 09	−4.5	8	42	13 31	18 33	18 26

VENUS

Day	R.A.	Dec.	Diam.	Phase	Transit	5° high	
						52°	56°
	h m	°	″	%	h m	h m	h m
1	6 00	+21.8	15	74	9 21	1 57	1 40
6	6 25	+21.9	14	75	9 26	2 01	1 44
11	6 50	+21.8	14	77	9 32	2 07	1 51
16	7 15	+21.5	14	79	9 37	2 15	1 59
21	7 40	+20.9	13	80	9 43	2 24	2 08
26	8 05	+20.0	13	81	9 48	2 34	2 20
31	8 30	+19.0	13	83	9 53	2 46	2 33

MARS

Day	R.A.	Dec.	Diam.	Phase	Transit	5° high	
						52°	56°
	h m	°	″	%	h m	h m	h m
1	4 50	+22.2	5	91	8 10	0 44	0 27
6	5 04	+22.6	5	91	8 05	0 36	0 19
11	5 18	+22.9	5	90	8 00	0 29	0 11
16	5 33	+23.2	6	90	7 54	0 22	0 03
21	5 47	+23.4	6	90	7 49	0 15	23 55
26	6 01	+23.5	6	90	7 43	0 08	23 48
31	6 15	+23.6	6	90	7 37	0 02	23 42

SUNRISE AND SUNSET

	London				*Bristol*				*Birmingham*				*Manchester*				*Newcastle*				*Glasgow*				*Belfast*			
	0° 05′		*51° 30′*		*2° 35′*		*51° 28′*		*1° 55′*		*52° 28′*		*2° 15′*		*53° 28′*		*1° 37′*		*54° 59′*		*4° 14′*		*55° 52′*		*5° 56′*		*54° 35′*	
d	*h*	*m*	*h*	*m*	*h*	*m*	*h*	*m*	*h*	*m*	*h*	*m*	*h*	*m*	*h*	*m*	*h*	*m*	*h*	*m*	*h*	*m*	*h*	*m*	*h*	*m*	*h*	*m*
1	4	24	19	48	4	34	19	58	4	28	19	59	4	25	20	05	4	15	20	09	4	22	20	24	4	35	20	24
2	4	26	19	47	4	36	19	56	4	29	19	58	4	26	20	03	4	17	20	07	4	24	20	22	4	36	20	22
3	4	27	19	45	4	37	19	55	4	31	19	56	4	28	20	01	4	19	20	05	4	25	20	20	4	38	20	21
4	4	29	19	43	4	39	19	53	4	32	19	54	4	30	19	59	4	21	20	03	4	27	20	17	4	40	20	19
5	4	30	19	41	4	40	19	51	4	34	19	52	4	31	19	57	4	23	20	01	4	29	20	15	4	42	20	17
6	4	32	19	40	4	42	19	49	4	36	19	50	4	33	19	55	4	24	19	59	4	31	20	13	4	43	20	15
7	4	33	19	38	4	43	19	48	4	37	19	49	4	35	19	53	4	26	19	57	4	33	20	11	4	45	20	13
8	4	35	19	36	4	45	19	46	4	39	19	47	4	37	19	52	4	28	19	55	4	35	20	09	4	47	20	10
9	4	36	19	34	4	47	19	44	4	40	19	45	4	38	19	50	4	30	19	53	4	37	20	07	4	49	20	08
10	4	38	19	32	4	48	19	42	4	42	19	43	4	40	19	48	4	32	19	51	4	39	20	04	4	51	20	06
11	4	40	19	30	4	50	19	40	4	44	19	41	4	42	19	45	4	34	19	48	4	41	20	02	4	52	20	04
12	4	41	19	28	4	51	19	38	4	45	19	39	4	43	19	43	4	35	19	46	4	43	20	00	4	54	20	02
13	4	43	19	27	4	53	19	36	4	47	19	37	4	45	19	41	4	37	19	44	4	45	19	58	4	56	20	00
14	4	44	19	25	4	54	19	34	4	49	19	35	4	47	19	39	4	39	19	42	4	46	19	55	4	58	19	58
15	4	46	19	23	4	56	19	32	4	50	19	33	4	49	19	37	4	41	19	39	4	48	19	53	5	00	19	55
16	4	47	19	21	4	58	19	31	4	52	19	31	4	50	19	35	4	43	19	37	4	50	19	51	5	02	19	53
17	4	49	19	19	4	59	19	28	4	54	19	29	4	52	19	33	4	45	19	35	4	52	19	48	5	03	19	51
18	4	51	19	17	5	01	19	26	4	55	19	26	4	54	19	31	4	47	19	33	4	54	19	46	5	05	19	49
19	4	52	19	14	5	02	19	24	4	57	19	24	4	56	19	28	4	49	19	30	4	56	19	43	5	07	19	46
20	4	54	19	12	5	04	19	22	4	59	19	22	4	57	19	26	4	50	19	28	4	58	19	41	5	09	19	44
21	4	55	19	10	5	06	19	20	5	00	19	20	4	59	19	24	4	52	19	26	5	00	19	39	5	11	19	42
22	4	57	19	08	5	07	19	18	5	02	19	18	5	01	19	22	4	54	19	23	5	02	19	36	5	13	19	39
23	4	59	19	06	5	09	19	16	5	04	19	16	5	03	19	19	4	56	19	21	5	04	19	34	5	14	19	37
24	5	00	19	04	5	10	19	14	5	05	19	13	5	04	19	17	4	58	19	18	5	06	19	31	5	16	19	35
25	5	02	19	02	5	12	19	12	5	07	19	11	5	06	19	15	5	00	19	16	5	08	19	29	5	18	19	32
26	5	03	19	00	5	13	19	10	5	09	19	09	5	08	19	13	5	02	19	14	5	10	19	26	5	20	19	30
27	5	05	18	58	5	15	19	07	5	10	19	07	5	10	19	10	5	04	19	11	5	12	19	24	5	22	19	27
28	5	07	18	55	5	17	19	05	5	12	19	05	5	11	19	08	5	05	19	09	5	14	19	21	5	24	19	25
29	5	08	18	53	5	18	19	03	5	14	19	02	5	13	19	06	5	07	19	06	5	16	19	19	5	25	19	23
30	5	10	18	51	5	20	19	01	5	15	19	00	5	15	19	03	5	09	19	04	5	18	19	16	5	27	19	20
31	5	11	18	49	5	21	18	59	5	17	18	58	5	17	19	01	5	11	19	01	5	20	19	13	5	29	19	18

JUPITER

Day	*R.A.*		*Dec.*		*Transit*		*5° high*			
							52°		*56°*	
	h	*m*	°	′	*h*	*m*	*h*	*m*	*h*	*m*
1	21	46.0	−14	34	1	07	5	12	4	54
11	21	41.1	−15	01	0	23	4	25	4	06
21	21	36.0	−15	27	23	34	3	37	3	18
31	21	31.1	−15	51	22	50	2	51	2	31

Diameters – equatorial 49″ polar 46″

SATURN

Day	*R.A.*		*Dec.*		*Transit*		*5° high*			
							52°		*56°*	
	h	*m*	°	′	*h*	*m*	*h*	*m*	*h*	*m*
1	11	24.0	+6	03	14	43	20	40	20	42
11	11	28.0	+5	36	14	08	20	03	20	04
21	11	32.2	+5	09	13	32	19	25	19	26
31	11	36.6	+4	40	12	58	18	48	18	48

Diameters – equatorial 16″ polar 14″
Rings – major axis 36″ minor axis 1″

URANUS

Day	*R.A.*		*Dec.*		*Transit*		*10° high*			
							52°		*56°*	
	h	*m*	°	′	*h*	*m*	*h*	*m*	*h*	*m*
1	23	47.5	−2	13	3	08	22	22	22	31
11	23	46.6	−2	19	2	28	21	43	21	52
21	23	45.4	−2	27	1	47	21	03	21	12
31	23	44.1	−2	35	1	07	20	23	20	32

Diameter 4″

NEPTUNE

Day	*R.A.*		*Dec.*		*Transit*		*10° high*			
							52°		*56°*	
	h	*m*	°	′	*h*	*m*	*h*	*m*	*h*	*m*
1	21	51.7	−13	24	1	13	4	46	4	23
11	21	50.7	−13	30	0	32	4	05	3	42
21	21	49.7	−13	35	23	48	3	24	3	01
31	21	48.6	−13	41	23	08	2	43	2	20

Diameter 2″

SEPTEMBER 2009

NINTH MONTH, 30 DAYS. *Septem* (seven), seventh month of Roman pre-Julian calendar

1	*Tuesday*	Germany invaded Poland 1939	day 244
2	*Wednesday*	The first Automatic Teller Machine made its debut in America 1969	245
3	*Thursday*	Cromwell defeated the Scots at the second battle of Dunbar 1650	246
4	*Friday*	The Forth Road Bridge was opened 1964	247
5	*Saturday*	Nine kidnapped Israeli athletes died in a gun battle at the Munich Olympics 1972	248
6	*Sunday*	The name St Petersburg was restored to Russia's second largest city Leningrad 1991	249
7	*Monday*	Desmond Tutu became the archbishop of Cape Town 1986	week 37 day 250
8	*Tuesday*	Germany was admitted to the League of Nations 1926	251
9	*Wednesday*	William the Conqueror died after falling from his horse 1087	252
10	*Thursday*	Hamida Djandoubi became the last person to be executed by guillotine in France 1977	253
11	*Friday*	Three aeroplanes hijacked by terrorists hit the USA's World Trade Centre and the Pentagon killing 3,000 2001	254
12	*Saturday*	Elizabeth Barrett and Robert Browning eloped 1846	255
13	*Sunday*	Quebec was captured by the British 1759	256
14	*Monday*	The first American saint was canonised by the Pope 1975	week 38 day 257
15	*Tuesday*	The *Sun* newspaper was published for the first time 1964	258
16	*Wednesday*	The Fire of Moscow broke out destroying three-quarters of the city 1812	259
17	*Thursday*	The constitution of the USA was signed 1787	260
18	*Friday*	Dag Hammarskjöld, the UN secretary-general, was killed in an air crash 1961	261
19	*Saturday*	Nikita Khrushchev was barred from visiting Disneyland 1959	262
20	*Sunday*	The first Cannes film festival took place 1946	263
21	*Monday*	Great Britain abandoned the gold standard 1931	week 39 day 264
22	*Tuesday*	The UK's first independent television station was launched 1955	265
23	*Wednesday*	Juan Peron was re-elected as president of Argentina after 18 years 1973	266
24	*Thursday*	Dougal Haston and Doug Scott became the first Britons to climb Everest 1975	267
25	*Friday*	The transatlantic telephone service was established 1956	268
26	*Saturday*	The *Golden Hind* returned to Plymouth after circumnavigating the Earth in over 33 months 1580	269
27	*Sunday*	The Stockton–Darlington railway opened 1825	270
28	*Monday*	William the Conqueror invaded England 1066	week 40 day 271
29	*Tuesday*	Pope John Paul I died after a 33-day reign 1978	272
30	*Wednesday*	The Munich Pact was signed annexing Czechoslovakia's Sudetenland to Germany 1938	273

ASTRONOMICAL PHENOMENA

d	*h*	
2	19	Jupiter in conjunction with Moon. Jupiter 3°S.
7	05	Mercury at stationary point
11	17	Pluto at stationary point
13	16	Mars in conjunction with Moon. Mars 1°S.
16	16	Venus in conjunction with Moon. Venus 3°N.
17	10	Uranus at opposition
17	18	Saturn in conjunction
18	17	Saturn in conjunction with Moon. Saturn 6°N.
19	00	Mercury in conjunction with Moon. Mercury 1°N.
20	10	Mercury in inferior conjunction
22	09	Saturn in conjunction with Mercury. Saturn 4°N.
22	21	Sun's longitude 180° ♎
29	13	Mercury at stationary point
29	22	Jupiter in conjunction with Moon. Jupiter 3°S.

MINIMA OF ALGOL

d	*h*	*d*	*h*	*d*	*h*
3	16.2	14	16.2	26	16.2
6	13.0	17	13.0	29	13.0
9	09.9	20	09.9		
12	06.7	23	06.7		

CONSTELLATIONS

The following constellations are near their meridian at

	d	*h*		*d*	*h*
August	1	24	September	15	21
August	16	23	October	1	20
September	1	22	October	16	19

Draco, Cepheus, Lyra, Cygnus, Vulpecula, Sagitta, Delphinus, Equuleus, Aquila, Aquarius and Capricornus

THE MOON

Phases, Apsides and Node	*d*	*h*	*m*
○ Full Moon	4	16	03
☾ Last Quarter	12	02	16
● New Moon	18	18	44
☽ First Quarter	26	04	50
Perigee (364,034 km)	16	07	48
Apogee (404,469 km)	28	03	29

Mean longitude of ascending node on September 1, 298°

THE SUN

s.d. 15′.9

Day	Right Ascension			Dec.		Equation of time		Rise 52°		Rise 56°		Transit		Set 52°		Set 56°		Sidereal time			Transit of first point of Aries		
	h	m	s	°	′	m	s	h	m	h	m	h	m	h	m	h	m	h	m	s	h	m	s
1	10	41	17	+8	18	−0	07	5	12	5	04	12	00	18	47	18	54	22	41	10	1	18	37
2	10	44	55	+7	57	+0	12	5	13	5	06	12	00	18	45	18	52	22	45	07	1	14	41
3	10	48	32	+7	35	+0	31	5	15	5	08	11	59	18	42	18	49	22	49	03	1	10	45
4	10	52	09	+7	13	+0	51	5	17	5	10	11	59	18	40	18	46	22	53	00	1	06	49
5	10	55	45	+6	50	+1	11	5	18	5	12	11	59	18	38	18	44	22	56	56	1	02	53
6	10	59	21	+6	28	+1	31	5	20	5	14	11	58	18	36	18	41	23	00	53	0	58	57
7	11	02	58	+6	06	+1	52	5	22	5	16	11	58	18	33	18	39	23	04	49	0	55	02
8	11	06	34	+5	43	+2	12	5	23	5	18	11	58	18	31	18	36	23	08	46	0	51	06
9	11	10	09	+5	21	+2	33	5	25	5	20	11	57	18	29	18	33	23	12	43	0	47	10
10	11	13	45	+4	58	+2	54	5	26	5	22	11	57	18	26	18	31	23	16	39	0	43	14
11	11	17	20	+4	35	+3	15	5	28	5	24	11	57	18	24	18	28	23	20	36	0	39	18
12	11	20	56	+4	12	+3	36	5	30	5	26	11	56	18	22	18	25	23	24	32	0	35	22
13	11	24	31	+3	49	+3	58	5	31	5	28	11	56	18	19	18	23	23	28	29	0	31	26
14	11	28	07	+3	26	+4	19	5	33	5	30	11	56	18	17	18	20	23	32	25	0	27	30
15	11	31	42	+3	03	+4	40	5	35	5	32	11	55	18	15	18	17	23	36	22	0	23	34
16	11	35	17	+2	40	+5	01	5	36	5	34	11	55	18	12	18	15	23	40	18	0	19	38
17	11	38	52	+2	17	+5	23	5	38	5	36	11	54	18	10	18	12	23	44	15	0	15	42
18	11	42	27	+1	54	+5	44	5	39	5	37	11	54	18	08	18	09	23	48	12	0	11	47
19	11	46	03	+1	31	+6	05	5	41	5	39	11	54	18	05	18	07	23	52	08	0	07	51
20	11	49	38	+1	07	+6	27	5	43	5	41	11	53	18	03	18	04	23	56	05	0	03	55
																					23	59	59
21	11	53	13	+0	44	+6	48	5	44	5	43	11	53	18	01	18	02	0	00	01	23	56	03
22	11	56	49	+0	21	+7	09	5	46	5	45	11	53	17	58	17	59	0	03	58	23	52	07
23	12	00	24	−0	03	+7	30	5	48	5	47	11	52	17	56	17	56	0	07	54	23	48	11
24	12	04	00	−0	26	+7	51	5	49	5	49	11	52	17	54	17	54	0	11	51	23	44	15
25	12	07	36	−0	49	+8	12	5	51	5	51	11	52	17	51	17	51	0	15	47	23	40	19
26	12	11	11	−1	13	+8	33	5	53	5	53	11	51	17	49	17	48	0	19	44	23	36	23
27	12	14	47	−1	36	+8	53	5	54	5	55	11	51	17	47	17	46	0	23	41	23	32	27
28	12	18	24	−1	59	+9	13	5	56	5	57	11	51	17	44	17	43	0	27	37	23	28	32
29	12	22	00	−2	23	+9	33	5	58	5	59	11	50	17	42	17	40	0	31	34	23	24	36
30	12	25	37	−2	46	+9	53	5	59	6	01	11	50	17	40	17	38	0	35	30	23	20	40

DURATION OF TWILIGHT (in minutes)

Latitude	*52°*	*56°*	*52°*	*56°*	*52°*	*56°*	*52°*	*56*
	1 September		*11 September*		*21 September*		*31 September*	
Civil	35	39	34	38	34	37	34	37
Nautical	79	89	76	85	74	82	73	80
Astronomical	127	147	120	136	116	129	113	125

THE NIGHT SKY

Mercury passes rapidly through inferior conjunction on the 20th and remains unobservable until the last two mornings of the month. Then it may be possible to see it very low in the eastern sky around the time of beginning of morning civil twilight. Mercury's magnitude is +1.0.

Venus, magnitude −3.9, continues to be visible as a brilliant object in the eastern sky in the mornings. By the end of September it is still visible for about two hours before sunrise. On the mornings of the 16th and 17th the old crescent Moon will be seen in the vicinity of the planet. Venus passes only 0.5 degrees north of Regulus, in Leo, on the 20th, 50 years since it occulted that star.

Mars, magnitude +0.9, is still visible as a morning object, but is now visible above the east-north-eastern horizon shortly after midnight. Mars is moving eastwards in the constellation of Gemini, passing south of Pollux early in October. The waning Moon, just after Last Quarter, will be seen near Mars on the 13th and 14th.

Jupiter continues to be visible as a brilliant object in the night sky in the evenings, magnitude −2.8, though by the end of the month the planet will not be visible for long after midnight. The waxing gibbous Moon passes two degrees north of Jupiter on the 2nd and again on the 29th.

Saturn continues to be too close to the Sun for observation.

Uranus is at opposition on the 17th, in the constellation of Pisces. The planet is barely visible to the naked eye as its magnitude is +5.7, but it is readily located with only small optical aid.

Zodiacal Light. The morning cone may be observed stretching up from the eastern horizon, along the ecliptic, before the beginning of morning twilight, from the 17th to the end of the month. This faint phenomenon is only visible under good conditions.

THE MOON

Day	R.A.		Dec.	Hor. Par.	Semi-diam.	Sun's Co-Long.	PA. of Br. Limb	Ph.	Age	Rise 52°		Rise 56°		Transit		Set 52°		Set 56°	
	h	m	°	′	′	°	°	%	d	h	m	h	m	h	m	h	m	h	m
1	20	01	−20.7	54.1	14.7	49	258	88	11.6	17	31	17	48	22	00	1	28	1	07
2	20	49	−16.8	54.2	14.8	61	256	93	12.6	17	47	18	00	22	43	2	39	2	24
3	21	35	−12.3	54.5	14.8	73	257	97	13.6	18	02	18	09	23	26	3	51	3	40
4	22	20	−7.3	54.8	14.9	86	270	100	14.6	18	14	18	17	–	–	5	02	4	57
5	23	04	−1.9	55.2	15.0	98	22	100	15.6	18	27	18	25	0	07	6	14	6	14
6	23	49	+3.6	55.6	15.1	110	51	98	16.6	18	40	18	34	0	49	7	27	7	32
7	0	35	+9.0	56.1	15.3	122	57	94	17.6	18	55	18	44	1	33	8	42	8	52
8	1	23	+14.2	56.5	15.4	134	62	89	18.6	19	14	18	57	2	18	10	00	10	15
9	2	14	+18.8	57.1	15.5	146	66	81	19.6	19	39	19	16	3	07	11	19	11	41
10	3	08	+22.6	57.6	15.7	159	72	72	20.6	20	13	19	45	4	00	12	38	13	06
11	4	06	+25.1	58.2	15.9	171	78	62	21.6	21	01	20	29	4	57	13	51	14	23
12	5	07	+26.3	58.7	16.0	183	85	51	22.6	22	05	21	33	5	57	14	53	15	25
13	6	10	+25.7	59.3	16.1	195	91	40	23.6	23	23	22	56	6	58	15	41	16	08
14	7	12	+23.5	59.7	16.3	207	98	29	24.6	—	—	—	—	7	58	16	15	16	37
15	8	12	+19.8	60.1	16.4	220	102	19	25.6	0	50	0	30	8	56	16	41	16	56
16	9	10	+14.8	60.2	16.4	232	105	11	26.6	2	19	2	06	9	51	17	01	17	10
17	10	05	+9.0	60.2	16.4	244	105	4	27.6	3	48	3	41	10	43	17	18	17	21
18	10	58	+2.7	59.9	16.3	256	94	1	28.6	5	15	5	14	11	33	17	33	17	32
19	11	50	−3.7	59.4	16.2	269	350	0	0.2	6	40	6	45	12	22	17	49	17	42
20	12	41	−9.8	58.8	16.0	281	310	2	1.2	8	04	8	15	13	12	18	06	17	54
21	13	34	−15.2	58.0	15.8	293	301	7	2.2	9	27	9	43	14	02	18	27	18	09
22	14	27	−19.7	57.2	15.6	305	294	13	3.2	10	47	11	10	14	54	18	53	18	29
23	15	21	−23.1	56.4	15.4	317	288	21	4.2	12	01	12	30	15	46	19	26	18	57
24	16	15	−25.3	55.6	15.2	330	282	29	5.2	13	06	13	38	16	39	20	10	19	37
25	17	10	−26.2	55.0	15.0	342	276	39	6.2	13	59	14	32	17	31	21	04	20	32
26	18	04	−25.8	54.6	14.9	354	270	48	7.2	14	40	15	09	18	21	22	06	21	38
27	18	56	−24.2	54.3	14.8	6	264	58	8.2	15	11	15	35	19	09	23	14	22	51
28	19	46	−21.5	54.2	14.8	18	260	67	9.2	15	34	15	53	19	55	—	—	—	—
29	20	34	−18.0	54.3	14.8	31	256	75	10.2	15	53	16	07	20	39	0	25	0	07
30	21	20	−13.7	54.5	14.8	43	254	83	11.2	16	08	16	17	21	22	1	36	1	24

MERCURY

Day	R.A.		Dec.	Diam.	Phase	Transit		5° high 52°		5° high 56°	
	h	m	°	″	%	h	m	h	m	h	m
1	12	11	−4.8	8	40	13	29	18	29	18	21
3	12	14	−5.4	9	36	13	23	18	21	18	12
5	12	16	−5.9	9	31	13	17	18	12	18	03
7	12	16	−6.2	9	26	13	09	18	03	17	54
9	12	16	−6.2	10	21	13	00	17	54	17	45
11	12	13	−6.0	10	16	12	50	17	45	17	36
13	12	10	−5.6	10	11	12	38	17	36	17	28
15	12	04	−4.9	10	7	12	25	17	27	17	19
17	11	58	−3.9	10	3	12	10	17	18	17	12
19	11	51	−2.7	10	1	11	56	6	43	6	48
21	11	44	−1.4	10	1	11	41	6	21	6	26
23	11	38	−0.1	10	2	11	27	6	00	6	04
25	11	33	+1.2	10	6	11	14	5	41	5	44
27	11	30	+2.3	9	12	11	04	5	25	5	27
29	11	29	+3.1	9	19	10	56	5	13	5	14
31	11	30	+3.5	8	28	10	50	5	05	5	05

VENUS

Day	R.A.		Dec.	Diam.	Phase	Transit		5° high 52°		5° high 56°	
	h	m	°	″	%	h	m	h	m	h	m
1	8	35	+18.7	13	83	9	54	2	48	2	35
6	9	00	+17.4	12	84	9	59	3	01	2	49
11	9	24	+15.8	12	86	10	04	3	14	3	04
16	9	48	+14.1	12	87	10	08	3	28	3	19
21	10	12	+12.2	12	88	10	12	3	42	3	35
26	10	35	+10.1	11	89	10	16	3	57	3	52
31	10	58	+ 7.9	11	90	10	19	4	11	4	08

MARS

Day	R.A.		Dec.	Diam.	Phase	Transit		5° high 52°		5° high 56°	
	h	m	°	″	%	h	m	h	m	h	m
1	6	17	+23.6	6	90	7	36	0	01	23	41
6	6	31	+23.5	6	89	7	30	23	54	23	35
11	6	44	+23.4	6	89	7	23	23	48	23	30
16	6	57	+23.3	6	89	7	16	23	42	23	24
21	7	10	+23.0	6	89	7	09	23	37	23	19
26	7	22	+22.8	6	89	7	02	23	31	23	14
31	7	34	+22.4	7	89	6	55	23	26	23	09

SUNRISE AND SUNSET

	London				*Bristol*				*Birmingham*				*Manchester*				*Newcastle*				*Glasgow*				*Belfast*			
	0° 05′		*51° 30′*		*2° 35′*		*51° 28′*		*1° 55′*		*52° 28′*		*2° 15′*		*53° 28′*		*1° 37′*		*54° 59′*		*4° 14′*		*55° 52′*		*5° 56′*		*54° 35′*	
d	*h*	*m*	*h*	*m*	*h*	*m*	*h*	*m*	*h*	*m*	*h*	*m*	*h*	*m*	*h*	*m*	*h*	*m*	*h*	*m*	*h*	*m*	*h*	*m*	*h*	*m*	*h*	*m*
1	5	13	18	47	5	23	18	56	5	19	18	55	5	18	18	58	5	13	18	59	5	22	19	11	5	31	19	15
2	5	15	18	44	5	25	18	54	5	20	18	53	5	20	18	56	5	15	18	56	5	24	19	08	5	33	19	13
3	5	16	18	42	5	26	18	52	5	22	18	51	5	22	18	54	5	17	18	54	5	25	19	06	5	35	19	10
4	5	18	18	40	5	28	18	50	5	24	18	49	5	23	18	51	5	18	18	51	5	27	19	03	5	36	19	08
5	5	19	18	38	5	29	18	47	5	25	18	46	5	25	18	49	5	20	18	49	5	29	19	01	5	38	19	05
6	5	21	18	35	5	31	18	45	5	27	18	44	5	27	18	47	5	22	18	46	5	31	18	58	5	40	19	03
7	5	23	18	33	5	33	18	43	5	29	18	41	5	29	18	44	5	24	18	44	5	33	18	55	5	42	19	00
8	5	24	18	31	5	34	18	41	5	30	18	39	5	30	18	42	5	26	18	41	5	35	18	53	5	44	18	58
9	5	26	18	28	5	36	18	38	5	32	18	37	5	32	18	39	5	28	18	39	5	37	18	50	5	46	18	55
10	5	27	18	26	5	37	18	36	5	34	18	34	5	34	18	37	5	30	18	36	5	39	18	47	5	47	18	53
11	5	29	18	24	5	39	18	34	5	35	18	32	5	36	18	34	5	31	18	33	5	41	18	45	5	49	18	50
12	5	30	18	22	5	41	18	32	5	37	18	30	5	37	18	32	5	33	18	31	5	43	18	42	5	51	18	48
13	5	32	18	19	5	42	18	29	5	39	18	27	5	39	18	30	5	35	18	28	5	45	18	40	5	53	18	45
14	5	34	18	17	5	44	18	27	5	40	18	25	5	41	18	27	5	37	18	26	5	47	18	37	5	55	18	43
15	5	35	18	15	5	45	18	25	5	42	18	23	5	43	18	25	5	39	18	23	5	49	18	34	5	57	18	40
16	5	37	18	12	5	47	18	22	5	44	18	20	5	44	18	22	5	41	18	21	5	51	18	32	5	58	18	38
17	5	38	18	10	5	49	18	20	5	45	18	18	5	46	18	20	5	43	18	18	5	53	18	29	6	00	18	35
18	5	40	18	08	5	50	18	18	5	47	18	15	5	48	18	17	5	44	18	15	5	54	18	26	6	02	18	32
19	5	42	18	05	5	52	18	15	5	49	18	13	5	50	18	15	5	46	18	13	5	56	18	24	6	04	18	30
20	5	43	18	03	5	53	18	13	5	50	18	11	5	51	18	12	5	48	18	10	5	58	18	21	6	06	18	27
21	5	45	18	01	5	55	18	11	5	52	18	08	5	53	18	10	5	50	18	08	6	00	18	18	6	08	18	25
22	5	46	17	59	5	56	18	09	5	54	18	06	5	55	18	07	5	52	18	05	6	02	18	16	6	09	18	22
23	5	48	17	56	5	58	18	06	5	55	18	04	5	57	18	05	5	54	18	03	6	04	18	13	6	11	18	20
24	5	50	17	54	6	00	18	04	5	57	18	01	5	58	18	03	5	56	18	00	6	06	18	10	6	13	18	17
25	5	51	17	52	6	01	18	02	5	59	17	59	6	00	18	00	5	58	17	57	6	08	18	08	6	15	18	15
26	5	53	17	49	6	03	17	59	6	00	17	57	6	02	17	58	6	00	17	55	6	10	18	05	6	17	18	12
27	5	55	17	47	6	05	17	57	6	02	17	54	6	04	17	55	6	01	17	52	6	12	18	03	6	19	18	10
28	5	56	17	45	6	06	17	55	6	04	17	52	6	05	17	53	6	03	17	50	6	14	18	00	6	20	18	07
29	5	58	17	42	6	08	17	52	6	05	17	49	6	07	17	50	6	05	17	47	6	16	17	57	6	22	18	05
30	5	59	17	40	6	09	17	50	6	07	17	47	6	09	17	48	6	07	17	45	6	18	17	55	6	24	18	02

JUPITER

Day	*R.A.*		*Dec.*		*Transit*		*5° high*			
							52°		*56°*	
	h	*m*	°	′	*h*	*m*	*h*	*m*	*h*	*m*
1	21	30.6	−15	54	22	45	2	46	2	26
11	21	26.4	−16	14	22	02	2	00	1	40
21	21	23.0	−16	29	21	19	1	16	0	55
31	21	20.8	−16	39	20	38	0	33	0	12

Diameters – equatorial 47″ polar 44″

SATURN

Day	*R.A.*		*Dec.*		*Transit*		*5° high*			
							52°		*56°*	
	h	*m*	°	′	*h*	*m*	*h*	*m*	*h*	*m*
1	11	37.1	+4	37	12	54	7	04	7	03
11	11	41.6	+4	08	12	19	6	32	6	31
21	11	46.2	+3	38	11	45	5	59	6	00
31	11	50.8	+3	09	11	10	5	27	5	28

Diameters – equatorial 16″ polar 14″
Rings – major axis 36″ minor axis 0″

URANUS

Day	*R.A.*		*Dec.*		*Transit*		*10° high*			
							52°		*56°*	
	h	*m*	°	′	*h*	*m*	*h*	*m*	*h*	*m*
1	23	44.0	−2	36	1	03	5	42	5	33
11	23	42.5	−2	46	0	22	5	01	4	51
21	23	41.1	−2	55	23	37	4	19	4	09
31	23	39.6	−3	04	22	56	3	37	3	28

Diameter 4″

NEPTUNE

Day	*R.A.*		*Dec.*		*Transit*		*10° high*			
							52°		*56°*	
	h	*m*	°	′	*h*	*m*	*h*	*m*	*h*	*m*
1	21	48.5	−13	41	23	04	2	39	2	15
11	21	47.5	−13	46	22	23	1	58	1	34
21	21	46.6	−13	51	21	43	1	17	0	53
31	21	45.9	−13	55	21	03	0	37	0	13

Diameter 2″

OCTOBER 2009

TENTH MONTH, 31 DAYS. *Octo* (eighth), eighth month of Roman pre-Julian calendar

1	*Thursday*	The People's Republic of China was formally proclaimed 1949	day 274
2	*Friday*	Britain's first live sextuplets were born 1968	275
3	*Saturday*	OJ Simpson was acquitted of the murder of his wife and her friend 1995	276
4	*Sunday*	Russia launched the world's first artificial satellite Sputnik 1957	277
5	*Monday*	Portugal was declared a republic 1910	week 41 day 278
6	*Tuesday*	International PEN was founded 1921	279
7	*Wednesday*	Arnold Schwarzenegger became the governor of California 2003	280
8	*Thursday*	The Great Chicago Fire broke out, killing hundreds 1871	281
9	*Friday*	Breathalyser tests came into force 1967	282
10	*Saturday*	Fiji became independent 1970	283
11	*Sunday*	The Second Boer War began 1899	284
12	*Monday*	A bomb exploded at the Conservative Party conference in Brighton 1984	week 42 day 285
13	*Tuesday*	Italy declared war on its former axis partner Germany 1943	286
14	*Wednesday*	The Norman army defeated the English at the battle of Hastings 1066	287
15	*Thursday*	China became the third country to send a manned spacecraft into orbit 2003	288
16	*Friday*	Marie Antoinette was guillotined 1793	289
17	*Saturday*	A high-speed train derailed at Hatfield, Hertfordshire, killing four 2000	290
18	*Sunday*	A major earthquake struck San Francisco and the coast of Northern California 1989	291
19	*Monday*	The first battle of Ypres began marking the end of the 'Race to the Sea' 1914	week 43 day 292
20	*Tuesday*	The naval battle of Navarino was fought in the Greek War of Independence 1827	293
21	*Wednesday*	Lord Nelson was mortally wounded 1805	294
22	*Thursday*	The first female peers were introduced into the House of Lords 1958	295
23	*Friday*	The royalists opposed the parliamentarians in the battle of Edgehill 1642	296
24	*Saturday*	The United Nations formally came into existence 1945	297
25	*Sunday*	Lord Cardigan led the charge of the Light Brigade against Russian guns at Balaclava 1854	298
26	*Monday*	The gunfight at the OK Corral took place between Ike Clanton's and Marshal Virgil Earp's gangs 1881	week 44 day 299
27	*Tuesday*	The Abortion Act was passed, allowing abortion for medical reasons 1967	300
28	*Wednesday*	The Statue of Liberty was unveiled 1886	301
29	*Thursday*	The US stock market collapsed, later known as the Wall Street Crash 1929	302
30	*Friday*	John Logie Baird made the first televised transmission of a moving image 1925	303
31	*Saturday*	Indira Gandhi, the Indian prime minister, was assassinated 1984	304

ASTRONOMICAL PHENOMENA

d	*h*	
6	01	Mercury at greatest elongation W.18°
8	07	Saturn in conjunction with Mercury. Saturn 0°.3N.
12	01	Mars in conjunction with Moon. Mars 1°N.
13	05	Jupiter at stationary point
13	11	Saturn in conjunction with Venus. Saturn 0°.5N.
16	08	Saturn in conjunction with Moon. Saturn 6° N
16	14	Venus in conjunction with Moon. Venus 6°N.
17	05	Mercury in conjunction with Moon. Mercury 7°N.
23	07	Sun's longitude 210° ♏
27	07	Jupiter in conjunction with Moon. Jupiter 3°S.

MINIMA OF ALGOL

d	*h*	*d*	*h*	*d*	*h*
2	16.2	13	16.2	25	16.2
4	13.0	16	13.0	27	13.0
7	09.9	19	09.9	30	09.9
10	06.7	22	06.7		

CONSTELLATIONS

The following constellations are near their meridian at

	d	*h*		*d*	*h*
September	1	24	October	16	21
September	15	23	November	1	20
October	1	22	November	15	19

Ursa Major (below the Pole), Cepheus, Cassiopeia, Cygnus, Lacerta, Andromeda, Pegasus, Capricornus, Aquarius and Piscis Austrinus

THE MOON

Phases, Apsides and Node	*d*	*h*	*m*
○ Full Moon	04	06	10
☾ Last Quarter	11	08	56
● New Moon	18	05	33
☽ First Quarter	26	00	42
Perigee (369,034 km)	13	12	16
Apogee (404,207 km)	25	23	18

Mean longitude of ascending node on October 1, 297°

THE SUN

s.d. 16′.1

Day	Right Ascension			Dec.		Equation of time		Rise 52°		Rise 56°		Transit		Set 52°		Set 56°		Sidereal time			Transit of first point of Aries		
	h	*m*	*s*	– °	′	*m*	*s*	*h*	*m*	*h*	*m*	*h*	*m*	*h*	*m*	*h*	*m*	*h*	*m*	*s*	*h*	*m*	*s*
1	12	19	14	3	09	+10	13	6	01	6	03	11	50	17	37	17	35	0	39	27	23	16	44
2	12	32	51	3	33	+10	32	6	03	6	05	11	49	17	35	17	32	0	43	23	23	12	48
3	12	36	28	3	56	+10	51	6	04	6	07	11	49	17	33	17	30	0	47	20	23	08	52
4	12	40	06	4	19	+11	10	6	06	6	09	11	49	17	30	17	27	0	51	16	23	04	56
5	12	43	44	4	42	+11	29	6	08	6	11	11	48	17	28	17	25	0	55	13	23	01	00
6	12	47	23	5	05	+11	47	6	09	6	13	11	48	17	26	17	22	0	59	09	22	57	04
7	12	51	02	5	28	+12	04	6	11	6	15	11	48	17	24	17	19	1	03	06	22	53	08
8	12	54	41	5	51	+12	21	6	13	6	17	11	48	17	21	17	17	1	07	03	22	49	12
9	12	58	21	6	14	+12	38	6	14	6	19	11	47	17	19	17	14	1	10	59	22	45	17
10	13	02	01	6	37	+12	54	6	16	6	21	11	47	17	17	17	12	1	14	56	22	41	21
11	13	05	42	6	59	+13	10	6	18	6	23	11	47	17	15	17	09	1	18	52	22	37	25
12	13	09	23	7	22	+13	26	6	20	6	25	11	46	17	12	17	07	1	22	49	22	33	29
13	13	13	05	7	44	+13	40	6	21	6	27	11	46	17	10	17	04	1	26	45	22	29	33
14	13	16	47	8	07	+13	55	6	23	6	29	11	46	17	08	17	02	1	30	42	22	25	37
15	13	20	30	8	29	+14	08	6	25	6	31	11	46	17	06	16	59	1	34	38	22	21	41
16	13	24	14	8	51	+14	21	6	27	6	33	11	46	17	04	16	57	1	38	35	22	17	45
17	13	27	58	9	13	+14	34	6	28	6	35	11	45	17	02	16	54	1	42	32	22	13	49
18	13	31	42	9	35	+14	46	6	30	6	38	11	45	16	59	16	52	1	46	28	22	09	53
19	13	35	27	9	57	+14	57	6	32	6	40	11	45	16	57	16	49	1	50	25	22	05	57
20	13	39	13	10	19	+15	08	6	34	6	42	11	45	16	55	16	47	1	54	21	22	02	02
21	13	43	00	10	40	+15	18	6	35	6	44	11	45	16	53	16	44	1	58	18	21	58	06
22	13	46	47	11	01	+15	28	6	37	6	46	11	44	16	51	16	42	2	02	14	21	54	10
23	13	50	35	11	22	+15	36	6	39	6	48	11	44	16	49	16	40	2	06	11	21	50	14
24	13	54	23	11	43	+15	44	6	41	6	50	11	44	16	47	16	37	2	10	07	21	46	18
25	13	58	12	12	04	+15	52	6	42	6	52	11	44	16	45	16	35	2	14	04	21	42	22
26	14	02	02	12	25	+15	59	6	44	6	54	11	44	16	43	16	33	2	18	01	21	38	26
27	14	05	53	12	45	+16	05	6	46	6	56	11	44	16	41	16	30	2	21	57	21	34	30
28	14	09	44	13	05	+16	10	6	48	6	59	11	44	16	39	16	28	2	25	54	21	30	34
29	14	13	36	13	25	+16	14	6	50	7	01	11	44	16	37	16	26	2	29	50	21	26	38
30	14	17	29	13	45	+16	18	6	51	7	03	11	44	16	35	16	24	2	33	47	21	22	42
31	14	21	22	14	05	+16	21	6	53	7	05	11	44	16	33	16	21	2	37	43	21	18	47

DURATION OF TWILIGHT (in minutes)

Latitude	52°	56°	52°	56°	52°	56°	52°	56°
	1 October		*11 October*		*21 October*		*31 October*	
Civil	34	37	34	37	34	38	35	39
Nautical	73	80	73	80	74	81	75	83
Astronomical	113	125	112	124	113	124	114	126

THE NIGHT SKY

Mercury reaches greatest western elongation (18 degrees) on the 6th and is visible low above the eastern horizon at the beginning of morning civil twilight. During its period of visibility its magnitude brightens from +0.4 to −1.0. For observers in the British Isles this is the most favourable morning apparition of the year, though it becomes too difficult to detect shortly after the middle of the month.

Venus continues to be visible as a brilliant object in the eastern sky, in the early mornings, magnitude −3.9, though it is gradually drawing closer to the Sun. The waning crescent Moon is in the vicinity of the planet on the mornings of the 16th and 17th. On the 13th Venus passes 0.5 degrees south of Saturn, a useful guide for locating the fainter planet.

Mars, magnitude +0.8 to +0.5, is a morning object. It continues to move eastwards, passing south of Pollux, in the constellation of Gemini, early in the month and crosses into Cancer in the middle of October. Even at the beginning of the month the planet will be visible in the eastern sky by midnight. Mars passes in front of the well-known Beehive open cluster between the 31st of October and the 2nd of November. The Moon, at Last Quarter, passes two degrees south of the planet on the morning of the 12th.

Jupiter, magnitude −2.6, is a splendid object in the south-western sky in the evenings. On the 13th the planet reaches its second stationary point and recommences its eastward motion. The waxing Moon, at First Quarter, is near the planet on the mornings of the 27th and 28th.

Saturn, after the first week of the month, is slowly emerging from the morning twilight and becomes visible low above the eastern horizon for a short while, before being lost in the brightening sky prior to sunrise. Saturn, magnitude +1.1, is in the constellation of Virgo. The waning crescent Moon passes seven degrees south of Saturn on the morning of the 16th.

THE MOON

Day	R.A.		Dec.	Hor. Par.	Semi-diam.	Sun's Co-Long.	PA. of Br. Limb	Ph.	Age	Rise				Transit		Set			
										52°		56°				52°		56°	
	h	*m*	°	′	′	°	°	%	*d*	*h*	*m*	*h*	*m*	*h*	*m*	*h*	*m*	*h*	*m*
1	22	06	−8.8	54.8	14.9	55	253	90	12.2	16	22	16	26	22	04	2	47	2	40
2	22	50	−3.6	55.2	15.1	67	255	95	13.2	16	35	16	34	22	46	3	59	3	57
3	23	35	+1.9	55.7	15.2	79	262	98	14.2	16	48	16	43	23	29	5	12	5	15
4	0	21	+7.5	56.3	15.3	92	304	100	15.2	17	03	16	53	—	—	6	27	6	35
5	1	09	+12.8	56.8	15.5	104	39	99	16.2	17	21	17	06	0	15	7	45	7	58
6	2	01	+17.6	57.3	15.6	116	57	96	17.2	17	44	17	23	1	04	9	05	9	24
7	2	55	+21.6	57.8	15.7	128	66	91	18.2	18	16	17	49	1	56	10	25	10	51
8	3	53	+24.5	58.2	15.9	140	74	84	19.2	18	59	18	29	2	52	11	41	12	12
9	4	53	+25.9	58.6	16.0	152	81	76	20.2	19	58	19	27	3	52	12	47	13	19
10	5	55	+25.8	58.9	16.0	165	89	65	21.2	21	12	20	44	4	52	13	38	14	07
11	6	57	+24.0	59.1	16.1	177	95	54	22.2	22	34	22	12	5	52	14	16	14	39
12	7	56	+20.7	59.3	16.2	189	101	43	23.2	—	—	23	45	6	49	14	44	15	01
13	8	53	+16.2	59.4	16.2	201	105	32	24.2	0	00	—	—	7	43	15	05	15	16
14	9	47	+10.8	59.4	16.2	213	108	22	25.2	1	26	1	17	8	34	15	23	15	28
15	10	40	+4.8	59.3	16.2	225	108	13	26.2	2	51	2	47	9	23	15	38	15	39
16	11	31	−1.4	59.0	16.1	238	106	6	27.2	4	14	4	16	10	12	15	54	15	49
17	12	21	−7.5	58.6	16.0	250	97	2	28.2	5	37	5	45	11	01	16	10	16	00
18	13	13	−13.1	58.1	15.8	262	53	0	29.2	7	00	7	13	11	50	16	29	16	14
19	14	06	−18.0	57.5	15.7	274	317	1	0.8	8	21	8	41	12	42	16	53	16	32
20	15	00	−21.8	56.8	15.5	287	298	4	1.8	9	39	10	05	13	34	17	23	16	57
21	15	55	−24.5	56.1	15.3	299	288	9	2.8	10	49	11	19	14	28	18	03	17	32
22	16	50	−25.8	55.5	15.1	311	280	15	3.8	11	48	12	20	15	21	18	54	18	22
23	17	45	−25.8	55.0	15.0	323	273	23	4.8	12	35	13	05	16	12	19	53	19	24
24	18	38	−24.6	54.6	14.9	335	267	31	5.8	13	10	13	35	17	02	21	00	20	35
25	19	29	−22.2	54.3	14.8	348	261	40	6.8	13	36	13	57	17	49	22	10	21	50
26	20	18	−19.0	54.2	14.8	360	257	50	7.8	13	56	14	12	18	33	23	20	23	06
27	21	05	−15.0	54.3	14.8	12	254	59	8.8	14	13	14	23	19	16	—	—	—	—
28	21	50	−10.3	54.6	14.9	24	251	68	9.8	14	27	14	33	19	58	0	31	0	21
29	22	34	−5.3	55.0	15.0	36	250	77	10.8	14	40	14	42	20	39	1	41	1	37
30	23	19	+0.1	55.6	15.1	48	251	85	11.8	14	53	14	51	21	22	2	53	2	54
31	0	04	+5.6	56.2	15.3	61	253	91	12.8	15	08	15	00	22	07	4	07	4	12

MERCURY

Day	R.A.		Dec.	Diam.	Phase	Transit		5° high			
								52°		56°	
	h	*m*	°	″	%	*h*	*m*	*h*	*m*	*h*	*m*
1	11	30	+ 3.5	8	28	10	50	5	05	5	05
3	11	34	+ 3.7	8	37	10	46	5	00	5	01
5	11	40	+ 3.5	7	47	10	45	5	00	5	00
7	11	48	+ 3.0	7	56	10	45	5	02	5	03
9	11	57	+ 2.2	6	65	10	47	5	08	5	09
11	12	07	+ 1.3	6	72	10	49	5	16	5	18
13	12	19	+ 0.1	6	78	10	53	5	25	5	28
15	12	30	− 1.1	6	84	10	57	5	35	5	40
17	12	42	− 2.4	5	88	11	01	5	46	5	52
19	12	55	− 3.8	5	91	11	05	5	58	6	05
21	13	07	− 5.2	5	94	11	10	6	10	6	18
23	13	19	− 6.7	5	96	11	14	6	23	6	32
25	13	32	− 8.1	5	97	11	19	6	35	6	46
27	13	44	− 9.5	5	98	11	23	6	48	7	00
29	13	57	−10.9	5	99	11	28	7	01	7	14
31	14	09	−12.2	5	100	11	33	7	13	7	28

VENUS

Day	R.A.		Dec.	Diam.	Phase	Transit		5° high			
								52°		56°	
	h	*m*	°	″	%	*h*	*m*	*h*	*m*	*h*	*m*
1	10	58	+7.9	11	90	10	19	4	11	4	08
6	11	21	+5.6	11	91	10	23	4	27	4	25
11	11	44	+3.3	11	92	10	26	4	42	4	42
16	12	07	+0.9	11	93	10	29	4	57	5	00
21	12	30	−1.6	11	94	10	32	5	13	5	18
26	12	53	−4.0	11	95	10	35	5	29	5	36
31	13	16	−6.4	10	95	10	39	5	46	5	55

MARS

Day	R.A.		Dec.	Diam.	Phase	Transit		5° high			
								52°		56°	
	h	*m*	°	″	%	*h*	*m*	*h*	*m*	*h*	*m*
1	7	34	+22.4	7	89	6	55	23	26	23	09
6	7	46	+22.1	7	88	6	47	23	20	23	03
11	7	57	+21.7	7	88	6	38	23	14	22	58
16	8	08	+21.3	7	88	6	29	23	07	22	52
21	8	19	+20.9	7	88	6	20	23	01	22	45
26	8	29	+20.4	8	89	6	10	22	53	22	39
31	8	38	+20.0	8	89	6	00	22	45	22	31

SUNRISE AND SUNSET

	London		*Bristol*		*Birmingham*		*Manchester*		*Newcastle*		*Glasgow*		*Belfast*	
	0° 05′	*51° 30′*	*2° 35′*	*51° 28′*	*1° 55′*	*52° 28′*	*2° 15′*	*53° 28′*	*1° 37′*	*54° 59′*	*4° 14′*	*55° 52′*	*5° 56′*	*54° 35′*
d	*h m*	*h m*	*h m*	*h m*	*h m*	*h m*	*h m*	*h m*	*h m*	*h m*	*h m*	*h m*	*h m*	*h m*
1	6 01	17 38	6 11	17 48	6 09	17 45	6 11	17 46	6 09	17 42	6 20	17 52	6 26	18 00
2	6 03	17 36	6 13	17 46	6 11	17 42	6 12	17 43	6 11	17 40	6 22	17 49	6 28	17 57
3	6 04	17 33	6 14	17 43	6 12	17 40	6 14	17 41	6 13	17 37	6 24	17 47	6 30	17 55
4	6 06	17 31	6 16	17 41	6 14	17 38	6 16	17 38	6 15	17 35	6 26	17 44	6 32	17 52
5	6 08	17 29	6 18	17 39	6 16	17 35	6 18	17 36	6 17	17 32	6 28	17 42	6 34	17 50
6	6 09	17 27	6 19	17 37	6 17	17 33	6 20	17 34	6 19	17 30	6 30	17 39	6 35	17 47
7	6 11	17 24	6 21	17 34	6 19	17 31	6 21	17 31	6 20	17 27	6 32	17 37	6 37	17 45
8	6 13	17 22	6 23	17 32	6 21	17 29	6 23	17 29	6 22	17 25	6 34	17 34	6 39	17 42
9	6 14	17 20	6 24	17 30	6 23	17 26	6 25	17 26	6 24	17 22	6 36	17 31	6 41	17 40
10	6 16	17 18	6 26	17 28	6 24	17 24	6 27	17 24	6 26	17 20	6 38	17 29	6 43	17 37
11	6 18	17 16	6 28	17 26	6 26	17 22	6 29	17 22	6 28	17 17	6 40	17 26	6 45	17 35
12	6 19	17 13	6 29	17 23	6 28	17 19	6 31	17 19	6 30	17 15	6 42	17 24	6 47	17 33
13	6 21	17 11	6 31	17 21	6 30	17 17	6 32	17 17	6 32	17 12	6 44	17 21	6 49	17 30
14	6 23	17 09	6 33	17 19	6 31	17 15	6 34	17 15	6 34	17 10	6 46	17 19	6 51	17 28
15	6 24	17 07	6 34	17 17	6 33	17 13	6 36	17 13	6 36	17 07	6 48	17 16	6 53	17 25
16	6 26	17 05	6 36	17 15	6 35	17 11	6 38	17 10	6 38	17 05	6 50	17 14	6 55	17 23
17	6 28	17 03	6 38	17 13	6 37	17 08	6 40	17 08	6 40	17 03	6 52	17 11	6 57	17 21
18	6 30	17 01	6 39	17 11	6 39	17 06	6 42	17 06	6 42	17 00	6 54	17 09	6 59	17 18
19	6 31	16 59	6 41	17 09	6 40	17 04	6 44	17 04	6 44	16 58	6 56	17 06	7 00	17 16
20	6 33	16 56	6 43	17 06	6 42	17 02	6 45	17 01	6 46	16 56	6 58	17 04	7 02	17 14
21	6 35	16 54	6 45	17 04	6 44	17 00	6 47	16 59	6 48	16 53	7 00	17 02	7 04	17 11
22	6 36	16 52	6 46	17 02	6 46	16 58	6 49	16 57	6 50	16 51	7 03	16 59	7 06	17 09
23	6 38	16 50	6 48	17 00	6 48	16 56	6 51	16 55	6 52	16 49	7 05	16 57	7 08	17 07
24	6 40	16 48	6 50	16 58	6 49	16 54	6 53	16 53	6 54	16 46	7 07	16 55	7 10	17 05
25	6 42	16 46	6 52	16 56	6 51	16 52	6 55	16 51	6 56	16 44	7 09	16 52	7 12	17 02
26	6 43	16 44	6 53	16 54	6 53	16 49	6 57	16 48	6 58	16 42	7 11	16 50	7 14	17 00
27	6 45	16 42	6 55	16 53	6 55	16 47	6 59	16 46	7 00	16 40	7 13	16 48	7 16	16 58
28	6 47	16 41	6 57	16 51	6 57	16 46	7 01	16 44	7 02	16 38	7 15	16 45	7 18	16 56
29	6 49	16 39	6 59	16 49	6 58	16 44	7 02	16 42	7 04	16 35	7 17	16 43	7 20	16 54
30	6 50	16 37	7 00	16 47	7 00	16 42	7 04	16 40	7 06	16 33	7 19	16 41	7 22	16 52
31	6 52	16 35	7 02	16 45	7 02	16 40	7 06	16 38	7 08	16 31	7 21	16 39	7 24	16 50

JUPITER

Day	*R.A.*		*Dec.*		*Transit*		*5° high*			
							52°		*56°*	
	h	*m*	°	′	*h*	*m*	*h*	*m*	*h*	*m*
1	21	20.8	−16	39	20	38	0	33	0	12
11	21	19.8	−16	42	19	58	23	49	23	27
21	21	20.2	−16	39	19	19	23	10	22	49
31	21	21.9	−16	31	18	41	22	34	22	13

Diameters – equatorial 43″ polar 41″

SATURN

Day	*R.A.*		*Dec.*		*Transit*		*5° high*			
							52°		*56°*	
	h	*m*	°	′	*h*	*m*	*h*	*m*	*h*	*m*
1	11	50.8	+3	09	11	10	5	27	5	28
11	11	55.3	+2	41	10	35	4	55	4	56
21	11	59.6	+2	14	10	00	4	22	4	23
31	12	03.8	+1	49	9	25	3	49	3	51

Diameters – equatorial 16″ polar 14″
Rings – major axis 36″ minor axis 1″

URANUS

Day	*R.A.*		*Dec.*		*Transit*		*10° high*			
							52°		*56°*	
	h	*m*	°	′	*h*	*m*	*h*	*m*	*h*	*m*
1	23	39.6	−3	04	22	56	3	37	3	28
11	23	38.2	−3	13	22	16	2	56	2	46
21	23	37.0	−3	21	21	35	2	15	2	05
31	23	36.0	−3	27	20	55	1	34	1	24

Diameter 4″

NEPTUNE

Day	*R.A.*		*Dec.*		*Transit*		*10° high*			
							52°		*56°*	
	h	*m*	°	′	*h*	*m*	*h*	*m*	*h*	*m*
1	21	45.9	−13	55	21	03	0	37	0	13
11	21	45.3	−13	58	20	23	23	52	23	28
21	21	44.9	−14	00	19	43	23	12	22	48
31	21	44.6	−14	01	19	04	22	33	22	09

Diameter 2″

NOVEMBER 2009

ELEVENTH MONTH, 30 DAYS. *Novem* (nine), ninth month of Roman pre-Julian calendar

1	*Sunday*	Premium bonds first went on sale 1956	day 305
2	*Monday*	President Kennedy announced the end of the Cuban Missile Crisis 1962	week 45 day 306
3	*Tuesday*	George W Bush was elected president of the USA for a second term 2004	307
4	*Wednesday*	Militant Islamic students stormed the US embassy in Tehran, taking 90 hostages 1979	308
5	*Thursday*	Guy Fawkes was arrested for attempting to blow up the Houses of Parliament 1605	309
6	*Friday*	Henry VI was crowned king of England 1429	310
7	*Saturday*	Vladimir Lenin seized power in a Bolshevik coup in Russia 1917	311
8	*Sunday*	Adolf Hitler led the Munich Putsch 1923	312
9	*Monday*	Demolition of the Berlin wall began 1989	week 46 day 313
10	*Tuesday*	Ken Saro-Wiwa, a human rights activist, was executed in Nigeria 1995	314
11	*Wednesday*	The First World War effectively ended with the signing of the Armistice 1918	315
12	*Thursday*	The Abbey Road recording studios in London were opened by Sir Edward Elgar 1931	316
13	*Friday*	Battle of the Somme ended 1916	317
14	*Saturday*	Princess Anne married Captain Mark Phillips 1973	318
15	*Sunday*	The German Luftwaffe bombed Coventry, damaging most of the city 1940	319
16	*Monday*	Benazir Bhutto was elected prime minister of Pakistan 1988	week 47 day 320
17	*Tuesday*	Sir Walter Raleigh was tried for treason 1604	321
18	*Wednesday*	William Caxton published the first dated book to be printed in England 1477	322
19	*Thursday*	The first National Lottery draw took place 1994	323
20	*Friday*	Trials of 20 Nazi leaders for war crimes began at Nuremberg 1945	324
21	*Saturday*	The first controlled manned flight in a hot air balloon took place in Paris 1783	325
22	*Sunday*	US President John F. Kennedy was assassinated 1963	326
23	*Monday*	Perkin Warbeck, a pretender to the English throne, was hanged at Tyburn 1499	week 48 day 327
24	*Tuesday*	Darwin's *On the Origin of Species* was published 1859	328
25	*Wednesday*	Alfred Nobel patented dynamite 1867	329
26	*Thursday*	The first Thanksgiving Day was celebrated nationally in America 1789	330
27	*Friday*	Charles de Gaulle vetoed Britain's application to join the European Common Market 1967	331
28	*Saturday*	The first female voters were allowed at a general election in New Zealand 1893	332
29	*Sunday*	Yugoslavia was proclaimed a republic 1945	333
30	*Monday*	The first international football match was played, with Scotland opposing England 1872	Week 49 day 334

ASTRONOMICAL PHENOMENA

d	*h*	
4	18	Neptune at stationary point
5	08	Mercury in superior conjunction
9	04	Mars in conjunction with Moon. Mars 3°N.
12	20	Saturn in conjunction with Moon. Saturn 7°N.
15	16	Venus in conjunction with Moon. Venus 6°N.
17	09	Mercury in conjunction with Moon. Mercury 3°N.
22	04	Sun's longitude 240° ♐
23	20	Jupiter in conjunction with Moon. Jupiter 3°S.

MINIMA OF ALGOL

d	*h*	*d*	*h*	*d*	*h*
2	16.2	14	16.2	25	16.2
5	13.0	16	13.0	28	13.0
8	09.9	19	09.9		
11	06.7	22	06.7		

CONSTELLATIONS

The following constellations are near their meridian at

	d	*h*		*d*	*h*
October	1	24	November	15	21
October	16	23	December	1	20
November	1	22	December	16	19

Ursa Major (below the Pole), Cepheus, Cassiopeia, Andromeda, Pegasus, Pisces, Aquarius and Cetus

THE MOON

Phases, Apsides and Node	*d*	*h*	*m*
○ Full Moon	2	19	14
☾ Last Quarter	9	15	56
● New Moon	16	19	14
☽ First Quarter	24	21	39
Perigee (368,870 km)	7	07	34
Apogee (404,770 km)	22	20	10

Mean longitude of ascending node on November 1, 295°

THE SUN

s.d. 16′.2

Day	Right Ascension h m s	Dec. – ° ′	Equation of time m s	Rise 52° h m	Rise 56° h m	Transit h m	Set 52° h m	Set 56° h m	Sidereal time h m s	Transit of first point of Aries h m s
1	14 25 16	14 24	+16 23	6 55	7 07	11 44	16 31	16 19	2 41 40	21 14 51
2	14 29 12	14 43	+16 25	6 57	7 09	11 44	16 30	16 17	2 45 36	21 10 55
3	14 33 07	15 02	+16 26	6 59	7 11	11 44	16 28	16 15	2 49 33	21 06 59
4	14 37 04	15 21	+16 25	7 00	7 13	11 44	16 26	16 13	2 53 30	21 03 03
5	14 41 02	15 39	+16 24	7 02	7 16	11 44	16 24	16 11	2 57 26	20 59 07
6	14 45 00	15 57	+16 23	7 04	7 18	11 44	16 23	16 09	3 01 23	20 55 11
7	14 48 59	16 15	+16 20	7 06	7 20	11 44	16 21	16 07	3 05 19	20 51 15
8	14 52 59	16 33	+16 16	7 08	7 22	11 44	16 19	16 05	3 09 16	20 47 19
9	14 57 00	16 50	+16 12	7 09	7 24	11 44	16 18	16 03	3 13 12	20 43 23
10	15 01 02	17 07	+16 07	7 11	7 26	11 44	16 16	16 01	3 17 09	20 39 27
11	15 05 05	17 24	+16 01	7 13	7 28	11 44	16 15	15 59	3 21 05	20 35 32
12	15 09 08	17 40	+15 54	7 15	7 30	11 44	16 13	15 57	3 25 02	20 31 36
13	15 13 13	17 56	+15 46	7 16	7 33	11 44	16 12	15 55	3 28 59	20 27 40
14	15 17 18	18 12	+15 37	7 18	7 35	11 44	16 10	15 54	3 32 55	20 23 44
15	15 21 24	18 28	+15 28	7 20	7 37	11 45	16 09	15 52	3 36 52	20 19 48
16	15 25 31	18 43	+15 17	7 22	7 39	11 45	16 07	15 50	3 40 48	20 15 52
17	15 29 39	18 58	+15 06	7 23	7 41	11 45	16 06	15 49	3 44 45	20 11 56
18	15 33 48	19 12	+14 54	7 25	7 43	11 45	16 05	15 47	3 48 41	20 08 00
19	15 37 57	19 26	+14 41	7 27	7 45	11 45	16 03	15 45	3 52 38	20 04 04
20	15 42 07	19 40	+14 27	7 29	7 47	11 46	16 02	15 44	3 56 34	20 00 08
21	15 46 19	19 54	+14 12	7 30	7 49	11 46	16 01	15 43	4 00 31	19 56 12
22	15 50 31	20 07	+13 57	7 32	7 51	11 46	16 00	15 41	4 04 28	19 52 17
23	15 54 43	20 19	+13 41	7 34	7 53	11 46	15 59	15 40	4 08 24	19 48 21
24	15 58 57	20 32	+13 24	7 35	7 55	11 47	15 58	15 38	4 12 21	19 44 25
25	16 03 11	20 44	+13 06	7 37	7 56	11 47	15 57	15 37	4 16 17	19 40 29
26	16 07 26	20 55	+12 48	7 38	7 58	11 47	15 56	15 36	4 20 14	19 36 33
27	16 11 41	21 06	+12 29	7 40	8 00	11 48	15 55	15 35	4 24 10	19 32 37
28	16 15 58	21 17	+12 09	7 41	8 02	11 48	15 54	15 34	4 28 07	19 28 41
29	16 20 15	21 28	+11 49	7 43	8 04	11 48	15 54	15 33	4 32 03	19 24 45
30	16 24 33	21 38	+11 28	7 44	8 05	11 49	15 53	15 32	4 36 00	19 20 49

DURATION OF TWILIGHT (in minutes)

Latitude	*52°*	*56°*	*52°*	*56°*	*52°*	*56°*	*52°*	*56°*
	1 November		*11 November*		*21 November*		*31 November*	
Civil	36	40	37	41	38	43	40	45
Nautical	75	84	78	87	80	90	82	93
Astronomical	115	127	117	130	120	134	123	138

THE NIGHT SKY

Mercury passes through superior conjunction on the 5th and remains unsuitably placed for observation throughout the month.

Venus, magnitude −3.9, is still visible as a brilliant object in the south-eastern sky before dawn. It is drawing closer to the Sun, the period available for observation shortening noticeably during the month. Venus passes four degrees north of Spica, in the constellation of Virgo, on the 2nd.

Mars is now more noticeable as its magnitude brightens from +0.4 to 0.0 during the month. The planet is now visible in the eastern sky well before midnight. The Moon, at Last Quarter, passes four degrees south of the planet on the morning of the 9th. At the very end of November Mars moves from Cancer into Leo.

Jupiter continues to be visible as a splendid evening object, magnitude −2.3, low in the south-western sky in the early evenings. By the end of the month it will be lost to view before 21h. During the evening of the 23rd the waxing crescent Moon passes about two degrees north of the planet. The four Galilean satellites are readily observable with a small telescope or even a good pair of binoculars.

Saturn, magnitude +1.1, is still visible as a morning object in the south-eastern quadrant of the sky, in the constellation of Virgo. The waning crescent Moon is in the vicinity of the planet on the 12th–13th.

THE MOON

Day	R.A.		Dec.	Hor. Par.	Semi-diam.	Sun's Co-Long.	PA. of Br. Limb	Ph.	Age	Rise				Transit		Set			
										52°		56°				52°		56°	
	h	m	°	′	′	°	°	%	d	h	m	h	m	h	m	h	m	h	m
1	0	52	+11.0	56.9	15.5	73	259	96	13.8	15	25	15	12	22	55	5	24	5	35
2	1	43	+16.0	57.6	15.7	85	275	99	14.8	15	47	15	28	23	47	6	44	7	01
3	2	37	+20.3	58.2	15.9	97	10	100	15.8	16	16	15	52	—	—	8	06	8	29
4	3	35	+23.6	58.7	16.0	109	62	98	16.8	16	56	16	27	0	43	9	26	9	54
5	4	37	+25.5	59.1	16.1	121	76	94	17.8	17	51	17	20	1	43	10	37	11	08
6	5	40	+25.7	59.3	16.2	133	85	87	18.8	19	02	18	33	2	45	11	34	12	04
7	6	42	+24.3	59.4	16.2	146	93	79	19.8	20	23	20	00	3	46	12	16	12	41
8	7	43	+21.3	59.4	16.2	158	100	69	20.8	21	49	21	31	4	45	12	47	13	05
9	8	40	+17.0	59.3	16.2	170	105	58	21.8	23	14	23	03	5	39	13	10	13	23
10	9	35	+11.8	59.1	16.1	182	109	46	22.8	—	—	—	—	6	31	13	28	13	36
11	10	26	+6.1	58.8	16.0	194	110	35	23.8	0	37	0	32	7	20	13	44	13	46
12	11	17	+0.1	58.5	15.9	206	111	25	24.8	1	58	1	59	8	07	14	00	13	57
13	12	06	−5.9	58.1	15.8	219	109	16	25.8	3	19	3	25	8	54	14	15	14	07
14	12	56	−11.5	57.7	15.7	231	105	9	26.8	4	40	4	51	9	42	14	33	14	20
15	13	48	−16.5	57.2	15.6	243	99	4	27.8	6	00	6	17	10	32	14	55	14	36
16	14	41	−20.6	56.7	15.5	255	82	1	28.8	7	18	7	42	11	24	15	22	14	58
17	15	35	−23.6	56.2	15.3	267	344	0	0.2	8	31	9	00	12	17	15	58	15	29
18	16	31	−25.3	55.7	15.2	280	292	2	1.2	9	35	10	07	13	10	16	44	16	13
19	17	26	−25.8	55.2	15.0	292	279	5	2.2	10	27	10	58	14	03	17	41	17	10
20	18	20	−24.9	54.8	14.9	304	270	10	3.2	11	07	11	34	14	54	18	46	18	19
21	19	12	−22.9	54.4	14.8	316	263	16	4.2	11	36	11	59	15	42	19	54	19	33
22	20	02	−19.9	54.2	14.8	328	258	24	5.2	11	59	12	16	16	27	21	05	20	48
23	20	49	−16.2	54.2	14.8	341	254	33	6.2	12	17	12	29	17	10	22	15	22	04
24	21	34	−11.7	54.3	14.8	353	251	42	7.2	12	32	12	39	17	52	23	24	23	18
25	22	18	−6.9	54.6	14.9	5	249	51	8.2	12	45	12	48	18	33	—	—	—	—
26	23	02	−1.7	55.0	15.0	17	248	61	9.2	12	58	12	57	19	14	0	34	0	33
27	23	46	+3.7	55.6	15.2	29	249	70	10.2	13	12	13	06	19	57	1	45	1	49
28	0	33	+9.0	56.4	15.4	41	250	79	11.2	13	27	13	17	20	43	2	59	3	08
29	1	21	+14.1	57.2	15.6	53	254	87	12.2	13	47	13	31	21	33	4	17	4	31
30	2	14	+18.7	58.1	15.8	66	259	93	13.2	14	12	13	51	22	28	5	38	5	58

MERCURY

Day	R.A.		Dec.	Diam.	Phase	Transit		5° high			
								52°		56°	
	h	m	°	′	%	h	m	h	m	h	m
1	14	15	−12.9	5	100	11	35	7	20	7	36
3	14	28	−14.1	5	100	11	40	7	32	7	50
5	14	41	−15.4	5	100	11	44	7	45	8	04
7	14	53	−16.5	5	100	11	49	7	57	8	18
9	15	06	−17.6	5	100	11	54	8	10	8	33
11	15	18	−18.7	5	100	11	58	8	22	8	47
13	15	31	−19.7	5	99	12	03	15	31	15	04
15	15	44	−20.6	5	99	12	08	15	29	15	00
17	15	57	−21.5	5	98	12	13	15	27	14	56
19	16	10	−22.3	5	98	12	18	15	26	14	52
21	16	23	−23.0	5	97	12	24	15	25	14	49
23	16	36	−23.7	5	96	12	29	15	25	14	47
25	16	49	−24.2	5	96	12	34	15	25	14	45
27	17	02	−24.7	5	94	12	40	15	26	14	44
29	17	16	−25.1	5	93	12	45	15	28	14	43
31	17	29	−25.4	5	92	12	50	15	30	14	45

VENUS

Day	R.A.		Dec.	Diam.	Phase	Transit		5° high			
								52°		56°	
	h	m	°	′	%	h	m	h	m	h	m
1	13	21	−6.9	10	96	10	39	5	49	5	59
6	13	44	−9.2	10	96	10	43	6	06	6	18
11	14	08	−11.5	10	97	10	47	6	23	6	38
16	14	32	−13.6	10	97	10	52	6	41	6	58
21	14	57	−15.7	10	98	10	57	6	59	7	18
26	15	22	−17.5	10	98	11	02	7	17	7	39
31	15	47	−19.1	10	99	11	08	7	34	8	00

MARS

Day	R.A.		Dec.	Diam.	Phase	Transit		5° high			
								52°		56°	
	h	m	°	′	%	h	m	h	m	h	m
1	8	40	+19.9	8	89	5	58	22	44	22	30
6	8	49	+19.5	8	89	5	47	22	35	22	22
11	8	57	+19.1	8	89	5	35	22	26	22	13
16	9	05	+18.8	9	89	5	23	22	16	22	03
21	9	11	+18.4	9	90	5	10	22	04	21	52
26	9	17	+18.2	9	90	4	57	21	52	21	40
31	9	23	+18.0	10	91	4	42	21	38	21	26

SUNRISE AND SUNSET

	London 0° 05′		51° 30′		*Bristol* 2° 35′		51° 28′		*Birmingham* 1° 55′		52° 28′		*Manchester* 2° 15′		53° 28′		*Newcastle* 1° 37′		54° 59′		*Glasgow* 4° 14′		55° 52′		*Belfast* 5° 56′		54° 35′	
d	*h*	*m*	*h*	*m*	*h*	*m*	*h*	*m*	*h*	*m*	*h*	*m*	*h*	*m*	*h*	*m*	*h*	*m*	*h*	*m*	*h*	*m*	*h*	*m*	*h*	*m*	*h*	*m*
1	6	54	16	33	7	04	16	43	7	04	16	38	7	08	16	36	7	10	16	29	7	24	16	37	7	26	16	48
2	6	56	16	31	7	06	16	41	7	06	16	36	7	10	16	34	7	12	16	27	7	26	16	34	7	28	16	46
3	6	57	16	30	7	07	16	40	7	08	16	34	7	12	16	32	7	14	16	25	7	28	16	32	7	30	16	44
4	6	59	16	28	7	09	16	38	7	09	16	32	7	14	16	31	7	16	16	23	7	30	16	30	7	32	16	42
5	7	01	16	26	7	11	16	36	7	11	16	31	7	16	16	29	7	18	16	21	7	32	16	28	7	34	16	40
6	7	03	16	25	7	13	16	35	7	13	16	29	7	18	16	27	7	20	16	19	7	34	16	26	7	36	16	38
7	7	05	16	23	7	14	16	33	7	15	16	27	7	20	16	25	7	22	16	17	7	36	16	24	7	38	16	36
8	7	06	16	21	7	16	16	31	7	17	16	25	7	21	16	23	7	24	16	15	7	38	16	22	7	40	16	34
9	7	08	16	20	7	18	16	30	7	19	16	24	7	23	16	22	7	27	16	13	7	41	16	20	7	42	16	32
10	7	10	16	18	7	20	16	28	7	20	16	22	7	25	16	20	7	29	16	12	7	43	16	18	7	44	16	30
11	7	12	16	17	7	21	16	27	7	22	16	21	7	27	16	18	7	31	16	10	7	45	16	17	7	46	16	29
12	7	13	16	15	7	23	16	25	7	24	16	19	7	29	16	17	7	33	16	08	7	47	16	15	7	48	16	27
13	7	15	16	14	7	25	16	24	7	26	16	17	7	31	16	15	7	35	16	06	7	49	16	13	7	50	16	25
14	7	17	16	12	7	27	16	22	7	28	16	16	7	33	16	13	7	37	16	05	7	51	16	11	7	52	16	24
15	7	18	16	11	7	28	16	21	7	29	16	15	7	35	16	12	7	39	16	03	7	53	16	09	7	54	16	22
16	7	20	16	10	7	30	16	20	7	31	16	13	7	37	16	10	7	40	16	01	7	55	16	08	7	56	16	20
17	7	22	16	08	7	32	16	18	7	33	16	12	7	38	16	09	7	42	16	00	7	57	16	06	7	58	16	19
18	7	24	16	07	7	33	16	17	7	35	16	10	7	40	16	08	7	44	15	58	7	59	16	05	8	00	16	17
19	7	25	16	06	7	35	16	16	7	36	16	09	7	42	16	06	7	46	15	57	8	01	16	03	8	02	16	16
20	7	27	16	05	7	37	16	15	7	38	16	08	7	44	16	05	7	48	15	56	8	03	16	02	8	04	16	15
21	7	29	16	04	7	38	16	14	7	40	16	07	7	46	16	04	7	50	15	54	8	05	16	00	8	05	16	13
22	7	30	16	02	7	40	16	13	7	41	16	06	7	47	16	03	7	52	15	53	8	07	15	59	8	07	16	12
23	7	32	16	01	7	42	16	12	7	43	16	05	7	49	16	01	7	54	15	52	8	09	15	57	8	09	16	11
24	7	33	16	00	7	43	16	10	7	45	16	04	7	51	16	00	7	56	15	50	8	11	15	56	8	11	16	10
25	7	35	15	59	7	45	16	10	7	46	16	03	7	52	15	59	7	57	15	49	8	13	15	55	8	13	16	08
26	7	36	15	59	7	46	16	09	7	48	16	02	7	54	15	58	7	59	15	48	8	14	15	54	8	14	16	07
27	7	38	15	58	7	48	16	08	7	50	16	01	7	56	15	57	8	01	15	47	8	16	15	53	8	16	16	06
28	7	39	15	57	7	49	16	07	7	51	16	00	7	57	15	56	8	03	15	46	8	18	15	51	8	18	16	05
29	7	41	15	56	7	51	16	06	7	53	15	59	7	59	15	55	8	04	15	45	8	20	15	50	8	19	16	04
30	7	42	15	55	7	52	16	06	7	54	15	58	8	00	15	55	8	06	15	44	8	21	15	49	8	21	16	04

JUPITER

Day	*R.A.*		*Dec.*		*Transit*		*5° high* 52°		56°	
	h	*m*	°	′	*h*	*m*	*h*	*m*	*h*	*m*
1	21	22.1	−16	29	18	38	22	30	22	09
11	21	25.1	−16	14	18	01	21	56	21	35
21	21	29.3	−15	53	17	26	21	23	21	03
31	21	34.5	−15	27	16	52	20	52	20	33

Diameters – equatorial 39″ polar 37″

SATURN

Day	*R.A.*		*Dec.*		*Transit*		*5° high* 52°		56°	
	h	*m*	°	′	*h*	*m*	*h*	*m*	*h*	*m*
1	12	04.2	+1	47	9	21	3	45	3	47
11	12	08.0	+1	24	8	46	3	12	3	14
21	12	11.4	+1	04	8	10	2	38	2	40
31	12	14.4	+0	47	7	33	2	03	2	05

Diameters – equatorial 16″ polar 15″
Rings– major axis 37″ minor axis 2″

URANUS

Day	*R.A.*		*Dec.*		*Transit*		*10° high* 52°		56°	
	h	*m*	°	′	*h*	*m*	*h*	*m*	*h*	*m*
1	23	35.9	−3	28	20	51	1	30	1	20
11	23	35.1	−3	32	20	11	0	49	0	39
21	23	34.6	−3	35	19	31	0	09	23	55
31	23	34.4	−3	36	18	51	23	26	23	15

Diameter 4″

NEPTUNE

Day	*R.A.*		*Dec.*		*Transit*		*10° high* 52°		56°	
	h	*m*	°	′	*h*	*m*	*h*	*m*	*h*	*m*
1	21	44.6	−14	01	19	00	22	29	22	05
11	21	44.7	−14	01	18	21	21	50	21	26
21	21	44.9	−14	00	17	42	21	11	20	47
31	21	45.4	−13	57	17	03	20	32	20	08

Diameter 2″

DECEMBER 2009

TWELFTH MONTH, 31 DAYS. *Decem* (ten), tenth month of Roman pre-Julian calendar

1	*Tuesday*	British and French workers joined the two halves of the Channel tunnel 1990	day 335
2	*Wednesday*	St Paul's cathedral opened 1697	336
3	*Thursday*	The first human heart-transplant operation was performed 1967	337
4	*Friday*	*The Observer* was published for the first time 1791	338
5	*Saturday*	The *Mary Celeste* was found abandoned 1872	339
6	*Sunday*	Thomas Edison made the first known sound recording 1877	340
7	*Monday*	The USA was brought into the Second World War with the battle of Pearl Harbor 1941	week 50 day 341
8	*Tuesday*	John Lennon was shot dead by a fan 1980	342
9	*Wednesday*	The Hubble telescope was successfully repaired 1993	343
10	*Thursday*	The first Nobel prizes were awarded in Stockholm, Sweden 1901	344
11	*Friday*	Edward VIII abdicated 1936	345
12	*Saturday*	Spain declared war on Britain 1804	346
13	*Sunday*	Francis Drake began his voyage around the world 1577	347
14	*Monday*	Roald Amundsen reached the South Pole 1911	week 51 day 348
15	*Tuesday*	Road speed limits were reduced to save fuel 1974	349
16	*Wednesday*	Battle of the Bulge began in Ardennes, France 1944	350
17	*Thursday*	Orville Wright made the first powered flight 1903	351
18	*Friday*	The Battle of Verdun ended 1916	352
19	*Saturday*	Ted Hughes was appointed poet laureate 1984	353
20	*Sunday*	Admiral Luis Carrero Blanco, the Spanish prime minister, was assassinated 1973	354
21	*Monday*	Pilgrims from the *Mayflower* landed on Plymouth Rock 1620	week 52 day 355
22	*Tuesday*	Fourteen survivors were found ten weeks after a plane crash in the Andes 1972	356
23	*Wednesday*	Vincent Van Gogh cut off part of his right ear 1888	357
24	*Thursday*	The Treaty of Ghent was signed by Great Britain and the USA 1814	358
25	*Friday*	King George V made the first royal Christmas day broadcast 1932	359
26	*Saturday*	A tsunami hit southern Asia, killing over 200,000 people 2004	360
27	*Sunday*	Leon Trotsky was expelled from the Russian Communist party 1927	361
28	*Monday*	The Tay bridge in Scotland blew down, killing over 70 people 1879	week 53 day 362
29	*Tuesday*	St Thomas à Becket was murdered 1170	363
30	*Wednesday*	Israel and the Vatican agreed to establish full diplomatic ties 1993	364
31	*Thursday*	The farthing ceased to be legal tender 1960	365

ASTRONOMICAL PHENOMENA

d	*h*	
1	20	Uranus at stationary point
7	00	Mars in conjunction with Moon. Mars 5°N.
10	05	Saturn in conjunction with Moon. Saturn 7°N.
15	22	Venus in conjunction with Moon. Venus 3°N.
18	08	Mercury in conjunction with Moon. Mercury 1°S.
18	18	Mercury at greatest elongation E.20°
20	13	Mars at stationary point
21	12	Jupiter in conjunction with Moon. Jupiter 4°S.
21	18	Sun's longitude 270° ♑
24	17	Pluto in conjunction
26	15	Mercury at stationary point
31	19	Partial eclipse of Moon

MINIMA OF ALGOL

d	*h*	*d*	*h*	*d*	*h*
1	16.2	12	16.2	24	16.2
4	13.0	15	13.0	27	13.0
7	09.9	18	09.9	29	09.9
9	06.7	21	06.7		

CONSTELLATIONS

The following constellations are near their meridian at

	d	*h*		*d*	*h*
November	1	24	January	1	20
December	16	21	December	1	22
November	15	23	January	16	19

Ursa Major (below the Pole), Ursa Minor (below the Pole), Cassiopeia, Andromeda, Perseus, Triangulum, Aries, Taurus, Cetus and Eridanus

THE MOON

Phases, Apsides and Node	*d*	*h*	*m*
○ Full Moon	2	07	30
☾ Last Quarter	9	00	13
● New Moon	16	12	02
☽ First Quarter	24	17	36
○ Full Moon	31	19	13
Perigee (363,461 km)	4	14	26
Apogee (405,760 km)	20	15	01

Mean longitude of ascending node on December 1, 293°

THE SUN

s.d. 16′.3

Day	Right Ascension			Dec. –		Equation of time		Rise 52°		Rise 56°		Transit		Set 52°		Set 56°		Sidereal time			Transit of first point of Aries		
	h	m	s	°	′	m	s	h	m	h	m	h	m	h	m	h	m	h	m	s	h	m	s
1	16	28	51	21	47	+11	06	7	46	8	07	11	49	15	52	15	31	4	39	57	19	16	53
2	16	33	10	21	56	+10	43	7	47	8	09	11	49	15	51	15	30	4	43	53	19	12	57
3	16	37	30	22	05	+10	20	7	48	8	10	11	50	15	51	15	29	4	47	50	19	09	02
4	16	41	50	22	13	+9	56	7	50	8	12	11	50	15	50	15	28	4	51	46	19	05	06
5	16	46	11	22	21	+9	32	7	51	8	13	11	51	15	50	15	28	4	55	43	19	01	10
6	16	50	32	22	29	+9	07	7	52	8	15	11	51	15	50	15	27	4	59	39	18	57	14
7	16	54	54	22	36	+8	42	7	54	8	16	11	52	15	49	15	27	5	03	36	18	53	18
8	16	59	17	22	42	+8	16	7	55	8	17	11	52	15	49	15	26	5	07	33	18	49	22
9	17	03	40	22	48	+7	49	7	56	8	19	11	52	15	49	15	26	5	11	29	18	45	26
10	17	08	03	22	54	+7	23	7	57	8	20	11	53	15	49	15	25	5	15	26	18	41	30
11	17	12	27	22	59	+6	55	7	58	8	21	11	53	15	48	15	25	5	19	22	18	37	34
12	17	16	51	23	04	+6	27	7	59	8	22	11	54	15	48	15	25	5	23	19	18	33	38
13	17	21	16	23	08	+5	59	8	00	8	23	11	54	15	48	15	25	5	27	15	18	29	42
14	17	25	41	23	12	+5	31	8	01	8	24	11	55	15	48	15	25	5	31	12	18	25	46
15	17	30	06	23	16	+5	02	8	02	8	25	11	55	15	49	15	25	5	35	08	18	21	51
16	17	34	32	23	19	+4	33	8	03	8	26	11	56	15	49	15	25	5	39	05	18	17	55
17	17	38	58	23	21	+4	04	8	03	8	27	11	56	15	49	15	25	5	43	02	18	13	59
18	17	43	24	23	23	+3	34	8	04	8	28	11	57	15	49	15	25	5	46	58	18	10	03
19	17	47	50	23	25	+3	05	8	05	8	29	11	57	15	50	15	26	5	50	55	18	06	07
20	17	52	16	23	26	+2	35	8	05	8	29	11	58	15	50	15	26	5	54	51	18	02	11
21	17	56	43	23	26	+2	05	8	06	8	30	11	58	15	50	15	27	5	58	48	17	58	15
22	18	01	09	23	26	+1	35	8	06	8	30	11	59	15	51	15	27	6	02	44	17	54	19
23	18	05	35	23	26	+1	05	8	07	8	31	11	59	15	52	15	28	6	06	41	17	50	23
24	18	10	02	23	25	+0	36	8	07	8	31	12	00	15	52	15	28	6	10	37	17	46	27
25	18	14	28	23	24	+0	06	8	07	8	31	12	00	15	53	15	29	6	14	34	17	42	31
26	18	18	54	23	22	–0	24	8	08	8	31	12	01	15	54	15	30	6	18	31	17	38	36
27	18	23	21	23	20	–0	53	8	08	8	32	12	01	15	54	15	31	6	22	27	17	34	40
28	18	27	47	23	17	–1	23	8	08	8	32	12	02	15	55	15	32	6	26	24	17	30	44
29	18	32	12	23	14	–1	52	8	08	8	32	12	02	15	56	15	33	6	30	20	17	26	48
30	18	36	38	23	10	–2	21	8	08	8	32	12	03	15	57	15	34	6	34	17	17	22	52
31	18	41	03	23	06	–2	50	8	08	8	31	12	03	15	58	15	35	6	38	13	17	18	56

DURATION OF TWILIGHT (in minutes)

Latitude	52°	56°	52°	56°	52°	56°	52°	56°
	1 December		*11 December*		*21 December*		*31 December*	
Civil	40	45	41	47	41	47	41	47
Nautical	82	93	84	96	85	97	84	96
Astronomical	123	138	125	141	126	142	125	141

THE NIGHT SKY

Mercury, although it reaches greatest eastern elongation (20 degrees) on the 18th, remains too close to the Sun for observation throughout December.

Venus, magnitude –4.1, is a morning object, but only for the first ten days of the month, visible low above the south-eastern horizon for a short while before dawn.

Mars continues to be visible, technically as a morning object, but now visible in the eastern sky by late evening. It is moving slowly eastwards in the constellation of Leo until the 20th when it reaches its first stationary point, and commences its retrograde motion only seven degrees short of Regulus. During the month its magnitude brightens from –0.1 to –0.7. The waning gibbous Moon passes six degrees south of Mars on the night of the 6th.

Jupiter, magnitude –2.2, is still visible as a splendid early evening object low in the south-western sky: by the end of the month it is lost to view after about 19h. The waxing crescent Moon will be seen near the planet on the evening of the 21st. Another good opportunity for using Jupiter to assist in locating Neptune occurs around the 20th when Neptune will be found about 0.5 degrees north of Jupiter.

Saturn, magnitude +1.1, can now be seen in the south-eastern quadrant of the sky after about 02h at the beginning of the month and shortly after midnight by the end of the month. The Moon, just after Last Quarter, is in the vicinity of Saturn on the morning of the 10th, but never closer than about eight degrees.

Meteors. The maximum of the well known Geminid meteor shower occurs on the 13th, and will be best seen in the late evening of that day without interference from moonlight.

THE MOON

Day	R.A.		Dec.	Hor. Par.	Semi-diam.	Sun's Co-Long.	PA. of Br. Limb	Ph.	Age	Rise 52°		Rise 56°		Transit		Set 52°		Set 56°	
	h	*m*	°	′	′	°	°	%	*d*	*h*	*m*	*h*	*m*	*h*	*m*	*h*	*m*	*h*	*m*
1	3	11	+22,5	58.9	16.0	78	268	98	14.2	14	47	14	20	23	27	7	00	7	27
2	4	12	+24.9	59.5	16.2	90	301	100	15.2	15	37	15	07	—		8	18	8	48
3	5	17	+25.8	60.0	16.4	102	70	99	16.2	16	44	16	14	0	30	9	23	9	53
4	6	22	+24.8	60.3	16.4	114	89	96	17.2	18	05	17	39	1	34	10	12	10	39
5	7	25	+22.2	60.3	16.4	126	98	90	18.2	19	32	19	13	2	35	10	48	11	08
6	8	25	+18.1	60.1	16.4	138	105	82	19.2	21	00	20	47	3	33	11	14	11	28
7	9	21	+13.0	59.7	16.3	151	109	72	20.2	22	25	22	19	4	27	11	34	11	43
8	10	14	+7.2	59.3	16.1	163	112	61	21.2	23	48	23	47	5	17	11	51	11	55
9	11	05	+1.2	58.7	16.0	175	113	50	22.2	—		—		6	05	12	07	12	05
10	11	55	–4.7	58.1	15.8	187	112	39	23.2	1	08	1	13	6	52	12	22	12	15
11	12	44	–10.4	57.5	15.7	199	111	29	24.2	2	28	2	38	7	39	12	39	12	27
12	13	34	–15.4	57.0	15.5	211	108	20	25.2	3	46	4	02	8	28	12	59	12	42
13	14	26	–19.7	56.5	15.4	224	103	12	26.2	5	04	5	26	9	18	13	23	13	01
14	15	19	–22.9	56.0	15.3	236	97	6	27.2	6	18	6	45	10	09	13	56	13	28
15	16	14	–25.0	55.5	15.1	248	88	2	28.2	7	25	7	56	11	02	14	38	14	07
16	17	09	–25.8	55.1	15.0	260	69	0	29.2	8	21	8	52	11	55	15	30	14	59
17	18	03	–25.3	54.7	14.9	272	288	0	0.5	9	05	9	33	12	46	16	33	16	04
18	18	56	–23.6	54.4	14.8	284	267	2	1.5	9	37	10	02	13	36	17	41	17	17
19	19	46	–20.8	54.2	14.8	297	259	6	2.5	10	02	10	21	14	22	18	51	18	33
20	20	34	–17.3	54.1	14.7	309	254	11	3.5	10	22	10	36	15	06	20	01	19	48
21	21	20	–13.0	54.0	14.7	321	250	17	4.5	10	37	10	47	15	48	21	10	21	02
22	22	04	–8.3	54.2	14.8	333	248	25	5.5	10	51	10	56	16	28	22	19	22	16
23	22	47	–3.3	54.5	14.8	345	246	34	6.5	11	04	11	05	17	09	23	28	23	29
24	23	31	+2.0	54.9	15.0	358	246	43	7.5	11	17	11	13	17	50	—		—	
25	0	15	+7.2	55.5	15.1	10	247	53	8.5	11	31	11	23	18	33	0	39	0	45
26	1	02	+12.3	56.3	15.3	22	249	63	9.5	11	48	11	35	19	20	1	53	2	04
27	1	52	+17.0	57.1	15.6	34	252	72	10.5	12	09	11	51	20	11	3	10	3	28
28	2	46	+21.1	58.1	15.8	46	256	81	11.5	12	39	12	14	21	07	4	31	4	54
29	3	44	+24.1	59.0	16.1	58	262	89	12.5	13	20	12	51	22	08	5	50	6	19
30	4	47	+25.6	59.9	16.3	70	270	95	13.5	14	18	13	47	23	12	7	02	7	33
31	5	52	+25.5	60.6	16.5	83	280	99	14.5	15	34	15	05	—		8	00	8	29

MERCURY

Day	R.A.		Dec.	Diam.	Phase	Transit		5° high 52°		5° high 56°	
	h	*m*	°	″	%	*h*	*m*	*h*	*m*	*h*	*m*
1	17	29	–25.4	5	92	12	50	15	30	14	45
3	17	42	–25.6	5	90	12	56	15	34	14	47
5	17	55	–25.7	5	88	13	01	15	38	14	51
7	18	08	–25.8	5	86	13	06	15	43	14	56
9	18	21	–25.7	6	83	13	11	15	49	15	02
11	18	34	–25.5	6	80	13	15	15	56	15	10
13	18	45	–25.3	6	77	13	19	16	03	15	18
15	18	57	–24.9	6	72	13	23	16	10	15	27
17	19	07	–24.5	6	67	13	25	16	16	15	36
19	19	17	–24.0	7	61	13	26	16	22	15	44
21	19	24	–23.4	7	53	13	25	16	26	15	51
23	19	30	–22.8	8	45	13	23	16	29	15	55
25	19	34	–22.2	8	36	13	17	16	29	15	56
27	19	34	–21.6	8	27	13	09	16	25	15	54
29	19	31	–21.1	9	18	12	58	16	17	15	48
31	19	25	–20.7	9	10	12	43	16	05	15	37

VENUS

Day	R.A.		Dec.	Diam.	Phase	Transit		5° high 52°		5° high 56°	
	h	*m*	°	″	%	*h*	*m*	*h*	*m*	*h*	*m*
1	15	47	–19.1	10	99	11	08	7	34	8	00
6	16	13	–20.6	10	99	11	14	7	51	8	20
11	16	40	–21.8	10	99	11	21	8	08	8	39
16	17	07	–22.7	10	99	11	28	8	23	8	57
21	17	34	–23.3	10	100	11	36	8	35	9	12
26	18	01	–23.6	10	100	11	44	8	46	9	24
31	18	29	–23.7	10	100	11	51	8	54	9	31

MARS

Day	R.A.		Dec.	Diam.	Phase	Transit		5° high 52°		5° high 56°	
	h	*m*	°	″	%	*h*	*m*	*h*	*m*	*h*	*m*
1	9	23	+18.0	10	91	4	42	21	38	21	26
6	9	27	+17.9	10	92	4	27	21	23	21	11
11	9	30	+17.8	11	92	4	10	21	07	20	55
16	9	32	+17.9	11	93	3	52	20	48	20	36
21	9	33	+18.0	12	94	3	33	20	28	20	16
26	9	32	+18.3	12	95	3	13	20	06	19	54
31	9	30	+18.7	13	96	2	52	19	42	19	30

SUNRISE AND SUNSET

	London				*Bristol*				*Birmingham*				*Manchester*				*Newcastle*				*Glasgow*				*Belfast*			
	0° 05′		*51° 30′*		*2° 35′*		*51° 28′*		*1° 55′*		*52° 28′*		*2° 15′*		*53° 28′*		*1° 37′*		*54° 59′*		*4° 14′*		*55° 52′*		*5° 56′*		*54° 35′*	
d	*h*	*m*	*h*	*m*	*h*	*m*	*h*	*m*	*h*	*m*	*h*	*m*	*h*	*m*	*h*	*m*	*h*	*m*	*h*	*m*	*h*	*m*	*h*	*m*	*h*	*m*	*h*	*m*
1	7	44	15	55	7	54	16	05	7	56	15	58	8	02	15	54	8	08	15	43	8	23	15	49	8	23	16	03
2	7	45	15	54	7	55	16	04	7	57	15	57	8	03	15	53	8	09	15	42	8	25	15	48	8	24	16	02
3	7	46	15	54	7	56	16	04	7	58	15	56	8	05	15	53	8	11	15	42	8	26	15	47	8	26	16	01
4	7	48	15	53	7	58	16	03	8	00	15	56	8	06	15	52	8	12	15	41	8	28	15	46	8	27	16	01
5	7	49	15	53	7	59	16	03	8	01	15	55	8	08	15	51	8	14	15	40	8	29	15	46	8	28	16	00
6	7	50	15	52	8	00	16	02	8	02	15	55	8	09	15	51	8	15	15	40	8	31	15	45	8	30	15	59
7	7	51	15	52	8	01	16	02	8	04	15	55	8	10	15	51	8	16	15	39	8	32	15	44	8	31	15	59
8	7	53	15	52	8	02	16	02	8	05	15	54	8	11	15	50	8	18	15	39	8	34	15	44	8	32	15	59
9	7	54	15	52	8	04	16	02	8	06	15	54	8	13	15	50	8	19	15	39	8	35	15	44	8	34	15	58
10	7	55	15	51	8	05	16	01	8	07	15	54	8	14	15	50	8	20	15	38	8	36	15	43	8	35	15	58
11	7	56	15	51	8	06	16	01	8	08	15	54	8	15	15	50	8	21	15	38	8	37	15	43	8	36	15	58
12	7	57	15	51	8	07	16	01	8	09	15	54	8	16	15	49	8	22	15	38	8	38	15	43	8	37	15	58
13	7	58	15	51	8	08	16	01	8	10	15	54	8	17	15	49	8	23	15	38	8	39	15	43	8	38	15	58
14	7	59	15	51	8	09	16	01	8	11	15	54	8	18	15	49	8	24	15	38	8	40	15	43	8	39	15	58
15	8	00	15	51	8	09	16	02	8	12	15	54	8	19	15	50	8	25	15	38	8	41	15	43	8	40	15	58
16	8	00	15	52	8	10	16	02	8	13	15	54	8	20	15	50	8	26	15	38	8	42	15	43	8	41	15	58
17	8	01	15	52	8	11	16	02	8	13	15	54	8	20	15	50	8	27	15	38	8	43	15	43	8	42	15	58
18	8	02	15	52	8	12	16	02	8	14	15	54	8	21	15	50	8	28	15	39	8	44	15	43	8	42	15	58
19	8	02	15	53	8	12	16	03	8	15	15	55	8	22	15	51	8	28	15	39	8	45	15	44	8	43	15	59
20	8	03	15	53	8	13	16	03	8	15	15	55	8	22	15	51	8	29	15	39	8	45	15	44	8	44	15	59
21	8	04	15	53	8	13	16	04	8	16	15	56	8	23	15	51	8	29	15	40	8	46	15	44	8	44	16	00
22	8	04	15	54	8	14	16	04	8	17	15	56	8	23	15	52	8	30	15	40	8	46	15	45	8	45	16	00
23	8	05	15	54	8	14	16	05	8	17	15	57	8	24	15	53	8	30	15	41	8	47	15	46	8	45	16	01
24	8	05	15	55	8	15	16	05	8	17	15	57	8	24	15	53	8	31	15	42	8	47	15	46	8	46	16	01
25	8	05	15	56	8	15	16	06	8	18	15	58	8	24	15	54	8	31	15	42	8	47	15	47	8	46	16	02
26	8	06	15	57	8	15	16	07	8	18	15	59	8	25	15	55	8	31	15	43	8	48	15	48	8	46	16	03
27	8	06	15	57	8	16	16	07	8	18	16	00	8	25	15	55	8	31	15	44	8	48	15	49	8	46	16	04
28	8	06	15	58	8	16	16	08	8	18	16	00	8	25	15	56	8	32	15	45	8	48	15	50	8	46	16	05
29	8	06	15	59	8	16	16	09	8	18	16	01	8	25	15	57	8	32	15	46	8	48	15	51	8	46	16	05
30	8	06	16	00	8	16	16	10	8	18	16	02	8	25	15	58	8	32	15	47	8	48	15	52	8	46	16	06
31	8	06	16	01	8	16	16	11	8	18	16	03	8	25	15	59	8	31	15	48	8	47	15	53	8	46	16	08

JUPITER

Day	*R.A.*		*Dec.*		*Transit*		*5° high*			
							52°		*56°*	
	h	*m*	°	′	*h*	*m*	*h*	*m*	*h*	*m*
1	21	34.5	–15	27	16	52	20	52	20	33
11	21	40.6	–14	56	16	19	20	22	20	04
21	21	47.4	–14	20	15	47	19	53	19	36
31	21	54.9	–13	41	15	15	19	26	19	09

Diameters – equatorial 36″ polar 34″

SATURN

Day	*R.A.*		*Dec.*		*Transit*		*5° high*			
							52°		*56°*	
	h	*m*	°	′	*h*	*m*	*h*	*m*	*h*	*m*
1	12	14.4	+0	47	7	33	2	03	2	05
11	12	16.9	+0	34	6	56	1	27	1	30
21	12	18.8	+0	24	6	19	0	50	0	53
31	12	20.1	+0	19	5	41	0	13	0	16

Diameters – equatorial 17″ polar 15″
Rings – major axis 39″ minor axis 3″

URANUS

Day	*R.A.*		*Dec.*		*Transit*		*10° high*			
							52°		*56°*	
	h	*m*	°	′	*h*	*m*	*h*	*m*	*h*	*m*
1	23	34.4	–3	36	18	51	23	26	23	15
11	23	34.5	–3	35	18	12	22	46	22	36
21	23	35.0	–3	32	17	33	22	08	21	58
31	23	35.7	–3	26	16	55	21	30	21	20

Diameter 4″

NEPTUNE

Day	*R.A.*		*Dec.*		*Transit*		*10° high*			
							52°		*56°*	
	h	*m*	°	′	*h*	*m*	*h*	*m*	*h*	*m*
1	21	45.4	–13	57	17	03	20	32	20	08
11	21	46.1	–13	54	16	24	19	54	19	30
21	21	46.9	–13	49	15	46	19	16	18	52
31	21	48.0	–13	44	15	07	18	39	18	15

Diameter 2″

RISING AND SETTING TIMES

TABLE 1. SEMI-DIURNAL ARCS (HOUR ANGLES AT RISING/SETTING)

Dec.	*Latitude* 0°	10°	20°	30°	40°	45°	50°	52°	54°	56°	58°	60°	*Dec.*
	h m	*h m*	*h m*	*h m*	*h m*	*h m*	*h m*	*h m*	*h m*	*h m*	*h m*	*h m*	
0°	6 00	6 00	6 00	6 00	6 00	6 00	6 00	6 00	6 00	6 00	6 00	6 00	0°
1°	6 00	6 01	6 01	6 02	6 03	6 04	6 05	6 05	6 06	6 06	6 06	6 07	1°
2°	6 00	6 01	6 03	6 05	6 07	6 08	6 10	6 10	6 11	6 12	6 13	6 14	2°
3°	6 00	6 02	6 04	6 07	6 10	6 12	6 14	6 15	6 17	6 18	6 19	6 21	3°
4°	6 00	6 03	6 06	6 09	6 13	6 16	6 19	6 21	6 22	6 24	6 26	6 28	4°
5°	6 00	6 04	6 07	6 12	6 17	6 20	6 24	6 26	6 28	6 30	6 32	6 35	5°
6°	6 00	6 04	6 09	6 14	6 20	6 24	6 29	6 31	6 33	6 36	6 39	6 42	6°
7°	6 00	6 05	6 10	6 16	6 24	6 28	6 34	6 36	6 39	6 42	6 45	6 49	7°
8°	6 00	6 06	6 12	6 19	6 27	6 32	6 39	6 41	6 45	6 48	6 52	6 56	8°
9°	6 00	6 06	6 13	6 21	6 31	6 36	6 44	6 47	6 50	6 54	6 59	7 04	9°
10°	6 00	6 07	6 15	6 23	6 34	6 41	6 49	6 52	6 56	7 01	7 06	7 11	10°
11°	6 00	6 08	6 16	6 26	6 38	6 45	6 54	6 58	7 02	7 07	7 12	7 19	11°
12°	6 00	6 09	6 18	6 28	6 41	6 49	6 59	7 03	7 08	7 13	7 20	7 26	12°
13°	6 00	6 09	6 19	6 31	6 45	6 53	7 04	7 09	7 14	7 20	7 27	7 34	13°
14°	6 00	6 10	6 21	6 33	6 48	6 58	7 09	7 14	7 20	7 27	7 34	7 42	14°
15°	6 00	6 11	6 22	6 36	6 52	7 02	7 14	7 20	7 27	7 34	7 42	7 51	15°
16°	6 00	6 12	6 24	6 38	6 56	7 07	7 20	7 26	7 33	7 41	7 49	7 59	16°
17°	6 00	6 12	6 26	6 41	6 59	7 11	7 25	7 32	7 40	7 48	7 57	8 08	17°
18°	6 00	6 13	6 27	6 43	7 03	7 16	7 31	7 38	7 46	7 55	8 05	8 17	18°
19°	6 00	6 14	6 29	6 46	7 07	7 21	7 37	7 45	7 53	8 03	8 14	8 26	19°
20°	6 00	6 15	6 30	6 49	7 11	7 25	7 43	7 51	8 00	8 11	8 22	8 36	20°
21°	6 00	6 16	6 32	6 51	7 15	7 30	7 49	7 58	8 08	8 19	8 32	8 47	21°
22°	6 00	6 16	6 34	6 54	7 19	7 35	7 55	8 05	8 15	8 27	8 41	8 58	22°
23°	6 00	6 17	6 36	6 57	7 23	7 40	8 02	8 12	8 23	8 36	8 51	9 09	23°
24°	6 00	6 18	6 37	7 00	7 28	7 46	8 08	8 19	8 31	8 45	9 02	9 22	24°
25°	6 00	6 19	6 39	7 02	7 32	7 51	8 15	8 27	8 40	8 55	9 13	9 35	25°
26°	6 00	6 20	6 41	7 05	7 37	7 57	8 22	8 35	8 49	9 05	9 25	9 51	26°
27°	6 00	6 21	6 43	7 08	7 41	8 03	8 30	8 43	8 58	9 16	9 39	10 08	27°
28°	6 00	6 22	6 45	7 12	7 46	8 08	8 37	8 52	9 08	9 28	9 53	10 28	28°
29°	6 00	6 22	6 47	7 15	7 51	8 15	8 45	9 01	9 19	9 41	10 10	10 55	29°
30°	6 00	6 23	6 49	7 18	7 56	8 21	8 54	9 11	9 30	9 55	10 30	12 00	30°
35°	6 00	6 28	6 59	7 35	8 24	8 58	9 46	10 15	10 58	12 00	12 00	12 00	35°
40°	6 00	6 34	7 11	7 56	8 59	9 48	12 00	12 00	12 00	12 00	12 00	12 00	40°
45°	6 00	6 41	7 25	8 21	9 48	12 00	12 00	12 00	12 00	12 00	12 00	12 00	45°
50°	6 00	6 49	7 43	8 54	12 00	12 00	12 00	12 00	12 00	12 00	12 00	12 00	50°
55°	6 00	6 58	8 05	9 42	12 00	12 00	12 00	12 00	12 00	12 00	12 00	12 00	55°
60°	6 00	7 11	8 36	12 00	12 00	12 00	12 00	12 00	12 00	12 00	12 00	12 00	60°
65°	6 00	7 29	9 25	12 00	12 00	12 00	12 00	12 00	12 00	12 00	12 00	12 00	65°
70°	6 00	7 56	12 00	12 00	12 00	12 00	12 00	12 00	12 00	12 00	12 00	12 00	70°
75°	6 00	8 45	12 00	12 00	12 00	12 00	12 00	12 00	12 00	12 00	12 00	12 00	75°
80°	6 00	12 00	12 00	12 00	12 00	12 00	12 00	12 00	12 00	12 00	12 00	12 00	80°

Note: If latitude and declination are of the same sign, take out the respondent directly. If they are of opposite signs, subtract the respondent from 12h.

Table 1 gives the complete range of declinations in case any user wishes to calculate semi-diurnal arcs for bodies other than the Sun and Moon.

Example:

Lat.	Dec.	Semi-diurnal arc
+52°	+20°	7h 51m
+52°	−20°	4h 09m

TABLE 2. CORRECTION FOR REFRACTION AND SEMI-DIAMETER

	m	*m*	*m*	*m*	*m*	*m*	*m*	*m*	*m*	*m*	*m*	*m*	*m*
0°	3	3	4	4	4	5	5	5	6	6	6	7	0°
10°	3	3	4	4	4	5	5	6	6	6	7	7	10°
20°	4	4	4	4	5	5	6	7	7	8	8	9	20°
25°	4	4	4	4	5	6	7	8	8	9	11	13	25°
30°	4	4	4	5	6	7	8	9	11	14	21	—	30°

SUNRISE AND SUNSET

The local mean time of sunrise or sunset may be found by obtaining the hour angle from Table 1 and applying it to the time of transit. The hour angle is negative for sunrise and positive for sunset. A small correction to the hour angle, which always has the effect of increasing it numerically, is necessary to allow for the Sun's semi-diameter (16′) and for refraction (34′); it is obtained from Table 2. The resulting local mean time may be converted into the standard time of the country by taking the difference between the longitude of the standard meridian of the country and that of the place, adding it to the local mean time if the place is west of the standard meridian, and subtracting it if the place is east.

Example – Required the New Zealand Mean Time (12h fast on GMT) of sunset on May 23 at Auckland, latitude 36° 50′ S. (or minus), longitude 11h 39m E. Taking the declination as +20°.6 (page 1245), we find

		h	*m*
New Zealand Standard Time	+	12	00
Longitude	–	11	39
Longitudinal Correction	+	0	21
Tabular entry for Lat. 30° and Dec. 20°, opposite signs	+	5	11
Proportional part for 6° 50′ of Lat.	–		15
Proportional part for 0°.6 of Dec.	–		2
Correction (Table 2)	+		4
Hour angle		4	58
Sun transits (page 1245)		11	57
Longitudinal correction	+		21
New Zealand Mean Time		17	16

MOONRISE AND MOONSET

It is possible to calculate the times of moonrise and moonset using Table 1, though the method is more complicated because the apparent motion of the Moon is much more rapid and also more variable than that of the Sun.

TABLE 3. LONGITUDE CORRECTION

X / *A*	*40m*	*45m*	*50m*	*55m*	*60m*	*65m*	*70m*
h	*m*	*m*	*m*	*m*	*m*	*m*	*m*
1	2	2	2	2	3	3	3
2	3	4	4	5	5	5	6
3	5	6	6	7	8	8	9
4	7	8	8	9	10	11	12
5	8	9	10	11	13	14	15
6	10	11	13	14	15	16	18
7	12	13	15	16	18	19	20
8	13	15	17	18	20	22	23
9	15	17	19	21	23	24	26
10	17	19	21	23	25	27	29
11	18	21	23	25	28	30	32
12	20	23	25	28	30	33	35
13	22	24	27	30	33	35	38
14	23	26	29	32	35	38	41
15	25	28	31	34	38	41	44
16	27	30	33	37	40	43	47
17	28	32	35	39	43	46	50
18	30	34	38	41	45	49	53
19	32	36	40	44	48	51	55
20	33	38	42	46	50	54	58
21	35	39	44	48	53	57	61
22	37	41	46	50	55	60	64
23	38	43	48	53	58	62	67
24	40	45	50	55	60	65	70

The parallax of the Moon, about 57′, is near to the sum of the semi-diameter and refraction but has the opposite effect on these times. It is thus convenient to neglect all three quantities in the method outlined below.

Notation

ϕ = latitude of observer
λ = longitude of observer (measured positively towards the west)
T_{-1} = time of transit of Moon on previous day
T_0 = time of transit of Moon on day in question
T_1 = time of transit of Moon on following day
δ_0 = approximate declination of Moon
δ_R = declination of Moon at moonrise
δ_S = declination of Moon at moonset
h_0 = approximate hour angle of Moon
h_R = hour angle of Moon at moonrise
h_S = hour angle of Moon at moonset
t_R = time of moonrise
t_S = time of moonset

Method

1. With arguments ϕ, δ_0 enter Table 1 on page 1276 to determine h_0 where h_0 is negative for moonrise and positive for moonset.
2. Form approximate times from
   $t_R = T_0 + \lambda + h_0$
   $t_S = T_0 + \lambda + h_0$
3. Determine δ_R, δ_S for times t_R, t_S respectively.
4. Re-enter Table 1 (as above) with
   (*a*) arguments ϕ, δ_R to determine h_R
   (*b*) arguments ϕ, δ_S to determine h_S
5. Form $t_R = T_0 + \lambda + h_R + AX$
   $t_S = T_0 + \lambda + h_S + AX$

where $A = (\lambda + h)$

and $X = (T_0 - T_{-1})$ if $(\lambda + h)$ is negative
$X = (T_1 - T_0)$ if $(\lambda + h)$ is positive

AX is the respondent in Table 3.

Example – To find the times of moonrise and moonset at Vancouver (ϕ = +49°, λ = +8h 12m) on 2009 January 21. The starting data (page 1230) are

T_{-1} = 7h 26m
T_0 = 8h 15m
T_1 = 9h 06m
δ_0 = –26°

1. h_0 = 3h 43m
2. Approximate values
   t_R = 21d 08h 15m + 8h 12m + (–3h 43m)
   = 21d 12h 44m
   t_S = 21d 08h 15m + 8h 12m + (+3h 43m)
   = 21d 20h 10m
3. δ_R = –26°.3
   δ_S = –26°.8
4. h_R = – 3h 41m
   h_S = +3h 37m
5. t_R = 21d 08h 15m + 8h 12m + (–3h 41m) + 9m
   = 21d 12h 55m
   t_S = 21d 08h 15m + 8h 12m + (+3h 37m) + 26m
   = 21d 20h 30m

To get the LMT of the phenomenon the longitude is subtracted from the GMT thus:

Moonrise = 21d 12h 55m – 8h 12m = 21d 04h 43m
Moonset = 21d 20h 30m – 8h 12m = 21d 12h 18m

ECLIPSES 2009

ECLIPSES

During 2009 there will be three eclipses, two of the Sun and one of the Moon. (Penumbral eclipses of the Moon are not mentioned in this section as they are so difficult to observe.)

1. An annular eclipse of the Sun on January 26 is visible as a partial eclipse from southern Africa, the southern Ocean, part of Antarctica, the Indian Ocean, Madagascar, southern and eastern India, part of southwest Asia, Indonesia, and Australia. The partial phase begins at 04h 57m and ends at 11h 01m. The track of annularity begins in the Southern Ocean, south of south Africa, at 06h 03m. It then crosses the Indian Ocean, southern Sumatra and Borneo before ending in the Celebes Sea at 09h 55m. The maximum duration of annularity is 7m 53s.

2. A total eclipse of the Sun on July 21–22 is visible as a partial eclipse from the eastern part of Africa, Madagascar, Asia, part of Indonesia, the north-eastern tip of Australia, and the extreme northern part of North Island, New Zealand. The partial phase begins at 21d 23h 58m and ends at 22d 05h 12m. The path of totality begins just off the west coast of India, crosses India, the extreme north of Burma, China, and ends in the Pacific Ocean among the Hawaiian Islands. Totality begins at 22d 00h 51m and ends at 22d 04h 19m. The maximum duration of totality is 6m 39s.

3. A partial eclipse of the Moon on December 31 is visible from Australasia, Asia, the Indian Ocean, Africa, Europe, Iceland, the Atlantic Ocean, Greenland, northern Canada, Alaska and part of eastern Brazil. The eclipse begins at 18h 52m and ends at 21h 30m. Only 8 per cent of the Moon's surface is obscured at maximum eclipse.

POSITIONS OF STARS

The positions of heavenly bodies on the celestial sphere are defined by two co-ordinates, right ascension and declination, which are analogous to longitude and latitude on the surface of the Earth. If we imagine the plane of the terrestrial equator extended indefinitely, it will cut the celestial sphere in a great circle known as the celestial equator. Similarly the plane of the Earth's orbit, when extended, cuts in the great circle called the ecliptic. The two intersections of these circles are known as the First Point of Aries and the First Point of Libra. If from any star a perpendicular is drawn to the celestial equator, the length of this perpendicular is the star's declination. The arc, measured eastwards along the equator from the First Point of Aries to the foot of this perpendicular, is the right ascension. An alternative definition of right ascension is that it is the angle at the celestial pole (where the Earth's axis, if prolonged, would meet the sphere) between the great circles to the First Point of Aries and to the star.

The plane of the Earth's equator has a slow movement, so that our reference system for right ascension and declination is not fixed. The consequent alteration in these quantities from year to year is called precession. In right ascension it is an increase of about 3 seconds a year for equatorial stars, and larger or smaller changes in either direction for stars near the poles, depending on the right ascension of the star. In declination it varies between +20″ and −20″ according to the right ascension of the star.

A star or other body crosses the meridian when the sidereal time is equal to its right ascension. The altitude is then a maximum, and may be deduced by remembering that the altitude of the elevated pole is numerically equal to the latitude, while that of the equator at its intersection with the meridian is equal to the co-latitude, or complement of the latitude.

Thus in London (lat. 51° 30′) the meridian altitude of Sirius is found as follows:

	°	′
Altitude of equator	38	30
Declination south	16	43
Difference	21	47

The altitude of Capella (Dec. +46° 00′) at lower transit is:

Altitude of pole	51	30
Polar distance of star	44	00
Difference	7	30

The brightness of a heavenly body is denoted by its magnitude. Omitting the exceptionally bright stars Sirius and Canopus, the twenty brightest stars are of the first magnitude, while the faintest stars visible to the naked eye are of the sixth magnitude. The magnitude scale is a precise one, as a difference of five magnitudes represents a ratio of 100 to 1 in brightness. Typical second magnitude stars are Polaris and the stars in the belt of Orion. The scale is most easily fixed in memory by comparing the stars with Norton's *Star Atlas*. The stars Sirius and Canopus and the planets Venus and Jupiter are so bright that their magnitudes are expressed by negative numbers. A small telescope will show stars down to the ninth or tenth magnitude, while stars fainter than the twentieth magnitude may be photographed by long exposures with the largest telescopes.

MEAN AND SIDEREAL TIME

The length of a sidereal day in mean time is 23h 56m 04s.09. Hence 1h MT = 1h+$9^{s}.86$ ST and 1h ST = 1h − $9^{s}.83$ MT.

Acceleration

h	*m*	*s*	*m*	*s*	*s*
1	0	10	0	00	
2	0	20	3	02	0
3	0	30	9	07	1
4	0	39	15	13	2
5	0	49	21	18	3
6	0	59	27	23	4
7	1	09	33	28	5
8	1	19	39	34	6
9	1	29	45	39	7
10	1	39	51	44	8
11	1	48	57	49	9
12	1	58	60	00	10
13	2	08			
14	2	18			
15	2	28			
16	2	38			
17	2	48			
18	2	57			
19	3	07			
20	3	17			
21	3	27			
22	3	37			
23	3	47			
24	3	57			

Retardation

h	*m*	*s*	*m*	*s*	*s*
1	0	10	0	00	
2	0	20	3	03	0
3	0	29	9	09	1
4	0	39	15	15	2
5	0	49	21	21	3
6	0	59	27	28	4
7	1	09	33	34	5
8	1	19	39	40	6
9	1	28	45	46	7
10	1	38	51	53	8
11	1	48	57	59	9
12	1	58	60	00	10
13	2	08			
14	2	18			
15	2	27			
16	2	37			
17	2	47			
18	2	57			
19	3	07			
20	3	17			
21	3	26			
22	3	36			
23	3	46			
24	3	56			

To convert an interval of mean time to the corresponding interval of sidereal time, enter the acceleration table with the given mean time (taking the hours and the minutes and seconds separately) and add the acceleration obtained to the given mean time. To convert an interval of sidereal time to the corresponding interval of mean time, take out the retardation for the given sidereal time and subtract.

The columns for the minutes and seconds of the argument are in the form known as critical tables. To use these tables, find in the appropriate left-hand column the two entries between which the given number of minutes and seconds lies; the quantity in the right-hand column between these two entries is the required acceleration or retardation. Thus the acceleration for 11m 26s (which lies between the entries 9m 07s and 15m 13s) is 2s. If the given number of minutes and seconds is a tabular entry, the required acceleration or retardation is the entry in the right-hand column above the given tabular entry, eg the retardation for 45m 46s is 7s.

Example – Convert 14h 27m 35s from ST to MT

	h	*m*	*s*
Given ST	14	27	35
Retardation for 14h		2	18
Retardation for 27m 35s			5
Corresponding MT	14	25	12

EXPLANATION OF ASTRONOMICAL DATA

Positions of the heavenly bodies are given only to the degree of accuracy required by amateur astronomers for setting telescopes, or for plotting on celestial globes or star atlases. Where intermediate positions are required, linear interpolation may be employed.

Definitions of the terms used cannot be given here. They must be sought in astronomical literature and textbooks.

A special feature has been made of the times when the various heavenly bodies are visible in the British Isles. Since two columns, calculated for latitudes 52° and 56°, are devoted to risings and settings, the range 50° to 58° can be covered by interpolation and extrapolation. The times given in these columns are Greenwich Mean Times for the meridian of Greenwich. An observer west of this meridian must add his/her longitude (in time) and vice versa.

In accordance with the usual convention in astronomy, + and – indicate respectively north and south latitudes or declinations.

All data are, unless otherwise stated, for 0h Greenwich Mean Time (GMT), ie at the midnight at the beginning of the day named. Allowance must be made for British Summer Time during the period that this is in operation.

PAGE ONE OF EACH MONTH

The calendar for each month is explained on page 1227.

Under the heading Astronomical Phenomena will be found particulars of the more important conjunctions of the Sun, Moon and planets with each other, and also the dates of other astronomical phenomena of special interest.

Times of Minima of Algol are approximate times of the middle of the period of diminished light.

The Constellations listed each month are those that are near the meridian at the beginning of the month at 22h local mean time. Allowance must be made for British Summer Time if necessary. The fact that any star crosses the meridian 4m earlier each night or 2h earlier each month may be used, in conjunction with the lists given each month, to find what constellations are favourably placed at any moment. The table preceding the list of constellations may be extended indefinitely at the rate just quoted.

The principal phases of the Moon are the GMTs when the difference between the longitude of the Moon and that of the Sun is 0°, 90°, 180° or 270°. The times of perigee and apogee are those when the Moon is nearest to, and farthest from, the Earth, respectively. The nodes or points of intersection of the Moon's orbit and the ecliptic make a complete retrograde circuit of the ecliptic in about 19 years. From a knowledge of the longitude of the ascending node and the inclination, whose value does not vary much from 5°, the path of the Moon among the stars may be plotted on a celestial globe or star atlas.

PAGE TWO OF EACH MONTH

The Sun's semi-diameter, in arc, is given once a month.

The right ascension and declination (Dec.) is that of the true Sun. The right ascension of the mean Sun is obtained by applying the equation of time, with the sign given, to the right ascension of the true Sun, or, more easily, by applying 12h to the Sidereal Time. The direction in which the equation of time has to be applied in different problems is a frequent source of confusion and error. Apparent Solar Time is equal to the Mean Solar Time plus the Equation of Time. For example, at 12h GMT on August 8 the Equation of Time is –5m 37s and thus at 12h Mean Time on that day the Apparent Time is 12h – 5m 37s = 11h 54m 23s.

The Greenwich Sidereal Time at 0h and the Transit of the First Point of Aries (which is really the mean time when the sidereal time is 0h) are used for converting mean time to sidereal time and vice versa.

The GMT of transit of the Sun at Greenwich may also be taken as the local mean time (LMT) of transit in any longitude. It is independent of latitude. The GMT of transit in any longitude is obtained by adding the longitude to the time given if west, and vice versa.

LIGHTING-UP TIME

The legal importance of sunrise and sunset is that the Road Vehicles Lighting Regulations 1989 (SI 1989 No. 1796) as amended make the use of front and rear position lamps on vehicles compulsory during the period between sunset and sunrise. Headlamps on vehicles are required to be used during the hours of darkness on unlit roads, on lit roads with a speed limit exceeding 30mph, or whenever visibility is seriously reduced. The hours of darkness are defined in these regulations as the period between half an hour after sunset and half an hour before sunrise.

In all laws and regulations 'sunset' refers to the local sunset, ie the time at which the Sun sets at the place in question. This common-sense interpretation has been upheld by legal tribunals. Thus the necessity for providing for different latitudes and longitudes, as already described, is evident.

SUNRISE AND SUNSET

The times of sunrise and sunset are those when the Sun's upper limb, as affected by refraction, is on the true horizon of an observer at sea-level. Assuming the mean refraction to be 34′, and the Sun's semi-diameter to be 16′, the time given is that when the true zenith distance of the Sun's centre is 90°+34′+16′ or 90° 50′, or, in other words, when the depression of the Sun's centre below the true horizon is 50′. The upper limb is then 34′ below the true horizon, but is brought there by refraction. An observer on a ship might see the Sun for a minute or so longer, because of the dip of the horizon, while another viewing the sunset over hills or mountains would record an earlier time. Nevertheless, the moment when the true zenith distance of the Sun's centre is 90° 50′ is a precise time dependent only on the latitude and longitude of the place, and independent of its altitude above sea-level, the contour of its horizon, the vagaries of refraction or the small seasonal change in the Sun's semi-diameter; this moment is suitable in every way as a definition of sunset (or sunrise) for all statutory purposes.

TWILIGHT

Light reaches us before sunrise and continues to reach us for some time after sunset. The interval between darkness and sunrise or sunset and darkness is called twilight. Astronomically speaking, twilight is considered to begin or end when the Sun's centre is 18° below the horizon, as no light from the Sun can then reach the observer. As thus defined twilight may last several hours; in high latitudes at the summer solstice the depression of 18° is not reached, and twilight lasts from sunset to sunrise.

The need for some sub-division of twilight is met by dividing the gathering darkness into four stages.

(1) *Sunrise or Sunset,* defined as above
(2) *Civil twilight,* which begins or ends when the Sun's centre is 6° below the horizon. This marks the time when operations requiring daylight may commence or must cease. In England it varies from about 30 to 60 minutes after sunset and the same interval before sunrise
(3) *Nautical twilight,* which begins or ends when the Sun's centre is 12° below the horizon. This marks the time when it is, to all intents and purposes, completely dark
(4) *Astronomical twilight,* which begins or ends when the Sun's centre is 18° below the horizon. This marks theoretical perfect darkness. It is of little practical importance, especially if nautical twilight is tabulated

To assist observers the durations of civil, nautical and astronomical twilights are given at intervals of ten days. The beginning of a particular twilight is found by subtracting the duration from the time of sunrise, while the end is found by adding the duration to the time of sunset. Thus the beginning of astronomical twilight in latitude 52°, on the Greenwich meridian, on March 11 is found as 06h 23m − 113m = 04h 30m and similarly the end of civil twilight as 17h 58m +34m = 18h 32m. The letters TAN (twilight all night) are printed when twilight lasts all night.

Under the heading The Night Sky will be found notes describing the position and visibility of the planets and other phenomena.

PAGE THREE OF EACH MONTH

The Moon moves so rapidly among the stars that its position is given only to the degree of accuracy that permits linear interpolation. The right ascension (RA) and declination (Dec.) are geocentric, ie for an imaginary observer at the centre of the Earth. To an observer on the surface of the Earth the position is always different, as the altitude is always less on account of parallax, which may reach 1°.

The lunar terminator is the line separating the bright from the dark part of the Moon's disk. Apart from irregularities of the lunar surface, the terminator is elliptical, because it is a circle seen in projection. It becomes the full circle forming the limb, or edge, of the Moon at New and Full Moon. The selenographic longitude of the terminator is measured from the mean centre of the visible disk, which may differ from the visible centre by as much as 8°, because of libration.

Instead of the longitude of the terminator the Sun's selenographic co-longitude (Sun's co-long.) is tabulated. It is numerically equal to the selenographic longitude of the morning terminator, measured eastwards from the mean centre of the disk. Thus its value is approximately 270° at New Moon, 360° at First Quarter, 90° at Full Moon and 180° at Last Quarter.

The Position Angle (PA) of the Bright Limb is the position angle of the midpoint of the illuminated limb, measured eastwards from the north point on the disk. The Phase column shows the percentage of the area of the Moon's disk illuminated; this is also the illuminated percentage of the diameter at right angles to the line of cusps. The terminator is a semi-ellipse whose major axis is the line of cusps, and whose semi-minor axis is determined by the tabulated percentage; from New Moon to Full Moon the east limb is dark, and vice versa.

The times given as moonrise and moonset are those when the upper limb of the Moon is on the horizon of an observer at sea-level. The Sun's horizontal parallax (Hor. par.) is about 9″, and is negligible when considering sunrise and sunset, but that of the Moon averages about 57′. Hence the computed time represents the moment when the true zenith distance of the Moon is 90° 50′ (as for the Sun) minus the horizontal parallax. The time required for the Sun or Moon to rise or set is about four minutes (except in high latitudes).

See also page 1277 and footnote on page 1281.

The GMT of transit of the Moon over the meridian of Greenwich is given; these times are independent of latitude but must be corrected for longitude. For places in the British Isles it suffices to add the longitude if west, and vice versa. For other places a further correction is necessary because of the rapid movement of the Moon relative to the stars. The entire correction is conveniently determined by first finding the west longitude λ of the place. If the place is in west longitude, λ is the ordinary west longitude; if the place is in east longitude λ is the complement to 24h (or 360°) of the longitude and will be greater than 12h (or 180°). The correction then consists of two positive portions, namely λ and the fraction λ/24 (or λ°/360) multiplied by the difference between consecutive transits. Thus for Christchurch, New Zealand, the longitude is 11h 31m east, so λ = 12h 29m and the fraction λ/24 is 0.52. The transit on the local date 16 January 2009 is found as follows:

		d	*h*	*m*
GMT of transit at Greenwich	January	15	03	37
λ			12	29
0.52 × (3h 37m − 2h 49m)				25
GMT of transit at Christchurch		15	16	31
Corr. to NZ Standard Time			12	00
Local standard time of transit	January	16	04	31

As is evident, for any given place the quantities λ and the correction to local standard time may be combined permanently, being here 24h 29m.

Positions of Mercury are given for every second day, and those of Venus and Mars for every fifth day; they may be interpolated linearly. The diameter (Diam.) is given in seconds of arc. The phase is the illuminated percentage of the disk. In the case of the inner planets this approaches 100 at superior conjunction and 0 at inferior conjunction.

When the phase is less than 50 the planet is crescent-shaped or horned; for greater phases it is gibbous. In the case of the exterior planet Mars, the phase approaches 100 at conjunction and opposition, and is a minimum at the quadratures.

Since the planets cannot be seen when on the horizon, the actual times of rising and setting are not given; instead, the time when the planet has an apparent altitude of 5° has been tabulated. If the time of transit is between 00h and 12h the time refers to an altitude of 5° above the eastern horizon; if between 12h and 24h, to the western horizon. The phenomenon tabulated is the one that occurs between sunset and sunrise. The times given may be interpolated for latitude and corrected for longitude, as in the case of the Sun and Moon.

PAGE FOUR OF EACH MONTH

The GMTs of sunrise and sunset for seven cities, whose adopted positions in longitude (W.) and latitude (N.) are given immediately below the name, may be used not only for these phenomena, but also for lighting-up times (*see* page 1279 for a fuller explanation).

The particulars for the four outer planets resemble those for the planets on Page Three of each month, except that, under Uranus and Neptune, times when the planet is 10° high instead of 5° high are given; this is because of the inferior brightness of these planets. The diameters given for the rings of Saturn are those of the major axis (in the plane of the planet's equator) and the minor axis respectively. The former has a small seasonal change due to the slightly varying distance of the Earth from Saturn, but the latter varies from zero when the Earth passes through the ring plane every 15 years to its maximum opening half-way between these periods. The rings were last open at their widest extent (and Saturn at its brightest) in 2002; this will occur again in 2017. The Earth passed through the ring plane in 1995–6 and will do so again in 2009.

TIME

From the earliest ages, the natural division of time into recurring periods of day and night has provided the practical time-scale for the everyday activities of the human race. Indeed, if any alternative means of time measurement is adopted, it must be capable of adjustment so as to remain in general agreement with the natural time-scale defined by the diurnal rotation of the Earth on its axis. Ideally the rotation should be measured against a fixed frame of reference; in practice it must be measured against the background provided by the celestial bodies. If the Sun is chosen as the reference point, we obtain Apparent Solar Time, which is the time indicated by a sundial. It is not a uniform time but is subject to variations which amount to as much as a quarter of an hour in each direction. Such wide variations cannot be tolerated in a practical time-scale, and this has led to the concept of Mean Solar Time in which all the days are exactly the same length and equal to the average length of the Apparent Solar Day.

The positions of the stars in the sky are specified in relation to a fictitious reference point in the sky known as the First Point of Aries (or the Vernal Equinox). It is therefore convenient to adopt this same reference point when considering the rotation of the Earth against the background of the stars. The time-scale so obtained is known as Apparent Sidereal Time.

GREENWICH MEAN TIME

The daily rotation of the Earth on its axis causes the Sun and the other heavenly bodies to appear to cross the sky from east to west. It is convenient to represent this relative motion as if the Sun really performed a daily circuit around a fixed Earth. Noon in Apparent Solar Time may then be defined as the time at which the Sun transits across the observer's meridian. In Mean Solar Time, noon is similarly defined by the meridian transit of a fictitious Mean Sun moving uniformly in the sky with the same average speed as the true Sun. Mean Solar Time observed on the meridian of the transit circle telescope of the Royal Observatory at Greenwich is called Greenwich Mean Time (GMT). The mean solar day is divided into 24 hours and, for astronomical and other scientific purposes, these are numbered 0 to 23, commencing at midnight. Civil time is usually reckoned in two periods of 12 hours, designated am (*ante meridiem,* ie before noon) and pm (*post meridiem,* ie after noon), although the 24 hour clock is increasingly being used.

UNIVERSAL TIME

Before 1925 January 1, GMT was reckoned in 24 hours commencing at noon; since that date it has been reckoned from midnight. To avoid confusion in the use of the designation GMT before and after 1925, since 1928 astronomers have tended to use the term Universal Time (UT) or Weltzeit (WZ) to denote GMT measured from Greenwich Mean Midnight.

In precision work it is necessary to take account of small variations in Universal Time. These arise from small irregularities in the rotation of the Earth. Observed astronomical time is designated UT0. Observed time corrected for the effects of the motion of the poles (giving rise to a 'wandering' in longitude) is designated UT1. There is also a seasonal fluctuation in the rate of rotation of the Earth arising from meteorological causes, often called the annual fluctuation. UT1 corrected for this effect is designated UT2 and provides a time-scale free from short-period fluctuations. It is still subject to small secular and irregular changes.

APPARENT SOLAR TIME

As mentioned above, the time shown by a sundial is called Apparent Solar Time. It differs from Mean Solar Time by an amount known as the Equation of Time, which is the total effect of two causes which make the length of the apparent solar day non-uniform. One cause of variation is that the orbit of the Earth is not a circle but an ellipse, having the Sun at one focus. As a consequence, the

---

SUNRISE, SUNSET, MOONRISE AND MOONSET

The tables have been constructed for the meridian of Greenwich and for latitudes 52° and 56°. They give Greenwich Mean Time (GMT) throughout the year. To obtain the GMT of the phenomenon as seen from any other latitude and longitude in the British Isles, first interpolate or extrapolate for latitude by the usual rules of proportion. To the time thus found, the longitude (expressed in time) is to be added if west (as it usually is in Great Britain) or subtracted if east. If the longitude is expressed in degrees and minutes of arc, it must be converted to time at the rate of 1° = 4m and 15′ = 1m. A method of calculating rise and set time for other places in the world is given on page 1277.

The GMT at which the planet transits the Greenwich meridian is also given. The times of transit are to be corrected to local meridians in the usual way, as already described.

angular speed of the Earth in its orbit is not constant; it is greatest at the beginning of January when the Earth is nearest the Sun.

The other cause is due to the obliquity of the ecliptic; the plane of the equator (which is at right angles to the axis of rotation of the Earth) does not coincide with the ecliptic (the plane defined by the apparent annual motion of the Sun around the celestial sphere) but is inclined to it at an angle of 23° 26′. As a result, the apparent solar day is shorter than average at the equinoxes and longer at the solstices. From the combined effects of the components due to obliquity and eccentricity, the equation of time reaches its maximum values in February (−14 minutes) and early November (+16 minutes). It has a zero value on four dates during the year, and it is only on these dates (approximately April 15, June 14, September 1 and December 25) that a sundial shows Mean Solar Time.

SIDEREAL TIME

A sidereal day is the duration of a complete rotation of the Earth with reference to the First Point of Aries. The term sidereal (or 'star') time is a little misleading since the time-scale so defined is not exactly the same as that which would be defined by successive transits of a selected star, as there is a small progressive motion between the stars and the First Point of Aries due to the precession of the Earth's axis. This makes the length of the sidereal day shorter than the true period of rotation by 0.008 seconds. Superimposed on this steady precessional motion are small oscillations (nutation), giving rise to fluctuations in apparent sidereal time amounting to as much as 1.2 seconds. It is therefore customary to employ Mean Sidereal Time, from which these fluctuations have been removed. The conversion of GMT to Greenwich sidereal time (GST) may be performed by adding the value of the GST at 0h on the day in question (page two of each month) to the GMT converted to sidereal time using the table on page 1278.

Example – To find the GST at August 8d 02h 41m 11s GMT

	h	*m*	*s*
GST at 0h	21	06	33
GMT	2	41	11
Acceleration for 2h			20
Acceleration for 41m 11s			7
Sum = GST =	23	48	11

If the observer is not on the Greenwich meridian then his/her longitude, measured positively westwards from Greenwich, must be subtracted from the GST to obtain Local Sidereal Time (LST). Thus, in the above example, an observer 5h east of Greenwich, or 19h west, would find the LST as 4h 48m 11s.

EPHEMERIS TIME

An analysis of observations of the positions of the Sun, Moon and planets taken over an extended period is used in preparing ephemerides. (An ephemeris is a table giving the apparent position of a heavenly body at regular intervals of time, eg one day or ten days, and may be used to compare current observations with tabulated positions.) Discrepancies between the positions of heavenly bodies observed over a 300-year period and their predicted positions arose because the time-scale to which the observations were related was based on the assumption that the rate of rotation of the Earth is uniform. It is now known that this rate of rotation is variable. A revised time-scale, Ephemeris Time (ET), was devised to bring the ephemerides into agreement with the observations.

The second of ET is defined in terms of the annual motion of the Earth in its orbit around the Sun (1/31556925.9747 of the tropical year for 1900 January 0d 12h ET). The precise determination of ET from astronomical observations is a lengthy process as the requisite standard of accuracy can only be achieved by averaging over a number of years.

In 1976 the International Astronomical Union adopted Terrestrial Dynamical Time (TDT), a new dynamical time-scale for general use whose scale unit is the SI second (*see* Atomic Time, below). TDT was renamed Terrestrial Time (TT) in 1991. ET is now of little more than historical interest.

TERRESTRIAL TIME

The uniform time system used in computing the ephemerides of the solar system is Terrestrial Time (TT), which has replaced ET for this purpose. Except for the most rigorous astronomical calculations, it may be assumed to be the same as ET. During 2009 the estimated difference TT − UT is about 66 seconds.

ATOMIC TIME

The fundamental standards of time and frequency must be defined in terms of a periodic motion adequately uniform, enduring and measurable. Progress has made it possible to use natural standards, such as atomic or molecular oscillations. Continuous oscillations are generated in an electrical circuit, the frequency of which is then compared or brought into coincidence with the frequency characteristic of the absorption or emission by the atoms or molecules when they change between two selected energy levels. Since the 13th General Conference on Weights and Measures in October 1967, the unit of time, the second, has been defined in the International System of units (SI) as 'the duration of 9 192 631 770 periods of the radiation corresponding to the transition between the two hyperfine levels of the ground state of the caesium-133 atom.'

In the UK, the national time scale is maintained by the National Physical Laboratory (NPL), using an ensemble of atomic clocks based on either caesium or hydrogen atoms. In addition the NPL (along with several other national laboratories) has constructed and operates a caesium fountain primary frequency standard, which utilises the cooling of caesium atoms by laser light to determine the duration of the SI second at the highest attainable level of accuracy. Caesium fountain primary standards typically achieve an accuracy of around 1 part in 1,000 000 000 000 000, which is equivalent to one second in 30 million years.

Timekeeping worldwide is based on two closely related atomic time scales that are established through international collaboration. International Atomic Time (TAI) is formed by combining the readings of more than 250 atomic clocks located in about 55 institutes and was set close to the astronomically-based Universal Time (UT) near the beginning of 1958. It was formally recognised in 1971 and since 1988 January 1 has been maintained by the International Bureau of Weights and Measures (BIPM). Civil time in almost all countries is now based on Coordinated Universal Time (UTC), which differs from TAI by an integer number of seconds and was designed to make both atomic time and UT available with accuracy appropriate for most users. On 1 January 1972 UTC was set to be exactly 10 seconds behind TAI, and since then the UTC time-scale has been adjusted by the insertion (or, in principle, omission) of leap seconds in order to keep it within ±0.9 s of UT. These leap seconds are introduced, when necessary, at the same instant throughout the world, either at the end of December or at the end of June. The last leap second occurred immediately prior to 0h UTC on 2006 January 1 and was the 23rd leap second. All leap seconds so far have been positive, with 61 seconds in the final minute of the UTC month. The time 23h 59m 60s UTC is followed one second later by 0h 0m 00s of the first day of the following month. Notices concerning the insertion of leap seconds are issued by the International Earth Rotation and Reference Systems Service at the Observatoire de Paris.

The computation of UTC is carried out monthly by the BIPM and takes place in three stages. First, a weighted average known as Echelle Atomique Libre (EAL) is calculated from all of the contributing atomic clocks. In the second stage, TAI is generated by applying small corrections, derived from the results contributed by primary frequency standards, to the scale interval of EAL to maintain its value close to that of the SI second. Finally, UTC is formed from TAI by the addition of an integer number of seconds. The results are published monthly in the BIPM Circular T in the form of offsets at 5-day intervals between UTC and the time scales of contributing organisations.

RADIO TIME-SIGNALS

UTC is made generally available through time-signals and standard frequency broadcasts such as MSF in the UK, CHU in Canada and WWV and WWVH in the USA. These are based on national time-scales that are maintained in close agreement with UTC and provide traceability to the national time-scale and to UTC. The markers of seconds in the UTC scale coincide with those of TAI.

To disseminate the national time-scale in the UK, special signals (call-sign MSF) are broadcast by the National Physical Laboratory. From 2007 April 1 the MSF service, previously broadcast from British Telecom's radio station at Rugby, has been transmitted from Anthorn radio station in Cumbria. The signals are controlled from a caesium beam atomic frequency standard and consist of a precise frequency carrier of 60 kHz which is switched off, after being on for at least half a second, to mark every second. The first second of the minute begins with a period of 500 ms with the carrier switched off, to serve as a minute marker. In the other seconds the carrier is always off for at least one tenth of a second at the start and then it carries an on-off code giving the British clock time and date, together with information identifying the start of the next minute. Changes to and from summer time are made following government announcements. Leap seconds are inserted as announced by the IERS and information provided by them on the difference between UTC and UT is also signalled. Other broadcast signals in the UK include the BBC six pips signal, the BT Timeline ('speaking clock'), the NPL telephone and internet time services for computers, and a coded time-signal on the BBC 198 kHz transmitters which is used for timing in the electricity supply industry. From 1972 January 1 the six pips on the BBC have consisted of five short pips from second 55 to second 59 (six pips in the case of a leap second) followed by one lengthened pip, the start of which indicates the exact minute. From 1990 February 5 these signals have been controlled by the BBC with seconds markers referenced to the satellite-based US navigation system GPS (Global Positioning System) and time and day referenced to the MSF transmitter. Formerly they were generated by the Royal Greenwich Observatory. The NPL telephone and internet services are directly connected to the national time scale.

Accurate timing may also be obtained from the signals of international navigation systems such as the ground-based LORAN-C, or the satellite-based American GPS or Russian GLONASS systems.

STANDARD TIME

Since 1880 the standard time in Britain has been Greenwich Mean Time (GMT); a statute that year enacted that the word 'time' when used in any legal document relating to Britain meant, unless otherwise specifically stated, the mean time of the Greenwich meridian. Greenwich was adopted as the universal meridian on 13 October 1884. A system of standard time by zones is used worldwide, standard time in each zone differing from that of the Greenwich meridian by an integral number of hours or, exceptionally, half-hours or quarter-hours, either fast or slow. The large territories of the USA and Canada are divided into zones approximately 7.5° on either side of central meridians.

Variations from the standard time of some countries occur during part of the year; they are decided annually and are usually referred to as Summer Time or Daylight Saving Time.

At the 180th meridian the time can be either 12 hours fast on Greenwich Mean Time or 12 hours slow, and a change of date occurs. The internationally recognised date or calendar line is a modification of the 180th meridian, drawn so as to include islands of any one group on the same side of the line, or for political reasons. The line is indicated by joining up the following coordinates:

Lat.	*Long.*	*Lat.*	*Long.*
90° S.	180°	48° N.	180°
51° S.	180°	53° N.	170° E.
45° S.	172.5° W.	65.5° N.	169° W.
15° S.	172.5° W.	68° N.	169° W.
5° S.	180°	90° N.	180°

Changes to the date line would require an international conference.

BRITISH SUMMER TIME

In 1916 an Act ordained that during a defined period of that year the legal time for general purposes in Great Britain should be one hour in advance of Greenwich Mean Time. The Summer Time Acts 1922 and 1925 defined the period during which Summer Time was to be in force, stabilising practice until the Second World War.

During World War 2 (1941–5) and in 1947 Double Summer Time (two hours in advance of Greenwich Mean Time) was used for the period in which ordinary Summer Time would have been in force. During these years clocks were also kept one hour in advance of Greenwich Mean Time in the winter. After the war, ordinary Summer Time was invoked each year from 1948–68.

Between 1968 October 27 and 1971 October 31 clocks were kept one hour ahead of Greenwich Mean Time throughout the year. This was known as British Standard Time.

The most recent legislation is the Summer Time Act 1972, which enacted that 'the period of summer time for the purposes of this Act is the period beginning at two o'clock, Greenwich mean time, in the morning of the day after the third Saturday in March or, if that day is Easter Day, the day after the second Saturday in March, and ending at two o'clock, Greenwich mean time, in the morning of the day after the fourth Saturday in October.'

The duration of Summer Time can be varied by Order in Council and in recent years alterations have been made to synchronise the period of Summer Time in Britain with that used in Europe. The rule for 1981–94 defined the period of Summer Time in the UK as from the last Sunday in March to the day following the fourth Saturday in October and the hour of changeover was altered to 01h Greenwich Mean Time.

There was no rule for the dates of Summer Time between 1995–7. Since 1998 the 9th European Parliament and Council Directive on Summer Time has harmonised the dates on which Summer Time begins and ends across member states as the last Sundays in March and October respectively. Under the directive Summer Time begins and ends at 01hr Greenwich Mean Time in each member state. Amendments to the Summer Time Act to implement the directive came into force in 2002.

The duration of Summer Time in 2009 is:
March 29 01h GMT to October 25 01h GMT

MEAN REFRACTION

Alt. ° ′	Ref. ′	Alt. ° ′	Ref. ′	Alt. ° ′	Ref. ′
1 20		3 12		7 54	
	21		13		6
1 30		3 34		9 27	
	20		12		5
1 41		4 00		11 39	
	19		11		4
1 52		4 30		15 00	
	18		10		3
2 05		5 06		20 42	
	17		9		2
2 19		5 50		32 20	
	16		8		1
2 35		6 44		62 17	
	15		7		0
2 52		7 54		90 00	
	14				
3 12					

The refraction table is in the form of a critical table (*see* page 1278).

ASTRONOMICAL CONSTANTS

Solar parallax	8″.794
Astronomical unit	149597870 km
Precession for the year 2009	50″.291
Precession in right ascension	3ˢ.075
Precession in declination	20″.043
Constant of nutation	9″.202
Constant of aberration	20″.496
Mean obliquity of ecliptic (2009)	23° 26′ 17″
Moon's equatorial hor. parallax	57′ 02″.70
Velocity of light in vacuo per second	299792.5 km
Solar motion per second	20.0 km
Equatorial radius of the Earth	6378.140 km
Polar radius of the Earth	6356.755 km
North galactic pole (IAU standard)	RA 12h 49m (1950.0). Dec.+27°.4 N.
Solar apex	RA 18h 06m Dec. +30°
Length of year (in mean solar days)	
Tropical	365.24219
Sidereal	365.25636
Anomalistic (perihelion to perihelion)	365.25964
Eclipse	346.62003

Length of month (mean values)	*d*	*h*	*m*	*s*
New Moon to New	29	12	44	02.9
Sidereal	27	07	43	11.5
Anomalistic (perigee to perigee)	27	13	18	33.2

THE EARTH

The shape of the Earth is that of an oblate spheroid or solid of revolution whose meridian sections are ellipses not differing much from circles, whilst the sections at right angles are circles. The length of the equatorial axis is about 12,756 km, and that of the polar axis is 12,714 km. The mean density of the Earth is 5.5 times that of water, although that of the surface layer is less. The Earth and Moon revolve about their common centre of gravity in a lunar month; this centre in turn revolves round the Sun in a plane known as the ecliptic, that passes through the Sun's centre. The Earth's equator is inclined to this plane at an angle of 23.4°. This tilt is the cause of the seasons. In mid-latitudes, and when the Sun is high above the Equator, not only does the high noon altitude make the days longer, but the Sun's rays fall more directly on the Earth's surface; these effects combine to produce summer. In equatorial regions the noon altitude is large throughout the year, and there is little variation in the length of the day. In higher latitudes the noon altitude is lower, and the days in summer are appreciably longer than those in winter.

The average velocity of the Earth in its orbit is 30 km a second. It makes a complete rotation on its axis in about 23h 56m of mean time, which is the sidereal day. Because of its annual revolution round the Sun, the rotation with respect to the Sun, or the solar day, is more than this by about four minutes. The extremity of the axis of rotation, or the North Pole of the Earth, is not rigidly fixed, but wanders over an area roughly 20 metres in diameter.

ELEMENTS OF THE SOLAR SYSTEM

Orb	Mean distance from Sun (Earth = 1)	km 10^6	Sidereal period days	Synodic period days	Incl. of orbit to ecliptic ° ′	Diameter km	Mass (Earth = 1)	Period of rotation on axis days
Sun	—	—	—	—	—	1,392,530	332,981	25–35*
Mercury	0.39	58	88.0	116	7 00	4,879	0.0553	58.646
Venus	0.72	108	224.7	584	3 24	12,104	0.8150	243.019*r*
Earth	1.00	150	365.3	—	—	12,756*e*	1.0000	0.997
Mars	1.52	228	687.0	780	1 51	6,794*e*	0.1074	1.026
Jupiter	5.20	778	4,332.6	399	1 18	142,984*e* 133,708*p*	317.83	0.410*e*
Saturn	9.55	1429	10,759.2	378	2 29	120,536*e* 108,728*p*	95.16	0.426*e*
Uranus	19.22	2875	30,684.6	370	0 46	51,118*e*	14.54	0.718*r*
Neptune	30.11	4504	60,191.2	367	1 46	49,528*e*	17.15	0.671
Pluto †	39.80	5954	91,708.2	367	17 09	2,302	0.002	6.387

e equatorial, *p* polar, *r* retrograde, * depending on latitude, † reclassified as a dwarf planet since August 2006

THE SATELLITES

Name		Star mag.	Mean distance from primary km	Sidereal period of revolution d
EARTH				
I	Moon	—	384,400	27.322
MARS				
I	Phobos	11	9,378	0.319
II	Deimos	12	23,459	1.262
JUPITER				
XVI	Metis	17	127,960	0.295
XV	Adrastea	19	128,980	0.298
V	Amalthea	14	181,300	0.498
XIV	Thebe	16	221,900	0.675
I	Io	5	421,600	1.769
II	Europa	5	670,900	3.551
III	Ganymede	5	1,070,000	7.155
IV	Callisto	6	1,883,000	16.689
XIII	Leda	20	11,165,000	240.92
VI	Himalia	15	11,460,000	250.57
X	Lysithea	18	11,717,000	259.22
VII	Elara	17	11,741,000	259.65
XII	Ananke	19	21,276,000	629.77*r*
XI	Carme	18	23,404,000	734.17*r*
VIII	Pasiphae	17	23,624,000	743.68*r*
IX	Sinope	18	23,939,000	758.90*r*
SATURN				
XVIII	Pan	20	133,583	0.575
XV	Atlas	18	137,640	0.602
XVI	Prometheus	16	139,353	0.613
XVII	Pandora	16	141,700	0.629
XI	Epimetheus	15	151,422	0.694
X	Janus	14	151,472	0.695
I	Mimas	13	185,520	0.942
II	Enceladus	12	238,020	1.370
III	Tethys	10	294,660	1.888
XIII	Telesto	19	294,660	1.888
XIV	Calypso	19	294,660	1.888
IV	Dione	10	377,400	2.737
XII	Helene	18	377,400	2.737
V	Rhea	10	527,040	4.518
VI	Titan	8	1,221,850	15.945
VII	Hyperion	14	1,481,000	21.277
VIII	Iapetus	11	3,561,300	79.330
IX	Phoebe	16	12,952,000	550.48*r*
URANUS				
VI	Cordelia	24	49,770	0.335
VII	Ophelia	24	53,790	0.376
VIII	Bianca	23	59,170	0.435
IX	Cressida	22	61,780	0.464
X	Desdemona	22	62,680	0.474
XI	Juliet	21	64,350	0.493
XII	Portia	21	66,090	0.513
XIII	Rosalind	22	66,940	0.558
XIV	Belinda	22	75,260	0.624
XV	Puck	20	86,010	0.762
V	Miranda	16	129,390	1.413
I	Ariel	14	191,020	2.520
II	Umbriel	15	266,300	4.144
III	Titania	14	435,910	8.706
IV	Oberon	14	583,520	13.463
XVI	Caliban	22	7,230,000	579.5*r*
XX	Stephano	24	8,002,000	676.5*r*
XVII	Sycorax	21	12,179,000	1,283.4*r*
XVIII	Prospero	23	16,418,000	1,992.8*r*
XIX	Setebos	23	17,459,000	2,202.2*r*
NEPTUNE				
III	Naiad	25	48,230	0.294
IV	Thalassa	24	50,080	0.311
V	Despina	23	52,530	0.335
VI	Galatea	22	61,950	0.429
VII	Larissa	22	73,550	0.555
VIII	Proteus	20	117,650	1.122
I	Triton	13	354,760	5.877
II	Nereid	19	5,513,400	360.136
PLUTO				
I	Charon	17	19,600	6.387

Currently the total number of satellites of the outer planets are: Jupiter 62, Saturn 60, Uranus 27, Neptune 13, Pluto 3.

TERRESTRIAL MAGNETISM

The Earth's main magnetic field corresponds approximately to that of a very strong small bar magnet near the centre of the Earth, but with appreciable smooth spatial departures. The origin of the main field is generally ascribed to electric currents associated with fluid motions in the Earth's core. As a result not only does the main field vary in strength and direction from place to place, but also with time. Superimposed on the main field are local and regional anomalies whose magnitudes may in places approach that of the main field; these are due to the influence of mineral deposits in the Earth's crust. A small proportion of the field is of external origin, mostly associated with electric currents in the ionosphere. The configuration of the external field and the ionisation of the atmosphere depend on the incident particle and radiation flux from the Sun. There are, therefore, short-term and non-periodic as well as diurnal, 27-day, seasonal and 11-year periodic changes in the magnetic field, dependent upon the position of the Sun and the degree of solar activity.

A magnetic compass points along the horizontal component of a magnetic line of force. These lines of force converge on the 'magnetic dip-poles', the places where the Earth's magnetic field is vertical. These poles move with time, and their present approximate adopted mean positions are 84.9° N., 129.6° W. and 64.5° S., 137.5° E.

There is also a 'magnetic equator', at all points of which the vertical component of the Earth's magnetic field is zero and a magnetised needle remains horizontal. This line runs between 2° and 12° north of the geographical equator in Asia and Africa, turns sharply south off the west African coast, and crosses South America through Brazil, Bolivia and Peru; it re-crosses the geographical equator in mid-Pacific.

Reference has already been made to secular changes in the Earth's field. The following table indicates the changes in magnetic declination (or variation of the compass). Declination is the angle in the horizontal plane between the direction of true north and that in which a magnetic compass points. Similar, though much smaller, changes have occurred in 'dip' or magnetic inclination. Secular changes differ throughout the world. Although the London observations suggest a cycle with a period of several hundred years, an exact repetition is unlikely.

London		*Greenwich*	
1580	11° 15′ E.	1900	16° 29′ W.
1622	5° 56′ E.	1925	13° 10′ W.
1665	1° 22′ W.	1950	9° 07′ W.
1730	13° 00′ W.	1975	6° 39′ W.
1773	21° 09′ W.	1998	3° 32′ W.
1850	22° 24′ W.		

In order that up-to-date information on declination may be available, many governments publish magnetic charts on which there are lines (isogonic lines) passing through all places at which specified values of declination will be found at the date of the chart.

In the British Isles, isogonic lines now run approximately north-east to south-west. Though there are considerable local deviations due to geological causes, a rough value of magnetic declination may be obtained by assuming that at 50° N. on the meridian of Greenwich, the value in 2009 is 1° 15′ west and allowing an increase of 14′ for each degree of latitude northwards and one of 27′ for each degree of longitude westwards. For example, at 53° N., 5° W., declination will be about 1°15′ + 42′ + 135′, ie 4° 12′ west. The average annual change at the present time is about 10′ decrease.

The number of magnetic observatories is about 180, irregularly distributed over the globe. There are three in Great Britain, run by the British Geological Survey: at Hartland, north Devon; at Eskdalemuir, Dumfries and Galloway; and at Lerwick, Shetland Islands. The following are some recent annual mean values of the magnetic elements for Hartland.

Year	*Declination West* ° ′	*Dip or inclination* ° ′	*Horizontal intensity nanoTesla (nT)*	*Vertical intensity nT*
1960	9 58.8	66 43.9	18707	43504
1965	9 30.1	66 34.0	18872	43540
1970	9 06.5	66 26.1	19033	43636
1975	8 32.3	66 17.0	19212	43733
1980	7 43.8	66 10.3	19330	43768
1985	6 56.1	66 07.9	19379	43796
1990	6 15.0	66 09.7	19539	43896
1995	5 33.2	66 07.3	19457	43951
2000	4 43.6	66 06.9	19508	44051
2005	3 56.4	66 06.0	19576	44177
2007	3 39.1	66 04.1	19619	44208

As well as navigation at sea, in the air and on land by compass the oil industry depends on the Earth's magnetic field as a directional reference. They use magnetic survey tools when drilling well-bores and require accurate estimates of the local magnetic field, taking into account the crustal and external fields.

MAGNETIC STORMS

Occasionally, sometimes with great suddenness, the Earth's magnetic field is subject for several hours to marked disturbance. During a severe storm in October 2003 the declination at Eskdalemuir changed by over 5° in six minutes. In many instances such disturbances are accompanied by widespread displays of aurorae, marked changes in the incidence of cosmic rays, an increase in the reception of 'noise' from the Sun at radio frequencies, and rapid changes in the ionosphere and induced electric currents within the Earth which adversely affect satellite operations, telecommunications and electric power transmission systems. The disturbances are caused by changes in the stream of ionised particles which emanates from the Sun and through which the Earth is continuously passing. Some of these changes are associated with visible eruptions on the Sun, usually in the region of sun-spots. There is a marked tendency for disturbances to recur after intervals of about 27 days, the apparent period of rotation of the Sun on its axis, which is consistent with the sources being located on particular areas of the Sun.

TIME MEASUREMENT AND CALENDARS

MEASUREMENTS OF TIME

Measurements of time are based on the time taken by the earth to rotate on its axis (day); by the moon to revolve around the earth (month); and by the earth to revolve around the sun (year). From these, which are not commensurable, certain average or mean intervals have been adopted for ordinary use.

THE DAY

The day begins at midnight and is divided into 24 hours of 60 minutes, each of 60 seconds. The hours are counted from midnight up to 12 noon (when the sun crosses the meridian), and these hours are designated am *(ante meridiem)*; and again from noon up to 12 midnight, which hours are designated pm *(post meridiem),* except when the 24-hour reckoning is employed. The 24-hour reckoning ignores am and pm, numbering the hours 0 to 23 from midnight.

Colloquially the 24 hours are divided into day and night, day being the time while the sun is above the horizon (including the four stages of twilight defined in the Astronomy section). Day is subdivided into morning, the early part of daytime, ending at noon; afternoon, from noon to about 6pm; and evening, which may be said to extend from 6pm until midnight. Night begins at the close of astronomical twilight (*see* the Astronomy section) and extends beyond midnight to sunrise the next day.

The names of the days are derived from Old English translations or adaptations of the Roman titles.

Sunday	Sol	Sun
Monday	Luna	Moon
Tuesday	Tiw/Tyr (god of war)	Mars
Wednesday	Woden/Odin	Mercury
Thursday	Thor	Jupiter
Friday	Frigga/Freyja (goddess of love)	Venus
Saturday	Saeterne	Saturn

THE MONTH

The month in the ordinary calendar is approximately the twelfth part of a year, but the lengths of the different months vary from 28 (or 29) days to 31.

THE YEAR

The equinoctial or tropical year is the time that the earth takes to revolve around the sun from equinox to equinox, ie 365.24219 mean solar days, or 365 days 5 hours 48 minutes and 45 seconds.

The calendar year usually consists of 365 days but a year containing 366 days is called a bissextile (*see* Roman calendar) or leap year, one day being added to the month of February so that a date 'leaps over' a day of the week. In the Roman calendar the day that was repeated was the sixth day before the beginning of March, the equivalent of 24 February.

A year is a leap year if the date of the year is divisible by four without remainder, unless it is the last year of the century. The last year of a century is a leap year only if its number is divisible by 400 without remainder, eg the years 1800 and 1900 had only 365 days but the year 2000 had 366 days.

THE SOLSTICE

A solstice is the point in the tropical year at which the sun attains its greatest distance, north or south, from the Equator. In the northern hemisphere the furthest point north of the Equator marks the summer solstice and the furthest point south marks the winter solstice.

The date of the solstice varies according to locality. For example, if the summer solstice falls on 21 June late in the day by Greenwich time, that day will be the longest of the year at Greenwich though it may be by only a second, but it will fall on 22 June, local date, in Japan, and so 22 June will be the longest day there. The date of the solstice is also affected by the length of the tropical year, which is 365 days 6 hours less about 11 minutes 15 seconds. If a solstice happens late on 21 June in one year, it will be nearly 6 hours later in the next (unless the next year is a leap year), ie early on 22 June, and that will be the longest day.

This delay of the solstice does not continue because the extra day in a leap year brings it back a day in the calendar. However, because of the 11 minutes 15 seconds mentioned above, the additional day in a leap year brings the solstice back too far by 45 minutes, and the time of the solstice in the calendar is earlier, in a four-year pattern, as the century progresses. The last year of a century is in most cases not a leap year, and the omission of the extra day puts the date of the solstice later by about 6 hours. Compensation for this is made by the fourth centennial year being a leap year. The solstice has become earlier in date throughout the last century and, because the year 2000 was a leap year, the solstice will get earlier still throughout the 21st century.

The date of the winter solstice, the shortest day of the year, is affected by the same factors as the longest day.

At Greenwich the sun sets at its earliest by the clock about ten days before the shortest day. The daily change in the time of sunset is due in the first place to the sun's movement southwards at this time of the year, which diminishes the interval between the sun's transit and its setting. However, the daily decrease of the Equation of Time causes the time of apparent noon to be continuously later day by day, which to some extent counteracts the first effect. The rates of the change of these two quantities are not equal or uniform; their combination causes the date of earliest sunset to be 12 or 13 December at Greenwich. In more southerly latitudes the effect of the movement of the sun is less, and the change in the time of sunset depends on that of the Equation of Time to a greater degree, and the date of earliest sunset is earlier than it is at Greenwich, eg on the Equator it is about 1 November.

THE EQUINOX

The equinox is the point at which the sun crosses the Equator and day and night are of equal length all over the world. This occurs in March and September.

DOG DAYS

The days about the heliacal rising of the Dog Star, noted from ancient times as the hottest period of the year in the northern hemisphere, are called the Dog Days. Their incidence has been variously calculated as depending on the Greater or Lesser Dog Star (Sirius or Procyon) and their duration has been reckoned as from 30 to 54 days. A generally accepted period is from 3 July to 15 August.

CHRISTIAN CALENDAR

In the Christian chronological system the years are distinguished by cardinal numbers before or after the birth of Christ, the period being denoted by the letters BC (Before Christ) or, more rarely, AC *(Ante Christum)*, and AD (*Anno Domini* – In the Year of Our Lord). The correlative dates of the epoch are the fourth year of the 194th Olympiad, the 753rd year from the foundation of Rome, AM 3761 in Jewish chronology, and the 4714th year of the Julian period. The actual date of the birth of Christ is somewhat uncertain.

The system was introduced into Italy in the sixth century. Though first used in France in the seventh century, it was not universally established there until about the eighth century. It has been said that the system was introduced into England by St Augustine (AD 596), but it was probably not generally used until some centuries later. It was ordered to be used by the bishops at the Council of Chelsea (AD 816).

THE JULIAN CALENDAR

In the Julian calendar (adopted by the Roman Empire in 45 BC) all the centennial years were leap years, and for this reason towards the close of the 16th century there was a difference of ten days between the tropical and calendar years; the equinox fell on 11 March of the calendar, whereas at the time of the Council of Nicaea (AD 325), it had fallen on 21 March. In 1582 Pope Gregory ordained that 5 October should be called 15 October and that of the end-century years only the fourth should be a leap year.

THE GREGORIAN CALENDAR

The Gregorian calendar was adopted by Italy, France, Spain and Portugal in 1582, by Prussia, the Roman Catholic German states, Switzerland, Holland and Flanders on 1 January 1583, by Poland in 1586, Hungary in 1587, the Protestant German and Netherland states and Denmark in 1700, and by Great Britain and its Dominions (including the North American colonies) in 1752, by the omission of 11 days (3 September being reckoned as 14 September). Sweden omitted the leap day in 1700 but observed leap days in 1704 and 1708, and reverted to the Julian calendar by having two leap days in 1712; the Gregorian calendar was adopted in 1753 by the omission of 11 days (18 February being reckoned as 1 March). Japan adopted the calendar in 1872, China in 1912, Bulgaria in 1915, Turkey and Soviet Russia in 1918, Yugoslavia and Romania in 1919, and Greece in 1923.

In the same year that the change was made in England from the Julian to the Gregorian calendar, the beginning of the new year was also changed from 25 March to 1 January.

THE ORTHODOX CHURCHES

Some Orthodox churches still use the Julian reckoning but the majority of Greek Orthodox churches and the Romanian Orthodox Church have adopted a modified 'New Calendar', observing the Gregorian calendar for fixed feasts and the Julian for movable feasts.

The Orthodox Church year begins on 1 September. There are four fast periods and, in addition to Pascha (Easter), twelve great feasts, as well as numerous commemorations of the saints of the Old and New Testaments throughout the year.

THE DOMINICAL LETTER

The dominical letter is one of the letters A–G which are used to denote the Sundays in successive years. If the first day of the year is a Sunday the letter is A; if the second, B; the third, C; and so on. A leap year requires two letters, the first for 1 January to 29 February, the second for 1 March to 31 December.

EPIPHANY

The feast of the Epiphany, commemorating the manifestation of Christ, later became associated with the offering of gifts by the Magi. The day was of great importance from the time of the Council of Nicaea (AD 325), as the primate of Alexandria was charged at every Epiphany feast with the announcement in a letter to the churches of the date of the forthcoming Easter. The day was also of importance in Britain as it influenced dates, ecclesiastical and lay, eg Plough Monday, when work was resumed in the fields, fell on the Monday in the first full week after Epiphany.

LENT

The Teutonic word *Lent,* which denotes the fast preceding Easter, originally meant no more than the spring season; but from Anglo-Saxon times, at least, it has been used as the equivalent of the more significant Latin term *Quadragesima*, meaning the 'forty days' or, more literally, the fortieth day. Ash Wednesday is the first day of Lent, which ends at midnight before Easter Day.

PALM SUNDAY

Palm Sunday, the Sunday before Easter and the beginning of Holy Week, commemorates the triumphal entry of Christ into Jerusalem and is celebrated in Britain (when palm is not available) by branches of willow gathered for use in the decoration of churches on that day.

MAUNDY THURSDAY

Maundy Thursday is the day before Good Friday, the name itself being a corruption of *dies mandati* (day of the mandate) when Christ washed the feet of the disciples and gave them the mandate to love one another.

EASTER DAY

Easter Day is the first Sunday after the full moon which happens on, or next after, the 21st day of March; if the full moon happens on a Sunday, Easter Day is the Sunday after.

This definition is contained in an Act of Parliament (24 Geo. II c. 23) and explanation is given in the preamble to the Act that the day of full moon depends on certain tables that have been prepared. These tables are summarised in the early pages of the Book of Common Prayer. The moon referred to is not the real moon of the heavens, but a hypothetical moon on whose 'full' the date of Easter depends, and the lunations of this 'calendar' moon consist of 29 and 30 days alternately, with certain necessary modifications to make the date of its full agree as nearly as possible with that of the real moon, which is known as the Paschal Full Moon.

A FIXED EASTER

In 1928 the House of Commons agreed to a motion for the third reading of a bill proposing that Easter Day shall, in the calendar year next but one after the commencement of the Act and in all subsequent years, be the first Sunday after the second Saturday in April. Easter would thus fall on the second or third Sunday in April, ie between 9 and 15 April (inclusive). A clause in the bill provided that before it shall come into operation, regard shall be had to any opinion expressed officially by the various Christian churches. Efforts by the World Council of Churches to secure a unanimous choice of date for Easter by its member churches have so far been unsuccessful.

ROGATION DAYS

Rogation Days are the Monday, Tuesday and Wednesday preceding Ascension Day and from the fifth century were observed as public fasts with solemn processions and supplications. The processions were discontinued as religious observances at the Reformation, but survive in the ceremony known as 'beating the parish bounds'. Rogation Sunday is the Sunday before Ascension Day.

EMBER DAYS

The Ember days occur on the Wednesday, Friday and Saturday of the same week, four times a year. Used for the ordination of clergy, these days are set aside for fasting and prayer. The weeks in which they fall are: *(a)* after the third Sunday in Advent, *(b)* before the second Sunday in Lent, *(c)* before Trinity Sundays and *(d)* after Holy Cross day.

TRINITY SUNDAY

Trinity Sunday is eight weeks after Easter Day, on the Sunday following Pentecost (Whit Sunday). Subsequent Sundays are reckoned in the Book of Common Prayer calendar of the Church of England as 'after Trinity'.

Thomas Becket (1118–70) was consecrated Archbishop of Canterbury on the Sunday after Whit Sunday and his first act was to ordain that the day of his consecration should be held as a new festival in honour of the Holy Trinity. This observance spread from Canterbury throughout the whole of Christendom.

MOVEABLE FEASTS TO THE YEAR 2035

Year	*Ash Wednesday*	*Easter*	*Ascension*	*Pentecost (Whit Sunday)*	*Advent Sunday*
2009	25 February	12 April	21 May	31 May	29 November
2010	17 February	4 April	13 May	23 May	28 November
2011	9 March	24 April	2 June	12 June	27 November
2012	22 February	8 April	17 May	27 May	2 December
2013	13 February	31 March	9 May	19 May	1 December
2014	5 March	20 April	29 May	8 June	30 November
2015	18 February	5 April	14 May	24 May	29 November
2016	10 February	27 March	5 May	15 May	27 November
2017	1 March	16 April	25 May	4 June	3 December
2018	14 February	1 April	10 May	20 May	2 December
2019	6 March	21 April	30 May	9 June	1 December
2020	26 February	12 April	21 May	31 May	29 November
2021	17 February	4 April	13 May	23 May	28 November
2022	2 March	17 April	26 May	5 June	27 November
2023	22 February	9 April	18 May	28 May	3 December
2024	14 February	31 March	9 May	19 May	1 December
2025	5 March	20 April	29 May	8 June	30 November
2026	18 February	5 April	14 May	24 May	29 November
2027	10 February	28 March	6 May	16 May	28 November
2028	1 March	16 April	25 May	4 June	3 December
2029	14 February	1 April	10 May	20 May	2 December
2030	6 March	21 April	30 May	9 June	1 December
2031	26 February	13 April	22 May	1 June	30 November
2032	11 February	28 March	6 May	16 May	28 November
2033	2 March	17 April	26 May	5 June	27 November
2034	22 February	9 April	18 May	28 May	3 December
2035	7 February	25 March	3 May	13 May	2 December

NOTES

Ash Wednesday (first day in Lent) can fall at earliest on 4 February and at latest on 10 March

Mothering Sunday (fourth Sunday in Lent) can fall at earliest on 1 March and at latest on 4 April

Easter Day can fall at earliest on 22 March and at latest on 25 April

Ascension Day is forty days after Easter Day and can fall at earliest on 30 April and at latest on 3 June

Pentecost (Whit Sunday) is seven weeks after Easter and can fall at earliest on 10 May and at latest on 13 June

Trinity Sunday is the Sunday after Whit Sunday

Corpus Christi falls on the Thursday after Trinity Sunday

Sundays after Pentecost – there are not less than 18 and not more than 23

Advent Sunday is the Sunday nearest to 30 November

EASTER DAYS AND DOMINICAL LETTERS 1500 TO 2035

Dates up to and including 1752 are according to the Julian calendar. For dominical letters in leap years, *see* note below

		1500–1599	1600–1699	1700–1799	1800–1899	1900–1999	2000–2035
March							
d	22	1573	1668	1761	1818		
e	23	1505/16	1600	1788	1845/56	1913	2008
f	24	1611/95	1706/99	1940			
g	25	1543/54	1627/38/49	1722/33/44	1883/94	1951	2035
A	26	1559/70/81/92	1654/65/76	1749/58/69/80	1815/26/37	1967/78/89	
b	27	1502/13/24/97	1608/87/92	1785/96	1842/53/64	1910/21/32	2005/16
c	28	1529/35/40	1619/24/30	1703/14/25	1869/75/80	1937/48	2027/32
d	29	1551/62	1635/46/57	1719/30/41/52	1807/12/91	1959/64/70	
e	30	1567/78/89	1651/62/73/84	1746/55/66/77	1823/34	1902/75/86/97	
f	31	1510/21/32/83/94	1605/16/78/89	1700/71/82/93	1839/50/61/72	1907/18/29/91	2002/13/24
April							
g	1	1526/37/48	1621/32	1711/16	1804/66/77/88	1923/34/45/56	2018/29
A	2	1553/64	1643/48	1727/38	1809/20/93/99	1961/72	
b	3	1575/80/86	1659/70/81	1743/63/68/74	1825/31/36	1904/83/88/94	
c	4	1507/18/91	1602/13/75/86/97	1708/79/90	1847/58	1915/20/26/99	2010/21
d	5	1523/34/45/56	1607/18/29/40	1702/13/24/95	1801/63/74/85/96	1931/42/53	2015/26
e	6	1539/50/61/72	1634/45/56	1729/35/40/60	1806/17/28/90	1947/58/69/80	
f	7	1504/77/88	1667/72	1751/65/76	1822/33/44	1901/12/85/96	
g	8	1509/15/20/99	1604/10/83/94	1705/87/92/98	1849/55/60	1917/28	2007/12
A	9	1531/42	1615/26/37/99	1710/21/32	1871/82	1939/44/50	2023/34
b	10	1547/58/69	1631/42/53/64	1726/37/48/57	1803/14/87/98	1955/66/77	
c	11	1501/12/63/74/85/96	1658/69/80	1762/73/84	1819/30/41/52	1909/71/82/93	2004
d	12	1506/17/28	1601/12/91/96	1789	1846/57/68	1903/14/25/36/98	2009/20
e	13	1533/44	1623/28	1707/18	1800/73/79/84	1941/52	2031
f	14	1555/60/66	1639/50/61	1723/34/45/54	1805/11/16/95	1963/68/74	
g	15	1571/82/93	1655/66/77/88	1750/59/70/81	1827/38	1900/06/79/90	2001
A	16	1503/14/25/36/87/98	1609/20/82/93	1704/75/86/97	1843/54/65/76	1911/22/33/95	2006/17/28
b	17	1530/41/52	1625/36	1715/20	1808/70/81/92	1927/38/49/60	2022/33
c	18	1557/68	1647/52	1731/42/56	1802/13/24/97	1954/65/76	
d	19	1500/79/84/90	1663/74/85	1747/67/72/78	1829/35/40	1908/81/87/92	
e	20	1511/22/95	1606/17/79/90	1701/12/83/94	1851/62	1919/24/30	2003/14/25
f	21	1527/38/49	1622/33/44	1717/28	1867/78/89	1935/46/57	2019/30
g	22	1565/76	1660	1739/53/64	1810/21/32	1962/73/84	
A	23	1508	1671		1848	1905/16	2000
b	24	1519	1603/14/98	1709/91	1859		2011
c	25	1546	1641	1736	1886	1943	

No dominical letter is placed against the intercalary day 29 February, but since it is still counted as a weekday and given a name, the series of letters moves back one day every leap year after intercalation. Thus, a leap year beginning with the dominical letter C will change to a year with the dominical letter B on 1 March

HINDU CALENDAR

The Hindu calendar is a luni-solar calendar of 12 months, each containing 29 days, 12 hours. Each month is divided into a light fortnight (Shukla or Shuddha) and a dark fortnight (Krishna or Vadya) based on the waxing and waning of the moon. In most parts of India the month starts with the light fortnight, ie the day after the new moon, although in some regions it begins with the dark fortnight, ie the day after the full moon.

The new year according to the civil calendar begins in the month of Chaitra (March/April) and ends in the month of Phalgun (March). The 12 months – Chaitra, Vaishakh, Jyeshtha, Ashadh, Shravan, Bhadrapad, Ashvin, Kartik, Margashirsh, Paush, Magh and Phalgun – have Sanskrit names derived from 12 asterisms (constellations). There are regional variations to the names of the months but the Sanskrit names are understood throughout India.

Every lunar month that has a solar transit is termed pure *(shuddha)*. The lunar month without a solar transit is impure *(mala)* and called an intercalary month. An intercalary month occurs approximately every 32 lunar months, whenever the difference between the Hindu year of 360 lunar days (354 days 8 hours solar time) and the 365 days 6 hours of the solar year reaches the length of one Hindu lunar month (29 days 12 hours).

The leap month may be added at any point in the Hindu year. The name given to the month varies according to when it occurs but is taken from the month immediately following it. There is no leap month in 2009.

The days of the week are called Raviwar (Sunday), Somawar (Monday), Mangalwar (Tuesday), Budhawar (Wednesday), Guruwar (Thursday), Shukrawar (Friday) and Shaniwar (Saturday). The names are derived from the Sanskrit names of the sun, the moon and five planets, Mars, Mercury, Jupiter, Venus and Saturn.

Most fasts and festivals are based on the lunar calendar but a few are determined by the apparent movement of the sun, eg Sankranti and Pongal (in southern India), which are celebrated on 14/15 January to mark the start of the Sun's apparent journey northwards and a change of season.

Festivals celebrated throughout India are Chaitra (the New Year), Raksha-bandhan (the renewal of the kinship bond between brothers and sisters), Navaratri (a nine-night festival dedicated to the goddess Parvati), Dasara (the victory of Rama over the demon army), Diwali (a festival of lights), Makara Sankranti, Shivaratri (dedicated to Shiva), and Holi (a spring festival). British Hindus commonly celebrate the festival of Diwali as the start of the new year instead of observing it at the beginning of Chaitra.

Regional festivals are Durga-puja (dedicated to the goddess Durga (Parvati)), Sarasvati-puja (dedicated to the goddess Sarasvati), Ganesh Chaturthi (worship of Ganesh on the fourth day (Chaturthi) of the light half of Bhadrapad), Ramanavami (the birth festival of the god Rama) and Janmashtami (the birth festival of the god Krishna).

The main festivals celebrated in Britain are Navaratri, Dasara, Durga-puja, Diwali, Holi, Sarasvati-puja, Ganesh Chaturthi, Raksha-bandhan, Ramanavami and Janmashtami.

For dates of the main festivals in 2009, *see* page 9.

JEWISH CALENDAR

The story of the Flood in the Book of Genesis indicates the use of a calendar of some kind and that the writers recognised 30 days as the length of a lunation. However, after the diaspora, Jewish communities were left in considerable doubt as to the times of fasts and festivals. This led to the formation of the Jewish calendar as used today. It is said that this was done in AD 358 by Rabbi Hillel II, though some assert that it did not happen until much later.

The calendar is luni-solar, and is based on the lengths of the lunation and of the tropical year as found by Hipparchus (*c*.120 BC), which differ little from those adopted at the present day. The year AM 5769 (2008–9) is the 12th year of the 304th Metonic (Minor or Lunar) cycle of 19 years and the 1st year of the 207th Solar (or Major) cycle of 28 years since the Era of the Creation. Jews hold that the Creation occurred at the time of the autumnal equinox in the year known in the Christian calendar as 3760 BC (954 of the Julian period). The epoch or starting point of Jewish chronology corresponds to 7 October 3761 BC. At the beginning of each solar cycle, the Tekufah of Nisan (the vernal equinox) returns to the same day and to the same hour.

The hour is divided into 1,080 minims, and the month between one new moon and the next is reckoned as 29 days 12 hours 793 minims. The normal calendar year, called a Regular Common year, consists of 12 months of 30 days and 29 days alternately. Since 12 months such as these comprise only 354 days, in order that each of them shall not diverge greatly from an average place in the solar year, a 13th month is occasionally added after the fifth month of the civil year (which commences on the first day of the month Tishri), or as the penultimate month of the ecclesiastical year (which commences on the first day of the month Nisan). The years when this happens are called Embolismic or leap years.

Of the 19 years that form a Metonic cycle, seven are leap years; they occur at places in the cycle indicated by the numbers 3, 6, 8, 11, 14, 17 and 19, these places being chosen so that the accumulated excesses of the solar years should be as small as possible.

A Jewish year is of one of the following six types:

Minimal Common	353 days
Regular Common	354 days
Full Common	355 days
Minimal Leap	383 days
Regular Leap	384 days
Full Leap	385 days

The Regular year has alternate months of 30 and 29 days. In a Full year, whether common or leap, Marcheshvan, the second month of the civil year, has 30 days instead of 29; in Minimal years Kislev, the third month, has 29 instead of 30. The additional month in leap years is called Adar I and precedes the month called Adar in common years. Adar II is called Adar Sheni in leap years, and the usual Adar festivals are kept in Adar Sheni. Adar I and Adar II always have 30 days, but neither this, nor the other variations mentioned, is allowed to change the number of days in the other months, which still follow the alternation of the normal 12.

These are the main features of the Jewish calendar, which must be considered permanent because as a Jewish law it cannot be altered except by a Great Sanhedrin.

The Jewish day begins between sunset and nightfall. The time used is that of the meridian of Jerusalem, which is 2h 21m in advance of Greenwich Mean Time. Rules for the beginning of sabbaths and festivals were laid down for the latitude of London in the 18th century and hours for nightfall are now fixed annually by the Chief Rabbi.

JEWISH CALENDAR 5769–70

AM 5769 (769) is a Regular Common year of 12 months, 50 sabbaths and 354 days. AM 5770 is a Full Common year of 12 months, 51 sabbaths and 355 days.

Month (length)	AM 5769	AM 5770
Tishri 1 (30)	30 September 2008	19 September
Marcheshvan 1 (30)	30 October	19 October
Kislev 1 (30)	28 November	18 November
Tebet 1 (29)	28 December	18 December
Shebat 1 (30)	26 January 2009	16 January 2010
**Adar 1* (29)	25 February	
Nisan 1 (30)	26 March	
Iyar 1 (29)	25 April	
Sivan 1 (30)	24 May	
Tammuz 1 (29)	23 June	
Ab 1 (30)	22 July	
Elul 1 (29)	21 August	

* Known as Adar Rishon in leap years

JEWISH FASTS AND FESTIVALS

For dates of principal festivals in 2009, *see* page 9.

Tishri 1–2	Rosh Hashanah (New Year)
Tishri 3	*Fast of Gedaliah
Tishri 10	Yom Kippur (Day of Atonement)
Tishri 15–21	Succoth (Feast of Tabernacles)
Tishri 21	Hoshana Rabba
Tishri 22	Shemini Atseret (Solemn Assembly)
Tishri 23	Simchat Torah (Rejoicing of the Law)
Kislev 25	Hanukkah (Dedication of the Temple) begins
Tebet 10	Fast of Tebet
†*Adar* 13	§Fast of Esther
†*Adar* 14	Purim
†*Adar* 15	Shushan Purim
Nisan 15–22	Pesach (Passover)
Sivan 6–7	Shavuoth (Feast of Weeks)
Tammuz 17	*Fast of Tammuz
Ab 9	*Fast of Ab

* If these dates fall on the sabbath the fast is kept on the following day

† Adar Sheni in leap years

§ This fast is observed on Adar 11 (or Adar Sheni 11 in leap years) if Adar 13 falls on a sabbath

MUSLIM CALENDAR

The Muslim era is dated from the *Hijrah,* or flight of the Prophet Muhammad from Mecca to Medina, the corresponding date of which in the Julian calendar is 16 July AD 622. The lunar *hijri* calendar is used principally in Iran, Egypt, Malaysia, Pakistan, Mauritania, various Arab states and certain parts of India. Iran uses the solar hijri calendar as well as the lunar hijri calendar. The dating system was adopted about AD 639, commencing with the first day of the month Muharram.

The lunar calendar consists of 12 months containing an alternate sequence of 30 and 29 days, with the intercalation of one day at the end of the 12th month at stated intervals in each cycle of 30 years. The object of the intercalation is to reconcile the date of the first day of the month with the date of the actual new moon.

Some adherents still take the date of the evening of the first physical sighting of the crescent of the new moon as that of the first of the month. If cloud obscures the moon the present month may be extended to 30 days, after which the new month will begin automatically regardless of whether the moon has been seen. (Under religious law a month must have less than 31 days.) This means that the beginning of a new month and the date of religious festivals can vary from the published calendars.

In each cycle of 30 years, 19 years are common and contain 354 days, and 11 years are intercalary (leap years) of 355 days, the latter being called *kabisah.* The mean length of the Hijrah years is 354 days 8 hours 48 minutes and the period of mean lunation is 29 days 12 hours 44 minutes.

To ascertain if a year is common or kabisah, divide it by 30: the quotient gives the number of completed cycles and the remainder shows the place of the year in the current cycle. If the remainder is 2, 5, 7, 10, 13, 16, 18, 21, 24, 26 or 29, the year is kabisah and consists of 355 days.

MUSLIM CALENDAR 1430–31

Hijrah 1429 AH (remainder 19) and 1430 AH (remainder 20) are common years. Calendar dates below are estimates based on calculations of moon phases.

Month (length)	1430 AH	1431 AH
Muharram 1 (30)	29 December 2008	18 December
Safar 1 (29)	28 January 2009	17 January 2010
Rabi' I 1 (30)	26 February	
Rabi' II 1 (29)	28 March	
Jumada I 1 (30)	26 April	
Jumada II 1 (29)	26 May	
Rajab 1 (30)	24 June	
Sha'ban 1 (29)	24 July	
Ramadan 1 (30)	22 August	
Shawwal 1 (29)	21 September	
Dhu'l-Qa'da 1 (30)	20 October	
Dhu'l-Hijjah 1 (29)	19 November	

MUSLIM FESTIVALS

Ramadan is a month of fasting for all Muslims because it is the month in which the revelation of the *Qur'an* (Koran) began. During Ramadan, Muslims abstain from food, drink and sexual pleasure from dawn until after sunset throughout the month.

The two major festivals are *Eid ul-Fitr* and *Eid ul-Adha.* Eid ul-Fitr marks the end of the Ramadan fast and is celebrated on the day after the sighting of the new moon of the following month. Eid ul-Adha, the festival of sacrifice (also known as the great festival), celebrates the submission of the Prophet Ibrahim (Abraham) to God. Eid ul-Adha falls on the tenth day of Dhu'l-Hijjah, coinciding with the day when those on *hajj* (pilgrimage to Mecca) sacrifice animals.

Other days accorded special recognition are:

Muharram 1	New Year's Day
Muharram 10	Ashura (the day Prophet Noah left the Ark and Prophet Moses was saved from Pharaoh (Sunni), the death of the Prophet's grandson Husain (Shi'ite))
Rabi'u-l-Awwal (Rabi' I) 12	Mawlid ul-Nabi (birthday of the Prophet Muhammad)
Rajab 27	Laylat ul-Isra' wa'l-Mi'raj (The Night of Journey and Ascension)
*Ramadan**	Laylat ul-Qadr (Night of Power)
Dhu'l-Hijjah 10	Eid ul-Adha (Festival of Sacrifice)

* Moveable feast

For dates of the major celebrations in 2009, *see* page 9.

SIKH CALENDAR

The Sikh calendar is a lunar calendar of 365 days divided into 12 months. The length of the months varies between 29 and 32 days.

There are no prescribed feast days and no fasting periods. The main celebrations are Baisakhi Mela (the new year and the anniversary of the founding of the Khalsa), Diwali Mela (festival of light), Hola Mohalla Mela (a spring festival held in the Punjab), and the Gurpurbs (anniversaries associated with the ten Gurus).

For dates of the major celebrations in 2009, *see* page 9.

THAI CALENDAR

Thailand adopted the Suriyakati calendar, a modified version of the Gregorian calendar during the reign of King Rama V in 1888, using 1 April as the first day of the year. In 1940 the date of the new year was changed to 1 January. The years are counted from the beginning of the Buddhist era (BE), which is calculated to have commenced upon the death of the Lord Buddha, taken to have occurred in 543 BC, so AD 2009 is BE 2552. The Chinese system of associating years with one of twelve animals is also in use in Thailand. The Chantarakati lunar calendar is used to determine religious holidays; the new year begins on the first day of the waxing moon in November or, if there is a leap month, in December.

CIVIL AND LEGAL CALENDAR

THE HISTORICAL YEAR

Before 1752, two calendar systems were used in England. The civil or legal year began on 25 March and the historical year on 1 January. Thus the civil or legal date 24 March 1658 was the same day as the historical date 24 March 1659; a date in that portion of the year is written as 24 March 1658/9, the earlier date showing the civil or legal year.

THE NEW YEAR

In England in the seventh century, and as late as the 13th, the year was reckoned from Christmas Day, but in the 12th century the Church in England began the year with the feast of the Annunciation of the Blessed Virgin ('Lady Day') on 25 March, and this practice was adopted generally in the 14th century. The civil or legal year in the

British dominions (exclusive of Scotland) began with Lady Day until 1751. But in and since 1752 the civil year has begun with 1 January. New Year's Day in Scotland was changed from 25 March to 1 January in 1600.

Elsewhere in Europe, 1 January was adopted as the first day of the year by Venice in 1522, German states in 1544, Spain, Portugal and the Roman Catholic Netherlands in 1556, Prussia, Denmark and Sweden in 1559, France in 1564, Lorraine in 1579, the Protestant Netherlands in 1583, Russia in 1725, and Tuscany in 1751.

REGNAL YEARS

Regnal years are the years of a sovereign's reign and each begins on the anniversary of his or her accession, eg regnal year 58 of the present queen begins on 6 February 2009.

The system was used for dating Acts of Parliament until 1962. The Summer Time Act 1925, for example, is quoted as 15 and 16 Geo. V c. 64, because it became law in the parliamentary session which extended over part of both of these regnal years. Acts of a parliamentary session during which a sovereign died were usually given two year numbers, the regnal year of the deceased sovereign and the regnal year of his or her successor, eg those passed in 1952 were dated 16 Geo. VI and 1 Elizabeth II. Since 1962 Acts of Parliament have been dated by the calendar year.

QUARTER AND TERM DAYS

Holy days and saints days were the usual means in early times for setting the dates of future and recurrent appointments. The quarter days in England and Wales are the feast of the Nativity (25 December), the feast of the Annunciation (25 March), the feast of St John the Baptist (24 June) and the feast of St Michael and All Angels (29 September).

The term days in Scotland are Candlemas (the feast of the Purification), Whitsunday, Lammas (Loaf Mass) and Martinmas (St Martin's Day). These fell on 2 February, 15 May, 1 August and 11 November respectively. However, by the Term and Quarter Days (Scotland) Act 1990, the dates of the term days were changed to 28 February (Candlemas), 28 May (Whitsunday), 28 August (Lammas) and 28 November (Martinmas).

RED-LETTER DAYS

Red-letter days were originally the holy days and saints days indicated in early ecclesiastical calendars by letters printed in red ink. The days to be distinguished in this way were approved at the Council of Nicaea in AD 325.

These days still have a legal significance, as judges of the Queen's Bench Division wear scarlet robes on red-letter days falling during the law sittings. The days designated as red-letter days for this purpose are:

Holy and saints days
The Conversion of St Paul, the Purification, Ash Wednesday, the Annunciation, the Ascension, the feasts of St Mark, SS Philip and James, St Matthias, St Barnabas, St John the Baptist, St Peter, St Thomas, St James, St Luke, SS Simon and Jude, All Saints, St Andrew.

Civil calendar (for dates, *see* page 9)
The anniversaries of the Queen's accession, the Queen's birthday and the Queen's coronation, the Queen's official birthday, the birthday of the Duke of Edinburgh, the birthday of the Prince of Wales, St David's Day and Lord Mayor's Day.

PUBLIC HOLIDAYS

Public holidays are divided into two categories, common law and statutory. Common law holidays are holidays 'by habit and custom'; in England, Wales and Northern Ireland these are Good Friday and Christmas Day.

Statutory public holidays, known as bank holidays, were first established by the Bank Holidays Act 1871. They were, literally, days on which the banks (and other public institutions) were closed and financial obligations due on that day were payable the following day. The legislation currently governing public holidays in the UK, which is the Banking and Financial Dealings Act 1971, stipulates the days that are to be public holidays in England, Wales, Scotland and Northern Ireland.

For dates of public holidays in 2009 and 2010, *see* pages 10–11. The public holidays are:

England and Wales
*New Year's Day
Good Friday
Easter Monday
*The first Monday in May
The last Monday in May
The last Monday in August
26 December, if it is not a Sunday
27 December when 25 or 26 December is a Sunday

Scotland
New Year's Day, or if it is a Sunday, 2 January
2 January, or if it is a Sunday, 3 January
Good Friday
The first Monday in May
*The last Monday in May
The first Monday in August
Christmas Day, or if it is a Sunday, 26 December
*Boxing Day – if Christmas Day falls on a Sunday, 26 December is given in lieu and an alternative day is given for Boxing Day

Northern Ireland
*New Year's Day
17 March, or if it is a Sunday, 18 March
Easter Monday
*The first Monday in May
The last Monday in May
†12 July, or if it is a Sunday, 13 July
The last Monday in August
26 December, if it is not a Sunday
27 December if 25 or 26 December is a Sunday

* Granted annually by royal proclamation
† Subject to proclamation by the secretary of state for Northern Ireland

CHRONOLOGICAL CYCLES AND ERAS

SOLAR (OR MAJOR) CYCLE

The solar cycle is a period of 28 years; in any corresponding year of each cycle the days of the week recur on the same day of the month.

METONIC (LUNAR, OR MINOR) CYCLE

In 432 BC, Meton, an Athenian astronomer, found that 235 lunations are very nearly, though not exactly, equal in duration to 19 solar years and so after 19 years the phases of the Moon recur on the same days of the month (nearly). The dates of full moon in a cycle of 19 years were inscribed in figures of gold on public monuments in

Athens, and the number showing the position of a year in the cycle is called the golden number of that year.

JULIAN PERIOD

The Julian period was proposed by Joseph Scaliger in 1582. The period is 7,980 Julian years, and its first year coincides with the year 4713 BC. The figure of 7980 is the product of the number of years in the solar cycle, the Metonic cycle and the cycle of the Roman indiction (28 × 19 × 15).

ROMAN INDICTION

The Roman indiction is a period of 15 years, instituted for fiscal purposes about AD 300.

EPACT

The epact is the age of the calendar Moon, diminished by one day, on 1 January, in the ecclesiastical lunar calendar.

CHINESE CALENDAR

A lunar calendar was the sole calendar in use in China until 1911, when the government adopted the new (Gregorian) calendar for official and most business activities. The Chinese tend to follow both calendars, the lunar calendar playing an important part in personal life, eg birth celebrations, festivals, marriages; and in rural villages the lunar calendar dictates the cycle of activities, denoting the change of weather and farming activities.

The lunar calendar is used in Hong Kong, Singapore, Malaysia, Tibet and elsewhere in south-east Asia. The calendar has a cycle of 60 years. The new year begins at the first new moon after the sun enters the sign of Aquarius, ie the new year falls between 21 January and 19 February in the Gregorian calendar.

Each year in the Chinese calendar is associated with one of 12 animals: the rat, the ox, the tiger, the rabbit, the dragon, the snake, the horse, the goat or sheep, the monkey, the chicken or rooster, the dog, and the pig.

The date of the Chinese new year and the astrological sign for the years 2009–12 are:

2009	26 January	Ox
2010	14 February	Tiger
2011	3 February	Rabbit
2012	23 January	Dragon

COPTIC CALENDAR

In the Coptic calendar, which is used in parts of Egypt and Ethiopia, the year is made up of 12 months of 30 days each, followed, in general, by five complementary days. Every fourth year is an intercalary or leap year and in these years there are six complementary days. The intercalary year of the Coptic calendar immediately precedes the leap year of the Julian calendar. The era is that of Diocletian or the Martyrs, the origin of which is fixed at 29 August AD 284 (Julian date).

INDIAN ERAS

In addition to the Muslim reckoning, other eras are used in India. The Saka era of southern India, dating from 3 March AD 78, was declared the national calendar of the Republic of India with effect from 22 March 1957, to be used concurrently with the Gregorian calendar. As revised, the year of the new Saka era begins at the spring equinox, with five successive months of 31 days and seven of 30 days in ordinary years, and six months of each length in leap years. The year AD 2009 is 1931 of the revised Saka era.

The year AD 2009 corresponds to the following years in other eras:

Year 2066 of the Vikram Samvat era
Year 1416 of the Bengali San era
Year 1185 of the Kollam era
Year 5110 of the Kaliyuga era
Year 2552 of the Buddha Nirvana era

JAPANESE CALENDAR

The Japanese calendar is essentially the same as the Gregorian calendar, the years, months and weeks being of the same length and beginning on the same days as those of the Gregorian calendar. The numeration of the years is different, based on a system of epochs or periods, each of which begins at the accession of an emperor or other important occurrence. The method is not unlike the British system of regnal years, except that each year of a period closes on 31 December. The Japanese chronology begins about AD 650 and the three latest epochs are defined by the reigns of emperors, whose actual names are not necessarily used:

Epoch
Taisho – 1 August 1912 to 25 December 1926
Showa – 26 December 1926 to 7 January 1989
Heisei – 8 January 1989

The year Heisei 21 begins on 1 January 2009.

The months are known as First Month, Second Month, etc, First Month being equivalent to January. The days of the week are Nichiyobi (Sun-day), Getsuyobi (Moon-day), Kayobi (Fire-day), Suiyobi (Water-day), Mokuyobi (Wood-day), Kinyobi (Metal-day) and Doyobi (Earth-day).

THE MASONIC YEAR

Two dates are quoted in warrants, dispensations, etc, issued by the United Grand Lodge of England, those for the current year being expressed as *Anno Domini* 2009 – *Anno Lucis* 6009. This *Anno Lucis* (year of light) is based on the Book of Genesis 1:3, the 4,000-year difference being derived, in modified form, from *Ussher's Notation,* published in 1654, which places the Creation of the World in 4004 BC.

OLYMPIADS

Ancient Greek chronology was reckoned in Olympiads, cycles of four years corresponding with the periodic Olympic Games held on the plain of Olympia, in Elis, once every four years. The intervening years were the first, second, etc, of the Olympiad, which received the name of the victor at the Games. The first recorded Olympiad is that of Choroebus, 776 BC.

ZOROASTRIAN CALENDAR

Zoroastrians, followers of the Iranian prophet Zarathushtra (known to the Greeks as Zoroaster) are mostly to be found in Iran and in India, where they are known as Parsees.

The Zoroastrian era dates from the coronation of the last Zoroastrian Sasanian king in AD 631. The Zoroastrian calendar is divided into 12 months, each comprising 30 days, followed by five holy days of the Gathas at the end of each year to make the year consist of 365 days.

In order to synchronise the calendar with the solar year of 365 days, an extra month was intercalated once every

120 years. However, this intercalation ceased in the 12th century and the new year, which had fallen in the spring, slipped back to August. Because intercalation ceased at different times in Iran and India, there was one month's difference between the calendar followed in Iran (Kadmi calendar) and that followed by the Parsees (Shenshai calendar). In 1906 a group of Zoroastrians decided to bring the calendar back in line with the seasons again and restore the new year to 21 March each year (Fasli calendar).

The Shenshai calendar (new year in August) is mainly used by Parsees. The Fasli calendar (new year, 21 March) is mainly used by Zoroastrians living in Iran, in the Indian subcontinent, or away from Iran.

ROMAN CALENDAR

Roman historians adopted as an epoch the foundation of Rome, which is believed to have happened in the year 753 BC. The ordinal number of the years in Roman reckoning is followed by the letters AUC *(ab urbe condita)*, so that the year 2009 is 2762 AUC (MMDCCLXII). The calendar that we know has developed from one said to have been established by Romulus using a year of 304 days divided into ten months, beginning with March. To this Numa added January and February, making the year consist of 12 months of 30 and 29 days alternately, with an additional day so that the total was 355. It is also said that Numa ordered an intercalary month of 22 or 23 days in alternate years, making 90 days in eight years, to be inserted after 23 February.

However, there is some doubt as to the origination and the details of the intercalation in the Roman calendar. It is certain that some scheme of this kind was inaugurated and not fully carried out, for in the year 46 BC Julius Caesar found that the calendar had been allowed to fall into some confusion. He sought the help of the Egyptian astronomer Sosigenes, which led to the construction and adoption (45 BC) of the Julian calendar, and, by a slight alteration, to the Gregorian calendar now in use. The year 46 BC was made to consist of 445 days and is called the Year of Confusion.

In the Roman (Julian) calendar the days of the month were counted backwards from three fixed points, or days, and an intervening day was said to be so many days before the next coming point, the first and last being counted. These three points were the Kalends, the Nones, and the Ides. Their positions in the months and the method of counting from them will be seen in the table below. The year containing 366 days was called *bissextilis annus*, as it had a doubled sixth day *(bissextus dies)* before the March Kalends on 24 February – *ante diem sextum Kalendas Martias*, or a.d. VI Kal. Mart.

Present days of the month	*March, May, July, October have thirty-one days*		*January, August, December have thirty-one days*		*April, June, September, November have thirty days*		*February has twenty-eight days, and in leap year twenty-nine*	
1	Kalendis		Kalendis		Kalendis		Kalendis	
2	VI		IV	ante	IV	ante	IV	ante
3	V	ante	III	Nonas	III	Nonas	III	Nonas
4	IV	Nonas	pridie Nonas		pridie Nonas		pridie Nonas	
5	III		Nonis		Nonis		Nonis	
6	pridie Nonas		VIII		VIII		VIII	
7	Nonis		VII		VII		VII	
8	VIII		VI	ante	VI	ante	VI	ante
9	VII		V	Idus	V	Idus	V	Idus
10	VI	ante	IV		IV		IV	
11	V	Idus	III		III		III	
12	IV		pridie Idus		pridie Idus		pridie Idus	
13	III		Idibus		Idibus		Idibus	
14	pridie Idus		XIX		XVIII		XVI	
15	Idibus		XVIII		XVII		XV	
16	XVII		XVII		XVI		XIV	
17	XVI		XVI		XV		XIII	
18	XV		XV		XIV		XII	
19	XIV		XIV		XIII		XI	
20	XIII		XIII		XII	ante Kalendas	X	ante Kalendas
21	XII		XII	ante Kalendas	XI	(of the month	IX	Martias
22	XI	ante Kalendas	XI	(of the month	X	following)	VIII	
23	X	(of the month	X	following)	IX		VII	
24	IX	following)	IX		VIII		*VI	
25	VIII		VIII		VII		V	
26	VII		VII		VI		IV	
27	VI		VI		V		III	
28	V		V		IV		pridie Kalendas Martias	
29	IV		IV		III			
30	III		III		pridie Kalendas (Maias, Quinctilis, Octobris, Decembris)			
31	pridie Kalendas (Aprilis, Iunias, Sextilis, Novembris)		pridie Kalendas (Februarias, Septembris, Ianuarias)					

* Repeated in leap year

CALENDAR FOR ANY YEAR 1780–2040

To select the correct calendar for any year between 1780 and 2040, consult the index below

*leap year

1780 N*	1813 K	1846 I	1879 G	1912 D*	1945 C	1978 A	2011 M
1781 C	1814 M	1847 K	1880 J*	1913 G	1946 E	1979 C	2012 B*
1782 E	1815 A	1848 N*	1881 M	1914 I	1947 G	1980 F*	2013 E
1783 G	1816 D*	1849 C	1882 A	1915 K	1948 J*	1981 I	2014 G
1784 J*	1817 G	1850 E	1883 C	1916 N*	1949 M	1982 K	2015 I
1785 M	1818 I	1851 G	1884 F*	1917 C	1950 A	1983 M	2016 L*
1786 A	1819 K	1852 J*	1885 I	1918 E	1951 C	1984 B*	2017 A
1787 C	1820 N*	1853 M	1886 K	1919 G	1952 F*	1985 E	2018 C
1788 F*	1821 C	1854 A	1887 M	1920 J*	1953 I	1986 G	2019 E
1789 I	1822 E	1855 C	1888 B*	1921 M	1954 K	1987 I	2020 H*
1790 K	1823 G	1856 F*	1889 E	1922 A	1955 M	1988 L*	2021 K
1791 M	1824 J*	1857 I	1890 G	1923 C	1956 B*	1989 A	2022 M
1792 B*	1825 M	1858 K	1891 I	1924 F*	1957 E	1990 C	2023 A
1793 E	1826 A	1859 M	1892 L*	1925 I	1958 G	1991 E	2024 D*
1794 G	1827 C	1860 B*	1893 A	1926 K	1959 I	1992 H*	2025 G
1795 I	1828 F*	1861 E	1894 C	1927 M	1960 L*	1993 K	2026 I
1796 L*	1829 I	1862 G	1895 E	1928 B*	1961 A	1994 M	2027 K
1797 A	1830 K	1863 I	1896 H*	1929 E	1962 C	1995 A	2028 N*
1798 C	1831 M	1864 L*	1897 K	1930 G	1963 E	1996 D*	2029 C
1799 E	1832 B*	1865 A	1898 M	1931 I	1964 H*	1997 G	2030 E
1800 G	1833 E	1866 C	1899 A	1932 L*	1965 K	1998 I	2031 G
1801 I	1834 G	1867 E	1900 C	1933 A	1966 M	1999 K	2032 J*
1802 K	1835 I	1868 H*	1901 E	1934 C	1967 A	2000 N*	2033 M
1803 M	1836 L*	1869 K	1902 G	1935 E	1968 D*	2001 C	2034 A
1804 B*	1837 A	1870 M	1903 I	1936 H*	1969 G	2002 E	2035 C
1805 E	1838 C	1871 A	1904 L*	1937 K	1970 I	2003 G	2036 F*
1806 G	1839 E	1872 D*	1905 A	1938 M	1971 K	2004 J*	2037 I
1807 I	1840 H*	1873 G	1906 C	1939 A	1972 N*	2005 M	2038 K
1808 L*	1841 K	1874 I	1907 E	1940 D*	1973 C	2006 A	2039 M
1809 A	1842 M	1875 K	1908 H*	1941 G	1974 E	2007 C	2040 B*
1810 C	1843 A	1876 N*	1909 K	1942 I	1975 G	2008 F*	
1811 E	1844 D*	1877 C	1910 M	1943 K	1976 J*	2009 I	
1812 H*	1845 G	1878 E	1911 A	1944 N*	1977 M	2010 K	

A

	January	*February*	*March*
Sun.	1 8 15 22 29	5 12 19 26	5 12 19 26
Mon.	2 9 16 23 30	6 13 20 27	6 13 20 27
Tue.	3 10 17 24 31	7 14 21 28	7 14 21 28
Wed.	4 11 18 25	1 8 15 22	1 8 15 22 29
Thur.	5 12 19 26	2 9 16 23	2 9 16 23 30
Fri.	6 13 20 27	3 10 17 24	3 10 17 24 31
Sat.	7 14 21 28	4 11 18 25	4 11 18 25

	April	*May*	*June*
Sun.	2 9 16 23 30	7 14 21 28	4 11 18 25
Mon.	3 10 17 24	1 8 15 22 29	5 12 19 26
Tue.	4 11 18 25	2 9 16 23 30	6 13 20 27
Wed.	5 12 19 26	3 10 17 24 31	7 14 21 28
Thur.	6 13 20 27	4 11 18 25	1 8 15 22 29
Fri.	7 14 21 28	5 12 19 26	2 9 16 23 30
Sat.	1 8 15 22 29	6 13 20 27	3 10 17 24

	July	*August*	*September*
Sun.	2 9 16 23 30	6 13 20 27	3 10 17 24
Mon.	3 10 17 24 31	7 14 21 28	4 11 18 25
Tue.	4 11 18 25	1 8 15 22 29	5 12 19 26
Wed.	5 12 19 26	2 9 16 23 30	6 13 20 27
Thur.	6 13 20 27	3 10 17 24 31	7 14 21 28
Fri.	7 14 21 28	4 11 18 25	1 8 15 22 29
Sat.	1 8 15 22 29	5 12 19 26	2 9 16 23 30

	October	*November*	*December*
Sun.	1 8 15 22 29	5 12 19 26	3 10 17 24 31
Mon.	2 9 16 23 30	6 13 20 27	4 11 18 25
Tue.	3 10 17 24 31	7 14 21 28	5 12 19 26
Wed.	4 11 18 25	1 8 15 22 29	6 13 20 27
Thur.	5 12 19 26	2 9 16 23 30	7 14 21 28
Fri.	6 13 20 27	3 10 17 24	1 8 15 22 29
Sat.	7 14 21 28	4 11 18 25	2 9 16 23 30

EASTER DAYS

March 26	1815, 1826, 1837, 1967, 1978, 1989
April 2	1809, 1893, 1899, 1961
April 9	1871, 1882, 1939, 1950, 2023, 2034
April 16	1786, 1797, 1843, 1854, 1865, 1911 1922, 1933, 1995, 2006, 2017
April 23	1905

B (LEAP YEAR)

	January	*February*	*March*
Sun.	1 8 15 22 29	5 12 19 26	4 11 18 25
Mon.	2 9 16 23 30	6 13 20 27	5 12 19 26
Tue.	3 10 17 24 31	7 14 21 28	6 13 20 27
Wed.	4 11 18 25	1 8 15 22 29	7 14 21 28
Thur.	5 12 19 26	2 9 16 23	1 8 15 22 29
Fri.	6 13 20 27	3 10 17 24	2 9 16 23 30
Sat.	7 14 21 28	4 11 18 25	3 10 17 24 31

	April	*May*	*June*
Sun.	1 8 15 22 29	6 13 20 27	3 10 17 24
Mon.	2 9 16 23 30	7 14 21 28	4 11 18 25
Tue.	3 10 17 24	1 8 15 22 29	5 12 19 26
Wed.	4 11 18 25	2 9 16 23 30	6 13 20 27
Thur.	5 12 19 26	3 10 17 24 31	7 14 21 28
Fri.	6 13 20 27	4 11 18 25	1 8 15 22 29
Sat.	7 14 21 28	5 12 19 26	2 9 16 23 30

	July	*August*	*September*
Sun.	1 8 15 22 29	5 12 19 26	2 9 16 23 30
Mon.	2 9 16 23 30	6 13 20 27	3 10 17 24
Tue.	3 10 17 24 31	7 14 21 28	4 11 18 25
Wed.	4 11 18 25	1 8 15 22 29	5 12 19 26
Thur.	5 12 19 26	2 9 16 23 30	6 13 20 27
Fri.	6 13 20 27	3 10 17 24 31	7 14 21 28
Sat.	7 14 21 28	4 11 18 25	1 8 15 22 29

	October	*November*	*December*
Sun.	7 14 21 28	4 11 18 25	2 9 16 23 30
Mon.	1 8 15 22 29	5 12 19 26	3 10 17 24 31
Tue.	2 9 16 23 30	6 13 20 27	4 11 18 25
Wed.	3 10 17 24 31	7 14 21 28	5 12 19 26
Thur.	4 11 18 25	1 8 15 22 29	6 13 20 27
Fri.	5 12 19 26	2 9 16 23 30	7 14 21 28
Sat.	6 13 20 27	3 10 17 24	1 8 15 22 29

EASTER DAYS

April 1	1804, 1888, 1956, 2040
April 8	1792, 1860, 1928, 2012
April 22	1832, 1984

C

	January	*February*	*March*
Sun.	7 14 21 28	4 11 18 25	4 11 18 25
Mon.	1 8 15 22 29	5 12 19 26	5 12 19 26
Tue.	2 9 16 23 30	6 13 20 27	6 13 20 27
Wed.	3 10 17 24 31	7 14 21 28	7 14 21 28
Thur.	4 11 18 25	1 8 15 22	1 8 15 22 29
Fri.	5 12 19 26	2 9 16 23	2 9 16 23 30
Sat.	6 13 20 27	3 10 17 24	3 10 17 24 31

	April	*May*	*June*
Sun.	1 8 15 22 29	6 13 20 27	3 10 17 24
Mon.	2 9 16 23 30	7 14 21 28	4 11 18 25
Tue.	3 10 17 24	1 8 15 22 29	5 12 19 26
Wed.	4 11 18 25	2 9 16 23 30	6 13 20 27
Thur.	5 12 19 26	3 10 17 24 31	7 14 21 28
Fri.	6 13 20 27	4 11 18 25	1 8 15 22 29
Sat.	7 14 21 28	5 12 19 26	2 9 16 23 30

	July	*August*	*September*
Sun.	1 8 15 22 29	5 12 19 26	2 9 16 23 30
Mon.	2 9 16 23 30	6 13 20 27	3 10 17 24
Tue.	3 10 17 24 31	7 14 21 28	4 11 18 25
Wed.	4 11 18 25	1 8 15 22 29	5 12 19 26
Thur.	5 12 19 26	2 9 16 23 30	6 13 20 27
Fri.	6 13 20 27	3 10 17 24 31	7 14 21 28
Sat.	7 14 21 28	4 11 18 25	1 8 15 22 29

	October	*November*	*December*
Sun.	7 14 21 28	4 11 18 25	2 9 16 23 30
Mon.	1 8 15 22 29	5 12 19 26	3 10 17 24 31
Tue.	2 9 16 23 30	6 13 20 27	4 11 18 25
Wed.	3 10 17 24 31	7 14 21 28	5 12 19 26
Thur.	4 11 18 25	1 8 15 22 29	6 13 20 27
Fri.	5 12 19 26	2 9 16 23 30	7 14 21 28
Sat.	6 13 20 27	3 10 17 24	1 8 15 22 29

EASTER DAYS

March 25	1883, 1894, 1951, 2035
April 1	1866, 1877, 1923, 1934, 1945, 2018, 2029
April 8	1787, 1798, 1849, 1855, 1917, 2007
April 15	1781, 1827, 1838, 1900, 1906, 1979, 1990, 2001
April 22	1810, 1821, 1962, 1973

D (LEAP YEAR)

	January	*February*	*March*
Sun.	7 14 21 28	4 11 18 25	3 10 17 24 31
Mon.	1 8 15 22 29	5 12 19 26	4 11 18 25
Tue.	2 9 16 23 30	6 13 20 27	5 12 19 26
Wed.	3 10 17 24 31	7 14 21 28	6 13 20 27
Thur.	4 11 18 25	1 8 15 22 29	7 14 21 28
Fri.	5 12 19 26	2 9 16 23	1 8 15 22 29
Sat.	6 13 20 27	3 10 17 24	2 9 16 23 30

	April	*May*	*June*
Sun.	7 14 21 28	5 12 19 26	2 9 16 23 30
Mon.	1 8 15 22 29	6 13 20 27	3 10 17 24
Tue.	2 9 16 23 30	7 14 21 28	4 11 18 25
Wed.	3 10 17 24	1 8 15 22 29	5 12 19 26
Thur.	4 11 18 25	2 9 16 23 30	6 13 20 27
Fri.	5 12 19 26	3 10 17 24 31	7 14 21 28
Sat.	6 13 20 27	4 11 18 25	1 8 15 22 29

	July	*August*	*September*
Sun.	7 14 21 28	4 11 18 25	1 8 15 22 29
Mon.	1 8 15 22 29	5 12 19 26	2 9 16 23 30
Tue.	2 9 16 23 30	6 13 20 27	3 10 17 24
Wed.	3 10 17 24 31	7 14 21 28	4 11 18 25
Thur.	4 11 18 25	1 8 15 22 29	5 12 19 26
Fri.	5 12 19 26	2 9 16 23 30	6 13 20 27
Sat.	6 13 20 27	3 10 17 24 31	7 14 21 28

	October	*November*	*December*
Sun.	6 13 20 27	3 10 17 24	1 8 15 22 29
Mon.	7 14 21 28	4 11 18 25	2 9 16 23 30
Tue.	1 8 15 22 29	5 12 19 26	3 10 17 24 31
Wed.	2 9 16 23 30	6 13 20 27	4 11 18 25
Thur.	3 10 17 24 31	7 14 21 28	5 12 19 26
Fri.	4 11 18 25	1 8 15 22 29	6 13 20 27
Sat.	5 12 19 26	2 9 16 23 30	7 14 21 28

EASTER DAYS

March 24	1940
March 31	1872, 2024
April 7	1844, 1912, 1996
April 14	1816, 1968

E

	January	*February*	*March*
Sun.	6 13 20 27	3 10 17 24	3 10 17 24 31
Mon.	7 14 21 28	4 11 18 25	4 11 18 25
Tue.	1 8 15 22 29	5 12 19 26	5 12 19 26
Wed.	2 9 16 23 30	6 13 20 27	6 13 20 27
Thur.	3 10 17 24 31	7 14 21 28	7 14 21 28
Fri.	4 11 18 25	1 8 15 22	1 8 15 22 29
Sat.	5 12 19 26	2 9 16 23	2 9 16 23 30

	April	*May*	*June*
Sun.	7 14 21 28	5 12 19 26	2 9 16 23 30
Mon.	1 8 15 22 29	6 13 20 27	3 10 17 24
Tue.	2 9 16 23 30	7 14 21 28	4 11 18 25
Wed.	3 10 17 24	1 8 15 22 29	5 12 19 26
Thur.	4 11 18 25	2 9 16 23 30	6 13 20 27
Fri.	5 12 19 26	3 10 17 24 31	7 14 21 28
Sat.	6 13 20 27	4 11 18 25	1 8 15 22 29

	July	*August*	*September*
Sun.	7 14 21 28	4 11 18 25	1 8 15 22 29
Mon.	1 8 15 22 29	5 12 19 26	2 9 16 23 30
Tue.	2 9 16 23 30	6 13 20 27	3 10 17 24
Wed.	3 10 17 24 31	7 14 21 28	4 11 18 25
Thur.	4 11 18 25	1 8 15 22 29	5 12 19 26
Fri.	5 12 19 26	2 9 16 23 30	6 13 20 27
Sat.	6 13 20 27	3 10 17 24 31	7 14 21 28

	October	*November*	*December*
Sun.	6 13 20 27	3 10 17 24	1 8 15 22 29
Mon.	7 14 21 28	4 11 18 25	2 9 16 23 30
Tue.	1 8 15 22 29	5 12 19 26	3 10 17 24 31
Wed.	2 9 16 23 30	6 13 20 27	4 11 18 25
Thur.	3 10 17 24 31	7 14 21 28	5 12 19 26
Fri.	4 11 18 25	1 8 15 22 29	6 13 20 27
Sat.	5 12 19 26	2 9 16 23 30	7 14 21 28

EASTER DAYS

March 24	1799
March 31	1782, 1793, 1839, 1850, 1861, 1907 1918, 1929, 1991, 2002, 2013
April 7	1822, 1833, 1901, 1985
April 14	1805, 1811, 1895, 1963, 1974
April 21	1867, 1878, 1889, 1935, 1946, 1957, 2019, 2030

F (LEAP YEAR)

	January	*February*	*March*
Sun.	6 13 20 27	3 10 17 24	2 9 16 23 30
Mon.	7 14 21 28	4 11 18 25	3 10 17 24 31
Tue.	1 8 15 22 29	5 12 19 26	4 11 18 25
Wed.	2 9 16 23 30	6 13 20 27	5 12 19 26
Thur.	3 10 17 24 31	7 14 21 28	6 13 20 27
Fri.	4 11 18 25	1 8 15 22 29	7 14 21 28
Sat.	5 12 19 26	2 9 16 23	1 8 15 22 29

	April	*May*	*June*
Sun.	6 13 20 27	4 11 18 25	1 8 15 22 29
Mon.	7 14 21 28	5 12 19 26	2 9 16 23 30
Tue.	1 8 15 22 29	6 13 20 27	3 10 17 24
Wed.	2 9 16 23 30	7 14 21 28	4 11 18 25
Thur.	3 10 17 24	1 8 15 22 29	5 12 19 26
Fri.	4 11 18 25	2 9 16 23 30	6 13 20 27
Sat.	5 12 19 26	3 10 17 24 31	7 14 21 28

	July	*August*	*September*
Sun.	6 13 20 27	3 10 17 24 31	7 14 21 28
Mon.	7 14 21 28	4 11 18 25	1 8 15 22 29
Tue.	1 8 15 22 29	5 12 19 26	2 9 16 23 30
Wed.	2 9 16 23 30	6 13 20 27	3 10 17 24
Thur.	3 10 17 24 31	7 14 21 28	4 11 18 25
Fri.	4 11 18 25	1 8 15 22 29	5 12 19 26
Sat.	5 12 19 26	2 9 16 23 30	6 13 20 27

	October	*November*	*December*
Sun.	5 12 19 26	2 9 16 23 30	7 14 21 28
Mon.	6 13 20 27	3 10 17 24	1 8 15 22 29
Tue.	7 14 21 28	4 11 18 25	2 9 16 23 30
Wed.	1 8 15 22 29	5 12 19 26	3 10 17 24 31
Thur.	2 9 16 23 30	6 13 20 27	4 11 18 25
Fri.	3 10 17 24 31	7 14 21 28	5 12 19 26
Sat.	4 11 18 25	1 8 15 22 29	6 13 20 27

EASTER DAYS

March 23	1788, 1856, 2008
April 6	1828, 1980
April 13	1884, 1952, 2036
April 20	1924

G

	January	*February*	*March*
Sun.	5 12 19 26	2 9 16 23	2 9 16 23 30
Mon.	6 13 20 27	3 10 17 24	3 10 17 24 31
Tue.	7 14 21 28	4 11 18 25	4 11 18 25
Wed.	1 8 15 22 29	5 12 19 26	5 12 19 26
Thur.	2 9 16 23 30	6 13 20 27	6 13 20 27
Fri.	3 10 17 24 31	7 14 21 28	7 14 21 28
Sat.	4 11 18 25	1 8 15 22	1 8 15 22 29

	April	*May*	*June*
Sun.	6 13 20 27	4 11 18 25	1 8 15 22 29
Mon.	7 14 21 28	5 12 19 26	2 9 16 23 30
Tue.	1 8 15 22 29	6 13 20 27	3 10 17 24
Wed.	2 9 16 23 30	7 14 21 28	4 11 18 25
Thur.	3 10 17 24	1 8 15 22 29	5 12 19 26
Fri.	4 11 18 25	2 9 16 23 30	6 13 20 27
Sat.	5 12 19 26	3 10 17 24 31	7 14 21 28

	July	*August*	*September*
Sun.	6 13 20 27	3 10 17 24 31	7 14 21 28
Mon.	7 14 21 28	4 11 18 25	1 8 15 22 29
Tue.	1 8 15 22 29	5 12 19 26	2 9 16 23 30
Wed.	2 9 16 23 30	6 13 20 27	3 10 17 24
Thur.	3 10 17 24 31	7 14 21 28	4 11 18 25
Fri.	4 11 18 25	1 8 15 22 29	5 12 19 26
Sat.	5 12 19 26	2 9 16 23 30	6 13 20 27

	October	*November*	*December*
Sun.	5 12 19 26	2 9 16 23 30	7 14 21 28
Mon.	6 13 20 27	3 10 17 24	1 8 15 22 29
Tue.	7 14 21 28	4 11 18 25	2 9 16 23 30
Wed.	1 8 15 22 29	5 12 19 26	3 10 17 24 31
Thur.	2 9 16 23 30	6 13 20 27	4 11 18 25
Fri.	3 10 17 24 31	7 14 21 28	5 12 19 26
Sat.	4 11 18 25	1 8 15 22 29	6 13 20 27

EASTER DAYS

March 23	1845, 1913
March 30	1823, 1834, 1902, 1975, 1986, 1997
April 6	1806, 1817, 1890, 1947, 1958, 1969
April 13	1800, 1873, 1879, 1941, 2031
April 20	1783, 1794, 1851, 1862, 1919, 1930, 2003, 2014, 2025

I

	January	*February*	*March*
Sun.	4 11 18 25	1 8 15 22	1 8 15 22 29
Mon.	5 12 19 26	2 9 16 23	2 9 16 23 30
Tue.	6 13 20 27	3 10 17 24	3 10 17 24 31
Wed.	7 14 21 28	4 11 18 25	4 11 18 25
Thur.	1 8 15 22 29	5 12 19 26	5 12 19 26
Fri.	2 9 16 23 30	6 13 20 27	6 13 20 27
Sat.	3 10 17 24 31	7 14 21 28	7 14 21 28

	April	*May*	*June*
Sun.	5 12 19 26	3 10 17 24 31	7 14 21 28
Mon.	6 13 20 27	4 11 18 25	1 8 15 22 29
Tue.	7 14 21 28	5 12 19 26	2 9 16 23 30
Wed.	1 8 15 22 29	6 13 20 27	3 10 17 24
Thur.	2 9 16 23 30	7 14 21 28	4 11 18 25
Fri.	3 10 17 24	1 8 15 22 29	5 12 19 26
Sat.	4 11 18 25	2 9 16 23 30	6 13 20 27

	July	*August*	*September*
Sun.	5 12 19 26	2 9 16 23 30	6 13 20 27
Mon.	6 13 20 27	3 10 17 24 31	7 14 21 28
Tue.	7 14 21 28	4 11 18 25	1 8 15 22 29
Wed.	1 8 15 22 29	5 12 19 26	2 9 16 23 30
Thur.	2 9 16 23 30	6 13 20 27	3 10 17 24
Fri.	3 10 17 24 31	7 14 21 28	4 11 18 25
Sat.	4 11 18 25	1 8 15 22 29	5 12 19 26

	October	*November*	*December*
Sun.	4 11 18 25	1 8 15 22 29	6 13 20 27
Mon.	5 12 19 26	2 9 16 23 30	7 14 21 28
Tue.	6 13 20 27	3 10 17 24	1 8 15 22 29
Wed.	7 14 21 28	4 11 18 25	2 9 16 23 30
Thur.	1 8 15 22 29	5 12 19 26	3 10 17 24 31
Fri.	2 9 16 23 30	6 13 20 27	4 11 18 25
Sat.	3 10 17 24 31	7 14 21 28	5 12 19 26

EASTER DAYS

March 22	1818
March 29	1807, 1891, 1959, 1970
April 5	1795, 1801, 1863, 1874, 1885, 1931, 1942, 1953, 2015, 2026, 2037
April 12	1789, 1846, 1857, 1903, 1914, 1925, 1998, 2009
April 19	1829, 1835, 1981, 1987

H (LEAP YEAR)

	January	*February*	*March*
Sun.	5 12 19 26	2 9 16 23	1 8 15 22 29
Mon.	6 13 20 27	3 10 17 24	2 9 16 23 30
Tue.	7 14 21 28	4 11 18 25	3 10 17 24 31
Wed.	1 8 15 22 29	5 12 19 26	4 11 18 25
Thur.	2 9 16 23 30	6 13 20 27	5 12 19 26
Fri.	3 10 17 24 31	7 14 21 28	6 13 20 27
Sat.	4 11 18 25	1 8 15 22 29	7 14 21 28

	April	*May*	*June*
Sun.	5 12 19 26	3 10 17 24 31	7 14 21 28
Mon.	6 13 20 27	4 11 18 25	1 8 15 22 29
Tue.	7 14 21 28	5 12 19 26	2 9 16 23 30
Wed.	1 8 15 22 29	6 13 20 27	3 10 17 24
Thur.	2 9 16 23 30	7 14 21 28	4 11 18 25
Fri.	3 10 17 24	1 8 15 22 29	5 12 19 26
Sat.	4 11 18 25	2 9 16 23 30	6 13 20 27

	July	*August*	*September*
Sun.	5 12 19 26	2 9 16 23 30	6 13 20 27
Mon.	6 13 20 27	3 10 17 24 31	7 14 21 28
Tue.	7 14 21 28	4 11 18 25	1 8 15 22 29
Wed.	1 8 15 22 29	5 12 19 26	2 9 16 23 30
Thur.	2 9 16 23 30	6 13 20 27	3 10 17 24
Fri.	3 10 17 24 31	7 14 21 28	4 11 18 25
Sat.	4 11 18 25	1 8 15 22 29	5 12 19 26

	October	*November*	*December*
Sun.	4 11 18 25	1 8 15 22 29	6 13 20 27
Mon.	5 12 19 26	2 9 16 23 30	7 14 21 28
Tue.	6 13 20 27	3 10 17 24	1 8 15 22 29
Wed.	7 14 21 28	4 11 18 25	2 9 16 23 30
Thur.	1 8 15 22 29	5 12 19 26	3 10 17 24 31
Fri.	2 9 16 23 30	6 13 20 27	4 11 18 25
Sat.	3 10 17 24 31	7 14 21 28	5 12 19 26

EASTER DAYS

March 29	1812, 1964
April 5	1896
April 12	1868, 1936, 2020
April 19	1840, 1908, 1992

J (LEAP YEAR)

	January	*February*	*March*
Sun.	4 11 18 25	1 8 15 22 29	7 14 21 28
Mon.	5 12 19 26	2 9 16 23	1 8 15 22 29
Tue.	6 13 20 27	3 10 17 24	2 9 16 23 30
Wed.	7 14 21 28	4 11 18 25	3 10 17 24 31
Thur.	1 8 15 22 29	5 12 19 26	4 11 18 25
Fri.	2 9 16 23 30	6 13 20 27	5 12 19 26
Sat.	3 10 17 24 31	7 14 21 28	6 13 20 27

	April	*May*	*June*
Sun.	4 11 18 25	2 9 16 23 30	6 13 20 27
Mon.	5 12 19 26	3 10 17 24 31	7 14 21 28
Tue.	6 13 20 27	4 11 18 25	1 8 15 22 29
Wed.	7 14 21 28	5 12 19 26	2 9 16 23 30
Thur.	1 8 15 22 29	6 13 20 27	3 10 17 24
Fri.	2 9 16 23 30	7 14 21 28	4 11 18 25
Sat.	3 10 17 24	1 8 15 22 29	5 12 19 26

	July	*August*	*September*
Sun.	4 11 18 25	1 8 15 22 29	5 12 19 26
Mon.	5 12 19 26	2 9 16 23 30	6 13 20 27
Tue.	6 13 20 27	3 10 17 24 31	7 14 21 28
Wed.	7 14 21 28	4 11 18 25	1 8 15 22 29
Thur.	1 8 15 22 29	5 12 19 26	2 9 16 23 30
Fri.	2 9 16 23 30	6 13 20 27	3 10 17 24
Sat.	3 10 17 24 31	7 14 21 28	4 11 18 25

	October	*November*	*December*
Sun.	3 10 17 24 31	7 14 21 28	5 12 19 26
Mon.	4 11 18 25	1 8 15 22 29	6 13 20 27
Tue.	5 12 19 26	2 9 16 23 30	7 14 21 28
Wed.	6 13 20 27	3 10 17 24	1 8 15 22 29
Thur.	7 14 21 28	4 11 18 25	2 9 16 23 30
Fri.	1 8 15 22 29	5 12 19 26	3 10 17 24 31
Sat.	2 9 16 23 30	6 13 20 27	4 11 18 25

EASTER DAYS

March 28	1880, 1948, 2032
April 4	1920
April 11	1784, 1852, 2004
April 18	1824, 1976

K

	January	*February*	*March*
Sun.	3 10 17 24 31	7 14 21 28	7 14 21 28
Mon.	4 11 18 25	1 8 15 22	1 8 15 22 29
Tue.	5 12 19 26	2 9 16 23	2 9 16 23 30
Wed.	6 13 20 27	3 10 17 24	3 10 17 24 31
Thur.	7 14 21 28	4 11 18 25	4 11 18 25
Fri.	1 8 15 22 29	5 12 19 26	5 12 19 26
Sat.	2 9 16 23 30	6 13 20 27	6 13 20 27

	April	*May*	*June*
Sun.	4 11 18 25	2 9 16 23 30	6 13 20 27
Mon.	5 12 19 26	3 10 17 24 31	7 14 21 28
Tue.	6 13 20 27	4 11 18 25	1 8 15 22 29
Wed.	7 14 21 28	5 12 19 26	2 9 16 23 30
Thur.	1 8 15 22 29	6 13 20 27	3 10 17 24
Fri.	2 9 16 23 30	7 14 21 28	4 11 18 25
Sat.	3 10 17 24	1 8 15 22 29	5 12 19 26

	July	*August*	*September*
Sun.	4 11 18 25	1 8 15 22 29	5 12 19 26
Mon.	5 12 19 26	2 9 16 23 30	6 13 20 27
Tue.	6 13 20 27	3 10 17 24 31	7 14 21 28
Wed.	7 14 21 28	4 11 18 25	1 8 15 22 29
Thur.	1 8 15 22 29	5 12 19 26	2 9 16 23 30
Fri.	2 9 16 23 30	6 13 20 27	3 10 17 24
Sat.	3 10 17 24 31	7 14 21 28	4 11 18 25

	October	*November*	*December*
Sun.	3 10 17 24 31	7 14 21 28	5 12 19 26
Mon.	4 11 18 25	1 8 15 22 29	6 13 20 27
Tue.	5 12 19 26	2 9 16 23 30	7 14 21 28
Wed.	6 13 20 27	3 10 17 24	1 8 15 22 29
Thur.	7 14 21 28	4 11 18 25	2 9 16 23 30
Fri.	1 8 15 22 29	5 12 19 26	3 10 17 24 31
Sat.	2 9 16 23 30	6 13 20 27	4 11 18 25

EASTER DAYS

March 28	1869, 1875, 1937, 2027
April 4	1790, 1847, 1858, 1915, 1926, 1999, 2010, 2021
April 11	1819, 1830, 1841, 1909, 1971, 1982, 1993
April 18	1802, 1813, 1897, 1954, 1965
April 25	1886, 1943, 2038

L (LEAP YEAR)

	January	*February*	*March*
Sun.	3 10 17 24 31	7 14 21 28	6 13 20 27
Mon.	4 11 18 25	1 8 15 22 29	7 14 21 28
Tue.	5 12 19 26	2 9 16 23	1 8 15 22 29
Wed.	6 13 20 27	3 10 17 24	2 9 16 23 30
Thur.	7 14 21 28	4 11 18 25	3 10 17 24 31
Fri.	1 8 15 22 29	5 12 19 26	4 11 18 25
Sat.	2 9 16 23 30	6 13 20 27	5 12 19 26

	April	*May*	*June*
Sun.	3 10 17 24	1 8 15 22 29	5 12 19 26
Mon.	4 11 18 25	2 9 16 23 30	6 13 20 27
Tue.	5 12 19 26	3 10 17 24 31	7 14 21 28
Wed.	6 13 20 27	4 11 18 25	1 8 15 22 29
Thur.	7 14 21 28	5 12 19 26	2 9 16 23 30
Fri.	1 8 15 22 29	6 13 20 27	3 10 17 24
Sat.	2 9 16 23 30	7 14 21 28	4 11 18 25

	July	*August*	*September*
Sun.	3 10 17 24 31	7 14 21 28	4 11 18 25
Mon.	4 11 18 25	1 8 15 22 29	5 12 19 26
Tue.	5 12 19 26	2 9 16 23 30	6 13 20 27
Wed.	6 13 20 27	3 10 17 24 31	7 14 21 28
Thur.	7 14 21 28	4 11 18 25	1 8 15 22 29
Fri.	1 8 15 22 29	5 12 19 26	2 9 16 23 30
Sat.	2 9 16 23 30	6 13 20 27	3 10 17 24

	October	*November*	*December*
Sun.	2 9 16 23 30	6 13 20 27	4 11 18 25
Mon.	3 10 17 24 31	7 14 21 28	5 12 19 26
Tue.	4 11 18 25	1 8 15 22 29	6 13 20 27
Wed.	5 12 19 26	2 9 16 23 30	7 14 21 28
Thur.	6 13 20 27	3 10 17 24	1 8 15 22 29
Fri.	7 14 21 28	4 11 18 25	2 9 16 23 30
Sat.	1 8 15 22 29	5 12 19 26	3 10 17 24 31

EASTER DAYS

March 27	1796, 1864, 1932, 2016
April 3	1836, 1904, 1988
April 17	1808, 1892, 1960

M

	January	*February*	*March*
Sun.	2 9 16 23 30	6 13 20 27	6 13 20 27
Mon.	3 10 17 24 31	7 14 21 28	7 14 21 28
Tue.	4 11 18 25	1 8 15 22	1 8 15 22 29
Wed.	5 12 19 26	2 9 16 23	2 9 16 23 30
Thur.	6 13 20 27	3 10 17 24	3 10 17 24 31
Fri.	7 14 21 28	4 11 18 25	4 11 18 25
Sat.	1 8 15 22 29	5 12 19 26	5 12 19 26

	April	*May*	*June*
Sun.	3 10 17 24	1 8 15 22 29	5 12 19 26
Mon.	4 11 18 25	2 9 16 23 30	6 13 20 27
Tue.	5 12 19 26	3 10 17 24 31	7 14 21 28
Wed.	6 13 20 27	4 11 18 25	1 8 15 22 29
Thur.	7 14 21 28	5 12 19 26	2 9 16 23 30
Fri.	1 8 15 22 29	6 13 20 27	3 10 17 24
Sat.	2 9 16 23 30	7 14 21 28	4 11 18 25

	July	*August*	*September*
Sun.	3 10 17 24 31	7 14 21 28	4 11 18 25
Mon.	4 11 18 25	1 8 15 22 29	5 12 19 26
Tue.	5 12 19 26	2 9 16 23 30	6 13 20 27
Wed.	6 13 20 27	3 10 17 24 31	7 14 21 28
Thur.	7 14 21 28	4 11 18 25	1 8 15 22 29
Fri.	1 8 15 22 29	5 12 19 26	2 9 16 23 30
Sat.	2 9 16 23 30	6 13 20 27	3 10 17 24

	October	*November*	*December*
Sun.	2 9 16 23 30	6 13 20 27	4 11 18 25
Mon.	3 10 17 24 31	7 14 21 28	5 12 19 26
Tue.	4 11 18 25	1 8 15 22 29	6 13 20 27
Wed.	5 12 19 26	2 9 16 23 30	7 14 21 28
Thur.	6 13 20 27	3 10 17 24	1 8 15 22 29
Fri.	7 14 21 28	4 11 18 25	2 9 16 23 30
Sat.	1 8 15 22 29	5 12 19 26	3 10 17 24 31

EASTER DAYS

March 27	1785, 1842, 1853, 1910, 1921, 2005
April 3	1825, 1831, 1983, 1994
April 10	1803, 1814, 1887, 1898, 1955, 1966, 1977, 2039
April 17	1870, 1881, 1927, 1938, 1949, 2022, 2033
April 24	1791, 1859, 2011

N (LEAP YEAR)

	January	*February*	*March*
Sun.	2 9 16 23 30	6 13 20 27	5 12 19 26
Mon.	3 10 17 24 31	7 14 21 28	6 13 20 27
Tue.	4 11 18 25	1 8 15 22 29	7 14 21 28
Wed.	5 12 19 26	2 9 16 23	1 8 15 22 29
Thur.	6 13 20 27	3 10 17 24	2 9 16 23 30
Fri.	7 14 21 28	4 11 18 25	3 10 17 24 31
Sat.	1 8 15 22 29	5 12 19 26	4 11 18 25

	April	*May*	*June*
Sun.	2 9 16 23 30	7 14 21 28	4 11 18 25
Mon.	3 10 17 24	1 8 15 22 29	5 12 19 26
Tue.	4 11 18 25	2 9 16 23 30	6 13 20 27
Wed.	5 12 19 26	3 10 17 24 31	7 14 21 28
Thur.	6 13 20 27	4 11 18 25	1 8 15 22 29
Fri.	7 14 21 28	5 12 19 26	2 9 16 23 30
Sat.	1 8 15 22 29	6 13 20 27	3 10 17 24

	July	*August*	*September*
Sun.	2 9 16 23 30	6 13 20 27	3 10 17 24
Mon.	3 10 17 24 31	7 14 21 28	4 11 18 25
Tue.	4 11 18 25	1 8 15 22 29	5 12 19 26
Wed.	5 12 19 26	2 9 16 23 30	6 13 20 27
Thur.	6 13 20 27	3 10 17 24 31	7 14 21 28
Fri.	7 14 21 28	4 11 18 25	1 8 15 22 29
Sat.	1 8 15 22 29	5 12 19 26	2 9 16 23 30

	October	*November*	*December*
Sun.	1 8 15 22 29	5 12 19 26	3 10 17 24 31
Mon.	2 9 16 23 30	6 13 20 27	4 11 18 25
Tue.	3 10 17 24 31	7 14 21 28	5 12 19 26
Wed.	4 11 18 25	1 8 15 22 29	6 13 20 27
Thur.	5 12 19 26	2 9 16 23 30	7 14 21 28
Fri.	6 13 20 27	3 10 17 24	1 8 15 22 29
Sat.	7 14 21 28	4 11 18 25	2 9 16 23 30

EASTER DAYS

March 26	1780
April 2	1820, 1972
April 9	1944
April 16	1876, 2028
April 23	1848, 1916, 2000

GEOLOGICAL TIME

The earth is thought to have come into existence approximately 4,600 million years ago, but for nearly half this time, the Archean era, it was uninhabited. Life is generally believed to have emerged in the succeeding Proterozoic era. The Archean and the Proterozoic eras are often together referred to as the Precambrian.

Although primitive forms of life, eg algae and bacteria, existed during the Proterozoic era, it is not until the strata of Palaeozoic rocks are reached that abundant fossilised remains appear. Since the Precambrian, there have been three great geological eras:

PALAEOZOIC ('ANCIENT LIFE')

*c.*542–*c.*251 million years ago

Cambrian – Mainly sandstones, slate and shales; limestones in Scotland. Shelled fossils and invertebrates, eg trilobites and brachiopods appear, as do the earliest known vertebrates (jawless fish)
Ordovician – Mainly shales and mudstones, eg in north Wales; limestones in Scotland. First fishes
Silurian – Shales, mudstones and some limestones, found mostly in Wales and southern Scotland
Devonian – Old red sandstone, shale, limestone and slate, eg in south Wales and the West Country
Carboniferous – Coal-bearing rocks, millstone grit, limestone and shale. First traces of land-living creatures
Permian – Marls, sandstones and clays. First reptile fossils

There were two great phases of mountain building in the Palaeozoic era: the Caledonian, characterised in Britain by NE–SW lines of hills and valleys; and the later Hercyian, widespread in west Germany and adjacent areas, and in Britain exemplified in E–W lines of hills and valleys.

The end of the Palaeozoic era was marked by the extensive glaciations of the Permian period in the southern continents and the decline of amphibians. It was succeeded by an era of warm conditions.

MESOZOIC ('MIDDLE FORMS OF LIFE')

*c.*251–*c.*65.5 million years ago

Triassic – Mostly sandstone, eg in the West Midlands; primitive mammals appear
Jurassic – Mainly limestones and clays, typically displayed in the Jura mountains, and in England in a NE–SW belt from Lincolnshire and the Wash to the Severn and the Dorset coast
Cretaceous – Mainly chalk, clay and sands, eg in Kent and Sussex

Giant reptiles were dominant during the Mesozoic era, but it was at this time that marsupial mammals first appeared, as well as *Archaeopteryx lithographica*, the earliest known species of bird. Coniferous trees and flowering plants also developed during the era and, with the birds and the mammals, were the main species to survive into the Cenozoic era. The giant reptiles became extinct.

CENOZOIC ('RECENT LIFE')

from *c.*65.5 million years ago

Palaeocene, *Eocene* } The emergence of new forms of life, including existing species; primates appear
Oligocene – Fossils of a few still existing species
Miocene – Fossil remains show a balance of existing and extinct species
Pliocene – Fossil remains show a majority of still existing species
Pleistocene – The majority of remains are those of still existing species
Holocene – The present, post-glacial period. Existing species only, except for a few exterminated by humans

In the last 25 million years, from the Miocene through the Pliocene periods, the Alpine-Himalayan and the circum-Pacific phases of mountain building reached their climax. During the Pleistocene period ice-sheets repeatedly locked up masses of water as land ice; its weight depressed the land, but the locking-up of the water lowered the sea level by 100–200 metres. The glaciations and interglacials of the Ice Age are difficult to date and classify, but recent scientific opinion considers the Pleistocene period to have begun approximately 1.64 million years ago. The last glacial retreat, merging into the Holocene period, was *c.*10,000 years ago.

HUMAN DEVELOPMENT

Any consideration of the history of humans must start with the fact that all members of the human race belong to one species of animal, ie *Homo sapiens,* the definition of a species being in biological terms that all its members can interbreed. As a species of mammal it is possible to group humans with other similar types, known as the primates. Amongst these is found a sub-group, the apes, which includes, in addition to humans, the chimpanzees, gorillas, orang-utans and gibbons. All lack a tail, have shoulder blades at the back, and a Y-shaped chewing pattern on the surface of their molars, as well as showing the more general primate characteristics of four incisors, a thumb which is able to touch the fingers of the same hand, and finger and toe nails instead of claws. The factors available to scientific study suggest that human beings have chimpanzees and gorillas as their nearest relatives in the animal world. However, there remains the possibility that there once lived creatures, now extinct, which were closer to modern man than the chimpanzees and gorillas, and which shared with modern man the characteristics of having flat faces (ie the absence of a pronounced muzzle), being bipedal, and possessing large brains.

There are two broad groups of extinct apes recognised by specialists. The ramapithecines – the remains of which, mainly jaw fragments, have been found in east Africa, Asia and Turkey – lived about 14 to 8 million years ago, and from the evidence of their teeth it seems they chewed more in the manner of modern humans than the other presently living apes. The second group, the australopithecines, have left more numerous remains amongst which sub-groups may be detected, although the geographic spread is limited to south and east Africa. Living between 5 and 1.5 million years ago, they were closer relatives of modern humans to the extent that they walked upright, did not have an extensive muzzle and had similar types of pre-molars. The first australopithecine remains were recognised at Taung in South Africa in 1924 and named *Australopithecus africanus,* dating between 3.3 and 2.3 million years ago. The most impressive discovery was made at Hadar, Ethiopia, in 1974 when about half a skeleton of *Australopithecus afarensis,* known as 'Lucy', was found. Some 3.2 million years ago, 'Lucy' certainly walked upright.

Also in east Africa, especially at Olduvai Gorge in Tanzania, between *c.*2.5 and 1.8 million years ago, lived a hominid group which not only walked upright, had a flat face, and a large brain case, but also made simple pebble and flake stone tools. On present evidence these habilines seem to have been the first people to make tools, however crude. This facility is related to the larger brain size and human beings are the only animals to make implements to be used in other processes. These early pebble tool users, because of their distinctive characteristics, have been grouped as a separate sub-species, now extinct, of the genus *Homo* and are known as *Homo habilis* or 'handy man'.

The use of fire, again a human characteristic, is associated with another group of extinct hominids whose remains, about a million years old, are found in south and east Africa, China, Indonesia, north Africa and Europe. Mastery of the techniques of making fire probably helped the colonisation of the colder northern areas and in this respect the site of Vertesszollos in Hungary is of particular importance. *Homo ergaster* in Africa and *Homo erectus* in Asia are the names given to this group of fossils and they relate to a number of famous individual discoveries, eg Solo Man, Heidelberg Man, and especially Peking Man who lived at the cave site at Choukoutien which has yielded evidence of fire and burnt bone.

The well-known group Neanderthal Man, or *Homo neanderthalensis,* is an extinct form of man that lived between about 350,000 and 24,000 years ago, thus spanning the last Ice Age. Indeed, its ability to adapt to the cold climate on the edge of the ice-sheets is one of its characteristic features, the remains being found only in Europe, Asia and the Middle East. Complete neanderthal skeletons were found during excavations at Tabun in Israel, together with evidence of tool-making and the use of fire. Distinguished by very large brains, it seems that neanderthal man was the first to develop recognisable social customs, especially deliberate burial rites. Why the neanderthals became extinct is not clear but it may be connected with the climatic changes at the end of the Ice Ages, which would have seriously affected their food supplies; possibly they became too specialised for their own good.

The shin bone of Boxgrove Man found in 1993 – *Homo heidelbergensis* – and the Swanscombe skull are the best known early human fossil remains found in England. Some specialists prefer to group Swanscombe Man (or, more probably, woman) together with the Steinheim skull from Germany, seeing both as a separate sub-species. There is too little evidence as yet on which to form a final judgement.

Modern humans – *Homo sapiens* – had evolved to our present physical condition and had colonised much of the world by about 40,000 years ago. There are many previously distinguished individual specimens, eg Cromagnon Man, which may now be grouped together as *Homo sapiens.* It was modern humans who spread to the American continent by crossing the landbridge between Siberia and Alaska and thence moved south through North America and into South America. Equally it is modern humans who over the last 40,000 years have been responsible for the major developments in technology, art and civilisation generally.

One of the problems for those studying human fossils is the lack in many cases of sufficient quantities of fossil bone for analysis. It is important that theories should be tested against evidence, rather than the evidence being made to fit the theory. The Piltdown hoax of 1912 (and not fully exposed until the 1970s) is a well-known example of 'fossils' being forged to fit what was seen in some quarters as the correct theory of human evolution.

The discovery of the structure of DNA in 1953 has come to have a profound effect upon the study of human evolution. For example, it was claimed in 1987 that a common ancestor of all human beings was a person who lived in Africa some 200,000 years ago, thus encouraging the 'out of Africa' theory of hominid migration from east Africa to the Middle East and then throughout the world. There is no doubt that the studies based on DNA have vast potential to elucidate further the course of human evolution.

CULTURAL DEVELOPMENT

The Eurocentric bias of early archaeologists meant that the search for a starting point for the development and transmission of cultural ideas, especially by migration, trade and warfare, concentrated unduly on Europe and the Near East. The Three Age system, whereby prehistory was divided into a Stone Age, a Bronze Age and an Iron Age, was devised by Christian Thomsen, curator of the National Museum of Denmark in the early 19th century, to facilitate the classification of the museum's collections. The descriptive adjectives referred to the materials from which the implements and weapons were made and came to be regarded as the dominant features of the societies to which they related. The refinement of the Three Age system once dominated archaeological thought and remains a generally accepted concept in the popular mind. However, it is now seen by archaeologists as an inadequate model for human development.

Common sense suggests that there were no complete breaks between one so-called Age and another, any more than contemporaries would have regarded 1485 as a complete break between medieval and modern English history. Nor can the Three Age system be applied universally. In some areas it is necessary to insert a Copper Age, while in Africa south of the Sahara there would seem to be no Bronze Age at all; in Australia, Old Stone Age societies survived, while in South America, New Stone Age communities existed into modern times. The civilisations in other parts of the world clearly invalidate a Eurocentric theory of human development.

The concept of the 'Neolithic revolution', associated with the domestication of plants and animals, was a development of particular importance in the human cultural pattern. It reflected change from the primitive hunter/gatherer economies to a more settled agricultural way of life and therefore, so the argument goes, made possible the development of urban civilisation. However, it can no longer be argued that this 'revolution' took place only in one area from which all development stemmed. Though it appears that the cultivation of wheat and barley was first undertaken, together with the domestication of cattle and goats/sheep, in the Fertile Crescent (the area bounded by the rivers Tigris and Euphrates), there is evidence that rice was first deliberately planted and pigs domesticated in south-east Asia, maize first cultivated in Central America and llamas first domesticated in South America. It has been recognised in recent years that cultural changes can take place independently of each other in different parts of the world at different rates and different times. There is no need for a general diffusionist theory.

Although scholars will continue to study the particular societies which interest them, it may be possible to obtain a reliable chronological framework, in absolute terms of years, against which the cultural development of any particular area may be set. The development and refinement of radio-carbon dating and other scientific methods of producing absolute chronologies is enabling the cross-referencing of societies to be undertaken. As the techniques of dating become more rigorous in application and the number of scientifically obtained dates increases, the attainment of an absolute chronology for prehistoric societies throughout the world comes closer to being achieved.

GEOLOGICAL TIME

Era	*Period*	*Epoch*	*Dates*	*Evolutionary stages*
Cenozoic	Quaternary	Holocene	9,600 BC –present	Humans
		Pleistocene	1,808,000– 9,600 BC	
	Tertiary	Pliocene	5,332,000– 1,806,000	
		Miocene	23,030,000–5,332,000	
		Oligocene	34–23 Ma*	
		Eocene	55.8–33.9 Ma	
		Palaeocene	65.5–55.8 Ma	
Mesozoic	Cretaceous		145.5–65.5 Ma	
	Jurassic		199.6–145.5 Ma	First birds
	Triassic		251–199.6 Ma	First mammals
Palaeozoic	Permian		299–251 Ma	First reptiles
	Carboniferous		359.2–299 Ma	First amphibians and insects
	Devonian		416–359.2 Ma	
	Silurian		443.7–416 Ma	
	Ordovician		488.3–443.7 Ma	First fishes
	Cambrian		542–488.3 Ma	First invertebrates
Precambrian	Proterozoic		2,500–542 Ma	First primitive life forms, eg algae and bacteria
	Archaean		3,800–2,500 Ma	
	Hadean		4,500–3,800 Ma	

* Ma = millions of years ago

TIDAL PREDICTIONS

CONSTANTS

The constant tidal difference may be used in conjunction with the time of high water at a standard port shown in the predictions data below to find the time of high water at any of the ports or places listed.

These tidal differences are very approximate and should be used only as a guide to the time of high water at the places below. More precise local data should be obtained for navigational and other nautical purposes.

All data allow high water time to be found in Greenwich Mean Time: this applies to data for the months when British Summer Time is in operation and the hour's time difference should be allowed for. Ports marked * are in a different time zone and the standard time zone difference also needs to be added/subtracted to give local time.

EXAMPLE

Required: time of high water at Stranraer on 2 January 2009. Appropriate time of high water at Greenock

Afternoon tide 2 January	15h 48m
Tidal difference	- 00h 20m
High water at Stranraer	15h 28m

The columns headed 'Springs' and 'Neaps' show the height, in metres, of the tide above datum for mean high water springs and mean high water neaps respectively.

Port		*Diff.*		*Springs*	*Neaps*
		h	*min*	*m*	*m*
Aberdeen	*Leith*	–1	19	4.4	3.4
*Antwerp	*London*	+0	50	5.8	4.8
Ardrossan	*Greenock*	–0	15	3.2	2.6
Ayr	*Greenock*	–0	25	3.0	2.5
Belfast	*London*	–2	47	3.5	3.0
Blackpool	*Liverpool*	–0	10	8.9	7.0
*Boulogne	*London*	–2	44	8.9	7.2
*Calais	*London*	–2	04	7.2	5.9
*Cherbourg	*London*	–6	00	6.4	5.0
Cobh	*Liverpool*	–5	55	4.2	3.2
Cowes	*London*	–2	38	4.2	3.5
Dartmouth	*London*	+4	25	4.9	3.8
*Dieppe	*London*	–3	03	9.3	7.3
Douglas, IoM	*Liverpool*	–0	04	6.9	5.4
Dover	*London*	–2	52	6.7	5.3
Dublin	*London*	–2	05	4.1	3.4
Dun Loaghaire	*London*	–2	10	4.1	3.4
*Dunkirk	*London*	–1	54	6.0	4.9
Fishguard	*Liverpool*	–4	01	4.8	3.4
Fleetwood	*Liverpool*	0	00	9.2	7.3
*Flushing	*London*	–0	15	4.7	3.9
Folkestone	*London*	–3	04	7.1	5.7
Galway	*Liverpool*	–6	08	5.1	3.9
Glasgow	*Greenock*	+0	26	4.7	4.0
Harwich	*London*	–2	06	4.0	3.4
*Le Havre	*London*	–3	55	7.9	6.6
Heysham	*Liverpool*	+0	05	9.4	7.4
Holyhead	*Liverpool*	–0	50	5.6	4.4
*Hook of Holland	*London*	–0	01	2.1	1.7
Hull (Albert Dock)	*London*	–7	40	7.5	5.8
Immingham	*London*	–8	00	7.3	5.8
Larne	*London*	–2	40	2.8	2.5
Lerwick	*Leith*	–3	48	2.2	1.6
Londonderry	*London*	–5	37	2.7	2.1
Lowestoft	*London*	–4	25	2.4	2.1
Margate	*London*	–1	53	4.8	3.9
Milford Haven	*Liverpool*	–5	08	7.0	5.2
Morecambe	*Liverpool*	+0	07	9.5	7.4
Newhaven	*London*	–2	46	6.7	5.1
Oban	*Greenock*	+5	43	4.0	2.9
*Ostend	*London*	–1	32	5.1	4.2
Plymouth	*London*	+4	05	5.5	4.4
Portland	*London*	+5	09	2.1	1.4
Portsmouth	*London*	–2	38	4.7	3.8
Ramsgate	*London*	–2	32	5.2	4.1
Richmond Lock	*London*	+1	00	4.9	3.7
Rosslare Harbour	*Liverpool*	–5	24	1.9	1.4
Rosyth	*Leith*	+0	09	5.8	4.7
*Rotterdam	*London*	+1	45	2.0	1.7
*St Helier	*London*	+4	48	11.0	8.1
*St Malo	*London*	+4	27	12.2	9.2
St Peter Port	*London*	+4	54	9.3	7.0
Scrabster	*Leith*	–6	06	5.0	4.0
Sheerness	*London*	–1	19	5.8	4.7
Shoreham	*London*	–2	44	6.3	4.9
Southampton (1st high water)	*London*	–2	54	4.5	3.7
Spurn Head	*London*	–8	25	6.9	5.5
Stornoway	*Liverpool*	–4	16	4.8	3.7
Stranraer	*Greenock*	–0	20	3.0	2.4
Stromness	*Leith*	–5	26	3.6	2.7
Swansea	*London*	–7	35	9.5	7.2
Tees (River Entrance)	*Leith*	+1	09	5.5	4.3
Tilbury	*London*	–0	49	6.4	5.4
Tobermory	*Liverpool*	–5	11	4.4	3.3
Tyne River (North Shields)	*London*	–10	30	5.0	3.9
Ullapool	*Leith*	–7	40	5.2	3.9
Walton-on-the-Naze	*London*	–2	10	4.2	3.4
Wick	*Leith*	–3	26	3.5	2.8
*Zeebrugge	*London*	–0	55	4.8	3.9

PREDICTIONS

The following data are daily predictions of the time and height of high water at London Bridge, Liverpool, Greenock and Leith. The time of the data is Greenwich Mean Time; this applies also to data for the months when British Summer Time is in operation and the hour's time difference should be allowed for. The datum of predictions for each port shows the difference of height, in metres from Ordnance data (Newlyn).

The section was compiled with the assistance of Chris Stevens.

JANUARY 2009 *High Water* GMT

	LONDON BRIDGE *Datum of Predictions 3.20m below						LIVERPOOL (Alfred Dock) *Datum of Predictions 4.93m below						GREENOCK *Datum of Predictions 1.62m below						LEITH *Datum of Predictions 2.90m below					
	hr		*ht m*	*hr*		*ht m*	*hr*		*ht m*	*hr*		*ht m*	*hr*		*ht m*	*hr*		*ht m*	*hr*		*ht m*	*hr*		*ht m*
TH 1	04	11	6.5	16	49	6.5	01	43	8.5	14	01	8.8	03	00	3.2	15	10	3.6	05	23	5.0	17	25	5.1
F 2	04	47	6.5	17	28	6.5	02	21	8.4	14	40	8.7	03	39	3.2	15	48	3.5	06	03	4.9	18	03	5.0
SA 3	05	27	6.5	18	11	6.5	03	02	8.2	15	24	8.5	04	19	3.2	16	29	3.4	06	46	4.8	18	45	4.9
SU 4	06	11	6.4	18	58	6.3	03	48	8.0	16	14	8.3	05	01	3.1	17	14	3.3	07	33	4.7	19	34	4.8
M 5	07	04	6.3	19	53	6.1	04	44	7.8	17	13	8.1	05	46	3.1	18	08	3.2	08	29	4.6	20	34	4.7
TU 6	08	05	6.1	20	57	5.9	05	49	7.6	18	20	8.0	06	39	3.0	19	16	3.1	09	35	4.6	21	50	4.7
W 7	09	17	6.0	22	10	5.9	07	01	7.8	19	31	8.1	07	52	3.0	20	43	3.0	10	44	4.7	23	07	4.8
TH 8	10	32	6.1	23	21	6.1	08	13	8.1	20	43	8.5	09	18	3.1	22	03	3.1	11	50	4.9	—		—
F 9	11	44	6.4	—		—	09	16	8.7	21	47	8.9	10	25	3.2	23	08	3.3	00	16	5.1	12	50	5.1
SA 10	00	23	6.4	12	48	6.7	10	13	9.2	22	43	9.3	11	21	3.4	—		—	01	17	5.4	13	43	5.4
SU 11	01	19	6.7	13	45	7.0	11	04	9.6	23	35	9.5	00	06	3.4	12	12	3.6	02	12	5.6	14	32	5.7
M 12	02	11	6.8	14	39	7.2	11	54	9.9	—		—	01	02	3.4	13	01	3.7	03	02	5.8	15	19	5.8
TU 13	02	59	6.9	15	29	7.3	00	23	9.7	12	42	10.0	01	54	3.4	13	47	3.8	03	50	5.8	16	06	5.9
W 14	03	45	7.0	16	17	7.3	01	10	9.6	13	28	9.9	02	42	3.4	14	32	3.9	04	37	5.7	16	53	5.8
TH 15	04	28	7.0	17	02	7.2	01	55	9.4	14	12	9.7	03	27	3.4	15	15	3.8	05	24	5.5	17	41	5.6
F 16	05	09	6.9	17	44	7.0	02	38	9.0	14	56	9.2	04	09	3.3	15	57	3.7	06	12	5.2	18	31	5.4
SA 17	05	48	6.7	18	26	6.6	03	20	8.6	15	39	8.7	04	49	3.2	16	39	3.6	07	00	4.9	19	23	5.1
SU 18	06	28	6.5	19	08	6.3	04	05	8.1	16	27	8.1	05	29	3.1	17	22	3.4	07	52	4.6	20	21	4.8
M 19	07	15	6.1	19	56	5.9	04	57	7.6	17	24	7.5	06	12	3.0	18	09	3.1	08	47	4.4	21	22	4.5
TU 20	08	17	5.8	20	58	5.6	06	05	7.2	18	40	7.2	07	03	2.9	19	01	2.9	09	47	4.3	22	28	4.4
W 21	09	38	5.6	22	10	5.6	07	25	7.2	20	01	7.2	08	16	2.8	20	15	2.8	10	54	4.3	23	41	4.4
TH 22	10	52	5.7	23	15	5.8	08	33	7.6	21	05	7.6	09	45	2.9	22	05	2.8	12	06	4.5	—		—
F 23	11	53	6.0	—		—	09	27	8.0	21	54	7.9	10	45	3.2	23	04	2.9	00	47	4.5	13	04	4.7
SA 24	00	12	6.1	12	46	6.3	10	11	8.5	22	36	8.3	11	30	3.3	23	48	3.0	01	37	4.7	13	47	4.9
SU 25	01	01	6.3	13	31	6.5	10	50	8.8	23	12	8.5	12	09	3.5	—		—	02	16	4.9	14	23	5.1
M 26	01	43	6.5	14	11	6.6	11	26	9.0	23	46	8.7	00	26	3.1	12	44	3.5	02	49	5.1	14	55	5.2
TU 27	02	21	6.5	14	48	6.6	11	59	9.1	—		—	01	01	3.1	13	15	3.5	03	20	5.2	15	26	5.3
W 28	02	55	6.5	15	21	6.6	00	17	8.8	12	32	9.1	01	34	3.2	13	45	3.5	03	52	5.2	15	57	5.4
TH 29	03	26	6.5	15	55	6.6	00	50	8.8	13	05	9.2	02	06	3.2	14	16	3.6	04	24	5.2	16	28	5.4
F 30	03	56	6.6	16	29	6.7	01	23	8.9	13	39	9.2	02	39	3.3	14	50	3.6	04	59	5.2	17	01	5.4
SA 31	04	28	6.7	17	05	6.7	01	57	8.8	14	16	9.1	03	13	3.3	15	26	3.6	05	34	5.1	17	36	5.3

FEBRUARY 2009 *High Water* GMT

	LONDON BRIDGE						LIVERPOOL (Alfred Dock)						GREENOCK						LEITH					
SU 1	05	05	6.7	17	44	6.6	02	33	8.7	14	55	8.9	03	48	3.3	16	03	3.5	06	13	5.0	18	16	5.2
M 2	05	47	6.7	18	28	6.4	03	14	8.4	15	40	8.6	04	25	3.3	16	44	3.3	06	56	4.8	19	02	5.0
TU 3	06	35	6.5	19	17	6.1	04	04	8.0	16	37	8.1	05	05	3.1	17	32	3.1	07	47	4.6	19	59	4.8
W 4	07	32	6.1	20	17	5.7	05	10	7.6	17	48	7.7	05	53	3.0	18	33	2.9	08	52	4.5	21	18	4.6
TH 5	08	44	5.8	21	34	5.6	06	30	7.4	19	12	7.7	06	55	2.9	20	17	2.8	10	13	4.5	22	48	4.6
F 6	10	09	5.8	23	00	5.7	07	56	7.8	20	36	8.0	08	46	2.9	22	03	2.9	11	32	4.7	—		—
SA 7	11	34	6.1	—		—	09	09	8.4	21	43	8.6	10	15	3.1	23	10	3.1	00	08	4.9	12	40	5.0
SU 8	00	11	6.1	12	42	6.5	10	06	9.1	22	36	9.2	11	14	3.3	—		—	01	13	5.2	13	34	5.4
M 9	01	09	6.5	13	38	7.0	10	55	9.6	23	23	9.6	00	05	3.3	12	04	3.5	02	04	5.5	14	20	5.7
TU 10	01	59	6.8	14	27	7.2	11	40	10.0	—		—	00	55	3.4	12	50	3.7	02	49	5.7	15	04	5.9
W 11	02	44	7.0	15	13	7.3	00	07	9.7	12	24	10.1	01	41	3.4	13	35	3.7	03	32	5.8	15	47	6.0
TH 12	03	25	7.1	15	55	7.3	00	49	9.7	13	05	10.0	02	23	3.4	14	16	3.8	04	15	5.7	16	30	5.9
F 13	04	03	7.1	16	34	7.2	01	28	9.5	13	44	9.7	03	01	3.4	14	55	3.8	04	56	5.5	17	13	5.7
SA 14	04	38	7.1	17	09	7.0	02	05	9.2	14	22	9.3	03	34	3.3	15	32	3.7	05	38	5.2	17	57	5.4
SU 15	05	12	6.9	17	41	6.7	02	41	8.8	14	59	8.7	04	07	3.2	16	09	3.5	06	19	4.9	18	43	5.0
M 16	05	47	6.7	18	14	6.4	03	18	8.2	15	39	8.1	04	41	3.1	16	47	3.3	07	02	4.6	19	34	4.7
TU 17	06	27	6.3	18	52	6.0	04	01	7.7	16	28	7.4	05	20	3.0	17	29	3.0	07	53	4.4	20	34	4.3
W 18	07	16	5.8	19	40	5.6	04	59	7.1	17	41	6.8	06	06	2.8	18	18	2.8	08	53	4.2	21	42	4.1
TH 19	08	28	5.3	20	54	5.3	06	35	6.9	19	29	6.8	07	06	2.7	19	19	2.6	10	02	4.1	23	03	4.1
F 20	10	21	5.3	22	40	5.4	08	05	7.2	20	43	7.2	09	04	2.7	21	50	2.6	11	26	4.2	—		—
SA 21	11	29	5.7	23	45	5.8	09	04	7.7	21	34	7.7	10	22	3.0	22	49	2.8	00	26	4.3	12	39	4.5
SU 22	12	22	6.2	—		—	09	49	8.3	22	14	8.2	11	08	3.2	23	30	2.9	01	17	4.6	13	25	4.8
M 23	00	36	6.2	13	08	6.5	10	28	8.7	22	50	8.6	11	46	3.3	—		—	01	54	4.9	14	01	5.0
TU 24	01	21	6.5	13	48	6.6	11	03	9.0	23	23	8.8	00	06	3.0	12	21	3.4	02	26	5.1	14	32	5.2
W 25	01	59	6.5	14	24	6.7	11	36	9.2	23	54	9.0	00	41	3.1	12	53	3.4	02	56	5.2	15	03	5.4
TH 26	02	34	6.5	14	58	6.7	12	08	9.3	—		—	01	13	3.1	13	23	3.4	03	26	5.3	15	33	5.5
F 27	03	05	6.6	15	32	6.7	00	25	9.1	12	41	9.4	01	42	3.2	13	54	3.5	03	58	5.4	16	04	5.5
SA 28	03	35	6.7	16	05	6.7	00	58	9.1	13	15	9.4	02	12	3.3	14	29	3.5	04	31	5.3	16	37	5.5

MARCH 2009 *High Water* GMT

	LONDON BRIDGE *Datum of Predictions 3.20m below				LIVERPOOL (Alfred Dock) *Datum of Predictions 4.93m below				GREENOCK *Datum of Predictions 1.62m below				LEITH *Datum of Predictions 2.90m below			
	hr	*ht m*	*hr*	*ht m*	*hr*	*ht m*	*hr*	*ht m*	*hr*	*ht m*	*hr*	*ht m*	*hr*	*ht m*	*hr*	*ht m*
SU 1	04 08	6.8	16 40	6.7	01 31	9.1	13 52	9.3	02 45	3.4	15 05	3.5	05 07	5.3	17 14	5.4
M 2	04 45	6.9	17 18	6.6	02 07	8.9	14 31	9.0	03 19	3.4	15 43	3.5	05 45	5.1	17 56	5.3
TU 3	05 27	6.8	18 00	6.4	02 48	8.6	15 17	8.5	03 56	3.3	16 23	3.3	06 27	4.9	18 44	5.0
W 4	06 15	6.5	18 48	6.0	03 37	8.1	16 15	7.9	04 36	3.2	17 10	3.0	07 17	4.6	19 44	4.7
TH 5	07 12	6.0	19 47	5.6	04 45	7.5	17 33	7.4	05 23	3.0	18 12	2.8	08 24	4.4	21 07	4.5
F 6	08 26	5.6	21 10	5.4	06 15	7.3	19 09	7.4	06 24	2.8	20 26	2.6	09 55	4.4	22 42	4.5
SA 7	10 05	5.6	22 47	5.6	07 50	7.7	20 33	7.9	08 31	2.8	22 08	2.9	11 20	4.6	—	—
SU 8	11 30	6.1	23 57	6.1	09 00	8.4	21 34	8.6	10 06	3.0	23 04	3.1	00 03	4.8	12 28	5.0
M 9	12 31	6.6	—	—	09 53	9.1	22 22	9.2	11 01	3.3	23 52	3.3	01 03	5.2	13 19	5.4
TU 10	00 52	6.6	13 23	7.1	10 39	9.6	23 05	9.6	11 48	3.5	—	—	01 50	5.4	14 03	5.6
W 11	01 39	6.9	14 09	7.3	11 21	9.9	23 45	9.7	00 36	3.3	12 33	3.6	02 30	5.6	14 44	5.8
TH 12	02 21	7.1	14 50	7.3	12 01	10.0	—	—	01 18	3.4	13 15	3.6	03 09	5.6	15 24	5.9
F 13	03 00	7.2	15 28	7.2	00 22	9.6	12 39	9.8	01 55	3.3	13 54	3.6	03 48	5.6	16 05	5.8
SA 14	03 36	7.2	16 02	7.1	00 58	9.5	13 15	9.5	02 27	3.3	14 30	3.6	04 26	5.4	16 46	5.6
SU 15	04 09	7.1	16 32	6.9	01 31	9.2	13 49	9.1	02 57	3.3	15 04	3.5	05 04	5.2	17 27	5.3
M 16	04 42	7.0	17 01	6.7	02 05	8.8	14 24	8.6	03 29	3.3	15 39	3.4	05 42	4.9	18 10	4.9
TU 17	05 16	6.7	17 34	6.5	02 40	8.3	15 02	8.0	04 03	3.2	16 17	3.2	06 21	4.7	18 57	4.6
W 18	05 56	6.3	18 12	6.1	03 19	7.8	15 47	7.3	04 40	3.1	16 58	2.9	07 08	4.4	19 53	4.3
TH 19	06 43	5.8	18 59	5.7	04 10	7.2	16 51	6.7	05 25	2.9	17 48	2.7	08 05	4.2	20 57	4.1
F 20	07 44	5.3	20 00	5.3	05 37	6.8	18 46	6.5	06 22	2.7	18 49	2.5	09 15	4.1	22 13	4.0
SA 21	09 34	5.2	21 54	5.3	07 24	7.0	20 08	7.0	07 51	2.6	21 00	2.5	10 34	4.1	23 42	4.2
SU 22	10 56	5.6	23 10	5.7	08 28	7.5	21 01	7.6	09 44	2.8	22 15	2.7	11 54	4.4	—	—
M 23	11 50	6.1	—	—	09 16	8.1	21 42	8.1	10 33	3.0	22 57	2.9	00 40	4.5	12 47	4.7
TU 24	00 03	6.1	12 36	6.4	09 55	8.6	22 18	8.5	11 12	3.2	23 34	3.0	01 19	4.8	13 26	5.0
W 25	00 49	6.4	13 16	6.6	10 31	8.9	22 51	8.9	11 47	3.2	—	—	01 52	5.1	13 59	5.2
TH 26	01 28	6.5	13 54	6.7	11 05	9.2	23 24	9.1	00 09	3.1	12 21	3.3	02 24	5.3	14 32	5.4
F 27	02 04	6.6	14 30	6.8	11 39	9.4	23 57	9.2	00 41	3.2	12 55	3.3	02 56	5.4	15 04	5.5
SA 28	02 38	6.7	15 05	6.8	12 15	9.5	—	—	01 12	3.2	13 31	3.4	03 29	5.5	15 38	5.6
SU 29	03 13	6.8	15 41	6.8	00 32	9.3	12 53	9.5	01 44	3.4	14 09	3.5	04 04	5.4	16 16	5.6
M 30	03 50	7.0	16 18	6.8	01 09	9.3	13 32	9.3	02 19	3.5	14 48	3.5	04 41	5.4	16 57	5.5
TU 31	04 31	7.0	16 58	6.6	01 48	9.1	14 16	8.9	02 56	3.5	15 29	3.4	05 22	5.2	17 43	5.3

APRIL 2009 *High Water* GMT

	LONDON BRIDGE				LIVERPOOL (Alfred Dock)				GREENOCK				LEITH			
W 1	05 15	6.8	17 40	6.3	02 32	8.7	15 05	8.4	03 34	3.4	16 13	3.2	06 07	4.9	18 36	5.0
TH 2	06 06	6.4	18 29	5.9	03 26	8.1	16 08	7.8	04 15	3.3	17 04	2.9	07 01	4.7	19 42	4.7
F 3	07 07	5.9	19 33	5.5	04 37	7.6	17 31	7.3	05 05	3.0	18 21	2.7	08 15	4.4	21 07	4.5
SA 4	08 29	5.6	21 06	5.4	06 09	7.5	19 04	7.5	06 14	2.8	20 39	2.7	09 45	4.5	22 34	4.6
SU 5	10 03	5.8	22 30	5.8	07 34	7.8	20 17	8.0	08 23	2.8	21 52	2.9	11 03	4.7	23 48	4.8
M 6	11 14	6.3	23 33	6.3	08 39	8.5	21 13	8.6	09 46	3.1	22 43	3.1	12 07	5.0	—	—
TU 7	12 10	6.8	—	—	09 31	9.0	21 59	9.1	10 39	3.3	23 28	3.2	00 44	5.1	12 58	5.3
W 8	00 26	6.7	12 59	7.1	10 17	9.4	22 40	9.3	11 25	3.4	—	—	01 28	5.3	13 41	5.5
TH 9	01 13	7.0	13 43	7.2	10 58	9.6	23 18	9.4	00 10	3.3	12 09	3.5	02 07	5.4	14 22	5.6
F 10	01 55	7.1	14 23	7.2	11 36	9.5	23 53	9.4	00 48	3.3	12 50	3.5	02 44	5.4	15 02	5.6
SA 11	02 35	7.1	14 59	7.0	12 12	9.4	—	—	01 23	3.3	13 28	3.4	03 21	5.4	15 43	5.5
SU 12	03 11	7.0	15 30	6.9	00 27	9.2	12 46	9.1	01 53	3.4	14 03	3.4	03 58	5.3	16 23	5.3
M 13	03 45	6.9	15 59	6.8	01 01	9.0	13 20	8.8	02 24	3.4	14 37	3.3	04 34	5.1	17 03	5.1
TU 14	04 18	6.8	16 29	6.7	01 34	8.8	13 55	8.4	02 56	3.4	15 12	3.2	05 10	4.9	17 44	4.8
W 15	04 54	6.5	17 03	6.5	02 10	8.4	14 33	7.9	03 31	3.3	15 51	3.1	05 48	4.7	18 28	4.6
TH 16	05 33	6.2	17 43	6.2	02 50	7.9	15 17	7.4	04 08	3.1	16 34	2.9	06 32	4.5	19 19	4.3
F 17	06 19	5.9	18 29	5.8	03 38	7.4	16 14	6.9	04 51	2.9	17 24	2.7	07 26	4.3	20 17	4.1
SA 18	07 15	5.5	19 26	5.5	04 45	7.0	17 43	6.6	05 45	2.7	18 25	2.5	08 31	4.2	21 23	4.1
SU 19	08 28	5.3	20 46	5.4	06 23	7.0	19 14	6.9	06 57	2.6	19 50	2.5	09 44	4.2	22 34	4.2
M 20	10 01	5.5	22 17	5.6	07 36	7.4	20 13	7.4	08 37	2.7	21 19	2.7	10 54	4.3	23 39	4.4
TU 21	11 04	5.9	23 18	5.9	08 29	7.9	20 58	7.9	09 42	2.9	22 11	2.9	11 53	4.6	—	—
W 22	11 54	6.3	—	—	09 12	8.4	21 37	8.4	10 27	3.0	22 53	3.0	00 29	4.7	12 40	4.9
TH 23	00 06	6.3	12 38	6.6	09 52	8.8	22 14	8.8	11 06	3.2	23 30	3.1	01 10	5.0	13 20	5.1
F 24	00 50	6.5	13 20	6.8	10 31	9.1	22 51	9.1	11 45	3.2	—	—	01 48	5.2	13 58	5.4
SA 25	01 31	6.7	14 00	6.8	11 10	9.4	23 29	9.3	00 06	3.2	12 26	3.3	02 25	5.4	14 36	5.5
SU 26	02 12	6.9	14 40	6.9	11 51	9.5	—	—	00 42	3.3	13 08	3.4	03 01	5.5	15 16	5.6
M 27	02 53	7.0	15 20	6.8	00 09	9.4	12 35	9.4	01 20	3.4	13 52	3.4	03 40	5.5	15 59	5.6
TU 28	03 37	7.0	16 02	6.8	00 52	9.3	13 20	9.2	01 59	3.5	14 36	3.4	04 21	5.4	16 46	5.5
W 29	04 23	7.0	16 45	6.6	01 37	9.1	14 09	8.9	02 39	3.6	15 22	3.3	05 06	5.3	17 37	5.3
TH 30	05 12	6.8	17 31	6.3	02 27	8.8	15 03	8.4	03 20	3.5	16 13	3.1	05 56	5.0	18 34	5.0

MAY 2009 *High Water* GMT

	LONDON BRIDGE *Datum of Predictions 3.20m below				LIVERPOOL (Alfred Dock) *Datum of Predictions 4.93m below				GREENOCK *Datum of Predictions 1.62m below				LEITH *Datum of Predictions 2.90m below			
	hr	*ht m*	*hr*	*ht m*	*hr*	*ht m*	*hr*	*ht m*	*hr*	*ht m*	*hr*	*ht m*	*hr*	*ht m*	*hr*	*ht m*
F 1	06 07	6.4	18 25	6.0	03 25	8.3	16 08	7.9	04 06	3.3	17 15	2.9	06 55	4.8	19 42	4.8
SA 2	07 12	6.1	19 34	5.8	04 35	8.0	17 24	7.6	05 01	3.1	18 41	2.8	08 10	4.7	20 59	4.6
SU 3	08 29	6.0	20 54	5.8	05 53	7.9	18 41	7.7	06 17	3.0	20 13	2.8	09 29	4.7	22 13	4.7
M 4	09 43	6.2	22 03	6.1	07 06	8.0	19 47	8.0	07 57	2.9	21 19	2.9	10 39	4.8	23 21	4.8
TU 5	10 46	6.5	23 03	6.4	08 09	8.4	20 43	8.4	09 14	3.1	22 11	3.1	11 40	5.0	—	—
W 6	11 41	6.8	23 56	6.7	09 03	8.7	21 31	8.8	10 09	3.2	22 57	3.2	00 16	5.0	12 33	5.2
TH 7	12 30	7.0	—	—	09 51	9.0	22 13	9.0	10 57	3.3	23 39	3.2	01 03	5.1	13 19	5.3
F 8	00 45	6.9	13 15	7.0	10 33	9.0	22 51	9.1	11 41	3.3	—	—	01 43	5.2	14 02	5.3
SA 9	01 30	6.9	13 56	6.9	11 12	9.0	23 27	9.1	00 17	3.3	12 23	3.3	02 21	5.2	14 44	5.3
SU 10	02 12	6.9	14 32	6.8	11 48	8.9	—	—	00 52	3.3	13 01	3.3	02 58	5.2	15 24	5.3
M 11	02 51	6.7	15 04	6.6	00 01	9.0	12 23	8.7	01 24	3.4	13 36	3.2	03 34	5.2	16 03	5.2
TU 12	03 26	6.6	15 33	6.6	00 35	8.9	12 57	8.5	01 56	3.4	14 12	3.2	04 09	5.1	16 42	5.0
W 13	04 01	6.5	16 05	6.5	01 11	8.7	13 34	8.3	02 30	3.4	14 49	3.1	04 44	5.0	17 21	4.8
TH 14	04 37	6.4	16 40	6.4	01 48	8.4	14 12	8.0	03 04	3.4	15 29	3.0	05 22	4.8	18 03	4.7
F 15	05 16	6.2	17 20	6.2	02 28	8.1	14 55	7.6	03 41	3.2	16 12	2.9	06 04	4.7	18 48	4.5
SA 16	06 00	6.0	18 05	6.0	03 14	7.8	15 44	7.3	04 22	3.1	17 01	2.8	06 52	4.5	19 39	4.3
SU 17	06 49	5.8	18 56	5.8	04 08	7.5	16 45	7.0	05 11	2.9	17 56	2.7	07 48	4.4	20 36	4.3
M 18	07 47	5.7	19 58	5.6	05 13	7.3	17 59	7.1	06 10	2.8	18 58	2.7	08 51	4.3	21 38	4.3
TU 19	08 54	5.7	21 11	5.7	06 24	7.5	19 08	7.3	07 20	2.8	20 08	2.7	09 57	4.4	22 40	4.5
W 20	10 04	5.9	22 20	5.9	07 27	7.8	20 04	7.8	08 34	2.8	21 12	2.8	10 57	4.6	23 36	4.7
TH 21	11 05	6.2	23 19	6.2	08 21	8.2	20 52	8.3	09 34	3.0	22 04	3.0	11 52	4.8	—	—
F 22	11 58	6.5	—	—	09 10	8.6	21 37	8.7	10 25	3.1	22 50	3.1	00 27	4.9	12 42	5.1
SA 23	00 12	6.5	12 47	6.7	09 58	9.0	22 21	9.1	11 13	3.2	23 33	3.2	01 13	5.2	13 28	5.3
SU 24	01 02	6.8	13 33	6.9	10 45	9.2	23 06	9.3	12 01	3.3	—	—	01 56	5.3	14 14	5.5
M 25	01 50	7.0	14 19	6.9	11 33	9.4	23 52	9.4	00 16	3.4	12 50	3.3	02 38	5.5	15 00	5.6
TU 26	02 39	7.1	15 04	6.9	12 22	9.4	—	—	01 00	3.5	13 40	3.3	03 22	5.5	15 48	5.7
W 27	03 28	7.1	15 50	6.8	00 40	9.4	13 13	9.2	01 44	3.6	14 31	3.3	04 08	5.5	16 39	5.6
TH 28	04 18	7.1	16 38	6.7	01 31	9.3	14 05	9.0	02 28	3.6	15 23	3.2	04 56	5.4	17 32	5.4
F 29	05 11	6.9	17 27	6.5	02 24	9.1	14 59	8.7	03 14	3.6	16 19	3.1	05 49	5.3	18 29	5.2
SA 30	06 05	6.7	18 21	6.3	03 20	8.8	15 57	8.3	04 02	3.5	17 21	3.0	06 48	5.1	19 31	5.0
SU 31	07 05	6.5	19 22	6.2	04 20	8.5	17 00	8.0	04 58	3.3	18 26	2.9	07 56	5.0	20 37	4.8

JUNE 2009 *High Water* GMT

	LONDON BRIDGE				LIVERPOOL (Alfred Dock)				GREENOCK				LEITH			
M 1	08 09	6.4	20 27	6.2	05 25	8.2	18 06	7.9	06 03	3.1	19 32	2.9	09 04	4.9	21 43	4.7
TU 2	09 12	6.4	21 30	6.2	06 30	8.1	19 10	7.9	07 17	3.1	20 34	2.9	10 09	4.9	22 45	4.7
W 3	10 12	6.4	22 29	6.3	07 34	8.1	20 09	8.1	08 32	3.0	21 31	3.0	11 10	4.9	23 43	4.8
TH 4	11 08	6.5	23 26	6.5	08 33	8.2	21 01	8.3	09 36	3.1	22 22	3.0	12 07	4.9	—	—
F 5	12 00	6.6	—	—	09 25	8.4	21 47	8.5	10 29	3.1	23 08	3.1	00 35	4.9	12 59	5.0
SA 6	00 19	6.6	12 48	6.7	10 11	8.5	22 28	8.7	11 16	3.1	23 50	3.2	01 21	5.0	13 47	5.0
SU 7	01 08	6.6	13 31	6.7	10 53	8.5	23 06	8.8	11 59	3.1	—	—	02 02	5.0	14 30	5.1
M 8	01 54	6.6	14 10	6.6	11 30	8.5	23 42	8.8	00 28	3.3	12 39	3.1	02 40	5.1	15 09	5.1
TU 9	02 36	6.6	14 45	6.5	12 06	8.5	—	—	01 03	3.4	13 15	3.1	03 16	5.1	15 47	5.0
W 10	03 14	6.5	15 17	6.4	00 17	8.8	12 41	8.4	01 36	3.4	13 51	3.0	03 50	5.1	16 23	5.0
TH 11	03 48	6.4	15 49	6.4	00 54	8.7	13 17	8.3	02 09	3.4	14 29	3.0	04 25	5.1	16 59	4.9
F 12	04 23	6.3	16 23	6.4	01 31	8.6	13 54	8.2	02 43	3.4	15 09	3.0	05 01	5.0	17 38	4.8
SA 13	04 59	6.3	17 01	6.4	02 09	8.4	14 33	8.0	03 18	3.3	15 50	3.0	05 40	4.9	18 19	4.7
SU 14	05 39	6.3	17 41	6.3	02 50	8.2	15 15	7.8	03 56	3.2	16 34	2.9	06 21	4.8	19 03	4.6
M 15	06 23	6.2	18 27	6.1	03 35	8.0	16 03	7.6	04 38	3.1	17 20	2.9	07 06	4.6	19 52	4.5
TU 16	07 12	6.0	19 19	6.0	04 27	7.9	16 58	7.5	05 27	3.0	18 09	2.9	07 58	4.6	20 48	4.5
W 17	08 08	5.9	20 20	5.9	05 25	7.8	18 01	7.5	06 25	2.9	19 04	2.8	08 58	4.5	21 48	4.5
TH 18	09 13	5.9	21 28	5.9	06 27	7.9	19 06	7.7	07 32	2.9	20 06	2.9	10 04	4.6	22 50	4.6
F 19	10 20	6.1	22 36	6.1	07 31	8.1	20 09	8.1	08 45	2.9	21 14	2.9	11 08	4.7	23 49	4.8
SA 20	11 23	6.3	23 40	6.4	08 34	8.4	21 06	8.5	09 51	3.0	22 14	3.1	12 09	4.9	—	—
SU 21	12 20	6.6	—	—	09 32	8.7	21 58	9.0	10 49	3.1	23 08	3.2	00 43	5.0	13 06	5.2
M 22	00 38	6.7	13 13	6.8	10 28	9.1	22 49	9.3	11 44	3.2	23 57	3.4	01 34	5.3	13 59	5.5
TU 23	01 34	6.9	14 03	6.9	11 21	9.3	23 40	9.5	12 39	3.2	—	—	02 22	5.5	14 49	5.7
W 24	02 28	7.1	14 52	6.9	12 13	9.4	—	—	00 46	3.5	13 34	3.3	03 09	5.6	15 39	5.7
TH 25	03 20	7.2	15 41	7.0	00 31	9.6	13 04	9.4	01 34	3.6	14 28	3.2	03 57	5.7	16 29	5.7
F 26	04 11	7.2	16 28	6.9	01 22	9.6	13 54	9.3	02 20	3.7	15 21	3.2	04 46	5.7	17 20	5.6
SA 27	05 01	7.2	17 15	6.9	02 12	9.5	14 44	9.1	03 06	3.7	16 13	3.2	05 37	5.6	18 13	5.4
SU 28	05 51	7.0	18 02	6.7	03 02	9.2	15 33	8.7	03 53	3.6	17 03	3.1	06 31	5.4	19 07	5.1
M 29	06 42	6.8	18 53	6.6	03 54	8.8	16 25	8.3	04 42	3.5	17 52	3.0	07 30	5.2	20 05	4.8
TU 30	07 36	6.5	19 48	6.3	04 48	8.4	17 23	7.9	05 33	3.3	18 42	2.9	08 32	5.0	21 05	4.7

JULY 2009 *High Water* GMT

	LONDON BRIDGE *Datum of Predictions 3.20m below				LIVERPOOL (Alfred Dock) *Datum of Predictions 4.93m below				GREENOCK *Datum of Predictions 1.62m below				LEITH *Datum of Predictions 2.90m below			
	hr	*ht m*	*hr*	*ht m*	*hr*	*ht m*	*hr*	*ht m*	*hr*	*ht m*	*hr*	*ht m*	*hr*	*ht m*	*hr*	*ht m*
W 1	08 34	6.3	20 50	6.1	05 49	8.0	18 27	7.6	06 28	3.1	19 37	2.9	09 34	4.8	22 05	4.5
TH 2	09 34	6.1	21 54	6.1	06 55	7.7	19 32	7.6	07 34	2.9	20 42	2.8	10 37	4.7	23 07	4.5
F 3	10 33	6.1	22 57	6.1	08 03	7.7	20 33	7.8	08 54	2.8	21 47	2.9	11 42	4.6	—	—
SA 4	11 29	6.2	23 56	6.3	09 03	7.8	21 26	8.1	10 04	2.9	22 43	3.1	00 08	4.6	12 43	4.7
SU 5	12 22	6.3	—	—	09 54	8.0	22 11	8.4	10 59	2.9	23 31	3.2	01 03	4.8	13 35	4.8
M 6	00 50	6.4	13 10	6.5	10 38	8.2	22 51	8.7	11 46	2.9	—	—	01 48	4.9	14 18	4.9
TU 7	01 39	6.5	13 53	6.5	11 17	8.3	23 28	8.8	00 12	3.3	12 26	2.9	02 27	5.0	14 56	5.0
W 8	02 22	6.6	14 31	6.5	11 53	8.4	—	—	00 48	3.4	13 02	3.0	03 01	5.1	15 30	5.1
TH 9	03 00	6.5	15 05	6.5	00 03	8.8	12 27	8.4	01 21	3.4	13 36	3.0	03 33	5.2	16 02	5.1
F 10	03 33	6.4	15 36	6.4	00 38	8.8	13 00	8.5	01 52	3.4	14 11	3.0	04 06	5.2	16 36	5.1
SA 11	04 06	6.4	16 08	6.4	01 12	8.8	13 33	8.4	02 23	3.4	14 46	3.1	04 40	5.2	17 12	5.0
SU 12	04 39	6.5	16 40	6.5	01 47	8.7	14 08	8.4	02 56	3.4	15 23	3.1	05 15	5.1	17 49	4.9
M 13	05 15	6.5	17 16	6.5	02 24	8.6	14 44	8.3	03 31	3.4	16 01	3.1	05 51	5.0	18 28	4.8
TU 14	05 54	6.4	17 56	6.4	03 03	8.5	15 25	8.1	04 08	3.3	16 41	3.1	06 30	4.9	19 12	4.7
W 15	06 37	6.3	18 42	6.3	03 48	8.3	16 13	7.8	04 49	3.1	17 24	3.0	07 14	4.8	20 01	4.6
TH 16	07 28	6.1	19 38	6.1	04 41	8.0	17 12	7.6	05 38	3.0	18 12	2.9	08 07	4.7	21 01	4.5
F 17	08 28	5.9	20 45	5.9	05 44	7.9	18 22	7.6	06 41	2.9	19 10	2.9	09 15	4.6	22 09	4.5
SA 18	09 39	5.8	21 59	6.0	06 55	7.8	19 35	7.8	08 03	2.8	20 28	2.9	10 33	4.6	23 18	4.7
SU 19	10 53	6.0	23 15	6.2	08 09	8.1	20 44	8.3	09 29	2.9	21 47	3.0	11 46	4.8	—	—
M 20	11 59	6.3	—	—	09 18	8.5	21 44	8.9	10 39	3.0	22 50	3.2	00 22	4.9	12 52	5.1
TU 21	00 24	6.5	12 57	6.6	10 17	9.0	22 38	9.4	11 39	3.1	23 45	3.4	01 19	5.2	13 48	5.5
W 22	01 24	6.9	13 50	6.9	11 11	9.3	23 29	9.8	12 34	3.2	—	—	02 09	5.5	14 39	5.7
TH 23	02 18	7.2	14 39	7.1	12 01	9.6	—	—	00 35	3.5	13 28	3.2	02 55	5.8	15 26	5.8
F 24	03 08	7.3	15 26	7.1	00 17	9.9	12 49	9.6	01 23	3.7	14 19	3.3	03 41	5.9	16 13	5.8
SA 25	03 56	7.4	16 10	7.2	01 05	10.0	13 35	9.6	02 09	3.7	15 06	3.3	04 28	5.9	16 59	5.7
SU 26	04 42	7.3	16 52	7.1	01 51	9.8	14 19	9.3	02 53	3.7	15 49	3.2	05 15	5.8	17 47	5.4
M 27	05 25	7.2	17 33	7.0	02 35	9.5	15 01	8.9	03 35	3.7	16 29	3.2	06 05	5.6	18 35	5.1
TU 28	06 08	6.9	18 13	6.8	03 20	8.9	15 45	8.4	04 17	3.6	17 07	3.1	06 57	5.3	19 26	4.8
W 29	06 51	6.5	18 58	6.4	04 06	8.3	16 34	7.8	04 59	3.3	17 47	3.0	07 54	4.9	20 21	4.6
TH 30	07 40	6.1	19 55	6.0	05 01	7.7	17 36	7.4	05 43	3.1	18 33	2.9	08 57	4.6	21 21	4.4
F 31	08 42	5.7	21 13	5.7	06 13	7.2	18 55	7.2	06 34	2.8	19 34	2.8	10 03	4.4	22 27	4.4

AUGUST 2009 *High Water* GMT

	LONDON BRIDGE				LIVERPOOL (Alfred Dock)				GREENOCK				LEITH			
SA 1	09 54	5.6	22 31	5.7	07 36	7.1	20 09	7.5	07 43	2.6	21 11	2.8	11 16	4.4	23 40	4.4
SU 2	10 59	5.8	23 36	6.0	08 45	7.4	21 07	7.9	09 50	2.6	22 24	3.0	12 27	4.5	—	—
M 3	11 57	6.1	—	—	09 38	7.8	21 54	8.4	10 51	2.8	23 14	3.2	00 44	4.6	13 22	4.7
TU 4	00 31	6.3	12 49	6.4	10 22	8.1	22 34	8.7	11 36	2.9	23 55	3.3	01 32	4.9	14 03	4.9
W 5	01 20	6.6	13 33	6.6	11 00	8.4	23 11	8.9	12 13	2.9	—	—	02 10	5.1	14 38	5.0
TH 6	02 02	6.7	14 13	6.6	11 34	8.5	23 44	9.0	00 31	3.4	12 47	3.0	02 42	5.2	15 08	5.1
F 7	02 39	6.7	14 48	6.6	12 06	8.6	—	—	01 03	3.4	13 18	3.0	03 13	5.3	15 39	5.2
SA 8	03 12	6.6	15 19	6.5	00 16	9.0	12 37	8.7	01 31	3.4	13 48	3.1	03 44	5.4	16 10	5.2
SU 9	03 43	6.5	15 47	6.5	00 48	9.0	13 08	8.7	02 00	3.4	14 19	3.1	04 15	5.4	16 43	5.2
M 10	04 14	6.6	16 16	6.6	01 21	9.0	13 40	8.7	02 32	3.5	14 52	3.2	04 47	5.3	17 18	5.1
TU 11	04 47	6.6	16 49	6.7	01 55	8.9	14 13	8.6	03 06	3.5	15 27	3.2	05 21	5.2	17 55	5.0
W 12	05 23	6.5	17 27	6.7	02 31	8.8	14 51	8.4	03 42	3.4	16 04	3.2	05 59	5.1	18 35	4.9
TH 13	06 03	6.4	18 12	6.5	03 14	8.5	15 36	8.1	04 20	3.3	16 44	3.1	06 43	5.0	19 22	4.7
F 14	06 50	6.1	19 05	6.2	04 07	8.1	16 35	7.7	05 03	3.1	17 31	3.0	07 35	4.8	20 20	4.5
SA 15	07 47	5.7	20 11	5.9	05 14	7.7	17 51	7.5	06 01	2.9	18 28	2.9	08 45	4.6	21 37	4.5
SU 16	09 00	5.6	21 32	5.7	06 34	7.5	19 16	7.6	07 32	2.7	19 52	2.9	10 12	4.6	22 56	4.6
M 17	10 28	5.7	23 02	6.0	08 00	7.8	20 34	8.2	09 26	2.8	21 31	3.0	11 34	4.8	—	—
TU 18	11 44	6.1	—	—	09 11	8.4	21 35	9.0	10 40	3.0	22 40	3.2	00 07	4.9	12 43	5.2
W 19	00 15	6.5	12 44	6.6	10 08	9.0	22 26	9.6	11 35	3.2	23 34	3.5	01 05	5.3	13 37	5.5
TH 20	01 13	7.0	13 34	7.0	10 58	9.5	23 13	10.0	12 25	3.3	—	—	01 53	5.7	14 23	5.8
F 21	02 04	7.3	14 21	7.2	11 43	9.7	23 58	10.1	00 22	3.6	13 13	3.3	02 37	5.9	15 07	5.9
SA 22	02 50	7.4	15 04	7.3	12 26	9.8	—	—	01 08	3.7	13 57	3.3	03 20	6.1	15 50	5.8
SU 23	03 34	7.5	15 44	7.3	00 41	10.1	13 08	9.6	01 52	3.8	14 38	3.3	04 04	6.0	16 33	5.7
M 24	04 14	7.3	16 22	7.3	01 23	9.8	13 47	9.3	02 32	3.8	15 14	3.3	04 49	5.9	17 16	5.4
TU 25	04 52	7.1	16 58	7.1	02 03	9.4	14 25	8.9	03 11	3.7	15 47	3.3	05 35	5.6	18 00	5.1
W 26	05 26	6.8	17 34	6.9	02 42	8.8	15 03	8.4	03 48	3.6	16 21	3.2	06 24	5.2	18 46	4.8
TH 27	06 00	6.5	18 13	6.4	03 23	8.2	15 45	7.8	04 26	3.3	16 59	3.1	07 18	4.8	19 38	4.6
F 28	06 36	6.0	19 01	5.9	04 12	7.4	16 42	7.3	05 07	3.0	17 44	2.9	08 18	4.5	20 38	4.3
SA 29	07 24	5.6	20 17	5.4	05 27	6.9	18 15	7.0	05 55	2.7	18 40	2.8	09 26	4.2	21 46	4.3
SU 30	09 00	5.3	22 05	5.4	07 10	6.8	19 42	7.3	06 57	2.5	20 21	2.8	10 44	4.2	23 05	4.3
M 31	10 29	5.5	23 13	5.8	08 23	7.2	20 43	7.8	09 39	2.5	22 00	3.0	12 06	4.4	—	—

SEPTEMBER 2009 *High Water* GMT

	LONDON BRIDGE *Datum of Predictions 3.20m below				LIVERPOOL (Alfred Dock) *Datum of Predictions 4.93m below				GREENOCK *Datum of Predictions 1.62m below				LEITH *Datum of Predictions 2.90m below			
	hr	*ht m*	*hr*	*ht m*	*hr*	*ht m*	*hr*	*ht m*	*hr*	*ht m*	*hr*	*ht m*	*hr*	*ht m*	*hr*	*ht m*
TU 1	11 31	6.0	—	—	09 15	7.7	21 30	8.3	10 35	2.7	22 49	3.2	00 18	4.6	13 01	4.7
W 2	00 07	6.3	12 22	6.4	09 58	8.2	22 10	8.8	11 14	2.9	23 29	3.3	01 07	4.9	13 40	4.9
TH 3	00 54	6.6	13 07	6.6	10 34	8.5	22 46	9.0	11 48	3.0	—	—	01 44	5.1	14 11	5.1
F 4	01 35	6.8	13 46	6.7	11 08	8.7	23 18	9.2	00 04	3.4	12 21	3.1	02 16	5.3	14 40	5.2
SA 5	02 11	6.8	14 21	6.6	11 38	8.8	23 49	9.2	00 36	3.4	12 51	3.1	02 46	5.4	15 10	5.3
SU 6	02 44	6.7	14 52	6.6	12 08	8.9	—	—	01 05	3.4	13 19	3.2	03 16	5.5	15 41	5.4
M 7	03 15	6.6	15 20	6.6	00 20	9.2	12 39	9.0	01 35	3.5	13 48	3.3	03 47	5.5	16 13	5.4
TU 8	03 46	6.6	15 50	6.7	00 52	9.2	13 10	8.9	02 08	3.5	14 21	3.4	04 19	5.5	16 48	5.3
W 9	04 18	6.7	16 24	6.8	01 27	9.1	13 45	8.8	02 44	3.5	14 56	3.4	04 55	5.4	17 24	5.2
TH 10	04 54	6.6	17 04	6.8	02 05	8.9	14 23	8.6	03 20	3.5	15 33	3.4	05 36	5.2	18 05	5.0
F 11	05 33	6.4	17 50	6.6	02 49	8.5	15 10	8.2	03 59	3.3	16 14	3.3	06 22	5.0	18 53	4.8
SA 12	06 19	6.1	18 44	6.2	03 44	7.9	16 12	7.7	04 42	3.1	17 01	3.1	07 18	4.8	19 54	4.6
SU 13	07 15	5.7	19 51	5.7	04 57	7.5	17 34	7.4	05 41	2.8	18 00	3.0	08 32	4.6	21 17	4.5
M 14	08 31	5.4	21 21	5.6	06 28	7.4	19 08	7.7	07 28	2.7	19 33	2.9	10 03	4.6	22 42	4.7
TU 15	10 12	5.6	22 56	6.0	07 57	7.8	20 24	8.3	09 33	2.8	21 22	3.1	11 25	4.9	23 52	5.0
W 16	11 27	6.1	—	—	09 01	8.5	21 21	9.1	10 33	3.1	22 27	3.3	12 30	5.2	—	—
TH 17	00 03	6.6	12 24	6.7	09 53	9.1	22 09	9.7	11 21	3.3	23 17	3.6	00 47	5.4	13 20	5.5
F 18	00 56	7.1	13 12	7.1	10 38	9.6	22 53	10.0	12 06	3.4	—	—	01 33	5.8	14 02	5.7
SA 19	01 43	7.4	13 56	7.3	11 20	9.8	23 35	10.1	00 03	3.7	12 49	3.4	02 15	6.0	14 43	5.8
SU 20	02 27	7.5	14 37	7.3	12 00	9.7	—	—	00 47	3.7	13 28	3.4	02 57	6.1	15 23	5.8
M 21	03 07	7.4	15 16	7.3	00 15	9.9	12 38	9.6	01 29	3.8	14 03	3.4	03 40	6.0	16 04	5.6
TU 22	03 43	7.2	15 53	7.2	00 53	9.6	13 14	9.3	02 07	3.7	14 35	3.4	04 24	5.8	16 44	5.4
W 23	04 16	7.0	16 27	7.1	01 30	9.2	13 49	8.9	02 44	3.6	15 08	3.4	05 08	5.5	17 25	5.1
TH 24	04 46	6.8	17 03	6.8	02 07	8.6	14 25	8.4	03 20	3.5	15 43	3.3	05 54	5.1	18 08	4.9
F 25	05 17	6.5	17 41	6.4	02 46	8.0	15 05	7.9	03 57	3.3	16 22	3.2	06 45	4.7	18 56	4.6
SA 26	05 53	6.1	18 27	5.9	03 32	7.3	15 57	7.4	04 39	3.0	17 07	3.0	07 42	4.4	19 55	4.4
SU 27	06 37	5.7	19 29	5.4	04 39	6.8	17 24	7.0	05 28	2.7	18 03	2.9	08 47	4.2	21 05	4.3
M 28	07 41	5.3	21 27	5.3	06 33	6.6	19 05	7.1	06 31	2.5	19 25	2.8	10 00	4.2	22 20	4.3
TU 29	09 50	5.3	22 39	5.6	07 50	7.0	20 09	7.6	08 49	2.6	21 19	3.0	11 23	4.3	23 34	4.5
W 30	10 56	5.8	23 34	6.1	08 42	7.6	20 57	8.2	09 58	2.8	22 13	3.2	12 23	4.6	—	—

OCTOBER 2009 *High Water* GMT

	LONDON BRIDGE				LIVERPOOL (Alfred Dock)				GREENOCK				LEITH			
TH 1	11 48	6.2	—	—	09 24	8.1	21 37	8.7	10 39	3.0	22 53	3.3	00 27	4.8	13 03	4.9
F 2	00 20	6.5	12 33	6.5	10 01	8.6	22 13	9.0	11 14	3.1	23 28	3.4	01 07	5.1	13 35	5.1
SA 3	01 01	6.7	13 12	6.6	10 34	8.8	22 46	9.2	11 47	3.2	—	—	01 41	5.3	14 06	5.3
SU 4	01 37	6.8	13 48	6.7	11 06	9.0	23 18	9.3	00 01	3.4	12 18	3.3	02 13	5.4	14 38	5.4
M 5	02 11	6.8	14 21	6.7	11 37	9.1	23 51	9.4	00 35	3.5	12 47	3.4	02 46	5.6	15 10	5.5
TU 6	02 45	6.7	14 53	6.7	12 10	9.2	—	—	01 09	3.5	13 19	3.5	03 19	5.6	15 44	5.5
W 7	03 18	6.7	15 28	6.9	00 27	9.4	12 45	9.2	01 47	3.5	13 55	3.6	03 55	5.6	16 20	5.4
TH 8	03 53	6.7	16 07	6.9	01 05	9.2	13 24	9.0	02 25	3.5	14 32	3.6	04 35	5.5	16 59	5.3
F 9	04 31	6.6	16 50	6.8	01 48	8.9	14 07	8.7	03 05	3.5	15 11	3.6	05 20	5.3	17 43	5.1
SA 10	05 12	6.4	17 39	6.5	02 36	8.4	14 58	8.3	03 47	3.3	15 53	3.5	06 11	5.1	18 34	4.9
SU 11	05 58	6.1	18 36	6.1	03 35	7.9	16 02	7.8	04 36	3.1	16 42	3.3	07 11	4.8	19 39	4.7
M 12	06 56	5.7	19 47	5.8	04 52	7.5	17 26	7.6	05 44	2.9	17 47	3.1	08 28	4.6	21 05	4.6
TU 13	08 20	5.5	21 19	5.8	06 23	7.5	18 54	7.9	07 45	2.8	19 24	3.0	09 53	4.7	22 26	4.8
W 14	09 54	5.8	22 39	6.2	07 41	8.0	20 04	8.5	09 18	3.0	21 02	3.2	11 09	4.9	23 31	5.1
TH 15	11 02	6.3	23 40	6.7	08 41	8.6	21 00	9.1	10 12	3.2	22 04	3.4	12 10	5.2	—	—
F 16	11 56	6.7	—	—	09 30	9.1	21 48	9.5	10 58	3.4	22 54	3.6	00 25	5.5	12 58	5.4
SA 17	00 31	7.1	12 45	7.1	10 14	9.5	22 31	9.7	11 40	3.5	23 39	3.7	01 11	5.7	13 39	5.6
SU 18	01 18	7.3	13 29	7.2	10 54	9.6	23 11	9.8	12 19	3.5	—	—	01 54	5.8	14 19	5.7
M 19	02 00	7.3	14 11	7.2	11 32	9.6	23 49	9.6	00 23	3.7	12 57	3.5	02 36	5.9	14 58	5.6
TU 20	02 38	7.2	14 51	7.1	12 08	9.4	—	—	01 04	3.7	13 30	3.5	03 19	5.8	15 37	5.5
W 21	03 13	7.0	15 28	7.0	00 26	9.3	12 44	9.2	01 42	3.6	14 03	3.5	04 02	5.6	16 16	5.4
TH 22	03 44	6.8	16 04	6.8	01 02	8.9	13 19	8.9	02 18	3.5	14 37	3.5	04 45	5.3	16 54	5.2
F 23	04 13	6.7	16 40	6.6	01 38	8.5	13 56	8.5	02 55	3.4	15 13	3.5	05 29	5.0	17 34	4.9
SA 24	04 45	6.5	17 19	6.3	02 17	8.0	14 36	8.1	03 34	3.2	15 52	3.4	06 15	4.7	18 20	4.7
SU 25	05 22	6.2	18 03	5.9	03 02	7.5	15 24	7.6	04 16	3.0	16 36	3.2	07 07	4.5	19 15	4.5
M 26	06 06	5.9	18 57	5.6	03 59	7.0	16 29	7.2	05 06	2.8	17 30	3.0	08 05	4.3	20 19	4.4
TU 27	07 01	5.5	20 08	5.4	05 29	6.7	18 04	7.2	06 08	2.7	18 38	2.9	09 09	4.2	21 29	4.4
W 28	08 26	5.3	21 42	5.5	06 56	7.0	19 17	7.5	07 36	2.7	20 08	3.0	10 17	4.3	22 35	4.5
TH 29	10 03	5.6	22 45	5.9	07 56	7.4	20 11	7.9	08 59	2.9	21 19	3.1	11 21	4.5	23 33	4.7
F 30	11 01	5.9	23 35	6.2	08 42	8.0	20 55	8.4	09 52	3.1	22 07	3.3	12 11	4.8	—	—
SA 31	11 49	6.3	—	—	09 22	8.4	21 34	8.8	10 34	3.2	22 48	3.4	00 21	5.0	12 52	5.1

NOVEMBER 2009 *High Water* GMT

	LONDON BRIDGE *Datum of Predictions 3.20m below				LIVERPOOL (Alfred Dock) *Datum of Predictions 4.93m below				GREENOCK *Datum of Predictions 1.62m below				LEITH *Datum of Predictions 2.90m below			
	hr	*ht m*	*hr*	*ht m*	*hr*	*ht m*	*hr*	*ht m*	*hr*	*ht m*	*hr*	*ht m*	*hr*	*ht m*	*hr*	*ht m*
SU 1	00 19	6.5	12 32	6.5	09 58	8.8	22 11	9.1	11 11	3.3	23 26	3.4	01 02	5.2	13 30	5.3
M 2	01 00	6.7	13 12	6.7	10 32	9.1	22 48	9.3	11 45	3.4	—	—	01 40	5.4	14 06	5.5
TU 3	01 39	6.8	13 51	6.8	11 08	9.3	23 27	9.4	00 05	3.5	12 19	3.5	02 18	5.5	14 42	5.6
W 4	02 17	6.9	14 31	6.9	11 46	9.4	—	—	00 47	3.5	12 56	3.6	02 56	5.6	15 19	5.6
TH 5	02 56	6.9	15 13	7.0	00 08	9.4	12 27	9.3	01 29	3.5	13 35	3.7	03 38	5.7	15 59	5.5
F 6	03 35	6.8	15 58	7.0	00 52	9.2	13 11	9.2	02 13	3.5	14 15	3.8	04 22	5.6	16 42	5.4
SA 7	04 17	6.7	16 45	6.8	01 40	9.0	14 00	8.9	02 57	3.5	14 57	3.7	05 11	5.4	17 29	5.3
SU 8	05 01	6.5	17 37	6.6	02 32	8.6	14 54	8.6	03 45	3.3	15 43	3.6	06 04	5.2	18 23	5.1
M 9	05 50	6.2	18 36	6.3	03 32	8.1	15 57	8.2	04 40	3.1	16 35	3.5	07 06	5.0	19 30	4.9
TU 10	06 51	5.9	19 45	6.1	04 44	7.8	17 11	8.1	05 53	3.0	17 40	3.3	08 18	4.8	20 49	4.9
W 11	08 11	5.8	21 02	6.1	06 01	7.8	18 26	8.1	07 27	2.9	19 03	3.2	09 34	4.8	22 02	5.0
TH 12	09 27	6.0	22 11	6.3	07 12	8.0	19 34	8.4	08 44	3.1	20 29	3.3	10 43	4.9	23 05	5.1
F 13	10 31	6.3	23 10	6.7	08 13	8.4	20 33	8.8	09 41	3.2	21 35	3.4	11 43	5.1	—	—
SA 14	11 27	6.7	—	—	09 04	8.8	21 24	9.1	10 29	3.4	22 28	3.5	00 01	5.3	12 34	5.2
SU 15	00 02	6.9	12 18	6.9	09 50	9.1	22 09	9.2	11 12	3.5	23 15	3.6	00 51	5.5	13 17	5.4
M 16	00 50	7.0	13 05	7.0	10 31	9.3	22 51	9.2	11 52	3.5	—	—	01 37	5.5	13 58	5.4
TU 17	01 34	7.0	13 50	7.0	11 09	9.3	23 29	9.1	00 00	3.6	12 30	3.6	02 21	5.5	14 37	5.5
W 18	02 13	6.9	14 32	6.9	11 45	9.2	—	—	00 42	3.5	13 05	3.6	03 04	5.5	15 16	5.4
TH 19	02 48	6.7	15 11	6.7	00 05	9.0	12 21	9.1	01 20	3.5	13 39	3.7	03 46	5.4	15 53	5.3
F 20	03 19	6.6	15 48	6.6	00 41	8.7	12 57	8.9	01 57	3.4	14 14	3.7	04 26	5.2	16 30	5.2
SA 21	03 49	6.5	16 23	6.4	01 18	8.5	13 35	8.7	02 35	3.3	14 50	3.6	05 06	5.0	17 07	5.0
SU 22	04 22	6.5	17 01	6.3	01 56	8.1	14 15	8.4	03 15	3.2	15 28	3.5	05 48	4.8	17 49	4.9
M 23	04 59	6.3	17 42	6.1	02 38	7.8	14 59	8.0	03 58	3.1	16 10	3.4	06 33	4.6	18 36	4.7
TU 24	05 41	6.1	18 28	5.9	03 26	7.4	15 49	7.7	04 45	3.0	16 57	3.2	07 22	4.5	19 30	4.5
W 25	06 29	5.9	19 20	5.7	04 24	7.2	16 50	7.5	05 38	2.9	17 53	3.1	08 17	4.4	20 32	4.5
TH 26	07 28	5.7	20 21	5.7	05 35	7.1	17 59	7.5	06 40	2.9	18 56	3.0	09 17	4.4	21 35	4.5
F 27	08 40	5.6	21 31	5.8	06 47	7.3	19 05	7.7	07 50	2.9	20 06	3.0	10 18	4.5	22 36	4.6
SA 28	09 54	5.8	22 37	6.0	07 47	7.7	20 02	8.1	08 55	3.0	21 11	3.1	11 15	4.7	23 32	4.8
SU 29	10 56	6.1	23 33	6.3	08 36	8.1	20 52	8.5	09 49	3.2	22 06	3.3	12 08	4.9	—	—
M 30	11 50	6.4	—	—	09 20	8.6	21 38	8.9	10 34	3.3	22 54	3.4	00 23	5.0	12 55	5.2

DECEMBER 2009 *High Water* GMT

	LONDON BRIDGE				LIVERPOOL (Alfred Dock)				GREENOCK				LEITH			
TU 1	00 23	6.6	12 39	6.7	10 03	9.0	22 23	9.2	11 16	3.4	23 41	3.4	01 11	5.2	13 39	5.4
W 2	01 10	6.8	13 27	6.9	10 46	9.3	23 09	9.4	11 56	3.6	—	—	01 55	5.5	14 20	5.5
TH 3	01 55	6.9	14 14	7.0	11 30	9.5	23 56	9.4	00 29	3.5	12 38	3.7	02 40	5.6	15 01	5.6
F 4	02 39	6.9	15 03	7.1	12 16	9.5	—	—	01 17	3.5	13 21	3.8	03 26	5.7	15 44	5.7
SA 5	03 23	6.9	15 52	7.1	00 45	9.4	13 05	9.5	02 06	3.5	14 05	3.9	04 13	5.7	16 30	5.6
SU 6	04 09	6.8	16 42	7.0	01 35	9.2	13 55	9.4	02 55	3.4	14 50	3.9	05 03	5.6	17 19	5.5
M 7	04 56	6.6	17 34	6.9	02 27	8.9	14 48	9.1	03 46	3.3	15 37	3.8	05 56	5.4	18 13	5.4
TU 8	05 45	6.5	18 29	6.6	03 22	8.6	15 44	8.8	04 41	3.2	16 29	3.7	06 53	5.2	19 13	5.2
W 9	06 40	6.3	19 28	6.4	04 21	8.3	16 44	8.5	05 42	3.1	17 26	3.5	07 57	4.9	20 23	5.1
TH 10	07 45	6.2	20 32	6.3	05 26	8.0	17 50	8.3	06 49	3.1	18 31	3.4	09 04	4.8	21 32	5.0
F 11	08 52	6.1	21 36	6.3	06 34	7.9	18 58	8.2	07 56	3.1	19 44	3.3	10 10	4.8	22 36	5.0
SA 12	09 57	6.2	22 36	6.3	07 39	8.1	20 04	8.3	09 00	3.1	20 59	3.3	11 12	4.8	23 38	5.0
SU 13	10 57	6.4	23 32	6.4	08 38	8.3	21 02	8.4	09 57	3.2	22 02	3.3	12 09	4.9	—	—
M 14	11 53	6.5	—	—	09 28	8.6	21 52	8.6	10 47	3.4	22 56	3.3	00 34	5.1	13 00	5.1
TU 15	00 23	6.6	12 46	6.6	10 13	8.8	22 37	8.7	11 32	3.5	23 44	3.3	01 26	5.2	13 44	5.2
W 16	01 11	6.6	13 34	6.7	10 53	9.0	23 16	8.8	12 12	3.6	—	—	02 12	5.2	14 25	5.3
TH 17	01 53	6.6	14 19	6.6	11 30	9.1	23 52	8.7	00 28	3.3	12 50	3.6	02 54	5.2	15 02	5.3
F 18	02 31	6.5	14 59	6.6	12 06	9.1	—	—	01 07	3.3	13 25	3.7	03 32	5.2	15 37	5.3
SA 19	03 03	6.5	15 35	6.5	00 27	8.7	12 42	9.0	01 44	3.3	13 58	3.7	04 09	5.2	16 11	5.2
SU 20	03 34	6.5	16 08	6.4	01 02	8.6	13 19	8.9	02 21	3.2	14 33	3.7	04 45	5.1	16 46	5.2
M 21	04 06	6.4	16 42	6.4	01 38	8.4	13 56	8.7	02 58	3.2	15 08	3.6	05 21	5.0	17 23	5.1
TU 22	04 40	6.4	17 19	6.4	02 16	8.2	14 34	8.5	03 38	3.2	15 45	3.5	06 00	4.8	18 02	4.9
W 23	05 18	6.4	17 59	6.3	02 55	8.0	15 15	8.2	04 18	3.1	16 25	3.4	06 43	4.7	18 45	4.8
TH 24	06 00	6.2	18 43	6.2	03 39	7.7	16 02	8.0	05 01	3.1	17 10	3.2	07 29	4.5	19 33	4.6
F 25	06 47	6.1	19 33	6.0	04 30	7.5	16 56	7.8	05 47	3.0	18 02	3.1	08 22	4.5	20 30	4.5
SA 26	07 44	5.9	20 32	5.9	05 31	7.4	17 58	7.7	06 39	3.0	19 02	3.0	09 21	4.4	21 37	4.5
SU 27	08 51	5.8	21 39	5.9	06 39	7.4	19 05	7.8	07 43	2.9	20 14	3.0	10 24	4.5	22 44	4.6
M 28	10 03	5.9	22 49	6.0	07 47	7.8	20 11	8.1	08 55	3.0	21 27	3.1	11 26	4.7	23 47	4.8
TU 29	11 11	6.2	23 51	6.3	08 46	8.3	21 11	8.5	09 58	3.2	22 30	3.2	12 24	4.9	—	—
W 30	12 12	6.6	—	—	09 40	8.8	22 06	9.0	10 51	3.4	23 26	3.3	00 46	5.1	13 17	5.2
TH 31	00 46	6.6	13 09	6.9	10 30	9.2	—	—	11 38	3.5	—	—	01 40	5.4	14 04	5.5

GENERAL REFERENCE

WEIGHTS AND MEASURES

CONVERSION TABLES

THE PERIODIC TABLE

NOBEL PRIZE WINNERS

ABBREVIATIONS

WEIGHTS AND MEASURES

SI UNITS

The Système International d'Unités (SI) is an international and coherent system of units devised to meet all known needs for measurement in science and technology. The system was adopted by the eleventh Conférence Générale des Poids et Mesures (CGPM) in 1960. A comprehensive description of the system is given in *SI The International System of Units* (HMSO). The British Standards that describe the essential features of the International System of Units are *Specifications for SI units and recommendations for the use of their multiples and certain other units* (BS ISO 1000: 1992) and *Conversion factors for units* (BS 350: 2004).

The system consists of seven base units and the derived units formed as products or quotients of various powers of the base units. Together the base units and the derived units make up the coherent system of units. In the UK the SI base units, and almost all important derived units, are realised at the National Physical Laboratory and disseminated through the National Weights and Measures Laboratory.

BASE UNITS

Ampere (A) = unit of electric current
Candela (cd) = unit of luminous intensity
Kelvin (K) = unit of thermodynamic temperature
Kilogram (kg) = unit of mass
Metre (m) = unit of length
Mole (mol) = unit of amount of substance
Second (s) = unit of time

DERIVED UNITS

For some of the derived SI units, special names and symbols exist; those approved by the CGPM are as follows:

Becquerel (Bq) = unit of activity (of a radionuclide)
Coulomb (C) = unit of electric charge, quantity of electricity
Degree Celsius (°C) = unit of Celsius temperature
Farad (F) = unit of electric capacitance
Gray (Gy) = unit of absorbed dose, specific energy imparted, kerma, absorbed dose index
Henry (H) = unit of inductance
Hertz (Hz) = unit of frequency
Joule (J) = unit of energy, work, quantity of heat
Katal (kat) = unit of catalytic activity
Lumen (lm) = unit of luminous flux
Lux (lx) = unit of illuminance
Newton (N) = unit of force
Ohm (Ω) = unit of electric resistance
Pascal (Pa) = unit of pressure, stress
Radian (rad) = unit of plane angle
Siemens (S) = unit of electric conductance
Sievert (Sv) = unit of dose equivalent, dose equivalent index
Steradian (sr) = unit of solid angle
Tesla (T) = unit of magnetic flux density
Volt (V) = unit of electric potential, potential difference, electromotive force
Watt (W) = unit of power, radiant flux
Weber (Wb) = unit of magnetic flux

Other derived units are expressed in terms of base units. Below are some of the more commonly used derived units:

Ampere per metre ($A\ m^{-1}$) = unit of magnetic field strength
Candela per square metre ($cd\ m^{-2}$) = unit of luminance
Cubic metre (m^3) = unit of volume
Joule per kelvin ($J\ K^{-1}$) = unit of heat capacity
Joule per kilogram kelvin ($J\ kg^{-1}\ K^{-1}$) = unit of specific heat capacity
Kilogram per cubic metre ($kg\ m^{-3}$) = unit of density
Kilogram metre per second ($kg\ m\ s^{-1}$) = unit of momentum
Metre per second ($m\ s^{-1}$) = unit of velocity
Metre per second squared ($m\ s^{-2}$) = unit of acceleration
Newton per metre ($N\ m^{-1}$) = unit of surface tension
Pascal second (Pa s) = unit of dynamic viscosity
Square metre (m^2) = unit of area
Volt per metre ($V\ m^{-1}$) = unit of electric field strength
Watt per metre kelvin ($W\ m^{-1}\ K^{-1}$) = unit of thermal conductivity
Watt per square metre ($W\ m^{-2}$) = unit of heat flux density, irradiance

Non SI units accepted for use with the SI by the CGPM:

Minute Hour Day	measurement of time
Degree Minute Second	plane angle measurement
Hectare	measurement of area
Litre	measurement of volume
Tonne	measurement of mass

SI PREFIXES

Decimal multiples and submultiples of the SI units are indicated by SI prefixes. These are as follows:

Multiples	*Submultiples*
yotta (Y) × 10^{24}	deci (d) × 10^{-1}
zetta (Z) × 10^{21}	centi (c) × 10^{-2}
exa (E) × 10^{18}	milli (m) × 10^{-3}
peta (P) × 10^{15}	micro (μ) × 10^{-6}
tera (T) × 10^{12}	nano (n) × 10^{-9}
giga (G) × 10^{9}	pico (p) × 10^{-12}
mega (M) × 10^{6}	femto (f) × 10^{-15}
kilo (k) × 10^{3}	atto (a) × 10^{-18}
hecto (h) × 10^{2}	zepto (z) × 10^{-21}
deca (da) × 10	yocto (y) × 10^{-24}

METRIC UNITS

The metric primary standards are the metre as the unit of measurement of length, and the kilogram as the unit of measurement of mass. Other units of measurement are defined by reference to the primary standards.

MEASUREMENT OF LENGTH

Kilometre (km) = 1,000 metres
Metre (m) = the length of the path travelled by light in vacuum during a time interval of 1/299 792 458 of a second

Decimetre (dm) = 1/10 metre
Centimetre (cm) = 1/100 metre
Millimetre (mm) = 1/1,000 metre

MEASUREMENT OF AREA
Hectare (ha) = 100 ares
Decare = 10 ares
Are (a) = 100 square metres
Square metre = a superficial area equal to that of a square each side of which measures one metre
Square decimetre = 1/100 square metre
Square centimetre = 1/100 square decimetre
Square millimetre = 1/100 square centimetre

MEASUREMENT OF VOLUME
Cubic metre (m^3) = a volume equal to that of a cube each edge of which measures one metre
Cubic decimetre = 1/1,000 cubic metre
Cubic centimetre (cc) = 1/1,000 cubic decimetre
Hectolitre = 100 litres
Litre = a cubic decimetre
Decilitre = 1/10 litre
Centilitre = 1/100 litre
Millilitre = 1/1,000 litre

MEASUREMENT OF CAPACITY
Hectolitre (hl) = 100 litres
Litre (l or L) = a cubic decimetre
Decilitre (dl) = 1/10 litre
Centilitre (cl) = 1/100 litre
Millilitre (ml) = 1/1,000 litre

MEASUREMENT OF MASS OR WEIGHT
Tonne (t) = 1,000 kilograms
Kilogram (kg) = mass of the international prototype of the kilogram
Hectogram (hg) = 1/10 kilogram
Gram (g) = 1/1,000 kilogram
*Carat (metric) = 1/5 gram
Milligram (mg) = 1/1,000 gram

* Used only for transactions in precious stones or pearls

IMPERIAL UNITS

The imperial primary standards are the yard as the unit of measurement of length and the pound as the unit of measurement of mass. Other units of measurement are defined by reference to the primary standards.

MEASUREMENT OF LENGTH
Mile = 1,760 yards
Furlong = 220 yards
Chain = 22 yards
Yard (yd) = 0.9144 metre
Foot (ft *or* ′) = 1/3 yard
Inch (in *or* ″) = 1/36 yard

MEASUREMENT OF AREA
Square mile = 640 acres
Acre = 4,840 square yards
Rood = 1,210 square yards
Square yard (sq. yd) = a superficial area equal to that of a square each side of which measures one yard
Square foot (sq. ft) = 1/9 square yard
Square inch (sq. in) = 1/144 square foot

MEASUREMENT OF VOLUME
Cubic yard = a volume equal to that of a cube each edge of which measures one yard
Cubic foot = 1/27 cubic yard
Cubic inch = 1/1,728 cubic foot

MEASUREMENT OF CAPACITY
Bushel = 8 gallons
Peck = 2 gallons
Gallon (gal) = 4.54609 cubic decimetres
Quart (qt) = 1/4 gallon
Pint (pt) = 1/2 quart
Gill = 1/4 pint
Fluid ounce (fl oz) = 1/20 pint
Fluid drachm = 1/8 fluid ounce
Minim (min) = 1/60 fluid drachm

MEASUREMENT OF MASS OR WEIGHT
Ton = 2,240 pounds
Hundredweight (cwt) = 112 pounds
Cental = 100 pounds
Quarter = 28 pounds
Stone = 14 pounds
Pound (lb) = 0.453 592 37 kilogram
Ounce (oz) = 1/16 pound
*Ounce troy (oz tr) = 12/175 pound
Dram (dr) = 1/16 ounce
Grain (gr) = 1/7,000 pound
Pennyweight (dwt) = 24 grains
Ounce apothecaries' = 480 grains
Drachm (ʒ 1) = 1/8 ounce apothecaries
Scruple (℈ 1) = 1/3 drachm

* Used only for transactions in gold, silver or other precious metals, and articles made therefrom

MEASUREMENT OF ELECTRICITY

Units of measurement of electricity are defined by the Weights and Measures Act 1985 as follows:
Ampere (A) = that constant current which, if maintained in two straight parallel conductors of infinite length, of negligible circular cross-section and placed 1 metre apart in vacuum, would produce between these conductors a force equal to 2×10^{-7} newton per metre of length
Ohm (Ω) = the electric resistance between two points of a conductor when a constant potential difference of 1 volt, applied between the two points, produces in the conductor a current of 1 ampere, the conductor not being the seat of any electromotive force
Volt (V) = the difference of electric potential between two points of a conducting wire carrying a constant current of 1 ampere when the power dissipated between these points is equal to 1 watt
Watt (W) = the power which in one second gives rise to energy of 1 joule
Kilowatt (kW) = 1,000 watts
Megawatt (MW) = one million watts

MEASUREMENT OF SOUND

INTENSITY
Decibels are used to measure the power or intensity of sound. Decibel level is calculated on a logarithmic scale as a ratio against a standard power; each increase of 10db on the scale corresponds to ten times the intensity and twice the loudness. Some examples of decibel levels are:

Silence	0db
Noise level of ordinary conversation	60db
Damage threshold for noise	90db
Noise level of typical streetworks	110db
Pain threshold for noise	130db

FREQUENCY AND PITCH

Frequency is a measure of how many waves or sound waves pass through a medium over a certain period of time. It is measured in Hertz (Hz) (*see* Derived SI Units), and a frequency of one Hz equals one wave, or one vibration every second. The typical range for human hearing is between 20Hz and 20,000Hz.

Frequency is closely linked to pitch, which indicates how high or low a sound is; a high frequency will have a high pitch, and a frequency doubled sounds an octave higher.

WATER AND LIQUOR MEASURES

1 cubic foot = 62.32 pounds
1 gallon = 10 pounds
1 cubic cm = 1 gram
1,000 cubic cm = 1 litre; 1 kilogram
1 cubic metre = 1,000 litres; 1,000 kilograms; 1 tonne
An inch of rain on the surface of an acre (43,560 sq. feet) = 3,630 cubic feet = 100.992 tons
Cisterns: A cistern 4 × 2.5 feet and 3 feet deep will hold brimful 186.963 gallons, weighing 1,869.63 pounds in addition to its own weight

WATER FOR SHIPS

Kilderkin = 18 gallons
Barrel = 36 gallons
Puncheon = 72 gallons
Butt = 110 gallons
Tun = 210 gallons

BOTTLES OF WINE

Traditional equivalents in standard champagne bottles:
Magnum = 2 bottles
Jeroboam = 4 bottles
Rehoboam = 6 bottles
Methuselah = 8 bottles
Salmanazar = 12 bottles
Balthazar = 16 bottles
Nebuchadnezzar = 20 bottles
A quarter of a bottle is known as a *nip*
An eighth of a bottle is known as a *baby*

ANGULAR AND CIRCULAR MEASURES

60 seconds (") = 1 minute (′)
60 minutes = 1 degree (°)
90 degrees = 1 right angle or quadrant
Diameter of circle × 3.1416 = circumference
Diameter squared × 0.7854 = area of circle
Diameter squared × 3.1416 = surface of sphere
Diameter cubed × 0.523 = solidity of sphere
One degree of circumference × 57.3 = radius*
Diameter of cylinder × 3.1416; product by length or height, gives the surface
Diameter squared × 0.7854; product by length or height, gives solid content

* Or, one radian (the angle subtended at the centre of a circle by an arc of the circumference equal in length to the radius) = 57.3 degrees

MILLION, BILLION ETC

Value in the UK

Million	thousand × thousand	10^6
*Billion	million × million	10^{12}
Trillion	million × billion	10^{18}
Quadrillion	million × trillion	10^{24}

Value in the USA

Million	thousand × thousand	10^6
*Billion	thousand × million	10^9
Trillion	million × million	10^{12}
Quadrillion	million × billion US	10^{15}

* The American usage of billion (ie 10^9) is increasingly common, and is now universally used by statisticians

NAUTICAL MEASURES

DISTANCE

Distance at sea is measured in nautical miles. The British standard nautical mile was 6,080 feet but this measure has been obsolete since 1970 when the international nautical mile of 1,852 metres was adopted by the Hydrographic Department of the Ministry of Defence. The cable (600 feet or 100 fathoms) was a measure approximately one-tenth of a nautical mile. Such distances are now expressed in decimal parts of a sea mile or in metres.

Soundings at sea were recorded in fathoms (6 feet). Depths are now expressed in metres on Admiralty charts.

SPEED

Speed is measured in nautical miles per hour, called knots. A ship moving at the rate of 30 nautical miles per hour is said to be doing 30 knots.

Knots	*Mph*	*Knots*	*Mph*
1	1.1515	9	10.3636
2	2.3030	10	11.5151
3	3.4545	15	17.2727
4	4.6060	20	23.0303
5	5.7575	25	28.7878
6	6.9090	30	34.5454
7	8.0606	35	40.3030
8	9.2121	40	46.0606

TONNAGE

Under the Merchant Shipping Act 1854, the tonnage of UK-registered vessels was measured in tons of 100 cubic feet. The need for a universal method of measurement led to the adoption of the International Convention on Tonnage Measurements of Ships 1969, which measures, in cubic metres, all the internal spaces of a vessel for the gross tonnage and those of the cargo compartments for the net tonnage. The convention has applied since July 1982 to new ships, ships which needed to be remeasured because of substantial alterations, and ships whose owners requested remeasurement. On 18 July 1994 the convention became mandatory.

DISTANCE OF THE HORIZON

The distance to the horizon can be calculated, in metric units, using the equation $D = 3.8373\sqrt{H}$ where D is the distance in kilometres and H is the height of the observer in metres, and in imperial units using the equation $D = 1.3157\sqrt{H}$ where D is the distance in miles and H is the height of the observer in feet. The resulting distances are those following a straight line from the observer to the horizon; it is not the distance along the curvature of the Earth. The difference between these two figures, however, is minimal for heights below 100km (62 miles).

Height in metres (feet)	*Range in km (miles)*
*1.7 (5.6)	5.0 (3.1)
5 (16)	8.6 (5.3)
10 (32.8)	12.1 (7.5)
50 (164)	27.1 (16.8)
100 (328)	38.4 (23.8)
†509 (1,670)	86.6 (53.8)
1,000 (3,281)	121.34 (75.4)
5,000 (16,404)	271.3 (168.5)
‡8,850 (29,035)	361.0 (224.2)
§9,144 (30,000)	366.9 (228.0)

* Average human height in the UK
† Height of the tallest inhabited building (Taipei 101)
‡ Height of Mt Everest
§ Height of cruising aeroplane

TEMPERATURE SCALES

The SI (International System) unit of temperature is the kelvin, which is defined as the fraction 1/273.16 of the temperature of the triple point of water (ie where ice, water and water vapour are in equilibrium). The zero of the Kelvin scale is the absolute zero of temperature. The freezing point of water is 273.15 K and the boiling point (as adopted in the International Temperature Scale of 1990) is 373.124 K.

The Celsius scale (formerly centigrade) is defined by subtracting 273.15 from the Kelvin temperature. The Fahrenheit scale is related to the Celsius scale by the relationships:

$$\text{temperature °F} = (\text{temperature °C} \times 1.8) + 32$$
$$\text{temperature °C} = (\text{temperature °F} - 32) \div 1.8$$

It follows from these definitions that the freezing point of water is 0°C and 32°F. The boiling point is 99.974°C and 211.953°F.

The temperature of the human body varies from person to person and in the same person can be affected by a variety of factors. In most people body temperature varies between 36.5°C and 37.2°C (97.7–98.9°F).

Conversion between scales

°C	°F	°C	°F	°C	°F
100	212	60	140	20	68
99	210.2	59	138.2	19	66.2
98	208.4	58	136.4	18	64.4
97	206.6	57	134.6	17	62.6
96	204.8	56	132.8	16	60.8
95	203	55	131	15	59
94	201.2	54	129.2	14	57.2
93	199.4	53	127.4	13	55.4
92	197.6	52	125.6	12	53.6
91	195.8	51	123.8	11	51.8
90	194	50	122	10	50
89	192.2	49	120.2	9	48.2
88	190.4	48	118.4	8	46.4
87	188.6	47	116.6	7	44.6
86	186.8	46	114.8	6	42.8
85	185	45	113	5	41
84	183.2	44	111.2	4	39.2
83	181.4	43	109.4	3	37.4
82	179.6	42	107.6	2	35.6
81	177.8	41	105.8	1	33.8
80	176	40	104	*Zero*	32
79	174.2	39	102.2	−1	30.2
78	172.4	38	100.4	−2	28.4
77	170.6	37	98.6	−3	26.6
76	168.8	36	96.8	−4	24.8
75	167	35	95	−5	23
74	165.2	34	93.2	−6	21.2
73	163.4	33	91.4	−7	19.4
72	161.6	32	89.6	−8	17.6
71	159.8	31	87.8	−9	15.8
70	158	30	86	−10	14
69	156.2	29	84.2	−11	12.2
68	154.4	28	82.4	−12	10.4
67	152.6	27	80.6	−13	8.6
66	150.8	26	78.8	−14	6.8
65	149	25	77	−15	5
64	147.2	24	75.2	−16	3.2
63	145.4	23	73.4	−17	1.4
62	143.6	22	71.6	−18	0.4
61	141.8	21	69.8	−19	−2.2

PAPER MEASURES

Printing Paper		*Writing Paper*	
5 bundles	= 1 bale	480 sheets	= 1 ream
2 reams	= 1 bundle	20 quires	= 1 ream
516 sheets	= 1 ream	24 sheets	= 1 quire

INTERNATIONAL PAPER SIZES

The basis of the international series of paper sizes is a rectangle having an area of one square metre, the sides of which are in the proportion of 1:√2. The proportions 1:√2 have a geometrical relationship, the side and diagonal of any square being in this proportion. The effect of this arrangement is that if the area of the sheet of paper is doubled or halved, the shorter side and the longer side of the new sheet are still in the same proportion 1:√2. This feature is useful where photographic enlargement or reduction is used, as the proportions remain the same.

Description of the A series is by capital A followed by a figure. The basic size has the description A0 and the higher the figure following the letter, the greater is the number of sub-divisions and therefore the smaller the sheet. Half A0 is A1 and half A1 is A2. Where larger dimensions are required the A is preceded by a figure. Thus 2A means twice the size A0; 4A is four times the size of A0.

SUBSIDIARY SERIES

B sizes are sizes intermediate between any two adjacent sizes of the A series. There is a series of C sizes which is used much less. A is for magazines and books, B for posters, wall charts and other large items, C for envelopes particularly where it is necessary for an envelope (in C series) to fit into another envelope. The size recommended for business correspondence is A4.

Long sizes (DL) are obtainable by dividing any appropriate sizes from the two series above into three, four or eight equal parts parallel with the shorter side in such a manner that the proportion of 1:√2 is not maintained, the ratio between the longer and the shorter sides being greater than √2:1. In practice long sizes should be produced from the A series only.

It is an essential feature of these series that the dimensions are of the trimmed or finished size.

A SERIES

	mm		mm
A0	841 × 1189	A6	105 × 148
A1	594 × 841	A7	74 × 105
A2	420 × 594	A8	52 × 74
A3	297 × 420	A9	37 × 52
A4	210 × 297	A10	26 × 37
A5	148 × 210		

BOOK SIZES

Traditional		*Modern*	
	mm		mm
Royal Quarto	250 × 320	Crown Royal	210 × 280
Demy Quarto	220 × 290	Royal	191 × 235
Crown Quarto	190 × 250	Demy	152 × 229
Royal Octavo	150 × 250	C format	143 × 222
Demy Octavo	143 × 222	B format or trade	129 × 198
Large Crown Octavo	129 × 198	A format	111 × 175

OBSOLETE MEASURES

Length
Cubit, Digit, Ell, Finger, Hand (still in use for measurement of horses), League, Palm, Span
Capacity
Barrel, Bushel, Cask, Hogshead, Sester, Tun
Weight
Clove, Fother, Last, Mark, Nail, Sack, Tod
Area
Bovate, Carucate, Perch, Virgate, Yoke

CLOTHING SIZES

MEN'S

Item	*UK*	*USA*	*Europe*
Suits	36	36	46
	38	38	48
	40	40	50
	42	42	52
	44	44	54
	46	46	56
Shirts	12	12	30–31
	12½	12½	32
	13	13	33
	13½	13½	34–35
	14	14	36
	14½	14½	37
	15	15	38
	15½	15½	39–40
	16	16	41
	16½	16½	42
	17	17	43
	17½	17½	44–45
Shoes	6½	7	39
	7	7½	40
	7½	8	41
	8	8½	42
	8½	9	43
	9	9½	43
	9½	10	44
	10	10½	44
	10½	11	45

WOMEN'S

Item	*UK*	*USA*	*Europe*
Clothing	8	6	36
	10	8	38
	12	10	40
	14	12	42
	16	14	44
	18	16	46
	20	18	48
	22	20	50
	24	22	52
Shoes	4	5½	37
	4½	6	37
	5	6½	38
	5½	7	38
	6	7½	39
	6½	8	39
	7	8½	40
	7½	9	40
	8	9½	41

CONVERSION TABLES FOR WEIGHTS AND MEASURES

Bold figures equal units of either of the columns beside them; thus: 1 cm = 0.394 inches and 1 inch = 2.540 cm

LENGTH			AREA			VOLUME			WEIGHT (MASS)		
Centimetres		*Inches*	*Square cm*		*Square in*	*Cubic cm*		*Cubic in*	*Kilograms*		*Pounds*
2.540	**1**	0.394	6.452	**1**	0.155	16.387	**1**	0.061	0.454	**1**	2.205
5.080	**2**	0.787	12.903	**2**	0.310	32.774	**2**	0.122	0.907	**2**	4.409
7.620	**3**	1.181	19.355	**3**	0.465	49.161	**3**	0.183	1.361	**3**	6.614
10.160	**4**	1.575	25.806	**4**	0.620	65.548	**4**	0.244	1.814	**4**	8.819
12.700	**5**	1.969	32.258	**5**	0.775	81.936	**5**	0.305	2.268	**5**	11.023
15.240	**6**	2.362	38.710	**6**	0.930	98.323	**6**	0.366	2.722	**6**	13.228
17.780	**7**	2.756	45.161	**7**	1.085	114.710	**7**	0.427	3.175	**7**	15.432
20.320	**8**	3.150	51.613	**8**	1.240	131.097	**8**	0.488	3.629	**8**	17.637
22.860	**9**	3.543	58.064	**9**	1.395	147.484	**9**	0.549	4.082	**9**	19.842
25.400	**10**	3.937	64.516	**10**	1.550	163.871	**10**	0.610	4.536	**10**	22.046
50.800	**20**	7.874	129.032	**20**	3.100	327.742	**20**	1.220	9.072	**20**	44.092
76.200	**30**	11.811	193.548	**30**	4.650	491.613	**30**	1.831	13.608	**30**	66.139
101.600	**40**	15.748	258.064	**40**	6.200	655.484	**40**	2.441	18.144	**40**	88.185
127.000	**50**	19.685	322.580	**50**	7.750	819.355	**50**	3.051	22.680	**50**	110.231
152.400	**60**	23.622	387.096	**60**	9.300	983.226	**60**	3.661	27.216	**60**	132.277
177.800	**70**	27.559	451.612	**70**	10.850	1147.097	**70**	4.272	31.752	**70**	154.324
203.200	**80**	31.496	516.128	**80**	12.400	1310.968	**80**	4.882	36.287	**80**	176.370
228.600	**90**	35.433	580.644	**90**	13.950	1474.839	**90**	5.492	40.823	**90**	198.416
254.000	**100**	39.370	645.160	**100**	15.500	1638.710	**100**	6.102	45.359	**100**	220.464
Metres		*Yards*	*Square m*		*Square yd*	*Cubic m*		*Cubic yd*	*Metric tonnes*		*Tons (UK)*
0.914	**1**	1.094	0.836	**1**	1.196	0.765	**1**	1.308	1.016	**1**	0.984
1.829	**2**	2.187	1.672	**2**	2.392	1.529	**2**	2.616	2.032	**2**	1.968
2.743	**3**	3.281	2.508	**3**	3.588	2.294	**3**	3.924	3.048	**3**	2.953
3.658	**4**	4.374	3.345	**4**	4.784	3.058	**4**	5.232	4.064	**4**	3.937
4.572	**5**	5.468	4.181	**5**	5.980	3.823	**5**	6.540	5.080	**5**	4.921
5.486	**6**	6.562	5.017	**6**	7.176	4.587	**6**	7.848	6.096	**6**	5.905
6.401	**7**	7.655	5.853	**7**	8.372	5.352	**7**	9.156	7.112	**7**	6.889
7.315	**8**	8.749	6.689	**8**	9.568	6.116	**8**	10.464	8.128	**8**	7.874
8.230	**9**	9.843	7.525	**9**	10.764	6.881	**9**	11.772	9.144	**9**	8.858
9.144	**10**	10.936	8.361	**10**	11.960	7.646	**10**	13.080	10.161	**10**	9.842
18.288	**20**	21.872	16.723	**20**	23.920	15.291	**20**	26.159	20.321	**20**	19.684
27.432	**30**	32.808	25.084	**30**	35.880	22.937	**30**	39.239	30.481	**30**	29.526
36.576	**40**	43.745	33.445	**40**	47.840	30.582	**40**	52.318	40.642	**40**	39.368
45.720	**50**	54.681	41.806	**50**	59.799	38.228	**50**	65.398	50.802	**50**	49.210
54.864	**60**	65.617	50.168	**60**	71.759	45.873	**60**	78.477	60.963	**60**	59.052
64.008	**70**	76.553	58.529	**70**	83.719	53.519	**70**	91.557	71.123	**70**	68.894
73.152	**80**	87.489	66.890	**80**	95.679	61.164	**80**	104.636	81.284	**80**	78.737
82.296	**90**	98.425	75.251	**90**	107.639	68.810	**90**	117.716	91.444	**90**	88.579
91.440	**100**	109.361	83.613	**100**	119.599	76.455	**100**	130.795	101.605	**100**	98.421
Kilometres		*Miles*	*Hectares*		*Acres*	*Litres*		*Gallons*	*Metric tonnes*		*Tons (US)*
1.609	**1**	0.621	0.405	**1**	2.471	4.546	**1**	0.220	0.907	**1**	1.102
3.219	**2**	1.243	0.809	**2**	4.942	9.092	**2**	0.440	1.814	**2**	2.205
4.828	**3**	1.864	1.214	**3**	7.413	13.638	**3**	0.660	2.722	**3**	3.305
6.437	**4**	2.485	1.619	**4**	9.844	18.184	**4**	0.880	3.629	**4**	4.409
8.047	**5**	3.107	2.023	**5**	12.355	22.730	**5**	1.100	4.536	**5**	5.521
9.656	**6**	3.728	2.428	**6**	14.826	27.276	**6**	1.320	5.443	**6**	6.614
11.265	**7**	4.350	2.833	**7**	17.297	31.822	**7**	1.540	6.350	**7**	7.716
12.875	**8**	4.971	3.327	**8**	19.769	36.368	**8**	1.760	7.257	**8**	8.818
14.484	**9**	5.592	3.642	**9**	22.240	40.914	**9**	1.980	8.165	**9**	9.921
16.093	**10**	6.214	4.047	**10**	24.711	45.460	**10**	2.200	9.072	**10**	11.023
32.187	**20**	12.427	8.094	**20**	49.421	90.919	**20**	4.400	18.144	**20**	22.046
48.280	**30**	18.641	12.140	**30**	74.132	136.379	**30**	6.599	27.216	**30**	33.069
64.374	**40**	24.855	16.187	**40**	98.842	181.839	**40**	8.799	36.287	**40**	44.092
80.467	**50**	31.069	20.234	**50**	123.555	227.298	**50**	10.999	45.359	**50**	55.116
96.561	**60**	37.282	24.281	**60**	148.263	272.758	**60**	13.199	54.431	**60**	66.139
112.654	**70**	43.496	28.328	**70**	172.974	318.217	**70**	15.398	63.503	**70**	77.162
128.748	**80**	49.710	32.375	**80**	197.684	363.677	**80**	17.598	72.575	**80**	88.185
144.841	**90**	55.923	36.422	**90**	222.395	409.137	**90**	19.798	81.647	**90**	99.208
160.934	**100**	62.137	40.469	**100**	247.105	454.596	**100**	21.998	90.719	**100**	110.231

THE PERIODIC TABLE OF ELEMENTS

Key	
6	atomic number
Carbon	name of element
C	chemical number
12.01	atomic mass

Transition metals: groups III B to II B. Non-metals: groups III A to VII A.

	Alkali metals I A	Alkaline earth metals II A	III B	IV B	V B	VI B	V II	VIII			I B	II B	III A	IV A	V A	VI A	VII A	Noble gases
1	1 Hydrogen **H** 1.01																	2 Helium **He** 4.00
2	3 Lithium **Li** 6.94	4 Beryllium **Be** 9.01											5 Boron **B** 10.81	6 Carbon **C** 12.01	7 Nitrogen **N** 14.01	8 Oxygen **O** 16.00	9 Fluorine **F** 19.00	10 Neon **Ne** 20.18
3	11 Sodium **Na** 22.99	12 Magnesium **Mg** 24.31											13 Aluminium **Al** 26.98	14 Silicon **Si** 28.09	15 Phosphorus **P** 30.97	16 Sulphur **S** 32.07	17 Chlorine **Cl** 35.45	18 Argon **Ar** 39.95
4	19 Potassium **K** 39.10	20 Calcium **Ca** 40.08	21 Scandium **Sc** 44.96	22 Titanium **Ti** 47.88	23 Vanadium **V** 50.94	24 Chromium **Cr** 52.00	25 Manganese **Mn** 54.95	26 Iron **Fe** 55.85	27 Cobalt **Co** 58.93	28 Nickel **Ni** 58.70	29 Copper **Cu** 63.55	30 Zinc **Zn** 65.39	31 Gallium **Ga** 69.72	32 Germanium **Ge** 72.61	33 Arsenic **As** 74.92	34 Selenium **Se** 78.96	35 Bromine **Br** 79.904	36 Krypton **Kr** 83.80
5	37 Rubidium **Rb** 85.47	38 Strontium **Sr** 87.62	39 Yttrium **Y** 88.91	40 Zirconium **Zr** 91.22	41 Niobium **Nb** 92.91	42 Molybdenum **Mo** 95.94	43 Technetium **Tc** 97.91	44 Ruthenium **Ru** 101.07	45 Rhodium **Rh** 102.91	46 Palladium **Pd** 106.4	47 Silver **Ag** 107.87	48 Cadmium **Cd** 112.41	49 Indium **In** 114.82	50 Tin **Sn** 118.71	51 Antimony **Sb** 121.74	52 Tellurium **Te** 127.60	53 Iodine **I** 126.9045	54 Xenon **Xe** 131.29
6	55 Caesium **Cs** 132.91	56 Barium **Ba** 137.33	Lanthanide series *(see below)*	72 Hafnium **Hf** 178.49	73 Tantalum **Ta** 180.94	74 Tungsten **W** 183.85	75 Rhenium **Ru** 186.21	76 Osmium **Os** 190.23	77 Iridium **Ir** 192.22	78 Platinum **Pt** 195.08	79 Gold **Au** 196.97	80 Mercury **Hg** 200.59	81 Thallium **Tl** 204.38	82 Lead **Pb** 207.2	83 Bismuth **Bi** 208.98	84 Polonium **Po** 209	85 Astatine **At** 210	86 Radon **Rn** 222.02
7	87 Francium **Fr** 223.02	88 Radium **Ra** 226.03	Actinide series *(see below)*	104 Rutherfordium **Rf** 261.12	105 Dubnium **Db** 262.11	106 Seaborgium **Sg** 236.12	107 Bohrium **Bh** 262	108 Hassium **Hs** 265	109 Meitnerium **Mt** 266	110 Darmstadtium **Ds** 269	111 Roentgenium **Rg** 272							

Rare earth elements—Lanthanide series														
57 Lanthanum **La** 138.91	58 Cerium **Ce** 140.12	59 Praeseodymium **Pr** 140.91	60 Neodymium **Nd** 144.24	61 Promethium **Pm** 144.91	62 Samarium **Sm** 150.36	63 Europium **Eu** 151.96	64 Gadolinium **Gd** 157.25	65 Terbium **Tb** 158.93	66 Dysprosium **Dy** 162.50	67 Holmium **Ho** 164.93	68 Erbium **Er** 167.26	69 Thulium **Tm** 168.93	70 Ytterbium **Yb** 173.04	71 Lutetium **Lu** 174.97

Actinide series														
89 Actinium **Ac** 227.03	90 Thorium **Th** 232.04	91 Protactinium **Pa** 231.04	92 Uranium **U** 238.03	93 Neptunium **Np** 237.05	94 Plutonium **Pu** 244.06	95 Americium **Am** 243.06	96 Curium **Cm** 247.07	97 Berkelium **Bk** 247	98 Californium **Cf** 251.08	99 Eisteinium **Es** 252.08	100 Fermium **Fm** 257.10	101 Mendelevium **Md** 258.10	102 Nobelium **No** 259.10	103 Lawrencium **Lr** 260.11

The periodic table arranges the elements into horizontal rows (periods) and vertical columns (groups) according to their atomic number. The elements in a group all have similar properties; across each period, atoms are electropositive (form positive ions) to the left and electronegative to the right. The earliest version of the periodic table was devised in 1869 by Dmitriy Mendeleyev, who predicted the existence of several elements from gaps in the table.

NOBEL PRIZE WINNERS

For prize winners for the years 1901–2004, *see* earlier editions of *Whitaker's Almanack*.

The Nobel Prizes are awarded each year from the income of a trust fund established by the Swedish scientist Alfred Nobel, the inventor of dynamite, who died on 10 December 1896 leaving a fortune of £1,750,000. The prizes are awarded to those who have contributed most to the common good in the domain of:

Physics – awarded by the Royal Swedish Academy of Sciences
Chemistry – awarded by the Royal Swedish Academy of Sciences
Physiology or Medicine – awarded by the Karolinska Institute
Literature – awarded by the Swedish Academy of Arts
Peace – awarded by a five-person committee elected by the Norwegian Storting
Economic Sciences (instituted 1969) – awarded by the Royal Swedish Academy of Sciences

The prizes are awarded every year on 10 December, the anniversary of Nobel's death. The first awards were made on 10 December 1901. The Trust is administered by the board of directors of the Nobel Foundation, Stockholm, consisting of five members and three deputy members. The Swedish government appoints a chairman and a deputy chairman, the remaining members being appointed by the awarding authorities.

The awards in the last three years have been distributed as follows:

	2005	*2006*	*2007*
Physics	Roy J. Glauber *(USA)*, John L. Hall *(USA)*, Theodor W. Hänsch *(Germany)*	John C. Mather *(USA)*, George F. Smoot *(USA)*	Albert Fert *(France)*, Peter Grünberg *(Germany)*
Chemistry	Yves Chauvin *(France)*, Robert H. Grubbs *(USA)*, Richard R. Schrock *(USA)*	Roger D. Kornberg *(USA)*	Gerhard Ertl *(Germany)*
Physiology or Medicine	Barry J. Marshall *(Australia)*, J. Robin Warren *(Australia)*	Andrew Z. Fire *(USA)*, Craig C. Mello *(USA)*	Mario R. Capecchi *(USA)*, Sir Martin J. Evans *(UK)*, Oliver Smithies *(USA)*
Literature	Harold Pinter *(UK)*	Orhan Pamuk *(Turkey)*	Doris Lessing *(UK)*
Peace	IAEA *(Austria)*, Mohamed ElBaradei *(Egypt)*	Grameen Bank *(Bangladesh)*, Muhammad Yunus *(Bangladesh)*	IPCC *(international)*, Albert Arnold Gore Jr. *(USA)*
Economics	Robert J. Aumann *(Israel and USA)*, Thomas C. Schelling *(USA)*	Edmund S. Phelps *(USA)*	Leonid Hurwicz *(USA)*, Eric S. Maskin *(USA)*, Roger B. Myerson *(USA)*

ABBREVIATIONS AND ACRONYMS

Ψ	seaport

A

A	ampere
AA	Alcoholics Anonymous
	Automobile Association
AAA	Amateur Athletic Association
AAS	Annual Abstract of Statistics
ABA	Amateur Boxing Association
ABE	Association of Building Engineers
ABM	anti-ballistic missile
abr	abridged
ac	alternating current
a/c	account
AC	*(ante Christum)* before Christ
	Companion, Order of Australia
ACAS	Advisory, Conciliation and Arbitration Service
ACT	Australian Capital Territory
AD	*(anno Domini)* in the year of our Lord
ADB	Asian Development Bank
ADC	Aide-de-Camp
ADC (P)	Personal ADC to the Queen
Adj.	Adjutant
Adj. Gen.	Adjutant General
ad lib	*(ad libitum)* at pleasure
Adm.	Admiral
AE	Air Efficiency award
AEM	Air Efficiency Medal
aet	after extra time
AFC	Air Force Cross
AFM	Air Force Medal
AG	Attorney-General
AGM	air-to-ground missile
	annual general meeting
AH	*(anno Hegirae)* in the year of the Hegira
AI	artificial intelligence
AIDS	acquired immune deficiency syndrome
AIM	Alternative Investment Market
ALG	Adult Learning Grant
alt	altitude
am	*(ante meridiem)* before noon
AM	amplitude modulation
	(anno mundi) in the year of the world
	Assembly Member (Wales)
amp	amplifier
AMU	Arab Maghreb Union
ANC	African National Congress
anon	anonymous
ANZAC	Australian and New Zealand Army Corps
AO	Air Officer
	Officer, Order of Australia
AOC	Air Officer Commanding
AONB	area of outstanding natural beauty
APEC	Asia-Pacific Economic Cooperation
apptd	appointed
APR	annual percentage rate
AS	Anglo-Saxon
ASA	Advertising Standards Authority
	Amateur Swimming Association
ASAP	as soon as possible
ASBO	anti social behaviour order
ASEAN	Association of South-East Asian Nations
ASLEF	Associated Society of Locomotive Engineers and Firemen
ASLIB	Association for Information Management
ATC	Air Training Corps
AUC	*(ab urbe condita)* in the year from the foundation of Rome
	(anno urbis conditae) in the year of the founding of the city
AV	Authorised Version *(of Bible)*
AVR	Army Volunteer Reserve
AWOL	absent without (official) leave

B

b.	born
	bowled *(cricket)*
BA	Bachelor of Arts
BAA	British Airports Authority
	British Astronomical Association
BAF	British Athletics Federation
BAFTA	British Academy of Film and Television Arts
BAS	Bachelor in Agricultural Science
	British Antarctic Survey
BBA	British Bankers' Association
BBC	British Broadcasting Corporation
BBFC	British Board of Film Classification
BBSRC	Biotechnology and Biological Sciences Research Council
BC	before Christ
	borough council
	British Columbia *(Canada)*
BCH (D)	Bachelor of (Dental) Surgery
BCL	Bachelor of Civil Law
BCOM	Bachelor of Commerce
BD	Bachelor of Divinity
BDA	British Dental Association
BDS	Bachelor of Dental Surgery
BED	Bachelor of Education
BEM	British Empire Medal
BENG	Bachelor of Engineering
BERR	Department for Business, Enterprise and Regulatory Reform
BFI	British Film Institute
BFPO	British Forces Post Office
BLIT	Bachelor of Literature
BLITT	Bachelor of Letters
BM	Bachelor of Medicine
	British Museum
BMA	British Medical Association
BMI	body mass index
BMUS	Bachelor of Music
BNFL	British Nuclear Fuels
Bp	Bishop
BPHARM	Bachelor of Pharmacy
BPHIL	Bachelor of Philosophy
bpm	beats per minute
Brig	Brigadier
BSC	Bachelor of Science
BSE	bovine spongiform encephalopathy
BSI	British Standards Institution
BST	British Summer Time
Bt.	Baronet
BTEC	Business and Technology Education Council
BTI	British Trade International
BTU	British thermal unit
BVMS	Bachelor of Veterinary Medicine and Surgery

C

c.	*(circa)* about
	chapter (Public Acts)
C	Celsius
	centigrade
C.	Conservative
CA	chartered accountant *(Scotland)*
CAA	Civil Aviation Authority
CAB	Citizens' Advice Bureau
CAD	computer-aided design
Cadw	Ancient Monuments Board for Wales
Cantuar:	of Canterbury *(Archbishop)*
CAP	Common Agricultural Policy
Capt	Captain
CARICOM	Caribbean Community and Common Market
Carliol:	of Carlisle *(Bishop)*
CB	Companion, Order of the Bath
CBE	Commander, Order of the British Empire

CBI Confederation of British Industry
CBSS Council of the Baltic Sea States
CC Chamber of Commerce
city council
Companion, Order of Canada
county council
county court
CCC county cricket club
CCF Combined Cadet Force
CCHEM chartered chemist
CCTA City Colleges for Technology and the Arts
CD Civil Defence
Corps Diplomatique
Cdr Commander
Cdre Commodore
CDS Chief of the Defence Staff
CE civil engineer
Common (or Christian) Era
CEFAS Centre for Environment, Fisheries and Aquaculture Science
CENG chartered engineer
CEO chief executive officer
CERN European Organisation for Nuclear Research
Cestr: of Chester *(Bishop)*
CET Central European Time
Common External Tariff
cf *(confer)* compare
CF Chaplain to the Forces
CFC chlorofluorocarbon
CGC Conspicuous Gallantry Cross
CGEOL chartered geologist
CGI computer-generated imagery
CGM Conspicuous Gallantry Medal
cgs centimetre-gramme-second *(system)*
CGS Chief of General Staff
CH Companion of Honour
CHB/M Bachelor/Master of Surgery
CI Channel Islands
Imperial Order of the Crown of India
CIA Central Intelligence Agency
CICA Conference on Interaction and Confidence Building Measures in Asia
Criminal Injuries Compensation Authority
CICAP Criminal Injuries Compensation Appeals Panel
Cicestr: of Chichester *(Bishop)*
CID Criminal Investigation Department
CIE Companion, Order of the Indian Empire
cif cost, insurance and freight
C-in-C Commander-in-Chief
CIPFA Chartered Institute of Public Finance and Accountancy
CIS Commonwealth of Independent States
CJD Creutzfeld-Jakob disease
CLJ Commander, Order of St Lazarus of Jerusalem
CM *(Chirurgiae Magister)* Master of Surgery
CMG Companion, Order of St Michael and St George
CMEC Child Maintenance and Enforcement Commission
CND Campaign for Nuclear Disarmament
c/o care of
CO Commanding Officer
C of E Church of England
COI Central Office of Information
Col. Colonel
cons. consecrated
Cpl. Corporal
CPM Colonial Police Medal
CPRE Council for the Protection of Rural England
CPS Crown Prosecution Service
CSI Companion, Order of the Star of India
CTC City Technology Colleges
CVO Commander, Royal Victorian Order

D

d *(denarius)* penny
d. died
DBE Dame Commander, Order of the British Empire
dc direct current
DC District of Columbia *(USA)*
district council
DCA Department for Constitutional Affairs
DCB Dame Commander, Order of the Bath
D CH *(Doctor Chirurgiae)* Doctor of Surgery
DCL Doctor of Civil Law
DCM Distinguished Conduct Medal
DCMG Dame Commander, Order of St Michael and St George
DCMS Department for Culture, Media and Sport
DCSF Department for Children, Schools and Families
DCVO Dame Commander, Royal Victorian Order
DD Doctor of Divinity
DDS Doctor of Dental Surgery
DDT dichlorodiphenyl trichloroethane
del *(delineavit)* he/she drew it
DEFRA Department of the Environment, Food and Rural Affairs
DFC Distinguished Flying Cross
DFID Department for International Development
DFM Distinguished Flying Medal
DfT Department for Transport
DG *(Dei gratia)* by the grace of God
director general
DIP ED Diploma in Education
DIP HE Diploma in Higher Education
DIPHS Diploma of the Heraldry Society
DIUS Department for Innovation, Universities and Skills
DL Deputy Lieutenant
DLIT Doctor of Literature
DLITT Doctor of Letters
DLR Docklands Light Railway
DMUS Doctor of Music
DNA deoxyribonucleic acid
DNB *Dictionary of National Biography*
do *(ditto)* the same
DoH Department of Health
DPH *or* DPHIL Doctor of Philosophy
DPP Director of Public Prosecutions
Dr Doctor
DSC Distinguished Service Cross
Doctor of Science
DSM Distinguished Service Medal
DSO Companion, Distinguished Service Order
DTP desktop publishing
Dunelm: of Durham *(Bishop)*
DV *(Deo volente)* God willing
DVD digital versatile disc
DVLA Driver and Vehicle Licensing Agency
DVT deep vein thrombosis
DWI Drinking Water Inspectorate
DWP Department for Work and Pensions

E

E east
email
Ebor: of York *(Archbishop)*
EBRD European Bank for Reconstruction and Development
EC European Community
ECB England and Wales Cricket Board
European Central Bank
ECG electrocardiogram
ECGD Export Credits Guarantee Department
ECOWAS Economic Community of West African States

ECU	European Currency Unit
ED	Efficiency Decoration
EEC	European Economic Community
EEG	electroencephalogram
EFA	European Fighter Aircraft
EFTA	European Free Trade Association
eg	*(exempli gratia)* for the sake of example
EHRC	Equality and Human Rights Commission
EIB	European Investment Bank
EMS	European Monetary System
EMU	European Monetary Union
EPSRC	Engineering and Physical Sciences Research Council
ER	*(Elizabetha Regina)* Queen Elizabeth
ERM	exchange rate mechanism
ERNIE	electronic random number indicator equipment
ESA	European Space Agency
ESRC	Economic and Social Research Council
est	established estimate
ETA	*(Euzkadi ta Askatasuna)* Basque separatist organisation
et al	*(et alibi)* and elsewhere
	(et alii) and others
etc	*(et cetera)* and the other things/and so forth
et seq	*(et sequentia)* and the following
EU	European Union
EURATOM	European Atomic Energy Community
Exon:	of Exeter *(Bishop)*

F

f	*(forte)* loud
F	Fahrenheit
	Fellow of
FA	Football Association
FANY	First Aid Nursing Yeomanry
FAO	for the attention of
FAQ	frequently asked questions
Farc	*(Fuerzas Armadas Revolucionarias de Colombia)* Colombian rebel oranisation
FBA	Fellow, British Academy
FBAA	Fellow, British Association of Accountants and Auditors
FBI	Federal Bureau of Investigation
FBS	Fellow, Botanical Society
FBU	Fire Brigades Union
FC	football club
FCA	Fellow, Institute of Chartered Accountants in England and Wales
FCCA	Fellow, Chartered Association of Certified Accountants
FCGI	Fellow, City and Guilds of London Institute
FCIA	Fellow, Corporation of Insurance Agents
FCIARB	Fellow, Chartered Institute of Arbitrators
FCIB	Fellow, Chartered Institute of Bankers
	Fellow, Corporation of Insurance Brokers
FCIBSE	Fellow, Chartered Institution of Building Services Engineers
FCII	Fellow, Chartered Insurance Institute
FCIPS	Fellow, Chartered Institute of Purchasing and Supply
FCIS	Fellow, Institute of Chartered Secretaries and Administrators
FCIT	Fellow, Chartered Institute of Transport
FCMA	Fellow, Chartered Institute of Management Accountants
FCO	Foreign and Commonwealth Office
FCP	Fellow, College of Preceptors
FD	*(Fidei Defensor)* Defender of the Faith
FE	further education
fec	*(fecit)* made this
ff	*(fecerunt)* made this (pl)
	folios following
ff	*(fortissimo)* very loud
FFA	Fellow, Faculty of Actuaries *(Scotland)*
	Fellow, Institute of Financial Accountants
FFAS	Fellow, Faculty of Architects and Surveyors
FFCM	Fellow, Faculty of Community Medicine
FFPHM	Fellow, Faculty of Public Health Medicine
FGS	Fellow, Geological Society
FHS	Fellow, Heraldry Society
FHSM	Fellow, Institute of Health Service Management
FIA	Fellow, Institute of Actuaries
FIBIOL	Fellow, Institute of Biology
FICE	Fellow, Institution of Civil Engineers
FICS	Fellow, Institution of Chartered Shipbrokers
FIEE	Fellow, Institution of Electrical Engineers
FIERE	Fellow, Institution of Electronic and Radio Engineers
FIFA	*(Fédération Internationale de Football Association)* International Federation of Association Football
FIM	Fellow, Institute of Metals
FIMGT	Fellow, Institute of Management
FIMM	Fellow, Institution of Mining and Metallurgy
FINSTF	Fellow, Institute of Fuel
FINSTP	Fellow, Institute of Physics
FIQS	Fellow, Institute of Quantity Surveyors
FIS	Fellow, Institute of Statisticians
FJI	Fellow, Institute of Journalists
FLA	Fellow, Library Association
FLS	Fellow, Linnean Society
FM	Field Marshal
	frequency modulation
FMEDSCI	Fellow, Academy of Medical Sciences
fo	folio
FO	Flying Officer
fob	free on board
FPHS	Fellow, Philosophical Society
FRAD	Fellow, Royal Academy of Dancing
FRAES	Fellow, Royal Aeronautical Society
FRAI	Fellow, Royal Anthropological Institute
FRAM	Fellow, Royal Academy of Music
FRAS	Fellow, Royal Asiatic Society
	Fellow, Royal Astronomical Society
FRBS	Fellow, Royal Botanic Society
	Fellow, Royal Society of British Sculptors
FRCA	Fellow, Royal College of Anaesthetists
FRCGP	Fellow, Royal College of General Practitioners
FRCM	Fellow, Royal College of Music
FRCO	Fellow, Royal College of Organists
FRCOG	Fellow, Royal College of Obstetricians and Gynaecologists
FRCP	Fellow, Royal College of Physicians, London
FRCPATH	Fellow, Royal College of Pathologists
FRCPE *or* FRCPED	Fellow, Royal College of Physicians, Edinburgh
FRCPI	Fellow, Royal College of Physicians, Ireland
FRCPSYCH	Fellow, Royal College of Psychiatrists
FRCR	Fellow, Royal College of Radiologists
FRCS	Fellow, Royal College of Surgeons of England
FRCSE *or* FRCSED	Fellow, Royal College of Surgeons of Edinburgh
FRCSGLAS	Fellow, Royal College of Physicians and Surgeons of Glasgow
FRCSI	Fellow, Royal College of Surgeons in Ireland

FRCVS	Fellow, Royal College of Veterinary Surgeons
FRECONS	Fellow, Royal Economic Society
FRENG	Fellow, Royal Academy of Engineering
FRGS	Fellow, Royal Geographical Society
FRHISTS	Fellow, Royal Historical Society
FRHS	Fellow, Royal Horticultural Society
FRIBA	Fellow, Royal Institute of British Architects
FRICS	Fellow, Royal Institution of Chartered Surveyors
FRMETS	Fellow, Royal Meteorological Society
FRMS	Fellow, Royal Microscopical Society
FRNS	Fellow, Royal Numismatic Society
FRPHARMS	Fellow, Royal Pharmaceutical Society
FRPS	Fellow, Royal Photographic Society
FRS	Fellow, Royal Society
FRSA	Fellow, Royal Society of Arts
FRSC	Fellow, Royal Society of Chemistry
FRSE	Fellow, Royal Society of Edinburgh
FRSH	Fellow, Royal Society of Health
FRSL	Fellow, Royal Society of Literature
FRTPI	Fellow, Royal Town Planning Institute
FSA	Fellow, Society of Antiquaries
	Financial Services Authority
	Food Standards Agency
FSS	Fellow, Royal Statistical Society
FSVA	Fellow, Incorporated Society of Valuers and Auctioneers
FT	*Financial Times*
FTI	Fellow, Textile Institute
FTII	Fellow, Chartered Institute of Taxation
FZS	Fellow, Zoological Society

G

GATT	General Agreement on Tariffs and Trade
GBE	Dame/Knight Grand Cross, Order of the British Empire
GC	George Cross
GCB	Dame/Knight Grand Cross, Order of the Bath
GCC	Gulf Cooperation Council
GCE	General Certificate of Education
GCHQ	Government Communications Headquarters
GCIE	Knight Grand Commander, Order of the Indian Empire
GCLJ	Knight Grand Cross, Order of St Lazarus of Jerusalem
GCMG	Dame/Knight Grand Cross, Order of St Michael and St George
GCSE	General Certificate of Secondary Education
GCSI	Knight Grand Commander, Order of the Star of India
GCVO	Dame/Knight Grand Cross, Royal Victorian Order
GDP	gross domestic product
Gen.	General
GHQ	general headquarters
GLA	Greater London Authority
GM	genetically modified
	George Medal
GMB	Britain's General Union
GMT	Greenwich Mean Time
GNI	gross national income
GNVQ	General National Vocational Qualification
GOC	General Officer Commanding
GP	General Practitioner
GPS	Global Positioning System
Gp Capt.	Group Captain
GSA	Girls' Schools Association
GST	Greenwich Sidereal Time

H

HA	Health Authority
HAC	Honourable Artillery Company
HB	His Beatitude
HBM	Her/His Britannic Majesty('s)
HCF	Honorary Chaplain to the Forces
HD	High Definition *(television)*
HE	Her/His Excellency
	higher education
	His Eminence
HGV	heavy goods vehicle
HH	Her/His Highness
	Her/His Honour
	His Holiness
HIM	Her/His Imperial Majesty
HIP	Home Information Pack
HIV	human immunodeficiency virus
HJS	*(hic jacet sepultus)* here lies buried
HM	Her/His Majesty('s)
HMAS	Her/His Majesty's Australian Ship
HMC	Headmasters' and Headmistresses' Conference
HMI	Her/His Majesty's Inspector
HML	Her/His Majesty's Lieutenant
HMS	Her/His Majesty's Ship
HMSO	Her/His Majesty's Stationery Office
HNC	Higher National Certificate
HND	Higher National Diploma
Hon.	Honorary
	Honourable
HPA	Health Protection Agency
HQ	headquarters
HR	human resources
HRH	Her/His Royal Highness
HRT	hormone replacement therapy
HSE	Health and Safety Executive
	(hic sepultus est) here is buried
HSH	Her/His Serene Highness
HTA	Human Tissue Authority
HTML	hypertext mark-up language
HTTP	hypertext transfer protocol
HWM	high water mark

I

I	Island
IAEA	International Atomic Energy Agency
IATA	International Air Transport Association
IB	International Baccalaureate
IBF	International Boxing Federation
ibid	*(ibidem)* in the same place
IBRD	International Bank for Reconstruction and Development
ICAO	International Civil Aviation Organisation
ICC	International Cricket Council
ICFTU	International Confederation of Free Trade Unions
ICJ	International Court of Justice
ICOMOS	International Council on Monuments and Sites
ICRC	International Committee of the Red Cross
id	*(idem)* the same
IDA	International Development Association
IDD	international direct dialling
ie	*(id est)* that is
IEA	International Energy Agency
IFA	independent financial adviser
IFAD	International Fund for Agricultural Development
IFC	International Finance Corporation
ILO	International Labour Office/Organisation

IMF	International Monetary Fund
IMO	International Maritime Organisation
inc.	incorporated
INLA	Irish National Liberation Army
in loc	*(in loco)* in its place
INRI	*(Iesus Nazarenus Rex Iudaeorum)* Jesus of Nazareth, King of the Jews
inst	*(instant)* current month
Interpol	International Criminal Police Organisation
IOC	International Olympic Committee
IoM	Isle of Man
IOU	I owe you
IoW	Isle of Wight
IQ	intelligence quotient
IRA	Irish Republican Army
IRB	International Rugby Board
IRC	International Red Cross
Is	Islands
ISA	individual savings account
ISBN	International Standard Book Number
ISO	Imperial Service Order International Standards Organisation
ISP	internet service provider
ISSN	International Standard Serial Number
ITN	Independent Television News
ITU	International Telecommunication Union
ITV	Independent Television
IVF	in vitro fertilisation
IWC	International Whaling Commission

J

J	Judge Justice
JP	Justice of the Peace
Jr	Junior

K

KBE	Knight Commander, Order of the British Empire
KCB	Knight Commander, Order of the Bath
KCIE	Knight Commander, Order of the Indian Empire
KCLJ	Knight Commander, Order of St Lazarus of Jerusalem
KCMG	Knight Commander, Order of St Michael and St George
KCSI	Knight Commander, Order of the Star of India
KCVO	Knight Commander, Royal Victorian Order
KG	Knight of the Garter
KGB	*(Komitet Gosudarstvennoi Bezopasnosti)* Committee of State Security *(USSR)*
kHz	kilohertz
KLJ	Knight, Order of St Lazarus of Jerusalem
ko	knock out *(boxing)*
KP	Knight, Order of St Patrick
KStJ	Knight, Order of St John of Jerusalem
Kt.	Knight
KT	Knight of the Thistle
kV	kilovolt
kW	kilowatt
kWh	kilowatt hour

L

Lab.	Labour
Lat.	Latitude
lbw	leg before wicket *(cricket)*
lc	lower case *(printing)*
LCD	Liquid Crystal Display
LCJ	Lord Chief Justice
LCM	least/lowest common multiple
LD	Liberal Democrat
LDS	Licentiate in Dental Surgery
LEA	Local Education Authority
LHB	Local Health Board *(Wales)*
LHD	*(Literarum Humaniorum Doctor)* Doctor of Humane Letters/Literature
Lib.	Liberal
lit	literary
Lit Hum	*(Literae Humaniores)* classics course, Oxford University
LITT D	Doctor of Letters
LJ	Lord Justice
LLB	Bachelor of Laws
LLD	Doctor of Laws
LLM	Master of Laws
loc cit	*(loco citato)* in the place cited
Londin:	of London *(Bishop)*
Long.	longitude
LS	*(loco sigilli)* place of the seal
LSC	Learning and Skills Council Legal Services Commission
lsd	*(librae, solidi, denarii)* pounds, shillings and pence
LSE	London School of Economics and Political Science
LST	Local Sidereal Time
Lt.	Lieutenant
LTA	Lawn Tennis Association
LTTE	Liberation Tigers of Tamil Eelam
ltd	limited (liability)
LVO	Lieutenant, Royal Victorian Order
LW	long wave
LWM	low water mark

M

M	Member Monsieur
MA	Master of Arts
Maj.	Major
maj.	majority
max	maximum
MB	*(Medicinae Baccalaureus)* Bachelor of Medicine
MBA	Master of Business Administration
MBC	Metropolitan Borough Council
MBE	Member, Order of the British Empire
MBO	management buy-out
MC	Master of Ceremonies Military Cross
MCC	Marylebone Cricket Club
MCH(D)	Master of (Dental) Surgery
MD	managing director Doctor of Medicine
MDS	Master of Dental Surgery
ME	Middle English myalgic encephalomyelitis
MEC	Member of Executive Council
MED	Master of Education
mega	one million times
MEP	Member of the European Parliament
MFH	Master of Foxhounds
Mgr	Monsignor
MI	Military Intelligence
micro	one-millionth part
milli	one-thousandth part
min	minimum minutes
MIT	Massachusetts Institute of Technology
MLA	Member of Legislative Assembly *(Northern Ireland)* Museums, Libraries and Archives Council
MLC	Member of Legislative Council
MLITT	Master of Letters
Mlle	Mademoiselle
MLR	minimum lending rate
MM	Military Medal
Mme	Madame
MMR	measles, mumps and rubella (vaccine)
MN	Merchant Navy
MO	Medical Officer/Orderly
MoD	Ministry of Defence
MoJ	Ministry of Justice
MoT	Ministry of Transport
MP	Member of Parliament Military Police
mph	miles per hour

MPHIL	Master of Philosophy
MR	Master of the Rolls
MRC	Medical Research Council
MRI	magnetic resonance imaging
MRSA	methicillin-resistant staphylococcus aureus
MS	manuscript (*pl* MSS)
	Master of Surgery
	multiple sclerosis
MSC	Master of Science
MSP	Member of Scottish Parliament
MUS B/D	Bachelor/Doctor of Music
MV	merchant vessel
	motor vessel
MVO	Member, Royal Victorian Order
MW	medium wave
	megawatt

N

N	north
n/a	not applicable
	not available
NAAFI	Navy, Army and Air Force Institutes
NAFTA	North American Free Trade Agreement
NASA	National Aeronautics and Space Administration
NASUWT	National Association of Schoolmasters/Union of Women Teachers
NATO	North Atlantic Treaty Organisation
NB	New Brunswick
nb	*(nota bene)* note well
NCO	non-commissioned officer
NDPB	non-departmental public body
NEB	New English Bible
nem con	*(nemine contradicente)* no one contradicting
NERC	Natural Environment Research Council
nes	not elsewhere specified
NESTA	National Endowment for Science, Technology and the Arts
NFU	National Farmers' Union
NHS	National Health Service
NI	National Insurance
	Northern Ireland
no	*(numero)* number
non seq	*(non sequitur)* it does not follow
Norvic:	of Norwich *(Bishop)*
NP	Notary Public
NRA	National Rifle Association
NS	New Style *(calendar)*
	Nova Scotia
NSPCC	National Society for the Prevention of Cruelty to Children
NSW	New South Wales *(Australia)*
NT	National Theatre
	National Trust
	New Testament
	Northern Territory *(Australia)*
NUJ	National Union of Journalists
NUM	National Union of Mineworkers
NUS	National Union of Students
NUT	National Union of Teachers
NVQ	National Vocational Qualification
NWT	Northwest Territory *(Canada)*
NZ	New Zealand

O

OAP	old age pension(er)
OAPEC	Organisation of Arab Petroleum Exporting Countries
OAS	Organisation of American States
Ob *or* obit	died
OBE	Officer, Order of the British Empire
OC	Officer Commanding
OE	Old English
	omissions excepted
OECD	Organisation for Economic Cooperation and Development
OED	*Oxford English Dictionary*
OFCOM	Office of Communications
OFGEM	Office of Gas and Electricity Markets
OFM	Order of Friars Minor *(Franciscans)*
OFREG	Office for the Regulation of Electricity and Gas
OFSTED	Office for Standards in Education, Children's Services and Skills
OFT	Office of Fair Trading
OFWAT	Office of Water Services
OHMS	On Her/His Majesty's Service
OHP	overhead projector
OIC	Organisation of the Islamic Conference
OM	Order of Merit
ono	or near(est) offer
ONS	Office for National Statistics
op	*(opus)* work
OP	opposite prompt side *(of theatre)*
	Order of Preachers *(Dominicans)*
	out of print *(books)*
op cit	*(opere citato)* in the work cited
OPEC	Organisation of Petroleum Exporting Countries
OPSI	Office of Public Sector Information
ORR	Office of Rail Regulation
OS	Old Style *(calendar)*
	Ordnance Survey
OSA	Order of St Augustine
OSB	Order of St Benedict
OSCE	Organisation for Security and Cooperation in Europe
OStJ	Officer, Order of St John of Jerusalem
OT	Old Testament
OTC	Officers' Training Corps
Oxon	(of) Oxford
	Oxfordshire

P

p	page
PA	personal assistant
	Press Association
	public address (system)
PAYE	pay as you earn
PAYG	pay as you go
pc	*(per centum)* in the hundred
PC	personal computer
	Police Constable
	politically correct
	Privy Counsellor
PCT	Primary Care Trust
PDSA	People's Dispensary for Sick Animals
PE	physical education
Petriburg:	of Peterborough *(Bishop)*
PFI	Private Finance Initiative
PG	parental guidance
PGA	Professional Golfers Association
PGCE	Postgraduate Certificate of Education
PHD	Doctor of Philosophy
PIF	Pacific Islands Forum
pl	plural
PLA	Port of London Authority
plc	public limited company
PLO	Palestine Liberation Organisation
pm	*(post meridiem)* after noon
PM	post mortem
	Prime Minister
PMRAFNS	Princess Mary's Royal Air Force Nursing Service
PO	Petty Officer
	Pilot Officer
	post office
	postal order
POW	prisoner of war
pp	pages
	(per procurationem) by proxy
PPS	Parliamentary Private Secretary
PR	proportional representation
	public relations
PRA	President of the Royal Academy
pro tem	*(pro tempore)* for the time being
prox	*(proximo)* next month
PRS	President of the Royal Society

PRSE President of the Royal Society of Edinburgh
PS *(postscriptum)* postscript
psc passed staff college
PSNCR public sector net cash requirement
PSV public service vehicle
PTA Parent-Teacher Association
Pte. Private
PTO please turn over

Q

QARANC Queen Alexandra's Royal Army Nursing Corps
QARNNS Queen Alexandra's Royal Naval Nursing Service
QBD Queen's Bench Division
QC Queen's Counsel
QED *(quod erat demonstrandum)* which was to be proved
QGM Queen's Gallantry Medal
QHC Queen's Honorary Chaplain
QHDS Queen's Honorary Dental Surgeon
QHNS Queen's Honorary Nursing Sister
QHP Queen's Honorary Physician
QHS Queen's Honorary Surgeon
Qld Queensland *(Australia)*
QMG Quartermaster-General
QPM Queen's Police Medal
QS quarter sessions
Queen's Scholar
QSO quasi-stellar object (quasar)
Queen's Service Order
quango quasi-autonomous non-governmental organisation
qv *(quod vide)* which see

R

r. *(recto)* on the right-hand page
R *(Regina)* Queen
(Rex) King
RA Royal Academy/Academician
Royal Artillery
RAC Royal Armoured Corps
Royal Automobile Club
RADA Royal Academy of Dramatic Art
RADC Royal Army Dental Corps
RAEC Royal Army Educational Corps
RAES Royal Aeronautical Society
RAF Royal Air Force
RAM random-access memory
Royal Academy of Music
RAMC Royal Army Medical Corps
RAN Royal Australian Navy
RAOC Royal Army Ordnance Corps
RAPC Royal Army Pay Corps
RAVC Royal Army Veterinary Corps
R&B rhythm and blues
RBS Royal Society of British Sculptors
RC Red Cross
Roman Catholic
RCM Royal College of Music
RCN Royal Canadian Navy
RCT Royal Corps of Transport
R&D research and development
RD refer to drawer *(banking)*
Royal Naval and Royal Marine Forces Reserve Decoration
Rural Dean
RE Religious Education
Royal Engineers
REM rapid eye movement
REME Royal Electrical and Mechanical Engineers
Rep representative
Republican
Rep. Republic
Revd Reverend
RFL Rugby Football League
RFU Rugby Football Union
RGN Registered General Nurse
RGS Royal Geographical Society
RHS Royal Horticultural Society
RI Rhode Island *(USA)*
Royal Institute of Painters in Watercolours
Royal Institution
RIBA Royal Institute of British Architects
RIP *(requiescat in pace)* may he/she rest in peace
RIR Royal Irish Regiment
RL rugby league
RM Registered Midwife
Royal Marines
RMA Royal Military Academy
RMN Registered Mental Nurse
RMT National Union of Rail, Maritime and Transport Workers
RN Royal Navy
RNIB Royal National Institute for the Blind
RNID Royal National Institute for the Deaf
RNLI Royal National Lifeboat Institution
RNMH Registered Nurse for the Mentally Handicapped
RNR Royal Naval Reserve
RNVR Royal Naval Volunteer Reserve
RNXS Royal Naval Auxiliary Service
RNZN Royal New Zealand Navy
ROC Royal Observer Corps
Roffen: of Rochester *(Bishop)*
ROI Republic of Ireland
Royal Institute of Oil Painters
RoSPA Royal Society for the Prevention of Accidents
RP Received Pronunciation
Royal Society of Portrait Painters
RPA Rural Payments Agency
rpm revolutions per minute
RRC Lady of Royal Red Cross
RSA Royal Scottish Academician
Royal Society of Arts
RSC Royal Shakespeare Company
RSCN Registered Sick Children's Nurse
RSE Royal Society of Edinburgh
RSM Regimental Sergeant Major
RSPB Royal Society for the Protection of Birds
RSPCA Royal Society for the Prevention of Cruelty to Animals
RSV Revised Standard Version *(of Bible)*
RSVP *(répondez, s'il vous plaît)* please reply
RSW Royal Scottish Society of Painters in Watercolours
Rt. Hon. Right Honourable
RTPI Royal Town Planning Institute
RU rugby union
RUC Royal Ulster Constabulary
RV Revised Version *(of Bible)*
RWS Royal Water Colour Society
RYS Royal Yacht Squadron

S

s second *(also* sec)
section (Public Acts)
(solidus) shilling
S south
SA Salvation Army
South Africa
South America
South Australia
SAARC South Asian Association for Regional Cooperation
SAE stamped addressed envelope
Salop Shropshire
SARS severe acute respiratory syndrome
Sarum: of Salisbury (Bishop)
SAS Special Air Service
SBS Small Business Service
Special Boat Service
SCD Doctor of Science
SCM State Certified Midwife
SCO Shanghai Cooperation Organisation
SDLP Social Democratic Labour Party
SEAQ Stock Exchange Automated Quotations system
sec second *(also* s)
SEN special educational needs
State Enrolled Nurse

SERPS	State Earnings Related Pension Scheme
SFO	Serious Fraud Office
SHA	Strategic Health Authority
SHMIS	Society of Headmasters and Headmistresses of Independent Schools
SI	statutory instrument
	(Système International d'Unités) International System of Units
sic	*(sic)* so written
SIDS	sudden infant death syndrome
sig	signature
	Signor
SJ	Society of Jesus *(Jesuits)*
SLD	Social and Liberal Democrats
SMP	Statutory Maternity Pay
SNP	Scottish National Party
SOCA	Serious Organised Crime Agency
SOE	Special Operations Executive
sp	*(sine prole)* without issue
spgr	specific gravity
Sr	Senior
	Sister *(title)*
SRN	State Registered Nurse
SRO	self-regulating organisation
SS	Saints
	steamship
SSC	Solicitor before Supreme Court *(Scotland)*
SSN	standard serial number
SSP	statutory sick pay
SSSI	Site of Special Scientific Interest
ST	*Social Trends*
STD	*(Sacrae Theologiae Doctor)* Doctor of Sacred Theology
	subscriber trunk dialling
stet	*(stet)* let it stand *(printing)*
STFC	Science and Technology Facilities Council
STI	sexually transmitted infection
stp	standard temperature and pressure
STP	*(Sacrae Theologiae Professor)* Professor of Sacred Theology
Sub Lt.	sub-lieutenant
SVQ	Scottish Vocational Qualification

T

TA	Territorial Army
TB	tuberculosis
TD	Territorial Decoration
TEFL	teaching English as a foreign language
temp	temperature
	temporary employee
TES	*Times Educational Supplement*
THES	*Times Higher Education Supplement*
TLS	*Times Literary Supplement*
TNT	trinitrotoluene *(explosive)*
trans.	translated
TRH	Their Royal Highnesses
trs	transpose *(printing)*
TT	Tourist Trophy *(motorcycle races)*
	tuberculin tested
TUC	Trades Union Congress

U

U	Unionist
UAB	unitary awarding body
UAE	United Arab Emirates
uc	upper case *(printing)*
UC	Unitary Council
UCAS	Universities and Colleges Admissions Service
UCATT	Union of Construction, Allied Trades and Technicians
UCL	University College London
UCU	University and College Union
UDA	Ulster Defence Association
UDI	Unilateral Declaration of Independence
UDR	Ulster Defence Regiment
UEFA	Union of European Football Associations
UFF	Ulster Freedom Fighters
UFO	unidentified flying object
UHF	ultra-high frequency
UKAEA	UK Atomic Energy Authority
UN	United Nations
UNESCO	United Nations Educational, Scientific and Cultural Organisation
UNHCR	United Nations High Commissioner for Refugees
UNICEF	United Nations Children's Fund
UNIDO	United Nations Industrial Development Organisation
UNITA	National Union for the Total Independence of Angola
UNPO	Unrepresented Nations and Peoples Organisation
UPU	Universal Postal Union
USDAW	Union of Shop, Distributive and Allied Workers
USSR	Union of Soviet Socialist Republics
UTC	coordinated universal time system *(Temps Universel Coordonné)*
UVF	Ulster Volunteer Force

V

v	*(versus)* against
v.	*(verso)* on the left-hand page
V&A	Victoria and Albert Museum
VA	Vicar Apostolic
	Victoria and Albert Order
VAD	Voluntary Aid Detachment *(nursing)*
VAT	value added tax
VC	Victoria Cross
VD	venereal disease
	Volunteer Officers' Decoration
VDU	visual display unit
Ven.	Venerable
VHF	very high frequency
VRD	Royal Naval Volunteer Reserve Officers' Decoration
VSO	Voluntary Service Overseas

W

W	website
	west
WBC	World Boxing Council
WBO	World Boxing Organisation
WCC	World Council of Churches
WEA	Workers' Educational Association
WEU	Western European Union
WFTU	World Federation of Trade Unions
WHO	World Health Organisation
WI	West Indies
	Women's Institute
Winton:	of Winchester *(Bishop)*
WIPO	World Intellectual Property Organisation
WMD	weapons of mass destruction
WMO	World Meteorological Organisation
WO	Warrant Officer
WRAC	Women's Royal Army Corps
WRAF	Women's Royal Air Force
WRNS	Women's Royal Naval Service
WRVS	Women's Royal Voluntary Service
WS	Writer to the Signet
WTO	World Trade Organisation
WWW	World Wide Web

Y

YHA	Youth Hostels Association
YMCA	Young Men's Christian Association
YWCA	Young Women's Christian Association

INDEX

A
2009 calendar 10
2010 calendar 11
abbreviations 1321
Aberavon
  constituencies
    UK parliament 173
    Welsh assembly 241
Aberdeen 302
  airport 445, 446
  bishop (RC) 476
  constituencies
    Scottish parliament 248
    UK parliament 176
  museums and art galleries 529
  unitary authority 273, 304
  universities 377, 384
Aberdeen and Orkney, bishop 472
Aberdeenshire
  unitary authority 273, 304
Aberdeenshire West & Kincardine
  constituencies, Scottish parliament 248
  constituency, UK parliament 176
Abertay Dundee, university 377
Aberystwyth, University of Wales 386
ABI (Association of British Insurers) 552
abortion
  legal notes 581
  see also legal abortion
Abu Dhabi 1044, 1046
Abuja 952
abuse of children 421
academic staff 371
  see also teachers
academies (England only) 360
academies of scholarship 406
Academy of Medical Sciences 406
ACAS (Advisory, Conciliation and Arbitration Service) 206
ACCAC (Qualifications, Curriculum and Assessment Authority for Wales) 364
accession to the EU 703
accidents
  on railways 447
  road 450
accountancy, professional education 387
Accra 847
Achonry, bishop (RC) 476
acronyms 1321
Action of Churches Together in Scotland 455
acts of parliament (2007–8) 1176
actuarial science, professional education 387
acute trusts 413
Adamstown 1074
ADB (Asian Development Bank) 712
Addis Ababa 831
additional adoption leave 592
additional maternity leave 592
additional member system (AMS) 234
additional state pension 424
Adjudication Panel 263
Adjudicator's Office 206
administration court 316
Administrative Justice and Tribunals Council 206
admirals of the fleet 347
admiralty court 316
admissions and course information for education 372
Adopted Children Register 582
adoption 581
  local authority service 421
Adoption Contact Register 582
adoption orders 581
adoption pay 592
adult and continuing education *see* lifelong learning
adult learning grants (ALGs) 367
adults living with parents, statistics 20
Adur, district council 269, 284
advanced higher national course 366
'advanced skills teacher' grade 369
advanced subsidiary (AS) level examinations 365
Advent Sunday 1289
Advisory, Conciliation and Arbitration Service (ACAS) 206
Advisory Council on National Records and Archives 206
Advocate-General for Scotland, Office of 193
AEP (Association of Electricity Producers) 443
AFCS (armed forces compensation scheme) 426
Afghanistan 735
  role of NATO 723
Africa
  geographical statistics 677
  events (2007–8) 1097
African churches in the UK 477
African Union 711
Afro-Caribbean churches in the UK 477
Agricultural Land Tribunals 325
agricultural properties
  and inheritance tax 575
  tenancies 596
Agriculture and Horticulture Development Board 207
AHRC (Arts and Humanities Research Council) 408
AIM (Alternative Investment Market) 551
air, distances from London by 688
Airdrie & Shotts
  constituencies
    Scottish parliament 248
    UK parliament 176
air force *see* Royal Air Force
airlines 445, 446
airmail letter rates 487
air passenger numbers 445
air pollution 499
  UK targets 498
airports 445
Airsure 487
AIRTO (Association of Independent Research and Technology Organisations Limited) 412
air transport 445
AIT (Asylum and Immigration Tribunal) 325
Akmola *see* Astana
Alabama 1050
Alaska 1050
Albania 737
alcohol consumption, statistics 22
Alcohol Education and Research Council 408
aldermen 266, 291
  listing 292
Alderney 309
  airport 446
Aldershot, constituency 146
Aldridge-Brownhills, constituency 146
A-levels 365
Alexandra, Princess 25
  funding 29
  military ranks and titles 33
  private secretary 26
Alexandra Palace 534
Algeria 739
Algiers 739
algol, minima of *see months of the year* eg January, minima of algol
ALGs (adult learning grants) 367
aliens, status of 584
Allerdale, district council 269, 284
Alnwick, district council 269, 284
alpine skiing, sports results (2007–8) 1195
Alternative Investment Market (AIM) 551
Altrincham & Sale West, constituency 146
Alyn & Deeside
  constituencies
    UK parliament 173
    Welsh assembly 241
Amber Valley
  constituency 146
  district council 269, 284
ambulance service 418
american football
  representative body 641
  sports results (2007–8) 1195
American Samoa 1051, 1053
Americas
  events (2007–8) 1099
  see also Central America; North America; South America
Amman 884
amperes 1314
Amsterdam 944
  see also treaty of Amsterdam
AMU (Arab Maghreb Union) 711
Ancient Monuments Advisory Board for Wales *see* CADW
Andean Community 711
Andorra 740
Andorra la Vella 740
Andrew, Prince 24
  funding 29
  military ranks and titles 32
  private secretary 26

Anglesey
  constituencies
    UK parliament 175
    Welsh assembly 244
  unitary authority 273, 299
Anglia Ruskin University 377
Anglican churches 462
Anglican Communion 462
Anglican Consultative Council 462
angling
  representative body 641
  sports results (2007–8) 1195
Angola 741
Anguilla 1069
angular measures 1315
Angus
  constituencies
    Scottish parliament 248
    UK parliament 176
  unitary authority 273, 304
Animal Health 197
animals, protected 510
Anjou, house of 34
Ankara (Angora) 1035
Anne, Princess 24
  funding 29
  military ranks and titles 32
  private secretary 26
annulment of marriage 588
  in Scotland 591
Antananarivo 913
the Antarctic 685
  Australian 750
  British 1070
  French territory 840
  Norwegian 956
Antarctica, geographical statistics 678, 679
Antarctic treaty 686
Antigua and Barbuda 743
Antilles, Netherlands 946
Antrim
  constituencies
    Northern Ireland assembly 258
    UK parliament 179
  district council 273, 306
Aomen, *see* Macao
AONBs (areas of outstanding natural beauty) 504
APACS (Association for Payment Clearing Services) 544
APEC (Asia-Pacific Economic Cooperation) 712
Apia 985
apostolic nuncios 474
  to Great Britain 475
  to Ireland 476
apparent sidereal time 1281
apparent solar time 1281
appeal courts *see* court of appeal
applicants to the EU 703
apprenticeships 366, 367
appropriate personal pensions (APPs) 425
April 1240
  astronomical phenomena 1240
  calendar 1240
  constellations 1240
  duration of twilight 1241
  high water 1305
  minima of algol 1240
  night sky 1241
  sunrise and sunset 1243
  Moon 1240
    position 1242
  Sun 1241
  Jupiter in 1243
  Mars in 1242
  Mercury in 1242
  Neptune in 1243
  Saturn in 1243
  Uranus in 1243
  Venus in 1242
Arab Maghreb Union (AMU) 711
archaeology (2007–8) 1115
archbishop of Canterbury 462, 463
archbishop of Wales 472
archbishop of York 462, 463
archbishops
  Church of England 463
  Church of Ireland 472, 473
  lords spiritual 75
  overseas 473
  Roman Catholic Church
    England and Wales 475
    Ireland 476
    Scotland 476
Archbishops' Council 462
archdeacons, listing 463
archery, representative body 641
Architects Registration Board 388
architecture
  professional education 388
  year (2007–8) 1120
  see also listed buildings
Architecture and Design Scotland (A+DS) 207
Architecture and the Built Environment, Commission for (CABE) 212
the Arctic 685
Arctic Council 711
Ardagh and Clonmacnois, bishop (RC) 476
Ards, district council 273, 306
area
  conversion tables 1318
  measurement
    imperial 1314
    metric 1314
  of Africa 677
  of America 678
  of Antarctica 678
  of Asia 678
  of Australia 678
  of the Earth 677
  of Europe 678
  of oceans and seas 677
  of the UK 17
areas of outstanding natural beauty (AONBs) 504
areas of special scientific interest (ASSIs) 506
Argentina 744
Argyll and Bute
  constituencies
    Scottish parliament 248
    UK parliament 176
  unitary authority 273, 304
Argyll and the Isles
  bishop (Anglican) 472
  bishop (RC) 476
Arizona 1050
Arkansas 1050
Armagh
  archbishop 472
  archbishop (RC) 476
  district council 273, 306
armed forces 344
  pay and pensions 354
  relative rank 355
  strength 344
armed forces compensation scheme (AFCS) 426
Armed Forces' Pay Review Body 207
Armenia 746
Armenian Orthodox Church 480
arms control 345
army 349
  constitution 349
  equipment holdings 350
  ranks 355
  salaries 354
  staff appointments 349
  strength 344
art (2007–8) 1127
art galleries 523
  England 523
  Northern Ireland 530
  Scotland 529
  Wales 528
  see also names of individual art galleries eg National Gallery
arts academies, privately funded 407
Arts and Humanities Research Council (AHRC) 408
arts and the media, events (2007–8) 1082
arts councils
  England 207
  Northern Ireland 207
  Scotland 229
  Wales 208
Arts London, University of the 377
art therapies, professional education 390
Aruba 946
Arun, district council 269, 284
Arundel & South Downs, constituency 146
Arundel and Brighton, bishop (RC) 475
A+DS (Architecture and Design Scotland) 207
AS (advanced subsidiary) level examinations 365
Ascension Day 1289
Ascension Island 1075
ASEAN (Association of South-East Asian Nations) 712
the Ashes *see* cricket
Ashfield
  constituency 146
  district council 269, 284
Ashford
  constituency 146
  district council 269, 284
Ashgabat 1038
Ashmore Islands 750
Ashton under Lyne, constituency 146
Ash Wednesday 1289
Asia
  events (2007–8) 1102
  geographical statistics 678
Asia Cooperation Dialogue 712
Asian-African Legal Consultative Organisation 712
Asian Development Bank (ADB) 712
Asian Network 610

Asia-Pacific Economic Cooperation (APEC) 712
Asmara 828
assay office marks 539
assembly learning grants 368, 373
Assembly Ombudsman for Northern Ireland and Northern Ireland Commissioner for Complaints 331
Assessment Appeal Tribunals 328
assessment in education 363
 see also public examinations and qualifications
Assets Recovery Agency *see* Serious Organised Crime Agency
ASSIs (areas of special scientific interest) 506
Associated Presbyterian Churches of Scotland 477
association agreements 703
association football
 representative bodies 641
 sports results (2007–8) 1195
 see also FA Cup winners; World Cup winners
Association for Payment Clearing Services (APACS) 544
Association of British Insurers (ABI) 552
Association of Electricity Producers (AEP) 443
Association of Independent Research and Technology Organisations Limited (AIRTO) 412
Association of South-East Asian Nations (ASEAN) 712
Association of Train Operating Companies (ATOC) 446, 447
assured shorthold tenancies 595
Astana 885
Aston, bishop suffragan 464
Aston University 377
astronomical constants 1284
astronomical phenomena 1279
 see also months of the year eg January, astronomical phenomena
astronomical twilight 1280
 see also months of year eg January, twilight
astronomy 1227
 explanation of data 1279
Asunción 964
Asylum and Immigration Tribunal (AIT) 325
Athens 849
athletics
 national (UK) records 1223
 representative bodies 641
 sports results (2007–8) 1197
 world records 1222
Atholl, house of 36
ATOC (Association of Train Operating Companies) 446, 447
atomic time 1282
attendance allowance 432
 weekly rates 432
attorney-general 184
Attorney-General's Office 184
 executive agencies 196
Audit Commission 208
Audit Scotland 208
August 1256
 astronomical phenomena 1256
 calendar 1256
 constellations 1256
 duration of twilight 1257
 high water 1307
 meteors 1257
 minima of algol 1256
 night sky 1257
 sunrise and sunset 1259
 Moon 1256
  position 1258
 Sun 1257
 Jupiter in 1259
 Mars in 1258
 Mercury in 1258
 Neptune in 1259
 Saturn in 1259
 Uranus in 1259
 Venus in 1258
Australasia and the Pacific, events (2007–8) 1104
Australia 748
 external territories 750
 geographical statistics 678
 states and territories 748
Australian Antarctic Territory 750
Australian Capital Territory 748
Austria 751
 EU membership 700, 710
Autumn 1227
Aylesbury, constituency 146
Aylesbury Vale, district council 269, 284
Ayr, Carrick & Cumnock, UK parliament constituency 176
Ayr, Scottish parliament constituency 248
Ayrshire, UK parliament constituencies 176
Azerbaijan 753
Azores 973

B
BAA 445, 446
BA (Baltic Assembly) 713
Babergh, district council 269, 284
BACS Payment Schemes ltd 544
badminton
 representative bodies 641
 sports results (2007–8) 1198
Baghdad 870
Baha'i faith 456
Bahamas 754
Bahrain 756
Baki (Baku) 753
balance of payments, UK 559
Balearic Isles 1010
Balliol, house of 37
Ballymena, district council 273, 306
Ballymoney, district council 273, 306
Baltic Assembly (BA) 713
Bamako 919
Banbridge, district council 273, 306
Banbury, constituency 146
Bandar Seri Begawan 775
Banff & Buchan
 constituencies
  Scottish parliament 248
  UK parliament 176
Bangkok 1028
Bangladesh 757
Bangor
 bishop 472
 University of Wales 386
Bangui 788
Banjul 841
bank holidays *see* public holidays
banking and personal finance 544
 glossary of financial terms 545
banknotes 543
Bank of England 208, 544
 banknotes 543
bankruptcy court 316
banns, marriage by 599
Baptist church 477
the Bar 393
Barbados 759
Barbican Centre 534
Barbuda, Antigua and 743
Barking
 bishop suffragan 465
 constituency 146
Barking and Dagenham
 London borough council 271, 296
Barnet
 London borough council 271, 296
Barnet and Camden, GLA constituency 237
Barnsley
 constituencies 146
 metropolitan borough council 272, 288
baronesses
 forms of address 65, 66
 hereditary 65
 life 66, 72
baronetage and knightage 85
baronetcies, extinct 85
baronets
 forms of address 85
 listing 86
barons
 courtesy titles 76
 forms of address 56, 66
 hereditary 56
 life 66
Barrow and Furness, constituency 146
Barrow-in-Furness, district council 269, 284
BAS (British Antarctic Survey) 687
baseball
 representative body 641
 sports results (2007–8) 1199
base units, SI 1313
Basildon
 constituency 146
 district council 269, 284
Basingstoke
 bishop suffragan 464
 constituency 146
Basingstoke and Deane, district council 269, 284
basketball
 representative bodies 641
 sports results (2007–8) 1199
Basse-Terre (Guadeloupe) 838
Basseterre (St Kitts and Nevis) 982
Bassetlaw
 constituency 146
 district council 269, 284
Bath 276
 constituency 147
 museums and art galleries 523
 universities 377
Bath, Most Honourable Order 82
Bath and North-East Somerset
 unitary authority 272, 289
Bath and Wells, bishop 464

Bath Spa University 377
Batley & Spen, constituency 147
Battersea, constituency 147
BBC 209, 607, 609
 estimated audience share 609
 see also broadcasting 2007–8
BBC One 607
BBC Two 607
BBC Asian Network 610
BBC Radio 610
 local stations 611
 national services 611
 network services 610
 estimated audience share 609
BBC Radio 1 610
BBC Radio 1Xtra 611
BBC Radio 2 610
BBC Radio 3 610
BBC Radio 4 610
BBC Radio Five Live 610
BBC Radio Five Live Sports Extra 610
BBC Radio 6 Music 610
BBC six pips signal 1283
BBC Radio 7 610
BBC Television 607
BBC World Service 611
BBC Worldwide ltd 607, 609
BBSRC (Biotechnology and Biological Sciences Research Council) 408
Beaconsfield, constituency 147
Beckenham, constituency 147
Bedford
 bishop suffragan 470
 constituency 147
 district council 269, 284
Bedfordshire
 constituencies 147
 county council 269, 283
 university 377
Beijing 793
Beirut 900
Belarus 760
Belfast 305
 constituencies
  Northern Ireland assembly 259
  UK parliament 179
 district council 273, 306
 university 384
Belgium 762
 EU membership 700, 710
Belgrade 992
Belize 764
Belmopan 764
benefits 429
 claims and questions 435
 contributory *see* contributory benefits
 for industrial injuries and disablement 435
 non-contributory *see* non-contributory benefits
benefits in kind 568
Benin 765
bereavement allowance 430
 weekly rates 430
bereavement benefits 430
 weekly rates 430
bereavement payment 430
Berlin 845
Bermuda 1069
Bern 1019
Bern convention (1979) 509
BERR (Department for Business, Enterprise and Regulatory Reform) 184
Berwickshire, Roxburgh & Selkirk, UK parliament constituency 176
Berwick-upon-Tweed
 constituency 147
 district council 269, 284
Bethnal Green & Bow, constituency 147
Better Regulation Executive (BRE) 185
Beverley & Holderness, constituency 147
Beverley, bishop suffragan 463
Bexhill & Battle, constituency 147
Bexley
 London borough council 271, 296
Bexley and Bromley, GLA constituency 237
Bexleyheath & Crayford, constituency 147
BFC (British Film Commission) *see* UK Film Council International
BFI (British Film Institute) 209
BG Group 442
Bhutan 766
Big Bang (London Stock Exchange) 551
Big Ben 535
Big Lottery Fund 208
Billericay, constituency 147
billiards, representative bodies 642
billion, definition 1315
bills *see* consolidated fund bills; private bills; private member's bills; public bills
BIOA (British and Irish Ombudsman Association) 331
biodiversity 509
biomedical sciences, professional education 390
Biotechnology and Biological Sciences Research Council (BBSRC) 408
Birkenhead
 bishop suffragan 465
 constituency 147
Birmingham 276
 archbishop (RC) 475
 bishop 464
 constituencies 147
 metropolitan borough council 272, 288
 museums and art galleries 523
 universities 377
birth certificates 583
births
 registration 582
 statistics 19
 see also illegitimacy
Bishkek 896
Bishop Auckland, constituency 148
bishop of Rome 474
bishops
 Church of England 463
 Church of Ireland 472, 476
 Church in Wales 472
 lords spiritual 75
 Roman Catholic Church
  England and Wales 475
  Ireland 476
  Scotland 476
 Scottish Episcopal Church 472
Bishops' Conference of England and Wales 475
Bishops' Conference of Scotland 475
bishops suffragan, listing 463
Bissau 855
bissextile year 1287
Blaby
 constituency 148
 district council 269, 284
Blackburn
 bishop 465
 constituency 148
Blackburn with Darwen
 unitary authority 272, 289
Blackpool
 constituencies 148
 unitary authority 272, 289
Black Sea Economic Cooperation (BSEC) 725
Blaenau Gwent
 constituencies
  UK parliament 173
  by-election (2006) result 181
  Welsh assembly 241
 unitary authority 272, 299
Blaydon, constituency 148
Bloemfontein 1006
blood services 418
Blyth Valley
 constituency 148
 district council 269, 284
BNFL (British Nuclear Fuels) 442, 443
bobsleigh, representative bodies 642
body temperature of humans 1316
Bognor Regis & Littlehampton, constituency 148
Bogotá 798
Bolivia 768
Bolsover
 constituency 148
 district council 269, 284
Bolton
 bishop suffragan 468
 constituencies 148
 metropolitan borough council 272, 288
 university 377
Bonn convention (1979) 509
books
 publishers 630
 sizes 1317
 see also literature (2007–8)
Bootle, constituency 148
borough councils *see* London borough councils; metropolitan borough councils
Bosnia and Hercegovina 769
Boston & Skegness, constituency 148
Boston, district council 269, 284
Bosworth, constituency 149
Botswana 772
bottles of wine, measurements of 1315
boundary changes for Scottish parliamentary constituencies 145
Boundary Commission for Scotland 262
Boundary Commissions 209
Boundary Committee for England 262

Bournemouth
constituencies 149
unitary authority 272, 289
university 378
bowls
representative bodies 642
sports results (2007–8) 1199
boxing
representative bodies 642
sports results (2007–8) 1200
Bracknell, constituency 149
Bracknell Forest
unitary authority 272, 289
Bradford 276
bishop 465
constituencies 149
metropolitan borough council 272, 288
museums and art galleries 523
university 378
Bradwell, bishop suffragan 465
Braintree
constituency 149
district council 269, 284
Brasília 773
Bratislava 1000
Brazil 773
Brazzaville 803
BRE (Better Regulation Executive) 185
Brechin, bishop 472
Breckland, district council 269, 284
Brecon & Radnorshire
constituencies
UK parliament 173
Welsh assembly 241
Brecon Beacons national park 502
Brecqhou 308
Brent
constituencies 149
London borough council 271, 296
Brent and Harrow, GLA constituency 237
Brentford & Isleworth, constituency 149
Brentwood & Ongar, constituency 149
Brentwood
bishop (RC) 475
district council 269, 284
the Brethren 477
Bridgend
constituencies
UK parliament 173
Welsh assembly 241
unitary authority 272, 299
bridges
in London 531
longest 1227, 683
bridge towers, tallest 684
Bridgetown 759
bridgings, longest stretch 683
Bridgnorth, district council 269, 284
Bridgwater, constituency 149
Brigg & Goole, constituency 149
Brighton, university 378
Brighton and Hove 276
constituencies 149
museums and art galleries 523
unitary authority 272, 289
Bristol 276
bishop 465
constituencies 149
museums and art galleries 523
unitary authority 272, 289
universities 378, 386
Britain *see* UK
British Academy 406
British and Irish Ombudsman Association (BIOA) 331
British Antarctic Survey (BAS) 687
British Antarctic Territory 1070
British Broadcasting Corporation *see* BBC
British Channel tunnel rail link 448
British citizenship 583
British Council 209
British Dependent Territories citizenship 584
British Empire, Most Excellent Order 84
British Energy 442, 443
British Film Commission (BFC) *see* UK Film Council International
British Film Institute (BFI) 209
British Gas 441, 442
British Indian Ocean Territory 1070
British Library 210
British Museum 210
British nationals (overseas) 584
British Nuclear Fuels (BNFL) 442, 443
British overseas citizenship 584
British Pharmacopoeia Commission 210
British protected persons 584
British Sky Broadcasting (BSkyB) 607, 609
British sovereign base areas (Cyprus) 811
British Standards Institution 211
British summer time 1227, 1283
British Transport Police 337
British Virgin Islands 1070
British Waterways 211
Brixworth, bishop suffragan 469
broadband subscribers 491
broadcasting 607
complaints 607
year (2007–8) 1131
see also radio; television
Broadcasting Standards Commission's standards code 607
Broadland, district council 269, 284
Broads Authority 502
the Broads national park 502
Bromley
London borough council 271, 296
Bromley & Chislehurst, constituency 150, 181
by-election (2006) result 181
Bromsgrove
constituency 150
district council 269, 284
bronze coin 542
Broxbourne
constituency 150
district council 269, 284
Broxtowe
constituency 150
district council 269, 284
Bruce, house of 37
Brunei 775
Brunel University 378
Brussels 762
Brussels Treaty Organisation (BTO) *see* Western European Union (WEU)
BSEC (Black Sea Economic Cooperation) 725
BSkyB (British Sky Broadcasting) 607
BTEC qualifications 371
Bucharest 974
Buckingham
area bishop 469
constituency 150
university 378
Buckinghamshire
county council 269, 283
Budapest 860
Buddhism 457
adherents in the UK 455
budget
EU 704
year 2008 557
budgeting loans 435
Buenos Aires 744
buildings
listed *see* listed buildings
tallest inhabited 682
see also historic buildings and monuments
building societies 544
built environment, conservation 513
Bujumbura 780
Bulgaria 776
EU membership 700, 703, 710
burial 587
Burkina Faso 778
Burma *see* Myanmar
Burnley
bishop suffragan 465
constituency 150
district council 269, 284
Burton, constituency 150
Burundi 779
Bury
constituencies 150
metropolitan borough council 272, 288
Bury St Edmunds, constituency 150
Bushy Park 534
business and economic affairs (2007–8), events 1085
business and finance (2007–8) 1136
see also economic and business affairs
business lettings 596
business rates 263, 266
business services for postal needs 488
bus services 449
by-elections, UK parliament 181
Byzantine Orthodox Church *see* Eastern Orthodox Church

C
CAA (Civil Aviation Authority) 212, 325, 445, 446
CABE (Commission for Architecture and the Built Environment) 212
cabinet 133
listing 182
Cabinet Office 185
executive agencies 196
CAB International (CABI) 713
cable television 608
CAC (Central Arbitration Committee) 211
CADW (Ancient Monuments Advisory Board for Wales) 207
list of properties 520

Caernarfon
constituencies
UK parliament 173
Welsh assembly 241
Caerphilly
constituencies
UK parliament 174
Welsh assembly 241
unitary authority 272, 299
Caicos Islands, Turks and 1076
Cairngorms national park 504
Cairo 823
Caithness, Sutherland and Easter Ross
constituencies
Scottish parliament 248
UK parliament 176
Calderdale
metropolitan borough council 272, 288
Calder Valley, constituency 150
calendars 9, 1288
year 2009 10
year 2010 11
for any year 1780 to 2040 1296
civil and legal 1292
Chinese 1294
Christian 1288
Coptic 1294
Gregorian 1288
Hindu 1290
Japanese 1294
Jewish 1291
Julian 1288
Muslim 1292
Roman 1295
Sikh 1292
Thai 1292
Zoroastrian 1294
see also months of the year eg January, calendar
calendar year 1287
California 1050
Calvinistic Methodist Church of Wales 481
Camberwell & Peckham, constituency 150
Camberwell College of Arts 377
Cambodia 781
Cambridge 277
constituency 150
district council 269, 284
museums and art galleries 523
university 378
Cambridgeshire
constituencies 150
county council 269, 283
Camden
London borough council 271, 296
Cameroon 783
Camilla, Duchess of Cornwall 24
military ranks and titles 32
private secretary 26
Canada 784
Canada Square 534
canals, longest ship 684
Canary Islands 1010
Canary Wharf 534
Canberra 748
Cannock Chase
constituency 151
district council 269, 284
canoeing, representative body 642
Canterbury 277
archbishop of 463
constituency 151
district council 269, 284
Canterbury Christ Church University 379
cantilever bridges, longest 683
capacity
measurement
imperial 1314
metric 1314
CAP (Common Agricultural Policy) 705
Cape Town 1006
Cape Verde 787
capital gains tax 569
and companies 577
exemptions 570
liability 570
rates 571
relief 571
Caracas 1059
Caradon, district council 269, 284
carbon footprint 498
Cardiff 298
archbishop (RC) 475
constituencies
UK parliament 174
Welsh assembly 241
museums and art galleries 529
unitary authority 272, 299
university 379
University of Wales Institute 386
care programme approach 421
carer's allowance (CA) 432
weekly rates 432
Care Standards Tribunal 325
Caribbean Community and Common Market (CARICOM) 713
Carlisle 277
bishop 465
constituency 151
district council 269, 284
Carmarthen
constituencies
UK parliament 174
Welsh assembly 242
Trinity College 386
Carmarthenshire
unitary authority 272, 299
Carrick, Cumnock & Doon Valley, constituencies, Scottish parliament 248
Carrick, district council 269, 284
Carrickfergus, district council 273, 306
cars *see* motor vehicles
Carshalton & Wallington, constituency 151
Cartier Island 750
Cashel and Emly, archbishop (RC) 476
Cashel and Ossory, bishop 473
Castle Morpeth, district council 269, 284
Castle Point
constituency 151
district council 269, 284
Castlereagh, district council 273, 306
Castries 983
CAT (Competition Appeal Tribunal) 326
Catholic Church *see* Roman Catholic Church
CATS (credit accumulation and transfer systems) 371
Cayenne 838
Cayman Islands 1071
CBI (Confederation of British Industry) 635
CBSS (Council of the Baltic Sea States) 716
CCEA (Northern Ireland Council for the Curriculum, Examinations and Assessment) 365
CCLRC (Council for the Central Laboratory of the Research Councils) *see* STFC
CCTAs (city colleges for the technology of the arts) 360
CCW (Consumer Council for Water) 213
CCW (Countryside Council for Wales) 214, 504, 506
CDC Group 192
CD (Conference on Disarmament) 727
CEFAS (Centre for Environment, Fisheries and Aquaculture Science) 197
Celsius scale 1316
cemeteries in London 532
Cenotaph 532
Cenozoic era 1300
census results 17
centenaries
year 2009 14
year 2010 14
Central African Republic 788
Central America, geographical statistics 678
Central Arbitration Committee (CAC) 211, 637
central bank *see* Bank of England
central criminal court (Old Bailey) 534
Central England in Birmingham, university 377
Central Lancashire, university 379
Central London congestion charge scheme 449
Central Office of Information 196
Central Saint Martins College of Art & Design 377
Central Science Laboratory (CSL) 197
Central Sponsor for Information Assurance (CSIA) 187
Centre for Environment, Fisheries and Aquaculture Science (CEFAS) 197
Centrica plc 442
Cerdic and Denmark, houses of 34
Ceredigion
constituencies
UK parliament 174
Welsh assembly 242
unitary authority 273, 299
CERN (European Organisation for Nuclear Research) 717
certificate, marriage by 599
certificates of birth, death or marriage 583
Certification Office for Trade Unions and Employers' Associations 211
Ceuta 1010
CFSP (Common Foreign and Security Policy) 702, 732
Chad 789
the Chaffarinas 1010

chairman of ways and means 129
Chamberlains 291, 292
champagne bottles, measurement in 1315
chancellor of the exchequer 182
chancery division of the high court of justice 313, 315
Channel 4 607, 609
  estimated audience share 609
Channel 5 *see* Five
Channel Islands 308
  airports 446
  area 308
  currency 542, 543
  see also Guernsey; Jersey
Channel tunnel 448
  rail links 448
CHAPS ltd 544
charges, NHS 416
charitable donations, tax relief on 567
Charity Commission 201
Charles, Prince of Wales 24, 38
  funding 30
  military ranks and titles 31
  private secretary 26
  taxation 30
Charlotte Amalie 1051, 1053
Charnwood
  constituency 151
  district council 269, 284
Charterhouse 534
Chatham & Aylesford, constituency 151
Chatham, museums and art galleries 524
chattels (stamp duty) 580
Chatto, Lady Sarah 24
Cheadle
  constituency 151
    by-election (2005) result 181
Chelmsford
  bishop 465
  district council 269, 284
Chelmsford West, constituency 151
Chelsea College of Art & Design 377
Chelsea Physic Garden 534
Cheltenham
  constituency 151
  district council 269, 284
Cheque and Credit Clearing Company ltd 544
Cherwell, district council 269, 284
Chesham & Amersham, constituency 151
Cheshire
  county council 269, 283
chess
  representative body 642
  sports results (2007–8) 1200
Chester 277
  bishop 465
  constituency 151
  district council 269, 284
  university 379
Chesterfield
  constituency 151
  district council 269, 284
Chester-le-Street, district council 269, 284
Chichester
  bishop 466
  constituency 151
  district council 270, 284
  university 379
Chief Commoner 292
chief constables
  listing 336
  rates of pay 335
chief of the defence staff 344, 345
  salary 354
chiefs of clans 120
child benefit 432
  weekly rates 432
child care payments 428
child health services, NHS 417
child protection 421
children
  adoption 581
  local authority services 420
  percentage living in different family types 20
  registration of births 582
  with special education needs (SEN) 363
  tracing adopted 582
  see also infant mortality
children's bonus bonds 549
children's hearings 321
Child Support Agency (CSA) 201, 589
Child Support Commissioners 328
  for Northern Ireland 328
child tax credit 428
Chile 791
Chiltern, district council 270, 284
Chiltern Hundreds 131
China 793
  special administrative regions 796
China's grand canal 684
Chinese calendar 1294
Chinese new year 1294
Chingford & Woodford Green, constituency 151
Chipping Barnet, constituency 151
chiropody, professional education 390
chiropractic, professional education 389
Chisinau 929
chivalry, orders of 82
Chorley
  constituency 151
  district council 270, 284
Christ, Scientist, Church of 483
Christadelphian 483
Christchurch
  constituency 151
  district council 270, 284
Christian calendar 1288
  year 2009 9
Christianity 455
  adherents in UK 455
  early English 275
Christmas Island 750, 889
chronological cycles and eras 1293
  year 2009 9
Church Commissioners 211
churches 462
  cooperation between 455
  tallest 682
Churches Together in Britain and Ireland 455
Churches Together in England 455
Churches Together in Wales (CYTUN) 455
Church in Wales 472
  marriage in 599
Church of Christ, Scientist 483
Church of England 462
  dioceses 463
  marriage in 599
  membership 462
  provinces 463
  stipends 463
  structure 462
Church of Ireland 472
Church of Jesus Christ of Latter-Day Saints 483
Church of Scotland 473
CICA (Criminal Injuries Compensation Authority) 214
CICAP (Criminal Injuries Compensation Appeals Panel) 326
cinema *see* film
circuit judges 313, 314, 319
circular measures 1315
circulation
  banknotes 543
  newspapers 619
CIS (Commonwealth of Independent States) 715
CITES (convention on international trade in endangered species of wild fauna and flora (1973)) 509
Cities of London & Westminster, constituency 152
citizenship of the UK 583
City and East, GLA constituency 237
city colleges for the technology of the arts (CCTAs) 360
city guilds 267, 293
City Lands and Bridge House Estates Committee 291
City of London 291
City of London Corporation 266, 291, 296
City of London Corporation open spaces 533
City of London Police 337
  rates of pay 335
city technology colleges (CTCs) 360
City University 379
civic dignities, local government 264
civil aviation 445
Civil Aviation Authority (CAA) 212, 325, 445, 446
civil calendar 1292
  year 2009 9
civil cases
  England and Wales 314
  Northern Ireland 324
  Scotland 321
civil fees for marriages
  in England and Wales 600
  in Scotland 600
civil legal aid 597
Civil List 29
civil marriage 599, 600
Civil Nuclear Constabulary 338
civil partnership 590
civil service 184
Civil Service Capability Group 186
civil service commissioners 187
civil twilight 1280
  see also months of year eg January, twilight
civil year 1292
Clackmannanshire
  unitary authority 273, 304
clans, chiefs of 120
classical music 1157
  awards 1161

- class sizes in schools 358, 359
- Cleethorpes, constituency 152
- clergy
  - Church of England 462
  - Church of Ireland 472
  - Church of Scotland 473
  - Church in Wales 472
  - overseas 473
  - Roman Catholic Church 475
  - Scottish Episcopal Church 472
- Clifton, bishop (RC) 475
- climate change 499
- clinical science, professional education 390
- Clogher
  - bishop (Anglican) 472
  - bishop (RC) 476
- Clonfert, bishop (RC) 476
- clothing sizes 1317
- Cloyne, bishop (RC) 476
- clubs 646
- Clwyd
  - constituencies
    - UK parliament 174
    - Welsh assembly 242
- Clydebank & Milngavie, constituencies, Scottish parliament 248
- Clydesdale, constituencies, Scottish parliament 249
- CMC (Common Market Council) 721
- CMG (Common Market Group) 721
- coach services 449
- coal 441
- Coal Authority 212
- coastguards 452
- Coatbridge & Chryston, Scottish parliament constituency 249
- Coatbridge, Chryston & Bellshill, UK parliament constituency 176
- Cockburn Town 1076
- Cocos Islands 750
- cohabitation 590
  - marriage by 600
- 'cohabitation contracts' 590
- COI Communications 196
- coinage, UK 542
- Colchester
  - bishop suffragan 465
  - constituency 152
  - district council 270, 284
- cold weather payments 434
- Coleraine, district council 273, 306
- College of Arms 217
- colleges of higher education
  - and adult and continuing education 370
  - governance 370
- Colne Valley, constituency 152
- Colombia 798
- Colombo 1011
- Colorado 1050
- Columbia, District of (USA) 1050
- COMB (contracted-out mixed benefit) schemes 425
- commemorative marks 541
- commercial court 316
- commercial radio *see* independent radio
- Commercial Radio Companies Association (CRCA) 612
- Commissary Office, HM 322
- commissioner for public appointments 187
- commissioners, EC 707
- Commissioners of Irish Lights 453
- Commission for Architecture and the Built Environment (CABE) 212
- Commission for Equality and Human Rights (CEHR) *see* equality and Human Rights Commission
- Commission for Integrated Transport (CfIT) 212
- Commission for Racial Equality (CRE) *see* Equality and Human Rights Commission
- Commission for Rural Communities 212, 502, 504
- Commission for Social Care Inspection (CSCI) 420
- Committee of the Regions (CoR) 708
- Committee on Standards in Public Life 212
- Common Agricultural Policy (CAP) 705
- Common Clerk 291, 292
- common council 266, 291
  - listing of councilmen 292
- Common Foreign and Security Policy (CFSP) 702, 732
- common law holidays 1293
- common licence, marriage by 599
- Common Market Council (CMC) 721
- Common Market Group (CMG) 721
- Commons *see* House of Commons
- Commons Commissioners 325
- Commonwealth 713
  - intergovernmental and other links 714
  - membership 714
- Commonwealth Agricultural Bureau *see* CAB International (CABI)
- Commonwealth Foundation 714
- Commonwealth of Independent States (CIS) 715
- Commonwealth Secretariat 714
- Commonwealth War Graves Commission 213
- Communication, London College of 377
- communications 485
  - mobile *see* mobile communications
- community care grants 435
- community councils
  - Scotland 268
  - Wales 267
- community healthcare, primary and 416
- community legal service fund 597
- community schools 360
- the Comoros 799
- companies court 316
- Companies House 196
- Companions of Honour, Order of 84
- COMP (contracted-out money purchase) schemes 425
- compensation 547
  - postal 488
- Compensation Agency, Northern Ireland 199
- Competition Appeal Tribunal (CAT) 326
- Competition Commission 213
- Competition Service 213
- complaints *see* ombudsmen
- comptroller, lord chamberlain's office 28
- computers
  - ancestry and development 493
- Conakry 853
- conditional fees 597
- Confederation of British Industry (CBI) 635
- Conference on Disarmament (CD) 727
- confirmation of wills 604
- Congleton
  - constituency 152
  - district council 270, 284
- Congo
  - Democratic Republic of 801
  - Republic of 802
- Congregational Federation 478
- Connecticut 1050
- Connor, bishop 472
- conservation and heritage 502
  - year (2007–8) 513
    - the built environment 513
    - the natural environment 1140
  - *see also* habitat conservation; wildlife conservation
- Conservative party 134
  - development 134
  - financial support 134
  - representation in House of Commons 128
  - whips 135
- consolidated fund bills 131
- constellations 1279
  - *see also months of the year* eg January, constellations
- constituencies
  - UK parliament 128, 146
    - boundary changes 145
    - England 146
    - Northern Ireland 179
    - Scotland 176
    - Wales 173
  - GLA 237
  - Northern Ireland assembly 258
  - Scottish parliament 248
  - Welsh assembly 241
- Constitutional Affairs, Department for *see* Ministry of Justice
- Constitutional Reform Act 2005 313
- constitution of the UK 125
- Consumer Council for Water (CCW) 213
- consumer credit 585
- consumer law 584
  - Scotland 586
- consumer prices index (CPI) 562
- consumer protection 585
- continents
  - geographical statistics 677
  - *see also* Africa; Antarctica; Asia; Australia; Europe; North America; South America
- contingency fees 597
- contracted-out mixed benefit (COMB) schemes 425
- contracted-out money purchase (COMP) schemes 425
- contracted-out pension schemes 425
- contracted-out salary related (COSR) schemes 425
- contract services for mobiles 486
- contribution-based jobseeker's allowance (JSA) 429
- contributory benefits 429
- convenors 264

convention hallmarks 541
convention on international trade in endangered species of wild fauna and flora (CITES) (1973) 509
conversion tables
temperature scales 1316
weights and measures 1318
Conwy
constituencies
UK parliament 174
Welsh assembly 242
unitary authority 273, 299
Cook Islands 949
Cookstown, district council 273, 306
Cooperation Council for the Arab States of the Gulf 715
coordinated universal time (UTC) 1282
Copeland
constituency 152
district council 270, 284
Copenhagen 814
Coptic calendar 1294
Coptic Orthodox Church 480
copyright 605
Copyright Tribunal 326
Coral Sea Islands Territory 750
Corby
constituency 152
district council 270, 284
CoR (Committee of the Regions) 708
Cork, Cloyne and Ross, bishop 473
Cork and Ross, bishop (RC) 476
Cornwall
constituencies 152
county council 269, 283
see also Duchy of Cornwall
Cornwall, Duchess of *see* Camilla, Duchess of Cornwall
coroners' courts 314
Corporation of Trinity House 213, 453
corporation tax 576
payment 577
rates 577
Corps of Queen's Messengers 198
Corpus Christi 1289
COSR (contracted-out salary related) schemes 425
Costa Rica 804
cost of living 562
Côte d'Ivoire 805
Cotswold
constituency 152
district council 270, 284
Council for the Central Laboratory of the Research Councils (CCLRC) *see* STFC
Council for the Curriculum, Examinations and Assessment 365
Council of Christians and Jews 455
council of Europe 715
Council of the Baltic Sea States (CBSS) 716
council of the European Union (council of ministers) 706
Council on Tribunals *see* Administrative Justice and Tribunals Council
council tax 262, 265
see also individual councils, eg Westminster, London borough council
council tax benefit 434
counsellors of state 125
countesses in own right 53
forms of address 53
counties
England 282
map 290
Northern Ireland 306
Wales 298
countries of the world 735
web domain names 496
Countryside Agency *see* Natural England
Countryside Council for Wales (CCW) 214, 504, 506
county councils 262, 283
functions 265
map 290
political composition 269
county courts
England and Wales 314
Northern Ireland 324
courtesy titles 76
forms of address 76
court of aldermen 266
court of appeal
England and Wales 314, 315
House of Lords as final 126, 314, 315
Northern Ireland 324
in Scotland 321
court of common council *see* common council
court of first instance 708
court of justice of the European communities 707
court of session 322
Court of the Lord Lyon 218
courts *see* Inns of Court; law courts and offices
courts-martial appeal court 315
Covent Garden Market Authority 214
Coventry 278
bishop 466
constituencies 152
metropolitan borough council 272, 288
university 379
museums and art galleries 524
CPI (consumer prices index) 562
CPS (Crown Prosecution Service) 202, 314, 319
Craigavon, district council 273, 306
Cranborne money 134
Craven, district council 270, 284
Crawley
constituency 152
district council 270, 284
CRCA (Commercial Radio Companies Association) 612
credit 585
credit accumulation and transfer systems (CATS) 371
Crediton, bishop suffragan 466
cremation 587
Crewe and Nantwich
constituency 152
by-election (2008) result 181
district council 270, 284
cricket
forthcoming events 13
representative bodies 642
sports results (2007–8) 1201
crime and legal affairs, events (2007–8) 1087
criminal cases
England and Wales 314
Northern Ireland 324
Scotland 321
Criminal Cases Review Commission 214
Criminal Defence Service 597
Criminal Injuries Compensation Appeals Panel (CICAP) 326
Criminal Injuries Compensation Authority (CICA) 214
criminal legal aid 598
Criminal Records Bureau 198
crisis loans 435
Croatia 807
application for EU membership 703
Crofters Commission 215
croquet, representative body 642
Crosby, constituency 152
cross-media ownership 607, 619
crown, proceedings against 586
crown agent 321
crown court
England and Wales 313
centres 318
Northern Ireland 324
Crown Estate 201
Crown Office 321, 323
Crown of India (1877) for Ladies, Imperial Order 83
Crown Prosecution Service (CPS) 202, 314, 319
Crown Solicitor's Office, Northern Ireland 324
Croydon
area bishop 470
constituencies 152
London borough council 271, 296
Croydon and Sutton, GLA constituency 237
CSA (Child Support Agency) 201, 589
CSCI (Commission for Social Care Inspection) 420
CSIA (Central Sponsor for Information Assurance) 187
CSL (Central Science Laboratory) 197
CTCs (city technology colleges) 360
Cuba 808
cultural development of man 1301
Culture, Media and Sport, Department for 188
Cumbernauld & Kilsyth, Scottish parliament constituency 249
Cumbernauld, Kilsyth & Kirkintilloch East, UK parliament constituency 176
Cumbria
county council 269, 283
Cunninghame, Scottish parliament constituencies 249
curling
representative bodies 642
sports results (2007–8) 1202
currencies
of the world 693
currency, UK 542
curriculum 363
cycles and eras, chronological *see* chronological cycles and eras

cycling
representative bodies 642
sports results (2007–8) 1203
Cymru *see* Wales
Cynon Valley
constituencies
UK parliament 174
Welsh assembly 242
Cyprus 810
British sovereign base areas 811
EU membership 700, 710
CYTUN (Churches Together in Wales) 455
Czech Republic 812
EU membership 700, 710

D
DAB (digital audio broadcasting) 610
Dacorum, district council 270, 284
Dagenham, constituency 153
daily newspapers
national 620
circulation 619
regional 621
Dakar 991
Damascus 1021
dames 114
forms of address 114
Dames Commanders 114
Dames Grand Cross 114
dams 682
dance
year (2007–8) 1144
productions 1146
Darlington
constituency 153
unitary authority 272, 289
Dartford
constituency 153
district council 270, 284
Dartmoor national park 502
darts
representative body 642
sports results (2007–8) 1203
date letters 540
London (Goldsmiths' Hall) 540
Daventry
constituency 153
district council 270, 285
day care, local authority services 420
daylight saving time 1283
days
definition 1287
for flying flags 23
Hindu 1290
Jewish 1291
longest and shortest 1227
names of 1287
see also dog days; Easter Days; Ember Days; opposition days; quarter days; red-letter days; Rogation Days; term days
DCA *see* Ministry of Justice
DCI (defence capabilities initiative) 723
DCLG *see* Department for Communities and Local Government
DCSF (Department for Children, Schools and Families) 187
DE&S (Defence Equipment and Support) 346
deans, listing 463
death certificates 583
deaths
and inheritance tax 574
legal notes 586
statistics 19
analysis by cause 21
Debt Management Office, UK 201
December 1272
astrological phenomena 1272
calendar 1272
constellations 1272
duration of twilight 1273
high water 1309
meteors 1273
minima of algol 1272
night sky 1273
sunrise and sunset 1275
Moon 1272
position 1274
Sun 1273
Jupiter in 1275
Mars in 1274
Mercury in 1274
Neptune in 1275
Saturn in 1275
Uranus in 1275
Venus in 1274
decorations and medals 117
decree absolute 588
decree nisi 588
'deed of grant' 587
Deer Commission for Scotland 215
defence 344
budget 345
Ministry of 344, 345
defence capabilities initiative (DCI) 723
Defence Council 344, 345
Defence Equipment and Support (DE&S) 346
Defence Logistics Organisation (DLO) *see* Defence Equipment and Support
Defence Management Board (DMB) 344
Defence Procurement Agency (DPA) *see* Defence Equipment and Support
DEFRA *see* Department for Environment, Food and Rural Affairs
degree courses 371
Delaware 1050
Delaware aqueduct 684
Delyn
constituencies
UK parliament 174
Welsh assembly 242
Democratic People's Republic of Korea 891
Democratic Republic of Congo 801
Democratic Unionist party 135
development 134
financial support 134
representation in House of Commons 128
De Montfort University 379
Denbighshire
unitary authority 273, 299
Denmark 814
EU membership 700, 710
Denmark and Cerdic, houses of 34
dental services, NHS 417
dentists
professional education 389
salaries 415
Dentists' and Doctors' Remuneration Review Body 227
Denton & Reddish, constituency 153
Department for Business, Enterprise and Regulatory Reform 184
executive agencies 196
Department for Children, Schools and Families 187
Department for Communities and Local Government 188
executive agencies 197
Department for Constitutional Affairs *see* Ministry of Justice
Department for Culture, Media and Sport 188
executive agency 197
Department for Education, Lifelong Learning and Skills (DELLS) 357, 364
Department for Education and Skills *see* Department for Children, Schools and Families *or* Department for Innovation, Universities and Skills
Department for Environment, Food and Rural Affairs 189, 440
executive agencies 197
Department for Innovation, Universities and Skills 191
executive agencies 198
Department for International Development (DFID) 191
Department for Transport 194
executive agencies 200
Department for Work and Pensions 195
executive agencies 201
Department of Education Northern Ireland (DENI) 360
Department of Health 190
executive agencies 198
Department of HM Procurator-General and Treasury Solicitor 196
Department of Trade and Industry *see* Department for Business, Enterprise and Regulatory Reform *or* Department for Innovation, Universities and Skills
depressions, deepest 679
depth of oceans and seas 677
Derby
bishop 466
constituencies 153
museums and art galleries 524
unitary authority 272, 289
university 379
the Derby (horse race) 1207
Derbyshire
constituencies 153
county council 269, 283
Derbyshire Dales, district council 270, 285
derived units, SI 1313
Derry
bishop (RC) 476
district council 273, 306
Derry and Raphoe, bishop 472
Derwentside, district council 270, 285
descendants of Queen Victoria 40
deserts, largest 679

designated professional bodies (DPBs) 547
Design Council 215
design protection 605
design right 605
Devizes, constituency 153
devolution 126
devolved school management 357
Devon
  constituencies 153
  county council 269, 283
Dewsbury, constituency 153
DFID (Department for International Development) 191
Dhaka 757
Diana, Princess of Wales 24
dietetics, professional education 391
digital audio broadcasting (DAB) 610
digital multiplexes 610
digital penetration 608
digital radio 610
digital switchover 608
digital television 608
digital terrestrial television licence 608
Dili 820
diocesan clergy *see* clergy
dioceses of the Church of England 463
diploma development partnerships 367
diploma in higher education (DipHE) 371
Directorate of Judicial Offices for England and Wales 321
director of public prosecutions
  England and Wales 314, 319
  Northern Ireland 324
disability living allowance 432
  weekly rates 432
Disability Rights Commission (DRC) *see* Equality and Human Rights Commission
disabled people
  benefits for 435
  local authority services 420
disclaimer of peerages 45
discovery, science and *see* science and discovery (2007–8)
discretionary financial contingency funds 367
discretionary payments, social fund 435
discrimination in employment 593
distance, nautical measurement 1315
distance of the Earth from the Sun 677
distance of the horizon 1315
distances from London by air 688
Distinguished Service Order 84
district councils
  England 262, 264, 284
    functions 265
    political composition 269
  Northern Ireland 268, 306
    political composition 273
district courts 321
district judges 314, 319
district judges (magistrates' courts)
  England and Wales 314, 319
  Scotland 321
DIUS (Department for Innovation, Universities and Skills) 191
dividends 566
divorce 587, 588
  financial relief *see* financial relief in divorces
  Scotland 590
  statistics 19
Djibouti 816
Djibouti (capital city) 816
DLO (Defence Logistics Organisation) *see* Defence Equipment and Support
DMB (Defence Management Board) 344
DMO (Debt Management Office) 201
Doctors' and Dentists' Remuneration Review Body 227
Dodoma 1026
dog days 1287
Doha (Al-Dawhah) 973
'do-it-yourself' divorce 590
domain names *see* web domain names
Domestic Policy Group 186
domestic violence 590
Dominica 817
dominical letters 1288
  years 1500–2035 1290
Dominican Republic 818
Doncaster
  bishop suffragan 470
  constituencies 153
  metropolitan borough council 272, 288
Don Valley, constituency 153
Dorchester, area bishop 469
Dorking, bishop suffragan 467
Dorset
  constituencies 153
  county council 269, 283
Douglas 307
Dover
  bishop suffragan 463
  constituency 154
  district council 270, 285
Down
  constituencies
    Northern Ireland assembly 260
    UK parliament 180
  district council 273, 306
Down and Connor, bishop (RC) 476
Down and Dromore, bishop 472
Downing Street 534
DPA (Defence Procurement Agency) *see* Defence Equipment and Support
DPBs (designated professional bodies) 547
DPP *see* Director of Public Prosecutions
drama therapies, professional education 390
Drinking Water Inspectorate (DWI) 438
Drinking Water Quality Regulator for Scotland 439
Driver and Vehicle Licensing Agency (DVLA) 200, 450, 451
Driver and Vehicle Testing Agency (Northern Ireland) 450
driving licences 450
Driving Standards Agency 200, 451
driving tests 451
Dromore, bishop (RC) 476
DTI *see* Department for Business, Enterprise and Regulatory Reform *or* Department for Innovation, Universities and Skills
Dublin 872
  archbishop 473
  archbishop (RC) 476
duchesses *see individual duchesses* eg Kent, Duchess of
Duchy of Cornwall 30
Duchy of Lancaster 30
Dudley
  bishop suffragan 471
  constituencies 154
  metropolitan borough council 272, 288
dukes 46
  forms of address 46
  see also individual dukes eg Kent, Duke of
Dulwich & West Norwood, constituency 154
Dumbarton, Scottish parliament constituency 249
Dumfries, Scottish parliament constituency 249
Dumfries and Galloway
  UK parliament constituency 176
  unitary authority 273, 304
Dumfriesshire, Clydesdale & Tweeddale, UK parliament constituency 176
Dunbartonshire, UK parliament constituencies 176
Dundee 302
  constituencies
    Scottish parliament 249
    UK parliament 177
  unitary authority 273, 304
  universities 377, 379
Dunfermline & Fife West
  UK parliament constituency 177
    by-election (2006) result 181
Dunfermline, Scottish parliament constituencies 249
Dungannon and South Tyrone, district council 273, 306
Dunkeld, bishop (RC) 476
Dunwich, bishop suffragan 470
Durham 278
  bishop 464
  constituencies 154
  county council 269, 283
  district council 270, 285
  university 379
Dushanbe 1024
duty solicitors 598
DVLA (Driver and Vehicle Licensing Agency) 200, 450, 451
dwelling-houses
  average prices 560
  and capital gains tax 570
DWI (Drinking Water Inspectorate) 438

E

Ealing Southall
  constituencies 154
    by-election (2007) result 181
  London borough council 271, 296
Ealing and Hillingdon, GLA constituency 237

EAPC (Euro-Atlantic Partnership Council) 723
earls 48
courtesy titles 76
forms of address 48
early day motions 131
the Earth 1284
geographical statistics 677
satellites 1285
see also the World
Easington
constituency 154
district council 270, 285
East Anglia
bishop (RC) 475
university 379
East Ayrshire
unitary authority 273, 304
Eastbourne
constituency 154
district council 270, 285
East Cambridgeshire, district council 270, 285
East Devon, district council 270, 285
East Dorset, district council 270, 285
East Dunbartonshire
unitary authority 273, 304
Easter Day 1288
1500–2035 1290
Eastern Orthodox Church 480
East Ham, constituency 154
East Hampshire, district council 270, 285
East Herts, district council 270, 285
East Kilbride, Scottish parliament constituency 249
East Kilbride, Strathaven & Lesmahagow, UK parliament constituency 177
Eastleigh
constituency 154
district council 270, 285
East Lindsey, district council 270, 285
East London, university 380
East Lothian
constituencies
Scottish parliament 250
UK parliament 177
unitary authority 273, 304
East Midlands European parliament region 311
East Northamptonshire, district council 270, 285
East Renfrewshire
unitary authority 273, 304
East Riding of Yorkshire
unitary authority 272, 289
East Staffordshire, district council 270, 285
East Sussex
county council 269, 283
East Timor 820
Eastwood, Scottish parliament constituency 250
easy access savings accounts 549
Ebbsfleet, bishop suffragan 463
EBRD (European Bank for Reconstruction and Development) 716
EC 707
delegations 709
presidency 707
representation offices 709
ECB (European Central Bank) 702, 705, 708
Eccles, constituency 154
ecclesiastical fees for marriages 600
ECGD (Export Credit Guarantee Department) 202
eclipses 1278
economic and business affairs, events (2007–8) 1085
Economic and Social Council 730
Economic and Social Research Council (ESRC) 408
Economic Community of West African States (ECOWAS) 716
economic statistics 557
Ecuador 821
ECUK (Engineering Council (UK)) 388
Eddisbury, constituency 154
Eden, district council 270, 285
Edge Hill University 380
Edinburgh 303
airport 445, 446
bishop 472
constituencies
Scottish parliament 250
UK parliament 177
museums and art galleries 529
unitary authority 273, 304
universities 380, 383
Edinburgh, Duke of *see* Philip, Prince
Edinburgh of the Seven Seas 1075
Edmonton
area bishop 464
constituency 154
education 357
the curriculum 363
elective home 363
expenditure 357
fees 360
higher *see* higher education
inspection framework 359
lifelong learning 374
local education administration 357
pre-school 362
primary *see* primary education
post-16 *see* post-16 education
professional 387
responsibility for 357
schools and pupils 360
secondary *see* secondary education
special 363
statistics 357
education and library boards (ELBs) 357, 361
Education and Training Inspectorate 360
education authorities *see* LEAs
education maintenance allowance (EMA) 367
Edward, Prince 24
funding 29
military ranks and titles 32
private secretary 26
EDX London 551
EEA (European Economic Area) 704, 717
EEA (European Environment Agency) 709
EESC (European Economic and Social Committee) 709
EFTA (European Free Trade Association) 704, 716
Egypt 823
EH *see* English Heritage
EIB (European Investment Bank) 708
Eilean Siar *see* Western Isles
Eisteddfod 298
ELBs (education and library boards) 357, 361
elderly people, local authority services 420
elections
European parliament 310
local government 262
England 265
Scotland 268
London assembly and mayor of London 234
UK parliament 128
see also by-elections; general election (2005); voting
elective home education 363
electoral register 602
electoral registration officer (ERO) 602
electricity 442
measurement 1314
suppliers 443
Elizabeth II 24
funding 29
military ranks and titles 31
private secretary 26
taxation 30
Ellesmere Port and Neston
constituency 155
district council 270, 285
Elmbridge, district council 270, 285
Elmet, constituency 155
Elphin, bishop (RC) 476
El Salvador 825
Eltham, constituency 155
ELWa (National Council for Education and Training) 364
Ely, bishop 466
EMA (education maintenance allowance) 367
Ember Days 1289
employer payments 436
employers' associations 635
employment
discrimination 593
pay and conditions 591
termination 592
UK statistics 558
Employment and Support Allowance (ESA) 429
weekly rates 430
Employment Appeal Tribunal 326
employment law 591
Employment Tribunals (England and Wales) 326
Employment Tribunals (Scotland) 326
EMS (European monetary system) 704
ENA (Energy Networks Association) 443
endowment policies 555
energy 440
coal 441
electricity *see* electricity
environmental policies 501
gas *see* gas
nuclear power 443
oil *see* oil
ombudsman 332
renewable sources 444

Energy Networks Association (ENA) 443
Energy Retail Association 443
Energy Supply Ombudsman 332
Enfield
constituencies 155
London borough council 271, 296
Enfield and Haringey, GLA constituency 237
engineering, professional education 388
Engineering and Physical Sciences Research Council (EPSRC) 409
Engineering Council (UK) (ECUK) 388
England
area 17, 274
areas of outstanding natural beauty (AONBs) 504
banknotes 543
constituencies 146
early history 275
European parliament regions 311
flag 274
historic buildings and monuments 516
hydrography 274
islands 274
judicature 313
kings and queens (927 to 1603) 34
local government *see* local government
museums and art galleries 523
national parks 502
NHS structure 413
police forces 336
population statistics 17, 274
precedence 42
principal cities 276
prison establishments 340
public holidays 1293
relief 274
water industry 437
see also Bank of England; Church of England
English Heritage (EH) 215, 515
list of properties 516
English Nature (EN), *see* Natural England
English Regions Network 265
enterprise investment scheme 572
Entitlement Appeal Tribunals 328
Entrepreneurs' Relief 572
environment 498
air pollution *see* air pollution
climate change 499
contacts 501
and health 501
London issues 235
sustainable development 499
UK targets 498
waste *see* waste
water *see* water, quality targets
Environment, Fisheries and Aquaculture Science, Centre for 197
Environment, Food and Rural Affairs, Department for *see* Department for Environment, Food and Rural Affairs
Environment Agency 215, 438, 501
environment and science, events (2007–8) 1091
epact 1294
ephemeris time (ET) 1282
Epiphany 1288
Epping Forest
constituency 155
district council 270, 285
Epsom and Ewell
constituency 155
district council 270, 285
EPSRC (Engineering and Physical Sciences Research Council) 409
Equality and Human Rights Commission 215
Equality Commission for Northern Ireland 216
Equal Opportunities Commission *see* Equality and Human Rights Commission
equator, diameter and circumference 677
Equatorial Guinea 826
equestrianism
representative bodies 642
sports results (2007–8) 1203
equinoctial year 1287
equinox 1287
eras *see* chronological cycles and eras; Indian eras
Erewash
constituency 155
district council 270, 285
Erith & Thamesmead, constituency 155
Eritrea 828
ERM (exchange rate mechanism) 704
ERO (electoral registration officer) 602
Eryri/Snowdonia national park 503
ESA (Employment and Support Allowance) 429
ESA (European Space Agency) 717
ESDI (European security and defence identity) 723
Esher & Walton, constituency 155
ESRC (Economic and Social Research Council) 408
Essex
county council 269, 283
university 380
Essex North, constituency 155
Estonia 829
EU membership 700, 710
Ethiopia 831
ethnic groups in the UK 18
Eton fives
representative body 642
sports results (2007–8) 1203
EU
budget 704
chronology 701
constitution 702
enlargement and external relations 703
environmental measures 499
institutions 706
legislative process 701
member states 700
recognition of professional qualifications 387
the euro 705
Euro-Atlantic Partnership Council (EAPC) 723
Eurojust (European Union's Judicial Cooperation Unit) 709
Europe
events (2007–8) 1105
geographical statistics 678
European Bank for Reconstruction and Development (EBRD) 716
European Central Bank (ECB) 702, 705, 708
European commission *see* EC
European constitution 701, 702
European convention on human rights (1950) 716
European council 707
European court of auditors 708
European court of human rights 716
European Derivatives Exchange (EDX) 551
European Economic and Social Committee (EESC) 709
European Economic Area (EEA) 704, 717
European Environment Agency (EEA) 709
European Free Trade Association (EFTA) 704, 716
European Investment Bank (EIB) 708
European Monetary Institute *see* European Central Bank (ECB)
European monetary system (EMS) 704
European Ombudsman 331
European Organisation for Nuclear Research (CERN) 717
European parliament (EP) 310, 706
elections 310
and the legislative process 701
political groupings 706, 710
UK members 310
UK regions 311
European Patent Office 606
European security and defence identity (ESDI) 723
European Space Agency (ESA) 717
European Union *see* EU
European Union's Judicial Cooperation Unit (Eurojust) 709
European wildlife trade regulation 510
Europol (European Police Office) 709
Eurostar 448
Evangelical Alliance 455
events (2007–8)
UK affairs 1079
arts and the media 1082
business and economic affairs 1085
crime and legal affairs 1087
environment and science 1091
sport 1094
Africa 1097
Americas 1099
Asia 1102
Australasia and the Pacific 1104
British affairs *see* UK affairs
Europe 1105
Middle East 1107
see also forthcoming events
Everest 680
eviction 596
examinations and qualifications *see* public examinations and qualifications
'excellent teacher' scheme 369
exchange markets 551

exchange rate mechanism (ERM) 704
exchange rates 693
executive agencies 184
listing 196
executors of wills 602
exempt supplies 579
Exeter
bishop 466
constituency 155
district council 270, 285
university 380
Exmoor national park 503
expenditure
government 557
household 559
local government 266, 267, 268
Export Credit Guarantee Department (ECGD) 202
exports, UK statistics 559
eyesight tests 417

F
FAA (Fleet Air Arm) 348
Faculty of Actuaries 388
Faculty of Advocates 393
FA Cup winner 2007–8 1196
Faeroe Islands 815
Fahrenheit scale 1316
Fair Employment Tribunal (Northern Ireland) 327
fair trading 585
see also Office of Fair Trading
faith *see* religion
Falkirk
constituencies
Scottish parliament 250
UK parliament 177
unitary authority 273, 304
Falkland Islands 1072
Falmouth & Camborne, constituency 155
families
local authority services 420
see also children
family division of the high court of justice 313, 314, 316
Family Health Services Appeal Authority (FHSAA) 326
family health services authorities (FHSAs) 413
family proceedings cases 314
Family Records Centre 583
FAO (Food and Agricultural Organisation of the United Nations) 717
Fareham
constituency 155
district council 270, 285
Fashion, London College of 377
Fasli calendar 1294
fasts
Hindu 1290
Jewish 1291
Muslim 1292
Sikh 1292
father of the house 131
Faversham & Kent Mid, constituency 155
FCC (Foreign Compensation Commission) 216
FCO *see* Foreign and Commonwealth Office
FCO Services 198
feasts
moveable 1289
see also festivals
February 1232
astronomical phenomena 1232
calendar 1232
constellations 1232
duration of twilight 1233
high water 1304
minima of algol 1232
night sky 1233
sunrise and sunset 1235
zodiacal light 1233
Moon 1232
position 1234
Sun 1233
Jupiter in 1235
Mars in 1234
Mercury in 1234
Neptune in 1235
Saturn in 1235
Uranus in 1235
Venus in 1234
FE bursaries 368
Federated States of Micronesia 928
federations (schools) 361
Feltham & Heston, constituency 155
fencing
representative body 643
sports results (2007–8) 1203
Fenland, district council 270, 285
Ferguson, Sarah 24
Fermanagh & South Tyrone
constituencies
Northern Ireland assembly 260
UK parliament 180
Fermanagh, district council 273, 306
Ferns, bishop (RC) 476
festivals
Hindu 1290
Jewish 1291
Muslim 1292
Sikh 1292
FHSAA (Family Health Services Appeal Authority) 326
FHSAs (family health services authorities) 413
field events
men
national (UK) records 1223
world records 1222
women
national (UK) records 1224
world records 1223
field marshals 349
salaries 354
Fife
constituencies, Scottish parliament 250
unitary authority 273, 304
Fife North East, UK parliament constituency 177
Fiji 833
film
year (2007–8) 1148
finance
government 557
higher education 359
local government 262
England 265
Northern Ireland 268, 306
Scotland 268
Wales 267
Channel Islands 308
Isle of Man 307
NHS 415
opposition parties 134
personal *see* banking and personal finance
roads 448
royal family 29
year (2007–8) *see* business and finance (2007–8)
Financial Ombudsman Service 331, 426, 544, 548, 552
financial relief in divorces 589
in Scotland 590
Financial Reporting Council (FRC) 388
Financial Services and Markets Tribunal 326
Financial Services Authority *see* FSA
financial services compensation scheme (FSCS) 547
financial services regulation 547
financial terms, glossary 545
Finchley & Golders Green, constituency 155
fineness (purity) marks 539
Finland 834
EU membership 700, 710
Fire Service College 197
first class post 487
Five 607, 609
estimated audience share 609
fixed Easter 1288
fixed interest saving certificates 549
fixtures (stamp duty) 580
flags
England 274
Northern Ireland 305
Scotland 300
Wales 297
Guernsey 309
Isle of Man 307
Jersey 308
see also national flag of the UK
flat horse racing results (2007–8) 1207
Fleet Air Arm (FAA) 348
flexible working 592
Flintshire
unitary authority 273, 299
'floating' bridging 683
Florida 1050
flying the Union Flag (or Jack) 23
Folkestone & Hythe, constituency 155
Food, Department for Environment, Rural Affairs and *see* Department for Environment, Food and Rural Affairs
Food and Agriculture Organisation of the United Nations (FAO) 717
Food Standards Agency (FSA) 202
football *see* American football; association football
Foreign and Commonwealth Office 189
executive agencies 198
Foreign Compensation Commission (FCC) 216
foreign goods, hallmarks 541
Forensic Science Northern Ireland 199
Forensic Science Service (FSS) 335
Forest Enterprise 202

Forest Heath, district council 270, 285
forest nature reserves 507
Forest of Dean
 constituency 155
 district council 270, 285
Forest Research 203
Forestry Commission 202, 507
Forest Service 507
Fort-de-France 838
forthcoming events 12
foundation degrees 371
foundation schools 360
foundation trusts 413
fourth plinth 532
Foyle
 constituencies
  Northern Ireland assembly 260
  UK parliament 180
France 836
 EU membership 700, 710
 overseas departments 838
 overseas territories 840
 territorial collectivities 839
Free Churches Group 455
Free Church of England 478
Free Church of Scotland 478
Free Presbyterian Church of Scotland 479
Freetown 996
Freeview 608
French Community of States 840
French Guiana 838
French Polynesia 839
FSA (Financial Services Authority) 544, 547, 551, 552, 554
FSA (Food Standards Agency) 202
FSCS (financial services compensation scheme) 547
FSS (Forensic Science Service) 335
Fulham, bishop suffragan 464
Funafuti 1039
funding councils for education
 see Learning and Skills Council (LSC); Training and Development Agency for Schools (TDA)
funding of the royal family 29
funeral payments 434
further education *see* post-16 education
Futuna Islands, Wallis and 840
Fylde
 constituency 156
 district council 270, 285

G
Gabon 840
Gaborone 772
Gaelic languages 300, 307, 364
Gainsborough, constituency 156
Galápagos Islands 822
Galloway & Upper Nithsdale, Scottish parliament constituency 251
Galloway, bishop (RC) 476
Galway and Kilmacduagh, bishop (RC) 476
Gambia 841
Gambling Commission 216
gardens of London 533
Garter, Most Noble Order 82
gas 440, 441
 suppliers 443
Gateshead
 metropolitan borough council 272, 288
 museums and art galleries 524
Gateshead East & Washington West, constituency 156
GATT (general agreement on tariffs and trade) 734
Gatwick airport 445, 446
Gaza City 877
Gaza Strip 877
GCC (General Chiropractic Council) 389
GCC (Gulf Cooperation Council) 715
GCE A-level examinations *see* A-levels
GCHQ (Government Communications Headquarters) 204
GCSE 365
Gedling
 constituency 156
 district council 270, 285
Genealogists, Society of 583
general agreement on tariffs and trade (GATT) 734
general assembly 473, 727
 specialised bodies 727
general assembly of the Church of Scotland 473
general certificate of education (GCE) advanced (A-level) examinations *see* A-levels
general certificate of secondary education *see* GCSE
General Chiropractic Council (GCC) 389
General Commissioners of Income Tax 327
General Council of the Bar 393
General Council of the Bar of Northern Ireland 394
General Dental Council 389
general election (2005)
 results 145
general index of retail prices 562
general insurance 552
General Medical Council (GMC) 389
general medical services (GMS) 416
general national vocational qualification (GNVQ) 365
general ophthalmic services, NHS 417
General Optical Council (GOC) 392
General Osteopathic Council (GOsC) 392
general practitioners *see* GPs
General Register Office 583
General Register Office for Scotland 583
general synod
 Church of England 462
 Church of Ireland 472
 Scottish Episcopal Church 472
general teaching councils (GTCs) 368, 369
Gentleman Usher of the Black Rod, Department of 127
geographical statistics of the world 677
geological time 1300
George Cross 119
George Inn 534
Georgetown (Ascension Island) 1075
George Town (Cayman Islands) 1071
Georgetown (Guyana) 856
George V 39
Georgia 843
Georgia (USA) 1050
Germany 845
 EU membership 700, 710
Ghana 847
Giant Tortoise Islands 822
Gibraltar 1072
Gibraltar (capital) 1072
Gibraltar in Europe, bishop 467
gift aid scheme 567, 578
gifts
 and capital gains tax 572
 and inheritance tax 573, 574
Gillingham, constituency 156
GLA 234, 266
 constituencies 237
glaciated areas 678
Glamorgan, university 380
Glasgow 303
 airport 445, 446
 archbishop (RC) 476
 constituencies
  Scottish parliament 251
  UK parliament 177
 museums and art galleries 529
 Scottish parliament region 254
 unitary authority 273, 304
 universities 380, 385
Glasgow and Galloway, bishop 472
Glasgow East by-election (2008) result 181
Glasgow Caledonian University 380
Glenrothes, UK parliament constituency 178
gliding, representative body 643
Gloucester
 bishop 467
 constituency 156
 district council 270, 285
Gloucester, Duchess of 25
 funding 29
 military ranks and titles 33
 private secretary 26
Gloucester, Duke of 24
 funding 29
 military ranks and titles 33
 private secretary 26
Gloucestershire
 county council 269, 283
 university 380
GMC (General Medical Council) 389
GMS (general medical services) 416
GMT (Greenwich Mean Time) 1281, 1283
GMTV 609
GNI of the UK 1047
GNVQ (general national vocational qualification) 365
GOC (General Optical Council) 392
Godthåb (Nuuk) 816
gold coin 542
gold hallmarks 539
golf
 representative bodies 643
 sports results (2007–8) 1204
Good Friday agreement 305
goods
 sale 584
 supply 585
 transport
  by rail 447
  by road 449
  by sea 452

see also durable goods; foreign goods
Gordon
constituencies
Scottish parliament 251
UK parliament 178
GOsC (General Osteopathic Council) 392
Gosport
constituency 156
district council 270, 285
governing bodies of schools 361
governing body of the Church in Wales 472
government 133
current administration 182
departments 184
finance 557
formation 134
organs 125
see also local government; regional government
Government Actuary's Department 216
Government Car and Despatch Agency 200
Government Communications Headquarters (GCHQ) 204
Government Decontamination Service 197
Government Equalities Office 189
government grants to local authorities 263
Government Offices for the Regions (GOs) 216
government whips 183
Gower
constituencies
UK parliament 174
Welsh assembly 242
GPs 416
salaries 415
graduated retirement benefit (GRB) 424, 431
graduate teacher programme (GTP) 368, 394
Graduate Teacher Training Registry (GTTR) 372, 394
grand canal in China 684
grand committees 131
Grand National 13
Grand Turk 1076
grant-aided schools 357
Grantham & Stamford, constituency 156
Grantham, bishop suffragan 468
grants
for students 372
to local authorities 263
grants-in-aid 29
Gravesham
constituency 156
district council 270, 285
Gray's Inn 394, 535
GRB (graduated retirement benefit) 424, 431
Great Britain *see* UK
Greater London Authority *see* GLA
Greater London returning officer (GLRO) 235
Great Grimsby, constituency 156
Great Yarmouth
constituency 156
district council 270, 285
Greece 849
EU membership 700, 710
Greek Orthodox Church 480
calendar 1288
greenhouse gases, emissions 499
Greenland (Kalaallit Nunaat), 679, 816
Greenock & Inverclyde, Scottish parliament constituency 252
Green Park 534
Green party 136
Greenwich & Woolwich, constituency 156
Greenwich
London borough council 271, 296
sights 534, 535
university 380
Greenwich and Lewisham, GLA constituency 237
Greenwich Mean Time (GMT) 1281, 1283
Greenwich Park 534, 535
Gregorian calendar 1288
Grenada 851
Grenadines, St Vincent and 984
greyhound racing
sports results (2007–8) 1205
Grimsby, bishop suffragan 468
GTCs (general teaching councils) 368, 369
GTP (graduate teacher programme) 368, 394
GTTR (Graduate Teacher Training Registry) 372, 394
Guadeloupe 838
Guam 1051
guarantee credit 433
guaranteed equity bonds 549
guaranteed growth bonds 550
guaranteed income bonds 549
guardian's allowance 432
weekly rate 432
Guatemala 852
Guatemala City 852
Guernsey 308
airport 446
area 308
currency 543
flag 309
police force 337
population 17, 308
water authority 437
Guiana, French 838
Guildford
bishop 467
constituency 156
district council 270, 285
Guinea 853
Guinea-Bissau 855
Gulf Cooperation Council (GCC) 715
Guyana 856
Gwynedd
unitary authority 273, 299
gymnastics
representative body 643
sports results (2007–8) 1206

H
habitat conservation 509
UK legislation 510
Hackney
constituencies 156
London borough council 271, 296
Hagatna 1051, 1053
Haiti 857
Halesowen & Rowley Regis, constituency 156
half-mast, flags at 23
Halifax, constituency 156
Hallam, bishop (RC) 475
hallmarks 539
Haltemprice & Howden
constituency 156
by-election (2008) result 181
Halton
constituency 156
unitary authority 272, 289
Hambleton, district council 270, 285
Hamilton, Scottish parliament constituencies 252
Hamilton (Bermuda) 1069
Hammersmith and Fulham
constituency 157
London borough council 271, 296
Hampshire
constituencies 157
county council 269, 283
Hampstead & Highgate, constituency 157
Hampton Court Park and Gardens 534
handball, representative body 643
Hanoi 1061
Hanover, house of 36
Harare 1066
Harborough
constituency 157
district council 270, 285
harbour authorities 453
Haringey
London borough council 271, 296
Harlow
constituency 157
district council 270, 285
harmonised index of consumer prices (HICP) 562
Harrogate & Knaresborough, constituency 157
Harrogate, district council 270, 285
Harrow
constituencies 157
London borough council 271, 296
Harry, Prince *see* Henry, Prince
Hart, district council 270, 285
Hartlepool
constituency 157
unitary authority 272, 289
Harwich, constituency 157
Hastings & Rye, constituency 157
Hastings, district council 270, 285
Havana 808
Havant
constituency 157
district council 270, 285
Havering
London borough council 271, 296
Havering and Redbridge, GLA constituency 237
Hawaii 1050
Hayes & Harlington, constituency 157

Hazel Grove, constituency 157
headteachers
qualifications 368, 369
salary 369
health
advice for travel overseas 698
and the environment 501
and mobile phone use 486
statistics 21
Health, Department of *see* Department of Health
Health and Safety Executive 217
health and social services boards 415, 416
health boards 414, 416
healthcare, professional education 389
Health Commission Wales (Specialised Services) 414
health costs 416
Health Professions Council (HPC) 390
Health Protection Agency (HPA) 217
Health Service Ombudsman 332, 419
health services, NHS 416
Heard Island 751
Heathrow airport 445, 446
the Hebrides 301
HEFCs (higher education funding councils) 357, 369, 374
Helsinki 834
Hemel Hempstead, constituency 157
Hemsworth, constituency 157
Hendon, constituency 157
Henley
constituency 158
by-election (2008) result 181
Henley Royal Regatta 13, 1212
Henry, Prince 24
military ranks and titles 32
private secretary 26
Heralds' College 217
hereditary peers 44, 46
hereditary women peers 44
Hereford
bishop 467
constituency 158
Herefordshire
unitary authority 272, 289
Heriot-Watt University 380
heritage, conservation and *see* conservation and heritage
heritage sites, world *see* world heritage sites
Herm 308
Her Majesty's Courts Service (HMCS) 320
Her Majesty's Inspectorate for Education and Training in Wales 359
Her Majesty's Officers of Arms 217
Hertford & Stortford, constituency 158
Hertford, bishop suffragan 470
Hertfordshire
constituencies 158
county council 269, 283
university 380
Hertsmere
constituency 158
district council 270, 285
Hexham, constituency 158
Hexham and Newcastle, bishop (RC) 475
Heywood & Middleton, constituency 158
HFEA (Human Fertilisation and Embryology Authority) 219
HICP (harmonised index of consumer prices) 562
HIE (Highlands and Islands Enterprise) 218
high court judges 313, 315
high court of justice
England and Wales 313, 315
centres 318
Northern Ireland 324
high court of justiciary (Scotland) 321, 322
higher education 370
admissions 372
courses 371
expenditure 357
fees 372
finance 359
student support 372
types of institution 370
Higher Education Academy 371
higher education funding councils (HEFCs) 357, 369, 374
higher level teaching assistant (HLTA) status 369
higher national certificate (HNC) 367, 371
higher national course 366
higher national diploma (HND) 367, 371
higher national qualifications 367
Highland
unitary authority 273, 304
Highlands and Islands Enterprise (HIE) 218
Highlands and Islands Scottish parliament region 254
High Peak
constituency 158
district council 270, 285
high sheriffs 264
England 282
Northern Ireland 306
Wales 298
high water, predictions 1303
highway authorities 448
Highways Agency 200, 448
Hillingdon
London borough council 271, 296
Hinckley and Bosworth, district council 270, 285
Hindu calendar 1290
year 2009 9
Hinduism 457
adherents in UK 455
hire-purchase agreements 585
historical year 1292
historic buildings and monuments 515
England 516
Northern Ireland 522
Scotland 521
Wales 520
conservation (2007–8) 513
listing *see* listed buildings
Historic Buildings and Monuments Commission for England 215
Historic Environment Advisory Council for Scotland 218
Historic Royal Palaces 218
Historic Scotland
list of properties 521
Hitchin & Harpenden, constituency 158
HLTAs (higher level teaching assistants) 369
HM Coastguard (HMCG) 452
HM Commissary Office 322
HMCS (Her Majesty's Courts Service) 320
HM Fleet 348
HM Inspectorate of Education (HMIE) 360
HM inspectors (HMIs) 360
HM Prison Service 340
operating costs 340
salaries 340
HM Procurator-General and Treasury Solicitor, Department of 196
HM Revenue and Customs (HMRC) 203
HM Treasury 194
executive agencies 200
HNC (higher national certificate) 367, 371
HND (higher national diploma) 367, 371
hockey
representative bodies 643
sports results (2007–8) 1206
Holborn & St Pancras, constituency 158
hold-over relief on capital gains tax 572
holidays *see* public holidays
Holy Apostolic Catholic Assyrian Church of the East 479
holy days 1293
Holy See 1058, 474
home education 363
Home Office 190
executive agencies 198
home responsibilities protection (HRP) 424
homo sapiens, development 1300
Honduras 859
Hong Kong 796
Honiara 1003
Honorary Dames Commanders 114
honorary knights 85
the Honourable the Irish Society 292
clerk 292
horizon, distance of 1315
Hornchurch, constituency 158
Hornsey & Wood Green, constituency 158
Horse Guards 535
Horserace Totalisator Board (the Tote) 219
horse racing
representative bodies 643
sports results (2007–8) 1207
Horsham
bishop suffragan 466
constituency 158
district council 270, 285
hospices 418
hospitals
NHS 417
Houghton & Washington East, constituency 158
Hounslow
London borough council 271, 296

household
income and expenditure 559
ownership of durable goods 560
statistics 19
water bills 438
House of Commons 128, 535
business 128
elections 128
government whips 183
hours of meeting 131
members *see* MPs
officers and officials 129
party representation 128
select committees 130, 132
speaker 129, 132
House of Commons members' fund 129
House of Lords 126, 535
composition 126, 127, 44
as final court of appeal 126, 314, 315
government whips 183
officers 127
party representation 127
select committees 126, 127, 132
speaker 127
houses *see* dwelling-houses
Houses of Parliament
tours 535
see also House of Commons; House of Lords
housing benefit 434
Housing Corporation 219
Hove, constituency 158
HPA (Health Protection Agency) 217
HPC (Health Professions Council) 390
HRP (home responsibilities protection) 424
HTA (Human Tissue Authority) 219
Huddersfield
constituency 158
university 380
Hull *see* Kingston upon Hull
Hulme, bishop suffragan 468
human body temperature 1316
human development 1300
Human Fertilisation and Embryology Authority (HFEA) 219
Human Genetics Commission 219
Humanism 458
human rights 594
see also European convention on human rights
Human Tissue Authority (HTA) 219
Hungary 860
EU membership 700, 710
Huntingdon
bishop suffragan 466
constituency 159
Huntingdonshire, district council 270, 285
Hyde Park 534
Hyndburn
constituency 159
district council 270, 285

I
IAEA (International Atomic Energy Agency) 717
IBRD (International Bank for Reconstruction and Development) 733
ICA (Institute of Contemporary Arts) 535
ICAO (International Civil Aviation Organisation) 718
ice hockey
representative body 643
sports results (2007–8) 1209
Iceland 862
ice skating
representative body 643
sports results (2007–8) 1209
ICFTU (International Confederation of Free Trade Unions) 718
ICRC (International Committee of the Red Cross) 720
ICTR (International Criminal Tribunal for Rwanda) 730
Idaho 1050
IDA (International Development Association) 733
IDD (international direct dialling) codes 488
Identity and Passport Service 198
IEA (International Energy Agency) 718
IFAD (International Fund for Agricultural Development) 719
IFC (International Finance Corporation) 733
IHO (International Hydrographic Organisation) 719
Ilford, constituencies 159
illegitimacy 594
Illinois 1050
ILO (International Labour Organisation) 719
IMF (International Monetary Fund) 720
Immigration Services Tribunal 327
immigration statistics 18
immunisation
for travel overseas 698
IMO (International Maritime Organisation) 719
Imperial College London 380
Imperial Service Order 84
Imperial Society of Knights Bachelor 85
imperial units 1314
Imperial War Graves Commission *see* Commonwealth War Graves Commission
Imperial War Museum 219
imports, UK statistics 559
incapacity benefit 429
weekly rates 429
income, household 559
income-based jobseeker's allowance (JSA) 431
weekly rates 431
income bonds 549
income support 432
weekly rates 433
income support premiums 433
weekly rates 433
income tax 564
allowances 564
relief 567
self-assessment 569
Independent Housing Ombudsman 331
Independent Methodist churches 479
Independent Police Complaints Commission (IPCC) 331, 334
independent radio 612
estimated audience share 609
local stations 612
national stations 612
see also broadcasting (2007–8)
Independent Review Service for the Social Fund 220
independent schools 396
Independent Schools Council (ISC) 396
Independent Schools Inspectorate (ISI) 396
independent/state school partnerships 361
independent television *see* ITV
Independent Television News 609
indexation allowance 571
see also taper relief
index-linked savings certificates 549
India 863
Indiana 1050
Indian Empire, Most Eminent Order 83
Indian eras 1294
individual savings accounts *see* ISAs
Indonesia 866
indoor bowls, sports results (2007–8) 1199
industrial and technological research bodies 412
Industrial Injuries Advisory Council 220
industrial injuries disablement benefit 435
industrial stoppages 559
industrial tribunals (Northern Ireland) 327
in Europe, bishop suffragan 467
infant mortality 19
infectious diseases, notifications 22
inflation rate 562
Information Commissioner's Office 220
information management, professional education 393
information technology 491
Information Tribunal 327
inhabited buildings, tallest 682
inheritance tax 573
calculation 575
liability 573
payment 576
rates 576
relief 573
transfer 576
initial teacher education (ITE) 369
initial teacher training (ITT) 369
inland postal services 487
inner house, court of session 322
Inner Temple 394, 535
Inns of Court 394, 535
input tax 578
Insolvency Service 196
Institute of Actuaries 388
Institute of Contemporary Arts (ICA) 535
institutions 649
insurance 552
insurance companies
authorisation and regulation 552
investments 556
new business 556
takeovers and mergers 552
UK figures 553

integrated schools in Northern Ireland 361
Integrated Transport, Commission for (CfIT) 212
intellectual property 605
intellectual property organisations 606
intelligence and security services 204
inter-church cooperation 455
interest rates 544
Inter Faith Network for the United Kingdom 455
Inter-Governmental Maritime Consultative Organisation (IMCO) *see* International Maritime Organisation (IMO)
'internal market' in the NHS 413
International Atomic Energy Agency (IAEA) 717
international atomic time (TAI) 1282
international baccalaureate 366
International Bank for Reconstruction and Development (IBRD) 733
International Civil Aviation Organisation (ICAO) 718
International Committee of the Red Cross (ICRC) 720
International Confederation of Free Trade Unions (ICFTU) 718
International Conference of the Red Cross and Red Crescent 720
international court of justice 731
International Criminal Police Organisation (Interpol) 718
International Criminal Tribunal for Rwanda (ICTR) 730
International Criminal Tribunal for the Former Yugoslavia 730
International Development, Department for 191
International Development Association (IDA) 733
international direct dialling (IDD) codes 488
International Energy Agency (IEA) 718
International Federation of Red Cross and Red Crescent Societies 720
International Federation of Reproduction Rights Organisations 605
International Finance Corporation (IFC) 733
International Francophone Organisation 718
International Fund for Agricultural Development (IFAD) 719
International Hydrographic Organisation (IHO) 719
International Labour Organisation (ILO) 719
International Maritime Organisation (IMO) 719
International Meteorological Organisation *see* World Meteorological Organisation (WMO)
International Monetary Fund (IMF) 720
International Organisation for Migration (IOM) 720
international organisations 711
International Power plc 442
International Primary Curriculum 365
International Rail Regulator (IRR) 446
International Red Cross and Red Crescent Movement 720
international signed for (airmail services) 487
international system *see* SI
International Telecommunication Union (ITU) 720
International Underwriting Association (IUA) 553
International Whaling Commission 721
internet 492
  glossary of terms 494
  trends and statistics 491
  see also web domain names
Interpol (International Criminal Police Organisation) 718
intestacy 603, 604
Inverclyde
  UK parliament constituency 178
  unitary authority 273, 304
Inverness 303
Inverness, Nairn, Badenoch & Strathspey, UK parliament constituency 178
Inverness East, Nairn & Lochaber, Scottish parliament constituency 252
Investigatory Powers Tribunal 220
investment accounts 549
IOM (International Organisation for Migration) 720
Iowa 1050
IPCC (Independent Police Complaints Commission) 331, 334
Ipswich
  constituency 159
  district council 270, 285
Iran 868
Iraq 870
Iraq War, and NATO 723
Ireland 872
  EU membership 700, 710
  see also Church of Ireland; Northern Ireland
Irish Council of Churches 455
Irish Episcopal Conference 475
Irish-medium schools 361
IRR (International Rail Regulator) 446
ISAs (individual savings accounts) 549
  income tax on 566
Isla de Faisanes 1010
Islam 458
  adherents in UK 455
  see also Muslim calendar
Islamabad 958
Islamic Cultural Centre, London Central Mosque and 535
islands
  England 274
  Scotland 301
  largest 679
Isle of Anglesey *see* Anglesey
Isle of Man *see* Man, Isle of
Isle of Wight *see* Wight, Isle of
Isles of Scilly *see* Scilly, Isles of
Islington
  constituencies 159
  London borough council 271, 296
Islwyn
  constituencies
    UK parliament 174
    Welsh assembly 242
Israel 874
Italy 878
  EU membership 700, 710
ITE (initial teacher education) 369
ITT (initial teacher training) 369
ITU (International Telecommunication Union) 720
ITV 607, 609
  estimated audience share 609
  regions and companies 609
  see also broadcasting
ITV Network Centre/ITV Association 607, 609
IUA (International Underwriting Association) 553

J
Jainism 459
Jakarta 866
Jamaica 880
Jamestown 1074
January 1228
  astronomical phenomena 1228
  calendar 1228
  constellations 1228
  duration of twilight 1229
  high water 1304
  minima of algol 1228
  night sky 1229
  sunrise and sunset 1231
  Moon 1228
    position 1230
  Sun 1229
  Jupiter in 1231
  Mars in 1230
  Mercury in 1230
  Neptune in 1231
  Saturn in 1231
  Uranus in 1231
  Venus in 1230
Japan 881
Japanese calendar 1294
Jarrow
  bishop suffragan 464
  constituency 159
Jehovah's Witnesses 483
Jersey 308
  airport 446
  area 308
  currency 543
  flag 308
  police force 337
  population 17, 308
  water authority 437
Jerusalem 875
Jesus Christ of Latter-Day Saints, Church of 483
Jethou 308
Jewish calendar 1291
  year 2009 9
Jobcentre Plus 201
jobseeker's allowance (JSA)
  contribution-based 429
    weekly rates 429
  income-based 431
    weekly rates 431
Joint Nature Conservation Committee 220
Jordan 884
JSA *see* jobseeker's allowance

Judaism 459
adherents in UK 455
see also Jewish calendar
judge advocates 318
judges
circuit 313, 314, 319
district 314, 319
district (magistrates' courts) *see* district judges (magistrates' courts)
high court 313, 315
judicature
England and Wales 313
Northern Ireland 324
Scotland 321
Judicial Appointments Board for Scotland 323
Judicial Appointments Commission 320
Judicial Committee of the Privy Council 321
judicial separation 587, 588
in Scotland 590
judo
sports results (2007–8) 1209
see also martial arts
Julian calendar 1288
see also Roman calendar
Julian date 1227
Julian period 1294
July 1252
astronomical phenomena 1252
calendar 1252
constellations 1252
duration of twilight 1253
high water 1307
minima of algol 1252
night sky 1253
sunrise and sunset 1255
twilight 1253
Moon 1252
position 1254
Sun 1253
Jupiter in 1255
Mars in 1254
Mercury in 1254
Neptune in 1255
Saturn in 1255
Uranus in 1255
Venus in 1254
June 1248
astronomical phenomena 1248
calendar 1248
constellations 1248
duration of twilight 1249
high water 1306
minima of algol 1248
night sky 1249
sunrise and sunset 1251
Moon 1248
position 1250
Sun 1249
Jupiter in 1251
Mars in 1250
Mercury in 1250
Neptune in 1251
Saturn in 1251
Uranus in 1251
Venus in 1250
Jupiter 1285
satellites 1285
see also months of the year eg January, Jupiter in
jury service 595
justices of the peace
England and Wales 314
Northern Ireland 324
Scotland 321
juvenile courts 324

K

Kabul 735
Kadmi calendar 1294
Kalaallit Nunaat (Greenland), 679, 816
Kampala 1040
Kansas 1050
Kathmandu 942
Kazakhstan 885
Keele University 380
Keeling Islands 750
keeper of the privy purse 27
keepsafe 488
Keighley, constituency 159
Kelvin scale 1316
Kennet, district council 270, 285
Kensington, area bishop 464
Kensington and Chelsea
constituency 159
London borough council 271, 296
Kensington Gardens 534
Kent
county council 269, 283
Kent, Duchess of 25
funding 29
military ranks and titles 33
private secretary 26
Kent, Duke of 25
funding 29
military ranks and titles 33
private secretary 26
Kent, Prince Michael of 25
military ranks and titles 33
private secretary 26
Kent, Princess Michael of 25
private secretary 26
Kent at Canterbury, University of 380
Kentucky 1050
Kenya 887
Kerrier, district council 270, 285
Kerry, bishop (RC) 477
Kettering
constituency 159
district council 270, 285
Kew Royal Botanical Gardens (RBG) 228, 534
Khartoum 1012
Kiev (Kyiv) 1042
Kigali 980
Kildare and Leighlin, bishop (RC) 477
Killala, bishop (RC) 477
Killaloe, bishop (RC) 477
Kilmarnock & Loudoun
constituencies
Scottish parliament 252
UK parliament 178
Kilmore, bishop (RC) 477
Kilmore, Elphin and Ardagh, bishop 472
King Edward Point 1074
kings
British (since 1603) 35
of England (927 to 1603) 34
of Scotland (1016 to 1603) 36
King's Lynn and West Norfolk, district council 270, 285
Kingston & Surbiton, constituency 159
Kingston (Jamaica) 880
Kingston University 381
Kingston upon Hull 278
bishop suffragan 463
constituencies 158
museums and art galleries 524
unitary authority 272, 289
university 380
Kingston upon Thames
area bishop 470
London borough council 271, 296
Kingstown 984
Kingswood, constituency 159
Kinshasa 801
Kiribati 889
Kirkcaldy & Cowdenbeath, UK parliament constituency 178
Kirkcaldy, Scottish parliament constituency 252
Kirklees
metropolitan borough council 272, 288
Kirkwall 301
Knaresborough, bishop suffragan 469
knighthood, orders of 85
knights 85
forms of address 85
listing 86
Knights Bachelor 85
Knowsley
constituencies 159
metropolitan borough council 272, 288
Korea 890
Koror 960
Kuala Lumpur 916
Kuwait 894
Kuwait City (Al-Kuwayt) 894
Kyrgyzstan 896

L

Labour party 135
development 134
representation in House of Commons 128
lacrosse, representative body 643
ladies in their own right 65
forms of address 65
Laeken Declaration 702
La Francophonie 718
Lagan Valley
constituencies
Northern Ireland assembly 260
UK parliament 180
Lake District national park 503
lakes 680
largest 680
in UK 680
deepest 681
in England 274
in Scotland 300
in Wales 297
Lambeth
London borough council 271, 296
Lambeth and Southwark, GLA constituency 238
Lambeth conference 462
Lampeter, University of Wales 386

Lanark & Hamilton East, UK parliament constituency 178
Lancashire
county council 269, 283
Lancashire West, constituency 160
Lancaster & Wyre, constituency 160
Lancaster
bishop (RC) 475
bishop suffragan 465
district council 270, 285
university 381
Lancaster, house of 35
land, UK environmental targets 498
landlords 595
responsibilities 596
Land Registry 199
Lands Tribunal 327
Lands Tribunal for Scotland 327
languages
Manx Gaelic 307
Scottish 300, 364
Welsh 297, 364
Laos 897
La Paz 768
lapsed legatees 602
Larne, district council 273, 306
Latin Union 721
Latvia 899
EU membership 700, 710
Laurence, Timothy 24
law
professional education 393
see also consumer law; employment law
Law Commission 220
law courts and offices 313
England and Wales 313
Northern Ireland 324
Scotland 321
law lords *see* lords of appeal in ordinary
lawn tennis
representative body 643
sports results (2007–8) 1216
law officers 182, 184
law officers' departments 184
Law Society 394
law terms 9
lay magistrates *see* justices of the peace
LDA (London Development Agency) 235
Leader of the House of Commons, Office of 193
leader of the opposition 131
financial support 134
League of Arab States 721
leap year 1287
learndirect 371
learner support funds 367
Learning and Skills Council (LSC) 221, 366, 374
Learning and Teaching Scotland 364
learning disabilities, local authority services 421
leaseholders 596
LEAs (local education authorities) *see* local government
expenditure 357
Lebanon 900
Leeds 278
bishop (RC) 475
constituencies 160
metropolitan borough council 272, 288
museums and art galleries 525
universities 381
Leeds Metropolitan University 381
legal abortion, statistics 19
legal affairs *see* crime and legal affairs
legal aid 597
see also Legal Services Commission; Scottish Legal Aid Board
legal calendar 1292
year 2009 9
legal notes 581
Legal Services Commission 221, 597, 598
Legal Services Ombudsman 332
legal tender
banknotes 543
coins 542
legal year 1292
legatees, lapsed 602
legitimation 595
Leicester 278
bishop 467
constituencies 160
museums and art galleries 525
unitary authority 272, 289
universities 379, 381
Leicestershire
county council 269, 283
Leicestershire North West, constituency 160
Leigh, constituency 160
length
conversion tables 1318
measurement
imperial 1314
metric 1313
obsolete 1317
of roads 449
Lent 1288
Leominster, constituency 160
Lerwick 301
Lesotho 679, 902
letters of administration 603
lettings
business 596
residential 595
Lewes
bishop suffragan 466
constituency 160
district council 270, 285
Lewisham
constituencies 160
London borough council 271, 296
Leyton & Wanstead, constituency 160
LFEPA (London Fire and Emergency Planning Authority) 235
LHA (local housing allowance) 434
Lhasa 796
LHBs (local health boards) 414, 416
Liberal Democrats 135
development 134
financial support 134
representation in House of Commons 128
spokesmen 135
whips 135
Liberal party 134
Liberia 904
Libreville 840
Libya 905
licence, marriage by 599
licences
driving 450
motor vehicles 451
television 608
licensing use of copyright material 605
Lichfield
bishop 467
constituency 160
district council 270, 285
Liechtenstein 907
life expectancy 1046
life insurance 554
lifelong learning 374
life peers 44, 66
forms of address 66
LIFTs (local improvement finance trusts) 415
lighthouse authorities 453
lighting-up time 1279
light rail systems 448
Lihou 308
Lilongwe 914
Lima 966
Limavady, district council 273, 306
Limerick, bishop (RC) 477
Limerick and Killaloe, bishop 473
Lincoln 278
bishop 468
constituency 161
district council 270, 285
museums and art galleries 525
university 381
Lincolnshire
county council 269, 283
Lincoln's Inn 394, 535
Linley, Viscount David Albert Charles 24
Linlithgow & Falkirk East, UK parliament constituency 178
Linlithgow, Scottish parliament constituency 252
liquor, measures of 1315
Lisbon 971
Lisburn, district council 273, 306
listed buildings 515
literature (2007–8) 1152
see also books
Lithuania 908
EU membership 700, 710
Liverpool 279
archbishop (RC) 475
bishop 468
constituencies 161
metropolitan borough council 272, 288
museums and art galleries 525
universities 381
Liverpool Hope University 381
Liverpool John Moores University 381
livery companies 267, 293
Livingston
constituencies
Scottish parliament 252
UK parliament 178
by-election (2005) result 181
Ljubljana 1001
Llandaff, bishop 472
Llanelli
constituencies
UK parliament 174
Welsh assembly 242
Lloyd's List 554

Lloyd's of London 452, 535, 554
Lloyd's Shipping Index 452, 554
loans for students 372
local authority care 421
local education authorities *see* local government
local government 262
Channel Islands 308
civic dignities 264
complaints 263
elections 262
England 264, 274
changes 262
political composition of councils 269
finance 262
internal organisation 262
Isle of Man 307
London 266, 291
Northern Ireland 268, 305, 306
political composition of councils 273
Queen's representatives 264
Scotland 267, 300, 304
changes 262
political composition of councils 273
Wales 267, 297, 299
changes 262
political composition of councils 272
Local Government Boundary Commission for Wales 262
local government ombudsmen
England 263, 332
Wales 264, 333
Scotland 264, 333
local health boards (LHBs) 414, 416
local housing allowance (LHA) 434
local improvement finance trusts (LIFTs) 415
local nature reserves 506
local precedence in Scotland 43
local transport plan (LTP) 448
Loch Lomond and the Trossachs national park 504
lochs *see* lakes
Lomé 1030
London
airports 445, 446
art galleries 525
bishop 464
clubs 646
distances by air from 688
environmental issues 235
local government 266, 291
museums 526
regional government 234
sights 531
theatres 537
universities 377, 379, 380, 381, 384, 385
see also City of London; Corporation of London; Port of London
London assembly 234, 266
committees 235
constituencies 237
members 236
organisational structure 236
party representation 236
role 234
top-up members 238
voting system 234
London borough councils 262, 266, 296
map 290
political composition 271
London Central Mosque and the Islamic Cultural Centre 535
Londonderry (city) 305
Londonderry East
constituencies
Northern Ireland assembly 260
UK parliament 180
London Development Agency (LDA) 235
London European parliament region 311
London Eye 535
London Fire and Emergency Planning Authority (LFEPA) 235
London (Goldsmiths' Hall) date letters 540
London Insurance Market 553
London Marathon 13, 1198
London Metropolitan University 382
London Monument 532
London Planetarium 536
London South Bank University 382
London Stock Exchange 551
London Transport Users' Committee 447
London Underground 447
London Zoo 536
longest day 1227
long-term incapacity benefit 429
long-term insurance 554
lord advocate 321
Lord Chamberlain's Office 28
lord chancellor 127, 131, 313
Lord Chancellor's Department *see* Ministry of Justice
lord chief justice of England and Wales 313
lord great chamberlain 132
lord high admiral of the UK 347
lord high commissioner 473
lord justices of appeal
England and Wales 315
Northern Ireland 324
lord-lieutenants 264
England 282
Northern Ireland 306
Scotland 303
Wales 298
lord mayors 264
Lord Mayor's Day 291
lord mayors of London 266, 291, 292
lord president of the council 193
lord privy seal *see* Office of the Leader of the House of Commons
lord provosts 264, 303
lords 56
courtesy titles 76
forms of address 56
see also House of Lords
lords of appeal in ordinary 313, 315, 44
lords of session 322
lord speaker 131
lords spiritual 75
Lothians Scottish parliament region 254
Loughborough
constituency 161
university 382
Louisiana 1050
Louth & Horncastle, constituency 161
Lowland Scottish language 300
LSC (Learning and Skills Council) 221, 366, 374
LTP (local transport plan) 448
Luanda 741
Ludlow
bishop suffragan 467
constituency 161
luge, representative body 642
lunar cycle 1293
Lundy 274
Lusaka 1064
Lutheran Church 479
Luton
constituencies 161
unitary authority 272, 289
see Bedfordshire, university of
Luxembourg 910
EU membership 700, 710
Luxembourg (City of) 910
Lynn, bishop suffragan 468

M
Maastricht treaty 701, 702, 705, 706
Macao 797
Macclesfield
constituency 161
district council 270, 285
McDonald Islands 751
Macedonia 911
application for EU membership 703
Madagascar 913
Madame Tussaud's 536
Madeira 973
Madrid 1008
Magherafelt, district council 273, 306
magistrates *see* justices of the peace; resident magistrates; stipendiary magistrates
magistrates' courts
England and Wales 314
Northern Ireland 324
magnetic storms 1286
magnetism, terrestrial 1286
Maidenhead, constituency 161
Maidstone & the Weald, constituency 161
Maidstone
bishop suffragan 463
district council 270, 285
mail *see* postal services
Maine 1050
maintenance grant 372
maintenance payments 588
tax relief on 567, 574
major cycle 1293
Majuro 922
Makerfield, constituency 161
Malabo 826
Malankara Orthodox Syrian Church 481
Malawi 914, 919
Malaysia 916
Maldives 679, 918
Maldon & Chelmsford East, constituency 161
Maldon, district council 270, 285
Malé 918
Mali 919
Malta 920
EU membership 700, 710

Malvern Hills, district council 270, 285
Mamoudzou 839
man, development of 1300
Man, Isle of 307
area 307
currency 542, 543
flag 307
police force 337
population 17
water authority 437
Managua 949
Manama (Al-Manamah) 756
Manchester 279
bishop 468
constituencies 161
metropolitan borough council 272, 288
museums and art galleries 526
universities 382, 385
Manchester Metropolitan University 383
Manila 968
manmade lakes, largest 680
Manpower Economics, Office of (OME) 225
Mansfield
constituency 162
district council 270, 285
Manx Gaelic 307
Maputo 936
March 1236
astronomical phenomena 1236
calendar 1236
constellations 1236
duration of twilight 1237
high water 1305
minima of algol 1236
night sky 1237
sunrise and sunset 1239
zodiacal light 1237
Moon 1236
position 1238
Sun 1237
Jupiter in 1239
Mars in 1238
Mercury in 1238
Neptune in 1239
Saturn in 1239
Uranus in 1239
Venus in 1238
Marine and Fisheries Agency 198
Marinecall 453
marine nature reserves 507
marine safety 452
Maritime and Coastguard Agency (MCA) 200, 452
markets in London 532
Marlborough House 536
marquesses 47
courtesy titles 76
forms of address 47
marriage 598
certificates of 583
in England and Wales 599
fees 600
nullity of 588
notice of 599
prohibition 598
in Scotland 600
fees 600
nullity of 591
solemnisation 599
statistics 19
Mars 1285
satellites 1285
see also months of the year eg January, Mars in
Marshall Islands 922
marshals of the RAF 352
martial arts
representative bodies 643
see also judo
Martinique 838
Maryland 1050
Maseru 902
masonic year 1294
mass
conversion tables 1318
measurement
imperial 1314
metric 1314
of the Earth 677
Massachusetts 1050
master of the household's department 27
master of the rolls 314, 315
Mata-Utu 840
maternity allowance (MA) 431
weekly rates 431
maternity leave 592
maternity pay 592
maternity rights 592
Maundy money 542
Maundy Thursday 1288
Mauritania 923
Mauritius 924
May 1244
astronomical phenomena 1244
calendar 1244
constellations 1244
duration of twilight 1245
high water 1306
minima of algol 1244
night sky 1245
sunrise and sunset 1247
Moon 1244
position 1246
Sun 1245
Jupiter in 1247
Mars in 1246
Mercury in 1246
Neptune in 1247
Saturn in 1247
Uranus in 1247
Venus in 1246
mayor of London 234
election results (2008) 236
role 234
salary 235
voting system 234
mayors 264
Mayotte 839
Mbabane 1016
MCA (Maritime and Coastguard Agency) 200, 452
mean and sidereal time 1278
mean refraction 1284
mean solar time 1281
measurement of time 1287
measures *see* weights and measures
Meath, bishop (RC) 477
Meath and Kildare, bishop 473
Meat Hygiene Service 202
medals, decorations and 117
media 607
see also arts and the media
Media, Department for Culture, Sport and *see* Department for Culture, Media and Sport
medical insurance 555
Medical Research Council (MRC) 409
medical treatment abroad 698
medicine
professional education 389
professions supplementary to, professional education 390
Medicines and Healthcare Products Regulatory Agency (MHRA) 198
Medway
constituency 162
unitary authority 272, 289
Meirionnydd Nant Conwy
constituencies
UK parliament 174
Welsh assembly 242
Melilla 1010
Melton, district council 270, 285
members of parliament *see* MPs
members of the European parliament *see* MEPs
member states of the EU 700
Mendip, district council 270, 285
Menevia, bishop (RC) 476
mental handicaps *see* learning disabilities
Mental Health Act Commission 221
Mental Health Review Tribunals 327
mentally ill people, local authority services 421
MEPs 706
political groupings 706, 710
UK 310
MERCOSUR 721
Mercury 1285
see also months of the year eg January, Mercury in
Meriden, constituency 162
Merit, Order of 83
Mersey Queensway Tunnel 684
Merthyr Tydfil & Rhymney
constituencies
UK parliament 175
Welsh assembly 242
Merthyr Tydfil
unitary authority 273, 299
Merton
London borough council 271, 296
Merton and Wandsworth, GLA constituency 238
Mesozoic era 1300
meteors
in August 1257
in December 1273
Methodist Church 479
Methodist Church in Ireland 480
metonic (lunar, or minor) cycle 1293
metric units 1313
metropolitan borough councils 262, 265, 288
functions 265
map 290
political composition 272
Metropolitan Police Authority (MPA) 235
Metropolitan Police Service 337
rates of pay 335
metro systems 448
Mexico 926
Mexico City 926

MHRA (Medicines and Healthcare Products Regulatory Agency) 198
MI5 (Security Service) 204
MI6 (Secret Intelligence Service) 204
Michigan 1050
Micronesia, Federated States of 928
Mid and West Wales Welsh assembly region 244
Mid Bedfordshire, district council 270, 285
Mid Devon, district council 270, 285
Middle East, events (2007–8) 1107
Middlesbrough
  bishop (RC) 476
  constituencies 162
  unitary authority 272, 289
middle schools 362
Middlesex University 383
Middle Temple 394, 535
Middleton, bishop suffragan 468
Midlothian
  constituencies
    Scottish parliament 252
    UK parliament 178
  unitary authority 273, 304
Mid Suffolk, district council 270, 285
Mid Sussex, district council 270, 285
MIGA (Multilateral Investment Guarantee Agency) 733
military officers *see* officers
military ranks and titles of the royal family 31
million, definition 1315
Milton Keynes
  constituencies 162
  unitary authority 272, 289
minima of algol 1279
  see also months of the year eg January, minima of algol
ministers of state 182
  salaries 184
Ministry of Defence 344, 345
Ministry of Defence Police 338
Ministry of Justice (MoJ) 192
  executive agencies 199
Minnesota 1050
minor cycle 1293
Minsk 760
Miquelon, St Pierre and 839
Missing Persons Bureau 335
Mississippi 1050
Missouri 1050
Mitcham & Morden, constituency 162
MLA (Museums, Libraries and Archives Council) 221, 523
mobile communications 485
  health implications of mobile phone use 486
  phone use and driving 486
  regulation 486
MoD *see* Ministry of Defence
moderator of the general assembly 473
modern pentathlon, representative body 643
Mogadishu 1004
MoJ *see* Ministry of Justice
Moldova 929
Mole Valley
  constituency 162
  district council 270, 286
Monaco 930
Monaco (city of) 930
the monarchy 125
  see also royal family
Mongolia 931
Monmouth
  bishop 472
  constituencies
    UK parliament 175
    Welsh assembly 243
Monmouthshire
  unitary authority 273, 299
Monrovia 904
Montana 1050
Montenegro 933
Montevideo 1054
Montgomeryshire
  constituencies
    UK parliament 175
    Welsh assembly 243
months
  definition 1287
  Hindu 1290
  Jewish 1291
  Muslim 1292
Montserrat 1073
the Monument 532
monuments
  in London 532
  see also historic buildings and monuments
Moon 1279, 1280
  see also months of the year eg January, Moon
moonrise 1281
  calculation 1277
moonset 1281
  calculation 1277
Moray
  constituencies
    Scottish parliament 252
    UK parliament 178
  unitary authority 273, 304
Moray, Ross and Caithness, bishop 472
Morecambe & Lunesdale, constituency 162
Morley & Rothwell, constituency 162
Mormons 483
Morocco 934
Moroni 800
Moscow 976
Mothering Sunday 1289
Motherwell & Wishaw
  constituencies
    Scottish parliament 252
    UK parliament 178
Motherwell, bishop (RC) 476
motorcycling, sports results (2007–8) 1210
motor racing, sports results (2007–8) 1211
motor rallying, sports results (2007–8) 1211
motor sports, representative bodies 643
motor vehicles
  licences 450
  road use 449
MOT testing 452
mountaineering, representative body 643
mountain ranges, longest 679
mountains, highest 680
moveable feasts to year 2035 1289
Moyle, district council 273, 306
Mozambique 936
MPA (Metropolitan Police Authority) 235
MPs
  eligibility 128
  listing 137
  pay and allowances 128
  pensions 129
MRC (Medical Research Council) 409
MSPs 246
Mt Everest 680
Multilateral Investment Guarantee Agency (MIGA) 733
multi-sport bodies 644
Muscat (Masqat) 956
Museum of London 221
museums 523
  England 523
  Northern Ireland 530
  Scotland 529
  Wales 528
  see also names of individual museums eg British Museum
Museums Association 523
Museums, Libraries and Archives Council (MLA) 221
music
  year (2007–8) 1157
    classical music *see* classical music
    pop music *see* pop music
music therapies, professional education 390
Muslim calendar 1292
  year 2009 9
  see also Islam
Myanmar 938

N

NAA (National Assessment Agency) 364
NAC (North Atlantic Council) 722
NAFTA (North American free trade agreement) 722
Na h-Eileanan an Iar, constituency 178
Nairobi 887
Namibia 940
nanotechnology 493
Napier University 383
Nassau 754
national academies of scholarship 406
National Air Traffic Services (NATS) 445
National Archives 199
National Army Museum 221
national assembly for Wales *see* Welsh assembly
National Assessment Agency (NAA) 364
National Audit Office 130
National Care Standards Commission (NCSC) 420
National College for School Leadership 368
National Consumer Council (NCC) 221
National Council for Education and Training (ELWa) 364
national courses 366
National Crime Squad (NCS) *see* Serious Organised Crime Agency

National Criminal Intelligence Service (NCIS) *see* Serious Organised Crime Agency
national curriculum 363
  assessment 363
national daily newspapers
  circulation 619
  listing 620
National Endowment for Science, Technology and the Arts (NESTA) 222
National Film Theatre 536
national flag of the UK 23
National Forest 506
National Forest Company 506
National Galleries of Scotland 222
National Gallery 222
National Grid Transco plc 442
National Health Service *see* NHS
National Heritage Memorial Fund 222
national hunt horse racing results (2007–8) 1206
National Institute of Adult Continuing Education (NIACE) 374
national insurance (NI) 422
National Library of Scotland 222
National Library of Wales 223
National Lottery Commission 223
National Maritime Museum 223
national museums and art galleries 523
  see also names of individual museums and galleries eg British Museum
National Museums and Galleries Northern Ireland 223
National Museums Liverpool 223
National Museums Scotland 223
National Museum Wales – Amgueddfa Cymru 224
national nature reserves 506
National Offender Management Service (NOMS) 339
national park authorities (NPAs) 502
National Parking Adjudication Service 328
national parks 502
  funding 502
  membership 502
National Physical Laboratory (NPL) 1282, 1283
National Physical Laboratory (NPL) 410
National Policing Improvement Agency (NPIA) 335
National Portrait Gallery 224
national professional qualification for headship (NPQH) 368
National Public Health Service 414
national qualifications 366, 367
National Rail Enquiries 447
National Savings and Investments 200, 544, 549
national scenic areas 505
National School of Government 203
National Statistics, Office for 563
national Sunday newspapers, circulation 619
National Trust, list of properties 522
National Trust for Scotland, list of properties 521
national vocational qualifications (NVQs) 365
National Weights and Measures Laboratory 198
NATO 722
  and Afghanistan 723
  and the Iraq War 723
  post-Cold War developments 723
  structure 722
NATO-Russia Council (NRC) 723
NATS (National Air Traffic Services) 445
Natural England 224, 502, 504, 506
natural environment, conservation 1140
Natural Environment Research Council (NERC) 410
natural gas *see* gas
Natural History Museum 224
naturalisation 584
natural parents, tracing 582
nature reserves 506
Nauru 941
nautical measures 1315
nautical twilight 1280
  see also months of the year eg January, twilight
navy *see* Royal Navy
Naypyidaw 938
NCC (National Consumer Council) 221
NCSC (National Care Standards Commission) 420
NDA (Nuclear Decommissioning Authority) 444
N'Djaména 790
Neath
  constituencies
    UK parliament 175
    Welsh assembly 243
Neath Port Talbot
  unitary authority 273, 299
Nebraska 1050
Nepal 942
Neptune 1285
  satellites 1285
  see also months of the year eg January, Neptune in
NERC (Natural Environment Research Council) 410
NESTA (National Endowment for Science, Technology and the Arts) 222
NETA (new electricity trading arrangements) 442
netball
  representative bodies 644
  sports results (2007–8) 1211
Netherlands, 679, 944
  EU membership 700, 710
  overseas territories 946
Netherlands Antilles 946
network operators 485
Network Rail 446, 447
  timetabling service 447
Nevada 1050
Nevis, St Kitts and 982
Newark, constituency 162
Newark and Sherwood, district council 270, 286
Newbury, constituency 162
New Caledonia 839
Newcastle-under-Lyme
  constituency 162
  district council 270, 286
Newcastle upon Tyne 279
  bishop 468
  constituencies 162
  metropolitan borough council 272, 288
  museums and art galleries 527
  universities 383
New Church 482
new deal for lone parents 433
New Delhi 863
New Forest, constituencies 162
New Forest, district council 270, 286
New Forest national park 503
Newham
  London borough council 271, 296
New Hampshire 1050
New Jersey 1050
New Mexico 1050
Newport
  constituencies
    UK parliament 175
    Welsh assembly 243
  unitary authority 273, 299
  University of Wales 386
Newry & Armagh
  constituencies
    Northern Ireland assembly 261
    UK parliament 180
Newry and Mourne, district council 273, 306
New South Wales 748
newspapers 619
Newtownabbey, district council 273, 306
New Year 1292
New York (state) 1050
New Zealand 947
  associated states 949
  territories 948
next steps programme 184
NFFO (non-fossil fuel obligation renewables orders) 444
NHS 413
  complaints procedure 419
  employees and salaries 415
  finance 415
  health services 416
  reciprocal arrangements 419
  structure 413
  waiting lists 418
NHS 24 417
NHS charters 418
NHS Direct 417
NHS Pay Review Body 225
NHS plan 415
NHS Purchasing and Supply Agency 198
NHS Tribunal (Scotland) 328
NHS trusts 413
  in Wales 414
NHS walk-in centres 416
NIACE (National Institute of Adult Continuing Education) 374
Niamey 951
NIAUR (Northern Ireland Authority for Utility Regulation) 257
Nicaragua 949
NICF (Northern Ireland consolidated fund) 306
Nicosia 810
Niger 951
Nigeria 952

night, definition 1287
night sky *see months of the year* eg January, night sky
Niue 949
NMC (Nursing and Midwifery Council) 392
NOMS (National Offender Management Service) 339
Non-Christian religions and beliefs 456
non-contributary benefits 431
non-domestic rates 263, 266
non-fossil fuel obligation (NFFO) renewables orders 444
non-hereditary peers *see* life peers
non-ministerial government departments 201
non-Trinitarian churches 483
non-vehicular tunnelling, longest 684
Nordic Council 722
nordic events, sports results (2007–8) 1211
Norfolk
  constituencies 163
  county council 269, 283
Norfolk Island 751
Normandy, house of 34
Normanton, constituency 163
North America, geographical statistics 678
North American free trade agreement (NAFTA) 722
Northampton
  bishop (RC) 476
  constituencies 163
  district council 270, 286
  university 383
Northamptonshire
  county council 269, 283
North Atlantic Council (NAC) 722
North Atlantic treaty 722
North Atlantic Treaty Organisation *see* NATO
Northavon, constituency 163
North Ayrshire
  unitary authority 273, 304
North Carolina 1050
North Cornwall, district council 270, 286
North Dakota 1050
North Devon, district council 270, 286
North Dorset, district council 270, 286
North Down, district council 273, 306
North East, GLA constituency 238
North East Derbyshire, district council 270, 286
North East European parliament region 311
North East Lincolnshire
  unitary authority 272, 289
North East Wales Institute of Higher Education 386
Northern Cyprus, Turkish Republic of 812
Northern Ireland
  area 17, 305
  areas of outstanding natural beauty (AONBs) 505
  banknotes 543
  constituencies (UK parliament) 179
  constitutional history 305
  flag 305
  historic buildings and monuments 522
  judicature 324
  local government *see* local government
  museums and art galleries 530
  national parks 504
  NHS structure 415
  passenger transport services 449
  police force *see* Police Service of Northern Ireland
  population statistics 17, 305
  principal cities 305
  prison establishments 343
  public holidays 1293
  regional government 256
  water industry 439
Northern Ireland assembly 126, 257
  constituencies 258
  departments and executive agencies 256
  members 257
  political composition 258
  salaries 257
Northern Ireland Audit Office 256
Northern Ireland Authority for Utility Regulation (NIAUR) 257
Northern Ireland commissioner for complaints 264
Northern Ireland consolidated fund (NICF) 306
Northern Ireland Council for the Curriculum, Examinations and Assessment (CCEA) 365
Northern Ireland Court Service 324
Northern Ireland Democratic Unionist party *see* Democratic Unionist party
Northern Ireland Electricity plc 442
Northern Ireland Environment and Heritage Service, list of properties 522
Northern Ireland European parliament region 311
Northern Ireland Executive 256
Northern Ireland Human Rights Commission 225
Northern Ireland Office 192
  executive agencies 199
Northern Ireland Prison Service 343
  operating costs 340
  salaries 343
Northern Ireland Tourist Board 231
Northern Lighthouse Board 225, 453
Northern Mariana Islands 1051, 1054
Northern Territory 748
North Hertfordshire, district council 270, 286
North Kesteven, district council 270, 286
North Korea *see* Democratic People's Republic of Korea
North Lanarkshire
  unitary authority 273, 304
North Lincolnshire
  unitary authority 272, 289
North Norfolk, district council 270, 286
North Shropshire, district council 270, 286
North Somerset
  unitary authority 272, 289
North Tyneside
  metropolitan borough council 272, 288
Northumberland
  county council 269, 283
Northumberland national park 503
Northumbria University at Newcastle 383
North Wales Welsh assembly region 244
North Warwickshire, district council 270, 286
North West European parliament region 312
North West Leicestershire, district council 270, 286
North Wiltshire, district council 270, 286
North York Moors national park 503
North Yorkshire
  county council 269, 283
Norway 954
  territories 956
Norwegian Antarctic Territory 956
Norwich 279
  bishop 468
  constituencies 163
  district council 270, 286
notice of marriage 599
Nottingham 280
  bishop (RC) 476
  constituencies 163
  museums and art galleries 527
  unitary authority 272, 289
  universities 383
Nottinghamshire
  county council 269
Nottingham Trent University 383
Nouakchott 923
Nouméa 839
November 1268
  astronomical phenomena 1268
  calendar 1268
  constellations 1268
  duration of twilight 1269
  high water 1309
  minima of algol 1268
  night sky 1269
  sunrise and sunset 1271
  Moon 1268
    position 1270
  Sun 1269
  Jupiter in 1271
  Mars in 1271
  Mercury in 1270
  Neptune in 1271
  Saturn in 1271
  Uranus in 1271
  Venus in 1270
NPAs (national park authorities) 502
NPIA (National Policing Improvement Agency) 335
NPL (National Physical Laboratory) 410, 1282, 1283
NPQH (national professional qualification for headship) 368
NRC (NATO-Russia Council) 723
nuclear forces 345
nuclear power 443
Nuclear Safety Directorate 444
Nuku'alofa 1031
nullity of marriage 588
  in Scotland 591
Nuneaton, constituency 163

Nuneaton and Bedworth, district council 270, 286
Nursing and Midwifery Council (NMC) 392
Nursing and Other Health Professions Review Body *see* NHS Pay Review Body
nursing staff
  professional education 391
  salaries 416
NVQs (national vocational qualifications) 365
Nyasaland *see* Malawi

O

Oadby and Wigston, district council 270, 286
OAPEC (Organisation of Arab Petroleum Exporting Countries) 724
OAS (Organisation of American States) 724
OAU (Organisation of African Unity) 711
obituaries 1111
Occupational Pensions Regulatory Authority (OPRA) *see* Pensions Regulator
occupational therapy, professional education 391
oceans, area and depth 677
Ochil & Perthshire South, UK parliament constituency 178
Ochil, Scottish parliament constituency 252
OCPA (Office of the Commissioner for Public Appointments) 187
OCSC (Office of the Civil Service Commissioners) 187
October 1264
  astronomical phenomena 1264
  calendar 1264
  constellations 1264
  duration of twilight 1265
  high water 1308
  minima of algol 1264
  night sky 1265
  sunrise and sunset 1267
  Moon 1264
    position 1266
  Sun 1265
  Jupiter in 1267
  Mars in 1266
  Mercury in 1266
  Neptune in 1267
  Saturn in 1267
  Uranus in 1267
  Venus in 1266
OECD (Organisation for Economic Cooperation and Development) 723
OFCOM (Office of Communications) 225, 607, 612
Office for National Statistics (ONS) 563
Office for Standards in Education, Children's Services and Skills (OFSTED) 203, 359, 420
Office of Communications (OFCOM) 225, 607, 612
Office of Fair Trading (OFT) 203
Office of Gas and Electricity Markets (OFGEM) 203, 443
Office of Government Commerce (OGC) 195
Office of Manpower Economics (OME) 225
Office of Public Sector Information (OPSI) 199
Office of Rail Regulation (ORR) 203, 446, 447
Office of the Advocate-General for Scotland 193
Office of the Civil Service Commissioners (OCSC) 187
Office of the Commissioner for Public Appointments (OCPA) 187
Office of the Leader of the House of Commons 193
Office of the Legal Services Ombudsman 332
Office of the Public Guardian 199
Office of the Qualifications and Examinations Regulator (OFQUAL) 363, 364
Office of the Telecommunications Ombudsman (Otelo) 332
officers
  salaries 354
  service retired pay 356
offices of the royal household 27
Official Roll of the Baronetage 85
OFGEM (Office of Gas and Electricity Markets) 203, 443
Oflot (Office of the National Lottery) *see* National Lottery Commission
OFQUAL (Office of the Qualifications and Examinations Regulator) 363, 364
OFSTED (Office for Standards in Education, Children's Services and Skills) 203, 359, 420
OFT (Office of Fair Trading) 203
OFWAT (Water Services Regulation Authority) 205, 438
OGC Buying Solutions 200
OGC (Office of Government Commerce) 195
Ogilvy, the Hon. Lady *see* Alexandra, Princess
Ogilvy, the Rt. Hon. Sir Angus 25
Ogmore
  constituencies
    UK parliament 175
    Welsh assembly 243
Ohio 1050
ohms 1314
OIC (Organisation of the Islamic Conference) 725
oil 440
Ojos del Salado 680
Oklahoma 1050
'Old Bailey' 534
Old Bexley & Sidcup, constituency 163
older people, local authority services 420
Oldham
  constituencies 163
  metropolitan borough council 272, 288
Olympiads 1294
Olympic Games (2008) 1217
  gold medallists 1217
  medal table 1220
Omagh, district council 273, 306
Oman 956
The Ombudsman Service Limited (TOSL) 332
ombudsmen
  energy 332
  estate agents 332
  European 331
  financial 426, 544, 548, 552
  health service 332, 419
  housing 331
  local government 263, 332, 333
  Northern Ireland assembly 331
  Northern Ireland police 334
  parliamentary 332
  pensions 332, 426, 548
  prisons and probation 333
  public services
    Scotland 333
    Wales 333
  surveyors 332
  telecommunications 332
  legal services 332
  waterways 333
OME (Office of Manpower Economics) 225
online art museum 523
ONS (Office for National Statistics) 204
OPAS (Pensions Advisory Service) 426
OPEC (Organisation of the Petroleum Exporting Countries) 725
open spaces of London 533
Open University 370, 383
  admissions 372
opera (2007–8) 1165
  productions 1168
ophthalmic services, NHS 417
opposition 134
  leader *see* leader of the opposition
  shadow cabinet 134
opposition days 132
opposition parties, financial support 134
OPRA (Occupational Pensions Regulatory Authority) *see* Pensions Regulator
OPSI (Office of Public Sector Information) 199
optometry and dispensing optics, professional education 392
Oranjestad 946
order of succession 25
orders of chivalry 82
orders of knighthood 85
ordinary adoption leave 592
ordinary maternity leave 592
ordination of women 462
Ordnance Survey 197
Oregon 1050
Organisation for Economic Cooperation and Development (OECD) 723
Organisation for Security and Cooperation in Europe (OSCE) 724
Organisation of African Unity (OAU) 711
Organisation of American States (OAS) 724
Organisation of Arab Petroleum Exporting Countries (OAPEC) 724
Organisation of the Black Sea Economic Cooperation (BSEC) 725

Organisation of the Islamic Conference (OIC) 725
Organisation of the Petroleum Exporting Countries (OPEC) 725
Oriental Orthodox churches 480
orienteering, representative body 644
Orkney 301
  Scottish parliament constituency 253
  unitary authority 273, 304
Orkney & Shetland, UK parliament constituency 178
Orpington, constituency 163
ORR (Office of Rail Regulation) 203, 446, 447
Orthodox churches 480
  calendar 1288
orthoptics, professional education 391
orthotics, professional education 391
OSCE (Organisation for Security and Cooperation in Europe) 724
Oslo 954
Ossory, bishop (RC) 477
osteopathy, professional education 392
Oswestry, district council 270, 286
Otelo (Office of the Telecommunications Ombudsman) 332
Ottawa 784
Ouagadougou 778
outdoor bowls, sports results (2007–8) 1200
outer house, court of session 322
out-of-hours (OOH) care 416
output tax 578
overseas clergy 473
overseas postal services 487
overseas travel 697
Oxford 280
  bishop 469
  constituencies 164
  district council 270, 286
  museums and art galleries 527
  universities 383
Oxford Brookes University 384
Oxfordshire
  county council 269

P

Pacific, Australasia and, events (2007–8) 1104
Pacific Islands Forum (PIF) 725
Paganism 460
Pago Pago 1051, 1053
Paisley & Renfrewshire, UK parliament constituencies 179
Paisley
  bishop (RC) 476
  Scottish parliament constituencies 253
  university 384
Pakistan 958
Palaeozoic era 1300
Palau 960
Palestinian Autonomous Areas 877
Palikir 928
palliative care 418
Palma 1010
Palm Sunday 1288
PALS (patients advice and liaison service) 419
Panama 961
Panama City 961
Panel on Takeovers and Mergers 548
Papeete 839
paper measures 1316
Papua New Guinea 963
Parades Commission 225
Paraguay 964
Paramaribo 1014
paramedical services, professional education 391
Parcelforce Worldwide 486, 488
parcel rates 487
parental leave 592
parental responsibility 594
parental rights 592
parents
  adults living with 20
  tracing natural 582
Paris 836
parish councils 265
Parker Bowles, Camilla *see* Camilla, Duchess of Cornwall
parks of London 533
parliament 125
  glossary of aspects of work 131
  public acts (2007–8) 1176
  white papers (2007–8) 1178
  year (2007–8) 1170
  see also Houses of Parliament
Parliament Acts 1911 and 1949 132
parliamentary annuities 29
Parliamentary Archives 133
parliamentary commissioner for administration 332
parliamentary constituencies *see* constituencies
Parliamentary Ombudsman 332
parliamentary privilege 132
Parole Board for England and Wales 226
Parole Board for Scotland 226
Particle Physics and Astronomy Research Council (PPARC) *see* STFC
parties, political *see* political parties
partnership and cooperation agreements (PCAs) 703
partnership for peace programme (PFP) 723
partnerships for health 415
Partners in Population and Development 726
party of Wales *see* Plaid Cymru
passenger numbers
  by air 445
  by sea 453
passport applications and regulations 488, 697
Passport Service 198
Patent Office *see* UK Intellectual Property Office
patents 606
patents court 316
paternity leave 592
paternity pay 592
patients advice and liaison service (PALS) 419
patient's charter 418
patriarchates
  of the Eastern Orthodox Church 480
  of the Oriental Orthodox churches 480
pay as you earn (PAYE) system 568
payment clearings 544
PCAs (partnership and cooperation agreements) 703
PCC (Press Complaints Commission) 619
PCTs *see* primary care trusts
peacekeeping forces, UN 729
Peak District national park 503
peerage 44
  disclaimed 45
  extinct since last edition 44
  hereditary 44, 46
  hereditary women 44
  life 44, 66
  membership of the House of Lords 126
  minors 45
peers of the blood royal 46
  forms of address 46
peers' surnames 77
Pembrokeshire
  unitary authority 273, 299
Pembrokeshire Coast national park 503
Pendle
  constituency 164
  district council 270, 286
peninsulas, largest 678
Pennsylvania 1050
Peñôn de Alhucemas 1010
Peñôn de la Gomera (Peñôn de Velez) 1010
Penrith & the Border, constituency 164
Penrith, bishop suffragan 465
pension credit 432, 433
  weekly rates 434
Pension Protection Fund (PPF) 226, 547
pensions 424, 554
  armed forces 356
  complaints 426
  MPs 129
  tax relief on contributions 568
  see also state pension scheme; war pensions
Pensions, Department for Work and *see* Department for Work and Pensions
Pensions Advisory Service (OPAS) 426
Pensions Appeal Tribunals 328
Pensions Appeal Tribunals for Scotland 328
Pension Service 201, 425
Pensions Ombudsman 332, 426, 548
Pensions Regulator 226, 426
Pentecost 1289
  Sunday after 1289
Pentecostal churches 481
Penwith, district council 270, 286
people's question time 234
People's Republic of China *see* China
PEPs (personal equity plans) 566
periodicals 623
periodic table 1319
personal equity plans (PEPs) 566
personal medical service (PMS) pilots 416
personal pension schemes 425
personal social services 420
  staff 420
Perth & Perthshire North, UK parliament constituency 179

Perth, Scottish parliament
constituency 253
Perth and Kinross
unitary authority 273, 304
Peru 966
Peterborough
bishop 469
constituency 164
unitary authority 272, 289
PFI (private finance initiative) 415
PFP (partnership for peace programme) 723
PGCE (postgraduate certificate in education) 368, 373, 394
pharmaceutical services, NHS 416
pharmacy, professional education 392
Philip, Prince 24
funding 29
military ranks and titles 31
private secretary 26
Philippines 967
Philips, Mark 24
Phnom Penh 781
physiotherapy, professional education 391
PIF (Pacific Islands Forum) 725
Pitcairn Islands 1074
Plaid Cymru 135
development 134
financial support 134
representation in House of Commons 128
planets *see individual planets* eg Mercury; transit of
planning, town and country 600
Planning Inspectorate 197
Plantagenets 34
plants, protected 511
PLA (Port of London Authority) 536
platinum hallmarks 539
Pluto
satellites 1285
Plymouth
bishop (RC) 476
bishop suffragan 466
constituencies 164
unitary authority 272, 289
university 384
museums and art galleries 527
Plymouth Brethren 477
Plymouth (Montserrat) 1073
PMRAFNS (Princess Mary's Royal Air Force Nursing Service) 353
PMS (personal medical service) pilots 416
PNB (Police Negotiating Board) 226
pneumoconiosis, byssinosis and miscellaneous diseases benefit scheme 435
podcasting 610
Podgorica 933
podiatry, professional education 390
poet laureate 29
Poland 969
EU membership 700, 710
polar diameter and circumference 677
Police Advisory Board for England and Wales 226
Police Complaints Authority *see* Independent Police Complaints Commission (IPCC)
Police Complaints Commissioner for Scotland 334
Police Negotiating Board (PNB) 226
Police Ombudsman for Northern Ireland 334
police service 334
complaints 334
national police services 335
police authorities 334
police forces 336
rates of pay 335
staff associations 338
Police Service of Northern Ireland 337
rates of pay 335
political parties 133
development 134
in the European parliament 710
representation in House of Commons 128
representation in House of Lords 127
polo
representative body 644
sports results (2007–8) 1212
Polynesia, French 839
Ponta Delgada 973
Pontefract & Castleford, constituency 164
Pontefract, bishop suffragan 471
Pontypridd
constituencies
UK parliament 175
Welsh assembly 243
Poole
constituency 164
unitary authority 272, 289
the Pope 474
Poplar & Canning Town, constituency 164
pop music (2007–8) 1162
awards 1164
population
UK statistics 17
England 17, 274
Northern Ireland 17, 305
Scotland 17, 300
Wales 17, 297
of prisons 339
Port-au-Prince 857
Port Louis 924
Port Moresby 963
Port of London 536
Port of London Authority (PLA) 536
Port of Spain 1032
Porto Novo 765
ports 452
Portsmouth
bishop 469
bishop (RC) 476
constituencies 164
unitary authority 272, 289
university 384
museums and art galleries 527
Portugal 971
autonomous regions 973
EU membership 700, 710
Port Vila 1057
Porvoo declaration 456
post-16 education 366
expenditure 357
financial support 367
postal services 486
Postal Services Commission (Postcomm) 204, 486
postal votes 602
postcode enquiries 488
Postcomm (Postal Services Commission) 204, 486
post-experience short courses 372
postgraduate certificate in education (PGCE) 368, 394
postgraduate students' allowances scheme (PSAS) 373
postgraduate studies 371
admissions 372
awards 373
Post Office 488
Post Office (PO) box 488
Postwatch 486
pound sterling 542
purchasing power 563
Powys
unitary authority 273, 299
PPARC (Particle Physics and Astronomy Research Council) *see* STFC
PPF (Pension Protection Fund) 226, 547
PQH(NI) (professional qualification for headship in Northern Ireland) 369
Prague 812
Praia 787
precedence 42
premium bonds 549
Presbyterian Church in Ireland 481
Presbyterian Church of Wales 481
presbyteries of the Church of Scotland 474
pre-school education 362
prescription charge system 416
Preseli Pembrokeshire
constituencies
UK parliament 175
Welsh assembly 243
presidency of the EC 707
president of the courts of England and Wales 313
the press 619
complaints 619
newspapers 619
periodicals 623
self-regulation 619
Press Complaints Commission (PCC) 619
Preston
constituency 164
district council 270, 286
museums and art galleries 527
Pretoria 1006
pricing in proportion 486
Prikaspiyskaya Nizmennost' 679
primary and community healthcare 416
primary care trusts (PCTs) 413, 416
primary education 362
expenditure 357
primary fuels 440
primary medical services 416
primates
overseas 473
see also archbishops
prime minister 182
office of 133
residence 534
salary 184
Prime Minister's Office 187
prime minister's questions 132
primus of the Scottish Episcopal Church 472

princes *see individual princes* eg Andrew, Prince
princes of Wales 38
see also Charles, Prince of Wales
princesses *see individual princesses* eg Kent, Princess Michael of
princesses royal 38
see also Anne, Princess
Princess Mary's Royal Air Force Nursing Service (PMRAFNS) 353
Principe, Sao Tome and 987
printing paper, measures of 1316
Prisons and Probation Ombudsman for England and Wales 333
prison service 339
complaints 339
inmate population 339
inspectorates 339
operating costs 340
prison establishments 339, 340
private sector 339
self-inflicted deaths 340
Prison Service Pay Review Body (PSPRB) 226
private bills 132
private finance initiative (PFI) 415
private medical insurance 555
private member's bills 132
private notice questions 132
private patients in the NHS 418
private pension schemes 425
private secretaries to the royal family 26
Private Secretary's Office 27
privilege of parliament 132
Privy Council 122, 125
members 122
forms of address 122
see also Judicial Committee of the Privy Council
Privy Council Office 193
Privy Council of Northern Ireland 124
privy purse 27, 30
probate 603
proceedings against the crown 586
Procurator Fiscal Service 321, 322, 323
professional education 387
EU recognition 387
professional qualification for headship in Northern Ireland (PQH(NI)) 369
prosthetics, professional education 391
protection of children 421
provosts 264
proxy, voting by 602
PSAS (postgraduate students' allowances scheme) 373
PSPRB (Prison Service Pay Review Body) 226
Psychology, professional education 393
public acts of parliament (2007–8) 1176
public bills 132
public bodies 206
public examinations and qualifications
higher education 359
secondary education 365
for teachers 368
vocational 365, 366
Public Guardianship Office (PGO) *see* Office of the Public Guardian
public holidays 1293
year 2009 10
year 2010 11
public lending right system 227
public prosecutions, director of *see* director of public prosecutions
public sector finances 557
Public Services Ombudsman for Wales 333
publishers 630
Pudsey, constituency 164
Puerto Barquerizo Moreno 822
Puerto Rico 1051, 1053
Puffin Island 274
pupils 358
number at independent schools 396
with statements of special needs 363
pupil-teacher ratios 358
Purbeck, district council 270, 286
purchasing power of the pound 563
Putney, constituency 164
Pyongyang 891

Q
QAA (Quality Assurance Agency for Higher Education) 360, 371
QARANC (Queen Alexandra's Royal Army Nursing Corps) 351
QARNNS (Queen Alexandra's Royal Naval Nursing Service) 348
Qatar 973
QCA (Qualifications and Curriculum Authority) 363, 365
QTS (qualified teacher status) 368
quadrillion, definition 1315
Quakerism 481
qualifications *see* public examinations and qualifications
Qualifications, Curriculum and Assessment Authority for Wales (ACCAC) 364
Qualifications and Curriculum Authority (QCA) 363, 365
qualified teacher status (QTS) 368
Quality Assurance Agency for Higher Education (QAA) 360, 371
quarter days 1293
year 2009 9
Queen, the *see* Elizabeth II
Queen Alexandra's Royal Army Nursing Corps (QARANC) 351
Queen Alexandra's Royal Naval Nursing Service (QARNNS) 348
Queen Elizabeth II Conference Centre 197
Queen Maud Land 956
queens
of England (927–1603) 34
of Scotland (1016 to 1603) 36
British (since 1603) 35
Queen's bench division of the high court of justice 313, 316
Queensland 748
Queen's Messengers, Corps of 198
Queen's representatives in local government 264
Queen's University Belfast 384
question time 132
Quito 821

R
Rabat 934
RAB (Radio Advertising Bureau) 612
rackets
representative body 644
sports results (2007–8) 1212
radio 609
see also broadcasting (2007–8)
Radio 1 610
Radio 2 610
Radio 3 610
Radio 4 610
Radio Advertising Bureau (RAB) 612
Radio Authority (RA) 612
RadioCentre 612
Radio Five Live 610
Radio Five Live Sports Extra 610
radiography, professional education 391
radio time-signals 1283
RAF (Royal Air Force) 352
constitution 352
equipment 352
ranks 355
salaries 354
staff appointments 352
strength 344
Rail Passengers Council (RPC) 446, 447
Rail Regulator *see* ORR
railways 446
Channel tunnel link 448
freight 447
safety 447
services 446
tunnels 684
rainfall records (2007–8) 1191, 1192
Ramadan 1292
Ramsar convention (1971) 510
Ramsbury, bishop suffragan 470
Rangoon *see* Naypyidaw
ranks of the armed forces 355
Raphoe, bishop (RC) 477
rapid reaction force 702
rates
non-domestic 263, 266
Northern Ireland 268
RAUXAF (Royal Auxiliary Air Force) 353
Rayleigh
constituency 164
RBG (Royal Botanic Gardens) Kew 228, 534
RBGE (Royal Botanic Garden Edinburgh) 227
RCHs (recognised clearing houses) 548
RCPO (Revenue and Customs Prosecutions Office) 204
RDAs (Regional Development Agencies) 227
Reading
area bishop 469
constituencies 164
unitary authority 272, 289
university 384
real tennis
representative body 644
sports results (2007–8) 1212
recognised clearing houses (RCHs) 548
recognised investment exchanges (RIEs) 548
recorded signed for 487

recorders
 England and Wales 313
 Northern Ireland 324
Redbridge
 London borough council 271, 296
Redcar, constituency 165
Redcar and Cleveland
 unitary authority 272, 289
Red Crescent 720
Red Cross 720
Redditch
 constituency 165
 district council 270, 286
redirection of post 488
red-letter days 1293
redundancy 592
refraction, mean 1284
regencies 125
Regent's Park & Kensington North, constituency 165
Regent's Park and Primrose Hill 534
regional assemblies, establishment of 262
regional chambers/assemblies 265
regional daily newspapers 621
Regional Development Agencies (RDAs) 227
regional government 234
 London 234
 Northern Ireland 256
 Scotland 245
 Wales 239
regions
 European parliament 311
 Scottish parliament 254
 Welsh assembly 244
registered community design 605
registered design 605
registered teacher programme (RTP) 368
Registrar of Public Lending Right 227
registration
 of births 582
 of deaths 586
regnal years 1293
regular marriages 600
regulated payments, social fund 434
regulated tenancies 596
Reigate, constituency 165
Reigate and Banstead, district council 270, 286
relays
 men
  national (UK) records 1223
  world records 1222
 women
  national (UK) records 1224
  world records 1223
religion in the UK 455
religious calendars 9
 see also types of religion eg Hindu calendar
Religious Society of Friends 481
renewable energy sources 444
 targets for 498
Renfrewshire
 unitary authority 273, 304
Renfrewshire East, UK parliament constituency 179
Renfrewshire West, Scottish parliament constituency 253
Rent Service 201
Repton, bishop suffragan 466
Republic of Congo 802
Republic of Korea 892
research and technology organisations 412
research councils 408
Research Disclosure journal 606
research disclosures 606
resettlement grants 356
residential lettings 595
Residential Property Tribunal Service 328
resident magistrates 324
resident population statistics 18
Respect – the Unity Coalition 135
 representation in House of Commons 128
Restormel, district council 270, 286
retail banking 544
retail price index (RPI) 562
retirement pension *see* state pension scheme
Réunion 839
revenue, government 557
Revenue and Customs 203
Revenue and Customs Prosecutions Office (RCPO) 204
revocation of wills 602
Reykjavík 862
RFA (Royal Fleet Auxiliary Service) 348
Rhode Island 1050
Rhondda
 constituencies
  UK parliament 175
  Welsh assembly 243
Rhondda Cynon Taff
 unitary authority 273, 299
RIBA (Royal Institute of British Architects) 388
Ribble South, constituency 165
Ribble Valley
 constituency 165
 district council 270, 286
Richborough, bishop suffragan 463
Richmond Park 534
 constituency 165
Richmondshire, district council 270, 286
Richmond upon Thames
 London borough council 271, 296
Richmond (Yorks), constituency 165
RICS (Royal Institution of Chartered Surveyors) 394
RIEs (recognised investment exchanges) 548
Riga 899
Ripon and Leeds, bishop 469
rising and setting times 1276
rivers
 in England 274
 in Scotland 300
 in Wales 297
 longest 681
  in UK 681
Riyadh 989
RMR (Royal Marines Reserve) 348
RNR (Royal Naval Reserve) 348
roads 448
 finance 448
 length 449
 safety 450
Road Town 1070
road use 449
road user charging 449
Robert Gordon University 384
Rochdale
 constituency 165
 metropolitan borough council 272, 288
Rochester, bishop 469
Rochford & Southend East, constituency 165
Rochford, district council 270, 286
Roehampton University 384
Rogation Days 1289
roll-over relief on capital gains tax 572
Roman calendar 1295
 see also Julian calendar
Roman Catholic Church 474
 England and Wales 475
 Ireland 476
 Scotland 476
Romania 974
 EU membership 700, 703, 710
Romanian Orthodox Church calendar 1288
Roman indiction 1294
Roman remains
 in London 536
Rome 878
 see also treaty of Rome
Romford, constituency 165
Romsey, constituency 165
Roseau 817
Ross, Skye & Inverness West, Scottish parliament constituency 253
Ross, Skye & Lochaber, UK parliament constituency 179
Ross Dependency 949
Rossendale & Darwen, constituency 165
Rossendale, district council 270, 286
Rother, district council 270, 286
Rotherham
 constituency 165
 metropolitan borough council 272, 288
Rother Valley, constituency 165
rowing
 representative bodies 644
 sports results (2007–8) 1212
Roxburgh & Berwickshire, Scottish parliament constituency 253
Royal Academy of Arts 407
Royal Academy of Engineering 406
Royal Air Force *see* RAF
Royal Air Force Museum 227
Royal Albert Hall 536
royal archives 27
royal assent 132
Royal Auxiliary Air Force (RAUXAF) 353
Royal Botanic Garden Edinburgh (RBGE) 227
Royal Botanic Gardens (RBG) Kew 228, 534
Royal College of Art 384
Royal College of Music 385
Royal College of Veterinary Surgeons 395
Royal Commission on Environmental Pollution 228
Royal Commission on the Ancient and Historical Monuments of Scotland 228

Royal Commission on the Ancient and Historical Monuments of Wales 228
Royal Courts of Justice 536
royal family 24
finances 29
military ranks and titles 31
private secretaries 26
taxation 30
Royal Fleet Auxiliary Service (RFA) 348
Royal Hospital, Chelsea 536
royal household, offices of 27
Royal Institute of British Architects (RIBA) 388
Royal Institution of Chartered Surveyors (RICS) 394
Royal Mail Group 228, 486, 488
Royal Marines 347
Royal Marines Reserves (RMR) 348
Royal Mint 200
Royal National Theatre 537
Royal Naval College 534
Royal Naval Museum 229
Royal Naval Reserve (RNR) 348
Royal Navy 347
fleet 348
ranks 355
salaries 354
staff appointments 347
strength 344
Royal Observatory 534, 535
Royal Opera House 536
the Royal Parks 197, 534
royal peculiars 471
Royal Pharmaceutical Society of Great Britain 393
royal salutes 26
Royal Scottish Academy 407
Royal Society 406
Royal Society of Edinburgh (RSE) 407
Royal Standard 23
Royal Victorian Chain 84
Royal Victorian Order 83
RPC (Rail Passengers Council) 446, 447
RPI (retail price index) 562
RSE (Royal Society of Edinburgh) 407, 535
RTP (registered teacher programme) 368
Rugby & Kenilworth, constituency 165
Rugby, district council 270, 286
rugby fives
representative body 644
sports results (2007–8) 1213
rugby league
representative bodies 644
sports results (2007–8) 1213
rugby union
representative bodies 644
sports results (2007–8) 1213
Ruislip-Northwood, constituency 165
Runnymede & Weybridge, constituency 165
Runnymede, district council 270, 286
Rural Affairs, Department for Food, Environment and *see* Department for Environment, Food and Rural Affairs
Rushcliffe
constituency 165
district council 271, 286
Rushmoor, district council 271, 286
Russia 976
Russian Orthodox Church 480
Rutherglen & Hamilton West, UK parliament constituency 179
Rutland & Melton, constituency 166
Rutland
unitary authority 272, 289
Rwanda 980
see also International Criminal Tribunal for Rwanda (ICTR)
Ryedale
constituency 166
district council 271, 286

S

S4C Wales 609
SAA (stabilisation and association agreement) 703
SAARC (South Asian Association for Regional Cooperation) 726
SAAS (Student Award Agency for Scotland) 373
SADC (Southern African Development Community) 727
safety
marine 452
rail 447
on roads 450
Saffron Walden, constituency 166
St Albans 280
bishop 470
constituency 166
district council 271, 286
St Andrews and Edinburgh, archbishop (RC) 476
St Andrews, Dunkeld and Dunblane, bishop 472
St Andrews, university 385
St Anne 309
St Asaph, bishop 472
St Christopher and Nevis 982
St David's, bishop 472
St Denis 839
St Edmundsbury and Ipswich, bishop 470
St Edmundsbury, district council 271, 286
St George's (capital of Grenada) 851
St Germans, bishop suffragan 471
St Gotthard (rail) tunnel 684
St Helena and Dependencies 1074
St Helens
constituencies 166
metropolitan borough council 272, 288
St Helier 308
St Ives, constituency 166
St James's Palace 536
St James's Park 534
St John's 743
St Kitts and Nevis 982
St Lawrence canal 684
St Lawrence seaway 684
St Lucia 983
St Mary Axe 534
St Michael and St George, Most Distinguished Order 83
St Paul's Cathedral 536
St Peter Port 309
St Pierre 840
St Pierre and Miquelon 839
saints days 1293
St Vincent and the Grenadines 984
sailing *see* yachting
Saipan 1051, 1054
Saka era 1294
sale of goods 584
Salford
bishop (RC) 476
constituency 166
metropolitan borough council 272, 288
university 385
Salisbury 280
bishop 470
constituency 166
district council 271, 286
Saltire 300
salutes, royal 26
Salvation Army 482
same-sex couples 590
Samoa 985
Samoa, American 1051, 1053
Sana'a' 1063
Sandwell
metropolitan borough council 272, 288
San José 804
San Juan 1051, 1053
San Marino 986
San Marino (capital city) 987
San Salvador 825
Santa Cruz 768
Santiago 791
Santo Domingo 818
Sao Tome and Principe 987
Sao Tome (capital city) 987
SAP (statutory adoption pay) 436
Sarajevo 769
Sark 309
satellites 1285
Saturn 1285
satellites 1285
see also months of the year eg January, Saturn in
Saudi Arabia 989
savings
effect on social fund payments 435
income from 566
savings credit 433
Saxe-Coburg and Gotha, house of 36
Scarborough & Whitby, constituency 166
Scarborough, district council 271, 286
scheduled monuments 515
Schengen agreement 702
Schengen information system 702
scholarship, national academies of 406
school-centred initial teacher training 394
schools 360
class sizes 358, 359
grammar 362
independent *see* independent schools
middle 362
numbers by category 358, 361
primary 362
secondary 362
special 363
School Teachers' Review Body (STRB) 229

science
  government budget (2007–8) 408
  see also environment and science
science and discovery (2007–8) 1179
Science and Technology Facilities Council (STFC) 411
Science Museum 229
Scilly, Isles of 274
  unitary authority 289
  water authority 437
Scotland
  area 17, 300
  banknotes 543
  chiefs of clans 120
  constituencies (UK parliament) 176
  early history 301
  flag 300
  historic buildings and monuments 521
  hydrography 300
  islands 301
  judicature 321
  kings and queens (1016 to 1603) 36
  languages 300, 364
  local government *see* local government
  museums and art galleries 529
  national parks 504
  national scenic areas 505
  NHS structure 414
  police forces 336
  population statistics 17, 300
  precedence 43
  principal cities 302
  prison establishments 343
  public holidays 1293
  regional government 245
  relief 300
  water industry 439
  see also Church of Scotland
Scotland Central Scottish parliament region 254
Scotland European parliament region 312
Scotland Mid and Fife Scottish parliament region 255
Scotland North East Scottish parliament region 255
Scotland Office 194
Scotland South Scottish parliament region 255
Scotland West Scottish parliament region 255
Scottish and Southern Energy plc 442
Scottish Arts Council 229
Scottish Borders
  unitary authority 273, 304
Scottish Court Service 323
Scottish credit and qualifications framework (SCQF) 367
Scottish Criminal Cases Review Commission 229
Scottish Enterprise 230
Scottish Environment Protection Agency (SEPA) 230, 439
Scottish Episcopal Church 472
Scottish executive *see* Scottish government
Scottish Further and Higher Education Funding Council 367, 370
Scottish government 245
Scottish Government Rural Payments and Inspections Directorate (SGRPID) 245
Scottish group awards (SGAs) 367
Scottish land court 322
Scottish Law Commission 230
Scottish Legal Aid Board 230
Scottish National party *see* SNP
Scottish Natural Heritage (SNH) 230, 506
Scottish parliament 126, 246
  constituencies 248
  departments and executive agencies 245
  members 246
  political composition 247
  regions 254
  salaries 246
Scottish Power plc 442
Scottish Prisons Complaints Commission 230
Scottish Prison Service (SPS) 343
  operating costs 340
  salaries 343
Scottish Public Services Ombudsman 333
Scottish qualification for headship 369
Scottish Qualifications Authority (SQA) 364, 367
Scottish Solicitors' Discipline Tribunal 329
Scottish Trades Union Congress (STUC) 638
Scottish vocational qualifications (SVQs) 367
Scottish Water 437, 439
SCQF (Scottish credit and qualifications framework) 367
Scunthorpe, constituency 166
SDA *see* severe disablement allowance
SDLP (Social Democratic and Labour party) 136
  development 134
  financial support 134
  representation in House of Commons 128
SDRT (stamp duty reserve tax) 580
Seafish Industry Authority 230
seas
  area and depth 677
SEA (Single European Act) 701, 704, 706
seasons 1227
seats in House of Commons
  number 128
  vacancies 132
secondary education 362
  expenditure 357
  public examinations and qualifications 365
secondary health care services 417
secondary shortage subject scheme (SSSS) 368
second class post 487
Secretariat of the Pacific Community (SPC) 726
secretaries-general of the UN 731
secretaries of state 182
  salaries 184
Secret Intelligence Service (MI6) 204
secure tenancies 596
security and intelligence services 204
Security Council 729
Security Service (MI5) 204
Sedgefield
  constituency 166
    by-election (2007) result 181
  district council 271, 286
Sedgemoor, district council 271, 286
Sefton
  metropolitan borough council 272, 288
Selby
  bishop suffragan 463
  constituency 166
  district council 271, 286
select committees
  House of Commons 130, 132
  House of Lords 126, 127, 132
selective education in Northern Ireland 362
self-assessment
  for corporation tax 576
  for income tax 569
Senegal 991
senior civil service 184
senior judiciary of England and Wales 315
senior military officers pay system 354
Senior Salaries Review Body 231
Seoul 892
separation 588
'separation deeds' 590
SEPA (Scottish Environment Protection Agency) 230, 439
September 1260
  astronomical phenomena 1260
  calendar 1260
  constellations 1260
  duration of twilight 1261
  high water 1308
  minima of algol 1260
  night sky 1261
  sunrise and sunset 1263
  zodiacal light 1261
  Moon 1260
    position 1262
  Sun 1261
  Jupiter in 1263
  Mars in 1262
  Mercury in 1262
  Neptune in 1263
  Saturn in 1263
  Uranus in 1263
  Venus in 1262
Serbia 992
Serbian Orthodox Church 480
Serious Fraud Office 204
Serious Organised Crime Agency (SOCA) 231, 336
SERPS (state earnings-related pension scheme) 425
Service Personnel and Veterans Agency (SPVA) 426
service providers 485
service retired pay 356
services
  supply of 585
service salaries 354
setting times, rising and 1276
Sevenoaks
  constituency 166
  district council 271, 286
Seventh-day Adventist Church 482
severe disablement allowance (SDA) 432
  weekly rates 432

Severn river 274
Seychelles 995
SGAs (Scottish group awards) 367
SGRPID (Scottish Government Rural Payments and Inspections Directorate) 245
shadow cabinet 134
Shanghai Cooperation Organisation 726
Shareholder Executive 185
SHAs (strategic health authorities) 413, 414
Sheep Islands *see* Faeroe Islands
Sheffield 281
    bishop 470
    constituencies 166
    metropolitan borough council 272, 288
    museums and art galleries 527
    universities 385
Sheffield Hallam University 385
Shenshai calendar 1294
Shepway, district council 271, 286
Sherbourne, bishop suffragan 470
sheriff court of chancery 322
sheriff courts 321
sheriffdoms (Scottish judicature) 321, 323
sheriffs (City of London) 266, 291, 292
sheriffs (county) *see* high sheriffs
sheriffs (Scottish judicature) 323
Sherwood
    bishop suffragan 471
    constituency 167
Shetland 301
    Scottish parliament constituency 253
    unitary authority 273, 304
ship canals, longest 684
Shipley, constituency 167
shipping 452
    Lloyd's intelligence service 554
    UK-owned vessels 453
shipping forecast areas 454
ships, measurement of water for 1315
shires of England 282
    map 290
shooting
    representative bodies 644
    sports results (2007–8) 1214
shortest day 1227
Short money 134
short-term incapacity benefit 429
Shrewsbury & Atcham
    constituency 167
    district council 271, 286
Shrewsbury
    bishop (RC) 476
    bishop suffragan 467
Shropshire
    county council 269
Shropshire North, constituency 167
sick pay 592
sidereal time 1282
    conversion of mean time to 1278
Sierra Leone 996
sights of London 531
sight tests 417
Sikh calendar 1292
    year 2009 9
Sikhism 461
    adherents in UK 455
silver coin 542
silver hallmarks 539
Singapore 998
single currency 704
Single European Act (SEA) 701, 704, 706
single market 704
Sinn Fein 136
    representation in House of Commons 128
SI prefixes 1313
sites of special scientific interest (SSSIs) 506
Sittingbourne & Sheppey, constituency 167
SI units of measurement 1313
six pips signal 1283
sixth form colleges *see* post-16 education
skiing
    representative bodies 645
    see also alpine skiing
Skipton & Ripon, constituency 167
Skopje 911
Sky, estimated audience share 609
Sleaford & North Hykeham, constituency 167
Slough
    constituency 167
    unitary authority 272, 289
Slovakia 999
    EU membership 700, 710
Slovenia 1001
    EU membership 700, 710
SMP (statutory maternity pay) 436, 592
SNH (Scottish Natural Heritage) 230, 506
snooker
    representative bodies 642
    sports results (2007–8) 1214
snowboarding, representative bodies 645
Snowdonia/Eryri national park 503
SNP (Scottish National party) 135
    development 134
    financial support 134
    representation in House of Commons 128
SOCA (Serious Organised Crime Agency) 231, 336
Social Democratic and Labour party *see* SDLP
Social Democratic party (SDP) 134
social fund 434
social fund commissioner 220
Social Security and Child Support Appeals Tribunal 328
social security benefits *see* benefits
social security commissioners 328
    for Northern Ireland 328
social welfare 413
societies 649
Society of Genealogists 583
Society of Knights *see* Imperial Society of Knights Bachelor
Sodor and Man, bishop 470
Sofia 777
solar (or major) cycle 1293
solar system 1285
    see also individual planets eg Mars
soldiers
    salaries 355
    service retired pay 356
solemnisation of marriages 599
solicitors
    professional education 394
    see also duty solicitors
Solicitors' Disciplinary Tribunal 329
Solihull
    constituency 167
    metropolitan borough council 272, 288
Solomon Islands 1003
solstice 1287
Somalia 1004
Somerset
    county council 269
Somerset House 536
Somerton & Frome, constituency 167
Sophie, Countess of Wessex
    military ranks and titles 32
    private secretary 26
sound, measurement 1314
South Africa 1005
South America, geographical statistics 678
Southampton 281
    airport 445, 446
    bishop suffragan 464
    constituencies 167
    museums and art galleries 528
    unitary authority 272, 289
    universities 385
South Asian Association for Regional Cooperation (SAARC) 726
South Australia 748
South Ayrshire
    unitary authority 273, 304
South Bank 536
South Bedfordshire, district council 271, 286
South Bucks, district council 271, 286
South Cambridgeshire, district council 271, 286
South Carolina 1050
South Dakota 1050
South Derbyshire, district council 271, 286
South Downs, designation as a national park 503
South East European parliament region 312
Southend-on-Sea
    unitary authority 272, 289
Southend West, constituency 167
Southern African Development Community (SADC) 727
Southern and Antarctic territories 840
South Georgia 1074
South Gloucestershire
    unitary authority 272
South Hams, district council 271, 286
South Holland & the Deepings, constituency 167
South Holland, district council 271, 286
South Kesteven, district council 271, 286
South Korea *see* Republic of Korea
South Lakeland, district council 271, 286
South Lanarkshire
    unitary authority 273, 304
South Norfolk, district council 271, 286
South Northamptonshire, district council 271, 286

South Oxfordshire, district council 271, 286
South Pacific Commission *see* Secretariat of the Pacific Community (SPC)
Southport, constituency 167
South Ribble, district council 271, 286
South Sandwich Islands 1074
South Shields
constituency 167
museums and art galleries 528
South Shropshire, district council 271, 286
South Somerset, district council 271, 286
South Staffordshire, district council 271, 286
South Tyneside
metropolitan borough council 272, 288
South Wales Central Welsh assembly region 244
South Wales East Welsh assembly region 244
South Wales West Welsh assembly region 244
Southwark
archbishop (RC) 475
bishop 470
London borough council 271, 296
Southwark Cathedral 537
Southwark North & Bermondsey, constituency 167
Southwell and Nottingham, bishop 471
South West, GLA constituency 238
South West European parliament region 312
the sovereign 125
see also crown; Elizabeth II
sovereign in council *see* Privy Council
sovereign pontiff 474
sovereigns and princes of Wales 38
see also Charles, Prince of Wales
Spain 1008
EU membership 700, 710
islands and enclaves 1010
overseas territories 1010
SPC (Secretariat of the Pacific Community) 726
speakers
House of Commons 129, 132
House of Lords 127
special advisers to government ministers, salaries 184
special commissioners 329
special constabulary 338
special delivery next day 487
special delivery services 487
special education 363
Special Educational Needs and Disability Tribunal 329
Special Immigration Appeals Commission 329
specialist schools programme 361
specialist teacher assistant (STA) scheme 369
special licence, marriage by 599
speech and language therapy, professional education 391
speed, nautical measurement 1315
speed skating, sports results (2007–8) 1214
speedway, representative body 645
Spelthorne
constituency 167
district council 271, 286
sponsor's marks 539
Sport, Department for Culture, Media and *see* Department for Culture, Media and Sport
sports
events (2007–8) 1094
forthcoming events 13
records 1222
representative bodies 641
results (2007–8) 1195
sports councils 641
SPP (statutory paternity pay) 436, 592
Spring 1227
SPVA (Service Personnel and Veterans Agency) 426
SQA (Scottish Qualifications Authority) 364, 367
squash
representative bodies 645
sports results (2007–8) 1215
SRA (Strategic Rail Authority) 446
Sri Lanka 1010
SSMG (Sure Start maternity grant) 434
SSP (statutory sick pay) 436
SSSIs (sites of special scientific interest) 506
SSSS (secondary shortage subject scheme) 368
stabilisation and association agreement (SAA) 703
staff associations, police service 338
Stafford
bishop suffragan 468
constituency 167
district council 271, 286
Staffordshire
constituencies 168
by-election (2005) result 181
county council 269
university 385
Staffordshire Moorlands, district council 271, 286
stakeholder pension schemes 425
Stalybridge & Hyde, constituency 168
stamp duty 579
stamp duty land tax 579
stamp duty reserve tax (SDRT) 580
standard grade examinations 366
Standards Board 263
Standards in Public Life, Committee on 212
standard time 1283
see also Greenwich Mean Time (GMT)
Stanley 1072
Stansted airport 446
stars, position of 1278
state earnings-related pension scheme (SERPS) 425
state pension scheme 424, 430, 432
weekly rate 431, 432
state second pension 425
state system of education 361
State Veterinary Service (SVS) *see* Animal Health
statutory adoption pay (SAP) 436
statutory maternity pay (SMP) 436, 592
statutory paternity pay (SPP) 436, 592
statutory public holidays 1293
statutory sick pay (SSP) 436
steel arch bridges, longest 683
Stepney, area bishop 464
sterling *see* pound sterling
Stevenage
constituency 168
district council 271, 286
Stewart, house of 37
STFC (Science and Technology Facilities Council) 411
stipendiary magistrates
Scotland 323
see also district judges (magistrates' courts)
stipends
Church of England 463
Church of Scotland 474
Church in Wales 472
Scottish Episcopal Church 472
Stirling
constituencies
Scottish parliament 253
UK parliament 179
unitary authority 273, 304
university 385
Stock Exchange *see* London Stock Exchange
Stockholm 1017
Stockport
bishop suffragan 466
constituency 168
metropolitan borough council 272, 288
Stockton, constituencies 168
Stockton-on-Tees
unitary authority 272, 289
Stoke-on-Trent 281
constituencies 168
museums and art galleries 528
unitary authority 272, 289
Stone, constituency 168
storms, magnetic 1286
Stourbridge, constituency 168
Strabane, district council 273, 306
Strangford
constituencies
Northern Ireland assembly 261
UK parliament 180
strategic health authorities (SHAs) 413, 414
Strategic Rail Authority (SRA) 446
Stratford-on-Avon, district council 271, 287
Stratford-upon-Avon, constituency 168
Strathclyde, university 385
Strathkelvin & Bearsden, Scottish parliament constituency 253
STRB (School Teachers' Review Body) 229
Streatham, constituency 168
Stretford & Urmston, constituency 168
strikes 559
Stroud
constituency 168
district council 271, 287
structures, tallest 682, 683

Stuart, house of 35
STUC (Scottish Trades Union Congress) 638
Student Award Agency for Scotland (SAAS) 373
Student Finance Wales 373
Student Loans Company ltd 231
students
- higher education
  - financial support 357
  - number of 359
- post-16 education
  - financial support 357, 367
  - number of 366

sub-aqua, representative body 645
succession, order of 25
Sudan 1012
Suffolk
- constituencies 168
- county council 269

Suffolk Coastal, district council 271, 287
suffragan bishops, listing 463
Summer 1227
summer time 1283
Sun 1279
- distance from the Earth 677
- *see also months of the year* eg January, Sun

Sunday national newspapers, circulation 619
Sundays after Pentecost 1289
Sunday trading 592
Sunderland
- constituencies 169
- metropolitan borough council 272, 288
- university 385

sunrise 1279, 1281
- calculation of 1277
- *see also months of the year* eg January, sunrise and sunset

sunset 1279, 1281
- calculation of 1277
- *see also months of the year* eg January, sunrise and sunset

sunshine records (2007–8) 1191, 1192
superintendent registrar's offices 583
supplementary vote system (SVS) 234
supreme court of judicature
- England and Wales 313, 315
  - departments and offices 317
- Northern Ireland 324

Sure Start 361
Sure Start maternity grant (SSMG) 434
surface mail rates 487
Suriname 1014
Suriyakati calendar 1292
Surrey
- constituencies 169
- county council 269
- university 385

Surrey Heath, district council 271, 287
surveying, professional education 394
Surveyors Ombudsman Service 332
suspension bridges, longest 683
Sussex, university 385
Sussex Mid, constituency 169
sustainable development 499
Sutton & Cheam, constituency 169
Sutton
- London borough council 271, 296

Sutton Coldfield, constituency 169
Suva 833
Svalbard 956
SVQs (Scottish vocational qualifications) 367
Swale, district council 271, 287
Swansea 298
- constituencies
  - UK parliament 175
  - Welsh assembly 243
- museums and art galleries 529
- unitary authority 273, 299
- University of Wales 386
- Institute of Higher Education 386

Swansea and Brecon, bishop 472
Swaziland 1016
Sweden 1017
- EU membership 700, 710

Swedenborgian New Church 482
swimming
- representative bodies 645
- sports results (2007–8) 1215
- world records 1224

Swindon
- bishop suffragan 465
- constituencies 169
- unitary authority 272, 289

Switzerland 1019
Syria 1021
Syrian Orthodox Church 481
Système International d'Unités *see* SI units of measurement

T

table tennis
- representative bodies 645
- sports results (2007–8) 1216

TAI (international atomic time) 1282
Taipei 1023
Taiwan 1023
Tajikistan 1024
Takeover Panel, *see* Panel on Takeovers and Mergers
Tallinn 829
Tameside
- metropolitan borough council 272, 288

Tamworth
- constituency 169
- district council 271, 287

Tandridge, district council 271, 287
Tanzania 1026
taper relief 571
Tarawa 889
Tashkent 1055
Tasmania 748
Tate Britain 231
Tate Modern 231
TA (Territorial Army) 351
Tatton, constituency 169
Taunton
- bishop suffragan 464
- constituency 169

Taunton Deane, district council 271, 287
taxation 564
- capital gains tax *see* capital gains tax
- corporation tax *see* corporation tax
- council tax *see* individual councils eg Westminster, London borough council
- income tax *see* income tax
- inheritance tax *see* inheritance tax
- royal family 30
- stamp duty 579
- VAT (value added tax) *see* VAT (value added tax)

tax credits 428
- effect on income tax 569

tax exempt special savings accounts (TESSAs) 566
tax-free products, National Savings and Investments 549
taxis 449
tax return filing 569
Tayside North, Scottish parliament constituency 253
Tbilisi 843
TDA (Training and Development Agency for Schools) 232, 369
teachers 368
- numbers 358
- pupil–teacher ratios 358
- salaries 369
- training 368, 394
  - application for courses 372
  - financial incentives 368
- *see also* academic staff

Teacher Training Agency (TTA) *see* Training and Development Agency for Schools (TDA)
technological research bodies 412
technology and construction court 313, 316
Teesdale, district council 271, 287
Teesside, university 385
Tegucigalpa 859
Tehran 868
Teignbridge
- constituency 169
- district council 271, 287

Tel Aviv 875
Telecommunications Ombudsman, Office of the 332
Teletext ltd 609
television 607
- licences 608
- *see also* broadcasting (2007–8)

Telford, constituency 169
Telford and Wrekin
- unitary authority 272, 289

temperature
- measurement 1316
- records (2007–8) 1191, 1192

tenancies 595
Tendring, district council 271, 287
Tennessee 1050
tennis *see* lawn tennis; real tennis
tenure, type of accommodation by 20
term days 1293
- year 2009 9

termination of employment 592
terrestrial magnetism 1286
terrestrial time (TT) 1282
Territorial Army (TA) 351
TESSAs (tax exempt special savings accounts) 566
Test Valley, district council 271, 287
Tewkesbury
- bishop suffragan 467
- constituency 169
- district council 271, 287

Texas 1050
TfL (Transport for London) 232, 235
- bus services 449

Thai calendar 1292

Thailand 1028
Thames embankments 537
Thames Flood Barrier 537
Thames river 274
Thames Valley University 385
Thanet
  constituencies 169
  district council 271, 287
theatre (2007–8) 1185
  awards 1188
theatres in London 537
Thetford, bishop suffragan 468
Thimphu 766
Thistle, Most Ancient and Most Noble Order 82
Three Rivers, district council 271, 287
Thurrock
  constituency 169
  unitary authority 272, 289
Tibet 796
tidal predictions 1303
time 1281
  measurement of 1287
  see also lighting-up time
time-signals, radio 1283
time zones 690
Tirana 737
Tiverton & Honiton, constituency 169
Tobago, Trinidad and 1032
TOCs (train operating companies) 446
Togo 1030
Tokelau 948
Tokyo 882
toll roads 449
Tonbridge & Malling
  constituency 170
  district council 271, 287
Tonbridge, bishop suffragan 469
Tonga 1031
tonnage, nautical measurement 1315
Tooting, constituency 170
Top Salaries Review Body *see* Senior Salaries Review Body
Torbay
  constituency 170
  unitary authority 272, 289
Torfaen
  constituencies
    UK parliament 175
    Welsh assembly 243
  unitary authority 273, 299
Torridge, district council 271, 287
Torshavn 815
TOSL (The Ombudsman Service Limited) 332
the Tote (Horserace Totalisator Board) 219
Totnes, constituency 170
Tottenham, constituency 170
tourism bodies 231
Tower Hamlets
  London borough council 271, 296
town and country planning 600
town clerk 291, 292
town mayors 264
track and trace postal service 488
track events
  men
    national (UK) records 1223
    world records 1222
  women
    national (UK) records 1223
    world records 1222
trade, UK statistics 559
Trade and Industry, Department of *see* Department for Business Enterprise and Regulatory Reform *or* Department for Innovation, Universities and Skills
trade associations 635
trade descriptions 585
trade marks 606
Trades Union Congress (TUC) 637
trade unions 637
  listing of affiliated unions 637, 638
  listing of non-affiliated unions 640
  number and membership 559
Trafford
  metropolitan borough council 272, 288
Training and Development Agency for Schools (TDA) 232, 369
train operating companies (TOCs) 446
Transco *see* National Grid Transco
Transformational Government Team 185
transport 445
  air transport 445
  rail *see* railways
  roads *see* roads
  shipping *see* shipping
Transport, Department for *see* Department for Transport
Transport for London *see* TfL
Transport Tribunal 329
travel overseas 697
Treasurer's Office 27
Treasury *see* HM Treasury
Treasury Solicitor's Department 196
treaty of Amsterdam 701, 703, 706
treaty of Lisbon 702
treaty of Nice 703
treaty of Rome 701, 703, 704
treaty of Washington 722
Trial of the Pyx 543
triathlon, representative body 645
tribunals 325
Tribunals Service 325
trillion, definition 1315
Trinidad and Tobago 1032
Trinity House Lighthouse Service 213, 453
Trinity Sunday 1289
Tripoli 905
Tristan Da Cunha 1075
tropical year 1287
Truro & St Austell, constituency 170
Truro, bishop 471
trusts, NHS *see* NHS trusts
trust schools 360
Tshwane *see* Pretoria
TTA (Teacher Training Agency) *see* Training and Development Agency for Schools (TDA)
Tuam, archbishop (RC) 476
Tuam, Killala and Achonry, bishop 473
TUC (Trades Union Congress) 637
Tudor, house of 35
Tunbridge Wells
  constituency 170
  district council 271, 287
Tunis 1034
Tunisia 1034
tunnels
  longest 684
  see also Channel tunnel; Thames tunnels
Turkey 1035
  accession to the EU 703
Turkish Republic of Northern Cyprus 812
Turkmenistan 1038
Turks and Caicos Islands 1076
Tuvalu 1039
TV licensing 608
Tweeddale, Ettrick & Lauderdale, Scottish parliament constituency 253
Twickenham, constituency 170
twilight 1280
  see also months of the year eg January, twilight
twin towers, tallest 682
Tyne Bridge, constituency 170
Tynedale, district council 271, 287
Tynemouth, constituency 170
Tyneside North, constituency 170
Tynwald 307
Tynwald Day 307
Tyrone West
  constituencies
    Northern Ireland assembly 261
    UK parliament 180

U

UCAS (Universities and Colleges Admission Service) 372
UCEA (Universities and Colleges Employers Association) 371
Uganda 1040
UK
  area 17
  athletics records 1223
  citizenship 583
  constitution 125
  currency 542
  economic statistics 557
  environmental targets 498
  EU membership 700, 710
  European parliament regions 311
  events (2007–8) 1079
  flag 23
  kings and queens (since 1603) 35
  MEPs 310
  overseas territories 1069
  population 17
  religion 455
  shipping forecast areas 454
  statistics 17
  world heritage sites 508
  see also England; Northern Ireland; Scotland; Wales
UKAEA (UK Atomic Energy Authority) 232, 444
UK Atomic Energy Authority (UKAEA) 232, 444
UK Debt Management Office 201
UK Film Council 232
UK Independence party 136
UK Intellectual Property Office 199
UK Nirex 444

Ukraine 1042
UK Sports Council 232
UK Statistics Authority 204
UK Trade and Investment 205
Ulaanbaatar 931
Ulster, university 385
Ulster Mid
constituencies
Northern Ireland assembly 261
UK parliament 180
Ulster Unionist Council 134, 136
Ulster Unionist party 134, 136
representation in House of Commons 128
UN 727
membership 727
observers 727
peacekeeping forces 729
UN Children's Fund (UNICEF) 728
Undeb Yr Annibynwyr Cymraeg 482
undergraduate courses 371
underground systems 447
under-secretaries of state 183
salaries 184
UN development programme 728
UN Educational, Scientific and Cultural Organisation (UNESCO) 731
unemployment statistics 558
unfair dismissal 593
unfair terms 585
UN High Commissioner for Refugees (UNHCR) 729
UN Human Rights Council 729
UN Industrial Development Organisation (UNIDO) 731
Union Flag (or Jack) 23
Union of Welsh Independents 482
unions *see* trade unions
Unitarian and Free Christian churches 484
unitary authorities 262
England 264, 289
functions 265
map 290
political composition 272
Scotland 267, 304
map 304
political composition 273
Wales 267, 299
map 299
political composition 272
United Arab Emirates 1044
United Kingdom *see* UK
United Nations *see* UN
United Reformed Church 482
United States of America *see* USA
United States Virgin Islands 1051, 1053
Universal Postal Union (UPU) 732
universal time (UT) 1281
universities 370
governance 370
listing 376
Universities and Colleges Admission Service (UCAS) 372
Universities and Colleges Employers Association (UCEA) 371
University Boat Race 13, 1212
University for Industry (Ufi) ltd 370, 371
UN Monitoring, Verification and Inspection Commission (UNMOVIC) 730
UN Relief and Works Agency for Palestine Refugees in the Near East (UNRWA) 729
Unrepresented Nations and Peoples Organisation (UNPO) 732
UNRWA (UN Relief and Works Agency for Palestine Refugees in the Near East) 729
Upminster, constituency 170
Upper Bann
constituencies
Northern Ireland assembly 261
UK parliament 180
Uranus 1285
satellites 1285
see also months of the year eg January, Uranus in
Uruguay 1054
USA 1048
states 1050
territories 1052
Utah 1050
UTC (coordinated universal time) 1282
Uttlesford, district council 271, 287
Uxbridge, constituency 170
Uzbekistan 1055

V

vacant seats in the House of Commons 132
see also by-elections
Vaduz 907
Vale of Clwyd
constituencies
UK parliament 175
Welsh assembly 243
Vale of Glamorgan
constituencies
UK parliament 175
Welsh assembly 243
unitary authority 273, 299
Vale of White Horse, district council 271, 287
Vale of York, constituency 170
Vale Royal, district council 271, 287
Valletta 920
The Valley 1069
Valuation Office Agency 203
Valuation Tribunal Service for Wales (VTSW) 329
Valuation Tribunal Service (VTS) 329
Vanuatu 1057
VAT and Duties Tribunals 330
Vatican City 1058
Vatican City State 1058, 474
VAT (value added tax) 578
collection 579
Vauxhall, constituency 170
Vehicle and Operator Services Agency (VOSA) 200, 452
Vehicle Certification Agency 200
vehicle excise duty 451
vehicles *see* motor vehicles
vehicular tunnels, longest 684
velocity of the Earth 677
Venezuela 1059
Venus 1285
see also months of the year eg January, Venus in
Vermont 1050
Veterans Agency *see* Service Personnel and Veterans Agency
Veterinary Laboratories Agency 198
veterinary medicine, professional education 395
Veterinary Medicines Directorate 198
Victoria, Queen
descendants 40
Victoria and Albert Museum 232
Victoria (Australia) 748
Victoria Cross 118
Victoria (Seychelles) 995
Vienna 751
Vientiane 897
Vietnam 1061
Vilnius 908
Virginia 1050
Virgin Islands
British 1070
United States 1051, 1053
Virgin Media Television 607, 609
visa requirements 699
viscounts 53
courtesy titles 76
forms of address 53
Visit Britain 231
Visit Scotland 231
vocational qualifications 365
volcanoes, highest active 680
volleyball
representative bodies 645
volts 1314
volume
measurement
imperial 1314
metric 1314
conversion tables 1318
voluntary schools 360
VOSA (Vehicle and Operator Services Agency) 200, 452
voting
for the London assembly 234
for the mayor of London 234
qualifications 601
registration 602
see also elections
VTS (Valuation Tribunal Service) 329
VTSW (Valuation Tribunal Service for Wales) 329

W

waiting lists, NHS 418
Wakefield
bishop 471
constituency 170
metropolitan borough council 272, 288
museums and art galleries 528
Wales
archbishop 472
area 17, 297
areas of outstanding natural beauty (AONBs) 504
constituencies (UK parliament) 173
early history 297
flag 297
historic buildings and monuments 520
hydrography 297
judicature 313
language 297, 364

local government *see* local government
museums and art galleries 528
national parks 502
NHS structure 414
police forces 336
population statistics 17
precedence 42
princes of 38
principal cities 298
prison establishments 340
public holidays 1293
regional government 239
relief 297
university 386
water industry 437
see also Church in Wales
Wales, Prince of
title 38
see also Charles, Prince of Wales
Wales, Princess of *see* Diana, Princess of Wales
Wales European parliament region 312
Wales Office 195
Wales Tourist Board 231
Wales TUC 638
walk-in centres, NHS 416
walking, representative body 645
walking (track)
national (UK) records 1223
world records 1222
Wallace Collection 233
Wallasey, constituency 170
Wallis and Futuna Islands 840
Walsall
constituencies 170
metropolitan borough council 272, 288
Waltham Forest
London borough council 271, 296
Walthamstow, constituency 170
Wandsworth
London borough council 271, 296
Wansbeck
constituency 171
district council 271, 287
Wansdyke, constituency 171
Wantage, constituency 171
WAP (Wireless Application Protocol) 495
war disablement pension 426
Warley, constituency 171
war pensions 426
claims and questions 427
effect on benefits 427
supplementary allowances 426
Warrington
bishop suffragan 468
constituencies 171
unitary authority 272, 289
Warsaw 969
Warwick & Leamington, constituency 171
Warwick
bishop suffragan 466
district council 271, 287
university 386
Warwickshire
county council 269
Warwickshire North, constituency 171
war widow/widower's pension 426
Washington, treaty of *see* North Atlantic treaty
Washington DC 1048
Washington (state) 1050
waste 500
UK targets 498
water
boiling and freezing points 1316
measures of 1315
quality targets 500
see also high water
waterfalls
greatest 681
in British Isles 681
in Scotland 300
Waterford and Lismore, bishop (RC) 477
water industry 437
England and Wales 437
Northern Ireland 439
Scotland 439
Water Industry Commissioner for Scotland 439
Water Service 437, 439
Water Services Regulation Authority (OFWAT) 205
water skiing, representative body 645
Water UK 437
Waterways Ombudsman 333
Watford
constituency 171
district council 271, 287
watts 1314
Waveney
constituency 171
district council 271, 287
Waverley, district council 271, 287
WCO (World Customs Organisation) 733
Wealden
constituency 171
district council 271, 287
Wear Valley, district council 271, 287
weather (2007–8) 1189
Weaver Vale, constituency 171
WEA (Workers' Education Association) 374
the web *see* internet
web domain names 606
of countries 496
weekly newspapers 620
weight
conversion tables 1318
measurement
imperial 1314
metric 1314
obsolete 1317
weightlifting, representative body 645
weights and measures 1313
conversion tables 1318
obsolete 1317
Wellingborough
constituency 171
district council 271, 287
Wellington 947
Wells, constituency 171
Welsh assembly 126, 240
committees 239
constituencies 241
departments and offices 239
executive agencies 239
members 240
political composition 241
regions 244
salaries 240
Welsh assembly government 239
Welsh baccalaureate 365
Welsh Fourth Channel Authority *see* S4C Wales
Welsh language 297, 364
Welwyn & Hatfield, district council 271, 287
Welwyn Hatfield, constituency 171
Wentworth, constituency 171
Wesleyan Reform Union 483
Wessex, Countess of *see* Sophie, Countess of Wessex
Wessex, Earl of *see* Edward, Prince
West Bank 877
West Berkshire
unitary authority 272, 289
West Bromwich, constituencies 171
Westbury, constituency 171
West Central, GLA constituency 238
West Devon, district council 271, 287
West Dorset, district council 271, 287
West Dunbartonshire
unitary authority 273, 304
Western Australia 748
Western European Union (WEU) 732
Western Isles
Scottish parliament constituency 254
unitary authority 273, 304
Western Sahara 936
West Ham, constituency 171
West Lancashire, district council 271, 287
West Lindsey, district council 271, 287
West Lothian
unitary authority 273, 304
West Midlands European parliament region 312
Westminster
archbishop (RC) 475
London borough council 271, 296
royal peculiar 471
university 386
Westminster Abbey 537
Westminster Cathedral 537
Westminster Hall Sittings 132
Westmorland & Lonsdale, constituency 172
West of England, university 386
Weston-super-Mare, constituency 172
West Oxfordshire, district council 271, 287
West Somerset, district council 271, 287
West Sussex
county council 269
West Virginia 1050
West Wiltshire, district council 271, 287
wetlands, conservation 510
WEU (Western European Union) 732
Weymouth and Portland, district council 271, 287
whips 133
government 183
Liberal Democrat 135
opposition 135
whistleblowing legislation 593
Whitby, bishop suffragan 463
white papers (2007–8) 1178

Whit Sunday 1289
WHO (World Health Organisation) 733
widowed parent's allowance 430
  weekly rates 430
widow's benefits 430
Wigan
  constituency 172
  metropolitan borough council 272, 288
Wight, Isle of 274
  constituency 159
  unitary authority 272, 289
wildlife conservation 509
  UK legislation 510
Willemstad 946
Willesden, area bishop 464
William, Prince 24
  military ranks and titles 32
  private secretary 26
wills 602
  capacity to make 602
  execution 602
  revocation 602
  in Scotland 604
  where to find proved 603
Wilton Park Conference Centre 198
Wiltshire
  county council 269
Wiltshire North, constituency 172
Wimbledon, constituency 172
Wimbledon championships (2008) 1217
Wimbledon College of Art 377
Winchester 281
  bishop 464
  constituency 172
  district council 271, 287
  university 386
Windhoek 940
Windsor
  constituency 172
  royal peculiar 471
Windsor and Maidenhead
  unitary authority 272, 289
Windsor, house of 36, 39
wine bottles, measurement of 1315
Winter 1227
winter fuel payments 434
WIPO (World Intellectual Property Organisation) 605, 606, 733
Wirral
  constituencies 172
  metropolitan borough council 272, 288
Wisconsin 1050
witnesses for wills 602
Witney, constituency 172
WMO (World Meteorological Organisation) 734
Woking
  constituency 172
  district council 271, 287
Wokingham
  constituency 172
  unitary authority 272, 289
Wolverhampton
  bishop suffragan 468
  constituencies 172
  metropolitan borough council 272, 288
  university 386
women
  hereditary peers 44
  ordination 462
  precedence 42
Women's National Commission 233
Woodspring, constituency 172
Woolwich, area bishop 470
Worcester
  bishop 471
  constituency 172
  district council 271, 287
  museums and art galleries 528
  university 386
Worcestershire
  constituencies 172
  county council 269
Work and Pensions, Department for *see* Department for Work and Pensions
work-based learning 366
Workers Education Association (WEA) 374
workforce, distribution of 558
working tax credit 428
working time regulations 594
Workington, constituency 173
workmen's compensation scheme 435
workplace parking levy schemes 449
the world
  countries of 735
  in figures 677
World Bank Group 732
World Customs Organisation (WCO) 733
World Health Organisation (WHO) 733
world heritage sites 508
World Intellectual Property Organisation (WIPO) 605, 606, 733
World Meteorological Organisation (WMO) 734
world records
  athletics 1222
  swimming 1224
World Service *see* BBC World Service
World Tourism Organisation (WTO) 734
World Trade Centre towers 682
World Trade Organisation (WTO) 734
Worsley, constituency 173
Worthing
  constituencies 173
  district council 271, 287
Wrekin, the, constituency 173
wrestling, representative body 645
Wrexham
  bishop (RC) 476
  constituencies
    UK parliament 175
    Welsh assembly 244
  unitary authority 273, 299
writing paper, measures of 1316
WTO (World Tourism Organisation) 734
WTO (World Trade Organisation) 734
Wychavon, district council 271, 287
Wycombe
  constituency 173
  district council 271, 287
Wyoming 1050
Wyre, district council 271
Wyre Forest
  constituency 173
  district council 271, 287
Wythenshawe & Sale East, constituency 173

Y

yachting
  representative body 645
Yamoussoukro 805
Yaoundé 783
Yaren District 941
years
  definition 1287
  Hindu 1290
  Jewish 1291
  Muslim 1292
  Thai 1292
  see also civil year; historical year; legal year; masonic year; New Year; regnal years
Yemen 1063
Yeovil, constituency 173
Yerevan 746
Ynys Mon *see* Anglesey
York 281
  archbishop of 463
  constituency 173
  museums and art galleries 528
  unitary authority 272, 289
  university 386
York, Duchess of *see* Ferguson, Sarah
York, Duke of *see* Andrew, Prince
York, house of 35
Yorkshire and the Humber European parliament region 312
Yorkshire Dales national park 503
Yorkshire East, constituency 173
young students' bursaries 373
youth courts 314
Youth Justice Agency, Northern Ireland 199

Z

Zaffarines 1010
Zagreb 807
Zambia 1064
Zimbabwe 1066
zodiacal light
  in February 1233
  in March 1237
  in September 1261
Zoo, London 536
Zoroastrian calendar 1294
Zoroastrianism 461

STOP PRESS

CHANGES SINCE PAGES WENT TO PRESS

EVENTS OF THE YEAR

AFRICA

6 August. A bloodless military coup in Mauritania removed the country's first elected leader, president Sidi ould Cheikh Abdallahi. **14 August.** The new military junta in Mauritania named the former ambassador to the EU, Moulaye Ould Mohamed Laghdaf, as prime minister. **20 August.** The President of Zambia, Levy Mwanawasa, died at the age of 59 after suffering a stroke in June.

THE AMERICAS

7 August. The jury at the first US military trial at Guantanamo Bay found Osama bin Laden's former driver, Salim Hamdan, guilty of supporting terrorism but acquitted him of attempted murder; he was jailed for 66 months. **10 August.** The President of Bolivia, Evo Morales, won a recall referendum, enabling him to continue as president. **23 August.** The US presidential candidate, Barack Obama, named veteran senator Joe Biden as his running mate; John McCain chose Alaskan governor Sarah Palin as his potential vice-president on 29 August. **5 September.** Severe tropical storms struck Haiti killing over 120 people. **7 September.** The US government announced a takeover of mortgage firms Fannie Mae and Freddie Mac because their debts posed a risk to the country's economy.

ASIA

3 August. A stampede at a Hindu temple in the Indian state of Himachel Pradesh led to around 140 deaths. **18 August.** The President of Pakistan, Pervez Musharraf, resigned; Mr Musharraf was facing impeachment charges drawn up by the governing coalition. **25 August.** A plane crash in Bishkek, Kyrgyzstan, killed 68 people. **3 September.** Japanese prime minister Yasou Fukuda resigned less than a year after he took the post. **6 September.** Asif Zardari, widower of former prime minister Benazir Bhutto, was elected president of Pakistan; Mr Zardari won over 68 per cent of the vote.

EUROPE

7 August. Russian troops moved into the Georgian separatist region of South Ossetia. **12 August.** Russian soldiers began to pull out of South Ossetia after a truce was brokered by French president Nicholas Sarkozy; there were reports of around 2,000 deaths linked to the violence. **15 August.** Poland signed a preliminary deal with the USA to host a missile defence shield. **20 August.** A plane crashed shortly after take-off in Madrid, Spain, killing 154 people.

MIDDLE EAST

17 August. The Israeli government agreed to release 200 Palestinian prisoners as a goodwill gesture. **25 August.** A suicide bomber killed 25 people in the Abu Ghraib region of Baghdad.